Key

◇ capital city

○ other major city

—— international boundary

NORTH AND CENTRAL AMERICA

Abbr.	Nation	Capital city
A.	**Antigua and Barbuda**	St John's
	Barbados	Bridgetown
	Belize	Belmopan
	Costa Rica	San José
D.	**Dominica**	Roseau
	Dominican Republic	Santo Domingo
	El Salvador	San Salvador
G.	**Grenada**	St George's
	Guatemala	Guatemala
	Haiti	Port-au-Prince
	Honduras	Tegucigalpa
	Jamaica	Kingston
	Nicaragua	Managua
	Panama	Panamá
S.K.	**St Kitts and Nevis**	Basseterre
S.L.	**St Lucia**	Castries
S.V.	**St Vincent and the Grenadines**	Kingstown
	Trinidad and Tobago	Port-of-Spain

AFRICA

Abbr.	Nation	Capital city
BE.	**Benin**	Porto Novo
B.F.	**Burkina Faso**	Ouagadougou
B.	**Burundi**	Bujumbura
	Cape Verde	Praia
	Comoros	Moroni
C.I.	**Côte d'Ivoire**	Yamoussoukro
D.	**Djibouti**	Djibouti
E.G.	**Equatorial Guinea**	Malabo
	Eritrea	Asmara
	Gabon	Libreville
	Gambia	Banjul
G.	**Ghana**	Accra
	Guinea-Bissau	Bissau
	Liberia	Monrovia
	Mauritius	Port Louis
R.	**Rwanda**	Kigali
S.T.	**São Tomé and Príncipe**	São Tomé
	Senegal	Dakar
	Seychelles	Victoria
	Swaziland	Mbabane
T.	**Togo**	Lomé

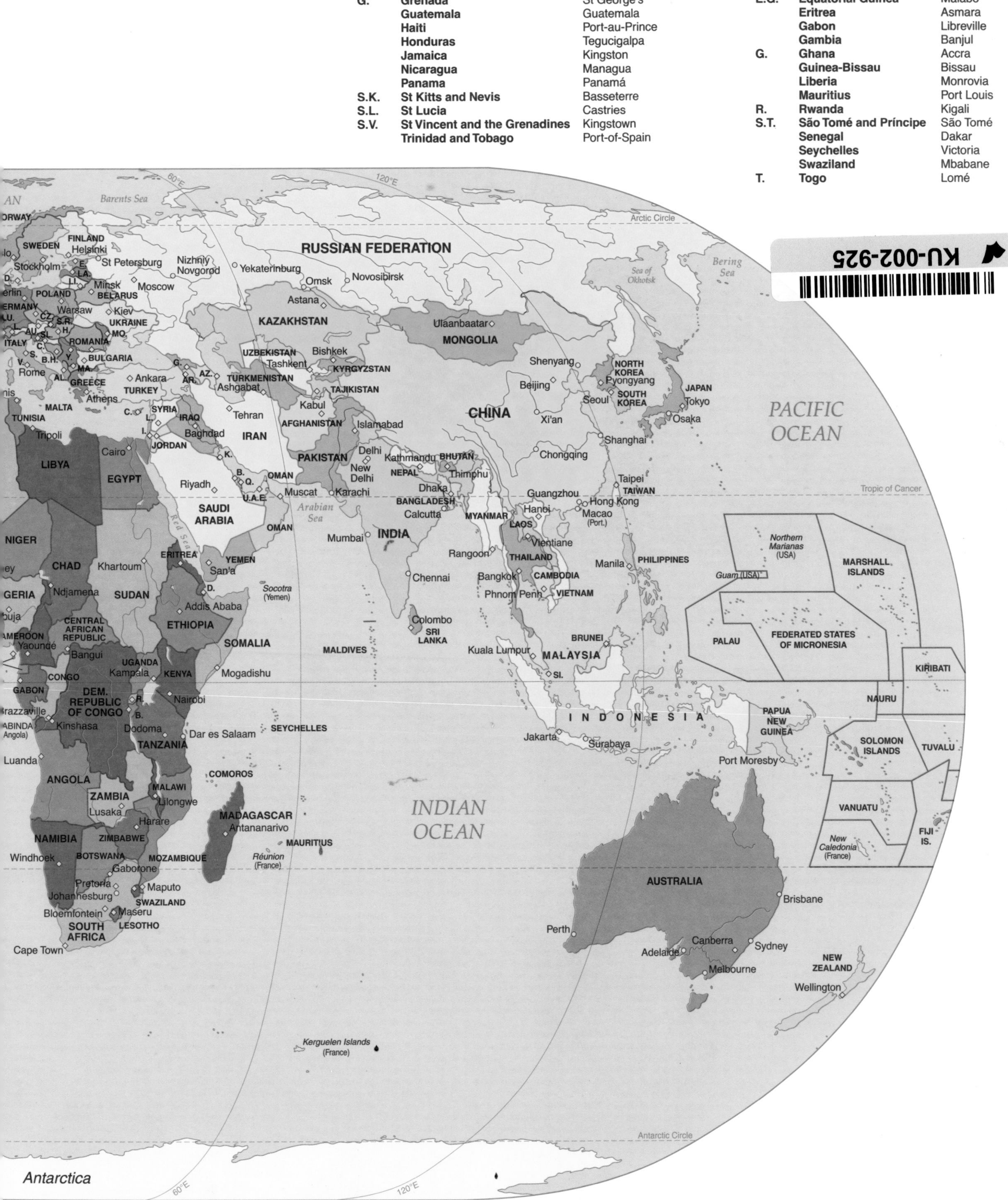

The HUTCHINSON ENCYCLOPEDIA

The HUTCHINSON ENCYCLOPEDIA

First published (as *Hutchinson's Twentieth Century Encyclopedia*) 1948
Second edition 1951
Third edition 1956
Fourth edition (as *Hutchinson's New 20th Century Encyclopedia*) 1964
Fifth edition 1970
Sixth edition (as *The New Hutchinson 20th Century Encyclopedia*) 1977
Seventh edition 1981
Eighth edition (as *The Hutchinson Encyclopedia*) 1988
Ninth edition 1990
Tenth edition 1992
1994 edition (revised and updated) 1993
Reprinted 1994
1995 edition (revised and updated) 1994
1996 edition (revised and updated) 1995
1997 edition (revised and updated) 1996
Reprinted 1997
Eleventh edition (1998 edition) 1997
Reprinted 1998
1999 edition (revised and updated) 1998
Reprinted 1999
2000 edition (revised and updated) 1999

This edition published in 1999 by
Best Sellers Direct
No 2 Harleston Units
Forncett Street
Sheffield S4 7QG

ISBN 1-85986-329-9

British Library Cataloguing in Publication Data
A catalogue record for this book is available from the British Library

Set in Times and Frutiger

Printed and bound by DeAgostini, Novara, Italy

Papers used by Helicon Publishing Ltd are natural recyclable products made from wood grown in sustainable forests. The manufacturing processes of both raw materials and paper conform to the environmental regulations of the country of origin.

Contents

FACTFILE

This section consists of tables arranged by subject. Entries in the main text have cross-references to these tables where relevant.

FOCUS FEATURES

These twenty features offer a more in-depth look at a subject than the average entry. Many have been selected with relevance to Key Stages 3 or 4 of the UK National Curriculum.

Introduction

The Hutchinson Encyclopedia 2000: The Millennium Edition has been very thoroughly revised and updated. As with its predecessors, this edition includes hundreds of updates and new entries. It also features an entirely new section – The Millennium Supplement – at the front of the Encyclopedia devoted to assessing the past century and the past millennium.

Eight specially commissioned features describe the discoveries, achievements, spirit, and attitudes of the past century. These features are followed by four concise chronologies which outline historic events of the past 1,000 years.

The aim of *The Hutchinson Encyclopedia* remains that of providing the reader with the widest possible range of material within the limitations of space, and to provide it in clear and accessible language. With each edition, the inclusion policy has to adapt to the needs of the times; the many changes seen in the past decade are reflected in the considerable number of entries in areas such as information technology and computing; the new countries and leaders of the post-Soviet world; advances in medicine and genetics; and popular culture and the arts.

This edition retains the twenty ***Focus Features*** on a selection of major topics, written by specialist contributors and selected with relevance to Key Stages of the National Curriculum; a thematically arranged ***Factfile*** at the back of the book with dozens of useful tables; a selection of illustrations and quotations, and additional cross-referencing to help link entries and features more clearly.

HOW TO USE THE BOOK

Arrangement of entries

Entries are ordered in strict alphabetical sequence, as if there were no spaces between words, thus: *Arab*, *arabesque*, *Arabia*, *Arabic language*, *Arab League*. But a purely mechanical alphabetization is avoided in cases where human logic demands otherwise: for example, sovereigns with the same name are grouped according to country first and then by number, so that King George II of England comes before King George III of England rather than next to King George II of Greece. Words beginning 'Mc' are treated the same as 'Mac', and 'St' as if it were spelt 'Saint'.

Foreign names and titles

Names of foreign sovereigns and places are usually shown in their English form, except where the foreign name is more familiar: thus, there are entries for Charles V of Spain, but for Juan Carlos (not John Charles). Entries for titled people are under the name by which they are best known to the general reader: thus, Anthony Eden, not Lord Avon.

Cross-references

Within entries, cross-references are shown by ◊ immediately preceding the reference. Cross-referencing is selective, with the aim of pointing the reader to an entry whose relevance to the subject may not be immediately obvious. Common alternative spellings or names are also given as cross-references: thus, there is a cross-reference from *Mohammed* to *Muhammad*, and from *Yangtze* to *Chang Jiang*. Cross-references are not given to neighbouring entries.

If names of people mentioned within an entry are not followed by their life dates, there is a separate entry for that person whether or not there is a cross-reference; if life dates are given after a name within text, there is no separate entry. Thus, in the entry for *Rembrandt:* 'He began his career in Leiden, where his work reflected knowledge of Adam Elsheimer (1578–1610) and ◊Caravaggio, among others.'

Normally falling at the end of an entry, the symbol ▷ indicates a cross-reference to a feature on the same or a related topic.

Bold type

Within entries, bold type is used for distinct types of the main term (for example, in the entry for *chemistry*, **organic chemistry**' and **'inorganic chemistry**' are in bold type), as well as for names of family members within the same entry (for example, *Brontë*).

SEE ALSO references

These are given in panels at the end of Focus Features and many country boxes. In the case of features, the reader is pointed to other entries most directly related to the subject of the feature; in country boxes, the pointers may be to less obviously related entries, or to people who had a considerable role in that country's history. Again, these cross-references are selective, and readers should also use the cross-referencing links between entries to explore areas of interest.

Chinese names

Pinyin, the preferred system for transcribing Chinese names for people and places, is generally used: thus, there is an entry at *Mao Zedong*, not *Mao Tse-Tung*; an exception is made for a few names which are more familiar in their former (Wade-Giles) form, such as *Sun-Yat-sen* and *Chiang Kai-shek*. (Where confusion is likely, Wade-Giles forms are given as cross-references.)

Comments and suggestions

The continuing success and accuracy of the *Hutchinson Encyclopedia* have been helped by the many readers who have taken the trouble to write in, whether with suggestions for new entries or additional information, or to correct existing entries. Your feedback is invaluable for the continual improvement of the encyclopedia.

Updates are included to January 1999, however, where possible, we have included subsequent developments and updated information within the constraints of the production process.

Abbreviations and symbols

km = kilometres
mi = miles
m = metres
C = century
Cs = centuries
c = circa
GDP = gross domestic product
GNP = gross national product
PPP = purchasing power parity
N, S, E, W = north, south, east, west
< 15 = up to and including 15
> 65 = over 65

Units: SI (metric) units are used for scientific entries; commonly used measurements include an imperial equivalent.

Acknowledgements

Contributors

Owen Adikibi PhD, CIM, IBIM
Lesley Adkins MPhil, FSA, MIFA
Roy Adkins MPhil, FSA, MIFA
Alain Anderton MA
Christine Avery MA, PhD
John Ayto MA
Paul Bahn PhD, FSA
Anne Baker, BA
Tallis Barker DPhil, ARCM
Malcolm Bradbury, MA, PhD, FRSL
Elizabeth Breuilly
Nigel Davis BSc
Ian Derbyshire MA, PhD, FCA
J D Derbyshire PhD, FInstM
Michael Dewar MA
Dougal Dixon MSc
Nigel Dudley BSc
Ingrid von Essen
Eric Farge
Anna Farkas MA
Peter W Fleming PhD
Karen Froud
Lawrence Garner BA
Wendy Grossman
Jackie Herald
Michael Hitchcock DPhil
Chris Holdsworth MA, PhD
Stuart Holroyd
Lisa Isenman Sullivan
Mawil Izzi Dien PhD
Sara Jenkins-Jones
Charles W Kidd
Peter Lafferty MSc
Graham K H Ley MPhil
Carol Lister PhD, FSS
Graham Littler MSc, FSS
Tom McArthur PhD
John Mapps
Richard Martin PhD
David M Munro, PhD, FSA (Scot)
Chris Murray
Joanne O'Brien MA
Maureen O'Connor BA
Robert Paisley PhD
Martin Palmer MA
Paulette Pratt
Tim Pulleine
Ben Ramos
Glyn Redworth MPhil
Ian Ridpath FRAS
Adrian Room MA, DipEd, FRGS
Simon Ross BA
Julian Rowe, PhD
Jack Schofield MA
Emma Shackleton MA
Andrew Skilton DPhil
Joe Staines BA
Callum Storrie BSc(Arch)
Catherine Thompson MA
Jason Tomes DPhil
Stephen Webster MPhil, PGCE
Elizabeth Whitelegg BSc
John Wright

Features Authors

Lord Asa Briggs MA, BSc(Econ), FBA Former Vice Chancellor of the University of Sussex (1967–76) and Provost of Worcester College, Oxford (1976–91). Chancellor of Oxford University (1978–94). Author of many books on social history and three volumes on the history of broadcasting

Michael Broers MA, DPhil Lecturer in Modern European History, University of Leeds; author of *Europe Under Napoleon* and *Europe After Napoleon 1814–1848*

Simon Buckby BA Journalist with the *Financial Times*, author, and broadcaster

Paul Davies BSc, PhD, FInstP, FAIP Visiting Professor of Physics at Imperial College London, and author of many books, including *The Fifth Miracle: The Search for the Origin of Life*

Ian Derbyshire MA, PhD, FCA Writer on history, government, and politics; coauthor of *Politics in Britain: from Callaghan to Thatcher* and *Political Systems of the World*

Nigel Dudley BSc Director, Equilibrium consultancy; formerly director, Soil Association

Wendy M. Grossman Author of *net.wars* and freelance writer specializing in technology and the Internet

Simon Hall MA Editor specializing in English and European history

Martin Henig MA, DPhil, FSA Visiting lecturer in Roman Art at the University of Oxford, and author of a number of books including *Classical Gems* and *The Art of Roman Britain*

Philip Hensher MA, PhD, FRSL Freelance journalist and author of several novels including *Kitchen Venom* and *The Bedroom of the Mister's Wife*

Chris Holdsworth MA, PhD Writer and researcher, specializing in anthropology

Peter Lafferty MSc Freelance writer on physical sciences

Patrick Maume MA, PhD British Academy Research Fellow, Department of Politics, The Queen's University of Belfast

Rosalind Miles MA Author of *The Women's History of the World*, broadcaster, and founder of the Centre for Women's Studies at Coventry University

Chris Murray Consultant and writer on the arts

Chris Partridge BD, PhD Lecturer in Theology and Religious Studies, University College Chester

Roy Porter MA, PhD, FBA Professor of history of medicine, The Wellcome Institute for the History of Medicine, London; author and broadcaster

Sue Rabbitt-Roff MA Cookson Senior Research Fellow at the Centre for Medical Education, University of Dundee

Peter Robinson BSc(Econ) Senior Economist, Institute for Public Policy Research

Robin Scagell Writer and broadcaster on astronomy; previously a telescope maker and astronomer

Andrew Skilton DPhil Author of *A Concise History of Buddism* and an ordained Buddhist

Chris Stringer MSc, PhD, DSc Palaeoanthropologist at the Natural History Museum, London; coauthor of *In Search of Neanderthals* and *African Exodus*

James Walvin MA, DPhil Professor of history at the University of York; author of *Questioning Slavery* and *Black Ivory: a history of British slavery*; coeditor of *Slavery and Abolition*

Stephen Webster MPhil, PGCE Teacher in science, King Alfred School, London

Editorial

Managing Editor
Roger Tritton

Editors
Jane Anson
Rachel Coldicutt
Chris Cowley
Sue Donaldson
Katia Hamza
Shereen Karmali
Peter Lewis
Nicky Matthews
Malgorzata Nawrocka-Colquhoun
Sue Purkis
Edith Summerhayes
Karen Young
Denise Dresner

Database Management
Nick Andrews
Tracey Auden
Lorraine Cotterell
Louise Richmond

Design and Production

Production
Tony Ballsdon

Art and Design
Terence Caven

Cartography
Olive Pearson

Picture Research
Elizabeth Loving

Typography
Roger Walker

Computer Typesetting and Page Make-up
Mendip Communications Ltd, Frome, Somerset

Repro and Film Output
Norton Matrix Ltd, Bath
Spectrum Colour, Ipswich

The Millennium Supplement

Specially created for the Millennium edition of *The Hutchinson Encyclopedia*, this supplement presents eight feature essays on subjects which have been of great importance in the twentieth century – from changes in society itself to our attempts to understand the composition of the universe to the renewed questioning about what constitutes art. The set of essays begins with a description of what the term 'millennium' means and of the ways in which previous millennia have been marked.

The essays are followed by four concise chronologies which identify moments of high significance in the past millennium. Special emphasis has been placed on happenings, discoveries, and achievements which illustrate broader developments, mark important 'firsts', and represent turning points within larger historical events.

FEATURE ESSAYS

CHRONOLOGIES OF THE MILLENNIUM

THE END OF A MILLENNIUM

The word 'millennium' – made more familiar than it ever has been as the 20th century reaches its end – has more than one meaning. One meaning, derived from the Latin word *mille*, meaning a thousand, is now used mainly chronologically. With the end of the 20th century the second Christian millennium will end also. Twenty centuries have come and gone since the birth of Christ. A second, far older use of the word was Christian too. Resting not on chronology but on eschatology – doctrines of first and last things – it referred to a thousand-year future rule of Christ following the Second Coming – his return to Earth.

The two meanings of 'millennium' have now been taken out of their specifically Christian context. The dating system of the Christian calendar, which derived from the Roman calendar, is now widely used throughout the world in non-Christian as well as Christian countries. The idea of a future state of bliss has long been secularized and the dream of a millennium need not involve belief in the Second Coming of Christ. Other religions too must be brought into the picture. Islam shares much with the Judeo-Christian vision, and anthropologists have identified non-Christian religious cults, particularly Melanesian cargo cults in the Pacific, which put their trust in a good time coming ahead – at a date unknown. The South American Tupi-Guarani searched for a 'Land without Evil'. New 20th-century sects and religions such as the Rastafarian movement focus on it.

Behind both meanings of the word 'millennium' there is a sense of the future, although it is a future that can be approached dramatically through apocalypse – divine intervention – or gradually through human action. The word need not carry a sense of progress. Moving into a third millennium is often conceived of simply as moving inexorably into the unknown through the passage of time. Yet there are politicians who have looked forward – and still look forward – to a golden age in the same way as religious prophets, some of them promising how to achieve this. The word of hope, 'millenarial', derived from the word millennium, still has more imaginative and emotive content than the word of time, 'millennial'.

The Second Coming. This depiction of the Second Coming dates from *c.* 980 and was made for St Aethelwold, Bishop of Winchester (963–984) by his chaplain Godeman. *The Bridgeman Art Library*

The first Christian millennium

At the end of the first Christian millennium there was little contemporary awareness of its chronological significance. Indeed, both the idea of a century as a unit of time and the idea of time as change were unformed. Medieval reckonings of time were different. Even at the end of the 14th century, when there were signs of increased awareness, the view prevailed that all time was running downhill from the Creation to the Day of Doom (Judgement).

Religious millenarianism had already taken shape within this context and computations were made, for example, by Joachim of Fiore in the 12th century, both about the Second Coming of Christ and about Antichrist – Christ's dark opponent. The English poet John Gower began his *Confessio Amantis/Lover's Confession* (1386–90) with the prophecy that 'the world will change ... till it to nought shall overpass.' Christian millenarians found their inspiration not only in the New Testament's Book of Revelation but also in the books of the Old Testament Hebrew prophets, particularly Daniel. There was parallel Judaic millenarianism which also incorporated different elements. King Simon would inaugurate a reign of peace and the 'Prince of Peace' would reign over the world.

Outside or on the edges of religious orthodoxy there was room for speculation and controversy concerning both the timing of future divine intervention and its relationship to the millennium. When would the Saviour come? During or after the millennium? What would be the signs? The questions continued to be asked – and answered in different fashion – after the Reformation of the 16th century had divided the Christian church. Indeed, millenarian sects were now provided with new opportunities for missionary organization, while remaining outside Protestant as well as Roman Catholic orthodoxy. They were prominent, for example, in 17th-century England under the Commonwealth, and there was a strong millenarial drive in England and Scotland in the 19th century.

A new context

By then, the social and cultural context was quite different from that of the 14th or the 16th century. The 18th-century Enlightenment, a European movement, pitted reason against revelation, and the idea of apocalyptic divine judgement was treated by many Enlightenment philosophers as superstition. Yet one writer, the Marquis de Condorcet, had the notion that human development was in nine phases and culminated in the French Revolution of 1789. He looked far into the future and predicted a tenth phase culminating in the realization of human perfectibility. The French revolutionaries devised a new calendar. The year 1800 was their Year IX. A chronological millennium based on that would have been far away. As it was, the calendar did not even survive Napoleon's empire.

In Condorcet's optimistic vision, and in the claims of the revolutionaries that a new world had been born, industrialization did not figure as an agency of change. But the steam engine had already been invented, and it was through unprecedented growth in wealth, made possible by the exploitation of materials, power, and labour that the world was to change most. In the 19th century Karl Marx appreciated the importance of industrialization, but, seeing history in terms of class struggles as he did, he focused on the conflict between capitalists and proletarians. He foresaw a proletarian revolution which the proletariat – the workers – would be bound to win. That was the first law of capitalist production. Yet the ultimate outcome (and Marx, a Jew by birth if not by faith, gave no date for it) was the millennium of a classless society. He did not conceive this as a Utopia – an ideal state. Indeed, he condemned utopian socialists such as Robert Owen with as much vigour as he condemned capitalists. Owen and his disciples, the Owenites, sometimes talked in millenarian language of 'crisis'. Marx and Marxists, by contrast, talked the language of science. The Marxists devoted most of their attention to the dynamics of the revolutionary struggle, not to talking about secular millennium. Marx described his task as that of changing the world, not merely explaining it. When the time is ripe men should act.

Revolution and evolution

Marx's fascination with the new powers of industrial production was shared by some other socialists, though not all of them believed in revolution. In fact the idea of 'revolution' did not dominate 19th-century scientific thinking. Instead, they were concerned with 'evolution', a concept developed independently by a variety of different thinkers in a variety of different versions. It was central to Charles Darwin, whose *Origin of Species* (1859) shaped nonscientific as well as scientific thought. Unlike revolutionary Marxism, evolutionary theory had no millenarian strand. Yet, like Marxism, it treated 'struggle' as the main theme in nature and in the 'descent of man', envisaging the emergence of 'forms of social life higher than any we have imagined.' A future orientation was fundamental, therefore, both to revolutionary and to evolutionary thought.

Nonetheless, in the evolutionary scenario there were implications also for the understanding of the past. By lengthening the timespan of the planet and of human beings, geologists and biologists effectively disposed of the chronology set out by a 17th-century Irish biblical scholar, Bishop James Usher, who had fixed the date of Creation precisely at 4004 BC.

Fin de Siècle

It was at the end of the 19th century, when a self-conscious sense of *fin de siècle* (end of century) coexisted with enthusiasm for all that was new, that for the first time people argued about just when centuries end, an argument which has continued a century after when not only a century but a millennium was ending. The German emperor Wilhelm II (1859–1941), defying arithmetic, settled it when he ordered a salute of 33 guns on 1 January 1900. And when in 1994 Henry Brooke, then British National Heritage Secretary, a post that did not exist a century earlier, announced that the 20th century – and the millennium – would end not on New Year's Eve 1999 but on 31 December 2000, he was immediately challenged and with the help of *The Times* successfully overruled. Already, indeed on both sides of the Atlantic, travel and hotel tickets had been booked for the millennial date preferred by *The Times* and apparently by the public.

Futurologies

Futurologists had begun writing during the 1960s about the world in 2000 or 2001 without necessarily mentioning the millennium. The American futurologist, Alvin Toffler, did warn the readers of his *Future Shock* in 1971, however, that in 'three short decades between now and the turn of the millennium millions of psychologically normal people will experience an abrupt collision with the future.' Toffler was thinking mainly, although not exclusively, of the continuing communications revolution which was affecting work, leisure, and the sense both of time and space which he wrote about elsewhere. As it was, some believers in the presence or the imminence of a New Age, many of them 20th-century millenarians, thinking in very different prophetic terms, with often apocalyptic images, had concluded that a new millennium, variously named, had already arrived. There were religious cults too in many different countries; their members sometimes believed in marking their Day of Judgement (not necessarily in 2000 or 2001) by committing collective suicide.

Evolutionary thought. English naturalist Charles Darwin, author of *Origin of Species* (1859). At a time when most people still believed in the literal truth of the Bible's account of creation, Darwin's idea that species had evolved gradually helped to shape our sense of the future. *Corbis*

The British millennium

In Britain, under the successive governments of John Major and Tony Blair, the millennium of 2000 was approached expensively, and controversially, largely in terms of festival, with the budget being borne not out of taxation but out of business sponsorship, ticket sales, and a grant from the recently founded National Lottery, handled by a Millennium Commission. In 1994 an exhibition in Greenwich was proposed. Two years later the architect Mike Davies of the Richard Rogers Partnership drew a sketch on the back of a napkin of the Dome which would house the festival. A contractor was appointed and work began. Millennial Central Ltd was set up as a government-owned company in February 1997 under the auspices of the Millennium Commission and, following the victory of the Labour Party at the general election of May of that year, changed its name to the New Millennium Experience Company.

What to put inside the Dome, subject to raising sponsorship funds, was decided after the decision to build it had been taken. History was to have a very small part in the allotted space, and there were to be difficulties in finding sponsors for a history zone or for a 'spirit' zone – called the 'Spirit Level' – which in a multi-religious society could not be permitted to proclaim exclusively Christian millennial messages. Meanwhile, a range of specific millennial projects had been approved in London and the provinces. The emphasis throughout was on 'benefits to Britain'. Yet it is clear that the next millennium will not be a distinctively British millennium (nor, despite empire, was the last). Modern technology, particularly communications and bio-based technology, is global. So too is economics, an economics of interdependence.

Millennial opportunities

Apart from the long-term value of some of the millennial projects, a number of them based on the local community, there are opportunities at the end of a millennium, as there are at national and international exhibitions, for social and cultural historical accounting. What were the most important events in the millennium that is ending? Who were its outstanding characters – poets, artists, and musicians as well as philosophers, scientists, and political leaders? What were the most significant breaks and continuities within it? How has it left religion and science?

The new media of the 20th century, recording as well as informing and entertaining, make it possible for the first time in history for everyone to share in the process of accounting. We could have done more to recapture in sound and vision the experience not of a millennium but of the last century within it. One proposed millennial project was to display a giant microchip on a hillside as horses used to be displayed in chalk. It would proclaim our digital revolution leading with no break into the next millennium far more proudly and pertinently than any dome.

Asa Briggs

The Individual in Society: A Hundred Years of Social Expectation

The dramatic jump in levels of personal education and income over the 20th century have greatly increased the life choices for the vast majority of people in the Western industrialized world – though by no means all. Knowledge and money have created industrialized countries in which most are able to enjoy an array of domestic comforts and leisure opportunities beyond the wildest dreams of even the richest living a hundred years ago. Yet this consumer culture has also spawned a glut of social problems unheard of at the beginning of the last century, such as traffic congestion and pollution, which are now taken for granted as the inevitable costs of modern life.

In just five generations this individual empowerment has ripped apart the traditional fabric of society. Institutions such as the family and the church have altered dramatically, global communications and international economics have challenged the authority even of governments, and the moral certainties which governed the relationship between individuals and communities for centuries have now been questioned.

We are all getting older

A century ago, when children were still sent up chimneys or down mines and infant deaths were common, women usually died before their late 40s and men were lucky to celebrate their 45th birthday. Thanks to social reforms, medical advances and healthier diets, babies born in 2000 can expect to live about 30 years longer than those born in 1900. Yet these changes in average life expectancy mask large and growing differences in lifespan between rich and poor. For instance, unskilled men are likely to die at least five years younger than those with professional careers. Unskilled workers are also three times more likely to admit to smoking, and an average 30-year-old smoker will die seven years sooner than a non-smoking contemporary.

Regardless of social class, children are no longer sent out to work. Instead, they are sent to school. Many infants now begin formal education from the age of 3, usually lasting at least until they are 16, and a rising proportion attend colleges and universities. The length of this education has delayed significantly the age at which people start work, and start a family. Thanks also to the widespread use of contraception since the 1960s, women are choosing to have their children later in life. Those over 30 are now more likely to give birth than those under 20, which was when their great grandparents probably first had children. Most are also choosing to have fewer children than their parents had, which means population growth in industrialized countries is beginning to slow down. In some countries, the total population size is actually set to fall for the first time.

As the birth rate has slowed and life lengths have increased, the average age of the population in developed societies is rising. The numbers over the common retirement age of 65 have shot up by 50% in the last 40 years of the 20th century, and in some countries within a decade or so of the beginning of the new millennium those aged over 65 will outnumber those under 16 for the first time.

These demographic shifts have had a profound impact on society. For example, as the number of old people escalates, so does the cost of providing pensions and health care. Perhaps even more importantly, as young adults increasingly decide not to have children but to exploit their independence, family structures have been transformed and an economically and socially powerful youth culture has been created.

At work and at home

Newborn babies are now far less likely to be raised in a traditional family unit, with their mother cooking and cleaning while their father goes out to work. They are also unlikely to be helped by a tightly knit support network of grandparents and other relatives living in the same town.

A hundred years ago, virtually all workers in industrialized economies were men. But equal education, equal pay, and equal opportunities legislation – coupled with the rise in service industry jobs – mean that about four in ten of the workforce are now female. The decline in heavy manufacturing and production-line factory working has also left larger numbers of men unemployed for longer periods of time. This restructuring of the workforce, with growing financial independence and civil rights for women, has helped transform the traditional roles in the family. Although most women still do most housework, the domestic responsibilities are less well defined.

As knowledge and money replace marriage as the main route to adult independence, so family structures have been revolutionized. In just one generation, the numbers marrying have halved, the numbers divorcing have trebled, and the proportion of children born outside marriage has quadrupled. In some

Women working in a cotton mill. At the beginning of the 20th century women made up only a small part of the paid workforce. However, by the end of the century that situation had changed greatly. *Private Collection*

countries there will soon be more unmarried than married adults for the first time. Consequently, about a third of births now take place outside of marriage. And an increasing proportion of people are choosing to live alone. Even those who do marry are no longer guaranteed to stay together until death do them part. Since reforms in the 1960s made divorce easier, the divorce rate has soared, so more children are raised by a single parent or in a stepfamily. As recently as 1970, fewer than one in ten families were headed by a lone parent, but in some countries that has already doubled to more than one in five.

High divorce rates, single parents, second generation families with parents and children from former marriages, and people choosing to live alone, with friends, or in same-sex relationships, mean that there is no longer a single 'model' family. This diversity, and the fact that people are having fewer children, has roughly halved the average household size over the century, down from 5 people per home in 1900 to about 2.5 today.

A hundred years ago, almost all children were raised by two parents whose marriage had been blessed by a religious ceremony. Indeed, the traditional family unit and the church were the very foundation of social life. Many people today will have virtually no contact with either.

Inner city life

Whatever the size and shape of people's families, they are now far more likely to live in a city than a century ago. To accommodate the rising population and the smaller family unit, the number of dwellings in the industrialized world grew by almost 50% in the last 40 years of the 20th century, with the majority of these concentrated in urban areas.

The move towards 'urbanization' is set to continue as people become more mobile, willing to leave their childhood home to look for jobs. At the turn of the last century, people began to move from one town to another, but since the 1950s they have moved in increasing numbers from one country to another. Importing with them different cultures and traditions, these immigrants have started to forge multicultural understanding and ethnic diversity.

Despite the projected slowdown in population growth, the need for more homes has left governments of densely populated countries with the difficult balance of allowing enough new houses to be built while also protecting green fields and the environment.

Overcrowding in cities has fostered a number of new social problems. Cities, for instance, are often the focus for racial tensions and illegal drug taking. Cities are also where the poorest are most visible, whether through street begging and sleeping rough or lower standards of housing and education. Cities usually have the worst traffic congestion, too. While virtually no one owned a motor car a hundred years ago, they are now so common that they often clog the streets reducing average speeds to little faster than those in the days of the horse and cart. Cities also suffer the highest rates of crime. More than half of property crimes and more than a third of property crime victims are found in a fifth of the communities in the developed world, and these tend to be in the poorer parts of urban areas.

Crime has risen throughout all the developed economies at the rate of about 5% a year since 1920. Yet in the early 1990s it stabilized and in some cases even started to fall. Although the fear of crime continues to rise, the reality is that people in the USA and European Union countries are now less likely to suffer a burglary or violent incident than ten years ago.

Consumer culture

Escalating incomes and wealth have allowed the widespread purchase of consumer durables since the 1950s. The consumer revolution over the past half century began with 'white goods' such as washing machines and refrigerators, followed by central heating, telephones, and other home comforts – appliances which were unknown at the beginning of the 20th century, luxuries by the middle of the century, and necessities by its end.

The individual at school. The experience of children in British primary schools in the 1990s is very different to that of children at the beginning of the 20th century. Today, education geared towards the child's viewpoint and learning through exploration and experiment has replaced rote learning within more regimented conditions. *Peter Arkell/Impact*

The advent of cheap package tours abroad changed the nature of people's holidays almost as much as the first television sets transformed their leisure activities. Televisions offered a rival entertainment to cinemas and theatres and they ushered in an information age which has seen homes and cars turned into electronic playpens. Video recorders, satellite dishes, compact disc players, and home computers are all now commonplace. The pace of change is increasing. By 1997, there were 75 million Internet subscribers world-wide, but by 2002 there are likely to be 400 million. Over the same period, the number of mobile phone owners will have increased from 250 million to 700 million.

It is no surprise that the availability of this glittering array of material possessions has taken a rising proportion of people's incomes, as have motoring and other leisure pursuits. Although the biggest weekly household bill is still for food and drink, the proportion of income spent on these basics has halved since the 1960s from about 30% to roughly 15%.

Yet these modern comforts are not available to all. As societies have become wealthier, the gap between the richest and the poorest has grown. In parts of Europe, for instance, the richest 1% of adults owns about 20% of the total marketable wealth, while the poorest half owns less than 10% of the total. While those in the middle third or richest third of the population have seen their incomes grow substantially in the past 20 years, those in the bottom third have not, leaving them relatively worse off. This has led to concern that those at the very bottom – the homeless, the unemployed, and those dependent on welfare payments – are becoming cut off from mainstream society in an 'underclass'.

Modern life

During the 20th century, the uniformity of life has been smashed by higher education and higher incomes, the advent of equal rights for women, the collapse of traditional family structures, the decline of factory working, a plurality of leisure lifestyles, and the proliferation of consumer gadgets. Although there have been negative consequences for society, including rising crime, this has helped to cause a positive and huge increase in individual freedom.

The pace of this change – technological and social – which has begun to accelerate over the past 40 years, is set to get even faster in the new millennium. Greater wealth and better educational standards are likely to offer even more independence and more choices for most people. With the extension of world-wide mobility, greater ethnic diversity, and equality of opportunities for the disabled, life styles are likely to become even more diverse.

Yet these increased personal freedoms have already often conflicted with the structures and rules which give order to society. Many institutions which helped bring individuals together in society are crumbling, and it is by no means clear how social stability and moral order will be maintained in the future.

The unanswered question for the 21st century is whether the declining institutions of the past will be capable of reform, or of being replaced by new means of binding society together, while also accommodating increased individual freedom. If not, and if the gap between the richest and poorest continues to grow as fast as it has in recent decades, individuals may have a less harmonious relationship with each other than they have had in the past.

Simon Buckby

THE WORLD VILLAGE: Living in a Global Economy

Most people are now familiar with the terms 'global economy' and 'global village'. Some observers see globalization as a wholly positive and liberating phenomenon indicating a breaking down of barriers between nations. Others perceive threats, to the ability of governments to control their economies and to the ability of individuals to control their lives. Others still believe that the global economy is nothing new and that the whole concept is overblown.

When some observers talk about the global economy they mean the apparent triumph of Western market capitalism as the main way of organizing economic life throughout most of the world, following the collapse of the Soviet bloc. The Western model of competing firms, usually privately owned, supplying goods and services to consumers in the marketplace, with the state confined to regulating this activity and providing those services the market cannot efficiently provide, does indeed appear to be dominant. In almost every country in the world one can see the products and trademarks of Western market capitalism, from familiar fast-food establishments and soft drinks through to cars, computers, and footwear. Allied to this are all the trappings of Western or, more accurately, American, pop culture.

However, some people use the term global economy to mean more than this. It implies a much greater role for flows of trade, investment, and finance across international boundaries. This in turn appears to imply a greater interdependence between countries. The downside of this is that if there is an economic crisis in one part of the world, the consequences are quickly felt elsewhere. At the end of the 1990s a number of Asian and Latin American countries faced economic difficulties, and the media in Europe and North America sounded warnings on what this might mean for economic prosperity in the West.

Multinational companies have establishments in many different nations. It is alleged that these companies can exploit their workforces or the environment and can threaten to pull out of countries whose governments do not follow the economic, taxation, and environmental policies which these multinationals desire. International financial institutions can apparently punish those countries that pursue policies they do not like by pulling out their funds. Some people worry that these unelected bodies have more power than elected governments. Moreover, these concerns are not confined to developing countries. The governments in rich developed countries are worried too that they may not be able to set the tax or environmental policies they would like for fear of being punished by multinational companies and international financial institutions.

YEARS OF DUST
DUST STORM
RESETTLEMENT ADMINISTRATION
Rescues Victims
Restores Land to Proper Use

A poster of a farmer facing ruin during the Great Depression, designed by US artist Bem Shahn. A world economy was in place at the start of the 20th century but the Depression helped to destroy it. *Corbis*

Why global economy?

If these worries are justified then why do we have a global economy in the first place? Of course people in different countries have been trading with each other for thousands of years. Economists first began to write about modern trade patterns in the 19th century as the spreading Industrial Revolution was associated with increased international commerce. They came up with a concept to explain why international trade took place. Countries would concentrate on producing the goods and services that they were relatively efficient at producing and would trade them for the goods and services that they were less efficient at producing. As each country concentrated on producing the things in which it had a comparative advantage and swapping them for things which other countries were better at producing, everyone would be better off.

At the most trivial level this seems obvious. Without international trade, people in Britain would not be able to eat types of food which cannot be grown here or use raw materials which are not available in this country. In addition, one economy might be better at producing cars and another at producing medical drugs, in which case both should concentrate on what they do well and trade for the other product. In fact, most trade, especially between industrialized countries, is now in the same products. Consumers in Britain, France, Germany, Italy, the USA, and Japan all buy cars made in all the other countries. This is because as countries grow richer consumers want to have a very wide range of choice of goods and services, and international trade facilitates this.

Also countries which want to invest more in, for example, developing their transport infrastructure, but which have limited domestic savings, can borrow the funds from institutions in other countries. And savers in lending countries can be better off if their overseas lending yields them a higher return than that from domestic borrowers.

Is the global economy new?

We may think that the concept of the global economy is new. In fact, a global economy was already in existence before World War I. In 1913 the UK exported a significantly greater proportion of the output of its factories than in the 1990s. It was the main source of funds for investment throughout the world and UK firms had establishments on most continents. A number of Western countries were integrated into the world economy in a fashion which matches patterns of economic

The Hong Kong stock exchange in the late 20th century. The world's largest stock exchanges are London, New York (Wall Street), and Tokyo. The oldest stock exchanges are Antwerp 1460, Hamburg 1558, Amsterdam 1602, New York 1790, and London 1801. *Julian Calder/Impact*

integration today, with extensive flows of trade and capital, and very extensive flows of immigration, and today's developing countries were integrated into this first global economy as the colonies of the richer nations.

World War I and the Great Depression of the interwar years shattered this first global economy. The way in which the depression that started in the USA in 1929 spread over the whole world in the early 1930s illustrates that vulnerability to outside economic events is nothing new. Unemployment rose sharply across the globe, and most countries retreated from the international economy by putting up barriers to trade with other nations. Nothing in the experience of countries since 1945 comes close to this global economic meltdown. After World War II the international economy had to be built up again almost from scratch. It was not until comparatively recently that the world economy once again reached the levels of integration which characterized the globe before World War I.

In 1973 another economic crisis hit the world following a sharp increase in the price of oil. This event emphasized once more the vulnerability of individual economies to events elsewhere in the world.

The organizations of the international economy

After World War II the nations of the world were determined not to repeat that terrible conflict or the economic dislocations of the 1930s which helped to produce it. Instead the key postwar international economic institutions were established by the victorious Western powers, primarily the USA and the UK, following a meeting at Bretton Woods in the US state of New Hampshire in 1944. These institutions were the International Monetary Fund (IMF) and what became known as the World Bank. The names of these institutions are in some ways deceptive. The IMF acts rather like a bank, in offering advice and loans to countries facing financial problems. The World Bank on the other hand is a fund that lends or gives grants to countries to foster their long-term economic development. Both organizations now deal mainly with developing countries, though originally they also interacted with the Western economies.

The IMF is the more controversial of the two institutions, as its loans come with advice or conditions attached, which, many critics argue, force governments in developing countries to introduce policies that hurt the most vulnerable in society. The IMF argues that it is more often the governments in those countries whose policies hurt their own people. The World Bank also offers advice to countries, at the same time as providing them with funds for development. Over time the more successful developing countries have been able to access more and more finance from private banks and other institutions, offering the World Bank the chance to concentrate on the poorest countries. Individual governments in rich developed countries also offer financial aid direct to developing countries and this aid too often comes with advice and other strings attached.

More recently these twin institutions have been joined by the World Trade Organization (WTO) which took over from another forum, the General Agreement on Tariffs and Trade (GATT), which played a major role in the postwar period in persuading governments to remove barriers to goods and services from other countries. The Organization for Economic Cooperation and Development (OECD) started life as the body which dispersed the funds made available by the USA under the Marshall Plan to help rebuild Europe's war-shattered economies. It now acts as a forum for debate for most of the richest countries on issues such as unemployment and taxation. The G-7 group of countries are the world's largest and richest: the USA, Japan, Germany, France, the UK, Italy, and Canada. Ministers and officials from these countries have been meeting regularly since the 1970s to discuss the main issues facing the global economy. More recently, Russia has been invited to attend these meetings.

What do all these world economic organizations have in common? They are all dominated by the rich developed countries. Most of the rules of the international economy are thus set by these countries and therefore many developing countries feel excluded. By virtue of their huge populations, China and Brazil have economies which are now bigger than Canada's and are certainly more important than Russia's. A major issue with regard to these international institutions is how to make them more representative of, and responsive to, the concerns of the developing countries.

Some of the most important institutions of the international economy are organized regionally rather than globally. The European Union (EU) certainly has a bigger impact on the lives of people in the 15 member states than any of the international institutions. The countries of North America and of the Asia-Pacific region have also fostered new links between the countries in their parts of the world. So alongside anything which may be described as globalization, we see the countries of particular regions coming closer together. This raises the issue of whether individual countries in those regions can afford to stay out of these arrangements, and, if they do, whether they pay a price for their independence.

The future

A number of unanswered questions remain about the course of the international economy as we enter the 21st century. Will regional coalitions of countries such as the EU become the main players in the world, and how far will international institutions such as the UN, the IMF, and the World Bank retain their importance? Do these institutions, which date from just after World War II, need overhauling to make them relevant for the new century and to increase their responsiveness to the needs of the developing countries?

Most people in the affluent developed countries have probably benefited from the global economy which has brought with it a wider choice of goods and services at more competitive prices. For many developing countries the benefits may seem less obvious, and, indeed, closing the gap between the relatively rich and the relatively poor countries remains the greatest challenge facing the international economy.

Peter Robinson

The Era of Mass Communication

The 20th century was good for utopian dreamers: a succession of new communications technologies regularly awakened the same set of dreams of freedom, openness, democracy, and equality that fuelled 17th-century thought. Communication technologies are shrinking the globe and forming an 'information revolution' expected to be as transforming as the Industrial Revolution before it.

Mass changes rarely fit neatly into the time classifications we would like, and the communications revolution is no exception – its roots are in the 18th century, in the discovery of electricity, and it first came to flower in the Victorian era, when the telegraph was built. The first transmission of speech via radio waves was in 1900, but mass radio broadcasting really emerged in the early 1920s. The first television transmission of recognizable human features was in 1925, and although the first scheduled television broadcasts took place in 1928 and the BBC started broadcasting in 1936, it was not until 1951 that television sets became widespread. In the USA there were 1.5 million sets in 1950, about 15 million only a year later.

Many things had to come together to create the mass communications revolution of the 20th century. First and foremost was electrification, completed in the USA by 1940. Second was mass production, required to build the many devices that enable communications. A huge leap forward in manufacturing, making devices both cheaper and faster to produce, was the development in 1948 of miniature transistors to replace the big, unwieldy, and delicate components, such as vacuum tubes and transistors, out of which early radios, televisions, and even computers were made. As we move into the 21st century, electronic devices are incredibly cheap and reliable by the standards of a hundred years ago, largely due to the development of printed circuit boards and silicon chips.

The advent of computers

The biggest development, however, was the advent of computers, first as giant, room-sized boxes, and eventually as desktop machines requiring a much lower level of skill. The first mechanical computer was conceived by Charles Babbage in 1835, but he never completed it. The first electronic computer, Colossus, was built in 1943. The first to use binary arithmetic and store instructions internally, the foundation of all of today's digital computing, was built in 1948 by John Von Neumann. In the mass market, the machine that had the biggest impact was the Apple Macintosh, released in 1984 as 'the computer for the rest of us', which turned computers from command-driven devices into machines ordinary people could interact with.

Computing and electronics generally are heavily indebted to the military establishment for the basic research that fuelled their development. During World War II the perceived need for faster calculating ability led the military to fund many experiments with large computers. In 1953 IBM began manufacturing large computers, which it saw as the business machines of the future. After the war was over, two major US Department of Defense agencies played key roles: first, the National Aeronautics and Space Administration (NASA), and second, the Advanced Research Projects Agency (ARPA). Both were set up in 1958 by President Eisenhower to rebuild America's scientific and technical leadership after Russia's successful 1957 launch of *Sputnik*, the first satellite ever to orbit the Earth. The chance acquisition of a large computer in 1961 led ARPA to hire psychologist J C R Licklider, who in 1960 published a seminal paper imagining a close partnership between humans and computers. Much of today's Internet was presaged in a memo he wrote shortly after joining ARPA, which posited the idea of a language of protocols that computers could share to enable them to talk to each other. By 1969 ARPA had started funding the first nationwide networking experiments that eventually became the Internet.

Looking in. Satellite image of Death Valley, California, USA, taken from the US Earth-survey satellite *Landsat* 1983. The author Arthur C Clarke predicted the key role of satellites in mass communication. *Corbis*

The Internet was restricted to academic and research use until 1993, when the US government allowed it to carry commercial traffic. This opened the way for business and consumer use of the Internet, which in turn sparked the creation of new businesses to provide Internet access as well as the opening of gateways onto the Internet from existing commercial online services and hobbyist bulletin board systems. By early 1999, it was estimated that 100 million users worldwide were on the Internet.

Science fiction becomes science fact

Many of the developments of the later half of the 20th century were foreseen by science fiction writers who thrived in the scientific and technological excitement of the 1950s. Arthur C Clarke, author of the original story that became the Stanley Kubrick film *2001*, imagined the Earth surrounded by communications satellites long before the 1980s when this fantasy became a reality. But science fiction characteristically deals with the obsessions and concerns of its own time. According to much of 1950s science fiction, the world of the year 2000 would have only one giant, planet-sized computer, stored on the Moon perhaps, and the Earth itself would be swarming with personal robots. No one imagined that robots would be nearly impossible to build while computers would proliferate everywhere. In the Western world today, even homes that do not have a personal computer, will often be populated with devices run by internal microprocessors such as microwave ovens and washing machines. It was not until computers became widespread and networking experiments became the Internet that science fiction writers, notably William Gibson in his 1984 novel *Neuromancer*, began to imagine a completely 'wired' world.

The impact of the Internet

All sorts of predictions have been made about the ultimate impact of the Internet: that it will

Looking out. Eight of the 27 radio telescopes at the National Radio Astronomy Observatory in New Mexico. Breakthroughs by large-scale scientific and technological projects have contributed massively to the development of everyday communications tools. *Corbis*

upend existing power structures, kill off the nation-state, bring about world peace, broaden public education, and enable developing nations to transform themselves and their economies. The same predictions were made, in their early days, about telegraphy, radio, and television. At least some of the predictions seem likely to come true. Some would argue that the individual power of nation-states is already being eaten away by global economic realities. The growth of the first global satellite news channel, CNN, for example, changed the way politicians handle wartime broadcasts. Now one message can be heard by everyone – troops, families back home, enemy leaders – when once military leaders could tailor individual messages for each of these groups. The media is independent of governments: the news of the 1989 student protest in Tiananmen Square escaped from China by fax; and the news from Kosovo, as the 1999 bombings began, escaped by e-mail and via Internet broadcasts of the banned Serbia-based radio station B92.

Few inventors really understand what the children of their thoughts will be good for. Thomas Edison imagined when he invented the gramophone that it would be used primarily for dictating office memos. Alexander Graham Bell, in inventing the telephone, imagined it would be used to broadcast music. The precursor of the Internet, ARPANET, was set up to enable researchers to share files, just as the World Wide Web, when invented by British physicist Tim Berners-Lee in 1984, was created to enable researchers to make information easily available to each other, not as a shopping medium. The early days of a new medium are invariably marked by a period of imitation, during which the new development is imagined to be almost, but not quite, like an existing one. So in the early days of movies, radio, and television many stage plays were broadcast, and in the early days of the World Wide Web, which we are still experiencing, there are numerous debates over whether the Web should be considered a new form of publishing or a new form of broadcasting, or perhaps just more computer software. The early wisdom was that the Internet was, and would always be, so anarchic and uncontrollable that it was hostile to commercial, especially large commercial, companies. While this may yet prove to be true, at the start of the 21st century much of the Internet is ultimately in the hands of relatively few telecommunications companies, and the desktop computer software market is dominated by a single manufacturer.

The Internet, however, unlike the earlier inventions that preceded it, has one major difference: where recording and broadcasting media enable one-to-many communication, and fax and the telephone enable fast one-to-one communication, the Internet in addition enables many-to-many communication. The plethora of online forums, chat groups, conferences, and cyber-communities that have sprung up on every online service, from the bulletin board systems of the 1970s onwards, are evidence that this unique feature of Web communication both meets a need and is able to thrive without commercial support.

Many other issues are raised by the convergence of mass communication and computers: the loss of privacy, problems of censorship and control, and the fear that real-world relationships will be replaced by virtual ones conducted at a safe distance. In addition, it could be argued that the mass communications of the 20th century have both destroyed elites (by giving everyone access to computing power and the ability to publish worldwide) and created new ones (by giving ever-greater power to those who understand and control technology and the media). The Internet, by speeding up communications and in combination with the ready availability of cheap computers and the growth of home-based 'knowledge worker' jobs, both drives and supports many trends. What is not clear is whether this will give people happier, more humane lives than working full-time in an office in a major corporation. As the century turns, we still have some choice over what the Internet will become and what impact it has on our lives.

Wendy M Grossman

A CHANGING SPIRITUALITY: The Progress of Religion in the 20th Century

The world we live in at the beginning of the third millennium is not the world of our grandparents and certainly not that of our great grandparents. The 20th century has been a century in which the religious landscape has dramatically changed.

In Judaism two 20th century events stand out as being of supreme importance, both of which have led to self-examination and tensions within the faith: the Holocaust – the Nazi regime's extermination of nearly 6 million Jews – and the establishment of the Jewish State of Israel on 14 May 1948.

Another very important religious development in the 20th century was the emergence of a revitalized and confident Islam. However, whereas the first half of the century saw Islamic countries united in a common struggle to overthrow colonialism, since then splits have emerged between 'progressive' and 'conservative' Muslims, the latter being increasingly strengthened by the emergence of 'fundamentalist' organizations – another significant religious development.

Unlike Islam, Western Christianity has moved from confidence to crisis. Although some individual churches may be experiencing growth, on the whole Christianity has witnessed a decline in attendance. Of particular significance is the shift of the centre of Christianity from the developed world to the developing world, from the West to Africa, Asia, Oceania, and Latin America. In these areas of the world Christianity has experienced remarkable growth.

When the British arrived in India in the 18th century Hinduism was lethargic. By the time the British left India in the middle of the 20th century Hinduism had become, like Islam, self-confident and assertive. Hindu confidence and the subsequent growth of political awareness and nationalism in India eventually led to Indian independence in 1947. For various reasons, the newly independent India did not become a Hindu state, but rather a secular state. This led to the passing of laws which have tended to undermine important aspects of Indian social and religious life (for example, the caste system). This in turn has led to the development of reactions and tensions within Hinduism. Also important for Hinduism has been its growth into a world religion, and in particular, the increasing appeal in the West of Hindu religious ideas.

Similarly, Buddhism in its various forms is experiencing a resurgence and, as a result of its very successful missionary activity, it too has emerged as a world religion. However, in its Asian homelands the experience of Buddhists in the 20th century has been very mixed. Although Buddhist nationalism helped secure the independence of Burma and Sri Lanka in 1948, and although Buddhism is the state religion of Thailand, it has suffered greatly under successive communist regimes, firstly in the Soviet Union and Mongolia and then in North Korea, China, Tibet, Vietnam, Laos, and Cambodia. Perhaps the most notable of these invasions was that of Tibet by communist China in 1950 and China's attempt wholly to destroy the Tibetan religion and culture.

Worshippers at the Great Mosque in Touba, Senegal. The 20th century has witnessed the emergence of a revitalized Islam. *Corbis*

The 20th century has also seen Sikhism emerge out of the Punjab to become a world religion. Although, in an attempt to secure employment, many Sikh men who travelled to the West earlier in the century abandoned their turbans and cut their hair, things changed in the 1960s when their families joined them. Sikh communities emerged in the West and, with them, a new confidence.

Religious plurality

For various reasons, people, sometimes whole communities, have travelled from the countries in which they were born to settle in other countries and cultures. This has led to a situation in which many people in the world live in religiously plural societies. Moreover, not only do modern methods of travel mean that the world's cultures are only a few hours away, but, thanks to radio and television, fewer and fewer people are able to avoid learning about other cultures and religious communities. As a result people at the turn of the third millennium are increasingly aware of and influenced by religious plurality.

Although it is hard to underestimate the impact of religious plurality, it is actually nothing new. There has always been religious diversity in the world and it has always been difficult for even the most isolated of tribes to remain ignorant of the fact that other people exist who hold different beliefs from their own. However, what is new in the 20th century is an increased exposure to and, consequently, a greater understanding of the beliefs of others. For example, whereas many in the West at the beginning of the 20th century would have known very little about non-Christian faiths, and probably regarded non-Christians as deluded and possibly backward, generally speaking this is not the case nowadays. Not only are people much more tolerant of and interested in the religious beliefs of others but, in some cases, they adopt those beliefs in preference to the dominant beliefs in their own culture.

Although some people have felt threatened by religious plurality, others celebrate it. Many people will argue that no one culture is superior and no one religion possesses the whole truth about God, humanity, and the world. Indeed, it is argued that there are no absolute standards of good or bad, right or wrong, truth or error which are applicable to all people everywhere – this is 'relativism'. Beliefs, morals, and values are relatively true only, not universally or absolutely true. Hence, the principal relativist response to other beliefs and practices is tolerance – 'live and let live'.

Secularization

In most industrial societies there has been a decline, not only of the social significance of religion, but also of its appeal. For example, European church membership has dropped by around 15% during the course of the 20th century. Although it is popular to claim that the declining significance of religion is a necessary feature of a modern educated society, there is too much evidence to the contrary to support the claim. Indeed, some sociologists have gone so far as to argue that religion will always be a feature of human society. Such is the human mind that it will never be satisfied with a purely physical explanation of the universe. As such, when mainstream religions become more secular and decline (as Christianity has done in the West) new forms of religion will emerge to satisfy this human religious need.

Perhaps the most prominent feature of 20th-century religion is the massive proliferation of new and alternative forms of religion.

As well as the alternative religious groups which can trace their origins directly back to one of the major world religions, there has been a proliferation of 'New Age' groups that tend to pick and mix from a variety of religious sources. The New Age is religion for late 20th-century consumer culture.

Apocalypticism

On the morning of 20 March 1995 five members of Aum Supreme Truth shocked the world with a nerve gas attack in the subways of rush-hour Tokyo. Their leader, Shoko Asahara, was a man who had visions of an Armageddon out of which a new Kingdom of Aum would emerge. Although there have always been such apocalyptic groups, they seem to have proliferated in the final decades of the 20th century.

Convinced that the emergence of Islam, New Age religion, the global economic system, and much else is evidence of the Antichrist, some fundamentalist Christians have insisted that humanity is now living in 'the last days'. David Koresh and the Branch Davidians, 86 of whom died in the fire at Ranch Apocalypse in April 1993, armed themselves for the end of the world which they believed was imminent.

Another feature of late 20th-century religion has been the emergence of UFO movements, some of which also have strong apocalyptic beliefs. For example, interpreting the arrival of the Hale-Bopp Comet as a sign of the end, the Heaven's Gate group committed mass suicide in March 1997 because they believed the comet's tail concealed a spacecraft which would transport them to another realm of existence.

Fundamentalisms

Conspicuous in 20th-century religion has been the emergence of increasingly vocal and active fundamentalisms. Although, strictly speaking, the term 'fundamentalism' refers to an American Protestant Christian movement which arose in the 1920s, more recently it has been applied to movements in other faiths (particularly Islam), which seek to protect traditional beliefs. Fundamentalists feel that the core traditional beliefs of their faith must be defended against modernist interpretations and the findings of critical scholarship, otherwise the faith itself collapses. For example, in Christianity, it is argued that if the early chapters of Genesis (which speak of God's creation of the world and humanity) are not literally and scientifically true in every respect, then the validity of the whole Bible is placed in doubt. Hence, many fundamentalists feel bound to do battle with evolutionary science, which is understood to cast doubt on aspects of the Creation narrative in the Bible.

Interfaith cooperation

In Chicago in 1893 the World Parliament of Religions (a gathering of representatives from the world religions) marked the beginning of the interfaith movement, the concern of which is to foster respectful and cooperative relationships between the religions of the world. From this gathering emerged the International Association for Religious Freedom, followed in 1936 by the World Congress of Faith. Since then, as the century progressed and religious plurality increased, there have been many interfaith initiatives including a second World Parliament of Religions (1993). Although relationships between religions are still competitive rather than cooperative, and although fundamentalisms are an increasingly powerful force in world religion, a century of global interfaith dialogue has borne fruit. Members of the world faiths are organizing local, national, and international networks to stimulate dialogue and interfaith understanding. More than any period in the history of religions, members of the world religions are reassessing their attitudes to other faiths.

Faith in the future

It seems clear that those who predict a secular future will be disappointed. From Neanderthal humanity to the present day, through philosophical and technological revolutions, religion has not simply survived, but thrived as a central characteristic of human culture. There is no indication that this will change.

It does seem likely that the major world religions, particularly where they are in decline (for instance, traditional Christianity in the West), will be increasingly challenged by an ever-greater variety of new and alternative religions, and particularly by New Age and eclectic forms of spirituality.

Along with this growing religious diversity, over the next couple of decades two broad streams of thought are likely to become more pronounced. First, a conservative stream, the extreme of which is fundamentalism, will feel the need to defend traditional orthodoxy. Second, a liberal stream of religious thought will increasingly question the dogmatism in the world religions, strive towards a common global understanding of religion, and possibly succumb to relativism. Although the first stream will tend to characterize religion in the developing world and the second stream will tend to characterize religion in developed societies, these different tendencies will be found throughout the world. Each will continue to emerge as a response to the assumptions of societies characterized by the opposite tendency. For example, conservative religion will continue to challenge relativism in the West, just as liberalizing tendencies will continue to challenge conservative and fundamentalist religion.

Chris Partridge

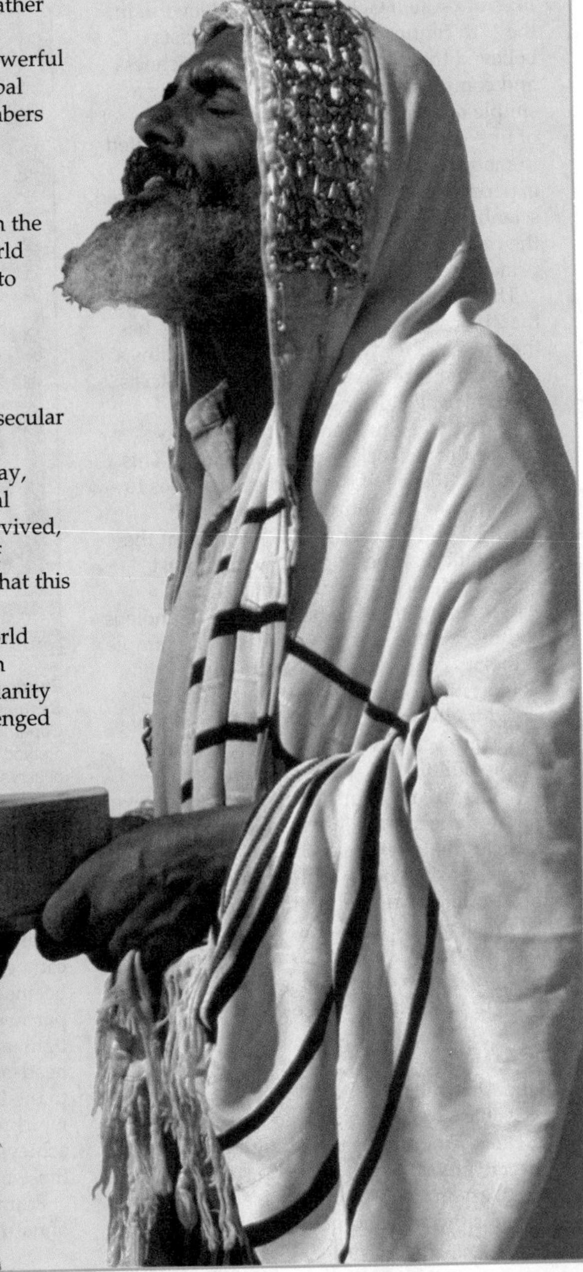

A supplicant prays near the Western ('wailing') Wall, Jerusalem, Israel in 1980. In Judaism two events mark the 20th century more than any others – the Holocaust and the creation of the Jewish state of Israel. *Gary Braasch/Corbis*

Understanding the Universe: From Atoms to M Theory

At the end of the last millennium science as we know it did not exist. Today our lives have been transformed by its dazzling successes. The scientific method seems like a golden path to truth, capable not only of explaining how the world works but, as a bonus, spawning countless technological marvels. Where will it all end? Is science a completable project, or will nature always present mysteries to baffle us?

The idea that humans could come to understand the world through rational reasoning began with the ancient Greek philosophers, two and a half millennia ago. They developed logic and mathematics, and pondered the great questions of existence, such as the nature of mind and matter, the organization of the heavens, and whether time had a beginning.

True science, however, had to await the likes of Galileo Galilei and Isaac Newton in the 17th century. These early physicists believed that beneath the stunning richness and complexity of the natural world lay a simple and elegant unity, in the form of a set of universal laws that could be encapsulated in mathematical equations. By conducting experiments and observations, they supposed, scientists might tease out the rules on which the cosmos runs, and thus unveil deep principles that link all physical things.

Three hundred years on, as we move into the 21st century, the dream that science has the power to unify all knowledge remains a tantalizing lure. Some theoretical physicists think they can glimpse a system of mathematical equations that will finally expose the bedrock of physical reality. This ultimate 'theory of everything' promises to explain how the entire universe is put together. If it succeeds, it will represent the culmination of the so-called reductionist programme begun by the Greeks.

Reductionism is the belief that the whole is nothing but the sum of its parts. For example, in the 5th century BC the philosopher Democritus conjectured that although the world might look complicated, all material things are actually composed of the same simple building blocks, or atoms.

What we call atoms today are not, however, the fundamental, indestructible, elementary particles that the Greeks had in mind. They are composite bodies with components inside them. Still, the central notion remains valid. If we break atoms apart, and probe inside their constituents, we might eventually find truly primitive, indecomposable entities that go to make up everything in the cosmos.

Particles

Belief that such a bottom level of structure exists has spurred a vast and expensive research programme called high-energy particle physics. This subject began with the discovery in the 1930s that the atomic nucleus contains protons and neutrons. In the decades that followed, many other particles were found too, most of them very unstable and short-lived. Today, scores of subatomic fragments have been created and studied in the laboratory using giant atom smashers. These gargantuan devices accelerate electrons and protons to enormous energies and then collide them. The debris from these violent encounters contains all manner of particles that exist only fleetingly. The jewel in the crown of this endeavour is the giant particle accelerator called the Large Electron Positron Collider (LEP) at the CERN Laboratory in Switzerland. A ring-shaped tube in a tunnel 3.8 m/12.5 ft wide and 27 km/16.7 mi long, it can be used to accelerate counter-rotating beams of electrons and their antimatter partners, positrons, to very near the speed of light, at which point they are brought into head-on collision. LEP will soon be converted to the Large Hadron Collider, which will whirl protons and antiprotons at each other, achieving collision energies millions of times those of familiar nuclear reactions.

Engraving from the original title page of Galileo's *De Systemate Mundi*, depicting Aristotle, Ptolemy, and Copernicus. Galileo's work founded the modern scientific method of deducing laws to explain the results of observation and experiment. *Corbis*

From accelerator experiments and the study of naturally occurring high-speed particles called cosmic rays, theorists have pieced together a detailed scheme of what structures lie buried in the deepest recesses of matter. So far, the smallest entities identified are the oddly named quarks, which cluster in triplets to make up nuclear particles such as protons. Together with electrons and neutrinos, which are collectively described as leptons, the total menagerie of apparently elementary particles runs to 12.

Physicists suspect, however, that they have as yet glimpsed only a fraction of the full complement of fundamental entities. One reason concerns the existence of so-called dark matter in the universe. Astronomers are convinced that stars make up only a small percentage of the total mass of the cosmos. Our Milky Way galaxy, for example, spins far too fast to hold itself together if the stars and luminous gas clouds are the only material exerting a gravitational pull. Some unseen matter must exist to augment the gravity of the shining objects. The nature of this invisible stuff remains contentious. Theories vary from small black holes to unknown subatomic particles created in the Big Bang and left inhabiting the spaces between the stars. Experiments are in progress to track down these mystery particles. If they exist, they will have to be incorporated into any unified theory of physics, along with the quarks and leptons.

Forces

Even if physicists finally identify all the basic particles of matter, both familiar and unfamiliar, the story does not end there. The rich diversity of material forms and physical phenomena depends upon the way these particles interact with each other through forces. At the time of Newton, three basic forces of nature were recognized: gravitation, electricity, and magnetism. In the 19th century, following the experiments of Michael Faraday and others, James Clerk Maxwell showed that electricity and magnetism were not, in fact, two separate forces, but deeply linked. He was able to demonstrate mathematically that they are actually two facets of a single electromagnetic force.

Further understanding came in the 20th century. In the 1920s it became apparent that the atomic nucleus is also subject to two more forces, dubbed weak and strong. Physicists therefore decided that there are four fundamental forces of nature: gravitation, electromagnetism, and the two nuclear forces. However, in 1967 Abdus Salam and Steven Weinberg proposed that there is a subtle connection between the electromagnetic and weak nuclear forces. They predicted that at very high energies these two normally distinct forces would merge in identity to form a single electroweak force. Some years later their theory was confirmed by collider experiments at CERN.

Following this triumph, theoretical physicists began to suspect that, at even higher energies, maybe the electroweak force would merge with the strong nuclear force, and perhaps even gravitation too. At the very highest energies, perhaps there is just one superforce. Cosmologists were quick to point out that, since the universe began with an ultra-high energy Big Bang, for a brief instant the superforce would have reigned supreme. Then, as the universe expanded and cooled, so the four familiar forces of nature would have frozen out one by one.

LEP, the Large Electron-Positron Collider at CERN, the European centre for particle physics near Geneva. This is the world's largest particle accelerator and has allowed notable advances to be made in particle physics. *Science Photo Library*

Our understanding of the unification of the forces of nature is incomplete. Although there is some evidence hinting at a connection between the strong force and the electroweak force, decisive experimental confirmation is still lacking, while gravitation remains something of a mystery. However, this has not prevented theorists from devising many imaginative mathematical models that seek to amalgamate all the forces and particles into a single scheme. In this quest they are guided by the fact that the forces of nature are transmitted between particles of matter by yet more particles, often called messengers, but technically known as bosons. Thus the familiar electrostatic force can be envisaged as acting across the space between two charged particles by virtue of the exchange of particles called photons, associated with light. Similarly, gravitation is transmitted by the exchange of gravitons.

Taking into account all four forces, the total number of these messenger bosons plus particles of matter amounts to some dozens. The hope is that this small army of subatomic denizens can be grouped into families and combined into a unified mathematical system. If such a scheme exists, it will join quarks, leptons, and bosons into a common theme, thus unifying not only matter, but matter and force too.

Superstrings

It was always Einstein's dream that he would be able to formulate some sort of unified field theory to achieve an amalgamation of all the forces and particles of nature. However, in spite of decades of work, he never came near to achieving his goal. One reason for this is because, until recently, all attempts at unification have been based on the assumption that the ultimate building blocks of matter are tiny particles. Now this assumption is being challenged by a bizarre set of ideas known as superstring theory. It takes as its starting point the notion that the smallest physical entities are not particles at all, but tiny loops of string, 20 powers of 10 smaller than an atomic nucleus. As the strings vibrate in different ways, so they present themselves to our instruments as different particles. Quarks, leptons, bosons – all are just alternative activities of the same basic stringy entities.

String theory has been described by Ed Witten of Princeton University, one of its leading proponents, as a 21st century theory that has dropped by accident into the late 20th century. So abstract and weird are the properties of superstrings that the theorists are having to invent the mathematics to describe them as they go.

One example of mathematical subtlety concerns the dimensions of space. In daily life we observe three space dimensions and one time dimension, making four dimensions of space-time in total. However, as long ago as the 1920s some theoretical physicists suggested that space might have additional unseen dimensions. To understand what this means, consider viewing a hosepipe from afar. It looks like a wiggly line, that is one-dimensional. On closer inspection, however, it is revealed to be a narrow tube. What one may have taken to be a point on a line turns out to be a tiny circle going around the tube. In the same way, perhaps what we normally take to be a point in three-dimensional space is actually a tiny circle going around a fourth space dimension.

Physicists find that when extra space dimensions are added to their theoretical models, marvellous mathematical simplifications occur, and otherwise hidden connections appear between different forces. In one popular version of string theory, space has nine dimensions, six of them being 'rolled up' (like the hosepipe) to a diameter of only about a billion-trillion-trillionth of a centimetre, which is why even our most powerful instruments cannot directly detect these extra dimensions.

If string theory is on the right track, then at the most fundamental level of structure, the physical universe would consist of nothing but string and space. The superstrings themselves are supposed to be absolutely elementary and primitive: they cannot be pulled apart to reveal interior parts. In that respect at least, they resemble the atoms of ancient Greece. But in terms of abstractness and mathematical elegance, we have come a long way since the first philosophical musings of Democritus.

At the time of writing, many technical obstacles obscure a full understanding of superstring theory, and there is much bewilderment that not only one but several contending string theories exist. Recently there has been a significant advance, with the development of something called M theory, where M stands for Mother, or Master or Membrane. This theory treats the basic entities not as strings, but two-dimensional sheets or membranes moving in an 11-dimensional space-time. There are suggestions that all the various string theories are in fact contained in the abstract mathematics of M theory.

Nobody knows whether these arcane investigations will finally realize the ancients' dream of yielding a fully unified description of reality, or whether they will peter out in intractable mathematical complexities. But even if M theory, or some yet more exotic variant, does succeed in giving us the master formula for the cosmos, it will not be the end of science. Reductionism is, after all, only half the story. A complete description of nature at the ultra-microscopic level will not explain sunspots or snowflakes, for example. And it certainly will not help us to understand life and consciousness, or why people fall in love.

Paul Davies

The Technology of Healing: A Century of Medicine

The detection of the X-ray in 1895 by Wilhelm Conrad Röntgen opened the modern era of technological medicine. The use of X-rays in hospitals and even on the battlefields of World War I for diagnostic purposes was one of the most rapid disseminations of a new medical technique. Wartime radar research was translated into ultrasound high-frequency sound-wave technology, which is now widely used in the monitoring of fetuses. The 1970s saw the development of computed tomography (CT or CAT) scanning. Magnetic resonance imaging (MRI) produces images of the body by beaming radio waves into a patient lying in a strong magnetic field. A consequence of the discovery of radioactivity by Antoine-Henri Becquerel in 1896 has been the use of radioactive isotopes for diagnosis and therapeutic purposes, especially for cancer, creating the new speciality of nuclear medicine.

In 1928, nearly fifty years after Louis Pasteur advanced the germ theory of infection, Alexander Fleming of St Mary's Hospital, London discovered the role of antibiotics in treating bacterial infections, when he observed the disinfecting properties of bread mould which proved to contain penicillin. In 1939 the Australian-born researcher Howard Florey and German-born Ernst Chain managed to isolate and manufacture penicillin which became an important asset to the Allies in World War II to keep the troops fit against tropical diseases and to hasten the healing of wounds. The range of antibacterial agents has proliferated greatly in the second half of the century, to the point where they are regarded as overused in many situations in both developed and developing countries. This increases the possibility of the emergence of resistance among new strains of bacteria and among patients who receive antibiotics too frequently or for the wrong purposes. Drugs as effective as penicillin, such as the sulphonamides, streptomycin, and aspirin have been developed and major pharmaceutical companies have emerged to manufacture them. Their production was often based on techniques used for the manufacture of chemical weapons during the two major wars of the century.

Vaccination

One of the triumphs of the century has been the eradication of the smallpox variola virus, the only naturally occurring disease to have been wiped out from the human population. This was achieved in 1980 (nearly two hundred years after Edward Jenner first introduced vaccination against smallpox) by massive immunization and case hunting. However this achievement was overshadowed for many by the appearance of what appear to be even more virulent viruses, such as Ebola and AIDS/HIV in the 1970s and 1980s.

Dr Jonas Salk had developed the inactivated polio vaccine and Dr Albert Sabin the live polio vaccine in the 1950s and by the end of the century the World Health Organization hoped to have eliminated the virus in Europe and the Eastern Mediterranean regions.

Vaccines were developed in the postwar period for measles, mumps, rubella, hepatitis B, and other diseases. Several anti-malarial drugs have been developed and the life cycle of the disease carrier – the mosquito – was studied closely to aid the fight against the various strains of malaria that still appear in both developed and developing countries. The growth of international travel has made diseases such as this hard to overcome and the goal at the end of the century is control of malaria rather than elimination.

Victims of research

An area of concern that emerged at the end of the century was the use of nonconsenting subjects in the development of these advances. The polio vaccines and many other medicines were tested on American prison inmates who were not fully informed of the dangers to which they were being subjected. Some experiments involved children with learning difficulties who had no one to protect their interests; many experiments involved poor African Americans who were not fully informed of their position. In May 1997 President Clinton apologized to the survivors of the Tuskegee Syphilis Study, where many participants were not offered appropriate treatment even after it was known that penicillin was an effective medication for this debilitating disease. Similarly, the president's Advisory Committee on Human Radiation Experiments reported in October 1995 that many individuals had been subjected to dangerous levels of radiation as part of medical research which they did not fully understand and to which they had not given informed consent. Some observers likened these activities to the medical experimentation in Nazi concentration camps

Scottish bacteriologist Alexander Fleming in his laboratory at St Mary's Hospital, London, where he discovered penicillin, the first antibiotic drug. Today, the original type of penicillin is limited by the increasing resistance of pathogens and by allergic reactions in patients. Since 1941 when penicillin came widely into use, numerous other antibiotics of the penicillin family have been discovered which are more selective against, or resistant to, specific microorganisms. *AKG Photo London* for which German doctors had been condemned at the Nürnberg Trials. President Clinton made more funding available for bioethical studies as part of his reparation for the offences against medical ethics that his government was acknowledging.

Stricter guidelines for the use of human subjects in medical research were advanced in various countries and by international agencies in the second half of the 20th century but there is still an awareness, as we move into the new millennium, that careful monitoring and vigilance is required by ethics committees overseeing this research.

Birth control

One of the great breakthroughs of the century was the development of the hormone-based birth control pill by Carl Djerassi and others in the 1950s, and the freedom it gave women to time their reproduction. Various forms of birth control have been disseminated in the effort to stem the growth of the world's population. In the last third of the century the understanding of the menstrual cycle and menopause led to the development of Hormone Replacement Therapy and other modifiers of the side effects of hormonal imbalances. Research at the turn of the 20th century in this field is especially focused on developing a contraceptive pill for men.

Genetics

At much the same time as Djerassi was developing the contraceptive pill, Crick and Watson identified the structure of DNA as a double helix. This new understanding – together with technical developments such as the electron microscope – ushered in an era of research into genes which culminated at the end of the century in the project to map the human genome – the sequence of genes on the 23 pairs of human chromosomes. Following the achievement of in vitro and ex utero human fertilization, and the transformation of fertility and reproductive treatments into a form of medical technology in the second half of the 20th century, there is some considerable apprehension about the prospects of genetic engineering and cloning that may become possible in the early years of the new millennium. The ethical considerations of such 'engineering' are already under close scrutiny.

A false-colour micrograph of the *Herpes simplex* or cold sore virus. Herpes is the name given to any of several infectious diseases – including cold sores, genital herpes, shingles, chickenpox, and glandular fever – caused by the viruses in the herpes group. In the 20th century many viruses have been eradicated but other more virulent viruses have appeared. *SmithKline Beecham Plc*

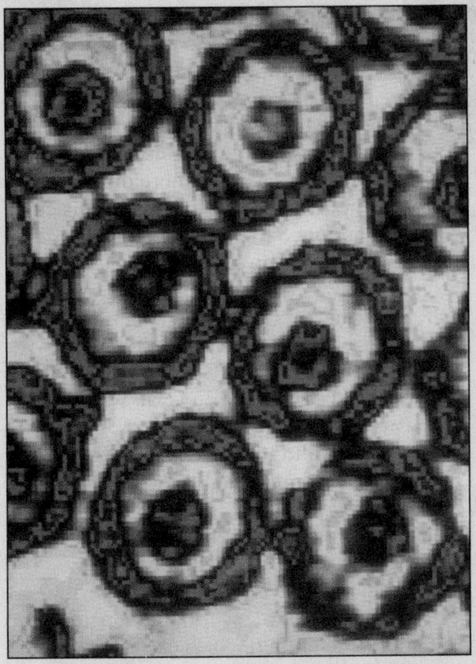

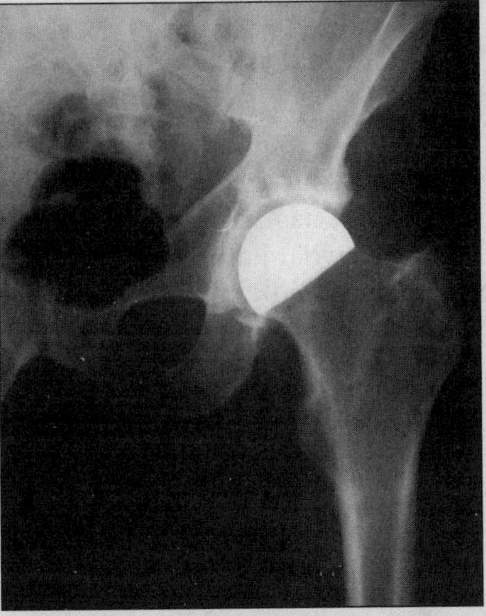

X-ray image showing a human hip joint that has been replaced with an artificial ball at the end of the femur, a successful treatment for hip joints damaged by arthritis. It was the detection of X-rays that set the stage for technological medicine in the 20th century. *Corbis*

Surgery

Advances in surgery too proceeded at a rapid pace, particularly as the 20th century was drawing to a close. The first heart transplant operation was performed by the South African surgeon Christiaan Barnard in 1967, and now major organ replacement surgery has become almost commonplace in the developed world. The development of laser surgery and 'keyhole' surgery has made day surgery more common and there has been increased access throughout the world to what were once major procedures. Replacement of hips, joints, and lenses have improved the quality of life for many people. These procedures, however, are still expensive and the health economists of developed countries in particular are now trying both to create new formulas for ensuring fair access to these treatments as older people live longer, and to resist any move to 'ration' medical procedures.

Work and ill health

Another area of great progress was the field of occupational health, as epidemiologists refined their techniques and the cause-and-effect relationships between various industries or occupations and particular illnesses were established in replicated studies. Environmental health hazards too were progressively identified, and this field of medicine grew after the publication of Rachel Carson's book *Silent Spring* alerted the world to the dangers of chemical and radiation pollutants. One of the areas of contention at the end of the century surrounded the hypothesis that men working in civilian and military nuclear plants might be exposed to radiation which could damage their sperm and therefore pass on birth defects to their children. New technologies such as cellular telephones will be subjected to close epidemiological investigation in the coming years.

Meeting new challenges

One of the clearest consequences of the increasing contribution of technology to medicine – including information technology – is the 'information explosion' which trainee doctors and those who are already in practice have to contend with. The UK General Medical Council observed in a major statement on undergraduate medical training, *Tomorrow's Doctors* (1991), that half of what a medical student learns at university will be out of date within a decade or two – and no one knows which half. This realization has deeply affected medical education, which now increasingly concentrates on teaching doctors how to learn and keep their knowledge up to date rather than expecting to cover the whole of medical knowledge in five years of university teaching. There has also been a shift towards more practical medical teaching. The old 'apprenticeship' model of the last century gave way to the emergence of university-based medical teaching rather than hospital observation in the first half of the 20th century, but as the new millennium approached some of the advantages of 'on the job learning' were more appreciated, and efforts were being made to structure the practical learning of undergraduates more coherently and to correlate it with classroom teaching and learning. Other changes in the profession of medicine continue to be triggered by the fact that, in the UK and USA at least, more than one-half of medical students are now women.

Patients too have changed. Mass media – from women's magazines to television health programmes – have educated patients to an unprecedented level and in many countries 'patients' charters' have emerged as people become more knowledgeable and assertive about medical care. While many of the challenges of the 19th century have been met, the 20th century has brought some of its own. Fair access to the best in medical care will probably be the first global challenge for medicine in the new millennium.

Sue Rabbitt-Roff

NEW ART: Culture in the 20th Century

At all times and in all places, the creative activities of a society's artists have seemed, to contemporary audiences, unprecedented in their novelty. It has always been left for posterity to discover the continuity with an artist's predecessors. In time, what had seemed audacious originality starts to be understood as audacious homage to the ancients, a link in the long chain of artistic tradition.

But the novelty which audiences perceived in the work of their contemporaries in the 20th century was perhaps more substantial than usual, the break with the past more complete. Thanks to the rapid development of technology, some art forms came into existence for the first time. Cinema, for instance, is an entirely 20th-century medium, and photography shrugged off the nervous imitation of graphic art which had previously characterized it.

Innovation

In more firmly established forms of culture, alterations of an unprecedented profundity were taking place. It is certainly true, of course, that some apparent innovations were less revolutionary than they at first seemed. This was particularly the case in literature. In the novel, the 'stream of consciousness' technique, by which such novelists as James Joyce or Carlo Emilio Gadda represented the unspoken thoughts of their characters, soon came to seem a fashionable device of the time. Much later in the century, South American novelists made a substantial impact on European and Indian novelists, who, struck by the apparent exoticism and fantasy in this previously neglected school, found a liberation from what had sometimes seemed the constraints of the realist novel. 'Magic realism', as it came to be called, was the term used to describe the realistic treatment of fantastic situations in the works of writers such as Gabriel García Márquez and Jorge Luis Borges.

In poetry, the possibilities of free verse – poetry without rhyme or regular rhythm – struck many poets across the world, after the beginning of the century, as a liberation and, unlike 'stream of consciousness', free verse continues to be a living force. But, like many previous apparent revolutions in poetic form, it became an additional element in a poetic vocabulary, and not a basis for a new understanding of form. Most of the best poets of the century chose to write within a formal metre or freely as it suited them. And many other much-hailed revolutions were very quickly discovered to be brilliant oddities, and no more. For instance, Marianne Moore's attempt to write syllabic verse – in which the number of syllables, not their length or stress, is important – in English provided, in the end, another possibility for poets, and not a new poetic language.

Revolution

A refinement of technique, mistaken for a fundamental revolution, is very much what the history of the arts would teach us to expect. But the 20th century was exceptional in that some of those proclaimed revolutions proved to be the real thing. After the composer Arnold Schoenberg or the artist Marcel Duchamp, music and the visual arts were altered as decisively as physics was by Max Planck. Some stylistic innovations, such as Igor Stravinsky's Neo-Classicism or Salvador Dali's Surrealism, are brilliant additions to the communal vocabulary. As well as these, however, music and the visual arts produced work which changed the nature of the art, and after Schoenberg's second string quartet, or Duchamp's sculpture *Fountain*, their respective arts were not added to, but altered.

***Arnold Schoenberg* (*c.*1905/06)** by Richard Gerstl. Schoenberg was a pioneer of atonal music, music of no apparent key, in which the sense of tonality is distorted or obscured. *AKG Photo London*

Western music had existed within a vast and flexible arena which had come to be termed 'tonality' for hundreds of years; a firmly hierarchic system, in which individual notes had inevitable and meaningful relationships with each other. From the beginning, these relationships had been stretched, in the name of expressiveness, to include dissonances and sounds of a piquant and sometimes alarming exoticism. By the end of the 19th century, the interest in the abstruse possibilities of the unfamiliar chord had begun to obscure the fundamental hieratic structure of tonal music.

It was left, however, for the Austrian-born composer Arnold Schoenberg to make a fundamental step, and write music in which the relations between notes which tonal music dictates are neglected. In his work, which has come to be taken as the epitome of 'atonality', the 12 notes of the chromatic scale do not form a hierarchy, but are formally equal. For some years, after 1908 or so, he and his followers wrote music which was guided principally by instinct. In the 1920s, he evolved a more systematic theory which provided a musical work with a fundamental order. This theory, the so-called 'twelve-tone' theory, gained many followers, and after World War II began to be extended to every element of music. But it was the liberation of his first atonal works which has had the more universal impact, and although great music has continued to be written in the tonal language, no serious musician after Schoenberg was untouched by his discoveries.

In the visual arts, other fundamental alterations began to be made. In the works of Vincent Van Gogh, Paul Gauguin, and Paul Cézanne we begin to see an acknowledgement of the artificiality of the painting. From this, Henri Matisse and the first Cubists, Pablo Picasso and Georges Braque, engineered a profound revolution. In their work, a painting boldly states that it is painted on canvas and, with flat sheets of colour and blunt juxtapositions, provides no illusion for the viewer. This is not the world, these paintings say, this is a painting, which exists in two dimensions, as painting, despite appearances, always has.

The work of the Cubists bears a curious, indirect relation to the world; using it, one might say, without representing it. It was left to others to break entirely with the burden of representation, and explore the possibilities of abstract painting. Entirely abstract painting and sculpture first made its appearance in the first decade of the century, making its point through formal relations of shape and colour. It remained a sporadic inspiration, from time to time throwing up a painter of genius, such as Vasily Kandinsky or Jackson Pollock.

Porte-chapeau/Fountain **(1917)** by French-born US artist Marcel Duchamp. Duchamp was a proponent of Dada, an artistic and literary movement founded in 1915 and characterized by a spirit of rebellion and disillusionment. *AKG Photo London, © ADAGP, Paris and DACS London 1999*

Conceptual art

The most profound rethinking of what the visual arts meant was initially taken as an offensive joke, and is still regarded by many intelligent viewers as an unacceptable development. When Duchamp, shortly before World War I, submitted a urinal which he had bought to be shown at a New York exhibition as a sculpture called *Fountain*, it could hardly be conceived of as art at all. The idea of the 'ready-made', as it came to be called, and 'conceptual art' as a whole, rejects deeply held convictions about the role of skill in art.

Art for everyone

The practitioners of conceptual art who followed Duchamp sometimes chose to explore his innovation in political terms. In a century in which national leaders abused authority to an unprecedented extent, it sometimes seemed inappropriate for artists to seek to elevate themselves above their audience by making a display of brilliance. To an artist such as Joseph Beuys, the 19th-century idea of the authority of the creative genius and the 19th-century idea of the authority of the great leader, both contemptuous of the common herd, seemed indissolubly linked. In his work and his teaching, Beuys attempted to answer the contemptuous dismissal of conceptual art that anyone could make such an object by agreeing with it. In Beuys's view, artistic creation was not something only available to a small and gifted elite, but a universal human quality, and one should celebrate the obvious truth that the act of placing a chair in an art gallery was within anybody's reach.

Woman with a Blue Hat **(1938)** a Cubist painting by Spanish artist Picasso. In Cubism objects are shown as they are known to be, rather than as they happen to look at a particular moment, so all three dimensions are visible within the two-dimensional painting. *AKG Photo London, © Succession Picasso/DACS 1999*

The inspiring egalitarianism of Beuys's art and teaching could only have arisen, perhaps, in a century where knowledge and appreciation of the arts spread throughout society to an unprecedented extent. The impact of the means of mechanical reproduction turned what had been bourgeois pleasures into universal ones, and, conversely, popular forms of art became so widespread as to threaten the previous dominance of high culture. In the course of the century, photography turned from an occasional occupation of the leisured classes to a universal interest. The possibilities of cinema and of television immediately fascinated creative minds, and some of the most sophisticated and elaborately inventive work of the century took place in what never ceased to be a mass medium. Books became cheaper, and both literacy rates and curiosity about literature steadily rose throughout the world. Music, too, through the technological advances of mechanical reproduction and transmission, became universally available, and works initially intended to be performed on rare and special occasions could be bought and played at whim.

Of course, there was a price to be paid when cultural activities spread beyond an elite. The first was that many creative artists began to develop a fastidiousness about these new audiences. Across the arts it can be argued that creative imaginations sought to develop a carapace of difficulty to protect themselves from the enthusiasms of the vulgar, not always to the benefit of the final result, and many serious artists who had no such inclination to be obscure or difficult found themselves unfairly castigated as second rate. The second consequence of this universal dissemination was that art, and particularly the popular arts, were increasingly designed for an international audience. As the century drew to a close, cinema in particular seemed to have lost its crucial desire to appeal to a local audience. The dominating US film industry's ambition to produce films comprehensible and profitable across the world resulted in some products of inevitable blandness.

But mass communication has also had beneficial results with Western exposure to the arts of other cultures such as Iranian cinema, West African drumming, or the Indian novel. As the new millennium begins, the cultural possibilities open to almost anyone in the world are wider than ever before. If the most fundamental creative revolutions of the 20th century are only slowly reaching wide understanding and appreciation, the thesaurus of individual cultural expression seems to be growing larger by the day, and its pleasures more bewilderingly various.

Philip Hensher

ARTS CHRONOLOGY

1000 *Makura no Soshi/The Pillow Book* of Sei Shonagon is written around this time. A Japanese lady's commonplace book with often mischievous reflections and anecdotes about court life, it is one of the masterpieces of Japanese literature.

***c.* 1025** Italian writer Guido d'Arezzo publishes his musical treatise *Micrologus de Disciplina Artis Musicae/Short Discourse on the Discipline of the Art of Music*. He establishes a system of precise pitch notation through the introduction of a four-line stave and the ut-re-mi-fa-so-la names for notes.

1078–1124 Work begins on the Romanesque cathedral of Santiago de Compostela, Spain, using French masons. It is built on a huge scale to accommodate the large number of pilgrims.

***c.* 1090**

The Bayeux tapestry, depicting the invasion of England by the Normans and the defeat of the English at the Battle of Hastings in 1066, is embroidered. It consists of 72 different scenes on 70 m/231 ft of linen. Here, Harold, king of England after the death of Edward the Confessor, is shown accepting an audience in his Rouen palace. *Corbis*

***c.* 1095** *Chanson de Roland/Song of Roland* is recorded. It is the earliest extant example of the chivalric epics known as *chanson de geste* ('song of exploits') which were sung and possibly composed by French *trouvères* (poets with a narrative style).

1140 *Poema di mío Cid/Poem of the Cid* is written. It is the most complete Spanish epic *chanson de geste* and tells of the fantastic deeds of the military commander Rodrigo or Ruy Díaz de Vivar (El Cid), who died in 1099.

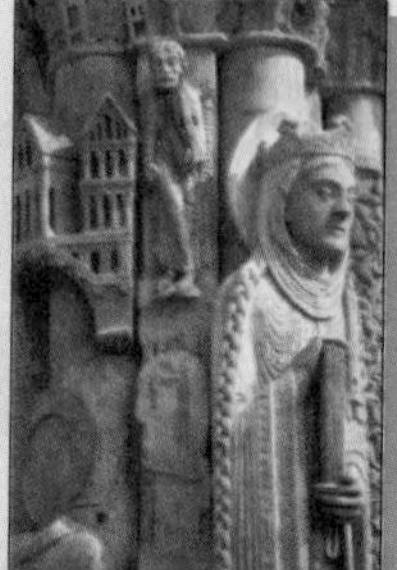

1145

Construction begins on the royal portal at the west end of Chartres Cathedral in France. These portal sculptures are among the masterpieces of Gothic architecture. The carvings, dating mostly from the 13th century, combine the sacred events, imaginary portraits of French kings, and homely depictions of everyday scenes to give a vigorous, elegant, and assured account of the medieval world. *Linda Proud*

1145 Construction begins on the 'Friday Mosque' at Isfahan, Persia, capital of the Seljuk Turks.

1150 A vast temple complex is built at Angkor Wat (in modern Cambodia) by the Khmer emperor Suryavarman II. The building is to be his mausoleum.

***c.* 1200** The *Five Icelandic Sagas: The Saga of Burnt Njal/Njal's Saga*; the *Laxdaela/Laxdale's Saga*; the *Eyrbyggja*, *Egil's Saga/Egla*; and *The Saga of Grettir the Strong/Grettis Saga* (legends and stories either about the deeds of the hero, or about events connected with a region) are compiled.

1202–1304 The Cloth Hall at Ypres, in Flanders (now part of Belgium), one of the finest Gothic secular buildings of the late Middle Ages, is built. It is destroyed in 1915.

***c.* 1210** Gottfried von Strassburg writes his unfinished epic poem *Tristan und Isolde/Tristan and Isolde* in Middle High German.

***c.* 1230** The long era of *Minnesingers* (German court lyric poets and singers who wrote love lyrics of a formal style and aristocratic beauty) ends. Among the most eminent names were Wolfram von Eschenbach who died in 1220, and Walter von der Vogelweide who may have died in this year.

1231 The mausoleum of 'Sultan Ghari' (Nasir-ad-Din Mahmud, son of Iltutmish) is built in Delhi, India.

***c.* 1237** Guillaume de Lorris writes the first 4,000 lines of the *Le Roman de la Rose/The Romance of the Rose*, an allegory of courtly love.

1260 Sculptor Nicola Pisano carves the pulpit in the baptistry of Pisa Cathedral, Italy. It marks the revival of a form of sculpture clearly based on classical models.

***c.* 1300** Chinese playwright Guan Han-qing is active. Regarded as China's greatest classical dramatist, his most important works include *Snow in Midsummer*.

***c.* 1321** Italian poet Dante Alighieri completes *Divine Comedy*.

1353 Italian writer Giovanni Boccaccio completes his *Decameron*.

***c.* 1360** English writer William Langland writes his long religious allegory *The Vision of Piers Plowman*.

1387

English writer Geoffrey Chaucer begins *The Canterbury Tales*. Told by a party of 30 pilgrims travelling from London to Canterbury, it consists of 24 tales, told in verse, that provide a vivid picture of 14th-century England. Chaucer was born in London, and travelled widely in France, and in Italy, where he was possibly influenced by the writers Boccaccio and Petrarch. *Philip Sauvain Picture Collection*

1421 Work begins on the Church of San Lorenzo in Florence, Italy. The design is by the Italian artist and architect Filippo Brunelleschi, whose aim is to construct the entire church in cubic units – a revolutionary approach that has a profound effect on Italian Renaissance architecture.

***c.* 1425** French writer Alain Chartier writes his poem *La Belle Dame sans merci/The Beautiful Lady without Pity*, one of the best-known medieval lyrics of courtly love.

***c.* 1427** Italian artist Masaccio paints the fresco *The Trinity*, one of the major works of the early Italian Renaissance, in the Church of Santa Maria Novella in Florence, Italy.

1434

Flemish artist Jan van Eyck paints *The Arnolfini Marriage* (National Gallery), a double portrait, full of complex symbolism. The candle, for example, represents God's all-seeing eye; the dog, fidelity; and the green of the bride's dress, fertility. Van Eyck was one of the first painters to use oil paint effectively and gained a Europe-wide reputation during his lifetime. *Corbis*

1443 Japanese dramatist Seami Motokiyo, perhaps the greatest of the No dramatists, dies. He wrote nearly half of the classic No repertoire.

1447 The Üç Serefeli Mosque in Edirne, the first centrally-planned mosque in the Ottoman Empire, is completed. Built in the Ottoman style, it is noted in particular for its fine minarets.

***c.* 1455** Italian artist Piero della Francesca completes his cycle of frescoes *The Legend of the True Cross* in the Church of San Francesco in Arezzo, Italy.

1470 Sir Thomas Malory completes *Le Morte d'Arthur/The Death of Arthur*. Based on French originals, it is the first prose account in English of the Arthurian legend.

***c.* 1485** Italian artist Sandro Botticelli paints *The Birth of Venus*.

***c.* 1500** The Inca town of Machu Picchu, built high in the mountains of Peru, reaches its final stage of building.

1500 German artist Albrecht Dürer paints *Self-portrait* (the Munich self-portrait).

1503 Italian artist Leonardo da Vinci paints *Mona Lisa* (*La Gioconda*).

1504 Italian artist Michelangelo (Buonarroti) completes his sculpture *David*, which is widely praised when set up in a square in Florence. He also paints his *Holy Family (Doni Tondo)*.

1523 Italian artist Titian paints *Bacchus and Ariadne*.

1553 Inca art comes to an end with the collapse of the Inca Empire in South America at the hands of Spanish conquistadors.

1554 The English composer Thomas Tallis writes the Mass *Puer natus est nobis/A Boy is Born to Us*.

1555 Italian Mannerist artist Tintoretto (Jacopo Robusti) paints *Saint George and the Dragon*.

1565 Dutch artist Pieter Brueghel completes a series of paintings depicting the seasons, including *Hunters in the Snow*, *Gloomy Day*, *Return of the Herd*, and *August*.

1572 The Fortress Palace at Ajmer in India, built by the Mogul king Akbar the Great, is completed.

1586 Greek-born Spanish artist El Greco paints *Burial of Count Orgaz*.

1589–1610 Shakespeare writes most of his plays.

1590–96 English poet Edmund Spenser publishes his vast poetic work *The Faerie Queene*.

c. 1595–1600 English metaphysical poet John Donne writes many of his best-known poems.

1605 Spanish writer Miguel de Cervantes (Saavedra) publishes part one of *Don Quixote*. The second part appears in 1615.

c. 1606 The comedy *Volpone, or The Fox* by the English dramatist Ben Jonson is first performed, in London, England, played by the King's Men. It is first published in 1607.

1607 The opera *La favola d'Orfeo/The Legend of Orpheus* by the Italian composer Claudio Monteverdi is first performed, in Mantua.

1611 Flemish Baroque artist Peter Paul Rubens paints *The Raising of the Cross*.

1618 The Queen's House at Greenwich, London, England, designed by the English Classical architect Inigo Jones, is completed. It is one of the first truly Renaissance buildings in Britain.

1642 Dutch artist Rembrandt paints *The Night Watch*.

1643 The Taj Mahal, at Agra, India, is completed. It was probably designed by the mogul architect Ustad Ahmad Lahori.

1656 Spanish artist Diego Rodriguez de Silva y Velázquez paints *Las meninas/Maids of Honour*.

1664 Two comedies, *Le Tartuffe, ou l'imposteur/Tartuffe, or the Impostor* (first published in 1669) and *Le Mariage forcé/The Enforced Marriage*, by the French dramatist Molière (Jean-Baptiste Poquelin) are first performed.

1667 English poet John Milton publishes his epic poem *Paradise Lost*.

1689 The opera *Dido and Aeneas* by the English Baroque composer Henry Purcell with a libretto by English dramatist Nathan Tate is first performed.

1697 French writer Charles Perrault publishes *Contes de ma mère l'oye/Mother Goose Stories*. This famous collection of fairy stories contains such classics as 'Sleeping Beauty', 'Little Red Riding Hood', 'Cinderella', and 'Bluebeard'.

c. 1700 The art of the Benin culture in Nigeria reaches its high point. From at least the mid-16th century fine sculptures in ivory and bronze have been produced, creating one of richest extant traditions of African art.

1710

The new St Paul's Cathedral, designed by the English architect Christopher Wren, built to replace the Gothic cathedral destroyed in the Great Fire of London in 1666, is completed. This is one of Sir Christopher Wren's unexecuted designs for St Paul's. *Philip Sauvain Picture Collection*

c. 1717 The German-born English composer George Frideric Handel writes his *Water Music*, a set of instrumental pieces.

1721 The German composer Johann Sebastian Bach completes *The Brandenburg Concertos*.

1725 The Italian Baroque composer and violinist Antonio Vivaldi publishes *Le quattro stagioni/The Four Seasons* (opus 8).

1726 Anglo-Irish churchman and writer Jonathan Swift publishes the prose satire *Gulliver's Travels*, anonymously.

1738 The Imperial Ballet School is founded in St Petersburg, Russia.

1748 The *kabuki* play *Chushingura* by the dramatist Takeda Izumo is first performed, in Japan. Based on an ancient legend, it becomes one of the best loved *kabuki* plays.

1749 English landscape and portrait painter Thomas Gainsborough paints *Mr and Mrs Robert Andrews*. English writer Henry Fielding publishes his novel *The History of Tom Jones, A Foundling*.

1759 French writer Voltaire (François-Marie Arouet) publishes his novel *Candide*, a satire on the thinkers and institutions he considers a hindrance to human progress.

1764 Mozart completes his Symphonies No 1 (K 16), No 2 (lost), No 3 (lost), and No 4 (K 19), and his Sonatas for Piano and Violin Nos 1 to 4 (K 6 to K 9).

1775 The comedy *The Rivals*, by the Irish dramatist Richard Brinsley Sheridan, is first performed, in London, England.

1786 The Scottish poet Robert Burns publishes *Poems Chiefly in the Scottish Dialect*, his first collection.

1793 The French Neo-Classicist artist Jacques-Louis David paints *The Death of Marat*, depicting the assassinated revolutionary leader Jean-Paul Marat dead in his bath.

1794 The English Romantic poet and artist William Blake publishes *Songs of Innocence and Experience*.

1801 Austrian composer Franz Josef Haydn completes his Mass No 11 in B flat, the *Schöpfungsmesse/The Creation Mass*, and his secular oratorio *Die Jahreszeiten/The Seasons*.

1805 The Spanish artist Francisco José de Goya y Lucientes paints *The Clothed Maja* and *The Nude Maja*.

1807 The English Romantic poet William Wordsworth publishes *Ode: Intimations of Immortality*, and *Poems, in Two Volumes*.

1808 The German poet Johann Wolfgang von Goethe publishes part one of his verse drama *Faust*. The second part appears in 1832.

1811 The English writer Jane Austen publishes her novel *Sense and Sensibility*. She began work on it in 1797.

c. 1812 The English artist J M W Turner paints *Snowstorm: Hannibal Crossing the Alps*.

1812 The German folklorists and philologists Jakob Ludwig Carl Grimm and his brother Wilhelm Carl Grimm publish the first volume of their famous *Kinder and Hausmärchen/Fairy Tales*. A second volume appears in 1815 and a third in 1822.

1820 The English Romantic poet John Keats publishes the first version of his epic poem *Hyperion*. He also publishes the poems *The Eve of Saint Agnes* and *Ode to a Nightingale*.

1821 The English artist John Constable paints *The Hay Wain*.

1823 Ludwig van Beethoven completes his Symphony No 9 in D minor, the *Choral* (Opus 125).

1824 The French Romantic artist Eugène Delacroix paints *The Massacre at Chios*, a depiction of a contemporary event from the Great War of Independence.

1832 The English poet Alfred, Lord Tennyson publishes *Poems*. Among its best-known poems are 'The Lotus-Eaters' and 'The Lady of Shalott'.

1835 The English pioneer of photography William Henry Fox Talbot creates *Picture of a Latticed Window*, the oldest existing photographic negative.

1836 The satire *Revizor/The Government Inspector* by the Russian writer Nikolay (Vasilyevich) Gogol is first performed, in Moscow, Russia.

1837 The English writer Charles Dickens publishes his first novel, *The Pickwick Papers*.

1839 The French writer Stendhal (Marie-Henri Beyle) publishes his novel *La Chartreuse de Parme/The Charterhouse of Parma*.

1847 The English writer Charlotte Brontë publishes *Jane Eyre*, under the name Currer Bell. The English writer Emily Brontë publishes her only novel, *Wuthering Heights*, under the name Ellis Bell.

1851 The US writer Herman Melville publishes *Moby Dick, or the Whale*, one of the great US novels of the 19th century.

1856 The French writer Gustave Flaubert publishes his novel *Madame Bovary* in serial form.

1857 English writer Anthony Trollope publishes *Barchester Towers*.

1858 The comic opera *Orphée aux enfers/Orpheus in the Underworld* by the German-born French composer Jacques Offenbach is first performed, in Paris. It popularizes the cancan.

1859 The French artist Jean-François Millet paints *The Angelus*.

1862 The French Romantic writer Victor Hugo publishes his novel *Les Misérables*. The Russian writer Ivan Sergeyevich Turgenev publishes his novel *Ottsy i deti/Fathers and Sons*.

1863 The French artist Edouard Manet paints *Déjeuner sur l'herbe/Luncheon on the Grass*.

1864
The Russian writer Leo Tolstoy publishes the first part of his epic novel *Voyna i mir/War and Peace*. The second part appears in 1869. This illustration by Ilya Repin is of Leo Tolstoy working in the fields. The great Russian writer Tolstoy was born a wealthy aristocrat and in his youth led a dissolute life, but after experiencing a religious conversion he condemned private property and lived like a peasant. Repin, the most famous Russian painter of the period, made several conventional portraits of Tolstoy as well as this striking picture of him living out his beliefs. *Corbis*

1866 The Russian writer Fyodor Mikhaylovich Dostoevsky publishes his novel *Prestupleniye i nakazaniye/Crime and Punishment*.

1867 The Norwegian dramatist Henrik Johan Ibsen publishes his verse play *Peer Gynt*. It is first performed in 1876.

1868 German composer Johannes Brahms completes his choral work *Ein deutsche Requiem/A German Requiem*.

1869 The opera *Das Rheingold* by the German composer Richard Wagner is first performed, in Munich, Germany. It is the first part of his *Der Ring des Nibelungen/The Ring of the Nibelung* cycle.

1871 The English writer George Eliot (pseudonym of Mary Anne Evans) publishes the first part of her novel *Middlemarch: A Study of Provincial Life*. The last part appears in 1872. The opera *Aïda* by the Italian Romantic composer Giuseppe Fortunino Francesco Verdi is first performed, in Cairo, Egypt (to celebrate the opening of the Suez Canal).

1872 The US artist James Abbot McNeill Whistler paints *Arrangement in Grey and Black No 1: The Artist's Mother*.

1876 The US writer Mark Twain (pseudonym of Samuel Langhorne Clemens) publishes his novel *The Adventures of Tom Sawyer*.

1884 The French Impressionist artist Pierre-Auguste Renoir paints *Umbrellas*.

1885 The French artist Auguste Rodin sculpts *Burghers of Calais*.

1888 Austrian composer Gustav Mahler completes his Symphony No 1.

1891 The English writer Thomas Hardy publishes his novel *Tess of the D'Urbervilles*.

1894 The French Impressionist artist Claude Monet paints his *Rouen Cathedral* series.

1895 A new version of the ballet *Lebedinoe ozero/Swan Lake*, written in 1877 by the Russian composer Pyotr Ilyich Tchaikovsky, is first performed, in St Petersburg, Russia.

1896 The French Post-Impressionist artist Paul Cézanne paints *The Great Pine* and *The Lake at Annecy*.

1897 The English writer Bram Stoker publishes *Dracula*. The French artist Henri Rousseau paints *Sleeping Gypsy*. The French artist Post-Impressionist Paul Gauguin paints *Where do we come from? What are we? Where are we going?*

1898 The US writer Henry James publishes *The Turn of the Screw*.

1899 English composer Edward Elgar completes *Enigma Variations*.

1900 The Polish-born English writer Joseph Conrad (Józef Teodor Konrad Korzeniowski) publishes his novel *Lord Jim*.

1901 The German writer Thomas Mann publishes his novel *Buddenbrooks*. The Russian composer Sergey Rachmaninov completes his Piano Concerto No. 2.

1902 The French writer André Gide publishes his novel *L'Immoraliste/The Immoralist*.

1904 The opera *Madame Butterfly*, by the Italian composer Giacomo Puccini, is first performed in Milan, Italy. The play *Vishnovy sad/The Cherry Orchard*, by the Russian writer Anton Chekhov, is first performed in Moscow, Russia.

1906 The Post Office Savings Bank in Vienna, Austria, designed by the Austrian architect Otto Wagner, is completed.

1907 The play *Playboy of the Western World*, by the Irish dramatist John Millington Synge, is first performed at the Abbey Theatre in Dublin, Ireland.

1908 The Scottish writer Kenneth Grahame publishes his children's novel *The Wind in the Willows*.

1909 The AEG Turbine Factory in Berlin, Germany, designed by the German architect Peter Behrens, is completed. It is one of the first steel and glass buildings. The School of Art, designed by the Scottish architect Charles Rennie Mackintosh, is completed in Glasgow, Scotland. It is one of the most original Art Nouveau buildings in Britain.

1910 The ballet *The Firebird*, by the Russian composer Igor Stravinsky and the Russian choreographer Mikhail Fokine, is first performed in Paris, France, under the Russian impressario Sergei Diaghilev. The French Fauvist artist Henri Matisse paints *The Dance*. The Indian writer Rabindranath Tagore publishes his Bengali poetry collection *Gitanjali/Song Offering*.

1911 The Russian-born French artist Marc Chagall paints *I and My Village*.

1912 The English composer Frederick Delius completes his orchestral work *On Hearing the First Cuckoo in Spring*, one of his *Two Mood Pictures*. The French artist Georges Braque creates the first *papiers-collés* (paintings that incorporate pieces of paper), exemplified by works such as *Fruit Dish and Glass*.

1913 The French writer Marcel Proust publishes *Du Côté de chez Swann/Swann's Way*, the first volume of *A la recherche du temps perdu/Remembrance of Things Past*.

1914 The US writer Robert Frost publishes his poetry collection *North of Boston*. It contains some of his best-known poems including 'The Death of the Hired Man' and 'Mending Wall'.

1915 The Bohemian-born German writer Franz Kafka publishes his novella *Die Verwandlung/Metamorphosis*.

1917 The Irish writer W B Yeats publishes his poetry collection *The Wild Swans at Coole*, which includes 'An Irish Airman Foresees his Death'.

1918 The *Poems* of the English Victorian writer Gerard Manley Hopkins are published posthumously.

1920 The *Collected Poems* of the English World War I poet Wilfred Owen are published posthumously, edited by Siegfried Sassoon.

1921 The Czech writer Jaroslav Hasek publishes the first volume of his satirical novel *Osudy dobrého vojáka Svejka za svetové války/The Good Soldier Schweik*. The last volume appears in 1923.

1922 The Irish writer James Joyce publishes his novel *Ulysses* in Paris. US-born English writer T S Eliot publishes his long poem *The Waste Land* in *The Criterion*.

1924 The English writer E M Forster publishes his novel *A Passage to India*. The play *Juno and the Paycock*, by the Irish dramatist Sean O'Casey, is first performed, at the Abbey Theatre in Dublin, Ireland. The US composer George Gershwin completes his orchestral work *Rhapsody in Blue*.

1925 The US writer F Scott Fitzgerald publishes *The Great Gatsby*.

1926 The English writer A A Milne publishes his children's story book *Winnie-the-Pooh*.

1927 The English writer Virginia Woolf publishes her novel *To the Lighthouse*. The German writer Hermann Hesse publishes his novel *Der Steppenwolf/Steppenwolf*.

1928 The English writer D H Lawrence publishes his novel *Lady Chatterley's Lover* privately in Florence, Italy. Thought obscene, the full text is not published until 1959 in the USA, and 1960 in Britain. The opera *Die Dreigroschenoper/The Threepenny Opera* by the German composer Kurt Weill is first performed, in Berlin.

1929 The Belgian Surrealist artist René Magritte paints *The Treachery of Images (Ceci n'est pas une pipe/This is not a Pipe)*. The Dutch artist Piet Mondrian paints *Composition with Yellow and Blue*. The French writer, filmmaker, and artist Jean Cocteau publishes his novel *Les Enfants terribles/The Incorrigible Children*. The Swiss artist Paul Klee draws *Fool in a Trance* with one continuous line. The US writer Ernest Hemingway publishes his novel *A Farewell to Arms*. The US writer William Faulkner publishes his novel *The Sound and the Fury*.

1930 The US artist Edward Hopper paints *Early Sunday Morning*.

1931 The Spanish Surrealist artist Salvador Dalí paints *The Persistence of Memory*.

1932 The English writer Aldous Huxley publishes his novel *Brave New World*, which presents a nightmarish vision of a utopia based on science and technology.

1933 The Spanish writer Federico García Lorca completes his play *Bodas de sangre/Blood Wedding*.

1935 The Bulgarian writer Elias Canetti publishes the novel *Die Blendung/The Blinding* in German. It will be translated in 1946 as *Auto-Da-Fé* in Britain and *The Tower of Babel* in the USA.

1936 Hungarian-born US photographer Frank Capa (pseudonym of André Friedman) takes *Death of a Loyalist* (also known as *Moment of Death*), one of the best-known images of the Spanish Civil War. The English writer W H Auden publishes his poetry collection *Look, Stranger!* and writes the verse commentary for the General Post Office documentary film *Night Mail*, directed by Harry Watt and Basil Wright.

1937 The English writer J R R Tolkien publishes his fantasy novel *The Hobbit*. The Russian composer Dmitry Shostakovich completes his Symphony No. 5 in D minor, *A Soviet Artist's Reply to Just Criticism*. The Spanish artist Pablo Picasso paints *Guernica*.

1938 French photographer Henri Cartier-Bresson takes *Sunday, Bank of the Marne*. The French philosopher and writer Jean-Paul Sartre publishes his novel *Nausée/Nausea*. It becomes one of the classics of the philosophy of Existentialism.

1939 The US crime writer Raymond Chandler publishes his classic novel *The Big Sleep*, the first of his novels to feature his detective Philip Marlowe. The US writer John Steinbeck publishes his novel *The Grapes of Wrath*, a vivid account of the Depression in California. Two major designs by the US architect Frank Lloyd Wright are completed in the USA: the Kaufman House, 'Falling Water', in Bear Run, Pennsylvania; and the Johnson Wax Factory (with umbrella columns), in Racine, Wisconsin.

1941 The English composer Michael Tippett completes his choral work *A Child of Our Time*. The play *Mutter Courage und ihre Kinder/Mother Courage and her Children*, by the German writer Bertolt Brecht, is first performed, in Zürich, Switzerland. The US writer Eugene O'Neill completes one of his best-known plays, *Long Day's Journey into Night*. It will not open until 1956.

1942 The Algerian-born French writer Albert Camus publishes his novel *L'Etranger/The Outsider*.

1943 The Hungarian composer Béla Bartók completes his Concerto for Orchestra.

1944 The Argentine writer Jorge Luis Borges publishes *Fictions*. The US composer Aaron Copland completes his score for the ballet *Appalachian Spring*, with choreography by Martha Graham. It is first performed the same year in Washington, DC.

1945 US photographer Alfred Eisenstaedt takes *The Kiss (V-J Day)*.

1947 The Swiss artist Alberto Giacometti sculpts *Man Pointing*. The US artist Jackson Pollock, an Abstract Expressionist, paints *Cathedral*. The play *A Streetcar Named Desire*, by the US writer Tennessee Williams, is first performed, in New York.

1948 The English writer Graham Greene publishes his novel *The Heart of the Matter*.

1949 The English writer George Orwell publishes his novel *Nineteen Eighty-Four*. The play *Death of a Salesman*, by the US writer Arthur Miller, is first performed, in New York. The US-born English artist Jacob Epstein sculpts *Lazarus*.

1950 The Chilean writer Pablo Neruda publishes his *Canto General/General Song*, a series of poems that give an epic account of the history of South America.

1951

The US writer J D Salinger publishes *The Catcher in the Rye*, which describes an adolescent's rejection of the 'phony' world of adults. It soon became a cult classic. Salinger became increasingly reclusive and published nothing after the mid 1960s.
Penguin Books Limited

1952 The Unité d'Habitation, an influential housing complex in Marseilles, France, designed by the Swiss-born French architect Le Corbusier (pseudonym of Charles Edouard Jeanneret), is completed. The US composer John Cage creates *4' 33''*, a piece for piano that consist of a pianist sitting silently at a piano for 4 minutes and 33 seconds.

1953 The Irish-born British artist Francis Bacon paints *Study After Velàzquez: Pope Innocent X*. The play *En attendant Godot/Waiting for Godot*, by the Irish writer Samuel Beckett, is first performed, in Paris, France. The play *Under Milk Wood*, by the Welsh writer Dylan Thomas is first performed, at Harvard University, Cambridge, Massachusetts.

1954 The English writer William Golding publishes his novel *Lord of the Flies*. The US artist Mark Rothko, a leading exponent of Abstract Expressionism, paints *Untitled: Yellow, Orange, Red on Orange*.

1955 The US rock 'n' roll group Bill Haley and the Comets release 'Rock Around the Clock'. Sales will exceed 17 million.

1956 The English artist Richard Hamilton creates the collage *What Is It That Makes Today's Homes So Different, So Appealing?*, one of the first works of British Pop Art. The Japanese writer Yukio Mishima publishes his novel *Kinkakuji/The Temple of the Golden Pavilion*. The play *Look Back in Anger*, by the English dramatist John Osborne, is first performed, in London, a classic text of the 'Angry Young Man' movement.

1957 The English artist Henry Moore sculpts *Reclining Figure* for the UNESCO building in Paris. The Russian writer Boris Pasternak publishes his novel *Doktor Zhivago/Dr Zhivago* in Italy, permission having been refused in the USSR. An English translation appears in 1958. The US writer Jack Kerouac publishes his novel *On the Road*, one of the major works of the 'Beat' movement of the 1950s and 1960s.

1959 The German writer Günther Grass publishes his novel *Die Blechtrommel/The Tin Drum*. The Solomon Guggenheim Museum, a modern art museum designed by US architect Frank Lloyd Wright, opens in New York.

1960 The absurdist play *Le Rhinocéros/The Rhinoceros*, by the Romanian-born French dramatist Eugène Ionesco, is first performed, in Paris, France. The German composer Karlheinz Stockhausen completes his electronic work *Kontakte/Contact*. The play *The Caretaker*, by the English dramatist Harold Pinter, is first performed, at the Arts Theatre in London, England. The US writer John Updike publishes his novel *Rabbit Run*.

1961 The Russian writer Yevgeny Yevtushenko publishes his long poem *Babi Yar*. Russian writer Alexander Solzhenitsyn publishes his novella *Odin den Ivana Denisovicha/One Day in the Life of Ivan Denisovich*.

1962 The Trans World Airlines Terminal at Idlewild (now John F Kennedy) Airport, in New York, designed by the Finnish architect Eero Saarinen, is completed. The US writer James Baldwin publishes his novel *Another Country*.

1963 The German writer Heinrich Böll publishes *Ansichten eines Clowns/The Clown*. The US Pop artist Roy Lichtenstein paints *I Know... Brad* and *Whaam!*.

1964 The English writer Philip Larkin publishes his poetry collection *The Whitsun Weddings*.

1966 The play *Rosencrantz and Guildenstern are Dead*, by the Czech-born English dramatist Tom Stoppard, is first performed, at the Edinburgh Festival, Scotland.

1967 The Colombian writer Gabriel García Márquez publishes his novel *Cien años de soledad/One Hundred Years of Solitude*. The Beatles release *Sergeant Pepper's Lonely Hearts Club Band*.

1969 US writer Philip Roth publishes his novel *Portnoy's Complaint*.

1971 The English artist David Hockney paints *Rubber Ring Floating in a Swimming Pool* and *Mr and Mrs Ossie Clark and Percy*.

1975 The play *American Buffalo*, by the US writer David Mamet, is first performed, in Chicago, Illinois.

1977 The Centre National d'Art et de Culture Georges Pompidou (Pompidou Centre) in Paris, France, designed by the High Tech architects Renzo Piano and Richard Rogers, is completed.

1979 Irish writer Seamus Heaney publishes his *Field Work*. The South African writer Nadine Gordimer publishes her novel *Burger's Daughter*. The Trinidadian writer V S Naipaul publishes his novel *A Bend in the River*.

1980 The Italian writer and scholar Umberto Eco publishes his novel *Il nome della rosa/The Name of the Rose*.

1981 The German-born English artist Lucian Freud paints *Naked Girl with Dog*. The Indian-born English writer Salman Rushdie publishes his novel *Midnight's Children*, which wins the Booker Prize.

1982 The US writer Alice Walker publishes her novel *The Color Purple*. It wins the Pulitzer Prize for Fiction in 1983.

1984 The Czech-born writer Milan Kundera publishes his novel *Nesnesitelná lehkost byti/The Unbearable Lightness of Being*. The Neue Staatsgalerie (an art gallery) in Stuttgart, West Germany, designed by the English architect James Stirling, is completed. It is one of the leading works of Post-Modernism.

1985 The Hong Kong and Shanghai Bank Headquarters in Hong Kong, designed by the English architect Norman Foster, is completed.

1989 A controversial glass pyramid entrance to the Louvre museum, designed by the Chinese-born US architect I M Pei, is completed in Paris, France. The West Indian poet Derek Walcott publishes his long poem *Omeros*.

1992 English artist Damien Hirst creates *The Physical Impossibility of Death in the Mind of Someone Living*, a shark preserved in a tank of formaldehyde.

1995 English writer Pat Barker publishes *Ghost Road*, the final volume in the *Regeneration* trilogy.

1997 The widely acclaimed futuristic branch of New York's Guggenheim Museum, designed by the US architect Frank Gehry, opens in Bilbao, Spain.

1998 The British poet Ted Hughes publishes *Birthday Letters*, previously unpublished poems about his late wife, US poet Sylvia Plath. It wins the 1998 Whitbread Book of the Year award.

Science Chronology

1050 The astrolabe arrives in Europe from the East, where Muslim scientists developed it two centuries before.

1120 The French-born Prior Walcher of Malvern Abbey, England, introduces the measurement of latitude and longitude in degrees, minutes, and seconds.

1193 Italian physician Burgundo of Pisa translates the works of ancient Greek physician Galen from Greek into Latin, thus reintroducing much of Galen's thinking into western Europe.

1248 Spanish-born Muslim Al-Baytar, 'chief of botanists' in Cairo, Egypt, writes *Kitab al-jami/Collection of Simple Drugs*, which lists 1,400 different remedies and is the largest and most popular Arab pharmacopoeia.

1260 The English friar and scholar Roger Bacon investigates the laws governing optical phenomena such as refraction and reflection.

1272 The *Alfonsine Tables* are completed and published by two Jewish astronomers working for King Alfonso X of Castile. They will be used to calculate planetary positions and eclipses for the next three centuries.

1288 The Jewish astronomer Jacob ben Makir ibn Tibbon writes a Hebrew treatise on the construction and use of an instrument called the quadrant. This is a considerably simpler device than the astrolabe for making astronomical measurements.

1305 King Edward I of England introduces measures to standardize certain weights and measures, including the yard and the acre.

1316 The Italian physician Mondino de Liuzzi conducts the first properly recorded dissection of a human corpse at Bologna University, Italy. His book *Anatomia* will become the standard work on anatomy for two centuries.

1330 English philosopher William of Occam proposes 'Occam's razor', the principle that the simplest explanation is most likely to be true – an idea that will be highly influential when applied to scientific theories.

1490 While visiting Milan, Italy, the Italian scholar Leonardo da Vinci begins to keep notebooks detailing his ideas and inventions. He discovers and describes capillarity, the way in which liquids rise up through small-bore tubes.

1522 German illustrator Albrecht Dürer designs a flying machine.

1530 A manual of dentistry is published at Leipzig, Germany – the first methodical approach to the subject.

1536 The Swiss physician Paracelsus (Theophrastus von Hohenheim) produces *Die grosse Wundartzney/Great Surgery Book*, a landmark break with Galenic medicine.

1540 Flemish anatomist Andreas Vesalius performs dissections on human cadavers at the University of Bologna.

1543 Polish astronomer and priest Nicolaus Copernicus outlines his theory that the Earth and other planets orbit the Sun.

1544 German mineralogist Agricola (Georg Bauer) writes *De ortu et causis subterraneis/On Subterranean Origin and Causes*, a founding work in geology, identifying the erosive power of water, and the origin of mineral veins as depositions from solution.

1568 Flemish cartographer Gerardus Mercator devises the cylindrical map projection named after him, for use on sea charts. It enables navigators to plot straight-line courses without having to continually adjust their compass readings.

***c.* 1600** The compound microscope, which uses two lenses to magnify objects, is invented – probably by Hans Lippershey or Hans Jansen and his son Zacharias, both spectacle makers from Middelburg in the Netherlands. The English physician William Gilbert writes *De magnete/On Magnetism*, a pioneering study of electricity and magnetism, which distinguishes between electrostatic and magnetic effects.

1602

Danish astronomer Tycho Brahe's *Astronomia instauratae progymnasmata/Introducing Exercises toward a Restored Astronomy* is published posthumously, giving accurate positions for 777 fixed stars. Tycho Brahe was the greatest astronomical observer of the era before the telescope. The invention of a refractor telescope is attributed to Hans Lippershey in 1608. Galileo improved this and was the first to use a telescope in astronomy in 1609. *Corbis.*

1604 Italian scientist Galileo Galilei discovers his law of falling bodies, proving that gravity acts with the same strength on all objects, independent of their mass.

1609 German astronomer Johannes Kepler publishes *Astronomia nova/New Astronomy*, which describes the orbit of Mars accurately. His first two laws of planetary motion state that all planets move in elliptical orbits around the Sun, and that they sweep out equal areas in equal times.

1610 French chemist Jean Beguin publishes *Tyrocinium chymicum/An introduction to chemistry*, the first textbook on chemistry (as opposed to alchemy). Italian astronomer Galileo Galilei publishes *Sidereus nuncius/The Starry Messenger*, revealing his telescopic discoveries, including the moons of Jupiter, the phases of Venus, sunspots, and the curious shape of Saturn.

1622 English mathematician William Oughtred invents an early form of circular slide rule, adapting the principle behind Scottish mathematician John Napier's 'bones'.

1623 English philosopher Francis Bacon, Baron Verulam, publishes *De augmentis scientarum/On the Increase of Knowledge*, an expanded version of an earlier work, dealing with the philosophy of science and the nature of scientific knowledge.

1643 Italian scientist Evangelista Torricelli invents the mercury barometer.

1658 Dutch microscopist Jan Swammerdam records oval particles in the blood of frogs – the first observation of red blood cells.

1660 German scientist Otto von Guericke discovers the sudden drop in air pressure preceding a violent storm – a discovery that will revolutionize weather forecasting.

1665 English scientist Robert Hooke publishes *Micrographia*, the first serious scientific work on microscopy, describing the function of the microscope, and coining the name 'cells' to describe cavities he has found in the structure of cork.

1666 In order to calculate the Moon's orbit accurately, English physicist Isaac Newton develops a new type of mathematics, calculus or 'fluxions'.

1674 Dutch microscopist Anton van Leeuwenhoek develops the single-lens microscope, and begins a series of important discoveries by observing protozoa.

1676 English physician Thomas Sydenham publishes *Observationes medicae/Medical Observations*, which will be a standard medical text for two centuries. In it, he analyses fevers and suggests cooling treatment for smallpox.

1679 German mathematician Gottfried von Leibniz introduces binary arithmetic, in which only combinations of two symbols are used to represent all numbers (later used in computing).

1682 English astronomer Edmond Halley observes the comet that he later concluded (in 1705) returns every 76 years, and which now bears his name.

1686 English mathematician and physicist Isaac Newton presents his great work, the *Philosophiae naturalis principia mathematica/Mathematical Principles and Natural Philosophy*, to the Royal Society. The work is published in 1687.

1709 Polish-born Dutch physicist Gabriel Fahrenheit creates a thermometer using the expansion of alcohol with temperature. He devises a temperature scale with the freezing point of water at 32° and boiling point at 212°.

1710 Irish philosopher George Berkeley publishes a treatise concerning sense perceptions, suggesting all knowledge is acquired by direct experience – the foundation of scientific empiricism.

1735 In his *Systema Naturae/System of Nature*, Swedish botanist Carolus Linnaeus introduces a system for classifying plants by genus and species – a taxonomy that will survive the upheavals of evolutionism and remains in use today.

1742 Swedish scientist Anders Celsius proposes an international fixed temperature scale to the Swedish Academy of Sciences, with 0° set as the boiling point of water, and 100° set as the freezing point. This was later reversed.

1763 English clergyman Edmund Stone describes the effective treatment of fever using willow bark, from which the active ingredient of aspirin is later derived. French surgeon Claudius Aymand performs the first successful appendectomy.

1766 English natural philosopher Henry Cavendish discovers the element hydrogen. Swiss biologist Albrecht von Haller shows that nerves stimulate muscles to contract, and that all nerves lead to the spinal column and brain. His work lays the foundation of modern neurology.

1769 English inventor Richard Arkwright patents a spinning machine (or 'water frame' because it operates by water) that produces cotton yarn suitable for warp; it is one of the key inventions of Britain's Industrial Revolution.

1777–1779

The cast-iron bridge over the River Severn at Ironbridge Gorge, Shropshire, England is built. It was the first iron bridge in the world and became a symbol of the Industrial Revolution. It was constructed by English engineer Abraham Darby (1750–1791), from castings made in his pioneering iron foundry nearby. *Linda Proud*

1774 English chemist Joseph Priestley discovers the element oxygen.

1777 French chemist Antoine-Laurent Lavoisier shows that air is made up of a mixture of gases, and that one of them (oxygen) is necessary for combustion and rusting to take place.

1781 German-born English astronomer William Herschel discovers the planet Uranus.

1782 Scottish engineer James Watt patents the double-acting steam engine, which provides power on both the upstroke and the downstroke of the piston.

1787 French physicist Jacques-Alexandre Charles demonstrates that different gases expand by the same amount for the same temperature rise. It becomes known as Charles's law.

1788 Scottish geologist James Hutton's paper *Theory of the Earth* expounds his uniformitarian theory of continual change in the Earth's geological features and marks a turning point in geology.

1790 French chemist Nicolas Leblanc develops an inexpensive process for making sodium carbonate from sodium chloride (common salt). Sodium carbonate is used in making paper, soap, glass, and porcelain.

1791 Italian physiologist Luigi Galvani announces his observations on the muscular contraction of dead frogs, which he argues are caused electrically.

1796 English physician Edward Jenner performs the first vaccination against smallpox. French astronomer Pierre-Simon Laplace enunciates the 'nebular hypothesis', that the Solar System formed from a cloud of gas.

1800 Italian physicist Alessandro Volta invents the voltaic pile made of discs of silver and zinc – the first battery.

1801 English chemist and physicist John Dalton formulates the law of partial pressure in gases – Dalton's Law – that states that each component of a gas mixture produces the same pressure as if it occupied the container alone. English physician and physicist Thomas Young discovers the interference of light when he observes that light passing through two closely spaced pinholes produces alternating bands of light and dark in the area of overlap. He thereby establishes the wave theory of light. German mathematician Karl Friedrich Gauss publishes *Disquisitiones Arithmeticae/Discourses on Arithmetic*, which deals with relationships and properties of integers and leads to the modern theory of algebraic equations.

1807 English chemist Humphry Davy invents the first arc lamp; a 2,000-cell battery creates an electric arc across a gap of 100 mm/4 in between two charcoal conductors.

1811 Swedish chemist Jöns Jakob Berzelius introduces the modern system of chemical symbols.

1814 English engineer George Stephenson constructs the first effective steam locomotive.

1819–1826 Scottish engineer Thomas Telford constructs the 177 m/580 ft Menai suspension bridge, the first modern suspension bridge.

1822 Mary Anning discovers the first fossil to be recognized as that of a dinosaur – an *Iguanodon* – in Devon, England.

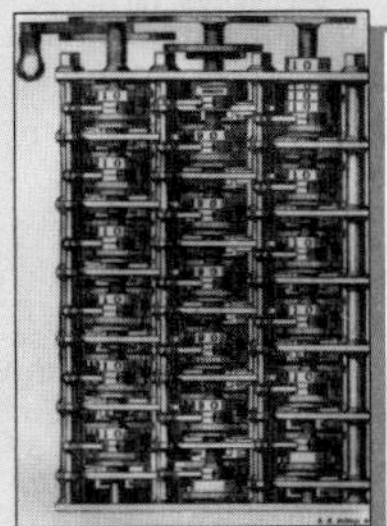

1823

English mathematician Charles Babbage begins construction of the 'difference' engine, a machine for calculating logarithms and trigonometric functions (shown here as a woodcut). He abandoned the difference engine for the analytical engine on which he worked for the rest of his life. The analytical engine was never actually built. *Corbis*

1828 German chemist Friedrich Wöhler synthesizes urea from ammonium cyanate. It is the first synthesis of an organic substance from an inorganic compound and signals the beginning of organic chemistry.

1830–1833 Scottish geologist Charles Lyell publishes his three-volume work *Principles of Geology* in which he argues that geological formations are the result of presently observable processes acting over millions of years.

1833 English physicist Michael Faraday announces the basic laws of electrolysis: that the amount of a substance deposited on an electrode is proportional to the amount of electric current passed through the cell, and that the amounts of different elements are proportional to their atomic weights.

1836 French physicist Edmund Becquerel discovers the photovoltaic effect when he observes the creation of a voltage between two electrodes, one of which is exposed to light.

1838 The US artist and inventor Samuel Finley Breese Morse and financier Alfred Louis Vail make the first successful public demonstration of an electric telegraph.

1843 English mathematician Ada Byron, Countess Lovelace, writes a programme for Charles Babbage's analytical engine – the first computer programme. English physicist James Joule determines the value for the mechanical equivalent of heat (now known as the joule), that is the amount of work required to produce a unit of heat.

1845–1858 German naturalist and explorer Alexander von Humboldt lays the basis of modern geography with the publication of *Kosmos/Cosmos*, in which he arranges geographic knowledge in a systematic fashion.

1846 US dentist William Thomas Morton gives the first successful demonstration of ether as an anaesthetic during a dental operation to extract a tooth.

1847 English physicist James Joule discovers the law of conservation of energy – the first law of thermodynamics.

1848 Scottish physicist William Thomson (Lord Kelvin), devises the absolute temperature scale. He defines absolute zero as –273°C/–459.67°F, where the molecular energy is zero.

1851 French scientist Jean-Bernard-Léon Foucault proves that the Earth rotates by using a pendulum 67 m/220 ft long (Foucault's pendulum), in Paris, France. The pendulum always swings in the same plane and the Earth rotates underneath it.

1855 French physiologist Claude Bernard discovers that ductless glands produce hormones, which he calls 'internal secretions'.

1856 French chemist and microbiologist Louis Pasteur establishes that microorganisms are responsible for fermentation, thus establishing the discipline of microbiology.

1858 British physician Henry Gray publishes *Anatomy of the Human Body, Descriptive and Surgical* (*Gray's Anatomy*). It remains the standard text in anatomy for over 100 years.

1859 Charles Darwin publishes *On the Origin of Species by Natural Selection*, which expounds his theory of evolution by natural selection, and by implication denies the truth of biblical creation and God's hand in Nature.

1863 French parasitologist Casimir-Joseph Davaine shows that anthrax is due to the presence of rodlike microorganisms in the blood. It is the first disease of animals and humans to be shown to be caused by a specific microorganism.

1864 Scottish physicist James Clerk Maxwell introduces mathematical equations that describe the electromagnetic field, and predict the existence of radio waves.

1865 Austrian monk and botanist Gregor Mendel publishes a paper that outlines the fundamental laws of heredity.

1869 Based on the fact that the elements exhibit recurring patterns of properties when placed in order of increasing atomic weight, Russian chemist Dmitry Ivanovich Mendeleyev develops the periodic classification of the elements. He leaves gaps for elements yet to be discovered.

1876 German engineer Nikolaus Otto patents the four-stroke internal combustion engine, the prototype of modern engines. Scottish-born US inventor Alexander Graham Bell patents a device for transmitting human speech over electric wires, the first telephone.

1877 German aeronautical engineer Otto Lilienthal begins to build successful gliders with arched wings he steers by moving his legs. English surgeon Joseph Lister performs the first operation conducted under antiseptic conditions. Its success convinces other surgeons of the value of antisepsis.

1877

US inventor Thomas Alva Edison (right) patents the phonograph. Recording involves the transmission of sound vibrations through a large horn and a diaphragm to a stylus, which inscribes a groove on a rotating wax cylinder. One of his other most important inventions was the electric light bulb in 1879. He is photographed here with Henry Ford, who was employed as chief engineer at the Edison Company before forming his own Ford Motor Company. *Corbis*

1881 French microbiologist Louis Pasteur vaccinates sheep against anthrax. It is the first infectious disease to be treated effectively with an antibacterial vaccine, and his success lays the foundations of immunology.

1882 German physician Robert Koch announces the discovery of *Mycobacterium tuberculosis*, the bacillus responsible for tuberculosis. This is the first time a microorganism has been definitively associated with a human disease.

1886 Swedish chemist Svante August Arrhenius explains the properties of acids and bases through their ability to yield ions.

1895 French inventors Auguste and Louis Lumière patent the cinématograph, a device for taking and projecting moving pictures. German physicist Wilhelm Röntgen discovers X-rays.

1897 English physicist John Joseph Thomson demonstrates the existence of the electron, the first known subatomic particle. It revolutionizes knowledge of atomic structure by indicating that the atom can be subdivided.

1898 French chemists Pierre and Marie Curie discover the radio-active elements radium and polonium. Radium is discovered in pitchblende and is the first element to be discovered radiochemically. Martinus Willem Beijerinck identifies the first virus; it is the cause of tobacco mosaic disease.

1899 British physicist Ernest Rutherford discovers alpha and beta rays, produced by the radioactivity of uranium.

1900 Austrian immunologist Karl Landsteiner discovers the ABO blood group. German physicist Max Planck suggests that black bodies (perfect absorbers) radiate energy in packets or quanta, rather than continuously, thus beginning the science of quantum physics.

1903 Russian physiologist Ivan Pavlov describes learning by conditioning. He trains dogs to expect food when they hear a bell and eventually they salivate every time the bell rings. US aviator Orville Wright makes the first successful flight in an aeroplane with a petrol engine at Kitty Hawk, North Carolina, covering 37 m/120ft in a flight lasting just 12 seconds.

1905 German physicist Albert Einstein develops his special theory of relativity in a series of four papers in Switzerland.

1906 English biochemist Frederick Gowland Hopkins suggests that necessary 'accessory factors' (vitamins) are contained in foods in addition to carbohydrates, fats, minerals, and water.

1909 Danish biochemist Søren Sørensen devises the pH scale for measuring acidity and alkalinity.

1911 New Zealand-born British physicist Ernest Rutherford proposes the concept of the nuclear atom, in which the mass of the atom is concentrated in a nucleus occupying 1/10,000 of the space of the atom and which has a positive charge balanced by surrounding electrons.

1912 German meteorologist Alfred Wegener suggests the idea of continental drift and proposes the existence of a supercontinent (Pangaea) in the distant past.

1912 Scottish physicist Charles Thomson Rees Wilson perfects the cloud chamber, which detects ion trails since water molecules condense on ions. It is used to study radioactivity, X-rays, cosmic rays, and other nuclear phenomena.

1917 The US inventor Edwin Armstrong invents the superheterodyne radio circuit. It allows easy tuning of weak radio waves, which it also amplifies. Its design becomes the basis of radar, television, and all AM radios.

1921 Canadian physiologists Frederick Banting, Charles Best, and John James MacLeod isolate insulin. German physicist Max Born develops a mathematical description of the first law of thermodynamics. Swiss psychologist Carl Jung differentiates two personality types: extroverted and introverted.

1923 Austrian psychiatrist Sigmund Freud publishes *The Ego and the Id*, in which he elaborates his division of the mind into the id, ego, and superego.

1924 US astronomer Edwin Hubble demonstrates that certain Cepheid variable stars are several hundred thousand light years away and thus outside the Milky Way galaxy. The nebulae they are found in are the first galaxies to be discovered that are proved to be independent of the Milky Way.

1925 The Scottish electrical engineer John Logie Baird transmits the first television images of recognizable human faces. US geneticists Thomas Hunt Morgan, Alfred Sturtevant, and Calvin Blackman Bridges publish the results of their genetic experiments with the fruit fly, showing that genes can be mapped onto chromosomes.

1926 Austrian physicist Erwin Schrödinger develops wave mechanics.

1927 Belgian astronomer Georges Lemaître proposes that the universe was created by an explosion of energy and matter from a 'primaeval atom' – the beginning of the Big Bang theory. German physicist Werner Heisenberg propounds the 'uncertainty principle' in quantum physics, which states that it is impossible to simultaneously determine the position and momentum of an atom. It explains why Newtonian mechanics is inapplicable at the atomic level.

1928 Scottish bacteriologist Alexander Fleming discovers penicillin when he notices that the mould *Penicillium notatum*, which has invaded a culture of staphylococci, inhibits bacterial growth.

1930 US electrical engineer Vannevar Bush builds the differential analyser. The first analogue computer, it is used to solve differential equations. US astronomer Clyde Tombaugh, at the Lowell Observatory, Arizona, discovers the ninth planet, Pluto.

1933 US engineer Edwin Armstrong patents frequency modulation (FM) in radio, which eliminates static.

1934 French physicists Frédéric and Irène Joliot-Curie bombard boron, aluminium, and magnesium with alpha particles and obtain radioactive isotopes of nitrogen, phosphorus, and aluminium – elements that are not normally radioactive. They are the first radioactive elements to be prepared artificially. German scientist Rudolf Kuhnold, using a 700-watt transmitter on 600 megacycles plus a receiver, succeeds in receiving echoes bounced off a battleship anchored 550 m/1,800 ft away. It is the first practical demonstration of radar.

1935 Austrian zoologist Konrad Lorenz founds the discipline of ethology by describing the learning behaviour of young ducklings; visual and auditory stimuli from the parent cause them to 'imprint' on the parent. Chemists working for the British company Imperial Chemical Industries (ICI) polymerize ethylene to make polyethylene, the first true plastic. US inventor Robert H Goddard launches a liquid-propelled rocket faster than the speed of sound.

1936 British mathematician Alan Turing supplies the theoretical basis for digital computers by describing a machine, now known as the Turing machine, capable of universal rather than special-purpose problem solving.

1937 French microbiologist Max Theiler develops a vaccine against yellow fever; it is the first antiviral vaccine. German-born British biochemist Hans Krebs describes the citric acid cycle in cells, which converts sugars, fats, and proteins into carbon dioxide, water, and energy – the 'Krebs cycle'. Nylon, developed by W H Carothers, is patented by the US chemicals company Du Pont and is commercially available the following year in the form of toothbrush bristles. English engineer Frank Whittle tests the first prototype jet engine.

1938 German inventor Konrad Zuse constructs the first binary calculator using a binary code; it is the first working computer.

1939 The first effective helicopter, the VS-300, designed by Ukranian-born US engineer Igor Sikorsky, makes its first test flight.

1942 Italian physicist Enrico Fermi and his colleagues at the University of Chicago, Illinois, use thin layers of uranium oxide and graphite to create the first nuclear pile and initiate a controlled chain-reaction – the first nuclear reactor.

1943 French oceanographer Jacques Cousteau invents the aqualung ('scuba'), the first fully automatic compressed-air breathing apparatus. It allows him to dive to a depth of 64 m/210 ft.

US biologist Selman A Waksman discovers the antibiotic streptomycin, which is used as a treatment for tuberculosis; he coins the term 'antibiotic'.

1944 British chemists Archer J P Martin and Richard L M Synge separate amino acids by using a solvent in a column of silica gel. The beginnings of partition chromatography, the technique leads to further advances in chemical, medical, and biological research.

1945 The first atomic explosion occurs when the nuclear device code-named 'Trinity' is exploded near Alamogordo, New Mexico in July. On 6 August and 9 August similar devices are dropped on Hiroshima and Nagasaki, Japan.

1947 US physicist Willard Libby develops carbon-14 dating. US-Hungarian mathematician John Von Neumann introduces the idea of a stored-program computer, in which both instruction codes and data are stored.

1948 Hungarian-British physicist Dennis Gabor invents holography, the production of three-dimensional images. US physicists George Gamow and Ralph Alpher develop the 'Big Bang' theory of the origins of the universe, which says that a primeval thermonuclear explosion led to the universe expanding rapidly from a highly compressed original state.

1949 BINAC is built by US scientists John W Mauchly and John Presper Eckert. It is the first electronic stored-program computer to store data on magnetic tape.

1952

The USA explodes the first thermonuclear fusion device, or hydrogen bomb, at Eniwetok island in the Marshall Islands, although this is not revealed until February 1954. The device had a yield of 10.4 megatons (the equivalent to 10.4 million tons of high explosive TNT). *Science Photo Library*

1953 English molecular biologist Francis Crick and US biologist James Watson announce the discovery of the double helix structure of DNA, the basic material of heredity.

1955 US radiophysicists at the Massachusetts Institute of Technology develop the use of ultra high-frequency (UHF) waves for television broadcasting.

1956 US engineers Charles Ginsburg and Ray Milton Dolby of Ampex Corporation demonstrate the first practical videotape recorder. It revolutionizes television broadcasting by permitting shows to be taped rather than shown live.

1957 Interferon, a natural protein that fights viruses, is discovered by Scottish virologist Alick Isaacs and Swiss virologist Jean Lindemann. The USSR launches the first artificial satellite, *Sputnik 1*, to study the cosmosphere. It weighs 84 kg/184 lb and circles the Earth in 95 minutes, inaugurating the space age.

1958 US electrical engineer Jack Kilby demonstrates the first integrated circuit. It consists of transistors, resistors, and capacitors contained within a silicon substrate. It leads to the third generation of computers.

1960 US physicist Theodore Maiman constructs the first laser (light amplification by stimulated emission of radiation), a device producing an intense beam of parallel or coherent light.

1961 US meteorologist Edward Lorenz discovers a mathematical system with chaotic behaviour, leading to a new branch of mathematics known as chaos theory.

1963 Dutch-born US astronomer Maarten Schmidt discovers the first quasar (3C 273), an extraordinarily distant object brighter than the largest known galaxy yet with a star-like image.

1965 Canadian geologist John Tuzo Wilson formulates the theory of plate tectonics to explain continental drift and seafloor spreading. The first international communication satellite, *Intelsat 1* (*Early Bird*), is launched into geostationary orbit over the Atlantic Ocean at the Equator. It provides 240 two-way telephone circuits or one television channel.

1966 British engineers Charles Kao and Georges Hockman of Standard Telecommunications Laboratories show that data can be carried on light transmitted over long distances in glass fibres rather than on electric currents in copper wire, leading to the development of fibre optic cables.

1967 US scientists Syukuvo Manabe and R T Wetherald warn that the increase in carbon dioxide in the atmosphere, produced by human activities, is causing a 'greenhouse effect', which will raise atmospheric temperatures and cause a rise in sea levels. Irish astronomer Jocelyn Bell and English astronomer Anthony Hewish discover the first pulsar (announced in 1968).

1968 The first supersonic airliner, the *Tupolev TU-144*, designed by Soviet engineer Alexey Tupolev, makes its first flight.

1969 US astronauts Neil Armstrong and Buzz Aldrin land on the Moon. The US Department of Defense establishes a computer network that becomes the basis of the Internet. US geneticist Jonathan Beckwith and associates at the Harvard Medical School isolate a single gene for the first time.

1970 IBM develops the floppy disk for storing computer data.

1972 English engineer Godfrey Hounsfield performs the first successful CAT (computerized axial tomography) scan, which provides cross-sectional X-rays of the human body. US palaeontologists Stephen Jay Gould and Nils Eldridge propose the punctuated equilibrium model – the idea that evolution progresses in fits and starts rather than at a uniform rate.

1974 English physicist Stephen Hawking suggests that black holes emit subatomic particles until their energy is diminished to the point where they explode.

1975 The Soviet spacecraft *Venera 9* and *10* land on Venus and transmit the first pictures from the surface of another planet.

1976 Indian-born US biochemist Har Gobind Khorana and his colleagues announce the construction of the first artificial gene to function naturally when inserted into a bacterial cell. This is a major breakthrough in genetic engineering.

1977 English biochemist Frederick Sanger describes the full sequence of 5,386 bases in the DNA (deoxyribonucleic acid) of virus *phi*X174 in Cambridge, England; the first sequencing of an entire genome.

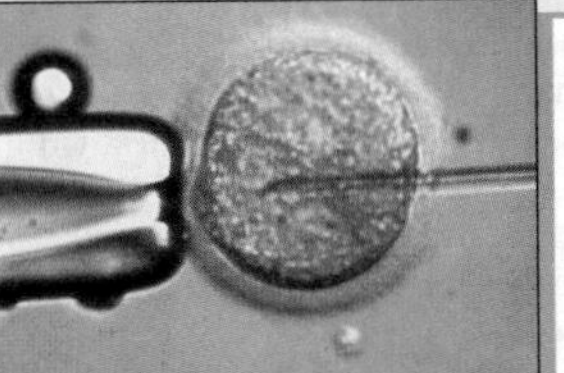

1978

Louise Brown, the first 'test tube' baby, is born. Having been unable to remove a blockage from her mother's Fallopian tube, gynaecologist Patrick Steptoe and physiologist Robert Edwards removed an egg from her ovary, fertilized it with her husband's sperm, and re-implanted it in her uterus. Intracytoplasmic sperm injection (ICSI), shown here, involves the injection of a sperm into an egg (held steady by a pipette). High fertilization rates are achieved as lack of sperm motility is no longer a handicap. *Science Photo Library*

1980 Mathematicians worldwide complete the classification of all finite and simple groups, a task that has taken over 100 mathematicians more than 35 years to complete. The results take up more than 14,000 pages in mathematical journals.

1982 US researcher Stanley Prusiner discovers prions (proteinaceous infectious particles); they are responsible for several neurological diseases including 'mad cow disease' (first identified in 1986).

1983 The US space probe *Pioneer 10* becomes the first artificial object to leave the Solar System.

1984 The Dutch company Philips and Japanese firm Sony introduce the CD-ROM, a laser-read, read-only disk.

1985 Harold Kroto and David Walton at the University of Sussex, England, discover a new unusually stable elemental form of solid carbon made up of closed cages of 60 carbon atoms shaped liked soccer balls; they call them buckminsterfullerines or 'buckyballs'. The British Antarctic Survey detects a hole in the ozone layer which opens each year in the spring over Antarctica.

1988 The Human Genome Organization (HUGO) is established in Washington, DC, USA; scientists announce a project to compile a complete 'map' of human genes.

1990 The space shuttle *Discovery* places the Hubble Space Telescope in Earth orbit; the main mirror proves to be defective.

1992 US biologist Philip Leder receives a patent for the first genetically engineered animal, the oncomouse, which is sensitive to carcinogens.

1995 US astronomers Alan Hale and Thomas Bopp discover the Hale-Bopp comet, the brightest periodic comet.

1997 Scottish researcher Ian Wilmut announces the cloning of a sheep from an adult baby cell.

1998 *Lunar Prospector* satellite detects 11 million tonnes of water on the Moon.

1999 US geneticist Craig Venter announces the possibility of creating a living, replicating organism from an artificial set of genes.

SOCIAL HISTORY CHRONOLOGY

c. 1000 References in the work of the Persian philosopher and physician Avicenna (ibn Sina) show that coffee is being drunk in Arabia and Persia and testify to its use being largely medicinal. Chess is widely played throughout Europe and backgammon is introduced by the Arabs.

1012 Rice is introduced into China from Champa (modern southern Vietnam) and becomes the staple diet.

1087 The *Domesday Book*, compiled for William I the Conqueror, King of England and Duke of Normandy, records 5,624 watermills for corn south of the rivers Trent and Severn, roughly one mill for every 400 people, some stamping-mills for crushing iron-ore, and hammer-mills. It estimates the population of England at between 1 and 1.5 million, with East Anglia the most populous region.

c. 1100 Old English, the common language of England, with strong roots in the Germanic languages of the early invaders, begins to be replaced by Middle English. Middle English embodies the Northern European origins of English, but is also starting to reflect the influence of Latin and Norman French. During this century the tournament (knightly contest) evolves in France as a formal event. *Jeu de paume*, a handball game and the forerunner of real-tennis, is first played in France by monks in monastery cloisters; it is later taken up and played on courts by the French monarchy and aristocracy but it is not played with rackets until around 1500. The board game draughts evolves in Europe, possibly in southern France.

1100–1532 The Inca empire dominates the Andes region of South America. Its population numbers as many as 12 million. Inca society is based on a strict hierarchy, with an emperor who rules with absolute power. Their religion is based on sun-worship, and they are skilled builders who create a system of roads and irrigation.

1120 Playing cards are used in China.

1151 Chess is introduced into England.

1170 The population of London, England, is around 30,000.

1190 English clerk William FitzStephen, clerk to Thomas à Becket, describes the sporting life of London, England, in the preface to his *Vita Sancti Thomae/Life of St Thomas*. Running, jumping, and throwing contests are held at Smithfield on holidays. On Shrove Tuesday the schoolboys of the city of London are permitted to watch cockfighting. At Easter the water quintain, a form of tilting on boats, is staged on the River Thames. In the winter bear- and bull-baiting and boar-fighting events are staged. He also describes horse racing at Smithfield. The races are run between two or three jockeys in the form of matches to prove the quality of a horse as a prerequisite for a sale.

1226 Glass bottles and windows are being manufactured in England.

1299 Italian tarot cards are first mentioned in a manuscript. They are used both for gaming and fortune telling, and the modern pack of playing cards derives from them.

1300 The game of battledore shuttlecock is played in England. It is a precursor of badminton in which players with racquets or paddles aim to keep a shuttlecock in the air for as long as possible. Calcio, a form of football, is played in Florence, Italy.

1333 The Black Death (a combination of bubonic and pneumonic plagues) appears in China, afflicting a population weakened by starvation. It will be spread in the West by travellers and merchants returning from the Far East to Europe.

1451–1456 German craftsman Johann Gutenberg produces the first printed Bible, in Mainz, Germany, using movable, reusable, metal type.

1475

William Caxton, first English printer, produced both the first printed book in English, *Recuyell of the Historyes of Troy* (1475), from a press in Belgium, and also the first book to be printed in England, *Dictes or Sayengis of the Philosophers* (1477). *Philip Sauvain Picture Collection*

1500 European settlers and explorers in North America witness the American Indian team game of *baggataway*, which French settlers later call *La Crosse* (lacrosse).

1518 The first known smallpox epidemic in the New World breaks out in the Caribbean islands. In the next hundred years, epidemics of smallpox, measles, and influenza kill over 90% of the indigenous American population.

1520 The Spanish explorer Hernán Cortés introduces chocolate, which had been used by the Aztecs in Central America, to the Spanish, who keep its existence secret for almost a century.

1540 The potato is introduced into Europe from the Spanish colonies in South America. Sir Francis Drake introduced potatoes to England a second time in 1586; the first time they didn't take.

1546 The population of England is more than 4 million.

1550 An English court case refers to 'crickett' being played in Guildford, Surrey. It is the first certain reference to cricket.

1550–1600 New agricultural products are exchanged between the New and Old Worlds. The Spanish introduce potatoes, tomatoes, quinine, cocoa, tapioca, and tobacco to Europe. From Europe, the New World gains barley, oats, rye, sugar cane, cattle, pigs, poultry, rabbits, and horses.

1556 Franciscan monk André Thevet from Rio de Janeiro introduces tobacco seeds into Europe. The plant is originally grown for decorative purposes, though it is also thought to have some medicinal properties.

1563 Italian physician and anatomist Gabriele Falloppio invents the condom, made of pig intestine, as a means to prevent the spread of syphilis.

1582 Pope Gregory XIII introduces the Gregorian Calendar, correcting errors in the Julian Calendar. 5 October 1582 becomes 15 October 1582 and the new year is confirmed as starting on 1 January. Protestant countries retained the Julian calendar until the beginning of the 18th century.

1584 Sir John Hawkins introduces tobacco into England, although there are a number of other claimants, including Sir Walter Raleigh.

c. 1610 Tea is introduced into Europe, by a Dutch East India Company ship returning from Macao, China.

1635 A postal service begins in Britain with the introduction of a mail coach service between London, England, and Edinburgh, Scotland. The cost of postage depends on the distance covered.

1653 The first postage stamps are produced, in Paris, enabling the sender rather than the receiver to pay the cost of postage.

1782 Ann Goddi, the last person officially executed for witchcraft, is hanged in Switzerland.

1790 Women's hairstyles in France become elaborate. Some shapes are known as 'a reclining dog on a hair cushion' and incorporate flowers and fruit baskets.

1793 The first metric weight system is introduced, in France.

1799 The British prime minister William Pitt the Younger introduces the first income tax in Britain, to finance the war against France, at a rate of 10% on all incomes over £200 per year.

1800–1850 A revolution in retail and wholesale trade occurs: specialization transforms the urban retail market, replacing the general store with individual stores for hardware, groceries, dry goods, furnishing, books, tobacco, etc. Cash-only sales policies are instituted around 1806.

1801 Populations in millions: China 295; India 130; Japan 15; France 27; the German states 14; Britain 10; Spain 10; USA 5.

1851 For the first time, more than 50% of the British population is urban. This is mainly caused by the growth of industries, particularly the textile industry.

1851

The Great Exhibition is held in Hyde Park, London, England. Devised by Prince Albert, it is the first exhibition to display the latest technical innovations in industry, from both Britain and Europe. It features the Crystal Palace, a large iron and glass structure, designed by English architect Joseph Paxton. *Science and Society Picture Library*

1857 The Matrimonial Causes Act sets up divorce courts in Britain, allowing divorcees to remarry without recourse to a private act of Parliament, and outlines permissible terms for divorce: men must prove adultery and women adultery and cruelty or desertion. The legislation also introduces the principle of a husband's responsibility for alimony.

1861–1865 The USA (the North), has a booming economy during the Civil War as production and profits soar. There is inflation, too; prices rise 117% and wages rise just 43%.

1863 The Football Association is founded in London.

1866 Three-quarters of US imports are manufactured goods, while three-quarters of US exports are crude materials or crude foodstuffs.

1871 Bank holidays are introduced in England, Wales, and Ireland, with the first on Whit Monday (the first Monday after Pentecost).

1875 Definitive legislation is passed outlawing the use of children as chimney sweeps in Britain. Russia has a standing army of 3,360,000 soldiers; Germany 2,800,000; France 412,000; Britain 114,000.

1880 Greenwich Mean Time is established as the legal time in the British Isles. The first telephone directory in Britain is published by the London Telephone Company in England: it contains just 255 listings.

1886

John S Pemberton invents the soft drink Coca-Cola in the USA: it goes on sale in Atlanta, Georgia, as 'the intellectual beverage and temperance drink', and is claimed to be a cure for headaches and dyspepsia. This Coca Cola advert is from 1941. Coca Cola was sold in every state of the USA by 1895, less than ten years after its invention, and in 155 countries by 1987. *AKG London*

1887 German immigrant Emile Berliner patents his gramophone, a machine which plays discs, in the USA. Commercial production begins in Germany in 1889 and in the USA in 1894. The first Test cricket match is played. Australia defeat England in Melbourne.

1889 The French corset-maker Hermine Cadolle creates the first bra, freeing women from the restrictions of corsets.

c. 1897 The development of the electric street car makes the suburbs more accessible, leading to an expansion of the cities in the USA.

1900 The world population stands at 1.6 billion.

1903 The first driving licences in Britain are introduced. They must be renewed annually. The problem of traffic congestion in London, England, leads to a review of the road network and extension of the recently opened underground system. The Ford Motor Company is established in Detroit.

1905 A regular motor omnibus service starts in London, England, and the Bakerloo and Piccadilly underground lines are opened. The population density in the slums of New York, reaches 1,000 persons an acre, higher than in Bombay, India.

1909 The suffragette Marion Wallace Dunlop becomes the first hunger striker in Britain: she is released after 91 hours. The first old-age pensions are paid out by the government in Britain. These are noncontributory: the payment is small and made on a restricted basis at the age of 70.

1913 The first domestic refrigerators appear on the market in the USA and Germany. The first stainless steel is cast in Britain, by Harry Brearley in Sheffield. Maternity, sickness, and unemployment benefits are introduced in Britain.

1915 The German company Bayer introduces aspirin in tablet form. Women in wartime Britain are increasingly taking on men's responsibilities in the workplace, and are proving more productive in many fields.

1916 The British government introduces British Summer Time. The clocks are put forward one hour to help save valuable resources such as coal during wartime.

1918–1919 A worldwide pandemic of Spanish influenza (so called because of its particular virulence in Spain) or *Encephalitis lethargica* (sleeping sickness) kills over 20 million people, more than were killed during the conflicts of World War I. The movement of the armed forces at the end of the war promotes its spread.

1920–1933 Prohibition (the ban on manufacturing, selling, or transporting alcohol) is carried out in the USA.

1924 The Ford Motor Company announces the production of its 10 millionth automobile.

1925 The celebrated Scopes monkey trial is held in Dayton, Tennessee. The case pits liberal lawyer Clarence Darrow against politician and fundamentalist William Jennings Bryan in the case of a schoolteacher, John T Scopes, arrested in May for teaching the theory of evolution contrary to state law. Scopes is convicted and fined $100, but this is waived on a technical point.

1927 A transatlantic telephone service begins between London, England, and New York, provided by the American Telephone and Telegraph company (AT&T).

1929 The USA now has 377 skyscrapers with more than 20 storeys.

1930 Pope Pius XI condemns contraception, but allows the use of the rhythm method for birth control.

1931 Populations (in millions): China 410; India 338; USSR 168; USA 122; Japan 75; Germany 64; Great Britain 46; France 42.

1932 The GPO (General Post Office) introduces the telephone service Directory Enquiries in the UK.

1933 The average life expectancy in the USA is 59 years (it was 49 years in 1900).

1934 The Road Traffic Act introduces driving tests in the UK.

1936 English economist John Maynard Keynes publishes *General Theory of Employment, Interest, and Money*, proposing that recession can be prevented if the government sponsors a full employment policy. It has a profound effect on economic thinking and government economic strategy worldwide.

1936 Adolf Hitler commissions Ferdinand Porsche to design a 'people's car' and the Volkswagen Beetle is born.

1937 The 999 emergency telephone number for police, fire, and ambulance services is introduced in the UK.

1937

English writer George Orwell publishes *Road to Wigan Pier*, an account of working class poverty. This photograph illustrating poverty in Wigan, England (1939) is by German photographer Kurt Hutton. *Corbis*

1938 During 1938, there are 32,000 automobile-related deaths in the USA, one-third involving pedestrians.

1939 The evacuation of around 650,000 children from London to rural England begins. Some 1.5 million people in total will move to the country for part of the war. The Citizens' Advice Bureaux scheme is launched in the UK with the opening of 200 offices.

1940 Social security payments start in the USA. The first cheque is for $22.54. US unemployment stands at 8 million: this represents 14.6% of the population. The population of the world is estimated at 2.229 billion.

1940

An all-night German bombing raid on London, England, begins the period of intense bombing known as the 'Blitz'. An estimated 40,000 civilians were killed. Here, Holborn Circus in London burns at the height of the Blitz. *Corbis*

1941 Unemployment is virtually eliminated in the UK. In the USA, food prices are 61% above prewar levels. President Roosevelt signs the Draft Act, which calls for all men 18 to 64 to register and all men 20 to 44 to be eligible for active duty.

1942 The T-shirt is produced, designed specifically for the US Navy to allow freedom of movement and to absorb sweat.

1942–1945 During the war, US women are recruited on a large scale for the war effort; between 1942 and 1945 the number of working women increases by 50%.

1943 Race riots break out in Detroit, Michigan, caused by the migration of 300,000 black Americans to the city for war industry jobs, leading to 35 deaths and injuring 600 people. Rioting also occurs in other US cities.

1944 The 1944 Education Act in England and Wales introduces primary, secondary, and further education, sanctions the Eleven Plus examination, provides for a raised school-leaving age of 15 (16 as soon as possible), and makes religious education compulsory. There are street riots in Damascus after the Syrian government permits women to remove their veils in public. Production of consumer goods, such as vacuum cleaners and stoves, resumes in the USA.

1945 Fees are abolished in state-maintained secondary schools in England and Wales. All rationing stops in the USA, with the exception of sugar. Food remains scarce everywhere else and the black market continues to exist throughout Europe. The Japanese parliament, under pressure from Allied occupation forces, grants women voting rights.

1946 Populations (in millions): China 455; India 311; USSR 194; US 140; Japan 73; West Germany 48; Italy 47; Britain 46; Brazil 45; France 40; Spain 27; Poland 24; Korea 24; Mexico 22; East Germany 18; Egypt 17. The report produced by the Reith Committee in the UK leads to the founding of New Towns as growth points in Britain, with Stevenage the first New Town to be built. Regular television broadcasts by the British Broadcasting Corporation (BBC), which have been interrupted for almost seven years by the war, are revived in the UK: at this stage there are fewer than 12,000 viewers.

1947 Prompted by the House Un-American Activities Committee (HUAC) hearings, which are intended to expose alleged communists working in Hollywood, the US film industry blacklists a number of writers and producers.

1948 One million homes have television sets in the USA, compared to 5,000 in 1945.

1949 The first weather forecast is broadcast on British television: it consists of a voice-over only.

1950 Dr Yoshiro Nakamata of the Imperial University, Tokyo, Japan, develops the floppy disk and licenses it to IBM. Life expectancy for men and women in India is 32 compared to 66 and 71 in the USA. Populations (in millions): London, England 8.3; New York, New York 7.8; Tokyo, Japan 5.3; Moscow, Russia 4.1; Chicago, Illinois 3.6; Shanghai, China 3.6; Calcutta, India 3.5; Berlin, Germany 3.3.

1954 Flashing directional indicator lights are made compulsory on cars in Britain.

1956 The general conference of the Methodist Church, meeting in Minneapolis, Minnesota, orders the abolishment of racial segregation in its churches.

1957 Detector vans are introduced in Britain by the General Post Office to identify television licence fee dodgers. The electronics company Sony markets the first pocket-sized transistor radio, in Japan. ERNIE (the 'Electronic Random Number Indicator Equipment') draws the first premium bond prizes in Britain.

1958 Radar is first used in Britain to catch speeding drivers. The first parking meters in Britain are introduced, in Mayfair, London. The first scheduled transatlantic jet services are launched, by British Overseas Airways Corporation flying a Comet IV between London and New York, followed by Pan-Am flying a Boeing 707 between Paris and New York.

1959 The Mini Minor car, designed by Alec Issigonis for the British Motor Corporation, is launched in Britain, costing less than £500. By 1965, 1 million Minis will have been produced. The car became a symbol of 'swinging London' in the late 1960s.

1960 A study by the American Heart Association finds that men who smoke are 50% to 150% more likely to die from coronary disease than nonsmokers.

1961 The first oral contraceptive pill, Conovid, goes on sale in Britain, manufactured by the British firm G D Searle. From 4 December is available on the NHS.

1962 Iron City Beer in Pittsburgh, Pennsylvania, produces the first aluminium can with a ring-pull. British weather reports start giving temperatures in centigrade as well as Fahrenheit.

1963 The USA has 6% of the world population and 66% of the world's cars. The muscle relaxant and antidepressant Valium, developed by Roche Laboratories as a more potent alternative to Librium, appears on the market in the USA.

1964 The infant mortality rate in Britain is 20 per 1,000, compared to 30 per 1,000 in 1951. Xerox develops the first office facsimile transmission system in the USA. It can only operate on dedicated phone lines. The term fax is not commonly used until the 1980s. The Dutch electronics company Philips launches the compact cassette in Britain. This is still the industry standard for analogue audio cassettes. The first family planning clinic in Britain to give advice to unmarried mothers opens.

1965 Britain decides to adopt metric measurements. The Japanese electronic company Sony launches the Sony CV-2000, the first home video recorder, using Sony's Betamax format. The first colour video recorder is available the following year. The world population is over 3 billion. Cigarette advertising is banned on British television.

1966 The first conviction for burning the draft card is obtained in the USA. The hallucinogenic drug LSD is declared illegal in the USA. The Midland Bank in Britain is the first to introduce cheque guarantee cards.

1967 Denmark is the first country to introduce VAT (Value Added Tax) on retail products. The British Broadcasting Corporation (BBC) replaces its Light, Home, and Third Programme radio services with four numbered stations. The Sexual Offences Act (affecting England and Wales) permits homosexual acts in private between consenting adults over the age of 21. Barclays Bank opens the world's first automatic cash machine. The Abortion Bill is passed in Britain, permitting abortion on medical and psychological grounds.

1968 The 911 emergency telephone system for police, fire, and ambulances is introduced in New York. It is the first such system in the USA. In Britain, figures show a drop of 23% in road deaths since the introduction of breath tests in 1967. The General Post Office in Britain introduces a two-tiered system of postal rates, at four pence and five pence.

1969 The television channel BBC1 begins to broadcast a colour service in Britain. Over 700 million people worldwide watch Neil Armstrong and Buzz Aldrin in the lunar module from the US spacecraft *Apollo 11* touch down on the moon.

1970 BBC2 begins broadcasting Open University programmes in Britain, to support students on the Open University distance learning courses. In the USA, 31% of white males and 39% of white females have completed four years of high school; the corresponding numbers for black males and females are 22% and 25%. The population of the world is approximately 3.7 billion. President Richard M Nixon signs a bill banning cigarette advertising on US radio and television. This takes effect the following year. The voting age in Britain is lowered from 21 to 18.

1971 Populations (in millions): China 789; India 548; USSR 244; USA 205; Japan 106; Brazil 95; Bangladesh 63; Pakistan 62; West Germany 61; Nigeria 57; Great Britain and Northern Ireland 56; Italy 54; France 51; Mexico 51. Telephone direct-dialling between London, England, and New York, USA, is introduced. Decimal currency is introduced in Britain: the half-crown and florin go out of use and the pound is now worth 100 rather than 240 pennies.

1972 Approximately 500 sex-change operations have been performed since Johns Hopkins University, Baltimore, Maryland, performed the first one in the USA in 1966.

1973 The US Supreme Court rules that advertisements for employment cannot specify gender. Women account for 44.7% of the US work force. Salaries differ as much as 20% between men and women performing the same job. In the case *Roe v Wade*, the US Supreme Court rules that state restrictions on abortion are unconstitutional and that a woman has the right to an abortion within the first six months of pregnancy. This provokes militant anti-abortion protests. The British government introduces a child-benefit scheme giving weekly cash payments of £2 per child to mothers.

1974 Women's pay as a percentage of men's pay is 53.9% in Japan; 86.7% in France; 80.1% in Australia; 77% in Denmark; 69.9% in Germany; and 60.7% in the UK. Free contraception is made universally available on the National Health Service in Britain. The first product barcode (on a pack of Wrigley's chewing gum) is scanned at the checkout of the Marsh Supermarket in Troy, Ohio.

1975 Adopted children in Britain over the age of 18 are granted the right to have information about their natural parents. Birth control becomes a priority in India; abortion is legalized and the government launches campaigns advocating sterilization for both sexes. Britain's birthrate falls to 12.2 per 1,000, the lowest rate since 1933. The percentage of government seats held by women is 4% in Africa; 13% in Asia; 3.4% in Latin America; 3.6% in North America; 13% in Europe; and 32% in the USSR. Tizer becomes the first soft drink to be packaged in an aluminium can.

1976 For the first time there are more colour than black and white TV licences in Britain. Legislation is passed permitting all-day pub opening (from 11 in the morning to 11 at night) in Scotland.

1977 84% of all travel in the USA is by private vehicle; 9% of the population walk to their destination, and only 2.4% use public transportation. For the first time, Britain imports more cars than it manufactures. In-vitro fertilization (IVF) is developed by the British gynaecologist and obstetrician Patrick Steptoe. The first IVF baby is born in 1978. Punk music comes to prominence in the UK, with the emergence of bands such as the Sex Pistols, the Clash, and the Stranglers.

1978 In the USA, 49% of all women work, up from 31% in 1950; 48% of married women work, double the percentage in 1950. Life expectancy in the USA is 70.2 years for men and 77.8 years for women, up from 64.4 and 69.5 in 1945. The birth rate in the USA is 15.3 per 1,000 population, a decline from 24.1 in 1950. The British take 48 million holidays: some 9 million of these are holidays abroad, with 30% of holidaymakers going to Spain. The Pregnancy Discrimination Act is passed in the USA, protecting women from being denied employment because of pregnancy. Regular radio broadcasts of the proceedings of the British Parliament begin.

1979 The British House of Lords has 51 women out of 1,107 members, and the House of Commons has 19 women out of 635 members.

1980 Divorce rates (divorces per 1,000 of the population): France 1.50; Germany 2.68; Great Britain and Northern Ireland 3.08; USA 5.19; USSR 3.50. Over 18% of births in the USA are to unmarried mothers; over 40% of births are to women under 20. Populations (in millions): Tokyo, Japan 11.6; Shanghai, China 10.0; Buenos Aires, Argentina 9.7; Mexico City, Mexico 8.9; Beijing, China 8.7; Seoul, South Korea 8.4; Cairo, Egypt 8.1; Moscow, Russia 8.0; New York, USA 7.1; Tientsin, China 7.0. The English Court of Appeal awards child custody to a lesbian mother for the first time. The population of the USA is 226.5 million compared to 76 million in 1900. A report shows that half of married British women go out to work, the largest proportion anywhere in the European Community.

1981 Strict population controls in China that limit families to one child lead to an increase in female infanticide. The IBM personal computer is introduced. The world population stands at 4.5 billion, up 2 billion since 1950. The classical music conductor Herbert von Karajan demonstrates the first compact discs, developed by the Dutch company Philips, at the Salzburg Festival, in Austria.

1982 Japanese car manufacturers control 22.6% of the market in the USA, compared to 3.7% in 1970. The population of China rises to over 1 billion. Women's pay as a percentage of men's pay: Kenya 84%; Singapore 63%; Australia 83%; France 80%; Switzerland 67%; UK 70%.

1983 Car drivers in Chicago, Illinois, try out cellular phones when Motorola introduce a test system of low-power transmitters across the city. The wearing of seat belts by front-seat car passengers is made compulsory in Britain.

1985 The average literacy rate of women worldwide is 97%. In developing countries, however, only 55% of women are literate on average.

1986 For the first time, the number of women in the USA holding professional jobs is greater than that of men, by 29,000.

1987 The British House of Commons is made up of 41 women and 609 men. The world population reaches 5 billion – double that of 1950. The Federal Communications Commission in the USA abandons its requirement that broadcasters must present all sides of controversial issues. Belgium becomes the first country to introduce a national smoking ban in all public buildings.

1988–1994 The amount of chlorofluorocarbons released into the air in the USA is reduced by 52%.

1988 The number of births in the USA is 3,829,000, the highest in 25 years. The number of farms in the USA reaches its lowest level since before the Civil War. Margaret Thatcher becomes the longest-serving British prime minister in the 20th century. The first EC passports in Britain are issued by the Glasgow Passport Office, Scotland.

1989 Satellite television is broadcast direct to homes in Britain via satellite dish decoders. Four Sky TV channels are available, featuring news, film, sport, and a general channel.

1990 According to the US Census Bureau, 28% of Americans are obese, including 30% of women and 38% of black Americans. Households in the USA headed by a single woman total 16.7%, compared to 9.3% in 1950. Life expectation at birth for men/women in selected countries: Australia 74/80; Brazil 62/68; Canada 73/80; China 68/71; France 73/78; Ghana 42/43; Great Britain and Northern Ireland 73/78; India 55/56; Japan 76/82; Kenya 55/60; Mexico 70/75; USA 72/79; USSR 65/74; West Germany 72/78. Percentage of workforce that is female: Austria 40%; France 39.9%; Italy 32%; Norway 41%; Spain 24.4%; Sweden 45%; UK 39%; USSR 48%. Populations (in millions): Mexico City, Mexico 18.7; Cairo, Egypt 14.0; Shanghai, China 12.8; Tokyo, Japan 11.9; Beijing, China 10.4; São Paulo, Brazil 10.1; Seoul, South Korea 10.0; Calcutta, India 9.2; Paris, France 9.1; Moscow, Russia 8.9.

1991 A nationwide poll in the USA indicates that 61% of women feel that they have been subjected to sexual harassment while at work; only 4% report the incidents. In the grip of the longest recession since the 1930s, unemployment in Britain stands at 2.5 million and house repossessions at 80,000 for the year. The number of black–white marriages in the USA has tripled since 1970. US federal health officials announce that 100,777 people have died from AIDS since the discovery of the disease in 1981.

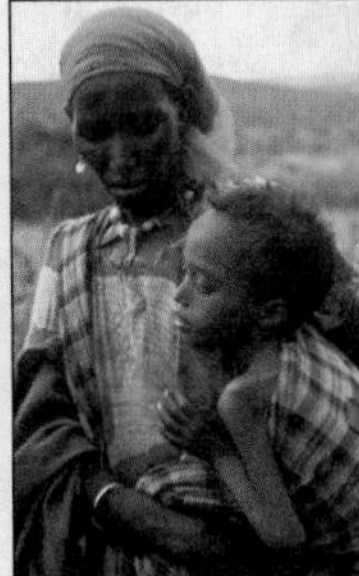

1992

A famine in Somalia kills more than 300,000 people. Though the broad causes of famine are overpopulation, drought, and war, the reasons why specific groups are affected – rarely more than 10% of a population – are still unclear. Governments and aid agencies are increasingly searching for solutions to famine by looking at the lives of those who can adapt to dramatic changes in their environment. Major famines of the 20th century include those of China 1920; Russia 1920–21, and 1932; India 1964; and Africa 1980 onwards. *Food and Agriculture Organization.*

1992 A study finds that Americans work 140 more hours a year than in 1970 and that vacation, sick leave, and days off have declined by 15% in the same period. The US Supreme Court opens the way for damage suits by cigarette smokers against the tobacco companies when it rules that the warning labels on cigarette packages do not exempt the manufacturers from lawsuits.

1993 A US survey reveals that 51.1 million workers (46% of the labour force) use computers for their work; the most popular application is word processing.

1994 In the USA, 38.1 million people (14.5% of the population) live below the government-defined poverty level. The USA's prisons hold 1,054,000 inmates, an all-time record. Of these, 2,890 are on death row. The National Lottery, the first regular British national lottery, is launched, under government control and run by Camelot. It is the largest lottery in the world.

1995 According to the US Census Bureau, the average size of a US household is 2.65 people, down from 3.33 people in 1960. In the USA, 64% of married women with children under six work, as opposed to 45% in 1980 and 19% in 1960. Less than 25% of people in the USA smoke, compared to around 40% in the 1960s.

1997

Death of Diana, Princess of Wales on 31 August. Her funeral was the biggest British televised event in history. Hundreds of thousands of bunches of flowers were left by mourners outside Kensington Palace, London after her death. *David Halford*

1998 An international test of education standards finds US high-school students among the worst in maths and science in the industrialized world. The UK Office for National Statistics indicates the highest level of teenage pregnancies – 9.4 per 1,000 – for more than a decade. The US Census Bureau reports that 26 million Americans, nearly one in ten, is an immigrant. Most come from Central or South America. Hurricane Mitch kills over 1,000 people in Central America and leaves at least 1 million people homeless.

POLITICS CHRONOLOGY

c. 1000 Traders and fishermen from Macassar in Sulawesi in Southeast Asia (modern Indonesia), make contact with the Aborigines of northern Australia.

1024 The Song dynasty government in China takes over the banks of Chengtu, in Szechwan. Their certificates of deposit then become official and thus become the first paper currency in the world.

1031 The caliphate of Córdoba comes to an end with the deposing of Hisham III, the last of the Umayyad dynasty. Dozens of independent Moorish and Arab kingdoms arise in Andalusia.

1066 King Harold Godwinson of England is defeated and killed by Duke William I of Normandy (William the Conqueror) at Hastings, England.

1085 William I the Conqueror orders a survey of the resources of England subsequently recorded in the *Domesday Book*.

1096–1291 The Crusades, a series of wars, are undertaken by European rulers to recover Palestine from the Muslims.

1154 Henry II Plantagenet is crowned as king of England, founding the Plantagenet dynasty.

1156 King Vikramanka of Rashtrakuta (in the Deccan) dies; his kingdom, which has been the most powerful in India for three centuries, collapses.

1168 The Toltec Empire of Mexico collapses after its capital at Tula is sacked by invaders.

1189 Richard I the Lionheart is crowned as king of England.

1206 Having unified most of the Mongol peoples, the Mongol conqueror Temüjin adopts the title Genghis (or Chingis) Khan ('Universal Khan') founding the Mongol Empire.

1215 King John of England signs the Magna Carta (Great Charter) in which he agrees to various curtailments of his powers.

c. 1250 The west African rainforest state of Benin is founded.

1300 A new wave of Turks, known as the 'Ottomans' after their founder Osman, are driven westwards by the Mongols. They defeat the Byzantines in Bithynia, and occupy western Anatolia. The Byzantine Empire holds on only in Nicaea, Heraclea, and Smyrna.

1314 Robert I the Bruce, King of Scotland, inflicts a disastrous defeat on King Edward II of England in the Battle of Bannockburn and so completes his expulsion of the English from Scotland.

1367 Chu Yüan-chang, having defeated rival rebel leaders, takes Beijing, China, and expels Toghan Temur, the last Yüan (Mongol) emperor. Chu Yüan-chang, under the name Hung-wu, founds the Ming Dynasty.

1381 During the 'peasants' revolt' against the poll tax in England, the rebels occupy London and kill the chancellor Archbishop Sudbury and the treasurer Robert Hales. On the following day, King Richard II of England meets the rebel leader Wat Tyler, who is later killed by the mayor of London, Sir William Walworth. The revolt is subsequently suppressed.

1400 Timur Leng (Tamerlane), the grand amir of the Mongols, defeats the Mameluke Egyptians at Aleppo and Damascus and sacks the cities of Syria.

1415 King Henry V of England inflicts a crushing defeat on the French at the Battle of Agincourt.

1417 The Great Schism (the period 1378–1417 of rival Popes in Rome, Italy and Avignon, France) ends with the election of Pope Martin V at the Council of Constance in Germany.

1453 The beleaguered port of Bordeaux, France, finally surrenders to the forces of King Charles VII of France, an event which sees the fall of the last English stronghold in Gascony and in France (excepting Calais) and ends the Hundred Years' War.

1455–1485 The Wars of the Roses, a series of English civil wars, takes place between the houses of Lancaster and York both of whom claimed the throne.

1474 Ming forces construct the present-day 'Great Wall' along the border of the Ordos desert in the Shensi province of China in order to hold back persistent Mongol incursions.

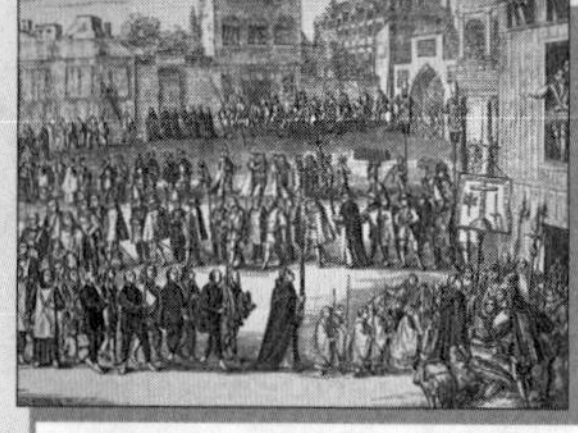

1481

The first *Auto da Fé/Act of Faith*, the pronouncement and enactment of sentences (including burning) on victims of the Spanish Inquisition, is carried out in Seville, Castile. *Philip Sauvain Picture Collection.*

1492 Granada, the last Muslim city in Spain, surrenders, completing the Christian *Reconquista* ('Reconquest') and unifying Spain (apart from Navarre) under its besiegers of nine months, Ferdinand V and Isabella I of Aragon and Castile.

1493 The Spanish expedition led by the explorer Christopher Columbus founds the first European city in the New World, on the island now comprising Haiti and the Dominican Republic.

1503 The Portuguese send African slaves to Brazil. These are the first Africans to be sent as slaves by Europeans to the New World and the journey marks the start of the Atlantic slave trade.

1517 The Ottomans take the Egyptian city of Cairo from its Mameluke rulers after bitter battles culminating in four days of vicious street fighting.

1521 The condemnation of church reformer Martin Luther at the Diet of Worms leads to schism and the emergence of the Protestant church.

1524 The *Bauernkrieg* ('Peasants' War'), the most extensive and revolutionary of European insurrections to date, begins in the Hegau at Stühlingen, against the landgrave's despotic demands that his peasants ignore the hay harvest to collect snail shells.

1529 The Ottoman army under Sultan Suleiman I the Magnificent besieges Vienna, the capital of the Habsburg archduke Ferdinand I of Austria.

1555 The Diet (legislative assembly) of Augsburg promulgates the religious Peace of Augsburg. The religious affiliations of Germany are to be decided on the principle of *Curia Regis*: the population must follow the religion of their ruler, or emigrate.

1567 The Russian tsar Ivan IV ('the Terrible') gains his epithet when, after hearing of plots by boyars (aristocratic landowners), he allocates half of Russia to an *oprichnina* (a separately administered royal territory) and unleashes his royal bodyguard, the *oprichniky*, on the boyars, the church, and the populace.

1574 Spanish Habsburg forces abandon the province of Holland in the Spanish Netherlands to the *stadtholder* (provincial executive officer) William the Silent, Prince of Orange, to the Dutch estates, and to Calvinism after failure in the siege of Leiden.

1588 The Spanish Armada is defeated by the combined English fleet under Lord Admiral Thomas Howard of Effingham off Gravelines, France.

1611 The first permanent British East India Company outpost 'factory' (trading station) in India is established.

1620 The Pilgrim Fathers land in Massachusetts to found the Plymouth Colony, with John Carver as governor.

1628 Shah Jahan becomes the Mogul emperor of India.

1642 The English Civil War officially begins when King Charles I raises his standard at Nottingham, England.

1649 King Charles I of Great Britain and Ireland is beheaded as a 'tyrant, traitor, murderer and enemy of the people' on 30 January. On 17 March 1649 the Rump Parliament officially abolishes the monarchy.

1660 Charles II is crowned: the restoration of the British monarchy.

1680 Tokugawa Tsunayoshi becomes shogun (military ruler) of Japan, ushering in one of the most tranquil and successful periods of Japanese history.

1707 The Act of Union unites England and Scotland as the United Kingdom of Great Britain.

1746 The Jacobite army under Prince Charles Edward Stuart ('Bonnie Prince Charlie'), the 'Young Pretender', is defeated in the Battle of Culloden in Scotland by the English military commander William Augustus, Duke of Cumberland, who subsequently abolishes the Scottish clan organization.

1776

The American Declaration of Independence, drafted by Thomas Jefferson (shown here) with revisions by Benjamin Franklin and John Adams, is approved by the Continental Congress on 4 July. The declaration stated a theory of government based on the right 'to life, liberty and the pursuit of happiness'. *Library of Congress*

1783 The Peace of Paris is signed between Britain on one side and France, Spain, and America on the other, ending the American Revolution.

1789 A large crowd of the common people storms and captures the Bastille in Paris. The emigration of French aristocrats begins. The French National Assembly adopts the Declaration of the Rights of Man.

1791 The first ten amendments to the US Constitution are ratified. They are known hereafter as the 'Bill of Rights'.

1801 The Act of Union creates the United Kingdom of Great Britain and Ireland, bringing Ireland under direct control of the Parliament in Westminster.

1804 The Civil Code (renamed the Code Napoleon in 1807) is promulgated in France, providing a uniform civil law (previously French law was split between Roman law in the south and custom law in the north). Napoleon Bonaparte crowns himself emperor as Napoleon I in Paris, France.

1819 The 'Peterloo Massacre' takes place in England when a crowd of 60,000 people gathered in St Peter's Fields, Manchester, to listen to speeches on parliamentary reform and repeal of the Corn Laws, is charged on by the yeomanry. Eleven people are killed and 400 injured.

1823 The 'Monroe Doctrine' is announced by the US president James Monroe. It excludes European powers from interfering in the politics of any of the American republics.

1824 The South American revolutionary leader Simón Bolívar is proclaimed emperor of Peru.

1834 Labourers from Tolpuddle in Dorset, England (the 'Tolpuddle Martyrs'), are sentenced to transportation to the colonies for forming a lodge (local branch) of the British socialist Robert Owen's Grand National Consolidated Trades Union. Slavery is abolished throughout the British Empire, thanks largely to the efforts of the English philanthropist and politician William Wilberforce. The Poor Law Amendment Act in Britain revises the provision of relief to the unemployed and elderly, establishing workhouses where conditions are to be made hard so that only the truly needy will submit themselves to them.

1836 The Communist League is founded in Paris, France, by emigré German intellectuals. Originally called the League of the Just, it becomes the Communist League after Karl Marx and Friedrich Engels join in 1847. Two hundred Texans are killed at the isolated fortress of Alamo in San Antonio, Texas, when 3,000 Mexicans commanded by general Antonio Lopes de Santa Anna overrun the Republic of Texas garrison.

1839 The First Opium War between China and Britain begins after the Chinese authorities seize and burn cargoes of opium due to be exported from China by British merchants, in an attempt to combat smuggling of the drug.

1846 The Irish potato crop fails for the second successive year and famine increases despite organized relief. British prime minister, Robert Peel, repeals the Corn Laws to allow unhindered importation of grain into Ireland to alleviate the famine.

1848 Revolutions break out in Hungary, Austria, Prussia, and some of the Italian states.

1853–1856 The Crimean War take place between Russia and the allied powers of England, France, Turkey and Sardinia.

1860 The Italian soldier and patriot Giuseppe Garibaldi and his Redshirts ('The Thousand') sail from Genoa, northwest Italy, to attempt to complete the unification of Italy.

1861–1865 The American Civil War is fought between the Southern or Confederate states and the Northern or United states.

1862 The US president, Abraham Lincoln, declares that all slaves will be free from 1 January 1863.

1870 The 15th Amendment to the US Constitution, guaranteeing black American voting rights, becomes law. The French defeat in the Franco-Prussian War leads to a revolt in Paris, France, against the government of Emperor Napoleon III. A provisional government of national defence is set up to continue the war against Prussia and a republic is proclaimed.

1875 Britain buys 176,602 shares in the Suez Canal – linking the Mediterranean with the Red Sea – from Khedive Ismail of Egypt, the canal being a vital part of the route to India.

1881 Violent pogroms against Jews begin in Russia and eastern Europe, forcing many Jews to emigrate westwards.

1885 The Congo State is established as a personal possession of King Leopold II of Belgium.

1893 New Zealand becomes the first country to extend the franchise to women.

1894 The Wilson–Gorman Tariff Act, introducing a 2% income tax, becomes law in the USA, passed by Congress without receiving the assent of US president Grover Cleveland. It is the nation's first graduated income tax.

1898 French novelist Emile Zola publishes his 'J'accuse!/I Accuse!', an open letter to the French president protesting that French army officer Alfred Dreyfus is the victim of an anti-Semitic plot.

1899–1902 The Boer War is fought between Dutch settlers in South Africa and the British.

1900 The Boxer Rising by supporters of the Society of Harmonious Fists begins in China, in opposition to the growth of European influence there.

1903 The Russian Social Democratic Party splits into the Mensheviks ('minority'), led by Grigory Plekhanov, and the Bolsheviks ('majority'), led by Vladimir Ilyich Lenin, at their London congress. The latter group favours a violent seizure of power.

1909 The British chancellor of the Exchequer, David Lloyd George, introduces his 'People's Budget', which proposes taxes on land values, profits on land sales, and a 'super-tax' on high incomes, in order to raise money for defence and social expenditure. The hereditary House of Lords rejects the 'People's Budget' generating a major constitutional crisis.

1913 Militant suffragist Emmeline Pankhurst is imprisoned in Britain for inciting persons to place explosives outside the house of the chancellor of the Exchequer, David Lloyd George.

1914–1918

World War I takes place between the Central European powers (Germany, Austria-Hungary, and allies) and the Triple Entente (Britain and the British Empire, France, and Russia). An estimated 10 million lives are lost. Here a British machine gun unit at the Somme is depicted. *Corbis.*

1916 With the support of Sinn Féin, members of the Irish Republican Brotherhood take part in the 'Easter Rising' in Dublin, Ireland, in an attempt to end British rule in Ireland. The rising is suppressed by British forces after heavy fighting, and its leaders are executed.

1917 The British foreign secretary, Arthur Balfour, issues the 'Balfour declaration' on Palestine, in which he favours the establishment of a national home for the Jewish people without prejudice to non-Jewish communities. The 'October Revolution' takes place in Russia, Vladimir Ilyich Lenin and the Bolsheviks seizing the Winter Palace in Petrograd and overthrowing the provisional government.

1919 Gurkha troops of the British Army fire on a protesting crowd in northern India in what becomes known as the 'Amritsar Massacre', killing 379 people and wounding over 1,200 more. US president Woodrow Wyatt lays the draft League of Nations covenant before the Paris Peace Conference.

1920 A new Turkish assembly opens at Ankara, Anatolia (modern Turkey), which elects the nationalist Mustafa Kemal as its president and proclaims a new constitution, the Law of Fundamental Organization.

1921 The British government and representatives of the Dáil Eireann sign the Anglo-Irish Treaty providing for an independent southern Ireland with dominion status (within the British Empire).

1922–1926 The Italian fascist leader Benito Mussolini forms a government of liberals, nationalists, and fascists at King Victor Emmanuel III's request. A general strike in Britain in support of the striking coal miners paralyses the country.

1928 The Soviet leader Joseph Stalin ends the New Economic Policy and introduces state-directed economic planning and distribution, the development of industry, and collectivization of agriculture, in accordance with the first Five-Year Plan.

1929 Share values crash on the Wall Street stock market, New York. Widespread panic results in the trading of some 16.4 million shares, a new record. The episode precipitates the Depression.

1930 The Indian nationalist leader Mahatma Gandhi opens a campaign of civil disobedience in India with his 'Salt March' (a march from Ahmedabad, Gujarat, to Dandi on the coast where, on 6 April, Gandhi seizes salt to protest at the levying of salt tax on poor people).

1930

Ras Tafari, regent of Ethiopia, becomes emperor on the death of Empress Zauditu; he assumes the name Haile Selassie ('Might of the Trinity'). He is finally deposed in a military coup in 1974. *Philip Sauvain Picture Collection.*

1934 The Long March of the Chinese communists begins, led by Mao Zedong and others. Driven out by a Nationalist offensive, some 100,000 people leave the Jiangxi Soviet in southern China and march 9,600 km/6,000 mi to the province of Shaanxi in the extreme northwest, where the survivors set up a new communist revolutionary base.

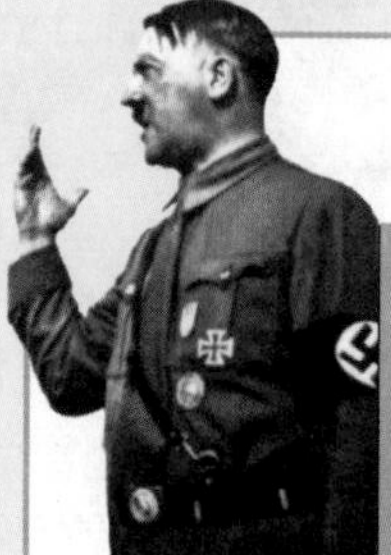

1935

The German Führer Adolf Hitler announces the racist 'Nuremberg Laws' against Jews at the Nazi Party Nuremberg rally. Legislation will define Jews, ban them from professions, and forbid their marriage or sexual relations with non-Jews. Here Hitler is portrayed in Nazi propaganda. *Philip Sauvain Picture Collection.*

1935 Jiang Jie Shi (Chiang Kai-shek) is elected chairman of the Guomindang (Nationalist Party) Executive Council, so becoming virtual ruler of China.

1936 The right-wing Spanish general Francisco Franco leads an army mutiny in Morocco against the Spanish Republican government marking the start of the Spanish Civil War that ends with the establishment of Franco's dictatorship. Britain's first woman Labour member of Parliament, Ellen Wilkinson, leads a 'hunger march' of workers from Jarrow in northeast England to London as a protest against unemployment following the closure of local shipyards.

1937 Guernica, the historic Basque capital in northern Spain, is heavily bombed by aircraft of the German Condor Legion supporting the Spanish Nationalist rebels.

1938 Austria is declared part of the German Reich, after the cancellation of a proposed referendum on unity with Germany (*Anschluss* or 'Annexation'). The Munich Agreement is signed in Munich, Germany, by the British prime minister, the French prime minister, the German Führer, and the Italian prime minister. It permits Germany to annex the Sudetenland in western Czechoslovakia. Chamberlain returns to London, England, speaking of 'peace with honour' and 'peace in our time'.

1939–1945 World War II between the Axis powers (Germany, Italy, and Japan) and the Allied powers (Britain, the Commonwealth, France, the USA, the USSR, and China). An estimated 55 million lives were lost including 6 million Jews killed in the Holocaust.

1945 At the Yalta Conference in the Crimea, USSR, the US president, Franklin D Roosevelt, the British prime minister, Winston Churchill, and the Soviet leader, Joseph Stalin, plan for the division of postwar Germany into four occupied zones, with four zones in Berlin, the capital. In August atomic bombs are dropped on Hiroshima and Nagasaki in Japan. The United Nations (UN), with headquarters in New York, comes into formal existence on the ratification of its Charter by 29 nations. The Federal Republic of Yugoslavia is proclaimed, under Marshal Josip Broz Tito, leader of the communist resistance against Germany during World War II.

1946 The French Indochina War (for Vietnamese independence) begins, and Ho Chi Minh, the leader of the Vietminh (Vietnam Independence League), seeks refuge in a remote area of North Vietnam.

1947

The US secretary of state, General George C Marshall, calls for a European Recovery Programme (the Marshall Plan) funded by the USA, to forestall the emergence of communist governments throughout the continent. This is the emblem used on all relief packages sent to Europe under the US Marshall Plan for economic recovery after World War II. *Corbis*

1947 British rule in India ends after 163 years and the two new independent countries of India and Pakistan are established. Jawaharlal Nehru becomes prime minister of India, and Mohammed Ali Jinnah governor general of Pakistan.

1948 The British mandate in Palestine ends, and the Jewish authorities proclaim the new state of Israel, with David Ben-Gurion as prime minister. Egypt, Transjordan, Iraq, and Syria invade Israel and occupy areas in the south and east.

1949 Social legislation in South Africa leads to apartheid being implemented. The Population Registration Act starts the process of defining people as white, coloured, or African. The North Atlantic Treaty Organization (NATO) is founded to provide mutual support against the Soviet military presence in eastern Europe. The treaty is signed by the USA, Canada, Britain, France, Luxembourg, Belgium, the Netherlands, Italy, Portugal, Denmark, Iceland, and Norway. Eire is formally proclaimed the Republic of Ireland and leaves the Commonwealth. The Federal Republic of Germany (West Germany) comes into being, with Bonn as its capital. West Berlin is excluded from the new state but associated with it. China's communist leader Mao Zedong proclaims the establishment of a People's Republic, with its government based in Beijing and with Zhou Enlai as prime minister and foreign minister.

1950 Communist North Korean forces invade South Korea, with several armies advancing southwards.

1953 A bus boycott in Baton Rouge, Louisiana, results in an amendment of the rules requiring blacks to sit at the back of buses; it is the first major action of the modern civil-rights movement.

1955 The Warsaw Treaty (of Friendship, Cooperation, and Mutual Assistance) is signed by the USSR, Albania, Bulgaria, Czechoslovakia, East Germany, Hungary, Poland, and Romania, establishing the 'Warsaw Pact' and providing for a unified military command (with headquarters in Moscow) and stationing of Soviet military units in member countries.

1956 The Egyptian president Gamal Abdel Nasser announces the nationalization of the Suez Canal precipitating the Suez Crisis.

1956 The Hungarian prime minister Imre Nagy promises free elections in Hungary, and Cardinal Mindszenty, the primate of Hungary, is released following eight years of captivity. The USSR responds by sending Soviet and satellite state troops to invade Hungary.

1957 Belgium, France, West Germany, Italy, Luxembourg, and the Netherlands sign the Treaty of Rome establishing the European Economic Community (EEC) or 'Common Market', and a second Rome Treaty establishing the European Atomic Energy Authority or 'Euratom' (to take effect from 1 January 1958).

1958 Communist China launches the 'Great Leap Forward', aiming to increase industrial output at great speed, especially the production of steel. The Campaign for Nuclear Disarmament (CND) is founded at a public meeting in London, England.

1960 The 'Sharpeville massacre' occurs in a township near Vereeniging (south of Johannesburg), South Africa, where members of the Pan-African Congress demonstrating against pass laws are fired on by police, killing 69 demonstrators.

1961 One thousand five hundred Cuban exiles, trained by US military instructors and supported by the CIA, land on Cuba in the 'Bay of Pigs' invasion. An expected sympathetic uprising fails to occur and the invaders are killed or captured. East German building workers begin constructing the Berlin Wall, a near-impregnable physical barrier sealing off West Berlin and preventing the escape of East Germans to the West.

1962 The Cuban Missile Crisis begins. The US president John F Kennedy announces that the USSR has installed a missile base in Cuba, and declares a naval blockade.

1963 The Organization of African Unity (OAU) is founded at a conference of African leaders in Addis Ababa, Ethiopia; it aims to maintain solidarity between African leaders and remove colonialism from the African continent. Two hundred thousand black Americans take part in the March on Washington, a peaceful demonstration for civil rights in Washington, DC. They are addressed by the civil-rights leader Martin Luther King, Jr, who makes his 'I have a dream …' speech.

1965

Two battalions of US Marines land to defend Danang airbase in South Vietnam. They are the first US combat troops to enter the Vietnam war. A peace treaty is finally negotiated in 1973. Here a family group flees from the fighting in the Cholon or Chinatown area of the city during the Battle of Saigon in 1968. In this part of the Vietnam War, the Vietcong communist guerrilla National Liberation Front was driven out of Saigon by South Vietnamese and US forces. *Corbis.*

1965 The Rhodesian prime minister Ian Smith makes a Unilateral Declaration of Independence. Britain declares the regime illegal and introduces exchange and trade restrictions.

1966 The Central Committee of the Chinese Communist Party, in its first plenary session since 1962, endorses the 'Great Proletarian Cultural Revolution', the movement to 'purify' Chinese communism through a purge of the intelligentsia.

1967 The Six Day War breaks out between Israel and the Arab states of the United Arab Republic (UAR), Syria, Jordan, Lebanon, and Iraq.

1968 The Czechoslovakian government announces a wide range of liberalizing reforms. Soviet and other Warsaw Pact forces invade Czechoslovakia and arrest reform leaders including Alexander Dubcek.

1971 The independence of East Pakistan as Bangladesh ('Bengali country') is declared. The split from Pakistan sparks a civil war.

1972 British troops shoot dead 13 civilians in Northern Ireland when violence erupts at a civil-rights march in Londonderry. It becomes known as 'Bloody Sunday'.

1972–1974 The Watergate affair, a series of US political scandals that eventually led to the resignation of President Nixon.

1973 The rise in the price of oil and restriction of its supply after war breaks out in the Middle East disrupts Western economies.

1974 General Antônio Ribeiro de Spínola leads a successful coup in Portugal. On 26 April, the junta vows to dismantle the authoritarian state and end the wars in Angola, Mozambique, and Portuguese Guinea (now Guinea-Bissau). A military coup in Ethiopia deposes Emperor Haile Selassie.

1975 Civil war erupts in Lebanon when clashes between Palestinians and Christian Phalangists outside a church in the capital, Beirut, leave 30 people dead. Communist Khmer Rouge revolutionaries in Cambodia capture the capital, Phnom Penh, in the civil war between the right-wing government and the Khmer Rouge. The last US personnel flee the South Vietnamese capital, Saigon (now Ho Ch Minh City), flying by helicopter from the US embassy compound, following a final North Vietnam offensive.

1976 The Race Relations Act in Britain, introduced in stages, makes the inciting of racial hatred an offence and in 1977 establishes the Commission for Racial Equality. South African police kill 76 students in Soweto and other townships during protests and riots about teaching in Afrikaans.

1977 The Chinese Communist Party expels the 'Gang of Four', who had tried to seize power after the death of Mao Zedong. Deng Xiaoping is reinstated as deputy premier.

1978 A summit at Camp David, Maryland, USA, between the US president, Jimmy Carter, the Egyptian president, Anwar Sadat, and the Israeli prime minister, Menachem Begin, concludes with a 'framework' peace treaty ending 30 years of hostility between Israel and Egypt. The USA and China normalize diplomatic relations with effect from 1 January 1979.

1979 Vietnamese troops and Cambodian rebels capture the Cambodian capital, Phnom Penh, and oust the Khmer Rouge regime. The British Conservative leader Margaret Thatcher becomes Britain's first woman prime minister. The civil war in Rhodesia ends with the introduction of majority rule. The new state of Zimbabwe becomes independent in April 1980.

1980–1988 The Iran–Iraq War is fought with a loss of over a million lives.

1980 Lech Walesa, leader of the Gdansk shipyard strikers, signs an agreement with the Polish government allowing the formation of independent trade unions and granting the release of political prisoners.

1981 The Irish Republican Army (IRA) hunger strike at the Maze prison in N. Ireland ends after seven months and ten deaths.

1982 Argentina invades and occupies the British-held Falkland Islands sparking the Falklands War which lasts for less than three months. More than 20,000 women encircle the Greenham Common air base in England in protest against the proposed siting of US cruise missiles there.

1983 The US president Ronald Reagan proposes a 'Star Wars' defence system for the USA, using satellites to detect and destroy incoming missiles.

1985 Mikhail Gorbachev is named first secretary of the Soviet Communist Party. He calls for more *glasnost* ('openness') in Soviet life and pursues a policy of *perestroika* ('reconstruction').

1987 The New York Dow Jones Industrial Average falls 508.32 points (23%) on 'Black Monday', precipitating large falls in stock prices across the world. A report of the joint US Senate/House of Representatives Iran–Contra Committee blames President Ronald Reagan for the administration's illegal activities. Eight Republicans refuse to sign the report.

1989 People's Liberation Army tanks in China move into Tiananmen Square in Beijing, killing 2,000 pro-democracy protesters. A Solidarity-dominated cabinet is formed in Poland under Tadeusz Mazowiecki, the first noncommunist government in Eastern Europe since 1948. East Germany announces the opening of its border with West Germany as unrest continues and refugees continue to reach the West through the neighbouring countries. The authorities begin demolishing sections of the Berlin Wall. The US president George Bush and the Soviet president Mikhail Gorbachev formally declare the Cold War to be over.

1990 The African National Congress (ANC) leader, Nelson Mandela, is released in South Africa after almost 26 years in prison.

1991

A US-led coalition commences air offensive 'Operation Desert Storm' to liberate Kuwait from Iraqi occupation, beginning the Gulf War. Here two British soldiers prepare their Challenger tank during the Gulf War, in preparation for a movement to retake Kuwait from the Iraqis. The war on land was swift and barely opposed, following weeks of US-led UN bombing of Iraqi positions. *Corbis*

1991 A summit of European Community heads of government in Maastricht, the Netherlands, agrees the Maastricht Treaty on closer economic and political union (Britain obtains the right to abstain from social legislation and a single currency).

1993 The European Community's single market comes into force, establishing the free movement of goods, capital, and services across national borders, with some restrictions.

1994 The presidents of Rwanda and Burundi, Juvénal Habyarimana and Cyprien Ntaryamira, are killed in an air crash; interethnic violence erupts on a huge scale. Nelson Mandela is sworn in as the first black president of South Africa. Israel withdraws its military forces from the Jericho area of the occupied West Bank to make way for self-rule by the Palestinian National Authority, as agreed in Washington, DC, in 1993.

1997 Antigovernment Tutsi rebels take Kinshasa, the capital of Zaire, and President Mobutu Sese Seko flees. The country is renamed the Democratic Republic of Congo. The former British colony of Hong Kong reverts to Chinese rule.

1998 At least 1,700 men, women, and children are massacred in Algeria by Islamic fundamentalists. Serbia sends troops into the southern province of Kosovo to flush out ethnic Albanian secessionist paramilitaries. Hundreds of men, women, and children are killed over the next few weeks. It is the worst bloodshed to date in the nine-year campaign by Kosovo's Albanian majority to regain their autonomy. Ireland, Britain, and the political parties in Northern Ireland reach a peace agreement over Northern Ireland involving the devolution of a wide range of executive and legislative powers to a Northern Ireland Assembly.

1999 The European Union's new single currency, the euro, is launched in 11 member states. The US senate votes to acquit President Clinton on two impeachment charges of lying under oath and obstructing justice in an effort to conceal a sexual relationship with former White House intern Monica Lewinsky.

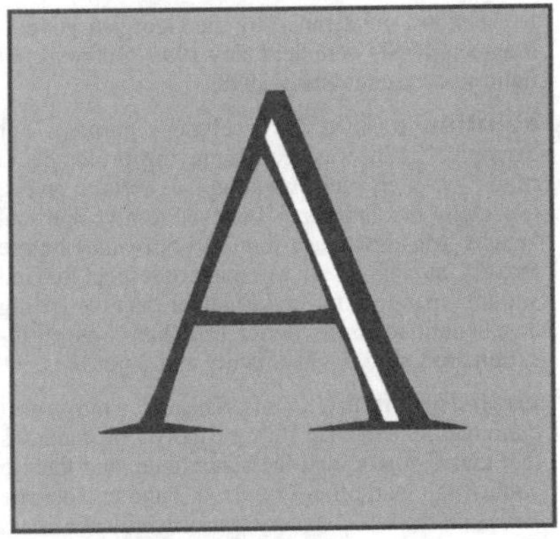

Aachen (French *Aix-la-Chapelle*) German cathedral city and spa in the administrative region (German *Land*) of North Rhine–Westphalia, 64 km/40 mi SW of Cologne; population (1993) 246,100. It has thriving electronic, glass, and rubber industries, and is one of Germany's principal railway junctions. Aachen was the Roman Aquisgranum and was the site of baths in the 1st century AD. Charlemagne was born and buried in Aachen, and founded the cathedral 796. The Holy Roman Emperors were crowned here 813–1531.

Aalborg (Danish *Aòlborg*) port in Denmark 32 km/20 mi inland from the Kattegat, on the south shore of the Limfjord; population (1995) 159,000. One of Denmark's oldest cities, it has a castle and the Budolfi cathedral (named after the English St Botolph), dating mainly from about 1400. It is the capital of Nordjylland county in Jylland (Jutland); the port is linked to Nørresundby on the north side of the fjord by a tunnel built 1969. Major industries include shipbuilding, cement, and textiles.

Aalto Alvar (Hugo Alvar Henrik) 1898–1976. Finnish architect and designer. He was a pioneer of the ◊Modern Movement in his native Finland. Initially working within the confines of the ◊International Style, he later developed a unique architectural style, characterized by asymmetry, curved walls, and contrast of natural materials. He invented a new form of laminated bent-plywood furniture 1932 and won many design awards for household and industrial items.

aardvark (Afrikaans 'earth pig') nocturnal mammal *Orycteropus afer*, the only species in the order Tubulidentata, found in central and southern Africa. A timid, defenceless animal about the size of a pig, it has a long head, a piglike snout, large ears, sparse body hair, a thick tail, and short legs.

It can burrow rapidly with its clawed front feet. It spends the day in its burrow, and at night digs open termite and ant nests, licking up the insects with its long sticky tongue. Its teeth are unique, without enamel, and are the main reason for the aardvark being placed in its own order. When fully grown, it is about 1.5 m/5 ft long and its tongue is 30 cm/12 in long.

aardwolf nocturnal mammal *Proteles cristatus* of the ◊hyena family, Hyaenidae. It is yellowish grey with dark stripes and, excluding its bushy tail, is around 70 cm/30 in long. It is found in eastern and southern Africa, usually in the burrows of the ◊aardvark. It feeds almost exclusively on termites, eating up to 300,000 per day, but may also eat other insects and small mammals.

Aarhus (Danish *Aòrhus*) second largest city of Denmark, on the east coast overlooking the Kattegat; population (1995) 277,500. It is the capital of Aarhus county in Jylland (Jutland) and a shipping and commercial centre.

abacus ancient calculating device made up of a frame of parallel wires on which beads are strung. The method of calculating with a handful of stones on a 'flat surface' (Latin *abacus*) was familiar to the Greeks and Romans, and used by earlier peoples, possibly even in ancient Babylon; it survives in the more sophisticated bead-frame form of the Russian *schoty* and the Japanese *soroban*. The abacus has been superseded by the electronic calculator.

The wires of a bead-frame abacus define place value (for example, in the decimal number system each successive wire, counting from right to left, would stand for ones, tens, hundreds, thousands, and so on) and beads are slid to the top of each wire in order to represent the digits of a particular number.

Abadan Iranian oil port on the east side of the Shatt-al-Arab waterway; population (1991) 84,800. Abadan is the chief refinery and shipping centre for Iran's oil industry, nationalized 1951. This measure was the beginning of the worldwide movement by oil-producing countries to assume control of profits from their own resources. Oil installations were badly damaged during the Iran–Iraq war 1980–88.

abalone edible marine snail of the worldwide genus *Haliotis*, family Haliotidae. Abalones have flattened, oval, spiralled shells, which have holes around the outer edge and a bluish mother-of-pearl lining. This lining is used in ornamental work.

Abba Swedish pop group 1973–81, one of the most successful groups in Europe during the 1970s. Their well-produced songs were characterized by the harmonies of the two female lead singers, and were aimed at a wide audience. Abba had a string of international hits beginning with 'Waterloo' (winner of the Eurovision Song Contest) 1974 and including 'SOS' 1974, 'Fernando' 1976, 'Dancing Queen' 1976, and 'The Winner Takes It All' 1980. There was a revival of interest in their music in the early 1990s.

Abbadid dynasty lived 11th century. Muslim dynasty based in Seville, Spain, which lasted from 1023 until 1091. The dynasty was founded by Abu-el-Kasim Muhammad Ibn Abbad, who led the townspeople against the Berbers when the Spanish caliphate fell. The dynasty continued under Motadid (1042–1069) and Motamid (1069–1091) when the city was taken by the ◊Almoravids.

Abbado Claudio 1933– . Italian conductor. He was principal director of the Vienna State Opera from 1986 and of the Berlin Philharmonic Orchestra from 1989. Associated early in his career with the La Scala Opera, Milan, his wide-ranging repertoire includes a significant number of 20th-century composers, among them Schoenberg, Prokofiev, Janáček, Bartók, and Stockhausen. He has also conducted the European Youth Orchestra from its inception 1977.

Abbās I ***the Great*** c. 1571–1629. Shah of Persia from 1587. He expanded Persian territory by conquest, defeating the Uzbeks near Herat 1597 and also the Turks. At his death his empire reached from the river Tigris to the Indus. He was a patron of the arts.

Abbās II or ***Abbās Hilmī Pasha*** 1874–1944. Last ◊khedive (viceroy) of Egypt, 1892–1914. On the outbreak of war between Britain and Turkey 1914, he sided with Turkey and was deposed following the establishment of a British protectorate over Egypt.

Abbado The conductor Claudio Abbado in rehearsal. Although his off-stage personality is somewhat reserved, his performances are highly charged through his attention to clarity, detail, and the immediate emotional needs of the music. He is also known for maintaining a scholarly attitude to the score. *Polygram*

Abbasid dynasty family of rulers of the Islamic empire, whose ◊caliphs reigned in Baghdad 750–1258. They were descended from Abbas, the prophet Muhammad's uncle, and some of them, such as Harun al-Rashid and Mamun (reigned 813–33), were outstanding patrons of cultural development. Later their power dwindled, and in 1258 Baghdad was burned by the Tatars. From then until 1517 the Abbasids retained limited power as caliphs of Egypt.

abbey in the Christian church, a building or group of buildings housing a community of monks or of nuns, all dedicated to a life of celibacy and religious seclusion, governed by an abbot or abbess respectively. The word is also applied to a building that was once the church of an abbey; for example, Westminster Abbey, London.

In England many abbeys were closed by Henry VIII, who turned from the Roman Catholic Church. In other countries many were closed in the 18th and 19th centuries as a result of political revolutions.

Abbey Theatre playhouse in Dublin, Ireland, associated with the Irish literary revival of the early 1900s. The theatre, opened 1904, staged the works of a number of Irish dramatists, including Lady Gregory, W B Yeats, J M Synge, and Sean O'Casey. Burned down 1951, the Abbey Theatre was rebuilt 1966.

Abbott and Costello Stage names of William Abbott (1895–1974) and Louis Cristillo (1906–1959) US comedy duo. They moved to films from vaudeville, and most, including *Buck Privates* 1941 and *Lost in a Harem* 1944, were showcases for their routines. They also appeared on radio and television.

Abd al-Hamid II 1842–1918. Last sultan of Turkey 1876–1909. In 1908 the ◊Young Turks under Enver Pasha forced Abd al-Hamid to restore the constitution of 1876 and in 1909 insisted on his deposition. He died in confinement. For his part in the ◊Armenian massacres suppressing the revolt of 1894–96 he was known as the 'Great Assassin'; his actions still motivate Armenian violence against the Turks.

Abd al-Karim (Abd al-Karim el-Khettabi) 1880–1963. Moroccan chief known as the 'Wolf of the ◊Riff'. With his brother Muhammad, he led the Riff revolt against the French and Spanish invaders, defeating the Spanish at Anual in 1921. For five years he ruled his own Republic of the Riff, centred on Melilla. Then the Spanish sought military assistance from the French (who governed northern Morocco); a joint army of 160,000 under Marshal Pétain subdued the rebellion 1925 and Abd al-Karim surrendered 1926.

Abd al-Malik Ibn Marwan 647–705. Fifth caliph of the Umayyad dynasty, who reigned 685–705, based in Damascus. He waged military campaigns to unite Muslim groups and battled against the Greeks. He instituted a purely Arab coinage and replaced Syriac, Coptic, and Greek with Arabic as the language for his lands. His reign was turbulent but succeeded in extending and strengthening the power of the dynasty. He was also a patron of the arts.

abdication crisis in British history, the constitutional upheaval of the period 16 Nov 1936 to 10 Dec 1936, brought about by the British king ◊Edward VIII's decision to marry Wallis ◊Simpson, a US divorcee. The marriage of the 'Supreme Governor' of the Church of England to a divorced person was considered unsuitable and the king abdicated on 10 Dec and left for voluntary exile in France. He was created Duke of Windsor and married Mrs Simpson 3 June 1937.

abdomen in vertebrates, the part of the body below the ◊thorax, containing the digestive organs; in insects and other arthropods, it is the hind part of the body. In mammals, the abdomen is separated from the thorax by the ◊diaphragm, a sheet of muscular tissue; in arthropods, commonly by a narrow constriction. In mammals, the female reproductive organs are in the abdomen. In insects and spiders, it is characterized by the absence of limbs.

‘Aberdeen impresses the stranger as a city of granite palaces … Nothing so time-defying has been built since the Temple of Karnak.’

On ABERDEEN
H V Morton *In Search of Scotland*

Abdullah Sheik Muhammad 1905–1982. Indian politician, known as the ‘Lion of Kashmir’. He headed the struggle for constitutional government against the Maharajah of Kashmir, and in 1948, following a coup, became prime minister. He agreed to the accession of the state to India, but was dismissed and imprisoned from 1953 (with brief intervals) until 1966, when he called for Kashmiri self-determination. He became chief minister of Jammu and Kashmir 1975, accepting the sovereignty of India.

Abdullah ibn Hussein 1882–1951. King of Jordan from 1946. He worked with the British guerrilla leader T E ◊Lawrence in the Arab revolt of World War I. Abdullah became king of Transjordan 1946; on the incorporation of Arab Palestine (after the 1948–49 Arab–Israeli War) he renamed the country the Hashemite Kingdom of Jordan. He was assassinated.

Abel in the Old Testament (Genesis 4), the second son of Adam and Eve; as a shepherd, he made burnt offerings of meat to God which were more acceptable than the fruits offered by his brother Cain; he was killed by the jealous Cain. This was the first death recounted in the Bible.

Abel John Jacob 1857–1938. US biochemist, discoverer of ◊adrenaline. He studied the chemical composition of body tissues, and this led, in 1898, to the discovery of adrenaline, the first hormone to be identified, which Abel called epinephrine. He later became the first to isolate ◊amino acids from blood.

Abelard Peter (English form of Pierre Abélard) 1079–1142. French scholastic philosopher who worked on logic and theology. His romantic liaison with his pupil ◊Héloïse caused a medieval scandal. Details of his life are contained in the autobiographical *Historia Calamitatum Mearum/The History of My Misfortunes*.

Abelard, born in Pallet, near Nantes, became canon of Notre Dame in Paris and master of the cathedral school 1115. When his seduction of Héloïse and secret marriage to her (shortly after the birth of a son) became known, she entered a convent. He was castrated at the instigation of her uncle Canon Fulbert, and became a monk. Resuming teaching a year later, he was cited for heresy and became a hermit at Nogent.

Aberconwy and Colwyn unitary authority of Wales created 1996 (*see United Kingdom map*).

Aberdeen city and seaport on the east coast of Scotland, administrative headquarters 1975–96 of Grampian region, and, from 1996, of local authorities of Aberdeen City and Aberdeenshire; population (1991) 189,700. Industries include agricultural machinery, paper, knitwear, carpets, and textiles; fishing; shipbuilding; granite-quarrying; and engineering. Oil discoveries in the North Sea in the 1960s–70s transformed Aberdeen into the European ‘offshore capital’, with an airport and heliport linking the mainland to the oil rigs, with shore-based maintenance and service depots. Aberdeen is Scotland’s third-largest city and its biggest resort. It is rich in historical interest and fine buildings, including the Municipal Buildings (1867); King’s College (1494) and Marischal College (founded 1593, and housed in one of the largest granite buildings in the world 1836), which together form Aberdeen University; St Machar Cathedral (1378); and the Auld Brig o’Balgownie (1320).

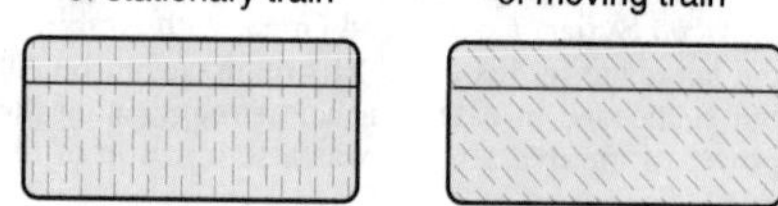

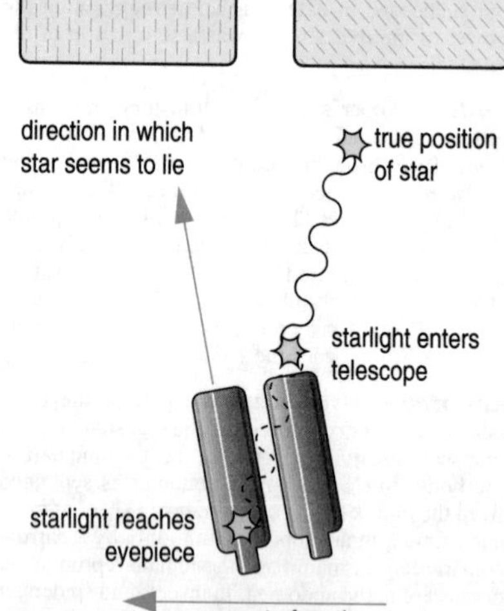

aberration of starlight The aberration of starlight is an optical illusion caused by the motion of the Earth. Rain falling appears vertical when seen from the window of a stationary train; when seen from the window of a moving train, the rain appears to follow a sloping path. In the same way, light from a star ‘falling’ down a telescope seems to follow a sloping path because the Earth is moving. This causes an apparent displacement, or aberration, in the position of the star.

Aberdeen George Hamilton Gordon, 4th Earl of Aberdeen 1784–1860. British Tory politician, prime minister 1852–55, when he resigned because of the criticism aroused by the miseries and mismanagement of the ◊Crimean War.

Aberdeen City local authority of E Scotland created 1996 (*see United Kingdom map*).

Aberdeenshire former county in E Scotland, merged 1975 into Grampian Region; became local authority of Scotland 1996 (*see United Kingdom map*).

Aberfan former coal-mining village in Mid Glamorgan, Wales. In 1966, coal waste from a slag heap overwhelmed a school and houses, killing 144 people, of whom 116 were children.

aberration of starlight apparent displacement of a star from its true position, due to the combined effects of the speed of light and the speed of the Earth in orbit around the Sun (about 30 km per sec/18.5 mi per sec).

Aberration, discovered 1728 by English astronomer James Bradley (1693–1762), was the first observational proof that the Earth orbits the Sun.

aberration, optical any of a number of defects that impair the image in an optical instrument. Aberration occurs because of minute variations in lenses and mirrors, and because different parts of the light ◊spectrum are reflected or refracted by varying amounts.

In chromatic aberration the image is surrounded by coloured fringes, because light of different colours is brought to different focal points by a lens. In spherical aberration the image is blurred because different parts of a spherical lens or mirror have different focal lengths. In astigmatism the image appears elliptical or cross-shaped because of an irregularity in the curvature of the lens. In coma the images appear progressively elongated towards the edge of the field of view. Elaborate computer programs are now used to design lenses in which the aberrations are minimized.

Aberystwyth resort and university town in Dyfed, Wales, on Cardigan Bay; population (1991) 11,150. The Welsh Plant Breeding Station and National Library of Wales are here. It is the unofficial capital of the Welsh-speaking area of Wales.

Abidjan port and former capital (until 1983) of the Republic of Côte d’Ivoire, W Africa; population (1990 est) 2,700,000. Products include coffee, palm oil, cocoa, and timber (mahogany). Yamoussoukro became the new capital 1983, but was not internationally recognized as such until 1992.

abiotic factor a nonorganic variable within the ecosystem, affecting the life of organisms. Examples include temperature, light, and soil structure. Abiotic factors can be harmful to the environment, as when sulphur dioxide emissions from power stations produce acid rain.

Abkhazia autonomous republic in Georgia, situated on the Black Sea
capital Sukhumi
area 8,600 sq km/3,320 sq mi
industries tin, fruit, tobacco, tea
population (1990) 537,500
history a Georgian kingdom from the 4th century, Abkhazia was inhabited traditionally by Abkhazis, an ethnic group converted from Christianity to Islam in the 17th century. By the 1980s some 17% of the population were Muslims and two-thirds were of Georgian origin. From 1989 the region was the scene of secessionist activity on the part of the minority Muslim Abkhazi community, culminating in the republic’s declaration of independence 1992. Georgian troops invaded and took control Aug 1992, but secessionists subsequently gained control of the northern half of the republic. In Oct 1993 they took the region’s capital, Sukhumi, as well as much of the republic’s remaining territory. A cease-fire was agreed 1994 and parliament adopted a new constitution, proclaiming Abkhazian sovereignty.

Elections, condemned by the Georgian government as illegal, were held Nov 1996. Outbreaks of fighting occurred during 1998.

ablution washing for a religious purpose. For example, Hindus wash before praying, preferably in running water, and washing in certain rivers, especially the Ganges, is believed to give spiritual benefit. Muslims wash themselves (*wudu*) before prayers, but this is seen as a mark of respect for God and a preparation for prayer rather than conferring any benefit in itself. Belief in ablution as purification are found in Christianity and Shinto.

abolitionism in UK and US history, a movement culminating in the late 18th and early 19th centuries that aimed first to end the slave trade, and then to abolish the institution of ◊slavery and emancipate slaves. In the USA, slavery was officially abolished by the ◊Emancipation Proclamation 1863 of President Abraham Lincoln, but it could not be enforced until 1865 after the Union victory in the Civil War. The question of whether newly admitted states would allow slavery had been a major issue in the break-up of the Union. In the UK, the leading abolitionist was William ◊Wilberforce, who secured passage of a bill abolishing the slave trade 1807. ▷ *See feature on pp. 982–983.*

abominable snowman or ***yeti*** legendary creature, said to resemble a human, with long arms and a thickset body covered with reddish-grey hair. Reports of its existence in the Himalayas have been made since 1832. In 1998 German mountaineer Reinhold Messner claimed that the abominable snowman is really a Tibetan bear that lives at altitudes between 12,000 and 18,000 feet.

aberration, optical The main defects, or aberrations, of optical systems. Chromatic aberration, or coloured fringes around images, arises because light of different colours is focused at different points by a lens, causing a blurred image. Spherical aberration arises because light that passes through the centre of the lens is focused at a different point from light passing through the edge of the lens. Astigmatism arises if a lens has different curvatures in the vertical and horizontal directions. Coma arises because light passing directly through a lens is focused at a different point to light entering the lens from an angle.

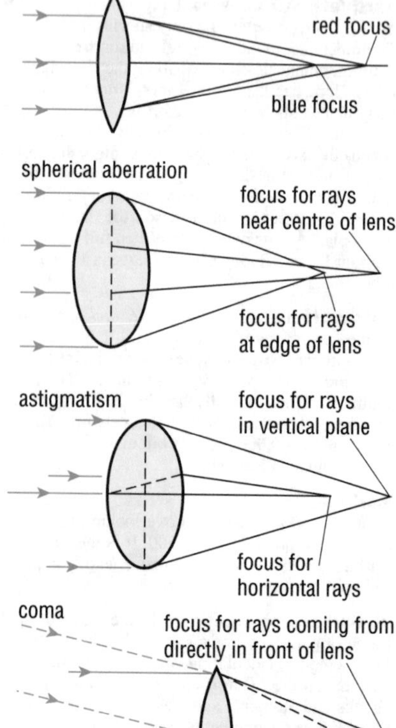

Aboriginal art art of the Australian Aborigines. Traditionally almost entirely religious and ceremonial, it was directed towards portraying stories of the ◊Dreamtime, a creation mythology reflecting the Aboriginal hunter-gatherer lifestyle. Perishable materials were used, as in bark painting and carved trees and logs, and few early works of this type survive. A great deal of rock art remains intact, however, and forms one of the richest continuing traditions in the world. Abstract patterns and stylized figures predominate. Ground and body painting were also practised, chiefly as part of secret initiation rites.

aborigine (Latin *ab origine* 'from the beginning') any indigenous inhabitant of a region or country. The word often refers to the original peoples of areas colonized by Europeans, and especially to ◊Australian Aborigines.

abortion (Latin *aborire* 'to miscarry') ending of a pregnancy before the fetus is developed sufficiently to survive outside the uterus. Loss of a fetus at a later gestational age is termed premature stillbirth. Abortion may be accidental (◊miscarriage) or deliberate (termination of pregnancy).

deliberate termination In the first nine weeks of pregnancy, medical termination may be carried out using the 'abortion pill' (◊mifepristone) in conjunction with a ◊prostaglandin. There are also various procedures for surgical termination, such as ◊dilatation and curettage, depending on the length of the pregnancy.

abortion as birth control Abortion as a means of birth control has long been controversial. The argument centres largely upon whether a woman should legally be permitted to have an abortion and, if so, under what circumstances. Another aspect is whether, and to what extent, the law should protect the fetus.

Those who oppose abortion generally believe that human life begins at the moment of conception, when a sperm fertilizes an egg. This is the view held, for example, by the Roman Catholic Church. Those who support unrestricted legal abortion may believe in a woman's right to choose whether she wants a child, and may take into account the large numbers of deaths and injuries from unprofessional back-street abortions.

Others approve abortion for specific reasons. For example, if a woman's life or health is jeopardized, abortion may be recommended; and if there is a strong likelihood that the child will be born with severe mental or physical disability. Other grounds for abortion include pregnancy resulting from sexual assault such as rape or incest.

1967 Abortion Act In the UK an abortion must be carried out under the terms of the 1967 Abortion Act, which states that two doctors must agree that termination of the pregnancy is necessary, and the operation must be performed on approved premises. In 1990, Parliament approved a measure to lower the time limit on abortions from 28 to 24 weeks. Pregnancy can still be terminated at a later date if the mother's life is in danger.

Aboukir Bay, Battle of also known as the ***Battle of the Nile***; naval battle during the Napoleonic Wars between Great Britain and France, in which Admiral Horatio Nelson defeated Napoleon Bonaparte's fleet at the Egyptian seaport of Aboukir on 1 Aug 1798. The defeat put an end to French designs in the Middle East.

Abraham lived c. 2300 BC. In the Old Testament, the founder of the Jewish nation. In his early life he was called Abram. God promised him heirs and land for his people in Canaan (Israel), renamed him Abraham ('father of many nations'), and tested his faith by a command (later retracted) to sacrifice his son Isaac.

Still childless at the age of 76, Abraham subsequently had a son (Ishmael) with his wife's maidservant Hagar, and then, at the age of 100, a son (Isaac) with his wife Sarah. God's promise to Abraham that his descendants would be a nation and Canaan their land was fulfilled when the descendants of Abraham's grandson Jacob were led out of Egypt by Moses.

Abraham, Plains of plateau near Quebec, Canada, where the British commander ◊Wolfe defeated the French under ◊Montcalm, 13 Sept 1759, during the French and Indian (or Seven Years) War (1754–63). The outcome of the battle established British supremacy in Canada.

abrasion in earth science, the effect of ◊corrasion, a type of erosion in which rock fragments scrape and grind away a surface. The rock fragments may be carried by rivers, wind, ice, or the sea. Striations, or grooves, on rock surfaces are common abrasions, caused by the scratching of rock debris embedded in glacier ice.

abrasive substance used for cutting and polishing or for removing small amounts of the surface of hard materials. There are two types: natural and artificial abrasives, and their hardness is measured using the ◊Mohs' scale. Natural abrasives include quartz, sandstone, pumice, diamond, emery, and corundum; artificial abrasives include rouge, whiting, and carborundum.

Abruzzi mountainous region of S central Italy, comprising the provinces of L'Aquila, Chieti, Pescara, and Teramo; area 10,800 sq km/4,169 sq mi; population (1992) 1,255,500; capital L'Aquila. Gran Sasso d'Italia, 2,914 m/9,564 ft, is the highest point of the ◊Apennines.

abscess collection of ◊pus in solid tissue forming in response to infection. Its presence is signalled by pain and inflammation.

abscissa in ◊coordinate geometry, the *x*-coordinate of a point – that is, the horizontal distance of that point from the vertical or *y*-axis. For example, a point with the coordinates (4, 3) has an abscissa of 4. The *y*-coordinate of a point is known as the ◊ordinate.

abscissin or ***abscissic acid*** plant hormone found in all higher plants. It is involved in the process of ◊abscission and also inhibits stem elongation, germination of seeds, and the sprouting of buds.

abscission in botany, the controlled separation of part of a plant from the main plant body – most commonly, the falling of leaves or the dropping of fruit controlled by ◊abscissin. In ◊deciduous plants the leaves are shed before the winter or dry season, whereas ◊evergreen plants drop their leaves continually throughout the year. Fruitdrop, the abscission of fruit while still immature, is a naturally occurring process.

absinthe green liqueur containing 60–80% alcohol and flavoured with herbs, mainly oil of wormwood and anise; when water is added it becomes cloudy. Owing to the harmful effect that wormwood has on the nervous system, the making of absinthe is banned in many countries and substitutes without wormwood, notably anis and pastis, have taken its place.

absolute zero lowest temperature theoretically possible, zero kelvin (0K), equivalent to −273.15°C/−459.67°F, at which molecules are in their lowest energy state. Although the third law of ◊thermodynamics indicates the impossibility of reaching absolute zero exactly, a temperature of 2.8×10^{-10}K (0.28 millionths of a degree above absolute zero) was produced 1993 at Lancaster University, England. Near absolute zero, the physical properties of some materials change substantially; for example, some metals lose their electrical resistance and become superconducting.

absolutism or ***absolute monarchy*** system of government in which the ruler or rulers have unlimited power and are subject to no constitutional safeguards or checks. The principle of an absolute monarch, given a right to rule by God (the ◊divine right of kings), was extensively used in Europe during the 17th and 18th centuries; it was based on an earlier theory of papal absolutism. Absolute monarchy is contrasted with limited or constitutional monarchy, in which the sovereign's powers are defined or limited.

absorption the taking up of one substance by another, such as a liquid by a solid (ink by blotting paper) or a gas by a liquid (ammonia by water). In physics, absorption is the phenomenon by which a substance retains radiation of particular wavelengths; for example, a piece of blue glass absorbs all visible light except the wavelengths in the blue part of the spectrum; it also refers to the partial loss of energy resulting from light and other electromagnetic waves passing through a medium. In nuclear physics, absorption is the capture by elements, such as boron, of neutrons produced by fission in a reactor.

abstract art nonrepresentational art. Ornamental art without figurative representation occurs in most cultures. The modern abstract movement in sculpture and painting emerged in Europe and North America between 1910 and 1920. Two approaches produce different abstract styles: images that have been 'abstracted' from nature to the point where they no longer reflect a conventional reality, and nonobjective, or 'pure', art forms, without any reference to reality.

history Abstract art began in the avant-garde movements of the late 19th century – ◊Impressionism, ◊Neo-Impressionism, and ◊Post-Impressionism. These styles of painting reduced the importance of the original subject matter and began to emphasize the creative process of painting itself. In the first decade of the 20th century, some painters in Europe began to abandon the established Western conventions of imitating nature and of storytelling and developed a new artistic form and expression.

abstract artists Wassily ◊Kandinsky is generally regarded as the first abstract artist. From 1910 to 1914 he worked on two series, *Improvisations* and *Compositions*, in which he moved gradually towards total abstraction. His highly coloured canvases influenced many younger European artists. In France around 1907, the Cubists Pablo ◊Picasso and Georges ◊Braque also developed a semi-abstract style; their pictures, some partly collage, were composed mainly of fragmented natural images. By 1912 Robert ◊Delaunay had pushed Cubism to complete abstraction.

Many variations of abstract art developed in Europe and Russia, as shown in the work of Piet ◊Mondrian, Kasimir Malevich, the ◊Futurists, the Vorticists, and the ◊Dadaists. Sculptors were inspired by the new freedom in form and content, and Constantin ◊Brancusi's versions of *The Kiss* 1907–12 are among the earliest semi-abstract sculptures. Cubist-inspired sculptors such as Raymond Duchamp-Villon (1876–1918) and Jacques Lipchitz moved further towards abstraction, as did the Dadaist Hans Arp.

US art Two exhibitions of European art, one in New York 1913 (the Armory Show), the other in San Francisco 1917, opened the way for abstraction in US art. Many painters, including the young Georgia ◊O'Keeffe, experimented with new styles. Morgan Russell (1886–1953) and Stanton Macdonald-Wright (1890–1973) invented their own abstract style, Synchromism, a rival to Orphism, a similar style developed in France by Delaunay. Both movements emphasized colour over form.

later developments Abstract art has dominated Western art from 1920 and has continued to produce many variations. In the 1940s it gained renewed vigour in the works of the Abstract Expressionists, and in the 1950s Minimal art developed as a more impersonal, simplified style of abstraction.

Abstract Expressionism US movement in abstract art that emphasized the act of painting, the expression inherent in the colour and texture of the paint itself, and the interaction of artist, paint, and canvas. Abstract Expressionism emerged in New York in the early 1940s. Arshile Gorky, Franz Kline, Jackson Pollock, and Mark Rothko are associated with the movement.

Abstract Expressionism may have been inspired by Hans Hofmann and Gorky, who were both working in the USA in the 1940s. Hofmann, who emigrated from Germany in the 1930s, had started to use dribbles and blobs of paint to create expressive abstract patterns, while Gorky, a Turkish Armenian refugee, was developing his highly coloured abstracts using wild organic forms. Abstract Expressionism was not a distinct school but rather a convergence of artistic personalities, each in revolt against the prevailing conventions in US art. The styles of the movement's exponents varied widely: Pollock's huge dripped and splashed work, Willem de Kooning's grotesque figures, Kline's strong calligraphic style, and Robert Motherwell's and Rothko's large, calm canvases. The movement made a strong impression on European painting in the late 1950s.

Absurd, Theatre of the avant-garde drama originating with a group of dramatists in the 1950s, including Samuel Beckett, Eugène Ionesco, Jean Genet, and Harold Pinter. Their work expressed the belief that in a godless universe human existence has no meaning or purpose and therefore all communication breaks down. Logical construction and argument gives way to irrational and illogical speech and to its ultimate conclusion, silence, as in Beckett's play *Breath* 1970.

Abu Bakr or ***Abu-Bekr*** 573–634. 'Father of the virgin', name used by Abd-al-Ka'aba from about 618 when the prophet Muhammad married his daughter Ayesha. Abu Bakr was a close adviser to Muhammad in the period 622–32. On the prophet's death, he became the first ◊caliph, adding Mesopotamia to the Muslim world and instigating expansion into Iraq and Syria.

Traditionally he is supposed to have encouraged some of those who had known Muhammad to memorize his teachings; these words were later written down to form the Koran.

Abu Dhabi sheikdom in SW Asia, on the Persian Gulf, capital of the ◊United Arab Emirates; area 67,350 sq km/26,000 sq mi; population (1985) 670,100. Formerly under British protection, it has been ruled since 1971 by Sheik Sultan Zayed bin al-Nahayan, who is also president of the Supreme Council of Rulers of the United Arab Emirates.

Abuja capital of Nigeria (formally designated as such 1982, although not officially recognized until 1992); population of Federal Capital District (1991) 378,700; population of city alone (1992 est) 305,900. Shaped like a crescent, the city was designed by Japanese architect Kenzo Tange; it began construction 1976 as a replacement for Lagos.

Abú Nuwás Hasan ibn Háni c.760–c. 815. Arab poet. Considered to be one of the greatest poets of the Abbasid period, he is celebrated for the freedom, eroticism, and ironic lightness of touch he brought to traditional forms, as manifested in his *Divan des Abu Nuwas*.

Abu Simbel site of two ancient temples cut into the rock on the banks of the Nile in S Egypt during the reign of Ramses II, commemorating him and his wife Nefertari. The temples were moved in sections 1966–67 and rebuilt 60 m/200 ft above their original location before the site was flooded by the waters of the Aswan High Dam.

abyssal plain broad expanse of sea floor lying 3–6 km/2–4 mi below sea level. Abyssal plains are found in all the major oceans, and they extend from bordering continental rises to mid-oceanic ridges.

abyssal zone dark ocean region 2,000–6,000 m/6,500–19,500 ft deep; temperature 4°C/39°F. Three-quarters of the area of the deep-ocean floor lies in the abyssal zone, which is too far from the surface for photosynthesis to take place. Some fish and crustaceans living there are blind or have their own light sources. The region above is the bathyal zone; the region below, the hadal zone.

Abyssinia former name of ◊Ethiopia.

abzyme in biotechnology, an artificially created antibody that can be used like an enzyme to accelerate reactions.

acacia any of a large group of shrubs and trees of the genus *Acacia* of the legume family Leguminosae. Acacias include the thorn trees of the African savanna and the gum arabic tree *A. senegal* of N Africa, and several North American species of the SW USA and Mexico. Acacias are found in warm regions of the world, particularly Australia.

The hardy tree commonly known as acacia is the false acacia or *Robinia pseudacacia*, which belongs to the subfamily Papilionoideae. The *A. dealbata* is grown in the open air in some parts of France and the warmer European countries, and is remarkable for its clusters of beautiful yellow flowers.

Academy Award annual film award in many categories, given since 1927 by the American Academy of Motion Picture Arts and Sciences (AMPAS). *See list of tables on p. 1177.*

Academy, French or ***Académie Française*** literary society concerned with maintaining the purity of the French language, founded by ◊Richelieu 1635.

acanthus any herbaceous plant of the genus *Acanthus*, in the family Acanthaceae, with handsome lobed leaves. Twenty species are found in the Mediterranean region and Old World tropics, including bear's-breech *Acanthus mollis*, whose leaves were used as a motif in classical architecture, especially on Corinthian columns.

a cappella (Italian 'in the style of the chapel') choral music sung without instrumental accompaniment. In modern music it is characteristic of ◊gospel music, ◊doo-wop, and the evangelical Christian church movement.

Acapulco or ***Acapulco de Juarez*** port and holiday resort in S Mexico; population (1990) 593,200. There is deep-sea fishing, and tropical products are exported. Acapulco was founded 1550 and was Mexico's major Pacific coast port until about 1815.

ACAS acronym for ◊***Advisory, Conciliation, and Arbitration Service***.

accelerated freeze drying common method of food preservation. See ◊food technology.

acceleration rate of change of the velocity of a moving body. It is usually measured in metres per second per second ($m\ s^{-2}$) or feet per second per second ($ft\ s^{-2}$). Because velocity is a ◊vector quantity (possessing both magnitude and direction) a body travelling at constant speed may be said to be accelerating if its direction of motion changes. According to Newton's second law of motion, a body will accelerate only if it is acted upon by an unbalanced, or resultant, ◊force.

Acceleration due to gravity is the acceleration of a body falling freely under the influence of the Earth's gravitational field; it varies slightly at different latitudes and altitudes. The value adopted internationally for gravitational acceleration is $9.806\ m\ s^{-2}/32.174\ fts^{-2}$.

acceleration, secular in astronomy, the continuous and nonperiodic change in orbital velocity of one body around another, or the axial rotation period of a body. An example is the axial rotation of the Earth. This is gradually slowing down owing to the gravitational effects of the Moon and the resulting production of tides, which have a frictional effect on the Earth. However, the angular ◊momentum of the Earth–Moon system is maintained, because the momentum lost by the Earth is passed to the Moon. This results in an increase in the Moon's orbital period and a consequential moving away from the Earth. The overall effect is that the Earth's axial rotation period is increasing by about 15 millionths of a second a year, and the Moon is receding from the Earth at about 4 cm/1.5 in a year.

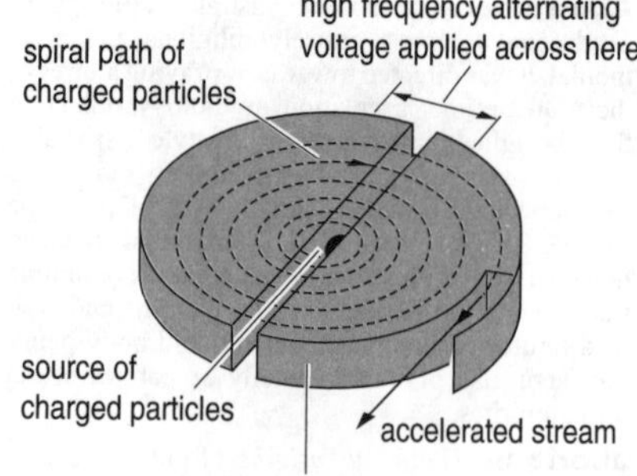

accelerator The cyclotron, an early accelerator, consisted of two D-shaped hollow chambers enclosed in a vacuum. An alternating voltage was applied across the gap between the hollows. Charged particles spiralled outward from the centre, picking up energy and accelerating each time they passed through the gap.

accelerator in physics, a device to bring charged particles (such as protons and electrons) up to high speeds and energies, at which they can be of use in industry, medicine, and pure physics. At low energies, accelerated particles can be used to produce the image on a television screen and generate X-rays (by means of a ◊cathode-ray tube), destroy tumour cells, or kill bacteria. When high-energy particles collide with other particles, the fragments formed reveal the nature of the fundamental forces of nature.

The first accelerators used high voltages (produced by ◊van de Graaff generators) to generate a strong, unvarying electric field. Charged particles were accelerated as they passed through the electric field. However, because the voltage produced by a generator is limited, these accelerators were replaced by machines where the particles passed through regions of alternating electric fields, receiving a succession of small pushes to accelerate them.

The first of these accelerators was the ***linear accelerator*** or ***linac***. The linac consists of a line of metal tubes, called drift tubes, through which the particles travel. The particles are accelerated by electric fields in the gaps between the drift tubes. Early accelerators directed the particle beam onto a stationary target; large modern accelerators usually collide beams of particles that are travelling in opposite directions. This arrangement doubles the effective energy of the collision.

The world's most powerful accelerator is the 2 km/1.25 mi diameter machine at ◊Fermilab near Batavia, Illinois, USA. This machine, the Tevatron, accelerates protons and antiprotons and then collides them at energies up to a thousand billion electron volts (or 1 TeV, hence the name of the machine). The largest accelerator is the ◊Large Electron Positron Collider at ◊CERN near Geneva, which has a circumference of 27 km/16.8 mi around which electrons and positrons are accelerated before being allowed to collide. The world's longest linac is also a colliding beam machine: the Stanford Linear Collider, in California, in which electrons and positrons are accelerated along a straight track, 3.2 km/2 mi long, and then steered to a head-on collision with other particles, such as protons and neutrons. Such experiments have been instrumental in revealing that protons and neutrons are made up of smaller elementary particles called ◊quarks.

accent way of speaking that identifies a person with a particular country, region, language, social class, or some mixture of these. Accent refers to features of pronunciation; variations from standard grammar and vocabulary are ◊dialects. People often describe only those who belong to groups other than their own as having accents and may give them

Abu Simbel One of the two temples built by Ramses II at Abu Simbel in the 13th century BC. This one was dedicated to his wife Nefertari and to Hathur, the goddess of love and beauty. The façade is adorned with six statues, two of Nefertari and four of Ramses. The temple consists of halls carved many metres into the sandstone cliff. *Egyptian Tourist Board*

special names; for example, an Irish brogue, a Southern accent.

accent mark (´, ˇ, ˆ) used to indicate stress on a particular syllable or a difference in the pronunciation of a letter. English does not use accents, except in some words of foreign origin such as 'cliché', 'café', and 'fête'.

accessory in law, a criminal accomplice who aids in commission of a crime committed by someone else. An accomplice may be either 'before the fact' (assisting, ordering, or procuring another to commit a crime) or 'after the fact' (giving assistance after the crime). An accomplice present when the crime is committed is an abettor.

access provider in computing, another term for ◊Internet Service Provider.

acclimation or ***acclimatization*** the physiological changes induced in an organism by exposure to new environmental conditions. When humans move to higher altitudes, for example, the number of red blood cells rises to increase the oxygen-carrying capacity of the blood in order to compensate for the lower levels of oxygen in the air. In evolutionary terms, the ability to acclimate is an important adaptation as it allows the organism to cope with the environmental changes occurring during its lifetime.

accommodation in biology, the ability of the ◊eye to focus on near or far objects by changing the shape of the lens. For an object to be viewed clearly its image must be precisely focused on the retina, the light-sensitive layer of cells at the rear of the eye. Close objects can be seen when the lens takes up a more spherical shape, far objects when the lens is flattened. These changes in shape are caused by the movement of ligaments attached to a ring of ciliary muscles lying beneath the iris. With age, the lens in the human eye becomes less flexible, causing the defect of vision known as presbyopia or lack of accommodation.

accomplice in law, a person who acts with another in the commission or attempted commission of a crime, either as a principal or as an ◊accessory.

accordion musical instrument of the free-reed organ type comprising left and right wind chests connected by flexible bellows. The right hand plays melody on a piano-style keyboard of 26 to 34 keys while the left hand has a system of push buttons for selecting single notes or chord harmonies.

accountant person responsible for drawing up accounts, usually for a business organization. Accountants have traditionally concentrated on recording what has happened financially in the past. In management accounting, accountants are increasingly involved in helping to formulate policy for business organizations, providing information for decision-makers and frameworks for making those decisions.

'Chartered accountants' spend at least three years training with a professional partnership and specialize in auditing and financial accountancy. 'Certified accountants' are trained while employed in industry, commerce, or the public service and are qualified to undertake audits of company accounts.

accounting the principles and practice of systematically recording, presenting, and interpreting financial accounts; financial record keeping and management of businesses and other organizations, from balance sheets to policy decisions, for tax or operating purposes. Forms of inflation accounting, such as CCA (current cost accounting) and CPP (current purchasing power), are aimed at providing valid financial comparisons over a period in which money values change.

Accra capital and port of Ghana; population (1988 est) 949,100. The port trades in cacao, gold, and timber. Industries include engineering, brewing, and food processing. Osu (Christiansborg) Castle is the presidential residence.

accumulator in electricity, a storage ◊battery – that is, a group of rechargeable secondary cells. A familiar example is the lead–acid car battery. An ordinary 12-volt car battery consists of six lead–acid cells which are continually recharged when the motor is running by the car's alternator or dynamo. It has electrodes of lead and lead oxide in an electrolyte of sulphuric acid. Another common type of accumulator is the 'nife' or Ni Fe cell, which has electrodes of nickel and iron in a potassium hydroxide electrolyte.

Acer genus of trees and shrubs of the temperate regions of the northern hemisphere with over 115 species, many of them popular garden specimens in Australia. The genus includes ◊sycamore and ◊maple. Some species have pinnate leaves, including *A. negundo* of North America, the box elder.

acetaldehyde common name for ◊ethanal.

acetate common name for ◊ethanoate.

acetic acid common name for ◊ethanoic acid.

acetone common name for ◊propanone.

acetylcholine (ACh) chemical that serves as a ◊neurotransmitter, communicating nerve impulses between the cells of the nervous system. It is largely associated with the transmission of impulses across the ◊synapse (junction) between nerve and muscle cells, causing the muscles to contract.

ACh is produced in the synaptic knob (a swelling at the end of a nerve cell) and stored in vesicles until a nerve impulse triggers its discharge across the synapse. When the ACh reaches the membrane of the receiving cell it binds with a specific site and brings about depolarization – a reversal of the electric charge on either side of the membrane – causing a fresh impulse (in nerve cells) or a contraction (in muscle cells). Its action is shortlived because it is quickly destroyed by the enzyme cholinesterase. Anticholinergic drugs have a number of uses in medicine by blocking the action of ACh, thereby disrupting the passage of nerve impulses and relaxing certain muscles, for example in premedication before surgery.

acetylene common name for ◊ethyne.

acetylsalicylic acid chemical name for the painkilling drug ◊aspirin.

Achaea or ***Achaia*** in ancient Greece, an area of the N Peloponnese. The Achaeans were the predominant society during the Mycenaean period and are said by Homer to have taken part in the siege of Troy. The larger Roman province of Achaea was created after the defeat of the Achaean League 146 BC; it included all mainland Greece south of a line drawn from the Ambracian to the Maliac Gulf.

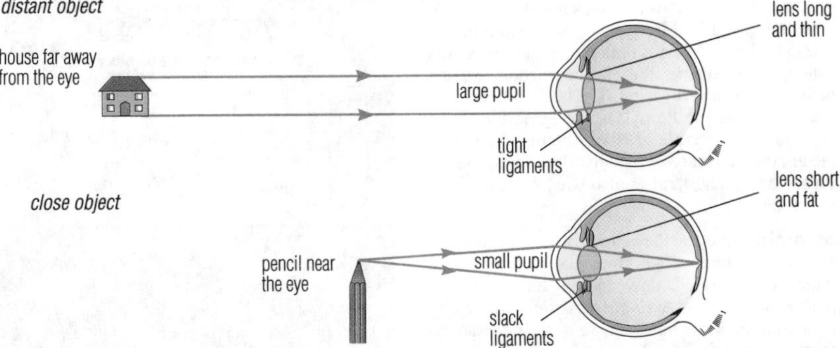

accommodation The mechanism by which the shape of the lens in the eye is changed so that clear images of objects, whether distant or near, can be focused on the retina.

Achaean League union 280 BC of most of the cities of the N Peloponnese, which managed to defeat ◊Sparta, but was itself defeated by the Romans 146 BC.

Achaemenid dynasty family ruling the Persian Empire 550–330 BC, named after Achaemenes, ancestor of ◊Cyrus the Great, founder of the empire. His successors included Cambyses, Darius I, Xerxes, and Darius III, who, as the last Achaemenid ruler, was killed after defeat in battle against Alexander the Great 330 BC.

Achebe Chinua (Albert Chinualumogo) 1930– . Nigerian novelist. His themes include the social and political impact of European colonialism on African people, and the problems of newly independent African nations. Among his works are the seminal *Things Fall Apart* 1958, one of the first African novels to achieve a global reputation, and *Anthills of the Savannah* 1987.

achene dry, one-seeded ◊fruit that develops from a single ◊ovary and does not split open to disperse the seed. Achenes commonly occur in groups – for example, the fruiting heads of buttercup *Ranunculus* and clematis. The outer surface may be smooth, spiny, ribbed, or tuberculate, depending on the species.

Achernar or ***Alpha Eridani*** brightest star in the constellation Eridanus, and the ninth brightest star in the night sky. It is a hot, luminous, blue star with a true luminosity 250 times that of the Sun. It is 125 light years away.

Acheson Dean (Gooderham) 1893–1971. US politician. As undersecretary of state 1945–47 in Harry Truman's Democratic administration, he was associated with George C Marshall in preparing the ◊Marshall Plan, and succeeded him as secretary of state 1949–53.

The first requirement of a statesman is that he be dull. This is not always easy to achieve.

DEAN ACHESON
Quoted in the *Observer* 21 June 1970

Achilles Greek hero of Homer's *Iliad*. He was the son of Peleus, King of the Myrmidons in Thessaly, and of the sea nymph Thetis, who rendered him invulnerable, except for the heel by which she held him, by dipping him in the river Styx. Achilles killed ◊Hector at the climax of the *Iliad*, and according to subsequent Greek legends was himself killed by ◊Paris, who shot a poisoned arrow into Achilles' heel.

Achilles tendon tendon at the back of the ankle attaching the calf muscles to the heel bone. It is one of the largest tendons in the human body, and can resist great tensional strain, but is sometimes ruptured by contraction of the muscles in sudden extension of the foot.

achromatic lens combination of lenses made from materials of different refractive indexes, constructed in such a way as to minimize chromatic aberration (which in a single lens causes coloured fringes around images because the lens diffracts the different wavelengths in white light to slightly different extents).

acid compound that, in solution in an ionizing solvent (usually water), gives rise to hydrogen ions (H^+ or protons). In modern chemistry, acids are defined as substances that are proton donors and accept electrons to form ◊ionic bonds. Acids react with ◊bases to form salts, and they act as solvents. Strong acids are corrosive; dilute acids have a sour or sharp taste, although in some organic acids this may be partially masked by other flavour characteristics.

Acids can be detected by using coloured indicators such as ◊litmus and methyl orange. The strength of an acid is measured by its hydrogen-ion concentration, indicated by the ◊pH value. Acids are classified as monobasic, dibasic, tribasic, and so forth, according to the number of hydrogen atoms, replaceable by bases, in a molecule. The first known acid was vinegar (ethanoic or acetic acid). Inorganic acids include boric, carbonic, hydrochloric, hydrofluoric, nitric, phosphoric, and sulphuric. Organic acids include acetic, benzoic, citric, formic, lactic, oxalic, and salicylic, as well as complex substances such as ◊nucleic acids and ◊amino acids.

acid house type of ◊house music. The derivation of the term is disputed but may be from 'acid burning', Chicago slang for ◊digital sampling, a recording technique much featured in acid house.

acid rain acidic precipitation thought to be caused principally by the release into the atmosphere of sulphur dioxide (SO_2) and oxides of nitrogen. Sulphur dioxide is formed by the burning of fossil fuels, such as coal, that contain high quantities of sulphur; nitrogen oxides are contributed from various industrial activities and from car exhaust fumes. Acid deposition occurs not only as wet precipitation (mist, snow, or rain), but also comes out of the atmosphere as dry particles or is absorbed directly by lakes, plants, and masonry as gases. Acidic gases can travel over 500 km/310 mi a day so acid rain can be considered an example of transboundary pollution.

Acid rain is linked with damage to and the death of forests and lake organisms in Scandinavia, Europe, and eastern North America. It also results in damage to buildings and statues. In the UK, reduction of emissions are being sought by using flue-gas desulphurization plants in power stations and by fitting more efficient burners; by using gas instead of coal as a power station fuel; and, with road transport rapidly becoming recognized as the single most important source of air pollution, the fitting of ◊catalytic converters to all new vehicles. ▷ *See feature on pp. 858–859.*

acid salt chemical compound formed by the partial neutralization of a dibasic or tribasic ◊acid (one that contains two or three hydrogen atoms). Although a salt, it contains replaceable hydrogen, so it may undergo the typical reactions of an acid. Examples are sodium hydrogen sulphate ($NaHSO_4$) and acid phosphates.

aclinic line the magnetic equator, an imaginary line near the equator, where a compass needle balances horizontally, the attraction of the north and south magnetic poles being equal.

acne skin eruption, mainly occurring among adolescents and young adults, caused by inflammation of the sebaceous glands which secrete an oily substance (sebum), the natural lubricant of the skin. Sometimes the openings of the glands become blocked, causing the formation of pus-filled swellings. Teenage acne is seen mainly on the face, back, and chest. There are other, less common types of acne, sometimes caused by contact with irritant chemicals; chloracne,for example, results from prolonged exposure to chlorinated hydrocarbons.

aconite or ***monkshood*** or ***wolfsbane*** herbaceous Eurasian plant *Aconitum napellus* of the buttercup family Ranunculaceae, with hooded blue-mauve flowers. It produces aconitine, a powerful alkaloid with narcotic and analgesic properties. There are about 100 species of the genus *Aconitum* throughout the northern temperate regions, hardy herbaceous plants, all of which contain poison.

acorn fruit of the ◊oak tree, a ◊nut growing in a shallow cup.

acouchi any of several small South American rodents, genus *Myoprocta*. They have white-tipped tails, and are smaller relatives of the ◊agouti.

acoustic term describing a musical instrument played without electrical amplification or assistance, for example an acoustic guitar or acoustic piano. It is also a term used by musicians to characterize room response, an important factor in performance. A so-called 'bright' acoustic provides a lively reverberation while a 'dry' or 'muddy' acoustic is lacking in response; see ◊acoustics.

acoustic coupler device that enables computer data to be transmitted and received through a normal telephone handset; the handset rests on the coupler to make the connection. A small speaker within the device is used to convert the computer's digital output data into sound signals, which are then picked up by the handset and transmitted through the telephone system. At the receiving telephone, a second acoustic coupler or modem converts the sound signals back into digital data for input into a computer. Unlike a ◊modem, an acoustic coupler does not require direct connection to the telephone system. However, the quality of transmission is poorer than with a modem.

north magnetic pole
earth's axis
north geographic pole
arctic circle
tropic of cancer
equator
tropic of capricorn
aclinic line (magnetic equator)
antarctic circle
south geographic pole

aclinic line The magnetic equator, or the line at which the attraction of both magnetic poles is equal. Along the aclinic line, a compass needle swinging vertically will settle in a horizontal position.

acoustics in general, the experimental and theoretical science of sound and its transmission; in particular, that branch of the science that has to do with the phenomena of sound in a particular space such as a room or theatre. In architecture, the sound-reflecting character of an internal space.

Acoustical engineering is concerned with the technical control of sound, and involves architecture and construction, studying control of vibration, soundproofing, and the elimination of noise. It also includes all forms of sound recording and reinforcement, the hearing and perception of sounds, and hearing aids.

acquired character feature of the body that develops during the lifetime of an individual, usually as a result of repeated use or disuse, such as the enlarged muscles of a weightlifter.

French naturalist Jean Baptiste ◊Lamarck's theory of evolution assumed that acquired characters were passed from parent to offspring.

Modern evolutionary theory does not recognize the inheritance of acquired characters because there is no reliable scientific evidence that it occurs, and because no mechanism is known whereby bodily changes can influence the genetic material. The belief that this does not occur is known as ◊central dogma.

acquired immune deficiency syndrome full name for the disease ◊AIDS.

acquittal in law, the setting free of someone charged with a crime after a trial. In English courts it follows a verdict of 'not guilty', but in Scotland the verdict may be either 'not guilty' or 'not proven'. Acquittal by the jury must be confirmed by the judge. If after an acquittal the person is again charged with the same offence he or she is entitled to be discharged.

acre traditional English land measure equal to 4,840 square yards (4,047 sq m/0.405 ha). Originally meaning a field, it was the size that a yoke of oxen could plough in a day. An acre may be subdivided into 160 square rods (one square rod equalling 25.29 sq m/30.25 sq yd).

Acre former name of the Israeli seaport of ◊Akko.

acridine $C_{13}H_9N$, a heterocyclic organic compound that occurs in coal tar. It is crystalline, melting at 108°C/226.4°F. Acridine is extracted by dilute acids but can also be obtained synthetically. It is used to make dyes and drugs.

acronym word formed from the initial letters and/or syllables of other words, intended as a pronounceable abbreviation; for example, NATO (*N*orth *A*tlantic *T*reaty *O*rganization), radar (*ra*dio *d*etecting *a*nd *r*anging), RAM (*r*andom-*a*ccess *m*emory) and FORTRAN (*for*mula *tran*slation).

acropolis (Greek 'high city') citadel of an ancient Greek town. The Acropolis of Athens contains the ruins of the ◊Parthenon and surrounding complexes, built there during the days of the Athenian empire, and stands on a rock about 45 m/150 ft high, 350 m/1,150 ft long, and 150 m/500 ft broad. The first kings of Athens built their palace here, and a temple of Athene, the Hecatompedon, existed before the Persian invasion. The later edifices were the Parthenon, the Propylaea, designed by Mnesicles 437 BC, a temple of Nike Apteros, the Erechtheum, the sanctuary of Artemis Brauronia, and the Pinacotheca. The term is also used for analogous structures.

acrostic (Greek 'at the extremity of a line or row') a number of lines of writing, usually verse, whose initial letters (read downwards) form a word, phrase, or sentence. A ***single acrostic*** is formed by the initial letters of lines only; a ***double acrostic*** is formed by the first and last letters.

acrylic acid common name for ◊propenoic acid.

acrylic fibre synthetic fibre often used as a substitute for wool. It was first developed in the mid-1940s but was not produced in large quantities until the 1950s. Strong and warm, acrylic fibre is often used for sweaters and tracksuits and as linings for boots and gloves, as well as in furnishing fabrics and carpets. It is manufactured as a filament, then cut into short staple lengths similar to wool hairs, and spun into yarn.

acrylic paint any of a range of synthetic substitutes for ◊oil paint, mostly soluble in water. Acrylic paints are used in a variety of painting techniques, from wash to impasto. They dry quicker than oil paint, are waterproof, and remain slightly flexible, but lack the translucency of natural substances.

actinide any of a series of 15 radioactive metallic chemical elements with atomic numbers 89 (actinium) to 103 (lawrencium). Elements 89 to 95 occur in nature; the rest of the series are synthesized elements only. Actinides are grouped together because of their chemical similarities (for example, they are all bivalent), the properties differing only slightly with atomic number. The series is set out in a band in the ◊periodic table of the elements, as are the ◊lanthanides.

actinium (Greek *aktis* 'ray') white, radioactive, metallic element, the first of the actinide series, symbol Ac, atomic number 89, relative atomic mass 227; it is a weak emitter of high-energy alpha particles. It occurs with uranium and radium in ◊pitchblende and other ores, and can be synthesized by bombarding radium with neutrons. The longest-lived isotope, Ac-227, has a half-life of 21.8 years (all the other isotopes have very short half-lives). Chemically, it is exclusively trivalent, resembling in its reactions the lanthanides and the other actinides. Actinium was discovered 1899 by French chemist André Debierne (1874–1949).

action in law, one of the proceedings whereby a person or agency seeks to enforce rights or redress a wrong in a civil court. In the UK, civil actions (for example, the enforcement of a debt) are distinguished from criminal proceedings (where the crown prosecutes a defendant accused of an offence). The person who brings the action is called the plaintiff and his or her opponent the defendant (in Scotland they are respectively known as the pursuer and the defender).

action painting or ***gesture painting*** in abstract art, a form of Abstract Expressionism that emphasized the importance of the physical act of painting. Jackson ◊Pollock, the leading exponent, threw, dripped, and dribbled paint on to canvases fastened to the floor. He was known to attack his canvas with knives and trowels and bicycle over it.

act of Parliament Title page of an Elizabethan act of Parliament 1585. *Philip Sauvain*

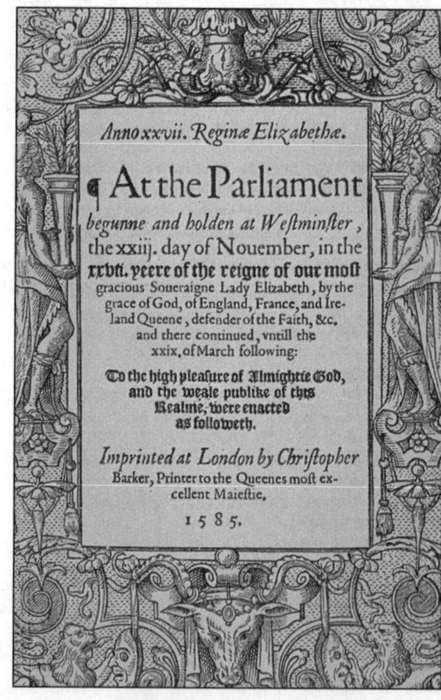

Anno xxvii. Reginæ Elizabethæ.

At the Parliament

begunne and holden at Westminster, the xxiij. day of Nouember, in the xxvi. yeere of the reigne of our most gracious Soueraigne Lady Elizabeth, by the grace of God, of England, France, and Ireland Queene, defender of the Faith, &c. and there continued, vntill the xxix, of March following:

To the high pleasure of Almightie God, and the weale publike of this Realme, were enacted as followeth.

Imprinted at London by Christopher Barker, Printer to the Queenes most excellent Maiestie.

1 5 8 5.

action potential in biology, a change in the ◊potential difference (voltage) across the membrane of a nerve cell when an impulse passes along it. A change in potential (from about −60 to +45 millivolts) accompanies the passage of sodium and potassium ions across the membrane.

Actium, Battle of naval battle (2 Sept 31 BC) in which Octavian defeated the combined fleets of ◊Mark Antony and ◊Cleopatra to become the undisputed ruler of the Roman world (as the emperor ◊Augustus). After their defeat, Antony and Cleopatra fled to Egypt but Octavian pursued them there the following year. The city of Alexandria surrendered without a fight and Antony and Cleopatra committed suicide. The site of the battle is at Akri, a promontory in W Greece.

activation energy in chemistry, the energy required in order to start a chemical reaction. Some elements and compounds will react together merely by bringing them into contact (spontaneous reaction). For others it is necessary to supply energy in order to start the reaction, even if there is ultimately a net output of energy. This initial energy is the activation energy.

active transport in cells, the use of energy to move substances, usually molecules or ions, across a membrane. Energy is needed because movement occurs against a concentration gradient, with substances being passed into a region where they are already present in significant quantities. Active transport thus differs from ◊diffusion, the process by which substances move towards a region where they are in lower concentration, as when oxygen passes into the blood vessels of the lungs. Diffusion requires no input of energy.

act of Congress in the USA, a bill or resolution passed by both houses of Congress, the Senate and the House of Representatives, which becomes law with the signature of the president. If vetoed by the president, it may still become law if it returns to Congress again and is passed by a majority of two-thirds in each house.

act of God legal term meaning some sudden and irresistible act of nature that could not reasonably have been foreseen or prevented, such as floods or exceptionally high tides, storms, lightning, earthquakes, sharp frosts, or sudden death. Damage by such an occurrence may be attributed to the act of God, and in the absence of any contract to the contrary, no person can be held liable for it. Nearly all insurance forms and shipping charter parties, and most contracts, have a clause relating to nonliability in the case of an act of God.

act of Parliament in Britain, a change in the law originating in Parliament and called a statute. Before an act receives the royal assent and becomes law it is a bill. The US equivalent is an ◊act of Congress.

An act of Parliament may be either public (of general effect), local, or private. The body of English statute law comprises all the acts passed by Parliament: the existing list opens with the Statute of Merton, passed 1235.

How an act of Parliament becomes law:

1 first reading of the bill The title is read out in the House of Commons (H of C) and a minister names a day for the second reading.
2 The bill is officially printed.
3 second reading A debate on the whole bill in the H of C followed by a vote on whether or not the bill should go on to the next stage.
4 committee stage A committee of MPs considers the bill in detail and makes amendments.
5 report stage The bill is referred back to the H of C which may make further amendments.
6 third reading The H of C votes whether the bill should be sent on to the House of Lords.
7 House of Lords The bill passes through much the same stages in the Lords as in the H of C. (Bills may be introduced in the Lords, in which case the H of C considers them at this stage.)
8 last amendments The H of C considers any Lords' amendments, and may make further amendments which must usually be agreed by the Lords.
9 royal assent The Queen gives her formal assent.
10 The bill becomes an act of Parliament at royal assent, although it may not come into force until a day appointed in the act.

actor or actress performer in a play or film who uses natural ability and/or taught skills to portray different characters and emotional states. Physical and (in unmasked drama) facial mobility, vocal control, and an ability to project characters and temperaments in front of an audience are skills that have been held in common by actors throughout the ages. See also ◊drama and ◊theatre.

Acts of the Apostles fifth book of the New Testament, attributed to ◊Luke, which describes the history of the early Christian church. The book was written in Greek and falls into two parts, the first 12 chapters dealing with the church in Jerusalem and Judaea, with Peter as the central figure, and the second 16 chapters dealing with the church among the gentiles and the journeys of Paul.

actuary mathematician who makes statistical calculations concerning human life expectancy and other risks, on which insurance, life assurance, and pension premiums are based.

acupuncture in alternative medicine, a system of inserting long, thin metal needles into the body at predetermined points to relieve pain, as an anaesthetic in surgery, and to assist healing. The needles are rotated manually or electrically. The method, developed in ancient China and increasingly popular in the West, is thought to work by stimulating the brain's own painkillers, the ◊endorphins.

Acupuncture is based on a theory of physiology that posits a network of life-energy pathways, or 'meridians', in the human body and some 800 'acupuncture points' where metal needles may be inserted to affect the energy flow for purposes of preventive or remedial therapy or to produce a local anaesthetic effect. Numerous studies and surveys have attested the efficacy of the method, which is widely conceded by orthodox practitioners despite the lack of acceptable scientific explanation.

acute angle an angle between 0° and 90°; that is, an amount of turn that is less than a quarter of a circle.

AD in the Christian chronological system, abbreviation for ◊*anno Domini*.

Ada high-level computer-programming language, developed and owned by the US Department of Defense, designed for use in situations in which a computer directly controls a process or machine, such as a military aircraft. The language took more than five years to specify, and became commercially available only in the late 1980s. It is named after English mathematician Ada Augusta ◊Byron.

Adam family of Scottish architects and designers. ***William Adam*** (1689–1748) was the leading Scottish architect of his day, and his son ***Robert Adam*** (1728–1792) is considered one of the greatest British architects of the late 18th century, responsible for transforming the prevailing Palladian fashion in architecture to a Neo-Classical style.

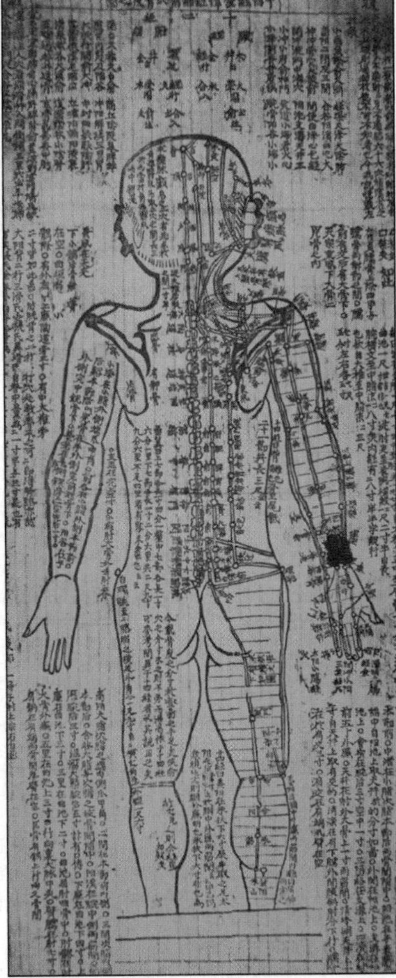

acupuncture A 19th-century Japanese acupuncture chart. Acupuncture, a traditional Chinese method of relieving pain and promoting healing, involves inserting needles into the body at points shown on such a chart. *Image Select (UK) Ltd*

'The world was all before them, where to choose / Their place of rest, and Providence their guide: / They hand in hand with wandering steps and slow, / Through Eden took their solitary way.'

Of ADAM AND EVE
John Milton *Paradise Lost* 1667

Adam (Hebrew *adham* 'man') in the Old Testament (Genesis 2, 3), the first human. Formed by God from dust and given the breath of life, Adam was placed in the Garden of Eden, where ◊Eve was created from his rib and given to him as a companion. Because she tempted him, he tasted the forbidden fruit of the Tree of Knowledge of Good and Evil, for which trespass they were expelled from the Garden.

Adam Adolphe Charles 1803–1856. French composer of light operas and founder of the Théâtre

Adam Park Crescent, at the northern end of Portland Place, Regent's Park, London. Portland Place was originally laid out by the Adam brothers in the 18th century. John Nash later added Park Crescent, a great sweep of stucco walls and Ionic columns. *Corbis*

❛When love's well-tim'd, 'tis not a fault to love; / The strong, the brave, the virtuous, and the wise, / Sink in the soft captivity together.❜

Joseph Addison
Cato

National, Paris, 1847. His stage works include *Le Postillion de Longjumeau/The Postillion of Longjumeau* 1836 and *Si j'étais roi/If I Were King* 1852, but he is best remembered for his ballet score for *Giselle* 1841. Around 80 of his works were staged.

Adams Ansel Easton 1902–1984. US photographer. He is known for his printed images of dramatic landscapes and organic forms of the American West. Light and texture were important elements in his photographs. He was associated with the ◊zone system of exposure estimation and was a founder member of the ◊'f/64' group which advocated precise definition.

In 1916 Adams made his first trip to the Yosemite National Park, California, a major focus of his work throughout his life. Aiming to establish photography as a fine art, he founded the first museum collection of photography, at New York City's Museum of Modern Art 1937.

Adams Gerry (Gerard) 1948– . Northern Ireland politician, president of Sinn Féin (the political wing of the Irish Republican Army, IRA) from 1978. He was interned 1973–76 on suspicion of involvement in terrorist activity. Elected member of Parliament for Belfast West 1983, he declined to take up his Westminster seat, stating that he did not believe in the British government. Having lost his seat 1992, he regained it 1997, but again refused to sit in Parliament. In Aug 1994, when Adams announced an IRA cease-fire, the British government removed all restrictions on his public appearances and freedom to travel to mainland Britain (in force since 1988).

The unwillingness of the IRA to decommission its arms prior to full British troop withdrawal from Northern Ireland led to a delay in the start of all-party peace talks 1995, and the resumption of IRA violence Feb 1996 damaged his credibility and cast doubt over the peace process.

Despite doubts about his ability to influence the IRA, he has been a key figure in Irish peace negotiations, and in 1997 he entered into multi-party talks with the British government.

Adams John 1735–1826. 2nd president of the USA 1797–1801, and vice president 1789–97. He was a member of the Continental Congress 1774–78 and signed the Declaration of Independence. In 1779 he went to France and negotiated the treaty of 1783 that ended the American Revolution. In 1785 he became the first US ambassador in London. ▷ *See feature on pp. 32–33.*

Adams John Couch 1819–1892. English astronomer. He mathematically deduced the existence of the planet Neptune 1845 from the effects of its gravitational pull on the motion of Uranus, although it was not found until 1846 by J G ◊Galle. Adams also studied the Moon's motion, the Leonid meteors, and terrestrial magnetism.

Adams John Quincy 1767–1848. 6th president of the USA 1825–29, eldest son of President John Adams. He negotiated the Treaty of Ghent to end the ◊War of 1812 (fought with Britain) on generous terms for the USA. In 1817 he became President James Monroe's secretary of state, formulating the ◊Monroe Doctrine 1823. As president, Adams was an advocate of strong federal government.

Adams John Quincy Adams, 6th president of the USA. During his long second career in Congress (1831–48), 'Old Man Eloquent', as he was called, won renewed respect throughout the North as an opponent of slavery. Although never an abolitionist, Adams fought the extension of slavery in the territories. *Library of Congress*

Adams Richard George 1920– . English novelist. He wrote *Watership Down* 1972, a story of rabbits who escape from a doomed warren and work together to establish a new one. As with all Adams' novels, there is an underlying social message. Later novels include *Shardik* 1974, *The Plague Dogs* 1977, *The Girl on a Swing* 1980, and *Traveller* 1988.

Adams Samuel 1722–1803. US politician, the chief instigator of the Boston Tea Party (see ◊American Revolution). He was a signatory to the Declaration of Independence, served in the ◊Continental Congress, and anticipated the French emperor Napoleon in calling the British a 'nation of shopkeepers'.

Adamson Robert 1821–1848. Scottish photographer. He collaborated with David Octavius ◊Hill.

Adana capital of Adana (Seyhan) province, S Turkey; population (1990) 916,150. It is a major cotton-growing centre and Turkey's fourth-largest city.

adaptation (Latin *adaptare* 'to fit to') in biology, any change in the structure or function of an organism that allows it to survive and reproduce more effectively in its environment. In ◊evolution, adaptation is thought to occur as a result of random variation in the genetic make-up of organisms coupled with ◊natural selection. Species become extinct when they are no longer adapted to their environment – for instance, if the climate suddenly becomes colder.

adaptive radiation in evolution, the formation of several species, with ◊adaptations to different ways of life, from a single ancestral type. Adaptive radiation is likely to occur whenever members of a species migrate to a new habitat with unoccupied ecological niches. It is thought that the lack of competition in such niches allows sections of the migrant population to develop new adaptations, and eventually to become new species.

addax light-coloured ◊antelope *Addax nasomaculatus* of the family Bovidae. It lives in N Africa around the Sahara Desert where it exists on scanty vegetation without drinking. It is about 1.1 m/3.5 ft at the shoulder, and both sexes have spirally twisted horns. Its hooves are broad, enabling it to move easily on soft sand.

adder (Anglo-Saxon *naedre* 'serpent') European venomous snake, the common ◊viper *Vipera berus*. Growing on average to about 60 cm/24 in in length, it has a thick body, triangular head, a characteristic V-shaped mark on its head and, often, zigzag markings along the back. It feeds on small mammals and lizards. The puff adder *Bitis arietans* is a large, yellowish, thick-bodied viper up to 1.6 m/5 ft long, living in Africa and Arabia.

addiction state of dependence caused by habitual use of drugs, alcohol, or other substances. It is characterized by uncontrolled craving, tolerance, and symptoms of withdrawal when access is denied. Habitual use produces changes in body chemistry and treatment must be geared to a gradual reduction in dosage.

Initially, only opium and its derivatives (morphine, heroin, codeine) were recognized as addictive, but many other drugs, whether therapeutic (for example, tranquillizers) or recreational (such as cocaine and alcohol), are now known to be addictive. Research points to a genetic predisposition to addiction; environment and psychological make-up are other factors.

Addington Henry, 1st Viscount Sidmouth 1757–1844. British Tory politician, prime minister 1801–04. As home secretary 1812–1822, he was responsible for much reprieve legislation, including the notorious ◊Six Acts.

Addis Ababa or ***Adis Abeba*** capital of Ethiopia; population (1992) 2,213,000. It was founded 1887 by Menelik, chief of Shoa, who ascended the throne of Ethiopia 1889. His former residence, Menelik Palace, is now occupied by the government.

Addison Joseph 1672–1719. English writer. In 1704 he celebrated ◊Marlborough's victory at Blenheim in a poem commissioned by the government, 'The Campaign', and subsequently held political appointments, including undersecretary of state 1706 and secretary to the Lord-Lieutenant of Ireland 1708. In 1709 he contributed to the *Tatler* magazine, begun by Richard ◊Steele, with whom he was cofounder 1711–12 of the *Spectator*.

adder The puff adder, from Africa and western Arabia, grows up to 1.6 m/5 ft long. Puff adders often bask in the sun during the day and, if disturbed, make a loud hissing or puffing sound, hence their name.

Addison's disease rare condition caused by destruction of the outer part of the ◊adrenal glands, leading to reduced secretion of corticosteroid hormones; it is treated by replacement of these hormones. The condition, formerly fatal, is mostly caused by autoimmune disease or tuberculosis. Symptoms include weight loss, anaemia, weakness, low blood pressure, digestive upset, and brownish pigmentation of the skin. Addison's disease is rare in children and in those over 60 years of age.

addition reaction chemical reaction in which the atoms of an element or compound react with a double bond or triple bond in an organic compound by opening up one of the bonds and becoming attached to it, for example

$$CH_2{=}CH_2 + HCl \rightarrow CH_3CH_2Cl$$

An example is the addition of hydrogen atoms to ◊unsaturated compounds in vegetable oils to produce margarine. Addition reactions are used to make useful polymers from ◊alkenes.

additive in food, any natural or artificial chemical added to prolong the shelf life of processed foods (salt or nitrates), alter the colour, texture, or flavour of food, or improve its food value (vitamins or minerals). Many chemical additives are used and they are subject to regulation, since individuals may be affected by constant exposure even to traces of certain additives and may suffer side effects ranging from headaches and hyperactivity to cancer. However, it can be difficult to know how to test the safety of such substances; many natural foods contain toxic substances which could not pass the tests applied today to new products.

Food companies in many countries are now required by law to list additives used in their products. Within the European Union, approved additives are given an official ◊E number.

Adelaide capital and industrial city of South Australia; population (1993) 1,071,100. Industries include oil refining, shipbuilding, and the manufacture of electrical goods and cars. Grain, wool, fruit, and wine are exported. Founded 1836, Adelaide was named after William IV's queen.

Adelaide 1792–1849. Queen consort of ◊William IV of England. Daughter of the Duke of Saxe-Meiningen, she married William, then Duke of Clarence, in 1818. No children of the marriage survived infancy.

Aden (Arabic ***'Adan***) main port and commercial centre of Yemen, on a rocky peninsula at the southwest corner of Arabia, commanding the entrance to the Red Sea; population (1995) 562,000. The city's economy is based on oil refining, fishing, and shipping. A British territory from 1839, Aden became part of independent South Yemen 1967; it was the capital of South Yemen until 1990. Aden comprises the new administrative centre Madinet al-Sha'ab, the commercial and business quarters of Crater and Tawahi, and the harbour area of Ma'alla.

history After annexation by Britain, Aden and its immediately surrounding area (121 sq km/47 sq mi) were developed as a ship-refuelling station following the opening of the Suez Canal 1869. It was a colony 1937–63 and then, after a period of transitional violence among rival nationalist groups and

British forces, was combined with the former Aden protectorate (290,000 sq km/112,000 sq mi) to create the Southern Yemen People's Republic 1967, which was renamed the People's Democratic Republic of Yemen 1970–90. Southern Yemen (calling itself the Democratic Republic of Yemen) declared independence May 1994, but its attempt to break away ended with the capture of Aden by government forces July 1994.

Adenauer Konrad 1876–1967. German Christian Democrat politician, chancellor of West Germany 1949–63. With the French president de Gaulle he achieved the postwar reconciliation of France and Germany and strongly supported all measures designed to strengthen the Western bloc in Europe. Adenauer was mayor of his native city of Cologne from 1917 until his imprisonment by Hitler 1933 for opposition to the Nazi regime. After the war he headed the Christian Democratic Union (CDU) and became chancellor, combining the office with that of foreign minister. He was re-elected chancellor 1953 and retained the post of foreign minister until 1955.

adenoids masses of lymphoid tissue, similar to ◊tonsils, located in the upper part of the throat, behind the nose. They are part of a child's natural defences against the entry of germs but usually shrink and disappear by the age of ten. Adenoids may swell and grow, particularly if infected, and block the breathing passages. If they become repeatedly infected, they may be removed surgically (adenoidectomy), usually along with the tonsils.

Adgeya autonomous republic of SW Russian Federation, in Krasnodar territory
area 7,600 sq km/2,934 sq mi
capital Maikop
physical extends from the Kuban River to the foothills of the Caucasus; mostly plain, with rich soil
industries timber, woodworking, food processing, engineering, cattle breeding, agriculture, flowers (especially Crimean roses and lavender)
population (1992) 442,000 (20% Cherkess)
history established as a region (*oblast*) 1922 for the Adyghian people; an autonomous republic from 1991

ADH (abbreviation for ***antidiuretic hormone***) in biology, part of the system maintaining a correct salt/water balance in vertebrates. Its release is stimulated by the ◊hypothalamus in the brain, which constantly receives information about salt concentration from receptors situated in the neck. In conditions of water shortage increased ADH secretion from the brain will cause more efficient conservation of water in the kidney, so that fluid is retained by the body. When an animal is able to take in plenty of water, decreased ADH secretion will cause the urine to become dilute and plentiful. The system allows the body to compensate for a varying fluid intake and maintain a correct balance.

adhesion in medicine, the abnormal binding of two tissues as a result of inflammation or damage. The moving surfaces of joints or internal organs may merge together if they have been inflamed and tissue fluid has been present between the surfaces. Adhesions sometimes occur after abdominal operations and may lead to colicky pains and intestinal obstruction.

adhesive substance that sticks two surfaces together. Natural adhesives (glues) include gelatin in its crude industrial form (made from bones, hide fragments, and fish offal) and vegetable gums. Synthetic adhesives include thermoplastic and thermosetting resins, which are often stronger than the substances they join; mixtures of ◊epoxy resin and hardener that set by chemical reaction; and elastomeric (stretching) adhesives for flexible joints. Superglues are fast-setting adhesives used in very small quantities.

adiabatic in physics, a process that occurs without loss or gain of heat, especially the expansion or contraction of a gas in which a change takes place in the pressure or volume, although no heat is allowed to enter or leave.

Adige second longest river (after the Po) in Italy, 410 km/255 mi in length. It crosses the Lombardy Plain and enters the Adriatic just N of the Po delta.

Adi Granth or ***Guru Granth Sahib*** the holy book of Sikhism; see ◊*Guru Granth Sahib*.

adipose tissue type of ◊connective tissue of vertebrates that serves as an energy reserve, and also pads some organs. It is commonly called fat tissue, and consists of large spherical cells filled with fat. In mammals, major layers are in the inner layer of skin and around the kidneys and heart. Fatty acids are transported to and from it via the blood system. An excessive amount of adipose tissue is developed in the course of some diseases, especially obesity.

Adirondacks mountainous area in NE New York State, USA, rising to 1,629 m/5,344 ft at Mount Marcy; the source of the Hudson and Ausable rivers. Named after a native American people, the area is thickly wooded and known for its scenery and sports facilities. The Adirondacks occupies about 25% of the state of New York.

adjutant in military usage, an army officer who assists the officer commanding a battalion or regiment. The adjutant has charge of the correspondence and official records, keeps the accounts, and prepares the officers' duty roster. By the authority of the commanding officer, the adjutant issues the daily orders and is generally responsible for the discipline and efficiency of the unit. When on active service he is also responsible for the unit's ammunition supply.

Adler Alfred 1870–1937. Austrian psychologist. He saw the 'will to power' as more influential in accounting for human behaviour than the sexual drive. A dispute over this theory led to the dissolution of his ten-year collaboration with psychiatry's founder Sigmund ◊Freud. The concepts of inferiority complex and overcompensation originated with Adler.

administrative law law concerning the powers and control of government agencies or those agencies granted statutory powers of administration. These powers include those necessary to operate the agency or to implement its purposes, and making quasi-judicial decisions (such as determining tax liability, granting licences or permits, or hearing complaints against the agency or its officers). The vast increase in these powers in the 20th century in many countries has been widely criticized.

admiral highest-ranking naval officer. In the UK Royal Navy and the US Navy the ranks of admiral are (in descending order): admiral of the fleet (fleet admiral in the USA), admiral, vice admiral, and rear admiral.

admiral any of several species of butterfly in the same family (Nymphalidae) as the tortoiseshells. The red admiral *Vanessa atalanta*, wingspan 6 cm/2.5 in, is found worldwide in the northern hemisphere. It either hibernates, or migrates south each year from northern areas to subtropical zones.

Adler Alfred Adler was a prominent member of the circle of psychologists surrounding Sigmund Freud during the early 1900s. In 1911, after professional disagreement concerning Freud's theories, he left, and developed his psychoanalytical theory of individual psychology. *Ann Ronan/Image Select (UK) Ltd*

admiral The red admiral butterfly *Vanessa atalanta* is widely distributed throughout Europe, Asia, and North America. It hibernates in warmer regions and migrates to northern regions in the summer. *Premaphotos Wildlife*

Admiral's Cup sailing series first held in 1957 and held biennially. National teams consisting of three boats compete over three inshore courses (in the Solent, off the English coast) and two offshore courses (378 km/235 mi across the English Channel from Cherbourg, France to the Isle of Wight; and 1,045 km/650 mi from Plymouth, England to Fastnet lighthouse off Ireland, and back). The highlight is the Fastnet race.

Admiralty, Board of the in the UK, the controlling department of state for the Royal Navy from the reign of Henry VIII until 1964, when most of its functions – apart from that of management – passed to the Ministry of Defence. The 600-year-old office of Lord High Admiral reverted to the sovereign.

Admiralty Court English court that tries and gives judgement in maritime causes. The court is now incorporated within the Queen's Bench Division of the High Court and deals with such matters as salvage and damages arising from collisions between ships.

Admiralty Islands group of small islands in the SW Pacific, part of Papua New Guinea; population (1980) 25,000. The main island is Manus. Exports are copra and pearls. The islands became a German protectorate 1884 and an Australian mandate 1920.

adobe in architecture, a building method employing sun-dried earth bricks; also the individual bricks. The use of earth bricks and the construction of walls by enclosing earth within moulds (*pisé de terre*) are the two principal methods of raw-earth building. The techniques are commonly found in Spain, Latin America, and SW USA.

Jericho is the site of the earliest evidence of building in sun-dried mud bricks, dating from the 8th millennium BC. Firing bricks was not practised until the 3rd millennium BC, and then only occasionally because it was costly in terms of fuel. The world's largest raw-earth building is the Great Mosque in Djenne, Mali, built 1907. The Great Wall of China is largely constructed of earth; whole cities of mud construction exist throughout the Middle East and N Africa – for example, San'a in Yemen and Yazd in Iran – and it remains a vigorous vernacular tradition in these areas.

adolescence in the human life cycle, the period between the beginning of puberty and adulthood.

Adonis (Semitic *Adon*, 'the Lord') in Greek mythology, a beautiful youth loved by the goddess ◊Aphrodite. He was killed while boar-hunting but was allowed to return from the underworld for a period every year to rejoin her. The anemone sprang from his blood. Worshipped as a god of vegetation, he seems also to have been identified with ◊Osiris, the Egyptian god of the underworld.

adoption permanent legal transfer of parental rights and duties from one person to another, usually to provide care for children who would otherwise lack family upbringing.

In the UK adoption can take place only by means of an order of the court, either with or without the natural parent's consent. It was first legalized in

'Whenever a child lies you will always find a severe parent. A lie would have no sense unless the truth were felt to be dangerous.'

ALFRED ADLER
Quoted in the *New York Times* 1949

Advertising may be described as the science of arresting human intelligence long enough to get money from it.

On ADVERTISING Stephen Leacock 'The Perfect Salesman', *Garden of Folly*

England 1926. In 1958 an adopted child was enabled to inherit on parental intestacy. The Children's Act 1975 enables an adopted child at the age of 18 to know his or her original name. See also ◊custody of children.

ADP abbreviation for ***adenosine diphosphate***, the chemical product formed in cells when ◊ATP breaks down to release energy.

adrenal gland or ***suprarenal gland*** triangular gland situated on top of the ◊kidney. The adrenals are soft and yellow, and consist of two parts: the cortex and medulla. The cortex (outer part) secretes various steroid hormones and other hormones that control salt and water metabolism and regulate the use of carbohydrates, proteins, and fats. The medulla (inner part) secretes the hormones adrenaline and noradrenaline.

adrenaline or ***epinephrine*** hormone secreted by the medulla of the adrenal glands. Adrenaline is synthesized from a closely related substance, noradrenaline, and the two hormones are released into the bloodstream in situations of fear or stress. Adrenaline's action on the ◊liver raises blood-sugar levels by stimulating glucose production and its action on adipose tissue raises blood fatty-acid levels; it also increases the heart rate, increases blood flow to muscles, reduces blood flow to the skin with the production of sweat, widens the smaller breathing tubes (bronchioles) in the lungs, and dilates the pupils of the eyes, generally preparing the body for 'fight or flight'.

Adrian IV (Nicholas Breakspear) c. 1100–1159. Pope 1154–59, the only English pope. He secured the execution of Arnold of Brescia (1100–1155), crowned Frederick I Barbarossa as German emperor, and was quarrelling with him over papal supremacy when he died. He allegedly issued the controversial bull giving Ireland to Henry II of England 1154. Attacked for false representation, the bull was subsequently refuted.

Adriatic Sea large arm of the Mediterranean Sea, lying NW to SE between the Italian and the Balkan peninsulas. The western shore is Italian; the eastern includes Croatia, Montenegro, and Albania, with a small strip of coastline owned by Slovenia. Bosnia has 20 km/12 mi of coastline, but no port. The sea is about 805 km/500 mi long, and its area is 135,250 sq km/52,220 sq mi.

ADSL abbreviation for ***asymmetric digital subscirber loop***, standard for transmitting video data through existing copper telephone wires, developed by US telephone companies as a way of competing with cable television companies in delivering both TV and phone services. ADSL is one of several types of digital subscriber loops (DSLs) in use.

adsorption taking up of a gas or liquid at the surface of another substance, most commonly a solid (for example, activated charcoal adsorbs gases). It involves molecular attraction at the surface, and should be distinguished from ◊absorption (in which a uniform solution results from a gas or liquid being incorporated into the bulk structure of a liquid or solid).

adult education in the UK, voluntary classes and courses for adults provided mainly in further-education colleges, adult-education institutes, and school premises. Courses are either vocational, designed to fill the gaps in earlier education and leading to examinations and qualifications, or non-vocational, to aid the adult's cultural development and contribute to his or her general education. Most adult education is provided by local education authorities (LEAs) and fees for classes are subsidized. The ◊Open College, ◊Open University, and ◊Workers' Educational Association are adult-education bodies.

adultery voluntary sexual intercourse between a married person and someone other than his or her legal partner. It is one factor that may prove 'irretrievable breakdown' of marriage in actions for judicial separation or ◊divorce in Britain.

Aduwa, Battle of defeat of the Italians by the Ethiopians at Aduwa in 1896 under Emperor Menelik II (1844–1913). It marked the end of Italian ambitions in this part of Africa until Mussolini's reconquest in 1935.

advanced gas-cooled reactor (AGR) type of ◊nuclear reactor widely used in W Europe. The AGR uses a fuel of enriched uranium dioxide in stainless-steel cladding and a moderator of graphite. Carbon dioxide gas is pumped through the reactor core to extract the heat produced by the ◊fission of the uranium. The heat is transferred to water in a steam generator, and the steam drives a turbogenerator to produce electricity.

I still sigh for the Aegean. Shall you not always love its bluest of waves and brightest of skies?

On the AEGEAN SEA Lord Byron, letter to Edward Daniel Clarke 26 June 1812

Advent (Latin *adventus* 'coming') in the Christian calendar, the preparatory season for Christmas, including the four Sundays preceding it. It begins with Advent Sunday, the Sunday that falls nearest (before or after) St Andrew's Day (30 Nov).

Adventist person who believes that Jesus will return to make a second appearance on Earth. Expectation of the Second Coming of Christ is found in New Testament writings generally. Adventist views are held by the Seventh-Day Adventists, Christadelphians, Jehovah's Witnesses, and the Four Square Gospel Alliance.

advertising any of various methods used by a company to increase the sales of its products or services or to promote a brand name. Advertising is also used by organizations and individuals to communicate an idea or image, to recruit staff, to publicize an event, or to locate an item or commodity.

Product advertising can be seen by economists as either beneficial (since it conveys information about a product and so brings the market closer to a state of perfect competition) or as a hindrance to perfect competition, since it attempts to make illusory distinctions (such as greater sex appeal) between essentially similar products.

Advertising Standards Authority (ASA) organization founded by the UK advertising industry 1962 to promote higher standards of advertising in the media (excluding television and radio, which have their own authority). It is financed by the advertisers, who pay a 0.1% supplement on the cost of advertisements. It recommends to the media that advertisements which might breach the British Code of Advertising Practice are not published, but has no statutory power.

Advisory, Conciliation, and Arbitration Service (ACAS) in the UK, government-funded independent body set up under the Employment Protection Act 1975 to improve ◊industrial relations through its advisory, conciliation, arbitration, and mediation services. Specifically, ACAS aims to encourage the extension of collective bargaining and, wherever possible, the reform of collective-bargaining machinery.

advocate (Latin *advocatus*, one summoned to a person's aid, especially in a court of law) professional pleader in a court of justice. More common terms are attorney, lawyer, barrister, or counsel, but advocate is retained in such countries as Scotland and France, whose legal systems are based on Roman law.

Advocates, Faculty of professional organization for Scottish advocates, the equivalent of English ◊barristers. It was incorporated 1532 under James V.

Aegean civilization the cultures of Bronze Age Greece, including the ◊Minoan civilization of Crete and the ◊Mycenaean civilization of the Peloponnese and mainland Greece.

Aegean Islands islands of the Aegean Sea, but more specifically a region of Greece comprising the Dodecanese islands, the Cyclades islands, Lesvos, Samos, and Chios; area 9,122 sq km/3,523 sq mi; population (1991) 460,800.

Aegean Sea branch of the Mediterranean between Greece and Turkey; the Dardanelles connect it with the Sea of Marmara. The numerous islands in the Aegean Sea include Crete, the Cyclades, the Sporades, and the Dodecanese. There is political tension between Greece and Turkey over sea limits claimed by Greece around such islands as Lesvos, Chios, Samos, and Kos.

Aelfric c. 955–1020. Anglo-Saxon writer and abbot. He was the author of two collections of *Catholic Homilies* 990–92, sermons, and the *Lives of the Saints* 996–97, written in vernacular Old English prose.

Aeneas in classical mythology, a Trojan prince who became the ancestral hero of the Romans. According to ◊Homer, he was the son of Anchises and the goddess Aphrodite. During the Trojan War he owed his life to the frequent intervention of the gods. The legend on which Virgil's epic poem the *Aeneid* is based describes his escape from Troy and his eventual settlement in Latium, on the Italian peninsula.

Aeolian harp wind-blown instrument consisting of a shallow soundbox supporting gut strings at low tension and tuned to the same pitch. It produces an eerie harmony that rises and falls with the changing pressure of the wind. It originated in India and China, becoming popular in parts of central Europe during the 19th century. The instrument is named after Aeolus, the god of the winds in Greek mythology.

Aeolian Islands another name for the ◊Lipari Islands.

Aeolus in Greek mythology, the ruler or keeper of the winds. He kept them imprisoned in a cave on the island of Aeolia, which came to be identified with ◊Lipari, one of the Aeolian islands that lie north of eastern Sicily.

aerenchyma plant tissue with numerous air-filled spaces between the cells. It occurs in the stems and roots of many aquatic plants where it aids buoyancy and facilitates transport of oxygen around the plant.

aerial or ***antenna*** in radio and television broadcasting, a conducting device that radiates or receives electromagnetic waves. The design of an aerial depends principally on the wavelength of the signal. Long waves (hundreds of metres in wavelength) may employ long wire aerials; short waves (several centimetres in wavelength) may employ rods and dipoles; microwaves may also use dipoles – often with reflectors arranged like a toast rack – or highly directional parabolic dish aerials. Because microwaves travel in straight lines, giving line-of-sight communication, microwave aerials are usually located at the tops of tall masts or towers.

aerial oxidation in chemistry, a reaction in which air is used to oxidize another substance, as in the contact process for the manufacture of sulphuric acid, and in the souring of wine.

$$2SO_2 + O_2 \rightleftharpoons 2SO_3$$

aerobic in biology, term used to describe those organisms that require oxygen (usually dissolved in water) for the efficient release of energy contained in food molecules, such as glucose. They include almost all organisms (plants as well as animals) with the exception of certain bacteria, yeasts, and internal parasites.

Aerobic reactions occur inside every cell and lead to the formation of energy-rich ◊ATP, subsequently used by the cell for driving its metabolic processes. Oxygen is used to convert glucose to carbon dioxide and water, thereby releasing energy.

Most aerobic organisms die in the absence of oxygen, but certain organisms and cells, such as those found in muscle tissue, can function for short periods anaerobically (without oxygen). ◊Anaerobic organisms can survive without oxygen.

aerobics (Greek 'air' and 'life') exercises to improve the performance of the heart and lungs, involving a strenuous application of movement to raise the heart rate to 120 beats per minute or more for sessions of 5–20 minutes' duration, 3–5 times per week.

For interest and pleasure, often a combination of dance, stretching exercises, and running aim to improve the performance of the heart and lungs system, but swimming, cycling and race-walking are preferred because they are less punishing to the joints and cause fewer sports-related injuries. Aerobics became a health and fitness pursuit in the 1980s.

aerodynamics branch of fluid physics that studies the forces exerted by air or other gases in motion. Examples include the airflow around bodies moving at speed through the atmosphere (such as land vehicles, bullets, rockets, and aircraft), the behaviour of gas in engines and furnaces, air conditioning of buildings, the deposition of snow, the operation of air-cushion vehicles (hovercraft), wind loads on buildings and bridges, bird and insect flight, musical wind instruments, and meteorology. For maximum efficiency, the aim is usually to design the shape of an object to produce a streamlined flow, with a minimum of turbulence in the moving air. The behaviour of aerosols or the pollution of the atmosphere by foreign particles are other aspects of aerodynamics.

aerogel light, transparent, highly porous material composed of more than 90% air. Such materials are formed from silica, metal oxides, and organic chemicals, and are produced by drying gels – networks of linked molecules suspended in a liquid – so that air fills the spaces previously occupied by the liquid. They are excellent heat insulators and have unusual optical, electrical, and acoustic properties.

aeronautics science of travel through the Earth's atmosphere, including aerodynamics, aircraft structures, jet and rocket propulsion, aerial navigation, and astronavigation (navigation by reference to the stars).

In ***subsonic aeronautics*** (below the speed of sound), aerodynamic forces increase at the rate of the square of the speed. ***Transsonic aeronautics*** covers the speed range from just below to just above the speed of sound and is crucial to aircraft design. Ordinary sound waves move at about 1,225 kph/760 mph at sea level, and air in front of an aircraft moving slower than this is 'warned' by the waves so that it can move aside. However, as the flying speed approaches that of the sound waves, the warning is too late for the air to escape, and the aircraft pushes the air aside, creating shock waves, which absorb much power and create design problems. On the ground the shock waves give rise to a ◊sonic boom. It was once thought that the speed of sound was a speed limit to aircraft, and the term ◊sound barrier came into use. ***Supersonic aeronautics*** concerns speeds above that of sound and in one sense may be considered a much older study than aeronautics itself, since the study of the flight of bullets, known as ◊ballistics, was undertaken soon after the introduction of firearms. ***Hypersonics*** is the study of airflows and forces at speeds above five times that of sound (Mach 5); for example, for guided missiles, space rockets, and advanced concepts such as HOTOL (horizontal takeoff and landing). For all flight speeds streamlining is necessary to reduce the effects of air resistance.

aeroplane (US ***airplane***) powered heavier-than-air craft supported in flight by fixed wings. Aeroplanes are propelled by the thrust of a jet engine or airscrew (propeller). They must be designed aerodynamically, since streamlining ensures maximum flight efficiency. For the history of aircraft and aviation, see ◊flight.

design Efficient streamlining prevents the formation of shock waves over the body surface and wings, which would cause instability and power loss. The wing of an aeroplane has the cross-sectional shape of an aerofoil, being broad and curved at the front, flat underneath, curved on top, and tapered to a sharp point at the rear. It is so shaped that air passing above it is speeded up, reducing pressure below atmospheric pressure. This follows from ◊Bernoulli's principle and results in a force acting vertically upwards, called lift, which counters the plane's weight. In level flight lift equals weight. The wings develop sufficient lift to support the plane when they move quickly through the air. The thrust that causes propulsion comes from the reaction to the air stream accelerated backwards by the propeller or the gases shooting backwards from the jet exhaust. In flight the engine thrust must overcome the air resistance, or ◊drag. Drag depends on frontal area (for example, large, airliner; small, fighter plane) and shape (drag coefficient); in level flight, drag equals thrust. The drag is reduced by streamlining the plane, resulting in higher speed and reduced fuel consumption for a given power. Less fuel need be carried for a given distance of travel, so a larger payload (cargo or passengers) can be carried.

The shape of a plane is dictated principally by the speed at which it will operate (see ◊aeronautics). A plane operating at well below the speed of sound (about 965 kph/600 mph) need not be particularly well streamlined, and it can have broad wings projecting at right angles from the fuselage. An aircraft operating close to the speed of sound must be well streamlined and have swept-back wings. This prevents the formation of shock waves over the body surface and wings, which would result in instability and high power loss. Supersonic planes (faster than sound) need to be severely streamlined, and require a needle nose, extremely swept-back wings, and what is often termed a 'Coke-bottle' (narrow-waisted) fuselage, in order to pass through the sound barrier without suffering undue disturbance. To give great flexibility of operation at low as well as high speeds, some supersonic planes are designed with variable geometry, or ◊swing wings. For low-speed flight the wings are outstretched; for high-speed flight they are swung close to the fuselage to form an efficient ◊delta-wing configuration.

Aircraft designers experiment with different designs in ◊wind tunnel tests, which indicate how their designs will behave in practice. Fighter jets are being deliberately designed to be aerodynamically unstable, to ensure greater agility. This is achieved by a main wing of continuously modifiable shape, the airflow over which is controlled by a smaller tilting foreplane. New aircraft are being made lighter and faster by the use of heat-resistant materials, some of which are also radar-absorbing, making the aircraft 'invisible' to enemy defences.

construction Planes are constructed from light but strong aluminium alloys such as duralumin (with copper, magnesium, and so on). For supersonic planes special stainless steel and titanium may be used in areas subjected to high heat loads. The structure of the plane, or the airframe (wings, fuselage, and so on), consists of a surface skin of alloy sheets supported at intervals by struts known as ribs and stringers. The structure is bonded together by riveting or by powerful adhesives such as ◊epoxy resins. In certain critical areas, which have to withstand very high stresses (such as the wing roots), body panels are machined from solid metal for extra strength.

On the ground a plane rests on wheels, usually in a tricycle arrangement, with a nose wheel and two wheels behind, one under each wing. For all except some light planes the landing gear, or undercarriage, is retracted in flight to reduce drag. Seaplanes, which take off and land on water, are fitted with nonretractable hydrofoils.

flight control Wings by themselves are unstable in flight, and a plane requires a tail to provide stability. The tail comprises a horizontal tailplane and vertical tailfin, called the horizontal and vertical stabilizer respectively. The tailplane has hinged flaps at the rear called elevators to control pitch (attitude). Raising the elevators depresses the tail and inclines the wings upwards (increases the angle of attack). This speeds the airflow above the wings until lift exceeds weight and the plane climbs. However, the steeper attitude increases drag, so more power is needed to maintain speed and the engine throttle must be opened up. Moving the elevators in the opposite direction produces the reverse effect. The angle of attack is reduced, and the plane descends. Speed builds up rapidly if the engine is not throttled back. Turning (changing direction) is effected by moving the rudder hinged to the rear of the tailfin, and by banking (rolling) the plane. It is banked by moving the ailerons, interconnected flaps at the rear of the wings which move in opposite directions, one up, the other down. In planes with a delta wing, such as ◊Concorde, the ailerons and elevators are combined. Other movable control surfaces, called flaps, are fitted at the rear of the wings closer to the fuselage. They are extended to increase the width and camber (curve) of the wings during takeoff and landing, thereby creating extra lift, while movable sections at the front, or leading edges, of the wing, called slats, are also extended at these times to improve the airflow. To land, the nose of the plane is brought up so that the angle of attack of the wings exceeds a critical point and the airflow around them breaks down; lift is lost (a condition known as stalling), and the plane drops to the runway. A few planes (for example, the Harrier) have a novel method of takeoff and landing, rising and dropping vertically by swivelling nozzles to direct the exhaust of their jet engines downwards. The ◊helicopter and ◊convertiplane use rotating propellers (rotors) to obtain lift to take off vertically.

operation The control surfaces of a plane are operated by the pilot on the flight deck, by means of a control stick, or wheel, and by foot pedals (for the rudder). The controls are brought into action by hydraulic power systems. An automatic pilot enables a plane to cruise on a given course at a fixed speed. Advanced experimental high-speed craft known as control-configured vehicles use a sophisticated computer-controlled system. The pilot instructs the computer which manoeuvre the plane must perform, and the computer, informed by a series of sensors around the craft about the altitude, speed, and turning rate of the plane, sends signals to the control surface and throttle to enable the manoeuvre to be executed.

aerosol particles of liquid or solid suspended in a gas. Fog is a common natural example. Aerosol cans contain a substance such as scent or cleaner packed under pressure with a device for releasing it as a fine spray. Most aerosols used chlorofluorocarbons (CFCs) as propellants until these were found to cause destruction of the ◊ozone layer in the stratosphere. The majority of so-called 'ozone-friendly' aerosols also use ozone-depleting chemicals, although they are not as destructive as CFCs. Some of the products sprayed, such as pesticides, can be directly toxic to humans.

Aeschylus c. 525–c. 456 BC. Athenian dramatist. He developed Greek tragedy by introducing the second actor, thus enabling true dialogue and dramatic action to occur independently of the chorus. Ranked with ◊Euripides and ◊Sophocles as one of the three great tragedians, Aeschylus composed some 90 plays between 500 and 456 BC, of which seven complete tragedies survive in his name: *Persians* 472 BC, *Seven Against Thebes* 467, *Suppliants* 463, the ◊*Oresteia* trilogy (*Agamemnon*, *Libation-Bearers*, and *Eumenides*) 458, and *Prometheus Bound* (the last, although attributed to him, is of uncertain date and authorship).

'Every ruler is harsh whose rule is new.'

AESCHYLUS *Prometheus Bound*

Aesculapius in Roman mythology, the god of medicine, equivalent to the Greek ◊Asclepius.

Aesop by tradition, a writer of Greek fables. According to the historian Herodotus, he lived in the mid-6th century BC and was a slave. The fables that are ascribed to him were collected at a later date and are anecdotal stories using animal characters to illustrate moral or satirical points.

Aesthetic Movement English artistic movement of the late 19th century, dedicated to the doctrine of aestheticism or 'art for art's sake' – that is, art as a self-sufficient entity concerned solely with beauty, and not with any moral, religious, political, social, or educational purpose. Associated with the movement were the artists Aubrey Beardsley and James McNeill Whistler and writers Walter Pater and Oscar Wilde.

The idea of art for art's sake, rooted in 18th-century philosophical thinking led by Immanuel Kant, was popularized by French writer Théophile Gautier 1832, and was taken up in mid-19th-century-France by the Symbolist poets and painters and spread throughout Europe. The English movement in the last two decades tended to advocate extremes of sensibility, which attracted much ridicule. John Ruskin and William Morris were staunch critics of the Aesthetic Movement.

aesthetics branch of philosophy that deals with the nature of beauty, especially in art. It emerged as a distinct branch of enquiry in the mid-18th century.

The subject of aesthetics was introduced by Plato and enlarged upon by Aristotle, but the term was first used by German philosopher Alexander Gottlieb Baumgarten (1714–1762). Other philosophers interested in this area were Immanuel ◊Kant, David

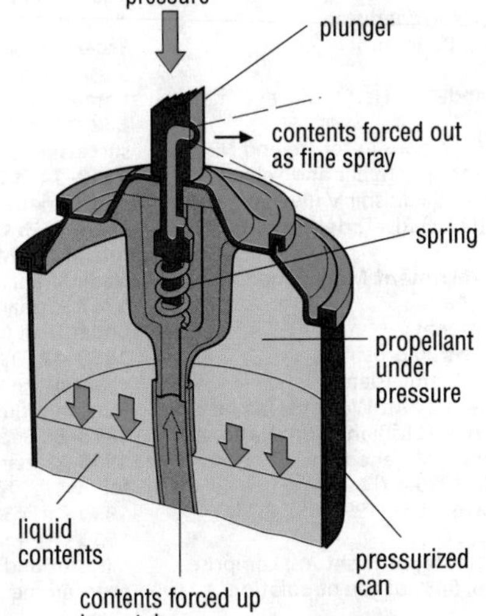

aerosol The aerosol can produces a fine spray of liquid particles, called an aerosol. When the top button is pressed, a valve is opened, allowing the pressurized propellant in the can to force out a spray of the liquid contents. As the liquid sprays from the can, the small amount of propellant dissolved in the liquid vaporizes, producing a fine spray of small droplets.

aestivation A group of snails in a state of aestivation (a dormancy which helps them to survive dry seasons) on coastal sand flats in Corfu. They may be so numerous as to completely envelop the plants on which they congregate. *Premaphotos Wildlife*

◊Hume, Benedetto ◊Croce, John ◊Dewey, and George ◊Santayana.

aestivation in zoology, a state of inactivity and reduced metabolic activity, similar to ◊hibernation, that occurs during the dry season in species such as lungfish and snails. In botany, the term is used to describe the way in which flower petals and sepals are folded in the buds. It is an important feature in ◊plant classification.

Aetolia district of ancient Greece on the northwest of the gulf of Corinth. The Aetolian League was a confederation of the cities of Aetolia formed AD 370 and which, following the death of Alexander the Great, became the chief rival of Macedonian power and the Achaean League. In 189 BC the Aetolians were forced to accept a treaty as subject allies of Rome.

affinity in chemistry, the force of attraction (see ◊bond) between atoms that helps to keep them in combination in a molecule. The term is also applied to attraction between molecules, such as those of biochemical significance (for example, between ◊enzymes and substrate molecules). This is the basis for affinity ◊chromatography, by which biologically important compounds are separated.

The atoms of a given element may have a greater affinity for the atoms of one element than for another (for example, hydrogen has a great affinity for chlorine and rapidly combines to form hydrochloric acid, but it has little affinity for argon).

affinity in law, relationship by marriage not blood (for example, between a husband and his wife's blood relatives, between a wife and her husband's blood relatives, or between step-parent and stepchild), which may legally preclude their marriage. It is distinguished from consanguinity or blood relationship.

affirmative action government policy of positive discrimination by the use of legal measures and moral persuasion that favours members of minority ethnic groups and women in such areas as employment and education. It is designed to counter the effects of long-term discrimination against these groups, and in Europe, Sweden, Belgium, the Netherlands, and Italy actively promote affirmative action through legal and financial incentives.

In the USA, the Equal Opportunities Act 1972 set up a commission to enforce the policy in organizations receiving public funds; many private institutions and employers adopted voluntary affirmative-action programmes at that time. President Clinton has demonstrated his commitment to affirmative-action programmes, but Republicans have pledged to end them.

affluent society society in which most people have money left over after satisfying their basic needs such as food and shelter. They are then able to decide how to spend their excess ('disposable') income, and become 'consumers'. The term was popularized by US economist John Kenneth ◊Galbraith, who used the term to describe the Western industrialized nations, particularly the USA, in his

AFGHANISTAN
Islamic Emirate of

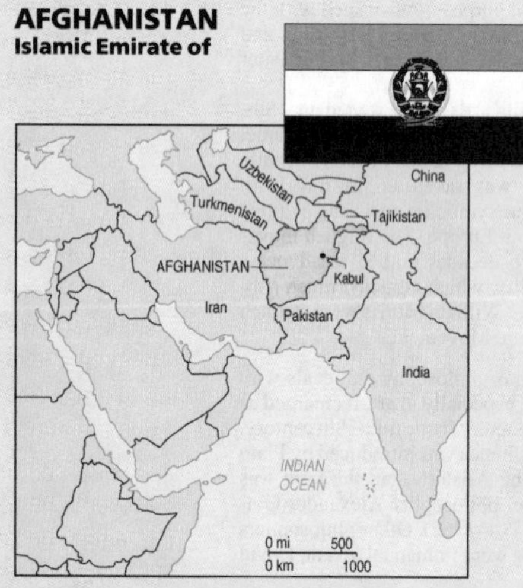

national name *Jamhuria Afghanistan*
area 652,090 sq km/251,707 sq mi
capital Kabul
major towns/cities Kandahar, Herat, Mazar-i-Sharif, Jalalabad
physical features mountainous in centre and NE (Hindu Kush mountain range; Khyber and Salang passes, Wakhan salient, and Panjshir Valley), plains in N and SW, Amu Darya (Oxus) River, Helmand River, Lake Saberi
head of state and government Mohammad Rabbani from 1996
political system transitional
administrative divisions 30 provinces
political parties Hezb-i-Islami, Islamic fundamentalist Mujaheddin, anti-Western; Jamiat-i-Islami, Islamic fundamentalist Mujaheddin; National Liberation Front, moderate Mujaheddin
population 20,883,000 (1996 est)
population growth rate 5.8% (1990–95); 2.7% (2000–05)
ethnic distribution Pathans, or Pushtuns, comprise the largest ethnic group, 54% of the population, followed by the Tajiks concentrated in the N (27%), the Uzbeks (8%), and Hazaras (7%)
life expectancy 43 (men), 44 (women)
literacy rate men 29% (1995 est)
languages Pushtu, Dari (Persian), Uzbek, Turkoman, Kirgiz
religions Muslim (85% Sunni, 15% Shi'ite)
currency afghâni
GDP (US $) 2.3 billion (1991 est)
growth rate −3.1% (1991)
exports dried fruit and nuts, natural gas, fresh fruits, carpets; small amounts of rare minerals, karakul lamb skins, Afghan coats, raw cotton and wool, opium and cannabis

HISTORY
6th C BC Part of Persian Empire under Cyrus II and Darius I.
329 BC Conquered by Alexander the Great.
323 BC Fell to the Seleucids who ruled from Babylon.
304 BC Ruled by Mauryan dynasty in the S and independent Bactria in the N.
135 BC Central Asian tribes established the Kusana dynasty.
3rd–7th Cs AD Decline of Kusana dynasty. Emergence of Sassanids as ruling power. Hepthalites (Central Asian nomads) and Western Turks also fighting for control.
642–11th C First Muslim invasion followed by a succession of Muslim dynasties.
1219–14th C Mongol invasions led by Genghis Khan and Tamerlane.
16th–18th Cs Much of Afghanistan came under the rule of the Mogul Empire under Babur (Zahir) and Nadir Shah.
1747 Afghanistan became an independent emirate under Dost Muhammad.
1838–42 First Afghan War, instigated by Britain to counter the threat to British India from expanding Russian influence in Afghanistan.
1878–80 Second Afghan War.
1919 Afghanistan recovered full independence following Third Afghan War.
1933 Zahir Shan became king of Afghanistan.
1953 Lt-Gen Mohammad Daud Khan became prime minister and introduced social and economic reform programme.
1963 Daud Khan forced to resign and constitutional monarchy established.
1973 Monarchy overthrown in coup staged by Daud Khan.
1978 Daud Khan assassinated in coup; Muhammad Taraki and the communist People's Democratic Party of Afghanistan (PDPA) took over. Start of Mujaheddin (Muslim guerrilla) resistance.
1979 Taraki ousted and murdered; replaced by Hafizullah Amin. USSR entered country installing Babrak Karmal. Amin executed.
1986 Replacement of Karmal as PDPA leader by Dr Najibullah Ahmadzai. Partial Soviet troop withdrawal.
1988 New non-Marxist constitution adopted.
1989 Withdrawal of Soviet troops; state of emergency imposed as Mujaheddin continued resistance to PDPA regime and civil war intensified.
1991 US and Soviet military aid withdrawn. Mujaheddin began talks with Russians and Kabul government.
1992 Najibullah government overthrown. Mujaheddin leader Burhanuddin Rabbani elected president. Hezb-i-Islami barred from government.
1993 Intensive fighting around Kabul. Peace agreement between Rabbani and dissident Hezb-i-Islami leader Gulbuddin Hekmatyar made Hekmatyar prime minister.
1994 Continuing rebel attacks on Kabul finally quelled. Hekmatyar dismissed from office.
1995 Talibaan Islamic fundamentalist army claimed town of Herat and advanced on Kabul.
1996 Country split between Talibaan-controlled fundamentalist south and more liberal north; six-member interim council of clerics, headed by Mohamad Rabbani installed; strict Islamic law imposed; new regime not recognized by international community.
1997 Talibaan controlled majority of provinces, and were recognized as legitimate government of Afghanistan by Pakistan and Saudi Arabia. New country name adopted: The Islamic Emirate of Afghanistan.
1998 10,000 people killed in earthquakes. Temporary cease-fire in civil war.

SEE ALSO Afghan Wars; Alexander the Great; Genghis Khan; Mujaheddin; Talibaan; Tamerlane book *The Affluent Society* 1958, in which he advocated using more of the nation's wealth for public spending and less for private consumption.

afforestation planting of trees in areas that have not previously held forests. (Reafforestation is the planting of trees in deforested areas.) Trees may be planted (1) to provide timber and wood pulp; (2) to provide firewood in countries where this is an energy source; (3) to bind soil together and prevent soil erosion; and (4) to act as windbreaks.

Afforestation is a controversial issue because while many ancient woodlands of mixed trees are being lost, the new plantations consist almost exclusively of conifers. It is claimed that such plantations acidify the soil and conflict with the interests of ◊biodiversity (they replace more ancient and ecologically valuable species and do not sustain wildlife).

Afghan people who are natives to or inhabitants of Afghanistan. The dominant group, particularly in Kabul, are the Pathans, most of whom are farmers, although some are nomadic. The Tajiks, a smaller ethnic group, are predominantly traders and farmers in the province of Herat and around Kabul; they were traditionally sedentary cereal cultivators and traders and were the original inhabitants of Afghanistan. The Hazaras, another farming group, are found in the southern mountain ranges of the Hindu Kush; they are traditionally nomadic herdsmen who came from Mongolia. The Uzbeks and Turkomen are farmers. The smallest Altaic minority are the Kirghiz, who live in the Pamir. Baluchi nomads live in the S, and Nuristani farmers live in the mountains of the NE.

The majority of the population are Sunni Muslims, the most recent converts being the Nuristanis.

Afghan hound breed of fast hunting dog resembling the ◊saluki in build, though slightly smaller. It can reach a speed of 56 kph/35 mph.

Afghanistan mountainous, landlocked country in S central Asia, bounded N by Tajikistan, Turkmenistan, and Uzbekistan, W by Iran, and S and E by Pakistan, India, and China. *See country box opposite.*

Afghan Wars three wars waged between Britain and Afghanistan to counter the threat to British India from expanding Russian influence in Afghanistan.

First Afghan War 1838–42, when the British garrison at Kabul was wiped out.

Second Afghan War 1878–80, when General Roberts (1832–1914) captured Kabul and relieved Kandahar.

Third Afghan War 1919, when peace followed the dispatch by the UK of the first aeroplane ever seen in Kabul.

Afonso six kings of Portugal, including Afonso I 1094–1185. King of Portugal from 1112, he made Portugal independent from León.

Africa second largest of the five continents. Africa is connected with Asia by the isthmus of Suez, and separated from Europe by the Mediterranean Sea. The name Africa was first given by the Romans to their African provinces with the city of Carthage, and it has since been extended to the whole continent. *See map on following page.*

area 30,097,000 sq km/11,620,451 sq mi (three times the area of Europe)

largest cities (population over 1 million) Cairo, Algiers, Lagos, Kinshasa, Abidjan, Cape Town, Nairobi, Casablanca, El Gîza, Addis Ababa, Luanda, Dar es Salaam, Ibadan, Mogadishu, Maputo, Johannesburg, Harare

features Great Rift Valley, containing most of the great lakes of E Africa (except Lake Victoria); Atlas Mountains in the NW; Drakensberg mountain range in the SE; Sahara Desert (world's largest desert) in the N; Namib, Kalahari, and Great Karoo deserts in the S; Nile, Zaïre, Niger, Zambezi, Limpopo, Volta, and Orange rivers

physical dominated by a uniform central plateau comprising a southern tableland with a mean altitude of 1,070 m/3,000 ft that falls northwards to a lower elevated plain with a mean altitude of 400 m/1,300 ft. Although there are no great alpine regions or extensive coastal plains, Africa has a mean altitude of 610 m/2,000 ft, two times greater than Europe. The highest points are Mount Kilimanjaro 5,900 m/19,364 ft, and Mount Kenya 5,200 m/17,058 ft; the lowest point is Lac Assal in Djibouti −144 m/−471 ft. Compared with other continents, Africa has few broad estuaries or inlets and therefore has proportionately the shortest coastline (24,000 km/15,000 mi). The geographical extremities of the continental mainland are Cape Hafun in the E, Cape Almadies in the W, Ras Ben Sekka in the N, and Cape Agulhas in the S. The Sahel is a narrow belt of savanna and scrub forest which covers 700 million hectares/1.7 billion acres of W and central Africa; 75% of the continent lies within the tropics

industries has 30% of the world's minerals including 51% of diamonds (Zaire, Botswana, South Africa) and 47% of gold (South Africa, Ghana, Zimbabwe); produces 11% of the world's crude petroleum, 58% of the world's cocoa (Côte d'Ivoire, Ghana, Cameroon, Nigeria), 23% of the world's coffee (Uganda, Côte d'Ivoire, Zaire, Ethiopia, Cameroon, Kenya), 20% of the world's groundnuts (Senegal, Nigeria, Sudan, Zaire), and 21% of the world's hardwood timber (Nigeria, Zaire, Tanzania, Kenya)

population (1988) 610 million; more than double the 1960 population of 278 million, and rising to an estimated 900 million by 2000; annual growth rate 3% (10 times greater than Europe); 27% of the world's undernourished people live in sub-Saharan Africa.

language over 1,000 languages spoken in Africa; Niger-Kordofanian languages including Mandinke, Kwa, Lingala, Bemba, and Bantu (Zulu, Swahili, Kikuyu), spoken over half of Africa from Mauritania in the W to South Africa; Nilo-Saharan languages, including Dinka, Shilluk, Nuer, and Masai, spoken in central Africa from the bend of the Niger River to the foothills of Ethiopia; Afro-Asiatic (Hamito-Semitic) languages, including Arabic, Berber, Ethiopian, and Amharic, N of the equator; Khoisan languages with 'click' consonants spoken in the SW by Kung, Khoikhoi, and Nama people of Namibia

religion Islam in the N and on the east coast as far S as N Mozambique; animism below the Sahara, which survives alongside Christianity (both Catholic and Protestant) in many central and southern areas.

Africa, Horn of projection constituted by Somalia and adjacent territories.

African art Africa has produced a rich diversity of art, reflecting marked differences of culture and environment. Nearly all African artworks, however, have important practical functions – as central elements in religious ceremonies and magical practices, and as markers of the social role and status of groups and individuals. Because many of these artworks are made of perishable materials, it is impossible to trace the origins and development of forms and styles: few of the many masks and carved figures, for example, are more than 150 years old. There is every reason to believe, however, that the visual arts of Africa form one of the oldest and richest traditions in the world. Among the many outstanding achievements are the masks of the Ashira Puna (W Africa), and the Dogon and the Dan (W Africa); the bronze sculptures of Benin and Ilf (W Africa); the wood carvings of the Yoruba (W Africa) and the Luba (central Africa); the ancient rock paintings of the San (S Africa); the textiles of the Berber (N Africa); and the jewellery of the Ashanti (NW Africa). In the early 20th century, African sculpture – particularly the carvings of W Africa – had a profound influence on the work of many European artists, in particular Pablo Picasso, Constantin Brancusi, Amedeo Modigliani, and Jacob Epstein.

African literature African literature was mainly oral until the 20th century and oral traditions of proverbs, mythological narratives, and poetry persist and influence contemporary writing. There exists a wide variety of narrative, dramatic, and lyric forms. In prose narrative, the folk tale, often featuring an animal hero, is one of the most common genres; stories of a trickster-hero (in the form of a spider, a tortoise, a rabbit, a human, or a god) are particularly popular. There are also many religious myths, and stories that preserve in legendary form the history and world-view of particular groups.

African literature in European languages Early works include those of the classical scholar Juan Latino, an enslaved African who later became a professor at the University of Granada 1557, the 18th-century Sengalese-American poet Phyllis ◊Wheatley, and the Nigerian Oloudah Equiana (also called Gustavus Vassa, c. 1750–1801), whose vivid account of his early life in Africa, his enslavement, his later adventures as a freed man, and his involvement in the abolitionist movement, went into eight editions in 18th-century England. Later writing has paid more attention to the themes of urban deprivation and political oppression and violence, particularly in South Africa, as in the work of writers such as the Nigerian Chinua ◊ Achebe.

Afro-American literature The considerable body of writing by Afro-Americans, especially in the 1920s, in turn influenced French-speaking writers from Africa and the Caribbean, including Senegal's president, Léopold ◊Senghor, who were advocates of the concept of *négritude* (blackness, belonging to a black culture), affirming a growing sense of African personality and political and cultural identity in the colonial and postcolonial period.

literature in English Africans who write in English have generally rejected négritude as an unrealistic idealization of the African past. Chinua ◊Achebe's widely acclaimed novels *Things Fall Apart* 1958 and *Arrow of God* 1964 draw on the language and forms of oral culture to recreate the conflicts within traditional Ibo society and to show how those conflicts were exacerbated by colonialism. The plays of the Nigerian author Wole ◊Soyinka also reject attempts to glamorize the past. *The Road* 1965 interweaves Yoruba and Christian metaphysics and rituals. In South Africa, drama has been an important instrument of political protest, particularly in the work of Athol ◊Fugard.

African National Congress (ANC) South African political party, founded 1912 as a multiracial nationalist organization with the aim of extending the franchise to the whole population and ending all racial discrimination. Its president from 1991–97 was Nelson ◊Mandela. Thabo Mbeki took over the presidency Dec 1997 with Jacob Zuma as vice president.

The ANC was banned by the government 1960–1990. Talks between the ANC and the South African government began Dec 1991 and culminated in the adoption of a nonracial constitution 1993 and the ANC's agreement to participate in a power-sharing administration, as a prelude to full majority rule. In the country's first universal suffrage elections April 1994, the ANC won a sweeping victory, capturing 62% of the vote, and Mandela was elected president.

Although originally nonviolent, in exile in Mozambique from 1960 the ANC developed a military wing, Umkhonto we Sizwe, which engaged in sabotage and guerrilla training. The armed struggle was suspended Aug 1990 after Mandela's release from prison and the organization's headquarters were moved from Zambia to Johannesburg.

The ANC's successes in constitutional negotiations from 1991 were seen as a threat by ◊Inkatha and by white, right-wing politicians, and during the early 1990s fighting between supporters of the ANC and Inkatha left hundreds dead.

The Truth and Reconciliation Commission published a retrospective report on apartheid in October 1998.

African nationalism political movement for the unification of Africa (◊Pan-Africanism) and for national self-determination. Early African political organizations included the Aborigines Rights Protection Society in the Gold Coast 1897, the African National Congress in South Africa 1912, and the National Congress of West Africa 1920. African nationalism has its roots among the educated elite (mainly 'returned' Americans of African descent and freed slaves or their descendants) in W Africa in the 19th century.

After World War I nationalists fostered moves for self-determination. The Fourteen Points of US president Woodrow Wilson, his terms proposed as a basis for the settlement of

> *The darkest thing about Africa has always been our ignorance of it.*
>
> On **Africa**
> George Kimble
> *Reporter* 15 May 1951

African art Portrait head of a king, 12th–14th century, Kimbell Art Museum, Fort Worth, Texas, USA. Heads like this one, made of terracotta or brass, have been discovered during the 20th century at the W Nigerian town of Ife. Similar, more stylized heads of brass or bronze were made in nearby Benin. *Corbis*

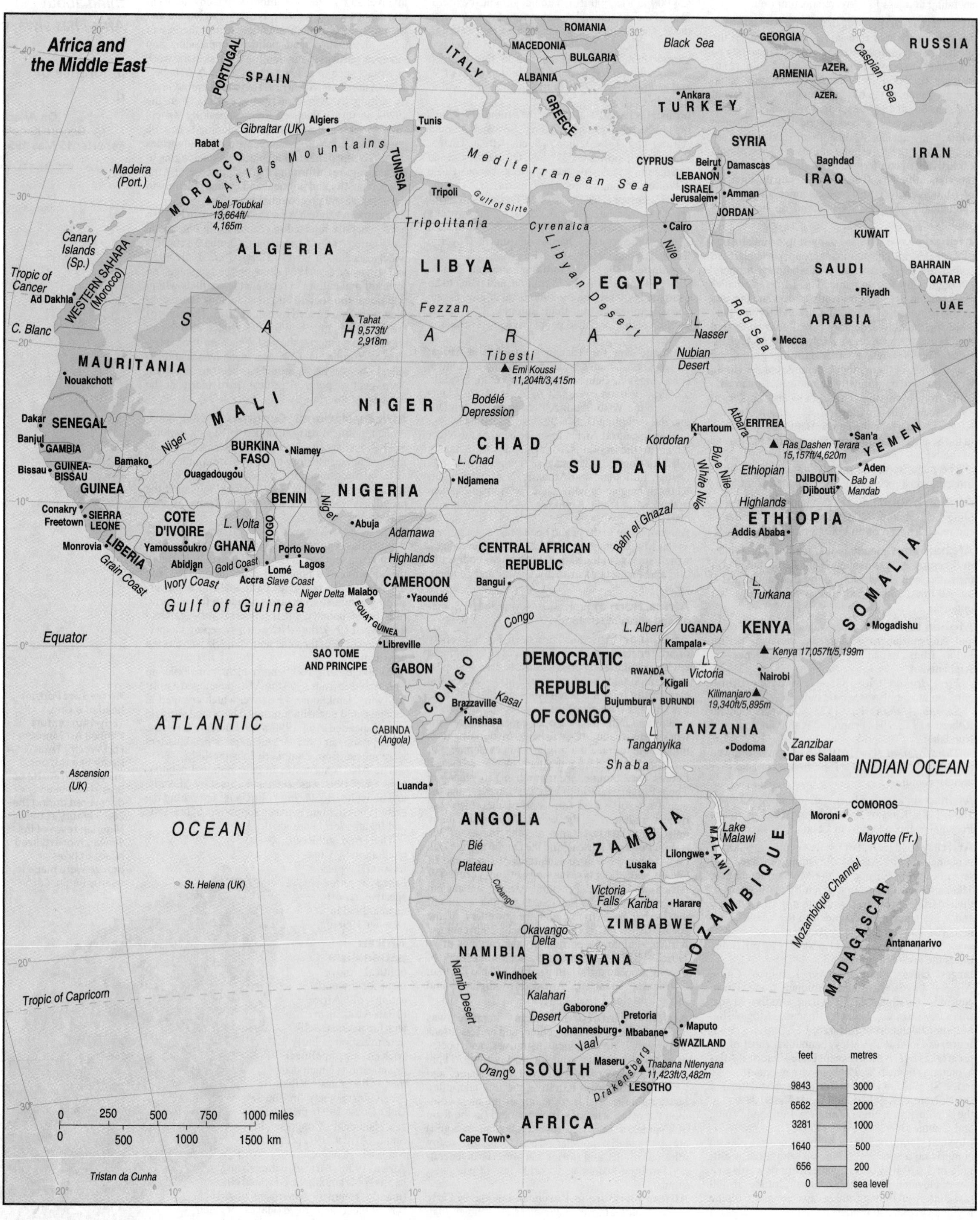
Africa and the Middle East
ROMANIA
MACEDONIA
BULGARIA
Black Sea
GEORGIA
RUSSIA
Caspian Sea
PORTUGAL
SPAIN
ITALY
ALBANIA
GREECE
ARMENIA
AZER.
Ankara
TURKEY
Gibraltar (UK)
Algiers
Tunis
Rabat
Atlas Mountains
TUNISIA
Mediterranean Sea
SYRIA
CYPRUS
Beirut
Damascus
LEBANON
ISRAEL
Jerusalem
Amman
JORDAN
Baghdad
IRAQ
IRAN
Madeira (Port.)
MOROCCO
Jbel Toubkal 13,664ft/ 4,165m
Tripoli
Gulf of Sirte
Tripolitania
Cyrenaica
Cairo
KUWAIT
Canary Islands (Sp.)
ALGERIA
LIBYA
Libyan Desert
EGYPT
Nile
SAUDI
ARABIA
BAHRAIN
QATAR
Riyadh
UAE
Tropic of Cancer
Ad Dakhla
WESTERN SAHARA (Morocco)
Fezzan
Tahat 9,573ft/ 2,918m
Red Sea
Mecca
C. Blanc
S A H A R A
L. Nasser
Tibesti
Emi Koussi 11,204ft/3,415m
Nubian Desert
MAURITANIA
Nouakchott
NIGER
Bodélé Depression
MALI
Atbara
ERITREA
Dakar
SENEGAL
Khartoum
San'a
YEMEN
Banjul
GAMBIA
Niger
BURKINA FASO
Niamey
CHAD
Kordofan
Ras Dashen Terara 15,157ft/4,620m
Aden
Bissau
GUINEA-BISSAU
Bamako
Ouagadougou
L. Chad
SUDAN
Blue Nile
White Nile
Ethiopian
Highlands
DJIBOUTI
Djibouti
Bab al Mandab
GUINEA
Ndjamena
Conakry
Freetown
SIERRA LEONE
BENIN
NIGERIA
Bahr el Ghazal
ETHIOPIA
COTE D'IVOIRE
L. Volta
TOGO
Abuja
Addis Ababa
Adamawa
Monrovia
LIBERIA
Yamoussoukro
GHANA
Porto Novo
Lagos
Highlands
CENTRAL AFRICAN REPUBLIC
Grain Coast
Abidjan
Gold Coast
Accra
Lomé
Slave Coast
L. Turkana
SOMALIA
Ivory Coast
CAMEROON
Bangui
Niger Delta
Malabo
Yaoundé
Gulf of Guinea
EQUAT GUINEA
Congo
Equator
L. Albert
UGANDA
KENYA
Mogadishu
Libreville
Kampala
Kenya 17,057ft/5,199m
SAO TOME AND PRINCIPE
GABON
DEMOCRATIC REPUBLIC OF CONGO
RWANDA
Kigali
L. Victoria
Nairobi
CONGO
Kasai
Brazzaville
Kinshasa
Bujumbura
BURUNDI
Kilimanjaro 19,340ft/5,895m
ATLANTIC
CABINDA (Angola)
L. Tanganyika
TANZANIA
Dodoma
Zanzibar
Dar es Salaam
Shaba
INDIAN OCEAN
Ascension (UK)
Luanda
COMOROS
Moroni
OCEAN
ANGOLA
Bié Plateau
ZAMBIA
MALAWI
Lake Malawi
Lilongwe
Mayotte (Fr.)
Lusaka
MOZAMBIQUE
St. Helena (UK)
Cubango
Victoria Falls
L. Kariba
Harare
Mozambique Channel
ZIMBABWE
Okavango Delta
MADAGASCAR
Antananarivo
NAMIBIA
BOTSWANA
Windhoek
Namib Desert
Kalahari Desert
Tropic of Capricorn
Gaborone
Pretoria
Johannesburg
Mbabane
Maputo
SWAZILAND
Vaal
Maseru
Thabana Ntlenyana 11,423ft/3,482m
Orange
SOUTH
Drakensberg
LESOTHO
AFRICA
Cape Town
0 250 500 750 1000 miles
0 500 1000 1500 km
Tristan da Cunha
feet metres
9843 3000
6562 2000
3281 1000
1640 500
656 200
0 sea level

World War I, encouraged such demands in Tunisia, and delegates to London 1919 from the Native National Congress in South Africa stressed the contribution to the war effort by the South African Native Labour Corps.

By 1939 African nationalist groups existed in nearly every territory of the continent. Africa's direct involvement in World War II, the weakening of the principal colonial powers, increasing anticolonialism from America (the ◊Atlantic Charter 1941 encouraged self-government), and Soviet criticism of imperialism inspired African nationalists.

African violet herbaceous plant *Saintpaulia ionantha* from tropical central and E Africa, with velvety green leaves and scentless purple flowers.

Afrikaans language an official language (with English) of the Republic of South Africa and Namibia. Spoken mainly by the Afrikaners – descendants of Dutch and other 17th-century colonists – it is a variety of the Dutch language, modified by circumstance and the influence of German, French, and other immigrant and local languages. It became a standardized written language about 1875.

Afrikaner (formerly known as ***Boer***) inhabitants of South Africa descended from the original Dutch, Flemish, and ◊Huguenot settlers of the 17th century. Comprising approximately 60% of the white population in South Africa, they were originally farmers but have now become mainly urbanized. Their language is Afrikaans.

Afro-Asiatic language any of a family of languages spoken throughout the world. There are two main branches, the languages of N Africa and the languages originating in Syria, Mesopotamia, Palestine, and Arabia, but now found from Morocco in the W to the Persian Gulf in the E.

The N African languages include ancient Egyptian, Coptic, and Berber, while the Asiatic languages include the largest number of speakers – modern Arabic – as well as Hebrew, Aramaic, and Syriac. The scripts of Arabic and Hebrew are written from right to left.

Afro-Caribbean West Indian people of African descent. Afro-Caribbeans are the descendants of W Africans captured or obtained in trade from African procurers. European slave traders then shipped them to the West Indies to English, French, Dutch, Spanish, and Portuguese colonies founded from the 16th century. Since World War II many Afro-Caribbeans have migrated to North America and to Europe, especially to the USA, the UK, and the Netherlands.

afterbirth in mammals, the placenta, umbilical cord, and ruptured membranes, which become detached from the uterus and expelled soon after birth.

afterburning method of increasing the thrust of a gas turbine (jet) aeroplane engine by spraying additional fuel into the hot exhaust duct between the turbojet and the tailpipe where it ignites. Used for short-term increase of power during takeoff, or during combat in military aircraft.

after-ripening process undergone by the seeds of some plants before germination can occur. The length of the after-ripening period in different species may vary from a few weeks to many months. It helps seeds to germinate at a time when conditions are most favourable for growth. In some cases the embryo is not fully mature at the time of dispersal and must develop further before germination can take place. Other seeds do not germinate even when the embryo is mature, probably owing to growth inhibitors within the seed that must be leached out or broken down before germination can begin.

Agadir resort and seaport in S Morocco, near the mouth of the river Sus; population (1990, urban area) 439,000. It was rebuilt after being destroyed by an earthquake 1960.

Agadir Incident or the ***Second Moroccan Crisis*** international crisis provoked by Kaiser Wilhelm II of Germany, July–Nov 1911. By sending the gunboat *Panther* to demand territorial concessions from the French, he hoped to drive a wedge into the Anglo-French entente. In fact, German aggression during the Second Moroccan Crisis merely served to reinforce Anglo-French fears of Germany's intentions. The crisis gave rise to the term 'gunboat diplomacy'.

Aga Khan IV (Karim) 1936– . Spiritual head (*imam*) of the Ismaili Muslim sect (see ◊Islam). He succeeded his grandfather 1957.

agama lizard of the Old World family Agamidae, especially the genus *Agama*. There are about 280 species, found throughout the warmer regions of the Old World. Many are brilliantly coloured and all are capable of changing the colour of their skin.

Agamemnon in Greek mythology, a Greek hero of the Trojan wars, son of Atreus, King of Mycenae, and brother of Menelaus. He sacrificed his daughter Iphigenia in order to secure favourable winds for the Greek expedition against Troy and after a ten-year siege sacked the city, receiving Priam's daughter Cassandra as a prize. On his return home, he and Cassandra were murdered by his wife Clytemnestra and her lover Aegisthus. His children Orestes and Electra later killed the guilty couple.

agar jellylike carbohydrate, obtained from seaweeds. It is used mainly in microbiological experiments as a culture medium for growing bacteria and other microorganisms. The agar is resistant to breakdown by microorganisms, remaining a solid jelly throughout the course of the experiment.

agaric fungus of typical mushroom shape. Agarics include the field mushroom *Agaricus campestris* and the cultivated edible mushroom *A. brunnesiens*. Closely related is the often poisonous ◊*Amanita* genus, including the fly agaric *Amanita muscaria*.

Agassi Andre 1970– . US tennis player. He won the Wimbledon men's singles title 1992, the US Open 1994, and the Australian Open 1994. Renowned for his service returns and hard-hitting forehand, he turned professional 1986 at the age of 16. He played in the US teams which won the Davis Cup in 1990, 1992, and 1995. He won the Olympic men's singles title at the Atlanta Games 1996.

Agassiz (Jean) Louis Rodolphe 1807–1873. Swiss-born US palaeontologist and geologist who developed the idea of the ice age. He established his name through his work on the classification of fossil fishes. Unlike Charles Darwin, he did not believe that individual species themselves changed, but that new species were created from time to time.

agate banded or cloudy type of ◊chalcedony, a silica, SiO_2, that forms in rock cavities. Agates are cryptocrystalline (with crystals too small to be seen with an optical microscope) and are used as ornamental stones, art objects, and also to burnish and polish gold applied to glass and ceramics.

agave any of several related plants with stiff sword-shaped spiny leaves arranged in a rosette. All species of the genus *Agave* come from the warmer parts of the New World. They include *A. sisalina*, whose fibres are used for rope making, and the Mexican century plant *A. americana*, which may take many years to mature (hence its common name). Alcoholic drinks such as ◊tequila and pulque are made from the sap of agave plants.

ageing in common usage, the period of deterioration of the physical condition of a living organism that leads to death; in biological terms, the entire life process.

Three current theories attempt to account for ageing. The first suggests that the process is genetically determined, to remove individuals that can no longer reproduce. The second suggests that it is due to the accumulation of mistakes during the replication of ◊DNA at cell division. The third suggests that it is actively induced by fragments of DNA that move between cells, or by cancer-causing viruses; these may become abundant in old cells and induce them to produce unwanted ◊proteins or interfere with the control functions of their DNA.

Agent Orange selective ◊weedkiller, notorious for its use in the 1960s during the Vietnam War by US forces to eliminate ground cover which could protect enemy forces. It was subsequently discovered to contain highly poisonous ◊dioxin. Thousands of US troops who had handled it, along with many Vietnamese people who came into contact with it, later developed cancer or produced deformed babies.

Agent Orange, named after the distinctive orange stripe on its packaging, combines equal parts of 2,4-D (2,4-dichlorophenoxyacetic acid) and 2,4,5-T (2,4,5-trichlorophenoxyacetic acid), both now banned in the USA.

Aggadah (or ***Haggadah***, Hebrew 'telling') the liturgical narration of the Israelites' slavery in Egypt and their liberation by God through Moses, which forms the heart of the Seder meal at the Jewish festival of *Pesach* (Passover). The story is dramatized by question and answer, and interspersed with songs, discussion, prayers, and psalms. *Aggadah* also refers to the book in which the words are written, often richly decorated or illustrated.

agglutination in biology, the clumping together of ◊antigens, such as red blood cells or bacteria, to form larger, visible clumps, under the influence of ◊antibodies. As each antigen clumps only in response to its particular antibody, agglutination provides a way of determining blood groups and the identity of unknown bacteria.

aggression in biology, behaviour used to intimidate or injure another organism (of the same or of a different species), usually for the purposes of gaining territory, a mate, or food. Aggression often involves an escalating series of threats aimed at intimidating an opponent without having to engage in potentially dangerous physical contact. Aggressive signals include roaring by red deer, snarling by dogs, the fluffing-up of feathers by birds, and the raising of fins by some species of fish.

Agincourt, Battle of battle of the ◊Hundred Years' War in which Henry V of England defeated the French 25 Oct 1415, mainly through the overwhelming superiority of the English longbow. The French lost more than 6,000 troops to about 1,600 English casualties. As a result of the battle, Henry gained France and the French princess Catherine of Valois as his wife.

Agni in Hindu mythology, god of fire, guardian of homes, and protector of humans against evil.

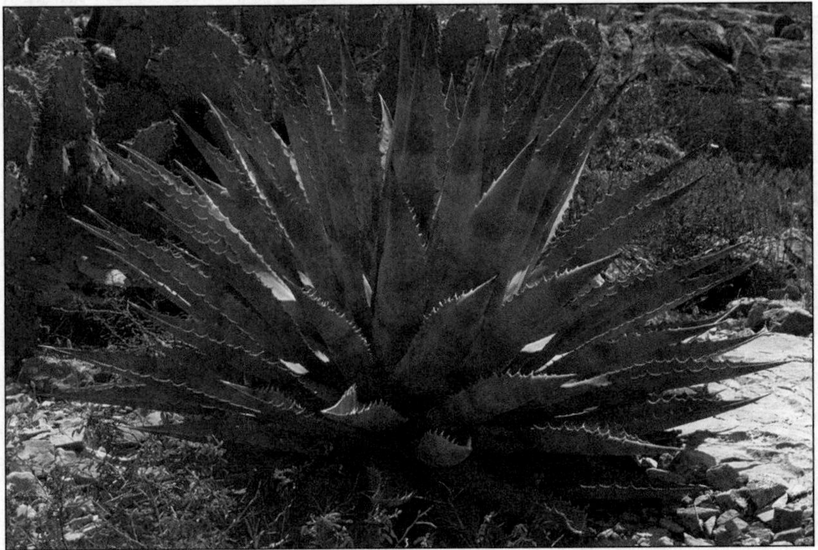

agave Agaves are desert plants from the New World. They normally flower once when they reach maturity – which in some species may take as long as 60 years – and then die. Fibres such as sisal can be produced from some species, and the alcoholic drink tequila is made from others. *Premaphotos Wildlife*

agnosticism belief that the existence of God cannot be proven; that in the nature of things the individual cannot know anything of what lies behind or beyond the world of natural phenomena. The term was coined 1869 by T H ◊Huxley.

Whereas an atheist (see ◊atheism) denies the existence of God or gods, an agnostic asserts that God or a First Cause is one of those concepts (others include the Absolute, infinity, eternity, and immortality) that lie beyond the reach of human intelligence, and therefore can be neither confirmed nor denied.

agoraphobia ◊fear of open spaces and public places. The anxiety produced can be so severe that some sufferers are unable to leave their homes for many years. Agoraphobia affects 1 person in 20 at some stage in their lives. The most common time of onset is between the ages of 18 and 28.

agouti small rodent of the genus *Dasyprocta*, family Dasyproctidae. It is found in the forests of Central and South America. The agouti is herbivorous, swift-running, and about the size of a rabbit.

Agra city of Uttar Pradesh, India, on the river Jumna, 160 km/100 mi SE of Delhi; population (1991) 892,000. A commercial and university centre, it was the capital of the Mogul empire 1566–69 and 1601–1658, from which period the Taj Mahal dates.

history ◊Babur, the first great Mogul ruler, made Agra his home 1527. The present city was founded 1566 as the capital of the Mogul empire. Akbar, grandson of Babur, rebuilt the Red Fort of Salim Shah 1566, and is buried outside the city in the tomb at Sikandra. In the 17th century the buildings of ◊Shah Jahan made Agra one of the most beautiful cities in the world. The Taj Mahal, erected as a tomb for the emperor's wife Mumtaz Mahal, was completed 1650. Agra's political importance dwindled from 1658, when Aurangzeb moved the capital back to Delhi. It was taken from the Marathas by Lord Lake 1803.

agribusiness commercial farming on an industrial scale, often financed by companies whose main interests lie outside agriculture; for example, multinational corporations. Agribusiness farms are mechanized, large in size, highly structured, and reliant on chemicals.

Agricola Gnaeus Julius AD 40–93. Roman general and politician. Born at Forum Julii (Fréjus) in Provence, he became consul 77, and then governor of Britain 78–85. He extended Roman rule to the Firth of Forth in Scotland and in 84 won the battle of Mons Graupius. His fleet sailed round the north of Scotland and proved Britain an island.

agricultural revolution sweeping changes that took place in British agriculture over the period 1750–1850 in response to the increased demand for food from a rapidly expanding population. Recent research has shown these changes to be only part of a much larger, ongoing process of development. Changes of the latter half of the 18th century included the enclosure of open fields, the introduction of four-course rotation together with new fodder crops such as turnips, and the development of improved breeds of livestock.

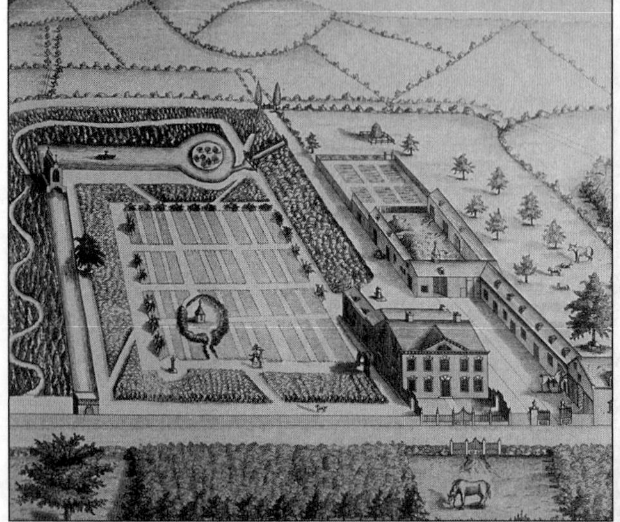

agricultural revolution An estate at Burbage, Leicestershire, c. 1750 showing some of the innovations of the agricultural revolution such as enclosed fields, a model farm, and separate parkland and woodland. *Image Select (UK) Ltd*

Pioneers of the new farming were Viscount ◊Townshend (known as 'Turnip' Townshend), Jethro ◊Tull, Robert Bakewell (1725–1795), and enlightened landowners such as Thomas Coke of Norfolk (1752–1842).

agriculture (Latin *ager* 'field', *colere* 'to cultivate') the practice of farming, including the cultivation of the soil (for raising ◊crops) and the raising of domesticated animals. The units for managing agricultural production vary from smallholdings and individually owned farms to corporate-run farms and collective farms run by entire communities.

Crops are for human or animal food, or commodities such as cotton and sisal. For successful production, the land must be prepared (ploughed, cultivated, harrowed, and rolled).

Seed must be planted and the growing plants nurtured. This may involve ◊fertilizers, ◊irrigation, pest control by chemicals, and monitoring of acidity or nutrients. When the crop has grown, it must be harvested and, depending on the crop, processed in a variety of ways before it is stored or sold.

Greenhouses allow cultivation of plants that would otherwise find the climate too harsh. ◊Hydroponics allows commercial cultivation of crops using nutrient-enriched solutions instead of soil. Special methods, such as terracing, may be adopted to allow cultivation in hostile terrain and to retain topsoil in mountainous areas with heavy rainfall.

Animals are raised for wool, milk, leather, dung (as fuel), or meat. They may be semi-domesticated, such as reindeer, or fully domesticated but nomadic (where naturally growing or cultivated food supplies are sparse), or kept in one location.

Animal farming involves accommodation (buildings, fencing, or pasture), feeding, breeding, gathering the produce (eggs, milk, or wool), slaughtering, and further processing such as tanning.

Agriculture, Fisheries, and Food, Ministry of (MAFF) UK government department established 1955, through combination of existing agriculture, fisheries, and food ministries. It is responsible for agriculture, horticulture, fisheries, and food policies.

agrimony herbaceous plant *Agrimonia eupatoria* of the rose family Rosaceae, with small yellow flowers on a slender spike. It grows along hedges and in fields.

Agrippa Marcus Vipsanius c. 63–12 BC. Roman general and admiral. He was instrumental in the successful campaigns and rise to power of the emperor ◊Augustus. He commanded the victorious fleet at the Battle of ◊Actium and married Augustus's daughter Julia.

agronomy study of crops and soils, a branch of agricultural science. Agronomy includes such topics as selective breeding (of plants and animals), irrigation, pest control, and soil analysis and modification.

AH in the Muslim calendar, abbreviation for ◊***anno hegirae***.

Ahab c. 875–854 BC. King of Israel. His empire included the suzerainty of Moab, and Judah was his subordinate ally, but his kingdom was weakened by constant wars with Syria. By his marriage with Jezebel, Princess of Sidon, Ahab introduced into Israel the worship of the Phoenician god Baal, thus provoking the hostility of Elijah and other prophets. Ahab died in battle against the Syrians at Ramoth Gilead.

Ahaggar or ***Hoggar*** mountainous plateau of the central Sahara, Algeria, whose highest point, Tahat, at 2,918 m/9,576 ft, lies between Algiers and the mouth of the Niger. It is the home of the formerly nomadic Tuareg.

Ahasuerus (Latinized Hebrew form of the Persian ***Khshayarsha***, Greek ***Xerxes***) name of several Persian kings in the Bible, notably the husband of Esther, whose story is told in the Old Testament book of the same name. Traditionally it was also the name of the ◊Wandering Jew.

Ahern Bertie 1951– . Prime minister (taoiseach) from 1997, leader of Fianna Fáil (FF) from 1994. He was elected to parliament (Dáil) in 1977 and was minister of state in the department of taoiseach and defence, 1982, in Charles Haughey's minority government. When Fianna Fáil returned to power, he was minister for Labour, 1987–91 and then minister for finance, 1991–94. In May 1997 the Fine Gael prime minister, John Bruton, called a general election which proved inconclusive but allowed Ahern to form a minority government as Ireland's youngest taoiseach.

agriculture Ancient Chinese farming implements. The upper panel shows mortars and pestles being used to pound rice. The central picture illustrates the use of a seed drill, and the lower drawing is of a plough. *Image Select (UK) Ltd*

ahimsa in Hinduism, Buddhism, and Jainism, the doctrine of respect for all life (including the lowest forms and even the elements themselves) and consequently an extreme form of nonviolence. It arises in part from the concept of *karma*, which holds that a person's actions (and thus any injury caused to any form of life) determine his or her experience and condition in this and future lives.

Ahmadiyya Islamic religious movement founded by Mirza Ghulam Ahmad (1839–1908). His followers reject the doctrine that Muhammad was the last of the prophets and accept Ahmad's claim to be the Mahdi and Promised Messiah. In 1974 the Ahmadis were denounced as non-Muslims by other Muslims.

Ahmad Shah Durrani 1724–1773. Founder and first ruler of Afghanistan. Elected shah 1745, he had conquered the Punjab by 1751 and defeated the ◊Maratha people's confederacy at Panipat, Punjab, 1761.

Ahmedabad or ***Ahmadabad*** city in India; population (1991) 3,298,000. It is a cotton-manufacturing centre, and has many sacred buildings of the Hindu, Muslim, and Jain faiths. Ahmedabad was founded in the reign of Ahmad Shah 1412, and came under the control of the East India Company 1818. In 1930 ◊Gandhi marched to the sea from here to protest against the government salt monopoly.

Ahriman in Zoroastrianism, the supreme evil spirit, lord of the darkness and death, waging war with his counterpart Ahura Mazda (Ormuzd) until a time when human beings choose to lead good lives and Ahriman is finally destroyed.

Ahtisaari Maarti 1939– . Finnish diplomat and politician, president from 1994. Prior to being chosen as the Social Democratic Party presidential candidate, he was undersecretary general of the United Nations, representing it in Namibia 1989–90 and in Yugoslavia 1993. He strongly supported Finland's membership of the European Union and pledged himself to work for better relations with Russia.

Ahura Mazda or ***Ormuzd*** in Zoroastrianism, the spirit of supreme good. As god of life and light he will finally prevail over his enemy, Ahriman.

aid money or resources given or lent on favourable terms to poorer countries. A distinction may be made between short-term aid (usually food and medicine), which is given to relieve conditions in emergencies such as famine, and long-term aid, which is intended to promote economic activity and improve the quality of life – for example, by funding irrigation, education, and communications programmes.

aid, development money given or lent on concessional terms to developing countries or spent on maintaining agencies for this purpose. In 1970, all industrialized United Nations (UN) member countries committed to giving at least 0.7% of GNP to aid. All the Scandinavian countries have met or exceeded this target, whereas the UK and the USA have not achieved it; in 1995, the UK aid budget was 0.28% and the US figure 0.15% of GNP. Each country spends more than half its contribution on direct bilateral assistance to countries with which they have historical or military links or hope to encourage trade. The rest goes to international organizations such as UN and ◊World Bank agencies, which distribute aid multilaterally. The World Bank is the largest dispenser of aid.

The United States Agency for International Development (USAID) is the State Department body responsible for bilateral aid. The USA is the largest contributor to, and thus the most powerful member of, the International Development Association. In the UK, the International Development Department (formerly the Overseas Development Administration) at the Foreign Office handles bilateral aid.

UK guidelines to concentrate aid and trade provision on countries with a gross national product of $700 or less per head of population were introduced 1993. Nonetheless, £16 million of aid was allocated to wealthier countries 1993–94. The European Development Fund (an arm of the European Union) and the International Development Association (an arm of the World Bank) receive approximately 5% and 8% respectively of the UK development-aid budget.

Aidan, St c. 600–651. Irish monk who converted Northumbria to Christianity and founded Lindisfarne monastery on Holy Island off the NE coast of England. His feast day is 31 Aug.

Aidid Muhammad Farah 1936–1996. Somali soldier and politician. A one-time colleague of the Somali president, Siad Barre, in 1990 he established an anti-Barre paramilitary organization, the United Somali Congress (USC), which eventually drove the president from office 1991. Rivalry subsequently developed within the ruling coalition and Somalia was again plunged into civil war. During 1993, United Nations peacekeeping forces (principally US Marines) targetted Aidid as the principal villain in the conflict and conducted an abortive mission to capture him. Aidid and Mahdi signed a peace agreement March 1994, however Aidid was ousted as factional leader June 1995. He was killed during faction fighting Aug 1996.

AIDS acronym for ***acquired immune deficiency syndrome***, the gravest of the sexually transmitted diseases, or ◊STDs. It is caused by the human immunodeficiency virus (HIV), now known to be a ◊retrovirus, an organism first identified 1983.

transmission Sexual transmission of the AIDS virus endangers heterosexual men and women as well as high-risk groups, such as homosexual and bisexual men, prostitutes, intravenous drug-users sharing needles, and haemophiliacs and other patients treated with contaminated blood products. The virus itself is not selective: worldwide, heterosexual activity accounts for three-quarters of all HIV infections. The virus has a short life outside the body, which makes transmission of the infection by methods other than sexual contact, blood transfusion, and shared syringes extremely unlikely.

diagnosis of AIDS The effect of the virus in those who become ill is the devastation of the immune system, leaving the victim susceptible to diseases that would not otherwise develop. Diagnosis of AIDS is based on the appearance of rare tumours or opportunistic infections in unexpected candidates. *Pneumocystis carinii* pneumonia, for instance, normally seen only in the malnourished or those whose immune systems have been deliberately suppressed, is common among AIDS victims and, for them, a leading cause of death.

the development of HIV Many people who have HIV in their blood are not ill; in fact, it was hitherto thought that during the delay between infection with HIV and the development of AIDS the virus lay dormant. However, results from 1995 research into the reproduction rate of HIV are likely to alter the approach to AIDS management; US researchers now estimate that HIV reproduces at a rate of a billion viruses a day, even in individuals with no symptoms, but is held at bay by the immune system producing enough white blood cells (CD4 cells) to destroy them. Gradually, the virus mutates so much that the immune system is unable to continue to counteract; people with advanced AIDS have virtually no CD4 cells remaining. These results indicate the importance of treating HIV-positive individuals before symptoms develop, rather than delaying treatment until the onset of AIDS.

treatment In the West the time-lag between infection with HIV and the development of AIDS seems to be about ten years, but progression is far more rapid in developing countries. Some AIDS victims die within a few months of the outbreak of symptoms, some survive for several years; roughly 50% are dead within three years. There is no cure for the disease and the four antivirals currently in use against AIDS have not lived up to expectations. Trials began 1994 using a new AIDS drug called

AGRICULTURE: TIMELINE

10000–8000 BC	Holocene (post-glacial) period of hunters and gatherers. Harvesting and storage of wild grains in SW Asia. Herding of reindeer in N Eurasia. Domestic sheep in N Iraq.
8000	Neolithic revolution with cultivation of domesticated wheats and barleys, sheep, and goats in SW Asia. Domestication of pigs in New Guinea.
7000–6000	Domestic goats, sheep, and cattle in Anatolia, Greece, Persia, and the Caspian basin. Planting and harvesting techniques transferred from Asia Minor to Europe.
5000	Beginning of Nile valley civilization. Millet cultivated in China.
3400	Flax used for textiles in Egypt. Widespread corn production in the Americas.
3200	Records of ploughing, raking, and manuring by Egyptians.
c. 3100	River Nile dammed during the rule of King Menes.
3000	First record of asses used as beasts of burden in Egypt. Sumerian civilization used barley as main crop with wheat, dates, flax, apples, plums, and grapes.
2900	Domestication of pigs in E Asia.
2640	Reputed start of Chinese silk industry.
2500	Domestic elephants in the Indus valley. Potatoes a staple crop in Peru.
2350	Wine-making in Egypt.
2250	First known irrigation dam.
1600	Important advances in the cultivation of vines and olives in Crete.
1500	*Shadoof* (mechanism for raising water) used for irrigation in Egypt.
1400	Iron ploughshares in use in India.
1300	Aqueducts and reservoirs used for irrigation in Egypt.
1200	Domestic camels in Arabia.
1000–500	Evidence of crop rotation, manuring, and irrigation in India.
600	First windmills used for grinding corn in Persia.
350	Rice cultivation well established in parts of W Africa. Hunting and gathering in the E, central, and S parts of the continent.
c. 200	Use of gears to create ox-driven water wheel for irrigation. Archimedes' screw used for irrigation.
100	Cattle-drawn iron ploughs in use in China.
AD 65	*De Re Rustica/On Rural Things*, Latin treatise on agriculture and irrigation.
500	'Three fields in two years' rotation used in China.
630	Cotton introduced to Arabia.
800	Origins of the 'open field' system in N Europe.
900	Wheeled ploughs in use in W Europe. Horse collar, originating in China, allowed horses to be used for ploughing as well as carrying.
1000	Frisians (NW Netherlands) began to build dykes and reclaim land. Chinese began to introduce Champa rice, which cropped much more quickly than other varieties.
11th C	Three-field system replaced the two-field system in W Europe. Concentration on crop growing.
1126	First artesian wells, at Artois, France.
12th C	Increasing use of water mills and windmills.
12th–14th Cs	Expansion of European population brought more land into cultivation. Crop rotations, manuring, and new crops such as beans and peas helped increase productivity. Feudal system at its height.
13th–14th Cs	Agricultural recession in W Europe with a series of bad harvests, famines, and pestilence.
1347	Black Death killed about a third of the European population.
16th C	Decline of the feudal system in W Europe. More specialist forms of production were now possible with urban markets. Manorial estates and serfdom remained in E Europe. Chinese began cultivation of non-indigenous crops such as corn, sweet potatoes, potatoes, and peanuts.
17th C	Potato introduced into Europe. Norfolk crop rotation became widespread in England, involving wheat, turnips, barley, and then ryegrass/clover.
1700–1845	Agricultural revolution began in England. Two million hectares of farmland in England enclosed. Removal of open fields in other parts of Europe followed.
c. 1701	Jethro Tull developed the seed drill and the horse-drawn hoe.
1747	First sugar extracted from sugar beet in Prussia.
1762	Veterinary school founded in Lyon, France.
1783	First plough factory in England.
1785	Cast-iron ploughshare patented.
1793	Invention of the cotton gin.
1800	Early threshing machines developed in England.
1820s	First nitrates for fertilizer imported from South America.
1830	Reaping machines developed in Scotland and the USA. Steel plough made by John Deere in Illinois, USA.
1840s	Extensive potato blight in Europe.
1850s	Use of clay pipes for drainage well established throughout Europe.
1862	First steam plough used in the Netherlands.
1850–1890s	Major developments in transport and refrigeration technology altered the nature of agricultural markets with crops, dairy products, and wheat being shipped internationally.
1890s	Development of stationary engines for ploughing.
1892	First petrol-driven tractor in the USA.
1921	First attempt at crop dusting with pesticides from an aeroplane near Dayton, Ohio, USA.
1938	First self-propelled grain combine harvester used in the USA.
1942–62	Huge increase in the use of pesticides, later curbed by disquiet about their effects and increasing resistance of pests to standard controls such as DDT.
1945 onwards	Increasing use of scientific techniques, crop specialization and larger scale of farm enterprises.
1995 onwards	Genetic engineering and testing of transgenic crops. Organic farming on the increase in EU countries.
1998	Use of some antibiotics in animal feed banned by EU.

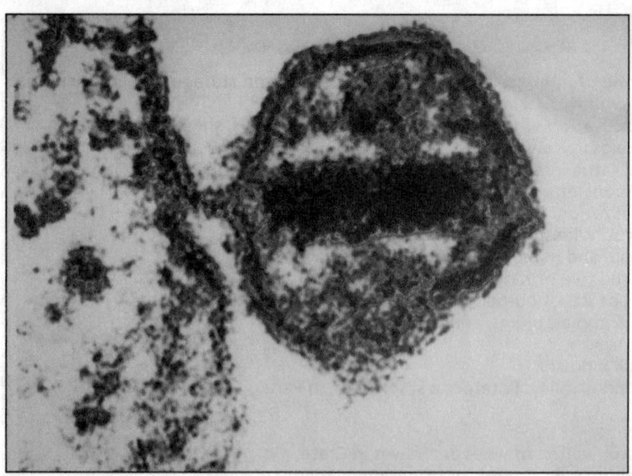

AIDS A 1985 electron micrograph picture of the human immunodeficiency virus (HIV), which causes acquired immune deficiency syndrome (AIDS). The virus, which was discovered in Paris in 1983 and independently in Maryland, USA in 1984, may have originated in African monkeys. *Corbis*

3TC in conjunction with ◊zidovudine (formerly AZT). Though individually the drugs produce little effect, together the 1995 results indicated some success; the levels of virus in the blood were 10 times lower than at the beginning of the trial.

the spread of AIDS Allowing for under-diagnosis, incomplete reporting, and reporting delay, and based on the available data on HIV infections around the world, it is estimated (1997) that approximately 8.4 million AIDS cases in adults and children have occurred worldwide since the pandemic began. The World Health Organization (WHO) estimates that of these cases, which include active AIDS cases and people who have died of AIDS, not HIV infections, more than 70% were in Africa, with about 9% in the USA, 9% in the rest of the Americas, 6% in Asia, and 4% in Europe.

HIV infections In Jan 1997 the WHO estimate of the number of HIV infections worldwide was 21.8 million adults and 830,000 children, a figure likely to rise to 40 million by the year 2000. Worst affected is sub-Saharan Africa (where the virus probably originated) with about 14 million people believed to be HIV-positive.

aikido Japanese art of self-defence (*Budo*, or 'martial way'), one of the ◊martial arts; it was created by Morihei Ueshiba (1883–1969). Many of the twisting and throwing techniques of aikido are derived from the samurai skills of jujitsu, while the striking techniques made with the open palm are similar to those used in karate. The central principle is that of *aiki*, or harmony of *ki* (which may approximately be translated as 'energy'). This can be interpreted physically, in the sense that force is never opposed by force (attacks are met with throws and immobilizations based on circular movements, to return the attacker's own force), and also morally, in that its ethos is essentially nonviolent and noncompetitive. Two main systems of aikido are *uyeshiba*, which is primarily defensive, and *tomiki*, which has developed into a competitive sport.

ailanthus any tree or shrub of the genus *Ailanthus* of the quassia family. All have compound leaves made up of pointed leaflets and clusters of small greenish flowers with an unpleasant smell. The tree of heaven *A. altissima*, native to E Asia, is grown worldwide as an ornamental. It can grow to 30 m/100 ft in height and 1 m/3 ft in diameter.

Ainu aboriginal people of Japan, driven north in the 4th century AD by ancestors of the Japanese. They now number about 25,000, inhabiting Japanese and Russian territory on Sakhalin, Hokkaido, and the Kuril Islands. Their language has no written form, and is unrelated to any other. The Ainu were recognized by the Japanese government as a minority people 1991.

air the mixture of gases making up the Earth's ◊atmosphere.

air conditioning system that controls the state of the air inside a building or vehicle. A complete air-conditioning unit controls the temperature and humidity of the air, removes dust and odours from it, and circulates it by means of a fan.

The air in an air conditioner is cooled by a type of ◊refrigeration unit comprising a compressor and a condenser. The air is cleaned by means of filters and activated charcoal. Moisture is extracted by condensation on cool metal plates. The air can also be heated by electrical wires or, in large systems, pipes carrying hot water or steam; and cool, dry air may be humidified by circulating it over pans of water or through a water spray.

aircraft any aeronautical vehicle capable of flying through the air. It may be lighter than air (supported by buoyancy) or heavier than air (supported by the dynamic action of air on its surfaces). ◊Balloons and ◊airships are lighter-than-air craft. Heavier-than-air craft include the ◊aeroplane, glider, autogiro, and helicopter.

aircraft carrier ocean-going naval vessel with a broad, flat-topped deck for launching and landing military aircraft; a floating military base for warplanes too far from home for refuelling, repairing, reconnaissance, escorting, and attack and defence operations. Aircraft are catapult-launched or take off and land on the flight-deck, a large expanse of unobstructed deck, often fitted with barriers and restraining devices to halt the landing aircraft.

The role of the carrier and its aircraft has included reconnaissance, torpedo, and bomb operations against hostile shipping, antisubmarine warfare, and air support of naval and amphibious operations. Aircraft carriers of the US Navy have formed the equivalent of mobile airfields, replacing fixed, shore-based fields for tactical and strategic attacks against land targets. The trend now seems to be towards antisubmarine warfare, although critics of the carrier emphasize how vulnerable carriers are against submarine and missile attack.

air-cushion vehicle (ACV) craft that is supported by a layer, or cushion, of high-pressure air. The ◊hovercraft is one form of ACV.

Airedale terrier breed of large terrier, about 60 cm/24 in tall, with a wiry red-brown coat and black saddle patch. It originated about 1850 in England, as a cross between the otterhound and Irish and Welsh terriers. The dog takes its name from the Aire and Wharfedale districts of Yorkshire, where it was first bred.

air force a nation's fleet of fighting aircraft and the organization that maintains them.

history A unified air force was established in the UK 1918, Italy 1923, France 1928, Germany 1935 (after repudiating the arms limitations of the Versailles treaty), and the USA 1947 (it began as the Aeronautical Division of the Army Signal Corps 1907, and evolved into the Army's Air Service Division by 1918; by 1926 it was the Air Corps and in World War II the Army Air Force). The main specialized groupings formed during World War I – such as combat, bombing (see ◊bomb), reconnaissance, and transport – were adapted and modified in World War II; activity was extended, with self-contained tactical air forces to meet the needs of ground commanders in the main theatres of land operations and for the attack on and defence of shipping over narrow seas.

From 1945 to 1960 piston-engine aircraft were superseded by jet aircraft. Computerized guidance systems lessened the difference between missile and aircraft, and flights of unlimited duration became possible with air-to-air refuelling. See also ◊Royal Air Force.

airglow faint and variable light in the Earth's atmosphere produced by chemical reactions (the recombination of ionized particles) in the ionosphere.

airlock airtight chamber that allows people to pass between areas of different pressure; also an air bubble in a pipe that impedes fluid flow. An airlock may connect an environment at ordinary pressure and an environment that has high air pressure (such as a submerged caisson used for tunnelling or building dams or bridge foundations).

An airlock may also permit someone wearing breathing apparatus to pass into an airless environment (into water from a submerged submarine or into the vacuum of space from a spacecraft).

air mass large body of air with particular characteristics of temperature and humidity. An air mass forms when air rests over an area long enough to pick up the conditions of that area. When an air mass moves to another area it affects the ◊weather of that area, but its own characteristics become modified in the process. For example, an air mass formed over the Sahara will be hot and dry, becoming cooler as it moves northwards.

air pollution contamination of the atmosphere caused by the discharge, accidental or deliberate, of a wide range of toxic airborne substances. Often the amount of the released substance is relatively high in a certain locality, so the harmful effects become more noticeable. The cost of preventing any discharge of pollutants into the air is prohibitive, so attempts are more usually made to reduce gradually the amount of discharge and to disperse this as quickly as possible by using a very tall chimney, or by intermittent release.

The greatest single cause of air pollution in the UK is the car, which is responsible for 85% of the carbon monoxide and 45% of the oxides of nitrogen present in the atmosphere. The air pollution caused by small particles, which results mainly from vehicle emissions, is a major health risk. ▷*See feature on pp. 858–859.*

air raid aerial attack, usually on a civilian target such as a factory, railway line, or communications centre (see also ◊bomb). Air raids began during World War I with the advent of military aviation, but it was the development of long-range bomber aircraft during World War II that made regular attacks on a large scale possible.

During the ◊Gulf War 1991 the UN coalition forces made thousands of air raids on Baghdad, Iraq, to destroy the Iraqi infrastructure and communications network (some 250,000 civilians were killed).

The first air raids in World War I were carried out by airships, since only they had the necessary range, but later in the war aeroplanes were also used as their performance improved. Bombing was generally indiscriminate due to the difficulty of accurately aiming the primitive bombs in use at the time. Despite the relatively limited nature of these early raids, there were 4,830 British and 2,589 German casualties in air raids 1914–18.

Many thousands died in attacks by both sides in World War II, notably the Blitz on London and other British cities 1940–41 and the firebombing of Dresden Feb 1945, and air raids by both bombers and rockets have been a standard military tactic ever since.

air sac in birds, a thin-walled extension of the lungs. There are nine of these and they extend into the abdomen and bones, effectively increasing lung capacity. In mammals, it is another name for the alveoli in the lungs, and in some insects, for widenings of the trachea. The sacs subdivide into further air spaces which partially replace the marrow in many of the bird's bones. The air space in these bones assists flight by making them lighter.

airship or ***dirigible*** any aircraft that is lighter than air and power-driven, consisting of an elliptical balloon that forms the streamlined envelope or hull and has below it the propulsion system (propellers), steering mechanism, and space for crew, passengers, and/or cargo. The balloon section is filled with lighter-than-air gas, either the nonflammable helium or, before helium was industrially available in large enough quantities, the easily ignited and flammable hydrogen. The envelope's form is maintained by internal pressure in the nonrigid (blimp) and semirigid (in which the nose and tail sections have a metal framework connected by a rigid keel) types. The rigid type (zeppelin) maintains its form using an internal metal framework. Airships have been used for luxury travel, polar exploration, warfare, and advertising.

Rigid airships predominated from about 1900 until 1940. As the technology developed, the size of the envelope was increased from about 45 m/150 ft to more than 245 m/800 ft for the last two zeppelins built. In 1852 the first successful airship was designed and flown by Henri ◊Giffard of France. In 1900 the first successful rigid type was designed by Count (*Graf*) Ferdinand von ◊Zeppelin of Germany. Airships were used by both sides during World War I, but they were not seriously used for military purposes after that as they were largely replaced by aeroplanes.

In 1919 the first nonstop transatlantic round trip flight was completed by a rigid airship, the British R34. In the early 1920s a large source of helium was discovered in the USA and was substituted for hydrogen, reducing the danger of fire. In the 1920s and early 1930s luxury zeppelin services took passengers across the Atlantic faster and in greater comfort than the great ocean liners. The successful German airship *Graf Zeppelin*, completed 1927, was used for transatlantic, cruise, and round-the-world trips. In 1929 it travelled 32,000 km/20,000 mi around the world. It was retired and dismantled after years of trouble-free service, and was replaced by the *Hindenburg* 1936.

Several airship accidents were caused by structural break-up during storms and by fire. The last and best known was the *Hindenburg*, which had been forced to return to the use of flammable hydrogen by a US embargo on helium; it exploded and burned at the mooring mast at Lakehurst, New Jersey, USA, 1937. The last and largest rigid airship was the German *Graf Zeppelin II*, completed just before World War II; it never saw commercial service but was used as a reconnaissance station off the English coast early in the war (it was the only zeppelin used in the war) and was soon retired and dismantled. Rigid airships, predominant from World War II, are no longer in use but blimps continued in use for coastal and antisubmarine patrol until the 1960s, and advertising blimps can be seen to this day. Recent interest in all types of airship has surfaced (including some with experimental and nontraditional shapes for the envelopes), since they are fuel-efficient, quiet, and capable of lifting enormous loads over great distances.

Airy George Biddell 1801–1892. English astronomer. He installed a transit telescope at the Royal Observatory at Greenwich, England, and accurately measured ◊Greenwich Mean Time by the stars as they crossed the meridian. He began the distribution of Greenwich time signals by telegraph, and Greenwich Mean Time as measured by Airy's telescope was adopted as legal time in Britain 1880.

Aix-en-Provence city in the *département* of Bouches-du-Rhône, France, 29 km/18 mi N of Marseille; population (1990) 126,800. It is the capital of Provence and dates from Roman times. It has a Gothic cathedral and a university founded 1409. The painter Paul Cézanne was born here.

Ajaccio capital and second largest port of Corsica; population (1990) 59,300. Founded by the Genoese 1492, it was the birthplace of Napoleon; it has been French since 1768.

Ajax Greek hero in Homer's *Iliad*. Son of Telamon, King of Salamis, he was second only to Achilles among the Greek heroes in the Trojan War. He fought ◊Hector single-handed, defended the ships, and killed many Trojans. According to subsequent Greek legends, Ajax went mad with jealousy when ◊Agamemnon awarded the armour of the dead Achilles to ◊Odysseus. He later committed suicide in shame.

Ajman smallest of the seven states that make up the ◊United Arab Emirates; area 250 sq km/96 sq mi; population (1985) 64,318.

Ajmer city in Rajasthan, India; population (1991) 402,000. Situated in a deep valley in the Aravalli Mountains, it is a commercial and industrial centre, notably of cotton manufacture. It has many ancient remains, including a Jain temple.

ajolote Mexican reptile of the genus *Bipes*. It and several other tropical burrowing species are placed in the Amphisbaenia, a group separate from lizards and snakes among the Squamata. Unlike the others, however, which have no legs, it has a pair of short but well-developed front legs. In line with its burrowing habits, the skull is very solid, the eyes small, and external ears absent. The scales are arranged in rings, giving the body a wormlike appearance.

Akbar Jalal ud-Din Muhammad 1542–1605. Mogul emperor of N India from 1556, when he succeeded his father Humayun. He gradually established his rule throughout N India. He is considered the greatest of the Mogul emperors, and the firmness and wisdom of his rule won him the title 'Guardian of Mankind'; he was a patron of the arts.

à Kempis Thomas see ◊Thomas à Kempis, religious writer.

Akhenaton or ***Ikhnaton*** King (pharaoh) of ancient Egypt of the 18th dynasty (c. 1353–1335 BC), who may have ruled jointly for a time with his father Amenhotep III. He developed the cult of the Sun, Aton, rather than the rival cult of Amen, and removed his capital to ◊Akhetaton. Akhenaton's favourite wife was Nefertiti, and two of their six daughters were married to his successors Smenkhkare and Tutankaton (later known as Tutankhamen).

Akhetaton capital of ancient Egypt established by the monotheistic pharaoh ◊Akhenaton as the centre for his cult of the Aton, the sun's disc; it is the modern Tell el Amarna 300 km/190 mi S of Cairo. Akhenaton's palace had formal enclosed gardens. After his death it was abandoned, and the Amarna tablets, clay tablets with cuneiform inscriptions found in the ruins in the 1880s, were probably discarded by his officials.

Akhmatova Anna. Pen name of Anna Andreevna Gorenko 1889–1966. Russian poet. She was a leading member of the Acmeist movement in Russian poetry. Among her works are the cycle *Requiem* 1963 (written in the 1930s), which deals with the Stalinist terror, and *Poem Without a Hero* 1962 (begun 1940).

Akihito 1933– . Emperor of Japan from 1989, succeeding his father Hirohito (Shōwa). His reign is called the Heisei ('achievement of universal peace') era.

Unlike previous crown princes, Akihito was educated alongside commoners at the elite Gakushuin school and in 1959 he married Michiko Shoda (1934–), the daughter of a flour-company president. Their three children, the Oxford University-educated Crown Prince Hiro, Prince Aya, and Princess Nori, were raised at Akihito's home instead of being reared by tutors and chamberlains in a separate imperial dormitory.

Akkad northern Semitic people who conquered the Sumerians 2350 BC and ruled Mesopotamia. Their language was Simitic (old Akkadian). Akkad was also the northern of the two provinces into which Babylonia was divided. The ancient city of Akkad in central Mesopotamia, founded by ◊Sargon I, was an imperial centre in the late 3rd millennium BC; the site is unidentified, but it was on the river Euphrates somewhere near Babylon.

Akko formerly ***Acre*** seaport in NW Israel, situated on the Mediterranean Sea; population (1994) 45,300. Taken by the Crusaders 1104, it was captured by Saladin 1187 and retaken by Richard the Lionheart 1191. Napoleon failed in a siege 1799. British field marshal Allenby captured the port 1918. From being part of British mandated Palestine, it became part of Israel 1948.

Akron (Greek 'summit') city in Ohio, USA, on the Cuyahoga River, 56 km/35 mi SE of Cleveland; population (1992) 223,600. Known as the 'Rubber Capital of the World', it is home to the headquarters of several major tyre and rubber companies, although production there had ended by 1982.

Aksum or ***Axum*** ancient Greek-influenced Semitic kingdom that flourished in the 1st–6th centuries AD and covered a large part of modern Ethiopia as well as the Sudan. The ruins of its capital, also called Aksum, lie NW of Aduwa, but the site has been developed as a modern city.

Aktyubinsk industrial city (chemicals, metals, electrical equipment) in Kazakhstan; population (1990) 267,000. Established 1869, it expanded after the opening of the Trans-Caspian railway 1905. It is the capital of Aktyubinsk Oblast.

al- for Arabic names beginning *al-*, see rest of name; for example, for 'al-Fatah', see ◊Fatah, al-.

Alabama state in S USA; nicknamed Heart of Dixie/Cotton State
area 134,700 sq km/51,994 sq mi

Alabama

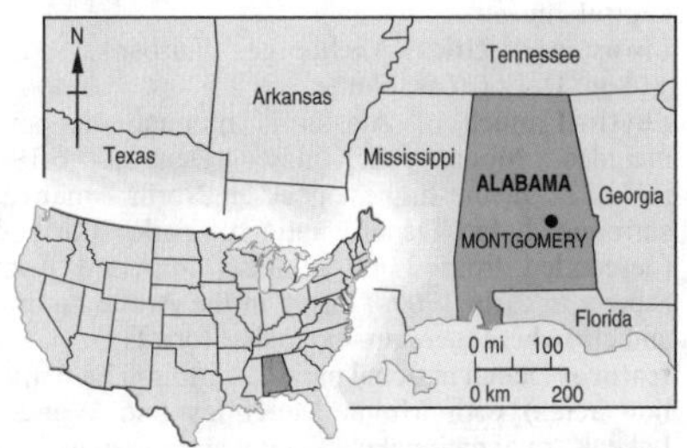

Akhmatova A portrait of the Russian poet Anna Akhmatova. Her works, such as *Requiem*, were severely criticized by the state. Her work was banned, and she was expelled from the Union of Writers 1946. *Corbis*

capital Montgomery
towns and cities Birmingham, Mobile, Huntsville, Tuscaloosa
physical the state comprises the Cumberland Plateau in the N; the Black Belt, or Canebrake, cotton-growing country in the centre; and S of this, the coastal plain of Piny Woods. The Alabama River is the largest in the state
features Alabama and Tennessee rivers; Appalachian Mountains; De Soto Caverns, onyx caves used as a Native American burial ground 2,000 years ago; US Space Camp, with NASA laboratories and shuttle test sites, at Huntsville
industries cotton (still important though no longer prime crop); soya beans, peanuts, wood products, coal, livestock, poultry, iron, chemicals, textiles, paper
population (1990) 4,040,600
famous people Hank Aaron, Tallulah Bankhead, Nat King Cole, W C Handy, Helen Keller, Joe Louis, Willie Mays, Jesse Owens, Leroy 'Satchel' Paige, George C Wallace, Booker T Washington, Hank Williams
history first settled by the French in the early 18th century, it was ceded to Britain 1763, passed to the USA 1783, and became a state 1819. It was one of the ◊Confederate States in the American Civil War, and Montgomery was the first capital of the Confederacy. Birmingham became the South's leading industrial centre in the late 19th century. Alabama was in the forefront of the civil-rights movement in the 1950s and 1960s: Martin Luther ◊King led a successful boycott of segregated Montgomery buses 1955; school integration began in the early 1960s despite the opposition of Governor George C Wallace; the 1965 Selma march resulted in federal voting-rights legislation.

alabaster naturally occurring fine-grained white or light-coloured translucent form of ◊gypsum, often streaked or mottled. A soft material, it is easily carved, but seldom used for outdoor sculpture.

Alain-Fournier pen name of Henri-Alban Fournier 1886–1914. French novelist. His haunting semi-autobiographical fantasy *Le Grand Meaulnes/The Lost Domain* 1913 was a cult novel of the 1920s and 1930s. His life is intimately recorded in his correspondence with his brother-in-law Jacques Rivière. He was killed in action on the Meuse in World War I.

Alamein, El, Battles of in World War II, two decisive battles in the western desert, N Egypt. In the First Battle of El Alamein 1–27 July 1942, the British 8th Army under ◊Auchinleck held off the German and Italian forces under ◊Rommel. In the

'It may almost be said, 'Before Alamein we never had a victory. After Alamein we never had a defeat.''

On El Alamein
Winston Churchill
The Second World War 1948–54

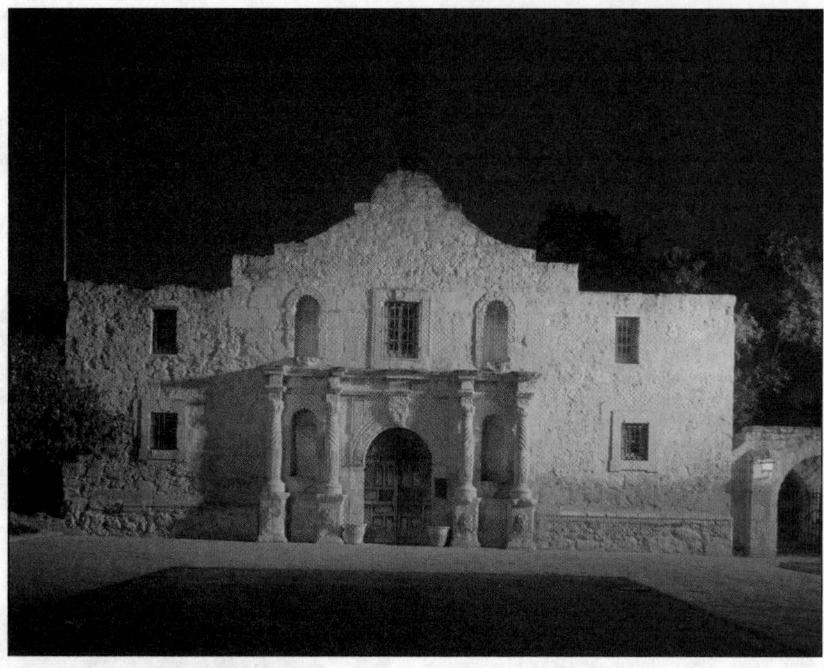
Alamo, the The Franciscan mission of the Alamo in San Antonio, Texas, USA. The defeat of the US defenders of the Alamo in 1836 – they survived for 11 days though outnumbered 20 to 1 – marked a turning point in the struggle for control of Texas, rousing a deep resentment against Mexican claims to the region. *Corbis*

Second Battle of El Alamein 23 Oct–4 Nov 1942, ◊Montgomery defeated Rommel.

The first battle was inconclusive but strategically vital: Rommel attacked the British line in a series of engagements, but Auchinleck kept him at bay. Neither side can be said to have won, but the British had the strategic advantage of short supply lines and so could reinforce faster than the Germans.

Montgomery began the second battle with a diversionary attack in the south to draw Axis forces into the area so that the main attack in the north could create a gap for the British armoured divisions to pass through German minefields. Progress was slow however and Montgomery changed tactics, constantly switching the main emphasis of his attack to wear down Rommel's front line. The decisive phase of the battle came with an Australian attack along the coastal road 26 Oct which diverted Axis forces while Montgomery launched a fresh attack further south which developed into a major tank battle. By 3 Nov Rommel had only 30 serviceable tanks in action and on the following day began organizing his withdrawal. He was able to escape, as the British were hampered by heavy rain and a shortage of fuel, but this was a crushing blow for the Axis campaign in North Africa.

Alamo, the mission fortress in San Antonio, Texas, USA. It was besieged 23 Feb–6 March 1836 by ◊Santa Anna and 4,000 Mexicans; they killed the garrison of about 180, including Davy ◊Crockett and Jim Bowie (1796–1836).

Alanbrooke Alan Francis Brooke, 1st Viscount Alanbrooke 1883–1963. British army officer. He was Chief of Staff in World War II and largely responsible for the strategy that led to the German defeat. Alanbrooke served in the artillery in World War I, and in World War II, as commander of the 2nd Corps 1939–40, did much to aid the extrication of the British Expeditionary Force from Dunkirk. He was commander in chief of the Home Forces 1940–41 and chief of the Imperial General Staff 1941–46.

Alaska

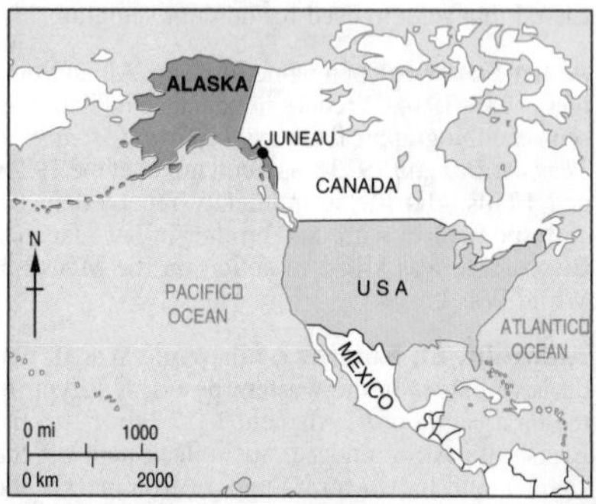

Åland Islands (Finnish ***Ahvenanmaa*** 'land of waters') group of some 6,000 islands in the Baltic Sea, at the southern extremity of the Gulf of Bothnia; area 1,481 sq km/572 sq mi; population (1992) 25,000. Only 80 are inhabited; the largest island has a small town, Mariehamn. The main sectors of the island economy are tourism, agriculture, and shipping.
history The islands were Swedish until 1809, when they came (with Finland) under Russian control. The Swedes tried, unsuccessfully, to recover the islands at the time of the Russian Revolution 1917. In 1921 the League of Nations ruled that the islands remain under Finnish sovereignty, be demilitarized, and granted autonomous status. Although the islands' assembly voted for union with Sweden 1945, the 1921 declaration remains valid. The islands became a member of the Nordic Council 1970.

Alania (formerly ***North Ossetia***) autonomous republic of SW Russian Federation. A new constitution was adopted 1994 and the republic took its former name of Alania
area 8,000 sq km/3,088 sq mi
capital Vladikavkaz (formerly Ordzhonikidze)
physical in the Caucasus, between the Russian Federation and Georgia
industries mining and metallurgy, maize processing, timber and woodworking, textiles, building materials, distilleries, food processing
population (1994) 650,400 (53% Ossetian)
history annexed by Russia 1774; an autonomous region 1924; an autonomous republic from 1936. See ◊Ossetia.

Alaric c. 370–410. King of the Visigoths. In 396 he invaded Greece and retired with much booty to Illyria. In 401 and 408 he invaded Italy, and in 410 captured and sacked Rome, but died the same year on his way to invade Sicily.

Alaska largest state of the USA, on the northwest extremity of North America, separated from the lower 48 states by British Columbia; nickname Last Frontier; territories include ◊Aleutian Islands
total area 1,530,700 sq km/591,004 sq mi
land area 1,478,457 sq km/570,833 sq mi
capital Juneau
towns and cities Anchorage, Fairbanks, Fort Yukon, Holy Cross, Nome
physical much of Alaska is mountainous and includes Mount McKinley (Denali), 6,194 m/20,322 ft, the highest peak in North America, surrounded by Denali national park. Caribou (descended from 2,000 reindeer imported from Siberia in early 1900s) thrive in the Arctic tundra, and elsewhere there are extensive forests
features Denali national park (2.4 million ha/6 million acres) with Mount McKinley and Wonder Lake; Katmai national park, a volcanic area, including Mount Katmai, which erupted 1912 and formed the Valley of Ten Thousand Smokes; Wrangell-St Alias national park, the largest in the USA
products oil, natural gas, coal, copper, iron, gold, tin, fur, salmon fisheries and canneries, lumber
population (1990) 550,000; including 9% American Indians, Aleuts, and Inuits
history various groups of Indians crossed the Bering land bridge about 15,000 years ago; the Inuit began to settle the Arctic coast from Siberia about 2000 BC; the Aleuts settled the Aleutian archipelago about 1000 BC. The first European to visit Alaska was Vitus Bering 1741. Alaska was a Russian colony from 1744 until purchased by the USA 1867 for $7,200,000; gold was discovered five years later. It became a state 1959.

albacore name loosely applied to several species of fishes found in warm regions of the Atlantic and Pacific oceans, in particular to a large tuna, *Thunnus alalunga*, and to several other species of the mackerel family.

Albania country in SE Europe, bounded N by Yugoslavia, E by the Former Yugoslav Republic of Macedonia, S by Greece, and W and SW by the Adriatic Sea. *See country box opposite.*

Albanian people of Albanian culture from Albania and the surrounding area. There are both Christian and Muslim Albanians, the latter having been converted by the Ottoman Turks. Albanians comprise the majority of Kosovo in Serbia and are in conflict with the Serbs, for whom the province is historically and culturally significant.

The Albanian language belongs to a separate group within the Indo-European family and has an estimated 3–4 million speakers.

Alban, St first Christian martyr in England. In 793 King Offa founded a monastery on the site of Alban's martyrdom, around which the city of St Albans grew up. His feast day is 20 June.

Albany capital of New York State, USA, situated on the west bank of the Hudson River, about 225 km/140 mi N of New York City; population (1992) 99,700. With Schenectady and Troy it forms a metropolitan area, population (1980) 794,298.

albatross large seabird, genus *Diomedea*, with long narrow wings adapted for gliding and a wingspan of up to 3 m/10 ft, mainly found in the southern hemisphere. It belongs to the family Diomedeidae, order Procellariiformes, the same group as petrels and shearwaters. The external nostrils of birds in this order are more or less tubular, and the bills are hooked. Albatrosses feed mainly on squid and fish, and nest on remote oceanic islands. Albatrosses can cover enormous distances, flying as far as 16,100 km/10,000 mi in 33 days, or up to 640 km/600 mi in one day. They continue flying even after dark. Albatrosses are becoming increasingly rare, and are in danger of extinction.

albedo the fraction of the incoming light reflected by a body such as a planet. A body with a high

albatross The wandering albatross *Diomedea exulans* is the largest member of the albatross family. The young are cared for by both parents for almost a year, so breeding takes place every two years. Courtship involves elaborate displays of dancing, bill-rubbing, and wing-spreading.

ALBANIA
Republic of

national name *Republika e Shqipërisë*
area 28,748 sq km/11,097 sq mi
capital Tiranë (Tirana)
major towns/cities Shkodër, Elbasan, Vlorë, Korçë
major ports Durrës
physical features mainly mountainous, with rivers flowing E–W, and a narrow coastal plain
head of state Rexhep Mejdani from 1997
head of government Fatos Nano from 1997
political system emergent democracy
administrative divisions 26 districts
political parties Democratic Party of Albania (PDS; formerly the Democratic Party: DP), moderate, market-oriented; Socialist Party of Albania (PSS), ex-communist; Human Rights Union (HMU), Greek minority party
population 3,441,000 (1995 est)
population growth rate 0.9% (1990–95); 1.1% (2000–05)
ethnic distribution 90% of Albanian, non-Slavic, descent; 8% ethnic Greek (concentrated in the S)
life expectancy 70 (men), 75 (women)
literacy rate 85%
languages Albanian, Greek
religions Muslim, Orthodox, Roman Catholic
currency lek
GDP (US $) 1.75 billion (1994)
growth rate 7.4% (1994)
exports crude oil, bitumen, chrome, iron ore, nickel, coal, copper wire, tobacco, fruit, vegetables

HISTORY
2000 BC Part of Illyria.
168 BC Conquest of Illyria by Romans.
AD 395 Became part of the Byzantine Empire.
6th–14th Cs Byzantine decline exploited by Serbs, Normans, Slavs, Bulgarians, and Venetians.
1381 Ottoman invasion of Albania followed by years of resistance to Turkish rule.
1468 Resistance led by Skanderbeg largely collapsed. Albania passed to Ottoman Empire.
15th–16th Cs Thousands fled to southern Italy to escape Ottoman rule; over half of the rest of the population converted to Islam.
1878 Foundation of Albanian League promoted emergence of nationalism.
1912 Achieved independence from Turkey as a result of the First Balkan War and the end of the Ottoman Empire in Europe.
1914–20 Occupied by Italy.
1925 Declared itself a republic.
1928–39 Monarchy of King Zog.
1939 Italian occupation led by Benito Mussolini.
1943–44 Under German rule following Italian surrender.
1946 Proclaimed the Communist People's Republic of Albania, with Enver Hoxha as premier.
1949 Developed close links with Joseph Stalin in the USSR and entered Comecon (Council for Mutual Economic Assistance).
1961 Broke with USSR in wake of Nikita Khrushchev's denunciation of Stalin, and withdrew from Comecon.
1978 Severed diplomatic links with China.
1982 Hoxha made Ramiz Alia head of state.
1985 Death of Hoxha. Alia became head of the Party of Labour of Albania (PLA).
1987 Normal diplomatic relations restored with Canada, Greece, and West Germany.
1988 Attendance of conference of Balkan states for the first time since the 1930s.
1990 One-party system abandoned in face of popular protest; first opposition party formed.
1991 Communist PLA won first multiparty elections; Alia re-elected president. PLA renamed PSS.
1992 Presidential elections won by Sali Berisha of the Democratic Party (DP). Alia and other former communist officials charged with corruption and abuse of power. Totalitarian and communist parties banned.
1993 Open conflict began between ethnic Greeks and Albanians, followed by a purge of ethnic Greeks from senior positions in the civil service and army. Alia sentenced to eight years' imprisonment. DP renamed the PDS.
1995 Alia released from prison following appeal court ruling. Communist-era MPs and Communist Party officials banned from national and local elections until 2002.
1996 Ruling PDS accused of ballot-rigging following overwhelming victory in elections.
1997 Anti-government riots followed collapse of bogus pyramid 'investment' schemes. Southern Albania fell under rebel control. General election was won by the PSS; Rexhep Mejdani was elected president and ex-communist Fatos Nano became prime minister at the head of a broad coalition.

SEE ALSO Byzantine Empire; Ottoman Empire

albedo, near 1, is very bright, while a body with a low albedo, near 0, is dark. The Moon has an average albedo of 0.12, Venus 0.76, Earth 0.37.

Albee Edward Franklin 1928– . US dramatist. His internationally performed plays are associated with the Theatre of the ◊Absurd and include *The Zoo Story* 1960, *The American Dream* 1961, *Who's Afraid of Virginia Woolf?* 1962 (his most successful play; also filmed with Elizabeth Taylor and Richard Burton as the quarrelling, alcoholic, academic couple 1966), and *Tiny Alice* 1965. *A Delicate Balance* 1966 and *Seascape* 1975 both won Pulitzer prizes, and *Three Tall Women* 1994 marked his return to critical acclaim.

> *I have a fine sense of the ridiculous, but no sense of humour.*
>
> **Edward Albee** *Who's Afraid of Virginia Woolf?*

Albert The Consort photographed with Queen Victoria in 1854; he received the title 'Prince Consort' in 1857. Victoria adored him, but government ministers resented his involvement in politics, and the British public mistrusted him because of his German origins. After his death the Queen was inconsolable and spent the next 40 years as a virtual recluse. *Corbis*

Albéniz Isaac 1860–1909. Spanish nationalist composer and pianist. His works include numerous zarzuelas (Spanish musical dramas) and operas, the orchestral suites *Española* 1886 and *Catalonia* 1899–1908 (with the assistance of Paul Dukas), and 250 piano works including the *Iberia* suite 1906–09.

Albert Prince Consort 1819–1861. Husband of British Queen ◊Victoria from 1840. A patron of the arts, science, and industry, Albert was the second son of the Duke of Saxe Coburg-Gotha and first cousin to Queen Victoria, whose chief adviser he became. He planned the Great Exhibition of 1851; the profit was used to buy the sites in London of all the South Kensington museums and colleges and the Royal Albert Hall, built 1871. He died of typhoid. The queen never fully recovered from his premature death, and remained in mourning for him for the rest of her life.

Albert I 1875–1934. King of the Belgians from 1909, the younger son of Philip, Count of Flanders, and the nephew of Leopold II. In 1900 he married Duchess Elisabeth of Bavaria. In World War I he commanded the Allied army that retook the Belgian coast 1918 and re-entered Brussels in triumph on 22 Nov.

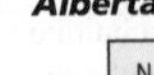

Alberta province of W Canada
area 661,200 sq km/255,223 sq mi
capital Edmonton
towns and cities Calgary, Lethbridge, Medicine Hat, Red Deer
physical Rocky Mountains; dry, treeless prairie in the centre and S; towards the N this merges into a zone of poplar, then mixed forest. The valley of the Peace River is the most northerly farming land in Canada (except for Inuit pastures), and there are good grazing lands in the foothills of the Rockies
features Banff, Elk Island, Jasper, Waterton Lake, and Wood Buffalo national parks; annual Calgary stampede; extensive dinosaur finds near Drumheller
industries coal; wheat, barley, oats, sugar beet in the S; more than a million head of cattle; oil and natural gas; lumbering
population (1991) 2,501,400
history in the 17th century much of its area was part of a grant to the ◊Hudson's Bay Company for the fur trade, and the first trading posts were established in the late 18th century. The grant was bought by Canada 1869, and Alberta became a province 1905. After an oil strike in 1947, Alberta became a major oil and gas producer.

Alberti Leon Battista 1404–1472. Italian Renaissance architect and theorist. He set out the principles of Classical architecture, as well as covering their modification for Renaissance practice, in *De re aedificatoria/On Architecture*, which he started 1452 and worked on until his death (published 1485; translated as *Ten Books on Architecture* 1955). Alberti's designs for the churches of San Sebastiano, begun 1460, and San Andrea 1470 (both in Mantua) – the only two extant buildings entirely of his design – are bold in their use of Classical language but to a certain extent anticipate ◊Mannerism.

Albertus Magnus, St 1206–1280. German scholar of Christian theology, philosophy (especially Aristotelian), natural science, chemistry, and physics. He was known as 'doctor universalis' because of the breadth of his knowledge.

He studied at Bologna and Padua, and entered the Dominican order 1223. He taught at Cologne and

Alberta

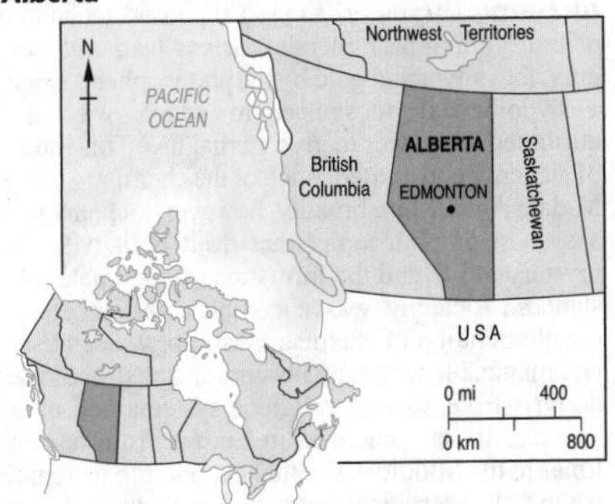

"The voice of the people is the voice of God."

ALCUIN
Letter to Emperor Charlemagne AD 800

lectured from 1245 at Paris University. St Thomas ◊Aquinas was his pupil there, and followed him to Cologne 1248.

Albigenses heretical sect of Christians (also known as the ◊Cathars) who flourished in S France near Albi and Toulouse during the 11th–13th centuries. They adopted the Manichean belief in the duality of good and evil and pictured Jesus as being a rebel against the cruelty of an omnipotent God. The Albigenses showed a consistently anti-Catholic attitude with distinctive sacraments, especially the *consolamentum*, or baptism of the spirit. An inquisition was initiated against the Albigenses 1184 by Pope Lucius III and a crusade (1208–29) was launched against them under the elder Simon de Montfort. Thousands were killed before the movement was crushed 1244.

albinism rare hereditary condition in which the body has no tyrosinase, one of the enzymes that form the pigment ◊melanin, normally found in the skin, hair, and eyes. As a result, the hair is white and the skin and eyes are pink. The skin and eyes are abnormally sensitive to light, and vision is often impaired. The condition occurs among all human and animal groups.

Albion ancient name for Britain used by the Greeks and Romans. It was mentioned by Pytheas of Massilia (4th century BC), and is probably of Celtic origin, but the Romans, having in mind the white cliffs of Dover, assumed it to be derived from *albus* (white).

Albright Madeleine 1937– . Czech-born US diplomat and Democrat politician, secretary of state from 1997. She was a university professor of international affairs and an advisor to leading Democrat politicians from the early 1970s onwards. In 1993 she was appointed US ambassador to the United Nations by President Bill Clinton, and in 1997 she became secretary of state – the first female to hold the post.

albumin or ***albumen*** any of a group of sulphur-containing ◊proteins. The best known is in the form of egg white; others occur in milk, and as a major component of serum. They are soluble in water and dilute salt solutions, and are coagulated by heat.

The presence of serum albumin in the urine, termed albuminuria or proteinuria, may be indicative of kidney or heart disease.

Albuquerque largest city of New Mexico, USA, situated E of the Rio Grande, in the Pueblo district; population (1992) 398,500. Founded 1706, it was named after Afonso de Albuquerque. It is a resort and industrial centre, specializing in electronic products and aerospace equipment.

Albuquerque Afonso de 1453–1515. Viceroy and founder of the Portuguese East Indies with strongholds in Ceylon, Goa, and Malacca 1508–15. In 1515 the king of Portugal recalled him, putting Albuquerque's personal enemy Lopes Soares in his place. He died at sea on the way home when his ship *Flor del Mar* was lost between Malaysia and India.

alcázar (Arabic 'fortress') any one of several fortified palaces built by the Moors in Spain. The one in Toledo was defended by the Nationalists against the Republicans for 71 days in 1936 during the Spanish ◊Civil War.

Alcazarquivir, Battle of battle 4 Aug 1578 between the forces of Sebastian, King of Portugal (1554–1578), and those of the Berber kingdom of Fez. Sebastian's death on the field of battle paved the way for the incorporation of Portugal into the Spanish kingdom of Philip II.

alchemy (Arabic *al-Kimya*) supposed technique of transmuting base metals, such as lead and mercury, into silver and gold by the philosopher's stone, a hypothetical substance, to which was also attributed the power to give eternal life. This aspect of alchemy constituted much of the chemistry of the Middle Ages. More broadly, however, alchemy was a system of philosophy that dealt both with the mystery of life and the formation of inanimate substances. Alchemy was a complex and indefinite conglomeration of chemistry, astrology, occultism, and magic, blended with obscure and abstruse ideas derived from various religious systems and other sources. It was practised in Europe from ancient times to the Middle Ages but later fell into disrepute when ◊chemistry and ◊physics developed.

Alcibiades 450–404 BC. Athenian politician and general. He organized a confederation of Peloponnesian states against Sparta that collapsed after the battle of Mantinea 418 BC. Although accused of profaning the ◊Eleusinian Mysteries, he was eventually accepted as the commander of the Athenian fleet against Sicily 415 BC. He was recalled to Athens but escaped to Sparta. After losing their confidence, he resumed command of the Athenian fleet and achieved several victories, such as Cyzicus 410 BC, before his forces were defeated at Notium 406. He was murdered in Phrygia by the Persians.

Alcock John William 1892–1919. British aviator. On 14 June 1919, he and Arthur Whitten Brown (1886–1948) made the first nonstop transatlantic flight, from Newfoundland to Ireland.

alcohol any member of a group of organic chemical compounds characterized by the presence of one or more aliphatic OH (hydroxyl) groups in the molecule, and which form ◊esters with acids. The main uses of alcohols are as solvents for gums, resins, lacquers, and varnishes; in the making of dyes; for essential oils in perfumery; and for medical substances in pharmacy. The alcohol produced naturally in the ◊fermentation process and consumed as part of alcoholic beverages is called ◊ethanol.

Alcohols may be liquids or solids, according to the size and complexity of the molecule. The five simplest alcohols form a series in which the number of carbon and hydrogen atoms increases progressively, each one having an extra CH_2 (methylene) group in the molecule: methanol or wood spirit (methyl alcohol, CH_3OH); ethanol (ethyl alcohol, C_2H_5OH); propanol (propyl alcohol, C_3H_7OH); butanol (butyl alcohol, C_4H_9OH); and pentanol (amyl alcohol, $C_5H_{11}OH$). The lower alcohols are liquids that mix with water; the higher alcohols, such as pentanol, are oily liquids immiscible with water; and the highest are waxy solids – for example, hexadecanol (cetyl alcohol, $C_{16}H_{33}OH$) and melissyl alcohol ($C_{30}H_{61}OH$), which occur in sperm-whale oil and beeswax respectively. Alcohols containing the CH_2OH group are primary; those containing CHOH are secondary; while those containing COH are tertiary.

alcoholic beverage any drink containing alcohol, often used for its intoxicating effects. ◊Ethanol (ethyl alcohol), a colourless liquid (C_2H_5OH) is the basis of all common intoxicants. Foods rich in sugars, such as grapes, produce this alcohol as a natural product of decay, called fermentation.

Wines, ciders, and sherry contain alcohol produced by direct fermentation with yeasts of the sugar in the fruit forming the basis of the drink.

Malt liquors are beers, ales, and stouts, in which the starch of the grain is converted to sugar by malting, and the sugar then fermented into alcohol by yeasts. Fermented drinks contain less than 20% alcohol.

Spirits are distilled from malted liquors or wines, and can contain up to 55% alcohol. Examples include whisky, rum, and brandy.

When consumed, alcohol is rapidly absorbed from the stomach and upper intestine and affects nearly every tissue, particularly the central nervous system. Tests have shown that the feeling of elation usually associated with drinking alcoholic liquors is caused by the loss of inhibitions through removal of the restraining influences of the higher cerebral centres. It also results in dilatation of the blood vessels, including those of the skin. The resulting loss of heat from the skin causes the body to cool, although the drinker feels warm. A concentration of 0.15% alcohol in the blood causes mild intoxication; 0.3% definite drunkenness and partial loss of consciousness; 0.6% endangers life.

Alcoholics Anonymous (AA) voluntary self-help organization established 1934 in the USA to combat alcoholism; branches now exist in many other countries, including the UK.

alcoholism dependence on alcohol. It is characterized as an illness when consumption of alcohol interferes with normal physical or emotional health. Excessive alcohol consumption, whether through sustained ingestion or irregular drinking bouts or binges, may produce physical and psychological addiction and lead to nutritional and emotional disorders. Long-term heavy consumption of alcohol leads to diseases of the heart, liver, and peripheral nerves. Support groups include Alcoholics Anonymous.

alcohol strength measure of the amount of alcohol in a drink. Wine is measured as the percentage volume of alcohol at 20°C; spirits in litres of alcohol at 20°C, although the percentage volume measure is also commonly used. A 75 cl bottle at 40% volume is equivalent to 0.3 litres of alcohol. See also ◊proof spirit.

Alcott Louisa May 1832–1888. US author. Her children's classic *Little Women* 1869 drew on her own home circumstances; the principal character Jo was a partial self-portrait. Sequels to *Little Women* were *Good Wives* 1869, *Little Men* 1871, and *Jo's Boys* 1886.

Alcuin (Flaccus Albinus Alcuinus) 735–804. English scholar. Born in York, he went to Rome 780, and in 782 took up residence at Charlemagne's court in Aachen. From 796 he was abbot of St Martin at Tours. He disseminated Anglo-Saxon scholarship, organized education and learning in the Frankish empire, gave a strong impulse to the Carolingian Renaissance, and was a prominent member of Charlemagne's academy.

Aldebaran or ***Alpha Tauri*** brightest star in the constellation Taurus and the 14th brightest star in the night sky; it marks the eye of the 'bull'. Aldebaran is a red giant 60 light years away, shining with a true luminosity of about 100 times that of the Sun.

Aldeburgh small town and coastal resort in Suffolk, England; population (1991) 2,700. It is the site of the Aldeburgh Festival, annual music festival founded by the English composer Benjamin ◊Britten, and is also the home of the Britten–Pears School for Advanced Musical Studies.

Aldeburgh Festival annual festival of operas and other concerts, established 1948 at Aldeburgh, Suffolk. The events have centred on the works of

alcohol The systematic naming of simple straight-chain organic molecules.

Alkane	Alcohol	Aldehyde	Ketone	Carboxylic acid	Alkene
CH_4 methane	CH_3OH methanol	HCHO methanal	—	HCO_2H methanoic acid	—
CH_3CH_3 ethane	CH_3CH_2OH ethanol	CH_3CHO ethanal	—	CH_3CO_2H ethanoic acid	CH_2CH_2 ethene
$CH_3CH_2CH_3$ propane	$CH_3CH_2CH_2OH$ propanol	CH_3CH_2CHO propanal	CH_3COCH_3 propanone	$CH_3CH_2CO_2H$ propanoic acid	CH_2CHCH_3 propene
methane	methanol	methanal	propanone	methanoic acid	ethene

Benjamin Britten, who lived at Aldeburgh, and take place at The Maltings, a concert hall at nearby Snape. First performances of Britten's works to be given here include the operas *A Midsummer Night's Dream* 1960 and *Death in Venice* 1973.

aldehyde any of a group of organic chemical compounds prepared by oxidation of primary alcohols, so that the OH (hydroxyl) group loses its hydrogen to give an oxygen joined by a double bond to a carbon atom (the aldehyde group, with the formula CHO). The name is made up from alcohol dehydrogenation – that is, alcohol from which hydrogen has been removed. Aldehydes are usually liquids and include methanal (formaldehyde), ethanal (acetaldehyde), and benzaldehyde.

alder any tree or shrub of the genus *Alnus*, in the birch family Betulaceae, found mainly in cooler parts of the northern hemisphere and characterized by toothed leaves and catkins. About 30 species of alder occur in the N hemisphere and South America.

alderman (Old English *ealdor mann* 'older man') Anglo-Saxon term for the noble governor of a shire; after the Norman Conquest the office was replaced with that of sheriff. From the 19th century aldermen were the senior members of the borough or county councils in England and Wales, elected by the other councillors, until the abolition of the office 1972; the title is still used in the City of London, and for members of a municipal corporation in certain towns in the USA.

Aldermaston village in Berkshire, England; site of an atomic and biological weapons research establishment, which employs some 7,000 people to work on the production of nuclear warheads. During 1958–63 the Campaign for Nuclear Disarmament (CND) made it the focus of an annual Easter protest march.

Alderney third largest of the ◊Channel Islands, with its capital at St Anne's; area 8 sq km/3 sq mi; population (1991) 2,300. It gives its name to a breed of cattle, better known as the Guernsey. It exports early potatoes.

Aldershot town in Hampshire, England, SW of London; population (1991) 51,400. It has a military camp and barracks dating from 1854.

Aldrin Edwin Eugene ('Buzz') 1930– . US astronaut who landed on the Moon with Neil ◊Armstrong during the *Apollo 11* mission in July 1969, becoming the second person to set foot on the Moon.

aleatory music (Latin *alea* 'dice') method of composition practised by postwar avant-garde composers in which the performer or conductor chooses the order of succession of the composed pieces. Examples of aleatory music include Pierre Boulez's *Piano Sonata No 3* 1956–57, Earle Brown's *Available Forms I* 1961, and Stockhausen's *Momente/Moments* 1961–72. Another term for aleatory music is 'mobile form'.

Alemanni or ***Alamanni*** (Gothic 'united men' or 'men from all parts') Germanic people who from the 2nd century AD occupied an area bounded by the rivers Rhine, Danube, and Main. They were part of the medieval western German grouping of peoples that also included Franks, Saxons, Frisians, and Thuringians. Late in the 5th century they crossed the Rhine and Danube and settled in what is now Alsace and N Switzerland, where they introduced the German language. They were fully absorbed into the East Frankish kingdom in the 9th century.

Alembert Jean le Rond d' 1717–1783. French mathematician, encyclopedist, and theoretical physicist. In association with Denis ◊Diderot, he helped plan the great ◊*Encyclopédie* , for which he also wrote the 'Discours préliminaire' 1751. He framed several theorems and principles – notably d'Alembert's principle – in dynamics and celestial mechanics (an extension of Isaac ◊Newton's laws of motion), and devised the theory of partial differential equations.

Aleppo (Syrian ***Halab***) ancient city in NW Syria; population (1993) 1,494,000. There has been a settlement on the site for at least 4,000 years.

Aletsch most extensive glacier in Europe, 23.6 km/14.7 mi long, beginning on the southern slopes of the Jungfrau in the Bernese Alps, Switzerland.

Aleut a people who are indigenous to the Aleutian Islands; a few thousand remain worldwide, most in the Aleutian Islands and mainland Alaska. They were exploited by Russian fur traders in the 18th and 19th centuries, and their forced evacuation 1942–45 earned the USA a United Nations reprimand 1959; compensation was paid 1990.

Aleutian Islands volcanic island chain in the N Pacific, stretching 1,200 mi/1,900 km SW of Alaska, of which it forms part; population 6,000 Aleuts (most of whom belong to the Orthodox Church. There are 14 large and more than 100 small islands running along the Aleutian Trench. The islands are mountainous, barren, and treeless; they are ice-free all year but are often foggy, with only about 25 days of sunshine recorded annually.

history The islands were settled by the Aleuts around 1000 BC and discovered by a Russian expedition 1741; they passed to the USA with the purchase of Alaska 1867. The Japanese occupied Attu and Kiska islands 1942–43; Attu was retaken May 1943 in the only ground fighting on North American soil during World War II.

A level or ***Advanced level*** in the UK, examinations taken by some students in no more than four subjects at one time, usually at the age of 18 after two years' study. Two A-level passes are normally required for entry to a university degree course.

Alexander Harold Rupert Leofric George, 1st Earl Alexander of Tunis 1891–1969. British field marshal, a commander in World War II in France, Burma (now Myanmar), N Africa, and the Mediterranean. He was governor general of Canada 1946–52 and UK minister of defence 1952–54.

In World War II he was the last person to leave in the evacuation of Dunkirk. In Burma he fought a delaying action for five months against superior Japanese forces. In Aug 1942 he went to N Africa, and in 1943 became deputy to Eisenhower in charge of the Allied forces in Tunisia. After the Axis forces in N Africa surrendered, Alexander became supreme Allied commander in the Mediterranean, and, in 1944, field marshal.

Alexander eight popes, including:

Alexander III (Orlando Bandinelli) died 1181. Pope 1159–81. His authority was opposed by Frederick I Barbarossa, but Alexander eventually compelled him to render homage 1178. He held the third Lateran Council 1179. He supported Henry II of England in his invasion of Ireland, but imposed penance on him after the murder of Thomas à ◊Becket.

Alexander VI (Rodrigo Borgia) 1431–1503. Pope 1492–1503. Of Spanish origin, he bribed his way to the papacy, where he furthered the advancement of his illegitimate children, who included Cesare and Lucrezia ◊Borgia. When ◊Savonarola preached against his corrupt practices Alexander had him executed. Alexander was a great patron of the arts in Italy.

Alembert From scandalous beginnings – he was found on a church doorstep, the illegitimate son of a courtesan – Jean le Rond d'Alembert went on to become an eminent mathematician and philosopher. He discovered the calculus of partial differences, and, in 1743, developed the principle that now bears his name, by extending the Newtonian theory of dynamics to include mobile bodies. *Ann Ronan/Image Select (UK) Ltd*

Alexander I 1777–1825. Tsar from 1801. Was defeated by Napoleon at Austerlitz 1805; he made peace at Tilsit 1807, but an ensuing economic crisis led to a break with Napoleon's ◊Continental System and the opening up of Russian ports to British trade; this led to Napoleon's ill-fated invasion of Russia 1812. After the Congress of Vienna 1815, Alexander hoped through the Holy Alliance with Austria and Prussia to establish a new Christian order in Europe. ▷ *See feature on pp. 748–749.*

Alexander II Tsar of Russia Alexander II. Despite efforts to remove the repressive institutions of his father Nicholas I's reign, continued civil unrest forced his return to despotism. He was killed by a bomb thrown by a Polish revolutionary. *Philip Sauvain*

Alexander II 1818–1881. Tsar from 1855. He embarked on reforms of the army, the government, and education, and is remembered as 'the Liberator' for his emancipation of the serfs 1861, but he lacked the personnel to implement his reforms. However, the revolutionary element remained unsatisfied, and Alexander became increasingly autocratic and reactionary. He was assassinated by an anarchistic terrorist group, the ◊Nihilists.

Alexander III 1845–1894. Tsar from 1881, when he succeeded his father, Alexander II. He pursued a reactionary policy, promoting Russification and persecuting the Jews. He married Dagmar (1847–1928), daughter of Christian IX of Denmark and sister of Queen Alexandra of Britain, 1866.

Alexander I c. 1078–1124. King of Scotland from 1107, known as the Fierce. He ruled to the north of the rivers Forth and Clyde while his brother and successor David ruled to the south. He assisted Henry I of England in his campaign against Wales 1114, but defended the independence of the church in Scotland. Several monasteries, including the abbeys of Inchcolm and Scone, were established by him.

Alexander II 1198–1249. King of Scotland from 1214, when he succeeded his father William the Lion. Alexander supported the English barons in their struggle with King John after ◊Magna Carta. The accession of Henry III of England allowed a rapprochement between the two countries, and the boundaries between England and Scotland were agreed by the Treaty of York 1237. Alexander consolidated the royal authority in Scotland and was a generous patron of the church. In 1221 he married Joanna, the sister of Henry III. After her death he married Marie de Coucy 1239 with whom he had a son, Alexander III.

Alexander III 1241–1286. King of Scotland from 1249, son of Alexander II. In 1263, by military defeat of Norwegian forces, he extended his authority over the Western Isles, which had been dependent on Norway. The later period of his reign brought a period of peace and prosperity to Scotland. He died as the result of a fall from his horse, leaving his granddaughter Margaret, the Maid of Norway, to become queen of Scotland.

Alexander I Karageorgevich 1888–1934. Regent of Serbia 1912–21 and king of Yugoslavia 1921–34, as dictator from 1929. Second son of ◊Peter I, King of Serbia, he was declared regent for his father 1912 and on his father's death became king of the state of South Slavs – Yugoslavia – that had come into being 1918. He was assassinated on a state visit to France, and Mussolini's government was later declared to have instigated the crime.

Alexander Nevski, St 1220–1263. Russian military leader, son of the grand duke of Novgorod. In 1240 he defeated the Swedes on the banks of the

‘I will not steal a victory.’

Alexander the Great
Remark on refusing to attack the Persian army before the Battle of Gaugamela 331 BC

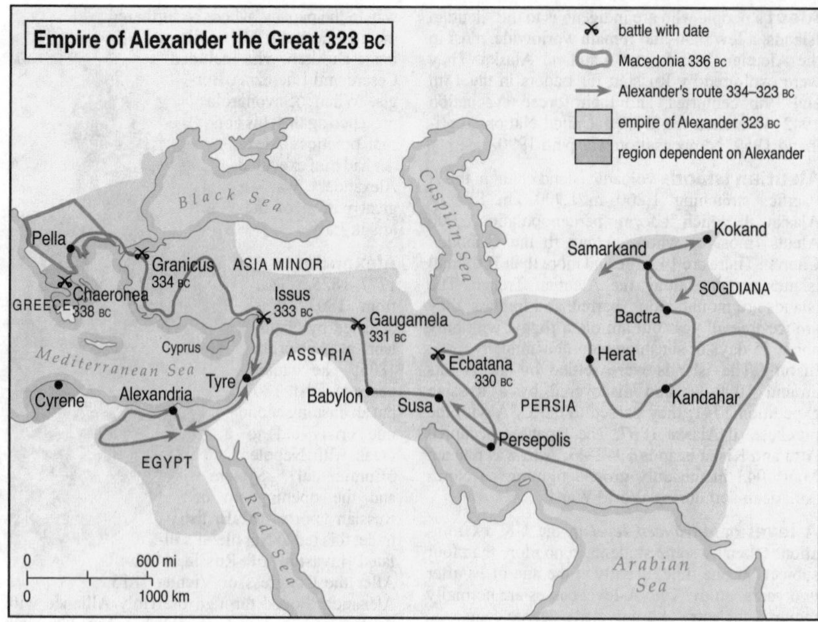

Neva (hence Nevski), and in 1242 defeated the Teutonic Knights on the frozen Lake Peipus.

Alexander Severus (in full Marcus Aurelius Severus Alexander) AD 208–235. Roman emperor from 222, when he succeeded his cousin Heliogabalus. He attempted to involve the Senate more closely in administration, and was the patron of the jurists Ulpian and Paulus, and the historian Cassius Dio. His campaign against the Persians 232 achieved some success, but in 235, on his way to defend Gaul against German invaders, he was killed in a mutiny.

Alexander technique in alternative medicine, a method of correcting bad habits of posture, breathing, and muscular tension, which Australian therapist F M Alexander (1869–1955) maintained cause many ailments. The technique is also used to promote general health and relaxation and enhance vitality.

Alexander the Great Head of a statue representing Alexander the Great, 2nd century BC, Kanellopoulos Museum, Athens, Greece. After inheriting the throne of tiny Macedonia at the age of 20, Alexander set about building an empire that, by the time of his death 13 years later, included Babylon, Samarkand, and the Punjab. *Corbis*

Alexander the Great 356–323 BC. King of Macedon from 336 BC and conqueror of the large Persian empire. As commander of the vast Macedonian army he conquered Greece 336, defeated the Persian king Darius in Asia Minor 333, then moved on to Egypt, where he founded Alexandria. He defeated the Persians again in Assyria 331, then advanced further east to reach the Indus. He conquered the Punjab before diminished troops forced his retreat.

The son of King Philip II of Macedon and Queen Olympias, Alexander was educated by the philosopher Aristotle. He first saw fighting 340, and at the battle of Chaeronea 338 contributed to the victory by a cavalry charge. At the age of 20, when his father was murdered, he assumed command of the throne and the army. He secured his northern frontier, suppressing an attempted rising in Greece by his capture of Thebes, and in 334 crossed the Dardanelles for the campaign against the vast Persian empire; at the river Granicus near the Dardanelles he won his first victory. In 333 he routed Darius at ◊Issus, and then set out for Egypt, where he was greeted as pharaoh. Meanwhile, Darius assembled half a million men for a final battle at Gaugamela, near Arbela on the Tigris, 331 but Alexander, with 47,000 men, drove the Persians into retreat. After the victory he stayed a month in Babylon, then marched to Susa and Persepolis and in 330 to Ecbatana (now Hamadán, Iran). Soon after, he learned that Darius was dead. In Afghanistan he founded colonies at Herat and Kandahar, and in 328 reached the plains of Sogdiana, where he married Roxana, daughter of King Oxyartes. India was his next objective, and he pressed on to the Indus. Near the river Hydaspes (now Jhelum) he fought one of his fiercest battles against the rajah Porus. At the river Hyphasis (now Beas) his depleted troops refused to go farther, and reluctantly he turned back down the Indus and along the coast. They reached Susa 324, where Alexander made Darius's daughter his second wife. He died in Babylon of a malarial fever.

Alexandra 1936– . Princess of the UK. Daughter of the Duke of Kent and Princess Marina, she married Angus Ogilvy (1928–), younger son of the earl of Airlie. They have two children, James (1964–) and Marina (1966–).

Alexandra Feodorovna 1872–1918. Last tsarina of Russia 1894–1917. She was the former Princess Alix of Hessen and granddaughter of Britain's Queen Victoria. She married ◊Nicholas II and, from 1907, fell under the spell of ◊Rasputin, a ‘holy man’ brought to the palace to try to cure her son of haemophilia. She was shot with the rest of her family by the Bolsheviks in the Russian Revolution.

Alexandria or *El Iskandariya* city, chief port, and second-largest city of Egypt, situated between the Mediterranean and Lake Maryut; population (1994 est) 3,419,000. It is linked by canal with the Nile and is an industrial city (oil refining, gas processing, and cotton and grain trading). Founded 331 BC by Alexander the Great, Alexandria was the capital of Egypt for over 1,000 years.

history The principal centre of Hellenistic culture, Alexandria has since the 4th century AD been the seat of a Christian patriarch. In 641 it was captured by the Muslim Arabs, and after the opening of the Cape route its trade rapidly declined. Early in the 19th century it began to recover its prosperity, and its growth was encouraged by its use as the main British naval base in the Mediterranean during both world wars. Of the large European community, most were expelled after the Suez Crisis 1956 and their property confiscated.

Few relics of antiquity remain. Pompey's Pillar is a column erected, as a landmark visible from the sea, by the emperor Diocletian. Two obelisks that once stood before the Caesarum temple are now in London (Cleopatra's Needle) and New York respectively.

Alexandria, Library of the world's first state-funded scientific institution, founded 330 BC in Alexandria, Egypt, by Ptolemy I and further expanded by Ptolemy II. It comprised a museum, teaching facilities, and a library that contained up to 700,000 scrolls, including much ancient Greek literature. It sustained significant damage AD 391, when Theodosius I ordered its destruction. It was burned down 640 at the time of the Arab conquest.

Alexandria, school of group of writers and scholars of Alexandria, Egypt, who made the city the chief centre of culture in the Western world from about 331 BC to AD 642. They include the poets Callimachus, Apollonius of Rhodes, and Theocritus; ◊Euclid, pioneer of geometry; ◊Eratosthenes, a geographer; Hipparchus, who developed a system of trigonometry; Ptolemy, whose system of astronomy endured for over 1,000 years; and the Jewish philosopher Philo. The Gnostics and Neo-Platonists also flourished in Alexandria.

Alexius five emperors of Byzantium, including:

Alexius I (Comnenus) 1048–1118. Byzantine emperor 1081–1118. The Latin (W European) Crusaders helped him repel Turkish invasions, and he devoted great skill to buttressing the threatened empire. His daughter ◊Anna Comnena chronicled his reign.

Alexius III (Angelos) died 1210. Byzantine emperor 1195–1203. He gained power by deposing and blinding his brother Isaac II, but Isaac's Venetian allies enabled him and his son Alexius IV to regain power as coemperors.

Alexandria The 15th-century fort of Qait Bay, now a naval museum, dominates the eastern harbour of Alexandria, Egypt. Built on a narrow strip of land between the Mediterranean and Lake Maryut, Alexandria has been a major port for centuries. It has been fought over and occupied many times since it was founded by Alexander the Great 331 BC. *Egyptian Tourist Board*

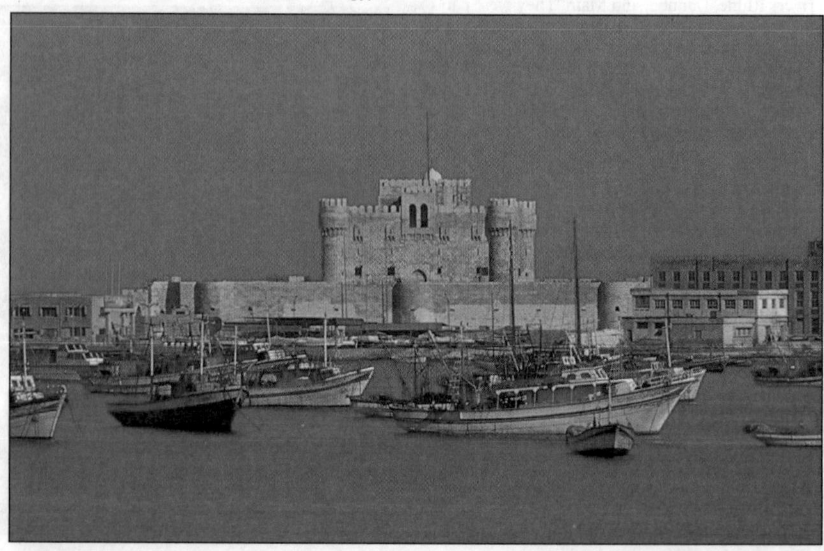

Alexius IV (Angelos) 1182–1204. Byzantine emperor from 1203, when, with the aid of the army of the Fourth Crusade, he deposed his uncle Alexius III. He soon lost the support of the Crusaders (by that time occupying Constantinople), and was overthrown and murdered by another Alexius, Alexius Mourtzouphlus (son-in-law of Alexius III) 1204, an act which the Crusaders used as a pretext to sack the city the same year.

alfalfa or ***lucerne*** perennial tall herbaceous plant *Medicago sativa* of the pea family Leguminosae. It is native to Eurasia and bears spikes of small purple flowers in late summer. It is now a major fodder crop, generally processed into hay, meal, or silage. Alfalfa sprouts, the sprouted seeds, are a popular salad ingredient.

Alfonsín Foulkes Raúl Ricardo 1927– . Argentine politician, president 1983–89. Becoming president at the time of the country's return to civilian government, he set up an investigation of the army's human-rights violations. Economic problems caused him to seek help from the International Monetary Fund and introduce austerity measures.

Alfonso thirteen kings of León, Castile, and Spain, including:

Alfonso VII c. 1107–1157. King of León and Castile from 1126 who attempted to unite Spain. Although he protected the Moors, he was killed trying to check a Moorish rising.

Alfonso (XI) ***the Avenger*** 1311–1350. King of Castile and León from 1312. He ruled cruelly, repressed a rebellion by his nobles, and defeated the last Moorish invasion 1340.

Alfonso XII 1857–1885. King of Spain from 1875, son of ◊Isabella II. He assumed the throne after a period of republican government following his mother's flight and effective abdication 1868. His rule was peaceful. He ended the civil war started by the Carlists and drafted a constitution, both 1876.

Alfonso XIII 1886–1941. King of Spain 1886–1931. He assumed power 1906 and married Princess Ena, granddaughter of Queen Victoria of the United Kingdom, in the same year. He abdicated 1931 soon after the fall of the Primo de Rivera dictatorship 1923–30 (which he supported), and Spain became a republic.

Alfred ***the Great*** c. 849–c. 901. King of Wessex from 871. He defended England against Danish invasion, founded the first English navy, and put into operation a legal code. He encouraged the translation of works from Latin (some he translated himself), and promoted the development of the Anglo-Saxon Chronicle, a history of England from the Roman invasion to the 11th century.

Alfred was born at Wantage, Oxfordshire, the youngest son of Ethelwulf (died 858), king of the West Saxons. In 870 Alfred and his brother Ethelred fought many battles against the Danes. He gained a victory over the Danes at Ashdown 871, and succeeded Ethelred as king April 871 after a series of defeats. Five years of uneasy peace followed while the Danes were occupied in other parts of England. In 876 the Danes attacked again, and in 878 Alfred was forced to retire to the stronghold of Athelney, near Taunton in Somerset, from where he finally emerged to win the victory of Edington, Wiltshire. By the Peace of Wedmore 878 the Danish leader Guthrum (died 890) agreed to withdraw from Wessex and from Mercia west of Watling Street. A new landing in Kent encouraged a revolt of the East Anglian Danes, which was suppressed 884–86, and after the final foreign invasion was defeated 892–96, Alfred strengthened the navy to prevent fresh incursions.

algae (singular ***alga***) diverse group of plants (including those commonly called seaweeds) that shows great variety of form, ranging from single-celled forms to multicellular seaweeds of considerable size and complexity.

Marine algae help combat global warming by removing carbon dioxide from the atmosphere during photosynthesis.

Algae were formerly included within the division Thallophyta, together with fungi and bacteria. Their classification changed with increased awareness of the important differences existing between the algae and Thallophyta, and also between the groups of algae themselves; many botanists now place each algal group in a separate class or division of its own.

They can be classified into 12 divisions, largely to be distinguished by their pigmentation, including the ***green algae*** Chlorophyta, freshwater or terrestrial; ***stoneworts*** Charophyta; ***golden-brown algae*** Chrysophyta; ***brown algae*** Phaeophyta, mainly marine and including the ***kelps*** Laminariales and allies, the largest of all algae; ***red algae*** Rhodophyta, mainly marine and often living parasitically or as epiphytes on other algae; ***diatoms*** Bacillariophyta; ***yellow-green algae*** Xanthophyta, mostly freshwater and terrestrial; and ***blue-green algae*** Cyanophyta, of simple cell structure and without sexual reproduction, mostly freshwater or terrestrial.

Algarve (Arabic *al-gharb* 'the west') ancient kingdom in S Portugal, the modern district of Faro, a popular holiday resort; population (1991) 341,400. Industries include agriculture, fishing, wine, mining, and tourism. The Algarve began to be wrested from the ◊Moors in the 12th century and was united with Portugal as a kingdom 1253. It includes the SW extremity of Europe, Cape St Vincent, where the British fleet defeated the Spanish 1797.

algebra system of mathematical calculations applying to any set of non-numerical symbols (usually letters), and the axioms and rules by which they are combined or operated upon; sometimes known as generalized arithmetic.

'Algebra' was originally the name given to the study of equations. In the 9th century, the Arab mathematician Muhammad ibn-Mūsā al-◊Khwārizmī used the term *al-jabr* for the process of adding equal quantities to both sides of an equation. When his treatise was later translated into Latin, *al-jabr* became 'algebra' and the word was adopted as the name for the whole subject.

In ordinary algebra the same operations are carried on as in arithmetic, but, as the symbols are capable of a more generalized and extended meaning than the figures used in arithmetic, it facilitates calculation where the numerical values are not known, or are inconveniently large or small, or where it is desirable to keep them in an analysed form.

Algeciras port in S Spain, to the W of Gibraltar across the Bay of Algeciras; population (1994) 104,000. Founded by the ◊Moors 713, it was taken from them by Alfonso XI of Castile 1344. Virtually destroyed in a fresh attack by the Moors, Algeciras was re-founded 1704 by Spanish refugees who had fled from Gibraltar after it had been captured by the British. Following a conference of European Powers held here 1906, France and Spain were given control of Morocco.

Algeria country in N Africa, bounded E by Tunisia and Libya, SE by Niger, SW by Mali and Mauritania, NW by Morocco, and N by the Mediterranean Sea. *See country box on p. 26.*

Algiers (Arabic ***al-Jazair***; French ***Alger***) capital of Algeria, situated on the narrow coastal plain between the Atlas Mountains and the Mediterranean; population (1989) 1,722,000. Founded by the Arabs AD 935, Algiers was taken by the Turks 1518 and by the French 1830. The old town is dominated by the Kasbah, the palace and prison of the Turkish rulers. The new town, constructed under French rule, is in European style. The Battle of Algiers, between the Algerian nationalist population and the French army and settlers, took place here during the Algerian War of Independence; independence was achieved 1962.

Algiers, Battle of bitter conflict in Algiers 1954–62 between the Algerian nationalist population and the French colonial army and French settlers. The conflict ended with Algerian independence 1962.

alginate salt of alginic acid, $(C_6H_8O_6)_n$, obtained from brown seaweeds and used in textiles, paper, food products, and pharmaceuticals.

ALGOL (acronym for algorithmic language) in computing, an early high-level programming language, developed in the 1950s and 1960s for scientific applications. A general-purpose language, ALGOL is best suited to mathematical work and has an algebraic style. Although no longer in common use, it has greatly influenced more recent languages, such as Ada and PASCAL.

Algol or ***Beta Persei*** ◊eclipsing binary, a pair of orbiting stars in the constellation Perseus, one of which eclipses the other every 69 hours, causing its brightness to drop by two-thirds.

The brightness changes were first explained 1782 by English amateur astronomer John Goodricke (1764–1786). He pointed out that the changes between magnitudes 2.2 and 3.5 repeated themselves exactly after an interval of 2.867 days and supposed this to be due to two stars orbiting round and eclipsing each other.

Algonquin the Algonquian-speaking hunting and fishing people who once lived around the Ottawa River in E Canada. Many now live on reservations in NE USA, E Ontario, and W Quebec; others have chosen to live among the general populations of Canada and the USA.

algorithm procedure or series of steps that can be used to solve a problem. In computer science, it describes the logical sequence of operations to be performed by a program.

Alhambra fortified palace in Granada, Spain, built by Moorish kings, mainly between 1248 and 1354. It stands on a rocky hill and is a fine example of Moorish architecture.

Ali c. 598–661. 4th ◊caliph of ◊Islam. He was born in Mecca, the son of Abu Talib, and was the cousin and close friend and supporter of the prophet Muhammad, who gave him his daughter Fatima in marriage. He was one of the first to believe in Islam. On Muhammad's death 632, Ali had a claim to succeed him, but this was not conceded until 656, following the murder of the third caliph, Uthman. After a brief and stormy reign, Ali was assassinated. Controversy has raged around Ali's name between the Sunni Muslims and the Shi'ites, the former denying his right to the caliphate and the latter supporting it.

Ali Muhammad. Adopted name of Cassius Marcellus Clay, Jr 1942– . US boxer. Olympic light-heavyweight champion 1960, he went on to become world professional heavyweight champion 1964, and was the only man to regain the title twice. He was known for his fast footwork and extrovert nature.

'Float like a butterfly, sting like a bee.'

MUHAMMAD ALI
Catchphrase

Alia Ramiz 1925– . Albanian communist politician, head of state 1982–92. He gradually relaxed the isolationist policies of his predecessor Enver Hoxha and following public unrest introduced political and economic reforms, including free elections 1991, when he was elected executive president. In Sept 1994 Alia was convicted of abuse of power while in office and sentenced to eight years' imprisonment, but was released July 1995 following an appeal court ruling.

aliasing or ***jaggies*** effect seen on computer screen or printer output, when smooth curves appear to be made up of steps because the resolution is not high enough. The steps are caused by clumps of pixels that become visible when the monitor's definition is lower than that of the image that it is trying to show. ◊Anti-aliasing reduces this effect by using intermediate shades of colour to create a smoother curve.

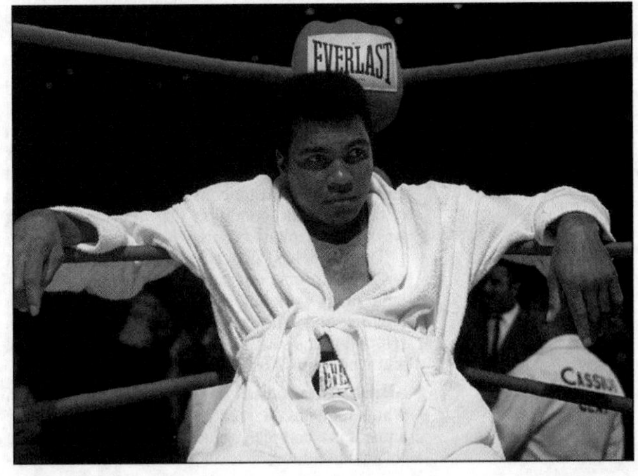

Ali US boxer Muhammad Ali, three times world heavyweight champion. He won an Olympic gold medal in 1960 and became world champion for the first time in 1964. A skilled and elegant boxer, he outmanoeuvred rather than outpunched his opponents. Born Cassius Clay, he changed his name when he became a Muslim. *Topham*

ALGERIA
Democratic and Popular Republic of

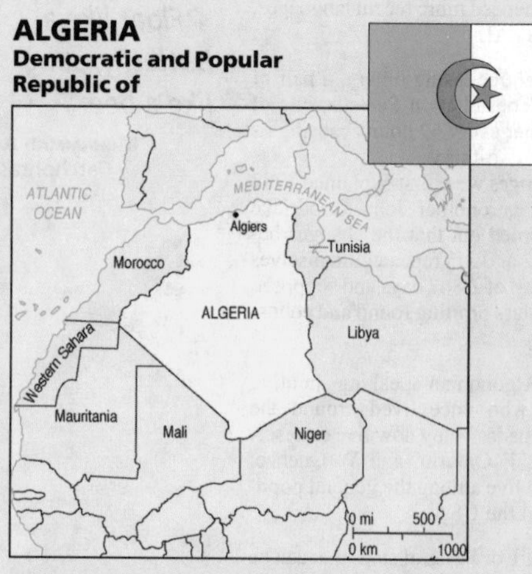

national name *al-Jumhuriya al-Jazairiya ad-Dimuqratiya ash-Shabiya*
area 2,381,741 sq km/919,352 sq mi
capital Algiers (al-Jaza'ir)
major towns/cities Constantine (Qacentina)
major ports Oran (Ouahran), Annaba (Bône)
physical features coastal plains backed by mountains in N, Sahara desert in S; Atlas mountains, Barbary Coast, Chott Melrhir depression, Hoggar mountains
head of state Liamine Zeroual from 1994
head of government Ahmed Ouyahia from 1995
political system military rule
administrative divisions 48 departments
political parties National Liberation Front (FLN), nationalist, socialist; Socialist Forces Front (FSS), Berber-based, left of centre; Islamic Front for Salvation (FIS), Islamic fundamentalist (banned from 1992)
population 27,939,000 (1995 est)
population growth rate 2.3% (1990–95); 2.0% (2000–05)
ethnic distribution 99% of Arab Berber origin, the remainder of European descent, mainly French
life expectancy 59 (men), 62 (women)
literacy rate men 70%, women 45%
languages Arabic (official); Berber, French
religion Sunni Muslim (state religion)
currency Algerian dinar
GDP (US $) 40.4 billion (1994)
growth rate 0.6% (1994)
exports oil, natural gas, iron, wine, olive oil

HISTORY
9th C BC Part of Carthaginian Empire, centred around Tunisia to the E, with Annaba, Algiers, and Skikda emerging as important trading posts en route to Spain.
146 BC Conquered by Rome, who called the area Numidia.
AD 396 St Augustine, one of the great early Christian leaders, became Bishop of Hippo, modern Annaba.
6th C Part of the Byzantine Empire.
late 7th C Conquered by Muslim Arabs, who spread Islam as the basis of a new Berberized Arab-Islamic civilization.
1516 Ottoman Turks expelled recent Christian Spanish invaders: under Ottoman rule much influence was left to local Arab tribes, Berbers, Barbary pirates, and deys, administrative officers who were elected for life.
1816 Anglo-Dutch forces bombarded Algiers as a reprisal against the Barbary pirates' attacks on Mediterranean shipping.
1830–47 French occupation of Algiers, followed by extension of control to the N, overcoming fierce resistance from Amir Abd al-Qadir, a champion of Arab Algerian nationalism, and from Morocco.
1850–70 Mountainous inland region, inhabited by the Kabyles, occupied by French.
1871 Major rebellion against French rule as French settlers began to immigrate and take over the best agricultural land.
1900–09 Sahara region subdued by France, who kept it under military rule.
1937 Algerian People's Party (PPA) formed by the charismatic separatist, Messali Hadj.
1940 Following France's defeat by Nazi Germany, Algeria became allied to the pro-Nazi Vichy Regime during World War II.
1945 8,000 died following the ruthless suppression of an abortive PPA-supported uprising against French rule.
1954–62 Battle of Algiers: bitter war of independence fought between the National Liberation Front (FLN) and the French colonial army.
1958 French inability to resolve the escalating civil war in Algeria, where French settlers had risen in favour of integration with France, toppled the Fourth Republic and brought to power, in Paris, General Charles de Gaulle, who accepted the principle of national self-determination.
1962 Independence achieved from France. Republic declared. Ahmed Ben Bella of the FLN elected prime minister; many French settlers fled.
1963 Ben Bella elected Algeria's first president and one-party state established.
1965 Ben Bella deposed by military, led by Col Houari Boumédienne (FLN).
1971 Oil and gas industry nationalized.
1976 New Islamic-socialist constitution approved.
1978 Death of Boumédienne.
1979 Benjedid Chadli (FLN) elected president. Ben Bella freed after 14 years of house arrest.
1981 Algeria helped secure release of US hostages in Iran.
1988 Riots in protest at austerity policies; 170 killed. Reform programme introduced. Diplomatic relations restored with Morocco after a 12-year break.
1989 Constitutional changes introduced limited political pluralism.
1991 Elections cancelled after Islamic fundamentalist Islamic Salvation Front (FIS) won first round of multiparty elections.
1992 Chadli resigned; military took control of government; Muhammad Boudiaf became president. State of emergency declared and FIS ordered to disband. Boudiaf assassinated, allegedly by fundamentalists, and was replaced by Ali Kafi.
1993 Worsening civil strife; assassinations of politicians and other public figures; foreigners murdered.
1994 General Lamine Zeroual replaced Kafi as president. Fundamentalists' campaign of violence intensified.
1996 Constitution amended to increase president's powers and counter religious fundamentalism.
1997 Widespread killings by fundamentalists.

SEE ALSO Berber

alibi (Latin 'elsewhere') in law, a provable assertion that the accused was at some other place when a crime was committed. In Britain it can usually only be used as a defence in a ◊crown court trial if the prosecution is supplied with details before the trial.

Alicante city and seaport in E Spain on the Mediterranean Sea, 123 km/77 mi S of Valencia; population (1994) 275,000. It is the commercial port for Madrid, exporting wine, olive oil, and fruit; there are manufacturing industries. Believed to occupy the site of the ancient Roman city of Lucentum, Alicante was captured by the Moors 713, retaken by James I of Aragon 1265, and besieged by the French 1709 and 1812.

alien (Latin *alienus* 'foreign') in law, a person who is not a citizen of a particular nation.

In the UK, under the British Nationality Act 1981, an alien is anyone who is neither a British Overseas citizen (for example Commonwealth) nor a member of certain other categories; citizens of the Republic of Ireland are not regarded as aliens. Aliens may not vote or hold public office in the UK.

alienation sense of isolation, powerlessness, and therefore frustration; a feeling of loss of control over one's life; a sense of estrangement from society or even from oneself. As a concept it was developed by German philosophers G W F Hegel and Karl Marx; the latter used it as a description and criticism of the condition that developed among workers in capitalist society.

The term has also been used by non-Marxist writers and sociologists (in particular Emile Durkheim in his work *Suicide* 1897) to explain unrest in factories and to describe the sense of powerlessness felt by groups such as young people, black people, and women in Western industrial society.

alimentary canal in animals, the tube through which food passes; it extends from the mouth to the anus. It is a complex organ, adapted for ◊digestion. In human adults, it is about 9 m/30 ft long, consisting of the mouth cavity, pharynx, oesophagus, stomach, and the small and large intestines.

A constant stream of enzymes from the canal wall and from the pancreas assists the breakdown of food molecules into smaller, soluble nutrient molecules, which are absorbed through the canal wall into the bloodstream and carried to individual cells. The muscles of the alimentary canal keep the incoming food moving, mix it with the enzymes and other juices, and slowly push it in the direction of the anus, a process known as ◊peristalsis. The wall of the canal receives an excellent supply of blood and is folded so as to increase its surface area. These two adaptations ensure efficient absorption of nutrient molecules.

Ali Pasha Mehmed Emin 1815–1871. Grand vizier (chief minister) of the Ottoman Empire 1855–56, 1858–59, 1861, and 1867–71, noted for his attempts to westernize the Ottoman Empire.

After a career as ambassador to the UK, minister of foreign affairs 1846, delegate to the Congress of ◊Vienna 1855 and of Paris 1856, he was grand vizier a total of five times. While promoting friendship with Britain and France, he defended the vizier's powers against those of the sultan.

aliphatic compound any organic chemical compound in which the carbon atoms are joined in straight chains, as in hexane (C_6H_{14}), or in branched chains, as in 2-methylpentane ($CH_3CH(CH_3)CH_2CH_2CH_3$).

Aliphatic compounds have bonding electrons localized within the vicinity of the bonded atoms. ◊Cyclic compounds that do not have delocalized electrons are also aliphatic, as in the alicyclic compound cyclohexane (C_6H_{12}) or the heterocyclic piperidine ($C_5H_{11}N$). Compare ◊aromatic compound.

alkali metal any of a group of six metallic elements with similar chemical properties: lithium, sodium, potassium, rubidium, caesium, and francium. They form a linked group (Group One) in the ◊periodic table of the elements. They are univalent (have a valency of one) and of very low density (lithium, sodium, and potassium float on water); in general they are reactive, soft, low-melting-point metals. Because of their reactivity they are only found as compounds in nature.

alkaline-earth metal any of a group of six metallic elements with similar bonding properties: beryllium, magnesium, calcium, strontium, barium, and radium. They form a linked group in the ◊periodic table of the elements. They are strongly basic, bivalent (have a valency of two), and occur in nature only in compounds.

They and their compounds are used to make alloys, oxidizers, and drying agents.

alkaloid any of a number of physiologically active and frequently poisonous substances contained in some plants. They are usually organic bases and contain nitrogen. They form salts with acids and, when soluble, give alkaline solutions. Substances in this group are included by custom rather than by scientific rules. Examples include morphine, cocaine, quinine, caffeine, strychnine, nicotine, and atropine.

In 1992, epibatidine, a chemical extracted from the skin of an Ecuadorian frog, was identified as a member of an entirely new class of alkaloid. It is an organochlorine compound, which is rarely found in animals, and a powerful painkiller, about 200 times as effective as morphine.

alkane member of a group of ◊hydrocarbons having the general formula C_nH_{2n+2}, commonly known as paraffins. As they contain only single ◊covalent bonds, alkanes are said to be saturated. Lighter alkanes, such as methane, ethane, propane, and butane, are colourless gases; heavier ones are liquids or solids. In nature they are found in natural gas and petroleum.

alkene member of the group of ◊hydrocarbons having the general formula C_nH_{2n}, formerly known as olefins. Alkenes are unsaturated compounds, characterized by one or more double bonds between adjacent carbon atoms. Lighter alkenes, such as ethene and propene, are gases, obtained from the ◊cracking of oil fractions. Alkenes react by addition, and many useful compounds, such as poly (ethene) and bromoethane, are made from them.

alkyne member of the group of ◊hydrocarbons with the general formula C_nH_{2n-2}, formerly known as the acetylenes. They are unsaturated compounds, characterized by one or more triple bonds between adjacent carbon atoms. Lighter alkynes, such as ethyne, are gases; heavier ones are liquids or solids.

Allah (Arabic *al-Ilah* 'the God') Islamic name for God. Evidence for the worship of Allah in pre-Islamic times is found as early as the 3rd century BC. The Koranic concept of Allah lays stress on his uniqueness and his role as the omniscient authority over humans, but he is also merciful and compassionate. Uncreated and eternal, he is the creator of all things, not least of the ◊Koran, of which Muhammad was merely the voice and messenger.

Allahabad ('city of god') historic city in Uttar Pradesh state, NE India, 580 km/360 mi SE of Delhi, on the Jumna River where it meets the Ganges and the mythical Seraswati River; population (1991) 806,000. A Hindu religious event, the festival of the jar of nectar of immortality (Khumbh Mela), is held here every 12 years with the participants washing away sin and sickness by bathing in the rivers.

Allegheny Mountains range over 800 km/500 mi long extending from Pennsylvania to Virginia, USA, rising to more than 1,500 m/4,900 ft and averaging 750 m/2,500 ft. The mountains are a major source of timber, coal, iron, and limestone. They initially hindered western migration, the first settlement to the west being Marietta 1788.

allegory in literature, the description or illustration of one thing in terms of another, or the personification of abstract ideas. The term is also used for a work of poetry or prose in the form of an extended metaphor or parable that makes use of symbolic fictional characters.

An example of the use of symbolic fictional character in allegory is the romantic epic *The Faerie Queene* 1590–96 by Edmund Spenser in homage to Queen Elizabeth I. Allegory is often used for moral purposes, as in John Bunyan's *Pilgrim's Progress* 1678. Medieval allegory often used animals as characters; this tradition survives in such works as *Animal Farm* 1945 by George Orwell.

allele one of two or more alternative forms of a ◊gene at a given position (locus) on a chromosome, caused by a difference in the ◊DNA. Blue and brown eyes in humans are determined by different alleles of the gene for eye colour. Organisms with two sets of chromosomes (diploids) will have two copies of each gene. If the two alleles are identical the individual is said to be ◊homozygous at that locus; if different, the individual is ◊heterozygous at that locus. Some alleles show ◊dominance over others.

Allen Woody. Adopted name of Allen Stewart Konigsberg 1935– . US film writer, director, and actor. He is known for his cynical, witty, often self-deprecating parody and offbeat humour. His film *Annie Hall* 1977 won him three Academy Awards. From the late 1970s, Allen mixed his output of comedies with straight dramas, such as *Interiors* 1978 and *Another Woman* 1988, but recent works such as *Manhattan Murder Mystery* 1994 and *Bullets over Broadway* 1994 have emphasized humour.

Allen, Bog of wetland E of the river Shannon in the Republic of Ireland, comprising some 96,000 ha/240,000 acres of the counties of Offaly, Leix, and Kildare; the country's main source of peat fuel.

Allenby (Edmund) Henry Hynman, 1st Viscount Allenby 1861–1936. British field marshal. In World War I he served in France before taking command 1917–19 of the British forces in the Middle East. His defeat of the Turkish forces at Megiddo in Palestine Sept 1918 was followed almost at once by the capitulation of Turkey. He was high commissioner in Egypt 1919–35.

Allende Isabel 1942– . Chilean novelist. She is one of the leading exponents of ◊magic realism. After the assassination 1973 of her uncle, Chile's socialist president Salvador Allende, exile in Venezuela released memories of family and country which emerged in her first novel *La casa de los espiritus/The House of the Spirits* 1982, now filmed in English. Her later novels *De amor y de sombra/Of Love and Shadows* 1984 and *Eva Luna* 1987 combine fantasy with the 'real' worlds of investigative journalism, filmmaking, and politics.

Allende (Gossens) Salvador 1908–1973. Chilean left-wing politician. Elected president 1970 as the candidate of the Popular Front alliance, Allende never succeeded in keeping the electoral alliance together in government. His failure to solve the country's economic problems or to deal with political subversion allowed the army, backed by the CIA, to stage the 1973 coup which brought about the death of Allende and many of his supporters.

Allende Chilean politician Salvador Allende. He became the first freely elected Marxist leader in the Western hemisphere 1970, at his fourth attempt. However, his efforts to build a socialist society within the framework of parliamentary democracy were opposed by US-backed business interests, and he died during a coup led by General Pinochet. *Associated Press/Topham*

allergy special sensitivity of the body that makes it react with an exaggerated response of the natural immune defence mechanism to the introduction of an otherwise harmless foreign substance (allergen).

All Fools' Day another name for ◊April Fools' Day.

Alliance, the in UK politics, a loose union 1981–87 formed by the ◊Liberal Party and ◊Social Democratic Party (SDP) for electoral purposes. The difficulties of presenting two separate parties to the electorate as if they were one proved insurmountable, and after the Alliance's poor showing in the 1987 general election the majority of the SDP voted to merge with the Liberals to form the Social and Liberal Democrats.

Allied Coordination Committee or ***Operation Stay Behind*** or ***Gladio*** secret right-wing paramilitary network in W Europe, set up in the 1950s to arm guerrillas chosen from the civilian population in the event of Soviet invasion or communist takeover. Initiated and partly funded by the US Central Intelligence Agency (CIA), it is linked to the North Atlantic Treaty Organization. Its past or present existence was officially acknowledged 1990 by Belgium, France, (West) Germany, Greece, Italy, the Netherlands, Norway, and Portugal; in the UK the matter is covered by the Official Secrets Act. In 1990 those governments that confirmed their countries' participation said that the branches had been or would be closed down; the European Parliament set up a commission of inquiry.

Allies, the in World War I, the 23 countries allied against the Central Powers (Germany, Austria-Hungary, Turkey, and Bulgaria), including France, Italy, Russia, the UK, Australia and other Commonwealth nations, and, in the latter part of the war, the USA; and in World War II, the 49 countries allied against the ◊Axis Powers (Germany, Italy, and Japan), including France, the UK, Australia and other Commonwealth nations, the USA, and the USSR.

alligator (Spanish *el lagarto* 'the lizard') reptile of the genus *Alligator*, related to the crocodile. There are only two living species: *A. mississipiensis*, the Mississippi alligator of the southern states of the USA, and *A. sinensis* from the swamps of the lower Chang Jiang River in China. The former grows to about 4 m/12 ft, but the latter only to 1.5 m/5 ft. Alligators lay their eggs in waterside nests of mud and vegetation and are good mothers. They swim well with lashing movements of the tail and feed on fish and mammals but seldom attack people. The skin is of value for fancy leather goods.

alliteration in poetry and prose, the use, within a line or phrase, of words beginning with the same sound, as in 'Two tired toads trotting to Tewkesbury'. It was a common device in Old English poetry, and its use survives in many traditional phrases, such as *dead as a doornail* and *pretty as a picture*.

Allium genus of plants belonging to the lily family Liliaceae. Members of the genus are usually strong-smelling with a sharp taste, but form bulbs in which sugar is stored. Cultivated species include onion, garlic, chive, and leek. Certain species are grown in gardens for their decorative globular heads of white, pink, or purple flowers.

Several species are native in Britain, the commonest being the woodland wild garlic or ramsons *A. ursinum* and the crow garlic *A. vineale* which is widespread in fields and hedgerows.

allometry in biology, a regular relationship between a given feature (for example, the size of an organ) and the size of the body as a whole, when this relationship is not a simple proportion of body size. Thus, an organ may increase in size proportionately faster, or slower, than body size does. For example, a human baby's head is much larger in relation to its body than is an adult's.

allotropy property whereby an element can exist in two or more forms (allotropes), each possessing different physical properties but the same state of matter (gas, liquid, or solid). The allotropes of carbon are diamond and graphite. Sulphur has several allotropes (flowers of sulphur, plastic, rhombic, and monoclinic). These solids have different crystal structures, as do the white and grey forms of tin and the black, red, and white forms of phosphorus.

Oxygen exists as two gaseous allotropes: one used by organisms for respiration (O_2), and the other a poisonous pollutant, ozone (O_3).

alloy metal blended with some other metallic or nonmetallic substance to give it special qualities, such as resistance to corrosion, greater hardness, or tensile strength. Useful alloys include bronze, brass, cupronickel, duralumin, German silver, gunmetal, pewter, solder, steel, and stainless steel.

Complex alloys are now common; for example, in dentistry, where a cheaper alternative to gold is made of chromium, cobalt, molybdenum, and titanium. Among the most recent alloys are superplastics: alloys that can stretch to double their length at specific temperatures, permitting, for example, their injection into moulds as easily as plastic.

All Saints' Day or ***All-Hallows*** or ***Hallowmas*** festival on 1 Nov for all Christian saints and martyrs who have no special day of their own. It was instituted 835.

All Souls' Day festival in the Roman Catholic Church, held on 2 Nov (following All Saints' Day) in the conviction that through prayer and self-denial the faithful can hasten the deliverance of souls expiating their sins in purgatory.

It was instituted by Odilo in the monastery of Cluny 998. The day is also observed by some sections of the Anglican Church.

allspice spice prepared from the dried berries of the evergreen pimento tree or West Indian pepper tree *Pimenta dioica* of the myrtle family, cultivated chiefly in Jamaica. It has an aroma similar to that of a mixture of cinnamon, cloves, and nutmeg.

alluvial deposit layer of broken rocky matter, or sediment, formed from material that has been carried in suspension by a river or stream and dropped as the velocity of the current changes. River plains and deltas are made entirely of alluvial

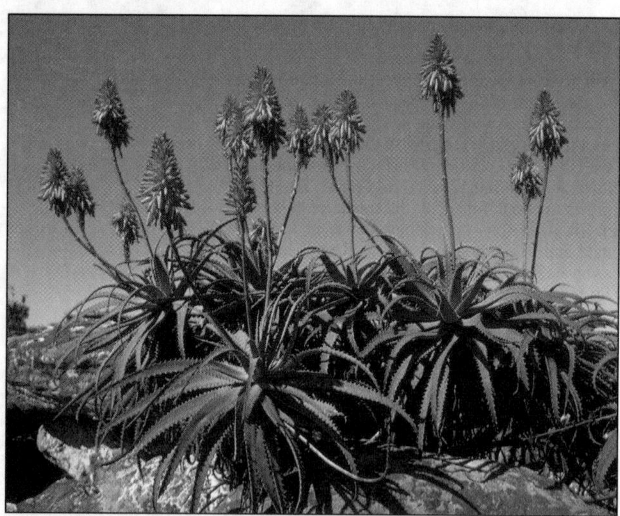

aloe Aloes vary in size from dwarf species, no more than a few centimetres in diameter (such as the popular houseplant *Aloe variegata*), to species as large as a small tree. This *Aloe arborescens* from South Africa is of intermediate size. In their natural habitat most aloes flower during winter. *Premaphotos Wildlife*

deposits, but smaller pockets can be found in the beds of upland torrents.

Alluvial deposits can consist of a whole range of particle sizes, from boulders down through cobbles, pebbles, gravel, sand, silt, and clay. The raw materials are the rocks and soils of upland areas that are loosened by erosion and washed away by mountain streams. Much of the world's richest farmland lies on alluvial deposits. These deposits can also provide an economic source of minerals. River currents produce a sorting action, with particles of heavy material deposited first while lighter materials are washed downstream. Hence heavy minerals such as gold and tin, present in the original rocks in small amounts, can be concentrated and deposited on stream beds in commercial quantities. Such deposits are called 'placer ores'.

alluvial fan roughly triangular sedimentary formation found at the base of slopes. An alluvial fan results when a sediment-laden stream or river rapidly deposits its load of gravel and silt as its speed is reduced on entering a plain. The surface of such a fan slopes outward in a wide arc from an apex at the mouth of the steep valley. A small stream carrying a load of coarse particles builds a shorter, steeper fan than a large stream carrying a load of fine particles. Over time, the fan tends to become destroyed piecemeal by the continuing headward and downward erosion leveling the slope.

Alma-Tadema Lawrence 1836–1912. Dutch painter who worked in England from 1870. He painted romantic, idealized scenes from ancient Greek, Roman, and Egyptian life in a style that combined Victorian sentiment and detailed historical accuracy. He studied painting first at the Antwerp academy, and later under the Dutch historical painter Baron Hendrik Leys (1815–69). He followed Leys in devoting himself to the reconstruction of the past, painting chiefly classical subjects such as *Phidias at Work on the Parthenon* 1869 (Tate Gallery, London) and the *Pyrrhic Dance* 1869 (Guildhall, London).

Almaty (*Vernyi* to 1921; *Alma-Ata* to 1994) former capital of Kazakhstan; population (1991) 1,151,300. Industries include engineering, printing, tobacco processing, textile manufacturing, and leather products.

Almería Spanish city, chief town of a province of the same name on the Mediterranean; population (1994) 167,000. The province is famous for its white grapes, and in the Sierra Nevada are rich mineral deposits.

Almohad Berber dynasty 1130–1269 founded by the Berber prophet Muhammad ibn Tumart (c. 1080–1130). The Almohads ruled much of Morocco and Spain, which they took by defeating the ◊Almoravids; they later took the area that today forms Algeria and Tunis. Their policy of religious 'purity' involved the forced conversion and massacre of the Jewish population of Spain. The Almohads were themselves defeated by the Christian kings of Spain 1212, and in Morocco 1269.

almond tree *Prunus amygdalus*, family Rosaceae, related to the peach and apricot. Dessert almonds are the kernels of the fruit of the sweet variety *P. amygdalus dulcis*, which is also the source of a low-cholesterol culinary oil. Oil of bitter almonds, from the variety *P. amygdalus amara*, is used in flavouring. Almond oil is also used for cosmetics, perfumes, and fine lubricants.

Almoravid Berber dynasty 1056–1147 founded by the prophet Abdullah ibn Tashfin, ruling much of Morocco and Spain in the 11th–12th centuries. The Almoravids came from the Sahara and in the 11th century began laying the foundations of an empire covering the whole of Morocco and parts of Algeria; their capital was the newly founded Marrakesh. In 1086 they defeated Alfonso VI of Castile to gain much of Spain. They were later overthrown by the ◊Almohads.

aloe plant of the genus *Aloe* of African plants, family Liliaceae, distinguished by their long, fleshy, spiny-edged leaves. The drug usually referred to as 'bitter aloes' is a powerful cathartic prepared from the juice of the leaves of several of the species.

alpaca domesticated South American hoofed mammal *Lama pacos* of the camel family, found in Chile, Peru, and Bolivia, and herded at high elevations in the Andes. It is bred mainly for its long, fine, silky wool, and stands about 1 m/3 ft tall at the shoulder with neck and head another 60 cm/2 ft. Like the ◊llama, it was probably bred from the wild ◊guanaco and is a close relative of the ◊vicuna.

alphabet set of conventional symbols used for writing, based on a correlation between individual symbols and spoken sounds, so called from *alpha* (α) and *beta* (β), the names of the first two letters of the classical Greek alphabet. The earliest known alphabet is from Palestine, about 1700 BC. Alphabetic writing now takes many forms – for example, the Hebrew *aleph-beth* and the Arabic script, both written from right to left; the Devanagari script of the Hindus, in which the symbols 'hang' from a line common to all the symbols; and the Greek alphabet, with the first clearly delineated vowel symbols.

Each letter of the alphabets descended from Greek represents a particular sound or sounds, usually grouped into vowels (*a*, *e*, *i*, *o*, *u*, in the English version of the Roman alphabet), consonants (*b*, *p*, *d*, *t*, and so on), and semivowels (*w*, *y*). Letters may be combined to produce distinct sounds (for example, *a* and *e* in words like *tale* and *take*, or *o* and *i* together to produce a 'wa' sound in the French *loi*), or may have no sound whatsoever (for example, the silent letters *gh* in *high* and *through*).

Alpha Centauri or ***Rigil Kent*** brightest star in the constellation Centaurus and the third brightest star in the night sky. It is actually a triple star (see ◊binary star); the two brighter stars orbit each other every 80 years, and the third, Proxima Centauri, is the closest star to the Sun, 4.2 light years away, 0.1 light years closer than the other two.

alpha decay disintegration of the nucleus of an atom to produce an ◊alpha particle. See also ◊radioactivity.

alpha particle positively charged, high-energy particle emitted from the nucleus of a radioactive atom. It is one of the products of the spontaneous disintegration of radioactive elements (see ◊radioactivity) such as radium and thorium, and is identical with the nucleus of a helium atom – that is, it consists of two protons and two neutrons. The process of emission, alpha decay, transforms one element into another, decreasing the atomic (or proton) number by two and the atomic mass (or nucleon number) by four.

Because of their large mass alpha particles have a short range of only a few centimetres in air, and can be stopped by a sheet of paper. They have a strongly ionizing effect on the molecules that they strike, and are therefore capable of damaging living cells. Alpha particles travelling in a vacuum are deflected slightly by magnetic and electric fields.

Alphege, St 954–1012. Anglo-Saxon priest, bishop of Winchester from 984, archbishop of Canterbury from 1006. When the Danes attacked Canterbury he tried to protect the city, was thrown into prison, and, refusing to deliver the treasures of his cathedral, was stoned and beheaded at Greenwich 19 April, his feast day.

alphorn wind instrument consisting of a straight, usually wooden tube terminating in a conical endpiece with an upturned bell, sometimes up to 4 m/12 ft in length. It is used to summon cattle and serenade tourists in the highlands of central Europe.

Alps mountain chain, the barrier between N Italy and France, Germany and Austria. Skiing and summer tourism are important. Skiing is damaging the Alpine environment; high forest is cut down to create pistes, increasing the risk of avalanches. Acid rain is destroying trees.

Peaks include Mont Blanc, the highest at 4,809 m/15,777 ft, first climbed by Jacques Balmat and Michel Paccard 1786; Matterhorn in the Pennine Alps, 4,479 m/14,694 ft, first climbed by Edward Whymper 1865 (four of the party of seven were killed when a rope broke during their descent); Eiger in the Bernese Alps/Oberland, 3,970 m/13,030 ft, with a near-vertical rock wall on the north face, first climbed 1858; Jungfrau, 4,166 m/13,673 ft; and Finsteraarhorn 4,275 m/14,027 ft.

Passes include Brenner, the lowest, Austria/Italy;

Alps The Glacier du Chardonnet, in the French Alps. The glacier moves slowly down between the Aiguille du Chardonnet (3,680 m/12,267 ft) on the right, and the Aiguille d'Argentière (3,878 m/12,927 ft) on the left. *Corbis*

Great St Bernard, one of the highest, 2,472 m/8,113 ft, Italy/Switzerland (by which Napoleon marched into Italy 1800); Little St Bernard, Italy/France (which Hannibal is thought to have used); and St Gotthard, S Switzerland, which Suvorov used when ordered by the tsar to withdraw his troops from Italy. All have been superseded by all-weather road/rail tunnels. The Alps extend down the Adriatic coast into Slovenia, Croatia, Bosnia-Herzegovina, Yugoslavia, and N Albania with the Julian and Dinaric Alps.

Alps, Australian highest area of the E Highlands in Victoria/New South Wales, Australia, noted for winter sports. They include the Snowy Mountains and Mount Kosciusko, Australia's highest mountain, 2,229 m/7,316 ft, first noted by Polish-born Paul Strzelecki 1829 and named after a Polish hero.

Alps, Lunar conspicuous mountain range on the Moon, NE of the Sea of Showers (Mare Imbrium), cut by a valley 150 km/93 mi long. The highest peak is Mont Blanc, about 3,660 m/12,000 ft.

Alps, Southern range of mountains running the entire length of South Island, New Zealand. They are forested to the west, with scanty scrub to the east. The highest point is Mount Cook, 3,764 m/12,349 ft. Scenic features include gorges, glaciers, lakes, and waterfalls. Among its lakes are those at the southern end of the range: Manapouri, Te Anau, and the largest, Wakatipu, 83 km/52 mi long, which lies about 300 m/1,000 ft above sea level and has a depth of 378 m/1,242 ft.

Alsace region of France; area 8,300 sq km/3,204 sq mi; population (1990) 1,624,400. It consists of the *départements* of Bas-Rhin and Haut-Rhin, and its capital is Strasbourg.

Alsace-Lorraine area of NE France, lying west of the river Rhine. It forms the French regions of ◊Alsace and ◊Lorraine. The former iron and steel industries are being replaced by electronics, chemicals, and precision engineering. The German dialect spoken does not have equal rights with French, and there is autonomist sentiment.
history Alsace-Lorraine formed part of Celtic Gaul in Caesar's time, was invaded by the Alemanni and other Germanic tribes in the 4th century, and remained part of the German Empire until the 17th century. In 1648 part of the territory was ceded to France; in 1681 Louis XIV seized Strasbourg. The few remaining districts were seized by France after the French Revolution. Conquered by Germany 1870–71 (chiefly for its iron ores), it was regained by France 1919, then again annexed by Germany 1940–44, when it was liberated by the Allies.

Alsatian another name for the ◊German shepherd dog.

Altai autonomous republic of S Russian Federation, in Altai territory
area 92,600 sq km/35,740 sq mi
capital Gorno-Altaisk
physical in the foothills of the Altai Mountains, bordered in the S by Mongolia and China; forested mountains and high plateaus
industries gold, mercury, and coal mining, timber, chemicals, dairying, cattle breeding
population (1992) 198,000
history colonized by the Russians from the 18th century. Established 1922 as Oirot Autonomous region for the Mongol Oirot people; renamed 1948. An autonomous republic from 1991, renamed 1992.

Altai Mountains mountain system of Kazakhstan, W Siberian Russia, W Mongolia, and N China. It is divided into two parts, the Russian Altai, which includes the highest peak, Mount Belukha, 4,506 m/14,783 ft, and the Mongolian or Great Altai.

Altair or *Alpha Aquilae* brightest star in the constellation Aquila and the 12th brightest star in the night sky. It is a white star 16 light years away and forms the so-called Summer Triangle with the stars Deneb (in the constellation Cygnus) and Vega (in Lyra).

Altamira cave decorated with Palaeolithic wall paintings, the first such to be discovered, 1879. The paintings are realistic depictions of bison, deer, and horses in polychrome (several colours). The cave is near the village of Santillana del Mar in Santander province, N Spain; other well-known Palaeolithic cave paintings are in ◊Lascaux, SW France.

Altamira Amazonian city in the state of Pará, NE Brazil, situated at the junction of the Trans-Amazonian Highway with the Xingu River, 700 km/400 mi SW of Belém; population (1991) 157,900.

altarpiece a painting (more rarely a sculpture) placed on, behind, or above an altar in a Christian church. Altarpieces vary greatly in size, construction, and number of images (a diptych has two hinged panels, a triptych three, and a polyptych more than three). Some are small and portable; some (known as a retable or reredos, there is no clear distinction) are fixed.

A typical Italian altarpiece has a large central panel, flanked by subsidiary panels, with a predella, or strip of scenes, across the bottom. Spanish altarpieces tend to be architecturally elaborate retables. A popular form in northern Europe was the winged altarpiece, in which outer wings are hinged so that they can be closed to cover the centre panel. Outstanding altarpieces include Duccio's *Maestà* 1308–11 (Cathedral Museum, Siena), Grünewald's *Isenheim Altarpiece* about 1515 (Unterlinden Museum, Colmar), and van Eyck's *Adoration of the Mystical Lamb* 1432 (St Bavon, Ghent).

Altamira A prehistoric painting of a bison in the caves at Altamira, northern Spain. Such cave paintings probably had a religious or magical function – to ensure a successful hunt. There are about 150 animal paintings at Altamira, all of them executed with a remarkable sensitivity to an animal's character. *Corbis*

Altdorfer Albrecht c. 1480–1538. German painter, architect, and printmaker. He was active in Regensburg, Bavaria. He is best known for his vast panoramic battle scenes in which his use of light creates movement and drama. On a smaller scale, he also painted some of the first true landscapes (see ◊landscape painting). With Albrecht Dürer and Lucas Cranach, Altdorfer is regarded as one of the leaders of the German Renaissance.

His engravings on wood and copper are second only to those of Dürer. *St George and the Dragon* 1510 (Alte Pinakothek, Munich) is an example of his landscape style; *The Battle of Issus* 1529 (also Munich) is a dramatic panorama.

alternate angles a pair of angles that lie on opposite sides and at opposite ends of a transversal (a line that cuts two or more lines in the same plane). The alternate angles formed by a transversal of two parallel lines are equal.

alternating current (AC) electric current that flows for an interval of time in one direction and then in the opposite direction, that is, a current that flows in alternately reversed directions through or around a circuit. Electric energy is usually generated as alternating current in a power station, and alternating currents may be used for both power and lighting.

The advantage of alternating current over direct current (DC), as from a battery, is that its voltage can be raised or lowered economically by a transformer: high voltage for generation and transmission, and low voltage for safe utilization.

alternation of generations typical life cycle of terrestrial plants and some seaweeds, in which there are two distinct forms occurring alternately: diploid (having two sets of chromosomes) and haploid (one set of chromosomes). The diploid generation produces haploid spores by ◊meiosis, and is called the sporophyte, while the haploid generation produces gametes (sex cells), and is called the gametophyte. The gametes fuse to form a diploid ◊zygote which develops into a new sporophyte; thus the sporophyte and gametophyte alternate.

alternative medicine see ◊medicine, alternative.

alternator electricity ◊generator that produces an alternating current.

Althing parliament of Iceland, established about 930, the oldest in the world. It was dissolved 1800, revived 1843 as an advisory body, and became a legislative body again 1874. It has 63 members who serve a four-year term.

Althusser Louis 1918–1990. French philosopher and Marxist, born in Algeria, who argued that the idea that economic systems determine family and political systems is too simple. He attempted to show how the ruling class ideology of a particular era is a crucial form of class control.

Althusser divides each mode of production into four key elements – the economic, political, ideological, and theoretical – all of which interact. His structuralist analysis of capitalism sees individuals and groups as agents or bearers of the structures of social relations, rather than as independent influences on history. His works include *For Marx* 1965, *Lenin and Philosophy* 1969, and *Essays in Self-Criticism* 1976.

altimeter instrument used in aircraft that measures altitude, or height above sea level. The common type is a form of aneroid ◊barometer, which works by sensing the differences in air pressure at different altitudes. This must continually be recalibrated because of the change in air pressure with changing weather conditions. The ◊radar altimeter measures the height of the aircraft above the ground, measuring the time it takes for radio pulses emitted by the aircraft to be reflected. Radar altimeters are essential features of automatic and blind-landing systems.

Altiplano densely populated upland plateau of the Andes of South America, stretching from S Peru to NW Argentina. The height of the Altiplano is 3,000–4,000 m/10,000–13,000 ft. *See illustration on following page.*

altitude in geometry, the perpendicular distance from a ◊vertex (corner) of a figure, such as a triangle, to the base (the side opposite the vertex).

altiplano, Chile Lake and marsh in altiplano in Lauca National Park, Chile. *K G Preston-Mafham/Premaphotos Wildlife*

altitude measurement of height, usually given in metres above sea level.

altitude sickness condition caused by sudden exposure to low atmospheric pressure and reduced oxygen at altitudes above 3,000 m/10,000 ft. Symptoms include nausea, breathlessness, and exhaustion. Treatment includes rest, analgesics, oxygen, and return to lower altitudes.

Altman Robert 1925– . US film director and producer. His films vary in tone from the comic to the elegiac, but are frequently ambitious in both content and form, taking a quizzical view of American life and culture and utilizing a complex and sometimes fragmentary style. His antiwar comedy *M*A*S*H* 1970 was a critical and commercial success. Subsequent films include *The Player* 1992, *Short Cuts* 1993, and *Prêt-à-Porter* 1994.

Altman, Sidney 1938– . Canadian-born US biochemist who shared the Nobel Prize for Chemistry in 1989 with Thomas Cech for his research on the catalytic activities of RNA (the nucleic acid involved in translating DNA into proteins).

Altman studied ribonuclease-P, an enzyme that catalyses the depolymerization (decoupling of molecules) of RNA in the formation of transfer RNA (tRNA). Ribonuclease-P is comprised of RNA and a protein. Altman showed that the RNA component is all that is required to catalyse the formation of tRNA with the protein playing no part in this process.

alto (Italian 'high') voice or instrument between tenor and soprano, of approximate range G3–D5. The traditional male alto voice of early opera, also known as countertenor, is trumpetlike and penetrating; the low-register female contralto ('contra-alto'), exemplified by English singer Kathleen ◊Ferrier, is rich and mellow in tone. Alto is also the French name for the ◊viola.

‘I have tamed men of iron and why then shall I not be able to tame these men of butter?’

Ferdinand Alvarez de Toledo Alva
Reply to King Philip II of Spain on being appointed governor general of the Netherlands 1567

altruism in biology, helping another individual of the same species to reproduce more effectively, as a direct result of which the altruist may leave fewer offspring itself. Female honey bees (workers) behave altruistically by rearing sisters in order to help their mother, the queen bee, reproduce, and forgo any possibility of reproducing themselves.

altruism term coined by the French positivist philosopher Auguste Comte, briefly defined as 'living for others'. The altruistic instinct is a social instinct or impulse, and is evidenced in kindness, veneration, and affection.

It was this instinct or tendency in human beings that Comte wished to raise to a conscious principle, or an ethical ideal, making it the chief aim of human action to seek the welfare of others. Herbert Spencer in his *Data of Ethics* 1879 sought to show that in the course of social evolution egoism and altruism would be reconciled.

ALU abbreviation for ◊***arithmetic and logic unit***.

alum any double sulphate of a monovalent metal or radical (such as sodium, potassium, or ammonium) and a trivalent metal (such as aluminium, chromium, or iron). The commonest alum is the double sulphate of potassium and aluminium, $K_2Al_2(SO_4)_4.24H_2O$, a white crystalline powder that is readily soluble in water. It is used in curing animal skins. Other alums are used in papermaking and to fix dye in the textile industry.

alumina or ***corundum*** Al_2O_3 oxide of aluminium, widely distributed in clays, slates, and shales. It is formed by the decomposition of the feldspars in granite and used as an abrasive. Typically it is a white powder, soluble in most strong acids or caustic alkalis but not in water. Impure alumina is called 'emery'. Rubies and sapphires are corundum gemstones.

aluminium lightweight, silver-white, ductile and malleable, metallic element, symbol Al, atomic number 13, relative atomic mass 26.9815, melting point 658°C. It is the third most abundant element (and the most abundant metal) in the Earth's crust, of which it makes up about 8.1% by mass. It is non-magnetic, an excellent conductor of electricity, and oxidizes easily, the layer of oxide on its surface making it highly resistant to tarnish.

pure aluminium Aluminium is a reactive element with stable compounds, so a great deal of energy is needed in order to separate aluminium from its ores, and the pure metal was not readily obtainable until the middle of the 19th century. Commercially, it is prepared by the electrolysis of alumina (aluminium oxide), which is obtained from the ore ◊bauxite. In its pure state aluminium is a weak metal, but when combined with elements such as copper, silicon, or magnesium it forms alloys of great strength.

uses Because of its light weight (relative density 2.70), aluminium is widely used in the shipbuilding and aircraft industries. It is also used in making cooking utensils, cans for beer and soft drinks, and foil. It is much used in steel-cored overhead cables and for canning uranium slugs for nuclear reactors. Aluminium is an essential constituent in some magnetic materials.

Alva Ferdinand Alvarez de Toledo. Duke of Alva (or ***Alba***) 1508–1582. Spanish politician and general. He successfully commanded the Spanish armies of the Holy Roman emperor Charles V and his son Philip II of Spain. In 1567 he was appointed governor of the Netherlands, where he set up a reign of terror to suppress Protestantism and the revolt of the Netherlands. In 1573 he was recalled at his own request. He later led a successful expedition against Portugal 1580–81.

Alvarado Pedro de c. 1485–1541. Spanish conquistador, ruler of Guatemala 1524–41. Alvarado joined Hernán ◊Cortés' army 1519 and became his principal captain during the conquest of New Spain. Left in command at Tenochtitlán, Mexico, he provoked the Aztec rebellion that resulted in the death of ◊Montezuma II 1520. He conquered Guatemala 1523–24 and was its governor and captain general until his death.

Alvarez Luis Walter 1911–1988. US physicist. He led the research team that discovered the Ξ_0 subatomic particle 1959. He also made many other breakthroughs in fundamental physics, accelerators, and radar. He worked on the US atom bomb for two years, at Chicago and at Los Alamos, New Mexico, during World War II. Nobel prize 1968.

extinction of the dinosaurs In 1980 Alvarez was responsible for the theory that dinosaurs disappeared because a meteorite crashed into Earth 70 million years ago, producing a dust cloud that blocked out the Sun for several years, causing dinosaurs and plants to die. The first half of the hypothesis is now widely accepted.

Alvarez Quintero Serafin (1871–1938) and Joaquin (1873–1944) Spanish dramatists. The brothers, born near Seville, always worked together and from 1897 produced about 200 comedies, principally dealing with local life in Andalusia. Among them are *Papá Juan: centenario* 1909 and *Los mosquitos* 1928.

Other well known plays are *Los galeotes* 1900, *Las flores* 1901, *Malvaloca* 1912, and *La calumniada* 1919. Genial and sentimental, they are not concerned with serious moral or social issues.

alveolus (plural ***alveoli***) one of the many thousands of tiny air sacs in the ◊lungs in which exchange of oxygen and carbon dioxide takes place between air and the bloodstream.

Alzheimer Alois (1864–1915). German neuropathologist who was the first to describe the degenerative illness affecting the nerve cells of the frontal and temporal lobes of the cerebrum of the brain, characterized by severe memory impairment.

Alzheimer's disease common manifestation of ◊dementia, thought to afflict one in 20 people over 65. After heart disease, cancer, and strokes it is the most common cause of death in the Western world. Attacking the brain's 'grey matter', it is a disease of mental processes rather than physical function, characterized by memory loss and progressive intellectual impairment. It was first described by Alois Alzheimer 1906. It affects up to 4 million people in the USA and around 600,000 in Britain.

causes Various factors have been implicated in causing Alzheimer's disease including high levels of aluminium in drinking water and the presence in the brain of an abnormal protein, known as beta-amyloid. In 1993 the gene coding for apolipoprotein (APoE) was implicated. US researchers established that people who carry a particular version of this gene are at greatly increased risk of developing the disease. Although there is no cure, trials of anti-inflammatory drugs have shown promising results. Also under development are drugs which block the toxic effects of beta-amyloid.

alveolus The tiny air sacs, called alveoli, in the lungs are covered with a network of blood capillaries, allowing oxygen to enter the blood. The alveoli of an adult have a total surface area of 70 sq m/750 sq ft.

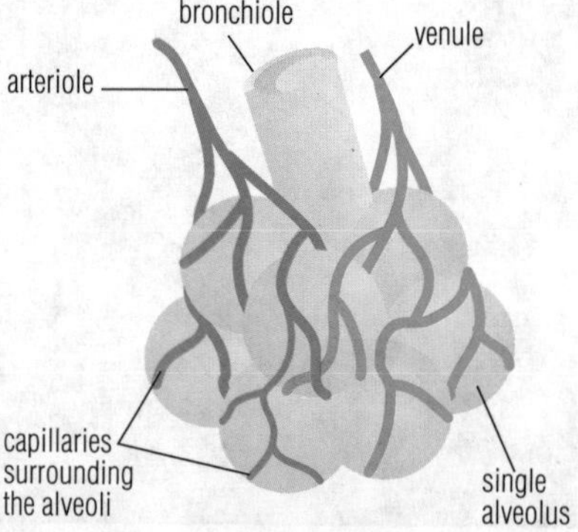

AM abbreviation for ◊***amplitude modulation***.

amadavat or ***avadavat*** small singing bird *Amandava amandava*, of the family Estrildidae, order Passeriformes. It is about 13 cm/5 in long and is found in the Malay Archipelago and throughout the Indian subcontinent. The breeding male is carmine coloured, with the upper parts brownish grey and wings spotted white. At other times the male is brownish olive, like the female.

Amal radical Lebanese ◊Shi'ite military force, established by Musa Sadr in the 1970s; its headquarters are in Borj al-Barajneh. The movement split into extremist and moderate groups 1982, but both sides agreed on the aim of increasing Shi'ite political representation in Lebanon.

Amalfi port 39 km/24 mi SE of Naples, Italy, situated at the foot of Monte Cerrato, on the Gulf of Salerno; population 7,000. For 700 years it was an independent republic. It is an ancient archiepiscopal see (seat of an archbishop) and has a Romanesque cathedral.

amalgam any alloy of mercury with other metals. Most metals will form amalgams, except iron and platinum. Amalgam is used in dentistry for filling teeth, and usually contains copper, silver, and zinc as the main alloying ingredients.

Amalgamation, the process of forming an amalgam, is a technique sometimes used to extract gold and silver from their ores. The ores are ground to a fine sand and brought into contact with mercury, which dissolves the gold and silver particles. The amalgam is then heated to distil the mercury, leaving a residue of silver and gold. The mercury is recovered and reused.

Amanita genus of fungi (see ◊fungus), of the family Agaricaceae, distinguished by a ring, or volva, round the stem, warty patches on the cap, and the clear white colour of the gills. Many of the species are brightly coloured and highly poisonous.

The fly agaric *A. muscaria*, a poisonous toadstool with a white-spotted red cap, which grows under birch or pine, and the deadly buff-coloured ◊death cap *A. phalloides* are both found in Britain. The fly agaric is the 'magic mushroom' used in religious ritual by early peoples of Siberia, Europe, and India. Edible species include the false death cap *A. citrina*, and the blusher *A. rubescens*. *A. pantherina* is not edible, causing very unpleasant though nonfatal poisoning.

Amanullah Khan 1892–1960. Emir (ruler) of Afghanistan 1919–29, who assumed the title of king 1926. Third son of Habibullah Khan, he seized the throne on his father's assassination and concluded a treaty with the British, but his policy of westernization led to rebellion 1928. Amanullah had to flee, abdicated 1929, and settled in Rome, Italy.

Amar Das 1495–1574. Indian religious leader, third guru (teacher) of Sikhism 1552–74. He laid emphasis on equality and opposed the caste system. He initiated the custom of the *langar* (communal meal).

Amarillo city in the Texas panhandle, USA; population (1992) 161,100. The centre of the world's largest cattle-producing area, it processes the live animal into frozen supermarket packets in a single continuous operation on an assembly line.

Amazon (Indian ***Amossona*** 'destroyer of boats') South American river, the world's second longest, 6,570 km/4,080 mi, and the largest in volume of water. Its main headstreams, the Marañón and the Ucayali, rise in central Peru and unite to flow east across Brazil for about 4,000 km/2,500 mi. It has 48,280 km/30,000 mi of navigable waterways, draining 7,000,000 sq km/2,750,000 sq mi, nearly half the South American landmass. It reaches the Atlantic on the equator, its estuary 80 km/50 mi wide, discharging a volume of water so immense that 64 km/40 mi out to sea, fresh water remains at the surface. The Amazon basin covers 7.5 million sq km/3 million sq mi, of which 5 million sq km/2 million sq mi is tropical forest containing 30% of all known plant and animal species (80,000 known species of trees, 3,000 known species of land vertebrates, 2,000 species of freshwater fish). It is the wettest region on Earth; average rainfall 2.54 m/8.3 ft a year.

The opening up of the Amazon river basin to settlers has resulted in a massive burning of tropical forest to create both arable and pasture land. The problems of soil erosion, the disappearance of potentially useful plant and animal species, and the possible impact of large-scale forest clearance on global warming of the atmosphere have become environmental issues of international concern. By 1990, at least 8% of the Brazilian Amazonian rainforest had been destroyed by deforestation, amounting to 404,000 sq km/155,944 sq mi (nearly the size of Sweden). ▷ *See feature on pp. 896–897.*

Amazon in Greek mythology, a member of a group of female warriors living near the Black Sea, who cut off their right breasts to use the bow more easily. Their queen Penthesilea was killed by Achilles at the siege of Troy. The Amazons attacked ◊Theseus and besieged him at Athens, but were defeated, and Theseus took the Amazon Hippolyta captive; she later gave birth to Hippolytus. The term Amazon has come to mean a large, strong woman.

Amazonia those regions of Brazil, Colombia, Ecuador, Peru, and Bolivia lying within the basin of the Amazon River.

Amazonian Indian indigenous inhabitants of the Amazon River Basin in South America. The majority of the societies are kin-based; traditional livelihood includes hunting and gathering, fishing, and shifting cultivation. A wide range of indigenous languages are spoken. Numbering perhaps 2.5 million in the 16th century, they had been reduced to perhaps one-tenth of that number by the 1820s. Rainforests are being destroyed for mining and ranching and Amazonian Indians are being transported or assimilated.

In June 1998 a previously unknown tribe of about 200 hunters and gatherers was discovered in Brazil's Amazon rainforest. The destruction of rainforest threatens the survival of such societies.

ambassador officer of the highest rank in the diplomatic service, who represents the head of one sovereign state at the court or capital of another.

amber fossilized resin from coniferous trees of the Middle Tertiary period. It is often washed ashore on the Baltic coast with plant and animal specimens preserved in it; many extinct species have been found preserved in this way. It ranges in colour from red to yellow, and is used to make jewellery.

Amber has been coveted for its supposed special properties since prehistoric times. Archaeologists have found amulets made of amber dating back as far as 35000 BC. When amber is rubbed with cloth, it attracts light objects, such as feathers. The effect, first noticed by the ancient Greeks, is due to acquisition of negative electric charge, hence the adaptation of the Greek word for amber, *elektron*, for electricity (see ◊static electricity).

Amber's preservative properties were demonstrated 1995 when US scientists succeeded in extracting and germinating bacterial spores from a bee in amber that was 40 million years old.

ambergris fatty substance, resembling wax, found in the stomach and intestines of the sperm ◊whale. It is found floating in warm seas, and is used in perfumery as a fixative.

Amazon

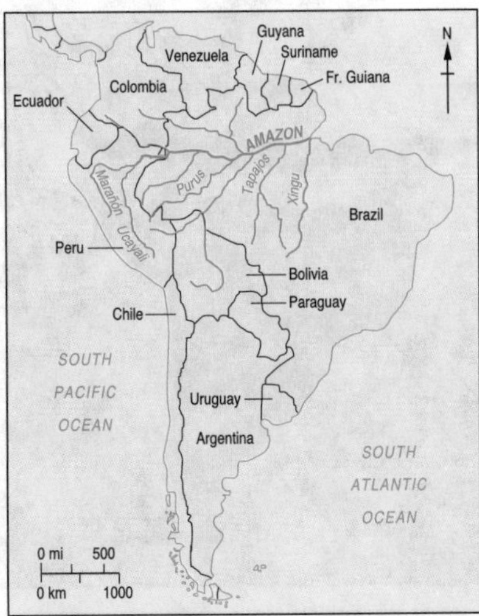

Ambrose Curtly Elconn Lynwall 1963– . West Indies cricketer, born in Antigua. A tall right-arm opening bowler, whose ability to bowl fast and accurately whilst extracting bounce and movement from even the most benign pitches made him the world's most feared pace bowler in the 1990s. In 1997 he became only the eleventh player to take 300 or more Test wickets.

Ambrose, St c. 340–397. One of the early Christian leaders and theologians known as the Fathers of the Church. Feast day 7 Dec.

Born at Trèves, in S Gaul, the son of a Roman prefect, Ambrose became governor of N Italy. In 374 he was chosen bishop of Milan, although he was not yet a member of the church. He was then baptized and consecrated. He wrote many hymns, and devised the regulation of Christian church music known as the Ambrosian chant, which retains many features of Middle Eastern religious chants.

ambrosia (Greek 'immortal') in Greek mythology, food of the gods which was supposed to confer eternal life upon all who ate it.

Amenhotep four Egyptian pharaohs, including ***Amenhotep III*** 1391–1353 BC, king (pharaoh) of ancient Egypt. He built great monuments at Thebes, including the temples at Luxor. Two portrait statues at his mortuary temple were known to the Greeks as the colossi of Memnon; one was cracked, and when the temperature changed at dawn it gave out an eerie sound, then thought supernatural. His son ***Amenhotep IV*** changed his name to ◊Akhenaton.

America western hemisphere of the Earth, containing the continents of ◊North America and ◊South America, with ◊Central America in between. This great landmass extends from the Arctic to the Antarctic, from beyond 75° N to past 55° S. The area is about 42,000,000 sq km/16,000,000 sq mi, and the estimated population is over 500 million. Politically, it consists of 36 nations and US, British, French, and Dutch dependencies.

The name America is derived from Amerigo Vespucci, the Florentine navigator who was falsely supposed to have been the first European to reach the American mainland 1497. The name is also popularly used to refer to the ◊United States of America, a usage which many Canadians, South Americans, and other non-US Americans dislike.

'The Discovery of America was the occasion of the greatest outburst of cruelty and reckless greed known in history.'

On **America**
Joseph Conrad
Last Essays

American Ballet Theater (ABT) US company founded 1939 (as the Ballet Theater), aiming to present both classical and contemporary American ballet. ABT has a repertoire of exemplary range and quality with celebrity guest appearances. Based in New York, the company tours annually, and is considered one of the top six ballet companies in the world.

Among ABT's first ballerinas were Alicia Markova and Alicia Alonso. In the 1970s ABT opened its doors to the Soviet dancers who defected to the West, such as Rudolf Nureyev, Natalia Makarova, and Mikhail Baryshnikov (artistic director 1980–90).

American Civil War 1861–65; see ◊Civil War, American.

American Federation of Labor and Congress of Industrial Organizations (AFL–CIO) federation of North American trade unions, representing (1995) 13 million workers, or about 14% of the workforce in North America.

The AFL was founded 1886 by Samuel Gompers (1850–1924) and was initially a union of skilled craftworkers. The CIO, representing unskilled workers, broke away from the AFL in the mid-1930s. A merger reunited them 1955, bringing most unions into the national federation. In 1995 John Sweeney became the leader of the AFL–CIO.

American football see ◊football, American.

American Independence, War of alternative name of the ◊American Revolution, the revolt 1775–83 of the British North American colonies that resulted in the establishment of the United States of America.

American literature see ◊United States literature.

American Revolution revolt 1775–83 of the British North American colonies, resulting in the establishment of the United States of America. It was caused by colonial opposition to British economic exploitation and by the unwillingness of the

cont. on p. 34

The Birth of the USA

Benjamin Franklin and the Declaration of Independence. Franklin helped draft the 1776 Declaration, the manifesto of the 13 American colonies which rejected British rule and became the foundation of the US constitution. Reflecting Enlightenment ideas on social and political justice, the Declaration based government on the consent of the governed, and on the right to 'life, liberty and the pursuit of happiness'. *(Franklin) Ann Ronan/Image Select (UK) Ltd; (Declaration) Library of Congress*

The American Revolution can be presented narrowly as simply the breakaway of the American colonists from the British colonial empire – achieved, after an eight-year war, at the Treaty of Paris 1783. A broader view presents it as a far-reaching revolution in the social, political, and economic order which began before and continued after the military conflict and independence. In the course of the revolution, America threw off its subordinate role as a colony of Britain – 5,000 km/2,000 mi away, with a hereditary monarchy and a parliamentary system corrupted by court patronage – and became the world's first modern political regime.

Post-revolutionary America became the United States, a federal republic based on representative democracy, in which three-quarters of adult males had the right to vote and civil rights were enshrined in the 1791 Bill of Rights. As a colony, America was economically dependent on Britain through the constraints on trade imposed by the Navigation Acts. By achieving independence, America secured autonomy to develop its own shipping and modern industries. From this perspective, the American Revolution can be seen as extending over nearly 30 years, beginning in the early 1760s. It was generated by an ever-widening gulf in outlooks and interests between the parent country and its colonial offshoot.

Background and causes

Permanent English settlements were founded in North America in 1607, at Jamestown, on the Chesapeake Bay, Virginia, and in 1620, at Plymouth, in Massachusetts Bay, by Puritan Pilgrim refugees. By the end of the century twelve colonies had been established, and in 1733 Georgia, founded to resettle imprisoned debtors, became the thirteenth.These Thirteen Colonies stretched 2,000 km/1,200 mi along the east coast. Resistance from native Americans made settlement inland more difficult, and

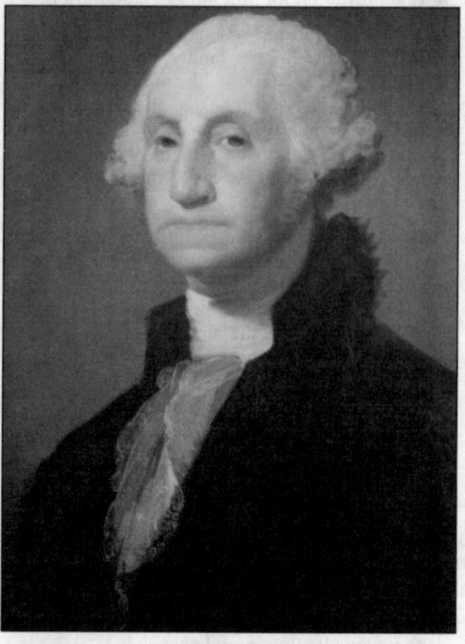

A portrait of George Washington, 1796, by Gilbert Stuart. Stuart was the best portraitist working in America in the period after it won independence from Britain. He painted many revolutionary heroes, above all the first president, George Washington, whom he depicted several times. Another American painter, Benjamin West, was greatly impressed by Stuart's power of characterization; he said that he 'nailed the face to the canvas'. *Corbis*

nowhere did the settlers penetrate more than 300 km/190 mi from the coast. Nevertheless, by the third quarter of the 18th century there were nearly three million American colonists. In the south they had established a thriving economy, based on tobacco plantations worked by black slaves, and in the north a largely self-sufficient farming-, craft-, and fishing-based economy. With abundant land and low taxes, they were one of the most prosperous communities in the world and, although there was a powerful and wealthy trading and landowning elite, American society was relatively egalitarian. America's remoteness from Britain made it possible for colonists to establish influential local representative assemblies, and these attracted politicians who

The Boston Tea Party. US colonists, dressed as Native Americans, throwing tea into Boston Harbour, Massachusetts, 1773, in protest at high British taxes. The illustration is from W D Cooper's *History of America*, published in London 1789, just six years after the end of the American War of Independence. *Corbis*

were influenced by radical, anti-monarchist thinking.

By 1763, following success against France and Spain in the Seven Years' War (known in America as the French and Indian War), Britain had extended its influence to Canada in the north and Florida in the south, and appeared to have gained complete control of North America. However, this prolonged global conflict placed a huge strain on the British economy, doubling the national debt to £130 million. This prompted the British government to rethink imperial policy and reorganize and rationalize the administration of America on more centralized lines, with a permanent standing army and professional administration paid for by taxing the colonists. A series of measures was introduced 1763–75 in support of this programme. This antagonized the colonies' elites, who feared that Britain intended to curb their autonomy and suppress their local assemblies. Initially, Americans responded with acts of disobedience, carried out by patriotic gangs known as the Sons of Liberty. In 1775 this escalated into armed conflict and, from 1776, became a demand for independence, drawing committed support from a third of the colonists and unspoken agreement from many more.

Military conflict: 1775–83

The first military engagement of the American War of Independence took place in April 1775 at Lexington and Concord, Massachusetts. British troops were sent to seize illegal military stores near Boston and arrest rebel leaders John Hancock and Samuel Adams; they were attacked by armed farmers – the minutemen militia – and forced to retreat. Further engagements followed at Fort Ticonderoga, New York and Bunker Hill, Massachusetts, in May and June 1775, won respectively by the Americans and the British. On 4 July 1776 the colonists formally issued a declaration of independence, drafted by Thomas Jefferson, and revised by Benjamin Franklin and John Adams.

The war soon escalated, as large numbers of British Redcoat troops, supported by German mercenaries, were sent across the Atlantic. The early fighting was concentrated in the more densely populated north, where the British anticipated swift success. They were disappointed, however, since they had overestimated the extent of American loyalist support they would receive. In addition, they were hampered by overextended supply lines, and were fighting in unfamiliar terrain. Facing them were highly motivated American 'Patriot' troops led by able commanders, notably George Washington (later the country's first president), a veteran of the French and Indian Wars, who adopted novel guerrilla tactics. These contributed to a crucial early defeat of the British, in Oct 1777, at Saratoga Springs, New York, when General John Burgoyne, surrounded in woods, was forced to surrender. This reverse in Britain's fortunes persuaded France in Feb 1778, followed later by the Spanish and Dutch, to form a military alliance with the American colonists. This alliance provided the Americans with vital naval support and distracted British forces.

From 1778, after the Americans had rejected an offer of peace negotiations, the British campaign moved south. They enjoyed initial successes at Savannah, Georgia and Charleston, South Carolina, but from early 1781 the tide began to turn and on 19 Oct 1781, besieged by 17,000 American and French troops, and blockaded by the French navy, Lord Charles Cornwallis surrendered ignominiously at Yorktown, Virginia. This was the decisive defeat that destroyed Britain's will to continue the struggle. Hostilities formally ceased in Feb 1783 and on 3 Sept 1783, at the Treaty of Paris, Britain formally recognized America's independence and its rights to the American interior. The last British troops left New York in Nov 1783.

Political settlement: the Constitution of 1787

The revolt against British rule took the form of a rebellion by individual colonies united in self-interest, rather than a concerted national uprising. In Sept 1774 delegates from the Thirteen Colonies met in Philadelphia in a Continental Congress to frame the Articles of Confederation. These delegated a restricted number of functions to a small federal, or national, legislature, but most powers were retained by the states. However, this contributed towards political instability, highlighted by Shays' Rebellion in western Massachusetts in 1786, when farmers protested against taxes.

Prompted by the nationally-minded professional and gentry elite, known as the Federalists, 55 delegates from 12 states met at Philadelphia in May 1787 to draft a new constitution. The leading Federalist, James Madison, put foward the Virginia Plan for a stronger central government. Eventually, following a compromise with anti-Federalist regional interests, a constitution was adopted by the Thirteen Colonies between 1787–90, providing for the sharing of power between the individual states and a federal government. This government was to be a powerful national legislature, the two-chamber Congress with a directly elected lower house; a relatively weak executive (the president) who was indirectly elected until after 1804; and an independent judiciary. Powers were deliberately balanced, with citizens' rights enshrined in a Bill of Rights.

The Boston Massacre took place on 5 March 1770, when a British officer ordered his troops to fire into a crowd who were voicing their resentment of the British military presence. Five men were killed, and all troops were withdrawn from the town. The incident fuelled anti-British feeling among the American colonists. *Corbis*

The repercussions of the American Revolution

For Britain, the loss of its American empire was humiliating, but the effects were surprisingly short-lived. British prime minister Lord North was immediately toppled, but national resurgence was swift. Over the next half century a new, larger, and more tightly controlled 'Second British Empire' was established, centred on India, and embracing a quarter of the world's population. Meanwhile, although economic ties with the new United States remained close, the colonists were free to develop the continent's vast interior and harness its rich natural resources.

The deeper consequences of the American Revolution were in the area of political ideology. The United States, with its representative republican democracy, provided a blueprint for future political developments both in Europe and in colonial Spanish America. With its rhetorical emphasis on people's intrinsic equality and rights, the Revolution has inspired liberals and radicals down the centuries, from the French Revolution and early 19th-century anti-colonial revolts in Haiti, Venezuela, and Colombia through to the abortive pro-democracy demonstrations that took place in Tiananmen Square, Beijing, China in 1989. However, not until 1920 and 1964, when the franchise was finally extended to women and southern blacks respectively, could America claim to have fully completed its democratic revolution.

IAN DERBYSHIRE

The uniforms of the American Revolutionary army in 1782. The American troops were probably not as well turned out as this picture suggests. However, they had weapons and knew the terrain better than the British, and their success was mainly due to their skill in guerrilla tactics. *Corbis*

SEE ALSO

Adams, John; American Revolution: timeline; Bill of Rights; Boston Tea Party; Continental Congress; Franklin, Benjamin; Jefferson, Thomas; Madison, James; Navigation Acts; Stamp Acts; Thirteen Colonies; Washington, George

I do not know the method of drawing up an indictment against an whole people.

American Revolution Edmund Burke on conciliation with America, at the start of the American Revolution 1775

AMERICAN REVOLUTION: TIMELINE

1773	A government tax on tea led Massachusetts citizens disguised as North American Indians to board British ships carrying tea and throw it into Boston harbour: the Boston Tea Party.
1774–75	The First Continental Congress was held in Philadelphia to call for civil disobedience in reply to British measures such as the Intolerable Acts, which closed the port of Boston and quartered British troops in private homes.
1775	19 April: Hostilities began at Lexington and Concord, Massachusetts. The first shots were fired when British troops, sent to seize illegal military stores and arrest rebel leaders John Hancock and Samuel Adams, were attacked by the local militia (minutemen). 10 May: Fort Ticonderoga, New York, was captured from the British. 17 June: The colonists were defeated in the first battle of the Revolution, the Battle of Bunker Hill (which actually took place on Breed's Hill, nearby); George Washington was appointed colonial commander in chief soon afterwards.
1776	4 July: The Second Continental Congress issued the Declaration of Independence, which specified some of the colonists' grievances and proclaimed an independent government. 27 Aug: Washington was defeated at Long Island and was forced to evacuate New York and retire to Pennsylvania. 26 Dec: Washington recrossed the Delaware River and defeated the British at Trenton, New Jersey.
1777	3 Jan: Washington defeated the British at Princeton, New Jersey. 11 Sept–4 Oct: British general William Howe defeated Washington at Brandywine and Germantown, and occupied Philadelphia. 17 Oct: British general John Burgoyne surrendered at Saratoga, New York, and was therefore unable to link up with Howe.
1777–78	Washington wintered at Valley Forge, Pennsylvania, enduring harsh conditions and seeing many of his troops leave to return to their families.
1778	France entered the war on the US side (John Paul Jones led a French-sponsored naval unit).
1780	12 May: The British captured Charleston, South Carolina, one of a series of British victories in the South, but alienated support by enforcing conscription.
1781	19 Oct: British general Charles Cornwallis, besieged in Yorktown, Virginia, by Washington and the French fleet, surrendered.
1782	Peace negotiations opened.
1783	3 Sept: The Treaty of Paris recognized American independence.

colonists to pay for a standing army. It was also fuelled by the colonists' antimonarchist sentiment and their desire to participate in the policies affecting them. ▷ *See feature on pp. 32–33.*

American Samoa see ◊Samoa, American.

America Online (AOL) US commercial information service, launched 1986. In 1995 it overtook the then market leader, ◊CompuServe, and by 1996 had more than 5 million users worldwide. America Online combined with the German publishing conglomerate Bertelsmann to launch a UK version of the service, known as AOL, in early 1996.

America's Cup international yacht-racing trophy named after the US schooner *America*, owned by J L Stevens, who won a race around the Isle of Wight 1851. Offered for a challenge in 1870, it is a seven-race series. The USA monopolized the race until 1983, when an Australian crew won the trophy. All races were held at Newport, Rhode Island, until 1987 when the Perth Yacht Club, Australia, hosted the series. Yachts are very expensive to produce and only syndicates can afford to provide a yacht capable of winning the trophy.

americium radioactive metallic element of the ◊actinide series, symbol Am, atomic number 95, relative atomic mass 243.13; it was first synthesized 1944. It occurs in nature in minute quantities in ◊pitchblende and other uranium ores, where it is produced from the decay of neutron-bombarded plutonium, and is the element with the highest atomic number that occurs in nature. It is synthesized in quantity only in nuclear reactors by the bombardment of plutonium with neutrons. Its longest-lived isotope is Am-243, with a half-life of 7,650 years.

Ames Research Center US space-research (NASA) installation at Mountain View, California, USA, for the study of aeronautics and life sciences. It has managed the Pioneer series of planetary probes and is involved in the search for extraterrestrial life.

amethyst variety of ◊quartz, SiO_2, coloured violet by the presence of small quantities of impurities such as manganese or iron; used as a semiprecious stone. Amethysts are found chiefly in the Ural Mountains, India, the USA, Uruguay, and Brazil.

It was no wonder that people were so horrible when they started life as children.

Kingsley Amis *Lucky Jim*

Amhara an ethnic group comprising approximately 25% of the population of Ethiopia; 13 million (1987). The Amhara are traditionally farmers. They speak Amharic, a language of the Semitic branch of the Hamito-Semitic (Afro-Asiatic) family. Most are members of the Ethiopian Christian Church.

Amida Buddha (Sanskrit *Amitābha*, Japanese *Amida Nyorai*) the 'Buddha of immeasurable light', venerated especially in ◊Pure Land Buddhism. He presides over the Western Paradise (the Buddha-land of his own creation), and through his unlimited compassion and power to save, devotees can be reborn there to achieve enlightenment.

Japanese paintings often show Amida towering over a landscape or descending on a cloud, greeting the soul of the dying believer. In sculpture, Amida is generally seated in meditation; standing figures of Amida show him making the gesture of bestowing fearlessness, right hand raised. He is often flanked by the bodhisattvas Kannon and Seishi.

amide any organic chemical derived from a fatty acid by the replacement of the hydroxyl group (–OH) by an amino group ($–NH_2$). One of the simplest amides is acetamide (CH_3CONH_2), which has a strong mousy odour.

Amiens ancient city of NE France at the confluence of the rivers Somme and Avre; capital of Somme *département* and centre of a market-gardening region irrigated by canals; population (1990) 136,200. It has a magnificent Gothic cathedral with a spire 113 m/370 ft high and gave its name to the battles of Aug 1918, when British field marshal Douglas Haig launched his victorious offensive in World War I.

Amin (Dada) Idi 1925– . Ugandan politician, president 1971–79. He led the coup that deposed Milton Obote 1971, expelled the Asian community 1972, and exercised a reign of terror over his people. He fled to Libya when insurgent Ugandan and Tanzanian troops invaded the country 1979.

amine any of a class of organic chemical compounds in which one or more of the hydrogen atoms of ammonia (NH_3) have been replaced by other groups of atoms.

Methyl amines have unpleasant ammonia odours and occur in decomposing fish. They are all gases at ordinary temperature. Aromatic amine compounds include aniline, which is used in dyeing.

amino acid water-soluble organic ◊molecule, mainly composed of carbon, oxygen, hydrogen, and nitrogen, containing both a basic amino group (NH_2) and an acidic carboxyl (COOH) group. They are small molecules able to pass through membranes. When two or more amino acids are joined together, they are known as ◊peptides; ◊proteins are made up of peptide chains folded or twisted in characteristic shapes.

Many different proteins are found in the cells of living organisms, but they are all made up of the same 20 amino acids, joined together in varying combinations (although other types of amino acid do occur infrequently in nature). Eight of these, the essential amino acids, cannot be synthesized by humans and must be obtained from the diet. Children need a further two amino acids that are not essential for adults. Other animals also need some preformed amino acids in their diet, but green plants can manufacture all the amino acids they need from simpler molecules, relying on energy from the Sun and minerals (including nitrates) from the soil.

Amis Kingsley (William) 1922–1995. English novelist and poet. He was associated early on with the ◊Angry Young Men group of writers. His sharply ironic works frequently debunk pretentious mediocrity; his first novel, the best-selling *Lucky Jim* 1954, is a comic portrayal of life at a provincial university.

amino acid Amino acids are natural organic compounds that make up proteins and can thus be considered the basic molecules of life. There are 20 different amino acids. They consist mainly of carbon, oxygen, hydrogen, and nitrogen. Each amino acid has a common core structure (consisting of two carbon atoms, two oxygen atoms, a nitrogen atom, and four hydrogen atoms) to which is attached a variable group, known as the R group. In glycine, the R group is a single hydrogen atom; in alanine, the R group consists of a carbon and three hydrogen atoms.

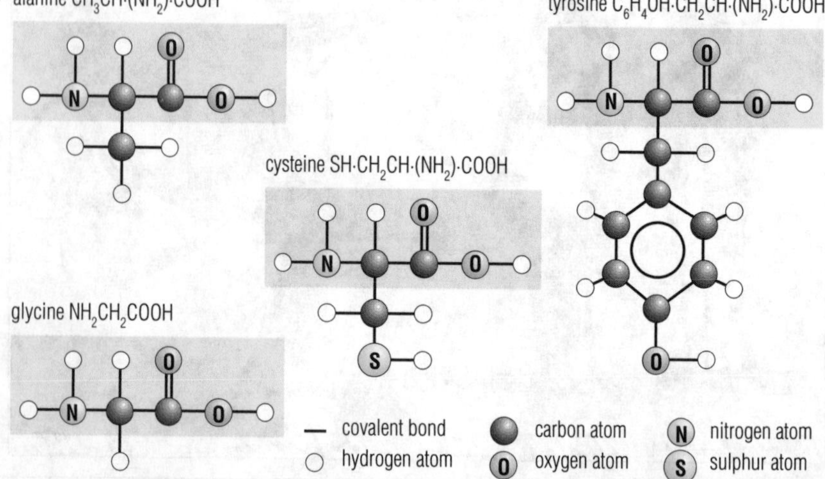

His other novels, written in a variety of genres, include the spy story *The Anti-Death League* 1966, the ghost story *The Green Man* 1969, *The Riverside Villas Murder* 1973, and *The Alteration* 1976, which imagines a 20th-century society dominated by the Roman Catholic Church. His fascination with middle-aged sexuality is demonstrated in such novels as *Stanley and the Women* 1984 and *The Old Devils* 1986 (Booker Prize). His poetry includes *A Case of Samples: Poems 1946–56* 1956 and *Collected Poems 1944–79* 1979. He is the father of writer Martin Amis.

Amis Martin Louis 1949– . English novelist. His works are characterized by their acerbic black humour and include *The Rachel Papers* 1973, a memoir of adolescence told through flashbacks, *Dead Babies* 1975, which addresses decadence and sadism, *Money* 1984, *London Fields* 1989, and *Time's Arrow* 1991.

Amis English novelist Martin Amis. His darkly satirical, sometimes macabre novels depict the contemporary world as being in a period of moral decadence and decay. *Penguin Books Ltd*

Amman capital and chief industrial centre of Jordan; population (1994 est) 1,300,000. It is a major communications centre, linking historic trade routes across the Middle East. Amman is built on the site of the Old Testament Rabbath-Ammon (Philadelphia), capital of the Ammonites.

ammeter instrument that measures electric current, usually in ◊amperes.

Ammon in Egyptian mythology, the king of the gods, the equivalent of Zeus (Roman Jupiter). The name is also spelled Amen/Amun, as in the name of the pharaoh Tutankh*amen*. In art, he is represented as a ram, as a man with a ram's head, or as a man crowned with feathers. He had temples at Siwa oasis, Libya, and at Thebes, Egypt; his oracle at Siwa was patronized by the classical Greeks.

ammonia NH_3 colourless pungent-smelling gas, lighter than air and very soluble in water. It is made on an industrial scale by the ◊Haber (or Haber-Bosch) process, and used mainly to produce nitrogenous fertilizers, nitric acid, and some explosives.

In aquatic organisms and some insects, nitrogenous waste (from the breakdown of amino acids and so on) is excreted in the form of ammonia, rather than as urea in mammals.

Ammonite member of an ancient Semitic people, mentioned in the Old Testament or Jewish Bible, who lived NW of the Dead Sea. Their capital was Amman, in present-day Jordan. They worshipped the god Moloch, to whom they offered human sacrifices. They were frequently at war with the Israelites.

ammonite extinct marine ◊cephalopod mollusc of the order Ammonoidea, related to the modern nautilus. The shell was curled in a plane spiral and made up of numerous gas-filled chambers, the outermost containing the body of the animal. Many species flourished between 200 million and 65 million years ago, ranging in size from that of a small coin to 2 m/6 ft across.

amnesia loss or impairment of memory. As a clinical condition it may be caused by disease or injury to the brain, by some drugs, or by shock; in some cases it may be a symptom of an emotional disorder.

amnesty release of political prisoners under a general pardon, or a person or group of people from criminal liability for a particular action.

For example, there are occasional amnesties in the UK for those who surrender firearms that they hold illegally.

Amnesty International human-rights organization established in the UK 1961 to campaign for the release of prisoners of conscience worldwide; fair trials for all political prisoners; an end to the death penalty, torture, and other inhuman treatment of all prisoners; and the cessation of extrajudicial executions and 'disappearances'. It is politically and economically unaligned. Amnesty International has 1.1 million members, and section offices over 50 countries (1997). The organization was awarded the Nobel Prize for Peace 1977.

amniocentesis sampling the amniotic fluid surrounding a fetus in the womb for diagnostic purposes. It is used to detect Down's syndrome and other genetic abnormalities.

amoeba (plural ***amoebae***) one of the simplest living animals, consisting of a single cell and belonging to the ◊protozoa group. The body consists of colourless protoplasm. Its activities are controlled by the nucleus, and it feeds by flowing round and engulfing organic debris. It reproduces by ◊binary fission. Some species of amoeba are harmful parasites.

Amorites ancient people of Semitic or Indo-European origin who were among the inhabitants of ◊Canaan at the time of the Israelite invasion. They provided a number of Babylonian kings.

ampere SI unit (abbreviation amp, symbol A) of electrical current. Electrical current is measured in a similar way to water current, in terms of an amount per unit time; one ampere represents a flow of about 6.28×10^{18} ◊electrons per second, or a rate of flow of charge of one coulomb per second. The ampere is defined as the current that produces a specific magnetic force between two long, straight, parallel conductors placed 1m/3.3 ft apart in a vacuum. It is named after the French scientist André Ampère.

Ampère André Marie 1775–1836. French physicist and mathematician who made many discoveries in electromagnetism and electrodynamics. He followed up the work of Hans ◊Oersted on the interaction between magnets and electric currents, developing a rule for determining the direction of the magnetic field associated with an electric current. The unit of electric current, the ampere, is named after him.

Ampère's law is an equation that relates the magnetic force produced by two parallel current-carrying conductors to the product of their currents and the distance between the conductors. Today Ampère's law is usually stated in the form of calculus: the line integral of the magnetic field around an arbitrarily chosen path is proportional to the net electric current enclosed by the path.

amphetamine or ***speed*** powerful synthetic ◊stimulant. Benzedrine was the earliest amphetamine marketed, used as a 'pep pill' in World War II to help soldiers overcome fatigue, and until the 1970s amphetamines were prescribed by doctors as an appetite suppressant for weight loss; as an antidepressant, to induce euphoria; and as a stimulant, to increase alertness. Indications for its use today are very restricted because of severe side effects, including addiction. It is a sulphate or phosphate form of $C_9H_{13}N$.

amphibian (Greek 'double life') member of the vertebrate class Amphibia, which generally spend their larval (tadpole) stage in fresh water, transferring to land at maturity (after ◊metamorphosis) and generally returning to water to breed. Like fish and reptiles, they continue to grow throughout life, and cannot maintain a temperature greatly differing from that of their environment. The class contains 4,553 known species, 4,000 of which are frogs and toads, 390 salamanders, and 163 caecilians (worm-like in appearance). *See illustration on following page.*

amphibole any one of a large group of rock-forming silicate minerals with an internal structure based on double chains of silicon and oxygen, and with a general formula $X_2Y_5Si_8O_{22}(OH)_2$; closely related to ◊pyroxene. Amphiboles form orthorhombic, monoclinic, and triclinic ◊crystals. They occur in a wide range of igneous and metamorphic rocks. Common examples are ◊hornblende (X = Ca, Y = Mg, Fe, Al) and tremolite (X = Ca, Y = Mg).

amphitheatre (Greek *amphi* 'around') large oval or circular building used by the Romans for gladiatorial contests, fights of wild animals, and other similar events. It is an open structure with a central arena surrounded by rising rows of seats. The ◊Colosseum in Rome, completed AD 80, held 50,000 spectators.

amphoteric term used to describe the ability of some chemical compounds to behave either as an ◊acid or as a ◊base depending on their environment. For example, the metals aluminium and zinc, and their oxides and hydroxides, act as bases in acidic solutions and as acids in alkaline solutions. Amino acids and proteins are also amphoteric, as they contain both a basic (amino, $-NH_2$) and an acidic (carboxyl, $-COOH$) group.

amplifier electronic device that magnifies the strength of a signal, such as a radio signal. The ratio of output signal strength to input signal strength is called the gain of the amplifier. As well as achieving high gain, an amplifier should be free from distortion and able to operate over a range of frequencies. Practical amplifiers are usually complex circuits, although simple amplifiers can be built from single transistors or valves.

amplitude maximum displacement of an oscillation from the equilibrium position. For a wave motion, it is the height of a crest (or the depth of a trough). With a sound wave, for example, amplitude corresponds to the intensity (loudness) of the sound. In AM (amplitude modulation) radio broadcasting, the required audio-frequency signal is made to modulate (vary slightly) the amplitude of a continuously transmitted radio carrier wave.

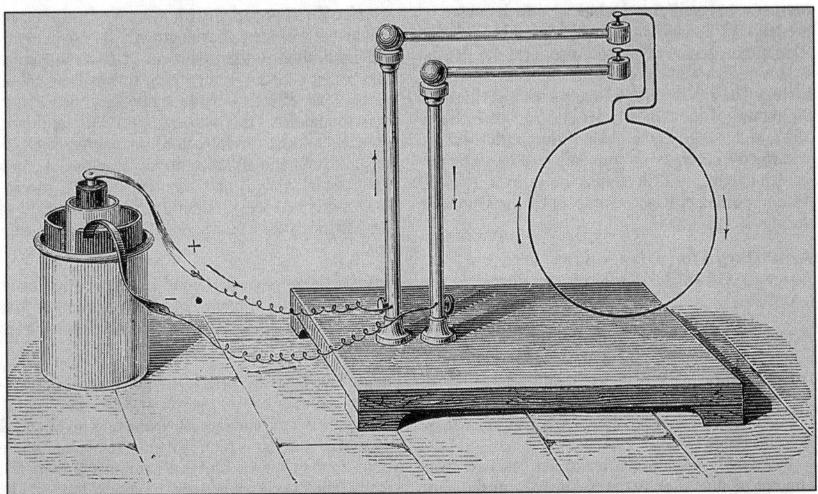

Ampère A drawing of Ampère's stand, an experimental investigation into the behaviour of an electric current in a magnetic field. The loop of wire is suspended in two small cups of mercury so that it can pivot freely, while a battery, connected to the supporting arms, provides a constant electrical current. *Ann Ronan/Image Select (UK) Ltd*

amphibian Toads are among the commonest amphibians. This striking green toad *Bufo viridis* is distributed in a number of habitats in the E Mediterranean area, such as these coastal sand flats on the island of Corfu. *Premaphotos Wildlife*

amplitude modulation (AM) method by which radio waves are altered for the transmission of broadcasting signals. AM waves are constant in frequency, but the amplitude of the transmitting wave varies in accordance with the signal being broadcast.

Amritsar industrial city in the Punjab, India; population (1991) 709,000. It is the holy city of ◊Sikhism, with the Guru Nanak University (named after the first Sikh guru), and the Golden Temple. The city was the scene of the ◊Amritsar Massacre 1919. Armed Sikh demonstrators were evicted from the Golden Temple by the Indian army 1984, in Operation Bluestar, led by General Dayal.

Over 300 were killed. Later in 1984, Indian prime minister Indira Gandhi was assassinated in reprisal by Sikh extremists wanting an independent Sikh state in Punjab. The whole of Punjab was put under presidential control 1987 following riots.

Amritsar Massacre also called ***Jallianwallah Bagh massacre*** the killing of 379 Indians (and wounding of 1,200) in Amritsar, at the site of a Sikh religious shrine in the Punjab 1919. British troops under General Edward Dyer (1864–1927) opened fire without warning on a crowd of some 10,000, assembled to protest against the arrest of two Indian National Congress leaders (see ◊Congress Party). Dyer was subsequently censured and resigned his commission, but gained popular support in the UK for his action, spurring Mahatma ◊Gandhi to a policy of active noncooperation with the British. ▷ *See feature on pp. 432–433.*

Amsterdam capital of the Netherlands; population (1994) 724,100. Canals cut through the city link it with the North Sea and the Rhine, and as a Dutch port it is second only to Rotterdam. There is shipbuilding, printing, food processing, banking, and insurance.
features Art galleries include the Rijksmuseum, Stedelijk, Vincent van Gogh Museum, and the Rembrandt house. Notable also are the Royal Palace 1655 and the Anne Frank house.
history The city developed out of a fishing village at the mouth of the Amstel; became part of Holland 1317; and passed to the duke of Burgundy 1428. It was freed from Spanish domination 1579. After the golden age of the 17th century it declined in maritime importance. It was occupied by the Germans during World War II.

Amu Darya formerly ***Oxus*** river in central Asia, flowing 2,530 km/1,578 mi from the ◊Pamirs to the ◊Aral Sea.

Amundsen Roald Engelbrecht Gravning 1872–1928. Norwegian explorer who in 1903–06 became the first person to navigate the ◊Northwest Passage. Beaten to the North Pole by US explorer Robert Peary 1910, he reached the South Pole ahead of Captain Scott 1911.

In 1918, Amundsen made an unsuccessful attempt to drift across the North Pole in the ship *Maud* and in 1925 tried unsuccessfully to fly from Spitsbergen, in the Arctic Ocean north of Norway, to the Pole by aeroplane. The following year he joined the Italian explorer Umberto Nobile (1885–1978) in the airship *Norge*, which circled the North Pole twice and landed in Alaska. Amundsen was killed in a plane crash over the Arctic Ocean while searching for Nobile and his airship *Italia*.

Amur river in E Asia. Formed by the Argun and Shilka rivers, the Amur enters the Sea of Okhotsk. At its mouth at Nikolevsk it is 16 km/10 mi wide. For much of its course of over 4,400 km/2,730 mi it forms, together with its tributary, the Ussuri, the boundary between Russia and China.

Under the treaties of Aigun 1858 and Peking 1860, 984,200 sq km/380,000 sq mi of territory north and east of the two rivers were ceded by China to the tsarist government. From 1963 China raised the question of its return and there have been border clashes.

amyl alcohol former name for ◊pentanol.

amylase one of a group of ◊enzymes that break down starches into their component molecules (sugars) for use in the body. It occurs widely in both plants and animals. In humans, it is found in saliva and in pancreatic juices.

Human amylase has an optimum pH of 7.2–7.4. Like most enzymes amylase is denatured by temperatures above 60°C.

Anabaptist (Greek 'baptize again') member of any of various 16th-century radical Protestant sects. They believed in adult rather than child baptism, and sought to establish utopian communities. Anabaptist groups spread rapidly in N Europe, particularly in Germany, and were widely persecuted. In Münster, Germany, Anabaptists controlled the city 1534–35.

anabolic steroid any ◊hormone of the ◊steroid group that stimulates tissue growth. Its use in medicine is limited to the treatment of some anaemias and breast cancers; it may help to break up blood clots. Side effects include aggressive behaviour, masculinization in women, and, in children, reduced height. Widely used in sports, such as weightlifting and athletics, to increase muscle bulk for greater strength and stamina, the UK government outlawed the production, import, or sale of anabolic steroids 1996 under the Misuse of Drugs act.

anabolism process of building up body tissue, promoted by the influence of certain hormones. It is the constructive side of ◊metabolism, as opposed to ◊catabolism.

anaconda South American snake *Eunectes murinus*, a member of the python and boa family, the Boidae. One of the largest snakes, growing to 9 m/30 ft or more, it is found in and near water, where it lies in wait for the birds and animals on which it feeds. The anaconda is not venomous, but kills its prey by coiling round it and squeezing until the creature suffocates.

anaemia condition caused by a shortage of haemoglobin, the oxygen-carrying component of red blood cells. The main symptoms are fatigue, pallor, breathlessness, palpitations, and poor resistance to infection. Anaemia arises either from abnormal loss or defective production of haemoglobin. Excessive loss occurs, for instance, with chronic slow bleeding or with accelerated destruction (haemolysis) of red blood cells. Defective production may be due to iron deficiency, vitamin B_{12} deficiency (pernicious anaemia), certain blood diseases (sickle-cell disease and thalassaemia), chronic infection, kidney disease, or certain kinds of poisoning. Untreated anaemia taxes the heart and may prove fatal.

anaerobic (of living organisms) not requiring oxygen for the release of energy from food molecules such as glucose. Anaerobic organisms include many bacteria, yeasts, and internal parasites.

Obligate anaerobes, such as certain primitive bacteria, cannot function in the presence of oxygen; but facultative anaerobes, like the fermenting yeasts and most bacteria, can function with or without oxygen. Anaerobic organisms release much less of the available energy from their food than do ◊aerobic organisms.

In plants, yeasts, and bacteria, anaerobic respiration results in the production of alcohol and carbon dioxide, a process that is exploited by both the brewing and the baking industries (see ◊fermentation). Normally aerobic animal cells can respire anaerobically for short periods of time when oxygen levels are low, but are ultimately fatigued by the build-up of the lactic acid produced in the process. This is seen particularly in muscle cells during intense activity, when the demand for oxygen can outstrip supply (see ◊oxygen debt).

Although anaerobic respiration is a primitive and inefficient form of energy release, deriving from the period when oxygen was missing from the atmosphere, it can also be seen as an ◊adaptation. To survive in some habitats, such as the muddy bottom of a polluted river, an organism must be to a large extent independent of oxygen; such habitats are said to be anoxic.

anaesthetic drug that produces loss of sensation or consciousness; the resulting state is anaesthesia, in which the patient is insensitive to stimuli. Anaesthesia may also happen as a result of nerve disorder.

Ever since the first successful operation 1846 on a patient rendered unconscious by ether, advances have been aimed at increasing safety and control. Sedatives may be given before the anaesthetic to make the process easier. The level and duration of unconsciousness are managed precisely. Where general anaesthesia may be inappropriate (for example, in childbirth, for a small procedure, or in the elderly), many other techniques are available. A topical substance may be applied to the skin or tissue surface; a local agent may be injected into the tissues under the skin in the area to be treated; or a regional block of sensation may be achieved by

anaconda The anaconda is a climber as well as a swimmer, and may be found in trees along river banks. Males attract mates by making booming noises. The young develop in thin-shelled eggs inside the mother, hatching as she lays them and emerging as live young; up to 40 are produced in a litter, each one about 60 cm/24 in long.

injection into a nerve. Spinal anaesthetic, such as epidural, is injected into the tissues surrounding the spinal cord, producing loss of feeling in the lower part of the body. ▷ *See feature on pp. 1024–1025.*

analects or ***analecta*** any collection of literary fragments taken from one or more sources. More specifically, the *Analects* are a selection of writings by Chinese philosopher Confucius and his followers, the most important of the four books containing the teachings and ideas of ◊Confucianism.

analgesic agent for relieving ◊pain. ◊Opiates alter the perception or appreciation of pain and are effective in controlling 'deep' visceral (internal) pain. Non-opiates, such as ◊aspirin, ◊paracetamol, and ◊NSAIDs (nonsteroidal anti-inflammatory drugs), relieve musculoskeletal pain and reduce inflammation in soft tissues.

Pain is felt when electrical stimuli travel along a nerve pathway, from peripheral nerve fibres to the brain via the spinal cord. An anaesthetic agent acts either by preventing stimuli from being sent (local), or by removing awareness of them (general). Analgesic drugs act on both.

analogous in biology, term describing a structure that has a similar function to a structure in another organism, but not a similar evolutionary path. For example, the wings of bees and of birds have the same purpose – to give powered flight – but have different origins. Compare ◊homologous.

analogue (of a quantity or device) changing continuously; by contrast a ◊digital quantity or device varies in series of distinct steps. For example, an analogue clock measures time by means of a continuous movement of hands around a dial, whereas a digital clock measures time with a numerical display that changes in a series of discrete steps.

Most computers are digital devices. Therefore, any signals and data from an analogue device must be passed through a suitable ◊analogue-to-digital converter before they can be received and processed by computer. Similarly, output signals from digital computers must be passed through a digital-to-analogue converter before they can be received by an analogue device.

analog computer computing device that performs calculations through the interaction of continuously varying physical quantities, such as voltages (as distinct from the more common ◊digital computer, which works with discrete quantities). An analog computer is said to operate in real time (corresponding to time in the real world), and can therefore be used to monitor and control other events as they happen.

Although common in engineering since the 1920s, analog computers are not general-purpose computers, but specialize in solving ◊differential calculus and similar mathematical problems. The earliest analog computing device is thought to be the flat, or planispheric, astrolabe, which originated in about the 8th century.

analogue signal in electronics, current or voltage that conveys or stores information, and varies continuously in the same way as the information it represents (compare ◊digital signal). Analogue signals are prone to interference and distortion.

analogue-to-digital converter (ADC) electronic circuit that converts an analogue signal into a digital one. Such a circuit is needed to convert the signal from an analogue device into a digital signal for input into a computer. For example, many sensors designed to measure physical quantities, such as temperature and pressure, produce an analogue signal in the form of voltage and this must be passed through an ADC before computer input and processing. A ◊digital-to-analogue converter performs the opposite process.

analytical chemistry branch of chemistry that deals with the determination of the chemical composition of substances. Qualitative analysis determines the identities of the substances in a given sample; quantitative analysis determines how much of a particular substance is present.

Simple qualitative techniques exploit the specific, easily observable properties of elements or compounds – for example, the flame test makes use of the different flame colours produced by metal cations when their compounds are held in a hot flame.

More sophisticated methods, such as those of ◊spectroscopy, are required where substances are present in very low concentrations or where several substances have similar properties.

Most quantitative analyses involve initial stages in which the substance to be measured is extracted from the test sample, and purified. The final analytical stages (or 'finishes') may involve measurement of the substance's mass (gravimetry) or volume (volumetry, titrimetry), or a number of techniques initially developed for qualitative analysis, such as fluorescence and absorption spectroscopy, chromatography, electrophoresis, and polarography. Many modern methods enable quantification by means of a detecting device that is integrated into the extraction procedure (as in gas–liquid chromatography).

analytical geometry another name for ◊coordinate geometry.

anaphylaxis in medicine, a severe allergic response. Typically, the air passages become constricted, the blood pressure falls rapidly, and the victim collapses. A rare condition, anaphylaxis most often occurs following wasp or bee stings, or treatment with some drugs.

anarchism (Greek *anarkhos* 'without ruler') political belief that society should have no government, laws, police, or other authority, but should be a free association of all its members. It does not mean 'without order'; most theories of anarchism imply an order of a very strict and symmetrical kind, but they maintain that such order can be achieved by cooperation. Anarchism must not be confused with nihilism (a purely negative and destructive activity directed against society); anarchism is essentially a pacifist movement.

Religious anarchism, claimed by many anarchists to be exemplified in the early organization of the Christian church, has found expression in the social philosophy of Russian writer Leo Tolstoy and Indian nationalist Mahatma Gandhi.

The theory of anarchism is expressed for example in the works of Russian revolutionary Peter ◊Kropotkin. Perhaps the most influential anarchist of the 20th century has been US linguist Noam Chomsky.

From the 1960s there were outbreaks of politically motivated violence popularly identified with anarchism; in the UK, the bombings and shootings carried out by the Angry Brigade 1968–71, and in the 1980s actions directed towards peace and animal-rights issues, and to demonstrate against large financial and business corporations.

Anatolia (Turkish ***Anadolu***) Asian part of Turkey, consisting of a mountainous peninsula with the Black Sea to the N, the Aegean Sea to the W, and the Mediterranean Sea to the S.

analogue-to-digital converter An ADC converts a continuous analogue signal produced by a sensor to a digital ('off and on') signal for computer processing.

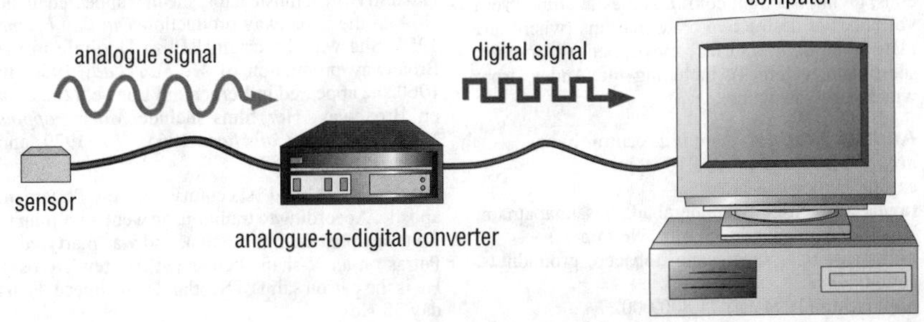

ancestor worship A Chinese shrine for ancestor worship. Under Confucianism, sacrifices were made to a family's ancestors, but this custom was abolished in China at the Revolution in 1912. However, reverence and remembrance of one's ancestors remain a regular practice in the home. *Corbis*

anatomy study of the structure of the body and its component parts, especially the ◊human body, as distinguished from physiology, which is the study of bodily functions.

Herophilus of Chalcedon (c. 330–c. 260 BC) is regarded as the founder of anatomy. In the 2nd century AD, the Graeco-Roman physician Galen produced an account of anatomy that was the only source of anatomical knowledge until *On the Working of the Human Body* 1543 by Belgian physician Andreas Vesalius. In 1628, English physician William Harvey published his demonstration of the circulation of the blood. With the invention of the microscope, Italian physiologist Marcello Malpighi and Dutch microscopist Anton van Leeuwenhoek were able to found the study of ◊histology. In 1747, Albinus (1697–1770), with the help of the artist Wandelaar (1691–1759), produced the most exact account of the bones and muscles, and in 1757–65 Swiss biologist Albrecht von Haller gave the most complete and exact description of the organs that had yet appeared. Among the anatomical writers of the early 19th century are the surgeon Charles Bell (1774–1842), Jonas Quain (1796–1865), and Henry Gray (1825–1861). Radiographic anatomy (using X-rays; see ◊radiography) has been one of the triumphs of the 20th century.

Anaximander c. 610–c. 546 BC. Greek astronomer and philosopher. He claimed that the Earth was a cylinder three times wider than it is deep, motionless at the centre of the universe, and that the celestial bodies were fire seen through holes in the hollow rims of wheels encircling the Earth. According to Anaximander, the first animals came into being from moisture and the first humans grew inside fish, emerging once fully developed.

ANC abbreviation for ◊***African National Congress***, a South African political party and former nationalist organization.

ancestor worship religious rituals and beliefs oriented towards deceased members of a family or group as a symbolic expression of values or in the belief that the souls of the dead remain involved in this world and are capable of influencing current events.

Zulus used to invoke the spirits of their great warriors before engaging in battle; the Greeks deified their early heroes; and the ancient Romans held in reverential honour the ◊Manes, or departed spirits of their forebears. Ancestor worship is a part of ◊Confucianism, and recent ancestors are venerated in the Shinto religion of Japan.

Anchorage port and largest city of Alaska, USA, at the head of Cook Inlet; population (1992) 245,900. Established 1918, Anchorage is an important centre of administration, communication, and commerce. Oil and gas extraction and fish canning are also important to the local economy.

anchovy small fish *Engraulis encrasicholus* of the ◊herring family. It is fished extensively, being abundant in the Mediterranean, and is also found on the Atlantic coast of Europe and in the Black Sea. It grows to 20 cm/8 in.

Pungently flavoured, it is processed into fish pastes and essences, and used as a garnish, rather than eaten fresh.

ancien régime the old order; the feudal, absolute monarchy in France before the French Revolution 1789.

Ancona Italian city and naval base on the Adriatic Sea, capital of Marche region; population (1992) 100,700. It has a Romanesque cathedral and a former palace of the popes.

Andalusia (Spanish *Andalucía*) fertile autonomous region of S Spain, including the provinces of Almería, Cádiz, Córdoba, Granada, Huelva, Jaén, Málaga, and Seville; area 87,300 sq km/33,698 sq mi; population (1991) 6,940,500. Málaga, Cádiz, and Algeciras are the chief ports and industrial centres. The Costa del Sol on the south coast has many tourist resorts, including Marbella and Torremolinos. Andalusia has Moorish architecture, having been under Muslim rule from the 8th to the 15th centuries.

andalusite aluminium silicate, Al_2SiO_5, a white to pinkish mineral crystallizing as square- or rhombus-based prisms. It is common in metamorphic rocks formed from clay sediments under low pressure conditions. Andalusite, kyanite, and sillimanite are all polymorphs of Al_2SiO_5.

Andaman and Nicobar Islands two groups of islands in the Bay of Bengal, between India and Myanmar, forming a Union Territory of the Republic of India; capital Port Blair; area 8,300 sq km/3,204 sq mi; population (1994 est) 322,000. The economy is based on fishing, timber, rubber, fruit, nuts, coffee, and rice.

The ***Andamans*** consist of five principal islands (forming the Great Andaman), the Little Andaman, and about 204 islets; area 6,340 sq km/2,447 sq mi; population (1991) 240,100. They were used as a penal settlement 1857–1942. The main items of trade here are timber, coconut, coffee, and rubber. The ***Nicobars***, consisting of 19 islands (7 of which are uninhabited), are 120 km/75 mi S of Little Andaman; area 1,953 sq km/754 sq mi; population (1991) 39,200. The main trade here is in coconuts and areca nuts. The Nicobars were British 1869–1947.

Andean Indian any indigenous inhabitant of the Andes range in South America, stretching from Ecuador to Peru to Chile, and including both the coast and the highlands. Many Andean civilizations developed in this region from local fishing-hunting-farming societies, all of which predated the ◊Inca, who consolidated the entire region and ruled from about 1200, imposing the Quechua language which is now spoken by over 10 million people.

Andersen Hans Christian 1805–1875. Danish writer of fairy tales. Examples include 'The Ugly Duckling', 'The Snow Queen', 'The Little Mermaid', and 'The Emperor's New Clothes'. Their inventiveness, sensitivity, and strong sense of wonder have given these stories universal appeal; they have been translated into many languages.

Anderson Elizabeth Garrett 1836–1917. English physician, the first English woman to qualify in medicine. Unable to attend medical school, Anderson studied privately and was licensed by the Society of Apothecaries in London 1865. She was physician to the Marylebone Dispensary for Women and Children (later renamed the Elizabeth Garrett Anderson Hospital), a London hospital now staffed by women and serving female patients.

Andersen The tales of the Danish writer Hans Christian Andersen earned him international acclaim. An innovator in his method of storytelling, Andersen sometimes reveals a deep pessimism beneath the charm and childlike wonder of his stories. He also wrote novels, plays, and travel books. *Danish Tourist Board*

Andes The western range of the Andes in Peru. The Andes are the longest system of mountains above sea level in the world. The snowy peaks are a source of water for local people and also a major attraction for the growing tourist industry. *Sally Jenkins*

Anderson Marian 1902–1993. US contralto, whose voice was remarkable for its range and richness. She toured Europe 1930, but in 1939 was barred from singing at Constitution Hall, Washington DC because she was black. In 1955 she sang at the Metropolitan Opera, the first black singer to appear there. In 1958 she was appointed an alternate (deputizing) delegate to the United Nations. She was one of the most important nonpolitical figures in the civil-rights movement and fight against racism in the USA.

Andes great mountain system or *cordillera* that forms the western fringe of South America, extending through some 67° of latitude and the republics of Colombia, Venezuela, Ecuador, Peru, Bolivia, Chile, and Argentina. The mountains exceed 3,600 m/12,000 ft for half their length of 6,500 km/4,000 mi.

Geologically speaking, the Andes are new mountains, having attained their present height by vertical upheaval of the entire strip of the Earth's crust as recently as the latter part of the Tertiary era and the Quaternary. But they have been greatly affected by weathering; rivers have cut deep gorges, and glaciers have produced characteristic valleys. The majority of the individual mountains are volcanic; some are still active.

The whole system may be divided into two almost parallel ranges. The southernmost extremity is Cape Horn, but the range extends into the sea and forms islands. Among the highest peaks are Cotopaxi and Chimborazo in Ecuador, Cerro de Pasco and Misti in Peru, Illampu and Illimani in Bolivia, Aconcagua (the highest mountain in the New World) in Argentina, and Ojos del Salado in Chile.

Andean mineral resources include gold, silver, tin, tungsten, bismuth, vanadium, copper, and lead.

andesite volcanic igneous rock, intermediate in silica content between rhyolite and basalt. It is characterized by a large quantity of feldspar ◊minerals, giving it a light colour. Andesite erupts from volcanoes at destructive plate margins (where one plate of the Earth's surface moves beneath another; see ◊plate tectonics), including the Andes, from which it gets its name.

Andhra Pradesh state in E central India
area 275,100 sq km/106,216 sq mi
capital Hyderabad
towns and cities Secunderabad, Visakhapatnam, Vijayawada, Kakinda, Guntur, Nellore
industries rice, sugar cane, tobacco, groundnuts, cotton
population (1994 est) 71,800,000
language Telugu, Urdu, Tamil
history formed 1953 from the Telegu-speaking areas of Madras, and enlarged 1956 from the former Hyderabad state.

Andorra landlocked country in the east Pyrenees, bounded north by France and south by Spain. *See country box opposite.*

Andrea del Sarto (Andrea d'Agnolo di Francesco) 1486–1530. Italian Renaissance painter. Active in Florence, he was one of the finest portraitists and religious painters of his time. His frescoes in Florence, such as the *Birth of the Virgin* 1514 (Sta Annunziata), rank among the greatest of the Renaissance. Chiefly influenced by ◊Masaccio and ◊Michelangelo, his style is serene and noble, characteristic of High Renaissance art.

Andreotti Giulio 1919– . Italian Christian Democrat politician, a fervent European. He headed seven postwar governments: 1972–73, 1976–79 (four successive terms), and 1989–92 (two terms). In addition he was defence minister eight times, and foreign minister five times. In 1995 Andreotti went on trial for protecting Mafia leaders in exchange for political support. In Nov 1995 he and four others were charged with the 1979 murder of journalist Carmine Pecorelli; and in Feb 1996 he was arraigned on further corruption charges.

Andrew (full name Andrew Albert Christian Edward) 1960– . Prince of the UK, Duke of York, second son of Queen Elizabeth II. He married Sarah Ferguson 1986; their two daughters are Princess Beatrice, born 1988, and Princess Eugenie, born 1990. The couple separated 1992, and divorced 1996. Prince Andrew is a naval helicopter pilot.

Andrew Rob (Christopher Robert) 1963– . English rugby union player. He is England's record points-scorer with 396 points in 71 internationals between 1985 and 1997. He also played five times for the British Lions, and is the most capped fly-half in international rugby. In 1995, he scored all of England's 24 points in their Grand Slam decider with Scotland. He retired from international rugby after the 1995 World Cup, but came back for one game 1997.

Andrews Julie. Stage name of Julia Elizabeth Wells 1935– . English-born US actress and singer. A child performer with her mother and stepfather in British music halls, she first appeared in the USA in the Broadway production *The Boy Friend* 1954. She was the original Eliza Doolittle in the Broadway production of *My Fair Lady* 1956. In 1960 she appeared in Lerner and Loewe's *Camelot* on Broadway. Her films include *Mary Poppins* 1964, *The Sound of Music* 1965, *'10'* 1979, and *Victor/Victoria* 1982.

Andrew, St lived 1st century AD. New Testament apostle. According to tradition, he went with John to Ephesus, preached in Scythia, and was martyred at Patras on an X-shaped cross (St Andrew's cross). He is the patron saint of Scotland and Greece. Feast day 30 Nov.

ANDORRA
Principality of

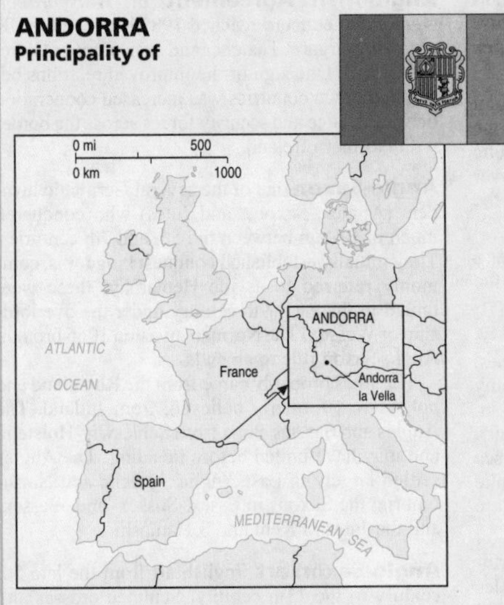

national name *Principat d'Andorra*
area 453 sq km/175 sq mi
capital Andorra-la-Vella
major towns/cities Les Escaldes
physical features mountainous, with narrow valleys; the E Pyrenees, Valira River
heads of state Joan Marti i Alanis (bishop of Urgel, Spain) and Jacques Chirac (president of France)
head of government Marc Forne from 1994
political system co-principality
administrative divisions seven parishes
political parties National Democratic Grouping (AND; formerly the Democratic Party of Andorra: PDA) moderate, centrist; National Democratic Initiative (IND), left of centre; New Democracy Party (ND), centrist; National Andorran Coalition (CNA), centrist; Liberal Union (UL), right of centre
population 62,500 (1994 est)
population growth rate 5.5% (1990–95)
ethnic distribution 25% Andorrans, 75% immigrant Spanish workers
literacy rate 100% (1987)
languages Catalan (official); Spanish, French
religion Roman Catholic
currency French franc and Spanish peseta
GDP (US $) 836 million (1992)
growth rate 0.8% (1992)
exports main industries tourism and tobacco

HISTORY
AD 803 Holy Roman Emperor Charlemagne liberated Andorra from Muslim control.
819 Louis I, 'the Pious', the son of Charlemagne, granted control over the area to the Spanish bishop of Urgel.
1278 Treaty signed making Spanish bishop and French count joint rulers of Andorra (through marriage the king of France later inherited the count's right).
1806 After temporary suspension during the French Revolution, from 1789 the feudal arrangement of dual allegiance to the co-princes (French and Spanish rulers) was re-established by the French emperor Napoleon Bonaparte.
1970 Extension of franchise to third-generation female and second-generation male Andorrans.
1976 First political organization, Democratic Party of Andorra, formed.
1977 Franchise extended to first-generation Andorrans.
1981 First prime minister appointed by General Council.
1991 Links with European Community formalized.
1993 New constitution legalized political parties and introduced first direct elections, leading to coalition government being formed under acting prime minister, Oscar Ribas Reig. Became member of United Nations.
1994 Reig resigned and was succeeded by Marc Forne; joined Council of Europe.
1997 Liberal Union (UL) won assembly majority in general election.

Androcles traditionally, a Roman slave who fled from a cruel master into the African desert, where he encountered a crippled lion and withdrew a thorn from its paw. The lion later recognized the recaptured slave in the arena and spared his life. The emperor Tiberius was said to have freed them both.

androecium male part of a flower, comprising a number of ◊stamens.

androgen general name for any male sex hormone, of which ◊testosterone is the most important. They are all ◊steroids and are principally involved in the production of male ◊secondary sexual characteristics (such as beard growth).

Andromache in Greek mythology, the loyal wife of ◊Hector. After the fall of Troy she was awarded to Neoptolemus, Achilles' son; she later married a Trojan seer called Helenus. Andromache is the heroine of Homer's *Iliad* and the subject of a play by ◊Euripides.

Andromeda major constellation of the northern hemisphere, visible in autumn. Its main feature is the Andromeda galaxy. The star Alpha Andromedae forms one corner of the Square of Pegasus. It is named after the princess of Greek mythology.

Andromeda galaxy galaxy 2.2 million light years away from Earth in the constellation Andromeda, and the most distant object visible to the naked eye. It is the largest member of the ◊Local Group of galaxies. Like the Milky Way, the Andromeda galaxy is a spiral orbited by several companion galaxies but contains about twice as many stars. It is about 200,000 light years across.

Andromeda galaxy Infrared image of the Andromeda galaxy produced by satellite. Astronomers think that it may have a double nucleus but this could be the result of a shadow caused by a lane of dust, for example. *Image Select (UK) Ltd*

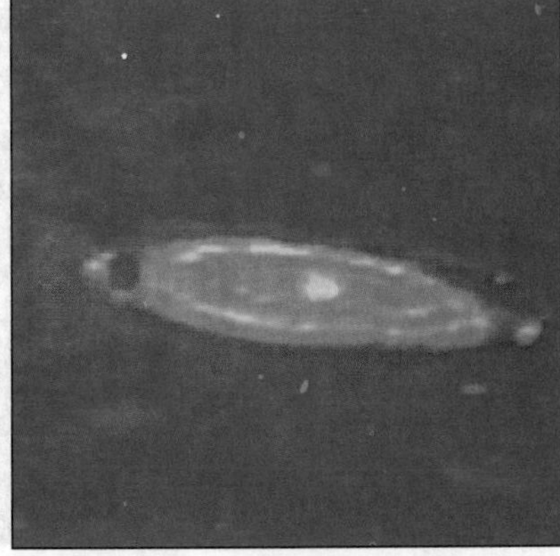

Andropov Yuri 1914–1984. Soviet communist politician, president of the USSR 1983–84. As chief of the KGB 1967–82, he established a reputation for efficiently suppressing dissent. He became a member of the Politburo 1973 and succeeded Brezhnev as party general secretary 1982. Elected president 1983, he instituted economic reforms.

anechoic chamber room designed to be of high sound absorbency. All surfaces inside the chamber are covered by sound-absorbent materials such as rubber. The walls are often covered with inward-facing pyramids of rubber, to minimize reflections. It is used for experiments in ◊acoustics and for testing audio equipment.

anemometer device for measuring wind speed and liquid flow. The most basic form, the ***cup-type anemometer***, consists of cups at the ends of arms, which rotate when the wind blows. The speed of rotation indicates the wind speed. ***Vane-type anemometers*** have vanes, like a small windmill or propeller, that rotate when the wind blows. ***Pressure-tube anemometers*** use the pressure generated by the wind to indicate speed. The wind blowing into or across a tube develops a pressure, proportional to the wind speed, that is measured by a manometer or pressure gauge. ***Hot-wire anemometers*** work on the principle that the rate at which heat is transferred from a hot wire to the surrounding air is a measure of the air speed.

anemone any plant of the genus *Anemone* of the buttercup family Ranunculaceae. The function of petals is performed by its sepals.

The Eurasian white wood anemone *A. nemorosa*, or windflower, grows in shady woods, flowering in spring. *Hepatica nobilis*, once included within *Anemone*, is common in the Alps. The ◊pasqueflower is now placed in a separate genus.

aneurysm weakening in the wall of an artery, causing it to balloon outwards with the risk of rupture and serious, often fatal, blood loss. If detected in time, some accessible aneurysms can be repaired by bypass surgery.

Angad 1504–1552. Indian religious leader, second guru (teacher) of Sikhism 1539–52, succeeding Nanak. He popularized the alphabet known as Gurmukhi, in which the Sikh scriptures are written.

angel (Greek *angelos* 'messenger') in Jewish, Christian, and Muslim belief, a supernatural being intermediate between God and humans. The Christian hierarchy has nine orders, from the top down: Seraphim, Cherubim, Thrones (who contemplate God and reflect his glory), Dominations, Virtues, Powers (who regulate the stars and the universe), Principalities, Archangels, and Angels (who minister to humanity). In traditional Catholic belief every human being has a guardian angel. The existence of angels was reasserted by Pope John Paul II 1986.

angel dust popular name for the anaesthetic phencyclidine (or PCP), a depressant drug.

Angel Falls highest waterfalls in the world, on the river Caroní in the tropical rainforest of Bolívar Region, Venezuela; total height 978 m/3,210 ft.

angelfish any of a number of unrelated fishes. The freshwater angelfish, genus *Pterophyllum*, of South America, is a tall, side-to-side flattened fish with a striped body, up to 26 cm/10 in long, but usually smaller in captivity. The angelfish or monkfish of the genus *Squatina* is a bottom-living shark up to 1.8 m/6 ft long with a body flattened from top to bottom. The marine angelfishes, *Pomacanthus* and others, are long narrow-bodied fish with spiny fins, often brilliantly coloured, up to 60 cm/2 ft long, living around coral reefs in the tropics.

angelica any plant of the genus *Angelica* of the carrot family Umbelliferae. Mostly Eurasian in distribution, they are tall, perennial herbs with divided leaves and clusters of white or greenish flowers. The roots and fruits have long been used in cooking and for medicinal purposes. *A. archangelica* is a culinary herb, the stems of which are preserved in sugar and used for cake decoration. *A. sylvestris*, the species found in Britain, has wedge-shaped leaves and clusters of white, pale violet, or pinkish flowers. The oil is used in perfume and liqueurs.

Angelico Fra (Guido di Pietro) c. 1400–1455. Italian painter. He was a monk, active in Florence, and painted religious scenes. His series of frescoes at the monastery of San Marco, Florence, begun after 1436, and in the Nicholas Chapel of the Vatican are his most important works. He also produced several altarpieces in a style characterized by a delicacy of line and colour. *See illustration on following page.*

Angelou Maya (born Marguerite Annie Johnson) 1928– . US writer and black activist. She became noted for her powerful autobiographical works, *I Know Why the Caged Bird Sings* 1970 and its four sequels up to *All God's Children Need Travelling Shoes* 1986. Based on her traumatic childhood, they tell of the struggles towards physical and spiritual liberation of a black woman from growing up in the South to emigrating to Ghana. She also wrote *Wouldn't Take Nothing for My Journey Now* 1993.

'Angels can fly because they take themselves lightly.'

On ANGELS
GK Chesterton
Orthodoxy

Angers ancient French city, capital of Maine-et-Loire *département*, on the river Maine; population (1990) 146,100. Products include electrical machinery and Cointreau liqueur. It has a 12th–13th-century cathedral and castle and was formerly the capital of the duchy and province of Anjou.

Angelico *Descent From the Cross*, Convento di San Marco, Florence, Italy. Fra Angelico was so called because of the visionary quality of his paintings, which aimed to inspire religious feeling in people who saw them, and led the 19th-century art critic John Ruskin to say of him 'Fra Angelico is not an artist properly so called, but an inspired saint'. *Corbis*

Angevin relating to the reigns of the English kings Henry II and Richard I (also known, with the later English kings up to Richard III, as the Plantagenets). Angevin derives from Anjou, a region in N France. The Angevin Empire comprised the territories (including England) that belonged to the Anjou dynasty.

angina or ***angina pectoris*** severe pain in the chest due to impaired blood supply to the heart muscle because a coronary artery is narrowed. Faintness and difficulty in breathing accompany the pain. Treatment is by drugs or bypass surgery.

angiosperm flowering plant in which the seeds are enclosed within an ovary, which ripens into a fruit. Angiosperms are divided into ◊monocotyledons (single seed leaf in the embryo) and ◊dicotyledons (two seed leaves in the embryo). They include the majority of flowers, herbs, grasses, and trees except conifers.

Angkor site of the ancient capital of the Khmer Empire in NW Cambodia, north of Tonle Sap. The remains date mainly from the 10th–12th centuries AD, and comprise temples originally dedicated to the Hindu gods, shrines associated with Theravāda Buddhism, and royal palaces. Many are grouped within the enclosure called Angkor Thom, but the great temple of Angkor Wat (early 12th century) lies outside.

Angle member of the Germanic tribe that invaded Britain in the 5th century; see ◊Anglo-Saxon.

angle in mathematics, the amount of turn or rotation; it may be defined by a pair of rays (half-lines) that share a common endpoint but do not lie on the same line. Angles are measured in ◊degrees (°) or ◊radians (rads) – a complete turn or circle being 360° or 2π rads.

Angles are classified generally by their degree measures: ***acute angles*** are less than 90°; ***right angles*** are exactly 90° (a quarter turn); ***obtuse angles*** are greater than 90° but less than 180°; ***reflex angles*** are greater than 180° but less than 360°.

angle The four types of angle, as classified by their degree measures. No angle is classified as having a measure of 180°, as by definition such an 'angle' is actually a straight line.

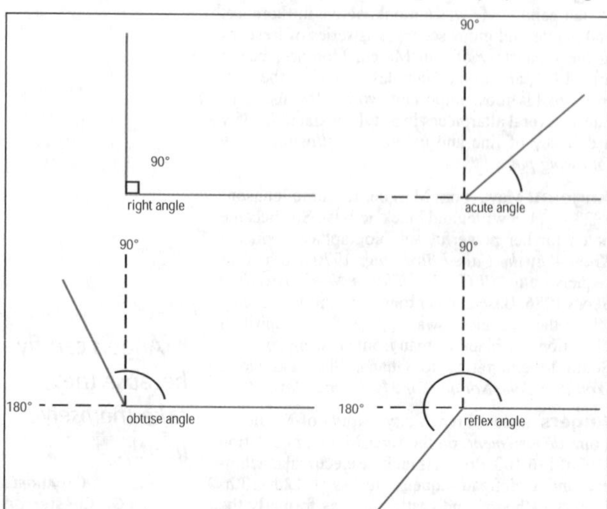

angle of declination angle at a particular point on the Earth's surface between the direction of the true or geographic North Pole and the magnetic north pole. The angle of declination has varied over time because of the slow drift in the position of the magnetic north pole.

angle of dip or ***angle of inclination*** angle at a particular point on the Earth's surface between the direction of the Earth's magnetic field and the horizontal; see ◊magnetic dip.

angler any of an order of fishes Lophiiformes, with flattened body and broad head and jaws. Many species have small, plantlike tufts on their skin. These act as camouflage for the fish as it waits, either floating among seaweed or lying on the sea bottom, twitching the enlarged tip of the threadlike first ray of its dorsal fin to entice prey. There are over 200 species of angler fish.

Anglesey (Welsh ***Ynys Môn***) island off the northwest coast of Wales, unitary authority of Wales created 1996 (*see United Kingdom map*); area 720 sq km/278 sq mi; population (1991) 67,800. It is separated from the mainland by the Menai Straits, which are crossed by the Britannia tubular railway bridge and Telford's suspension bridge, built 1819–26 but since rebuilt. It is a holiday resort with rich fauna (notably bird life) and flora, and many buildings and relics of historic interest.

Sheep farming and agriculture are the main occupations. Anglesey was the ancient granary of Wales, but now has industries such as toy-making, electrical goods, and bromine extraction from the sea. Wylfa nuclear power station is here. Holyhead is the principal town and port; Llangefni is the administrative headquarters. There is a ferry service to Ireland.

Anglican Communion family of Christian churches including the Church of England, the US Episcopal Church, and those holding the same essential doctrines, that is the Lambeth Quadrilateral 1888 Holy Scripture as the basis of all doctrine, the Nicene and Apostles' Creeds, Holy Baptism and Holy Communion, and the historic episcopate.

In England the two archbishops head the provinces of Canterbury and York, which are subdivided into bishoprics. The Church Assembly 1919 was replaced 1970 by a General Synod with three houses (bishops, other clergy, and laity) to regulate church matters, subject to Parliament. A decennial Lambeth Conference (so called because the first was held there 1867), attended by bishops from all parts of the Anglican Communion, is presided over by the archbishop of Canterbury; it is not legislative but its decisions are often put into practice. In 1988 it passed a resolution paving the way for the consecration of women bishops.

Anglicanism see ◊Anglican Communion.

angling fishing with rod and line. It is widespread and ancient in origin, fish hooks having been found in prehistoric cave dwellings. Competition angling exists and world championships take place for most branches of the sport. The oldest is the World Freshwater Championship, inaugurated 1957.

Freshwater fishing embraces coarse fishing, in which members of the carp family, pike, perch, and eels are taken by baits or lures, and (in the UK) are returned to the water virtually unharmed; and game fishing, in which members of the salmon family, such as salmon and trout, are taken by spinners (revolving lures) and flies (imitations of adult or larval insects).

In sea fishing the catch includes flatfish, bass, and mackerel; big-game fishes include shark, tuna or tunny, marlin, and swordfish.

Anglo-American War war between the USA and Britain 1812–1814; see ◊War of 1812.

Anglo-Catholicism in the Anglican Church, the Catholic heritage of faith and liturgical practice which was stressed by the founders of the ◊Oxford Movement. The term was first used 1838 to describe the movement, which began in the wake of pressure from the more Protestant wing of the Church of England. Since the Church of England voted 1992 to ordain women as priests, some Anglo-Catholics have found it difficult to remain within the Church of England.

Anglo-Irish Agreement or ***Hillsborough Agreement*** concord reached 1985 between the UK premier Margaret Thatcher and Irish premier Garret FitzGerald. One sign of the improved relations between the two countries was increased cooperation between police and security forces across the border with Northern Ireland.

Anglo-Saxon one of the several Germanic invaders (Angles, Saxons, and Jutes) who conquered much of Britain between the 5th and 7th centuries. They initially established conquest kingdoms, commonly referred to as the Heptarchy; these were united in the early 9th century under the overlordship of Wessex. The Norman invasion 1066 brought Anglo-Saxon rule to an end.

The Jutes probably came from the Rhineland and not, as was formerly believed, from Jutland. The Angles and Saxons came from Schleswig-Holstein, and may have united before invading. The Angles settled largely in East Anglia, Mercia, and Northumbria; the Saxons in Essex, Sussex, and Wessex; and the Jutes in Kent and S Hampshire.

Anglo-Saxon art English art from the late 5th century to the 11th century. Sculpted crosses and ivories, manuscript painting, and gold and enamel jewellery survive, all showing a love of intricate, interwoven designs. The relics of the ◊Sutton Hoo ship burial, 7th century, and the *Lindisfarne Gospels*, about 690 (both British Museum, London), have typical Celtic ornamental patterns. In the manuscripts of southern England, in particular those produced at Winchester and Canterbury, a different style emerged in the 9th century, with delicate, lively pen-and-ink figures and heavily decorative foliage borders. Anglo-Saxon art was influenced by the Celtic arts of the native Britons, by Roman influences brought by the Christian church, and by Norse arts following the Viking invasions of the 8th century.

Anglo-Saxon language group of dialects spoken by the ◊Anglo-Saxon peoples who, in the 5th–7th centuries, invaded and settled in Britain (in what became England and Lowland Scotland). The term Anglo-Saxon, coined in the 17th century, is rather misleading; it is sometimes used in opposition to 'continental Saxon'. Anglo-Saxon is traditionally known as Old English. See ◊English language; ◊Old English literature.

Anglo-Saxon literature another name for ◊Old English literature.

Angkor Angkor in Cambodia, the capital of the medieval Khmer empire and the site of several important Hindu and Buddhist remains. Angkor Wat is probably the largest religious structure in the world. Built in the form of a stupa, it is covered in Hindu carvings and decoration. Angkor Thom was built around AD 1200, and is primarily Buddhist in its imagery. *Corbis*

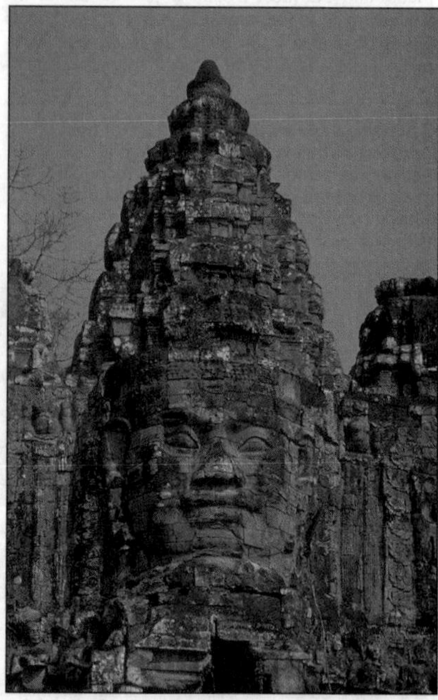

Angola country in SW Africa, bounded W by the Atlantic ocean, N and NE by the Democratic Republic of Congo, E by Zambia, and S by Namibia. The Cabinda enclave, a district of Angola, is bounded W by the Atlantic Ocean, N by the river Congo, and E and S by the Democratic Republic of Congo. *See country box below.*

Angora earlier form of ◊Ankara, Turkey, which gave its name to the Angora goat (see ◊mohair), and hence to other species of long-haired animal, such as the Angora rabbit (a native of the island of Madeira) and the Angora cat. Angora 'wool' from these animals has long, smooth fibres, and the demand for the fibre has led to wool farming in Europe, Japan, and the USA.

angostura flavouring prepared from oil distilled from the bitter, aromatic bark of either of two South American trees, *Galipea officinalis* or *Cusparia trifoliata*, of the rue family. It is blended with herbs and other flavourings to give angostura bitters, which was first used as a stomach remedy and is now used to season food, fruit, and alcoholic drinks.

Angry Young Men journalistic term applied to a loose group of British writers who emerged in the 1950s after the creative hiatus that followed World War II. They expressed dissatisfaction with and revolted against the prevailing social mores, class distinction, and 'good taste'. It was typified by such works as John Osborne's *Look Back in Anger* 1956, Kingsley Amis's *Lucky Jim* 1954, Colin Wilson's *The Outsider* 1956, John Braine's *Room at the Top* 1957, and John Wain's *Hurry on Down* 1953.

angst (German 'anxiety') emotional state of anxiety without a specific cause. In ◊existentialism, the term refers to general human anxiety about free will, and of being responsible for one's actions.

angstrom unit (symbol Åò) of length equal to 10^{-10} metres or one-ten-millionth of a millimetre, used for atomic measurements and the wavelengths of electromagnetic radiation.

Ångström Anders Jonas 1814–1874. Swedish astrophysicist who worked in spectroscopy and solar physics. In 1861 he identified the presence of hydrogen in the Sun. His outstanding *Recherches sur le spectre solaire* 1868 presented an atlas of the solar spectrum with measurements of 1,000 spectral lines expressed in units of one-ten-millionth of a millimetre, the unit which later became the angstrom.

Anguilla

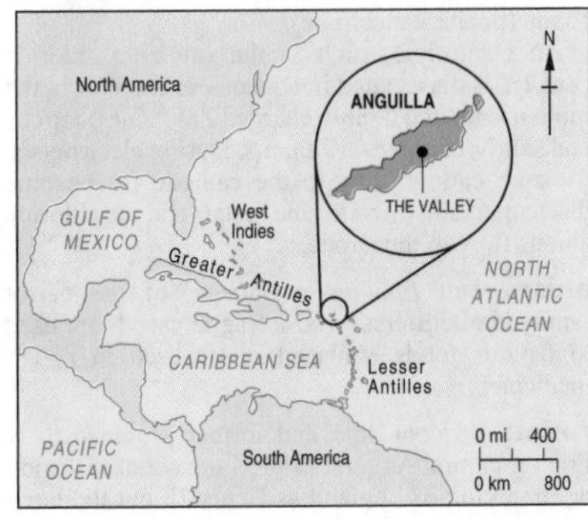

Anguilla island in the E Caribbean
area 160 sq km/62 sq mi
capital The Valley
features white coral-sand beaches; 80% of its coral reef has been lost through tourism (pollution and souvenir sales)
exports lobster, salt
currency Eastern Caribbean dollar
population (1992) 8,960
language English, Creole
government from 1982, governor, executive council, and legislative house of assembly
history a British colony from 1650, Anguilla was long associated with St Christopher–Nevis but revolted against alleged domination by the larger island and seceded 1967. A small British force restored order 1969, and Anguilla retained a special position at its own request; since 1980 it has been a separate dependency of the UK.

Angus former county and modern district on the east coast of Scotland, part of Tayside Region 1975–96; created as new local authority of Scotland 1996 (*see United Kingdom map*).

Anhui or ***Anhwei*** province of E China, watered by the Chang Jiang (Yangtze River)
area 139,900 sq km/54,000 sq mi
capital Hefei
industries cereals in the N; cotton, rice, tea in the S
population (1990) 52,290,000.

anhydride chemical compound obtained by the removal of water from another compound; usually a dehydrated acid. For example, sulphur (VI) oxide (sulphur trioxide, SO_3) is the anhydride of sulphuric acid (H_2SO_4).

anhydrous of a chemical compound, containing no water. If the water of crystallization is removed from blue crystals of copper(II) sulphate, a white powder (anhydrous copper sulphate) results. Liquids from which all traces of water have been removed are also described as being anhydrous.

aniline (Portuguese *anil* 'indigo') $C_6H_5NH_2$ or ***phenylamine*** one of the simplest aromatic chemicals (a substance related to benzene, with its carbon atoms joined in a ring). When pure, it is a colourless oily liquid; it has a characteristic odour, and turns brown on contact with air. It occurs in coal tar, and is used in the rubber industry and to make drugs and dyes. It is highly poisonous. Aniline was discovered 1826, and was originally prepared by the dry distillation of ◊indigo, hence its name.

animal (Latin *anima* 'breath', 'life') or ***metazoan*** member of the ◊kingdom Animalia, one of the major categories of living things, the science of which is zoology. Animals are all ◊heterotrophs (they obtain their energy from organic substances produced by other organisms); they have eukaryotic cells (the genetic material is contained within a

angler Angler fish entice their prey into their large mouths by means of a fishing rod – a modified dorsal ray with a fleshy lure at its tip. The female of this species (13 cm/5 in long) is very much larger than the male (4 cm/1.75 in long).

ANGOLA
People's Republic of

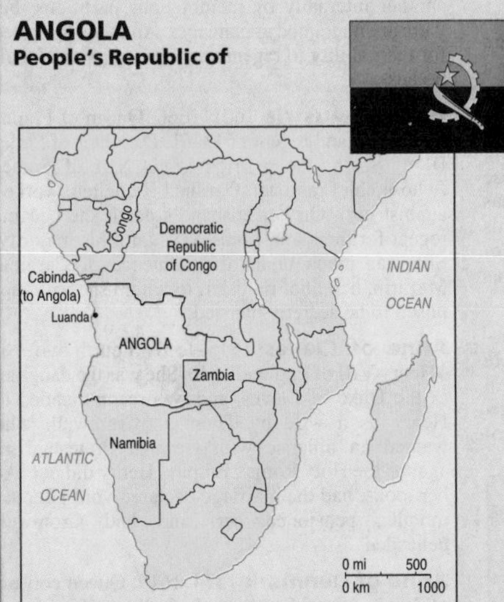

national name *República Popular de Angola*
area 1,246,700 sq km/481,226 sq mi
capital (and chief port) Luanda
major towns/cities Lobito and Benguela
major ports Huambo, Lubango, Malange
physical features narrow coastal plain rises to vast interior plateau with rainforest in NW; desert in S; Cuanza, Cuito, Cubango, and Cunene rivers
head of state José Eduardo dos Santos from 1979
head of government Fernando Franca van Dunem from 1996
political system emergent democracy
administrative divisions 18 provinces
political parties People's Movement for the Liberation of Angola–Workers' Party (MPLA–PT), Marxist-Leninist; National Union for the Total Independence of Angola (UNITA); National Front for the Liberation of Angola (FNLA)
population 11,185,000 (1996 est)
population growth rate 3.7% (1990–95); 3.1% (2000–05)
ethnic distribution eight main ethnic groups (Bakonga, Mbunda, Ovimbundu, Lunda-Tchokwe, Nganguela, Nyaneka-Humbe, Hiriro, and Ambo), and about 100 subgroups. A major exodus of Europeans in the 1970s left around 30,000, mainly Portuguese
life expectancy 45 (men), 48 (women)
literacy rate men 56%, women 29%
languages Portuguese (official); Bantu dialects
religions Roman Catholic 68%, Protestant 20%, animist 12%
currency kwanza
GDP (US $) 3.72 billion (1995)
growth rate 8.6% (1994)
exports oil, coffee, diamonds, palm oil, sisal, iron ore, fish, maize, mahogany and other hardwoods

HISTORY
14th C Under Wene, the powerful Kongo kingdom extended control over much of N Angola.
early 16th C The Kongo ruler, King Afonso I, adopted Christianity, and sought constructive relations with Portuguese traders.
1575 and 1617 Portugal secured control over the ports of Luanda and Benguela and began to pentetrate inland, meeting resistance from Queen Nzinga, the Ndonga ruler.
17th–18th Cs Inland, the Lunda peoples established powerful kingdoms which stretched into S Zaire; the Portuguese made Angola a key centre for the export of slaves.
1836 Slave trade officially abolished.
1885–1915 Military campaigns waged by Portugal to conquer the interior.
1926 Modern borders delineated.
1951 Angola became an overseas territory of Portugal.
1956 Formation of People's Movement for the Liberation of Angola (MPLA), a socialist guerrilla independence movement based in the Congo to the N.
1961 50,000 massacred in rebellion on coffee plantations; forced labour abolished, but armed struggle for independence now waged.
1962 Second nationalist guerrilla movement formed, the National Front for the Liberation of Angola (FNLA), based in N.
1966 National Union for the Total Independence of Angola (UNITA) formed in SE Angola as a breakaway from the FNLA.
1975 Independence achieved from Portugal and Soviet Union. MPLA (backed mainly by Cuba) proclaimed People's Republic of Angola under the presidency of Dr Agostinho Neto. FNLA and UNITA (backed by South Africa and the USA) proclaimed People's Democratic Republic of Angola.
1976 MPLA gained control of most of the country. South African troops withdrew, but Cuban units remained as civil war continued.
1979 Death of Neto, succeeded by José Eduardo dos Santos.
1980 UNITA guerrillas, aided by South Africa, continued raids against the Luanda government and bases of the Namibian South West Africa People's Organization (SWAPO) in Angola.
1988 Peace treaty, providing for the withdrawal of all foreign troops, signed with South Africa and Cuba.
1989 Cease-fire agreed with UNITA broke down and guerrilla activity restarted.
1991 Peace agreement ended civil war. Amnesty for all political prisoners. New multiparty constitution.
1992 MPLA general election victory, led by dos Santos, was fiercely disputed by UNITA, and plunged the country into renewed civil war.
1993 MPLA government recognized by USA. United Nations sanctions imposed against UNITA.
1994 Peace treaty signed by government and UNITA.
1995 UN peacekeepers drafted in.
1996 UNITA leader Jonas Savimbi rejected offer of vice presidency.
1997 National unity government sworn in.
1998 New agreement leading to the demilitarization of UNITA and its transformation into a political party.
1999 UNITA rebels shot down two United Nations (UN) aircraft.

SEE ALSO MPLA; UNITA

distinct nucleus) bounded by a thin cell membrane rather than the thick cell wall of plants. Most animals are capable of moving around for at least part of their life cycle. In the past, it was common to include the single-celled ◊protozoa with the animals, but these are now classified as protists, together with single-celled plants. Thus all animals are multicellular. The oldest land animals known date back 440 million years. ▷*See feature on pp. 704–705.*

animation films in which drawings are photographed to create the illusion of movement, usually by means of exposing the film frame by frame. Alternative forms include use of puppets or other objects. More recently, computer techniques have been used to produce animation. The key exponent of cartoon animation was Walt ◊Disney, who inspired the first wave of the large Japanese animation industry, but a reaction to his representational style subsequently produced a more graphic approach by both North American rivals and Eastern European practitioners.

In the USA Winsor McCay, creator of the newspaper cartoon hero 'Little Nemo', showed a series of ten animated films 1911–21 featuring 'Gertie the Dinosaur', which pioneered the modern cartoon film.

animation, computer computer-generated graphics that appear to move across the screen. Traditional animation involves a great deal of drudgery in creating the 24 frames per second needed to fool the human eye into seeing a moving picture on film. In computer-generated animation, while humans still create the key frames which specify the starting and ending points of a particular sequence – a character running through a landscape, for example – computers are faster and more accurate at calculating the in-between positions and generating the frames. The first feature film created entirely by computer animation was *Toy Story* 1996.

animism in anthropology, the belief that everything, whether animate or inanimate, possesses a soul or spirit. It is a fundamental system of belief in certain religions, particularly those of some pre-industrial societies. Linked with this is the worship of natural objects such as stones and trees, thought to harbour spirits (naturism); fetishism; and ancestor worship.

In psychology and physiology, animism is the view of human personality that attributes human life and behaviour to a force distinct from matter. In developmental psychology, an animistic stage in the early thought and speech of the child has been described, notably by Swiss psychologist Jean Piaget. In philosophy, animisim is the view that in all things consciousness or something mindlike exists; in religious theory, it is the conception of a spiritual reality behind the material one: for example, beliefs in the soul as a shadowy duplicate of the body capable of independent activity, both in life and death.

Ankara The Citadel of Ankara, the capital of Turkey. The foundations were laid by the Galatians in the 3rd century BC and completed by the Romans. The turreted double walls of the Citadel are still standing, as are 15 of the 20 original towers. The houses in the warren of lanes surrounding the Citadel are adorned with broken marble slabs and columns removed from the Roman ruins. *Turkish Embassy*

anion ion carrying a negative charge. During electrolysis, anions in the electrolyte move towards the anode (positive electrode).

An electrolyte, such as the salt zinc chloride ($ZnCl_2$), is dissociated in aqueous solution or in the molten state into doubly charged Zn^{2+} zinc ◊cations and singly-charged Cl^- anions. During electrolysis, the zinc cations flow to the cathode (to become discharged and liberate zinc metal) and the chloride anions flow to the anode.

anise plant *Pimpinella anisum*, of the carrot family Umbelliferae, whose fragrant seeds are used to flavour foods. Aniseed oil is used in cough medicines.

Anjou old countship and former province in N France; capital Angers. In 1154 the count of Anjou became king of England as Henry II, but the territory was lost by King John 1204. In 1480 the countship was annexed to the French crown. The *départements* of Maine-et-Loire and part of Indre-et-Loire, Mayenne, and Sarthe cover the area. The people are called Angevins – a name also applied by the English to the ◊Plantagenet kings.

Ankara formerly ***Angora*** capital of Turkey; population (1990) 2,559,500. Industries include cement, textiles, and leather products. It replaced Istanbul (then in Allied occupation) as capital 1923. It has the largest mosque in Turkey at Kocatepe.

Annaba formerly ***Bône*** seaport in Algeria; population (1989) 348,000. The name means 'city of jujube trees'. There are metallurgical industries, and iron ore and phosphates are exported.

Anna Comnena 1083–after 1148. Byzantine historian, daughter of the emperor ◊Alexius I, who was the historian of her father's reign. After a number of abortive attempts to alter the imperial succession in favour of her husband, Nicephorus Bryennius (c. 1062–1137), she retired to a convent to write her major work, the *Alexiad*. It describes the Byzantine view of public office, as well as the religious and intellectual life of the period.

Annam former country of SE Asia, incorporated in Vietnam 1946 as Central Vietnam. Its capital was Hué. A Bronze Age civilization was flourishing in the area when China conquered it late 2nd century BC. The Chinese named their conquest An-Nam, 'peaceful south'. Independent from 1428, Annam signed a treaty with France 1787 and became a French protectorate, part of Indochina 1884. During World War II, Annam was occupied by Japan.

Annamese the majority ethnic group in Vietnam, comprising 90% of the population. The Annamese language is distinct from Vietnamese, though it has been influenced by Chinese and has loan words from Khmer. Their religion combines elements of Buddhism, Confucianism, and Taoism, as well as ancestor worship.

Annan Kofi 1938– . Ghanaian diplomat, secretary general of the United Nations from 1997. He joined the World Health Organization (WHO) in 1962 and later oversaw the UN peacekeeping operations in Somalia from 1993 and Bosnia-Herzegovina from 1995. He became secretary general after the USA vetoed the re-election of his predecessor Boutros ◊Boutros-Ghali. He was the first UN official to rise through the ranks to the post.

Annapurna mountain 8,075 m/26,502 ft in the Himalayas, Nepal. The north face was first climbed by a French expedition (Maurice Herzog) 1950 and the south by a British team 1970.

Anne 1665–1714. Queen of Great Britain and Ireland 1702–14. She was the second daughter of James, Duke of York, who became James II, and Anne Hyde. She succeeded William III 1702. Events of her reign include the War of the Spanish Succession, Marlborough's victories at Blenheim, Ramillies, Oudenarde, and Malplaquet, and the union of the English and Scottish parliaments 1707. Anne was succeeded by George I.

She received a Protestant upbringing, and in 1683 married Prince George of Denmark (1653–1708). Of their many children only one survived infancy, William, Duke of Gloucester (1689–1700).

Anne (full name Anne Elizabeth Alice Louise) 1950– . Princess of the UK, second child of Queen Elizabeth II, declared Princess Royal 1987. She is actively involved in global charity work, especially for children. An excellent horsewoman, she won silver medals in both individual and team events in the 1975 European Championships, and competed in the 1976 Olympics.

In 1973 she married Capt Mark Phillips (1949–); they separated 1989 and were divorced 1992. In Dec 1992 she married Commander Timothy Laurence. Her son Peter (1977–) was the first direct descendant of the Queen not to bear a title. She also has a daughter, Zara (1981–).

annealing process of heating a material (usually glass or metal) for a given time at a given temperature, followed by slow cooling, to increase ductility and strength. It is a common form of ◊heat treatment.

annelid any segmented worm of the phylum Annelida. Annelids include earthworms, leeches, and marine worms such as lugworms. They have a distinct head and soft body, which is divided into a number of similar segments shut off from one another internally by membranous partitions, but there are no jointed appendages. Annelids are noted for their ability to regenerate missing parts of their bodies.

Anne of Austria 1601–1666. Queen of France from 1615 and regent 1643–61. Daughter of Philip III of Spain, she married Louis XIII of France (whose chief minister, Cardinal Richelieu, worked against her). On her husband's death she became regent for their son, Louis XIV, until his majority. She was much under the influence of Cardinal Mazarin, her chief minister, to whom she was supposed to be secretly married.

Anne of Cleves 1515–1557. Fourth wife of ◊Henry VIII of England 1540. She was the daughter of the Duke of Cleves, and was recommended to Henry as a wife by Thomas ◊Cromwell, who wanted an alliance with German Protestantism against the Holy Roman Empire. Henry did not like her looks, had the marriage declared void after six months, pensioned her, and had Cromwell beheaded.

Anne of Denmark 1574–1619. Queen consort of James VI of Scotland (later James I of Great Britain 1603). She was the daughter of Frederick II of Denmark and Norway, and married James 1589. Anne was suspected of Catholic leanings and was notably extravagant.

annihilation in nuclear physics, a process in which a particle and its 'mirror image' particle called an antiparticle collide and disappear, with the creation of a burst of energy. The energy created is equivalent to the mass of the colliding particles in accordance with the ◊mass–energy equation. For example, an electron and a positron annihilate to produce a burst of high-energy X-rays.

Not all particle–antiparticle interactions result in annihilation; the exception concerns the group called ◊mesons, which are composed of ◊quarks and their antiquarks. See ◊antimatter.

anno Domini (Latin 'in the year of our Lord') in the Christian chronological system, a reference to dates since the birth of Jesus, denoted by the letters

annelid Annelids are worms with segmented bodies. The ragworm, lugworm, and peacock worm shown here are all marine species. Ragworms commonly live in mucous-lined burrows on muddy shores or under stones, and lugworms occupy U-shaped burrows. The peacock worm, however, builds a smooth, round tube from fine particles of mud.

AD. There is no year 0, so AD 1 follows immediately after the year 1 BC (before Christ). The system became the standard reckoning in the Western world after being adopted by English historian Bede in the 8th century. The abbreviations CE (Common Era) and BCE (before Common Era) are often used instead by scholars and writers as objective, rather than religious, terms. The system is based on the calculations made 525 by Dionysius Exiguus, a Scythian monk, but the birth of Jesus should more correctly be placed about 4 BC.

anno hegirae (Latin 'year of the flight') first year of the Muslim calendar, the year of the flight of Muhammad from Mecca to Medina AD 622. In dates it is often abbreviated to AH.

annual percentage rate (APR) the true annual rate of ◊interest charged for a loan. Lenders usually increase the return on their money by compounding the interest payable on a loan to that loan on a monthly or even daily basis. This means that each time that interest is payable on a loan it is charged not only on the initial sum (principal) but also on the interest previously added to that principal. As a result, APR is usually approximately double the flat rate of interest, or simple interest.

annual plant plant that completes its life cycle within one year, during which time it germinates, grows to maturity, bears flowers, produces seed, and then dies. Examples include the common poppy *Papaver rhoeas* and groundsel *Senecio vulgaris*. Among garden plants, some that are described as 'annuals' are actually perennials, although usually cultivated as annuals because they cannot survive winter frosts. See also ◊biennial plant and ◊perennial plant.

annual rings or ***growth rings*** concentric rings visible on the wood of a cut tree trunk or other woody stem. Each ring represents a period of growth when new ◊xylem is laid down to replace tissue being converted into wood (secondary xylem). The wood formed from xylem produced in the spring and early summer has larger and more numerous vessels than the wood formed from xylem produced in autumn when growth is slowing down. The result is a clear boundary between the pale spring wood and the denser, darker autumn wood. Annual rings may be used to estimate the age of the plant (see ◊dendrochronology), although occasionally more than one growth ring is produced in a given year.

Annunciation in the New Testament, the announcement to Mary by the archangel Gabriel that she was to be the mother of Christ; the feast of the Annunciation is 25 March (also known as Lady Day).

anode in chemistry, the positive electrode of an electrolytic ◊cell, towards which negative particles (anions), usually in solution, are attracted. See ◊electrolysis. An anode is given its positive charge by the application of an external electrical potential, unlike the positive electrode of an electrical (battery) cell, which acquires its charge in the course of a spontaneous chemical reaction taking place within the cell.

anodizing process that increases the resistance to ◊corrosion of a metal, such as aluminium, by building up a protective oxide layer on the surface. The natural corrosion resistance of aluminium is provided by a thin film of aluminium oxide; anodizing increases the thickness of this film and thus the corrosion protection.

anomie in the social sciences, a state of 'normlessness' created by the breakdown of commonly agreed standards of behaviour and morality; the term often refers to situations where the social order appears to have collapsed. The concept was developed by French sociologist Emile ◊Durkheim who used 'anomie' to describe societies in transition during industrialization.

anorexia lack of desire to eat, or refusal to eat, especially the pathological condition of anorexia nervosa, most often found in adolescent girls and young women. Compulsive eating, or ◊bulimia, distortions of body image, and depression often accompany anorexia.

Anorexia nervosa is characterized by severe self-imposed restriction of food intake. The consequent weight loss may lead, in women, to absence of menstruation. Anorexic patients sometimes commit suicide. Anorexia nervosa is often associated with increased physical activity and symptoms of mental disorders. Psychotherapy is an important part of the treatment.

Anouilh Jean 1910–1987. French dramatist. His plays, which are often studies in the contrast between purity and cynical worldliness, include *Antigone* 1944, *L'Invitation au château/Ring Round the Moon* 1947, *Colombe* 1950, and *Becket* 1959, about St Thomas à Becket and Henry II.

anoxaemia or ***hypoxaemia*** shortage of oxygen in the blood; insufficient supply of oxygen to the tissues. It may be due to breathing air deficient in oxygen (for instance, at high altitude or where there are noxious fumes), a disease of the lungs, or some disorder where the oxygen-carrying capacity of the blood is impaired.

anoxia or ***hypoxia*** in biology, deprivation of oxygen, a condition that rapidly leads to collapse or death, unless immediately reversed.

Anschluss (German 'union') the annexation of Austria with Germany, accomplished by the German chancellor Adolf Hitler 12 March 1938.

Anselm, St c. 1033–1109. Italian priest and philosopher. He was born in Piedmont and educated at the abbey of Bec in Normandy, which, as abbot from 1078, he made a centre of scholarship in Europe. He was appointed archbishop of Canterbury by William II of England 1093, but was later forced into exile. He holds an important place in the development of ◊scholasticism. Feast day 21 April.

Anouilh The French dramatist Jean Anouilh. He wrote around 40 plays, and was also involved in cinema. The film version of his stage comedy *Becket* 1964, was nominated for several Academy Awards. *Corbis*

Anshan Chinese city in Liaoning province, 89 km/55 mi SE of Shenyang (Mukden); population (1991) 1,390,000. The iron and steel centre started here 1918, was expanded by the Japanese, dismantled by the Russians, and restored by the communist government of China.

Anson George, 1st Baron Anson 1697–1762. English admiral who sailed around the world 1740–44. In 1740 he commanded the squadron attacking the Spanish colonies and shipping in South America; he returned home by circumnavigating the world, with £500,000 of Spanish treasure. He carried out reforms at the Admiralty, which increased the efficiency of the British fleet and contributed to its success in the Seven Years' War (1756–63) against France.

ant insect belonging to the family Formicidae, and to the same order (Hymenoptera) as bees and wasps. Ants are characterized by a conspicuous 'waist' and elbowed antennae. Ant behaviour is complex, and serves the colony rather than the individual. Ants are found in all parts of the world, except the polar regions. About 10,000 different species are known; all are social in habit, and all construct nests of various kinds. Remarkable species include army (South American) and driver (African) ants, which march nomadically in huge columns, devouring even tethered animals in their path.

antacid any substance that neutralizes stomach acid, such as sodium bicarbonate or magnesium hydroxide ('milk of magnesia'). Antacids are weak ◊bases, swallowed as solids or emulsions. They may be taken between meals to relieve symptoms of hyperacidity, such as pain, bloating, nausea, and 'heartburn'. Excessive or prolonged need for antacids should be investigated medically.

Antall Jozsef 1932–1993. Hungarian politician, prime minister 1990–93. He led the centre-right Hungarian Democratic Forum (MDF) to electoral victory April 1990, becoming Hungary's first post-communist prime minister. He promoted gradual, and successful, privatization and encouraged inward foreign investment.

Antalya Mediterranean port on the west coast of Turkey and capital of a province of the same name; population (1990) 378,200. The port trades in grain and timber. Industries include canning and flour milling. It is a popular coastal resort. Founded in the 2nd century BC, it has two Roman amphitheatres and the ruins of Perga nearby. It flourished under the Seljuk Turks in the 13th century.

Antananarivo formerly ***Tananarive*** capital of Madagascar, on the interior plateau, with a rail link to Tamatave; population (1993) 1,053,000. Industries include tobacco, food processing, leather goods, and clothing.

Antarctica continent surrounding the South Pole, arbitrarily defined as the region lying S of the Antarctic Circle. Occupying 10% of the world's surface, Antarctica contains 90% of the world's ice, representing 90% of its fresh water
area 13,900,000 sq km/5,400,000 sq mi
features Mount Erebus on Ross Island is the world's southernmost active volcano; the Ross Ice Shelf is formed by several glaciers coalescing in the Ross Sea
physical formed of two blocs of rock with an area of about 8 million sq km/3 million sq mi, Antarctica is covered by a cap of ice that flows slowly towards its 22,400 km/14,000 mi coastline, reaching the sea in high ice cliffs. The most southerly shores are near the 78th parallel in the Ross and Weddell seas. E Antarctica is a massive bloc of ancient rocks that surface in the Transantarctic Mountains of Victoria Land, much of it over 3,000 m/10,000 ft high.

Separated by a deep channel, W Antarctica is characterized by the mountainous regions of Graham Land, the Antarctic Peninsula, Palmer Land, and Ellsworth Land; the highest peak is Vinson Massif (5,139 m/16,866 ft).
Antarctic ice around 2% of the land is ice-free. With an estimated volume of 30 million cu km/7.2 million cu mi, the ice-cap has an average thickness of 2,450 m/7,100 ft, in places reaching depths of 4,000 m/13,000 ft or more. The ice is so thick that whole mountain ranges are hidden by it; the few peaks that are visible above the ice are known as

'Tragedy is restful and the reason is that hope, that foul, deceitful thing, has no part in it.'

JEAN ANOUILH
Antigone

nunataks. Each annual layer of snow preserves a record of global conditions, and where no melting at the surface of the bedrock has occurred the ice can be a million years old.

Solid ice attached to the Antarctic land-mass is known as fast ice. If the ice forms a ridge more than 2 m/6 ft above sea level, it is known as an ice shelf. Pack ice is a mixture of ice floes in water. A lead is a navigable passage through pack ice. A polynya is a small area of open water surrounded by ice. The Antarctic Convergence is the point at which colder water from Antarctica meets and flows beneath warmer subantarctic water. The position of the Convergence may vary by up to 100 km/62 mi.

climate winds are strong and temperatures are cold, particularly in the interior where temperatures can drop to −70°C/−94°F and below; the average winter temperature is −60°C/−76°F. The lowest temperature ever recorded in the world was here in 1983: −89°C/−128°F. Precipitation is largely in the form of snow or hoar-frost rather than rain which rarely exceeds 50 mm/2 in per year (less than the Sahara Desert). Average temperature on the Antarctic Peninsula has risen by 2.5°C/36.5°F since monitoring started in the 1950s. Dry valleys are unique areas that remain snow-free all the year round because the katabatic winds (cool winds that blow down valleys on calm clear nights) remove moisture. The Antarctic summer (the period during which the ice melts) has lengthened from 60 to 90 days since the 1970s.

flora and fauna the Antarctic ecosystem is characterized by large numbers of relatively few species of higher plants and animals, and a short food chain from tiny marine plants to whales, seals, penguins, and other sea birds.

Only two species of flowering plant are known – the Antarctic pearlwort and the Antarctic hairgrass; both of which are rapidly increasing – but there are about 60 species of moss, 100 species of lichen, and 400 species of algae. As the Antarctic ice shelves disintegrate with the lengthening summers, new lichens are appearing in soil uncovered by the retreating glaciers.

animals there are only 67 species of insect; the largest resident animal in Antarctica is a midge 12 mm/0.5 in long. There are no native land mammals (the Arctic has 40); no resident land birds (the Arctic has 8); and fewer than 50 species of seabirds, only 13 of which breed in Antarctica. Because of the cold conditions, animals live longer, produce fewer eggs, and protect them for longer. The oceans around the Antarctic contain relatively few fish; it is estimated that there are six times as many squid by weight in Antarctic seas as fish. Three-quarters of the Antarctic fish belong to the order Nototheniidae, comprising five families, of which four are found only in Antarctica, reflecting the need for specialization to survive in such hostile conditions. Most of them are deepwater fish. There is a high level of parental care, unusual in fish.

Fish have lower levels of haemoglobin, and some have a specialized 'antifreeze' glycoprotein in their blood, which lowers its freezing point, enabling them to survive without freezing in the sea at −1.9°C/28.6°F. One family has no haemoglobin at all, with blood an anaemic pale colour; the fish survive because the cold water can contain higher levels of oxygen.

products cod, Antarctic icefish, and krill are fished in Antarctic waters. Whaling, which began in the early 20th century, ceased during the 1960s as a result of overfishing, although Norway and Iceland defied the ban 1992 to recommence whaling. Petroleum, coal, and minerals such as palladium and platinum exist, but their exploitation is prevented by a 50-year ban on commercial mining agreed by 39 nations 1991

population no permanent residents and no indigenous inhabitants; settlement limited to scientific research stations with maximum population of 10,000 (including 3,000 tourists) during the summer months. Sectors of Antarctica are claimed by Argentina, Australia, Chile, France, the UK, Norway, and New Zealand.

exploration the first to explore Antarctica was Captain James Cook, who reached 71° S. In 1819 William Smith landed on and claimed for Britain the South Shetland Islands.

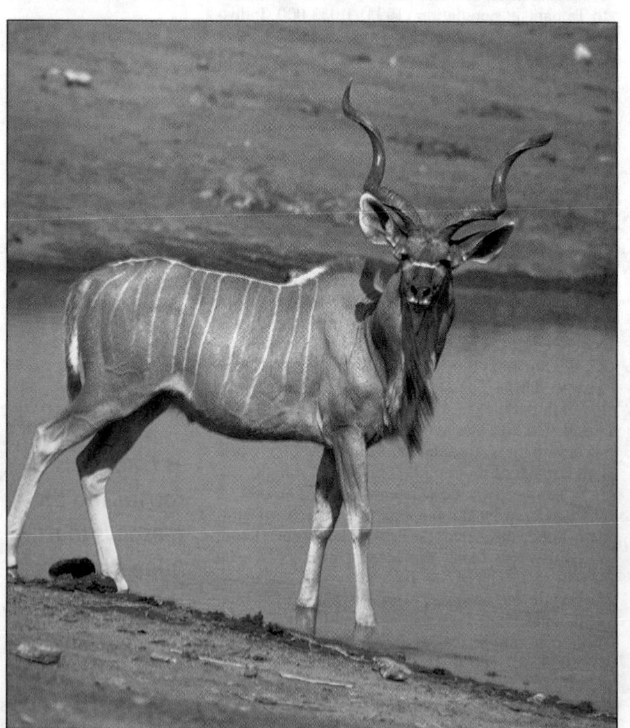

antelope **One of the largest of the antelopes, the greater kudu** ***Tragelaphus strepsiceros*** **lives mainly on the African savannas. In many species of antelope both sexes are fully horned, but the spirally twisted horns of the greater kudu are, with rare exceptions, found only on the males.** ***Premaphotos Wildlife***

Antarctic Circle imaginary line that encircles the South Pole at latitude 66° 32′ S. The line encompasses the continent of Antarctica and the Antarctic Ocean. The region S of this line experiences at least one night in the southern summer during which the Sun never sets, and at least one day in the southern winter during which the Sun never rises.

Antarctic Ocean popular name for the reaches of the Atlantic, Indian, and Pacific oceans extending S of the Antarctic Circle (66° 32′S). The term is not used by the International Hydrographic Bureau.

Antares or ***Alpha Scorpii*** brightest star in the constellation Scorpius and the 15th brightest star in the night sky. It is a red supergiant several hundred times larger than the Sun and perhaps 10,000 times as luminous, lies about 300 light years away, and fluctuates slightly in brightness.

anteater mammal of the family Myrmecophagidae, order Edentata, native to Mexico, Central America, and tropical South America. The anteater lives almost entirely on ants and termites. It has toothless jaws, an extensile tongue, and claws for breaking into the nests of its prey. Species include the giant anteater *Myrmecophaga tridactyla*, about 1.8 m/6 ft long including the tail, the tamandua or collared anteater *Tamandua tetradactyla*, about 90 cm/3.5 ft long, and the silky anteater *Cyclopes didactyla*, about 35 cm/14 in long.

antelope any of numerous kinds of even-toed, hoofed mammals belonging to the cow family, Bovidae. Most antelopes are lightly built and good runners. They are grazers or browsers, and chew the cud. They range in size from the dik-diks and duikers, only 30 cm/1 ft high, to the eland, which can be 1.8 m/6 ft at the shoulder.

The majority of antelopes are African, including the eland, gnu, kudu, springbok, and waterbuck, although other species live in parts of Asia, including the deserts of Arabia and the Middle East.

antenna in radio and television, another name for ◊aerial.

antenna in zoology, an appendage ('feeler') on the head. Insects, centipedes, and millipedes each have one pair of antennae but there are two pairs in crustaceans, such as shrimps. In insects, the antennae are involved with the senses of smell and touch; they are frequently complex structures with large surface areas that increase the ability to detect scents.

anthem in music, a short, usually elaborate, religious choral composition, sometimes accompanied by the organ; also a song of loyalty and devotion. Composers of anthems include Byrd, Gibbons, Purcell, Blow, and Handel.

anther in a flower, the terminal part of a stamen in which the ◊pollen grains are produced. It is usually borne on a slender stalk or filament, and has two lobes, each containing two chambers, or pollen sacs, within which the pollen is formed.

antheridium organ producing the male gametes, ◊antherozoids, in algae, bryophytes (mosses and liverworts), and pteridophytes (ferns, club mosses, and horsetails). It may be either single-celled, as in most algae, or multicellular, as in bryophytes and pteridophytes.

antherozoid motile (or independently moving) male gamete produced by algae, bryophytes (mosses and liverworts), pteridophytes (ferns, club mosses, and horsetails), and some gymnosperms (notably the cycads). Antherozoids are formed in an antheridium and, after being released, swim by means of one or more ◊flagella, to the female gametes. Higher plants have nonmotile male gametes contained within ◊pollen grains.

Anthony Susan B(rownell) 1820–1906. US pioneering campaigner for women's rights who also worked for the antislavery and temperance movements. Her causes included equality of pay for women teachers, married women's property rights, and women's suffrage. In 1869, with Elizabeth Cady ◊Stanton, she founded the National Woman Suffrage Association.

Anthony edited and published a radical women's newspaper, *The Revolution* 1868–70, and co-edited with Elizabeth Cady Stanton *History of Woman Suffrage* 1881–86. She organized the International Council of Women and founded the International Woman Suffrage Alliance in Berlin 1904.

anteater **The anteater is a relative of the sloths, armadillos, and pangolins. There are four species, native to South and Central America. The giant anteater** ***Myrmecophaga tridactyla*** **is 1.8 m/6 ft long with an elongated face, hairy coat, and bushy tail. It lives in forests and savanna.**

Anthony, St or ***Anthony of Thebes*** c. 251–356. Egyptian founder of Christian monasticism. At the age of 20, he renounced all his possessions and began a hermetic life of study and prayer, later seeking further solitude in a cave in the desert. In 305 Anthony founded the first cenobitic order, a community of Christians following a rule of life under a superior. Late in his life he went to Alexandria and preached against ◊Arianism. He lived to over 100, and a good deal is known about his life since a biography (by St Athanasius) has survived. Anthony's temptations in the desert were a popular subject in art; he is also often depicted with a pig and a bell.

anthracene white, glistening, crystalline, tricyclic, aromatic hydrocarbon with a faint blue fluorescence when pure. Its melting point is about 216°C/421°F and its boiling point 351°C/664°F. It occurs in the high-boiling-point fractions of coal tar, where it was discovered 1832 by the French chemists Auguste Laurent (1808–1853) and Jean Dumas (1800–1884).

anthracite (from Greek *anthrax*, 'coal') hard, dense, shiny variety of ◊coal, containing over 90% carbon and a low percentage of ash and impurities, which causes it to burn without flame, smoke, or smell. Because of its purity, anthracite gives off relatively little sulphur dioxide when burnt.

Anthracite gives intense heat, but is slow-burning and slow to light; it is therefore unsuitable for use in open fires. Its characteristic composition is thought to be due to the action of bacteria in disintegrating the coal-forming material when it was laid down during the ◊Carboniferous period.

anthrax disease of livestock, occasionally transmitted to humans, usually via infected hides and fleeces, caused by *Bacillus anthracis*. It may develop as black skin pustules or severe pneumonia. Treatment is with antibiotics. Vaccination is effective.

ANTARCTICA: TIMELINE

1773–74	English explorer James Cook first sailed in Antarctic seas.
1819–21	Antarctica was circumnavigated by Russian explorer Fabian Bellingshausen.
1823	British navigator James Weddell sailed into the sea now named after him.
1841–42	Scottish explorer James Ross sighted the Great Ice Barrier now named after him.
1895	Norwegian explorer Carsten Borchgrevink was one of the first landing party on the continent.
1898	Borchgrevink's British expedition first wintered in Antarctica.
1901–04	English explorer Robert Scott first penetrated the interior of the continent.
1907–08	English explorer Ernest Shackleton came within 182 km/113 mi of the Pole.
1911	Norwegian explorer Roald Amundsen reached the Pole 14 Dec, overland with dogs.
1912	Scott reached the Pole 18 Jan, initially aided by ponies.
1928–29	US naval officer Richard Byrd made the first flight to the Pole.
1935	US explorer Lincoln Ellsworth first flew across Antarctica.
1946–48	US explorer Finn Ronne's expedition proved the Antarctic to be one continent.
1957–58	International Geophysical Year, involving 12 countries setting up research stations; this led to the 1959 Antarctic Treaty. English explorer Vivian Fuchs made the first overland crossing.
1959	A Soviet expedition crossed from the West Ice Shelf to the Pole. The International Antarctic Treaty was signed by 39 countries, and suspended all territorial claims, reserving an area south of 60° S latitude for peaceful and scientific purposes only.
1961–62	The Bentley Trench was discovered, suggesting that there may be an Atlantic–Pacific link beneath the continent.
1966–67	Specially protected areas established internationally for animals and plants.
1979	Fossils of apelike humanoids resembling E Africa's Proconsul were found 500 km/300 mi from the Pole.
1980	International Convention on the exploitation of resources – oil, gas, fish, and krill.
1982	The first circumnavigation of Earth (2 Sept 1979–29 Aug 1982) via the Poles was completed by English explorers Ranulph Fiennes, Charles Burton, and Oliver Shepard.
1985	A hole in the ozone layer over Antarctica was discovered by the British Antarctic Survey.
1990	The longest unmechanized crossing (6,100 km/3,182 mi) was made by a six-person international team, using only skis and dogs.
1991	The Antarctic Treaty imposing a 50-year ban on mineral exploitation was secured, signed by the 39 signatories of the 1959 treaty.
1992	US geologists found evidence of active volcanoes beneath the ice.
1992–93	Norwegian lawyer Erling Kagge skied unassisted to the Pole from Berkner Island in Weddell Sea; Ranulph Fiennes and Michael Stroud crossed the Antarctic continent on foot, unassisted, but had to be rescued before reaching their ultimate destination of Scott's Base.
1994	The International Whaling Commission voted to establish a whale sanctuary in Antarctica.
1995	The disintegration of the Prince Gustav Ice Shelf and the northern Larsen Ice Shelf – as a result of global warming – was discovered.
1996	A 14,000 sq km/5,400 sq mi freshwater lake was discovered beneath the Antarctic ice. It was estimated to be 5 million years old.

anthropoid (Greek *anthropos* 'man', *eidos* 'resemblance') any primate belonging to the suborder Anthropoidea, including monkeys, apes, and humans.

anthropology (Greek *anthropos* 'man', *logos* 'discourse') the science of the nature of man. It investigates the physical, cultural, and social aspects, both past and present, of the human species. It is divided into two broad categories. Biological or physical anthropology attempts to explain human biological variation from an evolutionary perspective and is concerned with human ◊palaeontology, primatology, human adaptation, ◊demography, population genetics, and human growth and development. Social or cultural anthropology attempts to explain the variety of human cultures and societies and is divided into three subfields: social or cultural anthropology proper, ◊prehistory or prehistoric archaeology, and anthropological linguistics. It differs from sociology in that anthropologists are concerned with 'other' cultures and societies.

Anthropology's primary method is called participant observation and involves the researcher living for a year or more in another culture, speaking the local language and participating in all aspects of everyday life. This experience is then recounted in an ethnographic monograph. By comparing these accounts anthropologists hope to understand who we are.

anthropomorphism (Greek *anthropos* 'man', *morphe* 'shape') the attribution of human characteristics to animals, inanimate objects, or deities. It appears in the mythologies of many cultures and as a literary device in fables and allegories.

anthroposophy system of mystical philosophy developed by Austrian educationist Rudolf ◊Steiner, who claimed to possess a power ofintuition giving him access to knowledge not attain able by scientific means. Designed to develop the whole human being, anthroposophy stresses the importance of awakening latent spiritual perception by training the mind to rise above material things. Anthroposophists believe that an appreciation of art is one of the keys to spiritual development, and that music and colours have curative properties.

anti-aliasing in computer graphics, a software technique for diminishing ◊aliasing ('jaggies') – steplike lines that should be smooth. Jaggies occur because the output device, the monitor or printer, does not have a high enough resolution to represent a smooth line. Anti-aliasing reduces the prominence of jaggies by surrounding the steps with intermediate shades of grey or colour. This reduces the jagged appearance of the lines but makes them fuzzier.

anti-art in the visual arts, work that is exhibited in a conventional context but makes fun of serious art or challenges the nature of art; it is characteristic of ◊Dada. Marcel Duchamp is credited with introducing the term around 1914, and its spirit is summed up in his attempt to exhibit a urinal (*Fountain* 1917). The term is also used to describe other intentionally provocative art forms, for example, nonsense poetry.

antibiotic drug that kills or inhibits the growth of bacteria and fungi. It is derived from living organisms such as fungi or bacteria, which distinguishes it from synthetic antimicrobials.

The earliest antibiotics, the ◊penicillins, came into use from 1941 and were quickly joined by chloramphenicol, the ◊cephalosporins, erythromycins, tetracyclines, and aminoglycosides. A range of broad-spectrum antibiotics, the 4-quinolones, was developed 1989, of which ciprofloxacin was the first. Each class and individual antibiotic acts in a different way and may be effective against either a broad spectrum or a specific type of disease-causing agent. Use of antibiotics has become more selective as side effects, such as toxicity, allergy, and resistance, have become better understood. Bacteria have the ability to develop resistance following repeated or subclinical (insufficient) doses, so more advanced and synthetic antibiotics are continually required to overcome them.

antibody protein molecule produced in the blood by ◊lymphocytes in response to the presence of foreign or invading substances (◊antigens); such substances include the proteins carried on the surface of infecting microorganisms. Antibody production is only one aspect of ◊immunity in vertebrates.

Each antibody acts against only one kind of antigen, and combines with it to form a 'complex'. This action may render antigens harmless, or it may destroy microorganisms by setting off chemical changes that cause them to self-destruct. In other cases, the formation of a complex will cause antigens to form clumps that can then be detected and engulfed by white blood cells, such as ◊macrophages and ◊phagocytes.

Each bacterial or viral infection will bring about the manufacture of a specific antibody, which will then fight the disease. Many diseases can only be contracted once because antibodies remain in the blood after the infection has passed, preventing any further invasion. Vaccination boosts a person's resistance by causing the production of antibodies specific to particular infections.

Antibodies were discovered 1890 by German physician Emil von ◊Behring and Japanese bacteriologist Shibasaburo ◊Kitasato.

Antichrist in Christian theology, the opponent of Christ. The appearance of the Antichrist was believed to signal the Second Coming, at which Christ would conquer his opponent. The concept may stem from the idea of conflict between Light and Darkness, present in Persian, Babylonian, and Jewish literature, which influenced early Christian thought. The Antichrist may be a false messiah, or be connected with false teaching, or be identified with an individual; for example, Nero at the time of the persecution of Christians, and the pope and Napoleon in later Christian history.

anticlericalism hostility to the influence of the clergy in affairs outside the sphere of the church. Identifiable from the 12th century onwards, it became increasingly common in France in the 16th century and especially after the French Revolution of 1789.

More recently apparent in most western European states, anticlericalism takes many forms; for example, opposition to the clergy as reactionary and against the principles of liberalism and the Enlightenment, also opposition to clerics as representatives of religion or as landowners, tax-gatherers, or state servants.

anticline in geology, a fold in the rocks of the Earth's crust in which the layers or beds bulge upwards to form an arch (seldom preserved intact). The fold of an anticline may be undulating or steeply curved. A steplike bend in otherwise gently dipping or horizontal beds is a monocline. The opposite of an anticline is a syncline.

anticoagulant substance that inhibits the formation of blood clots. Most anticoagulants prevent the production of thrombin, an enzyme that induces the formation from blood plasma of fibrinogen, to which blood platelets adhere and form clots. Common anticoagulants are heparin, produced by the liver and some white blood cells, and derivatives of coumarin. Anticoagulants are used medically in the prevention and treatment of thrombosis and heart attacks. Anticoagulant substances are also produced by blood-feeding animals, such as mosquitoes, leeches, and vampire bats, to keep the victim's blood flowing.

Anti-Corn Law League an extra-parliamentary pressure group formed 1838, led by British Liberals Richard ◊Cobden and John ◊Bright, which argued for free trade and campaigned successfully against duties on the import of foreign corn to Britain imposed by the ◊Corn Laws, which were repealed 1846.

Formed Sept 1838 by Manchester industrialists and campaigning on a single issue, the league initiated strategies for popular mobilization and agitation including mass meetings, lecture tours, pamphleteering, opinion polls, and parliamentary lobbying. Reaction by the conservative landed interests was organized with the establishment of

'The true Republic: men, their rights and nothing more; women, their rights and nothing less.'

Susan B Anthony
Motto of her newspaper *Revolution*

"The steamer carried us past a shifting diorama of scenery which may be likened to Vesuvius and the Bay of Naples, repeated again and again with every possible variation of the same type of delicate loveliness."

On the **Lesser Antilles**
Charles Kingsley
At Last 1871

the Central Agricultural Protection Society, nicknamed the Anti-League. In June 1846 political pressure, the state of the economy, and the Irish situation prompted Prime Minister ◊Peel to repeal the Corn Laws.

anticyclone area of high atmospheric pressure caused by descending air, which becomes warm and dry. Winds radiate from a calm centre, taking a clockwise direction in the northern hemisphere and an anticlockwise direction in the southern hemisphere. Anticyclones are characterized by clear weather and the absence of rain and violent winds. In summer they bring hot, sunny days and in winter they bring fine, frosty spells, although fog and low cloud are not uncommon in the UK. ***Blocking anticyclones***, which prevent the normal air circulation of an area, can cause summer droughts and severe winters.

antidepressant any drug used to relieve symptoms in depressive illness. The two main groups are the tricyclic antidepressants (TCADs) and the monoamine oxidase inhibitors (MAOIs), which act by altering chemicals available to the central nervous system. Both may produce serious side effects and are restricted.

antidiarrhoeal any substance that controls diarrhoea. Choice of treatment depends on the underlying cause. One group, including opiates, codeine, and atropine, produces constipation by slowing down motility (muscle activity of the intestine wall).

Bulking agents, such as vegetable fibres (for example, methylcellulose), absorb fluid. Antibiotics may be appropriate for certain systemic bacterial infections, such as ◊typhoid fever, salmonella, and infective enteritis (inflammation of the small intestine). Current therapy of acute diarrhoea is based on fluid and ◊electrolyte replacement. Chronic diarrhoea, a feature of some bowel disorders (for example, Crohn's disease, colitis, coeliac disease) responds to drugs such as ◊antispasmodics and corticosteroids, and special diet.

antifreeze substance added to a water-cooling system (for example, that of a car) to prevent it freezing in cold weather. The most common types of antifreeze contain the chemical ethylene ◊glycol, an organic alcohol with a freezing point of about −15°C/5°F.

antigen any substance that causes the production of ◊antibodies by the body's immune system. Common antigens include the proteins carried on the surface of bacteria, viruses, and pollen grains. The proteins of incompatible blood groups or tissues also act as antigens, which has to be taken into account in medical procedures such as blood transfusions and organ transplants.

Antigone in Greek mythology, a daughter of Jocasta by her son ◊Oedipus. She is the subject of a tragedy by ◊Sophocles.

Antigonus 382–301 BC. General of Alexander the Great after whose death 323 BC Antigonus made himself master of Asia Minor. He was defeated and killed by ◊Seleucus I at the battle of Ipsus.

Antigua and Barbuda country comprising three islands in the E Caribbean (Antigua, Barbuda, and uninhabited Redonda). *See country box below.*

antihistamine any substance that counteracts the effects of ◊histamine. Antihistamines may occur naturally or they may be synthesized.

H_1 antihistamines are used to relieve allergies, alleviating symptoms such as runny nose, itching, swelling, or asthma. H_2 antihistamines suppress acid production by the stomach, and are used in the treatment of peptic ulcers, often making surgery unnecessary.

anti-inflammatory any substance that reduces swelling in soft tissues. Antihistamines relieve allergic reactions; aspirin and ◊NSAIDs are effective in joint and musculoskeletal conditions; and rubefacients (counterirritant liniments) ease painful joints, tendons, and muscles.

◊Steroids, because of their severe side effects, are only prescribed if other therapy is ineffective, or if a condition is life-threatening. A ◊corticosteroid injection into the affected joint usually gives prolonged relief from inflammation.

antiknock substance added to ◊petrol to reduce knocking in car engines. It is a mixture of dibromoethane and tetraethyl lead. Its use in leaded petrol has resulted in atmospheric pollution by lead compounds.

Antilles group of West Indian islands, divided N–S into the ***Greater Antilles*** (Cuba, Jamaica, Haiti–Dominican Republic, Puerto Rico) and ***Lesser Antilles***, subdivided into the Leeward Islands (Virgin Islands, St Christopher–Nevis, Antigua and Barbuda, Anguilla, Montserrat, and Guadeloupe) and the Windward Islands (Dominica, Martinique, St Lucia, St Vincent and the Grenadines, Barbados, and Grenada).

antimatter in physics, a form of matter in which most of the attributes (such as electrical charge, magnetic moment, and spin) of ◊elementary particles are reversed. Such particles (◊antiparticles) can be created in particle accelerators, such as those at ◊CERN in Geneva, Switzerland, and at ◊Fermilab in the USA. In 1996 physicists at CERN created the first atoms of antimatter: nine atoms of antihydrogen survived for 40 nanoseconds.

Antilles

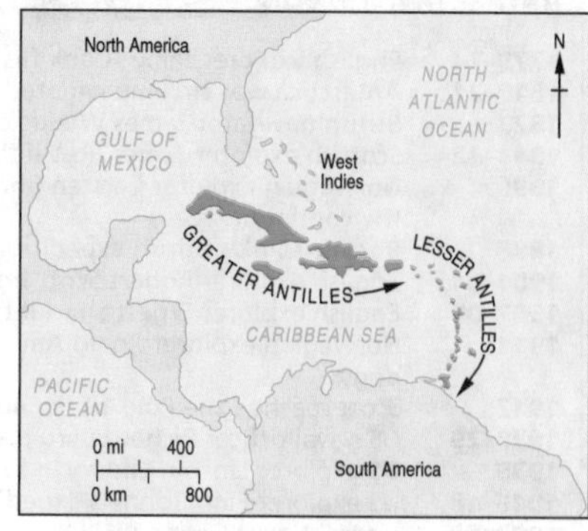

antimony silver-white, brittle, semimetallic element (a metalloid), symbol Sb (from Latin *stibium*), atomic number 51, relative atomic mass 121.75. It occurs chiefly as the ore stibnite, and is used to make alloys harder; it is also used in photosensitive substances in colour photography, optical electronics, fireproofing, pigment, and medicine. It was employed by the ancient Egyptians in a mixture to protect the eyes from flies.

antinode in physics, the position in a ◊standing wave pattern at which the amplitude of vibration is greatest (compare ◊node). The standing wave of a stretched string vibrating in the fundamental mode has one antinode at its midpoint. A vibrating air column in a pipe has an antinode at the pipe's open end and at the place where the vibration is produced.

Antioch ancient capital of the Greek kingdom of Syria, founded 300 BC by ◊Seleucus I in memory of his father Antiochus, and famed for its splendour and luxury. Under the Romans it was an early centre of Christianity. St Paul set off on his missionary journeys from here. It was captured by the Arabs 637. After a five-month siege 1098 Antioch was taken by the crusaders, who held it until 1268. The site is now occupied by the Turkish town of Antakya.

Antiochus thirteen kings of Syria of the Seleucid dynasty, including:

Antiochus I c. 324–c. 261 BC. King of Syria from 281 BC, son of Seleucus I, one of the generals of

ANTIGUA AND BARBUDA
State of

USA
ATLANTIC OCEAN
BARBUDA
St. John's
ANTIGUA
Mexico
Cuba
St Kitts-Nevis
Montserrat
CARIBBEAN SEA
Venezuela
PACIFIC OCEAN
0 mi 500
0 km 1000

area Antigua 280 sq km/108 sq mi, Barbuda 161 sq km/62 sq mi, plus Redonda 1 sq km/0.4 sq mi (440 sq km/170 sq mi altogether)
capital (and chief port) St John's (on Antigua)
major towns/cities Codrington (on Barbuda)
physical features low-lying tropical islands of limestone and coral with some higher volcanic outcrops; no rivers and low rainfall result in frequent droughts and deforestation. Antigua is the largest of the Leeward Islands; Redonda is an uninhabited island of volcanic rock rising to 305 m/1,000 ft
head of state Elizabeth II from 1981, represented by governor general James B Carlisle from 1993
head of government Lester Bird from 1994
political system liberal democracy
administrative divisions seven parishes
political parties Antigua Labour Party (ALP), moderate left of centre; United Progressive Party (UPP), centrist; Barbuda People's Movement (BPM), left of centre
population 64,166 (1994 est)
population growth rate 0.6% (1990–95)
ethnic distribution population almost entirely of black African descent
life expectancy 70 years
literacy rate 96%
language English
religion Christian (mostly Anglican)
currency Eastern Caribbean dollar
GDP (US $) 494 million (1994)
growth rate 5.3% (1994)
exports sea-island cotton, rum, lobsters, tourism

HISTORY
1493 Antigua, then peopled by Amerindian (American Indian) Caribs, visited by Christopher Columbus; he named it after a painting in the Church of Sante Maria la Antigua, in Seville.
1632 Antigua colonized by British settlers from St Kitts.
1667 Treaty of Breda formally ceded Antigua to Britain, ending French claim.
1674 Christopher Codrington, a sugar planter from Barbados, established sugar plantations and acquired Barbuda island on lease from the British monarch in 1685; Africans brought in as slaves.
1834 Antigua's slaves were freed.
1860 Annexation of Barbuda.
1871–1956 Antigua and Barbuda administered as part of the Leeward Islands federation.
1946 Antigua Labour Party (ALP) formed by Vere Bird.
1958–62 Part of the West Indies Federation.
1967 Antigua and Barbuda became an associated state within the Commonwealth, with full internal independence, but Britain responsible for defence and foreign affairs.
1969 Separatist movement developed on Barbuda.
1971 Progressive Labour Movement (PLM) won the general election, defeating ALP, and George Walter replaced Bird as prime minister.
1973 Entered the Caribbean Community and Common Market (CARICOM).
1976 PLM called for early independence, but ALP urged caution. ALP, led by Bird, won the general election.
1981 Independence from Britain achieved.
1983 Assisted US invasion of Grenada, despite policy on nonalignment.
1991 Bird remained in power despite calls for his resignation.
1993 Lester Bird succeeded his father as ALP leader.

SEE ALSO Carib; Caribbean Community and Common Market; West Indies, Federation of

Alexander the Great. He earned the title of Antiochus Soter, or Saviour, by his defeat of the Gauls in Galatia 276.

Antiochus II c. 286–c. 246 BC. King of Syria 261–246 BC, son of Antiochus I. He was known as Antiochus Theos, the Divine. During his reign the eastern provinces broke away from Graeco-Macedonian rule and set up native princes. He made peace with Egypt by marrying the daughter of Ptolemy Philadelphus, but was a tyrant among his own people.

Antiochus (III) the Great c. 241–187 BC. King of Syria from 223 BC, nephew of Antiochus II. He secured a loose control over Armenia and Parthia 209, overcame Bactria, received the homage of the Indian king of the Kabul valley, and returned by way of the Persian Gulf 204. He took possession of Palestine, entering Jerusalem 198. He crossed into NW Greece, but was decisively defeated by the Romans at Thermopylae 191 and at Magnesia 190. The Peace of Apamea 188 BC confined Seleucid rule to Asia.

Antiochus IV c. 215–164 BC. King of Syria from 175 BC, known as Antiochus Epiphanes, the Illustrious, son of Antiochus III. He occupied Jerusalem about 170, seizing much of the Temple treasure, and instituted worship of the Greek type in the Temple in an attempt to eradicate Judaism. This produced the revolt of the Hebrews under the Maccabees; Antiochus died before he could suppress the uprising.

Antiochus VII c. 159–129 BC. King of Syria from 138 BC. The last strong ruler of the Seleucid dynasty, he took Jerusalem 134, reducing the Maccabees to subjection. He was defeated and killed in battle against the ◊Parthians.

Antiochus XIII lived 1st century BC. King of Syria 69–65 BC, the last of the Seleucid dynasty. During his reign Syria was made a Roman province by Pompey the Great.

anti-oxidant any substance that prevents deterioration of fats, oils, paints, plastics, and rubbers by oxidation. When used as food ◊additives, anti-oxidants prevent fats and oils from becoming rancid when exposed to air, and thus extend their shelf life.

Vegetable oils contain natural anti-oxidants, such as vitamin E, which prevent spoilage, but anti-oxidants are nevertheless added to most oils. They are not always listed on food labels because if a food manufacturer buys an oil to make a food product, and the oil has anti-oxidant already added, it does not have to be listed on the label of the product.

antiparticle in nuclear physics, a particle corresponding in mass and properties to a given ◊elementary particle but with the opposite electrical charge, magnetic properties, or coupling to other fundamental forces. For example, an electron carries a negative charge whereas its antiparticle, the positron, carries a positive one. When a particle and its antiparticle collide, they destroy each other, in the process called 'annihilation', their total energy being converted to lighter particles and/or photons. A substance consisting entirely of antiparticles is known as ◊antimatter.

antiphony music exploiting directional and canonic opposition of widely spaced choirs or groups of instruments to create perspectives in sound. It was developed in 17th-century Venice by Giovanni Gabrieli and in Germany by his pupil Heinrich Schütz and Roland de Lassus; an example is the double choir motet *Alma Redemptoris Mater* 1604. The practice was revived in the 20th century by Bartók, Stockhausen, and Berio.

antipodes (Greek 'opposite feet') places at opposite points on the globe. In the UK, Australia and New Zealand are called the Antipodes.

antipope rival claimant to the elected pope for the leadership of the Roman Catholic Church, for instance in the Great Schism 1378–1417 when there were rival popes in Rome and Avignon.

antirrhinum any of several plants, genus *Antirrhinum*, in the figwort family Scrophulariaceae, including the ◊snapdragon, *A. majus*. ◊Foxglove and ◊toadflax are relatives. Antirrhinums are native to the Mediterranean region and W North America.

anti-Semitism prejudice or discrimination against, and persecution of, the Jews as an ethnic group. Historically this has been practised for almost 2,000 years by European Christians. Anti-Semitism was a tenet of Nazi Germany, and in the ◊Holocaust 1933–45 about 6 million Jews died in concentration camps and in local extermination ◊pogroms.

The destruction of Jerusalem AD 70 led many Jews to settle in Europe and throughout the Roman Empire. In the 4th century Christianity was adopted as the official religion of the Empire, which reinforced existing prejudice (dating back to pre-Christian times and referred to in the works of Seneca and Tacitus) against Jews who refused to convert. Legislation in the Middle Ages forbade Jews to own land or be members of a craft guild; to earn a living they had to become moneylenders and traders (and were then resented when they prospered). Britain expelled many Jews 1290, but they were formally readmitted 1655 by Cromwell.

Late 18th- and early 19th-century liberal thought improved the position of Jews in European society. In the Austro-Hungarian Empire, for example, they were allowed to own land, and after the French Revolution the 'rights of man' were extended to French Jews 1790. The rise of 19th-century nationalism and unscientific theories of race instigated new resentments, and the term 'anti-Semitism' was coined 1860. Literally it means prejudice against Semitic people (see ◊Semite), but in practice it has been directed only against Jews. Anti-Semitism became strong in Austria, France (epitomized by the ◊Dreyfus affair 1894–1906), and Germany, and from 1881 pogroms in Poland and Russia caused refugees to flee to the USA, to the UK, and to other European countries as well as Palestine (see ◊Zionism).

In the 20th century, fascism and the Nazi Party's application of racial theories led to organized persecution and the genocide of over six million Jews in the ◊Holocaust. Other forms of anti-Semitism were also common, such as the routine exclusion of Jews from academic posts in US universities prior to 1945. After World War II, the creation of Israel 1948 provoked Palestinian anti-Zionism, backed by the Arab world. Anti-Semitism is still fostered by extreme right-wing groups, such as the National Front in the UK and France, and the neo-Nazis in, particularly, the USA and Germany. It is a form of ◊racism.

antiseptic any substance that kills or inhibits the growth of microorganisms. The use of antiseptics was pioneered by Joseph ◊Lister. He used carbolic acid (◊phenol), which is a weak antiseptic; antiseptics such as TCP are derived from this. ▷ *See feature on pp. 1024–1025.*

antispasmodic any drug that reduces motility, the spontaneous action of the intestine wall. Anticholinergics are a type of antispasmodic that act indirectly by way of the autonomic nervous system, which controls involuntary movement. Other drugs act directly on the smooth muscle to relieve spasm (contraction).

antitrust laws in economics, regulations preventing or restraining trusts, monopolies, or any business practice considered to be unfair or uncompetitive. In the US, antitrust laws prevent mergers and acquisitions that might create a monopoly situation or ones in which restrictive practices might be stimulated.

antler 'horn' of a deer, often branched, and made of bone rather than horn. Antlers, unlike true horns, are shed and regrown each year. Reindeer of both sexes grow them, but in all other types of deer, only the males have antlers.

ant lion larva of one of the insects of the family Myrmeleontidae, order Neuroptera, which traps ants by waiting at the bottom of a pit dug in loose, sandy soil. Ant lions are mainly tropical, but also occur in parts of Europe, where there are more than 40 species, and in the USA, where they are called doodlebugs.

Antonello da Messina c. 1430–1479. Italian painter. He was a pioneer in his country of the technique of oil painting developed by Flemish artists; he probably acquired his knowledge of it in Naples. Flemish influence is reflected in his brushwork, his use of light, and sometimes in his imagery, although his sense of structure is entirely Italian. Surviving works *St Jerome in His Study* about 1460 (National Gallery, London).

anti-Semitism Jews being burnt alive in medieval Cologne after confessing under torture to profanity, from *Liber chronicum mundi* 1493. These unfortunates were condemned on the accusation of a woman who testified that they had forced her to carry stolen holy artefacts for use in profane rituals. Such pretexts were common in medieval Europe, especially after the Inquisition gave anti-Semitism the legitimacy of papal backing. *Image Select (UK) Ltd*

Antonescu Ion 1882–1946. Romanian general and politician. He headed a pro-German government during World War II which enforced the Nazis' anti-Semitic policies and was executed for war crimes 1946.

Antonine Wall Roman line of fortification built AD 142 in the reign of Antoninus Pius. It was the Roman Empire's northwest frontier, between the Clyde and Forth rivers, Scotland. It was defended until about 200.

Antoninus Pius (Titus Aurelius Fulvus) AD 86–161. Roman emperor. He was adopted 138 as Hadrian's heir, and succeeded him later that year. He enjoyed a prosperous reign, during which the ◊Antonine Wall was built. His daughter Faustina the Younger married his successor ◊Marcus Aurelius.

Antonioni Michelangelo 1912– . Italian film director. He is known for his subtle presentations of neuroses and personal relationships among the leisured classes. His elliptical approach to narrative is best seen in *L'Avventura* 1960. His other films include *Blow-Up* 1966, *Zabriskie Point* 1970, *The Passenger* 1975.

Antrim county of Northern Ireland
area 2,830 sq km/1,092 sq mi
towns and cities Belfast (county town), Larne (port)
features Giant's Causeway of natural hexagonal basalt columns on the N coast, which, according to legend, was built to enable the giants to cross between Ireland and Scotland; peat bogs; Antrim borders Lough Neagh, and is separated from Scotland by the North Channel, 30 km/20 mi wide
industries potatoes, oats, linen, synthetic textiles, flax, shipbuilding. Manufacture of man-made fibres has largely replaced traditional linen production.

ant lion There are about 1,000 species of ant lion; all larvae, and many adults, are carnivorous, feeding on insects and spiders. Eggs are laid singly in sand or dry soil. Larvae of the genus *Myrmeleon* live in funnel-shaped sandy pits, with their strong, toothed jaws ready to trap any insect that stumbles in.

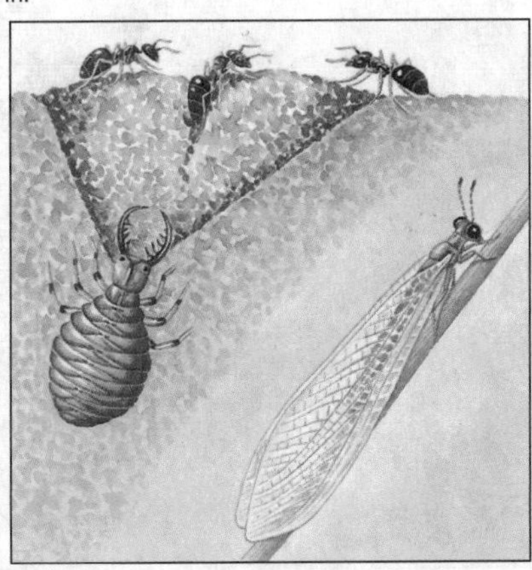

'Antoninus Pius' reign is marked by the rare advantage of furnishing very few materials for history; which is, indeed, little more than the register of the crimes, follies, and misfortunes of mankind.'

On **Antoninus Pius**
Edward Gibbon
Decline and Fall of the Roman Empire
1776–88

Antwerp The harbour and city centre of Antwerp, a port and trading centre since the late 15th century. The city rose to prominence after the silting-up of the river at Bruges, to the west. The riverside wharves were built in the early 1800s by Napoleon, who cleared the town's slums for the purpose. *Corbis*

‘Every little yielding to anxiety is a step away from the natural heart of man.’

on **ANXIETY**
Japanese proverb

ANZAC Australian troops charge the Turks during the abortive Dardanelles campaign in 1915. This was an early test for the ANZAC corps – the combined forces of Australia and New Zealand. *Corbis*

Antwerp (Flemish ***Antwerpen***, French ***Anvers***) port in Belgium on the river Scheldt, capital of the province of Antwerp; population (1995) 459,000. One of the world's busiest ports, it has shipbuilding, oil-refining, petrochemical, textile, and diamond-cutting industries. The home of the artist Rubens is preserved, and many of his works are in the Gothic cathedral. The province of Antwerp has an area of 2,900 sq km/1,119 sq mi; population (1995) 1,628,700.

Antwerp rose to prosperity in the 15th century and from 1500 to 1560 it was the richest port in N Europe. Later Antwerp was beset by religious troubles and the Netherlands' revolt against Spain. In 1648 the Treaty of Westphalia gave both shores of the Scheldt estuary to the United Provinces, which closed it to Antwerp trade. The Treaty of Paris 1814 opened the estuary to all nations on payment of a small toll to the Dutch, abandoned 1863. During World War I Antwerp was occupied by Germany Oct 1914–Nov 1918; during World War II, May 1940–Sept 1944.

Anubis in Egyptian mythology, the jackal-headed god of the dead, son of Osiris. Anubis presided over the funeral cult, including the weighing of the heart and embalming, and led the dead to judgement.

anus or ***anal canal*** the opening at the end of the alimentary canal that allows undigested food and other waste materials to pass out of the body, in the form of faeces. In humans, the term is also used to describe the last 4 cm/1.5 in of the alimentary canal. The anus is found in all types of multicellular animal except the coelenterates (sponges) and the platyhelminths (flatworms), which have a mouth only. It is normally kept closed by rings of muscle called sphincters.

anxiety unpleasant, distressing emotion usually to be distinguished from fear. Fear is aroused by the perception of actual or threatened danger; anxiety arises when the danger is imagined or cannot be identified or clearly perceived. It is a normal response in stressful situations, but is frequently experienced in many mental disorders.

Anxiety is experienced as a feeling of suspense, helplessness, or alternating hope and despair together with excessive alertness and characteristic bodily changes such as tightness in the throat, disturbances in breathing and heartbeat, sweating, and diarrhoea.

In psychiatry, an anxiety state is a type of neurosis in which the anxiety either seems to arise for no reason or else is out of proportion to what may have caused it. ‘Phobic anxiety’ refers to the irrational fear that characterizes ◊phobia.

Anyang city in Henan province, E China; population (1990) 420,000. It was the capital of the Shang dynasty (13th–12th centuries BC). Rich archaeological remains have been uncovered since the 1930s.

ANZAC (acronym for ***Australian and New Zealand Army Corps***) general term for all troops of both countries serving in World War I, particularly one who fought at ◊Gallipoli, and to some extent in World War II. It began as a code name based on the initials of the Corps in Jan 1915.

Anzio seaport and resort on the W coast of Italy, 53 km/33 mi SE of Rome; population (1984) 25,000. It is the site of the Roman town of Antium, birthplace of the emperor Nero.

Anzio, Battle of in World War II, the beachhead invasion of Italy 22 Jan–23 May 1944 by Allied troops; failure to use information gained by deciphering German codes (see ◊Ultra) led to Allied troops being stranded temporarily after German attacks.

aorta the body's main ◊artery, arising from the left ventricle of the heart in birds and mammals. Carrying freshly oxygenated blood, it arches over the top of the heart and descends through the trunk, finally splitting in the lower abdomen to form the two iliac arteries. Loss of elasticity in the aorta provides evidence of ◊atherosclerosis, which may lead to heart disease.

In fish a ventral aorta carries deoxygenated blood from the heart to the ◊gills, and the dorsal aorta carries oxygenated blood from the gills to other parts of the body.

Aouita Said 1960– . Moroccan runner. Outstanding at middle and long distances, he won the 1984 Olympic and 1987 World Championship 5,000-metres title, and has set many world records.

In 1985 he held world records at both 1,500 and 5,000 metres, the first person for 30 years to hold both. He has since broken the 2 miles, 3,000 metres, and 2,000 metres world records.

Aoun Michel 1935– . Lebanese soldier and Maronite Christian politician, president 1988–90. As commander of the Lebanese army, he was made president without Muslim support, his appointment precipitating a civil war between Christians and Muslims. His unwillingness to accept a 1989 Arab League-sponsored peace agreement increased his isolation until the following year when he surrendered to military pressure. He left the country 1991 and was pardoned by the new government in the same year.

Apache group of ◊Native American peoples who lived as hunters in SW North America. They are related to the Navajo, and now number about 10,000, living in reservations in Arizona, SW Oklahoma, and New Mexico. They were known as fierce raiders and horse warriors in the 18th and 19th centuries. Apache also refers to any of several southern Athabaskan languages and dialects spoken by these people.

apartheid (Afrikaans ‘apartness’) racial-segregation policy of the government of South Africa 1948–94. Nonwhites – classified as Bantu (black), coloured (mixed), or Indian – did not share full rights of citizenship with the white minority (for example, black people could not vote in parliamentary elections), and many public facilities and institutions were until 1990 restricted to the use of one race only. The establishment of ◊Black National States was another manifestation of apartheid.

Internally, organizations opposed to apartheid – for example, the African National Congress (ANC) and the United Democratic Front (UDF) – were banned, and some leading campaigners for its abolition were, like Steve Biko, killed, or, like Archbishop Tutu, harassed. Anger at the policy sparked off many uprisings, from ◊Sharpeville 1960 and ◊Soweto 1976 to the Crossroads squatter camps 1986.

Abroad, anti-apartheid movements sprang up in many countries. In 1961 South Africa was forced to withdraw from the British Commonwealth because of apartheid; during the 1960s and 1970s there were calls for international ◊sanctions, especially boycotts of sporting and cultural links; and in the 1980s advocates of sanctions extended them into trade and finance.

The South African government's reaction to internal and international pressure was twofold: it abolished some of the more hated apartheid laws (the ban on interracial marriages was lifted 1985 and the pass laws, which restricted the movement of nonwhites, were repealed 1986); and it sought to replace the term ‘apartheid’ with ‘plural democracy’. In 1989 President de Klerk permitted anti-apartheid demonstrations. In 1990 Nelson ◊Mandela, a leading figure in the ANC, was finally

Apache An Apache Indian boy with painted face and legs. Fiercely independent, the semi-nomadic Apaches fought long and hard against the attempts by the US government to confine them within reservations. The capture of their leader Geronimo 1886 marked the end of their resistance. *Library of Congress*

released. In 1991 the remaining major discriminating laws embodied in apartheid were repealed. Finally, multiracial elections were held for both the state presidency and the new nonracial assembly April 1994. The Truth and Reconciliation Commission published their retrospective report on apartheid in October 1998.

apastron the point at which an object travelling in an elliptical orbit around a star is at its furthest from the star. The term is usually applied to the position of the minor component of a ◊binary star in relation to the primary. Its opposite is periastron.

apatite common calcium phosphate mineral, $Ca_5(PO_4)_3(F,OH,Cl)$. Apatite has a hexagonal structure and occurs widely in igneous rocks, such as pegmatite, and in contact metamorphic rocks, such as marbles. It is used in the manufacture of fertilizer and as a source of phosphorus. Carbonate hydroxyapatite, $Ca_5(PO_4CO_3)_3(OH)_2$, is the chief constituent of tooth enamel and the chief inorganic constituent of bone marrow. Apatite ranks 5 on the ◊Mohs' scale of hardness.

apatosaurus large plant-eating dinosaur, formerly called ***brontosaurus***, which flourished about 145 million years ago. Up to 21 m/69 ft long and 30 tonnes in weight, it stood on four elephantlike legs and had a long tail, long neck, and small head. It probably snipped off low-growing vegetation with peglike front teeth, and swallowed it whole to be ground by pebbles in the stomach.

ape ◊primate of the family Pongidae, closely related to humans, including gibbon, orang-utan, chimpanzee, and gorilla.

Apennines chain of mountains stretching the length of the Italian peninsula. A continuation of the Maritime Alps, from Genoa it swings across the peninsula to Ancona on the east coast, and then back to the west coast and into the 'toe' of Italy. The system is continued over the Strait of Messina along the N Sicilian coast, then across the Mediterranean Sea in a series of islands to the Atlas Mountains of N Africa. The highest peak is Gran Sasso d'Italia at 2,914 m/9,560 ft.

aperture in photography, an opening in the camera that allows light to pass through the lens to strike the film. Controlled by the iris diaphragm, it can be set mechanically or electronically at various diameters.

The aperture ratio or relative aperture, more commonly known as the ◊f-number, is a number defined as the focal length of the lens divided by the effective diameter of the aperture. A smaller f-number implies a larger diameter lens and therefore more light available for high-speed photography, or for work in poorly illuminated areas. However, small f-numbers involve small depths of focus.

aphelion the point at which an object, travelling in an elliptical orbit around the Sun, is at its furthest from the Sun. The Earth is at its aphelion on 5 July.

aphid any of the family of small insects, Aphididae, in the order Hemiptera, suborder Homoptera, that live by sucking sap from plants. There are many species, often adapted to particular plants; some are agricultural pests. In some stages of their life cycle, wingless females rapidly produce large numbers of live young by ◊parthenogenesis, leading to enormous infestations, and numbers can approach 2 billion per hectare/1 billion per acre. They can also cause damage by transmitting viral diseases.

aphid A colony of aphids *Cavariella konoi*, commonly known as greenfly, feeding on green stems of the almond willow. Ants often attend such colonies to feed on the honeydew that aphids excrete. *Premaphotos Wildlife*

aphorism (Greek *apo* 'from', *horos* 'limit') short, sharp, witty saying, usually making a general observation. 'Experience is the name everyone gives to their mistakes' is one of many aphorisms by Irish playwright Oscar Wilde. The term derives from the *Aphorisms* ascribed to Greek writer Hippocrates. An aphorism which has become universally accepted is a proverb.

aphrodisiac (from Aphrodite, the Greek goddess of love) any substance that arouses or increases sexual desire. Sexual activity can be stimulated in humans and animals by drugs affecting the pituitary gland. Preparations commonly sold for the purpose can be dangerous (cantharidin) or useless (rhinoceros horn), and alcohol and cannabis, popularly thought to be effective because they lessen inhibition, may have the opposite effect.

Aphrodite in Greek mythology, the goddess of love (Roman Venus, Phoenician Astarte, Babylonian Ishtar). She is said to be either a daughter of Zeus (in Homer) or sprung from the foam of the sea (in Hesiod). She was the unfaithful wife of Hephaestus, the god of fire, and the mother of Eros.

Apia capital and port of ◊Samoa, on the north coast of Upolu Island, in the W Pacific; population (1986) 32,200. It was the final home of the writer Robert Louis Stevenson 1888–94, who is buried on Mount Vaea.

Apis ancient Egyptian deity, a manifestation of the creator god Ptah of Memphis, in the form of a black bull with a small white triangle on the forehead, often bearing a sun-disc between its horns. The cult of Apis originated in the early 3rd millennium BC. Apis was a fertility god, associated also with Osiris and Sokaris, gods of the dead and the underworld.

Apocrypha (Greek *apokryptein* 'to hide away') appendix to the Old Testament of the Bible, 14 books not included in the final Hebrew canon but recognized by Roman Catholics. There are also disputed New Testament texts known as Apocrypha.

Apollinaire Guillaume. Pen name of Guillaume Apollinaire de Kostrowitsky 1880–1918. French poet of aristocratic Polish descent. He was a leader of the avant-garde in Parisian literary and artistic circles. His novel *Le Poète assassiné/The Poet Assassinated* 1916, followed by the experimental poems *Alcools/Alcohols* 1913 and *Calligrammes/Word Pictures* 1918, show him as a representative of the Cubist and Futurist movements. He coined the term 'Surrealism' to describe his play *Les Mamelles de Tirésias/The Breasts of Tiresias* 1917.

Apollo in Greek and Roman mythology, the god of sun, music, poetry, prophecy, agriculture, and pastoral life, and leader of the Muses. He was the twin child (with ◊Artemis) of Zeus and Leto. Ancient statues show Apollo as the embodiment of the Greek ideal of male beauty. His chief cult centres were his supposed birthplace on the island of Delos, in the Cyclades, and Delphi.

Apollo asteroid member of a group of ◊asteroids whose orbits cross that of the Earth. They are named after the first of their kind, Apollo, discovered 1932 and then lost until 1973. Apollo asteroids are so small and faint that they are difficult to see except when close to Earth (Apollo is about 2 km/1.2 mi across).

Apollonius of Perga c. 262–c. 190 BC. Greek mathematician, called 'the Great Geometer'. In his work *Konica/The Conics* he showed that a plane intersecting a cone will generate an ellipse, a parabola, or a hyperbola, depending on the angle of intersection. In astronomy, he used a system of circles called epicycles and deferents to explain the motion of the planets; this system, as refined by Ptolemy, was used until the Renaissance.

Apollonius of Rhodes or ***Apollonius Rhodius*** lived 3rd century BC. Greek poet. He was the author of the epic *Argonautica*, which tells the story of Jason and the Argonauts and their quest for the Golden Fleece. A pupil of ◊Callimachus, he was for a time head of the library at Alexandria.

Apollo project One of the *Apollo 12* astronauts walking on the Moon, Nov 1969. The Apollo project sent 17 spacecraft to the Moon 1969–72. Six of these missions involved landing astronauts on the Moon and featured space walks during which they collected rocks and soil, took photographs, and set up scientific equipment. *NASA*

Apollo project US space project to land a person on the Moon, achieved 20 July 1969, when Neil ◊Armstrong was the first to set foot there. He was accompanied on the Moon's surface by 'Buzz' ◊Aldrin; Michael Collins remained in the orbiting command module.

The programme was announced 1961 by President Kennedy. After three other preparatory flights, *Apollo 11* made the first lunar landing. Five more crewed landings followed, the last 1972.

apologetics (Greek *apologia* 'a defendant's personal reply to an accuser') philosophical writings that attempt to refute attacks on the Christian faith. Apologists include St Justin, Origen, St Augustine, Thomas Aquinas, Blaise Pascal, and Joseph Butler. The questions raised by scientific, historical, and archaeological discoveries have widened the field of apologetics.

Apo, Mount active volcano and highest peak in the Philippines, rising to 2,954 m/9,692 ft on the island of Mindanao.

aposematic coloration in biology, the technical name for warning coloration markings that make a dangerous, poisonous, or foul-tasting animal particularly conspicuous and recognizable to a

aposematic coloration A *Phymateus morbillosus* foaming grasshopper from South Africa. A member of the subfamily Pyrgomorphinae, it exhibits aposematic (warning) colours when provoked to indicate to predators that it will exude copious quantities of foul-tasting foam if attacked. *Premaphotos Wildlife*

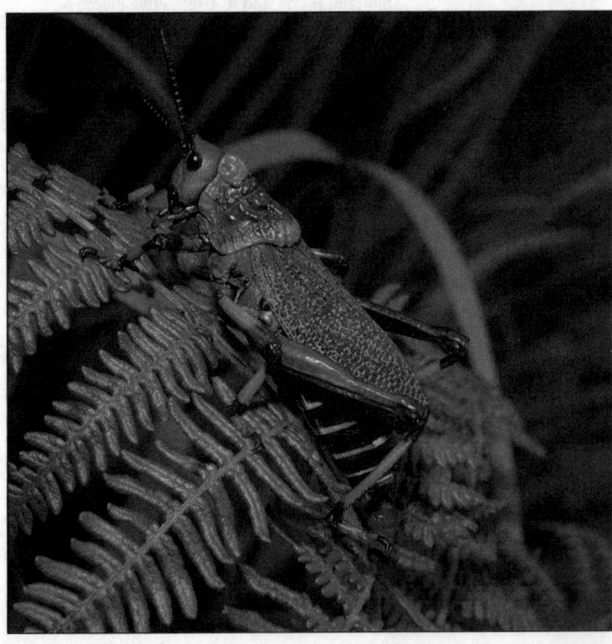

predator. Examples include the yellow and black stripes of bees and wasps, and the bright red or yellow colours of many poisonous frogs. See also ◊mimicry.

apostle (Greek 'messenger') in the New Testament, any of the chosen 12 ◊disciples sent out by Jesus after his resurrection to preach the Gospel.

The qualifications for an apostle, in the full sense, are indicated in Acts 1.21–22: personal eyewitness to the life and resurrection of Jesus. An apostle also had to receive a commission either direct from Jesus or mediately through the other apostles, as in the case of Matthias who took the place of Judas. In the earliest days of Christianity the term was extended to include some who had never known Jesus in the flesh, notably St Paul.

Apostles' creed one of the three ancient ◊creeds of the Christian church. It probably dates from the 2nd century.

apostolic succession doctrine in the Christian church that certain spiritual powers were received by the first apostles directly from Jesus, and have been handed down in the ceremony of 'laying on of hands' from generation to generation of bishops.

apothecaries' weights obsolete units of mass, formerly used in pharmacy: 20 grains equal one scruple; three scruples equal one dram; eight drams equal an apothecary's ounce (oz apoth.), and 12 such ounces equal an apothecary's pound (lb apoth.). There are 7,000 grains in one pound avoirdupois (0.454 kg).

apothecary traditional term for person who prepares and dispenses medicines; a pharmacist. The word 'apothecary' retains its original meaning in the USA and other countries, but in England it came to mean a licensed medical practitioner. An Act of Parliament 1815 gave the Society of Apothecaries of London the power to examine all apothecaries in England and Wales and grant them licences to practise medicine; to this day a medical student may qualify by passing the Society's licensing examination, which is recognized by the General Medical Council for purposes of registration.

Appalachians mountain system of E North America, stretching about 2,400 km/1,500 mi from Alabama to Quebec, composed of ancient eroded rocks and rounded peaks. The chain includes the Allegheny, Catskill, and Blue Ridge mountains, the last-named having the highest peak, Mount Mitchell, 2,045 m/6,712 ft. The eastern edge has a fall line to the coastal plain where Philadelphia, Baltimore, and Washington stand.

apparent depth depth that a transparent material such as water or glass appears to have when viewed from above. This is less than its real depth because of the ◊refraction that takes place when light passes into a less dense medium. The ratio of the real depth to the apparent depth of a transparent material is equal to its ◊refractive index.

appeal in law, an application for rehearing of all or part of an issue that has already been dealt with by a lower court or tribunal. The outcome can be a new decision on all or part of the points raised, or the previous decision may be upheld. Appeals against conviction in the ◊magistrates' court are heard in the ◊crown court. Appeal against conviction or sentence in the crown court is heard by the criminal division of the Court of Appeal. The highest and final court of appeal is the House of Lords. Further appeal may lie to either the ◊European Court of Justice or the ◊European Court of Human Rights.

appeasement historically, the conciliatory policy adopted by the British government, in particular under Neville Chamberlain, towards the Nazi and Fascist dictators in Europe in the 1930s in an effort to maintain peace. It was strongly opposed by Winston Churchill, but the ◊Munich Agreement 1938 was almost universally hailed as its justification. Appeasement ended when Germany occupied Bohemia–Moravia March 1939.

appendicitis inflammation of the appendix, a small, blind extension of the bowel in the lower right abdomen. In an acute attack, the pus-filled appendix may burst, causing a potentially lethal spread of infection. Treatment is by removal (appendicectomy).

appendix a short, blind-ended tube attached to the ◊caecum. It has no known function in humans, but in herbivores it may be large, containing millions of bacteria that secrete enzymes to digest grass (as no vertebrate can secrete enzymes that will digest cellulose, the main constituent of plant cell walls).

apple fruit of several species of the genus *Malus* in the family Rosaceae. There are several hundred varieties of cultivated apples, grown all over the world, which may be divided into eating, cooking, and cider apples. All are derived from the wild crab apple.

Apple US computer company, manufacturer of the ◊Macintosh range of computers.

applet mini-software application. Examples of applets include the cut-down word processor WordPad in Windows 95 or the single-purpose applications that in 1996 were beginning to appear on the World Wide Web, written in ◊Java. These include small animations such as a moving ticker tape of stock prices.

Appleton layer band containing ionized gases in the Earth's upper atmosphere, above the ◊E layer (formerly the Kennelly–Heaviside layer). It can act as a reflector of radio signals, although its ionic composition varies with the sunspot cycle. It is named after the English physicist Edward Appleton (1892–1965).

application in computing, a program or job designed for the benefit of the end user, such as a payroll system or a word processor. The term is used to distinguish such programs from those that control the computer (systems programs) or assist the programmer, such as a compiler.

appliqué embroidery used to create pictures or patterns by 'applying' pieces of material onto a background fabric. The pieces are cut into the appropriate shapes and sewn on, providing decoration for wall hangings, furnishing textiles, and clothes.

Appomattox village in Virginia, USA, scene of the surrender 9 April 1865 of the Confederate army under Robert E Lee to the Union army under Ulysses S Grant, which ended the American Civil War.

apricot fruit of *Prunus armeniaca*, a tree of the rose family Rosaceae, closely related to the almond, peach, plum, and cherry. It has yellow-fleshed fruit. Although native to the Far East, it has long been cultivated in Armenia, from where it was introduced into Europe and the USA.

April Fools' Day the first day of April, when it is customary in W Europe and the USA to expose people to ridicule by a practical joke, causing them to believe some falsehood or to go on a fruitless errand.

The victim is known in England as an April Fool; in Scotland as a gowk (cuckoo or fool); and in France as a *poisson d'avril* (April fish). There is a similar Indian custom on the last day of the Holi festival in late March.

Apuleius Lucius lived 2nd century AD. Roman lawyer, philosopher, and writer. He was the author of ◊*The Golden Ass*, or *Metamorphoses*, a prose fantasy. It is the only complete Latin novel to survive.

Apulia English form of ◊Puglia, a region of Italy.

Aqaba, Gulf of gulf extending for 160 km/100 mi between the Negev and the Red Sea; its coastline is uninhabited except at its head, where the frontiers of Israel, Egypt, Jordan, and Saudi Arabia converge.

The two ports of Eilat (Israeli 'Elath') and Aqaba, Jordan's only port, are situated here. A border crossing near the two ports was opened 1994, for non-Israelis and non-Jordanians, to encourage the E Mediterannean tourist industry.

aquaculture the cultivation of fish and shellfish for human consumption; see ◊fish farming.

aqualung or ***scuba*** underwater breathing apparatus worn by divers, developed in the early 1940s by French diver Jacques Cousteau. Compressed-air cylinders strapped to the diver's back are regulated by a valve system and by a mouth tube to provide air to the diver at the same pressure as that of the surrounding water (which increases with the depth).

aquamarine blue variety of the mineral ◊beryl. A semiprecious gemstone, it is used in jewellery.

aqua regia (Latin 'royal water') mixture of three parts concentrated hydrochloric acid and one part concentrated nitric acid, which dissolves all metals except silver.

aquarium tank or similar container used for the study and display of living aquatic plants and animals. The same name is used for institutions that exhibit aquatic life. These have been common since Roman times, but the first modern public aquarium was opened in Regent's Park, London, 1853. A recent development is the oceanarium or seaquarium, a large display of marine life forms.

Aquarius zodiacal constellation a little south of the celestial equator near Pegasus. Aquarius is represented as a man pouring water from a jar. The Sun passes through Aquarius from late Feb to early March. In astrology, the dates for Aquarius, the 11th sign of the zodiac, are between about 20 Jan and 18 Feb (see ◊precession).

aquatic living in water. All life on Earth originated in the early oceans, because the aquatic environment has several advantages for organisms. Dehydration is almost impossible, temperatures usually remain stable, and the density of water provides physical support. Life forms that cannot exist out of water, amphibians that take to the water on occasions, animals that are also perfectly at home on land, and insects that spend a stage of their life cycle in water can all be described as aquatic. Aquatic plants are known as ◊hydrophytes.

aquatint printmaking technique. When combined with ◊etching it produces areas of subtle tone as well as more precisely etched lines. Aquatint became common in the late 18th century.

An etching plate is covered with a fine layer of resin and then immersed in acid, which bites through the resin, causing tiny pits on the surface of the plate. When printed, a fine, grainy tone is apparent. Lighter tones are created by using acid-resistant varnishes, darker tones by longer exposure to the acid. English painter Thomas Gainsborough experimented with aquatint, but the first artist to become proficient in the technique was J B Le Prince (1733–1781).

aqueduct any artificial channel or conduit for water, often an elevated structure of stone, wood, or iron built for conducting water across a valley. The Greeks built a tunnel 1,280 m/4,200 ft long near Athens some 2,500 years ago. Many Roman aqueducts are still standing, for example the one carried by the Pont du Gard at Nîmes in S France (48 m/160 ft high).

aqueous humour watery fluid found in the chamber between the cornea and lens of the vertebrate eye. Similar to blood serum in composition, it is constantly renewed.

aquifer any rock formation containing water. The rock of an aquifer must be porous and permeable (full of interconnected holes) so that it can absorb water. Aquifers are an important source of fresh water, for example, for drinking and irrigation, in many arid areas of the world and are exploited by the use of ◊artesian wells. An aquifer may be underlain, overlain, or sandwiched between impermeable layers, called aquicludes, which impede water movement. Sandstones and porous limestones make the best aquifers.

Aquila constellation on the celestial equator (see ◊celestial sphere). Its brightest star is first-magnitude ◊Altair, flanked by the stars Beta and Gamma Aquilae. It is represented by an eagle.

Aquinas, St Thomas 1225–1274. Italian philosopher and theologian, the greatest figure of the school of ◊scholasticism. He was a Dominican monk, known as the 'Angelic Doctor'. In 1879 his works were recognized as the basis of Catholic theology. His *Summa contra Gentiles/Against the Errors of the Infidels* 1259–64 argues that reason and faith are compatible. He assimilated the philosophy of Aristotle into Christian doctrine. He was canonized 1323.

His unfinished *Summa Theologica*, begun 1265, deals with the nature of God, morality, and the work of Jesus. The philosophy of Aquinas is known as Thomism.

aqueduct A Roman aqueduct, the Pont du Gard, in southern France. It was built in 19 BC and carried water almost 48 km/30 mi from the rivers Eure and Ayran to the Roman town at Nîmes. An even earlier aqueduct was constructed around 2000 BC to supply the palace of Knossos, Crete, with fresh water from a spring 5 km/7 mi away. *Corbis*

Aquino (Maria) Corazon (born Cojuangco) 1933– . President of the Philippines 1986–92. Widow of the opposition leader Benigno Aquino (who was assassinated on his return from exile 1983), she was instrumental in the nonviolent 'people's power' campaign which overthrew President Ferdinand Marcos 1986. As president, she sought to rule in a conciliatory manner, but encountered opposition from left (communist guerrillas) and right (army coup attempts), and her land reforms were seen as inadequate.

Aquitaine region of SW France; capital Bordeaux; area 41,300 sq km/15,942 sq mi; population (1990) 2,795,800. It comprises the *départements* of Dordogne, Gironde, Landes, Lot-et-Garonne, and Pyrénées-Atlantiques. Red wines (Margaux, St Julien) are produced in the Médoc district, bordering the Gironde.
history Aquitaine was conquered by the Goths in the early 5th century, by the Franks in the 6th century, and was an independent duchy under the Merovingians. The name was corrupted to Guienne by the 10th century and, until 1258, the two terms were used interchangeably. Aquitaine was an English possession 1152–1453.

Arab any of the Semitic (see ◊Semite) people native to the Arabian peninsula, but now settled throughout North Africa and the nations of the Middle East.

Arab Common Market organization providing for the abolition of customs duties on agricultural products, and reductions on other items, between the member states: Egypt, Iraq, Jordan, Libya, Mauritania, Syria, and Yemen. It was founded 1964.

Arab Emirates see ◊United Arab Emirates.

arabesque in the visual arts, a linear decoration based on plant forms. It is a feature of ancient Greek and Roman art and is particularly common in Islamic art (hence the term).

arabesque in ballet, a pose in which the dancer stands on one leg, straight or bent, with the other leg raised behind, fully extended. The arms are held in a harmonious position to give the longest possible line from fingertips to toes. It is one of the fundamental positions in ballet.

Arabia peninsula between the Persian Gulf and the Red Sea, in SW Asia; area 2,600,000 sq km/1,000,000 sq mi. The peninsula contains the world's richest gas reserves and half the world's oil reserves. It comprises the states of Bahrain, Kuwait, Oman, Qatar, Saudi Arabia, the United Arab Emirates, and Yemen.
physical A sandy coastal plain of varying width borders the Red Sea, behind which a mountain chain rises to about 2,000–2,500 m/6,600–8,200 ft. Behind this range is the plateau of the Nejd, averaging 1,000 m/3,300 ft. The interior comprises a vast desert area: part of the Al-Hamad (Syrian) Desert in the far north, Nafud in N Saudi Arabia, and Rub'al Khali in S Saudi Arabia.
history Conquered in part by the Romans, the Christian Abyssinians, and the Persians, the Arabian civilization was revived by Muhammad during the 7th century, but in the new empire created by militant Islam, Arabia became a subordinate state, and its cities were eclipsed by Damascus, Baghdad, and Cairo. The British established protectorates in the Persian Gulf from the end of the 18th century; Muscat 1798, the Trucial States and Bahrain 1820, Aden 1839, Kuwait 1899, and Saudia Arabia 1915. The British finally left the peninsula 1971.

Nominally part of the Ottoman Empire from the 16th century to 1919, until the 20th century the interior was unknown to Europeans. Nationalism began actively to emerge at the period of World War I (1914–18), and the oil discoveries from 1953 gave the peninsula significant economic power.

Arabian Sea northwestern branch of the ◊Indian Ocean.

Arabic language major Semitic language of the Hamito-Semitic family of W Asia and N Africa, originating among the Arabs of the Arabian peninsula. It is spoken today by about 120 million people in the Middle East and N Africa. Arabic script is written from right to left.

The language has spread by way of conquest and trade as far west as Morocco and as far east as Malaysia, Indonesia, and the Philippines, and is also spoken in Arab communities scattered across the western hemisphere. Forms of colloquial Arabic vary in the countries where it is the dominant language: Algeria, Bahrain, Egypt, Iraq, Jordan, Kuwait, Lebanon, Libya, Mali, Mauritania, Morocco, Oman, Saudi Arabia, Sudan, Syria, Tunisia, the United Arab Emirates, and Yemen. Arabic is also a language of religious and cultural significance in Bangladesh, India, Iran, Israel, Pakistan, and Somalia. Arabic-speaking communities are growing in the USA and the West Indies.

Arab League see ◊League of Arab States.

Arab–Israeli Wars series of wars between Israel and various Arab states in the Middle East since the founding of the state of Israel 1948.

First Arab–Israeli War 15 May 1948–13 Jan/24 March 1949. As soon as the independent state of Israel had been proclaimed by the Jews, it was invaded by combined Arab forces. The Israelis defeated them and went on to annex territory until they controlled 75% of what had been Palestine under British mandate.

Second Arab–Israeli War 29 Oct–4 Nov 1956. After Egypt had taken control of the Suez Canal and blockaded the Straits of Tiran, Israel, with British and French support, invaded and captured Sinai and the Gaza Strip, from which it withdrew under heavy US and United Nations pressure.

Third Arab–Israeli War 5–10 June 1967, the ***Six-Day War***. It resulted in the Israeli capture of the Golan Heights from Syria; the eastern half of Jerusalem and the West Bank from Jordan; and, in the south, the Gaza Strip and Sinai peninsula as far as the Suez Canal.

Fourth Arab–Israeli War 6–24 Oct 1973, the 'October War' or ***Yom Kippur War***, so called because the Israeli forces were taken by surprise on the Day of ◊Atonement, a Jewish holy day. It started with the recrossing of the Suez Canal by Egyptian forces who made initial gains, though there was some later loss of ground by the Syrians in the north. The war had 19,000 casualties.

Fifth Arab–Israeli War From 1978 the presence of Palestinian guerrillas in Lebanon led to Arab raids on Israel and Israeli retaliatory incursions, but on 6 June 1982 Israel launched a full-scale invasion. By 14 June Beirut was encircled, and ◊Palestine Liberation Organization (PLO) and Syrian forces were evacuated (mainly to Syria) 21–31 Aug, but in Feb 1985 there was a unilateral Israeli withdrawal from the country without any gain or losses incurred. Israel maintains a 'security zone' in S Lebanon and supports the South Lebanese Army militia as a buffer against Palestinian guerrilla incursions.
background Arab opposition to an Israeli state began after the Balfour Declaration 1917, which supported the idea of a Jewish national homeland. In the 1920s there were anti-Zionist riots in Palestine, then governed by the UK under a League of Nations mandate. In 1936 an Arab revolt led to a British royal commission that recommended partition (approved by the United Nations 1947, but rejected by the Arabs).

Tension in the Middle East remained high, and the conflict was sharpened and given East–West overtones by Soviet adoption of the Arab cause and US support for Israel. Several wars only increased the confusion over who had a claim to what territory. Particularly in view of the area's strategic sensitivity as an oil producer, pressure grew for a settlement, and in 1978 the ◊Camp David Agreements brought peace between Egypt and Israel, but this was denounced by other Arab countries. Israel withdrew from Sinai 1979–82, but no final agreement on Jerusalem and the establishment of a Palestinian state on the West Bank was reached. Israeli occupation of the Gaza Strip and the West Bank continued into the 1990s in the face of a determined uprising (◊Intifada), but hope of a settlement emerged Sept 1993 with the signing of an Israeli–PLO peace accord.

arable farming cultivation of crops, as opposed to the keeping of animals. Crops may be ◊cereals, vegetables, or plants for producing oils or cloth. Arable farming generally requires less attention than livestock farming. In a mixed farming system, crops may therefore be found farther from the farm centre than animals.

In the UK a major arable farming area is East Anglia, where it is favoured by flat land, fertile well-drained soils and a warm and sunny climate. Many arable farms practise ◊crop rotation to maintain soil fertility.

Arab Monetary Fund (AMF) money reserve established 1976 by 20 Arab states plus the Palestine Liberation Organization (PLO) to provide a mechanism for promoting greater stability in exchange rates and to coordinate Arab economic and monetary policies. It operates mainly by regulating petrodollars within the Arab community to make member countries less dependent on the West for the handling of their surplus money. The fund's headquarters are in Abu Dhabi in the United Arab Emirates.

Arachne (Greek 'spider') in Greek mythology, a Lydian woman who was so skilful a weaver that she challenged the goddess ◊Athena to a contest. Athena tore Arachne's beautiful tapestries to pieces and Arachne hanged herself. She was transformed into a spider, and her weaving became a cobweb.

arachnid or ***arachnoid*** type of arthropod of the class Arachnida, including spiders, scorpions, ticks,

The function of genius is to furnish cretins with ideas twenty years later.

Louis Aragon
'Le Porte-Plume'
Traité du Style

and mites. They differ from insects in possessing only two main body regions, the cephalothorax and the abdomen, and in having eight legs.

Arafat Yassir, born Mohammed Abed Ar'ouf Arafat 1929– . Palestinian nationalist politician, cofounder of al-◊Fatah 1957, and president of the ◊Palestine Liberation Organization (PLO) from 1969. In 1993 he participated in the historic peace accord of mutual recognition with Israel, under which the Gaza Strip and Jericho were transferred to PLO control. He returned to the former occupied territories 1994 as head of an embryonic Palestinian state, and in 1995 reached agreement on further Israeli troop withdrawals from areas in the West Bank. The assassination of Yitzhak Rabin Nov 1995 by an Israeli extremist and the ensuing campaign of violence in Israel threatened the peace process; however, Arafat continued his efforts for a lasting peace throughout 1996, and in December of that year the West Bank town of Hebron was handed over to Palestinian control.

He was elected president, with almost 90% of the popular vote, of the self-governing Palestinian National Council 1996.

Arafat received the 1994 Nobel Prize for Peace jointly with the then Israeli prime minister Yitzhak Rabin and foreign minister Shimon Peres.

Arafura Sea area of the Pacific Ocean between N Australia and Indonesia, bounded by the Timor Sea in the W and the Coral Sea in the E. It is 1,290 km/800 mi long and 560 km/350 mi wide.

Law is a bottomless pit.

John Arbuthnot
The History of John Bull

Aragon Spanish ***Aragón*** autonomous region of NE Spain including the provinces of Huesca, Teruel, and Zaragoza; area 47,700 sq km/18,412 sq mi; population (1991) 1,188,800. Its capital is Zaragoza, and products include almonds, figs, grapes, and olives. Aragon was an independent kingdom 1035–1479.
history A Roman province until taken in the 5th century by the Visigoths, who lost it to the Moors in the 8th century; it became a kingdom 1035. It was united with Castile 1479 under Ferdinand and Isabella.

Aragon Louis 1897–1982. French poet and novelist. Beginning as a Dadaist, he became one of the leaders of Surrealism, published volumes of verse, and in 1930 joined the Communist Party. Taken prisoner in World War II, he escaped to join the Resistance; his experiences are reflected in the poetry of *Le Crève-coeur/Heart-break* 1941 and *Les Yeux d'Elsa/Elsa's Eyes* 1942.

His novels include the Surrealist *Le Paysan de Paris/The Nightwalker* 1926 and the later social-realistic *Les Communistes/The Communists* 1949–51, *La Semaine sainte/Holy Week* 1958, *La Mise à mort/The Kill* 1965, and *Blanche, ou l'oubli/Blanche or Forgetting* 1967.

Arakan state of Myanmar (formerly Burma) on the Bay of Bengal coast, some 645 km/400 mi long and strewn with islands; population (1983) 2,046,000. The chief town is Sittwe. It is bounded along its eastern side by the Arakan Yoma, a mountain range rising to 3,000 m/10,000 ft. The ancient kingdom of Arakan was conquered by Burma 1785.

Aral Sea inland sea divided between Kazakhstan and Uzbekistan, the world's fourth largest lake; former area 62,000 sq km/24,000 sq mi, but decreasing. Water from its tributaries, the Amu

Arafat Palestinian leader Yassir Arafat, who was a controversial figure from the late 1960s when he advocated terrorism to destroy Israel. He was often treated as a national leader, and in 1994, with Israeli prime minister Yiztak Shamir, he made a peace agreement that led to both men winning the Nobel Peace prize. When the Palestinians won a degree of self-government in 1995, he became the head of the government and won the 1996 elections. *Corbis*

Aral Sea

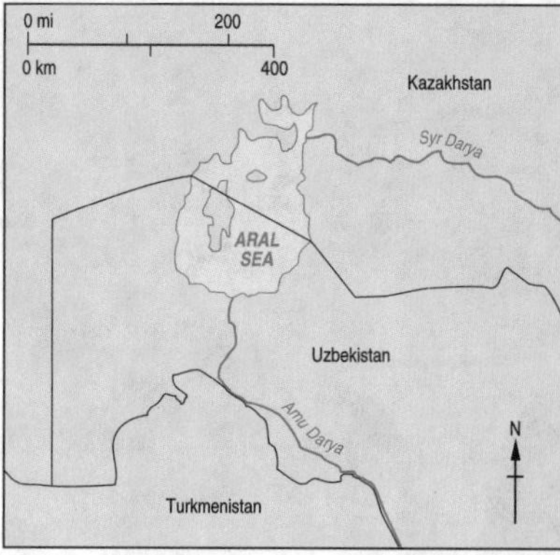

Darya and Syr Darya, has been diverted for irrigation and city use, and the sea is disappearing, with long-term consequences for the climate. This shrinkage has led to hotter, drier summers and longer, colder winters. Of the 24 fish species in the lake all 20 native species have disappeared, and winds drop 43 million tonnes of salt a year on the surrounding cropland.

Aramaic language Semitic language of the Hamito-Semitic family of W Asia, the everyday language of Palestine 2,000 years ago, during the Roman occupation and the time of Jesus. Aramaic dialects survive among small Christian communities in various parts of W Asia, although Arabic spread widely with the acceptance of Islam.

Aran Islands three rocky islands (Inishmore, Inishmaan, Inisheer) in the mouth of Galway Bay, Republic of Ireland; population approximately 4,600. The capital is Kilronan.

Ararat, Mount double-peaked mountain in Turkey near the Iranian border; Great Ararat, at 5,137 m/16,854 ft, is the highest mountain in Turkey.

Araucanian Indian (Araucanian ***Mapuche***) member of a group of South American peoples native to central Chile and the Argentine pampas. They were agriculturalists and hunters, as well as renowned warriors, defeating the Incas and resisting the Spanish for 200 years. Originally, they lived in small villages; some 200,000 still survive in reserves. Scholars are divided over whether the Araucanian language belongs to the Penutian or the Andean-Equatorial family.

araucaria coniferous tree of the genus *Araucaria*, allied to the firs, with flat, scalelike needles. Once widespread, it is now native only to the southern hemisphere. Some grow to gigantic size. Araucarias include the monkey-puzzle tree *A. araucana*, the Australian bunya bunya pine *A. bidwillii*, and the Norfolk Island pine *A. heterophylla*.

Arawak indigenous American people of the Caribbean and NE Amazon Basin. Arawaks lived mainly by shifting cultivation in tropical forests. They were driven out of many West Indian islands by another Native American people, the Caribs, shortly before the arrival of the Spanish in the 16th century. Subsequently, their numbers on ◊Hispaniola declined from some 4 million in 1492 to a few thousand after their exploitation by the Spanish in their search for gold; the remaining few were eradicated by disease (smallpox was introduced 1518). Arawakan languages belong to the Andean-Equatorial group.

Arbenz Guzmán Jácobo 1913–1971. Guatemalan social democratic politician and president from 1951 until his overthrow 1954 by rebels operating with the help of the US Central Intelligence Agency.

Arbīl (or Irbīl) Kurdish capital city, in a province of the same name in N Iraq; population (1985) 334,000. Occupied since Assyrian times, it was the site of a battle 331 BC at which Alexander the Great defeated the Persians under Darius III. In 1974 Arbīl became the capital of a Kurdish autonomous region set up by the Iraqi government. It was captured by the Kurdish Democratic Party 1996 with the help of Saddam Hussein.

arbitration submission of a dispute to a third, unbiased party for settlement. It may be personal litigation, a trade-union issue, or an international dispute.

Following the Hague Conventions of 1899 and 1907, the first permanent international court was established in The Hague in the Netherlands, and the League of Nations set up an additional Permanent Court of International Justice 1921 to deal with frontier disputes and the like. The latter was replaced 1945 with the International Court of Justice under the United Nations. The UN Commission on International Trade Law adopted a model law 1985 on international commercial arbitration. Another arbiter is the European Court of Justice, which rules on disputes arising out of the Rome treaties regulating the European Union. The Council of Europe adopted the European Convention for the Peaceful Settlement of Disputes 1977.

In the UK, the ◊Advisory, Conciliation and Arbitration Service (ACAS) offers an arbitration service. The Consumer Arbitration Agreement Act 1988 governs proceedings concerning differences between trader and consumer, and arbitration with respect to terms in a trader's standard contract.

arboretum collection of trees. An arboretum may contain a wide variety of species or just closely related species or varieties – for example, different types of pine tree.

arbor vitae any of several coniferous trees or shrubs of the genus *Thuja* of the cypress family, having flattened branchlets covered in overlapping aromatic green scales. In North America, the northern white cedar *Thuja occidentalis* and the western red cedar *T. plicata* are representatives. The Chinese or Oriental species *T. orientalis*, reaching 60 ft/18 m in height, is grown widely as an ornamental.

Arbroath fishing town in Tayside, Scotland; population (1991) 23,500. In 1320 the Scottish Parliament asserted Scotland's independence here in a letter to the pope. There are engineering, sailmaking, and knitwear industries. The town is famous for its smoked haddock.

Arbus Diane 1923–1971. US photographer. Although she practised as a fashion photographer for 20 years, Arbus is best known for her later work which examined the fringes of American society: the misfits, the eccentrics, and the bizarre. *A Box of Ten Photographs*, a limited edition of her work, was published 1970.

Arbuthnot John 1667–1735. Scottish writer and physician. He attended Prince George and then Queen Anne 1705–14. He was a friend of Alexander Pope, Thomas Gray, and Jonathan Swift and was the chief author of the satiric *Memoirs of Martinus Scriblerus* 1741. He created the English national character of John Bull, a prosperous farmer, in his 'History of John Bull' 1712, pamphlets advocating peace with France.

arbutus any evergreen shrub of the genus *Arbutus* of the heath family Ericaceae. The strawberry tree *A. unedo* is grown for its ornamental, strawberrylike fruit.

arc in geometry, a section of a curved line or circle. A circle has three types of arc, measured in degrees: a ***semicircle***, which is 180°, exactly half of the circle; ***minor arcs***, which are less than the semicircle and therefore always less than 180° (acute or obtuse); and ***major arcs***, which are greater than the semicircle, and therefore always greater than 180° but less than 360° (reflex).

Arcadia (Greek ***Arkadhia***) central plateau and department of S Greece; area 4,419 sq km/1,706 sq mi; population (1991) 103,800. Tripolis is the capital town. The English poet Philip ◊Sidney idealized the life of shepherds here in antiquity.

Arc de Triomphe arch at the head of the Champs Elysées in the Place de l'Etoile, Paris, France, begun by Napoleon 1806 and completed 1836. It was intended to commemorate Napoleon's victories of 1805–06 and commissioned from Jean Chalgrin (1739–1811). Beneath it rests France's 'Unknown Soldier'.

Arc de Triomphe, Prix de l' French horse race run over 2,400 m/1.5 mi at Longchamp, near Paris. It is the leading 'open age' race in Europe, and one of the richest. It was first run 1920.

arch in geomorphology, any natural bridgelike land feature formed by erosion. A sea arch is formed from the wave erosion of a headland where the backs of two caves have met and broken through. The roof of the arch eventually collapses to leave part of the headland isolated in the sea as a ◊stack. A natural bridge is formed by wind or water erosion and spans a valley or ravine.

arch in masonry, a curved structure that supports the weight of material over an open space, as in a bridge or doorway. The first arches consisted of several wedge-shaped stones supported by their mutual pressure. The term is also applied to any curved structure that is an arch in form only, such as the Arc de Triomphe, Paris, 1806–36.

The Romans are credited with engineering the earliest round keystone arches, used for aqueducts. Other forms of arch include the pointed arch, the corbelled arch of the Maya Indians, the medieval lancet and ogee arches, and the Islamic horseshoe arch.

Archaea group of microorganisms that are without a nucleus and have a single chromosome. All are strict anaerobes, that is, they are killed by oxygen. This is thought to be a primitive condition and to indicate that Archaea are related to the earliest life forms, which appeared about 4 billion years ago, when there was little oxygen in the Earth's atmosphere. They are found in undersea vents, hot springs, the Dead Sea, and salt pans, and have even adapted to refuse tips. Archaea was originally classified as bacterial, but in 1996 when the genome of *Methanococcus jannaschii*, an archaeaon that lives in undersea vents at temperatures around 100°C/212°, was sequenced US geneticists found that 56% of its genes were unlike those of any other organism, making Archaea unique.

Archaean or ***Archaeozoic*** the earliest eon of geological time; the first part of the Precambrian, from the formation of Earth up to about 2,500 million years ago. It was a time when no life existed, and with every new discovery of ancient life its upper boundary is being pushed further back.

archaeology (Greek *archaia* 'ancient things', *logos* 'study') study of prehistory and history, based on the examination of physical remains. Principal activities include preliminary field (or site) surveys, ◊excavation (where necessary), and the classification, ◊dating, and interpretation of finds. Since 1958 ◊radiocarbon dating has been used to establish the age of archaeological strata and associated materials.

Archer Jeffrey Archer, best-selling English author and playwright who turned to writing political thrillers as a way of overcoming bankruptcy. Several of his works have been dramatized for television. Though only serving briefly as an MP, he pursued a high-profile career with the Conservative Party. *HarperCollins*

history Interest in the physical remains of the past began in the Renaissance among dealers in and collectors of ancient art. It was further stimulated by discoveries made in Africa, the Americas, and Asia by Europeans during the period of imperialist colonization in the 16th–19th centuries, such as the antiquities discovered during Napoleon's Egyptian campaign in the 1790s. Towards the end of the 19th century archaeology became an academic study, making increasing use of scientific techniques and systematic methodologies. Since World War II new developments within the discipline include medieval, post-medieval, and industrial archaeology; underwater archaeology (the excavation of wrecks and other underwater sites, made possible by the development of the aqualung); and rescue archaeology (excavation of sites at risk from deep ploughing, quarrying, and road laying). *See timeline on following page*.

archaeopteryx (Greek *archaios* 'ancient', *pterux* 'wing') extinct primitive bird, known from fossilized remains, about 160 million years old, found in limestone deposits in Bavaria, Germany. It is popularly known as 'the first bird', although some earlier bird ancestors are now known. It was about the size of a crow and had feathers and wings, with three clawlike digits at the end of each wing, but in many respects its skeleton is reptilian (teeth and a long, bony tail) and very like some small meat-eating dinosaurs of the time.

Archangel (Russian ***Arkhangel'sk***) port in N Russian Federation; population (1994) 407,000. It is the chief timber-exporting port of Russia. Formerly blocked by ice for half the year, it has been kept open constantly since 1979 by icebreakers. Archangel was made an open port by Boris ◊Godunov and was of prime importance until Peter the Great built St Petersburg.

archbishop in the Christian church, a bishop of superior rank who has authority over other bishops in his jurisdiction and often over an ecclesiastical province. The office exists in the Roman Catholic, Eastern Orthodox, and Anglican churches.

In the Church of England there are two archbishops – the archbishop of Canterbury ('Primate of All England') and the archbishop of York ('Primate of England').

archdeacon originally an ordained dignitary of the Christian church charged with the supervision of the deacons attached to a cathedral. Today in the Roman Catholic Church the office is purely titular; in the Church of England an archdeacon, directly subordinate to the bishop, still has many business duties, such as the periodic inspection of churches. The office is not found in other Protestant churches.

archegonium (Greek *arche* 'origin', *gonos* 'offspring') female sex organ found in bryophytes (mosses and liverworts), pteridophytes (ferns, club mosses, and horsetails), and some gymnosperms. It is a multicellular, flask-shaped structure consisting of two parts: the swollen base or venter containing the egg cell, and the long, narrow neck. When the egg cell is mature, the cells of the neck dissolve, allowing the passage of the male gametes, or ◊antherozoids.

Archer Frederick 1857–1886. English jockey. He rode 2,748 winners in 8,084 races 1870–86, including 21 classic winners.

He won the Derby five times, Oaks four times, St Leger six times, the Two Thousand Guineas four times, and the One Thousand Guineas twice. He rode 246 winners in the 1885 season, a record that stood until 1933 (see Gordon ◊Richards). Archer shot himself in a fit of depression.

Archer Jeffrey Howard, Baron Archer of Weston-super-Mare 1940– . English writer and politician. A Conservative member of Parliament 1969–74, he lost a fortune in a disastrous investment, but recouped it as a best-selling novelist and dramatist. His books, which often concern the rise of insignificant characters to high political office or great business success, include *Not a Penny More, Not a Penny Less* 1975 and *First Among Equals* 1984.

archerfish surface-living fish of the family Toxotidae, such as the genus *Toxotes*, native to SE Asia and Australia. The archerfish grows to about 25 cm/10 in and is able to shoot down insects up to 1.5 m/5 ft above the water by spitting a jet of water from its mouth.

archery use of the bow and arrow, originally in hunting and warfare, now as a competitive sport.

Arc de Triomphe The Arc de Triomphe, Paris, erected to commemorate Napoleon's victories. It was designed by Jean Chalgrin, and built 1806–36. The arch incorporates relief sculptures by J P Cartot and François Rude. Beneath it lies France's 'Tomb of the Unknown Soldier' and the eternal flame. *Corbis*

The world governing body is the Fédération Internationale de Tir à l'Arc (FITA) founded 1931. In competitions, results are based on double FITA rounds; that is, 72 arrows at each of four targets at 90, 70, 50, and 30 metres (70, 60, 50, and 30 for women). The best possible score is 2,880. Archery was reintroduced to the Olympic Games 1972.

archetype typical or perfect specimen of its kind. In the psychology of Carl ◊Jung, it refers to one of the basic roles or situations, received from the ◊collective unconscious, in which people tend to cast themselves – such as the Hero, the Terrible Mother (stepmother, witch); death and rebirth. Archetypes are recurring motifs in myth, art, and literature.

Archimedes c. 287–212 BC. Greek mathematician who made major discoveries in geometry, hydrostatics, and mechanics. He formulated a law of fluid displacement, Archimedes' principle, and is credited with the invention of the Archimedes screw, a cylindrical device for raising water.

Archimedes' principle in physics, law stating that an object totally or partly submerged in a fluid displaces a volume of fluid that weighs the same as the apparent loss in weight of the object (which, in turn, equals the upwards force, or upthrust, experienced by that object). It was discovered by the Greek mathematician Archimedes.

If the weight of the object is less than the upthrust exerted by the fluid, it will float partly or completely above the surface; if its weight is equal to the upthrust, the object will come to equilibrium below the surface; if its weight is greater than the upthrust, it will sink.

Archimedes screw one of the earliest kinds of pump, thought to have been invented by Archimedes. It consists of an enormous spiral screw revolving inside a close-fitting cylinder. It is used, for example, to raise water for irrigation.

The lowest portion of the screw just dips into the

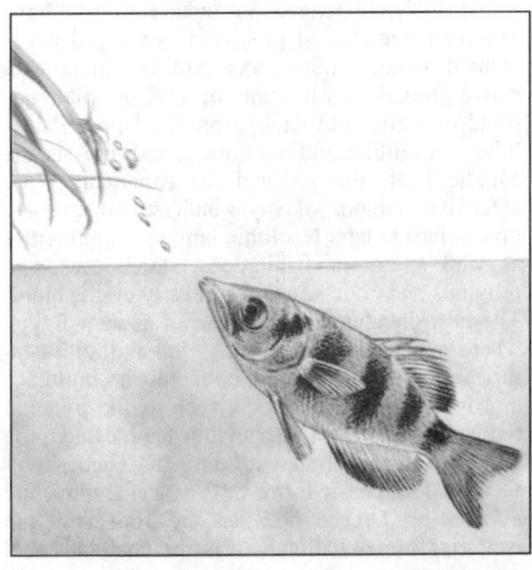

archerfish The archerfish inhabits the brackish waters of river estuaries around the coasts of S Asia and N Australia. It can squirt a jet of water from its mouth to knock down insects as much as 1.5 m/5 ft above the surface of the water.

Archimedes screw The Archimedes screw, a spiral screw turned inside a cylinder, was once commonly used to lift water from canals. The screw is still used to lift water in the Nile delta in Egypt, and is often used to shift grain in mills and powders in factories.

water, and as the cylinder is turned a small quantity of water is scooped up. The inclination of the cylinder is such that at the next revolution the water is raised above the next thread, whilst the lowest thread scoops up another quantity. The successive revolutions, therefore, raise the water thread by thread until it emerges at the top of the cylinder.

archipelago group of islands, or an area of sea containing a group of islands, usually volcanic in origin.

Volcanic islands are formed either when a hot spot within the Earth's mantle produces a chain of volcanoes on the surface, such as the Hawaiian Archipelago, or at a destructive plate margin (see ◊plate tectonics) where the subduction of one plate beneath another produces an arc-shaped island group, such as the Aleutian Archipelago. Novaya Zemlya in the Arctic Ocean, the northern extension of the Ural Mountains, resulted from continental flooding.

Archipenko Alexander 1887–1964. Ukrainian-born abstract sculptor. He pioneered Cubist sculpture, producing geometrically stylized forms, as in *Woman Combing Her Hair* 1915 (Tate Gallery, London). He also experimented with polychrome reliefs (which he called 'sculpto-paintings'), with clear plastics and other materials, and sculptures incorporating lights. These experiments with form, colours, and materials had a profound influence on the development of 20th-century sculpture.

architecture art of designing structures. The term covers the design of the visual appearance of structures; their internal arrangements of space; selection of external and internal building materials; design or selection of natural and artificial lighting systems, as well as mechanical, electrical, and plumbing systems; and design or selection of decorations and furnishings. Architectural style may emerge from evolution of techniques and styles particular to a culture in a given time period with or without identifiable individuals as architects, or may be attributed to specific individuals or groups of architects working together on a project.

early architecture Little remains of the earliest forms of architecture, but archaeologists have examined remains of prehistoric sites and documented villages of wooden-post buildings with above-ground construction of organic materials (mud or wattle and daub) from the Upper Paleolithic, Mesolithic, and Neolithic periods in Asia, the Middle East, Europe, and the Americas. More extensive remains of stone-built structures have given clues to later Neolithic farming communities as well as to the habitations, storehouses, and religious and civic structures of early civilizations. The best documented are those of ancient Egypt, where exhaustive work in the 19th and 20th centuries revealed much about both ordinary buildings and monumental structures, such as the pyramid tombs near modern Cairo and the temple and tomb complexes concentrated at Luxor and Thebes.

Classical The basic forms of Classical architecture evolved in Greece between the 16th and 2nd centuries BC. A hallmark was the post-and-lintel

'No person who is not a great sculptor or painter can be an architect. If he is not a sculptor or painter, he can only be a builder.'

On ARCHITECTURE
John Ruskin *Lectures on Architecture and Painting* 1854

ARCHAEOLOGY: TIMELINE

14th–16th Cs	Interest revived in Classical Greek and Roman art and architecture, including ruins and buried art and artefacts.
1748	The Roman city of Pompeii was discovered buried under volcanic ash from Vesuvius.
1784	Thomas Jefferson excavated an American Indian burial mound on the Rivanna River in Virginia and wrote a report on his finds.
1790	John Frere identified Old Stone Age (Palaeolithic) tools together with large extinct animals.
1822	Jean François Champollion deciphered Egyptian hieroglyphics.
1836	Christian Thomsen devised the Stone, Bronze, and Iron Age classification (Three Age System).
1840s	Austen Layard excavated the Assyrian capital of Nineveh.
1868	The Great Zimbabwe ruins in E Africa were first seen by Europeans.
1871	Heinrich Schliemann began excavations at Troy.
1879	Ice Age paintings were first discovered at Altamira, Spain.
1880s	Augustus Pitt-Rivers developed the concept of stratigraphy (identification of successive layers of soil within a site with successive archaeological stages, the most recent being at the top).
1891	Flinders Petrie began excavating Akhetaton in Egypt.
1899–1935	Arthur Evans excavated Minoan Knossos in Crete.
1900–44	Max Uhle began the systematic study of the civilizations of Peru.
1911	The Inca city of Machu Picchu was discovered by Hiram Bingham in the Andes.
1911–12	The Piltdown skull was 'discovered'; it was proved to be a fake 1949.
1914–18	Osbert Crawford developed the technique of aerial survey of sites.
1917–27	John Eric Thompson (1898–1975) investigated the great Maya sites in Yucatán, Mexico.
1922	Tutankhamen's tomb in Egypt was opened by Howard Carter.
1926	A kill site in Folsom, New Mexico, USA, was found with chipped stone spearpoints in association with ancient bison.
1935	Dendrochronology (dating events in the distant past by counting tree rings) was developed by A E Douglass.
1939	An Anglo-Saxon ship-burial treasure was found at Sutton Hoo, England.
1947	The first of the Dead Sea Scrolls was discovered.
1948	The Proconsul prehistoric ape was discovered by Mary Leakey in Kenya.
1950s–1970s	Several early hominid fossils were found by Louis and Mary Leakey in Olduvai Gorge.
1953	Michael Ventris deciphered Minoan Linear B.
1960s	Radiocarbon and thermoluminescence measurement techniques were developed as aids for dating remains.
1961	The Swedish warship *Wasa* was raised at Stockholm.
1963	Walter Emery pioneered rescue archaeology at Abu Simbel before the site was flooded by the Aswan Dam.
1969	Human remains found at Lake Mungo, Australia, were dated at 26,000 years; earliest evidence of ritual cremation.
1974	The tomb of Shi Huangdi, with its terracotta army, was discovered in China; the partial skeleton of a 3.18-million year old hominid nicknamed 'Lucy' was found in Ethiopia, and hominid footprints, 3.8 million years old, at Laetoli in Tanzania.
1978	The tomb of Philip II of Macedon (Alexander the Great's father) was discovered in Greece.
1979	The Aztec capital Tenochtitlán was excavated beneath a zone of Mexico City.
1982	English king Henry VIII's warship *Mary Rose* of 1545 was raised and studied with new techniques in underwater archaeology.
1985	The tomb of Maya, Tutankhamen's treasurer, was discovered at Sakkara, Egypt.
1988	The Turin Shroud was established as being of medieval origin by radiocarbon dating.
1989	The remains of the Globe and Rose Theatres, where many of Shakespeare's plays were originally performed, were discovered in London.
1991	Clothed body of man from 5,300 years ago, with bow, arrows, copper axe, and other implements, was found preserved in ice in the Italian Alps.
1992	The world's oldest surviving wooden structure, a well 15 m/49 ft deep made of huge oak timbers at Kückhoven, Germany, was dated by tree-rings to 5090 BC. The world's oldest sea-going vessel, dating from about 1400 BC, was discovered at Dover, southern England.
1993	Drawings done in charcoal on the walls of the Cosquer Cave (near Marseille, France, discovered 1991) were dated by radiocarbon to be 27,110 and around 19,000 years old; a fragment of cloth found on a tool handle unearthed in Çayönü, SE Turkey 1988 was carbon-dated at 9,000 years old, making it the oldest cloth ever found.
1994	The earliest known ancestral human, *Ardipithecus ramidus*, from Ethiopia, was announced (4.4 million years old); and a major new Ice Age cave, the Grotte Chauvet, was found in SE France, decorated with hundreds of Palaeolithic cave drawings. Rivalling those of Lascaux and Altamira, they included depictions of a panther and an owl – hitherto unknown in Palaeolithic art. Scientific tests in 1995 revealed that certain of the paintings within the Chauvet complex were between 30,340 and 32,410 years old, making them the world's oldest known paintings.
1995	A vast underground tomb believed to be the burial site of 50 of the sons of Ramses II was discovered. It was the largest yet found in the Valley of the Kings. Researchers in Spain found human remains dating back more than 780,000 years, in a cave site at Gran Dolina at Atapuerca in northern central Spain. Previously it was thought humans reached Europe around 300,000 years later than this.

construction of temples and public structures, classified into the Doric, Ionic, and Corinthian ◊orders and defined by simple, scrolled, or acanthus-leaf capitals for support columns. The Romans copied and expanded on Greek Classical forms, notably introducing bricks and concrete and developing the vault, arch, and dome for public buildings and aqueducts.
Byzantine This form of architecture developed primarily in the Eastern Roman Empire from the 4th century, with its centre at Byzantium (later named Constantinople, now Istanbul). It is dominated by the arch and dome, with the Classical orders reduced in importance. Its most notable features are churches, some very large, based on the Greek cross plan (Hagia Sophia, Istanbul; St Mark's, Venice), with formalized painted and mosaic decoration.
Islamic This developed from the 8th century, when the Islamic religion spread from its centre in the Middle East west to Spain and east to China and parts of the Philippine Islands. Notable features are the development of the tower with dome and the pointed arch. Islamic architecture, chiefly through Spanish examples such as the Great Mosque at Córdoba and the Alhambra in Granada, profoundly influenced Christian church architecture, for example, the adoption of the pointed arch in ◊Gothic architecture.
Romanesque This style flourished in Western European Christianity from the 10th to the 12th centuries. It is marked by churches with massive walls for structural integrity, rounded arches, small windows, and resulting dark volumes of interior space. In England the style is generally referred to as ◊Norman architecture (an example is Durham Cathedral). Romanesque enjoyed a renewal of interest in Europe and the USA in the late 19th and early 20th centuries.
Gothic Gothic architecture emerged out of Romanesque. The development of the pointed arch and flying buttress made it possible to change from thick supporting walls to lighter curtain walls with extensive expansion of window areas (and stained-glass artwork) and resulting increases in interior light. Gothic architecture was developed mainly in France from the 12th to 16th centuries. The style is divided into Early Gothic (for example, Sens Cathedral), High Gothic (Chartres Cathedral), and Late or ◊Flamboyant Gothic. In England the corresponding divisions are Early English (Salisbury Cathedral), Decorated (Wells Cathedral), and ◊Perpendicular (Kings College Chapel, Cambridge). Gothic was also developed extensively in Germany and Italy.
Renaissance The 15th and 16th centuries in Europe saw the rebirth of Classical form and motifs in the Italian Neo-Classical movement. A major source of inspiration for the great Renaissance architects – Andrea ◊Palladio, Leon Battista ◊Alberti, Filippo ◊Brunelleschi, Donato ◊Bramante, and ◊Michelangelo Buonarotti – was the work of the 1st-century BC Roman engineer Marcus ◊Vitruvius Pollio. The Palladian style was later used extensively in England by Inigo Jones; Christopher ◊Wren also worked in the Classical idiom. Classicism, or Neo-Classicism as it is also known, has been popular in the USA from the 18th century.
Baroque European architecture of the 17th and 18th centuries elaborated on Classical models with exuberant and extravagant decoration. In large-scale public buildings, the style is best seen in the innovative works of Giovanni Lorenzo ◊Bernini and Francesco ◊Borromini in Italy and later in those of John Vanbrugh, Nicholas Hawksmoor, and Christopher Wren in England. There were numerous practitioners in France and the German-speaking countries, and notably in Vienna.
Rococo This architecture extends the Baroque style with an even greater extravagance of design motifs, using a new lightness of detail and naturalistic elements, such as shells, flowers, and trees.
Neo-Classical European architecture of the 18th and 19th centuries again focused on the more severe Classical idiom (inspired by archaeological finds), producing, for example, the large-scale rebuilding of London by Robert Adam and John Nash and later of Paris by Georges Haussman.
Neo-Gothic The late 19th century saw a Gothic revival in Europe and the USA, which was evident in churches and public buildings, such as the Houses of Parliament in London, designed by Charles Barry and A W Pugin.
Art Nouveau This architecture, arising at the end of the 19th century, countered Neo-Gothic with sinuous, flowing shapes for buildings, room plans, and interior decoration. The style is characterized by the work of Charles Rennie Mackintosh in Scotland (Glasgow Art School) and Antonio ◊Gaudí in Spain (Church of the Holy Family, Barcelona).
Modernist This style of architecture, referred to as the Modern Movement, began in the 1900s with the Vienna School and the German ◊Bauhaus and was also developed in the USA, Scandinavia, and France. With ◊Functionalism as its central precept, its hallmarks are the use of spare line and form, an emphasis on rationalism, and the elimination of ornament. It makes great use of technological advances in materials such as glass, steel, and concrete and of construction techniques that allow flexibility of design. Notable practitioners include Frank Lloyd Wright, Mies van der Rohe, and Charles Edouard Jeanneret, known as ◊Le Corbusier. Modern architecture has furthered the notion of the planning of extensive multibuilding projects and of whole towns or communities.
Post-Modernist This style, which emerged in the 1980s in the USA, the UK, and Japan, rejected the Functionalism of the Modern Movement in favour of an eclectic mixture of styles and motifs, often Classical. Its use of irony, parody, and illusion is in sharp distinction to the Modernist ideals of truth to materials and form following function.
High Tech This building style also developed in the 1980s. It took the ideals of the Modern Movement and expressed them through highly developed structures and technical innovations. Examples include Norman ◊Foster's Hong Kong and Shanghai Bank, Hong Kong, and Richard ◊Rogers's Lloyds Building in the City of London.
Deconstructionism An architectural debate as much as a style, Deconstructionism fragments forms and space by taking the usual building elements of floors, walls, and ceilings and sliding them apart to create a sense of disorientation and movement.

archive collection of historically valuable records, ranging from papers and documents to photographs, films, videotapes, and sound recordings. In the UK, the Public Record Office (London and Kew) has documents of law and government departments from the Norman Conquest, including the ◊Domesday Book and ◊Magna Carta. Some government documents remain closed, normally for 30 years, but some for up to 100 years.

archon (Greek 'ruler') in ancient Greece, title of the chief magistrate in many cities. In Athens, there were originally three; their numbers were later increased to nine, with the extra six keeping a record of judgements.

Arcimboldo Giuseppe c. 1530–1593. Italian painter and designer. He is known for his fantastical portraits, human in form but composed of fruit, plant, and animal details. He also designed tapestries and was a successful portrait painter at the court of Rudolf II in Prague. The Surrealists helped to revive interest in his symbolic portraits, which were considered in bad taste at the time of their conception.

arc lamp or ***arc light*** electric light that uses the illumination of an electric arc maintained between two electrodes. The British scientist Humphry Davy developed an arc lamp 1808, and its main use in recent years has been in cinema projectors. The lamp consists of two carbon electrodes, between which a very high voltage is maintained. Electric current arcs (jumps) between the two, creating a brilliant light.

arc minute, arc second units for measuring small angles, used in geometry, surveying, map-making, and astronomy. An arc minute (symbol ′) is one-sixtieth of a degree, and an arc second (symbol ″) is one-sixtieth of an arc minute. Small distances in the sky, as between two close stars or the apparent width of a planet's disc, are expressed in minutes and seconds of arc.

Arctic, the that part of the northern hemisphere surrounding the North Pole; arbitrarily defined as the region lying N of the Arctic Circle (66° 32′N) or N of the tree line. There is no Arctic continent; the greater part of the region comprises the Arctic Ocean, which is the world's smallest ocean. Arctic climate, fauna, and flora extend over the islands and northern edges of continental land masses that surround the Arctic Ocean (Svalbard, Iceland, Greenland, Siberia, Scandinavia, Alaska, and Canada)
area 36,000,000 sq km/14,000,000 sq mi
physical pack-ice floating on the Arctic Ocean occupies almost the entire region between the North Pole and the coasts of North America and Eurasia, covering an area that ranges in diameter from 3,000 km/1,900 mi to 4,000 km/2,500 mi. The pack-ice reaches a maximum extent in Feb when its outer limit (influenced by the cold Labrador Current and the warm Gulf Stream) varies from 50°N along the coast of Labrador to 75°N in the Barents Sea N of Scandinavia. In spring the pack-ice begins to break up into ice floes which are carried by the south-flowing Greenland Current to the Atlantic Ocean. Arctic ice is at its minimum area in Aug. The greatest concentration of icebergs in Arctic regions is found in Baffin Bay. They are derived from the glaciers of W Greenland, then carried along Baffin Bay and down into the N Atlantic where they melt off Labrador and Newfoundland.

The Bering Straits are icebound for more than six months each year, but the Barents Sea between Scandinavia and Svalbard is free of ice and is navigable throughout the year. Arctic coastlines, which have emerged from the sea since the last Ice Age, are characterized by deposits of gravel and disintegrated rock. The area covered by the Arctic icecap shrank 2% 1978–87
climate permanent ice sheets and year-round snow cover are found in regions where average monthly temperatures remain below 0°C/32°F, but on land areas where one or more summer months have average temperatures between freezing point and 10°C/50°F, a stunted, treeless tundra vegetation is found. Mean annual temperatures range from −23°C/−9.4°F at the North Pole to −12°C/10.4°F on the coast of Alaska. In winter the Sun disappears below the horizon for a time, but the cold is less severe than in parts of inland Siberia or Antartica. During the short summer season there is a maximum of 24 hours of daylight at the summer solstice on the Arctic Circle and six months' constant light at the North Pole. Countries with Arctic coastlines established the International Arctic Sciences Committee 1987 to study ozone depletion and climatic change
flora and fauna the plants of the relatively infertile Arctic tundra (lichens, mosses, grasses, cushion plants, and low shrubs) spring to life during the short summer season and remain dormant for the remaining ten months of the year. There are no annual plants, only perennials. Animal species include reindeer, caribou, musk ox, arctic fox, hare, lemming, arctic wolf, polar bear, seal, and walrus. The birds are chiefly sea birds, such as petrels, eider ducks, cormorants, auks, gulls, puffins, and guillemots, and most are migratory. Other birds include terns, ptarmigams, snowy owls, and geese (Greenland). There are no reptiles. Bees, flies, and butterflies are found in small numbers; mosquitoes and blackflies are plentiful in summer. Freshwater fish include whitefish, trout, and Atlantic salmon; seawater fish include arctic char and polar and arctic cod
natural resources the Arctic is rich in coal (Svalbard, Russia), oil and natural gas (Alaska, Canadian Arctic, Russia), and mineral resources including gold, silver, copper, uranium, lead, zinc, nickel, and bauxite. Because of climatic conditions, the Arctic is not suited to navigation and the exploitation of these resources. Murmansk naval base on the Kola Peninsula is the largest in the world
population there are about 1 million aboriginal people including 26 minority peoples in Russia and Siberia, the Aleuts of Alaska, North American Indians, the Lapps of Scandinavia and Russia, the Yakuts, Samoyeds, Komi, Chukchi, Tungus, and Dolgany of Russia, and the Inuit of Siberian Russia, the Canadian Arctic, and Greenland.

'The great open spaces of the North are God's sanatorium.'

On the ARCTIC Jessica Bortwick, interview 7 May 1914

Arctic Circle imaginary line that encircles the North Pole at latitude 66° 32′ N. Within this line there is at least one day in the summer during which the Sun never sets, and at least one day in the winter during which the Sun never rises.

Arctic Ocean ocean surrounding the North Pole; area 14,000,000 sq km/5,400,000 sq mi. Because of the Siberian and North American rivers flowing into it, it has comparatively low salinity and freezes readily.

ARCTIC EXPLORATION: TIMELINE

60000–35000 BC	Ancestors of the Inuit and American Indians began migration from Siberia to North America by the 'lost' land bridge of Beringia.
320 BC	Pytheas, a Greek sailor contemporary with Alexander the Great, possibly reached Iceland.
9th–10th Cs AD	Vikings colonized Iceland and Greenland, which at that time had a much warmer climate.
***c.* 1000**	Norwegian sailor Leif Ericsson reached Baffin Island (NE of Canada) and Labrador.
1497	Genoese pilot Giovanni Caboto first sought the Northwest Passage as a trade route around North America for Henry VII of England.
1553	English navigator Richard Chancellor tried to find the Northeast Passage around Siberia and first established direct English trade with Russia.
1576	English sailor Martin Frobisher reached Frobisher Bay, but found only 'fools' gold' (iron pyrites) for Elizabeth I of England.
1594–97	Dutch navigator Willem Barents made three expeditions in search of the Northeast Passage.
1607	English navigator Henry Hudson failed to cross the Arctic Ocean, but his reports of whales started the northern whaling industry.
1670	Hudson's Bay Company started the fur trade in Canada.
1728	Danish navigator Vitus Bering passed the Bering Strait.
1829–33	Scottish explorer John Ross discovered the North Magnetic Pole.
1845	The mysterious disappearance of English explorer John Franklin's expedition to the Northwest Passage stimulated further exploration.
1878–79	Swedish navigator Nils Nordenskjöld was the first European to discover the Northeast Passage.
1893–96	Norwegian explorer Fridtjof Nansen's ship *Fram* drifted across the Arctic while locked in the ice, proving that no Arctic continent existed.
1903–06	Norwegian explorer Roald Amundsen sailed through the Northwest Passage.
1909	US explorers Robert Peary, Matt Henson, and four Inuit reached the North Pole on 2 April.
1926	US explorers Richard Byrd and Floyd Bennett flew to the Pole on 9 May.
1926	Italian aviator Umberto Nobile and Amundsen crossed the Pole (Spitzbergen–Alaska) in the airship *Norge* on 12 May.
1954	Scandinavian Airlines launched the first regular commercial flights over the short-cut polar route.
1958	The US submarine *Nautilus* crossed the Pole beneath the ice.
1960	From this date a Soviet nuclear-powered icebreaker kept open a 4,000 km/2,500 mi Asia–Europe passage along the north coast of Siberia for 150 days a year.
1969	Wally Herbert of the British Transarctic Expedition made the first surface crossing, by dog sled, of the Arctic Ocean (Alaska–Spitsbergen).
1977	The Soviet icebreaker *Arktika* made the first surface voyage to the Pole.
1982	English explorers Ranulph Fiennes and Charles Burton completed the first circumnavigation of the Earth via the Poles, 2 Sept 1979–29 Aug 1982.
1988	Canadian and Soviet skiers attempted the first overland crossing from the USSR to Canada via the Pole.

The ocean comprises:

Beaufort Sea off Canada/Alaska coast, named after British admiral Francis Beaufort (1774–1857); oil drilling allowed only in winter because the sea is the breeding and migration route of the bowhead whales, staple diet of the local Inuit people;

Greenland Sea between Greenland and Svalbard;

Norwegian Sea between Greenland and Norway.

From W to E along the north coast of Russia:

Barents Sea named after Willem ◊Barents, which has oil and gas reserves and was strategically significant as the meeting point of the NATO and Warsaw Pact forces. The ◊White Sea is its southernmost gulf;

Kara Sea renowned for bad weather and known as the 'great ice cellar';

Laptev Sea between Taimyr Peninsula and New Siberian Island;

East Siberian Sea and ***Chukchi Sea*** between Russia and the USA; the semi-nomadic Chukchi people of NE Siberia finally accepted Soviet rule in the 1930s.

The Arctic Ocean has the world's greatest concentration of nuclear submarines, but at the same time there is much scientific cooperation on exploration, especially since Russia needs Western aid to develop oil and gas in its areas.

What exists here is a ludicrous form of nationalism. Our entire country is imported. Everyone here is really from somewhere else.

On ARGENTINA
Jorge Luis Borges quoted in the *New Yorker* 7 Aug 1978

Arcturus or ***Alpha Boötis*** brightest star in the constellation Boötes and the fourth brightest star in the night sky. Arcturus is a red giant about 28 times larger than the Sun and 70 times more luminous, 36 light years away from Earth.

Ardennes wooded plateau in NE France, SE Belgium, and N Luxembourg, cut through by the river Meuse; also a *département* of ◊Champagne-Ardenne.

area the size of a surface. It is measured in square units, usually square centimetres (cm^2), square metres (m^2), or square kilometres (km^2). Surface area is the area of the outer surface of a solid.

The areas of geometrical plane shapes with straight edges are determined using the area of a rectangle. Integration may be used to determine the area of shapes enclosed by curves.

areca any palm tree of the genus *Areca*, native to Asia and Australia. The ◊betel nut comes from the species *A. catechu*.

Arecibo site in Puerto Rico of the world's largest single-dish ◊radio telescope, 305 m/1,000 ft in diameter. It is built in a natural hollow and uses the rotation of the Earth to scan the sky. It has been used both for radar work on the planets and for conventional radio astronomy, and is operated by Cornell University, USA.

Arendt Hannah 1906–1975. German-born US political philosopher. Her concerns included totalitarianism, the nature of evil, and the erosion of public participation in the political process. Her works include *Eichmann in Jerusalem* 1963 and *On Violence* 1972.

In *The Origins of Modern Totalitarianism* 1951, she pointed out the similarities between Nazism and Soviet communism, and in her report of the trial of a leading Nazi war criminal, *Eichmann in Jerusalem*, she coined the phrase 'the banality of evil' to describe how bureaucratic efficiency can facilitate the acceptance of the most terrible deeds.

Arequipa city in Peru at the base of the volcano El Misti; population (1993) 619,200. Founded by Pizarro 1540 on the site of an ancient Inca city, it is the cultural focus of S Peru and a busy commercial centre (soap, textiles).

Ares in Greek mythology, the god of war, equivalent to the Roman ◊Mars. The son of Zeus and Hera, he was worshipped chiefly in Thrace. Ares loved ◊Aphrodite, whose husband Hephaestus made the pair the laughing stock of the gods.

arête (German ***grat***; North American ***combe-ridge***) sharp narrow ridge separating two ◊glacial troughs (valleys), or ◊corries. The typical U-shaped cross sections of glacial troughs give arêtes very steep sides. Arêtes are common in glaciated mountain regions such as the Rockies, the Himalayas, and the Alps.

Arezzo town in the Tuscan region of Italy; 80 km/50 mi SE of Florence; population (1981) 92,100. It is a mining town and also trades in textiles, olive oil, and antiques. The writers Petrarch and Aretino were born here. There is a fresco series by Renaissance painter Piero della Francesca.

argali wild sheep *Ovis ammon* of Central Asia. The male can grow to 1.2 m/4 ft at the shoulder, and has massive spiral horns.

Argentina country in South America, bounded W and S by Chile, N by Bolivia, and E by Paraguay, Brazil, Uruguay, and the Atlantic Ocean. *See country box on p. 58.*

argon (Greek *argos* 'idle') colourless, odourless, nonmetallic, gaseous element, symbol Ar, atomic number 18, relative atomic mass 39.948. It is grouped with the ◊inert gases, since it was long believed not to react with other substances, but observations now indicate that it can be made to combine with boron fluoride to form compounds. It constitutes almost 1% of the Earth's atmosphere, and was discovered 1894 by British chemists John Rayleigh (1842–1919) and William Ramsay after all oxygen and nitrogen had been removed chemically from a sample of air. It is used in electric discharge tubes and argon lasers.

argonaut or ***paper nautilus*** octopus living in the open sea, genus *Argonauta*. The female of the common paper nautilus, *A. argo*, is 20 cm/8 in across, and secretes a spiralled papery shell for her eggs from the web of the first pair of arms. The male is a shell-less dwarf, 1 cm/0.4 in across.

Argonauts in Greek mythology, the band of heroes who accompanied ◊Jason when he set sail in the *Argo* to find the ◊Golden Fleece.

Argos city in ancient Greece, at the head of the Gulf of Nauplia, which was once a cult centre of the goddess Hera; her celebrated sanctuary lay outside the city. In the Homeric age the name 'Argives' was sometimes used instead of 'Greeks'. Although one of the most important cities in the Peloponnese, Argos was dominated by ◊Corinth and ◊Sparta. During the classical period the city repeatedly, but unsuccessfully, contested supremacy in S Greece with Sparta.

argument in mathematics, a specific value of the independent variable of a ◊function of *x*.

Argus in Greek mythology, a giant with 100 eyes. When he was killed by Hermes, Hera transplanted

Arendt, Hannah German-born political philosopher Hannah Arendt, photographed in 1963. She emigrated to the USA in 1941, where she held teaching posts in several universities. Her study of the Jerusalem trial of Nazi Adolf Eichmann aroused great controversy when it was published. *Corbis*

Argentina Cerro Fitz Roy in the Parque Nacional los Glaciares, SW Argentina. The national park is an area of great natural beauty and has become one of Argentina's main tourist attractions. *Sally Jenkins*

his eyes into the tail of her favourite bird, the peacock.

Argyll and Bute local authority of Scotland created 1996 (*see United Kingdom map*).

aria (Italian 'air') melodic solo song of reflective character, often with a contrasting middle section, expressing a moment of truth in the action of an opera or oratorio. By the early 18th century an aria was a song in three sections, of which the third repeated the first, while the second introduced variety of subject matter, key, and mood. This is known more exactly as the 'da capo aria'.

Ariadne in Greek mythology, the daughter of Minos, King of Crete. When ◊Theseus came from Athens as one of the sacrificial victims offered to the ◊Minotaur, she fell in love with him and gave him a ball of thread, which enabled him to find his way out of the labyrinth. When Theseus abandoned her on the island of Naxos, she married ◊Dionysus.

Arianism system of Christian theology that denied the complete divinity of Jesus. It was founded about 310 by ◊Arius, and condemned as heretical at the Council of Nicaea 325.

Some 17th- and 18th-century theologians held Arian views akin to those of ◊Unitarianism (that God is a single being, and that there is no such thing as the Trinity). In 1979 the heresy again caused concern to the Vatican in the writings of such theologians as Edouard Schillebeeckx of the Netherlands.

Arica port in Chile; population (1992) 169,200. Much of Bolivia's trade passes through it, and there is contention over the use of Arica by Bolivia to allow access to the Pacific Ocean. It is Chile's northernmost city.

arid region in earth science, a region that is very dry and has little vegetation. Aridity depends on temperature, rainfall, and evaporation, and so is difficult to quantify, but an arid area is usually defined as one that receives less than 250 mm/10 in of rainfall each year. (By comparison, New York City receives 1,120 mm/44 in per year). There are arid regions in North Africa, Pakistan, Australia, the USA, and elsewhere. Very arid regions are ◊deserts.

Ariège river in S France, a tributary of the Garonne, which rises in the Pyrenees; length 170 km/106 mi. It gives its name to a *département*.

Aries zodiacal constellation in the northern hemisphere between Pisces and Taurus, near Auriga, represented as the legendary ram whose golden fleece was sought by Jason and the Argonauts.

Its most distinctive feature is a curve of three stars of decreasing brightness. The brightest of these is Hamal or Alpha Arietis, 65 light years from Earth.

aril accessory seed cover other than a ◊fruit; it may be fleshy and sometimes brightly coloured, woody, or hairy. In flowering plants (◊angiosperms) it is often derived from the stalk that originally attached the ovule to the ovary wall. Examples of arils include the bright-red, fleshy layer surrounding the yew seed (yews are ◊gymnosperms so they lack true fruits), and the network of hard filaments that partially covers the nutmeg seed and yields the spice known as mace.

Ariosto Ludovico 1474–1533. Italian poet. He wrote Latin poems and comedies on Classical lines. His major work is the poem ◊*Orlando furioso* 1516, published 1532, an epic treatment of the ◊Roland story, the perfect poetic expression of the Italian Renaissance.

Ariosto was born in Reggio, and joined the household of Cardinal Ippolito d'Este 1503. He was frequently engaged in ambassadorial missions and diplomacy for the Duke of Ferrara, whose service he entered 1518. He was governor of Garfagnana 1522–25, a province in the Apennines, where he was mostly occupied in suppressing bandits and enforcing order. After three years he retired to Ferrara to work on the final revision of *Orlando furioso*.

Aristarchus of Samos c. 320–c. 250 BC. Greek astronomer. The first to argue that the Earth moves around the Sun, he was ridiculed for his beliefs. He was also the first astronomer to estimate (quite inaccurately) the sizes of the Sun and Moon and their distances from the Earth.

Aristide Jean-Bertrand 1953– . President of Haiti Dec 1990–Oct 1991 and Oct 1994–Dec 1995. A left-wing Catholic priest opposed to the right-wing regime of the Duvalier family, he relinquished his priesthood to concentrate on the presidency. He campaigned for the National Front for Change and Democracy, representing a loose coalition of peasants, trade unionists, and clerics, and won 70% of the vote. He was deposed by the military Sept 1991 and took refuge in the USA. In Sept 1994, under an agreement brokered by former US president Jimmy Carter, the military stepped down and allowed Aristide to return. Constitutionally barred from seeking a second term Dec 1995, he was succeeded by his preferred candidate René Préval.

Aristides c. 530–468 BC. Athenian politician. He was one of the ten Athenian generals at the Battle of ◊Marathon 490 BC and was elected chief archon, or magistrate. Later he came into conflict with the democratic leader Themistocles, and was exiled about 483 BC. He returned to fight against the Persians at Salamis 480 BC and in the following year commanded the Athenians at Plataea. As commander of the Athenian fleet he established the alliance of Ionian states known as the Delian League.

Aristippus c. 435–356 BC. Greek philosopher. He was the founder of the ◊Cyrenaic or hedonist school. A pupil of Socrates, he developed the doctrine that pleasure is the highest good in life. He lived at the court of ◊Dionysius of Syracuse and then with Laïs, a courtesan, in Corinth.

aristocracy (Greek *aristos* 'best', *kratos* 'power') social elite or system of political power associated with landed wealth, as in western Europe; with monetary wealth, as in Carthage and Venice; or with religious superiority, as were the Brahmans in India. Aristocracies are also usually associated with monarchy but have frequently been in conflict with the sovereign over their respective rights and privileges. In Europe, their economic base was undermined during the 19th century by inflation and falling agricultural prices, leading to their demise as a political force after 1914.

Aristophanes c. 445–c. 380 BC. Greek comedy dramatist. Of his 11 extant plays (of a total of over 40), the early comedies are remarkable for the violent satire with which he ridiculed the democratic war leaders. He also satirized contemporary issues such as the new learning of Socrates in *The Clouds* 423 BC and the obsession with war, with the sex-strike of women in *Lysistrata* 411 BC. The chorus plays a prominent role, frequently giving the play its title, as in *The Wasps* 422 BC, *The Birds* 414 BC, and *The Frogs* 405 BC.

Aristotle 384–322 BC. Greek philosopher who advocated reason and moderation. He maintained that sense experience is our only source of knowledge, and that by reasoning we can discover the essences of things, that is, their distinguishing qualities. In his works on ethics and politics, he suggested that human happiness consists in living in conformity with nature. He derived his political theory from the recognition that mutual aid is natural to humankind, and refused to set up any one constitution as universally ideal. Of Aristotle's works, around 22 treatises survive, dealing with logic, metaphysics, physics, astronomy, meteorology, biology, psychology, ethics, politics, and literary criticism.

‘Man by nature is a political animal.’

ARISTOTLE *Politics*

arid region The Negev Desert in Israel. Although superficially barren, arid regions such as the Negev Desert support a remarkable diversity of plants and animals, all of which have developed highly specialized ways of coping with the harsh conditions. *Premaphotos Wildlife*

ARGENTINA
Republic of

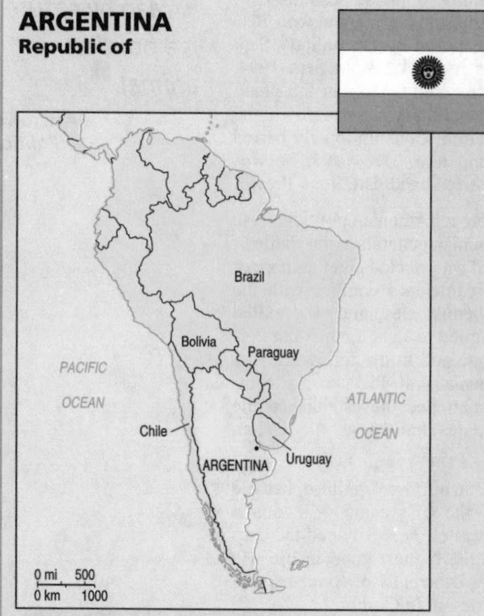

national name *República Argentina*
area 2,780,092 sq km/1,073,116 sq mi
capital Buenos Aires (to move to Viedma)
major towns/cities Rosario, Córdoba, St Miguel de Tucumán, Mendoza, Santa Fé
major ports La Plata and Bahía Blanca
physical features mountains in W, forest and savanna in N, pampas (treeless plains) in E central area, Patagonian plateau in S; rivers Colorado, Salado, Paraná, Uruguay, Río de La Plata estuary; Andes mountains, with Aconcagua the highest peak in the W hemisphere; Iguaçú Falls
territories claims Falkland Islands (*Islas Malvinas*), South Georgia, the South Sandwich Islands, and part of Antarctica
head of state Carlos Menem from 1989
head of government Carlos Menem from 1989
political system democratic federal republic
administrative divisions 23 provinces and one federal district (Buenos Aires)
political parties Radical Civic Union Party (UCR), moderate centrist; Justicialist Party (PJ), right-wing Perónist; Movement for Dignity and Independence (Modin), right-wing; Front for a Country in Solidarity (Frepaso), centre-left
armed forces 67,300 plus paramilitary gendarmerie of 18,000 run by Ministry of Defence (June 1995)
conscription abolished 1995
defence spend (% GDP) 1.7 (1994)
education spend (% GNP) 3.1 (1992)
health spend (% GDP) 4.2 (1990)
death penalty reintroduced 1976
population 35,219,000 (1996 est)
population growth rate 1.2% (1990–95); 1.1% (2000–05)
age distribution (% of total population) <15 28.7%; 15–65 61.8%; >65 9.5% (1995)
ethnic distribution 85% of European descent, mainly Spanish; 15% mestizo (offspring of Spanish–American and American–Indian parents)
population density (per sq km) 12 (1994)
urban population (% of total) 88 (1995)
labour force 38% of population: 12% agriculture, 32% industry, 55% services
unemployment 18.6% (May 1995)
child mortality rate (under 5, per 1,000 live births) 27 (1993)
life expectancy 68 (men), 75 (women)
education (compulsory years) 7; age limits 7–16
literacy rate 96% (men); 95% (women)
languages Spanish 95% (official); Italian 3%
religion Roman Catholic (state-supported)
TV sets (per 1,000 people) 220 (1993)
currency peso = 10,000 australs (which it replaced 1992)
GDP (US $) 281.9 billion (1994)
GDP per capita (PPP) (US $) 8,350 (1993)
growth rate 7.4% (1994)
average annual inflation 374.3% (1980–93); 4.2% (1994)
trading partners USA, Brazil, the Netherlands, Germany, Italy, Uruguay, Chile
resources coal, crude oil, natural gas, iron ore, lead ore, zinc ore, tin, gold, silver, uranium ore, marble, borates, granite. Crude oil reserves: 310 million metric tons; natural gas reserves: 517 billion cubic metres (1993)
industries petroleum and petroleum products, primary iron, crude steel, sulphuric acid, synthetic rubber, paper and paper products, crude oil, cement, cigarettes, motor vehicles
exports meat and meat products, prepared animal fodder, cereals, petroleum and petroleum products, soya beans, vegetable oils and fats. Principal market: Brazil 21.5% (1993)
imports machinery and transport equipment, chemicals and mineral products. Principal sources: USA 23%, Brazil 21.3% (1993)
arable land 9.0% (1993)
agricultural products wheat, maize, soya beans, sugar cane, rice, sorghum, potatoes, tobacco, sunflowers, cotton, vine fruits, citrus fruit; livestock production (chiefly cattle)

HISTORY
1516 Spanish navigator Juan Diaz de Solis discovered Río de La Plata.
1536 Buenos Aires founded, but soon abandoned because of attacks by American Indians.
1580 Buenos Aires re-established as part of Spanish province of Asunción.
1617 Buenos Aires became a separate province within Spanish viceroyalty of Lima.
1776 Spanish South American Empire reorganized: Atlantic regions became viceroyalty of La Plata, with Buenos Aires as capital.
1810 After French conquest of Spain, Buenos Aires junta took over government of viceroyalty.
1816 Independence proclaimed as United Provinces of Río de La Plata, but Bolivia and Uruguay soon seceded; civil war followed between federalists and those who wanted a unitary state.
1835–52 Dictatorship of General Juan Manuel Rosas.
1853 Adoption of federal constitution based on US model; Buenos Aires refused to join confederation.
1861 Buenos Aires incorporated into Argentine confederation by force.
1865–70 Argentina took part in War of Triple Alliance against Paraguay.
late 19th C Large-scale European immigration and rapid economic development; Argentina became a major world supplier of meat and grain.
1880 Buenos Aires became a special federal district and national capital.
1880–1916 Government dominated by oligarchy of conservative landowners; each president effectively chose his own successor.
1916 Following introduction of secret ballot, Radical Party of Hipólito Irigoyen won election victory, beginning a period of 14 years in government.
1930 Military coup ushered in a series of conservative governments sustained by violence and fraud.
1943 Group of pro-German army officers seized power; Colonel Juan Perón emerged as a leading figure.
1946 Perón won free presidential election; he secured working-class support by through welfare measures, trade unionism, and the popularity of his wife, Eva Perón (Evita).
1949 New constitution abolished federalism and increased powers of president.
1952 Death of Evita. Support for Perón began to decline.
1955 Perón overthrown; constitution of 1853 restored.
1966–70 Dictatorship of General Juan Carlos Ongania.
1973 Perónist Party won free elections; Perón returned from exile in Spain to become president.
1974 Perón died; succeeded by his third wife, Isabel Perón.
1976 Coup resulted in rule by military junta headed by Lt-Gen Jorge Videla (until 1978; succeeded by General Roberto Viola 1978–81 and General Leopoldo Galtieri 1981–82).
1976–83 Military regime conducted murderous campaign ('Dirty War') against left-wing elements.
1982 Invasion of Falkland Islands by Argentina. Intervention and defeat by UK; Galtieri replaced by General Reynaldo Bignone.
1983 Return to civilian rule under President Rául Alfonsín; investigation launched into 'disappearance' of more than 8,000 people during 'Dirty War'.
1985 Economic austerity programme failed to halt hyperinflation.
1989 Perónist candidate Carlos Menem won presidential election. Annual inflation rate reached 12,000%.
1990 Full diplomatic relations with UK restored.
1995 President Menem re-elected.
1997 PJ lost its assembly majority. Britain announces that is to partially lift its 16-year ban on the sale of arms to Argentina.

SEE ALSO Falkland Islands; Perón, Juan; Perón, María

Aristotle was born in Stagira in Thrace and studied in Athens, where he became a distinguished member of the Academy founded by Plato; at this time he regarded himself as a Platonist. His subsequent thought led him further from the traditions that had formed his early background and he became critical of Plato.

In 342 he accepted an invitation from Philip II of Macedon to go to Pella as tutor to Philip's son ◊Alexander the Great. In 335 he opened a school in the Lyceum (grove sacred to Apollo) in Athens. It became known as the 'peripatetic school' because he walked up and down as he talked, and his works are a collection of his lecture notes. When Alexander died 323, Aristotle was forced to flee to Chalcis, where he died.

Among his many contributions to political thought were the first systematic attempts to distinguish between different forms of government, ideas about the role of law in the state, and the conception of a science of politics.

In the *Poetics*, Aristotle defines tragic drama as an imitation (mimesis) of the actions of human beings, with character subordinated to plot. The audience is affected by pity and fear, but experiences a purgation (catharsis) of these emotions through watching the play. The three books of the *Rhetoric* form the earliest analytical discussion of the techniques of persuasion.

In the Middle Ages, Aristotle's philosophy first became the foundation of Islamic philosophy, and was then incorporated into Christian theology; medieval scholars tended to accept his vast output without question. Aristotle held that all matter consisted of a single 'prime matter', which was always determined by some form. The simplest kinds of matter were the four elements – earth, water, air, and fire – which in varying proportions constituted all things. According to Aristotle's laws of motion, bodies moved upwards or downwards in straight lines. Earth and water fell, air and fire rose. To explain the motion of the heavenly spheres, Aristotle introduced a fifth element, ether, whose natural movement was circular.

arithmetic branch of mathematics concerned with the study of numbers and their properties. The fundamental operations of arithmetic are addition, subtraction, multiplication, and division. Raising to powers (for example, squaring or cubing a number), the extraction of roots (for example, square roots), percentages, fractions, and ratios are developed from these operations.

arithmetic and logic unit (ALU) in a computer, the part of the ◊central processing unit (CPU) that performs the basic arithmetic and logic operations on data.

arithmetic mean the average of a set of n numbers, obtained by adding the numbers and dividing by n. For example, the arithmetic mean of the set of 5 numbers 1, 3, 6, 8, and 12 is $(1 + 3 + 6 + 8 + 12)/5 = 30/5 = 6$.

The term 'average' is often used to refer only to the arithmetic mean, even though the mean is in fact only one form of average (the others include ◊median and ◊mode).

arithmetic progression or ***arithmetic sequence*** sequence of numbers or terms that have a common difference between any one term and the next in the sequence. For example, 2, 7, 12, 17, 22, 27, ... is an arithmetic sequence with a common difference of 5.

The nth term in any arithmetic progression can be found using the formula:

$$n\text{th term} = a + (n - 1)d$$

where *a* is the first term and *d* is the common difference.

An ***arithmetic series*** is the sum of the terms in an arithmetic sequence. The sum *S* of *n* terms is given by:

$$S = n/2\ [2a + (n - 1)d]$$

Arius c. 250–336. Egyptian priest whose ideas gave rise to ◊Arianism, a Christian belief that denied the complete divinity of Jesus.

Arizona

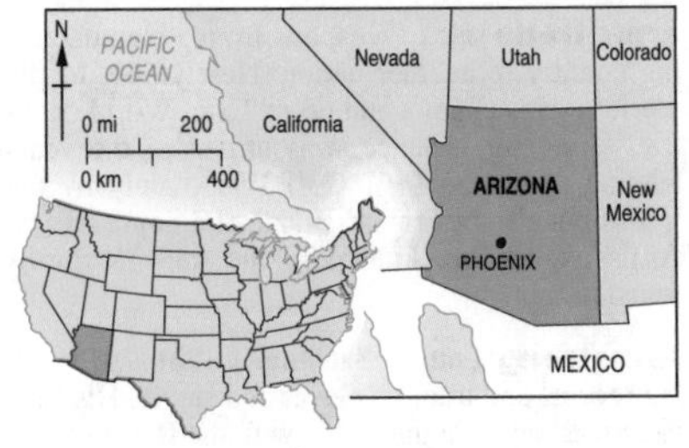

Arizona state in southwestern USA; nicknamed Grand Canyon State
area 294,100 sq km/113,500 sq mi
capital Phoenix
towns and cities Tucson, Scottsdale, Tempe, Mesa, Glendale, Flagstaff
physical Colorado Plateau in the N and E, desert basins and mountains in the S and W, Colorado River, Grand Canyon
features the Grand Canyon, the rock gorge through which the Colorado River flows, 350 km/217 mi long, 6–28 km/4–18 mi wide, and up to over 1.6 km/1 mi deep, in the Grand Canyon national park; Monument Valley; Navajo national monument, the largest ruin in Arizona, abandoned before 1300; Tombstone, site of the famous gunfight at the OK Corral
industries cotton under irrigation, livestock, copper, molybdenum, silver, electronics, aircraft
population (1990) 3,665,000; including 4.5% Native Americans (Navajo, Hopi, Apache), who by treaty own 25% of the state
famous people Wyatt Earp, Geronimo, Barry Goldwater, Zane Grey, Percival Lowell, Frank Lloyd Wright
history part of New Spain 1752; part of Mexico 1824; passed to the USA after the Mexican War 1848; territory 1863; statehood achieved 1912.

Arjan Indian religious leader, fifth guru (teacher) of Sikhism 1581–1606. He built the Golden Temple in ◊Amritsar and compiled the *Adi Granth*, the first volume of Sikh scriptures. He died in Muslim custody.

Arkansas

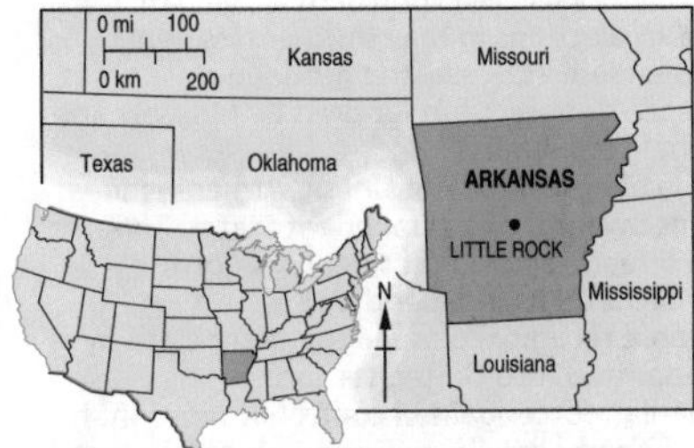

Arkansas state in S central USA; nicknamed Wonder State/Land of Opportunity
area 137,800 sq km/53,191 sq mi
capital Little Rock
towns and cities Fort Smith, Pine Bluff, Fayetteville
physical Ozark Mountains and plateau in the W, lowlands in the E; Arkansas River; many lakes
features the Ozark Mountains and Ozark national forest; Arkansas and Mississippi rivers; Buffalo national river; Hot Springs, the boyhood home of President Bill Clinton; Hope, the birthplace of President Clinton
industries cotton, soya beans, rice, oil, natural gas, bauxite, timber, processed foods
population (1990) 2,350,700
famous people Johnny Cash, Bill Clinton, J William Fulbright, Douglas MacArthur, Winthrop Rockefeller
history explored by Hernando de Soto 1541; European settlers 1648, who traded with local Indians; part of Louisiana Purchase 1803; statehood achieved 1836.

The first European settlement was Arkansas Post, founded by some of the companions of the French explorer La Salle. After seceding from the Union 1861 (see ◊Confederacy), it was readmitted 1868.

Ark of the Covenant in the Old Testament, the chest that contained the Tablets of the Law as given to Moses. It is now the cupboard in a synagogue in which the ◊Torah scrolls are kept.

The original ark was built under Moses' direction when the Israelites were wandering in the desert, and was carried on poles by the priests. King David brought the Ark to Jerusalem, where it was subsequently kept in the Holy of Holies in the Temple.

Arkwright Richard 1732–1792. English inventor and manufacturing pioneer who developed a machine for spinning cotton (he called it a 'spinning frame') 1768. He set up a water-powered spinning factory 1771 and installed steam power in a Nottingham factory 1790.

Arles town in Bouches-du-Rhône *département*, SE France, on the left bank of the Rhône; population (1990) 52,600. It is an important fruit- and vine-growing district. Roman relics include an amphitheatre for 25,000 spectators. The cathedral of St Trophime is a notable Romanesque structure. The painter Van Gogh lived here 1888–89, during which period he painted some of his major works.

Arlington county in Virginia, USA, and suburb of Washington DC; population (1990) 170,900. It is the site of the National Cemetery for the dead of the US wars. The grounds were first used as a military cemetery 1864 during the American Civil War. By 1975, 165,142 military, naval, and civilian persons had been buried, including the Unknown Soldier (memorial to all unidentified soldiers killed) of both world wars, President John F Kennedy, and his brother Robert Kennedy.

Armada fleet sent by Philip II of Spain against England 1588. See ◊Spanish Armada.

armadillo mammal of the family Dasypodidae, with an armour of bony plates along its back or, in some species, almost covering the entire body. Around 20 species live between Texas and Patagonia and range in size from the fairy armadillo, or pichiciego, *Chlamyphorus truncatus*, at 13 cm/5 in, to the giant armadillo *Priodontes giganteus*, 1.5 m/4.5 ft long. Armadillos feed on insects, snakes, fruit, and carrion. Some can roll into an armoured ball if attacked; others defend themselves with their claws or rely on rapid burrowing for protection.

They belong to the order Edentata ('without teeth') which also includes sloths and anteaters. However, only the latter are toothless. Some species of armadillos can have up to 90 peglike teeth.

Armageddon in the New Testament (Revelation 16:16), the site of the final battle between the nations that will end the world; it has been identified with ◊Megiddo in Israel.

Armagh county of Northern Ireland
area 1,250 sq km/483 sq mi
towns and cities Armagh (county town), Lurgan, Portadown, Keady
features smallest county of Northern Ireland; flat in the N, with many bogs; low hills in the S; the rivers Bann and Blackwater, flowing into Lough Neagh, and the Callan tributary of the Blackwater
industries chiefly agricultural: apples, potatoes, flax; linen manufacture.

Armagh town of Armagh, Northern Ireland; population (1991) 14,300. Industries include textiles (its chief product), engineering, whiskey, shoes, optical instruments, chemicals, and food processing. It became the religious centre of Ireland in the 5th century when St Patrick was made archbishop. For 700 years it was the seat of the kings of Ulster. It is the seat of both the Roman Catholic and Anglican archbishops of Ireland, who each bear the title 'Archbishop of Armagh and Primate of All Ireland'.

Armagnac deep-coloured brandy named after the district of Armagnac in Gascony, SW France, where it is produced.

armadillo The horny bands and plates of the armadillo serve as armour. Many species can draw in their feet beneath the shell when attacked. The three-banded armadillo can roll itself into a ball. In spite of all this protection, however, many species of armadillo are more likely to run or burrow if threatened by a predator. *Corbis*

Armani Giorgio 1935– . Italian fashion designer. He launched his first menswear collection 1974 and the following year started designing women's clothing. His work is known for understated styles, and fine fabrics. He pioneered the 'unstructured jacket' and his designs are marketed under different labels, from exclusive models to the less expensive diffusion range.

armed forces state military organizations; see ◊army, ◊navy, ◊air force.

Armenia country in W Asia, bounded E by Azerbaijan, N by Georgia, W by Turkey, and S by Iran. *See country box on p. 60.*

Armenian the largest ethnic group inhabiting Armenia. There are Armenian minorities in Azerbaijan (see ◊Nagorno-Karabakh), as well as in Turkey and Iran. Christianity was introduced to the ancient Armenian kingdom in the 3rd century. There are 4–5 million speakers of Armenian, which belongs to the Indo-European family of languages.

Armenian language one of the main divisions of the Indo-European language family. Old Armenian, the classical literary language, is still used in the liturgy of the Armenian Church. Armenian was not written down until the 5th century AD, when an alphabet of 36 (now 38) letters was evolved. Literature flourished in the 4th to 14th centuries, revived in the 18th, and continued throughout the 20th.

Contemporary Armenian is used in Armenia, Iran, Turkey, Lebanon, and wherever Armenian emigrants have settled in significant numbers.

Armenian massacres series of massacres of Armenians by Turkish soldiers between 1895 and 1915. In 1894–96 demands for better treatment led to massacres of Armenians in eastern Asia Minor. Over 50,000 Armenians were killed by Kurdish irregulars and Ottoman troops. The killing was stopped by the major European powers, but in 1915 Ottoman suspicions of Armenian loyalty led to further massacres and deportations. The Turks deported 1.75 million Armenians to Syria and Palestine; 600,000 were either killed or died of starvation during the journey.

armillary sphere earliest known astronomical device, in use from 3rd century BC. It showed the Earth at the centre of the universe, surrounded by a number of movable metal rings representing the Sun, Moon, and planets. The armillary sphere was originally used to observe the heavens and later for teaching navigators about the arrangements and movements of the heavenly bodies.

Arminius Jacobus. Latinized name of Jakob Harmensen 1560–1609. Dutch Protestant priest who founded Arminianism, a school of Christian theology opposed to John Calvin's doctrine of predestination. His views were developed by Simon Episcopius (1583–1643). Arminianism is the basis of Wesleyan ◊Methodism.

Arminius was born in S Holland, ordained in Amsterdam 1588, and from 1603 was professor of theology at Leiden. He asserted that forgiveness and eternal life are bestowed on all who repent of their sins and sincerely believe in Jesus Christ. He was drawn into many controversies, and his followers were expelled from the church and persecuted.

‘A lot of cats copy the Mona Lisa, but people still line up to see the original.’

Louis Armstrong
Reply when asked whether he objected to people copying his style

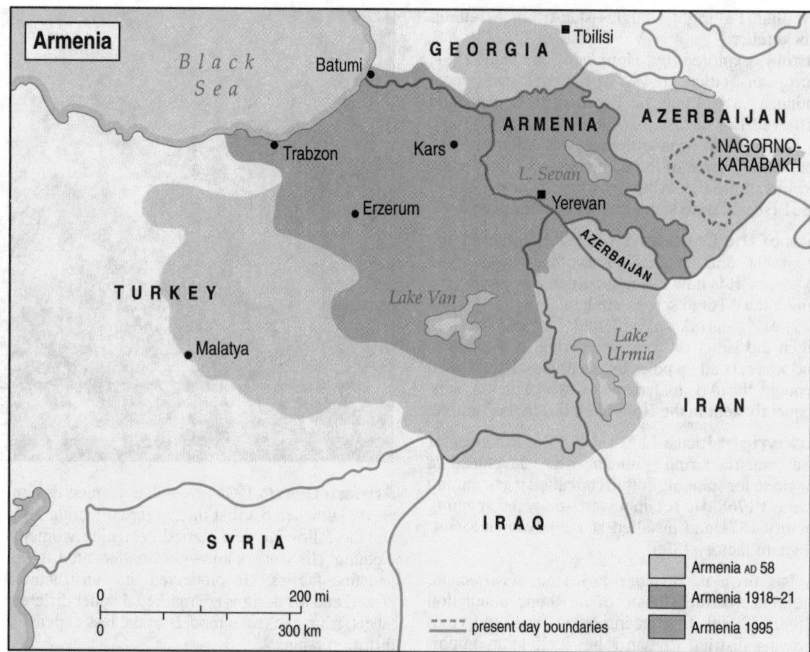

armistice cessation of hostilities while awaiting a peace settlement. ‘The Armistice’ refers specifically to the end of World War I between Germany and the Allies 11 Nov 1918. On 22 June 1940 French representatives signed an armistice with Germany in the same railway carriage at Compiègne as in 1918. No armistice was signed with either Germany or Japan 1945; both nations surrendered and there was no provision for the suspension of fighting. The Korean armistice, signed at Panmunjom 27 July 1953, terminated the Korean War 1950–53.

Armistice Day anniversary of the armistice signed 11 Nov 1918, ending World War I. In the UK it is commemorated on the same day as ◊Remembrance Sunday.

armour body protection worn in battle. Body armour is depicted in Greek and Roman art. Chain mail was developed in the Middle Ages but the craft of the armourer in Europe reached its height in design in the 15th century, when knights were completely encased in plate armour that still allowed freedom of movement. Medieval Japanese armour was articulated, made of iron, gilded metal, leather, and silk. Contemporary bulletproof vests and riot gear are forms of armour. Modern armour, used by the army, police, security guards, and people at risk from assassination, uses nylon and fibreglass and is often worn beneath their clothing. The term is also used in a modern context to refer to a mechanized armoured vehicle, such as a tank.

armoured personnel carrier (APC) wheeled or tracked military vehicle designed to transport up to ten people. Armoured to withstand small-arms fire and shell splinters, it is used on battlefields.

arms control attempts to limit the arms race between the superpowers by reaching agreements to restrict the production of certain weapons; see ◊disarmament.

arms trade sale of weapons from a manufacturing country to another nation. Nearly 56% of the world's arms exports end up in Third World countries. Iraq, for instance, was armed in the years leading up to the 1991 Gulf War mainly by the USSR but also by France, Brazil, and South Africa. Arms exports are known in the trade as ‘arms transfers’.

Armstrong Louis (‘Satchmo’) 1901–1971. US jazz cornet and trumpet player and singer. His Chicago recordings in the 1920s with the Hot Five and Hot Seven brought him recognition for his warm and pure trumpet tone, his skill at improvisation, and his quirky, gravelly voice. From the 1930s he also appeared in films.

Armstrong was born in New Orleans. In 1923 he joined the Creole Jazz Band led by the cornet player Joe ‘King’ ◊Oliver in Chicago, but soon broke away and fronted various bands of his own. In 1947 he formed the Louis Armstrong All-Stars. He firmly established the pre-eminence of the virtuoso jazz soloist. He is also credited with the invention of scat singing, jazz singing with nonsense syllables.

Armstrong Neil Alden 1930– . US astronaut. With Edwin ‘Buzz’ ◊Aldrin and Michael Collins (1930–) in *Apollo 11* on 16 July 1969, he lifted off from Cape Kennedy and four days later was the first person to set foot on the Moon. The Moon landing was part of the ◊Apollo project.

army organized military force for fighting on the ground. A national army is used to further a political

ARMENIA
Republic of

national name *Haikakan Hanrapetoutioun*
area 29,800 sq km/11,500 sq mi
capital Yerevan
major towns/cities Kumayri (formerly Leninakan), Kirovakan
physical features mainly mountainous (including Mount Ararat), wooded
head of state and government Robert Kocharyan from 1998
political system authoritarian nationalist
administrative divisions 68 districts
political parties Armenian Pan-National Movement (APM), nationalist, left of centre; Armenian Revolutionary Federation (ARF), centrist (banned 1994); Communist Party of Armenia (banned 1991–92); National Unity, opposition coalition
population 3,638,000 (1996 est)
population growth rate 1.4% (1990–95); 1.0% (2000–05)
ethnic distribution 91% of Armenian ethnic descent, 5% Azeri, 2% Russian, and 2% Kurdish
life expectancy 78 (men), 73 (women)
literacy rate 99%
language Armenian
religion Armenian Christian
currency dram (replaced Russian rouble 1993)
GDP (US $) 3 billion (1994)
growth rate 5.4% (1994)
exports copper, molybdenum, cereals, cotton, silk

HISTORY
6th C BC Armenian peoples moved into the area, which was then part of the Persian Empire.
c. 94–56 BC Under King Tigranes II ‘the Great’, Armenia reached height of its power, expanding S to become strongest state in the Roman E, controlling area from the Caucasus to the Mediterranean.
c. AD 300 Christianity became the state religion when the local ruler was converted by St Gregory the Illuminator.
c. AD 390 Became divided between Byzantine Armenia, which became part of Byzantine Empire, and Persarmenia, under Persian control.
886–1045 Independent under the Bagratid monarchy.
13th C After being overrun by the Mongols, a substantially independent Little Armenia survived until 1375.
early 16th C Conquered by Muslim Ottoman Turks.
1813–28 Russia took control of E Armenia.
late 19th C Revival in Armenian culture and national spirit, provoking Ottoman backlash in W Armenia and international concern at Armenian maltreatment.
1894–96 Massacre of Armenians by Turkish soldiers to suppress unrest.
1915 Suspected of pro-Russian sympathies, two-thirds of Armenian population of 2 million were deported to Syria and Palestine. Around 600,000–1 million died en route: the survivors contributed towards an Armenian diaspora in Europe and North America.
1916 Conquered by Tsarist Russia. A brief ‘Transcaucasian Alliance’ with Georgia and Azerbaijan.
1918 Became an independent republic.
1920 Occupied by the Red Army of the Soviet Union (USSR), but W Armenia remained part of Turkey and NW Iran.
1936 Became a constituent republic of the USSR; rapid industrial development.
later 1980s Armenian ‘national reawakening’, encouraged by *glasnost* (openness) initiative of Soviet leader Mikhail Gorbachev.
1988 Earthquake claimed around 20,000 lives.
1989 Strife-torn Nagorno-Karabakh placed under direct rule from Moscow; civil war erupted with Azerbaijan over Nagorno-Karabakh and Nakhichevan, an Azerbaijani-peopled enclave in Armenia.
1990 Nationalists secured control of Armenian parliament in elections in May; former dissident Ter-Petrossian indirectly elected president; independence declared, but ignored by Moscow and international community.
1991 After collapse of Soviet Union, Armenia joined new Commonwealth of Independent States. Ter-Petrossian directly elected president. Nagorno-Karabakh declared its independence.
1992 Armenia recognized as independent state by USA and admitted into United Nations.
1993 Armenian forces gained control of more than one-fifth of Azerbaijan, including much of Nagorno-Karabakh.
1994 Nagorno-Karabakh cease-fire ended conflict.
1995 Privatization and price liberalization programme launched. Ruling APM re-elected, amid reports of intimidation of opposition candidates.
1996 Ter-Petrossian re-elected president.
1997 Border fighting with Azerbaijan. Arkady Gukasyan elected president of Nagorno-Karabakh.
1998 Ter-Petrossian resigned following opposition to his moderate approach to resolving the dispute with Azerbaijan over Nagorno-Karabakh. Prime minister Kocharyan, a hardliner, elected president.

SEE ALSO Armenian massacres; Azerbaijan; Nagorno-Karabakh; Union of Soviet Socialist Republics

Armstrong, Louis US jazz player and singer Louis Armstrong. As well as performing and recording jazz music, Armstrong appeared in a number of films, including *Pennies from Heaven* 1936, *Cabin in the Sky* 1943, and *High Society* 1956. *Corbis*

policy by force either within the state or on the territory of another state. Most countries have a national army, maintained by taxation, and raised either by conscription (compulsory military service) or voluntarily (paid professionals). Private armies may be employed by individuals and groups.

Arne Thomas Augustine 1710–1778. English composer. He wrote incidental music for theatre and introduced opera in the Italian manner to the London stage with works such as *Artaxerxes* 1762, revised 1777. He is remembered for the songs 'Where the bee sucks' from *The Tempest* 1746, 'Blow, blow thou winter wind' from *As You Like It* 1740, and 'Rule Britannia!' from the masque *Alfred* 1740.

Arnhem, Battle of in World War II, airborne operation by the Allies, 17–26 Sept 1944, to secure a bridgehead over the Rhine, thereby opening the way for a thrust towards the Ruhr and a possible early end to the war. It was only partially successful, with 7,600 casualties.

Arnhem Land plateau of the central peninsula in Northern Territory, Australia. It is named after a Dutch ship which dropped anchor here 1618.

The chief town is Nhulunbuy. It is the largest of the Aboriginal reserves, and a traditional way of life is maintained, now threatened by mineral exploitation.

Arnim Ludwig Achim von 1781–1831. German Romantic poet and novelist. He wrote short stories, a romance (*Armut, Schuld und Busse der Gräfin Dolores/Countess Dolores* 1810), and plays, but left the historical novel *Die Kronenwächter* 1817 unfinished. With Clemens ◊Brentano he collected the German folk songs in *Des Knaben Wunderhorn/The Boy's Magic Horn* 1805–08, several of which were set to music by Mahler.

Arno Italian river 240 km/150 mi long, rising in the Apennines, and flowing westwards to the Mediterranean Sea. Florence and Pisa stand on its banks. A flood 1966 damaged virtually every Renaissance landmark in Florence.

Arnold Benedict 1741–1801. US soldier and military strategist who, during the American Revolution, won the turning-point battle at Saratoga 1777 for the Americans. He is chiefly remembered as a traitor to the American side, having plotted to betray the strategic post at West Point to the British.

Arnold Malcolm Henry 1921– . English composer. His work is tonal and includes a large amount of orchestral, chamber, ballet, and vocal music. His overtures *Beckus the Dandipratt* 1948, *A Sussex Overture* 1951, and *Tam O'Shanter* 1955 are well known. His operas include *The Dancing Master* 1951, and he has written music for more than 80 films, including *The Bridge on the River Kwai* 1957, for which he won an Academy Award.

Arnold Matthew 1822–1888. English poet and critic. His poem 'Dover Beach' 1867 was widely regarded as one of the most eloquent expressions of the spiritual anxieties of Victorian England. The critical essays collected in *Culture and Anarchy* 1869 were highly influential.

Arnold's poems, characterized by their elegiac mood and pastoral themes, include 'The Forsaken Merman' 1849, 'Sohrab and Rustum' 1853, 'Thyrsis' 1867 (commemorating his friend Arthur Hugh Clough), and 'The Scholar-Gipsy' 1853. His *Essays in Criticism* were published 1865 and 1888, and *Literature and Dogma*, on biblical interpretation, 1872. In *Culture and Anarchy* he attacked the smugness and philistinism of the Victorian middle classes, and argued for a new culture based on the pursuit of artistic and intellectual values.

Arnold Thomas 1795–1842. English schoolmaster, father of the poet and critic Matthew Arnold. He was headmaster of Rugby School 1828–42. His regime has been graphically described in Thomas Hughes's *Tom Brown's Schooldays* 1857. He emphasized training of character, and had a profound influence on public school education.

aromatherapy in alternative medicine, use of oils and essences derived from plants, flowers, and wood resins. Bactericidal properties and beneficial effects upon physiological functions are attributed to the oils, which are sometimes ingested but generally massaged into the skin.

army A regiment of the French infantry going to battle 1917. World War I employed enormous armies in trench warfare. The British army, for example, expanded from 750,000 to 5.5 million troops. *Image Select (UK) Ltd*

Aromatherapy was first used in ancient Greece and Egypt, but became a forgotten art until the 1930s, when a French chemist accidentally spilt lavender over a cut and found that the wound healed without a scar. However, it was not until the 1990s that aromatherapy gained a degree of acceptance in mainstream health treatment.

aromatic compound organic chemical compound in which some of the bonding electrons are delocalized (shared among several atoms within the molecule and not localized in the vicinity of the atoms involved in bonding). The commonest aromatic compounds have ring structures, the atoms comprising the ring being either all carbon or containing one or more different atoms (usually nitrogen, sulphur, or oxygen). Typical examples are benzene (C_6H_6) and pyridine (C_5H_5N). *See illustration on following page.*

Arp Hans, or Jean 1887–1966. French abstract painter, sculptor, and poet. He was one of the founders of the ◊Dada movement 1916, and was later associated with the Surrealists. Using chance and ◊automatism, Arp developed an abstract sculpture whose sensuous shapes suggest organic forms. In many of his works, in particular his early collages, he collaborated with his wife ***Sophie Taeuber-Arp*** (1889–1943).

'The pursuit of perfection, then, is the pursuit of sweetness and light.'

MATTHEW ARNOLD
Culture and Anarchy

Arran large mountainous island in the Firth of Clyde, Scotland, in Strathclyde; area 427 sq km/165 sq mi; population (1991) 4,500. It is popular as a holiday resort. The chief town is Brodick.

Arras French town on the Scarpe River NE of Paris; population (1990) 42,700. It is the capital of Pas-de-Calais *département*, and was formerly known for tapestry. It was the birthplace of the French revolutionary leader Robespierre.

Arras, Battle of battle of World War I, April–May 1917; an effective but costly British attack on

Arnhem Land The Arnhem Land Escarpment, a stark sandstone wall, marks the western edge of Arnhem Land, Northern Territory, Australia. Rich in uranium, bauxite, and manganese, Arnhem Land was threatened with ruthless exploitation. The 1976 Aboriginal Land Act gave the land rights to the Aboriginal groups of the area, and permission to mine must be obtained from them. *Australian High Commission*

Arnold, Matthew English poet and literary critic Matthew Arnold, photographed in about 1860. He was professor of poetry at Oxford University 1857–67, and wrote such memorable poems as 'Dover Beach' 1867. He also wrote essays on culture and religion. *Corbis*

aromatic compound Compounds whose molecules contain the benzene ring, or variations of it, are called aromatic. The term was originally used to distinguish sweet-smelling compounds from others.

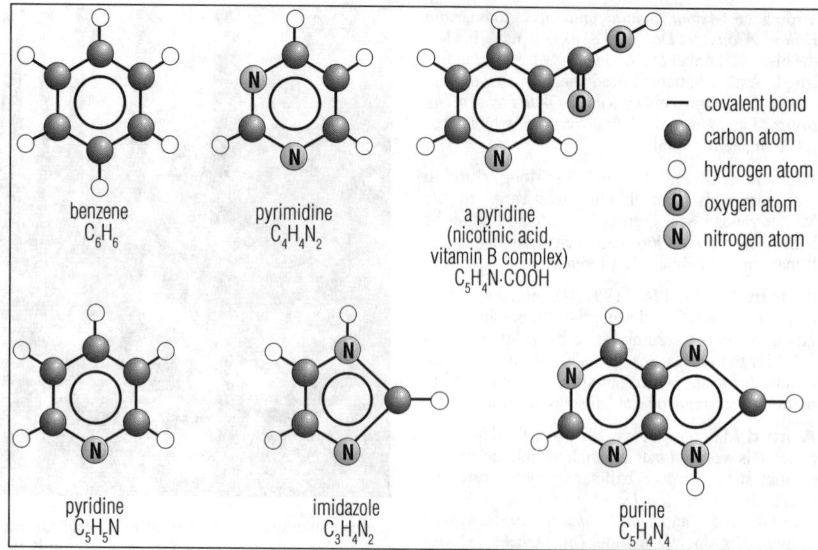

German forces in support of a French offensive, which was only partially successful, on the ◊Siegfried Line. British casualties totalled 84,000 as compared to 75,000 German casualties.

Arrau Claudio 1903–1991. Chilean-born US pianist. A concert performer from the age of five, he specialized in 19th-century music and was known for his magisterial interpretations of Chopin, Beethoven, and Brahms.

'Without tradition, art is a flock of sheep without a shepherd. Without innovation, it is a corpse.'

On **ART**
Winston Churchill, quoted in *Time* 11 May 1954

arrest apprehension and detention of a person suspected of a crime. In Britain, an arrest may be made on a magistrate's warrant, but a police constable is empowered to arrest without warrant in all cases where he or she has reasonable ground for thinking a serious offence has been committed. A private citizen may arrest anyone committing a serious offence or breach of the peace in their presence. A person who makes a citizen's arrest must inform the arrested person of the grounds of arrest and take him or her to the police or a magistrate as soon as is practicable or they may be guilty of false imprisonment. In the USA police officers and private persons have similar rights and duties.

Arrhenius Svante August 1859–1927. Swedish scientist, the founder of physical chemistry. For his study of electrolysis, he received the Nobel Prize for Chemistry 1903. In 1905 he predicted global warming as a result of carbon dioxide emission from burning fossil fuels.

Arrhenius explained that in an ◊electrolyte the dissolved substance is dissociated into electrically charged ions. The electrolyte conducts electricity because the ions migrate through the solution.

Arrhenius Swedish scientist Svante August Arrhenius's doctoral thesis was almost rejected by the University of Uppsala, because of his innovative and novel ideas. He was highly regarded by several prominent chemists, such as Ostwald and van't Hoff, and was able to continue his pioneering work in Europe on a travelling scholarship. In 1887, by consolidating and extending his doctoral thesis, Arrhenius published his theory of electrolytic dissociation, which is still largely accepted today. In 1903 he was awarded the Nobel Prize for Chemistry. *Ann Ronan/ Image Select (UK) Ltd*

arrhythmia disturbance of the normal rhythm of the heart. There are various kinds of arrhythmia, some benign, some indicative of heart disease. In extreme cases, the heart may beat so fast as to be potentially lethal and surgery may be used to correct the condition. Extra beats between the normal ones are called extrasystoles; abnormal slowing is known as bradycardia and speeding up is known as tachycardia.

Arrian lived 2nd century AD. Greek historian. His *Anabasis/Expedition* is the chief literary source of information on the campaigns of ◊Alexander the Great, drawn with care from much earlier material. Arrian was a governor and commander under Roman emperor Hadrian.

arrowroot starchy substance derived from the roots and tubers of various tropical plants with thick, clumpy roots. The true arrowroot *Maranta arundinacea* was used by the Indians of South America as an antidote against the effects of poisoned arrows.

The West Indian island of St Vincent is the main source of supply today. The roots and tubers are dried, finely powdered, and filtered. Because of the small size of the starch particles, the powder becomes translucent when cooked. Hence, it is often used as a glaze. The edible starch is easily digested and is often prescribed in the diet of invalids and young children.

Arsacid dynasty rulers of ancient Parthia c. 250 BC–AD 226, who took their titles from their founder Arsaces. At its peak the dynasty controlled a territory from E India to W Mesopotamia, with a summer capital at Ecbatana and a winter palace at ◊Ctesiphon. Claiming descent from the Persian ◊Achaemenids, but adopting Hellenistic Greek methods of administration, they successfully challenged Roman expansion, defeating the Roman general Crassus at the battle of Carrhae 53 BC. The Arsacid dynasty came to an end with the overthrow of Parthia by Ardashir AD 226; it was succeeded by the ◊Sassanian Empire.

arsenic brittle, greyish-white, semimetallic element (a metalloid), symbol As, atomic number 33, relative atomic mass 74.92. It occurs in many ores and occasionally in its elemental state, and is widely distributed, being present in minute quantities in the soil, the sea, and the human body. In larger quantities, it is poisonous. The chief source of arsenic compounds is as a by-product from metallurgical processes. It is used in making semiconductors, alloys, and solders.

As it is a cumulative poison, its presence in food and drugs is very dangerous. The symptoms of arsenic poisoning are vomiting, diarrhoea, tingling and possibly numbness in the limbs, and collapse. It featured in some drugs, including Salvarsan, the first specific treatment for syphilis. Its name derives from the Latin *arsenicum*.

arson malicious and wilful setting fire to property. In English law arson is covered by the Criminal Damage Act 1971. In Scotland arson is known as 'wilful fire-raising'.

art in the broadest sense, all the processes and products of human skill, imagination, and invention; the opposite of nature. In contemporary usage, definitions of art usually reflect aesthetic criteria, and the term may encompass literature, music, drama, painting, and sculpture. Popularly, the term is most commonly used to refer to the visual arts. In Western culture, aesthetic criteria introduced by the ancient Greeks still influence our perceptions and judgements of art.

Two currents of thought run through our ideas about art. In one, derived from Aristotle, art is concerned with mimesis (imitation), the representation of appearances, and gives pleasure through the accuracy and skill with which it depicts the real world. The other view, derived from Plato, holds that the artist is inspired by the Muses (or by God, or by the inner impulses, or by the collective unconscious) to express that which is beyond appearances – inner feelings, eternal truths, or the essence of the age. In the Middle Ages the term 'art' was used, chiefly in the plural, to signify a branch of learning which was regarded as an instrument of knowledge. The seven liberal arts consisted of the *trivium*, that is grammar, logic, and rhetoric, and the *quadrivium*, that is arithmetic, music, geometry, and astronomy. In the visual arts of Western civilizations, painting and sculpture have been the dominant forms for many centuries. This has not always been the case in other cultures. ◊Islamic art, for example, is one of ornament, for under the Muslim religion artists were forbidden to usurp the divine right of creation by portraying living creatures. In some cultures masks, tattoos, pottery, and metalwork have been the main forms of visual art. Recent technology has made new art forms possible, such as photography and cinema, and today electronic media have led to entirely new ways of creating and presenting visual images. See also ◊prehistoric art; the arts of ancient civilizations, for example ◊Egyptian art; indigenous art traditions, for example ◊Oceanic art; ◊medieval art; the arts of individual countries, such as ◊French art; individual movements, such as ◊Romanticism, ◊Cubism, and ◊Impressionism; and ◊painting and ◊sculpture. ▷*See feature on pp. 200–201.*

Artaud Antonin 1896–1948. French actor, theatre director, and theorist. Although his play *Les Cenci/ The Cenci* 1935 was a failure, his passionate manifestos in *Theatre of ◊Cruelty*, advocating the release of feelings usually repressed in the unconscious, have been an important influence on modern dramatists and directors, such as Brook and Grotowski.

Art Deco style in the decorative arts which influenced design and architecture. It emerged in Europe in the 1920s and continued through the 1930s, becoming particularly popular in the USA and France. A self-consciously modern style, originally called 'Jazz Modern', it is characterized by angular, geometrical patterns and bright colours, and by the use of materials such as enamel, chrome, glass, and plastic. The graphic artist Erté was a fashionable exponent.

Artemis in Greek mythology, the goddess of chastity, the young of all creatures, the Moon, and the hunt (Roman Diana). She is the twin sister of ◊Apollo and was worshipped at cult centres throughout the Greek world, one of the largest of which was at Ephesus. Her great temple there, reconstructed several times in antiquity, was one of the ◊Seven Wonders of the World.

arteriosclerosis hardening of the arteries, with thickening and loss of elasticity. It is associated with smoking, ageing, and a diet high in saturated fats. The term is used loosely as a synonym for ◊atherosclerosis.

artery vessel that carries blood from the heart to the rest of the body. It is built to withstand considerable pressure, having thick walls which contain smooth muscle fibres. During contraction of the heart muscle, arteries expand in diameter to allow for the sudden increase in pressure that occurs; the resulting ◊pulse or pressure wave can be felt at the wrist. Not all arteries carry oxygenated (oxygen-rich) blood; the pulmonary arteries convey deoxygenated (oxygen-poor) blood from the heart to the lungs. Arteries are flexible, elastic tubes, consisting of three layers, the middle of which is muscular; its rhythmic contraction aids the pumping of blood around the body. Research indicates that a typical Western diet, high in saturated fat, increases the

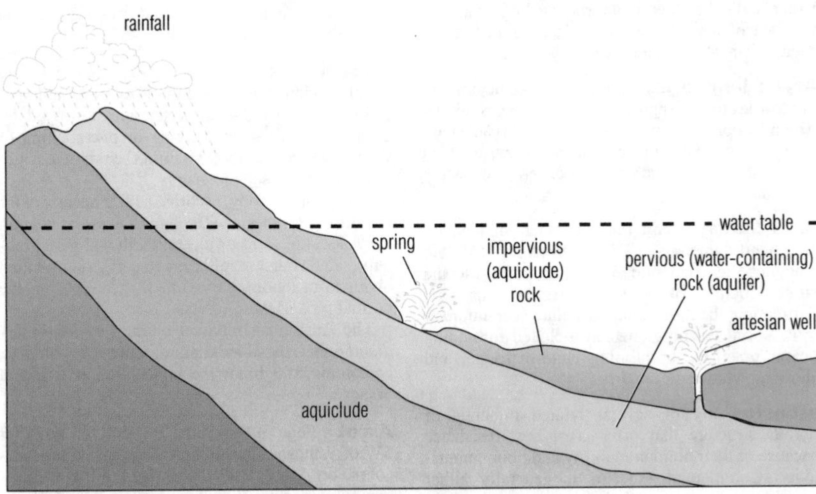

artesian well In an artesian well, water rises from an underground water-containing rock layer under its own pressure. Rain falls at one end of the water-bearing layer, or aquifer, and percolates through the layer. The layer fills with water up to the level of the water table. Water will flow from a well under its own pressure if the well head is below the level of the water table.

chances of arterial disease developing, especially in middle and old age. See ◊atherosclerosis and ◊atheroma.

artesian well well that is supplied with water rising naturally from an underground water-saturated rock layer (◊aquifer). The water rises from the aquifer under its own pressure. Such a well may be drilled into an aquifer that is confined by impermeable rocks both above and below. If the water table (the top of the region of water saturation) in that aquifer is above the level of the well head, hydrostatic pressure will force the water to the surface.

Artesian wells are often overexploited because their water is fresh and easily available, and they eventually become unreliable. There is also some concern that pollutants such as pesticides or nitrates can seep into the aquifers.

arthritis inflammation of the joints, with pain, swelling, and restricted motion. Many conditions may cause arthritis, including gout, infection, and trauma to the joint. There are three main forms of arthritis: rheumatoid arthritis, osteoarthritis, and septic arthritis.

arthropod member of the phylum Arthropoda; an invertebrate animal with jointed legs and a segmented body with a horny or chitinous casing (exoskeleton), which is shed periodically and replaced as the animal grows. Included are arachnids such as spiders and mites, as well as crustaceans, millipedes, centipedes, and insects.

Arthur lived 6th century AD. Legendary British king and hero in stories of ◊Camelot and the quest for the ◊Holy Grail. Arthur is said to have been born in Tintagel, Cornwall, and buried in Glastonbury, Somerset. He may have been a Romano-Celtic leader against pagan Saxon invaders.

The legends of Arthur and the knights of the Round Table were developed in the 12th century by Geoffrey of Monmouth, Chrétien de Troyes, and the Norman writer Wace. Later writers on the theme include the anonymous author of *Sir Gawayne and the Greene Knight* 1346, Thomas Malory, Tennyson, T H White, and Mark Twain.

Arthur Chester Alan 1830–1886. 21st president of the USA 1881–85, a Republican. In 1880 he was chosen as James ◊Garfield's vice president, and was his successor when Garfield was assassinated the following year.

artichoke either of two plants of the composite or sunflower family Compositae. The common or globe artichoke *Cynara scolymus* is native to the Mediterranean, and is a form of thistle. It is tall, with purplish blue flowers; the bracts of the unopened flower are eaten. The Jerusalem artichoke *Helianthus tuberosus* is a sunflower, native to North America. It has edible tubers, and its common name is a corruption of the Italian for sunflower, *girasole*.

articles of association in the UK, the rules governing the relationship between a registered company, its members (the shareholders), and its directors. The articles of association are deposited with the Registrar of Companies along with the memorandum of association, the document that defines the purpose of a company and the amount and different classes of share capital. In the USA the articles of association are called ***by-laws***.

artificial insemination (AI) introduction by instrument of semen from a sperm bank or donor into the female reproductive tract to bring about fertilization. Originally used by animal breeders to improve stock with sperm from high-quality males, in the 20th century it has been developed for use in humans, to help the infertile. The sperm for artificial insemination may come from the husband (AIH) or a donor (AID); an AID child is illegitimate under British law. See ◊in vitro fertilization.

artificial intelligence (AI) branch of science concerned with creating computer programs that can perform actions comparable with those of an intelligent human. Current AI research covers such areas as planning (for robot behaviour), language understanding, pattern recognition, and knowledge representation. One notably successful AI project is IBM's Deep Blue, which in 1996 was the first chess-playing computer to defeat a human grand master, the Russian Gary Kasparov.

The possibility of artificial intelligence was first proposed by the English mathematician Alan ◊Turing in 1950. Early AI programs, developed in the 1960s, attempted simulations of human intelligence or were aimed at general problem-solving techniques. By the mid-1990s, scientists were concluding that AI was more difficult to create than they had imagined. It is now thought that intelligent behaviour depends as much on the knowledge a system possesses as on its reasoning power. Present emphasis is on ◊knowledge-based systems, such as ◊expert systems, while research projects focus on ◊neural networks, which attempt to mimic the structure of the human brain.

Arthur During his term as 21st president of the USA, Chester Arthur became a determined enemy of the corrupt use of patronage to gain political support. Prior to his selection as Garfield's vice-presidential running mate, Arthur had headed an eminent law firm and was the leader of the Republican Party in New York State. *Library of Congress*

artificial respiration emergency procedure to restart breathing once it has stopped; in cases of electric shock or apparent drowning, for example, the first choice is the expired-air method, the kiss of life by mouth-to-mouth breathing until natural breathing is restored.

artificial selection in biology, selective breeding of individuals that exhibit the particular characteristics that a plant or animal breeder wishes to develop. In plants, desirable features might include resistance to disease, high yield (in crop plants), or attractive appearance. In animal breeding, selection has led to the development of particular breeds of cattle for improved meat production (such as the Aberdeen Angus) or milk production (such as Jerseys).

artillery collective term for military ◊firearms too heavy to be carried. Artillery can be mounted on tracks, wheels, ships, or aeroplanes and includes cannons and rocket launchers.

Art Nouveau in the visual arts, interior design, and architecture, a decorative style flourishing 1890–1910 and characterized by organic, sinuous patterns and ornamentations based on plant forms. In England, it appears in the illustrations of Aubrey Beardsley; in Scotland, in the interior and exterior designs of Charles Rennie Mackintosh; in France, in the glass of René Lalique and the posters of Alphonse Mucha; and in the USA, in the lamps and metalwork of Louis Comfort Tiffany.

Art Nouveau is an element in the work of many painters and graphic artists of the period, among them Edvard Munch, Gustav Klimt, Ferdinand Hodler, and even Henri de Toulouse-Lautrec, Paul Gauguin, and Vincent van Gogh.

In architecture, both interior and exterior, a new simplicity of design produced linear constructions of glass and iron which often combines with more decorative elements. Architects strongly influenced by Art Nouveau include Antonio Gaudí (Spain); Hector Guimard, who designed the entrances to the Paris Métro stations (France); and Victor Horta (Belgium).

Artois former province of N France, bounded by Flanders and Picardie and almost corresponding with the modern *département* of Pas-de-Calais. Its capital was Arras. Its Latin name *Artesium* lent its name to the artesian well first sunk at Lillers 1126.

Arts and Crafts movement English social and aesthetic movement that stressed the importance of crafts and the dignity of labour. In 1861 a group of artists headed by William ◊Morris founded the design company Morris, Marshall, Faulkner and Company (known as 'the Firm'). Their designs – by such artists as Ford Madox Brown, William Holman Hunt, Philip Webb, Dante Gabriel Rossetti, Edward Burne-Jones, and Morris himself – were for stained glass, furniture, fabrics, wallpaper, and so on. The movement was supported by architect A W Pugin and critic John Ruskin and expressed a rejection of Victorian industrialization and mass production, and a nostalgic desire to return to a medieval way of life. The Arts and Crafts movement influenced Art Nouveau and, less directly, the Bauhaus school of design.

Arts Council of Great Britain former name of the UK organization that aids music, drama, and visual arts with government funds. In April 1994 it was divided into the Arts Council of England, the Scottish Arts Council, and the Arts Council of Wales; the latter two became autonomous at that time, and are funded directly by the Scottish Office and Welsh Office respectively.

The Councils' main objectives are to develop and improve the knowledge, understanding, and practice of the arts; to increase their accessibility to the

‘Art Nouveau ... was brought up in Germany, fostered by what are called decadent artists. These are artists whose works are a mixture of beer and sausage and Aubrey Beardsley.’

On ART NOUVEAU
Maurice Baring
Round the World in Any Number of Days

He that will write well in any tongue must follow the counsel of Aristotle: to speak as the common people do, to think as wise men do.

Roger Ascham
Toxophilus

public, and to advise and cooperate with Government departments, local authorities, and other organizations to achieve these objectives.

The Arts Council of England distributes an annual grant from the Department of National Heritage; the grant for 1995–6 was £191.1 million. The 1995–6 grant for the Scottish Arts Council was £24.47 million, and for the Arts Council of Wales was £14.19 million. The Arts Council of Northern Ireland is funded by the Department of Education for Northern Ireland; its 1995–6 grant was £6.66 million.

The Arts Councils receive one-fifth of the proceeds of the National Lottery that are allocated to 'good causes'.

Aruba island in the Caribbean, the westernmost of the Lesser Antilles; an overseas territory of the Netherlands
area 193 sq km/75 sq mi
population (1991) 68,900 (half of Indian descent)
language Dutch (official), Papiamento (a Creole language)
economy the economy is based largely on tourism
history Part of the Dutch West Indies from 1828, and part of the Netherlands Antilles from 1845, Aruba obtained separate status from the other Netherlands Antilles 1986 and has full internal autonomy. It was due to become fully independent 1996, but a 1990 agreement deleted references to eventual independence.

arum any of a group of mainly European plants with narrow leaves and a single, usually white, special leaf (spathe) surrounding the spike of tiny flowers. The ornamental arum called the trumpet lily (*Zantedeschia aethiopica*) is a native of South Africa. The species *Arum maculatum*, known as cuckoopint or lords-and-ladies, is a common British hedgerow plant.

Arunachal Pradesh state of India, in the Himalayas on the borders of Tibet and Myanmar
area 83,700 sq km/32,316 sq mi
capital Itanagar
industries rubber, coffee, spices, fruit, timber
population (1994 est) 965,000; over 80 ethnic groups
language 50 different dialects
history formerly part of the state of Assam, it became a state of India 1987.

Arup Ove 1895–1988. Danish engineer. He founded the British-based architectural practice, Arup Associates, a firm noted for the considered and elegant manner in which modern materials, especially concrete, are employed in its designs. Set up 1963, the practice represented Arup's ideal of interdisciplinary cooperation. Examples of its work are at Somerville College, Oxford, 1958–62, and Corpus Christi, Cambridge, 1961–64.

Aryan the hypothetical parent language of an ancient people who are believed to have lived between central Asia and E Europe and to have reached Persia and India in one direction and Europe in another, some time in the 2nd century BC, diversifying into the various ◊Indo-European language speakers of later times. In ◊Nazi Germany Hitler and other theorists erroneously propagated the idea of the Aryans as a white-skinned, blue-eyed, fair-haired master race.

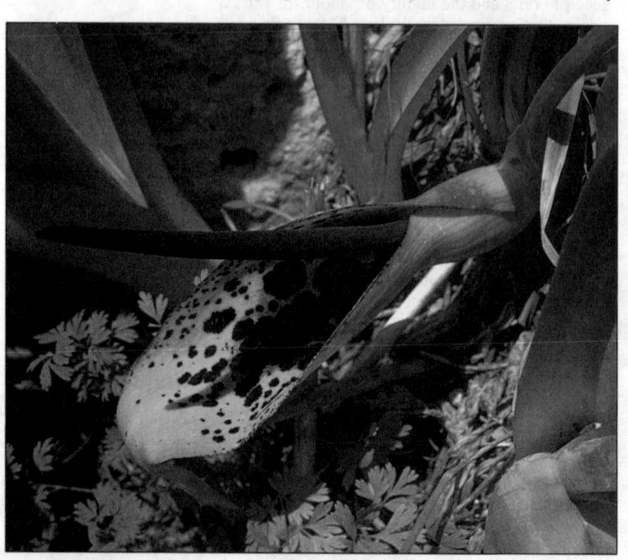

arum *Arum dioscoridis* comes from the Mediterranean region, where arum lilies grow in abundance. What appears to be a single flower is in fact a flower head, the spadix, bearing separate rings of male and female flowers enclosed in a leaflike spathe. *Premaphotos Wildlife*

Aryan languages 19th-century name for the ◊Indo-European languages; the languages of the Aryan peoples of India. The name Aryan is no longer used by language scholars because of its association with the Nazi concept of white supremacy.

Arya Samaj Hindu religious sect founded by Dayanand Saraswati (1825–1888) about 1875. He renounced idol worship and urged a return to the purer principles of the Vedas (Hindu scriptures). For its time the movement was quite revolutionary in its social teachings, which included forbidding ◊caste practices, prohibiting child-marriage, and allowing widows to remarry.

asbestos any of several related minerals of fibrous structure that offer great heat resistance because of their nonflammability and poor conductivity. Commercial asbestos is generally either made from serpentine ('white' asbestos) or from sodium iron silicate ('blue' asbestos). The fibres are woven together or bound by an inert material. Over time the fibres can work loose and, because they are small enough to float freely in the air or be inhaled, asbestos usage is now strictly controlled.

Exposure to asbestos is a recognized cause of industrial cancer (mesothelioma), especially in the 'blue' form (from South Africa), rather than the more common 'white'. Asbestosis is a chronic lung inflammation caused by asbestos dust.

Ascension British island of volcanic origin in the S Atlantic, a dependency of ◊St Helena since 1922; area 88 sq km/34 sq mi; population (1993) 1,117 (excluding military personnel). The chief settlement is Georgetown.

A Portuguese navigator landed there on Ascension Day 1501, but it remained uninhabited until occupied by Britain 1815. There are sea turtles and sooty terns. It is known for its role as a staging post to the Falkland Islands, and is chiefly used as a relay and cable station.

Ascension Day or ***Holy Thursday*** in the Christian calendar, the feast day commemorating Jesus' ascension into heaven. It is the 40th day after Easter.

asceticism the renunciation of physical pleasure, for example, in eating, drinking, sexuality, and human company. Often for religious reasons, discomfort or pain may be sought.

Ascham Roger c. 1515–1568. English scholar and royal tutor. He wrote *Toxophilus* 1545, a treatise on archery (King Henry VIII's favourite sport). Written in dialogue form, it provided the model for later treatises, including *The Compleat Angler*. His chief work is *The Scholemaster*, published by his widow 1570, a humane and attractively written treatise on education.

In 1548 Ascham was appointed tutor to Princess Elizabeth. He retained favour under Edward VI and Queen Mary (despite his Protestant views), and returned to Elizabeth's service as her secretary after she became queen.

ASCII (acronym for ***American standard code for information interchange***) in computing, a coding system in which numbers are assigned to letters, digits, and punctuation symbols. Although computers work in code based on the ◊binary number system, ASCII numbers are usually quoted as decimal or ◊hexadecimal numbers. For example, the decimal number 45 (binary 0101101) represents a hyphen, and 65 (binary 1000001) a capital A. The first 32 codes are used for control functions, such as carriage return and backspace.

Strictly speaking, ASCII is a 7-bit binary code, allowing 128 different characters to be represented, but an eighth bit is often used to provide ◊parity or to allow for extra characters. The system is widely used for the storage of text and for the transmission of data between computers.

Asclepius in Greek mythology, the god of medicine (Roman Aesculapius) and son of ◊Apollo. His emblem was a winged staff with two snakes coiled around it, since snakes appeared to renew life by shedding their skin. His cult originated in Thessaly in N Greece, but the major sanctuary of the classical period was at ◊Epidaurus. Patients slept in his temple overnight, and treatment was based on the visions they saw in their sleep.

ascorbic acid $C_6H_8O_6$ or ***vitamin C*** a relatively simple organic acid found in citrus fruits and vegetables. It is soluble in water and destroyed by prolonged boiling, so soaking or overcooking of vegetables reduces their vitamin C content. Lack of ascorbic acid results in scurvy.

In the human body, ascorbic acid is necessary for the correct synthesis of ◊collagen. Lack of vitamin C causes skin sores or ulcers, tooth and gum problems, and burst capillaries (scurvy symptoms) owing to an abnormal type of collagen replacing the normal type in these tissues.

The Australian billygoat plum, *Terminalia ferdiandiana*, is the richest natural source of vitamin C, containing 100 times the concentration found in oranges.

Ascot village in Berkshire, England 9.5 km/6 mi SW of Windsor. Queen Anne established the racecourse on Ascot Heath 1711, and the Royal Ascot meeting is a social as well as a sporting event. Horse races include the Gold Cup, Ascot Stakes, Coventry Stakes, and King George VI and Queen Elizabeth Stakes.

ASEAN acronym for ◊***Association of South East Asian Nations***.

asexual reproduction in biology, reproduction that does not involve the manufacture and fusion of sex cells, nor the necessity for two parents. The process carries a clear advantage in that there is no need to search for a mate nor to develop complex pollinating mechanisms; every asexual organism can reproduce on its own. Asexual reproduction can therefore lead to a rapid population build-up.

In evolutionary terms, the disadvantage of asexual reproduction arises from the fact that only identical individuals, or clones, are produced – there is no variation.

In the field of horticulture, where standardized production is needed, this is useful, but in the wild, an asexual population that cannot adapt to a changing environment or evolve defences against a new disease is at risk of extinction. Many asexually

asexual reproduction Asexual reproduction is the simplest form of reproduction, occurring in many simple plants and animals. Binary fission, shown here occurring in an amoeba, is one of a number of asexual reproduction processes

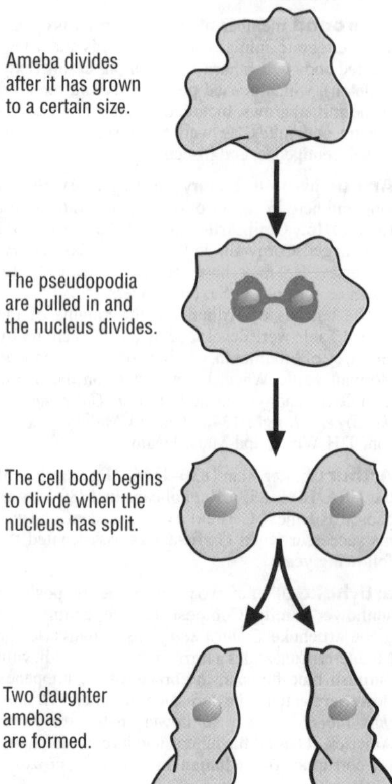
Ameba divides after it has grown to a certain size.
The pseudopodia are pulled in and the nucleus divides.
The cell body begins to divide when the nucleus has split.
Two daughter amebas are formed.

reproducing organisms are therefore capable of reproducing sexually as well.

Asexual processes include ◊binary fission, in which the parent organism splits into two or more 'daughter' organisms, and ◊budding, in which a new organism is formed initially as an outgrowth of the parent organism. The asexual reproduction of spores, as in ferns and mosses, is also common and many plants reproduce asexually by means of runners, rhizomes, bulbs, and corms; see also ◊vegetative reproduction.

Asgard in Scandinavian mythology, the home of the gods and of the heroes who died in battle. One of its halls was ◊Valhalla. Asgard was reached by a bridge called Bifrost, the rainbow.

ash any tree of the worldwide genus *Fraxinus*, belonging to the olive family Oleaceae, with winged fruits. The ◊***mountain ash*** or ***rowan*** belongs to the family Rosaceae. *F. excelsior* is the European species; its timber is of importance.

Ashanti or ***Asante*** region of Ghana, W Africa; area 25,100 sq km/9,700 sq mi; population (1984) 2,089,683. Kumasi is the capital. Most Ashanti are cultivators and the main crop is cocoa, but the region is also noted for its metalwork and textiles. For more than 200 years Ashanti was an independent kingdom.

During the 19th century the Ashanti and the British fought for control of trade in West Africa. The British sent four expeditions against the Ashanti and formally annexed their country 1901. Otomfuo Sir Osei Agyeman, nephew of the deposed king, Prempeh I, was made head of the re-established Ashanti confederation 1935 as Prempeh II. The Golden Stool (actually a chair), symbol of the Ashanti peoples since the 17th century, was returned to Kumasi 1935 (the rest of the Ashanti treasure is in the British Museum). The Asantahene (King of the Ashanti) still holds ceremonies in which this stool is ceremonially paraded.

Ashbee Charles Robert 1863–1942. English designer, architect, and writer. He was one of the major figures of the ◊Arts and Crafts movement. He founded a Guild and School of Handicraft in the East End of London 1888, but later modified his views, accepting the importance of machinery and design for industry.

Ashbery John Lawrence 1927– . US poet and art critic. His collections of poetry – including *Self-Portrait in a Convex Mirror* 1975, which won a Pulitzer prize – are distinguished by their exuberant artifice and strong visual and musical elements. His most experimental work, *Europe* (in *The Tennis Court Oath* 1962), uses montage and collage methods derived from Cubist painting. Other volumes include *Some Trees* 1956, *Houseboat Days* 1977, *As We Know* 1979, *A Wave* 1984, and *And the Stars Were Shining* 1994.

Ashcan School group of US Realist painters active about 1908–14. The School's central figures were Robert Henri, George Luks, William Glackens, Everett Shinn (1876–1953), and John Sloan, all former members of The Eight (a group of realist painters who exhibited together 1908 outside of the official circuit). Their subjects were taken from city life, depicting in particular the poor and the outcast. They organized the Armory Show of 1913, which introduced modern European art to the USA.

ash Ash is the name given to a few northern European trees and shrubs of the *Fraxinus* genus. They belong to the same family as the olive, lilac, and jasmine. Ashes generally have a compound leaf with leaflets arranged on either side of a stem and a winged fruit.

Ashcroft The English actress Peggy Ashcroft. In addition to her accomplishments in Shakespearean roles on stage, she appeared in films, notably *The Thirty-Nine Steps* 1935 and *A Passage to India* (for which she won an Academy Award) 1984. *Corbis*

Ashcroft Peggy 1907–1991. English actress. Her Shakespearean roles included Desdemona in *Othello* (with Paul Robeson) and Juliet in *Romeo and Juliet* 1935 (with Laurence Olivier and John Gielgud), and she appeared in the British TV play *Caught on a Train* 1980 (BAFTA award), the series *The Jewel in the Crown* 1984, and the film *A Passage to India* 1984.

Ashdod deep-water port of Israel, on the Mediterranean 32 km/20 mi S of Tel-Aviv, which it superseded 1965; population (1994) 120,100. It stands on the site of the ancient Philistine site of Ashkelon.

Ashdown Paddy (Jeremy John Durham) 1941– . English politician, leader of the merged Social and Liberal Democrats 1988–99. He served in the Royal Marines as a commando, and was a member of the Diplomatic Service 1971–76. He became a Liberal member of Parliament 1983 for the constituency of Yeovil, Somerset. In the 1997 general election his party significantly increased its number of Parliamentary seats.

Ashes, the cricket trophy theoretically held by the winners in the England–Australia test series.

The trophy is permanently held at ◊Lord's cricket ground no matter who wins the series. It is an urn containing the ashes of stumps and bails used in a match when England toured Australia 1882–83. The urn was given to the England captain Ivo Bligh by a group of Melbourne women. The action followed the appearance of an obituary notice in the *Sporting Times* the previous summer announcing the 'death' of English cricket after defeat by the Australians in the Oval test match.

Ashgabat formerly ***Ashkhabad*** capital of Turkmenistan; population (1990) 407,000. The spelling was changed 1992 to reflect the Turkmen origin of the name. Industries include glass, carpets ('Bukhara' carpets are made here), and cotton; the spectacular natural setting has been used by the film-making industry.

Ashikaga in Japanese history, the family who held the office of ◊shogun 1338–1573, a period of civil wars. Nō drama evolved under the patronage of Ashikaga shoguns. Relations with China improved intermittently and there was trade with Korea. The last (15th) Ashikaga shogun was ousted by Oda Nobunaga at the start of the ◊Momoyama period. The Ashikaga belonged to the Minamoto clan.

Ashkenazi (plural ***Ashkenazim***) any Jew of German or E European descent, as opposed to a Sephardi, of Spanish, Portuguese, or N African descent.

Ashkenazim developed European customs and the ◊Yiddish language during the centuries they remained outside the influence of the Middle East. They were the ◊Zionists who resettled Palestine and who now run the government of Israel, resettling Jews from anywhere in the world.

Ashkenazy Vladimir 1937– . Russian-born pianist and conductor. He was music director of the Royal Philharmonic, London, from 1987 and of the Berlin Radio Symphony Orchestra from 1989. He excels in Rachmaninov, Prokofiev, and Liszt.

After studying in Moscow, he toured the USA 1958. In 1962 he was joint winner of the Tchaikovsky Competition with John Ogdon. He settled in England 1963 and moved to Iceland 1968.

Ashley Laura, (born Mountney) 1925–1985. Welsh designer. She established and gave her name to a Neo-Victorian country style in clothes and furnishings manufactured by her company from 1953. She founded a highly successful international chain of shops.

Ashmole Elias 1617–1692. English antiquary. His collection forms the basis of the Ashmolean Museum, Oxford, England. He wrote books on alchemy, astrology, and on antiquarian subjects, and amassed a fine library and a collection of curiosities, both of which he presented to Oxford University 1682. His collection was housed in the 'Old Ashmolean' (built 1679–83); the present Ashmolean Museum was erected 1897.

Ashmore and Cartier Islands group of uninhabited Australian islands comprising Middle, East, and West Islands (the Ashmores), and Cartier Island, in the Indian Ocean, about 190 km/120 mi off the northwest coast of Australia; area 5 sq km/2 sq mi. They were transferred to the authority of Australia by Britain 1931. Formerly administered as part of the Northern Territory, they became a separate territory 1978. West Ashmore has an automated weather station. Ashmore reef was declared a national nature reserve 1983.

Ashton Frederick William Mallandaine 1904–1988. English choreographer and dancer. He was director of the Royal Ballet, London, 1963–70. He studied with Marie Rambert before joining the Sadler's Wells (now Royal) Ballet 1935 as chief choreographer. His choreography is marked by a soft, pliant, classical lyricism. His many works and long association with Margot Fonteyn, for whom he created her most famous roles, contributed to the worldwide reputation of British ballet and to the popularity of ballet in the mid-20th century. His major works include *Façade* 1931 and *Les Rendezvous* 1933 for Rambert; *Symphonic Variations* 1946, *Cinderella* 1948, *Ondine* 1958, *La Fille mal*

Ashikaga Portrait of the 14th-century Japanese shogun Ashikaga Yoshiteru, wearing a ceremonial hat and court robe. The shoguns, originally military leaders, became hereditary military rulers 1192–1868. The Ashikaga shogunate was in power 1336–1573, following the Minamoto and preceding the Tokugawa shogunates. *Corbis*

Asia is not going to be civilized after the methods of the West. There is too much Asia and she is too old.

On Asia
Rudyard Kipling
Life's Handicap

gardée 1960, *Marguerite and Armand* – for Margot Fonteyn and Rudolf Nureyev – 1963, and *A Month in the Country* 1976.

Ash Wednesday first day of Lent, the period in the Christian calendar leading up to Easter; in the Roman Catholic Church the foreheads of the congregation are marked with a cross in ash, as a sign of penitence.

Asia largest of the continents, occupying one-third of the total land surface of the world. The origin of the name is unknown, though it seems probable that it was at first used with a restricted local application, gradually extended to the whole continent.
area 44,000,000 sq km/17,000,000 sq mi
largest cities (population over 5 million) Tokyo, Shanghai, Osaka, Beijing, Seoul, Calcutta, Bombay, Jakarta, Bangkok, Tehran, Hong Kong, Delhi, Tianjin, Karachi
features Mount Everest, at 8,872 m/29,118 ft is the world's highest mountain; Dead Sea at −394 m/−1,293 ft is the world's lowest point below sea level; rivers (over 3,200 km/2,000 mi) include Chiang Jiang (Yangtze), Huang He (Yellow River), Ob-Irtysh, Amur, Lena, Mekong, Yenisei; lakes (over 18,000 sq km/7,000 sq mi) include Caspian Sea (the largest lake in the world), Aral Sea, Baikal (largest freshwater lake in Eurasia), Balkhash; deserts include the Gobi, Takla Makan, Syrian Desert, Arabian Desert, Negev
physical lying in the eastern hemisphere, Asia extends from the Arctic Circle to just over 10° S of the equator. The Asian mainland, which forms the greater part of the Eurasian continent, lies entirely in the northern hemisphere and stretches from Cape Chelyubinsk at its northern extremity to Cape Piai at the southern tip of the Malay Peninsula. From Dezhneva Cape in the E, the mainland extends W over more than 165° longitude to Cape Baba in Turkey.

Asia Minor historical name for ***Anatolia***, the Asian part of Turkey.

Assassination has never changed the history of the world.

On assassination
Benjamin Disraeli,
Speech in the House of Commons
1 May 1865

Asian Republics, Central see ◊Central Asian Republics.

Asimov Isaac 1920–1992. Russian-born US author and editor of science fiction and nonfiction. He published more than 400 books, including his science-fiction novels *I, Robot* 1950 and the *Foundation* trilogy 1951–53, continued in *Foundation's Edge* 1983. His two-volume work *The Intelligent Man's Guide to Science* 1960 gained critical acclaim.

Asmara or ***Asmera*** capital of Eritrea; 64 km/40 mi SW of Massawa on the Red Sea; population (1991) 367,100. Products include beer, clothes, and textiles. It has a naval school. The population is half Christian and half Muslim.

It became the capital of the Italian colony of Eritrea 1900, and was the base for the Italian invasion of Ethiopia 1935. It was under British administration 1941–52 until the federation of Eritrea and Ethiopia formed. In 1974 unrest here precipitated the end of the Ethiopian Empire.

Asimov
Science-fiction author Isaac Asimov. Asimov published more than 400 books and gained much of his recognition through his adeptness at presenting science to the general public. He won the Hugo award for his *Foundation* trilogy published 1951–53. *Image Select (UK) Ltd*

Aśoka lived c. 273–228 BC. ◊Mauryan emperor of India c. 268–232 BC, the greatest of the Mauryan rulers. He inherited an empire covering most of north and south-central India which, at its height, had a population of at least 30 million, with its capital at ◊Pataliputra. A devout Buddhist, he renounced militarism and concentrated on establishing an efficient administration with a large standing army and a secret police.

asp any of several venomous snakes, including *Vipera aspis* of S Europe, allied to the adder, and the Egyptian cobra *Naja haje*.

asparagus any plant of the genus *Asparagus*, family Liliaceae, with small scalelike leaves and many needlelike branches. Native to Eurasia, *A. officinalis* is cultivated, and the young shoots are eaten as a vegetable.

aspartame noncarbohydrate sweetener used in foods under the tradename Nutrasweet. It is about 200 times as sweet as sugar and, unlike saccharine, has no aftertaste.

The aspartame molecule consists of two amino acids (aspartic acid and phenylalanine) linked by a methylene ($-CH_2-$) group. It breaks down slowly at room temperature and rapidly at higher temperatures. It is not suitable for people who suffer from ◊phenylketonuria.

aspen any of several species of ◊poplar tree, genus *Populus*. The European quaking aspen *P. tremula* has flattened leafstalks that cause the leaves to flutter with every breeze. The soft, light-coloured wood is used for matches and paper pulp.

asphalt mineral mixture containing semisolid brown or black ◊bitumen, used in the construction industry. Asphalt is mixed with rock chips to form paving material, and the purer varieties are used for insulating material and for waterproofing masonry. It can be produced artificially by the distillation of ◊petroleum.

The availability of recycled coloured glass led 1988 to the invention of glassphalt, asphalt that is 15% crushed glass. It is used to pave roads in New York.

Considerable natural deposits of asphalt occur around the Dead Sea and in the Philippines, Cuba, Venezuela, and Trinidad. Bituminous limestone occurs at Neufchâtel, France.

asphodel either of two related Old World genera (*Asphodeline* and *Asphodelus*) of plants of the lily family Liliaceae. *Asphodelus albus*, the white asphodel or king's spear, is found in Italy and Greece, sometimes covering large areas, and providing grazing for sheep. *Asphodeline lutea* is the yellow asphodel.

asphyxia suffocation; a lack of oxygen that produces a potentially lethal build-up of carbon dioxide waste in the tissues.

Asphyxia may arise from any one of a number of causes, including inhalation of smoke or poisonous gases, obstruction of the windpipe (by water, food, vomit, or a foreign object), strangulation, or smothering. If it is not quickly relieved, brain damage or death ensues.

aspidistra Asiatic plant of the genus *Aspidistra* of the lily family Liliaceae. The Chinese *A. elatior* has broad, lanceolate leaves and, like all members of the genus, grows well in warm indoor conditions.

aspirin acetylsalicylic acid, a popular pain-relieving drug (◊analgesic) developed in the late 19th century as a household remedy for aches and pains. It relieves pain and reduces inflammation and fever. It is derived from the white willow tree *Salix alba*, and is the world's most widely used drug.

Aspirin was first refined from salicylic acid by German chemist Felix Hoffman, and marketed 1899. Although salicylic acid occurs naturally in willow bark (and has been used for pain relief since 1763) the acetyl derivative is less bitter and less likely to cause vomiting.

Regular use of aspirin is recommended for people at increased risk of heart attack, thrombosis, and some kinds of stroke. However, aspirin may cause stomach bleeding, kidney damage, and hearing defects. It is no longer considered suitable for children under 12 because of a suspected link with a rare disease, ◊Reye's syndrome (consequently, acetaminophen is often substituted).

Asquith Herbert Henry, 1st Earl of Oxford and Asquith 1852–1928. British Liberal politician, prime minister 1908–16. As chancellor of the Exchequer he introduced old-age pensions 1908. He limited the powers of the House of Lords and attempted to give Ireland Home Rule.

Asquith was born in Yorkshire. Elected a member of Parliament 1886, he was home secretary in Gladstone's 1892–95 government. He was chancellor of the Exchequer 1905–08 and succeeded Campbell-Bannerman as prime minister. Forcing through the radical budget of his chancellor ◊Lloyd George led him into two elections 1910, which resulted in the Parliament Act 1911, limiting the right of the Lords to veto legislation. His endeavours to pass the Home Rule for Ireland Bill led to the Curragh 'Mutiny', in which British forces refused to take part in forcing Protestant Ulster to participate in Home Rule, and incipient civil war. Unity was re-established by the outbreak of World War I 1914, and a coalition government was formed May 1915. However, his attitude of 'wait and see' was not adapted to all-out war, and in Dec 1916 he was replaced by Lloyd George.

ass any of several horselike, odd-toed, hoofed mammals of the genus *Equus*, family Equidae. Species include the African wild ass *E. asinus*, and the Asian wild ass *E. hemionus*. They differ from horses in their smaller size, larger ears, tufted tail, and characteristic bray. Donkeys and burros are domesticated asses.

Assad Hafez al 1930– . Syrian Ba'athist politician, president from 1971. He became prime minister after a bloodless military coup 1970, and the following year was the first president to be elected by popular vote. Having suppressed dissent, he was re-elected 1978, 1985, and 1991. He is a Shia (Alawite) Muslim.

He has ruthlessly suppressed domestic opposition, and was Iran's only major Arab ally in its war against Iraq. He steadfastly pursued military parity with Israel, and made himself a key player in any settlement of the Lebanese civil war or Middle East conflict generally. His support for United Nations action against Iraq following its invasion of Kuwait 1990 raised his international standing. In 1995, following intense US diplomatic pressure, he was close to reaching a mutual peace agreement with Israel. However, the assassination of Yitzhak Rabin Nov 1995 and the return of a Likud-led government in Israel seriously threatened the peace process.

Assam state of NE India
area 78,400 sq km/30,262 sq mi
capital Dispur
towns and cities Guwahati, Dibrugarh, Silchar
industries half of India's tea is grown and half its oil produced here; rice, jute, sugar, cotton, coal, petrochemicals, paper, cement
population (1994 est) 24,200,000, including 12 million Assamese (Hindus), 5 million Bengalis (chiefly Muslim immigrants from Bangladesh), Nepalis, and 2 million indigenous people (Christian and traditional religions)
language Assamese
history a thriving region from 1000 BC, Assam migrants came from China and Myanmar (Burma). After Burmese invasion 1826, Britain took control and made Assam a separate province 1874; it was included in the Dominion of India, except for most of the Muslim district of Silhet, which went to Pakistan 1947. Ethnic unrest started in the 1960s when Assamese was declared the official language. After protests, the Gara, Khasi, and Jainitia tribal hill districts became the state of Meghalaya 1971; the Mizo hill district became the Union Territory of Mizoram 1972. There were massacres of Muslim Bengalis by Hindus 1983. In 1987 members of the Bodo ethnic group began fighting for a separate homeland. In the early 1990s the Marxist-militant United Liberation Front of Assam (ULFA), which had extorted payments from tea-exporting companies, spearheaded a campaign of separatist terrorist violence.

assassination murder, usually of a political, royal, or public person. The term derives from the order of the Assassins, a Muslim sect that, in the 11th and 12th centuries, murdered officials to further its political ends.

assay in chemistry, the determination of the quantity of a given substance present in a sample.

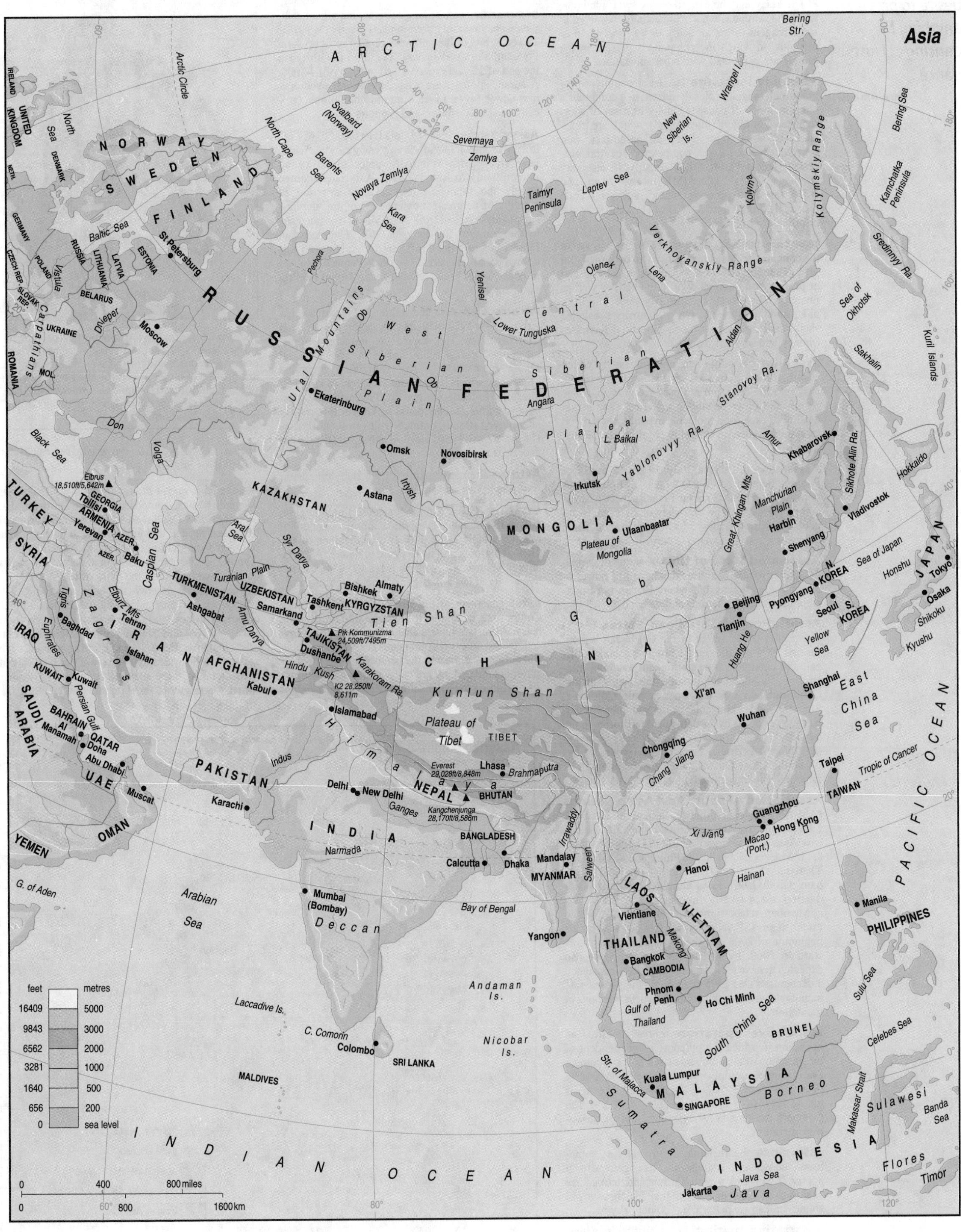
Asia
ARCTIC OCEAN
RUSSIAN FEDERATION
NORWAY
SWEDEN
FINLAND
KAZAKHSTAN
MONGOLIA
CHINA
INDIA
PAKISTAN
AFGHANISTAN
IRAN
TURKMENISTAN
UZBEKISTAN
KYRGYZSTAN
TAJIKISTAN
NEPAL
BHUTAN
BANGLADESH
MYANMAR
THAILAND
LAOS
VIETNAM
CAMBODIA
MALAYSIA
INDONESIA
PHILIPPINES
JAPAN
N. KOREA
S. KOREA
TAIWAN
BRUNEI
SINGAPORE
SRI LANKA
MALDIVES
OMAN
UAE
YEMEN
SAUDI ARABIA
QATAR
BAHRAIN
KUWAIT
IRAQ
SYRIA
TURKEY
GEORGIA
ARMENIA
AZER.
UKRAINE
BELARUS
MOL.
ROMANIA
ESTONIA
LATVIA
LITHUANIA
RUSSIA
POLAND
CZECH REP.
SLOVAK REP.
GERMANY
NETH.
DENMARK
UNITED KINGDOM
IRELAND
Moscow
St Petersburg
Ekaterinburg
Omsk
Novosibirsk
Astana
Irkutsk
Ulaanbaatar
Khabarovsk
Vladivostok
Harbin
Shenyang
Beijing
Tianjin
Pyongyang
Seoul
Tokyo
Osaka
Xi'an
Shanghai
Wuhan
Chongqing
Taipei
Guangzhou
Hong Kong
Macao (Port.)
Hanoi
Vientiane
Bangkok
Phnom Penh
Ho Chi Minh
Yangon
Mandalay
Dhaka
Calcutta
Lhasa
Delhi
New Delhi
Mumbai (Bombay)
Colombo
Karachi
Islamabad
Kabul
Dushanbe
Tashkent
Samarkand
Bishkek
Almaty
Ashgabat
Tehran
Isfahan
Baghdad
Kuwait
Al Manamah
Doha
Abu Dhabi
Muscat
Baku
Yerevan
Tbilisi
Kuala Lumpur
Jakarta
Manila
Elbrus 18,510ft/5,642m
Pik Kommunizma 24,509ft/7495m
K2 28,250ft/8,611m
Everest 29,028ft/8,848m
Kangchenjunga 28,170ft/8,586m
Bering Str.
Bering Sea
Wrangel I.
New Siberian Is.
Severnaya Zemlya
Svalbard (Norway)
North Cape
Barents Sea
Novaya Zemlya
Kara Sea
Taimyr Peninsula
Laptev Sea
Kolyma
Kolymskiy Range
Kamchatka Peninsula
Sredinnyy Ra.
Verkhoyanskiy Range
Olenek
Lena
Sea of Okhotsk
Kuril Islands
Sakhalin
Aldan
Stanovoy Ra.
Central Siberian Plateau
Lower Tunguska
Angara
L. Baikal
Yablonovyy Ra.
Amur
Sikhote Alin Ra.
Hokkaido
Honshu
Shikoku
Kyushu
Sea of Japan
Yellow Sea
East China Sea
Manchurian Plain
Great Khingan Mts.
Plateau of Mongolia
Gobi
Huang He
Chang Jiang
Xi Jiang
Tropic of Cancer
PACIFIC OCEAN
Hainan
Arctic Circle
North Sea
Baltic Sea
Vistula
Pechora
Ural Mountains
Ob
West Siberian Plain
Yenisei
Irtysh
Dnieper
Carpathians
Don
Volga
Black Sea
Caspian Sea
Aral Sea
Syr Darya
Amu Darya
Turanian Plain
Tien Shan
Elburz Mts
Zagros
Tigris
Euphrates
Persian Gulf
Hindu Kush
Karakoram Ra.
Kunlun Shan
Plateau of Tibet
TIBET
Himalaya
Brahmaputra
Indus
Ganges
Narmada
Irrawaddy
Salween
Mekong
Deccan
G. of Aden
Arabian Sea
Bay of Bengal
Andaman Is.
Nicobar Is.
Laccadive Is.
C. Comorin
Gulf of Thailand
South China Sea
Sulu Sea
Celebes Sea
Str. of Malacca
Sumatra
Borneo
Sulawesi
Makassar Strait
Banda Sea
Java
Java Sea
Flores
Timor
INDIAN OCEAN
feet metres
16409 5000
9843 3000
6562 2000
3281 1000
1640 500
656 200
0 sea level
0 400 800 miles
0 800 1600 km

I have no desire to prove anything by dancing ... I just dance.

FRED ASTAIRE

Usually it refers to determining the purity of precious metals.

The assay may be carried out by 'wet' methods, when the sample is wholly or partially dissolved in some reagent (often an acid), or by 'dry' or 'fire' methods, in which the compounds present in the sample are combined with other substances.

assembly language low-level computer-programming language closely related to a computer's internal codes. It consists chiefly of a set of short sequences of letters (mnemonics), which are translated, by a program called an assembler, into ◊machine code for the computer's ◊central processing unit (CPU) to follow directly. In assembly language, for example, 'JMP' means 'jump' and 'LDA' means 'load accumulator'. Assembly code is used by programmers who need to write very fast or efficient programs.

asset in accounting, anything owned by or owed to the company that is either cash or can be turned into cash. The term covers physical assets such as land or property of a company or individual, as well as financial assets such as cash, payments due from bills, and investments. On a company's balance sheet, total assets must be equal to total liabilities (money and services owed).

assimilation in animals, the process by which absorbed food molecules, circulating in the blood, pass into the cells and are used for growth, tissue repair, and other metabolic activities. The actual destiny of each food molecule depends not only on its type, but also on the body requirements at that time.

Assisi town in Umbria, Italy, 19 km/12 mi SE of Perugia; population (1991) 24,600. St Francis was born here and is buried in the Franciscan monastery, completed 1253. The churches of St Francis are adorned with frescoes by Giotto, Cimabue, and others.

Associated State of the UK status of certain ◊Commonwealth countries that have full power of internal government, but where Britain is responsible for external relations and defence.

Association of Caribbean States (ACS) association of 25 states in the Caribbean region, formed 1994 in Colombia to promote social, political, and economic cooperation and eventual integration. Its members include the states of the Caribbean and Central America plus Colombia, Surinam, and Venezuela. Associate membership has been adopted by 12 dependent territories in the region. Its creation was seen largely as a reaction to the ◊North American Free Trade Agreement between the USA, Canada, and Mexico, although its far smaller market raised doubts about its vitality.

Association of South East Asian Nations (ASEAN) regional alliance formed in Bangkok 1967; it took over the nonmilitary role of the Southeast Asia Treaty Organization 1975. Its members are Indonesia, Malaysia, the Philippines, Singapore, Thailand, (from 1984) Brunei, (from 1995) Vietnam, (from 1997) Laos and Myanmar; its headquarters are in Jakarta, Indonesia.

Member states signed an agreement 1992 to establish an ASEAN free trade area (AFTA) by the beginning of 2008; the date was later brought forward to 2000, by which time Cambodia is also expected to have joined the alliance. Leaders signed a declaration Dec 1995 prohibiting the possession, manufacture, and acquisition of nuclear weapons in the region.

associative operation in mathematics, an operation in which the outcome is independent of the grouping of the numbers or symbols concerned. For example, multiplication is associative, as $4 \times (3 \times 2) = (4 \times 3) \times 2 = 24$; however, division is not, as $12 \div (4 \div 2) = 6$, but $(12 \div 4) \div 2 = 1.5$. Compare ◊commutative operation and ◊distributive operation.

assonance the matching of vowel (or, sometimes, consonant) sounds in a line, generally in poetry. 'Load' and 'moat', 'farther' and 'harder' are examples of assonance, since they match in vowel sounds and stress pattern, but do not ◊rhyme.

assortative mating in population genetics, selective mating in a population between individuals that are genetically related or have similar characteristics. If sufficiently consistent, assortative mating can theoretically result in the evolution of new species without geographical isolation.

assurance form of long-term saving where individuals pay monthly premiums, typically over 10 or 25 years, and at the end receive a large lump sum. For example, a person may save £50 a month and at the end of 25 years receive a lump sum of £40,000. Assurance policies are offered by assurance companies which invest savers' monthly premiums, typically in stocks, shares, and property.

Assyria empire in the Middle East c. 2500–612 BC, in N Mesopotamia (now Iraq); early capital Ashur, later Nineveh. It was initially subject to Sumer and intermittently to Babylon. The Assyrians adopted largely the Sumerian religion and structure of society. At its greatest extent the empire included Egypt and stretched from the E Mediterranean coast to the head of the Persian Gulf. The Assyrian Empire began to decline from 671 BC; Ninevah was destroyed 612 BC and Assyria became a Median province and subsequently a principality of the Persian Empire.

Astaire Fred. Adopted name of Frederick Austerlitz 1899–1987. US dancer, actor, singer, and choreographer. He starred in numerous films, including *Top Hat* 1935, *Easter Parade* 1948, and *Funny Face* 1957, many containing inventive sequences which he designed and choreographed himself. He made ten classic films with the most popular of his dancing partners, Ginger Rogers. He later played straight dramatic roles in such films as *On the Beach* 1959. He was the greatest popular dancer of his time.

Astarte alternative name for the Babylonian and Assyrian goddess ◊Ishtar.

astatine (Greek *astatos* 'unstable') nonmetallic, radioactive element, symbol At, atomic number 85, relative atomic mass 210. It is a member of the ◊halogen group, and is very rare in nature. Astatine is highly unstable, with at least 19 isotopes; the longest lived has a half-life of about eight hours.

aster any plant of the large genus *Aster*, family Compositae, belonging to the same subfamily as the daisy. All asters have starlike flowers with yellow centres and outer rays (not petals) varying from blue and purple to white and the genus comprises a great variety of size. Many are cultivated as garden flowers, including the Michaelmas daisy *A. nova-belgii*.

Astaire US dancer Fred Astaire and his partner, Ginger Rogers. The sophisticated, intimate style of dancing, its grace and technical excellence, and the integration of plot and music in the Rogers–Astaire films revolutionized the musical comedy. Astaire's later co-stars included Judy Garland, Leslie Caron, and Audrey Hepburn.

The sea aster *A. tripolium* grows wild on sea cliffs in the south of England.

asteroid or ***minor planet*** any of many thousands of small bodies, composed of rock and iron, that orbit the Sun. Most lie in a belt between the orbits of Mars and Jupiter, and are thought to be fragments left over from the formation of the ◊Solar System. About 100,000 may exist, but their total mass is only a few hundredths the mass of the Moon.

They include ◊Ceres (the largest asteroid, 940 km/584 mi in diameter), Vesta (which has a light-coloured surface, and is the brightest as seen from Earth), ◊Eros, and ◊Icarus. Some asteroids are in orbits that bring them close to Earth, and some, such as the ◊Apollo asteroids, even cross Earth's orbit; at least some of these may be remnants of former comets. One group, the Trojans, moves along the

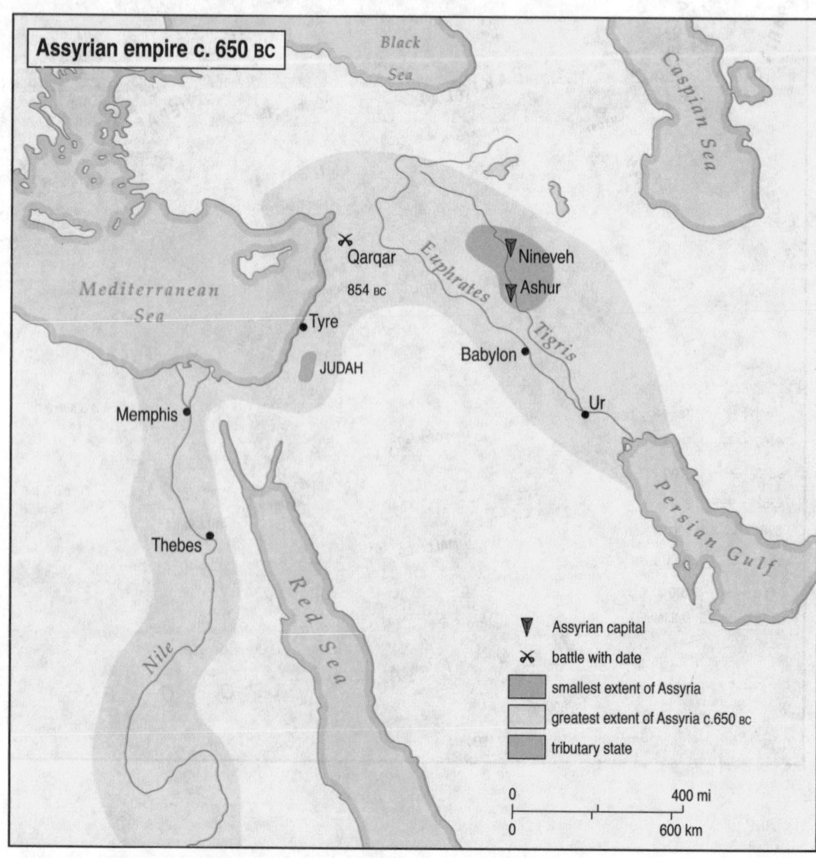

same orbit as Jupiter, 60° ahead and behind the planet. One unusual asteroid, Chiron, orbits beyond Saturn.

NASA's Near Earth Asteroid Rendezvous (NEAR) was launched Feb 1996 to study Eros to ascertain what asteroids are made of and whether they are similar in structure to meteorites.

asthenosphere division of the Earth's structure lying beneath the ◊lithosphere, at a depth of approximately 70 km/45 mi to 260 km/160 mi. It is thought to be the soft, partially molten layer of the ◊mantle on which the rigid plates of the Earth's surface move to produce the motions of ◊plate tectonics.

asthma chronic condition characterized by difficulty in breathing due to spasm of the bronchi (air passages) in the lungs. Attacks may be provoked by allergy, infection, and stress. The incidence of asthma may be increasing as a result of air pollution and occupational hazard. Treatment is with ◊bronchodilators to relax the bronchial muscles and thereby ease the breathing, and in severe cases by inhaled ◊steroids that reduce inflammation of the bronchi.

Extrinsic asthma, which is triggered by exposure to irritants, such as pollen and dust, is more common in children and young adults. Less common, intrinsic asthma tends to start in the middle years. Approximately 5–10% of children suffer from asthma, but about a third of these will show no symptoms after adolescence, while another 5–10% of people develop the condition as adults. Growing evidence that the immune system is involved in both forms of asthma has raised the possibility of a new approach to treatment. Although the symptoms are similar to those of bronchial asthma, cardiac asthma is an unrelated condition and is a symptom of heart deterioration.

astigmatism aberration occurring in the lens of the eye. It results when the curvature of the lens differs in two perpendicular planes, so that rays in one plane may be in focus while rays in the other are not. With astigmatic eyesight, the vertical and horizontal cannot be in focus at the same time; correction is by the use of a cylindrical lens that reduces the overall focal length of one plane so that both planes are seen in sharp focus.

Astor prominent US and British family. ***John Jacob Astor*** (1763–1848) was a US millionaire. His great-grandson ***Waldorf Astor***, 2nd Viscount Astor (1879–1952), was a British politician, and served as Conservative member of Parliament for Plymouth 1910–19, when he succeeded to the peerage. His US-born wife Nancy Witcher Langhorne (1879–1964), ***Lady Astor***, was the first woman member of Parliament to take a seat in the House of Commons 1919, when she succeeded her husband for the constituency of Plymouth.

William Backhouse Astor (1792–1875) was known as the 'landlord of New York'. John Jacob Astor's grandson ***William Waldorf Astor*** (1848–1919), a US diplomat and writer, became naturalized British 1899.

astrolabe ancient navigational instrument, forerunner of the sextant. Astrolabes usually consisted of a flat disc with a sighting rod that could be pivoted to point at the Sun or bright stars.

From the altitude of the Sun or star above the horizon, the local time could be estimated.

astrology (Greek *astron* 'star', *legein* 'speak') study of the relative position of the planets and stars in the belief that they influence events on Earth. The astrologer casts a ◊horoscope based on the time and place of the subject's birth. Astrology has no proven scientific basis, but has been widespread since ancient times. Western astrology is based on the 12 signs of the zodiac; Chinese astrology is based on a 60-year cycle and lunar calendar.

history A strongly held belief in ancient Babylon, astrology spread to the Mediterranean world, and was widely used by the Greeks and Romans. In Europe during the Middle Ages it had a powerful influence, since kings and other public figures had their own astrologers; astrological beliefs are reflected in Elizabethan and Jacobean literature.

In Chinese and Hindu thought, the universe is seen as forming a pattern in which everything is linked. Human life should be lived in harmony with this pattern, and astrology is seen as one way of helping to do this.

astrometry measurement of the precise positions of stars, planets, and other bodies in space. Such information is needed for practical purposes including accurate timekeeping, surveying and navigation, and calculating orbits and measuring distances in space. Astrometry is not concerned with the surface features or the physical nature of the body under study.

Before telescopes, astronomical observations were simple astrometry. Precise astrometry has shown that stars are not fixed in position, but have a ◊proper motion caused as they and the Sun orbit the Milky Way Galaxy. The nearest stars also show ◊parallax (apparent change in position), from which their distances can be calculated. Above the distorting effects of the atmosphere, satellites such as ◊*Hipparcos* can make even more precise measurements than ground telescopes, so refining the distance scale of space.

astronaut person making flights into space; the term cosmonaut is used in the West for any astronaut from the former Soviet Union.

astronautics science of space travel. See ◊rocket; ◊satellite; ◊space probe.

Astronomer Royal honorary post in British astronomy. Originally it was held by the director of the Royal Greenwich Observatory; since 1972 the title of Astronomer Royal has been awarded separately as an honorary title to an outstanding British astronomer. The Astronomer Royal from 1995 is Martin Rees. There is a separate post of Astronomer Royal for Scotland.

astronomical unit unit (symbol AU) equal to the mean distance of the Earth from the Sun: 149,597,870 km/92,955,800 mi. It is used to describe planetary distances. Light travels this distance in approximately 8.3 minutes.

astronomy science of the celestial bodies: the Sun, the Moon, and the planets; the stars and galaxies; and all other objects in the universe. It is concerned with their positions, motions, distances, and physical conditions and with their origins and evolution. Astronomy thus divides into fields such as astrophysics, celestial mechanics, and ◊cosmology. See also ◊gamma-ray astronomy, ◊infrared astronomy, ◊radio astronomy, ◊ultraviolet astronomy, and ◊X-ray astronomy.

Greek astronomers Astronomy is perhaps the oldest recorded science; there are observational records from ancient Babylonia, China, Egypt, and Mexico. The first true astronomers, however, were the Greeks, who deduced the Earth to be a sphere and attempted to measure its size. Ancient Greek astronomers included ◊Thales and ◊Pythagoras. ◊Eratosthenes of Cyrene measured the size of the Earth with considerable accuracy. Star catalogues were drawn up, the most celebrated being that of Hipparchus. The *Almagest*, by ◊Ptolemy of Alexandria, summarized Greek astronomy and survived in its Arabic translation. The Greeks still regarded the Earth as the centre of the universe, although this was doubted by some philosophers, notably ◊Aristarchus of Samos, who maintained that the Earth moves around the Sun.

Ptolemy, the last famous astronomer of the Greek school, died about AD 180, and little progress was made for some centuries.

Arab revival The Arabs revived the science, developing the astrolabe and producing good star catalogues. Unfortunately, a general belief in the pseudoscience of astrology continued until the end of the Middle Ages (and has been revived from time to time).

the Sun at the centre The dawn of a new era came 1543, when a Polish canon, ◊Copernicus, published a work entitled *De revolutionibus orbium coelestium/On the Revolutions of the Heavenly Spheres*, in which he demonstrated that the Sun, not the Earth, is the centre of our planetary system. (Copernicus was wrong in many respects – for instance, he still believed that all celestial orbits must be perfectly circular.) Tycho ◊Brahe, a Dane, increased the accuracy of observations by means of improved instruments allied to his own personal skill, and his observations were used by German mathematician Johannes ◊Kepler to prove the validity of the Copernican system. Considerable opposition existed, however, for removing the Earth from its central position in the universe; the Catholic church was openly hostile to the idea, and, ironically, Brahe never accepted the idea that the Earth could move around the Sun. Yet before the end of the 17th century, the theoretical work of Isaac ◊Newton had established celestial mechanics.

Galileo and the telescope The refracting telescope was invented about 1608, by Hans ◊Lippershey in Holland, and was first applied to astronomy by Italian scientist ◊Galileo in the winter of 1609–10. Immediately, Galileo made a series of spectacular discoveries.

He found the four largest satellites of Jupiter, which gave strong support to the Copernican theory; and he saw the craters of the Moon, the phases of Venus, and the myriad faint stars of our ◊Galaxy, the Milky Way.

astrolabe An astrolabe from 1574. The astrolabe was invented 200 BC. It is an instrument used to calculate the time, latitude, and longitude from the position of the Sun and stars. *Image Select (UK) Ltd*

Galileo's most powerful telescope magnified only 30 times, but it was not long before larger telescopes were built and official observatories were established.

Galileo's telescope was a refractor; that is to say, it collected its light by means of a glass lens or object glass. Difficulties with his design led Newton, in 1671, to construct a reflector, in which the light is collected by means of a curved mirror.

further discoveries In the 17th and 18th centuries astronomy was mostly concerned with positional measurements. Uranus was discovered 1781 by William ◊Herschel, and this was soon followed by the discovery of the first four asteroids, Ceres 1801, Pallas 1802, Juno 1804, and Vesta 1807. In 1846 Neptune was located by Johann ◊Galle, following calculations by British astronomer John Couch ◊Adams and French astronomer Urbain Jean Joseph ◊Leverrier. Also significant was the first measurement of the distance of a star, when in 1838 the German astronomer Friedrich ◊Bessel measured the ◊parallax of the star 61 Cygni, and calculated that it lies at a distance of about 6 light years (about half the correct value).

Astronomical spectroscopy was developed, first by Fraunhofer in Germany and then by people such as Pietro Angelo Secchi (1818–1878) and William Huggins, while Gustav ◊Kirchhoff successfully interpreted the spectra of the Sun and stars. By the 1860s good photographs of the Moon had been obtained, and by the end of the century photographic methods had started to play a leading role in research.

galaxies William Herschel, probably the greatest observer in the history of astronomy, investigated the shape of our Galaxy during the latter part of the 18th century and concluded that its stars are arranged roughly in the form of a double-convex lens. Basically Herschel was correct, although he placed our Sun near the centre of the system; in fact, it is well out towards the edge, and lies 25,000 light years from the galactic nucleus. Herschel also studied the luminous 'clouds' or nebulae, and made the tentative suggestion that those nebulae capable of resolution into stars might be separate galaxies, far outside our own Galaxy.

It was not until 1923 that US astronomer Edwin Hubble, using the 2.5 m/100 in reflector at the Mount Wilson Observatory, was able to verify this suggestion. It is now known that the 'spiral nebulae' are galaxies in their own right, and that they lie at immense distances. The most distant galaxy visible to the naked eye, the Great Spiral in ◊Andromeda, is 2.2 million light years away; the most remote galaxy so far measured lies over 10 billion light years away. It was also found that galaxies tended to form groups, and that the groups were apparently receding from each other at speeds proportional to their distances.

a growing universe This concept of an expanding and evolving universe at first rested largely on ◊Hubble's law, relating the distance of objects to the amount their spectra shift towards red – the ◊red shift. Subsequent evidence derived from objects studied in other parts of the electromagnetic

cont. on p. 72

Seeing the Universe

Three astronomers making observations in Flamsteed House, Greenwich, London, in the latter half of the 17th century. The astronomer on the right is using a refracting telescope while the one on the left is using an arc to determine the elevation of an object. The most accurate clocks of the day are mounted on the end wall. *Image Select (UK) Ltd*

To most people, astronomy means telescopes, whether the traditional ground-based type housed in domes or the modern space-borne variety such as the Hubble Space Telescope. It is true that progress in astronomy over the centuries has gone hand in hand with the development of new telescopes, but the real advances have been made using other instruments and, crucially, new means of detecting the light from astronomical bodies.

Astronomy before telescopes

The first detector – and the one we all still rely on more than any other – is often fondly called the 'Mk 1 eyeball'. For thousands of years, the human eye observed the movements of the stars and planets through the sky, the fall of shooting stars, the dramas of eclipses, comets, and new stars, and the basic apparent turning of the heavens.

People often suppose that it was Galileo's telescope which proved that the Earth goes round the Sun, though Copernicus had published the theory 20 years before Galileo's birth. The real proof came from Tycho Brahe's naked-eye observations of the movement of the planets. Although Tycho himself believed that the Sun moved around the Earth, it was his particularly accurate measurements that effectively laid the foundation for the biggest revolution in astronomical thinking – the heliocentric theory, or the understanding that the Sun, not the Earth, lies at the centre of the system of planets. Tycho's assistant and successor, Johannes Kepler, used Tycho's data to derive the laws of planetary motion within the same decade that the telescope was first turned on the skies. What Galileo saw provided only circumstantial evidence for the heliocentric theory.

For the next 200 years or so, astronomy progressed only slowly. During this time its main purpose was to provide mariners with an accurate means of navigation by the stars, and telescopes were used more to improve the precision of star catalogues than to reveal fainter objects and finer detail.

Astronaut Edward H White II is shown performing the first space walk by an American during the third orbit of the *Gemini–Titan 4* flight 1965. *Image Select (UK) Ltd*

The arrival of astrophysics

Then in the 19th century the second great instrumental development took place – the invention of the spectroscope. For the first time, it was possible to discover not only what the stars and other bodies are made of, but also a great deal about their true sizes and motions. The science of astrophysics, which deals with the stars as physical bodies in space rather than mere points of light, was born.

At first the spectroscope was used by eye, but during the second half of the 19th century came an advance as important to astronomy as the invention of the telescope: photography. As a new type of detector, the camera had two valuable features – its ability to carry on building up light for several hours if necessary, revealing objects too faint for the eye to see; and its ability to record permanently what previously had to be remembered and sketched.

Ironically, one of the enduring myths of astronomy – life on Mars – was fostered by visual observations at a time when photography was well into its stride. The claims of US astronomer Percival Lowell, in the early years of the 20th century, that the fine 'canals' which he saw on Mars were artificially created, gave rise to a widespread belief in intelligent Martians. Lowell's observations are now put down to optical illusions, but the myth lives on.

Exploring our galaxy and beyond

The first half of the 20th century saw a transformation in our understanding of the scale and content of the universe. In 1900 the sky contained a mystifying collection of cloudy patches lumped together as 'nebulae'. Some shone with starlight, while others were gaseous, but the links between them were largely unknown. By the 1950s, as a result of the combination of large reflecting telescopes, increasingly sensitive photographic plates, and spectroscopy, astronomers knew that the gaseous nebulae are gas clouds within our own Milky Way galaxy or star system, while the others are much more distant individual galaxies. What's more, all the galaxies share in a uniform expansion of space which can be run backwards to an actual beginning of the universe as we know it – what became known in the 1960s as the Big Bang.

At about this time came the next instrumental advances – space travel, and astronomy at wavelengths other than that of light. With the advent of the Space Age in 1957, astronomers were in effect able to reach out and touch the nearest celestial bodies – the Moon and planets. Automatic probes began a series of epic voyages which have now sent back close-up pictures of all the major planets except Pluto, while humans have actually travelled to the Moon and brought back pieces of it.

Riding the wavelengths

Meanwhile, new parts of the spectrum were being exploited, notably radio waves. New objects were discovered: for example, quasars – powerful emitters of light and radio waves, often

Radio telescopes, like this one (the world's largest) at Arecibo, Puerto Rico, allow astronomers to analyse a broad range of low-frequency electromagnetic waves – visible light is only a small part of the electromagnetic spectrum. Pulsars and quasars were first discovered by radio telescopes. *National Aeronautical Space Agency*

***Liftoff of the space shuttle* Atlantis** on 18 Oct 1989. *National Aeronautical Space Agency*

further away than any visible galaxy; and pulsars – the tiny, spinning remnants of dying stars within our own galaxy. High-energy astrophysics was born, in which black holes of varying sizes are often found to cause vast outpourings of energy.

One particularly valuable technique developed by radio astronomers is aperture synthesis. This uses comparatively small receiving dishes some distance apart to record the same detail as a single receiving dish the size of the distance between them. Very long baselines, up to the diameter of the Earth, yield highly detailed radio images of objects half a universe away.

Today, astronomers make use of observations at a wide variety of wavelengths, from gamma rays to infrared, using observatories above the atmosphere. The best known of these is the Hubble Space Telescope (HST), but a vast amount of data comes from such satellites as the European Space Agency's Infrared Space Observatory and NASA's Rossi X-ray Timing Explorer. While the quality of observations from the HST is very high, and the regular HST servicing missions by the Space Shuttle allow it to be upgraded, so is its cost. Some astronomers maintain that smaller, cheaper satellites would be more cost-effective, and view crewed spaceflight as having political rather than scientific value. Others point to the quality of work done by the HST, and the waste of effort put into uncrewed satellites which fail because of trivial faults.

The giant cloud of cold gas and dust which is thought to fuel a black hole. The image was produced by the Hubble Space Telescope, using visible wavelengths. *Image Select (UK) Ltd*

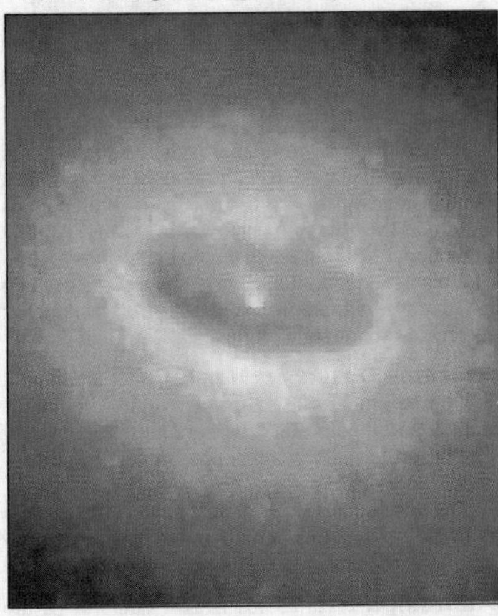

The computer age and future aims

Photography has now been almost entirely replaced in all branches of astronomy by electronic light detectors called charge-coupled devices (CCDs). These are grown-up versions of the ones used in camcorders, and have the advantage over photography that they give a digital output, so that the data can be stored and manipulated in computers. The development of the computer has had a great effect on astronomy, allowing sophisticated digital models of stars, galaxies, and even the universe as a whole to be explored from a desk. Astronomers use electronic mail to disseminate discoveries and plan joint observations, and some observing is now carried out by remote control – instead of the telescope being adjacent to the control room, it can now be on the other side of the world.

The greatest challenges for astronomers today include deciding on the scale of the universe, its rate of expansion, and eventual fate, and finding out what makes up the dark matter which affects the motion of galaxies. But for the public, the goals are different – they want to know if there is life elsewhere in the universe. The possible discovery of fossils in a meteorite believed to have come from Mars made headline news in 1996; and optical astronomers are eagerly adapting aperture synthesis in the hope of seeing new planets around nearby stars, so far known only through their effects on the motions of the stars. Such newsworthy investigations ensure that astronomy continues to enjoy public support while also giving it a valuable role as a window into science as a whole.

ROBIN SCAGELL

The Hubble Space Telescope was launched in 1990 by the space shuttle *Discovery*. It was subsequently found to have numerous electrical and mechanical problems, which were repaired on an instrument-upgrade mission in Dec 1993. The telescope has produced images of astral objects far superior to any taken from Earth. *Image Select (UK) Ltd*

SEE ALSO

astrophotography; Brahe, Tycho; Copernicus; Galileo; Hubble Space Telescope; Kepler, Johannes; nebula; radio astronomy; universe

ASTRONOMY: TIMELINE

2300 BC	Chinese astronomers made their earliest observations.
2000	Babylonian priests made their first observational records.
1900	Stonehenge was constructed: first phase.
434	Anaxagoras claimed the Sun is made up of hot rock.
365	The Chinese observed the satellites of Jupiter with the naked eye.
3rd C	Aristarchus argued that the Sun is the centre of the Solar System.
2nd C AD	Ptolemy's complicated Earth-centred system was promulgated, which dominated the astronomy of the Middle Ages.
1543	Copernicus revived the ideas of Aristarchus in *De Revolutionibus*.
1572	Brilliant new star (now known as a supernova) appeared in Cassiopeia, and encouraged Tycho Brahe to make detailed measurements of star positions, later used by Johannes Kepler.
1608	Hans Lippershey invented the telescope, which was first used by Galileo 1609.
1609	Johannes Kepler's first two laws of planetary motion were published (the third appeared 1619).
1632	The world's first official observatory was established in Leiden in the Netherlands.
1633	Galileo's theories were condemned by the Inquisition.
1675	The Royal Greenwich Observatory was founded in England.
1687	Isaac Newton's *Principia* was published, including his 'law of universal gravitation'.
1705	Edmond Halley correctly predicted that the comet that had passed the Earth in 1682 would return in 1758; the comet was later to be known by his name.
1781	William Herschel discovered Uranus and recognized stellar systems beyond our Galaxy.
1796	Pierre Laplace elaborated his theory of the origin of the Solar System.
1801	Giuseppe Piazzi discovered the first asteroid, Ceres.
1814	Joseph von Fraunhofer first studied absorption lines in the solar spectrum.
1846	Neptune was identified by Johann Galle, following predictions by John Adams and Urbain Leverrier.
1859	Gustav Kirchhoff explained dark lines in the Sun's spectrum.
1887	The earliest photographic star charts were produced.
1889	Edward Barnard took the first photographs of the Milky Way.
1908	Fragment of comet fell at Tunguska, Siberia.
1920	Arthur Eddington began the study of interstellar matter.
1923	Edwin Hubble proved that the galaxies are systems independent of the Milky Way, and by 1930 had confirmed the concept of an expanding universe.
1930	The planet Pluto was discovered by Clyde Tombaugh at the Lowell Observatory, Arizona, USA.
1931	Karl Jansky founded radio astronomy.
1945	Radar contact with the Moon was established by Z Bay of Hungary and the US Army Signal Corps Laboratory.
1948	The 5-m/200-in Hale reflector telescope was installed at Mount Palomar, California, USA.
1957	The Jodrell Bank telescope dish in England was completed.
1957	The first *Sputnik* satellite (USSR) opened the age of space observation.
1962	The first X-ray source was discovered in Scorpius.
1963	The first quasar was discovered.
1967	The first pulsar was discovered by Jocelyn Bell and Antony Hewish.
1969	The first crewed Moon landing was made by US astronauts.
1976	A 6 m/240 in reflector telescope was installed at Mount Semirodniki, USSR.
1977	Uranus was discovered to have rings.
1977	The spacecraft *Voyager 1* and *2* were launched, passing Jupiter and Saturn 1979–1981.
1978	The spacecraft *Pioneer Venus 1* and *2* reached Venus.
1978	A satellite of Pluto, Charon, was discovered by James Christy of the US Naval Observatory.
1986	Halley's comet returned. *Voyager 2* flew past Uranus and discovered six new moons.
1987	Supernova SN1987A flared up, becoming the first supernova to be visible to the naked eye since 1604. The 4.2 m/165 in William Herschel Telescope on La Palma, Canary Islands, and the James Clerk Maxwell Telescope on Mauna Kea, Hawaii, began operation.
1988	The most distant individual star was recorded – a supernova, 5 billion light years away, in the AC118 cluster of galaxies.
1989	*Voyager 2* flew by Neptune and discovered eight moons and three rings.
1990	The Hubble Space Telescope was launched into orbit by the US space shuttle.
1991	The space probe *Galileo* flew past the asteroid Gaspra, approaching it to within 26,000 km/16,200 mi.
1992	COBE satellite detected ripples from the Big Bang that mark the first stage in the formation of galaxies.
1994	Fragments of comet Shoemaker–Levy struck Jupiter.
1996	A number of planets were discovered in orbit around several stars. A meteorite from Mars was claimed to contain microfossils.
1997	Release of data from Hipparcos satellite, revising distances of many nearby stars and improving estimates of the age of the Universe and of our galaxy.

spectrum, at radio and X-ray wavelengths, has provided confirmation. ◊Radio astronomy established its place in probing the structure of the universe by demonstrating 1954 that an optically visible distant galaxy was identical with a powerful radio source known as Cygnus A. Later analysis of the comparative number, strength, and distance of radio sources suggested that in the distant past these, including the ◊quasars discovered 1963, had been much more powerful and numerous than today. This fact suggested that the universe has been evolving from an origin, and is not of infinite age as expected under a ◊steady-state theory.

The discovery 1965 of microwave background radiation was direct evidence for the enormous temperature of the giant explosion, or Big Bang, that brought the universe into existence.

further exploration The 1990s have seen great developments in telescope power. The launch by the USA of the Hubble Space Telescope in 1990 freed astronomy from the confines of Earth's unsteady and murky atmosphere, and allowed detailed images to be built up for many hours. Its 2.4 m/94.5 in mirror is exceeded in light-gathering power by many Earth-based telescopes, however. Notable among these are the Keck Telescopes on Hawaii, with two 10 m/400 in mirrors, each built up from smaller segments. Experiments to overcome the unsteadiness of the atmosphere have been successful, either by actively altering the light path through the telescope or by linking two separate telescopes in an interferometer. Space observatories have access to wavelengths blocked by the atmosphere, such as gamma rays and x-rays, while space probes have photographed most of the major solar-system bodies in close-up.

See also ◊black hole and ◊infrared radiation. ▷*See feature on pp. 70–71.*

astrophysics study of the physical nature of stars, galaxies, and the universe. It began with the development of spectroscopy in the 19th century, which allowed astronomers to analyse the composition of stars from their light. Astrophysicists view the universe as a vast natural laboratory in which they can study matter under conditions of temperature, pressure, and density that are unattainable on Earth. ▷*See feature on pp. 70–71.*

Asturias autonomous region of N Spain; area 10,600 sq km/4,092 sq mi; population (1991) 1,093,900. Half of Spain's coal comes from the mines of Asturias. Agricultural produce includes maize, fruit, and livestock. Oviedo and Gijón are the main industrial towns. It was once a separate kingdom.

Asunción capital and port of Paraguay, on the Paraguay River; population (1992) 502,400 (metropolitan area 637,700). It produces textiles, footwear, and food products.

history Founded by the Spanish 1537. It was the first Spanish settlement in the La Plata region, and centre of the Spanish in South America until the refounding of Buenos Aires 1580. It declined in importance in the 17th century.

features 19th-century Pantheon of Heroes; Hotel Guaraní, designed by Oscar Niemayer; National University, founded 1890; Catholic University, founded 1960.

asylum, political in international law, refuge granted in another country to a person who, for political reasons, cannot return to his or her own country without putting himself or herself in danger. A person seeking asylum is a type of ◊refugee.

Under British immigration rules, asylum is granted only in cases where refugees can prove that if they return to their country of origin they will be persecuted for reasons of race, religion, nationality, membership of a particular group, or political opinion; this excludes the vast majority of refugees currently allowed to stay in the UK under exceptional leave.

asymptote in ◊coordinate geometry, a straight line that a curve approaches more and more closely but never reaches. The x and y axes are asymptotes to the graph of xy = constant (a rectangular ◊hyperbola).

If a point on a curve approaches a straight line such that its distance from the straight line is d, then the line is an asymptote to the curve if limit d tends to zero as the point moves towards infinity. Among ◊conic sections (curves obtained by the intersection of a plane and a double cone), a hyperbola has two asymptotes, which in the case of a rectangular hyperbola are at right angles to each other.

Atacama Desert desert in N Chile; area about 80,000 sq km/31,000 sq mi. There are mountains inland, and the coastal area is rainless and barren. The desert has silver and copper mines, and extensive nitrate deposits.

The world's largest and most powerful telescope is being built at the Cerro Paranal Space Observatory, for the European Southern Observatory.

Atahualpa c. 1502–1533. Last emperor of the Incas of Peru. He was taken prisoner 1532 when the

Atatürk Turkish soldier and statesman Mustafa Kemal Atatürk (left). He led the Turkish nationalist movement from 1909, opposing the British in World War I and expelling the Greeks. As president 1923–38 he pursued a thoroughgoing programme of westernization that affected all aspects of Turkish life – women were given the vote, the traditional Turkish fez was prohibited, Roman lettering replaced Arabic, and European legal systems such as the Swiss code of civil law were adopted wholesale. *Topham*

Spaniards arrived and agreed to pay a substantial ransom, but he was accused of plotting against the conquistador Pizarro and was sentenced to be burned. On his consenting to Christian baptism, the sentence was commuted to strangulation.

Atalanta in Greek mythology, a woman hunter who challenged each of her suitors to a foot race; if they lost they were killed. The goddess ◊Aphrodite gave one of the suitors, Hippomenes, three golden apples to drop so that when Atalanta stopped to pick them up, she lost the race and became his wife.

AT&T abbreviation for ***American Telephone and Telegraph***, US telecommunications company that owns four out of five telephones in the USA. It was founded 1877 by the inventor of the telephone, Alexander Graham Bell, as the Bell Telephone Company; it took its present name 1899.

Atatürk Mustafa Kemal. Name assumed 1934 by Mustafa Kemal Pasha, (Turkish 'Father of the Turks') 1881–1938. Turkish politician and general, first president of Turkey from 1923. After World War I he established a provisional rebel government and in 1921–22 the Turkish armies under his leadership expelled the Greeks who were occupying Turkey. He was the founder of the modern republic, which he ruled as virtual dictator, with a policy of consistent and radical westernization.

Atatürk Dam dam on the river Euphrates, in the province of Gaziantep, S Turkey, completed 1989. The lake, 550 km/340 mi SE of Ankara, covers 815 sq km/315 sq mi (when full, it holds four times the annual flow of the Euphrates). In 1990 it was filled for the first time, submerging 25 villages, all of whose 55,000 inhabitants were relocated. It is the world's fifth largest dam. The impact of the dam on river flow has caused tension with Iraq and Syria.

atavism (Latin *atavus* 'ancestor') in genetics, the reappearance of a characteristic not apparent in the immediately preceding generations; in psychology, the manifestation of primitive forms of behaviour.

Athanasian creed one of the three ancient ◊creeds of the Christian church. Mainly a definition of the Trinity and Incarnation, it was written many years after the death of Athanasius, but was attributed to him as the chief upholder of Trinitarian doctrine.

Athanasius, St 298–373. Bishop of Alexandria, Egypt, supporter of the doctrines of the Trinity and Incarnation. He was a disciple of St Anthony the hermit, and an opponent of ◊Arianism in the great Arian controversy. Following the official condemnation of Arianism at the Council of Nicaea 325, Athanasius was appointed bishop of Alexandria 328. The Athanasian creed was not actually written by him, although it reflects his views.

atheism nonbelief in, or the positive denial of, the existence of a God or gods. A related concept is ◊agnosticism. Like theism, its opposite, atheism cannot be proved or disproved conclusively.

Perhaps the strongest atheistic argument concerns the existence of evil, which is hard to reconcile with the notion (in Christianity and other religions) that the world was created by an omnipotent, all-loving God. Theologians have responded with a variety of theodicies, or justifications for the existence of evil.

Buddhism has been called an atheistic religion since it does not postulate any supreme being. The Jains are similarly atheistic, and so are those who adopt the Sankhya system of philosophy in Hinduism. Following the revolution of 1917 the USSR and later communist states, such as Albania, adopted an atheist position.

Athelstan c. 895–939. King of the Mercians and West Saxons. Son of Edward the Elder and grandson of Alfred the Great, he was crowned king 925 at Kingston upon Thames. He subdued parts of Cornwall and Wales, and defeated the Welsh, Scots, and Danes at Brunanburh 937.

Athena in Greek mythology, the goddess of war, wisdom, and the arts and crafts (Roman Minerva), who was supposed to have sprung fully grown from the head of Zeus. In Homer's *Odyssey*, she is the protector of ◊Odysseus and his son Telemachus. Her chief cult centre was Athens, where the ◊Parthenon was dedicated to her.

Athens (Greek ***Athinai***) capital city of Greece and of ancient Attica; population (1991) 784,100, metropolitan area (1991) 3,096,800. Situated 8 km/5 mi NE of its port of Piraeus on the Gulf of Aegina, it is built around the rocky hills of the Acropolis 169 m/555 ft and the Areopagus 112 m/368 ft, and is overlooked from the NE by the hill of Lycabettus, 277 m/909 ft high. It lies in the S of the central plain of Attica, watered by the mountain streams of Cephissus and Ilissus. It has less green space than any other European capital (4%) and severe air and noise pollution.

features The Acropolis dominates the city. Remains of ancient Greece include the Parthenon, the Erechtheum, and the temple of Athena Nike. Near the site of the ancient Agora (marketplace) stands the Theseum, and south of the Acropolis is the theatre of Dionysus. To the SE stand the gate of Hadrian and the columns of the temple of Olympian Zeus. Nearby is the marble stadium built about 330 BC and restored 1896.

history The site was first inhabited about 3000 BC with Athens as the capital of a united Attica before 700 BC. Captured and sacked by the Persians 480 BC, it became the first city of Greece in power and culture under ◊Pericles. After the death of Alexander the Great the city fell into comparative decline, but it flourished as an intellectual centre until AD 529 when the philosophical schools were closed by Justinian. In 1458 it was captured by the Turks, who held it until 1833; it was chosen as the capital of Greece 1834. During World War II, it was occupied by the Germans April 1941–Oct 1944 and was then the scene of fierce street fighting between monarchist and communist partisan factions until Jan 1945.

atheroma furring-up of the interior of an artery by deposits, mainly of cholesterol, within its walls. Associated with atherosclerosis, atheroma has the effect of narrowing the lumen (channel) of the artery, thus restricting blood flow. This predisposes to a number of conditions, including thrombosis, angina, and stroke.

atherosclerosis thickening and hardening of the walls of the arteries. In middle and old age, the walls of the arteries degenerate and are vulnerable to damage by the build-up of fatty deposits. These reduce elasticity, hardening the arteries and decreasing the internal bore leading high blood pressure, loss of circulation, heart disease, and death. The condition is associated with atheroma.

Atherton, Michael Andrew 1968– . English cricketer. A right-handed opening batsman from Lancashire who captained England in a record 52 Tests 1993–98. He made his Test debut in 1989 and took over as England captain in 1993. In his 68th Test in 1997 be became the 12th England cricketer to score 5,000 test runs.

athletics competitive track and field events consisting of running, throwing, and jumping disciplines. Running events range from sprint races (100 metres) and hurdles to cross-country running and the ◊marathon (26 miles 385 yards). Jumping events are the high jump, long jump, triple jump, and pole vault. ◊Throwing events are javelin, discus, shot put, and hammer throw.

history Among the Greeks, vase paintings show that competitive athletics were established at least by 1600 BC. Greek and Roman athletes were well paid and sponsored. The philosopher Aristotle paid the expenses of a boxer contestant at Olympia, and chariot races were sponsored by the Greek city-states. Today athletes are supposed to be unpaid amateurs. The concept of the unpaid amateur was popularized following the founding of the modern Olympic Games 1896. However, athletes in the USA and Eastern bloc nations have become full-time, their incomes coming from commercial or state sponsorship, so that the status of athletics as an amateur sport is today rapidly disappearing at the senior level. *See list of tables on p. 1177.*

Athos mountainous peninsula on the Macedonian coast of Greece. Its peak is 2,033 m/6,672 ft high. The promontory is occupied by a group of 20 Orthodox monasteries, inhabited by some 3,000 monks and lay brothers. A council of representatives from the monasteries runs the affairs of the peninsula as a self-governing republic under the protection of the Greek government.

‘Let there be light! said Liberty / And like sunrise from the sea, Athens arose!’

On ATHENS
Percy Bysshe Shelley, *Hellas*

Athens The ruins of the Parthenon rise from the Acropolis in Athens, seen from the northeast. A settlement existed around the Acropolis as early as 3000 BC. Two thousand years later a walled palace existed there, with a community clustered around it. The Parthenon dates from 447–438 BC. *Corbis*

Atlanta capital and largest city of Georgia, USA, in the foothills of the Blue Ridge Mountains; population (1992) 394,850, metropolitan area (1992) 3,143,000. It is the headquarters of Coca-Cola. Atlanta hosted the 1996 Olympic Games.
history Originally named Terminus, Atlanta was founded 1837 after the site was chosen as the southern terminus of the Western and Atlantic Railroad; the name was changed to Atlanta 1845. During the American Civil War it was captured and partly destroyed by General ◊Sherman 1864. At the Atlanta Exposition of 1895 Booker T Washington made the declaration known as the Atlanta Compromise. The city grew in importance after 1900 and became the financial, trade, and convention centre for the SE United States. Atlanta was the first large city in the South to elect a black mayor 1973.
features A few sites from the earliest settlement are preserved in the Underground Atlanta complex; the State Capitol 1889; Stone Mountain Memorial, the world's largest sculpture memorial, commemorating the Confederate war heroes Jefferson Davis, Robert E Lee, and Stonewall Jackson; the Martin Luther King Jr National Historic District – sites include his birthplace and his grave.

Atlantic, Battle of the German campaign during World War I to prevent merchant shipping from delivering food supplies from the USA to the Allies, chiefly the UK. By 1917, some 875,000 tons of shipping had been lost. The odds were only turned by the belated use of naval convoys and depth charges to deter submarine attack.

Notable action included the British defeat at Coronel off Chile 1 Nov 1914, the subsequent British success at the Falkland Islands 8 Dec 1914, and the battle in the North Sea at Jutland 31 May 1916, which effectively neutralized the German surface fleet for the rest of the war.

Atlantic, Battle of the during World War II, continuous battle fought in the Atlantic Ocean by the sea and air forces of the Allies and Germany, to control the supply routes to the UK. The Allies destroyed nearly 800 U-boats during the war and at least 2,200 convoys of 75,000 merchant ships crossed the Atlantic, protected by US naval forces.

The battle opened 4 Sept 1939, the first night of the war, when the ocean liner *Athenia*, sailing from Glasgow to New York, was torpedoed by a German U-boat off the Irish coast. The Germans employed a variety of tactics in the course of the campaign such as U-boats, surface-raiders, indiscriminate minelaying, and aircraft, but the Allies successfully countered all of them, although they suffered some significant reverses such as the sinking of the armed merchant ships *Rawalpindi* (23 Nov 1939) and *Jervis Bay* (5 Nov 1940) by German warships.

Atlantic Charter declaration issued during World War II by the British prime minister Winston Churchill and the US president Franklin Roosevelt after meetings Aug 1941. It stressed their countries' broad strategy and war aims and was largely a propaganda exercise to demonstrate public solidarity among the Allies.

Atlantic City seaside resort in New Jersey; population (1990) 38,000. Formerly a family resort, Atlantic City has become a centre for casino gambling, which was legalized 1978.

It is known for its 'boardwalk' (a wooden pavement along the beach).

Atlantic Ocean ocean lying between Europe and Africa to the E and the Americas to the W, probably named after the legendary island continent of Atlantis; area of basin 81,500,000 sq km/31,500,000 sq mi; including the Arctic Ocean and Antarctic seas, 106,200,000 sq km/41,000,000 sq mi. The average depth is 3 km/2 mi; greatest depth the Milwaukee Depth in the Puerto Rico Trench 8,648 m/28,374 ft. The Mid-Atlantic Ridge, of which the Azores, Ascension, St Helena, and Tristan da Cunha form part, divides it from N to S. Lava welling up from this central area annually increases the distance between South America and Africa. The N Atlantic is the saltiest of the main oceans and has the largest tidal range.

In the 1960s–80s average wave heights increased by 25%, the largest from 12 m/39 ft to 18 m/59 ft.

Atlantis in Greek mythology, an island continent, said to have sunk following an earthquake. Although the Atlantic Ocean is probably named after it, the structure of the sea bottom rules out its ever having existed there. The Greek philosopher Plato created an imaginary early history for it and described it as a utopia.

Legends about the disappearance of Atlantis may have some connection with the volcanic eruption that devastated Santorini in the ◊Cyclades islands, north of Crete, about 1500 BC. The ensuing earthquakes and tidal waves are believed to have been one cause of the collapse of the empire of Minoan Crete.

Atlas in Greek mythology, one of the ◊Titans who revolted against the gods; as a punishment, he was compelled to support the heavens on his head and shoulders. Growing weary, he asked ◊Perseus to turn him into stone, and he was transformed into Mount Atlas.

Atlas Mountains mountain system of NW Africa, stretching 2,400 km/1,500 mi from the Atlantic coast of Morocco to the Gulf of Gabes, Tunisia, and lying between the Mediterranean on the N and the Sahara on the S. The highest peak is Mount Toubkal 4,167 m/13,670 ft.

atman in Hinduism, the individual soul or the eternal essential self.

atmosphere mixture of gases surrounding a planet. The Earth's atmosphere is prevented from escaping by the pull of the Earth's gravity.

Atmospheric pressure decreases with height in the atmosphere. In its lowest layer, the atmosphere consists of nitrogen (78%) and oxygen (21%), both in molecular form (two atoms bonded together). The other 1% is largely argon, with very small quantities of other gases, including water vapour and carbon dioxide. The atmosphere plays a major part in the various cycles of nature (the ◊water cycle, ◊carbon cycle, and ◊nitrogen cycle). It is the principal industrial source of nitrogen, oxygen, and argon, which are obtained by fractional distillation of liquid air.

The lowest level of the atmosphere, the ◊troposphere, is heated by the Earth, which is warmed by infrared and visible radiation from the Sun. Warm air cools as it rises in the troposphere, causing rain and most other weather phenomena. However, infrared and visible radiations form only a part

atmosphere All but 1% of the Earth's atmosphere lies in a layer 30 km/19 mi above the ground. At a height of 5,500 m/18,000 ft, air pressure is half that at sea level. The temperature of the atmosphere varies greatly with height; this produces a series of layers, called the troposphere, stratosphere, mesosphere, and thermosphere.

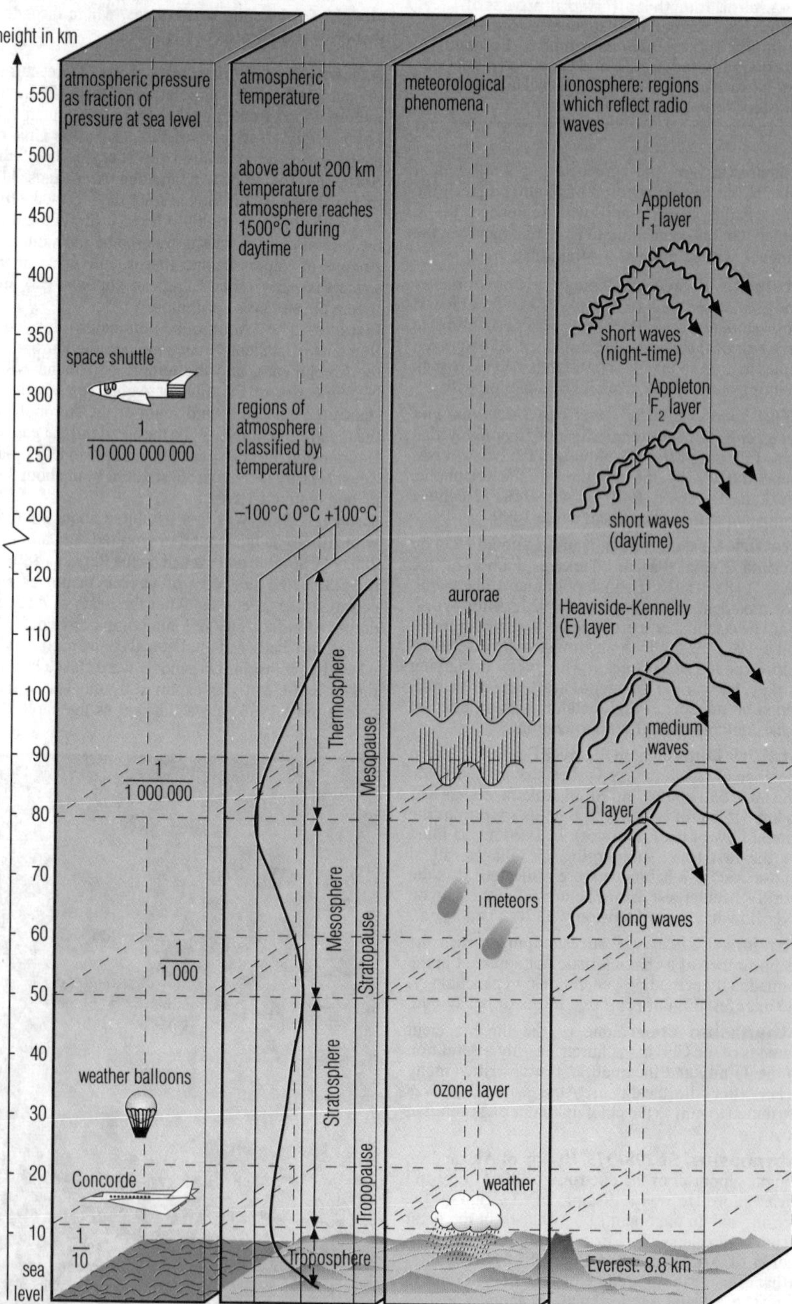

of the Sun's output of electromagnetic radiation. Almost all the shorter-wavelength ultraviolet radiation is filtered out by the upper layers of the atmosphere. The filtering process is an active one: at heights above about 50 km/31 mi ultraviolet photons collide with atoms, knocking out electrons to create a ◊plasma of electrons and positively charged ions. The resulting ionosphere acts as a reflector of radio waves, enabling radio transmissions to 'hop' between widely separated points on the Earth's surface.

Waves of different wavelengths are reflected best at different heights. The collisions between ultraviolet photons and atoms lead to a heating of the upper atmosphere, although the temperature drops from top to bottom within the zone called the thermosphere as high-energy photons are progressively absorbed in collisions. Between the thermosphere and the tropopause (at which the warming effect of the Earth starts to be felt) there is a 'warm bulge' in the graph of temperature against height, at a level called the stratopause. This is due to longer-wavelength ultraviolet photons that have survived their journey through the upper layers; now they encounter molecules and split them apart into atoms. These atoms eventually bond together again, but often in different combinations. In particular, many ◊ozone molecules (oxygen atom triplets, O_3) are formed. Ozone is a better absorber of ultraviolet than ordinary (two-atom) oxygen, and it is the ozone layer that prevents lethal amounts of ultraviolet from reaching the Earth's surface.

Far above the atmosphere, as so far described, lie the Van Allen radiation belts. These are regions in which high-energy charged particles travelling outwards from the Sun (as the so-called solar wind) have been captured by the Earth's magnetic field. The outer belt (at about 1,600 km/1,000 mi) contains mainly protons, the inner belt (at about 2,000 km/1,250 mi) contains mainly electrons. Sometimes electrons spiral down towards the Earth, noticeably at polar latitudes, where the magnetic field is strongest. When such particles collide with atoms and ions in the thermosphere, light is emitted. This is the origin of the glows visible in the sky as the aurora borealis (northern lights) and the aurora australis (southern lights).

A fainter, more widespread, airglow is caused by a similar mechanism.

During periods of intense solar activity, the atmosphere swells outwards; there is a 10–20% variation in atmosphere density. One result is to increase drag on satellites. This effect makes it impossible to predict exactly the time of re-entry of satellites.

atmosphere or ***standard atmosphere*** in physics, a unit (symbol atm) of pressure equal to 760 torr, 1013.25 millibars, or 1.01325×10^5 newtons per square metre. The actual pressure exerted by the atmosphere fluctuates around this value, which is assumed to be standard at sea level and 0°C/32°F, and is used when dealing with very high pressures.

atmospheric pollution contamination of the atmosphere with the harmful by-products of human activity; see ◊air pollution.

atmospheric pressure the pressure at any point on the Earth's surface that is due to the weight of the column of air above it; it therefore decreases as altitude increases. At sea level the average pressure is 101 kilopascals (1,013 millibars, 760 mmHg, or 14.7 lb per sq in).

Changes in atmospheric pressure, measured with a barometer, are used in weather forecasting. Areas of relatively high pressure are called ◊anticyclones; areas of low pressure are called ◊depressions.

atoll continuous or broken circle of ◊coral reef and low coral islands surrounding a lagoon.

atom (Greek *atomos* 'undivided') smallest unit of matter that can take part in a chemical reaction, and which cannot be broken down chemically into anything simpler. An atom is made up of protons and neutrons in a central nucleus surrounded by electrons (see ◊atomic structure). The atoms of the various elements differ in atomic number, relative atomic mass, and chemical behaviour. There are 112 different types of atom, corresponding with the 112 known elements as listed in the ◊periodic table of the elements.

Atoms are much too small to be seen even by even the most powerful optical microscope (the largest, caesium, has a diameter of 0.0000005 mm/0.00000002 in), and they are in constant motion. However, modern electron microscopes, such as the ◊scanning tunnelling microscope (STM) and the ◊atomic force microscope (AFM), can produce images of individual atoms and molecules.

atom bomb bomb deriving its explosive force from nuclear fission (see ◊nuclear energy) as a result of a neutron chain reaction, developed in the 1940s in the USA into a usable weapon.

Research began in the UK 1940 and was transferred to the USA after its entry into World War II the following year. Known as the Manhattan Project, the work was carried out under the direction of the US physicist J Robert Oppenheimer at Los Alamos, New Mexico.

After one test explosion, two atom bombs were dropped on the Japanese cities of Hiroshima (6 Aug 1945) and Nagasaki (9 Aug 1945); the bomb dropped on Hiroshima was as powerful as 12,700 tonnes of TNT, that on Nagaskai was equivalent to 22,000 tonnes of TNT. The USSR first detonated an atom bomb 1949 and the UK 1952.

The test site used by the UK was in the Monte Bello Islands off Australia. The development of the hydrogen bomb in the 1950s rendered the early atom bomb obsolete. See ◊nuclear warfare.

atomic clock timekeeping device regulated by various periodic processes occurring in atoms and molecules, such as atomic vibration or the frequency of absorbed or emitted radiation.

The first atomic clock was the ammonia clock, invented at the US National Bureau of Standards 1948. It was regulated by measuring the speed at which the nitrogen atom in an ammonia molecule vibrated back and forth. The rate of molecular vibration is not affected by temperature, pressure, or other external influences, and can be used to regulate an electronic clock.

A more accurate atomic clock is the caesium clock. Because of its internal structure, a caesium atom produces or absorbs radiation of a very precise frequency (9,192,631,770 Hz) that varies by less than one part in 10 billion. This frequency has been used to define the second, and is the basis of atomic clocks used in international timekeeping.

Hydrogen maser clocks, based on the radiation from hydrogen atoms, are the most accurate. The hydrogen maser clock at the US Naval Research Laboratory, Washington DC, is estimated to lose one second in 1,700,000 years. Cooled hydrogen maser clocks could theoretically be accurate to within one second in 300 million years.

Atomic clocks are so accurate that minute adjustments must be made periodically to the length of the year to keep the calendar exactly synchronized with the Earth's rotation, which has a tendency to speed up or slow down. There have been 17 adjustments made since 1972. In 1992 the northern hemisphere's summer was longer than usual – by one second. An extra second was added to the world's time at precisely 23 hours, 59 minutes, and 60 seconds on 30 June 1992. The adjustment was called for by the International Earth Rotation Service in Paris, which monitors the difference between Earth time and atomic time.

atom bomb The atomic explosion over the Japanese city of Nagasaki, 9 Aug 1945. Known as 'Fat Man', the Nagasaki bomb exploded at about 245 m/800 ft above the city, its 1.13 kg/2.5 lb of plutonium producing an explosion equivalent to some 22,000 tonnes of TNT. *Library of Congress*

atomic energy another name for ◊nuclear energy.

atomic force microscope (AFM) microscope developed in the late 1980s that produces a magnified image using a diamond probe, with a tip so fine that it may consist of a single atom, dragged over the surface of a specimen to 'feel' the contours of the surface. In effect, the tip acts like the stylus of a record player, reading the surface. The tiny up-and-down movements of the probe are converted to an image of the surface by computer and displayed on a screen. The AFM is useful for examination of biological specimens since, unlike the ◊scanning tunnelling microscope, the specimen does not have to be electrically conducting.

atomicity number of atoms of an ◊element that combine together to form a molecule. A molecule of oxygen (O_2) has atomicity 2; sulphur (S_8) has atomicity 8.

atomic mass see ◊relative atomic mass.

atomic mass unit or ***dalton unit*** (symbol amu or u) unit of mass that is used to measure the relative mass of atoms and molecules. It is equal to one-twelfth of the mass of a carbon-12 atom, which is equivalent to the mass of a proton or 1.66×10^{-27} kg. The ◊relative atomic mass of an atom has no units; thus oxygen-16 has an atomic mass of 16 daltons but a relative atomic mass of 16.

atomic number or ***proton number*** the number (symbol *Z*) of protons in the nucleus of an atom. It is equal to the positive charge on the nucleus.

In a neutral atom, it is also equal to the number of electrons surrounding the nucleus. The 112 elements are arranged in the ◊periodic table of the elements according to their atomic number. See also ◊nuclear notation.

atomic radiation energy given out by disintegrating atoms during ◊radioactive decay, whether natural or synthesized. The energy may be in the form of fast-moving particles, known as ◊alpha particles and ◊beta particles, or in the form of high-energy electromagnetic waves known as ◊gamma radiation. Overlong exposure to atomic radiation can lead to ◊radiation sickness.

Radiation biology studies the effect of radiation on living organisms. Exposure to atomic radiation is linked to chromosomal damage, cancer, and, in laboratory animals at least, hereditary disease.

atomic size or ***atomic radius*** size of an atom expressed as the radius in ◊angstroms or other units of length.

The sodium atom has an atomic radius of 1.57 angstroms (1.57×10^{-8} cm). For metals, the size of the atom is always greater than the size of its ion. For non-metals the reverse is true.

atomic structure internal structure of an ◊atom.

the nucleus The core of the atom is the ***nucleus***, a dense body only one ten-thousandth the diameter of the atom itself. The simplest nucleus, that of hydrogen, comprises a single stable positively charged particle, the ***proton***. Nuclei of other elements contain more protons and additional particles, called ***neutrons***, of about the same mass as the proton but with no electrical charge. Each element has its own characteristic nucleus with a unique number of protons, the atomic number. The number of neutrons may vary. Where atoms of a single element have different numbers of neutrons, they are called ◊isotopes.

Although some isotopes tend to be unstable and exhibit ◊radioactivity, they all have identical chemical properties.

electrons The nucleus is surrounded by a number of moving ***electrons***, each of which has a negative charge equal to the positive charge on a proton, but

'Anyone who spends any time watching animals has to conclude that the overriding purpose of an individual's existence is to pass on some part of it to the next generation.'

DAVID ATTENBOROUGH
The Trials of Life

which weighs only 1/1,839 times as much. In a neutral atom, the nucleus is surrounded by the same number of electrons as it contains protons. According to ◊quantum theory, the position of an electron is uncertain; it may be found at any point. However, it is more likely to be found in some places than others. The region of space in which an electron is most likely to be found is called an orbital (see ◊orbital, atomic). The chemical properties of an element are determined by the ease with which its atoms can gain or lose electrons from its outer orbitals.

attraction and repulsion Atoms are held together by the electrical forces of attraction between each negative electron and the positive protons within the nucleus. The latter repel one another with enormous forces; a nucleus holds together only because an even stronger force, called the strong nuclear force, attracts the protons and neutrons to one another. The strong force acts over a very short range – the protons and neutrons must be in virtual contact with one another (see ◊forces, fundamental). If, therefore, a fragment of a complex nucleus, containing some protons, becomes only slightly loosened from the main group of neutrons and protons, the natural repulsion between the protons will cause this fragment to fly apart from the rest of the nucleus at high speed. It is by such fragmentation of atomic nuclei (nuclear ◊fission) that nuclear energy is released.

atomic time time as given by ◊atomic clocks, which are regulated by natural resonance frequencies of particular atoms, and display a continuous count of seconds.

In 1967 a new definition of the second was adopted in the SI system of units: the duration of 9,192,631,770 periods of the radiation corresponding to the transition between two hyperfine levels of the ground state of the caesium-133 atom. The International Atomic Time Scale is based on clock data from a number of countries; it is a continuous scale in days, hours, minutes, and seconds from the origin on 1 Jan 1958, when the Atomic Time Scale was made 0 h 0 min 0 sec when Greenwich Mean Time was at 0 h 0 min 0 sec.

atomic weight another name for ◊relative atomic mass.

atonality music in which the sense of ◊tonality is distorted or obscured; music of no apparent key. It is used by film and television composers for situations of mystery or horror, exploiting dissonance for its power to disturb.

For Schoenberg, pioneer of atonal music from 1909, the intention was to liberate tonal expression and not primarily to disturb, and he rejected the term as misleading. Other exponents of atonality include Berg, Webern, Stockhausen, and Boulez.

atonement in Christian theology, the doctrine that Jesus suffered on the cross to bring about reconciliation and forgiveness between God and humanity.

Atonement is an action that enables a person separated from God by sin to be reconciled ('at one') with him. In ancient Judaism this was achieved through the sacrificial killing of animals.

Atonement, Day of Jewish holy day (***Yom Kippur***) held on the tenth day of Tishri (Sept–Oct), the first month of the Jewish year. It is a day of fasting, penitence, and cleansing from sin, ending the Ten Days of Penitence that follow Rosh Hashanah, the Jewish New Year.

ATP abbreviation for ***adenosine triphosphate***, a nucleotide molecule found in all cells. It can yield large amounts of energy, and is used to drive the thousands of biological processes needed to sustain life, growth, movement, and reproduction. Green plants use light energy to manufacture ATP as part of the process of ◊photosynthesis. In animals, ATP is formed by the breakdown of glucose molecules, usually obtained from the carbohydrate component of a diet, in a series of reactions termed ◊respiration. It is the driving force behind muscle contraction and the synthesis of complex molecules needed by individual cells.

Atreus in Greek mythology, the father of Agamemnon and Menelaus (the Atridae), son of Pelops, and brother of ◊Thyestes, with whom he contested the throne of ◊Mycenae. As part of the feud, Atreus served the flesh of Thyestes' children to their father at a banquet held to confirm the reconciliation of the two brothers.

atrium either of the two upper chambers of the heart. The left atrium receives freshly oxygenated blood from the lungs via the pulmonary vein; the right atrium receives deoxygenated blood from the ◊vena cava. Atrium walls are thin and stretch easily to allow blood into the heart. On contraction, the atria force blood into the thick-walled ventricles, which then give a second, more powerful beat.

atrium in architecture, an open inner courtyard. An atrium was originally the central court or main room of an ancient Roman house, open to the sky, often with a shallow pool to catch rainwater.

atrophy in medicine, a diminution in size and function, or output, of a body tissue or organ. It is usually due to nutritional impairment, disease, or disuse (muscle).

atropine alkaloid derived from ◊belladonna, a plant with toxic properties. It acts as an anticholinergic, inhibiting the passage of certain nerve impulses. It is used in premedication, to reduce bronchial and gastric secretions. It is also administered as a mild antispasmodic drug, and to dilate the pupil of the eye.

attempt in law, a partial or unsuccessful commission of a crime. An attempt must be more than preparation for a crime; it must involve actual efforts to commit a crime. In the UK, attempt is covered under the Criminal Attempts Act 1981, which repealed the 'suspected person offence', commonly known as the 'sus' law.

Attenborough David Frederick 1926– . English traveller and zoologist who has made numerous wildlife films for television. He was the writer and presenter of the television series *Life on Earth* 1979, *The Living Planet* 1983, *The Trials of Life* 1990, and *The Private Life of Plants* 1995.

Attenborough Richard, Baron Attenborough 1923– . English director, actor, and producer. He made his screen acting debut in *In Which We Serve* 1942, and later appeared in such films as *Brighton Rock* 1947 and *10 Rillington Place* 1970. He co-produced the socially-conscious *The Angry Silence* 1960, and directed *Oh! What a Lovely War* 1969. He subsequently concentrated on directing, including the epic biographies of *Gandhi* (which won eight Academy Awards) 1982, *Cry Freedom* 1987, and *Chaplin* 1992. He is the brother of naturalist David Attenborough.

attention-deficit hyperactivity disorder (ADHD) psychiatric condition occurring in young children characterized by impaired attention and hyperactivity. The disorder, associated with disruptive behaviour, learning difficulties, and under-achievement, is more common in boys. It is treated with methylphenidate (Ritalin).

In 1996, US researchers found that 50% of children diagnosed as ADHD sufferers carry a gene that effects brain cell response to the neurotransmitter dopamine. The same gene has also been linked to impulsiveness in adults. The outlook for ADHD sufferers varies, with up to a quarter being diagnosed with antisocial personality disorder as adults.

Attica (Greek ***Attiki***) region of Greece comprising Athens and the district around it; area 3,381 sq km/1,305 sq mi; population (1991) 3,522,800. It is renowned for its language, art, and philosophical thought in Classical times. It is a prefecture of modern Greece with Athens as its capital.

Attila c. 406–453. King of the Huns in an area from the Alps to the Caspian Sea from 434, known to later Christian history as the 'Scourge of God'. He twice attacked the Eastern Roman Empire to increase the quantity of tribute paid to him, 441–443 and 447–449, and then attacked the Western Roman Empire 450–452.

Attila first ruled jointly with his brother Bleda, whom he murdered 444. In 450 Honoria, the sister of the western emperor Valentinian III, appealed to him to rescue her from an arranged marriage, and Attila used her appeal to attack the West. He was forced back from Orléans by Aetius and Theodoric, King of the Visigoths, and defeated by them on the Catalaunian Fields 451. In 452 he led the Huns into Italy, and was induced to withdraw by Pope ◊Leo I.

He died on the night of his marriage to the German Ildico, either by poison or, as Chaucer represents it in his *Pardoner's Tale*, from a nasal haemorrhage induced by drunkenness.

Attis in classical mythology, a Phrygian god whose death and resurrection symbolized the end of winter and the arrival of spring. Beloved by the goddess ◊Cybele, who drove him mad as a punishment for his infidelity, he castrated himself and bled to death.

Attlee Clement (Richard), 1st Earl Attlee 1883–1967. British Labour politician. In the coalition government during World War II he was Lord Privy Seal 1940–42, dominions secretary 1942–43, and Lord President of the Council 1943–45, as well as deputy prime minister from 1942. As prime minister 1945–51 he introduced a sweeping programme of nationalization and a whole new system of social services.

Attlee was educated at Oxford and practised as a barrister 1906–09. Social work in London's East End and cooperation in poor-law reform led him to become a socialist; he joined the Fabian Society and the Independent Labour Party 1908. He became lecturer in social science at the London School of Economics 1913. After service in World War I he was mayor of Stepney, E London, 1919–20, and Labour member of Parliament for Limehouse 1922–50 and for W Walthamstow 1950–55. In the first and second Labour governments he was under-secretary for war 1924 and chancellor of the Duchy of Lancaster and postmaster general 1929–31. In 1935 he became leader of the opposition. In July 1945 he became prime minister after a Labour landslide in the general election. The government was returned to power with a much reduced majority 1950 and was defeated 1951.

attorney person who represents another in legal matters. In the USA, attorney is the formal title for a lawyer. Use of the term is largely obsolete in the UK except in Attorney General. See also ◊power of attorney.

Attorney General in the UK, principal law officer of the crown and head of the English Bar; the post is one of great political importance. In the USA, it is the chief law officer of the government and head of the Department of Justice.

In England, Wales, and Northern Ireland, the consent of the Attorney General is required for bringing certain criminal proceedings where offences against the state or public order are at issue (for example, the *Spycatcher* litigation, in which the UK government attempted to suppress the publication of the memoirs of former intelligence officer Peter Wright). Under the Criminal Justice Act 1988, cases can be referred to the Court of Appeal by the Attorney General if it appears to him or her that the sentencing of a person convicted of a serious offence has been unduly lenient.

Attlee, Clement British Labour politician Clement Attlee, photographed in about 1950. Attlee was prime minister 1945–51, and reforms under his leadership included the introduction of the National Health Service, mass nationalization, and the independence of India and Burma. *Corbis*

Auden English-born US poet W H Auden photographed at 'Poetry International 72'. Auden dominated the 1930s literary scene in Britain and was a member of a left-wing literary group with Stephen Spender and Christopher Isherwood. After his conversion to Christianity in 1941, Auden rewrote many of the left-wing poems that had been a feature of his early work. *Corbis*

attrition in earth science, the process by which particles of rock being transported by river, wind, or sea are rounded and gradually reduced in size by being struck against one another.

The rounding of particles is a good indication of how far they have been transported. This is particularly true for particles carried by rivers, which become more rounded as the distance downstream increases.

Atwood Margaret Eleanor 1939– . Canadian novelist, short-story writer, and poet. Her novels, which often treat feminist themes with wit and irony, include *The Edible Woman* 1969, *Life Before Man* 1979, *Bodily Harm* 1981, *The Handmaid's Tale* 1986, *Cat's Eye* 1989, and *The Robber Bride* 1993. Collections of poetry include *Power Politics* 1971, *You are Happy* 1974, and *Interlunar* 1984.

aubergine or ***eggplant*** plant *Solanum melongena*, a member of the nightshade family Solanaceae. The aubergine is native to tropical Asia. Its purple-skinned, sometimes white, fruits are eaten as a vegetable.

Aubrey John 1626–1697. English biographer and antiquary. He was the first to claim Stonehenge as a Druid temple. His *Lives*, begun 1667, contains gossip, anecdotes, and valuable insights into the celebrities of his time. It was published as *Brief Lives* 1898. *Miscellanies* 1696, a work on folklore and ghost stories, was the only work to be published during his lifetime.

aubrieta any spring-flowering dwarf perennial plant of the genus *Aubrieta* of the cress family Cruciferae. All are trailing plants with showy, purple flowers. Native to the Middle East, they are cultivated widely in rock gardens.

Auchinleck Claude John Eyre 1884–1981. British commander in World War II. He won the First Battle of El ◊Alamein 1942 in N Egypt. In 1943 he became commander in chief in India and founded the modern Indian and Pakistani armies. In 1946 he was promoted to field marshal; he retired 1947.

Auchinleck, nicknamed 'the Auk', succeeded Wavell as commander in chief Middle East July 1941, and in the summer of 1942 was forced back to the Egyptian frontier by the German field marshal Rommel, but his victory at the First Battle of El Alamein is regarded by some as more important to the outcome of World War II than the Second Battle. From India he gave background support to the Burma campaign.

Auckland largest city in New Zealand, situated in N North Island; population (1993) 910,200. It fills the isthmus that separates its two harbours (Waitemata and Manukau), and its suburbs spread N across the Harbour Bridge. It is the country's chief port and leading industrial centre, having iron and steel plants, engineering, car assembly, textiles, food processing, sugar refining, and brewing. There was a small whaling settlement on the site in the 1830s, and Auckland was officially founded as New Zealand's capital 1840, remaining so until 1865. The university was founded 1882.

auction bridge card game played by two pairs of players using all 52 cards in a standard deck. The chief characteristic is the selection of trumps by a preliminary bid or auction. It has been succeeded by ◊contract bridge.

Auden W(ystan) H(ugh) 1907–1973. English-born US poet. He wrote some of his most original poetry, such as *Look, Stranger!* 1936, in the 1930s when he led the influential left-wing literary group that included Louis MacNeice, Stephen Spender, and C Day Lewis. He moved to the USA 1939, became a US citizen 1946, and adopted a more conservative and Christian viewpoint, for example in *The Age of Anxiety* 1947.

He also wrote verse dramas with Christopher ◊Isherwood, such as *The Dog Beneath the Skin* 1935 and *The Ascent of F6* 1936, and opera librettos, notably for Igor Stravinsky's *The Rake's Progress* 1951. Auden was professor of poetry at Oxford 1956–61. His last works, including *Academic Graffiti* 1971 and *Thank You, Fog* 1973, are light and mocking in style and tone, but are dazzling virtuoso performances by a poet who recognized his position as the leading writer in verse of his time.

audit official inspection of a company's accounts by a qualified accountant as required by law each year to ensure that the company balance sheet reflects the true state of its affairs.

Audit Commission independent body in the UK established by the Local Government Finance Act 1982. It administers the District Audit Service (established 1844) and appoints auditors for the accounts of all UK local authorities. The Audit Commission consists of 15 members: its aims include finding ways of saving costs, and controlling illegal local-authority spending.

auditory canal tube leading from the outer ◊ear opening to the eardrum. It is found only in animals whose eardrums are located inside the skull, principally mammals and birds.

Audubon John James 1785–1851. US naturalist and artist. In 1827, after extensive travels and observations of birds, he published the first part of his *Birds of North America*, with a remarkable series of colour plates. Later he produced a similar work on North American quadrupeds.

Augean stables in Greek mythology, the stables of Augeas, king of Elis in southern Greece. One of the labours of ◊Heracles was to clean out the stables, which contained 3,000 cattle and had never been cleaned before. He was given only one day to do the labour and so diverted the river Alpheus through their yard.

Augsburg industrial city in Bavaria, Germany, at the confluence of the Wertach and Lech rivers, 52 km/32 mi NW of Munich; population (1993) 265,000. It is named after the Roman emperor Augustus, who founded it 15 BC.

Augsburg, Confession of statement of the Protestant faith as held by the German Reformers, composed by Philip ◊Melanchthon. Presented to the holy Roman emperor Charles V, at the conference known as the Diet of Augsburg 1530, it is the creed of the modern Lutheran church.

Augsburg, Peace of religious settlement following the Diet of Augsburg 1555, which established the right of princes in the Holy Roman Empire (rather than the emperor himself, Ferdinand I) to impose a religion on their subjects – later summarized by the maxim *cuius regio, eius religio* ('those who live in a country shall adopt the religion of its leader'). It initially applied only to Lutherans and Catholics.

augur member of a college of Roman priests who interpreted the will of the gods from signs or 'auspices' such as the flight of birds, the condition of entrails of sacrificed animals, and the direction of thunder and lightning. Their advice was sought before battle and on other important occasions. Consuls and other high officials had the right to consult the auspices themselves, and a campaign was said to be conducted 'under the auspices' of the general who had consulted the gods.

Augustan Age golden age of the Roman emperor ◊Augustus, during which art and literature flourished. The name is also given to later periods which used Classical ideals, such as that of Queen Anne in England.

Augustine of Hippo, St (Aurelius Augustinus) 354–430. One of the early Christian leaders and writers known as the Fathers of the Church. He was converted to Christianity by Ambrose in Milan and became bishop of Hippo (modern Annaba, Algeria) 396. Among Augustine's many writings are his *Confessions*, a spiritual autobiography, and *De Civitate Dei/The City of God*, vindicating the Christian church and divine providence in 22 books.

Augustine, St died 605. First archbishop of Canterbury, England. He was sent from Rome to convert England to Christianity by Pope Gregory I. He landed at Ebbsfleet in Kent 597 and soon after baptized Ethelbert, King of Kent, along with many of his subjects. He was consecrated bishop of the English at Arles in the same year, and appointed archbishop 601, establishing his see at Canterbury. Feast day 26 May.

Augustine was originally prior of the Benedictine monastery of St Andrew, Rome. In 603 he attempted unsuccessfully to unite the Roman and native Celtic churches at a conference on the Severn. He founded Christ Church, Canterbury, 603, and the abbey of Saints Peter and Paul.

Augustinian member of a religious community that follows the Rule of St ◊Augustine of Hippo. It includes the Canons of St Augustine, Augustinian Friars and Hermits, Premonstratensians, Gilbertines, and Trinitarians.

Augustus 63 BC–AD 14. Title of Octavian (born Gaius Octavius), first of the Roman emperors. He joined forces with Mark Antony and Lepidus in the Second Triumvirate. Following Mark Antony's liaison with the Egyptian queen Cleopatra, Augustus defeated her troops at Actium 31 BC. As emperor (from 27 BC) he reformed the government of the empire, the army, and Rome's public services and was a patron of the arts. The period of his rule is known as the ◊Augustan Age.

The son of a senator who married a niece of Julius Caesar, he became Caesar's adopted son and principal heir, and took the name Gaius Julius Caesar Octavianus. Following Caesar's murder, Octavian formed with Mark Antony and Lepidus the Triumvirate that divided the Roman world between them and proceeded to eliminate the opposition. Antony's victory 42 BC over Brutus and Cassius had

Augustine, St
Saint Augustine by the Italian painter Tiepolo (National Gallery, London). Early depictions of Augustine show him as a scholar in a library. With the Counter-Reformation he was increasingly shown – in grandiose terms, as in this picture – as a pillar of the True Church, its principal defender against heresy. *Corbis*

One half of the world cannot understand the pleasures of the other.

JANE AUSTEN
Emma

brought the republic to an end. Antony then became enamoured of Cleopatra and spent most of his time at Alexandria, while Octavian consolidated his hold on the western part of the Roman dominion. War was declared against Cleopatra, and the naval victory at Actium left Octavian in unchallenged supremacy, since Lepidus had been forced to retire.

After his return to Rome 29 BC, Octavian was created *princeps senatus*, and in 27 BC he was given the title of Augustus ('venerable'). He then resigned his extraordinary powers and received from the Senate, in return, the proconsular command, which gave him control of the army, and the tribunician power, whereby he could initiate or veto legislation. In his programme of reforms Augustus received the support of three loyal and capable helpers, Agrippa, Maecenas, and his wife, Livia, while Virgil and Horace acted as the poets laureate of the new regime.

A firm frontier for the empire was established: to the north, the friendly Batavians held the Rhine delta, and then the line followed the course of the Rhine and Danube; to the east, the Parthians were friendly, and the Euphrates gave the next line; to the south, the African colonies were protected by the desert; to the west were Spain and Gaul. The provinces were governed either by imperial legates responsible to the *princeps* or by proconsuls appointed by the Senate. The army was made a profession, with fixed pay and length of service, and a permanent fleet was established. Finally, Rome itself received an adequate water supply, a fire brigade, a police force, and a large number of public buildings.

The years after 12 BC were marked by private and public calamities: the marriage of Augustus' daughter Julia to his stepson ◊Tiberius proved disastrous; a serious revolt occurred in Pannonia AD 6; and in Germany three legions under Varus were annihilated in the Teutoburg Forest AD 9. Augustus ensured the stability of the empire by handing his powers intact to his successor Tiberius.

auk oceanic bird belonging to the family Alcidae, order Charadriiformes, consisting of 22 species of marine diving birds including razorbills, puffins, murres, and guillemots. Confined to the northern hemisphere, their range extends from well inside the Arctic Circle to the lower temperate regions. They feed on fish, and use their wings to 'fly' underwater in pursuit.

Most auks are colonial, breeding on stack tops or cliff edges, although some nest in crevices or holes. With the exception of one species they all lay a single large, very pointed egg.

'Auld Lang Syne' song written by the Scottish poet Robert Burns about 1789, which is often sung at New Year's Eve gatherings. The title means 'old long since' or 'long ago'.

Aum Shinrikyō (Japanese 'Om teaching the truth') millennial Buddhist–Hindu sect founded 1987 in Japan. Members believe that the world will end in 1997 or 1999 with a bloody war or nuclear explosion. Its leaders were held responsible for the ◊sarin nerve-gas attack on the Tokyo underground 1995. At that time the sect claimed 10,000 followers in Japan, as well as branches in Russia, the USA, and Germany.

Aung San 1916–1947. Burmese (Myanmar) politician. He was a founder and leader of the Anti-Fascist People's Freedom League, which led Burma's fight for independence from Great Britain. During World War II he collaborated first with Japan and then with the UK. In 1947 he became head of Burma's provisional government but was assassinated the same year by political opponents. His daughter ◊Suu Kyi spearheaded a nonviolent prodemocracy movement in Myanmar from 1988.

Aung San Suu Kyi Burmese (Myanmar) politician; see ◊Suu Kyi.

Aurangzeb or ***Aurungzebe*** 1618–1707. Mogul emperor of N India from 1658. Third son of ◊Shah Jahan, he made himself master of the court by a palace revolution. His reign was the most brilliant period of the Mogul dynasty, but his despotic tendencies and Muslim fanaticism aroused much opposition. His latter years were spent in war with the princes of Rajputana and the Marathas and Sikhs. His drive south into the Deccan overextended Mogul resources.

Aurelian (Lucius Domitius Aurelianus) c. 215–275 AD. Roman emperor from 270. A successful soldier, he was chosen emperor by his troops on the death of Claudius II. He defeated the Goths and Vandals, defeated and captured ◊Zenobia of Palmyra, and was planning a campaign against Parthia when he was murdered. The Aurelian Wall, a fortification surrounding Rome, was built by Aurelian 271. It was made of concrete, and substantial ruins exist. The Aurelian Way ran from Rome through Pisa and Genoa to Antipolis (Antibes) in Gaul.

Aurelius Marcus. Roman emperor; see ◊Marcus Aurelius Antoninus.

auricula species of primrose *Primula auricula*, a plant whose leaves are said to resemble a bear's ears. It is native to the Alps but popular in cool-climate areas and often cultivated in gardens.

Auriga constellation of the northern hemisphere, represented as a charioteer. Its brightest star is the first-magnitude ◊Capella, about 45 light years from Earth; Epsilon Aurigae is an ◊eclipsing binary star with a period of 27 years, the longest of its kind (last eclipse 1983).

Aurignacian in archaeology, an Old Stone Age culture in Europe that came between the Mousterian and the Solutrean in the Upper Palaeolithic. The name is derived from a rock-shelter at Aurignac in the Pyrenees of France. The earliest cave paintings and figurines are attributed to the Aurignacian peoples of W Europe about 30,000 BC.

Auriol Vincent 1884–1966. French Socialist politician. He was president of the two Constituent Assemblies of 1946 and first president of the Fourth Republic 1947–54.

aurochs (plural ***aurochs***) extinct species of long-horned wild cattle *Bos primigenius* that formerly roamed Europe, SW Asia, and N Africa. It survived in Poland until 1627. Black to reddish or grey, it was up to 1.8 m/6 ft at the shoulder. It is depicted in many cave paintings, and is considered the ancestor of domestic cattle.

aurora coloured light in the night sky near the Earth's magnetic poles, called ***aurora borealis*** ('northern lights') in the northern hemisphere and ***aurora australis*** in the southern hemisphere. Although aurorae are usually restricted to the polar skies, fluctuations in the ◊solar wind occasionally cause them to be visible at lower latitudes. An aurora is usually in the form of a luminous arch with its apex towards the magnetic pole followed by arcs, bands, rays, curtains, and coronas, usually green but often showing shades of blue and red, and sometimes yellow or white. Aurorae are caused at heights of over 100 km/60 mi by a fast stream of charged particles from solar flares and low-density 'holes' in the Sun's corona. These are guided by the Earth's magnetic field towards the north and south magnetic poles, where they enter the upper atmosphere and bombard the gases in the atmosphere, causing them to emit visible light.

Austen English novelist Jane Austen, whose uneventful life belied her ability to produce insightful novels concerning relationships and the nuances of social interaction amongst the landed gentry. Although she had several suitors, Austen never married. She died in 1817 of Addison's disease. *Corbis*

Aurora in Roman mythology, the goddess of the dawn. Her Greek equivalent is Eos.

Auschwitz (Polish ***Oswiecim***) town near Kraków in Poland, the site of a notorious ◊concentration camp used by the Nazis in World War II to exterminate Jews and other political and social minorities, as part of the 'final solution'. Each of the four gas chambers could hold 6,000 people.

The site was originally established as a transit camp but from March 1941 was expanded to a capacity of 130,000 to function as a labour camp: the nearby IG Farben factory was to use 10,000 Auschwitz prisoners as slave labour. In Sept 1941, mass executions began in the four gas chambers. Total numbers who died at Auschwitz are usually cited as between 1 million and 2.5 million, but some estimates reach 4 million.

Ausgleich compromise between Austria and Hungary 8 Feb 1867 that established the Austro-Hungarian Dual Monarchy under Habsburg rule. It endured until the collapse of Austria–Hungary 1918.

Austen Jane 1775–1817. English novelist. She described her raw material as 'three or four families in a Country Village'. *Sense and Sensibility* was published 1811, *Pride and Prejudice* 1813, *Mansfield Park* 1814, *Emma* 1815 (dated 1816), and

aurora The aurora australis or southern lights. Auroras are called aurora australis in the southern hemisphere and aurora borealis, or northern lights, in the northern hemisphere. *Image Select (UK) Ltd*

Northanger Abbey and *Persuasion* together 1817 (dated 1818), all anonymously. She observed speech and manners with wit and precision, revealing her characters' absurdities in relation to high standards of integrity and appropriateness.

Jane Austen was born in Steventon, Hampshire, where her father was rector. She was sent to school in Reading with her elder sister Cassandra, who was her lifelong friend and confidante, but she was mostly taught by her father. She began writing early; the burlesque *Love and Freindship* (sic), published 1922, was written 1790. In 1801 the family moved to Bath and after the death of her father in 1805, to Southampton, settling in 1809 with her mother and sisters in a house in Chawton, Hampshire, provided by her brother Edward (1768–1852).

Between 1795 and 1798 she worked on three novels. The first to be published was *Sense and Sensibility* (rewritten 1797–98 from an earlier draft in letter form). *Pride and Prejudice* (written 1796–97) followed, but *Northanger Abbey*, a skit on the contemporary Gothic novel (written 1798, sold to a publisher in Bath 1803, and bought back 1816), did not appear until 1817. The fragmentary *The Watsons* and *Lady Susan*, written about 1806, remained unfinished. The small success of her published works, however, stimulated Jane Austen to finish *Mansfield Park*, and to write *Emma*, *Persuasion*, and the final fragment *Sanditon* 1817, published 1825. She died in Winchester, and is buried in the cathedral.

Austerlitz, Battle of battle on 2 Dec 1805, in which the French forces of Emperor Napoleon Bonaparte defeated those of Alexander I of Russia and Francis II of Austria at a small town in the Czech Republic (formerly in Austria), 19 km/12 mi E of Brno. The battle was one of Napoleon's greatest victories, resulting in the end of the coalition against France – the Austrians signed the Treaty of Pressburg and the Russians retired to their own territory. ▷ *See feature on pp. 748–749.*

Austin capital of Texas, on the Colorado River; population (1992) 492,300. It is a centre for electronic and scientific research.

Austin Alfred 1835–1913. English poet. His satirical poem *The Season* 1861 was followed by plays and volumes of poetry little read today. *The Garden that I Love* 1894 is a prose idyll. He was poet laureate 1896–1913.

Austin J(ohn) L(angshaw) 1911–1960. British philosopher, a pioneer in the investigation of the way words are used in everyday speech. His later work was influential on the philosophy of language and his books include *How to do Things with Words* 1962.

Australasia and Oceania two geographical terms; Australasia is applied somewhat loosely to the islands of the South Pacific, including Australia, New Zealand, and their adjacent islands, while Oceania is a general or collective name for the groups of islands in the southern and central Pacific Ocean, comprising all those intervening between the southeastern shores of Asia and the western shores of America. The 10,000 or more Pacific Islands offer a great diversity of environments, from almost barren, waterless coral atolls to vast, continental islands.

area 8,500,000 sq km/3,300,000 sq mi (land area)

largest cities (population over 500,000) Sydney, Melbourne, Brisbane, Perth, Adelaide, Auckland

features the Challenger Deep in the Mariana Trench −11,034 m/−36,201 ft is the greatest known depth of sea in the world; Ayers Rock in Northern Territory, Australia, is the world's largest monolith; the Great Barrier Reef is the longest coral reef in the world; Mount Kosciusko 2,229 m/7,316 ft in New South Wales is the highest peak in Australia; Mount Cook 3,764 m/12,349 ft is the highest peak in New Zealand

physical Oceania can be broadly divided into groups of volcanic and coral islands on the basis of the ethnic origins of their inhabitants: Micronesia (Guam, Kiribati, Mariana, Marshall, Caroline Islands), Melanesia (Papua New Guinea, Vanuatu, New Caledonia, Fiji Islands, Solomon Islands) and Polynesia (Tonga, Samoa, Line Islands, Tuvalu, French Polynesia, Pitcairn); the highest point is Mount Wilhelm, Papua New Guinea 4,509 m/14,793 ft; the lowest point is Lake Eyre, South Australia −16m/−52 ft; the longest river is the Murray in SE Australia 2,590 km/1,609 mi; Australia is the largest island in the world. Most of the small islands are coral atolls, though some are of volcanic origin.

industries with a small home market, the region has a manufacturing sector dedicated to servicing domestic requirements and a large export-oriented sector, 70% of which is based on exports of primary agricultural or mineral products. Australia is a major producer of bauxite, nickel, silver, cobalt, gold, iron ore, diamonds, lead, and uranium; New Caledonia is a source of cobalt, chromite, and nickel; Papua New Guinea produces gold and copper. Agricultural products include coconuts, copra, palm oil, coffee, cocoa, phosphates (Nauru), rubber (Papua New Guinea), 40% of the world's wool (Australia, New Zealand); New Zealand and Australia are, respectively, the world's second and third largest producers of mutton and lamb; fishing and tourism are also major industries

population 26 million, rising to 30 million by the year 2000; annual growth rate from 1980 to 1985 1.5%; Australia accounts for 65% of the population

language English, French (French Polynesia, New Caledonia, Wallis and Futuna, Vanuatu); a wide range of indigenous Aboriginal, Maori, Melanesian, Micronesian, and Polynesian languages and dialects (over 700 in Papua New Guinea) are spoken

religion predominantly Christian; 30% of the people of Tonga adhere to the Free Wesleyan Church; 70% of the people of Tokelau adhere to the Congregational Church; French overseas territories are largely Roman Catholic

history there is a mixed diversity of race, language, and culture. The islands of Melanesia, dominated by New Guinea, were the first to be settled. Human prehistory may stretch back some 40,000 years in New Guinea, and recent archaeology in the highlands suggests that agriculture was practised there as long as 9,000 years ago. But the settlement of the remainder of the Pacific occurred only during the last 6,000 years, and in Polynesia as recently as 2,000 years ago. Food crops (notably yam, taro, banana, and coconut) and domestic animals (pig, dog, chicken) are all of Southeast Asian origin, with the exception of the sweet potato (important in the New Guinea highlands and Polynesia), which was probably introduced into the Pacific from America. ▷ *See map on p. 80; see feature on pp. 806–807.*

Australia country occupying all of the Earth's smallest continent, situated S of Indonesia, between the Pacific and Indian oceans. *See country box on p. 81 and table on p. 80.*

Australia Day Australian national day and public holiday in Australia, the anniversary of Captain Phillip's arrival on 26 Jan 1788 at Sydney Cove in Port Jackson and the founding of the colony of New South Wales.

Australian Aboriginal religions beliefs associated with the creation legends recorded in the ◊Dreamtime stories.

Australian Aborigine any of the 500 groups of indigenous inhabitants of the continent of Australia, who migrated to this region from S Asia about 40,000 years ago. They were hunters and gatherers, living throughout the continent in small kin-based groups before European settlement. Several hundred different languages developed, including Aranda (Arunta), spoken in central Australia, and Murngin, spoken in Arnhem Land.

In recent years a movement for the recognition of Aborigine rights has begun, with campaigns against racial discrimination in housing, education, wages, and medical facilities. Since 1984 aboriginal culture has been protected by federal law under the Aboriginal and Torres Islander Heritage Protection Act.

There are about 228,000 Aborigines in Australia, making up about 1.5% of Australia's population of 16 million. 12% of Australia is owned by Aborigines and many live in reserves as well as among the general population (65% of Aborigines live in cities or towns). The unemployment rate among Aborigines is three times the national average, and their average income is about half (1995). They have an infant mortality rate three times the national average, a suicide rate six times higher, and an adult life expectancy 20 years below the average for Australians generally; Aborigines living in remote areas of northern Australia face extremely high death rates – three and four times the national average for men and women respectively (1995).

Under an 'assimilation' policy in force 1918–53, thousands of Aborigine children, known as the 'stolen generation', were removed from their homes in Northern Territory and either given to white families or sent to orphanages.

In 1995, the Australian Senate dropped its opposition to the controversial Aboriginal Land Fund Bill, created to establish a fund enabling Aborigines to purchase land and housing. It was intended to supplement the 1993 Native Title Act, aimed at protecting land claims where indigenous people could prove continuing association – applicable to only a small minority of Aborigines.

Australian Antarctic Territory islands and territories south of 60° S, between 160° and 45° E longitude, excluding Adélie Land; area 6,044,000 sq km/2,332,984 sq mi of land and 75,800 sq km/29,259 sq mi of ice shelf. The population on the Antarctic continent is limited to research personnel.

Australian architecture the architecture of the Australian continent. Traditionally, Aboriginal settlements tended to be based around caves, or a construction of bark huts, arranged in a circular group; there was some variation in different areas.

Architecture of the early settlers includes Vaucluse House and the Sydney home of Australian politician William Charles Wentworth. Queensland has old-style homes built on stilts for coolness beneath their floors. Outstanding examples of modern architecture include the layout of the town of Canberra, by Walter Burley Griffin (1876–1937); Victoria Arts Centre, Melbourne, by Roy Grounds (1905–1981), who also designed the Academy of Science, Canberra, 1958–59; and the Sydney Opera House 1956–73, by Jorn Utzon (1918–).

'I dare not alter these things, they come to me from above.'

ALFRED AUSTIN
Remark rejecting the accusation of writing ungrammatical verse

Australian Aborigine
Australian Aborigine boys awaiting circumcision at an initiation ceremony. Aboriginal religious beliefs are based on the Dreamtime, a mythical past in which the land was created and rituals and laws established. Many of their rituals are to do with the land, and with the special meaning associated with particular sites such as mountains and rocks. *Corbis*

AUSTRALIA, COMMONWEALTH OF

State	Capital	Area in sq km/sq mi
New South Wales	Sydney	801,600/309,497
Queensland	Brisbane	1,727,200/666,871
South Australia	Adelaide	984,000/379,922
Tasmania	Hobart	67,800/26,177
Victoria	Melbourne	227,600/87,876
Western Australia	Perth	2,525,500/975,095
Territories		
Northern Territory	Darwin	1,346,200/519,767
Capital Territory	Canberra	2,400/926
External territories		
Ashmore and Cartier Islands		5/2
Australian Antarctic Territory		6,044,000/233,358
Christmas Island		135/52
Cocos (Keeling) Islands		14/5.5
Coral Sea Islands		1,000,000/386,100
Heard Island and McDonald Islands		410/158
Norfolk Island		40/15.5

Australian art art in Australia appears to date back at least 40,000 years, judging by radiocarbon dates obtained from organic material trapped in varnish that is covering apparently abstract rock engravings in South Australia, but may be even older, since worn crayons of ochre have been found in occupation layers of more than 50,000 years ago. Aboriginal art is closely linked with religion and mythology and includes rock and bark paintings. True Aboriginal art is now rare. European-style art developed in the 18th century, with landscape painting predominating.

precolonial art Pictures and decorated objects were produced in nearly all settled areas. Subjects included humans, animals, and geometric ornament. The 'X-ray style', showing the inner organs in an animal portrait, is unique to Australian ◊Aboriginal art.

18th century The first European paintings were documentary, depicting the Aborigines, the flora and fauna, and topographical scenes of Sydney and the surrounding area, showing the progress of development. They were executed by immigrant artists, mostly from Britain, France, and Germany.

late 19th–early 20th century The landscape painters of the Heidelberg School, notably Tom Roberts and later Arthur Streeton (1867–1943), became known outside Australia.

20th century The figurative painters William Dobell, Russell Drysdale, Sidney Nolan, and Albert Namatjira are among Australia's best-known modern artists. Sidney Nolan created a highly individual vision of the Australian landscape and of such folk heroes as Ned Kelly.

Australian Capital Territory territory ceded to Australia by New South Wales 1911 to provide the site of ◊Canberra, with its port at Jervis Bay, ceded 1915; area 2,400 sq km/926 sq mi; population (1993) 299,400.

Australian literature Australian literature begins with the letters, journals, and memoirs of early settlers and explorers. The first poet of note was Charles Harpur (1813–1868); idioms and rhythms typical of the country were developed by, among others, Henry Kendall (1841–1882) and Andrew Barton (Banjo) Paterson (1864–1941). More recent poets include Christopher Brennan (1870–1932) and Judith Wright (1915–), Kenneth Slessor (1901–1971), R D (Robert David) Fitzgerald (1902–), A D (Alec Derwent) Hope (1907–), James McAuley (1917–1976), and poet and novelist David ◊Malouf. Among early Australian novelists are Marcus Clarke (1846–1881), Rolfe Boldrewood (1826–1915), and Henry Handel Richardson (1870–1946). Striking a harsh vein in contemporary themes are the dramatist Ray Lawler (1921–) and novelist Patrick ◊White; the latter received the Nobel Prize for Literature 1973. Thomas ◊Keneally won the Booker Prize 1982 for *Schindler's Ark*.

Austria landlocked country in central Europe, bounded E by Hungary, S by Slovenia and Italy, W by Switzerland and Liechtenstein, NW by Germany, N by the Czech Republic, and NE by the Slovak Republic. *See country box on p. 82.*

Australian Capital Territory

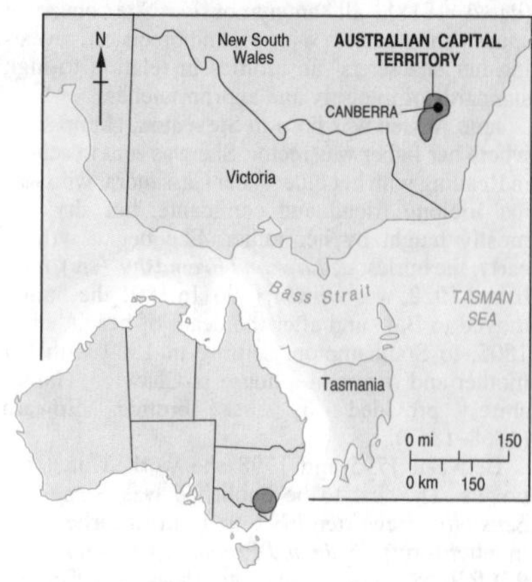

Austrian Succession, War of the war 1740–48 between Austria (supported by England and Holland) and Prussia (supported by France and Spain).

1740 The Holy Roman emperor Charles VI died and the succession of his daughter Maria Theresa was disputed by a number of European powers. Frederick the Great of Prussia seized Silesia from Austria.

1743 At Dettingen an army of British, Austrians, and Hanoverians under the command of George II was victorious over the French.

1745 An Austro-English army was defeated at Fontenoy but British naval superiority was confirmed, and there were gains in the Americas and India.

1748 The war was ended by the Treaty of Aix-la-Chapelle.

Austro-Hungarian Empire the Dual Monarchy established by the Habsburg Franz Joseph 1867 between his empire of Austria and his kingdom of

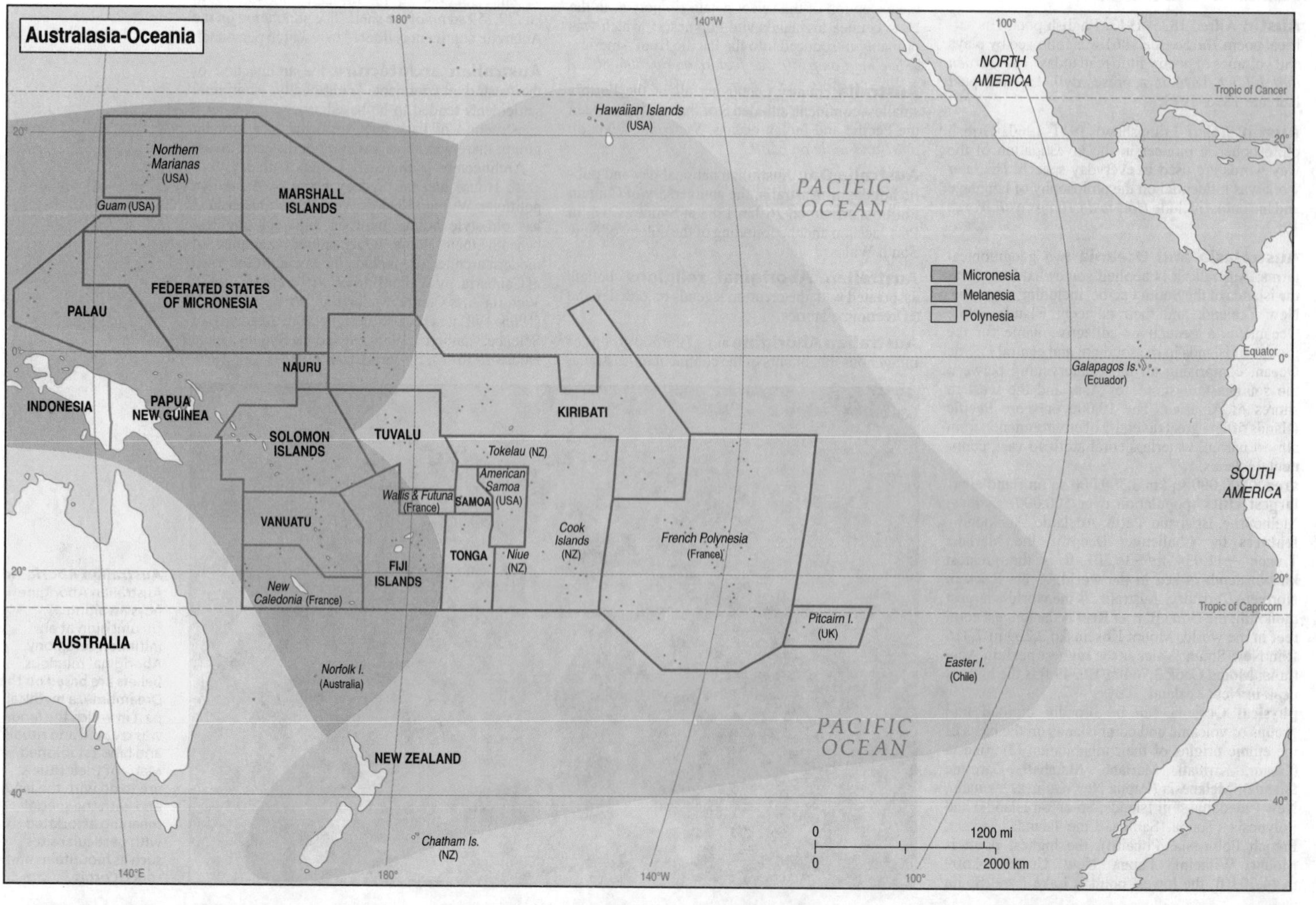

Australasia-Oceania

Hungary (including territory that became Czechoslovakia as well as parts of Poland, the Ukraine, Romania, Yugoslavia, and Italy).

It collapsed autumn 1918 with the end of World War I. Only two king-emperors ruled: Franz Joseph 1867–1916 and Charles 1916–18.

The Austro-Hungarian Empire came into being with an agreement known as the ◊Ausgleich. The two countries retained their own legal and administrative systems but shared foreign policy. In 1910 the empire had an area of 261,239 sq km/100,838 sq mi with a population of 51 million.

Austronesian languages (also known as ***Malayo-Polynesian***) family of languages spoken in Malaysia, the Indonesian archipelago, parts of the region that was formerly Indochina, Taiwan, Madagascar, Melanesia, and Polynesia (excluding Australia and most of New Guinea). The group contains some 500 distinct languages, including Malay in Malaysia, Bahasa in Indonesia, Fijian, Hawaiian, and Maori. ▷*See feature on pp. 806–807.*

autarchy national economic policy that aims at achieving self-sufficiency and eliminating the need for imports (by imposing tariffs, for example). Such a goal may be difficult, if not impossible, for a small country. Countries that take protectionist measures and try to prevent free trade are sometimes described as autarchical.

authoritarianism rule of a country by a dominant elite who repress opponents and the press to maintain their own wealth and power. They are frequently indifferent to activities not affecting their security, and rival power centres, such as trade unions and political parties, are often allowed to exist, although under tight control. An extreme form is ◊totalitarianism.

autism, infantile rare disorder, generally present from birth, characterized by a withdrawn state and a failure to develop normally in language or social behaviour. Although the autistic child may, rarely, show signs of high intelligence (in music or with numbers, for example), many have impaired intellect. The cause is unknown, but is thought to involve a number of factors, possibly including an inherent abnormality of the child's brain. Special education may bring about some improvement.

autobiography a person's own biography, or written account of his or her life, distinguished from the journal or diary by being a connected narrative, and from memoirs by dealing less with contemporary events and personalities. *The Boke of Margery Kempe* about 1432–36 is the oldest known autobiography in English.

Forms of autobiography include the confessional, attempting faithful description of moral weakness and the inner life, as in the influential *Confessions* of St Augustine (early 5th century) and Rousseau (1781); the would-be exemplary, seeking to promote a particular cause or outlook espoused by the writer, as in Hitler's *Mein Kampf* (written in the 1920s) or the autobiography of John Stuart Mill (1873); and military and political memoirs, intended as contributions to history.

AUSTRALIA
Commonwealth of

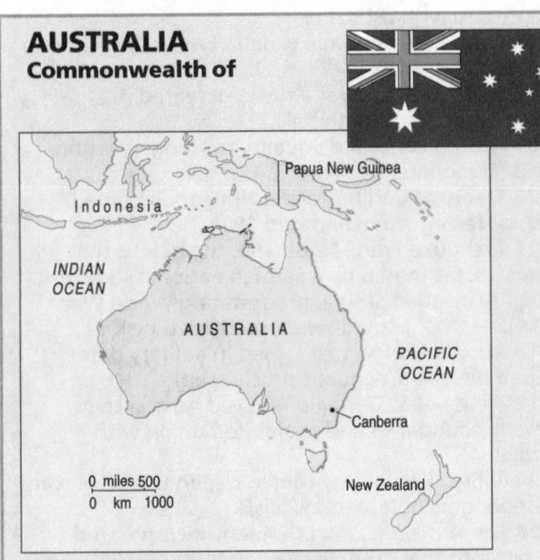

area 7,682,300 sq km/2,966,136 sq mi
capital Canberra
major towns/cities Adelaide, Alice Springs, Brisbane, Darwin, Melbourne, Perth, Sydney, Hobart, Geelong, Newcastle, Townsville, Wollongong
physical features Ayers Rock; Arnhem Land; Gulf of Carpentaria; Cape York Peninsula; Great Australian Bight; Great Sandy Desert; Gibson Desert; Great Victoria Desert; Simpson Desert; the Great Barrier Reef; Great Dividing Range and Australian Alps in the E (Mount Kosciusko, 2,229 m/7,136 ft, Australia's highest peak). The fertile SE region is watered by the Darling, Lachlan, Murrumbridgee, and Murray rivers. Lake Eyre basin and Nullarbor Plain in the S
territories Norfolk Island, Christmas Island, Cocos (Keeling) Islands, Ashmore and Cartier Islands, Coral Sea Islands, Heard Island and McDonald Islands, Australian Antarctic Territory
head of state Elizabeth II from 1952, represented by governor general William George Hayden from 1989
head of government John Howard from 1996
political system federal constitutional monarchy
administrative divisions six states and two territories
political parties Australian Labor Party, moderate left of centre; Liberal Party of Australia, moderate, liberal, free enterprise; National Party of Australia (formerly Country Party), centrist non-metropolitan
armed forces 56,100 (1995)
conscription none
defence spend (%GDP) 2.3 (1994)
education spend (%GDP) 5.5% (1992)
health spend (%GNP) 5.8 (1993)
death penalty abolished 1985
population 18,088,000 (1995 est)
population growth rate 1.4% (1990–95); 1.1% (2000–05)
age distribution (% of total population) <15 21.6%, 15–65 66.8%, >65 11.6% (1995)
ethnic distribution 99% of European descent; remaining 1% Aborigine or Asian
population density (per sq km) 2 (1994)
urban population (% of total) 85 (1995)
labour force 50% of total population: 6% agriculture, 26% industry, 68% services (1990)
unemployment 8.5% (1995)
child mortality rate (under 5, per 1,000 live births) 8 (1993)
life expectancy 74 (men), 80 (women)
education (compulsory years) 10 or 11 (states vary)
literacy rate 99%
languages English, Aboriginal languages
religions Anglican 26%, other Protestant 17%, Roman Catholic 26%
TV sets (per 1,000 people) 482 (1992)
currency Australian dollar
GDP (US $) 347.4 billion (1995)
GDP per capita (PPP) (US $) 19,102 (1995)
growth rate 3.1% (1994/95)
average annual inflation 1.9% (1994)
major trading partners USA, Japan, UK, New Zealand, Republic of Korea, China, Taiwan, Singapore
resources coal, iron ore (world's third-largest producer), bauxite, copper, zinc (world's second-largest producer), nickel (world's fifth-largest producer), uranium, gold, diamonds
industries mining, metal products, textiles, wood and paper products, chemical products, electrical machinery, transport equipment, printing, publishing and recording media, tourism, electronic communications
exports major world producer of raw materials: iron ore, aluminium, coal, nickel, zinc, lead, gold, tin, tungsten, uranium, crude oil; wool, meat, cereals, fruit, sugar, wine. Principal markets: Japan 25%, USA 8.1% (1993)
imports processed industrial supplies, transport equipment and parts, road vehicles, petroleum and petroleum products, medicinal and pharmaceutical products, organic chemicals, consumer goods
arable land 6%
agricultural products wheat, barley, oats, rice, sugar cane, fruit, grapes; livestock (chiefly cattle and sheep) and dairy products

HISTORY
c. 40,000 BC Aboriginal immigration from S India, Sri Lanka, and SE Asia.
AD 1606 First recorded sightings of Australia by Europeans including discovery of Cape York by Dutch explorer Willem Jansz in *Duyfken*.
1770 Captain James Cook claimed New South Wales for Britain.
1788 Sydney founded as British penal colony.
late 18th–19th Cs Great age of exploration: coastal surveys by George Bass and Matthew Flinders; interior by Charles Sturt, Edward Eyre, Robert Burke and William Wills, John McDouall Stuart, and John Forrest. Overlanders and squatters also opened up new territory as did bushrangers, including Ned Kelly.
1804 Castle Hill Rising by Irish convicts.
1813 Crossing of Blue Mountains removed major barrier to exploration of interior.
1825 Tasmania seceded from New South Wales.
1829 Western Australia colonized.
1836 South Australia colonized.
1840–68 End of convict transportation.
1850 British Act of Parliament permitted Australian colonies to draft their own constitutions and achieve virtual self-government.
1851–61 Gold rushes contributed to exploration and economic growth.
1851 Victoria seceded from New South Wales.
1855 Victoria achieved self-government.
1856 New South Wales, South Australia, and Tasmania achieved self-government.
1859 Queensland formed from New South Wales and achieved self-government.
1860 (National) Country Party founded.
1890 Western Australia achieved self-government.
1891 Depression gave rise to Australian Labor Party.
1899–1900 South African War – forces offered by individual colonies.
1901 Creation of Commonwealth of Australia.
1902 Immigration Restriction Act introduced language tests for potential settlers; women gained right to vote.
1914–18 World War I: over 300,000 Australian volunteers fought in Middle East and on Western Front.
1919 Australia given mandates over Papua New Guinea and Solomon Islands.
1927 Seat of federal government moved to Canberra.
1931 Statute of Westminster confirmed Australian independence.
1933 Western Australia's vote to secede overruled.
1939–45 World War II: Australian troops fought in Greece, N Africa, and SW Pacific.
1941 Curtin's appeal to USA for military help marked shift away from exclusive relationship with Britain.
1944 Liberal Party founded by Menzies.
1948–75 Influx of around two million new immigrants, chiefly from continental Europe.
1950–53 Australia contributed troops to United Nations (UN) forces in Korean War.
1951 Australia joined USA and New Zealand in ANZUS Pacific security alliance.
1965–72 Australian troops participated in Vietnam War.
1967 Referendum gave Australian Aborigines full citizenship rights. Australia became a member of the Association of South East Asian Nations (ASEAN).
1973 Britain entered European Economic Community (EEC), and in 1970s Japan became Australia's chief trading partner.
1974 'White Australia' immigration restrictions abolished.
1975 Constitutional crisis: Governor General John Kerr dismissed Prime Minister Gough Whitlam after senate blocked financial legislation. Papua New Guinea became independent.
1978 Northern Territory achieved self-government.
1983 Labor Party returned to power under Bob Hawke.
1986 Australia Act passed by British Parliament eliminating last vestiges of British legal authority in Australia.
1988 Free Trade Agreement signed with New Zealand.
1992 Citizenship Act removed oath of allegiance to British crown.
1993 Labor Party won record fifth election victory.
1996 Liberal-National coalition, headed by John Howard, won general election.
1998 Howard's coalition retained power in general election, despite a reduced majority.

SEE ALSO Australian Aborigine; Cook, James; New South Wales

AUSTRIA
Republic of

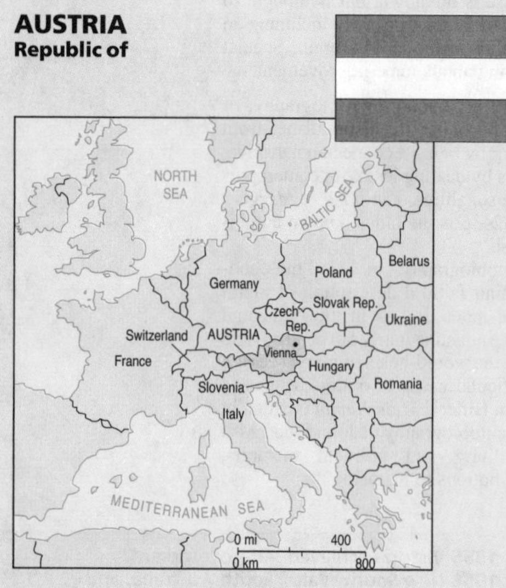

national name *Republik Österreich*
area 83,500 sq km/32,374 sq mi
capital Vienna
major towns/cities Graz, Linz, Salzburg, Innsbruck
physical features landlocked mountainous state, with Alps in W and S (Austrian Alps, including Grossglockner and Brenner and Semmering passes, Lechtaler and Allgauer Alps N of river Inn, Carnic Alps on Italian border) and low relief in E where most of the population is concentrated; river Danube
head of state Thomas Klestil from 1992
head of government Franz Vranitzky from 1986
political system democratic federal republic
administrative divisions nine federal states
political parties Social Democratic Party of Austria (SPÖ), democratic socialist; Austrian People's Party (ÖVP), progressive centrist; Freedom (formerly Freedom Party of Austria: FPÖ), right-wing; United Green Party of Austria (VGÖ), conservative ecological; Green Alternative Party (ALV), radical ecological
armed forces 55,750 (1995)
conscription 6 months
defence spend (% GDP) 0.9 (1994)
education spend (% GNP) 5.8 (1992)
health spend (% GDP) 6.0 (1993)
death penalty abolished 1968
population 8,106,000 (1996 est)
population growth rate 0.7% (1990–95); 0.2% (2000–05)
age distribution (% of total population) <15 17.8%, 15–65 67.3%, >65 14.9% (1995)
ethnic distribution 98% German, 0.7% Croatian, 0.3% Slovene
population density (per sq km) 94 (1994)
urban population (% of total) 56 (1995)
labour force 46% of population: 8% agriculture, 38% industry, 55% services (1990)
unemployment 6.6% (1995)
child mortality rate (under 5, per 1,000 live births) 8 (1993)
life expectancy 72 (men), 79 (women)
education (compulsory years) 9
literacy rate 99%
language German
religions Roman Catholic 78%, Protestant 5%
TV sets (per 1,000 people) 480 (1992)
currency schilling
GDP (US $) 226.1 billion (1996)
GDP per capita (PPP) (US $) 20,907 (1995)
growth rate 1.8% (1994/95)
average annual inflation 2.8% (1995)
major trading partners EU, Switzerland, USA, Japan
resources lignite, iron, kaolin, gypsum, talcum, magnetite, lead, zinc, forests
industries raw and rolled steel, machinery, cellulose, paper, cardboard, cement, fertilizers, viscose staple yarn, sawn wood, flat glass, salt, sugar, milk, margarine
exports dairy products, food products, wood and paper products, machinery and transport equipment, metal and metal products, chemical products. Principal market for exports: EU countries 63.6% (1993)
imports petroleum and petroleum products, food and live animals, chemicals and related products, textiles, clothing. Principal source: EU countries 67% (1993)
arable land 16.9% (1993)
agricultural products wheat, barley, rye, oats, potatoes, maize, sugar beet; dairy products

HISTORY
14 BC Country S of river Danube conquered by the Romans.
5th C AD Region occupied by Vandals, Huns, Goths, Lombards, and Avars.
791 Charlemagne conquered the Avars and established the East Mark, the nucleus of the future Austrian Empire.
976 Holy Roman Emperor Otto II granted the East Mark to the House of Babenburg, which ruled until 1246.
1156 Margrave of Austria raised to a duke.
1282 Holy Roman Emperor Rudolf of Habsburg seized Austria and invested his son as its duke; for over 500 years most rulers of Austria were elected Holy Roman emperor.
1453 Austria became an archduchy.
1519–56 Emperor Charles V was both archduke of Austria and king of Spain; Habsburgs dominant in Europe.
1526 Bohemia came under Habsburg rule.
1529 Vienna besieged by the Ottoman Turks.
1618–48 Thirty Years' War: Habsburgs weakened by failure to secure control over Germany.
1683 Polish-Austrian force led by Jan Sobieski defeated the Turks at Vienna.
1699 Treaty of Karlowitz: Austrians expelled Turks from Hungary, which came under Habsburg rule.
1713 By the Treaty of Utrecht, Austria obtained the Spanish Netherlands (Belgium) and political control over most of Italy.
1740–48 War of Austrian Succession: Prussia (supported by France and Spain) attacked Austria (supported by Holland and England) on the pretext of disputing rights of Maria Theresa; Austria lost Silesia to Prussia.
1772 Austria joined in partition of Poland, annexing Galicia.
1780–90 'Enlightened despotism': Joseph II tried to impose radical reforms.
1792 Austria went to war with revolutionary France.
1804 Francis II took the title Emperor of Austria.
1806 Holy Roman Empire abolished.
1809–48 Guided by foreign minister Prince Klemens von Metternich, Austria took a leading role in resisting liberalism and nationalism in Europe.
1815 After the Napoleonic Wars, Austria lost its Netherlands but received Lombardy and Venetia.
1848 Outbreak of liberal-nationalist revolts throughout the Austrian Empire; Ferdinand I abdicated in favour of Franz Joseph; revolutions suppressed with difficulty.
1859 France and Sardinia expelled Austrians from Lombardy by force.
1866 Seven Weeks' War: Prussia defeated Austria, which ceded Venetia to Italy.
1867 Austria conceded equality to Hungary within the dual monarchy of Austria-Hungary.
1878 Treaty of Berlin: Austria-Hungary occupied Bosnia-Herzegovina; annexed 1908.
1914 Archduke Franz Ferdinand, the heir to the throne, assassinated by a Serbian nationalist; Austria-Hungary invaded Serbia, precipitating World War I.
1916 Death of Franz Joseph; succeeded by Karl I.
1918 Austria-Hungary collapsed in military defeat; empire dissolved; republic proclaimed.
1919 Treaty of St Germain reduced Austria to its present boundaries and prohibited union with Germany.
1934 Political instability culminated in brief civil war; right-wingers defeated socialists.
1938 The *Anschluss*: Nazi Germany incorporated Austria into the Third Reich.
1945 Following World War II, the victorious Allies divided Austria into four zones of occupation (US, British, French, and Soviet); Second Republic established under Karl Renner.
1955 Austrian State Treaty ended occupation; Austria regained independence on condition of neutrality.
1960–70s Austria experienced rapid industrialization and prosperity under governments dominated by moderate socialists and centrists.
1986 Election of Kurt Waldheim as president, despite allegations of war crimes during World War II, led to a measure of diplomatic isolation until Waldheim's replacement 1992.
1995 Became a full European Union (EU) member.
1998 President Klestil re-elected.

SEE ALSO Austrian Succession, War of the; Austro-Hungarian Empire; Metternich, Klemens von; Napoleonic Wars; World War I

autochrome in photography, a single-plate additive colour process devised by the ◊Lumière brothers 1903. It was the first commercially available process, in use 1907–35.

autocracy form of government in which one person holds absolute power. The autocrat has uncontrolled and undisputed authority. Russian government under the tsars was an autocracy extending from the mid-16th century to the early 20th century. The title *Autocratix* (a female autocrat) was assumed by Catherine II of Russia in the 18th century.

AUSTRIA: PROVINCES

Province	Capital	Area in sq km/sq mi
Burgenland	Eisenstadt	4,000/1,544
Carinthia	Klagenfurt	9,500/3,667
Lower Austria	St Pölten	19,200/7,413
Salzburg	Salzburg	7,200/2,779
Styria	Graz	16,400/6,332
Tirol	Innsbruck	12,600/4,864
Upper Austria	Linz	12,000/4,633
Vienna	Vienna	420/162
Vorarlberg	Bregenz	2,600/1,003

auto-da-fé (Portuguese 'act of faith') religious ceremony, including a procession, solemn mass, and sermon, which accompanied the sentencing of heretics by the Spanish ◊Inquisition before they were handed over to the secular authorities for punishment, usually burning.

autogiro or ***autogyro*** heavier-than-air craft that supports itself in the air with a rotary wing, or rotor. The Spanish aviator Juan de la Cierva (1895–1936) designed the first successful autogiro 1923. The autogiro's rotor provides only lift and not propulsion; it has been superseded by the helicopter, in which the rotor provides both. The autogiro is propelled by an orthodox propeller.

The three- or four-bladed rotor on an autogiro spins in a horizontal plane on top of the craft, and is not driven by the engine. The blades have an aerofoil cross section, as a plane's wings. When the autogiro moves forward, the rotor starts to rotate by itself, a state known as autorotation. When travelling fast enough, the rotor develops enough lift from its aerofoil blades to support the craft.

autoimmunity in medicine, condition where the body's immune responses are mobilized not against 'foreign' matter, such as invading germs, but against the body itself. Diseases considered to be of autoimmune origin include myasthenia gravis, rheumatoid arthritis, and lupus erythematous.

In autoimmune diseases T-lymphocytes reproduce to excess to home in on a target (properly a foreign disease-causing molecule); however, molecules of the body's own tissue that resemble the target may also be attacked, for example insulin-producing cells, resulting in insulin-dependent diabetes; if certain joint membrane cells are attacked, then rheumatoid arthritis may result; and if myelin, the basic protein of the nervous system, then multiple sclerosis results. In 1990 in Israel a T-cell vaccine was produced that arrests the excessive reproduction of T-lymphocytes attacking healthy target tissues.

Autolycus in Greek mythology, an accomplished thief and trickster, son of the god ◊Hermes, who gave him the power of invisibility.

autolysis in biology, the destruction of a ◊cell after its death by the action of its own ◊enzymes, which break down its structural molecules.

automatic pilot control device that keeps an aeroplane flying automatically on a given course at a given height and speed. Devised by US business executive Lawrence Sperry 1912, the automatic pilot contains a set of ◊gyroscopes that provide references for the plane's course. Sensors detect when the plane deviates from this course and send signals to the control surfaces – the ailerons, elevators, and rudder – to take the appropriate action. Autopilot is also used in missiles. Most airliners cruise on automatic pilot, also called autopilot and gyropilot, for much of the time.

automation widespread use of self-regulating machines in industry. Automation involves the addition of control devices, using electronic sensing and computing techniques, which often follow the pattern of human nervous and brain functions, to already mechanized physical processes of production and distribution; for example, steel processing, mining, chemical production, and road, rail, and air control.

automatism in the arts, an act of creation which either allows chance to play a major role or which draws on the unconscious mind through free association, states of trance, or dreams. Automatism was fundamental to Surrealism, whose practitioners experimented with automatic writing and automatic drawing, producing streams of words or doodles from the unconscious. It has been taken up other abstract painters, such as the Canadian Automatistes, a group working in Montreal in the 1940s, and the Abstract Expressionist Jackson ◊Pollock.

automaton mechanical figure imitating human or animal performance. Automatons are usually designed for aesthetic appeal as opposed to purely functional robots. The earliest recorded automaton is an Egyptian wooden pigeon of 400 BC.

autonomic nervous system in mammals, the part of the nervous system that controls those functions not controlled voluntarily, including the heart rate, activity of the intestines, and the production of sweat.

There are two divisions of the autonomic nervous system. The ***sympathetic*** system responds to stress, when it speeds the heart rate, increases blood pressure, and generally prepares the body for action. The ***parasympathetic*** system is more important when the body is at rest, since it slows the heart rate, decreases blood pressure, and stimulates the digestive system.

automation Industrial automation has led to greater productivity and improved quality control. On this production line at a Rover car plant in England, car bodies are welded by computer-controlled robots, a task that is complex yet boring and potentially hazardous for human workers. *Rover Group*

At all times, both types of autonomic nerves carry signals that bring about adjustments in visceral organs. The actual rate of heartbeat is the net outcome of opposing signals. Today, it is known that the word 'autonomic' is misleading – the reflexes managed by this system are actually integrated by commands from the brain and spinal cord (the central nervous system).

autonomy in politics, a term used to describe political self-government of a state or, more commonly, a subdivision of a state. Autonomy may be based upon cultural or ethnic differences and often leads eventually to independence.

autopsy or ***postmortem*** examination of the internal organs and tissues of a dead body, performed to try to establish the cause of death.

autoradiography in biology, a technique for following the movement of molecules within an organism, especially a plant, by labelling with a radioactive isotope that can be traced on photographs. It is used to study ◊photosynthesis, where the pathway of radioactive carbon dioxide can be traced as it moves through the various chemical stages.

autosome any ◊chromosome in the cell other than a sex chromosome. Autosomes are of the same number and kind in both males and females of a given species.

autosuggestion conscious or unconscious acceptance of an idea as true, without demanding rational proof, but with potential subsequent effect for good or ill. Pioneered by French psychotherapist Emile Coué (1857–1926) in healing, it is sometimes used in modern psychotherapy to conquer nervous habits and dependence on addictive substances such as tobacco and alcohol.

autotroph any living organism that synthesizes organic substances from inorganic molecules by using light or chemical energy. Autotrophs are the primary producers in all food chains since the materials they synthesize and store are the energy sources of all other organisms. All green plants and many planktonic organisms are autotrophs, using sunlight to convert carbon dioxide and water into sugars by ◊photosynthesis.

The total ◊biomass of autotrophs is far greater than that of animals, reflecting the dependence of animals on plants, and the ultimate dependence of all life on energy from the Sun – green plants convert light energy into a form of chemical energy (food) that animals can exploit. Some bacteria use the chemical energy of sulphur compounds to synthesize organic substances. It is estimated that 10% of the energy in autotrophs can pass into the next stage of the ◊food chain, the rest being lost as heat or indigestible matter. See also ◊heterotroph.

autumnal equinox see ◊equinox.

autumn crocus any member of the genus *Colchicum*, family Liliaceae. One species, the mauve meadow saffron *C. autumnale*, yields colchicine, which is used in treating gout and in plant breeding (it causes plants to double the numbers of their chromosomes, forming ◊polyploids).

Auvergne ancient province of central France and modern region comprising the *départements* of Allier, Cantal, Haute-Loire, and Puy-de-Dôme; capital Clermont-Ferrand; area 26,000 sq km/10,036 sq mi; population (1990) 1,321,200. It is a mountainous area, composed chiefly of volcanic rocks in several masses. Industries include cattle, wheat, wine, and cheese.

history a Roman province, it was named after the ancient Gallic Avenni tribe whose leader, Vercingetorix, led a revolt against the Romans 52 BC. In the 14th century the Auvergne was divided into a duchy, dauphiny, and countship. The duchy and dauphiny were united by the dukes of Bourbon before being confiscated by Francis I 1527. The countship united with France 1615.

Auxerre capital of Yonne *département*, France, 170 km/106 mi SE of Paris, on the river Yonne; population (1990) 40,600. The Gothic cathedral, founded 1215, has exceptional sculptures and stained glass.

auxin plant ◊hormone that promotes stem and root growth in plants. Auxins influence many aspects of plant growth and development, including cell enlargement, inhibition of development of axillary buds, ◊tropisms, and the initiation of roots. ***Synthetic auxins*** are used in rooting powders for cuttings, and in some weedkillers, where high auxin concentrations cause such rapid growth that the plants die. They are also used to prevent premature fruitdrop in orchards.

The most common naturally occurring auxin is known as indoleacetic acid, or IAA. It is produced in the shoot apex and transported to other parts of the plant.

Ava former capital of Burma (now Myanmar), on the river Irrawaddy, founded by Thadomin Payä 1364. Thirty kings reigned there until 1782, when a new capital, Amarapura, was founded by Bodaw Payä. In 1823 the site of the capital was transferred back to Ava by King Baggidaw.

avalanche (from French *avaler* 'to swallow') fall or flow of a mass of snow and ice down a steep slope under the force of gravity. Avalanches occur because of the unstable nature of snow masses in mountain areas.

Changes of temperature, sudden sound, or earth-borne vibrations may trigger an avalanche, particularly on slopes of more than 35°. The snow compacts into ice as it moves, and rocks may be carried along, adding to the damage caused.

Avalokiteśvara in Mahāyāna Buddhism, one of the most important ◊bodhisattvas, seen as embodying compassion. He is an emanation of Amida Buddha. In China, as Kuan Yin, and Japan, as Kannon, he is confused with his female consort, becoming the popular goddess of mercy.

Avalon in Celtic mythology, the island of the blessed, or paradise; and in the legend of King ◊Arthur, the land of heroes, ruled over by ◊Morgan le Fay to which King Arthur is conveyed after his final battle with ◊Mordred. It has been identified since the Middle Ages with Glastonbury in Somerset, SW England.

avant-garde (French 'forward guard') in the arts, those artists or works that are in the forefront of new developments in their media. The term was introduced (as was 'reactionary') after the French Revolution, when it was used to describe any socialist political movement.

avant-garde dance experimental dance form that rejects the conventions of classical ballet and modern dance. It is often performed in informal spaces – museums, rooftops, even scaling walls.

In the USA, avant-garde dance has been mainly represented by the work of Merce ◊Cunningham, and by the performances held by artists at the Judson Memorial Church during the 1960s. While retaining technique and rhythm, Cunningham abolished narrative, explicit emotional statements, and any direct connection between dance and music.

In the UK, leading exponents of avant-garde dance techniques include Michael ◊Clark from the mid-1980s, Rosemary Butcher (1947–), and Lloyd Newson (1954–). In Japan, experimental dance is represented by butoh dance companies.

Avar member of a Central Asian nomadic people who in the 6th century invaded the area of Russia north of the Black Sea previously held by the Huns. They extended their dominion over the Bulgarians and Slavs in the 7th century and were finally defeated by Charlemagne 796.

avatar in Hindu mythology, the descent of a deity to Earth in a visible form, for example the ten avatars of ◊Vishnu.

Avebury Europe's largest stone circle (diameter 412 m/1,352 ft), in Wiltshire, England. It was probably constructed in the Neolithic period 3,500 years ago, and is linked with nearby ◊Silbury Hill.

The village of Avebury was built within the circle, and many of the stones were used for building material.

Avedon Richard 1923– . US photographer. A fashion photographer with *Harper's Bazaar* magazine in New York from the mid-1940s, he moved to *Vogue* 1965. He became associated with the *New Yorker* 1993. Using large-format cameras, his work consists of intensely realistic images, chiefly portraits.

Avignon The Palais des Papes, or palace of the popes, at Avignon, France. This palace was built 1334–52, after the papacy moved to Avignon from Rome 1309. The magnificence of the palace and of the popes' lifestyle caused anger at such extravagance in a time of poverty. *Philip Sauvain*

avens any of several low-growing plants of the genus *Geum*, family Rosaceae. Species are distributed throughout Eurasia and N Africa.

Mountain avens *Dryas octopetala* belongs to a different genus and grows in mountain and arctic areas of Eurasia and North America. A creeping perennial, it has white flowers with yellow stamens.

Averroës (Arabic ***Ibn Rushd***) 1126–1198. Arabian philosopher who argued for the eternity of matter and against the immortality of the individual soul. His philosophical writings, including commentaries on Aristotle and on Plato's *Republic*, became known to the West through Latin translations. He influenced Christian and Jewish writers into the Renaissance, and reconciled Islamic and Greek thought in asserting that philosophic truth comes through reason. St Thomas Aquinas opposed this position.

Averroës was born in Córdoba, Spain, trained in medicine, and became physician to the caliph as well as judge of Seville and Córdoba. He was accused of heresy by the Islamic authorities and banished 1195. Later he was recalled, and died in Marrakesh, N Africa.

'Averroism' was taught in Paris and elsewhere in the 13th century by the 'Averroists', who defended a distinction between philosophical truth and revealed religion.

aviation term used to describe both the science of powered ◊flight and also aerial navigation by means of an aeroplane.

Avicenna (Arabic ***Ibn Sina***) 979–1037. Persian philosopher and physician. He was the most renowned philosopher of medieval Islam. His *Canon Medicinae* was a standard work for many centuries. His philosophical writings were influenced by al-Farabi, Aristotle, and the neo-Platonists, and in turn influenced the scholastics of the 13th century.

Aviemore winter sports centre, in the Highlands, Scotland, SE of Inverness among the Cairngorm Mountains.

Avignon city in Provence, France, capital of Vaucluse *département*, on the river Rhône NW of Marseilles; population (1990) 89,400. An important Gallic and Roman city, it has a 12th-century bridge (only half still standing), a 13th-century cathedral, 14th-century walls, and the Palais des Papes, built during the residence here of the popes, comprised of Le Palais Vieux (1334–42) to the north, and Le Palais Nouveau (1342–52) to the south. Avignon was papal property 1348–1791.

Avila city in Spain, 90 km/56 mi NW of Madrid; population (1986) 45,000. It is the capital of a province of the same name. It has the remains of a Moorish castle, a Gothic cathedral, and the convent and church of St Teresa, who was born here. The medieval town walls are among the best preserved in Europe.

avocado tree *Persea americana* of the laurel family, native to Central America. Its dark-green, thick-skinned, pear-shaped fruit has buttery-textured flesh and is used in salads.

avocet wading bird, with a characteristic long, narrow, upturned bill, which it uses to sift water as it feeds in the shallows. It is about 45 cm/18 in long, and has long legs, partly webbed feet, and black and white plumage. There are four species of avocet, genus *Recurvirostra*, family Recurvirostridae, order Charadriiformes. They are found in Europe, Africa, and central and southern Asia. Stilts belong to the same family.

Avogadro Amedeo, Conte di Quaregna 1776–1856. Italian physicist, one of the founders of physical chemistry, who proposed Avogadro's hypothesis on gases 1811. His work enabled scientists to calculate Avogadro's number, and still has relevance for atomic studies.

Avogadro made it clear that the gas particles need not be individual atoms but might consist of molecules, the term he introduced to describe combinations of atoms. No previous scientists had made this fundamental distinction between the atoms of a substance and its molecules.

Avogadro's hypothesis in chemistry, the law stating that equal volumes of all gases, when at the same temperature and pressure, have the same numbers of molecules. It was first propounded by Amedeo Avogadro.

Avogadro's number or ***Avogadro's constant*** the number of carbon atoms in 12 g of the carbon-12 isotope (6.022045×10^{23}). The relative atomic mass of any element, expressed in grams, contains this number of atoms. It is named after Amedeo Avogadro.

avoirdupois system of units of mass based on the pound (0.45 kg), which consists of 16 ounces (each of 16 drams) or 7,000 grains (each equal to 65 mg).

Avon former county of SW England, formed 1974 and reorganized in 1996 as part of local government changes which included splitting the county into unitary authorities.

Avon any of several rivers in England and Scotland. The Avon in Warwickshire is associated with Shakespeare.

The Upper, or Warwickshire, Avon, 154 km/96 mi, rises in the Northampton uplands near Naseby and joins the Severn at Tewkesbury. The Lower, or Bristol, Avon, 121 km/75 mi, rises in the Cotswolds and flows into the Bristol Channel at Avonmouth.

The East, or Salisbury, Avon, 104 km/65 mi, rises S of the Marlborough Downs and flows into the English Channel at Christchurch.

AWACS acronym for ***Airborne Warning And Control System***, surveillance system that incorporates a long-range surveillance and detection radar mounted on a Boeing E-3 sentry aircraft.

Awash river that rises to the S of Addis Ababa in Ethiopia and flows NE to Lake Abba on the frontier with Djibouti; length 800 km/500 mi. Although deep inside present-day Ethiopia, the Awash River was considered by Somalis to mark the eastern limit of Ethiopian sovereignty prior to the colonial division of Somaliland in the 19th century.

Awe longest (37 km/23 mi) of the Scottish freshwater lochs, in Strathclyde, SE of Oban. It is drained by the river Awe into Loch Etive.

Axelrod Julius 1912– . US neuropharmacologist who shared the 1970 Nobel Prize for Physiology or Medicine with the biophysicists Bernard ◊Katz and Ulf von Euler (1905–1983) for his work on neurotransmitters (the chemical messengers of the brain).

Axelrod wanted to know why the messengers, once transmitted, should stop operating. Through his studies he found a number of specific ◊enzymes that rapidly degraded the neurotransmitters.

axil upper angle between a leaf (or bract) and the stem from which it grows. Organs developing in the axil, such as shoots and buds, are termed axillary, or lateral.

axiom in mathematics, a statement that is assumed to be true and upon which theorems are proved by using logical deduction; for example, two straight lines cannot enclose a space. The Greek mathematician Euclid used a series of axioms that he considered could not be demonstrated in terms of simpler concepts to prove his geometrical theorems.

axis (plural ***axes***) in geometry, one of the reference lines by which a point on a graph may be located. The horizontal axis is usually referred to as the x-axis, and the vertical axis as the y-axis. The term is also used to refer to the imaginary line about which an object may be said to be symmetrical (axis of symmetry) – for example, the diagonal of a square – or the line about which an object may revolve (axis of rotation).

Axis alliance of Nazi Germany and Fascist Italy before and during World War II. The ***Rome–Berlin Axis*** was formed 1936, when Italy was being threatened with sanctions because of its invasion of Ethiopia (Abyssinia). It became a full military and political alliance May 1939. A ten-year alliance between Germany, Italy, and Japan (***Rome–Berlin–Tokyo Axis***) was signed Sept 1940 and was subsequently joined by Hungary, Bulgaria, Romania, and the puppet states of Slovakia and Croatia. The Axis collapsed with the fall of Mussolini and the surrender of Italy 1943 and Germany and Japan 1945.

axolotl (Aztec 'water monster') aquatic larval form ('tadpole') of the Mexican salamander *Ambystoma mexicanum*, belonging to the family Ambystomatidae. Axolotls may be up to 30 cm/12 in long. They are remarkable because they can breed without changing to the adult form, and will metamorphose into adults only in response to the drying-up

axolotl The rare axolotl *Ambystoma mexicanum* lives in mountain lakes in Mexico. The capture of specimens as pets and the introduction of predatory fish has led to a decline in numbers. Axolotls spend most of their lives in water in a larval state, breathing by means of three pairs of feathery gills and having undeveloped legs and feet. Occasionally, individuals may develop into the adult, land-living form.

of their ponds. The adults then migrate to another pond.

axon long threadlike extension of a ◊nerve cell that conducts electrochemical impulses away from the cell body towards other nerve cells, or towards an effector organ such as a muscle. Axons terminate in ◊synapses, junctions with other nerve cells, muscles, or glands.

axonometric projection three-dimensional drawing of an object, such as a building, in which the floor plan provides the basis for the visible elevations, thus creating a diagram that is true to scale but incorrect in terms of perspective. Vertical lines are projected up from the plan at the same scale; the usual angle of projection is 45°. An isometric projection is a slightly flattened variation.

Axum variant spelling of ◊Aksum, a kingdom that flourished in the 1st–6th centuries AD.

ayatollah (Arabic 'sign of God') honorific title awarded to Shi'ite Muslims in Iran by popular consent, as, for example, to Ayatollah Ruhollah ◊Khomeini.

Ayckbourn Alan 1939– . English playwright, and artistic director of the Stephen Joseph Theatre, Scarborough, from 1970. His prolific output, characterized by comic dialogue and teasing experiments in dramatic structure, includes *Relatively Speaking* 1967, *Absurd Person Singular* 1972, a trilogy *The Norman Conquests* 1974, *Intimate Exchanges* 1982, *A Woman in Mind* 1986, and *Haunting Julia* 1994. He has recently written a number of plays for children, including *Invisible Friends* 1989 and *This Is Where We Came In* 1990.

aye-aye nocturnal tree-climbing prosimian *Daubentonia madagascariensis* of Madagascar, related to the lemurs. It is just over 1 m/3 ft long, including a tail 50 cm/20 in long. The aye-aye has an exceptionally long middle finger with which it probes for insects and their larvae under the bark of trees, and gnawing, rodentlike front teeth, with which it tears off the bark to get at its prey. The aye-aye has become rare through loss of its forest habitat, and is now classified as an endangered species.

Ayer A(lfred) J(ules) 1910–1989. English philosopher. He wrote *Language, Truth and Logic* 1936, an exposition of the theory of 'logical positivism', presenting a criterion by which meaningful statements (essentially truths of logic, as well as statements derived from experience) could be distinguished from meaningless metaphysical utterances (for example, claims that there is a God or that the world external to our own minds is illusory). He was professor of logic at Oxford 1959–78. Other works include *Probability and Evidence* 1972 and *Philosophy in the Twentieth Century* 1982.

Ayers Rock (Aboriginal ***Uluru***) vast ovate mass of pinkish rock in Northern Territory, Australia; 335 m/1,110 ft high and 9 km/6 mi around. For the Aboriginals, whose paintings decorate its caves, it has magical significance. It is named after Henry Ayers, a premier of South Australia.

Ayesha 611–678. Third and favourite wife of the prophet Muhammad, who married her when she was nine. Her father, Abu Bakr, became ◊caliph on Muhammad's death 632. She bitterly opposed the later succession to the caliphate of Ali, who had once accused her of infidelity.

aye-aye The aye-aye is a nocturnal animal that lives in the dense forests of Madagascar. Closely related to the lemur, the aye-aye has large forward-looking eyes, powerful rodentlike teeth, large ears, and a particularly long middle finger which is used to dig insects out of tree trunks.

Ayers Rock The largest rock mass in the world, Ayers Rock, or Uluru, in Australia, is composed of a sandstone containing particles of quartz and feldspar, and appears to change from red to purple at sunset. It has been a centre of aboriginal spiritual life for thousands of years, and has many aboriginal rock paintings on its surface. *Corbis*

Aymara the Native American people of Bolivia and Peru, builders of a great culture, who were conquered first by the Incas and then by the Spaniards. Today 1.4 million Aymara farm and herd llamas and alpacas in the highlands; their language, belonging to the Andean-Equatorial language family, survives, and their Roman Catholicism incorporates elements of their old beliefs.

Ayr administrative headquarters of South Ayrshire, Scotland, at the mouth of the river Ayr; population (1991) 48,000. Auld Bridge was built in the 5th century, the New Bridge 1788 (rebuilt 1879). Ayr has associations with Robert Burns. Industries include fishing, machinery, woollens, silicon chips, and aircraft.

Aytoun Robert, or ***Ayton*** 1570–1638. Scottish poet. He was employed and knighted by James I and was noted for his love poems. Aytoun is the reputed author of the lines on which Robert Burns based 'Auld Lang Syne'.

Ayub Khan Muhammad 1907–1974. Pakistani soldier and president 1958–69. He served in the Burma Campaign 1942–45, and was commander in chief of the Pakistan army 1951. In 1958 Ayub Khan assumed power after a bloodless army coup. He won the presidential elections 1960 and 1965, and established a stable economy and achieved limited land reforms. His militaristic form of government was unpopular, particularly with the Bengalis. He resigned 1969 after widespread opposition and civil disorder, notably in Kashmir.

Ayurveda basically naturopathic system of medicine widely practised in India and based on principles derived from the ancient Hindu scriptures, the ◊Vedas. Hospital treatments and remedial prescriptions tend to be nonspecific and to coordinate holistic therapies for body, mind, and spirit.

azalea any of various deciduous flowering shrubs, genus *Rhododendron*, of the heath family Ericaceae. There are several species native to Asia and North America, and from these many cultivated varieties have been derived. Azaleas are closely related to the evergreen ◊rhododendrons of the same genus.

Azaña Manuel 1880–1940. Spanish politician and first prime minister 1931–33 of the second Spanish republic. He was last president of the republic during the Civil War 1936–39, before the establishment of a dictatorship under Franco.

Azerbaijan country in W Asia, bounded S by Iran, E by the Caspian Sea, W by Armenia and Georgia, and N by Russia. *See country box on p. 86.*

Azerbaijan, Iranian two provinces of NW Iran, ***Eastern Azerbaijan*** (capital Tabriz), population (1991) 3,278,700, and ***Western Azerbaijan*** (capital Orúmiyeh), population (1991) 2,284,200. Azerbaijanis in Iran, as in the Republic of Azerbaijan, are mainly Shi'ite Muslim ethnic Turks, descendants of followers of the Khans from the Mongol Empire.

There are about 5 million Azerbaijanis in E and W Azerbaijan, and 3 million in the rest of Iran, where they form a strong middle class. In 1946, with Soviet backing, they briefly established their own republic. Denied autonomy under the Shah, they rose 1979–80 against the supremacy of Ayatollah Khomeini and were forcibly repressed, although a degree of autonomy was promised.

Azeri or ***Azerbaijani*** native of the Azerbaijan region of Iran (population 5,500,000) or of the Republic of Azerbaijan (formerly a Soviet republic) (population 7,145,600). Azeri is a Turkic language belonging to the Altaic family. Of the total population of Azeris, 70% are Shi'ite Muslims and 30% Sunni Muslims.

Azhar, El Muslim university and mosque in Cairo, Egypt. Founded 970 by Jawhar, commander in chief of the army of the Fatimid caliph, it is claimed to be the oldest university in the world. It became the centre of Islamic learning, with several subsidiary foundations, and is now primarily a school of Koranic teaching.

Azilian archaeological period following the close of the Old Stone (Palaeolithic) Age and regarded as the earliest culture of the Mesolithic Age in W Europe. It was first recognized at Le Mas d'Azil, a cave in Ariège, France.

azimuth in astronomy, the angular distance of an object eastwards along the horizon, measured from due north, between the astronomical ◊meridian (the vertical circle passing through the centre of the sky and the north and south points on the horizon) and the vertical circle containing the celestial body whose position is to be measured. ◊meridian (the vertical circle passing through the centre of the sky and the north and south points on the horizon) and the vertical circle containing the celestial body whose position is to be measured.

Aziz, Tariq 1936– born Mikhail Yuhanna. Iraqi politician, deputy prime minister from 1979, and foreign minister 1983–91. Saddam Hussein's right-hand man, Aziz was a loyalist who remained staunchly faithful to the Iraqi leader. After 1983, and especially during the Gulf War, Aziz was the chief international spokesman for Iraqi policy. He visited Egypt in 1983 in the first formal contact between the two nations since 1978. In the summer of 1990 he led Iraq's intimidation of its erstwhile Arab allies, culminating in the invasion of Kuwait in August of that year.

Aznar José Maria 1953– . Spanish politician, prime minister from 1996. He became premier of the Castile-Léon region 1987. Elected leader of the right-of-centre Popular Party (PP) 1989, Aznar and the PP lost to the ruling Social Workers' Party (PSOE) in elections 1989 and 1993. A minority PP government headed by Aznar was installed 1996.

azo dye synthetic dye containing the azo group of two nitrogen atoms (N=N) connecting aromatic ring compounds. Azo dyes are usually red, brown, or yellow, and make up about half the dyes produced. They are manufactured from aromatic ◊amines.

Azores group of nine islands in the N Atlantic, belonging to Portugal; area 2,247 sq km/867 sq mi; population (1991) 237,800. They are outlying peaks of the Mid-Atlantic Ridge and are volcanic in origin. The capital is Ponta Delgada on the main island, San Miguel.

Portuguese from 1430, the Azores were granted

'If I had been someone not very clever, I would have done an easier job like publishing. That's the easiest job I can think of.'

A J Ayer

AZERBAIJAN
Republic of

national name *Azarbaijchan Respublikasy*
area 86,600 sq km/33,400 sq mi
capital Baku
major towns/cities Gyandzha (formerly Kirovabad), Sumgait
physical features Caspian Sea with rich oil reserves; the country ranges from semi-desert to the Caucasus Mountains
head of state Geidar Aliyev from 1993
head of government Artur Rasizade from 1996
political system authoritarian nationalist
administrative divisions two autonomous regions, nine independent cities, and 54 districts
political parties Popular Front of Azerbaijan (FPA), democratic nationalist; New Azerbaijan, ex-communist; Communist Party of Azerbaijan (banned 1991–93); Muslim Democratic Party (Musavat), Islamic, pro-Turkic unity
population 7,594,000 (1996 est)
population growth rate 1.2% (1990–95); 1.0% (2000–05)
ethnic distribution 83% of Azeri descent, 6% Russian, 6% Armenian
life expectancy 67 (men), 75 (women)
literacy rate 97%
language Azeri
religions Shi'ite Muslim 62%, Sunni Muslim 26%, Orthodox Christian 12%
currency manat (left rouble zone 1993)
GDP (US $) 4 billion (1994)
growth rate −21.9% (1994)
exports oil, iron, copper, fruit, vine fruits, cotton, silk, carpets

HISTORY
4th C BC Established as an independent state for the first time by Atrophates, a vassal of Alexander III of Macedon.
7th C Spread of Islam.
11th C Immigration by Oghuz Seljuk races, from the steppes to the NE.
13th–14th Cs Incorporated within Mongol Empire; the Mongol ruler Tamerlane had his capital at Samarkand.
16th C Baku besieged and incorporated within Ottoman Empire, before falling under Persian dominance.
1805 Khanates (chieftaincies), including Karabakh and Shirvan, which had won independence from Persia, gradually became Russian protectorates, being confirmed by the Treaty of Gulistan, which concluded the 1804–13 First Russo-Iranian War.
1828 Under Treaty of Turkmenchai, which concluded the Second Russo-Iranian War begun in 1826, Persia was granted control over the S and Russia over N Azerbaijan.
late 19th C Petroleum industry developed, resulting in large influx of Slav immigrants to Baku, which supplied half of Russia's oil needs by 1901.
1906 Himmat ('Effort') Party, linked to the Russian Social-Democrat Labour Party (Bolshevik), founded in Baku.
1912 Himmat Party banned; Islamic nationalist Musavat ('Equality') Party formed in Baku.
1917–18 Member of the anti-Bolshevik Transcaucasian Federation.
1918 Became an independent republic.
1920 Occupied by the Red Army and subsequently forcibly secularized.
1922–36 Became part of the Transcaucasian Federal Republic with Georgia and Armenia.
early 1930s Peasant uprisings against agricultural collectivization and Stalinist purges of the local Communist Party.
1936 Became a constituent republic of the USSR.
late 1980s Growth in nationalist sentiment, taking advantage of the *glasnost* initiative of the reformist Soviet leader Mikhail Gorbachev.
1988 Riots followed the request of Nagorno-Karabakh, an Armenian-peopled enclave within Azerbaijan, for transfer to Armenia.
1989 Nagorno-Karabakh placed under direct rule from Moscow; civil war broke out with Armenia over Nagorno-Karabakh.
1990 Soviet troops sent to Baku to restore order, amid Azeri calls for secession from the Soviet Union.
1991 Independence declared after collapse of anti-Gorbachev coup in Moscow, which had been supported by Azeri communist leadership. Joined new Commonwealth of Independent States (CIS); Nagorno-Karabakh declared independence.
1992 Admitted into United Nations and accorded diplomatic recognition by the USA; Albulfaz Elchibey, leader of the nationalist Popular Front, elected president; renewed campaign in Nagorno-Karabakh.
1993 Elchibey fled military revolt, replaced in a coup by former Communist Party leader Geidar Aliyev, later elected president. Rebel military leader Surat Huseynov appointed prime minister. Nagorno-Karabakh overtaken by Armenian forces.
1994 Nagorno-Karabakh cease-fire agreed. After coup attempt, Huseynov replaced as premier by Fuad Kuliyev. State of emergency imposed.
1995 Attempted coup foiled. Pro-Aliyev legislature elected and market-centred economic reform programme introduced.
1996 Kuliyev replaced by Artur Rasizade.
1997 Border fighting with Armenia. Arkady Gukasyan elected president of Nagorno-Karabakh. Sharp rise in Caspian Sea oil extraction. Former president Elchibey returned from exile to lead opposition coalition.
1998 New pro-government grouping, Democratic Azerbaijan, formed.

SEE ALSO Armenia; Nagorno-Karabakh; Union of Soviet Socialist Republics

partial autonomy 1976, but remain a Portuguese overseas territory. The islands have a separatist movement. The Azores command the Western shipping lanes.

Azov (Russian ***Azovskoye More***) inland sea of Europe forming a gulf in the NE of the Black Sea, between Ukraine and Russia; area 37,555 sq km/14,500 sq mi. Principal ports include Rostov-on-Don, Kerch, and Taganrog. Azov is a good source of freshwater fish.

AZT drug used in the treatment of AIDS; see ◊zidovudine.

Aztec member of a Mexican Native American people that migrated south into the valley of Mexico in the 12th century, and in 1325 began reclaiming lake marshland to build their capital, Tenochtitlán, on the site of present-day Mexico City. Under Montezuma I (reigned from 1440), the Aztecs created a tribute empire in central Mexico. After the conquistador ◊Cortés landed 1519, ◊Montezuma II (reigned from 1502) was killed and Tenochtitlán subsequently destroyed. ◊Nahuatl is the Aztec language; it belongs to the Uto-Aztecan family of languages.

The ancient Aztecs are known for their architecture, jewellery (gold, jade, and turquoise), sculpture, and textiles. Their form of writing combined hieroglyphs and pictographs, and they used a complex calendar that combined a sacred period of 260 days with the solar year of 365 days. Propitiatory rites were performed at the intersection of the two, called the 'dangerous' period, every 52 years, when temples were rebuilt. Their main god in a pantheon of gods was Huitzilopochtli (Hummingbird Wizard), but they also worshipped the feathered serpent ◊Quetzalcoatl, inherited from earlier Mexican civilizations. Religious ritual included human sacrifice on a large scale, the priests tearing the heart from the living victim or flaying people alive. War captives were obtained for this purpose, but their own people were also used. The Aztec state was a theocracy with farmers, artisans, and merchants taxed to support the priestly aristocracy. Tribute was collected from a federation of conquered nearby states.

Aztec empire 1519

Aztec city
route of Cortés 1519
extent of Aztec empire 1519

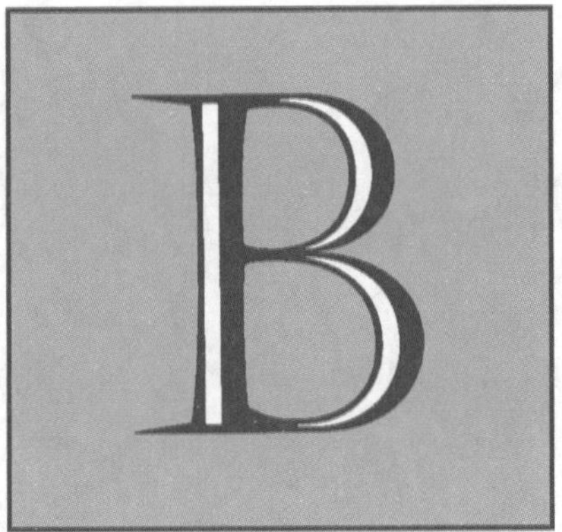

BA in education, abbreviation for the degree of *Bachelor of Arts*.

Baade (Wilhelm Heinrich) Walter 1893–1960. German-born US astronomer who made observations that doubled the distance, scale, and age of the universe. He discovered that stars are in two distinct populations according to their age, known as Population I (the younger) and Population II (the older). Later, he found that ◊Cepheid variable stars of Population I are brighter than had been supposed and that distances calculated from them were wrong.

Baader–Meinhof gang popular name for the West German left-wing guerrilla group the *Rote Armee Fraktion/Red Army Faction*, active from 1968 against what it perceived as US imperialism. The three main founding members were Andreas Baader (1943–1977), Gudrun Ensslin, and Ulrike Meinhof (1934–1976).

Baal (Semitic 'lord' or 'owner') divine title given to their chief male gods by the Phoenicians, or Canaanites, of the E Mediterranean coast about 1200–332 BC. Their worship as fertility gods, often orgiastic and of a phallic character, was strongly denounced by the Hebrew prophets.

Baalbek city of ancient Syria, now in Lebanon, 60 km/36 mi NE of Beirut. It was originally a centre of Baal worship. The Greeks identified Baal with Helios, the Sun, and renamed Baalbek Heliopolis. Its ruins, including Roman temples, survive, notably the Temple of Jupiter Heliopolitanus and the Temple of Bacchus, built in the 2nd century AD, which is still almost intact.

Ba'ath Party (full name ***Party of Arab Renaissance***) ruling political party in Iraq and Syria. Despite public support of pan-Arab unity and its foundation 1943 as a party of Arab nationalism, its ideology has been so vague that it has fostered widely differing (and often opposing) parties in Syria and Iraq.

The Ba'ath Party was founded in Damascus, Syria, 1943 by Michel Aflaq (1910–89), who became its chief ideologist, and Salah Eddin Bitar (1912–1980), later prime minister of Syria 1961–66, in opposition to both French rule and the older generation of Syrian Arab nationalists. Its constitution is a blend of neo-Marxist socialism and nationalism. Its influence spread to other Arab countries 1954–58, and branches were established in Iraq, Jordan, and Lebanon. The movement split into several factions after 1958 and again 1966. In Iraq, the Ba'ath Party took control briefly 1963 and again from 1968, although its support there has always been limited.

Bab, the (Arabic 'gate'). Adopted name of Mirza Ali Muhammad 1819–1850. Persian religious leader, born in Shiraz, founder of ◊Babism, an offshoot of Islam. In 1844 he proclaimed that he was a gateway to the Hidden Imam, a new messenger of Allah who was to come. He gained a large following whose activities caused the Persian authorities to fear a rebellion, and who were therefore persecuted. The Bab was executed for heresy.

Babangida Ibrahim 1941– . Nigerian politician and soldier, president 1985–93. He became head of the Nigerian army 1983 and in 1985 led a coup against President Buhari, assuming the presidency himself. From 1992 he promised a return to civilian rule but resigned 1993, after allegations of fraud.

Babbage Charles 1792–1871. English mathematician who devised a precursor of the computer. He designed an analytical engine, a general-purpose mechanical computing device for performing different calculations according to a program input on punched cards (an idea borrowed from the Jacquard loom). This device was never built, but it embodied many of the principles on which digital computers are based.

Babbage was a founder member of the Royal Astronomical Society, the British Association, the Cambridge Philosophical Society, and the Statistical Society of London. He was elected Fellow of the Royal Society 1816. His book *On the Economy of Machinery and Manufactures* 1832 is an analysis of industrial production systems and their economics.

In 1991, the British Science Museum completed Babbage's second difference engine (to demonstrate that it would have been possible with the materials then available). It evaluates polynomials up to the seventh power, with 30-figure accuracy.

Babbitt Milton 1916– . US composer and theorist. He pioneered the application of information theory to music in the 1950s, introducing set theory to series manipulations and the term 'pitch class' to define every octave identity of a note name. His works include four string quartets, works for orchestra, *Philomel* for soprano and electronic tape 1963–64, and *Ensembles for Synthesizer* 1967, both composed using the 1960 RCA Princeton-Columbia Mark II Synthesizer, which he helped to design.

babbler bird of the thrush family Muscicapidae with a loud babbling cry. Babblers, subfamily Timaliinae, are found in the Old World, and there are some 250 species in the group.

Babel Hebrew name for the city of ◊Babylon, chiefly associated with the Tower of Babel which, in the Genesis story in the Old Testament, was erected in the plain of Shinar by the descendants of Noah. It was a ziggurat, or staged temple, seven storeys high (100 m/328 ft) with a shrine of Marduk on the summit. It was built by Nabopolassar, father of Nebuchadnezzar, and was destroyed when Sennacherib sacked the city 689 BC.

Babel Isaak Emmanuilovich 1894–1941. Russian writer. Born in Odessa, he was an ardent supporter of the Revolution and fought with Budyenny's cavalry in the Polish campaign of 1921–22, an experience which inspired *Red Cavalry* 1926. His other works include *Stories from Odessa* 1924, which portrays the life of the Odessa Jews.

Babeuf François-Noël 1760–1797. French revolutionary journalist, a pioneer of practical socialism. In 1794 he founded a newspaper in Paris, later known as the *Tribune of the People*, in which he demanded the equality of all people. He was guillotined for conspiring against the ruling Directory during the French Revolution.

Babbitt US musician Milton Babbitt, who is known as a writer and teacher as well as for his compositions. He is an exponent of serialism and his works are very elaborately structured, reflecting his interest in mathematics. *Corbis*

Baalbek The Temple of Bacchus, Baalbek, Lebanon. Built in the 2nd century AD, the temple is exceptionally well preserved. Bacchus was the Roman god of fertility and wine (his Greek equivalent is Dionysus). *Corbis*

Babi faith faith from which the ◊Baha'i faith grew.

Babington Anthony 1561–1586. English traitor who hatched a plot to assassinate Elizabeth I and replace her with ◊Mary Queen of Scots; its discovery led to Mary's execution and his own.

babirusa wild pig *Babirousa babyrussa*, becoming increasingly rare, found in the moist forests and by the water of Sulawesi, Buru, and nearby Indonesian islands. The male has large upper tusks which grow upwards through the skin of the snout and curve back towards the forehead. The babirusa is up to 80 cm/2.5 ft at the shoulder. It is nocturnal, and swims well.

Babism religious movement founded during the 1840s by Mirza Ali Mohammad ('the ◊Bab'). An offshoot of Islam, it differs mainly in the belief that Muhammad was not the last of the prophets. The movement split into two groups after the death of the Bab; Baha'u'llah, the leader of one of these groups, founded the ◊Baha'i faith.

Babi Yar ravine near Kiev, Ukraine, where more than 100,000 people (80,000 Jews; the others were Poles, Russians, and Ukrainians) were killed by the Nazis 1941. The Soviet poet Yevtushenko wrote a poem called 'Babi Yar' 1961 in protest at plans for a sports centre on the site.

baboon large monkey of the genus *Papio*, with a long doglike muzzle and large canine teeth, spending much of its time on the ground in open country. Males, with head and body up to 1.1 m/3.5 ft long, are larger than females, and dominant males rule the 'troops' in which baboons live. They inhabit Africa and SW Arabia.

Babur (Arabic 'lion') (Zahir ud-Din Muhammad) 1483–1530. First Great Mogul of India from 1526. He was the great-grandson of the Mogul conqueror Tamerlane and, at the age of 11, succeeded his father, Omar Sheik Mirza, as ruler of Ferghana (Turkestan). In 1526 he defeated the emperor of Delhi at Panipat in the Punjab, captured Delhi and ◊Agra (the site of the Taj Mahal), and established a dynasty that lasted until 1858.

Babylon capital of ancient Babylonia, on the bank of the lower Euphrates River. The site is now in Iraq, 88 km/55 mi S of Baghdad and 8 km/5 mi N of Hilla, which is built chiefly of bricks from the ruins of Babylon. The Hanging Gardens of Babylon, one of the ◊Seven Wonders of the World, were probably erected on a vaulted stone base, the only stone construction in the mud-brick city. They formed a series of terraces, irrigated by a hydraulic system.

In ◊Rastafarianism, Babylon refers to the non-African world.

Babylonian captivity exile of Jewish deportees to Babylon after Nebuchadnezzar II's capture of Jerusalem 586 BC. According to tradition, the captivity lasted 70 years, but Cyrus of Persia, who conquered Babylon, actually allowed them to go home in 536 BC. By analogy, the name has also

'Baalbeck is the triumph of stone; of lapidary magnificence on a scale whose language, being still the language of the eye, dwarfs New York into a home of ants.'

On BAALBEK
Robert Byron
The Road to Oxiana
1937

To make divine things human, and human things divine; such is Bach, the greatest and purest moment in music of all times.

On BACH
Pablo Casals
Speech at Prades Bach Festival 1950

been applied to the papal exile to Avignon, France, 1309–77.

Bacall Lauren. Stage name of Betty Joan Perske 1924– . US actress. She became an overnight star when cast by Howard Hawks opposite Humphrey Bogart in *To Have and Have Not* 1944. She and Bogart married 1945 and starred together in *The Big Sleep* 1946. She returned to Hollywood after an eight-year absence with *Murder on the Orient Express* 1974 and two years later appeared in *The Shootist* 1976, subsequently playing occasional cameo roles.

baccalaureate or 'Bac'. French examination providing the school-leaving certificate and qualification for university entrance, as well as vocational options. It is also available in 52 countries as the international baccalaureate (IB).

Bacchus in Greek and Roman mythology, the god of fertility (see ◊Dionysus) and of wine; his rites (the Bacchanalia) were orgiastic.

Bach Carl Philip Emmanuel 1714–1788. German composer. He was the third son of J S Bach. He introduced a new 'homophonic' style, light and easy to follow, which influenced Mozart, Haydn, and Beethoven.

In the service of Frederick the Great 1740–67, he left to become master of church music at Hamburg 1768. He wrote over 200 pieces for keyboard instruments, and published a guide to playing the piano. Through his music and concert performances he helped to establish a leading solo role for the piano in Western music.

Bach Johann Christian 1735–1782. German composer. The eleventh son of J S Bach, he became celebrated in Italy as a composer of operas. In 1762 he was invited to London, where he became music master to the royal family. He remained in England until his death, enjoying great popularity as both a composer and a performer.

They are ill discoverers that think there is no land, when they can see nothing but sea.

FRANCIS BACON
Advancement of Learning

Bach Johann Sebastian 1685–1750. German composer. A master of ◊counterpoint, his music epitomizes the Baroque polyphonic style. His orchestral music includes the six Brandenburg Concertos 1721, other concertos for keyboard instrument and violin, four orchestral suites, sonatas for various instruments, six violin partitas, and six unaccompanied cello suites. Bach's keyboard music, for clavier and organ, his fugues, and his choral music are of equal importance. He also wrote chamber music and songs.

Born at Eisenach, Bach came from a distinguished musical family. At 15 he became a chorister at Lüneburg, and at 19 he was organist at Arnstadt. His appointments included positions at the courts of Weimar and Anhalt-Köthen, and from 1723 until his death he was musical director at St Thomas' choir school in Leipzig. He married twice and had over 20 children (although several died in infancy). His second wife, Anna Magdalena Wülkens, was a soprano; she also worked for him when his sight failed in later years.

Bach's sacred music includes 200 church cantatas; the Christmas and Easter oratorios 1734 and 1736; the two great Passions, of St John and St Matthew, first performed 1723 and 1729; and the Mass in B minor 1749. His keyboard music includes a collection of 48 preludes and fugues known as *Das wohltemperierte Clavier/The Well-Tempered Clavier* 1742, the Goldberg Variations 1742, and the Italian Concerto 1735. Of his organ music the finest examples are the chorale preludes. Two works written in his later years illustrate the principles and potential of his polyphonic art – *Das Musikalische Opfer/The Musical Offering* 1747 and *Die Kunst der Fuge/The Art of Fugue*, published posthumously 1751.

Bach German composer J S Bach represented in his later years in a painting by Gemäide von Elias Gottlieb Haussmann (1746). The seminal figure of the Baroque period, Bach's greatest legacy was his extensive oeuvre of sacred and keyboard works; as a composer for the organ he is unrivalled. *Image Select (UK) Ltd*

Bach Wilhelm Friedemann 1710–1784. German composer. He was also an organist, improviser, and master of ◊counterpoint. He was the eldest son of J S Bach.

Bach flower healing a homoeopathic system of medical therapy developed in the 1920s by English physician Edward Bach. Based on the healing properties of wild flowers, it seeks to alleviate mental and emotional causes of disease rather than their physical symptoms.

bacille Calmette-Guérin tuberculosis vaccine ◊BCG.

bacillus member of a group of rodlike ◊bacteria that occur everywhere in the soil and air. Some are responsible for diseases such as ◊anthrax or for causing food spoilage.

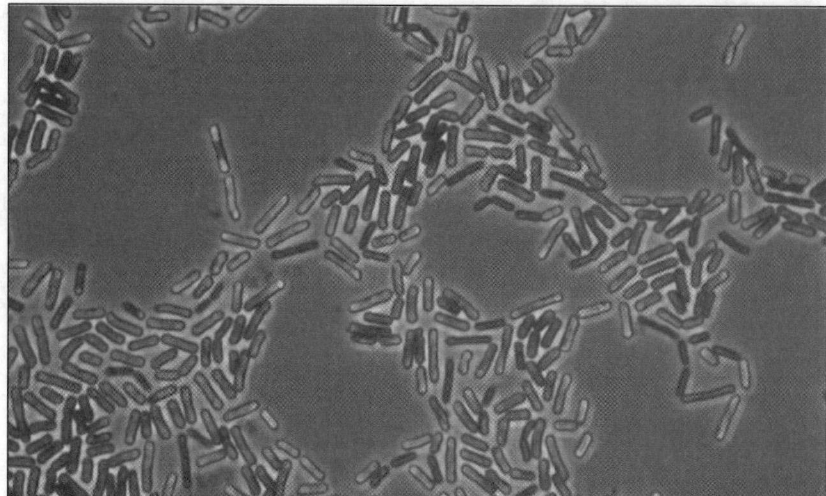

bacillus Bacillus bacteria under magnification. The group of bacteria known as bacilli includes many types of bacteria, some disease-causing. They are rod-shaped, typically move by the use of flagella (small hairlike organs), and are found in air, soil, and water. *Corbis*

backgammon board game for two players, often used in gambling. It was known in Mesopotamia, Greece, and Rome and in medieval England. Players have included Tutankhamun, Geoffrey Chaucer, Henry VIII, and Samuel Pepys.

The board is marked out in 24 triangular points of alternating colours, 12 to each side. Throwing two dice, the players move their 15 pieces around the board to the 6 points that form their own 'inner table'; the first player to move all his or her pieces off the board is the winner.

background radiation radiation that is always present in the environment. By far the greater proportion (87%) of it is emitted from natural sources. Alpha and beta particles, and gamma radiation are radiated by the traces of radioactive minerals that occur naturally in the environment and even in the human body, and by radioactive gases such as radon and thoron, which are found in soil and may seep upwards into buildings. Radiation from space (◊cosmic radiation) also contributes to the background level.

back pain aches in the region of the spine. Low back pain can be caused by a very wide range of medical conditions. About half of all episodes of back pain will resolve within a week, but severe back pain can be chronic and disabling. The causes include muscle sprain, a prolapsed intervertebral disc, and vertebral collapse due to ◊osteoporosis or cancer. Treatment methods include rest, analgesics, physiotherapy, osteopathy, and exercises.

backup system in computing, a duplicate computer system that can take over the operation of a main computer system in the event of equipment failure. A large interactive system, such as an airline's ticket-booking system, cannot be out of action for even a few hours without causing considerable disruption. In such cases a complete duplicate computer system may be provided to take over and run the system should the main computer develop a fault or need maintenance.

Bacon Francis, 1st Baron Verulam and Viscount St Albans 1561–1626. English philosopher, politician, and writer, a founder of modern scientific research. His works include *Essays* 1597 (revised and augmented 1612 and 1625), characterized by pith and brevity; *The Advancement of Learning* 1605, a seminal work discussing scientific method; *Novum organum* 1620, in which he redefined the task of natural science, seeing it as a means of empirical discovery and a method of increasing human power over nature; and *The New Atlantis* 1626, describing a utopian state in which scientific knowledge is systematically sought and exploited. He was briefly Lord Chancellor 1618 but lost his post through corruption.

Bacon Francis 1909–1992. Irish painter. Self-taught, he practised abstract art, then developed a stark Expressionist style characterized by distorted, blurred figures enclosed in loosely defined space. One of his best-known works is *Study after Velázquez's Portrait of Pope Innocent X* 1953 (Museum of Modern Art, New York).

Bacon moved to London 1925, began to paint about 1930, and held his first show in London 1949. He destroyed much of his early work. *Three Studies for Figures at the Base of a Crucifixion* about 1944 (Tate Gallery, London) is an early example of his mature style, which is often seen as a powerful expression of the existential anxiety and nihilism of 20th-century life.

Bacon Roger c. 1214–1294. English philosopher and scientist. He was interested in alchemy, the biological and physical sciences, and magic. Many discoveries have been credited to him, including the magnifying lens. He foresaw the extensive use of gunpowder and mechanical cars, boats, and planes.

In 1266, at the invitation of his friend Pope Clement IV, he began his *Opus majus/Great Work*, a compendium of all branches of knowledge. In 1277 Bacon was condemned and imprisoned by the Christian church for 'certain novelties' (heresy) and not released until 1292. He followed the maxim 'Cease to be ruled by dogmas and authorities; look at the world!'.

bacteria (singular ***bacterium***) microscopic single-celled organisms lacking a nucleus. Bacteria are widespread, present in soil, air, and water, and as parasites on and in other living things. Some parasitic bacteria cause disease by producing toxins, but others are harmless and may even benefit their hosts. Bacteria usually reproduce by ◊binary fission (dividing into two equal parts), and this may occur approximately every 20 minutes. It is thought that 1–10% of the world's bacteria have been identified.

classification Bacteria are now classified biochemically, but their varying shapes provide a rough classification; for example, cocci are round or oval, bacilli are rodlike, spirilla are spiral, and vibrios are shaped like commas. Exceptionally, one bacterium has been found, *Gemmata obscuriglobus*, that does have a nucleus. Unlike ◊viruses, bacteria do not necessarily need contact with a live cell to become active.

Bacteria can be classified into two broad classes (called Gram positive and negative) according to their reactions to certain stains, or dyes, used in microscopy. The staining technique, called the Gram test after Danish bacteriologist Hans Gram, allows doctors to identify many bacteria quickly.

Bacteria have a large loop of ◊DNA, sometimes called a bacterial chromosome. In addition there are often small, circular pieces of DNA known as ◊plasmids that carry spare genetic information. These plasmids can readily move from one bacterium to another, even though the bacteria may be of different species. In a sense, they are parasites within the bacterial cell, but they survive by coding characteristics that promote the survival of their hosts. For example, some plasmids confer antibiotic resistance on the bacteria they inhabit. The rapid and problematic spread of antibiotic resistance among bacteria is due to plasmids, but they are also useful to humans in ◊genetic engineering. There are ten times more bacterial cells than human cells in the human body.

functions Certain types of bacteria are vital in many food and industrial processes, while others play an essential role in the ◊nitrogen cycle, which maintains soil fertility. For example, bacteria are used to break down waste products, such as sewage; make butter, cheese, and yoghurt; cure tobacco; tan leather; and (by virtue of the ability of certain bacteria to attack metal) clean ships' hulls and derust their tanks, and even extract minerals from mines. Bacteria cannot normally survive temperatures above 100°C/212°F, such as those produced in pasteurization, but those in deep-sea hot vents in the eastern Pacific are believed to withstand temperatures of 350°C/662°F. *Thermus aquaticus*, or taq, grows freely in the boiling waters of hot springs, and an enzyme derived from it is used in genetic engineering to speed up the production of millions of copies of any DNA sequence, a reaction requiring very high temperatures.

Bacterial spores 40 million years old were extracted from a fossilized bee and successfully germinated by US scientists 1995. It is hoped that prehistoric bacteria can be tapped as a source of new chemicals for use in the drugs industry. Any bacteria resembling extant harmful pathogens will be destroyed, and all efforts are being to made to ensure no bacteria escape the laboratory.

bacteriology the study of ◊bacteria.

bacteriophage virus that attacks ◊bacteria. Such viruses are now of use in genetic engineering.

Bactria former region of central Asia (now divided among Afghanistan, Pakistan, and Tajikistan) which was partly conquered by ◊Alexander the Great. During the 6th–3rd centuries BC it was a centre of East–West trade and cultural exchange.

Bactrian species of ◊camel *Camelus bactrianus* found in the Gobi Desert in Central Asia. Body fat is stored in two humps on the back. It has very long winter fur which is shed in ragged lumps. The head and body length is about 3 m/10 ft, and the camel is up to 2.1 m/6.8 ft tall at the shoulder. Most Bactrian camels are domesticated and are used as beasts of burden in W Asia.

Baden former state of SW Germany, which had Karlsruhe as its capital. Baden was captured from the Romans 282 by the Alemanni; later it became a margravate and, in 1806, a grand duchy. A state of the German empire 1871–1918, then a republic, and under Hitler a *Gau* (province), it was divided between the *Länder* of Württemberg-Baden and Baden 1945 and in 1952 made part of ◊Baden-Württemberg.

Baden-Powell British general Robert Baden-Powell. He fought at Mafeking in the Second South African War, and later started the Scout movement 1907. *Image Select (UK) Ltd*

Baden town in Aargau canton, Switzerland, near Zurich; at an altitude of 388 m/1,273 ft; population (1990) 14,780. Its hot sulphur springs and mineral waters have been visited since Roman times.

Baden-Baden Black Forest spa in Baden-Württemberg, Germany; population (1991) 52,500. Fashionable in the 19th century, it is now a conference centre.

Baden-Powell Agnes 1854–1945. Sister of Robert Baden-Powell, she helped him found the ◊Girl Guides.

Baden-Powell Robert Stephenson Smyth, 1st Baron Baden-Powell 1857–1941. British general, founder of the Scout Association. He fought in defence of Mafeking (now Mafikeng) during the Second South African War. After 1907 he devoted his time to developing the Scout movement, which rapidly spread throughout the world.

Baden-Württemberg administrative region (German *Land*) of Germany
area 35,800 sq km/13,819 sq mi
capital Stuttgart
towns and cities Mannheim, Karlsruhe, Freiburg, Heidelberg, Heilbronn, Pforzheim, Ulm
physical Black Forest; Rhine boundary S and W; source of the river Danube; see also ◊Swabia
industries wine, jewellery, watches, clocks, musical instruments, textiles, chemicals, iron, steel, electrical equipment, surgical instruments
population (1994 est) 10,234,000
history formed 1952 (following a plebiscite) by the merger of the *Länder* Baden, Württemberg-Baden, and Württemberg-Hohenzollern.

Bader Douglas Robert Steuart 1910–1982. British fighter pilot. He lost both legs in a flying accident 1931, but had a distinguished flying career in World War II before being shot down and captured Aug 1941. He was twice decorated for his war service and was knighted 1976 for his work with disabled people.

badger large mammal of the weasel family with molar teeth of a crushing type adapted to a partly vegetable diet, and short strong legs with long claws suitable for digging. The Eurasian common badger *Meles meles* is about 1 m/3 ft long, with long, coarse, greyish hair on the back, and a white face with a broad black stripe along each side. Mainly a woodland animal, it is harmless and nocturnal, and spends the day in a system of burrows called a 'sett'. It feeds on roots, a variety of fruits and nuts, insects, worms, mice, and young rabbits.

The American badger *Taxidea taxus* is slightly smaller than the Eurasian badger, and lives in open country in North America. Various species of hog badger, ferret badger, and stink badger occur in S and E Asia, the last having the well developed anal scent glands characteristic of the weasel family.

badlands barren landscape cut by erosion into a maze of ravines, pinnacles, gullies and sharp-edged ridges. Areas in South Dakota and Nebraska, USA, are examples.

> *Such a place the Fallen Angels might have built as a spite to Heaven, dry and sharp, desolate and dangerous.*
>
> On the BADLANDS
> John Steinbeck
> *Travels with Charley*

badminton racket game similar to lawn ◊tennis but played on a smaller court and with a shuttlecock (a half sphere of cork or plastic with a feather or nylon skirt) instead of a ball. The object of the game is to prevent the opponent from being able to return the shuttlecock. Badminton is played by two or four players. The court measures 6.1 m/20 ft by 13.4 m/44 ft. A net, 0.8 m/2.5 ft deep, is stretched across the middle of the court and at a height of 1.52 m/5 ft above the ground to the top of the net. The shuttlecock must be volleyed. Only the server can win points.

The sport is named after Badminton House, the seat of the duke of Beaufort, where the game was played in the 19th century.

The invention of a cheap and durable synthetic shuttlecock 1952 gave the game a wider appeal, though synthetic shuttlecocks are not accepted in top-level badminton games. World championships have existed since 1977 in singles, doubles, and mixed doubles and are now held every two years.

Badoglio Pietro 1871–1956. Italian soldier and Fascist politician. He served as a general in World War I and subsequently in the campaigns against the peoples of Tripoli and Cyrenaica. In 1935 he became commander in chief in Ethiopia, adopting ruthless measures to break patriot resistance. He was created viceroy of Ethiopia and duke of Addis Ababa in 1936. He resigned during the disastrous campaign into Greece 1940 and succeeded Mussolini as prime minister of Italy from July 1943 to June 1944, negotiating the armistice with the Allies.

Baedeker Karl 1801–1859. German editor and publisher of foreign travel guides; the first was for Coblenz 1829. These are now published from Hamburg (before World War II from Leipzig).

Baekeland Leo Hendrik 1863–1944. Belgian-born US chemist. He invented ◊Bakelite, the first commercial plastic, made from formaldehyde (methanal) and phenol. He also made a photographic paper, Velox, which could be developed in artificial light.

Baez Joan 1941– . US folk singer and pacifist activist. Her pure soprano in the early 1960s popularized traditional English and American folk songs such as 'Silver Dagger' and 'We Shall Overcome' (an anthem of the civil-rights movement). She helped Bob Dylan at the start of his career and has recorded many of his songs.

Baffin William 1584–1622. English explorer and navigator. In 1616 he and Robert Bylot explored Baffin Bay, NE Canada, and reached latitude 77° 45′ N, which for 236 years remained the 'furthest north'.

In 1612, Baffin was chief pilot of an expedition in search of the Northwest Passage, and in 1613–14 commanded a whaling fleet near Spitsbergen, Norway. He piloted the *Discovery* on an expedition to Hudson Bay led by Bylot 1615. After 1617, Baffin worked for the ◊East India Company and made surveys of the Red Sea and Persian Gulf. In 1622 he was killed in an Anglo-Persian attack on Hormuz.

Baffin Island island in the Northwest Territories, Canada
area 507,450 sq km/195,875 sq mi
features largest island in the Canadian Arctic; mountains rise above 2,000 m/6,000 ft, and there

badger The American badger is slightly smaller than its Eurasian cousin. Unlike the Eurasian badger, it is a solitary creature, and lives mainly on small rodents. It usually spends the day in its burrow or sett, emerging at night to hunt for mice, eggs, and reptiles. It is an excellent digger and can rapidly dig out burrowing rodents.

Prejudice is planted in childhood, learnt like table manners and cadences of speech.

BERYL BAINBRIDGE
Forever England

are several large lakes. The northernmost part of the strait separating Baffin Island from Greenland forms Baffin Bay, the southern end is Davis Strait.

It is named after William Baffin, who carried out research here 1614 during his search for the ◊Northwest Passage.

BAFTA acronym for ***British Academy of Film and Television Arts***, formed 1959 as a result of the amalgamation of the British Film Academy (founded 1948) and the Guild of Television Producers (founded 1954). *See list of tables on p. 1177.*

Bagehot Walter 1826–1877. British writer and economist. His *English Constitution* 1867, a classic analysis of the British political system, is still a standard work.

Baghdad historic city and capital of Iraq, on the river Tigris; population (1987) 3,850,000. Industries include oil refining, distilling, tanning, tobacco processing, and the manufacture of textiles and cement. Founded 762, it became Iraq's capital 1921. During the Gulf War 1991, the UN coalition forces bombed it in repeated air raids and destroyed much of the city.

To the SE, on the river Tigris, are the ruins of Ctesiphon, capital of Parthia about 250 BC–AD 226 and of the ◊Sassanian Empire about 226–641; the remains of the Great Palace include the world's largest single-span brick arch 26 m/85 ft wide and 29 m/95 ft high. A transportation hub from the earliest times, it was developed by the 8th-century caliph Harun al-Rashid, although little of the *Arabian Nights* city remains.

It was overrun 1258 by the Mongols, who destroyed the irrigation system. In 1639 it was taken by the Turks. During World War I it was part of the Turkish Empire until it was captured March 1917 by General Sir Frederick Maude (1864–1917).

Bagnold Enid (Algerine) 1889–1981. English novelist and dramatist. Her novel *National Velvet* 1935, about a girl who wins the Grand National on a horse won in a raffle, was made into a film 1944 starring Elizabeth Taylor. Her most notable play was *The Chalk Garden* 1954.

bagpipes any of an ancient family of double-reed folk woodwind instruments employing a bladder or bellows as an air reservoir to a 'chanter' or melody pipe, and optional 'drones' providing a continuous accompanying harmony.

Examples include the old French musette, Scottish and Irish pipes, smaller Northumbrian pipes, Breton *biniou*, Spanish *gaita*, and numerous variants in Eastern Europe, the Middle East, and North Africa.

Bahadur Shah II 1775–1862. Last of the Mogul emperors of India. He reigned, though in name only, as king of Delhi 1837–57, when he was hailed by the mutineers of the ◊Indian Mutiny as an independent emperor at Delhi. After the rebellion he was exiled to Burma with his family.

Baha'i religion founded in the 19th century from a Muslim splinter group,by the Persian Baha'u'llah (1817–1892). His message in essence was that all great religious leaders are manifestations of the unknowable God and all scriptures are sacred. There is no priesthood: all Baha'is are expected to teach, and to work towards world unification. There are about 6 million Baha'is worldwide.

Great stress is laid on equality regardless of religion, race, or gender. Drugs and alcohol are forbidden. Marriage is strongly encouraged; there is no arranged marriage, but parental approval must be given. Baha'is are expected to pray daily, but there is no set prayer. During 2–20 March, adults under 70 fast from sunrise to sunset. Administration is carried out by an elected body, the Universal House of Justice.

Bahamas country comprising a group of about 700 islands and about 2,400 uninhabited islets and cays in the Caribbean, 80 km/50 mi from the SE coast of Florida. They extend for about 1,223 km/760 mi from NW to SE, but only 22 of the islands are inhabited. *See country box below.*

Bahrain country comprising a group of islands in the Persian Gulf, between Saudi Arabia and Iran. *See country box opposite.*

Baikal (Russian ***Baykal Ozero***) freshwater lake in S Siberia, Russia, the largest in Asia, and the eighth largest in the world (area 31,500 sq km/12,150 sq mi); also the deepest in the world (up to 1,640 m/5,700 ft). Fed by more than 300 rivers, it is drained only by the Lower Angara. It has sturgeon fisheries and is rich in fauna.

The lake has 1,155 species of animals and 1,085 species of plants – more than 1,000 of these are not found anywhere else in the world. The water at the bottom of the lake holds sufficient oxygen to allow animals to live at depths of over 1,600m/5,200 ft. It has its own breed of seals, and is severely threatened by pollution.

Baikonur launch site for spacecraft, located at Tyuratam, Kazakhstan, near the Aral Sea: the first satellites and all Soviet space probes and crewed Soyuz missions were launched from here. It covers an area of 12,200 sq km/4,675 sq mi, much larger than its US equivalent, the ◊Kennedy Space Center in Florida.

bail the setting at liberty of a person in legal custody on an undertaking (usually backed by some security, given either by that person or by someone else) to attend at a court at a stated time and place. If the person does not attend, the bail may be forfeited.

Baile Atha Cliath official Gaelic name of ◊Dublin, capital of the Republic of Ireland, from 1922.

bailey an open space or court of a stone-built castle.

Bailey David 1938– . English fashion photographer. His work for *Vogue* magazine in the 1960s and his black-and-white portraits of fashionable celebrities did much to define the image of 'swinging London'. He has published several books, including *Box of Pin-ups* 1965 and *Goodbye Baby and Amen* 1969.

bailiff officer of the court whose job, usually in the county courts, is to serve notices and enforce the court's orders involving seizure of the goods of a debtor.

Baily's beads bright spots of sunlight seen around the edge of the Moon for a few seconds immediately before and after a total ◊eclipse of the Sun, caused by sunlight shining between mountains at the Moon's edge. Sometimes one bead is much brighter than the others, producing the so-called 'diamond ring' effect. The effect was described 1836 by the English astronomer Francis Baily (1774–1844), a wealthy stockbroker who retired in 1825 to devote himself to astronomy.

Bainbridge Beryl 1934– . English novelist. Her writing has dramatic economy and pace. Acutely observed, peppered with ironic black humour, and often dealing with the tragedy and comedy of human self-delusion, her works include *The Dressmaker* 1973, *The Bottle Factory Outing* 1974, *An Awfully Big Adventure* 1989, *The Birthday Boys* 1991, and *Master Georgie* 1998 (shortlisted for the 1998 Booker Prize).

Baird John Logie 1888–1946. Scottish electrical engineer who pioneered television. He took out his first provisional patent 1923 and in 1925 he gave the first public demonstration of television. In 1926 he pioneered fibre optics, radar (in advance of Robert Watson-Watt (1892–1973)), and 'noctovision', a system for seeing at night by using infrared rays.

Baird also developed video recording on both wax records and magnetic steel discs (1926–27), colour TV (1925–28), 3-D colour TV (1925–46), and transatlantic TV (1928). In 1936 his mechanically scanned 240-line system competed with EMI-Marconi's 405-line, but the latter was preferred for the BBC service from 1937, partly because it used electronic scanning, partly because it handled live indoor scenes with smaller, more manoeuvrable

BAHAMAS
Commonwealth of the

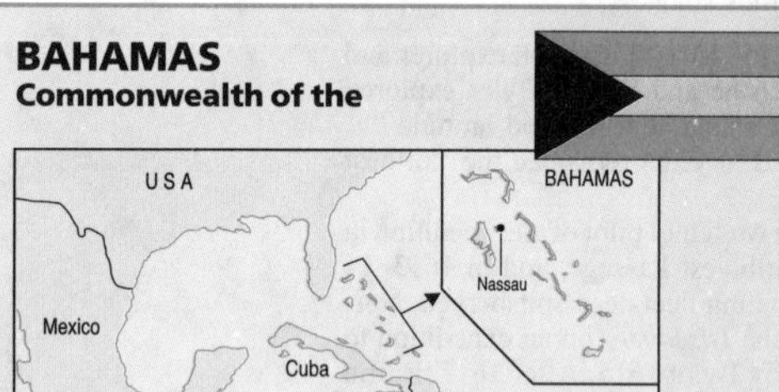

area 13,864 sq km/5,352 sq mi
capital Nassau (on New Providence Island)
major towns/cities Freeport (on Grand Bahama)
physical features comprises 700 tropical coral islands and about 1,000 cays; the Exumas are a narrow spine of 365 islands; only 30 of the desert islands are inhabited; Blue Holes of Andros, the world's longest and deepest submarine caves
principal islands Andros, Grand Bahama, Abaco, Eleuthera, New Providence, Berry Islands, Bimini Islands, Great Inagua, Acklins Island, Exuma Islands, Mayguana, Crooked Island, Long Island, Cat Islands, Rum Cay, Watling (San Salvador) Island, Inagua Islands
head of state Elizabeth II from 1973, represented by governor general Orville Turnquest from 1995
head of government Hubert Ingraham from 1992
political system constitutional monarchy
administrative divisions based on 18 natural island groupings
political parties Progressive Liberal Party (PLP), centrist; Free National Movement (FNM), centre-left
population 284,000 (1996 est)
population growth rate 1.5% (1990–95)
ethnic distribution about 85% of the population is of African origin, 15% European (mostly British, American, and Canadian)
literacy rate 99%
languages English and some Creole
religions Christian 94% (Roman Catholic 26%, Anglican 21%, other Protestant 48%)
currency Bahamian dollar
GDP (US $) 3.4 billion (1994)
growth rate 0.3% (1994)
exports cement, pharmaceuticals, petroleum products, crawfish, salt, aragonite, rum, pulpwood; over half the islands' employment comes from tourism

HISTORY
8th–9th Cs AD Arawak Indians driven northwards to the islands by the Caribs.
1492 First visited by Christopher Columbus; Arawaks deported to provide cheap labour for the gold and silver mines of Cuba and Hispaniola (Haiti).
1629 The English king Charles I granted the islands to Robert Heath.
1666 Colonization of New Providence island began.
1783 Recovered after brief Spanish occupation and became a British colony, being settled by American Loyalists during the American War of Independence, who brought with them black slaves.
1838 Slaves were emancipated.
1940–45 The Duke of Windsor, the former King Edward VIII, was governor of Bahamas.
from 1950s Major development of the tourist trade, especially from the USA.
1964 Became internally self-governing.
1967 First national assembly elections; Lynden Pindling, of the centrist Progressive Liberal Party (PLP), became prime minister.
1973 Full independence achieved, within the British Commonwealth.
1983 Allegations of drug trafficking by government ministers.
1984 Deputy prime minister and two cabinet ministers resigned. Pindling denied any personal involvement and was endorsed as party leader.
1992 Centre-left Free National Movement (FNM) led by Hubert Ingraham won absolute majority in assembly elections, ending 25 years of rule by Pindling.

SEE ALSO Arawak; Carib

BAHRAIN
State of

national name *Dawlat al Bahrayn*
area 688 sq km/266 sq mi
capital Manama on the largest island (also called Bahrain)
major towns/cities Muharraq, Jiddhafs, Isa Town, Hidd, Rifa'a
major ports Mina Sulman
physical features archipelago of 35 islands in Arabian Gulf, composed largely of sand-covered limestone; generally poor and infertile soil; flat and hot; causeway linking Bahrain to mainland Saudi Arabia
head of state Sheik Isa bin Sulman al-Khalifa from 1961
head of government Sheik Khalifa bin Sulman al-Khalifa from 1970
political system absolute emirate
administrative divisions no local government system
political parties none
population 570,000 (1996 est)
population growth rate 2.8% (1990–95)
ethnic distribution about 73% Arabic and 9% Iranian; Pakistani and Indian minorities
life expectancy 70 (men), 74 (women)
literacy rate men 82%, women 69%
languages Arabic (official); Farsi, English, Urdu
religions 85% Muslim (Shi'ite 60%, Sunni 40%), Christian; Islam is the state religion
currency Bahraini dinar
GDP (US $) 7.3 billion (1995 est)
growth rate 4% (1993)
exports oil, natural gas, aluminium, fish, refined petroleum, machinery

HISTORY
4th C AD Became part of Persian (Iranian) Sassanian Empire.
7th C Adopted Islam.
8th C Came under Arab Abbasid control.
1521 Seized by Portugal and held for eight decades, despite local unrest.
1602 Fell under the control of a Persian Shi'ite dynasty.
1783 Persian rule overthrown and became a sheikdom under the Sunni Muslim al-Khalifa dynasty, which originated from the same tribal federation, the Anaza, as the al-Saud family, who now rule Saudi Arabia.
1816–20 Friendship and peace treaties signed with Britain, which sought to end piracy in the Gulf.
1861 Became British protectorate, government shared between the ruling sheik (Arab leader) and a British adviser.
1923 British influence increased when Sheik Isa al-Khalifa was deposed and Charles Belgrave was appointed as the dominating 'adviser' to the new ruler.
1928 Sovereignty claimed by Persia (Iran).
1930s Oil discovered, providing backbone for country's wealth.
1953–56 Council for National Unity was formed by Arab nationalists, but suppressed after large demonstrations against British participation in the Suez War.
1968 Britain announced its intention to withdraw its forces. Bahrain formed, with Qatar and the Trucial States of the United Arab Emirates, the Federation of Arab Emirates.
1970 Iran accepted a United Nations report showing that Bahrain's inhabitants preferred independence to Iranian control.
1971 Qatar and the Trucial States withdrew from the federation; Bahrain became an independent state under Sheik Sulman al-Khalifa.
1973 New constitution adopted, with an elected national assembly dominated by left-nationalist Bahrain National Liberation Front (BNLF).
1975 Prime minister Sheik al-Khalifa resigned; national assembly dissolved and political activists driven underground. Emir and his family assumed virtually absolute power.
early 1980s Tensions between the Sunni and Shi'ite Muslim communities heightened by Iranian Shi'ite Revolution of 1979.
1986 Gulf University established in Bahrain. Causeway opened linking the island with Saudi Arabia.
1991 Bahrain joined United Nations coalition that ousted Iraq from its occupation of Kuwait; signed defence cooperation agreement with USA.
1994 Antimonarchy protests by Shi'ite Muslim majority community.
1995 Sheik al-Khalifa re-appointed prime minister. Prodemocracy demonstrations violently suppressed, with 11 deaths.
1996 Emir proposed an expanded consultative assembly in move towards democracy.

SEE ALSO Sassanian Empire; United Arab Emirates

cameras. In 1944 he developed facsimile television, the forerunner of ◊Ceefax, and demonstrated the world's first all-electronic colour and 3-D colour receiver (500 lines).

Baja California mountainous peninsula that forms the twin northwestern states of Lower (Spanish *baja*) California, Mexico; Baja California Norte in the north, and Baja California Sur in the south.

Bakelite first synthetic ◊plastic, created by Leo ◊Baekeland 1909. Bakelite is hard, tough, and heatproof, and is used as an electrical insulator. It is made by the reaction of phenol with formaldehyde, producing a powdery resin that sets solid when heated. Objects are made by subjecting the resin to compression moulding (simultaneous heat and pressure in a mould). It is one of the thermosetting plastics, which do not remelt when heated, and is often used for electrical fittings.

Baker Chet (Chesney) 1929–1988. US jazz trumpeter. His good looks, occasional vocal performances, and romantic interpretations of ballads helped make him a cult figure. He became known with the Gerry Mulligan Quartet 1952 and formed his own quartet 1953. Recordings include 'My Funny Valentine' and 'The Thrill Is Gone'.

Baker James Addison III 1930– . US Republican politician. Under President Reagan, he was White House Chief of Staff 1981–85 and Treasury secretary 1985–88. After managing George Bush's successful presidential campaign, Baker was appointed secretary of state 1989 and played a prominent role in the 1990–91 Gulf crisis and the subsequent search for a lasting Middle East peace settlement. In 1992 he left the State Department to become White House Chief of Staff and to oversee Bush's unsuccessful re-election campaign.

Baker Janet Abbott 1933– . English mezzo-soprano noted for the emotional strength and richness of her interpretations of lieder (musical settings for poems), oratorio, and opera from Purcell to Britten, including a notable Dido in Purcell's *Dido and Aeneas*. She retired from the stage 1981.

Baker Kenneth Wilfrid 1934– . British Conservative politician, home secretary 1990–92. He was environment secretary 1985–86, education secretary 1986–89, and chair of the Conservative Party 1989–90, retaining his cabinet seat, before becoming home secretary in John Major's government. He was dismissed in 1992.

Baker Samuel White 1821–1893. English explorer, in 1864 the first European to sight Lake Albert Nyanza (now Lake Mobutu Sese Seko) in central Africa, and discover that the river Nile flowed through it.

Bakhtaran formerly (until 1980) ***Kermanshah*** capital of Bakhtaran province, NW Iran; population (1986) 624,100. The province (area 23,700 sq km/9,148 sq mi; population 1,463,000) is on the Iraqi border and is mainly inhabited by Kurds. Industries include oil refining, carpets, and textiles.

baking powder mixture of ◊bicarbonate of soda, an acidic compound, and a nonreactive filler (usually starch or calcium sulphate), used in baking as a raising agent. It gives a light open texture to cakes and scones, and is used as a substitute for yeast in making soda bread.

Several different acidic compounds (for example, tartaric acid, cream of tartar, sodium or calcium acid phosphates, and glucono-delta-lactone) may be used, any of which will react with the sodium hydrogen carbonate, in the presence of water and heat, to release the carbon dioxide that causes the cake mix or dough to rise.

Bakst Leon. Assumed name of Leon Rosenberg 1866–1924. Russian painter and theatrical designer. He combined intense colours and fantastic images adapted from Oriental and folk art with an Art Nouveau tendency toward graceful surface pattern. His designs for Diaghilev's touring Ballets Russes made a deep impression in Paris 1909–14.

He studied for a time at the Imperial Academy of Arts, and was associated with Benois and Diaghilev in the World of Art group and the movement for reviving native Russian art. He exhibited in Paris 1906, and became famous as designer of settings and costumes for Diaghilev's ballets, *Scheherazade*, 1909, being one of his triumphs. He went to Russia 1922 but returned to Paris soon after. His brilliant and exotic *décors* for ballet had an influence extending to fashion in dress and interior decoration.

Baku capital city of the Republic of Azerbaijan, industrial port (oil refining) on the Caspian Sea; population (1993) 1,700,000. It is a major oil centre and is linked by pipelines with Batumi on the Black Sea. In Jan 1990 there were violent clashes between the Azeri majority and the Armenian minority, and Soviet troops were sent to the region; over 13,000 Armenians subsequently fled from the city. In March 1992, opposition political forces sponsored protests in the city that led to the resignation of President Mutalibov.

Bakunin Mikhail 1814–1876. Russian anarchist, active in Europe. In 1848 he was expelled from France as a revolutionary agitator. In Switzerland in the 1860s he became recognized as the leader of the anarchist movement. In 1869 he joined the First International (a coordinating socialist body) but, after stormy conflicts with Karl Marx, was expelled 1872.

Born of a noble family, Bakunin served in the Imperial Guard but, disgusted with tsarist methods

Baird Scottish television pioneer John Logie Baird (centre) recording the matinée idol Jack Buchanan (left) 1929. He had given the first public demonstration of his television system four years earlier. *Topham*

❛There is more felicity on the far side of baldness than young men can possibly imagine.❜

On BALDNESS
Logan Pearsall Smith
All Trivia 1933

in Poland, resigned his commission and travelled abroad. For his share in a brief revolt at Dresden 1849 he was sentenced to death. The sentence was commuted to imprisonment, and he was handed over to the tsar's government and sent to Siberia 1855. In 1861 he managed to escape to Switzerland. He had a large following, mainly in the Latin American countries.

Balaclava, Battle of in the Crimean War, Russian attack on British positions 25 Oct 1854, near a town in Ukraine, 10 km/6 mi SE of Sevastopol. It was the scene of the ill-timed Charge of the Light Brigade of British cavalry against the Russian entrenched artillery. Of the 673 soldiers who took part, there were 272 casualties. Balaclava helmets were knitted hoods worn here by soldiers in the bitter weather.

Balakirev Mily Alexeyevich 1837–1910. Russian composer. He wrote orchestral works including the fantasy *Islamey* 1869/1902, piano music, songs, and a symphonic poem *Tamara*, all imbued with the Russian national character and spirit. He was leader of the group known as 'The Five' and taught its members, Mussorgsky, Cui, Rimsky-Korsakov, and Borodin.

balalaika Russian musical instrument, resembling a guitar. It has a triangular sound box, frets, and two, three, or four strings played by strumming with the fingers.

Bala Lake (Welsh ***Llyn Tegid***) lake in Gwynedd, N Wales, about 6.4 km/4 mi long and 1.6 km/1 mi wide. Bala Lake has a unique primitive species of fish, the gwyniad (a form of ◊whitefish), a protected species from 1988.

balance apparatus for weighing or measuring mass. The various types include the ***beam balance***, consisting of a centrally pivoted lever with pans hanging from each end, and the ***spring balance***, in which the object to be weighed stretches (or compresses) a vertical coil spring fitted with a pointer that indicates the weight on a scale. Kitchen and bathroom scales are balances.

balance of nature in ecology, the idea that there is an inherent equilibrium in most ◊ecosystems, with plants and animals interacting so as to produce a stable, continuing system of life on Earth. The activities of human beings can, and frequently do, disrupt the balance of nature.

Organisms in the ecosystem are adapted to each other – for example, waste products produced by one species are used by another and resources used by some are replenished by others; the oxygen needed by animals is produced by plants while the waste product of animal respiration, carbon dioxide, is used by plants as a raw material in photosynthesis. The nitrogen cycle, the water cycle, and the control of animal populations by natural predators are other examples.

balance of payments in economics, an account of a country's debit and credit transactions with other countries. Items are divided into the *current account*, which includes both visible trade (imports and exports of goods) and invisible trade (services such as transport, tourism, interest, and dividends), and the *capital account*, which includes investment in and out of the country, international grants, and loans. Deficits or surpluses on these accounts are brought into balance by buying and selling reserves of foreign currencies.

balance of power in politics, the theory that the best way of ensuring international order is to have power so distributed among states that no single state is able to achieve a dominant position. The term, which may also refer more simply to the actual distribution of power, is one of the most enduring concepts in international relations.

balance of trade the balance of trade transactions of a country recorded in its current account; it forms one component of the country's ◊balance of payments.

Balanchine George, born Georgi Melitonovich Balanchivadze 1904–1983. Russian-born US choreographer. After leaving the USSR 1924, he worked with ◊Diaghilev in France. Moving to the USA 1933, he became a major influence on dance, starting the New York City Ballet 1948. He was the most influential 20th-century choreographer of ballet in the USA. He developed an 'American Neo-Classic' dance style and made the New York City Ballet one of the world's great companies. His ballets are usually plotless and are performed in practice clothes to modern music. He also choreographed dances for five Hollywood films.

His many works include *Apollon Musagète* 1928 and *The Prodigal Son* 1929 for Diaghilev; *Serenade* 1934; several works with music by Stravinsky, such as *Agon* 1957 and *Duo Concertante* 1972; and Broadway musicals, such as *On Your Toes* 1936 and *The Boys from Syracuse* 1938.

Balboa Vasco Núñez de 1475–1519. Spanish ◊conquistador. He founded a settlement at Darien (now Panama) 1511 and crossed the Isthmus in search of gold, reaching the Pacific Ocean (which he called the South Sea) on 25 Sept 1513, after a 25-day expedition. He was made admiral of the Pacific and governor of Panama but was removed by Spanish court intrigue, imprisoned, and executed.

Balcon Michael Elias 1896–1977. English film producer. He was responsible for the influential Ealing comedies of the 1940s and early 1950s (see ◊Ealing Studios), such as *Kind Hearts and Coronets* 1949, *Whisky Galore!* 1949, and *The Lavender Hill Mob* 1951.

Balder in Norse mythology, the son of Odin and Freya and husband of Nanna, and the best, wisest, and most loved of all the gods. He was killed, at ◊Loki's instigation, by a twig of mistletoe shot by the blind god Hodur.

baldness loss of hair from the scalp, common in older men. Its onset and extent are influenced by genetic make-up and the level of male sex ◊hormones. There is no cure, and expedients such as hair implants may have no lasting effect. Hair loss in both sexes may also occur as a result of ill health or radiation treatment, such as for cancer. Alopecia, a condition in which the hair falls out, is different from the 'male-pattern baldness' described above.

Baldwin James Arthur 1924–1987. US writer and civil-rights activist. He portrayed with vivid intensity the suffering and despair of black Americans in contemporary society. After his first novel, *Go Tell It On The Mountain* 1953, set in Harlem, and *Giovanni's Room* 1956, about a homosexual relationship in Paris, his writing became more politically indignant with *Another Country* 1962 and *The Fire Next Time* 1963, a collection of essays.

Baldwin Stanley, 1st Earl Baldwin of Bewdley 1867–1947. British Conservative politician, prime minister 1923–24, 1924–29, and 1935–37. He weathered the general strike 1926, secured complete adult suffrage 1928, and handled the ◊abdication crisis of Edward VIII 1936, but failed to prepare Britain for World War II.

Baldwin I 1058–1118. King of Jerusalem from 1100. A French nobleman, he joined his brother Godfrey de Bouillon (c. 1060–1100) on the First Crusade 1096 and established the kingdom of Jerusalem 1100. It was destroyed by Islamic conquest 1187. ▷ *See feature on pp. 280–281.*

Balearic Islands (Spanish ***Baleares***) group of Mediterranean islands forming an autonomous region of Spain; including ◊Majorca, ◊Minorca, ◊Ibiza, Cabrera, and Formentera
area 5,000 sq km/1,930 sq mi
capital Palma de Mallorca
industries figs, olives, oranges, wine, brandy, coal, iron, slate; tourism is crucial
population (1991) 709,100
history a Roman colony from 123 BC, the Balearic Islands were an independent Moorish kingdom 1009–1232; they were conquered by Aragon 1343.

Balearic Islands

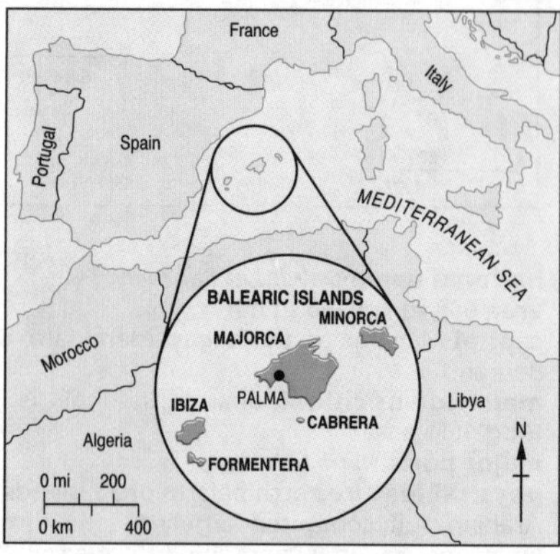

Balenciaga Cristóbal 1895–1972. Spanish couturier. His influential innovations in women's clothing included drop shoulder lines, nipped-in waists, and rounded hips, followed by three-quarter length sleeves and the pillbox hat.

Balfour Arthur James, 1st Earl of Balfour 1848–1930. British Conservative politician, prime minister 1902–05, and foreign secretary 1916–19. He issued the Balfour Declaration 1917 and was involved in peace negotiations after World War I, signing the Treaty of Versailles.

Balfour was elected a Conservative member of Parliament 1874, and secretary for Ireland 1887. In 1891 and again in 1895 he became First Lord of the Treasury and leader of the Commons, and in 1902 he succeeded Salisbury as prime minister; he suffered a crushing defeat in the 1905 elections. He retired from the party leadership 1911, and in 1915 joined the Asquith coalition as First Lord of the Admiralty. As foreign secretary 1916–19 he issued the Balfour Declaration in favour of a national home in Palestine for the Jews. He was Lord President of the Council 1919–22 and 1925–29.

Balfour Declaration letter, dated 2 Nov 1917, from British foreign secretary A J Balfour to Lord Rothschild (chair, British Zionist Federation) stating: 'HM government view with favour the establishment in Palestine of a national home for the Jewish people.' It helped form the basis for the foundation of Israel 1948.

Bali island of Indonesia, E of Java, one of the Sunda Islands; area 5,800 sq km/2,240 sq mi; population (1990) 2,777,800. The capital is Denpasar. The island features volcanic mountains. Industries include gold and silver work, woodcarving, weaving, copra, salt, coffee, and tourism, with 1 million tourists a year (1990); arts include Balinese dancing, music, and drama. Bali's Hindu culture goes back to the 7th century; the Dutch gained control of the island by 1908.

Baliol John de, or ***Balliol*** c. 1249–1315. King of Scotland 1292–96. As an heir to the Scottish throne on the death of Margaret, the Maid of Norway, his cause was supported by the English king, Edward I, against 12 other claimants. Having paid homage to Edward, Baliol was proclaimed king but soon rebelled and gave up the kingdom when English forces attacked Scotland.

Balkans (Turkish 'mountains') peninsula of SE Europe, stretching into the Mediterranean Sea between the Adriatic and Aegean seas, comprising Albania, Bosnia-Herzegovina, Bulgaria, Croatia, Greece, Romania, the part of Turkey in Europe, and Yugoslavia. It is joined to the rest of Europe by an isthmus 1,200 km/750 mi wide between Rijeka on the west and the mouth of the Danube on the Black Sea to the east.

Balakirev The Russian composer Balakirev as drawn by the Russian painter Leon Bakst. Balakirev's tyrannical character earned him many enemies, especially amongst his musical opponents who followed the traditional German school of composition. His works are reminiscent of Mikhail Glinka, with whom he helped to establish a Russian national style. *Image Select (UK) Ltd*

Ethnic diversity has made the Balkans a byword for political dissension. Political differences have led, for example, to the confrontation of Greece and Turkey over Cyprus, and the differing types of communism that prevailed until the early 1990s. More recently, ethnic interfighting has dominated the peninsula as first Slovenia and Croatia, and then Bosnia-Herzegovina, have battled to win independence from the Serb-dominated Yugoslav federation. Despite international recognition being awarded to all three republics early 1992, fierce fighting between Serb, Croat, and Muslim factions continued in Bosnia-Herzegovina into the 1990's.

Balkan Wars two wars 1912–13 and 1913 (preceding World War I) which resulted in the expulsion by the Balkan states of Ottoman Turkey from Europe, except for a small area around Istanbul.

The ***First Balkan War***, 1912, of Bulgaria, ◊Serbia, Greece, and Montenegro against Turkey, forced the Turks to ask for an armistice, but the London-held peace negotiations broke down when the Turks, while agreeing to surrender all Turkey-in-Europe W of the city of Edirne (formerly Adrianople), refused to give up the city itself. In Feb 1913 hostilities were resumed. Edirne fell on 26 March, and on 30 May, by the Treaty of London, Turkey retained in Europe only a small piece of E Thrace and the Gallipoli peninsula.

The ***Second Balkan War***, June–July 1913, took place when the victors fought over acquisitions in Macedonia, from most of which Bulgaria was excluded. Bulgaria attacked Greece and Serbia, which were joined by Romania. Bulgaria was defeated, and Turkey retained Thrace.

Balkhash salt lake in Kazakhstan; area 17,300 sq km/6,678 sq mi. It is 600 km/375 mi long and receives several rivers, but has no outlet. It is very shallow and is frozen throughout the winter.

Ball John died c. 1381. English priest. He was one of the leaders of the ◊Peasants' Revolt 1381, known as 'the mad priest of Kent'. A follower of John ◊Wycliffe and a believer in social equality, he was imprisoned for disagreeing with the archbishop of Canterbury. During the revolt he was released from prison, and when in Blackheath, London, incited people against the ruling classes by preaching from the text 'When Adam delved and Eve span, who was then the gentleman?' When the revolt collapsed he escaped but was captured near Coventry and executed.

Ball Lucille Desirée 1911–1989. US comedy actress. She began her film career as a bit player 1933, and appeared in dozens of movies over the next few years, including *Room Service* 1938 (with the Marx Brothers) and *Fancy Pants* 1950 (with Bob Hope). From 1951 to 1957 she starred with her husband, Cuban bandleader Desi Arnaz, in the television sitcom *I Love Lucy*, the first US television show filmed before an audience. It was followed by *The Lucy Show* 1962–68 and *Here's Lucy* 1968–74.

ballad (Latin *ballare* 'to dance') form of traditional narrative poetry, widespread in Europe and the USA. Ballads are metrically simple, sometimes (as in Russia) unstrophic and unrhymed or (as in Denmark) dependent on assonance. Concerned with some strongly emotional event, the ballad is halfway between the lyric and the epic. Most English ballads date from the 15th century but may describe earlier events.

Poets of the Romantic movement both in England and in Germany were greatly influenced by the ballad revival, as seen in, for example, the *Lyrical Ballads* 1798 of ◊Wordsworth and ◊Coleridge. *Des Knaben Wunderhorn/The Boy's Magic Horn* 1805–08, a collection edited by Clemens ◊Brentano and Achim von ◊Arnim, was a major influence on 19th-century German poetry. The ballad form was adapted in 'broadsheets', with a satirical or political motive, and in the 'hanging' ballads purporting to come from condemned criminals.

ballade in literature, a poetic form developed in France in the later Middle Ages from the ballad, generally consisting of one or more groups of three stanzas of seven or eight lines each, followed by a shorter stanza or envoy, the last line being repeated as a chorus. In music, a ballade is an instrumental piece based on a story; a form used in piano works by Chopin and Liszt.

Balladur Edouard 1929– . French Conservative politician, prime minister 1993–95. He is a supporter of the European Union and of maintaining close relations between France and Germany.

ball-and-socket joint joint allowing considerable movement in three dimensions, for instance the joint between the pelvis and the femur. To facilitate movement, such joints are rimmed with cartilage and lubricated by synovial fluid. The bones are kept in place by ligaments and moved by muscles.

Ballarat town in Victoria, Australia; population (1993) 81,200. It was founded in the 1851 gold rush, and the mining village and workings have been restored for tourists. The ◊Eureka Stockade miners' revolt took place here 1854.

Ballard J(ames) G(raham) 1930– . English novelist. His works include science fiction on the theme of catastrophe and collapse of the urban landscape, such as *The Drowned World* 1962, *Crash!* 1973, and *High-Rise* 1975; the partly autobiographical *Empire of the Sun* 1984, dealing with his internment in China during World War II; and the autobiographical novel *The Kindness of Women* 1991. His fundamentally moral vision is expressed with an untrammelled imagination and pessimistic irony.

Ballesteros Seve(riano) 1957– . Spanish golfer. He came to prominence 1976 and has won several leading tournaments in the USA, including the Masters Tournament 1980 and 1983. He has also won the British Open three times: in 1979, 1984, and 1988.

ballet (Italian *balletto* 'a little dance') theatrical representation in ◊dance form in which music also plays a major part in telling a story or conveying a mood. Some such form of entertainment existed in ancient Greece, but Western ballet as we know it today first appeared in Renaissance Italy, where it was a court entertainment. From there it was brought by Catherine de' Medici to France in the form of a spectacle combining singing, dancing, and declamation. During the 18th century, there were major developments in technique and ballet gradually became divorced from opera, emerging as an art form in its own right.

In the 20th century Russian ballet has had a vital influence on the classical tradition in the West, and ballet developed further in the USA through the work of George Balanchine and the American Ballet Theater, and in the UK through the influence of Marie Rambert.

◊Modern dance is a separate development.

history The first important dramatic ballet, the *Ballet comique de la reine*, was produced 1581 by the Italian Balthasar de Beaujoyeux at the French court and was performed by male courtiers, with ladies of the court forming the *corps de ballet*. In 1661 Louis XIV founded the Académie Royale de Danse, to which all subsequent ballet activities throughout the world can be traced. Long, flowing court dress was worn by the dancers until the 1720s when Marie-Anne Camargo, the first great ballerina, shortened her skirt to reveal her ankles, thus allowing greater movement *à terre* and the development of dancing *en l'air*.

During the 18th century, ballet spread to virtually every major capital in Europe. Vienna became an important centre and was instrumental in developing the dramatic aspect of the art as opposed to the athletic qualities, which also evolved considerably during this century, particularly among male dancers. In the early 19th century a Paris costumier, Maillot, invented tights, which allowed complete muscular freedom. The first of the great ballet masters was Jean-Georges ◊Noverre, and great contemporary dancers were Teresa Vestris (1726–1808), Anna Friedrike Heinel (1753–1808), Jean Dauberval (1742–1806), and Maximilien Gardel (1741–1787).

Carlo ◊Blasis is regarded as the founder of classical ballet, since he defined the standard conventional steps and accompanying gestures.

Romantic ballet The great Romantic era of the dancers Marie Taglioni (1804–1884), Fanny Elssler, Carlotta Grisi, Lucile Grahn, and Fanny Cerrito began about 1830 but survives today only in the ballets *Giselle* 1841 and *La Sylphide* 1832. Characteristics of this era were the new calf-length Romantic white dress and the introduction of dancing on the toes, *sur les pointes*. The technique of the female dancer was developed, but the role of the male dancer was reduced to that of being her partner. Important choreographers of the period were Jules Joseph Perrot (1810–1894), Arthur Saint-Léon (1821–1871), and August Bournonville. From 1860 ballet declined rapidly in popular favour in Europe, but its importance was maintained in St Petersburg under Marius Petipa (1818–1910).

Russian ballet was introduced to the West by Sergei ◊Diaghilev, who set out for Paris 1909 and founded the Ballets Russes (Russian Ballet), at about the same time that Isadora ◊Duncan, a fervent opponent of classical ballet, was touring Europe. Associated with Diaghilev were Mikhail Fokine, Enrico Cecchetti (1850–1928), Vaslav ◊Nijinsky, Anna Pavlova, Tamara Karsavina (1885–1978), Léonide Massine, Bronislava Nijinska, George Balanchine, and Serge Lifar. Ballets presented by his company, before its break-up after his death 1929, included *Les Sylphides*, *Schéhérazade*, *Petrouchka*, *Le Sacre du printemps/The Rite of Spring*, and *Les Noces*.

Diaghilev and Fokine pioneered a new and exciting combination of the perfect technique of imperial Russian dancers and the appealing naturalism favoured by Isadora Duncan. In Russia ballet continues to flourish, the two chief companies being the ◊Kirov and the ◊Bolshoi. Best-known ballerinas are Galina Ulanova and Maya Plisetskaya, and male dancers include Mikhail ◊Baryshnikov, Irek Mukhamedov, and Alexander Godunov, now dancing in the West.

American ballet was firmly established by the founding of Balanchine's School of American Ballet 1934, and by de Basil and René Blum's (1878–1942) Ballets Russes de Monte Carlo and Massine's Ballets Russes de Monte Carlo, which also carried on the Diaghilev tradition. In 1939 dancer Lucia Chase (1897–1986) and ballet director Richard Pleasant (1906–1961) founded the American Ballet Theater. From 1948 the New York City Ballet, under the guiding influence of Balanchine, developed a genuine American Neo-Classic style.

British ballet Marie Rambert initiated 1926 the company that developed into the Ballet Rambert, and launched the careers of choreographers such as Frederick Ashton and Anthony Tudor. The national company, the ◊Royal Ballet (so named 1956), grew from foundations laid by Ninette de Valois and Frederick Ashton 1928. British dancers include Alicia Markova, Anton Dolin (1904–1983), Margot ◊Fonteyn, Antoinette Sibley, Lynn Seymour, Beryl Grey, Anthony Dowell, David Wall, Merle Park, and Lesley Collier; choreographers include Kenneth MacMillan. Fonteyn's partners included Robert Helpmann and Rudolf ◊Nureyev.

ballet music During the 16th and 17th centuries there was not always a clear distinction between opera and ballet, since ballet during this period often included singing, and operas often included dance. The influence of the court composer Jean Baptiste Lully on the development of ballet under Louis XIV in France was significant (Lully was a dancer himself, as was the king). During this period many courtly dances originated, including the gavotte, passepied, bourrée, and minuet. In the 19th century, as public interest in ballet increased, Russia produced composers of international reputation such as Peter Ilich Tchaikovsky whose ballet scores include *Swan Lake* 1876, *Sleeping Beauty* 1890, and *The Nutcracker* 1892.

With the modern era of ballet which began 1909 with the founding of the Ballets Russes, innovative choreography transformed the visual aspects of ballet and striking new compositions by Achille Claude Debussy, Maurice Ravel, and especially Igor Stravinsky left their mark not only on the ballet composers who followed, but on the course of music history itself. Later in the century, the formal tradition of ballet was upset by the influence of jazz, jazz rhythms, and modern dance originating in the USA, which introduced greater freedom of bodily expression.

Today there exists a wide range of musical and choreographic styles, ranging from the classical to the popular. Many full ballet scores have been reduced by composers to ballet ◊suites or purely orchestral works, which incorporate the essential musical elements, tending to omit musically non-thematic and transitional passages which may be, nevertheless, essential to the choreography and visual narration. Examples include Stravinsky's *The Firebird* 1910 and Ravel's *Boléro* 1928. *See table on following page.*

'Anyone who has ever struggled with poverty knows how extremely expensive it is to be poor.'

James Baldwin
Nobody Knows My Name

'A platitude is simply a truth repeated until people get tired of hearing it.'

Stanley Baldwin
Hansard 29 May 1924

BALLET: REPERTORY

Date and place of first performance.

	Ballet	Composer	Choreographer	Place
1670	*Le Bourgeois Gentilhomme*	Lully	Beauchamp	Chambord
1735	*Les Indes galantes*	Rameau	Blondy	Paris
1761	*Don Juan*	Gluck	Angiolini	Vienna
1778	*Les Petits Riens*	Mozart	Noverre	Paris
1801	*The Creatures of Prometheus*	Beethoven	Viganò	Vienna
1828	*La Fille mal gardée*	Hérold	Aumer	Paris
1832	*La Sylphide*	Schneitzhoeffer	F Taglioni	Paris
1841	*Giselle*	Coralli	Perrot	Paris
1842	*Napoli*	Gade/Helsted/Lumbye/Paulli	Bournonville	Copenhagen
1844	*La Esmeralda*	Pugni	Perrot	London
1869	*Don Quixote*	Minkus	M Petipa	Moscow
1870	*Coppélia*	Delibes	Saint-Léon	Paris
1877	*La Bayadère*	Minkus	M Petipa	St Petersburg
1877	*Swan Lake*	Tchaikovsky	Reisinger	Moscow
1890	*The Sleeping Beauty*	Tchaikovsky	M Petipa	St Petersburg
1892	*Nutcracker*	Tchaikovsky	M Petipa/Ivanov	St Petersburg
1898	*Raymonda*	Glazunov	M Petipa	St Petersburg
1905	*The Dying Swan*	Saint-Saëns	Fokine	St Petersburg
1909	*Les Sylphides/Chopiniana*	Chopin	Fokine	St Petersburg
1910	*The Firebird*	Stravinsky	Fokine	Paris
1911	*Petrushka*	Stravinsky	Fokine	Paris
1911	*Le Spectre de la rose*	Weber	Fokine	Monte Carlo
1912	*L'Après-midi d'un faune*	Debussy	Nijinsky	Paris
1913	*Le Sacre du printemps*	Stravinsky	Nijinsky	Paris
1917	*Parade*	Satie	Massine	Paris
1919	*The Three-Cornered Hat*	Falla	Massine	London
1923	*Les Noces*	Stravinsky	Nijinska	Paris
1924	*Les Biches*	Poulenc	Nijinska	Monte Carlo
1927	*The Red Poppy*	Glière	Lashchilin/Tikhomirov	Moscow
1928	*Apollo*	Stravinsky	Balanchine	Paris
1929	*The Prodigal Son*	Prokofiev	Balanchine	Paris
1929	*La Valse*	Ravel	Nijinska	Monte Carlo
1931	*Façade*	Walton	Ashton	London
1937	*Checkmate*	Bliss	de Valois	Paris
1937	*Les Patineurs*	Meyerbeer/Lambert	Ashton	London
1938	*Billy the Kid*	Copland	Loring	Chicago
1940	*Romeo and Juliet*	Prokofiev	Lavrovsky	Leningrad
1942	*The Miraculous Mandarin*	Bartók	Milloss	Milan
1942	*Rodeo*	Copland	deMille	New York
1944	*Fancy Free*	Bernstein	Robbins	New York
1949	*Carmen*	Bizet	Petit	London
1951	*Pineapple Poll*	Sullivan/Mackerras	Cranko	London
1956	*Spartacus*	Khachaturian	Jacobson	Leningrad
1957	*Agon*	Stravinsky	Balanchine	New York
1962	*Pierrot lunaire*	Schoenberg	Tetley	New York
1964	*The Dream*	Mendelssohn/Lanchbery	Ashton	London
1965	*The Song of the Earth*	Mahler	MacMillan	Stuttgart
1966	*Romeo and Juliet*	Prokofiev	MacMillan	London
1968	*Enigma Variations*	Elgar	Ashton	London
1969	*The Taming of the Shrew*	Scarlatti/Stolze	Cranko	Stuttgart
1972	*Duo Concertante*	Stravinsky	Balanchine	New York
1974	*Elite Syncopations*	Joplin and others	MacMillan	London
1976	*A Month in the Country*	Chopin/Lanchbery	Ashton	London
1978	*Mayerling*	Liszt/Lanchbery	MacMillan	London
1978	*Symphony of Psalms*	Stravinsky	Kylían	Scheveningen
1980	*Gloria*	Poulenc	MacMillan	London
1980	*Rhapsody*	Rachmaninov	Ashton	London
1982	*The Golden Age*	Shostakovich	Grigorovich	Moscow
1984	*Different Drummer*	Webern/Schoenberg	MacMillan	London
1986	*The Snow Queen*	Tovey/Mussorgsky	Bintley	Birmingham
1988	*L'allegro, il penseroso ed il moderato*	Handel	Morris	Brussels
1989	*The Prince of the Pagodas*	Britten	MacMillan	London
1991	*Winter Dreams*	Tchaikovsky	MacMillan	London

balloon **The first free ascent from Earth on 21 Nov 1783. Pilatre de Rozier and Marquis d'Arlandes wave from the gallery of their Montgolfier balloon as they set out from Paris. They were airborne for 20 minutes, and travelled 9 km/6 mi.** ***Corbis***

ballistics study of the motion and impact of projectiles such as bullets, bombs, and missiles. For projectiles from a gun, relevant exterior factors include temperature, barometric pressure, and wind strength; and for nuclear missiles these extend to such factors as the speed at which the Earth turns.

balloon lighter-than-air craft that consists of a gasbag filled with gas lighter than the surrounding air and an attached basket, or gondola, for carrying passengers and/or instruments.

In 1783, the first successful human ascent was in Paris, in a hot-air balloon designed by the ◊Montgolfier brothers Joseph Michel and Jacques Etienne. In 1785, a hydrogen-filled balloon designed by French physicist Jacques Charles travelled across the English Channel.

ballot the process of voting in an election. In political elections in democracies ballots are usually secret: voters indicate their choice of candidate on a voting slip that is placed in a sealed ballot box. Ballot rigging is a term used to describe elections that are fraudulent because of interference with the voting process or the counting of ◊votes.

❛The ballot is stronger than the bullet.❜

On the BALLOT
Abraham Lincoln
speech 19 May 1856

ballroom dancing collective term for social dances such as the ◊foxtrot, quickstep, ◊tango, and ◊waltz.

Balmaceda José Manuel 1840–1891. Chilean president 1886–91. He inaugurated a vast reform programme including education, railways, communications, and public utilities, and invested revenue from Chile's nitrate fields in public works. The volatility of this key market led him to denounce foreign interests in Chile.

Balmoral Castle residence of the British royal family in Scotland on the river Dee, 10.5 km/6½ mi NE of Braemar, Grampian region. The castle, built of granite in the Scottish baronial style, is dominated by a square tower and circular turret rising 30 m/100 ft. It was rebuilt 1853–55 by Prince Albert, who bought the estate in 1852.

balsam any of various garden plants of the genus *Impatiens* of the balsam family. They are usually annuals with spurred red or white flowers and pods that burst and scatter their seeds when ripe. In medicine and perfumery, balsam refers to various oily or gummy aromatic plant resins, such as balsam of Peru from the Central American tree *Myroxylon pereirae*.

Balthus (Balthazar Klossowksi de Rola) 1908– . Polish-born French painter. He is famed for his enigmatic paintings of interiors featuring languid, prepubescent girls, both clothed and nude, for example *Nude with Cat* about 1954 (National Gallery of Victoria, Melbourne). The studied, intense realism with which his self-absorbed figures are depicted lends his pictures a dreamlike quality.

Baltic, Battle of the naval battle fought off Copenhagen on 2 April 1801, in which a British fleet under Sir Hyde Parker, with ◊Nelson as second-in-command, annihilated the Danish navy.

Baltic Sea large shallow arm of the North Sea, extending NE from the narrow Skagerrak and Kattegat, between Sweden and Denmark, to the Gulf of Bothnia between Sweden and Finland. Its coastline is 8,000 km/5,000 mi long, and its area, including the gulfs of Riga, Finland, and Bothnia, is 422,300 sq km/163,000 sq mi.

Its shoreline is shared by Denmark, Germany, Poland, the Baltic States, Russia, Finland, and Sweden.

Many large rivers flow into it, including the Oder, Vistula, Niemen, Western Dvina, Narva, and Neva. Tides are hardly perceptible, and salt content is low; weather is often stormy and navigation dangerous. Most ports are closed by ice from Dec until May. The Kiel canal links the Baltic and North seas; the Göta canal connects the two seas by way of the S Swedish lakes. Since 1975 the Baltic Sea has been linked by the St Petersburg–Belomorsk seaway with the White Sea. A waterway system links the Baltic Sea (at St Petersburg) to the Caspian Sea (at Astrakhan).

Baltic States collective name for the states of ◊Estonia, ◊Latvia, and ◊Lithuania, former constituent republics of the USSR (from 1940). They regained independence Sept 1991.

Baltimore industrial port and largest city in Maryland, USA, on the western shore of Chesapeake Bay, NE of Washington DC; population (1992) 726,100; metropolitan area (1992) 2,434,000. Industries include shipbuilding, oil refining, food processing, and the manufacture of steel, chemicals, and aerospace equipment.

Baltic Sea

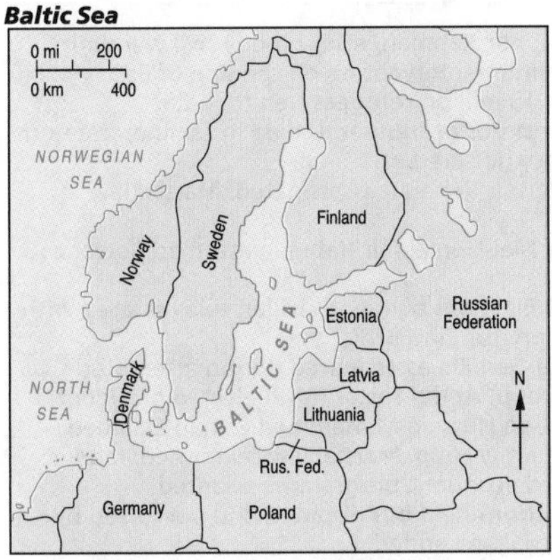

Baltistan region in the Karakoram range of NE Kashmir, held by Pakistan since 1949. It is the home of Balti Muslims of Tibetan origin.

Baluchistan mountainous desert area, comprising a province of Pakistan, part of the Iranian province of Sistán and Balúchestan, and a small area of Afghanistan. The Pakistani province has an area of 347,200 sq km/134,019 sq mi and a population (1981 census) of 4,332,000; its capital is Quetta. Sistán and Balúchestan has an area of 181,600 sq km/70,098 sq mi and a population (1986) of 1,197,000; its capital is Zahedan. The port of Gwadar in Pakistan is strategically important, situated on the Indian Ocean and the Strait of Hormuz. The common religion of the Baluch (or Baluchi) people is Islam, and they speak Baluchi, a member of the Iranian branch of the Indo-European language family. In the drier areas they make use of tents, moving when it becomes too arid. Although they practise nomadic pastoralism, many are settled agriculturalists.

Balzac Honoré de 1799–1850. French writer. He was one of the major novelists of the 19th century. His first success was *Les Chouans/The Chouans*, inspired by Walter Scott. This was the beginning of the long series of novels *La Comédie humaine/The ◊Human Comedy* which includes *Eugénie Grandet* 1833, *Le Père Goriot* 1834, and *Cousine Bette* 1846. He also wrote the Rabelaisian *Contes drolatiques/Ribald Tales* 1833.

Born in Tours, Balzac studied law and worked as a notary's clerk in Paris before turning to literature. A venture in printing and publishing 1825–28 involved him in a lifelong web of debt. His patroness, Madame de Berny, figures in *Le Lys dans la vallée/The Lily in the Valley* 1836. Balzac intended his major work *La Comédie humaine* to comprise 143 volumes, depicting every aspect of society in 19th-century France, of which he completed 80. Balzac corresponded constantly with the Polish countess Evelina Hanska after meeting her 1833, and they married four months before his death in Paris. He was buried in Père Lachaise cemetery, Paris.

banana The banana plant grows as a series of suckers from a rhizome. Each stem gradually droops downwards and produces at its tip the male flowers, which are sterile. The female flowers, which produce the edible fruit without fertilization, are found further along the stem. After a stem has produced a crop of fruit, it dies and is replaced by a new stem from a bud further along the rhizome. A banana plant may live for over 60 years.

Bamako capital and port of Mali on the river Niger; population (1992) 746,000. It produces pharmaceuticals, chemicals, textiles, tobacco, and metal products.

bamboo any of numerous plants of the subgroup Bambuseae within the grass family Gramineae, mainly found in tropical and subtropical regions. Some species grow as tall as 36 m/120 ft.

The stems are hollow and jointed and can be used in furniture, house, and boat construction. The young shoots are edible; paper is made from the stem. Bamboo flowers and seeds only once before the plant dies, sometimes after growing for as long as 120 years.

banana any of several treelike tropical plants of the genus *Musa*, family Musaceae, which grow up to 8 m/25 ft high. The edible banana is the fruit of a sterile hybrid form. The curved yellow fruits of the commercial banana, arranged in rows of 'hands', form cylindrical masses of a hundred or more.

They are picked and exported green and ripened aboard refrigerated ships. The plant is destroyed after cropping. The plantain, a larger, coarser hybrid variety that is used green as a cooked vegetable, is a dietary staple in many countries. In the wild, bananas depend on bats for pollination.

Banbury town in Oxfordshire, England, on the river Cherwell; population (1991) 39,900. Industries include car components, electrical goods, aluminium, food processing, and printing. The Banbury Cross of the nursery rhyme was destroyed by the Puritans 1602, but replaced 1858. Banbury cakes are criss-cross pastry cases with a mince-pie-style filling.

band music group, usually falling into a special category: for example, military, comprising woodwind, brass, and percussion; brass, solely brass and percussion; marching, a variant of brass; dance and swing, often like a small orchestra; jazz, with no fixed instrumentation; rock and pop, generally electric guitar, bass, and drums, variously augmented; and steel, from the West Indies, in which percussion instruments made from oil drums sound like marimbas.

Band, the North American rock group 1961–76. They acquired their name when working as Bob Dylan's backing band, and made their solo debut 1968 with *Music from Big Pink*. In their appearance and mysterious lyrics they often reflected a fascination for past American culture and history, as in the song 'The Night They Drove Old Dixie Down'. Their albums include *The Band* 1969, *Stage Fright* 1970, and *Northern Lights – Southern Cross* 1975. Their farewell concert was filmed by Martin Scorsese as *The Last Waltz* 1978.

Banda Hastings Kamuzu 1905–1997. Malawi politician, president 1966–94. He led his country's independence movement and was prime minister of Nyasaland (the former name of Malawi) from 1964. He became Malawi's first president 1966 and was named president for life 1971; his rule was authoritarian. Having bowed to opposition pressure and opened the way for a pluralist system, Banda stood in the first free presidential elections for 30 years 1994, but was defeated by Bakili Muluzi. In Jan 1996 he and his former aide, John Tembo, were acquitted of the murders of three senior politicians and a lawyer in 1983.

Bandaranaike Sirimavo (born Ratwatte) 1916– . Sri Lankan politician who succeeded her husband Solomon Bandaranaike to become the world's first female prime minister, 1960–65 and 1970–77, but was expelled from parliament 1980 for abuse of her powers while in office. She became prime minister in the 1994 elections, with her daughter Chandrika Bandaranaike ◊Kumaratunga as president.

Bandaranaike Solomon West Ridgeway Dias 1899–1959. Sri Lankan nationalist politician. In 1952 he founded the Sri Lanka Freedom party and in 1956 became prime minister, pledged to a socialist programme and a neutral foreign policy. He was assassinated by a Buddhist monk.

Bandar Seri Begawan formerly (until 1970) ***Brunei Town*** capital and largest town of Brunei, 14 km/9 mi from the mouth of the Brunei River; population (1992) 55,000. Features include the Omar Ali Saifuddin Mosque 1958, one of the largest and most splendid in Asia, and the Kampong Ayer water village. Since 1972 the town's main trade outlet has been the deepwater port of Muara at the mouth of the Brunei.

bandicoot small marsupial mammal inhabiting Australia and New Guinea. There are about 11 species, family Peramelidae, rat- or rabbit-sized, living in burrows. They have long snouts, eat insects, and are nocturnal. A related group, the rabbit bandicoots or bilbies, is reduced to a single species that is now endangered and protected by law.

bandicoot The rabbit bandicoot or bilby is the single surviving species of its family, Thylacomyidae. It lives in the arid scrubland of central and NW Australia. Sleeping in its burrow during the heat of the day, it emerges at night to feed on termites and beetle larvae.

Bandung commercial city and capital of Jawa Barat province on the island of Java, Indonesia; population (1990) 2,026,900. Bandung is the third-largest city in Indonesia and was the administrative centre when the country was the Netherlands East Indies.

Bandung Conference first conference 1955 of the Afro-Asian nations, proclaiming anticolonialism and neutrality between East and West.

bandy-bandy venomous Australian snake *Vermicella annulata* of the cobra family, which grows to about 75 cm/2.5 ft. It is banded in black and white. It is not aggressive toward humans.

Bangladesh country in southern Asia, bounded N, W, and E by India, SE by Myanmar, and S by the Bay of Bengal. *See country box on p. 96.*

Bangalore capital of Karnataka state, S India; population (1991) 4,087,000. Industries include electronics, aircraft and machine-tools construction, and coffee.

Bangka or ***Banka*** or ***Banca*** Indonesian island off the east coast of Sumatra; area 12,000 sq km/4,600 sq mi. The capital is Pangkalpinang. It is one of the world's largest producers of tin.

Bangkok (Thai *Krung Thep* 'City of Angels') capital and port of Thailand, on the river Chao Phraya; population (1993) 5,572,700. Products include paper, ceramics, cement, textiles, aircraft, and silk. It is the headquarters of the Southeast Asia Treaty Organization (SEATO).

Bangkok was established as the capital by Phra Chao Tak 1782, after the Burmese had burned down the former capital, Avuthia, about 65 km/40 mi to the N. Features include the temple of the Emerald Buddha and the vast palace complex.

Bangor resort town in County Down, N Ireland, on the shore of Belfast Lough; population (1991) 52,400. It is the site of a famous missionary abbey of the Celtic church founded by St Comgall 555 and sacked by the Danes in the 9th century. The abbey was the home of St Columbanus and St Gall.

Bangor cathedral city in Gwynedd, N Wales, on the Menai Strait; population (1991) 12,300. The cathedral was begun 1495. Industries include chemicals, electrical goods, and engineering. Slate from Penrhyn quarries is exported.

Bangui capital and port of the Central African Republic, on the river Ubangi; population (1988) 597,000. Industries include beer, cigarettes, office machinery, and timber and metal products.

'It is more like an English town than most of its transatlantic brethren, and the ways of its inhabitants are English.'

On **Baltimore**
Anthony Trollope
North America

'Equality may be perhaps a right, but no power on earth can turn it into a fact.'

Honoré de Balzac
La Duchesse de Langeais

BANGLADESH
People's Republic of (formerly *East Pakistan*)

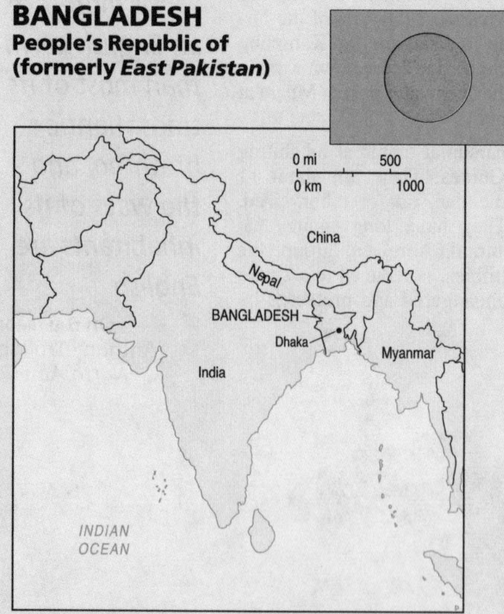

national name *Gana Prajatantri Bangladesh*
area 144,000 sq km/55,585 sq mi
capital Dhaka (formerly Dacca)
major ports Chittagong, Khulna
physical features flat delta of rivers Ganges (Padma) and Brahmaputra (Jamuna), the largest estuarine delta in the world; annual rainfall of 2,540 mm/100 in; some 75% of the land is less than 3 m/10 ft above sea level; hilly in extreme SE and NE
head of state Abdur Rahman Biswas from 1991
head of government Sheikha Hasina Wazed from 1996
political system emergent democratic republic
administrative divisions four divisions and 64 districts
political parties Bangladesh Nationalist Party (BNP), Islamic, right of centre; Awami League (AL), secular, moderate socialist; Jatiya Dal (National Party), Islamic nationalist
population 120,073,000 (1996 est)
population growth rate 2.2% (1990–95); 2.0% (2000–05)
ethnic distribution 98% of Bengali descent, half a million Bihari, and around 1 million belonging to 'tribal' communities
life expectancy 53 (men), 53 (women)
literacy rate men 47%, women 22%
languages Bengali (official); English
religions Sunni Muslim 85%, Hindu 12%; Islam is the state religion
currency taka
GDP (US $) 26.2 billion (1994)
growth rate 4.6% (1994)
exports jute, tea, garments, fish products, newsprint, hides and skins

HISTORY
c. 1000 BC Arrival of Bang tribe in lower Ganges valley, establishing the kingdom of Banga (Bengal).
8th–12th Cs AD Period of rule in Bengal, successively, by the Buddhist Pala and Hindu Senha dynasties.
1199 Bengal was invaded and briefly ruled by the Muslim Khiljis from Central Asia.
1517 Portuguese merchants arrived in Chittagong.
1576 Bengal conquered by Muslim Mogul emperor Akbar.
1651 British East India Company established a commercial factory in Bengal.
1757 Bengal came under de facto British rule after Robert Clive defeated the nawab (ruler) of Bengal at Battle of Plassey.
1905–12 Bengal briefly partitioned by the British Raj between a Mulsim-dominated E and Hindu-dominated W.
1906 Muslim League (ML) founded in Dhaka.
1947 Bengal formed into E province of Pakistan on partition of British India, with ML administration.
1952 12 students killed by troops in anti-Urdu and pro-Bengali language riots in Dhaka.
1954 The opposition United Front, dominated by the Awami League (AL) and campaigning for East Bengal's autonomy, trounced ML in elections.
1955 East Bengal renamed East Pakistan.
1966 Sheik Mujibur Rahman of AL announced a Six-Point Programme of autonomy for East Pakistan.
1970 500,000 people killed in cyclone. Pro-autonomy AL secured crushing electoral victory in East Pakistan.
1971 Bangladesh ('land of the Bangla speakers') emerged as independent nation, under leadership of Sheik Mujibur Rahman, after bloody civil war with Indian military intervention on the side of East Pakistan; 10 million refugees fled to India.
1974 Hundreds of thousands died in famine; state of emergency declared.
1975 Mujibur Rahman assassinated. Martial law imposed.
1976–77 Maj-Gen Zia ur-Rahman assumed power as president.
1978–79 Elections held and civilian rule restored with clear victory for Zia's BNP.
1981 Maj-Gen Zia assassinated during attempted military coup. Abdul Sattar (BNP) elected president.
1982 Lt-Gen Hussain Mohammed Ershad assumed power in army coup. Martial law reimposed; market-orientated economic programme adopted.
1986 Elections held but disputed and boycotted by BNP. Martial law ended.
1987 State of emergency declared in response to opposition demonstrations and violent strikes.
1988 Assembly elections boycotted by main opposition parties. State of emergency lifted. Islam made state religion. Monsoon floods left 30 million homeless and thousands dead.
1989 Power devolved to Chittagong Hill Tracts to end 14-year conflict between local people and army-protected settlers.
1990 Following mass anti-government protests, President Ershad resigned; chief justice Shahabuddin Ahmad became interim president.
1991 Cyclone killed around 139,000 and left up to 10 million homeless. Elections resulted in coalition government with BNP dominant. Parliamentary government restored, with Abdur Rahman Biswas as president and Begum Khaleda Zia prime minister.
1994–95 Opposition boycotted parliament, charging government with fraud.
1996 Zia handed over power to neutral caretaker government. General election won by AL, led by Sheika Hasina Wazed, daughter of Sheik Mujibur Rahman. BNP boycotted parliament.
1997 BNP boycotted parliament and called a one-day strike in protest against government 'repression'.
1998 Opposition BNP ended boycott of parliament.

SEE ALSO East India Company; Pakistan

banjo resonant stringed musical instrument with a long fretted neck and circular drum-type sound box covered on the topside only by stretched skin (now usually plastic). It is played with a plectrum.

The banjo originated in the American South among black slaves (based on a similar instrument of African origin). It was introduced to Britain 1846.

Banjul capital and chief port of Gambia, on an island at the mouth of the river Gambia; population of urban area (1986) 150,000; city 44,200 (1983). Established 1816 as a settlement for freed slaves, it was known as Bathurst until 1973.

Bankhead Tallulah 1903–1968. US actress. She was renowned for her wit and flamboyant lifestyle. Her stage appearances include *Dark Victory* 1934, Lillian Hellman's *The Little Foxes* 1939, and Thornton Wilder's *The Skin of Our Teeth* 1942. Her films include Alfred Hitchcock's *Lifeboat* 1943, *A Royal Scandal* 1945, and *Die! Die! My Darling!* 1965.

Bank of England UK central bank founded by act of Parliament 1694. It was entrusted with issuing bank notes 1844 and nationalized 1946. It is banker to the clearing banks and the UK government.

As the government's bank, it manages and arranges the financing of the ◊public sector borrowing requirement and the national debt, implements monetary policy and exchange-rate policy by intervening in foreign-exchange markets, and supervises the UK banking system.

Bangkok Although Bangkok has grown rapidly to become one of the leading industrial and financial centres of SE Asia, it has preserved much of its cultural heritage. This Buddhist temple – one of over 400 in the city – is in the industrial district of Thon Buri. *Anthony Lambert*

bank rate interest rate fixed by the Bank of England as a guide to mortgage, hire purchase rates, and so on, which was replaced 1972 by the minimum lending rate (lowest rate at which the Bank acts as lender of last resort to the money market), which from 1978 was again a 'bank rate' set by the Bank.

bankruptcy process by which the property of a person (in legal terms, an individual or corporation) unable to pay debts is taken away under a court order and divided fairly among the person's creditors, after preferential payments such as taxes and wages. Proceedings may be instituted either by the debtor (voluntary bankruptcy) or by any creditor for a substantial sum (involuntary bankruptcy). Until 'discharged', a bankrupt is severely restricted in financial activities.

When 'discharged', the person becomes free of most debts dating from the time of bankruptcy. The largest financial-services bankruptcy, with liabilities of $3 billion, was filed by US securities firm Drexel Burnham Lambert 1990.

Banks Joseph 1743–1820. British naturalist and explorer. He accompanied Capt James ◊Cook on his voyage around the world 1768–71 and brought back 3,600 plants, 1,400 of them never before classified. The *Banksia* genus of shrubs is named after him.

banksia any shrub or tree of the genus *Banksia*, family Proteaceae, native to Australia and including the honeysuckle tree. The genus is named after Joseph Banks.

Bannister Roger Gilbert 1929– . English track and field athlete. He was the first person to run a mile in under four minutes. He achieved this feat at Oxford, England, on 6 May 1954, in a time of 3 min 59.4 sec. At the 1954 Commonwealth Games in Vancouver, Canada, he was involved with John Landy (1930–) from Australia, in the 'Mile of the Century', so called because it was a clash between the only two people to have broken the four-minute barrier for the mile at that time.

Bannockburn, Battle of battle on 24 June 1314 in which ◊Robert (I) the Bruce of Scotland defeated the English under Edward II, who had come to relieve the besieged Stirling Castle. Named after the town of Bannockburn, S of Stirling, central Scotland.

banshee in Gaelic folklore, a female spirit whose wailing outside a house foretells the death of one of its inhabitants.

bantam small ornamental variety of domestic chicken weighing about 0.5–1 kg/1–2 lb. Bantams can either be a small version of one of the larger breeds, or a separate type. Some are prolific egg layers. Bantam cocks have a reputation as spirited fighters.

banteng wild species of cattle *Bos banteng*, now scarce, but formerly ranging from Myanmar (Burma) through SE Asia to Malaysia and Java, inhabiting hilly forests. Its colour varies from pale brown to blue-black, usually with white stockings and rump patch; height up to 1.5 m/5 ft at the shoulder.

Banting Frederick Grant 1891–1941. Canadian physician. He discovered a technique for isolating the hormone insulin 1921 when he and his colleague Charles ◊Best tied off the ducts of the ◊pancreas to determine the function of the cells known as the ◊islets of Langerhans. This made possible the treatment of diabetes. Banting and John J R Macleod (1876–1935), his mentor, shared the 1923 Nobel Prize for Physiology or Medicine, and Banting divided his prize with Best.

Banting Canadian physician Frederick Banting who, with Charles Best, opened the way to a treatment for diabetes by discovering a technique for isolating insulin. *Topham*

Bantu languages group of related languages belonging to the Niger-Congo family, spoken widely over the greater part of Africa south of the Sahara, including Swahili, Xhosa, and Zulu. Meaning 'people' in Zulu, the word Bantu itself illustrates a characteristic use of prefixes: *mu-ntu* 'man', *ba-ntu* 'people'.

banyan tropical Asian fig tree *Ficus benghalensis*, family Moraceae. It produces aerial roots that grow down from its spreading branches, forming supporting pillars that have the appearance of separate trunks.

baobab tree of the genus *Adansonia*, family Bombacaceae. It has rootlike branches, hence its nickname 'upside-down tree', and a disproportionately thick girth, up to 9 m/30 ft in diameter. The pulp of its fruit is edible and is known as monkey bread.

Baobabs may live for 1,000 years and are found in Africa (*A. digitata*) and Australia (*A. gregorii*), a relic of the time when these continents were both part of ◊Gondwanaland.

baptism (Greek 'to dip') immersion in or sprinkling with water as a religious rite of initiation. It was practised long before the beginning of Christianity. In the Christian baptism ceremony, sponsors or godparents make vows on behalf of the child, which are renewed by the child at confirmation. It is one of the seven sacraments. The *amrit* ceremony in Sikhism is sometimes referred to as baptism.

Baptist member of any of several Protestant and evangelical Christian sects that practise baptism by immersion only upon profession of faith. Baptists seek their authority in the Bible. They originated among English Dissenters who took refuge in the Netherlands in the early 17th century, and spread by emigration and, later, missionary activity. Of the world total of approximately 31 million, some 26.5 million are in the USA and 265,000 in the UK.

The Baptist Missionary Society, formed 1792 in Britain, pioneered the 19th-century missionary movement which spread the Baptist creed through Europe and to British colonies. The first Baptist church in America was organized in Rhode Island 1639. Baptism grew rapidly during the Great Awakening religious revival of the 18th century. After the American Revolution, Baptism spread into the South and among blacks, both slave and free. In 1905 the Baptist World Alliance was formed.

Bar, the in law, the profession of ◊barristers collectively. To be 'called to the Bar' is to become a barrister. Prospective barristers in the UK must complete a course of study in law and also be admitted to one of the four Inns of Court before they can be 'called'. The General Council of the Bar and of the Inns of Court (known as the Bar Council) is the professional governing body of the Bar.

bar modular segment of music incorporating a fixed number of beats, as in the phrase 'two/three/four beats to the bar'. It is shown in notation by vertical 'barring' of the musical continuum. The US term is measure.

bar unit of pressure equal to 10^5 pascals or 10^6 dynes/cm^2, approximately 750 mmHg or 0.987 atm. Its diminutive, the millibar (one-thousandth of a bar), is commonly used by meteorologists.

Bara Theda. Stage name of Theodosia Goodman 1890–1955. US silent-film actress. She became known as the 'the vamp', and the first movie sex symbol, after appearing in *A Fool There Was* 1915, based on a poem by Rudyard Kipling, 'The Vampire'.

Barabbas in the New Testament, a condemned robber released by Pilate at Passover instead of Jesus to appease a mob.

Barbados island country in the Caribbean, one of the Lesser Antilles. It is about 483 km/300 mi N of Venezuela. *See country box on p. 98.*

Barbarossa nickname 'red beard' given to the Holy Roman emperor Frederick I (1657–1713), and also to two brothers, Horuk and Khair-ed-Din, who were Barbary pirates. Horuk was killed by the Spaniards 1518; Khair-ed-Din took Tunis 1534 and died in Constantinople 1546.

Barbary ape tailless, yellowish-brown macaque monkey *Macaca sylvanus*, 55–75 cm/20–30 in long. Barbary apes are found in the mountains and wilds of Algeria and Morocco, especially in the forests of the Atlas Mountains. They were introduced to Gibraltar, where legend has it that the British will leave if the ape colony dies out.

Barbary Coast North African coast of the Mediterranean Sea (named after the ◊Berbers) from which pirates operated against US and European shipping (taking hostages for ransom) from the 16th up to the 19th century.

barbastelle insect-eating bat *Barbastella barbastellus* with hairy cheeks and lips, 'frosted' black fur, and a wingspan of about 25 cm/10 in. It lives in hollow trees and under roofs, and is occasionally found in the UK but more commonly in Europe.

barbel freshwater fish *Barbus barbus* found in fast-flowing rivers with sand or gravel bottoms in Britain and Europe. Long-bodied, and up to 1 m/3 ft long in total, the fish has four barbels ('little beards' – sensory fleshy filaments) near the mouth.

Barber Samuel 1910–1981. US composer. He worked in a Neo-Classical, astringent style. Compositions include *Adagio for Strings* 1936 and the opera *Vanessa* 1958, which won one of his two Pulitzer prizes. Another opera, *Antony and Cleopatra* 1966, was commissioned for the opening of the new Metropolitan Opera House at the Lincoln Center, New York City. Barber's music is lyrical and fastidiously worked. His later works include *The Lovers* 1971.

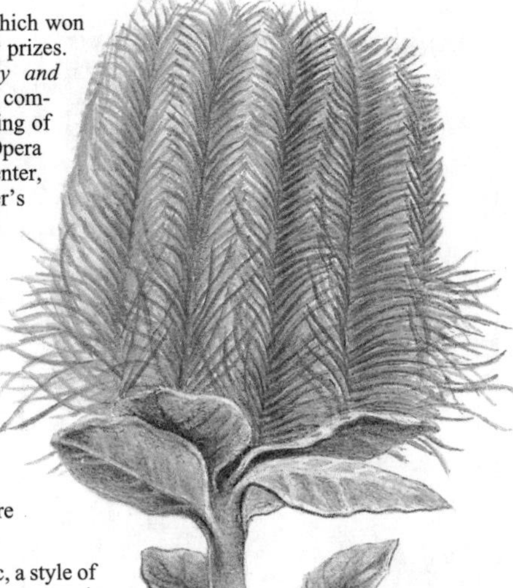

banksia Banksias vary from prostrate shrubs to large trees, but have in common a large flower spike made up of about 1,000 individual flowers formed around a central axis.

barberry any spiny shrub of the genus *Berberis* of the barberry family (Berberidaceae), having sour red berries and yellow flowers. These shrubs are often used as hedges.

barbershop in music, a style of unaccompanied close-harmony singing of sentimental ballads, revived in the USA during the 19th century. Traditionally sung by four male voices, since the 1970s it has developed as a style of ◊a cappella choral singing for both male and female voices.

barbet (Latin *barbatus*, 'bearded') small, tropical bird, often brightly coloured. There are about 78 species of barbet in the family Capitonidae, order Piciformes, common to tropical Africa, Asia, and America. Barbets eat insects and fruit and, being distant relations of woodpeckers, drill nest holes with their beaks. The name comes from the 'little beard' of bristles about the mouth that assists them in catching insects.

barbet Barbets are tropical birds most commonly found in Africa. They are named after the 'little beard' of bristles found around the beak.

Barbican, the arts and residential complex in the City of London. The Barbican Arts Centre (1982) contains theatres, cinemas, and exhibition and concert halls. The architects were Powell, Chamberlin, and Bon.

Barbie Klaus 1913–1991. German Nazi, a member of the ◊SS from 1936. During World War II he was involved in the deportation of Jews from the occupied Netherlands 1940–42 and in tracking down Jews and Resistance workers in France 1942–45. He was arrested 1983 and convicted of crimes against humanity in France 1987. He died in prison.

Barbirolli John (Giovanni Battista) 1899–1970. English conductor. He was noted for his interpretation of Vaughan Williams and Sibelius symphonies. Trained as a cellist, he succeeded Toscanini as conductor of the New

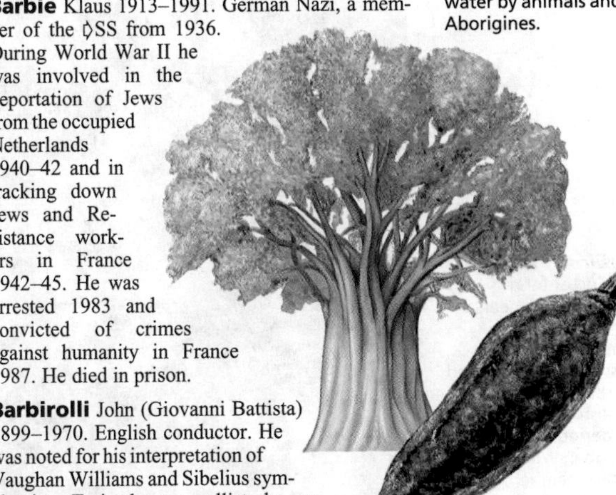

baobab The Australian baobab, or gourd tree, grows in NW Australia. It has edible seeds, and the massive trunk is used as a source of water by animals and Aborigines.

BARBADOS

area 430 sq km/166 sq mi
capital Bridgetown
major towns/cities Speightstown, Holetown, Oistins
physical features most easterly island of the West Indies; surrounded by coral reefs; subject to hurricanes June–Nov; highest point Mount Hillaby 340 m/1,115 ft
head of state Elizabeth II from 1966, represented by Denys Williams from 1995
head of government Owen Arthur from 1994
political system constitutional monarchy
administrative divisions 11 parishes
political parties Barbados Labour Party (BLP), moderate left of centre; Democratic Labour Party (DLP), moderate left of centre; National Democratic Party (NDP), centrist
population 264,300 (1994 est)
population growth rate 0.3% (1990–95)
ethnic distribution about 80% of African descent, about 16% mixed race, and 4% of European origin (mostly British)
life expectancy 73 (men), 78 (women)
literacy rate 99%
languages English and Bajan (Barbadian English dialect)
religions 33% Anglican, 13% Pentecostalist, 6% Methodist, 4% Roman Catholic
currency Barbados dollar
GDP (US $) 1.7 billion (1994)
growth rate 4.1% (1994)
exports sugar, rum, electronic components, clothing, cement, chemicals, foodstuffs. Tourism is important

HISTORY
1536 Visited by Portuguese explorer Pedro a Campos and the name Los Barbados ('The Bearded Ones') given in reference to its 'bearded' fig trees; indigineous Arawak Indians were virtually wiped out, via epidemics, after contact with Europeans.
1627 British colony established; developed as a sugar-plantation economy, initially on basis of black slaves brought in from W Africa.
1639 Island's first parliament, the House of Assembly, established.
1816 Last and largest ever revolt by slaves led by Bussa.
1834 Slaves freed.
1937 Outbreak of riots, which were followed within a year by the establishment of the BLP by Grantley Adams, and moves towards a more independent political system.
1951 Universal adult suffrage introduced. BLP won general election.
1954 Ministerial government established, with BLP leader Adams as first prime minister.
1961 Independence achieved from Britain. Democratic Labour Party (DLP), led by Errol Barrow, in power.
1966 Barbados achieved full independence within Commonwealth, with Barrow as prime minister.
1967 Became a member of the United Nations.
1972 Diplomatic relations with Cuba established.
1976 BLP, led by Tom Adams, the son of Grantley Adams, returned to power.
1983 Barbados supported US invasion of Grenada.
1985 Adams died; Bernard St John became prime minister.
1986 DLP, led by Barrow, returned to power.
1987 Barrow died; Erskine Lloyd Sandiford became prime minister.
1994 BLP, led by Owen Arthur, won decisive election victory.

SEE ALSO Arawak; West Indies

York Philharmonic Orchestra 1937–43 and was conductor of the Hallé Orchestra, Manchester, England, 1943–70.

barbiturate hypnosedative drug, commonly known as a 'sleeping pill', consisting of any salt or ester of barbituric acid $C_4H_4O_3N_2$. It works by depressing brain activity. Most barbiturates, being highly addictive, are no longer prescribed and are listed as controlled substances.

Tolerance develops quickly in the user so that increasingly large doses are required to induce sleep. A barbiturate's action persists for hours or days, causing confused, aggressive behaviour or disorientation. Overdosage causes death by inhibiting the breathing centre in the brain.

'I gave my beauty and youth to men. I am going to give my wisdom and experience to animals.'
BRIGITTE BARDOT
Quoted in *The Guardian* 1987

Barbizon School French school of landscape painters of the mid-19th century, based at Barbizon in the forest of Fontainebleau. They aimed to paint fresh, realistic scenes, sketching and painting their subjects in the open air and in this respect were the forerunners of the Impressionists. Members included Jean François Millet, Théodore Rousseau, and Charles Daubigny (1817–1878).

Barbour John c. 1320–1395. Scottish poet. His epic 13,000-line poem *The Brus* (written 1374–75, printed 1571) chronicles the war of Scottish independence and includes a vivid account of Robert Bruce's victory over the English at Bannockburn 1314. It is among the earliest known works of Scottish poetry.

Barbirolli The conductor John Barbirolli in rehearsal. An exponent of Romantic music, he passionately supported works by the pastoral English composers of his period: Elgar, Delius, Vaughan Williams. He is best remembered for his fine recordings of English music. *EMI*

Barbuda one of the islands that form the state of ◊Antigua and Barbuda.

Barcelona capital, industrial city (textiles, engineering, chemicals), and port of Catalonia, NE Spain; population (1994) 1,631,000. As the chief centre of anarchism and Catalonian nationalism, it was prominent in the overthrow of the monarchy 1931 and was the last city of the republic to surrender to Franco 1939. In 1992 the city hosted the Summer Olympics.
features The Ramblas, tree-lined promenades leading from the Plaza de Cataluña, the largest square in Spain; ◊Gaudí's unfinished church of the Holy Family 1883; the Pueblo Español 1929, with specimens of Spanish architecture; a replica of Columbus's flagship the *Santa Maria*, in the Maritime Museum; a large collection of art by Picasso.
history Founded in the 3rd century BC, Barcelona was ruled independently by the Counts of Barcelona from the 9th century, becoming a commercial centre for Aragon and Catalonia in the 13th–14th centuries and one of the leading ports of the Mediterranean. The city was devastated in the Catalonian Revolt 1652 and again during the War of the Spanish Succession 1714. At the forefront of the fight for regional autonomy during the Spanish Civil War, it suffered as a result of insurrections 1835, 1856, and 1909, and was held by the Republicans 1936–39.

bar code pattern of bars and spaces that can be read by a computer. Bar codes are widely used in retailing, industrial distribution, and public libraries. The code is read by a scanning device; the computer determines the code from the widths of the bars and spaces.

bard Celtic minstrel who, in addition to composing songs, usually at a court, often held important political posts. Originating in the pre-Christian era, bards were persecuted in Wales during the 13th century on political grounds. Since the 19th century annual meetings and competitions in Wales have attempted to revive the musical tradition of the bard.

Bardeen John 1908–1991. US physicist. He won a Nobel prize 1956, with Walter Brattain (1902–1987) and William Shockley (1910–1989), for the development of the ◊transistor 1948. In 1972 he became the first double winner of a Nobel prize in the same subject (with Leon ◊Cooper and Robert Schrieffer [1931–]) for his work on ◊superconductivity.

Bardot Brigitte, born Camille Javal 1934– . French film actress. A celebrated sex symbol of the 1960s, she did much to popularize French cinema internationally. Her films include *Et Dieu créa la femme/And God Created Woman* 1950, *Viva Maria* 1965, and *Shalako* 1968. She has subsequently devoted herself to animal welfare.

Bardo Thödol or ***Book of the Dead*** Tibetan Buddhist text giving instructions to the newly dead about the Bardo, or state between death and rebirth.

Barebones Parliament English assembly called by Oliver ◊Cromwell to replace the 'Rump Parliament' July 1653. It consisted of 140 members nominated by the army and derived its name from one of its members, Praise-God Barbon. Although they attempted to pass sensible legislation (civil marriage; registration of births, deaths, and marriages; custody of lunatics), its members' attempts to abolish tithes, patronage, and the court of chancery, and to codify the law, led to the resignation of the moderates and its dissolution Dec 1653.

Barenboim Daniel 1942– . Israeli pianist and conductor. He was pianist/conductor with the English Chamber Orchestra from 1964, conductor of the New York Philharmonic Orchestra 1970, musical director of the Orchestre de Paris 1975, and director of the Chicago Symphony Orchestra 1991. As a pianist he specialized in the German classic and romantic repertoire; as a conductor he has extended into 19th- and 20th-century French music,

bar code The bars of varying thicknesses and spacings represent two series of numbers, identifying the manufacturer and the product. Two longer, thinner bars mark the beginning and end of the manufacturer and product codes. The bar code is used on groceries, books, and most articles for sale in shops.

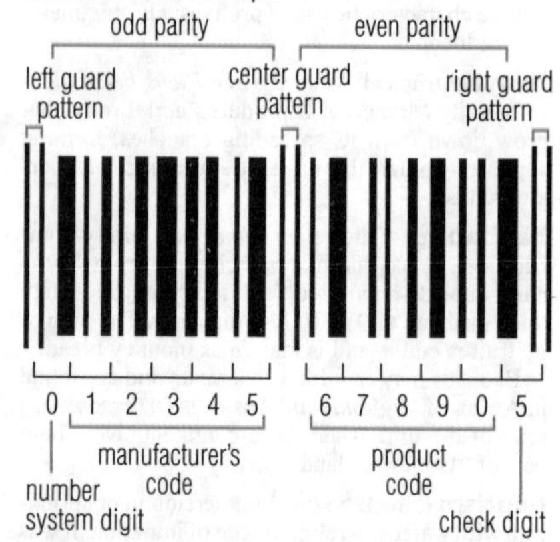

including Boulez. He was married to the cellist Jacqueline Du Pré.

Barents Willem c. 1550–1597. Dutch explorer and navigator. He made three expeditions to seek the ◊Northeast Passage; he died on the last voyage. The Barents Sea, part of the Arctic Ocean N of Norway, is named after him.

Bari capital of Puglia region, S Italy, and industrial port on the Adriatic Sea; population (1992) 342,100. It is the site of Italy's first nuclear power station; the part of the town known as Tecnopolis is the Italian equivalent of ◊Silicon Valley.

baritone male voice pitched between bass and tenor, of approximate range G2–F4, well suited to lieder (musical settings for poems). Dietrich Fischer-Dieskau (1925–) and Hermann Prey (1929–) are well-known German baritones.

barium (Greek *barytes* 'heavy') soft, silver-white, metallic element, symbol Ba, atomic number 56, relative atomic mass 137.33. It is one of the alkaline-earth metals, found in nature as barium carbonate and barium sulphate. As the sulphate it is used in medicine: taken as a suspension (a 'barium meal'), its movement along the gut is followed using X-rays. The barium sulphate, which is opaque to X-rays, shows the shape of the gut, revealing any abnormalities of the alimentary canal. Barium is also used in alloys, pigments, and safety matches and, with strontium, forms the emissive surface in cathode-ray tubes. It was first discovered in barytes or heavy spar.

bark protective outer layer on the stems and roots of woody plants, composed mainly of dead cells. To allow for expansion of the stem, the bark is continually added to from within, and the outer surface often becomes cracked or is shed as scales. Trees deposit a variety of chemicals in their bark, including poisons. Many of these chemical substances have economic value because they can be used in the manufacture of drugs. Quinine, derived from the bark of the cinchona tree, is used to fight malarial infections; curare, an anaesthetic used in medicine, comes from the *Strychnus toxifera* tree in the Amazonian rainforest.

Barking and Dagenham outer London borough of E Greater London
population (1991) 143,700
features 15th–16th-century St Margaret's Church; Barking Abbey, with its 15th-century tower; Cross Keys Inn at Dagenham (about 1500); Quaker burial ground where Elizabeth Fry is buried
industries Ford motor industry at Dagenham; paint; telephone cables.

barley cereal belonging to the grass family Gramineae. It resembles wheat but is more tolerant of cold and draughts. Cultivated barley *Hordeum vulgare* comprises three main varieties – six-rowed, four-rowed, and two-rowed.

Barley was one of the earliest cereals to be cultivated, about 5000 BC in Egypt, and no other cereal can thrive in so wide a range of climatic conditions; polar barley is sown and reaped well within the Arctic Circle in Europe. Barley is no longer much used in bread-making, but it is used in soups and stews and as a starch. Its high-protein form finds a wide use as animal feed, and its low-protein form is used in brewing and distilling alcoholic beverages.

bar mitzvah (Hebrew 'son of the commandment') in Judaism, initiation of a boy, which takes place at the age of 13, into the adult Jewish community; less common is the ***bat mitzvah*** or ***bat*** for girls aged 12. The child reads a passage from the Torah in the synagogue on the Sabbath and is subsequently regarded as a full member of the congregation.

barn farm building traditionally used for the storage and processing of cereal crops and hay. On older farmsteads, the barn is usually the largest building. It is often characterized by ventilation openings rather than windows and has at least one set of big double doors for access. Before mechanization, wheat was threshed by hand on a specially prepared floor inside these doors.

Tithe barns were used in feudal England to store the produce paid as a tax to the parish priest by the local occupants of the land. In the Middle Ages, monasteries often controlled the collection of tithes over a wide area and, as a result, constructed some enormous tithe barns.

Barnabas, St lived 1st century AD. In the New Testament, a 'fellow labourer' with St Paul; he went with St Mark on a missionary journey to Cyprus, his birthplace. Feast day 11 June.

barnacle marine crustacean of the subclass Cirripedia. The larval form is free-swimming, but when mature, it fixes itself by the head to rock or floating wood. The animal then remains attached, enclosed in a shell through which the cirri (modified legs) protrude to sweep food into the mouth. Barnacles include the stalked goose barnacle *Lepas anatifera* found on ships' bottoms, and the acorn barnacles, such as *Balanus balanoides*, common on rocks.

Barnard Christiaan Neethling 1922– . South African surgeon who performed the first human heart transplant 1967 at Groote Schuur Hospital in Cape Town. The 54-year-old patient lived for 18 days.

Barnardo Thomas John 1845–1905. British philanthropist. He was known as Dr Barnardo, although he was not medically qualified. He opened the first of a series of homes for destitute children 1867 in Stepney, E London.

Barnard's star second-closest star to the Sun, six light years away in the constellation Ophiuchus. It is a faint red dwarf of 10th magnitude, visible only through a telescope. It is named after the US astronomer Edward E Barnard (1857–1923), who discovered 1916 that it has the fastest proper motion of any star, crossing 1 degree of sky every 350 years.

Some observations suggest that Barnard's star may be accompanied by planets.

Barnes Thomas 1785–1841. British journalist, forthright and influential editor of *The Times* of London from 1817, during whose editorship it became known as 'the Thunderer'.

Barnet outer London borough of NW Greater London. It includes the district of Hendon
population (1991) 293,600
features site of the Battle of Barnet 1471 in one of the Wars of the ◊Roses; Lawrence Campe almshouses 1612; Hadley Woods; department for newspapers and periodicals of the British Library at Colindale; Metropolitan Police Training Centre and Royal Air Force Battle of Britain and Bomber Command museums in Hendon.

Barnsley administrative headquarters of Barnsley unitary authority; population (1991) 220,900. It is an industrial town (iron and steel, glass, paper, carpets, clothing) on one of Britain's richest coal fields; the headquarters of the National Union of Mineworkers is here.

Barnum P(hineas) T(aylor) 1810–1891. US showman. In 1871 he established the 'Greatest Show on Earth', which included the midget 'Tom Thumb', a circus, a menagerie, and an exhibition of 'freaks', conveyed in 100 railway carriages. In 1881, it merged with its chief competitor and has continued to this day as the Ringling Brothers and Barnum and Bailey Circus.

His American Museum in New York (1843–68) contained a theatre alongside numerous curiosities. He coined the phrase 'there's a sucker born every minute'.

barograph device for recording variations in atmospheric pressure. A pen, governed by the movements of an aneroid ◊barometer, makes a continuous line on a paper strip on a cylinder that rotates over a day or week to create a barogram, or permanent record of variations in atmospheric pressure.

barometer instrument that measures atmospheric pressure as an indication of weather. Most often used are the mercury barometer and the aneroid barometer.

In a mercury barometer a column of mercury in a glass tube, roughly 0.75 m/2.5 ft high (closed at one end, curved upwards at the other), is balanced by the pressure of the atmosphere on the open end; any change in the height of the column reflects a change in pressure. In an aneroid barometer, a shallow cylindrical metal box containing a partial vacuum expands or contracts in response to changes in pressure.

baron rank in the ◊peerage of the UK, above a baronet and below a viscount. Historically, any member of the higher nobility, a direct vassal (feudal servant) of the king, not bearing other titles such as duke or count. The term originally meant the vassal of a lord, but acquired its present meaning in the 12th century. The wife of a baron, or a woman holding a title in her own right, is a baroness.

baronet British order of chivalry below the rank of baron, but above that of knight, created 1611 by James I to finance the settlement of Ulster. It is a hereditary honour, although women cannot succeed to a baronetcy. A baronet does not have a seat in the House of Lords but is entitled to the style *Sir* before his name. The sale of baronetcies was made illegal 1937.

Barons' Wars civil wars in England:

1215–17 between King ◊John and his barons, over his failure to honour ◊Magna Carta;

1264–67 between ◊Henry III (and the future ◊Edward I) and his barons (led by Simon de ◊Montfort);

1264 14 May Battle of Lewes at which Henry III was defeated and captured.

1265 4 Aug Simon de Montfort was defeated by Edward at Evesham and killed.

Baroque in the visual arts, architecture, and music, a style flourishing in Europe 1600–1750, broadly characterized as expressive, flamboyant, and dynamic. Playing a central role in the crusading work of the Catholic Counter-Reformation, the Baroque used elaborate effects to appeal directly to the emotions. In some of its most characteristic works – such as Giovanni Bernini's Cornaro Chapel (Sta Maria della Vittoria, Rome), containing his sculpture *Ecstasy of St Theresa* 1645–52 – painting, sculpture, decoration, and architecture were designed to create a single, dramatic effect.
architecture The Baroque style in architecture emerged as a revolt against the rigid conventions of Italian Renaissance classicism – straight lines gave way to curved and broken lines; decoration became more important and elaborate; and spaces became more complex, their impact highlighted by the dramatic use of light and shade. Designs were often large-scale, as in Bernini's piazza for St Peter's in Rome.
painting Michelangelo Merisi da Caravaggio, with his bold use of light and forceful compositions, was an early exponent, but the Carracci family and Guido Reni were more typical of the early Baroque style, producing grandiose visions in ceiling paintings that deployed illusionistic displays of florid architectural decoration. The works of Pietro da Cortona and Il Guercino exemplify the mature or 'High' Baroque style. In Catholic Flanders the Baroque is represented by Peter Paul Rubens and Anthony van Dyck, and in Spain by Diego Velázquez and José Ribera. In Protestant Holland, where patronage had moved from the church to the middle classes, it is represented by Rembrandt Harmensz van Rijn, Jan Vermeer, and Frans Hals.
sculpture The master of Baroque sculpture was Bernini, whose *Ecstasy of St Theresa* is a fine example of overt emotionalism. Other Baroque sculptors are Pierre Puget and Antoine Coysevox, both French.
music In music, the Baroque can be traced to the Camerata, a society of poets and musicians who revived elements of Greek drama and developed the opera form in Florence; Claudio Monteverdi and Giovanni Gabrieli were important figures in early Baroque music, introducing exclamatory and polychoral effects. The sonata, suite, and concerto grosso emerged during the period; the vocal forms of opera, oratorio, and cantata were also developed. Baroque composers include Girolamo Frescobaldi and Antonio Vivaldi in Italy, Johann Pachelbel and Johann Sebastian Bach in Germany, and George Handel in England.

The 19th-century Swiss art historian Jacob Burckhardt was the first to use the term 'baroque'; he applied it derogatively, meaning 'bizarre', 'irregular', but the word was absorbed into the language of art history.

Barra southernmost island of the larger Outer Hebrides, Scotland; area 90 sq km/35 sq mi; population (1991) 1,250. It is separated from South Uist by the Sound of Barra. The main town is Castlebay. The main industries are fishing and tourism.

barracuda large predatory fish *Sphyraena barracuda* found in the warmer seas of the world. It can grow over 2 m/6 ft long and has a superficial

‘Today, conducting is a question of ego: a lot of people believe they are actually playing the music.’

DANIEL BARENBOIM
Quoted in Jacobson *Reverberations* 1975

resemblance to a pike. Young fish shoal, but the older ones are solitary.

Barranquilla seaport in N Colombia, on the Magdalena River; population (1994) 1,049,000. Products include chemicals, tobacco, textiles, furniture, and footwear. It is Colombia's chief port on the Caribbean and the site of Latin America's first air terminal 1919.

Barras Paul François Jean Nicolas, Count 1755–1829. French revolutionary. He was elected to the National Convention 1792 and helped to overthrow Robespierre 1794. In 1795 he became a member of the ruling Directory (see ◊French Revolution). In 1796 he brought about the marriage of his former mistress, Joséphine de Beauharnais, with Napoleon and assumed dictatorial powers. After Napoleon's coup d'état 19 Nov 1799, Barras fell into disgrace.

Barrault Jean-Louis 1910–1994. French actor and stage director. He appeared in such films as *La Symphonie fantastique* 1942 and *La Ronde* 1950, and is perhaps best known for his role as the mime, Baptiste, in Marcel Carné's classic of the cinema *Les Enfants du Paradis* 1945.

He was producer and director to the ◊Comédie Française 1940–46, and set up the Compagnie Renaud-Barrault 1946 with his wife Madeleine Renaud, the company's leading actress. He became director of the Théâtre de France (formerly Odéon) from 1958, and presented a wide repertory, including a production of Eugène Ionesco's *Rhinocéros*, playing the lead himself.

Barre Raymond 1924– . French politician, member of the centre-right Union pour la Démocratie Française; prime minister 1976–81, when he also held the Finance Ministry portfolio and gained a reputation as a tough and determined budget-cutter.

barrel unit of liquid capacity, the value of which depends on the liquid being measured. It is used for petroleum, a barrel of which contains 159 litres/35 imperial gallons; a barrel of alcohol contains 189 litres/41.5 imperial gallons.

barrel organ portable pipe organ, played by turning a handle. The handle works a pump and drives a replaceable cylinder upon which music is embossed as a pattern of ridges controlling the passage of air to the pipes. It is often confused with the barrel or street piano used by buskers, which employed a barrel-and-pin mechanism to control a piano hammer action.

Bartók The composer Béla Bartók. As one of the first ethnomusicologists he drew upon the music of his native Hungary for inspiration; his knowledge of Bach is also evident in his own often complex contrapuntal procedures. Bartók's music, often very dissonant, is nevertheless highly individual. *Image Select (UK) Ltd*

Barrett Browning Elizabeth. English poet; see ◊Browning, Elizabeth Barrett.

Barrie J(ames) M(atthew) 1860–1937. Scottish dramatist and novelist. His work includes *The Admirable Crichton* 1902 and the children's fantasy *Peter Pan* 1904.

After early studies of Scottish rural life in plays such as *A Window in Thrums* 1889, his reputation as a dramatist was established with *The Professor's Love Story* 1894 and *The Little Minister* 1897. Later plays include *Quality Street* 1901 and *What Every Woman Knows* 1908.

barrier island long island of sand, lying offshore and parallel to the coast. Some are over 100 km/60 mi in length. Most barrier islands are derived from marine sands piled up by shallow longshore currents that sweep sand parallel to the seashore. Others are derived from former spits, connected to land and built up by drifted sand, that were later severed from the mainland. The Frisian Islands are barrier islands along the coast of the Netherlands.

barrier reef ◊coral reef that lies offshore, separated from the mainland by a shallow lagoon.

Barrios de Chamorro Violeta c. 1939– . President of Nicaragua from 1990. With strong US support, she was elected to be the candidate for the National Opposition Union (UNO) 1989, winning the presidency from David Ortega Saavedra Feb 1990 and thus ending the period of ◊Sandinista rule and the decade-long ◊Contra war.

barrister in the UK, a lawyer qualified by study at the ◊Inns of Court to plead for a client in court. In Scotland such lawyers are called ◊advocates. Traditionally, in the highest courts, only barristers could represent litigants, but this distinction between barristers and solicitors was abolished in the 1990s. When pupil barristers complete their training they are 'called to the Bar': this being the name of the ceremony in which they are admitted as members of the profession. Barristers remain outside the bar until they become ◊Queen's Counsel, appointed on the recommendation of the Lord Chancellor, when they 'take silk' (wear a silk instead of a stuff gown) and are called 'within the Bar'.

In Britain, a barrister is obliged to accept instructions from any client who wants their services, provided the case is within the lawyer's expertise and the client can pay the fee – the 'cab rank rule'. The barrister is not, therefore, personally vouching for a client's case, and cannot turn down a case because of their perception of a client's guilt or innocence.

barrow burial mound, usually composed of earth but sometimes of stones, examples of which are found in many parts of the world. The two main types are ***long***, dating from the New Stone Age, or Neolithic, and ***round***, dating from the later Mesolithic peoples of the early Bronze Age.

Long barrows may be mere mounds, but usually they contain a chamber of wood or stone slabs in which were placed the bodies of the deceased. They are common in southern England from Sussex to Dorset. The earthen (or unchambered) long barrows belong to the early and middle Neolithic, while others were constructed over Megalithic tombs.

Round barrows belong mainly to the Bronze Age, although in historic times some of the Saxon and most of the Danish invaders were barrow-builders. The commonest type is the bell barrow, consisting of a circular mound enclosed by a ditch and an outside bank of earth. Other types include the bowl barrow, pond barrow, and saucer barrow, all of which are associated with the Wessex culture (the Early Bronze Age culture of southern England dating to approximately 2000–1500 BC).

Barrow most northerly town in the USA, at Point Barrow, Alaska; the world's largest Inuit settlement. There is oil at nearby Prudhoe Bay.

Barrow Isaac 1630–1677. British mathematician, theologian, and classicist. His *Lectiones geometricae* 1670 contains the essence of the theory of ◊calculus, which was later expanded by Isaac ◊Newton and Gottfried ◊Leibniz.

Barry Charles 1795–1860. English architect. He designed the Neo-Gothic Houses of Parliament at Westminster, London, 1840–60, in collaboration with Augustus ◊Pugin. His early designs for the Travellers Club 1829–31 and for the Reform Club 1837, both in London, were in Renaissance style.

Barrymore US family of actors, the children of British-born Maurice Barrymore and Georgie Drew, both stage personalities.

Lionel Barrymore (1878–1954) first appeared on the stage with his grandmother, Mrs John Drew, 1893. He played numerous film roles from 1909, including *A Free Soul* 1931 and *Grand Hotel* 1932, but was perhaps best known for his annual radio portrayal of Scrooge in Dickens' *A Christmas Carol*.

John Barrymore (1882–1942), a flamboyant actor who often appeared on stage and screen with his brother and sister. In his early years he was a Shakespearean actor. From 1923 he acted almost entirely in films, including *Dinner at Eight* 1933, and became a screen idol, nicknamed 'the Profile'.

Ethel Barrymore (1879–1959) played with the British actor Henry Irving in London 1898 and opened the Ethel Barrymore Theater in New York 1928; she also appeared in many films from 1914, including *None but the Lonely Heart* 1944.

Barstow Stan 1928– . English novelist. His realist novels describe northern working-class life and include *A Kind of Loving* 1960 (filmed 1962), a first-person, present tense narrative of a young man forced to marry his pregnant girlfriend.

Barth Heinrich 1821–1865. German geographer and explorer who in explorations of N Africa between 1844 and 1855 established the exact course of the river Niger. He spent five years exploring the country between Lake Chad and Cameroon which he described in the five-volume *Travels and Discoveries in Central Africa* 1857–58.

Barth John Simmons 1930– . US novelist and short-story writer. He was influential in the 'academic' experimental movement of the 1960s. His works, typically encyclopedic in scale, are usually interwoven fictions based on language games, his principal concerns being the nature of narrative and the relationship of language to reality. His novels include *The Sot-Weed Factor* 1960, *Giles Goat-Boy* 1966, *Letters* 1979, *Sabbatical: A Romance* 1982, and *The Last Voyage of Somebody the Sailor* 1991.

Barth Karl 1886–1968. Swiss Protestant theologian. A socialist in his political views, he attacked the Nazis. His *Church Dogmatics* 1932–62 makes the resurrection of Jesus the focal point of Christianity.

Barthes Roland 1915–1980. French critic and theorist of ◊semiology, the science of signs and symbols. One of the French 'new critics' and an exponent of ◊structuralism, he attacked traditional literary criticism in his first collection of essays, *Le Degré zéro de l'écriture/Writing Degree Zero* 1953.

Barthes's main aim was to expose the bourgeois values and ideology he saw as implicit in the seemingly 'natural' and innocent language of French literature. For Barthes, a text was not a depiction of the world or the expression of an author's personality, but a system of signs in which meanings are generated solely by the interplay of these signs.

In *Mythologies* 1957 he used this structuralist approach to the study of signs in everyday life, looking at such things as toys, advertisements, and wrestling. This and similar studies had a profound influence on the study of popular culture.

Bartholomew, Massacre of St see ◊St Bartholomew, Massacre of.

Bartholomew, St in the New Testament, one of the apostles. Some legends relate that after the Crucifixion he took Christianity to India; others that he was a missionary in Anatolia and Armenia, where he suffered martyrdom by being flayed alive. Feast day 24 Aug.

Bartók Béla 1881–1945. Hungarian composer. His works combine folk elements with mathematical concepts of tonal and rhythmic proportion. His large output includes six string quartets, a *Divertimento* for string orchestra 1939, concertos for piano, violin, and viola, the *Concerto for Orchestra* 1942–45, a one-act opera *Duke Bluebeard's Castle* 1918, and graded teaching pieces for piano.

A child prodigy, Bartók studied music at the Budapest Conservatory, later working with Zoltán Kodály in recording and transcribing folk music of Hungary and adjoining countries. His ballet *The Miraculous Mandarin* 1919 was banned because of its subject matter (it was set in a brothel). Bartók died in the USA, having fled from Hungary 1940.

Bartolommeo Fra, also called ***Baccio della Porta*** c. 1472–1517. Italian religious painter of the High Renaissance, active in Florence. He introduced Venetian artists to the Florentine High Renaissance style during a visit to Venice 1508, and took back with him to Florence a Venetian sense of colour. His style is one of classic simplicity and order, as in *The Mystical Marriage of St Catherine* 1511 (Louvre, Paris).

Greatly affected by the preaching of the revivalist Savonarola, he burned all his nude studies, and on Savonarola's death became a Dominican monk at S Marco. After an interval due to this disturbance he resumed religious painting, and when Raphael visited Florence 1506 he made Fra Bartolommeo's acquaintance, each artist influencing the other's work.

Barton Edmund 1849–1920. Australian politician; first prime minister 1901–03. A member of the New South Wales Legislative Assembly from 1879, he was an ardent federalist and one of the key figures in the drafting of the federal bill. Barton became prime minister and minister for external affairs when the Commonwealth was inaugurated in 1901. In his term of office much of the machinery of the new government was created. In 1903 he resigned to become a judge of the newly-created High Court of Australia and remained on the bench until his death in 1920.

baryon in nuclear physics, a heavy subatomic particle made up of three indivisible elementary particles called quarks. The baryons form a subclass of the ◊hadrons and comprise the nucleons (protons and neutrons) and hyperons.

Baryshnikov Mikhail Nikolayevich 1948– . Latvian-born dancer, now based in the USA. He joined the Kirov Ballet 1967 and, after defecting from the Soviet Union 1974, joined the American Ballet Theater (ABT) as principal dancer, partnering Gelsey Kirkland. He left to join the New York City Ballet 1978–80, but rejoined ABT as director 1980–90. From 1990 he has danced for various companies including his own modern dance company, White Oak Project. His physical prowess and amazing aerial feats have combined with an impish sense of humour and dash to make him one of the most accessible of dancers.

baryte barium sulphate, $BaSO_4$, the most common mineral of barium. It is white or light-coloured, and has a comparatively high density (specific gravity 4.6); the latter property makes it useful in the production of high-density drilling muds (muds used to cool and lubricate drilling equipment). Baryte occurs mainly in ore veins, where it is often found with calcite and with lead and zinc minerals. It crystallizes in the orthorhombic system and can form tabular crystals or radiating fibrous masses.

baryton complex bowed stringed instrument producing an intense singing tone. It is based on an 18th-century viol and modified by the addition of sympathetic (freely vibrating) strings.

basal metabolic rate (BMR) minimum amount of energy needed by the body to maintain life. It is measured when the subject is awake but resting, and includes the energy required to keep the heart beating, sustain breathing, repair tissues, and keep the brain and nerves functioning. Measuring the subject's consumption of oxygen gives an accurate value for BMR, because oxygen is needed to release energy from food.

A cruder measure of BMR estimates the amount of heat given off, some heat being released when food is used up. BMR varies from one species to another, and from males to females. In humans, it is highest in children and declines with age. Disease, including mental illness, can make it rise or fall. Hormones from the ◊thyroid gland control BMR.

basalt commonest volcanic ◊igneous rock, and the principal rock type on the ocean floor; it is basic, that is, it contains relatively little silica: about 50%. It is usually dark grey but can also be green, brown, or black.

The groundmass may be glassy or finely crystalline, sometimes with large ◊crystals embedded. Basaltic lava tends to be runny and flows for great distances before solidifying. Successive eruptions of basalt have formed the great plateaus of Colorado and the Indian Deccan. In some places, such as Fingal's Cave in the Inner Hebrides of Scotland and the Giant's Causeway in Antrim, Northern Ireland, shrinkage during the solidification of the molten lava caused the formation of hexagonal columns.

bascule bridge type of drawbridge in which one or two counterweighted deck members pivot upwards to allow shipping to pass underneath. One example is the double bascule Tower Bridge, London.

base in chemistry, a substance that accepts protons, such as the hydroxide ion (OH^-) and ammonia (NH_3). Bases react with acids to give a salt. Those that dissolve in water are called alkalis.

Inorganic bases are usually oxides or hydroxides of metals, which react with dilute acids to form a salt and water. A number of carbonates also react with dilute acids, additionally giving off carbon dioxide. Many organic compounds that contain nitrogen are bases.

base in mathematics, the number of different single-digit symbols used in a particular number system. In our usual (decimal) counting system of numbers (with symbols 0, 1, 2, 3, 4, 5, 6, 7, 8, 9) the base is 10. In the ◊binary number system, which has only the symbols 1 and 0, the base is two. A base is also a number that, when raised to a particular power (that is, when multiplied by itself a particular number of times as in $10^2 = 10 \times 10 = 100$), has a ◊logarithm equal to the power. For example, the logarithm of 100 to the base ten is 2.

In geometry, the term is used to denote the line or area on which a polygon or solid stands.

In general, any number system subscribing to a place-value system with base value b may be represented by ... $b^4, b^3, b^2, b^1, b^0, b^{-1}, b^{-2}, b^{-3}$, ...

Hence in base ten the columns represent ... 10^4, 10^3, 10^2, 10^1, 10^0, 10^{-1}, 10^{-2}, 10^{-3} ..., in base two ...2^4, 2^3, 2^2, 2^1, 2^0, 2^{-1}, 2^{-2}, 2^{-3} ..., and in base eight ...8^4, 8^3, 8^2, 8^1, 8^0, 8^{-1}, 8^{-2}, 8^{-3} .... For bases beyond 10, the denary numbers 10, 11, 12, and so on must be replaced by a single digit. Thus in base 16, all numbers up to 15 must be represented by single-digit 'numbers', since 10 in hexadecimal would mean 16 in decimal. Hence decimal 10, 11, 12, 13, 14, 15 are represented in hexadecimal by letters A, B, C, D, E, F.

baseball national summer game of the USA, derived in the 19th century from the English game of ◊rounders. Baseball is a bat-and-ball game played between two teams, each of nine players, on a pitch ('field') marked out in the form of a diamond, with a base at each corner. The ball is struck with a cylindrical bat, and the players try to score ('make a run') by circuiting the bases. A 'home run' is a circuit on one hit.

rules The game is divided into nine innings, each with two halves, with each team taking turns to bat while the other team takes the field, pitching, catching, and fielding. Essentially an offensive player attempts to get on base and advance around the bases, to score a run by crossing home plate. Batters appear in an assigned order. Assuming a batting stance in front of the catcher, the batter faces the pitcher, who throws the baseball to home plate to the catcher.

'strikes' and 'balls' Standing behind the catcher is an umpire (major-league games have four umpires at various vantage points), who calls out a 'ball' or 'strike' ruling for each unhit pitch. A pitch that fails to cross the plate within the batter's 'strike zone' (it must pass between the batter's armpits and knees) is called a ball. However, if such a pitch is swung at and missed, a strike is ruled against the batter. Any unhit pitch that is within the strike zone, whether or not the batter swings, is called a strike. Hit balls that fall outside playing-field bounds are called 'foul balls' and are counted as strikes, unless it would be a third strike. A three-strike count is an 'out'. If the count reaches four balls before the third strike is called, the batter earns a 'walk' and proceeds to first base.

making a run Having hit the ball into fair territory, the batter tries to make a run, either in stages from home base to first, second, and third base, and back to home base, or in a 'home run', a hit that usually goes beyond the outfield wall, so the batter (and any baserunners) completes the circuit of base paths that leads back to home plate.

getting out Batters are declared out if (1) they fail to hit the ball after three 'strikes', (2) they hit the ball into the air and it is caught by a fielder (a 'fly ball'), (3) they are touched by the ball in the hand of one of their opponents while they are between bases, and (4) a fielder standing on one of the bases catches the ball before the batter reaches the base.

During each inning, a team's offensive play continues until three outs occur. After nine innings, the team with the most runs wins. If the game is tied

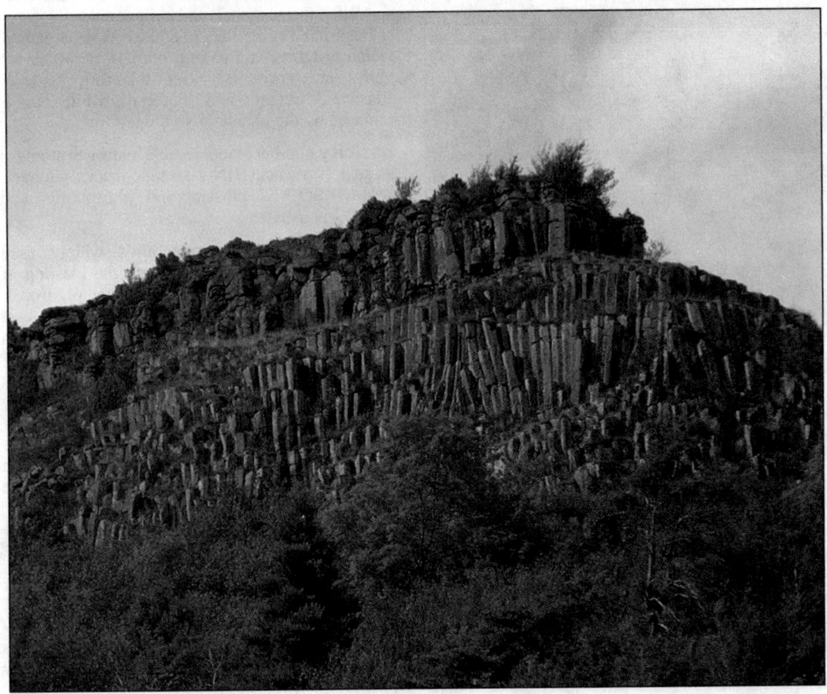

basalt A basalt outcrop in the French Auvergne. Basalt is a volcanic rock which when it cools sometimes cracks along its natural planes of cleavage to produce distinctive hexagonal columns. *Premaphotos Wildlife*

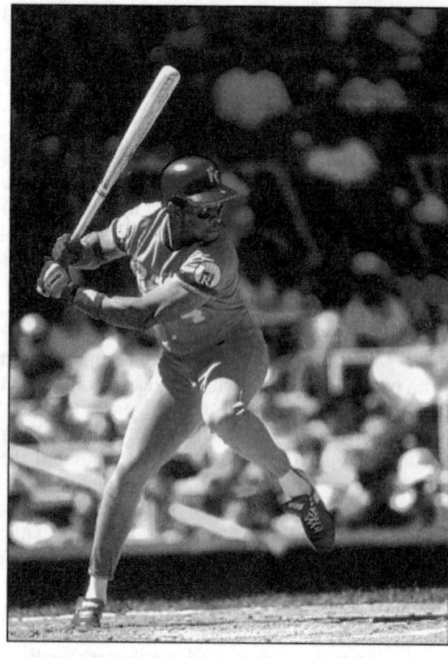

baseball Danny Tartabull of the Kansas City Royals. *Image Select (UK) Ltd*

after nine innings, extra innings are played until the tie is broken.

competition The World Series was first held as an end-of-season game between the winners of the two professional leagues of the USA, the National League and the American League 1903, and was established as a series of seven games 1905. Besides these there are over 60 minor professional leagues and many more amateur ones. The average salary in 1990 of a Major League baseball player in the USA was $890,844. *See list of tables on p. 1177.*

Basel or ***Basle*** (French ***Bâle***) financial, commercial, and industrial city (dyes, vitamins, agrochemicals, dietary products, genetic products) in Switzerland; population (1994) 179,600. Basel was a strong military station under the Romans. In 1501 it joined the Swiss confederation and later developed as a centre for the Reformation.

Bashō The Japanese poet Matsuo Bashō pausing on his travels. He was influenced by Zen Buddhism, and travelled extensively, staying in temples and with other poets, in search of enlightenment. *Corbis*

basenji breed of dog originating in Central Africa, where it is used for hunting. About 41 cm/16 in tall, it has pointed ears, curled tail, and short glossy coat of black or red, often with white markings. It is remarkable because it has no true bark.

base pair in biochemistry, the linkage of two base (purine or pyrimidine) molecules in ◊DNA. They are found in nucleotides, and form the basis of the genetic code.

One base lies on one strand of the DNA double helix, and one on the other, so that the base pairs link the two strands like the rungs of a ladder. In DNA, there are four bases: adenine and guanine (purines) and cytosine and thymine (pyrimidines). Adenine always pairs with thymine, and cytosine with guanine.

Bashkir the majority ethnic group of the autonomous republic of Bashkir in Russia. The Bashkirs are agriculturalists and have been Muslims since the 13th century. The Bashkir language belongs to the Turkic branch of the Altaic family, and has about 1 million speakers.

Bashkir autonomous republic of the Russian Federation
area 143,600 sq km/55,430 sq mi
capital Ufa
physical Ural Mountains in the east
industries minerals, oil, natural gas
population (1992) 4,008,000
language Russian, Bashkir (about 25%)
history annexed by Russia 1557; became the first Soviet autonomous republic 1919. Declared independence 1992. According to the 1993 constitution it is part of the Russian Federation on a voluntary and equal basis.

Bashō pen name of Matsuo Munefusa 1644–1694. Japanese poet. He was a master of the haiku, a 17-syllable poetic form with lines of 5, 7, and 5 syllables, which he infused with subtle allusiveness. His *Oku-no-hosomichi/The Narrow Road to the Deep North* 1694, an account of a visit to northern and western Honshū, consists of haiku interspersed with prose passages.

BASIC (acronym for ***beginner's all-purpose symbolic instruction code***) high-level computer-programming language, developed 1964, originally designed to take advantage of multiuser systems (which can be used by many people at the same time). The language is relatively easy to learn and is popular among microcomputer users.

Basic English simplified form of English devised and promoted by C K Ogden (1889–1957) in the 1920s and 1930s as an international auxiliary language; as a route into Standard English for foreign learners; and as a reminder to the English-speaking world of the virtues of plain language. Its name derives from the initial letters of British, American, scientific, international, and commercial.

Basic has a vocabulary of 850 words (plus names, technical terms, and so on), only 18 of which are verbs or 'operators'. *Get* therefore replaces 'receive', 'obtain', and 'become', while *buy* is replaced by the phrase 'give money for'.

basicity number of replaceable hydrogen atoms in an acid. Nitric acid (HNO_3) is monobasic, sulphuric acid (H_2SO_4) is dibasic, and phosphoric acid (H_3PO_4) is tribasic.

basic–oxygen process most widely used method of steelmaking, involving the blasting of oxygen at supersonic speed into molten pig iron.

Pig iron from a blast furnace, together with steel scrap, is poured into a converter, and a jet of oxygen is then projected into the mixture. The excess carbon in the mix and other impurities quickly burn out or form a slag, and the converter is emptied by tilting. It takes about 45 minutes to refine 350 tonnes/400 tons of steel. The basic–oxygen process was developed 1948 at a steelworks near the Austrian towns of Linz and Donawitz. It is a version of the ◊Bessemer process.

basidiocarp spore-bearing body, or 'fruiting body', of all basidiomycete fungi (see ◊fungus), except the rusts and smuts. A well known example is the edible mushroom *Agaricus brunnescens*. Other types include globular basidiocarps (puffballs) or flat ones that project from tree trunks (brackets). They are made up of a mass of tightly packed, intermeshed ◊hyphae.

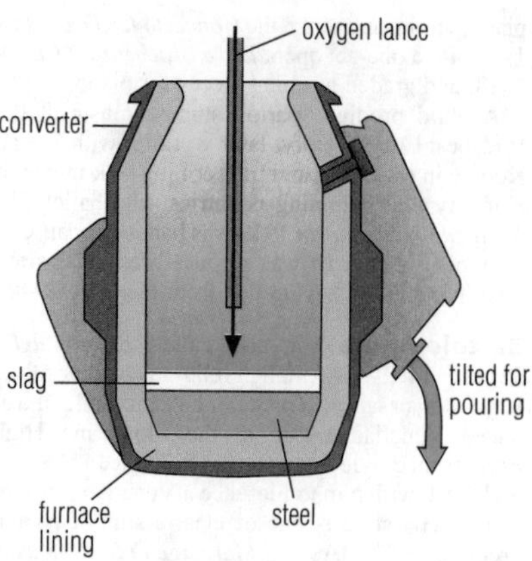

basic–oxygen process The basic–oxygen process is the primary method used to produce steel. Oxygen is blown at high pressure through molten pig iron and scrap steel in a converter lined with basic refractory materials. The impurities, principally carbon, quickly burn out, producing steel.

Basie Count (William) 1904–1984. US jazz band leader and pianist. He developed the big-band sound and a simplified, swinging style of music. He led impressive groups of musicians in a career spanning more than 50 years. Basie's compositions include 'One O'Clock Jump' and 'Jumpin' at the Woodside'.

basil or ***sweet basil*** plant *Ocimum basilicum* of the mint family Labiatae. A native of the tropics, it is cultivated in Europe as a culinary herb.

Basil II c. 958–1025. Byzantine emperor from 976. His achievement as emperor was to contain, and later decisively defeat, the Bulgarians, earning for himself the title 'Bulgar-Slayer' after a victory 1014. After the battle he blinded almost all 15,000 of the defeated, leaving only a few men with one eye to lead their fellows home.

Basildon industrial town in Essex, England; population (1991) 157,500. It was designated a new town 1949 from several townships to accommodate overspill population from London. Industries include chemicals, clothing, printing, engineering, and tobacco.

basilica Roman public building; a large roofed hall flanked by columns, generally with an aisle on each side, used for judicial or other public business. The earliest known basilica, at Pompeii, dates from the 2nd century BC. This architectural form was adopted by the early Christians for their churches.

Basilicata mountainous region of S Italy, comprising the provinces of Potenza and Matera; area 10,000 sq km/3,860 sq mi; population (1992 est) 610,800. Its capital is Potenza. It was the Roman province of Lucania.

basilisk Central and South American lizard, genus *Basiliscus*. It is about 50 cm/20 in long and

basilisk The basilisk of Central and South America is a lizard of the iguana family. It can run on its hind legs and has been known to do so over water, aided by flaps of skin on its toes.

Basie, Count US pianist, bandleader, and composer Count Basie in concert in London. One of the most durable of the great jazz musicians, he led a big band virtually continuously for almost half a century, from 1935 until his death in 1984. The singers with whom he toured and recorded included Bing Crosby and Frank Sinatra. *Corbis*

weighs about 90 g/0.2 lb. Its rapid speed (more than 2 m/6.6 ft per second) and the formation of air pockets around the feet enable it to run short distances across the surface of water. The male has a well-developed crest on the head, body, and tail.

Basil, St c. 330–379. Cappadocian monk, known as 'the Great', founder of the Basilian monks. Elected bishop of Caesarea 370, Basil opposed the heresy of ◊Arianism. He wrote many theological works and composed the *Liturgy of St Basil*, in use in the Eastern Orthodox Church. Feast day 2 Jan.

Basingstoke industrial town (light engineering, scientific instruments, leather goods, agricultural machinery, electronics, printing, publishing) in Hampshire, England, 72 km/45 mi WSW of London; population (1991) 77,800.

Baskerville John 1706–1775. English printer and typographer. He experimented in casting types from 1750 onwards. The Baskerville typeface is named after him.

basketball ball game between two teams of five players on an indoor enclosed court. The object is, via a series of passing moves, to throw the large inflated ball through a circular hoop and net positioned at each end of the court, 3.05 m/10 ft above the ground. The first world championship for men was held 1950, and 1953 for women. They are now held every four years.

the court In the USA the standard court is 28.7 m/94 ft long and 16.5 m/54 ft wide, with a backboard at the centre of each end of the court, to which a circular metal hoop is attached.

rules The object of the game is to score the most points by throwing the ball through the hoop, also called a basket, with two points scored for each field goal, or basket, shot from the field. Under certain rules, three points are awarded for field goals made beyond a specified distance from the basket.

One point is scored for each foul shot (awarded after certain types of rules infractions by the opposing teams). Foul shots, also called free throws, are taken from a line 4.6 m/15 ft from the backboard. The court has lines from the foul line to the court's base line. The lane between the lines cannot be entered by players until the foul shot has been released by the shooter. During regular play, offensive players may remain in the lane for only three consecutive seconds. Under professional rules a player must leave the game after committing six fouls.

The court dimensions and markings vary slightly among US amateur, US professional, and international rules. If a regulation game ends in a tie, overtime periods are played until one team wins. Under professional rules a game is made up of 4 quarters each lasting 12 minutes. Under some rules the team with possession of the ball must shoot within a certain time period: 24 seconds in professional games. *See list of tables on p. 1177.*

Basle alternative form of ◊Basel, a city in Switzerland.

Basov, Nikolai Gennadievich 1922– . Soviet physicist who, with his compatriot Aleksandr Prokhorov, developed the microwave amplifier called a maser. Nobel Prize for physics 1964.

Basque the people inhabiting the Basque Country of central N Spain and the extreme SW of France. The Basques are a pre-Indo-European people whose language (Euskara) is unrelated to any other language. Although both the Romans and, later, the Visigoths conquered them, they largely maintained their independence until the 19th century. During the Spanish Civil War 1936–39, they were on the republican side defeated by Franco. The Basque separatist movement ◊Euskadi ta Askatasuna (ETA; 'Basque Nation and Liberty') and the French organization Iparretarrak ('ETA fighters from the

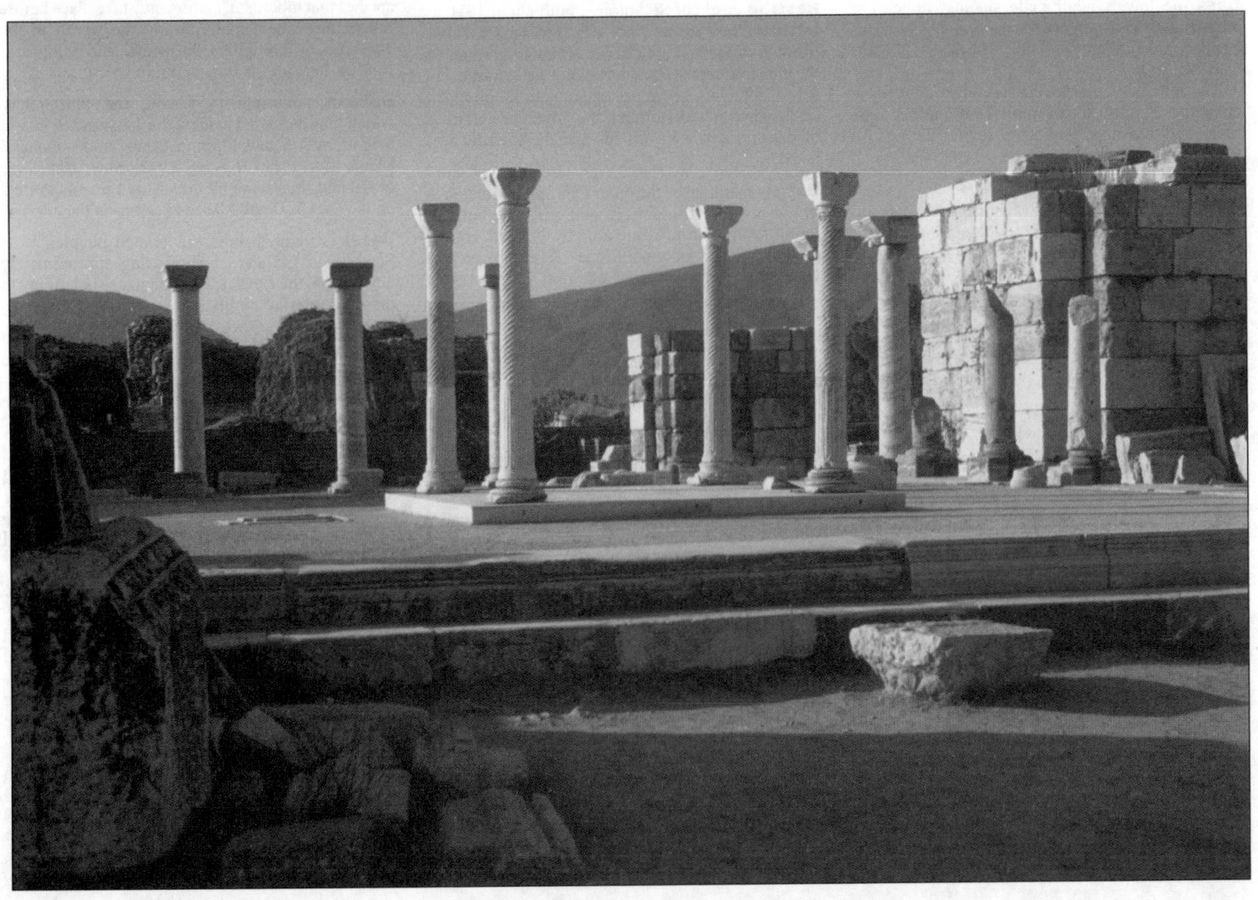

basilica The ruins of the early Christian church of St John's Basilica at Selçuk, near Ephesus in Turkey. It was built by the Byzantine emperor Justinian I in the 6th century AD in the belief that it was the site of the tomb of St John. *Corel*

❛Basra was about the hottest place on earth in summer ... the place where the fable of frying eggs on the street came true.❜

On **Basra**
Cedric Belfrage
Away from it All

North Side') have engaged in guerrilla activity from 1968 in an attempt to secure a united Basque state.

Basque Country (Basque ***Euskal Herria***) homeland of the Basque people in the W Pyrenees, divided by the Franco-Spanish border. The Spanish Basque Country (Spanish *País Vasco*) is an autonomous region (created 1979) of central N Spain, comprising the provinces of Vizcaya, Alava, and Guipúzcoa (Basque *Bizkaia*, *Araba*, and *Gipuzkoa*); area 7,300 sq km/2,818 sq mi; population (1991) 2,104,000.

The French Basque Country (French *Pays Basque*) is the area occupied by Basques in the département of Pyrenees-Atlantiques. It is estimated that there are about 170,000 Basques in France. To Basque nationalists *Euskal Herria* also includes the autonomous Spanish province of Navarre.

Basque language language of W Europe known to its speakers, the Basques, as *Euskara*, and apparently unrelated to any other language on Earth. It is spoken by some half a million people in central N Spain and SW France, around the Bay of Biscay, as well as by emigrants in both Europe and the Americas. The language is of central importance to the Basque nationalist movement.

Although previously forbidden in all public places for most of Franco's rule, Basque was permitted in church and primary schools from 1968 and taught in all schools from 1979. The first Basque parliament was elected 1980 and the language officially recognized along with Spanish in the Basque provinces.

Basra (Arabic ***al-Basrah***) principal port in Iraq, in the Shatt-al-Arab delta, 97 km/60 mi from the Persian Gulf, founded in the 7th century; population (1991) 850,000. Exports include wool, oil, cereal, and dates. The city was bombed during the 1991 Gulf War. A Shi'ite rebellion March 1991 was crushed by the Iraqi army, causing further death and destruction.

bas relief see ◊relief.

bass long-bodied scaly sea fish *Morone labrax* found in the N Atlantic and Mediterranean. They grow to 1 m/3 ft, and are often seen in shoals.

Other fish of the same family (Serranidae) are also called bass, as are North American freshwater fishes of the family Centrarchidae, such as black bass and small-mouthed bass.

bass the lowest adult male singing voice. The best-known bass singers have been the Russians Fyodor ◊Chaliapin and Boris Christoff (1919–1993).

The term also covers the bass instrument of a consort or family, for example bass clarinet, bass tuba, and bassoon, having a similar range. An instrument an octave lower than bass is a contrabass.

Bass George 1763–c. 1808. English naval surgeon who with Matthew ◊Flinders explored the coast of New South Wales and the strait that bears his name between Tasmania and Australia 1795–99.

Basse-Normandie or ***Lower Normandy*** coastal region of NW France lying between Haute-Normandie and Brittany (Bretagne). It includes the *départements* of Calvados, Manche, and Orne; area 17,600 sq km/6,794 sq mi; population (1990) 1,391,300. Its capital is Caen. Apart from stock farming, dairy farming, and textiles, the area produces Calvados (apple brandy).

basset any of several breeds of hound with a long low body and long pendulous ears, of a type originally bred in France for hunting hares by scent.

Basse-Terre main island of the French West Indian island group of Guadeloupe; area 848 sq km/327 sq mi; population (1991) 149,900. It has an active volcano, Grande Soufrière, rising to 1,484 m/4,870 ft.

basset horn musical woodwind instrument, a wide-bore alto clarinet pitched in F, invented about 1765 and used by Mozart in his *Masonic Funeral Music* 1785, for example, and by Richard Strauss. It was revived 1981 by Stockhausen and features prominently as a solo in the opera cycle *LICHT*. Performers include Alan Hacker and Suzanne Stephens.

bassoon double-reed woodwind instrument in C, the bass of the oboe family. It doubles back on itself in a tube about 2.5 m/7.5 ft long and has a rich and deep tone. The bassoon concert repertoire extends from the early Baroque via Vivaldi, Mozart, and Dukas to Stockhausen.

The bassoon was developed from the Renaissance curtal about 1660 as a continuo instrument to provide bassline support. Further development in the 18th century led to the double bassoon or contrabassoon, an octave lower.

Bass Rock islet in the Firth of Forth, Scotland, about 107 m/350 ft high, with a lighthouse. It is a seabird sanctuary.

Bass Strait channel between Australia and Tasmania, named after British explorer George Bass; oil was discovered here in the 1960s.

Bastia (Italian *bastiglia* 'fortress') port and commercial centre in NE Corsica, France; capital of the *département* of Haute-Corse; population (1990) 38,700. Founded by the Genoese 1380, it was the capital of Corsica until 1811. There are several fine churches.

Bastille castle of St Antoine, built about 1370 as part of the fortifications of Paris. It was made a state prison by Cardinal ◊Richelieu and was stormed by the mob that set the French Revolution in motion 14 July 1789. Only seven prisoners were found in the castle when it was stormed; the governor and most of the garrison were killed, and the Bastille was razed.

bat any mammal of the order Chiroptera, related to the Insectivora (hedgehogs and shrews), but differing from them in being able to fly. Bats are the only true flying mammals. Their forelimbs are developed as wings capable of rapid and sustained flight. There are two main groups of bats: ***megabats***, which eat fruit, and ***microbats***, which mainly eat insects. Although by no means blind, many microbats rely largely on ◊echolocation for navigation and finding prey, sending out pulses of high-pitched sound and listening for the echo. Bats are nocturnal, and those native to temperate countries hibernate in winter. There are about 977 species forming the order Chiroptera, making this the second-largest mammalian order; bats make up nearly one-quarter of the world's mammals. Although bats are widely distributed, populations have declined alarmingly and many species are now endangered.

megabats The Megachiroptera live in the tropical regions of the Old World, Australia, and the Pacific, and feed on fruit, nectar, and pollen. The hind feet have five toes with sharp hooked claws which suspend the animal head downwards when resting. There are 162 species of Megachiroptera. Relatively large, weighing up to 900 g/2 lb and with a wingspan as great as 1.5 m/5 ft, they have large eyes and a long face, earning them the name 'flying fox'. Most orient by sight.

microbats Most bats are Microchiroptera, mainly small and insect-eating. Some eat fish as well as insects; others consume small rodents, frogs, lizards, or birds; a few feed on the blood of mammals (◊vampire bats). There are about 750 species. They roost in caves, crevices, and hollow trees. A single bat may eat 3,000 insects in one night. The bumblebee bat, inhabiting SE Asian rainforests, is the smallest mammal in the world.

ancestors The difference in the two bat groups is so marked that many biologists believe that they must have had different ancestors: microbats descending from insectivores and megabats descending from primates. Analysis of the proteins in blood serum from megabats and primates by German biologists 1994 showed enough similarities to suggest a close taxonomic relationship between the two groups.

biology A bat's wings consist of a thin hairless skin expansion, stretched between the four fingers of the hand, from the last finger down to the hindlimb, and from the hindlimb to the tail. The thumb is free and has a sharp claw to help in climbing. The shoulder girdle and breastbone are large, the latter being keeled, and the pelvic girdle is small. The bones of the limbs are hollow, other bones are slight, and the ribs are flattened.

An adult female bat usually rears only one pup a year, which she carries with her during flight. In species that hibernate, mating may take place before hibernation, the female storing the sperm in the genital tract throughout the winter and using it to fertilize her egg on awakening in spring.

Bataan peninsula in Luzon, the Philippines, which was defended against the Japanese in World War II by US and Filipino troops under General MacArthur 1 Jan–9 April 1942. MacArthur was evacuated, but some 67,000 Allied prisoners died on the Bataan Death March to camps in the interior.

Batak several distinct but related peoples of N Sumatra in Indonesia. Numbering approximately 2.5 million, the Batak speak languages belonging to the Austronesian family.

Bateman H(enry) M(ayo) 1887–1970. Australian cartoonist who lived in England. His cartoons were based on themes of social embarrassment and confusion, in such series as *The Man who* ... (as in *The Guardsman who Dropped his Rifle*).

Bates Alan 1934– . English actor. He has proved himself a versatile male lead in over 60 plays and films. His films include *Zorba the Greek* 1965, *Far from the Madding Crowd* 1967, *Women in Love* 1970, *The Go-Between* 1971, *The Shout* 1978, and *Duet for One* 1986.

Bates H(enry) W(alter) 1825–1892. English naturalist and explorer. He spent 11 years collecting animals and plants in South America and identified 8,000 new species of insects. He made a special study of ◊camouflage in animals, and his observation of insect imitation of species that are unpleasant to predators is known as 'Batesian mimicry'.

Bates H(erbert) E(rnest) 1905–1974. English writer. Of his many novels and short stories, *The Purple Plain* 1947 and *The Jacaranda Tree* 1949 particularly demonstrate his observation, compassionate characterization, and taste for exotic as well as rural places and events. *Fair Stood the Wind*

Bastille The storming of the Bastille 14 July 1789. The Bastille, built in about 1370, was destroyed when it was attacked by the mob at the beginning of the French Revolution. A new opera house was built on the site 1989. *Image Select (UK) Ltd*

Bates During a two-year insect hunting expedition to the Amazon, H W Bates collected over 14,000 specimens, many of which were new to science. On his return, he published a paper describing the phenomenon of insect mimicry, now known as Batesian mimicry. His theory proposes that edible species of insects may gradually evolve markings which are very similar to poisonous species in an attempt to deceive predators. *Ann Ronan/Image Select (UK) Ltd*

for France 1944 reflects his service as a squadron leader in World War II, during which he also wrote stories under the pseudonym Flying Officer X.

Bates eyesight training method developed by US ophthalmologist William Bates (1860–1931) to enable people to correct problems of vision without wearing glasses. The method is of proven effectiveness in relieving all refractive conditions, correcting squints, lazy eyes, and similar problems, but does not claim to treat eye disease.

Bath historic city in Bath and North East Somerset, England; population (1991) 78,700
features hot springs; the ruins of the baths after which it is named, as well as a great temple, are the finest Roman remains in Britain. Excavations 1979 revealed thousands of coins and 'curses', offered at a place which was thought to be the link between the upper and lower worlds. The Gothic Bath Abbey has an unusually decorated west front and fan vaulting. There is much 18th-century architecture, notably the Royal Crescent by John Wood. The Assembly Rooms 1771 were destroyed in an air raid 1942 but reconstructed 1963. The Bath Festival Orchestra is based here
history the Roman spa town of Aquae Sulis ('waters of Sul' – the British goddess of wisdom) was built in the first 20 years after the Roman invasion. In medieval times the hot springs were crown property, administered by the church, but the city was transformed in the 18th century to a fashionable spa, presided over by 'Beau' Nash (1674–1762).

Bath and North East Somerset unitary authority of England created 1996 (*see United Kingdom map*).

batholith large, irregular, deep-seated mass of intrusive ◊igneous rock, usually granite, with an exposed surface of more than 100 sq km/40 sq mi. The mass forms by the intrusion or upswelling of magma (molten rock) through the surrounding rock. Batholiths form the core of all major mountain ranges.

According to plate tectonic theory, magma rises in subduction zones along continental margins where one plate sinks beneath another. The solidified magma becomes the central axis of a rising mountain range, resulting in the deformation (folding and overthrusting) of rocks on either side.

Bath, Order of the British order of knighthood, believed to have been founded in the reign of Henry IV (1399–1413). Formally instituted 1815, it included civilians from 1847 and women from 1970.

bathyal zone upper part of the ocean, which lies on the continental shelf at depths between 200 m/650 ft and 2,000 m/6,500 ft.

Bathyal zones (both temperate and tropical) have greater biodiversity than coral reefs, according to a 1995 study by the Natural History Museum in London. Maximum biodiversity occurs between 1,000 m/3,280 ft and 3,000 m/9,800 ft.

bathyscaph or ***bathyscaphe*** or ***bathyscape*** deep-sea diving apparatus used for exploration at great depths in the ocean. In 1960, Jacques Piccard and Don Walsh took the bathyscaph *Trieste* to a depth of 10,917 m/35,820 ft in the Challenger Deep in the ◊Mariana Trench off the island of Guam in the Pacific Ocean.

batik Javanese technique of dyeing fabrics in which areas to be left undyed are sealed with wax. Practised throughout Indonesia, the craft was introduced to the West by Dutch traders.

Batista Fulgencio 1901–1973. Cuban dictator. He ruled 1933–44, when he stood down, and again 1952–59, after seizing power in a coup. His authoritarian methods enabled him to jail his opponents and amass a large personal fortune. He was overthrown by rebel forces led by Fidel ◊Castro 1959.

Batman comic-strip character created 1939 by US cartoonist Bob Kane and his collaborator Bill Finger. A crime-busting superhero, disguised by a black batlike mask and cape, Batman and his sidekick Robin were long a staple of the DC Comics group.

Baton Rouge deepwater port on the Mississippi River, USA, the capital of Louisiana; population (1992) 224,700. Industries include oil refining, petrochemicals, and iron.

battalion or ***unit*** basic personnel unit in the military system, usually consisting of four or five companies. A battalion is commanded by a lieutenant colonel. Several battalions form a ◊brigade.

Batten Jean 1909–1982. New Zealand aviator who made the first return solo flight by a woman Australia–Britain 1935, and established speed records.

Battenberg title (conferred 1851) of German noble family; its members included Louis (1854–1921), Prince of Battenberg, and Louis Alexander, Prince of Battenberg, the father of Louis ◊Mountbatten, who anglicized his name to Mountbatten 1917 due to anti-German feeling in Britain during World War I.

Battersea district of the Inner London borough of Wandsworth on the south bank of the Thames. It has a park (including a funfair 1951–74), Battersea Dogs' Home (opened 1860) for strays, and Battersea Power Station (1937, designed by Sir Giles Gilbert Scott, with an Art Deco interior), closed 1983. A listed building from 1980, the power station was sold in 1993 to the Kwang family, Hong Kong property developers.

battery any energy-storage device allowing release of electricity on demand. It is made up of one or more electrical ◊cells. Primary-cell batteries are disposable; secondary-cell batteries, or ◊accumulators, are rechargeable. Primary-cell batteries are an extremely uneconomical form of energy, since they produce only 2% of the power used in their manufacture.

The common ***dry cell*** is a primary-cell battery based on the Georges Leclanché (1839–1882) cell and consists of a central carbon electrode immersed in a paste of manganese dioxide and ammonium chloride as the electrolyte. The zinc casing forms the other electrode. It is dangerous to try to recharge a primary-cell battery.

The lead–acid ***car battery*** is a secondary-cell battery. The car's generator continually recharges the battery. It consists of sets of lead (positive) and lead peroxide (negative) plates in an electrolyte of sulphuric acid (◊battery acid). Hydrogen cells and sodium–sulphur batteries are under development 1995 to allow cars to run entirely on battery power for up to 60 km/100 mi.

The introduction of rechargeable nickel–cadmium batteries has revolutionized portable electronic news gathering (sound recording, video) and information processing (computing). These batteries offer a stable, short-term source of power free of noise and other electrical hazards.

battery The common dry cell relies on chemical changes occurring between the electrodes – the central carbon rod and the outer zinc casing – and the ammonium chloride electrolyte to produce electricity. The mixture of carbon and manganese is used to increase the life of the cell.

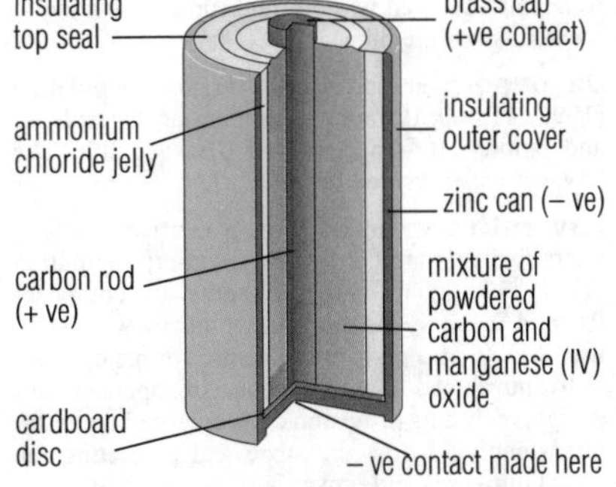

battery acid ◊sulphuric acid of approximately 70% concentration used in lead–acid cells (as found in car batteries). The chemical reaction within the battery that is responsible for generating electricity also causes a change in the acid's composition. This can be detected as a change in its specific gravity: in a fully charged battery the acid's specific gravity is 1.270–1.290; in a half-charged battery it is 1.190–1.210; in a flat battery it is 1.110–1.130.

battleship class of large warships with the biggest guns and heaviest armour. In 1991, four US battleships were in active service. They are now all decommissioned.

Batumi Black Sea port and capital of the autonomous republic of Adzhar, in Georgia; population (1991) 138,000. Main industries include oil refining, food canning, engineering, clothing, drug factories. There is a shipyard.

baud in computing, a unit that measures the speed of transmission of data over an asynchronous connection, in which data are transmitted irregularly rather than as a steady stream.

baud in engineering, a unit of electrical signalling speed equal to one pulse per second, measuring the rate at which signals are sent between electronic devices such as telegraphs and computers; 300 baud is about 300 words a minute.

Baudelaire Charles Pierre 1821–1867. French poet. His immensely influential work combined rhythmical and musical perfection with a morbid romanticism and eroticism, finding beauty in decadence and evil. His first and best-known book of verse was *Les Fleurs du mal/Flowers of Evil* 1857. He was one of the main figures in the development of ◊Symbolism.

Baudouin 1930–1993. King of the Belgians 1951–93. In 1950 his father, ◊Leopold III, abdicated and Baudouin was known until his succession 1951 as *Le Prince Royal*. During his reign he succeeded in holding together a country divided by religion and language, while presiding over the dismemberment of Belgium's imperial past. In 1960 he married Fabiola de Mora y Aragón (1928–), member of a Spanish noble family. They were unable to have any children, and he was succeeded by his brother, Albert, 1993.

Bauhaus influential German school of architecture and design founded 1919 in Weimar by the architect Walter ◊Gropius in an attempt to fuse art, design, architecture, and crafts into a unified whole. Moved to Dessau under political pressure 1925, the school was closed by the Nazis 1933. Among the artists associated with the Bauhaus were the painters Paul Klee and Wassily Kandinsky and the architect Ludwig Mies van der Rohe.

Teaching at the Bauhaus was a radical departure from existing art-school training, stressing the intimate link between architecture and such crafts as stained glass, mural decoration, metalwork, carpentry, weaving, pottery, typography, and graphics. Gropius and Marcel ◊Breuer worked together in the USA 1937–40 and the ◊International Style (of which Gropius's Bauhaus building 1925–26 is a hallmark) spread worldwide from there.

'But the real travellers are only those who leave / For the sake of leaving.'

Charles Baudelaire 'The Voyage'

❛'The road to the City of Emeralds is paved with yellow brick,' said the Witch, 'so you cannot miss it.'❜

L FRANK BAUM
The Wonderful Wizard of Oz

Baum L(yman) Frank 1856–1919. US writer. He was the author of the children's fantasy *The Wonderful Wizard of Oz* 1900 and its 13 sequels.

Bausch Pina 1940– . German avant-garde dance choreographer, director from 1974 of the Wuppertal Tanztheater (dance theatre). Her works incorporate dialogue, elements of psychoanalysis, comedy, and drama, and have been performed on floors covered with churned earth (*Le Sacre du printemps* 1975), water (*Arien* 1979), and rose petals (*Nelken* 1982).

bauxite principal ore of ◊aluminium, consisting of a mixture of hydrated aluminium oxides and hydroxides, generally contaminated with compounds of iron, which give it a red colour. It is formed by the chemical weathering of rocks in tropical climates. Chief producers of bauxite are Australia, Guinea, Jamaica, Russia, Kazakhstan, Surinam, and Brazil.

To extract aluminium from bauxite, high temperatures (about 800°C/1,470°F) are needed to make the ore molten. Strong electric currents are then passed through the molten ore. The process is only economical if cheap electricity is readily available, usually from a hydroelectric plant.

Bavaria (German ***Bayern***) administrative region (German *Land*) of Germany
area 70,600 sq km/27,252 sq mi
capital Munich
towns and cities Nuremberg, Augsburg, Würzburg, Regensburg
features largest of the German *Länder*; forms the Danube basin; festivals at Bayreuth and Oberammergau
industries beer, electronics, electrical engineering, optics, cars, aerospace, chemicals, plastics, oil refining, textiles, glass, toys
population (1994 est) 11,863,000 (25% Czechs and Slovaks)
famous people Lucas Cranach, Franz Josef Strauss, Richard Strauss
religion 70% Roman Catholic, 26% Protestant
history the last king, Ludwig III, abdicated 1918, and Bavaria declared itself a republic.

The original Bavarians were Teutonic invaders from Bohemia who occupied the country at the end of the 5th century. From about 555 to 788 Bavaria was ruled by Frankish dukes of the Agilolfing family. In the 7th and 8th centuries the region was christianized by Irish and Scottish monks. In 788 Charlemagne deposed the last of the Agilolfing dukes and incorporated Bavaria into the Carolingian Empire, and in the 10th century it became part of the Holy Roman Empire. The house of Wittelsbach ruled parts or all of Bavaria 1181–1918; Napoleon made the ruler a king 1806. In 1871 Bavaria became a state of the German Empire.

Bawa Geoffrey 1919– . Sri Lankan architect. His buildings are a contemporary interpretation of vernacular traditions, and include houses, hotels, and gardens. He has designed public buildings such as the new parliamentary complex, near Colombo, 1982, and Ruhuana University, Matara, 1984.

Bay of Pigs Cuban militiamen in Escaubry just after the unsuccessful Bay of Pigs invasion 1961. Badly planned and ill executed, the invasion was a major failure of US foreign policy, illustrating how a small country, largely defended by militiamen, could defy a world power. *Corbis*

Bax Arnold Edward Trevor 1883–1953. English composer. His works, often based on Celtic legends, include seven symphonies and *The Garden of Fand* 1913–16 and *Tintagel* 1917–19 (both tone poems).

bay various species of ◊laurel, genus *Laurus*. The aromatic evergreen leaves are used for flavouring in cookery. There is also a golden-leaved variety.

Bayer (Farbenfabriken Bayer AG) German chemical and pharmaceutical company, the largest chemical multinational in Europe, founded 1863. Its headquarters are in Leverkusen, Germany.

The company was founded by industrialist Friedrich Bayer (1825–1880), initially to manufacture dyestuffs. It was a chemist employed by Bayer, C Witthauer, who developed and patented ◊aspirin 1899.

Bayern German name for ◊Bavaria, a region of Germany.

Bayes' theorem in statistics, a theorem relating the ◊probability of particular events taking place to the probability that events conditional upon them have occurred.

For example, the probability of picking an ace at random out of a pack of cards is 4/52. If two cards are picked out, the probability of the second card being an ace is conditional on the first card: if the first card is an ace the probability of drawing a second ace will be 3/51; if not it will be 4/51. Bayes' theorem gives the probability that given that the second card is an ace, the first card is also.

Bayeux town in N France. Its museum houses the Bayeux Tapestry. There is a 13th-century Gothic cathedral.

Bayeux Tapestry linen hanging made about 1067–70 which gives a vivid pictorial record of the invasion of England by William I (the Conqueror) 1066. It is an embroidery rather than a true tapestry, sewn with woollen threads in blue, green, red, and yellow, 70 m/231 ft long and 50 cm/20 in wide, and containing 72 separate scenes with descriptive wording in Latin.

Bayle Pierre 1647–1706. French critic and philosopher. In *Dictionnaire historique et critique/Historical and Critical Dictionary* 1696, he wrote learned and highly sceptical articles attacking almost all the contemporary religious, philosophical, moral, scientific, and historical views. His scepticism greatly influenced the French *Encyclopédistes* and most Enlightenment thinkers.

Baylis Lilian Mary 1874–1937. English theatre manager. She was responsible for re-opening Sadler's Wells Theatre, London, 1931. From 1934 Sadler's Wells specialized in productions of opera and ballet: the resultant companies eventually became the Royal Ballet and the English National Opera.

Bay of Pigs inlet on the S coast of Cuba about 145 km/90 mi SW of Havana. It was the site of an unsuccessful invasion attempt by 1,500 US-sponsored Cuban exiles 17–20 April 1961; 1,173 were taken prisoner. In 1962 most of the Cuban prisoners were ransomed for $53 million in food and medicine. The incident served to strengthen Cuba's links with the USSR.

bayonet short sword attached to the muzzle of a firearm. The bayonet was placed inside the barrel of the muzzleloading muskets of the late 17th century. The sock or ring bayonet, invented 1700, allowed a weapon to be fired without interruption, leading to the demise of the pike.

Bayonne river port in SW France; population (1990) 41,800. It trades in timber, steel, fertilizer, and brandy. It is a centre of ◊Basque life. The bayonet was invented here.

Bayreuth town in Bavaria, S Germany, where opera festivals are held every summer; population (1991) 72,800. It was the home of composer Richard Wagner, and the Wagner theatre was established 1876 as a performing centre for his operas.

It introduced new concepts of opera house design, including provision of an enlarged orchestra pit extending below the stage and projecting the sound outwards and upwards.

Bazalgette Joseph William 1819–1890. British civil engineer who, as chief engineer to the London Board of Works, designed London's sewer system, a total of 155 km/83 mi of sewers, covering an area of 256 sq km/100 sq mi. It was completed 1865.

BBC abbreviation for ◊***British Broadcasting Corporation***.

BC in the Christian calendar, abbreviation for ***before Christ***, used with dates.

BCE abbreviation for ***before the Common Era***, used with dates instead of BC.

B cell or *B lymphocyte* immune cell that produces antibodies. Each B cell produces just one type of ◊antibody, specific to a single ◊antigen. Lymphocytes are related to ◊T cells.

BCG abbreviation for ***bacille Calmette-Guérin***, bacillus injected as a vaccine to confer active immunity to ◊tuberculosis (TB).

BCG was developed by Albert Calmette and Camille Guérin in France 1921 from live bovine TB bacilli. These bacteria were bred in the laboratory over many generations until they became attenuated (weakened). Each inoculation contains just enough live, attenuated bacilli to provoke an immune response: the formation of specific antibodies. The vaccine provides protection for 50–80% of infants vaccinated.

beach strip of land bordering the sea, normally consisting of boulders and pebbles on exposed coasts or sand on sheltered coasts. It is usually defined by the high- and low-water marks. A berm, a ridge of sand and pebbles, may be found at the farthest point that the water reaches.

The material of the beach consists of a rocky debris eroded from exposed rocks and headlands, or carried in by rivers. The material is transported to the beach, and along the beach, by waves that hit the coastline at an angle, resulting in a net movement of the material in one particular direction. This movement is known as longshore drift. Attempts are often made to halt longshore drift by erecting barriers (◊groynes), at right angles to the movement. Pebbles are worn into round shapes by being battered against one another by wave action and the result is called shingle. The finer material, the sand, may be subsequently moved about by the wind forming sand dunes. Apart from the natural process of longshore drift, a beach may be threatened by the commercial use of sand and aggregate, by the mineral industry – since particles of metal ore are often concentrated into workable deposits by the wave action – and by pollution (for example, by oil spilled or dumped at sea).

Beach Boys, the US pop group formed 1961. They began as exponents of vocal-harmony surf music with Chuck Berry guitar riffs (their hits include 'Surfin' USA' 1963 and 'Help Me, Rhonda' 1965), but the compositions, arrangements, and production by Brian Wilson (1942–) became highly complex under the influence of psychedelic rock, as in 'Good Vibrations' 1966. Wilson spent most of the next 20 years in retirement but returned with a solo album 1988.

Beachy Head (French ***Béveziers***) loftiest chalk headland (162 m/532 ft high) on the south coast of England, between Seaford and Eastbourne in Sussex, the eastern end of the South Downs. The lighthouse off the shore is 38 m/125 ft high.

Beaconsfield title taken by Benjamin ◊Disraeli, prime minister of Britain 1868 and 1874–80.

beagle short-haired hound with pendant ears, sickle tail, and a bell-like voice for hunting hares on foot ('beagling').

Beagle Channel channel to the S of Tierra del Fuego, South America, named after the ship of Charles ◊Darwin's voyage. Three islands at its eastern end, with krill and oil reserves within their 322 km/200 mi territorial waters, and the dependent sector of the Antarctic with its resources, were disputed between Argentina and Chile and awarded to Chile 1985.

Beaker people people thought to be of Iberian origin who spread out over Europe from the 3rd millennium BC. They were skilled in metalworking, and are identified by their use of distinctive earthenware beakers with various designs, of which the bell-beaker type was widely distributed throughout

Europe. They favoured inhumation (burial of the intact body), often round ◊barrows, or secondary burials in some form of chamber tomb. A beaker accompanied each burial, possibly to hold a drink for the deceased on their final journey.

Beale Dorothea 1831–1906. British pioneer in women's education whose work helped to raise the standard of women's education and the status of women teachers.

beam engine engine that works by providing an up and down motion to one end of a beam, which is translated into working machinery at the other end. Beam machines may be powered by a number of sources, including steam and water.

Beamon, Bob 1946– . US athlete. His leap of 8.90 metres in the long jump final at the 1968 Olympic Games in Mexico City represents one of the great achievements in the history of sport, beating the previous world record by a remarkable 55 cm. Prior to the Games his best leap was 8.33 metres and after then he never exceeded 8.20 metres. For many years it seemed doubtful that his record would ever be broken, but 1991 at the World Championships in Tokyo, US athlete Mike Powell jumped 8.95 metres.

beam weapon weapon capable of destroying a target by means of a high-energy beam. Beam weapons similar to the 'death ray' of science fiction have been explored, most notably during Ronald Reagan's presidential term in the 1980s in the USA.

The high-energy laser (HEL) produces a beam of high accuracy that burns through the surface of its target. The charged particle beam uses either electrons or protons, which have been accelerated almost to the speed of light, to slice through its target.

bean any seed of numerous leguminous plants. Beans are rich in nitrogenous or protein matter and are grown both for human consumption and as food for cattle and horses. Varieties of bean are grown throughout Europe, the USA, South America, China, Japan, SE Asia, and Australia.

The broad bean *Vicia faba* has been cultivated in Europe since prehistoric times. The French bean, kidney bean, or haricot *Phaseolus vulgaris* is probably of South American origin; the runner bean *Phaseolus coccineus* is closely allied to it, but differs in its climbing habit. Among beans of warmer countries are the lima or butter bean *Phaseolus lunatus* of South America; the soya bean *Glycine max*, extensively used in China and Japan; and the winged bean *Psophocarpus tetragonolobus* of SE Asia. The tuberous root of the winged bean has potential as a main crop in tropical areas where protein deficiency is common. The Asian mung bean *Phaseolus mungo* yields the bean sprouts used in Chinese cookery. Canned baked beans are usually a variety of *Phaseolus vulgaris*, which grows well in the USA.

bear in business, a speculator who sells stocks or shares on the stock exchange expecting a fall in the price in order to buy them back at a profit, the opposite of a ◊bull.

In a bear market, prices fall, and bears prosper.

bear large mammal with a heavily built body, short powerful limbs, and a very short tail. Bears breed once a year, producing one to four cubs. In northern regions they hibernate, and the young are born in the winter den. They are found mainly in North America and N Asia. The skin of the polar bear is black to conserve 80–90% of the solar energy trapped and channelled down the hollow hairs of its fur.

Bears walk on the soles of the feet and have long, nonretractable claws. The bear family, Ursidae, is related to carnivores such as dogs and weasels, and all are capable of killing prey. (The panda is probably related to both bears and raccoons.)

species There are seven species of bear. The ***brown bear*** *Ursus arctos* formerly ranged across most of Europe, N Asia, and North America, but is now reduced in number. It varies in size from under 2 m/7 ft long in parts of the Old World to 2.8 m/9 ft long and 780 kg/1,700 lb in Alaska. The ***grizzly bear*** is a North American variety of this species, and another subspecies, the ***Kodiak bear*** of Alaska, is the largest living land carnivore. The white ***polar bear*** *Thalarctos maritimus* is up to 2.5 m/8 ft long, has furry undersides to the feet, and feeds mainly on seals. It is found in the north polar region. The North American ***black bear*** *Euarctos americanus* and the ***Asian black bear*** *Selenarctos thibetanus* are smaller, only about 1.6 m/5 ft long. The latter has a white V-mark on its chest. The ***spectacled bear*** *Tremarctos ornatus* of the Andes is similarly sized, as is the ***sloth bear*** *Melursus ursinus* of India and Sri Lanka, which has a shaggy coat and uses its claws and protrusile lips to obtain termites, one of its preferred foods. The smallest bear is the Malaysian ***sun bear*** *Helarctos malayanus*, rarely more than 1.2 m/4 ft long, a good climber, whose favourite food is honey.

threat of extinction Of the seven species of bear, five are currently reckoned to be endangered and all apart from the polar bear and the American black bear are in decline. The population of brown bears in the Pyrenees was estimated at eight in 1994, and it is feared they will be extinct in 20 years unless new bears are introduced. In May 1996 two female Slovenian brown bears were released into the central Pyrenees; the Slovenian brown bear is closest genetically to the Pyrenean one.

In 1992, American black bears were upgraded to Appendix 2 of CITES (Convention on International Trade in Endangered Species) to stem the trade in their gall bladders, which are used in Asian traditional medicine to treat liver disease. The gall bladders contain an active substance, ursodiol, which is tapped through surgically-implanted tubes. Although an inexpensive synthetic version of ursodiol is available, in 1995 there were at least 10,000 bears being kept in farms in China for their gall bladders, for which many people still prefer to pay thousands of dollars. Trade in Asian black bears and their parts is illegal.

bear Grizzly bears *Ursus arctos* will hunt for fish in rivers or lakes. Their diet may include fruit, nuts, and roots, as well as insects, fish, and small vertebrates. Grizzly bears can grow up to 2.5 m/8.3 ft in length. They have no tail. *Corel*

bearberry any of several species of evergreen trailing shrub, genus *Arctostaphylos*, of the heath family, found on uplands and rocky places. Most bearberries are North American but *A. uva-ursi* is also found in Asia and Europe in northern mountainous regions. It bears small pink flowers in spring, followed by red berries that are edible but dry.

Beard, Charles Austin 1874–1948. US historian and a leader of the Progressive movement, active in promoting political and social reform. As a chief exponent of critical economic history, he published *An Economic Interpretation of the Constitution of the United States* 1913 and *The Economic Origins of Jeffersonian Democracy* 1915. With his wife Mary, he wrote *A Basic History of the United States* 1944, long a standard textbook in the USA.

bearded collie breed of British sheepdog with shaggy hair on its muzzle. Standing about 53 cm/21 in tall, it has a long coat, comprised of a soft furry undercoat and a harsh shaggy top coat and a shaggy beard. The coat is often grey, or sometimes sandy, with white on the head, chest, and feet. Bearded collies are kept as both working dogs and domestic companions.

Beardsley Aubrey Vincent 1872–1898. English illustrator and leading member of the ◊Aesthetic Movement. His meticulously executed black-and-white drawings show the influence of Japanese prints and French Rococo, and also display the sinuous line and decorative mannerisms of Art Nouveau. His work was often charged with being grotesque and decadent.

Bear, Great and Little common names (and translations of the Latin) for the constellations ◊Ursa Major and ◊Ursa Minor respectively.

bearing device used in a machine to allow free movement between two parts, typically the rotation

Beardsley A drawing of St John the Baptist and Salome by the English artist Aubrey Beardsley. His bold and original use of line and pattern, combined with his fascination with the erotic and the grotesque, made him a leading and controversial member of the Aesthetic Movement at the end of the 19th century. *Linda Proud*

Blessed are the meek: for they shall inherit the earth.

BEATITUDES
New Testament, Matthew 5:5

of a shaft in a housing. ***Ball bearings*** consist of two rings, one fixed to a housing, one to the rotating shaft. Between them is a set, or race, of steel balls. They are widely used to support shafts, as in the spindle in the hub of a bicycle wheel.

The ***sleeve***, or ***journal bearing***, is the simplest bearing. It is a hollow cylinder, split into two halves. It is used for the big-end and main bearings on a car ◊crankshaft. In some machinery the balls of ball bearings are replaced by cylindrical rollers or thinner ***needle bearings***.

In precision equipment such as watches and aircraft instruments, bearings may be made from material such as ruby and are known as ***jewel bearings***.

For some applications bearings made from nylon and other plastics are used. They need no lubrication because their surfaces are naturally waxy.

bearing the direction of a fixed point, or the path of a moving object, from a point of observation on the Earth's surface, expressed as an angle from the north. Bearings are taken by ◊compass and are measured in degrees (°), given as three-digit numbers increasing clockwise. For instance, north is 000°, northeast is 045°, south is 180°, and southwest is 225°.

True north differs slightly from magnetic north (the direction in which a compass needle points), hence NE may be denoted as 045M or 045T, depending on whether the reference line is magnetic (M) or true (T) north. True north also differs slightly from grid north since it is impossible to show a spherical Earth on a flat map.

Beat Generation or ***Beat movement*** US social and literary movement of the 1950s and early 1960s. Members of the Beat Generation, called beatniks, responded to the conformist materialism of the period by adopting lifestyles derived from Henry David Thoreau's social disobedience and Walt Whitman's poetry of the open road. The most influential writers were Jack ◊Kerouac (who is credited with coining the term), Allen ◊Ginsberg, and William ◊Burroughs.

Other cultural reference points were contemporary jazz, Buddhist philosophy, and the use of psychotropic drugs to heighten experience. The movement had no shared artistic credo beyond breaking the current literary orthodoxy, and its definition was largely historical. Most representative and influential were Kerouac's novel ◊*On the Road* 1957 and Ginsberg's poem *Howl* 1956, which used less conventionally structured forms alternately to celebrate the 'beatific' spirit of Beat and to indict the repressiveness of modern society.

There's something wrong with our bloody ships today, Chatfield.

DAVID BEATTY
Remark during the Battle of Jutland 1916

beatification in the Catholic church, the first step towards ◊canonization. Persons who have been beatified can be prayed to, and the title 'Blessed' can be put before their names.

Beatitudes in the New Testament, the sayings of Jesus reported in Matthew 5: 3–11 and Luke 6: 20–22, depicting the spiritual qualities that characterize members of the Kingdom of God.

Beatles, the English pop group 1960–70. The members, all born in Liverpool, were John Lennon (1940–1980, rhythm guitar, vocals), Paul McCartney (1942– , bass, vocals), George Harrison (1943– , lead guitar, vocals), and Ringo Starr (formerly Richard Starkey, 1940– , drums). Using songs written largely by Lennon and McCartney, the Beatles dominated rock music and pop culture in the 1960s.

The Beatles gained early experience in Liverpool and Hamburg, West Germany. They had a top-30 hit with their first record, 'Love Me Do' 1962, followed by 'Please Please Me' which reached number one. Every subsequent single and album released until 1967 reached number one in the UK charts.

At the peak of Beatlemania they starred in two films, *A Hard Day's Night* 1964 and *Help!* 1965, and provided songs for the animated film *Yellow Submarine* 1968. Their ballad 'Yesterday' 1965 was covered by 1,186 different performers in the first ten years. The album *Sgt Pepper's Lonely Hearts Club Band* 1967, recorded on two four-track machines, anticipated subsequent technological developments.

The Beatles were the first British group to challenge the US dominance of rock and roll, and continued to influence popular music beyond their break-up in 1970. Of the 30 songs most frequently broadcast in the USA 1955–91, 13 were written by members of the Beatles. They pursued separate careers with varying success. See separate entries for John ◊Lennon and Paul ◊McCartney.

'Tis virtue, and not birth that makes us noble: / Great actions speak great minds.

FRANCIS BEAUMONT AND JOHN FLETCHER
The Prophetess

beat music pop music that evolved in the UK in the early 1960s, known in its purest form as ◊Mersey beat, and as British Invasion in the USA. The beat groups characteristically had a simple, guitar-dominated line-up, vocal harmonies, and catchy tunes. They included the Beatles (1960–70), the Hollies (1962–), and the Zombies (1962–67).

Beaton Cecil Walter Hardy 1904–1980. English photographer. His elegant and sophisticated fashion pictures and society portraits often employed exotic props and settings. He adopted a more simple style for his wartime photographs of bomb-damaged London. He also worked as a stage and film designer, notably for the musicals *Gigi* 1959 and *My Fair Lady* 1965.

Beaton David 1494–1546. Scottish nationalist cardinal and politician, adviser to James V. Under Mary Queen of Scots, he was opposed to the alliance with England and persecuted reformers such as George Wishart, who was condemned to the stake; he was killed by Wishart's friends.

Beatrix (Wilhelmina Armgard) 1938– . Queen of the Netherlands. The eldest daughter of Queen ◊Juliana, she succeeded to the throne on her mother's abdication 1980. In 1966 she married West German diplomat Claus von Amsberg (1926–), who was created Prince of the Netherlands. Her heir is Prince Willem Alexander (1967–).

Beatty David, 1st Earl Beatty 1871–1936. British admiral in World War I. He commanded the cruiser squadron 1912–16 and bore the brunt of the Battle of ◊Jutland 1916.

Beatty Warren. Stage name of Warren Beaty 1937– . US actor, director, and producer. He attracted attention as a young man in such films as *Splendour in the Grass* 1961, then produced and starred as gangster Clyde Barrow in the hugely successful *Bonnie and Clyde* 1967. Later, he directed *Reds* 1981, *Dick Tracy* 1990, and co-produced *Bugsy* 1992, in which he played the gangster Bugsy Siegel. He is the brother of actress Shirley MacLaine.

Beaufort Henry 1375–1447. English priest, bishop of Lincoln from 1398, of Winchester from 1405. As chancellor of England, he supported his half-brother Henry IV and made enormous personal loans to Henry V to finance war against France. As a guardian of Henry VI from 1421, he was in effective control of the country until 1426. In the same year he was created a cardinal. In 1431 he crowned Henry VI as king of France in Paris.

Beaufort scale system of recording wind velocity (speed), devised by Francis Beaufort (1774–1857) in 1806. It is a numerical scale ranging from 0 to 17, calm being indicated by 0 and a hurricane by 12; 13–17 indicate degrees of hurricane force.

In 1874 the scale received international recognition; it was modified 1926. Measurements are made at 10 m/33 ft above ground level. *See list of tables on p. 1177.*

Beaufort Sea section of the Arctic Ocean off Alaska and Canada, named after Francis Beaufort (1774–1857).

Beauharnais Alexandre, Vicomte de 1760–1794. French liberal aristocrat and general who served in the American Revolution and became a member of the National Convention in the early days of the French Revolution. He was the first husband of Josephine (consort of Napoleon I). Their daughter Hortense (1783–1837) married Louis, a younger brother of Napoleon, and their son became ◊Napoleon III. Beauharnais was guillotined during the Terror for his alleged lack of zeal for the revolutionary cause and his lack of success as Commander of the Republican Army of the North.

Beaujolais light, fruity red wine produced in the area S of Burgundy in E France. Beaujolais is best drunk while young; the broaching date is the third Thursday in Nov, when the new vintage is rushed to the USA, the UK, Japan, and other countries, so that the Beaujolais *nouveau* (new Beaujolais) may be marketed.

Beaulieu village in Hampshire, England, 9 km/6 mi SW of Southampton. The former abbey is the home of Lord Montagu of Beaulieu and has the Montagu Museum of vintage cars.

Beaumarchais Pierre Augustin Caron de 1732–1799. French dramatist. His great comedies, *Le Barbier de Seville/The Barber of Seville* 1775 and *Le Mariage de Figaro/The Marriage of Figaro* (1778, but prohibited until 1784), form the basis of operas by ◊Rossini and ◊Mozart, with their blend of social criticism and sharp humour.

Louis XVI entrusted Beaumarchais with secret missions, notably for the profitable shipment of arms to the American colonies during the War of Independence. Accused of treason 1792, he fled to Holland and England, but in 1799 he returned to Paris.

Beaumont Francis 1584–1616. English dramatist and poet. About 1606–13 he collaborated with John ◊Fletcher. Their joint plays include the tragicomedies *Philaster* 1610, *A King and No King* about 1611, and *The Maid's Tragedy* about 1611. *The Woman Hater* about 1606 and *The Knight of the Burning Pestle* about 1607, which is a satire on the audience, are ascribed to Beaumont alone.

Beaumont William 1785–1853. US surgeon who conducted pioneering experiments on the digestive system. In 1822 he saved the life of a Canadian trapper wounded in the side by a gun blast; the wound only partially healed, and through an opening in the stomach wall, Beaumont was able to observe the workings of the stomach. His *Experiments and Observations on the Gastric Juice and the Physiology of Digestion* was published 1833.

Beaune city SW of Dijon, France; population (1990) 22,100. It is the centre of the Burgundian wine trade, and has a wine museum. Other products include agricultural equipment and mustard.

Beauregard Pierre Gustave Toutant 1818–1893. US military leader and Confederate general whose opening fire on Fort Sumter, South Carolina, started the American Civil War 1861. His military successes were clouded by his conflicts with Confederate president Jefferson Davis.

Beauvais city 76 km/47 mi NW of Paris, France; population (1990) 56,300. It is a trading centre for fruit, dairy produce, and agricultural machinery. Beauvais has a Gothic cathedral, the tallest in France (68 m/223 ft), and is renowned for tapestries (which are now made at the ◊Gobelins factory, Paris).

Beauvoir Simone de 1908–1986. French socialist, feminist, and writer. She played a large role in

Beauregard Remembered as the Confederate general who fired on Fort Sumter and so opened the American Civil War, Pierre Beauregard had a distinguished career, fighting at Bull Run, Shiloh, and Charleston. *Library of Congress*

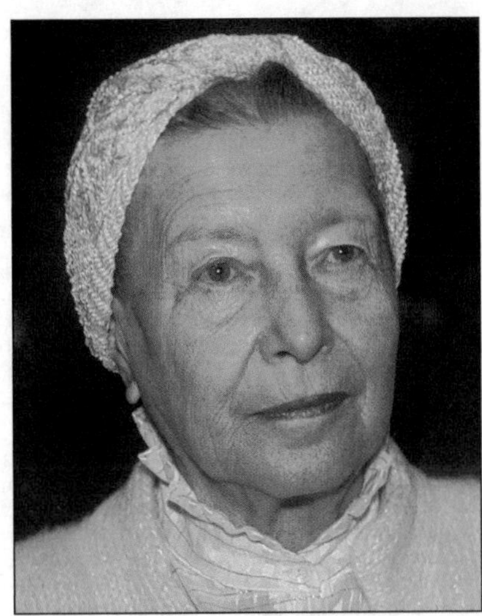

Beauvoir French writer and feminist Simone de Beauvoir. A close collaborator with the philosopher Jean-Paul Sartre, de Beauvoir applied existentialism to postwar moral and political issues. In *The Second Sex* 1949 – which became a feminist classic – she analysed the role of women in a male-dominated society. Her novels and her series of autobiographies give a vivid account of French intellectual life from the 1940s to the 1980s. *Topham*

French intellectual life from the 1940s to the 1980s. Her book *Le Deuxième Sexe/The Second Sex* 1949, one of the first major feminist texts, is an encyclopedic study of the role of women in society, drawing on literature, myth, and history. In this work she argues that the subservient position of women is the result of their systematic repression by a male-dominated society that denies their independence, identity, and sexuality.

She also published novels, including *Les Mandarins/The Mandarins* 1954 (winner of the Prix Goncourt), and many autobiographical volumes. She taught philosophy at the University of Paris 1931–43 and was a lifelong companion of the philosopher Jean-Paul ◊Sartre; *La Cérémonie des Adieux/Adieux: A Farewell to Sartre* 1981 gives an intimate insight into their relationship.

beaver aquatic rodent with webbed hind feet, a broad flat scaly tail, and thick waterproof fur. It has very large incisor teeth and fells trees to feed on the bark and to use the logs to construct the 'lodge', in which the young are reared, food is stored, and much of the winter is spent. There are two species, the Canadian *Castor canadensis* and the European *C. fiber*. They grow up to 1.4 m/4.6 ft in length and weigh about 20 kg/44 lb.

Beavers are monogamous and a pair will produce a litter of twins each year. Their territory consists of about 3 km/2 mi of river. Beavers can construct dams on streams, and thus modify the environment considerably; beaver ponds act as traps for minerals and provide fertile living conditions for other species – zooplankton biomass may be 1,000 times greater within a beaver pond than elsewhere. Beavers once ranged across Europe, N Asia, and North America, but in Europe now only survive where they are protected, and are reduced elsewhere, partly through trapping for their fur.

Beaverbrook (William) Max(well) Aitken, 1st Baron Beaverbrook 1879–1964. British financier, newspaper proprietor, and politician, born in Canada. He bought a majority interest in the *Daily Express* 1919, founded the *Sunday Express* 1921, and bought the London *Evening Standard* 1923. He served in Lloyd George's World War I cabinet and Churchill's World War II cabinet.

Between the wars he used his newspapers, in particular the *Daily Express*, to campaign for empire and free trade and against Prime Minister Baldwin.

bebop or ***bop*** hot jazz style, rhythmically complex, virtuosic, and highly improvisational. It was developed in New York in the 1940s and 1950s by Charlie Parker, Dizzy Gillespie, Thelonius Monk, and other black musicians reacting against ◊swing music.

Bechet Sidney Joseph 1897–1959. US jazz musician. He played clarinet and was the first to forge an individual style on soprano saxophone. Bechet was based in Paris in the late 1920s and the 1950s, where he was recognized by classical musicians as a serious artist.

Beckenbauer Franz 1945– . German footballer who captained West Germany to the 1972 European Championship and the 1974 World Cup, and was twice European Footballer of the Year. After retiring as a player, he became West Germany's team manager, taking them to the runners-up spot in the 1986 World Cup and victory in the 1990 World Cup. He is the only person both to captain and manage a winning World Cup team.

Becker Boris 1967– . German tennis player. In 1985, at the age of 17, he became the youngest winner of a singles title at Wimbledon. He has won the title three times and helped West Germany to win the Davis Cup 1988 and 1989. He also won the US Open 1989 and the Grand Prix Masters/ATP Tour World Championship 1992.

Becket St Thomas à 1118–1170. English priest and politician. He was chancellor to ◊Henry II 1155–62, when he was appointed archbishop of Canterbury.

A friend of Henry II, Becket was a loyal chancellor, but on becoming archbishop of Canterbury transferred his allegiance to the church. In 1164 he opposed Henry's attempt to regulate the relations between church and state, and had to flee the country; he returned 1170, but the reconciliation soon broke down. Encouraged by a hasty outburst from the king, four knights murdered Becket before the altar of Canterbury cathedral. He was declared a saint 1172, and his shrine became the busiest centre of pilgrimage in England until the Reformation.

Beckett Samuel (Barclay) 1906–1989. Irish dramatist and novelist. He wrote in both French and English. His play *En attendant Godot* – first performed in Paris 1952, and then in his own translation as *Waiting for Godot* 1955 in London, 1956 in New York – is possibly the best-known example of Theatre of the ◊Absurd, in which life is taken to be meaningless. This genre is taken to further extremes in *Fin de partie/Endgame* 1957 and *Happy Days* 1961. Nobel Prize for Literature 1969.

As a novelist, Beckett was strongly influenced by James Joyce, in such works as *Molloy* 1951 and *Malone meurt/Malone Dies* 1951. He also wrote plays for radio, among them *All That Fall* 1957 and *Embers* 1959. As well as paring character to its grimmest essentials, Beckett honed his prose with meticulous precision to a painful articulateness, scrupulously cautious of redundancy. Composition in French, before translating into English, helped towards this refining of style.

Beckmann Max 1884–1950. German Expressionist painter and graphic artist. He was influenced both by medieval art and by the *Neue Sachlichkeit* movement and after World War I his art concentrated on themes of cruelty in human society, as in *Night* 1918–19 (Kunstsammlung Nardrheim-Westfalen, Düsseldorf).

Beckmann was born in Leipzig. He fought in World War I and was discharged following a breakdown, reflected in the agony of his work. Denounced by the Nazi regime (see ◊Degenerate Art), he moved to Amsterdam where he began a series of complex allegorical works. He spent the last three years of his life in the USA.

becquerel SI unit (symbol Bq) of ◊radioactivity, equal to one radioactive disintegration (change in the nucleus of an atom when a particle or ray is given off) per second.

The becquerel is much smaller than the previous standard unit, the curie (3.7×10^{10} Bq). It is named after French physicist Henri Becquerel.

Becquerel (Antoine) Henri 1852–1908. French physicist. He discovered penetrating radiation coming from uranium salts, the first indication of ◊radioactivity, and shared a Nobel prize with Marie and Pierre ◊Curie 1903.

bedbug flattened wingless red-brown insect *Cimex lectularius* with piercing mouthparts. It hides by day in crevices or bedclothes and emerges at night to suck human blood.

Bede c. 673–735. English theologian and historian, known as ***the Venerable Bede***. Active in Durham and Northumbria, he wrote many scientific, theological, and historical works. His *Historia Ecclesiastica Gentis Anglorum/Ecclesiastical History of the English People* 731 is a seminal source for early English history.

Born at Monkwearmouth, Durham, he entered the local monastery at the age of seven, later transferring to Jarrow, where he became a priest about 703. He devoted his life to writing and teaching; among his pupils was Egbert, archbishop of York.

Bedford administrative headquarters of Bedfordshire, England, on the river Ouse; population (1991) 73,900. Industries include agricultural machinery, airships, diesel engines, pumps, foodstuffs, bricks, and electronic equipment. John Bunyan wrote *The Pilgrim's Progress* (1678) while imprisoned here.

bedford level peat portion of the ◊Fens.

Bedfordshire county of S central England (*see United Kingdom map*).

towns and cities Bedford (administrative headquarters), Dunstable

features low lying with Chiltern Hills in the SW; Whipsnade Zoo 1931, near Dunstable, a zoological park (200 ha) belonging to the London Zoological Society; Woburn Abbey, seat of the duke of Bedford

industries cereals, vegetables, agricultural machinery, electrical goods, cement, clay, chalk, sand, gravel, motor vehicles. Agriculture is important, especially wheat and barley. It has one of the world's largest brickworks

famous people John Bunyan, John Howard, Joseph Paxton.

Bedlam (abbreviation of ***Bethlehem***) the earliest mental hospital in Europe. The hospital was opened in the 14th century in London and is now sited in Surrey. It is now used as a slang word meaning chaos.

'One is not born a woman. One becomes one.'

SIMONE DE BEAUVOIR *The Second Sex*

'Vladimir: 'That passed the time.' / Estragon: 'It would have passed in any case.' / Vladimir: 'Yes, but not so rapidly.''

SAMUEL BECKETT *Waiting for Godot*

Becket The murder of Thomas à Becket, Archbishop of Canterbury, depicted by the artist and chronicler Matthew Paris. After his death, Becket's tomb in Canterbury became one of the most important English pilgrimage sites of the Middle Ages. *Philip Sauvain*

bee The honey bee lives in colonies of 40,000–80,000 workers, 200 drones, and one queen. The queen lays about 1,500 eggs each day; fertilized eggs give rise to workers or queens, unfertilized ones produce drones. The sole function of the male, or drone, is to fertilize the queen. The sterile worker has a pollen sac to carry pollen back to the hive.

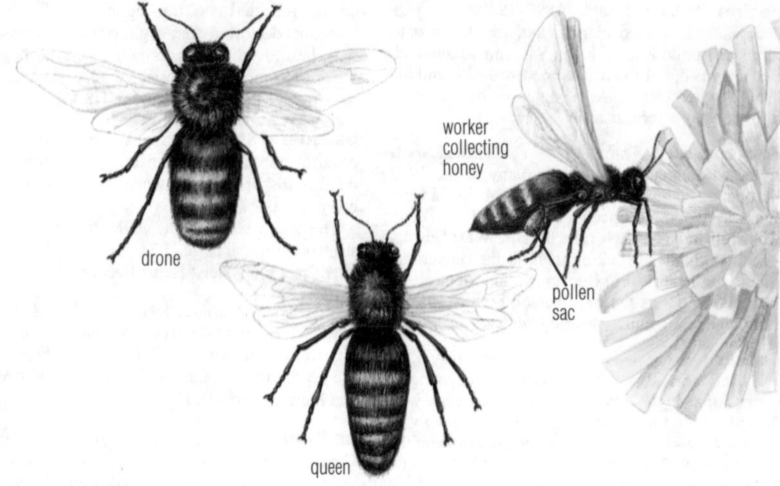

Bedouin (Arabic 'desert-dweller') any of the nomadic, Arabic peoples occupying the desert regions of Arabia and N Africa, now becoming increasingly settled. Their traditional trade was the rearing of horses and camels.

bee four-winged insect of the superfamily Apoidea in the order Hymenoptera, usually with a sting. There are over 12,000 species, of which fewer than 1 in 20 are social in habit. The ***hive bee*** or ***honey bee*** *Apis mellifera* establishes perennial colonies of about 80,000, the majority being infertile females (workers), with a few larger fertile males (drones), and a single very large fertile female (the queen). Worker bees live for no more than a few weeks, while a drone may live a few months, and a queen several years. Queen honey bees lay two kinds of eggs: fertilized, female eggs, which have two sets of chromosomes and develop into workers or queens, and unfertilized, male eggs, which have only one set of chromosomes and develop into drones.

Bees transmit information to each other about food sources by 'dances', each movement giving rise to sound impulses which are picked up by tiny hairs on the back of the bee's head, the orientation of the dance also having significance. They use the Sun in navigation (see ◊migration). Besides their use in crop pollination and production of honey and wax, bees (by a measure of contaminants brought back to their hives) can provide an inexpensive and effective monitor of industrial and other pollution of the atmosphere and soil.

At a rehearsal I let the orchestra play as they like. At the concert I make them play as I like.

Thomas Beecham
N Cardus *Sir Thomas Beecham*

The most familiar species is the ***bumblebee***, genus *Bombus*, which is larger and stronger than the hive bee and so is adapted to fertilize plants in which the pollen and nectar lie deep, as in red clover; they can work in colder weather than the hive bee.

Social bees, apart from the bumblebee and the hive bee, include the stingless South American ***vulture bee*** *Trigona hypogea*, discovered 1982, which is solely carnivorous.

Solitary bees include species useful in pollinating orchards in spring, and may make their nests in tunnels under the ground or in hollow plant stems; 'cuckoo' bees lay their eggs in the nests of bumblebees, which they closely resemble.

Most bees are pacific unless disturbed, but some species are aggressive. One bee sting may be fatal to a person who is allergic to them, but this is comparatively rare (about 1.5% of the population), and most adults can survive 300–500 stings without treatment. A vaccine treatment against bee stings, which uses concentrated venom, has been developed.

The killer bees of South America are a hybrid type, created when an African subspecies of honey bee escaped from a research establishment in Brazil 1957. They mated with, and supplanted, the honey bees of European origin in most of South and Central America, and by 1990 had spread as far north as Texas, USA. As well as being more productive and resistant to disease than European honey bees, they also defend their hives more aggressively, in larger numbers, and for a greater length of time than other honeybees. However, their stings are no more venomous, and although they have killed hundreds of thousands of animals and probably more than 1,000 people, most individuals survive an attack, and almost all deaths have occurred where the victim has somehow been prevented from fleeing.

Good ale, the true and proper drink of Englishmen.

On **beer**
George Borrow
Lavengro 1851

beech any tree of the genera *Fagus* and *Nothofagus*, family Fagaceae. The common beech *F. sylvaticus*, found in European forests, has a smooth grey trunk and edible nuts, or 'mast', which are used as animal feed or processed for oil. The timber is used in furniture.

Beecham Thomas 1879–1961. English conductor and impresario. He established the Royal Philharmonic Orchestra 1946 and fostered the works of composers such as Delius, Sibelius, and Richard Strauss.

Beecher Harriet. Unmarried name of Harriet Beecher ◊Stowe, author of *Uncle Tom's Cabin*.

Beecher Henry Ward 1813–1887. US Congregational minister and militant opponent of slavery, son of the pulpit orator Lyman ◊Beecher and brother of the writer Harriet Beecher ◊Stowe.

Beecher Lyman 1775–1863. US Congregational and Presbyterian minister, one of the most popular pulpit orators of his time. He was the father of Harriet Beecher ◊Stowe and Henry Ward Beecher.

bee-eater brightly-coloured bird *Merops apiaster*, family Meropidae, order Coraciiformes, found in Africa, S Europe, and Asia. Bee-eaters are slender, with chestnut, yellow, and blue-green plumage, a long bill and pointed wings, and a flight like that of the swallow, which they resemble in shape. They feed on bees, wasps, and other insects, and nest in colonies in holes dug out with their long bills in sandy river banks.

The European bee-eater migrates from Africa, where it also breeds, to southern and central Europe. It is a rare visitor to the UK.

Beelzebub (Hebrew 'lord of the flies') in the New Testament, the leader of the devils, sometimes identified with Satan and sometimes with his chief assistant (see ◊devil). In the Old Testament Beelzebub was a fertility god worshipped by the Philistines and other Semitic groups (◊Baal).

bee-eater The bee-eater is one of the most colourful birds found in Europe. Bee-eaters live in colonies, feeding on a variety of insects, chiefly wasps and bees. They catch their prey in mid-flight and rub it on the ground or on a branch before eating it, either to kill it or to remove its sting.

beer alcoholic drink made from water and malt (fermented barley or other grain), flavoured with hops. Beer contains between 1% and 6% alcohol. One of the oldest alcoholic drinks, it was brewed in ancient China, Egypt, and Babylon.

The medieval distinction between beer (containing hops) and ***ale*** (without hops) has now fallen into disuse and beer has come to be used strictly as a generic term including ale, stout, and lager. ***Stout*** is top fermented, but is sweet and strongly flavoured with roasted grain; ***lager*** is a light beer, bottom fermented and matured over a longer period (German *Lager* 'store').

Beerbohm (Henry) Max(imilian) 1872–1956. English caricaturist and author. A perfectionist in style, he contributed to *The Yellow Book* 1894; wrote a novel of Oxford undergraduate life, *Zuleika Dobson* 1911; and published volumes of caricature, including *Rossetti and His Circle* 1922. He succeeded George Bernard Shaw as critic to the *Saturday Review* 1898.

Beersheba industrial city in Israel; population (1994) 147,900. It is the chief centre of the Negev Desert and has been a settlement from the Stone Age.

beet plant of the genus *Beta* of the goosefoot family Chenopodiaceae. The common beet *B. vulgaris* is used in one variety to produce sugar, and another, the mangelwurzel, is grown as cattle fodder. The beetroot, or red beet, *B. rubra* is a salad plant. The family also includes ◊spinach; spinach beet, used as a spinach substitute, is *B. vulgaris cicle*, commonly known as goosefoot.

Beethoven Ludwig van 1770–1827. German composer and pianist. His mastery of musical expression in every genre made him the dominant influence on 19th-century music. Beethoven's repertoire includes concert overtures; the opera *Fidelio* 1805, revised 1814; five piano concertos and two for violin (one unfinished); 32 piano sonatas, including the *Moonlight* 1801 and *Appassionata* 1804–05; 17 string quartets; the Mass in D (*Missa solemnis*) 1824; and nine symphonies, as well as many youthful works. He usually played his own piano pieces and conducted his orchestral works until he was hampered by deafness 1801; nevertheless he continued to compose.

Born in Bonn, the son and grandson of musicians, Beethoven became deputy organist at the court of the Elector of Cologne at Bonn before he was 12; later he studied under Haydn and possibly Mozart, whose influence dominated his early work. From 1809, he received a small allowance from aristocratic patrons.

Beethoven's career spanned the transition from Classicism to Romanticism. Of his symphonies the best-known are the Third (*Eroica*) 1803–04, originally intended to be dedicated to Napoleon with whom Beethoven became disillusioned, the Fifth 1807–08, the Sixth (*Pastoral*) 1803–08, and the Ninth (*Choral*) 1815–24, which includes the passage from Schiller's 'Ode to Joy' chosen as the national anthem of Europe.

beetle common name of insects in the order Coleoptera (Greek 'sheath-winged') with leathery forewings folding down in a protective sheath over the membranous hindwings, which are those used for flight. They pass through a complete metamorphosis. They include some of the largest and smallest of all insects: the largest is the Hercules beetle *Dynastes hercules* of the South American rainforests, 15 cm/6 in long; the smallest is only 0.05 cm/0.02 in long. Comprising more than 50% of the animal kingdom, beetles number some 370,000 named species, with many not yet described.

Beetles are found in almost every land and freshwater habitat and feed on almost anything edible. Examples include ***click beetle*** or ***skipjack*** species of the family Elateridae, so called because if they fall on their backs they right themselves with a jump and a loud click; the larvae, known as wireworms, feed on the roots of crops. In some tropical species of Elateridae the beetles have luminous organs between the head and abdomen and are known as ***fireflies***. The potato pest ***Colorado beetle*** *Leptinotarsa decemlineata* is striped in black and yellow. The ***blister beetle*** *Lytta vesicatoriaf*, a shiny green species from S Europe, was once sold pulverized as an aphrodisiac and contains the toxin cantharidin. The larvae of the ***furniture beetle*** *Anobium punctatum* and the ***deathwatch beetle*** *Xestobium rufovillosum* and their relatives are serious pests of structural timbers and furniture (see ◊woodworm).

Beeton Mrs, (Isabella Mary Mayson) 1836–1865. British writer on cookery and domestic management. She produced *Beeton's Household Management* 1859, the first comprehensive work on domestic science.

Begin Menachem 1913–1992. Israeli politician. He was leader of the extremist Irgun Zvai Leumi organization in Palestine from 1942 and prime minister of Israel 1977–83, as head of the right-wing Likud party. In 1978 Begin shared a Nobel Peace Prize with President Sadat of Egypt for work on the ◊Camp David Agreements for a Middle East peace settlement.

begonia any plant of the genus *Begonia* of the tropical and subtropical family Begoniaceae. Begonias have fleshy and succulent leaves, and some have large, brilliant flowers. There are numerous species native to the tropics, in particular South America and India.

Behan Brendan Francis 1923–1964. Irish dramatist. His early experience of prison and knowledge of the workings of the ◊IRA (recounted in his autobiography *Borstal Boy* 1958) provided him with two recurrent themes in his plays. *The Quare Fellow* 1954 was followed by the tragicomedy *The Hostage* 1958, first written in Gaelic.

behaviourism school of psychology originating in the USA, of which the leading exponent was John B ◊Watson.

Behaviourists maintain that all human activity can ultimately be explained in terms of conditioned reactions or reflexes and habits formed in consequence. Leading behaviourists include Ivan ◊Pavlov and B F ◊Skinner.

behaviour therapy in psychology, the application of behavioural principles, derived from learning theories, to the treatment of clinical conditions such as ◊phobias, ◊obsessions, and sexual and interpersonal problems. The symptoms of these disorders are regarded as learned patterns of behaviour that therapy can enable the patient to unlearn.

Behn Aphra 1640–1689. English novelist and dramatist. She was the first woman in England to earn her living as a writer. Her works were criticized for their explicitness; they frequently present events from a woman's point of view. Her novel *Oroonoko* 1688 is an attack on slavery.

Between 1670 and 1687 fifteen of her plays were produced, including *The Forced Marriage* 1670 and *The Rover* 1677. Condemnation of forced and mercenary marriages was a recurring theme in her work. She had the patronage of James I and was employed as a government spy in Holland 1666.

Behan Irish dramatist Brendan Behan in a Dublin bar, 1952. Drawing upon his experiences as a political prisoner, and using the racy speech of the Dublin working classes, Behan brought a new vitality, honesty, and lyricism to the theatre of the 1950s. *Corbis*

beetle Although having the appearance of a normal beetle, click beetles, such as this *Chalcolepidius porcatus* from Trinidad, have a unique escape mechanism when attacked. Using the click mechanism on its underside, the beetle is able to spring away if touched. *Premaphotos Wildlife*

Behrens Peter 1868–1940. German architect. He pioneered the adaptation of architecture to industry and designed the AEG turbine factory in Berlin 1909, a landmark in industrial architecture. He taught Le Corbusier, Walter Gropius, and Mies van der Rohe.

Behring Emil von 1854–1917. German physician. He discovered that the body produces antitoxins, substances able to counteract poisons released by bacteria. Using this knowledge, he developed new treatments for such diseases as ◊diphtheria. He won the first Nobel Prize for Physiology or Medicine, 1901.

Behring discovered the diphtheria antitoxin and developed serum therapy together with Japanese bacteriologist Shibasaburō ◊Kitasato, and they went on to apply the technique to tetanus. Behring also introduced early vaccination techniques against diphtheria and tuberculosis.

Beiderbecke Bix (Leon Bismarck) 1903–1931. US jazz cornetist, composer, and pianist. A romantic soloist with the bands of King Oliver, Louis Armstrong, and Paul Whiteman, Beiderbecke was the first acknowledged white jazz innovator. He was influenced by the classical composers Debussy, Ravel, and Stravinsky.

Beijing or ***Peking*** capital of China; part of its northeast border is formed by the Great Wall of China; population (1993) 6,560,000. The municipality of Beijing has an area of 17,800 sq km/6,871 sq mi and a population (1994) of 12,000,000. Industries include textiles, petrochemicals, steel, and engineering

features Tiananmen Gate (Gate of Heavenly Peace) and Tiananmen Square, where, in 1989, Chinese troops massacred over 1,000 students and civilians demonstrating for greater freedom and democracy; the Forbidden City, built between 1406 and 1420 as Gu Gong (Imperial Palace) of the Ming Emperors, where there were 9,000 ladies-in-waiting and 10,000 eunuchs in service (it is now the seat of the government); the Great Hall of the People 1959 (used for official banquets); museums of Chinese history and of the Chinese revolution; Chairman Mao Memorial Hall 1977 (shared from 1983 with Zhou Enlai, Zhu De, and Liu Shaoqi); the Summer Palace built by the dowager empress Zi Xi (damaged by European powers 1900, but restored 1903); Temple of Heaven (Tiantan); and Ming tombs 50 km/30 mi to the northwest

history Beijing, founded 2,000 years ago, was the 13th-century capital of the Mongol emperor Kublai Khan. Later replaced by Nanking, it was again capital from 1421, except from 1928 to 1949, when it was renamed Peiping. Beijing was held by Japan 1937–45. The UN Conference on Women was held here 1995.

Beirut or ***Beyrouth*** capital and port of ◊Lebanon, devastated by civil war in the 1970s and 1980s, when it was occupied by armies of neighbouring countries; population (1993) 1,200,000.

history Beirut dates back to at least 1400 BC. Before the civil war 1975–90, Beirut was an international financial and educational centre, with four universities (Lebanese, Arab, French, and US); it was also a centre of espionage. Subsequent struggles for power among Christian and Muslim factions caused widespread destruction.

From July to Sept 1982 the city was besieged and sections virtually destroyed by the Israeli army to enforce the withdrawal of the forces of the Palestinian Liberation Organization (PLO). After the cease-fire, 500 Palestinians were massacred in the Sabra–Shatila camps 16–18 Sept 1982, by dissident ◊Phalangist and ◊Maronite troops. In 1987 Syrian troops entered the city and remained; intensive fighting broke out between Christian and Syrian troops. In Oct 1990 President Elias Hwari formally invited Syrian troops to remove the Maronite Christian leader General Michel ◊Aoun from his E Beirut stronghold; the troops then went on to dismantle the 'Green Line' separating Muslim western and Christian eastern Beirut. The Syrian-backed 'Greater Beirut Security Plan' was subsequently implemented by the Lebanese government, enforcing the withdrawal of all militias from greater Beirut. In April 1996, following the firing of rockets by Hezbollah into northern Israel, which injured 36 people, Israeli gunships rocketed Beirut for the first time since 1982, killing 26 people.

Béjart Maurice. Adopted name of Maurice Jean Berger 1927– . French choreographer and ballet director. Believing dance to be 'total theatre', he has staged huge, spectacular productions, for example *Romeo and Juliet* 1966. As director of his Ballet of the 20th Century 1960, based in Brussels until 1987, Béjart's productions included *The Firebird* 1970 (where the ballerina's role is taken by a male leader of a band of partisans) and *Kabuki* 1986, which features the suicide of 47 samurai in the finale. Other ballets include *Bolero* 1961 and *Notre Faust* 1975.

He is also the founder of Mudra 1970, a school he named after the Hindu hand gestures, the full title of which is *Centre européen de perfectionnement et de recherche des interprètes du spectacle/European Centre for Perfection and Research for Performing Artists*. His choreography generally centres on the male dancers in his company.

Bekaa, the or ***El Beqa'a*** governorate of E Lebanon separated from Syria by the Anti-Lebanon Mountains. Zahlé and the ancient city of Baalbek are the chief settlements. The Bekaa Valley was of strategic importance in the Syrian struggle for

'I was court-martialled in my absence, and sentenced to death in my absence, so I said they could shoot me in my absence.'

Brendan Behan
The Hostage

BELARUS
Republic of

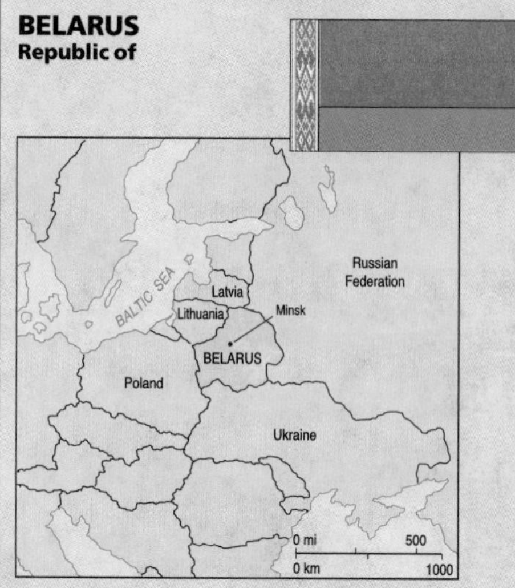

national name *Respublika Belarus*
area 207,600 sq km/80,100 sq mi
capital Minsk (Mensk)
major towns/cities Gomel, Vitebsk, Mogilev, Bobruisk, Grodno, Brest
physical features more than 25% forested; rivers Dvina, Dnieper and its tributaries, including the Pripet and Beresina; the Pripet Marshes in the E; mild and damp climate
head of state Alexandr Lukashenko from 1994
head of government Syargey Ling from 1996
political system emergent democracy
administrative divisions six districts and the capital city
political parties Belarus Communist Party (BCP, banned 1991–92); Belarus Patriotic Movement (BPM), populist; Belarussian Popular Front (BPFs), moderate nationalist; Christian Democratic Union of Belarus, centrist; Socialist Party of Belarus, left of centre
population 10,141,00 (1995 est)
population growth rate −0.1% (1990–95); −0.1% (2000–05)
ethnic distribution 75% of Belarussian ('eastern Slav') descent, 13% ethnic Russian, 4% Polish, 3% Ukranian, and 1% Jewish
life expectancy men 64, women 75
literacy rate 98%
languages Byelorussian (official), Russian, Polish
religions Russian Orthodox, Roman Catholic, with Baptist and Muslim minorities
currency rouble and zaichik
GDP (US $) 20.2 billion (1994)
growth rate −21.5% (1994)
exports peat, agricultural machinery, fertilizers, glass, textiles, leather, salt, electrical goods, meat, dairy produce

HISTORY
5th–8th Cs Settled by East Slavic tribes, the ancestors of the present-day Belarussians.
11th C Minsk founded.
12th C Part of Kievan Russia, to the S, with an independent Belarus state developing around Polotsk, on the Dvina river.
14th C Incorporated within the Slavonic Grand Duchy of Lithuania, to the W.
1569 Union with Poland.
late 18th C Came under the control of tsarist Russia as Belarussia ('White Russia'), following the three partitions of Poland in 1772, 1793, and 1795.
1812 Minsk was destroyed by the French emperor Napoleon Bonaparte during his military campaign against Russia.
1839 Belarussian Catholic Church forcibly abolished.
1914–18 The site of fierce fighting between Germany and Russia during World War I.
1918–19 Briefly independent from Russia.
1919–20 Wars between Poland and Soviet Russia over control of Belarus.
1921 West Belarus ruled by Poland; East Belarus became a Soviet republic.
1930s Agriculture collectivized despite peasant resistance; more than 100,000 people, chiefly writers and intellectuals, shot in mass executions ordered by Soviet dictator Joseph Stalin.
1939 West Belarus occupied by Soviet troops.
1941–44 Occupied by Nazi Germany, resulting in the death of 1.3 million people, including many Jews; Minsk destroyed.
1945 Became a founding member of the United Nations; much of West Belarus incorporated into the Soviet republic.
1950s–60s Large-scale immigration of ethnic Russians and 'Russification'.
1986 Fallout from the nearby Chernobyl nuclear reactor in Ukraine rendered a fifth of agricultural land unusable.
1989 Belarussian Popular Front established as national identity revived under *glasnost* initiative of Soviet leader Mikhail Gorbachev.
1990 Belarussian established as state language and republican sovereignty declared.
1991 Strikes and unrest in Minsk; BCP suspended following attempted coup against Gorbachev in Moscow; moderate nationalist Stanislav Shushkevich elected president. Independence recognized by USA; Commonwealth of Independent States (CIS) formed in Minsk.
1993 BCP re-established.
1994 President Shushkevich ousted; Alexandr Lukashenko, a pro-Russian populist, elected president.
1995 Friendship and cooperation pact signed with Russia.
1996 Agreement on 'economic union' with Russia. Lukashenka's impeachment averted following his agreement to compromise over increased presidential powers.
1997 Treaty with Russia signed, providing for closer links.

SEE ALSO Byelorussian; Lithuania; Union of Soviet Socialist Republics

control of N Lebanon. In the early 1980s the valley was penetrated by Shia Muslims who established an extremist Hezbollah stronghold with the support of Iranian Revolutionary Guards.

bel unit of sound measurement equal to ten ◊decibels. It is named after Scottish scientist Alexander Graham Bell.

Belarus or ***Byelorussia*** or ***Belorussia*** country in E central Europe, bounded S by Ukraine, E by Russia, W by Poland, and N by Latvia and Lithuania. *See country box above.*

Belau former name for the Republic of ◊Palau.

Belaúnde Terry Fernando 1913– . President of Peru 1963–1968 and 1980–1985. He championed land reform and the construction of roads to open up the Amazon valley. His second term in office was marked by rampant inflation, enormous foreign debts, terrorism, mass killings, and human-rights violations by the armed forces.

bel canto (Italian 'beautiful song') in music, an 18th-century Italian style of singing with emphasis on perfect technique and beautiful tone. The style reached its peak in the operas of Rossini, Donizetti, and Bellini.

Belém port and naval base in N Brazil; population (1991) 1,235,600 (metropolitan area 1,620,600). The chief trade centre of the Amazon basin, it is also known as Pará, the name of the state of which it is capital. It was founded about 1615 as Santa Maria de Belém do Grãs Pará.

Belfast city and industrial port in County Antrim and County Down, Northern Ireland, at the mouth of the river Lagan on Belfast Lough; the capital of Northern Ireland since 1920. It is the county town of County Antrim. The city was heavily damaged by civil disturbances from 1968 until the cessation of violence 1994.
population (1985) 300,000 (Protestants form the majority in E Belfast, Catholics in the W)
industries shipbuilding, engineering, electronics, aircraft, textiles, tobacco, linen, rope, and fertilizers
features 19th-century City Hall; Stormont (site of N Ireland parliament 1932 until suspended 1972)
history Belfast grew up around a castle built 1177 by John de Courcy. With the settlement of English and Scots, Belfast became a centre of Irish Protestantism in the 17th century. An influx of Huguenots after 1685 extended the linen industry, and the 1800 Act of Union with England resulted in the promotion of Belfast as an industrial centre. It was created a city 1888, with a lord mayor from 1892.

Belgae name given by Roman authors to people who lived in Gaul, north of the Seine and Marne rivers. They were defeated by Caesar 57 BC. Many of the Belgae settled in SE England during the 2nd century BC. Belgic remains in Britain include coins, minted in Gaul, pottery made on a wheel, and much of the finest Iron Age Celtic art.

Belgium country in W Europe, bounded N by the Netherlands, NW by the North Sea, S and W by France, E by Luxembourg and Germany. *See country box opposite.*

Belgrade (Serbo-Croatian ***Beograd***) capital of Yugoslavia and Serbia, and Danube river port linked with the port of Bar on the Adriatic Sea; population (1991) 1,168,500. Industries include light engineering, food processing, textiles, pharmaceuticals, and electrical goods.

Belgravia residential district of W central London, laid out in squares by Thomas Cubitt (1788–1855) 1825–30, and bounded to the N by Knightsbridge.

Belisarius c. 505–565. Roman general under Emperor ◊Justinian I. He won major victories over the Persians 530 and the Vandals 533 when he sacked Carthage. Later he invaded Sicily and fought a series of campaigns against the Goths in Italy.

Belize country in Central America, bounded N by Mexico, W and S by Guatemala, and E by the Caribbean Sea. *See country box on p. 114.*

Belize City chief port of Belize, and capital until 1970; population (1991) 44,000. After the city was destroyed by a hurricane 1961 it was decided to move the capital inland, to Belmopan.

bell musical instrument, made in many sizes, comprising a suspended resonating vessel swung by a handle or from a pivoted frame to make contact with a beater which hangs inside the bell. Church bells are among the most massive structures to be cast in bronze in one piece. Their shape, a flared bowl with a thickened rim, is engineered to produce a clangorous mixture of tones. Miniature handbells are tuned to resonate harmoniously. Orchestral tubular bells, of brass or steel, are tuned to a chromatic scale of pitches and are played by striking with a wooden

Bell **The Scottish-born US scientist and inventor Alexander Graham Bell opening the New York telephone exchange 1882. Bell invented the telephone 1876, and also worked on many other innovations such as a type of phonograph, a photophone, and a device for locating bullets in the body, which was used until the invention of X-rays.** ***Image Select (UK) Ltd***

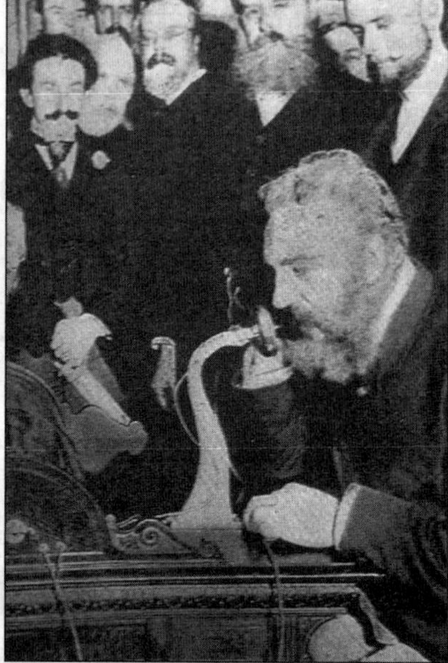

'Belgrade is blessed as few cities are with natural beauty, lying high on the confluence of two great rivers, Danube and Save.'

On BELGRADE
John Gunther
Inside Europe

BELGIUM
Kingdom of

national name French *Royaume de Belgique*, Flemish *Koninkrijk België*
area 30,510 sq km/11,784 sq mi
capital Brussels
major towns/cities Ghent, Liège, Charleroi, Bruges, Mons, Namur, Leuven
major ports Antwerp, Ostend, Zeebrugge
physical features fertile coastal plain in NW, central rolling hills rise eastwards, hills and forest in SE; Ardennes Forest; rivers Scheldt and Meuse
head of state King Albert from 1993
head of government Jean-Luc Dehaene from 1992
political system federal constitutional monarchy
administrative divisions ten provinces within three regions
political parties Flemish Christian Social Party (CVP), centre-left; French Social Christian Party (PSC), centre-left; Flemish Socialist Party (SP), left of centre; French Socialist Party (PS), left of centre; Flemish Liberal Party (PVV), moderate centrist; French Liberal Reform Party (PRL), moderate centrist; Flemish People's Party (VU), federalist; Flemish Vlaams Blok, right-wing; Flemish Green Party (Agalev); French Green Party (Ecolo)
armed forces 47,200 (1994)
conscription abolished 1995
defence spend (% GDP) 1.7 (1994)
education spend (% GNP) 5.2 (1992)
health spend (% GDP) 7.3 (1993)
death penalty retained for ordinary crimes, but considered abolitionist in practice; last execution 1950
population 10,113,000 (1995 est)
population growth rate 0.3% (1990–95); 0.1% (2000–05)
age distribution (% of total population) <15 17.8%, 15–65 66.4%, >65 15.8%
ethnic distribution mainly Flemings in the N, Walloons in S
population density (per sq km) 330 (1994)
urban population (% of total) 97 (1995)
labour force 41% of population: 3% agriculture, 28% industry, 70% services (1990)
unemployment 9.4% (1995)
child mortality rate (under 5, per 1,000 live births) 10 (1993)
life expectancy 72 (men), 79 (women)
education (compulsory years) 12
literacy rate 99%
languages in the N (Flanders) Flemish (a Dutch dialect, known as *Vlaams*) 55%; in the S (Wallonia) Walloon (a French dialect) 32%; bilingual 11%; German (E border) 0.6%. Dutch is official in the N, French in the S; Brussels is officially bilingual
religions Roman Catholic 75%, various Protestant denominations
TV sets (per 1,000 people) 453 (1992)
currency Belgian franc
GDP (US $) 269.4 billion (1995)
GDP per capita (PPP) (US $) 20,852 (1995)
growth rate 1.9% (1994/95)
average annual inflation 2.9% (1995)
trading partners Germany, the Netherlands, France, UK, USA
resources coal, coke, natural gas, iron
industries wrought and finished steel, cast iron, sugar refinery, glassware, chemicals and related products, beer, textiles, rubber and plastic products
exports food, livestock and livestock products, gem diamonds, iron and steel manufacturers, machinery and transport equipment, chemicals and related products. Principal markets: Germany, the Netherlands, France 53% (1993)
imports food and live animals, machinery and transport equipment, precious metals and stones, mineral fuels and lubricants, chemicals and related products. Principal source: Germany, the Netherlands, France 55.5% (1993)
arable land 39.6%
agricultural products wheat, barley, potatoes, beet (sugar and fodder), fruit, tobacco; livestock (chiefly pigs and cattle) and dairy products

HISTORY
57 BC Romans conquered the Belgae (the indigenous Celtic people), and formed province of Belgica.
3rd–4th Cs AD Region overrun by Franks and Saxons.
8th–9th Cs Part of Frankish Empire; peace and order fostered growth of Ghent, Bruges, and Brussels.
843 Division of Holy Roman Empire; became part of Lotharingia, but frequent repartitioning followed.
10th–11th Cs Seven feudal states emerged: Flanders, Hainaut, Namur, Brabant, Limburg, and Luxembourg, all nominally subject to French king or Holy Roman emperor, but in practice independent.
12th C Economy began to flourish: textiles in Bruges, Ghent, and Ypres; copper and tin in Dinant and Liège.
15th C One by one, states came under rule of dukes of Burgundy.
1477 Passed into Habsburg dominions through marriage of Mary of Burgundy to Maximilian, archduke of Austria.
1555 Division of Habsburg dominions; Low Countries allotted to Spain.
1648 Independence of Dutch Republic recognized; S retained by Spain.
1713 Treaty of Utrecht transferred Spanish Netherlands to Austrian rule.
1792–97 Austrian Netherlands invaded by revolutionary France and finally annexed.
1815 Congress of Vienna reunited N and S Netherlands as one kingdom under House of Orange.
1830 Largely French-speaking people in S rebelled against union with Holland and declared Belgian independence.
1831 Leopold of Saxe-Coburg-Gotha became first king of Belgium.
1839 Treaty of London recognized independence of Belgium and guaranteed its neutrality.
1847–70 Government dominated by Liberals; growth of heavy industry.
1870–1914 Catholic Party predominant.
1914–18 Invaded and occupied by Germany. Belgian forces under King Albert I fought in conjunction with Allies.
1919 Acquired Eupen-Malmédy region from Germany.
1940 Second invasion by Germany; King Leopold III ordered Belgian army to capitulate.
1944–45 Belgium liberated.
1948 Belgium formed Benelux customs union with Luxembourg and the Netherlands.
1949 Belgium was a founding member of North Atlantic Treaty Organization (NATO).
1951 Leopold III abdicated in favour of his son Baudouin.
1958 Belgium was a founding member of European Economic Community (EEC) which made Brussels its headquarters.
1967 NATO made Brussels its headquarters.
1971 Constitution amended to safeguard cultural rights of the Flemish (in Flanders in the N) and French-speaking communities (Walloons in the SE) in an effort to ease the linguistic dispute.
1974 Separate regional councils and ministerial committees established for Flemings and Walloons.
1980 Open violence over language divisions; regional assemblies for Flanders and Wallonia and a three-member executive for Brussels created.
1993 Federal system adopted, based on Flanders, Wallonia, and Brussels. King Baudouin died, succeeded by his brother, Albert.
1995 Dehaene-led coalition re-elected.

SEE ALSO Charlemagne; Flanders; Netherlands

mallet. A set of steeple bells played from a keyboard is called a carillon.

The world's largest bell is the 'Tsar Kolokol' or 'King of Bells', 220 tonnes, cast 1734, which stands on the ground of the Kremlin, Moscow, where it fell when being hung. The 'Peace Bell' at the United Nations headquarters, New York, was cast 1952 from coins presented by 64 countries.

Bell Alexander Graham 1847–1922. Scottish-born US scientist and inventor. He was the first person to transmit speech from one point to another by electrical means. This invention – the telephone – was made 1876. Later Bell experimented with a type of phonograph and, in aeronautics, invented the tricycle undercarriage. Bell also invented a photophone, which used selenium crystals to apply the telephone principle to transmitting words in a beam of light. He thus achieved the first wireless transmission of speech.

belladonna or ***deadly nightshade*** poisonous plant *Atropa belladonna*, found in Europe and Asia. The dried powdered leaves contain ◊alkaloids from which the drugs atropine and hyoscine are extracted. Belladonna extract acts medicinally as an anticholinergic (blocking the passage of certain nerve impulses), and is highly toxic in large doses.

Belladonna is of the nightshade family, Solanaceae. It grows to 5 ft/1.5 m, with dull green leaves 8 in/20 cm in length, and solitary greenish flowers that produce deadly black berries. *See illustration on following page.*

Bellerophon in Greek mythology, a victim of slander who was sent against the monstrous ◊chimera, which he killed with the help of his winged horse Pegasus. After further trials, he ended his life as a beggar. His story was dramatized by ◊Euripides.

bellflower general name for many plants of the family Campanulaceae, notably those of the genus *Campanula*. The Canterbury bell *C. medium* is the garden variety, originally from S Europe. The ◊harebell is also a *Campanula*. The clustered bellflower *C. glomerata* is characteristic of chalk grassland, and found in Europe and N Asia. Erect and downy, it has tight clusters of violet bell-shaped flowers in late summer.

Bellingshausen Fabian Gottlieb von 1778–1852. Russian Antarctic explorer, the first to sight and circumnavigate the Antarctic continent 1819–21, although he did not realize what it was.

Bellini Venetian family of artists, founders of the Venetian School in the 15th and early 16th centuries. ***Jacopo Bellini*** (c. 1400–1470/71) worked in Venice, Padua, Verona, and Ferrara. ***Gentile Bellini*** (c. 1429–1507) was probably the elder son of Jacopo and was trained by him. Although now overshadowed by his brother, he was no less famous in his own day. ***Giovanni Bellini*** (c. 1430–1516) contributed more than any other painter of his time to the creation of the great Venetian School.

Gentile's great ability in portraiture is shown by the *Man with a Pair of Dividers* about 1500 (National Gallery, London), though the superb *St Dominic* about 1515 (National Gallery), long attributed to him, is now assigned to Giovanni.

The numerous works attributed to Giovanni, and coming from the workshop where he employed many assistants, show wide variations of style. A sculptural firmness derived from his brother-in-law Andrea Mantegna, appears in the impressive early work *The Agony in the Garden* (National Gallery). Antonello da Messina, who visited Venice 1475–76, contributed no doubt to the richness of colour and the development of his oil technique (as seen in the portrait of *The Doge Leonardo Loredan*, about 1500, National Gallery). One of the great Renaissance compositions is the altarpiece of San Giobbe 1479 (Accademia, Venice), and in its soft fullness of modelling the *Madonna degli Alberetti* (Accademia) links Bellini with his pupils Giorgione and Titian.

Bellini Mario 1935– . Italian architect and industrial designer. He was one of the figures who helped establish Italy as a leading nation in

> *Mr Watson, come here; I want you.*
>
> **Alexander Graham Bell**
> First complete sentence spoken over the telephone March 1876

BELIZE
(formerly *British Honduras*)

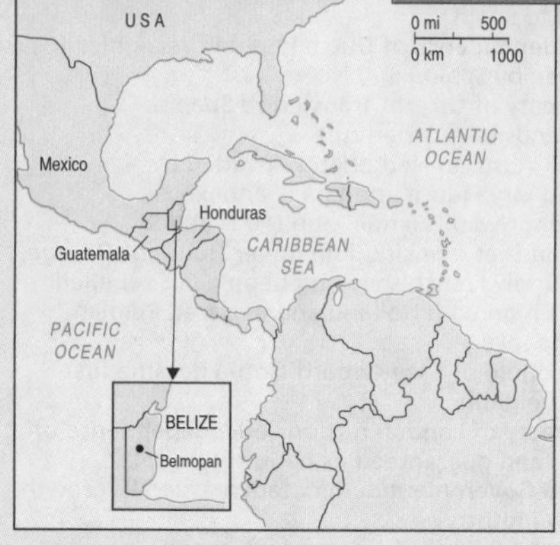

area 22,963 sq km/8,864 sq mi
capital Belmopan
major towns/cities Orange Walk, Corozal
major ports Belize City, Dangriga, Punta Gorda
physical features tropical swampy coastal plain, Maya Mountains in S; over 90% forested
head of state Elizabeth II from 1981, represented by governor general Dr Norbert Colville Young from 1993
head of government Manuel Esquivel from 1993
political system constitutional monarchy
administrative divisions six districts
political parties People's United Party (PUP), left of centre; United Democratic Party (UDP), moderate conservative
population 215,000 (1995 est)
population growth rate 2.6% (1990–95); 2.3% (2000–05)
ethnic distribution a wide mix of races, comprising Creoles, mestizos, Caribs, East Indians, and Europeans, including Spanish, British, and Canadian Mennonites
life expectancy 60 years
literacy rate 95%
languages English (official); Spanish (widely spoken), native Creole dialects
religions Roman Catholic 60%, Protestant 35%
currency Belize dollar
GDP (US $) 552 million (1994)
growth rate 1.6% (1994)
exports sugar, citrus fruits, rice, fish products, bananas, lobsters, timber, garments, molasses, honey

HISTORY
325–925 AD Part of the American Indian Maya civilization.
1600s Colonized by British bucanneers and log-cutters
1862 Formally declared a British colony, known as British Honduras.
1893 Mexico renounced its long-standing claim to the territory.
1954 Constitution adopted, providing for limited internal self-government. General election won by PUP led by George Price.
1964 Self-government achieved from the UK. Universal adult suffrage and a two-chamber legislature introduced.
1970 Capital moved from Belize City to new town of Belmopan.
1973 Name changed to Belize.
1975 British troops sent to defend the long-disputed frontier with Guatemala.
1980 United Nations called for full independence.
1981 Full independence achieved, with Price as prime minister.
1984 Price defeated in general election. Manuel Esquivel of the right-of-centre United Democratic Party (UDP) formed government. The UK reaffirmed its undertaking to defend the frontier.
1989 Price and PUP won general election.
1991 Diplomatic relations re-established with Guatemala, who finally recognized Belize's sovereignty.
1993 UDP defeated PUP in general election; Esquivel returned as prime minister. UK announced intention to withdraw troops following the resolution of the border dispute with Guatemala.

SEE ALSO Guatemala; Maya

industrial design from the 1960s. He is known for his elegant pieces of office machinery for the ◊Olivetti company (from 1962) and his sophisticated furniture designs for the Italian furniture-manufacturing company Cassina (from 1964).

Bellini Vincenzo 1801–1835. Italian composer of operas. He collaborated with the tenor Giovanni Battista Rubini (1794–1854) to develop a new simplicity of melodic expression in romantic evocations of classic themes, as in *La Sonnambula/The Sleepwalker* and *Norma*, both 1831. In *I Puritani/The Puritans* 1835, his last work, he discovered a new boldness and vigour of orchestral effect.

Belloc (Joseph) Hilaire (René Pierre) 1870–1953. French-born British writer. His verses for children include *The Bad Child's Book of Beasts* 1896 and *Cautionary Tales for Children* 1907. With G K ◊Chesterton, he advocated a return to the late medieval ◊guild system of commercial association in place of capitalism or socialism.

Bellow Saul 1915– . Canadian-born US novelist. From his first novel, *Dangling Man* 1944, Bellow has typically set his naturalistic narratives in Chicago and made his central character an anxious, Jewish-American intellectual. In *The Adventures of Augie March* 1953 and *Henderson the Rain King* 1959, he created confident and comic picaresque heroes, before *Herzog* 1964, which pitches a comic but distressed scholar into a world of darkening humanism. Later works, developing Bellow's depiction of an age of urban disorder and indifference, include the near-apocalyptic *Mr Sammler's Planet* 1970, *Humboldt's Gift* 1975, *The Dean's December* 1982, *More Die of Heartbreak* 1987, and the novella *A Theft* 1989. His finely styled works and skilled characterizations won him the Nobel Prize for Literature 1976.

bell ringing or ***campanology*** the art of ringing church bells individually or in sequence by rhythmically drawing on a rope fastened to a wheel rotating the bell, so that it falls back and strikes in time. Change ringing is an English art, dating from the 17th century, of ringing a patterned sequence of permutations of 5–12 church bells, using one player to each bell.

bells nautical term applied to half-hours of watch. A day is divided into seven watches, five of four hours each and two, called dogwatches, of two hours. Each half-hour of each watch is indicated by the striking of a bell, eight bells signalling the end of the watch.

Belmondo Jean-Paul 1933– . French film actor who became a star in Jean-Luc Godard's *A bout de souffle/Breathless* 1959. He is best known for his racy personality in French vehicles.

Belmopan capital of ◊Belize from 1970; population (1991) 3,558. It replaced Belize City as the administrative centre of the country.

Belorussia see ◊Belarus.

Belsen site of a Nazi ◊concentration camp in Lower Saxony, Germany. Established 1943 it was not officially an extermination camp, but an outbreak of typhus 1945 caused thousands of deaths. When captured by British troops 13 April 1945 several thousand bodies lay around the camp and the remaining inmates were barely alive. It was the first camp to be taken by the Allies.

Belshazzar in the Old Testament, the last king of Babylon, son of Nebuchadnezzar. During a feast (known as 'Belshazzar's Feast') he saw a message, interpreted by ◊Daniel as prophesying the fall of Babylon and death of Belshazzar.

Ben Ali Zine el Abidine 1936– . Tunisian politician, president from 1987. He was made minister of the interior and then prime minister under the ageing president for life, Habib ◊Bourguiba, whom he deposed 1987. He ended the personality cult established by Bourguiba and moved towards a pluralist political system. He was re-elected 1994, with 99% of the popular vote.

His hardline stance against Islamic militancy provoked criticism from human-rights organizations.

Benares alternative transliteration of ◊Varanasi, a holy Hindu city in Uttar Pradesh, India.

Ben Bella Mohammed Ahmed 1916– . Algerian politician. He was leader of the National Liberation Front (FLN) from 1952, the first prime minister of independent Algeria 1962–63, and its first president 1963–65. In 1965 Ben Bella was overthrown by Col Houari ◊Boumédienne and detained until 1979. In 1985 he founded a new party, Mouvement pour la Démocratie en Algérie, and returned to Algeria 1990 after nine years in exile.

belladonna Although the belladonna (deadly nightshade) is of the same family as the potato and the tomato (Solanaceae), its black berries are extremely poisonous. As tiny amounts of the poison cause the pupils of the eyes to dilate, it was once used as a cosmetic, hence the name belladonna – meaning beautiful woman in Italian. *Premaphotos Wildlife*

benchmark in computing, a measure of the performance of a piece of equipment or software, usually consisting of a standard program or suite of programs. Benchmarks can indicate whether a computer is powerful enough to perform a particular task, and so enable machines to be compared.

bends or *compressed-air sickness* or *caisson disease* popular name for a syndrome seen in deep-sea divers, arising from too rapid a release of nitrogen from solution in their blood. If a diver surfaces too quickly, nitrogen that had dissolved in the blood under increasing water pressure is suddenly released, forming bubbles in the bloodstream and causing pain (the 'bends') and paralysis. Immediate treatment is gradual decompression in a decompression chamber, whilst breathing pure oxygen.

Benedict 15 popes, including:

Benedict XV (Giacomo della Chiesa) 1854–1922. Pope from 1914. During World War I he endeavoured to bring about a peace settlement, and it was during his papacy that British, French, and Dutch official relations were renewed with the Vatican.

Benedictine order religious order of monks and nuns in the Roman Catholic Church, founded by St ◊Benedict at Subiaco, Italy, in the 6th century. It had a strong influence on medieval learning and reached the height of its prosperity early in the 14th century.

St Augustine brought the order to England. A number of Oxford and Cambridge colleges have a Benedictine origin. At the Reformation there were nearly 300 Benedictine monasteries and nunneries in England, all of which were suppressed. The English novice house survived in France, and in the 19th century monks expelled from France moved to England and built abbeys at Downside, Ampleforth, and Woolhampton. The monks from Pierre-qui-vive, who went to England 1882, rebuilt Buckfast Abbey in Devon on the ruins of a Cistercian monastery.

Benedict, St c. 480–c. 547. Founder of Christian monasticism in the West and of the ◊Benedictine order. He founded the monastery of Monte Cassino and others in Italy. His feast day is 11 July.

benefice in the early Middle Ages, a donation of land or money to the Christian church as an act of devotion; from the 12th century, the term came to mean the income enjoyed by clergy.

Benelux (acronym for ***Belgium, the Netherlands, and Luxembourg***) customs union agreed by Belgium, the Netherlands, and Luxembourg 1948, fully effective 1960. It was the precursor of the European Community.

Beneš Edvard 1884–1948. Czechoslovak politician. He worked with Tomáš ◊Masaryk towards Czechoslovak nationalism from 1918 and was foreign minister and representative at the League of Nations. He was president of the republic from 1935 until forced to resign by the Germans; he headed a government in exile in London during World War II. He returned home as president 1945 but resigned again after the Communist coup 1948.

Benét Stephen Vincent 1898–1943. US poet, novelist, and short-story writer. He won a Pulitzer prize 1929 for his narrative poem of the Civil War, *John Brown's Body* 1928. One of his short stories, 'The Devil and Daniel Webster', became a classic and was made into a play, an opera, and a film (*All That Money Can Buy*). He published more than 17 volumes of verse and prose.

Bengal former province of British India, divided 1947 into ◊West Bengal, a state of India, and East Bengal, from 1972 ◊Bangladesh. A famine in 1943, caused by a slump in demand for jute and a bad harvest, resulted in over 3 million deaths.

Bengal, Bay of part of the Indian Ocean lying between the east coast of India and the west coast of Myanmar and the Malay Peninsula. The Irrawaddy, Ganges, and Brahmaputra rivers flow into the bay. The principal islands are to be found in the Andaman and Nicobar groups.

Bengali people of Bengali culture from Bangladesh and India (W Bengal, Tripura). There are 80–150 million speakers of Bengali, an Indo-Iranian language belonging to the Indo-European family. It is the official language of Bangladesh and of the state of Bengal and is also used by emigrant Bangladeshi and Bengali communities in such countries as the UK and the USA. Bengalis in Bangladesh are predominantly Muslim, whereas those in India are mainly Hindu.

Benghazi or ***Banghazi*** historic city and industrial port in N Libya on the Gulf of Sirte; population (1984) 485,000. It was controlled by Turkey between the 16th century and 1911, and by Italy 1911–42; it was a major naval supply base during World War II. With Tripoli, it was co-capital of Libya 1951–72.

Ben-Gurion David. Adopted name of David Gruen 1886–1973. Israeli statesman and socialist politician. He was one of the founders of the state of Israel, the country's first prime minister 1948–53, and again 1955–63. He was a leader of the Zionist movement, and as defence minister he presided over the development of Israel's armed forces into one of the strongest armies in the Middle East. *See illustration on following page.*

Benin country in W Africa, bounded E by Nigeria, N by Niger and Burkina Faso, W by Togo, and S by the Gulf of Guinea. *See country box below.*

Benin former African kingdom 1200–1897, now a province of Nigeria. It reached the height of its power in the 14th–17th centuries when it ruled the area between the Niger Delta and Lagos.

Benin traded in spices, ivory, palm oil, and slaves until its decline and eventual incorporation into Nigeria. The oba (ruler) of Benin continues to rule his people as a divine monarch. The present oba is considered an enlightened leader and one who is helping his people to become part of modern Nigeria.

Artworks honouring the Oba of Benin were looted by a British military expedition 1897. They included cast bronzes and carved ivories and have since found their way into museums and into the hands of collectors worldwide. See ◊African art.

Benjedid Chadli 1929– . Algerian socialist politician, president 1979–92. An army colonel, he supported Boumédienne in the overthrow of Ben Bella 1965, and succeeded Boumédienne 1979, pursuing more moderate policies. Benjedid resigned Jan 1992 following a victory for Islamic fundamentalists in the first round of assembly elections.

Benn Tony (Anthony Neil Wedgwood) 1925– . British Labour politician, formerly the leading figure on the party's left wing. He was minister of technology 1966–70 and secretary of state for industry 1974–75, but his campaign against entry to the European Community (EC; now the European

'When I am dead, I hope it may be said: / 'His sins were scarlet, but his books were read.''

HILAIRE BELLOC
'On His Books'

'Death is the dark backing a mirror needs if we are to see anything.'

SAUL BELLOW
Quoted in the *Observer* Dec 1983

BENIN

People's Republic of (formerly known as *Dahomey* 1904–75)

national name *République Populaire du Bénin*
area 112,622 sq km/43,472 sq mi
capital Porto Novo (official), Cotonou (de facto)
major towns/cities Abomey, Natitingou, Parakou, Kandi, Ouidah
major ports Cotonou
physical features flat to undulating terrain; hot and humid in S; semiarid in N; coastal lagoons with fishing villages on stilts; Niger River in NE
head of state and government Mathieu Kerekou from 1996
political system socialist pluralist republic
administrative divisions six provinces, subdivided into 78 districts
political parties Union for the Triumph of Democratic Renewal (UTDR); National Party for Democracy and Development (PNDD); Party for Democratic Renewal (PRD); Social Democratic Party (PSD); National Union for Solidarity and Progress (UNSP); National Democratic Rally (RND). The general orientation of most parties is left of centre
population 5,409,000 (1995 est)
population growth rate 3.1% (1990–95); 2.8% (2000–05)
ethnic distribution 98% indigenous African, distributed among 42 ethnic groups, the largest being the Fon, Adja, Yoruba, and Braiba; small European (mainly French) community
life expectancy 46 (males), 50 (females)
literacy rate men 32%, women 16%
languages French (official); Fon 47% and Yoruba 9% in S; six major tribal languages in N
religions animist 60%, Muslim, Roman Catholic
currency franc CFA
GDP (US $) 1.52 billion (1994)
growth rate 4.8% (1994)
exports cocoa, peanuts, cotton, palm oil, petroleum, cement, sea products, palm kernel cake, cotton cake

HISTORY

12th–13th Cs Settled by Ewe-speaking people, called the Aja, who mixed with local peoples to gradually form the Fon ethnic group.
16th C Aja kingdom, called Great Ardha, at its peak.
early 17th C Kingdom of Dahomey established in S by Fon peoples, who defeated the neighbouring Dan; following contact with European traders, the kingdom became became an intermediary in the slave trade, which was particularly active along the Bight (Bay) of Benin, between Ghana and Nigeria during the 16th–19th centuries.
1800–50 King Dezo of Dahomey raised regiments of female soldiers to attack the Yoruba ('land of the big cities') kingdom of E Benin and SW Nigeria to obtain slaves; palm oil trade developed.
1857 French base established at Grand-Popo.
1892–94 War between the French and Dahomey, after which the victorious French established a protectorate.
1899 Incorporated in federation of French West Africa as Dahomey.
1914 French troops from Dahomey participated in conquest of German-ruled Togoland to W, during World War I.
1940–44 Along with the rest of French West Africa, supported the 'Free French' anti-Nazi resistance cause during World War II.
1960 Independence achieved from France.
1960–72 Acute political instability, with frequent switches from civilian to military rule, and regional ethnic disputes.
1972 Military regime established by Major Mathieu Kerekou.
1974 Kerekou announced that the country would follow a path of 'scientific socialism'.
1975 Name of country changed from Dahomey to Benin.
1977 Return to civilian rule under a new constitution, but with Kerekou as president.
1989 Army deployed against antigovernment strikers and protesters, inspired by E European revolutions; Marxist-Leninism dropped as official ideology and market-centred economic reform programme adopted.
1990 Referendum backed establishment of multiparty politics.
1991 In multiparty elections, President Kerekou was replaced by the leader of the new Benin Renaissance Party (PRB), Nicéphore Soglo, who formed a ten-party coalition government.
1996 Kerekou defeated Soglo in presidential election run-off despite opposition claims of fraud.

SEE ALSO Fon; Free French

Ben-Gurion David Ben-Gurion, the first prime minister of Israel. Emigrating to Palestine 1906, he was active against the Turks in World War I. He became leader of the Mapai (Labour) Party between the wars and as prime minister 1948–53 and 1955–63 was one of the principal architects of the modern state of Israel. *Topham*

Union) led to his transfer to the Department of Energy 1975–79.

Born the son of the 1st Viscount Stansgate, Benn was member of Parliament for Bristol SE 1950–60, when he succeeded to his father's title. Despite refusing to accept the title and being re-elected in Bristol 1961, he was debarred from sitting in the House of Commons. His campaign to enable those inheriting titles to disclaim them led to the passing of the Peerage Act 1963.

He was again MP for Bristol SE 1963–83; he became a member of the cabinet 1966 as minister of technology, and secretary of state for industry 1974. At the time of the 1975 referendum he campaigned against the renegotiated terms of British membership of the EC, and in June 1975 was appointed secretary of state for energy.

His diaries *Out of the Wilderness* 1987, *Office Without Power* 1988, *Against the Tide* 1989, and *Conflicts of Interest* 1990 cover in enormous detail the events of the 1970s and 1980s .

‘We started off trying to set up a small anarchist community, but people wouldn't obey the rules.’

ALAN BENNETT
Getting On

Bennett (Enoch) Arnold 1867–1931. English novelist. His main books are set in the industrial Five Towns of the Midlands (Tunstall, Burslem, Hanley, Stoke, and Longton) and are concerned with the manner in which the environment dictates the pattern of his characters' lives. They include *Anna of the Five Towns* 1902, *The Old Wives' Tale* 1908, and the trilogy *Clayhanger*, *Hilda Lessways*, and *These Twain* 1910–15.

Bennett Alan 1934– . English dramatist, screenwriter, and actor. His works (often set in his native north of England) treat subjects such as class, senility, illness, and death with macabre comedy. They include *Talking Heads* 1988, a series of monologues for television, and the play *The Madness of George III* 1991, made into the film *The Madness of King George* 1995.

Bennett Richard Rodney 1936– . English composer of jazz, film music, symphonies, and operas. His film scores for *Far from the Madding Crowd* 1967, *Nicholas and Alexandra* 1971, and *Murder on the Orient Express* 1974 all received Oscar nominations. His operas include *The Mines of Sulphur* 1963 and *Victory* 1970.

Ben Nevis highest mountain in the British Isles (1,343 m/4,406 ft), in the Grampian Mountains, Scotland.

Benny Jack. Stage name of Benjamin Kubelsky 1894–1974. US comedian notable for his perfect timing and lugubrious manner. Over the years, Benny appeared on the stage, in films, and on radio and television. His radio programme, *The Jack Benny Show* from 1932, made him a national institution. Featuring his wife Mary Livingston, singer Dennis Day, announcer Don Wilson, and valet Eddie ‘Rochester’ Anderson, it was produced for television in the 1950s. His film appearances, mostly in the 1930s and 1940s, included *To Be or Not to Be* 1942. He also played in *Charley's Aunt* 1941, *It's In the Bag* 1945, and *A Guide for the Married Man* 1967.

‘All punishment is mischief: all punishment in itself is evil.’

JEREMY BENTHAM
Principles of Morals and Legislation

Bentham Jeremy 1748–1832. English philosopher, legal and social reformer, and founder of ◊utilitarianism. The essence of his moral philosophy is found in the pronouncement of his *Principles of Morals and Legislation* (written 1780, published 1789): that the object of all legislation should be ‘the greatest happiness for the greatest number’.

Bentham declared that the ‘utility’ of any law is to be measured by the extent to which it promotes the pleasure, good, and happiness of the people concerned. In 1776 he published *Fragments on Government*. He made suggestions for the reform of the poor law 1798, which formed the basis of the reforms enacted 1834, and in his *Catechism of Parliamentary Reform* 1817 he proposed annual elections, the secret ballot, and universal male suffrage. He was also a pioneer of prison reform.

In economics he was an apostle of *laissez-faire*, and in his *Defence of Usury* 1787 and *Manual of Political Economy* 1798 he contended that his principle of ‘utility’ was best served by allowing every man (sic) to pursue his own interests unhindered by restrictive legislation. He was made a citizen of the French Republic 1792.

Bentinck Lord William Henry Cavendish 1774–1839. British colonial administrator, first governor general of India 1828–35. He acted against the ancient Indian rituals of thuggee and suttee, and established English as the medium of instruction. He was the son of the 3rd Duke of Portland.

Bentley Edmund Clerihew 1875–1956. English writer. He invented the four-line humorous verse form known as the ◊clerihew, first collected in *Biography for Beginners* 1905 and then in *More Biography* 1929. He was also the author of the classic detective story *Trent's Last Case* 1913, introducing a new naturalistic style that replaced Sherlock Holmesian romanticism.

Benz Karl Friedrich 1844–1929. German automobile engineer. He produced the world's first petrol-driven motor vehicle. He built his first model engine 1878 and the petrol-driven car 1885.

Benz made his first four-wheeled prototype 1891 and by 1895, he was building a range of four-wheeled vehicles that were light, strong, inexpensive, and simple to operate. These vehicles ran at speeds of about 24 kph/15 mph. In 1926, the thriving company merged with the German firm of Daimler to form Daimler-Benz.

benzaldehyde C_6H_5CHO colourless liquid with the characteristic odour of almonds. It is used as a solvent and in the making of perfumes and dyes. It occurs in certain leaves, such as the cherry, laurel, and peach, and in a combined form in certain nuts and kernels. It can be extracted from such natural sources, but is usually made from ◊toluene.

Benzedrine trade name for ◊amphetamine, a stimulant drug.

benzene C_6H_6 clear liquid hydrocarbon of characteristic odour, occurring in coal tar. It is used as a solvent and in the synthesis of many chemicals.

The benzene molecule consists of a ring of six carbon atoms, all of which are in a single plane, and it is one of the simplest ◊cyclic compounds. Benzene is the simplest of a class of compounds collectively known as aromatic compounds. Some are considered carcinogenic (cancer-inducing).

In the UK levels of airborne benzene in urban areas were declared a health risk 1994. Benzene pollution comes from combustion of petrol (80%), diesel exhausts, and evaporation from petrol pumps. One part per billion was recommended as a safe level. According to the World Health Organization, there is no safe level.

benzene The molecule of benzene consists of six carbon atoms arranged in a ring, with six hydrogen atoms attached. The benzene ring structure is found in many naturally occurring organic compounds.

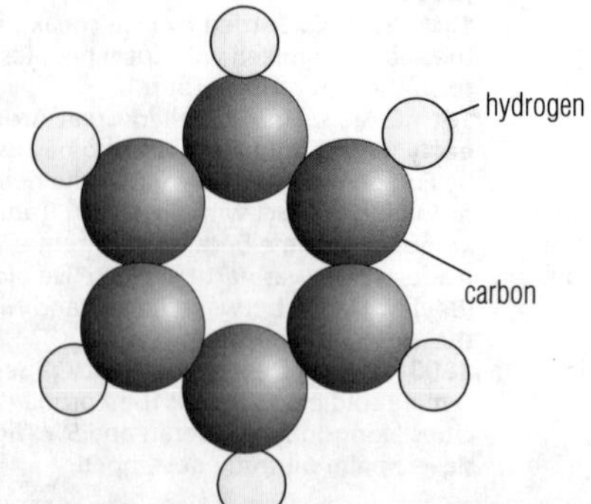

benzodiazepine any of a group of mood-altering drugs (tranquillizers), for example Librium and Valium. They are addictive and interfere with the process by which information is transmitted between brain cells, and various side effects arise from continued use. They were originally developed as muscle relaxants, and then excessively prescribed in the West as anxiety-relieving drugs.

Today the benzodiazepines are recommended only for short-term use in alleviating severe anxiety or insomnia.

benzoic acid C_6H_5COOH white crystalline solid, sparingly soluble in water, that is used as a preservative for certain foods and as an antiseptic. It is obtained chemically by the direct oxidation of benzaldehyde and occurs in certain natural resins, some essential oils, and as hippuric acid.

benzoin resin obtained by making incisions in the bark of *Styrax benzoin*, a tree native to the East Indies. Benzoin is used in the preparation of cosmetics, perfumes, and incense.

benzpyrene one of a number of organic compounds associated with a particular polycyclic ring structure. Benzpyrenes are present in coal tar at low levels and are considered carcinogenic (cancer-inducing). Traces of benzpyrenes are present in wood smoke, and this has given rise to some concern about the safety of naturally smoked foods.

Beowulf Anglo-Saxon poem of over 3,000 lines (composed c. 700), the only complete surviving example of Germanic folk epic. It exists in a single manuscript copied in England about 1000, housed in the Cottonian collection of the British Museum, London.

The hero Beowulf delivers the Danish king Hrothgar from the water demon Grendel and its monstrous mother, and, returning home, succeeds his cousin Heardred as king of the Geats. After 50 years of prosperity, he is killed slaying a dragon.

Berber non-Semitic people of North Africa who since prehistoric times have inhabited Barbary – the Mediterranean coastlands from Egypt to the Atlantic. Their language, present-day Berber (a member of the Hamito-Semitic or Afro-Asiatic language family), is written in both Arabic and Berber characters and is spoken by about 10 million people: about one-third of Algerians and nearly two-thirds of Moroccans. Berbers are mainly agricultural, but some are still nomadic.

The Berber, who include the ◊Tuareg, the ◊Kabyles, and the Shawiya, were progressively Islamized from the time of the Arab invasion in the 7th century. They are mainly mixed pastoralists and agriculturalists, some groups being nomadic pastoralists. Although some desert groups have a hierarchical social structure, most are remarkably egalitarian. Today many have moved to the towns to become traders and labourers.

Bérégovoy Pierre Eugène 1925–1993. French socialist politician, prime minister 1992–93. A close ally of François ◊Mitterrand, he was named Chief of Staff 1981 after managing the successful presidential campaign. He was social affairs minister 1982–84 and finance minister 1984–86 and 1988–92. He resigned as premier following the Socialists' defeat in the March 1993 general election, and shortly afterwards committed suicide.

Berengaria of Navarre 1165–c. 1230. Queen of England. The only English queen never to set foot in England, she was the daughter of King Sancho VI of Navarre. She married Richard I of England in Cyprus 1191, and accompanied him on his crusade to the Holy Land.

Berg Alban 1885–1935. Austrian composer. He studied under Arnold Schoenberg and developed a personal 12-tone idiom of great emotional and stylistic versatility. His relatively small output includes two operas: *Wozzeck* 1920, a grim story of working-class life, and the unfinished *Lulu* 1929–35; and chamber music incorporating coded references to friends and family. His music is emotionally expressive, and sometimes anguished, but it can also be lyrical, as in the Violin Concerto 1935.

Berg Paul 1926– . US molecular biologist. In 1972, using gene-splicing techniques developed by others, Berg spliced and combined into a single hybrid the ◊DNA from an animal tumour virus (SV40) and the DNA from a bacterial virus. For his work on recombinant DNA, he shared the 1980 Nobel Prize for Chemistry.

Bergamo city in Lombardy, Italy, 48 km/30 mi NE of Milan; population (1992) 115,100. Industries include silk and metal. The Academia Carrara holds a fine collection of paintings.

bergamot small, evergreen tree *Citrus bergamia* of the rue family Rutaceae. From the rind of its fruit a fragrant orange-scented essence used as a perfume is obtained.

Bergen industrial port (shipbuilding, engineering, fishing) in SW Norway; population (1994) 195,000. Founded 1070, Bergen was a member of the ◊Hanseatic League.

Bergman (Ernst) Ingmar 1918– . Swedish stage producer (from the 1930s) and film director (from the 1940s). He is regarded by many as one of the great masters of modern cinema. His work deals with complex moral, psychological, and metaphysical problems and is often strongly pessimistic. His films include *Wild Strawberries* 1957, *The Seventh Seal* 1957, *Persona* 1966, *Autumn Sonata* 1978 and *Fanny and Alexander* 1982.

Bergman Ingrid 1915–1982. Swedish-born actress. She went to the USA 1939 to appear in David Selznick's *Intermezzo* 1939 and later appeared in *Casablanca* 1942, *For Whom the Bell Tolls* 1943, and *Gaslight* 1944, for which she won an Academy Award. She projected a combination of radiance, refined beauty, and fortitude.

By leaving her husband to have a child with director Roberto Rossellini, she broke an unofficial moral code of Hollywood star behaviour and was ostracized for many years. During her 'exile', she made films in Europe such as *Stromboli* 1949 (directed by Rossellini). Returning to the USA, she made such films as *Anastasia* 1956, and *Murder on the Orient Express* 1974.

Bergson Henri Louis 1859–1941. French philosopher. He believed that time, change, and development were the essence of reality. He thought that time was a continuous process in which one period merged imperceptibly into the next. In *Creative Evolution* 1907 he attempted to prove that all evolution and progress are due to the working of the *élan vital*, or life force. Nobel Prize for Literature 1928.

Beria Lavrenti Pavlovich 1899–1953. Soviet politician. In 1938 he became minister of the interior and head of the Soviet police force that imprisoned, liquidated, and transported millions of Soviet citizens. On Stalin's death 1953, he attempted to seize power but was foiled and shot after a secret trial. Apologists for Stalin have blamed Beria for the atrocities committed by Soviet police during Stalin's dictatorship.

beriberi nutritional disorder occurring mostly in the tropics and resulting from a deficiency of vitamin B_1 (◊thiamine). The disease takes two forms: in one ◊oedema (waterlogging of the tissues) occurs; in the other there is severe emaciation. There is nerve degeneration in both forms and many victims succumb to heart failure.

Bering Vitus Jonassen 1681–1741. Danish explorer. He was the first European to sight Alaska. He died on Bering Island in the Bering Sea, both named after him, as is the Bering Strait, which separates Asia (Russia) from North America (Alaska).

Beringia or ***Bering Land Bridge*** former land bridge 1,600 km/1,000 mi wide between Asia and North America; it existed during the ice ages that occurred before 35,000 BC and during the period 24,000–9000 BC. It is now covered by the Bering Strait and Chukchi Sea.

Bering Sea section of the N Pacific between Alaska and Siberia, from the Aleutian Islands north to the Bering Strait.

Bering Strait strait between Alaska and Siberia, linking the N Pacific and Arctic oceans.

Berio Luciano 1925– . Italian composer. His work combines serial techniques with commedia dell'arte and antiphonal practices, as in *Alleluiah II* 1958 for five instrumental groups. His prolific output includes nine *Sequenzas/Sequences* 1957–75 for various solo instruments or voice, *Sinfonia* 1969 for voices and orchestra, *Formazioni/Formations* 1987 for orchestra, and the opera *Un re in ascolto/A King Listens* 1984.

Berisha Sali 1944– . Albanian political leader, president from 1992. He cofounded the Democratic Party (DP), the country's first opposition party, which came to power in the 1992 general election. Berisha became Albania's first noncommunist president since the end of World War II. His presidency oversaw market-centred economic reform and entry into the Council of Europe. Following anti-government riots in early 1997, due to the collapse of bogus investment schemes in which almost half the population participated, Berisha declared a state of emergency; by March, the country was in a state of anarchy.

Berkeley city on San Francisco Bay in California; population (1992) 101,100. It is the site of an acclaimed branch of the University of California, noted for its nuclear research at the Lawrence Berkeley Laboratory.

Berkeley Busby. Stage name of William Berkeley Enos 1895–1976. US choreographer and film director. He used ingenious and extravagant sets and teams of female dancers to create song and dance sequences that formed large-scale kaleidoscopic patterns when filmed from above, as in *Gold Diggers of 1933* and *Footlight Parade* 1933.

Berkeley George 1685–1753. Irish philosopher and cleric who believed that nothing exists apart from perception, and that the all-seeing mind of God makes possible the continued apparent existence of things. For Berkeley, everyday objects are collections of ideas or sensations, hence the dictum *esse est percipi* ('to exist is to be perceived'). He became bishop of Cloyne 1734.

Berkeley Lennox Randal Francis 1903–1989. English composer. His works for the voice include *The Hill of the Graces* 1975, verses from Spenser's *Faerie Queene* set for eight-part unaccompanied chorus; and his operas *Nelson* 1953 and *Ruth* 1956.

berkelium synthesized, radioactive, metallic element of the actinide series, symbol Bk, atomic number 97, relative atomic mass 247. It was first produced 1949 by Glenn Seaborg and his team, at the University of California at Berkeley, USA, after which it is named.

Berkoff Steven 1937– . English dramatist and actor. His abrasive and satirical plays include *East* 1975, *Greek* 1979, and *West* 1983. Berkoff's production of Oscar Wilde's *Salome* was staged 1991.

Bergman Swedish film actress Ingrid Bergman. She established herself as a Hollywood star with films such as *Casablanca* 1942, starring with Humphrey Bogart, and the two Hitchcock films *Spellbound* 1945 and *Notorious* 1946. In 1948 her romance with Italian director Roberto Rossellini took her to Italy but she returned to Hollywood 1956. Her last film was *Autumn Sonata* 1978, directed by Ingmar Bergman (no relation). *British Film Institute*

His *Collected Plays* (2 vols) were published 1994.

He formed the London Theatre Group 1968 as a vehicle for his own productions, which have included his adaptations of Kafka's *Metamorphosis* 1969 and *The Trial* 1970, and Poe's *The Fall of the House of Usher* 1974.

Berkshire or ***Royal Berkshire*** county of S central England

area 1,260 sq km/486 sq mi (*see United Kingdom map*)

towns and cities Reading (administrative headquarters), Eton, Slough, Maidenhead, Ascot, Bracknell, Newbury, Windsor, Wokingham

features rivers Thames and Kennet; Inkpen Beacon, 297 m/975 ft; Bagshot Heath; Ridgeway Path, walkers' path (partly prehistoric) running from Wiltshire across the Berkshire Downs into Hertfordshire; Windsor Forest and Windsor Castle; Eton College; Royal Military Academy at Sandhurst; atomic-weapons research establishment at Aldermaston; the former main UK base for US cruise missiles at Greenham Common, Newbury

industries general agricultural and horticultural goods, electronics, plastics, pharmaceuticals, engineering, paints, biscuits, pigs, poultry, barley, dairy products

population (1991) 734,200

famous people William Laud, Jethro Tull, Stanley Spencer.

Berlin industrial city (machine tools, electrical goods, paper, printing) and capital of the Federal Republic of Germany; population (1993) 3,471,500. After the division of Germany 1949, East Berlin became the capital of East Germany and Bonn was made the provisional capital of West Germany. The Berlin Wall divided the city from 1961 until it was dismantled 1989. Following reunification East and West Berlin were once more

The Balkans after the Congress of Berlin 1878–1913

'Sir Christopher Wren / Said, 'I am going to dine with some men. / If anybody calls / Say I am designing St Paul's.'

EDMUND CLERIHEW BENTLEY
Biography for Beginners, 'Sir Christopher Wren'

'No art passes our conscience in the way film does, and goes directly to our feelings, deep down into the dark rooms of our souls.'

INGMAR BERGMAN
Quoted in *Sight and Sound*

Berlin US songwriter Irving Berlin. Beginning with ragtime at the turn of the century, he wrote successful songs over a period of nearly 50 years, many of them becoming familiar worldwide. Bing Crosby's version of Irving Berlin's 'White Christmas' is the world's biggest selling record, and 'God Bless America' is considered as the unofficial US anthem. *Topham*

reunited as the 16th *Land* (state) of the Federal Republic.

features Unter den Linden, the tree-lined avenue once the whole city's focal point, has been restored in what was formerly East Berlin. The fashionable Kurfürstendamm and the residential Hansa quarter (1957) form part of what was once West Berlin. Prominent buildings include the Reichstag (parliament building); Schloss Bellevue (Berlin residence of the president); Schloss Charlottenburg (housing several museums); Congress Hall; restored 18th-century State Opera; the National Gallery (1968), designed by Mies van der Rohe; and Dahlem picture gallery.

The Reichstag is to be rebuilt under the direction of Sir Norman Foster. In 1995 the *Wrapping of the Reichstag* by the artist Christo Javacheff attracted 5 million tourists. Friedrichstrasse, the Alexanderplatz, and No Man's Land are being redeveloped. The Tiergarten is a fine park. The environs of Berlin include the Grünewald forest and the Wannsee and Havel lakes. In the Grünewald is the Trümmerbery, an artificial hill 130 m/427 ft high, formed out of 18 million cubic metres/70 million cubic feet of war debris, and now used as an artificial ski slope.

The city contains several research institutes including the Hahn-Meitner Institute for Nuclear Research, the Max Planck Institute, and the Research Institute for Marine Engineering and Shipbuilding. It is also the home of the world-famous Berlin Philharmonic Orchestra.

history First mentioned about 1230, the city grew out of a fishing village, joined the Hanseatic League in the 15th century, became the permanent seat of the Hohenzollerns, and was capital of the Brandenburg electorate 1486–1701, of the kingdom of Prussia 1701–1871, and of united Germany 1871–1945. From the middle of the 18th century it developed into a commercial and cultural centre. After the Napoleonic Wars, Friedrich Wilhelm III was responsible for the squares, avenues, and Neo-Classical buildings, many designed by Karl Friedrich Schinkel, including the Altes Museum and the Schauspielhaus.

In World War II air raids and conquest by the Soviet army 23 April–2 May 1945, destroyed much of the city. After the war, Berlin was divided into four sectors – British, US, French, and Soviet – and until 1948 was under quadripartite government by the Allies. Following the ◊Berlin blockade the city was divided, with the USSR maintaining a separate municipal government in its sector. The other three sectors (West Berlin) were made a *Land* of the Federal Republic May 1949 and Bonn became the provisional capital; in Oct 1949 East Berlin was proclaimed capital of East Germany. On 13th August 1961 the Soviet zone was sealed off by the Russians, and the ◊Berlin Wall was built along the zonal boundary. Access to East Berlin was severely restricted, although restrictions were lifted occasionally, and a pass system was introduced 1964.

In June 1991 the Bundestag (the lower chamber of government) voted to restore Berlin as the capital of a unified Germany. The move of the Bundestag offices went ahead despite a campaign by some politicians to delay it until 2010 or stop it altogether.

Berlin blockade Berliners watch Allied planes arriving with supplies during the Soviet blockade of 1948–49. After World War II, Berlin was an isolated enclave in Soviet-held territory and the Communist authorities hoped that a ban on land traffic would persuade the Western powers to leave. However, supplies were flown in, and on 12 May 1949 the blockade was lifted. *Corbis*

Berlin Irving. Adopted name of Israel Baline 1888–1989. Russian-born US songwriter. His songs include hits such as 'Alexander's Ragtime Band' 1911, 'Always' 1925, 'God Bless America' 1917 (published 1939), and 'White Christmas' 1942, and the musicals *Top Hat* 1935, *Annie Get Your Gun* 1946, and *Call Me Madam* 1950. He also provided songs for films like *Blue Skies* 1946 and *Easter Parade* 1948.

Berlin grew up in New York and had his first song published 1907. He began providing songs for vaudeville and revues and went on to own a theatre, the Music Box, where he appeared in his own revues 1921 and 1923. Generally writing both lyrics and music, he was instrumental in the development of the popular song, taking it from jazz and ragtime to swing and romantic ballads.

Berlin, Battle of final battle of the European phase of World War II, 16 April–2 May 1945; Soviet forces captured Berlin, the capital of Germany and seat of government and site of most German military and administrative headquarters. Hitler committed suicide 30 April as the Soviets closed in and General Karl Weidling surrendered the city 2 May. Soviet casualties came to about 100,000 dead; German casualties are unknown but some 136,000 were taken prisoner and it is believed over 100,000 civilians died in the course of the fighting.

Berlin blockade the closing of entry to Berlin from the west by Soviet forces June 1948–May 1949. It was an attempt to prevent the other Allies (the USA, France, and the UK) unifying the western part of Germany. The British and US forces responded by sending supplies to the city by air for over a year (the Berlin airlift). In May 1949 the blockade was lifted; the airlift continued until Sept. The blockade marked the formal division of the city into Eastern and Western sectors.

Berlin, Conference of conference 1884–85 of the major European powers (France, Germany, the UK, Belgium, and Portugal) called by Chancellor Otto von Bismarck to decide on the colonial partition of Africa. Also discussed were a neutral Congo Basin with free trade, and an independent Congo Free State; the slave trade was forbidden.

Berlin, Congress of congress of the European powers (Russia, Turkey, Austria–Hungary, the UK, France, Italy, and Germany) held in Berlin 1878 to determine the boundaries of the Balkan states after the Russo-Turkish war 1877–78.

Prime Minister Disraeli attended as the UK's chief envoy, and declared on his return to England that he had brought back 'peace with honour'.

Berlin Wall dividing barrier between East and West Berlin 1961–89, erected by East Germany to prevent East Germans from leaving for West Germany. Escapers were shot on sight.

From 13 Aug 1961, the East German security forces sealed off all but 12 of the 80 crossing points to West Berlin with a barbed wire barrier. It was reinforced with concrete by the Russians to prevent the escape of unwilling inhabitants of East Berlin to the rival political and economic system of West Berlin. The interconnecting link between East and West Berlin was Checkpoint Charlie, where both sides exchanged captured spies. On 9 Nov 1989 the East German government opened its borders to try to halt the mass exodus of its citizens to the West via other Eastern bloc countries, and the wall was gradually dismantled, with portions of it sold off as souvenirs.

Berlioz The French composer Hector Berlioz. At a time in France when literature was considered the greatest art form, Berlioz achieved more than any other composer in placing music on a par with it. He prepared the way for the later Romantics in France and abroad, including Liszt (who settled in Paris) and Wagner. *Image Select (UK) Ltd*

Berlioz (Louis) Hector 1803–1869. French Romantic composer. He is noted as the founder of modern orchestration. Much of his music was inspired by drama and literature and has a theatrical quality. He wrote symphonic works, such as *Symphonie fantastique* 1830–31 and *Roméo et Juliette* 1839; dramatic cantatas including *La Damnation de Faust* 1846 and *L'Enfance du Christ* 1854; sacred music; and three operas: *Benvenuto Cellini* 1838, *Les Troyens* 1856–58, and *Béatrice et Bénédict* 1862.

Berlioz studied music at the Paris Conservatoire. He won the Prix de Rome 1830, and spent two years in Italy. In 1833 he married Harriet Smithson, an Irish actress playing Shakespearean parts in Paris, but they separated 1842. After some years of poverty and public neglect, he went to Germany 1842.

Bermuda British colony in the NW Atlantic Ocean

area 54 sq km/21 sq mi

capital and chief port Hamilton

features consists of about 150 small islands, of which 20 are inhabited, linked by bridges and causeways; Britain's oldest colony

industries Easter lilies, pharmaceuticals; tourism and banking are important

currency Bermuda dollar

Bermuda

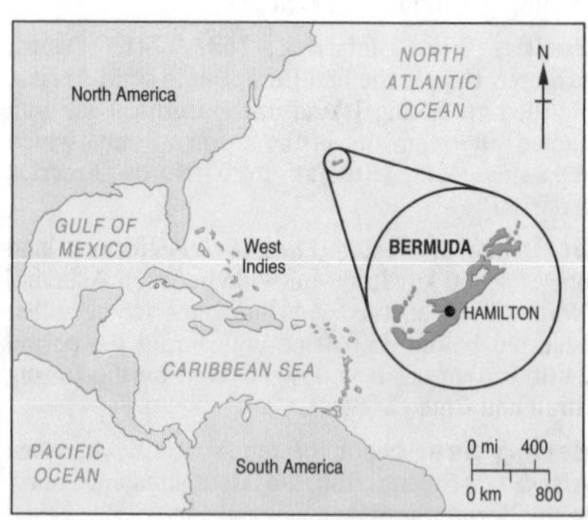

population (1992 est) 72,000
language English
religion Christian
government under the constitution of 1968, Bermuda is a fully self-governing British colony, with a governor (Lord Waddington from 1992), senate, and elected House of Assembly (premier from 1982 John Swan, United Bermuda Party)
history the islands were named after Juan de Bermudez, who visited them 1515, and were settled by British colonists 1609. Indian and African slaves were transported from 1616 and soon outnumbered the white settlers. Racial violence 1977 led to intervention, at the request of the government, by British troops.

Bermuda Triangle sea area bounded by Bermuda, Florida, and Puerto Rico, which gained the nickname 'Deadly Bermuda Triangle' 1964 when it was suggested that unexplained disappearances of ships and aircraft were exceptionally frequent there. Analysis of the data has not confirmed the idea.

Bern (French ***Berne***) capital of Switzerland and of Bern canton, in W Switzerland on the Aare River; population (1994) 134,100; canton (1994 est) 943,600. It joined the Swiss confederation 1353 and became the capital 1848. Industries include textiles, chocolate, pharmaceuticals, and light metal and electrical goods.

It was founded 1191 and made a free imperial city by Frederick II 1218. Its name is derived from the bear in its coat of arms, and there has been a bear pit in the city since the 16th century. The minster was begun 1421, the town hall 1406, and the university 1834. It is the seat of the Universal Postal Union.

Bernadette, St of Lourdes (originally Marie Bernard Soubirous) 1844–1879. French saint, born in Lourdes in the French Pyrenees. In Feb 1858 she had a vision of the Virgin Mary in a grotto, and it became a centre of pilgrimage. Many sick people who were dipped in the water of a spring there were said to have been cured. Canonized 1933. Her feast day is 16 April.

The grotto of Massabielle was opened to the public by command of Napoleon III, and a church built on the rock above became a shrine. At the age of 20 Bernadette became a nun at Nevers, and nursed the wounded of the Franco-Prussian War.

Bernadotte Count Folke 1895–1948. Swedish diplomat and president of the Swedish Red Cross. In 1945 he conveyed Nazi commander Himmler's offer of capitulation to the British and US governments, and in 1948 was United Nations mediator in Palestine, where he was assassinated by Israeli Stern Gang guerrillas. He was a nephew of Gustaf VI of Sweden.

Bernadotte Jean-Baptiste Jules 1763–1844. Marshal in Napoleon's army who in 1818 became ◊Charles XIV of Sweden. Hence, Bernadotte is the family name of the present royal house of Sweden.

Bernard Claude 1813–1878. French physiologist and founder of experimental medicine. Bernard first demonstrated that digestion is not restricted to the stomach, but takes place throughout the small intestine. He discovered the digestive input of the pancreas, several functions of the liver, and the vasomotor nerves which dilate and contract the blood vessels and thus regulate body temperature. This led him to the concept of the *milieu intérieur* ('internal environment') whose stability is essential to good health.

Bernard of Clairvaux, St 1090–1153. Christian founder in 1115 of Clairvaux monastery in Champagne, France. He reinvigorated the ◊Cistercian order, preached in support of the Second Crusade in 1146, and had the scholastic philosopher Abelard condemned for heresy. He is often depicted with a beehive. Canonized 1174. His feast day is 20 Aug.

Berners-Lee Tim(othy) 1955– . English inventor of the World Wide Web 1990. He developed the Web whilst working as a consultant at ◊CERN.

Bernese Oberland or ***Bernese Alps*** mountainous area in the S of Bern canton. It includes the Jungfrau, Eiger, and Finsteraarhorn peaks. Interlaken is the chief town.

Bernhard Leopold Prince of the Netherlands 1911– . Formerly Prince Bernhard of Lippe-Biesterfeld, he married Princess ◊Juliana in 1937. When Germany invaded the Netherlands in 1940, he escaped to England and became liaison officer for the Dutch and British forces, playing a part in the organization of the Dutch Resistance.

Bernhardt Sarah. Stage name of Henriette Rosine Bernard 1844–1923. French actress. She dominated the stage in her day, frequently performing at the Comédie Française in Paris. She excelled in tragic roles, including Cordelia in Shakespeare's *King Lear*, the title role in Racine's *Phèdre*, and the male roles of Hamlet and of Napoleon's son in Edmond Rostand's *L'Aiglon*.

Bernini Gianlorenzo (Giovanni Lorenzo) 1598–1680. Italian sculptor, architect, and painter. He was a leading figure in the development of the ◊Baroque style. His work in Rome includes the colonnaded piazza in front of St Peter's Basilica 1656, fountains (as in the Piazza Navona), and papal monuments. His sculpture includes *The Ecstasy of St Theresa* 1645–52 (Sta Maria della Vittoria, Rome) and numerous portrait busts.

Bernini's sculptural style is full of movement and drama, captured in billowing drapery and facial expressions. His subjects are religious and mythological. A fine example is the marble *Apollo and Daphne* for Cardinal Borghese 1622–25 (Borghese Palace, Rome), with the figures shown in full flight. Inside St Peter's, he created several marble monuments and the elaborate canopy over the high altar. His many fine portrait busts include one of Louis XIV of France.

Bernoulli Daniel 1700–1782. Swiss mathematical physicist. He made important contributions to trigonometry and differential equations. In hydrodynamics he proposed Bernoulli's principle, an early formulation of the idea of conservation of energy.

Bernoulli Jakob 1654–1705. Swiss mathematician who with his brother Johann pioneered German mathematician Gottfried ◊Leibniz's calculus. Jakob used calculus to study the forms of many curves arising in practical situations, and studied mathematical probability (*Ars conjectandi* 1713); Bernoulli numbers are named after him.

Bernoulli Johann 1667–1748. Swiss mathematician who with his brother Jakob Bernoulli pioneered German mathematician Gottfried ◊Leibniz's calculus. He was the father of Daniel Bernoulli. Johann also contributed to many areas of applied mathematics, including the problem of a particle moving in a gravitational field. He found the equation of the ◊catenary 1690 and developed exponential ◊calculus 1691.

Bernoulli's principle law stating that the speed of a fluid varies inversely with pressure, an increase in speed producing a decrease in pressure (such as a drop in hydraulic pressure as the fluid speeds up flowing through a constriction in a pipe) and vice versa. The principle also explains the pressure differences on each surface of an aerofoil, which gives lift to the wing of an aircraft. The principle was named after Swiss mathematician and physicist Daniel Bernoulli.

Bernstein Leonard 1918–1990. US composer, conductor, and pianist. He is one of the most energetic and versatile 20th-century US musicians. His works, which established a vogue for realistic, contemporary themes, include symphonies such as *The Age of Anxiety* 1949, ballets such as *Fancy Free* 1944, and scores for musicals, including *Wonderful Town* 1953, *West Side Story* 1957, and *Mass* 1971 in memory of President J F Kennedy.

berry fleshy, many-seeded ◊fruit that does not split open to release the seeds. The outer layer of tissue, the exocarp, forms an outer skin that is often brightly coloured to attract birds to eat the fruit and thus disperse the seeds. Examples of berries are the tomato and the grape.

Berry Chuck (Charles Edward Anderson) 1926– . US rock-and-roll singer, songwriter, and guitarist. His characteristic guitar riffs became staples of rock music, and his humorous storytelling lyrics were also emulated. He had a string of hits in the 1950s and 1960s beginning with 'Maybellene' 1955.

Born in St Louis, Missouri, Berry began as a blues guitarist in local clubs. Early songs like 'Roll Over Beethoven' 1956, 'Rock 'n' Roll Music' 1957, 'Sweet Little Sixteen' 1958, and 'Johnny B Goode' 1958 are classics of the genre, and one of them was chosen as a sample of Earth music for the *Voyager* space probes. He was the subject of a film tribute, *Hail! Hail! Rock 'n' Roll* 1987. *See illustration on following page.*

Bernini *The Ecstasy of Saint Teresa* by Bernini, the Cornaro Chapel in the church of Sta Maria della Vittoria, Rome. One of the finest Baroque sculptures, *The Ecstasy of Saint Teresa* gives full expression to Bernini's technical virtuosity, his flair for the theatrical, and his ability to convey intense emotion. *Corbis*

Berryman John 1914–1972. US poet. His emotionally intense, witty, and personal works often deal with sexual torments and are informed by a sense of suffering. After collections of short poems and sonnets, he wrote *Homage to Mistress Broadstreet* 1956, a romantic narrative featuring the first American poet, Anne Dudley (born 1612), and then introduced his guilt-ridden, anti-heroic alter-ego, Henry, in *77 Dream Songs* 1964 (Pulitzer prize) and *His Toy, His Dream, His Rest* 1968. His poetry has much in common with that of the 'confessional' poets, but his use of humour sets it apart. He also wrote short stories.

berserker legendary Scandinavian warrior whose frenzy in battle transformed him into a wolf or bear howling and foaming at the mouth (hence 'to go berserk'), and rendered him immune to sword and flame.

Bertolucci Bernardo 1940– . Italian film director. His work combines political and historical perspectives with an elegant and lyrical visual appeal. His films include *The Spider's Stratagem* 1970, *Last Tango in Paris* 1972, *1900* 1976, *The Last Emperor* 1987 (which won nine Academy Awards), *Little Buddha* 1992, and *Stealing Beauty* 1996.

Bernstein US composer, conductor, and pianist Leonard Bernstein juxtaposed a Romantic intensity with jazz and Latin American elements in his large instrumental and choral works. He wrote in widely different styles, from *West Side Story* 1957, a musical based on the *Romeo and Juliet* theme, to the *Chichester Psalms* 1965. *CBS*

Berry US pop singer Chuck Berry, one of the leading figures in the development of rock and roll. His career was cut short by a prison sentence for transporting a minor across state lines for immoral purposes, but revived again when British rock stars such as Keith Richards, the Beatles, and Eric Clapton acknowledged his importance. *Associated Press/ Topham*

Berwick-upon-Tweed town in NE England, at the mouth of the Tweed, Northumberland, 5 km/ 3 mi SE of the Scottish border; population (1991) 13,500.

beryl mineral, beryllium aluminium silicate, $Be_3Al_2Si_6O_{18}$, which forms crystals chiefly in granite. It is the chief ore of beryllium. Two of its gem forms are aquamarine (light-blue crystals) and emerald (dark-green crystals).

beryllium hard, light-weight, silver-white, metallic element, symbol Be, atomic number 4, relative atomic mass 9.012. It is one of the ◊alkaline-earth metals, with chemical properties similar to those of magnesium; in nature it is found only in combination with other elements. It is used to make sturdy, light alloys and to control the speed of neutrons in nuclear reactors. Beryllium oxide was discovered in 1798 by French chemist Louis-Nicolas Vauquelin (1763–1829), but the element was not isolated until 1828, by Friedrich Wöhler and Antoine-Alexandre-Brutus Bussy independently.

In 1992 large amounts of beryllium were unexpectedly discovered in six old stars in the Milky Way.

Berzelius Jöns Jakob 1779–1848. Swedish chemist. He accurately determined more than 2,000 relative atomic and molecular masses. He devised 1813–14 the system of chemical symbols and formulae now in use and proposed oxygen as a reference standard for atomic masses. His discoveries include the elements cerium 1804, selenium 1817, and thorium 1828; he was the first to prepare silicon in its amorphous form and to isolate zirconium. The words 'isomerism', 'allotropy', and 'protein' were coined by him.

Berzelius noted that some reactions appeared to work faster in the presence of another substance which itself did not appear to change, and postulated that such a substance contained a catalytic force.

Besançon city on the river Doubs, France; population (1990) 119,200. It is the capital of Franche-Comté. The first factory to produce artificial fibres was established here 1890. Industries include textiles and clock-making. It has fortifications by ◊Vauban, Roman remains, and a Gothic cathedral.

The writer Victor Hugo and the Lumière brothers, inventors of cinematography, were born here.

‘Think of what our Nation stands for, / Books from Boots' and country lanes, / Free speech, free passes, class distinction.’

John Betjeman
'In Westminster Abbey'

Besant Annie, born Wood 1847–1933. English socialist and feminist activist. She was associated with the radical atheist Charles Bradlaugh and the socialist ◊Fabian Society. In 1889 she became a disciple of Madame ◊Blavatsky. She thereafter preached theosophy, went to India, and became president of the Indian National Congress in 1917.

She was the sister-in-law of Walter Besant.

Besant Walter 1836–1901. English writer. He wrote novels in partnership with James Rice (1843–1882), and produced an attack on the social evils of the East End of London, *All Sorts and Conditions of Men* 1882, and an unfinished *Survey of London* 1902–12. He was the brother-in-law of Annie Besant.

Bessarabia region in SE Europe, divided between Moldova and Ukraine. Bessarabia was annexed by Russia 1812, but broke away at the Russian Revolution to join Romania. The cession was confirmed by the Allies, but not by Russia, in a Paris treaty of 1920; the USSR reoccupied it 1940 and divided it between the Moldavian and Ukrainian republics (now independent Moldova and Ukraine). Romania recognized the position in the 1947 peace treaty.

Bessel Friedrich Wilhelm 1784–1846. German astronomer and mathematician. He was the first person to find the approximate distance to a star by direct methods when he measured the ◊parallax (annual displacement) of the star 61 Cygni 1838. In mathematics, he introduced the series of functions now known as Bessel functions. Bessel's work laid the foundations for a more accurate calculation of the scale of the universe and the sizes of stars, galaxies, and clusters of galaxies.

Bessemer process the first cheap method of making ◊steel, invented by Henry Bessemer in England 1856. It has since been superseded by more efficient steel-making processes, such as the ◊basic–oxygen process. In the Bessemer process compressed air is blown into the bottom of a converter, a furnace shaped like a cement mixer, containing molten pig iron. The excess carbon in the iron burns out, other impurities form a slag, and the furnace is emptied by tilting.

Bessel Friedrich Wilhelm Friedrich Bessel developed the technique of stellar parallax, by means of which distances to nearby stars can be calculated by observing their apparent change in position when viewed from opposite ends of a long baseline such as the diameter of the Earth's

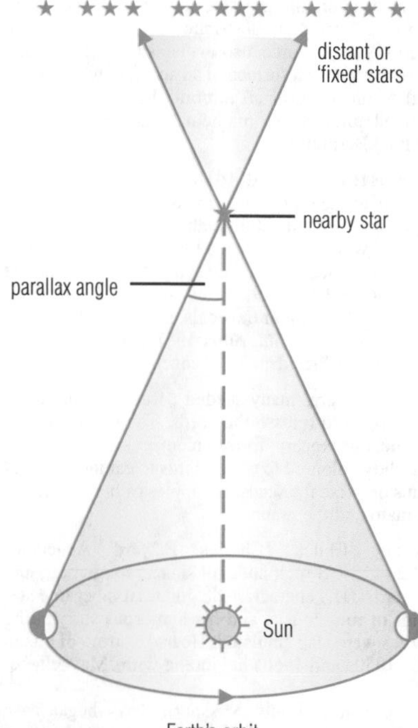

Best Charles H(erbert) 1899–1978. Canadian physiologist. He was one of the team of Canadian scientists including Frederick ◊Banting whose research resulted 1922 in the discovery of insulin as a treatment for diabetes.

Best also discovered the vitamin choline and the enzyme histaminase, and introduced the use of the anticoagulant heparin.

bestiary in medieval times, a book with stories and illustrations which depicted real and mythical animals or plants to illustrate a (usually Christian) moral. The stories were initially derived from the Greek *Physiologus*, a collection of 48 such stories, written in Alexandria around the 2nd century AD.

beta-blocker any of a class of drugs that block impulses that stimulate certain nerve endings (beta receptors) serving the heart muscle. This reduces the heart rate and the force of contraction, which in turn reduces the amount of oxygen (and therefore the blood supply) required by the heart. Beta-blockers may be useful in the treatment of angina, arrhythmia (abnormal heart rhythms), and raised blood pressure, and following heart attacks. They must be withdrawn from use gradually.

beta decay the disintegration of the nucleus of an atom to produce a beta particle, or high-speed electron, and an electron-antineutrino. During beta decay, a neutron in the nucleus changes into a proton, thereby increasing the atomic number by one while the mass number stays the same. The mass lost in the change is converted into kinetic (movement) energy of the beta particle.

Beta decay is caused by the weak nuclear force, one of the fundamental ◊forces of nature operating inside the nucleus.

beta particle electron ejected with great velocity from a radioactive atom that is undergoing spontaneous disintegration. Beta particles do not exist in the nucleus but are created on disintegration, beta decay, when a neutron converts to a proton to emit an electron.

Beta particles are more penetrating than ◊alpha particles, but less so than ◊gamma radiation; they can travel several metres in air, but are stopped by 2–3 mm of aluminium. They are less strongly ionizing than alpha particles and, like cathode rays, are easily deflected by magnetic and electric fields.

Betelgeuse or ***Alpha Orionis*** red supergiant star in the constellation of ◊Orion. It is the tenth brightest star in the night sky, although its brightness varies. It is 1,100 million km/700 million mi across, about 800 times larger than the Sun, roughly the same size as the orbit of Mars. It is over 10,000 times as luminous as the Sun, and lies 650 light years from Earth. Light takes 60 minutes to travel across the giant star.

Its magnitude varies irregularly between 0.4 and 1.3 in a period of 5.8 years. It was the first star whose angular diameter was measured with the Mount Wilson ◊interferometer 1920. The name is a corruption of the Arabic, describing its position in the shoulder of Orion.

betel nut fruit of the areca palm *Areca catechu*, used together with lime and betel pepper as a masticatory stimulant by peoples of the East and Papua New Guinea. Chewing it results in blackened teeth and a mouth stained deep red.

Bethlehem (Hebrew ***Beit-Lahm***) town on the west bank of the river Jordan, S of Jerusalem; population about 20,000. It was occupied by Israel 1967. In the Bible it is mentioned as the birthplace of King David and Jesus, and in 326 AD the Church of the Nativity was built over the grotto said to be the birthplace of Jesus.

Betjeman John 1906–1984. English poet and essayist. He wrote a peculiarly English form of romantic and nostalgic light verse, as well as prose works on architecture and social history which reflect his interest in the ◊Gothic Revival. His *Collected Poems* appeared 1958 and a verse autobiography, *Summoned by Bells*, 1960. He became poet laureate 1972.

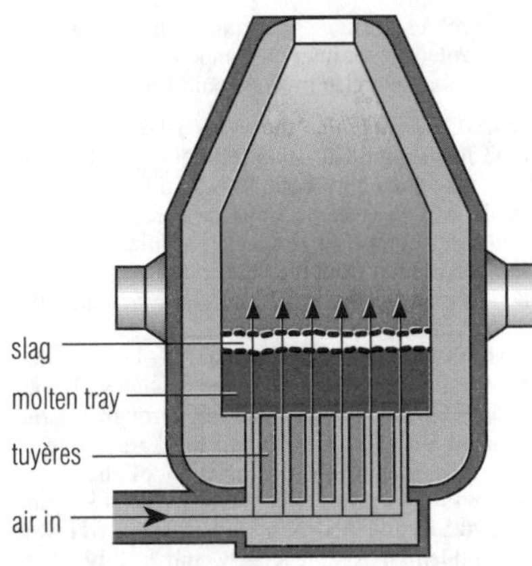

Bessemer process In a Bessemer converter, a blast of high-pressure air oxidizes impurities in molten iron and converts it to steel.

betony plant, *Stachys* (formerly *Betonica*) *officinalis*, of the mint family, formerly used in medicine and dyeing. It has a hairy stem and leaves, and reddish-purple flowers. Betony is found growing as a hedgerow weed in Britain.

Bettelheim Bruno 1903–1990. Austrian-born US child psychologist. At the University of Chicago he founded a treatment centre for emotionally disturbed children based on the principle of a supportive home environment. Among his books are *Love Is Not Enough* 1950 and *The Uses of Enchantment: The Meaning and Importance of Fairy Tales* 1976.

Imprisoned in the Dachau and Buchenwald concentration camps for ten months 1938–39, he emigrated to the USA in 1939. His other books include *Truants from Life* 1954, *Children of the Dream* 1962, and *A Good Enough Parent* 1987. He took his own life.

Betti Ugo 1892–1953. Italian dramatist. Some of his most important plays, such as *Frana allo scalo nord/Landslide at the North Station* 1936, concern the legal process (Betti was a judge for many years) and focus on the themes of justice and moral responsibility. Of his many other plays, often austere, even pessimistic, the best known include *La padrone/The Mistress* 1927, *Delitto all'isola delle capre/Crime on Goat Island* 1948 and *La Regina e gli insorte/The Queen and the Rebels* 1949.

Beuys Joseph 1921–1986. German sculptor and performance artist. He was one of the leaders of the European avant-garde during the 1970s and 1980s. An exponent of Arte Povera, he made use of so-called 'worthless', unusual materials such as felt and fat. His best-known performance was *How to Explain Pictures to a Dead Hare* 1965. He was also an influential exponent of video art, for example, *Felt TV* 1968. Beuys saw the artist as a shaman and art as an agent of social and spiritual change.

Bevan Aneurin (Nye) 1897–1960. British Labour politician. Son of a Welsh miner, and himself a miner at 13, he became member of Parliament for Ebbw Vale 1929–60. As minister of health 1945–51, he inaugurated the National Health Service (NHS); he was minister of labour Jan–April 1951, when he resigned (with Harold Wilson) on the introduction of NHS charges and led a Bevanite faction against the government. In 1956 he became chief Labour spokesperson on foreign affairs, and deputy leader of the Labour party 1959. He was an outstanding speaker.

Beveridge William Henry, 1st Baron Beveridge 1879–1963. British economist. A civil servant, he acted as Lloyd George's lieutenant in the social legislation of the Liberal government before World War I. The Beveridge Report 1942 formed the basis of the welfare state in Britain.

Beveridge Report, the popular name of *Social Insurance and Allied Services*, a report written by William Beveridge 1942 that formed the basis for the social-reform legislation of the Labour government of 1945–50.

Also known as the *Report on Social Security*, it identified five 'giants': illness, ignorance, disease, squalor, and want. It proposed a scheme of social insurance from 'the cradle to the grave', and recommended a national health service, social insurance and assistance, family allowances, and full-employment policies.

Beverly Hills residential city and a part of greater Los Angeles, California, USA; population (1990) 31,900. It is known as the home of Hollywood film stars.

Bevin Ernest 1881–1951. British Labour politician. Chief creator of the Transport and General Workers' Union, he was its general secretary from 1921 to 1940, when he entered the war cabinet as minister of labour and national service. He organized the 'Bevin boys', chosen by ballot to work in the coal mines as war service, and was foreign secretary in the Labour government 1945–51.

Bewick Thomas 1753–1828. English wood engraver. He excelled in animal subjects, some of his finest works appearing in his illustrated *A General History of Quadrupeds* 1790 and *A History of British Birds* 1797–1804.

Bexley outer borough of SE Greater London. It includes the suburbs of Crayford, Erith, Sidcup
population (1991) 215,600
features 16th-century Hall Palace; Red House (1859), home of William Morris 1860–65; 18th-century Danson Park, with grounds landscaped by 'Capability' ◊Brown
industries armaments manufacture (important since the 19th century at Crayford, site of Vickers Factory)

Bezier curve curved line invented by Pierre Bézier that connects a series of points (or 'nodes') in the smoothest possible way. The shape of the curve is governed by a series of complex mathematical formulae. They are used in ◊computer graphics and ◊CAD.

BFI abbreviation for ◊***British Film Institute***.

Bhagavad-Gītā (Hindi 'the Song of the Blessed') religious and philosophical Sanskrit poem, dating from around 300 BC, forming an episode in the sixth book of the *Mahābhārata*, one of the two great Hindu epics. It is the supreme religious work of Hinduism.

bhakti (Sanskrit 'devotion') in Hinduism, a tradition of worship that emphasizes devotion to a personal god as the sole necessary means for achieving salvation. It developed in S India in the 6th–8th centuries and in N India from the 14th century.

In N India bhakti was in part a social protest movement. The poet Kabir (1440–1518) synthesized Hinduism and Islam to produce a new mystic philosophy. Nanak, influenced by Kabir, founded the Sikh religion. In Bengal, Caitanya (1486–1533) led a popular bhakti movement which later gave rise to the Hare Krishna sect.

bhangra pop music evolved in the UK in the late 1970s from traditional Punjabi music, combining electronic instruments and ethnic drums. Bhangra bands include Holle Holle, Alaap, and Heera. A 1990s development is bhangramuffin, a reggae-rap-bhangra fusion popularized by Apache Indian (stage name of Steve Kapur, 1967–).

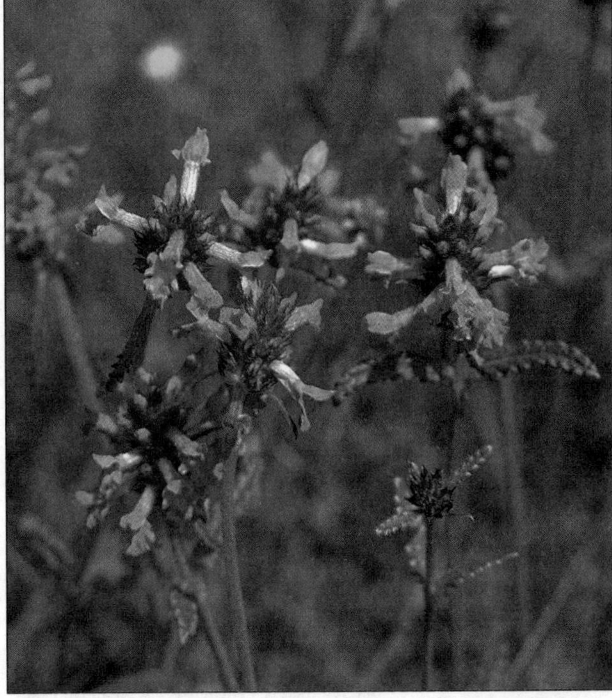

betony Betony is a plant of light soils, found in hedgerows, open woodland, grassland, and heaths. It is distributed across much of Europe, except the far north, and is also present in Algeria. *Premaphotos Wildlife*

Bharat Natyam one of the four main Indian Classical dancing styles (others are ◊Kathak, ◊Kathakali, and ◊Manipuri). It is a female dance solo, over 2,000 years old, performed by Hindu temple dancers, today practised mainly in S India. It is characterized by great strength and austerity and its performances can last up to three hours. The dancer wears a richly decorated brocade blouse and silk sari and is accompanied by cymbals and singing.

It is based on *Bharata Natya Shastra*, a book written c. 200 BC–AD 300, on drama for the dance actor.

Bhindranwale Sant Jarnail Singh 1947–1984. Indian Sikh fundamentalist leader who campaigned for the creation of a separate state of Khalistan during the early 1980s, precipitating a bloody Hindu–Sikh conflict in the Punjab. Having taken refuge in the Golden Temple complex in Amritsar and built up an arms cache for guerrilla activities, Bhindranwale, along with around 500 followers, died at the hands of Indian security forces who stormed the temple in 'Operation Blue Star' June 1984.

Bhopal industrial city (textiles, chemicals, electrical goods, jewellery) and capital of Madhya Pradesh, central India; population (1991) 1,064,000. Nearby Bhimbetka Caves, discovered 1973, have the world's largest collection of prehistoric paintings, about 10,000 years old. In 1984 some 2,600 people died from an escape of the poisonous gas methyl isocyanate from a factory owned by US

'This island is made mainly of coal and surrounded by fish. Only an organizing genius could produce a shortage of coal and fish at the same time.'

ANEURIN BEVAN
Speech at Blackpool 18 May 1945

Bewick Woodcut of a spaniel putting up duck during wildfowling, from Thomas Bewick's *Select Fables* 1820. Bewick's birthplace, Cherryburn, in Northamptonshire, is a museum of wood-engraving, with many of his original blocks. Although he was trained in metal engraving, he made many improvements in wood-engraving techniques. *Image Select (UK) Ltd*

The weak have one weapon: the errors of those who think they are strong.

GEORGES BIDAULT
Quoted in the *Observer* July 1962

company Union Carbide; another 300,000 suffer from long-term health problems.

The city was capital of the former princely state of Bhopal, founded 1723, which became allied to Britain 1817. It was merged with Madhya Pradesh 1956.

Bhumibol Adulyadej 1927– . King of Thailand from 1946. Born in the USA and educated in Bangkok and Switzerland, he succeeded to the throne on the assassination of his brother. In 1973 he was active, with popular support, in overthrowing the military government of Marshal Thanom Kittikachorn and thus ended a sequence of army-dominated regimes in power from 1932.

Bhutan mountainous, landlocked country in the eastern Himalayas (SE Asia), bounded N and W by Tibet (China) and to the S and E by India. *See country box below.*

Bhutto Benazir 1953– . Pakistani politician, leader of the Pakistan People's Party (PPP) from 1984 (in exile until 1986), prime minister of Pakistan 1988–90 and 1993–96.

Benazir Bhutto was educated at Harvard and Oxford universities. She returned to Pakistan 1977 but was placed under house arrest after General ◊Zia ul-Haq seized power from her father, Prime Minister Zulfikar Ali Bhutto who was hanged 1979. On her release she moved to the UK and became, with her mother Nusrat (1934–), the joint leader in exile of the opposition PPP.

She returned to Pakistan 1986 to launch a campaign for open elections. She became the first female leader of a Muslim state 1988. In 1990, she was removed from office by presidential decree. Charges of corruption and abuse of power were levelled against her and her husband Asif Ali Zardari, and her party was defeated in the subsequent general election. In 1993 she became prime minister for a second time, but was removed from office by President Farooq Leghari in Nov 1996 amidst further concern over government corruption.

Bhutto Zulfikar Ali 1928–1979. Pakistani politician, president 1971–73; prime minister from 1973 until the 1977 military coup led by General ◊Zia ul-Haq. In 1978 Bhutto was sentenced to death for conspiring to murder a political opponent and was hanged the following year. He was the father of Benazir Bhutto.

Biafra, Republic of African state proclaimed 1967 when fears that Nigerian central government was increasingly in the hands of the rival Hausa tribe led the predominantly Ibo Eastern Region of Nigeria to secede under Lt-Col Odumegwu Ojukwu. On the proclamation of Biafra, civil war ensued with the rest of the federation. In a bitterly fought campaign federal forces confined the Biafrans to a shrinking area of the interior by 1968, and by 1970 Biafra ceased to exist.

Bhutto Pakistani politician Benazir Bhutto. As prime minister of Pakistan 1988–90 she was the first woman leader of a Muslim country. She is the daughter of the former prime minister Zulfikar Ali Bhutto, who was deposed by General Zia ul-Haq 1977 and executed. She won the post-Zia elections 1988, lost power two years later, and served again as prime minister 1993–96. *Topham*

biathlon athletic competition that combines cross-country skiing with rifle marksmanship. Basic equipment consists of cross-country skis, poles, and boots, and bolt-action (nonautomatic) rifles.

It involves accurate shooting with rifles at prepared targets at set intervals, and is used as a military training exercise in some countries.

Bible (Greek *ta biblia* 'the books') the sacred book of the Jewish and Christian religions. The Hebrew Bible, recognized by both Jews and Christians, is called the ◊Old Testament by Christians. The ◊New Testament comprises books recognized by the Christian church from the 4th century as canonical. The Roman Catholic Bible also includes the ◊Apocrypha.

translations It was only in the 13th century that single-volume Bibles with a fixed content and order of books became common, largely through a Paris-produced Vulgate of 1200 and the Paris Bible of 1230. The first English translation of the entire Bible was by a priest, Miles Coverdale, 1535; the Authorized Version, or King James Bible 1611, was long influential for the clarity and beauty of its language. A revision of the Authorized Version carried out 1959 by the British and Foreign Bible Society produced the widely used American translation, the Revised Standard Version. A conference of British churches 1946 recommended a completely new translation into English from the original Hebrew and Greek texts; work on this was carried out over the following two decades, resulting in the publication of the New English Bible (New Testament 1961, Old Testament and Apocrypha 1970). Another recent translation is the Jerusalem Bible, completed by Catholic scholars 1966.

Missionary activity led to the translation of the Bible into the languages of people they were trying to convert, and by 1993 parts of the Bible had been translated into over 2,000 different languages, with 329 complete translations.

bicarbonate common name for ◊hydrogen-carbonate

bicarbonate of soda or ***baking soda*** (technical name ***sodium hydrogencarbonate***) $NaHCO_3$ white crystalline solid that neutralizes acids and is used in medicine to treat acid indigestion. It is also used in baking powders and effervescent drinks.

Bichat Marie François Xavier 1771–1802. French physician and founder of ◊histology, the study of tissues. He studied the organs of the body, their structure, and the ways in which they are affected by disease. This led to his discovery and naming of 'tissue', a basic biological and medical concept; he identified 21 types. He argued that disease does not affect the whole organ but only certain of its constituent tissues.

BHUTAN
Kingdom of

BHUTAN
Thimphu
China
Nepal
India
INDIAN OCEAN
0 mi 500
0 km 1000

national name *Druk-yul*
area 46,500 sq km/17,954 sq mi
capital Thimbu (Thimphu)
major towns/cities Paro, Punakha, Mongar
physical features occupies southern slopes of the Himalayas; Gangkar Punsum (7,529 m/24,700 ft) is one of the world's highest unclimbed peaks; cut by valleys formed by tributaries of the Brahmaputra; thick forests in the S
head of state and government Jigme Singye Wangchuk from 1972
political system absolute monarchy
administrative divisions 20 districts; seven are divided into subdistricts
political parties none officially; illegal Bhutan People's Party (BPP) and Bhutan National Democratic Party (BNDP), both ethnic Nepali
population 1,812,000 (1996 est)
population growth rate 1.2% (1990–95); 2.3% (2000–05)
ethnic distribution 54% Bhotia, residing principally in the N and E; 32% of Tibetan descent; a substantial Nepali minority lives in the S – they are prohibited from moving into the Bhotia-dominated N
life expectancy 51 (males), 49 (females)
languages Dzongkha (official, a Tibetan dialect), Sharchop, Bumthap, Nepali, and English
literacy rate men 51%, women 25%
religions 70% Mahayana Buddhist (state religion), 25% Hindu
currency ngultrum; also Indian currency
GDP (US $) 1.3 billion (1995 est)
growth rate 6.4% (1983–93)
exports timber, talc, fruit and vegetables, cement, distilled spirits, calcium carbide, cardamoms

HISTORY
to 8th C Under effective Indian control.
16th C Came under Tibetan rule.
1616–51 Unified by Ngawang Namgyal, leader of the Drukpa Kagyu (Thunder Dragon) Tibetan Buddhist branch.
1720 Came under Chinese rule.
1774 Treaty signed with East India Company.
1865 Trade treaty with Britain signed after invasion.
1907 Ugyen Wangchuk, the governor of Tongsa, became Bhutan's first hereditary monarch.
1910 Anglo-Bhutanese Treaty signed, placing foreign relations under the 'guidance' of the British government in India.
1926 Jigme Wangchuk succeeded to the throne.
1949 Indo-Bhutan Treaty of Friendship signed, giving India continued influence over Bhutan's foreign relations, but returning territory annexed in 1865.
1950 Became a member of the Colombo Plan for economic and social development in Asia and the Pacific.
1952 Reformist king Jigme Dorji Wangchuk came to power.
1953 National assembly (Tshogdu) established.
1958 Slavery abolished.
1959 4,000 Tibetan refugees given asylum after Chinese annexation of Tibet.
1968 King established first cabinet.
1972 King died and was succeeded by his Western-educated son Jigme Singye Wangchuk.
1973 Became an adherent of the nonaligned movement.
1979 Tibetan refugees told to take Bhutanese citizenship or leave; most stayed.
1983 Bhutan became a founding member of the South Asian Regional Association for Cooperation.
1988 Buddhist Dzongkha/Drukpa king imposed 'code of conduct' suppressing the customs of the large Hindu-Nepali community in the S.
1990 Hundreds of people allegedly killed during prodemocracy demonstrations.
1993 Leader of banned Bhutan People's Party (BPP) sentenced to life imprisonment for 'antinational activities'.

bicycle pedal-driven two-wheeled vehicle used in ◊cycling. It consists of a metal frame mounted on two large wire-spoked wheels, with handlebars in front and a seat between the front and back wheels. The bicycle is an energy-efficient, nonpolluting form of transport, and it is estimated that 800 million bicycles are in use throughout the world – outnumbering cars three to one. China, India, Denmark, and the Netherlands are countries with a high use of bicycles.

The first bicycle was seen in Paris 1791 and was a form of hobby-horse. The first treadle-propelled cycle was designed by Scottish blacksmith Kirkpatrick Macmillan 1839. By the end of the 19th century wire wheels, metal frames (replacing wood), and pneumatic tyres (invented by Scottish veterinary surgeon John B Dunlop 1888) had been added. Among the bicycles of that time was the front-wheel-driven penny farthing with a large front wheel.

Recent technological developments have been related to reducing wind resistance caused by the frontal area and the turbulent drag of the bicycle. Most of an Olympic cyclist's energy is taken up in fighting wind resistance in a sprint. The first major innovation was the solid wheel, first used in competitive cycling 1984, but originally patented as long ago as 1878. Further developments include handle bars that allow the cyclist to crouch and use the shape of the hands and forearms to divert air away from the chest. Modern racing bicycles now have a monocoque structure produced by laying carbon fibre around an internal mould and then baking them in an oven. Using all of these developments Chris Boardman set a speed record of 54.4 km/h (34 mph) on his way to winning a gold medal at the 1992 Barcelona Olympics.

Bidault Georges Augustin 1899–1983. French politician, prime minister 1946, 1949–50. He was a leader of the French Resistance during World War II and foreign minister and president in de Gaulle's provisional government. He left the Gaullists over Algerian independence, and in 1962 he became head of the Organisation de l'Armée Secrète (OAS), formed 1961 by French settlers devoted to perpetuating their own rule in Algeria. He was charged with treason 1963 and left the country, but was allowed to return 1968.

Biedermeier early- to mid-19th-century Germanic style of art and furniture design, derogatorily named after Gottlieb Biedermeier, a humorous pseudonym used by several German poets, embodying bourgeois taste.

biennial plant plant that completes its life cycle in two years. During the first year it grows vegetatively and the surplus food produced is stored in its ◊perennating organ, usually the root. In the following year these food reserves are used for the production of leaves, flowers, and seeds, after which the plant dies. Many root vegetables are biennials, including the carrot *Daucus carota* and parsnip *Pastinaca sativa*. Some garden plants that are grown as biennials are actually perennials, for example, the wallflower *Cheiranthus cheiri*.

Bierce Ambrose Gwinnett 1842–c. 1914. US author. After service in the American Civil War, he established his reputation as a master of the short story, his themes being war and the supernatural, as in *Tales of Soldiers and Civilians* 1891 and *Can Such Things Be?* 1893. He also wrote *The Devil's Dictionary* 1911 (first published as *The Cynic's Word Book* 1906), a collection of ironic definitions showing his sardonic humour. He disappeared in Mexico 1913.

bigamy in law, the offence of marrying a person while already lawfully married to another. In some countries marriage to more than one wife or husband is lawful; see also ◊polygamy.

big-band jazz ◊swing music created in the late 1930s and 1940s by bands of 13 or more players, such as those of Duke ◊Ellington and Benny ◊Goodman. Big-band jazz relied on fixed arrangements, where there is more than one instrument to some of the parts, rather than improvisation. Big bands were mainly dance bands, and they ceased to be economically viable in the 1950s. *See illustration on following page.*

Big Bang in astronomy, the hypothetical 'explosive' event that marked the origin of the universe as we know it. At the time of the Big Bang, the entire universe was squeezed into a hot, superdense state. The Big Bang explosion threw this compact material outwards, producing the expanding universe (see ◊red shift). The cause of the Big Bang is unknown; observations of the current rate of expansion of the universe suggest that it took place about 12 billion years ago. The Big Bang theory began modern ◊cosmology.

According to a modified version of the Big Bang, called the inflationary theory, the universe underwent a rapid period of expansion shortly after the Big Bang, which accounts for its current large size and uniform nature. The inflationary theory is supported by the most recent observations of the ◊cosmic background radiation.

Scientists have calculated that one 10^{-36} second (equivalent to one million-million-million-million-million-millionth of a second) after the Big Bang, the universe was the size of a pea, and the temperature was 10 billion million million million°C (18 billion million million million°F). One second after the Big Bang, the temperature was about 10 billion°C (18 billion°F).

Big Bang in economics, popular term for the changes instituted in late 1986 to the organization and practices of the City of London which were intended to ensure that London retained its place as one of the world financial centres and involving the liberalization of the London ◊Stock Exchange. This involved merging the functions of jobber (dealer in stocks and shares) and broker (who mediates between the jobber and the public), introducing negotiated commission rates, and allowing foreign banks and financial companies to own British brokers/jobbers, or themselves to join the London Stock Exchange.

In the year before and after the Big Bang the City of London was marked by hyperactivity: there were many takeovers, mergers, and acquisitions as companies sought to improve their competitiveness. Share prices rose sharply and trading was helped by the introduction of highly sensitive computerized systems and on-line communications. The level of activity could not be sustained, and in Oct 1987 the frenzied trading halted abruptly and share prices fell sharply around the world on what became known as ◊Black Monday.

Big Ben popular name for the bell in the clock tower of the Houses of Parliament in London, cast at the Whitechapel Bell Foundry 1858, and known as 'Big Ben' after Benjamin Hall, First Commissioner of Works at the time. It weighs 13.7 tonnes.

Big Dipper North American name for the Plough, the seven brightest and most prominent stars in the constellation ◊Ursa Major.

bight coastal indentation, crescent-shaped or gently curving, such as the Bight of Bonny in W Africa and the Great Australian Bight.

Bihar or ***Behar*** state of NE India
area 173,900 sq km/67,125 sq mi
capital Patna
features river Ganges in the N, Rajmahal Hills in the S
industries copper, iron, coal, rice, jute, sugar cane, grain, oilseed, tobacco, potatoes; 40% of India's mineral production
language Hindi, Bihari
population (1994 est) 93,080,000
famous people Chandragupta, Aśoka
history the ancient kingdom of Magadha roughly corresponded to central and S Bihar. Many Bihari people were massacred as a result of their protest at the establishment of Bangladesh 1971. Elections were postponed and direct rule imposed after public disturbances 1995.

Bihari a N Indian people, also living in Bangladesh, Nepal, and Pakistan, and numbering over 40 million. The Bihari are mainly Muslim. The Bihari language is related to Hindi and has several widely varying dialects. It belongs to the Indic branch of the Indo-European family. Many Bihari were massacred during the formation of Bangladesh, which they opposed.

Bikini atoll in the ◊Marshall Islands, W Pacific, where the USA carried out 23 atomic- and hydrogen-bomb tests (some underwater) 1946–58.

The islanders were relocated by the USA before 1946. Some returned after Bikini was declared safe for habitation 1969, but they were again removed in the late 1970s because of continuing harmful levels of radiation. In 1990 a US plan was announced to remove radioactive topsoil, allowing 800 islanders to return home.

BIBLE: BOOKS

Name of book	Chapters	Date written
Books of the Old Testament		
Genesis	50	mid-8th century BC
Exodus	40	950–586 BC
Leviticus	27	mid-7th century BC
Numbers	36	850–650 BC
Deuteronomy	34	mid-7th century BC
Joshua	24	c. 550 BC
Judges	21	c. 550 BC
Ruth	4	end 3rd century BC
1 Samuel	31	c. 900 BC
2 Samuel	24	c. 900 BC
1 Kings	22	550–600 BC
2 Kings	25	550–600 BC
1 Chronicles	29	c. 300 BC
2 Chronicles	36	c. 300 BC
Ezra	10	c. 450 BC
Nehemiah	13	c. 450 BC
Esther	10	c. 200 BC
Job	42	600–400 BC
Psalms	150	6th–2nd century BC
Proverbs	31	350–150 BC
Ecclesiastes	12	c. 200 BC
Song of Solomon	8	3rd century BC
Isaiah	66	end 3rd century BC
Jeremiah	52	604 BC
Lamentations	5	586–536 BC
Ezekiel	48	6th century BC
Daniel	12	c. 166 BC
Hosea	14	c. 732 BC
Joel	3	c. 500 BC
Amos	9	775–750 BC
Obadiah	1	6th–3rd century BC
Jonah	4	600–200 BC
Micah	7	end 3rd century BC
Nahum	3	c. 626 BC
Habakkuk	3	c. 600 BC
Zephaniah	3	3rd century BC
Haggai	2	c. 520 BC
Zechariah	14	c. 520 BC
Malachi	4	c. 430 BC
Books of the New Testament		
Matthew	28	before AD 70
Mark	16	before AD 70
Luke	24	AD 70–80
John	21	AD 90–100
Acts	28	AD 70–80
Romans	16	AD 120
1 Corinthians	16	AD 57
2 Corinthians	13	AD 57
Galatians	6	AD 53
Ephesians	6	AD 140
Philippians	4	AD 63
Colossians	4	AD 140
1 Thessalonians	5	AD 50–54
2 Thessalonians	3	AD 50–54
1 Timothy	6	before AD 64
2 Timothy	4	before AD 64
Titus	3	before AD 64
Philemon	1	AD 60–62
Hebrews	13	AD 80–90
James	5	before AD 52
1 Peter	5	before AD 64
2 Peter	3	before AD 64
1 John	5	AD 90–100
2 John	1	AD 90–100
3 John	1	AD 90–100
Jude	1	AD 75–80
Revelation	22	AD 81–96

Biko Steve (Stephen) 1946–1977. South African civil-rights leader. An active opponent of ◊apartheid, he was arrested Sept 1977; he died in detention six days later. Following his death in the custody of South African police, he became a symbol of the anti-apartheid movement.

He founded the South African Students Organization (SASO) 1968 and was cofounder 1972 of the Black People's Convention, also called the Black Consciousness movement, a radical association of South African students that aimed to develop black pride. His death in the hands of the police caused much controversy.

bilateralism in economics, a trade agreement between two countries or groups of countries in

'Patience – A minor form of despair, disguised as a virtue.'

AMBROSE BIERCE
The Devil's Dictionary

bilberry Also referred to as the blaeberry, whortleberry, or huckleberry, the bilberry has blue-grey edible berries which appear in autumn. The common bilberry *Vaccinium myrtillus*, shown here, is found across Europe and N Asia. *K G Preston-Mafham/Premaphotos Wildlife*

which they give each other preferential treatment. Usually the terms agreed result in balanced trade and are favoured by countries with limited foreign exchange reserves. Bilateralism is incompatible with free trade.

Bilbao industrial port (iron and steel, chemicals, cement, food) in N Spain, capital of Biscay province; population (1994) 372,000. Work began 1993 on the Guggenheim Museum Bilbao.

bilberry several species of shrubs of the genus *Vaccinium* of the heath family Ericaceae, closely related to North American blueberries.

bilby rabbit-eared bandicoot *Macrotis lagotis*, a lightly built marsupial with big ears and long nose. This burrowing animal is mainly carnivorous, and its pouch opens backwards.

Bildt, Carl 1949– . Swedish politician, prime minister 1991–94. Leader of the Moderate Party (MS) from 1986, in 1991 he formed a right-of-centre coalition after decades of social democratic politics, heading what was, in effect, a government of national unity. In 1995 he succeeded David Owen as European Union negotiator in the former Yugoslavia, and in 1996 was appointed 'High representative' of Bosnia-Herzegovina, overseeing the reconstruction side of the Dayton peace agreement.

Bildungsroman (German 'education novel') novel that deals with the psychological and emotional development of its protagonist, tracing his or her life from inexperienced youth to maturity. The first example of the type is generally considered to be C M ◊Wieland's *Agathon* 1765–66, but it was ◊Goethe's *Wilhelm Meisters Lehrjahre/Wilhelm Meister's Apprenticeship* 1795–96 that established the genre. Although taken up by writers in other languages, it remained chiefly a German form; later examples include Thomas ◊Mann's *Der Zauberberg/The Magic Mountain* 1924.

bile brownish alkaline fluid produced by the liver. Bile is stored in the gall bladder and is intermittently released into the duodenum (small intestine) to aid digestion. Bile consists of bile salts, bile pigments, cholesterol, and lecithin. Bile salts assist in the breakdown and absorption of fats; bile pigments are the breakdown products of old red blood cells that are passed into the gut to be eliminated with the faeces.

bilharzia or ***schistosomiasis*** disease that causes anaemia, inflammation, formation of scar tissue, dysentery, enlargement of the spleen and liver, cancer of the bladder, and cirrhosis of the liver. It is contracted by bathing in water contaminated with human sewage. Some 200 million people are thought to suffer from this disease in the tropics, and 750,000 people a year die.

Freshwater snails act as host to the first larval stage of blood flukes of the genus *Schistosoma*; when these larvae leave the snail in their second stage of development, they are able to pass through human skin, become sexually mature, and produce quantities of eggs, which pass to the intestine or bladder. Numerous eggs are excreted from the body in urine or faeces to continue the cycle. Treatment is by means of drugs, usually containing antimony, to kill the parasites.

bill in birds, the projection of the skull bones covered with a horny sheath. It is not normally sensitive, except in some aquatic birds, rooks, and woodpeckers, where the bill is used to locate food that is not visible. The bills of birds are adapted by shape and size to specific diets, for example, shovellers use their bills to sieve mud in order to extract food and birds of prey have hooked bills adapted to tearing flesh. The bill is also used by birds for preening, fighting, display, and nest-building.

billet in Romanesque architecture, an ornamental moulding formed of short cylindrical blocks, suggesting miniature wooden 'billets', and set in a concave moulding.

billiards indoor game played, normally by two players, with tapered poles (cues) and composition balls (one red, two white) on a rectangular table covered with a green, feltlike cloth (baize). The table has six pockets, one at each corner and in each of the long sides at the middle. Scoring strokes are made by potting the red ball, potting the opponent's ball, or potting another ball off one of these two. The cannon (when the cue ball hits the two other balls on the table) is another scoring stroke.

Billiards is played in many different forms. The most popular is the three-ball game played on a standard English billiards table, which is approximately 3.66 m/12 ft by 1.83 m/6 ft in size.

Carom, played on a table without pockets, is popular in Europe. Another form is ◊pool, popular in the USA and Britain. The World Professional Championship was instituted 1870 and organized on a challenge basis. It was restored as an annual tournament 1980.

billion the cardinal number represented by a 1 followed by nine zeros (1,000,000,000 or 10^9), equivalent to a thousand million.

In Britain, this number was formerly known as a milliard, and a million million (1,000,000,000,000) as a billion, but the first definition is now internationally recognized.

bill of exchange form of commercial credit instrument, or IOU, used in international trade. In Britain, a bill of exchange is defined by the Bills of Exchange Act 1882 as an unconditional order in writing addressed by one person to another, signed by the person giving it, requiring the person to whom it is addressed to pay on demand or at a fixed or determinable future time a certain sum in money to or to the order of a specified person, or to the bearer.

Bill of Rights in the USA, the first ten amendments to the US ◊Constitution, incorporated 1791:

1 guarantees freedom of worship, of speech, of the press, of assembly, and to petition the government;

2 grants the right to keep and bear arms;

3 prohibits billeting of soldiers in private homes in peacetime;

4 forbids unreasonable search and seizure;

5 guarantees none be 'deprived of life, liberty or property without due process of law' or compelled in any criminal case to be a witness against himself or herself;

6 grants the right to speedy trial, to call witnesses, and to have defence counsel;

7 grants the right to trial by jury of one's peers;

8 prevents the infliction of excessive bail or fines, or 'cruel and unusual punishment';

9, 10 provide a safeguard to the states and people for all rights not specifically delegated to the central government.

Not originally part of the draft of the Constitution, the Bill of Rights was mooted during the

bill The yellow-billed hornbill *Tockus flavirostris*, common in dry bush country from Ethiopia to South Africa, illustrates one of the extremes to which bills have evolved. This species lacks the prominent casque found in some of the larger members of the family. There is, as yet, no satisfactory explanation for the adaptation of this particular hornbill. *K G Preston-Mafham/Premaphotos Wildlife*

Billy the Kid US outlaw Billy the Kid (left) being shot dead by sheriff Pat Garrett at Fort Sumner. A contemporary woodcut. Though he was a ruthless and brutal killer, his short life became part of the Wild West's mythology, portrayals of him becoming increasingly sympathetic. A ballet based on his life, with music by Aaron Copeland, appeared 1938. *Corbis*

period of ratification. Twelve amendments were proposed by Congress 1789; the ten now called the Bill of Rights were ratified 1791. ◊*See feature on pp. 32–33.*

Bill of Rights in Britain, an act of Parliament 1689 which established it as the primary governing body of the country. The Bill of Rights embodied the Declaration of Rights which contained the conditions on which William and Mary were offered the throne. It made provisions limiting ◊royal prerogative with respect to legislation, executive power, money levies, courts, and the army and stipulated Parliament's consent to many government functions.

The act made illegal the suspension of laws by royal authority without Parliament's consent; the power to dispense with laws; the establishment of special courts of law; levying money by royal prerogative without Parliament's consent; and the maintenance of a standing army in peacetime without Parliament's consent. It also asserted a right to petition the sovereign, freedom of parliamentary elections, freedom of speech in parliamentary debates, and the necessity of frequent parliaments.

Billy the Kid nickname of William H Bonney 1859–1881. US outlaw. A leader in the 1878 Lincoln County cattle war in New Mexico, he allegedly killed his first victim at 12 and was reputed to have killed 21 men by age 22, when he died.

Born in Brooklyn, New York, Bonney moved west with his family to Kansas and then New Mexico. He was sentenced to death for murdering a sheriff, but escaped (killing two guards), and was finally shot by Sheriff Pat Garrett while trying to avoid recapture.

bimetallism monetary system in which two metals, traditionally gold and silver, both circulate at a ratio fixed by the state, are coined by the ◊mint on equal terms, and are legal tender to any amount. The system was in use in the 19th century.

Advocates of bimetallism have argued that the 'compensatory action of the double standard' makes for a currency more stable than one based only on gold, since the changes in the value of the two metals taken together may be expected to be less than the changes in one of them. One of the many arguments against the system is that the ratio of the prices of the metals is frozen regardless of the supply and demand.

binary fission in biology, a form of ◊asexual reproduction, whereby a single-celled organism, such as the amoeba, divides into two smaller 'daughter' cells. It can also occur in a few simple multicellular organisms, such as sea anemones, producing two smaller sea anemones of equal size.

binary form in music, a composition in symmetrical halves, the first modulating to the ◊dominant key, the second modulating back to the starting ◊tonic key.

binary number system system of numbers to ◊base two, using combinations of the digits 1 and 0. Codes based on binary numbers are used to represent instructions and data in all modern digital computers, the values of the binary digits (contracted to 'bits') being stored or transmitted as, for example, open/closed switches, magnetized/unmagnetized discs and tapes, and high/low voltages in circuits.

The value of any position in a binary number increases by powers of 2 (doubles) with each move from right to left (1, 2, 4, 8, 16, and so on). For example, 1011 in the binary number system means $(1 \times 8) + (0 \times 4) + (1 \times 2) + (1 \times 1)$, which adds up to 11 in the decimal system. *See list of tables on p. 1177.*

binary star pair of stars moving in orbit around their common centre of mass. Observations show that most stars are binary, or even multiple – for example, the nearest star system to the Sun, ◊Alpha Centauri.

One of the stars in the binary system Epsilon Aurigae may be the largest star known. Its diameter is 2,800 times that of the Sun. If it were in the position of the Sun, it would engulf Mercury, Venus, Earth, Mars, Jupiter, and Saturn. A spectroscopic binary is a binary in which two stars are so close together that they cannot be seen separately, but their separate light spectra can be distinguished by a spectroscope.

Another type is the ◊eclipsing binary.

binary weapon in chemical warfare, weapon consisting of two substances that in isolation are harmless but when mixed together form a poisonous nerve gas. They are loaded into the delivery system separately and combine after launch.

With conventional chemical weapons, chemical stockpiles deteriorate, and the handling and security of such unstable compounds present serious problems. The development of binary chemical weapons in the USA served to minimize these risks, since the principle on which they are based is the combination of two individually harmless compounds into a deadly chemical agent only in the shell or bomb they are housed in, and then only when the projectile is armed or fired.

bind over in law, a UK court order that requires a person to carry out some act, usually by an order given in a magistrates' court. A person may be bound over to appear in court at a particular time if bail has been granted or, most commonly, be bound over not to commit some offence; for example, causing a breach of the peace.

There is no power for the court to impose any conditions, but an order may be made in terms such as 'to keep the peace towards all Her Majesty's subjects, and especially towards X'.

history The origins of the power to bind over can be traced back to the 10th century. Statutory powers for justices of the peace to take recognizance were introduced 1361. This act empowered justices to bind over all those who were of 'good fame' so long as they were prepared to give sufficient surety of their good behaviour towards the king and his people. The Justices of the Peace Act 1361, parts of which are still in force, included provisions for dealing with 'vagabonds' and was used to regulate the behaviour of troops who had been living on the spoils of war and were returning to England looting and pillaging along the highways.

Binet Alfred 1857–1911. French psychologist who introduced the first ◊intelligence tests 1905. They were standardized so that the last of a set of graded tests the child could successfully complete gave the level described as 'mental age'. If the test was passed by most children over 12, for instance, but failed by those younger, it was said to show a mental age of 12. Binet published these in collaboration with Théodore Simon.

bingo game of chance played with numbered balls and cards each divided into 27 squares, 15 of them containing random numbers between 1 and 90. As the numbers are called out, also at random, the corresponding numbers are marked off the players' card(s). The first person to complete a line across or full card (known as a 'full house') wins a prize.

binoculars optical instrument for viewing an object in magnification with both eyes; for example, field glasses and opera glasses. Binoculars consist of two telescopes containing lenses and prisms, which produce a stereoscopic effect as well as magnifying the image. Use of prisms has the effect of 'folding' the light path, allowing for a compact design. The first binocular telescope was made by the Dutch inventor Hans Lippershey 1608. *See illustration on following page.*

binomial system of nomenclature in biology, the system in which all organisms are identified by a two-part Latinized name. Devised by the biologist ◊Linnaeus, it is also known as the Linnaean system. The first name is capitalized and identifies the ◊genus; the second identifies the ◊species within that genus.

binomial theorem formula whereby any power of a binomial quantity may be found without performing the progressive multiplications. It was discovered by Isaac ◊Newton and first published in 1676.

binturong shaggy-coated mammal *Arctitis binturong*, the largest member of the mongoose family, nearly 1 m/3 ft long excluding a long muscular tail with a prehensile tip. Mainly nocturnal and tree-dwelling, the binturong is found in the forests of SE Asia, feeding on fruit, eggs, and small animals.

Binyon (Robert) Laurence 1869–1943. English poet. His ode 'For the Fallen' 1914 is frequently quoted in war memorial services and was set to music by English composer Edward ◊Elgar. Binyon's verse volumes include *London Visions* 1896; his art criticism includes *Painting in the Far East* 1908.

biochemistry science concerned with the chemistry of living organisms: the structure and reactions of proteins (such as enzymes), nucleic acids, carbohydrates, and lipids.

Its study has led to an increased understanding of life processes, such as those by which organisms synthesize essential chemicals from food materials, store and generate energy, and pass on their characteristics through their genetic material. A great deal of medical research is concerned with the ways in which these processes are disrupted. Biochemistry also has applications in agriculture and in the food industry (for instance, in the use of enzymes). *See timeline on p. 127.*

biodegradable capable of being broken down by living organisms, principally bacteria and fungi. In biodegradable substances, such as food and sewage, the natural processes of decay lead to compaction and liquefaction, and to the release of nutrients that are then recycled by the ecosystem.

This process can have some disadvantageous side effects, such as the release of methane, an explosive greenhouse gas. However, the technology now exists for waste tips to collect methane in underground pipes, drawing it off and using it as a cheap source of energy. Nonbiodegradable substances, such as glass, heavy metals, and most types of plastic, present serious problems of disposal.

binary number system The capital letter A represented in binary form.

data A

binary code 0 1 0 0 0 0 0 1

digital signal in the computer

They shall grow not old, as we that are left grow old: / Age shall not weary them, nor the years condemn. / At the going down of the sun and in the morning / We will remember them.

LAURENCE BINYON
'Poem for the Fallen'

binoculars An optical instrument that allows the user to focus both eyes on the magnified image at the same time. The essential components of binoculars are objective lenses, eye pieces, and a system of prisms to invert and reverse the image. A focusing system provides a sharp image by adjusting the relative positions of these components.

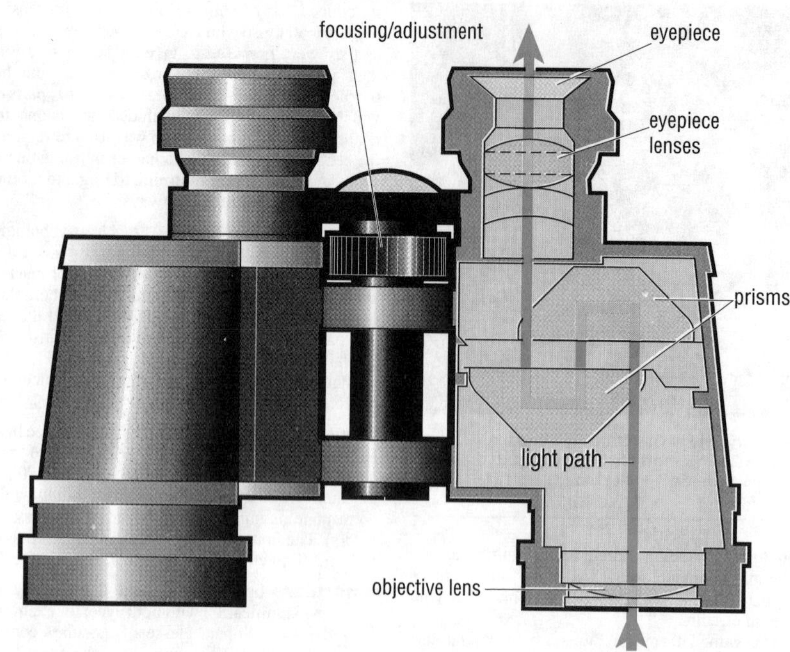

biodiversity (contraction of ***biological diversity***) measure of the variety of the Earth's animal, plant, and microbial species; of genetic differences within species; and of the ecosystems that support those species. Its maintenance is important for ecological stability and as a resource for research into, for example, new drugs and crops. In the 20th century, the destruction of habitats is believed to have resulted in the most severe and rapid loss of biodiversity in the history of the planet.

Estimates of the number of species vary widely because many species-rich ecosystems, such as tropical forests, contain unexplored and unstudied habitats. Especially among small organisms, many are unknown; for instance, it is thought that only 1–10% of the world's bacterial species have been identified.

The most significant threat to biodiversity comes from the destruction of rainforests and other habitats in the southern hemisphere. It is estimated that 7% of the Earth's surface hosts 50–75% of the world's biological diversity. Costa Rica, for example, has an area less than 10% of the size of France but possesses three times as many vertebrate species. ◊*See feature on pp. 896–897.*

bioenergetics in alternative medicine, extension of the principles of Reichian therapy (see ◊Reich, Wilhelm) developed in the 1960s by US physician Alexander Lowen, and designed to promote, by breathing, physical exercise, and the elimination of muscular blockages, the free flow of energy in the body and thus restore optimum health and vitality.

bioengineering the application of engineering to biology and medicine. Common applications include the design and use of artificial limbs, joints, and organs, including hip joints and heart valves.

biofeedback in biology, modification or control of a biological system by its results or effects. For example, a change in the position or ◊trophic level of one species affects all levels above it.

Many biological systems are controlled by negative feedback. When enough of the hormone thyroxine has been released into the blood, the hormone adjusts its own level by 'switching off' the gland that produces it. In ecology, as the numbers in a species rise, the food supply available to each individual is reduced. This acts to reduce the population to a sustainable level.

biofeedback in medicine, the use of electrophysiological monitoring devices to 'feed back' information about internal processes and thus facilitate conscious control. Developed in the USA in the 1960s, independently by neurophysiologist Barbara Brown and neuropsychiatrist Joseph Kamiya, the technique is effective in alleviating hypertension and preventing associated organic and physiological dysfunctions.

‘Biography should be written by an acute enemy.’

On **BIOGRAPHY** Arthur Balfour Quoted in the *Observer* 30 Jan 1927

biofuel any solid, liquid, or gaseous fuel produced from organic (once living) matter, either directly from plants or indirectly from industrial, commercial, domestic, or agricultural wastes. There are three main methods for the development of biofuels: the burning of dry organic wastes (such as household refuse, industrial and agricultural wastes, straw, wood, and peat); the fermentation of wet wastes (such as animal dung) in the absence of oxygen to produce biogas (containing up to 60% methane), or the fermentation of sugar cane or corn to produce alcohol and esters; and energy forestry (producing fast-growing wood for fuel).

Fermentation produces two main types of biofuels: alcohols and esters. These could theoretically be used in place of fossil fuels but, because major alterations to engines would be required, biofuels are usually mixed with fossil fuels. The EU allows 5% ethanol, derived from wheat, beet, potatoes, or maize, to be added to fossil fuels. A quarter of Brazil's transportation fuel 1994 was ethanol. ◊*See feature on pp. 360–361.*

biogenesis biological term coined 1870 by English scientist Thomas Henry Huxley to express the hypothesis that living matter always arises out of other similar forms of living matter. It superseded the opposite idea of ◊spontaneous generation or abiogenesis (that is, that living things may arise out of nonliving matter).

biogeography study of how and why plants and animals are distributed around the world, in the past as well as in the present; more specifically, a theory describing the geographical distribution of ◊species developed by Robert MacArthur and US zoologist Edward O ◊Wilson. The theory argues that for many species, ecological specializations mean that suitable habitats are patchy in their occurrence. Thus for a dragonfly, ponds in which to breed are separated by large tracts of land, and for edelweiss adapted to alpine peaks the deep valleys between cannot be colonized.

biography account of a person's life. When it is written by that person, it is an ◊autobiography. Biography may consist simply of the factual details of a person's life told in chronological order, but has generally become a matter of interpretation as well as historical accuracy. Unofficial biographies (not sanctioned by the subject) have frequently led to legal disputes over both interpretation and facts.

Among ancient biographers are Xenophon, Plutarch, Tacitus, Suetonius, and the authors of the Gospels of the New Testament. Medieval biography was mostly devoted to religious edification and produced chronicles of saints and martyrs; among secular biographies are *Charlemagne* by Frankish monk Einhard (c. 770–840), *Alfred* by Welsh monk Asser (died c. 910), and *Petrarch* by ◊Boccaccio.

In England true biography begins with the early Tudor period and such works as *Sir Thomas More* 1626, written by his son-in-law William Roper (1498–1578). By the 18th century it became a literary form in its own right through Samuel Johnson's *Lives of the Most Eminent English Poets* 1779–81 and James Boswell's biography of Johnson 1791. Nineteenth-century biographers include Robert Southey, Elizabeth Gaskell, G H Lewes, J Morley, and Thomas Carlyle. The general tendency was to provide irrelevant detail and suppress the more personal facts. Lytton Strachey's *Eminent Victorians* opened a new era of frankness in the history of biography.

Twentieth-century biographers include Richard Ellmann (1918–1987) (James Joyce and Oscar Wilde), Michael Holroyd (1935–) (Lytton Strachey and George Bernard Shaw), and Elizabeth Longford (Queen Victoria and Wellington).

The earliest biographical dictionary in the accepted sense was that of Pierre Bayle 1696, followed during the 19th century by the development of national biographies in Europe, and the foundation of the *English Dictionary of National Biography* 1882 and the *Dictionary of American Biography* 1928.

biological clock regular internal rhythm of activity, produced by unknown mechanisms, and not dependent on external time signals. Such clocks are known to exist in almost all animals, and also in many plants, fungi, and unicellular organisms; the first biological clock gene in plants was isolated 1995 by a US team of researchers. In higher organisms, there appears to be a series of clocks of graded importance. For example, although body temperature and activity cycles in human beings are normally 'set' to 24 hours, the two cycles may vary independently, showing that two clock mechanisms are involved.

biological control control of pests such as insects and fungi through biological means, rather than the use of chemicals. This can include breeding resistant crop strains; inducing sterility in the pest; infecting the pest species with disease organisms; or introducing the pest's natural predator. Biological control tends to be naturally self-regulating, but as ecosystems are so complex, it is difficult to predict all the consequences of introducing a biological controlling agent.

biological oxygen demand (BOD) the amount of dissolved oxygen taken up by microorganisms in a sample of water. Since these microorganisms live by decomposing organic matter, and the amount of oxygen used is proportional to their number and metabolic rate, BOD can be used as a measure of the extent to which the water is polluted with organic compounds.

biological shield shield around a nuclear reactor that is intended to protect personnel from the effects of ◊radiation. It usually consists of a thick wall of steel and concrete.

biological warfare the use of living organisms, or of infectious material derived from them, to bring about death or disease in humans, animals, or plants. At least ten countries have this capability.

Biological warfare, together with ◊chemical warfare, was originally prohibited by the Geneva Protocol 1925, to which the United Nations has urged all states to adhere. Nevertheless research in this area continues; the Biological Weapons Convention 1972 permits research for defence purposes but does not define how this differs from offensive weapons development. In 1990 the US Department of Defense allocated $60 million to research, develop, and test defence systems. Russian president Boris Yeltsin signed a decree to comply with the Protocol 1992. Although the treaty was ratified by the Kremlin three months after its original signing, national laws ensuring compliance were never passed.

Advances in genetic engineering make the development of new varieties of potentially offensive biological weapons more likely.

biological weathering form of ◊weathering caused by the activities of living organisms – for example, the growth of roots or the burrowing of animals. Tree roots are probably the most significant agents of biological weathering as they are capable of prising apart rocks by growing into cracks and joints.

BIOCHEMISTRY: TIMELINE

c. 1830	Johannes Müller discovered proteins.
1833	Anselme Payen and J F Persoz first isolated an enzyme.
1862	Haemoglobin was first crystallized.
1869	The genetic material DNA (deoxyribonucleic acid) was discovered by Friedrich Mieschler
1899	Emil Fischer postulated the 'lock-and-key' hypothesis to explain the specificity of enzyme action.
1913	Leonor Michaelis and M L Menten developed a mathematical equation describing the rate of enzyme-catalysed reactions
1915	The hormone thyroxine was first isolated from thyroid gland tissue.
1920	The chromosome theory of heredity was postulated by Thomas H Morgan; growth hormone was discovered by Herbert McLean Evans and J A Long.
1921	Insulin was first isolated from the pancreas by Frederick Banting and Charles Best.
1926	Insulin was obtained in pure crystalline form.
1927	Thyroxine was first synthesized.
1928	Alexander Fleming discovered penicillin.
1931	Paul Karrer deduced the structure of retinol (vitamin A); vitamin D compounds were obtained in crystalline form by Adolf Windaus and Askew, independently of each other.
1932	Charles Glen King isolated ascorbic acid (vitamin C).
1933	Tadeus Reichstein synthesized ascorbic acid.
1935	Richard Kuhn and Karrer established the structure of riboflavin (vitamin B_2).
1936	Robert Williams established the structure of thiamine (vitamin B_1); biotin was isolated by Kogl and Tonnis.
1937	Niacin was isolated and identified by Conrad Arnold Elvehjem.
1938	Pyridoxine (vitamin B_6) was isolated in pure crystalline form.
1939	The structure of pyridoxine was determined by Kuhn.
1940	Hans Krebs proposed the Krebs (citric acid) cycle; Hickman isolated retinol in pure crystalline form; Williams established the structure of pantothenic acid; biotin was identified by Albert Szent-Györgyi, Vincent Du Vigneaud, and co-workers.
1941	Penicillin was isolated and characterized by Howard Florey and Ernst Chain.
1943	The role of DNA in genetic inheritance was first demonstrated by Oswald Avery, Colin MacLeod, and Maclyn McCarty.
1950	The basic components of DNA were established by Erwin Chargaff; the alpha-helical structure of proteins was established by Linus Pauling and R B Corey.
1953	James Watson and Francis Crick determined the molecular structure of DNA.
1956	Mahlon Hoagland and Paul Zamecnick discovered transfer RNA (ribonucleic acid); mechanisms for the biosynthesis of RNA and DNA were discovered by Arthur Kornberg and Severo Ochoa.
1957	Interferon was discovered by Alick Isaacs and Jean Lindemann.
1958	The structure of RNA was determined.
1960	Messenger RNA was discovered by Sidney Brenner and François Jacob.
1961	Marshall Nirenberg and Ochoa determined the chemical nature of the genetic code.
1965	Insulin was first synthesized.
1966	The immobilization of enzymes was achieved by Chibata.
1968	Brain hormones were discovered by Roger Guillemin and Andrew Schally.
1975	J Hughes and Hans Kosterlitz discovered encephalins.
1976	Guillemin discovered endorphins.
1977	J Baxter determined the genetic code for human growth hormone.
1978	Human insulin was first produced by genetic engineering.
1979	The biosynthetic production of human growth hormone was announced by Howard Goodman and J Baxter of the University of California, and by D V Goeddel and Seeburg of Genentech.
1982	Louis Chedid and Michael Sela developed the first synthesized vaccine.
1983	The first commercially available product of genetic engineering (Humulin) was launched.
1985	Alec Jeffreys devised genetic fingerprinting.
1993	UK researchers introduced a healthy version of the gene for cystic fibrosis into the lungs of mice with induced cystic fibrosis, restoring normal function.
1996	Japanese chemists synthesized cellulose.

biology (Greek *bios* 'life', *logos* 'discourse') science of life. Biology includes all the life sciences – for example, anatomy and physiology (the study of the structure of living things), cytology (the study of cells), zoology (the study of animals) and botany (the study of plants), ecology (the study of habitats and the interaction of living species), animal behaviour, embryology, and taxonomy, and plant breeding. Increasingly in the 20th century biologists have concentrated on molecular structures: biochemistry, biophysics, and genetics.

Biological research has come a long way towards understanding the nature of life, and during the 1990s our knowledge will be further extended as the international ◊Human Genome Project attempts to map the entire genetic code contained in the 23 pairs of human chromosomes. *See timeline on following page.*

BIODIVERSITY: NUMBER OF SPECIES WORLDWIDE

	Number identified	% of estimated total number of species
microorganisms	5,800	3–27
invertebrates	1,021,000	3–27
plants	322,500	67–100
fish	19,100	83–100
birds	9,100	94–100
reptiles and amphibians	12,000	90–95
mammals	4,000	90–95
total	1,393,500	
	Number of species	**% identified**
low estimate of all species	4.4 million	31
high estimate of all species	80 million	2

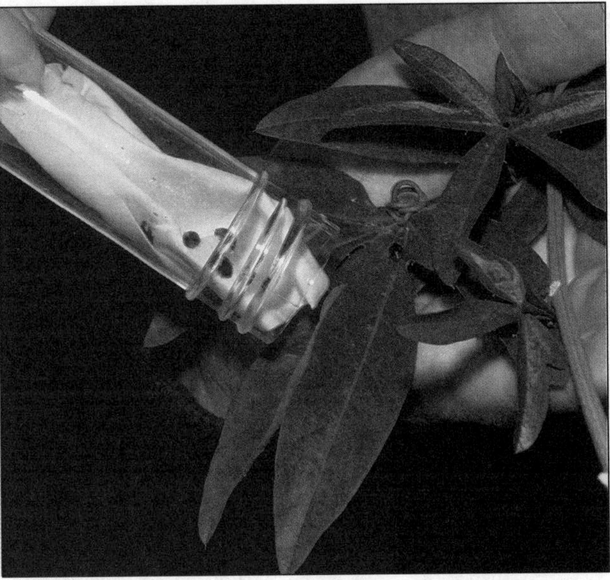

biological control The beetle *Cryptolaemus montrouzieri* being released on to a mealybug-infested passion flower. Because mealybugs, which are a serious pest, have a waxy coating and so are resistant to insecticides, biological control agents are used against them. *Premaphotos Wildlife*

bioluminescence production of light by living organisms. It is a feature of many deep-sea fishes, crustaceans, and other marine animals. On land, bioluminescence is seen in some nocturnal insects such as glow-worms and fireflies, and in certain bacteria and fungi. Light is usually produced by the oxidation of luciferin, a reaction catalysed by the ◊enzyme luciferase. This reaction is unique, being the only known biological oxidation that does not produce heat. Animal luminescence is involved in communication, camouflage, or the luring of prey, but its function in other organisms is unclear.

biomass the total mass of living organisms present in a given area. It may be specified for a particular species (such as earthworm biomass) or for a general category (such as herbivore biomass). Estimates also exist for the entire global plant biomass. Measurements of biomass can be used to study interactions between organisms, the stability of those interactions, and variations in population numbers. Where dry biomass is measured, the material is dried to remove all water before weighing.

Some two-thirds of the world's population cooks and heats water by burning biomass, usually wood. Plant biomass can be a renewable source of energy as replacement supplies can be grown relatively quickly. Fossil fuels however, originally formed from biomass, accumulate so slowly that they cannot be considered renewable. The burning of biomass (defined either as natural areas of the ecosystem or as forest, grasslands, and fuelwoods) produces 3.5 million tonnes of carbon in the form of carbon dioxide each year, accounting for up to 40% of the world's annual carbon dioxide production.

biome broad natural assemblage of plants and animals shaped by common patterns of vegetation and climate. Examples include the tundra biome and the desert biome.

biomechanics application of mechanical engineering principles and techniques in the field of medicine and surgery, studying natural structures to improve those produced by humans. For example, mother-of-pearl is structurally superior to glass fibre, and deer antlers have outstanding durability because they are composed of microscopic fibres. Such natural structures may form the basis of high-tech composites. Biomechanics has been responsible for many recent advances in ◊orthopaedics, anaesthesia, and intensive care. Biomechanical assessment of the requirements for replacement of joints, including evaluation of the stresses and strains between parts, and their reliability, has allowed development of implants with very low friction and long life.

bionics (from 'biological electronics') design and development of electronic or mechanical artificial systems that imitate those of living things. The bionic arm, for example, is an artificial limb (◊prosthesis) that uses electronics to amplify minute electrical signals generated in body muscles to work electric motors, which operate the joints of the fingers and wrist.

BIOLOGY: TIMELINE

c. 500 BC	First studies of the structure and behaviour of animals, by the Greek Alcmaeon of Croton.
c. 450	Hippocrates of Kos undertook the first detailed studies of human anatomy.
c. 350	Aristotle laid down the basic philosophy of the biological sciences and outlined a theory of evolution.
c. 300	Theophrastus carried out the first detailed studies of plants.
c. AD 175	Galen established the basic principles of anatomy and physiology.
c. 1500	Leonardo da Vinci studied human anatomy to improve his drawing ability and produced detailed anatomical drawings.
1628	William Harvey described the circulation of the blood and the function of the heart as a pump.
1665	Robert Hooke used a microscope to describe the cellular structure of plants.
1672	Marcelle Malphigi undertook the first studies in embryology by describing the development of a chicken egg.
1677	Anton van Leeuwenhoek greatly improved the microscope and used it to describe spermatozoa as well as many microorganisms.
1736	Carolus Linnaeus published his systematic classification of plants, so establishing taxonomy.
1768–79	James Cook's voyages of discovery in the Pacific revealed an undreamed-of diversity of living species, prompting the development of theories to explain their origin.
1796	Edward Jenner established the practice of vaccination against smallpox, laying the foundations for theories of antibodies and immune reactions.
1809	Jean-Baptiste Lamarck advocated a theory of evolution through inheritance of acquired characteristics.
1839	Theodor Schwann proposed that all living matter is made up of cells.
1857	Louis Pasteur established that microorganisms are responsible for fermentation, creating the discipline of microbiology.
1859	Charles Darwin published *On the Origin of Species*, expounding his theory of the evolution of species by natural selection.
1865	Gregor Mendel pioneered the study of inheritance with his experiments on peas, but achieved little recognition.
1883	August Weismann proposed his theory of the continuity of the germ plasm.
1900	Mendel's work was rediscovered and the science of genetics founded.
1935	Konrad Lorenz published the first of many major studies of animal behaviour, which founded the discipline of ethology.
1953	James Watson and Francis Crick described the molecular structure of the genetic material, DNA.
1964	William Hamilton recognized the importance of inclusive fitness, so paving the way for the development of sociobiology.
1975	Discovery of endogenous opiates (the brain's own painkillers) opened up a new phase in the study of brain chemistry.
1976	Har Gobind Khorana and his colleagues constructed the first artificial gene to function naturally when inserted into a bacterial cell, a major step in genetic engineering.
1982	Gene databases were established at Heidelberg, Germany, for the European Molecular Biology Laboratory, and at Los Alamos, USA, for the US National Laboratories.
1985	The first human cancer gene, retinoblastoma, was isolated by researchers at the Massachusetts Eye and Ear Infirmary and the Whitehead Institute, Massachusetts.
1988	The Human Genome Organization (HUGO) was established in Washington DC with the aim of mapping the complete sequence of DNA.
1991	Biosphere 2, an experiment attempting to reproduce the world's biosphere in miniature within a sealed glass dome, was launched in Arizona, USA.
1992	Researchers at the University of California, USA, stimulated the multiplication of isolated brain cells of mice, overturning the axiom that mammalian brains cannot produce replacement cells once birth has taken place. The world's largest organism, a honey fungus with underground hyphae (filaments) spreading across 600 hectares/1,480 acres, was discovered in Washington State, USA.
1994	Scientists from Pakistan and the USA unearthed a 50-million-year-old fossil whale with hind legs that would have enabled it to walk on land.
1995	New phylum identified and named Cycliophora. It contains a single known species, *Symbion pandora*, a parasite of the lobster.
1996	The sequencing of the genome of brewer's yeast *Saccharomyces cerevisiae* was completed, the first time this had been achieved for an organism more complex than a bacterium. The 12 million base pairs took 300 scientists six years to map.
1997	'Dolly', the first mammal (a sheep) to be cloned from an adult body cell, was born in Scotland.

biophysics application of physical laws to the properties of living organisms. Examples include using the principles of ◊mechanics to calculate the strength of bones and muscles, and ◊thermodynamics to study plant and animal energetics.

biopsy removal of a living tissue sample from the body for diagnostic examination.

biorhythm rhythmic change, mediated by ◊hormones, in the physical state and activity patterns of certain plants and animals that have seasonal activities. Examples include winter hibernation, spring flowering or breeding, and periodic migration. The hormonal changes themselves are often a response to changes in day length (◊photoperiodism); they signal the time of year to the animal or plant. Other biorhythms are innate and continue even if external stimuli such as day length are removed. These include a 24-hour or ◊circadian rhythm, a 28-day or circalunar rhythm (corresponding to the phases of the Moon), and even a year-long rhythm in some organisms. Such innate biorhythms are linked to an internal or ◊biological clock, whose mechanism is still poorly understood.

Often both types of rhythm operate; thus many birds have a circalunar rhythm that prepares them for the breeding season, and a photoperiodic response. There is also a nonscientific and unproven theory that human activity is governed by three biorhythms: the intellectual (33 days), the emotional (28 days), and the physical (23 days). Certain days in each cycle are regarded as 'critical', even more so if one such day coincides with that of another cycle.

biosensor device based on microelectronic circuits that can directly measure medically significant variables for the purpose of diagnosis or monitoring treatment. One such device measures the blood sugar level of diabetics using a single drop of blood, and shows the result on a liquid crystal display within a few minutes.

biosphere the narrow zone that supports life on our planet. It is limited to the waters of the Earth, a fraction of its crust, and the lower regions of the atmosphere.

BioSphere 2 (BS2) ecological test project, a 'planet in a bottle', in Arizona, USA. Under a sealed glass dome, several different habitats are recreated, with representatives of nearly 4,000 species, including man, to see how well air, water, and waste can be recycled in an enclosed environment and whether a stable ecosystem can be created.

BS2 is not in fact the second in a series: the Earth is considered to be BioSphere 1. The sealed area covers a total of 3.5 acres and contains tropical rainforest, salt marsh, desert, coral reef, and savanna habitats, as well as a section for intensive agriculture. The major problem has been in maintaining satisfactory oxygen levels. The rainforest was thriving 1994 but the plankton levels in the ocean were too low to sustain the corals; the climate was too moist for the desert plants and the desert was being overrun by grasses and shrubs.

The people within are entirely self-sufficient, except for electricity, which is supplied by a 3.7 megawatt power station on the outside (solar panels were considered too expensive). The original team of eight in residence 1991–1993 was replaced March 1994 with a new team of six people for 10 months; in 1995 it was decided that further research would not involve sealing people within the biosphere.

The cost of setting up and maintaining the project has been estimated at $100 million, some of which will be covered by paying visitors, who can view the inhabitants through the geodesic glass dome.

biosynthesis synthesis of organic chemicals from simple inorganic ones by living cells – for example, the conversion of carbon dioxide and water to glucose by plants during ◊photosynthesis. Other biosynthetic reactions produce cell constituents including proteins and fats.

Biosynthesis requires energy; in the initial or light-dependent stages of photosynthesis this is obtained from sunlight, but in all other instances, it is supplied chemically by ◊ATP and NADPH. The term is also used in connection with the products achieved through biotechnology processes.

biotechnology industrial use of living organisms to manufacture food, drugs, or other products. The brewing and baking industries have long relied on the yeast microorganism for ◊fermentation purposes, while the dairy industry employs a range of bacteria and fungi to convert milk into cheeses and yoghurts. ◊Enzymes, whether extracted from cells or produced artificially, are central to most biotechnological applications.

Recent advances include ◊genetic engineering, in which single-celled organisms with modified ◊DNA are used to produce insulin and other drugs.

In 1993 two-thirds of biotechnology companies were concentrating on human health developments, whilst only 1 in 10 were concerned with applications for food and agriculture.

biotin or ***vitamin H*** vitamin of the B complex, found in many different kinds of food; egg yolk, liver, legumes, and yeast contain large amounts. Biotin is essential to the metabolism of fats. Its absence from the diet may lead to dermatitis.

biotite dark mica, $K(Mg, Fe)_3Al\,Si_3O_{10}(OH, F)_2$, a common silicate mineral. It is brown to black with shiny surfaces, and like all micas, it splits into very thin flakes along its one perfect cleavage. Biotite is a mineral found in igneous rocks, such as granites, and metamorphic rocks such as schists and gneisses.

birch any tree of the genus *Betula*, including about 40 species found in cool temperate parts of the northern hemisphere. Birches grow rapidly, and their hard, beautiful wood is used for veneers and cabinet work.

The white or silver birch *Betula pendula* is of great use to industry because its timber is quick-

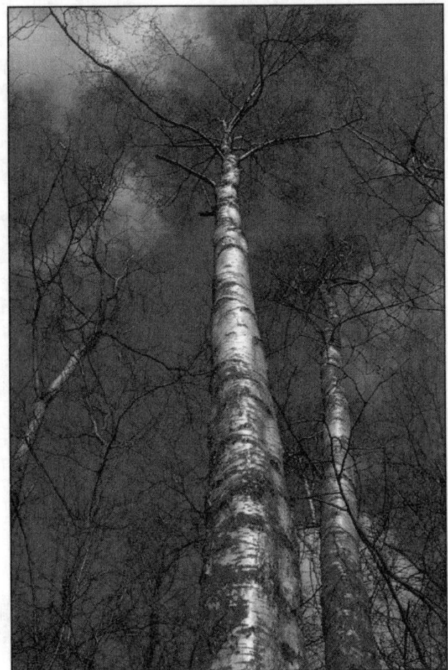

birch The familiar silver birch is widely distributed across Europe, Siberia, and parts of Asia and is also found in Morocco. It likes light soils and often colonizes heathland. Despite its delicate appearance, it is one of the hardiest trees and can grow in very cold climates. *Premaphotos Wildlife*

growing and durable. The bark is used for tanning and dyeing leather, and an oil is obtained from it.

bird backboned animal of the class Aves, the biggest group of land vertebrates, characterized by warm blood, feathers, wings, breathing through lungs, and egg-laying by the female. Birds are bipedal; feet are usually adapted for perching and never have more than four toes. Hearing and eyesight are well developed, but the sense of smell is usually poor. No existing species of bird possesses teeth.

Most birds fly, but some groups (such as ostriches) are flightless, and others include flightless members. Many communicate by sounds (nearly half of all known species are songbirds) or by visual displays, in connection with which many species are brightly coloured, usually the males. Birds have highly developed patterns of instinctive behaviour. There are nearly 8,500 species of birds.

wing structure The wing consists of the typical bones of a forelimb, the humerus, radius and ulna, carpus, metacarpus, and digits. The first digit is the pollex, or thumb, to which some feathers, known as ala spuria, or bastard wing, are attached; the second digit is the index, which bears the large feathers known as the primaries or manuals, usually ten in number. The primary feathers, with the secondaries or cubitals, which are attached to the ulna, form the large wing-quills, called remiges, which are used in flight.

anatomy The sternum, or breastbone, of birds is affected by their powers of flight: those birds which are able to fly have a keel projecting from the sternum and serving as the basis of attachment of the great pectoral muscles which move the wings. In birds that do not fly the keel is absent or greatly reduced. The vertebral column is completed in the tail region by a flat plate known as the pygostyle, which forms a support for the rectrices, or steering tailfeathers.

The legs are composed of the femur, tibia and fibula, and the bones of the foot; the feet usually have four toes, but in many cases there are only three. In swimming birds the legs are placed well back.

The uropygial gland on the pygostyle (bone in the tail) is an oil gland used by birds in preening their feathers, as their skin contains no sebaceous glands. The eyes have an upper and a lower eyelid and a semi-transparent nictitating membrane with which the bird can cover its eyes at will.

The vascular system contains warm blood, which is kept usually at a higher temperature (about 41°C/106°F) than that of mammals; death from cold is rare unless the bird is starving or ill. The aortic arch (main blood vessel leaving the heart) is on the right side of a bird, whereas it is on the left in a mammal. The heart of a bird consists of a right and a left half with four chambers.

The lungs are small and prolonged into air-sacs connected to a number of air-spaces in the bones. These air-spaces are largest in powerful fliers, but they are not so highly developed in young, small, aquatic, and terrestrial birds. These air-spaces increase the efficiency of the respiratory system and reduce the weight of the bones. The lungs themselves are more efficient than those of mammals; the air is circulated through a system of fine capillary tubes, allowing continuous gas exchange to take place, whereas in mammals the air comes to rest in blind air sacs.

The organ of voice is not the larynx, but usually the syrinx, a peculiarity of this class formed at the bifurcation of the trachea (windpipe) and the modulations are effected by movements of the adjoining muscles.

digestion Digestion takes place in the oesophagus, stomach, and intestines in a manner basically similar to mammals. The tongue aids in feeding, and there is frequently a crop, a dilation of the oesophagus, where food is stored and softened. The stomach is small with little storage capacity and usually consists of the proventriculus, which secretes digestive juices, and the gizzard, which is tough and muscular and grinds the food, sometimes with the aid of grit and stones retained within it. Digestion is completed, and absorption occurs, in the intestine and the digestive caeca. The intestine ends in a cloaca through which both urine and faeces are excreted.

nesting and eggs Typically eggs are brooded in a nest and, on hatching, the young receive a period of parental care. The collection of nest material, nest building, and incubation may be carried out by the male, female, or both. The cuckoo neither builds a nest nor rears its own young, but places the eggs in the nest of another bird and leaves the foster parents to care for them.

The study of birds is called ◊ornithology.

Bird Isabella Lucy, (Mrs Bishop) 1831–1904. British traveller and writer who wrote extensively of her journeys in the USA, Persia, Tibet, Kurdistan, China, Japan, and Korea. A fearless horsewoman, she generally travelled alone and in later life undertook medical missionary work.

Her published works include *The Englishwoman in America* 1856, *A Lady's Life in the Rocky Mountains* 1874, *Unbeaten Tracks in Japan* 1880, *Among the Tibetans* 1894, and *Pictures from China* 1900. Her last great journey was made 1901 when she travelled over 1,600 km/1,000 mi in Morocco.

bird of paradise one of 40 species of crowlike birds in the family Paradiseidae, native to New Guinea and neighbouring islands. Females are generally drably coloured, but the males have bright and elaborate plumage used in courtship display. Hunted almost to extinction for their plumage, they are now subject to conservation.

They are smallish birds, extremely active, and have compressed beaks, large toes, and strong feet. Their food consists chiefly of fruits, seeds, and nectar, but it may also include insects and small animals, such as worms. The Australian ◊bowerbirds are closely related.

Birdseye Clarence 1886–1956. US inventor who pioneered food refrigeration processes. While working as a fur trader in Labrador 1912–16 he was struck by the ease with which food could be preserved in an Arctic climate. Back in the USA he found that the same effect could be obtained by rapidly freezing prepared food between two refrigerated metal plates. To market his products he founded the General Sea Foods Company 1924, which he sold to General Foods 1929.

Birinus, St died c. 650. English saint and first bishop of Dorchester, Oxon, who in 635 converted and baptized the Saxon king Cynegils.

Birkenhead seaport in Merseyside, England, on the Mersey estuary opposite Liverpool; population (1981) 128,900. Chief industries include engineering, and flour milling. The rail Mersey Tunnel 1886 and road Queensway Tunnel 1934 link Birkenhead with Liverpool.

history The first settlement grew up round a Benedictine priory. William Laird established a small shipbuilding yard, the forerunner of the immense Cammell Laird yards and in1829 the first iron vessel in the UK was built at Birkenhead. Wallasey dock, the first of the series, was opened 1847. The last Cammell Laird shipyard closed 1993.

Birkenhead F(rederick) E(dwin) Smith, 1st Earl of Birkenhead 1872–1930. British lawyer and Conservative politician. A flamboyant and ambitious character, known as 'FE', he played a major role in securing the Anglo-Irish Treaty 1921 which created the Irish Free State (now the Republic of Ireland). As a lawyer, his greatest achievement was the Law of Property Act 1922, which formed the basis of current English land law.

Birmingham industrial city, administrative headquarters of Birmingham unitary authority and second largest city of the UK; population (1993 est) 1,017,000. It is an important manufacturing and commercial centre. Industries include engineering, motor vehicles, machine tools, aerospace control systems, plastics, chemicals, food, chocolates, jewellery, tyres, glass, and guns.

features The National Exhibition Centre and National Indoor Arena; Barber Institute of Fine Arts; City of Birmingham Symphony Orchestra (conductor Simon Rattle); Birmingham Conservatoire, now part of the University of Central England; the City Art Gallery containing a Pre-Raphaelite collection; the repertory theatre founded 1913 by Sir Barry Jackson (1897–1961) (since 1990 it has been the home of the ◊Royal Ballet); Symphony Hall (holding over 4,000) opened 1991; the Bull Ring Centre, a large shopping complex designed by Sydney Greenwood, built 1961–64 on the site of the old centre of the town; Sutton Park, in the residential suburb of Sutton Coldfield, has been a public country recreational area since the 16th century; canals ('Britain's Canal City') – a World Waterways Centre is proposed.

history Its location on the edge of the S Staffordshire coalfields and its reputation for producing small arms allowed Birmingham to develop rapidly during the 18th–19th centuries It has continued to expand in the 20th century due to a gradual change from heavy to high-tech industries.

Birmingham commercial and industrial city (iron, steel, chemicals, building materials,

bird of paradise The male blue bird of paradise displays to the female high up in the tree canopy. It swings upside down, exposing its bright blue plumage and tail streamers, at the same time uttering low mechanical-sounding cries.

computers, cotton textiles) and largest city in Alabama, USA; population (1992) 265,000.

Biró Lazlo 1900–1985. Hungarian-born Argentine who invented a ballpoint pen 1944. His name became generic for ballpoint pens in the UK.

Birmingham Six Irish victims of a miscarriage of justice who spent nearly 17 years in British prisons convicted of an IRA terrorist bombing in Birmingham 1974. They were released 1991 when the Court of Appeal quashed their convictions. The methods of the police and prosecution were called into question.

Birt John 1944– . English television executive, since 1993 director general (chief executive) of the BBC. His initial television work was in current affairs, especially *World In Action*, and with Peter Jay (1937–) he proposed an approach to reporting that placed emphasis on giving greater context to news and opinion.

birth act of producing live young from within the body of female animals. Both viviparous and ovoviviparous animals give birth to young. In viviparous animals, embryos obtain nourishment from the mother via a ◊placenta or other means.

In ovoviviparous animals, fertilized eggs develop and hatch in the oviduct of the mother and gain little or no nourishment from maternal tissues. See also ◊pregnancy.

birth control another name for ◊family planning; see also ◊contraceptive.

birth rate the number of live births per thousand of the population over a period of time, usually a year (sometimes it is also expressed as a percentage). For example, a birth rate of 20 per thousand (or 2%) would mean that 20 babies were being born per thousand of the population. It is sometimes called crude birth rate because it takes in the whole population, including men and women who are too old to bear children.

Birtwistle Harrison 1934– . English avant-garde composer. He has specialized in chamber music, for example, his chamber opera *Punch and Judy* 1967 and *Down by the Greenwood Side* 1969.

Birtwistle's early music was influenced by US composer Igor Stravinsky and by the medieval and Renaissance masters, and for many years he worked alongside Peter Maxwell ◊Davies. Orchestral works include *The Triumph of Time* 1972 and *Silbury Air* 1977; he has also written operas including *The Mask of Orpheus* 1986 (with electronic music by Barry Anderson (1935–1987)) and *Gawain* 1991 a reworking of the medieval English poem 'Sir Gawain and the Green Knight'. His tape composition *Chronometer* 1972 (assisted by Peter Zinovieff (1934–)) is based on clock sounds.

Bismarck The imperialist 'Iron Chancellor' Prince Otto von Bismarck, from a photograph published c. 1880. Bismarck's expansionist policies and autocratic rule secured Prussia's dominance in his new German Empire. *Image Select (UK) Ltd*

Biscay, Bay of bay of the Atlantic Ocean between N Spain and W France, known for rough seas and exceptionally high tides.

biscuit small, flat, brittle cake of baked dough. The basic components of biscuit dough are weak flour and fat; other ingredients, such as eggs, sugar, chocolate, and spices, may be added to vary the flavour and texture. In the USA, 'biscuit' means something between a bread roll and a Yorkshire pudding, and 'cookie' means biscuit. Originally made from slices of unleavened bread baked until hard and dry, biscuits could be stored for several years, and were a useful, though dull, source of carbohydrate on long sea voyages and military campaigns.

bishop (Greek 'overseer') priest next in rank to an archbishop in the Roman Catholic, Eastern Orthodox, Anglican or episcopal churches. A bishop has charge of a district called a diocese.

Originally bishops were chosen by the congregation, but in the Roman Catholic church they are appointed by the pope, although in some countries, such as Spain, the political authority nominates appointees. In the Eastern Orthodox church bishops are always monks. In the Church of England the prime minister selects bishops on the advice of the archbishop of Canterbury; when a diocese is very large, assistant (suffragan) bishops are appointed. Bishops are responsible for meeting to settle matters of belief or discipline; they ordain priests and administer confirmation (as well as baptism in the Orthodox church). In the Methodist and Lutheran churches the bishop's role is mostly that of a supervisory official.

Bismarck Otto Eduard Leopold von 1815–1898. German politician, prime minister of Prussia 1862–90 and chancellor of the German Empire 1871–90. He pursued an aggressively expansionist policy, waging wars against Denmark 1863–64, Austria 1866, and France 1870–71, which brought about the unification of Germany. He became Prince 1871.

Bismarck was ambitious to establish Prussia's leadership within Germany and eliminate the influence of Austria. He secured Austria's support for his successful war against Denmark then, in 1866, went to war against Austria and its allies (the ◊Seven Weeks' War), his victory forcing Austria out of the German Bund and unifying the N German states into the North German Confederation under his own chancellorship 1867. He then defeated France, under Napoleon III, in the Franco-Prussian War 1870–71, proclaimed the German Empire 1871, and annexed Alsace-Lorraine. He tried to secure his work by the ◊Triple Alliance 1881 with Austria and Italy but ran into difficulties at home with the Roman Catholic church and the socialist movement and was forced to resign by Wilhelm II 18 March 1890.

Bismarck Archipelago group of over 200 islands in the SW Pacific Ocean, part of ◊Papua New Guinea; area 49,660 sq km/19,200 sq mi. The largest island is New Britain.

bismuth hard, brittle, pinkish-white, metallic element, symbol Bi, atomic number 83, relative atomic mass 208.98. It has the highest atomic number of all the stable elements (the elements from atomic number 84 up are radioactive). Bismuth occurs in ores and occasionally as a free metal (◊native metal). It is a poor conductor of heat and electricity, and is used in alloys of low melting point and in medical compounds to soothe gastric ulcers. The name comes from the Latin *besemutum*, from the earlier German *Wismut*.

bison large, hoofed mammal of the bovine family. There are two species, both brown. The ***European bison*** or ***wisent*** *Bison bonasus*, of which only a few protected herds survive, is about 2 m/7 ft high and weighs up to 1,100 kg/2,500 lb. The ***North American bison*** (often known as 'buffalo') *Bison bison* is slightly smaller, with a heavier mane and more sloping hindquarters. Formerly roaming the prairies in vast numbers, it was almost exterminated in the 19th century, but survives in protected areas.

Bissau capital and chief port of Guinea-Bissau, on an island at the mouth of the Geba River; population (1992) 145,000. Originally a fortified slave-trading centre, Bissau became a free port 1869.

bit (contraction of ***binary digit***) in computing, a single binary digit, either 0 or 1. A bit is the smallest unit of data stored in a computer; all other data must be coded into a pattern of individual bits. A ◊byte represents sufficient computer memory to store a single character of data, and usually contains eight bits. For example, in the ◊ASCII code system used by most microcomputers the capital letter A would be stored in a single byte of memory as the bit pattern 01000001.

Microcomputers are often described according to how many bits of information they can handle at once. The higher the number of bits a computer can process simultaneously, the more powerful the computer is said to be. However, other factors influence the overall speed of a computer system, such as the clock rate of the processor (the frequency of its internal electronic clock) and the amount of ◊RAM available. Tasks that require a high processing speed include sorting a database or doing long, complex calculations in spreadsheets. A system running slowly with a ◊graphical user interface may benefit more from the addition of extra RAM than from a faster processor.

bit map in computing, a pattern of ◊bits used to describe the organization of data. Bit maps are used to store typefaces or graphic images, with 1 representing black (or a colour) and 0 white. Bit maps may be used to store a typeface or ◊font, but a separate set of bit maps is required for each typesize. A vector font, by contrast, can be held as one set of data and scaled as required. Bit-mapped graphics are not recommended for images that require scaling (compare ◊vector graphics – those stored in the form of geometric formulas).

bittern any of several species of small herons, in particular the common bittern *Botaurus stellaris* of Europe and Asia. It is shy, stoutly built, buff-coloured, speckled with black and tawny brown, with a long bill and a loud, booming call. Its habit of holding its neck and bill in a vertical position conceals it among the reeds, where it rests by day, hunting for frogs, reptiles, and fish towards nightfall. An inhabitant of marshy country, it is now quite rare in Britain.

bitumen impure mixture of hydrocarbons, including such deposits as petroleum, asphalt, and natural gas, although sometimes the term is restricted to a soft kind of pitch resembling asphalt.

Solid bitumen may have arisen as a residue from the evaporation of petroleum. If evaporation took place from a pool or lake of petroleum, the residue might form a pitch or asphalt lake, such as Pitch Lake in Trinidad. Bitumen was used in ancient times as a mortar, and by the Egyptians for embalming.

bivalent in biology, a name given to the pair of homologous chromosomes during reduction division (◊meiosis). In chemistry, the term is sometimes used to describe an element or group with a ◊valency of two, although the term 'divalent' is more common.

bivalve marine or freshwater mollusc whose body is enclosed between two shells hinged together by a ligament on the dorsal side of the body.

The shell is closed by strong 'adductor' muscles. Ventrally, a retractile 'foot' can be put out to assist movement in mud or sand. Two large platelike gills are used for breathing and also, with the ◊cilia present on them, make a mechanism for collecting the small particles of food on which bivalves depend. The bivalves form one of the five classes of molluscs, the Lamellibranchiata, otherwise known as Bivalvia or Pelycypoda, containing about 8,000 species.

Bizet Georges (Alexandre César Léopold) 1838–1875. French composer of operas. Among his works are *Les Pêcheurs de perles/The Pearl Fishers* 1863 and *La Jolie Fille de Perth/The Fair Maid of Perth* 1866. He also wrote the concert overture *Patrie* and incidental music to Alphonse Daudet's play *L'Arlésienne*. His operatic masterpiece *Carmen* was produced a few months before his death 1875.

Björnson Björnstjerne Martinius 1832–1910. Norwegian novelist, playwright, poet, and journalist. His plays include *The Newly Married Couple* 1865 and *Beyond Human Power* 1883, dealing with

Bismarck Archipelago

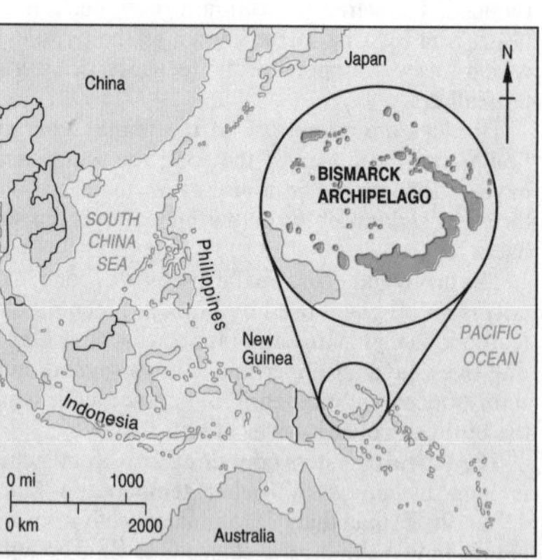

politics and sexual morality. Among his novels is *In God's Way* 1889. Nobel Prize for Literature 1903.

black English term first used 1625 to describe West Africans, now used to refer to Africans south of the Sahara and to people of African descent living outside Africa. In some countries such as the UK (but not in North America) the term is sometimes also used for people originally from the Indian subcontinent, for Australian Aborigines, and peoples of Melanesia.

The term 'black', at one time considered offensive by many people, was first adopted by militants in the USA in the mid-1960s to emphasize ethnic pride; they rejected the terms 'coloured' and 'Negro' as derogatory. 'Black' has since become the preferred term in the USA and largely in the UK. Currently, US blacks often prefer the term 'African-American'.

history Black Africans were first taken to the West Indies in large numbers as slaves by the Spanish in the early 16th century and to the North American mainland in the early 17th century. They were transported to South America by both the Spanish and Portuguese from the 16th century. African blacks were also taken to Europe to work as slaves and servants. Some of the indigenous coastal societies in W Africa were heavily involved in the slave trade and became wealthy on its proceeds. Sometimes, black sailors settled in European ports on the Atlantic seaboard, such as Liverpool and Bristol, England. Although blacks fought beside whites in the American Revolution, the US Constitution (ratified 1788) did not redress the slave trade, and slaves were given no ◊civil rights. ▷*See feature on pp. 982–983.*

Slavery was gradually abolished in the northern US states during the early 19th century, but as the South's economy had been based upon slavery, it was one of the issues concerning states' rights that led to the secession of the South, which provoked the American Civil War 1861–65. During the Civil War about 200,000 blacks fought in the Union (Northern) army, but in segregated units led by white officers.

The Emancipation Proclamation 1863 of President Abraham Lincoln officially freed the slaves (about 4 million), but it could not be enforced until the Union victory 1865 and the period after the war known as the ◊Reconstruction. Freed slaves were often resented by poor whites as economic competitors, and vigilante groups in the South, such as the ◊Ku Klux Klan were formed to intimidate them. In addition, although freed slaves had full US citizenship under the 14th Amendment to the Constitution, and were thus entitled to vote, they were often disenfranchised in practice by state and local literacy tests and poll taxes.

A 'separate but equal' policy was established when the US Supreme Court ruled 1896 (*Plessy* v. *Ferguson*) that segregation was legal if equal facilities were provided for blacks and whites. The ruling was overturned 1954 (*Brown* v. *Board of Education*) with the Supreme Court decision outlawing segregation in state schools. This led to a historic confrontation in Little Rock, Arkansas, 1957 when Governor Orval Faubus attempted to prevent black students from entering Central High School, and President Eisenhower sent federal troops to enforce their right to attend.

Another landmark in the blacks' struggle for civil rights was the ◊Montgomery bus boycott in Alabama 1955, which first brought Martin Luther ◊King Jr to national attention. In the early 1960s the civil-rights movement had gained impetus, largely under the leadership of King, who in 1957 had founded the Southern Christian Leadership Conference (SCLC), a coalition group advocating nonviolence. Moderate groups such as the National Association for the Advancement of Colored People (NAACP) had been active since early in the century; for the first time they were joined in large numbers by whites, in particular students, as in the historic march converging on Washington DC 1963 from all over the USA. At about this time, impatient with the lack of results gained through moderation, the militant ◊Black Power movements began to emerge, such as the Black Panther Party founded 1966, and black separatist groups such as the ◊Black Muslims gained support.

Increasing pressure led to the passage of federal legislation, the Civil Rights acts of 1964 and 1968, and the Voting Rights Act of 1965, under President Lyndon Johnson; they guaranteed equal rights under the law and prohibited discrimination in public facilities, schools, employment, and voting. However, in the 1980s, despite some advances, legislation, and affirmative action (positive discrimination), blacks, who comprise some 12% of the US population, continued to suffer discrimination and inequality of opportunities in practice in such areas as education, employment, and housing. Despite these obstacles, many blacks have made substantial contributions in the arts, the sciences, and politics.

blacks in Britain Unlike the USA, Britain does not have a recent history of slavery at home, though slaves were used in Roman Britain. The UK outlawed the slave trade 1807 and abolished slavery in the British Empire 1833. In the UK only a tiny proportion of the population was black until after World War II, when immigration from Commonwealth countries increased. Legislation such as the Race Relations Act 1976 specifically outlawed discrimination on grounds of race and emphasized the official policy of equality of opportunity in all areas. The Commission for Racial Equality was established 1977 to work towards eliminating discrimination; nevertheless, there is still considerable evidence of ◊racism in British society as a whole. The Swann Report on education 1985 emphasized that Britain was a multicultural society, and suggested various ways in which teachers could ensure that black children were able to reach their full potential. Black people are now beginning to take their place in public life in the UK; the election of Diane Abbott (1953–) as Britain's first black woman member of Parliament 1987 was an example.

Black James Whyte 1924– . British physiologist, director of therapeutic research at Wellcome Laboratories (near London) from 1978. He was active in the development of ◊beta-blockers (which reduce the rate of heartbeat) and anti-ulcer drugs. He shared the Nobel Prize for Physiology or Medicine 1988 with US scientists George Hitchings (1905–) and Gertrude Elion (1918–).

Black and Tans nickname of a special auxiliary force of the Royal Irish Constabulary employed by the British 1920–21 to combat the Sinn Féiners (Irish nationalists) in Ireland; the name derives from the colours of the uniforms, khaki with black hats and belts. ▷*See feature on pp. 550–551.*

black beetle another name for ◊cockroach, although cockroaches belong to an entirely different order of insects (Dictyoptera) from the beetles (Coleoptera).

blackberry prickly shrub *Rubus fruticosus* of the rose family, closely allied to raspberries and dewberries, that is native to northern parts of Europe. It produces pink or white blossoms and edible, black, compound fruits.

blackbird bird *Turdus merula* of the thrush family, Muscicapidae, order Passeriformes, about 25 cm/10 in long. The male is black with a yellow bill and eyelids, the female dark brown with a dark beak. It lays three to five blue-green eggs with brown spots in a nest of grass and moss, plastered with mud, built in thickets or creeper-clad trees. The blackbird feeds on fruit, seeds, worms, grubs, and snails. Its song is rich and flutelike.

Found across Europe, Asia, and North Africa, the blackbird adapts well to human presence and gardens, and is one of the most common British birds. North American 'blackbirds' belong to a different family of birds, the Icteridae.

black box popular name for the unit containing an aeroplane's flight and voice recorders. These monitor the plane's behaviour and the crew's conversation, thus providing valuable clues to the cause of a disaster. The box is nearly indestructible and usually painted orange for easy recovery. The name also refers to any compact electronic device that can be quickly connected or disconnected as a unit.

The maritime equivalent is the voyage recorder, installed in ships from 1989. It has 350 sensors to record the performance of engines, pumps, navigation lights, alarms, radar, and hull stress.

blackbuck antelope *Antilope cervicapra* found in central and NW India. It is related to the gazelle, from which it differs in having spirally-twisted horns. The male is black above and white beneath, whereas the female and young are fawn-coloured above. It is about 76 cm/2.5 ft in height.

Blackburn industrial city in Lancashire, England, on the Leeds–Liverpool canal, 32 km/20 mi NW of Manchester; population (1991) 106,000. Textiles, electronics, paint, paper, and compact discs are produced, and there are other high-tech industries.

blackcap ◊warbler *Sylvia atricapilla*, family Muscicapidae, order Passeriformes. The male has a black cap, the female a reddish-brown one. The general colour of the bird is an ashen-grey, turning to an olive-brown above and pale or whitish-grey below. About 14 cm/5.5 in long, the blackcap likes wooded areas, and is a summer visitor to N Europe, wintering in Africa.

blackcock or ***heathcock*** large grouse *Lyrurus tetrix* found on moors and in open woods in N Europe and Asia. The male is mainly black with a lyre-shaped tail, and grows up to 54 cm/1.7 ft in height. The female is speckled brown and only 40 cm/1.3 ft tall. Their food consists of buds, young shoots, berries, and insects.

Blackcocks are polygamous, and in the spring males attract females by curious crowings. In males a piece of bright red skin above the eyes also becomes more intense during the pairing season.

They are related to the quail, partridge, and capercaillie, in the order Galliformes.

Black Country central area of England, around and to the W of Birmingham. Heavily industrialized, it gained its name in the 19th century from its belching chimneys and mining spoil. Antipollution laws have changed its aspect, and coal mining in the region ceased 1968.

blackcurrant variety of ◊currant.

Black Death great epidemic of bubonic ◊plague that ravaged Europe in the mid-14th century, killing between one-third and half of the population (about 75 million people). The cause of the plague was the bacterium *Yersinia pestis*, transmitted by fleas borne by migrating Asian black rats. The name Black Death was first used in England in the early 19th century.

black economy unofficial economy of a country, which includes undeclared earnings from a second job ('moonlighting'), and enjoyment of undervalued goods and services (such as company 'perks'), designed for tax evasion purposes. In industrialized countries, it has been estimated to equal about 10% of ◊gross domestic product.

blackfly plant-sucking insect, a type of ◊aphid.

Blackfoot the members of a Plains ◊Native American people, numbering about 10,000 and consisting of three subtribes: the Blackfoot proper, the Blood, and the Piegan, who live in Montana, USA, and Saskatchewan and Alberta, Canada. They were skilled, horse-riding buffalo hunters until their territories were settled by Europeans. Their name derives from their black moccasins. Their language belongs to the Algonquian family.

Black Forest (German ***Schwarzwald***) mountainous region of coniferous forest in Baden-Württemberg, W Germany. Bounded to the W and S by the Rhine, which separates it from the Vosges, it has an area of 4,660 sq km/1,800 sq mi and rises to 1,493 m/4,905 ft in the Feldberg. Parts of the forest have recently been affected by ◊acid rain.

Black Friday 24 Sept 1869, a day on which Jay Gould (1836–1892) and James Fisk (1834–1872), stock manipulators, attempted to corner the gold market by trying to prevent the government from selling gold. President Grant refused to agree, but they spread the rumour that the president was opposed to the sales.

George S Boutweel (1818–1905), with Grant's approval, ordered the sale of $4 million in gold. The gold price plunged and many speculators were ruined. Gould and Fisk made about $11 million out of their manipulation of the market.

Blackheath suburb of London, lying S of Greenwich Park on the London–Dover road. It falls within the Greater London boroughs of Greenwich and Lewisham and takes its name from the common, where Wat Tyler encamped during the 1381 Peasants' Revolt. It developed as a residential suburb from the late 18th century.

Black Power A march in New York 1968 by the Black Panthers, the most potent expression of the US Black Power movement. Willing to support armed struggle, the Panthers were involved in several violent incidents. This demonstration was to protest against the imprisonment of their founder, Huey P Newton, for murder. *Corbis*

For centuries the common was used as a place of assembly: Henry V was welcomed here after the Battle of Agincourt 1415; Henry VIII met Anne of Cleves at a Blackheath pageant; Charles II was welcomed here 1660; and the Methodist John Wesley held religious meetings on the heath in the 18th century.

Black Hills mountains in the Dakotas and Wyoming, USA. They occupy about 15,500 sq km/6,000 sq mi and rise to 2,207 m/7,242 ft at Harney Peak, South Dakota.

black hole object in space whose gravity is so great that nothing can escape from it, not even light. Thought to form when massive stars shrink at the end of their lives, a black hole sucks in more matter, including other stars, from the space around it. Matter that falls into a black hole is squeezed to infinite density at the centre of the hole. Black holes can be detected because gas falling towards them becomes so hot that it emits X-rays.

Black holes containing the mass of millions of stars are thought to lie at the centres of ◊quasars. Satellites have detected X-rays from a number of objects that may be black holes, but only four likely black holes in our Galaxy had been identified by 1994. ▷ *See feature on pp. 70–71.*

Black Hole of Calcutta incident in Anglo-Indian history: according to tradition, the nawab (ruler) of Bengal confined 146 British prisoners on the night of 20 June 1756 in one small room, of whom only 23 allegedly survived. Later research reduced the death count to 43, assigning negligence rather than intention.

black humour humour based on the grotesque, morbid, or macabre. It is often an element of satire. A classic example is Jonathan Swift's 'A Modest Proposal' 1729, in which he argues that eating Irish children would help to alleviate Ireland's poverty. Twentieth-century examples can be found in the works of Samuel Beckett, the routines of the US comic Lenny Bruce (1925–1966), and the drawings of the English caricaturist Gerald Scarfe (1936–). It is also an important element of Theatre of the ◊Absurd.

blacking in an industrial dispute, the refusal of workers to handle particular goods or equipment, or to work with particular people.

Blacking John Anthony Randoll 1928–1990. British anthropologist and ethnomusicologist who researched the relationship between music and body movement, and the patterns of social and musical organization. His most widely read book is *How Musical is Man?* 1973.

blackmail criminal offence of extorting money with menaces or threats of detrimental action, such as exposure of some misconduct on the part of the victim.

Black Monday worldwide stockmarket crash that began 19 Oct 1987, prompted by the announcement of worse-than-expected US trade figures and the response by US Secretary of the Treasury, James Baker, who indicated that the sliding dollar needed to decline further. This caused a world panic as fears of the likely impact of a US recession were voiced by the major industrialized countries. Between 19 and 23 Oct, the New York Stock Exchange fell by 33%, the London Stock Exchange Financial Times 100 Index by 25%, the European index by 17%, and Tokyo by 12%. The expected world recession did not occur; by the end of 1988 it was clear that the main effect had been a steadying in stock market activity and only a slight slowdown in world economic growth.

Blackmore R(ichard) D(oddridge) 1825–1900. English novelist. His romance *Lorna Doone* 1869, set on Exmoor, SW England, in the late 17th century, became a classic.

His first novel, *Clara Vaughan* 1864, was successful and *Lorna Doone* won him lasting popularity. He published 13 other novels.

Black Mountain ridge of hills in the Brecon Beacons National Park in Dyfed and Powys, S Wales, stretching 19 km/12 m N from Swansea. The hills are composed of limestone and red sandstone.

Black Mountains upland massif with cliffs and steep-sided valleys in Powys and Gwent, SE Wales, lying to the W of ◊Offa's Dyke. The highest peak is Waun Fach (811 m/2,660 ft).

Black Muslims religious group founded 1930 in the USA. Members adhere to Muslim values and believe in economic independence for black Americans. Under the leadership of Louis ◊Farrakhan and the group's original name of the ◊Nation of Islam, the movement has undergone a resurgence of popularity in recent years. In Oct 1995 more than 400,000 black males attended a 'Million Man March' to Washington DC., the largest ever civil rights demonstration in US history.

black nationalism movement towards black separatism in the USA during the 1960s; see ◊Black Power.

Black National State area in the Republic of South Africa set aside, 1971–94, for development towards self-government by black Africans, in accordance with ◊apartheid. Before 1980 these areas were known as black homelands or bantustans. Those that achieved nominal independence were Transkei 1976, Bophuthatswana 1977, Venda 1979, and Ciskei 1981. They were not recognized outside South Africa because of their racial basis.

Outbreaks of violence resulted in the overthrow of the governments in Ciskei and Venda 1990, and calls for reintegration within South Africa in all of the four independent states. Bophuthatswana was annexed by South Africa March 1994 after a popular uprising.

The repeal of the Land Acts and Group Areas Acts 1991 promised progressively to change the status of Black National States. Under South Africa's nonracial constitution, which came into effect April 1994, the states became part of the republic's provincial structure, with guaranteed legislative and executive power.

Blackpool seaside resort in Lancashire, England, 45 km/28 mi N of Liverpool; population (1987 est) 144,100. The largest resort in N England, the amusement facilities include 11 km/7 mi of promenades, known for their 'illuminations' of coloured lights, a tower 152 m/500 ft high, and funfairs, including the world's largest roller-coaster, 75 m/235 ft high and 1.5 km/1 mi long, opened 1994. Political party conferences are often held here.

Black Power movement towards black separatism in the USA during the 1960s, embodied in the Black Panther Party founded 1966 by Huey Newton and Bobby Seale. Its declared aim was the creation of a separate black state in the USA to be established by a black plebiscite under the aegis of the United Nations. Following a National Black Political Convention 1972, a National Black Assembly was established to exercise pressure on the Democratic and Republican parties.

The Black Power concept arose when existing ◊civil rights organizations, such as the National Association for the Advancement of Colored People and the Southern Christian Leadership Conference, were perceived to be ineffective in producing significant change in the status of black people. Stokely Carmichael then advocated the exploitation of political and economic power and abandonment of nonviolence, with a move towards the type of separatism first developed by the ◊Black Muslims. Such leaders as Martin Luther ◊King rejected this approach, but the Black Panther Party (so named because the panther, though not generally aggressive, will fight to the death under attack) adopted it fully and, for a time, achieved nationwide influence.

Black Prince nickname of ◊Edward, Prince of Wales, eldest son of Edward III of England.

Black Sea (Russian ***Chernoye More***) inland sea in SE Europe, linked with the seas of Azov and Marmara, and via the Dardanelles strait with the Mediterranean. Uranium deposits beneath it are among the world's largest. About 90% of the water is polluted, mainly by agricultural fertilizers.

Black Sea

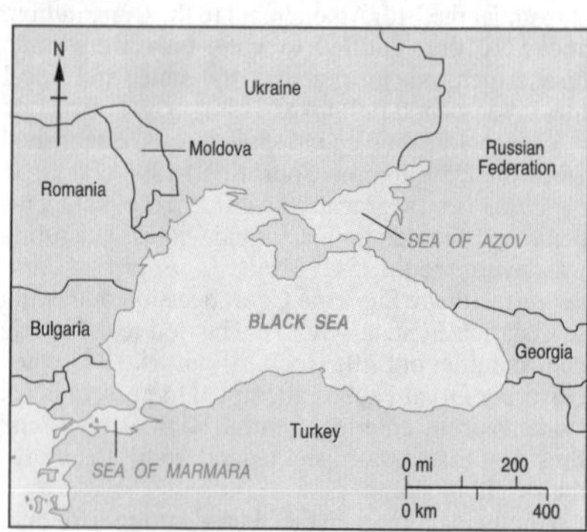

The Black Sea is Europe's most polluted sea; rivers feeding it bring raw sewage, nitrates, phosphates, pesticides, heavy metals, and other pollutants from 13 countries. This is accelerating the natural accumulation at the bottom of the sea of a layer of hydrogen sulphide, ammonia, methane, and ethane, which is rising by 2 m/7 ft a year. Below a depth of 150 m/500 ft 90% of the water is anoxic (lacking in oxygen), mixing little with the surface water, and supporting little life.

In addition to pollution, the comb jellyfish *Mnemiopsis leidyi* has contributed significantly to a reduction in marine biodiversity. It entered the Black Sea in the early 1980s in ballast water from a US ship. Without predators it thrived, feeding on fish eggs and larvae. Fish catches were reduced by 90% in only six years. By 1990 the estimated biomass of *Mnemiopsis* peaked at 900 million tonnes.

Blackshirts term widely used to describe fascist paramilitary organizations. Originating with Mussolini's fascist Squadristi in the 1920s, it was also applied to the Nazi SS (*Schutzstaffel*) and to the followers of Oswald Mosley's British Union of Fascists.

blacksnake any of several species of snake. The blacksnake *Pseudechis porphyriacus* is a venomous snake of the cobra family found in damp forests and swamps in E Australia. The blacksnake, *Coluber constrictor* from the eastern USA, is a relative of the European grass snake, growing up to 1.2 m/4 ft long, and without venom.

Black Stone in Islam, the sacred stone built into the east corner of the ◊Kaaba which is a focal point of the *hajj*, or pilgrimage, to Mecca.

blackthorn densely branched spiny European bush *Prunus spinosa*, family Rosaceae. It produces white blossom on black and leafless branches in early spring. Its sour, plumlike, blue-black fruit, the sloe, is used to make sloe gin.

Black Thursday day of the Wall Street stock market crash 24 Oct 1929, which precipitated the Depression in the USA and throughout the world.

Blackwall Tunnel road tunnel under the river Thames, London, linking the Bugsby Marshes (south) with the top end of the Isle of Dogs (north). The northbound tunnel, 7,056 km/4,410 ft long with an internal diameter of 7.2 m/24 ft, was built 1891–97 to a design by Alexander Binnie; the southbound tunnel, 4,592 km/2,870 ft long with an internal diameter of 8.25 m/27.5 ft, was built 1960–67 to a design by Mott, Hay, and Anderson.

Blackwell Elizabeth 1821–1910. English-born US physician, the first woman to qualify in medicine in the USA 1849, and the first woman to be recognized as a qualified physician in the UK 1869.

black widow North American spider *Latrodectus mactans*. The male is small and harmless, but the female is 1.3 cm/0.5 in long with a red patch below the abdomen and a powerful venomous bite. The bite causes pain and fever in human victims, but they usually recover.

bladder hollow elastic-walled organ which stores the urine produced in the kidneys. It is present in the ◊urinary systems of some fishes, most amphibians, some reptiles, and all mammals. Urine enters the bladder through two ureters, one leading from each kidney, and leaves it through the urethra.

bladderwort any of a large genus *Utricularia* of carnivorous aquatic plants of the family Lentibulariaceae. They have leaves with bladders that entrap small aquatic animals.

Blaenau Gwent unitary authority of Wales created 1996 (*see United Kingdom map*).

Blair Tony (Anthony Charles Lynton) 1953– . British politician, leader of the Labour Party from 1994, prime minister from 1997. A centrist in the manner of his predecessor John ◊Smith, he became Labour's youngest leader by a large majority in the first fully democratic elections to the post July 1994. In 1995 he won approval of a new Labour Party charter, intended to distance the party from its traditional socialist base and promote 'social market' values. In the 1997 general election he and his party secured a landslide victory.

Blair practised as a lawyer before entering the House of Commons 1983 as member for the Durham constituency of Sedgfield. He was elected to Labour's shadow cabinet 1988 and given the energy portfolio; he shadowed employment from 1991 and home affairs from 1992. Like John Smith, he did not ally himself with any particular faction and, in drawing a distinction between 'academic and ethical socialism', succeeded in winning over most sections of his party, apart from the extreme left.

Blake George 1922–1994. British double agent who worked for MI6 (see ◊intelligence) and also for the USSR. Blake was unmasked by a Polish defector 1960 and imprisoned, but escaped to the Eastern bloc 1966. He is said to have betrayed at least 42 British agents to the Soviet side.

Blake Quentin Saxby 1932– . English book illustrator. His animated pen-and-ink drawings are instantly recognizable. A prolific illustrator of children's books written by others, he has also written and illustrated his own books, including *The Marzipan Pig* 1986.

Blake Robert 1599–1657. British admiral of the Parliamentary forces during the English ◊Civil War. Appointed 'general-at-sea' 1649, he destroyed Prince Rupert's privateering fleet off Cartagena, Spain, in the following year. In 1652 he won several engagements against the Dutch navy. In 1654 he bombarded Tunis, the stronghold of the Barbary corsairs, and in 1657 captured the Spanish treasure fleet in Santa Cruz.

Blake William 1757–1827. English poet, artist, engraver, and visionary. He was one of the most important figures of English Romanticism. His lyrics, as in *Songs of Innocence* 1789 and *Songs of Experience* 1794, express a spiritual vision in radiant imagery and symbolism. In his 'prophetic books' like *The Marriage of Heaven and Hell* 1790, *America* 1793, and *Milton* 1804, he created a vast personal mythology. He illustrated his own works with hand-coloured engravings.

Blake was born in London and apprenticed to an engraver 1771–78. He illustrated the Bible, works by Dante and Shakespeare, and later began to illustrate his own poems, his highly individual style ultimately based on Michelangelo and Raphael, with slender and ethereal figures. Central themes in his work are the importance of passion and imagination, his visionary spirituality – he often claimed that he saw angels – and a political radicalism that made him a keen supporter of the French Revolution and of Mary Wollstonecraft's views on the rights of women. The frequent targets of his bitter scorn were physical and mental oppression, hypocrisy (particularly religious hypocrisy), and the materialistic rationalism of his age. These themes found their fullest expression in his prophetic books, though their elaborate imagery and complex personal mythology are often obscure.

Blakey Art(hur). Muslim name Abdullah Ibn Buhaina 1919–1990. US jazz drummer and bandleader. His dynamic, innovative style made him one of the jazz greats. He contributed to the development of bebop in the 1940s and subsequently to hard bop, and formed the Jazz Messengers in the mid-1950s, continuing to lead the band for most of his life and discovering many talented musicians.

Blamey Thomas Albert 1884–1951. Australian field marshal. Born in New South Wales, he served at Gallipoli, Turkey, and on the Western Front in World War I. After his appointment as commander in chief, Allied Land Forces, he commanded operations on the Kokoda Trail and the recapture of Papua.

Blanc (Jean Joseph Charles) Louis 1811–1882. French socialist and journalist. In 1839 he founded the *Revue du progrès*, in which he published his *Organisation du travail*, advocating the establishment of cooperative workshops and other socialist schemes. He was a member of the provisional government of 1848 (see ◊revolutions of 1848) and from its fall lived in the UK until 1871.

Blanchard Jean Pierre François 1753–1809. French balloonist who made the first hot air balloon flight across the English Channel with John Jeffries 1785. He made the first balloon flight in the USA 1793.

Blanche of Castile 1188–1252. Queen of France, wife of ◊Louis VIII of France, and regent for her son Louis IX (St Louis of France) from the death of her husband 1226 until Louis IX's majority 1234, and again from 1247 while he was on a Crusade.

Blanco Serge 1958– . French rugby union player, renowned for his pace, skill, and ingenuity on the field. Blanco played a world-record 93 internationals before his retirement in 1991, scoring 38 tries of which 34 were from full back – another world record. He was instrumental in France's Grand Slam wins of 1981 and 1987.

blank verse in literature, the unrhymed iambic pentameter or ten-syllable line of five stresses. First used by the Italian Gian Giorgio Trissino in his tragedy *Sofonisba* 1514–15, it was introduced to England about 1540 by the Earl of Surrey, who used it in his translation of Virgil's *Aeneid*. It was developed by Christopher Marlowe and Shakespeare, becoming the distinctive verse form of Elizabethan and Jacobean drama. It was later used by Milton in *Paradise Lost* 1667 and by Wordsworth in *The Prelude* 1805. More recent exponents of blank verse in English include Thomas Hardy, T S Eliot, and Robert Frost.

blackthorn The flowering of the blackthorn *Prunus spinosa*, before the leaves appear, is one of the early signs of spring. A plant of hedgerows, thickets, and woodland edges on most types of soil it does, however, avoid deep shade and acid, peaty soils. *Premaphotos Wildlife*

Blanqui (Louis) Auguste 1805–1881. French revolutionary politician. He formulated the theory of the 'dictatorship of the proletariat', used by Karl Marx, and spent a total of 33 years in prison for insurrection. Although in prison, he was elected president of the Commune of Paris 1871. His followers, the Blanquists, joined with the Marxists 1881.

Blarney small town in County Cork, Republic of Ireland, possessing, inset in the wall of the 15th-century castle, the Blarney Stone, reputed to give persuasive speech to those kissing it.

Blashford-Snell John 1936– . British explorer and soldier. His expeditions have included the first descent and exploration of the Blue Nile 1968; the journey N to S from Alaska to Cape Horn, crossing the Darien Gap between Panama and Colombia for the first time 1971–72; and the first complete navigation of the Zaïre River, Africa 1974–75.

From 1963 he organized adventure training at Sandhurst military academy. He was director of Operation Drake 1977–81 and Operation Raleigh 1978–82. His books include *A Taste for Adventure* 1978.

Blasis Carlo 1795–1878. Italian ballet teacher of French extraction. He was successful as a dancer in Paris and in Milan, where he established a dancing school 1837. His celebrated treatise on the art of dancing, *Traité élémentaire, théoretique et pratique de l'art de la danse/Treatise on the Dance* 1820, forms the basis of classical dance training.

blasphemy (Greek 'evil-speaking') written or spoken insult directed against religious belief or sacred things with deliberate intent to outrage believers.

blast furnace smelting furnace used to extract metals from their ores, chiefly pig iron from iron ore. The temperature is raised by the injection of an air blast. In the extraction of iron the ingredients of the furnace are iron ore, coke (carbon), and limestone. The coke is the fuel and provides the carbon monoxide for the reduction of the iron ore; the limestone acts as a flux, removing impurities.

blastula early stage in the development of a fertilized egg, when the egg changes from a solid mass of cells (the morula) to a hollow ball of cells (the blastula), containing a fluid-filled cavity (the blastocoel). See also ◊embryology.

Blaue Reiter, der (German 'the Blue Rider') loose association of German Expressionist painters formed 1911 in Munich. They were united by an interest in the expressive qualities of colour, in primitive and folk art, and in the necessity of painting 'the inner, spiritual side of nature', though their individual styles varied greatly. Two central figures were ◊Kandinsky and Franz ◊Marc.

'And did those feet in ancient time / Walk upon England's mountains green? / And was the holy Lamb of God / On England's pleasant pastures seen?'

WILLIAM BLAKE
Milton, preface

A book explaining *Blaue Reiter* objectives, the *Almanach*, was published 1912, and there were two exhibitions, 1911 and 1912. Other members of the group were Gabriele Münter, August Macke, Alfred Kubin, Alexei von Jawlensky, Heinrich Campendonck (1889–1957), and Paul Klee.

Blavatsky Helena Petrovna, (born Hahn) 1831–1891. Russian spiritualist and mystic, cofounder of the Theosophical Society (see ◊theosophy) 1875, which has its headquarters near Madras, India. In Tibet she underwent spiritual training and later became a Buddhist. Her books include *Isis Unveiled* 1877 and *The Secret Doctrine* 1888. She was declared a fraud by the London Society for Psychical Research 1885.

bleaching decolorization of coloured materials. The two main types of bleaching agent are the oxidizing bleaches, which bring about the ◊oxidation of pigments and include the ultraviolet rays in sunshine, hydrogen peroxide, and chlorine in household bleaches, and the reducing bleaches, which bring about ◊reduction and include sulphur dioxide.

bleak freshwater fish *Alburnus alburnus* of the carp family. It is up to to 20 cm/8 in long, and lives in still or slow-running clear water in Britain and Europe. In Eastern Europe its scales are used in the preparation of artificial pearls.

Blenheim, Battle of in the War of the Spanish Succession, decisive victory 13 Aug 1704 of Allied troops under ◊Marlborough over French and Bavarian armies near the Bavarian village of Blenheim (now in Germany) on the left bank of the Danube, about 25 km/18 mi northwest of Augsburg. Although the war was to continue for a further eight years, Blenheim marked the turning point at which the power of France was first broken.

blenny any fish of the family Blenniidae, mostly small fishes found near rocky shores, with elongated slimy bodies tapering from head to tail, no scales, and long pelvic fins set far forward.

Blériot Louis 1872–1936. French aviator. In a 24-horsepower monoplane of his own construction, he made the first flight across the English Channel 25 July 1909.

blesbok African antelope *Damaliscus albifrons*, about 1 m/3 ft high, with curved horns, brownish body, and a white blaze on the face. It was seriously depleted in the wild at the end of the 19th century. A few protected herds survive in South Africa. It is farmed for meat.

blesbok Blesbok antelopes, which live on the African savanna, are now scarce. Blesbok males are highly territorial and spend a great deal of time standing near a central dung-heap attracting females to their harem and driving off rival males. *Premaphotos Wildlife*

Bligh William 1754–1817. English sailor who accompanied Captain James ◊Cook on his second voyage around the world 1772–74, and in 1787 commanded HMS *Bounty* on an expedition to the Pacific.

On the return voyage the crew mutinied 1789, and Bligh was cast adrift in a boat with 18 men with no map and few provisions. They survived, after many weeks reaching Timor, near Java, having drifted 5,822 km/3,618 mi. Many of the crew members settled in the ◊Pitcairn Islands. He was appointed governor of New South Wales 1805, where his discipline again provoked a mutiny 1808 (the Rum Rebellion). He returned to Britain, and was made an admiral 1811.

blight any of a number of plant diseases caused mainly by parasitic species of ◊fungus, which produce a whitish appearance on leaf and stem surfaces; for example, potato blight *Phytophthora infestans*. General damage caused by aphids or pollution is sometimes known as blight.

blimp airship: any self-propelled, lighter-than-air craft that can be steered. A blimp with a soft frame is also called a dirigible; a ◊zeppelin is rigid-framed.

British lighter-than-air aircraft were divided in World War I into A-rigid and B-limp (that is, without rigid internal framework), a barrage balloon therefore becoming known as a blimp. The cartoonist David Low adopted the name for his stuffy character Colonel Blimp.

blindness complete absence or impairment of sight. It may be caused by heredity, accident, disease, or deterioration with age.

Age-related macular degeneration (AMD), the commonest form of blindness, occurs as the retina gradually deteriorates with age. It affects 1% of people over the age of 70, with many more experiencing marked reduction in sight.

Retinitis pigmentosa, a common cause of blindness, is a hereditary disease affecting 1.2 million people worldwide.

Education of the blind was begun by Valentin Haüy, who published a book with raised lettering 1784, and founded a school. Aids to the blind include the use of the ◊Braille and Moon alphabets in reading and writing. Guide dogs for the blind were first trained in Germany for soldiers blinded in World War I.

blind spot area where the optic nerve and blood vessels pass through the retina of the ◊eye. No visual image can be formed as there are no light-sensitive cells in this part of the retina. Thus the organism is blind to objects that fall in this part of the visual field.

Bliss Arthur Edward Drummond 1891–1975. English composer and conductor. He became Master of the Queen's Musick 1953. Among his works are *A Colour Symphony* 1922; music for the ballets *Checkmate* 1937, *Miracle in the Gorbals* 1944, and *Adam Zero* 1946; an opera *The Olympians* 1949; and dramatic film music, including *Things to Come* 1935. He conducted the first performance of US composer Igor Stravinsky's *Ragtime* for 11 instruments 1918.

Blitzkrieg (German 'lightning war') swift military campaign, as used by Germany at the beginning of World War II 1939–41. It was characterized by rapid movement by mechanized forces, supported by tactical air forces acting as 'flying artillery' and is best exemplified by the campaigns in Poland 1939 and France 1940.

The abbreviated 'Blitz' was applied to the attempted saturation bombing of London by the German air force between Sept 1940 and May 1941.

Blixen Karen (Christentze), Baroness Blixen, born Dinesen 1885–1962. Danish writer. She wrote mainly in English and is best known for her short stories, Gothic fantasies with a haunting, often mythic quality, published in such collections as *Seven Gothic Tales* 1934 and *Winter's Tales* 1942 under the pen name Isak Dinesen. Her autobiography *Out of Africa* 1937 (filmed 1985) is based on her experience of running a coffee plantation in Kenya.

Bloch Ernest 1880–1959. Swiss-born US composer. Among his works are the lyrical drama *Macbeth* 1910, *Schelomo* for cello and orchestra 1916, five string quartets, and *Suite Hébraique* for viola and orchestra 1953. He often used themes based on Jewish liturgical music and folk song.

Bloch Marc 1886–1944. French historian, leading member of the Annales school that pioneered new methods of historical enquiry. Most of his research was into medieval European history. He held that economic structures and systems of belief were just as important to the study of history as legal norms and institutional practices, and pioneered the use of comparative history.

blockade cutting-off of a place by hostile forces by land, sea, or air so as to prevent any movement to or fro, in order to compel a surrender without attack or to achieve some other political aim (for example, the ◊Berlin blockade 1948). Economic sanctions are sometimes used in an attempt to achieve the same effect.

No nation has the right to declare a blockade unless it has the power to enforce it, according to international law. The Declaration of London 1909 laid down that a blockade must not be extended beyond the coasts and ports belonging to or occupied by an enemy.

Bloemfontein capital of the ◊Orange Free State and judicial capital of the Republic of South Africa; population (1991) 300,150. Founded 1846, the city produces canned fruit, glassware, furniture, plastics, and railway engineering.

Blok Alexander Alexandrovich 1880–1921. Russian poet. As a follower of the French Symbolist movement, he used words for their symbolic rather than actual meaning. He backed the 1917 Revolution, as in his poems *The Twelve* 1918 and *The Scythians* 1918, the latter appealing to the West to join in the revolution.

Blondin Charles. Assumed name of Jean François Gravelet 1824–1897. French tightrope walker who walked across a rope suspended above Niagara Falls, USA. He first crossed the falls 1859 at a height of 49 m/160 ft, and later repeated the feat blindfold and then pushing a wheelbarrow.

blood fluid circulating in the arteries, veins, and capillaries of vertebrate animals; the term also refers to the corresponding fluid in those invertebrates that possess a closed ◊circulatory system. Blood carries nutrients and oxygen to each body cell and removes waste products, such as carbon dioxide. It is also important in the immune response and, in many animals, in the distribution of heat throughout the body.

In humans blood makes up 5% of the body weight, occupying a volume of 5.5 l/10 pt in the average adult. It is composed of a colourless, transparent liquid called ***plasma***, in which are suspended microscopic cells of three main varieties:

Red cells (erythrocytes) form nearly half the volume of the blood, with about 6 million red cells in every millilitre of an adult's blood. Their red colour is caused by ◊haemoglobin.

White cells (leucocytes) are of various kinds. Some (phagocytes) ingest invading bacteria and so protect the body from disease; these also help to repair injured tissues. Others (lymphocytes) produce antibodies, which help provide immunity.

Blood ***platelets*** (thrombocytes) assist in the clotting of blood.

Blood cells constantly wear out and die and are replaced from the bone marrow. Red blood cells die at the rate of 200 billion per day but the body produces new cells at an average rate of 9,000 million per hour.

Blood Thomas 1618–1680. Irish adventurer, known as Colonel Blood, who attempted to steal the crown jewels from the Tower of London, England, 1671.

blood–brain barrier theoretical term for the defence mechanism that prevents many substances circulating in the bloodstream (including some germs) from invading the brain.

blood clotting complex series of events (known as the blood clotting cascade) that prevents excessive bleeding after injury. It is triggered by ◊vitamin K. The result is the formation of a meshwork of protein fibres (fibrin) and trapped blood cells over the cut blood vessels.

When platelets (cell fragments) in the bloodstream come into contact with a damaged blood vessel, they and the vessel wall itself release the enzyme thrombokinase, which brings about the conversion of the inactive enzyme prothrombin into the active thrombin. Thrombin in turn catalyses the conversion of the soluble protein fibrinogen, present in blood plasma, to the insoluble fibrin. This fibrous protein forms a net over the wound that traps red blood cells and seals the wound; the resulting jellylike clot hardens on exposure to air to form a scab. Calcium, vitamin K, and a variety of enzymes called factors are also necessary for efficient blood clotting. ◊Haemophilia is one of several diseases in which the clotting mechanism is impaired.

blood group any of the types into which blood is classified according to the presence or otherwise of certain ◊antigens on the surface of its red cells. Red blood cells of one individual may carry molecules on their surface that act as antigens in another individual whose red blood cells lack these molecules. The two main antigens are designated A and B. These give rise to four blood groups: having A only (A), having B only (B), having both (AB), and having neither (O). Each of these groups may or may not contain the ◊rhesus factor. Correct typing of blood groups is vital in transfusion, since incompatible types of donor and recipient blood will result in coagulation, with possible death of the recipient.

The ABO system was first described by Austrian scientist Karl ◊Landsteiner 1902. Subsequent research revealed at least 14 main types of blood group systems, 11 of which are involved with induced ◊antibody production.

bloodhound breed of dog originated as a hunting dog in Belgium in the Middle Ages. Black and tan in colour, it has long, pendulous ears and distinctive wrinkled head and face. It grows to a height of about 65 cm/26 in. Its excellent powers of scent have been employed in tracking and criminal detection from very early times.

blood poisoning presence in the bloodstream of quantities of bacteria or bacterial toxins sufficient to cause serious illness.

blood pressure pressure, or tension, of the blood against the inner walls of blood vessels, especially the arteries, due to the muscular pumping activity of the heart. Abnormally high blood pressure (◊hypertension) may be associated with various conditions or arise with no obvious cause; abnormally low blood pressure (hypotension) occurs in ◊shock and after excessive fluid or blood loss from any cause.

In mammals, the left ventricle of the ◊heart pumps blood into the arterial system. This pumping is assisted by waves of muscular contraction by the arteries themselves, but resisted by the elasticity of the inner and outer walls of the same arteries. Pressure is greatest when the heart ventricle contracts (systole) and lowest when the ventricle relaxes (diastole), and pressure is solely maintained by the elasticity of the arteries. Blood pressure is measured in millimetres of mercury (the height of a column on the measuring instrument, a sphygmomanometer). Normal human blood pressure varies with age, but in a young healthy adult it is around 120/80 mm Hg; the first number represents the systolic pressure and the second the diastolic. Large deviations from this reading usually indicate ill health.

blood test laboratory evaluation of a blood sample. There are numerous blood tests, from simple typing to establish the ◊blood group to sophisticated biochemical assays of substances, such as hormones, present in the blood only in minute quantities.

The majority of tests fall into one of three categories: haematology (testing the state of the blood itself), microbiology (identifying infection), and blood chemistry (reflecting chemical events elsewhere in the body). Before operations, a common test is haemoglobin estimation to determine how well a patient might tolerate blood loss during surgery.

blood transfusion see ◊transfusion.

blood vessel tube that conducts blood either away from or towards the heart in multicellular animals. Freshly oxygenated blood is carried in the arteries – major vessels which give way to the arterioles (small arteries) and finally capillaries; deoxygenated blood is returned to the heart by way of capillaries, then venules (small veins) and veins.

bloom whitish powdery or waxlike coating over the surface of certain fruits that easily rubs off when handled. It often contains ◊yeasts that live on the sugars in the fruit. The term bloom is also used to describe a rapid increase in number of certain species of algae found in lakes, ponds, and oceans. This type of bloom can lead to the death of almost every other organism in the water; because light cannot penetrate the algal growth, the plants beneath can no longer photosynthesize and therefore do not release oxygen into the water. Only those organisms that are adapted to very low levels of oxygen survive.

Bloomer Amelia, born Jenks 1818–1894. US campaigner for women's rights. In 1849, when unwieldy crinolines were the fashion, she introduced a knee-length skirt combined with loose trousers gathered at the ankles, which became known as bloomers (also called 'rational dress'). She published the magazine *The Lily* 1849–54, which campaigned for women's rights and dress reform, and lectured with Susan B ◊Anthony in New York, USA.

Blücher, Gebhard Leberecht von The Prussian general Gebhard Leberecht von Blücher. He fought in the Napoleonic Wars, defeating Napoleon at Leipzig in Oct 1813 and at Laon in March 1814. He was made prince of Wahlstadt and received the Grand Cross of the Order of the Iron Cross in 1815. *Corbis*

Bloomsbury Group intellectual circle of writers and artists based in Bloomsbury, London, which flourished in the 1920s. It centred on the house of publisher Leonard Woolf (1880–1969) and his wife, novelist Virginia ◊Woolf, and included the artists Duncan ◊Grant and Vanessa Bell (1879–1961), the biographer Lytton ◊Strachey, art critics Roger Fry and Clive Bell (1881–1964), and the economist John Maynard ◊Keynes. Typically Modernist, their innovatory artistic contributions represented an important section of the English avant-garde.

Blow John 1648–1708. English composer. He taught English composer Henry Purcell and wrote church music, for example the anthem 'I Was Glad When They Said Unto Me' 1697. His masque *Venus and Adonis* 1685 is sometimes called the first English opera.

blowfly any fly of the genus *Calliphora*, also known as bluebottle, or of the related genus *Lucilia*, when it is greenbottle. It lays its eggs in dead flesh, on which the maggots feed.

blubber thick layer of ◊fat under the skin of marine mammals, which provides an energy store and an effective insulating layer, preventing the loss of body heat to the surrounding water. Blubber has been used (when boiled down) in engineering, food processing, cosmetics, and printing, but all of these products can now be produced synthetically.

Blücher Gebhard Leberecht von 1742–1819. Prussian general and field marshal, popularly known as 'Marshal Forward'. He took an active part in the patriotic movement, and in the War of German Liberation defeated the French as commander in chief at Leipzig 1813, crossed the Rhine to Paris 1814, and was made prince of Wahlstadt (Silesia).

In 1815 he was defeated by Napoleon at Ligny but came to the aid of British commander Wellington at ◊Waterloo. *See feature on pp. 748–749.*

Bluebeard folk-tale character, popularized by the writer Charles ◊Perrault in France about 1697, and historically identified with Gilles de Rais, a 15th-century French nobleman executed for murdering children. Bluebeard murdered six wives for disobeying his command not to enter a locked room, but was himself killed before he could murder the seventh.

bluebell name given in Scotland to the harebell *Campanula rotundifolia*, and in England to the wild hyacinth *Endymion nonscriptus*, belonging to the family Liliaceae.

blueberry any of various North American acid-soil shrubs of the genus *Vaccinium* of the heath family. The genus also includes huckleberries, bilberries, deerberries, and cranberries, many of which resemble each other and are difficult to distinguish from blueberries. All have small, elliptical short-stalked leaves, slender green or reddish twigs, and whitish bell-like blossoms. Only true blueberries, however, have tiny granular speckles on their twigs. Blueberries have black or blue edible fruits, often covered with a white bloom.

bluebird or ***blue robin*** or ***blue warbler*** three species of a North American bird, genus *Sialia*, belonging to the thrush subfamily, Turdinae, order Passeriformes. The eastern bluebird *Sialia sialis* is regarded as the herald of spring as it returns from migration. About 18 cm/7 in long, it has a reddish breast, the upper plumage being sky-blue, and a distinctive song. It lays about six pale-blue eggs.

bluebuck any of several species of antelope, including the blue ◊duiker *Cephalophus monticola* of South Africa, about 33 cm/13 in high. The male of the Indian ◊nilgai antelope is also known as the bluebuck.

The bluebuck or blaubok, *Hippotragus leucophaeus*, was a large blue-grey South African antelope. Once abundant, it was hunted to extinction, the last being shot 1800.

blue chip in business and finance, a stock that is considered strong and reliable in terms of the dividend yield and capital value. Blue-chip companies are favoured by stock-market investors more interested in security than risk taking.

bluegrass dense, spreading grass of the genus *Poa*, which is blue-tinted and grows in clumps. Various species are known from the northern hemisphere. Kentucky bluegrass *P. pratensis*, introduced to the USA from Europe, provides pasture for horses.

blue-green algae or ***cyanobacteria*** single-celled, primitive organisms that resemble bacteria in their internal cell organization, sometimes joined together in colonies or filaments. Blue-green algae are among the oldest known living organisms and, with bacteria, belong to the kingdom Monera; remains have been found in rocks up to 3.5 billion years old. They are widely distributed in aquatic habitats, on the damp surfaces of rocks and trees, and in the soil.

Blue-green algae and bacteria are prokaryotic organisms. Some can fix nitrogen and thus are necessary to the nitrogen cycle, while others follow a symbiotic existence – for example, living in association with fungi to form lichens. Fresh water can become polluted by nitrates and phosphates from fertilizers and detergents. This eutrophication, or over-enrichment, of the water causes multiplication of the algae in the form of algae blooms.

bluebird The eastern bluebird is found throughout the eastern part of North America, where it may be seen perching on fences. Bluebirds nest in holes in tree trunks; both male and female build the nest. The female lays four or five eggs and incubates them for about two weeks. The young leave the nest after two to three weeks. Usually two broods are produced each year.

❛Cricket to us, like you, was more than play, / It was a worship in the summer sun.❜

EDMUND BLUNDEN *Pride of the Village*

blue gum either of two Australian trees: Tasmanian blue gum *Eucalyptus globulus* of the myrtle family, with bluish bark, a chief source of eucalyptus oil; or Sydney blue gum *E. saligna*, a tall, straight tree. The former is cultivated extensively in California and has also been planted in South America, India, parts of Africa, and S Europe.

Blue Mountains part of the ◊Great Dividing Range, New South Wales, Australia, ranging 600–1,100 m/2,000–3,600 ft and blocking Sydney from the interior until the crossing 1813 by surveyor William Lawson, Gregory Blaxland, and William Wentworth.

Blue Nile (Arabic *Bahr el Azraq*) river rising in the mountains of Ethiopia. Flowing west then north for 2,000 km/1,250 mi, it eventually meets the White Nile at Khartoum. The river is dammed at Roseires where a hydroelectric scheme produces 70% of Sudan's electricity.

blueprint photographic process used for copying engineering drawings and architectural plans, so called because it produces a white copy of the original against a blue background.

blue riband or ***blue ribbon*** the highest distinction in any sphere.

The Blue Riband of the Atlantic is held by the vessel making the fastest crossing without refuelling. The *Queen Mary* won it 1938 and held the record until the *United States* created a new record of 3 dy 10 hr 31 min 1952. Richard Branson's time of 3 dy 8hr 31 min in *Virgin Atlantic Challenger* 1985 was a new record time but failed to win the trophy because he refuelled three times. On 27 July 1989, Tom Gentry of the USA in his craft *Gentry Eagle* broke the record with a time of 67 hr 7 min. He was presented with the Blue Riband Trophy by Richard Branson. The catamaran *Hoverspeed Great Britain* made the crossing in 3 dy 7 hr 25 min in July 1990, and was awarded the Hales Trophy until after litigation.

Blue Ridge Mountains range extending from West Virginia to Georgia, USA, and including Mount Mitchell 2,045 m/6,712 ft; part of the ◊Appalachians.

blues African-American music that originated in the work songs and Negro spirituals of the rural American South in the late 19th century. It is characterized by a 12-bar, or occasionally 16-bar, construction and melancholy lyrics which relate tales of woe or unhappy love. The guitar has been the dominant instrument; harmonica and piano are also common. Blues guitar and vocal styles have played a vital part in the development of jazz, rock, and pop music in general.

1920s–1930s The ***rural*** or ***delta blues*** was usually performed solo with guitar or harmonica, by such artists as Robert Johnson (c. 1912–1938) and Bukka White (1906–1977), but the earliest recorded style, ***classic blues***, by such musicians as W C Handy (1873–1958) and Bessie ◊Smith, was sung with a small band.

1940s–1950s The ***urban blues***, using electric amplification, emerged in the northern cities, chiefly Chicago. As exemplified by ◊Howlin' Wolf, ◊Muddy Waters, and John Lee ◊Hooker, urban blues became ◊***rhythm and blues***.

1960s The jazz-influenced guitar style of B B ◊King inspired many musicians of the ***British blues boom***, including Eric ◊Clapton.

1980s The 'blues *noir*' of Robert Cray (1953–) contrasted with the rock-driven blues playing of Stevie Ray Vaughan (1955–1990).

In classical music, composers such as Ravel, Copland, and Michael Tippett have used the term loosely to refer to mood rather than a strict musical form.

blue shift in astronomy, a manifestation of the ◊Doppler effect in which an object appears bluer when it is moving towards the observer or the observer is moving towards it (blue light is of a higher frequency than other colours in the spectrum). The blue shift is the opposite of the ◊red shift.

bluestocking learned woman; the term is often used disparagingly. It originated 1750 in England with the literary gatherings of Elizabeth Vesey (1715–1791), the wife of an Irish MP, in Bath, and Elizabeth Montagu, a writer and patron, in London. According to the novelist Fanny Burney, the term arose when the poet Benjamin Stillingfleet protested that he had nothing formal to wear. She told him to come in his 'blue stockings' – that is, ordinary clothes. The regulars at these gatherings became known as the Blue Stocking Circle.

Blum Léon 1872–1950. French politician. He was converted to socialism by the ◊Dreyfus affair 1899 and in 1936 became the first socialist prime minister of France. He was again premier for a few weeks 1938. Imprisoned under the ◊Vichy government 1942 as a danger to French security, he was released by the Allies 1945. He again became premier for a few weeks 1946.

Blunden Edmund (Charles) 1896–1974. English poet and critic. He served in World War I and published the prose work *Undertones of War* 1928. His poetry is mainly about rural life. Among his scholarly contributions was the discovery and publication of some poems by the 19th-century poet John ◊Clare.

Blunt Anthony Frederick 1907–1983. British art historian and double agent. As a Cambridge lecturer, he recruited for the Soviet secret service and, as a member of the British Secret Service 1940–45, passed information to the USSR. In 1951 he assisted the defection to the USSR of the British agents Guy ◊Burgess and Donald Maclean (1913–1983). He was the author of many respected works on French and Italian art. Unmasked 1964, he was given immunity after his confession, but was stripped of his knighthood 1979 when the affair became public.

Blunt Wilfrid Scawen 1840–1922. English poet. He travelled in the Middle East, becoming a supporter of Arab nationalism. He also supported Irish Home Rule (he was imprisoned 1887–88), and wrote anti-imperialist books as well as poetry and diaries.

Blur English pop group. Their album *Parklife* 1994 won wide admiration for its catchy melodies and quirky 'Cockney' attitude. Members are singer Damon Albarn (1968–), guitarist Graham Coxon (1969–), bassist Alex James (1968–), and drummer Dave Rowntree (1963–).

Blyton Enid Mary 1897–1968. English writer of children's books. She created the character Noddy and the adventures of the 'Famous Five' and 'Secret Seven'. She has been criticized for social, racial, and sexual stereotyping.

boa any of various nonvenomous snakes of the family Boidae, found mainly in tropical and subtropical parts of the New World. Boas feed mainly on small mammals and birds. They catch these in their teeth or kill them by constriction (crushing the creature within their coils until it suffocates). The boa constrictor *Constrictor constrictor* can grow up to 5.5 m/18.5 ft long, but rarely reaches more than 4 m/12 ft. Other boas include the anaconda and the emerald tree boa *Boa canina*, about 2 m/6 ft long and bright green.

boa The emerald tree boa is the fastest-moving member of the boa family. It lives in trees, where it lies in wait for its prey – chiefly parrots, monkeys, and bats. It kills these with its teeth, not by constriction.

Boadicea alternative spelling of British queen ◊Boudicca.

boar wild member of the pig family, such as the Eurasian wild boar *Sus scrofa*, from which domestic pig breeds derive. The wild boar is sturdily built, being 1.5 m/4.5 ft long and 1 m/3 ft high, and possesses formidable tusks. Of gregarious nature and mainly woodland-dwelling, it feeds on roots, nuts, insects, and some carrion.

The dark coat of the adult boar is made up of coarse bristles with varying amounts of underfur, but the young are striped. The male domestic pig is also known as a boar, the female as a sow.

Boardman Chris 1968– . English cyclist. He first came to prominence in 1992 when he won the individual pursuit gold medal at the Barcelona Olympics. In 1996 he won back the world pursuit title and regained the world one-hour record, extending the distance by 1.089 km to 56.38 km.

boardsailing another name for ◊windsurfing, a watersport combining elements of surfing and sailing, also called sailboarding.

Boas Franz 1858–1942. German-born US anthropologist. He stressed the need to study 'four fields' – ethnology, linguistics, physical anthropology, and archaeology – before generalizations might be made about any one culture or comparisons about any number of cultures.

In 1886 he travelled to the Pacific Northwest to study the culture of the Kwakiutl Indian people, including their language. Joining the faculty of Clark University 1888, Boas became one of America's first academic anthropologists. In 1896 he was appointed professor at Columbia University, where he trained the first generation of US anthropologists, including Alfred Kroeber (1876–1960) and Margaret ◊Mead. From 1901 to 1905 he was also curator of the American Museum of Natural History in New York City. His books include *The Mind of Primitive Man* 1911, *Primitive Art* 1927, and *Race, Language and Culture* 1940.

boat people illegal emigrants travelling by sea, especially those Vietnamese who left their country after the takeover of South Vietnam 1975 by North Vietnam. Around 160,000 Vietnamese fled to Hong Kong, many being attacked at sea by Thai pirates. The UK government began forced repatriation 1990, leaving only 18,000 in Hong Kong by 1996. A UN-backed plan to accelerate the repatriation of around 38,000 boat people living in SE Asia was announced Jan 1996.

The term 'boat people' has also been used for Cuban and Haitian refugees who reach Florida, USA, by boat. More than 2,400 entered the USA from Cuba 1991; there was a further influx from Cuba 1994.

Boat Race, the annual UK ◊rowing race between the crews of Oxford and Cambridge universities. It is held during the Easter vacation over a 6.8 km/4.25 mi course on the river Thames between Putney and Mortlake, SW London.

bobcat wild cat *Felis rufa* living in a variety of habitats from S Canada through to S Mexico. It is similar to the lynx, but only 75 cm/2.5 ft long, with reddish fur and less well-developed ear tufts.

bobolink North American songbird *Dolichonyx oryzivorus*, family Icteridae, order Passeriformes, that takes its common name from the distinctive call of the male. It has a long middle toe and pointed tail-feathers. Breeding males are mostly black, with a white rump; females are buff-coloured with dark streaks. Bobolinks are about 18 cm/7 in long and build their nests on the ground in hayfields and weedy meadows.

bobsleighing or ***bobsledding*** sport of racing steel-bodied, steerable toboggans, crewed by two or four people, down mountain ice chutes at speeds of up to 130 kph/80 mph. It was introduced as an Olympic event 1924 and world championships have been held every year since 1931. Included among the major bobsleighing events are the Olympic Championships (the four-crew event was introduced at the 1924 Winter Olympics and the two-crew 1932) and the World Championships, the four-crew championship introduced 1924 and the two-crew 1931.

Boccaccio Giovanni 1313–1375. Italian writer and poet. He is chiefly known for the collection of tales called the ◊*Decameron* 1348–53. Equally at home with tragic and comic narrative, he laid the foundations for the humanism of the Renaissance and raised vernacular literature to the status enjoyed by the ancient classics.

He was born in Florence but lived in Naples 1328–41, where he fell in love with the unfaithful

'Fiammetta' who inspired his early poetry. Before returning to Florence 1341 he had written the romance *Filostrato* and the verse narrative *Teseide* (used by Chaucer in his *Troilus and Criseyde* and 'The Knight's Tale'). *Teseide* is the first romantic narrative to appear in the Italian language in *ottava rima*, the metre adopted by ◊Ariosto and ◊Tasso. The narrative poem *Filostrato* is also written in *ottava rima*. Boccaccio was much influenced by the poet ◊Petrarch, whom he met 1350.

Bode Johann Elert 1747–1826. German astronomer and mathematician. He contributed greatly to the popularization of astronomy. He published the first atlas of all stars visible to the naked eye, *Uranographia* 1801, and devised ◊Bode's law.

Bode's law numerical sequence that gives the approximate distances, in astronomical units (distance between Earth and Sun = one astronomical unit), of the planets from the Sun by adding 4 to each term of the series 0, 3, 6, 12, 24, ... and then dividing by 10. Bode's law predicted the existence of a planet between ◊Mars and ◊Jupiter, which led to the discovery of the asteroids.

The 'law' breaks down for ◊Neptune and ◊Pluto. The relationship was first noted 1772 by the German mathematician Johann Titius (1729–1796) 1772 (it is also known as the Titius–Bode law).

Bodhidharma lived 6th century AD. Indian Buddhist and teacher. He entered China from S India about 520 and was the founder of the Ch'an school. Ch'an focuses on contemplation leading to intuitive meditation, a direct pointing to and stilling of the human mind. In the 20th century, the Japanese variation, ◊Zen, has attracted many followers in the West. ▷ *See feature on pp. 162–163.*

bodhisattva in Mahāyāna Buddhism, someone who seeks ◊enlightenment in order to help other living beings. A bodhisattva is free to enter ◊nirvana but voluntarily chooses to be reborn until all other beings have attained that state. Bodhisattvas are seen as intercessors to whom believers may pray for help.

Bodmin market town in Cornwall, England, 48 km/30 m from Plymouth; population (1991) 12,500. It is the centre of a farming area. Bodmin Moor to the NE is a granite upland, culminating in Brown Willy 419 m/1,375 ft.

Boeotia ancient district of central Greece, of which ◊Thebes was the chief city. The Boeotian League (formed by ten city states in the 6th century BC) superseded ◊Sparta in the leadership of Greece in the 4th century BC.

Boer Dutch settler or descendant of Dutch and Huguenot settlers in South Africa.

Boer War the second of the ◊South African Wars 1899–1902, waged between Dutch settlers in South Africa and the British.

Boethius Anicius Manlius Severinus AD 480–524. Roman philosopher. He wrote treatises on music and mathematics and *De Consolatione Philosophiae/The Consolation of Philosophy*, written while imprisoned on suspicion of treason by Emperor ◊Theodoric the Great. In it, a lady, Philosophy, responds to Boethius' account of his misfortunes with stoic, Platonic, and Christian advice. English translations were written by Alfred the Great, Geoffrey Chaucer, and Queen Elizabeth I. Boethius also translated Aristotle's works on logic and wrote treatises on Christian philosophy.

bog type of wetland where decomposition is slowed down and dead plant matter accumulates as ◊peat. Bogs develop under conditions of low temperature, high acidity, low nutrient supply, stagnant water, and oxygen deficiency. Typical bog plants are sphagnum moss, rushes, and cotton grass; insectivorous plants such as sundews and bladderworts are common in bogs (insect prey make up for the lack of nutrients).

Large bogs are found in Ireland and northern Scotland.

Bogarde Dirk. Stage name of Derek Niven van den Bogaerde 1921– . English actor. He appeared in comedies and adventure films such as *Doctor in the House* 1954 and *Campbell's Kingdom* 1957, before acquiring international recognition for complex roles in Joseph Losey's *The Servant* 1963 and *Accident* 1967, and Luchino Visconti's *Death in Venice* 1971. His other films include *A Bridge Too Far* 1977.

He has also written autobiographical books and novels including *A Postillion Struck by Lightning* 1977, *Backcloth* 1986, *A Particular Friendship* 1989, and *A Short Walk from Harrods* 1993.

Bogart Humphrey De Forest 1899–1957. US film actor. He achieved fame as the gangster in *The Petrified Forest* 1936. He became an international cult figure as the tough, romantic 'loner' in such films as *The Maltese Falcon* 1941 and *Casablanca* 1942, a status resurrected in the 1960s and still celebrated today. He won an Academy Award for his role in *The African Queen* 1952.

He co-starred in *To Have and Have Not* 1944 and *The Big Sleep* 1946 with Lauren Bacall, who became his fourth wife. *See illustration on following page.*

bogbean or ***buckbean*** aquatic or bog plant *Menyanthes trifoliata* of the gentian family, with a creeping rhizome and leaves and pink flower spikes held above water. It is found over much of the northern hemisphere.

Bogotá capital of Colombia, South America; 2,640 m/8,660 ft above sea level on the edge of the plateau of the E Cordillera; population (1994) 5,132,000. Main industries are textiles, chemicals, food processing, and tobacco.

history Founded by the Spanish 1538 on the site of the Indian settlement of Bacatá. It became the capital of the viceroyalty of New Granada, which became the republic of Columbia 1718.

features Home of Simon Bolívar; world's largest collection of pre-Columbian gold objects in its Gold Museum; its two oldest universities were founded 1580 and 1622.

Bohemia area of the Czech Republic, a fertile plateau drained by the Elbe and Vltava rivers. It is rich in mineral resources, including uranium, coal, lignite, iron ore, silver, and graphite. The main cities are Prague and Plzeň. The name Bohemia derives from the Celtic Boii, its earliest known inhabitants.

history It became part of the Holy Roman Empire as the result of Charlemagne's establishment of a protectorate over the Celtic, Germanic, and Slav tribes settled in this area. Christianity was introduced in the 9th century, the See of Prague being established 975, and feudalism was introduced by King Ottokar I of Bohemia (1197–1230). From the 12th century onwards, mining attracted large numbers of German settlers, leading to a strong Germanic influence in culture and society. In 1310, John of Luxemburg (died 1346) founded a German-Czech royal dynasty that lasted until 1437. His son, Charles IV, became Holy Roman Emperor 1355, and during his reign the See of Prague was elevated to an archbishopric and a university was founded here. During the 15th century, divisions within the nobility and religious conflicts culminated in the Hussite Wars 1420–36. It was under Habsburg rule 1526–1918, when it was included in Czechoslovakia.

Bohr Niels Henrik David 1885–1962. Danish physicist. His theoretical work produced a new model of atomic structure, now called the Bohr model, and helped establish the validity of ◊quantum theory. He also explained the process of nuclear fission. Nobel Prize for Physics 1922.

Bohr's first model of the atom was developed working with Ernest ◊Rutherford in Manchester, UK. He was director of the Institute of Theoretical Physics in Copenhagen from 1920. During World War II he took part in work on the atomic bomb in the USA. In 1952 he helped to set up ◊CERN, the European nuclear research organization in Geneva. He proposed the doctrine of complementarity: that a fundamental particle is neither a wave nor a particle, because these are complementary modes of description.

Bohr model model of the atom conceived by Danish physicist Neils Bohr 1913. It assumes that the following rules govern the behaviour of electrons: (1) electrons revolve in orbits of specific radius around the nucleus without emitting radiation; (2) within each orbit, each electron has a fixed amount of energy; electrons in orbits farther away from the nucleus have greater energies; (3) an electron may 'jump' from one orbit of high energy to another of lower energy causing the energy difference to be emitted as a ◊photon of electromagnetic radiation such as light. The Bohr model has been superseded by wave mechanics (see ◊quantum theory).

bobsleighing A modern two-seated bob on the Cresta Run in St Moritz, Switzerland, the site of the first organized bobsleigh competition 1898. The name of the sport comes from the technique, used in the early days, of team members bobbing their bodies back and forth to increase speed. *Swiss National Tourist Office*

Boiardo Matteo Maria, Count of Scandiano 1434–1494. Italian poet. He is famed for his *Orlando innamorato/Roland in Love* 1487, a chivalrous epic glorifying military honour, patriotism, and religion. ◊Ariosto's *Orlando furioso* 1516 was conceived as a sequel to this work.

boiler any vessel that converts water into steam. Boilers are used in conventional power stations to generate steam to feed steam ◊turbines, which drive the electricity generators. They are also used in steamships, which are propelled by steam turbines, and in steam locomotives. Every boiler has a furnace in which fuel (coal, oil, or gas) is burned to produce hot gases, and a system of tubes in which heat is transferred from the gases to the water.

The common kind of boiler used in ships and power stations is the water-tube type, in which the water circulates in tubes surrounded by the hot furnace gases. The water-tube boilers at power stations produce steam at a pressure of up to 300 atmospheres and at a temperature of up to 600°C/1,100°F to feed to the steam turbines. It is more efficient than the fire-tube type that is used in steam locomotives. In this boiler the hot furnace gases are drawn through tubes surrounded by water.

Boer War A Boer picket on Spion Kop at the start of the Boer War. General Buller occupied this vantage point Jan 1900 but, after a fierce counter-attack by the Boers, British forces were compelled to abandon the ground they had gained. *Corbis*

Bogart US actor Humphrey Bogart with Lauren Bacall in *To Have and Have Not* 1944. Playing gangster roles in the 1930s, Bogart had by the 1940s developed the role of the tough, laconic loner that made him a cult figure. He and Bacall married 1945 and went on to make several more films together, notably *The Big Sleep* 1946 and *Key Largo* 1948. *British Film Institute*

boiling point for any given liquid, the temperature at which the application of heat raises the temperature of the liquid no further, but converts it into vapour. The boiling point of water under normal pressure is 100°C/212°F. The lower the pressure, the lower the boiling point and vice versa.

Bokassa Jean-Bédel 1921–1996. President of the Central African Republic 1966–79 and later self-proclaimed emperor 1977–79. Commander in chief from 1963, in Dec 1965 he led the military coup that gave him the presidency. On 4 Dec 1976 he proclaimed the Central African Empire and one year later crowned himself as emperor for life. His regime was characterized by arbitrary state violence and cruelty. Overthrown 1979, Bokassa was in exile until 1986. Upon his return he was sentenced to death, but this was commuted to life imprisonment 1988.

bolero Spanish dance in moderate triple time (3/4), invented in the late 18th century. It is performed by a solo dancer or a couple, usually with castanet accompaniment, and is still a contemporary form of dance in Caribbean countries. In music, Ravel's one-act ballet score *Boléro* 1928 is the most famous example, consisting of a theme which is constantly repeated and varied instrumentally, building to a powerful climax. The ballet was choreographed by Nijinsky for Ida Rubinstein 1928.

boletus genus of fleshy fungi belonging to the class Basidiomycetes, with thick stems and caps of various colours. The European *Boletus edulis* is edible, but some species are poisonous.

boletus The red crack boletus *Boletus chrysenteron*. Like other members of the genus, it releases its spores through a mass of pores beneath the cap, rather than from the more familiar gills seen beneath the cap of an edible mushroom. *Premaphotos Wildlife*

Boleyn Anne c. 1501–1536. Queen of England 1533–36. Henry VIII broke with the pope (see ◊Reformation) in order to divorce his first wife and marry Anne. She was married to him 1533 and gave birth to the future Queen Elizabeth I in the same year. Accused of adultery and incest with her half-brother (a charge invented by Thomas ◊Cromwell), she was beheaded.

Bolger Jim (James Brendan) 1935– . New Zealand politician, prime minister 1990–96. He held a variety of cabinet posts under Robert Muldoon's leadership 1977–84 and was leader of the opposition from March 1986, taking the National Party to electoral victory Oct 1990. His subsequent failure to honour election pledges, leading to cuts in welfare provision, led to a sharp fall in his popularity. He retained power in the 1993 general election with a majority of one, but lost it in 1996 after an inconclusive general election result.

Bolingbroke title of Henry of Bolingbroke, ◊Henry IV of England.

Bolingbroke Henry St John, 1st Viscount Bolingbroke 1678–1751. British Tory politician and political philosopher. He was foreign secretary 1710–14 (he negotiated the Treaty of Utrecht 1713) and a Jacobite conspirator. His books, such as *Idea of a Patriot King* 1738 and *The Dissertation upon Parties* 1735, laid the foundations for 19th-century Toryism. His plans to restore the 'Old Pretender' James Francis Edward Stuart were ruined by Queen Anne's death only five days after he had secured the dismissal of Harley 1714. He fled abroad, returning 1723, when he worked to overthrow Robert Walpole.

Bolívar Simón 1783–1830. South American nationalist, leader of revolutionary armies, known as 'the Liberator'. He fought the Spanish colonial forces in several uprisings and eventually liberated his native Venezuela 1821, Colombia 1819 and Ecuador 1822, Peru 1824, and Bolivia (a new state named after him, formerly Upper Peru) 1825.

Born in Venezuela, he joined that country's revolution against Spain 1810, and in the following year he declared Venezuela independent. His army was soon defeated by the Spanish, however, and he was forced to flee.It was not until 1819 that Bolívar won his first major victory, defeating the Spanish in Colombia and winning independence for that country. He went on to liberate Venezuela 1821 and (along with Antonio ◊Sucre) Ecuador 1822. These three countries were united into the republic of Gran Colombia with Bolívar as its president. In 1824 Bolívar helped bring about the defeat of Spanish forces in Peru, and the area known as Upper Peru was renamed 'Bolivia' in Bolívar's honour. Within the next few years, Venezuela and Ecuador seceded from the union, and in 1830 Bolívar resigned as president. He died the same year, despised by many for his dictatorial ways but since revered as South America's greatest liberator.

Bolivia landlocked country in central Andes mountains in South America, bounded N and E by Brazil, SE by Paraguay, S by Argentina, and W by Chile and Peru. *See country box opposite.*

Bolkiah Hassanal 1946– . Sultan of Brunei from 1967, following the abdication of his father, Omar Ali Saifuddin (1916–1986). As absolute ruler, Bolkiah also assumed the posts of prime minister and defence minister on independence 1984.

As head of an oil- and gas-rich microstate, the sultan is reputedly the world's richest individual, with an estimated total wealth of $22 billion, which includes the Dorchester and Beverly Hills hotels in London and Los Angeles and, at a cost of $40 million, the world's largest palace. He was educated at a British military academy.

Böll Heinrich (Theodor) 1917–1985. German novelist. A radical Catholic and anti-Nazi, he attacked Germany's political past and the materialism of its contemporary society. His many publications include poems, short stories, and novels which satirized West German society, for example *Billard um Halbzehn/Billiards at Half-Past Nine* 1959 and *Gruppenbild mit Dame/Group Portrait with Lady* 1971. Nobel Prize for Literature 1972.

boll weevil small American beetle *Anthonomus grandis* of the weevil group. The female lays her eggs in the unripe pods or 'bolls' of the cotton plant, and on these the larvae feed, causing great destruction.

Bolívar, Simón The South American soldier, statesman, and revolutionary leader Simón Bolívar. He was involved in many wars of independence in South America, and is revered as a national hero in Bolivia (which was named after him), Colombia, Ecuador, Peru, and Venezuela. *Corbis*

Bologna industrial city and capital of Emilia-Romagna, Italy, 80 km/50 mi N of Florence; population (1992) 401,300. It was the site of an Etruscan town, later of a Roman colony, and became a republic in the 12th century. It came under papal rule 1506 and was united with Italy 1860.

The city has a cathedral and medieval towers, and the university, which dates from the 11th century, laid the foundations of the study of anatomy and was attended by the poets Dante, Petrarch, and Tasso, and the astronomer Copernicus.

Bolshevik (from Russian *bolshinstvo* 'a majority') member of the majority of the Russian Social Democratic Party who split from the ◊Mensheviks 1903. The Bolsheviks, under ◊Lenin, advocated the destruction of capitalist political and economic institutions, and the setting-up of a socialist state with power in the hands of the workers. The Bolsheviks set the ◊Russian Revolution 1917 in motion.

They changed their name to the Russian Communist Party 1918.

Bolshoi Ballet (Russian 'great') Russian ballet company founded 1776 and based at the Bolshoi Theatre in Moscow. With their mixed repertory of classics and new works, the Bolshoi is noted for its grand scale productions and the dancers' dramatic and eloquent technique. From 1964 its artistic director was the choreographer Yuri Grigorovich (1927–).

The Bolshoi was formed by English entrepreneur Michael Maddox and Prince Urusov. Its dancers were recruited from the Moscow Orphanage where the first classes were conducted 1773. The present Bolshoi Theatre was opened 1825. In contrast to the ◊Kirov Ballet, the Bolshoi tended to be earthier and more contemporary in style and theme. The Bolshoi came into its own in the late 19th century with the first staging of ◊Petipa's *Don Quixote* 1877 and *Swan Lake* 1877. Under Alexander Gorsky (died 1942), the Bolshoi's style of highly dramatic action woven into the dance, innovative stage designs, and symphonic music, was developed. It was not until Leonid Lavrovsky (1905–1967) transferred as artistic director from the Kirov to the Bolshoi 1944, along with prima ballerinas Galina Ulanova and Maya Plisetskaya that the creative emphasis shifted to Moscow. Since the 1960s the Bolshoi has concentrated on spectacular and heroic productions of the classics and modern works, such as *Spartacus* 1968 and *The Golden Age* 1982.

Bolt Robert Oxton 1924–1995. English dramatist and screenwriter. He is known for his historical

BOLIVIA
Republic of

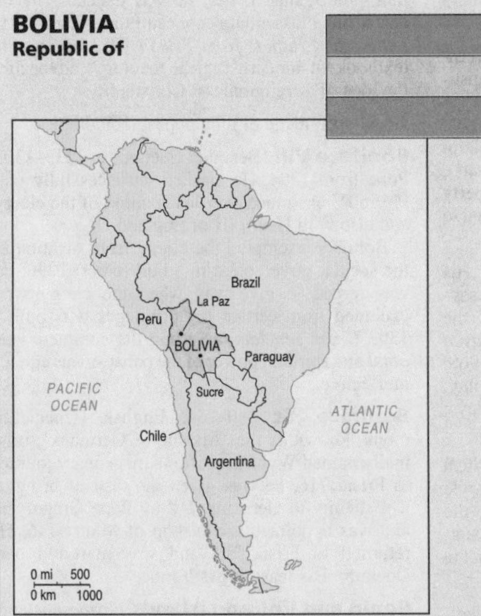

national name *República de Bolivia*
area 1,098,581 sq km/424,052 sq mi
capital La Paz (seat of government), Sucre (legal capital and seat of judiciary)
major towns/cities Santa Cruz, Cochabamba, Oruro, El Alto
physical features high plateau (Altiplano) between mountain ridges (cordilleras); forest and lowlands (llano) in the E; Andes; lakes Titicaca (the world's highest navigable lake, 3,800 m/12,500 ft) and Poopó
head of state and government Hugo Banzer Suarez from 1997
political system emergent democratic republic
administrative divisions nine departments
political parties National Revolutionary Movement (MNR), centre right; Movement of the Revolutionary Left (MIR), left of centre; Nationalist Democratic Action Party (ADN), right-wing; Solidarity and Civic Union (UCS), populist, free market
population 7,414,000 (1995 est)
population growth rate 2.4% (1990–95); 2.2% (2000–05)
ethnic distribution 30% Quechua Indians, 25% Aymara Indians, 25–30% mixed race, and 5–15% of European descent
life expectancy 54 (males), 58 (females)
literacy rate men 85%, women 71%
languages Spanish (official), Aymara, Quechua
religion Roman Catholic 95% (state-recognized)
currency boliviano
GDP (US $) 6.35 billion (1994)
growth rate 4.2% (1994)
exports tin, antimony (second largest world producer), other nonferrous metals, zinc, gold, oil, gas (piped to Argentina), agricultural products, coffee, sugar, cotton, soyabeans, beef, cowhides

HISTORY
c. AD 600 Development of sophisticated civilization at Tiahuanaco, S of Lake Titicaca.
c. 1200 Tiahuanaco culture was succeeded by smaller Aymara-speaking kingdoms.
16th C Became incorporated within westerly Quechua-speaking Inca civilization, centred in Peru.
1538 Conquered by Spanish and, known as 'Upper Peru', became part of the Viceroyalty of Peru, whose capital was at Lima (Peru); Charcas (now Sucre) became the local capital.
1545 Silver discovered at Potosi in the SW, which developed into chief silver-mining town and most important city in South America in the 17th and 18th centuries.
1776 Transferred to the Viceroyalty of La Plata, with its capital in Buenos Aires.
late 18th C Increasing resistance of Amerindians and mixed-race Mestizos to Spanish rule; silver production slumped.
1825 Liberated from Spanish rule by the Venezuelan freedom fighter Simón Bolívar, after whom the country was named, and his general, Antonio José de Sucre, after battle of Tumulsa; Sucre became Bolivia's first president.
1836–39 Part of a federation with Peru, headed by Bolivian president Andres Santa Cruz, but it dissolved following defeat in war with Chile.
1879–84 Lost coastal territory in the Atacama, containing valuable minerals, after defeat in war with Chile.
1880 Start of a period of civilian rule which lasted until 1936.
1903 Lost territory to Brazil.
1932–35 Lost further territory after defeated by Paraguay in the Chaco War, fought over control of the Chaco Boreal.
1952 After military regime overthrown by peasants and mineworkers in the Bolivian National Revolution, the formerly exiled Dr Victor Paz Estenssoro of the centrist National Revolutionary Movement (MNR) became president and introduced social and economic reforms, including universal suffrage, nationalization of tin mines, and land redistribution.
1956 Dr Hernán Siles Zuazo (MNR) became president, defeating Paz.
1960 Paz returned to power.
1964 Army coup led by Vice President General René Barrientos.
1967 Peasant uprising, led by Ernesto 'Che' Guevara, put down with US help; Guevara was killed.
1969 Barrientos killed in plane crash, replaced by Vice President Siles Salinas, who was soon deposed in army coup.
1971 Col Hugo Banzer Suárez came to power after further military coup.
1974 Attempted coup prompted Banzer to postpone promised elections and ban political and trade-union activity.
1980 Inconclusive elections were followed by the country's 189th coup, led by General Luis García. Allegations of corruption and drug trafficking led to cancellation of US and European Community (EC) aid.
1981 García forced to resign. Replaced by General Celso Torrelio Villa.
1982 Torrelio resigned and, with the economy worsening, junta handed power over to civilian administration headed by Dr Siles Zuazo.
1983 US and EC economic aid resumed as austerity measures introduced.
1985 President Siles resigned after general strike and attempted coup. Election result inconclusive; veteran Dr Paz Estenssoro (MNR) chosen by congress as president. Inflation rate 23,000%.
1989 Jaime Paz Zamora, of the left-wing Movement of Revolutionary Left (MIR) chosen as president in power-sharing arrangement with Banzer.
1993 Gonzalo Sanchez de Lozada (MNR) elected president after Banzer withdrew his candidacy. Foreign investment encouraged as inflation fell to single figures.
1997 Banzer elected president.

SEE ALSO Bolívar, Simón; Guevara, Che; Inca

plays, such as *A Man for All Seasons* 1960 (filmed 1966), and for his screenplays, including *Lawrence of Arabia* 1962, *Dr Zhivago* 1965 (both Academy Awards), *Ryan's Daughter* 1970, and *The Bounty* 1984.

Bolton administrative headquarters of Bolton unitary authority, 18 km/11 mi NW of Manchester; population (1991) 253,300. Industries include engineering, chemicals, textiles, and the manufacture of missiles. It was a former cotton-spinning town.

Boltzmann Ludwig Eduard 1844–1906. Austrian physicist who studied the kinetic theory of gases, which explains the properties of gases by reference to the motion of their constituent atoms and molecules. He established the branch of physics now known as statistical mechanics.

He derived a formula, the Boltzmann distribution, which gives the number of atoms or molecules with a given energy at a specific temperature. The constant in the formula is called the Boltzmann constant.

Boltzmann constant in physics, the constant (symbol k) that relates the kinetic energy (energy of motion) of a gas atom or molecule to temperature. Its value is 1.38066×10^{-23} joules per Kelvin. It is equal to the gas constant R, divided by ◊Avogadro's number.

bomb container filled with explosive or chemical material and generally used in warfare. There are also ◊incendiary bombs and nuclear bombs and missiles (see ◊nuclear warfare). Any object designed to cause damage by explosion can be called a bomb (car bombs, letter bombs). Initially dropped from aeroplanes (from World War I), bombs were in World War II also launched by rocket (◊V1, V2). The 1960s saw the development of missiles that could be launched from aircraft, land sites, or submarines. In the 1970s laser guidance systems were developed to hit small targets with accuracy.

Aerial bombing started in World War I (1914–18) when the German air force carried out 103 raids on Britain, dropping 269 tonnes of bombs. In 1939 bombs were commonly about 115 kg/250 lb and 230 kg/500 lb, but by the end of the war the ten-tonner was being produced. The fission or ◊***atom bomb*** was developed in the 1940s and the USA exploded three during World War II: first a test explosion on 16 July 1945, at Alamogordo, New Mexico, USA, then on 6 Aug the first to be used in actual warfare was dropped over ◊Hiroshima and three days later another over Nagasaki, Japan. The force of the bomb on Hiroshima was equivalent to 12,700 tonnes of TNT, and on Nagasaki, 22,000 tonnes of TNT. The fusion or ◊***hydrogen bomb*** was developed in the 1950s, and by the 1960s intercontinental 100-megatonne nuclear warheads could be produced (5,000 times more powerful than those of World War II). More recent bombs produce less fallout, a 'dirty' bomb being one that produces large quantities of radioactive debris from a U-238 (uranium isotope) casing. The danger of nuclear weapons increases with the number of nations possessing them, and nuclear-arms verification has been complicated by the ban on above-ground testing. Testing grounds include Lop Nor (China); Mururoa Atoll in the S Pacific (France); Nevada Desert, Amchitka Islands in the Aleutians (USA); Semipalatinsk (Kazakhstan); and Novaya Zemlya Islands in the Arctic (Russia). Under the Outer Space Treaty 1966 nuclear warheads may not be sent into orbit, but this measure has been circumvented by more sophisticated weapons. The Fractional Orbital Bombardment System (FOBS) sends a warhead into a low partial orbit, followed by a rapid descent to Earth. This renders it both less vulnerable to ballistic missile defence systems and cuts the warning time to three minutes. The rapid development of laser guidance systems in the 1970s meant that precise destruction of small but vital targets could be more effectively achieved with standard 450 kg/1,000 lb high-explosive bombs. The laser beam may be directed at the target by the army from the ground, or alternatively from high-performance aircraft accompanying the bombers, for example, the Laser Ranging Marker Target System (LRMTS). These systems' effectiveness was demonstrated during the Gulf War of 1991.

Bombay industrial port (textiles, engineering, pharmaceuticals, diamonds), commercial centre, and capital of Maharashtra, W India; population (1994) 14,500,000. It is the centre of the Hindi film industry
features World Trade Centre 1975; National Centre for the Performing Arts 1969. The port handles half of India's foreign trade. Its factories generate 30% of India's GDP
history Bombay was founded in the 13th century, came under Mogul rule, was occupied by Portugal 1530, and passed to Britain 1662 as part of Catherine of Braganza's dowry. It was the headquarters of the East India Company 1685–1708. The city expanded rapidly with the development of the cotton trade and the railway in the 1860s.

A bewitching place, a bewildering place, an enchanting place – the Arabian nights come again!
On Bombay
Mark Twain *More Tramps Abroad*

Bombay duck or ***bummalow*** small fish *Harpodon nehereus* found in the Indian Ocean. It has a thin body, up to 40 cm/16 in long, and sharp, pointed teeth. It feeds on shellfish and other small fish. It is valuable as a food fish, and is eaten, salted and dried, with dishes such as curry.

Bomberg David (Garshen) 1890–1957. English painter. He applied forms inspired by Cubism and

We have only one thing to keep us sane, pity; and the man without pity is mad.

EDWARD BOND
Lear

Vorticism to figurative subjects in such early works as *The Mud Bath* 1914 (Tate Gallery, London). Moving away from semi-abstraction in the mid-1920s, his work became more representational.

bona fide (Latin 'in good faith') legal phrase used to signify that a contract is undertaken without intentional misrepresentation.

Bonaparte Corsican family of Italian origin that gave rise to the Napoleonic dynasty: see ◊Napoleon I, ◊Napoleon II, and ◊Napoleon III. Others were the brothers and sister of Napoleon I: ***Joseph*** (1768–1844) whom Napoleon made king of Naples 1806 and Spain 1808; ***Lucien*** (1775–1840) whose handling of the Council of Five Hundred on 10 Nov 1799 ensured Napoleon's future; ***Louis*** (1778–1846) the father of Napoleon III, who was made king of Holland 1806–10; also called (from 1810) Comte de Saint Leu; ***Caroline*** (1782–1839) who married Joachim ◊Murat 1800; full name Maria Annunciata Caroline; ***Jerome*** (1784–1860) made king of Westphalia 1807.

Bonar Law British Conservative politician; see ◊Law, Andrew Bonar.

bona vacantia (Latin 'empty goods') in law, the property of a person who dies without making a will and without relatives or dependants who would be entitled or might reasonably expect to inherit. In the UK, in such a case the property goes to either the Crown or the duchies of Lancaster and Cornwall.

Bonaventura, St (Giovanni di Fidanza) 1221–1274. Italian Roman Catholic theologian. He entered the Franciscan order 1243, became professor of theology in Paris, and in 1256 general of his order. In 1273 he was created cardinal and bishop of Albano. Canonized 1482. Feast day 15 July.

bond in chemistry, the result of the forces of attraction that hold together atoms of an element or elements to form a molecule. The principal types of bonding are ◊ionic, ◊covalent, ◊metallic, and ◊intermolecular (such as hydrogen bonding).

The type of bond formed depends on the elements concerned and their electronic structure. In an ionic or electrovalent bond, common in inorganic compounds, the combining atoms gain or lose electrons to become ions; for example, sodium (Na) loses an electron to form a sodium ion (Na^+) while chlorine (Cl) gains an electron to form a chloride ion (Cl^-) in the ionic bond of sodium chloride (NaCl).

In a covalent bond, the atomic orbitals of two atoms overlap to form a molecular orbital containing two electrons, which are thus effectively shared between the two atoms. Covalent bonds are common in organic compounds, such as the four carbon-hydrogen bonds in methane (CH_4). In a dative covalent or coordinate bond, one of the combining atoms supplies both of the valence electrons in the bond.

A metallic bond joins metals in a crystal lattice; the atoms occupy lattice positions as positive ions, and valence electrons are shared between all the ions in an 'electron gas'.

In a hydrogen bond, a hydrogen atom joined to an electronegative atom, such as nitrogen or oxygen, becomes partially positively charged, and is weakly attracted to another electronegative atom on a neighbouring molecule.

bond in commerce, a security issued by a government, local authority, company, bank, or other institution on fixed interest. Usually a long-term security, a bond may be irredeemable (with no date of redemption), secured (giving the investor a claim on the company's property or on a part of its assets), or unsecured (not protected by a lien). Property bonds are nonfixed securities with the yield fixed to property investment.

Bond Edward 1934– . English dramatist. His early work aroused controversy because of the savagery of some of his imagery, for example, the brutal stoning of a baby by bored youths in *Saved* 1965. Other works include *Early Morning* 1968; *Lear* 1972, a reworking of Shakespeare's play; *Bingo* 1973, an account of Shakespeare's last days; and *The War Plays* 1985.

Bondi Hermann 1919– . Austrian-born British cosmologist. In 1948 he joined with Fred ◊Hoyle and Thomas Gold (1920–) in developing the steady-state theory of cosmology 1948, which suggested that matter is continuously created in the universe.

bone hard connective tissue comprising the ◊skeleton of most vertebrate animals. Bone is composed of a network of collagen fibres impregnated with mineral salts (largely calcium phosphate and calcium carbonate), a combination that gives it great density and strength, comparable in some cases with that of reinforced concrete. Enclosed within this solid matrix are bone cells, blood vessels, and nerves. The interior of the long bones of the limbs consists of a spongy matrix filled with a soft marrow that produces blood cells.

There are two types of bone: those that develop by replacing ◊cartilage and those that form directly from connective tissue. The latter, which includes the bones of the cranium, are usually platelike in shape and form in the skin of the developing embryo. Humans have about 206 distinct bones in the skeleton, of which the smallest are the three ossicles in the middle ear.

bone china or ***softpaste*** semiporcelain made of 5% bone ash added to 95% kaolin. It was first made in the West in imitation of Chinese porcelain, whose formula was kept secret by the Chinese.

bone marrow substance found inside the cavity of bones. In early life it produces red blood cells but later on lipids (fat) accumulate and its colour changes from red to yellow. Bone marrow may be transplanted in the treatment of some diseases, such as leukaemia, using immunosuppressive drugs in the recipient to prevent rejection.

bongo Central African antelope *Boocercus eurycerus*, living in dense humid forests. Up to 1.4 m/4.5 ft at the shoulder, it has spiral horns which may be 80 cm/2.6 ft or more in length. The body is rich chestnut, with narrow white stripes running vertically down the sides, and a black belly.

Bonhoeffer Dietrich 1906–1945. German Lutheran theologian and opponent of Nazism. Involved in a plot against Hitler, he was executed by the Nazis in Flossenburg concentration camp. His *Letters and Papers from Prison* 1953 became the textbook of modern radical theology, advocating the idea of a 'religionless' Christianity.

Boniface name of nine popes, including:

Boniface VIII (Benedict Caetani) c. 1235–1303. Pope from 1294. He clashed unsuccessfully with Philip IV of France over his taxation of the clergy, and also with Henry III of England.

Boniface exempted the clergy from taxation by the secular government in a bull (edict) 1296, but was forced to give way when the clergy were excluded from certain lay privileges. His bull of 1302 *Unam sanctam*, asserting the complete temporal and spiritual power of the papacy, was equally ineffective.

Boniface, St 680–754. English Benedictine monk, known as the 'Apostle of Germany'; originally named Wynfrith. After a missionary journey to Frisia 716, he was given the task of bringing Christianity to Germany 718 by Pope Gregory II, and was appointed archbishop of Mainz 746. He returned to Frisia 754 and was martyred near Dockum. His feast day is 5 June.

Bonin and Volcano islands Japanese islands in the Pacific, N of the Marianas and 1,300 km/800 mi E of the Ryukyu Islands. They were under US control 1945–68. The ***Bonin Islands*** (Japanese *Ogasawara Gunto*) number 27 (in three groups), the largest being Chichijima: area 104 sq km/40 sq mi, population (1991) 2,430. The ***Volcano Islands*** (Japanese *Kazan Retto*) number three, including ◊Iwo Jima, scene of some of the fiercest fighting of World War II; total area 28 sq km/11 sq mi.

Bonington Chris(tian John Storey) 1934– . British mountaineer. He took part in the first ascent of Annapurna II 1960, Nuptse 1961, and the first British ascent of the north face of the Eiger 1962, climbed the central Tower of Paine in Patagonia 1963, and was the leader of an Everest expedition 1975 and again 1985, reaching the summit.

bonito any of various species of medium-sized tuna, predatory fish of the genus *Sarda*, in the mackerel family. The ocean bonito *Katsuwonus pelamis* grows to 1 m/3 ft and is common in tropical seas. The Atlantic bonito *Sarda sarda* is found in the Mediterranean and tropical Atlantic and grows to the same length but has a narrower body.

Bonn industrial city (chemicals, textiles, plastics, aluminium) in North Rhine–Westphalia in the Federal Republic of Germany, 18 km/15 mi SSE of Cologne, on the left bank of the Rhine; population (1993) 297,900. It was the seat of government of West Germany 1949–90 and of the Federal Republic of Germany from 1990. In 1991 the Bundestag voted to move the capital to Berlin. This is being done in phases.

Once a Roman outpost, Bonn was captured by the French 1794, annexed 1801, and was allotted to Prussia 1815. Beethoven was born here. There are three new museums, including the Museum of the History of the Federal Republic of Germany (opened 1994).

Bonnard Pierre 1867–1947. French painter, designer, and graphic artist. Influenced by Gauguin and Japanese prints, he specialized in intimate domestic scenes and landscapes, his paintings shimmering with colour and light. With other members of *les ◊Nabis*, he explored the decorative arts (posters, stained glass, furniture), but is most widely known for his series of nudes, for example, *Nude in the Bath* 1938 (Petit Palais, Paris).

Bonnie and Clyde Bonnie Parker (1911–1934) and Clyde Barrow (1909–1934). Infamous US criminals who carried out a series of small-scale robberies in Texas, Oklahoma, New Mexico, and Missouri between Aug 1932 and May 1934. They were eventually betrayed and then killed in a police ambush.

Bonnie Prince Charlie Scottish name for ◊Charles Edward Stuart, pretender to the throne.

bonsai (Japanese 'bowl cultivation') art of producing miniature trees by selective pruning. It originated in China many centuries ago and later spread to Japan. Some specimens in China are about 1,000 years old and some in the imperial Japanese collection are more than 300 years old.

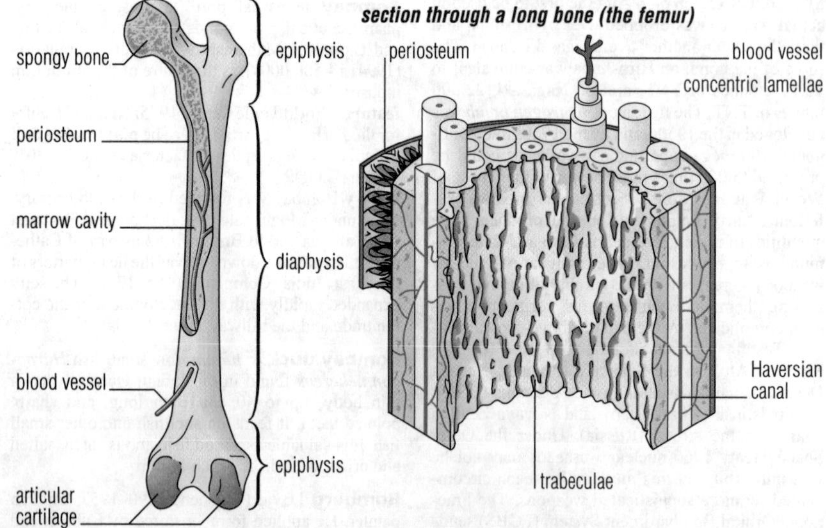

bone Bone is a network of fibrous material impregnated with mineral salts and as strong as reinforced concrete. The upper end of the thighbone or femur is made up of spongy bone, which has a fine lacework structure designed to transmit the weight of the body. The shaft of the femur consists of hard compact bone designed to resist bending. Fine channels carrying blood vessels, nerves, and lymphatics interweave even the densest bone.

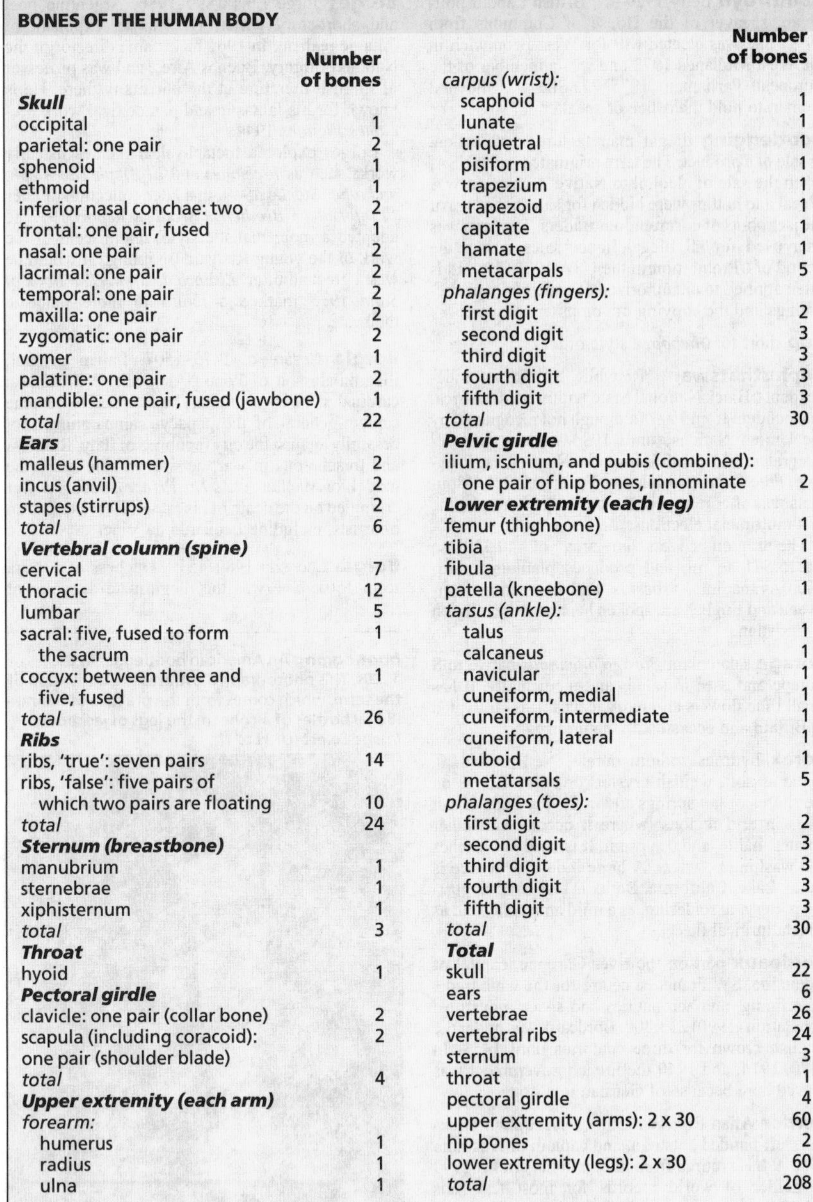

BONES OF THE HUMAN BODY

	Number of bones
Skull	
occipital	1
parietal: one pair	2
sphenoid	1
ethmoid	1
inferior nasal conchae: two	2
frontal: one pair, fused	1
nasal: one pair	2
lacrimal: one pair	2
temporal: one pair	2
maxilla: one pair	2
zygomatic: one pair	2
vomer	1
palatine: one pair	2
mandible: one pair, fused (jawbone)	1
total	22
Ears	
malleus (hammer)	2
incus (anvil)	2
stapes (stirrups)	2
total	6
Vertebral column (spine)	
cervical	7
thoracic	12
lumbar	5
sacral: five, fused to form the sacrum	1
coccyx: between three and five, fused	1
total	26
Ribs	
ribs, 'true': seven pairs	14
ribs, 'false': five pairs of which two pairs are floating	10
total	24
Sternum (breastbone)	
manubrium	1
sternebrae	1
xiphisternum	1
total	3
Throat	
hyoid	1
Pectoral girdle	
clavicle: one pair (collar bone)	2
scapula (including coracoid): one pair (shoulder blade)	2
total	4
Upper extremity (each arm)	
forearm:	
humerus	1
radius	1
ulna	1
carpus (wrist):	
scaphoid	1
lunate	1
triquetral	1
pisiform	1
trapezium	1
trapezoid	1
capitate	1
hamate	1
metacarpals	5
phalanges (fingers):	
first digit	2
second digit	3
third digit	3
fourth digit	3
fifth digit	3
total	30
Pelvic girdle	
ilium, ischium, and pubis (combined): one pair of hip bones, innominate	2
Lower extremity (each leg)	
femur (thighbone)	1
tibia	1
fibula	1
patella (kneebone)	1
tarsus (ankle):	
talus	1
calcaneus	1
navicular	1
cuneiform, medial	1
cuneiform, intermediate	1
cuneiform, lateral	1
cuboid	1
metatarsals	5
phalanges (toes):	
first digit	2
second digit	3
third digit	3
fourth digit	3
fifth digit	3
total	30
Total	
skull	22
ears	6
vertebrae	26
vertebral ribs	24
sternum	3
throat	1
pectoral girdle	4
upper extremity (arms): 2 x 30	60
hip bones	2
lower extremity (legs): 2 x 30	60
total	208

boobook owl *Ninox novaeseelandiae* found in Australia, so named because of its call.

booby tropical seabird of the genus *Sula*, in the same family, Sulidae, as the northern ◊gannet, order Pelicaniformes. There are six species, including the circumtropical brown booby *S. leucogaster*. Plumage is white and black or brown, with no feathers on the throat and lower jaw. They inhabit coastal waters, and dive to catch fish. The name was given by sailors who saw the bird's tameness as stupidity.

boogie-woogie jazz played on the piano, using a repeated motif for the left hand. It was common in the USA from around 1900 to the 1950s. Boogie-woogie players included Pinetop Smith (1904–1929), Meade 'Lux' Lewis (1905–1964), and Jimmy Yancey (1898–1951). Rock-and-roll pianist Jerry Lee Lewis adapted the style.

book portable written record. Substances used to make early books included leaves, bark, linen, silk, clay, leather, and papyrus. In about AD 100–150, the codex or paged book, as opposed to the roll or scroll, began to be adopted. Vellum (parchment of calfskin, lambskin, or kidskin) was generally used for book pages by the beginning of the 4th century, and its use lasted until the 15th. It was superseded by paper, which came to Europe from China. Books became widely available only after the invention of the ◊printing press in the 15th century. Printed text is also reproduced and stored in ◊microform.

bookbinding securing of the pages of a book between protective covers by sewing and/or gluing. Cloth binding was first introduced 1822, but from the mid-20th century synthetic bindings were increasingly employed, and most hardback books are bound by machine.

Bookbinding did not emerge as a distinct craft until printing was introduced to Europe in the 15th century. Until that time scrolls and (from around 1200) codices (see ◊codex) were usual. Gold tooling, the principal ornament of leather bookbinding, was probably introduced to Europe from the East by the Venetian Aldus Manutius (1450–1515).

Booker Prize for Fiction British literary prize. *See list of tables on p. 1177.*

book-keeping process of recording commercial transactions in a systematic and established procedure. These records provide the basis for the preparation of accounts. The first English work on the subject, by the schoolmaster Hugh Oldcastle, appeared 1543.

booklouse any of numerous species of tiny wingless insects of the order Psocoptera, especially *Atropus pulsatoria*, which lives in books and papers, feeding on starches and moulds. Most of the other species live in bark, leaves, and lichens. They thrive in dark, damp conditions.

Book of Hours see ◊Hours, Book of.

Book of the Dead ancient Egyptian book, known as the *Book of Coming Forth by Day*, buried with the dead as a guide to reaching the kingdom of Osiris, the god of the underworld.

Similar practices were observed by Orphic communities (6th–1st century BC) in S Italy and Crete, who deposited gold laminae, inscribed with directions about the next world, in the graves of their dead. An ancient Buddhist example is the ◊Bardo Thödol from Tibet. In medieval times, Christians could obtain advice about dying from a book entitled *Ars Morendi/The Art of Dying*.

Bonnard *Dining Room* by French artist Pierre Bonnard. Painting in a richly decorative style, Bonnard concentrated on depicting the small, intimate scenes of everyday middle-class life. *Corbis*

Boole George 1815–1864. English mathematician. His work *The Mathematical Analysis of Logic* 1847 established the basis of modern mathematical logic, and his Boolean algebra can be used in designing computers.

Boole's system is essentially two-valued. By subdividing objects into separate classes, each with a given property, his algebra makes it possible to treat different classes according to the presence or absence of the same property. Hence it involves just two numbers, 0 and 1 – the binary system used in the computer. *See illustration on following page.*

Boolean algebra set of algebraic rules, named after mathematician George Boole, in which TRUE and FALSE are equated to 0 and 1. Boolean algebra includes a series of operators (AND, OR, NOT, NAND (NOT AND), NOR, and XOR (exclusive OR)), which can be used to manipulate TRUE and FALSE values. It is the basis of computer logic because the truth values can be directly associated with ◊bits. These rules are used in searching databases.

boomerang hand-thrown, flat wooden hunting missile shaped in a curved angle, formerly used throughout the world but developed by the Australian Aborigines to a great degree of diversity and

Bonnie and Clyde US outlaw Bonnie Parker, who with her partner Clyde Barrow held up small-town gas stations and banks in the early 1930s. They killed 12 people before being shot dead by police on 23 May, 1934. *Corbis*

Boole George Boole was the founder of the modern science of symbolic logic and the first mathematician to consider logic algebraically. Boolean algebra, applied to binary addition and subtraction, is important today in the design and construction of circuits and computers. *Ann Ronan/ Image Select (UK) Ltd*

elaboration. It is used to kill game and as a weapon or, in the case of the returning boomerang, as recreation.

Boone Daniel 1734–1820. US pioneer. He explored the Wilderness Road (East Virginia–Kentucky) 1775 and paved the way for the first westward migration of settlers.

Boorman John 1933– . English film director. He started out in television, and has directed successful films both in Hollywood (*Point Blank* 1967, *Deliverance* 1972) and in Britain (*Excalibur* 1981, *Hope and Glory* 1987).

booster first-stage rocket of a space-launching vehicle, or an additional rocket strapped to the main rocket to assist takeoff.

The US Delta rocket, for example, has a cluster of nine strap-on boosters that fire on lift off. Europe's Ariane 3 rocket uses twin strap-on boosters, as does the US space shuttle.

‘Tell mother – tell mother – I died for my country.’

JOHN WILKES BOOTH
Remark after having assassinated President Lincoln 1865

boot or ***bootstrap*** in computing, the process of starting up a computer. Most computers have a small, built-in boot program that starts automatically when the computer is switched on – its only task is to load a slightly larger program, usually from a hard disc, which in turn loads the main ◊operating system.

Boot Jesse, 1st Baron Trent 1850–1931. British entrepreneur and founder of the Boots pharmacy chain. In 1863 Boot took over his father's small Nottingham shop trading in medicinal herbs and concentrated on selling cheaply, advertising widely, and offering a wide range of medicines. In 1892, Boot also began to manufacture drugs. He had 126 shops by 1900 and more than 1,000 by his death.

Boötes constellation of the northern hemisphere represented by a herdsman driving a bear (◊Ursa Major) around the pole. Its brightest star is ◊Arcturus (or Alpha Boötis), which is about 37 light years from Earth. The herdsman is assisted by the neighbouring ◊Canes Venatici, ‘the Hunting Dogs’.

Booth John Wilkes 1838–1865. US actor and fanatical Confederate sympathizer who assassinated President Abraham ◊Lincoln 14 April 1865; he escaped with a broken leg and was later shot in a barn in Virginia when he refused to surrender.

Booth William 1829–1912. British founder of the ◊Salvation Army 1878, and its first ‘general’. Booth experienced religious conversion at the age of 15. In 1865 he founded the Christian Mission in Whitechapel, E London, which became the Salvation Army 1878. His wife Catherine (1829–1890, born Mumford), whom he married 1855, became a public preacher about 1860, initiating the ministry of women. Their eldest son, ***William Bramwell Booth*** (1856–1929), became chief of staff of the Salvation Army 1880 and was general from 1912 until his deposition 1929.

Evangeline Cora Booth (1865–1950), seventh child of General William Booth, was a prominent Salvation Army officer, and was general 1934–39. She became a US citizen.

Catherine Bramwell Booth (1884–1987), a granddaughter of William Booth, was a commissioner in the Salvation Army.

‘Writing is nothing more than a guided dream.’

JORGE LUIS BORGES
Dr Brodie's Report

Boothroyd Betty 1929– . British Labour politician, speaker of the House of Commons from 1992. She was elected MP for West Bromwich in the West Midlands 1973 and was a member of the European Parliament 1975–77. She was the first woman to hold the office of speaker.

bootlegging illegal manufacture, distribution, or sale of a product. The term originated in the USA, when the sale of alcohol to Native Americans was illegal and bottles were hidden for sale in the legs of the jackboots of unscrupulous traders. The term was later used for all illegal liquor sales during the period of ◊Prohibition in the USA 1920–33, and is often applied to unauthorized commercial tape recordings and the copying of computer software.

bop short for ◊***bebop***, a style of jazz.

Bophuthatswana Republic of; former independent ◊Black National State within South Africa, independent from 1977 (although not recognized by the United Nations) until 1994 when it was reintegrated into South Africa (in North West Province, Free State, and Eastern Transvaal, now Mpumalanga) after rioting broke out in the run-up to the first multiracial elections.

The region covers an area of 40,330 sq km/15,571 sq mi, and produces platinum, chromium, vanadium, asbestos, and manganese. Setswana and English are spoken here, and the religion is Christian.

borage salad plant *Borago officinalis* native to S Europe and used in salads and medicinally. It has small blue flowers and hairy leaves. It is cultivated in Britain and occasionally naturalized.

borax hydrous sodium borate, $Na_2B_4O_7.10H_20$, found as soft, whitish crystals or encrustations on the shores of hot springs and in the dry beds of salt lakes in arid regions, where it occurs with other borates, halite, and ◊gypsum. It is used in bleaches and washing powders. A large industrial source is Borax Lake, California. Borax is also used in glazing pottery, in soldering, as a mild antiseptic, and as a metallurgical flux.

Bordeaux port on the river Garonne, capital of Aquitaine, SW France, a centre for the wine trade, oil refining, and aeronautics and space industries; population (1990) 213,300. Bordeaux was under the English crown for three centuries until 1453. In 1870, 1914, and 1940 the French government was moved here because of German invasion.

Border Allan Robert 1955– . Australian cricketer, left-handed batsman, and captain of Australia 1985–94. He retired from international cricket 1994 as holder of world records for most test runs (11,174), most test matches as captain (93), most appearances in test matches (156), most consecutive appearances in test matches (153), most catches in test matches by an outfielder (156), and most appearances in one-day internationals (263). Border played for Queensland after starting his career with New South Wales and has played in England for Gloucestershire and Essex.

Borders local authority of Scotland, created 1975, renamed ◊Scottish Borders in reorganization of local authorities 1996. (*See United Kingdom map.*)

Bordet Jules Jean Baptiste Vincent 1870–1961. Belgian bacteriologist and immunologist who researched the role of blood serum in the human immune response. He was the first to isolate 1906 the whooping-cough bacillus.

bore surge of tidal water up an estuary or a river, caused by the funnelling of the rising tide by a narrowing river mouth. A very high tide, possibly fanned by wind, may build up when it is held back by a river current in the river mouth. The result is a broken wave, a metre or a few feet high, that rushes upstream.

Famous bores are found in the rivers Severn (England), Seine (France), Hooghly (India), and Chiang Jiang (China), where bores of over 4 m/13 ft have been reported.

Borg Björn Rune 1956– . Swedish tennis player. He won the men's singles title at Wimbledon five times 1976–80, a record since the abolition of the challenge system 1922. He also won six French Open singles titles 1974–75 and 1978–81 inclusive. In 1990 Borg returned to professional tennis, but he enjoyed little competitive success.

Borges Jorge Luis 1899–1986. Argentine poet and short-story writer. He was an exponent of ◊magic realism. In 1961 he became director of the National Library, Buenos Aires, and was professor of English literature at the university there. He is known for his fantastic and paradoxical work *Ficciones/Fictions* 1944.

Borges explored metaphysical themes in early works such as *Ficciones* and *El Aleph/The Aleph, and other Stories* 1949. In a later collection of tales *El informe de Brodie/Dr Brodie's Report* 1972 he adopted a more realistic style, reminiscent of the work of the young Rudyard ◊Kipling, of whom he was a great admirer. *El libro de arena/The Book of Sand* 1975 marked a return to more fantastic themes.

Borgia Cesare c. 1475–1507. Italian general, illegitimate son of Pope ◊Alexander VI. Made a cardinal at 17 by his father, he resigned to become captain-general of the papacy, campaigning successfully against the city republics of Italy. Ruthless and treacherous in war, he was an able ruler (the model for Machiavelli's *The Prince*), but his power crumbled on the death of his father. He was a patron of artists, including Leonardo da Vinci.

Borgia Lucrezia 1480–1519. Duchess of Ferrara from 1501. She was the illegitimate daughter of

bootlegging An American bootlegger in the 1920s. This photograph illustrates the derivation of the term, which comes from the practice of hiding illegal bottles of alcohol in the legs of jackboots. *Image Select (UK) Ltd*

Pope ◊Alexander VI and sister of Cesare Borgia. She was married at 12 and again at 13 to further her father's ambitions, both marriages being annulled by him. At 18 she was married again, but her husband was murdered 1500 on the order of her brother, with whom (as well as with her father) she was said to have committed incest. Her final marriage was to the Duke of Este, the son and heir of the Duke of Ferrara. She made the court a centre of culture and was a patron of authors and artists such as Ariosto and Titian.

boric acid or *boracic acid* H_3BO_3, acid formed by the combination of hydrogen and oxygen with nonmetallic boron. It is a weak antiseptic and is used in the manufacture of glass and enamels. It is also an efficient insecticide against ants and cockroaches.

Boris Godunov 1552–1605. Tsar of Russia from 1598; see Boris ◊Godunov.

Borlaug Norman Ernest 1914– . US microbiologist and agronomist. He developed high-yielding varieties of wheat and other grain crops to be grown in Third World countries, and was the first to use the term 'Green Revolution'. Nobel Prize for Peace 1970.

Bormann Martin 1900–1945. German Nazi leader. He took part in the abortive Munich beer-hall putsch (uprising against the government of Bavaria) 1923 and rose to high positions in the Nazi (National Socialist) Party, becoming deputy party leader May 1941.

In 1943 Hitler made him his personal secretary, a position in which he exercised enormous influence over Hitler's decisions. Bormann was believed to have escaped the fall of Berlin May 1945 and was tried in his absence and sentenced to death at the ◊Nuremberg trials 1945–46, but a skeleton uncovered in Berlin 1972 was officially recognized as his 1973.

Born Max 1882–1970. German-born British physicist. He received a Nobel prize 1954 for fundamental work on the ◊quantum theory, especially his 1926 discovery that the wave function of an electron is linked to the probability that the electron is to be found at any point.

In 1924 Born coined the term 'quantum mechanics'. He made Göttingen a leading centre for theoretical physics and together with his students and collaborators – notably Werner ◊Heisenberg – he devised 1925 a system called matrix mechanics that accounted mathematically for the position and momentum of the electron in the atom. He also devised a technique, the Born approximation method, for computing the behaviour of subatomic particles.

Borneo third-largest island in the world, one of the Sunda Islands in the W Pacific; area 754,000 sq km/290,000 sq mi. It comprises the Malaysian territories of ◊Sabah and ◊Sarawak; ◊Brunei; and, occupying by far the largest part, the Indonesian territory of ◊Kalimantan. It is mountainous and densely forested. In coastal areas the people of Borneo are mainly of Malaysian origin, with a few Chinese, and the interior is inhabited by the indigenous Dyaks. It was formerly under both Dutch and British colonial influence until Sarawak was formed 1841.

Bornu kingdom of the 9th–19th centuries to the west and south of Lake Chad, W central Africa. Converted to Islam in the 11th century, Bornu reached its greatest strength in the 15th–18th centuries. From 1901 it was absorbed in the British, French, and German colonies in this area, which became the states of Niger, Cameroon, and Nigeria. The largest section of ancient Bornu is now the state of Bornu in Nigeria.

Borodin Alexander Porfiryevich 1833–1887. Russian composer. Born in St Petersburg, the illegitimate son of a Russian prince, he became by profession an expert in medical chemistry, but in his spare time devoted himself to writing music. His principal work is the opera *Prince Igor*, left unfinished; it was completed by Rimsky-Korsakov and Glazunov and includes the Polovtsian Dances. His other works include symphonies, songs, and chamber music, using traditional Russian themes.

Borodino, Battle of French victory over Russian forces under Kutusov 7 Sept 1812 near the village of Borodino, 110km/70 mi NW of Moscow, during Napoleon Bonaparte's invasion of Russia. This was one of the bloodiest battles of the Napoleonic years: the Russians lost 15,000 dead and 25,000 wounded; the French lost about 28,000, including 12 generals. ▷*See feature on pp. 748–749.*

boron nonmetallic element, symbol B, atomic number 5, relative atomic mass 10.811. In nature it is found only in compounds, as with sodium and oxygen in borax. It exists in two allotropic forms (see ◊allotropy): brown amorphous powder and very hard, brilliant crystals. Its compounds are used in the preparation of boric acid, water softeners, soaps, enamels, glass, and pottery glazes. In alloys it is used to harden steel. Because it absorbs slow neutrons, it is used to make boron carbide control rods for nuclear reactors. It is a necessary trace element in the human diet. The element was named by Humphry Davy, who isolated it 1808, from *bor*ax + -on, as in carb*on*.

borough unit of local government in the UK from the 8th century until 1974, when it continued as an honorary status granted by royal charter to a district council, entitling its leader to the title of mayor.

Borromini Francesco, originally Francesco Castelli 1599–1667. Swiss-born Italian Baroque architect. He was one of the two most important architects (with ◊Bernini, his main rival) in 17th-century Rome. Whereas Bernini designed in a florid, expansive style, his pupil Borromini developed a highly idiosyncratic and austere use of the Classical language of architecture. His genius may be seen in the cathedrals of San Carlo alle Quatro Fontane 1637–41, San Ivo della Sapienza 1643–60, and the Oratory of St Philip Neri 1638–50.

borstal in the UK, formerly a place of detention for offenders aged 15–21, first introduced 1908. From 1983 borstal institutions were officially known as youth custody centres, and have been replaced by young offender institutions.

borzoi (Russian 'swift') breed of large dog originating in Russia. It is of the greyhound type, white with darker markings, with a thick, silky coat, and stands 75 cm/30 in or more at the shoulder. The borzoi's original quarry was hares and foxes, but it was selectively bred in the 19th century to produce a larger, stronger dog suitable for hunting wolves.

Bosch Hieronymus (Jerome) c. 1460–1516. Early Dutch painter. His fantastic visions, often filled with bizarre and cruel images, depict a sinful world in which people are tormented by demons and weird creatures, as in *Hell*, a panel from the triptych *The Garden of Earthly Delights* about 1505–10 (Prado, Madrid). In their richness, complexity, and sheer strangeness, his pictures foreshadow Surrealism.

Bosch is named after his birthplace, 's-Hertogenbosch, in North Brabant, the Netherlands. His work, which strongly influenced ◊Brueghel the Elder, may have been inspired by a local religious brotherhood. However, he seems to have been an orthodox Catholic and a prosperous painter, not a heretic, as was once believed. His work was collected by Philip II of Spain, who shared Bosch's dark vision of the world.

Bose–Einstein condensate hypothesis put forward 1925 by Albert Einstein and Indian physicist Satyendra Bose (1894–1974), suggesting that when a dense gas is cooled to a little over absolute zero it will condense and its atoms will lose their individuality and act as an organized whole. The first Bose–Einstein condensate was produced June 1995 by US physicists cooling rubidinum atoms to 10 billionths of a degree above zero. The condensate existed for about a minute before becoming rubidinum ice.

Bosnia-Herzegovina Serbo-Croatian ***Bosna-Hercegovina*** country in central Europe, bounded N and W by Croatia, E by the Yugoslavian republic of Serbia, and E and S by the Yugoslavian republic of Montenegro. *See country box on p. 144.*

boson in physics, an elementary particle whose spin can only take values that are whole numbers or zero. Bosons may be classified as ◊gauge bosons (carriers of the four fundamental forces) or ◊mesons. All elementary particles are either bosons or ◊fermions.

Unlike fermions, more than one boson in a system (such as an atom) can possess the same energy state. When developed mathematically, this

Bosch *Ship of Fools* by Hieronymus Bosch (Louvre, Paris). A member of a devout religious group, Bosch painted works which satirized human vanity and weakness. In this picture he has drawn upon the legend of the Ship of Fools, a well-known Medieval satire. *Corbis*

statement is known as the Bose–Einstein law, after its discoverers Indian physicist Satyendra Bose and Albert Einstein.

Bosporus (Turkish ***Karadeniz Boğazi***) strait 27 km/17 mi long, joining the Black Sea with the Sea of Marmara and forming part of the water division between Europe and Asia. Istanbul stands on its west side. The Bosporus Bridge 1973, 1,621 m/5,320 ft, links Istanbul and Anatolia (the Asian part of Turkey). In 1988 a second bridge across the straits was opened, linking Asia and Europe.

Bossuet Jacques Bénigne 1627–1704. French Roman Catholic priest and theologian. Appointed to the Chapel Royal, Paris 1662, he became known for his funeral orations.

Bossuet was tutor to the young dauphin (crown prince). He became involved in a controversy between Louis XIV and the pope and did his best to effect a compromise. He wrote an 'Exposition de la foi catholique' 1670 and 'Histoire des variations des églises protestantes' 1688.

Boston seaport and market town in Lincolnshire, England, on the river Witham; population (1991) 34,600. St Botolph's is England's largest parish church, and its tower 'Boston stump' is a landmark for sailors.

Boston industrial and commercial centre, capital of Massachusetts, USA; population (1992) 551,700; metropolitan area (1992) 5,439,000. A publishing centre and industrial port on Massachusetts Bay, its economy is dominated by financial and health services and government. The subway system (begun 1897) was the first in the USA. Boston's famous baseball team, the Red Sox, are based at Fenway Park.

history Founded by Puritans 1630, Boston was a centre of opposition to British trade restrictions, culminating in the Boston Tea Party 1773. After the first shots of the American Revolution 1775 at nearby Lexington and Concord, the Battle of Bunker Hill was fought outside the city; the British withdrew 1776. In the 19th century, Boston became the metropolis of New England. Urban redevelopment and the growth of service industries have compensated for the city's industrial decline.

features The Freedom trail (2.4km/1.5mi) covers 16 sites connected with the American Revolution, including Paul Revere House, which was built in the 17th century, and is the oldest house in Boston.

Notable museums are the Museum of Fine Arts; the Isabella Stewart Gardner Museum, and the Museum of Science. The John F Kennedy Library

'Music is a pastime, a relaxation from more serious occupations.'

Alexander Borodin
Letter to Krylov 1867

BOSNIA-HERZEGOVINA
Republic of

national name *Republika Bosna i Hercegovina*
area 51,129 sq km/19,745 sq mi
capital Sarajevo
major towns/cities Banja Luka, Mostar, Prijedor, Tuzla, Zenica
physical features barren, mountainous country, part of the Dinaric Alps; limestone gorges; 20 km/12 mi of coastline with no harbour
heads of state Alija Izetbegović (from 1990), Momcilo Krajisnik, and Kerismir Zubak from 1996
heads of government Haris Silajdzic and Boro Bosic from 1997
political system emergent democracy
administrative divisions military rule by locally dominant ethnic militias
political parties Party of Democratic Action (PDA), Muslim-oriented; Serbian Renaissance Movement (SPO), Serbian nationalist; Croatian Christian Democratic Union of Bosnia-Herzegovina (CDU), Croatian nationalist; League of Communists (LC) and Socialist Alliance (SA), left-wing
population 3,366,000 (1998 est)
population growth rate −4.4% (1990–95); 0.2% (2000–05)
ethnic distribution 44% ethnic Muslim, 31% Serb, 17% Croat, and 6% 'Yugoslav'. Croats are most thickly settled in SW Bosnia and W Herzegovina, Serbs in E and W Bosnia. From the start of the civil war 1992 there were large-scale population movements, with many Croats and Muslims fleeing to nearby states
life expectancy 68 (males), 73 (females)
literacy rate 86%
language Serbian variant of Serbo-Croatian
religions Sunni Muslim, Serbian Orthodox, Roman Catholic
currency dinar
exports citrus fruits and vegetables; iron, steel, and leather goods; textiles

HISTORY

1st C AD Part of Roman province of Illyricum.
395 On division of Roman Empire, stayed in W, along with Croatia and Slovenia, whereas Serbia to E became part of the Byzantine Empire.
7th C Settled by Slav tribes.
12–15th Cs Independent state.
1463 and 1482 Bosnia and Herzegovina, in S, successively conquered by Ottoman Turks; many Slavs were converted to Sunni Islam.
1878 Became an Austrian protectorate, following Bosnian revolt against Turkish rule in 1875–76.
1908 Annexed by Austrian Habsburgs in wake of Turkish Revolution.
1914 Archduke Franz Ferdinand, the Habsburg heir, assassinated in Sarajevo by a Bosnian-Serb extremist, precipitating World War I.
1918 Part of Serb-dominated 'Kingdom of Serbs, Croats and Slovenes', known as Yugoslavia from 1929.
1941 Occupied by Nazi Germany; became 'Greater Croatia' fascist puppet state, a scene of fierce fighting.
1943–44 Liberated by the communist Partisans, led by Marshal Tito.
1945 Became republic within Yugoslav Socialist Federation.
1980 Upsurge in Islamic nationalism.
1990 Ethnic violence erupted between Muslims and Serbs. Communists defeated in multiparty elections; coalition formed by Serb, Muslim, and Croatian parties, with Muslim, Alija Izetbegovic, as president.
1991 Serb-Croat civil war in Croatia spread disorder into Bosnia. Fears that Serbia aimed to annex Serb-dominated parts of the republic led to 'sovereignty' declaration by parliament. Serbs within Bosnia established own autonomous enclaves.
1992 In a Serb-boycotted referendum, Bosnian Muslims and Croats voted overwhelmingly for independence, which was recognized by USA and European Community (EC); admitted into United Nations (UN). Violent civil war broke out, as independent 'Serbian Republic of Bosnia-Herzegovina', proclaimed by Bosnian-Serb militia leader Radovan Karadzic, with Serbian backing. UN forces drafted into Sarajevo to break Serb siege of city; accusations of 'ethnic cleansing', particularly of Muslims, by Bosnian Serbs.
1993 UN–EC peace plan failed. USA began airdrops of food and medical supplies. Six UN 'safe areas' created as havens for Muslim civilians. Croat-Serb partition plan rejected by Muslims.
1994 Serb siege of Sarajevo lifted after UN–NATO ultimatum and Russian diplomatic intervention. Croat-Muslim federation formed after cease-fire negotiated by former US president Jimmy Carter.
1995 Hostilities resumed; 'safe areas' of Srebrenica (where more than 4,000 Muslims were massacred) and Zepa were overrun before the Serbs were halted by Croatians near Bihac. US-sponsored peace accord, providing for two sovereign states (one Muslim–Croat, one Serb) and cease-fire agreed at Dayton, Ohio, USA, leading to the Dayton peace accord; 60,000-strong NATO peacekeeping force deployed.
1996 Arms-control accord signed. Karadic resigned as president of the Republika Srpska (Serb-controlled Bosnia). A three-person presidency was elected: Alija Izetbegovic (incumbent Muslim president), Momcilo Krajisnik (Serb), and Kresimir Zubak (Croat). Herceg-Bosna para-state and Bosnian republic government replaced by Muslim-Croat federation.
1997 Haris Silajdzic (Muslim) and Boro Bosic (Serb) appointed co-chairs of all-Bosnian Council of Ministers. Serb-dominated part of Bosnia signed joint customs agreement with Yugoslavia. Croat Vladimir Soljic elected president of Muslim-Croat Federation, with Muslim Ejup Ganic as his deputy. Implementation of Dayton Peace Accord delayed. Municipal elections held after 12-month delay; nationalist parties successful. Three-man presidency agreed common passport and citizenship law.
1998 Moderate, pro-western government formed in Republika Srpska, headed by Milorad Dodik.

SEE ALSO Habsburg Empire; Ottoman Empire; Serbia; World War I; Yugoslavia

and Museum are in South Boston. Universities include Harvard University 1636, the oldest in the country, Massachusetts Institute of Technology (MIT), Boston University, Northeastern University, Brandeis University, Tufts University, and Wellesley College.

Boston Tea Party protest 1773 by colonists in Massachusetts, America, against the tea tax imposed on them by the British government before the ◊American Revolution.

When a consignment of tea (belonging to the East India Company and intended for sale in the American colonies) arrived in Boston Harbor, it was thrown overboard by a group of Bostonians disguised as Indians during the night of 16 Dec 1773. The British government, angered by this and other colonial protests against British policy, took retaliatory measures 1774, including the closing of the port of Boston. *See feature on pp. 32–33.*

Boswell James 1740–1795. Scottish biographer and diarist. He was a member of Samuel ◊Johnson's Literary Club and the two men travelled to Scotland together 1773, as recorded in Boswell's *Journal of a Tour to the Hebrides* 1785. His *Life of Samuel Johnson LL.D* was published 1791. Boswell's ability to record Johnson's pithy conversation verbatim makes this a classic of English biography.

> *Now we can go to the polling booth without a bad conscience.*
>
> P W Botha
> *The Independent* 28 April 1994

Bosworth, Battle of last battle of the Wars of the ◊Roses, fought on 22 Aug 1485. Richard III, the Yorkist king, was defeated and slain by Henry of Richmond, who became Henry VII. Henry later married Edward IV's daughter Elizabeth, uniting the houses of York and Lancaster to bring the Wars to an end. The battlefield is near the village of Market Bosworth, 19 km/12 mi W of Leicester, England.

botanical garden place where a wide range of plants is grown, providing the opportunity to see a botanical diversity not likely to be encountered naturally. Among the earliest forms of botanical garden was the 'physic garden', devoted to the study and growth of medicinal plants; an example is the Chelsea Physic Garden in London, established 1673. Following increased botanical exploration, botanical gardens were used to test the commercial potential of new plants being sent back from all parts of the world.

Today a botanical garden serves many purposes: education, science, and conservation. Many are associated with universities and also maintain large collections of preserved specimens (see ◊herbarium), libraries, research laboratories, and gene banks. There are 1,600 botanical gardens worldwide.

botany (Greek *botane* 'herb') the study of living and fossil ◊plants, including form, function, interaction with the environment, and classification.

Botany is subdivided into a number of specialized studies, such as the identification and classification of plants (taxonomy), their external formation (plant morphology), their internal arrangement (plant anatomy), their microscopic examination (plant histology), their functioning and life history (plant physiology), and their distribution over the Earth's surface in relation to their surroundings (plant ecology). Palaeobotany concerns the study of fossil plants, while economic botany deals with the utility of plants. ◊Horticulture, ◊agriculture, and ◊forestry are branches of botany.

Botany Bay inlet on the east coast of Australia, 8 km/5 mi S of Sydney, New South Wales. Chosen 1787 as the site for a penal colony, it proved unsuitable. Sydney now stands on the site of the former settlement. The name Botany Bay continued to be popularly used for any convict settlement in Australia.

botfly any fly of the family Oestridae. The larvae are parasites that feed on the skin (warblefly of cattle) or in the nasal cavity (nostrilflies of sheep and deer). The horse botfly belongs to another family, the Gasterophilidae. It has a parasitic larva that feeds in the horse's stomach.

Botha Louis 1862–1919. South African soldier and politician. He was a commander in the Second South African War (Boer War). In 1907 Botha became premier of the Transvaal and in 1910 of the first Union South African government. On the outbreak of World War I 1914 he rallied South Africa to the Commonwealth, suppressed a Boer revolt, and conquered German South West Africa. He represented South Africa at the Versailles peace conference 1919 .

Botha P(ieter) W(illem) 1916– . South African politician, prime minister from 1978–89. He initiated a modification of ◊apartheid, which later slowed in the face of Afrikaner (Boer) opposition. In 1984 he became the first executive state president. In 1989 he unwillingly resigned both party leadership and presidency after suffering a stroke, and was succeeded by F W de Klerk.

Botham Ian Terence 1955– . English cricketer. His Test record places him among the world's greatest all-rounders. He has played county cricket for Somerset, Worcestershire, and Durham, as well as playing in Australia. He played for England 1977–89 and returned to the England side 1991.

Bothwell James Hepburn, 4th Earl of Bothwell c. 1536–1578. Scottish nobleman. The third husband of ◊Mary Queen of Scots, 1567–70, he was alleged to have arranged the explosion that killed Darnley, her previous husband, 1567. Tried and acquitted a few weeks after the assassination, he abducted Mary and married her on 15 May. A revolt ensued, and Bothwell was forced to flee. In 1570

Mary obtained a divorce, and Bothwell was confined in a castle in the Netherlands where he died insane.

bo tree or *peepul* Indian ◊fig tree *Ficus religiosa*, said to be the tree under which the Buddha became enlightened.

Botswana landlocked country in central southern Africa, bounded S and SE by South Africa, W and N by Namibia, and NE by Zimbabwe. *See country box below.*

Botticelli Sandro, born Alessandro Filipepi 1445–1510. Florentine painter. He depicted religious and mythological subjects. He was patronized by the ruling ◊Medici family and was deeply influenced by their Neo-Platonic circle. It was for the Medicis that he painted *Primavera* 1478 and *The Birth of Venus* about 1482–84. From the 1490s he was influenced by the religious fanatic ◊Savonarola, and developed a harshly expressive and emotional style, as seen in his *Mystic Nativity* 1500.

His work for the Medicis was designed to cater to the educated classical tastes of the day. As well as his sentimental and beautiful young Madonnas, he produced a series of inventive compositions, including *tondi* (circular paintings) and illustrations for Dante's ◊*Divine Comedy*. He broke with the Medicis after their execution of Savonarola.

bottlebrush any of several trees or shrubs common in Australia, belonging to the genus *Callistemon* of the myrtle family, with characteristic cylindrical, composite flower heads in green, yellow, white, various shades of red, and violet.

botulism rare, often fatal type of ◊food poisoning. Symptoms include vomiting, diarrhoea, muscular paralysis, breathing difficulties and disturbed vision.

It is caused by a toxin produced by the bacterium *Clostridium botulinum*, found in soil and sometimes in improperly canned foods. Thorough cooking destroys the toxin. In neurology, botulinum toxin is sometimes used to treat rare movement disorders.

Boucher François 1703–1770. French Rococo painter. Court painter to Louis XV from 1765, he was much patronized for his light-hearted, decorative scenes which often convey a playful eroticism, as in *Diana Bathing* 1742 (Louvre, Paris).

He was appointed first painter to Louis XV on the death of van Loo and was also chief designer to the Royal Beauvais Tapestry works, designer for the Opéra and the favourite artist of Mme de Pompadour, whom he taught drawing and of whom he made a number of portraits, notable being the full-length in the Wallace Collection (where also are the panels of gods and goddesses he designed for her boudoir).

***Botticelli** Primavera* 1478 by Botticelli (Uffizi Gallery, Florence). The scene is an allegory of Spring based on Greek mythology. On the right, the figure of Chloris is being transformed by the touch of her husband Zephyr (the Wind) into Flora, the goddess of flowers (the third figure from the right). In the centre is Venus, the goddess of love. On the left are the three Graces and Mercury, the messenger of the gods. *Corbis*

Boudicca died AD 61. Queen of the Iceni (native Britons), often referred to by the Latin form ***Boadicea***. Her husband, King Prasutagus, had been a tributary of the Romans, but on his death AD 60 the territory of the Iceni was violently annexed. Boudicca was scourged and her daughters raped. Boudicca raised the whole of SE England in revolt, and before the main Roman armies could return from campaigning in Wales she burned Londinium (London), Verulamium (St Albans), and Camulodunum (Colchester). Later the Romans under governor Suetonius Paulinus defeated the British between London and Chester; they were virtually annihilated and Boudicca poisoned herself.

Boudin (Louis) Eugène 1824–1898. French artist. A forerunner of the Impressionists, he is known for his luminous seaside scenes such as *Harbour of Trouville* (National Gallery, London).

The son of a ship's captain at Honfleur, he was encouraged to paint by artists of the Barbizon School. He worked mainly on the Normandy coast and in Brittany, rendering vividly the breezy atmosphere and restless sea and sky of the region. He initiated Claude Monet into open-air painting in 1858. He contributed to the first Impressionist exhibition in 1874.

Bougainville island province of Papua New Guinea; largest of the Solomon Islands archipelago
area 10,620 sq km/4,100 sq mi
capital Kieta
industries copper, gold, and silver
population (1989) 128,000
history named after the French navigator Louis de Bougainville who arrived 1768. It was occupied by the Japnese during World War II from March 1942 until liberated by US troops 1943 and then held by the Australians until the end of the war. In 1976 Bougainville became a province (with substantial autonomy) of Papua New Guinea. A state of emergency was declared 1989 after secessionist violence. In 1990 the secessionist Bougainville Revolutionary Army took control of the island, declaring it

BOTSWANA
Republic of

area 582,000 sq km/225,000 sq mi
capital Gaborone
major towns/cities Mahalapye, Serowe, Tutume, Bobonong Francistown
physical features Kalahari Desert in SW (70–80% of national territory is desert), plains (Makgadikgadi salt pans) in E, fertile lands and Okavango Swamp in N
head of state and government Festus Mogae from 1998
political system democratic republic
administrative divisions nine districts and six independent townships
political parties Botswana Democratic Party (BDP), moderate centrist; Botswana National Front (BNF), moderate left of centre
population 1,484,000 (1996 est)
population growth rate 3.1% (1990–95); 2.7% (2000–05)
ethnic distribution about 90% Tswana and 5% Kung and other hunter-gatherer groups; the remainder is European
life expectancy 58 (males), 64 (females)
literacy rate men 84%, women 65%
languages English (official), Setswana (national)
religions Christian 50%, animist, Baha'i, Muslim, Hindu
currency franc CFA
GDP (US $) 4 billion (1994)
growth rate 4.1% (1994)
exports diamonds (third largest producer in world), copper, nickel, meat products, textiles

HISTORY
18th C Formerly inhabited by nomadic hunter-gatherer groups, including the Kung, the area was settled by the Tswana people, from whose eight branches the majority of the people are descended.
1872 Khama III 'the Great', a converted Christian, became chief of the Bamangwato, the largest Tswana group. He developed a strong army and greater unity among the Botswana peoples.
1885 Became the British protectorate of Bechuanaland at the request of Chief Khama, who feared invasion by Boers from the Transvaal (South Africa) following the discovery of gold.
1895 The southern part of the Bechuanaland Protectorate was annexed by Cape Colony (South Africa).
1960 New constitution created a legislative council controlled (until 1963) by a British High Commissioner.
1965 Capital transferred from Mafeking to Gaborone. Internal self-government achieved, with Seretse Khama, the grandson of Khama III and leader of the centrist Democratic Party (BDP), elected head of government.
1966 Independence achieved from Britain. Name changed to Botswana; Seretse Khama elected president under new presidentialist constitution.
mid-1970s The economy grew rapidly as diamond mining expanded.
1980 Seretse Khama died, and was succeeded by Vice President Quett Masire (BDP).
1985 South African raid on Gaborone, allegedly in search of African National Congress (ANC) guerrillas.
1993 Relations with South Africa fully normalized following ending of apartheid and establishment of a multiracial government.
1997 Major constitutional changes reduced voting age to 18.
1998 Festus Mogae (BDP) succeeded President Masire, who retired.

SEE ALSO Khama, Seretse; Kung; Tswana

❛Those expressions are omitted which can not with propriety be read aloud in the family.❜

THOMAS BOWDLER
Family Shakespeare, preface 1818

independent; government troops regained control 1992. A peace agreement 1994 set up four neutral zones occupied by the Pacific peacekeeping force (from Fiji Islands, Tonga, and Vanuatu).

Bougainville Louis Antoine de 1729–1811. French navigator. After service with the French in Canada during the Seven Years' War, he made the first French circumnavigation of the world 1766–69 and the first systematic observations of longitude.

Several Pacific islands are named after him, as is the climbing plant bougainvillea.

bougainvillea any plant of the genus of South American tropical vines *Bougainvillea*, of the four o'clock family Nyctaginaceae, now cultivated in warm countries throughout the world for the red and purple bracts that cover the flowers. They are named after the French navigator Louis Bougainville.

Boulanger Nadia Juliette 1887–1979. French music teacher and conductor. A pupil of Fauré, and admirer of Stravinsky, she included among her composition pupils at the American Conservatory in Fontainebleau, France, (from 1921) Aaron Copland, Roy Harris, Walter Piston, and Philip Glass.

boulder clay another name for ◊till, a type of glacial deposit.

boules (French 'balls') French game (also called *boccie* and *pétanque*) between two players or teams; it is similar to bowls.

Boules is derived from the ancient French game *jeu provençal*. The object is to deliver a boule (or boules) from a standing position to land as near the jack (target) as possible. The boule is approximately 8 cm/3 in in diameter and weighs 620–800 g/22–28 oz. The standard length of the court, normally with a sand base, is 27.5 m/90 ft.

Boulez Pierre 1925– . French composer and conductor. He is the founder and director of IRCAM, a music research studio in Paris opened 1977. His music, strictly serial and expressionistic in style, includes the cantatas *Le Visage nuptial* 1946–52 and *Le Marteau sans maître* 1955, both to texts by René Char; *Pli selon pli* 1962 for soprano and orchestra; and *Répons* 1981 for soloists, orchestra, tapes, and computer-generated sounds.

Boulogne-sur-Mer town on the English Channel in the *département* of Pas-de-Calais, France; population (1990) 44,200. Industries include oil refining, food processing, and fishing. It is also a ferry port (connecting with Dover and Folkestone) and seaside resort. Boulogne was a medieval countship, but became part of France 1477.

Boumédiene Houari. Adopted name of Mohammed Boukharouba 1925–1978. Algerian politician who brought the nationalist leader Ben Bella to power by a revolt 1962 and superseded him as president 1965 by a further coup.

Bourbon Charles, 8th Duke of Bourbon 1490–1527. Constable of France, honoured for his courage at the Battle of Marignano 1515. Later he served the Holy Roman Emperor Charles V, and helped to drive the French from Italy. In 1526 he was made duke of Milan, and in 1527 allowed his troops to sack Rome. He was killed by a shot the artist Cellini claimed to have fired.

Boulez Composer and conductor Pierre Boulez. Working first as a mathematician and then as a composer, Boulez has been at the leading edge of musical developments since World War II. His uncompromising brand of modernism has ignored current populist trends. Since the 1970s he has also been influential as a conductor of 20th-century music. *Polygram*

Bourbon, duchy of originally a seigneury (feudal domain) created in the 10th century in the county of Bourges, central France, held by the Bourbon family. It became a duchy 1327.

The lands passed to the Capetian dynasty (see ◊Capet) as a result of the marriage of the Bourbon heiress Beatrix to Robert of Clermont, son of Louis IX. Their son Pierre became the first duke of Bourbon 1327. The direct line ended with the death of Charles, Duke of Bourbon, in 1527.

Bourbon dynasty French royal house (succeeding that of ◊Valois), beginning with Henry IV and ending with Louis XVI, with a brief revival under Louis XVIII, Charles X, and Louis Philippe. The Bourbons also ruled Spain almost uninterruptedly from Philip V to Alfonso XIII and were restored 1975 (◊Juan Carlos); at one point they also ruled Naples and several Italian duchies. The Grand Duke of Luxembourg is also a Bourbon by male descent.

bourgeoisie (French) the middle classes. The French word originally meant 'the freemen of a borough'. It came to mean the whole class above the workers and peasants, and below the nobility. 'Bourgeoisie' (and 'bourgeois') has also acquired a contemptuous sense, implying commonplace, philistine respectability. By socialists it is applied to the whole propertied class, as distinct from the proletariat.

Bourgogne French name of ◊Burgundy, a region of E France.

Bourguiba Habib ben Ali 1903– . Tunisian politician, first president of Tunisia 1957–87. He became prime minister 1956 and president (for life from 1975) and prime minister of the Tunisian republic 1957; he was overthrown in a bloodless coup 1987.

Bournemouth unitary authority of England created 1997 (*see United Kingdom map*). The town is a seaside resort; population (1991) 151,300.

Boutros-Ghali Boutros 1922– . Egyptian diplomat and politician, deputy prime minister 1991–92, secretary general of the United Nations (UN) 1992–96. He worked towards peace in the Middle East in the foreign ministry posts he held 1977–91. At the UN he faced a series of challenges regarding the organization's role in conflict areas such as Bosnia-Herzegovina, Somalia, Haiti, and Rwanda. In 1996 he was succeeded by Kofi ◊Annan.

Bouts Dirk (Dierick) c. 1420–1475. Dutch painter. Born in Haarlem, he settled in Louvain, painting portraits and religious scenes influenced by Rogier van der Weyden and Petrus Christus. *The Last Supper* 1464–68 (St Pierre, Louvain) is one of his finest works.

bovine spongiform encephalopathy (BSE) or ***mad cow disease*** disease of cattle, allied to ◊scrapie in sheep, which attacks the nervous system, causing aggression, lack of coordination, and collapse. First identified 1986, it is almost entirely confined to the UK. By 1996 it had claimed 158,000 British cattle.

BSE is one of a group of diseases known as the transmissible spongiform encephalopathies, since they are characterized by the appearance of spongy changes in brain tissue. Some scientists believe that all these conditions, including ◊Creutzfeldt-Jakob disease (CJD) in humans, are in effect the same disease, and in 1996 a link was established between deaths from CJD and the consumption of beef products. The cause of these universally fatal diseases is not fully understood, but they may be the result of a rogue protein called a ◊prion. A prion may be inborn or it may be transmitted in contaminated tissue.

The source of the disease has been traced to manufactured protein feed incorporating the rendered brains of scrapie-infected sheep. Following the ban on the use of offal in feed 1988, the epidemic continued, indicating that the disease could be transmitted from cows to their calves. It was not till 1996 that government scientists admitted that this was so.

Bow Clara 1905–1965. US film actress. She was known as a 'Jazz Baby' and the 'It Girl' after her portrayal of a glamorous flapper in the silent film *It* 1927.

bower bird The regent bower bird *Sericulus chrysocephalus* is found in the rainforests of NE Australia and New Guinea. The male is brightly coloured and seeks to impress his mate by building a colourfully decorated bower. It is the female who builds the nest; her dull plumage camouflages her while she is sitting on her eggs and feeding her young.

Bow Bells the bells of St Mary-le-Bow church, Cheapside, London; a person born within the sound of Bow Bells is traditionally considered a true Cockney. The bells also feature in the legend of Dick ◊Whittington.

The church was nearly destroyed by bombs in 1941. The bells, recast from the old metal, were restored in 1961.

Bowdler Thomas 1754–1825. English editor. His prudishly expurgated versions of Shakespeare and other authors gave rise to the verb bowdlerize.

Bowen Elizabeth (Dorothea Cole) 1899–1973. Irish novelist and short-story writer. She published her first volume of short stories, *Encounters*, 1923. Her novels include *The Death of the Heart* 1938, *The Heat of the Day* 1949, and *The Little Girls* 1964. Her collections of short stories include *Ann Lee's* 1928, *Joining Charles* 1929, *The Cat Jumps* 1934, *The Demon Lover* 1946, and *Collected Stories* 1980.

bower bird New Guinean and N Australian bird of the family Ptilonorhynchidae, order Passeriformes, related to the ◊bird of paradise. The males are dull-coloured, and build elaborate bowers of sticks and grass, decorated with shells, feathers, or flowers, and even painted with the juice of berries, to attract the females. There are 17 species.

bowfin North American fish *Amia calva* with a swim bladder highly developed as an air sac, enabling it to breathe air. It is the only surviving member of a primitive group of bony fishes.

bowhead Arctic whale *Balaena mysticetus* with strongly curving upper jawbones supporting the plates of baleen with which it sifts planktonic crustaceans from the water. Averaging 15 m/50 ft long and 90 tonnes/100 tons in weight, these slow-moving, placid whales were once extremely common, but by the 17th century were already becoming scarce through hunting. Only an estimated 3,000 remain, and continued hunting by the Inuit may result in extinction.

Bowie David. Stage name of David Robert Jones 1947– . English pop singer, songwriter, and actor. His career has been a series of image changes. His hits include 'Jean Genie' 1973, 'Rebel, Rebel' 1974, 'Golden Years' 1975, and 'Underground' 1986. In 1989 he formed the hard-rock band Tin Machine. He has acted in plays and films, including Nicolas Roeg's *The Man Who Fell to Earth* 1976.

Bowie's albums include *Aladdin Sane* 1973, *Station to Station* 1976, *Heroes* 1977, *Let's Dance* 1983, and *Black Tie/White Noise* 1993.

bowls outdoor and indoor game popular in Commonwealth countries. It has been played in Britain since the 13th century and was popularized by Francis Drake, who is reputed to have played bowls on Plymouth Hoe as the Spanish Armada approached 1588.

The outdoor game is played on a finely cut grassed area called a rink, with biased bowls

13 cm/5 in in diameter. It is played as either singles, pairs, triples, or fours. The object is to get one's bowl (or bowls) as near as possible to the jack (target).

There are two popular forms: ***lawn bowls***, played on a flat surface, and ***crown green bowls***, played on a rink with undulations and a crown at the centre of the green. This latter version is more popular in the Midlands and N England. The major events include the World Outdoor Championship first held 1966 for men and 1969 for women, the World Indoor Championship first held 1979 for men and 1988 for women, and the Waterloo Handicap, Crown Green bowling's principal tournament, which was first held 1907 at the Waterloo Hotel, Blackpool, England.

box any of several small evergreen trees and shrubs, genus *Buxus*, of the family Buxaceae, with small, leathery leaves. Some species are used as hedge plants and for shaping into garden ornaments.

The common box *B. sempervirens* is slow-growing and ideal for hedging.

boxer breed of dog, about 60 cm/24 in tall, with a smooth coat and a set-back nose. The tail is usually docked. A boxer is usually brown, often with white markings, but may be fawn or brindled.

Boxer member of the *I ho ch'üan* ('Righteous Harmonious Fists'), a society of Chinese nationalists dedicated to fighting European influence. The Boxer Rebellion or Uprising 1900 was instigated by the empress ◊Zi Xi. European and US legations in Beijing were besieged and thousands of Chinese Christian converts and missionaries murdered. An international punitive force was dispatched, Beijing was captured 14 Aug 1900, and China agreed to pay a large indemnity.

boxfish or ***trunkfish***,any fish of the family Ostraciodontidae, with scales that are hexagonal bony plates fused to form a box covering the body, only the mouth and fins being free of the armour. Boxfishes swim slowly. The cowfish, genus *Lactophrys*, with two 'horns' above the eyes, is a member of this group.

boxing fighting with gloved fists, almost entirely a male sport. The sport dates from the 18th century, when fights were fought with bare knuckles and untimed rounds. Each round ended with a knockdown. Fighting with gloves became the accepted form in the latter part of the 19th century after the formulation of the Queensberry Rules 1867.

Jack Broughton (1704–1789) was one of the early champions and in 1743 drew up the first set of boxing rules. The last bare-knuckle championship fight was between John L Sullivan and Jake Kilrain 1899. Today all boxing follows the original Queensberry Rules, but with modifications. Contests take place in a roped ring 4.3–6.1 m/14–20 ft square. All rounds last three minutes. Amateur bouts last three rounds; professional championship bouts last as many as 12 or 15 rounds. Boxers are classified according to weight and may not fight in a division lighter than their own. The weight divisions in professional boxing range from strawweight (also known as paperweight and mini-flyweight), under 49 kg/108 lb, to heavyweight, over 88 kg/195 lb. *See list of tables on p. 1177.*

Boycott Charles Cunningham 1832–1897. English land agent in County Mayo, Ireland, who strongly opposed the demands for agrarian reform by the Irish Land League 1879–81, with the result that the peasants refused to work for him; hence the word boycott.

Boycott Geoffrey 1940– . English cricketer. He was England's most prolific run-maker with 8,114 runs in Test cricket until overtaken by David Gower 1992. He was banned as a Test player 1982 for taking part in matches against South Africa.

He played in 108 Test matches and in 1981 overtook Gary Sobers' world record total of Test runs. Twice, in 1971 and 1979, his average was over 100 runs in an English season. He was released by Yorkshire after a dispute 1986.

Boyle Robert 1627–1691. Irish chemist and physicist who published the seminal *The Sceptical Chymist* 1661. He formulated Boyle's law 1662. He was a pioneer in the use of experiment and scientific method.

Boyle questioned the alchemical basis of the chemical theory of his day and taught that the proper object of chemistry was to determine the compositions of substances. The term 'analysis' was coined by Boyle and many of the reactions still used in qualitative work were known to him. He introduced certain plant extracts, notably litmus, for the indication of acids and bases. He was also the first chemist to collect a sample of gas.

Boyle's law law stating that the volume of a given mass of gas at a constant temperature is inversely proportional to its pressure. For example, if the pressure of a gas doubles, its volume will be reduced by a half, and vice versa. The law was discovered 1662 by Irish physicist and chemist Robert Boyle. See also ◊gas laws.

Boyne river in the Republic of Ireland. Rising in the Bog of Allen in County Kildare, it flows 110 km/69 mi NE to the Irish Sea near Drogheda. The Battle of the Boyne was fought at Oldbridge near the mouth of the river 1690.

Boyne, Battle of the battle fought 1 July 1690 in E Ireland, in which the exiled king James II was defeated by William III and fled to France. It was the decisive battle of the War of English Succession, confirming a Protestant monarch. It took its name from the river Boyne which rises in County Kildare and flows 110 km/69 mi NE to the Irish Sea.

Brabant (Flemish ***Braband***) former duchy of W Europe, comprising the Dutch province of ◊North Brabant and the Belgian provinces of Brabant and Antwerp. They were divided when Belgium became independent 1830. The present-day Belgian Brabant is comprised of two provinces: Flemish Brabant (capital Leuven), with an area of 2,106 sq km/813 sq mi and a population of 995,300 (1995); and Wallern Brabant (capital Wavre), with an area of 1,091 sq km/421 sq mi and a population of 336,500 (1995).

history During the Middle Ages Brabant was an independent duchy, and after passing to Burgundy, and thence to the Spanish crown, was divided during the Dutch War of Independence. The southern portion was Spanish until 1713, then Austrian until 1815, when the whole area was included in the Netherlands. In 1830 the French-speaking part of the population in the S Netherlands rebelled, and when Belgium was recognized 1839, S Brabant was included in it.

Brabham Grand Prix racing team started 1962 by the twice-world champion Australian driver Jack Brabham (1926–). Their first car, designed by Ron Tauranac, had its first win 1964, and in 1966 Brabham won the world title for the third time in his own Repco engine-powered car. The team withdrew from Formula One racing 1992.

brachiopod or ***lamp shell*** any member of the phylum Brachiopoda, marine invertebrates with two shells, resembling but totally unrelated to bivalves.

There are about 300 living species; they were much more numerous in past geological ages. They are suspension feeders, ingesting minute food particles from water. A single internal organ, the lophophore, handles feeding, aspiration, and excretion.

bracken large fern, especially *Pteridium aquilinum*, abundant in the northern hemisphere. A perennial rootstock throws up coarse fronds.

It causes cancer in sheep and cattle, and harbours a sheep tick that transmits ◊lyme disease to humans. It is invasive and endemic in upland regions, and has spread because its only enemy, cattle that trample on young shoots, are no longer kept on hillsides. It is estimated that some 3,000 sq km/1,160 sq mi of countryside in England and Wales is now covered by bracken.

bracket fungus any ◊fungus of the class Basidiomycetes, with fruiting bodies that grow like shelves from trees.

bract leaflike structure in whose ◊axil a flower or inflorescence develops. Bracts are generally green and smaller than the true leaves. However, in some plants they may be brightly coloured and conspicuous, taking over the role of attracting pollinating insects to the flowers, whose own petals are small; examples include poinsettia *Euphorbia pulcherrima* and bougainvillea.

A whorl of bracts surrounding an ◊inflorescence is termed an involucre. A bracteole is a leaf-like organ that arises on an individual flower stalk, between the true bract and the ◊calyx.

Bradbury Malcolm (Stanley) 1932– . English novelist and critic. His fiction includes comic and satiric portrayals of provincial British and US campus life: *Eating People is Wrong* 1959 (his first novel), *Stepping Westward* 1965, and *The History Man* 1975. His critical works include *The Modern American Novel* (new edition 1992) and *The Modern British Novel* 1993.

'I like the English. They have the most rigid code of immorality in the world.'

MALCOLM BRADBURY
Eating People is Wrong

Bradford industrial city (engineering, chemicals, machine tools, electronics, printing) and administrative headquarters of Bradford unitary authority; population (1991) 457,300. It is the main city for wool textile in the UK.

features A 15th-century cathedral; Cartwright Hall art gallery; the National Museum of Photography, Film, and Television 1983 (with Britain's largest cinema screen 14 × 20 m/46 × 66 ft); and the Alhambra, built as a music hall and restored for ballet, plays, and pantomime.

history From the 13th century, Bradford developed as a great wool- and, later, cloth-manufacturing centre, but the industry declined from the 1970s with competition from developing countries and the European Economic Community (now European Union). The city has received a succession of immigrants, Irish in the 1840s, German merchants in the mid-19th century, then Poles and Ukrainians, and more recently West Indians and Asians; 10% of the population are Pakistani. In 1985 Bradford City Football Club was the scene of a disaster when the stand caught fire, killing 56 people.

Areas of the city experienced severe rioting 9–10 June 1995 after local vigilante groups backed two

bracket fungus This varicoloured *Coriolus versicolor* is one of a large number of often unrelated fungi referred to collectively as bracket fungi because they form bracketlike growths on trees and timber. *Premaphotos Wildlife*

Brahms The German composer Brahms, pictured in 1860. During this early period he fell in love with Clara Schumann, who, along with husband Robert, gave him the encouragement and support needed to help launch his career. He became the greatest Romantic composer still to adhere to traditional formal models. *Image Select (UK) Ltd*

Asian youths in a confrontation with police. More than 300 police from throughout the UK were called in before order was restored.

Bradlaugh Charles 1833–1891. British free-thinker and radical politician. In 1880 he was elected Liberal member of Parliament for Northampton, but was not allowed to take his seat until 1886 because, as an atheist, he (unsuccessfully) claimed the right to affirm instead of taking the oath. He was associated with the feminist Annie Besant.

Bradley James 1693–1762. English astronomer. In 1728 he discovered the ◊aberration of starlight. From the amount of aberration in star positions, he was able to calculate the speed of light. In 1748, he announced the discovery of ◊nutation (variation in the Earth's axial tilt).

Bradley Omar Nelson 1893–1981. US general in World War II. In 1943 he commanded the 2nd US Corps in their victories in Tunisia and Sicily, leading to the surrender of 250,000 Axis troops, and in 1944 led the US troops in the invasion of France. His command, as the 12th Army Group, grew to 1.3 million troops, the largest US force ever assembled.

Bradman Don(ald George) 1908– . Australian Test cricketer. From 52 Test matches he averaged 99.94 runs per innings, the highest average in Test history. He only needed four runs from his final Test innings to average 100 but was dismissed second ball.

Bradman was born in Cootamundra, New South Wales, and brought up in Bowral, New South Wales. He came to prominence at an early age, and made his Test debut 1928. He played for Australia for 20 years and was captain 1936–48.

He twice scored triple centuries against England and in 1930 scored 452 not out for New South Wales against Queensland, the highest first-class innings until 1959. In 1989 a Bradman Museum was opened in his home town.

Braemar village in Grampian, Scotland, where the most celebrated of the ◊Highland Games, the Braemar Gathering, takes place every August.

Braganza the royal house of Portugal whose members reigned 1640–1910; members of another branch were emperors of Brazil 1822–89.

Brahe Tycho 1546–1601. Danish astronomer. His accurate observations of the planets enabled German astronomer and mathematician Johannes ◊Kepler to prove that planets orbit the Sun in ellipses. Brahe's discovery and report of the 1572 supernova brought him recognition, and his observations of the comet of 1577 proved that it moved in an orbit among the planets, thus disproving Aristotle's view that comets were in the Earth's atmosphere.

Brahe was a colourful figure who wore a silver nose after his own was cut off in a duel, and who took an interest in alchemy. In 1576 Frederick II of Denmark gave him the island of Hven, where he set up an observatory. Brahe was the greatest observer in the days before telescopes, making the most accurate measurements of the positions of stars and planets. He moved to Prague as imperial mathematician 1599, where he was joined by Kepler, who inherited his observations when he died. ▷ *See feature on pp. 70–71.*

Brahma in Hinduism, the creator of the cosmos, who forms with Vishnu and Siva the Trimurti, or three aspects of the absolute spirit.

In the Hindu creation myth, Brahma, the demiurge, is born from the unfolding lotus flower that grows out of Vishnu's navel; after Brahma creates the world, Vishnu wakes and governs it for the duration of the cosmic cycle *kalpa*, the 'day of Brahma', which lasts for 4,200 million earthly years. Unlike Brahman, which is an impersonal principle and of neuter gender, Brahma is a personified god and of masculine gender.

Brahman in Hinduism, the supreme being, an abstract, impersonal world soul into whom the *atman*, or individual soul, will eventually be absorbed when its cycle of rebirth is ended.

Brahmanism earliest stage in the development of ◊Hinduism. Its sacred scriptures are the ◊Vedas, with their accompanying literature of comment and explanation known as Brahmanas, Aranyakas, and Upanishads.

Brahmaputra river in Asia 2,900 km/1,800 mi long, a tributary of the Ganges. It rises in the Himalayan glaciers as Zangbo and runs east through Tibet, to the mountain mass of Namcha Barwa. Turning south, as the Dihang, it enters India and flows into the Assam Valley near Sadiya, where it is now known as the Brahmaputra. It flows generally west until, shortly after reaching Bangladesh, it turns south and divides into the Brahmaputra proper, without much water, and the main stream, the Jamuna, which joins the Padma arm of the Ganges. The river is navigable for 1,285 km/800 mi from the sea.

Brahms Johannes 1833–1897. German composer, pianist, and conductor. Considered one of the greatest composers of symphonic music and of songs, his works include four symphonies, lieder (songs), concertos for piano and for violin, chamber music, sonatas, and the choral *Ein Deutsches Requiem/A German Requiem* 1868. He performed and conducted his own works.

In 1853 the violinist Joachim introduced him to Liszt and Schumann, who encouraged his work. From 1868 Brahms made his home in Vienna. Brahms saw himself as continuing the classical tradition from the point to which Beethoven had brought it. To his contemporaries, he was a strict formalist, in opposition to the romantic sensuality of Wagner. His influence on Mahler and Schoenberg was profound.

Braille system of writing for the blind. Letters are represented by a combination of raised dots on paper or other materials, which are then read by touch. It was invented in 1829 by Louis Braille (1809–1852), who became blind at the age of three.

brain in higher animals, a mass of interconnected ◊nerve cells forming the anterior part of the ◊central nervous system, whose activities it coordinates and controls. In ◊vertebrates, the brain is contained by the skull. At the base of the ◊brainstem, the medulla oblongata contains centres for the control of respiration, heartbeat rate and strength, and blood pressure. Overlying this is the cerebellum, which is concerned with coordinating complex muscular processes such as maintaining posture and moving limbs.

The cerebral hemispheres (cerebrum) are paired outgrowths of the front end of the forebrain, in early vertebrates mainly concerned with the senses, but in higher vertebrates greatly developed and involved in the integration of all sensory input and motor output, and in thought, emotions, memory, and behaviour.

In vertebrates, many of the nerve fibres from the two sides of the body cross over as they enter the brain, so that the left cerebral hemisphere is associated with the right side of the body and vice versa. In humans, a certain asymmetry develops in the two halves of the cerebrum. In right-handed people, the left hemisphere seems to play a greater role in controlling verbal and some mathematical skills, whereas the right hemisphere is more involved in spatial perception. In general, however, skills and abilities are not closely localized. In the brain, nerve impulses are passed across ◊synapses by neurotransmitters, in the same way as in other parts of the nervous system.

brain The structure of the human brain. At the back of the skull lies the cerebellum, which coordinates reflex actions that control muscular activity. The medulla controls respiration, heartbeat, and blood pressure. The hypothalamus is concerned with instinctive drives and emotions. The thalamus relays signals to and from various parts of the brain. The pituitary gland controls the body's hormones. Distinct areas of the large convoluted cerebral hemispheres that fill most of the skull are linked to sensations, such as hearing and sight, and voluntary activities, such as movement.

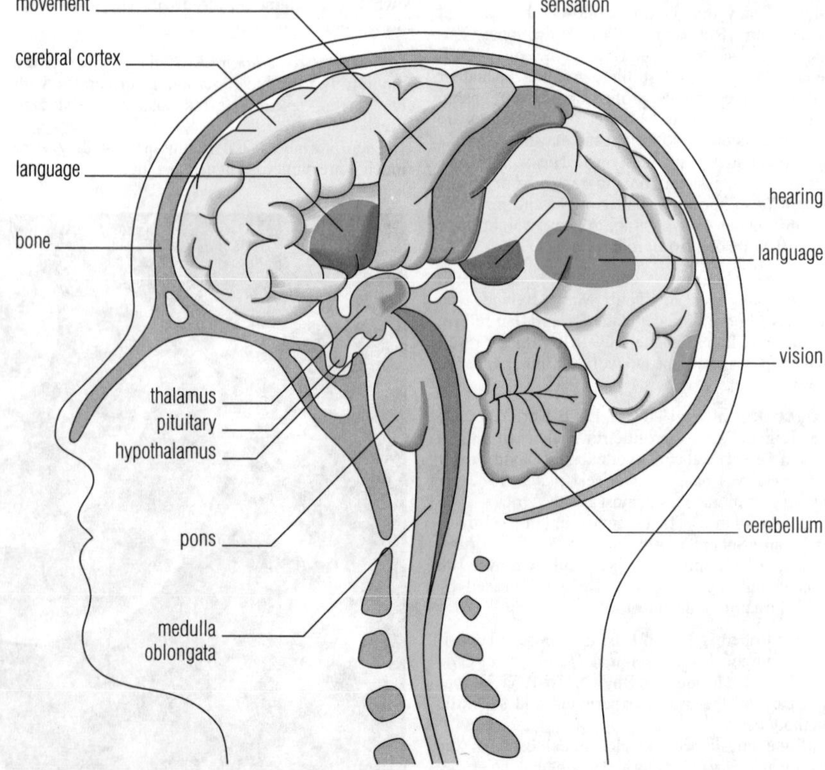

In mammals the cerebrum is the largest part of the brain, carrying the cerebral cortex. This consists of a thick surface layer of cell bodies (grey matter), below which fibre tracts (white matter) connect various parts of the cortex to each other and to other points in the central nervous system. As cerebral complexity grows, the surface of the brain becomes convoluted into deep folds. In higher mammals, there are large unassigned areas of the brain that seem to be connected with intelligence, personality, and higher mental faculties. Language is controlled in two special regions usually in the left side of the brain: Broca's area governs the ability to talk, and Wernicke's area is responsible for the comprehension of spoken and written words. In 1990, scientists at Johns Hopkins University, Baltimore, succeeded in culturing human brain cells.

brain damage impairment which can be caused by trauma (for example, accidents) or disease (such as encephalitis), or which may be present at birth. Depending on the area of the brain that is affected, language, movement, sensation, judgement, or other abilities may be impaired.

Braine John (Gerard) 1922–1986. English novelist. His novel *Room at the Top* 1957 created the character of Joe Lampton, one of the first of the northern working-class antiheroes, who reappears in *Life at the Top* 1962.

brainstem region where the top of the spinal cord merges with the undersurface of the brain, consisting largely of the medulla oblongata and midbrain.

The oldest part of the brain in evolutionary terms, the brainstem is the body's life-support centre, containing regulatory mechanisms for vital functions such as breathing, heart rate, and blood pressure. It is also involved in controlling the level of consciousness by acting as a relay station for nerve connections to and from the higher centres of the brain.

In many countries, death of the brainstem is now formally recognized as death of the person as a whole. Such cases are the principal donors of organs for transplantation. So-called 'beating-heart donors' can be maintained for a limited period by life-support equipment.

brake Two common braking systems: the disc brake (right) and the drum brake (left). In the disc brake, increased hydraulic pressure of the brake fluid in the pistons forces the brake pads against the steel disc attached to the wheel. A self-adjusting mechanism balances the force on each pad. In the drum brake, increased pressure of the brake fluid within the slave cylinder forces the brake pad against the brake drum attached to the wheel.

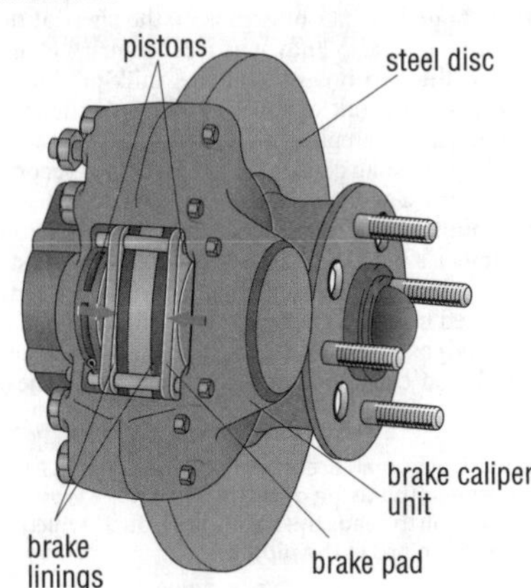

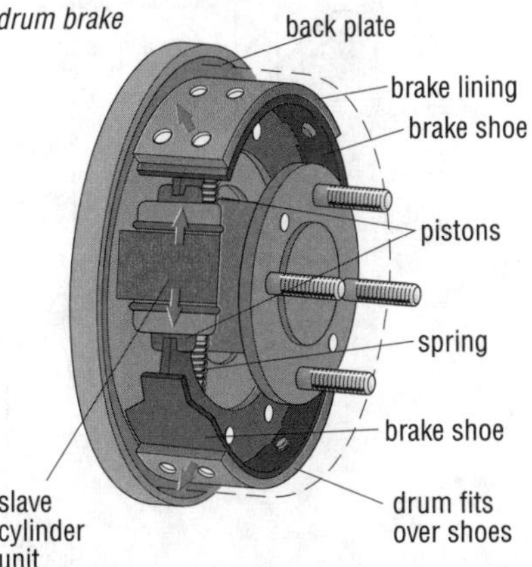

brake device used to slow down or stop the movement of a moving body or vehicle. The mechanically applied calliper brake used on bicycles uses a scissor action to press hard rubber blocks against the wheel rim. The main braking system of a car works hydraulically: when the driver depresses the brake pedal, liquid pressure forces pistons to apply brakes on each wheel.

Two types of car brakes are used. ***Disc brakes*** are used on the front wheels of some cars and on all wheels of sports and performance cars, since they are the more efficient and less prone to fading (losing their braking power) when they get hot. Braking pressure forces brake pads against both sides of a steel disc that rotates with the wheel. ***Drum brakes*** are fitted on the rear wheels of some cars and on all wheels of some passenger cars. Braking pressure forces brake shoes to expand outwards into contact with a drum rotating with the wheels. The brake pads and shoes have a tough ◊friction lining that grips well and withstands wear.

Many trucks and trains have ***air brakes***, which work by compressed air. On landing, jet planes reverse the thrust of their engines to reduce their speed quickly. Space vehicles use retrorockets for braking in space and use the air resistance, or drag of the atmosphere, to slow down when they return to Earth.

Bramante Donato 1444–1514. Italian Renaissance architect and artist. Inspired by Classical designs and by the work of Leonardo da Vinci, he was employed by Pope Julius II in rebuilding part of the Vatican and St Peter's in Rome. The circular Tempietto of San Pietro in Montorio, Rome (commissioned 1502; built about 1510), is possibly his most important completed work. Though small in size, this circular colonnaded building possesses much of the grandeur of ancient Roman buildings.

bramble any prickly bush of a genus *Rubus* belonging to the rose family Rosaceae. Examples are ◊blackberry, raspberry, and dewberry.

There are over 400 types of bramble found in Britain. In the past some have been regarded as distinct species.

brambling or ***bramble finch*** bird *Fringilla montifringilla* belonging to the finch family Fringillidae, order Passeriformes. It is about 15 cm/6 in long, and breeds in N Europe and Asia.

Branagh Kenneth Charles 1960– . Northern Irish stage and film actor, director, and producer. He cofounded the Renaissance Theatre Company 1987. His first film as both actor and director was *Henry V* 1989; he returned to Shakespeare with lavish film versions of *Much Ado About Nothing* 1993 and *Hamlet* 1996.

Branagh's first Hollywood film was *Dead Again* 1992, a stylish *film noir* in which he played two roles. He also demonstrated a deft comic touch with *Peter's Friends* 1992 and *In the Bleak Midwinter* 1995, although his extravagant interpretation of *Mary Shelley's Frankenstein* 1994 was coolly received.

Brancusi Constantin 1876–1957. Romanian sculptor. Active in Paris from 1904, he was a pioneer of abstract sculpture, reducing a few basic themes such as birds, fishes, and the human head to simple essential forms appropriate to the special quality of his material, whether stone, bronze, or wood. His works include *Sleeping Muse* 1910 (Musée National d'Art Moderne, Paris) and *Bird in Space* 1928 (Museum of Modern Art, New York).

Brancusi was one of the first sculptors in the 20th century to carve directly from his material. He departed from convention in his treatment of wood, shaping it with axe or saw cuts, as in *Prodigal Son* 1915 (Philadelphia Museum of Art). By contrast, his bronzes, such as *Maiastra* 1911 (Tate Gallery, London), are sleek and highly polished.

Branagh Hailed by some as a new Olivier, Northern Irish actor and director Kenneth Branagh has played a wide variety of Shakespearean and contemporary roles on stage, film, and television. The film *Dead Again* 1991 was a major box office hit on both sides of the Atlantic. Other films which he has both directed and starred in include *Much Ado About Nothing* 1993 and *Mary Shelley's Frankenstein* 1994. *Topham*

Brandenburg administrative *Land* (state) of Germany
area 25,000 sq km/10,000 sq mi
capital Potsdam
towns and cities Cottbus, Brandenburg, Frankfurt-an-der-Oder
industries iron and steel, paper, pulp, metal products, semiconductors
population (1994 est) 2,538,000
history the Hohenzollern rulers who took control of Brandenburg 1415 later acquired the powerful duchy of Prussia and became emperors of Germany. At the end of World War II, Brandenburg lost over 12,950 sq km/5,000 sq mi of territory when Poland advanced its frontier to the line of the Oder and Neisse rivers. The remainder, which became a region of East Germany, was divided 1952 into the districts of Frankfurt-an-der-Oder, Potsdam, and Cottbus. When Germany was reunited 1990, Brandenburg reappeared as a state of the Federal Republic.

Brando Marlon 1924– . US actor. His powerful presence, mumbling speech, and use of ◊Method acting earned him a place as a distinctive actor. He won best-actor Academy Awards for *On the Waterfront* 1954 and *The Godfather* 1972.

He made his Broadway debut in *I Remember Mama* 1944, and achieved fame in *A Streetcar Named Desire* 1947. Other films include *The Men* 1950, *Julius Caesar* 1953, *The Wild One* 1954, *Mutiny on the Bounty* 1962, *Last Tango in Paris* 1973, *Apocalypse Now* 1979, *The Freshman* 1990, and *Don Juan De Marco* 1995.

Brandt Bill (Hermann Wilhelm) 1904–1983. English photographer. During the 1930s he made a series of social records contrasting the lives of the rich and the poor, some of which were presented in his book *The English at Home* 1936. During World War II he documented conditions in London in the Blitz. The strong contrasts in his black-and-white prints often produced a gloomy and threatening atmosphere. His outstanding creative work was his treatment of the nude, published in *Perspective of Nudes* and *Shadows of Light*, both 1966.

Brandt Willy. Adopted name of Karl Herbert Frahm 1913–1992. German socialist politician, federal chancellor (premier) of West Germany 1969–74. He played a key role in the remoulding of the Social Democratic Party (SPD) as a moderate socialist force (leader 1964–87). As mayor of West Berlin 1957–66, Brandt became internationally known during the Berlin Wall crisis 1961. He was awarded the Nobel Peace Prize 1971.

In the 'grand coalition' 1966–69, Brandt served as foreign minister and introduced ***Ostpolitik***, a policy of reconciliation between East and West Europe, which was continued when he became federal chancellor 1969 and culminated in the 1972 signing of the Basic Treaty with East Germany. He chaired the Brandt Commission on Third World

Brandt German politician Willy Brandt. A fervent anti-Nazi, he fled Germany before World War II broke out and entered politics when Germany was divided and the Cold War was intense – the Berlin Wall was built when he was mayor of Berlin. He was chancellor of West Germany 1969–74 and later played a major role in the reconstruction of Germany. *Topham*

problems 1977–83 and was a member of the European Parliament 1979–83.

Brandt Commission international committee 1977–83 set up to study global development issues. It produced two reports, stressing the interdependence of the countries of the wealthy, industrialized North and the poor South (or Third World), and made detailed recommendations for accelerating the development of poorer countries (involving the transfer of resources to the latter from the rich countries).

Its main report was published 1980 under the title *North–South: A Programme for Survival*. Both reports noted that measures taken in the past had met with limited success; this was also the fate of the commission's recommendations. The commission was disbanded 1983.

brandy (Dutch ***brandewijn*** 'burnt wine') alcoholic drink distilled from fermented grape juice (wine). The best-known examples are produced in France, notably Armagnac and Cognac. Brandy can also be prepared from other fruits, for example, apples (Calvados) and cherries (Kirschwasser). Brandies contain up to 55% alcohol.

'Claret is the liquor for boys; port for men; but he who aspires to be a hero must drink brandy.'

On BRANDY
Samuel Johnson quoted in Boswell's *Life of Johnson* 1791

Branson Richard 1950– . British entrepreneur whose Virgin company developed quickly, diversifying from retailing records to the airline business.

'Borrow fivers off everyone you meet.'

RICHARD BRANSON
Answer on being asked what is the quickest way to become a millionaire

Braque Georges 1882–1963. French painter. With Picasso, he played a decisive role in the development of Cubism 1907–1910.

Braque was the first to exhibit a Cubist work, at the Salon des Indépendants 1908. The idea behind Cubism led logically to abstraction, a path that Braque pursued without losing a sense of pictorial beauty. In his many still lifes he shows how from some quite simple object, such as a dish of fruit, a whole set of novel relationships and harmonies can be derived. Still active in his last years, he produced a series of studio interiors which are among the finest of his works in their highly original conception of space.

Brasília capital of Brazil from 1960, 1,000 m/3,000 ft above sea level; population (1991) 1,601,100. The main area of employment is in government service

history designed by Lucio Costa, with Oscar Niemeyer as chief architect, as a completely new city to bring life to the interior. The idea of a capital city in the interior was first discussed 1789, but the present site was not chosen until 1956. Inaugurated 1960

features National Congress building; cathedral; Central Square of Three Powers; the University of Brasília, founded 1962; the city is surrounded by an artificial lake.

brass metal ◊alloy of copper and zinc, with not more than 5% or 6% of other metals. The zinc content ranges from 20% to 45%, and the colour of brass varies accordingly from coppery to whitish yellow. Brasses are characterized by the ease with which they may be shaped and machined; they are strong and ductile, resist many forms of corrosion, and are used for electrical fittings, ammunition cases, screws, household fittings, and ornaments.

Brasses are usually classed into those that can be worked cold (up to 25% zinc) and those that are better worked hot (about 40% zinc).

Brassäi adopted name of Gyula Halasz 1899–1984. French photographer of Hungarian origin. He chronicled, mainly by flash, the nightlife of Paris: the prostitutes, street cleaners, and criminals. These pictures were published as *Paris by Night* 1933. Later he turned to more abstract work.

brass instrument any of a class of musical instruments made of brass or other metal, including trumpets, bugles, trombones, and horns. The function of a reed is served by the lips, shaped and tensed by the mouthpiece, acting as a valve releasing periodic pulses of pressurized air into the tube. Orchestral brass instruments are derived from signalling instruments that in their natural or valveless form produce a directionally focused range of tones from the harmonic series by overblowing to as high as the 16th harmonic. They are powerful and efficient generators, and produce tones of great depth and resonance.

In the symphony orchestra the brass instruments are the French horn, trumpet, trombone, and tuba. In the brass band (in descending order of pitch) they comprise the cornet, flugelhorn, tenor horn, B-flat baritone, euphonium, trombone, and bombardon (bass tuba).

Bratislava (German ***Pressburg***) industrial port (engineering, chemicals, oil refining) and capital of the Slovak Republic, on the river Danube; population (1991) 441,500. It was the capital of Hungary 1526–1784 and capital of Slovakia (within Czechoslovakia) until 1993.

Braun Eva 1912–1945. German mistress of Adolf Hitler. Secretary to Hitler's photographer and personal friend, Heinrich Hoffmann, she became Hitler's mistress in the 1930s and married him in the air-raid shelter of the Chancellery in Berlin on 29 April 1945. The next day they committed suicide together.

Braunschweig German form of ◊Brunswick, a city in Lower Saxony, Germany.

Brazil largest country in South America (almost half the continent), bounded SW by Uruguay, Argentina, Paraguay and Bolivia; W by Peru and Colombia; N by Venezuela, Guyana, Surinam, and French Guiana; and NE and SE by the Atlantic Ocean. *See country box opposite.*

Brazzaville capital of the Congo, industrial port (foundries, railway repairs, shipbuilding, shoes, soap, furniture, bricks) on the river Zaïre, opposite Kinshasa; population (1992) 938,000. There is a cathedral 1892 and the Pasteur Institute 1908. It stands on Pool Malebo (Stanley Pool).

Brazzaville was founded by the French count Pierre Savorgnan de Brazza (1852–1905), employed in African expeditions by the French government. It was the African headquarters of the Free (later Fighting) French during World War II.

bread food baked from a kneaded dough or batter made with ground cereals, usually wheat, and water; many other ingredients may be added. The dough may be unleavened or raised (usually with yeast).

Bread has been a staple of human diet in many civilizations as long as agriculture has been practised, and some hunter-gatherer peoples made it from crushed acorns or beech nuts. Potato, banana, and cassava bread are among some local varieties, but most breads are made from fermented cereals which form glutens when mixed with water.

The earliest bread was unleavened and was made from a mixture of flour and water and dried in the sun on flat stones. Leavened bread was first made in the ancient Near East and Egypt in brick ovens similar to ceramic kilns. The yeast creates gas, making the dough rise. Traditionally bread has been made from whole grains: wheat, barley, rye, and oats, ground into a meal which varied in quality. Modern manufacturing processes have changed this to optimize the profit and shorten the manufacturing time. Fermentation is speeded up using ascorbic acid and potassium bromide with fast-acting flour improvers. White bread was developed by the end of the 19th century. Roller-milling, which removed wheat germ, satisfied consumer demand for finer flour, but it removed important fibre and nutrient content at the same time. Today, some of the nutrients removed in the modern processing of bread, such as vitamins, are synthetically replaced.

breadfruit fruit of the tropical trees *Artocarpus communis* and *A. altilis* of the mulberry family Moraceae. It is highly nutritious and when baked is said to taste like bread. It is native to many South Pacific islands.

breadfruit Breadfruit trees, native to Polynesia, are now a familiar sight in many tropical countries around the world, where they have been planted for their large nutritious fruits. When cooked, the fruit has a breadlike texture, hence the name. *Premaphotos Wildlife*

bream deep-bodied, flattened fish *Abramis brama* of the carp family, growing to about 50 cm/1.6 ft, typically found in lowland rivers across Europe.

The sea-breams are also deep-bodied flattened fish, but belong to the family Sparidae, and are unrelated to the true breams. The red sea-bream *Pagellus bogaraveo*, up to 45 cm/1.5 ft, is heavily exploited as a food fish in the Mediterranean.

Bream Julian Alexander 1933– . English guitar and lute virtuoso. He has revived much Elizabethan lute music and encouraged composition by contemporaries for both instruments. Benjamin Britten and Hans Henze have written for him.

breast one of a pair of organs on the chest of the human female, also known as a ◊mammary gland. Each of the two breasts contains milk-producing cells and a network of tubes or ducts that lead to openings in the nipple.

Milk-producing cells in the breast do not become active until a woman has given birth to a baby. Breast milk is made from substances extracted from the mother's blood as it passes through the breasts, and contains all the nourishment a baby needs. Breast-fed newborns develop fewer infections than bottle-fed babies because of the antibodies and white blood cells contained in breast milk. These

breast The human breast or mammary gland. Milk produced in the tissue of the breast after a woman has given birth feeds the baby along ducts which lead to openings in the nipple.

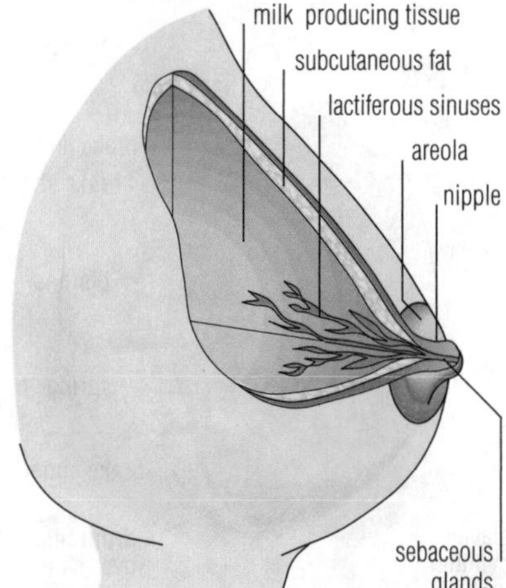

BRAZIL
Federative Republic of

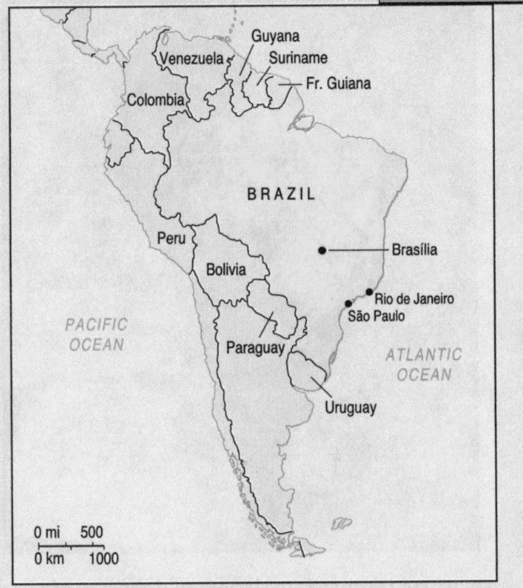

national name *República Federativa do Brasil*
area 8,511,965 sq km/3,285,618 sq mi
capital Brasília
major towns/cities São Paulo, Belo Horizonte, Nova Iguaçu, Curitiba, Manaus, Fortaleza
major ports Rio de Janeiro, Belém, Recife, Pôrto Alegre, Salvador
physical features the densely forested Amazon basin covers the northern half of the country with a network of rivers; the S is fertile; enormous energy resources, both hydroelectric (Itaipú dam on the Paraná, and Tucuruí on the Tocantins) and nuclear (uranium ores); mostly tropical climate
head of state and government Fernando Henrique Cardoso from 1994
political system democratic federal republic
administrative divisions 26 states and one federal district
political parties Workers' Party (PT), left of centre; Social Democratic Party (PSDB), moderate, left of centre; Brazilian Democratic Movement Party (PMDB), centre-left; Liberal Front Party (PFL), right-wing; National Reconstruction Party (PRN), centre-right
armed forces 295,000; public security forces under army control 385,600 (1995)
conscription 12 months
defence spend (% GDP) 1.6 (1994)
education spend (% GNP) 4.6 (1992)
health spend (% GDP) 2.8 (1990)
death penalty for exceptional crimes only; last execution 1855
population 161,087,000 (1996 est)
population growth rate 1.7% (1990–95); 1.4% (2000–05)
age distribution (% of total population) <15 32.3%, 15–65 62.5%, >65 5.2% (1995)
ethnic distribution wide range of ethnic groups, including 55% of European origin (mainly Portuguese, Italian, and German), 38% of mixed parentage, 6% of Black African origin, as well as Native Americans and Japanese
population density (per sq km) 18.3 (1995)
urban population (% of total) 78 (1995)
labour force 44% of population: 23% agriculture, 23% industry, 54% services (1990)
unemployment 4.9% (1993)
child mortality rate (under 5, per 1,000 live births) 61 (1994)
life expectancy 64 (men), 69 (women)
education (compulsory years) 8
literacy rate literacy 83% (men), 80% (women)
languages Portuguese (official); 120 Indian languages
religions Roman Catholic 89%; Indian faiths
TV sets (per 1,000 people) 208 (1992)
currency real
GDP (US $) 554.6 billion (1994)
GDP per capita (PPP) (US $) 5,500 (1993)
growth rate 5.8% (1994)
average annual inflation 26.4% (1995); 2,668.5% (1985–94)
major trading partners USA, Germany, Japan, Iran, the Netherlands, France, Argentina, UK
resources iron ore (world's second-largest producer), tin (world's fourth-largest producer), aluminium (world's fourth-largest producer), gold, phosphates, platinum, bauxite, uranium, manganese, coal, copper, petroleum, natural gas, hydroelectric power, forests
industries mining, steel, machinery and transport equipment, food processing, textiles and clothing, chemicals, petrochemicals, cement, lumber
exports steel products, transport equipment, coffee, iron ore and concentrates, aluminium, iron, tin, soya beans, orange juice (85 % of world's concentrates), tobacco, leather footwear, sugar, beef, textiles. Principal market: USA 20.7% (1993)
imports mineral fuels, machinery and mechanical appliances, chemical products, foodstuffs, coal, wheat, fertilizers, cast iron and steel. Principal source: USA 23.7% (1993)
arable land 4.9% (1993)
agricultural products soya beans, coffee (world's largest producer), tobacco, sugar cane (world's third-largest producer), cocoa beans (world's second-largest producer), maize, rice, cassava, oranges; livestock (beef and poultry)

HISTORY
1500 Originally inhabited by South American Indians, Portuguese explorer Pedro Alvares Cabral sighted and claimed Brazil for Portugal.
1530 Start of Portuguese colonization; Portugal monopolized trade but colonial government was decentralized.
1580–1640 Brazil, with Portugal, under Spanish rule.
17th C Huge sugar-cane plantations established with slave labour; cattle ranching inland.
1695 Discovery of gold in central highlands.
1763 Colonial capital moved from Bahia to Rio de Janeiro.
1770 Brazil's first coffee plantations established in Rio de Janeiro.
18th C Population 1798 totalled 3.3 million, of which around 1.9 million were slaves, mainly of African origin; significant growth of gold mining industry.
19th C Rapid expansion in coffee growing.
1808 Following Napoleon's invasion of Portugal, the Portuguese regent, Prince John, arrived in Brazil and established his court at Rio de Janeiro; Brazilian trade opened to foreign merchants.
1815 United Kingdom of Portugal, Brazil, and Algarve made Brazil co-equal with Portugal and Rio de Janeiro as capital.
1821 Political disorder in Portugal forced King John VI to return to Europe, leaving government of Brazil to his son, Crown Prince Pedro.
1822 Pedro defied orders from Portuguese parliament to return to Portugal; he declared Brazil's independence to avoid reversion to colonial status.
1825 King John VI recognized his son as Emperor Pedro I of Brazil.
1831 Pedro I abdicated in favour of his infant son, Pedro II; regency (to 1840) dominated by Brazilian politicians.
1847 First prime minister appointed, but emperor retained wide-ranging powers.
1865–70 Brazilian efforts to control Uruguay led to War of the Triple Alliance with Paraguay.
1888 Abolition of slavery in Brazil.
1889 Monarch overthrown by liberal revolt; federal republic established with central government controlled by coffee planters; by 1902 Brazil produced 65% of world's coffee.
1915–19 Lack of European imports during World War I led to rapid industrialization, especially in state of São Paulo.
1930 Revolution against planter oligarchy placed Getúlio Vargas in power; he introduced social reforms and economic planning.
1937 Vargas established authoritarian corporate state.
1942 Brazil entered World War II as ally of USA; small fighting force sent to Italy 1944.
1945 Vargas ousted by military coup, but General Eurico Gaspar Dutra soon forced to abandon free-market policies.
1951 Vargas elected president; continued to extend state control of economy.
1954 Vargas committed suicide.
1956–61 Juscelino Kubitschek became president, pursuing measures for rapid economic growth.
1960 Capital moved to Brasília.
1961 Janio Quadros elected president; controversial programme for radical reform; resigned after seven months; succeeded by Vice President João Goulart.
1964 Bloodless coup established technocratic military regime; free political parties abolished; intense concentration on industrial growth aided by foreign investment and loans.
1970s Economic recession and inflation undermined public support for military regime.
1985 After gradual democratization from 1979, Tancredo Neves became first civilian president in 21 years; on Neves's death, Vice President José Sarney took office.
1988 New constitution reduced powers of president.
1989 Fernando Collor (PRN) elected president, promising economic deregulation; Brazil suspended foreign debt payments.
1992 Collor charged with corruption and replaced by Vice President Itamar Franco.
1994 New currency introduced (third in eight years). Fernando Henrique Cardoso (PSDB) elected president. Collor cleared of corruption charges.
1997 Constitution amended to allow president to seek second term of office.
1998 Former president Collor acquitted on charges of illegal enrichment. In Dec, the central bank governor resigned and the currency was devalued.

SEE ALSO Amazon; American Indian; slavery

are particularly abundant in the colostrum, the clear yellowish fluid produced in the first few days of breast-feeding.

Breathalyzer trademark for an instrument for on-the-spot checking by police of the amount of alcohol consumed by a suspect driver. The driver breathes into a plastic bag connected to a tube containing a chemical (such as a diluted solution of potassium dichromate in 50% sulphuric acid) that changes colour in the presence of alcohol. Another method is to use a gas chromatograph, again from a breath sample.

Breath testing was introduced in the UK in 1967. The approved device is now the Lion Intoximeter 3000, which is used by police to indicate the proportion of alcohol in the blood.

breathing rate the number of times a minute the lungs inhale and exhale. The rate increases during exercise because the muscles require an increased supply of oxygen and nutrients. At the same time very active muscles produce a greater volume of carbon dioxide, a waste gas that must be removed by the lungs via the blood.

breccia coarse-grained clastic ◊sedimentary rock, made up of broken fragments (clasts) of pre-existing rocks held together in a fine-grained matrix. It is similar to ◊conglomerate but the fragments in breccia are jagged in shape.

Brecht Bertolt (Eugen Berthold Friedrich) 1898–1956. German dramatist and poet. He was one of the most influential figures in 20th-century theatre. A committed Marxist, he sought to develop an 'epic theatre' which aimed to destroy the 'suspension of disbelief' usual in the theatre and so encourage audiences to develop an active and critical attitude to a play's subject. He adapted John Gay's *The Beggar's Opera* as *Die Dreigroschenoper/The Threepenny Opera* 1928, set to music by Kurt Weill. Later plays include *Mutter Courage und ihre Kinder/Mother Courage and her Children* 1941, set during the Thirty Years' War, and *Der kaukasische Kreidekreis/The Caucasian Chalk Circle* 1945. *See illustration on following page.*

breed recognizable group of domestic animals, within a species, with distinctive characteristics that have been produced by ◊artificial selection.

breeder reactor or ***fast breeder*** alternative names for ◊fast reactor, a type of nuclear reactor.

breeding in biology, the crossing and selection of animals and plants to change the characteristics of an existing ◊breed or ◊cultivar (variety), or to produce a new one.

'Food comes first, then morals.'

Bertolt Brecht
The Threepenny Opera

breeding in nuclear physics, a process in a reactor in which more fissionable material is produced than is consumed in running the reactor.

For example, plutonium-239 can be made from the relatively plentiful (but nonfissile) uranium-238, or uranium-233 can be produced from thorium. The Pu-239 or U-233 can then be used to fuel other reactors. The French breeder reactor Superphénix, one of the most successful, generates 250 megawatts of electrical power.

Brel Jacques 1929–1978. Belgian singer and songwriter. He was active in France from 1953, where his fatalistic ballads made him a star. Of his more than 400 songs, many have been recorded in translation by singers as diverse as Frank Sinatra and David Bowie. 'Ne me quitte pas/If You Go Away' 1964 is one of his best-known songs. Other Brel songs are 'Marieke' 1964, 'Les Moribonds/Seasons in the Sun', 'La Colombe', 'Jackie', and 'Amsterdam'. The album *Brel* 1977 was his last work.

Bremen industrial port in Germany, on the river Weser 69 km/43 mi from the open sea; population (1993) 552,700. Industries include iron, steel, oil refining, chemicals, aircraft, cars, and shipbuilding. The Bremer Vulkan Shipyards closed 1996.

Bremen was a member of the ◊Hanseatic League, and a free imperial city from 1646. It became a member of the North German Confederation 1867 and of the German Empire 1871.

Bremen administrative region (German *Land*) of Germany, consisting of the cities of Bremen and Bremerhaven; area 400 sq km/154 sq mi; population (1994 est) 683,000.

Brenner Sidney 1927– . South African scientist, one of the pioneers of genetic engineering. Brenner discovered messenger ◊RNA (a link between ◊DNA and the ◊ribosomes in which proteins are synthesized) 1960.

Brenner became engaged in one of the most elaborate efforts in anatomy ever attempted: investigating the nervous system of nematode worms and comparing the nervous systems of different mutant forms of the animal. About 100 genes are involved in constructing the nervous system of a nematode and most of the mutations that occur affect the overall design of a section of the nervous system.

Brenner Pass lowest of the Alpine passes, 1,370 m/4,495 ft; it leads from Trentino-Alto Adige, Italy, to the Austrian Tirol, and is 19 km/12 mi long.

Brent outer borough of NW Greater London. It includes the suburbs of Wembley and Willesden
population (1991) 243,000.
features Wembley Stadium (1923); former State Cinema in Willesden (1937), the largest cinema in Europe when built; Brent Cross shopping centre (1976), first regional shopping centre in Europe

Brentano Clemens 1778–1842. German Romantic writer. He published a seminal collection of folk tales and songs with Ludwig von ◊Arnim (*Des Knaben Wunderhorn/The Boy's Magic Horn*) 1805–08, and popularized the legend of the Lorelei (a rock in the river ◊Rhine). He also wrote mystic religious verse, as in *Romanzen von Rosenkranz/Romances of the Rosary* 1852, and short novels.

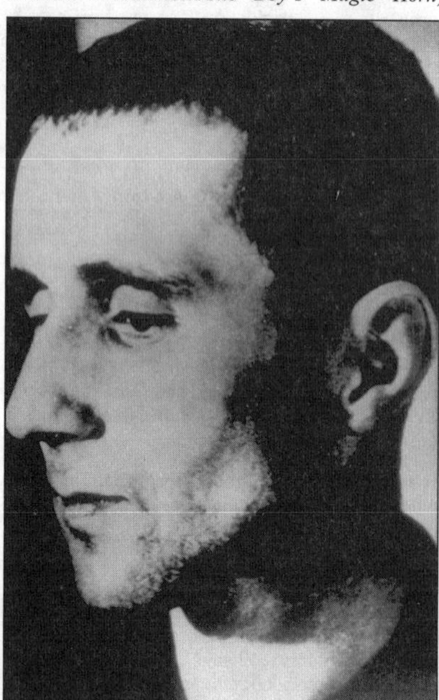

Brecht German playwright and poet Bertolt Brecht who developed drama as a social and ideological forum. Often regarded with suspicion in communist E Europe for his unorthodox theories and in the West for his left-wing politics, he had a great influence on 20th-century theatre, both as a writer and director. *Topham*

Brenton Howard 1942– . English dramatist. His political theatre, deliberately provocative, includes *The Churchill Play* 1974 and *The Romans in Britain* 1980. *Bloody Poetry* 1984 is an examination of the poet Shelley, and he co-wrote *Pravda* 1985 with David Hare and *Gold* 1990 with activist/writer Tariq Ali.

Brescia (ancient ***Brixia***) historic and industrial city (textiles, engineering, firearms, metal products) in N Italy, 84 km/52 mi E of Milan; population (1992) 192,900. It has medieval walls and two cathedrals (12th and 17th century).

Brest city in Belarus, on the river Bug and the Polish frontier; population (1991) 277,000. It was in Poland (***Brześć nad Bugiem***) until 1795 and again 1921–39. In World War I, the Russian truce with Germany, the Treaty of ◊Brest-Litovsk (an older Russian name of the city), was signed here March 1918.

Brest naval base and industrial port (electronics, engineering, chemicals) on ***Rade de Brest*** (Brest Roads), a great bay at the western extremity of Brittany, France; population (1990) 201,500. Occupied as a U-boat base by the Germans 1940–44, the city was destroyed by Allied bombing and rebuilt.

Brest-Litovsk, Treaty of bilateral treaty signed 3 March 1918 between Russia and Germany, Austria–Hungary, and their allies. Under its terms, Russia agreed to recognize the independence of Georgia, Ukraine, Poland, and the Baltic States, and to pay heavy compensation. Under the Nov 1918 Armistice that ended World War I, it was annulled, since Russia was one of the winning allies.

Breton André 1896–1966. French writer and poet. He was among the leaders of the ◊Dada art movement and was also a founder of Surrealism, publishing *Le Manifeste de surréalisme/Surrealist Manifesto* 1924. Influenced by communism and the theories of psychoanalyst Sigmund Freud, he believed that on both a personal and a political level Surrealist techniques could shatter the inhibiting order and propriety of the conscious mind (bourgeois society) and release deep reserves of creative energy.

Breton language member of the Celtic branch of the Indo-European language family; the language of Brittany in France, related to Welsh and Cornish, and descended from the speech of Celts who left Britain as a consequence of the Anglo-Saxon invasions of the 5th and 6th centuries. Officially neglected for centuries, Breton is now a recognized language of France.

Since 1985 Breton has received some encouragement from the central government. The Breton Liberation Movement claims equal status in Brittany for Breton and French.

Bretton Woods township in New Hampshire, USA, where the United Nations Monetary and Financial Conference was held 1944 to discuss postwar international payments problems. The agreements reached on financial assistance and measures to stabilize exchange rates led to the creation of the International Bank for Reconstruction and Development 1945 and the International Monetary Fund (IMF).

Breuer Marcel Lajos 1902–1981. Hungarian-born architect and designer. He studied and taught at the ◊Bauhaus school in Germany. His tubular steel chair 1925 was the first of its kind. He moved to England, then to the USA, where he was in partnership with Walter Gropius 1937–40. His buildings show an affinity with natural materials, as exemplified in the Bijenkorf, Rotterdam, the Netherlands (with Elzas) 1953.

brewing making of beer, ale, or other alcoholic beverage, from ◊malt and ◊barley by steeping (mashing), boiling, and fermenting.

Mashing the barley releases its sugars. Yeast is then added, which contains the enzymes needed to convert the sugars into ethanol (alcohol) and carbon dioxide. Hops are added to give a bitter taste.

Brezhnev Leonid Ilyich 1906–1982. Soviet leader. A protégé of Stalin and Khrushchev, he came to power (after he and ◊Kosygin forced Khrushchev to resign) as general secretary of the Soviet Communist Party (CPSU) 1964–82 and was president 1977–82. Domestically he was conservative; abroad the USSR was established as a military and political superpower during the Brezhnev era, extending its influence in Africa and Asia.

Bretton Woods English diplomat the Earl of Halifax signing the agreement reached at the Bretton Woods Conference 1944. The conference, held in New Hampshire, USA, was an important stage in the economic reconstruction of Europe after World War II. *Corbis*

Brezhnev, born in the Ukraine, joined the CPSU in the 1920s. Stalin inducted Brezhnev into the secretariat and Politburo 1952. Brezhnev was removed from these posts after Stalin's death 1953, but returned 1956. In 1960 Brezhnev was moved to the ceremonial post of state president and began to criticize Khrushchev's policies.

Brezhnev stepped down as president 1963 and returned to the Politburo and secretariat. He was elected CPSU general secretary 1964, when Khrushchev was ousted, and came to dominate the conservative and consensual coalition. In 1977 he regained the additional title of state president under the new constitution. He suffered an illness (thought to have been a stroke or heart attack) March–April 1976 that was believed to have affected his thought and speech severely.

Brian known as ***Brian Boru*** ('Brian of the Tribute') 926–1014. High king of Ireland from 976, who took Munster, Leinster, and Connacht to become ruler of all Ireland. He defeated the Norse at Clontarf, thus ending Norse control of Dublin, although he was himself killed. He was the last high king with jurisdiction over most of Scotland. His exploits were celebrated in several chronicles.

Briand Aristide 1862–1932. French radical socialist politician. He was prime minister 1909–11, 1913, 1915–17, 1921–22, 1925–26 and 1929, and foreign minister 1925–32. In 1925 he concluded the Pact of ◊Locarno (settling Germany's western frontier) and in 1928 the ◊Kellogg–Briand pact renouncing war; in 1930 he outlined a scheme for a United States of Europe.

brick common block-shaped building material, with all opposite sides parallel. It is made of clay that has been fired in a kiln. Bricks are made by kneading a mixture of crushed clay and other materials into a stiff mud and extruding it into a ribbon. The ribbon is cut into individual bricks, which are fired at a temperature of up to about 1,000°C/1,800°F. Bricks may alternatively be pressed into shape in moulds.

Sun-dried bricks of mud reinforced with straw were first used in Mesopotamia some 8,000 years ago. Similar mud bricks, called adobe, are still used today in Mexico and other areas where the climate is warm and dry.

brickwork method of construction using bricks made of fired clay or sun-dried earth (see ◊adobe).

In wall building, bricks are either laid out as stretchers (long side facing out) or as headers (short side facing out). The two principle patterns of brickwork are ***English bond*** in which alternate courses, or layers, are made up of stretchers or headers only, and ***Flemish bond*** in which stretchers and headers alternate within courses.

Some evidence exists of the use of fired bricks in ancient Mesopotamia and Egypt, although the Romans were the first to make extensive use of this technology. Today's mass-production of fired bricks tends to be concentrated in temperate regions where there are plentiful supplies of fuel available.

bridewealth or ***brideprice*** goods or property presented by a man's family to his prospective wife's as part of the marriage agreement. It was the usual practice among many societies in Africa, Asia, and the Pacific, and among many Native American groups. In most European and S Asian countries the alternative custom was ◊dowry.

Bridewealth is regarded as compensation to the woman's family for giving her away in marriage, and it usually means that the children she bears will belong to her husband's family group rather than her own. It may require a large amount of valuables such as livestock, shell items, or cash.

bridge structure that provides a continuous path or road over water, valleys, ravines, or above other roads. The basic designs and composites of these are based on the way they bear the weight of the structure and its load.

Beam, or ***girder***, bridges are supported at each end by the ground with the weight thrusting downwards. ***Cantilever*** bridges are a complex form of girder. ***Arch*** bridges thrust outwards but downwards at their ends; they are in compression. ***Suspension*** bridges use cables under tension to pull inwards against anchorages on either side of the span, so that the roadway hangs from the main cables by the network of vertical cables. The ***cable-stayed*** bridge relies on diagonal cables connected directly between the bridge deck and supporting towers at each end. Some bridges are too low to allow traffic to pass beneath easily, so they are designed with movable parts, like swing and draw bridges.

history In prehistory, people used logs or wove vines into ropes that were thrown across the obstacle. By 4000 BC arched structures of stone and/or brick were used in the Middle East, and the Romans built long arched spans, many of which are still standing. Wooden bridges proved vulnerable to fire and rot and many were replaced with cast and wrought iron, but these were disadvantaged by low tensile strength. The ◊Bessemer process produced steel that made it possible to build long-lived framed structures that support great weight over long spans.

Examples of the main types of bridges

beam or girder The Rio-Niteroi bridge, Guanabara Bay, Brazil, is the longest continuous box and plate girder bridge, with a centre span 300 m/984 ft; length 13,900 m/8 mi 3,380 ft.

cantilever Forth Rail Bridge, Scotland, 1,658 m/5,440 ft long with two main spans, two cantilevers each, one from each tower.

arch Sydney Harbour Bridge, Australia, a steel arch with a span of 503 m/1,650 ft.

suspension Humber Bridge, England, with a centre span of 1,410 m/4,628 ft.

cable-stayed Dartford Bridge, 30 km/19 mi downstream of central London, main span 450 m/1,476 ft. The longest cable-stayed bridge is the 2,200 m/7,216 ft Pont de Normandie bridge over the Seine estuary in France, completed 1995.

The single-span bridge designed to cross the Messina Straits between Sicily and the mainland of Italy will be 3,320 m/10,892 ft long, the world's largest by far. Steel is pre-eminent in the construction of long-span bridges because of its high strength-to-weight ratio, but in other circumstances reinforced concrete has the advantage of lower maintenance costs.

The Newport Transporter Bridge, Wales (1906) is a high-level suspension bridge which carries a car suspended a few feet above the water. It was used in preference to a conventional bridge where expensive high approach roads would have to be built.

bridge card game derived from whist. First played among members of the Indian Civil Service about 1900, bridge was brought to England 1903 and played at the Portland Club 1908. It is played in two forms: ◊auction bridge and ◊contract bridge.

Bridgend unitary authority of Wales created 1996 (*see United Kingdom map*).

Bridges Robert Seymour 1844–1930. English poet and critic. He was poet laureate 1913–30. His topographical poems and lyrics, which he began to publish 1873, demonstrate a great command of rhythm and melody. He wrote *The Testament of Beauty* 1929, a long philosophical poem. In 1918 he edited and published posthumously the poems of Gerard Manley ◊Hopkins.

Sensitivity to the influence of the English countryside and history characterized Bridges's work. His *Collected Poems* 1912 were widely acclaimed and enlarged editions followed 1936 and 1953.

Bridgetown port and capital of Barbados; population (1990) 6,700. Sugar is exported through the nearby deep-water port. Bridgetown was founded 1628.

Bridget, St 453–523. A patron saint of Ireland, also known as ***St Brigit*** or ***St Bride***. She founded a church and monastery at Kildare, and is said to have been the daughter of a prince of Ulster. Feast day 1 Feb.

Bridgewater Francis Egerton, 3rd Duke of Bridgewater 1736–1803. Pioneer of British inland navigation. With James Brindley (1716–1772) as his engineer, he constructed 1762–72 the Bridgewater canal from Worsley to Manchester and on to the Mersey, a distance of 67.5 km/42 mi. Initially built to carry coal, the canal crosses the Irwell Valley on an aqueduct.

brigade military formation consisting of a minimum of two battalions, but more usually three or more, as well as supporting arms. There are typically about 5,000 soldiers in a brigade, which is commanded by a brigadier. Two or more brigades form a ◊division.

An infantry brigade is one that contains more infantry than armour; it is said to be 'infantry-heavy'. A typical armoured brigade ('armour-heavy') consists of two armoured battalions and one infantry battalion supported by an artillery battalion and a field-engineer battalion as well as other logistic support.

Bright John 1811–1889. British Liberal politician. He was a campaigner for free trade, peace, and social reform. A Quaker millowner, he was among the founders of the Anti-Corn Law League 1839, and was largely instrumental in securing the passage of the Reform Bill of 1867.

Bright Richard 1789–1858. British physician who described many conditions and linked ◊oedema to kidney disease. Bright's disease, an acute inflammation of the kidneys (see ◊nephritis), is named after him.

Brighton seaside resort on the E Sussex coast, England, and administrative headquarters of Brighton and Hove unitary authority; population (1991) 143,600. It has Regency architecture and the Royal Pavilion 1782 in Oriental style. There are two piers and an aquarium.

Originally a fishing village called Brighthelmstone, it became known as Brighton at the beginning of the 19th century, when it was already a fashionable health resort patronized by the Prince Regent, afterwards George IV. In 1990 the Royal Pavilion reopened after nine years of restoration.

Brighton and Hove unitary authority of England (*see United Kingdom map*).

brill flatfish *Scophthalmus laevis*, living in shallow water over sandy bottoms in the NE Atlantic and Mediterranean. It is a freckled sandy brown, and grows to 60 cm/2 ft.

Brillat-Savarin Jean Anthelme 1755–1826. French gastronome, author of *La Physiologie du Goût*/*The Physiology of Taste* 1825, a compilation of observations on food and drink regarded as the first great classic of gastronomic literature. Most of his professional life was spent as a politician.

brine common name for a solution of sodium chloride (NaCl) in water. Brines are used extensively in the food-manufacturing industry for canning vegetables, pickling vegetables (sauerkraut manufacture), and curing meat. Industrially, brine is the source from which chlorine, caustic soda (sodium hydroxide), and sodium carbonate are made.

Brisbane industrial port (brewing, engineering, tanning, tobacco, shoes; oil pipeline from Moonie), capital of Queensland, E Australia, near the mouth of Brisbane River, dredged to carry ocean-going ships; population (1993) 1,421,600.

Brisbane Thomas Makdougall 1773–1860. Scottish soldier, colonial administrator, and astronomer. After serving in the Napoleonic Wars under Wellington, he was governor of New South Wales 1821–25. Brisbane in Queensland is named after him. He catalogued over 7,000 stars.

bristlecone pine the oldest living species of ◊pine.

bristletail primitive wingless insect of the order Thysanura. Up to 2 cm/0.8 in long, bristletails have a body tapering from front to back, two long antennae, and three 'tails' at the rear end. They include the silverfish *Lepisma saccharina* and the firebrat *Thermobia domestica*. Two-tailed bristletails constitute another insect order, the Diplura. They live under stones and fallen branches, feeding on decaying material.

'Force is not a remedy.'

JOHN BRIGHT
Speech in Birmingham 1880

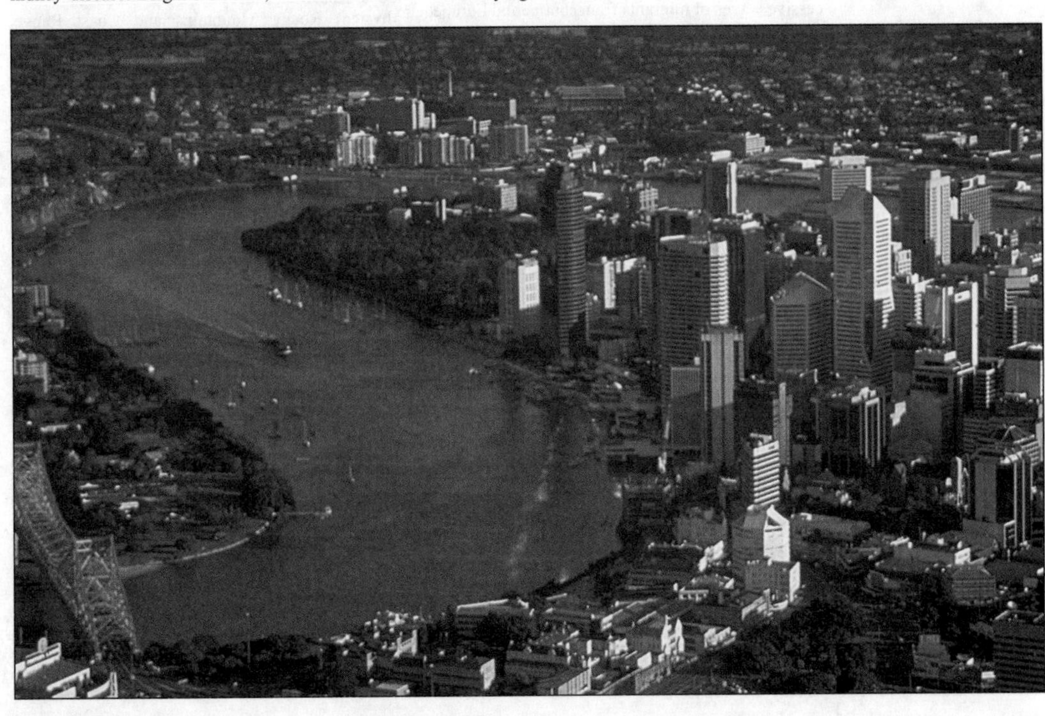

Brisbane The third largest city in Australia, Brisbane is the state capital of Queensland. Built around a bend in the Brisbane River, it was first settled as a penal colony 1824 and opened to colonists 1842. Much of the city was destroyed by fire 1864. *Australian Overseas Information Office*

❝In the middle of the street, as far as you can see, hundreds of Ships, their Masts as thick as they can stand by one another, which is the oddest and most surprising sight imaginable.❞

On Bristol
Alexander Pope, letter to Martha Blount 19 Nov 1739

Bristol industrial port in SW England and unitary authority created 1996; also administrative headquarters of Bath and North East Somerset unitary authority. The old docks have been redeveloped for housing, industry, yachting facilities, and the National Lifeboat Museum. Further developments include a new city centre, with Brunel's Temple Meads railway station at its focus, and a weir across the Avon nearby to improve the waterside environment
population (1991) 376,100
industries aircraft engines, engineering, microelectronics, tobacco, chemicals, paper, printing, soap, metal refining, chocolate, banking, and insurance
features 12th-century cathedral; 14th-century St Mary Redcliffe; 16th-century Acton Court, built by Sir Nicholas Poynz, a courtier of Henry VIII; Georgian residential area of Clifton; the Clifton Suspension Bridge (completed 1864) designed by Brunel, and his *SS Great Britain*, which is being restored in dry dock
history John Cabot sailed from here 1497 to Newfoundland, and there was a great trade with the American colonies and the West Indies in the 17th–18th centuries, including slaves. The poet Thomas Chatterton was born here.

Britain island off the NW coast of Europe, one of the British Isles. It comprises England, Scotland, and Wales (together officially known as ◊Great Britain), and is part of the ◊United Kingdom. The name is derived from the Roman name Britannia, which in turn is derived from the ancient Celtic name of the inhabitants, *Bryttas*.

Britain, ancient period in the British Isles (excluding Ireland) extending through prehistory to the Roman occupation (1st century AD). Settled agricultural life evolved in Britain during the 3rd millennium BC. Neolithic society reached its peak in southern England, where it was capable of producing the great stone circles of Avebury and Stonehenge early in the 2nd millennium BC. It was succeeded in central southern Britain by the Early Bronze Age Wessex culture, with strong trade links across Europe. The Iron Age culture of the Celts was predominant in the last few centuries BC, and the ◊Belgae (of mixed Germanic and Celtic stock) were partially Romanized in the century between the first Roman invasion of Britain under Julius Caesar (54 BC) and the Roman conquest (AD 43). For later history, see ◊Roman Britain; ◊United Kingdom.

At the end of the last Ice Age, Britain had a cave-dwelling population of Palaeolithic hunter-gatherers, whose culture was called Creswellian, after Creswell Crags, Derbyshire, where remains of flint tools were found. Throughout prehistory successive waves of migrants from continental Europe accelerated or introduced cultural innovations. Important Neolithic remains include: the stone houses of Skara Brae, Orkney; so-called causewayed camps in which hilltops such as Windmill Hill, Wiltshire, were enclosed by concentric fortifications of ditches and banks; the first stages of the construction of the ritual monuments known as henges (for example, Stonehenge, Woodhenge); and the flint mines at Grimes Graves, Norfolk. Burial of the dead was in elongated earth mounds (long barrows).

The ◊Beaker people probably introduced copper working to the British Isles. The aristocratic society of the Bronze Age Wessex culture of southern England is characterized by its circular burial mounds (round barrows); the dead were either buried or cremated, and cremated remains were placed in pottery urns. Later invaders were the ◊Celts, a warrior aristocracy with an Iron Age technology; they introduced horse-drawn chariots, had their own distinctive art forms (see ◊Celtic art), and occupied fortified hilltops. The Belgae, who buried the ashes of their dead in richly furnished flat graves, were responsible for the earliest British sites large and complex enough to be called towns; settled in southern Britain, the Belgae resisted the Romans from centres such as Maiden Castle, Dorset. ▷ *See feature on pp. 200–201.*

❝Never in the field of human conflict was so much owed by so many to so few.❞

Of the British aircrews at the Battle of Britain
Winston Churchill 20 Aug 1940

Britain, Battle of World War II air battle between German and British air forces over Britain 10 July–31 Oct 1940.

At the outset the Germans had the advantage because they had seized airfields in the Netherlands, Belgium, and France, which were basically safe from attack and from which SE England was within easy range. On 1 Aug 1940 the Luftwaffe had about 4,500 aircraft of all kinds, compared to about 3,000 for the RAF. The Battle of Britain had been intended as a preliminary to the German invasion plan *Seelöwe* (Sea Lion), which Hitler indefinitely postponed 17 Sept and abandoned 10 Oct, choosing instead to invade the USSR.

The main battle was between some 600 Hurricanes and Spitfires and the Luftwaffe's 800 Messerschmitt 109s and 1,000 bombers (Dornier 17s, Heinkel 111s, and Junkers 88s). Losses Aug–Sept were, for the RAF: 832 fighters totally destroyed; for the Luftwaffe: 668 fighters and some 700 bombers and other aircraft.

British Academy of Film and Television Arts see ◊BAFTA, ◊cinema.

British Antarctic Territory British dependent territory created 1962 and comprising all British territories south of latitude 60° S and between 20° and 80° W longitude: the South Orkney Islands, the South Shetland Islands, the Antarctic Peninsula and all adjacent lands, and Coats Land, extending to the South Pole; total land area 1,810,000 sq km/700,000 sq mi; population (exclusively scientific personnel) about 300.

British Broadcasting Corporation (BBC) the UK state-owned broadcasting network. It operates television and national and local radio stations, and is financed by the sale of television viewing licences; it is not allowed to carry advertisements but it has an additional source of income through its publishing interests and the sales of its programmes. Overseas radio broadcasts (World Service) have a government subsidy.

The World Service broadcasts in 42 languages, including English. Listeners increased from 130 million a week 1990 to 133 million 1996. Countries that have attempted to ban the World Service include the USSR, which jammed the airwaves for 24 years during the Cold War, and finally allowed BBC broadcasts to filter through Jan 1988. Since then Libya, Iran, and China have all attempted to stifle BBC transmissions.

The BBC was converted from a private company (established 1922) to a public body under royal charter 1927. Under the Charter, news programmes were required to be politically impartial. The first director-general 1922–1938 was John Reith.

British Columbia province of Canada on the Pacific Ocean
area 947,800 sq km/365,851 sq mi
capital Victoria
towns and cities Vancouver, Prince George, Kamloops, Kelowna, Surrey
physical Rocky Mountains and Coast Range; deeply indented coast; rivers include the Fraser and Columbia; over 80 lakes; more than half the land is forested
industries fruit and vegetables; timber and wood products; fish; coal, copper, iron, lead; oil and natural gas; hydroelectricity
population (1991) 3,185,900
history Captain Cook explored the coast 1778; a British colony was founded on Vancouver Island 1849, and the gold rush of 1858 extended settlement to the mainland; it became a province 1871. In 1885 the Canadian Pacific Railroad linking British Columbia to the east coast was completed.

British Columbia

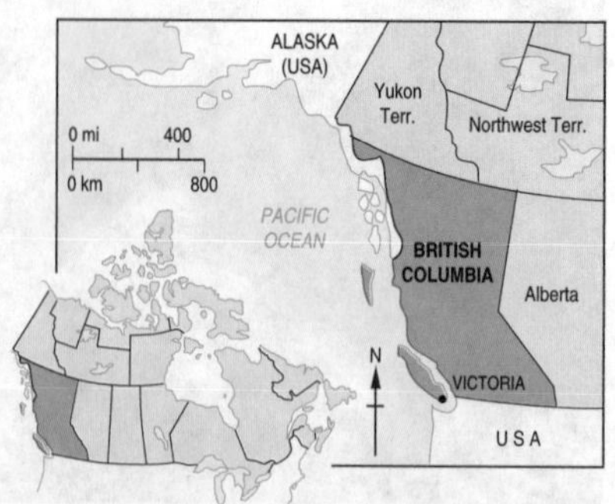

British Council semi-official organization set up 1935 (royal charter 1940) to promote a wider knowledge of the UK, excluding politics and commerce, and to develop cultural relations with other countries.

British Empire various territories conquered or colonized by Britain from about 1600, most now independent or ruled by other powers; the British Empire was at its largest at the end of World War I, consisting of over 25% of the world's population and area. The ◊Commonwealth is composed of former and remaining territories of the British Empire.

The British Empire lasted more than three and a half centuries – almost as long as the Roman Empire. By the time the British began colonizing overseas, the Portuguese and Spaniards had already divided a considerable part of the Earth's land surface between them.

The Empire grew comparatively quickly, initially with acquisitions in North America and India, as well as some marginal settlement in Africa, in the 17th and 18th centuries.

The 19th century saw the largest expansion of the Empire as the British took many former French possessions in the West Indies and began to settle in large numbers in Australia in the early part of the century and later competed fiercely with other European powers for territory in Africa. At the same time, there was serious expansion in Asia, notably the acquisition of Singapore 1824, Hong Kong 1841, and Burma 1886, and the South Pacific, particularly the settlement of New Zealand 1840. The only serious loss of territory was the loss of the 13 American colonies in the ◊American Revolution 1776.

The Empire faded gradually into the Commonwealth from the 1930s onwards as one by one former British colonies and protectorates gained independence but retained this last link with the crown.
building the Empire The first successful British colony was Jamestown, Virginia, founded 1607, although there was an earlier settlement at Newfoundland 1583. Settlements were made in Gambia and on the Gold Coast of Africa 1618; in Bermuda 1609 and other islands of the West Indies; Jamaica was taken from Spain 1655; in Canada, Acadia (Nova Scotia) was secured from France by the Treaty of Utrecht 1713, which recognized Newfoundland and Hudson Bay (as well as Gibraltar in Europe) as British. New France (Quebec), Cape Breton Island, and Prince Edward Island became British as a result of the Seven Years' War 1756–63.
West Indies Between 1623 and 1632 English settlers occupied St Kitts, Barbados, St Croix (later lost), Nevis, Antigua, and Montserrat. Cromwell's forces took Jamaica from the Spaniards 1655, although it was not officially ceded until 1760, and the tiny Atlantic island of St Helena was annexed 1673. Belize (British Honduras) was governed as part of Jamaica until 1884.
North America Following the early settlement in Virginia, British colonies spread up and down the east coast of North America and by 1664, when the British secured New Amsterdam (New York) from the Dutch, there was a continuous fringe of colonies from the present South Carolina in the south to what is now New Hampshire. The attempt of George III and his minister Lord North to coerce the colonists into paying special taxes to Britain roused them to resistance, which came to a head in the ◊American Revolution 1775–81 and led to the creation of the United States of America from the 13 English colonies then lost.

Constitutional development in Canada started with an act of 1791 which set up Lower Canada (Quebec), mainly French-speaking, and Upper Canada (Ontario), mainly English-speaking.

In the War of 1812, the USA wrongly assumed that Canada would join the union. But there was sufficient discontent there to lead to rebellion 1837 in both Canadas. After the suppression of these risings, the two Canadas were united 1840 and given a representative legislative council: the beginning of colonial self-government. With the British North America Act 1867, the self-governing dominion of Canada came into existence; to the original union of Ontario, Quebec, New Brunswick, and Nova Scotia were later added further territories until the federal government of Canada controlled all the northern part of the continent except Alaska.

India India was at the heart of the British Empire but it was initially controlled by the ◊East India Company. This huge company, chartered 1600, set up a number of factories, as their trading posts were called, and steadily increased its possessions and the territories over which it held treaty rights until its power extended from Aden in Arabia to Penang in Malaya. The East India Company was the most powerful private company in history, controlling India partly by direct rule and partly by a system of alliances with Indian princes, maintained by the Company's powerful army. The company's political power was ended by the ◊Indian Mutiny 1857. Although this revolt was put down, it resulted in the crown taking over the government of India 1858; Queen Victoria was proclaimed empress of India 1 Jan 1877. British India gained independence as the two dominions of India and Pakistan 1947.

East Asia Ceylon (now Sri Lanka) was annexed to the East India Company 1796. When the British government took over from the company it also acquired the ◊Straits Settlements and by 1914 all Malaya was under British control. Britain gained Hong Kong as a result of the ◊Opium Wars 1839–42 and Kowloon was added to the colony after a second Opium War (1856–58).

Burma became a province of British India 1886. In Borneo, Sarawak was ruled as a personal possession by James Brooke, a former soldier of the East India Company, and the British North Borneo Company acquired Sabah 1888. The sultanate of Brunei, which had formerly possessed Sarawak and Sabah, itself came under British protection in the same year. Burma and Ceylon became independent 1948 and the republic of Sri Lanka dates from 1972.

Australia In Australia, colonization began with the desire to find a place for penal settlement after the loss of the original American colonies. The first shipload of British convicts landed in Australia 1788 on the site of the future city of Sydney. New South Wales was opened to free settlers 1819, and in 1853 transportation of convicts was abolished. Before the end of the century five Australian colonies – New South Wales, Western Australia, South Australia, Victoria, Queensland – and the island colony of Tasmania had each achieved self-government; the federal commonwealth of Australia, an independent dominion, was created 1901. New Zealand, annexed 1840, was at first a dependency of New South Wales. It became a separate colony 1853 and a dominion 1907.

Southern Africa The Cape of Good Hope in South Africa was occupied by two English captains 1620, but the Dutch occupied it 1650 until 1795 when the British seized it to keep it from the French. Under the Treaty of Paris 1814, the UK bought Cape Town from the new kingdom of the Netherlands for $6 million. British settlement began 1824 on the coast of Natal, proclaimed a British colony 1843.

The need to find new farmland and establish independence from British rule led a body of Boers (Dutch 'farmers') from the Cape to make the Great Trek northeast 1836, to found Transvaal and Orange Free State. Conflict between the British government and the Boers culminated, after the discovery of gold in the Boer territories, in the South African War 1899–1902, which brought Transvaal and Orange Free State definitely under British sovereignty. Given self-government 1907, they were formed, with Cape Colony (self-governing 1872) and Natal (self-governing 1893), into the Union of South Africa 1910.

Cecil Rhodes's British South Africa Company, chartered 1889, extended British influence over Southern Rhodesia (a colony 1923) and Northern Rhodesia (a protectorate 1924); with Nyasaland, taken under British protection 1891, the Rhodesias were formed into a federation 1953–63 with representative government. Uganda was made a British protectorate 1894. Kenya, formerly a protectorate, became a colony 1920, but certain districts on the coast forming part of the sultan of Zanzibar's dominions remained a protectorate.

West Africa The British showed little interest in Africa outside the Cape until the scramble for territory of the 1880s, although a few forts were kept in West Africa, where gold and ivory remained important after the slave trade was ended by Britain 1807. An early exception was the colony of Sierra Leone founded 1788. British influence in Nigeria began through the activities of the National Africa Company (the Royal Niger Company from 1886), which bought Lagos from an African chief 1861 and steadily extended its hold over the Niger Valley until it surrendered its charter 1899; in 1900 the two protectorates of North and South Nigeria were proclaimed. In 1921–22, under a League of Nations mandate, Tanganyika was transferred to British administration, and SW Africa to South Africa; the Cameroons and Togoland, in West Africa, were divided between Britain and France.

East Africa Private companies under charter from the British government established their control over Kenya 1888 and Uganda 1890. Northern Somalia came under direct control of the British government 1884 and in 1890 Germany, which had already relinquished its interests in Uganda, ceded Zanzibar to Britain in exchange for Heligoland, an island off the German coast.

dominion status The concept of self-government for some of the colonies was first formulated in Lord Durham's 'Report on the Affairs of British North America' 1839 which recommended that responsible government (the acceptance by governors of the advice of local ministers) should be granted to Upper Canada (Ontario) and Lower Canada (Quebec). This pattern was subsequently applied to the other Canadian provinces and to the Australian colonies by 1859, except for Western Australia (1890). New Zealand obtained responsible government 1856 and the Cape colony 1872, followed by Natal 1893. A further intermediate form of government, dominion status, was devised in the late 19th and early 20th century at a series of Colonial Conferences (renamed Imperial Conferences 1907). Canada became a dominion 1867, Australia 1901, New Zealand 1907, and South Africa by 1910. These four self-governing countries were known as Dominions within the British Empire. Dominion status was very inexactly defined until the Statute of Westminster 1931 established it as synonymous with complete independence.

decline The first fatal challenge to the Empire came from Ireland, where the British Empire began when Henry II declared himself 'Lord of Ireland' 1171. After 750 years of English rule, most of Ireland became the Irish Free State 1922. The Free State had dominion status but only after centuries of hatred culminating in civil war. A new constitution adopted by the Free State 1937 dropped the name Irish Free State and declared Ireland (Eire) to be a 'sovereign independent state'. The break was completed 1949 when Eire became a republic outside the Commonwealth.

There were varying degrees of unrest throughout much of the Empire during the 1930s, notably in India, where Mahatma Gandhi led a campaign of 'civil disobedience' against British rule. World War II (1939–45) hastened the end of the former colonial empires. India gained complete independence 1947–48; Sudan, Ghana, and Malaya in the 1950s, and much of the rest of Africa in the 1960s. By 1970 the former British colonies in the West Indies were either independent or linked to Britain as associated states only by their own choice. Rhodesia declared itself independent 1965, but Britain declared its action illegal, and no other state recognized it.

By 1973, when Britain entered the European Economic Community (now European Union), only a few small possessions remained. Some did not want to end their colonial status. Gibraltar and Hong Kong, for example, felt they risked absorption by Spain and China respectively if Britain withdrew. However, the British Empire as a whole largely faded away, to be replaced by the Commonwealth of Nations. *See features on pp. 32–33, pp. 432–433, pp. 982–983.*

BRITISH EMPIRE

Current name	Colonial names and history	Colonized	Independent
India	British East India Company	18th C–1858	1947
Pakistan	British East India Company	18th C–1858	1947
Myanmar	Burma	1866	1948
Sri Lanka	Portuguese, Dutch 1602–1796; Ceylon 1802–1972	16th C	1948
Ghana	Gold Coast; British Togoland integrated 1956	1618	1957
Nigeria		1861	1960
Cyprus	Turkish to 1878, then British rule	1878	1960
Sierra Leone	British protectorate	1788	1961
Tanzania	German E Africa to 1921; British mandate from League of Nations/UN as Tanganyika	19th C	1961
Jamaica	Spanish to 1655	16th C	1962
Trinidad & Tobago	Spanish 1532–1797; British 1797–1962	1532	1962
Uganda	British protectorate	1894	1962
Kenya	British colony from 1920	1895	1963
Malaysia	British interests from 1786; Federation of Malaya 1957–63	1874	1963
Malawi	British protectorate of Nyasaland 1907–53; Federation of Rhodesia & Nyasaland 1953–64	1891	1964
Malta	French 1798–1814	1798	1964
Zambia	N Rhodesia – British protectorate; Federation of Rhodesia & Nyasaland 1953–64	1924	1964
The Gambia		1888	1965
Singapore	Federation of Malaya 1963–65	1858	1965
Guyana	Dutch to 1796; British Guiana 1796–1966	1620	1966
Botswana	Bechuanaland – British protectorate	1885	1966
Lesotho	Basutoland	1868	1966
Bangladesh	British East India Company 18th century–1858; British India 1858–1947; E Pakistan 1947–71	18th C	1971
Zimbabwe	S Rhodesia from 1923; UDI under Ian Smith 1965–79	1895	1980
Belize	British Honduras	17th C	1981

British Expeditionary Force (BEF) British army serving in France in World War I 1914–18. Also the 1939–40 army in Europe in World War II, which was evacuated from Dunkirk, France.

In World War I the BEF was first commanded by General J French and then General D Haig. The term 'BEF' strictly referred only to the forces intially sent to France in 1914, but it continued to be commonly applied to the British forces operating in France and Flanders.

In World War II General Gort commanded the BEF sent to France in 1939. After sustaining heavy losses during the French and Belgian campaigns of 1940 the remains were evacuated from Dunkirk in June, leaving much of their equipment behind.

British Film Institute (BFI) organization, founded 1933, to promote the cinema as a 'means of entertainment and instruction.' It includes the National Film Archive (1935) and the National Film Theatre (1951), and is involved in publishing books

Britten The composer Benjamin Britten pictured with his lifelong companion, the tenor Peter Pears. An essentially vocal composer, Britten left his mark on all such genres, especially opera: he is sometimes considered the greatest composer for the stage in the 20th century. *Image Select (UK) Ltd*

and periodicals, as well as in providing funding for film distribution and exhibition in Britain.

British Honduras former name (to 1973) of ◊Belize.

British Indian Ocean Territory British colony in the Indian Ocean directly administered by the Foreign and Commonwealth Office. It consists of the Chagos Archipelago some 1,900 km/1,200 mi NE of Mauritius
area 60 sq km/23 sq mi
features lagoons; US naval and air base on Diego Garcia
industries copra, salt fish, tortoiseshell
population there is no permanent population
history purchased 1965 for $3 million by Britain from Mauritius to provide a joint US/UK base. The islands of Aldabra, Farquhar, and Desroches, some 485 km/300 mi N of Madagascar, originally formed part of the British Indian Ocean Territory but were returned to the administration of the Seychelles 1976.

British Isles group of islands off the northwest coast of Europe, consisting of Great Britain (England, Wales, and Scotland), Ireland, the Channel Islands, the Orkney and Shetland islands, the Isle of Man, and many other islands that are included in various counties, such as the Isle of Wight, Scilly Isles, Lundy Island, and the Inner and Outer Hebrides. The islands are divided from Europe by the North Sea, Strait of Dover, and the English Channel, and face the Atlantic to the west.

British Legion organization to promote the welfare of British veterans of war service and their dependants. Established under the leadership of Douglas Haig in 1921 (royal charter 1925) it became the Royal British Legion 1971; it is nonpolitical.

British Library national library of the UK. It was announced in 1978 by the then secretary of state for education, Shirley Williams, and building work began in 1982. It was completed in Dec 1996, and was expected to be fully open to the public in 1999.

The library comprises the reference division (the former library departments of the British Museum, rehoused in Euston Road, St Pancras, London); lending division at Boston Spa, Yorkshire, from which full text documents and graphics can be sent by satellite link to other countries; bibliographic services division (incorporating the British National Bibliography); and the National Sound Archive in South Kensington, London.

The new library at St Pancras will store 12 million volumes, accommodate 1,200 readers, and includes a conference centre and exhibition facilities.

British Museum largest museum of the UK. Founded in 1753, it opened in London in 1759. Rapid additions led to the construction of the present buildings (1823–47). In 1881 the Natural History Museum was transferred to South Kensington.

The museum began with the purchase of Hans Sloane's library and art collection, and the subsequent acquisition of the Cottonian, Harleian, and other libraries. It was first housed at Montagu House in Bloomsbury. Its present buildings were designed by Robert Smirke, with later extensions in the circular reading room 1857, and the north wing or Edward VII galleries 1914.

British Petroleum (BP) one of the world's largest oil concerns and Britain's largest company, with more than 128,000 employees in 70 countries. It was formed as the Anglo-Persian Oil Company 1909 and acquired the chemical interests of the Distillers Company 1967.

In 1917 British Petroleum was established as a marketing subsidiary of the Anglo-Persian Oil Company (from 1935 the Anglo-Iranian Oil Company), and the latter was renamed the British Petroleum Company 1954.

British Somaliland British protectorate comprising over 176,000 sq km/67,980 sq mi of territory on the Somali coast of E Africa from 1884 until the independence of Somalia 1960.

British Standards Institute (BSI) UK national standards body. Although government funded, the institute is independent. The BSI interprets international technical standards for the UK, and also sets its own.

For consumer goods, it sets standards which products should reach (the BS standard), as well as testing products to see that they conform to that standard (as a result of which the product may be given the BSI 'kite' mark).

British thermal unit imperial unit (symbol Btu) of heat, now replaced in the SI system by the ◊joule (one British thermal unit is approximately 1,055 joules). Burning one cubic foot of natural gas releases about 1,000 Btu of heat.

One British thermal unit is defined as the amount of heat required to raise the temperature of 0.45 kg/1 lb of water by 1°F. The exact value depends on the original temperature of the water.

British Virgin Islands part of the ◊Virgin Islands group in the West Indies.

Brittain Vera (Mary) 1893–1970. English socialist writer. She was a nurse to the troops overseas 1915–19, as told in her *Testament of Youth* 1933; *Testament of Friendship* 1940 commemorates English novelist Winifred Holtby (1898–1935).

Brittan Leon 1939– . British Conservative politician and lawyer. Chief secretary to the Treasury 1981–83, home secretary 1983–85, secretary for trade and industry 1985–86, and senior European commissioner from 1988. He later became vice president of the European Commission.

Brittany (French *Bretagne*, Breton ***Breiz***) region of NW France in the Breton peninsula between the Bay of Biscay and the English Channel; area 27,200 sq km/10,499 sq mi; capital Rennes; population (1990) 2,795,600. A farming region, it includes the *départements* of Côtes-d'Armor, Finistère, Ille-et-Vilaine, and Morbihan.
history Brittany was the Gallo-Roman province of Armorica after being conquered by Julius Caesar 56 BC. It was devastated by Norsemen after the Roman withdrawal. Established under the name of Brittany in the 5th century AD by Celts fleeing the Anglo-Saxon invasion of Britain, it became a strong, expansionist state that maintained its cultural and political independence, despite pressure from the Carolingians, Normans, and Capetians. In 1171, the duchy of Brittany was inherited by Geoffrey, son of Henry II of England, and remained in the Angevin dynasty's possession until 1203, when Geoffrey's son Arthur was murdered by King ◊John, and the title passed to the Capetian Peter of Dreux. Under the Angevins, feudalism was introduced, and French influence increased under the Capetians. By 1547 it had been formally annexed by France, and the ◊Breton language was banned in education. A separatist movement developed after World War II, and there has been guerrilla activity.

Britten (Edward) Benjamin, Baron Britten 1913–1976. English composer. He often wrote for the individual voice; for example, the role in the opera *Peter Grimes* 1945, based on verses by George Crabbe, was created for his life companion Peter ◊Pears. Among his many works are the *Young Person's Guide to the Orchestra* 1946; the chamber opera *The Rape of Lucretia* 1946; *Billy Budd* 1951; *A Midsummer Night's Dream* 1960; and *Death in Venice* 1973.

Born in Lowestoft, Suffolk, he was educated at Gresham's School, Holt, Norfolk. He studied at the Royal College of Music. From 1939 to 1942 he worked in the USA, then returned to England and devoted himself to composing at his home in Aldeburgh, Suffolk, where he and Pears established an annual music festival. His oratorio *War Requiem* 1962 was written for the rededication of Coventry Cathedral.

brittle-star any member of the echinoderm class Ophiuroidea. A brittle-star resembles a starfish, and has a small, central, rounded body and long, flexible, spiny arms used for walking. The small brittle-star *Amphipholis squamata* is greyish, about 4.5 cm/2 in across, and found on sea bottoms worldwide. It broods its young, and its arms can be luminous.

Brno industrial city (chemicals, arms, textiles, machinery) in the Czech Republic; population (1993) 390,000. Now the second largest city in the Czech Republic, Brno was formerly the capital of the Austrian crown land of Moravia.

broadbill primitive perching bird of the family Eurylaimidae, found in Africa and S Asia. Broadbills are forest birds and are often found near water. They are gregarious and noisy, have brilliant coloration and wide bills, and feed largely on insects.

broadcasting the transmission of sound and vision programmes by ◊radio and ◊television. Broadcasting may be organized under private enterprise, as in the USA, or may operate under a compromise system, as in Britain, where a television and radio service controlled by the state-regulated ◊British Broadcasting Corporation (BBC) operates alongside the commercial Independent Television Commission (known as the Independent Broadcasting Authority before 1991 and Channel 5).

In the USA, broadcasting is limited only by the issue of licences from the Federal Communications Commission to competing commercial companies; in Britain, the BBC is a centralized body appointed by the state and responsible to Parliament, but with policy and programme content not controlled by the state; in Japan, which ranks next to the USA in the number of television sets owned, there is a semi-governmental radio and television broadcasting corporation (NHK) and numerous private television companies.

broad-leaved tree another name for a tree belonging to the ◊angiosperms, such as ash, beech, oak, maple, or birch. The leaves are generally broad and flat, in contrast to the needlelike leaves of most ◊conifers. See also ◊deciduous tree.

Broadmoor special hospital (established 1863) in Crowthorne, Berkshire, England, for those formerly described as 'criminally insane'. Patients are admitted if considered by a psychiatrist to be both mentally disordered and potentially dangerous.

broadbill The 14 species of broadbills are found only in the forests of S and E Africa and parts of SE Asia. Broadbills feed mainly on fruit and small invertebrates such as insects. They build domed nests usually suspended over water from tree branches.

Broads, Norfolk area of navigable lakes and rivers in England; see ◊Norfolk Broads.

Broadway major avenue in New York running northwest from the tip of Manhattan and crossing Times Square at 42nd Street, at the heart of the theatre district, where Broadway is known as 'the Great White Way'. New York theatres situated outside this area are described as off-Broadway; those even smaller and farther away are off-off-Broadway, the home of avant-garde and experimental works.

brocade rich woven fabric, produced on a Jacquard loom. It is patterned, normally with more than two colours. It was traditionally made from silk, sometimes with highlights in metal thread.

broderie anglaise (French 'English embroidery') embroidered fabric, usually white cotton, in which holes are cut in patterns and oversewn, often to decorate lingerie, shirts, and skirts.

Brodsky Joseph Alexandrovich 1940–1996. Russian poet. He emigrated to the USA 1972. His work, often dealing with themes of exile, is admired for its wit and economy of language, particularly in its use of understatement. Many of his poems, written in Russian, have been translated into English (*A Part of Speech* 1980). More recently he has also written in English. He was awarded the Nobel Prize for Literature 1987 and became US poet laureate 1991.

Broglie (Louis César Victor) Maurice de, 6th Duc de Broglie 1875–1960. French physicist. He worked on X-rays and gamma rays, and helped to establish the Einsteinian description of light in terms of photons. He was the brother of Louis de Broglie.

Broglie Louis Victor Pierre Raymond de, 7th Duc de Broglie 1892–1987. French theoretical physicist. He established that all subatomic particles can be described either by particle equations or by wave equations, thus laying the foundations of wave mechanics. He was awarded the 1929 Nobel Prize for Physics.

De Broglie's discovery of wave–particle duality enabled physicists to view Einstein's conviction that matter and energy are interconvertible as being fundamental to the structure of matter. The study of matter waves led not only to a much deeper understanding of the nature of the atom but also to explanations of chemical bonds and the practical application of electron waves in electron microscopes.

brome grass any annual grasses of the genus *Bromus* of the temperate zone; some are used for forage, but many are weeds.

bromeliad any tropical or subtropical plant of the pineapple family Bromeliaceae, usually with stiff leathery leaves and bright flower spikes.

Bromeliads are native to tropical America, where there are some 1,400 species. Some are terrestrial, growing in habitats ranging from scrub desert to tropical forest floor. Many, however, are epiphytes and grow on trees. The epiphytes are supported by the tree but do not take nourishment from it, using rain and decayed plant and animal remains for independent sustenance. Some species, such as Spanish moss *Tillandsia usneoides*, can even grow on telegraph wires.

bromide salt of the halide series containing the Br^- ion, which is formed when a bromine atom gains an electron. The term 'bromide' is sometimes used to describe an organic compound containing a bromine atom, even though it is not ionic. Modern naming uses the term 'bromo-' in such cases. For example, the compound C_2H_5Br is now called bromoethane; its traditional name, still used sometimes, is ethyl bromide.

bromine (Greek *bromos* 'stench') dark, reddish-brown, nonmetallic element, a volatile liquid at room temperature, symbol Br, atomic number 35, relative atomic mass 79.904. It is a member of the ◊halogen group, has an unpleasant odour, and is very irritating to mucous membranes. Its salts are known as bromides.

Bromine was formerly extracted from salt beds but is now mostly obtained from sea water, where it occurs in small quantities. Its compounds are used in photography and in the chemical and pharmaceutical industries.

Bromley outer borough of SE Greater London
population (1991) 290,600
features Crystal Palace, re-erected at Sydenham 1854 and burned down 1936, site now partly occupied by the National Sports Centre; 13th-century parish church of SS Peter and Paul; 17th-century Bromley College; Keston Common has a Roman cemetery and traces of a Roman villa; Holwood Park contains 'Caesar's Camp', the site of a British encampment with earthworks dating from c. 200 BC. It is the best surviving field monument in Greater London
famous people William Pitt, H G Wells, W G Grace.

bromocriptine drug that mimics the actions of the naturally occurring biochemical substance dopamine, a neurotransmitter. Bromocriptine acts on the pituitary gland to inhibit the release of prolactin, the hormone that regulates lactation, and thus reduces or suppresses milk production. It is also used in the treatment of ◊Parkinson's disease.

Bromocriptine may also be given to control excessive prolactin secretion and to treat prolactinoma (a hormone-producing tumour). Recent research has established its effectiveness in reversing some cases of infertility.

bronchiole small-bore air tube found in the vertebrate lung responsible for delivering air to the main respiratory surfaces. Bronchioles lead off from the larger bronchus and branch extensively before terminating in the many thousand alveoli that form the bulk of lung tissue.

bronchitis inflammation of the bronchi (air passages) of the lungs, usually caused initially by a viral infection, such as a cold or flu. It is aggravated by environmental pollutants, especially smoking, and results in a persistent cough, irritated mucus-secreting glands, and large amounts of sputum.

bronchodilator drug that relieves obstruction of the airways by causing the bronchi and bronchioles to relax and widen. It is most useful in the treatment of ◊asthma.

bronchus one of a pair of large tubes (bronchii) branching off from the windpipe and passing into the vertebrate lung. Apart from their size, bronchii differ from the bronchioles in possessing cartilaginous rings, which give rigidity and prevent collapse during breathing movements.

Numerous glands in the wall of the bronchus secrete a slimy mucus, which traps dust and other particles; the mucus is constantly being propelled upwards to the mouth by thousands of tiny hairs or cilia. The bronchus is adversely effected by several respiratory diseases and by smoking, which damages the cilia and therefore the lung-cleansing mechanism.

Brontë three English novelists, daughters of a Yorkshire parson. ***Charlotte*** (1816–1855), notably with *Jane Eyre* 1847 and *Villette* 1853, reshaped autobiographical material into vivid narrative. ***Emily*** (1818–1848) in *Wuthering Heights* 1847 expressed the intensity and nature mysticism which also pervades her poetry. The more modest talent of ***Anne*** (1820–1849) produced *Agnes Grey* 1847 and *The Tenant of Wildfell Hall* 1848.

The Brontës were brought up by an aunt in their father's rectory at Haworth (now a museum) in Yorkshire. In 1846 the sisters published a volume of poems under the pen names Currer (Charlotte), Ellis (Emily), and Acton (Anne) Bell. In 1847 (using the same names), they published the novels *Jane Eyre*, *Wuthering Heights*, and *Agnes Grey*, Anne's much weaker work. During 1848–49 Emily, Anne, and their brother Patrick Branwell (1817–1848) all died of tuberculosis, aided in Branwell's case by alcohol and opium addiction; his portrait of the sisters survives.

brontosaurus former name of a type of large, plant-eating dinosaur, now better known as ◊apatosaurus.

Bronx, the borough of New York City, USA, northeast of Harlem River; area 109 sq km/42 sq mi; population (1990) 1,169,000. Largely residential, it is named after an early Dutch settler, James Bronck. The New York Zoological Society and Gardens are here popularly called the Bronx Zoo and the Bronx Botanical Gardens.

bronze alloy of copper and tin, yellow or brown in colour. It is harder than pure copper, more suitable for ◊casting, and also resists ◊corrosion. Bronze may contain as much as 25% tin, together with small amounts of other metals, mainly lead.

Bronze is one of the first metallic alloys known and used widely by early peoples during the period of history known as the ◊Bronze Age.

Bell metal, the bronze used for casting bells, contains 15% or more tin. Phosphor bronze is hardened by the addition of a small percentage of phosphorus. Silicon bronze (for telegraph wires) and aluminium bronze are similar alloys of copper with silicon or aluminium and small amounts of iron, nickel, or manganese, but usually no tin.

Brontë English novelist Charlotte Brontë, who is best known for her novel *Jane Eyre*, which achieved great success when she published it under the pseudonym Currer Bell in 1847. She lived in Haworth, Yorkshire with her sisters Emily and Anne. *Corbis*

Bronze Age stage of prehistory and early history when copper and bronze became the first metals worked extensively and used for tools and weapons. It developed out of the ◊Stone Age, preceded the ◊Iron Age, and may be dated 5000–1200 BC in the Middle East and about 2000–500 BC in Europe. Recent discoveries in Thailand suggest that the Far East, rather than the Middle East, was the cradle of the Bronze Age.

Mining and metalworking were the first specialized industries, and the invention of the wheel during this time revolutionized transport.

Agricultural productivity (which began in the New Stone Age, or Neolithic period, about 6,000 BC), and hence the size of the population that could be supported, was transformed by the ox-drawn plough.

Bronzino Agnolo 1503–1572. Italian Mannerist painter. He is known for his cool, elegant portraits – *Lucrezia Panciatichi* about 1540 (Uffizi, Florence) is typical – and for the allegory *Venus, Cupid, Folly and Time* about 1545 (National Gallery, London). Bronzino's elegant portrait style earned him the appointment of court painter to Cosimo de' Medici, 1st Grand Duke of Tuscany, who commissioned many portraits, altarpieces, and frescoes.

Brook Peter Stephen Paul 1925– . English theatre director. His work with the Royal Shakespeare Company (joined 1962) included a production of Shakespeare's *A Midsummer Night's Dream* 1970, combining elements of circus and commedia dell'arte. His films include *Lord of the Flies* 1962 and *Meetings with Remarkable Men* 1979. He is the author of the influential study of contemporary theatre, *The Empty Space* 1968, and of the essays and observations published in *The Shifting Point* 1988.

Brooke Rupert (Chawner) 1887–1915. English poet. He stands as a symbol of the World War I 'lost generation'. His five war sonnets, including 'The Soldier', were published posthumously. Other notable poems are 'Grantchester' 1912 and 'The Great Lover', written 1914.

Brookeborough Basil Stanlake Brooke, Viscount Brookeborough 1888–1973. Unionist politician of Northern Ireland. He entered Parliament in 1929, held ministerial posts 1933–45, and was prime minister of Northern Ireland 1943–63. He was a staunch advocate of strong links with Britain.

Brooklyn borough of New York City, USA, occupying the southwest end of Long Island. It is linked to Manhattan Island by the Brooklyn-Battery Tunnel, the Brooklyn Bridge 1883, the Williamsburg and the Manhattan bridges, and to Staten Island by the Verrazano-Narrows Bridge 1964. There are more than 60 parks of which Prospect is the largest. There is also a museum, botanical garden, and a beach and amusement area at Coney Island.

Brookner Anita 1928– . English novelist. Her books include *Hotel du Lac* 1984 (Booker Prize), *A*

'There are worse crimes than burning books. One of them is not reading them.'

JOSEPH BRODSKY
Quoted in the *Independent on Sunday* 19 May 1991

'Good women always think it is their fault when someone else is being offensive. Bad women never take the blame for anything.'

ANITA BROOKNER
Hotel du Lac

Brooks **Louise Brooks as Lulu in *Pandora's Box* 1929. Brooks began her professional career at 15 as a dancer. Eventually her appearances in George White's *Scandals* and in the Ziegfeld Follies led to a Hollywood contract.**

Misalliance 1986, *Latecomers* 1988, *Family Romance* 1993, *Incidents in the rue Laugier* 1995, and *Altered States* 1996. Her skill is in the subtle portrayal of hopelessness and lack of vitality in her female characters.

No man can justly censure or condemn another, because indeed no man truly knows another.

THOMAS BROWNE
Religio Medici

Brooks Louise 1906–1985. US actress. She was known for her dark, enigmatic beauty and for her roles in silent films such as *A Girl in Every Port* 1928 and *Die Büchse der Pandora/Pandora's Box* and *Das Tagebuch einer Verlorenen/The Diary of a Lost Girl*, both 1929 and both directed by G W Pabst.

Brooks Mel. Stage name of Melvin Kaminsky 1926– . US film director and comedian. He is known for madcap and slapstick verbal humour. He became well known with his record album *The 2,000-Year-Old Man* 1960. His films include *The Producers* 1968, *Blazing Saddles* 1974, *Young Frankenstein* 1975, and *To Be or Not to Be* 1983.

broom any shrub of the family Leguminosae, especially species of the *Cytisus* and *Spartium*, often cultivated for their bright yellow flowers. In Britain the yellow-flowered Scots broom *Cytisus scoparius* predominates.

Brown Capability (Lancelot) 1715–1783. English landscape gardener. He acquired his nickname because of his continual enthusiasm for the 'capabilities' of natural landscapes. He advised on gardens of stately homes, including Blenheim, Oxfordshire; Stowe, Buckinghamshire; and Petworth, W Sussex, sometimes also contributing to the architectural designs.

Brown Earle 1926– . US composer. He pioneered ◊graph notation and mobile form during the 1950s, as in *Available Forms II* 1958. He was an associate of John ◊Cage.

Brown Ford Madox 1821–1893. English painter, associated with the ◊Pre-Raphaelite Brotherhood. His pictures, which include *The Last of England* 1855 (City Art Gallery, Birmingham) and *Work* 1852–65 (City Art Gallery, Manchester), are characterized by elaborate symbolism and abundance of realistic detail.

I love thee with the breath, / Smiles, tears, of all my life! – and, if God choose, / I shall but love thee better after death.

ELIZABETH BARRETT BROWNING
Sonnets from the Portuguese

Brown (James) Gordon 1951– . British Labour politician, chancellor of the Exchequer from 1997. He entered Parliament in 1983, rising quickly to the opposition front bench; he took over from John Smith as shadow chancellor 1992. On becoming chancellor of the Exchequer in May 1997, he ceded full control over interest rates to the Bank of England.

Brown James 1928– . US rhythm-and-blues and soul singer. He was a pioneer of ◊funk. His hits include 'Please, Please, Please' 1956, 'Papa's Got a Brand New Bag' 1965, and 'Say It Loud, I'm Black and I'm Proud' 1968.

Brown John 1800–1859. US slavery abolitionist. With 18 men, on the night of 16 Oct 1859, he seized the government arsenal at Harper's Ferry in W Virginia, apparently intending to distribute weapons to runaway slaves who would then defend a mountain stronghold, which Brown hoped would become a republic of former slaves. On 18 Oct the arsenal was stormed by US Marines under Col Robert E ◊Lee. Brown was tried and hanged on 2 Dec, becoming a martyr and the hero of the popular song 'John Brown's Body' about 1860.

brown dwarf in astronomy, an object less massive than a star, but heavier than a planet. Brown dwarfs do not have enough mass to ignite nuclear reactions at their centres, but shine by heat released during their contraction from a gas cloud. Some astronomers believe that vast numbers of brown dwarfs exist throughout the Galaxy. Because of the difficulty of detection, none were spotted until 1995, when US astronomers discovered a brown dwarf, GI229B, in the constellation Lepus. It is about 20–40 times as massive as Jupiter but emits only 1% of the radiation of the smallest known star.

Browne Robert 1550–1633. English Puritan leader, founder of the Brownists. He founded communities in Norwich, East Anglia, and in the Netherlands which developed into present-day ◊Congregationalism.

Browne Thomas 1605–1682. English writer and physician. His works display a richness of style and an enquiring mind. They include *Religio medici/The Religion of a Doctor* 1643, a justification of his profession; 'Vulgar Errors' 1646, an examination of popular legend and superstition; and *Urn Burial* and *The Garden of Cyrus* both 1658.

brownfield site site that has previously been developed; for example, a derelict area in the inner city. There is often a surprising level of biodiversity on brownfield sites – for example at one site in London, 300 species of flowering plant were found – and there is often a high proportion of invertebrate species.

Browning Elizabeth Barrett 1806–1861. English poet. In 1844 she published *Poems* (including 'The Cry of the Children'), which led to her friendship with and secret marriage to Robert ◊Browning 1846. *Sonnets from the Portuguese* 1850 were written during their courtship. Later works include *Casa Guidi Windows* 1851 and the poetic novel *Aurora Leigh* 1857, today regarded as a feminist work. She was a learned, fiery, and metrically experimental poet.

Browning Robert 1812–1889. English poet. His work is characterized by the use of dramatic monologue and an interest in obscure literary and historical figures. It includes *Pippa Passes* 1841 (written in dramatic form) and the poems 'The Pied Piper of Hamelin' 1842, 'My Last Duchess' 1842, 'Home Thoughts from Abroad' 1845, and 'Rabbi Ben Ezra' 1864.

In 1845 he met Elizabeth Barrett; they eloped the following year and went to Italy. There he wrote *Christmas Eve and Easter Day* 1850 and much of *Men and Women* 1855, the latter containing some of his finest love poems and dramatic monologues. He published no further collection of verse until *Dramatis Personae* 1864, which was followed by *The Ring and the Book* 1868–69. After his wife's death 1861 Browning settled in England.

Brownshirts the SA (*Sturmabteilung*) or Storm Troops, the private army of the German Nazi party, who derived their name from the colour of their uniform.

browser in computing, any program that allows the user to search for and view data. Browsers are usually limited to a particular type of data, so, for example, a graphics browser will display graphics files stored in many different file formats. Browsers do not permit the user to edit data, but are sometimes able to convert data from one file format to another.

Web browsers allow access to the ◊World Wide Web, acting as a graphical interface to information available on the Internet – they read HTML (hypertext markup language) documents and display them as graphical documents which may include images, video, sound, and ◊hypertext links to other documents.

Brubeck Dave (David Warren) 1920– . US jazz pianist and composer. He was the leader of the Dave Brubeck Quartet (formed 1951). A student of composers Darius Milhaud and Arnold Schoenberg, Brubeck combines improvisation with classical discipline. Included in his large body of compositions is the internationally popular *Take Five*.

Bruce Christopher 1945– . English choreographer and dancer. He became artistic director of the Rambert Dance Company 1992. Bruce often mixes modern and classical idioms with overtly political and social themes, as in *Ghost Dances* 1981, which treats the theme of political oppression. His other pieces include *Cruel Garden* 1977 and *The Dream is Over* 1987, a tribute to John Lennon.

Bruce James 1730–1794. Scottish explorer, the first European to reach the source of the Blue Nile 1770, and to follow the river downstream to Cairo 1773.

Bruce Robert. King of Scotland; see ◊Robert (I) the Bruce.

brucellosis disease of cattle, goats, and pigs, also known when transmitted to humans as ***undulant fever*** since it remains in the body and recurs. It was named after Australian doctor David Bruce (1855–1931), and is caused by bacteria (genus *Brucella*). It is transmitted by contact with an infected animal or by drinking contaminated milk.

It has largely been eradicated in the West through vaccination of livestock and pasteurization of milk. Brucellosis can be treated with antibacterial drugs.

Brücke, die (German 'the bridge') German Expressionist art movement 1905–13, formed in Dresden by Ernst Ludwig Kirchner, Schmidt-Rottluff, and others; Emil Nolde was a member 1906–07. Influenced by African art, van Gogh, and Fauvism, they strove for an art which expressed spiritual values, using raw colours and strong, angular lines derived from their highly original work in woodcut. In 1911 the ◊*Blaue Reiter* overtook them as the leading group in German art.

Bruckner (Josef) Anton 1824–1896. Austrian Romantic composer. He was cathedral organist at Linz 1856–68, and professor at the Vienna Conservatoire from 1868. His works include many choral pieces and 11 symphonies, the last unfinished. His compositions were influenced by Wagner and Beethoven.

Brüderhof (German 'Society of Brothers') Christian Protestant sect with beliefs similar to the ◊Mennonites. They live in groups of families (single persons are assigned to a family), marry only within the sect (divorce is not allowed), and retain a 'modest' dress for women (cap or headscarf, and long skirts). In the USA they are known as Hutterites.

Originally established in Germany, there are Brüderhof communities in the USA, and in Robertsbridge, E Sussex, UK.

Brueghel or ***Bruegel*** family of Flemish painters.

Pieter Brueghel the Elder (c. 1525–1569) was one of the greatest artists of his time. His pictures of peasant life helped to establish genre painting, and he also popularized works illustrating proverbs, such as *The Blind leading the Blind* 1568 (Museo di Capodimonte, Naples). A contemporary taste for the macabre can be seen in *The Triumph of Death* 1562 (Prado, Madrid), which clearly shows the influence of Hieronymus Bosch. One of his best-known works is *Hunters in the Snow* 1565 (Kunsthistorisches Museum, Vienna).

The elder Pieter was nicknamed 'Peasant' Brueghel, referring to the subjects of his paintings. Two of his sons were also painters.

Pieter Brueghel the Younger (1564–1638), called 'Hell' Brueghel, specialized in religious subjects, and another son,

Jan Brueghel (1568–1625), called 'Velvet' Brueghel, painted flowers, landscapes, and seascapes.

Bruges (Flemish ***Brugge***) historic city in NW Belgium; capital of W Flanders province, 16 km/10 mi from the North Sea, with which it is connected by canal; population (1995) 116,000. Bruges was the capital of medieval ◊Flanders and was the chief European wool manufacturing town as well as its chief market. The contemporary port handles coal, iron ore, oil, and fish; local industries include lace, textiles, paint, steel, beer, furniture, and motors.
features Among many fine buildings are the 14th-century cathedral, the church of Notre Dame with a Michelangelo statue of the Virgin and Child, the Gothic town hall and market hall; there are remarkable art collections. It was named for its many bridges. The College of Europe is the oldest centre of European studies.

Brummell Beau (George Bryan) 1778–1840. British dandy and leader of fashion. He introduced long trousers as conventional day and evening wear for men. A friend of the Prince of Wales, the future George IV, he later quarrelled with him. Gambling losses drove him in 1816 to exile in France, where he died in an asylum.

Brundtland Gro Harlem 1939– . Norwegian Labour politician. Environment minister 1974–76, she briefly took over as prime minister 1981, a post to which she was re-elected 1986, 1990, and again held 1993–96. Leader of the Norwegian Labour Party from 1981, she resigned 1992. She failed to secure backing for the European Union membership application in a 1994 national referendum. She resigned Oct 1996.

She chaired the World Commission on Environment and Development which produced the Brundtland Report, published as *Our Common Future* 1987.

Brunei country comprising two enclaves on the NW coast of the island of Borneo, bounded to the landward side by Sarawak and to the NW by the South China Sea. *See country box below.*

Brunel Isambard Kingdom 1806–1859. British engineer and inventor. In 1833 he became engineer to the Great Western Railway, which adopted the 2.1-m/7-ft gauge on his advice. He built the Clifton Suspension Bridge over the river Avon at Bristol and the Saltash Bridge over the river Tamar near Plymouth. His shipbuilding designs include the *Great Western* 1837, the first steamship to cross the Atlantic regularly; the *Great Britain* 1843, the first large iron ship to have a screw propeller; and the *Great Eastern* 1858, which laid the first transatlantic telegraph cable.

The son of Marc Brunel, he made major contributions in shipbuilding and bridge construction, and assisted his father in the Thames tunnel project. Brunel University in Uxbridge, London, is named after both father and son.

Brunel Marc Isambard 1769–1849. French-born British engineer and inventor, father of Isambard Kingdom Brunel. He constructed the tunnel under the river Thames in London from Wapping to Rotherhithe 1825–43.

Brunel fled to the USA 1793 to escape the French Revolution. He became chief engineer in New York. In 1799 he moved to England to mass-produce pulley blocks, which were needed by the navy. Brunel demonstrated that with specially designed machine tools 10 men could do the work of 100, more quickly, more cheaply, and yield a better product. Cheating partners and fire damage to his factory caused the business to fail and he was imprisoned for debt 1821. He spent the latter part of his life working on the Rotherhithe tunnel.

Brunel English engineer and inventor Isambard Kingdom Brunel. Perhaps the greatest of the 19th-century engineers, he designed railways for the Great Western Railway, with bridges, tunnels, and viaducts; ships, including the *Great Western* 1838, the first steamship to cross the Atlantic, and the *Great Britain* 1843; bridges, including the Clifton Suspension Bridge 1864; armaments; and docks. *Topham*

Brunelleschi Filippo 1377–1446. Italian Renaissance architect. The first and one of the greatest of the Renaissance architects, he pioneered the scientific use of perspective. He was responsible for the construction of the dome of Florence Cathedral (completed 1436), a feat deemed impossible by many of his contemporaries.

His use of simple geometries and a modified Classical language lend his buildings a feeling of tranquillity, to which many other early Renaissance architects aspired. His other works include the Ospedale degli Innocenti 1419 and the Pazzi Chapel 1429, both in Florence.

Bruno Frank 1961– . English heavyweight boxer. He won the World Boxing Association (WBA) world title after defeating Oliver McCall 1995. Bruno had made three previous unsuccessful attempts to win a world title, against Tim Witherspoon 1986 (WBA title), Mike Tyson 1989 (undisputed world title), and Lennox Lewis 1993 (World Boxing Council (WBC) title). He lost his WBA title to Mike Tyson 1996. An eye injury forced him to retire from boxing August 1996.

Bruno Giordano, born Filippo Bruno 1548–1600. Italian philosopher. He entered the Dominican order of monks 1563, but his sceptical attitude to Catholic doctrines forced him to flee Italy 1577. He was arrested by the ◊Inquisition 1593 in Venice and burned at the stake for his adoption of Copernican astronomy and his heretical religious views.

After visiting Geneva and Paris, he lived in England 1583–85, where he wrote some of his finest works. Drawing both on contemporary science (in particular the theories of Copernicus) and on magic and esoteric wisdom, he developed a radical form of pantheism in which all things are aspects of a single, infinite reality animated by God as the 'world soul'. His views had a profound influence on the philosophers Benedict Spinoza and Gottfried Leibniz.

Bruno, St c. 1030–1101. German founder of the monastic Catholic ◊Carthusian order. He was born in Cologne, became a priest, and controlled the cathedral school of Rheims 1057–76. Withdrawing to the mountains near Grenoble after an ecclesiastical controversy, he founded the monastery at Chartreuse in 1084. Canonized 1514. Feast day 6 Oct.

Brunswick (German ***Braunschweig***) industrial city (chemical engineering, precision engineering, food processing) in Lower Saxony, Germany; population (1993) 257,800. It was one of the chief cities of N Germany in the Middle Ages and a member of the ◊Hanseatic League. It was capital of the duchy of Brunswick from 1671.

Brussels (Flemish ***Brussel***, French ***Bruxelles***) capital of Belgium, industrial city (lace, textiles, machinery, and chemicals); population (1995) 952,000 (80% French-speaking, the suburbs Flemish-speaking). It is the headquarters of the European Union (EU) and since 1967 of the international secretariat of ◊NATO. First settled in the 6th century, and a city from 1312, Brussels became the capital of the Spanish Netherlands 1530 and of Belgium 1830.

features It has fine buildings including the 13th-century church of Sainte Gudule; the Hôtel de Ville, Maison du Roi, and others in the Grande Place; the royal palace. The Musées Royaux des Beaux-Arts de Belgique hold a large art collection.

Brussels, Treaty of pact of economic, political, cultural, and military alliance established 17 March

'Where the quiet-coloured end of evening smiles, / Miles and miles.'

ROBERT BROWNING
'Love Among the Ruins'

'When God finally calls me and asks 'What have you done with the talent I gave you, my lad?', I will present to him the score of my Te Deum and I hope he will judge me mercifully.'

ANTON BRUCKNER
Quoted in Sutton, *Introduction to the Te Deum* 1993

BRUNEI
State of

national name *Negara Brunei Darussalam*
area 5,765 sq km/2,225 sq mi
capital Bandar Seri Begawan
major towns/cities Seria, Kuala Balai
physical features flat coastal plain with hilly lowland in W and mountains in E (Mount Pagon 1,850 m/6,070 ft); 75% of the area is forested; the Limbang valley splits Brunei in two, and its cession to Sarawak 1890 is disputed by Brunei; tropical climate; Temburong, Tutong, and Belait rivers
head of state and government HM Muda Hassanal Bolkiah Mu'izzaddin Waddaulah, Sultan of Brunei, from 1967
political system absolute monarchy
administrative divisions four districts and four municipalities
political parties Brunei National Democratic Party (BNDP) and Brunei National United Party (BNUP) (both banned since 1988); Brunei People's Party (BPP) (banned since 1962)
population 284,500 (1994 est)
population growth rate 2.1% (1990–95)
ethnic distribution 68% indigenous Malays, predominating in government service and agriculture; more than 20% Chinese, predominating in the commercial sphere
life expectancy 74 years
literacy rate 86%
languages Malay (official), Chinese (Hokkien), English
religions Muslim 66%, Buddhist 14%, Christian 10%
currency Brunei dollar (ringgit)
GDP (US $) 6.47 billion (1993)
growth rate 1.6% (1993)
exports liquefied natural gas (world's largest producer) and crude oil, both expected to be exhausted by the year 2000

HISTORY
15th C Islamic monarchy established, ruling Brunei and North Borneo, including Sabah and Sarawak states of Malaysia.
1841 Lost control of Sarawak.
1888 Brunei became a British protectorate.
1906 Became a dependency when British Resident appointed as adviser to the Sultan.
1929 Oil was discovered.
1941–45 Occupied by Japan.
1950 Sir Omar became the 28th Sultan.
1959 Written constitution made Britain responsible for defence and external affairs.
1962 Sultan began rule by decree after plan to join Federation of Malaysia was opposed by a week-long rebellion organized by the Brunei People's Party (BPP).
1967 Sultan Omar abdicated in favour of his son, Hassanal Bolkiah, but remained chief adviser.
1971 Brunei given full internal self-government.
1975 United Nations resolution called for independence for Brunei.
1984 Independence achieved from Britain, with Britain maintaining a small force to protect the oil and gas fields.
1985 A 'loyal and reliable' political party, the Brunei National Democratic Party (BNDP), legalized.
1986 Death of former sultan, Sir Omar. Formation of multiethnic Brunei National United Party (BNUP); nonroyals given key cabinet posts for the first time.
1988 BNDP and BNUP banned.
1991 Joined nonaligned movement.

Brussels The capital city of Belgium, Brussels contains many fine buildings including these elaborate guild houses surrounding the Grand Place which mostly date from the late 17th century. The Grand Place is a public square, the site of tournaments, ceremonies, and public events. *Corbis*

1948, for 50 years, by the UK, France, and the Benelux countries, joined by West Germany and Italy 1955. It was the forerunner of the North Atlantic Treaty Organization and the European Community (now the European Union).

Brutalism architectural style of the 1950s and 1960s that evolved from the work of Le Corbusier and Mies van der Rohe. Uncompromising in its approach, it stresses functionalism and honesty to materials; steel and concrete are favoured. The term was coined by Alison and Peter ◊Smithson who developed the style in the UK.

Bruton John 1947– . Irish politician, leader of Fine Gael (United Ireland Party) from 1990 and prime minister 1994–97. The collapse of Albert ◊Reynolds's Fianna Fáil–Labour government Nov 1994 thrust Bruton, as a leader of a new coalition with Labour, into the prime ministerial vacancy. He pledged himself to the continuation of the Anglo-Irish peace process, and in 1995 he pressed for greater urgency in negotiations for a permanent peace agreement.

Brutus Marcus Junius c. 85–42 BC. Roman senator and general, a supporter of ◊Pompey (against ◊Caesar) in the civil war. Pardoned by Caesar and raised to high office by him, he nevertheless plotted Caesar's assassination to restore the purity of the Republic. Brutus committed suicide when he was defeated (with ◊Cassius) by ◊Mark Antony, Caesar's lieutenant, at Philippi 42 BC.

Bruxelles French form of ◊Brussels, the capital of Belgium.

bryony White bryony *Bryonia dioica*, found in Europe, is a wild vine that produces small, greenish-white flowers and red berries. It grows in hedges, scrub, and copses where its long stems climb over other plants, holding on with tendrils. *Premaphotos Wildlife*

Brynner Yul, originally Taidje Khan 1915–1985. Actor, in the USA from 1940, who had a distinctive stage presence and made a shaven head his trademark. He played the king in *The King and I* both on stage 1951 and on film 1956 (Academy Award), and was the leader of *The Magnificent Seven* 1960.

bryony either of two hedgerow climbing plants found in Britain: white bryony *Bryonia dioca* belonging to the gourd family Cucurbitaceae, and black bryony *Tamus communis* of the yam family Dioscoreaceae.

bryophyte member of the Bryophyta, a division of the plant kingdom containing three classes: the Hepaticae (◊liverwort), Musci (◊moss), and Anthocerotae (◊hornwort). Bryophytes are generally small, low-growing, terrestrial plants with no vascular (water-conducting) system as in higher plants. Their life cycle shows a marked ◊alternation of generations. Bryophytes chiefly occur in damp habitats and require water for the dispersal of the male gametes (◊antherozoids).

In bryophytes, the ◊sporophyte, consisting only of a spore-bearing capsule on a slender stalk, is wholly or partially dependent on the ◊gametophyte for water and nutrients. In some liverworts the plant body is a simple ◊thallus, but in the majority of bryophytes it is differentiated into stem, leaves, and ◊rhizoids.

BSc abbreviation for the degree of ***Bachelor of Science***. The US abbreviation is ***BS***.

BSE abbreviation for ◊***bovine spongiform encephalopathy***.

bubble chamber in physics, a device for observing the nature and movement of atomic particles, and their interaction with radiation. It is a vessel filled with a superheated liquid through which ionizing particles move and collide. The paths of these particles are shown by strings of bubbles, which can be photographed and studied. By using a pressurized liquid medium instead of a gas, it overcomes drawbacks inherent in the earlier ◊cloud chamber. It was invented by US physicist Donald Glaser 1952. See ◊particle detector.

Buber Martin 1878–1965. Austrian-born Israeli philosopher, a Zionist and advocate of the reappraisal of ancient Jewish thought in contemporary terms. His book *I and Thou* 1923 posited a direct dialogue between the individual and God; it had great impact on Christian and Jewish theology.

Bubka Sergey Nazarovich 1963– . Ukrainian pole vaulter who achieved the world's first six-metre vault in 1985. World champion in 1983, he was unbeaten in a major event from 1981 to 1990. From 1984 he has broken the world record on 32 occasions.

bubonic plague epidemic disease of the Middle Ages; see ◊plague and ◊Black Death.

buccaneer member of any of various groups of seafarers who plundered Spanish ships and colonies on the Spanish American coast in the 17th century. Unlike true pirates, they were acting on (sometimes spurious) commission.

Buchan John, 1st Baron Tweedsmuir 1875–1940. Scottish writer and politician. His popular adventure stories, today sometimes criticized for their alleged snobbery, sexism, and anti-Semitism, include *The Thirty-Nine Steps* 1915, *Greenmantle* 1916, and *The Three Hostages* 1924. He was governor general of Canada 1935–40.

Bucharest (Romanian ***Bucureşti***) capital and largest city of Romania; population (1993) 2,343,800. The conurbation of Bucharest district has an area of 1,520 sq km/587 sq mi. It was originally a citadel built by Vlad the Impaler (see ◊Dracula) to stop the advance of the Ottoman invasion in the 14th century. Bucharest became the capital of the princes of Wallachia 1698 and of Romania 1861. Savage fighting took place in the city during Romania's 1989 revolution.

Buchenwald site of a Nazi ◊concentration camp 1937–45 at a village NE of Weimar, E Germany.

It was established 1937 as a labour camp for political prisoners and criminals and was later used as a collection point for Jews and other victims en route to extermination camps.

Buchner Eduard 1860–1917. German chemist who researched the process of fermentation. In 1897 he observed that fermentation could be produced mechanically, by cell-free extracts. Buchner argued that it was not the whole yeast cell that produced fermentation, but only the presence of the enzyme he named zymase. Nobel Prize for Chemistry 1907.

Buck Pearl S(ydenstricker) 1892–1973. US novelist. Daughter of missionaries to China, she spent much of her life there and wrote novels about Chinese life, such as *East Wind–West Wind* 1930 and *The Good Earth* 1931, for which she received a Pulitzer prize 1932. She received the Nobel Prize for Literature 1938.

Buckingham George Villiers, 1st Duke of Buckingham 1592–1628. English courtier, adviser to James I and later Charles I. After Charles's accession, Buckingham attempted to form a Protestant coalition in Europe, which led to war with France, but he failed to relieve the Protestants besieged in La Rochelle 1627. This added to his unpopularity with Parliament, and he was assassinated.

Buckingham George Villiers, 2nd Duke of Buckingham 1628–1687. English politician, a member of the ◊Cabal under Charles II. A dissolute son of the first duke, he was brought up with the royal children. His play *The Rehearsal* satirized the style of the poet Dryden, who portrayed him as Zimri in *Absalom and Achitophel*.

Buckingham market town in Buckinghamshire, England, on the river Ouse; population (1991) 10,200. University College was established 1974, and was given a royal charter as the University of Buckingham 1983.

Buckingham Palace London home of the British sovereign, built 1703 for the duke of Buckingham, but bought by George III 1762 and reconstructed by John ◊Nash 1821–36; a new front was added 1913.

Buckinghamshire county of SE central England (*see United Kingdom map*)

towns and cities Aylesbury (administrative headquarters), Buckingham, High Wycombe, Beaconsfield, Olney

features Chiltern Hills; ◊Chequers (country seat of the prime minister); Burnham Beeches and the church of the poet Gray's 'Elegy' at Stoke Poges; Cliveden, a country house designed by Charles Barry (now a hotel, it was once the home of Nancy, Lady Astor); Bletchley Park, home of World War II code-breaking activities, now used as a training post for GCHQ (Britain's electronic surveillance centre); Open University at Walton Hall; homes of the poets William Cowper at Olney and John Milton at Chalfont St Giles, and of the Tory prime minister Disraeli at Hughenden; Stowe gardens

products furniture, chiefly beech; agricultural goods including barley, wheat, oats, sheep, cattle, poultry, pigs

famous people John Hampden, Edmund Waller, William Herschel, George Gilbert Scott, Ben Nicholson.

Buckley William F(rank) 1925– . US conservative political writer, novelist, and founder-editor of the *National Review* 1955. In such books as *Up from Liberalism* 1959, and in a weekly television debate *Firing Line*, he represented the 'intellectual' right-wing, antiliberal stance in US political thought.

buckminsterfullerene form of carbon, made up of molecules (buckyballs) consisting of 60 carbon atoms arranged in 12 pentagons and 20 hexagons to form a perfect sphere. It was named after the US architect and engineer Richard Buckminster Fuller because of its structural similarity to the geodesic dome that he designed. See ◊fullerene.

buckthorn any of several thorny shrubs of the family Rhamnaceae. The buckthorn *Rhamnus catharticus* is native to Britain, but found throughout Europe, W Asia, and N Africa. Its berries were formerly used in medicine as a purgative.

buckwheat any of several plants of the genus *Fagopyrum*, family Polygonaceae. The name usually refers to *F. esculentum*, which grows to about 1 m/3 ft and can grow on poor soil in a short summer. The highly nutritious black, triangular seeds (groats) are consumed by both animals and humans. They can be eaten either cooked whole or as a cracked meal (kasha) or ground into flour, often made into pancakes.

buckyballs popular name for molecules of ◊buckminsterfullerene.

bud undeveloped shoot usually enclosed by protective scales; inside is a very short stem and numerous undeveloped leaves, or flower parts, or both. Terminal buds are found at the tips of shoots, while axillary buds develop in the ◊axils of the leaves, often remaining dormant unless the terminal bud is removed or damaged. Adventitious buds may be produced anywhere on the plant, their formation sometimes stimulated by an injury, such as that caused by pruning.

Budapest capital of Hungary, industrial city (chemicals, textiles) on the river Danube; population (1993 est) 2,009,000. Buda, on the right bank of the Danube, became the Hungarian capital 1867 and was joined with Pest, on the left bank, 1872.
history The site of a Roman outpost in the 1st century AD, Buda was the seat of the Magyar kings from the 14th century. It was later occupied by the Turks, and was under Hapsburg rule from the end of the 17th century. In 1867 Hungary was given self-government, and the city of Budapest was created 1872 when the towns of Buda and Pest were joined. Hungary became independent 1918, with Budapest as capital. The city was occupied by German troops in World War II, and was the site of a seven-week siege by Soviet troops, finally being liberated Feb 1945. It was also the scene of fighting between the Hungarians and Soviet troops in the uprising of 1956.

Buddha 'enlightened one'. Title of Prince ***Gautama Siddhārtha*** lived 5th century BC. Religious leader, founder of Buddhism, born at Lumbini in Nepal. At the age of 29 he left his wife and son and a life of luxury, to resolve the problems of existence. After six years of austerity he realized that asceticism, like overindulgence, was futile, and chose the middle way of meditation. He became enlightened under a bo, or bodhi, tree near Buddh Gaya in Bihar, India. He began teaching at Varanasi, and founded the Sangha, or order of monks. He spent the rest of his life travelling around N India, and died at Kusinagara in Uttar Pradesh. He is not a god.

The Buddha's teaching is summarized as the Four Noble Truths: the fact of frustration or suffering; that suffering has a cause; that it can be ended; and that it can be ended by following the Noble Eightfold Path – right views, right intention, right speech, right action, right livelihood, right effort, right mindfulness, and right concentration – eventually arriving at nirvana, the extinction of all craving for things of the senses and release from the cycle of rebirth.

Buddhism one of the great world religions, which originated in India in the 5th century BC. It derives from the teaching of the ◊Buddha, who is regarded as one of a series of such enlightened beings. The chief doctrine is that all phenomena share three characteristics: they are impermanent, unsatisfactory, and lack a permanent essence (such as a soul). All beings, including gods, are subject to these characteristics, but can achieve freedom through enlightenment. The main forms of Buddhism are ◊Theravāda (or Hīnayāna) in SE Asia and ◊Mahāyāna in N and E Asia; ◊Lamaism in Tibet and ◊Zen in Japan are among the many Mahāyāna forms of Buddhism. There are over 300 million Buddhists worldwide (1994).
scriptures The only surviving complete canon of the Buddhist scriptures is that of the Sinhalese (Sri Lanka) Buddhists, in Pāli, but other schools had essentially the same canon in Sanskrit. The scriptures are divided into three groups, known as *pitakas* (baskets): vinaya (discipline), listing offences and rules of life; the sūtras (discourse), or dharma (doctrine), the exposition of Buddhism by the Buddha and his disciples; and abhidharma (further doctrine), later discussions on doctrine.
beliefs The self is not regarded as permanent, as it is subject to change and decay. It is attachment to the things that are essentially impermanent that causes delusion, suffering, greed, and aversion, and reinforce the sense of self. Actions which incline towards selflessness are called 'skilful' and constitute the path leading to enlightenment. In the ◊Four Noble Truths the Buddha acknowledged the existence and source of suffering and showed the way of deliverance from it through the Eightfold Path. The aim of following the Eightfold Path is to attain nirvana ('blowing out') – the eradication of all desires. Supreme reverence is accorded to the historical Buddha (Sakyamuni, or, when referred to by his clan name, Gautama), who is seen as one in a long and ongoing line of Buddhas, the next one (Maitreya) being due c. AD 3000.

Theravāda Buddhism, the School of the Elders, also known as Hīnayāna or Lesser Vehicle, prevails in SE Asia (Sri Lanka, Thailand, and Myanmar), and emphasizes the mendicant, meditative life as the way to break the cycle of samsāra, or death and rebirth. Its three possible goals are *arahat*: one who, under the guidance of a Buddha, has gained insight into the true nature of things; *Paccekabuddha*: an enlightened one who lives alone and does not teach; and fully awakened *Buddha*. Its scriptures are written in Pāli, an Indo-Aryan language with its roots in N India. In India itself Buddhism had virtually died out by the 13th century under pressure from Islam and Hinduism. However, it has 5 million devotees in the 20th century and is growing.

Mahāyāna Buddhism, or Greater Vehicle, arose at the beginning of the Christian era. It exhorts the individual not merely to attain personal nirvana, but to become a trainee Buddha, or ◊bodhisattva, and so save others. Cults of various Buddhas and bodhisattvas arose. Mahāyāna Buddhism also emphasizes śunyata, or the experiential understanding of the emptiness of all things, even Buddhist doctrine.

Mahāyāna Buddhism prevails in China, Korea, Japan, and Tibet. In the 6th century AD Mahāyāna spread to China with the teachings of ◊Bodhidharma and formed Ch'an, which became established in Japan from the 12th century as Zen Buddhism. Zen emphasizes silent meditation with sudden interruptions from a master to encourage awakening of the mind. Japan also has the lay organization Sōka Gakkai (Value Creation Society), founded 1930, which equates absolute faith with immediate material benefit; by the 1980s it was followed by more than 7 million households.

Esoteric Buddhism, also known as ◊Tantrism or Diamond Buddhism, became popular in Tibet and Japan, and holds that enlightenment is already within the disciple and with the proper guidance (that is privately passed on by a master) can be realized.

▷*See feature on pp. 162–163 and timeline on p. 164.*

budding type of ◊asexual reproduction in which an outgrowth develops from a cell to form a new individual. Most yeasts reproduce in this way.

In horticulture, the term is used for a technique of plant propagation whereby a bud (or scion) and a sliver of bark from one plant are transferred to an incision made in the bark of another plant (the stock). This method of ◊grafting is often used for roses.

buddleia any shrub or tree of the tropical genus *Buddleia*, family Buddleiaceae. The purple or white flower heads of the butterfly bush *B. davidii* attract large numbers of butterflies.

budgerigar small Australian parakeet *Melopsittacus undulatus* of the parrot family, Psittacidae, order Psittaciformes, that feeds mainly on grass seeds. Normally it is bright green, but yellow, white, blue, and mauve varieties have been bred for the pet market. It breeds freely in captivity.

Buenos Aires capital and industrial city and port of Argentina, on the south bank of the Río de la Plata; population (1992 est) 11,662,050. Its main exports are grain, beef, and wool
history founded 1536 by the Spaniard Pedro de Mendoza as Puerto de Santa Mariá del Buen Aire, it was abandoned after attacks by American Indians, and refounded 1580. It became the capital of the viceroyalty of Rió de la Plata 1776, and federal capital of Argentina 1880
features Congress building; cathedral, built 1804; presidential palace (called the Pink House) on the Plaza de Mayo; University of Buenos Aires, founded 1821; opera house, the Teatro Colón; avenues built in the early 20th century, modelled on those in Paris, including 9 de Julio, which was built 1937 and was modelled on the Champs Elysées.

Buber, Martin Religious philosopher Martin Buber, photographed around 1960. He saw Zionism as an opportunity for Jewish cultural renaissance. After studying philosophy and art history at Vienna and Berlin, he edited and founded several German-Jewish publications and worked on a translation of the Bible from Hebrew into German. *Corbis*

buffalo either of two species of wild cattle. The Asiatic water buffalo *Bubalis bubalis* is found domesticated throughout S Asia and wild in parts of India and Nepal. It likes moist conditions. Usually grey or black, up to 1.8 m/6 ft high, both sexes carry large horns. The African buffalo *Syncerus caffer* is found in Africa, south of the Sahara, where there is grass, water, and cover in which to retreat. There are a number of subspecies, the biggest up to 1.6 m/5 ft high, and black, with massive horns set close together over the head. The name is also commonly applied to the American ◊bison.

buffer in chemistry, mixture of compounds chosen to maintain a steady ◊pH. The commonest buffers consist of a mixture of a weak organic acid and one of its salts or a mixture of acid salts of phosphoric acid. The addition of either an acid or a base causes a shift in the chemical equilibrium (the condition in which the products of a reversible chemical reaction are formed at the same rate at which they decompose back to the reactants), thus keeping the pH constant.

buffer in computing, a part of the ◊memory used to store data temporarily while it is waiting to be used. For example, a program might store data in a printer buffer until the printer is ready to print it.

Buffon Georges-Louis Leclerc. Comte de Buffon 1707–1788. French naturalist and author of the 18th century's most significant work of natural history, the 44-volume *Histoire naturelle génerale et particulière* 1749–67. In *The Epochs of Nature*, one of the volumes, he questioned biblical chronology for the first time, and raised the Earth's age from the traditional figure of 6,000 years to the seemingly colossal estimate of 75,000 years.

bug in computing, an ◊error in a program. It can be an error in the logical structure of a program or a syntax error, such as a spelling mistake.

bug in entomology, an insect belonging to the order Hemiptera. All these have two pairs of wings with forewings partly thickened. They also have piercing mouthparts adapted for sucking the juices of plants or animals, the 'beak' being tucked under the body when not in use.

They include: the bedbug, which sucks human blood; the shieldbug, or stinkbug, which has a strong odour and feeds on plants; and the water boatman and other water bugs. *See illustration on p. 165.*

Bugatti racing and sports-car company, founded by the Italian Ettore Bugatti (1881–1947). The first car was produced 1908, but it was not until 1924 that one of the great Bugattis, the Type 35, was produced. Bugatti cars are credited with more race wins than any others. The company was taken over by Hispano Suiza after Bugatti's death.

For Brutus is an honourable man; / So are they all, all honourable men.

On BRUTUS
William Shakespeare
Julius Cæsar

buggery or ***sodomy*** anal intercourse by a man with another man or a woman, or sexual intercourse by a man or woman with an animal (bestiality).

In English law, buggery may be committed by a man with his wife, or with another man in private if both parties consent and are over 18 years old. In all other circumstances it is an offence.

bugle compact valveless brass instrument with a shorter tube and less flared bell than the trumpet.

cont. on p. 164

The Spread of Buddhism

A reclining Buddha figure at a temple in Thailand, to which Buddhism spread from India in the 2nd century AD. Buddhism is still the majority religion of the country, and there are many popular festivals and pilgrimage sites. *Corbis*

Since its beginnings 2,500 years ago, Buddhism has spread from India throughout Asia and the Far East, and in this century to Europe and the Americas. Like other world religions, Buddhism addresses universal human issues, and has evolved distinctive forms in each new culture in which it has taken root. Yet within this diversity, the main principles of Buddhism have remained constant – non-harming of other beings, compassion, wisdom, and the goal of transcendence of all worldly limitations. By observing these, Buddhists today maintain a link to the Buddha's personal disciples.

Initially the Teaching – the Dharma – was transmitted directly by the Buddha to disciples in Northeast India (Bihar and Uttar Pradesh) during the 5th century BC. Although he encouraged them to wander widely and teach their own disciples, Buddhism remained a regional religion practised in the Buddha's homelands until adopted by the emperor Aśoka (262–239 BC). He ordered Buddhist missions led by monks to be sent throughout India and abroad. Wherever they went, monks acted as the personal teachers of disciples and transmitted the words of the Buddha in the form of scriptures known as sūtras. The spread of Buddhist literature was therefore an integral part of the spread of Buddhism. As technology evolved so did the means for this transmission. Originally memorized and recited by individual monks, sūtras were later written down on palm leaves, tree bark, and eventually on paper. Printing was also used, and the oldest surviving printed book in the world is a Chinese translation of a Buddhist scripture, the *Diamond Sūtra*, produced in AD 868.

The first major expansion of Buddhism was therefore the result of royal decree, and was carried out by missionary monks, a pattern to be repeated in many other countries in Asia. As a result, Buddhism often began in a new country as the preserve of the ruling elite. In each case it took several centuries for distinctive indigenous forms to evolve. Another major influence in the spread of Buddhism was the patronage of traders and members of the business class. Even in the time of the Buddha there were many merchants attracted to his teaching. Since merchants have to travel for their business, Buddhism soon began to spread along the major trade routes, both within India and abroad.

India and Southeast Asia

In India the routes of expansion from the Buddhist homeland were northwest towards modern Afghanistan, northeast into Myanmar, and southwards. On the west coast rich merchants sponsored splendid monasteries and shrines such as the cave temples of Ajanta, cut into the rock of the Western Ghat hill range. From the western coast trade flourished with the Roman empire, as shown by Buddhist place names on the east coast of the Persian Gulf and Arabia. To the east, trade flourished with other countries in Southeast Asia. Sea trade routes were especially important in this spread, and there are even records of Chinese pilgrims who travelled from western China to India by land via Afghanistan and who returned home by sea from Sri Lanka, via Indonesia and Vietnam.

Buddhism was transmitted directly to Myanmar and Thailand. Although Buddhism was introduced to Southeast Asia by Aśoka's missions, later missions were invited by local monarchs who wished the Buddhists to legitimize their rule and who thus made Buddhism the state religion. This movement was dominated by the conservative Theravāda Buddhism of Sri Lanka, and this is the only form of Buddhism to survive in the region.

Buddhism as an institutional religion was eradicated in much of India after the 12th century, under the impact of Muslim invasions from the northwest, and later in the south by resurgent militant Hinduism. In the 20th century Buddhism has had a presence in the land of its origin through monks from Southeast Asia and Sri Lanka, and many Tibetan Buddhist refugees have escaped to India since the 1950s. Since 1956, India has also seen the mass conversion of millions of 'untouchable' Hindus to Buddhism following the leadership of the first Law Minister of modern India, Dr B R Ambedkar (1891–1956).

The Silk Road

In the northwest, Buddhism spread along trade routes that led northwards through the Himalayas into the kingdoms of central Asia and from there into Tibet and western China. These were a part of the system of trade routes known collectively as the 'Silk Road', the major trade artery that linked China with the eastern Mediterranean and along which goods travelled in both directions. The spread of Buddhism westwards along this artery was blocked, initially by persecution by the Zoroastrians of Persia and from the 7th century by the vigorous expansion of Islam. However, all forms of Buddhism freely spread eastwards along this route, and that which found the greatest success was the Mahāyāna. This is now the characteristic form of Buddhism in China, Japan, Korea, Mongolia, and Tibet.

Tibet

One of the major attractions of Buddhism was that monks were often educated and brought with them literary culture. This was certainly the case in Tibet. Even the Tibetan script was invented in order to translate and record the Buddhist scriptures in Tibetan. The transmission of Buddhism there began in the 7th century when Indian Buddhists were invited by the Tibetan king to establish a monastery. Subsequently Tibetan Buddhism was characterized by large monastic establishments copied from India, and which survived until the Chinese invasion of Tibet in 1959. These monasteries were affiliated to one or another of the Tibetan orders, each of which had developed from the teachings of distinct lineages of teachers. These include the Gelug-pa order, headed by the Dalai Lama. After the Chinese invasion, teachers from these Orders dispersed around the world, where they have established new Buddhist communities.

China

The reception of Buddhism in China was entirely different. China had a longstanding literary culture and religion, and traditionalists were not at all impressed by this strange new religion from the west (that is, from India).

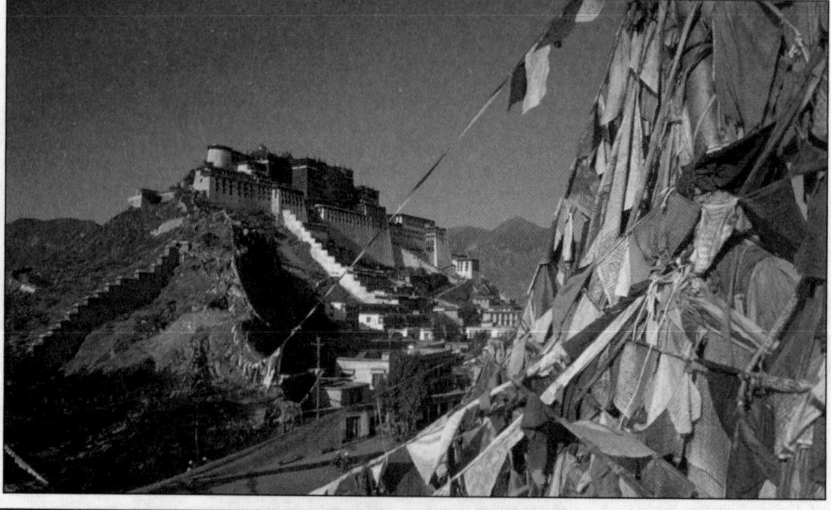

Prayer flags are strung across the road and up the hill towards Potala, the traditional home of the Dalai Lamas and the seat of the Tibetan government in the capital, Lhasa, prior to the Chinese invasion. *Corbis*

Hüan Tsang, a 7th-century Chinese Buddhist pilgrim, returning home from India. Hüan Tsang travelled 65,000 km/40,000 mi during his 16-year pilgrimage from China to India. He is said to have returned to China with nearly 650 Buddhist texts he collected in India. During the last 20 years of his life he translated over 75 of them into Chinese. *Philip Sauvain*

Monks blowing ritual horns at Tiksei Temple, Ladakh. A Buddhist country in the south of the Himalayas, Ladakh received its Buddhist tradition from Tibet. *Corel*

Initially Buddhism appealed to fringe elements in Chinese society, and it was only after the division of the country into two kingdoms (3rd–6th century) that Buddhism made much headway. In the northern kingdom, Buddhism was welcomed as a foreign religion which would endorse the foreign rulers who held power there. In the southern kingdom, Buddhism became the object of an intellectual interest among the Chinese aristocracy. The development of Chinese forms of Buddhism was characterized by attempts to simplify the body of teachings and scriptures brought to China from India. Some schools were more scholastic and concentrated on single scriptures which were regarded as the most authoritative, such as the T'ien-t'ai school based on the *Lotus Sūtra*. Other schools appealed more to ordinary people, such as Ching-t'u (Pure Land) – which emphasized worship of the Buddha Amitābha – and Ch'an, which stressed the importance of meditation. Later Chinese Buddhism merged to some degree with Confucianism and Taoism. The years of Communist rule have seen the suppression of Buddhism on the mainland, but it has survived in its characteristic Chinese form in Taiwan.

Japan

Buddhism, in its Chinese form, was brought to Japan in AD 552 from Korea and was welcomed as a stabilizing influence at a time of political turmoil. For the first centuries it remained an interest of a cultured aristocracy, but from the 13th century onwards distinctive and more popular Japanese schools appeared, most notably forms of Pure Land Buddhism taught by Hōnen and Shinran (1173–1263). Zen (Japanese for Ch'an), which appealed particularly to the warrior samurai class, was brought to Japan by the monk Bodhidharma in the 12th century. One school, founded by Nichiren in the 13th century and still flourishing, recommended repetition of the title of the *Lotus Sūtra*.

A painting from the Ajanta caves, India. These Buddhist cave temples, which date from 200 BC to the 7th century AD, are cut from solid granite, and are decorated with many paintings and sculptures. *Philip Sauvain*

The West

The European contact with Buddhism arose through missionary and colonial activity starting from the 17th century onwards. This in turn stimulated academic study in the 19th and 20th centuries. Buddhism was brought to the USA by large populations of Chinese and Japanese immigrants in the 19th century. The practice of Buddhism by westerners themselves was encouraged by the teachings of Buddhist academics in the west, such as the Japanese Zen scholar D T Suzuki (1870–1966), and the activities of the Theosophical Society, a western organization which sponsored the revival of Buddhism in India. The spread of Buddhism in the west was assisted by the dispersal of Tibetan and Chinese Buddhists following the communist revolution in China and China's subsequent invasion of Tibet. In the USA, which has the largest western population of Buddhists, contact with Japanese Buddhism increased during the American occupation of Japan after the World War II. The greatest growth in the practice of Buddhism by non-Asian westerners has occurred since the social revolution in the west in the 1960s.

Just as Buddhism developed distinctive forms in other cultures, a distinctive western form of Buddhism is likely to evolve in due course. Buddhism is still taught by personal instruction from teacher to pupil, but the means for its transmission are now more diverse than ever. The last two decades have seen a flowering of books and magazines on the subject, but these are augmented by more modern media, including video, CDs and the Internet. The increasing availability of information, teachings, and scriptures in electronic formats, and the existence of Internet networks of Buddhists, have made Buddhism a truly global religion for the 21st century.

ANDREW SKILTON

SEE ALSO
Buddhism; dharma; Lamaism; Mahāyāna; Nichiren; Pure Land Buddhism; Zen

BUDDHISM: TIMELINE

5th C BC	Life of Siddhartha Gautama, the historical Buddha. At the age of 35 he delivered his first sermon, and the remaining 45 years of his life were spent teaching in Northern India.
5th C–1st C BC	The Buddha's teachings survived orally in Middle Indian languages, and were gradually divided into the *Tipitaka*.
c. 300 BC	The Sangha met in council at Vesāli to discuss allegations of misconduct on the part of certain factions. The council ended in a schism between the minority Sthaviravada and majority Mahasangha groups. The roots of the division between the two major schools of Buddhism – the Theravāda and the Mahāyāna – are sometimes traced back to the council of Vesali.
3rd C BC	Emperor Aśoka, ruler of much of South Asia, embraced Buddhism as his state religion, and sent missionaries to introduce Buddhism to Burma and Afghanistan.
1st C BC	The Buddha's teachings were first committed to writing, in the Pāli language, in Sri Lanka. Buddhism began to spread along trading routes through central Asia. In India, the first versions of the Astasāhasrikā Prajñāpāramitā Sūtra, considered the first Mahāyāna Buddhist sūtra, were written.
1st C AD	Buddhism was taken to central Asia and China. In India Buddhism was patronized by the king Kanishka.
2nd C	Nāgārjuna, a south Indian monastic philospher and mystic, put forward the Sūnyatāvāda or 'Way of Emptiness', which later became one of the central Mahāyāna doctrines.
3rd C	Buddhism expanded into Southeast Asia.
399–413	The Chinese pilgrim Fa-hsien made his famous journey from China to India to obtain Indian sūtras.
4th C	Buddhism reached Korea and Indonesia, and was officially recognized in China. In India, a new wave of Mahāyāna sutras led the philosophers Asańga and Vasubandhu to propound the Vijñānavāda or 'Mind-Only' school, further developing Mahāyāna philosophy.
c. 520	According to tradition, Bodhidharma, founder of the Ch'an school, arrived in China.
6th C	Buddhism was introduced to Japan as the state religion, during the regency of Prince Shotoku Taishi.
618–907	During the T'ang dynasty Buddhism enjoyed a high level of importance in China and also in Korea and Japan. This period saw the beginnings of the Chinese form of Pure Land Buddhism, as well as the T'ien-t'ai, Hua-yen, and Ch'an schools.
early 7th C	Buddhism was first established in Tibet during the reign of Srong btsan sam po.
756–97	Buddhism in Tibet made significant advances during the reign of Khri srong lde brtsan, culminating in the founding of the first Tibetan monastery, called bSam yas.
842	On the death of King gLang dar ma, Tibet lost control of central Asia and northern Buddhism temporarily lost its political influence.
842–845	Towards the end of the T'ang dynasty, Buddhism was persecuted in China, signalling a decline in its importance and a revival of Confucian and Taoist belief.
971–983	The canon of Chinese Buddhism was first established.
11th C	Buddhism in Tibet was rejuvenated by the arrival from India of the teacher Atiśa, and also by the contemporary Tibetan religious teacher Milaraspa. Many of Tibet's most important Buddhist schools were founded.
11th–15th Cs	Sri Lankan monarchs unified the Theravadin Sangha (monastic orders), leading to a period of great prosperity for Theravāda, in both Sri Lanka and Southeast Asia.
12th C	Pure Land Buddhism was established in Japan by Hōnen.
1190s	Muslim Turkish invaders established control of northern India, destroying the Buddhist university at Nalanda and imposing forced conversions to Islam. Within two centuries, Buddhism had been driven out of northern India.
13th C	Efforts towards unification of the Sangha by the Buddhist monarchs of Southeast Asia led to a consolidation of Southeast Asian Buddhism.
11th–15th Cs	Sri Lankan monarchs unified the Theravadin Sangha under orthodox Mahavihara rules, leading to a period of great prosperity for Theravāda, both in Sri Lanka and in Southeast Asia.
14th C	The scholar Bu-ston collected together the Tibetan canon.
1357–1419	Tsong-kha pa reformed Tibetan Buddhism and founded the Gelug-pa school. The heads of this school later ruled Tibet under the title of Dalai Lama.
16th–17th Cs	Explorers, merchants, and military expeditions began to bring knowledge of Buddhism to the West. Tibetan scholar Tārānātha wrote a history of Buddhism in India.
19th C	The end of the Sri Lankan and Burmese monarchies, and their replacement by foreign powers, weakened the southern Buddhist Sangha considerably.
1839–1949	The Opium Wars and subsequent conflicts generally weakened the position of Buddhism in Chinese society – in particular, the T'ai-P'ing rebellion left many temples and monasteries destroyed.
1950s	Tibet was invaded by communist China. By 1959 all Tibetan self-rule was abolished, and the Dalai Lama fled to India along with thousands of refugees. In Tibet, the Chinese authorities attempted to eradicate Tibetan religious culture.
1960s and 1970s	The Chinese Cultural Revolution prohibited Buddhist practice in China, and many monasteries were damaged or destroyed. Conflicts in Southeast Asia resulted in a decline in the strength of the Southeast Asian Sangha.
1980s	The communist authorities of China and Southeast Asia gradually became more tolerant of Buddhist practice. In Europe and the USA Buddhism, particularly of the Theravāda, Tibetan, and Zen schools, became established as a significant minority religion.

Constructed of copper plated with brass, it has long been used as a military instrument for giving a range of signals based on the tones of a harmonic series. The bugle is conical whereas the trumpet is cylindrical.

bugle any of a genus *Ajuga* of low-growing plants of the mint family Labiatae, with spikes of white, pink, or blue flowers. They are often grown as ground cover. The leaves may be smooth-edged or faintly toothed, the lower ones with a long stalk. Bugle is found across Europe and N Africa, usually in damp woods or pastures.

bugloss any of several genera of plants of the family Boraginaceae, distinguished by their rough, bristly leaves and small blue flowers.

building society in the UK, a financial institution that attracts investment in order to lend money, repayable at interest, for the purchase or building of a house on security of a ◊mortgage. Building societies originated 1781 from the ◊friendly societies in England.

Bujones Fernando 1955– . US ballet dancer. He joined the American Ballet Theater 1972. A virtuoso performer, he has danced leading roles both in the major classics and in contemporary ballets, including *Swan Lake*, *La Bayadère*, and *Fancy Free*.

Bujumbura capital of Burundi; population (1994 est) 300,000. Formerly called ***Usumbura*** (until 1962), it was founded 1899 by German colonists. The university was established 1960.

Bukhara or ***Bokhara*** central city in Uzbekistan; population (1990) 228,000. It is the capital of Bukhara region, which has given its name to carpets (made in Ashgabat). It is an Islamic centre, with a Muslim theological training centre. An ancient city in central Asia, it was formerly the capital of the independent emirate of Bukhara, annexed to Russia 1868. It was included in Bukhara region 1924.

Bukharin Nikolai Ivanovich 1888–1938. Soviet politician and theorist. A moderate, he was the chief Bolshevik thinker after Lenin. Executed on Stalin's orders for treason 1938, he was posthumously rehabilitated 1988.

Bulawayo industrial city and railway junction in Zimbabwe; population (1992) 620,900. It lies at an altitude of 1,355 m/4,450 ft on the river Matsheumlope, a tributary of the Zambezi, and was founded on the site of the kraal (enclosed village), burned down 1893, of the Matabele chief, Lobenguela. It produces agricultural and electrical equipment. The former capital of Matabeleland, Bulawayo developed with the exploitation of gold mines in the neighbourhood.

bulb underground bud with fleshy leaves containing a reserve food supply and with roots growing from its base. Bulbs function in vegetative reproduction and are characteristic of many monocotyledonous plants such as the daffodil, snowdrop, and onion. Bulbs are grown on a commercial scale in temperate countries, such as England and the Netherlands.

bulbil small bulb that develops above ground from a bud. Bulbils may be formed on the stem from axillary buds, as in members of the saxifrage family, or in the place of flowers, as seen in many species of onion *Allium*. They drop off the parent plant and develop into new individuals, providing a means of ◊vegetative reproduction and dispersal.

bulbul fruit-eating bird of the family Pycnonotidae, order Passeriformes, that ranges in size from that of a sparrow to a blackbird. They are mostly rather dull coloured and very secretive, living in dense forests. They are widely distributed throughout Africa and Asia; there are about 120 species.

Bulganin Nikolai Aleksandrovich 1895–1975. Soviet politician and military leader. His career began 1918 when he joined the Cheka, the Soviet secret police. He helped to organize Moscow's defence in World War II, became a marshal of the USSR 1947, and was minister of defence 1947–49 and 1953–55. On the fall of Malenkov he became prime minister (chair of Council of Ministers) 1955–58 until ousted by Khrushchev.

Bulgaria country in SE Europe, bounded N by Romania, W by Yugoslavia and the Former Yugoslav Republic of Macedonia, S by Greece, SE by Turkey, and E by the Black Sea. *See country box opposite.*

Bulgarian an ethnic group living mainly in Bulgaria. There are 8–8.5 million speakers of Bulgarian, a Slavic language belonging to the Indo-European family. The Bulgarians use the Cyrillic alphabet.

Known in E Europe since the 6th century AD, the Bulgarians were unified under Kurt or Kubrat in the 7th century. In 864 Boris I adopted the Eastern Orthodox faith. Between 1018 and 1185 the Bulgarians were ruled by the Byzantines, and between 1396 and 1878 by the Ottomans. To suppress an uprising against the Ottoman Empire 1876 the Turks massacred thousands of Bulgarians.

Bulge, Battle of the (or ***Ardennes offensive***) in World War II, Hitler's plan for a breakthrough in the Ardennes 16 Dec 1944–28 Jan 1945. Hitler aimed to isolate the Allied forces north of the corridor which would be created by a drive through the Ardennes, creating a German salient or 'bulge'. There were 77,000 Allied casualties and 130,000 German, including Hitler's last powerful reserve of elite Panzer units. Although US troops were encircled for some weeks at Bastogne, the German counteroffensive failed.

bulgur wheat or ***bulgar*** or ***burghul*** cracked whole wheat, made by cooking the grains, then drying and cracking them. It is widely eaten in the Middle East. Coarse bulgur may be cooked in the same way as rice; more finely ground bulgur is mixed with minced meat to make a paste that may be eaten as a dip with salad, or shaped and stuffed before being grilled or fried.

bug Bugs of the family Pyrrhocoridae are commonly called 'cotton stainers' since certain species damage cotton bolls while feeding on the seeds. This cotton stainer *Dysdercus flavidus* is feeding on kapok seeds in Madagascar. *Premaphotos Wildlife*

bulimia (Greek 'ox hunger') eating disorder in which large amounts of food are consumed in a short time ('binge'), usually followed by depression and self-criticism. The term is often used for bulimia nervosa, an emotional disorder in which eating is followed by deliberate vomiting and purging. This may be a chronic stage in ◊anorexia nervosa.

bull or ***papal bull*** document or edict issued by the pope; so called from the circular seals (medieval Latin *bulla*) attached to them. Some of the most celebrated bulls include Leo X's condemnation of Luther 1520 and Pius IX's proclamation of papal infallibility 1870.

Bull John. Imaginary figure personifying England; see ◊John Bull.

Bull John c. 1562–1628. English composer, organist, and virginalist. Most of his output is for keyboard, and includes ◊'God Save the King'. He also wrote sacred vocal music.

bull speculator who buys stocks or shares on the stock exchange expecting a rise in the price in order to sell them later at a profit, the opposite of a ◊bear. In a bull market, prices rise and bulls profit.

bulldog British breed of dog of ancient but uncertain origin, formerly bred for bull-baiting. The head is broad and square, with deeply wrinkled cheeks, small folded ears, very short muzzle, and massive

BULGARIA
Republic of

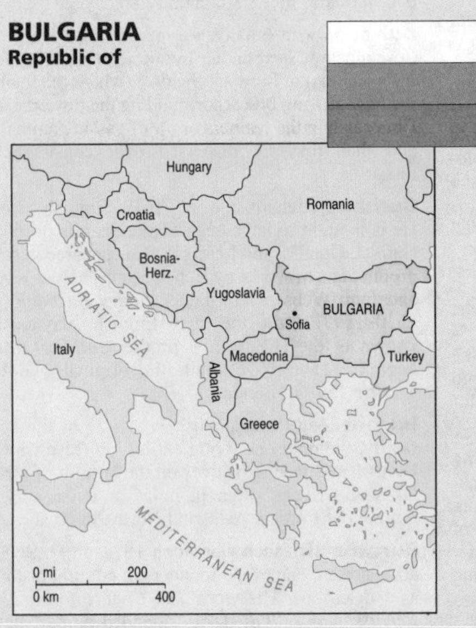

national name *Republika Bulgaria*
area 110,912 sq km/42,812 sq mi
capital Sofia
major towns/cities Plovdiv, Ruse
major ports Black Sea ports Burgas and Varna
physical features lowland plains in N and SE separated by mountains (Balkan and Rhodope) that cover three-quarters of the country; Danube river in N
head of state Petar Stoyanov from 1997
head of government Ivan Kostov from 1997
political system emergent democratic republic
administrative divisions nine regions
political parties Union of Democratic Forces (UDF), right of centre; Bulgarian Socialist Party (BSP), left-wing, ex-communist; Movement for Rights and Freedoms (MRF), Turkish-oriented, centrist; Civic Alliances for the Republic (CAR), left of centre
population 10,319,000 (1995 est)
population growth rate 2.8% (1990–95); 2.5 (2000–05)
ethnic distribution Southern Slavic Bulgarians constitute around 90% of the population; 9% are ethnic Turks, who during the later 1980s were subjected to government pressure to adopt Slavic names and to resettle elsewhere
life expectancy 70 (men), 76 (women)
literacy 93%
languages Bulgarian, Turkish
religions Eastern Orthodox Christian, Muslim, Roman Catholic, Protestant
currency lev
GDP (US $) 10.1 billion (1994)
growth rate 1.4% (1994)
exports textiles, leather, chemicals, nonferrous metals, timber, machinery, tobacco, cigarettes (world's largest exporter), meat, tomatoes, cheese, wine, soda ash, carbamide, ammonium nitrate, polyethylene, footwear, rolled iron and steel products, zinc, electric motors

HISTORY
c. 3500 BC onwards Settlement of semi-nomadic pastoralists from Central Asian steppes, who formed the Thracian community.
mid-5th C BC Thracian state formed, which was to extend over Bulgaria, N Greece, and N Turkey.
4th C BC Phillip II and Alexander the Great of Macedonia, to the SW, waged largely unsuccessful campaigns against the Thracian Empire.
AD 50 Thracians subdued and incorporated within Roman Empire as the province of Moesia Inferior.
3rd–6th Cs Successively invaded from the N and devastated by the Goths, Huns, Bulgars, and Avars.
681 The Bulgars, an originally Turkic group that had merged with earlier Slav settlers, revolted against the Avars and established, S of the Danube River, the first Bulgarian kingdom, with its capital at Pliska, in the Balkans.
864 Orthodox Christianity adopted by Boris I.
1018 Subjugated by the Byzantines, whose empire had its capital at Constantinople; led to Bulgarian Church breaking with Rome in 1054.
1185 Second independent Bulgarian Kingdom formed.
mid-13th C Bulgarian state destroyed by Mongol incursions.
1396 Bulgaria became the first European state to be absorbed into the Turkish Ottoman Empire; the imposition of a harsh feudal system and the sacking of monasteries followed.
1859 Bulgarian Catholic Church re-established links with Rome.
1876 Bulgarian nationalist revolt against Ottoman rule crushed brutally by Ottomans, with 15,000 massacred at Plovdiv ('Bulgarian Atrocities').
1878 At the Congress of Berlin, concluding a Russo-Turkish war in which Bulgarian volunteers had fought alongside the Russians, the area S of the Balkans, Eastern Rumelia, remained an Ottoman province, but the area to the N became the autonomous Principality of Bulgaria, with a liberal constitution and Alexander Battenberg as prince.
1885 Eastern Rumelia annexed by the Principality; Serbia defeated in war.
1908 Full independence proclaimed from Turkish rule, with Ferdinand I as tsar.
1913 Following defeat in the Second Balkan War, King Ferdinand I abdicated and was replaced by his son Boris III.
1919 Bulgarian Agrarian Union government, led by Alexander Stamboliiski, came to power and redistributed land to poor peasants.
1923 Agrarian government overthrown in right-wing coup and Stamboliiski murdered.
1934 Semi-fascist dictatorship established by King Boris III, who sided with Germany during World War II, but died mysteriously in 1943 following a visit to Adolf Hitler.
1944 Soviet invasion of German-occupied Bulgaria.
1946 Monarchy abolished and communist-dominated people's republic proclaimed following plebiscite.
1947 Gained South Dobruja in the NE, along the Black Sea, from Romania; Soviet-style constitution established a one-party state; industries and financial institutions nationalized and co-operative farming introduced.
1949 Death of Georgi Dimitrov, the communist government leader; replaced by Vulko Chervenkov.
1954 Election of Todor Zhivkov as Bulgarian Communist Party (BCP) general secretary; Bulgaria became a loyal and cautious satellite of the Soviet Union.
1968 Participated in the Soviet-led invasion of Czechoslovakia.
1971 Zhivkov became president, under new constitution.
1985–89 Haphazard administrative and economic reforms, known as *preustroistvo* ('restructuring'), introduced under stimulus of reformist Soviet leader Mikhail Gorbachev.
1989 Programme of enforced 'Bulgarianization' resulted in mass exodus of ethnic Turks to Turkey. Zhivkov ousted by foreign minister Petar Mladenov. Opposition parties tolerated.
1990 BCP reformed under new name Bulgarian Socialist Party (BSP). Zhelyu Zhelev of the centre-right Union of Democratic Forces (UDF) indirectly elected president. Following mass demonstrations and general strike, BSP government replaced by coalition.
1991 New liberal-democratic constitution adopted. UDF beat BSP in general election; formation of first noncommunist, UDF-minority government.
1992 Zhelev became Bulgaria's first directly elected president. Following industrial unrest, Lyuben Berov became head of a non-party government. Zhivkov sentenced to seven years' imprisonment for corruption whilst in government.
1993 Voucher-based 'mass privatization' programme launched.
1994 Berov resigned; general election won by BSP.
1996 High inflation; radical economic and industrial reforms imposed. Petar Stoyanov elected president.
1997 General election won by UDF; Ivan Kostov became prime minister.

SEE ALSO Balkan Wars; Byzantine Empire; Dobruja; Ottoman Empire; Thrace

bullfinch The bullfinch *Pyrrhula pyrrhula* is notorious for the damage it does by eating the buds of fruit trees and flowering shrubs in spring. Bullfinches prefer to stay in the safety of trees, and are rarely seen on the ground. A bullfinch's nest is made from small twigs, moss, and lichen, lined with root fibres. The female lays a clutch of four or five eggs, two or three times per year.

jaws, the peculiar set of the lower jaw making it difficult for the dog to release its grip. Thickset in build, the bulldog grows to about 45 cm/18 in and has a smooth beige, tawny, or brindle coat. The French bulldog is much lighter in build and has large upright ears.

bulletin board in computing, a centre for the electronic storage of messages, usually accessed over the telephone network via a ◊modem but also sometimes accessed across the Internet. Bulletin board systems (often abbreviated to BBSs) are usually dedicated to specific interest groups, and may carry public and private messages, notices, and programs.

He that is down needs fear no fall, / He that is low no pride.

JOHN BUNYAN
Pilgrim's Progress

bullfighting the national sport of Spain (where there are more than 400 bullrings), which is also popular in Mexico, Portugal, and much of Latin America. It involves the ritualized taunting of a bull in a circular ring, until its eventual death at the hands of the matador. Originally popular in Greece and Rome, it was introduced into Spain by the Moors in the 11th century.

bullfinch Eurasian finch with a thick head and neck, and short heavy bill, genus *Pyrrhula pyrrhula*, family Fringillidae, order Passeriformes. It is small and blue-grey or black in colour, the males being reddish and the females brown on the breast. Bullfinches are 15 cm/6 in long, and usually seen in pairs. They feed on tree buds as well as seeds and berries, and are usually seen in woodland. They also live in the Aleutians and on the Alaska mainland.

bullroarer musical instrument used by Australian Aborigines for communication and during religious rites. It consists of a weighted aerofoil (a piece of wood or stone) whirled on a long cord to make a deep whirring noise.

Bull Run, Battles of in the American Civil War, two victories for the Confederate army under General Robert E Lee at Manassas Junction, NE Virginia, named after the stream where they took place: First Battle of Bull Run 21 July 1861; Second Battle of Bull Run 29–30 Aug 1862.

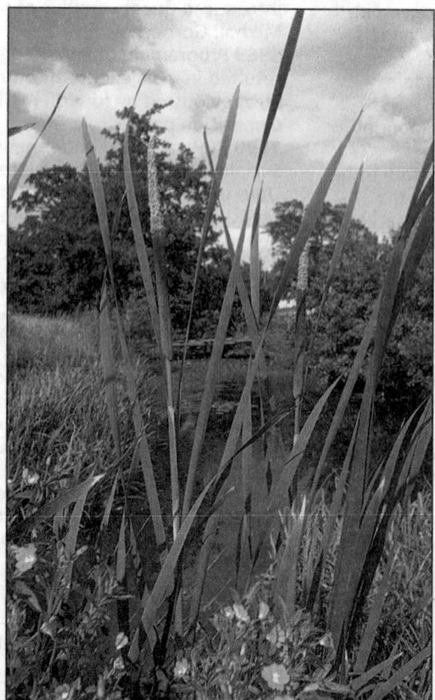

bulrush The true bulrush *Scirpus lacustris* is an inhabitant of ponds, lakes, and rivers, preferring those with an abundance of silt. Bulrushes were once gathered for making rush mats. A tall, virtually leafless plant, it produces clusters of small, reddish-brown flowers. *Premaphotos Wildlife*

bull terrier breed of dog, originating as a cross between a terrier and a bulldog. Very powerfully built, it grows to about 40 cm/16 in tall, and has a short, usually white, coat, narrow eyes, and distinctive egg-shaped head. It was formerly used in bull-baiting. Pit bull terriers are used in illegal dog fights. The Staffordshire bull terrier is a distinct breed.

Bülow Bernhard Heinrich Martin Karl, Prince von Bülow 1849–1929. German diplomat and politician. He was chancellor of the German Empire 1900–09 under Kaiser Wilhelm II and, holding that self-interest was the only rule for any state, adopted attitudes to France and Russia that unintentionally reinforced the trend towards opposing European power groups: the ◊Triple Entente (Britain, France, Russia) and the ◊Triple Alliance (Germany, Austria–Hungary, Italy).

bulrush either of two plants: the great reed mace or cat's tail *Typha latifolia* with chocolate-brown tight-packed flower spikes reaching up to 15 cm/6 in long; and a type of ◊sedge, *Scirpus lacustris*, with tufts of reddish-brown flowers at the top of a rounded, rushlike stem. Bulrushes are used in basket-making and thatching.

Bulwer-Lytton Edward George Earle, 1st Baron Lytton 1803–1873. see ◊Lytton.

bumblebee any large ◊bee, 2–5 cm/1–2 in, usually dark-coloured but banded with yellow, orange, or white, belonging to the genus *Bombus*.

Most species live in small colonies, usually underground. All the bees die at the end of the season except fertilized females, which hibernate and produce fresh colonies in the spring. Bumblebees are found naturally all over the world, with the exception of Australia, where they have been introduced to facilitate the pollination of some cultivated varieties of clover.

Bunche Ralph Johnson 1904–1971. US diplomat. Grandson of a slave, he was principal director of the UN Department of Trusteeship 1947–54, and UN undersecretary acting as mediator in Palestine 1948–49 and as special representative in the Congo 1960. In 1950 he was awarded the Nobel Prize for Peace, the first awarded to a black man.

bundling computer industry practice of selling different, often unrelated, products in a single package. Bundles may consist of hardware or software or both; for example, a modem or a selection of software may be bundled with a personal computer to make the purchase of the computer seem more attractive.

Bunin Ivan Alexeyevich 1870–1953. Russian writer. He was the author of *The Village* 1910, a novel which tells of the passing of peasant life; and the short story collection *The Gentleman from San Francisco* 1916 (about the death of a millionaire on Capri), for which he received a Nobel prize 1933. He was also a poet and translated Byron into Russian.

Bunker Hill, Battle of the first significant engagement in the ◊American Revolution, 17 June 1775, near a small hill in Charlestown (now part of Boston), Massachusetts, USA; the battle actually took place on Breed's Hill, but is named after Bunker Hill as this was the more significant of the two. Although the colonists were defeated they were able to retreat to Boston in good order and lost only 450 casualties against British losses of 226 killed and 828 wounded.

Bunsen Robert Wilhelm 1811–1899. German chemist credited with the invention of the Bunsen burner. His name is also given to the carbon–zinc electric cell, which he invented 1841 for use in arc lamps. In 1860 he discovered two new elements, caesium and rubidium.

Bunsen burner gas burner used in laboratories, consisting of a vertical metal tube through which a fine jet of fuel gas is directed. Air is drawn in through airholes near the base of the tube and the mixture is ignited and burns at the tube's upper opening.

bunting any of a number of sturdy, finchlike birds with short, thick bills, of the family Emberizidae, order Passeriformes, especially the genera *Passerim* and *Emberiza*. Most of these brightly coloured birds are native to the New World.

Buñuel Luis 1900–1983. Spanish Surrealist film director (see ◊Surrealism). He collaborated with Salvador Dali on *Un chien andalou* 1928 and *L'Age d'or/The Golden Age* 1930, and established his solo career with *Los olvidados/The Young and the Damned* 1950. His works are often anticlerical, with black humour and erotic imagery.

Bunyan John 1628–1688. English writer. A Baptist, he was imprisoned in Bedford 1660–72 for unlicensed preaching and wrote *Grace Abounding* 1666, which describes his early spiritual life. During a second jail sentence 1676–77 he started to write *The Pilgrim's Progress*, the first part of which was published 1678. This allegorical story of Christian's spiritual quest is written in straightforward language with fervour and imagination.

buoy floating object used to mark channels for shipping or warn of hazards to navigation. Buoys come in different shapes, such as a pole (spar buoy), cylinder (car buoy), and cone (nun buoy). Light buoys carry a small tower surmounted by a flashing lantern, and bell buoys house a bell, which rings as the buoy moves up and down with the waves. Mooring buoys are heavy and have a ring on top to which a ship can be tied.

buoyancy lifting effect of a fluid on a body wholly or partly immersed in it. This was studied by ◊Archimedes in the 3rd century BC.

bur or ***burr*** in botany, a type of 'false fruit' or ◊pseudocarp, surrounded by numerous hooks; for instance, that of burdock *Arctium*, where the hooks are formed from bracts surrounding the flowerhead. Burs catch in the feathers or fur of passing animals, and thus may be dispersed over considerable distances.

Burbage Richard c. 1567–1619. English actor. He is thought to have been Shakespeare's original Hamlet, Othello, and Lear. He also appeared in first productions of works by Ben Jonson, Thomas Kyd, and John Webster. His father ***James Burbage*** (c. 1530–1597) built the first English playhouse, known as 'the Theatre'; his brother ***Cuthbert Burbage*** (c. 1566–1636) built the original ◊Globe Theatre 1599 in London.

burbot long, rounded fish *Lota lota* of the cod family, the only one living entirely in fresh water. Up to 1 m/3 ft long, it lives on the bottom of clear lakes and rivers, often in holes or under rocks, throughout Europe, Asia, and North America.

Burckhardt Jacob Christoph 1818–1897. Swiss art historian, one of the founders of cultural history as a discipline. His work *The Civilization of the Renaissance in Italy* 1860, intended as part of a study of world cultural history, profoundly influenced thought on the Renaissance.

burdock any of the bushy herbs belonging to the genus *Arctium* of the family Compositae, characterized by hairy leaves and ripe fruit enclosed in ◊burs with strong hooks.

bureaucracy organization whose structure and operations are governed to a high degree by written rules and a hierarchy of offices; in its broadest sense, all forms of administration, and in its narrowest, rule by officials.

Burges William 1827–1881. English Gothic Revival architect and designer. His style is characterized by sumptuous interiors with carving, painting, and gilding. His chief works are Cork Cathedral 1862–76, and additions to and the remodelling of Cardiff Castle 1868–85 and Castle Coch near Cardiff 1875–91.

Burgess Anthony. Pen name of John Anthony Burgess Wilson 1917–1993. English novelist, critic, and composer. His work includes *A Clockwork Orange* 1962, a despairing depiction of high technology and violence set in a future London terrorized by teenage gangs, and the panoramic *Earthly Powers* 1980.

Burgess Guy Francis de Moncy 1911–1963. British spy, a diplomat recruited by the USSR as an agent. He was linked with Kim ◊Philby, Donald Maclean (1913–1983), and Anthony ◊Blunt.

Burgess Shale Site site of unique fossil-bearing rock formations created 530 million years ago by a

Bunker Hill, Battle of British ships bombarding American positions on Breed's Hill during the Battle of Bunker Hill 1775. Although the British won, they sustained heavy losses and the battle was a moral victory for the American rebels. *Image Select (UK) Ltd*

mud slide, in Yoho National Park, British Columbia, Canada. The shales in this corner of the Rocky Mountains contain more than 120 species of marine invertebrate fossils. Although discovered 1909 by US geologist Charles Walcott, the Burgess Shales have only recently been used as evidence in the debate concerning the evolution of life.

burgh former unit of Scottish local government, referring to a town enjoying a degree of self-government, abolished 1975; the terms burgh and royal burgh once gave mercantile privilege but are now only an honorary distinction.

Burgh Hubert de, died 1243. English ◊justiciar and regent of England. He began his career in the administration of Richard I, and was promoted to the justiciarship by King John. He was a supporter of King John against the barons. He reorganized royal administration and the Common Law.

burgher term used from the 11th century to describe a citizen of a burgh (the former unit of Scottish local government) who was a freeman of the burgh and had the right to participate in its government. Burghers usually had to possess a house within the burgh.

Bunsen burner The Bunsen burner, used for heating laboratory equipment and chemicals. The flame can reach temperatures of 1,500°C/2,732°F and is at its hottest when the collar is open.

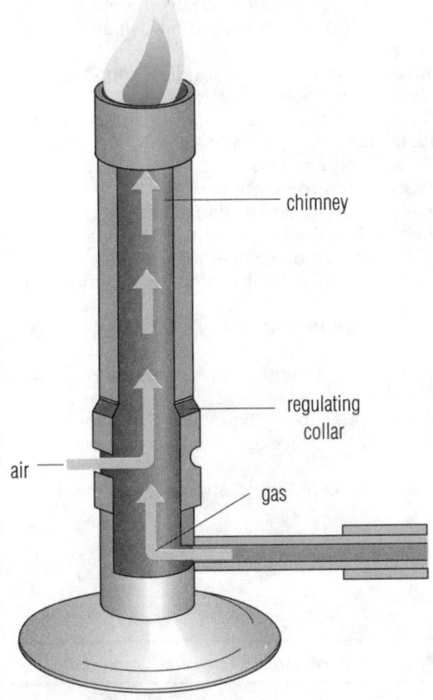

Burghley William Cecil, 1st Baron Burghley 1520–1598. English politician, chief adviser to Elizabeth I as secretary of state from 1558 and Lord High Treasurer from 1572. He was largely responsible for the religious settlement of 1559, and took a leading role in the events preceding the execution of Mary Queen of Scots 1587.

Burgundy ancient kingdom in the valleys of the rivers Rhône and Saône in E France and SW Germany, partly corresponding with modern-day Burgundy. Settled by the Teutonic Burgundi around AD 443, and brought under Frankish control 534, Burgundy played a central role in the medieval history of NW Europe.

It was divided among various groups between the 9th and 11th centuries, splitting into a duchy in the west (equivalent to the modern region), controlled by French ◊Carolingians, while the rest became a county in the ◊Holy Roman Empire. The duchy was acquired by the Capetian king Robert the Pious 1002, and until 1361 it was the most important and loyal fiefdom in the realm. Duchy and county were reunited 1384, and in the 15th century this wealthy region was the glittering capital of European court culture. The duchy was incorporated into France on the death of Duke ◊Charles the Bold 1477.

Burgundy (French ***Bourgogne***) modern region and former duchy of France that includes the *départements* of Côte-d'Or, Nièvre, Saône-et-Loire, and Yonne; area 31,600 sq km/12,198 sq mi; population (1990) 1,609,700. Its capital is Dijon.

It is renowned for its wines, such as Chablis and Nuits-Saint-Georges, and for its cattle (the Charolais herd-book is maintained at Nevers). A duchy from the 9th century, it was part of an independent medieval kingdom and was incorporated into France 1477.

Burke Edmund 1729–1797. British Whig politician and political theorist, born in Dublin, Ireland. In Parliament from 1765, he opposed the government's attempts to coerce the American colonists, for example in *Thoughts on the Present Discontents* 1770, and supported the emancipation of Ireland, but denounced the French Revolution, for example in *Reflections on the Revolution in France* 1790. Burke also wrote *A Philosophical Inquiry into the Origin of our Ideas on the Sublime and Beautiful* 1756, on aesthetics.

Burke was a skilled orator and is regarded by the British Conservatives as the greatest of their political theorists.

Burke Robert O'Hara 1821–1861. Irish-born Australian explorer who made the first south-north crossing of Australia (from Victoria to the Gulf of Carpentaria), with William Wills (1834–1861). Both died on the return journey, and only one of their party survived.

Burke William 1792–1829. Irish murderer. He and his partner William Hare, living in Edinburgh, sold the body of an old man who had died from natural causes in their lodging house. After that, they increased their supplies by murdering at least 15 people. Burke was hanged on the evidence of Hare. Hare is said to have died a beggar in London in the 1860s.

Burkina Faso (formerly ***Upper Volta***) landlocked country in W Africa, bounded E by Niger, NW and W by Mali, S by Côte d'Ivoire, Ghana, Togo, and Benin. *See country box on page 168.*

burlesque in the 17th and 18th centuries, a form of satirical comedy parodying a particular play or dramatic genre. For example, John ◊Gay's *The Beggar's Opera* 1728 is a burlesque of 18th-century opera, and Richard Brinsley ◊Sheridan's *The Critic* 1777 satirizes the sentimentality in contemporary drama. In the USA from the mid-19th century, burlesque referred to a sex-and-comedy show invented by Michael Bennett Leavitt 1866 with acts including acrobats, singers, and comedians. During the 1920s striptease was introduced in order to counteract the growing popularity of the movies.

Burlington Richard Boyle, 3rd Earl of Burlington 1695–1753. Anglo-Irish architectural patron and architect. He was one of the premier exponents of the Palladian style in Britain. His buildings are characterized by absolute adherence to the Classical rules. Chiswick House in London, built by Burlington 1725–29, is based on Palladio's Villa Rotonda, Italy. His major protégé was William ◊Kent.

Burman the largest ethnic group in Myanmar (formerly Burma). The Burmans, speakers of a Sino-Tibetan language, migrated from the hills of Tibet, settling in the areas around Mandalay by the 11th century AD.

burn in medicine, destruction of body tissue by extremes of temperature, corrosive chemicals, electricity, or radiation. ***First-degree burns*** may cause reddening; ***second-degree burns*** cause blistering and irritation but usually heal spontaneously; ***third-degree burns*** are disfiguring and may be life-threatening.

Burns cause plasma, the fluid component of the blood, to leak from the blood vessels, and it is this loss of circulating fluid that engenders ◊shock. Emergency treatment is needed for third-degree burns in order to replace the fluid volume, prevent infection (a dire threat to the severely burned), and reduce the pain. Plastic, or reconstructive, surgery, including skin grafting, may be required to compensate for damaged tissue and minimize disfigurement. If a skin graft is necessary, dead tissue must be removed from a burn (a process known as debridement) so that the patient's blood supply can nourish the graft.

Burne-Jones Edward Coley 1833–1898. English painter. In 1856 he was apprenticed to the Pre-Raphaelite painter and poet Dante Gabriel ◊Rossetti, who remained a dominant influence. His paintings, inspired by legend and myth, were

The greater the power, the more dangerous the abuse.

EDMUND BURKE
Speech on the Middlesex election 1771

Bunyan English 17th-century author John Bunyan, who is best known for his *Pilgrim's Progress*, an allegory of the spiritual quest as a journey. He spent 12 years in prison for unlicensed preaching and during this time he wrote numerous books including *The Holy City* 1665, which was inspired by a passage in the Book of Revelation. *Corbis*

Burne-Jones A page from the *Kelmscott Chaucer* 1896, illustrating *The Romaunt of the Rose*, by Edward Burne-Jones. A member of the Pre-Raphaelite movement, Burne-Jones was strongly influenced by the ideas of William Morris and the visual style of Dante Gabriel Rossetti. He stressed the spiritual side of the Pre-Raphaelite movement, creating an ethereal world of legend and fable.

characterized by elongated forms and subdued tones, as in *King Cophetua and the Beggar Maid* 1880–84 (Tate Gallery, London). He also designed tapestries and stained glass in association with William ◊Morris.

Travelling is the ruin of all happiness! There's no looking at a building here after seeing Italy.

Fanny Burney *Cecilia*

burnet herb *Sanguisorba minor* of the rose family, also known as ***salad burnet***. It smells of cucumber and can be used in salads. The term is also used for other members of the genus *Sanguisorba*.

Burnet (Frank) Macfarlane 1899–1985. Australian physician, an authority on immunology and viral diseases such as influenza, poliomyelitis, and cholera. He shared the 1960 Nobel Prize for Physiology or Medicine with the immunologist Peter ◊Medawar for his work on skin grafting.

Burnett Frances Eliza Hodgson 1849–1924. English writer. She emigrated with her family to the USA 1865. Her novels for children include the sentimental rags-to-riches tale *Little Lord Fauntleroy* 1886 and *The Secret Garden* 1911, which has its values anchored in nature mysticism.

Burney Fanny (Frances) 1752–1840. English novelist and diarist. She achieved success with *Evelina*, an epistolary novel published anonymously 1778, became a member of Samuel ◊Johnson's circle, and received a post at court from Queen Charlotte. She published three further novels, *Cecilia* 1782, *Camilla* 1796, and *The Wanderer* 1814.

burning common name for ◊combustion.

Burns Robert 1759–1796. Scottish poet. He used a form of Scots dialect at a time when it was not considered suitably 'elevated' for literature. Burns's first volume, *Poems, Chiefly in the Scottish Dialect*, appeared 1786. In addition to his poetry (such as 'To a Mouse'), Burns wrote or adapted many songs, including 'Auld Lang Syne'. 'Burns Night' is celebrated on 25 Jan, his birthday.

Burns wrote as well in English as he did in Scots. He is recognized as the culminating figure in two centuries' tradition of folk song and genre poetry and one of the greatest of all writers of love songs. He contributed some 300 songs to James Johnson's *Scots Musical Museum* 1787–1803 and Thomson's *Select Collection of Original Scottish Airs* 1793–1841.

Burr Aaron 1756–1836. US politician, Republican vice president 1800–04, in which year he killed his political rival Alexander ◊Hamilton in a duel. In 1807 Burr was tried and acquitted of treason charges, which implicated him variously in a scheme to conquer Mexico, or part of Florida, or to rule over a seceded Louisiana.

Burroughs Edgar Rice 1875–1950. US novelist. He wrote *Tarzan of the Apes* 1914, the story of an aristocratic child lost in the jungle and reared by apes, and followed it with over 20 more books about the Tarzan character. He also wrote a series of novels about life on Mars, including *A Princess of Mars* 1917 and *Synthetic Men of Mars* 1940.

Burroughs William S(eward) 1914–1997. US writer. His work is noted for its experimental methods, black humour, explicit homo-eroticism, and apocalyptic vision. In 1944 he met Allen Ginsberg and Jack Kerouac, all three becoming leading members of the ◊Beat Generation. His first novel, *Junkie* 1953, documented his heroin addiction and expatriation to Mexico, where in 1951 he accidentally killed his common-law wife. He settled in Tangier 1954 and wrote his celebrated anti-novel *Naked Lunch* 1959. In Paris, he developed collage-based techniques of writing, resulting in his 'cut-up' science-fiction trilogy, *The Soft Machine* 1961, *The Ticket That Exploded* 1962, and *Nova Express* 1964.

Burroughs US novelist William Burroughs, a leading figure of the Beat Generation, became notorious for his graphic depictions of the often sordid and sometimes violent world of drug addiction. His frank and innovative novels are regarded by some as dreary exercises in narcissism, and by others as strikingly original satires on the spiritual and emotional emptiness of contemporary life. *Picador*

BURKINA FASO

The People's Democratic Republic of (formerly *Upper Volta*)

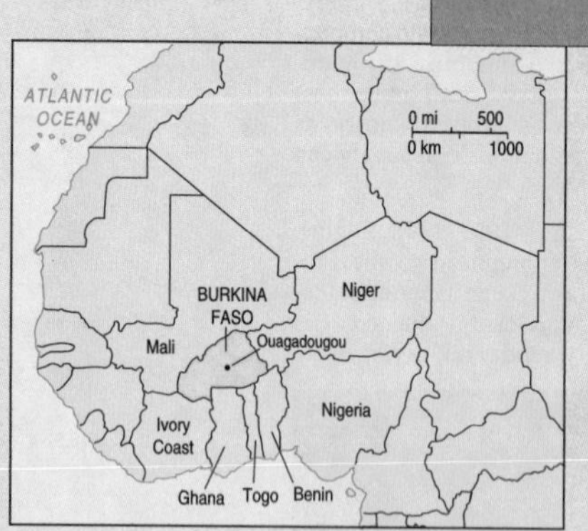

national name *République Démocratique Populaire de Burkina Faso*
area 274,122 sq km/105,811 sq mi
capital Ouagadougou
major towns/cities Bobo-Dioulasso, Koudougou
physical features landlocked plateau with hills in W and SE; headwaters of the river Volta; semiarid in N, forest and farmland in S; linked by rail to Abidja'n in Côte d'Ivoire, Burkina Faso's only outlet to the sea
head of state Blaise Compaoré from 1987
head of government Kadre Desire Ouedraogo from 1996
political system emergent democracy
administrative divisions 30 provinces
political parties Popular Front (FP), centre-left coalition grouping; National Convention of Progressive Patriots–Democratic Socialist Party (CNPP–PSD), left of centre
population 8,769,000 (1995 est)
population growth rate −0.5% (1990–95); −0.4% (2000–05)
ethnic distribution over 50 ethnic groups, including the nomadic Mossi (48%), the Fulani (10%), and the Gourma (5%). Settled tribes include: in the N the Lobi-Dagari (7%) and the Mande (7%); in the SE the Bobo (7%); and in the SW the Senoufu (6%) and Gourounsi (5%)
life expectancy 48 (males), 51 (females)
literacy rate men 28%, women 9%
languages French (official); about 50 native Sudanic languages spoken by 90% of population
religions animist 53%, Sunni Muslim 36%, Roman Catholic 11%
currency franc CFA
GDP (US $) 1.87 billion (1994)
growth rate 1.0% (1994)
exports cotton, livestock, hides, skins, sesame, cereals, karite nuts

HISTORY

13th–14th Cs Formerly settled by the Bobo, Lobi, and Gurunsi peoples, the E and centre were conquered by Mossi and Gurma peoples, who established powerful warrior kingdoms, some of which survived into the late 19th century.
1895–1903 France secured protectorates over the Mossi kingdom of Yatenga and the Gurma region, and annexed the Bobo and Lobi lands, meeting armed resistance.
1904 The French-controlled region, known as Upper Volta, was attached administratively to French Sudan; tribal chiefs were maintained in their traditional seats and the region was to serve as a labour reservoir for more developed colonies to S.
1919 Made a separate French colony.
1932 Partitioned between French Sudan, Ivory Coast, and Niger.
1947 Became a French Overseas Territory.
1959 Became a founder member (with Benin, Côte d'Ivoire, and Niger) of the Council of the Entente, which aimed to strengthen economic links between the members.
1960 Independence achieved, with Maurice Yaméogo as the first president.
1966 Military coup led by Lt-Col Sangoulé Lamizana, and a supreme council of the armed forces established.
1975 Became a member of the West African Economic Community.
1977 Ban on political activities removed. Referendum approved a new constitution based on civilian rule.
1978 Lamizana elected president.
1980 Lamizana overthrown in bloodless coup led by Col Saye Zerbo as economy deteriorated.
1982 Zerbo ousted in a coup by junior officers: Major Jean-Baptiste Ouédraogo became president and Capt Thomas Sankara prime minister.
1983 Sankara seized complete power.
1984 Upper Volta renamed Burkina Faso ('land of upright men') to signify break with colonial past; literacy and afforestation campaigns by radical Sankara, who established links with Libya, Benin, and Ghana.
1987 Sankara killed in coup led by Capt Blaise Compaoré.
1991 New constitution approved. Compaoré re-elected president.
1992 Multiparty elections won by pro-Compaoré Popular Front (FP), despite opposition claims of ballot-rigging.
1996 Kadre Desire Ouedraogo appointed prime minister.

SEE ALSO Mossi; West African Economic Community

Bursa city in NW Turkey, with a port at Mudania; population (1990) 834,600. It was the capital of the Ottoman Empire 1326–1423.

Burton Richard. Stage name of Richard Walter Jenkins 1925–1984. Welsh stage and screen actor. He had a rich, dramatic voice but his career was dogged by personal problems and an often poor choice of roles. Films in which he appeared with his wife, Elizabeth ◊Taylor, include *Cleopatra* 1962 and *Who's Afraid of Virginia Woolf?* 1966. Among his later films are *Equus* 1977 and *Nineteen Eighty-Four* 1984.

Burton Richard Francis 1821–1890. British explorer and translator (he knew 35 oriental languages). He travelled mainly in the Middle East and NE Africa, often disguised as a Muslim; made two attempts to find the source of the Nile, 1855 and 1857–58 (on the second, with John ◊Speke, he reached Lake Tanganyika); and wrote many travel books. He translated oriental erotica and the *Arabian Nights* 1885–88.

Burton upon Trent town in Staffordshire, England, NE of Birmingham; population (1991) 60,500. Industries include brewing, tyres, engineering, food processing, and rubber products. It is a former cotton-spinning town. The Benedictine monks of Burton Abbey (founded 1002) began its tradition of brewing in the 11th century.

Burundi country in E central Africa, bounded N by Rwanda, W by the Democratic Republic of Congo, SW by Lake Tanganyika, and SE and E by Tanzania. *See country box below.*

Bury administrative headquarters of Bury unitary authority on the river Irwell, 16 km/10 mi N of central Manchester; population (1991) 62,600. It is a textile town, concentrating on cotton spinning and weaving. Other industries include chemicals, engineering, textile machinery, felt, paint, printing, and paper making.

Buryat autonomous republic of the Russian Federation, in East Siberia
area 351,300 sq km/135,600 sq mi
capital Ulan-Ude
physical bounded S by Mongolia, W by Lake Baikal; mountainous and forested
industries coal, timber, building materials, fish, sheep, cattle
population (1992) 1,059,000
history settled by Russians 17th century; annexed from China by treaties 1689 and 1727; an autonomous republic from 1920.

Bury St Edmunds market town in Suffolk, England, on the river Lark; population (1991) 31,200. Industries include brewing, sugar beet refining, electronic equipment, cameras, lamps, and confectionery. It was named after St Edmund, and there are remains of a large Benedictine abbey.

bus in computing, the electrical pathway through which a computer processor communicates with some of its parts and/or peripherals. Physically, a bus is a set of parallel tracks that can carry digital signals.

Bush George Herbert Walker 1924– . 41st president of the USA 1989–93, a Republican. He was director of the Central Intelligence Agency (CIA) 1976–81 and US vice president 1981–89. As president, his response to the Soviet leader Gorbachev's diplomatic initiatives were initially criticized as inadequate, but his sending of US troops to depose his former ally, General Noriega of Panama, proved a popular move at home. Success in the 1991 Gulf War against Iraq further raised his standing. Domestic economic problems 1991–92 were followed by his defeat in the 1992 presidential elections by Democrat Bill Clinton.

bushbuck antelope *Tragelaphus scriptus* found over most of Africa south of the Sahara. Up to 1 m/3 ft high, the males have keeled horns twisted into spirals, and are brown to blackish. The females are generally hornless, lighter, and redder. All have white markings, including stripes or vertical rows of dots down the sides. Rarely far from water, bushbuck live in woods and thick brush. *See illustration on following page.*

bushel dry or liquid measure equal to eight gallons or four pecks (2,219.36 cu in/36.37 litres) in the UK; some US states have different standards according to the goods measured.

bushmaster large snake *Lachesis muta*. It is a type of pit viper, and is related to the rattlesnakes. Up to 4 m/12 ft long, it is found in wooded areas of South and Central America, and is the largest venomous snake in the New World. When alarmed, it produces a noise by vibrating its tail among dry leaves.

Bushmen former name for the ◊Kung, ◊San, and other hunting and gathering groups (for example, the Gikwe, Heikom, and Sekhoin) living in and around the Kalahari Desert in southern Africa. They number approximately 50,000 and speak San and other 'click' languages of the ◊Khoisan family. They are characteristically small-statured.

For much of the year the Bushmen live in small egalitarian bands of about 25 people, each band consisting of a few families living independently in a large territory within which it alone has hunting rights. They once occupied a larger area, but were driven into the Kalahari Desert in the 18th century by Bantu peoples (Sotho and Nguni). Their early art survives in cave paintings.

bushranger Australian armed robber of the 19th century. The first bushrangers were escaped convicts. The last gang was led by Ned Kelly (1855–1880) and his brother Dan in 1878–80. They form the subject of many Australian ballads.

business park low-density office development of a type often established by private companies on greenfield sites. The sites are often landscaped to create a pleasant working environment. Business parks tend to be located near motorway junctions and may have a high proportion of high-tech firms. They were introduced into the UK in the early 1980s, and by 1991 there were about 800 throughout the country.

business rate tax levied on commercial property in an area. Business rates are set and collected by central government and the money is then distributed to local authorities to help finance their expenditure. Business rates are an example of fixed or overhead costs for a business.

'Man's inhumanity to man / Makes countless thousands mourn!'

Robert Burns
'Man was made to Mourn'

BURUNDI
Republic of

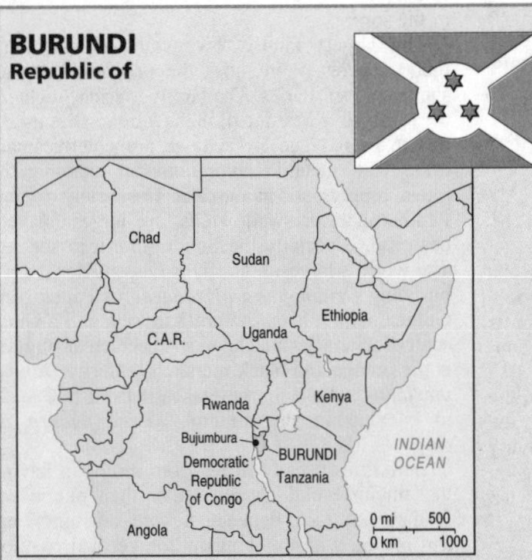

national name *Republika y'Uburundi*
area 27,834 sq km/10,744 sq mi
capital Bujumbura
major towns/cities Kitega, Bururi, Ngozi, Muhinga
physical features landlocked grassy highland straddling watershed of Nile and Congo; Lake Tanganyika, Great Rift Valley
head of state Pierre Buyoya from 1996
head of government Pascal-Firmin Ndimira from 1996
political system authoritarian nationalist
administrative divisions 15 provinces
political parties Front for Democracy in Burundi (FRODEBU), left of centre; Union for National Progress (UPRONA), nationalist socialist
population 6,393,000 (1995 est)
population growth rate 3.0% (1990–95); 2.6% (2000–05)
ethnic distribution two main groups: the agriculturalist Hutu, comprising about 85% of the population, and the predominantly pastoralist Tutsi, about 14%. There is a small Pygmy minority, comprising about 1% of the population, and a few Europeans and Asians
life expectancy 48 (males), 51 (females)
literacy rate men 61%, women 40%
languages Kirundi (a Bantu language) and French (both official), Kiswahili
religions Roman Catholic 62%, Pentecostalist 5%, Anglican 1%, Muslim 1%, animist
currency Burundi franc
GDP (US $) 1.06 billion (1994)
growth rate −18.0% (1994)
exports coffee, cotton, tea, nickel, hides, livestock, cigarettes, beer, soft drinks; there are 500 million tonnes of peat reserves in the basin of the Akanyaru River

HISTORY
10th C Formerly inhabited by the hunter-gatherer Twa Pygmies; Hutu peoples settled in the region and became peasant farmers.
15th–17th Cs The majority Hutu community came under the dominance of the cattle-owning Tutsi peoples, immigrants from the E, who became a semi-aristocracy; the minority Tutsis developed a feudalistic political system, organized around a nominal king (mwami), with royal princes (ganwa) in control of local areas.
1890 Known as Urundi, the Tutsi kingdom, along with neighbouring Rwanda, came under nominal German control, as Ruanda-Urundi.
1916 Occupied by Belgium during World War I.
1923 Belgium was granted a League of Nations mandate to administer Ruanda-Urundi; it was to rule 'indirectly' through the Tutsi chiefs.
1962 Separated from Ruanda-Urundi, as Burundi, and given independence as a monarchy under Tutsi King Mwambutsa IV.
1965 King refused to appoint a Hutu prime minister after an election in which Hutu candidates were victorious; attempted coup by Hutus brutally suppressed.
1966 King deposed by his teenage son Charles, who became Ntare V; he was in turn deposed by his Tutsi prime minister, Col Michel Micombero, who declared Burundi a republic; the Tutsi-dominated Union for National Progress (UPRUNA) declared only legal political party.
1972 Ntare V killed, allegedly by Hutus, provoking a massacre of 150,000 Hutus by Tutsi soldiers; 100,000 Hutus fled to Tanzania.
1976 Army coup deposed Micombero and appointed the Tutsi Col Jean-Baptiste Bagaza as president, who launched a drive against corruption and a programme of land reforms and economic development.
1987 Bagaza deposed in coup by the Tutsi Maj Pierre Buyoya.
1988 About 24,000 Hutus killed by Tutsis and 60,000 fled as refugees to Rwanda.
1992 New multiparty constitution adopted following referendum.
1993 Melchior Ndadaye, a Hutu, elected president in first-ever democratic contest but later killed in coup by Tutsi-dominated army; massacres followed, claiming 100,000 lives.
1994 Cyprien Ntaryamira, a Hutu, became president but later killed in air crash along with Rwandan president Juvenal Habyarimana. Ethnic violence; 750,000 Hutus fled to Rwanda. Hutu Sylvestre Ntibantunganya became head of state, serving with a Tutsi prime minister, as part of a four-year power-sharing agreement between main political parties.
1995 Renewed ethnic violence in the capital, Bujumbura, following massacre of Hutu refugees.
1996 Former Tutsi president Pierre Buyoya seized power amid renewed ethnic violence; coup provoked economic sanctions by other African countries. 'Government of national unity' appointed, with Pascal-Firmin Ndimira as premier. Bujumbura shelled by Hutu rebels.

SEE ALSO Hutu; Pygmy; Rwanda; Twa; Tutsi

bushbuck A male bushbuck in the Kruger National Park, South Africa. A small, shy antelope living in pairs on the African savanna, the bushbuck nibbles at the leaves of herbs, trees, and bushes, and also at buds, fruits, and the bark of trees. *Premaphotos Wildlife*

business school institution for training in management and marketing. In recent years, the emphasis has shifted to include study of such issues as environmental policy, corporate responsibility, business ethics, and internationalism. The master's in business administration (MBA) has become a highly prized degree in many professions. Major business schools include the London Business School (LBS), Harvard in the USA, and Insead in France.

Busoni Ferruccio Dante Benvenuto 1866–1924. Italian pianist, composer, and music critic. Much of his music was for the piano, but he also composed several operas including *Doktor Faust*, completed by Philipp Jarnach after his death. An apostle of Futurism, he encouraged the French composer Edgard Varèse.

‘In matters concerning art my feelings are those of an autocrat.’

Ferrucio Busoni
To Heinrich Burkard 1923

bustard bird of the family Otididae, order Gruiformes, related to ◊cranes but with a rounder body, thicker neck, and a relatively short beak. Bustards are found on the ground on open plains and fields.

The great bustard *Otis tarda* is one of the heaviest flying birds at 18 kg/40 lb, and the larger males may have a length of 1 m/3 ft and wingspan of 2.3 m/7.5 ft. It is found in N Asia and Europe, although there are fewer than 30,000 great bustards left in Europe; two-thirds of these live on the Spanish steppes.

It has been extinct in Britain for some time, although attempts are being made by the Great Bustard Trust (1970) to naturalize it again on Salisbury Plain. The little bustard *O. tetrax* is less than half the size of the great bustard, and is also found in continental Europe. The great Indian bustard is endangered because of hunting and loss of its habitat to agriculture; there are fewer than 1,000 individuals left.

butane C_4H_{10} one of two gaseous alkanes (paraffin hydrocarbons) having the same formula but differing in structure. Normal butane is derived from natural gas; isobutane is a by-product of petroleum manufacture. Liquefied under pressure, it is used as a fuel for industrial and domestic purposes (for example, in portable cookers).

bustard The Kori bustard *Ardeotis kori* is the largest member of the bustard family, measuring 130 cm/52 in in length. Bustards live in groups on grassy plains in S and E Africa, feeding on seeds, buds, insects, and small vertebrates. In spite of being clumsy fliers, they are powerful runners.

Bute island and resort in the Firth of Clyde, Scotland; area 120 sq km/46 sq mi. The chief town is Rothesay. There is farming and tourism. It is separated from the mainland in the N by a winding channel, the Kyles of Bute. With Arran and the adjacent islands it comprised the former county of Bute, merged 1975 into the region of Strathclyde.

Buthelezi Chief Mangosuthu Gatsha 1928– . South African Zulu leader and politician, president of the Zulu-based ◊Inkatha Freedom Party (IFP), which he founded as a paramilitary organization for attaining a nonracial democratic society 1975. Buthelezi's threatened boycott of South Africa's first multiracial elections led to a dramatic escalation in politically motivated violence, but he eventually agreed to register his party and in May 1994 was appointed home affairs minister in the country's first post-apartheid government.

Butler Richard Austen, (‘Rab’), Baron Butler of Saffron Walden 1902–1982. British Conservative politician. As minister of education 1941–45, he was responsible for the 1944 Education Act; he was chancellor of the Exchequer 1951–55, Lord Privy Seal 1955–59, and foreign minister 1963–64. As a candidate for the prime ministership, he was defeated by Harold Macmillan in 1957 (under whom he was home secretary 1957–62), and by Alec Douglas Home in 1963.

Butler Samuel 1612–1680. English satirist. His poem *Hudibras*, published in three parts 1663, 1664, and 1678, became immediately popular for its biting satire against the Puritans and on other contemporary issues.

Although the story line is a bare framework, the use of epigram and flippantly comic rhyme, the conversion of the tetrameter line to swift-moving semi-doggerel, and especially the virulence in expressing the contempt of a ‘good hater’, make it a memorable work.

Butler Samuel 1835–1902. English writer. He made his name 1872 with a satiric attack on contemporary utopianism, *Erewhon* (an anagram of *nowhere*), but is now remembered for his unfinished, semi-autobiographical discursive novel *The Way of All Flesh* written and frequently revised 1873–84 and posthumously published 1903.

Butlin Billy (William Heygate Edmund Colborne) 1899–1980. British holiday-camp entrepreneur. Born in South Africa, he went in early life to Canada, but later entered the fairground business in the UK. He originated a chain of camps (the first was at Skegness 1936) that provided accommodation, meals, and amusements at an inclusive price.

butte steep-sided, flat-topped hill, formed in horizontally layered sedimentary rocks, largely in arid areas. A large butte with a pronounced tablelike profile is a ◊mesa.

Buttes and mesas are characteristic of semi-arid areas where remnants of resistant rock layers protect softer rock underneath, as in the plateau regions of Colorado, Utah, and Arizona, USA.

butter solid, edible yellowish fat made from whole milk. Making butter by hand, which is done by skimming off the cream and churning it, was traditionally a convenient means of preserving milk.

The transfer of butter making from a farm-based to a factory-based process began in the last quarter of the 19th century, with the introduction of centrifugal separators for the instant separation of cream from milk. It could then be conveyed into large steam-powered churns. Today, most butter is made on a continuous system devised in Germany during World War II. Inside a single machine, the cream is churned, the buttermilk drawn off, and the butter washed, salted, and worked, to achieve an even consistency. Colour and flavouring may be added. A continuous stream of finished butter is extruded from the machine ready for wrapping.

buttercup plant of the genus *Ranunculus* of the buttercup family with divided leaves and yellow flowers. Species include the common buttercup *R. acris* and the creeping buttercup *R. repens*.

Butterfield William 1814–1900. English Gothic Revival architect. His work is characterized by vigorous, aggressive forms and multicoloured striped and patterned brickwork. His schools, parsonages, and cottages developed an appealing functional secular style that anticipated Philip ◊Webb and other ◊Arts and Crafts architects.

Typical buildings by Butterfield are the church of All Saints, Margaret Street, London, 1849–59, and Keble College and Chapel, Oxford, 1867–83. At Baldersby, Yorkshire, UK, he designed a whole village of church, rectory, almshouse, school, and cottages 1855–57.

butterfly insect belonging, like moths, to the order Lepidoptera, in which the wings are covered with tiny scales, often brightly coloured. There are some 15,000 species of butterfly, many of which are under threat throughout the world because of the destruction of habitat.

Butterflies have a tubular proboscis through which they suck up nectar, or, in some species, carrion, dung, or urine. ◊Metamorphosis is complete; the pupa, or chrysalis, is usually without the protection of a cocoon. Adult lifespan may be only a few weeks, but some species hibernate and lay eggs in the spring.

The largest family, Nymphalidae, has some 6,000 species; it includes the peacock, tortoiseshells, and fritillaries. The family Pieridae includes the cabbage white, one of the few butterflies injurious to crops. The Lycaenidae are chiefly small, often with metallic coloration, for example the blues, coppers, and hairstreaks. The mainly tropical Papilionidae, or swallowtails, are large and very beautiful, especially the South American species. The world's largest butterfly is Queen Alexandra's birdwing *Ornithoptera alexandrae* of Papua New Guinea, with a body 7.5 cm/3 in long and a wingspan of 25 cm/10 in. The most spectacular migrant is the orange and black monarch butterfly *Danaus plexippus*, whose journey takes it from N Canada to Mexico in the autumn. ▷*See feature on pp. 704–705.*

Butterflies usually differ from moths in having the antennae club-shaped rather than plumed or feathery, no ‘lock’ between the fore- and hindwing, and resting with the wings in the vertical position rather than flat or sloping.

butterfly fish any of several fishes, not all related. The freshwater butterfly fish *Pantodon buchholzi* of W Africa can leap from the water and glide for a short distance on its large winglike pectoral fins. Up to 10 cm/4 in long, it lives in stagnant water. The tropical marine butterfly fishes, family Chaetodontidae, are brightly coloured with laterally flattened bodies, often with long snouts.

butterwort insectivorous plant, genus *Pinguicula*, of the bladderwort family, with purplish flowers and a rosette of flat leaves covered with a sticky secretion that traps insects.

buttress in brickwork or masonry, a reinforcement built against a wall to give it strength. A flying buttress is an arc transmitting the force of the wall to be supported to an outer buttress, a feature common in Gothic architecture.

Buxtehude Dietrich 1637–1707. German composer. In 1668 he was appointed organist at the Marienkirche, Lübeck, Germany, where his fame attracted J S Bach and Handel. He is remembered for his organ works and cantatas, written for his evening concerts or *Abendmusiken*; he also wrote numerous trio sonatas for two violins, viola da gamba, and harpsichord.

Buxton former spa town in Derbyshire, England; population (1991) 19,900. Known from Roman times for its hot springs, it is today a source for bottled mineral water and a tourist centre.

Buzek Jerzy Karol 1940– . Polish politician, prime minister of Poland from 1997. Buzek, a chemical-engineering professor and a veteran trade union activist, was named prime minister of a new centre-right coalition in October 1997, after the Solidarity Electoral Action (AWS) emerged victorious in general elections. Outlining his new government's programme, he promised to push for rapid integration with the North Atlantic Treaty Organization (NATO) and the European Union (EU), to cut bureaucracy, to decentralize finances, and to expedite privatization plans.

buzzard species of medium-sized hawk with broad wings, often seen soaring. Buzzards are in the falcon family, Falconidae, order Falconiformes. The common buzzard *Buteo buteo* of Europe and Asia is about 55 cm/1.8 ft long with a wingspan of over 1.2 m/4 ft. It preys on a variety of small animals up to the size of a rabbit.

The rough-legged buzzard *B. lagopus* lives in the northern tundra and eats lemmings. The honey buzzard *Pernis apivora* feeds largely, as its name suggests, on honey and insect larvae. It spends the summer in Europe and W Asia and winters in Africa. The red-shouldered hawk *B. lineatus* and red-tailed hawk *B. jamaicensis* occur in North America.

Byatt A(ntonia) S(usan) 1936– . English novelist and critic. Her novels include *The Virgin in the Garden* 1978, its sequel *Still Life* 1985, *Possession* 1990 (winner of the Booker Prize), *The Djinn in the Nightingale's Eye* 1995, and *Babel Tower* 1996. She has also written *Passions of the Mind* 1991 (selected essays), *Angels and Insects* 1992 (novellas), and *The Matisse Stories* 1994 (short stories).

Byblos ancient Phoenician city (modern Jebeil), 32 km/20 mi N of Beirut, Lebanon. Known to the Assyrians and Babylonians as ***Gubla***, it had a thriving export of cedar and pinewood to Egypt as early as 1500 BC. In Roman times it boasted an amphitheatre, baths, and a temple, and was known for its celebration of the resurrection of Adonis, worshipped as a god of vegetation.

Byelorussia see ◊Belarus.

Byelorussian or ***Belorussian*** 'White Russian' natives of Belarus. Byelorussian, a Balto-Slavic language belonging to the Indo-European family, is spoken by about 10 million people, including some in Poland. It is written in the Cyrillic script. Byelorussian literature dates to the 11th century AD. The Byelorussians are descended from E Slavic tribes who moved into the region between the 6th and 8th centuries AD.

by-product substance formed incidentally during the manufacture of some other substance; for example, slag is a by-product of the production of iron in a ◊blast furnace. For industrial processes to be economical, by-products must be recycled or used in other ways as far as possible; in this example, slag is used for making roads.

Byrd Richard Evelyn 1888–1957. US aviator and explorer. The first to fly over the North Pole (1926), he also flew over the South Pole (1929) and led five overland expeditions in Antarctica.

Byrd William 1543–1623. English composer. His sacred and secular choral music, including over 200 motets and masses for three, four, and five voices, exemplifies the English polyphonic style.

Probably born in Lincoln, he became organist at the cathedral there 1563. He shared with Thomas Tallis the honorary post of organist in Queen Elizabeth's Chapel Royal, and in 1575 he and Tallis were granted a monopoly in the printing and selling of music.

Byron (Augusta) Ada, Countess of Lovelace 1815–1852. English mathematician, a pioneer in writing programs for Charles ◊Babbage's analytical engine. In 1983 a new, high-level computer language, Ada, was named after her. She was the daughter of the poet Lord Byron.

Byron George Gordon, 6th Baron Byron 1788–1824. English poet. He became the symbol of Romanticism and political liberalism throughout Europe in the 19th century. His reputation was established with the first two cantos of *Childe Harold* 1812. Later works include *The Prisoner of Chillon* 1816, *Beppo* 1818, *Mazeppa* 1819, and, most notably, the satirical *Don Juan* 1819–24. He left England 1816, spending most of his later life in Italy.

Byron A statue of the English poet Lord Byron in the Villa Borghese, Rome. Passionate, romantic, and sometimes scandalous, his poetry and personality captured the imagination of Europe. Deeply committed to the cause of freedom, he took part in political uprisings in Italy (hence this statue) and then in Greece, where he lost his life. *Corbis*

Childe Harold romantically describes Byron's tours in Portugal, Spain, and the Balkans. In S Europe, he became friendly with Percy and Mary ◊Shelley. He engaged in Italian revolutionary politics and sailed for Greece 1823 to further the Greek struggle for independence, but died of fever at Missolonghi.

> *'He has spent his life best who has enjoyed it most.'*
>
> SAMUEL BUTLER *Notebooks*

byte sufficient computer memory to store a single character of data. The character is stored in the byte of memory as a pattern of ◊bits (binary digits), using a code such as ◊ASCII. A byte usually contains eight bits – for example, the capital letter F can be stored as the bit pattern 01000110.

Byzantine Empire the ***Eastern Roman Empire*** 395–1453, with its capital at Constantinople (formerly Byzantium, modern Istanbul). It was the direct continuation of the Roman Empire in the East, and inherited many of its traditions and institutions.

BYZANTINE EMPIRE

330	Emperor Constantine converted to Christianity and moved his capital to Constantinople.
395	The Roman Empire was divided into eastern and western halves.
476	The Western Empire was overrun by barbarian invaders.
527–565	Emperor Justinian I temporarily recovered Italy, N Africa, and parts of Spain.
7th–8th Cs	Syria, Egypt, and N Africa were lost to the Muslims, who twice besieged Constantinople (673–77, 718), but the Christian Byzantines maintained their hold on Anatolia.
8th–11th Cs	The iconoclastic controversy brought the emperors into conflict with the papacy, and in 1054 the Greek Orthodox Church broke with the Roman.
867–1056	Under the Macedonian dynasty the Byzantine Empire reached the height of its prosperity; the Bulgars proved a formidable danger, but after a long struggle were finally crushed in 1018 by Basil II ('the Bulgar-Slayer'). After Basil's death the Byzantine Empire declined because of internal factions.
1071–73	The Seljuk Turks conquered most of Anatolia.
1204	The Fourth Crusade sacked Constantinople and set Baldwin of Flanders (1171–1205) on the throne of the new Latin (W European) Empire.
1261	The Greeks recaptured the Latin (W European) Empire and restored the Byzantine Empire, but it maintained a precarious existence.
1453	The Turks captured Constantinople and founded the Ottoman Empire.

Byzantine style style in the visual arts and architecture that originated in the 4th–5th centuries in Byzantium (the capital of the Eastern Roman Empire) and spread to Italy, throughout the Balkans, and to Russia, where it survived for many centuries. It is characterized by heavy stylization, strong linear emphasis, the use of rigid artistic stereotypes, and rich colours such as gold. Byzantine artists excelled in mosaic work, manuscript painting, and religious ◊icon painting. In architecture, the dome supported on pendentives was in widespread use. Classical examples of Byzantine architecture are the churches of Hagia Sophia 537–52, Istanbul, and St Mark's, Venice, 11th century.

Byzantium (modern Istanbul) ancient Greek city on the Bosporus, founded as a colony of the Greek city of Megara on an important strategic site at the entrance to the Black Sea about 660 BC. In AD 330 the capital of the Roman Empire was transferred there by Constantine the Great, who renamed it ◊Constantinople and it became the capital of the ◊Byzantine Empire to which it gave its name.

> *'There is no such thing as a life of passion any more than a continuous earthquake, or an eternal fever. Besides, who would ever shave themselves in such a state?'*
>
> GEORGE GORDON BYRON Letter to Thomas Moore 5 July 1821

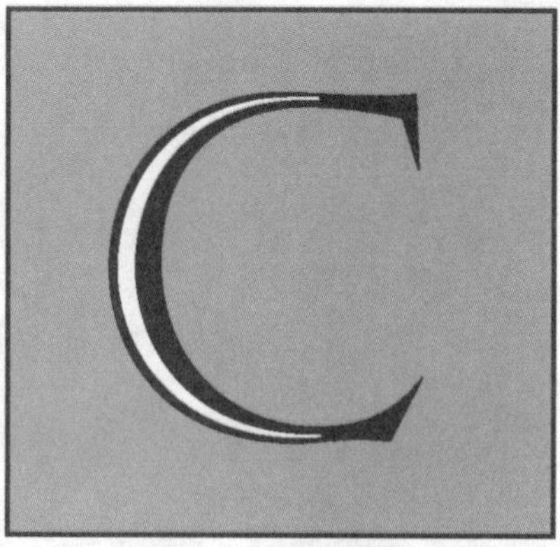

C abbreviation for ***centum*** (Latin 'hundred'); ***century***; ***centigrade***; ◊***Celsius***.

C in computing, a high-level, general-purpose programming language popular on minicomputers and microcomputers. Developed in the early 1970s from an earlier language called BCPL, C was first used as the language of the operating system ◊Unix. It is useful for writing fast and efficient systems programs.

Cabal, the (from *kabbala*) group of five politicians, the English king Charles II's counsellors 1667–73, whose initials made up the name. The word cabal, meaning 'club' or 'association of intriguers', is now applied to any intriguing faction that works in secret for private or political ends.

cabaret theatrical revue traditionally combining satire and song and performed in cafés or bars. Originating in Paris in the late 19th century in venues such as the Moulin Rouge, cabaret was embraced by avant-garde writers and artists. In Germany, Berlin became a centre for an increasingly political cabaret in the 1920s, which was later suppressed by the Nazis. In Britain, satirical revue was revived by the Cambridge Footlights theatre group in *Beyond the Fringe* 1961, before cabaret and alternative comedy combined to provide a new generation of stand-up entertainers during the 1980s, notably from the Comedy Store group in London.

cabbage plant *Brassica oleracea* of the cress family Cruciferae, allied to the turnip and wild mustard, or charlock. It is a table vegetable, cultivated as early as 2000 BC, and the numerous commercial varieties include kale, Brussels sprouts, common cabbage, savoy, cauliflower, sprouting broccoli, and kohlrabi.

caber, tossing the (Gaelic *cabar* 'pole') Scottish athletic sport, a ◊Highland Games event. The caber (a tapered tree trunk about 6 m/20 ft long, weighing about 100 kg/220 lb) is held in the palms of the cupped hands and rests on the shoulder. The thrower runs forward and tosses the caber, rotating it through 180 degrees so that it lands on its opposite end and falls forward. The best competitors toss the caber about 12 m/40 ft.

Cabinda or ***Kabinda*** African coastal enclave, a province of ◊Angola; area 7,770 sq km/3,000 sq mi; population (1992 est) 152,100. The capital is Cabinda. Attached to Angola 1886, the enclave has made claims to independence.

cabinet (a small room, implying secrecy) in politics, the group of ministers holding a country's highest executive offices who decide government policy. In Britain the cabinet system originated under the Stuarts. Under William III it became customary for the king to select his ministers from the party with a parliamentary majority. The US cabinet, unlike the British, does not initiate legislation, and its members, appointed by the president, must not be members of Congress.

The first British 'cabinet councils' or subcommittees of the ◊Privy Council undertook special tasks. When George I ceased to attend cabinet meetings, the office of prime minister, not officially recognized until 1905, came into existence to provide a chair (Robert Walpole was the first). Cabinet members are chosen by the prime minister; policy is collective and the meetings are secret, minutes being taken by the secretary of the cabinet, a high civil servant. Secrecy has been infringed in recent years by 'leaks', or unauthorized disclosures to the press. *See list of tables on p. 1177.*

cable unit of length, used on ships, originally the length of a ship's anchor cable or 120 fathoms (219 m/720 ft), but now taken as one-tenth of a ◊nautical mile (185.3 m/608 ft).

cable car method of transporting passengers up steep slopes by cable. In the cable railway, passenger cars are hauled along rails by a cable wound by a powerful winch. A pair of cars usually operates together on the funicular principle, one going up as the other goes down. The other main type is the aerial cable car, where the passenger car is suspended from a trolley that runs along an aerial cableway.

Cable News Network (CNN) international television news channel; the 24-hour service was founded 1980 by US entrepreneur Ted Turner (1938–) and has its headquarters in Atlanta, Georgia. It established its global reputation 1991 with eyewitness accounts from Baghdad of the beginning of the Gulf War.

In 1995, CNN's owner, Turner Broadcasting System Inc, was bought by Time Warner Inc, which subsequently became the largest media company in the world. Also that year, CNN signed an agreement with US telecommunications company ◊AT&T, which made CNN news available on a new on-line service.

cable television distribution of broadcast signals through cable relay systems. Narrow-band systems were originally used to deliver services to areas with poor regular reception; systems with wider bands, using coaxial and fibreoptic cable, are increasingly used for distribution and development of home-based interactive services, typically telephones.

Cabot Sebastian 1474–1557. Italian navigator and cartographer, the second son of Giovanni ◊Caboto. He explored the Brazilian coast and the Rio de la Plata for the Holy Roman Emperor Charles V 1526–30. Cabot was also employed by Henry VIII, Edward VI, and Ferdinand of Spain. He planned a voyage to China by way of the North-East Passage, the sea route along the N Eurasian coast, encouraged the formation of the Company of Merchant Adventurers of London 1551, and in 1553 and 1556 directed the company's expeditions to Russia, where he opened British trade.

Caboto Giovanni, or ***John Cabot*** c. 1450–c. 1498. Italian navigator. Commissioned, with his three sons, by Henry VII of England to discover unknown lands, he arrived at Cape Breton Island on 24 June 1497, thus becoming the first European to reach the North American mainland (he thought he was in NE Asia). In 1498 he sailed again, touching Greenland, and probably died on the voyage.

cacao tropical American evergreen tree *Theobroma cacao* of the Sterculia family, now also cultivated in W Africa and Sri Lanka. Its seeds are cocoa beans, from which ◊cocoa and chocolate are prepared.

The trees mature at five to eight years and produce two crops a year. The fruit is 17–25 cm/6.5–9.5 in long, hard and ridged, with the beans inside. The seeds are called cocoa nibs; when left to ferment, then roasted and separated from the husks, they contain about 50% fat, part of which is removed to make chocolate and cocoa. The Aztecs revered cacao and made a drink for the nobility only from cocoa beans and chillies, which they called chocolatl. In the 16th century Spanish traders brought cacao to Europe. It was used to make a drink, which came to rival coffee and tea in popularity.

cactus (plural ***cacti***) plant of the New World family Cactaceae, although the term is commonly applied to many different succulent and prickly plants. True cacti have a woody axis (central core) overlaid with an enlarged fleshy stem, which assumes various forms and is usually covered with spines (actually reduced leaves). They all have special adaptations to growing in dry areas. Cactus flowers are often large and brightly coloured; the fruit is fleshy and often edible, as in the case of the prickly pear.

CAD (acronym for ***computer-aided design***) the use of computers in creating and editing design drawings. CAD also allows such things as automatic testing of designs and multiple or animated three-dimensional views of designs. CAD systems are widely used in architecture, electronics, and engineering, for example in the motor-vehicle industry.

caddis fly insect of the order Trichoptera. Adults are generally dull brown, mothlike, with wings covered in tiny hairs. Mouthparts are poorly developed, and many caddis flies do not feed as adults. They are usually found near water; the larvae are aquatic.

Cadiz Spanish city and naval base, capital and seaport of the province of Cadiz, standing on Cadiz Bay, an inlet of the Atlantic, 103 km/64 mi S of Seville; population (1994) 155,000. After the discovery of the Americas 1492, Cadiz became one of Europe's most vital trade ports. The English adventurer Francis ◊Drake burned a Spanish fleet here 1587 to prevent the sailing of the ◊Armada.

cadmium soft, silver-white, ductile, and malleable metallic element, symbol Cd, atomic number 48, relative atomic mass 112.40. Cadmium occurs in nature as a sulphide or carbonate in zinc ores. It is a toxic metal that, because of industrial dumping, has become an environmental pollutant. It is used in batteries, electroplating, and as a constituent of alloys used for bearings with low coefficients of friction, and alloys with a very low melting point. Cadmium is also used in the control rods of nuclear reactors, because of its high absorption of neutrons.

Cadmus in Greek legend, a Phoenician from Tyre, brother of ◊Europa. He founded the city of Thebes in Greece. Obeying the oracle of ◊Athena, Cadmus killed the sacred dragon that guarded the spring of Ares. He sowed the teeth of the dragon, from which

cactus The strawberry cactus *Echinocereus enneacanthus*, which bears bright pink flowers and edible fruit. *Premaphotos Wildlife* sprang a multitude of fierce warriors who fought among themselves; the survivors were considered to be the ancestors of the Theban aristocracy.

Cadwalader lived 7th century. Welsh hero. The son of Cadwallon, King of Gwynedd, N Wales, he defeated and killed Eadwine of Northumbria 633. About a year later he was killed in battle.

caecilian tropical amphibian of wormlike appearance. There are about 170 species known in the family Caeciliidae, forming the amphibian order Apoda (also known as Caecilia or Gymnophiona). Caecilians have a grooved skin and no trace of limbs or pelvis. The body is 20–130 cm/8–50 in long, beige to black in colour. The eyes are very small and weak or blind. Some species bear live young, others lay eggs.

caecum in the ◊digestive system of animals, a blind-ending tube branching off from the first part of the large intestine, terminating in the appendix. It has no function in humans but is used for the digestion of cellulose by some grass-eating mammals.

Caedmon lived c. 660–70. Earliest known English Christian poet. According to the Northumbrian historian Bede, when Caedmon was a cowherd at the monastery of Whitby, he was commanded to sing by a stranger in a dream, and on waking produced a hymn on the Creation. The poem is preserved in some manuscripts. Caedmon became a monk and may have composed other religious poems.

Caen capital of Calvados *département*, France, on the river Orne; population (1990) 115,600. It is a business centre, with ironworks and electric and electronic industries; Caen building stone has a fine reputation. The city is linked by canal with the nearby English Channel to the NE. The church of St Etienne was founded by William the Conqueror, and the university by Henry VI of England 1432. In World War II Caen was one of the main objectives of the ◊D-Day landings and was finally captured by British forces 9 July 1944 after five weeks' fighting.

Caernarvon or ***Caernarfon*** town in N Wales, situated on the southwest shore of the Menai Strait, and administrative headquarters of Gwynedd unitary authority. Formerly a Roman station, it is now a market town and port. Industries include plastics and metal-working. The first Prince of Wales (later Edward II) was born in Caernarvon Castle; Edward VIII was invested here 1911 and Prince Charles 1969.

Caerphilly (Welsh ***Caerffili***) market town in Mid Glamorgan, Wales, 11 km/7 mi N of Cardiff; population (1991) 28,500. The castle was built by Edward I. The town gives its name to mild Caerphilly cheese.

Caerphilly unitary authority of Wales created 1996 (*see United Kingdom map*).

Caesar powerful family of ancient Rome, which included Gaius Julius Caesar, whose grand-nephew and adopted son ◊Augustus assumed the name of Caesar and passed it on to his adopted son ◊Tiberius. From then on, it was used by the successive emperors, becoming a title of the Roman rulers.

Caesar (Gaius) Julius 100–44 BC. Roman statesman and general. He formed with ◊Pompey and ◊Crassus the First Triumvirate 60 BC. He conquered Gaul 58–50 and invaded Britain 55 and 54. He fought against Pompey 49–48, defeating him at Pharsalus. After a period in Egypt Caesar returned to Rome as dictator from 46. He was assassinated by conspirators on the ◊Ides of March 44.

A patrician, Caesar allied himself with the popular party, and when elected to the office of aedile (magistrate) 65, nearly ruined himself with lavish amusements for the Roman populace. Although a free thinker, he was elected chief pontiff 63 and appointed governor of Spain 61. Returning to Rome 60, he formed with Pompey and Crassus the First Triumvirate. As governor of Gaul, he was engaged in its subjugation 58–50, defeating the Germans under Ariovistus and selling thousands of the Belgic tribes into slavery. In 55 he crossed into Britain, returning for a further campaigning visit 54. A revolt by the Gauls under ◊Vercingetorix 52 was crushed 51. His governorship of Gaul ended 49, and after the death of Crassus, Pompey became his rival. Declaring 'the die is cast', Caesar crossed the Rubicon (the small river separating Gaul from Italy) to meet the army raised against him by Pompey. In the ensuing civil war, he followed Pompey to Greece 48, defeated him at Pharsalus, and followed him to Egypt, where Pompey was murdered. Caesar stayed some months in Egypt, where ◊Cleopatra, Queen of Egypt, gave birth to his son, Caesarion. Caesar executed a lightning campaign 47 against King Pharnaces II (ruled 63–47 BC) in Asia Minor, which he summarized: *Veni vidi vici* 'I came, I saw, I conquered'. He was awarded a ten-year dictatorship 46, and with his final victory over the sons of Pompey at Munda in Spain 45, he was awarded the dictatorship for life 44. On 15 March 44, he was stabbed to death by conspirators (led by ◊Brutus and ◊Cassius) at the foot of Pompey's statue in the Senate house.

Caesarean section surgical operation to deliver a baby by way of an incision in the mother's abdominal and uterine walls. It may be recommended for almost any obstetric complication implying a threat to mother or baby. Caesarean section was named after the Roman emperor Julius Caesar, who was born this way.

caesium (Latin *caesius* 'bluish-grey') soft, silvery-white, ductile metallic element, symbol Cs, atomic number 55, relative atomic mass 132.905. It is one of the ◊alkali metals, and is the most electropositive of all the elements. In air it ignites spontaneously, and it reacts vigorously with water. It is used in the manufacture of photocells. The name comes from the blueness of its spectral line.

The rate of vibration of caesium atoms is used as the standard of measuring time. Its radioactive isotope Cs-137 (half-life 30.17 years) is a product of fission in nuclear explosions and in nuclear reactors; it is one of the most dangerous waste products of the nuclear industry.

caffeine ◊alkaloid organic substance found in tea, coffee, and kola nuts; it stimulates the heart and central nervous system. When isolated, it is a bitter crystalline compound, $C_8H_{10}N_4O_2$. Too much caffeine (more than six average cups of tea or coffee a day) can be detrimental to health.

Cage John 1912–1992. US composer. His interest in Indian classical music led him to the view that the purpose of music was to change the way people listen. From 1948 he experimented with instruments, graphics, and methods of random selection in an effort to generate a music of pure incident. For example, he used 24 radios, tuned to random stations, in *Imaginary Landscape No 4* 1951. His ideas profoundly influenced late 20th-century aesthetics.

Working in films during the 1930s, Cage assembled and toured a percussion orchestra incorporating ethnic instruments and noisemakers, for which *Double Music* 1941 was composed (with Lou Harrison). He invented the prepared piano to tour as accompanist with the dancer Merce Cunningham, a lifelong collaborator. In a later work, *4 Minutes and 33 Seconds* 1952, the pianist sits at the piano reading a score for that length of time but does not play.

Cagliari capital and port of Sardinia, Italy, on the Gulf of Cagliari; population (1992) 180,300.

Cagney James 1899–1986. US actor. His physical dynamism and staccato vocal delivery made him one of the first stars of talking pictures. Often associated with gangster roles (for example, *The Public Enemy* 1931), he was an actor of great versatility, playing Bottom in *A Midsummer Night's Dream* 1935 and singing and dancing in *Yankee Doodle Dandy* 1942.

Cain in the Old Testament, the first-born son of Adam and Eve. Motivated by jealousy, he murdered his brother Abel because the latter's sacrifice was more acceptable to God than his own.

Caine Michael. Stage name of Maurice Joseph Micklewhite 1933– . English actor. He is an accomplished performer with an enduring Cockney streak. His films include *Alfie* 1966, *Sleuth* 1972, *The Man Who Would Be King* 1975, *Educating Rita* 1983, *Hannah and Her Sisters* 1986, and many others.

Cairngorm Mountains granite mountain group in Scotland, northern part of the ◊Grampian Mountains. The central range includes four out of five of Britain's highest mountains: Ben Macdhui (1,309 m/4,294 ft), Braeriach (1,296 m/4,251 ft), Cairn Toul (1,291 m/4,235 ft), and Cairn Gorm (1,245 m/4,084 ft).

Cairo (Arabic *El Qahira*) capital of Egypt, on the east bank of the river Nile 13 km/8 mi above the apex of the delta and 160 km/100 mi from the Mediterranean; the largest city in Africa and in the Middle East; population (1994) 9,400,000; metropolitan area (1994 est) 13,000,000

history El Fustat (Old Cairo) was founded by Arabs about AD 642, Al Qahira about 1000 by the ◊Fatimid ruler Gowhar. Cairo was the capital of the Ayyubid dynasty, one of whose sultans, Saladin, built the Citadel in the late 1100s. Under the Mamelukes 1250–1517 the city prospered, but declined in the 16th century after conquest by the Turks. It became the capital of the virtually autonomous kingdom of Egypt established by Mehmet Ali 1805. During World War II it was the headquarters of the Allied forces in N Africa

features Cairo is the site of the mosque that houses the El Azhar university (972). The Mosque of Amr dates from 643; the 12th-century Citadel contains the 19th-century Muhammad Ali mosque. The city is 32 km/20 mi north of the site of the ancient Egyptian centre of ◊Memphis. The Great Pyramids and Sphinx are at nearby El Gîza. Cairo's industries include the manufacture of textiles, cement, vegetable oils, and beer. There are two secular universities: Cairo University (1908) and Ein Shams (1950).

Cajun member of a French-speaking community of Louisiana, USA, descended from French-Canadians who, in the 18th century, were driven there from Nova Scotia (then known as Acadia, from which the name Cajun comes). Cajun music has a lively rhythm and features steel guitar, fiddle, and accordion.

CAL (acronym for ***computer-assisted learning***) the use of computers in education and training: the computer displays instructional material to a student and asks questions about the information given; the student's answers determine the sequence of the lessons.

Calabria mountainous earthquake region occupying the 'toe' of Italy, comprising the provinces of Catanzaro, Cosenza, and Reggio; capital Catanzaro; area 15,100 sq km/5,829 sq mi; population (1992) 2,074,800. Reggio is the industrial centre.

Calais port in Pas-de-Calais *département*, N France; population (1990) 75,800. Taken by England's Edward III 1347, it was saved from destruction by the personal surrender of the burghers of Calais; the French retook it 1558. In World War II, following German occupation May 1940–Oct 1944, it was surrendered to the Canadians.

calamine $ZnCO_3$ zinc carbonate, an ore of zinc. The term also refers to a pink powder made of a mixture of zinc oxide and iron (II) oxide used in lotions and ointments as an astringent for treating, for example, sunburn, eczema, measles rash, and insect bites and stings.

calcite colourless, white, or light-coloured common rock-forming mineral, calcium carbonate, $CaCO_3$. It is the main constituent of ◊limestone and marble and forms many types of invertebrate shell. Calcite often forms ◊stalactites and stalagmites in caves and is also found deposited in veins through many rocks because of the ease with which it is dissolved and transported by groundwater. It rates 3 on the ◊Mohs' scale of hardness. It is a valuable resource, used in the making of iron, steel, cement, glass, slaked lime, bleaching powder, sodium carbonate and bicarbonate, and many other industrially useful substances.

calcium (Latin *calcis* 'lime') soft, silvery-white metallic element, symbol Ca, atomic number 20, relative atomic mass 40.08. It is one of the ◊alkaline-earth metals. It is the fifth most abundant element (the third most abundant metal) in the Earth's crust. It is found mainly as its carbonate $CaCO_3$, which occurs in a fairly pure

'Light was first / Through the Lord's word / Named day: / Beauteous, bright creation.'

Caedmon
'Creation. The First Day'

'I came, I saw, I conquered.'

Julius Caesar
On his campaign in Pontus, quoted in Suetonius *Lives of the Caesars*

Caesar A statue of the Roman statesman and general Gaius Julius Caesar. Caesar became dictator of Rome 46 BC, and was assassinated two years later. *Philip Sauvain*

Even in dreams a good deed is not wasted.

PEDRO CALDERÓN DE LA BARCA
Life is a Dream

condition as chalk and limestone (see ◊calcite). Calcium is an essential component of bones, teeth, shells, milk, and leaves, and it forms 1.5% of the human body by mass.

Calcium ions in animal cells are involved in regulating muscle contraction, blood clotting, hormone secretion, digestion, and glycogen metabolism in the liver. It is acquired mainly from milk and cheese, and its uptake is facilitated by vitamin D. Calcium deficiency leads to chronic muscle spasms (tetany); an excess of calcium may lead to the formation of stones (see ◊calculus) in the kidney or gall bladder.

The element was discovered and named by the English chemist Humphry Davy in 1808. Its compounds include slaked lime (calcium hydroxide, $Ca(OH)_2$); plaster of Paris (calcium sulphate, $CaSO_4\ 2H_2O$); calcium phosphate ($Ca_3(PO_4)_2$), the main constituent of animal bones; calcium hypochlorite ($CaOCl_2$), a bleaching agent; calcium nitrate ($Ca(NO_3)_2 4H_2O$), a nitrogenous fertilizer; calcium carbide (CaC_2), which reacts with water to give ethyne (acetylene); calcium cyanamide ($CaCN_2$), the basis of many pharmaceuticals, fertilizers, and plastics, including melamine; calcium cyanide ($Ca(CN)_2$), used in the extraction of gold and silver and in electroplating; and others used in baking powders and fillers for paints.

calcium carbonate $CaCO_3$ white solid, found in nature as limestone, marble, and chalk. It is a valuable resource, used in the making of iron, steel, cement, glass, slaked lime, bleaching powder, sodium carbonate and bicarbonate, and many other industrially useful substances.

calculus (Latin 'pebble') branch of mathematics which uses the concept of a derivative to analyse the way in which the values of a ◊function vary. Calculus is probably the most widely used part of mathematics. Many real-life problems are analysed by expressing one quantity as a function of another – position of a moving object as a function of time, temperature of an object as a function of distance from a heat source, force on an object as a function of distance from the source of the force, and so on – and calculus is concerned with such functions.

There are several branches of calculus. Differential and integral calculus, both dealing with small quantities which during manipulation are made smaller and smaller, compose the infinitesimal calculus. Differential equations relate to the derivatives of a set of variables and may include the variables. Many give the mathematical models for physical phenomena such as ◊simple harmonic motion. Differential equations are solved generally by integration, depending on their degree. If no analytical processes are available, integration can be performed numerically.

Calcutta city in India, on the river Hooghly, the westernmost mouth of the river Ganges, some 130 km/80 mi north of the Bay of Bengal. Calcutta is the capital of West Bengal; population (1994) 11,500,000. It is chiefly a commercial and industrial centre (engineering, shipbuilding, jute, and other textiles), and was the seat of government of British India 1773–1912

features Buildings include a magnificent Jain temple, the palaces of former Indian princes; and the Law Courts and Government House, survivals of the British Raj. Across the river is ◊Howrah, and between Calcutta and the sea there is a new bulk cargo port, Haldia, which is the focus of oil refineries, petrochemical plants, and fertilizer factories. There is a fine museum; educational institutions include the University of Calcutta (1857); the Visva Bharati at Santiniketan, founded by Rabindranath Tagore; and the Bose Research Institute

history Calcutta was founded 1686–90 by Job Charnock of the East India Company as a trading post. Captured by Suraj-ud-Dowlah 1756, during the Anglo-French wars in India, it was retaken 1757 by Robert Clive.

Calder Alexander (Stirling) 1898–1976. US abstract sculptor. He invented mobiles, sculptures consisting of flat, brightly coloured shapes, suspended from wires and rods and moved by motors or currents of air. Although he was not the first sculptor to exploit real movement, no one before him had used it consistently. Huge mobiles by Calder have been installed at Kennedy Airport, New York (1957) and the UNESCO headquarters in Paris (1962). He also created nonmoving sculptures called 'stabiles'.

caldera in geology, a very large basin-shaped ◊crater. Calderas are found at the tops of volcanoes, where the original peak has collapsed into an empty chamber beneath. The basin, many times larger than the original volcanic vent, may be flooded, producing a crater lake, or the flat floor may contain a number of small volcanic cones, produced by volcanic activity after the collapse. Typical calderas are Kilauea, Hawaii; Crater Lake, Oregon, USA; and the summit of Olympus Mons, on Mars.

Calderón, Alberto P 1920–1998. Argentinean mathematician who specialized in ◊ Fourier analysis and partial differential equations. With Antoni Zygmund he devised the Calderón–Zygmund theory of singular integrals.

Calderón de la Barca Pedro 1600–1681. Spanish dramatist and poet. After the death of Lope de Vega 1635, he was considered to be the leading Spanish dramatist. Most celebrated of the 118 plays is the philosophical *La vida es sueño/Life is a Dream* 1635. Other works include the tragedies *El pintor de su deshonra/The Painter of His Own Dishonour* 1645, *El alcalde de Zalamea/The Mayor of Zalamea* 1640, and *El médico de su honra/The Surgeon of His Honour* 1635.

Calderón was born in Madrid and 1613–19 studied law at Salamanca. In 1620 and 1622 he was successful in poetry contests in Madrid; while still writing dramas, he served in the army in Milan and the Netherlands (1625–35). By 1636 his first volume of plays was published and he had been made master of the revels at the court of Philip IV, receiving a knighthood in 1637. In 1640 he assisted in the suppression of the Catalan rebellion. He became a Franciscan 1650, was ordained 1651, and appointed as a prebendary of Toledo in 1653.

Caledonian Canal waterway in NW Scotland, 98 km/61 mi long, linking the Atlantic and the North Sea. Of its total length only a 37 km/23 mi stretch is artificial, the rest being composed of lochs Lochy, Oich, and Ness. The canal was built by Thomas ◊Telford 1803–23.

calendar division of the ◊year into months, weeks, and days and the method of ordering the years. From year one, an assumed date of the birth of Jesus, dates are calculated backwards (BC 'before Christ' or BCE 'before common era') and forwards (AD, Latin *anno Domini* 'in the year of the Lord', or CE 'common era'). The ***lunar month*** (period between one new moon and the next) naturally averages 29.5 days, but the Western calendar uses for convenience a ***calendar month*** with a complete number of days, 30 or 31 (Feb has 28). For adjustments, since there are slightly fewer than six extra hours a year left over, they are added to Feb as a 29th day every fourth year (leap year), century years being excepted unless they are divisible by 400: for example, 1896 was a leap year; 1900 was not.

The ***month names*** in most European languages were probably derived as follows: January from Janus, Roman god; February from *Februar*, Roman festival of purification; March from Mars, Roman god; April from Latin *aperire*, 'to open'; May from Maia, Roman goddess; June from Juno, Roman goddess; July from Julius Caesar, Roman general; August from Augustus, Roman emperor; September, October, November, December (originally the seventh to tenth months) from the Latin words meaning seventh, eighth, ninth, and tenth, respectively.

The ***days of the week*** are Monday named after the Moon; Tuesday from Tiu or Tyr, Anglo-Saxon and Norse god; Wednesday from Woden or Odin, Norse god; Thursday from Thor, Norse god; Friday from Freya, Norse goddess; Saturday from Saturn, Roman god; and Sunday named after the Sun.

All early calendars except the ancient Egyptian were lunar. The word calendar comes from the Latin *Kalendae* or *calendae*, the first day of each month on which, in ancient Rome, solemn proclamation was made of the appearance of the new moon.

The ***Western*** or ***Gregorian calendar*** derives from the ***Julian calendar*** instituted by Julius Caesar 46 BC. It was adjusted by Pope Gregory XIII 1582, who eliminated the accumulated error caused by a faulty calculation of the length of a year and avoided its recurrence by restricting century leap years to those divisible by 400. Other states only gradually changed from Old Style to New Style; Britain and its colonies adopted the Gregorian calendar 1752, when the error amounted to 11 days, and 3 Sept 1752 became 14 Sept (at the same time the beginning of the year was put back from 25 March to 1 Jan). Russia did not adopt it until the October Revolution of 1917, so that the event (then 25 Oct) is currently celebrated 7 Nov.

The ***Jewish calendar*** is a complex combination of lunar and solar cycles, varied by considerations of religious observance. A year may have 12 or 13 months, each of which normally alternates between 29 and 30 days; the New Year (Rosh Hashanah) falls between 5 Sept and 5 Oct. The calendar dates from the hypothetical creation of the world (taken as 7 Oct 3761 BC).

The ***Chinese calendar*** is lunar, with a cycle of 60 years. Both the traditional and, from 1911, the Western calendar are in use in China.

The ***Muslim calendar***, also lunar, has 12 months of alternately 30 and 29 days, and a year of 354 days. This results in the calendar rotating around the seasons in a 30-year cycle. The era is counted as beginning on the day Muhammad fled from Mecca AD 622. *See list of tables on p. 1177.*

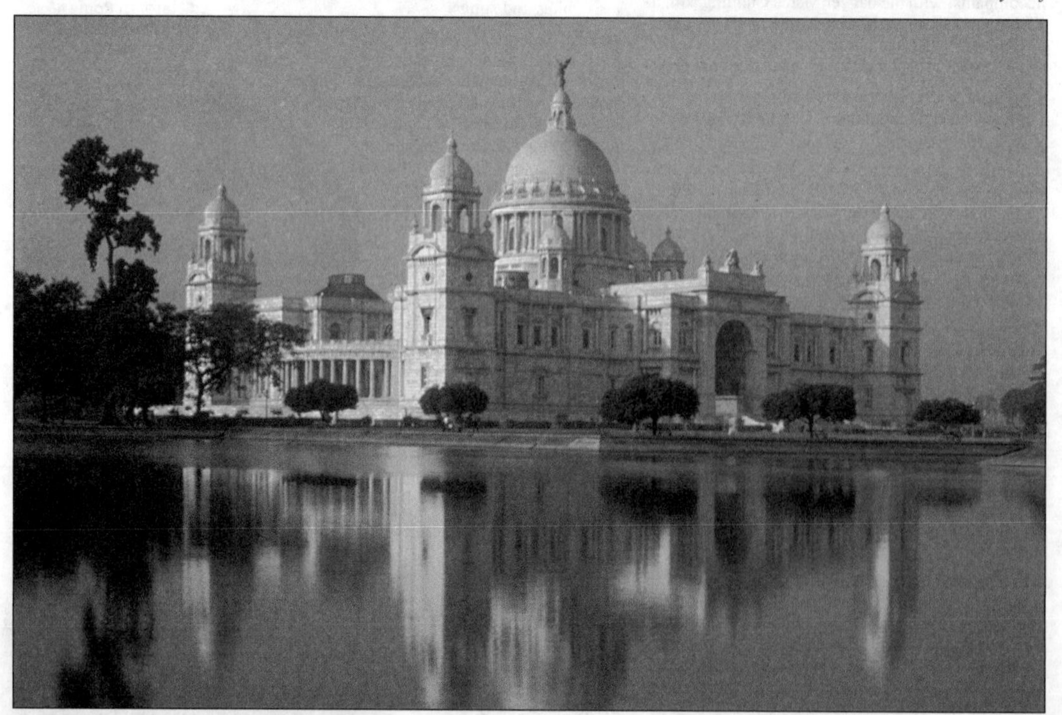

Calcutta The Victoria Memorial in Calcutta, a museum of Indian history, is a very visible reminder that the city was once the capital of British India. A blend of Western and Mogul styles, it was built 1906–21 as a monument to Queen Victoria, Empress of India from 1877. *Sally Jenkins*

Calgary city in Alberta, Canada, on the Bow River, in the foothills of the Rocky Mountains; at 1,048 m/3,440 ft it is one of the highest Canadian cities; population (1986) 671,000. It is the centre of a large agricultural region and is the oil and financial centre of Alberta and W Canada. The 1988 Winter Olympic Games were held here.

Founded as Fort Calgary by the North West Mounted Police 1875, it was reached by the Canadian Pacific Railway 1885 and developed rapidly after the discovery of oil 1914.

Calgary The Saddledome, Stampede Park, Calgary, Alberta, W Canada. The Saddledome, which is equipped for ice hockey and figure-skating, was built for the 1988 Winter Olympics. *Canadian Tourist Office*

calibration the preparation of a usable scale on a measuring instrument. A mercury ◊thermometer, for example, can be calibrated with a Celsius scale by noting the heights of the mercury column at two standard temperatures – the freezing point (0°C) and boiling point (100°C) of water – and dividing the distance between them into 100 equal parts and continuing these divisions above and below.

California Pacific-coast state of the USA; nicknamed the Golden State
area 411,100 sq km/158,685 sq mi
capital Sacramento
cities Los Angeles, San Diego, San Francisco, San José, Fresno
physical Sierra Nevada, including Yosemite and Sequoia national parks, Lake Tahoe, Mount Whitney (4,418 m/14,500 ft, the highest mountain in the lower 48 states); the Coast Range; Death Valley (86 m/282 ft below sea level, the lowest point in the Western hemisphere); Colorado and Mojave deserts; Monterey Peninsula; Salton Sea; the San Andreas fault; huge, offshore underwater volcanoes with tops 5 mi/8 km across
features Yosemite Falls (739 m/2,425 ft), the highest waterfall in North America; redwood trees in several state parks, including Humboldt Redwoods state park, and the Avenue of the Giants; Lava Beds national monument; Point Reyes national seashore; Anza-Borrego Desert state park; gold rush towns, including Downieville; Marshall Gold Discovery state historic park; Monterey, with the Custom House (1827) and Cannery Row; J Paul Getty Museum, Malibu; California Institute of Technology (Caltech); University of California, Berkeley; University of California, Los Angeles (UCLA); Stanford University, Palo Alto; Hollywood, with Universal Studios, Sunset Strip, and Beverly Hills; Napa Valley wine country; Orange County, with Disneyland; homes of celebrities at Malibu and Palm Beach
products leading agricultural state with fruit (peaches, citrus, grapes in the valley of the San Joaquin and Sacramento rivers), nuts, wheat, vegetables, cotton, and rice, all mostly grown by irrigation; beef cattle; timber; fish; oil; natural gas; aerospace technology; electronics (Silicon Valley); food processing; films and television programmes; great reserves of geothermal energy
population (1990) 29,760,000, the most populous state of the USA (69.9% white; 25.8% Hispanic; 9.6% Asian and Pacific islander, including many Vietnamese, 7.4% black; 0.8% Native American)
famous people Luther Burbank, Walt Disney, William Randolph Hearst, Jack London, Marilyn Monroe, Richard Nixon, Ronald Reagan, John Steinbeck
history colonized by Spain 1769; ceded to the USA after the Mexican War 1848; became a state 1850. The discovery of gold in the Sierra Nevada Jan 1848 was followed by the gold rush 1849–56. The completion of the first transcontinental railroad 1869 fostered economic development. The Los Angeles area flourished with the growth of the film industry after 1910, oil discoveries in the early 1920s, and the development of aircraft plants and shipyards during World War II. Devastating earthquakes occurred in the San Francisco Bay area 1989 and the San Fernando Valley–Los Angeles area 1994. Storms and floods Jan and March 1995 caused a total of 26 deaths and an estimated $3.3 billion in damage.

California

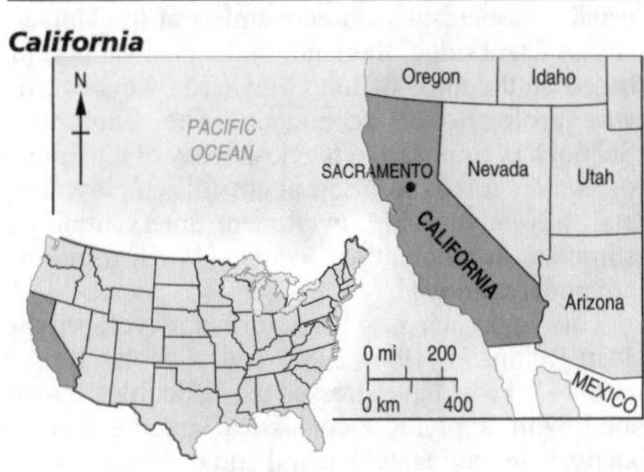

californium synthesized, radioactive, metallic element of the actinide series, symbol Cf, atomic number 98, relative atomic mass 251. It is produced in very small quantities and used in nuclear reactors as a neutron source. The longest-lived isotope, Cf-251, has a half-life of 800 years. It was first synthesized 1950 by US nuclear chemist Glenn Seaborg and his team at the University of California, Berkeley.

Caligula (Gaius Caesar) AD 12–41. Roman emperor, son of Germanicus and successor to Tiberius AD 37. Caligula was a cruel tyrant and was assassinated by an officer of his guard. He is believed to have been mentally unstable.

caliph title of civic and religious heads of the world of Islam. The first caliph was ◊Abu Bakr. Nominally elective, the office became hereditary, held by the Umayyad dynasty 661–750 and then by the ◊Abbasid dynasty. After the death of the last Abbasid (1258), the title was claimed by a number of Muslim chieftains in Egypt, Turkey, and India. The most powerful of these were the Turkish sultans of the Ottoman Empire.

The title was adopted by the prophet Muhammad's successors. During the 10th century the political and military power passed to the leader of the caliph's Turkish bodyguard; about the same time, an independent ◊Fatimid caliphate sprang up in Egypt. The last of the Turkish caliphs was deposed by Kemal ◊Atatürk 1924.

Callaghan (Leonard) James. Baron Callaghan of Cardiff 1912– . British Labour politician. As chancellor of the Exchequer 1964–67, he introduced corporation and capital-gains taxes, and resigned following devaluation. He was home secretary 1967–70 and prime minister 1976–79 in a period of increasing economic stress. As foreign secretary 1974, he renegotiated Britain's membership of the European Community (now the European Union).

In 1976 Callaghan succeeded Harold Wilson as prime minister and in 1977 entered into a pact with the Liberals to maintain his government in office. Strikes in the so-called 'winter of discontent' 1978–79 led to the government's losing a vote of no confidence in the Commons, forcing him to call an election May 1979, when his party was defeated by the Conservatives. He resigned the party leadership 1980 under left-wing pressure.

A lie can be halfway round the world before the truth has got its boots on.

James Callaghan
Speech in House of Commons 1976

Callao chief commercial and fishing port of Peru, 12 km/7 mi SW of Lima; population (1993) 369,800. Founded 1537, it was destroyed by an earthquake 1746. It is Peru's main naval base, and produces fertilizers.

Callas Maria. Adopted name of Maria Kalogeropoulos 1923–1977. US lyric soprano. She was born in New York of Greek parents. With a voice of fine range and a gift for dramatic expression, she excelled in operas including *Norma*, *La Sonnambula*, *Madame Butterfly*, *Aïda*, *Tosca*, and *Medea*.

She made her debut in Verona, Italy, 1947 and at New York's Metropolitan Opera 1956. Although her technique was not considered perfect, she helped to popularize classical coloratura roles through her expressiveness and charisma.

calligraphy art of handwriting, regarded in China and Japan as the greatest of the visual arts, and playing a large part in Islamic art because the depiction of the human and animal form is forbidden. The present letter forms have gradually evolved from originals shaped by the tools used to make them – the flat brush on paper, the chisel on stone, the stylus on wax and clay, and the reed and quill on papyrus and skin.

In Europe during the 4th and 5th centuries books were written in square capitals ('majuscules') derived from classical Roman inscriptions (Trajan's Column in Rome is the outstanding example). The rustic capitals of the same period were written more freely, the pen being held at a severe angle so that the scribe was less frequently inclined to change the angle for special flourishes. Uncial capitals, more rounded, were used from the 4th to the 8th centuries. During this period the cursive hand was also developing, and the interplay of this with the formal hands, coupled with the need for speedier writing, led to the small letter forms (minuscules). During the 7th century the half-uncial was developed with ascending and descending strokes and was adopted by all countries under Roman rule. The cursive forms developed differently in different countries. In Italy the italic script was evolved and became the model for italic typefaces. In the UK there was a 20th-century revival of interest in calligraphy inspired by Edward Johnston (1872–1944) and Irene Wellington (1904–1984).

Callimachus c. 310–c. 240 BC. Greek poet, critic, and scholar. Born in Cyrene, he taught in

Callaghan British Labour politician James Callaghan, prime minister 1976–79. His premiership, which began when Harold Wilson unexpectedly resigned, was marked by currency crises and the collapse of any kind of working relationship between government and trades unions. His government was forced into a general election when it lost a vote of no confidence in the Commons. *United Nations*

Alexandria, Egypt, where he is reputed to have been head of the great library. As a scholar he numbered among his pupils Aristophanes of Byzantium, Eratosthenes, the geographer and polymath, and Apollonius of Rhodes. His best-known work in antiquity was the *Aetia*, containing explanations, written in elegiac couplets, of familiar legends and customs; only fragments of this work survive. His epigrams and hymns reveal him as a poet of great craftsmanship, ingenuity, and elegance.

callipers measuring instrument used, for example, to measure the internal and external diameters of pipes. Some callipers are made like a pair of compasses, having two legs, often curved, pivoting about a screw at one end. The ends of the legs are placed in contact with the object to be measured, and the gap between the ends is then measured against a rule. The slide calliper looks like an adjustable spanner, and carries a scale for direct measuring, usually with a vernier scale for accuracy.

Callisto second-largest moon of Jupiter, 4,800 km/3,000 mi in diameter, orbiting every 16.7 days at a distance of 1.9 million km/1.2 million mi from the planet.

Callot Jacques c. 1592–1635. French engraver and painter. He was influenced by ◊Mannerism. His series of etchings *Great Miseries of War* 1633, prompted by his own experience of the Thirty Years' War, is arrestingly composed and full of horrific detail. He is regarded as one of the greatest etchers, and his enormous output includes over 1,400 prints and 1,500 drawings.

Calmette (Léon Charles) Albert 1863–1933. French bacteriologist. A student of ◊Pasteur, he developed, with Camille ◊Guérin, the ◊BCG vaccine against tuberculosis 1921.

calorie c.g.s. unit of heat, now replaced by the ◊joule (one calorie is approximately 4.2 joules). It is the heat required to raise the temperature of one gram of water by 1°C. In dietetics, the Calorie or kilocalorie is equal to 1,000 calories.

The kilocalorie measures the energy value of food in terms of its heat output: 28 g/1 oz of protein yields 120 kilocalories, of carbohydrate 110, of fat 270, and of alcohol 200.

calorimeter instrument used in physics to measure heat. A simple calorimeter consists of a heavy copper vessel that is polished (to reduce heat losses by radiation) and covered with insulating material (to reduce losses by convection and conduction).

In a typical experiment, such as to measure the heat capacity of a piece of metal, the calorimeter is filled with water, whose temperature rise is measured using a thermometer when a known mass of the heated metal is immersed in it. Chemists use a bomb calorimeter to measure the heat produced by burning a fuel completely in oxygen.

calotype paper-based photograph using a wax paper negative, the first example of the ◊negative/positive process invented by the English photographer Fox ◊Talbot around 1834.

Calvados French brandy distilled from apple cider, named after the *département* in the Basse-Normandie region of NW France where it is produced.

Calvin The Protestant theologian and reformer John Calvin. Calvin was born in France, and trained in theology and law before becoming a preacher in Paris. He then went to Geneva, Switzerland, where he became a prominent figure in the Reformation. *Philip Sauvain*

Calvary (Aramaic *Golgotha* 'skull') in the New Testament, the site of Jesus' crucifixion at Jerusalem. Two chief locations are suggested: the site where the Church of the Sepulchre now stands, and the hill beyond the Damascus gate.

Calvin John, (also known as ***Cauvin*** or ***Chauvin***) 1509–1564. French-born Swiss Protestant church reformer and theologian. He was a leader of the Reformation in Geneva and set up a strict religious community there. His theological system is known as Calvinism, and his church government as ◊Presbyterianism. Calvin wrote (in Latin) *Institutes of the Christian Religion* 1536 and commentaries on the New Testament and much of the Old Testament.

Calvin, born in Noyon, Picardie, studied theology and then law, and about 1533 became prominent in Paris as an evangelical preacher. In 1534 he was obliged to leave Paris and retired to Basel, where he studied Hebrew. In 1536 he accepted an invitation to go to Geneva, Switzerland, and assist in the Reformation, but was expelled 1538 because of public resentment against the numerous and too drastic changes he introduced. He returned to Geneva 1541 and, in the face of strong opposition, established a rigorous theocracy (government by priests). In 1553 he had the Spanish theologian Servetus burned for heresy. He supported the Huguenots in their struggle in France and the English Protestants persecuted by Queen Mary I.

Calvin Melvin 1911–1997. US chemist who, using radioactive carbon-14 as a tracer, determined the biochemical processes of ◊photosynthesis, in which green plants use ◊chlorophyll to convert carbon dioxide and water into sugar and oxygen. Nobel prize 1961.

Calvinism Christian doctrine as interpreted by John Calvin and adopted in Scotland, parts of Switzerland, and the Netherlands; by the ◊Puritans in England and New England, USA; and by the subsequent Congregational and Presbyterian churches in the USA. Its central doctrine is predestination, under which certain souls (the elect) are predestined by God through the sacrifice of Jesus to salvation, and the rest to damnation. The 20th century has seen a neo-Calvinist revival through the work of Karl ◊Barth.

calypso West Indian satirical ballad with a syncopated beat. Calypso is a traditional song form of Trinidad, a feature of its annual carnival, with roots in W African praise-singing. It was first popularized in the USA by Harry Belafonte (1927–) 1956.

Calypso in Greek legend, a sea ◊nymph who waylaid the homeward-bound ◊Odysseus for seven years.

calyx collective term for the ◊sepals of a flower, forming the outermost whorl of the perianth (the outer whorls of a flower). It surrounds the other flower parts and protects them while in bud. In some flowers the sepals are fused along their sides, forming a tubular calyx.

cam part of a machine that converts circular motion to linear motion or vice versa. The edge cam in a car engine is in the form of a rounded projection on a shaft, the camshaft. When the camshaft turns, the cams press against linkages (plungers or followers) that open the valves in the cylinders.

CAM (acronym for ***computer-aided manufacturing***) the use of computers to control production processes, in particular, the control of machine tools and ◊robots in factories. In some factories, the whole design and production system has been automated by linking ◊CAD (computer-aided design) to CAM.

Camargo Marie-Anne de Cupis de 1710–1770. French ballerina. She became a ballet star in Paris 1726 and was the first ballerina to attain the 'batterie' (movements involving beating the legs together) previously danced only by men. She shortened her skirt to expose her ankles and her brilliant footwork, thereby gaining more freedom of movement.

Camargue marshy area of the ◊Rhône delta, S of Arles, France; about 780 sq km/300 sq mi. Black bulls and white horses are bred here, and the nature reserve, which is known for its bird life, forms the southern part.

cambium in botany, a layer of actively dividing cells (lateral ◊meristem), found within stems and roots, that gives rise to ◊secondary growth in perennial plants, causing an increase in girth. There are two main types of cambium: ***vascular cambium***, which gives rise to secondary ◊xylem and ◊phloem tissues, and ***cork cambium*** (or phellogen), which gives rise to secondary cortex and cork tissues (see ◊bark).

Cambodia (formerly ***Khmer Republic*** 1970–76, ***Democratic Kampuchea*** 1976–79, and ***People's Republic of Kampuchea*** 1979–89) country in SE Asia, bounded N and NW by Thailand, N by Laos, E and SE by Vietnam, and SW by the Gulf of Thailand. *See country box opposite.*

Cambrai, Battles of two battles in World War I at Cambrai in NE France as British forces attempted to retake the town from the occupying Germans, eventually succeeding 5 Oct 1918.

First Battle 20–27 Nov 1917: the city was almost captured by the British in a major offensive but heavy losses and the lack of reserve troops left the British unable to resist the German counterattack and by the end of the action the British were almost back where they had started. This was the first battle in which large numbers of tanks were deployed.

Second Battle 26 Aug–5 Oct 1918: the town was attacked during the final British offensive, as part of the push to break the Hindenburg Line. A heavy artillery barrage and specially adapted Mark V tanks, which could span the broad trenches of the line, succeeded in forcing a 65 km/40 mi breach in the line and the town itself was recaptured 5 Oct.

Cambrian period of geological time 570–510 million years ago; the first period of the Palaeozoic era. All invertebrate animal life appeared, and marine algae were widespread. The Cambrian Explosion 530–520 million years ago saw the first appearance in the fossil record of all modern animal phyla; the earliest fossils with hard shells, such as trilobites, date from this period.

Cambridge city in England, on the river Cam (a river sometimes called by its earlier name, Granta), 80 km/50 mi N of London; population (1991) 91,900. It is the administrative headquarters of Cambridgeshire. The present-day city is centred on ◊Cambridge University (founded 12th century), some of whose outstanding buildings, including Kings College Chapel, back onto the river. Industries include the manufacture of scientific instruments, radios, electronics, paper, flour milling, fertilizers, printing, and publishing.

Apart from those of Cambridge University, fine buildings include St Benet's church, with a Saxon tower (about AD 1000), the oldest building in Cambridge; the Holy Sepulchre or Round Church (about 1130, restored 1841); and the Guildhall (1939). The Fitzwilliam Museum (1816) houses a fine art collection.

University colleges include Peterhouse, founded 1284, the oldest college; King's College 1441; Queen's College 1448; Jesus College 1496; St John's College 1511; and Trinity College 1546, the largest college. Emmanuel College chapel was built by Sir Christopher Wren 1666. Among the treasures of the university library (built 1931–34) is the first book ever printed in English.

Cambridge city in Massachusetts, USA; population (1992) 93,550. Industries include paper and publishing. Harvard University 1636 (the oldest educational institution in the USA), Massachusetts Institute of Technology (1861), and the John F Kennedy School of Government (part of Harvard) are here.

Cambridge School an approach to economics usually associated with economists at the University of Cambridge, England, in the postwar period, based on the ideas of John Maynard ◊Keynes who was professor of economics. The Cambridge School has emphasized the possibility of the failure of market forces to bring about full employment, and has advocated government intervention to stimulate investment and demand when resources are underemployed.

This approach has been further developed by Joan Robinson (1903–1983) and Nicholas Kalder (1908–) who have stressed the difficulties associated with applying neoclassical microeconomic analysis to aggregate demand and output.

Cambridgeshire county of E England
area 3,410 sq km/1,316 sq mi (*see United Kingdom map*)
towns and cities Cambridge (administrative headquarters), Ely, Huntingdon, Peterborough
features fens; flat with very fertile, fenland soil; rivers: Ouse, Cam, Nene; Isle of Ely; Cambridge University; at RAF Molesworth, near Huntingdon, Britain's second ◊cruise missile base was deactivated Jan 1989
products mainly agricultural, including cereals, fruit and vegetables; industries include electronics, food processing, and mechanical engineering
population (1991) 645,100
famous people Oliver Cromwell, Octavia Hill, John Maynard Keynes.

Cambridge University English university, one of the earliest in Europe, founded in the 12th century, though the earliest of the existing colleges, Peterhouse, was not founded until about 1284. The university was a centre of Renaissance learning and Reformation theology, and more recently has excelled in scientific research.

Famous students of the university include Rupert Brooke, Samuel Taylor Coleridge, Thomas Gray, Christopher Marlowe, John Milton, Samuel Pepys, and William Wordsworth.

Cambyses lived 6th century BC. King of Persia 529–522 BC. Succeeding his father Cyrus, he assassinated his brother Smerdis and conquered Egypt in 525 BC. There he outraged many of the local religious customs and was said to have become insane. He died in Syria.

camcorder another name for a ◊video camera.

Camden inner borough of NW Greater London. It includes the districts of Bloomsbury, Fitzrovia, Hampstead, Highgate, Holborn, and Somerton
population (1991) 170,400
features St Pancras station (1868), chosen 1994 as the international terminal for the high-speed rail link between the Channel Tunnel and London; Highgate Cemetery (1839), burial place of George Eliot, Michael Faraday, Karl Marx, and Herbert Spencer; new British Library premises (under construction near St Pancras station); Inns of Court; Hatton Garden, centre of the diamond trade; the London Silver Vaults; Camden lock street market; Hampstead Heath; the Roundhouse, Chalk Farm (1846), a former engine shed, to be converted into the British Architectural Library
famous people Francis Bacon, John Betjeman; Charles Dickens and A E Housman were residents; the early 20th-century Camden Town Group of artists, was based here, as was the ◊Bloomsbury Group of writers and artists, which flourished in the 1920s.

Camden Town Group school of British painters 1911–13, based in Camden, London, led by W R ◊Sickert. The work of Spencer Gore (1878–1914) and Harold Gilman (1876–1919) is typical of the group, rendering everyday town scenes in Post-Impressionist style. In 1913 they merged with another group to form the London Group.

camel large cud-chewing mammal of the even-toed hoofed order Artiodactyla. Unlike typical ruminants, it has a three-chambered stomach. It has two toes which have broad soft soles for walking on sand, and hooves resembling nails. There are two species, the single-humped ***Arabian camel*** *Camelus dromedarius* and the twin-humped ***Bactrian camel*** *C. bactrianus* from Asia. They carry a food reserve of fatty tissue in the hump, can go without drinking for long periods, can feed on salty vegetation, and withstand extremes of heat and cold, thus being well adapted to desert conditions.

The Arabian camel has long been domesticated, so that its original range is not known. It is used throughout Arabia and N Africa, and has been taken to other places such as North America and Australia, in the latter country playing a crucial part in the development of the interior. The ***dromedary*** is, strictly speaking, a lightly built, fast, riding variety of the Arabian camel, but often the name is applied to all one-humped camels. Arabian camels can be used as pack animals, for riding, racing, milk production, and for meat. The Bactrian camel is native to the central Asian deserts, where a small number still live wild, but most are domestic animals.

Camelot legendary seat of King ◊Arthur. A possible site is the Iron Age hill fort of South Cadbury Castle in Somerset, England, where excavations from 1967 have revealed remains dating from 3000 BC to AD 1100, including those of a large 6th-century settlement, the time ascribed to Arthur.

cameo small relief carving of semiprecious stone, shell, or glass, in which a pale-coloured surface layer is carved to reveal a darker ground. Fine cameos were produced in ancient Greece and

CAMBODIA

State of (formerly *Khmer Republic* 1970–75, *Kampuchea* 1975–79)

Laos
PACIFIC OCEAN
India
Philippines
Vietnam
Thailand
CAMBODIA
Phnom Penh
Malaysia
INDIAN OCEAN
Indonesia
0 mi 500
0 km 1000

national name *Roat Kampuchea*
area 181,035 sq km/69,880 sq mi
capital Phnom Penh
major towns/cities Battambang
major ports Kompong Cham
physical features mostly flat forested plains with mountains in SW and N; Mekong River runs N–S; Lake Tonle Sap
head of state Prince Norodom Sihanouk from 1991
head of government joint prime ministers Ung Huot and Hun Sen from 1997
political system limited constitutional monarchy
administrative divisions 21 provinces and two municipalities
political parties United Front for an Independent, Neutral, Peaceful, and Cooperative Cambodia (FUNCINPEC), nationalist, monarchist; Liberal Democratic Party (BLDP), republican, anticommunist (formerly the Khmer People's National Liberation Front [KPNLF]); Cambodian People's Party (CPP), reform socialist (formerly the communist Kampuchean People's Revolutionary Party [KPRP]); Cambodian National Unity Party (CNUP) (political wing of the Khmer Rouge), ultranationalist communist; Democratic National United Movement (DNUM)
population 10,273,000 (1996 est)
population growth rate 3.0% (1990–95); 2.3% (2000–05)
ethnic distribution 91% Khmer, 4% Vietnamese, 3% Chinese
life expectancy 50 (males), 52 (females)
literacy rate men 48%, women 22%
languages Khmer (official), French
religions Theravāda Buddhist 95%, Muslim, Roman Catholic
currency Cambodian riel
GDP (US $) 2.77 billion (1995)
growth rate 4.9% (1994)
exports rubber, rice, pepper, wood, cattle

HISTORY
1st C AD Part of the kingdom of Hindu-Buddhist Funan (Fou Nan), centred on Mekong delta region.
6th C Conquered by the Chenla kingdom.
9th C Establishment by Jayavarman II of extensive and sophisticated Khmer Empire, supported by an advanced irrigation system and architectural achievements, with a capital at Angkor in the NW.
14th C Theravāda Buddhism replaced Hinduism.
15th C Came under the control of Siam (Thailand), which made Phnom Penh the capital and, later, Champa (Vietnam).
1863 Became a French protectorate, but traditional political structures left largely intact.
1887 Became part of French Indo-China Union, which included Laos and Vietnam.
1941 Prince Norodom Sihanouk was elected king.
1941–45 Occupied by Japan during World War II.
1946 Recaptured by France; parliamentary constitution adopted.
1953 Independence achieved from France as the Kingdom of Cambodia.
1955 Norodom Sihanouk abdicated as king and became prime minister, representing the Popular Socialist Community mass movement.
1960 On the death of his father, Norodom Sihanouk became head of state.
later 1960s Mounting guerrilla insurgency, led by the communist Khmer Rouge, and civil war in neighbouring Vietnam.
1970 Prince Sihanouk overthrown by US-backed Lt-Gen Lon Nol in a right-wing coup; name of Khmer Republic adopted; Sihanouk, exiled in China, formed own guerrilla movement.
1975 Lon Nol overthrown by Khmer Rouge, which was backed by North Vietnam and China; name Kampuchea adopted, with Sihanouk as head of state.
1976–78 Khmer Rouge, led by Pol Pot, introduced an extreme Maoist communist programme, forcing urban groups into rural areas and resulting in over 2.5 million deaths from famine and maltreatment; Sihanouk removed from power.
1978–79 Vietnamese invasion; government headed by Heng Samrin, an anti-Pol Pot communist.
1980–82 Faced by guerrilla resistance from Pol Pot's Chinese-backed Khmer Rouge and Sihanouk's ASEAN and US-backed nationalists, more than 300,000 Cambodians fled to refugee camps in Thailand and thousands of soldiers were killed.
1985 Reformist Hun Sen appointed prime minister.
1987–89 Vietnamese troop withdrawal.
1989 Renamed State of Cambodia and Buddhism was re-established as state religion.
1991 Peace agreement signed in Paris provided for a cease-fire and a United Nations Transitional Authority in Cambodia (UNTAC) in conjunction with all-party Supreme National Council; communism abandoned. Sihanouk returned as head of state.
1992 Political prisoners released; refugees resettled; freedom of speech and party formation restored. Khmer Rouge refused to disarm.
1993 Free general elections (boycotted by Khmer Rouge) resulted in surprise win by FUNCINPEC; new constitution adopted. Sihanouk reinstated as constitutional monarch; Prince Norodom Ranariddh, FUNCINPEC leader, appointed executive prime minister, with reform-socialist CCP leader Hun Sen deputy premier. Khmer Rouge continued fighting.
1994 Antigovernment coup foiled. Surrender of 7,000 guerrillas of outlawed Khmer Rouge in amnesty.
1995 Prince Norodom Sirivudh, FUNCINPEC leader and half-brother of King Sihanouk, exiled for allegedly plotting to assassinate Hun Sen.
1996 Political instability exacerbated by assassination of opposition leader Sam Rainsy. Serious split in Khmer Rouge when its deputy leader formed the DNUM and was granted amnesty by Sihanouk.
1997 Divisions within Khmer Rouge. Pol Pot sentenced to life imprisonment after trial by Khmer Rouge. FUNCINPEC troops routed by CPP, led by Hun Sen. First prime minister Prince Norodom Ranariddh deposed and replaced by Ung Huot. Peace restored in Phnom Penh. Fighting between supporters of Hun Sen and Ranariddh.
1998 Ranariddh tried in absentia and found guilty of arms smuggling and colluding with Khmer Rouge. However, as part of Japanese-brokered peace deal, he was immediately pardoned by the King and returned home to prepare for July general election. Death of Pol Pot and defection of thousands of Khmer Rouge guerrillas.

SEE ALSO Buddhism; Khmer Rouge; Pol Pot; Sihanouk, Norodom

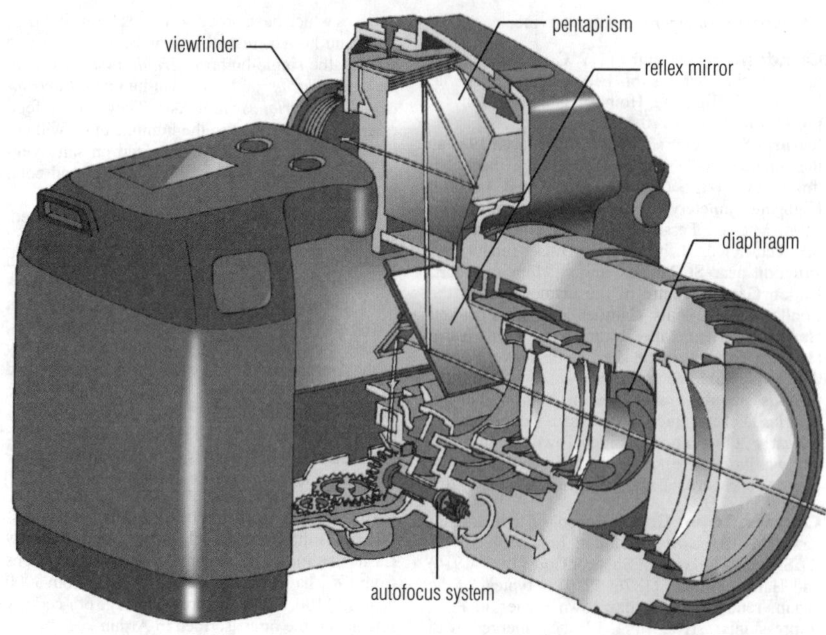

camera **The single-lens reflex (SLR) camera in which an image can be seen through the lens before a picture is taken. The reflex mirror directs light entering the lens to the viewfinder. The SLR allows different lenses, such as close-up or zoom, to be used because the photographer can see exactly what is being focused on.**

Rome, during the Renaissance, and in the Victorian era. They were used for decorating goblets and vases, and as jewellery.

camera apparatus used in ◊photography, consisting of a lens system set in a light-proof box inside of which a sensitized film or plate can be placed. The lens collects rays of light reflected from the subject and brings them together as a sharp image on the film; it has marked numbers known as ◊apertures, or f-stops, that reduce or increase the amount of light that can enter. Apertures also control depth of field. A shutter controls the amount of time light has to affect the film. There are small-, medium-, and large-format cameras; the format refers to the size of recorded image and the dimensions of the print obtained.

A simple camera has a fixed shutter speed and aperture, chosen so that on a sunny day the correct amount of light is admitted. More complex cameras allow the shutter speed and aperture to be adjusted; most have a built-in exposure meter to help choose the correct combination of shutter speed and aperture for the ambient conditions and subject matter. The most versatile camera is the single lens reflex (◊SLR).

camera obscura darkened box with a tiny hole for projecting the inverted image of the scene outside on to a screen inside. For its development as a device for producing photographs, see ◊photography.

Cameron Julia Margaret, (born Pattle) 1815–1879. British photographer. She made lively and dramatic portraits of the Victorian intelligentsia, often posed as historical or literary figures. Her sitters included her friends the English astronomer Sir John Herschel, the poet Alfred Lord Tennyson, and Charles Darwin. She used a large camera, five-minute exposures, and wet plates.

Cameroon country in W Africa, bounded NW by Nigeria, NE by Chad, E by the Central African Republic, S by Congo, Gabon, and Equatorial Guinea, and W by the Atlantic. *See country box below.*

Camoëns Luis Vaz de, or ***Camões*** 1524–1580. Portuguese poet and soldier. His poem *Os Lusiades/The Lusiads* 1572 tells the story of the explorer Vasco da Gama and incorporates much Portuguese history; it was immediately acclaimed and has become the country's national epic.

Camorra Italian secret society formed about 1820 by criminals in the dungeons of Naples and continued once they were freed. It dominated politics from 1848, was suppressed 1911, but many members eventually surfaced in the US ◊Mafia. The Camorra still operates in the Naples area.

camouflage colours or structures that allow an animal to blend with its surroundings to avoid detection by other animals. Camouflage can take the form of matching the background colour, of countershading (darker on top, lighter below, to counteract natural shadows), or of irregular patterns that break up the outline of the animal's body. More elaborate camouflage involves closely resembling a feature of the natural environment, as with the stick insect; this is closely akin to ◊mimicry.

Camouflage is also important as a military technique, disguising either equipment, troops, or a position in order to conceal them from an enemy.

Campaign for Nuclear Disarmament (CND) nonparty-political British organization advocating the abolition of nuclear weapons worldwide. Since its foundation 1958, CND has sought unilateral British initiatives to help start, and subsequently to accelerate, the multilateral process and end the arms race. The movement was launched by the philosopher Bertrand Russell and Canon John Collins and grew out of the demonstration held outside the government's Atomic Weapons Research Establishment at Aldermaston, Berkshire, at Easter 1956. From 1970 CND has also opposed nuclear power. Its membership peaked in the early 1980s, during the campaign against the presence of US Pershing and cruise nuclear missiles on British soil.

Campania agricultural region (wheat, citrus, wine, vegetables, tobacco) of S Italy, including the

CAMEROON
Republic of

Chad
Nigeria
Yaoundé
C.A.R.
CAMEROON
ATLANTIC OCEAN
Equatorial Guinea
Gabon
Congo
0 mi 500
0 km 1000

national name *République du Cameroun*
area 475,440 sq km/183,638 sq mi
capital Yaoundé
major towns/cities Garoua, Maroua, Bamenda, Bafoussam
major ports Douala
physical features desert in far N in the Lake Chad basin, mountains in W, dry savanna plateau in the intermediate area, and dense tropical rainforest in S; Mount Cameroon 4,070 m/13,358 ft, an active volcano on the coast, W of the Adamawa Mountains
head of state Paul Biya from 1982
head of government Simon Achidi Achu from 1992
political system emergent democratic republic
administrative divisions ten provinces
political parties Cameroon People's Democratic Movement (RDPC), nationalist, left of centre; Front of Allies for Change (FAC), centre-left
population 13,233,000 (1995 est)
population growth rate 2.8% (1990–95); 2.8% (2000–05)
ethnic distribution main groups include the Cameroon Highlanders (31%), Equatorial Bantu (19%), Kirdi (11%), Fulani (10%), Northwestern Bantu (8%), and Eastern Nigritic (7%)
life expectancy 54 (males), 57 (females)
literacy rate men 66%, women 43%
languages French and English in pidgin variations (official); there has been some discontent with the emphasis on French – there are 163 indigenous peoples with their own African languages (Sudanic languages in N, Bantu languages elsewhere)
religions Roman Catholic 35%, animist 25%, Muslim 22%, Protestant 18%
currency franc CFA
GDP (US $) 7.46 billion (1994)
growth rate −2.2% (1983–93)
exports cocoa, coffee, bananas, cotton, timber, rubber, groundnuts, gold, aluminium, crude oil

HISTORY
1472 First visited by the Portuguese, who named it the Rio dos Camaroes ('River of Prawns') after the giant shrimps they found in the Wouri river estuary, and later introduced slave-trading.
early 17th C The Douala people immigrated into the coastal region from E and came to serve as intermediaries between Portuguese, Dutch, and English traders and interior tribes.
1809–48 Northern savannas conquered by the Fulani, Muslim pastoral nomads from S Sahara, forcing forest and upland peoples southwards.
1856 Douala chiefs signed a commercial treaty with Britain and invited British protection.
1884 Treaty signed establishing German rule as the protectorate of Kamerun; cocoa, coffee, and banana plantations developed.
1916 Captured by Allied forces in World War I.
1919 Divided under League of Nations' mandates between Britain, which administered the SW and N, adjoining Nigeria, and France, which administered the E and S (comprising four-fifths of the area), and developed palm oil and cocoa plantations.
1946 French Cameroon and British Cameroons made UN trust territories.
1955 French crushed a revolt by the Union of the Cameroon Peoples (UPC), southern-based radical nationalists.
1960 French Cameroon became the independent Republic of Cameroon, with Ahmadou Ahidjo, a Muslim from the N, elected president; UPC rebellion in SW crushed, and a state of emergency declared.
1961 Following a UN plebiscite, northern part of British Cameroons merged with Nigeria and southern part joined the Republic of Cameroon to become the Federal Republic of Cameroon, with French and English as official languages.
1966 Autocratic one-party regime introduced; government and opposition parties merged to form Cameroon National Union (UNC).
1970s Petroleum exports made possible successful investment in education and agriculture.
1972 New constitution made Cameroon a unitary state.
1982 President Ahidjo resigned; succeeded by his prime minister Paul Biya, a Christian from the S.
1983 Biya began to remove the northern Muslim political 'barons' close to Ahidjo, who went into exile in France.
1984 Biya defeated a plot by Muslim officers from the N to overthrow him.
1985 UNC adopted the name RDPC.
1990 Widespread public disorder as living standards declined; Biya granted amnesty to political prisoners.
1992 Ruling RDPC won first multiparty elections in 28 years. Biya's presidential victory challenged by opposition, who claimed ballot-rigging.
1995 Cameroon admitted to Commonwealth.

volcano ◊Vesuvius; area 13,600 sq km/5,250 sq mi; population (1992) 5,668,900. The capital is ◊Naples; industrial centres include Benevento, Caserta, and Salerno. There are ancient sites at Pompeii, Herculaneum, and Paestum.

Campbell Colen 1676–1729. Scottish architect. He was one of the principal figures in British Palladian architecture. His widely influential book *Vitruvius Britannicus* was published 1712. Among his best-known works are Burlington House, London, 1718–19 and Merewith Castle, Kent, 1722–25.

Campbell Donald Malcolm 1921–1967. British car and speedboat enthusiast, son of Malcolm Campbell, who simultaneously held the land-speed and water-speed records. In 1964 he set the world water-speed record of 444.57 kph/276.3 mph on Lake Dumbleyung, Australia, with the turbojet hydroplane *Bluebird*, and achieved the land-speed record of 648.7 kph/403.1 mph at Lake Eyre salt flats, Australia. He was killed in an attempt to raise his water-speed record on Coniston Water, England.

Campbell Malcolm 1885–1948. British racing driver who once held both land- and water-speed records. He set the land-speed record nine times, pushing it up to 484.8 kph/301.1 mph at Bonneville Flats, Utah, USA, 1935, and broke the water-speed record three times, the best being 228.2 kph/141.74 mph on Coniston Water, England, 1939. His car and boat were both called *Bluebird*.

Campbell-Bannerman Henry, (born Henry Campbell) 1836–1908. British Liberal politician, prime minister 1905–08. It was during his term of office that the South African colonies achieved self-government, and the Trades Disputes Act 1906 was passed.

He was chief secretary for Ireland 1884–85, war minister 1886 and again 1892–95, and leader of the Liberals in the House of Commons from 1899. In 1905 he became prime minister and led the Liberals to an overwhelming electoral victory 1906. He began the conflict between Commons and Lords that led to the Parliament Act of 1911. He resigned 1908.

Camp David official country home of US presidents, situated in the Appalachian mountains, Maryland; it was originally named Shangri-la by F D Roosevelt, but was renamed Camp David by Eisenhower (after his grandson).

Camp David Agreements two framework accords agreed 1978 and officially signed March 1979 by Israeli prime minister Begin and Egyptian president Sadat at Camp David, Maryland, USA, under the guidance of US president Carter. They cover an Egypt–Israel peace treaty and phased withdrawal of Israel from Sinai, which was completed 1982, and an overall Middle East settlement including the election by the West Bank and Gaza Strip Palestinians of a 'self-governing authority'. The latter issue has stalled repeatedly over questions of who should represent the Palestinians and what form the self-governing body should take.

Campese David 1962– . Australian rugby union player, one of the outstanding entertainers of the game. He holds the world record for the most tries scored in international rugby and is the most-capped Australian international (91 by 15 July 1995). Campese was a member of the 1984 Australia team, which won all four internationals in Britain, and a key element in Australia's 1991 World Cup victory. He played for Randwick (New South Wales) and Milan (Italy), but has now retired from international rugby.

Campin Robert, also known as the ***Master of Flémalle*** c. 1378–1444. Early Netherlandish painter, active in Tournai from 1406. The few works attributed to him are almost as revolutionary in their naturalism as the van Eyck brothers' Ghent altarpiece, which they may antedate, and he ranks as one of the founders of the Netherlandish School.

Campin's outstanding work is the *Mérode Altarpiece* about 1425 (Metropolitan Museum of Art, New York), which shows a characteristic blend of naturalism and elaborate symbolism, together with a new subtlety in modelling and a grasp of pictorial space. Other works include the *Virgin and Child Before a Fire Screen* (National Gallery, London) and the *Werl Altar* (Prado, Madrid). His *Portrait of a Woman* (National Gallery, London) exemplifies the cool but precise tradition of Flemish portraiture.

Campion Jane 1954– . New Zealand film director and screenwriter. She made her feature debut with *Sweetie* 1989, then went on to make *An Angel at My Table* 1990, based on the autobiography of writer Janet Frame (1924–). Later films included *The Piano* 1993 (co-winner of the Cannes Film Festival Palme d'Or) and *Portrait of a Lady* 1996.

Campylobacter genus of bacteria that cause serious outbreaks of gastroenteritis. They grow best at 43°C, and so are well suited to the digestive tract of birds. Poultry is therefore the most likely source of a *Campylobacter* outbreak, although the bacteria can also be transmitted via beef or milk. *Campylobacter* can survive in water for up to 15 days, so may be present in drinking water if supplies are contaminated.

Camus Albert 1913–1960. Algerian-born French writer. His works, such as the novels *L'Etranger/The Outsider* 1942 and *La Peste/The Plague* 1948, owe much to ◊existentialism in their emphasis on the absurdity and arbitrariness of life. Other works include *Le Mythe de Sisyphe/The Myth of Sisyphus* 1943 and *L'Homme révolté/The Rebel* 1951. Nobel Prize for Literature 1957.

The plays *Le Malentendu/Cross Purpose* and *Caligula* both 1944, and the novel *L'Etranger* ('the study of an absurd man in an absurd world') explore various aspects of 'the Absurd', while *Le Mythe de Sisyphe* is a philosophical treatment of the same concept. With *Lettres à un ami allemand/Letters to a German Friend* 1945, *La Peste*, the play *L'Etat de siège/State of Siege* 1948, and *L'Homme révolté*, Camus began to explore the problem of suffering in its more historical manifestations, and the concept of revolt.

> *An intellectual is someone whose mind watches itself.*
>
> ALBERT CAMUS *Notebooks*

Canaan ancient region between the Mediterranean and the Dead Sea, called in the Bible the 'Promised Land' of the Israelites. It was occupied as early as the 3rd millennium BC by the Canaanites, a Semitic-speaking people who were known to the Greeks of the 1st millennium BC as Phoenicians. The capital was Ebla (now Tell Mardikh, Syria).

The Canaanite Empire included Syria, Palestine, and part of Mesopotamia. It was conquered by the Israelites during the 13th to 10th centuries BC. Ebla was excavated 1976–77, revealing an archive of inscribed tablets dating from the 3rd millennium BC, which includes place names such as Gaza and Jerusalem.

Canada country occupying the northern part of the North American continent, bounded S by the USA, N by the Arctic Ocean, NW by Alaska, E by the Atlantic Ocean, and W by the Pacific Ocean. *See country box on p. 180 and table on p. 181.*

Canadian art Since the 17th century Canadian art has been dominated by European styles, in particular those of Britain (especially in portraiture) and France. During the 19th century Canadian artists increasingly sought to develop a national artistic identity, often using landscape as the most appropriate form. In the 20th century European influences such as Post-Impressionism and then Surrealism have been felt, though US art – particularly Abstract Expressionism – has also become part of Canada's artistic development.

Canadian literature Canadian literature in English began early in the 19th century in the Maritime Provinces with the humorous tales of T C Haliburton (1796–1865). Charles Heavysege (1816–1876) published poems combining psychological insight with Puritan values. The late 19th century brought the lyrical output of Charles G D ◊Roberts, Bliss Carman (1861–1929), Archibald Lampman (1861–1899), and Duncan Campbell Scott (1862–1944). Realism in fiction developed with Frederick P Grove (1879–1948), Mazo de la Roche (1885–1961), creator of the 'Jalna' series, and Hugh MacLennan (1907–1990). Humour of worldwide appeal emerged in Stephen ◊Leacock; Brian Moore (1921–), author of *The Luck of Ginger Coffey* 1960; and Mordecai Richler (1931–). Also widely read outside Canada was L M Montgomery (1874–1942), whose *Anne of Green Gables* 1908 became a children's classic. US novelist Saul Bellow and the communication theorist Marshall McLuhan were both Canadian-born, as were contemporary novelists Robertson Davies (1913–1995) and Margaret ◊Atwood.

Recent poetry and fiction, stimulated by journals such as *The Canadian Forum* (founded 1920) and *Canadian Fiction Magazine* (founded 1971) and by a growing number of literary prizes, has become increasingly international in outlook while also drawing attention to contemporary Canadian issues such as racial and linguistic minorities and the environment.

canal artificial waterway constructed for drainage, irrigation, or navigation. ***Irrigation canals*** carry water for irrigation from rivers, reservoirs, or wells, and are designed to maintain an even flow of water over the whole length. ***Navigation and ship canals*** are constructed at one level between ◊locks, and frequently link with rivers or sea inlets to form a waterway system. The Suez Canal 1869 and the Panama Canal 1914 eliminated long trips around continents and dramatically shortened shipping routes.

Irrigation canals fed from the Nile have maintained life in Egypt since the earliest times; the

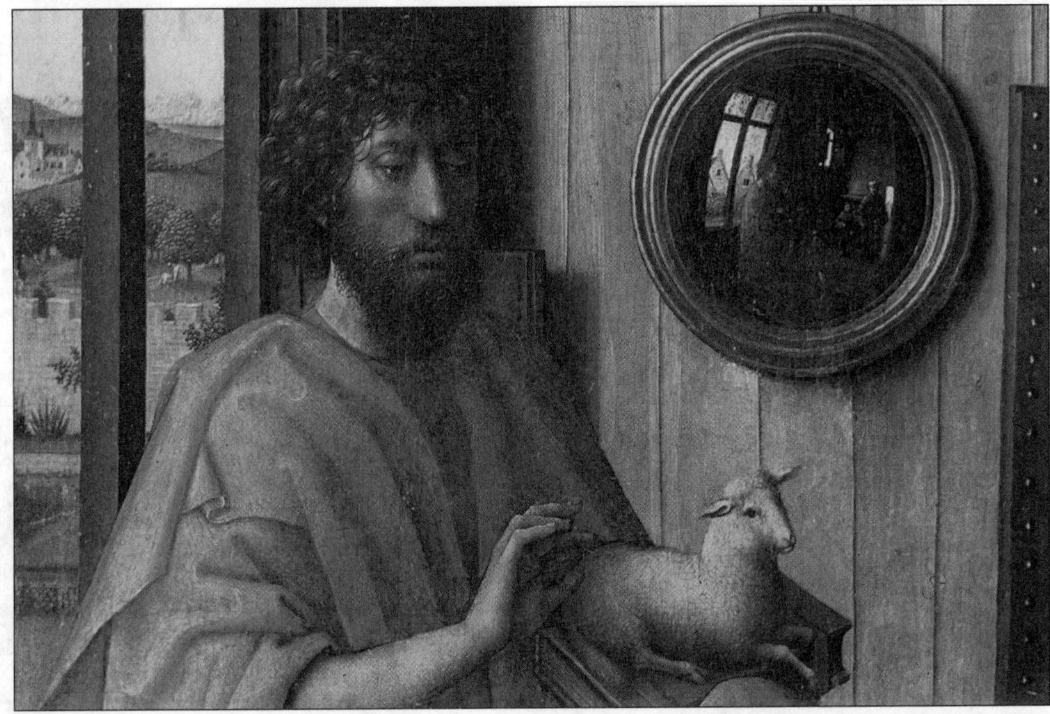

Campin A detail from *Saint John the Baptist and Heinrich Werl* by Robert Campin (Prado, Madrid). One of the earliest and most original Flemish masters, Campin created a style of elegant realism that had a profound influence on the development of Netherlandish art. *Corbis*

division of the waters of the Upper Indus and its tributaries, which form an extensive system in Pakistan and Punjab, India, was, for more than ten years, a major cause of dispute between India and Pakistan, settled by a treaty 1960; the Murray basin, Victoria, Australia, and the Imperial and Central Valley projects in California, USA, are examples of 19th- and 20th-century irrigation canal development.

Probably the oldest ***ship canal*** to be still in use, as well as the longest, is the Grand Canal in China, which links Tianjin and Hangzhou and connects the Huang He (Yellow River) and Chang Jiang. It was originally built in three stages 485 BC–AD 283, reaching a total length of 1,780 km/1,107 mi. Large sections silted up in later years, but the entire system was dredged, widened, and rebuilt 1958–72 in conjunction with work on flood protection, irrigation, and hydroelectric schemes. It carries millions of tonnes of freight every year.

Where speed is not a prime factor, the cost-effectiveness of transporting goods by canal has encouraged a revival; Belgium, France, Germany, and the countries of the former USSR are among countries that have extended and streamlined their canals. The Baltic–Volga waterway links the Lithuanian port of Klaipeda with Kahovka, at the mouth of the Dnieper on the Black Sea, a distance of 2,430 km/1,510 mi. A further canal cuts across the northern Crimea, thus shortening the voyage of ships from the Dnieper through the Black Sea to the Sea of Azov. In Central America, the Panama Canal 1904–14 links the Atlantic and Pacific oceans (64 km/40 mi). In North America, the Erie Canal 1825 links the Great Lakes with the Hudson River and opened up the northeast and Midwest to commerce; the St Lawrence Seaway 1954–59 extends from Montréal to Lake Ontario (290 km/180 mi) and, with the deepening of the Welland Ship Canal and some of the river channels, provides a waterway that enables ocean going vessels to travel (during the ice-free months) between the Atlantic and

CANADA

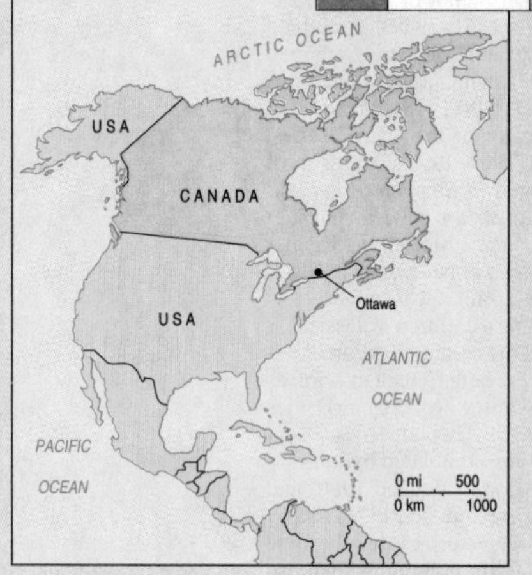

area 9,970,610 sq km/3,849,674 sq mi
capital Ottawa
major towns/cities Toronto, Montréal, Vancouver, Edmonton, Calgary, Winnipeg, Quebec, Hamilton, Saskatoon, Halifax, Regina, Windsor, Oshawa, London, Kitchener
physical features mountains in W, with low-lying plains in interior and rolling hills in E; St Lawrence Seaway, Mackenzie River; Great Lakes; Arctic Archipelago; Rocky Mountains; Great Plains or Prairies; Canadian Shield; Niagara Falls; climate varies from temperate in S to arctic in N; 45% of country forested
head of state Elizabeth II from 1952, represented by governor general Ramon John Hnatyshyn from 1990
head of government Jean Chrétien from 1993
political system federal constitutional monarchy
administrative divisions ten provinces and two territories
political parties Liberal Party, nationalist, centrist; Bloc Quebecois, Quebec-based, separatist; Reform Party, populist, right-wing; New Democratic Party (NDP), moderate left of centre; Progressive Conservative Party (PCP), free-enterprise, right of centre
armed forces 70,500 (1995)
conscription none
defence spend (% GDP) 1.7 (1994)
education spend (% GNP) 7.6 (1992)
health spend (% GDP) 7.4 (1993)
death penalty for exceptional crimes only; last execution 1962
population 29,463,000 (1995 est)
population growth rate 1.2% (1990–95); 0.9% (2000–05)
age distribution (% of total population) <15 20.8%, 15–65 67.3%, >65 11.8% (1995)
ethnic distribution about 45% of British origin, 29% French, 23% of other European descent, and about 3% indigenous Indians or Inuits
population density (per sq km) 3 (1994)
urban population (% of total) 77% (1995)
labour force 53% of population: 3% agriculture, 25% industry, 71% services (1990)
unemployment 9.5% (1995)
child mortality rate (under 5, per 1,000 live births) 8 (1993)
life expectancy 74 (men), 81 (women)
education (compulsory years) 10
literacy rate 99%
languages English, French (both official; 60% English mother tongue, 24% French mother tongue); there are also Native American languages and the Inuit Inuktitut
religions Roman Catholic, various Protestant denominations
TV sets (per 1,000 people) 640 (1992)
currency Canadian dollar
GDP (US $) 562.9 billion (1995)
GDP per capita (PPP) (US $) 21,000 (1995)
growth rate 2.2% (1994/95)
average annual inflation 8.3% (1994); 3.3% (1985–93)
major trading partners USA, EU countries, Japan, China, Mexico, South Korea
resources petroleum, natural gas, coal, copper (world's third-largest producer), nickel (world's second-largest producer), lead (world's fifth-largest producer), zinc (world's largest producer), iron, gold, uranium, timber
industries transport equipment, food products, paper and related products, wood industries, chemical products, machinery
exports motor vehicles and parts, lumber, wood pulp, paper and newsprint, crude petroleum, natural gas, aluminium and alloys, petroleum and coal products. Principal market: USA 81.7% (1994)
imports motor vehicle parts, passenger vehicles, computers, foodstuffs, telecommunications equipment. Principal source: USA 67.6% (1994)
arable land 4.6% (1993)
agricultural products wheat, barley, maize, oats, rapeseed, linseed; livestock production (chiefly cattle and pigs)

HISTORY

35,000 BC First evidence of people reaching North America from Asia by way of Beringia.
c. 2000 BC Inuit (Eskimos) began settling the Arctic coast from Siberia E to Greenland.
c. 1000 AD Vikings, including Leif Ericsson, established Vinland, a settlement in NE America that did not survive.
1497 John Cabot, an Italian navigator in the service of English king Henry VII, landed on Cape Breton Island and claimed the area for England.
1534 French navigator Jacques Cartier reached the Gulf of St Lawrence and claimed the region for France.
1608 Samuel de Champlain, a French explorer, founded Quebec; French settlers developed fur trade and fisheries.
1663 French settlements in Canada formed the colony of New France, which expanded southwards.
1670 Hudson's Bay Company established trading posts N of New France, leading to Anglo-French rivalry.
1689–97 King William's War: Anglo-French conflict in North America arising from the 'Glorious Revolution' in Europe.
1702–13 Queen Anne's War: Anglo-French conflict in North America arising from the War of Spanish Succession in Europe; Britain gained Newfoundland.
1744–48 King George's War: Anglo-French conflict in North America arising from the War of Austrian Succession in Europe.
1756–63 Seven Years' War: James Wolfe captured Quebec 1759; France ceded Canada to Britain by the Treaty of Paris.
1775–83 American Revolution caused influx of 40,000 United Empire Loyalists, who formed New Brunswick 1784.
1791 Canada divided into Upper Canada (much of modern Ontario) and Lower Canada (much of modern Quebec).
1793 British explorer Alexander Mackenzie crossed the Rocky Mountains to reach the Pacific coast.
1812–14 War of 1812 between Britain and USA; US invasions repelled by both provinces.
1820s Start of large-scale immigration from British Isles caused resentment among French Canadians.
1837 Rebellions led by Louis Joseph Papineau in Lower Canada and William Lyon Mackenzie in Upper Canada.
1841 Upper and Lower Canada united as Province of Canada; granted internal self-government 1848.
1867 British North America Act united Ontario, Quebec, Nova Scotia, and New Brunswick in Dominion of Canada.
1869 Red River Rebellion of métis (people of mixed French-Indian descent), led by Louis Riel, against British settlers in Rupert's Land.
1870 Manitoba (part of Rupert's Land) formed the fifth province of Canada; British Columbia became the sixth in 1871, and Prince Edward Island became the seventh in 1873.
late 19th C Growth of large-scale wheat farming, mining, and railways.
1885 Northwest Rebellion crushed and Riel hanged; Canadian Pacific Railway completed.
1896 Wilfred Laurier was the first French Canadian to become prime minister.
1905 Alberta and Saskatchewan formed from Northwest Territories and became provinces of Canada.
1914–18 Half a million Canadian troops fought for the British Empire on the western front in World War I.
1931 Statute of Westminster affirmed equality of status between Britain and Dominions.
1939–45 World War II: Canadian participation in all theatres.
1949 Newfoundland became the tenth province of Canada; Canada was a founding member of the North Atlantic Treaty Organization (NATO).
1950s Postwar boom caused rapid expansion of industry.
1957 Progressive Conservatives returned to power after 22 years in opposition.
1960 Quebec Liberal Party of Jean Lesage launched 'Quiet Revolution' to re-assert French Canadian identity.
1970 Pierre Trudeau invoked War Measures Act to suppress separatist terrorists of the Front de Libération du Québec.
1976 The Parti Québécois won control of Quebec provincial government; referendum rejected independence 1980.
1982 'Patriation' of constitution removed Britain's last legal control over Canada.
1987 Meech Lake Accord: constitutional amendment proposed to increase provincial powers (to satisfy Quebec); failed to be ratified 1990.
1989 Canada and USA agreed to establish free trade by 1999.
1992 Self-governing homeland for Inuit approved; constitutional reform package, the Charlottetown Accord, rejected in national referendum.
1993 Progressive Conservatives reduced to two seats in crushing election defeat.
1994 Canada formed the North American Free Trade Area with USA and Mexico.
1995 Quebec referendum narrowly rejected sovereignty proposal.

SEE ALSO British Columbia; Commonwealth, the British; Inuit; Quebec

Duluth, Minnesota, USA, at the western end of Lake Superior, some 3,770 km/2,342 mi.

The first major British canal was the Bridgewater Canal 1759–61, constructed for the 3rd Duke of Bridgewater to carry coal from his collieries to Manchester. The engineer, James Brindley (1716–1772), overcame great difficulties in the route. Today, many of Britain's canals form part of an interconnecting system of waterways some 4,000 km/2,500 mi long. Many that have become disused commercially have been restored for recreation and the use of pleasure craft.

Canaletto Antonio. Adopted name of Giovanni Antonio Canal 1697–1768. Italian painter. He painted highly detailed views (*vedute*) of Venice (his native city), and of London and the river Thames 1746–56. Typical of his Venetian works is *Venice: Regatta on the Grand Canal* about 1735 (National Gallery, London).

Much of his work is detailed and precise, with a warm light and a sparkling of tiny highlights on the green waters of canals and rivers. *The Upper Reaches of the Grand Canal* about 1738 (National Gallery, London) is an example. His drawings and etchings are often more lively than his paintings, but even where his paintings are at their most mechanical they show a strong sense of design and the ability to create the illusion of space. His presence in England was influential on topographical artists and others – his brushwork may well have given its example to William Hogarth and Richard Wilson, while his drawings were models followed by Thomas Girtin and J M W Turner.

canary bird *Serinus canaria* of the finch family Fringillidae, found wild in the Canary Islands and Madeira. In its wild state the plumage is green, sometimes streaked with brown. It builds its nest of moss, feathers, and hair in thick high shrubs or trees, and produces two to four broods in a season. Canaries have been bred as cage birds in Europe since the 15th century, and many domestic varieties are yellow or orange as a result of artificial selection.

Canary Islands (Spanish ***Canarias***) group of volcanic islands 100 km/60 mi off the NW coast of Africa, forming the Spanish provinces of Las Palmas and Santa Cruz de Tenerife; area 7,300 sq km/2,818 sq mi; population (1991) 1,493,800.

features The chief centres are Santa Cruz on Tenerife (which also has the highest peak in extracontinental Spain, Pico de Teide, 3,713 m/12,186 ft), and Las Palmas on Gran Canaria. The province of Santa Cruz comprises Tenerife, Palma, Gomera, and Hierro; the province of Las Palmas comprises Gran Canaria, Lanzarote, and Fuerteventura. There are also six uninhabited islets. The Northern Hemisphere Observatory (1981) is on the island of La Palma.

Canary Wharf 4.5 million-sq ft office development on the Isle of Dogs in London's ◊Docklands, the first phase of which was completed 1992, along with the foundations for a further 8 million sq ft. The complex of offices, surrounding landscaped squares, is best known for its central skyscraper, the second tallest in Europe at 244 m/800 ft. Designed by US architect Cesar Pelli (1926–), it sports a pyramid-shaped crown in stainless steel. The site has gained notoriety as a symbol of the economic recession in the UK, with much of its office space remaining unlet. By the end of 1995 75% had been let.

Canberra capital of Australia (since 1908), situated in the Australian Capital Territory, enclosed within New South Wales, on a tributary of the Murrumbidgee River; area (Australian Capital Territory including the port at Jervis Bay) 2,432 sq km/939 sq mi; population (1993) 324,600.

features It contains the Parliament House (first used by the Commonwealth Parliament 1927), the Australian National University (1946), the Canberra School of Music (1965), and the National War Memorial.

history The site for the new city was selected 1908, located between Sydney and Melbourne, rivals to be capital of the new country. The city was named Canberra 1913 and was designed by the architect Walter Burley Griffin. Parliament first convened there 1927, but the city's development was slow until after World War II. The new Parliament House was opened 1988.

Canary Islands

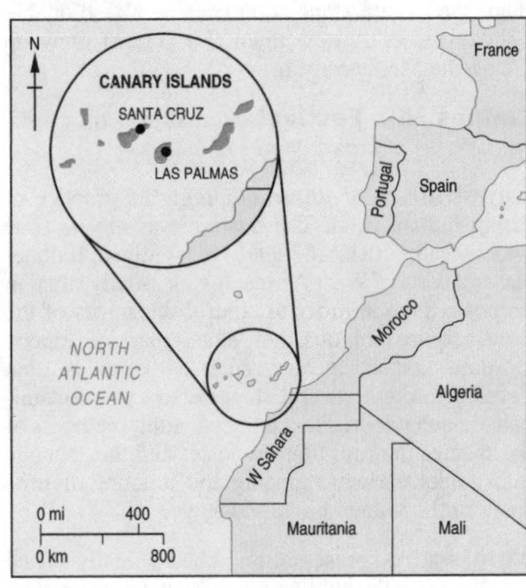

cancer group of diseases characterized by abnormal proliferation of cells. Cancer (malignant) cells are usually degenerate, capable only of reproducing themselves (tumour formation). Malignant cells tend to spread from their site of origin by travelling through the bloodstream or lymphatic system.

causes There are more than 100 types of cancer. Some, like lung or bowel cancer, are common; others are rare. The likely causes remain unexplained. Triggering agents (◊carcinogens) include chemicals such as those found in cigarette smoke, other forms of smoke, asbestos dust, exhaust fumes, and many industrial chemicals. Some viruses can also trigger the cancerous growth of cells (see ◊oncogenes), as can X-rays and radioactivity. Dietary factors are important in some cancers; for example, lack of fibre in the diet may predispose people to bowel cancer and a diet high in animal fats and low in fresh vegetables and fruit increases the risk of breast cancer. Psychological ◊stress may increase the risk of cancer, more so if the person concerned is not able to control the source of the stress.

cancer genes In some families there is a genetic tendency towards a particular type of cancer. In 1993 researchers isolated the first gene that predisposes individuals to cancer. About 1 in 200 people in the West carry the gene. If the gene mutates, those with the altered gene have a 70% chance of developing colon cancer, and female carriers have a 50% chance of developing cancer of the uterus. This accounts for an estimated 10% of all colon cancer.

In 1994 a gene that triggers breast cancer was identified, BRCA1 (found to be responsible for almost half the cases of inherited breast cancer, and most cases of ovarian cancer); and in 1995 a link between BRCA1 and non-inherited breast cancer was discovered. Women with the gene have an 85% chance of developing breast or ovarian cancer during their lifetime. A second breast cancer gene BRCA2 was identified 1995.

Cancer faintest of the zodiacal constellations (its brightest stars are fourth magnitude). It lies in the northern hemisphere between ◊Leo and ◊Gemini, and is represented as a crab. The Sun passes through the constellation during late July and early Aug. In astrology, the dates for Cancer are between about 22 June and 22 July (see ◊precession). Cancer's most distinctive feature is the open star cluster Praesepe, popularly known as the Beehive, visible to the naked eye as a nebulous patch.

candela SI unit (symbol cd) of luminous intensity, which replaced the old units of candle and standard candle. It measures the brightness of a light itself rather than the amount of light falling on an object, which is called illuminance and measured in ◊lux. One candela is defined as the luminous intensity in a given direction of a source that emits monochromatic radiation of frequency 540×10^{-12} Hz and whose radiant energy in that direction is 1/683 watt per steradian.

Candida albicans yeastlike fungus present in the human digestive tract and in the vagina, which causes no harm in most healthy people. However, it can cause problems if it multiplies excessively, as in vaginal candidiasis or ◊thrush, the main symptom of which is intense itching. The most common form of thrush is oral, which often occurs in those taking steroids or prolonged courses of antibiotics. Treatment is based on antifungal drugs.

Canes Venatici constellation of the northern hemisphere near ◊Ursa Major, identified with the hunting dogs of ◊Boötes, the herder. Its stars are faint, and it contains the Whirlpool galaxy (M51), the first spiral galaxy to be recognized. It contains many objects of telescopic interest, including the relatively bright ◊globular cluster M3. The brightest star, a third magnitude double, is called Cor Caroli or Alpha Canum Venaticorum.

cane toad toad of the genus *Bufo marinus*, family Bufonidae. Also known as the giant or marine toad, the cane toad is the largest in the world. It acquired its name after being introduced to Australia during the 1930s to eradicate the cane beetle, which had become a serious pest there. However, having few natural enemies, the cane toad itself has now

CANADA: PROVINCES

Province	Capital	Area in sq km/sq mi
Alberta	Edmonton	661,200/255,289
British Columbia	Victoria	947,800/365,945
Manitoba	Winnipeg	650,000/250,965
New Brunswick	Fredericton	73,400/28,339
Newfoundland	St John's	405,700/156,640
Nova Scotia	Halifax	55,500/21,428
Ontario	Toronto	1,068,600/412,586
Prince Edward Island	Charlottetown	5,700/2,200
Québec	Québec	1,540,700/594,864
Saskatchewan	Regina	652,300/251,853
Territory	**Capital**	**Area in sq km/sq mi**
Northwest Territories	Yellowknife	3,426,300/1,322,894
Yukon Territory	Whitehorse	483,500/186,679

canal View of the Paddington Canal, London, a stretch of the Grand Junction Canal. The Grand Junction, which extended from Paddington to Uxbridge, opened 1801 at the height of the canal-building boom. *Philip Sauvain*

Canetti The Bulgarian-born writer Elias Canetti. His writings, particularly his powerful autobiographical works, present in acute form the predicament of the isolated intellectual confronted by a totalitarian society. *Topham*

become a pest in Australia. The cane toad's defence system consists of highly-developed glands on each side of its neck which can squirt a poisonous fluid to a distance of around 1 m/3.3 ft.

Canetti Elias 1905–1994. Bulgarian-born writer. He was exiled from Austria 1937 and settled in England 1939. His books, written in German, include *Die Blendung/Auto da Fé* 1935. Nobel Prize for Literature 1981.

He was concerned with crowd behaviour and the psychology of power, and wrote the anthropological study *Masse und Macht/Crowds and Power* 1960. His three volumes of memoirs are *Die gerettete Zunge: Geschichte einer Jugend/The Tongue Set Free: Remembrance of a Childhood* 1977, in which he writes of his earliest years; *Die Fackel im Ohr: Lebensgeschichte 1921–31/The Torch in My Ear* 1980, set mainly in Vienna and covering the period when Canetti came under the spell of satirist Karl Kraus; and *Das Augenspeil/The Play of the Eyes* 1985, which covers the years 1931–37, and is rich in satirical insights into the artistic Viennese society of the time.

‘History portrays everything as if it could not have come otherwise. History is on the side of what happened.’

ELIAS CANETTI
The Human Province

canine in mammalian carnivores, any of the long, often pointed teeth found at the front of the mouth between the incisors and premolars. Canine teeth are used for catching prey, for killing, and for tearing flesh. They are absent in herbivores and are much reduced in humans.

Canis Major brilliant constellation of the southern hemisphere, represented (with Canis Minor) as one of the two dogs following at the heel of ◊Orion. Its main star, ◊Sirius, is the brightest star in the night sky. Epsilon Canis Majoris is also of the first magnitude, and there are three second magnitude stars.

Canis Minor small constellation along the celestial equator (see ◊celestial sphere), represented as the smaller of the two dogs of ◊Orion (the other dog being ◊Canis Major). Its brightest star is the first magnitude ◊Procyon. Procyon and Beta Canis Minoris form what the Arabs called ‘the Short Cubit’, in contrast to ‘the Long Cubit’ formed by ◊Castor and ◊Pollux (Alpha and Beta Geminorum).

cannabis dried leaves and female flowers (marijuana) and resin (hashish) of certain varieties of ◊hemp *Cannabis sativa*, which are smoked or swallowed to produce a range of effects, including euphoria and altered perception. Cultivation of cannabis is illegal in the UK and USA except under licence.

Cannabis is a soft drug in that any dependence is psychological rather than physical. It is illegal in many countries and has played little part in orthodox medicine since the 1930s. However, recent research has resulted in the discovery of cannabis receptors in the brain, and the discovery of a naturally occurring brain chemical which yields the same effects as smoking cannabis. Researchers believe this work could lead to the exploitation of cannabis-like compounds to treat physical illness without affecting the mind. Cannabis has alleged beneficial effects in treating chronic diseases such as AIDS and ◊multiple sclerosis.

Cannes resort in Alpes-Maritimes *département*, S France; population (1990) 69,400. Formerly only a small seaport, in 1834 it attracted the patronage of Lord Brougham (1778–1868) and other distinguished visitors and soon became a fashionable holiday resort. A new town (La Bocca) grew up facing the Mediterranean.

Cannes Film Festival international film festival. *See list of tables on p. 1177.*

cannibalism or ***anthropophagy*** the practice of eating human flesh. The custom was at one time widespread in the Americas, New Guinea, Indonesia, and parts of West Africa. It was usually ritual in purpose, done in order to control the spirits of the dead, acquire their qualities, or as a mark of respect.

Some animal species, such as tadpoles, that develop through several stages also exhibit cannibalistic behaviour. The young eat adult members of the species in order to grow faster and thus change into adults earlier, reducing the amount of time spent in the vulnerable larval stage.

canning food preservation in hermetically sealed containers by the application of heat. Originated by Nicolas Appert in France 1809 with glass containers, it was developed by Peter Durand in England 1810 with cans made of sheet steel thinly coated with tin to delay corrosion. Cans for beer and soft drinks are now generally made of aluminium.

Canneries were established in the USA before 1820, but the US canning industry expanded considerably in the 1870s when the manufacture of cans was mechanized and factory methods of processing were used. The quality and taste of early canned food was frequently inferior but by the end of the 19th century, scientific research made greater understanding possible of the food-preserving process, and standards improved. More than half the aluminium cans used in the USA are now recycled.

In Britain, imports of canned fruit, beef, vegetables, and condensed milk rose substantially after World War I. A British canning industry was slow to develop compared to the USA or Australia, but it began to grow during the 1920s, and by 1932, the Metal Box Company was producing over 100 million cans a year.

Canning Charles John, 1st Earl Canning 1812–1862. British administrator, first viceroy of India from 1858. As governor general of India from 1856, he suppressed the Indian Mutiny with a fair but firm hand which earned him the nickname ‘Clemency Canning’. He was the son of George Canning.

Canning George 1770–1827. British Tory politician, foreign secretary 1807–10 and 1822–27, and prime minister 1827 in coalition with the Whigs. He was largely responsible, during the ◊Napoleonic Wars, for the seizure of the Danish fleet and British intervention in the Spanish peninsula.

Cannizzaro Stanislao 1826–1910. Italian chemist who revived interest in the work of ◊Avogadro that had, in 1811, revealed the difference between ◊atoms and ◊molecules, and so established atomic and molecular weights as the basis of chemical calculations. Cannizzaro also worked in aromatic organic chemistry. In 1853 he discovered reactions (named after him) that make benzyl alcohol and benzoic acid from benzaldehyde.

Cannon Annie Jump 1863–1941. US astronomer. She carried out revolutionary work on the classification of stars by examining their spectra. Her system, still used today, has spectra arranged according to temperature into categories labelled O, B, A, F, G, K, M, R, N, and S. O-type stars are the hottest, with surface temperatures of over 25,000 K.

Cano Juan Sebastian del c. 1476–1526. Spanish voyager. It is claimed that he was the first sea captain to sail around the world. He sailed with Magellan 1519 and, after the latter's death in the Philippines, brought the *Victoria* safely home to Spain.

canoeing sport of propelling a lightweight, shallow boat, pointed at both ends, by paddles or sails. Present-day canoes are made from fibreglass, but original boats were of wooden construction covered in bark or skin. Canoeing was popularized as a sport in the 19th century.

Two types of canoe are used: the kayak and the Canadian-style canoe. The kayak, derived from the Inuit model, has a keel and the canoeist sits. The Canadian-style canoe has no keel and the canoeist kneels. In addition to straightforward racing, there are slalom courses, with up to 30 ‘gates’ to be negotiated through rapids and around artificial rock formations. Penalty seconds are added to course time for touching suspended gate poles or missing a gate. One to four canoeists are carried. The sport was introduced into the Olympic Games 1936. The Royal Canoe Club in Britain was founded 1866.

canon in music, an echo form for two or more parts employed in classical music, for example by two solo violins in an orchestral movement by Vivaldi or J S Bach, as a means of generating pace and advertising professional skill. Canonic variations may also introduce a difference in starting pitch between the voices, creating ambiguities of tonality; the highest expression is the ◊fugue.

canon in the Roman Catholic and Anglican churches, a type of priest. Canons, headed by the dean, are attached to a cathedral and constitute the chapter.

canonical hours in the Catholic church, seven set periods of devotion: matins and lauds, prime, terce, sext, nones, evensong or vespers, and compline. In the Anglican church, it is the period 8 am–6 pm within which marriage can be legally performed in a parish church without a special licence.

canonization in the Catholic church, the admission of one of its members to the Calendar of ◊Saints. The evidence of the candidate's exceptional piety is contested before the Congregation for the Causes of Saints by the Promotor Fidei, popularly known as the devil's advocate. Papal ratification of a favourable verdict results in ◊beatification, and full sainthood (conferred in St Peter's basilica, the Vatican) follows after further proof.

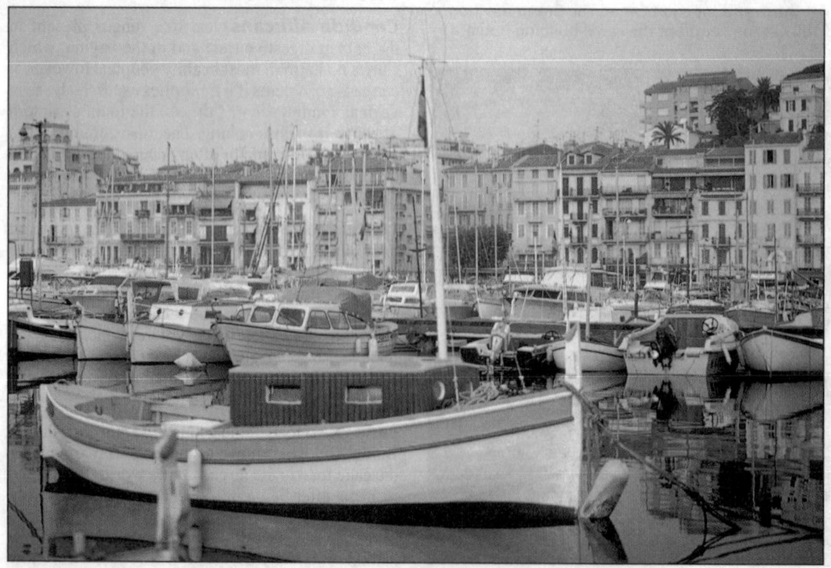

Cannes The old port of Cannes, SE France. Named after the cane reeds that used to grow along the coast, Cannes is now best known for its broad palm-lined streets and subtropical vegetation. The main industry is tourism, though there is still an important trade in perfumes, soap, and fruit. *Sally Jenkins*

canon law rules and regulations of the Christian church, especially the Greek Orthodox, Roman Catholic, and Anglican churches. Its origin is sought in the declarations of Jesus and the apostles. In 1983 Pope John Paul II issued a new canon law code reducing offences carrying automatic excommunication, extending the grounds for annulment of marriage, removing the ban on marriage with non-Catholics, and banning trade-union and political activity by priests. The canon law of the Church of England was completely revised 1969 and is kept under constant review by the Canon Law Commission of the General Synod.

Canopus or ***Alpha Carinae*** second brightest star in the night sky (after Sirius), lying in the southern constellation ◊Carina. It is a first-magnitude yellow-white supergiant about 120 light years from Earth, and thousands of times more luminous than the Sun.

Canova Antonio, Marquese d'Ischia 1757–1822. Italian Neo-Classical sculptor. Born near Treviso, he was based in Rome from 1781. He received commissions from popes, kings, and emperors for his highly finished marble portrait busts and groups of figures, and made several portraits of Napoleon.

His reclining marble *Pauline Borghese as Venus* 1805–07 (Borghese Gallery, Rome) is a fine example of his cool, polished Classicism. He executed the tombs of popes Clement XIII, Pius VII, and Clement XIV. His marble sculptures include *Cupid and Psyche* 1793 (Louvre, Paris) and *The Three Graces* (held in the Victoria and Albert Museum, London, from 1990 while efforts were made to raise the £7.6 million needed to keep it in the UK).

Cantabria autonomous region of N Spain; area 5,300 sq km/2,046 sq mi; population (1991) 527,300. The capital is Santander. From the coastline on the Bay of Biscay it rises to the Cantabrian Mountains. Mining is the major industry.

Cantabrian Mountains (Spanish ***Cordillera Cantábrica***) mountain range running along the N coast of Spain, reaching 2,648 m/8,688 ft in the Picos de Europa massif. The mountains contain coal and iron deposits.

cantata in music, an extended work for voices, from the Italian, meaning 'sung', as opposed to ◊sonata ('sounded') for instruments. A cantata can be sacred or secular, sometimes uses solo voices, and usually has orchestral accompaniment.

Canterbury historic cathedral city in Kent, England, on the river Stour, 100 km/62 mi SE of London; population (1991) 36,500. In 597 King Ethelbert welcomed ◊Augustine's mission to England here, and the city has since been the metropolis of the Anglican Communion and seat of the archbishop of Canterbury. The cathedral was begun in the 11th century. The Roman *Durovernum Cantiacorum*, Canterbury was the Saxon capital of Kent. The present name derives from *Cantwarabyrig* (Old English 'fortress of the men of Kent'). The foundations of a Saxon cathedral were uncovered 1992.

Canterbury, archbishop of primate of all England, archbishop of the Church of England (Anglican), and first peer of the realm, ranking next to royalty. He crowns the sovereign, has a seat in the House of Lords, and is a member of the Privy Council. He is appointed by the prime minister.

Formerly selected by political consultation, since 1980 the new archbishops have been selected by a church group, the Crown Appointments Commission (formed 1977). The first holder of the office was St Augustine 601–04; his 20th-century successors have been Randal T Davidson 1903, Cosmo Gordon Lang 1928, William Temple 1942, Geoffrey Fisher 1945, Michael Ramsey 1961, Donald Coggan 1974, Robert Runcie 1980, and George Carey 1991. The archbishop's official residence is at Lambeth Palace, London, and second residence at the Old Palace, Canterbury. *See list of tables on p. 1177.*

Canterbury Tales, The unfinished collection of stories in prose and verse (c. 1387) by Geoffrey ◊Chaucer, told in Middle English by a group of pilgrims on their way to Thomas à ◊Becket's tomb at Canterbury. The tales and preludes are remarkable for their vivid character portrayal and colloquial language. Each pilgrim had to tell two stories on the way to Canterbury, and two on the way back, but only 24 tales were written.

cantilever beam or structure that is fixed at one end only, though it may be supported at some point along its length; for example, a diving board. The cantilever principle, widely used in construction engineering, eliminates the need for a second main support at the free end of the beam, allowing for more elegant structures and reducing the amount of materials required. Many large-span bridges have been built on this principle, typically consisting of two beams cantilevered out from either bank, each supported part way along, with their free ends meeting in the middle.

canton in France, an administrative district, a subdivision of the *arrondissement*; in Switzerland, one of the 23 subdivisions forming the Confederation.

Canton alternative spelling of Kwangchow or ◊Guangzhou, a city in China.

Canute c. 995–1035. King of England from 1016, Denmark from 1018, and Norway from 1028. Having invaded England 1013 with his father, Sweyn, King of Denmark, he was acclaimed king on his father's death 1014 by his ◊Viking army. Canute defeated ◊Edmund (II) Ironside at Assandun, Essex, 1016, and became king of all England on Edmund's death. He succeeded his brother Harold as king of Denmark 1018, compelled King Malcolm to pay homage by invading Scotland about 1027, and conquered Norway 1028. He was succeeded by his illegitimate son Harold I.

Canute VI (***Cnut VI***) 1163–1202. King of Denmark from 1182, son and successor of Waldemar Knudsson. With his brother and successor, Waldemar II, he resisted Frederick I's northward expansion, and established Denmark as the dominant power in the Baltic.

canyon (Spanish *cañon* 'tube') deep, narrow valley or gorge running through mountains. Canyons are formed by stream down-cutting, usually in arid areas, where the rate of down-cutting is greater than the rate of weathering, and where the stream or river receives water from outside the area. There are many canyons in the western USA and in Mexico, for example the Grand Canyon of the Colorado River in Arizona, the canyon in Yellowstone National Park, and the Black Canyon in Colorado.

cap another name for a ◊diaphragm contraceptive.

CAP abbreviation for ◊***Common Agricultural Policy***.

Capa Robert. Adopted name of André Friedmann 1913–1954. US photographer, born in Hungary. He specialized in war photography. He covered the Spanish Civil War as a freelance and World War II for *Life* and *Collier's* magazines. His pictures emphasize the human tragedy of war. He was a founder member of the Magnum photographic agency. He died while on an assignment in Vietnam.

capacitor or ***condenser*** device for storing electric charge, used in electronic circuits; it consists of two or more metal plates separated by an insulating layer called a dielectric. Its capacitance is the ratio of the charge stored on either plate to the potential difference between the plates. The SI unit of capacitance is the farad, but most capacitors have much smaller capacitances, and the microfarad (a millionth of a farad) is the commonly used practical unit.

Cape Canaveral promontory on the Atlantic coast of Florida, USA, 367 km/228 mi N of Miami, used as a rocket launch site by ◊NASA. It was known as Cape Kennedy 1963–73. The ◊Kennedy Space Center is nearby.

Cape Cod hook-shaped peninsula in SE Massachusetts, USA, 100 km/60 mi long and 1.6–32 km/1–20 mi wide. Its beaches and woods make it a popular tourist area. It is separated from the rest of the state by the Cape Cod Canal. The islands of Martha's Vineyard and Nantucket are just S of the cape. Basque and Norse fisherfolk are believed to have visited Cape Cod many years before the English Pilgrims landed at Provincetown 1620.

Cape Horn southernmost point of South America, in the Chilean part of the archipelago of ◊Tierra del Fuego; notorious for gales and heavy seas. It was named 1616 by Dutch explorer Willem Schouten (1580–1625) after his birthplace (Hoorn).

Canterbury A view of Canterbury cathedral from the north-west. Historically and artistically, it is one of the most important buildings in England. The oldest part of the building is the crypt, dating from the late 11th century. Externally, the dominant feature is the majestic central tower (known as 'Bell Harry'), built in the 15th century. *Corbis*

Capella or ***Alpha Aurigae*** brightest star in the constellation ◊Auriga and the sixth brightest star in the night sky. It is a visual and spectroscopic binary that consists of a pair of yellow-giant stars 45 light years from Earth, orbiting each other every 104 days. It is a first-magnitude star, whose Latin name means the 'the Little Nanny Goat': its kids are the three adjacent stars Epsilon, Eta, and Zeta Aurigae.

Cape of Good Hope South African headland forming a peninsula between Table Bay and False Bay, Cape Town. The first European to sail around it was Bartolomeu ◊Diaz 1488. It was formerly named Cape of Storms.

Cape Province (Afrikaans ***Kaapprovinsie***) former province of the Republic of South Africa to 1994, named after the Cape of Good Hope. Dutch traders established the first European settlement on the Cape 1652, but it was taken by the British 1795, after the French Revolutionary armies had occupied the Netherlands, and was sold to Britain for £6 million 1814. The Cape achieved self-government 1872. It was an original province of the Union 1910.

Capet Hugh 938–996. King of France from 987, when he claimed the throne on the death of Louis V. He founded the Capetian dynasty, of which various branches continued to reign until the French Revolution, for example, ◊Valois and ◊Bourbon.

'Save me, oh, save me from the candid friend.'

George Canning
New Morality

Cape Town (Afrikaans ***Kaapstad***) port and oldest city (founded 1652) in South Africa, situated in the SW on Table Bay; population (1991) 2,350,200 (urban area). Industries include horticulture and trade in wool, wine, fruit, grain, and oil. It is the legislative capital of the Republic of South Africa and capital of ◊Western Cape province.

It includes the Houses of Parliament, City Hall, Cape Town Castle 1666, and Groote Schuur ('great barn'), the estate of Cecil Rhodes (he designated the house as the home of the premier, and a university and the National Botanical Gardens occupy part of the grounds). The naval base of Simonstown is to the SE; in 1975 Britain's use of its facilities was ended by the Labour government in disapproval of South Africa's racial policies.

Cape Verde group of islands in the Atlantic, W of Senegal (W Africa). *See country box on p. 184.*

Cape Wrath headland at the northwest extremity of Scotland, extending 159 m/523 ft into the Atlantic Ocean. Its lighthouse dates from 1828.

capillarity spontaneous movement of liquids up or down narrow tubes, or capillaries. The movement is due to unbalanced molecular attraction at the boundary between the liquid and the tube. If liquid molecules near the boundary are more strongly attracted to molecules in the material of the tube than to other nearby liquid molecules, the liquid will rise in the tube. If liquid molecules are less attracted to the material of the tube than to other liquid molecules, the liquid will fall.

capillary in biology, the narrowest type of blood vessel in vertebrates, 0.008–0.02 mm in diameter, barely wider than a red blood cell. Capillaries are distributed as beds, complex networks connecting arteries and veins. Capillary walls are extremely

'This fine old town, or rather city, is remarkable of cleanliness and niceness, notwithstanding it has a cathedral in it.'

On **Canterbury**
William Cobbett
Rural Rides
4 Sept 1823

Capone US mobster Al Capone leaving a court in Chicago, Oct 1931. Like several other Mafia leaders, he was brought to trial not for murder, extortion, or bootlegging, but for income tax evasion – his empire was thought to make $100 million a year. Shortly after this picture was taken he was sentenced to 11 years in prison. *Corbis*

‘I think that Capitalism, wisely managed, can probably be made more efficient for attaining economic ends than any alternative system yet in sight, but that in itself it is in many ways extremely objectionable.’

On CAPITALISM
J M Keynes *The End of Laissez-Faire*

thin, consisting of a single layer of cells, and so nutrients, dissolved gases, and waste products can easily pass through them. This makes the capillaries the main area of exchange between the fluid (◊lymph) bathing body tissues and the blood.

capillary in physics, a very narrow, thick-walled tube, usually made of glass, such as in a thermometer. Properties of fluids, such as surface tension and viscosity, can be studied using capillary tubes.

capital in architecture, a stone placed on the top of a column, pier, or pilaster, and usually wider on the upper surface than the diameter of the supporting shaft. A capital consists of three parts: the top member, called the abacus, a block that acts as the supporting surface to the superstructure; the middle portion, known as the bell or echinus; and the lower part, called the necking or astragal.

capital in economics, the stock of goods used in the production of other goods. Financial capital is accumulated or inherited wealth held in the form of assets, such as stocks and shares, property, and bank deposits. Fixed capital is durable, examples being factories, offices, plant, and machinery. Circulating capital is capital that is used up quickly, such as raw materials, components, and stocks of finished goods waiting for sale. Private capital is usually owned by individuals and private business organizations. Social capital is usually owned by the state and is the ◊infrastructure of the economy, such as roads, bridges, schools, and hospitals. Investment is the process of adding to the capital stock of a nation or business.

capitalism economic system in which the principal means of production, distribution, and exchange are in private (individual or corporate) hands and competitively operated for profit. A mixed economy combines the private enterprise of capitalism and a degree of state monopoly, as in nationalized industries and welfare services. Most capitalist economies are actually mixed economies, but some (such as the US and Japanese) have a greater share of the economy devoted to ◊free enterprise.

capital punishment punishment by death. Capital punishment is retained in 92 countries and territories (1990), including the USA (37 states), China, and Islamic countries. It was abolished in the UK 1965 for all crimes except treason. Ireland abolished the death penalty for all offences 1990. Methods of execution include electrocution, lethal gas, hanging, shooting, lethal injection, garrotting, and decapitation.

The reduction in the number of capital offences in Britain in the 19th century followed campaigns from 1810 onwards by Samuel Romilly (1757–1818) and others. Several acts were passed, each reducing the number of crimes liable to this penalty. From 1838 it was rarely used except for murder, and its use was subject to the royal prerogative of mercy.

Capone Al(phonse), (‘Scarface’) 1899–1947. US gangster. During the ◊Prohibition period, he built a formidable criminal organization in Chicago. He was brutal in his pursuit of dominance, killing seven members of a rival gang in the St Valentine’s Day massacre. He was imprisoned 1931–39 for income-tax evasion, the only charge that could be sustained against him.

Capote Truman. Pen name of Truman Streckfus Persons 1924–1984. US novelist, journalist, and playwright. After achieving early success as a writer of sparkling prose in the stories of *Other Voices, Other Rooms* 1948 and the novel *Breakfast at Tiffany’s* 1958, Capote’s career flagged until the sensational ‘nonfiction novel’ *In Cold Blood* 1965 made him a celebrity. Later works included *Music for Chameleons* 1980 and the posthumously published *Answered Prayers* 1986, an unfinished novel of scandalous socialite gossip.

Cappadocia ancient region of Asia Minor, in E central Turkey. It was conquered by the Persians 584 BC but in the 3rd century BC became an independent kingdom. The region was annexed as a province of the Roman Empire AD 17. The area includes over 600 Byzantine cave churches cut into volcanic rock, dating mainly from the 10th and 11th centuries.

Capra Frank 1897–1991. Italian-born US film director. His satirical comedies, which often have the common man pitted against corrupt institutions, were hugely successful in the Depression years of the 1930s. He won Academy Awards for the fairy-tale comedy romance *It Happened One Night* 1934, *Mr Deeds Goes to Town* 1936, and *You Can’t Take It with You* 1938. Among his other classic films are *Mr Smith Goes to Washington* 1939, and *It’s a Wonderful Life* 1946.

Capote US novelist Truman Capote, who explored the edge between documentary writing and fiction, most notably in his study of remorseless murder *In Cold Blood*. He was associated with the Beat Generation writers throughout the 1950s. *Corbis*

Capri Italian island at the southern entrance of the Bay of Naples; 32 km/20 mi S of Naples; area 13 sq km/5 sq mi. It has two towns, Capri and Anacapri, a profusion of flowers, beautiful scenery, and an ideal climate. The Blue Grotto on the north coast is an important tourist attraction.

Capricornus zodiacal constellation in the southern hemisphere next to ◊Sagittarius. It is represented as a fish-tailed goat, and its brightest stars are third magnitude. The Sun passes through it late Jan to mid-Feb. In astrology, the dates for Capricornus (popularly known as Capricorn) are between about 22 Dec and 19 Jan (see ◊precession).

capsicum any pepper plant of the genus *Capsicum* of the nightshade family Solanaceae, native to Central and South America. The differing species produce green to red fruits that vary in size. The small ones are used whole to give the hot flavour of chilli, or ground to produce cayenne pepper; the large pointed or squarish pods, known as sweet peppers, are mild-flavoured and used as a vegetable.

Capuchin member of the Franciscan order of monks in the Roman Catholic church, instituted by the Italian monk Matteo di Bassi (died 1552), who

CAPE VERDE
Republic of

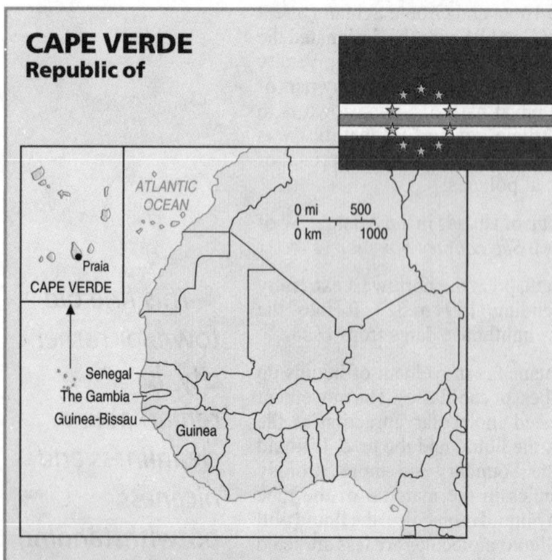

national name *República de Cabo Verde*
area 4,033 sq km/1,557 sq mi
capital Praia
major ports Mindelo
physical features archipelago of ten volcanic islands 565 km/350 mi W of Senegal; the windward (Barlavento) group includes Santo Antão, São Vicente, Santa Luzia, São Nicolau, Sal, and Boa Vista; the leeward (Sotovento) group comprises Maio, São Tiago, Fogo, and Brava; all but Santa Luzia are inhabited
head of state Monteiro Mascarenhas from 1991
head of government Carlos Viega from 1991
political system emergent democracy
administrative divisions two districts, each subdivided into seven councils
political parties African Party for the Independence of Cape Verde (PAICV), African nationalist; Movement for Democracy (MPD), moderate, centrist
population 359,500 (1995 est)
population growth rate 2.8% (1990–95)
ethnic distribution about 60% of mixed descent (Portuguese and African), known as *mestiços* or creoles; the remainder is mainly African. The European population is very small
life expectancy 67 (males), 69 (females)
literacy rate 53%
languages Portuguese (official), Creole
religions Roman Catholic 93%, Protestant (Nazarene church)
currency Cape Verde escudo
GDP (US $) 309.5 million (1994)
growth rate 4.0% (1994)
exports bananas, salt, fish, coffee

HISTORY
1462 Originally uninhabited; settled by Portuguese, who brought in slave labour from W Africa.
later 19th C Decline in prosperity as slave trade ended.
1950s Liberation movement developed on the islands and the Portuguese African mainland colony of Guinea-Bissau.
1951 Became an overseas territory of Portugal.
1975 Independence achieved. National people’s assembly elected, with Aristides of the PAICV as the first executive president; a policy of nonalignment followed.
1981 Goal of union with Guinea-Bissau abandoned; became one-party state.
1988 Rising unrest and demand for political reforms.
1991 In first multiparty elections, new MPD won majority and Monteiro Mascarenhas became president; market-centred economic reforms introduced.

SEE ALSO Guinea-Bissau

wished to return to the literal observance of the rule of St Francis. The Capuchin rule was drawn up 1529 and the order recognized by the pope 1619. The name was derived from the French term for the brown habit and pointed hood (*capuche*) that they wore. The order has been involved in missionary activity.

capybara world's largest rodent *Hydrochoerus hydrochaeris*, up to 1.3 m/4 ft long and 50 kg/110 lb in weight. It is found in South America, and belongs to the guinea-pig family. The capybara inhabits marshes and dense vegetation around water. It has thin, yellowish hair, swims well, and can rest underwater with just eyes, ears, and nose above the surface.

car small, driver-guided, passenger-carrying motor vehicle; originally the automated version of the horse-drawn carriage, meant to convey people and their goods over streets and roads.

Over 50 million motor cars are produced each year worldwide. Most are four-wheeled and have water-cooled, piston-type internal-combustion engines fuelled by petrol or diesel. Variations have existed for decades that use ingenious and often nonpolluting power plants, but the motor industry long ago settled on this general formula for the consumer market. Experimental and sports models are streamlined, energy-efficient, and hand-built.

origins Although it is recorded that in 1479 Gilles de Dom was paid 25 livres (the equivalent of 25 pounds of silver) by the treasurer of Antwerp in the Low Countries for supplying a self-propelled vehicle, the ancestor of the automobile is generally agreed to be the cumbersome steam carriage made by Nicolas-Joseph Cugnot 1769, still preserved in Paris. Steam was an attractive form of power to the English pioneers, and in 1808 Richard Trevithick built a working steam carriage. Later in the 19th century, practical steam coaches were used for public transport until stifled out of existence by punitive road tolls and legislation.

the first motorcars Although a Frenchman, Jean Etienne Lenoir, patented the first internal-combustion engine (gas-driven) 1860, and an Austrian, Siegfried Marcus, built a vehicle which was shown at the Vienna Exhibition (1873), two Germans, Gottlieb Daimler and Karl Benz are generally regarded as the creators of the motorcar. In 1885 Daimler and Benz built and ran the first petrol-driven motorcar. The pattern for the modern motorcar was set by Panhard 1890 (front radiator, engine under bonnet, sliding-pinion gearbox, wooden ladder-chassis) and Mercedes 1901 (honeycomb radiator, in-line four-cylinder engine, gate-change gearbox, pressed-steel chassis) set the pattern for the modern car. Emerging with Haynes and Duryea in the early 1890s, US demand was so fervent that 300 makers existed by 1895; only 109 were left by 1900.

In England, cars were still considered to be light locomotives in the eyes of the law and, since the Red Flag Act 1865, had theoretically required someone to walk in front with a red flag (by night, a lantern). Despite these obstacles, which put UK development another ten years behind all others, in 1896 Frederick Lanchester produced an advanced and reliable vehicle, later much copied.

motorcars as an industry The period 1905–06 inaugurated a world motorcar boom continuing to the present day. Among the legendary cars of the early 20th century are: De Dion Bouton, with the first practical high-speed engines; Mors, notable first for racing and later as a silent tourer; Napier, the 24-hour record-holder at Brooklands 1907, unbeaten for 17 years; the incomparable Silver Ghost Rolls-Royce; the enduring Model T ⇨Ford; and the many types of Bugatti and Delage, from record-breakers to luxury tourers. After World War I popular motoring began with the era of cheap, light (baby) cars made by Citroën, Peugeot, and Renault (France); Austin, Morris, Clyno, and Swift (England); Fiat (Italy); Volkswagen (Germany); and the cheap though bigger Ford, Chevrolet, and Dodge in the USA. During the interwar years a great deal of racing took place, and the experience gained benefited the everyday motorist in improved efficiency, reliability, and safety. There was a divergence between the lighter, economical European car, with its good handling, and the heavier US car,

'Then, to the scream of the horse, the change began. The brass-lamped motor-car came coughing up the road.'

On the CAR
Laurie Lee
Cider With Rosie 1959

CAR: TIMELINE

1769	Nicholas-Joseph Cugnot in France built a steam tractor.
1801	Richard Trevithick built a steam coach.
1860	Jean Etienne Lenoir built a gas-fuelled internal-combustion engine.
1865	The British government passed the Red Flag Act, requiring a person to precede a 'horseless carriage' with a red flag.
1876	Nikolaus August Otto improved the gas engine, making it a practical power source.
1885	Gottlieb Daimler developed a successful lightweight petrol engine and fitted it to a bicycle to create the prototype of the present-day motorcycle; Karl Benz fitted his lightweight petrol engine to a three-wheeled carriage to pioneer the motorcar.
1886	Gottlieb Daimler fitted his engine to a four-wheeled carriage to produce a four-wheeled motorcar.
1891	René Panhard and Emile Levassor established the present design of cars by putting the engine in front.
1896	Frederick Lanchester introduced epicyclic gearing, which foreshadowed automatic transmission.
1899	C Jenatzy broke the 100-kph barrier in an electric car *La Jamais Contente* at Achères, France, reaching 105.85 kph/65.60 mph.
1901	The first Mercedes took to the roads; it was the direct ancestor of the present car. Ransome Olds in the USA introduced mass production on an assembly line.
1904	Louis Rigolly broke the 100 mph barrier, reaching 166.61 kph/103.55 mph in a Gobron-Brillé at Nice, France.
1906	Rolls-Royce introduced the Silver Ghost, which established the company's reputation for superlatively engineered cars.
1908	Henry Ford also used assembly-line production to manufacture his celebrated Model T, nicknamed the Tin Lizzie because it used lightweight sheet steel for the body, which looked tinny.
1911	Cadillac introduced the electric starter and dynamo lighting.
1913	Ford introduced the moving conveyor belt to the assembly line, further accelerating production of the Model T.
1920	Duesenberg began fitting four-wheel hydraulic brakes.
1922	The Lancia Lambda featured unitary (all-in-one) construction and independent front suspension.
1927	Henry Segrave broke the 200 mph barrier in a Sunbeam, reaching 327.89 kph/203.79 mph.
1928	Cadillac introduced the synchromesh gearbox, greatly facilitating gear changing.
1934	Citroën pioneered front-wheel drive in their 7CV model.
1936	Fiat introduced their baby car, the Topolino, 500 cc.
1938	Germany produced its 'people's car', the Volkswagen Beetle.
1948	Jaguar launched the XK120 sports car; Michelin introduced the radial-ply tyre; Goodrich produced the tubeless tyre.
1950	Dunlop announced the disc brake.
1951	Buick and Chrysler introduced power steering.
1952	Rover's gas-turbine car set a speed record of 243 kph/152 mph.
1954	Carl Bosch introduced fuel injection for cars.
1955	Citroën produced the advanced DS-19 'shark-front' car with hydropneumatic suspension.
1957	Felix Wankel built his first rotary petrol engine.
1959	BMC (now Rover) introduced the Issigonis-designed Mini, with front-wheel drive, transverse engine, and independent rubber suspension.
1965	US car manufacturers were forced to add safety features after the publication of Ralph Nader's *Unsafe at Any Speed*.
1966	California introduced legislation regarding air pollution by cars.
1970	American Gary Gabelich drove a rocket-powered car, *Blue Flame*, to a new record speed of 1,001.473 kph/622.287 mph.
1972	Dunlop introduced safety tyres, which seal themselves after a puncture.
1979	American Sam Barrett exceeded the speed of sound in the rocket-engined *Budweiser Rocket*, reaching 1,190.377 kph/ 739.666 mph, a speed not officially recognized as a record because of timing difficulties.
1980	The first mass-produced car with four-wheel drive, the Audi Quattro, was introduced; Japanese car production overtook that of the USA.
1981	BMW introduced the on-board computer, which monitored engine performance and indicated to the driver when a service was required.
1983	British driver Richard Noble set an official speed record in the jet-engined *Thrust 2* of 1,019.4 kph/633.5 mph; Austin Rover introduced the Maestro, the first car with a 'talking dashboard' that alerted the driver to problems.
1987	The solar-powered *Sunraycer* travelled 3,000 km/1,864 mi from Darwin to Adelaide, Australia, in six days. Toyota Corona production topped 6 million in 29 years.
1988	California introduced stringent controls on car emissions, aiming for widespread use of zero emission vehicles by 1998.
1989	The first mass-produced car with four-wheel steering, the Mitsubishi Galant, was launched.
1990	Fiat of Italy and Peugeot of France launched electric passenger cars on the market.
1991	Satellite-based car navigation systems were launched in Japan. European Parliament voted to adopt stringent control of car emissions.
1992	Mazda and NEC of Japan developed an image-processing system for cars, which views the road ahead through a video camera, identifies road signs and markings, and helps the driver to avoid obstacles.
1993	A Japanese electric car, the *IZA*, built by the Tokyo Electric Power Company, reached a speed of 176 kph/109 mph (10 kph/6 mph faster than the previous record for an electric car).
1995	Greenpeace designed its own environmentally friendly car to show the industry how 'it could be done'. It produced a modified Renault Twingo with 30% less wind resistance, capable of doing 67–78 mi to the gallon (100 km per 3–3.5 litres).

cheap, rugged, and well adapted to long distances on straight roads at speed. By this time motoring had become a universal pursuit.

After World War II small European cars tended to fall into three categories, in about equal numbers: front engine and rear drive, the classic arrangement; front engine and front-wheel drive; and rear engine and rear-wheel drive. Racing cars have the engine situated in the middle for balance. From the 1950s a creative resurgence produced in practical form automatic transmission for small cars, rubber suspension, transverse engine mounting, self-levelling ride, disc brakes, and safer wet-weather tyres.

By the mid-1980s, Japan was building 8 million cars a year, on par with the USA. The largest Japanese manufacturer, Toyota, was producing 2.5 million cars per year.

A typical present-day medium-sized saloon car has a semi-monocoque construction in which the body panels, suitably reinforced, support the road loads through independent front and rear sprung suspension, with seats located within the wheelbase for comfort. It is usually powered by a ◊petrol engine using a carburettor to mix petrol and air for feeding to the engine cylinders (typically four or six), and the engine is usually water cooled.

In the 1980s high-performance diesel engines were being developed for use in private cars, and it is anticipated that this trend will continue for reasons of economy. From the engine, power is transmitted through a clutch to a four- or five-speed gearbox and from there, in a front-engine rear-drive car, through a drive (propeller) shaft to a ◊differential gear, which drives the rear wheels. In a front-engine, front-wheel drive car, clutch, gearbox, and final drive are incorporated with the engine unit. An increasing number of high-performance cars are being offered with four-wheel drive, giving superior roadholding in wet and icy conditions and allowing off-road driving.

cars and pollution Cars are responsible for almost a quarter of the world's carbon dioxide emissions. The drive against pollution from the 1960s and the fuel crisis from the 1970s led to experiments with steam cars (cumbersome), diesel engines (slow and heavy, though economical), solar-powered cars, and hybrid cars using both electricity (in town centres) and petrol (on the open road). The industry brought on the market the stratified-charge petrol engine, using a fuel injector to achieve 20% improvement in petrol consumption (the average US car in 1991 did only 27 mi/gal); weight reduction in the body by the use of aluminium and plastics; and 'slippery' body designs with low air resistance, or drag.

In 1996 Daimler-Benz unveiled the world's first car to be powered by fuel-cell, which may become the industry's most practical pollution-free alternative. It can cover 155 mi/250 km and reach speeds of over 100 mph/160 kph.

During the 1980s the number of cars in the UK increased by 34% to some 22 million; in 1950 there were only 4 million. There were 1.9 million new registrations 1995. In the UK, 85% of all passenger transport is by car. Cars are responsible for 85% of all UK carbon monoxide pollution and 45% of nitrogen oxide pollution.

Caracalla (Marcus Aurelius Antoninus) AD c. 186–217. Roman emperor, nicknamed after the Celtic cloak (*caracalla*) that he wore. He succeeded his father ◊Septimius Severus AD 211 and, with the support of the army, he murdered his brother Geta 212 to become sole ruler of the empire. During his reign in 212, Roman citizenship was given to all subjects of the empire. He built on a grandiose scale, and campaigned in Germany and against the ◊Parthians. He was assassinated.

Caracas chief city and capital of Venezuela, situated on the slopes of the Andes Mountains, 13 km/8 mi S of its port La Guaira on the Caribbean coast; population of metropolitan area (1990) 1,824,900 (Federal District 2,265,900). It is now a large industrial and commercial centre, notably for oil companies, developed since the 1950s.

history Founded by the Spanish in 1567 and sacked by the English in 1595, the city was destroyed by earthquakes in 1755 and 1812. It was expanded from the 1940s.

features Colonial buildings around the Plaza Bolívar, including the cathedral and the birthplace of Simon Bolívar; Central University of Venezuela, founded 1725.

Caractacus died c. 54. British chieftain who headed resistance to the Romans in SE England AD 43–51, but was defeated on the Welsh border. Shown in Claudius's triumphal procession, he was released in tribute to his courage and died in Rome.

Caravaggio *Salome Receives the Head of John the Baptist* by Caravaggio (National Gallery, London). Working in the early years of the 17th century, Caravaggio created a sensual and dramatic realism that was revolutionary. *Corbis*

carat (Arabic *quirrat* 'seed') unit for measuring the mass of precious stones; it is equal to 0.2 g/0.00705 oz, and is part of the troy system of weights. It is also the unit of purity in gold (US karat). Pure gold is 24-carat; 22-carat (the purest used in jewellery) is 22 parts gold and two parts alloy (to give greater strength). Originally, one carat was the weight of a carob seed.

Caravaggio Michelangelo Merisi da 1573–1610. Italian early Baroque painter. He was active in Rome 1592–1606, then in Naples, and finally in Malta. He created a forceful style, using contrasts of light and shade, dramatic foreshortening, and a meticulous attention to detail. His life was as dramatic as his art (he had to leave Rome after killing a man in a brawl).

The son of a mason in the village of Caravaggio near Milan, he had some early training in Milan, but was painting in Rome before he was 20, quickly developing that famous 'naturalism' which was in strong contrast to the prevailing Mannerism of Zuccaro and the Cavaliere d'Arpino. Instead of ideal figures, he painted the types he saw and knew, delighting in plebeian traits of character, contemporary dress and carefully delineated still life. Early examples are the *Bacchus* (Uffizi), the *Fortune Teller* (Louvre) and the *Fruit Basket* (Ambrosiana, Milan). The innovation that gave him fame and made him the centre of controversy was not only that he applied this realistic method to religious painting, but also intensified its effect by combining it with a depth and drama of light and shade that he may have adapted from Tintoretto. It appears in his first commission for the Contarelli Chapel of St Luigi dei Francesi, *St Matthew and the Angel*, the *Vocation of St Matthew*, and *Martyrdom of the Apostle*. These and other works in Rome, painted 1600–07, including the *Madonna of the Serpent* (Borghese Gallery), the *Death of the Virgin* (Louvre) and the *Madonna del Rosario* (Vienna), were either refused by his patrons or were the subject of fierce argument.

carbide compound of carbon and one other chemical element, usually a metal, silicon, or boron. Calcium carbide (CaC_2) can be used as the starting material for many basic organic chemical syntheses, by the addition of water and generation of ethyne (acetylene). Some metallic carbides are used in engineering because of their extreme hardness and strength. Tungsten carbide is an essential ingredient of carbide tools and high-speed tools.

carbohydrate chemical compound composed of carbon, hydrogen, and oxygen, with the basic formula $C_m(H_2O)_n$, and related compounds with the same basic structure but modified ◊functional groups. As sugar and starch, carbohydrates form a major energy-providing part of the human diet.

The simplest carbohydrates are sugars (***monosaccharides***, such as glucose and fructose, and ***disaccharides***, such as sucrose), which are soluble compounds, some with a sweet taste. When these basic sugar units are joined together in long chains or branching structures they form ***polysaccharides***, such as starch and glycogen, which often serve as food stores in living organisms. Even more complex carbohydrates are known, including ◊chitin, which is found in the cell walls of fungi and the hard outer skeletons of insects, and ◊cellulose, which makes up the cell walls of plants. Carbohydrates form the chief foodstuffs of herbivorous animals.

carbolic acid common name for the aromatic compound ◊phenol.

carbon (Latin *carbo, carbonaris* 'coal') nonmetallic element, symbol C, atomic number 6, relative atomic mass 12.011. It occurs on its own as diamond, graphite, and as fullerenes (the allotropes), as compounds in carbonaceous rocks such as chalk and limestone, as carbon dioxide in the atmosphere, as hydrocarbons in petroleum, coal, and natural gas, and as a constituent of all organic substances.

In its amorphous form, it is familiar as coal, charcoal, and soot. The atoms of carbon can link with one another in rings or chains, giving rise to innumerable complex compounds. Of the inorganic carbon compounds, the chief ones are ***carbon dioxide***, a colourless gas formed when carbon is burned in an adequate supply of air; and ***carbon monoxide*** (CO), formed when carbon is oxidized in a limited supply of air. ***Carbon disulphide*** (CS_2) is a dense liquid with a sweetish odour. Another group of compounds is the ***carbon halides***, including carbon tetrachloride (tetrachloromethane, CCl_4).

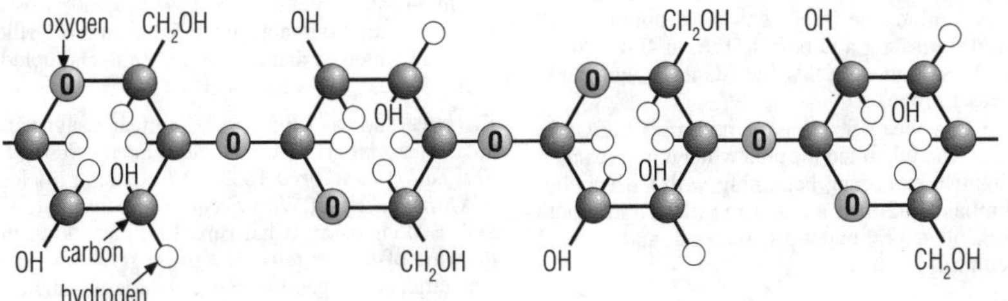

carbohydrate A molecule of the polysaccharide glycogen (animal starch) is formed from linked glucose ($C_6H_{12}O_6$) molecules. A typical glycogen molecule has 100–1,000 glucose units.

When added to steel, carbon forms a wide range of alloys with useful properties. In pure form, it is used as a moderator in nuclear reactors; as colloidal graphite it is a good lubricant and, when deposited on a surface in a vacuum, obviates photoelectric and secondary emission of electrons. Carbon is used as a fuel in the form of coal or coke. The radioactive isotope carbon-14 (half-life 5,730 years) is used as a tracer in biological research. Analysis of interstellar dust has led to the discovery of discrete carbon molecules, each containing 60 carbon atoms. The C_{60} molecules have been named ◊buckminsterfullerenes because of their structural similarity to the geodesic domes designed by US architect and engineer Buckminster Fuller.

carbonate CO_3^{2-} ion formed when carbon dioxide dissolves in water; any salt formed by this ion and another chemical element, usually a metal. Carbon dioxide (CO_2) dissolves sparingly in water (for example, when rain falls through the air) to form carbonic acid (H_2CO_3), which unites with various basic substances to form carbonates. Calcium carbonate ($CaCO_3$) (chalk, limestone, and marble) is one of the most abundant carbonates known, being a constituent of mollusc shells and the hard outer skeletons of crustaceans.

carbon cycle sequence by which ◊carbon circulates and is recycled through the natural world. The carbon element from carbon dioxide, released into the atmosphere by living things as a result of ◊respiration, is taken up by plants during ◊photosynthesis and converted into carbohydrates; the oxygen component is released back into the atmosphere. Some of this carbon becomes locked up in coal and petroleum and other sediments. The simplest link in the carbon cycle occurs when an animal eats a plant and carbon is transferred from, say, a leaf cell to the animal body. The oceans absorb 25–40% of all carbon dioxide released into the atmosphere.

Today, the carbon cycle is in danger of being disrupted by the increased consumption and burning of fossil fuels, and the burning of large tracts of tropical forests, as a result of which levels of carbon dioxide are building up in the atmosphere and probably contributing to the ◊greenhouse effect.

carbon dating alternative name for ◊radiocarbon dating.

carbon dioxide CO_2 colourless, odourless gas, slightly soluble in water and denser than air. It is formed by the complete oxidation of carbon. It is produced by living things during the processes of respiration and the decay of organic matter, and plays a vital role in the carbon cycle. It is used as a coolant in its solid form (known as 'dry ice'), and in the chemical industry. Its increasing density contributes to the ◊greenhouse effect and ◊global warming. Britain has 1% of the world's population, yet it produces 3% of CO_2 emissions; the USA has 5% of the world's population and produces 25% of CO_2 emissions.

Carboniferous period of geological time 363–290 million years ago, the fifth period of the Palaeozoic era. In the USA it is divided into two periods: the Mississippian (lower) and the Pennsylvanian (upper). Typical of the lower-Carboniferous rocks are shallow-water ◊limestones, while upper-Carboniferous rocks have ◊delta deposits with ◊coal (hence the name). Amphibians were abundant, and reptiles evolved during this period.

carbon monoxide CO colourless, odourless gas formed when carbon is oxidized in a limited supply of air. It is a poisonous constituent of car exhaust fumes, forming a stable compound with haemoglobin in the blood, thus preventing the haemoglobin from transporting oxygen to the body tissues.

In industry, carbon monoxide is used as a reducing agent in metallurgical processes – for example, in the extraction of iron in ◊blast furnaces – and is a constituent of cheap fuels such as water gas. It burns in air with a luminous blue flame to form carbon dioxide.

carboxyl group –COOH in organic chemistry, the acidic functional group that determines the properties of fatty acids (carboxylic acids) and amino acids.

carburation mixing of a gas, such as air, with a volatile hydrocarbon fuel, such as petrol, kerosene, or fuel oil, in order to form an explosive mixture. The process, which ensures that the maximum amount of heat energy is released during combustion, is used in internal-combustion engines. In most petrol engines the liquid fuel is atomized and mixed with air by means of a device called a carburettor.

Carcassonne city in SW France, capital of Aude *département*, on the river Aude, which divides it into the ancient and modern town; population (1990) 45,000. Its medieval fortifications (restored) are the finest in France.

Carchemish (now Karkamis, Turkey) centre of the ◊Hittite New Empire (c. 1400–1200 BC) on the river Euphrates, 80 km/50 mi NE of Aleppo, and taken by Sargon II of Assyria 717 BC. Nebuchadnezzar II of Babylon defeated the Egyptians here 605 BC.

carcinogen any agent that increases the chance of a cell becoming cancerous (see ◊cancer), including various chemical compounds, some viruses, X-rays, and other forms of ionizing radiation. The term is often used more narrowly to mean chemical carcinogens only.

carcinoma malignant ◊tumour arising from the skin, the glandular tissues, or the mucous membranes that line the gut and lungs.

Cardiff (Welsh ***Caerdydd***) seaport and capital of Wales (from 1955), at the mouth of the Taff, Rhymney, and Ely rivers; population (1996 est) 306,500. It was the administrative headquarters of South and Mid Glamorgan 1974–96 and the administrative headquarters of Cardiff unitary authority from 1996. Industries include car components, flour milling, ship repairs, electrical goods, paper, and cigars; there are also high-tech industries. The city dates from Roman times, the later town being built around a Norman castle. The castle was the residence of the earls and marquesses of Bute from the 18th century and was given to the city 1947 by the fifth marquess. Coal was exported until the 1920s. As coal declined, iron and steel exports continued to grow, and an import trade in timber, grain and flour, tobacco, meat, and citrus fruit developed.

The docks on the Bristol Channel were opened 1839 and greatly extended by the second marquess of Bute (1793–1848). They have now been redeveloped for industry. In Cathays Park is a group of public buildings including the Law Courts, City Hall, the National Museum of Wales, the Welsh Office (established 1964), and the Temple of Peace and Health. Llandaff, on the right bank of the river Taff, was included in Cardiff 1922; its cathedral, virtually rebuilt in the 19th century and restored 1948–57 after air-raid damage in World War II, has Jacob Epstein's sculpture *Christ in Majesty*. At St Fagan's is the Welsh National Folk Museum, containing small, rebuilt historical buildings from rural Wales in which crafts are demonstrated. The city is the headquarters of the Welsh National Opera.

Cardiff unitary authority of Wales created 1996 (*see United Kingdom map*).

Cardiff Arms Park (Welsh ***Parc yr Arfau***) Welsh rugby ground, officially known as the National Stadium, situated in Cardiff. The stadium became the permanent home of the Welsh national team 1964 and has a capacity of 64,000. It is to be replaced by a new stadium (the Milennium Stadium), which is to host the opening of the 1999 Rugby Union World Cup.

Cardin Pierre 1922– . French pioneering fashion designer. He was particularly influential in the 1960s, creating his 'Space Age Collection' of catsuits, tight leather trousers, jumpsuits with bat wings, and close-fitting helmet-style caps 1964, followed 1966 by shift dresses with ring collars from

The Cité and its population vaguely reminded me of an immense Noah's ark.

On **Carcassonne**
Henry James *A Little Tour in France* 1884

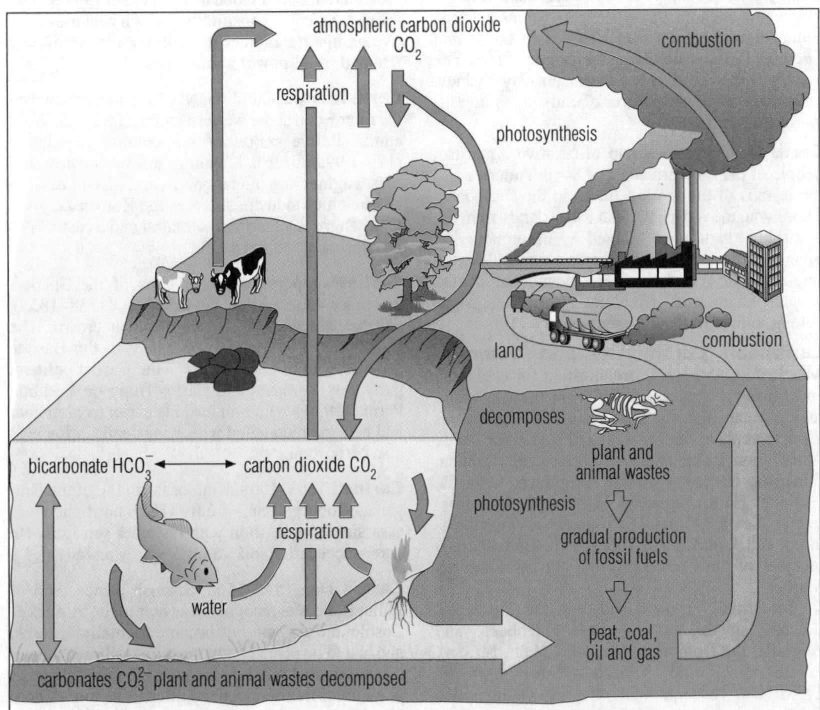

carbon cycle The carbon cycle is necessary for the continuation of life. Since there is only a limited amount of carbon in the Earth and its atmosphere, carbon must be continuously recycled if life is to continue. Other chemicals necessary for life – nitrogen, sulphur, and phosphorus, for example – also circulate in natural cycles.

Cardin French fashion designer Pierre Cardin. He was born in Italy and worked in Vichy as a tailor during World War II, and then in Paris, designing costumes for Jean Cocteau's film *Beauty and the Beast* 1947. First established in 1953 as a designer of women's clothes, he began designing men's wear in 1960 and later became the first designer to provide ready-to-wear clothes for department stores under his own label. *Associated Press/ Topham*

which the fabric was suspended. He was the first to launch menswear (1960) and designer ready-to-wear collections (1963).

cardinal in the Roman Catholic church, the highest rank next to the pope. Cardinals act as an advisory body to the pope and elect him. Their red hat is the badge of office.

cardinal number in mathematics, one of the series of numbers 0, 1, 2, 3, 4, … . Cardinal numbers relate to quantity, whereas ordinal numbers (first, second, third, fourth, … .) relate to order.

care order in Britain, a court order that places a child in the care of a local authority. Surveys show that 75% of those who have been in care leave school with no qualifications. They are less likely to find employment and more likely to go to prison, and one in three was homeless 1993.

Carew Thomas c. 1595–c. 1640. English poet. Often associated with the ◊'Cavalier poets', he was a courtier and gentleman of the privy chamber to Charles I, for whom he wrote the spectacular masque *Coelum Britannicum* 1634. *Poems* 1640 revealed his ability to weave metaphysical wit, eroticism, and a jewelled lyricism in his work.

Carey George Leonard 1935– . 103rd archbishop of Canterbury from 1991. A product of a liberal evangelical background, he was appointed bishop of Bath and Wells 1987. His support of the ◊ordination of women priests brought disagreement during his first meeting with Pope John Paul II 1992.

Carey Peter Philip 1943– . Australian novelist. His works include *Bliss* 1981, *Illywhacker* (Australian slang for 'con man') 1985, and *Oscar and Lucinda* 1988, which won the Booker Prize. *The Tax Inspector* 1991 is set in modern-day Sydney, and depicts an eccentric Greek family under investigation for tax fraud.

Carib member of a group of ◊Native American people of the northern coast of South America and the islands of the S West Indies in the Caribbean. Those who moved north to take the islands from the Arawak Indians were alleged by the conquering Spaniards to be fierce cannibals. In 1796, the English in the West Indies deported most of them to Roatan Island, off Honduras. Carib languages belong to the Ge-Pano-Carib family.

Caribbean Community and Common Market (CARICOM) organization for economic and foreign policy coordination in the Caribbean region, established by the Treaty of Chaguaramas 1973 to replace the former Caribbean Free Trade Association. Its members are Antigua and Barbuda, Bahamas, Barbados, Belize, Dominica, Grenada, Guyana, Haiti, Jamaica, Montserrat, St Christopher–Nevis, St Lucia, St Vincent and the Grenadines, and Trinidad and Tobago. The Bahamas is a member of the Community but not the Common Market.

The British Virgin Islands and the Turks and Caicos Islands are associate members, and Anguilla, the Dominican Republic, Haiti, Mexico, Puerto Rico, and Venezuela are observers. CARICOM headquarters are in Georgetown, Guyana.

'Man is a tool-using animal … Without tools he is nothing, with tools he is all.'

THOMAS CARLYLE
Sartor Resartus

Caribbean Sea western part of the Atlantic Ocean between the southern coast of North America and the northern coasts of South America. Central America is to the W and the West Indies are the islands within the sea, which is about 2,740 km/1,700 mi long and 650–1,500 km/400–900 mi wide. It is from here that the ◊Gulf Stream turns towards Europe.

The Caribbean Sea was named after the Carib Indians who inhabited the area when it was reached by Spanish explorers, beginning with Christopher Columbus 1492. It is a major maritime trade route for oil, other raw materials, seafood, and tropical agricultural products.

caribou the ◊reindeer of North America.

caricature in the arts or literature, an exaggerated portrayal of an individual or type, aiming to ridicule or otherwise expose the subject. Classical and medieval examples of pictorial caricatures survive. Artists of the 18th, 19th, and 20th centuries have often used caricature as a way of satirizing society and politics. Notable exponents include the French artist Honoré Daumier and the German George Grosz. In literature, caricatures have appeared since the comedies of Aristophanes in ancient Greece. Shakespeare and Dickens were adept at creating caricatures.

British caricaturists include James Gillray, William Hogarth, Thomas Rowlandson, George Cruikshank, Edward Lear, Richard Doyle, George Du Maurier, Max Beerbohm, David Low, 'Vicky' (Victor Weisz, 1913–1966), 'Giles' (Carl Ronald Giles), Ronald Searle, Osbert Lancaster, Mel Calman (1931–), Gerald Scarfe (1936–), Ralph Steadman (1936–), and Peter Fluck and Roger Law (who created the three-dimensional puppets for their satirical television series *Spitting Image*).

CARICOM acronym for ◊***Caribbean Community and Common Market***.

Carina constellation of the southern hemisphere, represented as a ship's keel. Its brightest star is ◊Canopus, the second brightest in the night sky; it also contains Eta Carinae, a massive and highly luminous star embedded in a gas cloud, perhaps 8,000 light years away. Carina is situated in one of the brightest parts of the ◊Milky Way.

Carinthia (German ***Kärnten***) federal province of Alpine SE Austria, bordering Italy and Slovenia in the S; area 9,500 sq km/3,667 sq mi; population (1994) 559,700. The capital is Klagenfurt. It was an independent duchy from 976 and a possession of the Habsburg dynasty 1276–1918.

Carl XVI Gustaf 1946– . King of Sweden from 1973. He succeeded his grandfather Gustaf VI, his father having been killed in an air crash 1947. Under the new Swedish constitution, which became effective on his grandfather's death, the monarchy was stripped of all power at his accession.

Carlisle city in Cumbria, NW England, situated on the river Eden at the western end of Hadrian's Wall, administrative centre of the county; population (1991) 99,800. It is a leading railway centre; textiles, engineering, metal goods, and biscuit making are the chief industries. It was the Roman *Luguvalium*. There is a Norman cathedral and a castle. The bishopric dates from 1133.

Carlist supporter of the claims of the Spanish pretender Don Carlos de Bourbon (1788–1855), and his descendants, to the Spanish crown. The Carlist revolt continued, primarily in the Basque provinces, until 1839. In 1977 the Carlist political party was legalized and Carlos Hugo de Bourbon Parma (1930–) renounced his claim as pretender and became reconciled with King Juan Carlos. See also ◊Bourbon.

Carlos I 1863–1908. King of Portugal, of the Braganza–Coburg line, from 1889 until he was assassinated in Lisbon with his elder son Luis. He was succeeded by his younger son Manuel.

Carlos Don 1545–1568. Spanish prince. Son of Philip II, he was recognized as heir to the thrones of Castile and Aragon but became mentally unstable and had to be placed under restraint following a plot to assassinate his father. His story was the subject of plays by Friedrich von Schiller, Vittorio Alfieri, Thomas Otway, and others.

Carlos four kings of Spain; see Charles.

Carlow county of the Republic of Ireland, in the province of Leinster; county town Carlow; area 900 sq km/347 sq mi; population (1991) 40,900. Mostly flat except for mountains in the S, the land is fertile, and well suited to dairy farming. Products include barley, wheat, and sugar beet.

Carlyle Thomas 1795–1881. Scottish essayist and social historian. His works include *Sartor Resartus/ The Tailor Retailored* 1833–34, reflecting his loss of Christian belief; *The French Revolution* 1837; and the long essay 'Chartism' 1839, attacking the doctrine of *laissez faire*. His prose style was idiosyncratic, encompassing grand, thunderous rhetoric and deliberate obscurity.

Carmarthenshire unitary authority of Wales created 1996 (*see United Kingdom map*).

Carmelite order mendicant order of friars in the Roman Catholic church. The order was founded on Mount Carmel in Palestine by Berthold, a crusader from Calabria, about 1155, and spread to Europe in the 13th century. The Carmelites have devoted themselves largely to missionary work and mystical theology. They are known as White Friars because of the white overmantle they wear (over a brown habit).

Carmichael Hoagy (Hoagland Howard) 1899–1981. US composer, pianist, singer, and actor. His songs include 'Stardust' 1927, 'Rockin' Chair' 1930, 'Lazy River' 1931, and 'In the Cool, Cool, Cool of the Evening' 1951 (Academy Award).

Carmina Burana medieval Latin verse miscellany compiled from the work of wandering 13th-century scholars and including secular (love songs and drinking songs) as well as religious verse. Carl Orff composed a cantata based on the material 1937.

Carnac Megalithic site in Brittany, France, where remains of tombs and stone alignments of the period 2000–1500 BC have been found. The largest of the latter has 1,000 stones up to 4 m/13 ft high arranged in 11 rows, with a circle at the western end. It is named after the village of Carnac; population about 4,000.

Carnarvon alternative spelling of ◊Caernarvon, a town in Wales.

Carné Marcel 1909–1996. French director. He is known for the romantic fatalism of such films as *Drôle de drame* 1936, *Hôtel du Nord* 1938, *Le Quai des brumes/Port of Shadows* 1938, and *Le Jour se lève/Daybreak* 1939. His masterpiece, *Les Enfants du paradis/The Children of Paradise* 1943–45, was made with his longtime collaborator, poet and screenwriter Jacques Prévert (1900–1977).

Carlyle Scottish essayist and historian Thomas Carlyle, who was acclaimed as one of the most brilliant and unconventional historians of his day. He became a fierce critic of Victorian values, arguing passionately for a moral, political, and intellectual renewal of society. *Corbis*

Carnegie Andrew 1835–1919. US industrialist and philanthropist, born in Scotland. He developed the Pittsburgh iron and steel industries, making the USA the world's leading producer. He endowed public libraries, education, and various research trusts. After his death the Carnegie trusts continued his philanthropic activities. Carnegie Hall in New York, opened 1891 as the Music Hall, was renamed 1898 because of his large contribution to its construction.

carnivore in zoology, mammal of the order Carnivora. Although its name describes the flesh-eating ancestry of the order, it includes pandas, which are herbivorous, and civet cats, which eat fruit. The characteristics of the Carnivora are sharp teeth, small incisors, a well-developed brain, a simple stomach, a reduced or absent caecum, and incomplete or absent clavicles (collarbones); there are never less than four toes on each foot; the scaphoid and lunar bones are fused in the hand; and the claws are generally sharp and powerful. The order includes cats, dogs, bears, badgers, and weasels.

Carnot (Nicolas Leonard) Sadi 1796–1832. French scientist and military engineer who founded the science of thermodynamics. His pioneering work was *Reflexions sur la puissance motrice du feu/On the Motive Power of Fire*, which considered the changes that would take place in an idealized, frictionless steam engine. Carnot's theorem showed that the amount of work that an engine can produce depends only on the temperature difference that occurs in the engine. He described the maximum amount of heat convertible into work by the formula $(T_1 - T_2)/T_2$, where T_1 is the temperature of the hottest part of the machine and T_2 is the coldest part.

Carnot Lazare Nicolas Marguerite 1753–1823. French general and politician. A member of the National Convention in the French Revolution, he organized the armies of the republic. He was war minister 1800–01 and minister of the interior 1815 under Napoleon. His work on fortification, *De la Défense de places fortes* 1810, became a military textbook. Minister of the interior during the ◊hundred days, he was proscribed at the restoration of the monarchy and retired to Germany.

Carnot cycle series of changes in the physical condition of a gas in a reversible heat engine, necessarily in the following order: (1) isothermal expansion (without change of temperature), (2) adiabatic expansion (without change of heat content), (3) isothermal compression, and (4) adiabatic compression. The principles derived from a study of this cycle are important in the fundamentals of heat and ◊thermodynamics.

Caro Anthony (Alfred) 1924– . English sculptor. His most typical work is brightly coloured abstract sculpture made from prefabricated metal parts, such as I-beams, angles, and mesh. An example is *Early One Morning* 1962 (Tate Gallery, London). He later experimented with unpainted works cast in bronze.

carob small Mediterranean tree *Ceratonia siliqua* of the legume family Leguminosae. Its pods, 20 cm/8 in long, are used as animal fodder; they are also the source of a chocolate substitute.

carol song that in medieval times was associated with a round dance; today carols are associated with festivals such as Christmas and Easter. Christmas carols were common as early as the 15th century. The custom of singing carols from house to house, collecting gifts, was called wassailing. Many carols, such as 'God Rest You Merry Gentlemen' and 'The First Noel', date from the 16th century or earlier.

Carol I 1839–1914. First king of Romania 1881–1914. A prince of the house of Hohenzollern-Sigmaringen, he was invited to become prince of Romania, then part of the Ottoman Empire, 1866. In 1877, in alliance with Russia, he declared war on Turkey, and the Congress of Berlin 1878 recognized Romanian independence. He promoted economic development and industrial reforms but failed to address rural problems. This led to a peasant rebellion 1907 which he brutally crushed. At the beginning of World War I, King Carol declared Romania's neutrality but his successor (his nephew King Ferdinand I) declared for the Allies.

Carol II 1893–1953. King of Romania 1930–40. Son of King Ferdinand, he married Princess Helen of Greece and they had a son, Michael. In 1925 he renounced the succession because of his affair with Elena Lupescu and went into exile in Paris. Michael succeeded to the throne 1927, but in 1930 Carol returned to Romania and was proclaimed king. In 1938 he introduced a new constitution under which he practically became an absolute ruler. He was forced to abdicate by the pro-Nazi ◊Iron Guard Sept 1940, went to Mexico, and married his mistress 1947.

Carnac The megalith site of Carnac in Brittany, NW France. It contains a spectacular and unique set of menhirs, or standing stones, consisting of 1,000 stones aligned in 11 rows with a circle at the western end. Dating from the Neolithic or Bronze Age, the alignment of stones was probably of astronomical and religious significance. *Corbis*

Carolina either of two separate states of the USA; see ◊North Carolina and ◊South Carolina.

Caroline of Anspach 1683–1737. Queen of George II of Great Britain and Ireland. The daughter of the Margrave of Brandenburg-Anspach, she married George, Electoral Prince of Hanover, 1705, and followed him to England 1714 when his father became King George I. She was the patron of many leading writers and politicians such as Alexander Pope, John Gay, and the Earl of Chesterfield. She supported Sir Robert Walpole and kept him in power and acted as regent during her husband's four absences.

Caroline of Brunswick 1768–1821. Queen of George IV of Great Britain, who unsuccessfully attempted to divorce her on his accession to the throne 1820. Second daughter of Karl Wilhelm, Duke of Brunswick, and Augusta, sister of George III, she married her first cousin, the Prince of Wales, 1795, but after the birth of Princess ◊Charlotte Augusta a separation was arranged. When her husband ascended the throne 1820 she was offered an annuity of £50,000 provided she agreed to renounce the title of queen and to continue to live abroad. She returned forthwith to London, where she assumed royal state. In July 1820 the government brought in a bill to dissolve the marriage, but Lord Brougham (1778–1868)'s brilliant defence led to the bill's abandonment. On 19 July 1821 Caroline was prevented by royal order from entering Westminster Abbey for the coronation. Her funeral was the occasion of popular riots.

Carolines scattered archipelago in Micronesia, Pacific Ocean, consisting of over 500 coral islets; area 1,200 sq km/463 sq mi. The chief islands are Ponape, Kusai, and Truk in the eastern group, and Yap and Palau in the western group. Occupied by Germany 1899, and Japan 1914, and mandated by the League of Nations to Japan 1919, they were fortified, contrary to the terms of the mandate. They remained in Japanese hands throughout World War II despite heavy Allied air attacks and then became part of the US Trust Territory of the Pacific Islands 1947–90. ▷ *See feature on pp. 806–807.*

Carolingian art the art of the reign of Charlemagne, the first Holy Roman Emperor (800–814), and his descendants until about 900. In line with his revival of learning and Roman culture, Charlemagne greatly encouraged the arts, which had been in eclipse. Illuminated manuscripts, metalwork, and small-scale sculpture survive from this period. See also ◊medieval art.

Carolingian dynasty Frankish dynasty descending from ◊Pepin the Short (died 768) and named after his son Charlemagne; its last ruler was Louis V of France (reigned 966–87), who was followed by Hugh ◊Capet, first ruler of the Capetian dynasty.

carotene naturally occurring pigment of the ◊carotenoid group. Carotenes produce the orange, yellow, and red colours of carrots, tomatoes, oranges, and crustaceans.

carotenoid any of a group of yellow, orange, red, or brown pigments found in many living organisms, particularly in the ◊chloroplasts of plants. There are two main types, the ***carotenes*** and the ***xanthophylls***. Some carotenoids act as accessory pigments in ◊photosynthesis, and in certain algae they are the principal light-absorbing pigments functioning more efficiently than ◊chlorophyll in low-intensity light. Carotenoids can also occur in organs such as petals, roots, and fruits, giving them their characteristic colour. They are also responsible for the autumn colours of leaves, persisting longer than the green chlorophyll, which masks them during the summer.

carp fish *Cyprinus carpio* found all over the world. It commonly grows to 50 cm/1.8 ft and 3 kg/7 lb, but may be even larger. It lives in lakes, ponds, and slow rivers. The wild form is drab, but cultivated forms may be golden, or may have few large scales (mirror carp) or be scaleless (leather carp). Koi carp are highly prized and can grow up to 1 m/3 ft long with a distinctive pink, red, white, or black colouring. A large proportion of European freshwater fish belong to the carp family, Cyprinidae, and related fishes are found in Asia, Africa, and North America.

Carpaccio Vittore 1450/60–1525/26. Italian painter. He is famous for scenes of his native Venice, for example, the series *The Legend of St Ursula* 1490–98 (Accademia, Venice). His paintings are a graceful blend of fantasy and closely observed details from everyday life. Other works include *The Miracle of the Cross at Rialto* (Accademia) and the so-called *Courtesans* (Correr Museum, Venice). *See illustration on following page.*

Carpathian Mountains central European mountain system, forming a semicircle through Slovakia–Poland–Ukraine–Moldova–Romania, 1,450 km/900 mi long. The central Tatra Mountains on the Slovak–Polish frontier include the highest peak, Gerlachovka, 2,663 m/8,737 ft.

carpe diem (Latin 'seize the day') live for the present.

carpel female reproductive unit in flowering plants (◊angiosperms). It usually comprises an ◊ovary containing one or more ovules, the stalk or style, and a ◊stigma at its top which receives the

Carpaccio The Annunciation by Vittore Carpaccio. A pupil of Bellini, Carpaccio became one of the leading painters of late 15th and early 16th-century Venice, his works noted for their charm and elegance. *Corbis*

pollen. A flower may have one or more carpels, and they may be separate or fused together. Collectively the carpels of a flower are known as the ◊gynoecium.

Carpenter John Howard 1948– . US director of horror and science-fiction films. He is notable for such films as *Dark Star* 1974 and *Assault on Precinct 13* 1976. His subsequent films include the low-budget thriller *Halloween* 1978, *The Fog* 1979, *The Thing* 1982, *Christine* 1983 (adapted from a Stephen King story about a vindictive car), *Starman* 1984, *They Live* 1988, and *Memoirs of an Invisible Man* 1992. He composes his own film scores, which have often added to the atmosphere of menace that often haunts his movies.

The rule is, jam to-morrow and jam yesterday – but never jam to-day.

LEWIS CARROLL
Alice Through the Looking-Glass

carpet thick textile fabric, generally made of wool, used for covering floors and stairs. There is a long tradition of fine handmade carpets in the Middle East, India, Pakistan, and China. Western carpets are machine-made. Carpets and rugs have also often been made in the home as a pastime, cross and tent stitch on canvas being widely used in the 18th and 19th centuries.

history The earliest known carpets date from c. 500 BC and were excavated at Passypych in SE Siberia, but it was not until the later Middle Ages that carpets reached W Europe from Turkey. Persian carpets (see ◊Islamic art), which reached a still unrivalled peak of artistry in the 15th and 16th centuries, were rare in Britain until the mid-19th century, reaching North America a little later. The subsequent demand led to a revival of organized carpetmaking in Persia. Europe copied oriental technique, but developed Western designs: France produced beautiful work at the Savonnerie and Beauvais establishments under Louis XIV and Louis XV; and Exeter, Axminster, London, and Wilton became British carpetmaking centres in the 18th century, though Kidderminster is the biggest centre today.

carpet An ornate carpet with animal figures and a floral motif from Kairouan, Morocco. Far more than floor coverings, genuine handmade carpets can be beautiful and valuable works of art in their own right. *Corbis*

carpetbagger in US history, derogatory name for any of the entrepreneurs and politicians from the North who moved to the Southern states during ◊Reconstruction 1861–65 after the Civil War, to exploit the chaotic conditions for their own benefit. They were so called because they were supposed to carry their ill-gotten gains in small satchels made of carpeting.

Carracci three Italian painters, ***Lodovico Carracci*** (1555–1619) and his two cousins, the brothers ***Agostino Carracci*** (1557–1602) and ***Annibale Carracci*** (1560–1609), who founded an influential school of painting in Bologna in the late 16th century, based on close study of the Renaissance masters and also life drawing. The three played a leading role in the development of the early Baroque.

Lodovico Carracci was the founder of the school of painting, but finding that he could not carry out his plan without help, he persuaded Agostino and Annibale to join him in running the school in Bologna, opened 1585. From 1600 he carried it on alone. An artist of scholarly inclination, he made an extensive study of Renaissance masters, especially of Antonio Correggio and Titian. *Susannah and the Elders* (National Gallery, London) is an important example of Lodovico's work.

Agostino took a leading place in the Bologna academy and in directing its teaching, which was designed to counteract Mannerism. He worked with his brother Annibale on the decorations for the Farnese Palace in Rome 1595–97, moving to Parma in 1600. His masterpiece is his *Communion of St Jerome* (Bologna).

Annibale was the most original artist of the three. He studied Correggio's work and was particularly good at drawing (a skill stressed by all the Carraccis). His principal work was the decoration of the Farnese Palace, commissioned by Cardinal Odoardo Farnese (1612–1646). Based on the theme of the loves of the gods, this set of paintings, exuberant in movement and with a light-hearted approach to its mythological subject, was one of the first major works of the early Baroque. Here Agostino joined him and assisted in the work till the two brothers quarrelled.

carragheen species of deep-reddish, branched seaweed *Chondrus crispus*. Named after Carragheen in Ireland, it is found on rocky shores on both sides of the Atlantic. It is exploited commercially in food and medicinal preparations and as cattle feed.

Carrel Alexis 1873–1944. US surgeon born in France, whose experiments paved the way for organ transplantation. Working at the Rockefeller Institute, New York City, he devised a way of joining blood vessels end to end (anastomosing). This was a key move in the development of transplant surgery, as was his work on keeping organs viable outside the body, for which he was awarded the Nobel Prize for Physiology or Medicine 1912.

Carreras José Maria 1947– . Spanish operatic tenor. His comprehensive repertoire includes Handel's Samson and his recordings include *West Side Story* 1984 under Leonard Bernstein. His vocal presence, charmingly insinuating rather than forceful, is favoured for Italian and French romantic roles. In 1987 he became seriously ill with leukaemia, but resumed his career 1988. Together with Placido Domingo and Luciano Pavarotti, he achieved worldwide fame in a recording of operatic hits released to coincide with the World Cup soccer series in Rome 1990.

carriage driving sport in which two- or four-wheeled carriages are pulled by two or four horses. Events include ◊dressage, obstacle driving, and the marathon. The Duke of Edinburgh is one of the sport's leading exponents.

Carrickfergus seaport on Belfast Lough, County Antrim, Northern Ireland; population (1991) 22,800. There is some light industry. The remains of the castle, built 1180, house two museums.

Carroll Lewis. Pen name of Charles Lutwidge Dodgson 1832–1898. English author of the children's classics *Alice's Adventures in Wonderland* 1865 and its sequel *Through the Looking-Glass* 1872. Among later works was the mock-heroic narrative poem *The Hunting of the Snark* 1876. He was fascinated by the limits and paradoxes of language and thought, the exploration of which leads to the apparent nonsense of Alice's adventures. He was a mathematics lecturer at Oxford 1855–81, where he first told the fantasy stories to Alice Liddell and her sisters, daughters of the dean of Christ Church. Dodgson was a prolific letter writer and one of the pioneers of portrait photography. He was also responsible, in his publication of mathematical games and problems requiring the use of logic, for a general upsurge of interest in such pastimes. He is said to be, after Shakespeare, the most quoted writer in the English language.

carrying capacity in ecology, the maximum number of animals of a given species that a particular area can support. When the carrying capacity is exceeded, there is insufficient food (or other resources) for the members of the population. The population may then be reduced by emigration, reproductive failure, or death through starvation.

Carson Rachel Louise 1907–1964. US biologist, writer, and conservationist. Her book *Silent Spring* 1962, attacking the indiscriminate use of pesticides, inspired the creation of the modern environmental movement.

Carson Willie (William Fisher Hunter) 1942– . Scottish jockey who has ridden four Epsom Derby winners as well as the winners of most major races worldwide. The top flat-race jockey on five occasions, he has ridden over 3,000 winners in Britain. For many years he rode for the royal trainer, Major Dick Hern. Since 1962 to the start of the 1994 season he has ridden 16 classic winners and 3,541 winners.

Carson City capital of Nevada, USA; population (1992) 42,800. Settled as a trading post 1851, it was named after the frontier guide Kit Carson 1858. It flourished as a boom town after the discovery of the nearby Comstock silver-ore lode 1859.

Cartagena or ***Cartagena de los Indes*** port, industrial centre, and capital of the department of Bolívar, NW Colombia; population (1994) 726,000. Plastics and chemicals are produced here. It was founded 1533 and taken by the English buccaneer Francis Drake 1586.

carte blanche (French 'white paper') no instructions, complete freedom to do as one wishes.

cartel (German *Kartell* 'a group') agreement among national or international firms to fix prices for their products. A cartel may restrict supply (output) to raise prices in order to increase member profits. It therefore represents a form of ◊oligopoly. ◊OPEC, for example, is an oil cartel. National laws concerning cartels differ widely, and international agreement is difficult to achieve. Both the Treaty of Rome and the Stockholm Convention, governing respectively the European Union (EU) and the European Free Trade Association (EFTA), contain provisions for control. In Germany, cartels are the most common form of monopolistic organization. In the USA, cartels are generally illegal.

Carter Angela 1940–1992. English writer of the ◊magic realist school. Her works are marked by elements of Gothic fantasy, a fascination with the erotic and the violent, tempered by a complex lyricism and a comic touch. Her novels include *The Magic Toyshop* 1967 (filmed 1987) and *Nights at the Circus* 1984. She co-wrote the script for the film *The Company of Wolves* 1984, based on one of her stories. Her last novel was *Wise Children* 1991.

Carter Elliott Cook 1908– . US composer. He created intricately structured works in Schoenbergian serial idiom, incorporating 'metrical modulation', an adaptation of standard notation allowing different instruments or groups to remain synchronized while playing at changing speeds. This practice was first employed in his *String Quartet No 1* 1950–51, and to dense effect in *Double Concerto* 1961 for harpsichord and piano. In his eighth decade, his music has shown a new tautness and vitality, as in *Three Occasions for Orchestra* 1986–89.

Carter Jimmy, (James Earl) 1924– . 39th president of the USA 1977–81, a Democrat. In 1976 he narrowly wrested the presidency from Gerald Ford. Features of his presidency were the return of the Panama Canal Zone to Panama, the introduction of an amnesty programme for deserters and draft dodgers of the Vietnam War, the Camp David Agreements for peace in the Middle East, and the Iranian seizure of US embassy hostages. He was defeated by Ronald Reagan 1980. During the 1990s he emerged as a leading mediator and peace negotiator, securing President Aristide's safe return to Haiti Oct 1994.

Carter Family US country- and folk-music group, active from the 1920s to 1943. Their material of old ballads and religious songs, and the guitar-picking technique of Maybelle Carter (1909–1978), influenced the development of country music, especially bluegrass. Songs they made popular include 'Keep on the Sunny Side', 'Wildwood Flower', and 'Will the Circle Be Unbroken'.

Cartesian coordinates in ◊coordinate geometry, components used to define the position of a point by its perpendicular distance from a set of two or more axes, or reference lines. For a two-dimensional area defined by two axes at right angles (a horizontal x-axis and a vertical y-axis), the coordinates of a point are given by its perpendicular distances from the y-axis and x-axis, written in the form (x,y). For example, a point P that lies three units from the y-axis and four units from the x-axis has Cartesian coordinates (3,4) (see ◊abscissa and ◊ordinate). In three-dimensional coordinate geometry, points are located with reference to a third, z-axis, mutually at right angles to the x and y axes.

The Cartesian coordinate system can be extended to any finite number of dimensions (axes), and is used thus in theoretical mathematics. It is named after the French mathematician, René Descartes. The system is useful in creating technical drawings of machines or buildings, and in computer-aided design (◊CAD).

Carthage ancient Phoenician port in N Africa founded by colonists from Tyre in the late 9th century BC; it lay 16 km/10 mi N of Tunis, Tunisia. A leading trading centre, it was in conflict with Greece from the 6th century BC, and then with Rome, and was destroyed by Roman forces 146 BC at the end of the ◊Punic Wars. About 45 BC, Roman colonists settled in Carthage, and it became the wealthy capital of the province of Africa. After its capture by the Vandals AD 439 it was little more than a pirate stronghold. From 533 it formed part of the Byzantine Empire until its final destruction by Arabs 698, during their conquest in the name of Islam.

Carthusian order Roman Catholic order of monks and, later, nuns, founded by St Bruno 1084 at Chartreuse, near Grenoble, France. Living chiefly in unbroken silence, they ate one vegetarian meal a day and supported themselves by their own labours; the rule is still one of severe austerity. The order was introduced into England about 1178, when the first Charterhouse was founded at Witham in Essex. They were suppressed at the Reformation, but there is a Charterhouse at Parkminster, Sussex, established 1833.

Cartier Jacques 1491–1557. French navigator who, while seeking a north-west passage to China, was the first European to sail up the St Lawrence River 1534. He named the site of Montréal.

Cartier-Bresson Henri 1908– . French photographer. He is considered one of the greatest photographic artists. His documentary work was shot in black and white, using a small-format Leica camera. His work is remarkable for its tightly structured composition and his ability to capture the decisive moment. He was a founder member of the Magnum photographic agency.

cartilage flexible bluish-white ◊connective tissue made up of the protein collagen. In cartilaginous fish it forms the skeleton; in other vertebrates it forms the greater part of the embryonic skeleton, and is replaced by ◊bone in the course of development, except in areas of wear such as bone endings (joints), and the discs between the backbones. It also forms structural tissue in the larynx, nose, and external ear of mammals. Cartilage does not heal itself, so where injury is severe the joint may need to be replaced surgically.

cartography art and practice of drawing ◊maps.

cartoon humorous or satirical drawing or ◊caricature; a strip cartoon or ◊comic strip; traditionally, the base design for a large fresco, mosaic, or tapestry, transferred to wall or canvas by tracing or pricking out the design on the cartoon and then dabbing with powdered charcoal to create a faint reproduction. Surviving examples include Leonardo da Vinci's *Virgin and St Anne* (National Gallery, London).

Cartwright Edmund 1743–1823. British inventor. He patented the power loom 1785, built a weaving mill 1787, and patented a wool-combing machine 1789.

Caruso Enrico 1873–1921. Italian operatic tenor. His voice was dark, with full-bodied tone and remarkable dynamic range. In 1902 he starred, with Australian soprano Nellie ◊Melba, in Puccini's *La Bohème/Bohemian Life*. He was among the first opera singers to achieve lasting fame through gramophone recordings. *See illustration on following page.*

Carter Former US president Jimmy Carter (centre), with Egypt's Anwar Sadat (left) and Israel's Menachem Begin, at the signing of the Camp David Agreements 1978, an early attempt to bring peace to the Middle East. Carter's record of well-meaning concern for human rights and the establishment of peace in the Middle East counted for little against the more charismatic and impulsive Ronald Reagan, who defeated him in the 1980 election. Such initiatives by Sadat isolated him from the rest of the Arab world, and in 1981 he was assassinated by Arab fundamentalists. *Topham*

carpetbagger Term of contempt for political or commercial interlopers. It originated in the Southern USA after the American Civil War and was applied to adventurers from the North. The term arose because the only property qualifications they required was their luggage, usually carried in a bag made out of carpet material. *Corbis*

Carver George Washington 1860–1943. US agricultural chemist. He devoted his life to improving the economy of the US South and the condition of blacks. He advocated the diversification of crops, promoted peanut production, and was a pioneer in the field of plastics.

Carver Raymond 1938–1988. US short-story writer and poet. His writing deals mainly with blue-collar middle America, depicting failed, empty lives in a spare prose. His major works include *Will You Please Be Quiet, Please* 1976, *What We Talk About When We Talk About Love* 1981, *Cathedral* 1983, and *In a Marine Light* 1988, a collection of poetry.

caryatid building support or pillar in the shape of a female figure, the name deriving from the Karyatides, who were priestesses at the temple of Artemis at Karyai; the male equivalent is a telamon or atlas. *See illustration on following page.*

Casablanca (Arabic ***Dar el-Beida***) port, commercial and industrial centre on the Atlantic coast of Morocco; population (1990, urban area) 3,079,000. It trades in fish, phosphates, and manganese. The Great Hassan II Mosque, completed 1989, is the world's largest; it is built on a platform (40,000 sq m/430,000 sq ft) jutting out over the Atlantic, with walls 60 m/200 ft high, topped by a hydraulic sliding roof, and a minaret 175 m/574 ft high. Casablanca was occupied by the French from 1907 until Morocco became independent 1956.

Casals Pablo (Pau) 1876–1973. Catalan cellist, composer, and conductor. He was largely self-taught. As a cellist, he was celebrated for his interpretations of J S Bach's unaccompanied suites. He wrote instrumental and choral works, including the Christmas oratorio *The Manger*. He was an outspoken critic of fascism who openly defied Franco, and a tireless crusader for peace.

Casals's pioneer recordings of Schubert and Beethoven trios 1905, with French violinist Jacques Thibaud and French pianist Alfred Cortot, launched his international career and established the popularity of the cello as a solo instrument, notably the solo suites of J S Bach recorded 1916. In 1919 he founded the Casals Orchestra in Barcelona, which he conducted until leaving Spain 1939 to live in Prades in the French Pyrenees, where he founded an annual music festival. In 1956 he moved to Puerto Rico, where he launched the Casals Festival 1957.

Casanova de Seingalt Giovanni Giacomo 1725–1798. Italian adventurer, spy, violinist, librarian, and, according to his *Memoires* (published 1826–38, although the complete text did not appear until 1960–61), one of the world's great lovers. From 1774 he was a spy in the Venetian police service. In 1782 a libel got him into trouble, and after more wanderings he was in 1785

'We should live our lives as though Christ were coming this afternoon.'

JIMMY CARTER
Speech to Bible class in Plains, Georgia, March 1976

'Carthage had not desired to create, but only to enjoy: therefore she left us nothing.'

On CARTHAGE
Hilaire Belloc
Esto Perpetua

Caruso The Italian tenor Enrico Caruso in one of his most famous roles, Canio in Leoncavallo's opera *Pagliacci/Clowns.* Immensely popular because of the warmth of his personality as well as the extraordinary beauty of his voice, Caruso was one of the first great stars of the gramophone. He made his first record in 1902. *Corbis*

appointed librarian to Count Waldstein at his castle of Dûx in Bohemia. It was here that Casanova wrote his *Memoires.*

'The British love permanence more than they love beauty.'

HUGH CASSON Quoted in the *Observer* 1964

case in grammar, the different forms (inflections) taken by nouns, pronouns, and adjectives depending on their function in a sentence. English is a language with four inflections; most words have no more than two forms. For example, six pronouns have one form when they are the subject of the verb, and a different form when they are either objects of the verb or governed by a preposition. The six are: *I/me, he/him, she/her, we/us, they/them, who/whom.* In 'I like cats', *I* is the subject of the sentence. In 'Cats hate me', *me* is the object. Latin has 6 cases, and Hungarian more than 25.

casein main protein of milk, from which it can be separated by the action of acid, the enzyme rennin, or bacteria (souring); it is also the main protein in cheese. Casein is used as a protein supplement in the treatment of malnutrition. It is used commercially in cosmetics, glues, and as a sizing for coating paper.

Casement Roger David 1864–1916. Irish nationalist. While in the British consular service, he exposed the ruthless exploitation of the people of the Belgian Congo and Peru, for which he was knighted 1911 (degraded 1916). In 1914 he went to Germany and attempted to induce Irish prisoners of war to form an Irish brigade to take part in a republican insurrection. He returned to Ireland in a submarine 1916 (actually to postpone, not start, the Easter Rising), was arrested, tried for treason, and hanged.

Cash Johnny 1932– . US country singer, songwriter, and guitarist. His work is distinguished by his gruff delivery and storytelling ability. His early hits, recorded for Sun Records in Memphis, Tennessee, include the million-selling 'I Walk the Line' 1956. Many of his songs have become classics. Cash is widely respected beyond the country-music field for his concern for the underprivileged, expressed on such albums as *Bitter Tears* 1964 about American Indians and *Live At Folsom Prison* 1968. He is known as the 'Man in Black' because of his penchant for dressing entirely in black.

caryatid The caryatid porch of the Erectheum, Athens, 421–406 BC. A caryatid is a carved female figure serving as a column, a device that was first used in Greek architecture. The caryatids on the Erectheum have suffered badly from pollution and have now been replaced with copies. One of the originals was removed by Lord Elgin in the early 19th century, and is now in the British Museum. It is in much better condition than the ones that remained on the building. *Corbis*

cash crop crop grown solely for sale rather than for the farmer's own use, for example, coffee, cotton, or sugar beet. Many Third World countries grow cash crops to meet their debt repayments rather than grow food for their own people. The price for these crops depends on financial interests, such as those of the multinational companies and the International Monetary Fund. In Britain, the most widespread cash crop is the potato.

cash flow input of cash required to cover all expenses of a business, whether revenue or capital. Alternatively, the actual or prospective balance between the various outgoing and incoming movements which are designated in total. Cash flow is positive if receipts are greater than payments; negative if payments are greater than receipts.

Caslavska Vera 1942– . Czechoslovak gymnast, the first of the great present-day stylists. She won a record 21 world, Olympic, and European gold medals 1959–68; she also won eight silver and three bronze medals.

Caspian Sea world's largest inland sea, divided between Iran, Azerbaijan, Russia, Kazakhstan, and Turkmenistan; area about 400,000 sq km/155,000 sq mi, with a maximum depth of 1,000 m/3,250 ft. The chief ports are Astrakhan and Baku. Drainage in the N and damming of the Volga and Ural rivers for hydroelectric power left the sea approximately 28 m/90 ft below sea level. In 1991 opening of sluices in the dams caused the water level to rise dramatically, threatening towns and industrial areas.

Cassandra in Greek mythology, the daughter of ◊Priam, king of Troy. Her prophecies (for example, of the fall of Troy) were never believed, because she had rejected the love of the god Apollo. She was murdered with ◊Agamemnon by his wife Clytemnestra, having been awarded as a prize to the Greek hero on his sacking of Troy.

Cassatt Mary 1845–1926. US Impressionist painter and printmaker, active in France. She excelled in etching and pastel, and her colourful pictures of mothers and children show the influence of Japanese prints, as in *The Bath* 1892 (Art Institute, Chicago). She contributed to the Impressionist exhibitions of 1879, 1880, 1881, and 1886, being admired by French Impressionist Edgar Degas, who encouraged her graphic work in particular. Her studies of women and children relate her work to that of Berthe ◊Morisot, though she was not so free and adventurous in style as her French contemporary. From 1912 she suffered from a partial but increasing blindness.

cassava or ***manioc*** plant *Manihot utilissima,* belonging to the spurge family Euphorbiaceae. Native to South America, it is now widely grown throughout the tropics for its starch-containing roots, from which tapioca and bread are made.

Cassavetes John 1929–1989. US director and actor. His independent experimental films include *Shadows* 1960 and *The Killing of a Chinese Bookie* 1980. His acting credits include *The Dirty Dozen* 1967 and *Rosemary's Baby* 1968.

Cassini Giovanni Domenico 1625–1712. Italian-born French astronomer. He discovered four moons of Saturn and the gap in the rings of Saturn now called the Cassini division.

Cassini joint space probe of the US agency NASA and the European Space Agency to the planet Saturn. *Cassini* is scheduled to be launched 1997 and to go into orbit around Saturn 2004, dropping off a sub-probe, *Huygens,* to land on Saturn's largest moon, Titan.

Cassiopeia prominent constellation of the northern hemisphere, named after the mother of Andromeda. It has a distinctive W-shape, and contains one of the most powerful radio sources in the sky, Cassiopeia A. This is the remains of a ◊supernova (star explosion) that occurred c. AD 1702, too far away to be seen from Earth.

Cassius (Gaius Cassius Longinus) died 42 BC. Roman soldier, one of the conspirators who killed Julius ◊Caesar 44 BC. He fought with Pompey against Caesar, and was pardoned after the battle of Pharsalus 48, but became a leader in the conspiracy of 44. After Caesar's death he joined Brutus, and committed suicide after their defeat at ◊Philippi 42.

Cassivelaunus chieftain of the British tribe, the Catuvellauni, who led the British resistance to the Romans under Caesar 54 BC.

Casson Hugh Maxwell 1910– . English architect. He was professor at the Royal College of Art 1953–75, and president of the Royal Academy 1976–84. He was director of architecture for the Festival of Britain on the South Bank in London 1948–51, in which pavilions designed by young architects helped to popularize the ◊Modern Movement. His books include *Victorian Architecture* 1948.

Caspian Sea

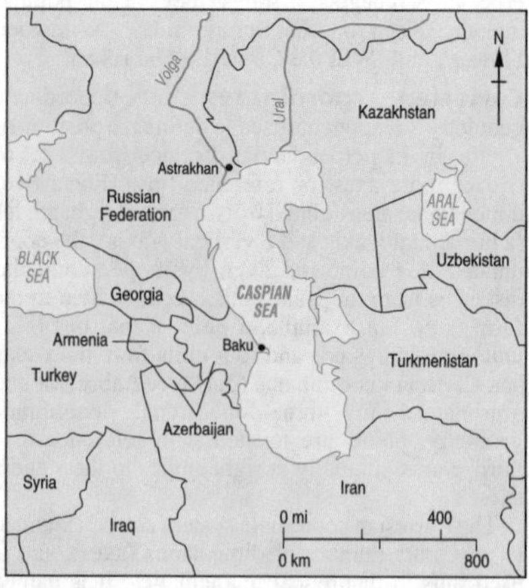

cassowary large flightless bird, genus *Casuarius,* of the family Casuariidae, order Casuariiformes, found in New Guinea and N Australia, usually in forests. Related to the emu, the cassowary has a bare head with a horny casque, or helmet, on top, and brightly-coloured skin on the neck. Its loose plumage is black and its wings tiny, but it can run and leap well and defends itself by kicking. Cassowaries stand up to 1.5 m/5 ft tall.

Castagno Andrea del. Adopted name of Andrea di Bartolo de Bargilla c. 1421–1457. Italian Renaissance painter, active in Florence. His work, which develops from that of ◊Masaccio, is powerful and sculptural in effect, showing clear outlines and an interest in foreshortening. His *David* about 1450–57 (National Gallery, Washington DC) is typical.

castanets Spanish percussion instrument made of two hollowed wooden shells, held in the palm and drummed together by the fingers to produce a rhythmic accompaniment to dance.

caste (Portuguese *casta* 'race') stratification of Hindu society into four main groups: Brahmans (priests), Kshatriyas (nobles and warriors), Vaisyas (traders and farmers), and Sudras (servants); plus a fifth group, Harijan (untouchables). No upward or downward mobility exists, as in classed societies. The system dates from ancient times, and there are more than 3,000 subdivisions.

In Hindu tradition, the four main castes are said to have originated from the head, arms, thighs, and feet respectively of Brahma, the creator; the members of the fifth were probably the aboriginal inhabitants of the country, known variously as Scheduled Castes, Depressed Classes, Untouchables, or Harijan (name coined by Gandhi, 'children of God'). This lowest caste handled animal products, garbage, and human wastes and so was considered to be polluting by touch, or even by sight, to others. Discrimination against them was made illegal 1947 when India became independent, but persists.

Castile kingdom founded in the 10th century, occupying the central plateau of Spain. Its union with ◊Aragon 1479, based on the marriage of Ferdinand and Isabella, effected the foundation of the Spanish state, which at the time was occupied and ruled by the ◊Moors. Castile comprised the two great basins separated by the Sierra de Gredos and the Sierra de Guadarrama, known traditionally as Old and New Castile. The area now forms the regions of ◊Castilla–León and ◊Castilla–La Mancha.

Cassatt *Sara Looking to the Right* c. 1901 by Mary Cassatt. In her early thirties Cassatt settled in France where she worked closely with the Impressionists. She excelled at depicting children and women, her style light and colourful, sensitive rather than sentimental. *Sotheby's*

Castilian language member of the Romance branch of the Indo-European language family, originating in NW Spain, in the provinces of Old and New Castile. It is the basis of present-day standard Spanish (see ◊Spanish language) and is often seen as the same language, the terms *castellano* and *español* being used interchangeably in both Spain and the Spanish-speaking countries of the Americas.

Castilla–La Mancha autonomous region of central Spain; area 79,200 sq km/30,571 sq mi; population (1991) 1,658,400. It includes the provinces of Albacete, Ciudad Real, Cuenca, Guadalajara, and Toledo. Irrigated land produces grain and chickpeas, and merino sheep graze here.

Castilla–León autonomous region of central Spain; area 94,100 sq km/36,323 sq mi; population (1991) 2,545,900. It includes the provinces of Ávila, Burgos, León, Palencia, Salamanca, Segovia, Soria, Valladolid, and Zamora. Irrigated land produces wheat and rye. Cattle, sheep, and fighting bulls are bred in the uplands.

casting process of producing solid objects by pouring molten material into a shaped mould and allowing it to cool. Casting is used to shape such materials as glass and plastics, as well as metals and alloys. The casting of metals has been practised for more than 6,000 years, using first copper and bronze, then iron, and now alloys of zinc and other metals. The traditional method of casting metal is sand casting. Using a model of the object to be produced, a hollow mould is made in a damp sand and clay mix. Molten metal is then poured into the mould, taking its shape when it cools and solidifies. The sand mould is broken up to release the casting. Permanent metal moulds called dies are also used for casting, in particular, small items in mass-production processes where molten metal is injected under pressure into cooled dies. Continuous casting is a method of shaping bars and slabs that involves pouring molten metal into a hollow, water-cooled mould of the desired cross section.

cast iron cheap but invaluable constructional material, most commonly used for car engine blocks. Cast iron is partly refined pig (crude) ◊iron, which is very fluid when molten and highly suitable for shaping by casting; it contains too many impurities (for example, carbon) to be readily shaped in any other way. Solid cast iron is heavy and can absorb great shock but is very brittle.

castle fortified building or group of buildings, characteristic of medieval Europe. The castle underwent many changes, its size, design, and construction being largely determined by changes in siege tactics and the development of artillery. Outstanding examples are the 12th-century Krak des Chevaliers, Syria (built by crusaders); 13th-century Caernarvon Castle, Wales; and 15th-century Manzanares el Real, Spain.

structure The main parts of a typical castle are the keep, a large central tower containing store rooms, soldiers' quarters, and a hall for the lord and his family; the inner bailey or walled courtyard surrounding the keep; the outer bailey or second courtyard, separated from the inner bailey by a wall; crenellated embattlements through which missiles were discharged against an attacking enemy; rectangular or round towers projecting from the walls; the portcullis, a heavy grating which could be let down to close the main gate; and the drawbridge crossing the ditch or moat surrounding the castle. Sometimes a tower called a barbican was constructed over a gateway as an additional defensive measure.

11th century The motte and bailey castle (the motte was a mound of earth, and the bailey a courtyard enclosed by a wall); the earliest example is on the river Loire in France, dated 1010. The first rectangular keep dates from this time; an example is the White Tower in the Tower of London.

12th century Developed more substantial defensive systems, based in part on the Crusaders' experiences of sieges during the First Crusade 1096; the first curtain walls with projecting towers were built (as at Framlingham, Suffolk).

13th century Introduction of the round tower, both for curtain walls (Pembroke, Wales) and for keeps (Conisborough, Yorkshire); concentric planning (in the castles of Wales, such as Beaumaris and Harlech); fortified town walls.

14th century First use of gunpowder; inclusion of gunports in curtain walls (Bodiam, Sussex).

15th century Fortified manor houses now adequate for private dwelling.

16th century End of castle as a practical means of defence; fortified coastal defences, however, continued to be built (Falmouth, Cornwall).

Castlereagh Robert Stewart, Viscount Castlereagh 1769–1822. British Tory politician. As chief secretary for Ireland 1797–1801, he suppressed the rebellion of 1798 and helped the younger Pitt secure the union of England, Scotland, and Ireland 1801. In Parliament he was secretary for war and the colonies 1805–06 and 1807–09, when he had to resign after a duel with foreign secretary George ◊Canning. As foreign secretary 1812–22, he coordinated European opposition to Napoleon and represented Britain at the Congress of Vienna 1814–15.

‘I met Murder in the way – / He had a mask like Castlereagh.’

On **Robert Castlereagh**
Percy Bysshe Shelley
The Mask of Anarchy
1832

Castor or ***Alpha Geminorum*** second brightest star in the constellation ◊Gemini and the 23rd brightest star in the night sky. Along with the brighter ◊Pollux, it forms a prominent pair at the eastern end of Gemini, representing the head of the twins. Second-magnitude Castor is 45 light years from Earth, and is one of the finest ◊binary stars in the sky for small telescopes. The two main components orbit each other over a period of 467 years. A third, much fainter, star orbits the main pair over a period probably exceeding 10,000 years. Each of the three visible components is a spectroscopic binary, making Castor a sextuple star system.

Castor and Pollux/Polydeuces in Greek mythology, twin sons of Leda (by Zeus), brothers of ◊Helen and ◊Clytemnestra. Protectors of mariners, they were transformed at death into the constellation Gemini.

castor-oil plant tall, tropical and subtropical shrub *Ricinus communis* of the spurge family Euphorbiaceae. The seeds yield the purgative castor oil and also ricin, one of the most powerful poisons known, which can be targeted to destroy cancer cells, while leaving normal cells untouched. *See illustration on following page.*

castration removal of the sex glands (either ovaries or testes). Male domestic animals, mainly stallions and bulls, may be castrated to prevent

castle Bodiam Castle and moat, Sussex, England. The castle was built 1385 by licence of Richard II. *Corbis*

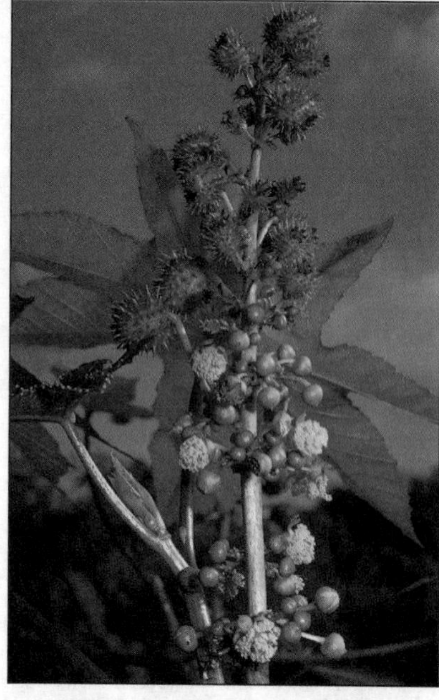

castor-oil plant The tall fruiting stems of the castor-oil plant *Ricinus communis* are a common sight throughout the tropical world, especially near human habitations and in disturbed ground generally. It is grown for ornament, and for the extraction of castor oil and ricin. *Premaphotos Wildlife*

reproduction, to make them larger or more docile, or to eradicate disease. Cockerels are castrated (capons) to improve their flavour and increase their size. Castration of humans was used in ancient and medieval times and occasionally later to preserve the treble voice of boy singers or, by Muslims, to provide eunuchs, trustworthy harem guards. If done in childhood, it inhibits sexual development: for instance, the voice remains high, and growth of hair on the face and body is reduced, owing to the absence of the hormones normally secreted by the testes. The effects of castration can also be achieved by administration of hormones.

All criticism is opposition. All opposition is counter-revolutionary.

FIDEL CASTRO
Quoted in the *New Yorker* 1992

castrato in music, a high male voice of unusual brilliance and power achieved by castration before puberty, regarded as the ideal timbre for heroic roles in opera by composers from Monteverdi to Wagner. Recordings preserve the voice of Alessandro Moreschi (1858–1922), the last male soprano of the Sistine Chapel.

Castries port and capital of St Lucia, on the northwest coast of the island in the Caribbean; population (1992) 53,900. It produces textiles, chemicals, tobacco, and wood and rubber products. The town was rebuilt after destruction by fire 1948.

Castro Cipriano 1858–1924. Venezuelan dictator 1899–1908, known as 'the Lion of the Andes'. When he refused to pay off foreign debts 1902, British, German, and Italian ships blockaded the country. He presided over a corrupt government. There were frequent rebellions during his rule, and opponents of his regime were exiled or murdered.

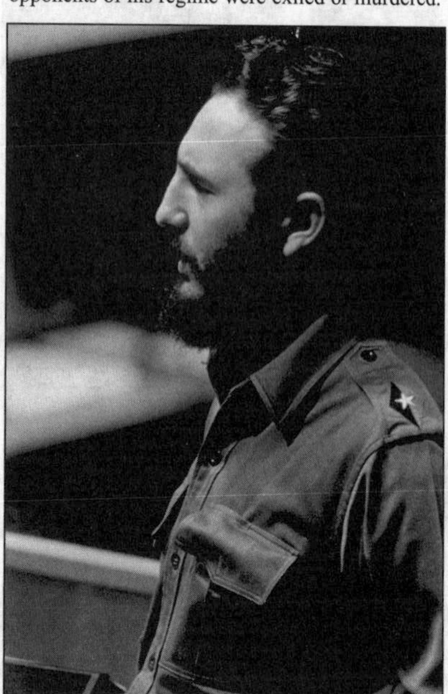

Castro (Ruz) The Cuban revolutionary leader Fidel Castro. After his overthrow of the right-wing Batista regime 1959, Castro maintained his leadership of Cuba despite the enmity of his powerful neighbour, the USA. Since 1990 events in E Europe and the former USSR have left Castro increasingly isolated. *United Nations*

Castro (Ruz) Fidel 1927– . Cuban communist politician, prime minister 1959–76 and president from 1976. He led two unsuccessful coups against the right-wing Batista regime and led the revolution that overthrew the dictator 1959. He raised the standard of living for most Cubans but dealt harshly with dissenters. From 1990, deprived of the support of the USSR and experiencing the long-term effects of a US trade embargo, Castro faced increasing pressure for reform; in 1995 he moved towards greater economic flexibility by permitting foreign ownership in major areas of commerce and industry. In 1996 the *rapprochement* between Cuba and the USA appeared to have progressed after a visit by Democratic members of the House of Representatives, although the US embargo was not lifted.

Of wealthy parentage, Castro was educated at Jesuit schools and, after studying law at the University of Havana, gained a reputation through his work for poor clients. He opposed the Batista dictatorship, and took part, with his brother Raúl, in an unsuccessful attack on the army barracks at Santiago de Cuba 1953. After some time in exile in the USA and Mexico, Castro attempted a secret landing in Cuba 1956 in which all but 11 of his supporters were killed. He eventually gathered an army of over 5,000 which overthrew Batista on 1 Jan 1959 and he became prime minister a few months later. Raúl Castro was appointed minister of armed forces.

Castro's administration introduced a centrally planned economy based on the production for export of sugar, tobacco, and nickel. He nationalized the property of wealthy Cubans, Americans, and other foreigners 1960, resulting in the severance of relations by the USA, an economic embargo, and US attempts to subvert Cuba's government (or invade and overthrow it; see ◊Bay of Pigs). This enmity came to a head in the ◊Cuban missile crisis 1962. Aid for development was provided by the USSR, which replaced the USA as Cuba's main trading partner, and Castro espoused Marxism-Leninism until, in 1974, he rejected Marx's formula 'from each according to his ability and to each according to his need' and decreed that each Cuban should 'receive according to his work'. He improved education, housing, and health care for the majority of Cubans but lost the support of the middle class, hundreds of thousands of whom fled the country. After 1990 events in E Europe and the disintegration of the USSR left Castro increasingly isolated, and by 1993 the US embargo had gravely weakened the country's economy, provoking increasing numbers of Cubans to flee the country.

casuistry the application of an ethical theory to particular cases or types of case, especially in theology and dogmatics. Casuistry is contrasted with situationism, which considers each moral situation as it arises and without reference to ethical theory or moral principles. Most ethical theories can be shown to be inadequate, if sufficient effort is devoted to identifying increasingly subtle features in a particular moral situation. Hence, casuistry has fallen into disrepute.

casus belli (Latin) justification for war, grounds for a dispute.

cat small, domesticated, carnivorous mammal *Felis catus*, often kept as a pet or for catching small pests such as rodents. Found in many colour variants, it may have short, long, or no hair, but the general shape and size is constant. Cats have short muzzles, strong limbs, and flexible spines which enable them to jump and climb. All walk on the pads of their toes (digitigrade) and have retractile claws, so are able to stalk their prey silently. They have large eyes and an acute sense of hearing. The canine teeth are long and well-developed, as are the shearing teeth in the side of the mouth.

origins Domestic cats have a common ancestor, the African wild cat *Felis libyca*, found across Africa and Arabia. This is similar to the European wild cat *F. silvestris*. Domestic cats can interbreed with either of these wild relatives. Various other species of small wild cat live in all continents except Antarctica and Australia. Large cats such as the lion, tiger, leopard, puma, and jaguar also belong to the cat family Felidae.

catabolism in biology, the destructive part of ◊metabolism where living tissue is changed into energy and waste products. It is the opposite of ◊anabolism. It occurs continuously in the body, but is accelerated during many disease processes, such as fever, and in starvation.

catacomb underground cemetery, such as the catacombs of the early Christians. Examples include those beneath the basilica of St Sebastian in Rome, where bodies were buried in niches in the walls of the tunnels.

Catalan language member of the Romance branch of the Indo-European language family, an Iberian language closely related to Provençal in France. It is spoken in Catalonia in NE Spain, the Balearic Islands, Andorra, and a corner of SW France. Since the end of the Franco regime in Spain 1975, Catalan nationalists have vigorously promoted their regional language as being equal in importance in Catalonia to Castilian Spanish, and it is now accepted as an official language of the European Union.

catalepsy in medicine, an abnormal state in which the patient is apparently or actually unconscious and the muscles become rigid.

Çatal Hüyük Neolithic site (6000 BC) in Turkey, SE of Konya. It was a fortified town and had temples with wall paintings, and objects such as jewellery, obsidian, and mirrors. Finds at Jericho and Catal Hüyük together indicated much earlier development of urban life in the ancient world than was previously imagined.

Catalonia (Spanish ***Cataluña***, Catalan ***Catalunya***) autonomous region of NE Spain; area 31,900 sq km/12,313 sq mi; population (1991) 6,059,500. It includes Barcelona (the capital), Gerona, Lérida, and Tarragona. Industries include wool and cotton textiles; hydroelectric power is produced. The north is mountainous, and the Ebro basin breaks through the Castellón Mountains in the south. The soil is fertile, but the climate in the interior is arid. Catalonia leads Spain in industrial development. Tourist resorts have developed along the Costa Brava

history the region has a long tradition of independence. It enjoyed autonomy 1932–39 but lost its privileges for supporting the republican cause in the ◊Spanish Civil War. Autonomy and official use of the ◊Catalan language were restored 1980.

catalyst substance that alters the speed of, or makes possible, a chemical or biochemical reaction but remains unchanged at the end of the reaction. ◊Enzymes are natural biochemical catalysts. In practice most catalysts are used to speed up reactions.

catalytic converter device fitted to the exhaust system of a motor vehicle in order to reduce toxic emissions from the engine. It converts harmful exhaust products to relatively harmless ones by passing the exhaust gases over a mixture of catalysts coated on a metal or ceramic honeycomb (a structure that increases the surface area and therefore the amount of active catalyst with which the exhaust gases will come into contact). ***Oxidation catalysts*** (small amounts of precious palladium and platinum metals) convert hydrocarbons (unburnt fuel) and carbon monoxide into carbon dioxide and water, but do not affect nitrogen oxide emissions. ***Three-way catalysts*** (platinum and rhodium metals) convert nitrogen oxide gases into nitrogen and oxygen.

Over the lifetime of a vehicle, a catalytic converter can reduce hydrocarbon emissions by 87%, carbon monoxide emissions by 85%, and nitrogen oxide emissions by 62%, but will cause a slight increase in the amount of carbon dioxide emitted.

catamaran (Tamil 'tied log') twin-hulled sailing vessel, based on the aboriginal craft of South America and the Indies, made of logs lashed together, with an outrigger. A similar vessel with three hulls is known as a trimaran. Car ferries with a wave-piercing catamaran design are also in use in parts of Europe and North America. They have a pointed main hull and two outriggers and travel at a speed of 35 knots (84.5 kph/52.5 mph).

cataract eye disease in which the crystalline lens or its capsule becomes cloudy, causing blindness. Fluid accumulates between the fibres of the lens and gives place to deposits of ◊albumin. These coalesce into rounded bodies, the lens fibres break down, and areas of the lens or the lens capsule become filled with opaque products of degeneration. In most cases, the treatment is replacement of the opaque lens with an artificial implant.

catastrophe theory mathematical theory developed by René Thom 1972, in which he showed that the growth of an organism proceeds by a series of gradual changes that are triggered by, and in turn trigger, large-scale changes or 'catastrophic' jumps. It also has applications in engineering – for example, the gradual strain on the structure of a bridge that can eventually result in a sudden collapse – and has been extended to economic and psychological events.

Catch-22 black-humour novel by Joseph ◊Heller, published 1961, about a US squadron that is ordered to fly an increased number of bombing missions in Italy in World War II; the crazed military justifications involved were described by the novel's phrase 'Catch-22', which has come to represent the dilemma of all false authoritarian logic.

catch crop crop such as turnip that is inserted between two principal crops in a rotation in order to provide some quick livestock feed or soil improvement at a time when the land would otherwise be lying idle.

Catcher in the Rye, The novel by US writer J D ◊Salinger, published 1951, about a young man growing up and his fight to maintain his integrity in a 'phoney' adult world; it has become an international classic.

catchment area in earth sciences, the area from which water is collected by a river and its tributaries. In the social sciences the term may be used to denote the area from which people travel to obtain a particular service or product, such as the area from which a school draws its pupils.

catechism teaching by question and answer on the Socratic method, but chiefly as a means of instructing children in the basics of the Christian creed. A person being instructed in this way in preparation for baptism or confirmation is called a catechumen.

A form of catechism was used for the catechumens in the early Christian church. Little books of catechism became numerous at the Reformation. Luther published simple catechisms for children and uneducated people, and a larger catechism for the use of teachers. The popular Roman Catholic catechism was that of Peter Canisius 1555; that with the widest circulation now is the *Explanatory Catechism of Christian Doctrine*. Protestant catechisms include Calvin's Geneva Catechism 1537; that composed by Cranmer and Ridley with additions by Overall 1549–1661, incorporated in the Book of Common Prayer; the Presbyterian Catechism 1647–48; and the Evangelical Free Church Catechism 1898. A new *Catechism of the Catholic Church* was published 1992, for bishops and teachers of religion.

catecholamine chemical that functions as a ◊neurotransmitter or a ◊hormone. Dopamine, adrenaline (epinephrine), and noradrenaline (norepinephrine) are catecholamines.

categorical imperative technical term in Immanuel ◊Kant's moral philosophy designating the supreme principle of morality for rational beings. The imperative orders us to act only in such a way that we can wish a maxim, or subjective principle, of our action to be a universal law.

category in philosophy, a fundamental concept applied to being that cannot be reduced to anything more elementary. Aristotle listed ten categories: substance, quantity, quality, relation, place, time, position, state, action, and passion.

catenary curve taken up by a flexible cable suspended between two points, under gravity; for example, the curve of overhead suspension cables that hold the conductor wire of an electric railway or tramway.

caterpillar larval stage of a ◊butterfly or ◊moth. Wormlike in form, the body is segmented, may be hairy, and often has scent glands. The head has strong biting mandibles, silk glands, and a spinneret. Caterpillars emerge from eggs that have been laid by the female insect on the food plant and feed greedily, increasing greatly in size and casting their skins several times, until the pupal stage is reached.

caterpillar track trade name for an endless flexible belt of metal plates on which certain vehicles such as tanks and bulldozers run, which takes the place of ordinary tyred wheels and improves performance on wet or uneven surfaces.

catfish fish belonging to the order Siluriformes, in which barbels (feelers) on the head are well-developed, so giving a resemblance to the whiskers of a cat. Catfishes are found worldwide, mainly but not exclusively in fresh water, and are plentiful in South America. The E European giant catfish or wels *Silurus glanis* grows to 1.5 m/5 ft long or more. It has been introduced to several places in Britain.

Cathar (medieval Latin 'the pure') member of a sect in medieval Europe usually numbered among the Christian heretics. Influenced by ◊Manichaeism, they started about the 10th century in the Balkans where they were called 'Bogomils', spread to SW Europe where they were often identified with the ◊Albigenses, and by the middle of the 14th century had been destroyed or driven underground by the Inquisition. The Cathars believed that this world is under the domination of Satan, and men and women are the terrestrial embodiment of spirits who were inspired by him to revolt and were driven out of heaven. At death, the soul will be reincarnated (whether in human or animal form) unless it has been united through the Cathar faith with Christ.

For someone who has become a Cathar, death brings release, the Beatific Vision, and immortality in Christ's presence. Baptism with the spirit – the *consolamentum* – was the central rite, believed to remedy the disaster of the Fall. The spirit received was the Paraclete, the Comforter, and it was imparted by imposition of hands. The Believers, or *Credentes*, could approach God only through the Perfect (the ordained priesthood), who were implicitly obeyed in everything, and lived lives of the strictest self-denial and chastity.

catharsis (Greek *katharsis* 'purification') emotional purging and purification brought about by the experience of pity and fear, as in tragic drama. Aristotle in his *Poetics* used the term to explain the audience's feelings of relief or pleasure in watching the suffering of characters in a tragedy brought low by their own mistakes or cruel fate.

cathedral (Latin *cathedra* 'seat' or 'throne') principal Christian church of a bishop or archbishop, containing his throne, which is usually situated on the south side of the choir. A cathedral is governed by a dean and chapter. Formerly, cathedrals were distinguished as either monastic or secular, the clergy of the latter not being members of a regular monastic order. Some British cathedrals, such as Southwell and York, are referred to as 'minsters', the term originating in the name given to the bishop and cathedral clergy who were often referred to as a *monasterium*. After the dissolution of the monasteries by Henry VIII, most of the monastic churches were refounded and are called Cathedrals of the New Foundation. Cathedrals of dioceses founded since 1836 include St Albans, Southwark, Truro, Birmingham, and Liverpool. There are cathedrals in most of the chief cities of Europe.

Because of their importance, cathedrals were for many centuries the main focus of artistic and architectural endeavour. Their artworks include stained glass, frescoes, mosaics, carvings in wood and stone, paintings (such as altarpieces), ironwork, and textiles. Most cathedrals were built during the Middle Ages and reflect the many styles of ◊Romanesque and ◊Gothic architecture.

Romanesque cathedrals include Durham (England), Worms (Germany), and Cefalù (Sicily). Gothic cathedrals include Canterbury, Ely, Exeter, Winchester, and York (England); Amiens, Chartres, Notre Dame, and Rouen (France); Cologne, Regensburg, and Ulm (Germany); Florence, Milan, Orvieto, and Siena (Italy); Ávila, Burgos, Léon, Salamanca, and Toledo (Spain); and Uppsala (Sweden). Among the few built since the Middle Ages are Valencia, Spain, 13th–15th century; St Paul's, London, 17th century; SS Peter and Paul, St Petersburg, Russia, both 18th century; Westminster, London, 19th century; Liverpool (Catholic), 20th century.

Cather Willa Sibert 1873–1947. US novelist and short-story writer. Her novels frequently explore life in the pioneer West, both in her own time and in past eras; for example, *O Pioneers!* 1913 and *My Antonia* 1918, and *A Lost Lady* 1923. She also wrote poetry and essays on fiction.

caterpillar A caterpillar of a notodontid moth from the rainforest of New Guinea. Its aposematic (warning) coloration is a signal to potential predators that it has an unpleasant taste. *Premaphotos Wildlife*

Catherine I 1684–1727. Empress of Russia from 1725. A Lithuanian peasant, born Martha Skavronsky, she married a Swedish dragoon and eventually became the mistress of Peter the Great. In 1703 she was rechristened Katarina Alexeievna. The tsar divorced his wife 1711 and married Catherine 1712. She accompanied him on his campaigns, and showed tact and shrewdness. In 1724 she was proclaimed empress, and after Peter's death 1725 she ruled capably with the help of her ministers. She allied Russia with Austria and Spain in an anti-English bloc.

Catherine (II) the Great 1729–1796. Empress of Russia from 1762, and daughter of the German prince of Anhalt-Zerbst. In 1745, she married the Russian grand duke Peter. Catherine dominated her husband; six months after he became Tsar Peter III in 1762, he was murdered in a coup and Catherine ruled alone. During her reign Russia extended its boundaries to include territory from wars with the Turks 1768–74, 1787–92, and from the partitions of Poland 1772, 1793, and 1795, as well as establishing hegemony over the Black Sea. Catherine's private life was notorious throughout Europe, but except for Grigory ◊Potemkin she did not permit her lovers to influence her policy. She admired and aided the French ◊Encyclopédistes, including d'Alembert, and corresponded with the radical writer Voltaire. *See illustration on following page.*

Catherine de' Medici 1519–1589. French queen consort of Henry II, whom she married 1533; daughter of Lorenzo de' Medici, Duke of Urbino; and mother of Francis II, Charles IX, and Henry III. At first outshone by Henry's mistress Diane de Poitiers (1490–1566), she became regent 1560–63 for Charles IX and remained in power until his death 1574. During the religious wars of 1562–69, she first supported the Protestant ◊Huguenots against the Roman Catholic Guises to ensure her own position as ruler; she later opposed them, and has been traditionally implicated in the Massacre of ◊St Bartholomew 1572.

Catherine of Alexandria, St lived early 4th century. Christian martyr. According to legend she disputed with 50 scholars, refusing to give up her faith and marry Emperor Maxentius. Her emblem is a wheel, on which her persecutors tried to kill her (the wheel broke and she was beheaded). Feast day 25 Nov; removed from church calendar 1969.

Catherine of Aragon 1485–1536. First queen of Henry VIII of England, 1509–33, and mother of Mary I. Catherine had married Henry's elder brother Prince Arthur 1501 and on his death 1502 was betrothed to Henry, marrying him on his accession. She failed to produce a male heir and Henry divorced her without papal approval, thus creating the basis for the English ◊Reformation. Of their six children, only Mary lived. Wanting a male heir, Henry sought an annulment 1526 when

'Religion and art spring from the same root and are close kin. Economics and art are strangers.'

WILLA CATHER
On Writing

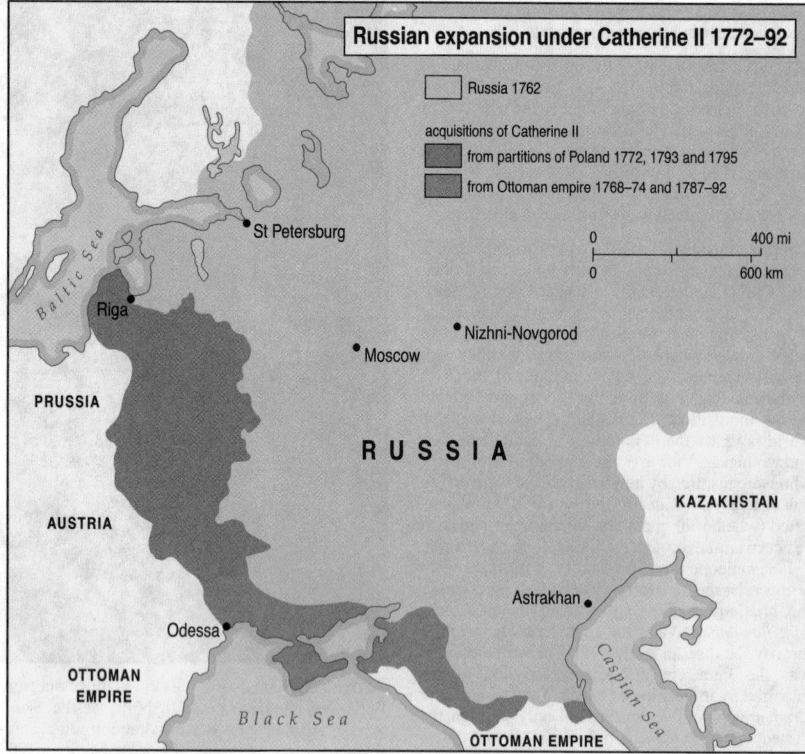

Catherine was too old to bear children. When the pope demanded that the case be referred to him, Henry married Anne Boleyn, afterward receiving the desired decree of nullity from Cranmer, the archbishop of Canterbury, in 1533. The Reformation in England followed, and Catherine went into retirement until her death.

Catherine of Braganza 1638–1705. Queen of Charles II of England 1662–85. Her childlessness and Catholic faith were unpopular, but Charles resisted pressure for divorce. She returned to Lisbon 1692 after his death. The daughter of John IV of Portugal (1604–1656), she brought the Portuguese possessions of Bombay and Tangier as her dowry and introduced tea drinking and citrus fruits to England.

Catherine of Valois 1401–1437. Queen of Henry V of England, whom she married 1420; the mother of Henry VI. After the death of Henry V, she secretly married Owen Tudor (c. 1400–1461) about 1425, and their son Edmund Tudor was the father of Henry VII.

catheter fine tube inserted into the body to introduce or remove fluids. The urinary catheter, passed by way of the urethra (the duct that leads urine away from the bladder) was the first to be used. In today's practice, catheters can be inserted into blood vessels, either in the limbs or trunk, to provide blood samples and local pressure measurements, and to deliver drugs and/or nutrients directly into the bloodstream.

cathode in chemistry, the negative electrode of an electrolytic ◊cell, towards which positive particles (cations), usually in solution, are attracted. See ◊electrolysis.

cathode in electronics, the part of an electronic device in which electrons are generated. In a thermionic valve, electrons are produced by the heating effect of an applied current; in a photocell, they are produced by the interaction of light and a semiconducting material. The cathode is kept at a negative potential relative to the device's other electrodes (anodes) in order to ensure that the liberated electrons stream away from the cathode and towards the anodes.

cathode-ray tube vacuum tube in which a beam of electrons is produced and focused onto a fluorescent screen. It is an essential component of television receivers, computer visual display units, and oscilloscopes. The electrons' kineteic energy is converted into light energy as they collide with the screen.

‘I would much rather have men ask why I have no statue than why I have one.’

Cato
Quoted in Plutarch, *Lives* 'Cato'

Catholic church the whole body of the Christian church, though usually referring to the Roman Catholic Church (see ◊Roman Catholicism).

Catholic Emancipation in British history, acts of Parliament passed 1780–1829 to relieve Roman Catholics of civil and political restrictions imposed from the time of Henry VIII and the Reformation.

Catiline (Lucius Sergius Catilina) c. 108–62 BC. Roman politician. Twice failing to be elected to the consulship in 64/63 BC, he planned a military coup, but ◊Cicero exposed his conspiracy. He died at the head of the insurgents.

cation ◊ion carrying a positive charge. During electrolysis, cations in the electrolyte move to the cathode (negative electrode).

catkin in flowering plants (◊angiosperms), a pendulous inflorescence, bearing numerous small, usually unisexual flowers. The tiny flowers are stalkless and the petals and sepals are usually absent or much reduced in size. Many types of trees bear catkins, including willows, poplars, and birches. Most plants with catkins are wind-pollinated.

Cato Marcus Porcius. Known as 'the Censor' 234–149 BC. Roman politician. Having significantly developed Roman rule in Spain, Cato was appointed ◊censor 184 BC. He acted severely, taxing luxuries and heavily revising the senatorial and equestrian lists. He was violently opposed to Greek influence on Roman culture and his suspicion of the re-emergence of Carthaginian power led him to remark: 'Carthage must be destroyed.'

CAT scan or *CT scan*(acronym for ***computerized axial tomography scan***) sophisticated method of X-ray imaging. Quick and noninvasive, CAT scanning is used in medicine as an aid to diagnosis, helping to pinpoint problem areas without the need for exploratory surgery. It is also used in archaeology to investigate mummies. The CAT scanner passes a narrow fan of X-rays through successive slices of the suspect body part. These slices are picked up by crystal detectors in a scintillator and converted electronically into cross-sectional images displayed on a viewing screen. Gradually, using views taken from various angles, a three-dimensional picture of the organ or tissue can be built up and irregularities analysed.

Catskills US mountain range, mainly in SE New York State, west of the Hudson River; the highest point is Slide Mountain, 1,281 m/4,204 ft.

cattle any large, ruminant, even-toed, hoofed mammal of the genus *Bos*, family Bovidae, including wild species such as the yak, gaur, gayal, banteng, and kouprey, as well as domestic breeds. Asiatic water buffaloes *Bubalus*, African buffaloes *Syncerus*, and American bison *Bison* are not considered true cattle. Cattle are bred for meat (beef cattle) or milk (dairy cattle).

Cattle were first domesticated in the Middle East during the Neolithic period, about 8000 BC. They were brought north into Europe by migrating Neolithic farmers. Fermentation in the four-chambered stomach allows cattle to make good use of the grass that is normally the main part of the diet. There are two main types of domesticated cattle: the European breeds, variants of *Bos taurus* descended from the ◊aurochs, and the various breeds of zebu *Bos indicus*, the humped cattle of India, which are useful in the tropics for their ability to withstand the heat and diseases to which European breeds succumb. The old-established beef breeds are mostly British in origin. The Hereford, for example, is the premier English breed, ideally suited to rich lowland pastures.

Of the Scottish beef breeds, the Aberdeen Angus, a black and hornless variety, produces high-quality meat through intensive feeding methods. Other breeds include the Devon, a hardy early-maturing type, and the Beef Shorthorn, now less important than formerly, but still valued for an ability to produce good calves when crossed with less promising cattle. In recent years, more interest has been shown in other European breeds, their tendency to have less fat being more suited to modern tastes. Examples include the Charolais and the Limousin from central France, and the Simmental, originally from Switzerland. For dairying purposes, a breed raised in many countries is variously known as the Friesian, Holstein, or Black and White. It can give enormous milk yields, up to 13,000 l/3,450 gal in a single lactation, and will produce calves ideally suited for intensive beef production. Other dairying types include the Jersey and Guernsey, whose milk has a high butterfat content, and the Ayrshire, a smaller breed capable of staying outside all year.

Catullus Gaius Valerius c. 84–54 BC. Roman lyric poet. He wrote in a variety of metres and forms, from short narratives and hymns to epigrams. He moved with ease through the literary and political society of late republican Rome. His love affair with the woman he called 'Lesbia' provided the inspiration for many of his poems.

Caucasoid or ***Caucasian*** former racial classification used for any of the light-skinned peoples; so named because the German anthropologist J F Blumenbach (1752–1840) theorized that they originated in the Caucasus.

Caucasus series of mountain ranges between the Caspian and Black seas, in the republics of Russia, Georgia, Armenia, and Azerbaijan; 1,200 km/750 mi long. The highest peak is Elbruz, 5,633 m/18,480 ft. The N Caucasus region is home to some 40 different ethnic groups.

causality in philosophy, a consideration of the connection between cause and effect, usually referred to as the 'causal relationship'. If an event is assumed to have a cause, two important questions arise: what is the relationship between cause and effect, and must it follow that every event is caused?

caustic soda former name for ◊sodium hydroxide (NaOH).

cauterization in medicine, the use of special instruments to burn or fuse small areas of body tissue to destroy dead cells, prevent the spread of infection, or seal tiny blood vessels to minimize blood loss during surgery.

Cauthen Steve 1960– . US jockey. He rode Affirmed to the US Triple Crown 1978 at the age of 18 and won 487 races 1977. He twice won the English Derby, on Slip Anchor 1985 and on Reference Point 1987, and was UK champion jockey 1984, 1985, and 1987.

caution legal term for a warning given by police questioning a suspect, which in the UK must be couched in the following terms: 'You do not have to say anything unless you wish to do so, but what you say may be given in evidence.' Persons not under arrest must also be told that they do not have to remain at the police station or with the police officer but that if they do, they may obtain legal advice if they wish. A suspect should be cautioned again after a break in questioning and upon arrest.

Cavaco Silva Anibal 1939– . Portuguese politician, finance minister 1980–81, and prime minister and Social Democratic Party (PSD) leader 1985–95. Under his leadership Portugal joined the European Community 1985 and the Western European Union 1988.

cavalier horseman of noble birth, but mainly used to describe a male supporter of Charles I in the English Civil War (Cavalier), typically with courtly dress and long hair (as distinct from a Roundhead); also a supporter of Charles II after the Restoration.

Cavalier poets poets of Charles I's court, including Thomas Carew, Robert Herrick, Richard Lovelace, and John Suckling. They wrote witty, lighthearted love lyrics.

Cavalli (Pietro) Francesco 1602–1676. Italian composer. He was organist at St Mark's, Venice, and the first to make opera a popular entertainment with such works as *Equisto* 1643 and *Xerxes* 1654, later performed in honour of Louis XIV's wedding in Paris. Twenty-seven of his operas survive.

Cavan county of the Republic of Ireland, in the province of Ulster; county town Cavan; area 1,890 sq km/730 sq mi; population (1991) 52,800. The river Erne divides it into a narrow, mostly low-lying peninsula, 30 km/20 mi long, between Leitrim and Fermanagh, and an eastern section of wild and bare hill country. The soil is generally poor and the climate moist and cold. The chief towns are Cavan, population about 3,000; Kilmore, seat of Roman Catholic and Protestant bishoprics; and Virginia.

cave roofed-over cavity in the Earth's crust usually produced by the action of underground water or by waves on a seacoast. Caves of the former type commonly occur in areas underlain by limestone, such as Kentucky and many Balkan regions, where the rocks are soluble in water. A pothole is a vertical hole in rock caused by water descending a crack; it is thus open to the sky.

Cave animals often show loss of pigmentation or sight, and under isolation, specialized species may develop. The scientific study of caves is called speleology. During the ◊ice age, humans began living in caves leaving many layers of debris that archaeologists have unearthed and dated in the Old World and the New. They also left cave art, paintings of extinct animals often with hunters on their trail. See also ◊Altamira. Celebrated caves include the Mammoth Cave in Kentucky, USA, 6.4 km/4 mi long and 38 m/125 ft high; the Caverns of Adelsberg (Postumia) near Trieste, Italy, which extend for many miles; Carlsbad Cave, New Mexico, the largest in the USA; the Cheddar Caves, England; Fingal's Cave, Scotland, which has a range of basalt columns; and Peak Cavern, England.

Cavell *English nurse Edith Cavell who ran a Red Cross hospital in Belgium during World War I which treated both Allied and German wounded soldiers. She was executed by the Germans Oct 1915 for helping Allied soldiers to escape to Holland. She became a national hero in Britain and a statue was erected in her honour in St Martin's Place, London. Image Select (UK) Ltd*

caveat emptor (Latin 'let the buyer beware') dictum that professes the buyer is responsible for checking that the goods or services they purchase are satisfactory.

Cavell Edith Louisa 1865–1915. English matron of a Red Cross hospital in Brussels, Belgium, in World War I, who helped Allied soldiers escape to the Dutch frontier. She was court-martialled by the Germans and condemned to death.

Cavendish family name of dukes of Devonshire; the family seat is at Chatsworth, Derbyshire, England.

Cavendish Henry 1731–1810. English physicist and chemist. He discovered hydrogen (which he called 'inflammable air') 1766, and determined the compositions of water and of nitric acid. The Cavendish experiment 1798 enabled him to discover the mass and density of the Earth. Cavendish demonstrated 1784 that water is produced when hydrogen burns in air, thus proving that water is a compound and not an element. He also worked on the production of heat and determined the freezing points for many materials, including mercury.

Cavendish Lord Frederick Charles 1836–1882. British administrator, second son of the 7th Duke of Devonshire. He was appointed chief secretary to the lord lieutenant of Ireland in 1882. On the evening of his arrival in Dublin he was murdered in Phoenix Park with Thomas Burke, the permanent Irish undersecretary, by members of the Irish Invincibles, a group of Irish Fenian extremists founded 1881.

Cavendish Spencer see ◊Hartington, Spencer Compton Cavendish, British politician.

caviar salted roe (eggs) of sturgeon, salmon, and other fishes. Caviar is prepared by beating and straining the egg sacs until the eggs are free from fats and then adding salt. Russia and Iran are the main exporters of the most prized variety of caviar, derived from Caspian Sea sturgeon.

Cavour Camillo Benso di, Count 1810–1861. Italian nationalist politician, a leading figure in the Italian ◊*Risorgimento*. As prime minister of Piedmont 1852–59 and 1860–61, he enlisted the support of Britain and France for the concept of a united Italy, achieved 1861; after expelling the Austrians 1859, he assisted Garibaldi in liberating southern Italy 1860.

cavy short-tailed South American rodent, family Caviidae, of which the guinea-pig *Cavia porcellus* is an example. Wild cavies are greyish or brownish with rather coarse hair. They live in small groups in burrows, and have been kept for food since ancient times.

Caxton William c. 1422–1491. The first English printer. He learned the art of ◊printing in Cologne, Germany, 1471 and set up a press in Belgium where he produced the first book printed in English, his own version of a French romance, *Recuyell of the Historyes of Troye* 1474. Returning to England 1476, he established himself in London, where he produced the first book printed in England, *Dictes or Sayengis of the Philosophres* 1477.

Caxton, born in Kent, was apprenticed to a London cloth dealer 1438, and set up his own business in Bruges 1441–70; he became governor of the English merchants there, negotiating on their behalf with the dukes of Burgundy. In 1471 he went to Cologne, where he learned the art of printing, and then set up his own press in Bruges in partnership with Colard Mansion, a calligrapher. The books from Caxton's press in Westminster included editions of the poets Chaucer, John Gower, and John Lydgate (c. 1370–1449). He translated many texts from French and Latin and revised some English ones, such as Malory's *Morte d'Arthur*. Altogether he printed about 100 books.

Cayenne capital and chief port of French Guiana, on Cayenne Island, NE South America, at the mouth of the river Cayenne; population (1990) 41,700. The main occupation is shrimping. It was founded 1634 by the French, and used as a penal settlement 1854–1946.

cayenne pepper condiment derived from the dried fruits of various species of ◊capsicum (especially *Capsicum frutescens*), a tropical American genus of plants of the family Solanaceae. It is wholly distinct in its origin from black or white pepper, which is derived from an East Indian plant (*Piper nigrum*).

cayman or ***caiman*** large reptile, resembling the ◊crocodile.

Cayman Islands British island group in the West Indies

area 260 sq km/100 sq mi

capital George Town (on Grand Cayman)

features comprises three low-lying islands: Grand Cayman, Cayman Brac, and Little Cayman

government governor, executive council, and legislative assembly

exports seawhip coral, a source of ◊prostaglandins; shrimps; honey; jewellery

currency Cayman Island dollar

population (1993 est) 31,150 (mostly on Grand Cayman)

language English

history first reached by Christopher Columbus 1503; acquired by Britain following the Treaty of Madrid 1670; became a dependency of Jamaica 1863. In 1959 the islands became a separate crown colony, although the inhabitants chose to remain British. From that date, changes in legislation attracted foreign banks and the Caymans are now an international financial centre and tax haven as well as a tourist resort, with emphasis on scuba diving.

Cayman Islands

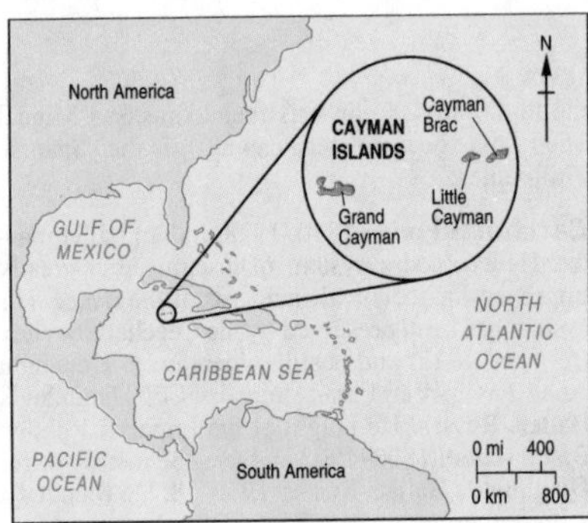

CD-I abbreviation for ***compact disc-interactive***, ◊compact disc developed by Philips for storing a combination of video, audio, text, and pictures. It is intended principally for the consumer market to be used in systems using a combination of computer and television.

CD-ROM (abbreviation for ***compact-disc read-only memory***) computer storage device developed from the technology of the audio ◊compact disc (CD). It consists of a plastic-coated metal disc, on which binary digital information is etched in the form of microscopic pits. This can then be read optically by passing a light beam over the disc. CD-ROMs typically hold about 650 ◊megabytes of data, and are used in distributing large amounts of text, graphics, audio, and video, such as encyclopedias, catalogues, technical manuals, and games.

High density CD's are being developed, that will be able to store many gigabytes of data, by using multiple layers on the surface of the disc and by using double-sided discs. *See illustration on following page.*

CE abbreviation for ***Common Era*** (see ◊calendar); ***Church of England*** (often ***C of E***).

Ceauşescu Nicolae 1918–1989. Romanian politician, leader of the Romanian Communist Party (RCP), in power 1965–89. He pursued a policy line independent of and critical of the USSR. He appointed family members, including his wife Elena Ceauşescu, to senior state and party posts, and governed in an increasingly repressive manner, implementing schemes that impoverished the nation. The Ceauşescus were overthrown in a bloody revolutionary coup Dec 1989 and executed. After his execution, the full extent of his repressive rule and personal extravagance became public. *See illustration on following page.*

Cebu chief city and port of the island of Cebu in the Philippines; population (1990) 610,400; area of the island 5,086 sq km/1,964 sq mi. The oldest city of

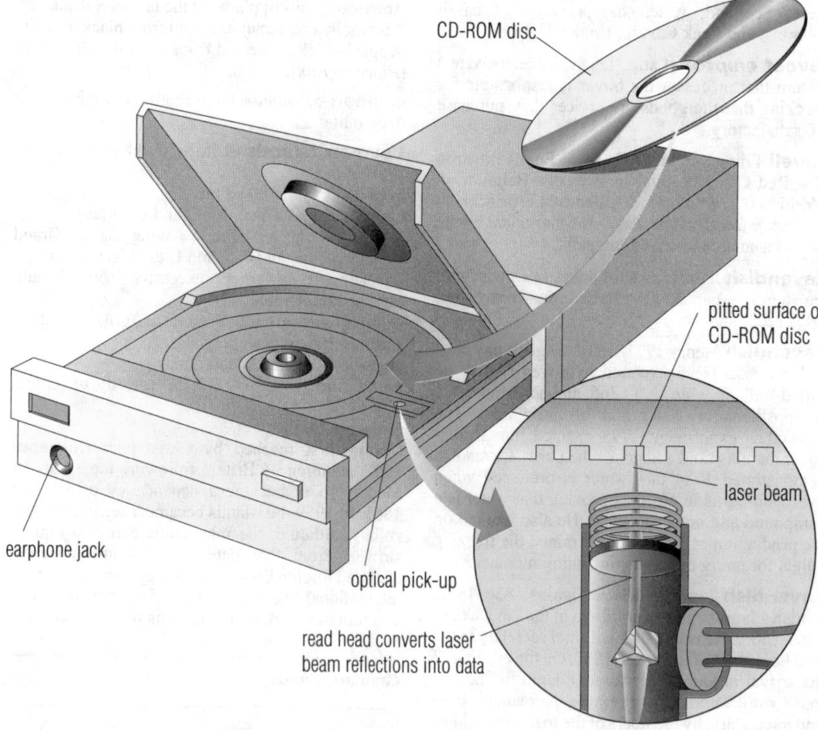

CD-ROM Data is obtained by the CD-ROM drive by converting the reflections from a disc's surface into digital form.

"The difference between a painting and a sculpture is the difference between a shadow and the thing that casts it."

Benvenuto Cellini
Letter to Benedetto Varchi 1547

the Philippines, Cebu was founded as San Miguel 1565 and became the capital of the Spanish Philippines.

Cecchetti Enrico 1850–1928. Italian ballet master. He evolved a system of teaching that greatly improved the technical standards of the dance. His system has been preserved by the Cecchetti Society (founded 1922) and is still widely used. He taught Anna Pavlova and many members of Diaghilev's Ballets Russes. He taught at the Imperial Russian Ballet school 1890–1902 and was the instructor for Diaghilev's Ballets Russes 1910–18. He founded a school in London 1918–25, and then became director of the La Scala ballet school in Milan 1925–28.

Cecil Robert, 1st Earl of Salisbury 1563–1612. Secretary of state to Elizabeth I of England, succeeding his father, Lord Burghley; he was afterwards chief minister to James I (James VI of Scotland) whose accession to the English throne he secured. He discovered the ◊Gunpowder Plot, the conspiracy to blow up the King and Parliament 1605. James I created him Earl of Salisbury 1605.

Cecilia, St lived 2nd or 3rd century AD. Christian patron saint of music. She was martyred in Rome in the 2nd or 3rd century, and is said to have sung hymns while undergoing torture. Feast day 22 Nov.

Ceauşescu Romanian politician Nicolae Ceauşescu. Becoming leader of the Romanian Communist Party 1965 and president 1974, Ceauşescu ruled Romania using stern neo-Stalinist methods for almost 25 years until his bloody overthrow and execution Dec 1989. The true extent of his corrupt nepotistic regime became apparent only after his death. *Topham*

cedar any of an Old World genus *Cedrus* of coniferous trees of the pine family Pinaceae. The cedar of Lebanon *C. libani* grows to great heights and age in the mountains of Syria and Asia Minor. Of the historic forests on Mount Lebanon itself, only a few stands of trees remain.

Ceefax ('see facts') one of Britain's two ◊teletext systems (the other is Teletext), or 'magazines of the air', developed by the BBC and first broadcast 1973.

Cela Camilo José 1916– Spanish novelist. Among his novels, characterized by their violence and brutal realism, are *La familia de Pascual Duarte/The Family of Pascal Duarte* 1942 and *La colmena/The Hive* 1951. He has written many other works of uneven merit, remarkable for their wit and frank treatment of sexual themes. Nobel Prize for Literature 1989.

celestial mechanics the branch of astronomy that deals with the calculation of the orbits of celestial bodies, their gravitational attractions (such as those that produce the Earth's tides), and also the orbits of artificial satellites and space probes. It is based on the laws of motion and gravity laid down by Isaac ◊Newton.

celestial sphere imaginary sphere surrounding the Earth, on which the celestial bodies seem to lie. The positions of bodies such as stars, planets, and galaxies are specified by their coordinates on the celestial sphere. The equivalents of latitude and longitude on the celestial sphere are called ◊declination and ◊right ascension (which is measured in hours from 0 to 24). The celestial poles lie directly above the Earth's poles, and the celestial equator lies over the Earth's equator. The celestial sphere appears to rotate once around the Earth each day, actually a result of the rotation of the Earth on its axis.

celibacy way of life involving voluntary abstinence from sexual intercourse. In some religions, such as Christianity and Buddhism, celibacy is sometimes a requirement for certain religious roles, such as the priesthood or a monastic life. Other religions, including Judaism, strongly discourage celibacy.

Céline Louis-Ferdinand. Pen name of Louis-Ferdinand Destouches 1894–1961. French novelist. His writings aroused controversy over their cynicism and misanthropy. His best-known work is *Voyage au bout de la nuit/Journey to the End of the Night* 1932.

cell in biology, a discrete, membrane-bound portion of living matter, the smallest unit capable of an independent existence. All living organisms consist of one or more cells, with the exception of ◊viruses. Bacteria, protozoa, and many other microorganisms consist of single cells, whereas a human is made up of billions of cells. Essential features of a cell are the membrane, which encloses it and restricts the flow of substances in and out; the jellylike material within, the ◊cytoplasm; the ◊ribosomes, which carry out protein synthesis; and the ◊DNA, which forms the hereditary material.

cell differentiation in developing embryos, the process by which cells acquire their specialization, such as heart cells, muscle cells, skin cells, and brain cells. The seven-day-old human pre-embryo consists of thousands of individual cells, each of which is destined to assist in the formation of individual organs in the body. Research has shown that the eventual function of a cell, in for example, a chicken embryo, is determined by the cell's position. The embryo can be mapped into areas corresponding with the spinal cord, the wings, the legs, and many other tissues. If the embryo is relatively young, a cell transplanted from one area to another will develop according to its new position. As the embryo develops the cells lose their flexibility and become unable to change their destiny.

cell division the process by which a cell divides, either ◊meiosis, associated with sexual reproduction, or ◊mitosis, associated with growth, cell replacement, or repair. Both forms involve the duplication of DNA and the splitting of the nucleus.

cell, electrical or ***voltaic cell*** or ***galvanic cell*** device in which chemical energy is converted into electrical energy; the popular name is ◊'battery', but this actually refers to a collection of cells in one unit. The reactive chemicals of a primary cell cannot be replenished, whereas secondary cells – such as storage batteries – are rechargeable: their chemical reactions can be reversed and the original condition restored by applying an electric current. It is dangerous to attempt to recharge a primary cell.

Each cell contains two conducting ◊electrodes immersed in an ◊electrolyte, in a container. A spontaneous chemical reaction within the cell generates a negative charge (excess of electrons) on one electrode, and a positive charge (deficiency of electrons) on the other. The accumulation of these equal but opposite charges prevents the reaction from continuing unless an outer connection (external circuit) is made between the electrodes allowing the charges to dissipate.

When this occurs, electrons escape from the cell's negative terminal and are replaced at the positive, causing a current to flow. After prolonged use, the cell will become flat (cease to supply current). The first cell was made by Italian physicist Alessandro Volta in 1800. Types of primary cells include the Daniell, Lalande, Leclanché, and so-called 'dry' cells; secondary cells include the Planté, Faure, and Edison. Newer types include the Mallory (mercury depolarizer), which has a very stable discharge curve and can be made in very small units (for example, for hearing aids), and the Venner accumulator, which can be made substantially solid for some purposes. Rechargeable nickel–cadmium dry cells are available for household use.

cell, electrolytic device to which electrical energy is applied in order to bring about a chemical reaction; see ◊electrolysis.

Cellini Benvenuto 1500–1571. Italian Mannerist sculptor and goldsmith. Among his works are a graceful bronze *Perseus* 1545–54 (Loggia dei Lanzi, Florence) and a gold salt cellar made for Francis I of France 1540–43 (Kunsthistorisches Museum, Vienna), topped by nude reclining figures. He wrote a frank autobiography (begun 1558), which gives a vivid picture both of him and his age.

cell membrane or ***plasma membrane*** thin layer of protein and fat surrounding cells that controls substances passing between the cytoplasm and the intercellular space. The cell membrane is semipermeable, allowing some substances to pass through and some not. Generally, small molecules such as water, glucose, and amino acids can penetrate the membrane, while large molecules such as starch cannot. Membranes also play a part in ◊active transport, hormonal response, and cell metabolism.

cedar The true cedars are evergreen conifers growing from the Mediterranean to the Himalayas. They have tufts of small needles and cones of papery scales which carry the seeds. The name has long also been applied to trees with a similar type of wood, for example the Spanish cedar, whose wood is used in cigar boxes.

cello common abbreviation for ***violoncello***, tenor member of the ◊violin family and fourth member of the string quartet. Its solo potential was recognized by J S Bach, and a concerto repertoire extends from Haydn (who also gave the cello a leading role in his string quartets), and Boccherini to Dvořák, Elgar, Britten, Ligeti, and Lukas Foss. The *Bachianas Brasilieras 1* by Villa-Lobos is scored for eight cellos, and Boulez's *Messagesquisse* 1977 for seven cellos.

cellophane transparent wrapping film made from wood ◊cellulose, widely used for packaging, first produced by Swiss chemist Jacques Edwin Brandenberger 1908. Cellophane is made from wood pulp, in much the same way that the artificial fibre ◊rayon is made: the pulp is dissolved in chemicals to form a viscose solution, which is then pumped through a long narrow slit into an acid bath where the emergent viscose stream turns into a film of pure cellulose.

cell sap dilute fluid found in the large central vacuole of many plant cells. It is made up of water, amino acids, glucose, and salts. The sap has many functions, including storage of useful materials, and provides mechanical support for non-woody plants.

cellular phone or ***cellphone*** mobile radio telephone, one of a network connected to the telephone system by a computer-controlled communication system.

cellulite fatty compound alleged by some dietitians to be produced in the body by liver disorder and to cause lumpy deposits on the hips and thighs. Medical opinion generally denies its existence, attributing the lumpy appearance to a type of subcutaneous fat deposit.

cellulitis inflammation of ◊connective tissue. It is usually due to bacterial infection.

celluloid transparent or translucent, highly flammable, plastic material (a ◊thermoplastic) made from cellulose nitrate and camphor. It was once used for toilet articles, novelties, and photographic film, but has now been replaced by the nonflammable substance cellulose acetate.

cellulose complex ◊carbohydrate composed of long chains of glucose units, joined by chemical bonds called glycosidic links. It is the principal constituent of the cell wall of higher plants, and a vital ingredient in the diet of many ◊herbivores. Molecules of cellulose are organized into long, unbranched microfibrils that give support to the cell wall. No mammal produces the enzyme cellulase, necessary for digesting cellulose; mammals such as rabbits and cows are only able to digest grass because the bacteria present in their gut can manufacture it. Cellulose forms a necessary part of the human diet as ◊fibre (roughage).

Cellulose is the most abundant substance found in the plant kingdom. It has numerous uses in industry: in rope-making; as a source of textiles (linen, cotton, viscose, and acetate) and plastics (cellophane and celluloid); in the manufacture of nondrip paint; and in such foods as whipped dessert toppings. Japanese chemists produced the first synthetic cellulose 1996.

cell wall in plants, the tough outer surface of the cell. It is constructed from a mesh of ◊cellulose and is very strong and relatively inelastic. Most living cells are turgid (swollen with water; see ◊turgor) and develop an internal hydrostatic pressure (wall pressure) that acts against the cellulose wall. The result of this turgor pressure is to give the cell, and therefore the plant, rigidity. Plants that are not woody are particularly reliant on this form of support.

Celsius scale of temperature, previously called centigrade, in which the range from freezing to boiling of water is divided into 100 degrees, freezing point being 0 degrees and boiling point 100 degrees. The degree centigrade (°) was officially renamed Celsius in 1948 to avoid confusion with the angular measure known as the centigrade (one hundredth of a grade). The Celsius scale is named after the Swedish astronomer Anders Celsius (1701–1744), who devised it in 1742 but in reverse (freezing point was 100°; boiling point 0°). *See list of tables on p. 1177.*

Celt (Greek *Keltoi*) the Indo-European people that originated in Alpine Europe and spread to the Iberian peninsula and beyond. They were ironworkers and farmers. In the 1st century BC they were defeated by the Roman Empire and by Germanic tribes and confined largely to Britain, Ireland, and N France. The Celts' first known territory was in central Europe about 1200 BC, in the basin of the upper Danube, the Alps, and parts of France and S Germany. In the 6th century they spread into Spain and Portugal. Over the next 300 years, they also spread into the British Isles (see ◊Britain, ancient), N Italy (sacking Rome 390 BC), Greece, the Balkans, and parts of Asia Minor, although they never established a united empire.

Between the Bronze and Iron Ages, in the 9th–5th centuries BC, they developed a transitional culture (named the Hallstatt culture after its archaeological site SW of Salzburg). They farmed, raised cattle, and were pioneers of ironworking, reaching their peak in the period from the 5th century to the Roman conquest (the La Tène culture). They had pronounced musical, literary, and poetical tastes, and were distinguished for their dramatic talents. Their Druids, or priests, performed ritual-magic ceremonies which survived in the forms of ◊ordeal, augury, and exorcism. Celtic languages survive in Ireland, Wales, Scotland, the Isle of Man, and Brittany, and have been revived in Cornwall.

Celt The Celtic cross, which was a distinctive feature of the Celtic Christianity that survived the fall of Rome in Ireland and Scotland, and spread to north Britain and flourished in Northumbria before the arrival of St Augustine from Rome. The design of the symbol, a cross in a circle, is said to derive ultimately from the ancient Egyptian symbol of life, known as the *ankh. Corbis*

Celtic art art of the Celtic peoples of western Europe, emerging about 500 BC, probably on the Rhine. It spread to most parts of Europe, but after the 1st century BC flourished only in Britain and Ireland, its influence being felt well into the 10th century AD. Pottery, woodwork, jewellery, and weapons are among its finest products, with manuscript illumination and stone crosses featuring in late Celtic art. Typically, Celtic art is richly decorated with flowing curves which, though based on animal and plant motifs, often form semi-abstract designs.

Early Celtic art, which reached its high point in 1st-century Britain, excelled in metalwork – in

cont. on p. 202

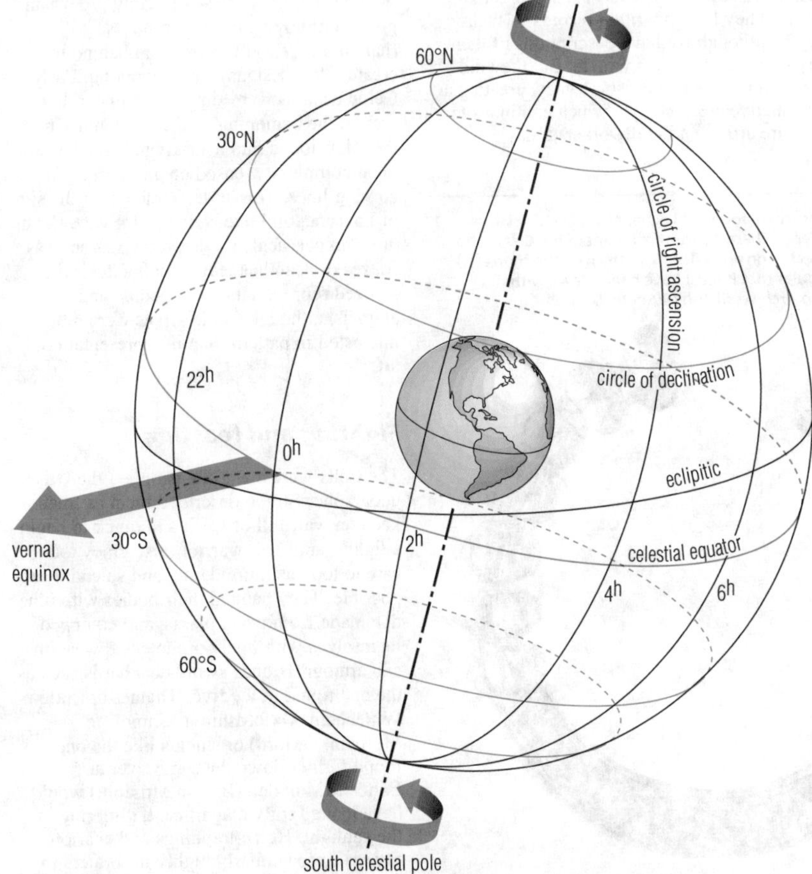

celestial sphere The main features of the celestial sphere. The equivalents of latitude and longitude on the celestial sphere are declination and right ascension. Declination runs from 0° at the celestial equator to 90° at the celestial poles. Right ascension is measured in hours eastwards from the vernal equinox, one hour corresponding to 15° of longitude.

The Art of the Celts

This Celtic bronze flagon, dating from the 5th or 4th century BC, was found in a burial mound at Basse Yutz, Moselle, France. Inlaid with coral and enamel in the form of an animal head, this jug would have been used at banquets by important figures. *Werner Forman Archive, British Museum, London*

The Celts were the most important of the peoples inhabiting prehistoric Europe. A society of warriors, farmers, and ironworkers, through the course of the first millenium BC they spread out from their original territory in central Europe westwards into France (Gaul), Spain, Portugal, and the British Isles; and eastwards into Italy, Greece, and parts of Asia. They left no written records of their own, although we have descriptions of them by Greek and Roman writers. But they did leave a remarkable artistic legacy, creating a distinctive abstract style which continues to inspire artists and craftworkers today.

A torque from the 1st century AD, found at Lochar Moss, Dumfriesshire, Scotland. Metal torques were a characteristic ornament of the Celts, who wore them around their necks and arms. The 'S' pattern on the central section of this one is so regular that it must have been drawn with compasses. *Werner Forman Archive, British Museum, London*

Masters of metal

Although the Celts in the Rhineland and southern Germany produced some sculpture in stone, and pottery decorated with Celtic designs is widespread, most Celtic art is in metal. Celtic smiths were highly skilled in working their materials – notably bronze and gold – employing casting, repoussé (hammering sheet bronze from behind to create relief designs), and engraving. Early Celtic designs were simple and linear, but around the beginning of the 5th century BC they developed into a striking abstract art of great complexity, based on an interplay of curving lines. This style, named after the site of La Tène, on Lake Neûchatel, Switzerland, drew on classical artistic prototypes such as friezes of acanthus leaves, palmettes, and stylized representations of people and animals, although Celtic artists were more interested in pattern than in representational art.

Fighting and feasting

The Celts were a warlike people – the Greek geographer Strabo described them as 'mad keen on war, full of spirit and quick to begin a fight'– and their warrior aristocracy took care to look as intimidating and splendid as possible. They painted their bodies with blue dye made from woad plants, and equipped themselves with finely ornamented weapons and armour. Bronze sword-scabbards such as the one found in the river Thames at Little Wittenham, Oxfordshire (Ashmolean Museum, Oxford) or shields like the one found further down the same river at Battersea, London (British Museum) would have looked truly magnificent, glittering in the sunlight. Horse-trappings and chariot-fittings were similarly highly decorated. In Britain the majority of such objects have been found in rivers or peat bogs, into which they were probably thrown as lavish offerings to the gods.

In Britain, the Celts found valuable sources of copper, lead, silver, and tin which they could mine and trade with mainland Europe for luxury goods such as gold, pottery, and wine. Apart from fighting, feasting seems to have been the Celts' favourite activity. Sometimes Greek, Etruscan, or Roman cups and flagons arrived in the Celtic world along with imported amphorae of wine. Frequently, however, such vessels were copied or adapted by Celtic artists in their own distinctive style. A pair of flagons from the 5th or 4th century BC found in Basse Yutz, Moselle (British Museum) is based on Etruscan designs but decorated in a far richer style. Each handle is in the form of a stylized wolf, whose two cubs crouch on the rim watching a little duck on the spout; these are far from the realistic creatures of classical art, and all their features are rendered as patterned shapes. Pieces of coral set around the bases and also in the spout add to the flagons' strange beauty.

Wine buckets were also decorated, such as those dating from perhaps 1st century BC found at Marlborough, Wiltshire (Devizes Museum) and at Aylesford, Kent (British Museum). The Marlborough bucket's body is covered in sheet bronze ornamented with repoussé masks, dancers wearing animal skins, horses, and panels of pattern; the Aylesford example is much simpler but the escutcheons into which the handle fits are in the form of helmeted heads. Such objects generally come from graves – presumably

This Celtic bronze shield, studded with red glass, was found in the river Thames at Battersea, London. Many pools and rivers were held sacred by the Celts, who often threw in metal objects as offerings to their gods. *Werner Forman Archive, British Museum, London*

placed there to ensure that their owners could enjoy the pleasures of the feast in the after life.

Ornaments for status and power

Status was immensely important to the Celts, and men and women of rank wore ornamented gold neck torques. Those from Waldalgesheim near Mainz, Germany (Romanisches Zentralmuseum, Mainz) date from the 4th century and are almost completely covered with decoration. Other examples, from what appears to be a deposit dedicated to the gods at Snettisham, Norfolk (British Museum), include many made of twisted gold wire, ornamented only at the terminals. The Roman historian Dio Cassius records that Boudicca, queen of the British tribe of the Iceni, wore such a torque a century later in AD 60, when rousing her people in revolt against Roman rule.

Perhaps the most beautiful examples of Celtic design from before the Roman conquest are the backs of mirrors, engraved with a linear design and cross-hatched infilling; dating from the second half of the 1st century BC and the beginning of the 1st century AD, these have been found only in Britain. One of the finest comes from a grave, probably that of a woman, at Birdlip, Gloucestershire (Gloucester City Museum) and there are other especially noteworthy examples from Holcombe, Devon and Desborough, Northamptonshire (both in the British Museum).

Later Celtic art

During the Roman period (in Britain approximately AD 43–410) Celtic art did not disappear. Brooches and horse-trappings ornamented with curvilinear devices and generally enamelled in bright colours were widely used in Roman Britain. The Celtic style also had a strong influence on bronzesmiths and sculptors working in the representational Roman manner, as shown by the mask of the male gorgon which embellished the pediment of the temple of Sulis Minerva at Bath (Roman Baths Museum, Bath) and the little bronze plaque depicting the goddess Minerva from Lavington, Wiltshire (Devizes Museum). Larger works in the purely Celtic style continued to be made outside the frontiers of the Roman empire, and especially in Ireland: for example, the Petrie crown (National Museum of Ireland, Dublin), possibly 2nd century AD, which has horns and discs ornamented with thin, flowing trumpet curves and stylized birds' heads.

This enamelled bronze plaque probably formed part of a horse's harness; it was found at a Gallo-Roman site at Paillard, Oise, France. Its symmetrical flowing curves and brightly coloured enamel are typical of Celtic design.
Werner Forman Archive, Musée Archéologique de Breteuil

Book of Kells Illumination depicting St Matthew from the 8th-century Book of Kells, Trinity College, Dublin. The intricately interlaced motifs surrounding the work are taken directly from early Celtic designs.
ET Archive

During the so-called Dark Ages that followed the end of the Roman empire there was a revival of Celtic art, exemplified by the 'hanging bowls' of the 5th and 6th centuries, which are frequently decorated with enamelled discs ornamented with S-curves and running scrolls. Perhaps the most magnificent is the great bronze bowl from the Anglo-Saxon ship burial at Sutton Hoo in Suffolk (British Museum) – decorated with scrolls and red enamel, it has a central pedestal surmounted by a finely decorated and enamelled fish.

The most splendid pieces of metalwork from this period come from Ireland, where Celtic art, untouched by Roman influence, was employed in the service of the Church. They include the superb chalice and paten from Derrynaflan, Co Tipperary (National Museum of Ireland, Dublin) and the Ardagh chalice from Co Limerick (also National Museum) made of silver and embellished with gold, amber, and enamels.

The influence of Celtic art was not restricted to metalwork, however. Although they incorporate classical and Ango-Saxon features, the finest and most accomplished examples of Celtic mastery of colour and pattern are the great illuminated Gospels from Lindisfarne, Northumberland (British Library), dating from the end of the 7th century, and the Book of Kells (Trinity College, Dublin) about a century later.

These manuscripts are truly examples of what the 12th-century traveller, Gerald of Wales, called 'the work of angels'.

MARTIN HENIG

SEE ALSO
Anglo-Saxon art; Britain, ancient; Celt; enamel; La Tène; metallurgy

particular weapons and jewellery. In Britain and Ireland, Celtic art flourished anew with the coming of Christianity, producing sculpture (stone crosses) and manuscript illumination, such as the Lindisfarne Gospels (British Museum, London) about AD 690. An outstanding example of Celtic art found in continental Europe is highly wrought metalwork, inlaid with coloured enamel and coral, found at La Tène, a site at Lake Neuchâtel, Switzerland. ▷ *See feature on pp. 200–201.*

Celtic languages branch of the Indo-European family, divided into two groups: the Brythonic or P-Celtic (Welsh, Cornish, Breton, and Gaulish) and the Goidelic or Q-Celtic (Irish, Scottish, and Manx Gaelic). Celtic languages once stretched from the Black Sea to Britain, but have been in decline for centuries, limited to the so-called 'Celtic fringe' of western Europe.

As their names suggest, a major distinction between the two groups is that where Brythonic has *p* (as in Old Welsh *map*, 'son') Goidelic has a *q* sound (as in Gaelic *mac*, 'son'). Gaulish is the long-extinct language of ancient Gaul. Cornish died out as a natural language in the late 18th century and Manx in 1974. All surviving Celtic languages have experienced official neglect in recent centuries and have suffered from emigration; currently, however, governments are more inclined than in the past to encourage their use.

Celtic League nationalist organization based in Ireland, aiming at an independent Celtic federation. It was founded 1961 with representatives from Alba (Scotland), Breizh (Brittany), Eire, Kernow (Cornwall), Cymru (Wales), and Ellan Vannin (Isle of Man).

Celtic Sea sea area bounded by Wales, Ireland, and SW England; the name is commonly used by workers in the oil industry to avoid nationalist significance. The Celtic Sea is separated from the Irish Sea by St George's Channel.

cembalo short form of ***clavicembalo***, an accompanying harpsichord. In classical orchestral music, such as that by Handel or Haydn, the cembalo part is taken by the conductor.

cement any bonding agent used to unite particles in a single mass or to cause one surface to adhere to another. Portland cement is a powder obtained from burning together a mixture of lime (or chalk) and clay, and when mixed with water and sand or gravel, turns into mortar or concrete.

In geology, cement refers to a chemically precipitated material such as carbonate that occupies the interstices of clastic rocks.

cenotaph (Greek 'empty tomb') monument to commemorate a person or persons not actually buried at the site, as in the Whitehall Cenotaph, London, designed by Edwin Lutyens to commemorate the dead of both world wars.

Cenozoic or ***Caenozoic*** era of geological time that began 65 million years ago and is still in process. It is divided into the Tertiary and Quaternary periods. The Cenozoic marks the emergence of mammals as a dominant group, including humans, and the formation of the mountain chains of the Himalayas and the Alps.

censor in ancient Rome, either of two senior magistrates, high officials elected every five years to hold office for 18 months. Their responsibilities included public morality, a census of the citizens, and a revision of the senatorial list.

censorship suppression by authority of material considered immoral, heretical, subversive, libellous, damaging to state security, or otherwise offensive. It is generally more stringent under totalitarian or strongly religious regimes and in wartime.

The British government uses the D-notice (a notice to the media prohibiting the publication of material alleged to be of importance to national security) and the ◊Official Secrets Act to protect itself. Laws relating to obscenity, libel, and blasphemy act as a form of censorship. The media exercise a degree of self-censorship. During the Gulf War 1991, access to the theatre of war was controlled by the US military: only certain reporters were allowed in and their movements were restricted. In the USA, despite First Amendment protection of free speech, attempts at censorship are made by government agencies or groups; the question is often tested in the courts, especially with respect to sexually explicit material. Recently, efforts have been made to suppress certain pieces of music and works of art, on such grounds as racial harassment and social depravity.

censorship, film control of the content and presentation of films. Film censorship dates back almost as far as the cinema. In Britain, censorship was established 1912, in the USA 1922. In some countries, self-regulation of the industry has not been regarded as sufficient; in the USSR, for example, state censorship forbade the treatment of certain issues.

Censorship in Britain is the responsibility of the British Board of Film Classification (formerly the British Board of Film Censors), run by the film industry, which gives each film a rating. There is a similar body, popularly called the Hays Office (after its first president, 1922–45, Will H Hays), in the USA.

census official count of the population of a country, originally for military call-up and taxation, later for assessment of social trends as other information regarding age, sex, and occupation of each individual was included. They may become unnecessary as computerized databanks are developed. The data collected are used by government departments in planning for the future in such areas as health, education, transport, and housing.

In the UK, a census has been conducted every ten years since 1801. Although the information about individual households remains secret for 100 years, data is available on groups of households down to about 200 (an enumeration district), showing such characteristics as age and sex structure, employment, housing types, car ownership, and qualifications held. The larger-scale information on population numbers, movements, and origins is published as a series of reports by the Office of Population Censuses and Surveys.

centipede A giant centipede of the species *Scolopendra*, active at night in the forests of Madagascar. Unlike millipedes, which have two pairs of legs to each body segment, centipedes have one pair of legs to a segment. They also have venomous fangs with which to immobilize their prey, mostly worms and insects but occasionally small vertebrates. *Premaphotos Wildlife*

centaur in Greek mythology, a creature half-human and half-horse. Centaurs were supposed to live in Thessaly, and be wild and lawless; the mentor of Heracles, Chiron, was an exception. The earliest representations of centaurs (about 1800–1000 BC) were excavated near Famagusta, Cyprus, 1962, and are two-headed. Some female representations also exist.

Centaurus large, bright constellation of the southern hemisphere, represented as a centaur. Its brightest star, ◊Alpha Centauri, is a triple star, and contains the closest star to the Sun, Proxima Centauri, which is only 4.3 light years away. Omega Centauri, which is just visible to the naked eye as a hazy patch, is the largest and brightest ◊globular cluster of stars in the sky, 16,000 light years away. Alpha and Beta Centauri are both of the first magnitude and, like Alpha and Beta Ursae Majoris, are known as 'the Pointers', as a line joining them leads to ◊Crux. Centaurus A, a galaxy 15 million light years away, is a strong source of radio waves and X-rays.

centigrade former name for the ◊Celsius temperature scale.

centipede jointed-legged animal of the group Chilopoda, members of which have a distinct head and a single pair of long antennae. Their bodies are composed of segments (which may number nearly 200), each of similar form and bearing a single pair of legs. Most are small, but the tropical *Scolopendra gigantea* may reach 30 cm/1 ft in length. Millipedes, class Diplopoda, have fewer segments (up to 100), but have two pairs of legs on each. Nocturnal, frequently blind, and all carnivorous, centipedes live in moist, dark places, and protect themselves by a poisonous secretion. They have a pair of poison claws, and strong jaws with poison fangs. The bite of some tropical species is dangerous to humans. Several species live in Britain, *Lithobius forficatus* being the most common.

Central African Republic landlocked country in Central Africa, bordered NE and E by Sudan, S by the Democratic Republic of Congo and the Congo, W by Cameroon, and NW by Chad. *See country box opposite.*

Central America the part of the Americas that links Mexico with the Isthmus of Panama, comprising Belize, Costa Rica, El Salvador, Guatemala, Honduras, Nicaragua, and Panama. It is crossed by mountains that form part of the Cordilleras, rising to a maximum height of 4,220 m/13,845 ft. There are numerous active volcanoes. Central America is about 523,000 sq km/200,000 sq mi in area and has a population (1980) estimated at 22,700,000, mostly Indians or mestizos (of mixed white-Indian ancestry). Tropical agricultural products and other basic commodities and raw materials are exported.

Much of Central America formed part of the ◊Maya civilization. Christopher Columbus first reached the isthmus 1502. Spanish settlers married indigenous women, and the area remained outside mainstream Spanish Empire history. When the Spanish Empire collapsed in the early 1800s, the area formed the Central American Federation, with a constitution based on that of the USA. The federation disintegrated 1840. Completion of the Panama Canal 1914 enhanced the region's position as a strategic international crossroads. Demand for cash crops (bananas, coffee, cotton), especially from the USA, created a strong landowning class controlling a serflike peasantry by military means. There has been US military intervention in the area, for example, in Nicaragua, where the dynasty of General Anastasio Somoza was founded. President Carter reversed support for such regimes, but in the 1980s, the Reagan and Bush administrations again favoured military and financial aid to right-wing political groups, including the ◊Contras in Nicaragua. Continuing US interest was underscored by its invasion of Panama Dec 1989.

Central American Common Market (CACM; ***Mercado Común Centroamericana*** MCCA) economic alliance established 1961 by El Salvador, Guatemala, Honduras (seceded 1970), and Nicaragua; Costa Rica joined 1962. Formed to encourage economic development and cooperation between the smaller Central American nations and to attract industrial capital, CACM failed to live up to early expectations: nationalist interests remained strong and by the mid-1980s political instability in the region and border conflicts between members were hindering its activities. Its offices are in Guatemala City, Guatemala.

Central Asian Republics group of five republics: ◊Kazakhstan, ◊Kyrgyzstan, ◊Tajikistan, ◊Turkmenistan, and ◊Uzbekistan. They were part of the Soviet Union until their independence was recognized 1991. They comprise a large part of the geographical region of ◊Turkestan and are the home of large numbers of Muslims. These areas were conquered by Russia as recently as 1866–73 and until 1917 were divided into the khanate of Khiva, the emirate of Bokhara, and the governor-generalship of Turkestan. The Soviet government became firmly established 1919, and in 1920 the Khan of Khiva and the Emir of Bokhara were overthrown and People's Republics set up. Turkestan became an Autonomous Soviet Socialist Republic 1921. Boundaries were redistributed 1925 along nationalist lines, and Uzbekistan, Tajikistan, and Turkmenistan became republics of the USSR, along with Bokhara and Khiva. The area populated by Kazakhs was united with Kazakhstan, which became a Union Republic 1936, the same year as Kyrgyzstan.

central bank the bank responsible for issuing currency in a country. Often it is also responsible for foreign-exchange dealings on behalf of the government and for supervising the banking system in the country (it holds the commercial reserves of the nation's clearing banks). Although typically independent of central government, a central bank will work closely with it, especially in implementing ◊monetary policy. The earliest bank to take on the role of central bank was the ◊Bank of England.

Central Command military strike force consisting of units from the US army, navy, and air force, which operates in the Middle East and North Africa. Its headquarters are in Fort McDill, Florida. It was established 1979, following the Iranian hostage crisis and the Soviet invasion of Afghanistan, and was known as the Rapid Deployment Force until 1983. It commanded coalition forces in the Gulf War 1991.

Central Criminal Court in the UK, crown court in the City of London, able to try all treasons and serious offences committed in the City or Greater London. First established 1834, it is popularly known as the Old Bailey after part of the medieval defences of London; the present building is on the site of Newgate Prison.

central dogma in genetics and evolution, the fundamental belief that ◊genes can affect the nature of the physical body, but that changes in the body (◊acquired character, for example, through use or accident) cannot be translated into changes in the genes.

Central Intelligence Agency (CIA) US intelligence organization established 1947. It has actively intervened overseas, generally to undermine left-wing regimes or to protect US financial interests. From 1980 all covert activity by the CIA had by law to be reported to Congress and to be authorized by the president. John M Deutch became CIA director 1995 after a scandal involving Aldrich Arnes, a CIA agent who had been a longtime mole for the KGB.

Developed from the wartime Office of Strategic Services and set up by Congress as part of the National Security Act, on the lines of the British Secret Service, the CIA was intended solely for use overseas in the Cold War. It was involved in the restoration of the Shah of Iran 1953, South Vietnam (during the Vietnam War), Chile (the coup against President Allende), and Cuba (the ◊Bay of Pigs). It was illegally involved in the ◊Watergate political scandal and in the 1970s lost public confidence when US influence collapsed in Iran, Afghanistan, Nicaragua, Yemen, and elsewhere.

CIA headquarters is in Langley, Virginia. Past directors include William Casey, Richard Helms, and George Bush. The CIA director is also coordinator of all the US intelligence organizations. Domestic intelligence functions are performed by the ◊Federal Bureau of Investigation. George Tenet became director 1997. He revealed the annual expenditure as $27 billion (£16.5 billion).

Central Lowlands one of the three geographical divisions of Scotland, occupying the fertile and densely populated plain that lies between two geological fault lines, which run nearly parallel NE–SW across Scotland from Stonehaven to Dumbarton and from Dunbar to Girvan.

central nervous system (CNS) the brain and spinal cord, as distinct from other components of the ◊nervous system. The CNS integrates all nervous functions. In invertebrates it consists of a paired ventral nerve cord with concentrations of nerve-cell bodies, known as ◊ganglia in each segment, and a small brain in the head. Some simple invertebrates, such as sponges and jellyfishes, have no CNS but a simple network of nerve cells called a nerve net.

Central Powers originally the signatories of the ◊Triple Alliance 1882: Germany, Austria–Hungary, and Italy; the name derived from the geographical position of the Germans and Austrians in Central Europe. During World War I, Italy remained neutral before joining the ◊Allies.

central processing unit (CPU) main component of a computer, the part that executes individual program instructions and controls the operation of other parts. It is sometimes called the central processor or, when contained on a single integrated circuit, a microprocessor. The CPU has three main components: the arithmetic and logic unit (ALU), where all calculations and logical operations are carried out; a control unit, which decodes, synchronizes, and executes program instructions; and the immediate access memory, which stores the data and programs on which the computer is currently working. All these components contain registers, which are rapidly accessible memory locations reserved for specific purposes. *See illustration on following page.*

Centre region of N central France; area 39,200 sq km/15,131 sq mi; population (1990) 2,371,000. Centre includes the *départements* of Cher, Eure-et-Loire, Indre, Indre-et-Loire, Loire-et-Cher, and Loiret. Its capital is Orléans.

CENTRAL AFRICAN REPUBLIC

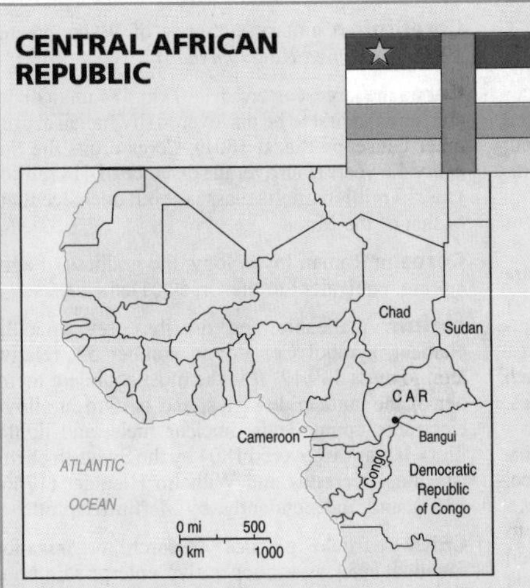

national name *République Centrafricaine*
area 622,436 sq km/240,260 sq mi
capital Bangui
major towns/cities Berbérati, Bouar, Bossangoa
physical features landlocked flat plateau, with rivers flowing N and S, and hills in NE and SW; dry in N, rainforest in SW; mostly wooded; Kotto and Mbali river falls; the Oubangui River rises 6 m/20 ft at Bangui during the wet season (June–Nov)
head of state Ange-Felix Patasse from 1993
head of government Gabriel Koyambounou from 1995
political system emergent democratic republic
administrative divisions 16 prefectures
political parties Central African People's Liberation Party (MPLC), left of centre; Central African Democratic Rally (RDC), nationalist, right of centre
population 3,315,000 (1995 est)
population growth rate 2.5% (1990–95); 2.3% (2000–05)
ethnic distribution over 80 ethnic groups, but 66% of the population falls into one of three: the Banda (30%), the Baya-Mandjia (29%), and the Mbaka (7%). There are clearly defined ethnic zones; the forest region, inhabited by Bantu groups, the Mbaka, Lissongo, Mbimu, and Babinga; the river banks, populated by the Sango, Yakoma, Baniri, and Buraka; and the savanna region, where the Banda, Sande, Sara, Ndle, and Bizao live. Europeans number less than 7,000, the majority being French
life expectancy 48 (males), 53 (females)
literacy rate men 52%, women 25%
languages French (official), Sangho (national), Arabic, Hunsa, and Swahili
religions Protestant, Roman Catholic, Muslim, animist
currency franc CFA
GDP (US $) 872 million (1994)
growth rate 5.8% (1994)
exports diamonds, uranium, coffee, cotton, hardwoods, tobacco

HISTORY

10th C Immigration by peoples from Sudan to E and Cameroon to W.
16th C Part of the Gaoga Empire.
16th–18th Cs Population reduced greatly by slave raids both by coastal traders and Arab empires in Sudan and Chad.
19th C The Zande nation of the Bandia peoples became powerful in E. Bantu speakers immigrated from Zaire and the Baya from N Cameroon.
1889–1903 The French established control over the area, quelling insurrections; a French colony known as Oubangi-Chari was formed and partitioned among commercial concessionaries.
1920–30 Series of rebellions against forced labour on coffee and cotton plantations savagely repressed by French.
1946 Given a territorial assembly and representation in French parliament.
1958 Granted self-government within French Equatorial Africa, with Barthélémy Boganda, founder of the pro-independence Movement for the Social Evolution of Black Africa (MESAN) prime minister.
1960 Achieved independence as Central African Republic; David Dacko, nephew of the late Boganda, elected president.
1962 The republic made a one-party state, dominated by MESAN and loyal to the French interest.
1965 Dacko ousted in military coup led by Col Jean-Bedel Bokassa as the economy deteriorated.
1972 Bokassa, a violent and eccentric autocrat, declared himself president for life.
1977 Bokassa made himself emperor of the 'Central African Empire'.
1979 Bokassa deposed by Dacko in French-backed bloodless coup, following violent repressive measures including the massacre of 100 children by the self-styled emperor, who went into exile.
1981 Dacko deposed in a bloodless coup, led by General André Kolingba, and military government established.
1983 Clandestine opposition movement formed.
1984 Amnesty for all political party leaders announced. President Mitterrand of France paid a state visit.
1988 Bokassa, who had returned from exile, found guilty of murder and embezzlement; he received death sentence, later commuted to life imprisonment.
1991 Opposition parties allowed to form.
1992 Multiparty elections promised, but cancelled with Kolingba in last place.
1993 Kolingba released several thousand prisoners, including Bokassa. Ange-Felix Patasse of the leftist African People's Labour Party (MLPC) elected president, ending twelve years of military dictatorship.
1996 Army revolt over pay; Patasse forced into hiding.

SEE ALSO Bokassa, Jean-Bédel

central processing unit The central processing unit is the 'brain' of a computer; it is here that all the computer's work is done. The arithmetic and logic unit (ALU) does the arithmetic, using the registers to store intermediate results, supervised by the control unit. Input and output circuits connect the ALU to external memory, input, and output devices.

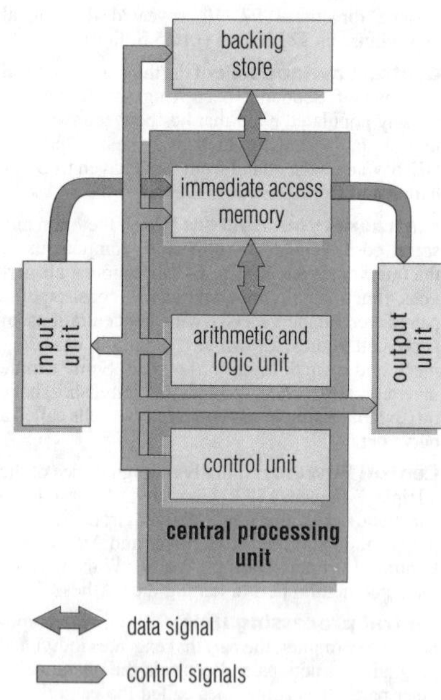

Every man is as God made him, and often even worse.

MIGUEL CERVANTES
Don Quixote

centre of mass point in or near an object about which the object would turn if allowed to rotate freely. A symmetrical homogeneous object such as a sphere or cube has its centre of mass at its geometrical centre; a hollow object (such as a cup) may have its centre of mass in space inside the hollow.

centrifugal force useful concept in physics, based on an apparent (but not real) force. It may be regarded as a force that acts radially outward from a spinning or orbiting object, thus balancing the ◊centripetal force (which is real). For an object of mass m moving with a velocity v in a circle of radius r, the centrifugal force F equals mv^2/r (outward).

centripetal force force that acts radially inward on an object moving in a curved path. For example, with a weight whirled in a circle at the end of a length of string, the centripetal force is the tension in the string. For an object of mass m moving with a velocity v in a circle of radius r, the centripetal force F equals mv^2/r (inward). The reaction to this force is the ◊centrifugal force.

cephalopod any predatory marine mollusc of the class Cephalopoda, with the mouth and head surrounded by tentacles. Cephalopods are the most intelligent, the fastest-moving, and the largest of all animals without backbones, and there are remarkable luminescent forms which swim or drift at great depths. They have the most highly developed nervous and sensory systems of all invertebrates, the eye in some closely paralleling that found in vertebrates. Examples include octopus, squid, and cuttlefish. Shells are rudimentary or absent in most cephalopods. Typically, they move by swimming with the mantle (fold of outer skin) aided by the arms, but can squirt water out of the siphon (funnel) to propel themselves backwards by jet propulsion.

cereal Wheat is the most widely cultivated cereal in the West, where bread forms the staple diet of many millions of people. Modern strains of wheat have been selectively bred to produce more grain, and to be resistant both to disease and to damage from wind and rain. Other major cereals include rice, maize, barley, and oats. *Premaphotos Wildlife*

cephalosporin any of a class of broad-spectrum antibiotics derived from a fungus (genus *Cephalosporium*). They are similar to penicillins and are used on penicillin-resistant infections.

Cepheid variable yellow supergiant star that varies regularly in brightness every few days or weeks as a result of pulsations. The time that a Cepheid variable takes to pulsate is directly related to its average brightness; the longer the pulsation period, the brighter the star. This relationship, the period luminosity law, allows astronomers to use Cepheid variables as 'standard candles' to measure distances in our Galaxy and to nearby galaxies. They are named after their prototype, Delta Cephei, whose light variations were observed 1784 by English astronomer John Goodricke (1764–1786).

Cepheus constellation of the north polar region. It contains the Garnet Star (Mu Cephei), a red supergiant of variable brightness that is one of the reddest-coloured stars known, and Delta Cephei, prototype of the ◊Cepheid variables.

ceramics objects made from clay, hardened into a permanent form by baking (firing) at very high temperatures in a kiln. Ceramics are used for building construction and decoration (bricks, tiles), for specialist industrial uses (linings for furnaces used to manufacture steel, fuel elements in nuclear reactors, and so on), and for plates and vessels used in the home. Different types of clay and different methods and temperatures of firing create a variety of results. Ceramics may be cast in a mould or hand-built out of slabs of clay, coiled, or thrown on a wheel. Technically, the main categories are ◊earthenware, ◊stoneware, and hard- and softpaste porcelain (see under ◊pottery and porcelain).

Examples through Western history:

Roman period potter's wheel; lead glazing; decorative use of slip (watered-down clay)

medieval period *sgraffito* (scratched) tiles and other products (earthenware decorated with slip of a contrasting colour, which is then scratched through) such as those made in Bologna, Italy. Lead-glazed jugs made in England and France, coloured bright green or yellow-brown with copper or iron oxides. Tin-glazed ware in S Italy and Spain by 13th century, influenced by established Islamic techniques

14th-century Germany stoneware developed from hard earthenwares; tin glazes developed; colour added by thin slips mixed with high-temperature colours. Later, mottled brown glaze recognized as characteristic of Cologne, referred to as 'tigerware' in Britain

15th century Hispano-Moresque painted ware imitated by Italians, developing into majolica by mid-century, using the full range of high-temperature colours; centres of the craft included Tuscany, Faenza, Urbino, and Venice. Some potteries, such as that at Gubbio, additionally used lustre glazes. Typical products are dishes and apothecary jars

16th century potters from Faenza spread tin-glazed earthenware (majolica) skills to France, Spain, and the Netherlands, where it became known as faience; from Antwerp the technique spread to England. The English in the 17th century named Dutch faience 'Delftware', after the main centre of production

17th century faience centres developed at Rouen and Moustiers in France, Alcora in Spain, and in Switzerland, Austria, and Germany. Blue underglaze was increasingly used, in imitation of Chinese blue and white designs, reflecting the growth of orientalism

18th century European developments in porcelain, also in using a rich palette of low-temperature enamel colours. The vitreous enamel process, first developed at Strasbourg about 1750, spread around N Europe.

Cerberus in Greek mythology, the three-headed dog guarding the entrance to ◊Hades, the underworld.

cereal grass grown for its edible, nutrient-rich, starchy seeds. The term refers primarily to wheat, oats, rye, and barley, but may also refer to maize (corn), millet, and rice. Cereals contain about 75% complex carbohydrates and 10% protein, plus fats and fibre (roughage). They store well. If all the world's cereal crop were consumed as whole-grain products directly by humans, everyone could obtain adequate protein and carbohydrate; however, a large proportion of cereal production in affluent nations is used as animal feed to boost the production of meat, dairy products, and eggs. The term also refers to breakfast foods prepared from the seeds of cereal crops.

cerebellum part of the brain of ◊vertebrate animals which controls muscle tone, movement, balance, and coordination. It is relatively small in lower animals such as newts and lizards, but large in birds since flight demands precise coordination. The human cerebellum is also well developed, because of the need for balance when walking or running, and for finely coordinated hand movements.

cerebral haemorrhage or ***apoplectic fit*** in medicine, a form of ◊stroke in which there is bleeding from a cerebral blood vessel into the surrounding brain tissue. It is generally caused by degenerative disease of the arteries and high blood pressure. Depending on the site and extent of bleeding, the symptoms vary from transient weakness and numbness to deep coma and death. Damage to the brain is permanent, though some recovery can be made. Strokes are likely to recur.

cerebral palsy any nonprogressive abnormality of the brain occurring during or shortly after birth. It is caused by oxygen deprivation, injury during birth, haemorrhage, meningitis, viral infection, or faulty development. Premature babies are at greater risk of being born with cerebral palsy, and in 1996 US researchers linked this to low levels of the thyroid hormone thyroxine. The condition is characterized by muscle spasm, weakness, lack of coordination, and impaired movement; or there may be spastic paralysis, with fixed deformities of the limbs. Intelligence is not always affected.

cerebrum part of the vertebrate ◊brain, formed from the two paired cerebral hemispheres, separated by a central fissure. In birds and mammals it is the largest and most developed part of the brain. It is covered with an infolded layer of grey matter, the cerebral cortex, which integrates brain functions. The cerebrum coordinates all voluntary activity.

Ceredigion unitary authority of Wales created 1996 (*see United Kingdom map*).

Ceres the largest asteroid, 940 km/584 mi in diameter, and the first to be discovered (by Italian astronomer Giuseppe Piazzi 1801). Ceres orbits the Sun every 4.6 years at an average distance of 414 million km/257 million mi. Its mass is about one-seventieth of that of the Moon.

Ceres in Roman mythology, the goddess of agriculture, equivalent to the Greek ◊Demeter.

cerium malleable and ductile, grey, metallic element, symbol Ce, atomic number 58, relative atomic mass 140.12. It is the most abundant member of the lanthanide series, and is used in alloys, electronic components, nuclear fuels, and lighter flints. It was discovered 1804 by the Swedish chemists Jöns Berzelius and Wilhelm Hisinger (1766–1852), and, independently, by Martin Klaproth.

CERN particle physics research organization founded 1954 as a cooperative enterprise among European governments. It has laboratories at Meyrin, near Geneva, Switzerland. It was originally known as the *Conseil Européen pour la Recherche Nucléaire* but subsequently renamed *Organisation Européenne pour la Recherche Nucléaire*, although still familiarly known as CERN. It houses the world's largest particle ◊accelerator, the ◊Large Electron Positron Collider (LEP), with which notable advances have been made in ◊particle physics.

In 1965 the original laboratory was doubled in size by extension across the border from Switzerland into France. In 1994 the 19 member nations of CERN approved the construction of the Large Hadron Collider. It is expected to cost £1.25 million and to be fully functional 2005.

Cervantes Saavedra, Miguel de 1547–1616. Spanish novelist, dramatist, and poet. His masterpiece ◊*Don Quixote de la Mancha* (in full *El ingenioso hidalgo Don Quixote de la Mancha*) was published 1605. In 1613 his *Novelas ejemplares/ Exemplary Novels* appeared, followed by *Viaje del*

Parnaso/The Voyage to Parnassus 1614. A spurious second part of *Don Quixote* prompted Cervantes to bring out his own second part 1615, often considered superior to the first in construction and characterization.

Cervantes entered the army in Italy, and was wounded in the sea battle of Lepanto 1571 against the Ottoman empire. On his way back to Spain 1575, he was captured by Barbary pirates and taken to Algiers, where he became a slave until ransomed 1580.

cervical cancer ◊cancer of the cervix (neck of the womb).

cervical smear removal of a small sample of tissue from the cervix (neck of the womb) to screen for changes implying a likelihood of cancer. The procedure is also known as the Pap test after its originator, George Papanicolau.

cervix (Latin 'neck') abbreviation for ***cervix uteri***, the neck of the womb; see ◊uterus.

Cesalpino Andrea 1519–1603. Italian botanist who showed that plants could be and should be classified by their anatomy and structure. In *De plantis* 1583, Cesalpino offered the first remotely modern classification of plants. Before this plants were classed by their location – for example marsh plants, moorland plants, and even foreign plants.

Cetewayo (Cetshwayo) c. 1826–1884. King of Zululand, South Africa, 1873–83, whose rule was threatened by British annexation of the Transvaal 1877. Although he defeated the British at Isandhlwana 1879, he was later that year defeated by them at Ulundi. Restored to his throne 1883, he was then expelled by his subjects.

Cetus (Latin 'whale') large constellation on the celestial equator (see ◊celestial sphere), represented as a sea monster or a whale. Cetus contains the long-period variable star ◊Mira, and Tau Ceti, one of the nearest stars visible with the naked eye. Mira is sometimes the most conspicuous object in the constellation, but it is more usually invisible to the naked eye.

Ceylon former name (to 1972) of ◊Sri Lanka.

Cézanne Paul 1839–1906. French Post-Impressionist painter. He was a leading figure in the development of modern art. He broke away from the Impressionists' concern with the ever-changing effects of light to develop a style that tried to capture the structure of natural forms, whether in landscapes, still lifes, or portraits. *Cardplayers* about 1890–95 (Louvre, Paris) is typical of his work.

Cézanne had no regular training, and his early work had an undisciplined and Romantic enthusiasm for Delacroix, Daumier and Courbet; his real apprenticeship began in the 1870s when his friendship with Camille ◊Pissarro brought him within the orbit of Impressionism.

CFC abbreviation for ◊***chlorofluorocarbon***.

Chablis white burgundy wine produced near the town of the same name in the Yonne *département* of central France.

Chabrol Claude 1930– . French film director. Originally a critic, he was one of the ◊New Wave directors. His works of murder and suspense, which owe much to Hitchcock, include *Les Cousins/The Cousins* 1959, *Les Biches/The Girlfriends* 1968, *Le Boucher/The Butcher* 1970, *Cop au Vin* 1984, and *L'Enfer*.

Chaco province of Argentina; area 99,633 sq km/38,458 sq mi; population (1991) 838,300. Its capital is Resistencia, in the SE. The chief crop is cotton, and there is forestry. It includes many lakes, swamps, and forests, producing timber and quebracho (a type of wood used in tanning). Until 1951 it was a territory, part of Gran Chaco, a great zone, mostly level, stretching into Paraguay and Bolivia. The N of Gran Chaco was the scene of the Chaco War.

Chaco War war between Bolivia and Paraguay 1932–35 over boundaries in the north of Gran Chaco, settled by arbitration 1938.

Chad landlocked country in central N Africa, bounded N by Libya, E by Sudan, S by the Central African Republic, and W by Cameroon, Nigeria, and Niger. *See country box on p. 206.*

Chad, Lake lake on the northeastern boundary of Nigeria. It once varied in extent between rainy and dry seasons from 50,000 sq km/20,000 sq mi to 20,000 sq km/7,000 sq mi, but a series of droughts 1979–89 reduced its area by 80%. The S Chad irrigation project used the lake waters to irrigate the surrounding desert, but the 4,000 km/2,500 mi of canals dug for the project are now permanently dry because of the shrinking size of the lake. The Lake Chad basin is being jointly developed for oil and natron by Cameroon, Chad, Niger, and Nigeria.

chador (Hindi 'square of cloth') all-enveloping black garment for women worn by some Muslims and Hindus. The origin of the chador dates to the 6th century BC under Cyrus the Great and the Achaemenian empire in Persia. Together with the ◊purdah (Persian 'veil') and the idea of female seclusion, it persisted under Alexander the Great and the Byzantine Empire, and was adopted by the Arab conquerors of the Byzantines. Its use was revived in Iran in the 1970s by Ayatollah Khomeini in response to the Koranic request for 'modesty' in dress.

Chaeronea, Battle of Macedonian victory over the confederated Greek army (Athenians and Thebans) 338 BC; this battle marked the end of Greek independence and its subjection to Philip II of Macedon.

chaffinch bird *Fringilla coelebs* of the finch family, common throughout much of Europe and W Asia. About 15 cm/6 in long, the male is olive-brown above, with a bright chestnut breast, a bluish-grey cap, and two white bands on the upper part of the wing; the female is duller. During winter they form single-sex flocks.

Chagall Marc 1887–1985. Belarusian-born French painter and designer. Much of his highly coloured, fantastic imagery was inspired by the village life of his boyhood and by Jewish and Russian folk traditions. He was an original figure, often seen as a precursor of Surrealism. *I and the Village* 1911 (Museum of Modern Art, New York) is characteristic.

Chagall studied painting under Leon Bakst in St Petersburg and then in Paris 1910–14, where, largely ignoring avant-garde movements, he concentrated on his highly personal fantasy. He worked in Russia during World War I but returned to Paris 1922 and lived mainly in France from then on. He designed mosaics (for Israel's Knesset in the 1960s), the ceiling of the Paris Opera House 1964, tapestries, stage sets, and stained glass. He also produced illustrated books, in particular editions of the Bible and La Fontaine's *Fables*.

Chagas's disease disease common in Central and South America, infecting approximately 18 million people worldwide. It is caused by a trypanosome parasite, *Trypanosoma cruzi*, transmitted by several species of blood-sucking insect; it results in incurable damage to the heart, intestines, and brain. In its first stage symptoms resemble flu but 20–30% of sufferers develop inflammation of the heart muscles up to 20 years later. It is named after Brazilian doctor Carlos Chagas (1879–1934).

Cetewayo Cetewayo, king of Zululand, South Africa. He was king from 1873 until he was captured after the defeat of the Zulus by the British 1879. *Corbis*

Chain Ernst Boris 1906–1979. German-born British biochemist. After the discovery of ◊penicillin by Alexander ◊Fleming, Chain worked to isolate and purify it. For this work, he shared the 1945 Nobel Prize for Medicine with Fleming and Howard ◊Florey. Chain also discovered penicillinase, an enzyme that destroys penicillin. *See illustration on following page.*

chain reaction in chemistry, a succession of reactions, usually involving ◊free radicals, where the products of one stage are the reactants of the next. A chain reaction is characterized by the continual generation of reactive substances. A chain reaction comprises three separate stages: initiation – the initial generation of reactive species; propagation – reactions that involve reactive species and generate similar or different reactive species; and termination – reactions that involve the reactive species but produce only stable, nonreactive substances. Chain reactions may occur slowly (for example, the oxidation of edible oils) or accelerate as the number of reactive species increases, ultimately resulting in explosion.

chain reaction in nuclear physics, a fission reaction that is maintained because neutrons released by the splitting of some atomic nuclei themselves go on to split others, releasing even more neutrons. Such a reaction can be controlled (as in a nuclear reactor) by using moderators to absorb excess neutrons. Uncontrolled, a chain reaction produces a nuclear explosion (as in an atom bomb).

Chaka alternative spelling of ◊Shaka, Zulu chief.

Cézanne *Still Life* 1900–06 by Paul Cézanne, J Paul Getty Museum, Malibu, California, USA. Painted towards the end of his life, this still life foreshadows the school of early 20th-century abstract painting that Cézanne inspired. In his still lifes and landscapes, he attempted to reduce all natural forms to the geometric basics of cone, sphere, or cube. *Royal Academy of Arts*

Chain Nobel laureate biochemist Ernst Chain. Chain won the prize for Physiology or Medicine 1945 after purifying penicillin in collaboration with Howard Florey at the William Dunn School of Pathology in Oxford. They shared the prize with Alexander Fleming, who identified the drug. *Image Select (UK) Ltd*

‘The day of small nations has long passed away. The day of Empires has come.’

JOSEPH CHAMBERLAIN
Speech in Birmingham
12 May 1904

Chalcedon, Council of ecumenical council of the early Christian church, convoked 451 by the Roman emperor Marcian, and held at Chalcedon (now Kadiköy, Turkey). The council, attended by over 500 bishops, resulted in the Definition of Chalcedon, an agreed doctrine for both the Eastern and Western churches.

chalcedony form of the mineral quartz, SiO_2, in which the crystals are so fine-grained that they are impossible to distinguish with a microscope (cryptocrystalline). Agate, onyx, and carnelian are ◊gem varieties of chalcedony.

chalcopyrite copper iron sulphide mineral, $CuFeS_2$, the most common ore of copper. It is brassy yellow in colour and may have an iridescent surface tarnish. It occurs in many different types of mineral vein, in rocks ranging from basalt to limestone.

Chaldaea ancient region of Babylonia.

Chaliapin Fyodor Ivanovich 1873–1938. Russian bass singer, born in Kazan (Tatar Republic). He achieved fame in the West through his charismatic recordings, notably as Boris in Mussorgsky's opera *Boris Godunov*. He specialized in Russian, French, and Italian roles.

chalice cup, usually of precious metal, used in celebrating the ◊Eucharist in the Christian church.

chalk soft, fine-grained, whitish sedimentary rock composed of calcium carbonate, $CaCO_3$, extensively quarried for use in cement, lime, and mortar, and in the manufacture of cosmetics and toothpaste. Blackboard chalk in fact consists of ◊gypsum (calcium sulphate, $CaSO_4.2H_2O$).

Chalk was once thought to derive from the remains of microscopic animals or foraminifera, but in 1953 it was seen to be composed chiefly of coccolithophores, unicellular lime-secreting algae, and hence primarily of plant origin. It is formed from deposits of deep-sea sediments called oozes. Chalk was laid down in the later ◊Cretaceous period and covers a wide area in Europe. In England it stretches in a belt from Wiltshire and Dorset, continuously across Buckinghamshire and Cambridgeshire to Lincolnshire and Yorkshire, and also forms the North and South Downs, and the cliffs of S and SE England.

Challenger orbiter used in the US ◊space shuttle programme which, on 28 Jan 1986, exploded on take-off, killing all seven crew members.

Chalmers Thomas 1780–1847. Scottish theologian. At the Disruption of the ◊Church of Scotland 1843, Chalmers withdrew from the church along with a large number of other priests, and became principal of the Free Church college, thus founding the ◊Free Church of Scotland.

Châlons-sur-Marne capital of the *département* of Marne, NE France; population (1990) 51,500. It is a market town and trades mainly in champagne. Tradition has it that Attila was defeated in his attempt to invade France at the Battle of Châlons 451 by the Roman general Aëtius and the Visigoth Theodoric.

Chamberlain (Joseph) Austen 1863–1937. British Conservative politician, elder son of Joseph Chamberlain; as foreign secretary 1924–29 he negotiated the Pact of ◊Locarno, for which he won the Nobel Peace Prize 1925, and signed the ◊Kellogg–Briand pact to outlaw war 1928.

He was elected to Parliament 1892 as a Liberal-Unionist, and after holding several minor posts was chancellor of the Exchequer 1903–06. During World War I he was secretary of state for India 1915–17 and member of the war cabinet 1918. He was chancellor of the Exchequer 1919–21 and Lord Privy Seal 1921–22, but failed to secure the leadership of the party 1922, as many Conservatives resented the part he had taken in the Irish settlement of 1921. He was foreign secretary in the Baldwin government 1924–29, and negotiated and signed the Locarno Pact 1925 to fix the boundaries of Germany, and the Kellogg–Briand pact 1928 to ban war and provide for peaceful settlement of disputes.

Chamberlain Joseph 1836–1914. British politician, reformist mayor of and member of Parliament for Birmingham; in 1886, he resigned from the cabinet over William Gladstone's policy of home rule for Ireland, and led the revolt of the Liberal-Unionists.

In 1876 he was elected to Parliament and joined the republican group led by Charles Dilke, the extreme left wing of the Liberal Party. In 1880 he entered Gladstone's cabinet as president of the Board of Trade. The climax of his radical period was reached with the unauthorized programme, advocating, among other things, free education, graduated taxation, and smallholdings of ‘three acres and a cow’.

Chamberlain (Arthur) Neville 1869–1940. British Conservative politician, prime minister 1937–40. His policy of appeasement toward the Italian fascist dictator Benito Mussolini and German Nazi Adolf Hitler (with whom he concluded

CHAD
Republic of

national name *République du Tchad*
area 1,284,000 sq km/495,624 sq mi
capital N'djaména (formerly Fort Lamy)
major towns/cities Sarh, Moundou, Abéché, Bongor, Doba
physical features landlocked state with mountains (Tibetsi) and part of Sahara Desert in N; moist savanna in S; rivers in S flow NW to Lake Chad
head of state Idriss Deby from 1990
head of government Nassour Ouaidou Guelendouksia from 1997
political system emergent democratic republic
administrative divisions 14 prefectures
political parties Patriotic Salvation Movement (MPS), centre-left; Alliance for Democracy and Progress (RDP), centre-left; Union for Democracy and Progress (UPDT), centre-left; Action for Unity and Socialism (ACTUS), centre-left; Union for Democracy and the Republic (UDR), centre-left
population 6,361,000 (1995 est)
population growth rate 2.7% (1990–95); 2.5%
ethnic distribution mainly Arabs in the N, and Pagan, or Kirdi, groups in the S. There is no single dominant group in any region, the largest are the Sara, who comprise about a quarter of the total population. Europeans, mainly French, constitute a very small minority
life expectancy 46 (males), 49 (females)
literacy rate men 62%, women 18%
languages French, Arabic (both official), over 100 African languages spoken
religions Muslim, Christian, animist
currency franc CFA
GDP (US $) 910 million (1994)
growth rate 4.0% (1994 est)
exports cotton, meat, livestock, hides, skins

HISTORY
7th–9th Cs Berber pastoral nomads, the Zaghawa, immigrated from north and became ruling aristocracy, dominating the Sao people, sedentary black farmers, and established Kanem state.
9th–19th Cs The Zaghawa's Saifi dynasty formed the kingdom of Bornu, which stretched to the W and S of Lake Chad, and converted to Islam in the 11th century. At its height between the 15th and 18th centuries, it raided the S for slaves, and faced rivalry from the 16th century from the Baguirmi and Ouadai Arab kingdoms.
1820s Visited by British explorers.
1890s–1901 Conquered by France, who ended slave raiding by Arab kingdoms.
1910 Became a colony in French Equatorial Africa and cotton production expanded in the S.
1944 The pro-Nazi Vichy government signed agreement giving Libya rights to the Aouzou Strip in N Chad.
1946 Became overseas territory of French Republic, with its own territorial assembly and representation in the French parliament.
1960 Independence achieved, with François Tombalbaye of the Chadian Progressive Party (CPT), dominated by Sara Christians from the S, as president.
1963 Violent opposition in the Muslim N, led by the Chadian National Liberation Front (Frolinat), backed by Libya following the banning of opposition parties.
1968 Revolt of northern militias quelled with France's help.
1973 Africanization campaign launched by Tombalbaye, who changed his first name to Ngarta.
1975 Tombalbaye killed in military coup led by southerner General Félix Malloum. Frolinat continued its resistance.
1978 Malloum tried to find a political solution by forming a coalition government with former Frolinat leader Hissène Habré, but it soon broke down.
1979 Malloum forced to leave the country; interim government set up under General Goukouni Oueddei (Frolinat). Habré continued his opposition with his Army of the North (FAN), and Libya provided support for Goukouni.
1981–82 Habré gained control of half the country. Goukouni fled and set up a ‘government in exile’.
1983 Habré's regime recognized by the Organization of African Unity (OAU) and France, but in the N, Goukouni's supporters, with Libya's help, fought on. Eventually a cease-fire was agreed, with latitude 16°N dividing the country.
1987 Chad, France, and Libya agreed on OAU cease-fire to end the civil war between the Muslim Arab N and Christian and animist black African S.
1988 Libya relinquished its claims to the Aouzu Strip on the Chad–Libya border.
1989 Signed peace agreement with Libya.
1990 President Habré ousted after army defeated by Libyan-backed Patriotic Salvation Movement (MPS) rebel troops based in the Sudan and led by Habré's former ally Idriss Deby.
1991–92 Several antigovernment coups foiled.
1993 Transitional charter adopted, as prelude to full democracy at a later date.
1996 Deby won Chad's first democratic presidential election.
1997 Nassour Ouiadou Guelendouksia appointed prime minister.

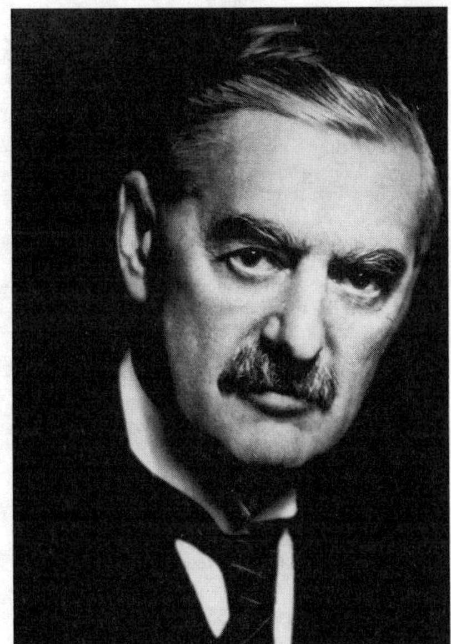

Chamberlain Neville Chamberlain, British prime minister after Stanley Baldwin. Chamberlain became prime minister in 1937, and is best known for his policy of appeasement. This policy did not prevent war, however, and Chamberlain resigned in 1940, to be succeeded by Winston Churchill. *Corbis*

the ◊Munich Agreement 1938) failed to prevent the outbreak of World War II. He resigned 1940 following the defeat of the British forces in Norway.

Chamberlain was born in Birmingham, of which he was lord mayor 1915. He was minister of health 1923 and 1924–29, and his policies centred on slum clearance. In 1931 he was chancellor of the Exchequer in the national government, and in 1937 succeeded Stanley Baldwin as prime minister. Trying to close the old Anglo-Irish feud, he agreed to return to Eire those ports that had been occupied by the navy. In 1938 he went to Munich and negotiated with Hitler the settlement of the Czechoslovak question. He was ecstatically received on his return, and claimed that the Munich Agreement brought 'peace in our time'. Within a year, however, Britain was at war with Germany.

Chamberlain, Lord in the UK, chief officer of the royal household who engages staff and appoints retail suppliers. Until 1968 the Lord Chamberlain licensed and censored plays before their public performance. The office is temporary, and appointments are made by the government.

chamber music music intended for performance in a small room or chamber, rather than in the concert hall, and usually written for instrumental combinations, played with one instrument to a part, as in the ◊string quartet. Chamber music developed as an instrumental alternative to earlier music for voices such as the madrigal, which allowed accompanying instruments little freedom for technical display.

chameleon any of 80 or so species of lizard of the family Chameleontidae. Some species have highly developed colour-changing abilities, caused by stress and changes in the intensity of light and temperature, which alter the dispersal of pigment granules in the layers of cells beneath the outer skin. The tail is long and highly prehensile, assisting the animal when climbing. Most chameleons live in trees and move very slowly. The tongue is very long, protrusile, and covered with a viscous secretion; it can be shot out with great rapidity to 20 cm/8 in for the capture of insects. The eyes are on 'turrets', move independently, and can swivel forward to give stereoscopic vision for 'shooting'. Most live in Africa and Madagascar, but the common chameleon *Chameleo chameleon* is found in Mediterranean countries; two species live in SW Arabia, and one species in India and Sri Lanka.

chamois goatlike mammal *Rupicapra rupicapra* found in mountain ranges of S Europe and Asia Minor. It is brown, with dark patches running through the eyes, and can be up to 80 cm/2.6 ft high. Chamois are very sure-footed, and live in herds of up to 30 members. Both sexes have horns which may be 20 cm/8 in long. These are set close together and go up vertically, forming a hook at the top. Chamois skin is very soft, and excellent for cleaning glass, but the chamois is now comparatively rare and 'chamois leather' is often made from the skin of sheep and goats.

Chamorro, Barrios de Violeta president of Nicaragua from 1990; see ◊Barrios de Chamorro.

champagne sparkling white wine invented by Dom Pérignon, a Benedictine monk, 1668. It is made from a blend of grapes (*pinot noir* and *chardonnay*) grown in the Marne River region around Reims and Epernay, in Champagne, NE France. After a first fermentation, sugar and yeast are added to the still wine, which, when bottled, undergoes a second fermentation to produce the sparkle. Sugar syrup may be added to make the wine sweet (*sec*) or dry (*brut*).

Increased demand has given rise to the production of similar wines outside France, in the USA, for example, and Spain. Although these wines imitate champagnes closely, only wines produced in the Champagne region of France can be termed 'champagne'. The pop when a bottle is opened is due to the sudden release of pressure that allows the accumulated carbon dioxide to escape: a bottle may contain up to five times its volume in gas.

Champagne-Ardenne region of NE France; area 25,600 sq km/9,882 sq mi; population (1990) 1,347,800. Its capital is Reims, and it comprises the *départements* of Ardennes, Aube, Marne, and Haute-Marne. It has sheep and dairy farming and vineyards. Its chief towns are Epernay, Troyes, and Chaumont. The region was the scene of bitter fighting in World War I, in particular the two Battles of Champagne Dec 1914–March 1915 and Sept–Oct 1915.

Champaigne Philippe de 1602–1674. French artist. He was the leading portrait painter of the court of Louis XIII. Of Flemish origin, he went to Paris 1621 and gained the patronage of Cardinal Richelieu. His style is elegant, cool, and restrained. *Ex Voto* 1662 (Louvre, Paris) is his best-known work.

champignon any of a number of edible fungi of the family Agaricaceae. The fairy ring champignon *Marasmius oreades* is so called because its fruiting bodies (mushrooms) occur in rings around the outer edge of the underground mycelium (threadlike tubes) of the fungus.

Champlain Samuel de 1567–1635. French pioneer, soldier, and explorer in Canada. In 1608 he founded and named Quebec, and was appointed lieutenant governor of French Canada 1612.

Champlain, Lake lake in northeastern USA (extending some 10 km/6 mi into Canada) on the New York–Vermont border; length 201 km/125 mi; area 692 sq km/430 sq mi. It is linked by canal to the St Lawrence and Hudson rivers. The largest city on its shores is Burlington, Vermont. Lake Champlain is named after explorer Samuel de ◊Champlain, who saw it 1609.

Champollion Jean François, le Jeune 1790–1832. French Egyptologist. In 1822 he deciphered Egyptian hieroglyphics with the aid of the ◊Rosetta Stone. He published his *Précis du système hiéroglyphique/Summary of the Hieroglyphic System* 1824.

chance likelihood, or ◊probability, of an event taking place, expressed as a fraction or percentage. For example, the chance that a tossed coin will land heads up is 50%.

chancel part of a Christian church where the choir and clergy sit, formerly kept separate from the nave.

Chancellor, Lord UK state official, originally the royal secretary, today a member of the cabinet, whose office ends with a change of government. The Lord Chancellor acts as Speaker of the House of Lords, may preside over the Court of Appeal, and is head of the judiciary.

chancellor of the Exchequer in the UK, senior cabinet minister responsible for the national economy. The office, established under Henry III, originally entailed keeping the Exchequer seal.

Chancery in the UK, a division of the High Court that deals with such matters as the administration of the estates of deceased persons, the execution of trusts, the enforcement of sales of land, and ◊foreclosure of mortgages.

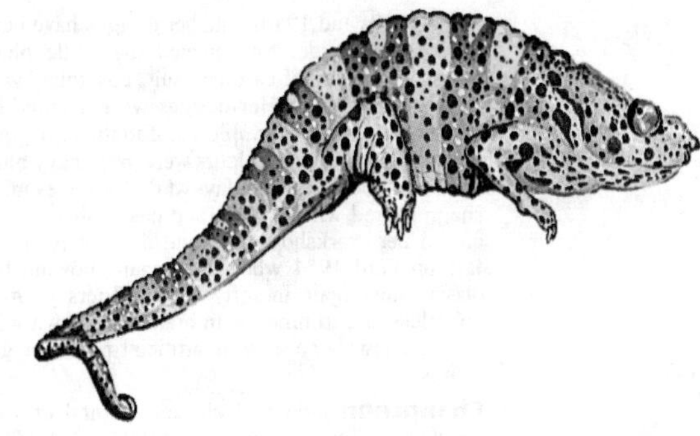

chameleon Meller's chameleon of the savanna of Tanzania and Malawi is the largest chameleon found outside Madagascar, about 55 cm/1.7 ft long. It feeds on small birds and insects, lying in wait on branches to ambush them. Its coloration makes it very hard to see among foliage.

Chandelā or ***Candella*** ◊Rajput dynasty that ruled the Bundelkhand region of central India from the 9th to the 11th century. The Chandelās fought against Muslim invaders, until they were replaced by the Bundelās. The Chandelā capital was Khajurāho.

Chandigarh city of N India, in the foothills of the Himalayas; population (1991) 511,000. It is also a union territory; area 114 sq km/44 sq mi; population (1991) 640,725. Planned by the architect Le Corbusier, the city was inaugurated 1953 to replace Lahore (capital of British Punjab), which went to Pakistan under partition 1947. Since 1966, when Chandigarh became a Union Territory, it has been the capital city of both Haryana and Punjab, pending the construction of a new capital for the former.

'Peace with honour. I believe it is peace for our time.'

NEVILLE CHAMBERLAIN
Speech from 10 Downing Street 30 Sept 1938

Chandler Raymond Thornton 1888–1959. US novelist. He turned the pulp detective mystery form into a successful genre of literature and created the quintessential private eye in the tough but chivalric loner, Philip Marlowe. Marlowe is the narrator of such books as *The Big Sleep* 1939 (filmed 1946), *Farewell My Lovely* 1940 (filmed 1944), *The Lady in the Lake* 1943 (filmed 1947), and *The Long Goodbye* 1954 (filmed 1975). He also wrote numerous screenplays.

Chandragupta Maurya ruler of N India c. 325–c. 297 BC, founder of the Mauryan dynasty. He overthrew the Nanda dynasty 325 and then conquered the Punjab 322 after the death of ◊Alexander the Great, expanding his empire west to Persia. He is credited with having united most of India.

Chandrasekhar Subrahmanyan 1910–1995. Indian-born US astrophysicist who made pioneering studies of the structure and evolution of stars. The Chandrasekhar limit is the maximum mass of a ◊white dwarf before it turns into a ◊neutron star. Nobel Prize for Physics 1983.

Chanel Coco (Gabrielle) 1883–1971. French fashion designer. She was renowned as a trendsetter

Chanel The French couturier Coco Chanel in 1937. The predominant influence on dress design for almost 60 years, she created simple, comfortable clothes that were a dramatically successful reaction to previous fashions in women's wear. *Chanel*

in the 1920s and 1930s, and her designs have been copied worldwide. She created the 'little black dress', the informal cardigan suit, costume jewellery, and perfumes. Her designs were inspired by her personal wish for simple, comfortable, and practical clothes. Popular colours were grey, navy blue, black, and beige for the day, while for the evening she preferred white, black, and pastel shades. She closed her workshop 1939 and did not return to fashion until 1954 when she began showing her classic suits again in soft tweed and jersey, often collarless and trimmed with braid and shown with costume jewellery such as artificial pearls or gilt chains.

Changchun industrial city and capital of Jilin province, China; population (1993) 2,400,000. Machinery and motor vehicles are manufactured. It is also the centre of an agricultural district. As Hsingking ('new capital') it was the capital of Manchukuo 1932–45 during Japanese occupation.

change of state in science, a change in the physical state (solid, liquid, or gas) of a material. For instance, melting, boiling, evaporation, and their opposites, solidification and condensation, are changes of state. The former set of changes are brought about by heating or decreased pressure; the latter by cooling or increased pressure. These changes involve the absorption or release of heat energy, called ◊latent heat, even though the temperature of the material does not change during the transition between states.

In the unusual change of state called sublimation, a solid changes directly to a gas without passing through the liquid state. For example, solid carbon dioxide (dry ice) sublimes to carbon dioxide gas.

Chang Jiang or ***Yangtze Kiang*** longest river of China, flowing about 6,300 km/3,900 mi from Tibet to the Yellow Sea. It is a main commercial waterway. Work began on the ◊ Three Gorges Dam on the river Dec 1994 (scheduled for completion 2003, it will be the world's largest dam and hydroelectric scheme). In the summer of 1998 the Chang Jiang flooded, killing 3,000 people and destroying 5 million homes.

Chang Jiang

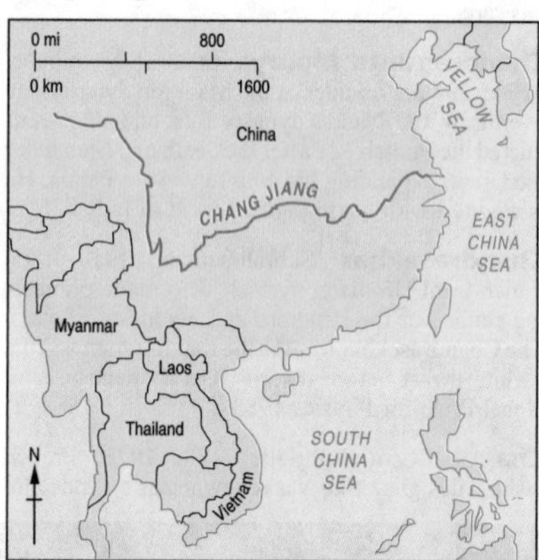

Channel, English see ◊English Channel.

Channel Five UK television channel. Launched 30 March 1997, it was set up by the 1990 Broadcasting Act, under which the ◊Independent Television Commission (ITC) was required to create a fifth national channel. It was awarded by competitive tender in 1995 to Channel 5 Broadcasting Ltd, a consortium of companies including Pearson, owners of the *Financial Times*, and United News and Media, owners of the *Daily Express* and Anglia Television.

Channel Four Britain's fourth national television channel, launched 2 Nov 1982 as a wholly-owned subsidiary of the IBA (Independent Broadcasting Authority; today known as the ITC or Independent Television Commission). Its brief was to serve minority interests, encourage innovation through the use of independent producers, and develop a character distinct from the other channels.

Channel Islands group of islands in the English Channel, off the northwest coast of France; they are a possession of the British crown. They comprise the islands of Jersey, Guernsey, Alderney, Great and Little Sark, with the lesser Herm, Brechou, Jethou, and Lihou.
area 194 sq km/75 sq mi

'All I need to make a comedy is a park, a policeman and a pretty girl.'
CHARLIE CHAPLIN
My Autobiography

Channel Islands

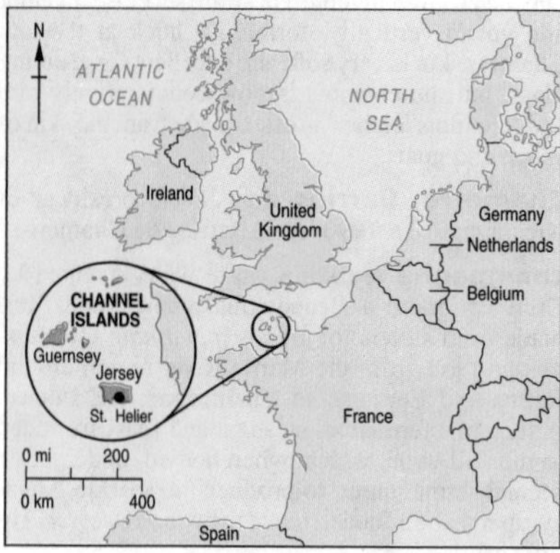

features very mild climate, productive soil; financially the islands are a tax haven
industries farming, fishing, and tourism; flowers, early potatoes, tomatoes, butterflies, and dairy cattle are exported
currency English pound, also local coinage
population (1991) 145,600
language official language French (◊Norman French) but English more widely used
religion chiefly Anglican
famous people Lillie Langtry
government the main islands have their own parliaments and laws. Unless specially signified, the Channel Islands are not bound by British acts of Parliament, though the British government is responsible for defence and external relations
history originally under the duchy of Normandy, they are the only part still held by Britain. The islands came under the same rule as England 1066, and are dependent territories of the British crown. Germany occupied the islands June 1940–May 1945, the only British soil to be occupied by the Germans during World War II.

Channel Tunnel tunnel built beneath the English Channel, linking Britain with mainland Europe. It comprises twin rail tunnels, 50 km/31 mi long and 7.3 m/24 ft in diameter, located 40 m/130 ft beneath the seabed. Construction began 1987, and the French and English sections were linked Dec 1990. It was officially opened 6 May 1994. The shuttle train service, Le Shuttle, opened to lorries May 1994 and to cars Dec 1994. The tunnel's high-speed train service, Eurostar, linking London to Paris and Brussels, opened Nov 1994. The estimated cost of the tunnel was continually revised upwards (reaching £8 billion 1995).
history In the 1880s British financier and railway promoter Edward Watkin started boring a tunnel near Dover, abandoning it 1894 because of governmental opposition after driving 1.6 km/1 mi out to sea. In 1973 Britain and France agreed to back a tunnel, but a year later Britain pulled out following a change of government.
high-speed link The contract to build the London–Dover high-speed rail link was awarded to the London and Continental Railways Consortium in 1996. The link, due to be completed 2003, would allow Eurostar trains to maintain their high speeds within Britain; under existing legislation, Eurostar trains that travel at up to 300 km/186 mi per hour in France are forced to slow to 80 km/50 mi per hour once in Britain. Transit time between London and Paris is three hours.

chanson de geste epic poetry of the High Middle Ages in Europe. It probably developed from oral poetry recited in royal or princely courts, and takes as its subject the exploits of heroes, such as those associated with Charlemagne and the Crusades. The best-known example is the *Chanson de Roland.*

Chanson de Roland 11th-century epic poem which tells of the real and imaginary deeds of Roland and other knights of Charlemagne, and their last stand against the Basques at Roncesvalles.

Chao Phraya chief river (formerly Menam) of Thailand, flowing 1,200 km/750 mi into the Bight of Bangkok, an inlet of the Gulf of Thailand.

chaos theory or ***chaology*** or ***complexity theory*** branch of mathematics that attempts to describe irregular, unpredictable systems – that is, systems whose behaviour is difficult to predict because there are so many variable or unknown factors. Weather is an example of a chaotic system.

Chaplin Charlie (Charles Spencer) 1889–1977. English film actor and director. He made his reputation as a tramp with a smudge moustache, bowler hat, and twirling cane in silent comedies, including *The Rink* 1916, *The Kid* 1921, and *The Gold Rush* 1925. His work combines buffoonery with pathos, as in *The Great Dictator* 1940 and *Limelight* 1952. He was one of cinema's most popular and greatest stars.

Chaplin was born in south London and first appeared on the music hall stage at the age of five. He joined Mack Sennett's Keystone Company in Los Angeles 1913. Along with Mary Pickford, Douglas Fairbanks, and D W ◊Griffith, Chaplin formed United Artists 1919 as an independent company to distribute their films. His other films include *City Lights* 1931, *Modern Times* 1936, and *Monsieur Verdoux* 1947. *Limelight* 1952 was awarded an Academy Award for Chaplin's musical theme. When accused of communist sympathies during the McCarthy witchhunt, he left the USA 1952 and moved to Switzerland. He received special Academy Awards 1928 and 1972.

Chapman George c. 1559–1634. English poet and dramatist. His translations of the Greek epics of Homer (completed 1616) were the earliest in England; his plays include the comedy *Eastward Hoe* (with Ben ◊Jonson and John ◊Marston) 1605 and the tragedy *Bussy d'Ambois* 1607.

chapter in the Christian church, the collective assembly of canons (priests) who together administer a cathedral.

chapterhouse in a cathedral, monastery, or other religious establishment, a meeting place. Access is usually via the cloisters. In England, chapterhouses are often polygonal in form.

characteristic in mathematics, the integral (whole-number) part of a ◊logarithm. The fractional part is the ◊mantissa. For example, in base ten, $10^0 = 1$, $10^1 = 10$, $10^2 = 100$, and so on; the powers to which 10 is raised are the characteristics. To determine the power to which 10 must be raised to obtain a number between 10 and 100, say 20 (2×10, or log 2 + log 10), the logarithm for 2 is found (0.3010), and the characteristic 1 added to make 1.3010.

charcoal black, porous form of ◊carbon, produced by heating wood or other organic materials in the absence of air. It is used as a fuel in the smelting of metals such as copper and zinc, and by artists for making black line drawings. Activated charcoal has been powdered and dried so that it presents a much increased surface area for adsorption; it is used for filtering and purifying liquids and gases – for example, in drinking-water filters and gas masks.

Charcoal was traditionally produced by burning dried wood in a kiln, a process lasting several days.

Chaplin English film actor and director Charlie Chaplin in *The Kid* 1921. He made a successful transition from silent films to those with soundtrack, such as *Limelight* 1952.
Image Select (UK) Ltd

charcoal Charcoal is produced in large quantities in S Madagascar, where whole villages are dependent on its production for their income. Charcoal is the most important fuel for cooking purposes over much of the Third World, leading to intensive exploitation of remaining native forests. *Premaphotos Wildlife*

The kiln was either a simple hole in the ground, or an earth-covered mound. Today kilns are of brick or iron, both of which allow the waste gases to be collected and used.

Charcot Jean-Martin 1825–1893. French neurologist who studied hysteria, sclerosis, locomotor ataxia, and senile diseases. One of the most influential neurologists of his day, he exhibited hysterical women at weekly public lectures, which became fashionable events. Among his pupils was the founder of psychiatry, Sigmund ◊Freud.

Chardin Jean-Baptiste-Siméon 1699–1779. French painter. He took as his subjects naturalistic still lifes and quiet domestic scenes that recall the Dutch tradition. His work is a complete contrast to that of his contemporaries, the Rococo painters. He developed his own technique, using successive layers of paint to achieve depth of tone, and is generally considered one of the finest exponents of genre painting.

Charente French river, rising in Haute-Vienne *département* and flowing past Angoulême and Cognac into the Bay of Biscay below Rochefort. It is 360 km/225 mi long. Its wide estuary is much silted up. It gives its name to two *départements*, Charente and Charente-Maritime (formerly Charente-Inférieure).

charge see ◊electric charge.

charge-coupled device (CCD) device for forming images electronically, using a layer of silicon that releases electrons when struck by incoming light. The electrons are stored in ◊pixels and read off into a computer at the end of the exposure. CCDs have now almost entirely replaced photographic film for applications such as astrophotography where extreme sensitivity to light is paramount.

Charge of the Light Brigade disastrous attack by the British Light Brigade of cavalry against the Russian entrenched artillery on 25 Oct 1854 during the Crimean War at the Battle of ◊Balaclava. Of the 673 soldiers who took part, there were 272 casualties. The fiasco came about as a result of a badly phrased order to 'prevent the enemy carrying away the guns'.

chariot horse-drawn carriage with two wheels, used in ancient Egypt, Greece, and Rome, for fighting, processions, and races; it is thought to have originated in Asia. Typically, the fighting chariot contained a driver and a warrior, who would fight on foot, with the chariot providing rapid mobility.

charismatic movement late 20th-century movement within the Christian church that emphasizes the role of the Holy Spirit in the life of the individual believer and in the life of the church. See ◊Pentecostal movement.

charity originally a Christian term meaning a selfless, disinterested form of love. This developed to include almsgiving or other actions performed by individuals to help the poor and needy. Today it refers to any independent agency (for example, Oxfam) that organizes such relief on a regular basis.

Charlemagne (Charles I the Great) 742–814. King of the Franks from 768 and Holy Roman emperor from 800. By inheritance (his father was ◊Pepin the Short) and extensive campaigns of conquest, he united most of W Europe by 804, when after 30 years of war the Saxons came under his control. He reformed the legal, judicial, and military systems; established schools; and promoted Christianity, commerce, agriculture, arts, and literature. In his capital, Aachen, scholars gathered from all over Europe.

Pepin had been mayor of the palace in Merovingian Neustria until he was crowned king by Pope Stephen II (died 757) in 754, and his sons Carl (Charlemagne) and Carloman were crowned as joint heirs. When Pepin died 768, Charlemagne inherited the N Frankish kingdom, and when Carloman died 771, he also took possession of his domains.

He was engaged in his first Saxon campaign when the Pope's call for help against the Lombards reached him; he crossed the Alps, captured Pavia, and took the title of king of the Lombards. The pacification and christianizing of the Saxon peoples occupied the greater part of Charlemagne's reign. From 792 N Saxony was subdued, and in 804 the whole region came under his rule.

In 777 the emir of Zaragoza asked for Charlemagne's help against the emir of Córdoba. Charlemagne crossed the Pyrenees 778 and reached the Ebro but had to turn back from Zaragoza. The rearguard action of Roncesvalles, in which ◊Roland, warden of the Breton March, and other Frankish nobles were ambushed and killed by Basques, was later glorified in the *Chanson de Roland*.

In 801 the district between the Pyrenees and the Llobregat was organized as the Spanish March. The independent duchy of Bavaria was incorporated in the kingdom 788, and the ◊Avar people were subdued 791–96 and accepted Christianity. Charlemagne's last campaign was against a Danish attack on his northern frontier 810.

The supremacy of the Frankish king in Europe found outward expression in the bestowal of the imperial title: in Rome, during Mass on Christmas Day 800, Pope Leo III crowned Charlemagne emperor. He enjoyed diplomatic relations with Byzantium, Baghdad, Mercia, Northumbria, and other regions. Jury courts were introduced, the laws of the Franks revised, and other peoples' laws written down. A new coinage was introduced, weights and measures were reformed, and communications were improved. Charlemagne also took a lively interest in theology, organized the church in his dominions, and furthered missionary enterprises and monastic reform.

The Carolingian Renaissance of learning began when he persuaded the Northumbrian scholar Alcuin to enter his service 781. Charlemagne gathered a kind of academy around him. Although he never learned to read, he collected the old heroic sagas, began a Frankish grammar, and promoted religious instruction in the vernacular. He died 28 Jan 814 in Aachen, where he was buried. Soon a cycle of heroic legends and romances developed around him, including epics by Ariosto, Boiardo, and Tasso.

Charles (Mary) Eugenia 1919– . Dominican politician, prime minister 1980–95; cofounder and first leader of the centrist Dominica Freedom Party (DFP). Two years after Dominica's independence the DFP won the 1980 general election and Charles became the Caribbean's first female prime minister. In 1993 she resigned the leadership of the DFP, but remained as prime minister until the 1995 elections, which were won by the opposition United Workers' Party (UNP).

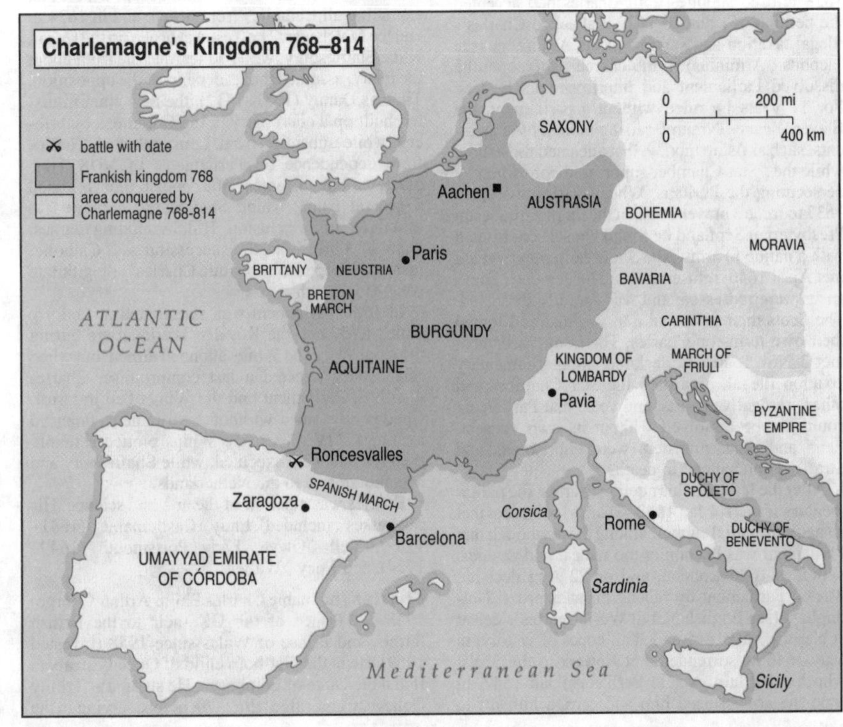

Charles I A contemporary engraving of the trial of Charles I at Westminster Hall Jan 1649. He was accused of having 'conceived a wicked design ... to overthrow the rights and liberties of the people'. The trial began 20 Jan and ended eight days later when the king was sentenced to death. *Philip Sauvain*

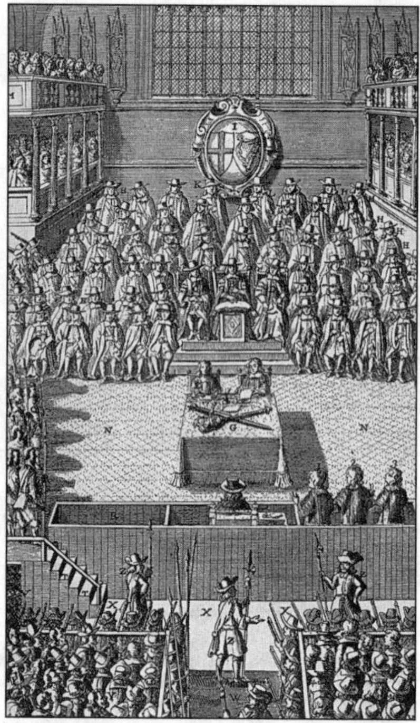

Charles Jacques Alexandre César 1746–1823. French physicist who studied gases and made the first ascent in a hydrogen-filled balloon 1783, ten days after the Montgolfiers' first flight in a hot-air balloon. His work on the expansion of gases led to the formulation of ◊Charles's law.

Charles I 1600–1649. King of Great Britain and Ireland from 1625, son of James I of England (James VI of Scotland). In 1628 he accepted the petition of right, whereby a subject could petition for legal relief against the crown, but then dissolved Parliament and ruled without it 1629–40. His advisers were ◊Strafford and ◊Laud, who persecuted the Puritans and provoked the Scots to revolt. The ◊Short Parliament, summoned 1640, refused funds, and the ◊Long Parliament later that year rebelled. Charles declared war on Parliament 1642 but surrendered 1646 and was beheaded 1649. He was the father of Charles II.

Charles was born at Dunfermline, and became heir to the throne on the death of his brother Henry 1612. He married Henrietta Maria, daughter of Henry IV of France. When he succeeded his father, friction with Parliament began at once. The parliaments of 1625 and 1626 were dissolved, and that of 1628 refused supplies until Charles had accepted the petition of right. In 1629 it attacked Charles's illegal taxation and support of the Arminians (see Jacobus ◊Arminius) in the church, whereupon he dissolved Parliament and imprisoned its leaders. For 11 years he ruled without a parliament, the Eleven Years' Tyranny, raising money by expedients, such as ◊ship money, that alienated the nation, while the ◊Star Chamber suppressed opposition by persecuting the Puritans. When Charles attempted 1637 to force a prayer book on the English model on Presbyterian Scotland he found himself confronted with a nation in arms. The Short Parliament, which met April 1640, refused to grant money until grievances were redressed, and was speedily dissolved. The Scots then advanced into England and forced their own terms on Charles. The Long Parliament met 3 Nov 1640 and declared extraparliamentary taxation illegal, abolished the Star Chamber and other prerogative courts, and voted that Parliament could not be dissolved without its own consent. Laud and other ministers were imprisoned, and Strafford condemned to death.

After the failure of his attempt to arrest the parliamentary leaders 4 Jan 1642, Charles, confident that he had substantial support among those who felt that Parliament was becoming too radical and zealous, withdrew from London, and on 22 Aug declared war on Parliament by raising his standard at Nottingham (see English ◊Civil War). Charles's defeat at Naseby June 1645 ended all hopes of victory; in May 1646 he surrendered at Newark to the Scots, who handed him over to Parliament Jan 1647. In June the army seized him and carried him off to Hampton Court. While the army leaders strove to find a settlement, Charles secretly intrigued for a Scottish invasion. In Nov he escaped, but was recaptured and held at Carisbrooke Castle; a Scottish invasion followed 1648, and was shattered by ◊Cromwell at Preston. In Jan 1649 the House of Commons set up a high court of justice, which tried Charles and condemned him to death. He was beheaded 30 Jan before the Banqueting House in Whitehall.

A merry monarch, scandalous and poor.

On **Charles II** John Wilmot, Earl of Rochester

Charles II 1630–1685. King of Great Britain and Ireland from 1660, when Parliament accepted the restoration of the monarchy after the collapse of Cromwell's Commonwealth; son of Charles I. His chief minister Edward ◊Clarendon, who arranged his marriage 1662 with Catherine of Braganza, was replaced 1667 with the ◊Cabal of advisers. His plans to restore Catholicism in Britain led to war with the Netherlands 1672–74 in support of Louis XIV of France and a break with Parliament, which he dissolved 1681. He was succeeded by James II.

Charles was born in St James's Palace, London; during the Civil War he lived with his father at Oxford 1642–45, and after the victory of Cromwell's Parliamentary forces withdrew to France. Accepting the ◊Covenanters' offer to make him king, he landed in Scotland 1650, and was crowned at Scone 1 Jan 1651. An attempt to invade England was ended 3 Sept by Cromwell's victory at Worcester. Charles escaped, and for nine years he wandered through France, Germany, Flanders, Spain, and Holland until the opening of negotiations by George Monk (1608–1670) 1660.

In April Charles issued the Declaration of Breda, promising a general amnesty and freedom of conscience. Parliament accepted the Declaration and he was proclaimed king 8 May 1660, landed at Dover on 26 May, and entered London three days later. Charles wanted to make himself absolute, and favoured Catholicism for his subjects as most consistent with absolute monarchy. The disasters of the Dutch war furnished an excuse for banishing Clarendon 1667, and he was replaced by the Cabal of Clifford and Arlington, both secret Catholics, and ◊Buckingham, Ashley (Lord ◊Shaftesbury), and ◊Lauderdale, who had links with the ◊Dissenters.

In 1670 Charles signed the Secret Treaty of Dover, the full details of which were known only to Clifford and Arlington, whereby he promised Louis XIV of France he would declare himself a Catholic, re-establish Catholicism in England, and support the French king's projected war against the Dutch; in return Louis was to finance Charles and in the event of resistance to supply him with troops. War with the Netherlands followed 1672, and at the same time Charles issued the Declaration of Indulgence, suspending all penal laws against Catholics and Dissenters. In 1673, Parliament forced Charles to withdraw the Indulgence and accept a Test Act excluding all Catholics from office, and in 1674 to end the Dutch war. The Test Act broke up the Cabal, while Shaftesbury, who had learned the truth about the treaty, assumed the leadership of the opposition. Thomas Danby (1631–1712), the new chief minister, built up a court party in the Commons by bribery, while subsidies from Louis relieved Charles from dependence on Parliament. In 1678 Titus ◊Oates's announcement of a 'popish plot' released a general panic, which Shaftesbury exploited to introduce his Exclusion Bill, excluding James, Duke of York, from the succession as a Catholic; instead he hoped to substitute Charles's illegitimate son ◊Monmouth.

In 1681 Parliament was summoned at Oxford, which had been the Royalist headquarters during the Civil War. The Whigs attended armed, but when Shaftesbury rejected a last compromise, Charles dissolved Parliament and the Whigs fled in terror. Charles now ruled without a parliament, financed by Louis XIV. When the Whigs plotted a revolt, their leaders were executed, while Shaftesbury and Monmouth fled to the Netherlands.

Charles was a patron of the arts and science. His mistresses included Lady Castlemaine (1641–1709), Nell ◊Gwyn, Lady Portsmouth (1649–1734), and Lucy ◊Walter.

Charles (full name Charles Philip Arthur George) 1948– . Prince of the UK, heir to the British throne, and Prince of Wales since 1958 (invested 1969). He is the first-born child of Queen Elizabeth II and the Duke of Edinburgh. He studied at Trinity College, Cambridge, 1967–70, before serving in the Royal Air Force and Royal Navy. The first royal heir since 1660 to have an English wife, he married Lady Diana Spencer, daughter of the 8th Earl Spencer, 1981. They have two sons and heirs, William (1982–) and Henry (1984–). Amid much publicity, Charles and Diana separated 1992 and were divorced 1996.

Prince Charles's concern for social and environmental issues has led to many self-help projects for the young and underprivileged, and he is a leading critic of unsympathetic features of contemporary architecture.

Charles I king of France, better known as the Holy Roman emperor ◊Charlemagne.

Charles (II) the Bald king of France, see ◊Charles II, Holy Roman emperor.

Charles (III) the Simple 879–929. King of France 893–922, son of Louis the Stammerer. He was crowned at Reims. In 911 he ceded what later became the duchy of Normandy to the Norman chief Rollo.

Charles (IV) the Fair 1294–1328. King of France from 1322, when he succeeded Philip V as the last of the direct Capetian line.

Charles (V) the Wise 1337–1380. King of France from 1364. He was regent during the captivity of his father, John II, in England 1356–60, and became king on John's death. He reconquered nearly all France from England 1369–80.

Charles (VI) the Mad or ***the Well-Beloved*** 1368–1422. King of France from 1380, succeeding his father Charles V; he was under the regency of his uncles until 1388. He became mentally unstable 1392, and civil war broke out between the dukes of Orléans and Burgundy. Henry V of England invaded France 1415, conquering Normandy, and in 1420 forced Charles to sign the Treaty of Troyes, recognizing Henry as his successor.

Charles VII 1403–1461. King of France from 1429. Son of Charles VI, he was excluded from the succession by the Treaty of Troyes, but recognized by the south of France. In 1429 Joan of Arc raised the siege of Orléans and had him crowned at Reims. He organized France's first standing army and by 1453 had expelled the English from all of France except Calais.

Charles VIII 1470–1498. King of France from 1483, when he succeeded his father, Louis XI. In 1494 he unsuccessfully tried to claim the Neapolitan crown, and when he entered Naples 1495 was forced to withdraw by a coalition of Milan, Venice, Spain, and the Holy Roman Empire. He defeated them at Fornovo, but lost Naples.

Charles IX 1550–1574. King of France from 1560. Second son of Henry II and Catherine de' Medici, he succeeded his brother Francis II at the age of ten but remained under the domination of his mother's regency for ten years while France was torn by religious wars. In 1570 he fell under the influence of the ◊Huguenot leader Gaspard de Coligny; alarmed by this, Catherine instigated his order for the Massacre of ◊St Bartholomew, which led to a new religious war.

Charles X 1757–1836. King of France from 1824. Grandson of Louis XV and brother of Louis XVI and Louis XVIII, he was known as the comte d'Artois before his accession. He fled to England at the beginning of the French Revolution, and when he came to the throne on the death of Louis XVIII, he attempted to reverse the achievements of the Revolution. A revolt ensued 1830, and he again fled to England.

Charles I Holy Roman emperor, better known as ◊Charlemagne.

Charles (II) the Bald 823–877. Holy Roman emperor from 875 and (as Charles II) king of France from 843. Younger son of Louis I (the Pious), he warred against his eldest brother, Emperor Lothair I. The Treaty of Verdun 843 made him king of the West Frankish Kingdom (now France and the Spanish Marches).

Charles (III) the Fat 839–888. Holy Roman emperor 881–87; he became king of the West Franks 885, thus uniting for the last time the whole of Charlemagne's dominions, but was deposed.

Charles IV 1316–1378. Holy Roman emperor from 1355 and king of Bohemia from 1346. Son of John of Luxembourg, king of Bohemia, he was elected king of Germany 1346 and ruled all Germany from 1347.

Charles V 1500–1558. Holy Roman emperor 1519–56. Son of Philip of Burgundy and Joanna of Castile, he inherited vast possessions, which led to rivalry from Francis I of France, whose alliance with the Ottoman Empire brought Vienna under siege 1529 and 1532. Charles was also in conflict with the Protestants in Germany until the Treaty of Passau 1552, which allowed the Lutherans religious liberty.

Charles was born in Ghent and received the Netherlands from his father 1506; Spain, Naples, Sicily, Sardinia, and the Spanish dominions in N Africa and the Americas on the death of his maternal grandfather, Ferdinand V of Castile (1452–1516); and from his paternal grandfather, Maximilian I, the Habsburg dominions 1519, when he was elected emperor. He was crowned in Aachen 1520. From 1517 the empire was split by the rise of Lutheranism, Charles making unsuccessful attempts to reach a settlement at Augsburg 1530 (see Confession of ◊Augsburg), and being forced by the Treaty of Passau to yield most of the Protestant demands. Worn out, he abdicated in favour of his son Philip II in the Netherlands 1555 and Spain 1556. He yielded the imperial crown to his brother Ferdinand I.

Charles VI 1685–1740. Holy Roman emperor from 1711, father of ◊Maria Theresa, whose succession to his Austrian dominions he tried to ensure, and himself claimant to the Spanish throne 1700, thus causing the War of the ◊Spanish Succession.

Charles VII 1697–1745. Holy Roman emperor from 1742, opponent of ◊Maria Theresa's claim to the Austrian dominions of Charles VI.

Charles (Karl Franz Josef) 1887–1922. Emperor of Austria and king of Hungary from 1916, the last of the Habsburg emperors. He succeeded his great-uncle Franz Josef 1916 but was forced to withdraw to Switzerland 1918, although he refused to abdicate. In 1921 he attempted unsuccessfully to regain the crown of Hungary and was deported to Madeira.

Charles I 1500–1558. Holy Roman emperor; see ◊Charles V.

Charles II 1661–1700. King of Spain from 1665. The second son of Philip IV, he was the last of the Spanish Habsburg kings. Mentally disabled from birth, he bequeathed his dominions to Philip of Anjou, grandson of Louis XIV, which led to the War of the ◊Spanish Succession.

Charles III 1716–1788. King of Spain from 1759. Son of Philip V, he became duke of Parma 1732 and conquered Naples and Sicily 1734. On the death of his half-brother Ferdinand VI (1713–1759), he became king of Spain, handing over Naples and Sicily to his son Ferdinand (1751–1825). At home, he reformed state finances, strengthened the armed forces, and expelled the Jesuits. During his reign, Spain was involved in the Seven Years' War with France against England. This led to the loss of Florida 1763, which was only regained when Spain and France supported the colonists during the American Revolution.

Charles IV 1748–1819. King of Spain from 1788, when he succeeded his father, Charles III; he left the government in the hands of his wife and her lover, the minister Manuel de Godoy (1767–1851). In 1808 Charles was induced to abdicate by Napoleon's machinations in favour of his son Ferdinand VII (1784–1833), who was subsequently deposed by Napoleon's brother Joseph.

Charles (Swedish ***Carl***) fifteen kings of Sweden (the first six were local chieftains), including:

Charles VIII 1408–1470. King of Sweden from 1448. He was elected regent of Sweden 1438, when Sweden broke away from Denmark and Norway. He stepped down 1441 when Christopher III of Bavaria (1418–1448) was elected king, but after his death became king. He was twice expelled by the Danes and twice restored.

Charles IX 1550–1611. King of Sweden from 1604, the youngest son of Gustavus Vasa. In 1568 he and his brother John led the rebellion against Eric XIV (1533–1577); John became king as John III and attempted to catholicize Sweden, and Charles led the opposition. John's son Sigismund, king of Poland and a Catholic, succeeded to the Swedish throne 1592, and Charles led the Protestants. He was made regent 1595 and deposed Sigismund 1599. Charles was elected king of Sweden 1604 and was involved in unsuccessful wars with Russia, Poland, and Denmark. He was the father of Gustavus Adolphus.

Charles X 1622–1660. King of Sweden from 1654, when he succeeded his cousin Christina. He waged war with Poland and Denmark and in 1657 invaded Denmark by leading his army over the frozen sea.

Charles XI 1655–1697. King of Sweden from 1660, when he succeeded his father Charles X. His mother acted as regent until 1672 when Charles took over the government. He was a remarkable general and reformed the administration.

Charles XII 1682–1718. King of Sweden from 1697, when he succeeded his father, Charles XI. From 1700 he was involved in wars with Denmark, Poland, and Russia. He won a succession of victories until, in 1709 while invading Russia, he was defeated at Poltava in the Ukraine, and forced to take refuge in Turkey until 1714. He was killed while besieging Fredrikshall, Norway.

Charles XIII 1748–1818. King of Sweden from 1809, when he was elected; he became the first king of Sweden and Norway 1814.

Charles XIV (Jean Baptiste Jules Bernadotte) 1763–1844. King of Sweden and Norway from 1818. A former marshal in the French army, in 1810 he was elected crown prince of Sweden under the name of Charles John (Carl Johan). Loyal to his adopted country, he brought Sweden into the alliance against Napoleon 1813, as a reward for which Sweden received Norway. He was the founder of the present dynasty.

Charles XV 1826–1872. King of Sweden and Norway from 1859, when he succeeded his father Oscar I. A popular and liberal monarch, his main achievement was the reform of the constitution.

Charles Albert 1798–1849. King of Sardinia from 1831. He showed liberal sympathies in early life, and after his accession introduced some reforms. On the outbreak of the 1848 revolution he granted a constitution and declared war on Austria. His troops were defeated at Custozza and Novara. In 1849 he abdicated in favour of his son Victor Emmanuel.

Charles Augustus 1757–1828. Grand Duke of Saxe-Weimar in Germany. He succeeded his father in infancy, fought against the French in 1792–94 and 1806, and was the patron and friend of the writer Goethe.

Charles Edward Stuart the ***Young Pretender*** or ***Bonnie Prince Charlie*** 1720–1788. British prince, grandson of James II and son of James, the Old Pretender. In the Jacobite rebellion 1745 Charles won the support of the Scottish Highlanders; his army invaded England to claim the throne but was beaten back by the duke of ◊Cumberland and routed at ◊Culloden 1746. Charles went into exile.

He was born in Rome, and created Prince of Wales at birth. In July 1745 he sailed for Scotland, and landed in Inverness-shire with seven companions. On 19 Aug he raised his father's standard, and within a week had rallied an army of 2,000 Highlanders. He entered Edinburgh almost without resistance, won an easy victory at Prestonpans, invaded England, and by 4 Dec had reached Derby, where his officers insisted on a retreat. The army returned to Scotland and won a victory at Falkirk, but was forced to retire to the Highlands before Cumberland's advance. On 16 April at Culloden Charles's army was routed by Cumberland, and he fled. For five months he wandered through the Highlands with a price of £30,000 on his head before escaping to France. He visited England secretly in 1750, and may have made other visits. He settled in Italy 1766.

Charles Martel c. 688–741. Frankish ruler (Mayor of the Palace) of the E Frankish kingdom from 717 and the whole kingdom from 731. His victory against the Moors at Moussais-la-Bataille near Tours 732 earned him his nickname of Martel, 'the Hammer', because he halted the Islamic advance by the ◊Moors into Europe.

Charles's law law stating that the volume of a given mass of gas at constant pressure is directly proportional to its absolute temperature (temperature in kelvin). It was discovered by French physicist Jacques Charles 1787, and independently by French chemist Joseph Gay-Lussac 1802.

The gas increases by 1/273 of its volume at 0°C for each °C rise of temperature. This means that the coefficient of expansion of all gases is the same. The law is only approximately true and the coefficient of expansion is generally taken as 0.003663 per °C.

Charles the Bold Duke of Burgundy 1433–1477. Son of Philip the Good, he inherited Burgundy and the Low Countries from him 1465. He waged wars attempting to free the duchy from dependence on France and restore it as a kingdom. He was killed in battle.

Charles' ambition was to create a kingdom stretching from the mouth of the Rhine to the mouth of the Rhône. He formed the League of the Public Weal against Louis XI of France, invaded France 1471, and conquered the country as far as Rouen. The Holy Roman emperor, the Swiss, and Lorraine united against him; he captured Nancy, but was defeated at Granson and again at Morat 1476. Nancy was lost, and he was killed while attempting to recapture it. His possessions in the Netherlands passed to the Habsburgs by the marriage of his daughter Mary to Maximilian I of Austria.

Charleston capital and chief city of West Virginia, USA, on the Kanawha River; population (1992) 57,100. It is the centre of a region that produces coal, natural gas, salt, clay, timber, and oil, and it is an important chemical-producing centre. Charleston developed from a fort built 1788.

Charleston main port and city of South Carolina, USA; population (1992) 81,300. Industries include textiles, clothing, and paper products. A nuclear-submarine naval base and an air-force base are nearby. The city dates from 1670.

Charlotte Amalie capital, tourist resort, and free port of the US Virgin Islands, on the island of St Thomas; population (1990) 12,331. Boatbuilding and rum distilling are among the economic activities. It was founded 1672 by the Danish West India Company.

Charlotte Augusta Princess 1796–1817. Only child of George IV and Caroline of Brunswick, and heir to the British throne. In 1816 she married Prince Leopold of Saxe-Coburg (later Leopold I of the Belgians), but died in childbirth 18 months later.

Charlotte Sophia 1744–1818. British queen consort. The daughter of the German duke of Mecklenburg-Strelitz, she married George III of Great Britain and Ireland 1761, and they had nine sons and six daughters.

Charlottetown capital of Prince Edward Island, Canada; population (1986) 16,000. The city trades in textiles, fish, timber, vegetables, and dairy produce. It was founded by French settlers in the 1720s.

Charlton Bobby (Robert) 1937– . English footballer, younger brother of Jack Charlton. He scored a record 49 goals in 106 appearances. An elegant midfield player who specialized in fierce long-range shots, he spent most of his playing career with Manchester United and played in the England team that won the World Cup 1966. On retiring Charlton had an unsuccessful spell as manager of Preston North End. He later became a director of Manchester United.

Charlton Jack (John) 1935– . English footballer, older brother of Bobby (Robert) and nephew of Jackie Milburn. He spent all his playing career with Leeds United

Charlotte Sophia A painting of the British queen consort Charlotte Sophia by Thomas Gainsborough. *Image Select (UK) Ltd*

The original writer is not the one who imitates nobody, but the one whom nobody can imitate.

François-René Chateaubriand
The Beauties of Christianity

and played more than 750 games for them. He appeared in the England team that won the World Cup 1966. After retiring, Charlton managed Middlesbrough to the 2nd division title. Appointed manager of the Republic of Ireland national squad in 1986, he took the team to the 1988 European Championship finals, after which he was made an 'honorary Irishman'. He led Ireland to the World Cup finals for the first time 1990 and again 1994.

charm in physics, a property possessed by one type of ◊quark (very small particles found inside protons and neutrons), called the charm quark. The effects of charm are only seen in experiments with particle ◊accelerators. See ◊elementary particles.

Charon in Greek mythology, the boatman who ferried the dead over the rivers Acheron and Styx to ◊Hades, the underworld. A coin placed on the tongue of the dead paid for their passage.

Chartism radical British democratic movement, mainly of the working classes, which flourished around 1838–48. It derived its name from the People's Charter, a six-point programme comprising universal male suffrage, equal electoral districts, secret ballot, annual parliaments, and abolition of the property qualification for, and payment of, members of Parliament. Greater prosperity, lack of organization, and rivalry in the leadership led to its demise.

Chartres capital of the *département* of Eure-et-Loir, NW France, 96 km/59 mi SW of Paris, on the river Eure; population (1990) 41,850. The city is an agricultural centre for the fertile Plaine de la Beauce. Its cathedral of Notre Dame, completed about 1240, is a masterpiece of Gothic architecture.

Go, litel book, go litel myn tragedie.

Geoffrey Chaucer
Troilus and Criseyde

Charybdis in Greek mythology, a whirlpool formed by a monster of the same name on one side of the narrow straits of Messina, Sicily, opposite the monster Scylla.

chasing indentation of a design on metal by small chisels and hammers. This method of decoration was familiar in ancient Egypt, Assyria, and Greece; it is used today on fine silverware.

château country house or important residence in France. The term originally applied to a French medieval castle. The château was first used as a domestic building in the late 15th century. By the reign of Louis XIII (1610–43) fortifications such as moats and keeps were no longer used for defensive purposes, but merely as decorative features. The Loire valley contains some fine examples of châteaux.

Chateaubriand François Auguste René, Vicomte de 1768–1848. French writer. He was a founder of Romanticism. Having lived in exile from the French Revolution 1794–1800, he wrote *Atala* 1801 (based on his encounters with North American Indians), *Le Génie du christianisme/The Genius of Christianity* 1802 – a defence of the Christian faith in terms of social, cultural, and spiritual benefits – and the autobiographical *René* 1805. He later wrote *Mémoires d'outre-tombe/Memoirs from Beyond the Tomb* 1848–50, an account, often imaginary, of his own life.

Chatham town in Kent, England, on the river Medway; population (1991) 71,700. The Royal Dockyard 1588–1984 was from 1985 converted to an industrial area, marina, and museum as a focus of revival for the whole Medway area. Industries include navigation equipment, cement, and electronics.

Chatterji Bankim Chandra 1838–1894. Indian novelist. Born in Bengal, where he established his reputation with his first book, *Durges-Nandini* 1864, he became a favourite of the nationalists. His book *Ananda Math* 1882 contains the Indian national song 'Bande-Mataram'.

Chatterton Thomas 1752–1770. English poet. His medieval-style poems and brief life were to inspire English Romanticism. Having studied ancient documents, he composed poems he ascribed to a 15th-century monk, 'Thomas Rowley', and these were at first accepted as genuine. He committed suicide after becoming destitute.

Chatwin (Charles) Bruce 1940–1989. English writer. His works include *The Songlines* 1987, written after living with Australian Aborigines; the novel *Utz* 1988, about a manic porcelain collector in Prague; and travel pieces and journalism collected in *What Am I Doing Here* 1989.

Chaucer Geoffrey c. 1340–1400. English poet. *The ◊Canterbury Tales*, a collection of stories told by a group of pilgrims on their way to Canterbury, reveals his knowledge of human nature and his stylistic variety, from urbane and ironic to simple and bawdy. His early work shows formal French influence, as in the dream-poem *The Book of the Duchess* and his adaptation of the French allegorical poem on courtly love, *The Romaunt of the Rose*. More mature works reflect the influence of Italian realism, as in *Troilus and Criseyde*, a substantial narrative poem about the tragic betrayal of an idealized courtly love, adapted from ◊Boccaccio. In *The Canterbury Tales* he shows his own genius for metre and characterization. Chaucer was the most influential English poet of the Middle Ages.

He was born in London, the son of a vintner. Taken prisoner in the French wars, he had to be ransomed by Edward III 1360. In 1366 he married Philippa Roet, sister of Katherine Swynford, the mistress and later third wife of ◊John of Gaunt, Duke of Lancaster. Payments during the period 1367–74 indicate a rising fortune and show that Chaucer made several journeys abroad, both on military service and public business. He was sent to Italy (where he may have met Boccaccio and ◊Petrarch), France, and Flanders. He was controller of wool customs 1374–86, and of petty customs 1382–86. He became justice of the peace for Kent 1385 and knight of the shire 1386. In 1389 he was made clerk of the king's works, and superintended undertakings at Woolwich and Smithfield. In 1391 he gave up the clerkship and accepted the position of deputy forester of North Petherton, Somerset. Late in 1399 he moved to Westminster and died the following year.

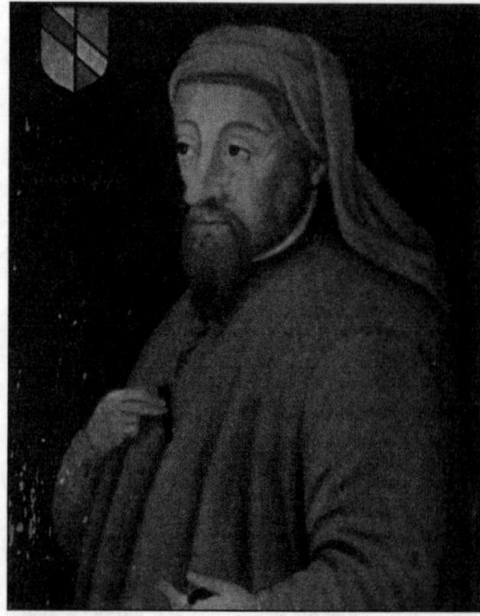

Chaucer Oil painting of English poet Geoffrey Chaucer, from the 14th century. Most of what we know of Chaucer comes from records of his court appointments and services to his patron John of Gaunt and, later, King Henry IV. Among his other offices, he sat in Parliament as knight of the shire of Kent from 1386. *Image Select (UK) Ltd*

Chaudhuri Nirad Chandra 1897– . Indian writer and broadcaster. He attracted attention with his *Autobiography of an Unknown Indian* 1950 which illuminates the clash of British and Indian civilizations. A first visit to England, previously known to him only through its literature, produced the quirky *A Passage to England* 1959. Later works include *The Continent of Circe* 1965, an erudite critique of Indian culture, and *Thy Hand Great Anarch* 1987, critical of the impact of British culture on India.

Chávez Carlos Antonio de Padua 1899–1978. Mexican composer and pianist. His music incorporates national and pre-Columbian folk elements, for example *Chapultepec: Republican Overture* 1935. He composed a number of ballets, seven symphonies, and concertos for both violin and piano. He was founder-director of the Mexico Symphony Orchestra 1928–48.

Chavín de Huantar archaeological site in the Peruvian Andes, 3,135 m/10,000 ft above sea level, thought to be 'the womb of Andean civilization'. Its influence peaked between 1000 and 300 BC.

Chayefsky Paddy (Sidney) 1923–1981. US screenwriter and dramatist of great passion and insight. He established his reputation with naturalistic television plays, at least two of which were adapted for cinema: *Marty* 1955 (for which he won an Oscar for the film screenplay) and *Bachelor Party* 1957. He also won Oscars for the bitterly satirical *The Hospital* 1971 and *Network* 1976. His stage plays include *The Tenth Man* 1959 and *Gideon* 1961. He wrote the screenplay for Ken Russell's *Altered States* 1980, which was very loosely based on Chayefsky's novel of the same name.

Chechnya or ***Chechenia*** breakaway part of the former Russian autonomous republic of Checheno-Ingush on the northern slopes of the Caucasus Mountains; official name *Noxcijn Republika Ickeriy* from 1994

area 17,300 sq km/6,680 sq mi

château Château de Chenonceau with its five-arch bridge. The château straddles the river Cher, France. *Corbis*

capital Grozny
industries oil extraction (at one of the largest Russian oilfields); engineering, chemicals, building materials; timber
population (1989) 1,070,000 (Chechen 90%)
religion Muslim
history After decades of resistance, the region was conquered by Russia 1859. It was an autonomous region of the USSR 1922–36 when it was joined to Ingushetia as the Autonomous Republic of Checheno-Ingush.

In Nov 1991, following the seizure of power by General Dzhokhar Dudayev, the region declared its independence. After a brief, unsuccessful attempt to quell the rebellion, Moscow entered into negotiations over the republic's future, and in 1992 Chechnya became an autonomous republic in its own right. Later the same year fighting broke out between forces loyal to Dudayev and anti-separatist opposition forces, backed by Russia. Civil war developed Aug 1994 and in Dec 1994 Russian forces entered Chechnya and bombed the capital. By March 1995 an estimated 40,000 civilians had been killed and 250,000 were refugees. By June 1995 Russian forces had overrun most of the republic's urban centres, forcing the Chechen rebels to resort to guerrilla warfare tactics; around 2,000 people were taken hostage by Chechen rebels, led by Shamil Basayev, in the town of Budennovsk 14 June. Following negotiations between Russian prime minister Chernomyrdin and Basayev for the hostages' release, peace talks began in Grozny, and an agreement was signed July 1995. Fighting broke out Dec 1995 as rebels attempted to disrupt local elections, and in Jan 1996 a further hostage crisis occurred in S Russia. The rebels were ambushed by Russian troops at the border town of Pervomayskoye with massive artillery and rocket bombardment. Many escaped under cover of darkness. In August 1996, on the eve of Boris Yeltsin's inauguration as president of the Russian Federation, the rebels stormed the capital city of Grozny. Chechnya's independence has not received international recognition. It was declared an Islamic Republic by President Aslan Maskhadov Nov 1997.

Checkpoint Charlie Western-controlled crossing point for non-Germans between West Berlin and East Berlin, opened 1961 as the only crossing point between the Allied and Soviet sectors. Its dismantling in June 1990 was seen as a symbol of the ending of the ◊Cold War.

Cheddar market town in Somerset, England, where Cheddar cheese was first produced. It is part of an agricultural area. Nearby are Cheddar Gorge (a limestone gorge) and caves with stalactites and stalagmites. In 1962 excavation revealed the site of a Saxon palace.

cheese food made from the curds (solids) of soured milk from cows, sheep, or goats, separated from the whey (liquid), then salted, put into moulds, and pressed into firm blocks. Cheese is ripened with bacteria or surface fungi, and kept for a time to mature before eating.

There are six main types of cheese. ***Soft cheeses*** may be ripe or unripe, and include cottage cheese and high-fat soft cheeses such as Bel Paese, Camembert, and Neufchatel. ***Semi-hard cheeses*** are ripened by bacteria (Munster) or by bacteria and surface fungi (Port Salut, Gouda, St Paulin); they may also have penicillin moulds injected into them (Roquefort, Gorgonzola, Blue Stilton, Wensleydale). ***Hard cheeses*** are ripened by bacteria, and include Cheddar, Cheshire, and Cucciocavallo; some have large cavities within them, such as Swiss Emmental and Gruyère. ***Very hard cheeses***, such as Parmesan and Spalen, are made with skimmed milk. ***Processed cheese*** is made with dried skim-milk powder and additives, and ***whey cheese*** is made by heat coagulation of the proteins from whey; examples are Mysost and Primost. In France (from 1980) a cheese has the same *appellation controlée* status as wine if it is made only in a special defined area – for example, Cantal and Roquefort are *appellation controlée* cheeses, but not Camembert and Brie, which are made in more than one region.

cheetah large wild cat *Acinonyx jubatus* native to Africa, Arabia, and SW Asia, but now rare in some areas. Yellowish with black spots, it has a slim lithe build. It is up to 1 m/3 ft tall at the shoulder, and up to 1.5 m/5 ft long. The world's fastest mammal, it can reach 110 kph/70 mph, but tires after about 400 yards. Cheetahs live in open country where they hunt small antelopes, hares, and birds.

Cheka secret police operating in the USSR 1917–23. It originated from the tsarist Okhrana (the security police under the tsar 1881–1917), and became successively the OGPU (GPU) 1923–34, NKVD 1934–46, MVD 1946–53, and the ◊KGB from 1954.

The name is formed from the initials *che* and *ka* of the two Russian words meaning 'extraordinary commission', formed for 'the repression of counter-revolutionary activities and of speculation', and extended to cover such matters as espionage and smuggling.

Chekhov Anton Pavlovich 1860–1904. Russian dramatist and writer of short stories. His plays concentrate on the creation of atmosphere and delineation of internal development, rather than external action. His first play, *Ivanov* 1887, was a failure, as was *The Seagull* 1896 until revived by Stanislavsky 1898 at the Moscow Art Theatre, for which Chekhov went on to write his finest plays: *Uncle Vanya* 1897, *The Three Sisters* 1901, and *The Cherry Orchard* 1904.

Chekhov was born in Taganrog, S Russia. He qualified as a doctor 1884, but devoted himself to writing short stories rather than practising medicine. The collection *Particoloured Stories* 1886 consolidated his reputation and gave him leisure to develop his style, as seen in *My Life* 1895, *The Lady with the Dog* 1898, and *In the Ravine* 1900.

Chekhov The Russian writer Anton Chekhov, whose plays are said to have made George Bernard Shaw want to destroy his own. As well as his major plays *The Seagull* 1895, *Uncle Vanya* 1900, *Three Sisters* 1901, and *The Cherry Orchard* 1904, Chekhov wrote many evocative and influential short stories. *Corbis*

chela in Hinduism, a follower or pupil of a guru (teacher).

chelate chemical compound whose molecules consist of one or more metal atoms or charged ions joined to chains of organic residues by coordinate (or dative covalent) chemical ◊bonds. Chelates are used in analytical chemistry, in agriculture and horticulture as carriers of essential trace metals, in water softening, and in the treatment of thalassaemia by removing excess iron, which may build up to toxic levels in the body.

Chelmsford market town in Essex, England, 48 km/30 mi NE of London; population (1991) 97,500. It is the administrative headquarters of the county, with radio, electrical, engineering, agricultural-machinery, flour-milling, and brewing industries. It was the Roman *Caesaromagus*.

Chelsea porcelain factory porcelain factory thought to be the first in England. Based in SW London, it dated from the 1740s, when it was known as the Chelsea Porcelain Works. It produced soft-paste porcelain in imitation of Chinese high-fired porcelain. Later items are distinguished by the anchor mark on the base. Chelsea porcelain includes plates and other items decorated with botanical, bird, and insect paintings. The factory was taken over by William Duesbury of Derby 1769 (after which the so-called 'Chelsea-Derby' was produced), and pulled down 1784.

Cheltenham spa town at the foot of the Cotswold Hills, Gloucestershire, England; population (1991) 91,300. There are annual literary and music festivals, a racecourse (the Cheltenham Gold Cup is held annually), and Cheltenham College (founded 1854). The town has light industries. The home of the composer Gustav Holst is now a museum, and to the SW is Prinknash Abbey, a Benedictine house that produces pottery. Cheltenham is the centre of the British government's electronic surveillance operations (◊GCHQ), as well as being Western Europe's most important electronic intelligence-gathering centre. The Universities and College Admission Service (UCAS) is here.

Chelyabinsk industrial city and capital of Chelyabinsk region, in the Russian Federation, in the S Ural Mountains; population (1994) 1,125,000. It has iron and engineering works and makes chemicals, motor vehicles, and aircraft. Waste from the plutonium plant makes it possibly the most radioactive place in the world. It lies E of the Ural Mountains, 240 km/150 mi SE of Ekaterinburg (Sverdlovsk). It was founded 1736 as a Russian frontier post.

chemical element alternative name for ◊element.

chemical equation method of indicating the reactants and products of a chemical reaction by using chemical symbols and formulae. A chemical equation gives two basic pieces of information: (1) the reactants (on the left-hand side) and products (right-hand side); and (2) the reacting proportions (stoichiometry) – that is, how many units of each reactant and product are involved. The equation must balance; that is, the total number of atoms of a particular element on the left-hand side must be the same as the number of atoms of that element on the right-hand side.

$$Na_2CO_3 + 2HCl \rightarrow 2NaCl + CO_2 + H_2O$$
$$\textit{reactants} \rightarrow \textit{products}$$

This equation states that one molecule of sodium carbonate combines with two molecules of hydrochloric acid to form two molecules of sodium chloride, one of carbon dioxide, and one of water. Double arrows indicate that the reaction is reversible – in the formation of ammonia from hydrogen and nitrogen, the direction depends on the temperature and pressure of the reactants.

$$3H_2 + N_2 \rightleftharpoons 2NH_3$$

chemical family collection of elements that have very similar chemical and physical properties. In the ◊periodic table of the elements such collections are to be found in the vertical columns (groups). The groups that contain the most markedly similar elements are group I, the ◊alkali metals; group II, the ◊alkaline-earth metals; group VII, the ◊halogens; and group 0, the noble or ◊inert gases.

chemical warfare use in ◊war of gaseous, liquid, or solid substances intended to have a toxic effect on humans, animals, or plants. Together with ◊biological warfare, it was banned by the Geneva Protocol 1925 and the United Nations in 1989 also voted for a ban. The total US stockpile 1989 was estimated at 30,000 tonnes and the Soviet stock-pile at 50,000 metric tons. In June 1990, the USA and USSR agreed bilaterally to reduce their stockpile to 5,000 tonnes each by 2002. The USA began replacing its stocks with new nerve-gas ◊binary weapons. In Jan 1993, over 120 nations, including the USA and Russia, signed a treaty outlawing the manufacture, stockpiling, and use of chemical weapons.

Some 20 nations currently hold chemical weapons, including Iraq, Iran, Israel, Syria, Libya, South Africa, China, Ethiopia, North Korea, Myanmar, Taiwan, and Vietnam. The Geneva Protocol 1925, as the only international legal mechanism for the control of chemical weapons, has not always been observed. In 1989 the 149-nation UN Conference on Disarmament unanimously voted to outlaw chemical weapons, and drew up a draft Convention on Chemical Weapons (CCW), intended as the basis for a new international agreement on chemical warfare, which was realized in the signing of the

'Medvedenko: 'Why do you wear black all the time?' / Masha: 'I'm in mourning for my life, I'm unhappy.''

Anton Chekhov
The Seagull

1993 treaty in Paris. The treaty was unique in establishing verification procedures (administered by a new body, the Organization for the Prohibition of Chemical Weapons, in the Hague, the Netherlands) and in allowing for sanctions against nations not party to the treaty. Iraq used chemical weapons during the 1980–88 Iran–Iraq war, inflicting massive casualties on largely unprotected Iranian Revolutionary Guards and on civilians; it threatened the use of chemical weapons during the 1991 Gulf War but did not use them. There are several types of chemical weapons.

Irritant gases may cause permanent injury or death. Examples include chlorine, phosgene (Cl_2CO), and mustard gas ($C_4H_8Cl_2S$), used in World War I (1914–18) and allegedly used by Soviet forces in Afghanistan, by Vietnamese forces in Laos, and by Iraq against Iran during their 1980–88 war.

Tear gases, such as CS gas, used in riot control, affect the lungs and eyes, causing temporary blindness.

Nerve gases are organophosphorus compounds similar to insecticides, which are taken into the body through the skin and lungs and break down the action of the nervous system. Developed by the Germans for World War II, they were not used.

Incapacitants are drugs designed to put an enemy temporarily out of action by, for example, impairing vision or inducing hallucinations. They have not so far been used.

Toxins are poisons to be eaten, drunk, or injected; for example, ricin (derived from the castor-oil plant) and the botulism toxin. Ricin has been used in individual cases, and other toxins were allegedly used by Soviet forces in Afghanistan and by Vietnamese forces in Cambodia.

Herbicides are defoliants used to destroy vegetation sheltering troops and the crops of hostile populations. They were used in Vietnam by the USA and in Malaya (now Malaysia) by the UK. ◊Agent Orange became notorious because it caused cancer and birth abnormalities among Vietnam War veterans and US factory staff.

Binary weapons are two chemical components that become toxic in combination, after the shell containing them is fired.

chemisorption the attachment, by chemical means, of a single layer of molecules, atoms, or ions of gas to the surface of a solid or, less frequently, a liquid. It is the basis of catalysis (see ◊catalyst) and is of great industrial importance.

chemistry branch of science concerned with the study of the structure and composition of the different kinds of matter, the changes which matter

CHEMISTRY: TIMELINE

c. 3000 BC	Egyptians were producing bronze – an alloy of copper and tin.
c. 450 BC	Greek philosopher Empedocles proposed that all substances are made up of a combination of four elements – earth, air, fire, and water – an idea that was developed by Plato and Aristotle and persisted for over 2,000 years.
c. 400 BC	Greek philosopher Democritus theorized that matter consists ultimately of tiny, indivisible particles, *atomoi*.
AD 1	Gold, silver, copper, lead, iron, tin, and mercury were known.
200	The techniques of solution, filtration, and distillation were known.
7th–17th Cs	Chemistry was dominated by alchemy, the attempt to transform nonprecious metals such as lead and copper into gold. Though misguided, it led to the discovery of many new chemicals and techniques, such as sublimation and distillation.
12thC	Alcohol was first distilled in Europe.
1242	Gunpowder introduced to Europe from the Far East.
1620	Scientific method of reasoning expounded by Francis Bacon in his *Novum Organum*.
1650	Leyden University in the Netherlands set up the first chemistry laboratory.
1661	Robert Boyle defined an element as any substance that cannot be broken down into still simpler substances and asserted that matter is composed of 'corpuscles' (atoms) of various sorts and sizes, capable of arranging themselves into groups, each of which constitutes a chemical substance.
1662	Boyle described the inverse relationship between the volume and pressure of a fixed mass of gas (Boyle's law).
1697	Georg Stahl proposed the erroneous theory that substances burn because they are rich in a certain substance, called phlogiston.
1755	Joseph Black discovered carbon dioxide.
1774	Joseph Priestley discovered oxygen, which he called 'dephlogisticated air'. Antoine Lavoisier demonstrated his law of conservation of mass.
1777	Lavoisier showed air to be made up of a mixture of gases, and showed that one of these – oxygen – is the substance necessary for combustion (burning) and rusting to take place.
1781	Henry Cavendish showed water to be a compound.
1792	Alessandra Volta demonstrated the electrochemical series.
1807	Humphry Davy passed electric current through molten compounds (the process of electrolysis) in order to isolate elements, such as potassium, that had never been separated by chemical means. Jöns Berzelius proposed that chemicals produced by living creatures should be termed 'organic'.
1808	John Dalton published his atomic theory, which states that every element consists of similar indivisible particles – called atoms – which differ from the atoms of other elements in their mass; he also drew up a list of relative atomic masses. Joseph Gay-Lussac announced that the volumes of gases that combine chemically with one another are in simple ratios.
1811	Publication of Amedeo Avogadro's hypothesis on the relation between the volume and number of molecules of a gas, and its temperature and pressure.
1813–14	Berzelius devised the chemical symbols and formulae still used to represent elements and compounds.
1828	Franz Wöhler converted ammonium cyanate into urea – the first synthesis of an organic compound from an inorganic substance.
1832–33	Michael Faraday expounded the laws of electrolysis, and adopted the term 'ion' for the particles believed to be responsible for carrying current.
1846	Thomas Graham expounded his law of diffusion.
1853	Robert Bunsen invented the Bunsen burner.
1858	Stanislao Cannizzaro differentiated between atomic and molecular weights (masses).
1861	Organic chemistry was defined by German chemist Friedrich Kekulé as the chemistry of carbon compounds.
1864	John Newlands devised the first periodic table of the elements.
1869	Dmitri Mendeleyev expounded his periodic table of the elements (based on atomic mass), leaving gaps for elements that had not yet been discovered.
1874	Jacobus van't Hoff suggested that the four bonds of carbon are arranged tetrahedrally, and that carbon compounds can therefore be three-dimensional and asymmetric.
1884	Swedish chemist Svante Arrhenius suggested that electrolytes (solutions or molten compounds that conduct electricity) dissociate into ions, atoms or groups of atoms that carry a positive or negative charge.
1894	William Ramsey and Lord Rayleigh discovered the first inert gas, argon.
1897	The electron was discovered by J J Thomson.
1901	Mikhail Tsvet invented paper chromatography as a means of separating pigments.
1909	Sören Sörensen devised the pH scale of acidity.
1912	Max von Laue showed crystals to be composed of regular, repeating arrays of atoms by studying the patterns in which they diffract X-rays.
1913–14	Henry Moseley equated the atomic number of an element with the positive charge on its nuclei, and drew up the periodic table, based on atomic numbers, that is used today.
1916	Gilbert Newton Lewis explained covalent bonding between atoms as a sharing of electrons.
1927	Nevil Sidgwick published his theory of valency, based on the numbers of electrons in the outer shells of the reacting atoms.
1930	Electrophoresis, which separates particles in suspension in an electric field, was invented by Arne Tiselius.
1932	Deuterium (heavy hydrogen), an isotope of hydrogen, was discovered by Harold Urey.
1940	Edwin McMillan and Philip Abelson showed that new elements with a higher atomic number than uranium can be formed by bombarding uranium with neutrons, and synthesized the first transuranic element, neptunium.
1942	Plutonium was first synthesized by Glenn T Seaborg and Edwin McMillan.
1950	Derek Barton deduced that some properties of organic compounds are affected by the orientation of their functional groups (the study of which became known as conformational analysis).
1954	Einsteinium and fermium were synthesized.
1955	Ilya Prigogine described the thermodynamics of irreversible processes (the transformations of energy that take place in, for example, many reactions within living cells).
1962	Neil Bartlett prepared the first compound of an inert gas, xenon hexafluoroplatinate; it was previously believed that inert gases could not take part in a chemical reaction.
1965	Robert B Woodward synthesized complex organic compounds.
1981	Quantum mechanics applied to predict course of chemical reactions by US chemist Roald Hoffmann and Kenichi Fukui of Japan.
1982	Element 109, unnilennium, synthesized.
1985	Fullerenes, a new class of carbon solids made up of closed cages of carbon atoms, were discovered by Harold Kroto and David Walton at the University of Sussex, England.
1987	US chemists Donald Cram and Charles Pederson, and Jean-Marie Lehn of France created artificial molecules that mimic the vital chemical reactions of life processes.
1990	Jean-Marie Lehn, Ulrich Koert, and Margaret Harding reported the synthesis of a new class of compounds, called nucleohelicates, that mimic the double helical structure of DNA, turned inside out.
1993	US chemists at the University of California and the Scripps Institute synthesized rapamycin, one of a group of complex, naturally occurring antibiotics and immunosuppressants that are being tested as anticancer agents.
1994	Elements 110 (ununnilium) and 111 (unununium) discovered at the GSI heavy-ion cyclotron, Darmstadt, Germany.
1995	German chemists built the largest-ever wheel molecule made up of 154 molybdenum atoms surrounded by oxygen atoms. It has a relative molecular mass of 24,000 and is soluble in water.
1996	Element 112 discovered at the GSI heavy-ion cyclotron, Darmstadt, Germany.

may undergo and the phenomena which occur in the course of these changes.

Organic chemistry is the branch of chemistry that deals with carbon compounds. ***Inorganic chemistry*** deals with the description, properties, reactions, and preparation of all the elements and their compounds, with the exception of carbon compounds. ***Physical chemistry*** is concerned with the quantitative explanation of chemical phenomena and reactions, and the measurement of data required for such explanations. This branch studies in particular the movement of molecules and the effects of temperature and pressure, often with regard to gases and liquids.

molecules, atoms, and elements All matter can exist in three states: gas, liquid, or solid. It is composed of minute particles termed molecules, which are constantly moving, and may be further divided into ◊atoms.

Molecules that contain atoms of one kind only are known as elements; those that contain atoms of different kinds are called compounds.

compounds and mixtures Chemical compounds are produced by a chemical action that alters the arrangement of the atoms in the reacting molecules. Heat, light, vibration, catalytic action, radiation, or pressure, as well as moisture (for ionization), may be necessary to produce a chemical change. Examination and possible breakdown of compounds to determine their components is analysis, and the building up of compounds from their components is synthesis. When substances are brought together without changing their molecular structures they are said to be mixtures.

formulas and equations Symbols are used to denote the elements. The symbol is usually the first letter or letters of the English or Latin name of the element – for example, C for carbon; Ca for calcium; Fe for iron (*ferrum*). These symbols represent one atom of the element; molecules containing more than one atom of an element are denoted by a subscript figure – for example, water is H_2O. In some substances a group of atoms acts as a single entity, and these are enclosed in parentheses in the symbol – for example $(NH_4)_2SO_4$ denotes ammonium sulphate. The symbolic representation of a molecule is known as a formula. A figure placed before a formula represents the number of molecules of a substance taking part in, or being produced by, a chemical reaction – for example, $2H_2O$ indicates two molecules of water. Chemical reactions are expressed by means of equations as in:

$$NaCl + H_2SO_4 \rightarrow NaHSO_4 + HCl$$

This equation states the fact that sodium chloride (NaCl) on being treated with sulphuric acid (H_2SO_4) is converted into sodium bisulphate (sodium hydrogensulphate, $NaHSO_4$) and hydrogen chloride (HCl). See also ◊chemical equation.

metals, nonmetals, and the periodic system Elements are divided into ***metals***, which have lustre and conduct heat and electricity, and ***nonmetals***, which usually lack these properties. The periodic system, developed by John Newlands in 1863 and established by Dmitri ◊Mendeleyev in 1869, classified elements according to their relative atomic masses. Those elements that resemble each other in general properties were found to bear a relation to one another by weight, and these were placed in groups or families. Certain anomalies in this system were later removed by classifying the elements according to their atomic numbers. The latter is equivalent to the positive charge on the nucleus of the atom.

Chemnitz industrial city (engineering, textiles, chemicals) in Saxony, Federal Republic of Germany, on the river Chemnitz, 65 km/40 mi SSE of Leipzig; population (1993) 282,000. As a former district capital of East Germany it was named Karl-Marx-Stadt 1953–90.

chemosynthesis method of making ◊protoplasm (contents of a cell) using the energy from chemical reactions, in contrast to the use of light energy employed for the same purpose in ◊photosynthesis. The process is used by certain bacteria, which can synthesize organic compounds from carbon dioxide and water using the energy from special methods of ◊respiration. Nitrifying bacteria are a group of chemosynthetic organisms which change free nitrogen into a form that can be taken up by plants; nitrobacteria, for example, oxidize nitrites to nitrates. This is a vital part of the ◊nitrogen cycle.

chemotherapy any medical treatment with chemicals. It usually refers to treatment of cancer with cytotoxic and other drugs. The term was coined by the German bacteriologist Paul Ehrlich for the use of synthetic chemicals against infectious diseases.

chemotropism movement by part of a plant in response to a chemical stimulus. The response by the plant is termed 'positive' if the growth is towards the stimulus or 'negative' if the growth is away from the stimulus.

Chengdu or ***Chengtu*** ancient city, capital of Sichuan province, China; population (1993) 2,670,000. It is a busy rail junction and has railway workshops, and textile, electronics, and engineering industries. It has well-preserved temples.

Chennai (formerly, to 1996, Madras) industrial port (cotton, cement, chemicals, iron, and steel) and capital of Tamil Nadu, India, on the Bay of Bengal; population (1991) 5,361,000. Fort St George 1639 remains from the East India Company when Chennai was the chief port on the E coast. Chennai was occupied by the French 1746–48, and was the only place in India to be attacked in World War I.

Chepstow (Welsh ***Casgwent***) market town in Gwent, Wales, on the river Wye. The high tides, sometimes 15 m/50 ft above low level, are the highest in Britain. There is a Norman castle, and the ruins of Tintern Abbey are 6.5 km/4 mi to the N. There are light industries, farming, and tourism.

Chequers country home of the prime minister of the UK. It is an Elizabethan mansion in the Chiltern hills near Princes Risborough, Buckinghamshire, and was given to the nation by Lord Lee of Fareham under the Chequers Estate Act 1917, which came into effect 1921.

Cher French river that rises in Creuse *département* and flows into the river Loire below Tours, length 355 km/220 mi. It gives its name to a *département*.

Cherbourg French port and naval station at the northern end of the Cotentin peninsula, in Manche *département*; population (1990) 28,800. There is an institute for studies in nuclear warfare, and large shipbuilding yards. During World War II, Cherbourg was captured June 1944 by US troops, who thus gained their first large port of entry into France. It was severely damaged and restoration of the harbour was only completed 1952. There are ferry links to England (Southampton, Weymouth, and Rosslare).

Cherenkov Pavel Alexeevich 1904–1990. Soviet physicist. In 1934 he discovered Cherenkov radiation; this occurs as a bluish light when charged atomic particles pass through water or other media at a speed in excess of that of light. He shared a Nobel prize 1958 with his colleagues Ilya Frank (1908–1990) and Igor Tamm (1895–1971) for work resulting in a cosmic-ray counter.

Chernenko Konstantin Ustinovich 1911–1985. Soviet politician, leader of the Soviet Communist Party (CPSU) and president 1984–85. He was a protégé of Brezhnev and from 1978 a member of the Politburo. He succeeded Andropov as leader of the CPSU and as president.

Chernobyl town in northern Ukraine; site of a nuclear power station. In April 1986 two huge explosions destroyed a central reactor, breaching the 1,000-tonne roof. In the immediate vicinity of Chernobyl, 31 people died (all firemen or workers at the plant) and 135,000 were permanently evacuated. It has been estimated that there will be an additional 20–40,000 deaths from cancer in the following 60 years; 600,000 are officially classified as at risk. According to World Health Organization figures of 1995, the incidence of thyroid cancer in children increased 200-fold in Belarus as a result of fallout from the disaster. The resulting clouds of radioactive isotopes were traced all over Europe, from Ireland to Greece.

Chernomyrdin Viktor Stepanovich 1938– . Russian politician, prime minister 1992–98. A communist party apparatchik, he became prime minister Dec 1992 after Russia's ex-communist dominated parliament had ousted the market reformer, Yegor Gaidar. He assumed temporary control over foreign and security policy after President Yeltsin suffered a heart attack Nov 1995, and again in Nov 1996 when Yeltsin underwent open-heart surgery.

Chernomyrdin emerged as a respected and pragmatic reformer who brought a measure of stability to the country. He formed the Russia is Our Home party 1995.

Cherokee the ◊Native American people, formerly living in the S Appalachian Mountains of North America, in what is now Alabama, the Carolinas, Georgia, and Tennessee. They sided with Britain against France in North America, and fought against the rebel colonists in the American War of Independence. The failure of the Royalist party led to their subjugation by the new republic and the loss of a large part of their territory. In 1829 they were transported to a reservation in Oklahoma by forced march, known as the Trail of Tears, by order of President Andrew Jackson as a punishment for aiding the British during the American Revolution. Until 1906, when they disbanded as a tribe to become US citizens, they had a constitutional government, consisting of an elected chief, a senate, and a house of representatives. They now live mainly in North Carolina and Oklahoma, where they established their capital at Tahlequah. In 1984, they were permitted to re-establish a tribal centre in North Carolina.

cherry any of various trees of the genus *Prunus*, belonging to the rose family. Cultivated cherries are derived from two species, the sour cherry *P. cerasus*, and the gean *P. avium*, which grow wild in Britain. Besides those varieties that are grown for their fruit, others are planted as ornamental trees.

Cherubini Luigi (Carlo Zanobi Salvadore Maria) 1760–1842. Italian composer. His first opera *Quinto Fabio* 1779 was produced at Alessandria. Following his appointment as court composer to King George III of England 1784–88, he settled in Paris where he produced a number of dramatic works including *Médée* 1797, *Les Deux Journées* 1800, and the ballet *Anacréon* 1803. After 1809 he devoted himself largely to church music.

Chesapeake Bay largest of the inlets on the Atlantic coast of the USA, bordered by Maryland and Virginia. It is about 320 km/200 mi in length and 6–64 km/4–40 mi in width. Among the rivers that flow into the bay are the James, York, Potomac, Rappahannock, Patuxent, and Susquehanna. Deep-water ports on the bay are Newport News, Norfolk, Portsmouth, and Baltimore. The Chesapeake and Delaware Canal links the bay to the Delaware River and the Wilmington-Philadelphia port area.

Cherubini The composer Luigi Cherubini, depicted here receiving divine inspiration from one of the Muses, painted by J A D Ingres 1842. Beethoven considered Cherubini his greatest contemporary. Although his reputation has declined this century, he greatly influenced a generation of Romantic composers. *Image Select (UK) Ltd*

chess The names of chess pieces reflect the game's long history. Behind the eight pawns (foot-soldiers) on the board stand the king and queen, two bishops, two knights and two rooks (or castles). The queen is the most powerful piece, being able to move any number of squares vertically or diagonally.

the way each piece can move
arrangement of the chessmen

Chess is ruthless: you've got to be prepared to kill people.

On CHESS
Nigel Short, quoted in the *Observer* 11 Aug 1991

Religion is by no means a proper subject of conversation in a mixed company.

PHILIP CHESTERFIELD
Letters to his Son

Cheshire county of NW England
area 2,320 sq km/896 sq mi (*see United Kingdom map*)
towns and cities Chester (administrative headquarters), Warrington, Crewe, Widnes, Macclesfield, Congleton
features chiefly a fertile plain, with the Pennines in the E; rivers: Mersey, Dee, Weaver; salt mines and geologically rich former copper workings at Alderley Edge (in use from Roman times until the 1920s); Little Moreton Hall; discovery of Lindow Man, the first 'bogman' to be found in mainland Britain, dating from around 500 BC; Quarry Bank Mill at Styal is a cotton-industry museum
industries textiles, chemicals, dairy products
famous people the novelist Elizabeth Gaskell lived at Knutsford (the locale of *Cranford*); Charles Dodgson (Lewis Carroll)
population (1991) 956,600.

chess board game originating as early as the 2nd century AD. Two players use 16 pieces each, on a board of 64 squares of alternating colour, to try to force the opponent into a position where the main piece (the king) is threatened and cannot move to another position without remaining threatened. Chess originated in India, and spread to Russia, China, Japan, and Iran, and from there was introduced to the Mediterranean area by Arab invaders. It reached Britain in the 12th century via Spain and Italy. The first official world championships were recognized in 1886.

The Fédération Internationale des Echecs (FIDE) was established 1924. Leading players are rated according to the Elo System, and Bobby Fischer (USA) is considered to be one of the greatest Grand Masters of all time with a rating of 2,785. The Professional Chess Association (PCA) introduced its championship 1993. *See list of tables on p. 1177.*

Chester city in Cheshire, England, on the river Dee 26 km/16 mi S of Liverpool; population (1991) 115,000. It is the administrative headquarters of Cheshire. There are engineering, metallurgical, and clothing industries, and car components are manufactured. It was a Roman legionary fortress *Deva* and there are many Roman remains, and a medieval town centre. It is the only English city to retain its city walls (2 mi/3 km long) intact. The cathedral dates from the 11th century but was restored 1876. The church of St John the Baptist is a well-known example of early Norman architecture. The 'Rows' are covered arcades dating from the Middle Ages.

Chesterfield market town of Derbyshire, England, near the Peak District National Park, 40 km/25 mi N of Derby, on the Rother River; population (1991) 71,900. Industries include iron founding, chemicals, pottery, engineering, and glass.

Chesterfield Philip Dormer Stanhope, 4th Earl of Chesterfield 1694–1773. English politician and writer. He was the author of *Letters to his Son* 1774, which gave voluminous instruction on aristocratic manners and morals. A member of the literary circle of Swift, Pope, and Bolingbroke, he incurred the wrath of Dr Samuel Johnson by failing to carry out an offer of patronage.

He was ambassador to Holland 1728–32 and 1744. In Ireland, he established schools, helped to reconcile Protestants and Catholics, and encouraged manufacturing. An opponent of Walpole, he was a Whig member of Parliament 1715–26, Lord Lieutenant of Ireland 1745–46, and secretary of state 1746–48.

Chesterton G(ilbert) K(eith) 1874–1936. English novelist, essayist, and poet. He wrote numerous short stories featuring a Catholic priest, Father Brown, who solves crimes by drawing on his knowledge of human nature. Other novels include the fantasy *The Napoleon of Notting Hill* 1904 and *The Man Who Was Thursday* 1908, a deeply emotional allegory about the problem of evil.

He was also active as a political essayist, and was president of the Distributist League, of which *G K's Weekly* 1925 was (more or less) the organ. 'Distributism' was a term invented by the writer Hilaire ◊Belloc to denote a revolt against capitalism in the direction opposite to socialism by strengthening the 'small man' and discouraging big business.

chestnut tree of the genus *Castanea*, belonging to the beech family Fagaceae. The Spanish or sweet chestnut *C. sativa* produces edible nuts inside husks; its timber is also valuable. ◊Horse chestnuts are quite distinct, belonging to the genus *Aesculus*, family Hippocastanaceae. The chestnut is native to the Balkans and Italy; it was introduced to Britain in Roman times.

Chetnik member of a Serbian nationalist group that operated underground during the German occupation of Yugoslavia in World War II. Led by Col Draza ◊Mihailovič, the Chetniks initially received aid from the Allies, but this was later transferred to the communist partisans led by Tito. The term was also popularly applied to Serb militia forces in the 1991–92 Yugoslav civil war.

Chevalier Maurice 1888–1972. French singer and actor. He began as dancing partner to the revue artiste ◊Mistinguett at the ◊Folies-Bergère, and made numerous films including *Innocents of Paris* 1929 (which revived his song 'Louise'), *The Merry Widow* 1934, and *Gigi* 1958.

Cheviot Hills range of hills 56 km/35 mi long, mainly in Northumberland, forming the border between England and Scotland for some 48 km/30 mi. The highest point is the Cheviot, 816 m/2,676 ft. For centuries the area was a battleground between the English and the Scots. It gives its name to a breed of sheep.

Chiang Ching alternative transliteration of ◊Jiang Qing, Chinese actress, third wife of Mao Zedong.

Chiang Ching-kuo 1910–1988. Taiwanese politician, son of Chiang Kai-shek, prime minister 1971–78, president 1978–88.

Chiang Kai-shek (Pinyin ***Jiang Jie Shi***) 1887–1975. Chinese nationalist ◊Guomindang (Kuomintang) general and politician, president of China 1928–31 and 1943–49, and of Taiwan from 1949, where he set up a US-supported right-wing government on his expulsion from the mainland by the communist forces.

Chiang took part in the revolution of 1911 that overthrew the Qing dynasty of the Manchus, and on the death of the Guomindang leader Sun Yat-sen was made commander in chief of the nationalist armies in S China 1925. Collaboration with the communists, broken 1927, was resumed after the ◊Xian Incident 1936 when China needed to pool military strength in the struggle against the Japanese invaders of World War II. After the Japanese surrender 1945, civil war between the nationalists and communists erupted, and in Dec 1949 Chiang and his followers took refuge on the island of Taiwan, maintaining a large army in the hope of reclaiming the mainland. His authoritarian regime enjoyed US support until his death. His son Chiang Ching-kuo then became president.

chestnut Chestnut trees come in two types: the sweet or Spanish chestnut (illustrated) and the horse chestnut. The sweet chestnut, native to S Europe, Asia, and N America, has toothed leaves and edible seeds, and can grow to a height of 21 m/70 ft.

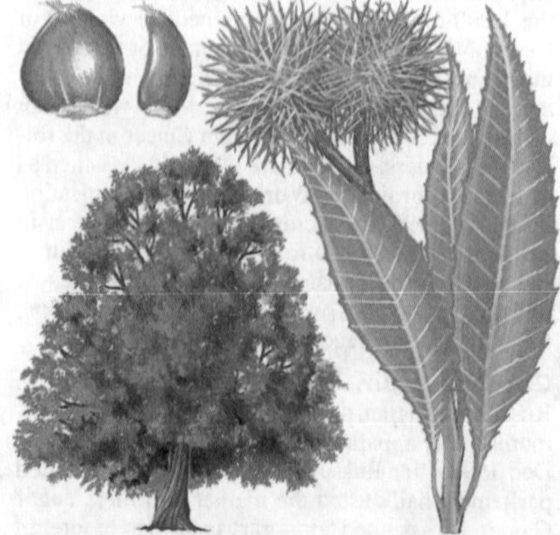

chiaroscuro (Italian 'light-dark') in painting and graphic art, the balanced use of light and shade, particularly where contrasting luminous and opaque materials are represented, for example, glinting metal and dark velvet. Masters of chiaroscuro include Leonardo da Vinci, Rembrandt, and Caravaggio. The term is also used to describe a monochromatic painting employing light and dark shades only.

Chibcha member of a Native American people of Colombia, whose high chiefdom was conquered by the Spanish in 1538. Their practice of covering their chief with gold dust, during rituals, fostered the legend of the 'Lost City' of El Dorado (the Golden Man), which was responsible for many failed expeditions into the interior of the continent.

Chicago (Ojibway 'wild onion place') financial and industrial city in Illinois, USA, on Lake Michigan. It is the third largest US city; population (1992) 2,768,500; metropolitan area (1992) 8,410,000. Industries include iron, steel, chemicals, electrical goods, machinery, meatpacking and food processing, publishing, and fabricated metals. The once famous stockyards are now closed.
features The world's first skyscraper was built here 1885 and some of the world's tallest skyscrapers, including the Sears Tower (443 m/1,454 ft), are in Chicago. It has a symphony orchestra, an art institute, the University of Chicago (site of the first controlled nuclear reaction), DePaul and Loyola universities, a campus of the University of Illinois, and the Illinois Institute of Technology.
history The site of Chicago was visited by Jesuit missionaries 1673, and Fort Dearborn, then a frontier fort, was built here 1803. As late as 1831 Chicago was still an insignificant village, but railroads from the east coast reached it by 1852, and by the time of the great fire of 1871 it was a city of more than 300,000 inhabitants. Around a third of the city was destroyed in the fire, producing rapid and innovative urban expansion, including the first telephone exchange 1878 and the first skyscrapers. By 1900 the population had reached 1.5 million and Chicago was the second largest city in the USA. Rapid development began again in the 1920s, and during the years of ◊Prohibition 1920–33, the city became notorious for the activities of its gangsters. The opening of the St Lawrence Seaway 1959 brought Atlantic shipping to its docks.

Chicago School in architecture, 19th-century North American movement, centred in Chicago, which heralded the arrival of the ◊skyscraper with its emphasis on verticality. The practice of Daniel H Burnham (1846–1912) and John Welbourn Root (1850–1891) produced two noted exemplars: the 16-storey Monadnock building 1889–91 and the Reliance building 1890–94, both in Chicago. The latter comprised a steel frame with glass infill – an obvious precursor of many 20th-century skyscrapers. The school's greatest exponent, however, was Louis ◊Sullivan.

Chicago School in economics, an approach that advocates strict control of the money supply to control inflation. Milton ◊Friedman, who advocated this approach, following the principles of ◊monetarism, was professor of economics at Chicago University, USA.

Chichen Itzá Toltec city situated among the Maya city-states of Yucatán, Mexico. It flourished AD 900–1200 and displays Classic and Post-Classic architecture of the Toltec style. The site has temples with sculptures and colour reliefs, an observatory, and a sacred well into which sacrifices, including human beings, were cast.

Chichester city and market town in West Sussex; 111 km/69 mi SW of London, near Chichester Harbour; population (1991) 26,600. It is the administrative headquarters of West Sussex. It was a Roman township (*Noviomagus Regnensium*), and the remains of the Roman palace built around AD 80 at nearby Fishbourne are unique outside Italy. There is a cathedral consecrated 1108, later much rebuilt and restored, and the Chichester Festival Theatre (1962). It lies in an agricultural area.

Chichester Francis Charles 1901–1972. English sailor and navigator. In 1931 he made the first east–west crossing of the Tasman Sea in *Gipsy Moth*, and in 1966–67 circumnavigated the world in his yacht *Gipsy Moth IV*.

chicken domestic fowl; see under ◊poultry.

chickenpox or ***varicella*** common, usually mild disease, caused by a virus of the ◊herpes group and transmitted by airborne droplets. Chickenpox chiefly attacks children under the age of ten. The incubation period is two to three weeks. One attack normally gives immunity for life. The temperature rises and spots (later inflamed blisters) develop on the torso, then on the face and limbs. The sufferer recovers within a week, but remains infectious until the last scab disappears.

chicory plant *Cichorium intybus*, family Compositae. Native to Europe and W Asia, it has large, usually blue, flowers. Its long taproot is used dried and roasted as a coffee substitute. As a garden vegetable, grown under cover, its blanched leaves are used in salads. It is related to ◊endive and grows wild in Britain, mainly on chalky soils.

chigger or ***harvest mite*** scarlet or rusty brown ◊mite genus *Trombicula*, family Trombiculidae, in the order Acarina, common in summer and autumn. Chiggers are parasitic, and their tiny red larvae cause intensely irritating bites in places where the skin is thin, such as behind the knees or between the toes. After a time they leave their host and drop to the ground where they feed upon minute insects.

chihuahua smallest breed of dog, 15 cm/10 in high, developed in the USA from Mexican origins. It may weigh only 1 kg/2.2 lb. The domed head and wide-set ears are characteristic, and the skull is large compared to the body. It can be almost any colour, and occurs in both smooth (or even hairless) and long-coated varieties.

chicory Native to Europe, W Asia, and N Africa, chicory is widely cultivated elsewhere as a salad vegetable and a coffee substitute. In the British Isles, the pale blue flowers of the chicory plant are most likely to be seen on roadside verges. *Premaphotos Wildlife*

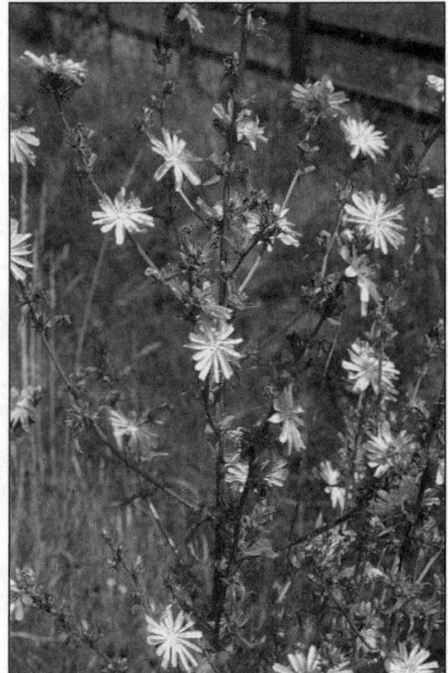

Chihuahua capital of Chihuahua state, Mexico, 1,285 km/800 mi NW of Mexico City; population (1990) 530,800. It was founded 1707. It is the centre of a mining district and has textile mills.

Chikamatsu Monzaemon, originally Sugimori Nobumori 1653–1725. Japanese dramatist. He wrote over 150 plays for the puppet and ◊kabuki theatres in Osaka. His plays for puppets were usually either domestic tragedies such as *The Love Suicides at Sonezaki* 1703, or heroic historical dramas like *The Battles of Coxinga* 1715. The plays are written in prose.

child abuse the molesting of children by parents and other adults. It can give rise to various criminal charges and has become a growing concern since the early 1980s. In the UK, a local authority can take abused children away from their parents by obtaining a care order from a juvenile court under the Children's and Young Persons Act 1969 (replaced by the Children's Act 1989). Controversial methods of diagnosing sexual abuse led to a public inquiry in Cleveland, England 1988, which severely criticized the handling of such cases. The standard of proof required for criminal proceedings is greater than that required for a local authority to take children into care. This led to highly publicized cases where children have been taken into care but prosecutions have eventually not been brought, as in Rochdale, Lancashire, and the Orkneys, Scotland in 1990.

Childe V(ere) Gordon 1892–1957. Australian archaeologist who was an authority on early European and Middle Eastern societies. He pioneered current methods of analytical archaeology. His books include *The Dawn of European Civilization* 1925 and *What Happened in History* 1942. He was professor of prehistoric archaeology at Edinburgh University 1927–46, and director of the London Institute of Archaeology 1946–57.

Children's Crusade ◊crusade by some 10,000 children from France, the Low Countries, and Germany, in 1212, to recapture Jerusalem for Christianity. Motivated by religious piety, many of them were sold into slavery or died of disease. ▷*See feature on pp. 280–281.*

children's literature works specifically written for children. The earliest known illustrated children's book in English is *Goody Two Shoes* 1765, possibly written by Oliver Goldsmith. Fairy tales were originally part of a vast range of oral literature, credited only to the writer who first recorded them, such as Charles Perrault. During the 19th century several writers, including Hans Christian Andersen, wrote original stories in the fairy-tale genre; others, such as the Grimm brothers, collected (and sometimes adapted) existing stories.

Early children's stories were written with a moral purpose; this was particularly true in the 19th century, apart from the unique case of Lewis Carroll's *Alice* books. The late 19th century was the great era of children's literature in the UK, with Lewis Carroll, Beatrix Potter, Charles Kingsley, and J M Barrie. It was also the golden age of illustrated children's books, with such artists as Kate Greenaway and Randolph Caldecott. In the USA, Louisa May Alcott's *Little Women* 1869 and its sequels found a wide audience. Among the most popular 20th-century children's writers in English have been Kenneth Grahame (*The Wind in the Willows* 1908) and A A Milne (*Winnie the Pooh* 1926) in the UK; and, in the USA, Laura Ingalls Wilder (*Little House on the Prairie* 1935), E B White (*Stuart Little* 1945, *Charlotte's Web* 1952), and Dr Seuss (*Cat in the Hat* 1957). Canadian Lucy Maud Montgomery's series that began with *Anne of Green Gables* 1908 was widely popular. Adventure stories have often appealed to children even when these were written for adults; examples include *Robinson Crusoe* by Daniel Defoe; the satirical *Gulliver's Travels* by Jonathan Swift, and *Tom Sawyer* 1876 and *Huckleberry Finn* 1884 by Mark Twain.

Many recent children's writers have been influenced by J R R ◊Tolkien whose *The Hobbit* 1937 and its sequel, the three-volume *Lord of the Rings* 1954–55, are set in the comprehensively imagined world of 'Middle-earth'. His friend C S ◊Lewis produced the allegorical chronicles of Narnia, beginning with *The Lion, the Witch and the Wardrobe* 1950. Rosemary Sutcliff's *The Eagle of the Ninth* 1954, Philippa Pearce's *Tom's Midnight Garden* 1958, and Penelope Lively's *The Wild Hunt of Hagworthy* 1971 are other outstanding books by children's authors who have exploited a perennial fascination with time travel. Writers for younger children combining stories and illustrations of equally high quality include Maurice Sendak (*Where the Wild Things Are* 1963) and Quentin Blake (*Mister Magnolia* 1980). Roald ◊Dahl's *James and the Giant Peach* 1961 is the first of his popular children's books, which summon up primitive emotions and have an imperious morality. More realistic stories for teenagers are written by US authors such as Judy Blume and S E Hinton.

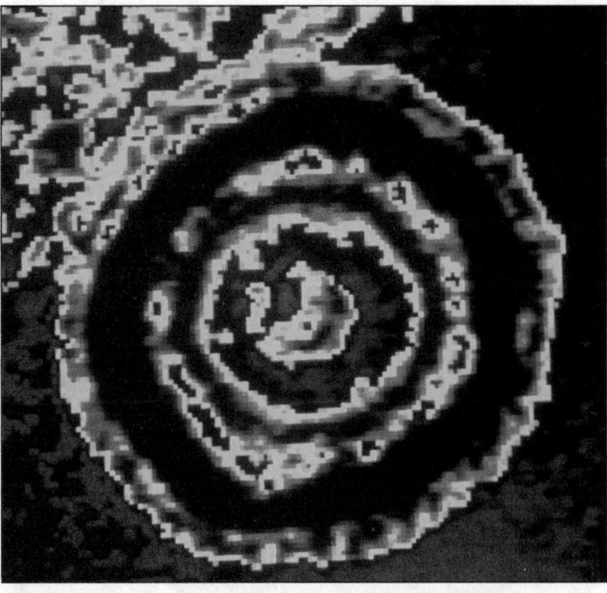

chickenpox A false-colour electron micrograph of the chickenpox virus *Varicella zoster*. Though highly contagious, chickenpox usually creates a lifelong immunity and children are therefore most commonly affected. The chickenpox virus is part of the herpes family of viruses. *SmithKline Beecham plc.*

Chile South American country, bounded N by Peru and Bolivia, E by Argentina, and S and W by the Pacific Ocean. *See country box on p. 218.*

Chilean Revolution in Chile, the presidency of Salvador ◊Allende 1970–73, the Western hemisphere's first democratically elected Marxist-oriented president of an independent state.

chilli (North American ***chili***) pod, or powder made from the pod, of a variety of ◊capsicum, *Capsicum frutescens*, a hot, red pepper. It is widely used in cooking. Capsaicin is the hot ingredient of chilli. It causes a burning sensation in the mouth by triggering nerve branches in the eyes, nose, tongue and mouth.

Chillida Eduardo 1924– . Spanish Basque sculptor. Influenced by ◊Cubism and ◊Constructivism, he developed an abstract style that characteristically features thick, interlocking bars of twisted iron. His carvings also often consist of several interlocking pieces which, regardless of their actual size, convey an impression of monumentality. He is widely considered to be Spain's most important living sculptor.

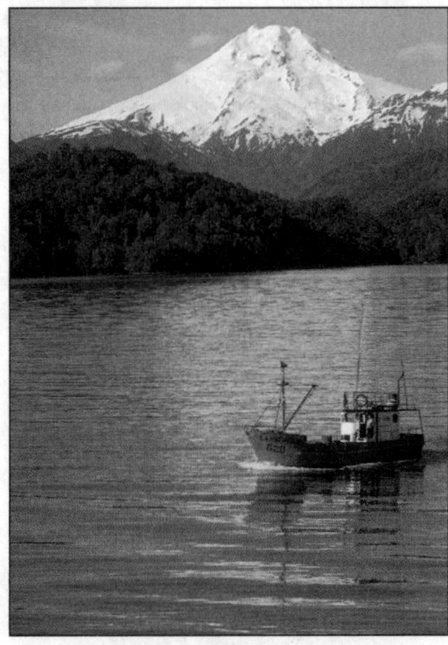

Chile The gulf of Ancud near Chaitén in Chile. The Andes mountain range dips down into the sea here, and ships have to navigate through the Chilean archipelago formed by the summits of submerged mountains. Sea transport is still very important in Chile, where the development of overland links has been slow. *Sally Jenkins*

CHILE
Republic of

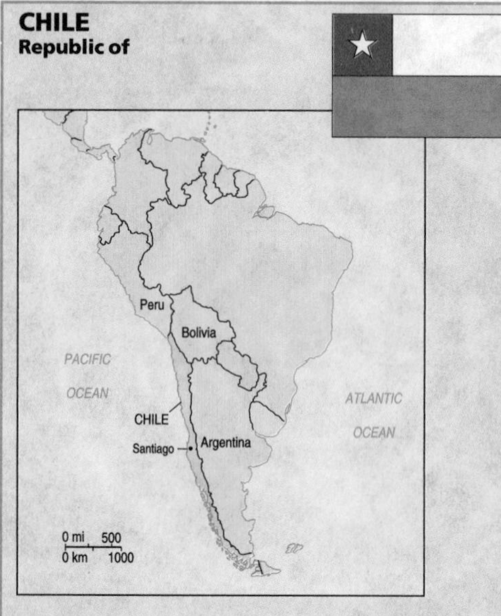

national name *República de Chile*
area 756,950 sq km/292,257 sq mi
capital Santiago
major towns/cities Concepción, Viña del Mar, Talcahuano, San Bernardo, Puente Alto, Chillán, Rancagua, Talca, Temuco
major ports Valparaíso, Antofagasta, Arica, Iquique, Punta Arenas
physical features Andes mountains along E border, Atacama Desert in N, fertile central valley, grazing land and forest in S
territories Easter Island, Juan Fernández Islands, part of Tierra del Fuego, claim to part of Antarctica
head of state Eduardo Frei from 1993
head of government Dante Cordova from 1995
political system emergent democratic republic
administrative divisions 12 regions and one metropolitan area
political parties Christian Democratic Party (PDC), moderate centrist; National Renewal Party (RN), right-wing; Socialist Party of Chile (PS), left-wing; Independent Democratic Union (UDI), right-wing; Party for Democracy (PPD), left of centre; Union of the Centre-Centre (UCC), right-wing; Radical Party (PR), left of centre
armed forces 54,000 (1995)
conscription one year (army) or two years (navy and air force)
defence spend (% GDP) 3.5 (1994)
education spend (% GNP) 2.9 (1992)
health spend (% GDP) 3.4 (1990)
death penalty retained and used for ordinary crimes
population 14,421,000 (1996 est)
population growth rate 1.6% (1990–95); 1.2% (2000–05)
age distribution (% of total population) <15 29.5%, 15–65 63.8%, >65 6.6% (1995)
ethnic distribution 65% mestizo (mixed Native American and Spanish descent), 30% European, remainder mainly American Indian
population density (per sq km) 18.8 (1995)
urban population (% of total) 84 (1995)
labour force 38% of population: 19% agriculture, 25% industry, 56% services (1990)
unemployment 5.1% (1993 est)
child mortality rate (under 5, per 1,000 live births) 15 (1994)
life expectancy 69 (men), 76 (women)
education (compulsory years) 8
literacy rate 94% (men), 93% (women)
language Spanish
religion Roman Catholic
TV sets (per 1,000 people) 210 (1992)
currency Chilean peso
GDP (US $) 52 billion (1994)
GDP per capita (PPP) (US $) 8,900 (1993)
growth rate 4.2% (1994)
average annual inflation 17.5% (1985–94); 11.4% (1994)
major trading partners USA, Japan, Brazil, Germany, Argentina, UK
resources copper (world's largest producer), gold, silver, iron ore, molybdenum, cobalt, iodine, saltpetre, coal, natural gas, petroleum, hydro-power
industries non-ferrous metals, food processing, petroleum refinery, chemicals, paper products (cellulose, newsprint, paper and cardboard), motor tyres, beer, glass sheets, motor vehicles
exports copper, fruits, timber products, fishmeal, vegetables, manufactured foodstuffs and beverages. Principal market: USA 17.3% (1994)
imports machinery and transport equipment, wheat, chemical and mineral products, consumer goods, raw materials. Principal source: USA 23.2% (1994)
arable land 5.3% (1993)
agricultural products wheat, sugar beet, potatoes, maize, fruit and vegetables; livestock

HISTORY
1535 First Spanish invasion of Chile abandoned in face of resistance from native Araucanian Indians.
1541 Pedro de Valdivia began Spanish conquest and founded Santiago.
1553 Valdivia captured and killed by Araucanian Indians led by Chief Lautaro.
17th C Spanish developed small agricultural settlements ruled by government subordinate to viceroy in Lima, Peru.
1778 King of Spain appointed a separate captain-general to govern Chile.
1810 Santiago junta proclaimed Chilean autonomy after Napoleon dethroned King of Spain.
1814 Spanish viceroy regained control of Chile.
1817 Army of the Andes, led by José de San Martín and Bernardo O'Higgins, defeated the Spanish.
1818 Achieved independence from Spain with O'Higgins as supreme director.
1823–30 O'Higgins forced to resign; civil war between conservative centralists and liberal federalists ended with conservative victory.
1833 Autocratic republican constitution created unitary Roman Catholic state with strong president and limited franchise.
1851–61 President Manuel Montt bowed to pressure to liberalize constitution.
1879–84 Chile defeated Peru and Bolivia in War of the Pacific and increased its territory by a third.
late 19th C Mining of nitrate and copper became major industry; large-scale European immigration followed 'pacification' of Araucanian Indians.
1891 Constitutional dispute between president and congress led to civil war; congressional victory reduced president to figurehead status.
1920 Election of liberal president Arturo Alessandri Palma; congress blocked his social reform programme.
1925 New constitution increased presidential powers, separated church and state, and made primary education compulsory.
1927 Military coup led to dictatorship of General Carlos Ibánez del Campo.
1931 Sharp fall in price of copper and nitrate caused dramatic economic and political collapse.
1932 Re-election of President Alessandri who restored order by harsh measures.
1938 Popular Front of Radicals, Socialists, and Communists took power under Pedro Aguirre Cedra.
1947 Communists organized violent strikes to exploit discontent over high inflation.
1948–58 Communist Party banned.
1952 General Ibánez elected president; austerity policies reduced inflation to 20%.
1958 Jorge Alessandri (son of former president) succeeded Ibánez as head of Liberal-Conservative coalition.
1964 Christian Democrat Eduardo Frei Montalva became president; he introduced 'communitarian' social reforms, but failed to combat inflation.
1970 Dr Salvador Allende, leader of Popular Unity coalition, became world's first democratically elected Marxist president; he embarked on a programme of nationalization and radical social reform.
1973 Allende killed in CIA-backed military coup; General Augusto Pinochet established dictatorship combining severe political repression with free-market economics.
1981 Pinochet began eight-year term as president under new constitution described as 'transition to democracy'.
1983 Economic recession provoked growing opposition to regime from all sides.
1988 Referendum on whether Pinochet should serve a further term resulted in a clear 'No' vote; he agreed to hold elections in following year.
1990 End of military regime; Christian Democrat Patricio Aylwin became president, with Pinochet as commander in chief of army; investigation into over 2,000 political executions during military regime.
1994 Eduardo Frei (son of former president), succeeded Aylwin as president.
1995 Frei introduced measures to reduce military influence in government.
1997 Pinochet's attempt to become senator for life thwarted.
1998 Pinochet retired from army and was made life senator.
1999 British home secretary Jack Straw authorized proceedings to extradite Pinochet to Spain.

SEE ALSO Allende, Salvador; Araucanian Indian; Pinochet, Augusto

Chiltern Hills range of chalk hills extending for some 72 km/45 mi in a curve from a point N of Reading to the Suffolk border. Coombe Hill, near Wendover, 260 m/852 ft high, is the highest point.

Chiluba Frederick 1943– . Zambian politician and trade unionist, president from 1991. In 1993 he was forced to declare a state of emergency, following the discovery of documents suggesting an impending coup. He later carried out a major reorganization of his cabinet but failed to silence his critics. He secured re-election Nov 1996.

When one-party rule officially ended 1990, Chiluba entered the political arena, becoming leader of the Movement for Multi-Party Democracy (MMD). As candidate for that party, he won the 1991 presidential elections with 75% of the votes.

chimera or ***chimaera*** in biology, an organism composed of tissues that are genetically different. Chimeras can develop naturally if a ◊mutation occurs in a cell of a developing embryo, but are more commonly produced artificially by implanting cells from one organism into the embryo of another.

chimera or ***chimaera*** in Greek mythology, a fire-breathing animal with a lion's head, a goat's body, and a tail in the form of a snake; hence any apparent hybrid of two or more creatures. The chimera was killed by the hero ◊Bellerophon on the winged horse Pegasus.

chimpanzee highly intelligent African ape *Pan troglodytes* that lives mainly in rain forests but sometimes in wooded savanna. Chimpanzees are covered in thin but long black body hair, except for the face, hands, and feet. They normally walk on all fours, supporting the front of the body on the knuckles of the fingers, but can stand or walk upright for a short distance. They can grow to 1.4 m/4.5 ft tall, and weigh up to 50 kg/110 lb. They are strong and climb well, but spend time on the ground, living in loose social groups. The bulk of the diet is fruit, with some leaves, insects, and occasional meat. Chimpanzees can use 'tools', for example they fashion twigs to extract termites from their nests.

They are found in an area from W Africa to W Uganda and Tanzania in the east. Studies of chromosomes suggest that chimpanzees are the closest apes to humans, perhaps sharing 99% of the same genes. Trained chimpanzees can learn to communicate with humans with the aid of machines or sign language, but are probably precluded from human speech by the position of the voicebox.

Chimú South American civilization that flourished on the coast of Peru from about 1250 to about 1470, when it was conquered by the ◊Incas. The Chimú people produced fine work in gold, realistic portrait pottery, savage fanged feline images in clay, and possibly a system of writing or recording by painting patterns on beans. They built aqueducts carrying water many miles, and the huge, mazelike city of Chan Chan, 36 sq km/14 sq mi, on the coast near Trujillo.

China the largest country in E Asia, bounded N by Mongolia; NW by Tajikistan, Kyrgyzstan, Kazakhstan, and Afghanistan; SW by India, Nepal, and Bhutan; S by Myanmar (Burma), Laos, and Vietnam; SE by the South China Sea; E by the East China Sea, North Korea, and Yellow Sea; NE by

Russia. *See country box on p. 220 and table on p. 221.*

china clay commercial name for ◊kaolin.

China Sea area of the Pacific Ocean bordered by China, Vietnam, Borneo, the Philippines, and Japan. Various groups of small islands and shoals, including the Paracels, 500 km/300 mi E of Vietnam, have been disputed by China and other powers because they lie in oil-rich areas. N of Taiwan it is known as the East China Sea and to the S as the South China Sea.

chinchilla South American rodent *Chinchilla laniger* found in high, rather barren areas of the Andes in Bolivia and Chile. About the size of a small rabbit, it has long ears and a long bushy tail, and shelters in rock crevices. These gregarious animals have thick, soft, silver-grey fur, and were hunted almost to extinction for it. They are now farmed and protected in the wild.

Chinese the native groups or inhabitants of China and Taiwan, and those people of Chinese descent. The Chinese comprise more than 25% of the world's population, and the Chinese language (Mandarin) is the largest member of the Sino-Tibetan family.

Chinese traditions are ancient, many going back to at least 3000 BC. They include a range of philosophies and religions, including Confucianism, Taoism, and Buddhism. The veneration of ancestors was an enduring feature of Chinese culture, as were patrilineal-based villages. The extended family was the traditional unit, the five-generation family being the ideal. Recent attempts by the People's Republic of China have included the restriction of traditions and the limit of one child to a married couple. The majority of Chinese are engaged in agriculture, cultivating irrigated rice fields in the south, and growing millet and wheat in the north. Many other Chinese work in commerce, industry, and government. Descendants of Chinese migrants are found throughout SE Asia, the Pacific, Australia, North and South America, and Europe. Within China many minorities speak non-Chinese languages belonging to the Sino-Tibetan family (such as Tibetan, Hmong, and Zhuang). Some peoples speak languages belonging to the Altaic (such as Uigur, Mongol, and Manchu) and Indo-European (such as Russian) families, while in the northeast there are Koreans. The Chinese were governed for long periods by the Mongol (AD 1271–1368) and Manchu (AD 1644–1911) dynasties.

Chinese architecture style of building in China. Traditionally of timber construction, few existing buildings predate the Ming dynasty (1368–1644), but records such as the *Ying Tsao Fa Shih/Method of Architecture* 1103 show that Chinese architecture changed little throughout the ages, both for the peasants and for the well-to-do. Curved roofs are a characteristic feature; also typical is the pagoda with a number of curved tiled roofs, one above the other. The Great Wall of China was built about 228–210 BC as a northern frontier defence, and Beijing's fine city walls, of which only a small section remains, date from the Ming period.

Chinese buildings usually face south, a convention which can be traced back to the 'Hall of Brightness', a building from the Zhou dynasty (1050–221 BC), and is still retained in the functionally Western-style Chinese architecture of the present day. Although some sections of Beijing have been destroyed by modernization, it still contains fine examples of buildings from the Ming dynasty, such as the Altar of Heaven, the ancestral temple of the Ming tombs, and the Five Pagoda Temple. The introduction of Buddhism from India exerted considerable influence on Chinese architecture.

Chinese art the painting and sculpture of China. From the Bronze Age to the Cultural Revolution, Chinese art shows a stylistic unity unparalleled in any other culture. From about the 1st century AD Buddhism inspired much sculpture and painting. The Han dynasty (206 BC–AD 220) produced outstanding metalwork, ceramics, and sculpture. The Song dynasty (960–1278) established standards of idyllic landscape and nature painting in a delicate calligraphic style.

Neolithic art Accomplished pottery dates back to about 2500 BC, already showing a distinctive Chinese approach to form.

Bronze Age art Rich burial goods, with bronzes and jade carvings, survive from the second millennium BC, decorated with hieroglyphs and simple stylized animal forms. Astonishing life-size terracotta figures from the Qin period (about 221–206 BC) guard the tomb of Emperor Shi Huangdi in the old capital of Xian. Bronze horses, naturalistic but displaying the soft curving lines of the Chinese style, are a feature of the Han dynasty.

early Buddhist art Once Buddhism was established in China it inspired a monumental art, with huge rock-cut Buddhas and graceful linear relief sculptures at the monasteries of Yungang, about 460–535, and Longmen. Bronze images show the same curving lines and rounded forms.

Tang dynasty (618–907) Increasing sophistication is evident in idealized images and naturalistic portraits, such as the carved figures of Buddhist monks (Luohan). This period also produced brilliant metalwork and delicate ceramics, particularly of robed figures and animals. It is known that the aims and, broadly speaking, the style of Chinese painting were already well established, but few paintings survive, with the exception of some Tang scrolls and silk paintings.

Song dynasty (960–1278) The golden age of painting was during the Song dynasty. The imperial court created its own workshop, fostering a fine calligraphic art, mainly devoted to natural subjects – landscape, mountains, trees, flowers, birds, and horses – though genre scenes of court beauties were also popular. Scrolls, albums, and fans of silk or paper were painted with watercolours and ink, using soft brushes that produced many different effects. Painting was associated with literature, and painters added poems or quotations to their work to intensify the effect. Ma Yuan and Xia Gui (active c. 1180–1230) are among the painters; Mu-Chi was a monk known for exquisite brushwork. The Song dynasty also produced the first true porcelain, achieving a classic simplicity and delicacy in colouring and form.

Ming dynasty (1368–1644) Painters continued the landscape tradition, setting new standards in idealized visions. The painter Dong Qichang wrote a history and theory of Chinese painting. The Song style of porcelain gradually gave way to increasingly elaborate decoration in rich, polychrome enamels and the famous Ming blue-and-white patterned ware.

Qing dynasty (1644–1911) The so-called Individualist Spirits emerged, painters who developed bolder, personal styles of brushwork.

20th century The strong spirit that supported traditional art began to fade in the 19th and 20th centuries, but attempts to incorporate modernist ideas have been frowned on by the authorities. Not directly concerned with the representation of political events, Chinese art took some years before responding to the political upheavals of this century. Subsequently, response to official directives produced a period of Soviet-style Realism followed by a reversion to a peasant school of painting, which was the officially favoured direction for art during the Cultural Revolution.

chimpanzee Chimpanzees use a wide variety of sounds, gestures, and facial expression to communicate with one another. Their flexible, protusible lips may be used to call another chimp, to show aggression, fear, excitement, subservience, or a desire to play, to be fed, or to be groomed. *Corbis*

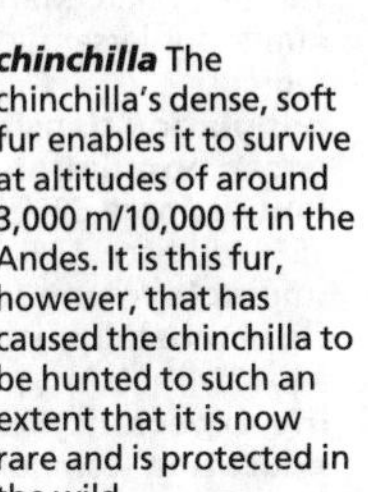

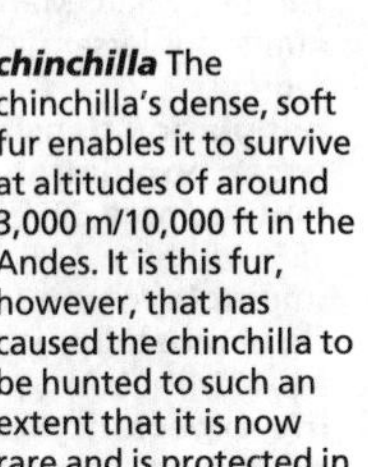

chinchilla The chinchilla's dense, soft fur enables it to survive at altitudes of around 3,000 m/10,000 ft in the Andes. It is this fur, however, that has caused the chinchilla to be hunted to such an extent that it is now rare and is protected in the wild.

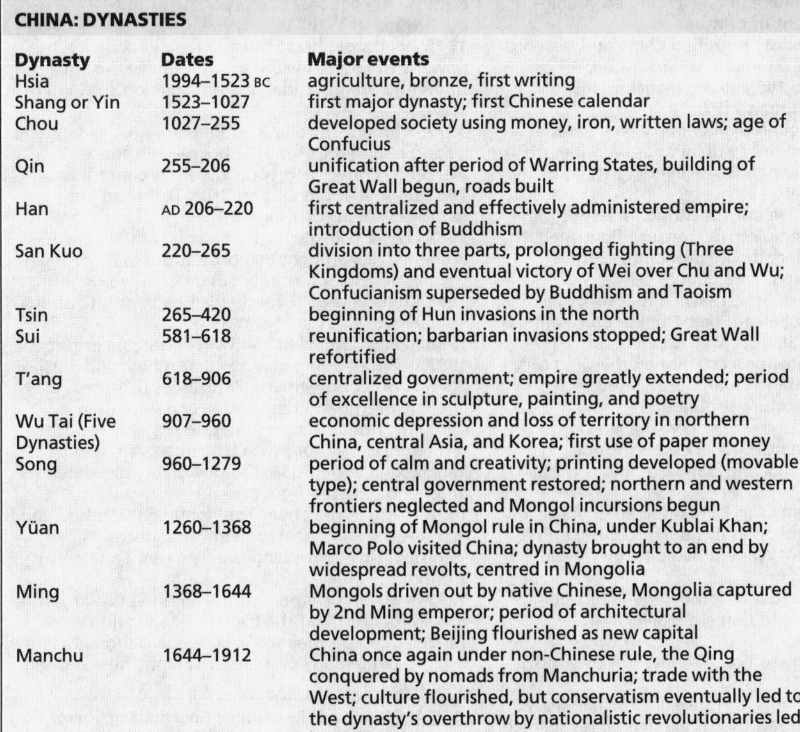

CHINA: DYNASTIES

Dynasty	Dates	Major events
Hsia	1994–1523 BC	agriculture, bronze, first writing
Shang or Yin	1523–1027	first major dynasty; first Chinese calendar
Chou	1027–255	developed society using money, iron, written laws; age of Confucius
Qin	255–206	unification after period of Warring States, building of Great Wall begun, roads built
Han	AD 206–220	first centralized and effectively administered empire; introduction of Buddhism
San Kuo	220–265	division into three parts, prolonged fighting (Three Kingdoms) and eventual victory of Wei over Chu and Wu; Confucianism superseded by Buddhism and Taoism
Tsin	265–420	beginning of Hun invasions in the north
Sui	581–618	reunification; barbarian invasions stopped; Great Wall refortified
T'ang	618–906	centralized government; empire greatly extended; period of excellence in sculpture, painting, and poetry
Wu Tai (Five Dynasties)	907–960	economic depression and loss of territory in northern China, central Asia, and Korea; first use of paper money
Song	960–1279	period of calm and creativity; printing developed (movable type); central government restored; northern and western frontiers neglected and Mongol incursions begun
Yüan	1260–1368	beginning of Mongol rule in China, under Kublai Khan; Marco Polo visited China; dynasty brought to an end by widespread revolts, centred in Mongolia
Ming	1368–1644	Mongols driven out by native Chinese, Mongolia captured by 2nd Ming emperor; period of architectural development; Beijing flourished as new capital
Manchu	1644–1912	China once again under non-Chinese rule, the Qing conquered by nomads from Manchuria; trade with the West; culture flourished, but conservatism eventually led to the dynasty's overthrow by nationalistic revolutionaries led by Sun Yat-sen

CHINA
People's Republic of

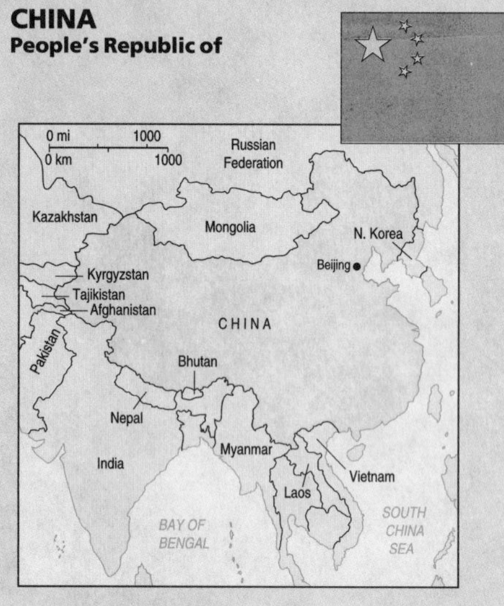

national name *Zhonghua Renmin Gonghe Guo*
area 9,596,960 sq km/3,704,426 sq mi
capital Beijing (Peking)
major towns/cities Chongqing (Chungking), Shenyang (Mukden), Wuhan, Nanjing (Nanking), Harbin
major ports Tianjin (Tientsin), Shanghai, Qingdao (Tsingtao), Guangzhou (Canton)
physical features two-thirds of China is mountains or desert (N and W); the low-lying E is irrigated by rivers Huang He (Yellow River), Chang Jiang (Yangtze-Kiang), Xi Jiang (Si Kiang)
head of state Jiang Zemin from 1993
head of government Zhu Rongji from 1998
political system communist republic
administrative divisions 22 provinces, five autonomous regions, and three municipalities
political party Chinese Communist Party (CCP), Marxist-Leninist-Maoist
armed forces 2,930,000; reserves approximately 1.2 million (1995 est)
conscription selective: 3 years (army and marines), 4 years (air force and navy)
defence spend (% GDP) 5.6 (1994)
education spend (% GNP) 2.0 (1992)
health spend (% GDP) 2.1 (1990)
death penalty retained and used for ordinary crimes
population 1,232,083 (1996 est)
population growth rate 1.1% (1990–95); 0.8% (2000–05)
age distribution (% of total population) <15 26.4%, 15–65 67.5%, >65 6.1% (1995)
ethnic distribution 94% Han Chinese, the remainder being Zhuang, Uygur, Hui (Muslims), Yi, Tibetan, Miao, Manchu, Mongol, Buyi, or Korean; numerous lesser nationalities reside mainly in border regions
population density (per sq km) 125.2 (1994)
urban population (% of total) 30 (1995)
labour force 59% of population: 72% agriculture, 15% industry, 13% services (1990)
unemployment 2.3% (1993)
child mortality rate (under 5, per 1,000 live births) 43 (1994)
life expectancy 69 (men), 73 (women)
education (compulsory years) 9
literacy rate 84% (men), 62% (women)
languages Chinese including Mandarin (official), Cantonese, Wu, and other dialects
religions Taoist, Confucianist, and Buddhist; Muslim 20 million; Catholic 3–6 million (divided between the 'patriotic' church established 1958 and the 'loyal' church subject to Rome); Protestant 3 million
TV sets (per 1,000 people) 31 (1992)
currency yuan
GDP (US $) 522.17 billion (1994)
GDP per capita (PPP) (US $) 2,330 (1993)
growth rate 10.2% (1995)
average annual inflation 14.8% (1995); 11.9% (1985–94)
major trading partners Japan, Hong Kong, USA, Taiwan
resources coal, graphite, tungsten, molybdenum, antimony, tin (world's largest producer), lead (world's fifth-largest producer), mercury, bauxite, phosphate rock, iron ore (world's largest producer), diamonds, gold, manganese, zinc (world's third-largest producer), petroleum, natural gas, fish
industries raw cotton and cotton cloth, cement, paper, sugar, salt, plastics, aluminium ware, steel, rolled steel, chemical fertilizers, silk, woollen fabrics, bicycles, cameras, electrical appliances; tourism is growing
exports basic manufactures, miscellaneous manufactured articles (particularly clothing and toys), crude petroleum, machinery and transport equipment, fishery products, cereals, canned food, tea, raw silk, cotton cloth. Principal market: Japan 17.8% (1994)
imports machinery and transport equipment, basic manufactures, chemicals, wheat, rolled steel, fertilizers. Principal source: Japan 22.8% (1994)
arable land 9.6% (1993)
agricultural products sweet potatoes, wheat, maize, soya beans, rice, sugar cane, tobacco, cotton, jute; world's largest fish catch (almost 17.6 tons in 1993)

HISTORY

c. 3000 BC Yangshao culture reached its peak in the Huang He Valley; displaced by Longshan culture in E China.
c. 1766–c.1122 BC First major dynasty, the Shang, arose from Longshan culture; writing and calendar developed.
c. 1122–256 BC Zhou people of W China overthrew Shang and set up new dynasty; development of money and written laws.
c. 500 BC Confucius expounded philosophy which guided Chinese government and society for the next 2,000 years.
403–221 BC 'Warring States Period': Zhou Empire broke up into small kingdoms.
221–206 BC Qin kingdom defeated all rivals and established first empire with strong central government; emperor Shi Huangdi built Great Wall of China.
202 BC–AD 220 Han dynasty expanded empire into Central Asia; first overland trade with Europe; art and literature flourished; Buddhism introduced from India.
220–581 Large-scale rebellion destroyed Han dynasty; empire split into three competing kingdoms; several short-lived dynasties ruled parts of China.
581–618 Sui dynasty reunified China and repelled Tatar invaders.
618–907 Tang dynasty enlarged and strengthened the empire; great revival of culture; major rebellion 875–84.
907–60 'Five Dynasties and Ten Kingdoms': disintegration of empire amid war and economic decline; development of printing.
960–1279 Song dynasty reunified China and restored order; civil service examinations introduced; population reached 100 million; Manchurians occupied northern China 1127.
1279 Mongols conquered all China, which became part of the vast empire of Kublai Khan, founder of the Yuan dynasty; Venetian traveller Marco Polo visited China 1275–92.
1368 Rebellions drove out the Mongols; native Ming dynasty expanded empire; architecture flourished in new capital of Beijing; dislike of Mongols led to contempt for all things foreign.
1516 Portuguese explorers reached Macao; other European traders followed; first Chinese porcelain arrived in Europe 1580.
1644 Manchurian invasion established the Qing (or Manchu) dynasty; Manchurians assimilated and Chinese trade and culture continued to thrive.
1796–1804 Anti-Manchu revolt weakened Qing dynasty; population increase in excess of food supplies led to falling living standards and cultural decline.
1839–42 First Opium War; Britain forced China to cede Hong Kong and open five ports to European trade; Second Opium War extracted further trade concessions 1856–60.
1850–64 Millions died in Taiping Rebellion; Taipings combined Christian and Chinese beliefs and demanded land reform.
1894–95 Sino-Japanese War: Chinese driven out of Korea.
1897–98 Germany, Russia, France, and Britain leased ports in China; conquest by European empires seemed likely.
1898 Hong Kong was secured by Britain on a 99-year lease (expired 1997).
1900 Anti-western Boxer Rebellion crushed by foreign intervention; jealousy between Great Powers prevented partition.
1911 Revolution broke out; Republic of China proclaimed by Sun Yat-sen of Guomindang (National People's Party).
1912 Abdication of infant emperor Pu-i; General Yuan Shih-K'ai became dictator.
1916 Power of central government collapsed on death of Yuan Shih-K'ai; N China dominated by local warlords.
1919 Beijing students formed May 4th movement to protest at transfer of German possessions in China to Japan.
1921 Sun Yat-sen elected president of nominal National Government; Chinese Communist Party founded; communists worked with Guomindang to reunite China from 1923.
1925 Death of Sun Yat-sen; leadership of Guomindang gradually passed to military commander Chiang Kai-shek.
1926–28 Revolutionary Army of Chiang Kai-shek reunified China; Guomindang broke with communists and tried to suppress them in civil war.
1932 Japan invaded Manchuria and established puppet state of Manchukuo.
1934–35 Communists undertook 'Long March' from Jiangxi and Fujian in S to Yan'an in N to escape encirclement by Guomindang.
1937–45 Japan renewed invasion of China; Chiang Kai-shek received help from USA and Britain from 1941.
1946 Civil war resumed between Guomindang and communists led by Mao Zedong.
1949 Victorious communists proclaimed People's Republic of China under Chairman Mao; Guomindang fled to Taiwan.
1950–53 China intervened heavily in Korean War.
1958 'Great Leap Forward': extremist five-year plan to accelerate output severely weakened economy.
1960 Sino-Soviet split: China accused USSR of betraying communism; USSR withdrew technical advisors; border clashes on Ussuri River 1969.
1962 Economic recovery programme under Liu Shaoqi caused divisions between 'rightists' and 'leftists'; brief border war with India.
1966–69 'Great Proletarian Cultural Revolution'; leftists overthrew Liu Shaoqi with support of Mao; Red Guards disrupted education, government, and daily life in attempt to enforce revolutionary principles.
1970 Mao supported efforts of Prime Minister Zhou Enlai to restore order.
1971 People's Republic of China admitted to United Nations; full diplomatic relations with USA established in 1979.
1976 Deaths of Zhou Enlai and Mao Zedong led to power struggle between rightists and leftists; Hua Guofeng became leader and arrested leftist 'Gang of Four'.
1977–81 Rightist Deng Xiaoping emerged as supreme leader; pragmatic economic policies introduced market incentives and encouraged foreign trade.
1987 Deng Xiaoping retired from Politburo but remained a dominant figure.
1989 Over 2,000 killed when army crushed prodemocracy student demonstrations in Tiananmen Square, Beijing; international sanctions imposed.
1991 China and USSR reached agreement on disputed border.
1996 Reunification with Taiwan declared a priority.
1997 Deng Xiaoping died aged 92. China and Russia signed border agreement. Reductions in armed forces. Government reported strong growth in economy. Hong Kong returned to Chinese sovereignty. Relations with USA improved; President Jiang Zemin visited USA. Pro-democracy dissident Wei Jingsheng released from prison.
1998 Economic reformer Zhu Rongji replaced Li Peng as prime minister; government reorganization launched. Dissident Wang Dan released on medical grounds.
1999 In an endorsement of the market economy, it was announced that the constitution would be amended to add the ideas of the late Deng Xiaoping to its state ideology of 'Marxist-Leninist-Mao Zedong thought'.

SEE ALSO Cultural Revolution; Guomindang; Hong Kong; Mao Zedong; Sino-Japanese Wars; Taiwan

CHINA: PROVINCES

Province	Alternative transcription	Capital	Area in sq km/sq mi
Anhui	Anhwei	Hefei	139,900/54,015
Fujian	Fukien	Fuzhou	123,100/47,528
Gansu	Kansu	Lanzhou	530,000/204,633
Guangdong	Kwantung	Guangzhou	231,400/89,343
Guizhou	Kweichow	Guiyang	174,000/67,181
Hainan		Haikou	34,000/13,127
Hebei	Hopei	Shijiazhuang	202,700/78,262
Heilongjiang	Heilungkiang	Harbin	463,600/178,995
Henan	Honan	Zhengzhou	167,000/64,478
Hubei	Hupei	Wuhan	187,500/72,393
Hunan		Changsha	210,500/81,274
Jiangsu	Kiangsu	Nanjing	102,200/39,459
Jiangxi	Kiangsi	Nanchang	164,800/63,629
Jilin	Kirin	Changchun	187,000/72,200
Liaoning		Shenyang	151,000/58,301
Qinghai	Tsinghai	Xining	721,000/278,378
Shaanxi	Shensi	Xian	195,800/75,598
Shandong	Shantung	Jinan	153,300/59,189
Shanxi	Shansi	Taiyuan	157,100/60,656
Sichuan	Szechwan	Chengdu	569,000/219,690
Yunnan		Kunming	436,200/168,416
Zhejiang	Chekiang	Hangzhou	101,800/39,304
Autonomous region			
Guangxi Zhuang	Kwangsi Chuang	Nanning	220,400/85,096
Nei Mongol	Inner Mongolia	Hohhot	450,000/173,745
Ningxia Hui	Ninghsia-Hui	Yinchuan	170,000/65,637
Xinjiang Uygur	Sinkiang Uighur	Urumqi	1,646,800/635,829
Xizang	Tibet	Lhasa	1,221,600/471,659
Municipality			
Beijing	Peking		17,800/6,872
Shanghai			5,800/2,239
Tianjin	Tientsin		4,000/1,544
		total	9,139,300/3,528,683

Chinese language language or group of languages of the Sino-Tibetan family, spoken in China, Taiwan, Hong Kong, Singapore, and Chinese communities throughout the world. Varieties of spoken Chinese differ greatly, but all share a written form using thousands of ideographic symbols – characters – which have changed little in 2,000 years. Nowadays, *putonghua* ('common speech'), based on the educated Beijing dialect known as Mandarin Chinese, is promoted throughout China as the national spoken and written language.

Because the writing system has a symbolic form (like numbers and music notes) it can be read and interpreted regardless of the reader's own dialect. The Chinese dialects are tonal; that is, they depend on the tone of a syllable to indicate its meaning: *ma* with one tone means 'mother', with another means 'horse'. The characters of Chinese script were traditionally written down the page from right to left. Today they are commonly written horizontally and read left to right, using 2,000 simplified characters. A variant of the Roman alphabet has been introduced and is used in schools to help with pronunciation. This, called *Pinyin*, is prescribed for international use by the People's Republic of China for personal and place names (as in *Beijing* rather than *Peking*). Pinyin spellings are generally used in this volume, but they are not accepted by the government of Taiwan.

Chinese literature the earliest written records in Chinese date from about 1500 BC; the earliest extant literary works date from about 800 BC.

poetry Chinese poems, often only four lines long, and written in the ancient literary language understood throughout China, consist of rhymed lines of a fixed number of syllables, ornamented by parallel phrasing and tonal pattern. The oldest poems are contained in the *Book of Songs* (800–600 BC). Some of the most celebrated Chinese poets are the nature poet T'ao Ch'ien (372–427), the master of technique Li Po, the autobiographical Bo Zhu Yi, and the wide-ranging Su Tung-p'o (1036–1101); and among the moderns using the colloquial language under European influence and experimenting in free verse are Hsu Chih-mo (1895–1931), and Pien Chih-lin (1910–).

prose Histories are not so much literary works as collections of edited documents with moral comment, whereas the essay has long been cultivated under strict rules of form and style. An example of the latter genre is 'Upon the Original Way' by Han Yü (768–824), recalling the nation to Confucianism. Until the 16th century the short story was confined to the anecdote, startling by its strangeness and written in the literary language – for example, the stories of the poetic Tuan Ch'eng-shih (died 863); but after that time the more novelistic type of short story, written in the colloquial tongue, developed by its side. The Chinese novel evolved from the street storyteller's art and has consequently always used the popular language. The early romances *Three Kingdoms*, *All Men Are Brothers*, and *Golden Lotus* are anonymous, the earliest known author of this genre being Wu Che'ng-en (c. 1505–1580); the most realistic of the great novelists is Ts'ao Chan (died 1763).

Twentieth-century Chinese novels have largely adopted European form, and have been influenced by Russia, as have the realistic stories of Lu Hsün. In typical Chinese drama, the stage presentation far surpasses the text in importance (the dialogue was not even preserved in early plays), but there have been experiments in the European manner. Some recent writing such as the stories of Bai Hua (1930–) has been energized by the tension between humanist individualism and the collectivist ideology of the communist state. Personal and family experience of China's social and political upheavals in the 20th century has been recorded in some distinguished autobiographical works such as *Wild Swans. Three Daughters of China* 1991 by Jung Chang (1952–).

Chinese Revolution series of great political upheavals in China 1911–49 that eventually led to Communist Party rule and the establishment of the People's Republic of China. In 1912, a nationalist revolt overthrew the imperial Manchu dynasty. Led by Sun Yat-sen 1923–25 and by Chiang Kai-shek 1925–49, the nationalists, or Guomindang, were increasing challenged by the growing communist movement. The 10,000 km/6,000 mi Long March to the NW by the communists 1934–35 to escape from attacks by the Guomindang forces resulted in ◊Mao Zedong's emergence as communist leader. During World War II 1939–45, the various Chinese political groups pooled military resources against the Japanese invaders. After World War II, the conflict reignited into open civil war 1946–49, until the Guomindang were defeated at Nanjing and forced to flee to Taiwan. Communist rule was established in the People's Republic of China under the leadership of Mao.

The Chinese revolution came about with the collapse of the Manchu dynasty, a result of increasing internal disorders, pressure from foreign governments, and the weakness of central government. A nationalist revolt in 1911–12 led to a provisional republican constitution being proclaimed and a government established in Beijing (Peking) headed by Yuan Shihai. The Guomindang were faced with the problems of restoring the authority of central government and meeting the challenges from militaristic factions (led by ◊warlords) and the growing communist movement.

After 1930, Chiang launched a series of attacks that encircled the communists in SE China and led to an attempt by communist army commander Chu Teh to break out. The resulting Long March to NW China Oct 1934–Oct 1935 reduced the communists' army from over 100,000 to little more than 8,000, mainly as a result of skirmishes with Chiang's forces and the severity of the conditions. During the march, a power struggle developed between Mao Zedong and Chang Kuo T'ao which eventually split the force. Mao's group finally based itself in Yan'an, where it remained throughout the war with the Japanese, forming an uneasy alliance with the nationalists to expel the invaders.

Mao's troops formed the basis of the Red Army that renewed the civil war against the nationalists 1946 and emerged victorious after defeating them at Nanjing 1949. As a result, communist rule was established in China under Mao's leadership.

chinoiserie in the decorative arts and architecture, the use of Chinese styles and motifs in Western art, especially in the late 17th- to early 19th-centuries. Chinese lacquerwork and porcelain were imported into Europe in the 17th century and became popular with Rococo designers.

chinook (American Indian 'snow-eater') warm dry wind that blows downhill on the E side of the Rocky Mountains of North America. It often occurs in winter and spring when it produces a rapid thaw, and so is important to the agriculture of the area.

chip or ***silicon chip*** another name for an ◊integrated circuit, a complete electronic circuit on a slice of silicon (or other semiconductor) crystal only a few millimetres square.

chipmunk any of several species of small ground squirrel with characteristic stripes along its side. Chipmunks live in North America and E Asia, in a variety of habitats, usually wooded, and take shelter in burrows. They have pouches in their cheeks for carrying food. They climb well but spend most of their time on or near the ground.

Chippendale Thomas 1718–1779. English furniture designer. He set up his workshop in St Martin's Lane, London, 1753. His book *The Gentleman and Cabinet Maker's Director* 1754, was a significant contribution to furniture design. Although many of his most characteristic designs are ◊Rococo, he also employed Louis XVI, Chinese, Gothic, and Neo-Classical styles. He worked mainly in mahogany.

Chirac Jacques René 1932– . French conservative politician, prime minister 1974–76 and

Chirac French president Jacques Chirac. He was prime minister under Giscard d'Estaing, but the relationship was an uneasy one as both sought the leadership of the French right. He lost the presidential election 1981 but was again prime minister under Mitterrand 1986–88, this time hampered by being a conservative prime minister under a socialist presidency. *Topham*

1986–88; became president 1995. He contested the 1981 presidential election, from which he emerged as the National Assembly leader for the parties of the right during the socialist administration of 1981–86. Following the rightist coalition's victory 1986, Chirac was appointed prime minister by President François Mitterrand in a 'cohabitation' experiment. He was defeated by Mitterand in the 1988 presidential elections, and was replaced as prime minister by the moderate socialist Michel Rocard.

Chirac's decision to resume nuclear-testing in the Pacific 1995–96 was widely condemned.

Chirico Giorgio de 1888–1978. Greek-born Italian painter. With Carlo Carrà (1881–1966), he founded the school of ◊Metaphysical Painting, which in its enigmatic imagery and haunted, dream-like settings presaged Surrealism, as in *Nostalgia of the Infinite* 1911 (Museum of Modern Art, New York). Between 1911 and 1915 he worked in Paris, where he produced a remarkable series of paintings in which an uneasy sense of mystery is created by empty squares, deeply shadowed colonnades and toylike trains in the far distance. *Melancholy and Mystery of a Street* (Museum of Modern Art, New York) is an example of his style. Chirico's style gradually changed and by the 1930s, having repudiated the modern movement in art, he was reworking the styles of the old masters.

chiropractic in alternative medicine, technique of manipulation of the spine and other parts of the body, based on the principle that physical disorders are attributable to aberrations in the functioning of the nervous system, which manipulation can correct.

Chişinău (Russian ***Kishinev***) capital of Moldova, situated in a rich agricultural area; population (1992) 667,000. It is a commercial and cultural centre; industries include cement, food processing, tobacco, and textiles. Founded 1436, it became Russian 1812. It was taken by Romania 1918, by the USSR 1940, and by Germany 1941, when it was totally destroyed. The USSR recaptured the site 1944, and rebuilding soon began. Nationalist demonstrations were held in the city 1989, prior to Moldova gaining independence 1991.

Chissano Joaquim 1939– . Mozambique nationalist politician, president from 1986; foreign minister 1975–86. In 1992 he signed a peace accord with the leader of the rebel Mozambique National Resistance (MNR) party, bringing to an end 16 years of civil war, and in 1994 won the first free presidential elections.

chitin complex long-chain compound, or ◊polymer; a nitrogenous derivative of glucose. Chitin is widely found in invertebrates. It forms the ◊exoskeleton of insects and other arthropods. It combines with protein to form a covering that can be hard and tough, as in beetles, or soft and flexible, as in caterpillars and other insect larvae. It is insoluble in water and resistant to acids, alkalis, and many organic solvents.

Chittagong city and port in Bangladesh, 16 km/10 mi from the mouth of the Karnaphuli River, on the Bay of Bengal; population (1991) 1,364,000. Industries include steel, engineering, chemicals, and textiles.

chivalry code of gallantry and honour that medieval knights were pledged to observe. Its principal virtues were piety, honour, valour, courtesy, chastity, and loyalty. The word originally meant the knightly class of the feudal Middle Ages. Chivalry originated in feudal France and Spain, spreading rapidly to the rest of Europe and reaching its height in the 12th and 13th centuries. It was strengthened by the Crusades. The earliest orders of chivalry were the Knights Hospitallers and Knights Templars, founded to serve pilgrims to the Holy Land. Secular literature of the period takes knighthood and chivalry as its theme.

chlamydia viruslike bacteria which live parasitically in animal cells, and cause disease in humans and birds. Chlamydiae are thought to be descendants of bacteria that have lost certain metabolic processes. In humans, a strain of chlamydia causes ◊trachoma, a disease found mainly in the tropics (a leading cause of blindness); venereally transmitted chlamydiae cause genital and urinary infections.

chlorate any salt derived from an acid containing both chlorine and oxygen and possessing the negative ion ClO^-, ClO_2^{2-}, ClO_3^{3-}, or ClO_4^{4-}. Common chlorates are those of sodium, potassium, and barium. Certain chlorates are used in weedkillers.

chloride Cl^- negative ion formed when hydrogen chloride dissolves in water, and any salt containing this ion, commonly formed by the action of hydrochloric acid (HCl) on various metals or by direct combination of a metal and chlorine. Sodium chloride (NaCl) is common table salt.

chlorine (Greek *chloros* 'green') greenish-yellow, gaseous, nonmetallic element with a pungent odour, symbol Cl, atomic number 17, relative atomic mass 35.453. It is a member of the ◊halogen group and is widely distributed, in combination with the ◊alkali metals, as chlorates or chlorides.

In nature it is always found in the combined form, as in hydrochloric acid, produced in the mammalian stomach for digestion. Chlorine is obtained commercially by the electrolysis of concentrated brine and is an important bleaching agent and germicide, used for both drinking and swimming-pool water. As an oxidizing agent it finds many applications in organic chemistry. The pure gas (Cl_2) is a poison and was used in gas warfare in World War I. Chlorine is a component of chlorofluorocarbons (CFCs) and is partially responsible for the depletion of the ◊ozone layer; it is released from the CFC molecule by the action of ultraviolet radiation in the upper atmosphere, making it available to react with and destroy the ozone. Chlorine was discovered 1774 by the German chemist Karl Scheele, but English chemist Humphry Davy first proved it to be an element 1810 and named it after its colour.

chlorofluorocarbon (CFC) synthetic chemical that is odourless, nontoxic, nonflammable, and chemically inert. The first CFC was synthesized 1892, but no use was found for it until the 1920s. Since then their stability and apparently harmless properties have made CFCs popular as ◊aerosol cans, as refrigerants in refrigerators and air conditioners, and in the manufacture of foam packaging. They are partly responsible for the destruction of the ◊ozone layer. In 1990 representatives of 93 nations, including the UK and the USA, agreed to phase out production of CFCs and various other ozone-depleting chemicals by the end of the 20th century.

When CFCs are released into the atmosphere, they drift up slowly into the stratosphere, where, under the influence of ultraviolet radiation from the Sun, they break down into chlorine atoms which destroy the ozone layer and allow harmful radiation from the Sun to reach the Earth's surface. CFCs can remain in the atmosphere for more than 100 years. Replacements for CFCs are being developed, and research into safe methods of destroying existing CFCs is being carried out. In Jan 1996 it was reported that US chemists at Yale University had developed a process for breaking down freons and other gases containing CFCs into nonhazardous compounds. ▷ *See feature on pp. 858–859.*

chloroform (technical name ***trichloromethane***) $CHCl_3$ clear, colourless, toxic, carcinogenic liquid with a characteristic pungent, sickly sweet smell and taste, formerly used as an anaesthetic (now superseded by less harmful substances). It is used as a solvent and in the synthesis of organic chemical compounds.

chlorophyll green pigment present in most plants; it is responsible for the absorption of light energy during ◊photosynthesis. The pigment absorbs the red and blue-violet parts of sunlight but reflects the green, thus giving plants their characteristic colour. Chlorophyll is found within chloroplasts, present in large numbers in leaves. Cyanobacteria (blue-green algae) and other photosynthetic bacteria also have chlorophyll, though of a slightly different type. Chlorophyll is similar in structure to ◊haemoglobin, but with magnesium instead of iron as the reactive part of the molecule.

chloroplast structure (◊organelle) within a plant cell containing the green pigment chlorophyll. Chloroplasts occur in most cells of the green plant that are exposed to light, often in large numbers. Typically, they are flattened and disclike, with a double membrane enclosing the stroma, a gel-like matrix. Within the stroma are stacks of fluid-containing cavities, or vesicles, where ◊photosynthesis occurs.

chocolate powder, syrup, confectionery, or beverage derived from cacao seeds. See ◊cocoa and chocolate.

choir in a cathedral, the area used by the choir, usually part of the chancel.

choir body of singers, usually of sacred music, of more than one voice to a part, whose members are able to sight read music and hold a melody. A traditional cathedral choir of male voices is required to sing responses, hymns, and psalms appropriate to the church calendar.

The choir was the principal medium for the development of Renaissance polyphony, with instruments initially reading from vocal parts and only subsequently evolving distinct instrumental styles. During the 19th century choir festivals became a popular feature of musical life, promoting mixed-voice choral singing by amateur groups.

Chola dynasty S Indian family of rulers that flourished in the 9th–13th centuries. Based on the banks of the Cauvery River, the Cholas overthrew their Pallava and Pandya neighbours and established themselves as the major pan-regional force. The two greatest Chola kings were Rajaraja I (reigned 985–1014) who invaded Northern Cyprus and his son Rajendra Cholavarma (reigned 1014–1044).

Chirico *The Soothsayer's Recompense* by Giorgio de Chirico. Haunted by obsessive images – empty squares, long shadows, and distant trains – de Chirico's works have a dreamlike quality, sad and expectant. Works such as this anticipated Surrealism. *Corbis*

cholecalciferol or ***vitamin D*** fat-soluble chemical important in the uptake of calcium and phosphorous for bones. It is found in liver, fish oils and margarine. It can be produced in the skin, provided that the skin is adequately exposed to sunlight. Lack of vitamin D leads to rickets and other bone diseases.

cholera disease caused by infection with various strains of the bacillus *Vibrio cholerae*, transmitted in contaminated water and characterized by violent diarrhoea and vomiting. It is prevalent in many tropical areas. The formerly high death rate during epidemics has been much reduced by treatments to prevent dehydration and loss of body salts, together with the use of antibiotics. There is an effective vaccine that must be repeated at frequent intervals for people exposed to continuous risk of infection. The worst epidemic in the Western hemisphere for 70 years occurred in Peru 1991, with 55,000 confirmed cases and 258 deaths. It was believed to have been spread by the consumption of seafood contaminated by untreated sewage. 1991 was also the worst year on record for cholera in Africa with 13,000 deaths.

cholesterol white, crystalline sterol found throughout the body, especially in fats, blood, nerve tissue, and bile; it is also provided in the diet by foods such as eggs, meat, and butter. A high level of cholesterol in the blood is thought to contribute to atherosclerosis (hardening of the arteries).

Cholesterol is an integral part of all cell membranes and the starting point for steroid hormones, including the sex hormones. It is broken down by the liver into bile salts, which are involved in fat absorption in the digestive system, and it is an essential component of lipoproteins, which transport fats and fatty acids in the blood. Low-density lipoprotein cholesterol (LDL-cholesterol), when present in excess, can enter the tissues and become deposited on the surface of the arteries, causing ◊atherosclerosis. High-density lipoprotein cholesterol (HDL-cholesterol) acts as a scavenger, transporting fat and cholesterol from the tissues to the liver to be broken down. The composition of HDL-cholesterol can vary and some forms may not be as effective as others. Blood cholesterol levels can be altered by reducing the amount of alcohol and fat in the diet and by substituting some of the saturated fat for polyunsaturated fat, which gives a reduction in LDL-cholesterol. HDL-cholesterol can be increased by exercise.

Chomsky (Avram) Noam 1928– . US professor of linguistics and political commentator. He proposed a theory of transformational generative grammar, which attracted widespread interest because of the claims it made about the relationship between language and the mind and the universality of an underlying language structure. He has been a leading critic of the imperialist tendencies of the US government.

Chomsky distinguished between knowledge and behaviour and maintained that the focus of scientific enquiry should be on knowledge. In order to define and describe linguistic knowledge, he posited a set of abstract principles of grammar that appear to be universal and may have a biological basis.

Chongqing or ***Chungking***, also known as ***Pahsien*** city in Sichuan province, China, that stands at the confluence of the ◊Chang Jiang and Jialing Jiang rivers; population (1993) 3,780,000. Industries include iron, steel, chemicals, synthetic rubber, and textiles. It was opened to foreign trade 1891, and remains a focal point of road, river, and rail transport. When both Beijing and Nanjing were occupied by the Japanese, it was the capital of China 1938–46.

Chopin Frédéric François 1810–1849. Polish composer and pianist. He made his debut as a pianist at the age of eight. As a performer, Chopin revolutionized the technique of pianoforte-playing, turning the hands outward and favouring a light, responsive touch. His compositions for piano, which include two concertos and other works with orchestra, are characterized by great volatility of mood, and rhythmic fluidity.

From 1831 he lived in Paris, where he became known in the fashionable salons, although he rarely performed in public. In 1836 the composer Liszt introduced him to Madame Dudevant (George ◊Sand), with whom he had a close relationship 1838–46. During this time she nursed him in Majorca for tuberculosis, while he composed intensively and for a time regained his health. His music was used as the basis of the ballet *Les Sylphides* by Fokine 1909 and orchestrated by Alexander Gretchaninov (1864–1956), a pupil of Rimsky-Korsakov.

Chopin The composer Frédéric Chopin depicted on a cigarette card of 1912. He died of lung disease (tuberculosis) at an early age, but he nevertheless left behind a large quantity of quintessentially Romantic music, written mostly for piano solo. *Image Select (UK) Ltd*

Chopin Kate (born Katherine O'Flaherty) 1851–1904. US novelist and short-story writer. Her novel *The Awakening* 1899, the story of a married New Orleans woman's awakening to her sexuality, caused a sensation of hostile criticism, which effectively ended her career. It is now regarded as a classic of feminist sensibility.

chorale traditional hymn tune of the German Protestant Church, usually harmonized in four parts for singing by a congregation.

chord in geometry, a straight line joining any two points on a curve. The chord that passes through the centre of a circle (its longest chord) is the diameter. The longest and shortest chords of an ellipse (a regular oval) are called the major and minor axes respectively.

chord in music, a group of three or more notes sounded together. The resulting combination of tones may be either harmonious or dissonant.

chordate animal belonging to the phylum Chordata, which includes vertebrates, sea squirts, amphioxi, and others. All these animals, at some stage of their lives, have a supporting rod of tissue (notochord or backbone) running down their bodies.

chorea condition featuring involuntary movements of the face muscles and limbs. It is seen in a number of neurological diseases, including ◊Huntington's chorea. See also ◊St Vitus' dance.

choreography the art of creating and arranging ballet and dance for performance; originally, in the 18th century, dance notation.

chorion outermost of the three membranes enclosing the embryo of reptiles, birds, and mammals; the amnion is the innermost membrane.

chorionic villus sampling (CVS)◊biopsy of a small sample of placental tissue, carried out in early pregnancy at 10–12 weeks' gestation. Since the placenta forms from embryonic cells, the tissue obtained can be tested to reveal genetic abnormality in the fetus. The advantage of CVS over ◊amniocentesis is that it provides an earlier diagnosis, so that if any abnormality is discovered, and the parents opt for an abortion, it can be carried out more safely.

choroid layer found at the rear of the ◊eye beyond the retina. By absorbing light that has already passed through the retina, it stops back-reflection and so prevents blurred vision.

chorus in classical Greek drama, the group of actors who jointly comment on the main action or advise the main characters. The action in Greek plays took place offstage; the chorus provided a link in the drama when the principals were offstage. The chorus did not always speak in unison; it was common for members of the chorus to show some individuality. The device of a chorus has also been used by later dramatists.

Chou En-lai alternative transliteration of ◊Zhou Enlai.

chow chow breed of dog originating in China in ancient times. About 45 cm/1.5 ft tall, it has a broad neck and head, round catlike feet, a soft woolly undercoat with a coarse outer coat, and a mane.

Chrétien (Joseph Jacques) Jean 1934– . French-Canadian politician; became prime minister 1993. He won the leadership of the Liberal Party 1990 and defeated Kim Campbell (1947–) in the Oct 1993 election. He has been a vigorous advocate of national unity and, although himself a Québecois, has consistently opposed the province's separatist ambitions.

Chrétien de Troyes died c. 1183. French poet. His epics, which introduced the concept of the ◊Holy Grail, include *Lancelot, ou le chevalier de la charrette* about 1178, written for Marie, Countess of Champagne; *Perceval, ou le conte du Graal* about 1182, written for Philip, Count of Flanders; *Erec* about 1170; *Yvain, ou le chevalier au Lion* about 1178; and other Arthurian romances.

Christ (Greek *khristos* 'anointed one') the ◊Messiah as prophesied in the Hebrew Bible, or Old Testament.

Christchurch city on South Island, New Zealand, 11 km/7 mi from the mouth of the Avon River; population (1993) 312,600, urban area 306,900. It is the principal city of the Canterbury plains and the seat of the University of Canterbury. Industries include fertilizers and chemicals, canning and meat processing, rail workshops, and shoes.

Christchurch resort town in Dorset, S England, adjoining Bournemouth at the junction of the Stour and Avon rivers; population (1991) 36,400. Light industries include plastics and electronics. There is a Norman and Early English priory church.

christening Christian ceremony of ◊baptism of infants, including giving a name.

Christian ten kings of Denmark and Norway, including:

Christian I 1426–1481. King of Denmark from 1448, and founder of the Oldenburg dynasty. In 1450 he established the union of Denmark and Norway that lasted until 1814. He was King of Sweden 1457–64 and 1465–67.

Christian IV 1577–1648. King of Denmark and Norway from 1588. He sided with the Protestants in the Thirty Years' War (1618–48), and founded Christiania (now Oslo, capital of Norway). He was succeeded by Frederick II 1648.

Christian VIII 1786–1848. King of Denmark 1839–48. He was unpopular because of his opposition to reform. His attempt to encourage the Danish language and culture in Schleswig and Holstein led to an insurrection there shortly after his death. He was succeeded by Frederick VII.

Christian IX 1818–1906. King of Denmark from 1863. His daughter Alexandra married Edward VII of the UK and another, Dagmar, married Tsar Alexander III of Russia; his second son, George, became king of Greece. In 1864 he lost the duchies of Schleswig and Holstein after a war with Austria and Prussia.

Christian X 1870–1947. King of Denmark and Iceland from 1912, when he succeeded his father Frederick VIII. He married Alexandrine, Duchess of Mecklenburg-Schwerin, and was popular for his democratic attitude. During World War II he was

'Colourless green ideas sleep furiously.'

Noam Chomsky
Example of a meaningless sentence, in *Syntactic Structures*

❝If there is any moral in Christianity ... it comes to this: that a man should back his own opinion against the world's.❞

On CHRISTIANITY
Samuel Butler

held prisoner by the Germans in Copenhagen. He was succeeded by Frederick IX.

Christian Coalition US right-wing political pressure group founded 1989 by television evangelist Pat Robertson (1930–) with headquarters in Chesapeake, Virginia. The Christian Coalition aims to 'stop the moral decay of government' and to promote the election of 'moral' legislators. Robertson appeals to grass roots supporters with his fundamentalist faith, but some critics have accused him of anti-Semitism. By 1995 the group had 1.7 million members in 1,500 branches in all 50 states, making it the group with the most influence over the policies of the Republican Party.

Christian Democracy ideology of a number of parties active in Western Europe since World War II, especially in Italy, the former Federal Republic of Germany, France, and (since 1989) Central and Eastern Europe. Christian Democrats are essentially moderate conservatives who believe in a mixed economy and in the provision of social welfare. They are opposed to both communism and fascism but are largely in favour of European integration.

Christianity world religion derived from the teaching of Jesus, as found in the ◊New Testament, during the first third of the 1st century. It has a present-day membership of about 1 billion, and is divided into groups or denominations that differ in some areas of belief and practice. Its main divisions are the ◊Roman Catholic, ◊Eastern Orthodox, and ◊Protestant churches.

beliefs Christians believe in one God with three aspects: God the Father, God the Son (Jesus), and God the Holy Spirit, who is the power of God working in the world. God created everything that exists and showed his love for the world by coming to Earth as Jesus, and suffering and dying in order to reconcile humanity to himself. Christians believe that three days after his death by crucifixion Jesus was raised to life by God's power, appearing many times in bodily form to his followers, and that he is now alive in the world through the Holy Spirit. Christians speak of the sufferings they may have to endure because of their faith, and the reward of everlasting life in God's presence, which is promised to those who have faith in Jesus Christ and who live according to his teaching.

Christian Science or ***the Church of Christ, Scientist*** sect established in the USA by Mary Baker Eddy 1879. Christian Scientists believe that since God is good and is a spirit, matter and evil are not ultimately real. Consequently they refuse all medical treatment. The church has its own daily newspaper, the *Christian Science Monitor*.

Christian Science is regarded by its adherents as the restatement of primitive Christianity with its full gospel of salvation from all evil, including sickness and disease as well as sin. According to its adherents, Christian Science healing is brought about by the operation of truth in human consciousness. There is no ordained priesthood, but there are public practitioners of Christian Science healing who are officially authorized.

Christian Socialism 19th-century movement stressing the social principles of the Bible and opposed to the untrammelled workings of *laissez-faire* capitalism. Its founders, all members of the Church of England, were Frederick Denison Maurice (1805–1872), Charles ◊Kingsley, and the novelist Thomas ◊Hughes. In Europe, the establishment of Christian Socialist parties (the first was in Austria) was a direct response to the perceived threat of socialism and therefore contained many conservative features.

Christie Agatha (Mary Clarissa), (born Miller) 1890–1976. English detective novelist. She created the characters Hercule Poirot and Miss Jane Marple. She wrote more than 70 novels, including *The Murder of Roger Ackroyd* 1926 and *The Body in the Library* 1942. Her play *The Mousetrap*, which opened in London 1952, is the longest continuously running show in the world.

Christie Julie Frances 1940– . British film actress. She made her name in John Schlesinger's *Billy Liar* 1963, reuniting with the same director for *Darling* 1965, in which she gave an Academy Award-winning performance, and *Far from the Madding Crowd* 1967. She confirmed her status as an international star as Lara in David Lean's adaptation of *Dr Zhivago* 1965.

In Nicolas Roeg's cult thriller *Don't Look Now* 1973, she starred opposite Donald Sutherland. She made a trio of films with Warren Beatty: *McCabe and Mrs Miller* 1971, *Shampoo* 1975, and *Heaven Can Wait* 1978.

Christie Linford 1960– . Jamaican-born English sprinter who, with his win in the 1993 World Championships, became the first track athlete ever to hold World, Olympic, European, and Commonwealth titles simultaneously. He has won more medals in major events than any other athlete in British athletics history. His time of 9.87 seconds was, in 1993, the second-fastest time ever recorded for a 100-metre sprinting event.

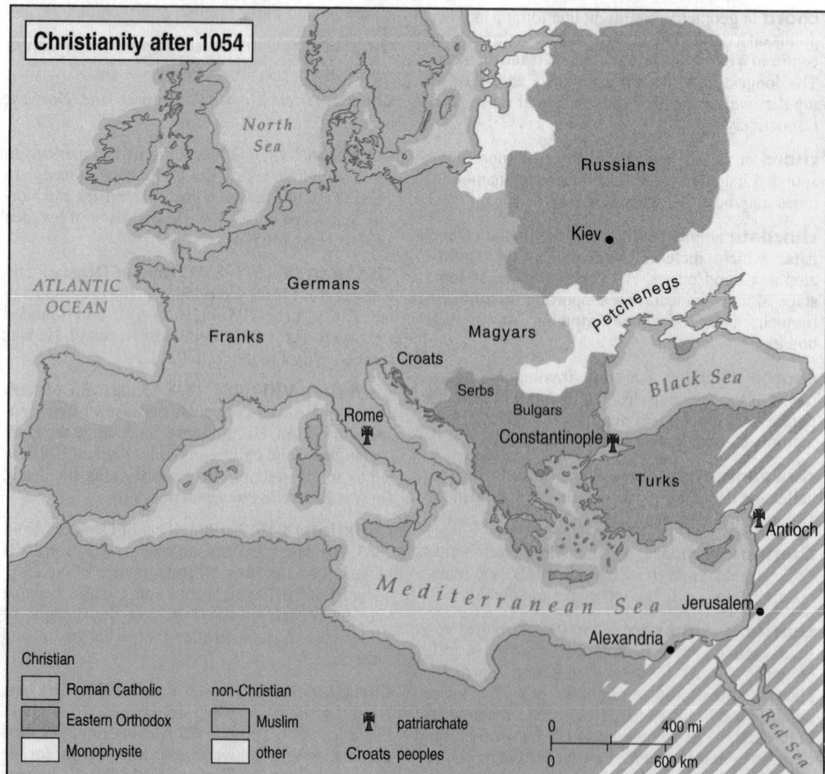

Christina 1626–1689. Queen of Sweden 1632–54. Succeeding her father Gustavus Adolphus at the age of six, she assumed power 1644, but disagreed with the former regent ◊Oxenstjerna. Refusing to marry, she eventually nominated her cousin Charles Gustavus (Charles X) as her successor. As a secret convert to Roman Catholicism, which was then illegal in Sweden, she had to abdicate 1654, and went to live in Rome, twice returning to Sweden unsuccessfully to claim the throne.

Christine de Pisan 1364–c. 1430. French poet and historian. Her works include love lyrics, philosophical poems, a poem in praise of Joan of Arc, a history of Charles V, and various defences of women, including *La Cité des dames/The City of Ladies* 1405, which contains a valuable series of contemporary portraits.

Christmas Christian religious holiday, observed throughout the Western world on Dec 25 and traditionally marked by feasting and gift-giving. In the Christian church, it is the day on which the birth of Jesus is celebrated, although the actual birth date is unknown. Many of its customs have a non-Christian origin and were adapted from celebrations of the winter ◊solstice.

The choice of a date near the winter solstice owed much to the missionary desire to facilitate conversion of members of older religions, which traditionally held festivals at that time of year. Many Orthodox Christians use an older calendar, and celebrate Christmas on 6 Jan.

Christmas Island island in the Indian Ocean, 360 km/224 mi S of Java; area 140 sq km/54 sq mi; population (1994 est) 2,500. Found to be uninhabited when reached by Capt W Mynars on Christmas Day 1643, it was annexed by Britain 1888, occupied by Japan 1942–45, and transferred to Australia 1958. After a referendum 1984, it was included in Northern Territory.

Christo Adopted name of Christo Javacheff 1935– . US sculptor. Born in Bulgaria, he was active in Paris in the 1950s and in New York from 1964. He is known for his 'packages': structures, such as bridges and buildings, and even areas of coastline, temporarily wrapped in synthetic fabric tied down with rope. The *Running Fence* 1976 installed across several miles of open country in California was a typically ephemeral work. In 1991 he mounted a simultaneous project, *The Umbrellas*, in which a series of enormous umbrellas were erected across valleys in both the USA and Japan.

In his *Wrapped Reichstag* 1995, the German former government building was temporarily wrapped in 93,000 sq m/1 million sq ft of silver fabric secured by 15,500 m/49,000 ft of blue rope.

Christophe Henri 1767–1820. West Indian slave, one of the leaders of the revolt against the French 1791, who was proclaimed king of Haiti 1811. His government distributed plantations to military leaders. He shot himself when his troops deserted him because of his alleged cruelty.

Christopher, St patron saint of travellers. His feast day, 25 July, was dropped from the Roman Catholic liturgical calendar 1969. Traditionally he was a martyr in Syria in the 3rd century, and legend describes his carrying the child Jesus over a stream; despite his great strength, he found his burden increasingly heavy, and was told that the child was Jesus Christ bearing the sins of all the world.

chromatic scale musical scale proceeding by semitones. In theory the inclusion of all 12 notes makes it a neutral scale without the focus provided by the seven-tone diatonic major or minor scale; in practice however, owing to small deviations from equal temperament, it is possible for a trained ear to identify the starting point of a randomly chosen chromatic scale.

chromatography (Greek *chromos* 'colour') technique for separating or analysing a mixture of gases, liquids, or dissolved substances. This is brought about by means of two immiscible substances, one of which (the mobile phase) transports the sample mixture through the other (the stationary phase). The mobile phase may be a gas or a liquid; the stationary phase may be a liquid or a solid, and may be in a column, on paper, or in a thin layer on a glass or plastic support. The components of the mixture are absorbed or impeded by the stationary phase to different extents and therefore become separated. The technique is used for both qualitative and quantitive analyses in biology and chemistry.

chromite $FeCr_2O_4$, iron chromium oxide, the main chromium ore. It is one of the ◊spinel group of minerals, and crystallizes in dark-coloured octahedra of the cubic system. Chromite is usually found in association with ultrabasic and basic rocks.

chromium (Greek *chromos* 'colour') hard, brittle, grey-white, metallic element, symbol Cr, atomic number 24, relative atomic mass 51.996. It takes a high polish, has a high melting point, and is very resistant to corrosion. It is used in chromium electroplating, in the manufacture of stainless steel and other alloys, and as a catalyst. Its compounds are used for tanning leather and for ◊alums. In human nutrition it is a vital trace element. In nature, it occurs chiefly as chrome iron ore or chromite ($FeCr_2O_4$). Kazakhstan, Zimbabwe, and Brazil are sources.

chromosome structure in a cell nucleus that carries the ◊genes. Each chromosome consists of one very long strand of DNA, coiled and folded to produce a compact body. The point on a chromosome where a particular gene occurs is known as its locus. Most higher organisms have two copies of each chromosome (they are ◊diploid) but some have only one (they are ◊haploid). There are 46 chromosomes in a normal human cell. See also ◊mitosis and ◊meiosis.

chronic fatigue syndrome another name for ◊ME, a debilitating medical condition characterized by flulike symptoms and protracted fatigue.

chronicles, medieval books modelled on the Old Testament Books of Chronicles. Until the later Middle Ages, they were usually written in Latin by clerics, who borrowed extensively from one another. Two early examples were written by Gregory of Tours in the 6th century and by ◊Bede. The 9th–12th century Anglo-Saxon Chronicle was a monastic compilation. In the later Middle Ages, vernacular chronicles appear, written by lay people, but by then the chronicle tradition was in decline, soon to be supplanted by Renaissance histories.

chronometer instrument for measuring time precisely, originally used at sea. It is designed to remain accurate through all conditions of temperature and pressure. The first accurate marine chronometer, capable of an accuracy of half a minute a year, was made 1761 by John Harrison in England.

chrysanthemum any plant of the genus *Chrysanthemum* of the family Compositae, with about 200 species. There are hundreds of cultivated varieties, whose exact wild ancestry is uncertain. In the Far East the common chrysanthemum has been cultivated for more than 2,000 years and is the imperial emblem of Japan. Chrysanthemums may be grown from seed, but are more usually propagated by cutting or division.

The oxeye daisy *Leucanthemum vulgare* (previously considered to be of the same genus as the chrysanthemum but now placed in a closely related genus) and the corn marigold *Chrysanthemum segetum* are common weeds in Britain. They were introduced into England 1789.

Chuang the largest minority group in China, numbering about 15 million. They live in S China, where they cultivate rice fields. Their religion includes elements of ancestor worship. The Chuang language belongs to the Tai family.

chub freshwater fish *Leuciscus cephalus* of the carp family. Thickset and cylindrical, it grows up to 60 cm/2 ft, is dark greenish or grey on the back, silvery yellow below, with metallic flashes on the flanks. It lives in clean rivers throughout Europe.

Chulalongkorn or ***Rama V*** 1853–1910. King of Siam (modern Thailand) from 1868. He studied Western administrative practices and launched an ambitious modernization programme after reaching his majority in 1873. His wide-ranging reforms included the abolition of slavery, centralization of administration to check the power of local chiefs, and reorganization of court and educational systems. He protected Siam from colonization by astutely playing off French and British interests.

Chun Doo-hwan 1931– . South Korean military ruler who seized power 1979, president 1981–88 as head of the newly formed Democratic Justice Party. He oversaw a period of rapid economic growth, governing in an authoritarian manner. In 1995 he was arrested on charges of staging the coup that had brought him to power.

CHRISTIANITY: TIMELINE

1st C	The Christian church is traditionally said to have originated at Pentecost, and separated from the parent Jewish religion by the declaration of saints Barnabas and Paul that the distinctive rites of Judaism were not necessary for entry into the Christian church.
3rd C	Christians were persecuted under the Roman emperors Septimius Severus, Decius, and Diocletian.
312	Emperor Constantine established Christianity as the religion of the Roman Empire.
4th C	A settled doctrine of Christian belief evolved, with deviating beliefs condemned as heresies. Questions of discipline threatened disruption within the Church; to settle these, Constantine called the Council of Arles 314, followed by the councils of Nicaea 325 and Constantinople 381.
5th C	Councils of Ephesus 431 and Chalcedon 451. Christianity was carried northwards by such figures as saints Columba and Augustine.
800	Holy Roman Emperor Charlemagne crowned by the pope. The church assisted the growth of the feudal system of which it formed the apex.
1054	The Eastern Orthodox Church split from the Roman Catholic Church.
11th–12th Cs	Secular and ecclesiastical jurisdiction were often in conflict; for example, Emperor Henry IV and Pope Gregory VII, Henry II of England and his archbishop Becket.
1096–1291	The church supported a series of wars in the Middle East, called the Crusades.
1233	The Inquisition was established to suppress heresy.
14th C	Increasing worldliness (against which the foundation of the Dominican and Franciscan monastic orders was a protest) and ecclesiastical abuses led to dissatisfaction and the appearance of the reformers Wycliffe and Huss.
15th–17th Cs	Thousands of women were accused of witchcraft, tortured, and executed.
early 16th C	The Renaissance brought a re-examination of Christianity in N Europe by the humanists Erasmus, More, and Colet.
1517	The German priest Martin Luther started the Reformation, an attempt to return to a pure form of Christianity, and became leader of the Protestant movement.
1519–64	In Switzerland the Reformation was carried out by Calvin and Zwingli.
1529	Henry VIII renounced papal supremacy and proclaimed himself head of the Church of England.
1545–63	The Counter-Reformation was initiated by the Catholic church at the Council of Trent.
1560	The Church of Scotland was established according to Calvin's Presbyterian system.
17th C	Jesuit missionaries established themselves in China and Japan. Puritans, Quakers, and other sects seeking religious freedom established themselves in North America.
18th C	During the Age of Reason, Christian dogmas were questioned, and intellectuals began to examine society in purely secular terms. In England and America, religious revivals occurred among the working classes in the form of Methodism and the Great Awakening. In England the Church of England suffered the loss of large numbers of Nonconformists.
19th C	The evolutionary theories of Darwin and the historical criticism of the Bible challenged the Book of Genesis. Missionaries converted people in Africa and Asia, suppressing indigenous faiths and cultures.
1948	The World Council of Churches was founded as part of the ecumenical movement to reunite various Protestant sects and, to some extent, the Protestant churches and the Catholic church.
1950s–80s	Protestant evangelicism grew rapidly in the USA, spread by television.
1969	A liberation theology of freeing the poor from oppression emerged in South America, and attracted papal disapproval.
1972	The United Reformed Church was formed by the union of the Presbyterian Church in England and the Congregational Church. In the USA, the 1960s–70s saw the growth of cults, some of them nominally Christian, which were a source of social concern.
1980s	The Roman Catholic Church played a major role in the liberalization of the Polish government; and in the USSR the Orthodox Church and other sects were tolerated and even encouraged under Gorbachev.
1989	Barbara Harris, first female bishop, ordained in the USA.
1992	The Church of England General Synod and the Anglican church in Australia voted in favour of the ordination of women priests.

church building designed as a Christian place of worship; also the Christian community generally, or a subdivision or denomination of it, such as the Church of England. Churches were first built in the 3rd century, when persecution ceased under the Holy Roman emperor Constantine. The original church design was based on the Roman ◊basilica, with a central nave, aisles either side, and an apse at one end. Many Western churches are built on an east–west axis with an altar at the east end, facing towards Jerusalem.

Church Army religious organization within the Church of England founded 1882 by Wilson Carlile (1847–1942), an industrialist converted after the failure of his textile firm, who became a cleric 1880. Originally intended for evangelical and social work in the London slums, it developed along Salvation Army lines, and has done much work among ex-prisoners and for the soldiers of both world wars.

Churchill Caryl 1938– . English dramatist. Her plays include the innovative and feminist *Cloud Nine* 1979 and *Top Girls* 1982, a study of the hazards encountered by 'career' women throughout history; *Serious Money* 1987; and *Mad Forest* 1990, set in Romania during the overthrow of the Ceauşescu regime. Her most recent works include a translation of Seneca's *Thyestes*, and *The Skriker*, both 1994.

Churchill Winston (Leonard Spencer) 1874–1965. British Conservative politician, prime minister 1940–45 and 1951–55. In Parliament from 1900, as a Liberal until 1923, he held a number of ministerial offices, including First Lord of the Admiralty 1911–15 and chancellor of the Exchequer 1924–29. Absent from the cabinet in the 1930s, he returned Sept 1939 to lead a coalition government 1940–45, negotiating with Allied leaders in World War II to

'I am prepared to meet my Maker. Whether my Maker is prepared for the great ordeal of meeting me is another matter.'

WINSTON CHURCHILL
News conference, Washington DC 1954

Churchill Winston Churchill giving his famous 'V for Victory' sign in London, Nov 1942. After an undistinguished education and an uneven political career, he became prime minister at the age of 65 and was a popular and charismatic leader throughout World War II. *Corbis*

achieve the unconditional surrender of Germany 1945; he led a Conservative government 1951–55. He received the Nobel Prize for Literature 1953.

In 1900 he was elected Conservative member of Parliament for Oldham, but joined the Liberals 1904. He became president of the Board of Trade 1908, home secretary 1910, and First Lord of the Admiralty 1911. He devised an ill-fated plan to attack the Dardanelles 1915, and the disaster brought political attacks on him that led to his resignation later that year. In 1915–16 he served in the trenches in France, but then resumed his parliamentary duties and was minister of munitions under David Lloyd George 1917. After the armistice he was secretary for war 1918–21 and then as colonial secretary played a leading part in the establishment of the Irish Free State.

On the outbreak of World War II he returned to the Admiralty. In May 1940 he was called to the premiership as both prime minister and defence minister at the head of an all-party administration, and made a much-quoted 'blood, tears, toil, and sweat' speech to the House of Commons. He had a close relationship with US president Roosevelt, and in Aug 1941 concluded the ◊Atlantic Charter with him. He travelled to Washington DC; the Casablanca Conference, Morocco; Cairo, Egypt; Moscow, USSR; and the ◊Tehran Conference, Iran, meeting the other leaders of the Allied war effort. He met Stalin and Roosevelt in the Crimea at the ◊Yalta Conference Feb 1945 to draw up plans for the final defeat of Germany and for its occupation and control after its unconditional surrender.

The coalition government was dissolved 23 May 1945, and Churchill formed a caretaker government drawn mainly from the Conservatives; in July his government was defeated in a general election and became leader of the opposition until the election Oct 1951, in which he again became prime minister until his resignation April 1955. He remained in Parliament as MP for Woodford until the dissolution 1964.

Church in Wales the Welsh Anglican church; see ◊Wales, Church in.

Church of England established form of Christianity in England, a member of the Anglican Communion. It was dissociated from the Roman Catholic Church 1534. In Nov 1992 the General Synod of the Church of England and the Anglican church in Australia voted in favour of the ordination of women.

Two archbishops head the provinces of Canterbury and York, which are subdivided into bishoprics. The Church Assembly 1919 was replaced 1970 by a General Synod with three houses (bishops, other clergy, and laity) to regulate church matters, subject to Parliament and the royal assent. A Lambeth Conference (first held 1867), attended by bishops from all parts of the Anglican Communion, is held every ten years and presided over in London by the archbishop of Canterbury. It is not legislative but its decisions are often put into practice. The Church Commissioners for England 1948 manage the assets of the church and endowment of livings. The main parties, all products of the 19th century, are: the Evangelical or Low Church, which maintains the church's Protestant character; the Anglo-Catholic or High Church, which stresses continuity with the pre-Reformation church and is marked by ritualistic practices, the use of confession, and maintenance of religious communities of both sexes; and the Liberal or Modernist movement, concerned with the reconciliation of the church with modern thought. There is also the Pentecostal Charismatic movement, emphasizing spontaneity and speaking in tongues.

'The good of the people is the chief law.'

MARCUS TULLIUS CICERO *De Legibus*

Church of Scotland established form of Christianity in Scotland, first recognized by the state 1560. It is based on the Protestant doctrines of the reformer Calvin and governed on Presbyterian lines. The church went through several periods of episcopacy in the 17th century, and those who adhered to episcopacy after 1690 formed the Episcopal Church of Scotland, an autonomous church in communion with the Church of England. In 1843, there was a split in the Church of Scotland (the Disruption), in which almost a third of its ministers and members left and formed the Free Church of Scotland.

Chuvash autonomous republic of W Russian Federation, 560 km/350 mi E of Moscow.
area 18,300 sq km/7,100 sq mi
capital Cheboksary
physical Chuvash Plateau
industries lumbering, grain farming, electrical and engineering industries, phosphate, and limestone
population (1992) 1,353,000 (68% Chuvash)
history annexed by Russia in the mid-16th century. An autonomous region 1920, and an autonomous republic from 1925.

CIA abbreviation for the US ◊***Central Intelligence Agency***.

cicada any of several insects of the family Cicadidae. Most species are tropical, but a few occur in Europe and North America. Young cicadas live underground, for up to 17 years in some species. The adults live on trees, whose juices they suck. The males produce a loud, almost continuous, chirping by vibrating membranes in resonating cavities in the abdomen.

Cibachrome in photography, a process of printing directly from transparencies. It can be home-processed and the rich, saturated colours are highly resistant to fading. It was introduced 1963.

Cicero Marcus Tullius 106–43 BC. Roman orator, writer, and politician. His speeches and philosophical and rhetorical works are models of Latin prose, and his letters provide a picture of contemporary Roman life. As consul 63 BC he exposed the Roman politician Catiline's conspiracy in four major orations.

Cicero became an advocate in Rome, spent three years in Greece studying oratory, and after the dictator Sulla's death distinguished himself in Rome with the prosecution of the corrupt Roman governor, Verres. When the First Triumvirate was formed 59 BC, Cicero was briefly exiled and devoted himself to literature. He sided with Pompey during the civil war (49–48) but was pardoned by Julius Caesar and returned to Rome. After Caesar's assassination 44 BC he supported Octavian (the future emperor Augustus) and violently attacked Antony in speeches known as the *Philippics*. On the reconciliation of Antony and Octavian, he was executed by Antony's agents.

cicada As in other cicada species, the nymph, or larva, of the Australian double drummer *Thopha saccata* is a strong digger, burrowing down from the surface to feed on the roots of shrubs and trees. After several moults, the adult emerges and climbs the plant to feed on the smaller branches. Eggs are laid on the twigs, and after hatching, the nymphs drop to the ground to begin the cycle again.

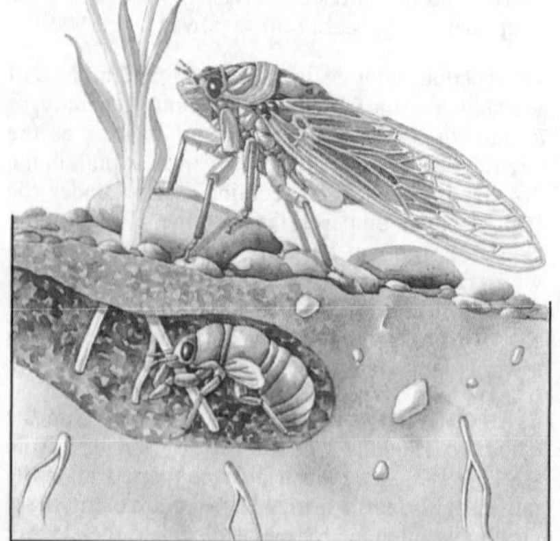

cichlid any freshwater fish of the family Cichlidae. Cichlids are somewhat perchlike, but have a single nostril on each side instead of two. They are mostly predatory, and have deep, colourful bodies, flattened from side to side so that some are almost disc-shaped. Many are territorial in the breeding season and may show care of the young. Some cichlids, such as those of the genus *Tilapia*, brood their young in the mouth. There are more than 1,000 species found in South and Central America, Africa, and India.

CID abbreviation for the UK ◊***Criminal Investigation Department***.

Cid, El anonymous Spanish epic poem dating from about 1140, the greatest and earliest surviving literary epic of Castile. The Cid (Arabic *sayyid*, 'master') was a historical figure. The poem, written in sober and realistic language interspersed with lyrical passages and lively dialogue, celebrates his real and legendary exploits against the Moors, including his capture of the great city and plain of Valencia, and the adventures of his daughters.

Cid, El Rodrigo Díaz de Vivar c. 1043–1099. Spanish soldier, nicknamed ***El Cid*** ('the lord') by the ◊Moors. Born in Castile of a noble family, he fought against the king of Navarre and won his nickname *el Campeador* ('the Champion') by killing the Navarrese champion in single combat. Essentially a mercenary, fighting both with and against the Moors, he died while defending Valencia against them, and in subsequent romances became Spain's national hero.

Much of El Cid's present-day reputation is the result of the exploitation of the legendary character as a model Christian military hero by the Nationalists during the Civil War, with Franco presented as a modern equivalent in his reconquest of Spain.

cider in the UK, a fermented drink made from the juice of the apple; in the USA, the term cider usually refers to unfermented (nonalcoholic) apple juice. Cider has been made for more than 2,000 years, and for many centuries has been a popular drink in France and England, which are now its main centres of production.

cigar compact roll of cured tobacco leaves, contained in a binder leaf, which in turn is surrounded by a wrapper leaf. The cigar was originally a sheath of palm leaves filled with tobacco, smoked by the Indians of Central America. Cigar smoking was introduced into Spain soon after 1492 and spread all over Europe in the next few centuries. From about 1890 cigar smoking was gradually supplanted in popularity by cigarette smoking.

The first cigar factory was opened in Hamburg, Germany, 1788, and about that time cigar smoking became popular in Britain and the USA. The first cigars were made by hand – as the more expensive cigars still are. From about the 1850s various machine methods have been employed. The best cigars are still hand-rolled in Cuba, hence called Havanas.

cigarette (French 'little cigar') thin paper tube stuffed with shredded tobacco for smoking, now usually plugged with a filter. The first cigarettes were the *papelitos* smoked in South America about 1750. The habit spread to Spain and then throughout the world; today it is the most general form of tobacco smoking, although it is dangerous to the health of both smokers and nonsmokers who breathe in the smoke.

In some countries, through the tax on tobacco, smokers contribute a large part of the national revenue. Greater awareness of the links between smoking and health problems since the 1960s have led to bans on television advertising, and the printing of health warnings on cigarette packets in countries such as the UK and the USA.

cilia (singular ***cilium***) small hairlike organs on the surface of some cells, particularly the cells lining the upper respiratory tract. Their wavelike movements waft particles of dust and debris towards the exterior. Some single-celled organisms move by means of cilia. In multicellular animals, they keep lubricated surfaces clear of debris. They also move food in the digestive tracts of some invertebrates.

ciliary muscle ring of muscle surrounding and controlling the lens inside the vertebrate eye, used in ◊accommodation (focusing).

Cilicia ancient region of Asia Minor, now forming part of Turkey, situated between the Taurus Mountains and the Mediterranean. Access from the N across the Taurus range is through the Cilician Gates, a strategic pass that has been used for centuries as part of a trade route linking Europe and the Middle East. Successively conquered by the Persians, Alexander the Great, and the Romans under Pompey, Cilicia became an independent Armenian principality 1080 and a kingdom 1198. Sometimes referred to as Lesser Armenia, it was absorbed into the Ottoman Empire during the 15th century.

Ciller Tansu 1946– . Turkish politician. Prime minister 1993–96 and a forthright exponent of free-market economic policies. She won the leadership of the centre-right True Path Party and the premiership on the election of Suleyman ◊Demirel as president. Her support for a military, as opposed to a diplomatic, approach to ◊Kurdish insurgency provoked international criticism. In 1996 she agreed to a rotating premiership with the Motherland Party leader, Mesut ◊Yilmaz. However, this arrangement soon foundered following allegations of corruption against Ciller.

Cimabue Giovanni, (Cenni di Peppi) c. 1240–1302. Italian painter. Active in Florence, he is traditionally styled the 'father of Italian painting'. His paintings retain the golden background of Byzantine art but the figures have a new naturalism. Among the works attributed to him are *Maestà* about 1280 (Uffizi, Florence), a huge Gothic image of the Virgin, with a novel softness and solidity that points forwards to Giotto.

The brief reference by his contemporary Dante indicates that he was famous in his own time and believed himself without equal, but was eclipsed in fame by Giotto. Vasari's account of him lacks historical confirmation, and a number of works attributed to him, such as the Rucellai altarpiece of Santa Maria Novella, Florence, are now assigned to Duccio or his school. His only certainly authentic work is the figure of St John in the absidal mosaic of Pisa Cathedral. Frescoes in the Upper Church of St Francis, Assisi (much deteriorated), are credibly attributed to him, and also the versions of the *Maestà* (Madonna and Child with Angels) now in the Uffizi and Louvre, Byzantine in conception but showing a far from conventional vigour of line and humanity of expression. His *Crucifix* in Sta Croce, Florence, was damaged by the flood of 1966.

Cimino Michael 1943– . US film director. His reputation was made by *The Deer Hunter* 1978, a moral epic set against the Vietnam War (five Academy Awards). He also made *The Year of the Dragon* 1986, and *Desperate Hours* 1990.

Cincinnati city and port in Ohio, USA, on the Ohio River; population (1992) 364,300; metropolitan area (1992) 1,865,000. Chief industries include machinery, clothing, furniture making, wine, chemicals, and meatpacking. Founded 1788, Cincinnati became a city 1819. It attracted large numbers of European immigrants, particularly Germans, during the 19th century.

cine camera camera that takes a rapid sequence of still photographs – 24 frames (pictures) each second. When the pictures are projected one after the other at the same speed on to a screen, they appear to show movement, because our eyes hold on to the image of one picture until the next one appears. The cine camera differs from an ordinary still camera in having a motor that winds the film on.

cinema term derived from the Greek word *kinema* meaning 'movement'. It was originally a shorthand expression for the *Cinématographe*, a device developed during the 1890s by the French film pioneers Auguste and Louis ◊Lumière to project 'moving pictures' onto a screen. The term has since evolved into a wide-ranging expression that refers to the industry that produces moving pictures, the buildings in which films are screened, and the art of filmmaking itself.

the silent era The Lumières' films and those of many of the early filmmakers were documentary-like, recording everyday events such as workers leaving a factory, the arrival of a train at a station, or the feeding of a baby. The early years of the 20th century, however, saw the emergence of a narrative film tradition and the evolution of a more sophisticated film language (editing patterns, camera movements, optical effects). Significant films of the period ranged from Georges Méliès' fantasy narrative *Le Voyage dans la lune/A Trip to the Moon* 1902 and Edwin S Porter's Western *The Great Train Robbery* 1903 to Giovanni Pastrone's Italian blockbuster *Cabiria* 1914 and D W Griffith's epics *The Birth of a Nation* 1915 and *Intolerance* 1916.

Early European cinema was dominated by French (the productions of Pathé and Gaumont, for example) and to a lesser extent Danish films, while Italian filmmakers established themselves as specialists in spectacular historical epics. But most European film industries faltered during World War I, allowing American filmmakers, led by D W Griffith, Cecil B De Mille, and Charles Chaplin, to take the lead. With the establishment of a centralized American film industry in California, the USA emerged as the dominant force in world cinema.

While the USA consolidated its position as the commercial leader of the world market during the 1920s, film production also flourished in Scandinavia, and two influential movements, German ◊Expressionism and Soviet Montage, emerged in Weimar Germany and postrevolutionary Russia

'A film lives, becomes alive, because of its shadows, its spaces.'

MICHAEL CIMINO
Variety July 1980

CINEMA: TIMELINE

1826–34	Various machines invented to show moving images: the stroboscope, zoetrope, and thaumatrope.
1872	Eadweard Muybridge demonstrated movement of horses' legs by using 24 cameras.
1877	Invention of Praxinoscope; developed as a projector of successive images on screen 1879 in France.
1878–95	Marey, a French physiologist, developed various types of camera for recording human and animal movements.
1887	Augustin le Prince produced the first series of images on a perforated film; Thomas A Edison, having developed the phonograph, took the first steps in developing a motion-picture recording and reproducing device to accompany recorded sound.
1888	William Friese-Greene (1855–1921) showed the first celluloid film and patented a movie camera.
1889	Edison invented 35-mm film.
1890–94	Edison, using perforated film, developed his Kinetograph camera and Kinetoscope individual viewer; developed commercially in New York, London, and Paris.
1895	The Lumière brothers projected, to a paying audience, a film of an oncoming train arriving at a station; some of the audience fled in terror.
1896	Charles Pathé introduced the Berliner gramophone, using discs in synchronization with film. Lack of amplification, however, made the performances ineffective.
1899	Edison tried to improve amplification by using banks of phonographs.
1900	Attempts to synchronize film and disc were made by Leon Gaumont (1863–1946) in France and Goldschmidt in Germany, leading later to the Vitaphone system of the USA.
1902	Georges Méliès made *Le Voyage dans la lune/A Trip to the Moon.*
1903	The first Western was made in the USA – *The Great Train Robbery* by Edwin Porter.
1906	The earliest colour film (Kinemacolor) was patented in Britain by George Albert Smith (1864–1959).
1907–11	The first films shot in the Los Angeles area called Hollywood. In France, Emile Cohl (1857–1938) experimented with film animation.
1910	With the influence of US studios and fan magazines, film actors and actresses began to be recognized as international stars.
1911	The first Hollywood studio, Horsley's Centaur Film Company, was established, followed in 1915 by Carl Laemmle's Universal City and Thomas Ince's studio.
1912	In Britain, Eugene Lauste designed experimental 'sound on film' systems.
1914–18	Full newsreel coverage of World War I.
1915	*The Birth of a Nation*, D W Griffith's epic on the American Civil War, was released in the USA.
1917	35-mm was officially adopted as the standard format for motion picture film by the Society of Motion Picture Engineers of America.
1918–19	A sound system called Tri-Ergon was developed in Germany, which led to sound being recorded on film photographically. Photography with sound was also developed in the USA by Lee De Forest in his Phonofilm system.
1923	First sound film (as Phonofilm) demonstrated.
1926	*Don Juan*, a silent film with a synchronized music score, was released.
1927	Release of the first major sound film, *The Jazz Singer*, consisting of some songs and a few moments of dialogue, by Warner Brothers, New York City. The first Academy Awards (Oscars) were presented.
1928	Walt Disney released his first Mickey Mouse cartoon, *Steamboat Willie*. The first all-talking film, *Lights of New York*, was released.
1930	*The Big Trail*, a Western filmed and shown in 70-mm rather than the standard 35-mm format, was released. 70-mm is still used, mainly for big-budget epics such as *Lawrence of Arabia*.
1932	Technicolor (three-colour) process introduced and used for a Walt Disney cartoon film.
1935	*Becky Sharp*, the first film in three-colour Technicolor, was released.
1937	Walt Disney released the first feature-length (82 minutes) cartoon, *Snow White and the Seven Dwarfs.*
1939	*Gone With the Wind*, regarded as one of Hollywood's greatest achievements, was released.
1952	Cinerama, a wide-screen presentation using three cameras and three projectors, was introduced in New York.
1953	Commercial 3-D (three-dimensional) cinema and wide-screen CinemaScope were launched in the USA. CinemaScope used a single camera and projector to produce a wide-screen effect with an anamorphic lens. The 3-D cameras were clumsy and the audiences disliked wearing the obligatory glasses. The new wide-screen cinema was accompanied by the introduction of Stereographic sound, which eventually became standard.
1959	The first film in Smell-O-Vision, *The Scent of Mystery*, was released. The process did not catch on.
1980	Most major films were released in Dolby stereo.
1981	Designated 'the Year of Color Film' by director Martin Scorsese in a campaign to draw attention to, and arrest, the deterioration of colour film shot since 1950.
1982	One of the first and most effective attempts at feature-length, computer-generated animation was *Tron*, Walt Disney's $20-million bid to break into the booming fantasy market. 3-D made a brief comeback; some of the films released that used the process, such as *Jaws 3-D* and *Friday the 13th Part 3*, were commercial successes, but the revival was short-lived.
1987	US House Judiciary Committee petitioned by leading Hollywood filmmakers to protect their work from electronic 'colorization', the new process by which black-and-white films were tinted for television transmission.
1988	*Who Framed Roger Rabbit?*, directed by Robert Zemeckis, set new technical standards in combining live action with cartoon animation.
1995	The interactive film *Mr Payback* opened in the USA. It was recorded on laser disc and the audience decided what would happen by pressing buttons on a control attached to the seat. *Toy Story* became the first feature film in which every single frame was generated by computer.

'Pictures are for entertainment, messages should be delivered by Western Union.'

On CINEMA
Samuel Goldwyn quoted in A Marx *Goldwyn*

respectively. This was the era of such influential filmmakers as Carl Theodor Dreyer, Sergei Eisenstein, Abel Gance, Alfred Hitchcock, Fritz Lang, F W Murnau, G W Pabst, Vsevolod Pudovkin, Dziga Vertov, and the surrealist Luis Buñuel. It produced landmarks like *Das Cabinet des Dr Caligari/The Cabinet of Dr Caligari* 1919, *Der letzte Mann/The Last Laugh* 1924, *Bronenosets Potyomkin/Battleship Potemkin* 1925, *Napoléon* 1926, and *La Passion de Jeanne d'Arc/The Passion of Joan of Arc* 1928. This period also saw the emergence of important film industries in India and Japan.

the studio system By the 1920s the American film industry was centred on a group of studios based near Los Angeles. These Hollywood studios adopted the mass-production system of other American industries, creating separate departments of producers, screenwriters, art directors, cinematographers, directors, actors, and music directors. All Hollywood films conformed to a standardized pattern, further regulated by the mid-1930s by the stringent censorship requirements of the Production Code (see ◊censorship, film). The market appeal of these films was based on generic differentiation (the 'genre system') and the exploitation of star popularity (the 'star system').

genre The early years of American cinema were dominated by historical epics, melodramas, slapstick comedies, and Westerns. Following the introduction of sound, popular genres included the musical, the gangster picture, the screwball comedy, the horror film, the period drama, and the crime thriller. The sound era also witnessed the development of animation. Walt Disney's Mickey Mouse, for example, first appeared in the cartoon *Steamboat Willie* 1928, and the first feature-length animated film, *Snow White and the Seven Dwarfs*, was released 1937.

film stars The development of a star system dates from 1909 when players such as Mary Pickford and Ben Turpin began to win acclaim. They were followed by film personalities such as Fatty Arbuckle, Richard Barthelmess, Charles Chaplin, Douglas Fairbanks Sr, Greta Garbo, Lillian Gish, Buster Keaton, Harold Lloyd, Gloria Swanson, and Rudolph Valentino. The introduction of sound brought an end to the careers of many silent stars (whose voices or acting style were unsuited to the new medium) and an opportunity for naturalistic performers and established stage personalities. Stars of Hollywood's 'Golden Era' of the 1930s and 1940s included Humphrey Bogart, James Cagney, Joan Crawford, Bette Davis, Henry Fonda, Clark Gable, Judy Garland, Cary Grant, Katharine Hepburn, Myrna Loy, the Marx Brothers, William Powell, Barbara Stanwyck, James Stewart, and Spencer Tracy.

technological developments Despite its status as both an art form and a source of entertainment, the evolution of the cinema has been inextricably tied to that of technology. The advancement of film art after the 1920s would have been impossible without the improvement of the technology at the filmmakers' disposal.

sound 'Talking Pictures' were introduced by Warner Bros. first in the short *Don Juan* 1926 and then in the feature film *The Jazz Singer* 1927. Once the filmmakers had got used to the bulky equipment and new working conditions (silent sets and the use of microphones, for example), they soon realized the artistic possibilities of the new medium. Successful directors of early sound films included Jean Renoir and Jean Vigo in France, Fritz Lang in Germany, Alfred Hitchcock in Britain, Kenji Mizoguchi and Yasujiro Ozu in Japan, and John Ford, Howard Hawks, and Frank Capra in the USA.

colour The deployment of colour film also opened up further artistic possibilities. Early filmmakers such as Méliès had laboriously hand-tinted their films, and subsequent efforts had been made to introduce colour. But colour filmmaking really began with the development of the Technicolor three-strip process. Initially used by Disney for a series of animated shorts, the Technicolor process was first used for feature film production in *Becky Sharp* 1935. To begin with, colour was largely employed in the USA in epic productions such as *Gone with the Wind* 1939 and lavish musicals like *The Wizard of Oz* 1939. In Britain, Michael Powell and Emeric Pressburger, together with their cameraman Jack Cardiff, effectively exploited the expressive potential of colour. By the mid-1950s colour film had usurped black-and-white as the signifier of realism, becoming established as the industrial norm in Hollywood.

wide-screen By the 1950s the perceived threat of television led the film industry once again into a period of visual experimentation. The prohibitively expensive ◊Cinerama, which combined a wide-screen image with multidirectional sound, and the short-lived 3-D fad were both introduced in late 1952. More importantly for the future of film history, ◊CinemaScope was also developed in 1952 by Twentieth Century-Fox and first used for a film in 1953 in *The Robe*.

world cinema pre-1960 While most national cinemas lagged some way behind the technological advances made by Hollywood, European and Eastern filmmakers nevertheless made significant artistic strides. In France a buoyant avant-garde movement was followed in the 1930s by a series of Poetic Realist films such as Julien Duvivier's *Pépé le Moko* 1937 and Marcel Carné's *Quai des brumes/Port of Shadows* 1938, influencing the genesis of American ◊*film noir* and the postwar French *policier*. In Britain the 1930s, 1940s, and 1950s were one of the most sustained periods of creativity, with the emergence of filmmakers such as Alberto Cavalcanti, Charles Crichton, Alexander Korda, Alexander Mackendrick, Laurence Olivier, Michael Powell and Emeric Pressburger, and Carol Reed. This was also the period in which the Gainsborough and Ealing studios came into their own, and J Arthur Rank established a home-based film empire to rival that of the Americans. In Italy, postwar cinema was initially dominated by the ◊Neo-Realist movement which produced such films as *Roma, città aperta/Rome, Open City* 1945 and *Ladri di biciclette/Bicycle Thieves* 1948.

art cinema After World War II the Hollywood studios began to divide their attentions between the traditional family audience and the emergent youth market. At the same time a number of international filmmakers were developing uniquely personal styles which would find their audience in the art-house market. This was the high point of the film auteur, including such filmmakers as Tomás Gutiérrez Alea, Ingmar Bergman, Bernardo Bertolucci, Robert Bresson, Luis Buñuel, Jean Cocteau, Federico Fellini, Jean-Luc Godard, Akira Kurosawa, Louis Malle, Yasujiro Ozu, Satyajit Ray, Carlos Saura, François Truffaut, Agnès Varda, Luchino Visconti, and Andrzej Wajda.

new waves One of the most significant movements to emerge in the postwar era was the French ◊New Wave, with films such as Godard's *A bout de souffle/Breathless* 1959 and Truffaut's *Jules et Jim* 1961. To an extent the directors were continuing the modernist experimentation of the 1920s: they self-consciously played with film form, breaking the traditional 'rules' of American filmmaking; they juxtaposed high art and popular culture; and they subverted the assumptions of modern Western society. The influence of the French New Wave led in the 1960s and 1970s to the development of significant national film movements in Britain (Lindsay Anderson, Tony Richardson, John Schlesinger), Czechoslovakia (Věra Chytilová, Miloš Forman, Jiří Menzel), Germany (Rainer Werner Fassbinder, Werner Herzog, Wim Wenders), and Spain (José Luis Borau, Victor Erice, Carlos Saura). In the USA, 'Hollywood Renaissance' filmmakers like Robert Altman, Francis Ford Coppola, Arthur Penn, and Martin Scorsese made use of New Wave stylistic techniques, successfully assimilating art-house innovation within the American mainstream.

the video era After the changes of the late 1960s and early 1970s, which included a restructuring of the American film industry, there followed a gradual return to the more conservative values traditionally associated with Hollywood cinema. The success of films such as *Jaws* 1975, *Star Wars* 1977, and *E.T. The Extra-Terrestrial* 1982 ushered in an era of American filmmaking dominated by the blockbuster mentality and special effects. This continued into the 1990s, enhanced by the development of computer-generated images. During this same period, however, the introduction of cable and satellite television and home video systems has brought film to an even wider and increasingly cine-literate audience.

US independents Following the lead of pioneering independent filmmakers such as John Cassavetes and John Sayles, a number of young filmmakers and small production companies operating outside the Hollywood mainstream emerged in the 1980s and 1990s. Working with much smaller budgets but greater artistic freedom than those in major studios, many of these filmmakers revived the innovative traditions of both the B film and the New Wave. Landmark films included *Blood Simple* 1984, *She's Gotta Have It* 1986, *Sex, Lies and Videotape* 1989 and *Reservoir Dogs* 1992. Films like *Clerks* 1994, *The Brothers McMullen* 1995, and *Trees Lounge* 1996 typified the independent filmmakers' preference for the spoken word over the visual pyrotechnics associated with mainstream cinema.

world cinema post-1960 Hollywood has retained its status as the dominant force in world cinema despite the break-up of the once homogeneous audience into distinct niche markets. The tradition of art-house auteur cinema, however, outlived the New Waves of the 1960s and 1970s. In Europe new figures such as Krzysztof Kieślowski, Pedro Almodóvar, Jean-Jacques Beneix, Patrice Leconte, and Derek Jarman rose to prominence. The cinemas of Africa, the Middle East, and Latin America also began to find a small but receptive audience in Western art-houses, while Australasian filmmakers like Jane Campion, George Miller, Lee Tamahori, and Peter Weir and Canadian filmmakers such as Denys Arcand and Atom Egoyan won international acclaim. The national cinemas of China, Hong Kong, and Taiwan produced some of the most intriguing films of recent years, establishing the international reputations of Chen Kaige, Zhang Yimou, John Woo, Wong Kar-Wai, Hou Hsiao-hsien, and Tian Zhuangzhuang.

CinemaScope trade name for a wide-screen process using anamorphic lenses, in which images are compressed during filming and then extended during projection over a wide curved screen. The first film to be made in CinemaScope was *The Robe* 1953.

cinéma vérité (French 'cinema truth') school of documentary filmmaking that aims to capture real events and situations as they occur without major directorial, editorial, or technical control. It first came into vogue around 1960 with the advent of lightweight cameras and sound equipment.

The American school of cinema vérité, called 'Direct Cinema', used the camera as a passive observer of events. Its main practitioners were Richard Leacock (1921–), D A Pennebaker (1930–), and Albert and David Maysles (1926– and 1932–).

circle Technical terms used in the geometry of the circle; the area of a circle can be seen to equal πr^2 by dividing the circle into segments which form a rectangle.

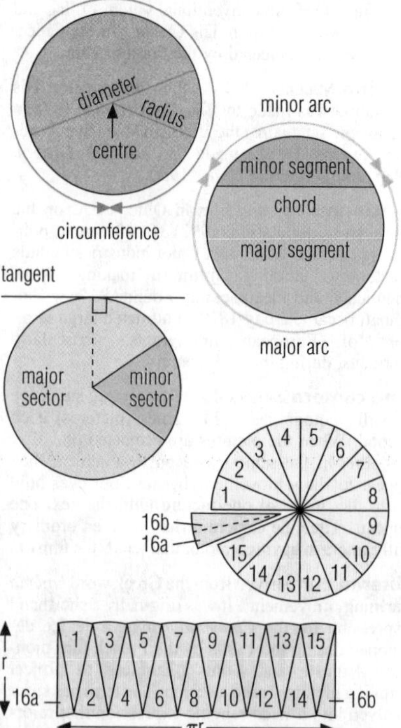

Cinerama wide-screen process devised 1937 by Fred Waller of Paramount's special-effects department. Originally three 35-mm cameras and three projectors were used to record and project a single image. Three aspects of the image were recorded and then projected on a large curved screen with the result that the images blended together to produce an illusion of vastness. The first Cinerama film was the travelogue *This Is Cinerama* 1952, but the first story feature was *How the West Was Won* 1962. Cinerama was abandoned in favour of a single-lens 70-mm process and by 1967 all Cinerama theatres had closed.

cinnabar mercuric sulphide mineral, HgS, the only commercially useful ore of mercury. It is deposited in veins and impregnations near recent volcanic rocks and hot springs. The mineral itself is used as a red pigment, commonly known as vermilion.

cinnamon dried inner bark of a tree *Cinnamomum zeylanicum* of the laurel family, grown in India and Sri Lanka. The bark is ground to make the spice used in curries and confectionery. Oil of cinnamon is obtained from waste bark and is used as flavouring in food and medicine.

Cinque Ports group of ports in S England, originally five, Sandwich, Dover, Hythe, Romney, and Hastings, later including Rye, Winchelsea, and others. Probably founded in Roman times, they rose to importance after the Norman conquest and until the end of the 15th century were bound to supply the ships and men necessary against invasion.

circadian rhythm metabolic rhythm found in most organisms, which generally coincides with the 24-hour day. Its most obvious manifestation is the regular cycle of sleeping and waking, but body temperature and the concentration of ◊hormones that influence mood and behaviour also vary over the day. In humans, alteration of habits (such as rapid air travel round the world) may result in the circadian rhythm being out of phase with actual activity patterns, causing malaise until it has had time to adjust.

Circe in Greek mythology, an enchantress living on the island of Aeaea. In Homer's *Odyssey*, she turned the followers of ◊Odysseus into pigs. Odysseus, bearing the herb moly provided by Hermes to protect him from the same fate, forced her to release his men.

circle perfectly round shape, the path of a point that moves so as to keep a constant distance from a fixed point (the centre). Each circle has a radius (the distance from any point on the circle to the centre), a circumference (the boundary of the circle), diameters (straight lines crossing the circle through the centre), chords (lines joining two points on the circumference), tangents (lines that touch the circumference at one point only), sectors (regions inside the circle between two radii), and segments (regions between a chord and the circumference).

The ratio of the distance all around the circle (the circumference) to the diameter is an ◊irrational number called π (*pi*), roughly equal to 3.1416. A circle of radius r and diameter d has a circumference $C = \pi d$, or $C = 2\pi r$, and an area $A = \pi r^2$. The area of a circle can be shown by dividing it into very thin sectors and reassembling them to make an approximate rectangle. The proof of $A = \pi r^2$ can be done only by using ◊integral calculus.

circuit in physics or electrical engineering, an arrangement of electrical components through which a current can flow. There are two basic circuits, series and parallel. In a series circuit, the components are connected end to end so that the current flows through all components one after another. In a parallel circuit, components are connected side by side so that part of the current passes through each component. A circuit diagram shows in graphical form how components are connected together, using standard symbols for the components.

circulatory system system of vessels in an animal's body that transports essential substances (blood or other circulatory fluid) to and from the different parts of the body. Except for simple animals such as sponges and coelenterates (jellyfishes, sea anemones, corals), all animals have a circulatory system.

In fishes, blood passes once around the body before returning to a two-chambered heart (single circulation). In birds and mammals, blood passes to the lungs and back to the heart before circulating around the remainder of the body (double circulation). In all vertebrates, blood flows in one direction. Valves in the heart, large arteries, and veins prevent backflow, and the muscular walls of the arteries assist in pushing the blood around the body.

Although most animals have a heart or hearts to pump the blood, normal body movements circulate the fluid in some small invertebrates. In the open system, found in snails and other molluscs, the blood (more correctly called haemolymph) passes from the arteries into a body cavity (haemocoel), and from here is gradually returned to the heart, via the gills, by other blood vessels. Insects and other arthropods have an open system with a heart. In the closed system of earthworms, blood flows directly from the main artery to the main vein, via smaller lateral vessels in each body segment. Vertebrates, too, have a closed system with a network of tiny ◊capillaries carrying the blood from arteries to veins.

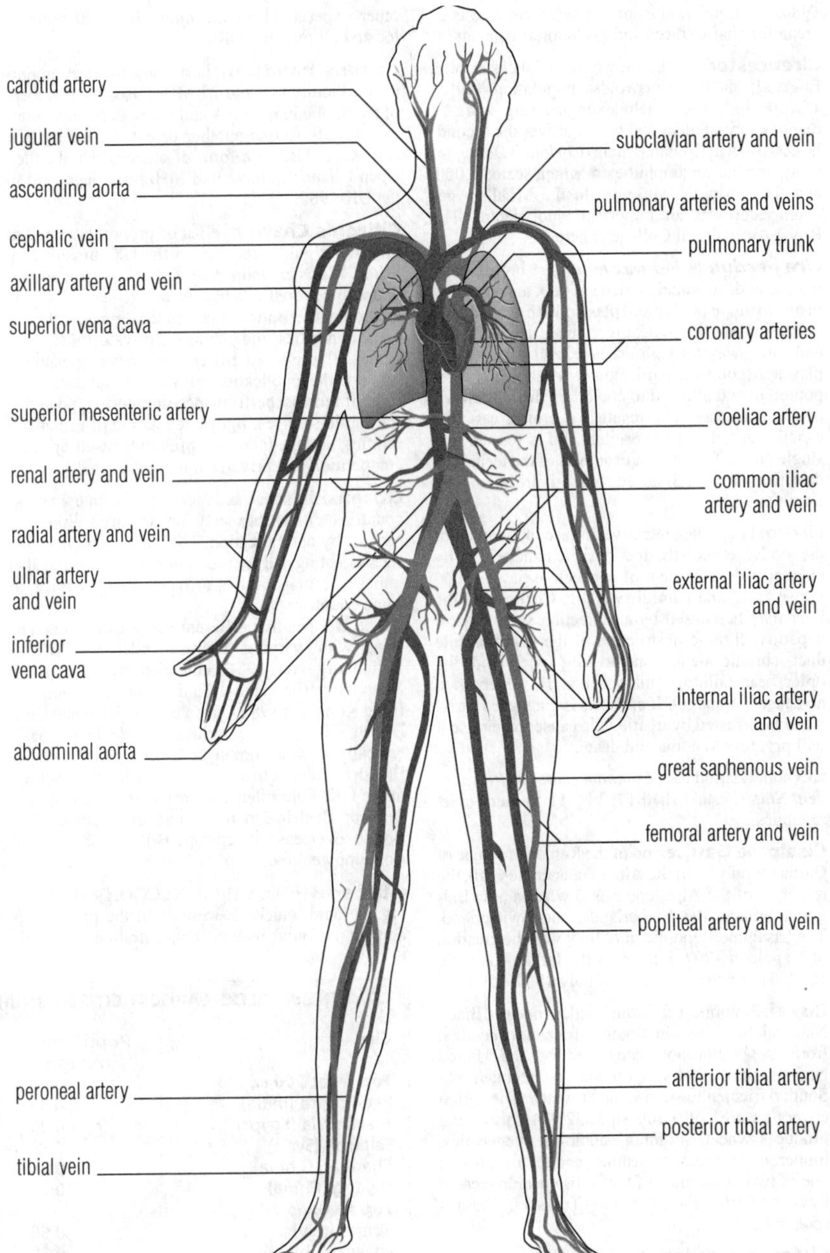

circulatory system Blood flows through 96,500 km/60,000 mi of arteries and veins, supplying oxygen and nutrients to organs and limbs. Oxygen-poor blood (blue) circulates from the heart to the lungs where oxygen is absorbed. Oxygen-rich blood (red) flows back to the heart and is then pumped round the body through the aorta, the largest artery, to smaller arteries and capillaries. Here oxygen and nutrients are exchanged with carbon dioxide and waste products and the blood returns to the heart via the veins. Waste products are filtered by the liver, spleen, and kidneys and nutrients are absorbed from the stomach and small intestine.

circumcision surgical removal of all or part of the foreskin (prepuce) of the penis, usually performed on the newborn; it is practised among Jews and Muslims. In some societies in Africa and the Middle East, female circumcision or clitoridectomy (removal of the labia minora and/or clitoris) is practised on adolescents as well as babies; it is illegal in the West.

Female circumcision has no medical benefit and often causes disease and complications in childbirth. Male circumcision too is usually carried out for cultural reasons and not as a medical necessity, apart from cases where the opening of the prepuce is so small as to obstruct the flow of urine.

circumference in geometry, the curved line that encloses a curved plane figure, for example a ◊circle or an ellipse. Its length varies according to the nature of the curve, and may be ascertained by the appropriate formula. The circumference of a circle is πd or $2\pi r$, where d is the diameter of the circle, r is its radius, and π is the constant pi, approximately equal to 3.1416.

circumnavigation sailing around the world. The first ship to sail around the world was the *Victoria*, one of a Spanish squadron of five vessels that sailed from Seville Aug 1519 under the Portuguese navigator Ferdinand Magellan. Four vessels were lost on the way, but the *Victoria* returned to Spain in Sept 1522 under Juan Cano. Magellan himself did not complete the voyage, but died in the Philippines 1521. The first English circumnavigator was Francis Drake 1577–80 in the *Golden Hind*.

circus (Latin 'circle') entertainment, often held in a large tent ('big top'), involving performing animals, acrobats, and clowns. In 1871 P T ◊Barnum created the 'Greatest Show on Earth' in the USA. The popularity of animal acts decreased in the

1980s. Originally, in Roman times, a circus was an arena for chariot races and gladiatorial combats.

Cirencester market town in Gloucestershire, England, in the Cotswolds; population (1991) 15,200. Industries include engineering and the manufacture of electrical goods. It was the second-largest town in Roman Britain (*Corinium Dobunnorum*), and has an amphitheatre which seated 8,000, and the Corinium Museum. In the Middle Ages Cirencester was an important wool centre. The Royal Agricultural College is here.

cire perdue or ***lost-wax technique*** bronze-casting method. A model is made of wax and enclosed in an envelope of clay and plaster, with a small hole in the bottom. When heat is applied, the wax melts and runs away through the hole, and the clay and plaster becomes a hard mould. Molten bronze is poured in and allowed to cool; then the clay envelope is cut away. The result is a bronze cast that exactly reproduces the original and is formed in a single piece. The earliest examples of the technique date from around 3000 BC, found both in Ancient Egypt and Ur.

cirrhosis any degenerative disease in an organ of the body, especially the liver, characterized by excessive development of connective tissue, causing scarring and painful swelling. Cirrhosis of the liver may be caused by an infection such as viral hepatitis, chronic obstruction of the common bile duct, chronic alcoholism or drug use, blood disorder, heart failure, or malnutrition. However, often no cause is apparent. If cirrhosis is diagnosed early, it can be arrested by treating the cause; otherwise it will progress to coma and death.

CIS abbreviation for ◊***Commonwealth of Independent States***, established 1992 by 11 former Soviet republics.

Cisalpine Gaul region of the Roman province of Gallia (N Italy) S of the Alps; Transalpine Gaul, the region N of the Alps, comprised what is now Belgium, France, the Netherlands, and Switzerland. The Cisalpine Republic in N Italy was the creation of Napoleon 1797, known as the Italian Republic 1802–04 and the Kingdom of Italy 1804–15.

Ciskei Republic of; former independent ◊Black National State within South Africa, independent from 1981 (but not recognized by the United Nations) until 1994 when it was re-integrated into South Africa, in Eastern Cape Province. The region covers an area of 7,700 sq km/2,974 sq mi, and produces wheat, sorghum, sunflower, vegetables, timber, metal products, leather, and textiles. It was one of two homelands of the Xhosa people created by South Africa, the other being Transkei; Xhosa is spoken here.

Cistercian order Roman Catholic monastic order established 1098 at Cîteaux, near Dijon, France, by St Robert de Champagne, abbot of Molesme, as a stricter form of the Benedictine order. Living mainly by agricultural labour, the Cistercians made many advances in farming methods in the Middle Ages. The ◊Trappists, so called from the original house at La Trappe in Normandy (founded by Dominique de Rancé 1664), followed a particularly strict version of the rule.

CITES abbreviation for ***Convention on International Trade in Endangered Species*** international agreement under the auspices of the ◊IUCN with the aim of regulating trade in ◊endangered species of animals and plants. The agreement came into force 1975 and by 1994 had been signed by 122 states. It prohibits any trade in a category of over 8,000 highly endangered species and controls trade in a further 30,000 species. Animals and plants listed in Appendix 1 of CITES are classified endangered; those listed in Appendix 2 are classified vulnerable.

cithara ancient musical instrument resembling a lyre but with a flat back. It was strung with wire and plucked with a plectrum or (after the 16th century) with the fingers. The bandurria and laud, still popular in Spain, are instruments of the same type.

Citizens' Advice Bureau (CAB) UK organization established 1939 to provide information and advice to the public on any subject, such as personal problems, financial, house purchase, or consumer rights. If required, the bureau will act on behalf of citizens, drawing on its own sources of legal and other experts. There are more than 900 bureaux located all over the UK.

citizens' band (CB) short-range radio communication facility (around 27 MHz) used by members of the public in the USA and many European countries to talk to one another or call for emergency assistance. Use of a form of citizens' band called Open Channel (above 928 MHz) was legalized in the UK 1980.

Citizen's Charter series of proposals aimed at improving public services in the UK, unveiled by Prime Minister John Major 1991. Major's programme covered a range of public-sector bodies, including the police, the health service, schools, local authorities, and public and private utility companies. It promised better quality for consumers through the publication of service standards, the right of redress, performance monitoring, penalties for public services, tighter regulation of privatized utilities, and the increased pressures resulting from competition and privatization.

citizenship status as a member of a state. In most countries citizenship may be acquired either by birth or by naturalization. The status confers rights such as voting and the protection of the law and also imposes responsibilities such as military service, in some countries.

The UK has five different categories of citizenship, with varying rights. Under the British Nationality Act 1981, amended by the British Nationality (Falkland Islands) Act 1983 and the Hong Kong Act 1985, only a person designated as a British citizen has a right of abode in the UK; basically, anyone born in the UK to a parent who is a British citizen, or to a parent who is lawfully settled in the UK. Four other categories of citizenship are defined: British dependent territories citizenship, British overseas citizenship, British subject, and Commonwealth citizen.

citric acid $HOOCCH_2C(OH)(COOH)CH_2COOH$ organic acid widely distributed in the plant kingdom; it is found in high concentrations in citrus fruits and has a sharp, sour taste. At one time it was commercially prepared from concentrated lemon juice, but now the main source is the fermentation of sugar with certain moulds.

Citroën French motor company founded 1913, acquired by ◊Peugeot 1974. Originally a gear-cutting firm founded by motor engineer André-Gustave Citroën (1878–1935), the company began making low-priced cars 1919, becoming France's first mass-producer. In 1934 Citroën made motoring history when it introduced cars with front-wheel drive.

citronella lemon-scented oil used in cosmetics and insect repellents, obtained from the S Asian grass *Cymbopogon nardus*.

citrus any tree or shrub of the genus *Citrus*, family Rutaceae. Citruses are found in Asia and other warm parts of the world. They are evergreen and aromatic, and several species – the orange, lemon, lime, citron, and grapefruit – are cultivated for fruit.

city generally, a large and important town. In the Middle East and ancient Europe, and in the ancient civilizations of Mexico and Peru, cities were states in themselves. In the early Middle Ages, European cities were usually those towns that were episcopal sees (seats of bishops).

Cities cover only 2% of the Earth's surface but use 75% of all resources. In 1996, the World Resources Report predicted that two-thirds of the world's population will live in cities by 2025.

In the UK, a city is a town, traditionally a cathedral town, awarded the title by the crown. UK cities occupy 7.7% of land and contain 89% of the population.

City, the financial centre of London, England.

city technology college (CTC) in the UK, one of a proposed network of schools, financed jointly by government and industry, designed to teach technological subjects in inner-city areas to students aged 11 to 18. CTCs have caused controversy because of: government plans to operate the schools

CITY: THE WORLD'S LARGEST CITIES/CONURBATIONS, 200 BC–AD 2000

City	Population (millions)	City	Population (millions)
Top five: 200 BC		***Top five: 1900***	
Pataliputra (India)	0.35	London (UK)	6.48
Alexandria (Egypt)	0.30	New York (USA)	4.24
Seleucia (Syria)	0.30	Paris (France)	3.33
Changan (China)	0.25	Berlin (Germany)	2.42
Loyang (China)	0.20	Chicago (USA)	1.72
Top five: AD 100		***Top five: 1950***	
Rome (Italy)	0.65	New York (USA)	12.30
Loyang (China)	0.50	London (UK)	8.86
Alexandria (Egypt)	0.40	Tokyo (Japan)	7.55
Seleucia (Persia)	0.30	Paris (France)	5.90
Changan (China)	0.25	Shanghai (China)	5.41
Top five: AD 622		***Top ten: 1985***	
Constantinople (Turkey)	0.50	Tokyo (Japan)	23.32
Changan (China)	0.45	New York (USA)	15.82
Loyang (China)	0.40	Mexico City (Mexico)	14.47
Ctesiphon (Persia)	0.25	São Paulo (Brazil)	13.42
Alexandria (Egypt)	0.20	Shanghai (China)	12.39
Top five: 1000		Los Angeles (USA)	10.44
Cordoba (Spain)	0.45	Osaka (Japan)	10.35
Constantinople (Turkey)	0.45	Buenos Aires (Argentina)	10.27
Kaifeng (China)	0.40	Bombay (India)	9.89
Xian (China)	0.30	Calcutta (India)	9.88
Kyoto (Japan)	0.20	***Top ten: 2000 (projected)***	
Top five: 1400		Tokyo (Japan)	27.85
Nanjing (China)	0.47	Bombay (India)	18.12
Cairo (Egypt)	0.45	São Paulo (Brazil)	17.80
Vijayanagar (India)	0.35	Shanghai (China)	17.21
Hangzhou (China)	0.33	New York (USA)	16.64
Beijing (China)	0.32	Mexico City (Mexico)	16.35
Top five: 1600		Beijing (China)	14.20
Beijing (China)	0.71	Jakarta (Indonesia)	14.09
Constantinople (Turkey)	0.70	Lagos (Nigeria)	13.45
Agra (India)	0.50	Los Angeles (USA)	13.15
Cairo (Egypt)	0.40		
Osaka (Japan)	0.40		
Top five: 1800			
Beijing (China)	1.10		
London (UK)	0.95		
Guangzhou (China)	0.80		
Constantinople (Turkey)	0.57		
Paris (France)	0.55		

civet The African palm civet *Nandinia binotata* spends most of its life in trees, resting among the branches during the day and searching for food at night. Its diet consists largely of fruit, but also includes insects and small mammals and reptiles.

independently of local education authorities; selection procedures; and the generous funds they receive compared with other schools. The government encouraged local authority and grant-maintained schools to opt for CTC status at reduced expense.

civet small to medium-sized carnivorous mammal found in Africa and Asia, belonging to the family Viverridae, which also includes ◊mongooses and genets. Distant relations of cats, they generally have longer jaws and more teeth. All have a scent gland in the groin region. Extracts from this gland are taken from the African civet *Civettictis civetta* and used in perfumery.

Civic Forum (Czech ***Občanske Forum***) Czech democratic movement, formed Nov 1989, led by Václav ◊Havel. In Dec 1989 it participated in forming a coalition government after the collapse of communist rule in Czechoslovakia. The party began to splinter during 1991: from it emerged the right-of-centre Civic Democratic Party, led by Václav Klaus, the social-democratic Civic Movement, and the centre-right Civic Democratic Alliance (CDA).

Its Slovak counterpart was Public Against Violence (*Verejnosť proti násiliu*), which also broke up 1991.

civil aviation operation of passenger and freight transport by air. With increasing traffic, control of air space is a major problem, and in 1963 Eurocontrol was established by Belgium, France, West Germany, Luxembourg, the Netherlands, and the UK to supervise both military and civil movement in the air space over member countries. There is also a tendency to coordinate services and other facilities between national airlines; for example, the establishment of Air Union 1963 by France (Air France), West Germany (Lufthansa), Italy (Alitalia), and Belgium (Sabena).

In the UK there are about 170 airports. Heathrow, City, Gatwick, and Stansted (all serving London), Prestwick, and Edinburgh are managed by the British Airports Authority (founded 1965). The British Airways Board supervises British Airways (BA), formerly British European Airways (BEA) and British Overseas Airways Corporation (BOAC); there are also independent companies. Close cooperation is maintained with authorities in other countries, including the Federal Aviation Agency, which is responsible for regulating development of aircraft, air navigation, traffic control, and communications in the USA. The Civil Aeronautics Board is the US authority prescribing safety regulations and investigating accidents. There are no state airlines in the USA, although many of the private airlines are large.

civil defence or ***civil protection*** organized activities by the civilian population of a state to mitigate the effects of enemy attack. During World War II civil-defence efforts were centred on providing adequate warning of air raids to permit the civilian population to reach shelter; then firefighting, food, rescue, communications, and ambulance services were needed. Subsequently, the threat of nuclear weapons led to the building of fallout shelters in the USA, the USSR, and elsewhere. China has networks of tunnels in cities that are meant to enable the population to escape nuclear fallout and reach the countryside, but which do not protect against the actual blast. Sweden and Switzerland have highly developed civil-defence systems.

In Britain the Ministry of Home Security was constituted 1939 to direct air-raid precautions in World War II. The country was divided into 12 regions, each under a commissioner to act on behalf of the central government in the event of national communications systems being destroyed. Associated with the air-raid wardens were ambulance and rescue parties, gas officers, breakdown gangs, and so on. The National Fire Service was based on existing local services, and about 5 million people enrolled as firewatchers and firefighters. The Civil Defence Corps and Auxiliary Fire Service were disbanded 1968. A new structure of 'Home Defence' is now being created in Britain, in which the voluntary services, local authorities, the Home Service Force, and the Territorial Army would cooperate. Regulations came into force 1983 compelling local authorities to take part in civil-defence exercises. Councils have to provide blast-proof bunkers and communication links, train staff, and take part in the exercises.

civil disobedience deliberate breaking of laws considered unjust, a form of nonviolent direct action; the term was coined by the US writer Henry Thoreau in an essay of that name 1849. It was advocated by Mahatma ◊Gandhi to prompt peaceful withdrawal of British power from India. Civil disobedience has since been employed by, for instance, the US civil-rights movement in the 1960s and the peace movement in the 1980s.

civil engineering branch of engineering that is concerned with the construction of roads, bridges, airports, aqueducts, waterworks, tunnels, canals, irrigation works, and harbours. The professional organization in Britain is the Institution of Civil Engineers. Founded 1818 (granted a royal charter 1828), it is the oldest engineering institution in the world. Its eight engineering boards cover the main subdivisions of civil engineering: airports; hydraulics and public health; maritime and waterways; offshore engineering; railways; roads; structures and buildings; and works construction.

civilization (Latin *civis* 'citizen') highly developed human society with structured division of labour. The earliest civilizations evolved in the Old World from advanced ◊Neolithic farming societies in the Middle East (Sumer in 3500 BC; Egypt in 3000 BC), the Indus Valley (in 2500 BC), and China (in 2200 BC). In the New World, similar communities evolved civilizations in Mesoamerica (the Olmec in 1200 BC) and Peru (the Chavin in 800 BC).

In anthropology, civilization is defined as an advanced sociopolitical stage of cultural evolution, whereby a centralized government (over a city, ceremonial centre, or larger region called a state) is supported by the taxation of surplus production, and rules the agricultural and, often, mercantile base. Those who do not produce food become specialists who govern, lead religious ritual, impose and collect taxes, record the past and present, plan and have executed monumental public works (irrigation systems, roads, bridges, buildings, tombs), and elaborate and formalize the style and traditions of the society. These institutions are based on the use of leisure time to develop writing, mathematics, the sciences, engineering, architecture, philosophy, and the arts.

civil law legal system based on ◊Roman law. It is one of the two main European legal systems, ◊English (common) law being the other. Civil law may also mean the law relating to matters other than criminal law, such as ◊contract and ◊tort.

During the Middle Ages, Roman law was adopted, with local modifications, all over Europe, mainly through the Christian church's influence; its later diffusion was due largely to the influence of the French *Code Napoléon*, based on Roman law, which was adopted in the 19th century by several states of E Europe and Asia, and in Egypt. Inside the Commonwealth, Roman law forms the basis of the legal systems of Scotland and Quebec and is also the basis of that of South Africa.

civil list in the UK, the annual sum provided from public funds to meet the official expenses of the sovereign and immediate dependents; private expenses are met by the ◊privy purse. Three-quarters of the civil list goes on wages for the royal household; the dependents it covers are the consort of a sovereign, children of a sovereign (except the Prince of Wales, who has the revenues from the Duchy of Cornwall), and widows of those children. Payments to other individual members of the royal family are covered by a contribution from the Queen.

civil-list pension in the UK, a pension paid to persons in need who have just claims on the royal beneficence, who have rendered personal service to the crown, or who have rendered service to the public by their discoveries in science and attainments in literature, art, or the like. The recipients are nominated by the prime minister, and the list is approved by Parliament. The pensions were originally paid out of the sovereign's civil list, but have been granted separately since the accession of Queen Victoria.

civil rights rights of the individual citizen. In many countries they are specified (as in the Bill of Rights of the US constitution) and guaranteed by law to ensure equal treatment for all citizens. In the USA, the struggle to obtain civil rights for former slaves and their descendants, both through legislation and in practice, has been a major theme since the Civil War. See ***history*** under ◊black.

civil-rights movement general term for efforts by American black people to improve their status in society after World War II. Having made a significant contribution to the national effort in wartime, they began a sustained campaign for full civil rights which challenged racial discrimination; the Civil Rights Commission was created by the Civil Rights Act of 1957. Despite further favourable legislation such as the Civil Rights Act 1964 and the 1965 Voting Rights Act, growing discontent among urban blacks in northern states led to outbreaks of civil disorder, such as the Watts riots in Los Angeles, Aug 1965. Another riot in the city 1992, following the acquittal of police charged with beating a black motorist, demonstrated continuing problems in US race relations. Other civil-rights movements have included women (see ◊women's movement) and homosexuals (see ◊homosexuality). *See illustration on following page.*

civil service body of administrative staff appointed to carry out the policy of a government. Members of the UK civil service may not take an active part in politics, and do not change with the government. The two main divisions are the Home and Diplomatic services, the latter created 1965 by amalgamation of the Foreign, Commonwealth, and Trade Commission services. All employees are paid out of funds voted annually for the purpose by Parliament. Since 1968 the Civil Service Department has been controlled by the prime minister (as minister for the civil service), but everyday supervision is exercised by the Lord Privy Seal. In 1981 the secretary to the cabinet was also made head of the Home Civil Service. The present emphasis is on the professional specialist, and the Civil Service College (Sunningdale Park, Ascot, Berkshire) was established 1970 to develop training.

Their permanence gives civil servants in the upper echelons an advantage over ministers, who are in office for a comparatively brief time, and in the 1970s and 1980s it was alleged that ministerial policies in conflict with civil-service views tended to be blocked from being put into practice. In 1988 it was decided to separate policy advice from executive functions in several departments, and there have been progressive moves towards 'hiving off' executive functions to outside agencies.

civil society part of a society or culture outside the government and state-run institutions. For Karl Marx and G W F Hegel, civil society was that part of society where self-interest and materialism were rampant, although Adam ◊Smith believed that enlightened self-interest would promote the general good. Classical writers and earlier political theorists such as John ◊Locke used the term to describe the whole of a civilized society.

Civil War, American also called the ***War Between the States*** war 1861–65 between the Southern or Confederate States of America and the

'To be able to fill leisure intelligently is the last product of civilization, and at present very few people have reached this level.'

On CIVILIZATION
Bertrand Russell
The Conquest of Happiness

civil-rights movement Civil-rights activists marching past a blockade of National Guards in Memphis, Tennessee, USA in 1968. Demonstrations like this eventually brought about the abolition of discrimination against blacks in education and employment. *Corbis*

Northern or Union States. The former wished to maintain certain 'states' rights', in particular the right to determine state law on the institution of slavery, and claimed the right to secede from the Union; the latter fought primarily to maintain the Union, with slave emancipation (proclaimed 1863) a secondary issue.

The war, and in particular its aftermath, when the South was occupied by Northern troops in the period known as the ◊Reconstruction, left behind much bitterness. Industry prospered in the North, while the economy of the South, which had been based on slavery, stagnated for some time. *See timeline on p. 234, and feature on pp. 982–983.*

Civil War, English the conflict between King Charles I and the Royalists (Cavaliers) on one side and the Parliamentarians (also called Roundheads) under Oliver ◊Cromwell on the other. Their differences centred on the king's unconstitutional acts but became a struggle over the relative powers of crown and Parliament. Hostilities began 1642 and a series of Royalist defeats (Marston Moor 1644, Naseby 1645) culminated in Charles's capture 1647 and execution 1649. The war continued until the final defeat of Royalist forces at Worcester 1651. Cromwell became Protector (ruler) from 1651 until his death 1658. *See timeline on p. 235.*

Civil War, Spanish war 1936–39 precipitated by a military revolt led by General Franco against the Republican government. Inferior military capability led to the gradual defeat of the Republicans by 1939, and the establishment of Franco's dictatorship.

Franco's insurgents (Nationalists, who were supported by Fascist Italy and Nazi Germany) seized power in the S and NW, but were suppressed in areas such as Madrid and Barcelona by the workers' militia. The loyalists (Republicans) were aided by the USSR and the volunteers of the International Brigade, which included several writers, among them George Orwell.

Clackmannanshire local authority of Scotland created 1996 (*see United Kingdom map*).

cladistics method of biological ◊classification (taxonomy) that uses a formal step-by-step procedure for objectively assessing the extent to which organisms share particular characters, and for assigning them to taxonomic groups. Taxonomic groups (for example, ◊species, ◊genus, family) are termed clades.

cladode in botany, a flattened stem that is leaflike in appearance and function. It is an adaptation to dry conditions because a stem contains fewer ◊stomata than a leaf, and water loss is thus minimized. The true leaves in such plants are usually reduced to spines or small scales. Examples of plants with cladodes are asparagus and certain cacti. Cladodes may bear flowers or fruit on their surface, and this distinguishes them from leaves.

Claes Willy 1938– . Belgian politician, secretary-general of the ◊North Atlantic Treaty Organization (NATO) 1994–95, with a proven reputation as a consensus-builder. He was a clear favourite for the post, but subsequent allegations about his involvement (while Belgian foreign minister) in illegal dealings with Agusta, the Italian aircraft manufacturer, eventually forced his resignation Nov 1995.

clam common name for a ◊bivalve mollusc. The term is usually applied to edible species, such as the North American hard clam *Venus mercenaria*, used in clam chowder, and whose shells were formerly used as money by North American Indians. The giant clam *Tridacna gigas* of the Indopacific can grow to 1 m/3 ft across in 50 years and weigh, with the shell, 500 kg/1,000 lb.

clan (Gaelic *clann* 'children') social grouping based on ◊kinship. Some traditional societies are organized by clans, which are either matrilineal or patrilineal, and whose members must marry into another clan in order to avoid in-breeding. Familiar examples are the Highland clans of Scotland. Theoretically each clan is descended from a single ancestor from whom the name is derived – for example, clan MacGregor ('son of Gregor').

Clapton Eric 1945– . English blues and rock guitarist, singer, and songwriter. Originally a blues purist, then one of the pioneers of heavy rock with Cream 1966–68, he returned to the blues after making the landmark album *Layla and Other Assorted Love Songs* 1970 by Derek and the Dominos. Solo albums include *Journeyman* 1989 and the acoustic *Unplugged* 1992, for which he received six Grammy awards 1993.

Clare county on the west coast of the Republic of Ireland, in the province of Munster; county town Ennis; area 3,190 sq km/1,231 sq mi; population (1991) 90,800. The coastline is rocky and dangerous, and inland Clare is an undulating plain, with mountains on the E, W, and NW, the chief range being the Slieve Bernagh Mountains in the SE rising to over 518 m/1,700 ft. The principal rivers are the Shannon and its tributary, the Fergus. There are over 100 lakes in the county, including Lough Derg on the eastern border.

Clare John 1793–1864. English poet. His work includes *Poems Descriptive of Rural Life and Scenery* 1820, *The Village Minstrel* 1821, *The Shepherd's Calendar* 1827, and *The Rural Muse* 1835. The dignified simplicity and truth of his descriptions of both landscape and emotions were rediscovered and appreciated in the 20th century.

Clarence English ducal title, which has been conferred on a number of princes. The last was Albert Victor 1864–92, eldest son of Edward VII.

Clarendon Edward Hyde, 1st Earl of Clarendon 1609–1674. English politician and historian, chief adviser to Charles II 1651–67. A member of Parliament 1640, he joined the Royalist side 1641. The Clarendon Code 1661–65, a series of acts passed by the government, was directed at Nonconformists (or Dissenters) and was designed to secure the supremacy of the Church of England.

In the ◊Short and ◊Long Parliaments Clarendon attacked Charles I's unconstitutional actions and supported the impeachment of Charles's minister Strafford. In 1641 he broke with the revolutionary party and became one of the royal advisers. When civil war began he followed Charles to Oxford, and was knighted and made chancellor of the Exchequer. On the king's defeat 1646 he followed Prince Charles to Jersey, where he began his *History of the Rebellion*, published 1702–04, which provides memorable portraits of his contemporaries. In 1651 he became chief adviser to the exiled Charles II. At the Restoration he was created Earl of Clarendon, while his influence was further increased by the marriage of his daughter Anne to James, Duke of York. His moderation earned the hatred of the extremists, however, and he lost Charles's support by openly expressing disapproval of the king's private life. After the disasters of the Dutch war 1667, he went into exile.

Clarendon George William Frederick Villiers, 4th Earl of Clarendon 1800–1870. British Liberal

Civil War, American Union soldiers in trenches before a battle, Petersburg, Virginia, 1865. Petersburg, a port on the Appomattox River, was under siege for ten months. Its fall April 1865 helped to hasten the end of the war. *Library of Congress*

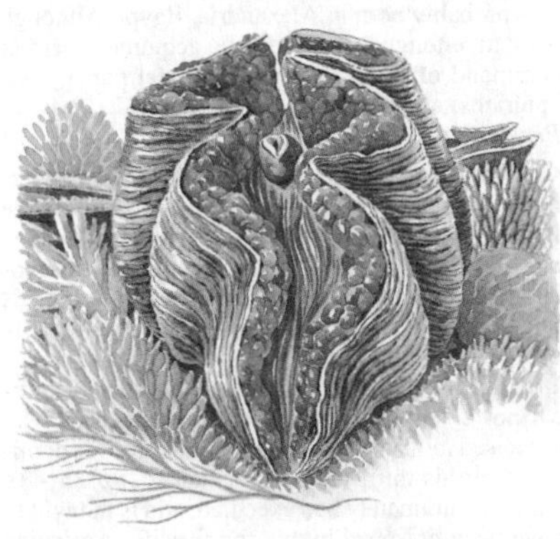

clam The giant clam has a siphon with two tubes: one to take in water, the other to expel waste. The water supplies the animal with oxygen and food in the form of tiny plankton.

diplomat, lord lieutenant of Ireland 1847–52, foreign secretary 1853–58, 1865–66, and 1868–70. His diplomatic skill was shown at the Congress of Paris 1856 and in the settlement of the dispute between Britain and the USA over the *Alabama* cruiser.

Clarendon, Constitutions of in English history, a series of resolutions agreed by a council summoned by Henry II at Clarendon in Wiltshire 1164. The Constitutions aimed at limiting the secular power of the clergy, and were abandoned after the murder of Thomas à Becket. They form an early English legal document of great historical value.

Clare, St c. 1194–1253. Christian saint. Born in Assisi, Italy, at 18 she became a follower of St Francis, who founded for her the convent of San Damiano. Here she gathered the first members of the Order of Poor Clares. In 1958 she was proclaimed the patron saint of television by Pius XII, since in 1252 she saw from her convent sickbed the Christmas services being held in the Basilica of St Francis in Assisi. Feast day 12 Aug. Canonized 1255.

claret English term since the 17th century for the dry red wines of Bordeaux, France.

clarinet any of a family of single-reed woodwind instruments of cylindrical bore. In their concertos for clarinet, Mozart and Weber exploited the instrument's range of tone from the dark low register rising to brilliance, and its capacity for sustained dynamic control. The ability of the clarinet both to blend and to contrast with other instruments make it popular for chamber music and as a solo instrument. It is also heard in military and concert bands and as a jazz instrument.

Clark Jim (James) 1936–1968. Scottish-born motor-racing driver who was twice world champion 1963 and 1965. He spent all his Formula One career with Lotus. He won 25 Formula One Grand Prix races, a record at the time, before losing his life at Hockenheim, West Germany during a Formula Two race 1968.

Clark Joe (Charles Joseph) 1939– . Canadian Progressive Conservative politician who became party leader 1976, and defeated Pierre ◊Trudeau at the polls 1979 to become the youngest prime minister in Canada's history. Following the rejection of his government's budget, he was defeated in a second election Feb 1980. He became secretary of state for external affairs (foreign minister) 1984 in the ◊Mulroney government.

Clark Kenneth (Mackenzie), Baron Clark 1903–1983. English art historian, director of the National Gallery, London, 1934–45, and chair of the Arts Council 1953–60. His books include *Leonardo da Vinci* 1939, *Landscape into Art* 1949, and *The Nude* 1956. He popularized the history of art through his television series *Civilization*, broadcast in the UK 1969, published as a book in the same year.

Clark Michael 1962– . Scottish avant-garde dancer. His outlandish costumes and stage props have earned him as much celebrity as his innovative dance technique. He formed his own company, the Michael Clark Dance Company, in the mid-1980s and became a leading figure in the British ◊avant-garde dance scene. In 1991 he played Caliban in Peter Greenaway's film *Prospero's Books*. He premiered his *Mmm... Modern Masterpiece* 1992.

Clarke Arthur C(harles) 1917– . English science-fiction and nonfiction writer. He originated the plan for a system of communications satellites in geostationary orbit 1945. His works include the short story 'The Sentinel' 1951 (filmed 1968 by Stanley Kubrick as *2001: A Space Odyssey*), and the novels *Childhood's End* 1953 and *2010: Odyssey Two* 1982.

> *Any sufficiently advanced technology is indistinguishable from magic.*
>
> **Arthur C Clarke**
> *The Lost Worlds of 2001*

Clarke Kenneth Harry 1940– . British Conservative politician. A cabinet minister 1985–1997, he held the posts of education secretary 1990–92; home secretary 1992–93; and chancellor of the Exchequer 1993–1997. Along with his colleagues Malcolm Rifkind, Tony Newton, and Patrick Mayhew, in 1996 he became the longest continuously serving minister since Palmerston in the early 19th century.

Clash, the English rock band 1976–85, a driving force in the British ◊punk movement. Reggae and rockabilly were important elements in their sound. Their albums include *The Clash* 1977, *London Calling* 1979, and *Combat Rock* 1982. The main songwriters were founder members Joe Strummer (John Mellors, 1952–) and Mick Jones (1955–).

class in biological classification, a group of related ◊orders. For example, all mammals belong to the class Mammalia and all birds to the class Aves. Among plants, all class names end in 'idae' (such as Asteridae) and among fungi in 'mycetes'; there are no equivalent conventions among animals. Related classes are grouped together in a ◊phylum.

class in sociology, the main grouping of social stratification in industrial societies, based primarily on economic and occupational factors, but also referring to people's style of living or sense of group identity. Within the social sciences, class has been used both as a descriptive category and as the basis of theories about industrial society. Theories of class may see such social divisions either as a source of social stability (Emile ◊Durkheim) or social conflict (Karl ◊Marx).

The most widely used descriptive classification in the UK divides the population into five main classes, with the main division between manual and nonmanual occupations. Such classifications have been widely criticized, however, on several grounds: they reflect a middle-class bias that brain is superior to brawn; they classify women according to their husband's occupation rather than their own; and they ignore the upper class, the owners of land and industry.

class action in law, a court procedure where one or more claimants represent a larger group of people who are all making the same kind of claim against the same defendant. The court's decision is binding on all the members of the group. This procedure is often used in the USA. The same effect is sometimes achieved in out-of-court settlements in Britain.

classical economics school of economic thought that dominated 19th-century thinking. It originated with Adam ◊Smith's *The Wealth of Nations* 1776, which embodied many of the basic concepts and principles of the classical school. Smith's theories were further developed in the writings of John Stuart Mill and David Ricardo. Central to the theory were economic freedom, competition, and *laissez-faire* government. The idea that economic growth could best be promoted by free trade, unassisted by government, was in conflict with mercantilism, the theory that a nation's wealth in the form of bullion or treasure was the key to its prosperity. The belief that agriculture was the chief determinant of economic health was also rejected in favour of manufacturing development, and the importance of labour productivity was stressed. The theories put forward by the classical economists still influence economists today.

Classicism in art, music, and literature, a style that emphasizes the qualities traditionally considered characteristic of ancient Greek and Roman art, that is, reason, balance, objectivity, restraint, and strict adherence to form. The term Classicism (also ◊Neo-Classicism) is often used to characterize the culture of 18th-century Europe, and contrasted with 19th-century Romanticism.

classification in biology, the arrangement of organisms into a hierarchy of groups on the basis of their similarities in biochemical, anatomical, or physiological characters. The basic grouping is a ◊species, several of which may constitute a ◊genus, which in turn are grouped into families, and so on up through orders, classes, phyla (in plants, sometimes called divisions), to kingdoms.

clathrate compound formed when the small molecules of one substance fill in the holes in the structural lattice of another, solid, substance – for example, sulphur dioxide molecules in ice crystals. Clathrates are therefore intermediate between mixtures and true compounds (which are held together by ◊ionic or covalent chemical bonds).

Claudel Paul (Louis Charles Marie) 1868–1955. French poet and dramatist. A fervent Catholic, he was influenced by the Symbolists (see ◊Symbolism and achieved an effect of mystic allegory in such plays as *L'Annonce faite à Marie/Tidings Brought to Mary* 1912 and *Le Soulier de satin/The Satin Slipper* 1929, set in 16th-century Spain. His verse includes *Cinq Grandes Odes/Five Great Odes* 1910.

Claude Lorrain (Claude Gelée) 1600–1682. French painter who worked in Rome. One of the leading Classical painters of the 17th century, he painted landscapes in a distinctive, luminous style

Civil War, Spanish Civilians line the barricades in Barcelona, 1936, during the Spanish Civil War. This war, in which air bombing focused on both civilian and military targets, marked the beginning of 'total war', with no distinction being made between combatants and noncombatants. *Corbis*

Claude Lorrain *Seaport with the Embarkation of the Queen of Sheba* 1648 by Claude Lorrain (National Gallery, London). More than any other artist, Claude expressed the nostalgia of the 17th- and 18th-century fascination with ancient Greece and Rome. Even when dealing with biblical subjects – as in this picture – the architecture is classical, and the world is bathed in a soft, romantic glow. *Corbis*

that had a great impact on late 17th- and 18th-century taste. In his paintings insignificant figures (mostly mythological or historical) are typically lost in great expanses of poetic scenery, as in *The Enchanted Castle* 1664 (National Gallery, London).

The poetic sense of wonder in a legendary land is seen in such works as this one, which inspired the poet John Keats, or in the great *Seaports* of the National Gallery, London, and the Louvre, Paris. The duality between realist and dreamer may be seen in the comparison of these with the direct drawings from nature such as the *View on the Tiber*.

Claudet Antoine François Jean 1797–1867. French-born pioneer of photography. Working in London, he made daguerreotype portraiture commercially viable when he discovered that chlorine and iodine vapour increased the sensitivity of the plate and greatly reduced exposure time. His other innovations include the earliest light meter and the introduction of painted backgrounds into studio portraits.

Claudian (Claudius Claudianus) c. 370–404. Last of the great Latin poets of the Roman Empire. He was probably born in Alexandria, Egypt. Although his native tongue was Greek he acquired a perfect command of Latin. He wrote official panegyrics, epigrams, and the mythological epic *The Rape of Proserpine*.

Claudius (Tiberius Claudius Drusus Nero Germanicus) 10 BC–AD 54. Nephew of ◊Tiberius, made Roman emperor by his troops AD 41, after the murder of his nephew ◊Caligula. Claudius was a scholar, historian, and able administrator. During his reign the Roman empire was considerably extended, and in 43 he took part in the invasion of Britain. His rule was marked by the increased political power enjoyed by his private secretaries who exercised ministerial functions. Claudius was dominated by his third wife, Messalina (c. AD 25–48), whom he ultimately had executed, and is thought to have been poisoned by his fourth wife, Agrippina the Younger.

Clause 28 in British law, section 28 of the Local Government Act 1988 that prohibits local authorities promoting homosexuality by publishing material, or by promoting the teaching in state schools of the acceptability of homosexuality as a 'pretended family relationship'. There was widespread opposition to the introduction of the provision.

claustrophobia ◊phobia involving fear of enclosed spaces

Clausewitz Karl Philipp Gottlieb von 1780–1831. Prussian officer whose book *Vom Kriege/On War* 1833 exerted a powerful influence on military strategists well into the 20th century. Although he advocated the total destruction of an enemy's forces as one of the strategic targets of warfare, his most important idea was to see war as an extension of political policy and not as an end in itself.

Claverhouse John Graham, Viscount Dundee c. 1649–1689. Scottish soldier. Appointed by Charles II to suppress the ◊Covenanters from 1677, he was routed at Drumclog 1679, but three weeks later won the battle of Bothwell Bridge, by which the rebellion was crushed. Until 1688 he was engaged in continued persecution and became known as 'Bloody Clavers'. His army then joined the first Jacobite rebellion and defeated the loyalist forces in the pass of Killiecrankie, where he was mortally wounded.

CIVIL WAR, AMERICAN: TIMELINE

1861 Feb	Having seceded from the Union, seven southern states (S Carolina, Mississippi, Florida, Alabama, Georgia, Louisiana, and Texas) sent representatives to Montgomery, Alabama, to form the rebel Confederate States of America under the presidency of Jefferson Davis. Their constitution legalized slavery.
April	Rebel forces attacked a Federal garrison at Fort Sumter, Charleston, S Carolina, capturing it 14 April. President Lincoln proclaimed a blockade of southern ports.
April–May	Four more states seceded from the Union: Virginia (part remaining loyal, eventually becoming W Virginia), Arkansas, Tennessee, and N Carolina.
July	Battle of Bull Run was first major military engagement of the war, near Manassas Junction, Virginia; Confederate army under generals P G T Beauregard and Thomas 'Stonewall' Jackson forced Union army to retreat to Washington DC.
1862 Feb	Union general Ulysses S Grant captured strategically located forts Henry and Donelson in Tennessee.
April	Battle of Shiloh, the bloodiest Americans had yet fought, when at terrible cost Grant's army forced rebel troops to withdraw. Confederate government introduced conscription of male white citizens aged 18–35.
June–July	Seven Days' battles in Virginia between Union army under George B McClellan and Confederate forces under generals Jackson and Robert E Lee; McClellan withdrew, but continued to threaten the Confederate capital at Richmond, Virginia.
Aug	At second Battle of Bull Run, Lee's troops forced Union army to fall back again to Washington DC.
Sept	At Battle of Antietam, near Sharpsburg, Maryland, McClellan forced Lee to give up his offensive, but failed to pursue the enemy. Lincoln removed him from his command.
Dec	Lee inflicted heavy losses on Federal forces attacking his position at Battle of Fredericksburg, Virginia.
1863 Jan	Lincoln's Emancipation Proclamation came into effect, freeing slaves in the Confederate states (but not those in border states which had remained loyal to the Union). Some 200,000 blacks eventually served in Union armies.
Mar	Federal government introduced conscription.
May	Battle of Chancellorsville, Virginia; Lee and Jackson routed Union forces.
July	Lee failed to break through Union lines at decisive Battle of Gettysburg, Pennsylvania, while Grant captured Vicksburg and the West and took control of the Mississippi, cutting the Confederacy in two.
Nov	Grant's victory at Chattanooga, Tennessee, led to his appointment as general in chief by Lincoln (March 1864). Lincoln's Gettysburg Address.
1864 May	Battle of the Wilderness, Virginia. Lee inflicted heavy casualties on Union forces, but Grant continued to move south through Virginia. They clashed again at Battle of Spotsylvania.
June	Battle of Cold Harbor claimed 12,000 casualties in a few hours. Grant wrote: 'I propose to fight it out along this line if it takes all summer'.
Sept	Union general William T Sherman occupied Atlanta, Georgia, and marched through the state to the sea, cutting a wide swathe of destruction.
Nov	Lincoln re-elected president.
Dec	Sherman marched into Savannah, Georgia, continuing over next three months into S and N Carolina.
1865 Mar	Lee failed to break through Union lines at Battle of Petersburg, Virginia.
April	Lee abandoned Confederate capital at Richmond, Virginia, and surrendered to Grant at Appomattox courthouse, Virginia. John Wilkes Booth assassinated President Lincoln at Ford's Theatre, Washington DC.
May	Last Confederate soldiers laid down their arms. The war had taken the lives of 359,528 Union troops and 258,000 Confederates, and cost $20 billion.

clavichord small domestic keyboard instrument of delicate tone developed in the 16th century on the principle of the single-stringed monochord. Notes are sounded by a metal blade striking the strings. The sound is clear and precise, and a form of vibrato (called bebung) is possible by varying finger pressure on the key. It was superseded in the 18th century by the fortepiano.

clavicle (Latin *clavis* 'key') the collar bone of many vertebrates. In humans it is vulnerable to fracture, since falls involving a sudden force on the arm may result in very high stresses passing into the chest region by way of the clavicle and other bones. It is connected at one end with the sternum (breastbone), and at the other end with the shoulder-blade, together with which it forms the arm socket.

clavier in music, general term for an early ◊keyboard instrument.

claw hard, hooked, pointed outgrowth of the digits of mammals, birds, and most reptiles. Claws are composed of the protein keratin, and grow continuously from a bundle of cells in the lower skin layer. Hooves and nails are modified structures with the same origin as claws.

clay very fine-grained ◊sedimentary deposit that has undergone a greater or lesser degree of consolidation. When moistened it is plastic, and it hardens on heating, which renders it impermeable. It may be white, grey, red, yellow, blue, or black, depending on its composition. Clay minerals consist largely of hydrous silicates of aluminium and magnesium together with iron, potassium, sodium, and organic substances. The crystals of clay minerals have a layered structure, capable of holding water, and are responsible for its plastic properties. According to international classification, in mechanical analysis of soil, clay has a grain size of less than 0.002 mm/0.00008 in.

Types of clay include adobe, alluvial clay, building clay, brick, cement, china clay (or kaolinite), ferruginous clay, fireclay, fusible clay, puddle clay, refractory clay, and vitrifiable clay. Clays have a variety of uses, some of which, such as pottery and bricks, date back to prehistoric times.

Clay Cassius Marcellus, Jr original name of boxer Muhammad ◊Ali.

clay mineral one of a group of hydrous silicate minerals that form most of the fine-grained particles in clays. Clay minerals are normally formed by weathering or alteration of other silicate minerals. Virtually all have sheet silicate structures similar to the ◊micas. They exhibit the following useful properties: loss of water on heating, swelling and shrinking in different conditions, cation exchange with other media, and plasticity when wet. Examples are kaolinite, illite, and montmorillonite.

cleavage in mineralogy, the tendency of a mineral to split along defined, parallel planes related to its internal structure. It is a useful distinguishing feature in mineral identification. Cleavage occurs where bonding between atoms is weakest, and cleavages may be perfect, good, or poor, depending on the bond strengths; a given mineral may possess one, two, three, or more orientations along which it will cleave.

Cleese John Harwood 1939– . English actor and comedian. He has written for and appeared in both television programmes and films. On British television, he is particularly associated with the comedy series *Monty Python's Flying Circus* and *Fawlty Towers*. His films include *Monty Python and the Holy Grail* 1974, *The Life of Brian* 1979, *A Fish Called Wanda* 1988, and *Fierce Creatures* 1997.

clef in music, a symbol prefixed to a five-line stave indicating the pitch range to which the written notes apply. Introduced as a visual aid in plainchant notation, it is based on the letter G (treble clef), establishing middle C (C4) as a prime reference pitch, G4 a fifth higher for higher voices, and F3 a fifth lower for lower voices. The C clef is now comparatively rare, except for viola, cello, and bassoon; for most other instruments the G and F clefs are standard.

cleft palate fissure of the roof of the mouth, often accompanied by a harelip, the result of the two halves of the palate failing to join properly during embryonic development. It can be remedied by plastic surgery.

Cleisthenes c. 570–c. 508 BC. Athenian statesman, the founder of Athenian democracy. He was exiled with his family, the Alcmaeonidae, and intrigued and campaigned against the Athenian tyrants, the Pisistratids. After their removal in 510 BC he developed a popular faction in favour of democracy, which was established by his reforms over the next decade.

cleistogamy production of flowers that never fully open and that are automatically self-fertilized. Cleistogamous flowers are often formed late in the year, after the production of normal flowers, or during a period of cold weather, as seen in several species of violet *Viola*.

clematis any temperate woody climbing plant of the genus *Clematis* with showy flowers. Clematis are members of the buttercup family, Ranunculaceae. The wild traveller's joy or old man's beard, *Clematis vitalba*, is the only native British species, although many have been introduced and garden hybrids bred.

'It is easier to make war than to make peace.'

GEORGES CLEMENCEAU
Speech at Verdun
20 July 1919

CIVIL WAR, ENGLISH: TIMELINE

1625	James I died, succeeded by Charles I, whose first parliament was dissolved after refusing to grant him tonnage and poundage (taxation revenues) for life.
1627	'Five Knights' case in which men who refused to pay a forced loan were imprisoned.
1628	Coke, Wentworth, and Eliot presented the Petition of Right, requesting the king not to tax without parliamentary consent, not to billet soldiers in private homes, and not to impose martial law on civilians. Charles accepted this as the price of parliamentary taxation to pay for war with Spain and France. Duke of Buckingham assassinated.
1629	Parliament dissolved following disagreement over religious policy, tonnage and poundage, beginning Charles' 'Eleven Years' Tyranny'. War with France ended.
1630	End of war with Spain.
1632	Strafford made lord deputy in Ireland.
1633	Laud became archbishop of Canterbury. Savage punishment of puritan William Prynne for his satirical pamphlet *Histriomastix*.
1634	Ship money first collected in London.
1634–37	Laud attempted to enforce ecclesiastical discipline by metropolitan visits.
1637	Conviction of John Hampden for refusal to pay ship money infringed Petition of Right.
1638	Covenanters in Scotland protested at introduction of Laudian Prayer Book into the Kirk.
1639	First Bishops' War. Charles sent army to Scotland after its renunciation of episcopacy. Agreement reached without fighting.
1640	Short Parliament April–May voted taxes for the suppression of the Scots, but dissolved to forestall petition against Scottish war.
	Second Bishops' War ended in defeat for English at Newburn-on-Tyne. Scots received pension and held Northumberland and Durham in Treaty of Ripon. Long Parliament called, passing the Triennial Act and abolishing the Star Chamber. High Commission and Councils of the North and of Wales set up.
1641	Strafford executed. English and Scots massacred at Ulster. Grand Remonstrance passed, appealing to mass opinion against episcopacy and the royal prerogative. Irish Catholic nobility massacred.
1642 Jan	Charles left Westminster after an unsuccessful attempt to arrest five members of the Commons united both Houses of Parliament and the City against him.
Feb	Bishop's Exclusion Bill passed, barring clergy from secular office and the Lords.
May–June	Irish rebels established supreme council. Militia Ordinance passed, assuming sovereign powers for parliament. Nineteen Propositions rejected by Charles.
Aug	Charles raised his standard at Nottingham. Outbreak of first Civil War.
Oct	General Assembly of the Confederate Catholics met at Kilkenny. Battle of Edgehill inconclusive.
1643	Irish truce left rebels in control of more of Ireland. Solemn League and Covenant, alliance between English Parliamentarians and Scots, pledged to establish Presbyterianism in England and Ireland, and to provide a Scottish army. Scots intervened in Civil War.
1643–49	Westminster Assembly attempted to draw up Calvinist religious settlement.
1644	Committee of Both Kingdoms to coordinate Scottish and Parliamentarians' military activities established. Royalists decisively beaten at Marston Moor.
1645	Laud executed. New Model Army created.
	Charles pulled out of Uxbridge negotiations on a new constitutional position. Cromwell and the New Model Army destroyed Royalist forces at Naseby.
1646	Charles fled to Scotland. Oxford surrendered to parliament. End of first Civil War.
1647 May	Charles agreed with parliament to accept Presbyterianism and to surrender control of the militia.
June–Aug	Army seized Charles and resolved not to disband without satisfactory terms. Army presented Heads of Proposals to Charles.
Oct–Dec	Army debated Levellers' Agreement of the People at Putney. Charles escaped to the Isle of Wight, and reached agreement with the Scots by Treaty of Newport.
1648 Jan	Vote of No Addresses passed by Long Parliament, declaring an end to negotiations with Charles.
Aug	Cromwell defeated Scots at Preston. Second Civil War began.
Nov–Dec	Army demanded trial of Charles I. Pride's Purge of parliament transferred power to the Rump of independent MPs.
1649 Jan–Feb	Charles tried and executed.
	Rump elected Council of State as its executive.
May	Rump declared England a Commonwealth. Cromwell landed in Dublin.
Sept–Oct	Massacres of garrisons at Drogheda and Wexford by Cromwell.

Clemenceau Georges 1841–1929. French politician and journalist (prominent in the defence of Alfred ◊Dreyfus). He was prime minister 1906–09 and 1917–20. After World War I he presided over the peace conference in Paris that drew up the Treaty of ◊Versailles, but failed to secure for France the Rhine as a frontier.

Clemenceau was mayor of Montmartre, Paris, in the war of 1870, and 1871 was elected a member of the National Assembly at Bordeaux. He was elected a deputy 1876 after the formation of the Third Republic. An extreme radical, he soon earned the nickname of 'the Tiger' on account of his ferocious attacks on politicians whom he disliked. He lost his seat 1893. When he became prime minister for the second time 1917, he made the decisive appointment of Marshal ◊Foch as supreme commander.

Clement VII 1478–1534. Pope 1523–34. He refused to allow the divorce of Henry VIII of England and Catherine of Aragon. Illegitimate son of a brother of Lorenzo de' Medici, the ruler of Florence, he commissioned monuments for the Medici chapel in Florence from the Renaissance artist Michelangelo.

Clementi Muzio 1752–1832. Italian pianist and composer. He settled in London 1782 as a teacher and then as proprietor of a successful piano and music business. He was the founder of the present-day technique of piano playing, and his series of studies, *Gradus ad Parnassum* 1817, is still in use.

clementine small orange, thought to be a hybrid between a tangerine and an orange or a variety of tangerine. It has a flowery taste and scent and is in season in winter. It is commonly grown in N Africa and Spain.

Clement of Rome, St lived late 1st century AD. One of the early Christian leaders and writers known as the fathers of the church. According to tradition he was the third or fourth bishop of Rome, and a disciple of St Peter. He was pope AD 88–97 or 92–101. He wrote a letter addressed to the church at Corinth (First Epistle of Clement), and many other writings have been attributed to him.

Cleon died 422 BC. Athenian politician and general in the ◊Peloponnesian War. He became 'leader of the people' (demagogue) after the death of ◊Pericles to whom he was opposed. He was an aggressive imperialist and advocated a vigorous war policy against the Spartans. He was killed by the Spartans at Amphipolis 422 BC.

Cleopatra c. 68–30 BC. Queen of Egypt 51–48 and 47–30 BC. When the Roman general Julius Caesar arrived in Egypt, he restored Cleopatra to the throne from which she had been ousted. Cleopatra and Caesar became lovers and she went with him to Rome. After Caesar's assassination 44 BC she returned to Alexandria and resumed her position as queen of Egypt. In 41 BC she was joined there by Mark Antony, one of Rome's rulers. In 31 BC Rome declared war on Egypt and scored a decisive victory in the naval Battle of Actium off the W coast of Greece. Cleopatra fled with her 60 ships to Egypt; Antony abandoned the struggle and followed her. Both he and Cleopatra committed suicide.

Clemenceau French prime minister Georges Clemenceau. An outspoken radical, his appointment of Marshal Foch secured the victory of the Allies in World War I. *Philip Sauvain*

Cleopatra was Macedonian, and the last ruler of the Macedonian dynasty, which ruled Egypt from 323 until annexation by Rome 31. She succeeded her father Ptolemy XII jointly with her brother Ptolemy XIII, and they ruled together from 51 to 49 BC, when she was expelled by him.

Her reinstatement in 48 BC by Caesar caused a war between Caesar and Ptolemy XIII, who was defeated and killed. The younger brother, Ptolemy XIV, was elevated to the throne and married to her, in the tradition of the pharaohs, although she actually lived with Caesar and they had a son, Ptolemy XV, known as Caesarion (he was later killed by Octavian).

After Caesar's death, Cleopatra and Mark Antony had three sons. He divorced in 32 BC his wife Octavia, the sister of Octavian, who then induced the Roman senate to declare war on Egypt. Shakespeare's play *Antony and Cleopatra* recounts that Cleopatra killed herself with an asp (poisonous snake) after Antony's suicide.

clerihew humorous verse form invented by Edmund Clerihew ◊Bentley, characterized by a first line consisting of a person's name. The four lines rhyme AABB, but the metre is often distorted for comic effect. An example, from Bentley's *Biography for Beginners* 1905, is: 'Sir Christopher Wren/ Said, I am going to dine with some men./If anybody calls/ Say I am designing St Paul's.'

Clermont-Ferrand city, capital of Puy-de-Dôme *département*, in the Auvergne region of France; population (1990) 140,200. It is a centre for agriculture, and its rubber industry is the largest in France. Car tyres are manufactured here; other products include chemicals, preserves, foodstuffs, and clothing. The Gothic cathedral is 13th century.

Cleveland former county of NE England, formed 1974 from parts of Durham and NE Yorkshire, and abolished 1996 as part of the local government changes, which split Cleveland into the unitary authorities of Hartlepool, Middlesbrough, Redcar and Cleveland, and Stockton-on-Tees.

Cleveland (Stephen) Grover 1837–1908. 22nd and 24th president of the USA, 1885–89 and 1893–97; the first Democratic president elected after the Civil War, and the only president to hold office for two nonconsecutive terms. He attempted to check corruption in public life, and in 1895 initiated arbitration proceedings that eventually settled a territorial dispute with Britain concerning the Venezuelan boundary.

An unswerving conservative, Cleveland refused to involve the government in economic affairs. Within a year of his taking office for the second time, 4 million were unemployed and the USA was virtually bankrupt.

click beetle beetle that can regain its feet from lying on its back by jumping into the air and turning over, clicking as it does so.

client-server architecture in computing, a system in which the mechanics of looking after data are separated from the programs that use the data. For example, the 'server' might be a central database, typically located on a large computer that is reserved for this purpose. The 'client' would be an ordinary program that requests data from the server as needed. Most Internet services are examples of client-server applications, including the World Wide Web.

Cliff Clarice 1899–1972. English pottery designer. Her Bizarre ware, characterized by brightly coloured floral and geometric decoration on often geometrically shaped china, became increasingly popular in the 1930s and increasingly collectable in the 1970s and 1980s.

Born in the ◊Potteries, she started as a factory apprentice at the age of 13, trained at evening classes and worked for many years at the Wilkinson factory. In 1963 she became art director of the factory, which was part of the Royal Staffordshire Pottery in Burslem.

Cleveland The 22nd and 24th president of the USA, Grover Cleveland, a Democrat. Cleveland is the only president to have served for two nonconsecutive terms of office. *Library of Congress*

Clift (Edward) Montgomery 1920–1966. US film and theatre actor. A star of the late 1940s and 1950s in films such as *Red River* 1948, *A Place in the Sun* 1951, and *From Here to Eternity* 1953, he was disfigured in a car accident in 1957 but continued to make films. He played the title role in *Freud* 1962.

climate weather conditions at a particular place over a period of time. Climate encompasses all the meteorological elements and the factors that influence them. The primary factors that determine the variations of climate over the surface of the Earth are: (a) the effect of latitude and the tilt of the Earth's axis to the plane of the orbit about the Sun (66.5°); (b) the large-scale movements of different wind belts over the Earth's surface; (c) the temperature difference between land and sea; (d) contours of the ground; and (e) location of the area in relation to ocean currents. Catastrophic variations to climate may be caused by the impact of another planetary body, or by clouds resulting from volcanic activity.

The most important local or global meteorological changes brought about by human activity are those linked with ◊ozone depleters and the ◊greenhouse effect.

How much heat the Earth receives from the Sun varies in different latitudes and at different times of the year. In the equatorial region the mean daily temperature of the air near the ground has no large seasonal variation. In the polar regions the temperature in the long winter, when there is no incoming solar radiation, falls far below the summer value. Climate types were first classified by Wladimir Köppen (1846–1940) in 1884. The temperature of the sea, and of the air above it, varies little in the course of day or night, whereas the surface of the land is rapidly cooled by lack of solar radiation. In the same way the annual change of temperature is relatively small over the sea and great over the land. Continental areas are thus colder than the sea in winter and warmer in summer. Winds that blow from the sea are warm in winter and cool in summer, while winds from the central parts of continents are hot in summer and cold in winter. On average, air temperature drops with increasing land height at a rate of 1°C/1.8°F per 90 m/300 ft. Thus places situated above mean sea level usually have lower temperatures than places at or near sea level. Even in equatorial regions, high mountains are snow-covered during the whole year. Rainfall is produced by the condensation of water vapour in air. When winds blow against a range of mountains so that the air is forced to ascend, rain results, the amount depending on the height of the ground and the dampness of the air.

The complexity of the distribution of land and sea, and the consequent complexity of the general circulation of the atmosphere, have a direct effect on the distribution of the climate. Centred on the equator is a belt of tropical ◊rainforest, which may be either constantly wet or monsoonal (seasonal with wet and dry seasons in each year). On each side of this is a belt of savannah, with lighter seasonal rainfall and less dense vegetation, largely in the

Clinton Bill Clinton, who defeated George Bush in the US presidential election of Nov 1992 to become the first Democratic president for 12 years. He had been governor of Arkansas since 1983. *American Embassy*

form of grasses. Usually there is then a transition through ◊steppe (semi-arid) to desert (arid), with a further transition through steppe to Mediterranean climate with dry summer, followed by the moist temperate climate of middle latitudes. Next comes a zone of cold climate with moist winter. Where the desert extends into middle latitudes, however, the zones of Mediterranean and moist temperate climates are missing, and the transition is from desert to a cold climate with moist winter. In the extreme east of Asia a cold climate with dry winters extends from about 70° N to 35° N. The polar caps have ◊tundra and glacial climates, with little or no ◊precipitation (rain or snow).

Climate changes over the last millennium can be detected by geophysicists using measurement through boreholes; heat travels so slowly that the first 500m/1,640 ft of the Earth's crust provides a record of the temperature for the last thousand years.

climatic change change in the climate of an area or of the whole world over an appreciable period of time. The geological record shows that climatic changes have taken place regularly, most notably during the ◊ice age. Modern climatic changes may be linked to increasing levels of pollution changing the composition of the atmosphere and producing a ◊greenhouse effect.

clinical ecology in medicine, ascertaining environmental factors involved in illnesses, particularly those manifesting nonspecific symptoms such as fatigue, depression, allergic reactions, and immune-system malfunctions, and prescribing means of avoiding or minimizing these effects.

clinical psychology branch of psychology dealing with the understanding and treatment of health problems, particularly mental disorders. The main problems dealt with include anxiety, phobias, depression, obsessions, sexual and marital problems, drug and alcohol dependence, childhood behavioural problems, psychoses (such as schizophrenia), mental disability, and brain disease (such as dementia) and damage. Other areas of work include forensic psychology (concerned with criminal behaviour) and health psychology.

clint one of a number of flat-topped limestone blocks that make up a ◊limestone pavement. Clints are separated from each other by enlarged joints called grykes.

Clinton Bill (William Jefferson) 1946– . 42nd president of the USA from 1993, a Democrat. He served as governor of Arkansas 1979–81 and 1983–93, establishing a liberal and progressive reputation. As president, he sought to implement a 'New Democrat' programme, combining social reform with economic conservatism as a means of bringing the country out of recession. He had initial successes in introducing legislation to reduce the federal deficit and cut crime, but the loss of Congress to the Republicans in the 1994 midterm elections hindered further social reform. He was re-elected president Nov 1996 with 49% of the popular vote, becoming the first Democrat since F D Roosevelt to be elected twice.

Born in the railway town of Hope, Arkansas, Clinton graduated from Georgetown University 1968, won a Rhodes scholarship to Oxford University 1968–70, and graduated from Yale University Law School 1973. He was elected attorney general for Arkansas 1975. With running mate Al ◊Gore, he won the 1992 presidential campaign by focusing on domestic issues and the ailing economy. He became the first Democrat in the White House for 13 years.

During his first year in office Clinton secured passage of an ambitious deficit-reduction plan, combining spending cuts with tax increases targeted against the rich, and won Congressional approval of the controversial North American Free Trade Agreement (NAFTA) and wide-ranging anticrime bills. Through 1995 he exercised vetoes against measures of the 'New Right' Republican extremism. The Israeli–PLO accord on the West Bank, the Bosnia-Herzegovina peace agreements in the former Yugoslavia, and the Northern Ireland cease-fire were significant foreign policy successes for the Clinton administration. He secured the Democratic presidential nomination in 1996 unopposed, and defeated his Republican challenger Bob Dole by a comfortable margin.

During his second term Clinton faced a judicial investigation into his role in fund-raising for the 1996 election campaign and allegations that he had had an improper relationship with a White House intern, Monica Lewinsky. Nevertheless, with the US economy booming, his public approval ratings remained high. He agreed to answer prosecutors' questions on his relationship with Monica Lewinsky, becoming the first sitting president to testify in a grand jury investigation into his own conduct. Clinton testified at the White House on 17 August 1998 and in an impeachment trial in 1999 Clinton was cleared of perjury and obstruction of justice regarding investigations into the Lewinsky affair.

Clive Robert, 1st Baron Clive 1725–1774. British soldier and administrator who established British rule in India by victories over French troops at Arcot 1751 and over the nawab of Bengal at Plassey 1757. He was governor of Bengal 1757–60 and 1765–66.

clo unit of thermal insulation of clothing. Standard clothes have an insulation of about 1 clo; the warmest clothing is about 4 clo per 2.5 cm/1 in of thickness. See also ◊tog.

cloaca the common posterior chamber of most vertebrates into which the digestive, urinary, and reproductive tracts all enter; a cloaca is found in most reptiles, birds, and amphibians; many fishes; and, to a reduced degree, marsupial mammals.

clock any device that measures the passage of time, usually shown by means of pointers moving over a dial or by a digital display. Traditionally a timepiece consists of a train of wheels driven by a spring or weight controlled by a balance wheel or pendulum. Many clocks now run by batteries rather than clockwork. The watch is a portable clock.

history In ancient Egypt the time during the day was measured by a shadow clock, a primitive form of ◊sundial, and at night the water clock was used. Up to the late 16th century the only clock available for use at sea was the sand clock, of which the most familiar form is the hourglass. During the Middle Ages various types of sundial were widely used, and portable sundials were in use from the 16th to the 18th century. Watches were invented in the 16th century – the first were made in Nuremberg, Germany, shortly after 1500 – but it was not until the 19th century that they became cheap enough to be widely available. The first known public clock was set up in Milan, Italy, in 1353. The timekeeping of both clocks and watches was revolutionized in the 17th century by the application of pendulums to clocks and of balance springs to watches.

types of clock The ***marine chronometer*** is a precision timepiece of special design, used at sea for giving Greenwich mean time (GMT). ***Electric timepieces*** were made possible by the discovery early in the 19th century of the magnetic effects of electric currents. The ***quartz crystal clock*** (made possible by the ◊piezoelectric effect of certain crystals) has great precision, with a short-term variation in accuracy of about one-thousandth of a second per day. More accurate still is the ◊***atomic clock***. This utilizes the natural resonance of certain atoms (for example, caesium) as a regulator controlling the frequency of a quartz crystal ◊oscillator. It is accurate to within one-millionth of a second per day.

cloisonné ornamental craft technique in which thin metal strips are soldered in a pattern onto a metal surface, and the resulting compartments (*cloisons*) filled with coloured ◊enamels and fired. The technique was probably developed in the Byzantine Middle East and traded to Asia and Europe. Cloisonné vases and brooches were made in medieval Europe, but the technique was perfected in Japan and China during the 17th, 18th, and 19th centuries.

cloister in a convent or monastery, a covered walkway, usually surrounding and opening on to a courtyard. The church would be linked to other areas of the convent or monastery via the cloisters.

clone an exact replica. In genetics, any one of a group of genetically identical cells or organisms. An identical ◊twin is a clone; so, too, are bacteria living in the same colony.

In Scotland in 1996, a sheep was successfully cloned from a single cell from the udder of a ewe. She was delivered as a healthy lamb in Feb 1997, after being implanted into the uterus of a surrogate mother. This was the first instance of a mammal being cloned from cells other than reproductive cells.

There is nothing wrong with America that cannot be cured by what is right with America.

Bill Clinton
Inaugural speech as US president 1993

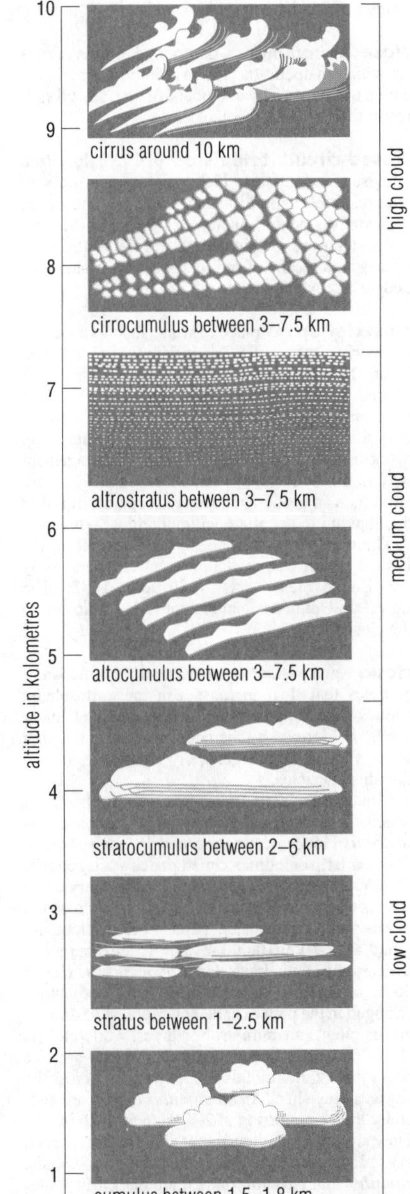

cloud Standard types of cloud. The height and nature of a cloud can be deduced from its name. Cirrus clouds are at high levels and have a wispy appearance. Stratus clouds form at low level and are layered. Middle-level clouds have names beginning with 'alto'. Cumulus clouds, ball or cottonwool clouds, occur over a range of height.

cloud A semi-vortex in clouds indicating the early stages of formation of a storm system. The Moon appears in the background settling over the Earth's limb. *Image Select (UK) Ltd*

Close Glenn 1947– . US actress. She received Academy Award nominations for her roles as the embittered 'other woman' in *Fatal Attraction* 1987 and as the scheming antiheroine of *Dangerous Liaisons* 1988. She played Gertrude in Franco Zeffirelli's film of *Hamlet* 1990 and appeared as an opera star in *Meeting Venus* 1991. She has also had roles on Broadway in Tom Stoppard's *The Real Thing* and Michael Frayn's *Benefactors*.

closed in mathematics, descriptive of a set of data for which an operation (such as addition or multiplication) done on any members of the set gives a result that is also a member of the set.

closed-circuit television (CCTV) localized television system in which programmes are sent over relatively short distances, the camera, receiver, and controls being linked by cable. Closed-circuit TV systems are used in department stores and large offices as a means of internal security, monitoring people's movements.

closed shop any place of work, such as a factory or an office, where all workers within a section must belong to a single, officially recognized trade union. Closed-shop agreements are negotiated between trade unions and management. Trade unions favour closed shops because 100% union membership gives them greater industrial power. Management may find it convenient because they can deal with workers as a group (◊collective bargaining) rather than having to negotiate with individual workers.

The practice became legally enforceable in the UK 1976, but was rendered largely inoperable by the Employment Acts 1980 and 1982. The European Union's social charter calls for an end to the closed shop.

cloud water vapour condensed into minute water particles that float in masses in the atmosphere. Clouds, like fogs or mists, which occur at lower levels, are formed by the cooling of air containing water vapour, which generally condenses around tiny dust particles.

Clouds are classified according to the height at which they occur and their shape. ***Cirrus*** and ***cirrostratus*** clouds occur at around 10 km/33,000 ft. The former, sometimes called mares'-tails, consist of minute specks of ice and appear as feathery white wisps, while cirrostratus clouds stretch across the sky as a thin white sheet. Three types of cloud are found at 3–7 km/10,000–23,000 ft: cirrocumulus, altocumulus, and altostratus. ***Cirrocumulus*** clouds occur in small or large rounded tufts, sometimes arranged in the pattern called mackerel sky. ***Altocumulus*** clouds are similar, but larger, white clouds, also arranged in lines. ***Altostratus*** clouds are like heavy cirrostratus clouds and may stretch across the sky as a grey sheet. ***Stratocumulus*** clouds are generally lower, occurring at 2–6 km/6,500–20,000 ft. They are dull grey clouds that give rise to a leaden sky that may not yield rain. Two types of clouds, ***cumulus*** and ***cumulonimbus***, are placed in a special category because they are produced by daily ascending air currents, which take moisture into the cooler regions of the atmosphere. Cumulus clouds have a flat base generally at 1.4 km/4,500 ft where condensation begins, while the upper part is dome-shaped and extends to about 1.8 km/6,000ft. Cumulonimbus clouds have their base at much the same level, but extend much higher, often up to over 6 km/20,000 ft. Short heavy showers and sometimes thunder may accompany them. ***Stratus*** clouds, occurring below 1–2.5 km/3,000–8,000 ft, have the appearance of sheets parallel to the horizon and are like high fogs.

In addition to their essential role in the water cycle, clouds are important in the regulation of radiation in the Earth's atmosphere. They reflect short-wave radiation from the Sun, and absorb and re-emit long-wave radiation from the Earth's surface. *See illustration on previous page.*

‘It is easier for a man to be loyal to his club than to his planet; the by-laws are shorter, and he is personally acquainted with the other members.’

On CLUBS
E B White
One Man's Meat

cloud chamber apparatus for tracking ionized particles. It consists of a vessel fitted with a piston and filled with air or other gas, saturated with water vapour. When the volume of the vessel is suddenly expanded by moving the piston outwards, the vapour cools and a cloud of tiny droplets forms on any nuclei, dust, or ions present. As fast-moving ionizing particles collide with the air or gas molecules, they show as visible tracks. Much information about interactions between such particles and radiations has been obtained from photographs of these tracks.

The system has been improved upon in recent years by the use of liquid hydrogen or helium instead of air or gas (see ◊particle detector).

Clouet French portrait painters and draughtsmen of the 16th century, father and son. The father, ***Jean*** (or Janet) (c. 1485–1541), is assumed to have been of Flemish origin. He became painter and *valet de chambre* to Francis I 1516. His son, ***François*** (c. 1520–1572), succeeded his father in Francis I's service 1541 and worked also under Henry II, Francis II, and Charles IX.

clove dried, unopened flower bud of the clove tree *Eugenia caryophyllus*. Cloves are used for flavouring in cookery and confectionery.

clover any of an Old World genus *Trifolium* of low-growing leguminous plants, usually with compound leaves of three leaflets and small flowers in dense heads. Sweet clover refers to various species belonging to the related genus *Melilotus*. Eighteen species are native to Britain. Many are cultivated as fodder plants for cattle, red clover being the most common. White or Dutch clover *Trifolium repens* is common in pastures.

Clovis 465–511. Merovingian king of the Franks from 481. He succeeded his father Childeric as king of the Salian (northern) Franks; defeated the Gallo-Romans (Romanized Gauls) near Soissons 486, ending their rule in France; and defeated the Alemanni, a confederation of Germanic tribes, near Cologne 496. He embraced Christianity and subsequently proved a powerful defender of orthodoxy against the Arian Visigoths, whom he defeated at Poitiers 507. He made Paris his capital.

club association of persons formed for leisure, recreational, or political purposes. Clubs based on political principles were common in the late 18th and early 19th centuries, for example the Jacobin Club in Paris in the 1790s and the English Carlton Club, founded in 1832 to oppose the Great Reform Bill.

Sports and recreational clubs also originated in the 19th century, with the creation of working men's clubs in Britain and workers' recreation clubs elsewhere in Europe. Many of the London men's clubs developed from the taverns and coffee houses of the 17th and 18th centuries. The majority of the older clubs have restrictions on access for women.

club moss or ***lycopod*** any non-seed-bearing plant of the order Lycopodiales belonging to the Pteridophyta family. Club mosses are allied to the ferns and horsetails and, like them, reproduce by spores. These plants have a wide distribution, but were far more numerous in Palaeozoic times, especially the Carboniferous period, when members of this group were large trees. The living species are all of small size. The common club moss or stag's horn moss *Lycopodium clavatum* is found on upland heaths.

Club of Rome informal international organization that aims to promote greater understanding of the interdependence of global economic, political, natural, and social systems. Members include industrialists, economists, and research scientists. Membership is limited to 100 people. It was established 1968.

Cluj-Napoca (German ***Klausenburg***; formerly ***Cluj***) city in Transylvania, Romania, located on the river Somes; population (1993) 322,000. It is a communications centre for Romania and the Hungarian plain. Industries include machine tools, furniture, and knitwear. There is a 14th-century cathedral, and Romanian (1872) and Hungarian (1945) universities.

clutch any device for disconnecting rotating shafts, used especially in a car's transmission system. In a car with a manual gearbox, the driver depresses the clutch when changing gear, thus disconnecting the engine from the gearbox. The clutch consists of two main plates, a pressure plate and a driven plate, which is mounted on a shaft leading to the gearbox. When the clutch is engaged, the pressure plate presses the driven plate against the engine ◊flywheel, and drive goes to the gearbox. Depressing the clutch springs the pressure plate away, freeing the driven plate.

Cars with automatic transmission have no clutch. Drive is transmitted from the flywheel to the automatic gearbox by a liquid coupling or torque converter.

Clwyd former region of Wales, created 1974, abolished 1996.

Clyde river in Strathclyde, Scotland; 170 km/103 mi long. The Firth of Clyde and Firth of Forth are linked by the Forth and Clyde Canal, 56 km/35 mi long. The shipbuilding yards have declined in recent years. The nuclear-submarine bases of Faslane (*Polaris*) and Holy Loch (USA *Poseidon*) are here.

Clydebank town on the river Clyde, West Dunbartonshire, Scotland, 10 km/6 mi NW of Glasgow; population (1991) 29,200. At the John Brown yard, liners such as the *Queen Elizabeth II* were built. Shipbuilding is now in decline.

Clytemnestra in Greek mythology, the wife of ◊Agamemnon, king of Mycenae. With the help of her lover Aegisthus, she murdered her husband and Cassandra, whom he brought back from the Trojan War, and was in turn killed by her son Orestes.

club moss Club mosses are named after their clublike fertile heads. Here the heads can be seen on a plant of *Lycopodium cernum* from the high mountain forests of Borneo. *Premaphotos Wildlife*

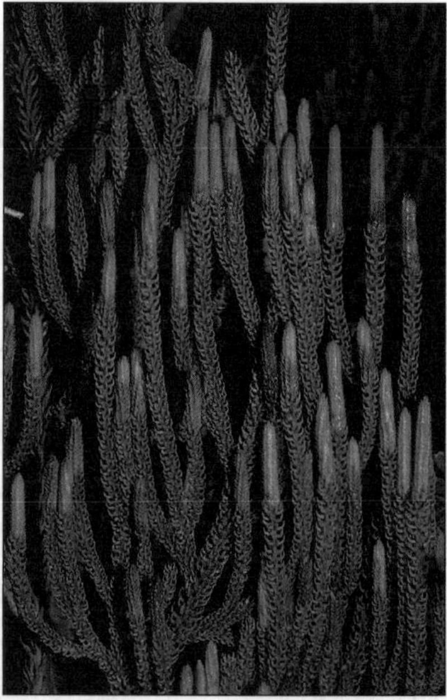

CND abbreviation for ◊*Campaign for Nuclear Disarmament.*

Cnossus alternative form of ◊Knossos, city of ancient Crete.

Cnut alternative spelling of ◊Canute.

coaching conveyance by coach – a horse-drawn passenger carriage on four wheels, sprung and roofed in. Public stagecoaches made their appearance in the middle of the 17th century; the first British mail coach began in 1784, and they continued until 1840 when railways began to take over the traffic. The main roads were kept in good repair by turnpike trusts, and large numbers of inns catered for stagecoach passengers and horses. In the UK, coaches still in use on ceremonial occasions include those of the Lord Mayor of London 1757 and the state coach built in 1761 for George III.

coal black or blackish mineral substance formed from the compaction of ancient plant matter in tropical swamp conditions. It is used as a fuel and in the chemical industry. Coal is classified according to the proportion of carbon it contains. The main types are ◊anthracite (shiny, with about 90% carbon), bituminous coal (shiny and dull patches, about 75% carbon), and lignite (woody, grading into peat, about 50% carbon). Coal burning is one of the main causes of ◊acid rain.

By 1700 Britain was the world's largest coal producer, and over 50% of the country's energy needs were met by coal. From about 1800, coal was carbonized commercially to produce ◊coal gas for gas lighting and ◊coke for smelting iron ore. By the second half of the 19th century, study of the byproducts (coaltar, pitch, and ammonia) formed the basis of organic chemistry, which eventually led to the development of the plastics industry in the 20th century. The York, Derby, and Notts coalfield is Britain's chief reserve, extending north of Selby. Under the Coal Industry Nationalization Act 1946 Britain's mines were administered by the National Coal Board, now known as British Coal. ▷*See feature on pp. 360–361.*

coal gas gas produced when coal is destructively distilled or heated out of contact with the air. Its main constituents are methane, hydrogen, and carbon monoxide. Coal gas has been superseded by ◊natural gas for domestic purposes.

coal mining extraction of coal (a ◊sedimentary rock) from the Earth's crust. Coal mines may be opencast (see ◊opencast mining), adit (in which a horizontal shaft reaches from the surface to the mineral seam), or deepcast. The least expensive is opencast but this may result in scars on the landscape.

history In Britain, coal was mined on a small scale from Roman times, but production expanded rapidly between 1550 and 1700. Coal was the main source of energy for the Industrial Revolution, and many industries were located near coalfields to cut transport costs. Competition from oil as a fuel, cheaper coal from overseas (USA, Australia), the decline of traditional users (town gas, railways), and the exhaustion of many underground workings resulted in the closure of mines (850 in 1955, 54 in 1992), but rises in the price of oil, greater productivity, and the discovery of new, deep coal seams suitable for mechanized extraction (for example, at Selby in Yorkshire) improved the position of the British coal industry 1973–90. It remains very dependent on the use of coal in electricity generation, however, and is now threatened by a trend towards using natural gas from the North Sea and Irish Sea gas fields for this purpose. The percentage of electricity generated from coal dropped from 74% 1992 to just over 50% in 1995.

pit closures In Oct 1992, Trade and Industry Secretary Michael Heseltine announced that 31 of the country's coal mines would be closed, putting some 30,000 miners out of work. After widespread protest from the public and from MPs from all parties, the government announced that 10 pits would close and the remaining 21 would be put under review. In March 1993 a revised closure programme reprieved 12 of the 21 collieries while they were assessed for economic viability. By August 1993, 18 collieries had closed. In 1995, 30 major deep mines and 35 opencast mines formerly owned by British coal, were still being worked.

coal tar black oily material resulting from the destructive distillation of bituminous coal. Further distillation of coal tar yields a number of fractions: light oil, middle oil, heavy oil, and anthracene oil; the residue is called pitch. On further fractionation a large number of substances are obtained, about 200 of which have been isolated. They are used as dyes and in medicines.

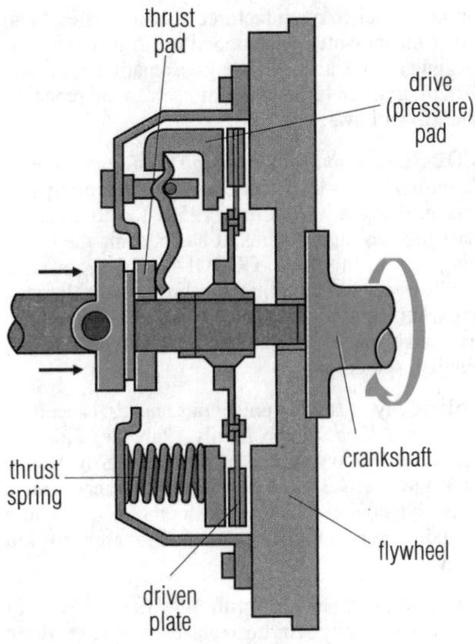

disengaged (pedal pressed down)

engaged (pedal up)

clutch The clutch consists of two main plates: a drive plate connected to the engine crankshaft and a driven plate connected to the wheels. When the clutch is disengaged, the drive plate does not press against the driven plate. When the clutch is engaged, the two plates are pressed into contact and the rotation of the crankshaft is transmitted to the wheels.

coastal erosion the erosion of the land by the constant battering of the sea's waves. This produces two effects. The first is a hydraulic effect, in which the force of the wave compresses air pockets in coastal rocks and cliffs, and the air then expands explosively. The second is the effect of ◊corrasion, in which rocks and pebbles are flung against the cliffs, wearing them away. Frost shattering (or freeze-thaw), caused by the expansion of frozen seawater in cavities, and ◊biological weathering, caused by the burrowing of rock-boring molluscs, also result in the breakdown of the rock. In areas where there are beaches, the waves cause longshore drift, in which sand and stone fragments are carried parallel to the shore, causing buildups (sandspits) in some areas and beach erosion in others.

In Britain, the southern half of the coastline is slowly sinking (on the east coast, at the rate of half a centimetre a year) whilst the northern half is rising, as a result of the land mass responding to the removal of ice from the last Ice Age. Some areas may be eroding at a rate of 6 m/20 ft per year.

coastguard governmental organization whose members patrol a nation's seacoast to prevent smuggling, assist distressed vessels, watch for oil slicks, and so on. In the UK HM Coastguard was formed to prevent smuggling after the Napoleonic Wars, and is now administered by the Department of Trade.

Coates Nigel 1949– . English architect. While teaching at the Architectural Association in London in the early 1980s, Coates and a group of students founded NATO (Narrative Architecture Today) and produced an influential series of manifestos and drawings on the theme of the imaginative regeneration of derelict areas of London.

coati or *coatimundi* any of several species of carnivores of the genus *Nasua*, in the same family, Procyonidae, as the raccoons. A coati is a good climber and has long claws, a long tail, a good sense of smell, and a long, flexible piglike snout used for digging. Coatis live in packs in the forests of South and Central America.

coaxial cable electric cable that consists of a solid or stranded central conductor insulated from and surrounded by a solid or braided conducting tube or sheath. It can transmit the high-frequency signals used in television, telephone, and other telecommunications transmissions.

cobalt (German *Kobalt* 'goblin') hard, lustrous, grey, metallic element, symbol Co, atomic number 27, relative atomic mass 58.933. It is found in various ores and occasionally as a free metal, sometimes in metallic meteorite fragments. It is used in the preparation of magnetic, wear-resistant, and high-strength alloys; its compounds are used in inks, paints, and varnishes. The isotope Co-60 is radioactive (half-life 5.3 years) and is produced in large amounts for use as a source of gamma rays in industrial radiography, research, and cancer therapy.

cobalt chloride $CoCl_2$ compound that exists in two forms: the hydrated salt ($CoCl_2.6H_2O$), which is pink, and the anhydrous salt, which is blue. The anhydrous form is used as an indicator because it turns pink if water is present. When the hydrated salt is gently heated the blue anhydrous salt is reformed.

cobalt ore cobalt is extracted from a number of minerals, the main ones being smaltite, $(CoNi)As_3$; linnaeite, Co_3S_4; cobaltite, CoAsS; and glaucodot, (CoFe)AsS. All commercial cobalt is obtained as a by-product of other metals, usually associated with other ores, such as copper. The Democratic Republic of Congo is the largest producer of cobalt. Other producers include Canada and Morocco.

Cobb Ty(rus Raymond), nicknamed 'the Georgia Peach' 1886–1961. US baseball player, one of the greatest batters and base runners of all time. He played for Detroit and Philadelphia 1905–28, and won the American League batting average championship 12 times. He holds the record for runs scored (2,254) and lifetime batting average (.367). He had 4,191 hits in his career – a record that stood for almost 60 years.

Cobbett William 1763–1835. English Radical politician and journalist, who published the weekly *Political Register* 1802–35. He spent much time in North America. His crusading essays on the conditions of the rural poor were collected as 'Rural Rides' 1830.

Born in Surrey, the self-taught son of a farmer, Cobbett enlisted in the army 1784 and served in Canada. He subsequently lived in the USA as a

❛From a very early age, I had imbibed the opinion, that it was every man's duty to do all that lay in his power to leave his country as good as he had found it.❜

WILLIAM COBBETT
Political Register
22 Dec 1832

coati The coati *Nasua nasua* is about 60 cm/24 in long, and has a tail of about the same length. It feeds on insects, fruit, and small vertebrates. Coatis live in groups of 30 or more, consisting of females and young; males live apart from the pack, and may only join a group for a short time during the mating season.

cobra The Indian cobra often lives in cultivated areas such as rice fields where, if disturbed, it may bite the perceived attacker. The powerful neurotoxins contained in cobra venom cause paralysis and respiratory failure. *Corbis*

teacher of English, and became a vigorous pamphleteer, at this time supporting the Tories. In 1800 he returned to England. With increasing knowledge of the sufferings of the farm labourers, he became a Radical and leader of the working-class movement.

He was imprisoned 1809–11 for criticizing the flogging of British troops by German mercenaries. He visited the USA again 1817–19. He became a strong advocate of parliamentary reform, and represented Oldham in the Reformed Parliament after 1832.

Cobden Richard 1804–1865. British Liberal politician and economist, co-founder with John Bright of the Anti-Corn Law League 1839. A member of Parliament from 1841, he opposed class and religious privileges and believed in disarmament and free trade.

A typical early Victorian radical, he believed in the abolition of privileges, a minimum of government interference, and the securing of international peace through free trade and by disarmament and arbitration. He opposed trade unionism and most of the factory legislation of his time, because he regarded them as opposed to liberty of contract. His opposition to the Crimean War made him unpopular. He was largely responsible for the commercial treaty with France in 1860.

Born in Sussex, the son of a farmer, Cobden became a calico manufacturer in Manchester. With other businessmen he founded the Anti-Corn Law League and began his lifelong association with John Bright, until 1845 devoting himself to the repeal of the ◊Corn Laws.

COBOL (acronym for ***common business-oriented language***) high-level computer-programming language, designed in the late 1950s for commercial data-processing problems; it has become the major language in this field. COBOL features powerful facilities for file handling and business arithmetic. Program instructions written in this language make extensive use of words and look very much like English sentences.

cobra any of several poisonous snakes, especially the genus *Naja*, of the family Elapidae, found in Africa and S Asia, species of which can grow from 1 m/3 ft to over 4.3 m/14 ft. The neck stretches into a hood when the snake is alarmed. Cobra venom contains nerve toxins powerful enough to kill humans.

coca South American shrub *Erythroxylon coca* of the coca family Erythroxylaceae, whose dried leaves are the source of cocaine. It was used as a holy drug by the Andean Indians.

Coca-Cola trade name of a sweetened, carbonated drink, originally made with coca leaves and flavoured with cola nuts, and containing caramel and caffeine. Invented in 1886, Coca-Cola was sold in every state of the USA by 1895 and in 155 countries by 1987. Coca-Cola & Schweppes Beverages, established 1987, is the largest company in the UK soft drinks market, controlling 40% of the country's soft drink sales. 49% of the company is owned by the US Coca-Cola Company and 51% by Cadbury Schweppes.

cocaine alkaloid $C_{17}H_{21}NO_4$ extracted from the leaves of the coca tree. It has limited medical application, mainly as a local anaesthetic agent that is readily absorbed by mucous membranes (lining tissues) of the nose and throat. It is both toxic and addictive. Its use as a stimulant is illegal. ◊Crack is a derivative of cocaine.

Most of the world's cocaine is produced from coca grown in Peru, Bolivia, Colombia, and Ecuador. Estimated annual production totals 215,000 tonnes, with most of the processing done in Colombia. Long-term use may cause mental and physical deterioration.

coccus (plural *cocci*) member of a group of globular bacteria, some of which are harmful to humans. The cocci contain the subgroups *streptococci*, where the bacteria associate in straight chains, and *staphylococci*, where the bacteria associate in branched chains.

Cochabamba city in central Bolivia, SE of La Paz; population (1992) 404,100. Its altitude is 2,550 m/8,370 ft; it is a centre of agricultural trading and oil refining. It is the third largest city in Bolivia.

Cochin seaport in Kerala state, India, on the Malabar coast; population (1991) 564,000. It is a fishing port, naval training base, and an industrial centre with oil refineries; ropes and clothing are also manufactured here. It exports coir, copra, tea, and spices. Vasco da Gama established a Portuguese factory at Cochin 1502, and St Francis Xavier made it a missionary centre 1530. The Dutch held Cochin from 1663 to 1795, when it was taken by the English.

Cochin-China region of SE Asia. With Cambodia it formed part of the ancient Khmer empire. In the 17th–18th centuries it was conquered by Annam. Together with Cambodia it became, 1863–67, the first part of the Indochinese peninsula to be occupied by France. Since 1949 it has been part of Vietnam.

cochineal red dye obtained from the cactus-eating Mexican ◊scale insect *Dactylopius coccus*, used in colouring food and fabrics.

Cochise c. 1812–1874. American Apache Indian leader who campaigned relentlessly against white settlement of his territory. Unjustly arrested by US authorities 1850, he escaped from custody and took American hostages, whom he later executed. A Chiricahua Apache, Cochise joined forces with the Mimbrẽno Apache and successfully fought off a large force of California settlers 1862. Finally apprehended by General George Crook 1871, Cochise made peace with the US government the following year.

cochlea part of the inner ◊ear. It is equipped with approximately 10,000 hair cells, which move in response to sound waves and thus stimulate nerve cells to send messages to the brain. In this way they turn vibrations of the air into electrical signals.

Cochran Eddie 1938–1960. US rock-and-roll singer, songwriter, and guitarist. He created classic rock songs like 'Summertime Blues' 1958 and 'C'mon Everybody' 1959 as well as slower romantic numbers ('Dark, Lonely Street' 1958, 'Three Steps to Heaven' 1960). His first record was 'Skinny Jim' 1956, and he appeared in the 1956 film *The Girl Can't Help It* singing 'Twenty Flight Rock'. He was killed in a car crash while touring the UK.

Cockaigne, Land of in medieval European folklore, a mythical country of leisure and idleness, where fine food and drink were plentiful and to be had for the asking.

cockatiel Australian parrot *Nymphicus hollandicus*, about 20 cm/8 in long, with greyish or yellow plumage, yellow cheeks, a long tail, and a crest like a cockatoo. Cockatiels are popular as pets and aviary birds.

cockatoo any of several crested parrots, especially of the genus *Cacatua*, family Psittacidae, of the order Psittaciformes. They usually have light-coloured plumage with tinges of red, yellow, or orange on the face, and an erectile crest on the head. They are native to Australia, New Guinea, and nearby islands.

cockchafer or ***maybug*** European beetle *Melolontha melolontha*, of the scarab family, up to 3 cm/1.2 in long, with clumsy, buzzing flight, seen on early summer evenings. Cockchafers damage trees by feeding on the foliage and flowers.

Cockerell Charles Robert 1788–1863. English architect. He built mainly in a Neo-Classical style derived from antiquity and from the work of Christopher Wren. His buildings include the Cambridge University Library (now the Cambridge Law Library) 1837–42 and the Ashmolean Museum and Taylorian Institute in Oxford 1841–45.

Cockerell Christopher Sydney 1910– . English engineer who invented the ◊hovercraft in the 1950s. Cockerell tested various ways of maintaining the air cushion. In 1957 he came up with the idea of a flexible skirt, which gave rise to much derision

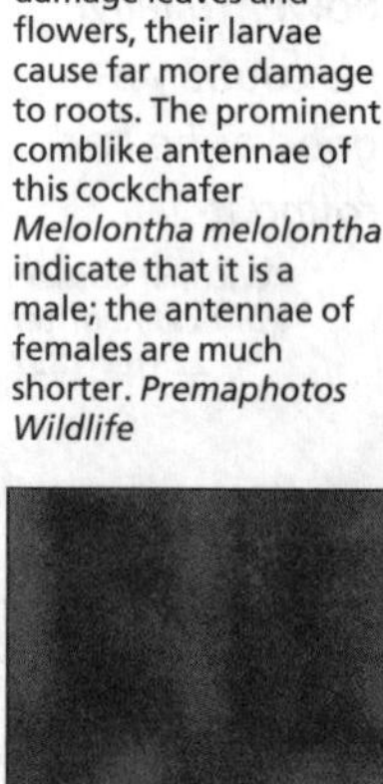

cockchafer Although adult cockchafers damage leaves and flowers, their larvae cause far more damage to roots. The prominent comblike antennae of this cockchafer *Melolontha melolontha* indicate that it is a male; the antennae of females are much shorter. *Premaphotos Wildlife* because nobody could believe that a piece of fabric could be made to support a large vessel.

cockfighting the pitting of gamecocks against one another to make sport for onlookers and gamblers; they have steel spurs attached to their legs. In most countries it is illegal because of its cruelty. The sport was very popular in feudal England. A royal cockpit was built in Whitehall by Henry VIII, and royal patronage continued in the next century. During the Cromwellian period it was banned, but at the Restoration it was revived until it was banned in 1849. Cockfighting is still legal in some countries and continues secretly in others.

cockle any of over 200 species of bivalve mollusc with ribbed, heart-shaped shells. Some are edible and are sold in W European markets. The common cockle *Cerastoderma edule* is up to 5 cm/2 in across, and is found in sand or mud on shores and in estuaries around N European and Mediterranean coasts.

cockney natives of the City of London. According to tradition cockneys must be born within sound of ◊Bow Bells in Cheapside. The term cockney is also applied to the dialect of the Londoner, of which a striking feature is rhyming slang.

cockroach any of numerous insects of the family Blattidae, distantly related to mantises and grasshoppers. There are 3,500 species, mainly in the tropics. They have long antennae and biting mouthparts. The common cockroach, or black-beetle *Blatta orientalis*, is found in human dwellings, is nocturnal, omnivorous, and contaminates food.

cocktail effect the effect of two toxic, or potentially toxic, chemicals when taken together rather than separately. Such effects are known to occur with some mixtures of drugs, with the active ingredient of one making the body more sensitive to the other. This sometimes occurs because both drugs require the same ◊enzyme to break them down.

Chemicals such as pesticides and food additives are only ever tested singly, not in combination with other chemicals that may be used at the same time, so no allowance is made for cocktail effects.

cocoa and chocolate (Aztec *xocolatl*) food products made from the ◊cacao (or cocoa) bean, fruit of a tropical tree *Theobroma cacao*, now cultivated mainly in Africa. Chocolate as a drink was introduced to Europe from the New World by the Spanish in the 16th century; eating-chocolate was first produced in the late 18th century. Cocoa and chocolate are widely used in confectionery and drinks.

preparation This takes place in the importing country and consists chiefly of roasting, winnowing, and grinding the nib (the edible portion of the bean). If cocoa for drinking is required, a proportion of the cocoa butter is removed by hydraulic pressure and the remaining cocoa is reduced by further grinding and sieving to a fine powder. In chocolate all the original cocoa butter remains. Sugar and usually milk are added; in the UK cheaper vegetable fats are widely substituted.

history The cacao tree is indigenous to the forests of the Amazon and Orinoco, and the use of the beans was introduced into Europe after the conquest of Mexico by Cortés. In Mexico cacao was mixed with hot spices, whisked to a froth and drunk cold by the ruling class, during ritual events. A 'cocoa-house' was opened in London in 1657; others followed and became fashionable meeting places. In 1828 a press was invented that removed two-thirds of the cocoa butter from the beans, leaving a cake-like mass which, when mixed with sugar and spices, made a palatable drink. Joseph Fry (1728–1787) combined the cocoa mass with sugar and cocoa butter to obtain a solid chocolate bar, which was turned into milk chocolate by a Swiss, Daniel Pieter, who added condensed milk developed by Henri Nestlé (1814–1890). Cocoa powder was a later development. Côte d'Ivoire is the world's top cocoa exporter (32% of the world total in 1986).

cocoa and chocolate Cocoa beans growing near Ibadan in Nigeria. Africa produces about two-thirds of the world's cocoa while the remainder is grown in South America. *Image Select (UK) Ltd*

coconut The coconut palm can grow up to 24 m/80 ft in height. Ripe nuts are harvested by climbing the tree – sometimes monkeys are trained for the job – or allowing the nuts to fall naturally. The outer fibrous husk of the fruit is removed to reveal the nut.

coconut fruit of the coconut palm *Cocos nucifera* of the family Arecaceae, which grows throughout the lowland tropics. The fruit has a large outer husk of fibres, which is split off and used for coconut matting and ropes. Inside this is the nut exported to temperate countries. Its hard shell contains white flesh and coconut milk, both of which are nourishing and palatable. The white meat can be eaten, or dried prior to the extraction of its oil, which is used in the making of soap and margarine and in cooking.

Cocos Islands or ***Keeling Islands*** group of 27 small coral islands in the Indian Ocean, about 2,770 km/1,720 mi NW of Perth, Australia; area 14 sq km/5.5 sq mi; population (1993) 593. They are owned by Australia. Discovered by William Keeling 1609, they were annexed by Britain 1857 and transferred to Australia as the Territory of Cocos (Keeling) Islands 1955. The Australian government purchased them from John Clunies-Ross 1978. In 1984 the islanders voted to become part of Australia.

Cocteau Jean 1889–1963. French poet, dramatist, and film director. A leading figure in European Modernism, he worked with the artist ◊Picasso, the choreographer ◊Diaghilev, and the composer ◊Stravinsky. He produced many volumes of poetry; ballets such as *Le Boeuf sur le toit/The Ox on the Roof* 1920; plays, for example, *Orphée/Orpheus* 1926; and a mature novel of bourgeois French life, *Les Enfants terribles/Children of the Game* 1929, which he made into a film 1950.

cod any fish of the family Gadidae, especially the Atlantic cod, *Gadus morhua* found in the N Atlantic and Baltic. It is brown to grey with spots, white below, and can grow to 1.5 m/5 ft. The main cod fisheries are in the North Sea, and off the coasts of Iceland and Newfoundland, Canada. Much of the catch is salted and dried. Formerly one of the cheapest fish, decline in numbers from overfishing has made it one of the most expensive.

codeine opium derivative that provides ◊analgesia in mild to moderate pain. It also suppresses the cough centre of the brain. It is an alkaloid, derived from morphine but less toxic and addictive.

codex (plural ***codices***) book from before the invention of printing: in ancient times wax-coated wooden tablets; later, folded sheets of parchment were attached to the boards, then bound together. The name 'codex' was used for all large works, collections of history, philosophy, poetry, and during the Roman Empire designated collections of laws. During the 2nd century AD codices began to replace the earlier rolls in the West. They were widely used by the medieval Christian church to keep records, from about 1200 onwards.

codominance in genetics, the failure of a pair of alleles, controlling a particular characteristic, to show the classic recessive-dominant relationship. Instead, aspects of both alleles may show in the phenotype.

codon in genetics, a triplet of bases (see ◊base pair) in a molecule of DNA or RNA that directs the placement of a particular amino acid during the process of protein (polypeptide) synthesis. There are 64 codons in the ◊genetic code.

Cody William Frederick, ('Buffalo Bill') 1846–1917. US scout and performer. From 1883 he toured the USA and Europe with a Wild West show which featured the recreation of Indian attacks and, for a time, the cast included Chief ◊Sitting Bull as well as Annie Oakley (1860–1926). His nickname derives from a time when he had a contract to supply buffalo carcasses to railway labourers (over 4,000 in 18 months).

Coe Sebastian Newbold 1956– . English middle-distance runner, Olympic 1,500-metres champion 1980 and 1984. He became Britain's most prolific world-record breaker with eight outdoor world records and three indoor world records 1979–81. After his retirement from running in 1990 he pursued a political career with the Conservative party, and in 1992 was elected member of Parliament for Falmouth and Camborne in Cornwall.

coeducation education of both boys and girls in one institution. In most countries coeducation is now favoured over single-sex education, although there is some evidence to suggest that girls perform better in a single-sex institution, particularly in maths and science. There has been a marked switch away from single-sex education and in favour of coeducation from the 1970s in the UK. In the USA, 90% of schools and colleges are coeducational. In Islamic countries, coeducation is discouraged beyond the infant stage on religious principles.

coefficient the number part in front of an algebraic term, signifying multiplication. For example, in the expression $4x^2 + 2xy - x$, the coefficient of x^2 is 4 (because $4x^2$ means $4 \times x^2$), that of xy is 2, and that of x is -1 (because $-1 \times x = -x$). In general algebraic expressions, coefficients are represented by letters that may stand for numbers; for example, in the equation $ax^2 + bx + c = 0$, a, b, and c are coefficients, which can take any number.

coefficient of relationship the probability that any two individuals share a given gene by virtue of being descended from a common ancestor. In sexual reproduction of diploid species, an individual shares half its genes with each parent, with its offspring, and (on average) with each sibling; but only a quarter (on average) with its grandchildren or its siblings' offspring; an eighth with its great-grandchildren, and so on.

coelenterate any freshwater or marine organism of the phylum Coelenterata, having a body wall composed of two layers of cells. They also possess stinging cells. Examples are jellyfish, hydra, and coral. *See illustration on following page.*

coeliac disease disease in which the small intestine fails to digest and absorb food. It is caused by an intolerance to gluten (a constituent of wheat, rye and barley) and characterized by diarrhoea and malnutrition. Treatment is by a gluten-free diet.

Coetzee J(ohn) M(ichael) 1940– . South African author. His novel *In the Heart of the Country*

'The worst tragedy for a poet is to be admired through being misunderstood.'

JEAN COCTEAU
Recall to Order

coelenterate Distributed along the west coasts of the British Isles, the snakelocks anemone *Anemonia sulcata* is found on the middle and lower shores. Along with the common beadlet anemone and the occasional stranded jellyfish, it is the coelenterate most likely to be discovered by the casual observer. *Premaphotos Wildlife*

1975 dealt with the rape of a white woman by a black man. In 1983 he won Britain's Booker Prize for *The Life and Times of Michael K.* Other works include *Waiting for the Barbarians* 1982, *Foe* 1987, and *The Master of Petersburg* 1994.

coelacanth lobe-finned fish *Latimeria chalumnae* up to 2 m/6 ft long. It has bone and muscle at the base of the fins, and is distantly related to the freshwater lobefins, which were the ancestors of all land animals with backbones. Coelacanths live in deep water (200 m/650 ft) around the Comoros Islands, although in Aug 1995 one was caught 1,300 km/808 mi away off the coast of Madagascar. They were believed to be extinct until one was caught in 1938. They are now threatened, and have been listed as endangered since 1991.

coelacanth The coelacanth is the sole survivor of an ancient group of fishes and is found only in deep trenches of the tropical W Indian Ocean. It is a heavy-bodied fish with fleshy fin lobes and small scales. It grows to a weight of 90 kg/200 lb and is dark brown to blue in colour.

coevolution evolution of those structures and behaviours within a species that can best be understood in relation to another species. For example, insects and flowering plants have evolved together: insects have produced mouthparts suitable for collecting pollen or drinking nectar, and plants have developed chemicals and flowers that will attract insects to them.

coffee drink made from the roasted and ground beanlike seeds found inside the red berries of any of several species of shrubs of the genus *Coffea*, originally native to Ethiopia and now cultivated throughout the tropics. It contains a stimulant, ◊caffeine.

cultivation The shrub is naturally about 5 m/17 ft high, is pruned to about 2 m/7 ft, is fully fruit-bearing in 5 or 6 years, and lasts for 30 years. Coffee grows best on frost-free hillsides with moderate rainfall. The world's largest producers are Brazil, Colombia, and Côte d'Ivoire; others include Indonesia (Java), Ethiopia, India, Hawaii, and Jamaica. In recent years the world coffee market has been dogged by over-supply, and in the early 1990s the price of coffee was well below the cost of production.

history Coffee drinking began in Arab regions in the 14th century but did not become common in Europe until 300 years later, when the first coffee houses were opened in Vienna, and soon after in Paris and London. In the American colonies, coffee became the substitute for tea when tea was taxed by the British.

cogito, ergo sum (Latin) 'I think, therefore I am'; quotation from French philosopher René Descartes. The concept formed the basis of the philosophical doctrine of ◊dualism.

Cognac town in Charente *département*, France, 40 km/25 mi W of Angoulême. Situated in a vine-growing district, Cognac has given its name to a brandy. Bottles, corks, barrels, and crates are manufactured here.

cognition in psychology, a general term covering the functions involved in synthesizing information – for example, perception (seeing, hearing, and so on), attention, memory, and reasoning.

cognitive therapy or ***cognitive behaviour therapy*** treatment for emotional disorders such as ◊depression and ◊anxiety states. It encourages the patient to challenge the distorted and unhelpful thinking that is characteristic of depression, for example. The treatment may include ◊behaviour therapy.

Cohan Robert Paul 1925– . US choreographer. He was founding artistic director of the ◊London Contemporary Dance Theatre (LCDT) 1969–89 and artistic adviser from 1992. A student of Martha ◊Graham and co-director of her company 1966–69, his choreography is a development of her style. Blending elements of American jazz dance and Graham's modern dance, Cohan's work is marked by a thematic vagueness and a willingness to utilize modern technology as in *Video-Life* 1987. His works include *Cell* 1969, a study on the loss of individuality; *Waterless Method of Swimming Instruction* 1974; and the television ballet *A Mass for Man* 1985.

cohesion in physics, a phenomenon in which interaction between two surfaces of the same material in contact makes them cling together (with two different materials the similar phenomenon is called adhesion). According to kinetic theory, cohesion is caused by attraction between particles at the atomic or molecular level. ◊Surface tension, which causes liquids to form spherical droplets, is caused by cohesion.

coil in medicine, another name for an ◊intrauterine device.

coin form of money. The right to make and issue coins is a state monopoly, and the great majority are tokens in that their face value is greater than that of the metal of which they consist. The invention of coinage is attributed to the Chinese in the 2nd millennium BC, the earliest types being small-scale bronze reproductions of barter objects such as knives and spades. In the Western world, coinage of stamped, guaranteed weight originated with the Lydians of Asia Minor (early 7th century BC) who used electrum, a local natural mixture of gold and silver; the first to issue gold and silver coins was Croesus of Lydia in the 6th century BC. The study of coins is called numismatics.

COIN acronym for ***counter insurgency***, the suppression by a state's armed forces of uprisings against the state. Also called internal security (IS) operations of counter-revolutionary warfare (CRW). The British army has been engaged in COIN operations in Northern Ireland since 1969.

coke clean, light fuel produced, along with town gas, when coal is strongly heated in an airtight oven. Coke contains 90% carbon and makes a useful domestic and industrial fuel (used, for example in the iron and steel industries). The process was patented in England 1622, but it was only in 1709 that Abraham Darby devised a commercial method of production.

Coke Edward 1552–1634. Lord Chief Justice of England 1613–17. He was a defender of common law against royal prerogative; against Charles I he drew up the petition of right 1628, which defines and protects Parliament's liberties.

Coke became a barrister 1578, and in 1592 speaker of the House of Commons and solicitor-general. As attorney-general from 1594, he conducted the prosecution of Elizabeth I's former favourites Essex and Raleigh, and of the Gunpowder Plot conspirators. In 1606 he became Chief Justice of the Common Pleas, and began his struggle, as champion of the common law, against James I's attempts to exalt the royal prerogative. An attempt to silence him by promoting him to the dignity of Lord Chief Justice proved unsuccessful, and from 1620 he led the parliamentary opposition and the attack on Charles I's adviser Buckingham. Coke's *Institutes* are a legal classic, and he ranks as the supreme common lawyer.

Coke Thomas William, 1st Earl of Leicester 1754–1842. English pioneer and promoter of the improvements associated with the Agricultural Revolution. His innovations included regular manuring of the soil, the cultivation of fodder crops in association with corn, and the drilling of wheat and turnips.

cola or ***kola*** any tropical tree of the genus *Cola*, especially *C. acuminata*, family Sterculiaceae. In W Africa, the nuts are chewed for their high caffeine content, and in the West are used to flavour soft drinks.

Colbert Jean-Baptiste 1619–1683. French politician, chief minister to Louis XIV, and controller-general (finance minister) from 1665. He reformed the Treasury, promoted French industry and commerce by protectionist measures, and tried to make France a naval power equal to England or the Netherlands, while favouring a peaceful foreign policy.

coffee The coffee plant *Coffea arabica* is a small tree, but is pruned into a large bush to make harvesting easier. It produces sweet-smelling white flowers; these are followed by green berries which turn red when ripe. Each berry contains two seeds, which are processed to make coffee for drinking.

Colbert succeeded Cardinal Mazarin as chief minister to Louis XIV. In 1661 he set to work to reform the Treasury. The national debt was largely repaid, and the system of tax collection was drastically reformed. Industry was brought under state control, shipbuilding was encouraged by bounties, companies were established to trade with India and America, and colonies were founded in Louisiana, Guiana, and Madagascar.

Colchester city and river port in England, on the river Colne, Essex; 80 km/50 mi NE of London; population (1991 est) 87,500. In an agricultural area, it is a market centre with clothing manufacture and engineering and printing works. It is famous for its oysters.

history Claiming to be the oldest town in England (the Roman *Camulodunum*), Colchester dates from the time of ◊Cymbeline (c. AD 10–43). It became a colony of Roman ex-soldiers AD 50, and one of the most prosperous towns in Roman Britain despite its burning by Boudicca (Boadicea) 61. Most of the Roman walls remain, as well as ruins of the Norman castle, and St Botolph's priory. Holly Tree Mansion (1718) is a museum of 18th-and 19th-century social life.

cold-blooded of animals, dependent on the surrounding temperature; see ◊poikilothermy.

cold fusion in nuclear physics, the fusion of atomic nuclei at room temperature. If cold fusion were possible it would provide a limitless, cheap, and pollution-free source of energy, and it has therefore been the subject of research around the world. In 1989, Martin Fleischmann (1927–) and Stanley Pons (1943–) of the University of Utah, USA, claimed that they had achieved cold fusion in the laboratory, but their results could not be substantiated. Most scientists now believe that cold fusion is impossible; however, research has continued in some laboratories.

Colditz city in E Germany, near Leipzig, site of a castle used as a high-security prisoner-of-war camp (Oflag IVC) in World War II. Among daring escapes was that of British Captain Patrick Reid (1910–1990) and others Oct 1942, whose story contributed much to its fame. It became a museum 1989. In 1990 the castle was converted to a hotel.

Cold War ideological, political, and economic tensions 1945–90 between the USSR and Eastern Europe on the one hand and the USA and Western Europe on the other. The Cold War was exacerbated by propaganda, covert activity by intelligence agencies, and economic sanctions; it intensified at times of conflict anywhere in the world. Arms-reduction agreements between the USA and USSR in the late 1980s, and a diminution of Soviet influence in Eastern Europe, symbolized by the opening of the Berlin Wall 1989, led to a reassessment of positions, and the 'war' officially ended 1990.

origins Mistrust between the USSR and the West dated from the Russian Revolution 1917 and contributed to the disagreements during and immediately after World War II over the future structure of Eastern Europe. The ◊Atlantic Charter signed 1941 by the USA and the UK favoured self-determination, whereas the USSR insisted on keeping the territory obtained as a result of the Hitler–Stalin pact of Aug 1939. After the war the USA was eager to have all of Europe open to Western economic interests, while the USSR, afraid of being encircled and attacked by its former allies, saw Eastern Europe as its own sphere of influence and, in the case of Germany, was looking to extract reparations. As the USSR increased its hold on the countries of Eastern Europe, the USA pursued a policy of 'containment' that involved offering material aid to Western Europe (the ◊Marshall Plan) and to Nazi-victimized countries such as Greece and Turkey. Berlin became the focal point of East–West tension (since it was zoned for military occupational governments of the USA, UK, France, and USSR, yet was situated within what was then Soviet-controlled East Germany). This culminated in the Soviet blockade of the US, British, and French zones of the city 1948, which was relieved by a sustained airlift of supplies (see ◊Berlin blockade). The increasing divisions between the capitalist and the communist worlds were reinforced by the creation of military alliances, the ◊North Atlantic Treaty Organization (NATO) 1949 in the West, and the ◊Warsaw Pact 1955 in the East. The formal end of the Cold War was declared in Nov 1990 at the Paris Conference on Security and Cooperation in Europe (CSCE). ▷ *See feature on pp. 1090–1091.*

coffee A contemporary picture of a coffee house from c. 1700. Coffee, chocolate, and tea were all introduced to England in the mid-17th century, and coffee houses rapidly became popular meeting places for the discussion of business affairs and literature. *Philip Sauvain*

cold, common minor disease of the upper respiratory tract, caused by a variety of viruses. Symptoms are headache, chill, nasal discharge, sore throat, and occasionally cough. Research indicates that the virulence of a cold depends on psychological factors and either a reduction or an increase of social or work activity, as a result of stress, in the previous six months. There is little immediate hope of an effective cure since the viruses transform themselves so rapidly.

Coleman Ornette 1930– . US alto saxophonist and jazz composer. In the late 1950s he rejected the established structural principles of jazz for free avant-garde improvisation. He has worked with small and large groups, ethnic musicians of different traditions, and symphony orchestras. His albums include *The Shape of Jazz to Come* 1959, *Chappaqua Suite* 1965, and *Skies of America* 1972.

Colenso John William 1814–1883. British cleric, Anglican bishop of Natal, South Africa, from 1853. He was the first to write down the Zulu language. He championed the Zulu way of life (including polygamy) in relation to Christianity, and applied Christian morality to race relations in South Africa.

coleoptile the protective sheath that surrounds the young shoot tip of a grass during its passage through the soil to the surface. Most coleoptiles are very sensitive to light, ensuring that seedlings grow upwards.

Coleridge Samuel Taylor 1772–1834. English poet. He was one of the founders of the Romantic movement. A friend of the poets Robert ◊Southey and William ◊Wordsworth, he collaborated with the latter on *Lyrical Ballads* 1798. His poems include 'The Rime of the Ancient Mariner', 'Christabel', and 'Kubla Khan' (all written 1797–98); critical works include *Biographia Literaria* 1817.

Coleridge was born in Ottery St Mary, Devon, and educated at Cambridge. During his time there he was driven by debt to enlist in the Dragoons. In 1795 he married Sarah Fricker (1779–1845), from whom he afterwards separated. Suffering from rheumatic pain, he became addicted to opium and from 1816 lived in Highgate, London, under medical care. As a philosopher, he argued that even in registering sense perceptions the mind was performing acts of creative imagination, rather than being a passive arena in which ideas interact mechanistically. A brilliant talker and lecturer, Coleridge was expected to produce some great work of philosophy or criticism. His *Biographia Literaria* is full of insight but its formlessness and the limited extent of his poetic output represents a partial failure of promise.

Colette Sidonie-Gabrielle 1873–1954. French writer. Her best novels reveal an exquisite sensitivity, largely centred on the joys and sorrows of love, and include *Chéri* 1920, *La Fin de Chéri/The End of Chéri* 1926, and *Gigi* 1944.

colic spasmodic attack of pain in the abdomen, usually coming in waves. Colicky pains are caused by the painful muscular contraction and subsequent distension of a hollow organ; for example, the bowels, gall bladder (biliary colic), or ureter (renal colic). Intestinal colic is due to partial or complete blockage of the intestine, or constipation; infantile colic is usually due to wind in the intestine.

❛Let us not be deceived – we are today in the midst of a cold war.❜

On the **Cold War**
Bernard Baruch, speech 16 April 1947

colitis inflammation of the colon (large intestine) with diarrhoea (often bloody). It is usually due to infection or some types of bacterial dysentery.

collage (French 'sticking', 'pasting' or 'paper-hanging') in art, the use of materials of any kind – pieces of newspaper, wallpaper, fabric – stuck on a canvas or other surface, usually in conjunction with a painted or drawn element of design. A technique first used by the Cubists and taken up by the Dadaists and Surrealists, collage became a familiar feature of 20th-century art.

collagen protein that is the main constituent of ◊connective tissue. Collagen is present in skin, cartilage, tendons, and ligaments. Bones are made up of collagen, with the mineral calcium phosphate providing increased rigidity.

collateral security available in return for a loan. Usually stocks, shares, property, or life insurance policies will be accepted as collateral.

collective bargaining process whereby management, representing an employer, and a trade union, representing employees, agree to negotiate jointly terms and conditions of employment. Agreements can be company-based or industry-wide.

collective farm (Russian ***kolkhoz***) farm in which a group of farmers pool their land, domestic animals, and agricultural implements, retaining as private property enough only for the members' own requirements. The profits of the farm are divided among its members. In cooperative farming, farmers retain private ownership of the land.

Collective farming was first developed in the USSR in 1917, where it became general after 1930. Stalin's collectivization drive 1929–33 wrecked a flourishing agricultural system and alienated the Soviet peasants from the land: 15 million people were left homeless, 1 million of whom were sent to labour camps and some 12 million deported to Siberia. In subsequent years, millions of those peasants forced into collectives died. Collective farming is practised in other countries; it was adopted from 1953 in China, and Israel has a large number of collective farms (see ◊kibbutz).

collective responsibility doctrine found in governments modelled on the British system of cabinet government. It is based on convention, or usage, rather than law, and requires that once a decision has been taken by the cabinet, all members of the government are bound by it and must support it or resign their posts.

collective security system for achieving international stability by an agreement among all states to unite against any aggressor. Such a commitment was embodied in the post-World War I ◊League of Nations and also in the ◊United Nations (UN),

❛No man was ever yet a great poet, without being at the same time a profound philosopher.❜

Samuel Coleridge
Biographia Literaria

although the League was not able to live up to the ideals of its founders, nor has the UN done so.

collective unconscious in psychology, a shared pool of memories, ideas, modes of thought, and so on, which, according to the Swiss psychiatrist Carl Jung, comes from the life experience of one's ancestors, indeed from the entire human race. It coexists with the personal ◊unconscious, which contains the material of individual experience, and may be regarded as an immense depository of ancient wisdom.

Primal experiences are represented in the collective unconscious by archetypes, symbolic pictures, or personifications that appear in dreams and are the common element in myths, fairy tales, and the literature of the world's religions.

collectivism in politics, a position in which the collective (such as the state) has priority over its individual members. It is the opposite of ◊individualism, which is itself a variant of anarchy.

College of Arms or ***Heralds' College*** English heraldic body formed 1484 by Richard III incorporating the heralds attached to the royal household; reincorporated by royal charter of Philip and Mary 1555. There are three kings of arms, six heralds, and four pursuivants, who specialize in genealogical and heraldic work. The college establishes the right to a coat of arms, and the kings of arms grant arms by letters patent. In Ireland the office of Ulster king of arms was transferred 1943 to the College of Arms in London and placed with that of Norroy king of arms, who now has jurisdiction in Northern Ireland as well as in the north of England.

college of higher education in the UK, a college in which a large proportion of the work undertaken is at degree level or above. Colleges of higher education are centrally funded by the Universities and Colleges Funding Council, and some of the largest became universities in 1992 at the same time as the former polytechnics.

collenchyma plant tissue composed of relatively elongated cells with thickened cell walls, in particular at the corners where adjacent cells meet. It is a supporting and strengthening tissue found in non-woody plants, mainly in the stems and leaves.

collie any of several breeds of sheepdog originally bred in Britain. They include the border collie, the bearded collie, and the rough collie and its smooth-haired counterpart.

Collier Lesley Faye 1947– . English ballerina. She became a principal dancer of the Royal Ballet 1972. She created roles in Kenneth MacMillan's *Anastasia* 1971, Hans van Manen's *Four Schumann Pieces* 1975, Frederick Ashton's *Rhapsody*, and Glen Tetley's *Dance of Albiar* both 1980.

Collins Michael 1890–1922. Irish nationalist. He was a ◊Sinn Féin leader, a founder and director of intelligence of the ◊Irish Republican Army 1919, minister for finance in the provisional government of the Irish Free State 1922 (see ◊Ireland, Republic of), commander of the Free State forces in the civil war, and for ten days head of state before being killed by Irishmen opposed to the partition treaty with Britain. ▷ *See feature on pp. 550–551.*

Collins Phil(lip David Charles) 1951– . English pop singer, drummer, and actor. A member of the group Genesis from 1970, he has also pursued a successful middle-of-the-road solo career since 1981, with hits (often new versions of old songs) including 'In the Air Tonight' 1981 and 'Groovy Kind of Love' 1988. He starred as the train robber Buster Edwards in the film *Buster* 1988.

Collins (William) Wilkie 1824–1889. English author of mystery and suspense novels. He wrote *The Woman in White* 1860 (with its fat villain Count Fosco), often called the first English detective novel, and *The Moonstone* 1868 (with Sergeant Cuff, one of the first detectives).

collision theory theory that explains how chemical reactions take place and why rates of reaction alter. For a reaction to occur the reactant particles must collide. Only a certain fraction of the total collisions cause chemical change; these are called fruitful collisions. The fruitful collisions have sufficient energy (activation energy) at the moment of impact to break the existing bonds and form new bonds, resulting in the products of the reaction. Increasing the concentration of the reactants and raising the temperature bring about more collisions and therefore more fruitful collisions, increasing the rate of reaction.

colloid substance composed of extremely small particles of one material (the dispersed phase) evenly and stably distributed in another material (the continuous phase). The size of the dispersed particles (1–1,000 nanometres across) is less than that of particles in suspension but greater than that of molecules in true solution. Colloids involving gases include aerosols (dispersions of liquid or solid particles in a gas, as in fog or smoke) and foams (dispersions of gases in liquids). Those involving liquids include emulsions (in which both the dispersed and the continuous phases are liquids) and sols (solid particles dispersed in a liquid). Sols in which both phases contribute to a molecular three-dimensional network have a jellylike form and are known as gels; gelatin, starch 'solution', and silica gel are common examples.

COLOMBIA
Republic of

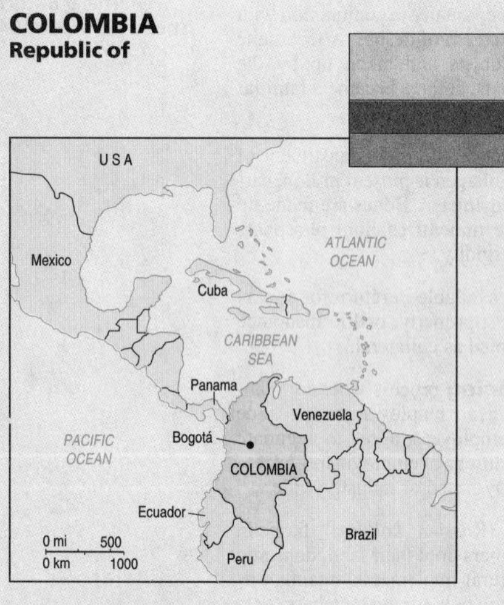

national name *República de Colombia*
area 1,141,748 sq km/440,715 sq mi
capital Bogotá
major towns/cities Medellín, Cali, Bucaramanga
major ports Barranquilla, Cartagena, Buenaventura
physical features the Andes mountains run N–S; flat coastland in W and plains (llanos) in E; Magdalena River runs N to Caribbean Sea; includes islands of Providencia, San Andrés, and Mapelo; almost half the country is forested
head of state and government Andres Pastrana from 1998
political system democratic republic
administrative divisions 23 departments, four intendencies, and five commissaries
political parties Liberal Party (PL), centrist; Conservative Party (PSC), right of centre; M-19 Democratic Alliance (ADM-19), left of centre; National Salvation Movement (MSN), right-of-centre coalition grouping
population 36,444 (1996 est)
population growth rate 1.7% (1990–95); 1.3% (2000–05)
ethnic distribution main ethnic groups are of mixed Spanish, Indian, and African descent; Spanish customs and values predominate
life expectancy 66 (males), 72 (females)
literacy rate men 88%, women 86%
language Spanish
religion Roman Catholic
currency Colombian peso
GDP (US $) 66.8 billion (1994)
growth rate 5.7% (1994)
exports emeralds (world's largest producer), coffee (world's second largest producer), cocaine (country's largest export), bananas, cotton, meat, sugar, oil, skins, hides, tobacco, petroleum, cut flowers

HISTORY
late 15th C S Colombia became part of the Inca Empire, whose core lay in Peru.
1522 The Spanish conquistador Pascual de Andagoya reached the San Juan River.
1536–38 Spanish conquest by Jimenez de Quesada, overcoming the powerful Chibcha Indian chiefdom, which had its capital in the uplands at Bogotá and was renowned for its gold crafts; became part of Spanish Viceroyalty of Peru, which covered much of South America.
1717 Bogotá became the capital of the new Spanish Viceroyalty of Nueva (New) Granada, which also ruled Ecuador and Venezuela.
1809 Struggle for independence from Spain began.
1819 The Venezuelan freedom fighter Simón Bolívar, 'The Liberator', who had withdrawn to Colombia in 1814, raised a force of 5,000 British mercenaries and defeated the Spanish at the battle of Boyaca, establishing Colombia's independence; Gran Colombia formed, also comprising Ecuador, Panama, and Venezuela.
1830 Became separate state, which included Panama, on dissolution of Republic of Gran Colombia.
1863 Became major coffee exporter and federalizing, anti-clerical Liberals came to power, with country divided into nine, largely autonomous 'sovereign' states, and church disestablished.
1885 Centralizing, pro-clerical Conservatives came to power, beginning a period of political dominance that was to last forty-five years; power was recentralized and the church restored to influence.
1899–1903 Civil war between Liberals and Conservatives, ended with Panama's separation as an independent state.
1930 Liberals returned to power at the time of the economic Depression; social legislation introduced and the labour movement encouraged.
1946 Conservatives returned to power after Liberal vote divided between rival candidates.
1948 Left-wing mayor of Bogotá assassinated; widespread outcry.
1949 Start of civil war, 'La Violencia', during which over 250,000 people died.
1957 Hoping to halt the violence, Conservatives and Liberals agreed to form a National Front, sharing the presidency.
1970 National Popular Alliance (ANAPO) formed as a left-wing opposition to the National Front.
1974 National Front accord temporarily ended.
1975 Civil unrest due to disillusionment with the government.
1978 Liberals, under Julio Turbay, revived the accord and began an intensive fight against drug dealers.
1982 Liberals maintained their control of congress but lost the presidency. The Conservative president, Belisario Betancur, granted guerrillas an amnesty and freed political prisoners.
1984 Minister of justice assassinated by drug dealers; campaign against them stepped up.
1986 Virgilio Barco Vargas, Liberal, elected president by record margin.
1989 Drug cartel assassinated leading presidential candidate; Vargas declared antidrug war; bombing campaign by drug traffickers killed hundreds; police killed José Rodríguez Gacha, one of the most wanted cartel leaders.
1990 Cesar Gaviria Trujillo elected president. Liberals maintained control of congress.
1991 New constitution prohibited extradition of Colombians wanted for trial in other countries; several leading drug traffickers arrested. Many guerrillas abandoned the armed struggle, but the Colombian Revolutionary Armed Forces (Farc) and National Liberation Army remained active. Liberals won general election.
1992 Medellín drug cartel leader Pablo Escobar escaped from prison. State of emergency declared.
1993 Escobar shot while attempting to avoid arrest.
1994 Liberals returned to power. Ernesto Samper Pizano, Liberal, elected president.
1995 Samper under pressure to resign over corruption allegations; state of emergency declared. Leaders of Cali drugs cartel imprisoned.
1998 Heavy army losses in clashes with left-wing guerrillas. Liberal Party secure assembly majority.
1999 Thousands killed and injured, and widespread devastation in major earthquake centred on the city of Armenia.

SEE ALSO Bolivár, Simón; Chibcha; Inca; Medellín cartel

Milk is a natural emulsion of liquid fat in a watery liquid; synthetic emulsions such as some paints and cosmetic lotions have chemical emulsifying agents to stabilize the colloid and stop the two phases from separating out.

Colman Ronald Charles 1891–1958. English film actor. In Hollywood from 1920, he played suave and dashing roles in *Beau Geste* 1924, *The Prisoner of Zenda* 1937, *Lost Horizon* 1937, and *A Double Life* 1947, for which he received an Academy Award.

Cologne (German ***Köln***) industrial and commercial port in North Rhine–Westphalia, Germany, on the left bank of the Rhine, 35 km/22 mi SE of Düsseldorf; population (1993) 961,600. To the N is the Ruhr coalfield, on which many of Cologne's industries are based. They include motor vehicles, railway wagons, chemicals, and machine tools. Cologne is an important transshipment centre.

Founded by the Romans 38 BC and made a colony AD 50 under the name *Colonia Claudia Arae Agrippinensis*, it became a leading Frankish city and during the Middle Ages was ruled by its archbishops. It was a free imperial city from 1288 until the Napoleonic age. In 1815 it passed to Prussia. The great Gothic cathedral was begun in the 13th century, but its towers were not built until the 19th century (completed 1880). Its university (1388–1797) was refounded 1919. Cologne suffered severely from aerial bombardment during World War II, notably the British 'thousand bomber raid' 30 May 1942; 85% of the city and its three Rhine bridges were destroyed.

Colombia country in South America, bounded N by the Caribbean Sea, W by the Pacific Ocean, NW corner by Panama, E and NE by Venezuela, SE by Brazil, and SW by Peru and Ecuador. *See country box opposite.*

Colombo capital and principal seaport of Sri Lanka, on the west coast near the mouth of the Kelani River; population (1993) 2,026,000. It trades in tea, rubber, andcacao. It has iron- and steelworks and an oil refinery. The Dutch seized it 1656 and surrendered it to Britain 1796. Since 1983 the chief government offices have been located at nearby Sri-Jayawardenapura, E of the city.

Colombo Joe Cesare 1930–1971. Italian industrial designer. He was a member of the postwar generation of designers who created a sophisticated, sculptural style for banal industrial goods. He is best known for his plastic chairs designed for Kartell, notable among them his 'Chair 4860' 1965 which brought a new respectability to the material.

Colombo Matteo Realdo c. 1516–1559. Italian anatomist who discovered pulmonary circulation, the process of blood circulating from the heart to the lungs and back. This showed that ◊Galen's teachings were wrong, and was of help to William ◊Harvey in his work on the heart and circulation.

Colón second largest city in Panama, at the Caribbean end of the Panama Canal; population (1990) 140,900. It has a special economic zone (created 1948) used by foreign companies to avoid taxes on completed products in their home countries.

colon in anatomy, the main part of the large intestine, between the caecum and rectum. Water and mineral salts are absorbed from undigested food in the colon, and the residue passes as faeces towards the rectum.

colonialism another name for ◊imperialism.

colonies, Greek overseas territories of the ancient Greek city-states. Greek colonization was mostly concerned with land, not trade. Greek cities on the western coast of modern Turkey may have been founded as early as 1000 BC. From the late 8th century BC population expansion prompted settlements in southern Italy (Taranto, by settlers from Sparta) and Sicily (Syracuse, by settlers from Corinth), followed by others in southern France (Marseilles), North Africa (◊Cyrenaica) and on the Black Sea coast.

colonies, Roman territories of the Roman empire. The earliest Roman citizen settlements guarded the local coast (◊Ostia) from the 4th century BC. In contrast, Latin colonies were independent and helped to secure Italy. In the later republic, colonies were founded to distribute land to army veterans or the poor. Overseas colonies were supported by Julius ◊Caesar and ◊Augustus in Spain, Gaul (France and Belgium), Africa and Asia. Imperial colonization continued to the end of the 1st century AD.

Colorado

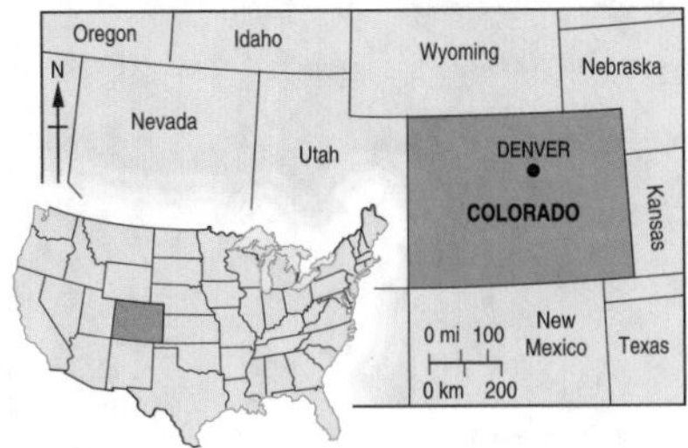

colonization in ecology, the spread of species into a new habitat, such as a freshly cleared field, a new motorway verge, or a recently flooded valley. The first species to move in are called pioneers, and may establish conditions that allow other animals and plants to move in (for example, by improving the condition of the soil or by providing shade). Over time a range of species arrives and the habitat matures; early colonizers will probably be replaced, so that the variety of animal and plant life present changes. This is known as ◊succession.

colonnade row of columns supporting arches or an entablature.

colophon decorative device on the title page or spine of a book, the trademark of the individual publisher. Originally a colophon was an inscription on the last page of a book giving the writer or printer's name and the place and year of publication.

Colorado river in North America, rising in the Rocky Mountains and flowing 2,333 km/1,450 mi to the Gulf of California through Colorado, Utah, Arizona (including the Grand Canyon), and N Mexico. The many dams along its course, including Hoover and Glen Canyon, provide power and irrigation water, but have destroyed wildlife and scenery, and very little water now reaches the sea. To the W of the river in SE California is the Colorado Desert, an arid area of 5,000 sq km/2,000 sq mi.

Colorado state of the W central USA; nicknamed Centennial State
area 269,700 sq km/104,104 sq mi
capital Denver
towns and cities Colorado Springs, Aurora, Lakewood, Fort Collins, Greeley, Pueblo, Boulder
physical Great Plains in the E; the main ranges of the Rocky Mountains; high plateaus of the Colorado Basin in the W
features Rocky Mountains, with peaks over 4,000 m/14,000 ft, in Rocky Mountain national park; Colorado River; Royal Gorge (the Grand Canyon of Colorado), carved by the Arkansas River, with the world's highest suspension bridge; Garden of the Gods (natural sandstone sculptures); Mesa Verde national park, with prehistoric cliff dwellings of the Anasazi Native Americans; goldmining 'ghost towns'; 19th-century towns; Denver, 1.6 km/1 mi high, with Denver Art Museum, containing a collection of Native American art, and the capitol building with its gold dome (1894); Colorado Springs; University of Colorado, Boulder; Aspen Music Festival; ski resorts, including Vail, the largest ski mountain in North America
products cereals, meat and dairy products, oil, coal, molybdenum, uranium, iron, steel, machinery
population (1990) 3,294,400
famous people Jack Dempsey, Douglas Fairbanks
history first visited by Spanish explorers in the 16th century; claimed for Spain 1706; east portion passed to the USA 1803 as part of the Louisiana Purchase, the rest 1845 and 1848 as a result of the Mexican War. It attracted fur traders, and Denver was founded following the discovery of gold 1858. Colorado became a state 1876. Irrigated agriculture, ranching, tourism and outdoor sports, energy development, and the establishment of military bases fuelled rapid growth after World War II.

Colorado Springs city in Colorado, USA, 120 km/75 mi SE of Denver; population (1992) 295,800. At an altitude of about 1,800 m/6,000 ft, and surrounded by magnificent scenery, it was founded as a health resort 1871. A gold strike at nearby Cripple Creek 1892 aided its growth. Colorado Springs is the home of the US Air Force Academy and the operations centre of the North American Air Defense Command (NORAD).

Colosseum amphitheatre in ancient Rome, begun by the emperor Vespasian to replace the one destroyed by fire during the reign of Nero, and completed by his son Titus AD 80. It was 187 m/615 ft long and 49 m/160 ft high, and seated 50,000 people. Early Christians were martyred there by lions and gladiators. It could be flooded for mock sea battles. *See illustration on following page.*

coloratura in music, a rapid ornamental vocal passage with runs and trills. A coloratura soprano is a light, high voice suited to such music.

Colossus of Rhodes bronze statue of Apollo erected at the entrance to the harbour at Rhodes 292–280 BC. Said to have been about 30 m/100 ft high, it was counted as one of the ◊Seven Wonders of the World, but in 224 BC fell as a result of an earthquake.

colour quality or wavelength of light emitted or reflected from an object. Visible white light consists of electromagnetic radiation of various wavelengths, and if a beam is refracted through a prism, it can be spread out into a spectrum, in which the various colours correspond to different wavelengths. From long to short wavelengths (from about 700 to 400 nanometres) the colours are red, orange, yellow, green, blue, indigo, and violet.

The light entering our eyes is either reflected from the objects we see, or emitted by hot or luminous objects. Sources of light have a characteristic ◊spectrum or range of wavelengths. Hot solid objects emit light with a broad range of wavelengths, the maximum intensity being at a wavelength which depends on the temperature. The

'The cathedral ... was the most beautiful of all the churches I have ever seen, If one could imagine the spirit of devotion embodied in any material form, it would be in such a building.'

On **Cologne**
Lewis Carroll *Diary* July 1867

Colorado The Colorado River running through the Grand Canyon, Arizona, USA. The river runs from the Rocky Mountains in Colorado down to the Gulf of California, USA. *Image Select (UK) Ltd*

Colosseum The Colosseum, Rome, Italy. It was begun AD 70 by the emperor Vespasian, and completed AD 80. It is four storeys high and could seat 50,000 people. Mock sea battles and animal and gladiator fights were staged here. Officially known as the Flavian Amphitheatre, the popular name 'Colosseum' probably derived from a statue of Nero that stood nearby, known as the Colossus. *Image Select (UK) Ltd*

hotter the object, the shorter the wavelengths emitted, as described by ◊Wien's displacement law. Hot gases, such as the vapour of sodium street lights, emit light at discrete wavelengths. The pattern of wavelengths emitted is unique to each gas and can be used to identify the gas (see ◊spectroscopy). When an object is illuminated by white light, some of the wavelengths are absorbed and some are reflected to the eye of an observer. The object appears coloured because of the mixture of wavelengths in the reflected light. For instance, a red object absorbs all wavelengths falling on it except those in the red end of the spectrum. This process of subtraction also explains why certain mixtures of paints produce different colours. Blue and yellow paints when mixed together produce green because between them the yellow and blue pigments absorb all wavelengths except those around green. A suitable combination of three pigments – cyan (blue–green), magenta (blue–red), and yellow – can produce any colour when mixed. This fact is used in colour printing, although additional black pigment is also added.

In the light-sensitive lining of our eyeball (the ◊retina), cells called cones are responsible for colour vision. There are three kinds of cones.

Each type is sensitive to one colour only, either red, green, or blue. The brain combines the signals sent from the set of cones to produce a sensation of colour. When all cones are stimulated equally the sensation is of white light. The three colours to which the cones respond are called the ***primary colours***. By mixing lights of these three colours it is possible to produce any colour. This process is called colour mixing by addition, and is used to produce the colour on a television screen where glowing phosphor dots of red, green, and blue combine. Pairs of colours that produce white light, such as yellow and blue, are called ***complementary colours***. Many schemes have been proposed for classifying colours. The most widely used is the Munsell scheme, which classifies colours according to their hue (dominant wavelength), saturation (the degree of whiteness), and brightness (intensity).

colour blindness hereditary defect of vision that reduces the ability to discriminate certain colours, usually red and green. The condition is sex-linked, affecting men more than women. In the most common types of colour blindness there is confusion among the red–yellow–green range of colours; for example, many colour-blind observers are unable to distinguish red from yellow or yellow from green. The physiological cause of congenital colour blindness is not known, although it probably arises from some defect in the retinal receptors.

‘To Castile and Aragon, Columbus gave another world.’

Epitaph to CHRISTOPHER COLUMBUS in Seville cathedral

Colt Samuel 1814–1862. US gunsmith who invented the revolver 1835 that bears his name. With its rotating cylinder which turned, locked, and unlocked by cocking the hammer, the Colt was superior to other revolving pistols, and it revolutionized military tactics.

Coltrane John William 1926–1967. US jazz saxophonist. He first came to prominence 1955 with the Miles ◊Davis quintet, later playing with Thelonious Monk 1957. He was a powerful and individual artist, whose performances featured much experimentation. His 1960s quartet was highly regarded for its innovations in melody and harmony.

Like Charlie Parker, Coltrane marked a watershed in jazz and has been deified by his fans. The free-jazz movement of the 1960s owed much to his extended exploratory solos, for example on 'Giant Steps' 1959, the year he traded tenor saxophone for soprano. A highly original musician, he has been much imitated, but the deeply emotional tone of his playing, for example on 'A Love Supreme' 1964, is impossible to copy.

coltsfoot perennial plant *Tussilago farfara*, family Compositae. The solitary yellow flower heads have many narrow rays, and the stems have large, purplish scales. The large leaf, up to 22 cm/9 in across, is shaped like a horse's foot and gives the plant its common name. Coltsfoot grows in Europe, N Asia, and N Africa, often on bare ground and in waste places, and has been introduced to North America. It was formerly used in medicine.

Colum Padraic 1881–1972. Irish poet and dramatist. He was associated with the foundation of the ◊Abbey Theatre, Dublin, where his plays *The Land* 1905 and *Thomas Muskerry* 1910 were performed. His *Collected Poems* 1953 shows his gift for lyrical expression.

Columba, St (Latin form of ***Colum-cille***, 'Colum of the cell') 521–597. Irish Christian abbot, missionary to Scotland. He was born in County Donegal of royal descent, and founded monasteries and churches in Ireland. In 563 he sailed with 12 companions to Iona, and built a monastery there that was to play a leading part in the conversion of Britain. From his base there he made missionary journeys to the mainland. Legend has it that he drove a monster from the river Ness, and he crowned Aidan, an Irish king of Argyll. His feast day is 9 June.

Columban, St 543–615. Irish Christian abbot. About 585 he went to the Vosges, France, with 12 other monks and founded the monastery of Luxeuil. Later, he preached in Switzerland, then went to Italy, where he built the abbey of Bobbio in the Apennines. Feast day 23 Nov.

Columbia river in W North America, over 1,950 km/1,218 mi long; it rises in British Columbia, Canada, and flows through Washington State, USA, to the Pacific below Astoria. It is harnessed for irrigation and power by the Grand Coulee and other great dams. It was listed 1994 as in danger of ecological collapse, along with its tributary the Snake River.

Columbia, District of seat of the federal government of the USA, coextensive with the city of ◊Washington, situated on the Potomac River; area 178 sq km/69 sq mi. It was ceded by Maryland as the national capital site 1790.

Columbia Pictures US film production and distribution company founded 1924. It grew out of a smaller company founded 1920 by Harry and Jack Cohn and Joe Brandt. Under Harry Cohn's guidance, Columbia became a major studio by the 1940s, producing such commercial hits as *Gilda* 1946. After Cohn's death 1958 the studio remained successful, producing such international films as *Lawrence of Arabia* 1962.

columbine any plant of the genus *Aquilegia* of the buttercup family Ranunculaceae. All are perennial herbs with divided leaves and flowers with spurred petals. In Britain *A. vulgaris* grows wild in woods and is a familiar garden plant.

Columbus capital of Ohio, USA, on the rivers Scioto and Olentangy; population (1992) 643,000; metropolitan area (1992) 1,394,000. It has coalfield and natural gas resources nearby; its industries include the manufacture of cars, aircraft, space equipment, missiles, and electrical goods.

Columbus Christopher, (Spanish ***Cristóbal Colón***) 1451–1506. Italian navigator and explorer who made four voyages to the New World: 1492 to San Salvador Island, Cuba, and Haiti; 1493–96 to Guadaloupe, Montserrat, Antigua, Puerto Rico, and Jamaica; 1498 to Trinidad and the mainland of South America; 1502–04 to Honduras and Nicaragua.

Believing that Asia could be reached by sailing westwards, he eventually won the support of King Ferdinand and Queen Isabella of Spain and set off on his first voyage from Palos 3 Aug 1492 with three small ships, the *Niña*, the *Pinta*, and his flagship the *Santa Maria*. Land was sighted 12 Oct, probably Watling Island (now San Salvador Island), and within a few weeks he reached Cuba and Haiti, returning to Spain March 1493.

Born in Genoa, Columbus went to sea at an early age, and settled in Portugal 1478. After his third voyage 1498, he became involved in quarrels among the colonists sent to Haiti, and in 1500 the governor sent him back to Spain in chains. Released and compensated by the king, he made his last voyage 1502–04, during which he hoped to find a strait leading to India. He died in poverty in Valladolid and is buried in Seville cathedral. In 1968 the

Columbus, Christopher Portrait of the Italian navigator Christopher Columbus by Sebastiano del Piombo. Columbus made four voyages to the New World, filled with hopes of discoveries, wealth, and high rank. He died in poverty, believing that the lands he had found were part of Asia, and never received the rewards the Spanish King and Queen had promised him. *Corbis*

site of the wreck of the *Santa Maria*, sunk off Hispaniola 25 Dec 1492, was located.

column in architecture, a structure, round or polygonal in plan, erected vertically as a support for some part of a building. Cretan paintings reveal the existence of wooden columns in Aegean architecture about 1500 BC. The Hittites, Assyrians, and Egyptians also used wooden columns, and they are a feature of the monumental architecture of China and Japan. In Classical architecture there are five principal types of column; see ◊order.

Colwyn Bay (Welsh ***Bae Colwyn***) seaside town in the former region of Clwyd, N Wales, known as the 'garden resort of Wales'; population (1991) 29,900.

coma in astronomy, the hazy cloud of gas and dust that surrounds the nucleus of a ◊comet.

coma in medicine, a state of deep unconsciousness from which the subject cannot be roused. Possible causes include head injury, brain disease, liver failure, cerebral haemorrhage, and drug overdose.

Comaneci Nadia 1961– . Romanian gymnast. She won three gold medals at the 1976 Olympics at the age of 14, and was the first gymnast to record a perfect score of 10 in international competition. Upon retirement she became a coach of the Romanian team, but defected to Canada 1989.

combe or ***coombe*** steep-sided valley found on the scarp slope of a chalk ◊escarpment. The inclusion of 'combe' in a placename usually indicates that the underlying rock is chalk.

Combination Acts laws passed in Britain 1799 and 1800 making trade unionism illegal, introduced after the French Revolution for fear that the unions would become centres of political agitation. The unions continued to exist, but claimed to be friendly societies or went underground, until the acts were repealed 1824.

combine harvester or ***combine*** machine used for harvesting cereals and other crops, so called because it combines the actions of reaping (cutting the crop) and threshing (beating the ears so that the grain separates). Combines, drawn by horses, were used in the Californian cornfields in the 1850s. Today's mechanical combine harvesters are capable of cutting a swath of up to 9 m/30 ft or more.

combustion burning, defined in chemical terms as the rapid combination of a substance with oxygen, accompanied by the evolution of heat and usually light. A slow-burning candle flame and the explosion of a mixture of petrol vapour and air are extreme examples of combustion.

Comecon (acronym for ***Council for Mutual Economic Assistance***, or ***CMEA***) economic organization 1949–91, linking the USSR with Bulgaria, Czechoslovakia, Hungary, Poland, Romania, East Germany (1950–90), Mongolia (from 1962), Cuba (from 1972), and Vietnam (from 1978), with Yugoslavia as an associated member. Albania also belonged 1949–61. Its establishment was prompted by the ◊Marshall Plan. Comecon was formally disbanded June 1991.

It was agreed 1987 that official relations should be established with the ◊European Community, and a free-market approach to trading was adopted 1990. In Jan 1991 it was agreed that Comecon should be effectively disbanded.

Comédie Française French national theatre (for both comedy and tragedy) in Paris, founded 1680 by Louis XIV. Its base is the Salle Richelieu on the right bank of the river Seine, and the Théâtre de l'Odéon, on the left bank, is a testing ground for avant-garde ideas.

comedy drama that aims to make its audience laugh, usually with a happy or amusing ending, as opposed to ◊tragedy. The comic tradition has undergone many changes since its Greek roots; the earliest comedy developed in ancient Greece, in the topical and fantastic satires of Aristophanes. Great comic dramatists include Shakespeare, Molière, Carlo Goldoni, Pierre de Marivaux, George Bernard Shaw, and Oscar Wilde. Genres of comedy include pantomime, satire, farce, black comedy, and ◊commedia dell'arte.

The comic tradition was established by the Greek dramatists Aristophanes and Menander, and the Roman writers Terence and Plautus. In medieval times, the Vices and Devil of the morality plays developed into the stock comic characters of the Renaissance ***comedy of humours*** with such notable villains as Ben Jonson's Mosca in *Volpone*. The timeless comedies of Shakespeare and Molière were followed in England during the 17th century by the witty ***comedy of manners*** of Restoration writers such as George Etherege, William Wycherley, and William Congreve. Their often coarse but always vital comedies were toned down in the later Restoration dramas of Richard Sheridan and Oliver Goldsmith. Sentimental comedy dominated most of the 19th century, though little is remembered in the late 20th century, which prefers the realistic tradition of Shaw and the elegant social comedies of Wilde. The polished comedies of Noël Coward and Terence Rattigan from the 1920s to 1940s were eclipsed during the late 1950s and the 1960s by a trend towards satire and cynicism as seen in the works of Joe Orton and Peter Nichols, alongside absurdist comedies by Samuel Beckett, Jean Genet, and Tom Stoppard. From the 1970s the 'black comedies' of Alan Ayckbourn have dominated the English stage, with the political satires of Dario ◊Fo affecting the radical theatre.

comet small, icy body orbiting the Sun, usually on a highly elliptical path. A comet consists of a central nucleus a few kilometres across, and has been likened to a dirty snowball because it consists mostly of ice mixed with dust. As a comet approaches the Sun its nucleus heats up, releasing gas and dust which form a tenuous coma, up to 100,000 km/60,000 mi wide, around the nucleus. Gas and dust stream away from the coma to form one or more tails, which may extend for millions of kilometres.

Comets are believed to have been formed at the birth of the Solar System. Billions of them may reside in a halo (the ◊Oort cloud) beyond Pluto. The gravitational effect of passing stars pushes some towards the Sun, when they eventually become visible from Earth. Most comets swing around the Sun and return to distant space, never to be seen again for thousands or millions of years, although some, called periodic comets, have their orbits altered by the gravitational pull of the planets so that they reappear every 200 years or less. Periodic comets are thought to come from the ◊Kuiper belt, a zone just beyond Neptune. Of the 800 or so comets whose orbits have been calculated, about 160 are periodic. The brightest is ◊Halley's comet. The one with the shortest known period is ◊Encke's comet, which orbits the Sun every 3.3 years. A dozen or more comets are discovered every year.

Comet Hale-Bopp *see table below.*

comfrey any plant of the genus *Symphytum*, borage family Boraginaceae, with rough, hairy leaves and small bell-shaped flowers (blue, purple-pink, or white), found in Europe and W Asia.

The European species *S. officinale* was once used to make ointment for treating wounds and various ailments, and is still sometimes used as a poultice.

comet An observation of Donati's comet in Oct 1858. Giovanni Donati, an Italian astronomer of the 19th century, discovered six comets. He also determined their gaseous composition using a spectroscope. *Image Select (UK) Ltd*

Up to 1.2 m/4 ft tall, it has hairy, winged stems, lanceolate (tapering) leaves, and white, yellowish, purple, or pink flowers in drooping clusters.

comic book publication in strip-cartoon form. Comic books are usually aimed at children, although in Japan, Latin America, and Europe millions of adults read them. Artistically sophisticated adult comics and graphic novels are produced in the USA and several European countries, notably France. Comic books developed from comic strips in newspapers or, like those of Walt ◊Disney, as spinoffs from animated cartoon films.

The first superhero, Superman, created 1938 by Jerome Siegel and Joseph Shuster, soon had his own periodical, and others followed; the Marvel Comics group, formed 1961, was selling 50 million copies a year worldwide by the end of the 1960s and found a cult readership among college students for such titles as *Spiderman* and *The Incredible Hulk*.

comic strip or ***strip cartoon*** sequence of several frames of drawings in ◊cartoon style. Strips, which may work independently or form instalments of a serial, are usually humorous or satirical in content. Longer stories in comic-strip form are published separately as ◊comic books. Some have been made into animated films; see ◊animation.

The first comic strip was 'The Yellow Kid' by Richard Felton Outcault, which appeared in the Sunday newspaper *New York World* 1896; it was

MAJOR COMETS

Name	First recorded sighting	Orbital period (years)	Interesting facts
Halley's comet	240 BC	76	parent of Eta Aquarid and Orionid meteor showers
Comet Tempel-Tuttle	AD 1366	33	parent of Leonid meteors
Biela's comet	1772	6.6	broke in two 1846; not seen since 1852
Encke's comet	1786	3.3	parent of Taurid meteors
Comet Swift-Tuttle	1862	130	parent of Perseid meteors; reappeared 1992
Comet Ikeya-Seki	1965	880	so-called 'Sun-grazing' comet, passed 500,000 km/300,000 mi above surface of Sun on 21 Oct 1965
Comet Kohoutek	1973		observed from space by Skylab astronauts
Comet West	1975	500,000	nucleus broke into four parts
Comet Bowell	1980		ejected from Solar System after close encounter with Jupiter
Comet IRAS-Araki-Alcock	1983		passed only 4.5 million km/2.8 million mi from Earth on 11 May 1983
Comet Austin	1989		passed 32 million km/20 million mi from Earth 1990
Comet Shoemaker-Levy 9	1993		made up of 21 fragments; crashed into Jupiter July 1994
Comet Hale-Bopp	1995	1,000	spitting out gas and debris producing a coma with greater volume than the Sun; the bright coma is due to the outgassing of carbon monoxide; passed 190 million km/118 million mi from Earth 1997
Comet Hyakutake	1996		passed 15 million km/9,300,000 mi from Earth

immediately successful and others soon followed. Some of the most admired early comic strips were the US 'Gertie the Dinosaur' and 'Happy Hooligan' as well as 'Krazy Kat', which began 1910 and ended with the death of its creator, Richard Herriman, 1944. Current comic strips include 'Peanuts' by Charles M Schulz (1922–), which began 1950 and was read daily by 60 million people by the end of the 1960s; the political 'Doonesbury' by Garry Trudeau; the British 'Andy Capp' by Reginald Smythe (1917–); and the French 'Astérix' by Albert Uderzo and René Goscinny, which began in the early 1960s.

Comintern acronym for *Communist* ◊*International*.

command economy or *planned economy* economy where resources are allocated to factories by the state through central planning. This system is unresponsive to the needs and whims of consumers and to sudden changes in conditions (for example, crop failure or fluctuations in the world price of raw materials). For example, in the former USSR, state planners decided what was to be produced. They passed orders down to factories, allocating raw materials, workers, and other factors of production to them. Factories were then told how much they should produce with these resources and where they should be sent. If there was a shortage of goods in the shops, then goods would be rationed through queueing.

In theory, the time and money expended on advertising and marketing in a market-led economy can in a command economy instead be devoted to producing something useful. However, historical experience in the 20th century suggests that planned economies have not produced as high growth as free-market or mixed economies.

commando member of a specially trained, highly mobile military unit. The term originated in South Africa in the 19th century, where it referred to Boer military reprisal raids against Africans and, in the South African Wars, against the British. Commando units have often carried out operations behind enemy lines.

In Britain, the first commando units were the British Combined Operations Command who raided enemy-occupied territory in World War II after the evacuation of Dunkirk 1940. Among the commando raids were those on the Lofoten Islands (3–4 March 1941), Vaagsö, Norway (27 Dec 1941), St Nazaire (28 March 1942), and Dieppe (19 Aug 1942). In 1940 commandos were sent to the Middle East. One of their most daring exploits was the raid Nov 1941 on Rommel's headquarters in the desert. At the end of the war the army commandos were disbanded, but the role was carried on by the Royal Marines.

commedia dell'arte popular form of Italian improvised comic drama in the 16th and 17th centuries, performed by trained troupes of actors and involving stock characters and situations. It exerted considerable influence on writers such as Molière and Carlo Goldoni, and on the genres of ◊pantomime, harlequinade, and the Punch and Judy show. It laid the foundation for a tradition of mime, strong in France, that has continued with the modern mime of Jean-Louis Barrault and Marcel Marceau.

commensalism in biology, a relationship between two ◊species whereby one (the commensal) benefits from the association, whereas the other neither benefits nor suffers. For example, certain species of millipede and silverfish inhabit the nests of army ants and live by scavenging on the refuse of their hosts, but without affecting the ants.

commercial bank bank that offers services to personal and corporate customers, such as current and deposit accounts as well as loans and overdrafts (unlike savings banks or merchant banks). They offer a range of other services including foreign currency dealing, insurance, and pensions. The activities of commercial banks are regulated by a ◊central bank. The four largest commercial banks in the UK are the National Westminster, Midland, Barclays, and Lloyds.

commissioner for oaths in English law, a person appointed by the Lord Chancellor with power to administer oaths or take affidavits. All practising solicitors have these powers but must not use them in proceedings in which they are acting for any of the parties or in which they have an interest.

committal proceedings in the UK, a preliminary hearing in a magistrate's court to decide whether there is a case to answer before a higher court. The media may only report limited facts about committal proceedings, such as the name of the accused and the charges, unless the defendant asks for reporting restrictions to be lifted.

commodity something produced for sale. Commodities may be consumer goods, such as radios, or producer goods, such as copper bars. Commodity markets deal in raw or semi-raw materials that are amenable to grading and that can be stored for considerable periods without deterioration.

Commodity markets developed to their present form in the 19th century, when industrial growth facilitated trading in large, standardized quantities of raw materials. Most markets encompass trading in commodity futures – that is, trading for delivery several months ahead. Major commodity markets exist in Chicago, Tokyo, London, and elsewhere. Although specialized markets exist, such as that for silkworm cocoons in Tokyo, most trade relates to cereals and metals. Soft is a term used for most materials other than metals.

Commodus Lucius Aelius Aurelius AD 161–192. Roman emperor from 177 (jointly with his father), sole emperor from 180, son of Marcus Aurelius Antoninus. He was a tyrant, spending lavishly on gladiatorial combats, confiscating the property of the wealthy, persecuting the Senate, and renaming Rome 'Colonia Commodiana'. There were many attempts against his life, and he was finally strangled at the instigation of his mistress and advisers, who had discovered themselves on the emperor's death list.

Common Agricultural Policy (CAP) system of financial support for farmers in ◊European Union (EU) countries. The most important way in which EU farmers are supported is through guaranteeing them minimum prices for part of what they produce. The CAP has been criticized for its role in creating overproduction, and consequent environmental damage, and for the high price of food subsidies.

aims The CAP permits the member countries of the EU jointly to organize and control agricultural production within their boundaries. The objectives of the CAP were outlined in the ◊Treaty of Rome: to increase agricultural productivity, to provide a fair standard of living for farmers and their employees, to stabilize markets, and to assure the availability of supply at a price that was reasonable to the consumer.

history The policy, applied to most types of agricultural product, was evolved and introduced between 1962 and 1967, and has since been amended to take account of changing conditions and the entry of additional member states. At the heart of the CAP is a price support system based on setting a target price for a commodity, imposing a levy on cheaper imports, and intervening to buy produce at a predetermined level to maintain the stability of the internal market. When the CAP was devised, the six member states were net importers of most essential agricultural products, and the intervention mechanism was aimed at smoothing out occasional surpluses caused by an unusually productive season.

overproduction The CAP became extremely expensive in the 1970s and 1980s due to overproduction of those agricultural products that were subsidized. In many years, far more was produced than could be sold and it had to be stored, creating 'mountains' and 'lakes' of produce. This put the CAP under intense financial and political strain, and led to mounting pressure for reform.

common denominator denominator that is a common multiple of, and hence exactly divisible by, all the denominators of a set of fractions, and which therefore enables their sums or differences to be found. For example, $\frac{2}{3}$ and $\frac{3}{4}$ can both be converted to equivalent fractions of denominator 12, $\frac{2}{3}$ being equal to $\frac{8}{12}$ and $\frac{3}{4}$ to $\frac{9}{12}$. Hence their sum is $\frac{17}{12}$ and their difference is $\frac{1}{12}$. The lowest common denominator (lcd) is the smallest common multiple of a given set of fractions.

common land unenclosed wasteland, forest, and pasture used in common by the community at large. Poor people have throughout history gathered fruit, nuts, wood, reeds, roots, game, and so on from common land; in dry regions of India, for example, the landless derive 20% of their annual income in this way, together with much of their food and fuel. Codes of conduct evolved to ensure that common resources were not depleted. But in the 20th century, in the Third World as elsewhere, much common land has been privatized or appropriated by the state, and what remains is overburdened by those dependent on it.

In the UK, ◊enclosure of common land by powerful landowners began in the 14th century, becoming widespread in the 15th–16th centuries. It caused poverty, homelessness, and rural depopulation, and led to several revolts. Under the Commons Registration Act 1965, all remaining common land (such as village greens) had to be registered by a certain date, otherwise the rights of common were lost.

common law that part of the English law not embodied in legislation. It consists of rules of law based on common custom and usage and on judicial decisions. English common law became the basis of law in the USA and many other English-speaking countries.

common logarithm another name for a ◊logarithm to the base ten.

Common Market popular name for the *European Economic Community*; see ◊European Union.

Common Prayer, Book of the service book of the Church of England and the Episcopal Church, based largely on the Roman breviary. The church's *Alternative Service Book* 1980, in contemporary language, is also in use.

Commons, House of the lower but more powerful of the two parts of the British and Canadian ◊parliaments. In the UK, the House of Commons consists of 659 elected members of parliament each of whom represents a constituency. Its functions are to debate and legislate, and to scrutinize the activities of government.

commonwealth body politic founded on law for the common 'weal' or good. Political philosophers of the 17th century, such as Thomas Hobbes and John Locke, used the term to mean an organized political community. In Britain it was specifically applied to the regime (the Commonwealth) of Oliver ◊Cromwell 1649–60.

Commonwealth conference any consultation between the prime ministers (or defence, finance, foreign, or other ministers) of the sovereign independent members of the British Commonwealth. These are informal discussion meetings, and the implementation of policies is decided by individual governments.

Commonwealth Day public holiday celebrated on the second Monday in March in many parts of the Commonwealth. It was called Empire Day until 1958 and celebrated on 24 May (Queen Victoria's birthday) until 1966.

Commonwealth Games multisport gathering of competitors from British Commonwealth countries, held every four years. The first meeting (known as the British Empire Games) was in Hamilton, Canada, Aug 1930. *See list of tables on p. 1177.*

Commonwealth Immigration Acts successive acts to regulate the entry into the UK of British subjects from the Commonwealth. The Commonwealth Immigration Act, passed by the Conservative government 1962, ruled that Commonwealth immigrants entering Britain must have employment or be able to offer required skills. Further restrictions have been added.

Commonwealth of Independent States (CIS) successor body to the ◊Union of Soviet Socialist Republics, initially formed as a new commonwealth of Slav republics on 8 Dec 1991 by the presidents of the Russian Federation, Belarus, and Ukraine. On 21 Dec, eight of the nine remaining non-Slav republics – Moldova, Tajikistan, Armenia, Azerbaijan, Turkmenistan, Kazakhstan, Kyrgyzstan, and Uzbekistan – joined the CIS at a meeting held in Kazakhstan's capital, Alma-Ata (now Almaty). The CIS formally came into existence Jan 1992 when President Gorbachev resigned and the Soviet government voted itself out of existence. It has no real, formal political institutions and its role is uncertain. Its headquarters are in Minsk (Mensk), Belarus. Georgia joined 1994.

The main objectives in founding the CIS were to ensure that some measure of cooperation continued in economic, financial, and monetary matters in order to avert a collapse in inter-republican trade and to coordinate price liberalization and market reform; to maintain some degree of coordination in foreign (and especially military) policy, and in such areas as transport and communications; and to ensure recognition of borders and thus prevent inter-republican conflicts. With no formal political institutions, CIS decisions are arrived at through the holding of regular summits of heads of state and through the formation of ministerial committees, with, in theory, all CIS members being equals; however, some members have complained of its domination by Russia.

Initially, the inherited Soviet army was placed under a unified command. However, the majority of the republics subsequently set up their own independent conventional forces, and in 1993 it was agreed that the unified defence structure should be abolished and replaced by a committee of joint staff responsible for coordinating military cooperation between the individual states. At a Dec 1993 summit Russia secured bilateral agreements with all members excepting Moldova, Ukraine, and Uzbekistan, giving it 'the right to oversee military policies'. In 1994 the CIS successfully negotiated cease-fires in Abkhazia, Georgia, and in the Nagorno-Karabakh dispute between Armenia and Azerbaijan, stationing peacekeeping forces in these regions, as well as in Tajikistan. In the same year Kazakhstan, Kyrgyzstan, and Uzbekistan created their own social, economic, and military union. In March 1996, Russia, Belarus, Kazakhstan, and Kyrgyzstan went on to establish even closer economic ties. ▷ *See feature on pp. 1090–1091.*

Commonwealth, the (British) voluntary association of 53 countries and their dependencies, the majority of which once formed part of the ◊British Empire and are now independent sovereign states. They are all regarded as 'full members of the Commonwealth'; the newest member being Mozambique which was admitted Nov 1995. Additionally, there are some 20 territories that are not completely sovereign and remain dependencies of the UK or one of the other fully sovereign members, and are regarded as 'Commonwealth countries'. Heads of government meet every two years, apart from those of Nauru and Tuvalu; however, Nauru and Tuvalu have the right to participate in all functional activities. The Commonwealth has no charter or constitution, and is founded more on tradition and sentiment than on political or economic factors. However, it can make political statements by withdrawing membership; a recent example was Nigeria's suspension in Nov 1995 because of human-rights abuses.

Queen Elizabeth II was the formal head but not the ruler of 17 member states in 1995; 5 member states had their own monarchs; and 31 were republics. The Commonwealth secretariat, headed from Oct 1989 by Nigerian Emeka Anyaoko (1933–) as secretary general, is based in London. The secretariat's staff come from a number of member countries, which also pay its operating costs.

On 15 May 1917 Jan Smuts, representing South Africa in the imperial war cabinet of World War I, suggested that 'British Commonwealth of Nations' was the right title for the British Empire. The name was recognized in the Statute of Westminster 1931, but after World War II a growing sense of independent nationhood led to the simplification of the title to the Commonwealth.

commune group of people or families living together, sharing resources and responsibilities. Communes developed from early 17th-century religious communities such as the Rosicrucians and Muggletonians, to more radical groups such as the ◊Diggers and the ◊Quakers. Many groups moved to America to found communes, such as the Philadelphia Society (1680s) and the Shakers, which by 1800 had ten groups in North America. The Industrial Revolution saw a new wave of utopian communities associated with the ideas of Robert ◊Owen and Charles Fourier. Communes had a revival during the 1960s, when many small groups were founded.

The term also refers to a communal division or settlement in a communist country. In China, a policy of Mao Zedong involved the grouping of villages within districts (averaging 30,000 people); thus were cooperatives amalgamated into larger units, the communes. 1958 (the ◊Great Leap Forward) saw the establishment of people's communes (workers' combines) with shared living quarters and shared meals. Communes organized workers' brigades and were responsible for their own nurseries, schools, clinics, and other facilities.

The term can also refer to the 11th-century to 12th-century association of ◊burghers in N and central Italy. The communes of many cities asserted their independence from the overlordship of either the Holy Roman emperor or the pope, only to fall under the domination of oligarchies or despots during the 13th and 14th centuries.

Commune, Paris two separate periods in the history of Paris 1789–94 and March–May 1871; see ◊Paris Commune.

communication in biology, the signalling of information by one organism to another, usually with the intention of altering the recipient's behaviour. Signals used in communication may be ***visual*** (such as the human smile or the display of colourful plumage in birds), auditory (for example, the whines or barks of a dog), olfactory (such as the odours released by the scent glands of a deer), electrical (as in the pulses emitted by electric fish), or tactile (for example, the nuzzling of male and female elephants).

communication the sending and receiving of messages. The messages can be verbal or nonverbal; verbal messages can be spoken or written, and transmitted in a variety of ways (see ◊telecommunications). Most nonverbal messages between human beings are in the form of body language.

communications satellite relay station in space for sending telephone, television, telex, and other messages around the world. Messages are sent to and from the satellites via ground stations. Most communications satellites are in ◊geostationary orbit, appearing to hang fixed over one point on the Earth's surface.

The first satellite to carry TV signals across the Atlantic Ocean was *Telstar* in July 1962. The world is now linked by a system of communications satellites called Intelsat. Other satellites are used by individual countries for internal communications, or for business or military use. A new generation of satellites, called direct broadcast satellites, are powerful enough to transmit direct to small domestic aerials. The power for such satellites is produced by solar cells (see ◊solar energy).

Communion, Holy in the Christian church, another name for the ◊Eucharist.

communism (French *commun* 'common, general') revolutionary socialism based on the theories of the political philosophers Karl ◊Marx and Friedrich ◊Engels, emphasizing common ownership of the means of production and a planned economy. The principle held is that each should work according to his or her capacity and receive according to his or her needs. Politically, it seeks the overthrow of capitalism through a proletarian revolution. The first communist state was the USSR after the revolution of 1917. Revolutionary socialist parties and groups united to form communist parties in other countries during the interwar years. After World War II, communism was enforced in those countries that came under Soviet occupation.

China emerged after 1961 as a rival to the USSR in world communist leadership, and other countries attempted to adapt communism to their own needs. The late 1980s saw a movement for more individual freedoms in many communist countries, culminating in the abolition or overthrow of communist rule in Eastern European countries and Mongolia, and further state repression in China. The failed hardline coup in the USSR against President Gorbachev 1991 resulted in the abandonment of communism there. However, in Dec 1995 the communists polled strongly in Russian parliamentary elections. Reform communist parties have also recovered some strength in central and Eastern Europe, forming governments in Hungary, Lithuania, and Poland from 1993.

Communism as the ideology of a nation state survives in only a few countries, notably China, Cuba, North Korea, Laos, and Vietnam, where market forces are being encouraged in the economic sphere.

communism and social democracy Marx and Engels in the *Communist Manifesto* 1848 put forward the theory that human society, having passed through successive stages of slavery, feudalism, and capitalism, must advance to communism. This combines with a belief in economic determinism to form the central communist concept of dialectical materialism. Marx believed that capitalism had become a barrier to progress and needed to be replaced by a dictatorship of the proletariat (working class), which would build a socialist society. The Social Democratic parties formed in Europe in the second half of the 19th century professed to be Marxist, but gradually began to aim at reforms of capitalist society rather than at the radical social change envisaged by Marx. The Russian Social Democratic Labour Party, led by Vladimir ◊Lenin, remained Marxist, and after the Nov 1917 revolution changed its name to Communist Party to emphasize its difference from Social Democratic parties elsewhere. The communal basis of feudalism was still strong in Russia, and Lenin and Joseph ◊Stalin were able to impose the communist system. China's communist revolution was completed 1949 under ◊Mao Zedong.

China and Russia Both China and the USSR took strong measures to maintain or establish their own types of 'orthodox' communism in countries on their borders (the USSR in Hungary and Czechoslovakia, and China in North Korea and Vietnam). In more remote areas (the USSR in the Arab world and Cuba, and China in Albania) and (both of them) in the newly emergent African countries, these orthodoxies were installed as the fount of doctrine and the source of technological aid.

uprisings and dissent In 1956 the Soviet premier Nikita ◊Khrushchev denounced Stalinism, and there were uprisings in Hungary and Poland. During the late 1960s and the 1970s it was debated whether the state required to be maintained as 'the dictatorship of the proletariat' once revolution on the economic front was achieved, or whether it then became the state of the entire people: Engels, Lenin, Khrushchev, and ◊Liu Shaoqi held the latter view; Stalin and Mao the former.

communist grip weakens After the 1960s communist parties in many capitalist countries (for example, Japan and the Eurocommunism of France, Italy, and the major part of the British Communist Party) rejected Soviet dominance. In the 1980s there was an expansion of political and economic freedom in Eastern Europe: the USSR remained a single-party state, but with a relaxation of strict party orthodoxy and a policy of *perestroika* ('restructuring'), while the other Warsaw Pact countries moved towards an end to communist rule and its replacement by free elections within more democratic political systems. However, the 1995 Russian parliamentary and presidential elections showed that the communists still had significant popular support.

Other manifestations of communism have included Libya's attempt to combine revolutionary socialism with Islam and the devastation of Cambodia (then called Kampuchea) by the extreme communist Khmer Rouge 1975–78. Latin America suffered from the US fear of communism, with the democratically elected Marxist regime in Chile violently overthrown 1973, and the socialist government of Nicaragua (until it fell 1990) involved in a prolonged civil war against US-backed guerrillas (Contras).

In 1991, the British Communist Party changed its name to the Democratic Left. The red and black logo was replaced by a red (traditional), purple (women's suffrage), and green (environment) one.

Communism Peak alternative form of Pik ◊Kommunizma, the highest mountain in the ◊Pamirs.

community in ecology, an assemblage of plants, animals, and other organisms living within a circumscribed area. Communities are usually named by reference to a dominant feature such as characteristic plant species (for example, a beech-wood community), or a prominent physical feature (for example, a freshwater-pond community).

community in the social sciences, the sense of identity, purpose, and companionship that comes from belonging to a particular place, organization, or social group. The concept dominated sociological thinking in the first half of the 20th century, and inspired the academic discipline of community studies.

'Communism is not love. Communism is a hammer which we use to crush the enemy.'

On COMMUNISM
Mao Zedong quoted in *Time* 18 Dec 1950

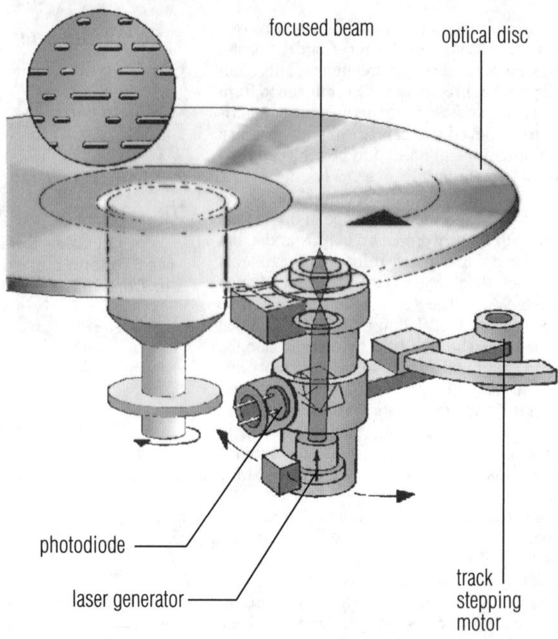

compact disc The compact disc is a digital storage device; music is recorded as a series of etched pits representing numbers in digital code. During playing, a laser scans the pits and the pattern of reflected light reveals the numbers representing the sound recorded. The optical signal is converted to electrical form by a photocell and sent to the amplifiers and loudspeakers.

community architecture movement enabling people to work directly with architects in the design and building of their own homes and neighbourhoods. Projects include housing at Byker, Newcastle, UK, by Ralph ◊Erskine, and the work of the Lewisham Self-Build Housing Association, London, 1977–80, pioneered by Walter Segal (1907–1985); the revitalization of the town of Bologna, Italy; and the University of Louvain, Belgium, by Lucien Kroll (1927–).

community council in Wales, name for a ◊parish council.

Community law law of the member states of the ◊European Union, as adopted by the Council of Ministers. The ◊European Court of Justice interprets and applies EU law. Community law forms part of the law of states and prevails over national law. In the UK, community law became effective after enactment of the European Communities Act 1972.

community school/education system based on the philosophy asserting that educational institutions are more effective if they involve all members of the surrounding community. It was pioneered by Henry Morris during his time as chief education officer for Cambridgeshire 1922–54.

community service in the penal systems of the UK and the USA, unpaid work in the service of the community (aiding children, the elderly, or the disabled), performed by a convicted person by order of the court as an alternative to prison. The scheme was introduced in Britain by the Criminal Justice Act 1972. In English law, the person must be over 16 years, have been convicted of a nonviolent offence punishable with imprisonment, and consent to the making of the order. Breach of a community service order may result in a fine or an alternative sentence.

commutative operation in mathematics, an operation that is independent of the order of the numbers or symbols concerned. For example, addition is commutative: the result of adding $4 + 2$ is the same as that of adding $2 + 4$; subtraction is not as $4 - 2 = 2$, but $2 - 4 = -2$. Compare ◊associative operation and ◊distributive operation.

commutator device in a DC (direct-current) electric motor that reverses the current flowing in the armature coils as the armature rotates.

Como city in Lombardy, Italy, on Lake Como at the foot of the Alps; population (1990) 90,000. Motorcycles, glass, silk, and furniture are produced here. The river Adda flows N–S through the lake, and the shores are extremely beautiful. Como has a marble cathedral, built 1396–1732, and is a tourist resort.

Comoros group of islands in the Indian Ocean between Madagascar and the east coast of Africa. Three of them – Njazidja, Nzwani, and Mwali – form the republic of Comoros; the fourth island, Mayotte, is a French dependency. *See country box below.*

compact disc (or ***CD***) disc for storing digital information, about 12 cm/4.5 in across, mainly used for music, when it can have over an hour's playing time. The compact disc is made of aluminium with a transparent plastic coating; the metal disc underneath is etched by a ◊laser beam with microscopic pits that carry a digital code representing the sounds. During playback, a laser beam reads the code and produces signals that are changed into near-exact replicas of the original sounds. Compact discs were launched 1983.

CD-ROM, or Compact-Disc Read-Only Memory, is used to store written text, pictures, and video clips in addition to music. The discs are ideal for large works, such as catalogues and encyclopedias. CD-I, or Compact-Disc Interactive, is a form of CD-ROM used with a computerized reader, which responds intelligently to the user's instructions. Recordable CDs, called WORMs ('write once, read many times'), are used as computer discs, but are as yet too expensive for home use. Video CDs store an hour of video. High-density video discs, first publicly demonstrated 1995, can hold full-length features. Erasable CDs, which can be erased and recorded many times, are also used by the computer industry. These are coated with a compound of cobalt and the rare earth metal gadolinium, which alters the polarization of light falling on it. In the reader, the light reflected from the disc is passed through polarizing filters and the changes in polarization are converted into electrical signals.

Companies Act 1980 act of Parliament which governs modern company law in the UK. In particular, it defines the difference between a ◊private limited company and a ◊public limited company.

Companion of Honour British order of chivalry, founded by George V 1917. It is of one class only, and carries no title, but Companions append 'CH' to their names. The number is limited to 65 and the award is made to both men and women.

company in the army, a subunit of a ◊battalion. It consists of about 120 soldiers, and is commanded by a major in the British army, a captain in the US army. Four or five companies make a battalion. In British tank and engineer battalions, a company is known as a squadron. In British artillery battalions, a company is known as a battery.

company in economics, a number of people grouped together as a business enterprise. Types of company include public limited companies, partnerships, joint ventures, sole proprietorships, and branches of foreign companies. Most companies are private and, unlike public companies, cannot offer their shares to the general public.

For most companies in Britain the liability of the members is limited to the amount of their

COMOROS
Federal Islamic Republic of

national name *Jumhurīyat al-Qumur al-Itthādīyah al-Islāmīyah* or *République Fédérale Islamique des Comoros*
area 1,862 sq km/719 sq mi
capital Moroni
major towns/cities Mutsamudu, Domoni, Fomboni
physical features comprises the volcanic islands of Njazídja, Nzwani, and Mwali (formerly Grande Comore, Anjouan, Moheli); at N end of Mozambique Channel in Indian Ocean between Madagascar and coast of Africa
head of state Said Massounde from 1998
head of government Ahmed Abdou from 1996
political system emergent democracy
administrative divisions each main island has a certain amount of autonomy in a very limited form of federalism
political parties National Union for Democracy in the Comoros (UNDC), Islamic, nationalist; Rally for Democracy and Renewal (RDR), left of centre
population 544,000 (1995 est)
population growth rate 3.7% (1990–95)
ethnic distribution population of mixed origin, with Africans, Arabs, and Malaysians predominating; the principal ethnic group is the Antalaotra
life expectancy 56 (males), 57 (females)
literacy rate 61%
languages Arabic (official), Comorian (Swahili and Arabic dialect), Makua, French
religion Muslim; Islam is the state religion
currency Comorian franc
GDP (US $) 360 million (1993 est)
growth rate 0.9% (1994)
exports copra, vanilla, sisal, coffee, cloves, essential oils

HISTORY
5th century AD First settled by Malay-Polynesian immigrants.
7th C Converted to Islam by Arab seafarers and fell under the rule of local sultans.
late 16th C First visited by European navigators.
mid to late 19th C Mayotte became a French protectorate (1843), followed by Grande Comore, Moheli island, and Anjouan (1886).
1904 Slave trade abolished, ending influx of Africans.
1912 Grande Comore and Anjouan, the main islands, joined Moheli to become a French colony, which was attached to Madagascar from 1914.
1947 Became a French Overseas Territory separate from Madagascar.
1961 Internal self-government achieved.
1975 Independence achieved from France (island of Mayotte to the SE had voted to remain part of France 1974). Comoros (with Mayotte) joined the United Nations.
1976 President Ahmed Abdallah overthrown in a coup by Ali Soilih; relations deteriorated with France as a Maoist-Islamic socialist programme was pursued.
1978 Soilih killed by French mercenaries led by Bob Denard. Federal Islamic republic proclaimed, with exiled Abdallah restored as president; diplomatic relations re-established with France.
1979 The Comoros became a one-party state; powers of the federal government increased.
1989 Abdallah killed by French mercenaries who, under French and South African pressure, turned authority over to French administration; Said Muhammad Djohar became president in a multiparty democracy.
1990–92 Antigovernment coups foiled.
1993 Djohar's supporters won overall majority in assembly elections.
1995 Djohar overthrown in coup led by Col Denard, who was persuaded to withdraw by French troops.
1996 Djohar allowed to return from exile in a non-political capacity and Muhammad Taki Abdoulkarim elected president. Ahmed Abdou appointed prime minister.
1998 Said Massounde becomes president.

SEE ALSO Mayotte

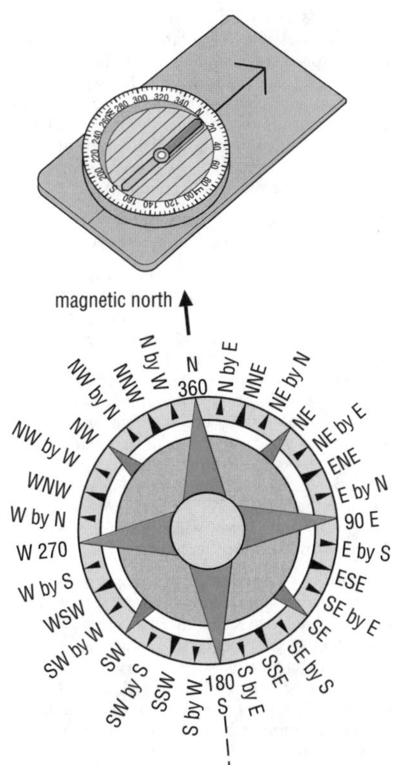

compass As early as 2500 BC, the Chinese were using pieces of magnetic rock, magnetite, as simple compasses. By the 12th century, European navigators were using compasses consisting of a needle-shaped magnet floating in a bowl of water.

subscription, under an act of 1855 promoted by Judge Lord Bramwell. This brought British law into line with European practice, which had already been largely adopted in the USA. This limitation of liability is essential when large capital sums must be raised by the contributions of many individuals. The affairs of companies are managed by directors, a public company having at least two, and their accounts must be audited.

compass any instrument for finding direction. The most commonly used is a magnetic compass, consisting of a thin piece of magnetic material with the north-seeking pole indicated, free to rotate on a pivot and mounted on a compass card on which the points of the compass are marked. When the compass is properly adjusted and used, the north-seeking pole will point to the magnetic north, from which true north can be found from tables of magnetic corrections.

Compasses not dependent on the magnet are gyrocompasses, dependent on the ◊gyroscope, and radiocompasses, dependent on the use of radio. These are unaffected by the presence of iron and by magnetic anomalies of the Earth's magnetic field, and are widely used in ships and aircraft. See ◊navigation.

compensation in law, money paid to a person who has suffered injury, loss, or damage. If a crime has been committed, compensation can be claimed from various official bodies and through the courts, depending on the circumstances.

competition in ecology, the interaction between two or more organisms, or groups of organisms (for example, species), that use a common resource which is in short supply. Competition invariably results in a reduction in the numbers of one or both competitors, and in ◊evolution contributes both to the decline of certain species and to the evolution of ◊adaptations.

competition in economics, rivalry in the marketplace between different business organizations, usually competition for custom between those who have the same commodities to dispose of. Firms can make their products competitive in price, quality, availability, and delivery dates, for example, or compete through advertising.

complement in mathematics, the set of the elements within the universal set that are not contained in the designated set. For example, if the universal set is the set of all positive whole numbers and the designated set S is the set of all even numbers, then the complement of S (denoted S') is the set of all odd numbers.

complementary angles two angles that add up to 90°.

complementary number in number theory, the number obtained by subtracting a number from its base. For example, the complement of 7 in numbers to base 10 is 3. Complementary numbers are necessary in computing, as the only mathematical operation of which digital computers (including pocket calculators) are directly capable is addition. Two numbers can be subtracted by adding one number to the complement of the other; two numbers can be divided by using successive subtraction (which, using complements, becomes successive addition); and multiplication can be performed by using successive addition.

complementation in genetics, the interaction that can occur between two different mutant alleles of a gene in a ◊diploid organism, to make up for each other's deficiencies and allow the organism to function normally.

complex in psychology, a group of ideas and feelings that have become repressed because they are distasteful to the person in whose mind they arose, but are still active in the depths of the person's unconscious mind, continuing to affect his or her life and actions.

complex number in mathematics, a number written in the form $a + ib$, where a and b are ◊real numbers and i is the square root of -1 (that is, $i^2 = -1$); i used to be known as the 'imaginary' part of the complex number. Some equations in algebra, such as those of the form $x^2 + 5 = 0$, cannot be solved without recourse to complex numbers, because the real numbers do not include square roots of negative numbers.

The sum of two or more complex numbers is obtained by adding separately their real and imaginary parts, for example:

$$(a + bi) + (c + di) = (a + c) + (b + d)i$$

Complex numbers can be represented graphically on an Argand diagram, which uses rectangular ◊Cartesian coordinates in which the x-axis represents the real part of the number and the y-axis the imaginary part. Thus the number $z = a + bi$ is plotted as the point (a, b). Complex numbers have applications in various areas of science, such as the theory of alternating currents in electricity.

complementary medicine systems of medical care based on methods of treatment or theories of disease that differ from those taught in most western medical schools. See ◊medicine, alternative.

component in physics, one of two or more vectors, normally at right angles to each other, that add together to produce the same effect as a single resultant vector. Any ◊vector quantity, such as force, velocity, or electric field, can be resolved into components chosen for ease of calculation. For example, the weight of a body resting on a slope can be resolved into two force components, one normal to the slope and the other parallel to the slope.

composite in industry, purpose-designed engineering material created by combining single materials with complementary properties into a composite form. Most composites have a structure in which one component consists of discrete elements, such as fibres, dispersed in a continuous matrix. For example, lengths of asbestos, glass, or carbon steel, or 'whiskers' (specially grown crystals a few millimetres long) of substances such as silicon carbide may be dispersed in plastics, concrete, or steel.

compost organic material decomposed by bacteria under controlled conditions to make a nutrient-rich natural fertilizer for gardening or farming.

compound chemical substance made up of two or more ◊elements bonded together, so that they cannot be separated by physical means. Compounds are held together by ionic or covalent bonds.

comprehensive school secondary school that admits pupils of all abilities, and therefore without any academic selection procedure. Most secondary education in the USA and the USSR has always been comprehensive, but most W European countries, including France and the UK, switched from a selective to a comprehensive system after about 1970.

In England, the 1960s and 1970s saw a slow but major reform of secondary education, in which most state-funded local authorities replaced selective grammar schools (taking only the most academic 20% of children) and secondary modern schools (for the remainder), with comprehensive schools capable of providing suitable courses for children of all abilities. Scotland and Wales have switched completely to comprehensive education, while Northern Ireland retains a largely selective system.

compressor machine that compresses a gas, usually air, commonly used to power pneumatic tools, such as road drills, paint sprayers, and dentist's drills.

Compton Denis Charles Scott 1918–1997. English cricketer and football player. In the 1947 English season he scored a record 3,816 runs (averaging 90.85) and 18 hundreds. As a footballer, he played for Arsenal, and in 12 wartime internationals for England.

Compton-Burnett Ivy 1884–1969. English novelist. She used dialogue to show reactions of small groups of characters dominated by the tyranny of family relationships. Her novels, set at the turn of the century, include *Pastors and Masters*

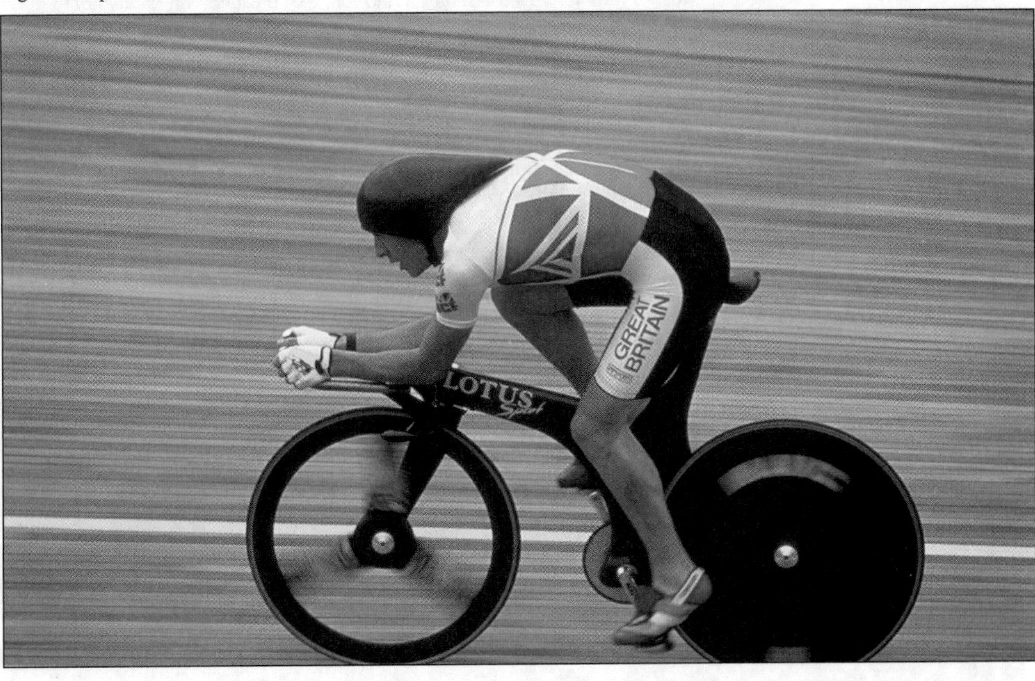

composite Chris Boardman breaking the 5-km/3.1-mi world-record time on a bicycle built from a composite material. In this instance the composite material has been designed to allow the lightest, most aerodynamic bicycle frame to be built, which is still strong enough to endure the stresses of racing. *Image Select (UK) Ltd*

‘Men are not allowed to think freely about chemistry and biology, why should they be allowed to think freely about political philosophy?’

Auguste Comte
Positive Philosophy

1925, *More Women than Men* 1933, and *Mother and Son* 1955.

compulsory purchase in the UK, the right of the state and authorized bodies to buy land required for public purposes even against the wishes of the owner. Under the Land Compensation Act 1973, fair recompense is payable.

CompuServe large (US-based) public on-line information service, established 1979. It is widely used for ◊electronic mail and ◊bulletin boards, as well as access to large periodical databases. It is easier to use than the Internet and most computer hardware and software suppliers provide support for their products on CompuServe.

computer programmable electronic device that processes data and performs calculations and other symbol-manipulation tasks. There are three types: the ◊***digital computer***, which manipulates information coded as binary numbers (see ◊binary number system); the ***analogue computer***, which works with continuously varying quantities (see ◊analogue); and the ***hybrid computer***, which has characteristics of both analogue and digital computers.

There are four types of digital computer, corresponding roughly to their size and intended use. ***Microcomputers*** are the smallest and most common, used in small businesses, at home, and in schools. They are usually single-user machines. ***Minicomputers*** are found in medium-sized businesses and university departments. They may support from 10 to 200 or so users at once. ***Mainframes***, which can often service several hundred users simultaneously, are found in large organizations, such as national companies and government departments. ***Supercomputers*** are mostly used for highly complex scientific tasks, such as analysing the results of nuclear physics experiments and weather forecasting.

Microcomputers now come in a range of sizes from battery-powered pocket PCs and electronic organizers, notebook and laptop PCs to floor-standing tower systems that may serve local area ◊networks or work as minicomputers. Indeed, most minicomputers are now built using low-cost microprocessors, and large-scale computers built out of multiple microprocessors are starting to challenge traditional mainframe and supercomputer designs.

computer-aided design use of computers to create and modify design drawings; see ◊CAD.

computer-aided manufacturing use of computers to regulate production processes in industry; see ◊CAM.

computer art art produced with the help of a computer. Since the 1950s the aesthetic use of computers has been increasingly evident in most artistic disciplines, including film animation, architecture, and music. ◊Computer graphics has been the most developed area, with the ‘paint-box’ computer liberating artists from the confines of the canvas. It is now also possible to programme computers in advance to generate graphics, music, and sculpture, according to ‘instructions’ which may include a preprogrammed element of unpredictability. In this last function, computer technology has been seen as a way of challenging the elitist nature of art by putting artistic creativity within relatively easy reach of anyone owning a computer.

computer-assisted learning use of computers in education and training; see ◊CAL.

computer game or ***video game*** any computer-controlled game in which the computer (sometimes) opposes the human player. Computer games typically employ fast, animated graphics on a ◊VDU (visual display unit) and synthesized sound.

Commercial computer games became possible with the advent of the ◊microprocessor in the mid-1970s and rapidly became popular as amusement-arcade games, using dedicated chips. Available games range from chess to fighter-plane simulations. Some of the most popular computer games in the early 1990s were id Software's *Wolfenstein 3D* and *Doom*, which are designed to be played across networks including the Internet.

computer graphics use of computers to display and manipulate information in pictorial form. Input may be achieved by scanning an image, by drawing with a mouse or stylus on a graphics tablet, or by drawing directly on the screen with a light pen. The output may be as simple as a pie chart, or as complex as an animated sequence in a science-fiction film, or a seemingly three-dimensional engineering blueprint. The drawing is stored in the computer as ◊raster graphics or ◊vector graphics. Computer graphics are increasingly used in computer-aided design (◊CAD), and to generate models and simulations in engineering, meteorology, medicine and surgery, and other fields of science.

computerized axial tomography medical technique, usually known as ◊CAT scan, for non-invasive investigation of disease or injury.

computer output on microfilm/microfiche (COM) technique for producing computer output in very compact, photographically reduced form (◊microform).

computer program coded instructions for a computer; see ◊program.

computer simulation representation of a real-life situation in a computer program. For example, the program might simulate the flow of customers arriving at a bank. The user can alter variables, such as the number of cashiers on duty, and see the effect. More complex simulations can model the behaviour of chemical reactions or even nuclear explosions. The behaviour of solids and liquids at high temperatures can be simulated using quantum simulation, the use of computer simulation to study the behaviour of matter. Computers also control the actions of machines – for example, a ◊flight simulator models the behaviour of real aircraft and allows training to take place in safety. Computer simulations are useful when it is too dangerous, time consuming, or simply impossible to carry out a real experiment.

computer terminal the device whereby the operator communicates with the computer; see ◊terminal.

Comte (Isidore) Auguste (Marie François Xavier) 1798–1857. French philosopher regarded as the founder of sociology, a term he coined 1830. He sought to establish sociology as an intellectual discipline, using a scientific approach (‘positivism’) as the basis of a new science of social order and social development.

In his six-volume *Cours de philosophie positive* 1830–42, Comte argued that human thought and social development evolve through three stages: the theological, the metaphysical, and the positive or scientific. Although he originally sought to proclaim society's evolution to a new golden age of science, industry, and rational morality, his radical ideas were increasingly tempered by the political and social upheavals of his time. His influence continued in Europe and the USA until the early 20th century.

Conakry capital and chief port of the Republic of Guinea; population (1992) 950,000. It is on the island of Tumbo, linked with the mainland by a

COMPUTER: TIMELINE

1614	John Napier invented logarithms.
1615	William Oughtred invented the slide rule.
1645	Blaise Pascal produced a calculator.
1672–74	Gottfried Leibniz built his first calculator, the Stepped Reckoner.
1801	Joseph-Marie Jacquard developed an automatic loom controlled by punch cards.
1820	The first mass-produced calculator, the Arithometer, was developed by Charles Thomas de Colmar (1785–1870).
1822	Charles Babbage completed his first model for the difference engine.
1830s	Babbage created the first design for the analytical engine.
1890	Herman Hollerith developed the punched-card ruler for the US census.
1936	Alan Turing published the mathematical theory of computing.
1939	US mathematician and physicist J V Atanasoff (1903–1995) became the first to use electronic means for mechanizing arithmetical operations.
1943	The Colossus electronic code-breaker was developed at Bletchley Park, England. The Harvard University Mark I or Automatic Sequence Controlled Calculator (partly financed by IBM) became the first program-controlled calculator.
1946	ENIAC (acronym for electronic numerator, integrator, analyser, and computer), the first general purpose, fully electronic digital computer, was completed at the University of Pennsylvania, USA.
1948	Manchester University (England) Mark I, the first stored-program computer, was completed. William Shockley of Bell Laboratories invented the transistor.
1951	Launch of Ferranti Mark I, the first commercially produced computer. Whirlwind, the first real-time computer, was built for the US air-defence system. Grace Murray Hopper of Remington Rand invented the compiler computer program.
1952	EDVAC (acronym for electronic discrete variable computer) was completed at the Institute for Advanced Study, Princeton, USA (by John Von Neumann).
1953	Magnetic core memory was developed.
1958	The first integrated circuit was constructed.
1963	The first minicomputer was built by Digital Equipment (DEC). The first electronic calculator was built by Bell Punch Company.
1964	Launch of IBM System/360, the first compatible family of computers. John Kemeny and Thomas Kurtz of Dartmouth College invented BASIC (Beginner's All-purpose Symbolic Instruction Code), a computer language.
1965	The first supercomputer, the Control Data CD6600, was developed.
1971	The first microprocessor, the Intel 4004, was announced.
1974	CLIP-4, the first computer with a parallel architecture, was developed by John Backus at IBM.
1975	Altair 8800, the first personal computer (PC), or microcomputer, was launched.
1981	The Xerox Star system, the first WIMP system (acronym for windows, icons, menus, and pointing devices), was developed. IBM launched the IBM PC.
1984	Apple launched the Macintosh computer. Internet begins as a means to allow US universities to share supercomputing centres.
1985	The Inmos T414 transputer, the first 'off-the-shelf' microprocessor for building parallel computers, was announced.
1988	An optical microprocessor, using light instead of electricity, was developed.
1989	Launch of wafer-scale silicon memory chips, able to store 200 million characters.
1990	Microsoft released Windows 3, a popular windowing environment for PCs.
1992	Philips launched the CD-I (Compact-Disc Interactive) player, based on CD audio technology, to provide interactive multimedia programs for the home user.
1993	Intel launched the Pentium chip containing 3.1 million transistors and capable of 100 MIPs (millions of instructions per second). The Personal Digital Assistant (PDA), which recognizes user's handwriting, went on sale.
1995	Intel launched the Pentium Pro microprocessor.
1997	In the USA, an attempt to bring legislation to control the Internet, intended to prevent access to sexual material, is rejected as unconstitutional.
1998	Plans announced in the USA for Internet2.

causeway and by rail with Kankan, 480 km/300 mi to the NE. Bauxite and iron ore are mined nearby.

concave of a surface, curving inwards, or away from the eye. For example, a bowl appears concave when viewed from above. In geometry, a concave polygon is one that has an interior angle greater than 180°. Concave is the opposite of ◊convex.

concave lens lens that possesses at least one surface that curves inwards. It is a diverging lens, spreading out those light rays that have been refracted through it. A concave lens is thinner at its centre than at its edges, and is used to correct short-sightedness. Common forms include the biconcave lens (with both surfaces curved inwards) and the plano-concave (with one flat surface and one concave). The whole lens may be further curved overall, making a convexo-concave or diverging meniscus lens, as in some lenses used for corrective purposes.

concave mirror curved mirror that reflects light from its inner surface. It may be either circular or parabolic in section. A concave mirror converges light rays to form a reduced, inverted, real image in front, or an enlarged, upright, virtual image seemingly behind it, depending on how close the object is to the mirror.

concentration in chemistry, the amount of a substance (solute) present in a specified amount of a solution. Either amount may be specified as a mass or a volume (liquids only). Common units used are ◊moles per cubic decimetre, grams per cubic decimetre, grams per 100 cubic centimetres, and grams per 100 grams.

The term also refers to the process of increasing the concentration of a solution by removing some of the substance (◊solvent) in which the solute is dissolved. In a concentrated solution, the solute is present in large quantities. Concentrated brine is around 30% sodium chloride in water; concentrated caustic soda (caustic liquor) is around 40% sodium hydroxide; and concentrated sulphuric acid is 98% acid.

concentration camp prison camp for civilians in wartime or under totalitarian rule. The first concentration camps were devised by the British during the Second Boer War in South Africa 1899 for the detention of Afrikaner women and children (with the subsequent deaths of more than 20,000 people). A system of hundreds of concentration camps was developed by the Nazis in Germany and occupied Europe (1933–45) to imprison Jews and political and ideological opponents after Adolf ◊Hitler became chancellor Jan 1933. The most infamous camps in World War II were the extermination camps of Auschwitz, Belsen, Dachau, Maidanek, Sobibor, and Treblinka. The total number of people who died at the camps exceeded 6 million, and some inmates were subjected to medical experimentation before being killed.

At Auschwitz, a vast camp complex was created for imprisonment and slave labour as well as the extermination of up to 4 million people in gas chambers or by other means. In addition to Jews, the victims included Gypsies, homosexuals, and 'misfits' or 'unwanted' people. At Maidanek, about 1.5 million people were exterminated, cremated, and their ashes used as fertilizer. Many camp officials and others responsible were tried after 1945 for war crimes, and executed or imprisoned. Foremost was Adolf ◊Eichmann, the architect of the extermination system, who was tried and executed by the state of Israel 1961.

concentric circles two or more circles that share the same centre.

Concepción city in Chile, near the mouth of the river Bió-Bió; population (1992) 330,400. It is the capital of the province of Concepción. It is in a rich agricultural district and is also an industrial centre for coal, steel, paper, and textiles.

Conceptual art or ***Concept art***, ***Conceptualism*** style of art, originating in the 1960s in the USA, that aims to express ideas rather than create visual images. Its materials include, among others, photographs, written information, diagrams, sound, and video tapes. Continuing the tradition of ◊Dada and ◊anti-art, Conceptual art aims to raise questions about the nature of art by flouting artistic conventions. As well as its theorist Sol LeWitt (1928–), its practitioners include Joseph Kosuth (1945–), Allan Krapow, and Bruce Nauman (1941–).

concertina portable reed organ related to the ◊accordion but smaller in size and hexagonal in shape, with buttons for keys. It was invented in England in the 19th century.

concerto composition, usually in three movements, for solo instrument (or instruments) and orchestra. It developed during the 18th century from the concerto grosso form for string orchestra, in which a group of solo instruments (concerto) is contrasted with a full orchestra (ripieno).

Conchobar in Celtic mythology, king of Ulster whose intended bride, Deirdre, eloped with Noísi. She died of sorrow when Conchobar killed her husband and his brothers.

conclave (Latin 'a room locked with a key') secret meeting, in particular the gathering of cardinals in Rome to elect a new pope. They are locked away in the Vatican Palace until they have reached a decision. The result of each ballot is announced by a smoke signal – black for an undecided vote and white when the choice is made.

Concord town in Massachusetts, USA, now a suburb of Boston; population (1990) 17,300. Concord was settled 1635 and was the site of the first battle of the American Revolution, 19 April 1775.

concordance book containing an alphabetical list of the important words in a major work, with reference to the places in which they occur. The first concordance was one for the Latin Vulgate Bible compiled by a Dominican monk in the 13th century.

concordat agreement regulating relations between the papacy and a secular government, for example, that for France between Pius VII and the emperor Napoleon, which lasted 1801–1905; Mussolini's concordat, which lasted 1929–78 and safeguarded the position of the church in Italy; and one of 1984 in Italy in which Roman Catholicism ceased to be the Italian state religion.

Concorde the only supersonic airliner, which cruises at Mach 2, or twice the speed of sound, about 2,170 kph/1,350 mph. Concorde, the result of Anglo-French cooperation, made its first flight 1969 and entered commercial service seven years later. It is 62 m/202 ft long and has a wing span of nearly 26 m/84 ft. Developing Concorde cost French and British taxpayers £2 billion.

concrete building material composed of cement, stone, sand, and water. It has been used since Egyptian and Roman times. Since the late 19th century, it has been increasingly employed as an economical alternative to materials such as brick and wood, and has been combined with steel to increase its tension capacity.

◊Reinforced concrete and ◊prestressed concrete are strengthened by combining concrete with another material, such as steel rods or glass fibres. The addition of carbon fibres to concrete increases its conductivity. The electrical resistance of the concrete changes with increased stress or fracture, so this 'smart concrete' can be used as an early indicator of structural damage.

concrete music (French ***musique concrète***) music created by reworking natural sounds recorded on disc or tape, developed 1948 by Pierre Schaeffer and Pierre Henry in the drama studios of Paris Radio. Concrete sound is pre-recorded natural sound used in electronic music, as distinct from purely synthesized tones or noises.

concurrent lines two or more lines passing through a single point; for example, the diameters of a circle are all concurrent at the centre of the circle.

concussion temporary unconsciousness resulting from a blow to the head. It is often followed by amnesia for events immediately preceding the blow.

Condé Louis de Bourbon, Prince of Condé 1530–1569. Prominent French ◊Huguenot leader, founder of the house of Condé and uncle of Henry IV of France. He fought in the wars between Henry II and the Holy Roman emperor Charles V, including the defence of Metz.

Condé Louis II 1621–1686. Prince of Condé, called the Great Condé. French commander who won brilliant victories during the Thirty Years' War at Rocroi 1643 and Lens 1648, but rebelled 1651 and entered the Spanish service. Pardoned 1660, he commanded Louis XIV's armies against the Spanish and the Dutch.

condensation in organic chemistry, a reaction in which two organic compounds combine to form a larger molecule, accompanied by the removal of a smaller molecule (usually water). This is also known as an addition–elimination reaction. Polyamides (such as nylon) and polyesters (such as Terylene) are made by condensation ◊polymerization.

condensation conversion of a vapour to a liquid. This is frequently achieved by letting the vapour come into contact with a cold surface. It is the process by which water vapour turns into fine water droplets to form ◊cloud. Condensation in the atmosphere occurs when the air becomes completely saturated and is unable to hold any more water vapour. As air rises it cools and contracts – the cooler it becomes the less water it can hold. Rain is frequently associated with warm weather fronts because the air rises and cools, allowing the water vapour to condense as rain. The temperature at which the air becomes saturated is known as the dew point. Water vapour will not condense in air if there are not enough condensation nuclei (particles of dust, smoke or salt) for the droplets to form on. It is then said to be supersaturated. Condensation is an important part of the ◊water cycle.

condensation polymerization ◊polymerization reaction in which one or more monomers, with more than one reactive functional group, combine to form a polymer with the elimination of water or another small molecule.

condenser laboratory apparatus used to condense vapours back to liquid so that the liquid can be recovered. It is used in ◊distillation and in reactions where the liquid mixture can be kept boiling without the loss of solvent.

condenser in electronic circuits, a former name for a ◊capacitor.

condenser in optics, a ◊lens or combination of lenses with a short focal length used for concentrating a light source onto a small area, as used in a slide projector or microscope substage lighting unit. A condenser can also be made using a concave mirror.

Condillac Étienne Bonnot de 1715–1780. French philosopher. He mainly followed English philosopher John ◊Locke, but his *Traité de sensations* 1754 claims that all mental activity stems from the transformation of sensations. He was a collaborator on the French ◊*Encyclopédie*.

'We cannot recollect the ignorance in which we were born.'
ÉTIENNE BONNOT DE CONDILLAC
Traité des Sensations

conditioning in psychology, two major principles of behaviour modification. In ***classical conditioning***, described by Russian psychologist Ivan Pavlov, a new stimulus can evoke an automatic response by being repeatedly associated with a stimulus that naturally provokes that response. For example, the sound of a bell repeatedly associated with food will eventually trigger salivation, even if sounded without food being presented. In ***operant conditioning***, described by US psychologists Edward Lee Thorndike (1874–1949) and B F Skinner, the frequency of a voluntary response can be increased by following it with a reinforcer or reward.

conditions of service or ***conditions of employment*** regulations which set out the rights and obligations of the employee. They are issued by employers and have to be accepted by employees. Conditions of service, for example, may lay down the rate of pay, how often the worker will be paid, and holiday entitlement, as well as the hours of work, dress that is expected, and a requirement for punctuality. Negotiating conditions of service, including pay, is arguably the most important function of a trade union in a place of work.

condom or ***sheath*** or ***prophylactic*** barrier contraceptive, made of rubber, which fits over an erect penis and holds in the sperm produced by ejaculation. It is an effective means of preventing pregnancy if used carefully, preferably with a ◊spermicide. A condom with spermicide is 97% effective; one without spermicide is 85% effective as a contraceptive. Condoms can also give some protection against sexually transmitted diseases, including AIDS.

condominium joint rule of a territory by two or more states, for example, Kanton and Enderbury islands in the South Pacific Phoenix group (under the joint control of Britain and the USA for 50 years from 1939). The term has also come into use in North America to describe a type of joint property ownership of, for example, a block of flats.

This is a Senate of equals, of men of individual honor and personal character, and of absolute independence. We know no masters, we acknowledge no dictators.

On the US CONGRESS Daniel Webster, speech 26 Jan 1830

condor name given to two species of birds in separate genera. The Andean condor *Vultur gryphus*, has a wingspan up to 3 m/10 ft, weighs up to 13 kg/28 lb, and can reach up to 1.2 m/3.8 ft in length. It is black, with some white on the wings and a white frill at the base of the neck. It lives in the Andes at heights of up to 4,500 m/14,760 ft, and along the South American coast, and feeds mainly on carrion. The Californian condor *Gymnogyps californianus* is a similar bird, with a wingspan of about 3 m/10 ft. It feeds entirely on carrion, and is on the verge of extinction.

Condorcet Marie Jean Antoine Nicolas de Caritat. Marquis de Condorcet 1743–1794. French philosopher, mathematician, and politician, associated with the ◊*Encyclopédistes* . In *Esquisse d'un tableau des progrès de l'esprit humain/Historical Survey of the Progress of Human Understanding* 1795, he traced human development from barbarity to the brink of perfection. As a mathematician he made important contributions to the theory of probability.

Although a keen supporter of the French Revolution, Condorcet opposed the execution of Louis XVI, and was imprisoned and poisoned himself.

conductance ability of a material to carry an electrical current, usually given the symbol *G*. For a direct current, it is the reciprocal of ◊resistance: a conductor of resistance *R* has a conductance of $1/R$. For an alternating current, conductance is the resistance *R* divided by the ◊impedance *Z*: $G = R/Z$. Conductance was formerly expressed in reciprocal ◊ohms (or mhos); the SI unit is the ◊siemens (S).

conduction, electrical flow of charged particles through a material giving rise to electric current. Conduction in metals involves the flow of negatively charged free ◊electrons. Conduction in gases and some liquids involves the flow of ◊ions that carry positive charges in one direction and negative charges in the other. Conduction in a ◊semiconductor such as silicon involves the flow of electrons and positive holes.

conduction, heat flow of heat energy through a material without the movement of any part of the material itself (compare ◊conduction, electrical). Heat energy is present in all materials in the form of the kinetic energy of their vibrating molecules, and may be conducted from one molecule to the next in the form of this mechanical vibration. In the case of metals, which are particularly good conductors of heat, the free electrons within the material carry heat around very quickly.

conductor any material that conducts heat or electricity (as opposed to an insulator, or nonconductor). A good conductor has a high electrical or heat conductivity, and is generally a substance rich in free electrons such as a metal. A poor conductor (such as the nonmetals glass and porcelain) has few free electrons. Carbon is exceptional in being nonmetallic and yet (in some of its forms) a relatively good conductor of heat and electricity. Substances such as silicon and germanium, with intermediate conductivities that are improved by heat, light, or voltage, are known as ◊semiconductors.

conductor in music, the director of an orchestra who beats time, cues entries, and controls the overall expression and balance of a performance. Conductors of ballet and opera are normally resident, on a fulltime contract, available for the ongoing preparation of new repertoire. Conductors for symphony orchestras are more often freelance, star performers in their own right, under temporary contract for concert or recording purposes and thus more reliant on the expertise of orchestras.

cone in botany, the reproductive structure of the conifers and cycads; also known as a ◊strobilus. It consists of a central axis surrounded by numerous, overlapping, scalelike, modified leaves (sporophylls) that bear the reproductive organs. Usually there are separate male and female cones, the former bearing pollen sacs containing pollen grains, and the larger female cones bearing the ovules that contain the ova or egg cells. The pollen is carried from male to female cones by the wind (anemophily). The seeds develop within the female cone and are released as the scales open in dry atmospheric conditions, which favour seed dispersal.

cone in geometry, a solid or surface consisting of the set of all straight lines passing through a fixed point (the vertex) and the points of a circle or ellipse whose plane does not contain the vertex.

A circular cone of perpendicular height, with its apex above the centre of the circle, is known as a right circular cone; it is generated by rotating an isosceles triangle or framework about its line of symmetry. A right circular cone of perpendicular height *h* and base of radius *r* has a volume $V = \frac{1}{3}\pi r^2 h$.

The distance from the edge of the base of a cone to the vertex is called the slant height. In a right circular cone of slant height *l*, the curved surface area is πrl, and the area of the base is πr^2. Therefore the total surface area $A = \pi rl + \pi r^2 = \pi r(l + r)$.

Coney Island seaside resort on a peninsula in Brooklyn, in the SW of Long Island, New York, USA. It has been popular for ocean bathing and its amusement parks since the 1840s.

Confederacy in US history, popular name for the ***Confederate States of America***, the government established by 7 (later 11) Southern states in Feb 1861 when they seceded from the Union, precipitating the American ◊Civil War. Richmond, Virginia, was the capital, and Jefferson Davis the president. The Confederacy fell after its army was defeated 1865 and General Robert E Lee surrendered.

The Confederacy suffered from a lack of political leadership as well as a deficit of troops and supplies. Nevertheless, Southern forces won many significant victories. Confederate leaders had hoped to enlist support from Britain and France, but the slavery issue and the Confederacy's uncertain prospects prompted the Europeans to maintain neutrality, although they provided supplies for a time. The Union's blockade and the grinding weight of superior resources made the outcome virtually inevitable 1865. The states of the Confederacy were South Carolina, Georgia, Florida, Alabama, Louisiana, Mississippi, Texas, Virginia, Tennessee, Arkansas, and North Carolina.

Confederation, Articles of in US history, the initial means by which the 13 former British colonies created a form of national government. Ratified 1781, the articles established a unicameral legislature, Congress, with limited powers of raising revenue, regulating currency, and conducting foreign affairs. But because the individual states retained significant autonomy, the confederation was unmanageable. The articles were superseded by the US Constitution 1788. ▷*See feature on pp. 32–33.*

Confederation of British Industry (CBI) UK organization of employers, established 1965, combining the former Federation of British Industries (founded 1916), British Employers' Confederation, and National Association of British Manufacturers. It acts as a pressure group for businesses, promoting their interests to government, overseas, and to workers.

confession in law, a criminal's admission of guilt. Since false confessions may be elicited by intimidation or ill treatment of the accused, the validity of confession in a court of law varies from one legal system to another. For example, in England and Wales a confession, without confirmatory evidence, is sufficient to convict; in Scotland it is not.

confession in religion, the confession of sins practised in Roman Catholic, Orthodox, and most Far Eastern Christian churches, and since the early 19th century revived in Anglican and Lutheran churches. The Lateran Council of 1215 made auricular confession (self-accusation by the penitent to a priest, who in Catholic doctrine is divinely invested with authority to give absolution) obligatory once a year.

condor The Californian condor is one of the largest and heaviest birds in the world. It can soar to great heights and glide as far as 16 km/10 mi without moving its wings.

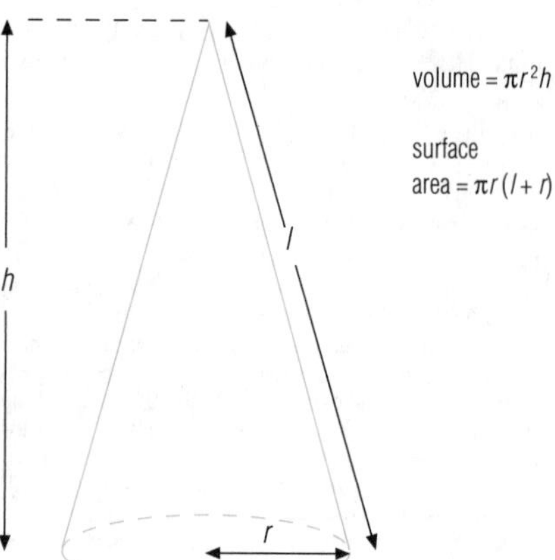

cone The volume and surface area of a cone are given by formulae involving a few simple dimensions.

confidence vote in politics, a test of support for the government in the legislature. In political systems modelled on that of the UK, the survival of a government depends on assembly support. The opposition may move a vote of 'no confidence'; if the vote is carried, it requires the government, by convention, to resign. The last prime minister to be defeated in the House of Commons and forced to resign was Labour prime minister James Callaghan 1979. He lost the subsequent general election to Margaret Thatcher.

confirmation rite practised by a number of Christian denominations, including Roman Catholic, Anglican, and Orthodox, in which a previously baptized person is admitted to full membership of the church. In Reform Judaism there is often a confirmation service several years after the bar or bat mitzvah (initiation into the congregation).

Christian confirmation is believed to give the participant the gift of the Holy Spirit. In the Anglican church it involves the laying on of hands by a bishop, while in the Roman Catholic and Orthodox churches the participant is anointed with oil. Except in the Orthodox churches, where infant confirmation is usual, the rite takes place around early adolescence.

Confucianism body of beliefs and practices based on the Chinese classics and supported by the authority of the philosopher Confucius. The origin of things is seen in the union of *yin* and *yang*, the passive and active principles. Human relationships follow the patriarchal pattern. For more than 2,000 years Chinese political government, social organization, and individual conduct was shaped by Confucian principles. In 1912, Confucian philosophy, as a basis for government, was dropped by the state.

The writings on which Confucianism is based include the ideas of a group of traditional books edited by Confucius, as well as his own works, such as the *Analects*, and those of some of his pupils. The ◊*I Ching* is included among the Confucianist texts.

doctrine Until 1912 the emperor of China was regarded as the father of his people, appointed by heaven to rule. The Superior Man was the ideal human and filial piety was the chief virtue. Accompanying a high morality was a kind of ancestor worship.

practices Under the emperor, sacrifices were offered to heaven and earth, the heavenly bodies, the imperial ancestors, various nature gods, and Confucius himself. These were abolished at the Revolution in 1912, but ancestor worship (better expressed as reverence and remembrance) remained a regular practice in the home. Under communism Confucianism continued. The defence minister Lin Biao was associated with the religion, and although the communist leader Mao Zedong undertook an anti-Confucius campaign 1974–76, this was not pursued by the succeeding regime.

Confucius (Latinized form of ***Kong Zi*** or ***K'ung Fu Tzu***, 'Kong the master') 551–479 BC. Chinese sage whose name is given to the ethical system of Confucianism. He placed emphasis on moral order and observance of the established patriarchal family and social relationships of authority, obedience, and mutual respect. His emphasis on tradition and ethics attracted a growing number of pupils during his lifetime. *The Analects of Confucius*, a compilation of his teachings, was published after his death.

Confucius was born in Lu, in what is now the province of Shangdong, and his early years were spent in poverty. Married at the age of 19, he worked as a minor official, then as a teacher. In 517 there was an uprising in Lu, and Confucius spent the next year or two in the adjoining state of Ch'i. As a teacher he was able to place many of his pupils in government posts butt a powerful position eluded him. Only in his fifties was he given an office, but he soon resigned because of the lack of power it conveyed. Then for 14 years he wandered from state to state looking for a ruler who could give him a post where he could put into practice his ideas for relieving suffering among the poor. At the age of 67 he returned to Lu and devoted himself to teaching. At his death five years later he was buried with great pomp, and his grave outside Qufu has remained a centre of pilgrimage. Within 300 years of his death, his teaching was adopted by the Chinese state.

congenital disease in medicine, a disease that is present at birth. It is not necessarily genetic in origin; for example, congenital herpes may be acquired by the baby as it passes through the mother's birth canal.

conger any large marine eel of the family Congridae, especially the genus *Conger*. Conger eels live in shallow water, hiding in crevices during the day and active by night, feeding on fish and crabs. They are valued for food and angling. The European conger *C. conger* is found in the N Atlantic and in the Mediterranean. It is often 1.8 m/6 ft long, and sometimes as much as 2.7 m/9 ft.

conglomerate company that has a number of subsidiaries in a number of nonrelated markets. For example, British American Tobacco (BAT) is a conglomerate owning a tobacco company and a Californian insurance company.

conglomerate in geology, coarse-grained clastic ◊sedimentary rock, composed of rounded fragments (clasts) of pre-existing rocks cemented in a finer matrix, usually sand.

Congo country in W central Africa, bounded N by Cameroon and the Central African Republic, E and S by Democratic Republic of Congo, W by the Atlantic Ocean, and NW by Gabon. *See country box on p. 256.*

Congo, Democratic Republic of country in central Africa, bounded W by Congo, N by the Central African Republic and Sudan, E by Uganda, Rwanda, Burundi and Tanzania, SE by Zambia, and SW by Angola. There is a short coastline on the Atlantic Ocean. *See country box below.*

Congregationalism form of church government adopted by those Protestant Christians known as Congregationalists, who let each congregation manage its own affairs. The first Congregationalists were the Brownists, named after Robert Browne, who defined the congregational principle 1580.

In the 17th century they were known as Independents – for example, the Puritan leader Cromwell and many of his Ironsides – and in 1662 hundreds of their ministers were driven from their churches and established separate congregations. The Congregational Church in England and Wales and the Presbyterian Church in England merged in 1972 to form the United Reformed Church. The latter, like its counterpart the Congregational Union of Scotland, has no control over individual churches but is simply consultative. Similar unions have been carried out in Canada (United Church of Canada, 1925) and USA (United Church of Christ, 1957).

congress in 19th-century European history, a formal meeting or assembly, usually for peace, where delegates assembled to discuss or settle a matter of international concern, such as the Congress of Vienna 1815, which divided up Napoleon's empire after the Napoleonic Wars; and the Congress of Paris 1856, which settled some of the problems resulting from the Crimean War.

Congress national legislature of the USA, consisting of the House of Representatives (435 members, apportioned to the states of the Union on the basis of population, and elected for two-year terms) and the Senate (100 senators, two for each state, elected for six years, one-third elected every two years). Both representatives and senators are elected by direct popular vote. Congress meets in Washington DC, in the Capitol Building. An ◊act of Congress is a bill passed by both houses. The Congress of the United States met for the first time on 4 March 1789. It was preceded by the Congress of the Confederation representing the several states under the Articles of Confederation 1781–89.

Congress of Racial Equality (CORE) US nonviolent civil-rights organization, founded in Chicago 1942.

Congress Party Indian political party, founded 1885 as the Indian National Congress. It led the movement to end British rule and was the governing party from independence 1947 until 1977, when Indira Gandhi lost the leadership she had held since 1966. Congress also held power 1980–89 and 1991–96. Heading a splinter group, known as Congress (I) ('I' for Indira), she achieved an overwhelming victory in the elections of 1980, and reduced the main Congress Party to a minority. The 'I' was dropped from the name in 1993 following

'Virtue is not left to stand alone. He who practises it will have neighbours.'

CONFUCIUS *Analects*

Congo
Democratic Republic of (formerly *Zaire*)

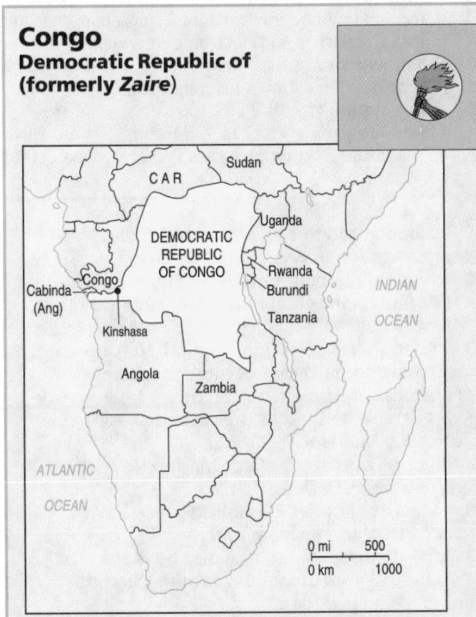

national name *République Démocratique du Congo*
area 2,344,900 sq km/905,366 sq mi
capital Kinshasa
major towns/cities Lubumbashi, Kananga, Mbuji-Mayi, Kisangani, Bukavu, Kikwit
major ports Matadi, Kalemie
physical features Zaïre/Congo River basin has tropical rainforest (second-largest remaining in world) and savanna; mountains in E and W; lakes Tanganyika, Albert, Edward; Ruwenzori Range; Victoria Falls
head of state and government Laurent Kabila from 1997
political system transitional
administrative divisions ten regions
political parties Popular Movement of the Revolution (MPR), African socialist; Democratic Forces of Congo–Kinshasa (formerly Sacred Union, an alliance of some 130 opposition groups), moderate, centrist; Union for Democracy and Social Progress (UPDS), left of centre; Congolese National Movement–Lumumba (MNC), left of centre
population 46,812,000 (1996 est)
population growth rate 3.2% (1990–95); 3% (2000–05)
ethnic groups almost entirely of African descent, distributed among over 200 ethnic groups, the most numerous being the Kongo, Luba, Lunda, Mongo, and Zande
life expectancy 50 (men); 53 (women) (1995–2000)
literacy rate 84% (men); 61% (women) (1995 est)
language French (official); Swahili, Lingala, Kikongo, and Tshiluba are recognized as national languages; over 200 other languages
religion Roman Catholic, Protestant, Kimbanguist; also half a million Muslims
currency zaïre
GDP (US $) 7.2 billion (1994 est)
GDP growth rate −0.6% (1995)
exports mineral products (mainly copper, cobalt, industrial diamonds, and petroleum), agricultural products (chiefly coffee).

HISTORY
13th century Rise of Kongo Empire, centred on banks of Zaïre/Congo river.
1483 First visited by Portuguese, who named the area Zaire (from Zadi, 'big water') and converted local rulers to Christianity.
16th–17th centuries Great development of slave trade by Portuguese, Dutch, British, and French merchants, initially supplied by Kongo intermediaries.
18th century Rise of Luba state, in southern copper belt of N Katanga, and Lunda, in Kasai region in central S.
mid-19th century Eastern Zaire invaded by Arab slave traders from E Africa.
1874–77 British explorer Henry Morton Stanley navigated Congo River to Atlantic Ocean.
1879–87 Stanley engaged by King Leopold II of Belgium to sign protection treaties with local chiefs and 'Congo Free State' awarded to Leopold by 1884–85 Berlin Conference; great expansion in rubber export, using forced labour.
1908 Leopold forced to relinquish personal control of Congo Free State, after international condemnation of human-rights abuses. Became colony of Belgian Congo and important exporter of minerals.
1959 Riots in Kinshasa (Leopoldville) persuaded Belgium to decolonize rapidly.
1960 Independence achieved as Republic of the Congo. Civil war broke out between central government based in Kinshasa (Leopoldville) with Joseph Kasavubu as president, and rich mining province of Katanga.
1961 Former prime minister Patrice Lumumba murdered in Katanga; fighting between mercenaries engaged by Katanga secessionist leader Moise Tshombe, and United Nations troops; Kasai and Kivu provinces also sought (briefly) to secede.
1963 Katanga secessionist war ended; Tshombe forced into exile.
1964 Tshombe returned from exile to become prime minister; pro-Marxist groups took control of E Zaire.
1965 Western-backed Col Sese Seko Mobutu seized power in coup, ousting Kasavubu and Tshombe.
1971 Country renamed Republic of Zaire, with Mobutu as president as *authenticité* (Africanization) policy launched.
1972 Mobutu's Popular Movement of the Revolution (MPR) became only legal political party. Katanga province renamed Shaba.
1974 Foreign-owned businesses and plantations seized by Mobutu and given to his political allies.
1977 Original owners of confiscated properties invited back. Zairean guerrillas, chiefly Lundas, invaded Shaba province from Angola, but were repulsed by Moroccan, French, and Belgian paratroopers.
1980s International creditors forced launch of series of austerity programmes, after level of foreign indebtedness had mounted with collapse in world copper prices.
1991 After antigovernment riots, Mobutu agreed to end ban on multiparty politics and share power with opposition; Etienne Tshisekedi appointed premier, but soon dismissed.
1992 Tshisekedi reinstated against Mobutu's wishes after renewed rioting.
1993 Rival pro- and anti-Mobutu governments created.
1994 Kengo Wa Dondo elected prime minister by interim parliament, with Mobutu's agreement. Mass influx of Rwandan refugees.
1995 Continuing secessionist activity in Shaba and Kasai provinces and interethnic warfare in Kivu, adjoining Rwanda in E.
1996 Zaire on brink of war with Rwanda after Rwandan support of Hutu killings by Tutsis in Zaire. Massive Hutu refugee crisis narrowly averted as thousands allowed to return to Rwanda.
1997 Mobutu ousted by rebel forces of Laurent Kabila, who declared himself president and renamed Zaire the Democratic Republic of Congo.

SEE ALSO Hutu; Kabila, Laurent; Mobutu, Sese Seko; Rwanda; Tutsi

Congreve A portrait of the English dramatist and poet William Congreve. One of the principal writers of Restoration comedy, which flourished on the reopening of the theatres after the restoration of Charles II to the throne, Congreve wrote witty and satirical plays about affectation and manners. *Corbis*

the assassination of Rajiv ◊Gandhi in 1991, and a small split occurred in the party in 1995. ▷*See feature on pp. 432–433.*

'Musick has charms to sooth a savage breast.'

WILLIAM CONGREVE *The Mourning Bride*

Congreve William 1670–1729. English dramatist and poet. His first success was the comedy *The Old Bachelor* 1693, followed by *The Double Dealer* 1694, *Love for Love* 1695, the tragedy *The Mourning Bride* 1697, and *The Way of the World* 1700. His plays, which satirize the social affectations of the time, are characterized by elegant wit and wordplay, and complex plots.

congruent in geometry, having the same shape and size, as applied to two-dimensional or solid figures. With plane congruent figures, one figure will fit on top of the other exactly, though this may first require rotation and/or rotation of one of the figures.

conic section curve obtained when a conical surface is intersected by a plane. If the intersecting plane cuts both extensions of the cone, it yields a ◊hyperbola; if it is parallel to the side of the cone, it produces a ◊parabola. Other intersecting planes produce ◊circles or ◊ellipses.

conifer tree or shrub of the order Coniferales, in the gymnosperm or naked-seed-bearing group of plants. They are often pyramidal in form, with leaves that are either scaled or made up of needles; most are evergreen. Conifers include pines, spruces, firs, yews, junipers, monkey puzzles, and larches.

The reproductive organs are the male and female cones, and pollen is distributed by the wind. The seeds develop in the female cones. The processes of maturation, fertilization, and seed ripening may extend over several years. Most conifers grow quickly and can tolerate poor soil, steep slopes, and short growing seasons. Coniferous forests are widespread in Scandinavia and upland areas of the UK such as the Scottish Highlands, and are often planted in ◊afforestation schemes. Conifers also grow in ◊woodland.

conjugate in mathematics, a term indicating that two elements are connected in some way; for example, $(a + ib)$ and $(a - ib)$ are conjugate complex numbers.

conjugation in biology, the bacterial equivalent of sexual reproduction. A fragment of the ◊DNA from one bacterium is passed along a thin tube, the pilus, into another bacterium.

conjugation in organic chemistry, the alternation of double (or triple) and single carbon–carbon bonds in a molecule – for example, in penta-1,3-diene, $H_2C{=}CH{-}CH{=}CH{-}CH_3$. Conjugation imparts additional stability as the double bonds are less reactive than isolated double bonds.

conjunction in astronomy, the alignment of two celestial bodies as seen from Earth. A superior planet (or other object) is in conjunction when it lies behind the Sun. An inferior planet (or other object) comes to inferior conjunction when it passes between the Earth and the Sun; it is at superior conjunction when it passes behind the Sun. Planetary conjunction takes place when a planet is closely aligned with another celestial object, such as the Moon, a star, or another planet.

conjunctiva membrane covering the front of the vertebrate ◊eye. It is continuous with the epidermis of the eyelids, and lies on the surface of the cornea.

conjunctivitis inflammation of the conjunctiva, the delicate membrane that lines the inside of the eyelids and covers the front of the eye. Symptoms include redness, swelling, and a watery or pus-filled discharge. It may be caused by infection, allergy, or other irritant.

Connacht province of the Republic of Ireland, comprising the counties of Galway, Leitrim, Mayo, Roscommon, and Sligo; area 17,130 sq km/6,612 sq mi; population (1991) 422,900. The chief towns are Galway, Roscommon, Castlebar, Sligo, and Carrick-on-Shannon. Mainly lowland, it is agricultural and stock-raising country, with poor land in the W. The chief rivers are the Shannon, Moy, and Suck, and there are a number of lakes. The Connacht dialect is the national standard.

Connecticut state in New England, USA; nicknamed Constitution State/Nutmeg State
area 13,000 sq km/5,018 sq mi
capital Hartford
towns and cities Bridgeport, New Haven, Waterbury
physical highlands in the NW; Connecticut River
features Connecticut River Valley; Housatonic Valley; Litchfield Hills; Litchfield village; Stonington; Mark Twain House, Hartford; Barnum Museum, Bridgeport, with a model of P T Barnum's three-ring circus; Yale University (1701); Trinity College, Hartford (1823); Wesleyan University (1831); US Coastguard Academy, New London; American Shakespeare Theatre, Stratford
products dairy, poultry, and market-garden products; tobacco, watches, clocks, silverware, helicopters, jet engines, nuclear submarines, hardware and locks, electrical and electronic equipment, guns and ammunition, optical instruments. Hartford is the centre of the nation's insurance industry
population (1990) 3,287,100
famous people Phineas T Barnum, George Bush, Katharine Hepburn, Charles Ives, Eugene O'Neill,

CONGO
Republic of

ATLANTIC OCEAN
CAR
Cameroon
Equatorial Guinea
Gabon
Democratic Republic of Congo
CONGO
Cabinda (to Angola)
Brazzaville
0 mi 500
0 km 1000

national name *République du Congo*
area 342,000 sq km/132,012 sq mi
capital Brazzaville
major towns/cities Nkayi, Loubomo
major ports Pointe-Noire
physical features narrow coastal plain rises to central plateau, then falls into northern basin; Zaïre/Congo River on the border with the Democratic Republic of Congo; half the country is rainforest
head of state Denis Sassou-Nguesso from 1997
head of government Bernard Kolelas from 1997
political system emergent democracy
administrative divisions nine provinces
political parties Pan-African Union for Social Democracy (UPADS), moderate, left of centre; Congolese Movement for Democracy and Integral Development (MCDDI), moderate, left of centre; Congolese Labour Party (PCT), left-wing
population 2,590,000 (1995 est)
population growth rate 3.0% (1990–95); 2.6% (2000–05)
ethnic distribution predominantly Bantus; population comprises 15 main ethnic groups and 75 tribes. The Kongo, or Bakongo, account for about 45% of the population, then come the Bateke, or Teke, at about 20%, and then the Mboshi, or Boubangui, about 16%
life expectancy 52 (males), 57 (females)
literacy rate men 70%, women 44%
languages French (official); Kongo languages; local patois Monokutuba and Lingala
religions animist, Christian, Muslim
currency franc CFA
GDP (US $) 1.45 billion (1994)
growth rate −4.9% (1994)
exports timber, petroleum, cocoa, sugar

HISTORY
late 15th C First visited by Portuguese explorers, at which time the Bakongo (a six-state confederation centred S of the Congo river in Angola) and Bateke, both Bantu groups, were the chief kingdoms.
16th C Portuguese, in collaboration with coastal peoples, exported slaves drawn from the interior to plantations in Brazil and São Tomé; missionaries spread Roman Catholic faith.
1880 French explorer Pierre Savorgnan de Brazza established French claims to coastal region. Makoko (king) of the Bateke accepted French protection.
1905 International outrage at revelations of the brutalities of forced labour, which decimated the population, as ivory and rubber resources were ruthlessly exploited by private concessionaries.
1910 As Moyen-Congo, became part of French Equatorial Africa, with the capital at Brazzaville.
1920s More than 17,000 were killed as forced labour used to build the Congo-Ocean railway; first Bakongo political organization founded.
1940–44 Supported the 'Free French' anti-Nazi resistance cause during World War II, Brazzaville serving as capital for General de Gaulle's forces.
1946 Became autonomous, with a territorial assembly and representation in French parliament.
1960 Achieved independence from France, with Abbé Fulbert Youlou, a moderate Catholic Bakongo priest, as the first president.
1963 Youlou forced to resign after labour unrest. Alphonse Massamba-Débat became president with Pascal Lissouba as prime minister, and a single-party state was established under the socialist National Revolutionary Movement (MNR).
1968 Military coup, led by Capt Marien Ngouabi, ousted Massamba-Débat.
1970 A Marxist People's Republic declared, with Ngouabi's PCT the only legal party.
1977 Ngouabi assassinated in a plot by Massamba-Débat, who was executed; Col Joachim Yhombi-Opango became president.
1979 Yhombi-Opango handed over the presidency to the PCT, who chose Col Denis Sassou-Nguessou as his successor.
early 1980s Petroleum production increased fivefold.
1990 With the collapse of eastern European communism, the PCT abandoned Marxist-Leninism and promised multiparty politics and market-centred reforms in an economy crippled by foreign debt.
1992 Multiparty elections gave the coalition dominated by the Pan-African Union for Social Democracy (UPADS) an assembly majority, with Pascal Lissouba elected president.
1993 Yhombi-Opango appointed prime minister; violent strikes and unrest after opposition disputed election results.
1994 International panel appointed to investigate results; UPADS-dominated coalition declared winner.
1995 New broad-based government formed, including opposition groups; market-centred economic reforms, including privatization.
1996 Charles David Ganao appointed prime minister.
1997 Violence between rival factions despite a unity government. Sassou-Nguesso took over the presidency. Bernard Kolelas appointed prime minister.

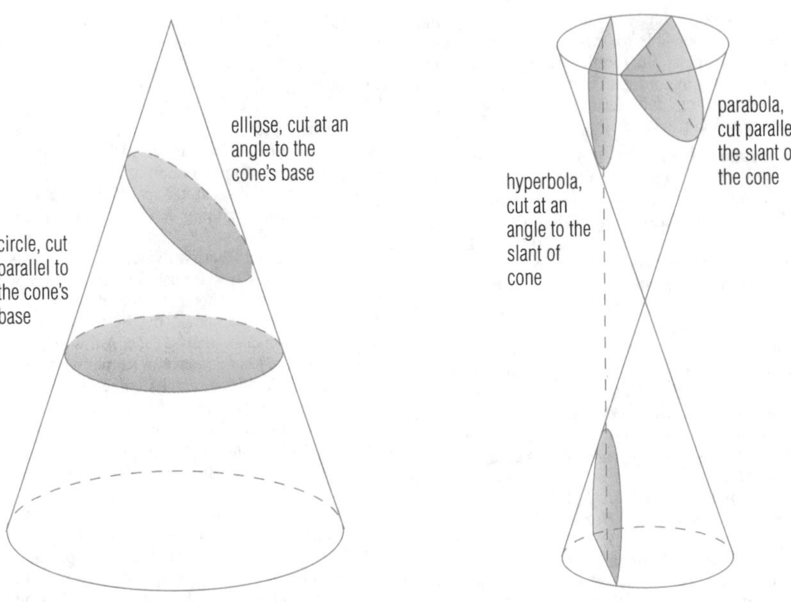

conic section The four types of curve that may be obtained by cutting a single or double right-circular cone with a plane (two-dimensional surface).

Wallace Stevens, Harriet Beecher Stowe, Mark Twain, Eli Whitney, Benedict Arnold, Jonathan Edwards, Nathan Hale, Edward H Land

history Dutch navigator Adriaen Block was the first European to record the area 1614, and in 1633 Dutch colonists built a trading post near modern Hartford but it soon was settled by Puritan colonists from Massachusetts 1635. It was one of the original 13 colonies and became a state 1788. It prospered in the 19th century from shipbuilding, whaling, and growing industry. In the 20th century it became an important supplier of military equipment. Connecticut is second to Alaska among states in personal income per capita. Many of New York City's most affluent residential suburbs are in SW Connecticut.

connective tissue in animals, tissue made up of a noncellular substance, the ◊extracellular matrix, in which some cells are embedded. Skin, bones, tendons, cartilage, and adipose tissue (fat) are the main connective tissues. There are also small amounts of connective tissue in organs such as the brain and liver, where they maintain shape and structure.

Connemara western part of County Galway, Republic of Ireland, an area of rocky coastline and mountainous scenery. There is fishing and tourism.

Connery Sean Thomas 1930– . Scottish film actor. He was the first interpreter of James Bond in several films based on the novels of Ian Fleming. His films include *Dr No* 1962, *From Russia with Love* 1963, *Marnie* 1964, *Goldfinger* 1964, *Diamonds Are Forever* 1971, *A Bridge Too Far* 1977, *The Name of the Rose* 1986, *The Untouchables* 1987 (Academy Award), and *Rising Sun* 1993.

Connolly Cyril (Vernon) 1903–1974. English critic and writer. As a founder and editor of the literary magazine *Horizon* 1939–50, he had considerable critical influence. His works include *The Rock Pool* 1936, a novel of artists on the Riviera, and *The Unquiet Grave* 1944, a series of reflections published under the pseudonym of Palinurus.

Connolly Maureen Catherine 1934–1969. US lawn-tennis player, nicknamed 'Little Mo' because she was just 157 cm/5 ft 2 in tall. In 1953 she became the first woman to complete the Grand Slam by winning all four major tournaments. All her singles titles (won at nine major championships) and her Grand Slam titles were won between 1951 and 1954. She also represented the USA in the Wightman Cup.

Connecticut

Connors Jimmy (James Scott) 1952– . US tennis player who won the Wimbledon title 1974 and 1982, and subsequently won ten Grand Slam events. He was one of the first players to popularize the two-handed backhand.

conquistador (Spanish 'conqueror') any of the early Spanish explorers and adventurers in the Americas, such as Hernán Cortés (Mexico) and Francisco Pizarro (Peru).

Conrad Joseph. Pen name of Teodor Jozef Konrad Korzeniowski 1857–1924. English novelist, born in Ukraine of Polish parents. His greatest works include the novels *Lord Jim* 1900, *Nostromo* 1904, *The Secret Agent* 1907, and *Under Western Eyes* 1911; the short story *Heart of Darkness* 1902; and the short novel 'The Shadow Line' 1917. These combine a vivid and sensuous evocation of various lands and seas with a rigorous, humane scrutiny of moral dilemmas, pitfalls, and desperation.

Conrad went to sea at the age of 17 and first learned English at 21. He is regarded as one of the greatest of modern novelists. His prose style varies from eloquently sensuous to bare and astringent.

Conrad I died 918. King of the Germans from 911, when he succeeded Louis the Child, the last of the German Carolingians. During his reign the realm was harassed by ◊Magyar invaders.

Conrad II c. 990–1039. King of the Germans from 1024, Holy Roman emperor from 1027. He ceded the Sleswick (Schleswig) borderland, S of the Jutland peninsula, to King Canute, but extended his rule into Lombardy and Burgundy.

Conrad III 1093–1152. King of Germany and Holy Roman emperor from 1138, the first king of the Hohenstaufen dynasty. Throughout his reign there was a fierce struggle between his followers, the ◊Ghibellines, and the ◊Guelphs, the followers of Henry the Proud, duke of Saxony and Bavaria (1108–1139), and later of his son Henry the Lion (1129–1195).

Conrad IV 1228–1254. Elected king of the Germans 1237. Son of the Holy Roman emperor Frederick II, he had to defend his right of succession against Henry Raspe of Thuringia (died 1247) and William of Holland (1227–56).

Conrad V (Conradin) 1252–1268. Son of Conrad IV, recognized as king of the Germans, Sicily, and Jerusalem by German supporters of the ◊Hohenstaufens 1254. He led ◊Ghibelline forces against Charles of Anjou at the battle of Tagliacozzo, N Italy 1266, and was captured and executed.

Conran Jasper Alexander Thirlby 1959– . English fashion designer. He is known for using quality fabrics to create comfortable garments. He launched his first collection 1978 and has rarely altered the simple, successful style he then adopted. He has also designed costumes for the stage. He is the son of Terence Conran.

Conran Terence Orby 1931– . English designer and retailer of furnishings, fashion, and household goods. He was founder of the Storehouse group of companies, including Habitat (1964) and Conran Design, with retail outlets in the UK, the USA, and elsewhere. The Storehouse group gained control of British Home Stores 1986. Conran also developed Mothercare. He has been influential in popularizing French country style in the UK.

consanguinity relationship by blood, whether lineal (for example by direct descent) or collateral (by virtue of a common ancestor). The degree of consanguinity is significant in laws relating to the inheritance of property and also in relation to marriage, which is forbidden in many cultures between parties closely related by blood. See also ◊affinity.

conscientious objector person refusing compulsory service, usually military, on moral, religious, or political grounds. During World War I, such objections were considered by tribunals and some objectors were given total exemption; others were directed to other work of national importance or were placed in noncombatant corps. Those who refused these alternatives were usually imprisoned or drafted into military service where, if they persisted in refusal, were court-martialled and imprisoned. Objectors were disenfranchised for five years after the war unless they had performed some work of national importance.

conscription legislation for all able-bodied male citizens (and female in some countries, such as Israel) to serve with the armed forces. It originated in France 1792, and in the 19th and 20th centuries became the established practice in almost all European states. Modern conscription systems often permit alternative national service for conscientious objectors.

In Britain conscription was introduced for single men between 18 and 41 in March 1916 and for married men two months later, but was abolished after World War I. It was introduced for the first time in peace April 1939, when all men aged 20 became liable to six months' military training. The National Service Act, passed Sept 1939, made all men between 18 and 41 liable to military service, and in 1941 women also became liable to be called up for the women's services as an alternative to industrial service. Men reaching the age of 18 continued to be called up until 1960.

consent, age of age at which consent may legally be given to sexual intercourse by a girl or boy. In the UK it is 16 (new legislation 1998 reduced it from 18 to 16 for male homosexual intercourse).

conservation in the life sciences, action taken to protect and preserve the natural world, usually from pollution, overexploitation, and other harmful features of human activity. The late 1980s saw a great increase in public concern for the environment, with membership of conservation groups, such as ◊Friends of the Earth, ◊Greenpeace, and the US Sierra Club, rising sharply. Globally the most important issues include the depletion of atmospheric ozone by the action of ◊chlorofluorocarbons (CFCs), the build-up of carbon dioxide in the atmosphere (thought to contribute to an intensification of the ◊greenhouse effect), and ◊deforestation.

Conservation groups in Britain originated in the 1860s; they include the Commons Preservation Society 1865, which fought successfully against the enclosure of Hampstead Heath (1865) and Epping Forest (1866) in London; the National Footpaths Preservation Society 1844; and the ◊National Trust 1895.

▷ *See feature on pp. 858–859.*

conservation, architectural attempts to maintain the character of buildings and historical areas. In England this is subject to a growing body of legislation that has designated more ◊listed buildings. There are now over 6,000 conservation areas throughout England alone.

'Greed, like the love of comfort, is a kind of fear.'

CYRIL CONNOLLY
The Unquiet Grave

'A belief in a supernatural source of evil is not necessary; men alone are quite capable of every wickedness.'

JOSEPH CONRAD
Under Western Eyes

❛Loyalty to petrified opinions never yet broke a chain or freed a human soul in this world – and never will.❜

On CONSERVATISM Mark Twain 'Consistency' 1884

conservation of energy in chemistry, the principle that states that in a chemical reaction, the total amount of energy in the system remains unchanged.

conservation of mass in chemistry, the principle that states that in a chemical reaction the sum of all the masses of the substances involved in the reaction (reactants) is equal to the sum of all of the masses of the substances produced by the reaction (products) – that is, no matter is gained or lost.

conservation of momentum in mechanics, a law that states that total ◊momentum is conserved (remains constant) in all collisions, providing no external resultant force acts on the colliding bodies.

conservatism approach to government favouring the maintenance of existing institutions and identified with a number of Western political parties, such as the British Conservative, US Republican, German Christian Democratic, and Australian Liberal parties. It tends to be explicitly nondoctrinaire and pragmatic but generally emphasizes free-enterprise capitalism, minimal government intervention in the economy, rigid law and order, and the importance of national traditions. In the UK, modern conservatism, under the ideological influence of ◊Thatcherism, has become increasingly radical, attacking entrenched institutions and promoting free-market economies.

conservative margin or ***passive margin*** in plate tectonics, a region on the Earth's surface in which one plate slides past another. An example is the San Andreas Fault, California, where the movement of the plates is irregular and sometimes takes the form of sudden jerks, causing ◊earthquakes.

Conservative Party UK political party, one of the two historic British parties; the name replaced Tory in general use from 1830 onwards. Traditionally the party of landed interests, it broadened its political base under Benjamin Disraeli's leadership in the 19th century. The present Conservative Party's free-market capitalism is supported by the world of finance and the management of industry.

In the 1980s the party's economic policies increased the spending power of the majority, but also the gap between rich and poor; nationalized industries were sold off (see ◊privatization); military spending and close alliance with the USA were favoured; and the funding of local government was overhauled with the introduction of the ◊poll tax. The Conservative government under John Major 1990–97 repudiated some of the extreme policies of Thatcherism, notably the poll tax, introduced the new ◊Citizen's Charter, and promoted further privatization of public services. In the May 1997 general election the party suffered a landslide defeat, and its parliamentary seats were reduced to the smallest number since 1906. John Major resigned and was succeeded by William Hague.

Conspicuous Gallantry Cross British military award, second only to the ◊Victoria Cross in honour, instituted in October 1993. It is awarded regardless of rank. It replaced the Conspicuous Gallantry Medal, the Distinguished Conduct Medal, and the Distinguished Service Order for particular acts of heroism.

conspiracy in law, an agreement between two or more people to do something unlawful. In the UK it is a complex offence and may be prosecuted under either the Criminal Law Act 1977 or common law.

constable (Latin *comes stabuli* 'count of the stable') low-ranking British police officer. In medieval Europe, a constable was an officer of the king, originally responsible for army stores and stabling, and later responsible for the army in the king's absence. In England the constable subsequently became an official at a sheriff's court of law, leading to the title's current meaning.

Constable John 1776–1837. English artist. He was one of the greatest landscape painters of the 19th century. He painted scenes of his native Suffolk, including *The Haywain* 1821 (National Gallery, London), as well as castles, cathedrals, landscapes, and coastal scenes in other parts of Britain. Constable inherited the Dutch tradition of sombre Realism, in particular the style of Jacob ◊Ruisdael. He aimed to capture the momentary changes of the weather as well as to create monumental images of British scenery, as in *The White Horse* 1819 (Frick Collection, New York) and *Salisbury Cathedral from the Bishop's Grounds* 1827 (Victoria and Albert Museum, London).

Constable's paintings are remarkable for their atmospheric effects and were admired by many French painters including Eugène Delacroix. Notable are *The Leaping Horse* 1825 (Royal Academy of Arts, London), *The Cornfield* 1826 (National Gallery, London), and *Dedham Vale* 1828 (National Gallery of Scotland, Edinburgh). His many oil sketches are often considered among his best work.

Constance, Lake (German ***Bodensee***) lake bounded by Germany, Austria, and Switzerland, through which the river Rhine flows; area 530 sq km/200 sq mi.

constant in mathematics, a fixed quantity or one that does not change its value in relation to ◊variables. For example, in the algebraic expression $y^2 = 5x - 3$, the numbers 3 and 5 are constants. In physics, certain quantities are regarded as universal constants, such as the speed of light in a vacuum.

Constanţa chief Romanian port on the Black Sea, capital of Constanţa region, and second largest city of Romania; population (1993) 349,000. It has refineries, shipbuilding yards, and food factories. It is the exporting centre for the Romanian oilfields, to which it is connected by pipeline. It was founded as a Greek colony in the 7th century BC, and later named after the Roman emperor Constantine I (4th century AD).

constantan or ***eureka*** high-resistance alloy of approximately 40% nickel and 60% copper with a very low coefficient of ◊thermal expansion (measure of expansion on heating). It is used in electrical resistors.

constant composition, law of in chemistry, the law that states that the proportions of the amounts of the elements in a pure compound are always the same and are independent of the method by which the compound was produced.

Constantine city in NE Algeria; population (1989) 449,000. Products include carpets and leather goods. It was one of the chief towns of the Roman province of Numidia, but declined and was ruined, then restored 313 by Constantine the Great, whose name it bears. It was subsequently ruled by Vandals, Arabs, and Turks and was captured by the French 1837.

Constantine II 1940– . King of the Hellenes (Greece). In 1964 he succeeded his father Paul I, went into exile 1967, and was formally deposed 1973.

Constantine the Great c. AD 285–337. First Christian emperor of Rome and founder of Constantinople. He defeated Maxentius, joint emperor of Rome AD 312, and in 313 formally recognized Christianity. As sole emperor of the west of the empire, he defeated Licinius, emperor of the east, to become ruler of the Roman world 324. He presided over the church's first council at Nicaea 325. Constantine moved his capital to Byzantium on the Bosporus 330, renaming it Constantinople (now Istanbul).

Constantine was born at Naissus (Niš, Yugoslavia), the son of Constantius. He was already well known as a soldier when his father died in York in 306 and he was acclaimed by the troops there as joint emperor in his father's place. A few years later Maxentius, the joint emperor in Rome (whose sister had married Constantine), challenged his authority and mobilized his armies to invade Gaul. Constantine won a crushing victory outside Rome in 312. During this campaign he was said to have seen a vision of the cross of Jesus superimposed upon the sun, accompanied by the words: 'In this sign, conquer'. By the Edict of Milan 313 he formally recognized Christianity as one of the religions legally permitted within the Roman Empire and in 314 he summoned the bishops of the Western world to the Council of Arles. However, there has never been agreement on whether Constantine adopted Christianity for reasons of faith or as an act of imperial absolutism to further his power. Constantine increased the autocratic power of the emperor, issued legislation to tie the farmers and workers to their crafts in a sort of caste system, and enlisted the support of the Christian church. He summoned, and presided over, the first general council of the church in Nicaea 325. In 337 he set out to defend the Euphrates frontier against the Persians, but he died before reaching it, at Nicomedia in Asia Minor.

Constantinople former name (330–1453) of Istanbul, Turkey. It was named after the Roman emperor Constantine the Great when he enlarged the Greek city of Byzantium 328 and declared it the capital of the ◊Byzantine Empire 330. Its elaborate fortifications enabled it to resist a succession of sieges, but it was captured by crusaders 1204, and was the seat of a Latin (Western European) kingdom until recaptured by the Greeks 1261. An attack by the Turks 1422 proved unsuccessful, but it was taken by another Turkish army 29 May 1453, after nearly a year's siege, and became the capital of the Ottoman Empire.

Constantinescu Emil 1940– . Romanian political leader, president from 1996. He unsuccessfully challenged Ion Iliescu for the presidency 1992, but led the centre-right Democratic Convention of Romania (DCR) coalition to victory in the parliamentary and presidential elections 1996. His victory was seen as a crucial stage in Romania's transition to democracy, which began with the 'partial revolution' of 1989.

constellation one of the 88 areas into which the sky is divided for the purposes of identifying and naming celestial objects. The first constellations were simple, arbitrary patterns of stars in which early civilizations visualized gods, sacred beasts, and mythical heroes. The constellations in use today are derived from a list of 48 known to the ancient Greeks, who inherited some from the Babylonians.

constitution body of fundamental laws of a state, laying down the system of government and defining the relations of the legislature, executive, and judiciary to each other and to the citizens. Since the French Revolution (1789–1799) almost all countries (the UK is an exception) have adopted written constitutions; that of the USA (1787) is the oldest. Of all the world's states, 69 have adopted their current constitutions in the period since 1989.

The proliferation of legislation during the 1970s, often carried on the basis of a small majority in the Commons and by governments elected by an overall minority of votes, led to demands such as those by the organization Charter 88 for the introduction of a written constitution as a safeguard for the liberty of the individual.

The constitution of the UK does not exist as a single document but as an accumulation of customs and precedents, together with laws defining certain of its aspects. Among the latter are ◊Magna Carta 1215, the petition of right 1628, and the Habeas Corpus Act 1679 (see ◊habeas corpus), limiting the

Constantinople An engraved impression of Constantinople, c. 1340. A fortified city, it survived a number of attempted sieges during its 850-year standing as capital of the Byzantine Empire. *Image Select (UK) Ltd*

royal powers of taxation and of imprisonment; the Bill of Rights 1689 and the Act of Settlement 1701, establishing the supremacy of ◊Parliament and the independence of the judiciary; and the Parliament Acts 1911 and 1949, limiting the powers of the Lords. The Triennial Act 1694, the Septennial Act 1716, and the Parliament Act 1911 limited the duration of Parliament, while the Reform Acts of 1832, 1867, 1884, 1918, and 1928 extended the electorate.

constitutional law that part of the law relating to the constitution. It sets out the rules defining the powers, limits, and rights of government. In countries without a written constitution, such as the United Kingdom, constitutional law is a mixture of legislation, judicial precedent, and accepted conventional behaviour.

constructive margin or ***divergent margin*** in plate tectonics, a region in which two plates are moving away from each other. Magma, or molten rock, escapes to the surface along this margin to form new crust, usually in the form of a ridge. Over time, as more and more magma reaches the surface, the sea floor spreads – for example, the upwelling of magma at the Mid-Atlantic Ridge causes the floor of the Atlantic Ocean to grow at a rate of about 5 cm/2 in a year.

Constructivism art movement that developed in Russia in the early years of the ◊Bolshevik Revolution, founded by Vladimir Tatlin. Inspired by ◊Cubism and ◊Futurism, Constructivists sought to produce abstract forms from industrial materials. By 1932 official Soviet disapproval had brought the movement effectively to a close, but its ideas had already spread to Europe, influencing the ◊Bauhaus and De ◊Stijl schools of architecture and design. Today, Deconstructionism and much high tech architecture reflect its influence.

Closely associated with the movement were the artists El Lissitzky, Naum Gabo, and Antoine Pevsner, and the architects Vladimir Melnikov and Alexander (1883–1959), Leonid (1880–1933), and Viktor (1882–1950) Vesnin.

consul chief magistrate of ancient Rome after the expulsion of the last king 510 BC. The consuls were two annually elected magistrates, both of equal power; they jointly held full civil power in Rome and the chief military command in the field. After the establishment of the Roman Empire the office became purely honorary.

consumer protection laws and measures designed to ensure fair trading for buyers. Responsibility for checking goods and services for quality, safety, and suitability has in the past few years moved increasingly away from the consumer to the producer.

In Britain, an early organization for consumer protection was the British Standards Institution, set up in 1901, which certifies with a 'kitemark' goods reaching certain standards. Statutory protection is now given by such acts as the ◊Weights and Measures Act 1963, the Trade Descriptions Act 1968 (making false descriptions of goods and services illegal) and 1972, the Fair Trading Act 1973, the Consumer Credit Act 1974, the Unfair Contract Terms Act 1977, the Consumer Safety Acts 1978 and 1987, the Supply of Goods and Services Act 1982, and the Data Protection Act 1984. In 1974 the government Department of Prices and Consumer Protection was set up.

A number of organizations are also concerned with consumers' interests, including the Consumers' Association, ◊Citizens' Advice Bureau, local-authority ◊trading standards departments, and regulatory bodies such as Oftel and Ofwat.

contact lens lens, made of soft or hard plastic, that is worn in contact with the cornea and conjunctiva of the eye, beneath the eyelid, to correct defective vision. In special circumstances, contact lenses may be used as protective shells or for cosmetic purposes, such as changing eye colour.

The earliest use of contact lenses in the late 19th century was protective, or in the correction of corneal malformation. It was not until the 1930s that simplification of fitting technique by taking eye impressions made general use possible. Recent developments are a type of soft lens that can be worn for lengthy periods without removal, and a disposable soft lens that needs no cleaning but should be discarded after a week of constant wear.

CONSTELLATIONS

Constellation	Abbreviation	Popular name
Andromeda	And	–
Antlia	Ant	Airpump
Apus	Aps	Bird of Paradise
Aquarius	Aqr	Water-bearer
Aquila	Aqi	Eagle
Ara	Ara	Altar
Aries	Ari	Ram
Auriga	Aur	Charioteer
Boötes	Boo	Herdsman
Caelum	Cae	Chisel
Camelopardalis	Cam	Giraffe
Cancer	Cnc	Crab
Canes Venatici	CVn	Hunting Dogs
Canis Major	CMa	Great Dog
Canis Minor	CMi	Little Dog
Capricornus	Cap	Sea-goat
Carina	Car	Keel
Cassiopeia	Cas	–
Centaurus	Cen	Centaur
Cepheus	Cep	–
Cetus	Cet	Whale
Chamaeleon	Cha	Chameleon
Circinus	Cir	Compasses
Columba	Col	Dove
Coma Berenices	Com	Berenice's Hair
Corona Australis	CrA	Southern Crown
Corona Borealis	CrB	Northern Crown
Corvus	Crv	Crow
Crater	Crt	Cup
Crux	Cru	Southern Cross
Cygnus	Cyn	Swan
Delphinus	Del	Dolphin
Dorado	Dor	Goldfish
Draco	Dra	Dragon
Equuleus	Equ	Foal
Eridanus	Eri	River
Fornax	For	Furnace
Gemini	Gem	Twins
Grus	Gru	Crane
Hercules	Her	–
Horologium	Hor	Clock
Hydra	Hya	Watersnake
Hydrus	Hyi	Little Snake
Indus	Ind	Indian
Lacerta	Lac	Lizard
Leo	Leo	Lion
Leo Minor	LMi	Little Lion
Lepus	Lep	Hare
Libra	Lib	Balance
Lupus	Lup	Wolf
Lynx	Lyn	–
Lyra	Lyr	Lyre
Mensa	Men	Table
Microscopium	Mic	Microscope
Monoceros	Mon	Unicorn
Musca	Mus	Southern Fly
Norma	Nor	Rule
Octans	Oct	Octant
Ophiuchus	Oph	Serpent-bearer
Orion	Ori	–
Pavo	Pav	Peacock
Pegasus	Peg	Flying Horse
Perseus	Per	–
Phoenix	Phe	Phoenix
Pictor	Pic	Painter
Pisces	Psc	Fishes
Piscis Austrinus	PsA	Southern Fish
Puppis	Pup	Poop
Pyxis	Pyx	Compass
Reticulum	Ret	Net
Sagitta	Sge	Arrow
Sagittarius	Sgr	Archer
Scorpius	Sco	Scorpion
Sculptor	Scl	–
Scutum	Sct	Shield
Serpens	Ser	Serpent
Sextans	Sex	Sextant
Taurus	Tau	Bull
Telescopium	Tel	Telescope
Triangulum	Tri	Triangle
Triangulum Australe	TrA	Southern Triangle
Tucana	Tuc	Toucan
Ursa Major	UMa	Great Bear
Ursa Minor	UMi	Little Bear
Vela	Vel	Sails
Virgo	Vir	Virgin
Volans	Vol	Flying Fish
Vulpecula	Vul	Fox

Contadora Group alliance formed between Colombia, Mexico, Panama, and Venezuela Jan 1983 to establish a general peace treaty for Central America and a Central American parliament (similar to the European parliament).

contempt of court behaviour that shows lack of respect for the authority of a court of law, such as disobeying a court order, breach of an injunction, or improper use of legal documents. Behaviour that disrupts, prejudices, or interferes with court proceedings either inside or outside the courtroom may also be contempt. The court may punish contempt with a fine or imprisonment.

continent any one of the seven large land masses of the Earth, as distinct from the oceans. They are Asia, Africa, North America, South America, Europe, Australia, and Antarctica. Continents are constantly moving and evolving (see ◊plate tectonics). A continent does not end at the coastline; its boundary is the edge of the shallow continental shelf, which may extend several hundred kilometres out to sea.

At the centre of each continental mass lies a shield or ◊craton, a deformed mass of old ◊metamorphic rocks dating from Precambrian times. The shield is thick, compact, and solid (the Canadian Shield is an example), having undergone all the mountain-building activity it is ever likely to, and is usually worn flat. Around the shield is a concentric pattern of fold mountains, with older ranges, such as the Rockies, closest to the shield, and younger ranges, such as the coastal ranges of North America, farther away. This general concentric pattern is modified when two continental masses have drifted together and they become welded with a great mountain range along the join, the way Europe and N Asia are joined along the Urals. If a continent is torn apart, the new continental edges have no fold mountains; for instance, South America has fold mountains (the Andes) along its western flank, but none along the east where it tore away from Africa 200 million years ago.

Continental Congress in US history, the federal legislature of the original 13 states, acting as a provisional government during the ◊American Revolution. It was responsible for drawing up the Declaration of Independence, July 1776, and the Articles of ◊Confederation 1777. The Continental Congress was convened in Philadelphia 1774–89, when the constitution was adopted. The congress authorized an army to resist the British and issued paper money to finance the war effort. ▷ *See feature on pp. 32–33.*

continental drift in geology, the theory that, about 250–200 million years ago, the Earth consisted of a single large continent (◊Pangaea), which subsequently broke apart to form the continents known today. The theory was proposed 1912 by

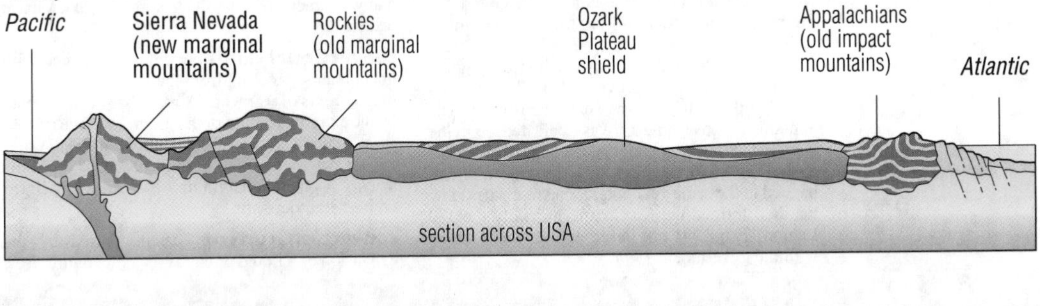

continent The North American continent is growing in the west as a result of collision with the Pacific plate. On the east of the wide area of the Ozark Plateau shield lie the Appalachian Mountains, showing where the continent once collided with another continent. The eastern coastal rifting formed when the continents broke apart. On the western edge, new impact mountains have formed.

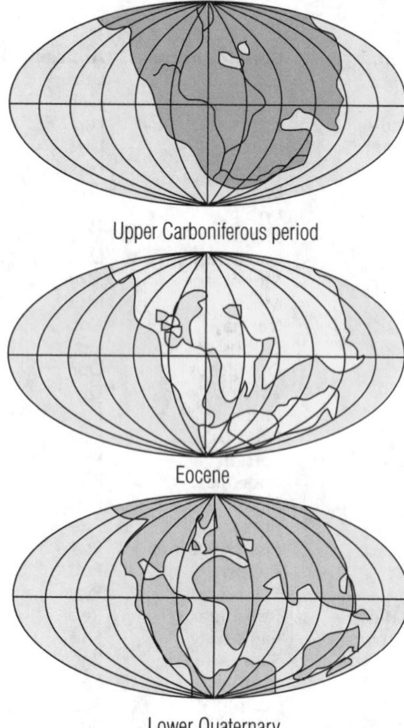

continental drift The drifting continents. The continents are slowly shifting their positions, driven by fluid motion beneath the Earth's crust. Over 200 million years ago, there was a single large continent called Pangaea. By 200 million years ago, the continents had started to move apart. By 50 million years ago, the continents were approaching their present positions.

German meteorologist Alfred Wegener, but such vast continental movements could not be satisfactorily explained until the study of ◊plate tectonics in the 1960s.

The term 'continental drift' is not strictly correct, since land masses do not drift through the oceans. The continents form part of a plate, and the amount of crust created at divergent plate margins must equal the amount of crust destroyed at subduction zones.

continental shelf the submerged edge of a continent, a gently sloping plain that extends into the ocean. It typically has a gradient of less than 1°. When the angle of the sea bed increases to 1°–5° (usually several hundred kilometres away from land), it becomes known as the continental slope.

Continental System system of economic preference and protection within Europe 1806–13 created by the French emperor Napoleon in order to exclude British trade. Apart from its function as economic warfare, the system also reinforced the French economy at the expense of other European states. It failed owing to British naval superiority. ▷ *See feature on pp. 748–749.*

continuity in cinema, the coordination of shots and sequences in the production of a film.

continuum in mathematics, a ◊set that is infinite and everywhere continuous, such as the set of points on a line.

contour on a map, a line drawn to join points of equal height. Contours are drawn at regular height intervals; for example, every 10 m. The closer together the lines are, the steeper the slope. Contour patterns can be used to interpret the relief of an area and to identify land forms.

Contra member of a Central American right-wing guerrilla force attempting to overthrow the democratically elected Nicaraguan Sandinista government 1979–90. The Contras, many of them mercenaries or former members of the deposed dictator Somoza's guard (see ◊Nicaraguan Revolution), operated mainly from bases outside Nicaragua, mostly in Honduras, with covert US funding, as revealed by the ◊Irangate hearings 1986–87.

In 1989 US president Bush announced an agreement with Congress to provide $41 million in 'non-lethal' aid to the Contras until Feb 1990. The Sandinista government was defeated by the National Opposition Union, a US-backed coalition, in the Feb 1990 elections. The Contras were disbanded in the same year but, fearing reprisals, a few hundred formed the Re-Contra (officially the 380 Legion) Feb 1991. A peace accord was reached with the government 1994.

contraceptive any drug, device, or technique that prevents pregnancy. The contraceptive pill (the ◊Pill) contains female hormones that interfere with egg production or the first stage of pregnancy. The 'morning-after' pill can be taken up to 72 hours after unprotected intercourse. Barrier contraceptives include ◊condoms (sheaths) and ◊diaphragms, also called caps or Dutch caps; they prevent the sperm entering the cervix (neck of the womb). ◊Intrauterine devices, also known as IUDs or coils, cause a slight inflammation of the lining of the womb; this prevents the fertilized egg from becoming implanted.

Other contraceptive methods include ◊sterilization (women) and ◊vasectomy (men); these are usually nonreversible. 'Natural' methods include withdrawal of the penis before ejaculation (coitus interruptus), and avoidance of intercourse at the time of ovulation (◊rhythm method). These methods are unreliable and normally only used on religious grounds. A new development is a sponge impregnated with spermicide that is inserted into the vagina. The use of any contraceptive (birth control) is part of ◊family planning.

contract legal agreement between two or more parties, where each party agrees to do something. For example, a contract of employment is a legal agreement between an employer and an employee and lays out the conditions of employment. Contracts need not necessarily be written; they can be verbal contracts. In consumer law, for example, a contract is established when a good is sold.

contract bridge card game first played 1925. From 1930 it quickly outgrew ◊auction bridge in popularity.

contractile root in botany, a thickened root at the base of a corm, bulb, or other organ that helps position it at an appropriate level in the ground. Contractile roots are found, for example, on the corms of plants of the genus *Crocus*. After they have become anchored in the soil, the upper portion contracts, pulling the plant deeper into the ground.

contracting out in business, putting out to tender the provision of goods or services. During the 1980s, the British government encouraged and then forced various parts of government to contract out the provision of services such as refuse collection and street cleaning. Instead of government workers providing these services directly, any company could bid to provide the service; the company which gives the lowest price in its bid wins the contract.

contracting out in industrial relations, an agreement between an employer and employee whereby the employee does not participate in a financial contributory scheme administered by the employer. This usually applies to pension and health insurance schemes, or payment of trade union or other subscriptions from the gross salary.

contralto in music, a low-register female voice, also called an ◊alto.

control experiment essential part of a scientifically valid experiment, designed to show that the factor being tested is actually responsible for the effect observed. In the control experiment all factors, apart from the one under test, are exactly the same as in the test experiments, and all the same measurements are carried out. In drug trials, a placebo (a harmless substance) is given alongside the substance being tested in order to compare effects.

convection heat energy transfer that involves the movement of a fluid (gas or liquid). According to ◊kinetic theory, molecules of fluid in contact with the source of heat expand and tend to rise within the bulk of the fluid. Less energetic, cooler molecules sink to take their place, setting up convection currents. This is the principle of natural convection in many domestic hot-water systems and space heaters.

convectional rainfall rainfall associated with hot climates, resulting from the uprising of convection currents of warm air. Air that has been warmed by the extreme heating of the ground surface rises to great heights and is abruptly cooled. The water vapour carried by the air condenses and rain falls heavily. Convectional rainfall is usually associated with a ◊thunderstorm.

convection current current caused by the expansion of a liquid or gas as its temperature rises. The expanded material, being less dense, rises above colder and therefore denser material. Convection currents arise in the atmosphere above warm land masses or seas, giving rise to sea breezes and land breezes respectively. In some heating systems, convection currents are used to carry hot water upwards in pipes.

convener in a trade union, the senior shop steward within an organization who is elected by other shop stewards.

conventional current direction in which an electric current is considered to flow in a circuit. By convention, the direction is that in which positive-charge carriers would flow – from the positive terminal of a cell to its negative terminal. It is opposite in direction to the flow of electrons. In circuit diagrams, the arrows shown on symbols for components such as diodes and transistors point in the direction of conventional current flow.

conventional forces in Europe (CFE) treaty signed by NATO and Warsaw Pact representatives Nov 1990, reducing the number of tanks, missiles, aircraft, and other forms of non-nuclear military hardware held by member states.

Talks between government representatives had begun in Vienna, Austria, March 1989 with the aim of reducing the 'conventional' – that is, non-nuclear – forces (US, Soviet, French, British, and German) in Europe. The dissolution of the Warsaw Pact 1991 left doubts over the verification of the treaty, but at the July 1992 Helsinki summit of the ◊Conference on Security and Cooperation in Europe a revised version of the 1990 treaty was signed by 29 states (all members of NATO or former Soviet republics).

conventionalism the view that a priori truths, logical axioms, or scientific laws have no absolute validity but are disguised conventions representing one of a number of possible alternatives. The French philosopher and mathematician Jules Henri Poincaré introduced this position into the philosophy of science.

convergence in mathematics, the property of a series of numbers in which the difference between consecutive terms gradually decreases. The sum of a converging series approaches a limit as the number of terms tends to ◊infinity.

convergent evolution in biology, the independent evolution of similar structures in species (or other taxonomic groups) that are not closely related, as a result of living in a similar way. Thus, birds and bats have wings, not because they are descended from a common winged ancestor, but because their respective ancestors independently evolved flight.

converging lens lens that converges or brings to a focus those light rays that have been refracted by it. It is a ◊convex lens, with at least one surface that curves outwards, and is thicker towards the centre than at the edge. Converging lenses are used to form real images in many ◊optical instruments, such as cameras and projectors. A converging lens that forms a virtual, magnified image may be used as a magnifying glass or to correct ◊long-sightedness.

converse in mathematics, the reversed order of a conditional statement; the converse of the statement 'if a, then b' is 'if b, then a'. The converse does not always hold true; for example, the converse of 'if $x = 3$, then $x^2 = 9$' is 'if $x^2 = 9$, then $x = 3$', which is not true, as x could also be -3.

convertiplane ◊vertical takeoff and landing craft (VTOL) with rotors on its wings that spin horizontally for takeoff, but tilt to spin in a vertical plane for forward flight. At takeoff it looks like a two-rotor helicopter, with both rotors facing skywards. As forward speed is gained, the rotors tilt slowly forward until they are facing directly ahead.

convex of a surface, curving outwards, or towards the eye. For example, the outer surface of a ball appears convex. In geometry, the term is used to describe any polygon possessing no interior angle greater than 180°. Convex is the opposite of ◊concave.

convex lens lens that possesses at least one surface that curves outwards. It is a ◊converging lens, bringing rays of light to a focus. A convex lens is thicker at its centre than at its edges, and is used to correct long-sightedness.

convolvulus Despite the beauty of its flowers, convolvulus or field bindweed is a pernicious weed. Moreover, it has underground stems and can, as here, send shoots up through asphalt pavements causing considerable damage. *Premaphotos Wildlife*

Common forms include the biconvex lens (with both surfaces curved outwards) and the plano-convex (with one flat surface and one convex). The whole lens may be further curved overall, making a concavo-convex or converging meniscus lens, as in some lenses used in corrective eyewear.

convex mirror curved mirror that reflects light from its outer surface. It diverges reflected light rays to form a reduced, upright, virtual image. Convex mirrors give a wide field of view and are therefore particularly suitable for car wing mirrors and surveillance purposes in shops.

conveyancing administrative process involved in transferring title to land, usually on its sale or purchase. In England and Wales, conveyancing is usually done by solicitors, but, since 1985, can also be done by licensed conveyancers. Conveyancing has been simplified by the registration of land with the ◊Land Registry. The English system has been criticized for the delays in its procedure, in particular before binding contracts are exchanged, which can lead to gazumping (the vendor accepting a higher offer). In Scotland, this is avoided because a formal offer is legally binding.

convocation in the Church of England, the synods (councils) of the clergy of the provinces of Canterbury and York. The General Synod, established 1970, took over the functions and authority of the Convocation of Canterbury and York which continued to exist only in a restricted form.

convolvulus or ***bindweed*** any plant of the genus *Convolvulus* of the morning-glory family Convolvulaceae. They are characterized by their twining stems and by their petals, which are united into a funnel-shaped tube. The field bindweed *C. arvensis*, a trailing plant with handsome white or pink-and-white-streaked flowers, is a common weed in Britain.

convoy system grouping of ships to sail together under naval escort in wartime. In World War I (1914–18) navy escort vessels were at first used only to accompany troopships, but the convoy system was adopted for merchant shipping when the unrestricted German submarine campaign began 1917. In World War II (1939–45) the convoy system was widely used by the Allies to keep the Atlantic sea lanes open.

convulsion series of violent contractions of the muscles over which the patient has no control. It may be associated with loss of consciousness. Convulsions may arise from any one of a number of causes, including brain disease (such as ◊epilepsy), injury, high fever, poisoning, and electrocution.

Conwy unitary authority of Wales created 1996 (*see United Kingdom map*).

Cooder Ry(land Peter) 1947– . US guitarist, singer, and composer. His explorations of various forms of American music (Tex-Mex, jazz, Hawaiian, and so on) and bottleneck slide playing have gained him much session work and a cult following. His records include *Into the Purple Valley* 1972, *Borderline* 1980, and *Get Rhythm* 1987; he has written music for many films, including *Paris, Texas* 1984.

Cook James 1728–1779. British naval explorer. After surveying the St Lawrence River in North America 1759, he made three voyages: 1768–71 to Tahiti, New Zealand, and Australia; 1772–75 to the South Pacific; and 1776–79 to the South and North Pacific, attempting to find the Northwest Passage and charting the Siberian coast. He was killed in Hawaii.

In 1768 Cook was given command of an expedition to the South Pacific to witness the transit of Venus across the Sun. He sailed in the *Endeavour* with Joseph ◊Banks and other scientists, reaching Tahiti in April 1769. He then sailed around New Zealand and made a detailed survey of the east coast of Australia, naming New South Wales and Botany Bay. He returned to England 12 June 1771.

Now a commander, Cook set out 1772 with the *Resolution* and *Adventure* to search for the southern continent. The location of Easter Island was determined, and the Marquesas and Tonga Islands plotted. He also went to New Caledonia and Norfolk Island. Cook returned 25 July 1775, having sailed 100,000 km/60,000 mi in three years.

On 25 June 1776, he began his third and last voyage with the *Resolution* and *Discovery*. On the way to New Zealand, he visited several of the Cook or Hervey Islands and revisited the Hawaiian or Sandwich Islands. The ships sighted the North American coast at latitude 45° N and sailed north hoping to discover the Northwest Passage. He made a continuous survey as far as the Bering Strait, where the way was blocked by ice. Cook then surveyed the opposite coast of the strait (Siberia), and returned to Hawaii early 1779, where he was killed when his expedition clashed with islanders.

Cook Peter Edward 1937–1995. English satirist and entertainer. With his partner Dudley Moore, he appeared in the revue *Beyond the Fringe* 1959–64. He opened London's first satirical nightclub, the Establishment, 1960, and backed the satirical magazine *Private Eye*. Cook's distinctive humour, best exemplified in the 'Pete and Dud' routines with Moore, was as little restrained by any concern for political correctness as by good taste, and frequently tended towards a kind of verbal surrealism.

Cook Robin (Robert Finlayson) 1946– . English Labour politician, foreign secretary from 1997. A member of the moderate-left Tribune Group, he entered Parliament 1974 and became a leading member of Labour's shadow cabinet, specializing in health matters. When John Smith assumed the party leadership 1992, Cook remained in the shadow cabinet as spokesman for trade and industry. In 1994 he became shadow foreign secretary under Smith's successor, Tony ◊Blair.

Cook Thomas 1808–1892. Pioneer British travel agent and founder of Thomas Cook & Son. He organized his first tour, to Switzerland, in 1863. He introduced traveller's cheques (then called 'circular notes') in the early 1870s.

Cooke Sam 1931–1964. US soul singer and songwriter. He began his career as a gospel singer and turned to pop music 1956. His hits include 'You Send Me' 1957 and 'Wonderful World' 1960 (re-released 1986). His smooth tenor voice gilded some indifferent material, but his own song 'A Change Is Gonna Come' 1965 is a moving civil-rights anthem.

Cook Islands group of six large and a number of smaller Polynesian islands 2,600 km/1,600 mi NE of Auckland, New Zealand; area 290 sq km/112 sq mi; population (1991) 19,000. Their main products include fruit, copra, and crafts. They became a self-governing overseas territory of New Zealand 1965.

The chief island, Rarotonga, is the site of Avarua, the seat of government. Niue, geographically part of the group, is separately administered. The Cook Islands were visited by Capt James Cook 1773, annexed by Britain 1888, and transferred to New Zealand 1901. They have common citizenship with New Zealand. ▷ *See feature on pp. 806–807.*

Cook Strait strait dividing North Island and South Island, New Zealand. A submarine cable carries electricity from South to North Island.

Coolidge (John) Calvin 1872–1933. 30th president of the USA 1923–29, a Republican. As governor of Massachusetts 1919, he was responsible for crushing a Boston police strike. As Warren ◊Harding's vice president 1921–23, he succeeded to the presidency on Harding's death (2 Aug 1923). He won the 1924 presidential election, and his period of office was marked by economic growth.

cooling-off period in industrial relations, the practice of allowing a period of time to elapse between the start of a dispute and the taking of industrial action by a trade union. The practice may be voluntary or compulsory; in the latter case it is written into an agreement or into legislation.

Cooper Grand Prix motor-racing team formed by John Cooper (1923–). They built Formula Two

'There is no right to strike against the public safety by anybody, anywhere, any time.'

CALVIN COOLIDGE
Telegram to US labour leader Samuel Gompers

Cook The British naval explorer Capt James Cook. Cook sailed to Tahiti in the *Endeavour* 1768 to observe the transit of Venus across the Sun. This done, he travelled on to explore New Zealand and Australia, returning to England 1771. He made two further exploratory voyages, and was killed in Hawaii 1779. *Image Select (UK) Ltd*

The tendency of democracies is, in all things, to mediocrity.

JAMES FENIMORE COOPER *The American Democrat* 1838

and Formula Three cars before building their revolutionary rear-engined Cooper T45 in 1958. Jack Brabham won the 1959 world title in a Cooper and the team won the Constructor's Championship. Both Brabham and Cooper retained their titles the following year. However, other rear-engined cars subsequently proved more successful and in 1968 Cooper left Formula One racing.

Cooper Gary (Frank James) 1901–1961. US film actor. He epitomized the lean, true-hearted American, slow of speech but capable of outdoing the 'bad guys'. His films include *Lives of a Bengal Lancer* 1935, *Mr Deeds Goes to Town* 1936, *Sergeant York* 1940 (Academy Award), and *High Noon* 1952 (Academy Award). In 1960 he received a special Academy Award for his lifetime contribution to cinema.

Cooper Henry 1934– . English heavyweight boxer, the only man to win three Lonsdale Belts outright, 1961, 1965, and 1970. He held the British heavyweight title 1959–71 and lost it to Joe Bugner. He fought for the world heavyweight title but lost in the sixth round to Muhammad Ali 1966.

Cooper James Fenimore 1789–1851. US writer. He wrote some 50 novels, becoming popular with *The Spy* 1821. His volumes of *Leatherstocking Tales* focused on the frontier hero Leatherstocking and the Native Americans before and after the American Revolution; they include *The Last of the Mohicans* 1826. Still popular as adventures, his novels have been reappraised for their treatment of social and moral issues in the settling of the American frontier.

Cooper Leon Niels 1930– . US physicist who in 1955 began work on the phenomenon of ◊superconductivity. He proposed that at low temperatures electrons would be bound in pairs (since known as Cooper pairs) and in this state electrical resistance to their flow through solids would disappear. He shared the 1972 Nobel Prize for Physics with John ◊Bardeen and J Robert Schrieffer (1931–).

Cooper Susie 1902–1995). English pottery designer. Her style has varied from colourful Art Deco to softer, pastel decoration on classical shapes. She started her own company 1929, which later became part of the Wedgwood factory, where she was senior designer from 1966.

Cooperation Council for the Arab States of the Gulf (CCASG) former name of the ◊Gulf Cooperation Council (GCC).

cooperative business organization with limited liability where each shareholder has only one vote however many shares they own. In a worker cooperative, it is the workers who are the shareholders and own the company. The workers decide on how the company is to be run. In a consumer cooperative, consumers control the company. Co-op shops and superstores are examples of consumer cooperatives. They are owned by regional cooperative retail groups.

cooperative movement the banding together of groups of people for mutual assistance in trade, manufacture, the supply of credit, housing, or other services. The original principles of the cooperative movement were laid down 1844 by the Rochdale Pioneers, under the influence of Robert ◊Owen, and by Charles Fourier in France.

Producers' cooperative societies, formed on a basis of co-partnership among the employees, exist on a large scale in France, Italy, Spain, and the ex-Soviet republics. (In 1988, Soviet economic cooperatives were given legal and financial independence and the right to appear in foreign markets and to set up joint ventures with foreign companies.) Agricultural cooperative societies have been formed in many countries for the collective purchase of seeds, fertilizers, and other commodities, while societies for cooperative marketing of agricultural produce are prominent in the USA, Ireland, Denmark, E Europe, and the ex-Soviet republics. Agricultural credit societies are strong in rural economies of Europe and Asia, including parts of India. The USA also has a cooperative farm credit system.

In the UK the 1970s and 1980s saw a growth in the number of workers' cooperatives, set up in factories otherwise threatened by closure due to economic depression.

Cooperative Party political party founded in Britain 1917 by the cooperative movement to maintain its principles in parliamentary and local government. A written constitution was adopted 1938. The party had strong links with the Labour Party; from 1946 Cooperative Party candidates stood in elections as Cooperative and Labour Candidates and, after the 1959 general election, agreement was reached to limit the party's candidates to 30.

Cooperative Wholesale Society (CWS) British concern, the largest cooperative organization in the world, owned and controlled by the numerous cooperative retail societies, which are also its customers. Founded 1863, it acts as wholesaler, manufacturer, and banker, and owns factories, farms, and estates, in addition to offices and warehouses.

coordinate in geometry, a number that defines the position of a point relative to a point or axis (reference line). ◊Cartesian coordinates define a point by its perpendicular distances from two or more axes drawn through a fixed point mutually at right angles to each other. ◊Polar coordinates define a point in a plane by its distance from a fixed point and direction from a fixed line.

coordinate geometry or ***analytical geometry*** system of geometry in which points, lines, shapes, and surfaces are represented by algebraic expressions. In plane (two-dimensional) coordinate geometry, the plane is usually defined by two axes at right angles to each other, the horizontal x-axis and the vertical y-axis, meeting at O, the origin. A point on the plane can be represented by a pair of ◊Cartesian coordinates, which define its position in terms of its distance along the x-axis and along the y-axis from O. These distances are respectively the x and y coordinates of the point.

Lines are represented as equations; for example, $y = 2x + 1$ gives a straight line, and $y = 3x^2 + 2x$ gives a ◊parabola (a curve). The graphs of varying equations can be drawn by plotting the coordinates of points that satisfy their equations, and joining up the points. One of the advantages of coordinate geometry is that geometrical solutions can be obtained without drawing but by manipulating algebraic expressions. For example, the coordinates of the point of intersection of two straight lines can be determined by finding the unique values of x and y that satisfy both of the equations for the lines, that is, by solving them as a pair of ◊simultaneous equations. The curves studied in simple coordinate geometry are the ◊conic sections (circle, ellipse, parabola, and hyperbola), each of which has a characteristic equation.

coot freshwater bird of the genus *Fulica* in the rail family, order Gruiformes. Coots are about 38 cm/1.2 ft long, and mainly black. They have a white bill, extending up the forehead in a plate, and big feet with four lobed toes.

coot The giant Andean coot *Fulica gigantea* inhabits the Altiplano, the high plateau between two chains of the Andes Mountains in South America, at a height of 4,300 m/14,100 ft. Males engage in vicious fights to establish and maintain territories. *Premaphotos Wildlife*

Coote Eyre 1726–1783. Irish general in British India. His victory 1760 at Wandiwash, followed by the capture of Pondicherry, ended French hopes of supremacy. He returned to India as commander in chief 1779, and several times defeated ◊Hyder Ali, sultan of Mysore.

Copenhagen (Danish ***København***) capital of Denmark, on the islands of Zealand and Amager; population (1995) 1,353,300 (including suburbs)

features to the E is the royal palace at Amalienborg; the 17th-century Charlottenborg Palace houses the Academy of Arts, and parliament meets in the Christiansborg Palace. The statue of Hans Christian Andersen's *Little Mermaid* (by Edvard Eriksen) is at the harbour entrance. The Tivoli amusement park is in the heart of the city

history Copenhagen was a fishing village until 1167, when the bishop of Roskilde built the castle on the site of the present Christiansborg palace. A settlement grew up, and it became the Danish capital 1443. The university was founded 1479. The city was under German occupation April 1940–May 1945.

Copenhagen, Battle of naval victory 2 April 1801 by a British fleet under Sir Hyde Parker (1739–1807) and ◊Nelson over the Danish fleet. Nelson put his telescope to his blind eye and refused to see Parker's signal for withdrawal.

Copernicus Nicolaus. Latinized form of Mikolaj Kopernik 1473–1543. Polish astronomer. He believed that the Sun, not the Earth, is at the centre of the Solar System, thus defying the Christian church doctrine of the time. For 30 years he worked on the hypothesis that the rotation and the orbital motion of the Earth were responsible for the apparent movement of the heavenly bodies. His great work *De revolutionibus orbium coelestium/On the Revolutions of the Heavenly Spheres* was not published until the year of his death.

Copernicus relegated the Earth from being the centre of the universe to being merely a planet (the centre only of its own gravity and the orbit of its solitary Moon). This forced a fundamental revision of the anthropocentric view of the universe and came as a psychological shock to European culture. Copernicus's model could not be proved right, because it contained several fundamental flaws, but it was the important first step to the more accurate picture built up by later astronomers. ▷ *See feature on pp. 70–71.*

coplanar in geometry, describing lines or points that all lie in the same plane.

Copland Aaron 1900–1990. US composer. His early works, such as his piano concerto 1926, were in the jazz idiom but he gradually developed a gentler style with a regional flavour drawn from

Copland US composer Aaron Copland. The many styles and forms in which he has worked have brought him wide recognition, including a Pulitzer Prize for music 1945, and an Academy Award for his film score for *The Heiresss* 1949.

American folk music. He wrote the ballets *Billy the Kid* 1939, *Rodeo* 1942, and *Appalachian Spring* 1944 (based on a poem by Hart Crane). Among his orchestral works is *Inscape* 1967.

Copland studied in France with Nadia Boulanger and taught from 1940 at the Berkshire Music Center, now the Tanglewood Music Center, near Lenox, Massachusetts. He took avant-garde European styles and gave them a distinctive American pitch. His eight film scores, including *The Heiress* 1949, set new standards for Hollywood.

copper orange-pink, very malleable and ductile, metallic element, symbol Cu (from Latin *cuprum*), atomic number 29, relative atomic mass 63.546. It is used for its durability, pliability, high thermal and electrical conductivity, and resistance to corrosion.

It was the first metal used systematically for tools by humans; when mined and worked into utensils it formed the technological basis for the Copper Age in prehistory. When alloyed with tin it forms bronze, which strengthens the copper, allowing it to hold a sharp edge; the systematic production and use of this was the basis for the prehistoric Bronze Age. Brass, another hard copper alloy, includes zinc.

copper ore any mineral from which copper is extracted, including native copper, Cu; chalcocite, Cu_2S; chalcopyrite, $CuFeS_2$; bornite, Cu_5FeS_4; azurite, $Cu_3(CO_3)_2(OH)_2$; malachite, $Cu_2CO_3(OH)_2$; and chrysocolla, $CuSiO_3.2H_2O$.

Native copper and the copper sulphides are usually found in veins associated with igneous intrusions. Chrysocolla and the carbonates are products of the weathering of copper-bearing rocks. The main producers are the USA, Russia, Kazakhstan, Georgia, Uzbekistan, Armenia, Zambia, Chile, Peru, Canada, and Democratic Republic of Congo.

coppicing woodland management practice of severe pruning where trees are cut down to near ground level at regular intervals, typically every 3–20 years, to promote the growth of numerous shoots from the base.

Coppola Francis Ford 1939– . US film director and screenwriter of wide-ranging ambition. He directed *The Godfather* 1972, and its sequels *The Godfather Part II* 1974, which won seven Academy Awards, and *The Godfather Part III* 1990. His other films include *Apocalypse Now* 1979, *One from the Heart* 1982, *Rumblefish* 1983, *The Outsiders* 1983, *Bram Stoker's Dracula* 1992, *Jack* 1996, and *The Rainmaker*, based on John Grisham's novel, 1997.

His first successes were *Finian's Rainbow* 1968 and *Patton* 1969, for which his screenplay won an Academy Award. Among his other films are *The Conversation* 1972 and *The Cotton Club* 1984.

copra dried meat from the kernel of the ◊coconut, used to make coconut oil.

Copt descendant of those ancient Egyptians who adopted Christianity in the 1st century and refused to convert to Islam after the Arab conquest. They now form a small minority (about 5%) of Egypt's population. Coptic is a member of the Hamito-Semitic language family. It is descended from the language of the ancient Egyptians and is the ritual language of the Coptic Christian church. It is written in the Greek alphabet with some additional characters derived from ◊demotic script.

The head of the Coptic church is the Patriarch of Alexandria, from 1971 Shenouda III (1923–), 117th pope of Alexandria. Imprisoned by President Sadat 1981, he is opposed by Muslim fundamentalists.

Coptic art the art of the indigenous Christian community of 5th–8th-century Egypt. Flat and colourful in style, with strong outlines and stylized forms, it shows the influence of Byzantine, late Roman, and ancient Egyptian art. Wall paintings, textiles, stone and ivory carvings, and manuscript illuminations remain, the most noted examples of which are in the Coptic Museum, Cairo. The influence of Coptic art was widespread in the Christian world, and Coptic interlacing patterns may have been the source for the designs of Irish and Northumbrian illuminated gospels. For the later period of Fatimid art, 10th–11th centuries, see ◊Islamic art.

copulation act of mating in animals with internal ◊fertilization. Male mammals have a ◊penis or other organ that is used to introduce spermatozoa into the reproductive tract of the female. Most birds transfer sperm by pressing their cloacas (the openings of their reproductive tracts) together.

copyright law applying to literary, musical, and artistic works (including plays, recordings, films, photographs, radio and television broadcasts, and, in the USA and the UK, computer programs), which prevents the reproduction of the work, in whole or in part, without the author's consent.

Copyright applies to a work, not an idea. For example, the basic plots of two novels might be identical, but copyright would be infringed only if it was clear that one author had copied from another. A translation is protected in its own right. The copyright holder may assign the copyright to another or license others to reproduce or adapt the work. In 1991, the US Supreme Court ruled that copyright does not exist in the information in a telephone directory since 'copyright rewards originality, not effort'.

In the UK and (since 1989) the USA, copyright lasts for a holder's lifetime plus 50 years, or (in the USA), a flat 75 years for a company copyright. An author's copyright was first recognized in Britain by Act of Parliament in 1709, and extended to cover public performance for gain by the Dramatic Copyright Act 1833. Copyright is internationally enforceable under the Berne Convention 1886 (ratified by the UK, among others) and the Universal Copyright Convention 1952 (more widely ratified, including the USA, the former USSR, and the UK). Both conventions have been revised, most recently in Paris 1971. Under the Universal Copyright Convention, works must be marked with the copyright symbol accompanied by the name of the copyright owner and the year of its first publication. The Berne Convention gives a longer minimum period of protection of copyright.

Under the UK Copyright, Designs, and Patents Act 1988, artists gained control of copyright over work commissioned by others; for example, additional payment must be made by the publisher commissioning the artwork if it is to be reused later. Artists were also enabled to object to the mutilation or distortion of their work. Photographers obtained the same 50-year copyright granted to other artists and the copyright itself was ruled to belong to whoever might have paid for the film used, as previously. Remedies for breach of copyright (piracy) include damages, account of profit, or an injunction.

Computer software is specifically covered in the USA under the Copyright Act 1976 and the Computer Software Act 1980, and in the UK the Copyright (Computer Software) Amendment Act 1985 extended copyright to computer programs.

coral marine invertebrate of the class Anthozoa in the phylum Cnidaria, which also includes sea anemones and jellyfish. It has a skeleton of lime (calcium carbonate) extracted from the surrounding water. Corals exist in warm seas, at moderate depths with sufficient light. Some coral is valued for decoration or jewellery, for example, Mediterranean red coral *Corallum rubrum*.

Corals live in a symbiotic relationship with microscopic ◊algae (zooxanthellae), which are incorporated into the soft tissue. The algae obtain carbon dioxide from the coral polyps, and the polyps receive nutrients from the algae. Corals also have a relationship to the fish that rest or take refuge within their branches, and which excrete nutrients that make the corals grow faster. The majority of corals form large colonies although there are species that live singly. Their accumulated skeletons make up large coral reefs and atolls. The Great Barrier Reef, to the NE of Australia, is about 1,600 km/1,000 mi long, has a total area of 20,000 sq km/7,700 sq mi, and adds 50 million tonnes of calcium to the reef each year. The world's reefs cover an estimated 620,000 sq km/240,000 sq mi.

Fringing reefs are so called because they build up on the shores of continents or islands, the living animals mainly occupying the outer edges of the reef. ***Barrier reefs*** are separated from the shore by a saltwater lagoon, which may be as much as 30 km/20 mi wide; there are usually navigable passes through the barrier into the lagoon. ***Atolls*** resemble a ring surrounding a lagoon, and do not enclose an island. They are usually formed by the gradual subsidence of an extinct volcano, the coral growing up from where the edge of the island once lay. *See illustrations on following page.*

Coppola US film director and screen writer Francis Ford Coppola. His film *Apocalypse Now* 1979 was the first major film to examine the US involvement in Vietnam. *Topham*

coral A coral reef off the coast of Kenya, E Africa. Formed from countless lime skeletons of generations of corals, these reefs take hundreds of years to form. The biggest threat to them is tourism: sewage discharged from hotels clouds the water and kills the coral by depriving it of sunlight.

Coral Sea (or ***Solomon Sea***) part of the ◊Pacific Ocean bounded by NE Australia, New Guinea, the Solomon Islands, Vanuatu, and New Caledonia. It contains numerous coral islands and reefs. The Coral Sea Islands are a territory of Australia; they comprise scattered reefs and islands over an area of about 1,000,000 sq km/386,000 sq mi. They are uninhabited except for a meteorological station on Willis Island. The ◊Great Barrier Reef lies along its western edge, just off the east coast of Australia.

The naval battle of the Coral Sea 7–8 May 1942, fought between the USA and Japan, mainly from aircraft carriers, checked the Japanese advance in the South Pacific in World War II. This was the first sea battle to be fought entirely by aircraft, launched from carriers, without any engagement between the actual warships themselves.

cor anglais or ***English horn*** alto ◊oboe in F with a distinctive tulip-shaped bell and warm nasal tone, heard to pastoral effect in Rossini's overture to *William Tell* 1829, and portraying a plaintive Sasha the duck in Prokofiev's *Peter and the Wolf* 1936.

Corbusier, Le French architect; see ◊Le Corbusier.

cord unit for measuring the volume of wood cut for fuel. One cord equals 128 cubic feet (3.456 cubic metres), or a stack 8 feet (2.4 m) long, 4 feet (1.2 m) wide, and 4 feet high.

Corday Charlotte, full name Marie-Anne Charlotte Corday d'Armont 1768–1793. French Girondin (right-wing republican during the French Revolution). After the overthrow of the Girondins by the extreme left-wing Jacobins May 1793, she stabbed to death the Jacobin leader, Jean Paul Marat, with a bread knife as he sat in his bath in July of the same year. She was guillotined.

‘I have done my task, let others do theirs.’

CHARLOTTE CORDAY
On being interrogated for the murder of Marat, July 1793

cordierite silicate mineral, $(Mg,Fe)_2Al_4Si_5O_{18}$, blue to purplish in colour. It is characteristic of metamorphic rocks formed from clay sediments under conditions of low pressure but moderate temperature; it is the mineral that forms the spots in spotted slate and spotted hornfels.

cordillera group of mountain ranges and their valleys, all running in a specific direction, formed by the continued convergence of two tectonic plates (see ◊plate tectonics) along a line.

Cordilleras, the mountainous western section of North America, with the Rocky Mountains and the coastal ranges parallel to the contact between the North American and the Pacific plates.

Córdoba city in central Argentina, on the Río Primero; population (1992 est) 1,179,400. It is the capital of Córdoba province. Main industries include cement, glass, textiles, and vehicles. Founded 1573, it has a university founded 1613, a military aviation college, an observatory, and a cathedral.

Córdoba capital of Córdoba province, Spain, on the river Guadalquivir; population (1994) 316,000. Paper, textiles, and copper products are manufactured here. It has many Moorish remains, including the mosque, now a cathedral, founded by 'Abd-ar-Rahman I 785, which is one of the largest Christian churches in the world. Córdoba was probably founded by the Carthaginians; it was held by the Moors 711–1236.

core in archaeology, a solid cylinder of sediment or soil collected with a coring device and used to evaluate the geological context and stratigraphy of archaeological material or to obtain palaeobotanical samples. Core can also mean the tool used to extract a core sample from the ground, or a stone blank from which flakes or blades are removed.

core in earth science, the innermost part of Earth. It is divided into an outer core, which begins at a depth of 2,898 km/1,800 mi, and an inner core, which begins at a depth of 4,982 km/3,095 mi. Both parts are thought to consist of iron-nickel alloy. The outer core is liquid and the inner core is solid. Evidence for the nature of the core comes from seismology (observation of the paths of earthquake waves through Earth), and calculations of Earth's density. The temperature of the core is estimated to be at least 4,000°C/7,232°F.

Corelli Arcangelo 1653–1713. Italian composer and violinist. He was one of the first virtuoso exponents of the Baroque violin and his music, marked by graceful melody, includes a set of *concerti grossi* and five sets of chamber sonatas.

Corfu (Greek ***Kérkyra***) northernmost and second largest of the Ionian islands of Greece, off the coast of Epirus in the Ionian Sea; area 1,072 sq km/414 sq mi; population (1991) 105,000. Its businesses include tourism, fruit, olive oil, and textiles. Its largest town is the port of Corfu (Kérkyra), population (1991) 36,900. Corfu was colonized by the Corinthians about 700 BC. Venice held it 1386–1797, Britain 1815–64.

Cori Carl Ferdinand (1896–1984) and Gerty (Theresa, born Radnitz) (1896–1957) US biochemists born in Austro-Hungary who, together with Argentine physiologist Bernardo Houssay (1887–1971), received a Nobel prize 1947 for their discovery of how ◊glycogen (animal starch) – a derivative of glucose – is broken down and resynthesized in the body, for use as a store and source of energy.

coriander pungent fresh herb, the Eurasian plant *Coriandrum sativum*, a member of the parsley family Umbelliferae, also a spice: the dried ripe fruit. The spice is used commercially as a flavouring in meat products, bakery goods, tobacco, gin, liqueurs, chilli, and curry powder. Both are much used in cooking in the Middle East, India, Mexico, and China.

Corinth (Greek ***Kórinthos***) port in Greece, on the isthmus connecting the Peloponnese with the mainland; population (1981) 22,650. The rocky isthmus is bisected by the 6.5 km/4 mi Corinth canal, opened 1893. The site of the ancient city-state of Corinth lies 7 km/4.5 mi SW of the port.

Corinth was already a place of some commercial importance in the 9th century BC. At the end of the 6th century BC it joined the Peloponnesian League, and took a prominent part in the ◊Persian and the ◊Peloponnesian Wars. In 146 BC it was destroyed by the Romans. It was established as a Roman colony by Julius Caesar 44 BC, and became the capital of the Roman province of Achaea. St Paul visited Corinth AD 51 and addressed two epistles to its churches. After many changes of ownership it became part of independent Greece 1822. Corinth's ancient monuments include the ruined temple of Apollo (6th century BC).

Corinthian in Classical architecture, one of the five types of column; see ◊order.

Coriolis effect the effect of the Earth's rotation on the atmosphere and on all objects on the Earth's surface. In the northern hemisphere it causes moving objects and currents to be deflected to the right; in the southern hemisphere it causes deflection to

coral Corals are marine animals related to jellyfishes and sea anemones. Most hard or stony corals live as colonies of polyps that secrete a rigid external skeleton of lime. But there are also those that live as solitary individuals. Corals grow in a wide variety of forms as the types here demonstrate. Sea fans, for example, have an internal skeleton linking the polyps, while the polyps of the brain coral are arranged in rows. The stagshorn coral gets its name from the resemblance of the colony to a male deer's antlers. The names of the plate and pillar corals also reflect their appearance.

Corelli The composer Arcangelo Corelli represented in a mezzotint by I Smith Anglus (after Hugh Howard). Although he was by no means a prolific composer, Corelli's influence spread far and wide as other composers copied his once-original gestures. *Image Select (UK) Ltd*

the left. The effect is named after its discoverer, the French mathematician Gaspard Coriolis (1792–1843).

cork light, waterproof outer layers of the bark of the stems and roots of almost all trees and shrubs. The cork oak *Quercus suber*, a native of S Europe and N Africa, is cultivated in Spain and Portugal; the exceptionally thick outer layers of its bark provide the cork that is used commercially.

Cork largest county of the Republic of Ireland, in the province of Munster; county town Cork; area 7,460 sq km/2,880 sq mi; population (1991) 409,800. It is agricultural, but there is also some copper and manganese mining, marble quarrying, and river and sea fishing. Natural gas and oil fields are found off the S coast at Kinsale. It includes Bantry Bay and the village of Blarney. There is a series of ridges and vales running NE–SW across the county. The Nagles and Boggeraph mountains run across the centre, separating the two main rivers, the Blackwater and the Lee. Towns are Cobh, Bantry, Youghal, Fermoy, and Mallow.

Cork city and seaport of County Cork, on the river Lee, at the head of the long inlet of Cork harbour; population (1991) 127,000. Cork is the second port of the Republic of Ireland. The lower section of the harbour can berth liners, and the city has distilleries, shipyards, and iron foundries. Other industries include tanning, food processing, and brewing. St Finbarr's 7th-century monastery was the original foundation of Cork. It was eventually settled by Danes who were dispossessed by the English 1172.

University College (1845) became the University of Cork 1968. The city hall was opened 1937. There is a Protestant cathedral dedicated to the city's patron saint, St Finbarr, and a Roman Catholic cathedral of St Mary and St Finbarr.

corm short, swollen, underground plant stem, surrounded by protective scale leaves, as seen in the genus *Crocus*. It stores food, provides a means of ◊vegetative reproduction, and acts as a ◊perennating organ. During the year, the corm gradually withers as the food reserves are used for the production of leafy, flowering shoots formed from axillary buds. Several new corms are formed at the base of these shoots, above the old corm.

Corman Roger William 1926– . US film director and producer whose films are mainly in the youth and science-fiction genres. He has over 200 films to his credit since 1954. Among his directed work was a series of Edgar Allan Poe adaptations, beginning with *The House of Usher* 1960.

cormorant any of various diving seabirds, mainly of the genus *Phalacrocorax*, order Pelecaniformes, about 90 cm/3 ft long, with webbed feet, a long neck, hooked beak, and glossy black plumage. Cormorants generally feed on fish and shellfish, which they catch by swimming and diving under water, sometimes to a considerable depth. They collect the food in a pouch formed by the dilatable skin at the front of the throat. Some species breed on inland lakes and rivers.

corn the main ◊cereal crop of a region – for example, wheat in the UK, oats in Scotland and Ireland, maize in the USA. Also, another word for ◊maize.

cornea transparent front section of the vertebrate ◊eye. The cornea is curved and behaves as a fixed lens, so that light entering the eye is partly focused before it reaches the lens. There are no blood vessels in the cornea and it relies on the fluid in the front chamber of the eye for nourishment. Further protection for the eye is provided by the ◊conjunctiva.

Corneille Pierre 1606–1684. French dramatist. His tragedies, such as *Horace* 1640, *Cinna* 1641, and *Oedipe* 1659, glorify the strength of will governed by reason, and established the French classical dramatic tradition. His first comedy, *Mélite*, was performed 1629, followed by others that gained him a brief period of favour with Cardinal Richelieu. His early masterpiece, *Le Cid* 1636, was attacked by the Academicians, although it received public acclaim, and was produced in the same year as *L'Illusion comique/The Comic Illusion*.

Although Corneille enjoyed public popularity, periodic disfavour with Richelieu marred his career, and it was not until 1639 that Corneille (again in favour) produced plays such as *Polyeucte* 1643, *Le Menteur* 1643, and *Rodogune* 1645, leading to his election to the Académie 1647. His later plays were approved by Louis XIV.

When there is no peril in the fight, there is no glory in the triumph.

Pierre Corneille
Le Cid

cornet three-valved brass band instrument, soprano member in B flat of a group of valved horns developed in Austria and Germany about 1820–50 for military band use. Of cylindrical bore, its compact shape and deeper conical bell allow greater speed and agility of intonation than the trumpet, at the expense of less tonal precision and brilliance.

cornflower plant *Centaurea cyanus* of the family Compositae. Formerly a common weed in N European wheat fields, it is now commonly grown in gardens as a herbaceous plant.

Cornish language extinct member of the ◊Celtic languages, a branch of the Indo-European language family, spoken in Cornwall, England, until 1777. In recent years the language has been revived in a somewhat reconstructed form by people interested in their Cornish heritage.

Corn Laws in Britain until 1846, laws used to regulate the export or import of cereals in order to maintain an adequate supply for consumers and a secure price for producers. For centuries the Corn Laws formed an integral part of the mercantile system in England; they were repealed because they became an unwarranted tax on food and a hindrance to British exports.

Although mentioned as early as the 12th century, the Corn Laws only became significant in the late 18th century. After the Napoleonic wars, with mounting pressure from a growing urban population, the laws aroused strong opposition because of their tendency to drive up prices. They were modified 1828 and 1842 and, partly as a result of the Irish potato famine, repealed by Prime Minister Robert ◊Peel 1846.

cornucopia (Latin 'horn of plenty') in Greek mythology, one of the horns of the goat Amaltheia, which was caused by Zeus to refill itself indefinitely with food and drink. In paintings, the cornucopia is depicted as a horn-shaped container spilling over with fruit and flowers.

Cornwall county in SW England including the Isles of ◊Scilly (Scillies).
area (excluding Scillies) 3,550 sq km/1,370 sq mi (*see United Kingdom map*)
towns and cities Truro (administrative headquarters), Camborne, Launceston; resorts of Bude, Falmouth, Newquay, Penzance, St Ives
features Bodmin Moor (including Brown Willy 419 m/1,375 ft); Land's End peninsula; St Michael's Mount; rivers Tamar, Fowey, Fal, Camel; Poldhu, site of first transatlantic radio signal 1901; the Stannary or Tinners' Parliament has six members from each of the four Stannary towns: Losthwithiel, Launceston, Helston, and Truro; Tate Gallery St Ives; the Mineral Tramways Project aims to preserve the mining landscape, once the centre of the world's hard-rock mining industry
industries electronics; spring flowers; dairy farming; market gardening; tourism; tin (mined since the Bronze Age, some workings renewed 1960s, but now only one mine remaining, at South Crofty); kaolin (St Austell); fish
population (1991) 469,300
famous people John Betjeman, Humphry Davy, Daphne Du Maurier, William Golding
history the Stannary, established in the 11th century, ceased to meet 1752 but its powers were never rescinded at Westminster, and it was revived 1974 as a separatist movement. The flag of St Piran, a white St George's cross on a black ground, is used by separatists.

This Cornwall is very primeval ... It is like the beginning of the world, wonderful: and so free and strong.

On **Cornwall**
D H Lawrence, letter to Lady Cynthia Asquith 7 Feb 1916

Cornwallis Charles, 1st Marquis and 2nd Earl 1738–1805. British general in the ◊American Revolution until 1781, when his defeat at Yorktown led to final surrender and ended the war. He then served twice as governor general of India and once as viceroy of Ireland.

corolla collective name for the petals of a flower. In some plants the petal margins are partly or completely fused to form a corolla tube, for example in bindweed *Convolvulus arvensis*.

corona faint halo of hot (about 2,000,000°C/ 3,600,000°F) and tenuous gas around the Sun, which boils from the surface. It is visible at solar ◊eclipses or through a coronagraph, an instrument that blocks light from the Sun's brilliant disc. Gas flows away from the corona to form the ◊solar wind.

Corona Australis or ***Southern Crown*** small constellation of the southern hemisphere, located near the constellation ◊Sagittarius. It is similar in size and shape to ◊Corona Borealis but is not as bright.

Corona Borealis or ***Northern Crown*** small but easily recognizable constellation of the northern hemisphere, between ◊Hercules and ◊Boötes. Its brightest star is Alphecca (or Gemma), which is 78 light years from Earth, and it contains several variable stars.

Coronado Francisco Vásquez de c. 1510–1554. Spanish explorer who sailed to the New World 1535 in search of gold. In 1540 he set out with several hundred men from the Gulf of California on an exploration of what are today the Southern states. Although he failed to discover any gold, his expedition came across the impressive Grand Canyon of the Colorado and introduced the use of the horse to the indigenous Indians.

coronary artery disease (Latin *corona* 'crown', from the arteries encircling the heart) condition in which the fatty deposits of ◊atherosclerosis form in the coronary arteries that supply the heart muscle, narrowing them and restricting the blood flow. These arteries may already be hardened (arteriosclerosis). If the heart's requirements are increased, as during exercise, the blood supply through the narrowed arteries may be

corona The solar corona, the gaseous outer layer of the Sun's atmosphere. It appears as a faint halo at solar eclipse. *Image Select (UK) Ltd*

inadequate, and the pain of ◊angina results. A ◊heart attack occurs if the blood supply to an area of the heart is cut off, for example because a blood clot (thrombus) has blocked one of the coronary arteries. The subsequent lack of oxygen damages the heart muscle (infarct), and if a large area of the heart is affected, the attack may be fatal.

Coronary artery disease tends to run in families and is linked to smoking, lack of exercise, and a diet high in saturated (mostly animal) fats, which tends to increase the level of blood ◊cholesterol. It is a common cause of death in many industrialized countries and is the biggest single cause of premature death in the UK; older men are the most vulnerable group. The condition is treated with drugs or bypass surgery.

coronation ceremony of investing a sovereign with the emblems of royalty, as a symbol of inauguration in office. Since the coronation of Harold 1066, English sovereigns have been crowned in Westminster Abbey, London. The kings of Scotland were traditionally crowned in Scone, and French kings in Reims.

The British coronation ceremony combines the Hebrew rite of anointing with customs of Germanic origin; for example, the actual crowning and the presentation of the monarch to his or her subjects to receive homage.

coroner official who investigates the deaths of persons who have died suddenly by acts of violence or under suspicious circumstances, by holding an inquest or ordering a postmortem examination (autopsy). The coroner's court aims not to establish liability but to find out how, where, and why the death occurred. In Scotland similar duties are performed by the procurator fiscal.

Corot Jean-Baptiste Camille 1796–1875. French painter. He created a distinctive landscape style using a soft focus and a low-key palette of browns, ochres, and greens. His early work, including Italian scenes of the 1820s, influenced the ◊Barbizon School of painters. Like them, Corot worked outdoors, but he also continued a conventional academic tradition with his romanticized paintings of women.

It is reasonable to suppose that he was impressed by Constable in the Salon of 1824; going to Rome the following year he showed in his first Italian landscapes a response to effects of sun and cloud that seems, as in the *Claudian Aqueduct* (National Gallery), related to the work of the English master. Their breadth and directness of style marked a new conception of landscape in French art. His first Salon picture, 1827, was the *Vue prise à Narni* (National Gallery of Canada), and he returned to France 1828, painting some of his best pictures in the following six years, and working in Paris and Normandy, at Fontainebleu, Ville d'Avray and elsewhere, the light of Italy giving place to harmonies of silvery grey. A second visit to Italy 1834, and another 1843 produced further masterly works, such as his *Villa d'Este*.

corporal punishment physical punishment of wrongdoers – for example, by whipping. It is still used as a punishment for criminals in many countries, especially under Islamic law. Corporal punishment of children by parents is illegal in some countries, including Sweden, Finland, Denmark, and Norway. Cyprus and Austria have comprehensive bans. In Britain, corporal punishment was abolished as a punishment for criminals 1967 but only became illegal for punishing schoolchildren in state schools 1986.

corporate strategy the way an organization intends to meet its objectives. This may be set out in a document of its principles, its situation, and the environment in which it expects to operate.

corporation tax tax levied on a company's profits. It is a form of income tax, and rates vary according to country, but there is usually a flat rate. It is a large source of revenue for governments.

corporatism belief that the state in capitalist democracies should intervene to a large extent in the economy to ensure social harmony. In Austria, for example, corporatism results in political decisions often being taken after discussions between chambers of commerce, trade unions, and the government.

corporative state state in which the members are organized and represented not on a local basis as citizens, but as producers working in a particular trade, industry, or profession. Originating with the syndicalist workers' movement, the idea was superficially adopted by the fascists during the 1920s and 1930s. Catholic social theory, as expounded in some papal encyclicals, also favours the corporative state as a means of eliminating class conflict. The concept arose in the political theories of the syndicalist movement of the early 20th century, which proposed that all industries should be taken over and run by the trade unions, a federation of whom should replace the state.

corps military formation consisting of two to five divisions. Its strength is between 50,000 and 120,000 people. All branches of the army are represented. A corps is commanded by a lieutenant general. Two or more corps form an army group.

corps de ballet dancers in a ballet company who usually dance in groups, in support of the soloists. At the Paris Opéra this is the name given to the whole company.

Corpus Christi feast celebrated in the Roman Catholic and Orthodox churches, and to some extent in the Anglican church, on the Thursday after Trinity Sunday. It was instituted in the 13th century through the devotion of St Juliana, prioress of Mount Cornillon, near Liège, Belgium, in honour of the Real Presence of Christ in the Eucharist.

corpus luteum glandular tissue formed in the mammalian ◊ovary after ovulation from the Graafian follicle, a group of cells associated with bringing the egg to maturity. It secretes the hormone progesterone in anticipation of pregnancy.

corrasion the grinding away of solid rock surfaces by particles carried by water, ice, and wind. It is generally held to be the most significant form of ◊erosion. As the eroding particles are carried along they become eroded themselves due to the process of ◊attrition.

Correggio assumed name of Antonio Allegri c. 1494–1534. Italian painter of the High Renaissance. His style followed the Classical grandeur of ◊Leonardo da Vinci and ◊Titian, but anticipated the ◊Baroque in its emphasis on movement, softer forms, and contrasts of light and shade. Based in Parma, he painted splendid illusionistic visions in the cathedral there, including the remarkable *Assumption of the Virgin* 1526–30. His religious paintings, for example, the night scene *Adoration of the Shepherds* about 1527–30 (Gemäldegalerie, Dresden), and mythological scenes, such as *Jupiter and Io* about 1532 (Wallace Collection, London), were much admired in the 18th century.

Correggio *Venus with Mercury and Cupid* c. 1525 by Correggio (National Gallery, London). A pupil of Leonardo da Vinci, Correggio developed a soft, sensual style that had a profound influence on the development of Baroque and Rococo painting. *Corbis*

correlation the degree of relationship between two sets of information. If one set of data increases at the same time as the other, the relationship is said to be positive or direct. If one set of data increases as the other decreases, the relationship is negative or inverse. Correlation can be shown by plotting a best-fit line on a scatter diagram.

correspondence in mathematics, the relation between two sets where an operation on the members of one set maps some or all of them onto one or more members of the other. For example, if A is the set of members of a family and B is the set of months in the year, A and B are in correspondence if the operation is: '... has a birthday in the month of ...'.

corresponding angles a pair of equal angles lying on the same side of a transversal (a line that cuts through two or more lines in the same plane), and making an interior and exterior angle with the intersected lines.

corresponding society in British history, one of the first independent organizations for the working classes, advocating annual parliaments and universal male suffrage. The London Corresponding Society was founded 1792 by politicians Thomas Hardy (1752–1832) and John Horne Tooke (1736–1812). It later established branches in Scotland and the provinces. Many of its activities had to be held in secret and government fears about the spread of revolutionary doctrines led to its banning 1799.

corrie (Welsh ***cwm***; French, North American ***cirque***) Scottish term for a steep-sided hollow in the mountainside of a glaciated area. The weight and movement of the ice has ground out the bottom and worn back the sides. A corrie is open at the front, and its sides and back are formed of ◊arêtes. There may be a lake in the bottom, called a tarn.

corroboree Australian Aboriginal ceremonial dance. Some corroborees record events in everyday life and are non-sacred, public entertainments; others have a religious significance and are of great ritual importance, relating to initiation, death, fertility, disease, war, and so on. The dancers' movements are prescribed by tribal custom and their bodies and faces are usually painted in clay in traditional designs. The dance is accompanied by song, and music is provided by clapping sticks and the didjeridu.

corrosion the eating away and eventual destruction of metals and alloys by chemical attack. The rusting of ordinary iron and steel is the most common form of corrosion. Rusting takes place in moist air, when the iron combines with oxygen and water to form a brown-orange deposit of ◊rust (hydrated iron oxide). The rate of corrosion is increased where the atmosphere is polluted with sulphur dioxide. Salty road and air conditions accelerate the rusting of car bodies.

Other examples of corrosion include the green deposit that forms on copper and bronze, called verdigris, a basic copper carbonate. The tarnish on silver is a corrosion product, a film of silver sulphide.

corrosion in earth science, an alternative name for ◊solution, the process by which water dissolves rocks such as limestone.

corsair pirate based on the N African Barbary Coast. From the 16th century onwards the corsairs plundered shipping in the Mediterranean and Atlantic, holding hostages for ransom or selling them as slaves. Although many punitive expeditions were sent against them, they were not suppressed until France occupied Algiers 1830. Most pirates were Turkish or North African, but there were also many Europeans.

Corsica (French ***Corse***) island region of France, in the Mediterranean off the west coast of Italy, N of Sardinia; it comprises the *départements* of Haute Corse and Corse du Sud

area 8,700 sq km/3,358 sq mi

capital Ajaccio (port)

Corsica

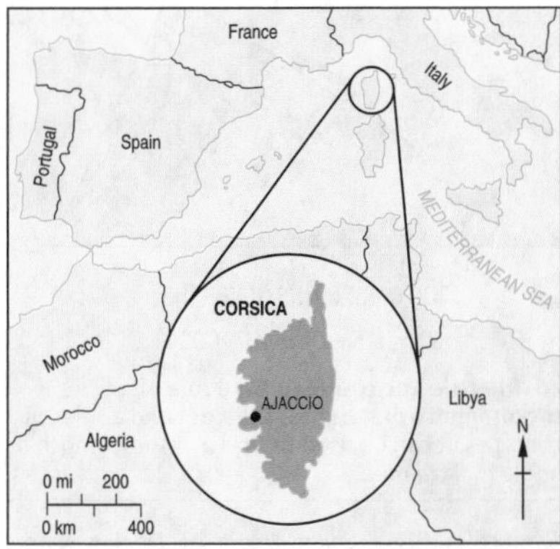

physical mountainous; ◊maquis vegetation
features ◊maquis vegetation. Corsica's mountain bandits were eradicated 1931, but the tradition of the vendetta or blood feud lingers. The island is the main base of the Foreign Legion
government its special status involves a 61-member regional parliament with the power to scrutinize French National Assembly bills applicable to the island and propose amendments
products wine, olive oil
population (1990) 250,400, including just under 50% native Corsicans. There are about 400,000 *émigrés*, mostly in Mexico and Central America, who return to retire
language French (official); the majority speak Corsican, an Italian dialect
famous people Napoleon
history the Phocaeans of Ionia founded Alalia about 570 BC, and were succeeded in turn by the Etruscans, the Carthaginians, the Romans, the Vandals, and the Arabs. In the 14th century Corsica fell to the Genoese, and in the second half of the 18th century a Corsican nationalist, Pasquale Paoli (1725–1807), led an independence movement.

Genoa sold Corsica to France 1768. In World War II Corsica was occupied by Italy 1942–43. From 1962, French *pieds noirs* (refugees from Algeria), mainly vine growers, were settled in Corsica, and their prosperity helped to fan nationalist feeling, which demands an independent Corsica. This fuelled the National Liberation Front of Corsica (FNLC), banned 1983, which has engaged in some terrorist bombings (a truce began June 1988 but ended 1991).

Cortés Hernán Ferdinand 1485–1547. Spanish conquistador. He conquered the Aztec empire 1519–21, and secured Mexico for Spain. Cortés went to the West Indies as a young man and in 1518 was given command of an expedition to Mexico. Landing with only 600 men, he was at first received as a god by the Aztec emperor ◊Montezuma II but was expelled from Tenochtitlán (Mexico City) when he was found not to be 'divine'. With the aid of Indian allies he recaptured the city 1521, and overthrew the Aztec empire. His conquests eventually included most of Mexico and N Central America.

cortex in biology, the outer part of a structure such as the brain, kidney, or adrenal gland. In botany the cortex includes non-specialized cells lying just beneath the surface cells of the root and stem.

corticosteroid any of several steroid hormones secreted by the cortex of the ◊adrenal glands; also synthetic forms with similar properties. Corticosteroids have anti-inflammatory and ◊immunosuppressive effects and may be used to treat a number of conditions, including rheumatoid arthritis, severe allergies, asthma, some skin diseases, and some cancers. Side effects can be serious, and therapy must be withdrawn very gradually.

cortisone natural corticosteroid produced by the ◊adrenal gland, now synthesized for its anti-inflammatory qualities and used in the treatment of rheumatoid arthritis, allergies, and certain cancers. The side effects of cortisone steroids include muscle wasting, fat redistribution, diabetes, bone thinning, and high blood pressure.

Cortona Pietro da Italian Baroque painter; see ◊Pietro da Cortona.

corundum native aluminium oxide, Al_2O_3, the hardest naturally occurring mineral known apart from diamond (corundum rates 9 on the Mohs' scale of hardness); lack of ◊cleavage also increases its durability. Its crystals are barrel-shaped prisms of the trigonal system. Varieties of gem-quality corundum are ruby (red) and sapphire (any colour other than red, usually blue). Poorer-quality and synthetic corundum is used in industry, for example as an ◊abrasive. Corundum forms in silica-poor igneous and metamorphic rocks.

Corunna (Spanish ***La Coruña***) city in the extreme NW of Spain; population (1991) 251,300. It is the capital of Corunna province. Industry is centred on the fisheries; tobacco, sugar refining, and textiles are also important. The ◊Armada sailed from Corunna 1588, and the town was sacked by Francis Drake 1589.

Cosby Bill (William Henry) 1937– . US comedian and actor. His portrayal of the dashing, handsome secret agent in the television series *I Spy* 1965–68, for which he won three Emmy awards, revolutionized the way in which blacks were presented on screen. His sardonic humour, based on wry observations of domestic life and parenthood, found its widest audience in *The Cosby Show* 1984–92. Among his other TV series was *Fat Albert and the Cosby Kids* 1972–84, and he began hosting the game show *You Bet Your Life* 1992.

cosecant in trigonometry, a ◊function of an angle in a right-angled triangle found by dividing the length of the hypotenuse (the longest side) by the length of the side opposite the angle. Thus the cosecant of an angle A, usually shortened to cosec A, is always greater than (or equal to) 1. It is the reciprocal of the sine of the angle, that is, cosec $A = 1/\sin A$.

Cosgrave Liam 1920– . Irish Fine Gael politician, prime minister of the Republic of Ireland 1973–77. As party leader 1965–77, he headed a Fine Gael–Labour coalition government from 1973. Relations between the Irish and UK governments improved under his premiership.

Cosgrave William Thomas 1880–1965. Irish politician. He took part in the ◊Easter Rising 1916 and sat in the Sinn Féin cabinet of 1919–21. Head of the Free State government 1922–33, he founded and led the Fine Gael opposition 1933–44. His eldest son is Liam Cosgrave.

cosine in trigonometry, a ◊function of an angle in a right-angled triangle found by dividing the length of the side adjacent to the angle by the length of the hypotenuse (the longest side). It is usually shortened to *cos*.

cosine rule in trigonometry, a rule that relates the sides and angles of triangles. The rule has the formula:

$$a^2 = b^2 + c^2 - 2bc \cos A$$

where a, b, and c are the sides of the triangle, and A is the angle opposite a.

cosmic background radiation or ***3° radiation*** electromagnetic radiation left over from the original formation of the universe in the Big Bang around 15 billion years ago. It corresponds to an

Corsica View of Tralonca, Corsica. Corsica is known as 'the scented isle' since much of it is covered in fragrant flowering maquis (dense scrub bush). At higher altitudes there are forests of beech, birch, chestnut, and pine. The economy is based on agricultural produce and tourism. *Sally Jenkins*

cosine **The cotangent of angle β is equal to the ratio of the length of the adjacent side to the length of the hypotenuse (the longest side, opposite to the right angle).**

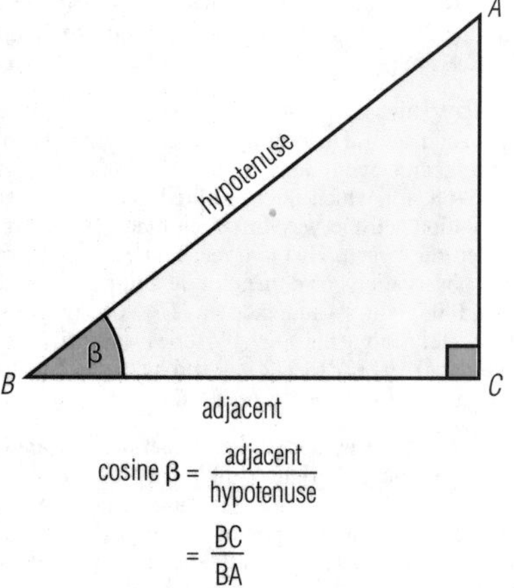

overall background temperature of 3K (−270°C/ −454°F), or 3°C above absolute zero. In 1992 the Cosmic Background Explorer satellite, COBE, detected slight 'ripples' in the strength of the background radiation that are believed to mark the first stage in the formation of galaxies.

Cosmic background radiation was first detected 1965 by US physicists Arno Penzias (1933–) and Robert Wilson (1936–), who in 1978 shared the Nobel Prize for Physics for their discovery.

cosmic radiation streams of high-energy particles from outer space, consisting of protons, alpha particles, and light nuclei, which collide with atomic nuclei in the Earth's atmosphere, and produce secondary nuclear particles (chiefly ◊mesons, such as pions and muons) that shower the Earth. Those of low energy seem to be galactic in origin, and those of high energy of extragalactic origin. The galactic particles may come from ◊supernova explosions or ◊pulsars. At higher energies, other sources are necessary, possibly the giants jets of gas which are emitted from some galaxies.

cosmology branch of astronomy that deals with the structure and evolution of the universe as an ordered whole. Its method is to construct 'model universes' mathematically and compare their large-scale properties with those of the observed universe.

Modern cosmology began in the 1920s with the discovery that the universe is expanding, which suggested that it began in an explosion, the ◊Big Bang. An alternative – now discarded – view, the ◊steady-state theory, claimed that the universe has no origin, but is expanding because new matter is being continually created.

Cossack people of S and SW Russia, Ukraine, and Poland, predominantly of Russian or Ukrainian origin, who took in escaped serfs and lived in independent communal settlements (military brotherhoods) from the 15th to the 19th century. Later they held land in return for military service in the cavalry under Russian and Polish rulers. After 1917, the various Cossack communities were incorporated into the Soviet administrative and collective system.

There are many Cossack settlements in the N Caucasus. Cossack movements demand the restoration of their traditional military role (granted in part by a 1993 decree) and collective ownership of land.

Costa Brava (Spanish 'Wild Coast') Mediterranean coastline of NE Spain, stretching from Port-Bou on the French border southwards to Blanes, NE of Barcelona. It is noted for its irregular rocky coastline, small fishing villages, and resorts such as Puerto de la Selva, Palafrugell, Playa de Aro, and Lloret del Mar.

Costa del Sol (Spanish 'Coast of the Sun') Mediterranean coastline of Andalucia, S Spain, stretching for nearly 300 km/190 mi from Algeciras to Almeria. Málaga is the principal port and Marbella, Torremolinos, and Nerja are the chief tourist resorts.

Costa Rica country in Central America, bounded N by Nicaragua, SE by Panama, E by the Caribbean Sea, and W by the Pacific Ocean. *See country box below.*

cost–benefit analysis process whereby a project is assessed for its social and welfare benefits in addition to considering the financial return on investment. For example, this might take into account the environmental impact of an industrial plant or convenience for users of a new railway. A major difficulty is finding a way to quantify net social costs and benefits.

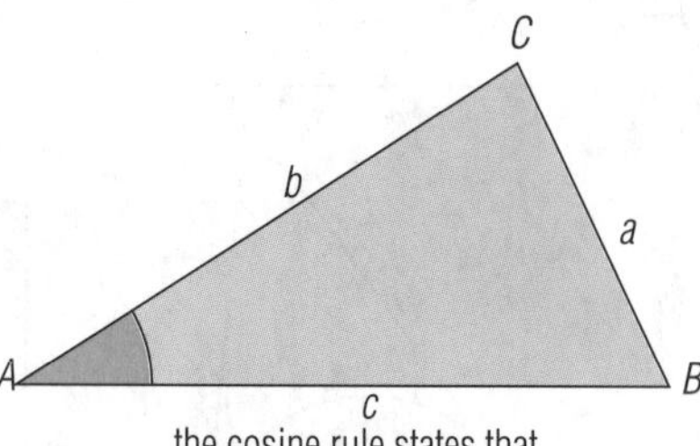

the cosine rule states that
$a^2 = b^2 + c^2 - 2bc \cos A$

cosine rule **The cosine rule is a rule of trigonometry that relates the sides and angles of triangles. It can be used to find a missing length or angle in a triangle.**

Costello Elvis. Stage name of Declan Patrick McManus 1954– . English rock singer, songwriter, and guitarist. He emerged as part of the ◊New Wave. His intricate yet impassioned lyrics have made him one of Britain's foremost songwriters, and he dominated the UK rock scene into the early 1980s. His hits range from the political rocker 'Oliver's Army' 1979 to the country weepy 'Good Year for the Roses' 1981 and the punning pop of 'Everyday I Write the Book' 1983.

Costner Kevin 1955– . US film actor. He emerged as a star in the late 1980s, with his role as law-enforcer Elliot Ness in *The Untouchables* 1987. He went on to direct and star in *Dances with Wolves* 1990, a Western sympathetic to the native American Indians, which won several Academy Awards. Subsequent films include *Robin Hood – Prince of Thieves* 1991, *JFK* 1991, *The Bodyguard* 1992, *A Perfect World* 1993, and *Waterworld* 1995.

cost of living cost of goods and services needed for an average standard of living. In Britain the cost-of-living index was introduced 1914 and based on the expenditure of a working-class family of a man, woman, and three children; the standard is 100. Known from 1947 as the Retail Price Index (RPI), it is revised to allow for inflation. Supplementary to the RPI are the Consumer's Expenditure Deflator (formerly Consumer Price Index) and the Tax and Price Index (TPI), introduced 1979. Comprehensive indexation has been advocated as a

COSTA RICA
Republic of

national name *República de Costa Rica*
area 51,100 sq km/19,735 sq mi
capital San José
major ports Limón, Puntarenas
physical features high central plateau and tropical coasts; Costa Rica was once entirely forested, containing an estimated 5% of the Earth's flora and fauna
head of state and government Miguel Ángel Rodríguez Echeverría from 1998
political system liberal democracy
administrative divisions seven provinces
political parties National Liberation Party (PLN), left of centre; Christian Socialist Unity Party (PUSC), centrist coalition; ten minor parties
population 3,500,000 (1996 est)
population growth rate 2.4% (1990–95); 1.8% (2000–05)
ethnic distribution about 97% of the population is of European descent, mostly Spanish, and about 2% is of African origin
life expectancy 73 (males), 78 (females)
literacy rate men 93%, women 93%
language Spanish (official)
religion Roman Catholic 90%
currency colón
GDP (US $) 8.33 billion (1994)
growth rate 4.5% (1994)
exports coffee, bananas, cocoa, sugar, beef, manufactured goods

HISTORY
1502 Visited by Christopher Columbus, who named the area Costa Rica (the rich coast), observing the gold decorations worn by the native Guaymi Indians.
1506 Colonized by Spain, but fierce guerrilla resistance was mounted by the Indian population, although many later died from exposure to European diseases.
18th C Settlements began to be established in the fertile central highlands, including San José and Alajuela.
1808 Coffee was introduced from Cuba and soon became the staple crop.
1821 Independence achieved from Spain, and was joined initially with Mexico.
1824 Became part of United Provinces (Federation) of Central America, also embracing El Salvador, Guatemala, Honduras, and Nicaragua.
1838 Became fully independent when it seceded from the Federation.
1849–59 Under presidency of Juan Rafuel Mora.
1870–82 Period of military dictatorship.
later 19th C Immigration by Europeans to run and work small coffee farms.
1917–19 Brief dictatorship by Frederico Tinoco.
1940–44 Liberal reforms, including recognition of workers' rights and minimum wages introduced by President Rafael Angel Calderón Guradia, founder of the United Christian Socialist Party (PUSC).
1948 Brief civil war following a disputed presidential election.
1949 New constitution adopted, giving women and blacks the vote. National army abolished and replaced by civil guard. José Figueres Ferrer, cofounder of the PLN, elected president; he embarked on ambitious socialist programme, nationalizing the banks and introducing a social security system.
1958–73 Mainly conservative administrations.
1974 PLN regained the presidency under Daniel Oduber and returned to socialist policies.
1978 Rodrigo Carazo, conservative, elected president. Sharp deterioration in the state of the economy.
1982 Luis Alberto Monge (PLN) elected president. Harsh austerity programme introduced. Pressure from the USA to abandon neutral stance and condemn Sandinista regime in Nicaragua.
1985 Following border clashes with Nicaraguan Sandinista forces, a US-trained antiguerrilla guard formed.
1986 Oscar Arias Sanchez (PLN) won the presidency on a neutralist platform.
1987 Arias won Nobel Prize for Peace for devising a Central American peace plan signed by leaders of Nicaragua, El Salvador, Guatemala, and Honduras.
1990 Rafael Calderón of the centrist PUSC elected president as economy deteriorated.
1994 José Maria Figueres Olsen, son of José Figueres Ferrer (PLN) elected president.
1998 Miguel Ángel Rodríguez Echeverría (PUSC) elected president.

SEE ALSO Central America

means of controlling inflation by linking all forms of income (such as wages and investment), contractual debts, and tax scales to the RPI. Index-linked savings schemes were introduced in the UK 1975.

In the USA a consumer price index, based on the expenditure of families in the iron, steel, and related industries, was introduced 1890. The present index is based on the expenditure of the urban wage-earner and clerical-worker families in 46 large, medium, and small cities, the standard being 100. Increases in social security benefits are linked to it, as are many wage settlements.

cotangent in trigonometry, a ◊function of an angle in a right-angled triangle found by dividing the length of the side adjacent to the angle by the length of the side opposite it. It is usually written as cotan, or cot and it is the reciprocal of the tangent of the angle, so that cot $A = 1/\tan A$, where A is the angle in question.

cot death or ***sudden infant death syndrome*** (SIDS) death of an apparently healthy baby, almost always during sleep. The cause is not known but risk factors that have been identified include prematurity, respiratory infection, overheating and sleeping position.

Côte d'Azur Mediterranean coast from Menton to St Tropez, France, renowned for its beaches; it is part of the region ◊Provence-Alpes-Côte d'Azur.

Côte d'Ivoire country in W Africa, bounded N by Mali and Burkino Faso, E by Ghana, S by the Gulf of Guinea, and W by Liberia and Guinea. *See country box below.*

Cotman John Sell 1782–1842. English landscape painter. With John Crome, he was a founder of the ◊Norwich School. His early watercolours were bold designs in simple flat washes of colour; for example, *Greta Bridge, Yorkshire* about 1805 (British Museum, London). In the simplification of design to broad, expressively silhouetted areas, he was highly original and unlike any of his contemporaries. His later work is unequal, but it included oil paintings in his own distinct manner as well as some drawings.

Cotonou chief port and largest city of Benin, on the Bight of Benin; population (1994) 537,000. Palm products and timber are exported. Although not the official capital, it is the seat of the president, and the main centre of commerce and politics.

Cotswold Hills or ***Cotswolds*** range of hills in Gloucestershire, England, 80 km/50 mi long, between Bath and Chipping Camden. They rise to 333 m/1,086 ft at Cleeve Cloud, near Cheltenham, but average about 200 m/600 ft. The area is known for its picturesque villages, built with the local honey-coloured stone.

cotton tropical and subtropical herbaceous plant of the genus *Gossypium* of the mallow family Malvaceae. Fibres surround the seeds inside the ripened fruits, or bolls, and these are spun into yarn for cloth. The fibres are separated from the seeds in a cotton gin. The seeds are used to produce cooking oil and livestock feed, and the pigment gossypol has potential as a male contraceptive in a modified form. Cotton disease (byssinosis), caused by cotton dust, affects the lungs of those working in the industry.

Cotton production uses 50% of world pesticides and represents 5% of world agricultural output.

cotyledon structure in the embryo of a seed plant that may form a 'leaf' after germination and is commonly known as a seed leaf. The number of cotyledons present in an embryo is an important character in the classification of flowering plants (◊angiosperms).

Monocotyledons (such as grasses, palms, and lilies) have a single cotyledon, whereas dicotyledons (the majority of plant species) have two. In seeds that also contain ◊endosperm (nutritive tissue), the cotyledons are thin, but where they are the primary food-storing tissue, as in peas and beans, they may be quite large. After germination the cotyledons either remain below ground (hypogeal) or, more commonly, spread out above soil level (epigeal) and become the first green leaves. In gymnosperms there may be up to a dozen cotyledons within each seed.

cougar another name for the ◊puma, a large North American cat.

coulomb SI unit (symbol C) of electrical charge. One coulomb is the quantity of electricity conveyed by a current of one ◊ampere in one second.

council in local government in England and Wales, a popularly elected local assembly charged with the government of the area within its boundaries. Under the Local Government Act 1972, they comprise three types: ◊county councils, ◊district councils, and ◊parish councils.

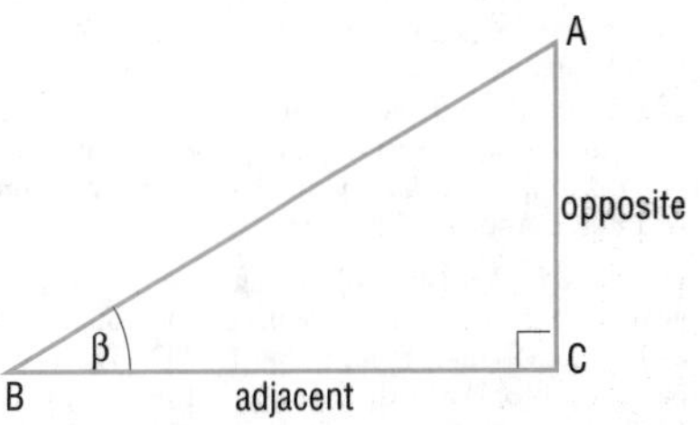

$$\text{cot(angent) } \beta = \frac{1}{\tan\beta} = \frac{\cos\beta}{\sin\beta} = \frac{\text{adjacent}}{\text{opposite}} = \frac{BC}{AC}$$

cotangent **The cotangent of angle β is equal to the ratio of the length of the adjacent side to the length of the opposite side.**

Council of Europe body constituted 1949 to achieve greater unity between European countries, to facilitate their economic and social progress, and to uphold the principles of parliamentary democracy and respect for human rights. It has a Committee of foreign ministers, a Consultative Assembly, a Parliamentary Assembly (with members from national parliaments), and, to fulfil one of its main functions, a European Commission on Human Rights, which examines complaints about human-rights abuses. If the commission is unable to achieve a friendly settlement after examining alleged violations, the case may be taken to the ◊European Court of Human Rights for adjudication. Its headquarters are in Strasbourg, France.

The founder members were the UK, France, Italy, Belgium, the Netherlands, Sweden, Denmark, Norway, the Republic of Ireland, Luxembourg, Greece, and Turkey; Iceland, Germany, Austria, Cyprus, Switzerland, Malta, Portugal, Spain, Liechtenstein, Finland, and San Marino joined subsequently. With the collapse of communism in E Europe, the council acquired a new role in assisting the establishment of Western-style democratic and accountable political systems in the region, and several former communist countries entered into membership. Hungary joined 1990, Czechoslovakia and Poland 1991 (the Czech and Slovak republics were given separate status 1993), Bulgaria 1992, Estonia, Lithuania, Romania, Slovakia, and Slovenia 1993, Andorra 1994, and Albania 1995. Latvia, Moldova, Ukraine, Macedonia, and Russia were admitted 1996, bringing the membership to 39.

In addition to its concern for human rights, the council is active in the fields of the mass media,

CÔTE D'IVOIRE

Republic of (also called Ivory Coast until 1986)

ATLANTIC OCEAN
0 mi 500
0 km 1000
Mali
Burkina Faso
Guinea
CÔTE D'IVOIRE
Ghana
Liberia
Yamoussoukro

national name *République de la Côte d'Ivoire*
area 322,463 sq km/124,471 sq mi
capital Yamoussoukro
major towns/cities Bouaké, Daloa, Man
major ports Abidjan, San Pedro
physical features tropical rainforest (diminishing as exploited) in S; savanna and low mountains in N; coastal plain; Vridi canal, Kossou dam, Monts du Toura
head of state Henri Konan Bedie from 1993
head of government Kablan Daniel Duncan from 1993
political system emergent democratic republic
administrative divisions 49 departments
political parties Democratic Party of the Ivory Coast (PDCI), nationalist, free enterprise; Rally of Republicans (RDR), nationalist; Ivorian Popular Front (FPI), left of centre; Ivorian Labour Party (PIT), left of centre
population 14,253,000 (1995 est)
population growth rate 3.5% (1990–95); 3.2% (2000–05)
ethnic distribution no single dominant ethnic group; main groups include the Agni, Baoule, Krou, Senoufou, and Mandingo. There are about 2 million Africans who have settled from neighbouring countries, particularly Burkina Faso. Europeans number about 70,000
life expectancy 53 (men), 56 (women)
literacy rate men 67%, women 40%
language French (official), over 60 local languages
religions animist, Muslim (mainly in N), Christian (mainly Roman Catholic in S)
currency franc CFA
GDP (US $) 7.4 billion (1994)
growth rate 1.7% (1994)
exports coffee, cocoa, timber, petroleum products

HISTORY

1460s Portuguese navigators arrived.
16th C Ivory export trade developed by Europeans and slave trade, though to a lesser extent than neighbouring areas; Krou people migrated from Liberia to the W and Senoufo and Lubi from the N.
late 17th C French coastal trading posts established at Assini and Grand Bassam.
18th–19th Cs Akan peoples, including the Baoulé, immigrated from the E and Malinke from the NW.
1840s French began to conclude commercial treaties with local rulers.
1893 Colony of Côte d'Ivoire created by French, after war with Mandinkas; Baoulé resistance was to continue until 1917.
1904 Became part of French West Africa; cocoa production encouraged.
1940–42 Under pro-Nazi French Vichy regime.
1946 Became overseas territory in French Union, with own territorial assembly and representation in French parliament: Felix Houphoüet-Boigny, a Western-educated Baoulé chief who had formed the Democratic Party (PDCI) to campaign for autonomy, was elected to the French assembly.
1947 A French-controlled area to the N, which had been added to Côte d'Ivoire in 1932, separated to create new state of Upper Volta (now Burkina Faso).
1950–54 Port of Abidjan constructed.
1958 Achieved internal self-government.
1960 Independence secured, with Houphouët-Boigny as president of a one-party state.
1960s–1980s Political stability, close links maintained with France and economic expansion of 10% per annum, as the country became one of the world's largest coffee producers.
1986 Name changed officially from Ivory Coast to Côte d'Ivoire.
1987–93 Per capita incomes fell by 25% as an IMF-promoted austerity programme implemented.
1990 Strikes and student unrest, but Houphouët-Boigny re-elected in a contested presidential election, as multiparty politics re-established.
1993 Houphouët-Boigny died and was succeeded by parliamentary speaker Baoulé Henri Konan Bedie.
1995 Bedie and PDCI re-elected in contest boycotted by opposition.

SEE ALSO Houphouët-Boigny, Félix

As hardly anyone has composed more than myself ... I hope that my family will find in my wallet something to make them regret my passing.

FRANÇOIS COUPERIN
Preface to *Pièces de Clavecin* 1730

social welfare, health, population trends, migration, social equality, crime, education and culture, youth affairs, sport, and the environment. It cooperates with the United Nations and other international organizations and has particularly close relations with the European Union.

council tax method of raising revenue for local government in Britain. It replaced the community charge, or ◊poll tax, from April 1993. The tax is based on property values at April 1991, but takes some account of the number of people occupying each property. It is levied by local authorities on the value of dwellings in their area. Each dwelling is valued and then placed into one of eight bands. The owners of properties worth more than £320,000 in the highest band pay three times as much in council tax as those in the lowest band of properties worth less than £40,000.

counterfeiting fraudulent imitation, usually of banknotes. It is countered by special papers, elaborate watermarks, skilled printing, and sometimes the insertion of a metallic strip. ◊Forgery is also a form of counterfeiting. The manufacture of, and trafficking in, counterfeit goods is a criminal offence.

counterpoint in music, the art of combining different forms of an original melody with apparent freedom while preserving a harmonious effect. Giovanni Palestrina and J S Bach were masters of counterpoint. It originated in ◊plainsong, with two independent vocal lines sung simultaneously (Latin *punctus contra punctum* 'note against note').

Counter-Reformation movement initiated by the Catholic church at the Council of Trent 1545–63 to counter the spread of the ◊Reformation. Extending into the 17th century, its dominant forces included the rise of the Jesuits as an educating and missionary group and the deployment of the Spanish ◊Inquisition in Europe and the Americas.

countertenor the highest natural male voice, also called an ◊alto. It was favoured by the Elizabethans for its heroic brilliance of tone. It was revived in the UK by Alfred Deller (1912–1979).

country and western or ***country music*** popular music of the white US South and West; it evolved from the folk music of the English, Irish, and Scottish settlers and has a strong blues influence. Characteristic instruments are slide guitar, mandolin, and fiddle. Lyrics typically extol family values and traditional sex roles, and often have a strong narrative element. Country music encompasses a variety of regional styles, from mournful ballads to fast and intricate dance music.

Countryside Commission official conservation body created for England and Wales under the Countryside Act 1968. It replaced the National Parks Commission, and had by 1980 created over 160 country parks.

Countryside Council for Wales Welsh nature conservation body formed 1991 by the fusion of the former ◊Nature Conservancy Council and the Welsh Countryside Commission. It is government-funded and administers conservation and land-use policies within Wales.

county administrative unit of a country or state. It was the name given by the Normans to Anglo-Saxon 'shires', and the boundaries of many present-day English counties date back to Saxon times.

In England, a major review overseen by the Local Government Commission (begun 1992 and completed 1994) put emphasis on the creation of unitary 'all purpose' authorities in some counties, and in others either retaining the existing structure or producing a blend of two-tier and unitary bodies. In Wales 22 unitary authorities were created 1996, divided equally between counties and county boroughs. In Scotland the two-tier system in the regions was abolished 1996 and replaced by 29 single-tier authorities; the island areas remained unchanged. Northern Ireland has six geographical counties, but under the Local Government Act 1973 administration is through twenty-six district councils (single-tier authorities), each based on a main town or centre. (*See map of United Kingdom.*)

The Republic of Ireland has twenty-six geographical and twenty-seven administrative counties.

In the USA a county is a subdivision of a state; the power of counties differs widely among states.

I deny that art can be taught.

GUSTAVE COURBET
Letter to prospective students 1861

county council in the UK, a unit of ◊local government whose responsibilities include broad planning policy, highways, education, personal social services, and libraries; police, fire, and traffic control; and refuse disposal.

Since the Local Government Act 1972, the county councils in England and Wales consist of a chair and councillors (the distinction between councillors and aldermen has been abolished). Councillors are elected for four years, the franchise being the same as for parliamentary elections, and elect the chair from among their own number. Metropolitan county councils, including the Greater London Council, were abolished 1986.

county court English court of law created by the County Courts Act 1846 and now governed by the Act of 1984. It exists to try civil cases, such as actions on ◊contract and ◊tort where the claim does not exceed £5,000, and disputes about land, such as between landlord and tenant. County courts are presided over by one or more circuit judges. An appeal on a point of law lies to the Court of Appeal.

county palatine in medieval England, a county whose lord held particular rights, in lieu of the king, such as pardoning treasons and murders. Under William I there were four counties palatine: Chester, Durham, Kent, and Shropshire.

coup d'état (French 'stroke of state') or ***coup*** forcible takeover of the government of a country by elements from within that country, generally carried out by violent or illegal means. It differs from a revolution in typically being carried out by a small group (for example, of army officers or opposition politicians) to install its leader as head of government, rather than being a mass uprising by the people.

Early examples include the coup of 1799, in which Napoleon overthrew the Revolutionary Directory and declared himself first consul of France, and the coup of 1851 in which Louis Napoleon (then president) dissolved the French national assembly and a year later declared himself emperor. Coups in more recent times include the overthrow of the socialist government of Chile 1973 by a right-wing junta, the military seizures of power in Myanmar 1988 and Gambia 1994, and the short-lived removal of Mikhail Gorbachev from power in the USSR by hardline communists Aug 1991.

Couperin François ***le Grand*** 1668–1733. French composer. He is the best-known member of a musical family which included his uncle Louis Couperin (1626–1661), composer for organ and harpsichord. A favoured composer of Louis XIV, Couperin composed numerous chamber concertos and harpsichord suites, and published a standard keyboard tutor *L'Art de toucher le clavecin/The Art of Playing the Harpsichord* 1716 in which he laid down guidelines for fingering, phrasing, and ornamentation.

Courbet Gustave 1819–1877. French artist. He was a portrait, genre, and landscape painter. Reacting against academic trends, both Classicist and Romantic, he became a major exponent of ◊Realism, depicting contemporary life with an unflattering frankness. His *Burial at Ornans* 1850 (Musée d'Orsay, Paris), showing ordinary working people gathered around a village grave, shocked the public and the critics with its 'vulgarity'.

His powerful genius found expression in portraiture, figure composition, landscape (the gorges and forests of his native Franche-Comté, and superb paintings of the Normandy coast, *The Wave* being famous in several versions), sensuous paintings of the nude, animal studies, and still life. He went to Paris 1841, his training mainly consisting in the study and imitation of old masters in the Louvre, especially Velázquez and Rembrandt. In defiance of both Romanticism and Classicism he evolved the idea of Realism, asserting, that is, that painting should consist in 'the representation of real and existing things', his aim therefore being, in his own words, to 'interpret the manners, ideas and aspect of our own time'.

courgette small variety of marrow, *Cucurbita pepo*, of the Cucurbitaceae family. It is cultivated as a vegetable and harvested before it is fully mature, at 15–20 cm/6–8 in. In the USA and Canada it is known as a zucchini.

Courrèges André 1923– . French fashion designer. He is credited with inventing the miniskirt 1964. His 'space-age' designs – square-shaped short skirts and trousers – were copied worldwide in the 1960s. Courrèges founded his own label 1961. From 1966 he produced both couture and ready-to-wear lines of well-tailored designs, often in pastel shades.

coursing chasing of hares by greyhounds, not by scent but by sight, as a sport and as a test of the greyhound's speed. It is one of the most ancient of field sports. Since the 1880s it has been practised in the UK on enclosed or park courses. The governing body in Great Britain is the National Coursing Club, formed 1858.

Court Margaret, (born Smith) 1942– . Australian tennis player. The most prolific winner in the women's game, she won a record 64 Grand Slam titles, including 25 at singles. Court was the first from her country to win the ladies title at Wimbledon 1963, and the second woman after Maureen Connolly to complete the Grand Slam 1970.

court martial court convened for the trial of persons subject to military discipline who are accused of violations of military laws. British courts martial are governed by the code of the service concerned – Naval Discipline, Army, or Air Force acts – and in 1951 an appeal court was established for all three services by the Courts Martial (Appeals) Act.

Court of Appeal UK law court comprising a Civil Division and a Criminal Division, set up under the Criminal Appeals Act 1968. The Criminal Division of the Court of Appeal has the power to revise sentences or quash a conviction on the grounds that in all the circumstances of the case the verdict is unsafe or unsatisfactory, or that the judgement of the original trial judge was wrong in law, or that there was a material irregularity during the course of the trial.

Court of Session supreme civil court in Scotland, established 1532. Cases come in the first place before one of the judges of the Outer House (corresponding to the High Court in England and Wales), and from that decision an appeal lies to the Inner House (corresponding to the Court of Appeal) which sits in two divisions called the First and the Second Division. From the decisions of the Inner House an appeal lies to the House of Lords. The court sits in Edinburgh.

courtship behaviour exhibited by animals as a prelude to mating. The behaviour patterns vary considerably from one species to another, but are often ritualized forms of behaviour not obviously related to courtship or mating (for example, courtship feeding in birds).

Cousteau Jacques Yves 1910–1997. French oceanographer who pioneered the invention of the aqualung 1943 and techniques in underwater filming. In 1951 he began the first of many research voyages in the ship *Calypso*. His film and television documentaries and books established him as a household name.

covalent bond chemical ◊bond produced when two atoms share one or more pairs of electrons (usually each atom contributes an electron). The bond is often represented by a single line drawn between the two atoms. Covalently bonded substances include hydrogen (H_2), water (H_2O), and most organic substances.

Covenanter in Scottish history, one of the Presbyterian Christians who swore to uphold their forms of worship in a National Covenant, signed 28 Feb 1638, when Charles I attempted to introduce a liturgy on the English model into Scotland.

A general assembly abolished episcopacy, and the Covenanters signed with the English Parliament the Solemn League and Covenant 1643, promising military aid in return for the establishment of Presbyterianism in England. A Scottish army entered England and fought at Marston Moor 1644. At the Restoration Charles II revived episcopacy in Scotland, evicting resisting ministers, so that revolts followed 1666, 1679, and 1685. However, Presbyterianism was again restored 1688.

Coventry industrial city in West Midlands, England; population (1991) 294,400. Industries include cars, electronic equipment, machine tools,

Coward English playwright, director, and songwriter Noël Coward in 1966. Coward evolved his distinct brand of satirical humour between the wars in a series of successful revues and plays, before turning to film scripts and, after World War II, becoming a successful performer of his own songs. *Topham*

agricultural machinery, man-made fibres, aerospace components, telecommunications equipment, and coal mining.

features Coventry cathedral, consecrated 1962, was designed by Basil Spence and retains the ruins of the old cathedral, which was destroyed in an air raid Nov 1940; St Mary's Hall, built 1394–1414 as a guild centre; two gates of the old city walls (1356); Belgrade Theatre (1958); Coventry Art Gallery and Museum; Museum of British Road Transport; and Lanchester Polytechnic.

history The city originated when Leofric, Earl of Mercia and husband of Lady ◊Godiva, founded a priory 1043. Industry began with bicycle manufacture 1870. The city was the target of a massive German air raid 14–15 Nov 1940 in which 550 people were killed and over 60,000 buildings destroyed.

Coverdale Miles 1488–1568. English Protestant priest whose translation of the Bible 1535 was the first to be printed in English. His translation of the psalms is that retained in the Book of Common Prayer. Coverdale became a Catholic priest, but turned to Protestantism and 1528 went to the continent to avoid persecution. In 1539 he edited the Great Bible which was ordered to be placed in churches. After some years in Germany, he returned to England 1548, and in 1551 was made bishop of Exeter. During the reign of Mary I he left the country.

Coward Noël Peirce 1899–1973. English dramatist, actor, revue-writer, director, and composer. He epitomized the witty and sophisticated man of the theatre. From his first success with *The Young Idea* 1923, he wrote and appeared in plays and comedies on both sides of the Atlantic such as *Hay Fever* 1925, *Private Lives* 1930 with Gertrude Lawrence, *Design for Living* 1933, *Blithe Spirit* 1941, and *A Song at Twilight* 1966. His revues and musicals included *On With the Dance* 1925 and *Bitter Sweet* 1929.

Coward also wrote for and acted in films, including the patriotic *In Which We Serve* 1942 and the sentimental *Brief Encounter* 1945. After World War II he became a nightclub and cabaret entertainer, performing songs like 'Mad Dogs and Englishmen'.

cow parsley or ***keck*** tall perennial plant, *Anthriscus sylvestris*, of the carrot family. It grows in Europe, N Asia, and N Africa. Up to 1 m/3 ft tall, with pinnate leaves, hollow furrowed stems, and heads of white flowers, it is widespread in hedgerows and shady places.

Cowper William 1731–1800. English poet. His verse anticipates ◊Romanticism and includes the six books of *The Task* 1785. He also wrote hymns (including 'God Moves in a Mysterious Way'). Cowper's work is important for its directness and descriptive accuracy, and it deals with natural themes later developed in Wordsworth's poetry. He was also among the finest of English letter writers.

cowrie marine snail of the family Cypreidae, in which the interior spiral form is concealed by a double outer lip. The shells are hard, shiny, and often coloured. Cowries are found in many parts of the world, particularly the tropical Indo-Pacific. Cowries have been used as ornaments and fertility charms, and also as currency, for example the Pacific money cowrie *Cypraea moneta*. The European cowrie *Trivia monacha* is fairly common on British shores.

cowslip European plant *Primula veris* of the same genus as the primrose and belonging to the family Primulaceae, with yellow flowers. It is native to temperate regions of the Old World.

coyote wild dog *Canis latrans*, in appearance like a small wolf, living from Alaska to Central America and east to New York. Its head and body are about 90 cm/3 ft long and brown, flecked with grey or black. Coyotes live in open country and can run at 65 kph/40 mph. Their main foods are rabbits and rodents.

coypu South American water rodent *Myocastor coypus*, about 60 cm/2 ft long and weighing up to 9 kg/20 lb. It has a scaly, ratlike tail, webbed hind feet, a blunt-muzzled head, and large orange incisors. The fur ('nutria') is reddish brown. It feeds on vegetation, and lives in burrows in rivers and lake banks.

CPU in computing, abbreviation for ◊***central processing unit***.

crab any decapod (ten-legged) crustacean of the division Brachyura, with a broad, rather round, upper body shell (carapace) and a small ◊abdomen tucked beneath the body. Crabs are related to lobsters and crayfish. Mainly marine, some crabs live in fresh water or on land. They are alert carnivores and scavengers. They have a typical sideways walk, and strong pincers on the first pair of legs, the other four pairs being used for walking. Periodically, the outer shell is cast to allow for growth. The name 'crab' is sometimes used for similar arthropods, such as the horseshoe crab, which is neither a true crab nor a crustacean.

There are many species of true crabs worldwide. The European shore crab *Carcinus maenas*, common on British shores between the tidemarks, is dull green, and grows to 4 cm/1.5 in or more. The edible crab *Cancer paqurus* grows to 14 cm/5.5 in long or more, lives down to 100 m/325 ft, and is extensively fished. Other true crabs include fiddler crabs (*Uca*),

Cowper Watercolour portrait of English poet William Cowper by William Blake. Cowper attempted to introduce everyday themes into English poetry after the period characterized by the heroic classical themes of Alexander Pope. He also produced his own translation of Homer, in rivalry to Pope's. *Image Select (UK) Ltd*

the males of which have one enlarged claw to wave at and attract females; the European river crab *Thelphusa fluviatilis*; and spider crabs with small bodies and very long legs, including the Japanese spider crab *Macrocheira kaempferi* with a leg span of 3.4 m/11 ft.

Hermit crabs (division Anomura) have a soft, spirally twisted abdomen and make their homes in empty shells of whelks and winkles for protection. The common hermit crab *Eupagurus bernhardus*, up to 10 cm/4 in long, is found off Atlantic and Mediterranean shores. Some tropical hermit crabs are found a considerable distance from the sea. The robber crab *Birgus latro* grows large enough to climb palm trees and feed on coconuts.

> *Mad dogs and Englishmen / Go out in the midday sun.*
>
> Noël Coward, 'Mad Dogs and Englishmen'

crab apple any of 25 species of wild ◊apple trees (genus *Malus*), native to temperate regions of the northern hemisphere. Numerous varieties of cultivated apples have been derived from *M. pumila*, the common native crab apple of SE Europe and central Asia.

The fruit of native species is smaller and more bitter than that of cultivated varieties and is used in crab-apple jelly. *M. sylvestris* is common in woods and hedgerows in southern Britain and varies from a mere bush to 10 m/30 ft in height.

Crabbe George 1754–1832. English poet. He wrote grimly realistic verse about the poor: *The Village* 1783, *The Parish Register* 1807, *The Borough* 1810 (which includes the story used in Benjamin Britten's opera *Peter Grimes*), and *Tales of the Hall* 1819.

Crab nebula cloud of gas 6,000 light years from Earth, in the constellation ◊Taurus. It is the remains

crab Crabs have adapted to many habitats. This *Sesarma* species crab from Kenya, E Africa, is adapted to the muddy tidal regions dominated by mangroves. *Premaphotos Wildlife*

crane The whooping crane *Grus americana* of North America is exceedingly rare in the wild. It breeds in Canada and migrates to the Texas coast in winter. Like all cranes, whooping cranes migrate in flocks, flying in V-formation or in lines, with necks forward and legs trailing.

of a star that according to Chinese records exploded as a ◊supernova observed as a brilliant point of light on Earth 4 July 1054. At its centre is a ◊pulsar that flashes 30 times a second.

crack street name for a chemical derivative (bicarbonate) of ◊cocaine in hard, crystalline lumps; it is heated and inhaled (smoked) as a stimulant. Crack was first used in San Francisco in the early 1980s, and is highly addictive. Its use has led to numerous deaths but it is the fastest-growing sector of the illegal drug trade, since it is less expensive than cocaine.

cracking reaction in which a large ◊alkane molecule is broken down by heat into a smaller alkane and a small ◊alkene molecule. The reaction is carried out at a high temperature (600°C or higher) and often in the presence of a catalyst. Cracking is a commonly used process in the ◊petrochemical industry.

Cracow alternative form of ◊Kraków, a Polish city.

crag in previously glaciated areas, a large lump of rock that a glacier has been unable to wear away. As the glacier passed up and over the crag, weaker rock on the far side was largely protected from erosion and formed a tapering ridge, or tail, of debris.

Craig (Edward Henry) Gordon 1872–1966. English director and stage designer. His innovations and theories on stage design and lighting effects, expounded in *On the Art of the Theatre* 1911, had a profound influence on stage production in Europe and the USA. He was the son of actress Ellen Terry.

Craig James, 1st Viscount Craigavon 1871–1940. Ulster Unionist politician, the first prime minister of Northern Ireland 1921–40. Craig became a member of Parliament 1906, and was a highly effective organizer of Unionist resistance to Home Rule. As prime minister he carried out systematic discrimination against the Catholic minority, abolishing proportional representation 1929 and redrawing constituency boundaries to ensure Protestant majorities.

crake any of several small birds of the family Rallidae, order Gruiformes, related to the corncrake. Another species which occurs annually in the UK, and sometimes nests, is the spotted crake, *Porzana porzana*. This species inhabits swamps, wet meadows, and the edges of lakes and rivers, but always where there is thick cover.

Cranach Lucas ***the Elder***, originally Lucas Müller 1472–1553. German painter, etcher, and woodcut artist. A leading figure in the German Renaissance, he painted religious scenes, allegories (many featuring full-length nudes), and precise and polished portraits, such as *Martin Luther* 1521 (Uffizi, Florence).

He is associated with the artists Albrecht Dürer and Albrecht Altdorfer and was a close friend of the religious reformer Martin Luther, whose portrait he painted several times. *The Flight into Egypt* 1504 (Staatliche Museum, Berlin) is typical in its combination of religious subject and sensitive landscape. His work shows the effect of the Reformation in changes of artistic direction, religious compositions gradually giving place to portraits of the Lutheran circle and to allegories from classical mythology, in which the sensuality of woman is freely expressed.

His second son, ***Lucas Cranach the Younger*** (1515–1586), succeeded him as director of the Cranach workshop.

cranberry any of several trailing evergreen plants of the genus *Vaccinium* in the heath family Ericaceae, allied to bilberries and blueberries. They grow in marshy places and bear small, acid, crimson berries, high in vitamin C, used for making sauce and jelly.

crane in engineering, a machine for raising, lowering, or placing in position heavy loads. The three main types are the jib crane, the overhead travelling crane, and the tower crane. Most cranes have the machinery mounted on a revolving turntable. This may be mounted on trucks or be self-propelled, often being fitted with ◊caterpillar tracks.

crane in zoology, a large, wading bird of the family Gruidae, order Gruiformes, with long legs and neck, short powerful wings, a naked or tufted head, and unwebbed feet. Cranes are marsh- and plains-dwelling birds, feeding on plants as well as insects and small animals. They are usually migratory. Their courtship includes frenzied, leaping dances. They are found in all parts of the world except South America.

The common crane *Grus grus* is still numerous in many parts of Europe, and winters in Africa and India.

Crane Stephen 1871–1900. US writer. He introduced grim realism into the US novel. His book *The Red Badge of Courage* 1895 deals vividly with the US Civil War in a prose of impressionist, visionary naturalism.

cranesbill any plant of the genus *Geranium*, which contains about 400 species. The plants are named after the beaklike protrusion attached to the seed vessels. When ripe, this splits into coiling spirals, which jerk the seeds out, assisting in their distribution. The genus includes ten species native to Britain, including herb Robert *G. robertianum* and bloody cranesbill *G. sanguineum*.

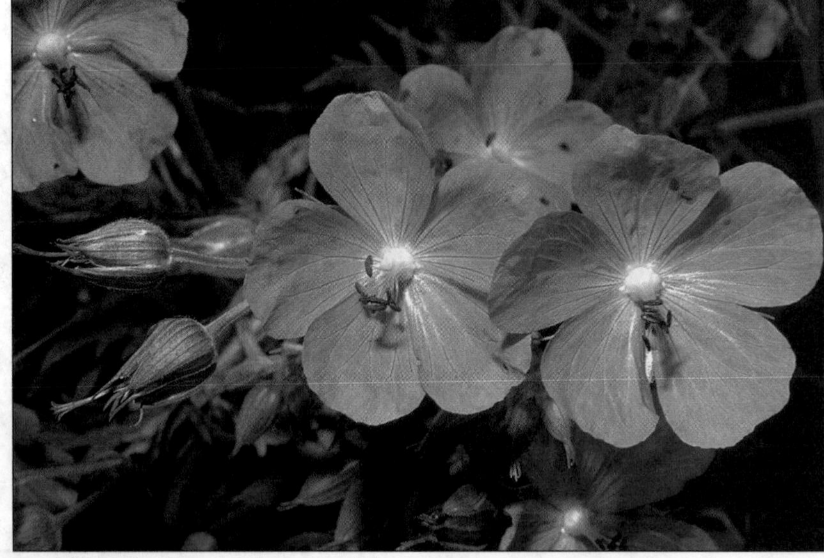

cranesbill The meadow cranesbill *Geranium pratense* is widespread in Europe, Asia, and North America. A distinctive meadow plant, it has large purple-blue flowers. Darker veins in the petals guide insects to the nectar in the flower. *Premaphotos Wildlife*

crane fly or ***daddy-longlegs*** any fly of the family Tipulidae, with long, slender, fragile legs. They look like giant mosquitoes, but the adults are quite harmless. The larvae live in soil or water; the soil-living larvae are known as leatherjackets and they cause crop damage by eating roots.

cranium the dome-shaped area of the vertebrate skull that protects the brain. It consists of eight bony plates fused together by sutures (immovable joints). Fossil remains of the human cranium have aided the development of theories concerning human evolution.

Cranko John Cyril 1927–1973. South African-born British choreographer. He was a pivotal figure in the ballet boom of the 1960s. He joined Sadler's Wells, London, 1946 as a dancer, becoming resident choreographer 1950. In 1961 he became director of the Stuttgart Ballet, where he achieved the 'Stuttgart Ballet Miracle', turning it into a world-class company with a vital and exhilarating repertory. He excelled in the creation of full-length narrative ballets, such as *Romeo and Juliet* 1958 and *Onegin* 1965. He is also known for his one-act ballets, peopled with comic characters, as in *Pineapple Poll* 1951 and *Jeu de cartes* 1965.

crankshaft essential component of piston engines that converts the up-and-down (reciprocating) motion of the pistons into useful rotary motion. The car crankshaft carries a number of cranks. The pistons are connected to the cranks by connecting rods and ◊bearings; when the pistons move up and down, the connecting rods force the offset crank pins to describe a circle, thereby rotating the crankshaft.

Cranmer Thomas 1489–1556. English cleric, archbishop of Canterbury from 1533. A Protestant convert, he helped to shape the doctrines of the Church of England under Edward VI. He suggested 1529 that the question of Henry VIII's marriage to Catherine of Aragon should be referred to the universities of Europe rather than to the pope, and in 1533 he declared it null and void.

He was responsible for the issue of the Prayer Books of 1549 and 1552, and supported the succession of Lady Jane Grey 1553. Condemned for heresy under the Catholic Mary Tudor, he at first recanted, but when his life was not spared, resumed his position and was burned at the stake.

Crassus Marcus Licinius c. 115–53 BC. Roman general who crushed the ◊Spartacus uprising 71 BC and became consul 70. In 60 BC he joined with Caesar and Pompey in the First Triumvirate and obtained a command in the east 55 BC. Eager to gain his own reputation for military glory, he invaded Parthia (Mesopotamia), but was defeated by the Parthians at the battle of Carrhae, captured, and put to death.

crater bowl-shaped depression in the ground, usually round and with steep sides. Craters are formed by explosive events such as the eruption of a volcano or a bomb, or by the impact of a meteorite. The Moon has more than 300,000 craters over 1 km/6 mi in diameter, formed by meteorite bombardment; similar craters on Earth have mostly been worn away by erosion. Craters are found on many other bodies in the Solar System.

craton or ***shield*** core of a continent, a vast tract of highly deformed ◊metamorphic rock around which the continent has been built. Intense mountain-building periods shook these shield areas in Precambrian times before stable conditions set in. Cratons exist in the hearts of all the continents, a typical example being the Canadian Shield.

Crawford Joan. Stage name of Lucille Le Sueur 1908–1977. US film actress. She became a star with her performance as a flapper (liberated young woman) in *Our Dancing Daughters* 1928. Later she appeared as a sultry, often suffering, mature woman. Her films include *Mildred Pierce* 1945 (Academy Award), *Sudden Fear* 1952, and *Whatever Happened to Baby Jane?* 1962.

crawling peg or ***sliding peg*** or ***sliding parity*** or ***moving parity*** in economics, a method of achieving a desired adjustment in a currency exchange rate (up or down) by small percentages over a given period, rather than by major revaluation or devaluation.

Craxi Bettino (Benedetto) 1934– . Italian socialist politician, leader of the Italian Socialist Party (PSI) 1976–93, and prime minister 1983–87. In 1993 he was one of many politicians suspected of involvement in Italy's corruption network. Between 1994 and 1996, he was sentenced to several prison sentences after being found guilty of corruption charges.

crayfish freshwater decapod (ten-limbed) crustacean belonging to several families structurally similar to, but smaller than, the lobster. Crayfish are brownish-green scavengers and are found in all parts of the world except Africa. They are edible, and some species are farmed.

The common crayfish *Astacus pallipes*, up to 10 cm/4 in long, is found in rivers in chalky areas of Britain, living in burrows in the mud and emerging, chiefly at night, to feed on small animals. The crawfish or spiny lobster *Palinurus vulgaris*, sometimes called crayfish, is a marine lobster without pincers.

Crazy Horse Sioux name ***Ta-Sunko-Witko*** 1849–1877. Sioux Indian chief, one of the Indian leaders at the massacre of ◊Little Bighorn. He was killed when captured.

creationism theory concerned with the origins of matter and life, claiming, as does the Bible in Genesis, that the world and humanity were created by a supernatural Creator, not more than 6,000 years ago. It was developed in response to Darwin's theory of ◊evolution; it is not recognized by most scientists as having a factual basis.

Crécy, Battle of first major battle of the Hundred Years' War 26 Aug 1346 in which Philip VI of France was defeated by Edward III of England at the village of Crécy-en-Ponthieu, now in Somme *département*, France, 18 km/11 mi NE of Abbeville. The English victory reinforced the lesson of Courtrai – that infantry were well capable of dealing with cavalry.

Edward's forces were arranged in three divisions, all dismounted, with Welsh archers and spearmen in the front ranks. The French arrived in the afternoon; their Genoese crossbowmen opened the battle, but rain had slacked their bowstrings and they were rapidly annihilated by the Welsh bowmen who had unstrung their bows and kept the strings dry. The French knights, impatient for victory, then rode forward but, clustered together by the confined battlefield, they were rapidly picked off by bowmen and spearmen. The battle then resolved itself into a series of charges by the French knights against the English lines, but they were eventually beaten off and before nightfall were in retreat.

credit in economics, a means by which goods or services are obtained without immediate payment, usually by agreeing to pay interest. The three main forms are ***consumer credit*** (usually extended to individuals by retailers), ***bank credit*** (such as overdrafts or personal loans), and ***trade credit*** (common in the commercial world both within countries and internationally).

credit in education, a system of evaluating courses so that a partial qualification or unit from one institution is accepted by another on transfer to complete a course.

credit card card issued by a credit company, retail outlet, or bank, which enables the holder to obtain goods or services on credit (usually to a specified limit), payable on specified terms. The first credit card was introduced 1947 in the USA.

Some credit cards also act as bank cards to enable customers to obtain money more easily from various bank branches. 'Intelligent' credit cards are now being introduced that contain coded information about the customer and the amount of credit still available. This can be read by a terminal connected with the company's central computer.

In the UK, the first credit card was introduced by Barclays Bank in 1966. By 1996, nearly 40% of adults in the UK held a credit card.

creditor individual or business organization that is owed money by another individual or business.

credit rating measure of the willingness or ability to pay for goods, loans, or services rendered by an individual, company, or country. The lower the credit rating of a firm, the higher the interest charged by banks and other ◊creditors is likely to be. A firm or country with a high credit rating will attract loans on favourable terms.

crayfish The spectacular blue mountain crayfish *Euastacus montanus* inhabits clear, swiftly-flowing mountain streams in the subtropical forests of S Queensland, Australia. *Premaphotos Wildlife*

Cree a Native American people whose language belongs to the Algonquian family. The Cree are distributed over a vast area in Canada from Alberta to Quebec, although in the latter their way of life is under threat from the expansion of a hydroelectric project. In the USA the majority of Cree live in the Rocky Boys reservation in Montana. Cree and Ojibwa languages are closely related and are spoken by around 50,000 people.

creed in general, any system of belief; in the Christian church the verbal confessions of faith expressing the accepted doctrines of the church. The different forms are the Apostles' Creed, the ◊Nicene Creed, and the ◊Athanasian Creed. The only creed recognized by the Orthodox Church is the Nicene Creed.

The oldest is the ***Apostles' Creed***, which, though not the work of the apostles, was probably first formulated in the 2nd century. The full version of the Apostles' Creed, as now used, first appeared about 750. The use of creeds as a mode of combating heresy was established by the appearance of the ***Nicene Creed***, introduced by the Council of Nicaea 325 when ◊Arianism was widespread, and giving the orthodox doctrine of the Trinity. The Nicene Creed used today is substantially the same as the version adopted at the church council in Constantinople 381, with a filioque clause (on the issue of whether the Holy Spirit proceeds from God the Father only or from God the Father and the Son) added during the 5th and 8th centuries in the Western church.

The ***Athanasian Creed*** is thought to be later in origin than the time of Athanasius (died 373), although it represents his views in a detailed exposition of the doctrines of the Trinity and the incarnation. Some authorities suppose it to have been composed in the 8th or 9th century but others place it as early as the 4th or 5th century.

creep in civil and mechanical engineering, the property of a solid, typically a metal, under continuous stress that causes it to deform below its yield point (the point at which any elastic solid normally stretches without any increase in load or stress). Lead, tin, and zinc, for example, exhibit creep at ordinary temperatures, as seen in the movement of the lead sheeting on the roofs of old buildings. Copper, iron, nickel, and their alloys also show creep at high temperatures.

cremation disposal of the dead by burning. The custom was universal among ancient Indo-European peoples, for example, the Greeks, Romans, and Teutons. It was discontinued among Christians until the late 19th century because of their belief in the bodily resurrection of the dead. Overcrowded urban cemeteries gave rise to its revival in the West. It has remained the usual method of disposal in the East.

Cremation was revived in Italy about 1870, and shortly afterwards introduced into the UK; the first crematorium was opened 1885 in Woking, Surrey. In the UK an application for cremation must be accompanied by two medical certificates. Cremation is usually carried out in gas-fired furnaces. Ashes are scattered in gardens of remembrance or elsewhere, or deposited in urns at the crematorium or in private graves.

Creole in the West Indies and Spanish America, originally someone of European descent born in the New World; later someone of mixed European and African descent. In Louisiana and other states on the Gulf of Mexico, it applies either to someone of French or Spanish descent or (popularly) to someone of mixed French or Spanish and African descent.

creole language any ◊pidgin language that has ceased to be simply a trade jargon in ports and markets and has become the mother tongue of a particular community. Many creoles have developed into distinct languages with literatures of their own; for example, Jamaican Creole, Haitian Creole, Krio in Sierra Leone, and Tok Pisin, now the official language of Papua New Guinea.

creosote black, oily liquid derived from coal tar, used as a wood preservative. Medicinal creosote, which is transparent and oily, is derived from wood tar.

cress any of several plants of the Cruciferae family, characterized by a pungent taste. The common European garden cress *Lepidium sativum* is cultivated worldwide.

crescent curved shape of the Moon when it appears less than half illuminated. It also refers to any object or symbol resembling the crescent Moon. Often associated with Islam, it was first used by the Turks on their standards after the capture of Constantinople 1453, and appears on the flags of many Muslim countries. The Red Crescent is the Muslim equivalent of the Red Cross.

Cretaceous (Latin *creta* 'chalk') period of geological time 146–65 million years ago. It is the last period of the Mesozoic era, during which angiosperm (seed-bearing) plants evolved, and dinosaurs reached a peak before their almost complete extinction at the end of the period. Chalk is a typical rock type of the second half of the period.

Crime and bad lives are the measure of a State's failure, all crime in the end is the crime of the community.

On **CRIME**
H G Wells *A Modern Utopia* 1905

Crete (Greek *Kríti*) largest Greek island in the E Mediterranean Sea, 100 km/62 mi SE of mainland Greece
area 8,378 sq km/3,234 sq mi
capital Iráklion (Heraklion)
towns and cities Khaniá (Canea), Rethymnon, Aghios Nikolaos
products citrus fruit, olives, wine
population (1991) 536,900
language Cretan dialect of Greek
history it has remains of the ◊Minoan civilization 3000–1400 BC (see ◊Knossos), and was successively under Roman, Byzantine, Venetian, and Turkish rule. The island was annexed by Greece 1913. In 1941 it was captured by German forces from Allied troops who had retreated from the mainland and was retaken by the Allies 1944.

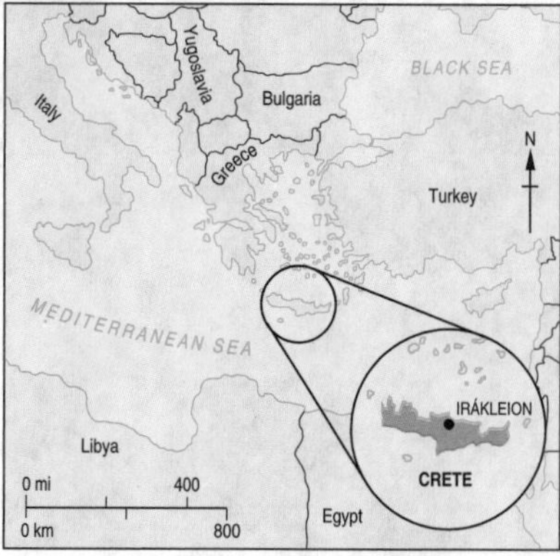

Creutzfeldt–Jakob disease (CJD) rare brain disease that causes progressive physical and mental deterioration, leading to death usually within a year of onset. It has been linked with ◊bovine spongiform encephalopathy (BSE), and there have also been occurrences in people treated with pituitary hormones derived from cows for growth or fertility problems.

CJD is one of a group of human and animal diseases known as the transmissible spongiform encephalopathies since they are characterized by the appearance of spongy changes in brain tissue. Some scientists believe that all these conditions, including BSE in cattle and ◊scrapie in sheep, are in effect the same disease. Like BSE, CJD is caused by the presence of an altered form of the brain protein PrP, that plays a role in sleep rhythms and in maintaining certain brain cells. Once a small amount of the abnormal protein is present it begins to convert all the normal PrP. In 1996 similarities in the PrP of humans and bovines were discovered.

Research published by British pathologists in 1997 proved that the new variant of CJD (vCJD) is caused by the same agent that causes BSE, indicating that the disease has jumped species, from cattle to humans.

crevasse deep crack in the surface of a glacier; it can reach several metres in depth. Crevasses often occur where a glacier flows over the break of a slope, because the upper layers of ice are unable to stretch and cracks result; they also form at the edges of glaciers owing to friction with the bedrock.

Crewe town in Cheshire, England; population (1991) 63,400. It owed its growth to its position as a railway junction; the chief construction workshops of British Rail are here. It is the centre of the dairy industry, providing cattle breeding, management, and animal health services. Other occupations include chemical works, clothing factories, and vehicle manufacture.

Crick Francis Harry Compton 1916– . English molecular biologist. From 1949 he researched the molecular structure of ◊DNA, and the means whereby characteristics are transmitted from one generation to another. For this work he was awarded a Nobel prize (with Maurice ◊Wilkins and James ◊Watson) 1962.

Using Wilkins's and others' discoveries, Crick and Watson postulated that DNA consists of a double helix consisting of two parallel chains of alternate sugar and phosphate groups linked by pairs of organic bases. They built molecular models which also explained how genetic information could be coded – in the sequence of organic bases. Crick and Watson published their work on the proposed structure of DNA in 1953. Their model is now generally accepted as correct.

Crick English molecular biologist Francis Crick. Crick shared the Nobel Prize for Physiology or Medicine with James Watson and Maurice Wilkins 1962, after discovering the molecular structure of the genetic material DNA, at the Cavendish Laboratory in Cambridge. He later turned his attention to investigating the nature of human consciousness. *Image Select (UK) Ltd*

cricket bat-and-ball game between two teams of 11 players each. It is played with a small solid ball and long flat-sided wooden bats, on a round or oval field, at the centre of which is a finely mown pitch, 20 m/22 yd long. At each end of the pitch is a wicket made up of three upright wooden sticks (stumps), surmounted by two smaller sticks (bails). The object of the game is to score more runs than the opposing team. A run is normally scored by the batsman striking the ball and exchanging ends with his or her partner until the ball is returned by a fielder, or by hitting the ball to the boundary line for an automatic four or six runs.
rules A batsman stands at each wicket and is bowled a stipulated number of balls (usually six), after which another bowler bowls from the other wicket. A batsman is usually got 'out' by being bowled, caught, run out, stumped, or l.b.w. (leg before wicket) – when the batsman's leg obstructs the wicket and is struck by the ball. A good captain will position fielders according to the strength of the opposition's batsman. Games comprise one or two innings, or turns at batting, per team. Two umpires arbitrate; one stands behind the wicket at the non-striker's end and makes decisions on l.b.w., close catches, and any infringements on the bowler's part; the other stands square of the wicket and is principally responsible for decisions on run-outs and stumpings. In Test matches, these officials are traditionally supplied by the host country, but recently there has been an increased call for neutral umpires.
history It became popular in southern England in the late 18th century. Rules were drawn up in 1774 and modified following the formation of the MCC 1787. The game's amateur status was abolished 1963; sponsored one-day cricket was introduced in the same year. From 1967 two overseas players were allowed in British first-class teams.
modern cricket and great players Every year a series of Test matches are played among member countries of the Commonwealth, where the game has its greatest popularity: Australia, India, New Zealand, Pakistan, England, Sri Lanka, and the West Indies. Test matches take several days, but otherwise the majority of matches last one, three, or four days. Famous grounds besides Lord's include the Oval (London), Old Trafford (Manchester), the Melbourne Ground and Sydney Oval (Australia), and the Wanderers' Ground (Johannesburg). Great cricketers have included the English players W G Grace, Jack Hobbs, and Len Hutton; the Australian Don Bradman; the Indian K S Ranjitsinhji; the South African A D Nourse; and the West Indians Leary Constantine, Frank Worrell, and Gary Sobers. Among the main events are the County Championship, first officially held 1890; the Refuge Assurance League (formerly John Player League), first held 1969; the NatWest Trophy (formerly called the Gillette Cup), first held 1963; the Benson and Hedges Cup, first held 1972; and the World Cup, first held 1975 and contested every four years. *See list of tables on p. 1177.*

cricket in zoology, an insect belonging to any of various families, especially the Gryllidae, of the order Orthoptera. Crickets are related to grasshoppers. They have somewhat flattened bodies and long antennae. The males make a chirping noise by rubbing together special areas on the forewings.

crime behaviour or action that is punishable by criminal law. A crime is a public, as opposed to a moral, wrong; it is an offence committed against (and hence punishable by) the state or the community at large. Many crimes are immoral, but not all actions considered immoral are illegal.

The laws of each country specify which actions or omissions are criminal. These include serious moral wrongs, such as murder; wrongs that endanger state security, such as treason; wrongs that endanger or disrupt an orderly society, such as evading taxes; and wrongs against the community, such as littering. Crime is socially determined and so what constitutes a crime may vary geographically and over time. Thus, an action may be considered a crime in one society but not in another; for example, drinking alcohol is not generally prohibited in the West but is a criminal offence in many Islamic countries. Certain categories of crime, though, such as violent crime and theft, are recognized almost universally.

Crime is dealt with in most societies by the judicial system, comprising the police, the courts, and so on. These may impose penalties ranging from a fine to imprisonment to, in some instances, death, depending upon the severity of the offence and the penalty laid down by the country where the offence was committed.

Crimea northern peninsula on the Black Sea, an autonomous republic of ◊Ukraine; formerly a region (1954–91)
area 27,000 sq km/10,425 sq mi
capital Simferopol
towns and cities Sevastopol, Yalta
features mainly steppe, but southern coast is a holiday resort; home of the Black Sea fleet (ownership of which has been the source of a dispute between Russia and Ukraine)
products iron, oil
population (1991 est) 2,549,800 (65% Russian, 25% Ukranian, despite return of 150,000 Tatars since 1989)
history Crimea was under Turkish rule 1475–1774; a subsequent brief independence was ended by Russian annexation 1783. Crimea was the republic of Taurida 1917–20 and the Crimean Autonomous Soviet Republic from 1920 until occupied by Germany 1942–44. It was then reduced to a region, its Tatar people being deported to Uzbekistan for collaboration. In 1954 Khrushchev made Crimea part of Ukraine. Although the Tatar people were exonerated 1967 and some were allowed to return, others were forcibly re-exiled 1979. A drift back to their former homeland began 1987 and a federal ruling 1988 confirmed their right to residency. Since 1991 the Crimea has sought to gain independence from the Ukraine; the latter has resisted all secessionist moves. A 1994 referendum in Crimea supported demands for greater autonomy and closer links with Russia.

Crimean War war 1853–56 between Russia and the allied powers of England, France, Turkey, and Sardinia. The war arose from British and French mistrust of Russia's ambitions in the Balkans. It began with an allied Anglo-French expedition to the Crimea to attack the Russian Black Sea city of Sevastopol. The battles of the river Alma, Balaclava (including the charge of the Light Brigade), and Inkerman 1854 led to a siege which, owing to military mismanagement, lasted for a year until Sept 1855. The war was ended by the Treaty of Paris 1856. The scandal surrounding French and British losses through disease led to the organization of proper military nursing services by Florence Nightingale.

1853 Russia invaded the Balkans (from which they were compelled to withdraw by Austrian intervention) and sank the Turkish fleet at the Battle of Sinope 30 Nov.

1854 Britain and France declared war on Russia, invaded the Crimea, and laid siege to Sevastopol (Sept 1854–Sept 1855). Battles of ◊Balaclava 25

Oct (including the Charge of the Light Brigade), Inkerman 5 Nov, and the Alma.

1855 Sardinia declared war on Russia.

1856 The Treaty of Paris in Feb ended the war.

crime fiction variant of ◊detective fiction distinguished by emphasis on character and atmosphere rather than solving a mystery. Examples are the works of US writers Dashiell Hammett and Raymond Chandler during the 1930s and, in the second half of the 20th century, Patricia Highsmith and English author Ruth Rendell.

criminal damage destruction of or damage to property belonging to another without lawful reason. Damaging property by fire is charged as arson.

Criminal Investigation Department (CID) detective branch of the London Metropolitan Police, established 1878, comprising a force of about 4,000 men and women recruited entirely from the uniformed police and controlled by an assistant commissioner. CID branches are also found in the regional police forces. In 1979 new administrative arrangements were introduced so that all police officers, including CID, came under the uniformed chief superintentendent of the regional division. Regional crime squads are composed of detectives drawn from local forces to deal with major crime, and are kept in touch by a London-based national coordinator.

The CID at New Scotland Yard: ***1*** Central Office: deals with international crime and serious crime throughout the country. It controls the Flying Squad (a rapid deployment force for investigating serious crimes). ***2*** Criminal Intelligence Department: studies criminals and their methods. ***3*** Fingerprint Department: holds some 2 million prints of convicted criminals. ***4*** Criminal Record Office: holds information on known criminals and publishes the *Police Gazette*. ***5*** The Scientific Laboratory. ***6*** The Stolen Car Squad. ***7*** Special Branch: deals with crimes against the state. ***8*** National coordinator for the Regional crime squads (detectives drawn from local forces to deal with major crime).

criminal law body of law that defines the public wrongs (crimes) that are punishable by the state and establishes methods of prosecution and punishment. It is distinct from ◊civil law, which deals with legal relationships between individuals (including organizations), such as contract law.

The laws of each country specify what actions or omissions are criminal. These include serious moral wrongs, such as murder; wrongs that endanger the security of the state, such as treason; wrongs that disrupt an orderly society, such as evading taxes; and wrongs against the community, such as dropping litter. An action may be considered a crime in one country but not in others, such as homosexuality or drinking alcohol. Some actions, such as assault, are both criminal and civil wrongs; the offender can be both prosecuted and sued for compensation.

In England and Wales crimes are either: indictable offences (serious offences triable by judge and jury in a crown court); summary offences dealt with in magistrates' courts; or hybrid offences tried in either kind of court according to the seriousness of the case and the wishes of the defendant. Crown courts have power to punish more severely those found guilty than a magistrates' court. Punishments include imprisonment, fines, suspended terms of imprisonment (which only come into operation if the offender is guilty of further offences during a specified period), probation, and ◊community service. Overcrowding in prisons and the cost of imprisonment have led to recent experiments with noncustodial sentences such as electronic tags fixed to the body to reinforce curfew orders on convicted criminals in the community.

crinoline stiff fabric, originally made of horsehair, widely used in 19th-century women's clothing. It was used to create skirts of great width in the 1850s when the cage-frame crinoline, made with steel hoops, was introduced. The frame was modified around 1865 when the skirts were flattened at the front, leaving a fuller skirt at the back. By the late 1860s many crinolines were discarded altogether in favour of a far narrower profile.

crith unit of mass used for weighing gases. One crith is the mass of one litre of hydrogen gas (H_2) at standard temperature and pressure.

cricket Most crickets are drably coloured in brown, grey, or black – this Kenyan species *Rhicnogryllus lepidus* is an exception. Its bright livery is probably an example of aposematic (warning) coloration. *Premaphotos Wildlife*

critical mass in nuclear physics, the minimum mass of fissile material that can undergo a continuous ◊chain reaction. Below this mass, too many ◊neutrons escape from the surface for a chain reaction to carry on; above the critical mass, the reaction may accelerate into a nuclear explosion.

critical path analysis procedure used in the management of complex projects to minimize the amount of time taken. The analysis shows which subprojects can run in parallel with each other, and which have to be completed before other subprojects can follow on. Complex projects may involve hundreds of subprojects, and computer ◊applications packages for critical path analysis are widely used to help reduce the time and effort involved in their analysis.

Croagh Patrick holy mountain rising to 765 m/2,510 ft in County Mayo, W Ireland, one of the three national places of pilgrimage in Ireland (with Lough Derg and Knock). An annual pilgrimage on the last Sunday of July commemorates St Patrick who fasted there for the 40 days of Lent 440 AD.

Croat the majority ethnic group in ◊Croatia. Their language is generally considered to be identical to that of the Serbs, hence ◊Serbo-Croatian. The Croats, who are mainly Roman Catholics, had a long association with the ◊Austro-Hungarian Empire. During World War II they were closely affiliated to the ◊Axis powers and Croatian fascists were involved in attacks on Serbs. Conflicting separatist demands provoked the outbreak of civil war in Yugoslavia 1991 and led to eventual recognition by the European Community (now the European Union) of Croatia's independence.

Croatia (Serbo-Croatian ***Hrvatska***) country in central Europe, bounded N by Slovenia and Hungary, W by the Adriatic Sea, and E by Bosnia-Herzegovina and the Yugoslavian republic of Serbia. *See country box on p. 276.*

Croce Benedetto 1866–1952. Italian philosopher, historian, and literary critic; an opponent of fascism. His *Filosofia dello spirito/Philosophy of the Spirit* 1902–17 was a landmark in idealism. Like the German philosopher G W F Hegel, he held that ideas do not represent reality but *are* reality; but unlike Hegel, he rejected every kind of transcendence.

crochet craft technique similar to both knitting and lacemaking, in which one hooked needle is used to produce a loosely looped network of wool or cotton.

Crockett Davy (David) 1786–1836. US folk hero, born in Tennessee. He served under Andrew ◊Jackson in the war with the Creek Native Americans 1813–14, then entered politics, serving on the state legislature 1821–24. He was a Democratic Congressman 1827–31 and 1833–35. A series of books, of which he may have been part-author, made him into a mythical hero of the frontier, but their Whig associations cost him his office. He clashed with Jackson, who he claimed had betrayed his frontier constituency, and left for Texas in bitterness. He died in the battle of the ◊Alamo during the War of Texan Independence.

crocodile large aquatic carnivorous reptile of the family Crocodiliae, related to alligators and caymans, but distinguished from them by a more pointed snout and a notch in the upper jaw into which the fourth tooth in the lower jaw fits. Crocodiles can grow up to 6 m/20 ft, and have long, powerful tails that propel them when swimming. They are fierce hunters, larger specimens attacking animals the size of antelopes or, occasionally, people. In some species, the female lays over 100 hard-shelled eggs in holes or nest mounds of vegetation, which she guards until the eggs hatch. When in the sun, crocodiles cool themselves by opening their mouths wide, which also enables scavenging birds to pick their teeth. They can stay underwater for long periods, but must surface to breathe. They ballast themselves with stones to adjust their buoyancy. They have remained virtually unchanged for 200 million years.

About a dozen species of crocodiles, all of them endangered, are found in tropical parts of Africa, Asia, Australia, and Central America. The largest is the saltwater crocodile *Crocodylus porosus*, which can grow to 6 m/20 ft or more, and is found in E India, Australia, and the W Pacific. The Nile crocodile *C. niloticus* is found in Africa and Madagascar. The American crocodile *C. acutus*, about 4.6 m/15 ft long, is found from S Florida to Ecuador. The gharial, or gavial, *Gavialis gangeticus* is sometimes placed in a family of its own. It is an Indian species which grows to 4.5m/15 ft or more, and has a very long narrow snout specialized for capturing and eating fish.

crocodile The estuarine or saltwater crocodile, of India, SE Asia, and Australasia, is one of the largest and most dangerous of its family. It has been known to develop a taste for human flesh. Hunted near to extinction for its leather, it is now protected by restrictions and the trade in skins is controlled.

❛Take away these baubles.❜

Oliver Cromwell Referring to the symbols of parliamentary power when he dismissed Parliament 1653

crocus any plant of the genus *Crocus* of the iris family Iridaceae, native to Northern parts of the Old World, especially S Europe and Asia Minor. It has single yellow, purple, or white flowers and narrow, pointed leaves. During the dry season of the year crocuses remain underground in the form of a corm, and produce fresh shoots and flowers in spring or autumn. At the end of the season of growth fresh corms are produced. Several species are cultivated as garden plants.

Croesus died 546 BC. Last king of Lydia c. 560–546 BC, famed for his wealth. Dominant over the Greek cities of the Asia Minor coast, he was defeated and captured by ◊Cyrus the Great and Lydia was absorbed into the Persian empire.

croft small farm in the Highlands of Scotland, traditionally farming common land cooperatively; the 1886 Crofters Act gave security of tenure to crofters. Today, although grazing land is still shared, arable land is typically enclosed.

Crohn's disease or ***regional ileitis*** chronic inflammatory bowel disease. It tends to flare up for a few days at a time, causing diarrhoea, abdominal cramps, loss of appetite, weight loss, and mild fever. The cause of Crohn's disease is unknown, although stress may be a factor. It is treated by surgical removal of badly affected segments of intestine, and by corticosteroids. Mild cases respond to rest, bland diet, and drug treatment. Crohn's disease first occurs most often in adults aged 20–40.

Cro-Magnon prehistoric human *Homo sapiens sapiens* believed to be ancestral to Europeans, the first skeletons of which were found 1868 in the Cro-Magnon cave near Les Eyzies, in the Dordogne region of France. They are thought to have superseded the Neanderthals in the Middle East, Africa, Europe, and Asia about 40,000 years ago. Although modern in skeletal form, they were more robust in build than some present-day humans. They hunted bison, reindeer, and horses, and are associated with Upper Palaeolithic cultures, which produced fine flint and bone tools, jewellery, and naturalistic cave paintings.

Crome John 1768–1821. English landscape painter. He was a founder of the ◊Norwich School with John Sell Cotman 1803. His works, which show the influence of Dutch landscape painting, include *The Poringland Oak* 1818 (Tate Gallery, London).

Cotman inspired him to produce some watercolours and he also made a number of etchings, but his main work is in oil paintings, broadly treated and with true grandeur of design. His masterpieces include *Boy Keeping Sheep* 1812 (Victoria and Albert Museum, London), *Mousehold Heath* c. 1814–16, *The Slate Quarries* c. 1802–5, and *Moonrise on the Yare* c. 1811–16 (all Tate Gallery, London).

As 'Old Crome' he is distinguished from his son ***John Bernay Crome*** (1794–1842), who also worked in Norwich as painter and art teacher and specialized in effects of moonlight.

Crompton Samuel 1753–1827. British inventor at the time of the Industrial Revolution. He invented the 'spinning mule' 1779, combining the ideas of Richard ◊Arkwright and James ◊Hargreaves. This span a fine, continuous yarn and revolutionized the production of high-quality cotton textiles.

Cromwell Oliver 1599–1658. English general and politician, Puritan leader of the Parliamentary side in the ◊Civil War. He raised cavalry forces (later called Ironsides) which aided the victories at Edgehill 1642 and ◊Marston Moor 1644, and organized the New Model Army, which he led (with General Fairfax) to victory at Naseby 1645. He declared Britain a republic ('the Commonwealth') 1649, following the execution of Charles I. As Lord Protector (ruler) from 1653, Cromwell established religious toleration and raised Britain's prestige in Europe on the basis of an alliance with France against Spain.

Cromwell was born at Huntingdon, NW of Cambridge, son of a small landowner. He entered Parliament 1629 and became active in events leading to the Civil War. Failing to secure a constitutional settlement with Charles I 1646–48, he defeated the 1648 Scottish invasion at Preston. A special commission, of which Cromwell was a member, tried the king and condemned him to death, and a republic, known as 'the Commonwealth', was set up.

The ◊Levellers demanded radical reforms, but he executed their leaders 1649. He used terror to crush Irish clan resistance 1649–50, and defeated the Scots (who had acknowledged Charles II) at Dunbar 1650 and Worcester 1651. In 1653, having forcibly expelled the corrupt 'Rump Parliament', he summoned a convention ('◊Barebones Parliament'), soon dissolved as too radical, and under a constitution (Instrument of Government) drawn up by the army leaders, became Protector (king in all but name). The parliament of 1654–55 was dissolved as uncooperative, and after a period of military dictatorship, his last parliament offered him the crown; he refused because he feared the army's republicanism.

Cromwell Richard 1626–1712. Son of Oliver Cromwell, he succeeded his father as Lord Protector but resigned May 1659, having been forced to abdicate by the army. He lived in exile after the Restoration until 1680, when he returned.

Cromwell Thomas. Earl of Essex c. 1485–1540. English politician who drafted the legislation that made the Church of England independent of Rome. Originally in Lord Chancellor Wolsey's service, he became secretary to ◊Henry VIII 1534 and the real director of government policy; he was executed for treason.

CROATIA
Republic of

national name *Republika Hrvatska*
area 56,538 sq km/21,824 sq mi
capital Zagreb
major towns/cities Osijek
major ports chief port: Rijeka (Fiume); other ports: Zadar, Sibenik, Split, Dubrovnik
physical features Adriatic coastline with large islands; very mountainous, with part of the Karst region and the Julian and Styrian Alps; some marshland
head of state Franjo Tudjman from 1990
head of government Zlatko Matesa from 1995
political system emergent democracy
administrative divisions 21 counties, 420 municipalities, and 61 towns
political parties Croatian Democratic Union (CDU), Christian Democrat, right-of-centre, nationalist; Croatian Social-Liberal Party (CSLP), centrist; Social Democratic Party of Change (SDP), reform socialist; Croatian Party of Rights (HSP), Croat-oriented, ultranationalist; Croatian Peasant Party (HSS), rural-based; Serbian National Party (SNS), Serb-oriented
population 4,501,000 (1996 est)
population growth rate −0.1% (1990–95); −0.1% (2000–05)
ethnic distribution in 1991, 77% of the population were ethnic Croats, 12% were ethnic Serbs,and 1% were Slovenes. Since the civil war began 1992, more than 300,000 Croats have been displaced from Serbian enclaves within the republic, and there are an estimated 500,000 refugees from Bosnia in the republic. Serbs are most thickly settled in areas bordering Bosnia-Herzegovina, and in Slavonia, although more than 150,000 fled from Krajina to Bosnia-Herzegovina and Serbia following the region's recapture by the Croatian army Aug 1995
life expectancy 67 (males), 74 (females)
literacy rate 96%
language Croatian variant of Serbo-Croatian (official); Serbian variant of Serbo-Croatian also widely spoken, particularly in border areas in E
religion Roman Catholic (Croats); Orthodox Christian (Serbs)
currency kuna
GDP (US $) 14 billion (1994 est)
growth rate 0.8% (1994)
exports machinery, transport equipment, chemicals, foodstuffs

HISTORY
early Cs AD Part of Roman region of Pannonia.
AD 395 On division of Roman Empire, stayed in W half, along with Slovenia and Bosnia.
7th C Settled by Carpathian Croats, from NE; Christianity adopted.
924 Formed by Tomislav into independent kingdom, which incorporated Bosnia from 10th century.
12th–19th Cs Enjoyed autonomy under Hungarian crown, following dynastic union in 1102.
1526–1699 Slavonia, in E, held by Ottoman Turks, while Serbs were invited by Austria to settle along the border with Ottoman-ruled Bosnia, in a Vojna Krajina (military frontier).
1797–1815 Dalmatia, in W, ruled by France.
19th C Part of Austro-Hungarian Habsburg Empire.
1918 On dissolution of Habsburg Empire, joined Serbia, Slovenia, and Montenegro in 'Kingdom of Serbs, Croats and Slovenes', under Serbian Karageorgevic dynasty.
1929 The Kingdom became Yugoslavia. Croatia continued its campaign for autonomy.
1930s Ustasa, a Croat terrorist organization, began a campaign against dominance of Yugoslavia by the non-Catholic Serbs.
1941–44 Following German invasion, a 'Greater Croatia' Nazi puppet state, including most of Bosnia and W Serbia, formed under Ustasa leader, Ante Pavelic; more than half a million Serbs, Jews, and members of the Romany community were massacred in extermination camps.
1945 Became constituent republic of Yugoslavia Socialist Federation after communist partisans, led by Croat Marshal Tito, overthrew Pavelic.
1970s Separatist demands provoked crackdown.
late 1980s Spiralling inflation and a deterioration in living standards sparked industrial unrest and a rise in nationalist sentiment, which affected the local communist party.
1989 Formation of opposition parties permitted.
1990 Communists defeated by conservative nationalist CDU led by ex-Partisan Franjo Tudjman in first free election since 1938. 'Sovereignty' declared.
1991 Serb-dominated region of Krajina in SW announced secession from Croatia. Croatia declared independence, leading to military conflict with Serbia, and internal civil war ensued.
1992 United Nations (UN) peace accord accepted; independence recognized by European Community and USA; Croatia entered UN. UN peacekeeping force stationed in Croatia. Tudjman directly elected president.
1993 Government offensive to retake parts of Serb-held Krajina, violating 1992 UN peace accord.
1994 Accord with Muslims and ethnic Croats within Bosnia, to the E, to link recently formed Muslim–Croat federation with Croatia.
1995 Serb-held W Slavonia and Krajina captured by government forces; mass exodus of Croatian Serbs. Offensive extended into Bosnia-Herzegovina to halt Bosnian Serb assault on Bihac in W Bosnia. Serbia agreed to cede control of E Slavonia to Croatia over a two-year period.
1996 Diplomatic relations between Croatia and Yugoslavia restored. Croatia entered Council of Europe.
1997 Opposition successes in local elections. Tudjman re-elected despite failing health. Constitution amended to prevent weakening of Croatia's national sovereignty.
1998 Croatia resumed control over East Slavonia.

SEE ALSO Austro-Hungarian Empire; Tito; Yugoslavia

Cromwell had Henry divorced from Catherine of Aragon by a series of acts that proclaimed him head of the church. From 1536 to 1540 Cromwell suppressed the monasteries, ruthlessly crushed all opposition, and favoured Protestantism, which denied the divine right of the pope. His mistake in arranging Henry's marriage to Anne of Cleves (to cement an alliance with the German Protestant princes against France and the Holy Roman Empire) led to his being accused of treason and beheaded.

Crookes William 1832–1919. English scientist whose many chemical and physical discoveries include the metallic element thallium 1861, the radiometer 1875, and the Crookes high-vacuum tube used in X-ray techniques.

crop any plant product grown or harvested for human use. Over 80 crops are grown worldwide, providing people with the majority of their food and supplying fibres, rubber, pharmaceuticals, dyes, and other materials. Crops grown for export are ◊cash crops. A ◊catch crop is one grown in the interval between two main crops.

There are four main groups of crops. ***Food crops*** provide the bulk of people's food worldwide. The main types are cereals, roots, pulses (peas, beans), vegetables, fruits, oil crops, tree nuts, sugar, and spices. Cereals make the largest contribution to human nutrition. ***Forage crops*** are those such as grass and clover which are grown to feed livestock. Forage crops cover a greater area of the world than food crops. Grasses, which dominate this group, form the world's most abundant crop, consisting mostly of wild species grown in an unimproved state. ***Fibre crops*** produce vegetable fibres. Temperate areas produce flax and hemp, but the most valuable fibre crops are cotton, jute, and sisal, which are grown mostly in the tropics. Cotton dominates fibre-crop production. ***Miscellaneous crops*** include tobacco, rubber, ornamental flowers, and plants that produce perfumes, pharmaceuticals, and dyes.

crop in birds, the thin-walled enlargement of the digestive tract between the oesophagus and stomach. It is an effective storage organ especially in seed-eating birds; a pigeon's crop can hold about 500 cereal grains. Digestion begins in the crop, by the moisturizing of food. A crop also occurs in insects and annelid worms.

crop circle circular area of flattened grain found in fields, especially in SE England, since 1980. More than 1,000 such formations were reported in the UK 1991. The cause is unknown.

Most of the research into crop circles has been conducted by dedicated amateur investigators rather than scientists. Physicists who have studied the phenomenon have suggested that an electromagnetic whirlwind, or 'plasma vortex', can explain both the crop circles and some UFO sightings, but this does not account for the increasing geometrical complexity of crop circles, nor for the fact that until 1990 they were unknown outside the UK. Crop circles began to appear in the USA only after a US magazine published an article about them. A few people have confessed publicly to having made crop circles that were accepted as genuine by investigators.

Cromwell Thomas Cromwell succeeded his mentor, Cardinal Wolsey, as chief minister to Henry VIII. He fell from power after he arranged Henry's fourth marriage to Anne of Cleves, which Henry found less than satisfactory. *Philip Sauvain*

crop rotation system of regularly changing the crops grown on a piece of land. The crops are grown in a particular order to utilize and add to the nutrients in the soil and to prevent the build-up of insect and fungal pests. Including a legume crop, such as peas or beans, in the rotation helps build up nitrate in the soil because the roots contain bacteria capable of fixing nitrogen from the air.

A simple seven-year rotation, for example, might include a three-year ley (temporary grassland) followed by two years of wheat and then two years of barley, before returning the land to temporary grass once more. In this way, the cereal crops can take advantage of the build-up of soil fertility that occurs during the period under grass. In the 18th century, a four-year rotation was widely adopted with autumn-sown cereal, followed by a root crop, then spring cereal, and ending with a leguminous crop. Since then, more elaborate rotations have been devised with two, three, or four successive cereal crops, and with the root crop replaced by a cash crop such as sugar beet or potatoes, or by a legume crop such as peas or beans.

croquet outdoor game played with mallets and balls on a level hooped lawn measuring 27 m/90 ft by 18 m/60 ft. Played in France in the 16th and 17th centuries, it gained popularity in the USA and England in the 1850s. Two or more players can play, and the object is to drive the balls though the hoops (wickets) in rotation. A player's ball may be advanced or retarded by another ball. The headquarters of croquet is the Croquet Association (founded 1897), based at the Hurlingham Club, London.

Crosby Bing (Harry Lillis) 1904–1977. US film actor and singer. He achieved world success with his distinctive style of crooning in such songs as 'Pennies from Heaven' 1936 (featured in a film of the same name) and 'White Christmas' 1942. He won an Academy Award for his acting in 'Going My Way' 1944, and made a series of 'road' film comedies with Dorothy Lamour (1914–1996) and Bob ◊Hope, the last being *Road to Hong Kong* 1962.

cross symbol of the Christian religion, in widespread use since the 3rd century. It is a symbol of the crucifixion of Jesus and the central significance of his suffering, death, and resurrection. The Latin cross is the most commonly used; other types are the Greek cross, St Anthony's cross, and St Andrew's cross. Symbolic crosses were used by pre-Christian cultures, for example the ancient Egyptian ankh (St Anthony's cross with a loop at the top), symbol of life, and the swastika, used by Hindus, Buddhists, Celts, and N American Indians before it was adopted by the Nazis.

crossbill species of ◊finch, genus *Loxia*, family Fringillidae, order Passeriformes, in which the hooked tips of the upper and lower beak cross one another, an adaptation for extracting the seeds from conifer cones. The red or common crossbill *Loxia curvirostra* is found in parts of Eurasia and North America, living chiefly in pine forests.

cross-section the surface formed when a solid is cut through by a plane at right angles to its axis.

crossword puzzle in which a grid of open and blacked-out squares must be filled with interlocking words, to be read horizontally and vertically, according to numbered clues. The first crossword was devised by Arthur Wynne of Liverpool, England, in the *New York World* 1913.

croup inflammation of the larynx in small children, with harsh, difficult breathing and hoarse coughing. Croup is most often associated with viral infection of the respiratory tract.

crow any of 35 species of omnivorous birds in the genus *Corvus*, family Corvidae, order Passeriformes, which also includes choughs, jays, and magpies. Crows are usually about 45 cm/1.5 ft long, black, with a strong bill feathered at the base. The tail is long and graduated, and the wings are long and pointed, except in the jays and magpies, where they are shorter. Crows are considered to be very intelligent. The common crows are *C. brachyrhynchos* in North America, and *C. corone* in Europe and Asia.

Cromwell Oliver Cromwell, a painting attributed to Van Dyck. Lord Protector and virtual dictator of England after the execution of Charles I, Cromwell inherited a divided and war-weary nation, to which he forcibly united Scotland and Ireland for the first time in their histories. His rule became associated with an unpopular type of Puritan zeal, and the Stuart Charles II was welcomed back by most of Britain after Cromwell's death. *Philip Sauvain*

Crowley Aleister (Edward Alexander) 1875–1947. British occultist, a member of the theosophical Order of the Golden Dawn; he claimed to practise black magic, and his books include the novel *Diary of a Drug Fiend* 1923. He designed a tarot pack that bears his name.

crown official headdress worn by a king or queen. The modern crown originated with the diadem, an embroidered fillet worn by Eastern rulers, for which a golden band was later substituted. A laurel crown was granted by the Greeks to a victor in the games, and by the Romans to a triumphant general. Crowns came into use among the Byzantine emperors and the European kings after the fall of the Western Empire. Perhaps the oldest crown in Europe is the Iron Crown of Lombardy, made in 591.

crown colony any British colony that is under the direct legislative control of the crown and does not possess its own system of representative government. Crown colonies are administered by a crown-appointed governor or by elected or nominated legislative and executive councils with an official majority. Usually the crown retains rights of veto and of direct legislation by orders in council.

crown court in England and Wales, any of several courts that hear serious criminal cases referred from ◊magistrates' courts after ◊committal proceedings. Appeals against conviction or sentence at magistrates' courts may be heard in crown

crossbill The crossbill *Loxia curvirostra* feeds almost exclusively on the seeds of coniferous trees. The crossed beak is more pronounced in birds that feed on the tougher seeds of trees such as Scots pine. Crossbills' beaks are not crossed when they first hatch, but become crossed a few weeks after the young leave the nest. Male and female crossbills are not alike – males are orange-red, while females are green.

courts. Appeal from a crown court is to the Court of Appeal.

Crown Estate title (from 1956) of land in UK owned by the monarch. The income from it was handed to Parliament by George III in 1760 in exchange for an annual payment (called the civil list). The Crown Estate owns valuable sites in central London, which, along with 268,400 acres in England and Scotland, are valued in excess of £1.2 billion.

crown jewels or ***regalia*** symbols of royal authority. The British set (except for the Ampulla and the Anointing Spoon) were broken up at the time of Oliver Cromwell, and now date from the Restoration. They are kept in the Tower of London in the Crown Jewel House (1967).

Main items include St Edward's Crown; the Imperial State Crown; the jewelled Sword of State, used only at the Coronation; the Sword of State used at the opening of Parliament and on other state occasions; the Curtana (Sword of Mercy); the Swords of Temporal and Spiritual Justice; the Orb; the Royal Sceptre or Sceptre with the Cross (containing the great Star of Africa, cut from the Cullinan diamond); the Rod with the Dove; St Edward's Staff; the Spurs; the Coronation Ring (the 'Wedding Ring of England'); the Armills (gold bracelets, given by the Commonwealth countries in 1953 for the coronation of Elizabeth II); the Ampulla (which contains oil for the anointing); and the Anointing Spoon.

Crown Prosecution Service body established by the Prosecution of Offences Act 1985, responsible for prosecuting all criminal offences in England and Wales. It is headed by the Director of Public Prosecutions (DPP), and brings England and Wales in line with Scotland (which has a procurator fiscal) in having a prosecution service independent of the police.

Croydon outer borough of S Greater London. It includes the suburbs of Purley and Coulsdon.
features 11th-century Addington Palace, former residence of archbishops of Canterbury; Whitgift School, founded 1599 by the then archbishop of Canterbury John Whitgift (c. 1530–1604), a resident of the borough; Whitgift's 16th-century almshouses; Surrey Street market (dating from the 13th century); Fairfield Halls (1962), including Ashcroft Theatre, Fairfield Hall, and Arnhem Gallery; overspill office development from central London
industries pharmaceuticals, electronics, engineering, foodstuffs
population (1991) 313,500.

crucifixion death by fastening to a cross, a form of capital punishment used by the ancient Romans, Persians, and Carthaginians, and abolished by the Roman emperor Constantine. Specifically, the Crucifixion refers to the execution by the Romans of ◊Jesus in this manner.

Cruelty, Theatre of theory advanced by Antonin ◊Artaud in his book *Le Théâtre et son double/Theatre and its Double* 1938 and adopted by a number of writers and directors. It aims to substitute gesture and sound for spoken dialogue, and to shock the audience into awareness through the release of feelings usually repressed by conventional behaviour. In the UK, Artaud's ideas particularly influenced the producer and director Peter Brook.

Cruikshank George 1792–1878. English painter and illustrator. He is remembered for his political cartoons and illustrations for Charles Dickens' *Oliver Twist* and Daniel Defoe's *Robinson Crusoe*. He began with political and social caricatures in the Gillray and Rowlandson style, but evolved a grotesque and humorous manner of his own in sketches of Victorian London life and in book illustration. Notable productions are his etchings, 1823–26, for Grimms' fairy-tales and the spirited melodrama of those for Dickens's *Oliver Twist* and Harrison Ainsworth's *Old St Paul's*. His brother Robert (1789–1856) was also a caricaturist and a miniature painter. They collaborated 1821 in illustrating the late-Georgian humours of Pierce Egan's *Life in London*.

cruise missile long-range guided missile that has a terrain-seeking radar system and flies at moderate speed and low altitude. It is descended from the German V1 of World War II. Initial trials in the 1950s demonstrated the limitations of cruise missiles, which included high fuel consumption and relatively slow speeds (when compared to intercontinental ballistic missiles – ICBMs) as well as inaccuracy and a small warhead. Improvements to guidance systems by the use of terrain-contour matching (TERCOM) ensured pinpoint accuracy on low-level flights after launch from a mobile ground launcher (ground-launched cruise missile – GLCM), from an aircraft (air-launched cruise missile – ALCM), or from a submarine or ship (sea-launched cruise missile – SLCM).

The 1972 Strategic Arms Limitation Talks (SALT I) excluded reference to cruise missiles, and thus research into improved systems continued. During the 1970s the USSR increased its intermediate nuclear force (INF) targeted upon W Europe and at the same time improved its own air defences. NATO therefore embarked in 1979 on a 'twin-track decision' to acquire additional cruise missiles while simultaneously offering to agree to an arms control treaty to withdraw them, provided the USSR did likewise. Tomahawk GLCMs were deployed from 1983 on. The 1987 INF Treaty resulted in GLCMs being withdrawn. Tomahawk cruise missiles were used in the 1991 Gulf War.

crusade (French *croisade*) European war against non-Christians and heretics, sanctioned by the pope; in particular, the Crusades, a series of wars 1096–1291 undertaken by European rulers to recover Palestine from the Muslims. Motivated by religious zeal, the desire for land, and the trading ambitions of the major Italian cities, the Crusades were varied in their aims and effects. ▷ *See feature on pp. 280–281.*

crust the outermost part of the structure of Earth, consisting of two distinct parts, the oceanic crust and the continental crust. The oceanic crust is on average about 10 km/6.2 mi thick and consists mostly of basaltic types of rock. By contrast, the continental crust is largely made of granite and is more complex in its structure. Because of the movements of ◊plate tectonics, the oceanic crust is in no place older than about 200 million years. However, parts of the continental crust are over 3 billion years old.

crustacean one of the class of arthropods that includes crabs, lobsters, shrimps, woodlice, and barnacles. The external skeleton is made of protein and chitin hardened with lime. Each segment bears a pair of appendages that may be modified as sensory feelers (antennae), as mouthparts, or as swimming, walking, or grasping structures.

Crux constellation of the southern hemisphere, popularly known as the Southern Cross, the smallest of the 88 constellations but one of the brightest, and one of the best known as it is represented on the flags of Australia and New Zealand. Its brightest stars are Alpha Crucis (or Acrux), a ◊double star about 400 light years from Earth, and Beta Crucis (or Mimosa).

Cruyff Johan 1947– . Dutch footballer, an outstanding European player in the 1970s. He was capped 48 times by his country, scoring 33 goals. He spent most of his career playing with Ajax and Barcelona and was named European Footballer of the Year three times. As coach, he took both clubs to domestic and European honours.

cryogenics science of very low temperatures (approaching ◊absolute zero), including the production of very low temperatures and the exploitation of special properties associated with them, such as the disappearance of electrical resistance (◊superconductivity).

Cryogenics has several practical applications. Cryotherapy is a process used in eye surgery, in which a freezing probe is briefly applied to the outside of the eye to repair a break in the retina. Electronic components, which could be used in very fast computers, need low temperatures to function. Magnetic levitation (◊maglev) systems must be maintained at low temperatures. Food can be frozen for years, and freezing eggs, sperm and pre-embryos is now routine.

cryonics practice of freezing a body at the moment of clinical death with the aim of enabling eventual resuscitation. The body, drained of blood, is indefinitely preserved in a thermos-type container filled with liquid nitrogen at −196°C/−321°F. The first human treated was James H Bedford, a lung-cancer patient of 74, in the USA in 1967.

cryptography science of creating and reading codes; for example, those produced by the Enigma coding machine used by the Germans in World War II and those used in commerce by banks encoding electronic fund-transfer messages, business firms sending computer-conveyed memos between headquarters, and in the growing field of electronic mail. The breaking and decipherment of such codes is known as 'cryptanalysis'.

cryptorchism or ***cryptorchidism*** condition marked by undescended testicles; failure of the testes to complete their descent into the scrotum before birth. When only one testicle has descended, the condition is known as monorchism.

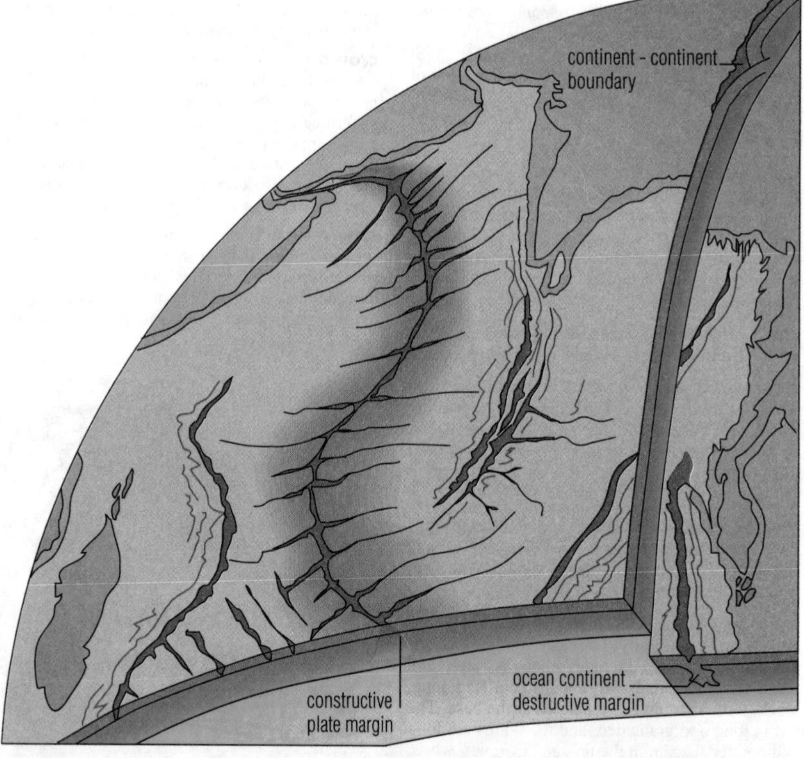

crust The crust of the Earth is made up of plates with different kinds of margins. In mid-ocean, there are constructive plate margins, where magma wells up from the Earth's interior, forming new crust. On continent–continent margins, mountain ranges are flung up by the collision of two continents. At an ocean–continent destructive margin, ocean crust is forced under the denser continental crust, forming an area of volcanic instability.

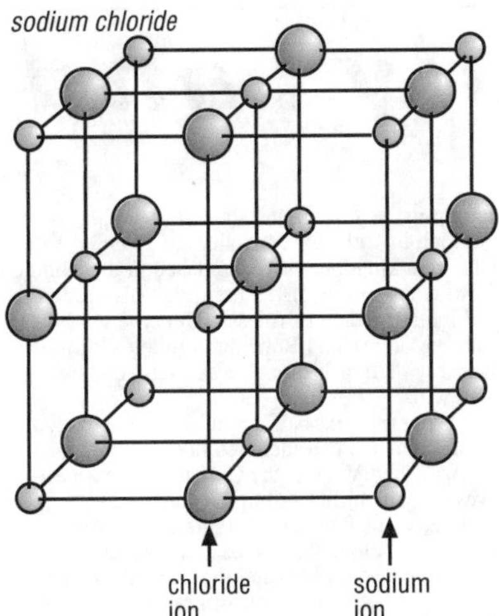

crystal The sodium chloride, or common salt, crystal is a regular cubic array of charged atoms (ions) – positive sodium atoms and negative chlorine atoms. Repetition of this structure builds up into cubic salt crystals.

crystal substance with an orderly three-dimensional arrangement of its atoms or molecules, thereby creating an external surface of clearly defined smooth faces having characteristic angles between them. Examples are table salt and quartz.

Each geometrical form, many of which may be combined in one crystal, consists of two or more faces – for example, dome, prism, and pyramid. A mineral can often be identified by the shape of its crystals and the system of crystallization determined. A single crystal can vary in size from a submicroscopic particle to a mass some 30 m/100 ft in length. Crystals fall into seven crystal systems or groups, classified on the basis of the relationship of three or four imaginary axes that intersect at the centre of any perfect, undistorted crystal.

crystallography the scientific study of crystals. In 1912 it was found that the shape and size of the repeating atomic patterns (unit cells) in a crystal could be determined by passing X-rays through a sample. This method, known as ◊X-ray diffraction, opened up an entirely new way of 'seeing' atoms. It has been found that many substances have a unit cell that exhibits all the symmetry of the whole crystal; in table salt (sodium chloride, NaCl), for instance, the unit cell is an exact cube.

crystal system all known crystalline substances crystallize in one of the seven crystal systems defined by symmetry. The elements of symmetry used for this purpose are: (1) planes of mirror symmetry, across which a mirror image is seen, and (2) axes of rotational symmetry, about which, in a 360° rotation of the crystal, equivalent faces are seen twice, three, four, or six times. To be assigned to a particular crystal system, a mineral must possess a certain minimum symmetry, but it may also possess additional symmetry elements. Since crystal symmetry is related to internal structure, a given mineral will always crystallize in the same system, although the crystals may not always grow into precisely the same shape. In cases where two minerals have the same chemical composition but different internal structures (for example graphite and diamond, or quartz and cristobalite), they will generally have different crystal systems.

CSCE abbreviation for ***Conference on Security and Cooperation in Europe***, known after Dec 1994 as the ◊Organization on Security and Cooperation in Europe (OSCE).

CSE abbreviation for ***Certificate of Secondary Education***, in the UK, the examinations taken by the majority of secondary school pupils who were not regarded as academically capable of GCE O level, until the introduction of the common secondary examination system, ◊GCSE, 1988.

Ctesiphon ruined royal city of the Parthians, and later capital of the Sassanian Empire, 19 km/12 mi SE of Baghdad, Iraq. A palace of the 4th century still has its throne room standing, spanned by a single vault of unreinforced brickwork some 24 m/80 ft across.

CT scanner medical device used to obtain detailed X-ray pictures of the inside of a patient's body. See ◊CAT scan.

Cuba island country in the Caribbean Sea, the largest of the West Indies, off the S coast of Florida and to the E of Mexico. *See country box on p. 282.*

Cuban missile crisis confrontation in international relations Oct 1962 when Soviet rockets were installed in Cuba and US president Kennedy compelled Soviet leader Khrushchev, by military threats and negotiation, to remove them. This event prompted an unsuccessful drive by the USSR to match the USA in nuclear weaponry.

Following reports that the USSR was constructing launching sites for nuclear missiles in Cuba, the USA imposed a naval 'quarantine' around the island 22 Oct 1962, and the two superpowers came closer to possible nuclear war than at any other time. Soviet inferiority in nuclear weapons forced a humiliating capitulation to Kennedy's demands 2 Nov, when Kennedy announced that Soviet missile bases in Cuba were being dismantled.

cube in geometry, a regular solid figure whose faces are all squares. It has six equal-area faces and 12 equal-length edges. If the length of one edge is l, the volume V of the cube is given by:

$$V = l^3$$

and its surface area A by:

$$A = 6l^2$$

cube to multiply a number by itself and then by itself again. For example, 5 cubed = $5^3 = 5 \times 5 \times 5 = 125$. The term also refers to a number formed by cubing; for example, 1, 8, 27, 64 are the first four cubes.

cubic equation any equation in which the largest power of x is x^3. For example, $x^3 + 3x^2y + 4y^2 = 0$ is a cubic equation.

Cubism revolutionary movement in early 20th-century art. Developed by Pablo ◊Picasso and Georges ◊Braque, it pioneered semi-abstract forms. In analytical Cubism (1907–12), painters built up a kaleidoscopic image of an object by combining several points of view. This austere early style, characterized by a multitude of intersecting facets painted in muted browns and greys, gradually gave way to synthetic Cubism (after 1912), in which the images became simpler, the colours brighter, and ◊collage was introduced. Cubism's message that an art work exists in its own right rather than as a representation of the world had a profound impact on 20th-century art.

The Cubists' aim was to show objects as they are known to be, rather than as they happen to look at a particular moment. The first painting to show the influence of these art forms was Picasso's *Les Demoiselles d'Avignon* 1907. Cubism did not long outlast World War I but it had far-reaching repercussions and led to much of the abstract art practised today. Leading Cubists include Juan Gris, Fernand Léger, Francis Picabia, and Robert Delaunay, and the sculptors Alexander Archipenko and Jacques Lipchitz.

cuckoo The cuckoo *Cuculus canorus* migrates northwards in spring to breed, and in April the characteristic call of the male can be heard in Britain. During May the female begins searching for suitable nests in which to lay her eggs. The host she chooses must be an insect-eater, and a female cuckoo always chooses nests belonging to one species to lay in, probably the same species that reared her. Before laying an egg, she removes one of the host's own eggs from the nest. She may lay up to 12 eggs in this way, each in a separate nest.

cubit earliest known unit of length, which originated between 2800 and 2300 BC. It is approximately 50.5 cm/20.6 in long, which is about the length of the human forearm measured from the tip of the middle finger to the elbow.

cuboid six-sided three-dimensional prism whose faces are all rectangles. A brick is a cuboid.

Cuchulain lived 1st century AD. Celtic hero, the chief figure in a cycle of Irish legends. He is associated with his uncle Conchobar, King of Ulster; his most famous exploits are described in *Taín Bó Cuailnge/The Cattle Raid of Cuchulain.*

cuckoo species of bird, any of about 200 members of the family Cuculidae, order Cuculiformes, especially the Eurasian cuckoo *Cuculus canorus*, whose name derives from its characteristic call. Somewhat hawklike, it is about 33 cm/1.1 ft long, bluish-grey and barred beneath (females sometimes reddish), and typically has a long, rounded tail. It lays its eggs in the nests of small insectivorous birds. As soon as the young cuckoo hatches, it ejects all other young birds or eggs from the nest and is tended by its 'foster parents' until fledging.

cuckoo-pint or ***lords-and-ladies*** perennial plant *Arum maculatum* of the Araceae family. The large arrow-shaped leaves appear in early spring, and the flower-bearing stalks are enveloped by a bract, or spathe. In late summer the bright red, berrylike fruits, which are poisonous, make their appearance.

cuckoo spit the frothy liquid surrounding and exuded by the larvae of the ◊froghopper.

cucumber trailing annual plant *Cucumis sativus* of the gourd family Cucurbitaceae, producing long, green-skinned fruit with crisp, translucent, edible

cont. on p. 282

'This was the first time I had met with Communism in a warm climate ... I had never before heard the 'Red Flag' played as a cha-cha-cha.'

On a visit to CUBA
James Cameron
What a Way to Run the Tribe

KASIMOV WITH IL-28 FUSELAGE CRATES ENROUTE TO CUBA
28 SEPTEMBER 1962

Cuban missile crisis The Soviet ship *Kasimov* photographed on its way to Cuba during the Cuban missile crisis, 1962. It was photographs like this, which clearly show the missile crates on the decks, which led to a swift and decisive response by the USA. *Corbis*

The Crusades to the Holy Land

Richard I and the Muslim warrior Saladin in battle, from the *Luttrell Psalter* 1338, British Museum, London. Richard embarked on the Third Crusade after Saladin had reunified the Muslim lands (1174–83) and recaptured Jerusalem from the crusaders. The crusaders' successes were minimal, and Richard ended the campaign by concluding a three-year truce with Saladin. *ET Archive*

The Crusades were a series of expeditions – part pilgrimage and part military campaign – mounted in the 12th and 13th centuries by European Christians, mainly against Muslims in the Middle East. The term 'crusade' also describes campaigns waged by European Christians against Muslims in North Africa and Spain, against non-Christians on Europe's northeastern frontiers, and against heretical Christians in Europe itself. They began at the end of the 11th century as a result of rising self-confidence and prosperity in Europe, and only came to an end in the 18th century.

The call for a crusade

Christians had lived and worshipped freely in Jerusalem since the Muslims conquered Palestine in the 7th century, despite regular wars between Muslims and the Christian Byzantine Empire. In 1071, however, the nomadic Seljuk Turks, who had recently become Sunni Muslims, decisively defeated the Byzantines at Manzikert, and expelled the last of the Ismaili Muslim Fatimids (known to the Europeans as Saracens) from Palestine and Syria. The Byzantine emperor and Christian pilgrims to the Holy Land (modern Israel and Lebanon) appealed to Pope Urban II for help in 1095. His solution was a holy war, in which Europeans could travel to Jerusalem as pilgrims and provide military assistance for their fellow Christians at the same time. The response among ordinary people and the military nobility alike was enthusiastic.

The earliest crusades

In 1095, several popular crusades, led by charismatic figures like Walter the Penniless and Peter the Hermit, set out for the Middle East. They were disorganized and undisciplined, and most of their participants died on the way. A more organized expedition was mounted 1096–97: a great army under Godfrey de Bouillon, Bohemund of Taranto, and other leaders fought its way through Asia Minor, taking Antioch in 1098 and Jerusalem in 1099. A Christian kingdom was established in the Middle East, with Godfrey as its first ruler, his brother Baldwin as Count of Edessa (Upper Mesopotamia), and Bohemund ruling at Antioch. Godfrey died in 1100 and was succeeded by Baldwin.

During the next half-century, in spite of reinforcements that included fleets from Genoa, Norway, and Venice, the Christians were hard-pressed. The military-religious orders of the Knights of St John and Knights Templar were formed to help defend Jerusalem. Nevertheless, Edessa was lost 1144, and the Second Crusade 1147–48, under Louis VII of France and Conrad III of Germany, ended disastrously in a failed attempt to capture Damascus. From the middle of the 12th century the Christian territories were constantly on the defensive, while the Seljuk regent of Mosul, Imad al-Din Zangi, and his son Nur al-Din steadily reunited the Muslim territories from Edessa to the Red Sea. In 1169 Nur al-Din destroyed Fatimid power in Egypt, and installed his Kurdish general Saladin as ruler there.

Saladin's conquests and European reaction

Saladin's impact on the region was tremendous, and his widespread conquests towards the end of the 12th century revived the Christians' crusading spirit. Having captured Damascus from his Zangid rivals in 1174 and Aleppo in 1183, Saladin swept down through Galilee with an immense force. He defeated a Christian army under Guy de Lusignan, King of Jerusalem, at the Horns of Hattin (near Lake Tiberias, in Palestine), and took Jerusalem in 1187. Tyre, Tripoli, and Antioch were the only towns that remained in Christian hands.

European Christians reacted to this news with a mixture of anger and fear, and mounted several

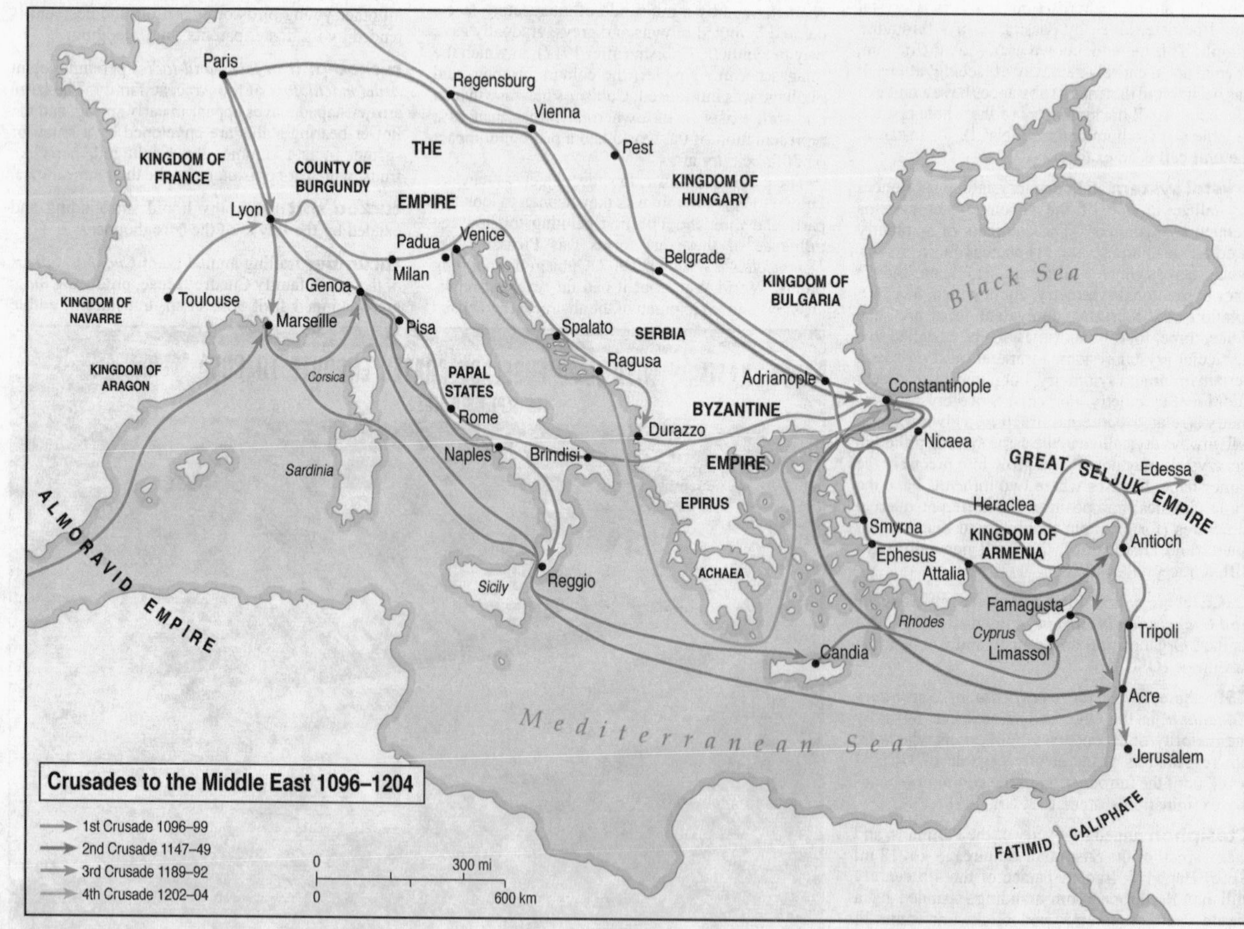

Embarking for the Crusades. European Christians waged a series of wars against the Muslims in Palestine 1096–1291, motivated by the desire to acquire land and goods as well as to deliver the Holy Land. *Philip Sauvain*

fresh expeditions. The most important of these was the Third Crusade, which set off in 1189 led by Philip II (Augustus) of France, Frederick I (Barbarossa) of Germany, and Richard I (the Lion-Heart) of England. The Germans went through Asia Minor, and the French and English went by sea to Acre, which had already been besieged for nearly two years by Guy de Lusignan. Under Richard's leadership, the Crusaders recovered a narrow strip of the Palestine coast, but were unable to recapture Jerusalem. Richard made a truce with Saladin, and returned to Europe.

13th-century crusades to the Middle East

The Fourth Crusade started from Venice in 1202. Instead of reaching Jerusalem, however, the crusaders became involved in Venetian and Byzantine political struggles, helping the deposed Byzantine emperor, Isaac Angelus, to regain his throne. A few months later the crusaders stormed and sacked Constantinople itself, and set up the Latin Empire of Constantinople under Baldwin of Flanders.

A contemporary Islamic miniature showing Saladin, sultan of Egypt. His recovery of Jerusalem from the Christians in 1187 led to the third Crusade. *Image Select (UK) Ltd*

The failure of these expeditions prompted several unofficial crusades, including the Children's Crusade of 1212 and the Shepherds' Crusade of 1251. The participants in these came mainly from Normandy, Flanders, and the Rhineland; their march through Europe was often accompanied by attacks on Jews, and few even reached the Mediterranean. Those members of the Children's Crusade who managed to sail for Alexandria, in Egypt, were captured and sold as slaves when they landed.

In 1217–18, King Andrew of Hungary and Duke Leopold IV of Austria led a new crusade to Palestine, with only limited success; an ambitious attack on Egypt (1218–21) led by John of Brienne, King of Jerusalem, ended in failure. Frederick II of Germany undertook a more successful crusade in 1228. Using diplomacy rather than force, he regained Jerusalem and southern Palestine. Jerusalem then remained in Christian hands until 1244. The crusade of Louis IX of France (St Louis) in 1249 was, like that of 1218–21, directed against Egypt, and proved even more disastrous. Louis was captured with the greater part of his army, and had to pay 800,000 pieces of gold as a ransom. In 1270 he led a further crusade to Tunis, but died of disease outside the city. Prince Edward of England (afterwards Edward I) led his own followers onwards to Acre a few months later, but achieved little. After a stunning victory at Ayn Jalut 1260 over the invading Mongols, the Mameluke Sultanate of Egypt reconquered all of Palestine and Syria, taking the last Christian outpost 1302.

Diminishing enthusiasm

The enthusiasm for crusades died down as European attention turned inwards in the grim 14th century, riven by war and the Black Death. Turkish power grew rapidly under the Ottomans, and crusades directed against them were no more than defensive actions against their incursions into the Balkans. Even the final capture of Constantinople by the Ottoman Sultan Mohammed II, in 1453, failed to prompt a European crusade for its recovery. The Knights Templar were suppressed 1307, but the Knights of St John, at Rhodes and later at Malta, continued to fight against Turkish advance in the Mediterranean.

Failure and benefits

Despite their military failure, the Crusades brought several benefits to Europe. Relations between European Christian settlers living in the Middle East and their Muslim neighbours were often much more friendly than the crusading ideal might suggest, and there was considerable exchange of knowledge between them. Trade between Europe and the Middle East increased greatly, particularly in the hands of Venetian and Genoese merchants. Sugar, cotton, and many other things now in everyday use first became known in Europe through the Crusades. European scholars gained access to learning from Classical Greece and Rome that had survived only thanks to Arabic scholars, and these and the works of the Arabic philosophers themselves helped pave the way for the Renaissance in Europe.

Simon Hall

The arrival of the crusaders at Damietta (Dumyat) in N Egypt, from a 15th-century edition of Vincent of Beauvais' *Speculum majus/Great Mirror*, Musée Condé, Chantilly, France. The port of Damietta was captured and then lost during the Fifth Crusade; it was captured again by French crusaders 1249. *ET Archive*

SEE ALSO
Children's Crusade; Islam; Richard I; St John, Knights of; Saladin; Templars

"Culture, the acquainting ourselves with the best that has been known and said in the world, and thus with the history of the human spirit."

On CULTURE
Matthew Arnold
Literature and Dogma, 1873

flesh. Small cucumbers, called gherkins, usually the fruit of *C. anguria*, are often pickled.

Cugnot Nicolas-Joseph 1725–1804. French engineer who produced the first high-pressure steam engine and, in 1769, the first self-propelled road vehicle. Although it proved the viability of steam-powered traction, the problems of water supply and pressure maintenance severely handicapped the vehicle.

Cukor George 1899–1983. US film director. He is known for sophisticated dramas and light comedies. He moved to the cinema from the theatre and was praised for his skilled handling of such stars as Greta ◊Garbo (in *Camille* 1937) and Katharine Hepburn (in *The Philadelphia Story* 1940). He won an Academy Award for the direction of *My Fair Lady* 1964.

Culloden, Battle of defeat 1746 of the ◊Jacobite rebel army of the British prince ◊Charles Edward Stuart (the 'Young Pretender') by the Duke of Cumberland on a stretch of moorland in Inverness-shire, Scotland. This battle effectively ended the military challenge of the Jacobite rebellion.

Although both sides were numerically equal (about 8,000 strong), the English were a drilled and disciplined force, while the Jacobites were a ragbag mixture of French, Irish, and Scots, ill-disciplined and virtually untrained. The English front line opened the battle with a volley of musketry, after which the Jacobites charged and broke through the first English line but were caught by the musket fire of the second line. They retired in confusion, pursued by the English cavalry which broke the Jacobite lines completely and shattered their force. About 1,000 were killed and a further 1,000 captured, together with all their stores and cannon.

cultivar variety of a plant developed by horticultural or agricultural techniques. The term derives from 'cultivated variety'.

cultural anthropology or ***social anthropology*** subdiscipline of anthropology that analyses human culture and society, the nonbiological and behavioural aspects of humanity. Two principal branches are ethnography (the study at first hand of living cultures) and ethnology (the comparison of cultures using ethnographic evidence).

Cultural Revolution Chinese mass movement 1966–69 begun by Communist Party leader ◊Mao Zedong, directed against the upper middle class – bureaucrats, artists, and academics – who were killed, imprisoned, humiliated, or 'resettled'. Intended to 'purify' Chinese communism, it was also an attempt by Mao to renew his political and ideological pre-eminence inside China. Half a million people are estimated to have been killed.

The 'revolution' was characterized by the violent activities of the semimilitary Red Guards, most of them students. Many established and learned people were humbled and eventually sent to work on the land, and from 1966 to 1970 universities were closed. Although the revolution was brought to an end in 1969, the resulting bureaucratic and economic chaos had many long-term effects. The ultra-leftist ◊Gang of Four, led by Mao's wife Jiang Qing and defence minister Lin Biao, played prominent roles in the Cultural Revolution. The chief political victims were ◊Liu Shaoqi and ◊Deng Xiaoping, who were depicted as 'bourgeois reactionaries'. After Mao's death, the Cultural Revolution was criticized officially and the verdicts on hundreds of thousands of people who were wrongly arrested and persecuted were reversed.

culture in biology, the growing of living cells and tissues in laboratory conditions.

culture in sociology and anthropology, the way of life of a particular society or group of people, including patterns of thought, beliefs, behaviour, customs, traditions, rituals, dress, and language, as well as art, music, and literature. Archaeologists use the word to mean the surviving objects or artefacts that provide evidence of a social grouping.

Cuman member of a powerful alliance of Turkic-speaking peoples of the Middle Ages, which dominated the steppes in the 11th and 12th centuries and built an empire reaching from the river Volga to the Danube.

Cumberland Ernest Augustus. Duke of Cumberland 1771–1851. King of Hanover from 1837, the fifth son of George III of Britain. A high Tory and an opponent of all reforms, he attempted to suppress the constitution but met with open resistance that had to be put down by force.

Cumberland William Augustus. Duke of Cumberland 1721–1765. British general who ended the Jacobite rising in Scotland with the Battle of Culloden 1746; his brutal repression of the Highlanders earned him the nickname of 'Butcher'. He was the third son of George II.

Cumbernauld ◊new town in Strathclyde, Scotland, 18 km/11 mi from Glasgow; population (1991) 48,800. It was founded 1956 to take in city overspill. In 1966 it won a prize as the world's best-designed community.

Cumbria county of NW England, created 1974 from Cumberland, Westmorland, and parts of NW Lancashire and NW Yorkshire
area 6,810 sq km/2,629 sq mi (*see United Kingdom map*)
towns and cities Carlisle (administrative headquarters), Barrow, Kendal, Whitehaven, Workington, Penrith

CUBA
Republic of

USA
Mexico
Havana
CUBA
ATLANTIC OCEAN
Dominican Republic
Haiti
CARIBBEAN SEA
PACIFIC OCEAN
0 mi 500
0 km 1000

national name *República de Cuba*
area 110,860 sq km/42,820 sq mi
capital Havana
major towns/cities Santiago de Cuba, Camagüey
physical features comprises Cuba and smaller islands including Isle of Youth; low hills; Sierra Maestra mountains in SE; Cuba has 3,380 km/2,100 mi of coastline, with deep bays, sandy beaches, coral islands and reefs
head of state and government Fidel Castro Ruz from 1959
political system communist republic
administrative divisions 14 provinces
political party Communist Party of Cuba (PCC), Marxist-Leninist
population 11,018,000 (1996 est)
population growth rate 0.8% (1990–95); 0.5% (2000–05)
ethnic distribution predominantly of mixed Spanish and African or Spanish and Indian origin
life expectancy 74 (males), 78 (females)
literacy rate men 95%, women 93%
language Spanish
religions Roman Catholic; also Episcopalians and Methodists
currency Cuban peso
GDP (US $) 11.9 billion (1994)
growth rate 0.7% (1994)
exports sugar, tobacco, coffee, nickel, fish and shellfish, minerals, citrus fruits, cigars.

HISTORY
3rd C AD The Ciboney, Cuba's earliest known inhabitants, were dislodged by the immigration of Taino, Arawak Indians from Venezuela.
1492 Christopher Columbus landed in Cuba and claimed it for Spain.
1511 Spanish settlement established at Baracoa by Diego Velazquez.
1523 Decline of Indian population and rise of sugar plantations led to import of slaves from Africa.
mid-19th C Cuba produced one-third of the world's sugar.
1868–78 Unsuccessful first war for independence from Spain.
1886 Slavery was abolished.
1895–98 Further uprising against Spanish rule, led by José Marti, who died in combat; 200,000 soldiers deployed by Spain.
1898 USA defeated Spain in Spanish-American War; Spain gave up all claims to Cuba, which was ceded to the USA.
1901 Cuba achieved independence; Tomás Estrada Palma became first president of the Republic of Cuba.
1906–09 Brief period of US administration after Estrada resigned in the face of an armed rebellion by political opponents.
1909 The Liberal, José Miguel Gomez, became president, but soon became tarred by corruption.
1924 Gerado Machado, an admirer of the Italian fascist leader Benito Mussolini, established a brutal dictatorship which lasted nine years.
1925 Socialist Party founded from which the communist party later developed.
1933 Army sergeant Fulgencio Batista seized power.
1934 USA abandoned its right to intervene in Cuba's internal affairs.
1944 Batista retired and was succeeded by the civilian Ramon Gray San Martin.
1952 Batista seized power again to begin an oppressive and corrupt regime.
1953 Fidel Castro Ruz led an unsuccessful coup against Batista on the 100th anniversary of the birth of Marti.
1956 Second unsuccessful coup by Castro.
1959 Batista overthrown by Castro and his 9,000-strong guerrilla army. Constitution of 1940 replaced by a 'Fundamental Law', making Castro prime minister, his brother Raúl Castro his deputy, and Argentinian-born Ernesto 'Che' Guevara as third in command.
1960 All US businesses in Cuba appropriated without compensation; USA broke off diplomatic relations.
1961 USA sponsored an unsuccessful invasion by Cuban exiles at the Bay of Pigs. Castro announced that Cuba had become a communist state, with a Marxist-Leninist programme of economic development, and became allied with the USSR.
1962 Cuban missile crisis: Cuba was expelled from the Organization of American States. Castro responded by tightening relations with the USSR which installed nuclear missiles in Cuba (subsequently removed at US insistence). US trade embargo imposed.
1965 Cuba's sole political party renamed Cuban Communist Party (PCC). With Soviet help, Cuba began to make considerable economic and social progress.
1972 Cuba became a full member of the Moscow-based Council for Mutual Economic Assistance (COMECON).
1976 New socialist constitution approved; Castro elected president.
1976–81 Castro became involved in extensive international commitments, sending troops as Soviet surrogates, particularly to Africa.
1982 Cuba joined other Latin American countries in giving moral support to Argentina in its dispute with Britain over the Falklands.
1984 Castro tried to improve US-Cuban relations by discussing exchange of US prisoners in Cuba for Cuban 'undesirables' in the USA.
1988 Peace accord with South Africa signed, agreeing to withdrawal of Cuban troops from Angola, as part of a reduction in Cuba's overseas military activities.
1991 Soviet troops withdrawn with the collapse of the Soviet Union.
1993 US trade embargo tightened; market-oriented reforms introduced in face of deteriorating economy.
1994 Mass refugee exodus; US policy on Cuban asylum seekers revised.
1998 Castro confirmed as president for a further five-year term. UN declined to condemn Cuba's human-rights record.

SEE ALSO Arawak; Bay of Pigs; Castro, Fidel; Spanish-American War

Cultural Revolution A Red Guard spreads the radical words of Chairman Mao to the people 1967 during the Chinese Cultural Revolution. (The mask is for protection against flu germs.) The young Red Guards played a prominent part in the revolution, attacking the power of the bureaucrats and intellectuals and disseminating Mao's political ideology, but their revolutionary zeal often led to violence. *Corbis*

features Lake District National Park, including Scafell Pike 978 m/3,210 ft, the highest mountain in England; Helvellyn 950 m/3,118 ft; Lake Windermere, the largest lake in England, 17 km/10.5 mi long, 1.6 km/1 mi wide; other lakes (Derwentwater, Ullswater); Grizedale Forest sculpture project; Furness peninsula; nuclear stations at Calder Hall (the world's first nuclear power station, 1956) and Sellafield (formerly Windscale); British Nuclear Fuels THORP nuclear reprocessing plant began operating 1994
products the traditional coal, iron, and steel industries of the coast towns have been replaced by newer industries including chemicals, plastics, marine engineering, and electronics; in the N and E there is dairying, and West Cumberland Farmers is the UK's largest agricultural cooperative; shipbuilding at Barrow-in-Furness (nuclear submarines and warships)
population (1991) 483,100
famous people birthplace of William Wordsworth at Cockermouth, and home at Grasmere; homes of Samuel Taylor Coleridge and Robert Southey at Keswick; Thomas de Quincey; John Ruskin's home, Brantwood, on Coniston Water; Beatrix Potter.

cumin seedlike fruit of the herb *Cuminum cyminum* of the carrot family Umbelliferae, with a bitter flavour. It is used as a spice in cooking.

cummings e(dward) e(stlin) 1894–1962. US poet. His work is marked by idiosyncratic punctuation and typography (for example, his own name is always written in lower case), and a subtle, lyric celebration of life. Before his first collection *Tulips and Chimneys* 1923, cummings published an avant-garde novel, *The Enormous Room* 1922, based on his internment in a French concentration camp during World War I. His typographical experiments were antecedents of the concrete and sound poetry of the 1960s.

cuneiform ancient writing system formed of combinations of wedge-shaped strokes, usually impressed on clay. It was probably invented by the Sumerians, and was in use in Mesopotamia as early as the middle of the 4th millennium BC. It was adopted and modified by the Assyrians, Babylonians, Elamites, Hittites, Persians, and many other peoples with different languages. In the 5th century BC it fell into disuse, but sporadically reappeared in later centuries. The decipherment of cuneiform scripts was pioneered by the German George Grotefend 1802 and the British orientalist Henry Rawlinson 1846.

Cunningham Merce 1919– . US choreographer and dancer. He is recognized as the father of post-modernist, or experimental, dance. He liberated dance from its relationship with music, allowing it to obey its own dynamics. Along with composer John ◊Cage, he introduced chance into the creative process, such as tossing coins to determine options. Influenced by Martha ◊Graham, with whose company he was soloist 1939–45, he formed his own avant-garde dance company and school in New York 1953. His works include *The Seasons* 1947, *Antic Meet* 1958, *Squaregame* 1976, and *Arcade* 1985.

Cunningham worked closely with composers, such as Cage, and artists, such as Robert Rauschenberg, when staging his works; among them *Septet* 1953, *Suite for Five* 1956, *Crises* 1960, *Winterbranch* 1964, *Scramble* 1967, *Signals* 1970, and *Sounddance* 1974.

Cupid in Roman mythology, the god of love, identified with the Greek ◊Eros.

cuprite Cu_2O ore (copper(I) oxide), found in crystalline form or in earthy masses. It is red to black in colour, and is often called ruby copper.

cupronickel copper alloy (75% copper and 25% nickel), used in hardware products and for coinage.

Curaçao island in the West Indies, one of the ◊Netherlands Antilles; area 444 sq km/171 sq mi; population (1993 est) 146,800. The principal industry, dating from 1918, is the refining of Venezuelan petroleum. Curaçao was colonized by Spain 1527, annexed by the Dutch West India Company 1634, and gave its name from 1924 to the group of islands renamed the Netherlands Antilles 1948. Its capital is the port of Willemstad.

curare black, resinous poison extracted from the bark and juices of various South American trees and plants. Originally used on arrowheads by Amazonian hunters to paralyse prey, it blocks nerve stimulation of the muscles. Alkaloid derivatives (called curarines) are used in medicine as muscle relaxants during surgery.

curate in the Christian church, literally, a priest who has the cure of souls in a parish, and the term is so used in mainland Europe. In the Church of England, a curate is an unbeneficed cleric who acts as assistant to a parish priest, more exactly an 'assistant curate'.

Curia Romana the judicial and administrative bodies through which the pope carries on the government of the Roman Catholic church. It includes certain tribunals; the chancellery, which issues papal bulls; various offices including that of the cardinal secretary of state; and the Congregations, or councils of cardinals, each with a particular department of work.

Curie Marie (born Manya Sklodowska) 1867–1934. Polish scientist. In 1898 she and her husband Pierre Curie (1859–1906) discovered two new radioactive elements in pitchblende ores: polonium and radium. They isolated the pure elements 1902. Both scientists refused to take out a patent on their discovery and were jointly awarded the Nobel Prize for Physics 1903, with Henri ◊Becquerel. Marie Curie wrote a *Treatise on Radioactivity* 1910, and was awarded the Nobel Prize for Chemistry 1911.

From 1896 the Curies worked together on radioactivity, building on the results of Wilhelm Röntgen (who had discovered X-rays) and Becquerel (who had discovered that similar rays are emitted by uranium salts). They took no precautions against radioactivity and Marie Curie died of radiation poisoning. Her notebooks, even today, are too contaminated to handle.

> *I have no dress except the one I wear every day. If you are going to be kind enough to give me one, please let it be practical and dark so that I can wear it afterwards to go to the laboratory.*
>
> MARIE CURIE
> Letter to a friend
> 1894

curium synthesized, radioactive, metallic element of the *actinide* series, symbol Cm, atomic number 96, relative atomic mass 247. It is produced by bombarding plutonium or americium with neutrons. Its longest-lived isotope has a half-life of 1.7×10^7 years. Curium is used to generate heat and power in satellites or in remote places. It was first synthesized 1944.

curlew wading bird of the genus *Numenius* of the sandpiper family, Scolopacidae, order Charadriiformes. The curlew is between 36 cm/14 in and 55 cm/1.8 ft long, and has pale brown plumage with dark bars and mainly white underparts, long legs, and a long, thin, downcurved bill. Several species live in N Europe, Asia, and North America. *See illustration on following page.*

curling game played on ice with stones; sometimes described as 'bowls on ice'. One of the national games of Scotland, it has spread to many countries. It can also be played on artificial (cement or tarmacadam) ponds. The first world championship for men was held in 1959 and in 1979 for women. *See illustration on following page.*

Curragh, the horse-racing course on the Curragh plain in County Kildare, Republic of Ireland, where all five Irish Classic races are run. At one time used for hurdle races, it is now used for flat racing only. It is also the site of the national stud.

currant berry of a small seedless variety of cultivated grape *Vitis vinifera*. Currants are grown on a large scale in Greece and California and used dried in cooking and baking. Because of the similarity of the fruit, the name currant is also given to several species of shrubs in the genus *Ribes*, family Grossulariaceae, including the redcurrant *Ribes rubrum* and blackcurrant *R. nigrum*.

current flow of a body of water or air, or of heat, moving in a definite direction. Ocean currents are fast-flowing currents of seawater generated by the wind or by variations in water density between two areas. They are partly responsible for transferring heat from the equator to the poles and thereby evening out the global heat imbalance. There are three basic types of ocean current: ***drift currents*** are broad and slow-moving; ***stream currents*** are narrow and swift-moving; and ***upwelling currents***

Curie Marie Curie and her husband Pierre in their Paris laboratory. They received the Nobel Prize for Physics 1903 for the discovery of radioactivity. In 1911 Marie Curie became the first person to be awarded the prize twice, when she was honoured for her discovery of radium. Some of her notebooks are so radioactive that they cannot be handled. *AEA Technology*

curlew The Eskimo curlew is one of eight species of large wading birds, streaked brown, buff, and white, of the genus *Numenius*. The species is extremely rare and may, indeed, be extinct. Curlews breed on moors and tundra. They winter on muddy and sandy shores, estuaries, and marshes.

bring cold, nutrient-rich water from the ocean bottom.

Stream currents include the ◊Gulf Stream and the ◊Japan (or Kuroshio) Current. Upwelling currents, such as the Gulf of Guinea Current and the Peru (Humboldt) current, provide food for plankton, which in turn supports fish and sea birds. At approximate five-to-eight-year intervals, the Peru Current that runs from the Antarctic up the W coast of South America, turns warm, with heavy rain and rough seas, and has disastrous results (as in 1982–83) for Peruvian wildlife and for the anchovy industry. The phenomenon is called *El Niño* (Spanish 'the Child') because it occurs towards Christmas.

current, electric see ◊electric current.

curriculum vitae (Latin 'the course of life') (CV) account of a person's education and previous employment, attached to a job application.

curry (Tamil *kari* 'sauce') traditional Indian mixture of spices used to flavour a dish of rice, meat, and/or vegetables. Spices include turmeric, fenugreek, cloves, chillies, cumin, cinnamon, ginger, black and cayenne pepper, coriander, and caraway. In S India curry dishes are made primarily with vegetables, seasoned with *sambar podi* or other hot spice mixtures; in N India *garam masala* is a milder curry, often used with lamb and poultry.

cursor on a computer screen, the symbol that indicates the current entry position (where the next character will appear). It usually consists of a solid rectangle or underline character, flashing on and off.

curtain wall in a building, an external, lightweight, non-loadbearing wall (either glazing or cladding) that is hung from a metal frame rather than built up from the ground like a brick wall; the framework it shields is usually of concrete or steel. Curtain walls are typically used in high-rise blocks, one of the earliest examples being the Reliance Building in Chicago 1890–94 by Daniel Burnham (1846–1912) and John Wellborn Root (1850–1891). In medieval architecture, the term refers to the outer wall of a castle.

Curtis Tony. Stage name of Bernard Schwartz 1925– . Versatile US film actor. His best work was characterized by a nervous energy, as the press agent in *Sweet Smell of Success* 1957 and the drag-disguised musician on the run from the Mob in *Some Like It Hot* 1959.

Curtiz Michael. Adopted name of Mihaly Kertész 1888–1962. Hungarian-born film director. He worked in Austria, Germany, and France before moving to the USA 1926, where he made several films with Errol Flynn (*Captain Blood* 1935). He directed *Mildred Pierce* 1945, which revitalized Joan Crawford's career, and *Casablanca* 1942 (Academy Award). His wide range of films include *The Private Lives of Elizabeth and Essex* 1939, *The Adventures of Robin Hood* 1938, *Yankee Doodle Dandy* 1942, and *White Christmas* 1954.

curling Curling, a game played on ice in which heavy stones are slid towards a target, has been played since the 16th century. It is especially popular in Scotland. *Image Select (UK) Ltd*

curve in geometry, the ◊locus of a point moving according to specified conditions. The circle is the locus of all points equidistant from a given point (the centre). Other common geometrical curves are the ◊ellipse, ◊parabola, and ◊hyperbola, which are also produced when a cone is cut by a plane at different angles.

Curzon George Nathaniel, 1st Marquess Curzon of Kedleston 1859–1925. British Conservative politician, viceroy of India 1899–1905. During World War I, he was a member of the cabinet 1916–19. As foreign secretary 1919–24, he set up a British protectorate over Persia.

Cusack Cyril James 1910–1993. Irish actor. He joined the Abbey Theatre, Dublin, 1932 and appeared in many of its productions, including Synge's *The Playboy of the Western World*, in which he played the naive and charming Christy Mahon. In Paris he won an award for his solo performance in Beckett's *Krapp's Last Tape*. In the UK he played many roles as a member of the Royal Shakespeare Company and the National Theatre Company. He also played a number of small parts in films.

Cushing Harvey Williams 1869–1939. US neurologist who pioneered neurosurgery. He developed a range of techniques for the surgical treatment of brain tumours, and also studied the link between the ◊pituitary gland and conditions such as dwarfism. He first described the disease now known as Cushing's syndrome.

Cushing's syndrome condition in which the body chemistry is upset by excessive production of ◊steroid hormones from the adrenal cortex. Symptoms include weight gain in the face and trunk, raised blood pressure, excessive growth of facial and body hair (hirsutism), demineralization of bone, and, sometimes, diabeteslike effects. The underlying cause may be an adrenal or pituitary tumour, or prolonged high-dose therapy with ◊corticosteroid drugs.

cusp point where two branches of a curve meet and the tangents to each branch coincide.

custard apple any of several tropical fruits produced by trees and shrubs of the family Annonaceae, often cultivated for their large, edible, heart-shaped fruits.

Custer George Armstrong 1839–1876. US Civil War general, who became the Union's youngest brigadier general 1863 as a result of a brilliant war record. He was made a major general 1865, but following the end of the Civil War, his rank was reduced to captain. He took part in an expedition against the Cheyennes 1867–68, and several times defeated other Native American groups in the West. He campaigned against the Sioux from 1874, and was killed with a detachment of his troops by the forces of Sioux chief Sitting Bull in the Battle of Little Bighorn, Montana, also known as Custer's last stand, 25 June 1876.

custody the state of being held in confinement by the police or prison authorities. Following an arrest, a person may either be kept in custody or released on bail.

custody of children the legal control of a minor by an adult. Parents often have joint custody of their children, but this may be altered by a court order, which may be made in various different circumstances. One parent may have 'care and control' over the day-to-day activities of the child while the other or both together have custody. In all cases, the court's role is to give the welfare of the child paramount consideration.

In matrimonial proceedings (such as divorce), the court decides which spouse shall have custody and provides for access by the other spouse. Custody can be transferred from parents to local authorities in care proceedings. An adoption order transfers custody to the adoptive parents.

Custer US general George A Custer (centre) during a Black Hills expedition 1874. Custer was now engaged on the campaign against the Sioux Indians that would lead to his famous 'last stand' at the Battle of Little Big Horn 1876. *Library of Congress*

Customs and Excise government department responsible for taxes levied on imports (◊customs duty). Excise duties are levied on goods produced domestically or on licences to carry on certain trades (such as sale of wines and spirits) or other activities (theatrical entertainments, betting, and so on) within a country. In the UK, both come under the Board of Customs and Excise, which also administers VAT generally, although there are independent tax tribunals for appeal against the decisions of the commissioners.

customs duty tax imposed on goods coming into the country from abroad. In the UK, it is the responsibility of the Customs and Excise to collect these duties. The taxes collected are paid directly to the European Union (EU) as part of the UK's contribution to the EU budget.

customs union organization of autonomous countries where trade between member states is free of restrictions, but where a ◊tariff or other restriction is placed on products entering the customs union from nonmember states. Examples include the ◊European Union (EU), the Caribbean Community (Caricom), the Central American Common Market, and the Central African Economic Community.

Cuthbert, St died 687. Christian saint. A shepherd in Northumbria, England, he entered the monastery of Melrose, Scotland, after receiving a vision. He travelled widely as a missionary and because of his alleged miracles was known as the 'wonder-worker of Britain'. He became prior of Lindisfarne 664, and retired 676 to Farne Island. In 684 he became bishop of Hexham and later of Lindisfarne. Feast day 20 March.

cuticle the horny noncellular surface layer of many invertebrates such as insects; in botany, the waxy surface layer on those parts of plants that are exposed to the air, continuous except for ◊stomata and ◊lenticels. All types are secreted by the cells of the ◊epidermis. A cuticle reduces water loss and, in arthropods, acts as an ◊exoskeleton.

cuttlefish any of a family, Sepiidae, of squidlike cephalopods with an internal calcareous shell (cuttlebone). The common cuttle *Sepia officinalis* of the Atlantic and Mediterranean is up to 30 cm/1 ft long. It swims actively by means of the fins into which the sides of its oval, flattened body are expanded, and jerks itself backwards by shooting a jet of water from its 'siphon'. Its ten arms are provided with suckers; two arms are longer than the others and are used to seize prey. It has an ink sac from which a dark fluid can be discharged into the water, distracting predators from the cuttle itself.

Cuvier Georges Léopold Chrétien Frédéric Dagobert. Baron Cuvier 1769–1832. French comparative anatomist, the founder of palaeontology. In 1799 he showed that some species have become extinct by reconstructing extinct giant animals that he believed were destroyed in a series of giant deluges. These ideas are expressed in *Recherches sur les ossiments fossiles de quadrupèdes/Researches on the Fossil Bones of Quadrupeds* 1812 and *Discours sur les révolutions de la surface du globe* 1825.

In 1798 Cuvier produced *Tableau élémentaire de l'histoire naturelle des animaux*, in which his scheme of classification is outlined. He was the first to relate the structure of ◊fossil animals to that of their living relatives. His great work *Le Règne animal/The Animal Kingdom* 1817 is a systematic survey.

Cuyp Aelbert 1620–1691. Dutch painter. His serene landscapes are bathed in a golden light; for example *A Herdsman with Cows by a River* about 1650 (National Gallery, London). He also painted seascapes and portraits. Both his father, ***Jacob Gerritsz Cuyp*** (1594–1652), and his uncle ***Benjamin Gerritsz*** (1612–1652) were painters.

Cuyp's works show the influence of the tonal paintings of Jan van Goyen (1596–1656) and, above all, ◊Claude Lorrain's luminous Italian landscapes. His subjects remained thoroughly Dutch, however, and well-observed cows, standing in the foreground of his paintings, are a hallmark of his work. Cuyp was very popular with English collectors from the mid-18th century onwards and most of his works are in England. His influence on English painting was enormous.

Cuzco city in S Peru, capital of Cuzco department, in the Andes Mountains, over 3,350 m/11,000 ft above sea level and 560 km/350 mi SE of Lima; population (1993) 255,600. It was founded c. AD 1200 as the ancient capital of the ◊Inca empire and was captured by the Spanish conqueror Francisco Pizarro 1533. The university was founded 1598. The city has a Renaissance cathedral and other relics of the early Spanish conquerors.

CV abbreviation for ◊***curriculum vitae***.

Cwmbran (Welsh 'Vale of the Crow') town in Wales, NW of Newport, on the Afon Lywel, a tributary of the river Usk; population (1991) 46,000. It was the administrative headquarters of Gwent (1974–96), and, from 1996, of Monmouthshire. It was established 1949 to provide a focus for new industrial growth in a depressed area, producing scientific instruments, car components, nylon, and biscuits. There are also engineering and electrical industries.

cwt symbol for ◊***hundredweight***, a unit of weight equal to 112 pounds (50.802 kg); 100 lb (45.36 kg) in the USA.

cyanide CN^- ion derived from hydrogen cyanide (HCN), and any salt containing this ion (produced when hydrogen cyanide is neutralized by alkalis), such as potassium cyanide (KCN). The principal cyanides are potassium, sodium, calcium, mercury, gold, and copper. Certain cyanides are poisons.

cyanobacteria (singular ***cyanobacterium***) alternative name for ◊blue-green algae.

cyanocobalamin chemical name for vitamin B_{12}, which is normally produced by microorganisms in the gut. The richest sources are liver, fish, and eggs. It is essential to the replacement of cells, the maintenance of the myelin sheath which insulates nerve fibres, and the efficient use of folic acid, another vitamin in the B complex. Deficiency can result in pernicious anaemia (defective production of red blood cells), and possible degeneration of the nervous system.

Cybele in Phrygian mythology, an earth goddess, identified by the Greeks with ◊Rhea and honoured in Rome.

cybernetics (Greek *kubernan* 'to steer') science concerned with how systems organize, regulate, and reproduce themselves, and also how they evolve and learn. In the laboratory, inanimate objects are created that behave like living systems. Applications range from the creation of electronic artificial limbs to the running of the fully automated factory where decisionmaking machines operate up to managerial level.

cyberspace the imaginary, interactive 'worlds' created by networked computers; often used interchangeably with 'virtual world'. The invention of the word 'cyberspace' is generally credited to US science-fiction writer William Gibson (1948–) and his first novel *Neuromancer* 1984.

As well as meaning the interactive environment encountered in a virtual reality system, cyberspace is 'where' the global community of computer-linked individuals and groups lives. From the mid-1980s, the development of computer networks and telecommunications, both international (such as the ◊Internet) and local (such as the services known as 'bulletin board' or conferencing systems), made possible the instant exchange of messages using ◊electronic mail and electronic conferencing systems directly from the individual's own home.

cycad plant of the order Cycadales belonging to the gymnosperms. Some have a superficial resemblance to palms, others to ferns. Their large cones contain fleshy seeds. There are ten genera and about 80–100 species, native to tropical and subtropical countries.

Cyclades (Greek ***Kikládhes***) group of about 200 Greek islands in the Aegean Sea, lying between mainland Greece and Turkey; area 2,579 sq km/996 sq mi; population (1991) 95,100. They include Andros, Melos, Paros, Naxos, and Siros, on which is the capital Hermoupolis.

Cycladic art art of the Bronze Age civilization in the Cyclades Islands, about 2500–1400 BC. It is exemplified by pottery with incised ornament and marble statuettes, usually highly stylized female nudes representing the Mother Goddess in almost abstract simplicity, her face reduced to an elongated oval with a triangular nose. The Cycladic culture preceded ◊Minoan, ran concurrently with it, and eventually shared its fate, becoming assimilated into the ◊Mycenaean culture.

cyclamen any plant of the genus *Cyclamen* of perennial plants of the primrose family Primulaceae, with heart-shaped leaves and petals that are twisted at the base and bent back. The flowers are usually white or pink, and several species are cultivated.

cycle in physics, a sequence of changes that moves a system away from, and then back to, its original state. An example is a vibration that moves a particle first in one direction and then in the opposite direction, with the particle returning to its original position at the end of the vibration.

cyclic compound any of a group of organic chemicals that have rings of atoms in their molecules, giving them a closed-chain structure. They may be alicyclic (cyclopentane), aromatic (benzene), or heterocyclic (pyridine). ***Alicyclic compounds*** (aliphatic cyclic) have localized bonding: all the electrons are confined to their own particular bonds, in contrast to ***aromatic compounds***, where certain electrons have free movement between different bonds in the ring. Alicyclic compounds have chemical properties similar to their straight-chain counterparts; aromatic compounds, because of their special structure, undergo entirely different chemical reactions. ***Heterocyclic compounds*** have a ring of carbon atoms with one or more carbons replaced by another element, usually nitrogen, oxygen, or sulphur. They may be aliphatic or aromatic in nature.

cycling riding a ◊bicycle for sport, pleasure, or transport. Cycle racing can take place on oval artificial tracks, on the road, or across country (cyclocross). Stage races are run over gruelling terrain and can last anything from three days to three and a half weeks, as in the ◊Tour de France, Tour of Italy, and Tour of Spain. Criteriums are fast, actionpacked races around the closed streets of town or city centres. Each race lasts about an hour. Road races are run over a prescribed circuit, which the riders will lap several times. Such a race will normally cover a distance of approximately 160 km/100 mi. Track racing takes place on a concrete or wooden banked circuit, either indoors or outdoors. In time trialling each rider races against the clock, with all the competitors starting at different intervals.

Among the main events are the Tour de France,

Cuyp *A Milkmaid and Cattle near Dordrecht* by Aelbert Cuyp. With the loss of church and court patronage during the Reformation, Dutch artists greatly extended the subject matter of painting, preferring cows to cardinals. Cuyp brought a romantic glow to even the most mundane scenes. *Corbis*

cycad The palmlike gymnosperm plants known as cycads have existed more or less unchanged for at least 200 million years. They are often referred to as living fossils. Each plant consists of an array of fronds growing from a single, stout trunk. There are ten living genera found mainly in tropical and subtropical regions. Cycads bear separate, conelike male and female reproductive structures.

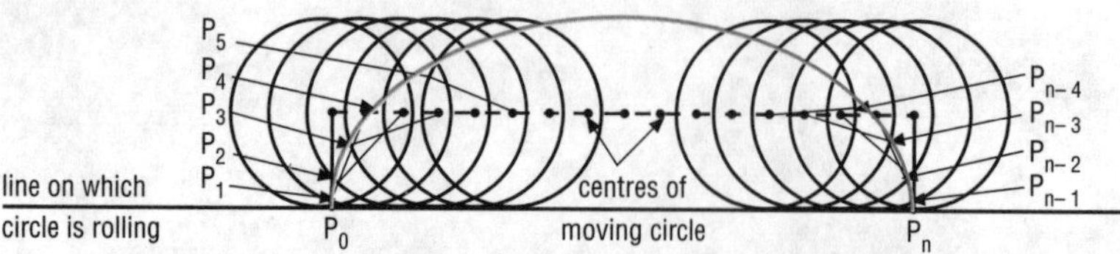

cycloid The cycloid is the curve traced out by a point on a circle as it rolls along a straight line. The teeth of gears are often cut with faces that are arcs of cycloids so that there is rolling contact when the gears are in use.

first held in 1903; the Tour of Britain (formerly called the Milk Race), first held in 1951; and the World Professional Road Race Championship, first held at the Neuburgring, Germany, in 1927. *See list of tables on p. 1177.*

cycloid in geometry, a curve resembling a series of arches traced out by a point on the circumference of a circle that rolls along a straight line. Its applications include the study of the motion of wheeled vehicles along roads and tracks.

cyclone alternative name for a ◊depression, an area of low atmospheric pressure. A severe cyclone that forms in the tropics is called a tropical cyclone or ◊hurricane.

Cyclops in Greek mythology, one of a race of Sicilian giants, who had one eye in the middle of the forehead and lived as shepherds. ◊Odysseus blinded the Cyclops ◊Polyphemus in Homer's *Odyssey*.

cyclosporin ◊immunosuppressive drug derived from a fungus (*Tolypocladium inflatum*). In use by 1978, it revolutionized transplant surgery by reducing the incidence and severity of rejection of donor organs.

cyclotron circular type of particle ◊accelerator.

Cygnus large prominent constellation of the northern hemisphere, represented as a swan. Its brightest star is first-magnitude Alpha Cygni or ◊Deneb. Beta Cygni (Albireo) is a yellow and blue ◊double star, visible through small telescopes. The constellation contains the North America nebula (named after its shape), the Veil nebula (the remains of a ◊supernova that exploded about 50,000 years ago), Cygnus A (apparently a double galaxy, a powerful radio source, and the first radio star to be discovered), and the X-ray source Cygnus X-1, thought to mark the position of a black hole. The area is rich in high luminosity objects, nebulae, and clouds of obscuring matter. Deneb marks the tail of the swan, which is depicted as flying along the Milky Way. Some of the brighter stars form the Northern Cross, the upright being defined by Alpha, Gamma, Eta, and Beta, and the crosspiece by Delta, Gamma, and Epsilon Cygni.

cylinder in geometry, a tubular solid figure with a circular base. In everyday use, the term applies to a right cylinder, the curved surface of which is at right angles to the base.

The volume V of a cylinder is given by the formula $V = \pi r^2 h$, where r is the radius of the base and h is the height of the cylinder. Its total surface area A has the formula $A = 2\pi r(h + r)$, where $2\pi rh$ is the curved surface area, and $2\pi r^2$ is the area of both circular ends.

cyclone A satellite picture of a cyclonic storm, or hurricane, off Hawaii. Tropical cyclones begin in the hot, moist air over tropical oceans. As an area of very low pressure develops, air is sucked in, creating a violent storm of spiralling winds. *National Aeronautical Space Agency*

cymbal ancient percussion instrument of indefinite pitch, consisting of a shallow circular brass dish suspended at the centre; either used in pairs clashed together or singly, struck with a beater. Smaller finger cymbals or crotala, used by Debussy and Stockhausen, are precise in pitch. Turkish or 'buzz' cymbals incorporate loose rivets to extend the sound.

Cymbeline or ***Cunobelin*** lived 1st century AD. King of the Catuvellauni AD 5–40, who fought unsuccessfully against the Roman invasion of Britain. His capital was at Colchester.

Cymru Welsh name for ◊Wales.

Cynewulf lived early 8th century. Anglo-Saxon poet. He is thought to have been a Northumbrian monk and is the undoubted author of 'Juliana' and part of the 'Christ' in the Exeter Book (a collection of poems now in Exeter Cathedral, England), and of the 'Fates of the Apostles' and 'Elene' in the Vercelli Book (a collection of Old English manuscripts housed in Vercelli, Italy), in all of which he inserted his name by using runic acrostics.

Cynic member of a school of Greek philosophy (Cynicism), founded in Athens about 400 BC by Antisthenes, a disciple of Socrates, who advocated a stern and simple morality and a complete disregard of pleasure and comfort. His followers, led by ◊Diogenes, not only showed a contemptuous disregard for pleasure, but despised all human affection as a source of weakness.

cypress any coniferous tree or shrub of the genera *Cupressus* and *Chamaecyparis*, family Cupressaceae. There are about 20 species, originating from temperate regions of the northern hemisphere. They have minute, scalelike leaves and cones made up of woody, wedge-shaped scales containing an aromatic resin.

Cyprian, St c. 210–258. Christian martyr, one of the earliest Christian writers, and bishop of Carthage about 249. He wrote a treatise on the unity of the church. Feast day 16 Sept.

Cyprus island in the Mediterranean Sea, off the S coast of Turkey and W coast of Syria. *See country box opposite.*

Cyrano de Bergerac Savinien 1619–1655. French writer. Joining a corps of guards at the age of 19, he performed heroic feats. He is the hero of a classic play by Edmond ◊Rostand, in which his excessively long nose is used as a counterpoint to his chivalrous character.

Cyrenaic member of a school of Greek ◊hedonistic philosophy founded about 400 BC by Aristippus of Cyrene. He regarded pleasure as the only absolutely worthwhile thing in life but taught that self-control and intelligence were necessary to choose the best pleasures.

Cyrenaica area of E Libya, colonized by the Greeks in the 7th century BC; later held by the Egyptians, Romans, Arabs, Turks, and Italians. Present cities in the region are Benghazi, Derna, and Tobruk. There are archaeological ruins at Cyrene and Apollonia.

Cyril and Methodius, Sts two brothers, both Christian saints: Cyril 826–869 and Methodius 815–885. Born in Thessalonica, they were sent as missionaries to what is today Moravia. They invented a Slavonic alphabet, and translated the Bible and the liturgy from Greek to Slavonic. The language (known as Old Church Slavonic) remained in use in churches and for literature among Bulgars, Serbs, and Russians up to the 17th century. The cyrillic alphabet is named after Cyril and may also have been invented by him. Feast day 14 Feb.

Cyrus the Great died 529 BC. Founder of the Persian Empire. As king of Persia, he was originally subject to the Medes, whose empire he overthrew 550 BC. He captured ◊Croesus 546 BC, and conquered ◊Lydia, adding Babylonia (including Syria and Palestine) to his empire 539 BC, allowing exiled Jews to return to Jersualem. He died fighting in Afghanistan.

cystic fibrosis hereditary disease involving defects of various tissues, including the sweat glands, the mucous glands of the bronchi (air passages), and the pancreas. The sufferer experiences repeated chest infections and digestive disorders and generally fails to thrive. In 1989 a gene for cystic fibrosis was identified by teams of researchers in Michigan, USA, and Toronto, Canada. This discovery enabled the development of a screening test for carriers; the disease can also be detected in the unborn child.

inheriting the disease One person in 22 is a carrier of the disease. If two carriers have children, each child has a one-in-four chance of having the disease, so that it occurs in about one in 2,000 pregnancies. Around 10% of newborns with cystic fibrosis develop an intestinal blockage (meconium ileus) which requires surgery.

treatment Cystic fibrosis was once universally fatal at an early age; now, although there is no definitive cure, treatments have raised both the quality and expectancy of life. Results in 1995 from a four-year US study showed that the painkiller ibuprofen, available over the counter, slowed lung deterioration in children by almost 90% when taken in large doses.

Management of cystic fibrosis is by diets and drugs, physiotherapy to keep the chest clear, and use of antibiotics to combat infection and minimize damage to the lungs. Some sufferers have benefited from heart-lung transplants.

cystitis inflammation of the bladder, usually caused by bacterial infection, and resulting in frequent and painful urination. It is more common in women, after sexual intercourse, and it is thought that intercourse encourages bacteria which are normally present on the skin around the anus and vagina, to enter the urethra and ascend to the bladder.Treatment is by antibiotics and copious fluids with vitamin C.

cytochrome protein responsible for part of the process of ◊respiration by which food molecules are broken down in ◊aerobic organisms. Cytochromes are part of the electron transport chain, which uses energized electrons to reduce molecular oxygen (O_2) to oxygen ions (O^{2-}). These combine with hydrogen ions (H^+) to form water (H_2O), the end product of aerobic respiration. As electrons are passed from one cytochrome to another, energy is released and used to make ◊ATP.

cytokine in biology, chemical messenger that carries information from one cell to another, for example the lymphokines, which carry messages between the cells of the immune system.

cytokinin ◊plant hormone that stimulates cell division. Cytokinins affect several different aspects of plant growth and development, but only if ◊auxin is also present. They may delay the process of senescence, or ageing, break the dormancy of certain seeds and buds, and induce flowering.

cytology the study of ◊cells and their functions. Major advances have been made possible in this field by the development of ◊electron microscopes.

cylinder The volume and area of a cylinder are given by simple formulae relating the dimensions of the cylinder.

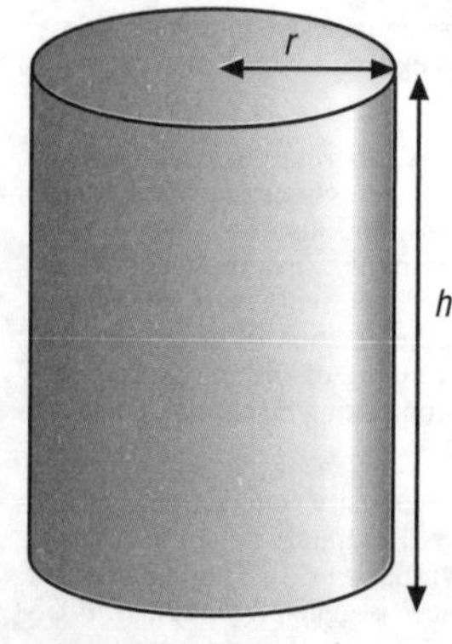

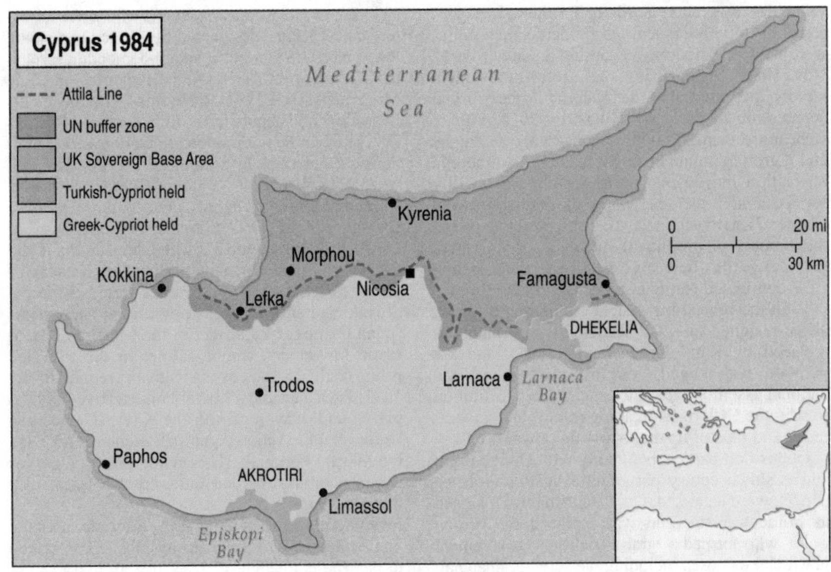

cytoplasm the part of the cell outside the ◊nucleus. Strictly speaking, this includes all the ◊organelles (mitochondria, chloroplasts, and so on), but often cytoplasm refers to the jellylike matter in which the organelles are embedded (correctly termed the cytosol). The cytoplasm is the site of protein synthesis.

cytoskeleton in a living cell, a matrix of protein filaments and tubules that occurs within the cytosol (the liquid part of the cytoplasm). It gives the cell a definite shape, transports vital substances around the cell, and may also be involved in cell movement.

cytotoxic drug any drug used to kill the cells of a malignant tumour; it may also damage healthy cells. Side effects include nausea, vomiting, hair loss, and bone-marrow damage. Some cytotoxic drugs are also used to treat other diseases and to suppress rejection in transplant patients.

czar alternative spelling of ◊*tsar*, an emperor of Russia.

Czech literature the literature of the Czechoslovakia and the Czech republic. Czech writing first flourished in the 14th century but was effectively suppressed by the Habsburg dynasty. The tradition revived in the 19th century and grew steadily until World War I. After the establishment of the independent state of Czechoslovakia 1918, literature flourished until the communist takeover 1948. In the 1960s, writers such as Milan ◊Kundera and Miroslav Holub (1923–) again gained attention both in Czechoslovakia and abroad. Kundera's *The Unbearable Lightness of Being* 1984 was made into an internationally successful film 1988.

In its early years, Czech literature was heavily associated with Hussite Protestantism and the early Renaissance. Hence, the emergence of the Catholic Habsburgs effectively drove the indigenous literary tradition into exile, where the polymath Ámos Komenský (Comenius) (1592–1670) wrote his prose masterpiece *Labyrint světa a ráj srdce/Labyrinth of the World and Paradise of the Heart* 1631. The romantic poetry of Karel Hynek Mácha (1810–1836) and the *Máj* group he inspired, which included the poet Vitězslaw Hálek (1835–1874), had a great impact in the 19th century. Czech literature flourished between the world wars with the plays of Karel Čapek (1890–1938) and František

CYPRUS

***Greek Republic of Cyprus* (S) and *Turkish Republic of Northern Cyprus* (N)**

national name *Kypriakí Dimokratía* (S), and *Kibris Cumhuriyeti* (N)
area 9,251 sq km/3,571 sq mi (3,335 sq km/1,287 sq mi is Turkish-occupied)
capital Nicosia (divided between Greek and Turkish Cypriots)
major towns/cities Morphou
major ports Limassol, Larnaca, and Paphos (Greek); Kyrenia and Famagusta (Turkish)
physical features central plain between two E–W mountain ranges
head of state and government Glafkos Clerides (Greek) from 1993, Rauf Denktaş (Turkish) from 1976
political system democratic divided republic
administrative divisions six districts
political parties *Greek zone*: Democratic Party (DEKO), federalist, centre-left; Progressive Party of the Working People (AKEL), socialist; Democratic Rally (DISY), centrist; Socialist Party–National Democratic Union of Cyprus (SK–EDEK), socialist; *Turkish zone*: National Unity Party (NUP), Communal Liberation Party (CLP), Republican Turkish Party (RTP), New British Party (NBP)
population 756,800 (1996 est)
population growth rate 1.1% (1990–95)
ethnic distribution about 80% of the population is of Greek origin, while about 18% are of Turkish descent, and live in the northern part of the island within the self-styled Turkish Republic of Northern Cyprus.
life expectancy 74 (males), 79 (females)
literacy rate 94%
languages Greek and Turkish (official), English
religions Greek Orthodox, Sunni Muslim
currency Cyprus pound and Turkish lira
GDP (US $) 7.19 billion (1994)
growth rate 5.1% (1994)
exports citrus, grapes, raisins, Cyprus sherry, potatoes, clothing, footwear

HISTORY

14th–11th Cs BC Colonized by Myceneans and Achaeans from Greece.
9th C BC Phoenicans settled in Cyprus.
7th C BC Several Cypriot kingdoms flourished under Assyrian influence.
414–374 BC Under Evagoras of Salamis (in eastern Cyprus) the island's ten city kingdoms were united into one state and Greek culture, including the Greek alphabet, was promoted.
333–58 BC Became part of the Greek Hellenistic and then, from 294 BC, the Egypt-based Ptolemaic empires.
58 BC Cyprus was annexed by the Roman Empire.
AD 45 Christianity introduced.
AD 395 When the Roman Empire divided, Cyprus was allotted to the Byzantine Empire.
7th–10th Cs Byzantines and Muslim Arabs fought for control of Cyprus.
1191 Richard I of England, 'the Lionheart', conquered Cyprus as a base for Crusades; he later sold it to a French noble, Guy de Lusignan, who established a feudal monarchy which ruled for three centuries.
1498 Venetian Republic took control of Cyprus.
1571 Conquered by Ottoman Turks, who introduced Turkish Muslim settlers, but permitted Christianity to continue in rural areas.
1821–33 Period of unrest, following execution of popular Greek Orthodox Archbishop Kyprianos.
1878 Anglo-Turkish Convention: Turkey ceded Cyprus to British administration in return for defensive alliance.
1914 Formally annexed by Britain after Turkey entered World War I as a Central Power.
1915 Greece rejected an offer of Cyprus in return for entry into World War I on Allied side.
1925 Cyprus became a Crown colony.
1931 Greek Cypriots rioted in support of demand for union with Greece (*enosis*); legislative council suspended.
1948 Greek Cypriots rejected new constitution because it did not offer links with Greece.
1951 Britain rejected Greek proposals for *enosis*.
1955 National Organization of Cypriot Fighters (EOKA), led by George Grivas, began terrorist campaign for *enosis*.
1956 British authorities deported Archbishop Makarios, head of the Cypriot Orthodox Church, for encouraging EOKA.
1958 Britain proposed autonomy for Greek and Turkish Cypriot communities under British sovereignty; plan accepted by Turks, rejected by Greeks; violence increased.
1959 Britain, Greece, and Turkey agreed to Cypriot independence; partition and *enosis* both ruled out.
1960 Cyprus became an independent republic with Archbishop Makarios as president; Britain retained two military bases.
1963 Makarios proposed major constitutional reforms; Turkish Cypriots withdrew from government and formed separate enclaves; communal fighting broke out.
1964 United Nations (UN) peacekeeping force installed.
1968 Intercommunal talks made no progress; Turkish Cypriots demanded federalism; Greek Cypriots insisted on unitary state.
1974 Coup by Greek officers in Cypriot National Guard installed Nikos Sampson as president; Turkey, fearing *enosis*, invaded northern Cyprus; military regime collapsed; President Makarios restored.
1975 Northern Cyprus declared itself the Turkish Federated State of Cyprus, with Rauf Denktaş as president.
1977 Makarios died; succeeded by Spyros Kyprianou.
1983 Denktaş proclaimed independent Turkish Republic of Cyprus; recognized only by Turkey.
1985 Summit meeting between Kyprianou and Denktaş failed to reach agreement; further peace talks failed 1989 and 1992.
1988 Kryprianou succeeded as Greek Cypriot president by Georgios Vassiliou.
1993 Glafkos Clerides (DISY) replaced Vassiliou.
1994 European Court of Justice declared trade with northern Cyprus illegal.
1996 Further peace talks jeopardized by boundary killing of Turkish Cypriot soldier; mounting tension between N and S.
1997 Decision to purchase Russian anti-aircraft missiles created tension. UN-mediated peace talks between Clerides and Denktaş collapsed.
1998 President Clerides re-elected. Denktaş refused to meet British envoy. US mediation failed.

SEE ALSO Assyria; EOKA; enosis; Turkey

Langer (1888–1965), the poetry of Jaroslav ◊Seifert, and the later fiction of Jaroslav ◊Hašek. After a brief stagnation in the early communist period, literature began to re-emerge in Czechoslovakia from the 1960s onward. From the 1970s until the fall of communism, writers played a prominent part in the democratic dissident movement, and the playwright Václav Havel (1936–) became the country's first post-communist president 1989.

Czechoslovakia former country in E central Europe, which came into existence as an independent republic 1918 after the break-up of the ◊Austro-Hungarian empire at the end of World War I. It consisted originally of the Bohemian crownlands (◊Bohemia, ◊Moravia, and part of ◊Silesia) and ◊Slovakia, the area of Hungary inhabited by Slavonic peoples; to this was added as a trust, part of Ruthenia when the Allies and associated powers recognized the new republic under the treaty of St Germain-en-Laye. Besides the Czech and Slovak peoples, the country included substantial minorities of German origin, long settled in the north, and of Hungarian (or Magyar) origin in the south. Despite the problems of welding into a nation such a mixed group of people, Czechoslovakia made considerable political and economic progress until the troubled 1930s. It was the only East European state to retain a parliamentary democracy throughout the interwar period, with five coalition governments (dominated by the Agrarian and National Socialist parties), with Thomas ◊Masaryk serving as president.

Munich Agreement The rise to power of the Nazi leader Hitler in Germany brought a revival of opposition among the German-speaking population, and nationalism among the Magyar speakers. In addition, the Slovak clerical party demanded autonomy for Slovakia. In 1938 the ◊Munich Agreement was made between Britain, France, Germany, and Italy, without consulting Czechoslovakia, resulting in the Sudetenland being taken from Czechoslovakia and given to Germany. Six months later Hitler occupied all Czechoslovakia. A government in exile was established in London under Eduard ◊Beneš until the liberation 1945 by Soviet and US troops.

Elections 1946 gave the left a slight majority, and in Feb 1948 the communists seized power, winning an electoral victory in May. The country was divided into 19 and, in 1960, into 10 regions plus Prague and Bratislava. There was a Stalinist regime during the 1950s, under presidents Klement Gottwald (1948–53), Antonin Zapotocky (1953–57), and Antonin Novotný (1957–68).

Prague Spring Pressure from students and intellectuals brought about policy changes from 1965. Following Novotný's replacement as the Communist Party (CCP) leader by Alexander ◊Dubček and as president by war hero General Ludvík Svoboda (1895–1979), and the appointment of Oldřich Černik as prime minister, a liberalization programme began 1968. This 'Socialist Democratic Revolution', as it was known, promised the return of freedom of assembly, speech, and movement, and the imposition of restrictions on the secret police, all with the goal of creating 'socialism with a human face'.

The USSR viewed these events with suspicion, and in Aug 1968 sent 600,000 troops from Warsaw Pact countries to restore the orthodox line. Over 70 deaths and some 266 injuries were inflicted by this invasion. After the invasion a purge of liberals began in the CCP, with Dr Gustáv ◊Husák replacing Dubček as CCP leader 1969 and Lubomír Štrougal becoming prime minister 1970. Svoboda remained as president until 1975 and negotiated the Soviet withdrawal. In 1973 an amnesty was extended to some of the 40,000 who had fled after the 1968 invasion, signalling a slackening of repression. But a new crackdown commenced 1977, triggered by a human-rights manifesto ('Charter 77') signed by over 700 intellectuals and former party officials.

> *The belief that security can be obtained by throwing a small state to the wolves is a fatal delusion.*
>
> On CZECHOSLOVAKIA Winston Churchill 21 Sept 1938

protest movement Czechoslovakia under Husák emerged as a loyal ally of the USSR during the 1970s and early 1980s. However, after Mikhail Gorbachev's accession to the Soviet leadership 1985, pressure for economic and administrative reform mounted. In 1987 Husák, while remaining president, was replaced as CCP leader by Miloš Jakeš (1923–). Working with prime minister Ladislav Adamec, he began to introduce a reform programme (*prestavba* 'restructuring') on the USSR's perestroika model. Influenced by events elsewhere in Eastern Europe, a series of initially student-led prodemocracy rallies were held in Prague's Wenceslas Square from 17 Nov 1989. Support for the protest movement rapidly increased after the security forces' brutal suppression of the early rallies; by 20 Nov there were more than 200,000 demonstrators in Prague and a growing number in Bratislava. An umbrella opposition movement, Civic Forum, was swiftly formed under the leadership of playwright and Charter 77 activist Václav ◊Havel, which attracted the support of prominent members of the small political parties that were members of the ruling CCP-dominated National Front coalition.

With the protest movement continuing to grow, Jakeš resigned as CCP leader 24 Nov and was replaced by Karel Urbanek (1941–), and the politburo was purged. Less than a week later, the national assembly voted to amend the constitution to strip the CCP of its 'leading role' in the government, and thus of its monopoly on power.

Opposition parties, beginning with Civic Forum and its Slovak counterpart, Public Against Violence (PAV), were legalized. On 7 Dec Adamec resigned as prime minister and was replaced by Marián Čalfa, who formed a 'grand coalition' government in which key posts, including the foreign, financial, and labour ministries, were given to former dissidents. Čalfa resigned from the CCP Jan 1990, but remained premier.

reform government On 27 Dec 1989 the rehabilitated Dubček was sworn in as chair of the federal assembly, and on 29 Dec Havel became president of Czechoslovakia. The new reform government immediately extended an amnesty to 22,000 prisoners, secured agreements from the CCP that it would voluntarily give up its existing majorities in the federal and regional assemblies and state agencies, and promised multiparty elections for June 1990. It also announced plans for reducing the size of the armed forces, called on the USSR to pull out its 75,000 troops stationed in the country, and applied for membership of the International Monetary Fund and World Bank. Václav Havel was re-elected president, unopposed, for a further two years by the assembly on 5 July 1990.

moves toward privatization Some devolution of power was introduced 1990 to ameliorate friction between the Czech and Slovak republics. A bill of rights was passed Jan 1991, and moves were made towards price liberalization and privatization of small businesses. In Feb 1991 a bill was passed to return property nationalized after 25 Feb 1948 to its original owners, the first such restitution measure in Eastern Europe, and legislation was approved May 1991. The name 'Czech and Slovak Federative Republic' was adopted April 1990. In Nov 1990 the Slovak Republic declared Slovak the official language of the republic.

new parties emerge During the opening months of 1991, Civic Forum began to split in two: a centre-right faction under the leadership of finance minister Václav Klaus, designated the Civic Democratic Party April 1991; and a social-democratic group, the Civic Forum Liberal Club, renamed the Civic Movement April 1991, led by foreign minister Jiri Dienstbier and deputy prime minister Pavel Rychetsky. The two factions agreed to work together until the next election. In March 1991 PAV also split when Slovak premier Vladimir Meciar formed a splinter grouping pledged to greater autonomy from Prague. In April 1991 he was dismissed as head of the Slovak government by the presidium of the Slovak National Council (parliament) because of policy differences. Protest rallies were held in the Slovak capital of Bratislava by Meciar supporters.

Jan Carnogursky, leader of the Christian Democratic Movement, junior partner in the PAV-led ruling coalition, took over as Slovak premier. In Oct 1991, PAV became a liberal-conservative political party, and was renamed the Civic Democratic Union–Public Action Against Violence (PAV), led by Martin Porubjak. The major political parties were becoming divided into separate Czech and Slovak groups.

foreign relations In July 1991, a month after the final withdrawal of Soviet troops, the USSR agreed to pay the equivalent of US$ 160 million to Czechoslovakia in compensation for damage done to the country since the 1968 Soviet invasion. In Aug, the phased privatization of Czech industry commenced, with 50 of its largest businesses put up for sale on international markets. Friendship treaties were signed with France, Germany, and the USSR in Oct 1991.

Czech and Slovak split A general election was held June 1992. Václav Klaus, leader of the CDP, became prime minister, and President Havel resigned. It was agreed that two separate Czech and Slovak states would be created from Jan 1993. In Oct 1992 the Slovakia-based political party, the new PAV, became the Civic Democratic Union (CDU). The Czech Republic and the ◊Slovak Republic became sovereign states 1 Jan 1993.

Czech Republic landlocked country in E central Europe, bounded N by Poland, NW and W by Germany, S by Austria, and E by the Slovak Republic. *See country box opposite.*

Czerny Carl 1791–1857. Austrian composer and pianist. He wrote an enormous quantity of religious and concert music, but is chiefly remembered for his books of graded studies and technical exercises used in piano teaching, including the *Complete Theoretical and Practical Pianoforte School* 1839 which is still in widespread use.

Częstochowa city in Poland, on the river Vistula, 193 km/120 mi SW of Warsaw; population (1993) 258,700. It produces iron goods, chemicals, paper, and cement. The basilica of Jasna Góra is a centre for Catholic pilgrims (it contains the painting known as the Black Madonna).

Czech Republic The old town square in Prague, Czech Republic, with the Baroque church of St Nicholas and the memorial to the religious reformer John Huss clearly visible. *Private collection*

CZECH REPUBLIC

national name *Česká Republika*
area 78,864 sq km/30,461 sq mi
capital Prague
major towns/cities Brno, Ostrava, Olomouc, Liberec, Plzeň, Ustí nad Labem, Hradec Králové
physical features mountainous; rivers: Morava, Labe (Elbe), Vltava (Moldau)
head of state Václav Havel from 1993
head of government (interim) Josef Tosovsky from 1997
political system emergent democracy
administrative divisions eight regions
political parties Civic Democratic Party (CDP), right of centre, free-market; Civic Democratic Alliance (CDA), right of centre, free-market; Civic Movement (CM), liberal, left of centre; Communist Party of Bohemia and Moravia (KSCM), reform socialist; Agrarian Party, centrist, rural-based; Liberal National Social Party (LNSP; formerly the Czech Socialist Party ÆCSPÅ), reform socialist; Czech Social Democratic Party (CSDP), moderate left of centre; Christian Democratic Union–Czech People's Party (CDU–CPP), centre-right; Movement for Autonomous Democracy of Moravia and Silesia (MADMS), Moravian and Silesian-based, separatist; Czech Republican Party, far-right
population 10,251,000 (1996 est)
population growth rate 0.0% (1990–95); −0.1% (2000–05)
ethnic distribution predominantly Western Slav Czechs; there is also a sizeable Slovak minority and small Polish, German, and Hungarian minorities
life expectancy 69 (men), 79 (women)
literacy 99%
language Czech (official)
religions Roman Catholic, Hussite, Presbyterian Evangelical Church of Czech Brethren, Orthodox
currency koruna (based on Czechoslovak koruna)
GDP (US $) 36.1 billion (1994)
growth rate 2.6% (1994)
exports machinery, vehicles, coal, iron and steel, chemicals, glass, ceramics, clothing

HISTORY

5th C Settled by West Slavs.
8th C Part of Charlemagne's Holy Roman Empire.
9th C Kingdom of Greater Moravia, in the eastern part of what is now the Czech Republic, founded by the Slavic prince Sviatopluk; Christianity adopted.
906 Moravia conquered by the Magyars (Hungarians).
995 Independent state of Bohemia in the NW, centred around Prague, formed under the Premysl rulers, who had broken away from Moravia; became kingdom in 12th century.
1029 Moravia became a fief of Bohemia.
1355 King Charles IV of Bohemia became Holy Roman Emperor.
early 15th C Nationalistic Hussite religion, opposed to German and papal influence, founded in Bohemia by John Huss.
1526 Bohemia came under the control of the Austrian Catholic Habsburgs.
1618 Hussite revolt precipitated the Thirty Years' War, which resulted in the Bohemians' defeat, more direct rule by the Habsburgs, and re-Catholicization.
1867 Austro-Hungarian monarchy created. Bohemia reduced to a province of Austria, leading to a growth in national consciousness.
1918 Austro-Hungarian Empire dismembered; Czechs joined Slovaks in forming Czechoslovakia as independent democratic nation, with Tomas Masaryk president.
1938 Under the Munich Agreement, Czechoslovakia was forced to surrender the Sudetenland German districts in the N to Germany.
1939 The remainder of Czechoslavakia annexed by Germany, Bohemia-Moravia being administered as a 'protectorate'; President Eduard Beneš set up a government-in-exile in London; liquidation campaigns against intelligentsia.
1945 Liberated by Soviet and American troops; communist-dominated government of national unity formed under Beneš; 2 million Sudeten Germans expelled.
1948 Beneš ousted; communists assumed full control under a Soviet-style single-party constitution.
1950s Political opponents purged; nationalization of industries.
1968 'Prague Spring' political liberalization programme, instituted by Communist Party leader Alexander Dubček, crushed by invasion of Warsaw Pact forces to restore the 'orthodox line'.
1969 New federal constitution, creating a separate Czech Socialist Republic; Gustáv Husák became Communist Party leader.
1977 Formation of the 'Charter '77' human-rights group by intellectuals, including the playwright Václav Havel, encouraged a crackdown against dissidents.
1987 Reformist Miloš Jakeš replaced Husák as communist leader, and introduced a *prestvaba* ('restructuring') reform programme on the Soviet leader Mikhail Gorbachev's *perestroika* model.
1989 Major prodemocracy demonstrations in Prague; new political parties formed and legalized, including Czech-based Civic Forum under Havel; Communist Party stripped of powers. New 'grand coalition' government formed; Havel appointed state president. Amnesty granted to 22,000 prisoners.
1990 Multiparty elections won by Civic Forum.
1991 Civic Forum split into centre-right Civic Democratic Party (CDP) and centre-left Civic Movement (CM); evidence of increasing Czech and Slovak separatism.
1992 Václav Klaus, leader of the Czech-based CDP, became prime minister; Havel resigned following nationalist Slovak gains in assembly elections. Creation of separate Czech and Slovak states and a customs union agreed. Market-centred economic-reform programme launched, including mass privatizations.
1993 Czech Republic became sovereign state within the United Nations, with Klaus as prime minister. Havel elected president.
1994 Joined NATO's 'partnership for peace' programme. Strong economic growth registered.
1996 Applied for EU membership. Klaus-led coalition lost its parliamentary majority after elections but remained in power. Ruling coalition successful in upper house elections.
1997 Former communist leader Miloš Jakeš charged with treason. Prime Minister Vaclav Klaus resigned after allegations of misconduct. Josef Tosovsky, governor of central bank, appointed as interim, non-party successor. Czech Republic invited to join NATO and to begin EU membership negotiations.
1998 Havel re-elected president. Split in former ruling Civic Democratic Party.

SEE ALSO Austro-Hungarian Empire; Bohemia; Czechoslovakia; Prague Spring; Slovak Republic; Thirty Years' War

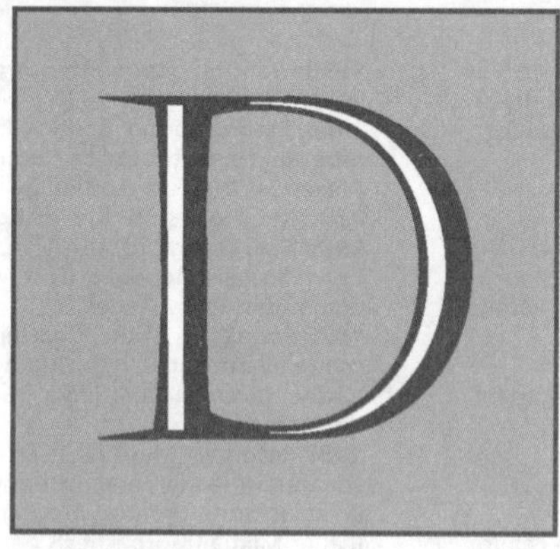

dab small marine flatfish of the flounder family, especially the genus *Limanda*. Dabs live in the N Atlantic and around the coasts of Britain and Scandinavia.

Dacca alternative name for ◊Dhaka, the capital of Bangladesh.

dace freshwater fish *Leuciscus leuciscus* of the carp family. Common in England and mainland Europe, it is silvery and grows up to 30 cm/1 ft.

Dachau site of a Nazi ◊concentration camp during World War II, in Bavaria, Germany. The first such camp to be set up, it opened early 1933 and functioned as a detention and forced labour camp until liberated 1945.

dachshund (German 'badger-dog') small dog of German origin, bred originally for digging out badgers. It has a long body and short legs. Several varieties are bred: standard size (up to 10 kg/22 lb), miniature (5 kg/11 lb or less), long-haired, smooth-haired, and wire-haired.

Dacia ancient region forming much of modern Romania. The various Dacian tribes were united around 60 BC, and for many years posed a threat to the Roman Empire; they were finally conquered by the Roman emperor Trajan AD 101–06, and the region became a province of the same name. It was abandoned to the invading Goths about 270.

Dada or ***Dadaism*** artistic and literary movement founded 1915 in Zürich, Switzerland, by the Romanian poet Tristan Tzara (1896–1963) and others in a spirit of rebellion and disillusionment during World War I. Other Dadaist groups were soon formed by the artists Marcel ◊Duchamp and Man ◊Ray in New York, Francis Picabia (1879–1953) in Barcelona, and Kurt ◊Schwitters in Germany. The Dadaists produced deliberately anti-aesthetic images, often using photomontages with worded messages to express their political views, and they directly scorned established art, as in Duchamp's *Mona Lisa* 1919, where a moustache and beard were added to Leonardo da Vinci's classic portrait.

With the German writers Hugo Ball and Richard Huelsenbeck, Tzara founded the Cabaret Voltaire in Zürich 1916, where works by Hans Arp, the pioneer Surrealist Max Ernst, and others were exhibited. In New York in the same period the artist Man Ray met Duchamp and Picabia and began to apply Dadaist ideas to photography. The first international Dada exhibition was in Paris 1922. Dada had a considerable impact on early 20th-century art, questioning established artistic conventions and values. In the 1920s it evolved into ◊Surrealism.

daddy-longlegs popular name for a ◊crane fly.

Dadra and Nagar Haveli since 1961, a union territory of W India; capital Silvassa; area 490 sq km/189 sq mi; population (1991) 138,500. It was formerly part of Portuguese Daman. It produces rice, wheat, and millet. 40% of the total area is forest.

Daedalus in Greek mythology, an Athenian artisan supposed to have constructed for King Minos of Crete the labyrinth in which the ◊Minotaur was imprisoned. When Minos became displeased with him, Daedalus fled from Crete with his son ◊Icarus using wings made by them from feathers fastened with wax.

daffodil any of several Old World species of the genus *Narcissus*, family Amaryllidaceae, distinguished by their trumpet-shaped flowers. The common daffodil of N Europe *N. pseudonarcissus* has large yellow flowers and grows from a large bulb. There are numerous cultivated forms.

Dafydd ap Gwilym c. 1340–c. 1400. Welsh poet. His work exhibits a complex but graceful style, concern with nature and love rather than with heroic martial deeds, and has references to Classical and Italian poetry.

Dagestan autonomous republic of S Russian Federation
area 50,300 sq km/19,421 sq mi
capital Makhachkala
physical E of the Caucasus, bordering the Caspian Sea; mountainous, with deep valleys
industries engineering, oil, chemicals, woodworking, textiles, and agriculture (wheat and grapes), sheep farming, and cattle breeding
population (1992) 1,890,000. Over 30 ethnic groups, including Avar, Dargin, and Kumyk
history annexed 1723 from Persia, which strongly resisted Russian conquest; an autonomous republic from 1921.

dahlia *Dahlia coccinea*, growing wild in a forest in Mexico. This species displays the simple flower from which all the complex and beautiful garden varieties have been derived. *Premaphotos Wildlife*

Daguerre Louis Jacques Mandé 1787–1851. French pioneer of photography. Together with Joseph Niépce, he is credited with the invention of photography (though others were reaching the same point simultaneously). In 1838 he invented the daguerreotype, a single image process using mercury vapour and an iodine-sensitized silvered plate. It was superseded ten years later by ◊Fox Talbot's negative/positive process.

Dahl Roald 1916–1990. British writer. His fiction includes short stories with a twist, for example, *Tales of the Unexpected* 1979, and children's books, including *Charlie and the Chocolate Factory* 1964. He also wrote the screenplay for the James Bond film *You Only Live Twice* 1967. His autobiography *Going Solo* 1986 recounted his experiences as a fighter pilot in the RAF.

dahlia any perennial plant of the genus *Dahlia*, family Compositae, comprising 20 species and many cultivated forms. Dahlias are stocky plants with showy flowers that come in a wide range of colours. They are native to Mexico and Central America.

Dahomey former name (until 1975) of the People's Republic of ◊Benin.

Dáil Éireann lower house of the legislature of the Republic of Ireland. It consists of 166 members elected by adult suffrage on a basis of proportional representation, for a five-year term.

Daimler Gottlieb Wilhelm 1834–1900. German engineer who pioneered the car and the internal-combustion engine together with Wilhelm Maybach (1846–1929). In 1885 he produced a motor bicycle and in 1889 his first four-wheeled motor vehicle. He combined the vaporization of fuel with the high-speed four-stroke petrol engine.

Daimler built his first petrol engines 1883. The Daimler Motoren Gesellschaft was founded 1890, and Daimler engines were also manufactured under licence; a Daimler-powered car won the first international car race: Paris to Rouen 1894.

dairying the business of producing ◊milk and milk products. In the UK and the USA, over 70% of the milk produced is consumed in its liquid form, whereas areas such as the French Alps and New Zealand rely on easily transportable milk products such as butter, cheese, and condensed and dried milk.

It is now usual for dairy farms to concentrate on the production of milk and for factories to take over the handling, processing, and distribution of milk as well as the manufacture of dairy products.

In Britain, the Milk Marketing Board (1933), to which all producers must sell their milk, forms a connecting link between farms and factories. Overproduction of milk in the European Union has led to the introduction of quotas, which set a limit on the amount of milk for which a farmer may be paid.

daisy any of numerous species of perennial plants in the family Compositae, especially the field daisy of Europe and North America *Chrysanthemum leucanthemum* and the English common daisy *Bellis perennis*, with a single white or pink flower rising from a rosette of leaves.

daisy bush any of several Australian and New Zealand shrubs of the genus *Olearia*, family Compositae, with flowers like daisies and felted or holly-like leaves.

Dakar capital and chief port of Senegal; population (1992 est) 1,729,800. It is an industrial centre, and there is a university, established 1957. Founded 1862, it was formerly the seat of government of ◊French West Africa.

Dakota see ◊North Dakota and ◊South Dakota.

Daladier Edouard 1884–1970. French Radical politician. As prime minister April 1938–March 1940, he signed the ◊Munich Agreement 1938 (by which the Sudeten districts of Czechoslovakia were ceded to Germany) and declared war on Germany 1939. He resigned 1940 because of his unpopularity for failing to assist Finland against Russia. He was arrested on the fall of France 1940 and was a prisoner in Germany 1943–45. Following the end of World War II he was re-elected to the Chamber of Deputies 1946–58.

Dalai Lama (Tibetan 'oceanic guru') 14th incarnation. Title of Tenzin Gyatso 1935– . Tibetan

Buddhist monk, political ruler of Tibet from 1940 until 1959, when he went into exile in protest against Chinese annexation and oppression. He has continued to campaign for self-government; Nobel Peace Prize 1989. Tibetan Buddhists believe that each Dalai Lama is a reincarnation of his predecessor and also of ◊Avalokiteśvara.

Dalai Lama is the title of the second hierarch of the Gelugpa monastic order. Tenzin Gyatso was chosen to be the 14th Dalai Lama in 1937 and enthroned in Lhasa 1940. He temporarily fled 1950–51 when the Chinese overran Tibet, and in March 1959 – when a local uprising against Chinese rule was suppressed – made a dramatic escape from Lhasa to India. He then settled at Dharmsala in the Punjab. The Chinese offered to lift the ban on his living in Tibet, providing he would refrain from calling for Tibet's independence. His deputy, the Panchen Lama, cooperated with the Chinese but failed to protect the monks. The Dalai Lama concerns himself closely with the welfare of the many Tibetans who have fled into exile.

In the 15th century, when the office was founded, Dalai Lama was purely a religious title. The fifth Dalai Lama (1617–1682) united Tibet politically and assumed temporal as well as spiritual powers.

▷ *See feature on pp. 162–163.*

Dalcroze Emile Jaques, Swiss composer. See ◊Jaques-Dalcroze.

Dale Henry Hallett 1875–1968. British physiologist who in 1936 shared the Nobel Prize for Physiology or Medicine with Otto Loewi (1873–1961) for proving that chemical substances are involved in the transmission of nerve impulses.

d'Alembert French mathematician. See Jean le Rond d' ◊Alembert.

Dales or ***Yorkshire Dales*** series of river valleys in N England, running E from the Pennines in West Yorkshire; a National Park was established 1954. The principal valleys are Airedale, Nidderdale, Swaledale, Teesdale, Wensleydale, and Wharfedale. The three main peaks are Ingleborough, Whernside, and Pen-y-Ghent. The Dales are highly scenic and popular with walkers and potholers; drystone walls and barns are features of the landscape.

Dalgarno George c. 1626–1687. Scottish schoolteacher and the inventor of the first sign-language alphabet 1680.

Dali Salvador Felipe Jacinto 1904–1989. Spanish painter and designer. In 1929 he joined the Surrealists and became notorious for his flamboyant eccentricity. Influenced by the psychoanalytic theories of Sigmund ◊Freud, he developed a repertoire of striking, hallucinatory images – such as distorted human figures, limp pocket watches, and burning giraffes – in superbly executed works, which he termed 'hand-painted dream photographs'. *The Persistence of Memory* 1931 (Museum of Modern Art, New York) is typical. By the late 1930s he had developed a more conventional style – this, and his apparent fascist sympathies, led to his expulsion from the Surrealist movement 1938.

Dali, born near Barcelona, initially came under the influence of the Italian Futurists. He is credited as co-creator of Luis Buñuel's Surrealist film *Un Chien andalou* 1928, but his role is thought to have been subordinate; he abandoned filmmaking after collaborating on the script for Buñuel's *L'Age d'or/The Golden Age* 1930. He also designed ballet costumes, scenery, jewellery, and furniture. The books *The Secret Life of Salvador Dali* 1942 and *Diary of a Genius* 1966 are autobiographical. He was buried beneath a crystal dome in the museum of his work at Figueras on the Costa Brava, Spain.

Dali Influenced by Freud's writings on the significance of subconscious imagery, Dali's art often represented explorations in this field. He developed a process, called 'paranoic critical', by which he could induce hallucinatory states and thereby bring up images from his subconscious mind. *Associated Press/Topham*

Daimler German engineer Gottlieb Daimler with one of his goods vehicles at the Paris Motor Show 1898. During the 1870s he worked on developing the gas engine, and in 1889 produced one of the earliest roadworthy cars. He also built motorcycles and goods vehicles. *Topham*

Dallapiccola Luigi 1904–1975. Italian composer. Initially a Neo-Classicist, he adopted a lyrical twelve-tone style after 1945. His works include the operas *Il prigioniero/The Prisoner* 1949 and *Ulisse/Ulysses* 1968, as well as many vocal and instrumental compositions.

Dallas commercial city on the Trinity River, in Texas, USA; population (1992) 1,022,500, metropolitan area (with Fort Worth) 4,215,000. Dallas is a cultural centre, with a symphony orchestra, opera, ballet, and theatre. Industries include banking, insurance, oil, aviation, aerospace, and electronics. The Cotton Bowl annual football game is played here. Dallas–Fort Worth Regional Airport (opened 1973) is one of the world's largest.

history Founded as a trading post 1841, it developed as the focus of a cotton area, and by the 1920s 40% of US cotton came from the area. The East Texas oilfield was discovered 1930, and the city became an important centre for the oil industry. It grew rapidly after World War II, with aircraft manufacturing, electronics, car assembly, and the manufacture of cotton-ginning machinery. It became a leading insurance centre, and the banking and financial centre for the Southwest.

President John F Kennedy was assassinated here 22 November 1963.

features One of the oldest buildings is the Old Red Courthouse 1892. At Fair Park there is a collection of Art Moderne buildings, mainly from the 1936 Texas Centennial Exhibition, with murals in the Hall of State depicting the history of Texas. Several of the skyscrapers, built mainly in the 1980s, were designed by the architect I M Pei, who also designed the Morton H Meyerson Symphony Center 1989. Museums include the Dallas Museum of Art. The Kalita Humphreys Theater was designed by Frank Lloyd Wright.

Dalmatia region divided between Croatia, Montenegro in Yugoslavia, and Bosnia-Herzegovina. The capital is Split. It lies along the eastern shore of the Adriatic Sea and includes a number of islands. The interior is mountainous. Important products are wine, olives, and fish. Notable towns in addition to the capital are Zadar, Sibenik, and Dubrovnik.

history Dalmatia became Austrian 1815 and by the treaty of Rapallo 1920 became part of the kingdom of the Serbs, Croats, and Slovenes (Yugoslavia from 1931), except for the town of Zadar (Zara) and the island of Lastovo (Lagosta), which, with neighbouring islets, were given to Italy until transferred to Yugoslavia 1947.

Dalmatian breed of dog, about 60 cm/24 in tall, with a distinctive smooth white coat with spots that are black or brown. Dalmatians are born white; the spots appear later. They were formerly used as coach dogs, running beside horse-drawn carriages to fend off highwaymen.

Dalton John 1766–1844. English chemist who proposed the theory of atoms, which he considered to be the smallest parts of matter. He produced the first list of relative atomic masses in 'Absorption of Gases' 1805 and put forward the law of partial pressures of gases (Dalton's law).

From experiments with gases, Dalton noted that the proportions of two components combining to form another gas were always constant. He suggested that if substances combine in simple numerical ratios, then the macroscopic weight proportions represent the relative atomic masses of those substances. He also propounded the law of partial pressures, stating that for a mixture of gases the total pressure is the sum of the pressures that would be developed by each individual gas if it were the only one present.

❛This grandiose tragedy that we call modern art.❜

SALVADOR DALI
Dali by Dali

dam structure built to hold back water in order to prevent flooding, to provide water for irrigation and storage, and to provide hydroelectric power. The biggest dams are of the earth- and rock-fill type, also called embankment dams. Early dams in Britain, built before about 1800, had a core made from puddled clay (clay which has been mixed with water

Dalton English chemist John Dalton whose work on the nature of matter provided the basis for modern atomic theories. He devised a system of classification by atomic weight, and his research work on gases led him to formulate the law of partial pressure of gases known as Dalton's law. *Topham*

dam There are two basic types of dam: the gravity dam and the arch dam. The gravity dam relies upon the weight of its material to resist the forces imposed upon it; the arch dam uses an arch shape to take the forces in a horizontal direction into the sides of the river valley. The largest dams are usually embankment dams. Buttress dams are used to hold back very wide rivers or lakes.

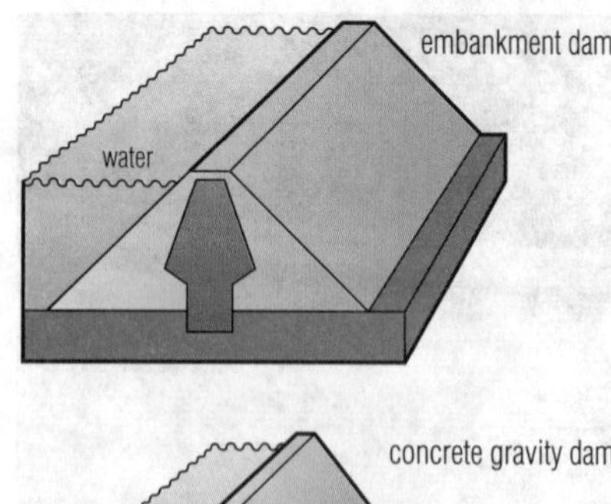

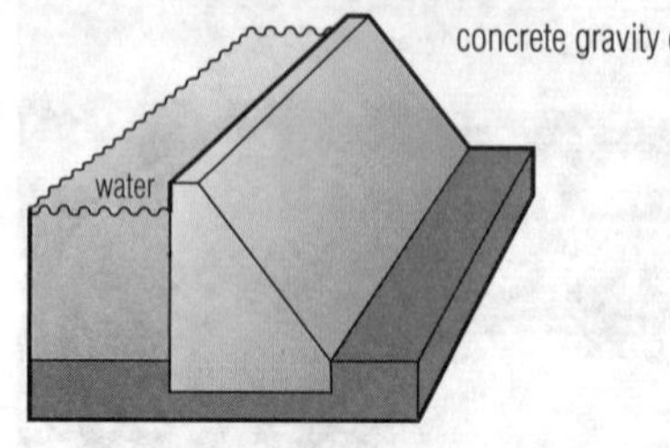

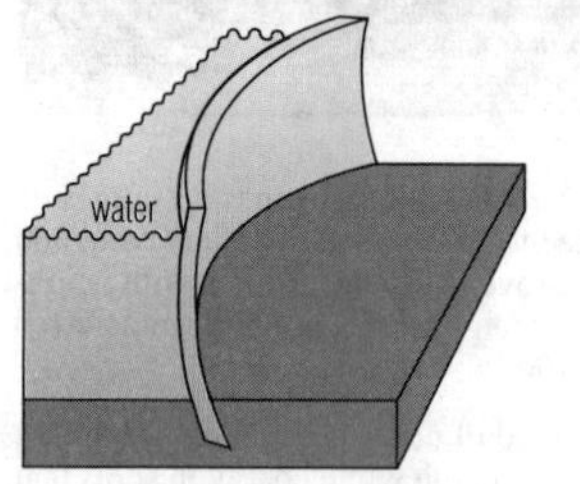

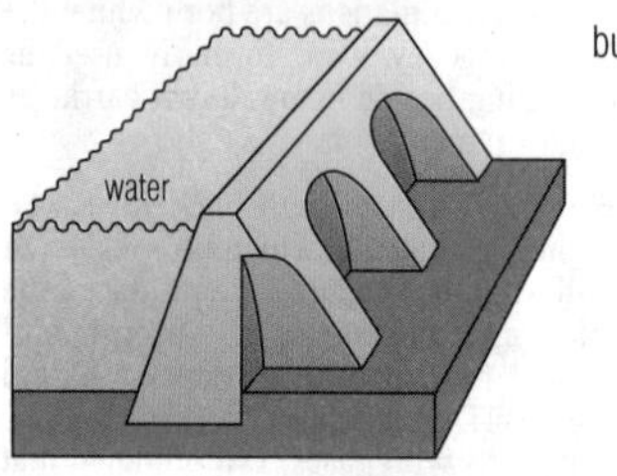

'When a dog bites a man that is not news, but when a man bites a dog that is news.'

CHARLES DANA 'What is News?' in the *New York Sun* 1882

to make it impermeable). Such dams are generally built on broad valley sites. Deep, narrow gorges dictate a concrete dam, where the strength of reinforced concrete can withstand the water pressures involved. *See list of tables on p. 1177.*

Dam Carl Peter Henrik 1895–1976. Danish biochemist who discovered vitamin K. For his success in this field he shared the 1943 Nobel Prize for Physiology or Medicine with US biochemist Edward Doisy (1893–1986).

damages in law, compensation for a ◊tort (such as personal injuries caused by negligence) or breach of contract. In the case of breach of contract the complainant can claim all the financial loss he or she has suffered. Damages for personal injuries include compensation for loss of earnings, as well as for the injury itself. In the majority of cases, the parties involved reach an out-of-court settlement (a compromise without going to court).

Daman and Diu union territory of W India; area 112 sq km/43 sq mi; capital Daman; population (1991) 101,400. ***Daman*** has an area of 72 sq km/28 sq mi. The port and capital, Daman, is on the west coast, 160 km/100 mi N of Bombay. The economy is based on tourism and fishing. ***Diu*** is an island off the Kathiawar peninsula with an area of 40 sq km/15 sq mi. The main town is also called Diu. The economy is based on tourism, coconuts, pearl millet, and salt.

history Daman was seized by Portugal 1531 and ceded to Portugal by the Shah of Gujarat 1539; Diu was captured by the Portuguese 1534. Both areas were annexed by India 1961 and were part of the Union Territory of ◊Goa, Daman, and Diu until Goa became a separate state 1987.

Damascus (Arabic ***Dimashq***) capital of Syria, on the river Barada, SE of Beirut; population (1993) 1,497,000. It produces silk, wood products, and brass and copperware. Said to be the oldest continuously inhabited city in the world, Damascus was an ancient city even in Old Testament times. Most notable of the old buildings is the Great Mosque, completed as a Christian church in the 5th century.

The Assyrians destroyed Damascus about 733 BC. In 332 BC it fell to one of the generals of Alexander the Great; in 63 BC it came under Roman rule. In AD 635 it was taken by the Arabs, and has since been captured many times, by Egyptians, Mongolians, and Turks. In 1918, during World War I, it was taken from the Turks by the British with Arab aid and in 1920 became the capital of French-mandated Syria. The 'street which is called straight' is associated with St Paul, who was converted while on the road to Damascus. The tomb of ◊Saladin is here. The fortress dates from 1219.

damask textile of woven linen, cotton, wool, or silk, with a reversible figured pattern. It was first made in the city of Damascus, Syria.

Dame in the UK honours system, the title of a woman who has been awarded the Order of the Bath, Order of St Michael and St George, Royal Victorian Order, or Order of the British Empire. It is also in law the legal title of the wife or widow of a knight or baronet, placed before her name.

Damocles lived 4th century BC. In Classical legend, a courtier of the elder Dionysius, ruler of Syracuse, Sicily. When Damocles made too much of his sovereign's good fortune, Dionysius invited him to a feast where he symbolically hung a sword over Damocles' head to demonstrate the precariousness of the happiness of kings.

Damon and Pythias in Greek mythology, devoted friends. When Pythias was condemned to death by the Sicilian tyrant Dionysius, Damon offered his own life as security to allow Pythias the freedom to go and arrange his affairs. When Pythias returned, they were both pardoned.

damper any device that deadens or lessens vibrations or oscillations; for example, one used to check vibrations in the strings of a piano. The term is also used for the movable plate in the flue of a stove or furnace for controlling the draught.

Dampier William 1651–1715. English explorer and hydrographic surveyor who circumnavigated the world three times. Born in Somerset, he went to sea in 1668. He led a life of buccaneering adventure, circumnavigated the globe, and published his *New Voyage Round the World* in 1697. In 1699 he was sent by the government on a voyage to Australia and New Guinea, and again circled the world. He accomplished a third circumnavigation 1703–07, and on his final voyage 1708–11 rescued Alexander Selkirk (1676–1721) (on whose life Daniel Defoe's *Robinson Crusoe* is based) from Juan Fernandez in the S Pacific.

damselfly long, slender, colourful ◊dragonfly of the suborder Zygoptera, with two pairs of similar wings that are generally held vertically over the body when at rest, unlike those of other dragonflies.

damson cultivated variety of plum tree *Prunus domestica* var. *institia*, distinguished by its small, oval, edible fruits, which are dark purple or blue to black in colour.

Dana Charles Anderson 1819–1897. US journalist who covered the European revolutions of 1848 and earned a reputation as one of America's most able foreign correspondents. During the US Civil War he served as assistant secretary of war 1863–65 and in 1868 purchased the *New York Sun*, with which he pioneered the daily tabloid format. He was later managing editor of the *New York Tribune* under Horace Greeley.

Danaë in Greek mythology, daughter of Acrisius, king of Argos. He shut her up in a bronze tower because of a prophecy that her son would kill his grandfather. Zeus became enamoured of her and descended in a shower of gold; she gave birth to ◊Perseus.

'We look at the dance to impart the sensation of living in an affirmation of life, to energize the spectator ....'

ON DANCE Martha Graham in *Modern Dance* 1935

dance rhythmic movement of the body, usually performed in time to music. Its primary purpose may be religious, magical, martial, social, or artistic – the last two being characteristic of nontraditional societies. The pre-Christian era had a strong tradition of ritual dance, and ancient Greek dance still exerts an influence on dance movement today. Although Western folk and social dances have a long history, the Eastern dance tradition long predates the Western. The European classical tradition dates from the 15th century in Italy, the first printed dance text from 16th-century France, and the first dance school in Paris from the 17th century. The 18th century saw the development of European classical ballet as we know it today, and the 19th century saw the rise of Romantic ballet. In the 20th century ◊modern dance firmly established itself as a separate dance idiom, not based on classical ballet, and many divergent styles and ideas have grown from a willingness to explore a variety of techniques and amalgamate different traditions.

Eastern history The oldest surviving dance forms are probably those of the East. Hindus believe the world was created by Shiva, a dancing god, and religious themes permeate their dances. The first Indian book on dancing, the *Natya Sastra*, existed a thousand years before its European counterpart. The *bugaku* dances of Japan, with orchestral accompaniment, date from the 7th century and are still performed at court. When the Peking (Beijing) Opera dancers first astonished Western audiences during the 1950s, they were representatives of a tradition stretching back to 740, the year in which Emperor Ming Huang established the Pear Garden Academy.

Western history The first comparable European institution, L'Académie Royale de Danse, was founded by Louis XIV 1661. In the European tradition social dances have always tended to rise upwards through the social scale; for example, the medieval court dances derived from peasant country dances. One form of dance tends to typify a whole period, thus the galliard represents the 16th century, the minuet the 18th, the waltz the 19th, and the quickstep represents ballroom dancing in the first half of the 20th century. The nine dances of the modern world championships in ◊ballroom dancing are the standard four (waltz, foxtrot, tango, and quickstep), the Latin-American styles (samba, rumba, cha-cha-cha, and paso doble), and the Viennese waltz.

popular dance Popular dance crazes have included the Charleston in the 1920s, jitterbug in the 1930s and 1940s, jive in the 1950s, the twist in the 1960s, disco and jazz dancing in the 1970s, and break dancing in the 1980s. In general, since the 1960s, popular dance in the West has moved away from any prescribed sequence of movements and physical contact between participants, the dancers performing as individuals with no distinction between the male and the female role. Dances requiring skilled athletic performance, such as the hustle and the New Yorker, have been developed.

classical dance In classical dance, the second half of the 20th century has seen a great cross-fertilization from dances of other cultures. Troupes visited the West, not only from the USSR and Eastern Europe, but from such places as Indonesia, Japan, South Korea, Nigeria, and Senegal. In the 1970s jazz dance, pioneered in the USA by Matt Mattox, became popular; it includes elements of ballet, modern, tap, Indian classical, Latin American, and Afro-American dance. Freestyle dance is loosely based on ballet with elements of jazz, ethnic, and modern dance. *See timeline on p. 295.*

Dance Charles 1946– . English film and television actor. He became known when he played the sympathetic Guy Perron in *The Jewel in the Crown* 1984. He has also appeared in *Plenty* 1986, *Good Morning Babylon*, *The Golden Child* both 1987, and *White Mischief* 1988.

dance of death (German ***Totentanz***, French ***danse macabre***) popular theme in painting of the late medieval period, depicting an allegorical representation of death (usually a skeleton) leading the famous and the not-so-famous to the grave. One of the best-known representations is a series of woodcuts (1523–26) by Hans Holbein the Younger. It has also been exploited as a theme in music, for example the *Danse macabre* of Saint-Saëns 1874, an orchestral composition in which the xylophone was introduced to represent dancing skeletons.

dandelion plant *Taraxacum officinale* belonging to the Compositae family. The stalk rises from a rosette of leaves that are deeply indented like a lion's teeth, hence the name (from French *dent de lion*). The flower heads are bright yellow. The fruit is surmounted by the hairs of the calyx which constitute the familiar dandelion 'clock'.

Dandolo Venetian family that produced four doges (rulers), of whom the most outstanding, Enrico (c. 1120–1205), became doge in 1193. He greatly increased the dominions of the Venetian republic and accompanied the crusading army that took Constantinople in 1203.

dandy male figure conspicuous for tasteful fastidiousness, particularly in dress. The famous Regency dandy George ('Beau') Brummell (1778–1840) helped to give literary currency to the figure of the dandy, particularly in England and France, providing a model and symbol of the triumph of style for the Francophile Oscar ◊Wilde and for 19th-century French writers such as Charles ◊Baudelaire, J K ◊Huysmans, and the extravagantly romantic novelist and critic Jules-Amédée Barbey d'Aurevilly (1808–1889), biographer of Brummell.

Dane people of Danish culture from Denmark and N Germany. There are approximately 5 million speakers of Danish (including some in the USA), a Germanic language belonging to the Indo-European family. The Danes are known for their seafaring culture, which dates back to the Viking age of expansion between the 8th and 10th centuries.

danegeld in English history, a tax imposed from 991 by Anglo-Saxon kings to pay tribute to the Vikings. After the Norman Conquest the tax continued to be levied until 1162, and the Normans used it to finance military operations.

Danelaw 11th-century name for the area of N and E England settled by the Vikings in the 9th century. It occupied about half of England, from the river Tees to the river Thames. Within its bounds, Danish law, customs, and language prevailed. Its linguistic influence is still apparent.

Daniel lived 6th century BC. Jewish folk hero and prophet at the court of Nebuchadnezzar; also the name of a book of the Old Testament, probably compiled in the 2nd century BC. It includes stories about Daniel and his companions Shadrach, Meshach, and Abednego, set during the Babylonian captivity of the Jews. One of the best-known stories is that of Daniel in the den of lions, where he was thrown for refusing to compromise his beliefs, and was preserved by divine intervention.

Danish language member of the North Germanic group of the Indo-European language family, spoken in Denmark and Greenland and related to Icelandic, Faroese, Norwegian, and Swedish. It has had a particularly strong influence on Norwegian. As one of the languages of the Vikings, who invaded and settled in parts of Britain during the 9th to 11th centuries, Old Danish had a strong influence on English. The English pronouns *they*, *their*, and *them*, as well as such *sk*-words as *sky*, *skill*, *skin*, *scrape*, and *scrub*, are of Danish origin. Danish place-name endings include *by* (a farm or town), as in Derby, Grimsby, and Whitby in England.

D'Annunzio Gabriele 1863–1938. Italian poet, novelist, and dramatist. Marking a departure from 19th-century Italian literary traditions, his use of language and style of writing earned him much criticism in his own time. His novels, often combining elements of corruption, snobbery, and scandal, include *L'innocente/The Intruder* 1891 and *Il triomfo della morte/The Triumph of Death* 1894.

During World War I, he was active in turning public opinion to the side of the Allies 1915. After serving in World War I, he led an expedition of volunteers 1919 to capture the Dalmatian port of Fiume, which he held until 1921. He became a national hero, and was created Prince of Montenevoso 1924. Influenced by the German philosopher Nietzsche's writings, he later became an ardent exponent of Fascism.

damselfly As in all members of the suborder Zygoptera, this common blue damselfly *Enallagma cyathigerum* male holds his wings closed above his back. Dragonflies (suborder Anisoptera) hold their wings out to their sides at 90 degrees to the body when at rest, and are generally stouter than damselflies. *Premaphotos Wildlife*

Dante Alighieri 1265–1321. Italian poet. His masterpiece *La divina commedia/The Divine Comedy* 1307–21 is an epic account in three parts of his journey through Hell, Purgatory, and Paradise, during which he is guided part of the way by the poet Virgil; on a metaphorical level, the journey is also one of Dante's own spiritual development. Other works include *De vulgari eloquentia/Concerning the Vulgar Tongue* 1304–06, an original Latin work on Italian, its dialects, and kindred languages; the philosophical prose treatise *Convivio/The Banquet* 1306–08, the first major work of its kind to be written in Italian rather than Latin; *De monarchia/On World Government* 1310–13, expounding his political theories; and *Canzoniere/Lyrics*.

Dante was born in Florence, where in 1274 he first met and fell in love with Beatrice Portinari (described in *La vita nuova/New Life* 1283–92). His love for her survived her marriage to another man and her death 1290 at the age of 24. According to the writer ◊Boccaccio, from 1283 to 1289 Dante was engaged in study, and after the death of Beatrice he seems to have entered into a period of intense philosophic study. In 1289 he fought in the battle of Campaldino, won by Florence against Arezzo, and from 1295 took an active part in Florentine politics. In 1300 he was one of the six priors of the Republic, favouring the moderate Guelph party rather than the extreme papal Ghibelline faction (see ◊Guelph and Ghibelline); when the Ghibellines seized power 1302, he was convicted in his absence of misappropriation of public money and sentenced to death. He escaped from Florence and spent the remainder of his life in exile, in central and N Italy. *See illustration on following page.*

Danton Georges Jacques 1759–1794. French revolutionary. Originally a lawyer, during the early years of the Revolution he was one of the most influential people in Paris. He organized the uprising 10 Aug 1792 that overthrew Louis XVI and the monarchy, roused the country to expel the Prussian invaders, and in April 1793 formed the revolutionary tribunal and the Committee of Public Safety, of which he was the leader until July of that year. Thereafter he lost power to the ◊Jacobins, and, when he attempted to recover it, was arrested and guillotined.

Danube (German ***Donau***) second longest of European rivers, rising on the eastern slopes of the

dance A wall painting of dancers, in an Etruscan tomb from about 475 BC. Dance has been used as a social, religious, and magical ritual for thousands of years. *Philip Sauvain*

Dante Alighieri A portrait of the Italian poet Dante Alighieri. In the foreground stands Dante holding his work *The Divine Comedy*. To one side a city is depicted, and to the other side is a vision of Hell. Behind Dante, human figures are attempting the difficult ascent to heaven. *Corbis*

Black Forest, and flowing 2,858 km/1,776 mi across Europe to enter the Black Sea in Romania by a swampy delta.

The head of river navigation is Ulm, in Baden-Württemberg; Braila, Romania, is the limit for ocean-going ships. Cities on the Danube include Linz, Vienna, Bratislava, Budapest, Belgrade, Ruse, Braila, and Galati. A canal connects the Danube with the river Main, and thus with the Rhine river system. In 1992 the river was diverted in Slovakia to feed the controversial Gabcikovo Dam.

Danzig German name for the Polish port of ◊Gdańsk.

Daphne in Greek mythology, a ◊nymph who was changed into a laurel tree to escape from ◊Apollo's amorous pursuit.

darcy c.g.s. unit (symbol D) of permeability, used mainly in geology to describe the permeability of rock (for example, to oil, gas, or water).

Dardanelles (ancient name ***Hellespont***, Turkish name ***Canakkale Boğazi***) Turkish strait connecting the Sea of Marmara with the Aegean Sea; its shores are formed by the ◊Gallipoli peninsula on the NW and the mainland of Anatolia on the SE. It is 75 km/47 mi long and 5–6 km/3–4 mi wide.

The Dardanelles was the scene of bitter fighting between Allied and Turkish troops during World War I, most notably the operations at ◊Gallipoli 1915.

Dardanelles

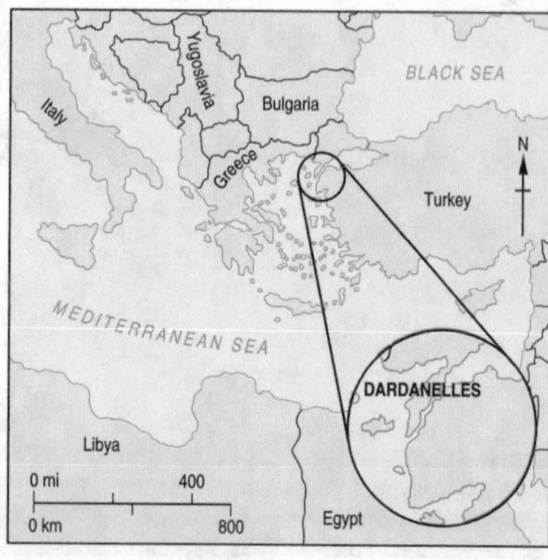

Dar es Salaam (Arabic 'haven of peace') chief seaport in Tanzania, on the Indian Ocean, and capital of Tanzania until its replacement by ◊Dodoma 1974; population (1988) 1,361,000.

Darío Rubén. Pen name of Félix Rubén García Sarmiento 1867–1916. Nicaraguan poet. His first major work *Azul/Azure* 1888, a collection of prose and verse influenced by French Symbolism, created a sensation. He went on to establish *modernismo*, the Spanish-American modernist literary movement, distinguished by an idiosyncratic and deliberately frivolous style that broke away from the prevailing Spanish provincialism and adapted French poetic models. His vitality and eclecticism influenced every poet writing in Spanish after him, both in the New World and in Spain.

Darius (I) the Great c. 558–486 BC. King of Persia 521–486 BC. A member of a younger branch of the Achaemenid dynasty, he won the throne from the usurper Gaumata (died 522 BC) and reorganized the government. In 512 BC he marched against the Scythians, a people N of the Black Sea, and subjugated Thrace and Macedonia.

Darjeeling town and health resort in West Bengal, India; situated 2,150 m/7,000 ft above sea level, on the southern slopes of the Himalayas; population (1981) 57,600. It is connected by rail with Calcutta, 595 km/370 mi to the S. It is the centre of a tea-producing district.

dark matter matter that, according to current theories of ◊cosmology, makes up 90–99% of the mass of the universe but so far remains undetected. Dark matter, if shown to exist, would explain many currently unexplained gravitational effects in the movement of galaxies. Theories of the composition of dark matter include unknown atomic particles (cold dark matter) or fast-moving neutrinos (hot dark matter) or a combination of both.

In 1993 astronomers identified part of the dark matter in the form of stray planets and ◊brown dwarfs, and possibly, stars that have failed to light up. These objects are known as MACHOs (massive astrophysical compact halo objects) and, according to US astronomers 1996, make up approximately half of the dark matter in the Milky Way's halo. ▷ *See feature on pp. 70–71.*

Darling river in SE Australia, a tributary of the river Murray, which it joins at Wentworth. It is 3,075 km/1,910 mi long, and its waters are conserved in Menindee Lake (155 sq km/60 sq mi) and others nearby. The name comes from Ralph Darling (1775–1858), governor of New South Wales 1825–31. The Darling Range, a ridge in W Australia, has a highest point of about 582 m/1,669 ft.

Darling Grace Horsley 1815–1842. British heroine. She was the daughter of a lighthouse keeper on the Farne Islands, off Northumberland. On 7 Sept 1838 the *Forfarshire* was wrecked, and Grace Darling and her father rowed through a storm to the wreck, saving nine lives. She was awarded a medal for her bravery.

Darlington industrial town in England, on the river Skerne, near its junction with the river Tees, and the administrative headquarters of Darlington unitary authority; population (1991) 96,700. It has coal and ironstone mines, and produces iron and steel goods, and knitting wool. The world's first passenger railway was opened between Darlington and Stockton 27 Sept 1825.

Unitary authority of England created 1997 (*see United Kingdom map*).

Darnley Henry Stewart or Stuart, Lord Darnley 1545–1567. British aristocrat, second husband of Mary Queen of Scots from 1565, and father of James I of England (James VI of Scotland).

On the advice of her secretary, David ◊Rizzio, Mary refused Darnley the crown matrimonial; in revenge, Darnley led a band of nobles who murdered Rizzio in Mary's presence. Darnley was assassinated 1567. Knighted and became Earl of Ross and Duke of Albany 1565.

Darrow Clarence Seward 1857–1938. US lawyer, born in Ohio, a champion of liberal causes and defender of the underdog. He defended many trade-union leaders, including Eugene ◊Debs 1894. He was counsel for the defence in the Nathan Leopold and Richard Loeb murder trial in Chicago 1924, and in the Scopes monkey trial, in which a science teacher was accused of teaching Charles Darwin's theory of evolution, contrary to a law of the state. Darrow matched wits in the latter trial with prosecution attorney William Jennings Bryan (1860–1925). He was an opponent of capital punishment.

Dart Raymond Arthur 1893–1988. Australian-born South African palaeontologist and anthropologist who in 1924 discovered the first fossil remains of the australopithecenes, early hominids, near Taungs in Botswana. Dart named them *Australopithecus africanus*, and spent many years trying to prove that they were early humans rather than apes. In the 1950s and 1960s, the ◊Leakey family found more fossils of this type and of related types in the Olduvai Gorge of E Africa, establishing that Australopithecines were hominids, walked erect, made tools, and lived as early as 5.5 million years ago. After further discoveries in the 1980s, they are today classified as *Homo sapiens australopithecus*, and Dart's assertions have been validated. ▷ *See feature on pp. 518–519.*

Dartford industrial town in Kent, England, 27 km/17 mi SE of London; population (1991) 28,400. Cement, chemicals, paper, and pharmaceuticals are manufactured. The Dartford Tunnel (1963) runs under the Thames to Purfleet, Essex. Congestion in the tunnel was relieved 1991 by the opening of the Queen Elizabeth II bridge.

Dartmoor plateau of SW Devon, England, over 1,000 sq km/400 sq mi in extent, of which half is some 300 m/1,000 ft above sea level. Most of Dartmoor is a National Park. The moor is noted for its wild aspect, and rugged blocks of granite, or 'tors', crown its higher points. The highest are ***Yes Tor*** 618 m/2,028 ft and ***High Willhays*** 621 m/2,039 ft. Devon's chief rivers have their sources on Dartmoor. There are numerous prehistoric remains. Near Hemerdon there are tungsten reserves.

Dartmouth English seaport at the mouth of the river Dart; 43 km/27 mi E of Plymouth, on the Devon coast; population (1996 est) 6,000. It is a centre for yachting and has an excellent harbour. The Britannia Royal Naval College dates from 1905.

darts indoor game played on a circular board. Darts (like small arrow shafts) about 13 cm/5 in long are thrown at segmented targets and score points according to their landing place.

The game may have derived from target practice with broken arrow shafts in days when archery was a compulsory military exercise. The Pilgrims are believed to have played darts aboard the *Mayflower* 1620.

DANCE: TIMELINE

1000 BC	King David danced 'with all his might' before the ark of the Covenant in Jerusalem – one of the earliest known instances of ritual dance.
405	*Bacchants* by Euripides was staged in Athens. The play demanded a considerable amount of dancing.
142	Consul Scipio Aemilianus Africanus closed the burgeoning dance schools of Rome in a drive against hedonism.
774 AD	Pope Zacharias forbade dancing.
1050	The *Ruodlieb*, a poem written by a monk at Tegernsee, Bavaria, contained the first European reference to dancing in couples.
1313	Rabbi Hacén ben Salomo of Zaragoza, in Aragon, like many other Jews in medieval times, was the local dancing master.
1489	A rudimentary allegorical ballet was performed in honour of the marriage of the Duke of Milan, at Tortona, Italy.
1581	In Paris, the first modern-style unified ballet, the *Ballet comique de la reine*, was staged at the court of Catherine de' Medici.
1588	Dance and ballet's first basic text, *L'Orchésographie*, by the priest Jehan Tabouret, was printed in Langres, near Dijon, France.
1651	In London, John Playford published *The English Dancing Master*. The 18th edition (1728) described 900 country dances.
1661	Louis XIV founded L'Académie Royale de Danse in Paris.
1670	The first classic ballet, *Le Bourgeois Gentilhomme*, was produced in Chambord, France.
1681	La Fontaine, the first professional female ballet dancer, made her debut in *Le Triomphe de L'amour* at the Paris Opéra.
1734	The dancer Marie Sallé adopted the gauze tunic, precursor to the Romantic tutu, and Marie Camargo shortened her skirts.
1738	The Kirov Ballet was established in St Petersburg, Russia.
1760	The great dancer and choreographer Jean-Georges Noverre published in Lyon *Lettres sur la danse et sur les ballets*, one of the most influential of all ballet books.
1776	The Bolshoi Ballet was established in Moscow.
1778	Noverre and Mozart collaborated on *Les Petits Riens* in Paris. The cast included the celebrated Auguste Vestris.
late 18th C	The waltz originated in Austria and Germany from a popular folk dance, the *Ländler*.
1820	Carlo Blasis, teacher and choreographer, published his *Traité élémentaire théoretique et pratique de l'art de la danse* in Milan which, together with his later works of dance theory, codified techniques for future generations of dancers.
1821	The first known picture of a ballerina *sur les pointes*, the French Fanny Bias by F Waldeck, dates from this year.
1832	The first performance of *La Sylphide* at the Paris Opéra opened the Romantic era of ballet and established the central significance of the ballerina. Marie Taglioni, the producer's daughter, who created the title role, wore the new-style Romantic tutu.
1841	Ballet's Romantic masterpiece *Giselle*, with Carlotta Grisi in the leading role, was produced in Paris.
1845	Four great rival ballerinas of the Romantic era – Taglioni, Grisi, Fanny Cerrito, and Lucile Grahn – appeared together in Perrot's *Pas de Quatre* in London.
1866	*The Black Crook*, the ballet extravaganza from which US vaudeville and musical comedy developed, began its run of 474 performances in New York.
1870	*Coppélia*, 19th-century ballet's comic masterpiece, was presented in Paris.
1877	*La Bayadère* and *Swan Lake* were premiered in Moscow, but the latter failed through poor production and choreography. The Petipa-Ivanov version, in which Pierina Legnani performed 32 *fouettés*, established the work 1895.
1897	Anna Pavlova made her debut in St Petersburg with the Imperial Russian Ballet.
1905	Isadora Duncan appeared in Russia, making an immense impression with her 'antiballet' innovations derived from Greek dance.
1906	Vaslav Nijinsky made his debut in St Petersburg.
1909	The first Paris season given by Diaghilev's troupe of Russian dancers, later to become known as the Ballets Russes, marked the beginning of one of the most exciting periods in Western ballet.
1913	The premiere of Nijinsky's *Le Sacre du printemps/The Rite of Spring* provoked a scandal in Paris.
1914	The foxtrot developed from the two-step in the USA.
1915	The Denishawn School of Modern Dance was founded in Los Angeles.
1926	Martha Graham, one of the most innovative figures in modern dance, gave her first recital in New York. In England, students from the Rambert School of Ballet, opened by Marie Rambert 1920, gave their first public performance in *A Tragedy of Fashion*, the first ballet to be choreographed by Frederick Ashton.
1928	The first performance of George Balanchine's *Apollo* in Paris, by the Ballets Russes, marked the birth of Neo-Classicism in ballet.
1931	Ninette de Valois' Vic-Wells Ballet gave its first performance in London. In 1956 the company became the Royal Ballet.
1933	The Hollywood musical achieved artistic independence through Busby Berkeley's kaleidoscopic choreography in *42nd Street* and Dave Gould's airborne finale in *Flying Down to Rio*, in which Fred Astaire and Ginger Rogers appeared together for the first time.
1939	The American Ballet Theater was founded in New York.
1940	The Dance Notation Bureau was established in New York for recording ballets and dances.
1948	The New York City Ballet was founded with George Balanchine as artistic director and principal choreographer. The film *The Red Shoes* appeared, choreographed by Massine and Robert Helpmann, starring Moira Shearer.
1950	The Festival Ballet, later to become the London Festival Ballet, was created by Alicia Markova and Anton Dolin, who had first danced together with the Ballets Russes de Monte Carlo 1929.
1952	Gene Kelly starred and danced in the film *Singin' in the Rain*.
1953	The US experimental choreographer Merce Cunningham, who often worked with the composer John Cage, formed his own troupe.
1956	The Bolshoi Ballet opened its first season in the West at Covent Garden in London, with Galina Ulanova dancing in *Romeo and Juliet*.
1957	Jerome Robbins conceived and choreographed the musical *West Side Story*, demonstrating his outstanding ability to work in both popular and classical forms.
1960	The progressive French choreographer Maurice Béjart became director of the Brussels-based Ballet du XXième Siècle company.
1961	Rudolf Nureyev defected from the USSR while dancing with the Kirov Ballet in Paris. He was to have a profound influence on male dancing in the West. The South African choreographer John Cranko became director and chief choreographer of the Stuttgart Ballet, transforming it into a major company.
1962	Glen Tetley's ballet *Pierrot lunaire*, in which he was one of the three dancers, was premiered in New York. In the same year he joined the Nederlands Dans Theater.
1965	US choreographer Twyla Tharp produced her first works.
1966–67	The London School of Contemporary Dance was founded from which entrepreneur Robin Howard and the choreographer Robert Cohan created the London Contemporary Dance Theatre, later to become an internationally renowned company.
1968	Arthur Mitchell, the first black principal dancer to join the New York City Ballet, founded the Dance Theatre of Harlem.
1974	Mikhail Baryshnikov defected from the USSR while dancing with the Kirov Ballet in Toronto, and made his US debut with the American Ballet Theater.
1977	The release of Robert Stigwood's film *Saturday Night Fever* popularized disco dancing worldwide.
1980	Natalia Makarova, who had defected from the USSR 1979, staged the first full-length revival of Petipa's *La Bayadère* in the West with the American Ballet Theater in New York.
1983	Peter Martins, principal dancer with the New York City Ballet, became choreographer and co-director with Jerome Robbins on the death of Balanchine.
1984	The avant-garde group Michael Clark and Company made its debut in London.
1988	Avant-garde choreographer Mark Morris and his company replaced Maurice Béjart's at the Théâtre de la Monnaie, Brussels.
1990	*Maple Leaf Rag*, Martha Graham's final work, was premiered in New York City. Classical dancer Peter Schaufuss became artistic director of the Berlin Ballet.
1991	The Sadler's Wells (Royal Ballet) moved to Birmingham, England, adopting the new name of the Birmingham Royal Ballet. British prima ballerina Dame Margot Fonteyn died in Panama after a long illness.
1993	Russian-born dancer and artistic director Rudolf Nureyev, who had transformed the role of the male dancer in the West, died in Paris.
1995	David Bintley became the artistic director of the Birmingham Royal Ballet. Riverdance, a troupe of 72 dancers performing hard- and soft-shoe traditional Irish dancing, opened to full houses in London.
1996	Matthew Bourne's company Adventures in Motion Pictures reached the West End with a new version of *Swan Lake*, featuring a flock of male cygnets.

Darwin Charles Darwin, the founder of modern evolutionary theory, photographed by Elliott G Fry on the verandah of his home, Down House, Kent, c. 1880. *Image Select (UK) Ltd*

❛We must, however, acknowledge … that man with all his noble qualities … still bears in his bodily frame the indelible stamp of his lowly origin.❜

CHARLES DARWIN
The Descent of Man

The present-day numbering system was designed by Brian Gamlin of Bury, Lancashire, England, in 1896. The world championship was inaugurated in 1978 and is held annually.

Darwin capital and port in Northern Territory, Australia, in NW Arnhem Land; population (1993) 77,900. It serves the uranium mining site at Rum Jungle to the south, and is the northern terminus of the rail line from Birdum. Founded 1869, under the name of Palmerston, the city was renamed after Charles Darwin 1911. During World War II it was an Allied base for action against the Japanese in the Pacific, and suffered repeated bombing – the only Australian town to do so. Destroyed 1974 by a cyclone, the city was rebuilt on the same site.

Darwin Charles Robert 1809–1882. English scientist who developed the modern theory of ◊evolution and proposed, with Alfred Russel ◊Wallace, the principle of ◊natural selection. After research in South America and the Galápagos Islands as naturalist on HMS *Beagle* 1831–36, Darwin published *On the Origin of Species by Means of Natural Selection or the Preservation of Favoured Races in the Struggle for Life* 1859. This explained the evolutionary process through the principles of natural and sexual selection. It aroused bitter controversy because it disagreed with the literal interpretation of the Book of Genesis in the Bible.

The theory of natural selection concerned the variation existing between members of a sexually reproducing population. According to Darwin, those members with variations better fitted to the environment would be more likely to survive and breed, subsequently passing on these favourable characteristics to their offspring.

On the Origin of Species also refuted earlier evolutionary theories, such as those of French naturalist J B de ◊Lamarck. Darwin himself played little part in the debates, but his *Descent of Man* 1871 added fuel to the theological discussion, in which English scientist T H ◊Huxley and German zoologist Ernst ◊Haeckel took leading parts.

Darwin also made important discoveries in many other areas, including the fertilization mechanisms of plants, the classification of barnacles, and the formation of coral reefs.

Darwin Erasmus 1731–1802. British poet, physician, and naturalist; he was the grandfather of Charles Darwin. He wrote *The Botanic Garden* 1792, which included a versification of the Linnaean system entitled *The Loves of the Plants*, and *Zoonomia* 1794–96, which anticipated aspects of evolutionary theory, but tended to French naturalist J B de ◊Lamarck's interpretation.

Darwinism, social in US history, an influential but contentious social theory, based on the work of Charles Darwin and Herbert Spencer, which claimed to offer a scientific justification for late 19th-century *laissez-faire* capitalism (the principle of unrestricted freedom in commerce).

Popularized by academics and by entrepreneurs such as Andrew ◊Carnegie, social Darwinism was used to legitimize competitive individualism and a market economy unregulated by government; it argued that only the strong and resourceful businesses and individuals would thrive in a free environment.

Dasam Granth collection of the writings of the tenth Sikh guru (teacher), Gobind Singh, and of poems by a number of other writers. It is written in a script called Gurmukhi, the written form of Punjabi popularized by Guru Angad. It contains a retelling of the Krishna legends, devotional verse, and amusing anecdotes.

dasyure any ◊marsupial of the family Dasyuridae, also known as a 'native cat', found in Australia and New Guinea. Various species have body lengths from 25 cm/10 in to 75 cm/2.5 ft. Dasyures have long, bushy tails and dark coats with white spots. They are agile, nocturnal carnivores, able to move fast and climb.

data facts, figures, and symbols, especially as stored in computers. The term is often used to mean raw, unprocessed facts, as distinct from information, to which a meaning or interpretation has been applied.

database in computing, a structured collection of data, which may be manipulated to select and sort desired items of information. For example, an accounting system might be built around a database containing details of customers and suppliers. In larger computers, the database makes data available to the various programs that need it, without the need for those programs to be aware of how the data are stored. The term is also sometimes used for simple record-keeping systems, such as mailing lists, in which there are facilities for searching, sorting, and producing records.

There are three main types (or 'models'): hierarchical, network, and relational, of which relational is the most widely used. A free-text database is one that holds the unstructured text of articles or books in a form that permits rapid searching.

A collection of databases is known as a databank. A database-management system (DBMS) program ensures that the integrity of the data is maintained by controlling the degree of access of the ◊applications programs using the data. Databases are normally used by large organizations with mainframes or minicomputers.

data communications sending and receiving data via any communications medium, such as a telephone line. The term usually implies that the data are digital (such as computer data) rather than analogue (such as voice messages). However, in the ISDN (◊Integrated Services Digital Network) system, all data – including voices and video images – are transmitted digitally. See also ◊telecommunications.

data compression in computing, techniques for reducing the amount of storage needed for a given amount of data. They include word tokenization (in which frequently used words are stored as shorter codes), variable bit lengths (in which common characters are represented by fewer ◊bits than less common ones), and run-length encoding (in which a repeated value is stored once along with a count).

data processing (DP) use of computers for performing clerical tasks such as stock control, payroll, and dealing with orders. DP systems are typically batch systems, in which there is little or no operator intervention, and run on mainframe computers. DP is sometimes called EDP (electronic data processing).

Data Protection Act UK Act of Parliament 1984 that gave the right to a copy of personal information held on computer files and to have inaccurate information corrected or erased. Individuals can complain to the Data Protection Registrar if the provisions of the Act have been broken and can claim compensation from the courts if damaged by inaccurate information or by the loss, unauthorized destruction, or disclosure of that information.

data security in computing, precautions taken to prevent the loss or misuse of data, whether accidental or deliberate. These include measures that ensure that only authorized personnel can gain entry to a computer system or file, and regular procedures for storing and backing up data, which enable files to be retrieved or recreated in the event of loss, theft, or damage.

A number of verification and validation techniques may also be used to prevent data from being lost or corrupted by misprocessing.

date palm tree of the genus *Phoenix*. The female tree produces the fruit, dates, in bunches weighing 9–11 kg/20–25 lb. Dates are an important source of food in the Middle East, being rich in sugar; they are dried for export. The tree also supplies timber, and materials for baskets, rope, and animal feed.

The most important species is *P. dactylifera*; native to N Africa, SW Asia, and parts of India, it grows up to 25 m/80 ft high. A single bunch can contain as many as 1,000 dates. Their juice is made into a kind of wine.

dating science of determining the age of geological structures, rocks, and fossils, and placing them in the context of geological time. The techniques are of two types: relative dating and absolute dating. ***Relative dating*** can be carried out by identifying fossils of creatures that lived only at certain times (marker fossils), and by looking at the physical relationships of rocks to other rocks of a known age. ***Absolute dating*** is achieved by measuring how much of a rock's radioactive elements have changed since the rock was formed, using the process of ◊radiometric dating.

datura any of several plants belonging to the genus *Datura*, family Solanaceae, such as the thornapple, with handsome trumpet-shaped blooms. They have narcotic properties.

Daudet (Alphonse Marie) Léon 1867–1942. French writer and journalist. He founded the militant right-wing royalist periodical *Action Française* 1899 after the Dreyfus case. During World War II he was a collaborator with the Germans. He was the son of Alphonse Daudet.

Daudet Alphonse 1840–1897. French novelist. He wrote about his native Provence in *Lettres de mon moulin/Letters from My Mill* 1866, and created the character Tartarin, a hero epitomizing southern temperament, in *Tartarin de Tarascon* 1872 and two sequels. Other works include the play *L'Arlésienne/The Woman from Arles* 1872, for which Georges Bizet composed the music; and *Souvenirs d'un homme de lettres/Recollections of a Literary Man* 1889.

Daumier Honoré Victorin 1808–1879. French artist. His sharply dramatic and satirical cartoons dissected Parisian society. He produced over 4,000 lithographs and, mainly after 1860, powerful,

Daumier *A Criminal Case* c. 1860 by Honoré Daumier, J Paul Getty Museum, Malibu, California, USA. Daumier was a witty social critic. He produced numerous lithographs for the satirical magazines of his day, much of his work focusing on the legal and medical professions in particular. *Royal Academy of Arts*

sardonic oil paintings that were little appreciated in his lifetime.

Daumier drew for *La Caricature*, *Charivari*, and other periodicals. He created several fictitious stereotypes of contemporary figures and was once imprisoned for an attack on King ◊Louis Philippe. His paintings show a fluent technique and a mainly monochrome palette. He also produced sculptures of his caricatures, such as the bronze statuette of *Ratapoil* about 1850 (Louvre, Paris).

dauphin title of the eldest son of the kings of France, derived from the personal name of a count, whose lands, known as the *Dauphiné*, traditionally passed to the heir to the throne from 1349 to 1830.

Dauphiné ancient province of France, comprising the modern *départements* of Isère, Drôme, and Hautes-Alpes.

After the collapse of the Roman Empire it belonged to Burgundy, then was under Frankish domination. Afterwards part of Arles, it was sold by its ruler to France in 1349 and thereafter was used as the personal fief of the heir to the throne (the dauphin) until 1560, when it was absorbed into the French kingdom. The capital was Grenoble.

David c. 1060–c. 970 BC. Second king of Israel. According to the Old Testament he played the harp for King Saul to banish Saul's melancholy; he later slew the Philistine giant Goliath with a sling and stone. After Saul's death David was anointed king at Hebron, took Jerusalem, and made it his capital.

In both Jewish and Christian belief, the messiah would be a descendant of David; Christians hold this prophecy to have been fulfilled by Jesus.

David statue in marble by ◊Michelangelo 1501–04 (Accademia, Florence). The subject of David, biblical boy hero who killed the giant Goliath, was a popular symbol of the small republic of Florence; that Michelangelo portrayed the diminutive hero as a giant was seen as a grand statement of civic confidence. The sculpture's size (about 5.5 m/18 ft) combined with the mastery of its execution has made it a symbol of the Renaissance itself.

David Elizabeth 1914–1992. British cookery writer. Her *Mediterranean Food* 1950 and *French Country Cooking* 1951 helped to spark an interest in foreign cuisine in Britain, and also inspired a growing school of informed, highly literate writing on food and wine.

David Gerard c. 1450–c. 1523. Netherlandish painter. He was active chiefly in Bruges from about 1484. His style follows that of Rogier van der ◊Weyden, but he was also influenced by the taste in Antwerp for Italianate ornament. *The Marriage at Cana* about 1503 (Louvre, Paris) is an example of his work.

David Jacques-Louis 1748–1825. French painter. One of the greatest of the Neo-Classicists, he sought to give his art a direct political significance. He was an active supporter of the republic during the French Revolution, and was imprisoned 1794–95. In his *Death of Marat* 1793 (Musées Royaux, Brussels), he turned political murder into Classical tragedy.

When Napoleon came to power, David became his official painter, creating such imperial images as *Napoleon Crossing the Alps* 1800 (Louvre, Paris) and *Napoleon Distributing the Eagles* 1810 (Versailles). David's major works also include portraits, one of the finest being *Mme Récamier* 1800 (Louvre, Paris).

His style, which was inherited by several of his pupils, most notably ◊Ingres, dominated French painting in the first half of the 19th century.

David I 1084–1153. King of Scotland from 1124. The youngest son of Malcolm III Canmore and St ◊Margaret, he was brought up in the English court of Henry I, and in 1113 married ◊Matilda, widow of the 1st earl of Northampton.

He invaded England 1138 in support of Queen Matilda, but was defeated at Northallerton in the Battle of the Standard, and again 1141.

David II 1324–1371. King of Scotland from 1329, son of ◊Robert (I) the Bruce. David was married at the age of four to Joanna, daughter of Edward II of England. In 1346 David invaded England, was captured at the battle of Neville's Cross, and imprisoned for 11 years. After the defeat of the Scots by Edward III at Halidon Hill 1333, the young David and Joanna were sent to France for safety. They returned 1341. On Joanna's death 1362 David married Margaret Logie, but divorced her 1370.

David, St or ***Dewi*** lived 5th–6th century. Patron saint of Wales, Christian abbot and bishop. According to legend he was the son of a prince of Dyfed and uncle of King Arthur; he was responsible for the adoption of the leek as the national emblem of Wales, but his own emblem is a dove. His feast day is 1 March.

Davies Peter Maxwell 1934– . English composer and conductor. His music combines medieval and serial codes of practice with a heightened Expressionism as in his opera *Taverner* 1962–68. Other works include the opera *The Lighthouse* 1980. He was appointed conductor of the BBC Scottish Symphony Orchestra 1985.

da Vinci see ◊Leonardo da Vinci, Italian Renaissance artist.

Davis Angela Yvonne 1944– . US left-wing activist for black rights, prominent in the student movement of the 1960s. In 1970 she went into hiding after being accused of supplying guns used in the murder of a judge who had been seized as a hostage in an attempt to secure the release of three black convicts. She was captured, tried, and acquitted. At the University of California she studied under Herbert ◊Marcuse, and was assistant professor of philosophy at UCLA 1969–70.

Davis Bette, assumed name of Ruth Elizabeth Davis 1908–1989. US actress. She entered films 1930, and established a reputation as a forceful dramatic actress with *Of Human Bondage* 1934. Later films included *Dangerous* 1935 and *Jezebel* 1938 (both won her Academy Awards); *All About Eve* 1950; and *Whatever Happened to Baby Jane?* 1962. She continued to make films throughout the 1980s such as *The Whales of August* 1987, in which she co-starred with Lillian Gish.

Davis Joe (Joseph) 1901–1978. British billiards and snooker player. He was world snooker champion a record 15 times 1927–46 and responsible for much of the popularity of the game. His brother Fred (1913–) was also a billiards and snooker world champion.

Davis John c. 1550–1605. English navigator and explorer. He sailed in search of the Northwest Passage through the Canadian Arctic to the Pacific Ocean 1585, and in 1587 sailed to Baffin Bay through the straits named after him. He was the first European to see the Falkland Islands 1592.

Davis Miles Dewey, Jr 1926–1991. US jazz trumpeter, composer, and bandleader. He was one of the most influential and innovative figures in jazz. He pioneered bebop with Charlie Parker 1945, cool jazz in the 1950s, and jazz-rock fusion from the late 1960s. His albums include *Birth of the Cool* 1957 (recorded 1949 and 1950), *Sketches of Spain* 1959, *Bitches Brew* 1970, and *Tutu* 1985.

Davis, born in Illinois, joined Charlie Parker's group 1946–48. In 1948 he began an association with composer and arranger Gil Evans (1912–1988) that was to last throughout his career. His quintet in 1955 featured the saxophone player John Coltrane, who recorded with Davis until 1961. In 1968 Davis introduced electric instruments, later adding electronic devices to his trumpet and more percussion to his band. He went on to use disco backings, and recorded pop songs and collaborated with rock musicians, remaining changeable to the end.

Davis Sammy, Jr 1925–1990. US entertainer. His starring role in the Broadway show *Mr Wonderful* 1956, his television work, and his roles in films with Frank Sinatra – among them, *Ocean's Eleven* 1960 and *Robin and the Seven Hoods* 1964 – made him a celebrity. He also appeared in the film version of the opera *Porgy and Bess* 1959. He published two memoirs, *Yes I Can* 1965 and *Why Me?* 1989.

Davis Steve 1957– . English snooker player who has won every major honour in the game since turning professional 1978. He has been world champion six times; he won his first major title 1980 when he won the Coral UK Championship. He has also won world titles at Pairs and with the England team.

Davis Stuart 1894–1964. US abstract painter. Much of his work shows the influence of both jazz tempos and Cubism in its use of hard-edged geometric shapes in primary colours and ◊collage. In the 1920s he produced paintings of commercial packaging, such as *Lucky Strike* 1921 (Museum of Modern Art, New York), that foreshadowed Pop art.

Davis Cup annual lawn tennis tournament for men's international teams, first held 1900 after Dwight Filley Davis (1879–1945) donated the trophy. The Davis Cup was held on a challenge basis up to 1971. Since then it has been organized on an elimination basis, with countries divided into zonal groups, with a promotion and relegation system. *See list of tables on p. 1177.*

Davison Emily Wilding 1872–1913. English militant suffragette. She joined the Women's Social and Political Union in 1906 and served several prison sentences for militant action such as stone throwing, setting fire to pillar boxes, and bombing Lloyd George's country house. She was trampled to death after throwing herself under the king's horse at the Derby at Epsom.

Davitt Michael 1846–1906. Irish nationalist. He joined the Fenians (forerunners of the Irish Republican Army) 1865, and was imprisoned for treason 1870–77. After his release, he and the politician Charles Parnell founded the ◊Land League 1879. Davitt was jailed several times for land-reform agitation. He was a member of Parliament 1895–99, advocating the reconciliation of extreme and constitutional nationalism.

Davy Humphry 1778–1829. English chemist. He discovered, by electrolysis, the metallic elements sodium and potassium in 1807, and calcium, boron, magnesium, strontium, and barium in 1808. In addition, he established that chlorine is an element and proposed that hydrogen is present in all acids. He invented the safety lamp for use in mines where methane was present, enabling miners to work in previously unsafe conditions.

Dawes Charles Gates 1865–1951. US Republican politician. In 1923 he was appointed by the Allied Reparations Commission president of the committee that produced the Dawes Plan, a $200 million loan that enabled Germany to pay enormous war debts after World War I. It reduced tensions temporarily in Europe but was superseded by the Young Plan (which reduced the total reparations bill) 1929. Dawes was made US vice president (under Calvin Coolidge) 1924, received the Nobel peace prize 1925, and was ambassador to Britain 1929–32.

Dawkins (Clinton) Richard 1941– . British zoologist whose book *The Selfish Gene* 1976 popularized the theories of sociobiology (social behaviour in humans and animals in the context of evolution). In *The Blind Watchmaker* 1986 he explained the modern theory of evolution. In 1995 he took the post of reader in the public understanding of science at Oxford.

day time taken for the Earth to rotate once on its axis. The ***solar day*** is the time that the Earth takes to rotate once relative to the Sun. It is divided into 24 hours, and is the basis of our civil day. The ***sidereal day*** is the time that the Earth takes to rotate once relative to the stars. It is 3 minutes 56 seconds

Davy Engraving of the English chemist Humphry Davy. A brilliant and successful chemist, Davy's many achievements include the discovery of seven previously unknown elements, and the invention of a safe miner's lamp. *Topham*

Day-Lewis English film actor Daniel Day-Lewis. A versatile performer, he is noted for his intelligent and sympathetic characterization, often of displaced figures. *Topham*

shorter than the solar day, because the Sun's position against the background of stars as seen from Earth changes as the Earth orbits it.

Day Doris. Stage name of Doris von Kappelhoff 1924– . US film actress and singing star of the 1950s and early 1960s. She appeared in musicals and, often with Rock Hudson, coy sex comedies. Her films include *Tea for Two* 1950, *Calamity Jane* 1953, *Love Me or Leave Me* 1955, and Alfred Hitchcock's *The Man Who Knew Too Much* 1956. In *Pillow Talk* 1959, *Lover Come Back* 1962, and other 1960s light sex comedies, she played a self-confident but coy woman who caused some of the biggest male stars to capitulate.

Dayan Moshe 1915–1981. Israeli general and politician. As minister of defence 1967 and 1969–74, he was largely responsible for the victory over neighbouring Arab states in the 1967 Six-Day War, but he was criticized for Israel's alleged unpreparedness in the 1973 October War and resigned along with Prime Minister Golda Meir. Foreign minister from 1977, Dayan resigned 1979 in protest over the refusal of the Begin government to negotiate with the Palestinians.

Day-Lewis Cecil 1904–1972. Irish poet who wrote under the name ***C Day Lewis***. With W H Auden and Stephen Spender, he was one of the influential left-wing poets of the 1930s. His later poetry moved from political concerns to a more traditional personal lyricism. He also wrote detective novels under the pseudonym ***Nicholas Blake***. He was British poet laureate 1968–1972.

His poetry, which includes *From Feathers to Iron* 1931 and *Overtures to Death* 1938, is marked by accomplished lyrics and sustained narrative power. *The Complete Poems* was published 1992.

Day-Lewis Daniel 1958– . English actor, noted for his chameleon-like versatility. He first came to prominence in *My Beautiful Laundrette* and *A Room With a View* both 1985. His other films include *My Left Foot* 1989 (for which he won an Academy Award), *The Last of the Mohicans* 1992, *The Age of Innocence*, *In the Name of the Father* (both 1993), and *The Crucible* 1996.

Dayton city in Ohio, USA; population (1992) 183,200. It produces precision machinery, household appliances, and electrical equipment. It has an aeronautical research centre and was the home of aviators Wilbur and Orville Wright.

Dazai Osamu. Pen name of Shuji Tsushima 1909–1948. Japanese novelist. The title of his novel *The Setting Sun* 1947 became identified in Japan with the dead of World War II.

dBASE family of microcomputer programs used for manipulating large quantities of data; also, a related fourth-generation language (a language designed for the rapid programming of applications). The first version, dBASE II, appeared in 1981; it has since become the basis for a recognized standard for database applications, known as Xbase.

DBE abbreviation for ***Dame Commander of the Order of the British Empire***.

D-day 6 June 1944, the day of the Allied invasion of Normandy under the command of General Eisenhower to commence Operation Overlord, the liberation of Western Europe from German occupation. The Anglo-US invasion fleet landed on the Normandy beaches on the stretch of coast between the Orne River and St Marcouf. Artificial harbours known as 'Mulberries' were constructed and towed across the Channel so that equipment and armaments could be unloaded on to the beaches. After overcoming fierce resistance the allies broke through the German defences; Paris was liberated on 25 Aug, and Brussels on 2 Sept. D-day is also military jargon for any day on which a crucial operation is planned. D+1 indicates the day after the start of the operation.

DDT abbreviation for ***dichloro-diphenyl-trichloroethane*** $(ClC_6H_5)_2CHC(HCl_2)$ insecticide discovered 1939 by Swiss chemist Paul Müller. It is useful in the control of insects that spread malaria, but resistant strains develop. DDT is highly toxic and persists in the environment and in living tissue. Its use is now banned in most countries, but it continues to be used on food plants in Latin America. ▷ *See feature on pp. 858–859.*

deacon in the Roman Catholic and Anglican churches, an ordained minister who ranks immediately below a priest. In the Protestant churches, a deacon is in training to become a minister or is a lay assistant.

The lay order of women deaconesses was revived 1962 (legally recognized 1968); in England they may not administer the sacraments, but may conduct public worship and preach. In 1985 the General Synod voted to allow ordination of women as deacons, enabling them to perform marriages and baptisms, but not to take communion or give absolution and the blessing. Deacons become priests after a year.

D-day US soldiers landing on the Normandy coast on D-day, 6 June 1944, the beginning of the Allied invasion of Europe. It was one of the largest and most complex movements of men and equipment in history. Over 5,000 ships were used, transporting 90,000 British, US, and Canadian troops (a further 20,000 were taken by air). *Library of Congress*

deadly nightshade another name for ◊belladonna, a poisonous plant.

Dead Sea large lake, partly in Israel and partly in Jordan, lying 394 m/1,293 ft below sea level; it is the lowest surface point on Earth; area 1,020 sq km/394 sq mi. The chief river entering it is the Jordan; it has no outlet and the water is very salty.

Since both Israel and Jordan use the waters of the Jordan River, the Dead Sea has now dried up in the centre and is divided into two halves. The Dead Sea Rift is part of the fault between the African and Arab plates.

Dead Sea

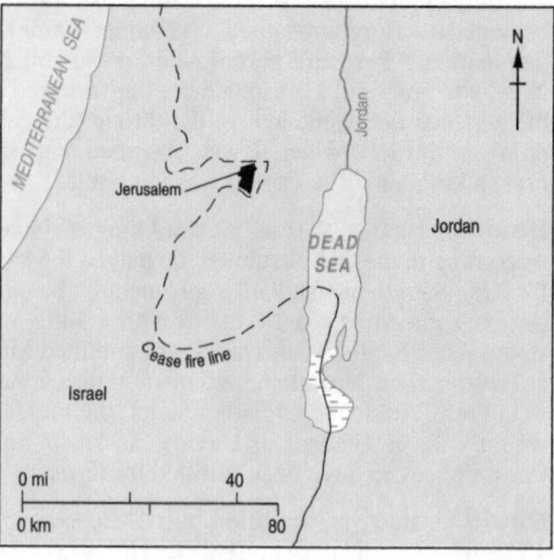

Dead Sea Scrolls collection of ancient scrolls (rolls of writing) and fragments of scrolls found 1947–56 in caves on the W side of the Jordan, at ◊Qumran. They include copies of Old Testament books a thousand years older than those previously known to be extant. The documents date mainly from about 150 BC–AD 68, when the monastic community that owned them, the Essenes, was destroyed by the Romans because of its support for a revolt against their rule.

The total of 800 manuscripts, containing all the books of the Old Testament except Esther, were publicly available for the first time 1986. Before this, only half the scrolls were published and only 15 scholars had access to them. They were made available for inspection on the Internet 1996, one of the first times ancient material was made available in this way.

deafness partial or total deficit of hearing in either ear. Of assistance are hearing aids, lip-reading, a cochlear implant in the ear in combination with a special electronic processor, sign language, and 'cued speech' (manual clarification of ambiguous lip movement during speech).

Conductive deafness is due to faulty conduction of sound inwards from the external ear, usually due to infection (see ◊otitis), or a hereditary abnormality of the bones of the inner ear (see ◊otosclerosis). ***Perceptive deafness*** may be inborn or caused by injury or disease of the cochlea, auditory nerve, or the hearing centres in the brain. It becomes more common with age.

Deakin Alfred 1856–1919. Australian politician, prime minister 1903–04, 1905–08, and 1909–10. In his second administration, he enacted legislation on defence and pensions.

dean in education, in universities and medical schools, the head of administration; in the colleges of Oxford and Cambridge, UK, the member of the teaching staff charged with the maintenance of discipline; in Roman Catholicism, senior cardinal bishop, head of the college of cardinals; in the Anglican Communion, head of the chapter of a cathedral or collegiate church (a rural dean presides over a division of an archdeaconry).

Dean James Byron 1931–1955. US actor. Killed in a car accident soon after the public showing of his first film, *East of Eden* 1955, he posthumously became a cult hero with *Rebel Without a Cause* 1955 and *Giant* 1956. His image has endured as the classic icon of teenage rebellion throughout the decades since his death.

Dearborn city in Michigan, USA, on the Rouge River 16 km/10 mi SW of Detroit; population

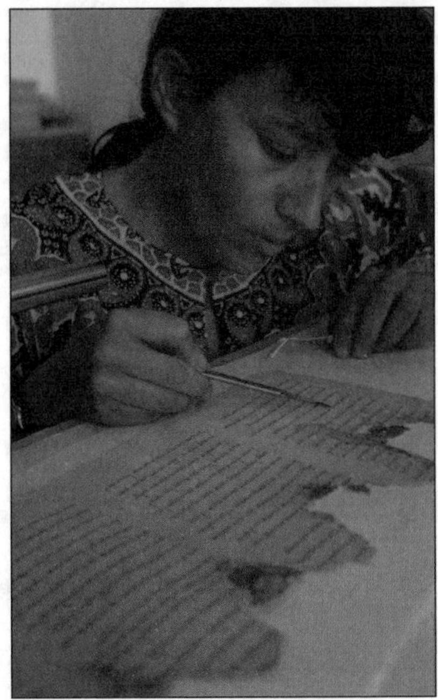

Dead Sea Scrolls An archaeologist at work restoring fragments of the Dead Sea Scrolls. The Hebrew and Aramaic manuscript scrolls were found in caves in the area of Khirbat Qumran, northwest of the Dead Sea. They are thought to be part of the library of an Essene monastic community which was destroyed by the Romans. *Corbis*

(1992) 88,300. Settled 1795, it was the birthplace and home of Henry ◊Ford, who built his first car factory here. Car manufacturing is still the main industry. Dearborn also makes aircraft parts, steel, and bricks.

death cessation of all life functions, so that the molecules and structures associated with living things become disorganized and indistinguishable from similar molecules found in nonliving things. In medicine, a person is pronounced dead when the brain ceases to control the vital functions, even if breathing and heartbeat are maintained artificially.

Death used to be pronounced with the permanent cessation of heartbeat, but the advent of life-support equipment has made this point sometimes difficult to determine. For removal of vital organs in transplant surgery, the World Health Organization in 1968 set out that a potential donor should exhibit no brain–body connection, muscular activity, blood pressure, or ability to breathe spontaneously.

In religious belief, death may be seen as the prelude to rebirth (as in Hinduism and Buddhism); under Islam and Christianity, there is the concept of a day of judgement and consignment to heaven or hell; Judaism concentrates not on an afterlife but on survival through descendants who honour tradition.

death cap fungus ◊*Amanita phalloides*, the most poisonous mushroom known. The fruiting body has a scaly white cap and a collarlike structure near the base of the stalk.

death penalty another name for ◊capital punishment.

Death Valley depression 225 km/140 mi long and 6–26 km/4–16 mi wide in SE California, USA. At 85 m/280 ft below sea level, it is the lowest point in North America. Bordering mountains rise to 3,000 m/10,000 ft. It is one of the world's hottest and driest places, with temperatures sometimes exceeding 51.7°C/125°F and an annual rainfall of less than 5 cm/2 in. Borax, iron ore, tungsten, gypsum, and salts are extracted.

deathwatch beetle any wood-boring beetle of the family Anobiidae, especially *Xestobium rufovillosum*. The larvae live in oaks and willows, and sometimes cause damage by boring in old furniture or structural timbers. To attract the female, the male beetle produces a ticking sound by striking his head on a wooden surface, and this is taken by the superstitious as a warning of approaching death.

de Bono Edward Francis Charles Publius 1933– . Maltese-born British medical doctor and psychologist whose concept of lateral thinking, first expounded in *The Use of Lateral Thinking* 1967, involves thinking round a problem rather than tackling it head on.

Deborah in the Old Testament, a prophet and judge (leader). She helped lead an Israelite army against the Canaanite general Sisera, who was killed trying to flee; her song of triumph at his death is regarded as an excellent example of early Hebrew poetry.

Debray Régis 1941– . French Marxist theorist. He was associated with Che ◊Guevara in the revolutionary movement in Latin America in the 1960s. In 1967 he was sentenced to 30 years' imprisonment in Bolivia but was released after three years. His writings on Latin American politics include *Strategy for Revolution* 1970. He became a specialist adviser to President Mitterrand of France on Latin American affairs.

Debrecen second largest city in Hungary, 193 km/120 mi E of Budapest, in the Great Plain (*Alföld*) region; population (1995) 211,000. It is a commercial centre and it produces tobacco, agricultural machinery, and pharmaceuticals. Lajos ◊Kossuth declared Hungary independent of the ◊Habsburgs here 1849.

Debrett's Peerage directory of the British peerage, first published in 1802 by John Debrett (1753–1822) under the title *Peerage of England, Scotland and Ireland*, but based on earlier compilations. Debrett aimed to avoid spurious genealogies and confine himself to authenticated facts.

de Broglie Maurice and Louis. French physicists; see ◊Broglie.

Debs Eugene V(ictor) 1855–1926. US labour leader and socialist who organized the Social Democratic Party 1897. He was the founder and first president of the American Railway Union 1893, and was imprisoned for six months in 1894 for defying a federal injunction to end the Pullman strike in Chicago. He was socialist candidate for the presidency in every election from 1900 to 1920, except that of 1916. In 1920 he polled nearly 1 million votes, the highest socialist vote ever in US presidential elections, despite having to conduct the campaign from a federal penitentiary in Atlanta, Georgia.

debt something that is owed by a person, organization, or country, usually money, goods, or services. Debt usually occurs as a result of borrowing ◊credit. Debt servicing is the payment of interest on a debt. The national debt of a country is the total money owed by the national government to private individuals, banks, and so on; international debt, the money owed by one country to another, began on a large scale with the investment in foreign countries by newly industrialized countries in the late 19th to early 20th centuries. International debt became a global problem as a result of the oil crisis of the 1970s.

debt crisis any situation in which an individual, company, or country owes more to others than it can repay or pay interest on; more specifically, the massive indebtedness of many developing countries that became acute in the 1980s, threatening the stability of the international banking system as many debtor countries became unable to service their debts.

debt-for-nature swap agreement under which a proportion of a country's debts are written off in exchange for a commitment by the debtor country to undertake projects for environmental protection. Debt-for-nature swaps were set up by environment groups in the 1980s in an attempt to reduce the debt problem of poor countries, while simultaneously promoting conservation. Most debt-for-nature swaps have concentrated on setting aside areas of land, especially tropical rainforest, for protection and have involved private conservation foundations. ◊*See feature on pp. 896–897.*

debugging finding and removing errors, or ◊bugs, from a computer program or system.

Debussy (Achille-) Claude 1862–1918. French composer. He broke with German Romanticism and introduced new qualities of melody and harmony based on the whole-tone scale, evoking oriental music. His work includes *Prélude à l'après-midi d'un faune/Prelude to the Afternoon of a Faun* 1894, illustrating a poem by Mallarmé, and the opera *Pelléas et Mélisande* 1902.

Among his other works are numerous piano pieces, songs, orchestral pieces such as *La Mer* 1903–05, and the ballet *Jeux* 1910–13. Debussy also published witty and humorous critical writing about the music of his day, featuring the fictional character Monsieur Croche 'antidilettante' (professional debunker), a figure based on Erik ◊Satie. *See illustration on following page.*

Deby Idriss. Chadian soldier and politician, president from 1990. As founder and leader of the Patriotic Salvation Movement (MPS), Deby seized power in an armed coup, ousting President Habré and making himself interim head of state. His presidency was constitutionally endorsed when he won Chad's first democratic presidential election 1996.

decadence in literary and artistic criticism, the decline that follows a time of great cultural achievement. It is typified by world-weariness, self-consciousness, and the search for new stimulation through artistic refinement and degenerate behaviour. The term is used especially in connection with

'I said then, I say now, that while there is a lower class, I am in it; while there is a criminal element, I am of it; while there is a soul in prison, I am not free.'

EUGENE DEBS
Speech at his trial 14 Sept 1918

'Art is the most beautiful of all lies.'

CLAUDE DEBUSSY
Monsieur Croche, antidilettante

Death Valley Death Valley, California, USA, was named by gold seekers, large numbers of whom perished there in the 1840s on their way to California. Though salt and alkali flats and briny pools abound in this arid region, rare desert plants and small animals have made this harsh environment their habitat. *David Pratt*

Debussy The composer Claude Debussy pictured with his first wife, Rosalie Texier. During the years they spent together (1899–1904) *Pelléas et Mélisande* 1902 was produced and Debussy consolidated his reputation as the leading impressionist composer. Following their separation his technique evolved in works such as *La Mer* 1903–05 and *Images* 1906–12. *Image Select (UK) Ltd*

the *fin-de-siècle* styles of the late 19th century (Symbolism, the Aesthetic Movement, and Art Nouveau). It has been applied to such artists and writers as Arthur Rimbaud, Oscar Wilde, and Aubrey Beardsley.

Decalogue ten commandments that, according to the Old Testament, were delivered by God to ◊Moses on Mount Sinai, stated in the books Exodus 20:1–17 and Deuteronomy 5:6–21. The Decalogue is recognized as the basis of morality by Jews and Christians.

Decameron, The collection of tales by the Italian writer Giovanni Boccaccio, brought together 1348–53. Ten young people, fleeing plague-stricken Florence, amuse their fellow travellers by each telling a story on the ten days they spend together. The work had a great influence on English literature, particularly on Chaucer's *Canterbury Tales*.

decathlon two-day athletic competition for men consisting of ten events: 100 metres, long jump, shot put, high jump, 400 metres (day one); 110 metres hurdles, discus, pole vault, javelin, 1,500 metres (day two). Points are awarded for performances, and the winner is the athlete with the greatest aggregate score. The decathlon is an Olympic event.

decay, radioactive see ◊radioactive decay.

decibel unit (symbol dB) of measure used originally to compare sound intensities and subsequently electrical or electronic power outputs; now also used to compare voltages. An increase of 10 dB is equivalent to a 10-fold increase in intensity or power, and a 20-fold increase in voltage. A whisper has an intensity of 20 dB; 140 dB (a jet aircraft taking off nearby) is the threshold of pain. *See list of tables on p. 1177.*

deciduous of trees and shrubs, that shed their leaves at the end of the growing season or during a dry season to reduce ◊transpiration (the loss of water by evaporation).

Most deciduous trees belong to the ◊angiosperms, plants in which the seeds are enclosed within an ovary, and the term 'deciduous tree' is sometimes used to mean 'angiosperm tree', despite the fact that many angiosperms are evergreen, especially in the tropics, and a few ◊gymnosperms, plants in which the seeds are exposed, are deciduous (for example, larches). The term 'broad-leaved' is now preferred to 'deciduous' for this reason. Examples of deciduous trees are oak and beech.

'We must indeed all hang together, or, most assuredly, we shall all hang separately.'

Declaration of Independence
Benjamin Franklin's remark at signing of the Declaration of Independence 4 July 1776

decimal fraction a ◊fraction in which the denominator is any higher power of 10. Thus $^{3}/_{10}$, $^{51}/_{100}$, and $^{23}/_{1,000}$ are decimal fractions and are normally expressed as 0.3, 0.51, 0.023. The use of decimals greatly simplifies addition and multiplication of fractions, though not all fractions can be expressed exactly as decimal fractions.

decimal number system or ***denary number system*** the most commonly used number system, to the base ten. Decimal numbers do not necessarily contain a decimal point; 563, 5.63, and −563 are all decimal numbers. Other systems are mainly used in computing and include the ◊binary number system, ◊octal number system, and ◊hexadecimal number system. Large decimal numbers may also be expressed in floating-point notation. *See list of tables on p. 1177.*

Declaration of Independence historic US document stating the theory of government on which the USA was founded, based on the right 'to life, liberty, and the pursuit of happiness'. The statement was issued by the ◊Continental Congress 4 July 1776, renouncing all allegiance to the British crown and ending the political connection with Britain.

Following a resolution moved 7 June, by Richard Henry Lee, 'that these United Colonies are, and of right ought to be, free and independent States', a committee including Thomas ◊Jefferson and Benjamin ◊Franklin was set up to draft a declaration; most of the work was done by Jefferson.

The resolution, coming almost a year after the outbreak of hostilities, was adopted by the representatives of 12 colonies (New York abstained initially) on 2 July, and the Declaration on 4 July; the latter date has ever since been celebrated as Independence Day in the USA. The representatives of New York announced their adhesion 15 July, and the Declaration was afterwards signed by the members of Congress 2 Aug.

The declaration enumerated the grievances the colonists harboured against the British crown, which included its use of Indians to attack colonists, taxation without representation, and denial of civil liberties. ▷ *See feature on pp. 32–33.*

Declaration of Rights in Britain, the statement issued by the Convention Parliament Feb 1689, laying down the conditions under which the crown was to be offered to ◊William III and Mary. Its clauses were later incorporated in the ◊Bill of Rights.

declination in astronomy, the coordinate on the ◊celestial sphere (imaginary sphere surrounding the Earth) that corresponds to latitude on the Earth's surface. Declination runs from 0° at the celestial equator to 90° at the north and south celestial poles.

decolonization gradual achievement of independence by former colonies of the European imperial powers, which began after World War I. The process of decolonization accelerated after World War II with 43 states achieving independence 1956–60, 51 1961–80 and 23 from 1981. The movement affected every continent: India and Pakistan gained independence from Britain 1947; Algeria gained independence from France 1962, the 'Soviet empire' broke up between 1989–91.

decomposer in biology, any organism that breaks down dead matter. Decomposers play a vital role in the ◊ecosystem by freeing important chemical substances, such as nitrogen compounds, locked up in dead organisms or excrement. They feed on some of the released organic matter, but leave the rest to filter back into the soil as dissolved nutrients, or pass in gas form into the atmosphere, for example as nitrogen and carbon dioxide.

The principal decomposers are bacteria and fungi, but earthworms and many other invertebrates are often included in this group. The ◊nitrogen cycle relies on the actions of decomposers.

decomposition process whereby a chemical compound is reduced to its component substances. In biology, it is the destruction of dead organisms either by chemical reduction or by the action of decomposers, such as bacteria and fungi.

decompression sickness illness brought about by a sudden and substantial change in atmospheric pressure. It is caused by a too rapid release of nitrogen that has been dissolved into the bloodstream under pressure; when the nitrogen bubbles it causes the ◊bends. The condition causes breathing difficulties, joint and muscle pain, and cramps, and is experienced mostly by deep-sea divers who surface too quickly.

deconstruction in literary theory, a radical form of ◊structuralism, pioneered by the French philosopher Jacques Derrida (1930–), which views text as a 'decentred' play of structures, lacking any ultimately determinable meaning.

Through analysis of the internal structure of a text, particularly its contradictions, deconstructionists demonstrate the existence of subtext meanings – often not those that the author intended – and hence illustrate the impossibility of attributing fixed meaning to a work. The French critic Roland ◊Barthes originated deconstruction in his book *Mythologies* 1957 in which he studied the inherent instability between sign and referent in a range of cultural phenomena, including not only literary works but also advertising, cookery, wrestling, and so on.

Deconstructionism in architecture, a style that fragments forms and space by taking the usual building elements of floors, walls, and ceilings and sliding them apart to create a sense of disorientation and movement. Essentially Modernist, it draws inspiration from the optimism of the Soviet avant-garde of the 1920s. Its proponents include Zaha Hadid in the UK, Frank Gehry and Peter Eisenman in the USA, and Coop Himmelbau in Austria.

Decorated in architecture, the second period of English Gothic, covering the latter part of the 13th century and the 14th century. Chief characteristics include ornate window tracery, the window being divided into several lights by vertical bars called mullions; sharp spires ornamented with crockets and pinnacles; complex church vaulting; and slender arcade piers.

The reconstruction of Exeter Cathedral (begun about 1270) is a notable example.

decree nisi conditional order of divorce. A ***decree absolute*** is normally granted six weeks after the decree nisi, and from the date of the decree absolute the parties cease to be husband and wife.

decretum collection of papal decrees. The best known is that collected by Gratian (died 1159) about 1140, comprising some 4,000 items. The decretum was used as an authoritative source of canon law (the rules and regulations of the church).

dedicated computer computer built into another device for the purpose of controlling or supplying information to it. Its use has increased dramatically since the advent of the ◊microprocessor: washing machines, digital watches, cars, and video recorders all now have their own processors. A dedicated system is a general-purpose computer system confined to performing only one function for reasons of efficiency or convenience. A word processor is an example.

deduction in philosophy, a form of argument in which the conclusion necessarily follows from the premises. It would be inconsistent ◊logic to accept the premises but deny the conclusion.

Dee river in Grampian Region, Scotland; length 139 km/87 mi. From its source in the Cairngorm

Mountains, it flows E into the North Sea at Aberdeen (by an artificial channel). It has salmon fishing.

There is also a river Dee in Wales and England; length 112 km/70 mi. Rising in Bala Lake, Gwynedd, it flows into the Irish Sea W of Chester. There is another Scottish river Dee (61 km/38 mi) in Kirkcudbright.

Dee John 1527–1608. English alchemist, astrologer, and mathematician who claimed to have transmuted metals into gold, although he died in poverty. He long enjoyed the favour of Elizabeth I, and was employed as a secret diplomatic agent.

deed legal document that passes an interest in property or binds a person to perform or abstain from some action. Deeds are of two kinds: indenture and deed poll. Indentures bind two or more parties in mutual obligations. A deed poll is made by one party only, such as when a person changes his or her name.

Deep Blue name given to the IBM chess-playing computer that first defeated a human grandmaster, the Russian Garry Kasparov, in 1996. This was the first match of a six-match series that Kasparov went on to win 4–2, but in 1997 Deep Blue won a rematch series 3.5–2.5, fuelling debate about the possibilities of artificial intelligence. The architect and principal designer of Deep Blue is Feng-Hsiung Hsu, who joined IBM in 1989.

deep freezing method of preserving food by lowering its temperature to −18°/0°F or below; see ◊food technology. It stops almost all spoilage processes, although there may be some residual enzyme activity in uncooked vegetables, which is why these are blanched (dipped in hot water to destroy the enzymes) before freezing. Microorganisms cannot grow or divide while frozen, but most remain alive and can resume activity once defrosted.

Deep Space I spacecraft launched Nov 1998 on a voyage to the distant asteroid 1992 KD. It is powered by an ion engine and is the first spacecraft to steer itself across the Solar System using a remote agent and autonomous navigation.

deer any of various ruminant, even-toed, hoofed mammals belonging to the family Cervidae. The male typically has a pair of antlers, shed and regrown each year. Most species of deer are forest-dwellers and are distributed throughout Eurasia and North America, but are absent from Australia and Africa S of the Sahara.

Native to Britain are red deer *Cervus elaphus* and roe deer *Capreolus capreolus*. Red deer are found across Europe and can be 1.2 m/4 ft or more at the shoulder, plain dark brown with yellowish rump, and may have many points to the antlers. The roe deer is smaller, only about 75 cm/2.5 ft at the shoulder, with small erect antlers with three points or fewer. Other species in the deer family include the ◊elk, ◊wapiti, ◊reindeer, and the ◊musk deer of central and NE Asia, the males of which yield musk and have no antlers.

deer Deer comprise a family of browsing and grazing mammals in which the males bear simple or complex antlers that are shed each year. Deer have four-toed feet. The Chinese water deer is the only true deer that does not have antlers but the male has enlarged upper canine teeth that grow as tusks.

Defender of the Faith one of the titles of the English sovereign, conferred on Henry VIII 1521 by Pope Leo X in recognition of the king's treatise against the Protestant Martin Luther. It appears on coins in the abbreviated form *F.D.* (Latin *Fidei Defensor*).

defibrillation use of electrical stimulation to restore a chaotic heartbeat to a rhythmical pattern. In fibrillation, which may occur in most kinds of heart disease, the heart muscle contracts irregularly; the heart is no longer working as an efficient pump. Paddles are applied to the chest wall, and one or more electric shocks are delivered to normalize the beat.

deflation in economics, a reduction in the level of economic activity, usually caused by an increase in interest rates and reduction in the money supply, increased taxation, or a decline in government expenditure. Deflation may be chosen as an economic policy to improve the balance of payments, by reducing demand and therefore cutting imports, and lowering inflation to stimulate exports. It can reduce wage increases but may also increase unemployment.

Defoe Daniel 1660–1731. English writer. His *Robinson Crusoe* 1719, though purporting to be a factual account of shipwreck and solitary survival, was influential in the development of the novel. The fictional *Moll Flanders* 1722 and the partly factual *A Journal of the Plague Year* 1722 are still read for their concrete realism. A prolific journalist and pamphleteer, he was imprisoned 1703 for the ironic *The Shortest Way with Dissenters* 1702.

Defoe was born in London and educated for the Nonconformist ministry, but became a hosier. He took part in ◊Monmouth's rebellion 1685, and joined William of Orange 1688. He wrote numerous pamphlets and the satirical poem *The True-Born Englishman* 1701. Serving five months in Newgate prison for *The Shortest Way with Dissenters*, he wrote his *Hymn to the Pillory* 1703 and made plans for a political periodical, which was published as the *Review* 1704–13. He travelled in Scotland 1706–07, working to promote the Union, and published *A History of the Union of Great Britain* 1709. During the next ten years he was almost constantly employed as a political controversialist and pamphleteer. *Robinson Crusoe*, based on the adventure of Alexander Selkirk (1676–1721), was followed by, among others, the pirate story *Captain Singleton* 1720 and the picaresque *Colonel Jack* 1722 and *Roxana* 1724. Since Defoe's death, an increasing number of works have been attributed to him, bringing the total to more than 560.

Defoe English writer Daniel Defoe, sometimes described as the first true novelist. A prolific journalist and pamphleteer, he travelled throughout Europe before settling as a hosiery merchant in London. His life was colourful; he was pilloried and imprisoned for his pamphlet *The Shortest Way with Dissenters* 1702, bankrupted three times, and spent 11 years as a secret agent for Tory politicians. His *Tour through the Whole Island of Great Britain* 1724–6 is a guide book and an account of the state of the country gained on his many travels. *Corbis*

> *One day, about noon, going towards my boat, I was exceedingly surprised with the print of a man's naked foot on the shore.*
>
> DANIEL DEFOE
> *Robinson Crusoe*

deforestation destruction of forest for timber, fuel, charcoal burning, and clearing for agriculture and extractive industries, such as mining, without planting new trees to replace those lost (reafforestation) or working on a cycle that allows the natural forest to regenerate. Deforestation causes fertile soil to be blown away or washed into rivers, leading to ◊soil erosion, drought, flooding, and loss of wildlife. It may also increase the carbon dioxide content of the atmosphere and intensify the ◊greenhouse effect, because there are fewer trees absorbing carbon dioxide from the air for photosynthesis.

Deforestation causes great damage to the habitats of plants and animals. It ultimately leads to famine, and is thought to be partially responsible for the flooding of lowland areas – for example, in Bangladesh – where there are no trees to help slow down water movement. ▷ *See feature on pp. 896–897.*

deforestation An area of Brazilian rainforest being cleared for agriculture. Such deforestation causes soil erosion, flooding, and loss of wildlife, and contributes to the greenhouse effect. *Image Select (UK) Ltd*

Degas (Hilaire Germain) Edgar 1834–1917. French Impressionist painter and sculptor. He devoted himself to lively, informal studies (often using pastels) of ballet, horse racing, and young women working. From the 1890s he turned increasingly to sculpture, modelling figures in wax in a fluent, naturalistic style.

Degas studied under a pupil of ◊Ingres and worked in Italy in the 1850s, painting Classical themes. In 1861 he met ◊Manet, and exhibited regularly with the Impressionists 1874–86. His characteristic style soon emerged, showing the influence of Japanese prints and photography in inventive compositions and unusual viewpoints, as in *Woman with Chrysanthemums* 1865 (Metropolitan Museum of Art, New York). An example of his sculpture is *The Little Dancer* 1881 (Tate Gallery, London).

de Gaulle Charles André Joseph Marie 1890–1970. French general and first president of the Fifth Republic 1958–69. He organized the ◊Free French troops fighting the Nazis 1940–44, was head of the provisional French government 1944–46, and leader of his own Gaullist party. In 1958 the national assembly asked him to form a government during France's economic recovery and to solve the crisis in Algeria. He became president at the end of 1958, having changed the constitution to provide for a presidential system, and served until 1969.

De Gaulle was wounded and captured by the Germans 1916. In June 1940 he refused to accept the new prime minister Pétain's truce with the Germans and 18 June made his historic broadcast calling on the French to continue the war against Germany. He based himself in England as leader of the Free French troops fighting the Germans 1940–44. In 1944 he entered Paris in triumph and was briefly head of the provisional government before resigning over the new constitution of the Fourth Republic 1946. In 1958, when national bankruptcy and civil war in Algeria loomed, de Gaulle was called to form a government. As prime minister he promulgated a constitution subordinating the legislature to the presidency and took office as president Dec 1958. Economic recovery followed, as well as Algerian independence after a bloody war. A nationalist, he opposed 'Anglo-Saxon' influence in Europe.

Re-elected president 1965, he pursued a foreign policy that opposed British entry to the European Economic Union (EEC), withdrew French forces from the North Atlantic Treaty Organization (NATO) 1966, and pursued the development of a French nuclear deterrent. He violently quelled student demonstrations May 1968 as soon as they were joined by workers. He resigned. in 1969 after the defeat of the government in a referendum on constitutional reform.

Until we learn the use of living words we shall continue to be waxworks inhabited by gramophones.

WALTER DE LA MARE in *The Observer* 1929

degaussing neutralization of the magnetic field around a body by encircling it with a conductor through which a current is maintained. Ships were degaussed in World War II to prevent them from detonating magnetic mines.

Degenerate Art (German ***Entartete Kunst***) art condemned by the Nazi regime in Germany from 1933. The name was taken from a travelling exhibition mounted by the Nazi Party 1937 to show modern art as 'sick' and 'decadent' – a view that fitted with Nazi racial theories. The exhibition was paralleled by the official Great German Art Exhibition to display officially approved artists. However, five times as many people (more than 3 million) saw the former as the latter. Artists condemned included Max Beckmann, Emil Nolde, Wassily Kandinsky, Henri Matisse, Ernst Barlach, and Pablo Picasso.

degree in mathematics, a unit (symbol °) of measurement of an angle or arc. A circle or complete rotation is divided into 360°. A degree may be subdivided into 60 minutes (symbol ′), and each minute may be subdivided in turn into 60 seconds (symbol ″). Temperature is also measured in degrees, which are divided on a decimal scale. See also ◊Celsius, and ◊Fahrenheit.

A degree of latitude is the length along a meridian such that the difference between its north and south ends subtend an angle of 1° at the centre of the Earth. A degree of longitude is the length between two meridians making an angle of 1° at the centre of the Earth.

Dehaene Jean-Luc 1940– . Belgian politician who became prime minister 1992. He successfully negotiated constitutional changes to make Belgium a federal state. His centre-left coalition was re-elected 1995. In 1994 his appointment as European Commission president was vetoed by UK prime minister John Major, in contrast to the other 11 European Union heads of government.

De Havilland Geoffrey 1882–1965. British aircraft designer who designed and whose company produced the Moth biplane, the Mosquito fighter-bomber of World War II, and in 1949 the Comet, the world's first jet-driven airliner to enter commercial service. Knighted 1944.

De Havilland Olivia Mary 1916– . US actress. She was a star in Hollywood from the age of 19, when she appeared in *A Midsummer Night's Dream* 1935. She later successfully played challenging dramatic roles in *Gone With the Wind* 1939, *To Each His Own* (Academy Award) and *Dark Mirror* 1946, and *The Snake Pit* 1948. She won her second Academy Award for *The Heiress* 1949, and played in *Lady in a Cage* and *Hush, Hush, Sweet Charlotte*, both 1964.

dehydration in chemistry, the removal of water from a substance to give a product with a new chemical formula; it is not the same as drying.

There are two types of dehydration. For substances such as hydrated copper sulphate ($CuSO_4.5H_2O$) that contain ◊water of crystallization, dehydration means removing this water to leave the anhydrous substance. This may be achieved by heating, and is reversible. Some substances, such as ethanol, contain the elements of water (hydrogen and oxygen) joined in a different form. Dehydrating agents such as concentrated sulphuric acid will remove these elements in the ratio 2:1.

dehydration process to preserve food. Moisture content is reduced to 10–20% in fresh produce, and this provides good protection against moulds. Bacteria are not inhibited by drying, so the quality of raw materials is vital.

The process was developed commercially in France about 1795 to preserve sliced vegetables, using a hot-air blast. The earliest large-scale application was to starch products such as pasta, but after 1945 it was extended to milk, potato, soups, instant coffee, and prepared baby and pet foods. A major benefit to food manufacturers is reduction of weight and volume of the food products, lowering distribution cost.

Deighton Len (Leonard Cyril) 1929– . English author of spy fiction. His novels include *The Ipcress File* 1963 and the trilogy *Berlin Game, Mexico Set,* and *London Match* 1983–85, featuring the spy Bernard Samson. Samson was also the main character in Deighton's trilogy *Spy Hook* 1988, *Spy Line* 1989, and *Spy Sinker* 1990.

Deimos one of the two moons of Mars. It is irregularly shaped, 15 × 12 × 11 km/9 × 7.5 × 7 mi, orbits at a height of 24,000 km/15,000 mi every 1.26 days, and is not as heavily cratered as the other moon, Phobos. Deimos was discovered 1877 by US astronomer Asaph Hall (1829–1907), and is thought to be an asteroid captured by Mars's gravity.

deism belief in a supreme being; but the term usually refers to a movement of religious thought in the 17th and 18th centuries, characterized by the belief in a rational 'religion of nature' as opposed to the orthodox beliefs of Christianity.

Deists believed that God is the source of natural law but does not intervene directly in the affairs of the world, and that the only religious duty of humanity is to be virtuous.

The founder of English deism was Lord Herbert of Cherbury (1583–1648), and the chief exponents were John Toland (1670–1722), Anthony Collins (1676–1729), Matthew Tindal (1657–1733), Thomas Woolston (1670–1733), and Thomas Chubb (1679–1747). In France, the writer Voltaire was the most prominent advocate of deism. In the USA, many of the country's founders, including Benjamin Franklin and Thomas Jefferson, were essentially deists. Later, deism came to mean a belief in a personal deity who is distinct from the world and not very intimately interested in its concerns. See also ◊theism.

Dekker Thomas c. 1572–c. 1632. English dramatist and pamphleteer. He wrote mainly in collaboration with others. His play *The Shoemaker's Holiday* 1600 was followed by collaborations with Thomas Middleton, John Webster, Philip Massinger, and others. His pamphlets include *The Gull's Hornbook* 1609, a lively satire on the fashions of the day. His plays include *The Honest Whore* 1604–05 and *The Roaring Girl* 1611 (both with Middleton), *Famous History of Sir Thomas Wyat* 1607 (with Webster), *Virgin Martyr* 1622 (with Massinger), and *The Witch of Edmonton* 1621 (with John Ford and William Rowley).

de Klerk F(rederik) W(illem) 1936– . South African National Party politician, president 1989–94. Projecting himself as a pragmatic conservative who sought gradual reform of the apartheid system, he won the Sept 1989 elections for his party, but with a reduced majority. In Feb 1990 he ended the ban on the ◊African National Congress (ANC) opposition movement and released its effective leader, Nelson ◊Mandela, and by June 1991 he had repealed all racially discriminating laws. After a landslide victory for Mandela and the ANC in the first universal suffrage elections April 1994, de Klerk became second executive deputy president. He was awarded the Nobel Peace Prize jointly with Mandela 1993.

de Klerk South African politician F W de Klerk. He succeeded P W Botha as leader of the National Party and then as state president 1989. His policy of rapid progress towards democracy began with the dramatic release from prison of Nelson Mandela 1990, with whom he shared the Nobel Peace Prize 1993. He ceded the presidency to Mandela 1994 when the ANC won 62% of the popular vote in the historic first South African multiracial elections. *Topham*

de Kooning Willem 1904–1997. Dutch-born US painter. He emigrated to the USA 1926 and worked as a commercial artist. After World War II he became, together with Jackson Pollock, one of the leaders of the Abstract Expressionist movement, although he retained figural images, painted with quick, violent brushstrokes. His *Women* series, exhibited 1953, was criticized for its grotesque depictions of women.

Delacroix (Ferdinand Victor) Eugène 1798–1863. French Romantic painter. His prolific output included religious and historical subjects and portraits of friends, among them the musicians Paganini and Chopin. Antagonistic to the French academic tradition, he evolved a highly coloured, fluid style, as in *The Death of Sardanapalus* 1829 (Louvre, Paris).

The *Massacre at Chios* 1824 (Louvre, Paris) shows Greeks enslaved by wild Turkish horse riders, a contemporary atrocity (his use of a contemporary theme recalls Géricault's example). His style was influenced by the English landscape painter Constable. He also produced illustrations for works by Shakespeare, Dante, and Byron. His *Journal* is a fascinating record of his times.

de la Mare Walter John 1873–1956. English poet and writer. His works include verse for children, such as *Peacock Pie* 1913, and the novels *The Three Royal Monkeys* 1910 (for children) and *The Memoirs of a Midget* 1921 (for adults). *The Listeners* 1912 established his reputation as a writer of delicately imaginative verse in the twin domains of childhood and dreamland. He excelled at creating a sense of eeriness and supernatural mystery.

Delaunay Robert 1885–1941. French painter. He was a pioneer of abstract art. With his wife Sonia Delaunay-Terk (1885–1979), he developed a style known as ◊Orphism, an early variation of Cubism, focusing on the effects of pure colour contrasts.

Working from the colour theories of the French chemist Michel Chevreul (1786–1889), Delaunay and his wife explored the simultaneous effects of light on disc-like planes of radiant, contrasting colour, their aim being to produce a visual equivalent to music. Delaunay painted several series 1912, notably *Circular Forms* and *Simultaneous Windows*. He carried out a huge decorative scheme for the Palace of Air and Railway Pavilion of the Paris Exposition of 1937.

De Laurentiis Dino 1919– . Italian film producer. His early films, including Fellini's *La strada/The Street* 1954, brought more acclaim than later epics such as *Waterloo* 1970. He then produced a series of undistinguished Hollywood films: *Death Wish* 1974, *King Kong* (remake) 1976, and *Dune* 1984.

Delaware state in northeastern USA; nicknamed First State/Diamond State
area 5,300 sq km/2,046 sq mi
capital Dover
towns and cities Wilmington, Newark
physical divided into two physical areas, one hilly and wooded, the other gently undulating
features one of the most industrialized states; headquarters of the Du Pont chemical firm; Delaware River; Atlantic beaches, including Rehobath Beach; the Piedmont; Bombay Hook and Prime Hook national wildlife refuges; New Castle, the restored colonial capital, site of William Penn's first landing in North America; Wilmington, the first permanent settlement in the Delaware Valley (1638), Delaware Art Museum; Henry Francis du Pont Winterthur Museum and Gardens, with a collection of American furniture and decorative arts; the University of Delaware
industries dairy, poultry, and market-garden produce; chemicals, motor vehicles, and textiles
population (1990) 666,200
famous people Du Pont family, J P Marquand
history the first settlers were Dutch 1631 and Swedes 1638, but in 1664 the area was captured by the British and transferred to William Penn. A separate colony from 1704, it fought in the

American Revolution as a state 1776, was one of the original 13 states, and was the first state to ratify the US Constitution 7 Dec 1787. In 1802 the Du Pont gunpowder mill was established near Wilmington. Completion of the Philadelphia–Baltimore railroad line 1838, through Wilmington, fostered development. Delaware was famous as a chemical centre by the early 1900s. Two auto-assembly plants and an oil refinery were built after World War II.

Delaware

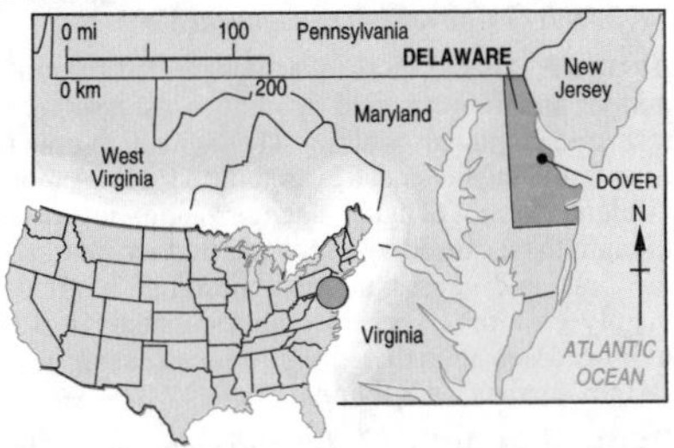

Delbruck Max 1906–1981. German-born US biologist who pioneered techniques in molecular biology, studying genetic changes occurring when viruses invade bacteria. He was awarded the Nobel Prize for Physiology or Medicine 1969, which he shared with Salvador ◊Luria and Alfred Hershey (1908–).

de Lesseps Ferdinand, VicomteFrench engineer; see ◊Lesseps, Ferdinand, Vicomte de Lesseps.

Delft town in South Holland province, the Netherlands, on the Schie Canal, 14 km/9 mi NW of Rotterdam; population (1994) 91,900. It is known worldwide for its pottery and porcelain; other industries include electronic equipment and cables. There is a technical university (1863). The Dutch nationalist leader William the Silent was murdered here 1584. It is the birthplace of the artist Jan Vermeer.

Delhi capital of India, comprising the walled city of ***Old Delhi*** (built 1639), situated on the west bank of the river Jumna, and ***New Delhi*** to the south, largely designed by English architect Edwin ◊Lutyens and chosen to replace Calcutta as the seat of government 1912 (completed 1929; officially inaugurated 1931). Delhi is the administrative centre of the state of Delhi and India's largest commercial and communications centre; population (1991) 8,375,000. Traditional handicrafts have been revived, including handwoven textiles and jewellery.

Delhi Union Territory of the Republic of India from 1956; capital Delhi; area 1,500 sq km/579 sq mi; population (1994) 9,500,000. It produces grain, sugar cane, fruit, and vegetables.

Delibes (Clément Philibert) Léo 1836–1891. French composer. His lightweight, perfectly judged works include the ballets *Coppélia* 1870 and *Sylvia* 1876, and the opera *Lakmé* 1883.

Delilah in the Old Testament, the Philistine mistress of ◊Samson. Following instructions from the lords of the Philistines she sought to find the source of Samson's great strength. When Samson eventually revealed that his physical power lay in the length of his hair, she shaved his head while he slept and then delivered him into the hands of the Philistines.

delirium in medicine, a state of acute confusion in which the subject is incoherent, frenzied, and out of touch with reality. It is often accompanied by delusions or hallucinations. Delirium may occur in feverish illness, some forms of mental illness, brain disease, and as a result of drug or alcohol intoxication. In chronic alcoholism, attacks of ***delirium tremens*** (DTs), marked by hallucinations, sweating, trembling, and anxiety, may persist for several days.

Delius Frederick Theodore Albert 1862–1934. English composer. His haunting, richly harmonious works include the opera *A Village Romeo and Juliet* 1901; the choral pieces *Appalachia* 1903, *Sea Drift* 1904, *A Mass of Life* 1905; orchestral works such as *In a Summer Garden* 1908 and *A Song of the High Hills* 1911; chamber music; and songs.

From 1890 Delius lived mainly in France and in 1903 married the artist Jelka Rosen. Although blind and paralysed for the last ten years of his life, he continued to compose.

della Robbia Italian family of artists; see ◊Robbia, della.

Delon Alain 1935– . French film actor. He graduated from youthful charmer to character roles, appearing in *Purple Noon* 1960, *Rocco e i suoi fratelli/Rocco and His Brothers* 1960, *Il gattopardo/The Leopard* 1963, *Texas Across the River* 1966, *Scorpio* 1972, and *Swann in Love* 1983.

Delors Jacques Lucien Jean 1925– . French socialist politician, finance minister 1981–84. As president of the European Commission 1984–94, he oversaw significant budgetary reform and the move towards a free European Community (now European Union) market, with increased powers residing in Brussels. His presidency saw the final ratification and implementation of the ◊Maastricht Treaty on European union, and negotiations for the Uruguay round of ◊General Agreement on Tariffs and Trade (GATT), concluded 1993.

Delphi city of ancient Greece, situated in a rocky valley north of the gulf of Corinth, on the southern slopes of Mount Parnassus, site of a famous ◊oracle in the temple of Apollo. The site was supposed to be the centre of the Earth and was marked by a conical stone, the *omphalos*. Towards the end of the 6th century BC the Athenian family of the Alcmaeonidae helped to rebuild the temple. The oracle was interpreted by priests from the inspired utterances of the Pythian priestess until it was closed down by the Roman emperor Theodosius I AD 390.

delphinium any plant of the genus *Delphinium* belonging to the buttercup family Ranunculaceae. There are some 250 species, including the butterfly or Chinese delphinium *D. grandiflorum*, an Asian form and one of the ancestors of the garden delphinium. Most species have blue, purple, or white flowers on a long spike.

del Sarto Andrea Italian Renaissance painter; see ◊Andrea del Sarto.

delta tract of land at a river's mouth, composed of silt deposited as the water slows on entering the sea. Familiar examples of large deltas are those of the Mississippi, Ganges and Brahmaputra, Rhône, Po, Danube, and Nile; the shape of the Nile delta is like the Greek letter *delta* Δ, and thus gave rise to the name.

delta wing aircraft wing shaped like the Greek letter *delta* Δ. Its design enables an aircraft to pass through the ◊sound barrier with little effect. The supersonic airliner ◊Concorde and the US ◊space shuttle have delta wings.

delusion in psychiatry, a false belief that is unshakeably held. Delusions are a prominent feature of schizophrenia and paranoia, but may also occur in other psychiatric states.

dementia mental deterioration as a result of physical changes in the brain. It may be due to degenerative change, circulatory disease, infection, injury, or chronic poisoning. Senile dementia, a progressive loss of mental faculties such as memory and orientation, is typically a disease process of old age, and can be accompanied by ◊depression.

demesne in the Middle Ages in Europe, land kept in the lord's possession, not leased out, but, under the system of ◊villeinage, worked by villeins to supply the lord's household.

Demeter in Greek mythology, the goddess of agriculture (Roman Ceres), daughter of Kronos and Rhea, and mother of Persephone by Zeus. Demeter and Persephone were worshipped in a sanctuary at Eleusis, where one of the foremost ◊mystery religions of Greece was celebrated. She was later identified with the Egyptian goddess ◊Isis.

DeMille Agnes George 1909–1993. US dancer and choreographer. She introduced popular dance idioms into ballet with such works as *Rodeo* 1942. One of the most significant contributors to the American Ballet Theater with dramatic ballets like *Fall River Legend* 1948, based on the Lizzie Borden murder case, she also led the change on Broadway to new-style musicals with her choreography of *Oklahoma!* 1943, *Carousel* 1945, and others. She was the daughter of playwright William C DeMille, and the niece of film director Cecil B DeMille.

DeMille Cecil B(lount) 1881–1959. US film director and producer. He entered films 1913 with Jesse L Lasky (with whom he later established Paramount Pictures), and was one of the founders of Hollywood. He specialized in lavish biblical epics, such as *The Sign of the Cross* 1932 and *The Ten Commandments* 1923; remade 1956. He also made the 1952 Academy Award-winning *The Greatest Show on Earth*.

Demirel Süleyman 1924– . Turkish politician who became president 1993. Leader from 1964 of the Justice Party, he was prime minister 1965–71, 1975–77, and 1979–80. He has favoured links with the West, full membership of the European Union, and foreign investment in Turkish industry.

democracy (Greek *demos* 'the community', *kratos* 'sovereign power') government by the people, usually through elected representatives. In the modern world, democracy has developed from the American and French revolutions.

‘What should have been evident at first hearing was the remotely alien sound of it, a note in English music stranger than any heard for over two hundred years.’

On **Delius**
Thomas Beecham
A Mingled Chime
1944

Delphi Ruins of the Temple of Apollo at Delphi. Situated on the slopes of Mount Parnassus, Delphi was one of the most important cultural centres in ancient Greece, the site of the famous oracle of Apollo (a shrine where the god was supposed to give an answer to questions asked of him). Three successive temples to Apollo have stood on the site, the final one dating from the 4th century BC. *Corbis*

> ‘Honey, I just forgot to duck.’
>
> **Jack Dempsey**
> Remark to his wife after losing his world heavyweight title 23 Sept 1926

Representative parliamentary government existed in Iceland from the 10th century and in England from the 13th century, but the British working classes were excluded almost entirely from the ◊vote until 1867, and women were admitted and property qualifications abolished only 1918.

In ***direct democracy*** the whole people meets for the making of laws or the direction of executive officers; for example, in Athens in the 5th century BC. Direct democracy today is represented mainly by the use of the ◊referendum, as in the UK, France, Italy. The populist instrument of citizen's initiatives or propositions is used in certain states of the USA whereby proposed laws and constitutional changes are put to the public for approval.

The two concepts underlying ***liberal democracy*** are the right to representative government and the right to individual freedom. In practice the features of a liberal democratic system include representative institutions based on majority rule, through free elections and a choice of political parties; accountability of the government to the electorate; freedom of expression, assembly, and the individual, guaranteed by an independent judiciary; and limitations on the power of government.

Democratic Party one of the two main political parties of the USA. It tends to be the party of the working person, as opposed to the Republicans, the party of big business, but the divisions between the two are not clear cut. Its stronghold since the Civil War has traditionally been industrial urban centres and the Southern states, but conservative Southern Democrats were largely supportive of Republican positions in the 1980s and helped elect President Reagan.

Originally called Democratic Republicans, the party was founded by Thomas Jefferson 1792 to defend the rights of the individual states against the centralizing policy of the Federalists. The party controlled all the Southern states that seceded from the Union 1860–61. In the 20th century, under the presidencies of Grover Cleveland, Woodrow Wilson, Franklin D Roosevelt, Harry Truman, John F Kennedy, Lyndon B Johnson, Jimmy Carter, and Bill Clinton, the party has adopted more liberal social-reform policies than the Republicans.

From the 1930s the Democratic Party pursued a number of policies that captured the hearts and minds of the US public, as well as making a significant contribution to their lives. They included Roosevelt's ‘New Deal’ and the ‘Great Society’ programme conceived by J F Kennedy and implemented by Lyndon Johnson. The ‘New Deal’ aimed at pulling the country out of the 1930s depression and putting it back to work, whereas the ‘Great Society’ programme – encompassing the Economic Opportunity Act, the Civil Rights Act 1964, the Medicare and Voting Rights Act 1965, and the Housing, Higher Education, and Equal Opportunities acts – sought to make the USA a better place for the ordinary, often disadvantaged, citizen.

In the 1990s the party comprised a number of significant factions: the southern conservative rump, the Conservative Democratic Forum (CDF); the northern liberals, moderate on military matters but interventionist on economic and social issues; the radical liberals of the Midwest agricultural states; the Trumanite ‘Defense Democrats’, liberal on economic and social matters but military hawks; and the non-Congressional fringe, seeking a ‘rainbow’ coalition of African-Americans, Hispanics, feminists, students, peace campaigners, and southern liberals.

Bill Clinton leads a reformist ‘New Democrat’ wing of the party, which is fiscally conservative, but liberal on social issues. Clinton became the first Democrat president for 13 years in 1993, and in 1996 the first Democrat president since F D Roosevelt to be elected for a second term.

Democritus c. 460–c. 370 BC. Greek philosopher and speculative scientist who made a significant contribution to metaphysics with his atomic theory of the universe: all things originate from a vortex of tiny, indivisible particles, which he called atoms, and differ according to the shape and arrangement of their atoms. Democritus' discussion of the constant motion of atoms to explain the origins of the universe was the most scientific theory proposed in his time. His concepts come to us through Aristotle's work in this area.

demodulation in radio, the technique of separating a transmitted audio frequency signal from its modulated radio carrier wave. At the transmitter the audio frequency signal (representing speech or music, for example) may be made to modulate the amplitude (AM broadcasting) or frequency (FM broadcasting) of a continuously transmitted radio-frequency carrier wave. At the receiver, the signal from the aerial is demodulated to extract the speech or sound component. See ◊modulation.

demography study of the size, structure, dispersement, and development of human ◊populations to establish reliable statistics on such factors as birth and death rates, marriages and divorces, life expectancy, and migration. It is significant in the social sciences as the basis for industry and for government planning in such areas as education, housing, welfare, transport, and taxation.

Demosthenes c. 384–322 BC. Athenian politician, famed for his oratory. From 351 BC he led the party that advocated resistance to the growing power of ◊Philip of Macedon, and in his *Philippics*, a series of speeches, incited the Athenians to war. This policy resulted in the defeat of Chaeronea 338, and the establishment of Macedonian supremacy. After the death of Alexander he organized a revolt; when it failed, he took poison to avoid capture by the Macedonians.

Demotic Greek common or vernacular variety of the modern ◊Greek language.

demotic script cursive (joined) writing derived from Egyptian hieratic script, itself a cursive form of ◊hieroglyphic. Demotic documents are known from the 6th century BC to about AD 470. It was written horizontally, from right to left.

Dempsey Jack (William Harrison) 1895–1983. US heavyweight boxing champion, nicknamed ‘the Manassa Mauler’. He beat Jess Willard 1919 to win the title and held it until 1926, when he lost it to Gene Tunney. He engaged in the ‘Battle of the Long Count’ with Tunney 1927.

Denbighshire unitary authority of Wales created 1996 (*see United Kingdom map*).

Dench Judi (Judith Olivia) 1934– . English actress. Her professional debut was as Ophelia in *Hamlet* 1957 with the Old Vic Company. Her Shakespearean roles include Viola in *Twelfth Night* 1969, Lady Macbeth 1976, and Cleopatra 1987; more recent plays include *The Seagull* 1994, *The Convent* 1995, and *A Little Night Music* 1995–96. Her films include *Wetherby* 1985, *A Handful of Dust* 1988, and *Goldeneye* 1995. She is also a versatile comedy actress and directed *Much Ado about Nothing* 1988 and John Osborne's *Look Back in Anger* 1989 for the Renaissance Theatre Company. In 1999 she won an Oscar for Best Supporting Actress for her role as Queen Elizabeth I in *Shakespeare in Love*.

dendrite part of a ◊nerve cell or neuron. The dendrites are slender filaments projecting from the cell body. They receive incoming messages from many other nerve cells and pass them on to the cell body. If the combined effect of these messages is strong enough, the cell body will send an electrical impulse along the axon (the threadlike extension of a nerve cell). The tip of the axon passes its message to the dendrites of other nerve cells.

dendrochronology analysis of the ◊annual rings of trees to date past events. Samples of wood are obtained by means of a narrow metal tube that is driven into a tree to remove a core extending from the bark to the centre. Samples taken from timbers at an archaeological site can be compared with a master core on file for that region or by taking cores from old, living trees; the year when they were felled can be determined by locating the point where the rings of the two samples correspond and counting back from the present.

Since annual rings are formed by variations in the water-conducting cells produced by the plant during different seasons of the year, they also provide a means of determining past climatic conditions in a given area (the rings are thin in dry years, thick in moist ones).

Deneb or ***Alpha Cygni*** brightest star in the constellation ◊Cygnus, and the 19th brightest star in the night sky. It is about 1,800 light years from Earth.

Deneuve Catherine (born Dorléac) 1943– . French actress. She was acclaimed for her performance in Roman Polanski's film *Repulsion* 1965. She also appeared in *Les Parapluies de Cherbourg/Umbrellas of Cherbourg* 1964, *Belle de jour* 1967, *Le Dernier Métro/The Last Metro* 1980, *Indochine* 1993, and *O Convento/The Convent* 1995.

dengue tropical viral fever transmitted by mosquitoes and accompanied by joint pains, headache, rash, and glandular swelling. The incubation time is a week and the fever also lasts about a week. A more virulent form, dengue haemorrhagic fever, is thought to be caused by a second infection on top of the first, and causes internal bleeding. It affects mainly children. There are an estimated 50–100 million cases annually in the tropics causing over 10,000 deaths (1998 figures).

Deng Xiaoping or *Teng Hsiao-ping* 1904–1997. Chinese political leader. A member of the Chinese Communist Party (CCP) from the 1920s, he took part in the ◊Long March 1934–36. He was in the Politburo from 1955 until ousted in the ◊Cultural Revolution 1966–69. Reinstated in the 1970s, he gradually took power and introduced a radical economic modernization programme. He retired from the Politburo 1987 and from his last official position 1990, but remained influential behind the scenes despite deteriorating health.

After the Cultural Revolution, during which Deng was sent to work in a tractor factory in Nanchang for ‘re-education’, he was rehabilitated by his patron Zhou Enlai 1973 and served as acting prime minister after Zhou's heart attack 1974. On Zhou's death Jan 1976 he was forced into hiding but returned to office as vice premier July 1977; by Dec 1978, Deng was the controlling force in China. His policy of ‘socialism with Chinese characteristics’, misinterpreted in the West as a drift to capitalism, had success in rural areas.

His reputation, both at home and in the West, was tarnished by his sanctioning of the army's massacre of more than 2,000 prodemocracy demonstrators in Tiananmen Square, Beijing, in June 1989.

denier unit used in measuring the fineness of yarns, equal to the mass in grams of 9,000 metres of yarn. Thus 9,000 metres of 15 denier nylon, used in nylon stockings, weighs 15 g/0.5 oz, and in this case the thickness of thread would be 0.00425 mm/0.0017 in.

denim cotton twill fabric with coloured warp (lengthwise yarns) and undyed weft, originating in France (hence the name ‘de Nîmes’). In its most classic form, indigo blue and heavyweight, it is used

Deng Xiaoping China's ‘paramount ruler’ Deng Xiaoping. Ousted during the Cultural Revolution, he returned to power in the 1970s. In effective charge of China throughout the 1980s, he promoted greater economic but not political liberalization. He remained influential behind the scenes in the early 1990s. *Topham*

De Niro US film actor Robert de Niro, seen here in the film *A Bronx Tale* 1993. Although he is a versatile actor, his most successful roles have been as psychotics. He has won critical acclaim for his striving for authenticity. *Rank Film Distributors*

for jeans and dungarees. It became fashionable in the early 1970s, and many variations followed, including lighter-weight dress fabrics and stonewashed, overdyed, and brushed finishes in many colours.

De Niro Robert 1943– . US actor of great magnetism and physical presence. He won Academy Awards for his performances in *The Godfather Part II* 1974 and *Raging Bull* 1980, in which he played a boxer gone to seed. His other films include *Mean Streets* 1973, *Taxi Driver* 1976, *The Deer Hunter* 1978, *Goodfellas* 1990, *Cape Fear* 1991, *Heat* 1995, and *Sleepers* 1996. He showed his versatility in *The King of Comedy* 1982 and other Martin Scorsese films. He directed *A Bronx Tale* 1993.

Denishawn School of Dancing and Related Arts US modern dance company and school founded 1915 by dancers Ruth St Denis (1879–1968) and Ted Shawn (1891–1972) in Los Angeles. It was designed to improve body, mind, and soul, and provided the training ground for numerous exponents of modern dance including Martha Graham, Doris Humphrey and Charles Weidman (1901–1975). The company toured extensively until 1931.

The school reflected the exotic influences of its two charismatic founders. Ruth St Denis' seductive interpretations of dances from India, Egypt, and Asia were hugely popular in both America and Europe. Shawn drew on Native American and aboriginal folklore for inspiration for his dances, which he toured with Ted Shawn and his Men Dancers through the 1930s. His efforts to raise the masculine role in dance from its secondary status paved the way for subsequent male stars, such as Nureyev, to emerge.

Denis, St first bishop of Paris and one of the patron saints of France, who was martyred by the Romans. Feast day 9 Oct.

St Denis is often confused with Dionysius the Areopagite, as well as with the original martyr of the 1st century AD. According to legend, he was sent as a missionary to Gaul in 250, and was beheaded several years later in Paris, during the reign of Emperor Valerian. He is often represented as carrying his head in his hands.

denitrification process occurring naturally in soil, where bacteria break down ◊nitrates to give nitrogen gas, which returns to the atmosphere.

Denktaş Rauf R 1924– . Turkish-Cypriot nationalist politician. In 1975 the Turkish Federated State of Cyprus (TFSC) was formed in the northern third of the island, with Denktaş as its head, and in 1983 he became president of the breakaway Turkish Republic of Northern Cyprus (TRNC); it was recognized internationally only by Turkey. He was re-elected 1995.

Denmark peninsula and islands in N Europe, bounded N by the Skagerrak, E by the Kattegat, S by Germany, and W by the North Sea. *See country box on p. 306.*

denominator in mathematics, the bottom number of a fraction, so called because it names the family of the fraction. The top number, or numerator, specifies how many unit fractions are to be taken.

Denpasar capital town of Bali in the Lesser Sunda Islands of Indonesia; population (1980) 261,300. Industries include food processing, machinery, papermaking and printing, and handicrafts. There is a university (1962) and, housed in the temple and palace, a museum of Balinese art.

density measure of the compactness of a substance; it is equal to its mass per unit volume and is measured in kg per cubic metre/lb per cubic foot. Density is a ◊scalar quantity. The average density D of a mass m occupying a volume V is given by the formula:

$$D = m/V$$

◊Relative density is the ratio of the density of a substance to that of water at 4°C.

In photography, density refers to the degree of opacity of a negative; in population studies, it is the quantity or number per unit of area; in electricity, current density is the amount of current passing through a cross-sectional area of a conductor (usually given in amperes per sq in or per sq cm).

dental formula way of showing the number of teeth in an animal's mouth. The dental formula consists of eight numbers separated by a line into two rows. The four above the line represent the teeth in one side of the upper jaw, starting at the front. If this reads 2 1 2 3 (as for humans) it means two incisors, one canine, two premolars, and three molars (see ◊tooth). The numbers below the line represent the lower jaw. The total number of teeth can be calculated by adding up all the numbers and multiplying by two.

dentistry care and treatment of the teeth and gums. ***Orthodontics*** deals with the straightening of the teeth for aesthetic and clinical reasons, and ***periodontics*** with care of the supporting tissue (bone and gums).

dentition type and number of teeth in a species. Different kinds of teeth have different functions; a grass-eating animal will have large molars for grinding its food, whereas a meat-eater will need powerful canines for catching and killing its prey. The teeth that are less useful to an animal's lifestyle may be reduced in size or missing altogether. An animal's dentition is represented diagramatically by a ◊dental formula.

Young children have ***deciduous dentition***, popularly known as 'milk teeth', the first ones erupting at about six months of age. ***Mixed dentition*** is present from the ages of about six (when the first milk teeth are shed) to about 12. ***Permanent dentition*** (up to 32 teeth) is usually complete by the mid-teens, although the third molars (wisdom teeth) may not appear until around the age of 21.

Denver city and capital of Colorado, USA, on the South Platte River, on the western edge of the Great Plains, near the foothills of the Rocky Mountains; population (1992) 483,900; Denver–Boulder metropolitan area (1992) 2,089,000. At 1,609 m/5,280 ft above sea level, it is known as 'Mile High City'.

history First settled 1858 following the discovery of gold, Denver became a centre for the mining camps. Silver was mined in the 1870s and 1880s, and created much wealth until the crash of the silver market 1893. Coal is mined nearby, and the city became the distribution centre for a large agricultural area as well as for natural resources, including minerals, oil, and gas.

features The Denver branch of the US Mint (1900) is the second largest gold depository in the United States, and produces 75% of the country's coinage. The State Capitol 1894, with its gold dome, is one of the oldest surviving buildings. The many museums include the Trianon Museum and Art Gallery (with 18th and 19th century European furniture), the Colorado History Museum, and the Black American West Museum and Heritage Center. The Denver Art Museum has important collections of Asian, pre-Columbian, and Spanish Colonial art.

deoxyribonucleic acid full name of ◊DNA.

De Palma Brian Russell 1940– . US film director, especially of thrillers. His films include *Sisters* 1973, *Carrie* 1976, *The Untouchables* 1987, and *Bonfire of the Vanities* 1990.

Depardieu Gérard 1948– . French actor. He has an imposing physique and screen presence. His films include *Deux Hommes dans la ville* 1973, *Le Camion* 1977, *Mon Oncle d'Amérique* 1980, *The Moon in the Gutter* 1983, *Jean de Florette* 1985, *Cyrano de Bergerac* 1990, and *Le Colonel Chabert* 1994. His English-speaking films include the US romantic comedy *Green Card* 1990, *1492 – Conquest of Paradise* 1992, and *My Father the Hero* 1994.

depreciation in economics, the decline of a currency's value in relation to other currencies. Depreciation also describes the fall in value of an asset (such as factory machinery) resulting from age, wear and tear, or other circumstances. It is an important factor in assessing company profits and tax liabilities.

depression in economics, a period of low output and investment, with high unemployment. Specifically, the term describes two periods of crisis in world economy: 1873–96 and 1929 to the mid-1930s.

The term is most often used to refer to the world economic crisis precipitated by the ◊Wall Street

'It's a recession when your neighbour loses his job; it's a depression when you lose yours.'

On DEPRESSION
Harry S Truman quoted in the *Observer* 13 April 1958

depression Farmers in Kaufman County, Texas, collecting benefit cheques during the Depression of the 1930s. The US Depression struck urban and rural communities alike, and benefit cheques, though small, were essential to alleviate the worst effects of poverty. *Corbis* crash of 29 Oct 1929 when millions of dollars were wiped off US share values in a matter of hours. This forced the closure of many US banks involved in stock speculation and led to the recall of US overseas investments. This loss of US credit had serious repercussions on the European economy, especially that of Germany, and led to a steep fall in the levels of international trade as countries attempted to protect their domestic economies. Although most European countries experienced a slow recovery during the mid-1930s, the main impetus for renewed economic growth was provided by rearmament programmes later in the decade.

depression in medicine, an emotional state characterized by sadness, unhappy thoughts, apathy, and dejection. Sadness is a normal response to major losses such as bereavement or unemployment. After childbirth, ◊postnatal depression is common. However, clinical depression, which is prolonged or unduly severe, often requires treatment, such as antidepressant medication, ◊cognitive therapy, or, in very rare cases, electroconvulsive therapy (ECT), in which an electrical current is passed through the brain.

Periods of depression may alternate with periods of high optimism, over-enthusiasm, and confidence. This is the manic phase in a disorder known as manic depression, in which a person switches repeatedly from one extreme to the other. Each mood can last for weeks or for months. Typically, the depressive state lasts longer than the manic phase.

depression or *cyclone* or *low* in meteorology, a region of low atmospheric pressure. In mid latitudes a depression forms as warm, moist air from the tropics mixes with cold, dry polar air, producing warm and cold boundaries (◊fronts) and unstable weather – low cloud and drizzle, showers, or fierce storms. The warm air, being less dense, rises above the cold air to produce the area of low pressure on the ground. Air spirals in towards the centre of the depression in an anticlockwise direction in the northern hemisphere, clockwise in the southern hemisphere, generating winds up to gale force. Depressions tend to travel eastwards and can remain active for several days.

A severe depression in the tropics is called a ◊hurricane, tropical cyclone, or typhoon, and is a great danger to shipping; a ◊tornado is a very intense, rapidly swirling depression, with a diameter of only a few hundred metres or so.

Deptford district in SE London, in the Greater London borough of Lewisham, on the river Thames W of Greenwich. It was a major royal naval dockyard 1513–1869, established by Henry VIII to build the flagship *Great Harry*. Now mainly residential, it has engineering and chemical industries.

Francis Drake was knighted at Deptford, and Peter the Great, tsar of Russia, studied shipbuilding here 1698. Deptford was the last stopping place for coaches on the Dover road.

De Quincey Thomas 1785–1859. English writer. His works include *Confessions of an English Opium-Eater* 1821 and the essays 'On the Knocking at the Gate in Macbeth' 1825 and 'On Murder Considered as One of the Fine Arts' 1827–54. He was a friend of the poets William ◊Wordsworth and Samuel Taylor ◊Coleridge, and his work had a powerful influence on Charles Baudelaire and Edgar Allan Poe, among others.

He succeeded in giving lasting expression to the fleeting pictures of his usually macabre dreams, and it could be said that he explored the subconscious before it was formally discovered.

Derain André 1880–1954. French painter. He experimented with the strong, almost primary colours associated with ◊Fauvism but later developed a more sombre landscape and figurative style. *Pool of London* 1906 (Tate Gallery, London) is a typical work.

He produced many stage designs as well as paintings, from the sets for Diaghilev's *La Boutique fantasque* 1919 to those for Rossini's *Le Barbier de Seville* 1953.

DENMARK
Kingdom of

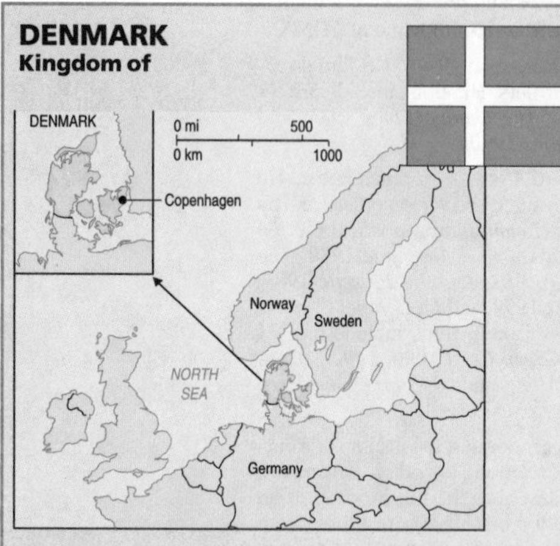

national name *Kongeriget Danmark*
area 43,075 sq km/16,627 sq mi
capital Copenhagen
major ports Aarhus, Odense, Aalborg, Esbjerg
physical features comprises the Jutland peninsula and about 500 islands (100 inhabited) including Bornholm in the Baltic Sea; the land is flat and cultivated; sand dunes and lagoons on the W coast and long inlets (fjords) on the E; the main island is Sja{lig}lland (Zealand), where most of Copenhagen is located (the rest is on the island of Amager)
territories the dependencies of Faroe Islands and Greenland
head of state Queen Margrethe II from 1972
head of government Poul Nyrup Rasmussen from 1993
political system liberal democracy
administrative divisions 14 counties, one city and one borough
political parties Social Democrats (SD), left of centre; Conservative People's Party (KF), moderate centre-right; Liberal Party (V), centre-left; Socialist People's Party (SF), moderate left-wing; Radical Liberals (RV), radical internationalist, left of centre; Centre Democrats (CD), moderate centrist; Progress Party (FP), radical antibureaucratic; Christian People's Party (KrF), interdenominational, family values
armed forces 33,100; 72,200 reservists and volunteer Home Guard of 65,200 (1994)
conscription 9–12 months (27 months for some ranks)
defence spend (% GDP) 1.9 (1994)
education spend (% GNP) 7.4 (1992)
health spend (% GDP) 5.5 (1993)
death penalty abolished 1978
population 5,215,718 (1995 est)
population growth rate 0.2% (1990–95); 0.0% (2000–05)
age distribution (% of total population) <17.2%, 15–65 67.6%, >65 15.2% (1995)
ethnic distribution all Danes are part of the Scandinavian race
population density (per sq km) 121 (1995)
urban population (% of total) 85 (1995)
labour force 57% of population: 6% agriculture, 28% industry, 66% services (1990)
unemployment 10.1% (1995)
child mortality rate (under 5, per 1,000 live births) 7 (1993)
life expectancy 73 (men), 79 (women)
education (compulsory years) 9
literacy rate 99%
languages Danish (official); there is a German-speaking minority
religion Lutheran 97%
TV sets (per 1,000 people) 537 (1992)
currency Danish krone
GDP (US $) 172.9 billion (1995)
GDP per capita (PPP) (US $) 21,502 (1995)
growth rate 2.6% (1994/95)
average annual inflation 2.9% (1995)
major trading partners EU (principally Germany, Sweden, and UK), Norway, USA
resources crude petroleum, natural gas, salt, limestone
industries mining, food processing, fisheries, machinery, textiles, furniture, electronic goods and transport equipment, chemicals and pharmaceuticals, printing and publishing
exports pig meat and pork products, food and food products, fish, industrial machinery, chemicals, transport equipment. Principal market: Germany 22.4% (1994)
imports food and live animals, machinery, transport equipment, iron, steel, electronics, petroleum, cereals, paper. Principal source: Germany 21.7% (1994)
arable land 58.9% (1993)
agricultural products wheat, rye, barley, oats, potatoes, sugar beet, dairy products; livestock production (chiefly pigs) and dairy products; fishing

HISTORY

5th–6th Cs Danes migrated from Sweden.
8th–10th Cs Viking raids throughout Europe.
c. 940–85 Harald Bluetooth unified Kingdom of Denmark and established Christianity.
1014–35 King Canute I created empire embracing Denmark, Norway, and England; empire collapsed after his death.
12th C Denmark re-emerged as dominant Baltic power.
1340–75 Valdemar IV restored order after period of civil war and anarchy.
1397 Union of Kalmar: Denmark, Sweden, and Norway (with Iceland) united under a single monarch.
1449 Sweden broke away from union.
1460 Christian I secured duchies of Schleswig and Holstein.
1523 Denmark recognized Sweden's independence.
1536 Lutheranism established as official religion of Denmark.
1563–70 Unsuccessful war to recover Sweden.
1625–29 Denmark sided with Protestants in Thirty Years War.
1643–45 Second attempt to reclaim Sweden ended in failure.
1657–60 Further failed attempt to reclaim Sweden.
1665 Frederick III made himself absolute monarch.
1729 Greenland became Danish province.
1780–81 Denmark, Russia, and Sweden formed 'Armed Neutrality' coalition to protect neutral shipping during War of American Independence.
1788 Serfdom abolished.
1800 France persuaded Denmark to revive Armed Neutrality against British blockade.
1801 First Battle of Copenhagen: much of Danish fleet destroyed by British navy.
1807 Second Battle of Copenhagen: British seized rebuilt fleet to pre-empt Danish entry into Napoleonic War on French side.
1814 Treaty of Kiel: Denmark ceded Norway to Sweden as penalty for supporting France in Napoleonic War; Denmark retained Iceland.
1848–50 Germans of Schleswig-Holstein revolted with Prussian support.
1849 Liberal pressure compelled Frederick VII to grant democratic constitution.
1864 Prussia seized Schleswig-Holstein after short war.
1914–1919 Denmark neutral during World War I.
1918 Iceland achieved full self-government.
1919 Denmark recovered northern Schleswig under peace settlement after World War I.
1929–40 Welfare state established under left-wing coalition government dominated by Social Democrat Party.
1940–45 German occupation.
1944 Iceland declared independence.
1949 Denmark became a founding member of North Atlantic Treaty Organization (NATO).
1960 Denmark joined European Free Trade Association (EFTA).
1973 Withdrew from EFTA and joined European Economic Community (EEC).
1981 Greenland achieved full self-government.
1992 Referendum rejected Maastricht Treaty on European union.
1993 Second referendum approved Maastricht Treaty after government negotiated a series of 'opt-out' clauses.

SEE ALSO Faroe Islands; Greenland; Maastricht Treaty; Norway; Sweden

Derby industrial city in England and the administrative headquarters of Derby unitary authority; population (1991) 218,800. Products include Rolls-Royce cars and aero engines, Toyota cars, train repair workshops, chemicals, paper, textiles, plastics, and electrical, mining, and engineering equipment. There is also a sugar-refining industry. The museum collections of Royal Crown Derby china, the Rolls-Royce collection of aero engines, and the Derby Playhouse are here.

Derby ◊blue riband of the English horseracing season, run over 2.4 km/1.5 mi at Epsom, Surrey, every June. It was established 1780 and named after the 12th Earl of Derby. The USA has an equivalent horse race, the Kentucky Derby.

Derby Edward (George Geoffrey Smith) Stanley, 14th Earl of Derby 1799–1869. British politician. He was leader of the Conservative Party 1846–68 and prime minister 1852, 1858–59, and 1866–68, each time as head of a minority government. He inherited the title of Lord Stanley 1834, became a peer 1844, and succeeded to the earldom 1851.

As chief secretary for Ireland 1830–33, he was responsible for much legislation, including the innovative Irish Education Act 1831. As colonial secretary 1833–34, he introduced the bill that abolished slavery in the British Empire.

Derby City unitary authority of England created 1997 (*see United Kingdom map*).

Derbyshire county of N central England (*see United Kingdom map*)
towns and cities Matlock (administrative headquarters), Chesterfield, Ilkeston
features Peak District National Park (including Kinder Scout 636 m/2,088 ft); rivers: Derwent, Dove, Rother, Trent; Chatsworth House, Bakewell (seat of the Duke of Devonshire); Haddon Hall
industries cereals; dairy and sheep farming; textiles; there have been pit and factory closures, but the area is being redeveloped, and there are large reserves of fluorite
famous people Samuel Richardson, Thomas Cook, Marquess Curzon of Kedleston.

deregulation action to abolish or reduce government controls and supervision of private economic activities, with the aim of improving competitiveness. In Britain, the major changes in the City of London 1986 (the ◊Big Bang) were in part deregulation. Another UK example was the Building Societies Act 1985, which enabled building societies to compete in many areas with banks.

Derg, Lough lake in County Donegal, NW Ireland. The island (Station Island or St Patrick's Purgatory) is the country's leading place of pilgrimage. Associated with St Patrick, a monastery flourished here from early times.

dermatitis inflammation of the skin (see ◊eczema), usually related to allergy. ***Dermatosis*** refers to any skin disorder and may be caused by contact or systemic problems.

dermatology medical speciality concerned with the diagnosis and treatment of skin disorders.

De Roburt Hammer 1923–1992. President of Nauru 1968–76, 1978–83, and 1987–89. During the country's occupation 1942–45, he was deported to Japan. He became head chief of Nauru 1956 and was elected the country's first president 1968. He secured only a narrow majority in the 1987 elections and in 1989 was ousted on a no-confidence motion.

derrick simple lifting machine consisting of a pole carrying a block and tackle. Derricks are commonly used on ships that carry freight. In the oil industry the tower used for hoisting the drill pipes is known as a derrick.

Derry district of the county of ◊Londonderry, Northern Ireland. The name is also commonly used in the Republic of Ireland and by Nationalists in Northern Ireland to refer to the city and county of Londonderry.

dervish in Iran and Turkey, a religious mendicant (one who depends on alms); throughout the rest of Islam a member of an Islamic religious brotherhood, not necessarily mendicant in character. The Arabic equivalent is *fakir*. There are various orders of dervishes, each with its rule and special ritual. The 'whirling dervishes' claim close communion with the deity through ecstatic dancing, reaching spiritual awareness with a trancelike state created by continual whirling. The spinning symbolizes the Earth's orbit of the Sun. 'Howling dervishes' gash themselves with knives to demonstrate the miraculous feats possible to those who trust in Allah.

Derwent river in North Yorkshire, NE England; length 112 km/70 mi. Rising in the North Yorkshire moors, it joins the river Ouse SE of Selby. Other rivers of the same name in the UK are found in Derbyshire (96 km/60 mi), Cumbria (56 km/35 mi), and Northumberland (26 km/16 mi).

Desai Morarji Ranchhodji 1896–1995. Indian politician. An early follower of Mahatma Gandhi, he was independent India's first non-Congress Party prime minister 1977–79, as leader of the ◊Janata party, after toppling Indira Gandhi. Party infighting led to his resignation of both the premiership and the party leadership.

desalination removal of salt, usually from sea water, to produce fresh water for irrigation or drinking. Distillation has usually been the method adopted, but in the 1970s a cheaper process, using certain polymer materials that filter the molecules of salt from the water by reverse osmosis, was developed.

Descartes René 1596–1650. French philosopher and mathematician. He believed that commonly accepted knowledge was doubtful because of the subjective nature of the senses, and attempted to rebuild human knowledge using as his foundation *cogito ergo sum* ('I think, therefore I am'). He also believed that the entire material universe could be explained in terms of mathematical physics, and founded coordinate geometry as a way of defining and manipulating geometrical shapes by means of algebraic expressions. ◊Cartesian coordinates, the means by which points are represented in this system, are named after him. Descartes also established the science of optics, and helped to shape contemporary theories of astronomy and animal behaviour.

Descartes identified the 'thinking thing' (*res cogitans*) or mind with the human soul or consciousness; the body, though somehow interacting with the soul, was a physical machine, secondary to, and in principle separable from, the soul. He believed that, although all matter is in motion, matter does not move of its own accord; the initial impulse comes from God. He also postulated two quite distinct substances: spatial substance, or matter, and thinking substance, or mind. This is called 'Cartesian dualism', and it preserved him from serious controversy with the church.

deselection in Britain, removal or withholding of a sitting member of Parliament's official status as a candidate for a forthcoming election. The term came into use in the 1980s with the efforts of many local Labour parties to revoke the candidature of MPs viewed as too right-wing.

Descartes French philosopher and mathematician René Descartes, who reformulated scientific thinking in the 17th century with his attempts to describe the whole of knowledge using mathematics. He devised the Cartesian system of coordinate geometry, which allows points to be described numerically on a set of perpendicular axes. *Ann Ronan/Image Select (UK) Ltd*

desert arid area with sparse vegetation (or in rare cases almost no vegetation). Soils are poor, and many deserts include areas of shifting sands. Deserts can be either hot or cold.

Characteristics common to all deserts include irregular rainfall of less than 250 mm per year, very high evaporation rates often 20 times the annual precipitation, and low relative humidity and cloud cover. Temperatures are more variable; tropical deserts have a big diurnal temperature range and very high daytime temperatures (58°C has been recorded at Azizia in Libya), whereas mid-latitude deserts have a wide annual range and much lower winter temperatures (in the Mongolian desert the mean temperature is below freezing point for half the year). ▷ *See feature on pp. 308–309 and table on p. 310.*

desertification spread of deserts by changes in climate, or by human-aided processes. Desertification can sometimes be reversed by special planting (marram grass, trees) and by the use of water-absorbent plastic grains, which, added to the soil, enable crops to be grown.

The processes leading to desertification include overgrazing, destruction of forest belts, and exhaustion of the soil by intensive cultivation without restoration of fertility – all of which may be prompted by the pressures of an expanding population or by concentration in land ownership. About 140 million people are directly affected by desertification, mainly in Africa, the Indian subcontinent, and South America.

desert Bedouin riding camels beside the Red Sea in the Sinai desert. The traditional Bedouin way of life is changing rapidly: since this photograph was taken in the early 1980s most Bedouin have changed their camels for four-wheel-drive vehicles, and many have changed their nomadic lives for settled ones. *Corbis*

Deserts and Desertification

The sand dunes of the Namib Desert, which stretches 1,290 km/800 mi along the coast of southwestern Africa and covers one-third of Namibia. It receives less than 1.3 cm/0.5 in of rainfall per year, and is barren except for succulents that survive by absorbing moisture from the fog that often rolls in from the Atlantic Ocean. *Premaphotos Wildlife*

What is a desert?

When people think about deserts, they usually imagine vast sand dunes under a burning sun, with nothing to break the monotony of the landscape except for an occasional palm-filled oasis. Although places like this certainly exist, the word 'desert' encompasses a wide range of landscapes, many of which are rich in wild plants, animals, and people, adapted to difficult conditions. Characteristics of deserts include very low rainfall and humidity, high evaporation rates, and little cloud cover. Many deserts are hot but some can be bitterly cold; there are ice deserts in the polar regions. Desert soils are generally poor because they contain little vegetable matter; if water is supplied, most deserts are capable of sustaining agriculture.

Natural deserts occur when geography and climate combine to prevent significant amounts of rain falling on an area. Tropical deserts are caused by the descent of air that is heated over warm land and has previously lost all its moisture. Continental deserts, such as the Gobi in Mongolia, are too far from the sea and large inland waters to receive any significant moisture. Rain-shadow deserts lie in the lee of mountains where the rain falls on the windward slope, as is the case in the Mojave Desert beyond the Sierra Nevada in California. Coastal deserts, such as the Namib in southern Africa, are formed when cold ocean currents cause local dry air masses to descend.

The location of deserts changes over time, and many of today's deserts were once covered with grassland or forest. In the middle of the Australian desert, for example, isolated valleys of palm trees survive as relics of a vast rainforest that once stretched south from the coast. Remnants of great civilizations in the deserts of Africa and the Middle East are reminders that these places once contained fields rich in agricultural crops.

Plants and animals adapt . . .

Any living plant or animal that makes its home in the desert has to adapt to some of the harshest conditions imaginable. Plants have to endure long periods of drought and often dramatic variations in temperature. Most either store water, like many cacti and succulents, or lie dormant until the rains come, like the sagebrush. Some desert trees are extremely deep-rooting, allowing them to reach underground water sources. Plants flower only very rarely, when conditions are suitable. Within a few hours of rainfall, plants that have not flowered for years burst into bloom, and the desert is a mass of colour for a few days.

Animals have also developed special adaptive strategies. In hot deserts, most lie dormant during the day; if the nights are cold, small mammals confine their activities to the hours of sunrise and sunset, and spend the rest of the time sheltering in their burrows. Birds migrating across desert regions follow routes that have remained the same for hundreds or thousands of years, stopping at occasional oases of water and vegetation along the way.

A lizard camouflaged against the white sand in the hollow of a sand dune of the White Sands National Park, south central New Mexico, USA. In the desert, even reptiles tend to avoid the hottest part of the day, coming out in the open only in the morning and evening. *Corbis*

. . . as do human cultures

Human societies also exist in deserts, although, like any other animal, they have had to adapt. Most live on the edges of desert regions, and the only settled communities are around oases. Truly desert cultures are nomadic, moving constantly to find food for their livestock or fresh supplies of water, and living in temporary accommodation. The Bedouin of Arabia and north Africa (the word *bedouin* means 'desert dweller' in Arabic) lived for centuries in tents made of animal skins, and traded in camels and horses, although they are now increasingly being forced to settle in one place. In the Gobi Desert in Mongolia, nomadic tribes lived in temporary structures known as yurts. The people of the Kalahari Desert in Botswana (formerly known as Bushmen) have no permanent dwellings at all and traditionally live a hunter-gatherer existence; their knowledge of desert survival is so acute that they spend only a small amount of time every day on gathering food and drink.

A nomadic lifestyle has a profound impact on culture. Artistic expression tends to be concentrated on portable objects, like jewellery and ornate clothes, and on dance music and an oral tradition of storytelling.

Deserts are expanding

Unfortunately, deserts can also be formed as a result of human mistakes. Degradation of a dry-land area – through deforestation, overgrazing, poorly designed irrigation systems, and soil erosion – can lead to a complex cycle of changes that results in desertification. Loss of trees and ground cover means that water is no longer trapped

Desert-dwellers, such as this woman digging for roots in the Kalahari Desert in southern Africa, have developed great skill in locating even the slightest source of water. Laurens Van der Post described the way of life of the Kung in *The Lost World of the Kalahari* and other books. *Corbis*

A group of nomads on the move in Iran. Pastoral nomads like these keep herds of camels, goats, cattle, sheep, or yaks, which provide them with milk, meat, leather, and wool. They travel with their animals, following the seasonal availability of grazing. *Corel*

by vegetation, increasing the evaporation rates and often also the frequency and severity of drought. Mismanagement of irrigation can lead to a raised salt content in the soil, preventing crop growth and adding to risks of desert formation. Overgrazing, particularly by animals like goats that can strip vegetation bare, is often a contributory factor. It is also possible that human-induced climate change, created by the release of carbon dioxide from fossil fuels, is helping to create conditions suitable for desert formation. Throughout the world, desertification is accelerating, and according to the United Nations, a hundred countries are affected.

Desertification is as old as history. The world's oldest known story, the Sumerian *Epic of Gilgamesh*, describes Mount Lebanon as being covered in vast forests of cedars, but overfelling starting in 3000 BC has left an area of desert. Similar changes have taken place as a result of mismanagement by many of the world's oldest human civilizations in the Tigris and Euphrates river basins of present-day Iraq, where the Sumerian, Mesopotamia, Assyrian, and Babylonian cultures all flourished but degraded the land. Further west, the hills of the Mediterranean coast long ago lost their forests and have degraded to semidesert and maquis scrub. In the 19th century, Italian travellers to the Horn of Africa left vivid accounts of the forests of Eritrea, but most of the country is now desert or semidesert and only a few tiny remnants of natural woodland remain.

Up to one-third of the world's land area could soon become desert unless urgent steps are taken to address the problem. However, solving it will not be easy. People in arid areas are fully aware of the risks of desertification, but are often forced into unsustainable lifestyles by such factors as lack of suitable land, population growth, poverty, and often also the impact of refugees and war. Most people who live in and around deserts only do so from necessity. Long-term solutions to desertification, including, for example, forest-restoration programmes and the introduction of techniques for stabilizing the soil, have to take place alongside actions to alleviate the immediate problems faced by desert societies. Solutions cannot just be imposed from above: they have a chance of working only if they have the backing of local desert communities. The importance of this has been recognized by the United Nations, which advises that 'public participation should be made an integral part of action to prevent and combat desertification and account should be taken of the needs, wisdom, and aspirations of people'.

NIGEL DUDLEY

A hairy-footed gerbil ***Gerbillurus paeba***, from the Kalahari Desert in southern Africa. Found in Africa and Asia, gerbils live in burrows and feed at night, mostly on seeds and roots. *Premaphotos Wildlife*

The Sonoran Desert, Arizona, southeastern USA. Deserts vary greatly in character and are difficult to define precisely. A commonly accepted definition is that a desert is an area with an average annual rainfall of 250 mm/10 in or less. Despite their apparently harsh conditions, deserts often support a surprising variety of highly adapted plants and animals. *United Nations*

Where the deserts are

The Earth has five main regions of natural desert. By far the largest is the ***Afro-Asian desert***, a vast belt that stretches from the Atlantic Ocean to China, and includes the African Sahara, the Arabian, Iranian, and Touranian deserts of the Middle East and central Asia, the Thar Desert in Pakistan and India, and the Takla Makan and Gobi deserts of China and Mongolia. Also in Africa, the ***Namib and Kalahari deserts*** cover a large area in the southwest. The ***North American desert*** covers much of the southern USA and northern Mexico. Further south, the Atacama Desert is a thin, arid strip on the coastal side of the Andes, and the ***Patagonian desert*** covers much of Argentina east of the Andes. The ***Australian desert*** covers much of the interior of the world's largest island.

DESERT: LARGEST DESERTS

Name/location	Area* in sq km/sq mi
Sahara, N Africa	8,600,000/3,320,000
Arabian, SW Asia	2,330,000/900,000
Gobi, Mongolia and NE China	1,166,000/450,000
Patagonian, Argentina	673,000/260,000
Great Victoria, SW Australia	647,000/250,000
Great Basin, SW USA	492,000/190,000
Chihuahuan, Mexico	450,000/175,000
Great Sandy, NW Australia	400,000/150,000
Sonoran, SW USA	310,000/120,000
Kyzyl Kum, SW USSR	300,000/115,000
Takla Makan, N China	270,000/105,000
Kalahari, SW Africa	260,000/100,000

* desert areas are very approximate, because clear physical boundaries may not occur

Desert Rats nickname of the British 8th Army in N Africa during World War II. Their uniforms had a shoulder insignia bearing a jerboa (N African rodent, capable of great leaps). The Desert Rats' most famous victories include the expulsion of the Italian army from Egypt in Dec 1940 when they captured 130,000 prisoners, and the Battle of El ◊Alamein. Their successors, the 7th Armoured Brigade, fought as part of the British 1st Armoured Division in the 1991 Gulf War.

Desert Storm, Operation code-name of the military action to eject the Iraqi army from Kuwait 1991. The build-up phase was code-named Operation Desert Shield and lasted from Aug 1990, when Kuwait was first invaded by Iraq, to Jan 1991 when Operation Desert Storm was unleashed, starting the ◊Gulf War. Desert Storm ended with the defeat of the Iraqi army in the Kuwaiti theatre of operations late Feb 1991.

De Sica Vittorio 1901–1974. Italian film director and actor. His *Bicycle Thieves* 1949 is a landmark of Italian neorealism. Later films included *Umberto D* 1955, *Two Women* 1960, and *The Garden of the Finzi-Continis* 1971. His considerable acting credits include *The Earrings of Madame de ...* 1953 and *The Millionaires* 1960.

desktop publishing (DTP) use of microcomputers for small-scale typesetting and page makeup. DTP systems are capable of producing camera-ready pages (pages ready for photographing and printing), made up of text and graphics, with text set in different typefaces and sizes. The page can be previewed on the screen before final printing on a laser printer.

Des Moines capital city of Iowa, USA, on the Des Moines River, a tributary of the Mississippi; population (1992) 194,500. It is a major road, railway, and air centre. Industries include printing, banking, insurance, and food processing.

De Sica Italian film director and actor Vittorio De Sica. After World War II, he emerged as one of the leading Italian neorealist directors with *Shoeshine* 1946, *Bicycle Thieves* 1949, and *Miracle in Milan* 1950. He continued to make films until the early 1970s. *British Film Institute*

Desmoulins (Lucie Simplice) Camille (Benoist) 1760–1794. French revolutionary who summoned the mob to arms on 12 July 1789, so precipitating the revolt that culminated in the storming of the Bastille. A prominent left-wing ◊Jacobin, he was elected to the National Convention 1792. His *Histoire des Brissotins* was largely responsible for the overthrow of the right-wing ◊Girondins, but shortly after he was sent to the guillotine as too moderate.

de Soto Hernando c. 1496–1542. Spanish explorer who sailed to Darien, Central America, 1519, explored the Yucatán Peninsula 1528, and travelled with Francisco Pizarro in Peru 1530–35. In 1538 he was made governor of Cuba and Florida. In his expedition of 1539, he explored Florida, Georgia, and the Mississippi River.

Desprez Josquin Franco-Flemish composer; see ◊Josquin Desprez.

Dessalines Jean Jacques c. 1758–1806. Emperor of Haiti 1804–06. Born in Guinea, he was taken to Haiti as a slave, where in 1802 he succeeded ◊Toussaint L'Ouverture as leader of the black revolt against the French. After defeating the French, he proclaimed Haiti's independence and made himself emperor. He was killed when trying to suppress an uprising provoked by his cruelty.

Dessau Paul 1894–1979. German composer. His work includes incidental music to Bertolt Brecht's theatre pieces; an opera, *Der Verurteilung des Lukullus/The Trial of Lucullus* 1949, also to a libretto by Brecht; and numerous choral works and songs.

destroyer small, fast warship designed for anti-submarine work. Destroyers played a critical role in the convoy system in World War II. Originally termed 'torpedo-boat destroyers', they were designed by Britain to counter the large flotillas built by the French and Russian navies in the late 19th century. They proved so effective that torpedo-boats were more or less abandoned in the early 1900s, but the rise of the submarine found a new task for the 'destroyer'. They proved invaluable as anti-submarine vessels in both World War I and World War II.

detective fiction novel or short story in which a mystery is solved mainly by the action of a professional or amateur detective. Where the mystery to be solved concerns a crime, the work may be called crime fiction. The earliest work of detective fiction as understood today was 'The Murders in the Rue Morgue' 1841 by Edgar Allan Poe, and his detective Dupin became the model for those who solved crimes by deduction from a series of clues. A popular deductive sleuth was Sherlock Holmes in the stories by Arthur Conan Doyle.

The 'golden age' of the genre was the period from the 1920s to the 1940s, when the leading writers were women – Agatha Christie, Margery Allingham, and Dorothy L Sayers. Types of detective fiction include the police procedural, where the mystery is solved by detailed police work; the inverted novel, where the identity of the criminal is known from the beginning and only the method or the motive remains to be discovered; and the hard-boiled school of private investigators begun by Raymond Chandler and Dashiell Hammett, which became known for its social realism and explicit violence.

détente (French) reduction of political tension and the easing of strained relations between nations; for example, the ending of the Cold War 1989–90. The term was first used in the 1970s to describe the easing of East–West relations in the form of trade agreements and cultural exchanges.

detention centre in the UK penal system, an institution where young offenders (aged 14–21) are confined for short periods. Treatment is designed to be disciplinary; for example, the 'short, sharp shock' regime introduced by the Conservative government 1982.

Detention centres were introduced to deal with young offenders for whom a long period of residential training away from home in a borstal was not thought necessary but who were considered inappropriate for noncustodial measures such as fines or probation.

detergent surface-active cleansing agent. The common detergents are made from ◊fats (hydrocarbons) and sulphuric acid, and their long-chain molecules have a type of structure similar to that of ◊soap molecules: a salt group at one end attached to a long hydrocarbon 'tail'. They have the advantage over soap in that they do not produce scum by forming insoluble salts with the calcium and magnesium ions present in hard water.

To remove dirt, which is generally attached to materials by means of oil or grease, the hydrocarbon 'tails' (soluble in oil or grease) penetrate the oil or grease drops, while the 'heads' (soluble in water but insoluble in grease) remain in the water and, being salts, become ionized. Consequently the oil drops become negatively charged and tend to repel one another; thus they remain in suspension and are washed away with the dirt.

Detergents were first developed from coal tar in Germany during World War I, and synthetic organic detergents were increasingly used after World War II.

Domestic powder detergents for use in hot water have alkyl benzene as their main base, and may also include bleaches and fluorescers as whiteners, perborates to free stain-removing oxygen, and water softeners. Environment-friendly detergents contain no phosphates or bleaches. Liquid detergents for washing dishes are based on epoxyethane (ethylene oxide). Cold-water detergents consist of a mixture of various alcohols, plus an ingredient for breaking down the surface tension of the water, so enabling the liquid to penetrate fibres and remove the dirt. When these surface-active agents (surfactants) escape the normal processing of sewage, they cause troublesome foam in rivers; phosphates in some detergents can also cause the excessive enrichment (◊eutrophication) of rivers and lakes.

determinant in mathematics, an array of elements written as a square, and denoted by two vertical lines enclosing the array. For a 2 × 2 matrix, the determinant is given by the difference between the products of the diagonal terms. Determinants are used to solve sets of ◊simultaneous equations by matrix methods.

When applied to transformational geometry, the determinant of a 2 × 2 matrix signifies the ratio of the area of the transformed shape to the original and its sign (plus or minus) denotes whether the image is direct (the same way round) or indirect (a mirror image).

For example, the determinant of the matrix

$$\begin{pmatrix} a & b \\ c & d \end{pmatrix} = \begin{vmatrix} a & b \\ c & d \end{vmatrix} = ad - bc$$

determinism in philosophy, the view that every event is an instance of some scientific law of nature; or that every event has at least one cause; or that nature is uniform. The thesis cannot be proved or disproved. Determinism is also the theory that we do not have free will, because our choices and actions are caused.

deterrence underlying conception of the nuclear arms race: the belief that a potential aggressor will be discouraged from launching a 'first strike' nuclear attack by the knowledge that the adversary is capable of inflicting 'unacceptable damage' in a retaliatory strike. This doctrine is widely known as that of ***mutual assured destruction (MAD)***.

de Tocqueville Alexis French politician; see ◊Tocqueville, Alexis de.

detonator or ***blasting cap*** or ***percussion cap*** small explosive charge used to trigger off a main charge of high explosive. The relatively unstable compounds mercury fulminate and lead azide are often used in detonators, being set off by a lighted fuse or, more commonly, an electric current.

detritus in biology, the organic debris produced during the ◊decomposition of animals and plants.

Detroit industrial city and port in Michigan, USA, situated on Detroit River; population (1992) 1,012,100, metropolitan area 5,246,000. It has the headquarters of Ford, Chrysler, and General Motors, hence its nickname, Motown, (from 'motor town').

history Founded 1701 by Frenchman Antoine de la Mothe Cadillac as a fur-trading centre, Detroit became the leading French settlement in the Great Lakes region. It was captured from the French by the British 1760, and passed to the United States 1796. It was destroyed by fire 1805 but soon rebuilt. The opening of the Erie Canal 1825 stimulated development. Henry Ford established the Ford Motor Company 1903, and the city grew rapidly after the building of the first car factories, becoming the headquarters of Chrysler and General Motors. During the 1960s and 1970s Detroit became associated with the '◊Motown Sound' of rock and soul music. Between 1950 and 1990 the population shrank by almost half as the car factories became automated.

features In nearby Dearborn, the Henry Ford Museum and Greenfield Village display 80 historic buildings, including Thomas Edison's laboratory and Henry Ford's birthplace. The Detroit Institute of Arts 1885 has a series of murals by the Mexican painter Diego Rivera. The Detroit Symphony Orchestra was founded 1914. Belle Isle Park, an island park in the Detroit River, has outdoor summer concerts, a zoo, and a botanical garden.

Dettori Frankie (Lanfranco) 1970– . Italian flat-racing jockey based in England. He was champion jockey in 1994 and 1995. He gained his first British classic success in the Oaks in 1994 and finished the season as champion jockey with 233 winners. On 28 Sept 1996 at Ascot he became the first rider to win all seven races at a single race meeting.

deus ex machina (Latin 'a god from the crane') far-fetched or unlikely event that resolves an intractable difficulty. The phrase was originally used in classical Greek and Roman tragedy to indicate a god lowered from 'heaven' on to the stage by machinery to resolve the plot.

deuterium naturally occurring heavy isotope of hydrogen, mass number 2 (one proton and one neutron), discovered by Harold Urey 1932. It is sometimes given the symbol D. In nature, about one in every 6,500 hydrogen atoms is deuterium. Combined with oxygen, it produces 'heavy water' (D_2O), used in the nuclear industry.

deuteron nucleus of an atom of deuterium (heavy hydrogen). It consists of one proton and one neutron, and is used in the bombardment of chemical elements to synthesize other elements.

Deuteronomy book of the Old Testament; fifth book of the ◊Torah. It contains various laws, including the laws for ◊kosher and the ten commandments, and gives an account of the death of Moses.

Dev Kapil 1959– . Indian cricketer who is one of the world's outstanding all-rounders. At the age of 20 he became the youngest player to complete the 'double' of 1,000 runs and 100 wickets in test cricket. In 1992 he followed Richard Hadlee as the second bowler to reach 400 wickets.

de Valera Éamon 1882–1975. Irish nationalist politician, prime minister of the Irish Free State/Eire/Republic of Ireland 1932–48, 1951–54, and 1957–59, and president 1959–73. Repeatedly imprisoned, he participated in the Easter Rising 1916 and was leader of the nationalist ◊Sinn Féin party 1917–26, when he formed the republican ◊Fianna Fáil party. He directed negotiations with Britain 1921 but refused to accept the partition of Ireland until 1937.

De Valera was born in New York and sent to Ireland as a child, where he became a teacher of mathematics. He was sentenced to death for his part in the Easter Rising, but the sentence was commuted, and he was released under an amnesty 1917. In the same year he was elected member of Parliament and president of Sinn Féin. He was rearrested May 1918, escaped to the USA 1919, and returned to Ireland 1920, where he directed the struggle against the British government from a hiding place in Dublin. He authorized the negotiations of 1921, but refused to accept the ensuing treaty which divided Ireland into the Free State and the North.

Civil war followed. De Valera was imprisoned for a year by the Free State government 1923. In 1926 he formed a new party, Fianna Fáil, which secured a majority in 1932. De Valera became prime minister and foreign minister of the Free State; in 1938 he negotiated an agreement with Britain, under which all outstanding points were settled. Throughout World War II he maintained a strict neutrality, rejecting an offer by Winston Churchill 1940 to recognize the principle of a united Ireland in return for Eire's entry into the war. He resigned after his defeat at the 1948 elections but was again prime minister in the 1950s, and then president of the republic. ◊*See feature on pp. 550–551.*

de Valois Ninette. Stage name of Edris Stannus 1898– . Irish choreographer, dancer, and teacher. In setting up the Vic-Wells Ballet 1931 (later the Royal Ballet and Royal Ballet School) she was, along with choreographer Frederick ◊Ashton, one of the architects of British ballet. Among her works are *Job* 1931 and *Checkmate* 1937.

devaluation in economics, the lowering of the official value of a currency against other currencies, so that exports become cheaper and imports more expensive. Used when a country is badly in deficit in its balance of trade, it results in the goods the country produces being cheaper abroad, so that the economy is stimulated by increased foreign demand.

Devaluation of important currencies upsets the balance of the world's money markets and encourages speculation. Significant devaluations include that of the German mark in the 1920s and Britain's devaluation of sterling in the 1960s. To promote greater stability, many countries have allowed the value of their currencies to 'float', that is, to fluctuate in value (see ◊exchange rate).

developed world or ***First World*** or ***the North*** the countries that have a money economy and a highly developed industrial sector. They generally also have a high degree of urbanization, a complex communications network, high GDP per person, low birth and death rates, high energy consumption, and a large proportion of the workforce employed in manufacturing or service industries. The developed world includes the USA, Canada, Europe, Japan, Australia, and New Zealand.

developing in photography, the process that produces a visible image on exposed photographic ◊film, involving the treatment of the exposed film with a chemical developer. The developing liquid consists of a reducing agent that changes the light-altered silver salts in the film into darker metallic silver. The developed image is made permanent with a fixer, which dissolves away any silver salts which were not affected by light. The developed image is a negative, or reverse image: darkest where the strongest light hit the film, lightest where the least light fell. To produce a positive image, the negative is itself photographed, and the development process reverses the shading, producing the final print.

developing world or ***Third World*** or ***the South*** countries with a largely subsistence economy where the output per person and the average income are both low. These countries typically have high population growth and mortality rates; poor educational and health facilities; poor communications; low energy consumption per person; heavy dependence on agriculture and commodities for which prices and demand fluctuate; high levels of underemployment; high national debt; and, in some cases, political instability. The developing world includes much of Africa and parts of Asia and South America. Terms like 'developing world' and 'less developed countries' are often criticized for implying that a highly industrialized economy (as in the ◊developed world) is a desirable goal.

The early 1970s saw the beginnings of attempts by developing countries to act together in confronting the powerful industrialized countries over such matters as the level of prices of primary products, with the nations regarding themselves as a group that had been exploited in the past by the developed nations and that had a right to catch up with them (see ◊nonaligned movement).

Developing countries are themselves divided into low-income countries, including China and India; middle-income countries, such as Nigeria, Indonesia, and Bolivia; and upper-middle-income countries, such as Brazil, Algeria, and Malaysia. Developing countries have 75% of the world's population but consume only 20% of its resources.

Failure by many countries in the developing world to meet their enormous foreign debt obligations has led to stringent terms being imposed on loans by industrialized countries, as well as rescheduling of loans (deferring payment).

development in biology, the process whereby a living thing transforms itself from a single cell into a vastly complicated multicellular organism, with structures, such as limbs, and functions, such as respiration, all able to work correctly in relation to each other. Most of the details of this process remain unknown, although some of the central features are becoming understood.

Apart from the sex cells (◊gametes), each cell within an organism contains exactly the same genetic code. Whether a cell develops into a liver cell or a brain cell depends therefore not on which ◊genes it contains, but on which genes are allowed to be expressed. The development of forms and patterns within an organism, and the production of different, highly specialized cells, is a problem of control, with genes being turned on and off according to the stage of development reached by the organism.

development in the social sciences, the acquisition by a society of industrial techniques and technology; hence the common classification of the 'developed' nations of the First and Second worlds and the poorer, 'developing' or 'underdeveloped' nations of the Third World. The assumption that development in the sense of industrialization is inherently good has been increasingly questioned since the 1960s.

development aid see ◊aid, development.

developmental psychology study of development of cognition and behaviour from birth to adulthood.

deviance abnormal behaviour; that is, behaviour that deviates from the norms or the laws of a society or group, and so invokes social sanctions, controls, or stigma.

Deviance is a relative concept: what is considered deviant in some societies may be normal in others; in a particular society the same act (killing someone, for example) may be either normal or deviant depending on the circumstances (in wartime or for money, for example). Some sociologists argue that the reaction of others, rather than the act itself, is what determines whether an act is deviant, and that deviance is merely behaviour other people so label.

devil in Jewish, Christian, and Muslim theology, the supreme spirit of evil (Beelzebub, Lucifer, Iblis), or an evil spirit generally.

The devil, or Satan, is mentioned only in the more recently written books of the Old Testament, but the later Jewish doctrine is that found in the New Testament. The concept of the devil passed into the early Christian church from Judaism, and theology until at least the time of St Anselm represented the Atonement as primarily the deliverance, through Christ's death, of mankind from the bondage of the devil. Jesus recognized as a reality the kingdom of evil, of which Satan or Beelzebub was the prince. In the Middle Ages the devil in popular superstition assumed the attributes of the horned fertility gods of paganism, and was regarded as the god of witches. The belief in a personal devil was strong during the Reformation, and the movement's leader Luther regarded himself as the object of a personal Satanic persecution. With the development of liberal Protestantism in the 19th century came a strong tendency to deny the existence of a positive spirit of evil, and to explain the devil as merely a personification.

In Muslim theology, Iblis is one of the jinn (beings created by Allah from fire), who refused to prostrate himself before Adam, and who tempted Adam and his wife Hawwa (Eve) to disobey Allah, an act which led to their expulsion from Paradise. He continues to try to lead people astray, but at the Last Judgement he and his hosts will be consigned to hell.

devil ray any of several large rays of the genera *Manta* and *Mobula*, fish in which two 'horns' project forwards from the sides of the huge mouth. These flaps of skin guide the plankton on which the fish feed into the mouth. The largest of these rays can be 7 m/23 ft across, and weigh 1,000 kg/2,200 lb. They live in warm seas.

Devil's Island (French ***Ile du Diable***) smallest of the Iles du Salut, off French Guiana, 43 km/27 mi NW of Cayenne. The group of islands was collectively and popularly known by the name Devil's Island and formed a penal colony notorious for its terrible conditions.

Alfred ◊Dreyfus was imprisoned here 1895–99. Political prisoners were held on Devil's Island, and dangerous criminals on St Joseph, where they were subdued by solitary confinement in tiny cells or subterranean cages. The largest island, Royale, now has a tracking station for the French rocket site at Kourou.

Devlin Patrick Arthur. Baron Devlin 1905–1992. British judge, a jurist and commentator on the English legal system. He was justice of the High Court in the Queen's Bench Division 1948–60, Lord Justice of Appeal 1960–61, and Lord of Appeal in Ordinary 1961–64.

devolution delegation of authority and duties; in the later 20th century, the movement to decentralize governmental power, as in the UK where a bill for the creation of Scottish and Welsh assemblies was introduced 1976 (rejected by referenda in Scotland and Wales 1979). The word was first widely used in this sense in connection with Ireland, with the Irish Nationalist Party leader John Redmond claiming 1898 that the Liberals wished to diminish Home Rule into 'some scheme of devolution or federalism'. The Labour government elected 1997 committed itself to devolving power to Scottish and Welsh assemblies and this was later supported by referenda.

Devolution, War of war waged unsuccessfully 1667–68 by Louis XIV of France to in an attempt to gain Spanish territory in the Netherlands, of which ownership had allegedly 'devolved' on his wife Maria Theresa. During the course of the war the French marshal Turenne (1611–1675) conducted a series of sieges. An alliance of England, Sweden, and the Netherlands threatened intervention, so peace was made at Aix-la-Chapelle.

Devon or ***Devonshire*** county of SW England
area 6,720 sq km/2,594 sq mi (*see United Kingdom map*)
towns and cities Exeter (administrative headquarters), Plymouth; resorts: Paignton, Torquay, Teignmouth, and Ilfracombe
features rivers: Dart, Exe, Tamar; National Parks: Dartmoor, Exmoor; Lundy bird sanctuary and marine nature reserve in the Bristol Channel
industries mainly agricultural, with sheep and dairy farming and beef cattle; cider and clotted cream; Honiton lace; Dartington glass
population (1991) 1,010,000
famous people Francis Drake, John Hawkins, Charles Kingsley, Robert F Scott.

Devonian period of geological time 408–360 million years ago, the fourth period of the Palaeozoic era. Many desert sandstones from North America and Europe date from this time. The first land plants flourished in the Devonian period, corals were abundant in the seas, amphibians evolved from air-breathing fish, and insects developed on land. Devonian rocks were first studied in the county of Devon in SW England.

De Vries Hugo Marie 1848–1935. Dutch botanist who conducted important research on osmosis in plant cells and was a pioneer in the study of plant evolution. His work led to the rediscovery of Austrian biologist Gregor ◊Mendel's laws and the discovery of spontaneously occurring ◊mutations.

dew precipitation in the form of moisture that collects on the ground. It forms after the temperature of the ground has fallen below the dew point (the temperature at which the air becomes saturated with water vapour) of the air in contact with it. As the temperature falls during the night, the air and its water vapour become chilled, and condensation takes place on the cooled surfaces.

'For one man who thanks God that he is not as other men there are a few thousand to offer thanks that they are as other men, sufficiently as others to escape attention.'

John Dewey
Human Nature and Conflict

Dewar James 1842–1923. Scottish chemist and physicist who invented the ◊vacuum flask (Thermos) 1872 during his research into the properties of matter at extremely low temperatures. Working on the liquefaction of gases, Dewar found, in 1891, that both liquid oxygen and ozone are magnetic. In 1895 he became the first to produce liquid hydrogen, and in 1899 succeeded in solidifying hydrogen at a temperature of −259°C/−434°F. He also invented the explosive cordite 1889.

Dewey John 1859–1952. US philosopher who believed that the exigencies of a democratic and industrial society demanded new educational techniques. He expounded his ideas in numerous writings, including *School and Society* 1899, and founded a progressive school in Chicago. A pragmatist thinker, influenced by William James, Dewey maintained that there is only the reality of experience and made 'inquiry' the essence of logic.

Dewey Melvil 1851–1931. US librarian. In 1876, he devised the Dewey decimal system of classification for accessing, storing, and retrieving books, widely used in libraries. The system uses the numbers 000 to 999 to designate the major fields of knowledge, then breaks these down into more specific subjects by the use of decimals.

Dewey founded the American Library Association 1876 and the first school of library science, at Columbia University, 1887.

Dhaka or ***Dacca*** capital of Bangladesh from 1971, in Dhaka region, W of the river Meghna; population (1991) 3,397,200. It trades in jute, oilseed, sugar, and tea and produces textiles, chemicals, glass, and metal products. A former French, Dutch, and English trading post, Dhaka became capital of East Pakistan 1947; it was handed over to Indian troops Dec 1971 to become capital of the new country of Bangladesh.

dharma (Sanskrit 'justice, order') in Hinduism, the consciousness of forming part of an ordered universe, and hence the moral duty of accepting one's station in life. In Buddhism, dharma is the teaching of the Buddha, both the words and the principles these express, that leads to enlightenment.

For Hindus, correct performance of dharma has a favourable effect on their ◊karma (fate); this may enable them to be reborn to a higher caste or on a higher plane of existence, thus coming closer to the final goal of liberation from the cycle of reincarnation.

Dhofar mountainous western province of ◊Oman, on the border with Yemen; population (1982) 40,000. South Yemen supported left-wing guerrilla activity here against the Oman government in the 1970s, while Britain and Iran supported the government's military operations. The guerillas were defeated 1975. The capital is Salalah, which has a port at Rasut.

dhole wild dog *Cuon alpinus* found in Asia from Siberia to Java. With head and body up to 1 m/39 in long, variable in colour but often reddish above and lighter below, the dhole lives in groups of from 3 to 30 individuals. The species is becoming rare and is protected in some areas.

diabetes disease *diabetes mellitus* in which a disorder of the islets of Langerhans in the ◊pancreas prevents the body producing the hormone ◊insulin, so that sugars cannot be used properly. Treatment is by strict dietary control and oral or injected insulin, depending on the type of diabetes.

There are two forms of diabetes: Type 1, or insulin-dependent diabetes, which usually begins in childhood (early onset) and is an autoimmune condition; and Type 2, or noninsulin-dependent diabetes, which occurs in later life (late onset).

Careful management of diabetes, including control of high blood pressure, can delay some of the serious complications associated with the condition, which include blindness, disease of the peripheral blood vessels and kidney failure.

diagenesis or ***lithification*** in geology, the physical and chemical changes by which a sediment becomes a ◊sedimentary rock. The main processes involved include compaction of the grains, and the cementing of the grains together by the growth of new minerals deposited by percolating groundwater.

Diaghilev Sergei Pavlovich 1872–1929. Russian ballet impresario. In 1909 he founded the Ballets Russes/Russian Ballet (headquarters in Monaco), which he directed for 20 years. Through this company he brought Russian ballet to the West, introducing and encouraging a dazzling array of dancers, choreographers, composers, and artists, such as Anna Pavlova, Vaslav Nijinsky, Bronislava Nijinksa, Mikhail Fokine, Léonide Massine, George Balanchine, Igor Stravinsky, Sergey Prokofiev, Pablo Picasso, and Henri Matisse.

dialect variation of a spoken language shared by those in a particular area or a particular social group or both. The term is used to indicate a geographical area ('northern dialects') or social group ('black dialect').

dialectic Greek term, originally associated with the philosopher Socrates' method of argument through dialogue and conversation. Hegelian dialectic, named after the German philosopher ◊Hegel, refers to an interpretive method in which the contradiction between a thesis and its antithesis is resolved through synthesis.

dialectical materialism political, philosophical, and economic theory of the 19th-century German thinkers Karl Marx and Friedrich Engels, also known as ◊Marxism.

dialysis technique for removing waste products from the blood in chronic or acute kidney failure. There are two main methods, haemodialysis and peritoneal dialysis.

In haemodialysis, the patient's blood is passed through a pump, where it is separated from sterile dialysis fluid by a semipermeable membrane. This allows any toxic substances which have built up in the bloodstream, and which would normally be filtered out by the kidneys, to diffuse out of the blood into the dialysis fluid. Haemodialysis is very expensive and usually requires the patient to attend a specialized unit.

Peritoneal dialysis uses one of the body's natural semipermeable membranes for the same purpose. About two litres of dialysis fluid is slowly instilled into the peritoneal cavity of the abdomen, and drained out again, over about two hours. During that time toxins from the blood diffuse into the peritoneal cavity across the peritoneal membrane. The advantage of peritoneal dialysis is that the patient can remain active while the dialysis is proceeding. This is known as continuous ambulatory peritoneal dialysis (CAPD).

In the long term, dialysis is expensive and debilitating, and ◊transplants are now the treatment of choice for patients in chronic kidney failure.

diameter straight line joining two points on the circumference of a circle that passes through the centre of that circle. It divides a circle into two equal halves.

diamond generally colourless, transparent mineral, an ◊allotrope of carbon. It is regarded as a precious gemstone, and is the hardest substance known (10 on the ◊Mohs' scale). Industrial diamonds, which may be natural or synthetic, are used for cutting, grinding, and polishing.

Diamond crystallizes in the cubic system as octahedral crystals, some with curved faces and striations. The high refractive index of 2.42 and the high dispersion of light, or 'fire', account for the spectral displays seen in polished diamonds.

Diana in Roman mythology, the goddess of chastity, hunting, and the Moon, daughter of Jupiter and twin of Apollo. Her Greek equivalent is the goddess ◊Artemis.

Diana Princess of Wales (born Diana Frances Spencer) 1961–1997. Daughter of the 8th Earl Spencer, Diana married Prince Charles in St Paul's Cathedral, London, in 1981. She had two sons, William and Harry, before her separation from Charles in 1992 and their subsequent divorce in 1996.

Following her divorce, Diana resigned as the patron of many British and Commonwealth charities and cut her workload to just six charities of her choice. In the last few years of her life, Diana became deeply involved in the anti-landmine campaign.

Diana died in a car crash in Paris on 31 August 1997 together with her companion, Dodi Fayed, and their chauffeur. The accident happened as their car was being pursued by paparazzi photographers on motorcycles. Her violent and tragic death shocked the British nation and led to calls for the introduction of tougher privacy laws.

Public response to Diana's death was unprecedented as hundreds of thousands paid tribute to her. The strength of public feeling led the Queen to make an extraordinary live television tribute to the late Princess of Wales, and to arrange Diana's funeral in a way that would accommodate the public's wishes to be involved.

The funeral of Diana, Princess of Wales, proved to be the biggest British televised event in history. A record 31.5 million people – three quarters of British adults – watched the ceremony. The BBC's coverage of the funeral was broadcast in 185 countries.

dianetics form of psychotherapy developed by the US science-fiction writer L Ron Hubbard (1911–1986), which formed the basis for ◊Scientology. Hubbard believed that all mental illness and

Díaz Porfirio Díaz, dictator of Mexico 1877–80 and 1884–1911. A ruthless but effective dictator, Díaz achieved peace and prosperity for Mexico. His complete disregard for the welfare of the peasants, however, led to the popular revolution that was his downfall. *Mexican Ministry of Tourism*

certain forms of physical illness are caused by 'engrams', or incompletely assimilated traumatic experiences, both pre- and postnatal. These engrams can be confronted during therapy with an auditor and thus exorcised. An individual free from engrams would be a 'clear' and perfectly healthy.

diapause period of suspended development that occurs in some species of insects, characterized by greatly reduced metabolism. Periods of diapause are often timed to coincide with the winter months, and improve the insect's chances of surviving adverse conditions.

diaphragm in mammals, a thin muscular sheet separating the thorax from the abdomen. It is attached by way of the ribs at either side and the breastbone and backbone, and a central tendon. Arching upwards against the heart and lungs, the diaphragm is important in the mechanics of breathing. It contracts at each inhalation, moving downwards to increase the volume of the chest cavity, and relaxes at exhalation.

diaphragm or ***cap*** or ***Dutch cap*** barrier ◊contraceptive that is passed into the vagina to fit over the cervix (neck of the uterus), preventing sperm from entering the uterus. For a cap to be effective, a ◊spermicide must be used and the diaphragm left in place for 6–8 hours after intercourse. This method is 97% effective if practised correctly.

diarrhoea frequent or excessive action of the bowels so that the faeces are liquid or semiliquid. It is caused by intestinal irritants (including some drugs and poisons), infection with harmful organisms (as in dysentery, salmonella, or cholera), or allergies.

Dehydration as a result of diarrhoeal disease can be treated by giving a solution of salt and glucose by mouth in large quantities (to restore the electrolyte balance in the blood). Since most diarrhoea is viral in origin, antibiotics are ineffective.

Diaspora (Greek 'dispersion') dispersal of the Jews, initially from Palestine after the Babylonian conquest 586 BC, and then following the Roman sack of Jerusalem AD 70 and their crushing of the Jewish revolt of 135. The term has come to refer to all the Jews living outside Israel. It is also sometimes applied to the enforced dispersal of other peoples.

diathermy generation of heat in body tissues by the passage of high-frequency electric currents between two electrodes placed on the skin. The heat engendered helps to relieve rheumatic and arthritic pain. The principle is also applied in surgery. The high-frequency current produces, at the tip of a diathermy knife, sufficient heat to cut tissues, or to coagulate and kill cells, with a minimum of bleeding.

diatom microscopic alga of the division Bacillariophyta found in all parts of the world. Diatoms consist of single cells, sometimes grouped in colonies.

The cell wall is made up of two overlapping valves known as frustules, which are usually impregnated with silica, and which fit together like the lid and body of a pillbox. Diatomaceous earths (diatomite) are made up of the valves of fossil diatoms, and are used in the manufacture of dynamite and in the rubber and plastics industries.

diatomic molecule molecule composed of two atoms joined together. In the case of an element such as oxygen (O_2), the atoms are identical.

diatonic scale in music, a scale consisting of the seven notes of any major or minor key.

Díaz (José de la Cruz) Porfirio 1830–1915. Dictator of Mexico 1877–80 and 1884–1911. After losing the 1876 election, he overthrew the government and seized power. He was supported by conservative landowners and foreign capitalists, who invested in railways and mines. He centralized the state at the expense of the peasants and Indians, and dismantled all local and regional leadership. He faced mounting and revolutionary opposition in his final years and was forced into exile 1911.

Diaz Bartolomeu c. 1450–1500. Portuguese explorer, the first European to reach the Cape of Good Hope 1488, and to establish a route around Africa. He drowned during an expedition with Pedro Cabral (1460–1526).

Di Caprio Leonardo (Wilhelm) 1974– . Actor who made his film debut as Tobias Wolff in *This Boy's Life* (1993), and starred in *Romeo+Juliet* (1996), *Titanic* (1997), and *The Man in the Iron Mask* (1998).

He was born in Los Angeles, California. His other films include *What's Eating Gilbert Grape* (1993), for which he received the Academy Award nomination for Best Supporting Actor, *The Quick and the Dead* (1995), *The Basketball Diaries* (1995), and *Total Eclipse* (1995).

Dick Philip K(endred) 1928–1982. US science-fiction writer. His protagonists are often alienated individuals struggling to retain their integrity in a technologically dominated world. His novels include *The Man in the High Castle* 1962, *The Simulacra* 1964, and *Do Androids Dream of Electric Sheep?* 1968 (filmed as *Blade Runner* 1982).

Dickens Charles (John Huffam) 1812–1870. English novelist. He is enduringly popular for his memorable characters and his portrayal of the social evils of Victorian England. In 1836 he published the first number of the *Pickwick Papers*, followed by *Oliver Twist* 1837, the first of his 'reforming' novels; *Nicholas Nickleby* 1838; *The Old Curiosity Shop* 1840; *Barnaby Rudge* 1841; and *David Copperfield* 1850. Among his later books are *Bleak House* 1853, *Hard Times* 1854, *Little Dorrit* 1857, *A Tale of Two Cities* 1859, and *Great Expectations* 1861. All his novels were written as serials.

The *Pickwick Papers* were originally intended merely as an accompaniment to a series of sporting illustrations, but the adventures of Pickwick outgrew their setting and established Dickens's reputation. In 1842 he visited the USA, where he was welcomed as a celebrity. On his return home, he satirized US democracy in *Martin Chuzzlewit* 1844. *David Copperfield*, his most popular novel and his own favourite, contains many autobiographical incidents and characters; Mr Micawber is usually recognized as a sketch of his father. Dickens inaugurated the weekly magazine *Household Words* 1850, reorganizing it 1859 as *All the Year Round*; many of his later stories were published serially in these periodicals.

Dickens English novelist Charles Dickens, whose immense creative energy made him the most popular novelist of his age. Born into a family on the fringes of gentility, he was always acutely conscious of the social and economic abysses of Victorian society. *Corbis*

Dickinson Photograph of US poet Emily Dickinson. Though she lived a quiet, obscure life, politely ignored by writers and critics, she produced a body of short lyrics – well over 1,700, though only seven were published in her lifetime – which makes her the most original US poet of the 19th century. *Corbis*

Dickens Monica Enid 1915–1992. English writer. Her first books were humorous accounts of her experiences in various jobs, beginning as a cook (*One Pair of Hands* 1939); she went on to become a novelist. A close friend of the Samaritans' founder, Chad Varah, she founded the Samaritans in the USA. She was a great-granddaughter of Charles Dickens.

Dickinson Emily Elizabeth 1830–1886. US poet. She wrote most of her poetry between 1850 and the late 1860s and was particularly prolific during the Civil War years. She experimented with poetic rhythms, rhymes, and forms, as well as language and syntax. Her work is characterized by a wit and boldness that seem to contrast sharply with the reclusive life she led. Very few of her many short, mystical poems were published during her lifetime, and her work became well known only in the 20th century. The first collection of her poetry, *Poems by Emily Dickinson*, was published 1890.

dicotyledon major subdivision of the ◊angiosperms, containing the great majority of flowering plants. Dicotyledons are characterized by the presence of two seed leaves, or ◊cotyledons, in the embryo, which is usually surrounded by an ◊endosperm. They generally have broad leaves with net-like veins, and may be small plants such as daisies and buttercups, shrubs, or trees such as oak and beech. The other subdivision of the angiosperms is the ◊monocotyledons.

dictatorship term or office of an absolute ruler, overriding the constitution. (In ancient Rome a dictator was a magistrate invested with emergency powers for six months.) Although dictatorships were common in Latin America during the 19th century, the only European example during this period was the rule of Napoleon III. The crises following World War I produced many dictatorships, including the regimes of Atatürk and

'It is a melancholy truth that even great men have their poor relations.'

CHARLES DICKENS
Bleak House

'The philosopher has never killed any priests, whereas the priest has killed a great many philosophers.'

Denis Diderot *Observations on Drawing Up of Laws* 1774

Piłsudski (nationalist); Mussolini, Hitler, Primo de Rivera, Franco, and Salazar (all right-wing); and Stalin (communist).

dictionary book that contains a selection of the words of a language, with their pronunciations and meanings, usually arranged in alphabetical order. The term is also applied to any usually alphabetic work of reference containing specialized information about a particular subject, art, or science; for example, a dictionary of music. Bilingual dictionaries provide translations of one language into another.

The first dictionaries of English (*glossa collectae*), in the 17th century, served to explain difficult words, generally of Latin or Greek origin, in everyday English. Samuel Johnson's *A Dictionary of the English Language* 1755 was one of the first dictionaries of standard English. In North America, Noah Webster's *An American Dictionary of the English Language* 1828 quickly became a standard reference work. The many-volume *Oxford English Dictionary*, begun 1884 and subject to continuous revision, provides a detailed historical record of each word and, therefore, of the English language.

Diderot Denis 1713–1784. French philosopher. He is closely associated with the Enlightenment, the European intellectual movement for social and scientific progress, and was editor of the enormously influential ◊*Encyclopédie* 1751–80.

An expanded and politicized version of the English encyclopedia 1728 of Ephraim Chambers (c. 1680–1740), this work exerted an enormous influence on contemporary social thinking with its materialism and anticlericalism. Its compilers were known as Encyclopédistes.

Diderot's materialism, most articulately expressed in *D'Alembert's Dream*, published after Diderot's death, sees the natural world as nothing more than matter and motion.

didgeridoo or *didjeridu* musical lip-reed wind instrument, made from a hollow eucalyptus branch 1.5 m/4 ft long and blown to produce rhythmic, booming notes of relatively constant pitch. It was first developed and played by Australian Aborigines.

Dido Phoenician princess. The legendary founder of Carthage, N Africa, she committed suicide to avoid marrying a local prince. In the Latin epic *Aeneid*, Virgil represents her death as the result of her desertion by the Trojan hero ◊Aeneas.

diecasting form of ◊casting in which molten metal is injected into permanent metal moulds or dies.

Diefenbaker John George 1895–1979. Canadian Progressive Conservative politician, prime minister 1957–63; he was defeated after criticism of the proposed manufacture of nuclear weapons in Canada.

He became a member of parliament 1940, leader of his party 1956, and prime minister 1957. In 1958 he achieved the greatest landslide in Canadian history. A 'radical' Tory, he was also a strong supporter of Commonwealth unity. He resigned the party leadership 1967.

dielectric insulator or nonconductor of electricity, such as rubber, glass, and paraffin wax. An electric field in a dielectric material gives rise to no net flow of electricity. However, the applied field causes electrons within the material to be displaced, creating an electric charge on the surface of the material. This reduces the field strength within the material by a factor known as the dielectric constant (or relative permittivity) of the material. Dielectrics are used in capacitors, to reduce dangerously strong electric fields, and have optical applications.

Diels Otto Paul Hermann 1876–1954. German chemist. In 1950 he and his former assistant Kurt Alder (1902–1958) were jointly awarded the Nobel Prize for Chemistry for their research into the synthesis of organic chemical compounds.

In 1927 Diels dehydrogenated cholesterol to produce 'Diels hydrocarbon' ($C_{18}H_{16}$), an aromatic hydrocarbon closely related to the skeletal structure of all steroids, of which cholesterol is one. In 1935 he synthesized it. This work proved to be a turning point in the understanding of the chemistry of cholesterol and other steroids.

Diemen Anthony van 1593–1645. Dutch admiral. In 1636 he was appointed governor general of Dutch settlements in the E Indies, and wrested Ceylon and Malacca from the Portuguese. In 1636 and 1642 he supervised expeditions to Australia, on the second of which the navigator Abel Tasman discovered land not charted by Europeans and named it ***Van Diemen's Land***, now Tasmania.

Dien Bien Phu, Battle of decisive battle in the ◊Indochina War at a French fortress in North Vietnam, near the Laotian border. French troops were besieged 13 March–7 May 1954 by the communist Vietminh and the eventual fall of Dien Bien Phu resulted in the end of French control of Indochina.

Dieppe channel port at the mouth of the river Arques, Seine-Maritime *département*, N France; population (1990) 36,600. There are ferry services from its harbour to Newhaven and elsewhere; industries include fishing, shipbuilding, and pharmaceuticals.

In World War II, it was the target of the disastrous Dieppe raid Aug 1942. Over 6,000 Allied troops, mainly Canadian, took part in the limited-objective raid but they were unable to dislodge the Germans from their well-defended positions and were soon forced to withdraw with heavy losses.

Diesel Rudolf Christian Karl 1858–1913. German engineer who patented the diesel engine. He began his career as a refrigerator engineer and, like many engineers of the period, sought to develop a better power source than the conventional steam engine. Able to operate with greater efficiency and economy, the diesel engine soon found a ready market.

Dietrich German film actress and singer Marlene Dietrich in the classic film *The Blue Angel* 1930. She created a mesmerizing and sexually alluring persona as a husky-voiced femme fatale through her collaboration with director Josef von Sternberg in films such as *The Blue Angel* and *Shanghai Express* 1932. She later developed this image as a singer and entertainer. *British Film Institute*

diesel engine ◊internal-combustion engine that burns a lightweight fuel oil. The diesel engine operates by compressing air until it becomes sufficiently hot to ignite the fuel. It is a piston-in-cylinder engine, like the ◊petrol engine, but only air (rather than an air-and-fuel mixture) is taken into the cylinder on the first piston stroke (down). The piston moves up and compresses the air until it is at a very high temperature. The fuel oil is then injected into the hot air, where it burns, driving the piston down on its power stroke. For this reason the engine is called a compression-ignition engine.

Diesel engines have sometimes been marketed as 'cleaner' than petrol engines because they do not need lead additives and produce fewer gaseous pollutants. However, they do produce high levels of the tiny black carbon particles called particulates, which are believed to be carcinogenic and may exacerbate or even cause asthma.

The principle of the diesel engine was first explained in England by Herbert Akroyd (1864–1937) in 1890, and was applied practically by Rudolf Diesel in Germany in 1892.

diet the range of foods eaten by an animal, also a particular selection of food, or the overall intake and selection of food for a particular person or people. The basic components of any diet are a group of chemicals: proteins, carbohydrates, fats, vitamins, minerals, and water. Different animals require these substances in different proportions, but the necessity of finding and processing an appropriate diet is a very basic drive in animal evolution. For instance, all guts are adapted for digesting and absorbing food, but different guts have adapted to cope with particular diets.

Dietary requirements may vary over the lifespan of an organism, according to whether it is growing, reproducing, highly active, or approaching death. For instance, increased carbohydrate for additional energy, or increased minerals, may be necessary during periods of growth. For humans, an adequate diet is one that fulfils the body's nutritional requirements and gives an energy intake proportional to the person's activity level. *See list of tables on p. 1177.*

diet meeting or convention of the princes and other dignitaries of the Holy Roman (German) Empire, for example, the Diet of Worms 1521 which met to consider the question of Luther's doctrines and the governance of the empire under Charles V.

dietetics specialized branch of human nutrition, dealing with the promotion of health through the proper kinds and quantities of food.

Dietrich Marlene (born Maria Magdalene Dietrich von Losch) 1901–1992. German-born US actress and singer. She appeared with Emil Jannings in both the German and American versions of the film *Der Blaue Engel/The Blue Angel* 1930, directed by Josef von Sternberg. She stayed in Hollywood, becoming a US citizen 1937. Her husky, sultry singing voice added to her appeal. Her other films include *Blonde Venus* 1932, *Destry Rides Again* 1939, and *Just a Gigolo* 1978.

difference engine mechanical calculating machine designed (and partly built 1822) by the British mathematician Charles ◊Babbage to produce reliable tables of life expectancy. A precursor of the analytical engine, it was to calculate mathematical functions by solving the differences between values given to ◊variables within equations. Babbage designed the calculator so that once the initial values for the variables were set it would produce the next few thousand values without error.

differential arrangement of gears in the final drive of a vehicle's transmission system that allows the driving wheels to turn at different speeds when cornering. The differential consists of sets of bevel gears and pinions within a cage attached to the crown wheel. When cornering, the bevel pinions rotate to allow the outer wheel to turn faster than the inner.

differential calculus branch of ◊calculus involving applications such as the determination of maximum and minimum points and rates of change.

differentiation in embryology, the process by which cells become increasingly different and specialized, giving rise to more complex structures that have particular functions in the adult organism. For instance, embryonic cells may develop into nerve, muscle, or bone cells.

diffraction the slight spreading of a light beam into a pattern of light and dark bands when it passes through a narrow slit or past the edge of an obstruction. A ***diffraction grating*** is a plate of glass or metal ruled with close, equidistant parallel lines used for separating a wave train such as a beam of incident light into its component frequencies (white light results in a spectrum).

The regular spacing of atoms in crystals are used to diffract X-rays, and in this way the structure of many substances has been elucidated, including recently that of proteins (see ◊X-ray diffraction). Sound waves can also be diffracted by a suitable array of solid objects.

diffusion spontaneous and random movement of molecules or particles in a fluid (gas or liquid) from a region in which they are at a high concentration to a region of lower concentration, until a uniform concentration is achieved throughout. No mechanical mixing or stirring is involved. For instance, if a drop of ink is added to water, its molecules will diffuse until their colour becomes evenly distributed throughout.

In biological systems, diffusion plays an essential role in the transport, over short distances, of molecules such as nutrients, respiratory gases, and neurotransmitters. It provides the means by which small molecules pass into and out of individual cells and microorganisms, such as amoebae, that possess no circulatory system. Diffusion of water across a semi-permeable membrane is termed ◊osmosis.

Laws of diffusion were formulated by Thomas ◊Graham 1829 (for gases) and Adolph Fick 1829–1901 (for solutions).

digestion process whereby food eaten by an animal is broken down mechanically, and chemically by ◊enzymes, mostly in the ◊stomach and ◊intestines, to make the nutrients available for absorption and cell metabolism.

In some single-celled organisms, such as amoebae, a food particle is engulfed by the cell and digested in a ◊vacuole within the cell.

digestive system mouth, stomach, intestine, and associated glands of animals, which are responsible for digesting food. The food is broken down by physical and chemical means in the ◊stomach; digestion is completed, and most nutrients are absorbed in the small intestine; what remains is stored and concentrated into faeces in the large intestine. In birds, additional digestive organs are the ◊crop and ◊gizzard.

In smaller, simpler animals such as jellyfishes, the digestive system is simply a cavity (coelenteron or enteric cavity) with a 'mouth' into which food is taken; the digestible portion is dissolved and absorbed in this cavity, and the remains are ejected back through the mouth.

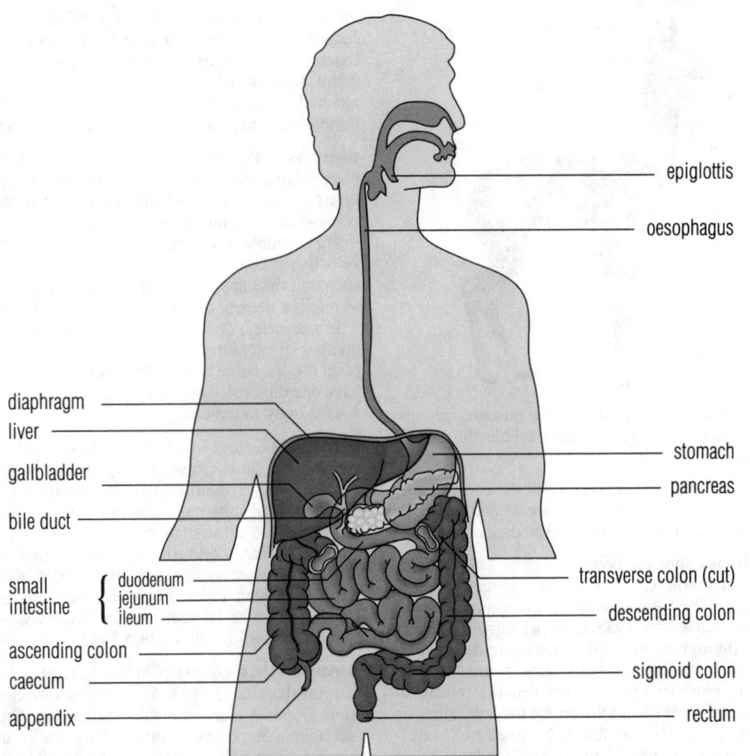

digestive system The human digestive system. When food is swallowed, it is moved down the oesophagus by the action of muscles (peristalsis) into the stomach. Digestion starts in the stomach as the food is mixed with enzymes and strong acid. After several hours, the food passes to the small intestine. Here more enzymes are added and digestion is completed. After all nutrients have been absorbed, the indigestible parts pass into the large intestine and thence to the rectum. The liver has many functions, such as storing minerals and vitamins and making bile, which is stored in the gall bladder until needed for the digestion of fats. The pancreas supplies enzymes. The appendix appears to have no function in human beings.

Digger or ***True Leveller*** member of an English 17th-century radical sect that attempted to seize and share out common land. The Diggers became prominent April 1649 when, headed by Gerrard Winstanley (c. 1609–1660), they set up communal colonies near Cobham, Surrey, and elsewhere. These colonies were attacked by mobs and, being pacifists, the Diggers made no resistance. The support they attracted alarmed the government and they were dispersed 1650. Their ideas influenced the early ◊Quakers.

digit in mathematics, any of the numbers from 0 to 9 in the decimal system. Different bases have different ranges of digits. For example, the ◊hexadecimal system has digits 0 to 9 and A to F, whereas the binary system has two digits (or ◊bits), 0 and 1.

digital in electronics and computing, a term meaning 'coded as numbers'. A digital system uses two-state, either on/off or high/low voltage pulses, to encode, receive, and transmit information. ***Digital electronics*** is the technology that underlies digital techniques. Low-power, miniature, integrated circuits (chips) provide the means for the coding, storage, transmission, processing, and reconstruction of information of all kinds. A ***digital display*** shows discrete values as numbers (as opposed to an analogue signal, such as the continuous sweep of a pointer on a dial).

digital audio tape (DAT) digitally recorded audio tape produced in cassettes that can carry up to two hours of sound on each side and are about half the size of standard cassettes. DAT players/recorders were developed 1987 but not marketed in the UK until 1989. Prerecorded cassettes are copy-protected. DAT is mainly used in recording studios for making master tapes. The system was developed by Sony. The first DAT for computer data was introduced 1988.

digital compact cassette (DCC) digitally recorded audio cassette that is roughly the same size as a standard cassette. It cannot be played on a normal tape recorder, though standard tapes can be played on a DCC machine; this is known as 'backwards compatibility'. A DCC player has a stationary playback and recording head similar to that in ordinary tape decks, though the tape used is chrome video tape. DCC was introduced in the UK 1992.

digital computer computing device that operates on a two-state system, using symbols that are internally coded as binary numbers (numbers made up of combinations of the digits 0 and 1); see ◊computer.

digital data transmission in computing, a way of sending data by converting all signals (whether pictures, sounds, or words) into numeric (normally binary) codes before transmission, then reconverting them on receipt. This virtually eliminates any distortion or degradation of the signal during transmission, storage, or processing.

digitalis medicinal substance derived from the leaves of the common European woodland plant *Digitalis purpurea* (foxglove). It is purified to digoxin, digitoxin, and lanatoside C, which are effective in cardiac regulation but induce the side effects of nausea, vomiting, and pulse irregularities. Pioneered in the late 1700s by William Withering, an English physician and botanist, digitalis was the first cardiac drug.

digitalis plant of the genus *Digitalis* of the figwort family Scrophulariaceae, which includes the ◊foxgloves. The leaves of the common foxglove *Digitalis purpurea* are the source of the drug digitalis used in the treatment of heart disease; it increases the efficiency of the heart by strengthening its muscle contractions and slowing its rate.

digital recording technique whereby the pressure of sound waves is sampled more than 30,000 times a second and the values converted by computer into precise numerical values. These are recorded and, during playback, are reconverted to sound waves. This technique gives very high-quality reproduction. The numerical values converted by computer represent the original sound-wave form exactly and are recorded on compact disc. When this is played back by ◊laser, the exact values are retrieved. When the signal is fed via an amplifier to a loudspeaker, sound waves exactly like the original ones are reproduced.

digital sampling electronic process used in ◊telecommunications for transforming a constantly varying (analogue) signal into one composed of discrete units, a digital signal. In the creation of recorded music, sampling enables the composer, producer, or remix engineer to borrow discrete vocal or instrumental parts from other recorded work (it is also possible to sample live sound).

A telephone microphone changes sound waves into an analogue signal that fluctuates up and down like a wave. In the digitizing process the waveform is sampled thousands of times a second and each part of the sampled wave is given a binary code number (made up of combinations of the digits 0 and 1) related to the height of the wave at that point, which is transmitted along the telephone line. Using digital signals, messages can be transmitted quickly, accurately, and economically.

digital-to-analogue converter electronic circuit that converts a digital signal into an ◊analogue (continuously varying) signal. Such a circuit is used to convert the digital output from a computer into the analogue voltage required to produce sound from a conventional loudspeaker.

digitizer in computing, a device that converts an analogue video signal into a digital format so that video images can be input, stored, displayed, and manipulated by a computer.

Dijon city in Côte-d'Or *département*, E central France, capital of Burgundy region; population (1990) 151,600. As well as metallurgical, chemical, and other industries, it has a wine trade and manufactures mustard.

dik-dik any of several species of tiny antelope, genus *Madoqua*, found in Africa south of the Sahara in dry areas with scattered brush. Dik-diks are about 60 cm/2 ft long and 35 cm/1.1 ft tall, and are often seen in pairs. Males have short, pointed horns. The dik-dik is so named because of its alarm call. *See illustration on following page.*

dilatation and curettage (D and C) common gynaecological procedure in which the cervix (neck of the womb) is widened, or dilated, giving access so that the lining of the womb can be scraped away (curettage). It may be carried out to terminate a

dik-dik Dik-diks are shy, secretive animals. At sunset and during the night, they browse on leaves, shoots, and buds. They also eat flowers (especially those of the acacia) and fruit, and dig up roots and tubers. They do not need to drink.

pregnancy, treat an incomplete miscarriage, discover the cause of heavy menstrual bleeding, or for biopsy.

dill herb *Anethum graveolens* of the carrot family Umbelliferae, whose bitter seeds and aromatic leaves are used for culinary and medicinal purposes.

Dillinger John Herbert 1903–1934. US bank robber and murderer. In 1923 he was convicted of armed robbery and spent the next ten years in state prison. Released in 1933, he led a gang on a robbery spree throughout the Midwest, staging daring raids on police stations to obtain guns. Named 'Public Enemy Number One' by the Federal Bureau of Investigation (FBI), Dillinger led the authorities on a long chase. He was finally betrayed by his mistress, the mysterious 'Lady in Red', and was killed by FBI agents in Chicago as he left a cinema.

Dilthey Wilhelm 1833–1911. German philosopher, a major figure in the interpretive tradition of ◊hermeneutics. He argued that the 'human sciences' (*Geisteswissenschaften*) could not employ the same methods as the natural sciences but must use the procedure of 'understanding' (*Verstehen*) to grasp the inner life of an alien culture or past historical period. Thus Dilthey extended the significance of hermeneutics far beyond the interpretation of texts to the whole of human history and culture.

dilution process of reducing the concentration of a solution by the addition of a solvent. The extent of a dilution normally indicates the final volume of solution required. A fivefold dilution would mean the addition of sufficient solvent to make the final volume five times the original.

DiMaggio Joe (Joseph Paul) 1914–1999. US baseball player with the New York Yankees 1936–51. In 1941 he set a record by getting hits in 56 consecutive games. He was an outstanding fielder, played centre field, hit 361 home runs, and had a career average of 325. DiMaggio was married to the actress Marilyn Monroe. He was elected to the Baseball Hall of Fame 1955.

Dimbleby Richard Frederick 1913–1965. British broadcaster. He joined the BBC in 1936 and became the foremost commentator on royal and state events and current affairs on radio and television. He is commemorated by the Dimbleby Lectures.

dime novel melodramatic paperback novel of a series started in the USA in the 1850s, published by Beadle and Adams of New York, which frequently dealt with Deadwood Dick and his frontier adventures. Authors included Edward L Wheeler, E Z C Judson, Prentiss Ingraham, and J R Coryell. The 'Nick Carter' Library added detective stories to the genre. Like British 'penny dreadfuls', dime novels attained massive sales and were popular with troops during the American Civil War and World War I.

dill Dill grows to a height of 45–90 cm/ 1.5–3 ft, and resembles fennel with feathery leaves and yellow flowers. A native plant of Asia and E Europe, it is now common throughout much of Europe.

dimension in science, any directly measurable physical quantity such as mass (M), length (L), and time (T), and the derived units obtainable by multiplication or division from such quantities.

For example, acceleration (the rate of change of velocity) has dimensions (LT^{-2}), and is expressed in such units as km s^{-2}. A quantity that is a ratio, such as relative density or humidity, is dimensionless.

In geometry, the dimensions of a figure are the number of measures needed to specify its size. A point is considered to have zero dimension, a line to have one dimension, a plane figure to have two, and a solid body to have three.

Dimitrov Georgi Mikhailovich 1882–1949. Bulgarian communist, prime minister from 1946. From 1919 he was a member of the executive of the Comintern, an international communist organization (see the ◊International). In 1933 he was arrested in Berlin and tried with others in Leipzig for allegedly setting fire to the parliament building (see ◊Reichstag Fire). Acquitted, he went to the USSR, where he became general secretary of the Comintern until its dissolution 1943.

Dinaric Alps extension of the European ◊Alps that runs parallel to the E Adriatic coast, stretching from Slovenia along the frontier between Croatia and Bosnia-Herzegovina into W Yugoslavia and N Albania. The highest peak is Durmitor at 2,522 m/8,274 ft.

Dine Jim (James) 1935– . US Pop artist. He experimented with combinations of paintings and objects, such as a bathroom sink attached to a canvas. Dine was a pioneer of ◊happenings in the 1960s and of ◊environment art.

Dinesen Isak. 1885–1962. Pen name of Danish writer Karen ◊Blixen, born Dinesen.

Dingaan 1795–c. 1843. Zulu chief who obtained the throne in 1828 by murdering his predecessor, Shaka, and became notorious for his cruelty. In warfare with the Boer immigrants into Natal he was defeated on 16 Dec 1838 – 'Dingaan's Day'. He escaped to Swaziland, where he was deposed by his brother Mpande and subsequently assassinated.

dingo wild dog of Australia. Descended from domestic dogs brought from Asia by Aborigines thousands of years ago, it belongs to the same species *Canis familiaris* as other domestic dogs. It is reddish brown with a bushy tail, and often hunts at night. It cannot bark.

Dinka Nilotic minority group in S Sudan. Primarily cattle herders, the Dinka inhabit the lands around the river system that flows into the White Nile. Their language belongs to the Nilo-Saharan family. The Dinka's animist beliefs conflict with those of Islam, the official state religion. This has caused clashes between the Dinka and the Sudanese army; by 1995 thousands had been massacred by one of the warring Sudanese factions, and more than 200,000 forced from their homes. The Dinka number around 1–2 million.

Dinkins David 1927– . Mayor of New York City 1990–93, a Democrat. He won a reputation as a moderate and consensual community politician and was Manhattan borough president before succeeding Edward Koch to become New York's first black mayor. He lost his re-election bid 1993 to Republican Rudolph Giuliani (1944–).

dinosaur (Greek *deinos* 'terrible', *sauros* 'lizard') any of a group (sometimes considered as two separate orders) of extinct reptiles living between 205 million and 65 million years ago. Their closest living relations are crocodiles and birds. Many species of dinosaur evolved during the millions of years they were the dominant large land animals. Most were large (up to 27 m/90 ft), but some were as small as chickens. They disappeared 65 million years ago for reasons not fully understood, although many theories exist.

classification Dinosaurs are divisible into two unrelated stocks, the orders Saurischia ('lizard-hip') and Ornithischia ('bird-hip'). Members of the former group possess a reptile-like pelvis and are mostly bipedal and carnivorous, although some are giant amphibious quadrupedal herbivores. Members of the latter group have a birdlike pelvis, are mainly four-legged, and entirely herbivorous.

The Saurischia are divided into: theropods ('beast-feet'), including all the bipedal carnivorous forms with long hindlimbs and short forelimbs (◊tyrannosaurus, megalosaurus); and sauropodomorphs ('lizard-feet forms'), including sauropods, the large quadrupedal herbivorous and amphibious types with massive limbs, long tails and necks, and tiny skulls (diplodocus, apatosaurus).

The Ornithischia were almost all plant-eaters, and eventually outnumbered the Saurischia. They are divided into four suborders: ornithopods ('bird-feet'), Jurassic and Cretaceous bipedal forms (iguanodon) and Cretaceous hadrosaurs with duck-bills; stegosaurs ('plated' dinosaurs), Jurassic quadrupedal dinosaurs with a double row of triangular plates along the back and spikes on the tail (stegosaurus); ankylosaurs ('armoured' dinosaurs), Cretaceous quadrupedal forms, heavily armoured with bony plates (nodosaurus); and ceratopsians ('horned' dinosaurs), Upper Cretaceous quadrupedal horned dinosaurs with very large skulls bearing a neck frill and large horns (triceratops).

These two main dinosaur orders form part of the superorder Archosaurus ('ruling reptiles'), comprising a total of five orders. The other three are pterosaurs ('winged lizards'), including ◊pterodactyls, of which no examples exist today, crocodilians, and birds. All five orders are thought to have evolved from a 'stem-order', the Thecondontia.

species Brachiosaurus, a long-necked plant-eater of the sauropod group, was about 12.6 m/40 ft to the top of its head, and weighed 80 tonnes. Compsognathus, a meat-eater, was only the size of a chicken, and ran on its hind legs. Stegosaurus, an armoured plant-eater 6 m/20 ft long, had a brain only about 3 cm/1.25 in long. Not all dinosaurs had small brains. At the other extreme, the hunting dinosaur stenonychosaurus, 2 m/6 ft long, had a brain size comparable to that of a mammal or bird of today, stereoscopic vision, and grasping hands. Many dinosaurs appear to have been equipped for a high level of activity. ◊Tyrannosaurus was a huge, two-footed, meat-eating theropod dinosaur of the Upper Cretaceous in North America and Asia. The largest carnivorous dinosaur was *Giganotosaurus carolonii*. It lived in Patagonia about 97 million years ago, was 12.5 m/41 ft long, and weighed 6–8 tonnes. Its skeleton was discovered 1995.

theories of extinction A popular theory of dinosaur extinction suggests that the Earth was struck by a giant meteorite or a swarm of comets 65 million years ago and this sent up such a cloud of debris and dust that climates were changed and the dinosaurs could not adapt quickly enough. The evidence for this includes a bed of rock rich in ◊iridium – an element rare on Earth but common in extraterrestrial bodies – dating from the time.

An alternative theory suggests that changes in geography brought about by the movements of continents and variations in sea level led to climate changes and the mixing of populations between previously isolated regions. This resulted in increased competition and the spread of disease.

archaeological findings The term 'dinosaur' was coined 1842 by Richard Owen (1804–1892), although there were findings of dinosaur bones as far back as the 17th century. In 1822 G A Mantell (1790–1852) found teeth of iguanodon in a quarry in Sussex. The first dinosaur to be described in a scientific journal was in 1824, when William Buckland, professor of geology at Oxford University, published his finding of a 'megalosaurus or great fossil lizard' found at Stonesfield, a village north-west of Oxford, although a megalosaurus bone had been found in 1677.

An almost complete fossil of a dinosaur skeleton was found in 1969 in the Andean foothills, South America; it had been a two-legged carnivore 2 m/6 ft tall and weighed more than 100 kg/220 lb. More than 230 million years old, it is the oldest known dinosaur. In 1982 a number of nests and eggs were found in 'colonies' in Montana, suggesting that some bred together like modern seabirds. In 1987 finds were made in China that may add much to the traditional knowledge of dinosaurs, chiefly gleaned from North American specimens. In 1989 and 1990 an articulated *Tyrannosaurus rex* was unearthed by a palaeontological team in Montana, with a full skull, one of only six known. Short stretches of dinosaur DNA were extracted 1994 from unfossilized bone retrieved from coal deposits approximately 80 million years old.

Dio Cassius c. AD 150–c. 235. Roman historian. He wrote, in Greek, a Roman history in 80 books (of which 26 survive), covering the period from the founding of the city to AD 229, including the only surviving account of the invasion of Britain by Claudius 43 BC.

Diocletian (Gaius Aurelius Valerius Diocletianus) AD 245–313. Roman emperor 284–305, when he abdicated in favour of Galerius. He reorganized and subdivided the empire, with two joint and two subordinate emperors, and in 303 initiated severe persecution of Christians.

diode combination of a cold anode and a heated cathode (or the semiconductor equivalent, which incorporates a *p–n* junction; see ◊semiconductor diode). Either device allows the passage of direct current in one direction only, and so is commonly used in a ◊rectifier to convert alternating current (AC) to direct current (DC).

dioecious of plants with male and female flowers borne on separate individuals of the same species. Dioecism occurs, for example, in the willows *Salix*. It is a way of avoiding self-fertilization.

Diogenes c. 412–c. 323 BC. Ascetic Greek philosopher who founded the ◊Cynic school. He believed in freedom and self-sufficiency for the individual, and that the virtuous life was the simple life; he did not believe in social mores. His writings do not survive. He is said to have wandered through the streets of Athens with a lantern, searching for an honest man.

Diomedes in Greek mythology, the son of Tydeus, and a prominent Greek leader in Homer's *Iliad*.

Dionysius two tyrants of the ancient Greek city of Syracuse in Sicily. ***Dionysius the Elder*** (c. 430–367 BC) seized power 405 BC. His first two wars with Carthage further extended the power of Syracuse, but in a third (383–378 BC) he was defeated. He was a patron of ◊Plato. He was succeeded by his son, ***Dionysius the Younger***, who was driven out of Syracuse by Dion 356; he was tyrant again 353, but in 343 returned to Corinth.

Dionysus in Greek mythology, the god of wine (son of Semele and Zeus), orgiastic excess, and mystic ecstasy. He was attended by women called maenads who were believed to be capable of tearing animals to pieces with their bare hands when under his influence. He was identified with the Roman ◊Bacchus, whose rites were less savage.

Diophantus lived AD 250. Greek mathematician in Alexandria whose *Arithmetica* is one of the first known works on problem-solving by algebra, in which both words and symbols are used.

His main mathematical study was in the solution of what are now known as 'indeterminate' or 'Diophantine' equations – equations that do not contain enough facts to give a specific answer but enough to reduce the answer to a definite type. These equations have led to the formulation of the theory of numbers, regarded as the purest branch of present-day mathematics.

Dior Christian 1905–1957. French couturier. He established his own Paris salon 1947 and made an impact with the 'New Look' – long, cinch-waisted, and full-skirted – after wartime austerity. His first collection 1947 was an instant success and he continued to be popular during the 1950s when he created elegant and sophisticated looks.

diorite igneous rock intermediate in composition between mafic (consisting primarily of dark-coloured minerals) and felsic (consisting primarily of light-coloured minerals); the coarse-grained plutonic equivalent of ◊andesite.

Dioscuri in classical mythology, title of ◊Castor and Pollux, meaning 'sons of Zeus'.

Diouf Abdou 1935– . Senegalese left-wing politician, first elected president 1980. He became prime minister 1970 under President Leopold Senghor and, on his retirement, succeeded him, being re-elected 1983, 1988, and 1993. His presidency has been characterized by authoritarianism.

dioxin any of a family of over 200 organic chemicals, all of which are heterocyclic hydrocarbons (see ◊cyclic compounds).

The term is commonly applied, however, to only one member of the family, 2,3,7,8-tetrachlorodibenzo-*p*-dioxin (2,3,7,8-TCDD), a highly toxic chemical that occurs, for example, as an impurity in the defoliant Agent Orange, used in the Vietnam War, and sometimes in the weedkiller 2,4,5-T. It has been associated with a disfiguring skin complaint (chloracne), birth defects, miscarriages, and cancer.

Disasters involving accidental release of large amounts of dioxin into the environment have occurred at Seveso, Italy, and Times Beach, Missouri, USA. Small amounts of dioxins are released by the burning of a wide range of chlorinated materials (treated wood, exhaust fumes from fuels treated with chlorinated additives, and plastics) and as a side effect of some techniques of paper-making.

diphtheria acute infectious disease in which a membrane forms in the throat (threatening death by ◊asphyxia), along with the production of a powerful toxin that damages the heart and nerves. The organism responsible is a bacterium (*Corynebacterium diphtheriae*). It is treated with antitoxin and antibiotics.

diploblastic in biology, having a body wall composed of two layers. The outer layer is the ectoderm, the inner layer is the endoderm. This pattern of development is shown by ◊coelenterates.

Diplock court in Northern Ireland, a type of court established 1972 by the British government under Lord Diplock (1907–1985) to try offences linked with guerrilla violence. The right to jury trial was suspended and the court consisted of a single judge, because potential jurors were allegedly being intimidated and were unwilling to serve. Despite widespread criticism, the Diplock courts continued in operation into the 1990s.

diplodocus plant-eating sauropod dinosaur that lived about 145 million years ago, the fossils of which have been found in the W USA. Up to 27 m/88 ft long, most of which was neck and tail, it weighed about 11 tonnes. It walked on four elephantine legs, had nostrils on top of the skull, and peglike teeth at the front of the mouth.

diploid having paired ◊chromosomes in each cell. In sexually reproducing species, one set is derived from each parent, the ◊gametes, or sex cells, of each parent being ◊haploid (having only one set of chromosomes) due to ◊meiosis (reduction cell division).

diplomacy process by which states attempt to settle their differences through peaceful means such as negotiation or ◊arbitration. See ◊foreign relations.

dip, magnetic angle at a particular point on the Earth's surface between the direction of the Earth's magnetic field and the horizontal. It is measured using a ***dip circle***, which has a magnetized needle suspended so that it can turn freely in the vertical plane of the magnetic field. In the northern hemisphere the needle dips below the horizontal, pointing along the line of the magnetic field towards its north pole. At the magnetic north and south poles, the needle dips vertically and the angle of dip is 90°. See also ◊angle of declination.

dipole the uneven distribution of magnetic or electrical characteristics within a molecule or substance so that it behaves as though it possesses two equal but opposite poles or charges, a finite distance apart.

The uneven distribution of electrons within a molecule composed of atoms of different ◊electronegativities may result in an apparent concentration of electrons towards one end of the molecule and a deficiency towards the other, so that it forms a dipole consisting of apparently separated but equal positive and negative charges. The product of one charge and the distance between them is the ***dipole moment***. A bar magnet behaves as though its magnetism were concentrated in separate north and south magnetic poles because of the uneven distribution of its magnetic field.

dipole, magnetic see ◊magnetic dipole.

dipper or ***water ouzel*** any of various birds of the genus *Cinclus*, family Cinclidae, order Passeriformes, found in hilly and mountainous regions across Eurasia and North America, where there are clear, fast-flowing streams. It can swim, dive, or walk along the bottom, using the pressure of water on its wings and tail to keep it down, while it searches for insect larvae and other small animals. Both wings and tail are short, the beak is fairly short and straight, and the general colour of the bird is brown, the throat and part of the breast being white.

Dirac Paul Adrien Maurice 1902–1984. British physicist who worked out a version of quantum mechanics consistent with special ◊relativity. The existence of antiparticles, such as the positron (positive electron), was one of its predictions. He shared the Nobel Prize for Physics 1933 with Austrian physicist Erwin ◊Schrödinger.

direct current (DC) electric current that flows in one direction, and does not reverse its flow as ◊alternating current does. The electricity produced by a battery is direct current.

Directoire style French decorative arts style of the period from about 1792 to 1799, following the Revolution. The style, which took its name from the Directory, the government of the day, introduces revolutionary art motifs, such as the pike of freedom, into ◊Neo-Classicism. A noted furniture designer working in the style was Georges Jacob (1739–1814).

Director of Public Prosecutions (DPP) in the UK, the head of the Crown Prosecution Service (established 1985), responsible for the conduct of all criminal prosecutions in England and Wales. The DPP was formerly responsible only for the prosecution of certain serious crimes, such as murder.

Directory the five-person ruling executive in France 1795–99. Established by the constitution of 1795, it failed to deal with the political and social tensions in the country and became increasingly unpopular after military defeats. It was overthrown by a military coup 9 Nov 1799 that brought Napoleon Bonaparte to power.

Members of the executive, known as the 'five majesties', included Paul-Jean Barras (1755–1829) and the Abbé Sieyès (1748–1836).

Dire Straits UK rock group formed 1977 by guitarist, singer, and songwriter Mark Knopfler (1949–). Their tasteful musicianship, influenced by American country rock, was tailor-made for the new compact-disc audience, and their 1985 LP *Brothers in Arms* went on to sell 20 million copies. Other albums include *On Every Street* 1991.

dirge (Latin *dirige*, from the office of the dead) song of lamentation for the dead. A poem of mourning is usually called an ◊elegy.

dirigible another name for ◊airship.

Dis in Roman mythology, the god of the underworld, also known as Orcus; he is equivalent to the Greek god ◊Pluto, ruler of Hades. Dis is also a synonym for the underworld itself.

disability limitation of a person's ability to carry out the activities of daily living, to the extent that he or she may need help in doing so.

Among adults the commonest disability is reduced mobility. Other common disabilities are in hearing, personal care, dexterity, and continence. Most disabilities arise from debilitating illness such as arthritis or stroke, although injury is also a leading cause. Other forms of disability are recognized in children: ***developmental disability*** is the failure to achieve a normal level of competence in some aspect of behaviour during infancy, childhood, or adolescence; a ***learning disability*** in a child of normal intelligence is a difficulty in acquiring one of the basic cognitive skills of speaking, reading, writing, or calculation.

disaccharide ◊sugar made up of two monosaccharides or simple sugars. Sucrose, $C_{12}H_{22}O_{11}$, or table sugar, is a disaccharide.

disarmament reduction of a country's weapons of war. Most disarmament talks since World War II have been concerned with nuclear-arms verification and reduction, but biological, chemical, and conventional weapons have also come under discussion at the United Nations and in other forums. Attempts to limit the arms race (initially between the USA and the USSR and since 1992 between the USA and

'Stand out of my sun a little.'

Diogenes
Response to Alexander the Great when asked whether he wanted anything

DISARMAMENT: TIMELINE

1930s	League of Nations attempt to achieve disarmament failed.
1968	US president Johnson's proposals for Strategic Arms Limitation Talks (SALT) were delayed by the Soviet invasion of Czechoslovakia.
1972–77	SALT I was in effect.
1979–85	SALT II, signed by the Soviet and US leaders Brezhnev and Carter, was never ratified by the US Senate, but both countries abided by it.
1986	US president Reagan revoked this pledge, against the advice of his European NATO partners.
1987	Reagan and the Soviet leader Gorbachev agreed to reduce their nuclear arsenals by 4% by scrapping intermediate-range nuclear weapons.
1990	Treaty signed between the USA and the USSR limiting both NATO and the Warsaw Pact to much-reduced conventional weapons systems in Europe.
1991 Jan	US president Bush announced decision to halve US military presence in Europe.
30–31 July	Bush and Gorbachev signed Strategic Arms Reduction Treaty (START), which limited both sides to no more than 6,000 nuclear warheads.
Sept–Oct	Bush announced the unilateral reduction of about 2,400 US nuclear weapons, asking the USSR to respond in kind. Gorbachev offered a package of unilateral cuts and proposals that surpassed the broad arms-control initiative presented by Bush.
1992 Jan	Bush and Russian president Yeltsin promised additional (60–80%) cuts in land- and sea-based long-range nuclear missiles. In addition, Bush promised an accelerated withdrawal of US troops from Europe and the halting of future production of the advanced B-2 bomber. Yeltsin announced that Russian long-range missiles would no longer be targeted on US cities.
June	Yeltsin consented to the abandonment of strategic parity (equal balance of arms) and announced, with Bush, bilateral cuts in long-term nuclear weapons that far surpassed the terms of the 1991 START treaty. By 2003, it was promised, US warheads would be cut from 9,986 to 3,500, and Russian warheads from 10,237 to 3,000.
1993 Jan	START II treaty signed by Bush and Yeltsin in Moscow, committing both countries to reduce long-range nuclear weapons by two-thirds by the year 2003 and to do away with land-based, multiple warheads.
1995 May	Negotiations to review Non-Proliferation Treaty (NPT) continued in New York. The treaty was originally signed in 1970 to limit the spread of nuclear weapons for 25 years; the 1995 negotiations aimed to renew the treaty on an indefinite basis, rather than for a limited period.

Russia) have included the ◊Strategic Arms Limitation Talks (SALT) of the 1970s and the ◊Strategic Arms Reduction Talks (START) of the 1980s–90s.

disc or ***disk*** in computing, a common medium for storing large volumes of data (an alternative is ◊magnetic tape). A ***magnetic disc*** is rotated at high speed in a disc-drive unit as a read/write (playback or record) head passes over its surfaces to record or read the magnetic variations that encode the data.

Recently, ***optical discs***, such as ◊CD-ROM (compact-disc read-only memory) and ◊WORM (write once, read many times), have been used to store computer data. Data are recorded on the disc surface as etched microscopic pits and are read by a laser-scanning device. Optical discs have an enormous capacity – about 550 megabytes (million ◊bytes) on a compact disc, and thousands of megabytes on a full-size optical disc.

Magnetic discs come in several forms:

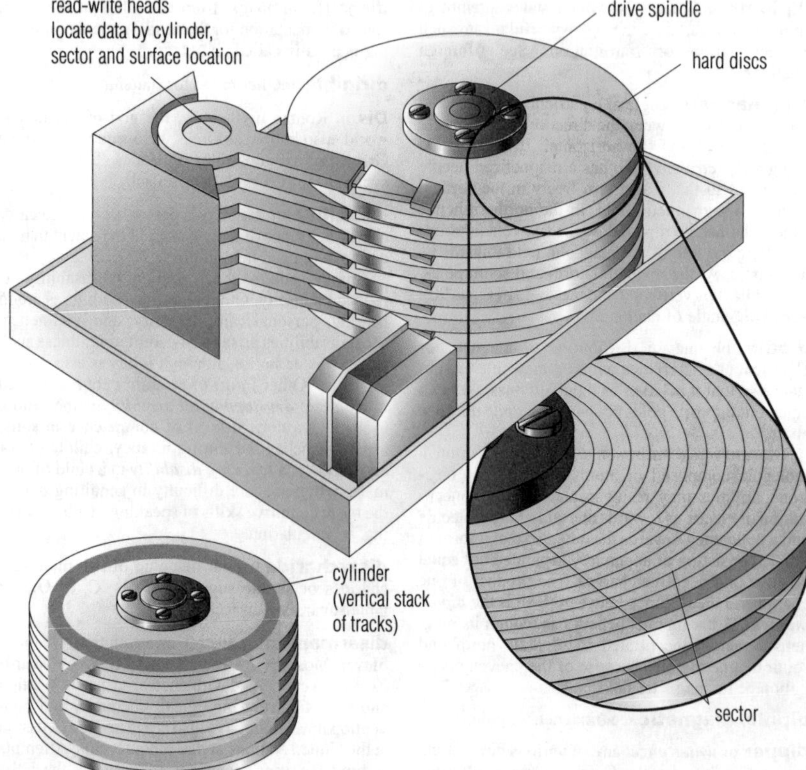

disc A hard disc. Data is stored in sectors within cylinders and is read by a head which passes over the spinning surface of each disc.

Fixed hard discs are built into the disc-drive unit, occasionally stacked on top of one another. A fixed disc cannot be removed: once it is full, data must be deleted in order to free space or a complete new disc drive must be added to the computer system in order to increase storage capacity. Large fixed discs, used with mainframe and minicomputers, provide up to 3,000 megabytes. Small fixed discs for use with microcomputers were introduced in the 1980s and typically hold 40–400 megabytes.

Removable hard discs are common in minicomputer systems. By swapping such discs around, a single hard-disc drive can be made to provide a potentially infinite storage capacity. However, access speeds and capacities tend to be lower than those associated with large fixed hard discs.

Floppy discs (or diskettes) are the most common form of backing store for microcomputers. They are much smaller in size and capacity than a hard disc, normally holding 0.5–2 megabytes of data. The floppy disc is so called because it is manufactured from thin flexible plastic coated with a magnetic material. All floppy discs can be removed from the drive unit.

disc drive mechanical device that reads data from and writes data to a magnetic ◊disc.

disc formatting in computing, preparing a blank magnetic disc in order that data can be stored on it. Data are recorded on a disc's surface on circular tracks, each of which is divided into a number of sectors. In formatting a disc, the computer's operating system adds control information such as track and sector numbers, which enables the data stored to be accessed correctly by the disc-drive unit.

Some floppy discs, called hard-sectored discs, are sold already formatted. However, because different makes of computer use different disc formats, discs are also sold unformatted, or soft-sectored, and computers are provided with the necessary utility program to format these discs correctly before they are used.

discharge tube device in which a gas conducting an electric current emits visible light. It is usually a glass tube from which virtually all the air has been removed (so that it 'contains' a near vacuum), with electrodes at each end. When a high-voltage current is passed between the electrodes, the few remaining gas atoms in the tube (or some deliberately introduced ones) ionize and emit coloured light as they conduct the current along the tube. The light originates as electrons change energy levels in the ionized atoms.

By coating the inside of the tube with a phosphor, invisible emitted radiation (such as ultraviolet light) can produce visible light; this is the principle of the fluorescent lamp.

disciple follower, especially of a religious leader. The word is used in the Bible for the early followers of Jesus. The 12 disciples closest to him are known as the ◊apostles.

disco music international style of dance music of the 1970s with a heavily emphasized beat, derived from ◊funk. It was designed to be played in discotheques rather than performed live; hence the production was often more important than the performer, and drum machines came to dominate.

Self-produced US disco group KC and the Sunshine Band (formed 1973) had five number-one hits, including 'Shake Your Booty' 1976. German producer Giorgio Moroder (1941–) created numerous disco hits, many of them with US singer Donna Summer (1948–), including 'Love to Love You, Baby' 1975 and 'I Feel Love' 1977. US producer Nile Rodgers (1952–) was a member of disco group Chic (1977–83), whose hits include 'Everybody Dance' 1978 and 'Good Times' 1979. Disco music was celebrated in the 1977 film *Saturday Night Fever*.

discrimination distinction made (social, economic, political, legal) between individuals or groups such that one has the power to treat the other unfavourably. Negative discrimination, often based on stereotype, includes anti-Semitism, apartheid, caste, racism, sexism, and slavery. Positive discrimination, or 'affirmative action', is sometimes practised in an attempt to counteract the effects of previous long-term discrimination. Minorities and, in some cases, majorities have been targets for discrimination.

Discrimination may be on grounds of difference of colour, nationality, religion, politics, culture, class, sex, age, or a combination of such factors. Legislation has been to some degree effective in forbidding racial discrimination, against which there is a United Nations convention 1969. National legislation in the UK includes the ◊race-relations acts 1965 and 1976 and the Sex Discrimination Act of 1975.

▷*See feature on pp. 1152–1153.*

discus circular disc thrown by athletes who rotate the body to gain momentum from within a circle 2.5 m/8 ft in diameter. The men's discus weighs 2 kg/4.4 lb and the women's 1 kg/2.2 lb. Discus throwing was a competition in ancient Greece at gymnastic contests, such as those of the Olympic Games. It is an event in the modern Olympics and athletics meetings.

disease any condition that impairs the normal state of an organism, and usually alters the functioning of one or more of its organs or systems. A disease is usually characterized by a set of specific symptoms and signs, although these may not always be apparent to the sufferer. Diseases may be inborn (see ◊congenital disease) or acquired through infection, injury, or other cause. Many diseases have unknown causes.

disinfectant agent that kills, or prevents the growth of, bacteria and other microorganisms. Chemical disinfectants include carbolic acid (phenol, used by Joseph ◊Lister in surgery in the 1870s), ethanol, methanol, chlorine, and iodine.

Disney Walt(er Elias) 1901–1966. US filmmaker and animator, a pioneer of family entertainment. He established his own studio in Hollywood 1923, and his first Mickey Mouse cartoons (*Plane Crazy*, which was silent, and *Steamboat Willie*, which had sound) appeared 1928.

In addition to short cartoons, the studio later made feature-length animated films, including *Snow White and the Seven Dwarfs* 1938, *Pinocchio* 1940, and *Dumbo* 1941. Disney's cartoon figures, such as Donald Duck, also appeared in comic books worldwide. In 1955, Disney opened the first theme park, Disneyland, in California.

Using the new medium of sound film, Disney developed the 'Silly Symphony', a type of cartoon based on the close association of music with visual images; the first was *The Skeleton Dance* 1929. He produced these in colour from 1932, culminating in the feature-length *Fantasia* 1940. The Disney studio also made nature-study films such as *The Living Desert* 1953, which have been criticized for their fictionalization of nature: wild animals were placed in unnatural situations to create 'drama'. Feature films with human casts were made from 1946, including *The Swiss Family Robinson* 1960 and *Mary Poppins* 1964. Disney also produced the first television series in colour 1961.

dispersal phase of reproduction during which gametes, eggs, seeds, or offspring move away from the parents into other areas. The result is that overcrowding is avoided and parents do not find themselves in competition with their own offspring. The mechanisms are various, including a reliance on wind or water currents and, in the case of animals, locomotion. The ability of a species to spread widely through an area and to colonize new habitats has survival value in evolution.

dispersion in physics, the separation of waves of different frequencies by passage through a dispersive medium, in which the speed of the wave depends upon its frequency or wavelength. In optics, the splitting of white light into a spectrum; for example, when it passes through a prism or diffraction grating. It occurs because the prism or grating bends each component wavelength through a slightly different angle. A rainbow is formed when sunlight is dispersed by raindrops.

displaced person originally, a refugee left without a home country by the border changes arising from World War II; later the term was also used to describe the millions of refugees who had been uprooted by the war and transported elsewhere, so that they had no home to which they could return.

Disraeli Benjamin, 1st Earl of Beaconsfield 1804–1881. British Conservative politician and novelist. Elected to Parliament 1837, he was chancellor of the Exchequer under Lord ◊Derby 1852, 1858–59, and 1866–68, and prime minister 1868 and 1874–80. His imperialist policies brought India directly under the crown, and he was personally responsible for purchasing control of the Suez Canal. The central Conservative Party organization is his creation. His popular, political novels reflect an interest in social reform and include *Coningsby* 1844 and *Sybil* 1845.

Excluded from ◊Peel's government of 1841–46, Disraeli formed his Young England group to keep a critical eye on Peel's Conservatism. When Peel decided in 1846 to repeal the Corn Laws, Disraeli opposed the measure in a series of witty and effective speeches; Peel's government fell soon after, and Disraeli gradually came to be recognized as the leader of the Conservative Party in the Commons. During the next 20 years the Conservatives formed short-lived minority governments in 1852, 1858–59, and 1866–68, with Lord Derby as prime minister and Disraeli as chancellor of the Exchequer and leader of the Commons. On Lord Derby's retirement in 1868 Disraeli became prime minister, but a few months later he was defeated by Gladstone in a general election. During the following six years of opposition he established Conservative Central Office, the prototype of modern party organizations. In 1874 Disraeli took office for the second time; some useful reform measures were carried, but the outstanding feature of the government's policy was its imperialism. It was Disraeli's personal initiative that purchased from the Khedive of Egypt a controlling interest in the Suez Canal, conferred on the Queen the title of Empress of India, and sent the Prince of Wales on the first royal tour of that country. The Bulgarian revolt of 1876 and the subsequent Russo-Turkish War of 1877–78 provoked one of many political duels between Disraeli and Gladstone, the Liberal leader, and was concluded by the Congress of Berlin 1878, where Disraeli was the principal British delegate and brought home 'peace with honour' and Cyprus. The government was defeated in 1880, and a year later Disraeli died.

dissection cutting apart of bodies to study their organization, or tissues to gain access to a site in surgery. Postmortem dissection was considered a sin in the Middle Ages. In the UK before 1832, hanged murderers were the only legal source of bodies, supplemented by graverobbing. The Anatomy Act 1832 authorized the use of deceased institutionalized paupers unclaimed by next of kin, and by the 1940s bequests of bodies had been introduced.

Dissenter former name for a Protestant refusing to conform to the established Christian church. For example, Baptists, Presbyterians, and Independents (now known as Congregationalists) were Dissenters.

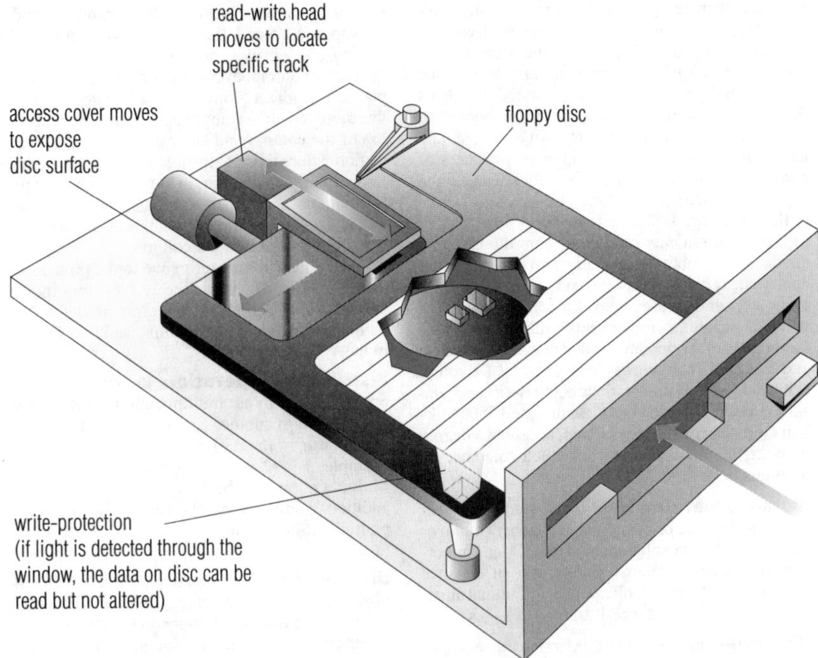

disc drive A floppy disc drive. As the disc is inserted into the drive, its surface is exposed to the read-write head, which moves over the spinning disc surface to locate a specific track.

'I love Mickey Mouse more than any woman I've ever known.'

WALT DISNEY
Quoted in W Wagner *You Must Remember This*

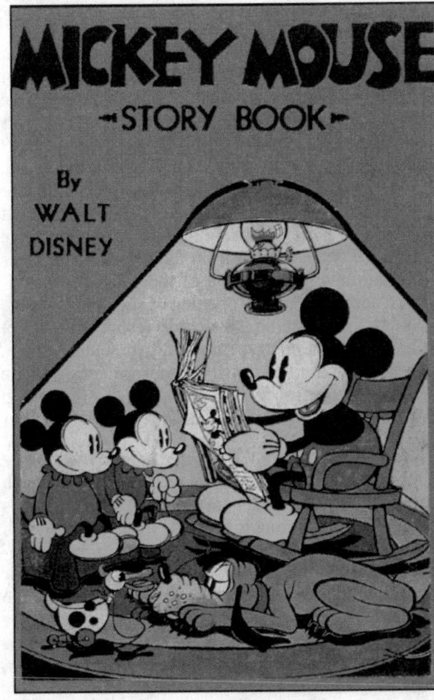

Disney Mickey Mouse, Disney's first and most famous cartoon character, made his debut in *Plane Crazy* 1928. *Sotheby's*

'Justice is truth in action.'

BENJAMIN DISRAELI
Speech in House of Commons
11 Feb 1851

Disraeli Cartoon from *Punch* 1872 depicting Disraeli (front) and Gladstone as two opposing lions making speeches in Lancashire. *Philip Sauvain*

'All hope abandon, ye who enter here.'

THE DIVINE COMEDY 'Inferno' Dante Alighieri

dissident in one-party states, a person intellectually dissenting from the official line. Dissidents have been sent into exile, prison, labour camps, and mental institutions, or deprived of their jobs. In the former USSR the number of imprisoned dissidents declined from more than 600 in 1986 to fewer than 100 in 1990, of whom the majority were ethnic nationalists. In China the number of prisoners of conscience increased after the 1989 Tiananmen Square massacre.

In the former USSR before the introduction of ◊glasnost, dissidents comprised communists who advocated a more democratic and humanitarian approach; religious proselytizers; Jews wishing to emigrate; and those who supported ethnic or national separatist movements within the USSR (among them Armenians, Lithuanians, Ukrainians, and Tatars). Their views were expressed through samizdat (clandestinely distributed writings) and sometimes published abroad. In the late 1980s Mikhail Gorbachev lifted censorship, accepted a degree of political pluralism, and extended tolerance to religious believers.

distance learning home-based study by correspondence course or by radio, television, or audio or video tape. The establishment of the ◊Open University1969 put the UK in the forefront of distance learning; the ◊Open College and individual institutions also offer distance-learning packages.

distemper any of several infectious diseases of animals characterized by catarrh, cough, and general weakness. Specifically, it refers to a virus disease in young dogs, also found in wild animals, which can now be prevented by vaccination. In 1988 an allied virus killed over 10,000 common seals in the Baltic and North seas.

distillation technique used to purify liquids or to separate mixtures of liquids possessing different boiling points. Simple distillation is used in the purification of liquids (or the separation of substances in solution from their solvents) – for example, in the production of pure water from a salt solution.

The solution is boiled and the vapours of the solvent rise into a separate piece of apparatus (the condenser) where they are cooled and condensed. The liquid produced (the distillate) is the pure solvent; the non-volatile solutes (now in solid form) remain in the distillation vessel to be discarded as impurities or recovered as required. Mixtures of liquids (such as ◊petroleum or aqueous ethanol) are separated by fractional distillation, or fractionation. When the mixture is boiled, the vapours of its most volatile component rise into a vertical ◊fractionating column where they condense to liquid form. However, as this liquid runs back down the column it is reheated to boiling point by the hot rising vapours of the next-most-volatile component and so its vapours ascend the column once more. This boiling-condensing process occurs repeatedly inside the column, eventually bringing about a temperature gradient along its length. The vapours of the more volatile components therefore reach the top of the column and enter the condenser for collection before those of the less volatile components. In the fractional distillation of petroleum, groups of compounds (fractions) possessing similar relative molecular masses and boiling points are tapped off at different points on the column.

The earliest known reference to the process is to the distillation of wine in the 12th century by Adelard of Bath. The chemical retort used for distillation was invented by Muslims, and was first seen in the West about 1570.

distillation Commercial distillation apparatus. Alcoholic liquor is prepared by distillation in the copper coloured vats whose long necks permit the efficient condensation and collection of the vapours to produce the distillate. *Image Select (UK) Ltd*

distributive operation in mathematics, an operation, such as multiplication, that bears a relationship to another operation, such as addition, such that $a \times (b + c) = (a \times b) + (a \times c)$. For example, $3 \times (2 + 4) = (3 \times 2) + (3 \times 4) = 18$. Multiplication may be said to be distributive over addition. Addition is not, however, distributive over multiplication because $3 + (2 \times 4) \neq (3 + 2) \times (3 + 4)$.

distributor device in the ignition system of a piston engine that distributes pulses of high-voltage electricity to the ◊spark plugs in the cylinders. The electricity is passed to the plug leads by the tip of a rotor arm, driven by the engine camshaft, and current is fed to the rotor arm from the ignition coil. The distributor also houses the contact point or breaker, which opens and closes to interrupt the battery current to the coil, thus triggering the high-voltage pulses. With electronic ignition it is absent.

district council unit of local government in England and Wales. District-council responsibilities cover housing, local planning and development, roads (excluding trunk and classified), bus services, environmental health (refuse collection, clean air, food safety and hygiene, and enforcement of the Offices, Shops and Railway Premises Act), council tax, museums and art galleries, parks and playing fields, swimming baths, cemeteries, and so on. In metropolitan district councils, education, personal social services, and libraries are also included. Following reorganization in 1997 and 1998 some district councils no longer exist, or have become 'single tier' ◊unitary authorities.

District of Columbia (DC) federal district of the USA, see ◊Washington DC.

diuretic any drug that increases the output of urine by the kidneys. It may be used in the treatment of high blood pressure and to relieve ◊oedema associated with heart, lung, kidney or liver disease, and some endocrine disorders.

diver The red-throated diver. Divers are primitive water birds usually known in the USA as loons. They are found in the high latitudes of the northern hemisphere where they inhabit estuaries, lakes, and wetland areas. Their eerie, wailing calls evoke the very essence of wild, uninhabited country. Divers can reach depths of up to 60 m/200 ft in pursuit of their fish prey.

diver or ***loon*** any of four species of marine bird of the order Gaviiformes, specialized for swimming and diving, found in northern regions of the northern hemisphere. The legs are set so far back that walking is almost impossible, but they are powerful swimmers and good flyers, and only come ashore to nest. They have straight bills, short tail-feathers, webbed feet, and long bodies; they feed on fish, crustaceans, and some water plants. During the breeding period they live inland and the female lays two eggs which hatch into down-covered chicks. Of the four species, the largest is the white-billed diver *Gavia adamsii*, an Arctic species 75 cm/2.5 ft long.

Two species regularly breed in Britain. They are the red-throated diver *Gavia stellata* and the black-throated diver *G. arctica*. The great northern diver or common loon *G. immer* also breeds sometimes in Britain.

diverticulitis inflammation of diverticula (pockets of herniation) in the large intestine. It is usually triggered by infection and causes diarrhoea or constipation, and lower abdominal pain. Usually it can be controlled by diet and antibiotics.

divertissement (French 'entertainment') dance, or suite of dances, within a ballet or opera, where the plot comes to a halt for a display of technical virtuosity, such as the character dances in the last act of *Coppélia* by Delibes, or the last acts of *Sleeping Beauty* and *A Midsummer Night's Dream*.

dividend in business, the amount of money that company directors decide should be taken out of net profits for distribution to shareholders. It is usually declared as a percentage or fixed amount per ◊share.

divination art of ascertaining future events or eliciting other hidden knowledge by supernatural or nonrational means. Divination played a large part in the ancient civilizations of the Egyptians, Greeks (see ◊oracle), Romans, and Chinese (using the ◊*I Ching*), and is still practised throughout the world.

Divination generally involves the intuitive interpretation of the mechanical operations of chance or natural law. Forms of divination have included omens drawn from the behaviour of birds and animals; examination of the entrails of sacrificed animals; random opening of such books as the Bible; fortune-telling by cards (especially ◊tarot cards) and palmistry; ◊dowsing; oracular trance-speaking; automatic writing; necromancy, or the supposed raising of the spirits of the dead; and dreams, often specially induced.

Divine Comedy, The epic poem by ◊Dante Alighieri 1307–21, describing a journey through Hell, Purgatory, and Paradise. The poet Virgil is Dante's guide through Hell and Purgatory; to each of the three realms, or circles, Dante assigns historical and contemporary personages according to their moral (and also political) worth. In Paradise Dante finds his lifelong love Beatrice. The poem makes great use of symbolism and allegory, and influenced many English writers, including Milton, Byron, Shelley, and T S Eliot.

Divine Light Mission religious movement founded in India in 1960, which gained a prominent following in the USA in the 1970s. It proclaims Guru Maharaj Ji (1957–) as the present age's successor to the gods or religious leaders Krishna, Buddha, Jesus, and Muhammad. He is believed to be able to provide his followers with the knowledge required to attain salvation.

divine right of kings Christian political doctrine that hereditary monarchy is the system approved by God, hereditary right cannot be forfeited, monarchs are accountable to God alone for their actions, and rebellion against the lawful sovereign is therefore blasphemous.

The doctrine had its origins in the anointing of Pepin in 751 by the pope after Pepin had usurped the throne of the Franks. It was at its peak in 16th- and 17th-century Europe as a weapon against the claims of the papacy – the court of Louis XIV of France pushed this to the limit – and was in 17th-century England maintained by the supporters of the Stuarts in opposition to the democratic theories of the Puritans and Whigs.

diving sport of entering water either from a springboard 1 m/3 ft or 3 m/10 ft above the water, or from a platform, or highboard, 10 m/33 ft above the water. Various differing starts are adopted, facing forwards or backwards, and somersaults, twists, and combinations thereof are performed in midair before entering the water. A minimum pool depth of 5 m/16.5 ft is needed for high or platform diving. Points are awarded and the level of difficulty of each dive is used as a multiplying factor.

diving apparatus any equipment used to enable a person to spend time underwater. Diving bells were in use in the 18th century, the diver breathing air trapped in a bell-shaped chamber. This was followed by cumbersome diving suits in the early 19th century. Complete freedom of movement came with the ◊aqualung, invented by Jacques ◊Cousteau in the early 1940s. For work at greater depths the technique of saturation diving was developed in the 1970s by which divers live for a week or more breathing a mixture of helium and oxygen at the pressure existing on the seabed where they work (as in work on North Sea platforms and tunnel building).

The first diving suit, with a large metal helmet supplied with air through a hose, was invented in the UK by the brothers John and Charles Deane in 1828. Saturation diving was developed for working in offshore oilfields. Working divers are ferried down to the work site by a pressurized submersible vessel. By this technique they avoid the need for lengthy periods of decompression after every dive. Slow decompression is necessary to avoid the dangerous consequences of an attack of the bends, or ◊decompression sickness.

division military formation consisting of two or more brigades. A major general at divisional headquarters commands the brigades and also additional artillery, engineers, attack helicopters, and other logistic support. There are 10,000 or more soldiers in a division. Two or more divisions form a corps.

divorce legal dissolution of a lawful marriage. It is distinct from an annulment, which is a legal declaration that the marriage was invalid. The ease with which a divorce can be obtained in different countries varies considerably and is also affected by different religious practices.

The Roman Catholic Church does not permit divorce among its members, and under Pope John Paul II conditions for annulment have been tightened. Among Muslims a wife cannot divorce her husband, but he may divorce her by repeating the formula 'I divorce you' three times (called *talaq*). In Shi'ite law this must be pronounced either once or three times in the presence of two witnesses; in Sunni law it can be either oral or in writing. No reason need be given, nor does the wife have to be notified (although some Muslim countries, for example Pakistan, have introduced such a requirement). Property settlements by careful parents make this a right infrequently exercised.

Diwali ('garland of lamps') Hindu festival in Oct/Nov celebrating Lakshmi, goddess of light and wealth, as well as the New Year and the story of the *Rāmāyana*. It is marked by the lighting of lamps and candles (inviting the goddess into the house), feasting, and the exchange of gifts. For Sikhs, Diwali celebrates Guru Hargobind's release from prison.

Dix Otto 1891–1969. German painter. He was a major exponent of the harsh Realism current in Germany in the 1920s and closely associated with the *Neue Sachlichkeit* group. He is known chiefly for his unsettling 1920s paintings of prostitutes and sex murders and for his powerful series of works depicting the hell of trench warfare, for example *Flanders: After Henri Barbusse 'Le Feu'* 1934–36 (Nationalgalerie, Berlin).

In 1933 Dix was dismissed from his teaching post at the Dresden Art Academy by the Nazis, and branded a decadent. His experiences as a serving soldier in World War I and as a prisoner of war 1945–46 instilled in him a profound horror of armed conflict.

Dixie southern states of the USA. The word probably derives from the ◊Mason–Dixon Line.

Dixieland jazz jazz style that originated in New Orleans, USA, in the early 20th century, dominated by cornet, trombone, and clarinet. The trumpeter Louis Armstrong emerged from this style. The ***trad jazz*** movement in the UK in the 1940s–50s was a Dixieland revival.

Djibouti chief port and capital of the Republic of Djibouti, on a peninsula 240 km/149 mi SW of Aden and 565 km/351 mi NE of Addis Ababa; population (1995) 383,000. The city succeeded Obock as capital of French Somaliland 1896 and was the official port of Ethiopia 1897–1949.

Djibouti country on the E coast of Africa, at the S end of the Red Sea, bounded E by the Gulf of Aden, SE by Somalia, S and W by Ethiopia, and NW by Eritrea. *See country box on p. 322.*

Djilas Milovan 1911–1995. Yugoslav dissident and political writer. A close wartime colleague of Marshal ◊Tito, he was dismissed from high office 1954 and twice imprisoned 1956–61 and 1962–66 because of his advocacy of greater political pluralism and condemnation of the communist bureaucracy. He was formally rehabilitated 1989.

DNA (abbreviation for ***deoxyribonucleic acid***) complex giant molecule that contains, in chemically coded form, the information needed for a cell to make proteins. DNA is a ladderlike double-stranded ◊nucleic acid which forms the basis of genetic inheritance in all organisms, except for a few viruses that have only ◊RNA. DNA is organized into ◊chromosomes and, in organisms other than bacteria, it is found only in the cell nucleus.

structure DNA is made up of two chains of ◊nucleotide subunits, with each nucleotide containing either a purine (adenine or guanine) or pyrimidine (cytosine or thymine) base.

The bases link up with each other (adenine linking with thymine, and cytosine with guanine) to form ◊base pairs that connect the two strands of the DNA molecule like the rungs of a twisted ladder.

heredity The specific way in which the pairs form means that the base sequence is preserved from generation to generation. Hereditary information is stored as a specific sequence of bases. A set of three bases – known as a codon – acts as a blueprint for the manufacture of a particular ◊amino acid, the subunit of a protein molecule.

blueprint for the organism The information encoded by the codons is transcribed (see ◊transcription) by messenger RNA and is then translated into amino acids in the ribosomes and cytoplasm. The sequence of codons determines the precise order in which amino acids are linked up during manufacture and, therefore, the kind of protein that is to be produced. Because proteins are the chief structural molecules of living matter and, as enzymes, regulate all aspects of metabolism, it may be seen that the genetic code is effectively responsible for building and controlling the whole organism.

laboratory techniques The sequence of bases along the length of DNA can be determined by cutting the molecule into small portions, using restriction enzymes. This technique can also be used for transferring specific sequences of DNA from one organism to another.

DNA fingerprinting or ***DNA profiling*** another name for ◊genetic fingerprinting.

Dnepropetrovsk city in Ukraine, on the right bank of the river Dnieper; population (1992) 1,190,000. It is the centre of a major industrial region, with iron, steel, chemical, and engineering industries. It is linked with the Dnieper Dam, 60 km/37 mi downstream.

Dnieper or ***Dnepr*** river rising in the Smolensk region of the Russian Federation and flowing S through Belarus and Ukraine to enter the Black Sea E of Odessa; total length 2,250 km/1,400 mi.

Dobell William 1899–1970. Australian portraitist and genre painter, born in New South Wales. He studied art in the UK and the Netherlands 1929–39. His portrait of *Joshua Smith* 1943 (Sir Edward Hayward, Adelaide, Australia) provoked a court case (Dobell was accused of caricaturing his subject).

Dobermann or ***Dobermann pinscher*** breed of smooth-coated dog with a docked tail, much used as a guard dog. It stands up to 70 cm/27.5 in tall, has a long head with a flat, smooth skull, and is often black with brown markings. It takes its name from the man who bred it in 19th-century Germany.

Döblin Alfred 1878–1957. German novelist. His *Berlin-Alexanderplatz* 1929 owes much to James Joyce's ◊*Ulysses* in its minutely detailed depiction of the inner lives of a city's inhabitants, scrutinizing the social and psychological pressures exerted by the city; it is considered by many to be the finest 20th-century German novel. Other works include *November 1918: Eine deutsche Revolution/A German Revolution* 1939–50 (published in four parts) about the formation of the Weimar Republic.

The question of reality was of persistent concern to Döblin, accounting for the uneasy tension in his works between realistic rationalism and elements of mystical religion.

The Right Divine of Kings to govern wrong.

DIVINE RIGHT OF KINGS Alexander Pope, *The Dunciad* 1728

We have discovered the secret of life!

Francis Crick on discovering the structure of **DNA**

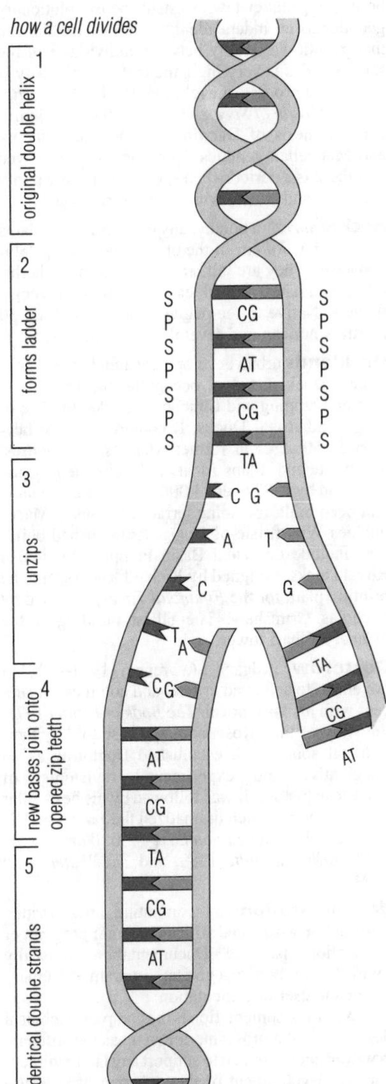

DNA How the DNA molecule divides. The DNA molecule consists of two strands wrapped around each other in a spiral or helix. The main strands consist of alternate sugar (S) and phosphate (P) groups, and attached to each sugar is a nitrogenous base – adenine (A), cytosine (C), guanine (G), or thymine (T). The sequence of bases carries the genetic code which specifies the characteristics of offspring. The strands are held together by weak bonds between the bases, cytosine to guanine, and adenine to thymine. The weak bonds allow the strands to split apart, allowing new bases to attach, forming another double strand.

DJIBOUTI
Republic of

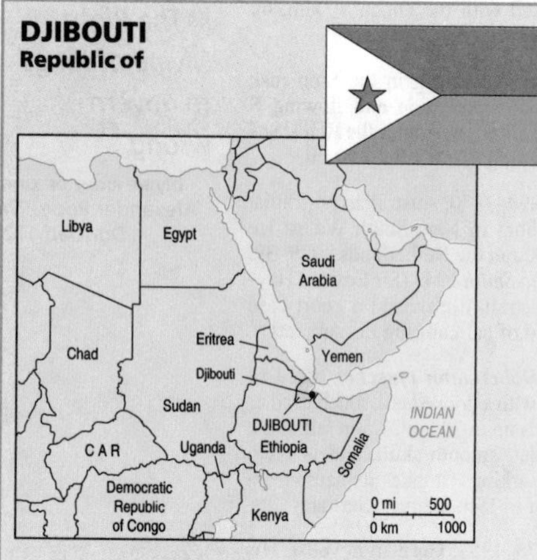

national name *Jumhouriyya Djibouti*
area 23,200 sq km/8,955 sq mi
capital (and chief port) Djibouti
major towns/cities Tadjoura, Obock, Dikhil
physical features mountains divide an inland plateau from a coastal plain; hot and arid
head of state Hassan Gouled Aptidon from 1977
head of government Barkat Gourad from 1981
political system emergent democracy
administrative divisions five districts
political parties People's Progress Assembly (RPP), nationalist; Democratic Renewal Party (PRD), moderate left of centre
population 586,000 (1995 est)
population growth rate 2.2% (1990–95)
ethnic distribution population divided mainly into two Hamitic groups; the Issas (Somalis) in the S, and the minority Afars (or Danakil) in the N and W. There are also minorities of Europeans (mostly French), as well as Arabs, Sudanese, and Indians
life expectancy 47 (males), 51 (females)
literacy rate 19%
languages French (official), Somali, Afar, Arabic
religion Sunni Muslim
currency Djibouti franc
GDP (US $) 468 million (1993 est)
growth rate 0.3% (1993)
exports acts mainly as a transit port for Ethiopia

HISTORY
3rd century BC The N settled by Able immigrants from Arabia, whose descendants are the Afars (Danakil).
early Christian era Somali Issas settled in coastal areas and S, ousting Afars.
825 Islam introduced by missionaries.
16th C Portuguese arrived to challenge trading monopoly of Arabs.
1862 French acquired a port at Obock.
1888 Annexed by France as part of French Somaliland.
1900s Railway linked Djibouti port with the Ethiopian hinterland.
1946 Became overseas territory within French Union, with own assembly and representation in French Parliament.
1958 Voted to become overseas territorial member of French Community.
1967 French Somaliland renamed the French Territory of the Afars and the Issas.
early 1970s Issas (Somali) peoples campaigned for independence, but the minority Afars, of Ethiopian descent, and Europeans sought to remain French.
1977 Independence achieved as Djibouti, with Hassan Gouled Aptidon, the leader of the independence movement, elected president.
1981 New constitution made the People's Progress Assembly (RPP) the only legal party. Treaties of friendship signed with Ethiopia, Somalia, Kenya, and Sudan.
1984 Policy of neutrality reaffirmed. Economy undermined by severe drought.
1992 New multiparty constitution adopted; fighting erupted between government forces and Afar Front for Restoration of Unity and Democracy (FRUD) guerrilla movement in the NE.
1993 Opposition parties allowed to operate, but Gouled re-elected president.
1994 Peace agreement reached with Afar FRUD militants, ending civil war.

Dobzhansky Theodosius, originally Feodosy Grigorevich Dobrzhansky 1900–1975. Ukrainian-born US geneticist who established evolutionary genetics as an independent discipline. He showed that genetic variability between individuals of the same species is very high and that this diversity is vital to the process of evolution. His book *Genetics and the Origin of Species* 1937 was the first significant synthesis of Darwinian evolutionary theory and Mendelian genetics. Dobzhansky also proved that there is a period when speciation is only partly complete and during which several races coexist.

dock or ***sorrel*** in botany, any of a number of plants of the genus *Rumex* of the buckwheat family Polygonaceae. They are tall, annual to perennial herbs, often with lance-shaped leaves and small, greenish flowers. Native to temperate regions, there are 30 North American and several British species.

Docklands urban development area E of St Katherine's Dock, London, occupying the site of the former Wapping and Limehouse docks, the Isle of Dogs, and Royal Docks. It comprises 2,226 hectares/5,550 acres of former wharves, warehouses, and wasteland. Plans for its redevelopment began 1981 and by 1993 over 13,000 private housing units had been built, including terraced houses at Maconochies Wharf, Isle of Dogs. Distinguished buildings include the Tidal Basin Pumping Station in Royal Docks, designed by Richard Rogers, and the printing plant for the *Financial Times*, designed by Nicholas Grimshaw. The tallest building is the ◊Canary Wharf tower.

Doctorow E(dgar) L(awrence) 1931– . US novelist. He achieved critical and commercial success with his third novel, *The Book of Daniel* 1971, the story of the ◊Rosenberg spy case told by their fictional son, which established Doctorow as an imaginative and experimental revisionist of American history. It was followed by his best-seller *Ragtime* 1975, which dramatized the Jazz Age. His other novels include *Loon Lake* 1980, *World's Fair* 1985, *Billy Bathgate* 1989, and *The Waterworks* 1994.

documentation in computing, the written information associated with a computer program or applications package. Documentation is usually divided into two categories: program documentation and user documentation.

Program documentation is the complete technical description of a program, drawn up as the software is written and intended to support any later maintenance or development of that program. It typically includes details of when, where, and by whom the software was written; a general description of the purpose of the software, including recommended input, output, and storage methods; a detailed description of the way the software functions, including full program listings and flow charts; and details of software testing, including sets of test data with expected results. ***User documentation*** explains how to operate the software. It typically includes a nontechnical explanation of the purpose of the software; instructions for loading, running, and using the software; instructions for preparing any necessary input data; instructions for requesting and interpreting output data; and explanations of any error messages that the program may produce.

document reader in computing, an input device that reads marks or characters, usually on preprepared forms and documents. Such devices are used to capture data by optical mark recognition (OMR), optical character recognition (OCR), and mark sensing.

dodder parasitic plant, genus *Cuscuta*, of the morning-glory family Convolvulaceae, without leaves or roots. The thin stem twines around the host, and penetrating suckers withdraw nourishment.

dodecahedron regular solid with 12 pentagonal faces and 12 vertices. It is one of the five regular ◊polyhedra, or Platonic solids.

Dodecanese (Greek *Dhodhekánisos* 'twelve islands') group of islands in the Aegean Sea; area 1,028 sq m/2,663 sq km; population (1991) 162,400. Once Turkish, the islands were Italian 1912–47, when they were ceded to Greece. They include ◊Rhodes and ◊Kos. Chief products include fruit, olives, and sponges.

Dodge City city in SW Kansas, USA, on the Arkansas River; population (1990) 21,100. It was a frontier cattle town in the days of the Wild West.

Dodgson Charles Lutwidge. Real name of writer Lewis ◊Carroll.

dodo extinct flightless bird *Raphus cucullatus*, order Columbiformes, formerly found on the island of Mauritius, but exterminated by early settlers around 1681. Although related to the pigeons, it was

dodder The large dodder *Cuscuta europaea*, a parasite of the nettle *Urtica dioica* and the hop *Humulus*, occurs mainly in the south of the British Isles and across Europe and Asia as far as the Himalayas. It also grows in N Africa and has been introduced into North America. *Premaphotos Wildlife*

Dodecanese

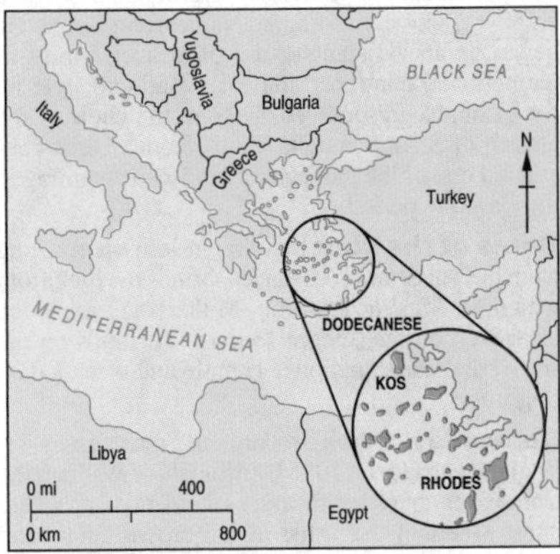

larger than a turkey, with a bulky body, rudimentary wings, and short curly tail-feathers. The bill was blackish in colour, forming a horny hook at the end.

Dodoma capital (replacing Dar es Salaam 1974) of Tanzania; 1,132 m/3,713 ft above sea level; population (1994) 203,800. It is a centre of communications, linked by rail with Dar es Salaam and Kigoma on Lake Tanganyika, and by road with Kenya to the N and Zambia and Malawi to the S.

Doe Samuel Kanyon 1950–1990. Liberian politician and soldier, head of state 1980–90. He seized power in a coup. In 1981 he made himself general and army commander in chief. In 1985 he was narrowly elected president, as leader of the newly formed National Democratic Party of Liberia. Having successfully put down an uprising April 1990, Doe was deposed and killed by rebel forces Sept 1990. His human-rights record was poor.

dog any carnivorous mammal of the family Canidae, including wild dogs, wolves, jackals, coyotes, and foxes. Specifically, the domestic dog *Canis familiaris*, the earliest animal descended from the wolf or jackal. Dogs were first domesticated over 10,000 years ago, and migrated with humans to all the continents. They have been selectively bred into many different varieties for use as working animals and pets.
characteristics The dog has slender legs and walks on its toes. The forefeet have five toes, the hind feet four, with non-retractile claws. The head is small and the muzzle pointed, but the shape of the head differs greatly in various breeds. The average life of a dog is from 10 to 14 years, though some live to be 20. The dog has a very acute sense of smell and can readily be trained, for it has a good intelligence.
wild dogs Of the wild dogs, some are solitary, such as the long-legged maned wolf *Chrysocyon brachurus* of South America, but others hunt in groups, such as the African hunting dog *Lycaonpictus* (classified as a vulnerable species) and the ◊wolf. ◊Jackals scavenge for food, and the raccoon dog *Nyctereutes procyonoides* of E Asia includes plant food as well as meat in its diet. The Australian wild dog is the ◊dingo.
breeds There are over 400 different breeds of dog throughout the world. The UK Kennel Club (1873) groups those eligible for registration (150 breeds) into sporting breeds (hound, gundog, and terrier) and nonsporting (utility, working, and toy). Numerous foreign dogs have been imported into the UK, including the dachshund, German shepherd, and boxer from Germany, the chow-chow from China, and the poodle from France.

dog, dangerous any of the breeds listed in a 1991 amendment to the UK Dangerous Dogs Act 1989, which have to be muzzled in public. These include pit-bull terriers (which must also be registered with the police) and the Japanese *tosa*. Earlier legislation includes the Dogs Act 1871, with regard to keeping dogs under proper control, and the Dogs (Protection of Livestock) Act 1953.

doge chief magistrate in the ancient constitutions of Venice and Genoa. The first doge of Venice was appointed 697 with absolute power (modified 1297), and from his accession dates Venice's prominence in history. The last Venetian doge, Lodovico Manin, retired 1797 and the last Genoese doge 1804.

Dōgen 1200–1253. Japanese Buddhist monk, pupil of Eisai; founder of the Sōtō school of Zen. He did not reject study, but stressed the importance of *zazen*, seated meditation, for its own sake.

dogfish any of several small sharks found in the NE Atlantic, Pacific, and Mediterranean. The sandy dogfish *Scyliorhinus caniculus* is found around the coasts of Britain, Scandinavia, and Europe. Bottom-living, it is sandy brown and covered with spots, and grows to about 75 cm/2.5 ft. It is edible, and is known in restaurants as 'rock eel' or 'rock salmon'. Various other species of small shark may also be called dogfish.

Dogger Bank submerged sandbank in the North Sea, about 115 km/70 mi off the coast of Yorkshire, England. In places the water is only 11 m/36 ft deep, but the general depth is 18–36 m/60–120 ft; it is a well-known fishing ground.

In World War I, it was the site of the Battle of Dogger Bank, a substantial naval engagement between British and German forces 24 Jan 1915.

Dogon people of W African Dogon culture from E Mali and NW Burkina Faso. The Dogon number approximately 250,000 and their language belongs to the Voltaic (Gur) branch of the Niger-Congo family.

Dogs, Isle of district of E London, England, part of the Greater London borough of ◊Tower Hamlets.

dogwood any of a genus *Cornus* of trees and shrubs of the dogwood family (Cornaceae), native to temperate regions of North America and Eurasia. The flowering dogwood *Cornus florida* of the E USA is often cultivated as an ornamental for its beautiful blooms consisting of clusters of small greenish flowers surrounded by four large white or pink petal-like ◊bracts. *C. sanguinea* is native to Britain and common in old hedgerows and woods. Its name derives from the redness of its twigs.

Doha (Arabic ***Ad Dawḩah***) capital and chief port of Qatar; population (1992) 243,000. Industries include oil refining, refrigeration plants, engineering, and food processing. It is the centre of vocational training for all the Persian Gulf states.

Dohnányi Ernst (Ernö) von 1877–1960. Hungarian pianist, conductor, composer, and teacher. His compositions include *Variations on a Nursery Song* 1914 and *Second Symphony for Orchestra* 1948.

doldrums area of low atmospheric pressure along the equator, in the intertropical convergence zone where the NE and SE trade winds converge. The doldrums are characterized by calm or very light winds, during which there may be sudden squalls and stormy weather. For this reason the areas are avoided as far as possible by sailing ships.

dogwood There are about 40 different types of shrubs called dogwoods found throughout the temperate parts of the northern hemisphere. Some kinds, such as the cornelian cherry, are grown for their decorative flowers and the wood of this species is also hard enough to be used for skewers. Dogwoods can be very invasive and, if left unchecked, may pose a threat to the survival of downland areas, for example.

Dole Bob (Robert Joseph) 1923– . US Republican politician, leader of his party in the Senate 1985–87 and 1995–96. He unsuccessfully stood as a candidate for the Republican presidential nomination 1980 and 1988; in 1996 he captured the nomination, but lost the election to Democrat Bill Clinton. Regarded initially as a hardline right-of-centre Republican, he later moderated his views, particularly in the social sphere.

dolerite igneous rock formed below the Earth's surface, a form of basalt, containing relatively little silica (mafic in composition). It is a medium-grained (hypabyssal) basalt and forms in shallow intrusions, such as dykes, which cut across the rock strata, and sills, which push between beds of sedimentary rock. When exposed at the surface, dolerite weathers into spherical lumps.

Dolin Anton. Stage name of (Sydney Francis) Patrick (Chippendall Healey) Kay 1904–1983. English dancer and choreographer. He was the first British male dancer to win an international reputation. As a dancer, his reputation rested on his commanding presence, theatricality, and gymnastic ability. His most famous partnership was with Alicia Markova. After studying under Nijinsky, he was a leading member of Diaghilev's company 1924–29. He formed the Markova–Dolin Ballet Company with Markova 1935–38, and was a guest soloist with the American Ballet Theater 1940–46.

Doll (William) Richard Shaboe 1912– . British physician who, with Bradford Hill, provided the first statistical proof of the link between smoking and lung cancer in 1950. In a later study, they showed that stopping smoking immediately reduces the risk of cancer.

dollar monetary unit containing 100 cents, adopted as the standard unit in the USA in 1785;

dodo The dodo, a native of the island of Mauritius, was reportedly last observed 1681. The bird was obliterated by human colonizers. *Image Select (UK) Ltd*

dolmen Neolithic burial chambers, or dolmens, found mainly in Western Europe. Constructed around 2000 BC, the chambers generally consisted of large stone slabs set upright with a capstone balanced on top. The chambers were concealed by earth barrows, which have now sometimes worn away to leave the stones standing freely. *Corbis*

also by Australia, Canada, Hong Kong, and a number of other countries.

Singapore became from 1968 the centre of the Asian dollar market, working in cooperation with London. Following the depreciation of the US dollar after the Vietnam War expenditure and the oil crisis of 1973, the European monetary system became anchored to the German mark, and in Asia the Japanese yen became important as a trading currency.

Dollfuss Engelbert 1892–1934. Austrian Christian Socialist politician. He was appointed chancellor in 1932, and in 1933 suppressed parliament and ruled by decree. In Feb 1934 he crushed a protest by the socialist workers by force, and in May Austria was declared a 'corporative' state. The Nazis attempted a coup d'état on 25 July; the Chancellery was seized and Dollfuss murdered.

dolmen prehistoric monument in the form of a chamber built of large stone slabs, roofed over by a flat stone which they support. Dolmens are grave chambers of the Neolithic period, found in Europe and Africa, and occasionally in Asia as far east as Japan.

dolomite in mineralogy, white mineral with a rhombohedral structure, calcium magnesium carbonate ($CaMg(CO_3)_2$).

dolphin any of various highly intelligent aquatic mammals of the family Delphinidae, which also includes porpoises. There are about 60 species. Most inhabit tropical and temperate oceans, but there are some freshwater forms in rivers in Asia, Africa, and South America. The name 'dolphin' is generally applied to species having a beaklike snout and slender body, whereas the name 'porpoise' is reserved for the smaller species with a blunt snout and stocky body. Dolphins use sound (see ◊echolocation) to navigate, to find prey, and for communication. The common dolphin *Delphinus delphis* is found in all temperate and tropical seas. It is up to 2.5 m/8 ft long, and is dark above and white below, with bands of grey, white, and yellow on the sides. It has up to 100 teeth in its jaws, which make the 15 cm/6 in 'beak' protrude forward from the rounded head. The corners of its mouth are permanently upturned, giving the appearance of a smile, though dolphins cannot actually smile. Dolphins feed on fish and squid.

river dolphins There are five species of river dolphin, two South American and three Asian, all of which are endangered. The two South American species are the Amazon river dolphin or boto *Inia geoffrensis*, the largest river dolphin (length 2.7 m/8.9 ft, weight 180 kg/396 lb) and the La Plata river dolphin *Pontoporia blainvillei* (length 1.8 m/5.9 ft, weight 50 kg/110 lb).

The Asian species are the Ganges river dolphin *Platanista gangetica*, the Indus river dolphin *Platanista minor* (length 2 m/6.6 ft, weight 70 kg/154 lb) (fewer than 500 remaining), and the Yangtze river dolphin or baiji *Lipotes vexillifer* (length 2 m/6.6 ft, weight 70 kg/154 lb) (fewer than 100 remaining).

As a result of living in muddy water, river dolphins' eyes have become very small. They rely on echolocation to navigate and find food. Some species of dolphin can swim at up to 56 kph/35 mph, helped by special streamlining modifications of the skin.

All dolphins power themselves by beating the tail up and down, and use the flippers to steer and stabilize. The flippers betray dolphins' land-mammal ancestry with their typical five-toed limb-bone structure. Dolphins have great learning ability and are popular performers in aquariums. The species most frequently seen is the bottle-nosed dolphin *Tursiops truncatus*, found in all warm seas, mainly grey in colour and growing to a maximum 4.2 m/14 ft. The US Navy began training dolphins for military purposes in 1962, and in 1987 six dolphins were sent to detect mines in the Persian Gulf. Marine dolphins are endangered by fishing nets, speedboats, and pollution.

Domagk Gerhard Johannes Paul 1895–1964. German pathologist, discoverer of antibacterial ◊sulphonamide drugs. He found in 1932 that a coal-tar dye called Prontosil red contains chemicals with powerful antibacterial properties. Sulphanilamide became the first of the sulphonamide drugs, used – before antibiotics were discovered – to treat a wide range of conditions, including pneumonia and septic wounds. Nobel prize 1939.

dome in architecture, roof form which is usually hemispherical and constructed over a circular, square, or octagonal space in a building. A feature of Islamic and Roman architecture, the dome was revived during the Renaissance.

The dome first appears in Assyrian architecture, later becoming a feature of Islamic mosques (after the notable example in the Byzantine church of Hagia Sophia, Istanbul, 532–37) and Roman ceremonial buildings: the Pantheon in Rome, about AD 112, is 43.5 m/143 ft in diameter. Rediscovered during the Renaissance, the dome features prominently in Brunelleschi's Florence Cathedral 1420–34, Bramante's Tempietto at San Pietro in Montorio, Rome, 1502–10, and St Peter's, Rome, 1588–90, by Giacomo della Porta (about 1537–1602). Other notable examples are St Paul's, London, 1675–1710, by Christopher Wren, and the Panthéon, Paris, 1757–90, by Jacques Soufflot (1709–1780). In the 20th century Buckminster Fuller developed the ◊geodesic dome (a type of space-frame).

Domenichino assumed name of Domenico Zampieri 1581–1641. Italian ◊Baroque painter and architect, active in Bologna, Naples, and Rome. He began as an assistant to the ◊Carracci family of painters and continued the early Baroque style in, for example, frescoes 1624–28 in the choir of the church of S Andrea della Valle, Rome. He is considered one of the pioneers of landscape painting in the Baroque period.

Dome of the Rock building in Jerusalem dating from the 7th century AD that enshrines the rock from which, in Muslim tradition, Muhammad ascended to heaven on his ◊Night Journey. It stands on the site of the Jewish national Temple and is visited by pilgrims.

Domesday Book record of the survey of England carried out 1086 by officials of William the Conqueror in order to assess land tax and other dues, ascertain the value of the crown lands, and enable the king to estimate the power of his vassal barons. Northumberland and Durham were omitted, and also London, Winchester, and certain other towns. The name is derived from the belief that its judgement was as final as that of Doomsday. The Domesday Book is preserved in two volumes at the Public Record Office, London.

domestic service paid employment in the household of another person, as maid, butler, cook, gardener, and so on. It is traditionally a poorly paid occupation, reserved for those without other job skills. The social and economic conditions of the 20th century, and the introduction of labour-saving technology, have narrowed this field of employment, and work by domestic cleaners, baby-sitters, and *au pairs* in the West is mostly part-time and unregulated. In the USA, undocumented foreign workers constitute a large proportion of domestic workers.

Before the Industrial Revolution domestic service was virtually the only form of employment open to women apart from work in the fields. In 19th-century Europe the increase in prosperity created a wealthy new middle class, whose ostentatious households demanded a number of servants for their upkeep. Domestic service was seen as a more 'respectable' occupation for women than industrial employment such as work in factories, until after World War I the shortage of available men meant that more women were able to choose nondomestic employment. The mobilization of women in World War II, the increase in labour-saving devices, and the growth of alternative employment opportunities for women, have meant that domestic service in Europe hardly exists today as a full-time occupation except for a tiny proportion of people working, generally in wealthy or aristocratic households.

dominance in genetics, the masking of one allele (an alternative form of a gene) by another allele. For example, if a ◊heterozygous person has one allele for blue eyes and one for brown eyes, his or her eye colour will be brown. The allele for blue eyes is described as ◊recessive and the allele for brown eyes as dominant.

dominant in music, the fifth note of the diatonic scale, for example, G in the C major scale. The chord of the dominant is related to the tonic chord by the dominant note, which corresponds to its third harmonic. Classical modulation involves a harmonic progression from the tonic to the dominant and back. The return may be a symmetrical journey, as in the binary form of a sonata by Scarlatti, or an abrupt resolution of dominant to tonic chords in a 'perfect' cadence.

Domingo Placido 1941– . Spanish lyric tenor. He specializes in Italian and French 19th-century operatic roles. As a youth in Mexico, he sang baritone roles in zarzuela (musical theatre), moving up to tenor as a member of the Israel National Opera 1961–64. He has established a world reputation as a leading tenor, and has made many films, including the 1988 version of Puccini's *Tosca* and the 1990 Zeffirelli production of Leoncavallo's *I Pagliacci/The Strolling Players*. He also sang with José ◊Carreras and Luciano ◊Pavarotti in a recording 1990, and again in the USA 1994.

Dominica island in the E Caribbean, between Guadeloupe and Martinique, the largest of the Windward Islands, with the Atlantic Ocean to the E and the Caribbean Sea to the W. *See country box on p. 326.*

Dominican order Roman Catholic order of friars founded 1215 by St Dominic. The Dominicans are also known as Friars Preachers, Black Friars, or Jacobins. The order is worldwide and there is also an order of contemplative nuns; the habit is black and white.

The first house was established in Toulouse, France, in 1215; in 1216 the order received papal recognition, and the rule was drawn up in 1220–21. They soon spread all over Europe, the first house in England being established in Oxford in 1221. The English Dominicans were suppressed in 1559, but were restored to a corporate existence in 1622. Dominicans have included Thomas Aquinas, Girolamo Savonarola, and Bartolome de las Casas. In 1983 there were 7,200 friars and 4,775 nuns.

Dominican Republic country in the West Indies (E Caribbean), occupying the eastern two-thirds of the island of Hispaniola, with Haiti covering the western third; the Atlantic Ocean is to the E and the Caribbean Sea to the W. *See country box on p. 327.*

Dominic, St c. 1170–1221. Founder of the Roman Catholic Dominican order of preaching friars. Feast day 7 Aug. Canonized 1234.

Born in Old Castile, Dominic was sent by Pope Innocent III in 1205 to preach to the heretic Albigensian sect in Provence. In 1208 the Pope instigated the Albigensian crusade to suppress the heretics by force, and this was supported by Dominic. In 1215 the Dominican order was given premises in Toulouse; during the following years Dominic established friaries in Bologna and elsewhere in Italy, and by the time of his death the order was established all over W Europe.

Dominions formerly, the self-governing divisions of the ◊British Empire – for example Australia, New Zealand, Canada, and South Africa.

Domino 'Fats' (Antoine) 1928– . US rock-and-roll pianist, singer, and songwriter. He was an exponent of the New Orleans style. His hits include 'Ain't That a Shame' 1955 and 'Blueberry Hill' 1956.

Domitian (Titus Flavius Domitianus) AD 51–96. Roman emperor from AD 81. He finalized the conquest of Britain (see ◊Agricola), strengthened the Rhine–Danube frontier, and suppressed immorality as well as freedom of thought in philosophy and religion. His reign of terror led to his assassination.

Don river in the Russian Federation, rising to the S of Moscow and entering the northeast extremity of the Sea of Azov; length 1,900 km/1,180 mi. In its lower reaches the Don is 1.5 km/1 mi wide, and for about four months of the year it is closed by ice. Its upper course is linked with the river Volga by a canal.

Domingo Spanish opera singer Placido Domingo, one of today's most popular tenors. He was brought up in Mexico and made his operatic debut there 1961. Besides numerous recordings, he has made film versions of operas and has also sung some popular music. *Colombia*

Donatello (Donato di Niccolo) c. 1386–1466. Italian sculptor of the early Renaissance. He was instrumental in reviving the Classical style, as in his graceful bronze statue of the youthful *David* about 1433 (Bargello, Florence) and his equestrian statue of the general *Gattamelata* 1447–50 (Piazza del Santo, Padua). The course of Florentine art in the 15th century was strongly influenced by his work.

Donatello introduced true perspective in his relief sculptures, such as the panel of *St George Slaying the Dragon* about 1415–17 (Or San Michele, Florence). He absorbed Classical influences during a stay in Rome 1430–32, and *David* is said to be the first life-size, free-standing nude since antiquity. In his later work, such as his wood-carving of the aged *Mary Magdalene* about 1456 (Baptistry, Florence), he sought dramatic expression through a distorted, emaciated figural style.

Donatism puritanical, schismatic Christian movement in 4th-and 5th-century N Africa, named after Donatus of Casae Nigrae, a 3rd-century bishop, later known as Donatus of Carthage.

The Donatists became for a time the main Christian movement in N Africa; following the tradition of ◊Montanism, their faith stressed the social revolutionary aspects of Christianity, the separation of church from state, and a belief in martyrdom and suffering. Their influence was ended by Bishop Augustine of Hippo; they were formally condemned 412.

Doncaster town in South Yorkshire, England, on the river Don; population (town, 1991) 71,600; (administrative district, 1995) 292,900. It has a racecourse; famous races here are the St Leger (1776) in Sept and the Lincolnshire Handicap in March. Coal, iron, and steel have been the dominant industries in this area for hundreds of years, though they have recently declined and are being replaced by other products, such as synthetic textiles.

Doncaster was originally a Roman station. Conisbrough, a ruined Norman castle to the SW, features in Walter Scott's novel *Ivanhoe* as Athelstan's stronghold.

Donegal mountainous county in Ulster province in the NW of the Republic of Ireland, surrounded on three sides by the Atlantic Ocean; area 4,830 sq km/1,864 sq mi; county town Lifford; population (1991) 127,900. The market town and port of Donegal is at the head of Donegal Bay in the SW. Commercial activities include sheep and cattle raising, tweed and linen manufacture, and some deep-sea fishing.

Donellan Declan 1953– . British theatre director. He was cofounder of the Cheek by Jowl theatre company 1981, and associate director of the National Theatre from 1989. His irreverent and audacious productions include many classics, such as Racine's *Andromaque* 1985, Corneille's *Le Cid* 1987, and Ibsen's *Peer Gynt* 1990.

Donen Stanley 1924– . US film director. Formerly a dancer, he co-directed two of Gene Kelly's best musicals, *On the Town* 1949 and *Singin' in the Rain* 1952. His other films include *Seven Brides for Seven Brothers* 1954, *Charade* 1963, *Two for the Road* 1968, and *Blame It on Rio* 1984.

Donets Basin (abbreviated to ***Donbas***) area in Ukraine, situated in the bend formed by the rivers Don and Donets, which holds one of Europe's richest coalfields, together with salt, mercury, and lead.

Donetsk city in Ukraine; capital of Donetsk region, situated in the Donets Basin, a major coal-mining area, 600 km/372 mi SE of Kiev; population (1992) 1,121,000. It has blast furnaces, rolling mills, and other heavy industries. It developed from 1871 when a Welshman, John Hughes, established a metallurgical factory, and the town was first called Yuzovka after him; it was renamed Stalino 1924 and Donetsk 1961.

Dongola town in the Northern Province of Sudan, above the third cataract on the river Nile. It was founded about 1812 to replace Old Dongola, 120 km/75 mi upriver, which was destroyed by the ◊Mamelukes. Old Dongola, a trading centre on a caravan route, was the capital of the Christian kingdom of ◊Nubia between the 6th and 14th centuries.

Dönitz Karl 1891–1980. German admiral, originator of the wolf-pack submarine technique, which sank 15 million tonnes of Allied shipping in World War II. He succeeded Hitler 1945, capitulated, and was imprisoned 1946–56.

Dome of the Rock The Dome of the Rock, the third most holy place of Islam after Mecca and Medina. A great Muslim mosque built on the same platform as the destroyed Temple of Jerusalem, the structure covers a bare rock, the summit of Mount Moriah, which was the legendary site of Mohammed's journey to heaven. The interior is decorated with marble panelling and spectacular mosaics. *Corbis*

Donizetti (Domenico) Gaetano (Maria) 1797–1848. Italian composer. He created more than 60 operas, including *Lucrezia Borgia* 1833, *Lucia di Lammermoor* 1835, *La Fille du régiment* 1840, *La Favorite* 1840, and *Don Pasquale* 1843. They show the influence of Rossini and Bellini, and are characterized by a flow of expressive melodies.

Don Juan (Italian ***Don Giovanni***) character of Spanish legend, Don Juan Tenorio, supposed to have lived in the 14th century and notorious for his debauchery. Molière, Mozart, Byron, and George Bernard Shaw have featured the legend in their works.

The prototype is found in the Spanish play *El burlador de Sevilla y convidado* 1630, attributed to Spanish dramatist Tirso de Molina (1584?–1648). The story is that Don Juan, of the noble Tenorio family, is an abandoned profligate living in the days of Pedro the Cruel in Seville. When Ulloa thwarts Don Juan's schemes to seduce his daughter, he is stabbed by the dissolute lover. An atheist, Don Juan mockingly challenges a stone image of his victim to a banquet in his tomb. The outraged Ulloa comes to life, accepts, and then carries his murderer off to hell.

donkey another name for ◊ass.

Donne John 1572–1631. English metaphysical poet. His work consists of love poems, religious poems, verse satires, and sermons. His sermons rank him with the century's greatest orators, and his fervent poems of love and hate, violent, tender, or abusive, give him a unique position among English poets. A Roman Catholic in his youth, he converted to the Church of England and finally became dean of St Paul's Cathedral, London.

His earliest poetry consisted of the 'conceited verses' (using elaborate metaphors to link seemingly dissimilar subjects) passed round in manuscript among his friends at the Inns of Court (finally published in the 1633 *Poems*). Most of these were apparently written in the 1590s. They record a series of actual or fictitious love affairs, in which the lover woos, not by praising his mistress's beauty, but by arguing, cajoling, and plunging off into philosophical speculation and flights of fancy. They show a strange blend of the

Donne The metaphysical poet John Donne. Donne is now recognized as one of the greatest English poets for his religious and love poems, but during his life he suffered for his Catholic faith, which he later renounced for the Church of England, and for his secret marriage to Ann More, as a result of which he lost his job and endured many years of poverty. *Image Select (UK) Ltd*

conversational (most of these poems open with a phrase that might come straight from colloquial speech) with the involved, and of the outspokenly erotic with theoretical digressions. His religious poems show the same passion and ingenuity as his love poetry.

Common to all the poems is the imaginative power of their imagery, which ransacks the post-Renaissance world for symbols, curious and sometimes far-fetched, but always compellingly apt. The sermons, in an elegant prose style less rugged and harsh than that of the poems, show the same preoccupation with humanity's place in the universe and its approaching end.

Donoghue Steve (Stephen) 1884–1945. British jockey. Between 1915 and 1925 he won the Epsom Derby six times, equalling the record of Jem Robinson (since beaten by Lester Piggott). Donoghue is the only jockey to have won the race in three successive years.

Don Quixote de la Mancha satirical romance by the Spanish novelist Miguel de Cervantes, published in two parts 1605 and 1615. Don Quixote, a self-styled knight, embarks on a series of chivalric adventures accompanied by his servant Sancho Panza. Quixote's imagination leads him to see harmless objects as enemies to be fought, as in his tilting at windmills. English translators include Tobias Smollett 1775.

Doomsday Book variant spelling of ◊Domesday Book, the English survey of 1086.

Doors, the US psychedelic rock group formed 1965 in Los Angeles by Jim Morrison (1943–1971, vocals), Ray Manzarek (1935– , keyboards), Robby Krieger (1946– , guitar), and John Densmore (1944– , drums). Their first hit was 'Light My Fire' from their debut album *The Doors* 1967. They were noted for Morrison's poetic lyrics and flamboyant performance.

doo-wop US pop-music form of the 1950s, a style of harmony singing without instrumental accompaniment or nearly so, almost exclusively by male groups. The name derives from the practice of having the lead vocalist singing the lyrics against a backing of nonsense syllables from the other members of the group.

Doo-wop had roots in the 1930s with rhythm-and-blues groups like the Ink Spots and in gospel music. It was practised by street-corner groups in the inner cities, some of whom went on to make hit records; for example, 'Earth Angel' by the Penguins 1954 and 'Why Do Fools Fall in Love' by Frankie Lymon and the Teenagers 1956.

Doré *Over London by Rail* 1872, an engraving by the French artist Gustave Doré. Though most of his works are book illustrations, in the 1870s Doré engraved a series depicting the grim realities of slum life in London. His images were so powerful they were used in British government reports on the conditions of the poor. *Corbis*

dopamine neurotransmitter, hydroxytyramine $C_8H_{11}NO_2$, an intermediate in the formation of adrenaline. There are special nerve cells (neurons) in the brain that use dopamine for the transmission of nervous impulses. One such area of dopamine neurons lies in the basal ganglia, a region that controls movement. Patients suffering from the tremors of Parkinson's disease show nerve degeneration in this region. Another dopamine area lies in the limbic system, a region closely involved with emotional responses. It has been found that schizophrenic patients respond well to drugs that limit dopamine excess in this area.

doppelgänger (German 'double-goer') apparition of a living person, a person's double, or a guardian spirit. The German composer and writer E T A Hoffman wrote a short story called 'Die Doppelgänger' in 1821. English novelist Charles Williams (1886–1945) used the idea to great effect in his novel *Descent into Hell* 1937.

Doppler effect change in the observed frequency (or wavelength) of waves due to relative motion between the wave source and the observer.

DOMINICA
Commonwealth of

area 751 sq km/290 sq mi
capital Roseau, with a deepwater port
major towns/cities Portsmouth, Marigot
physical features second largest of the Windward Islands, mountainous central ridge with tropical rainforest
head of state Clarence Seignoret from 1983
head of government Edison James from 1995
political system liberal democracy
administrative divisions ten parishes
political parties Dominica Freedom Party (DFP), centrist; Labour Party of Dominica (LPD), left-of-centre coalition; Dominica United Workers' Party (DUWP), left of centre
population 71,000 (1996 est)
population growth rate −0.1 (1990–95)
ethnic distribution majority descended from African slaves; a small number of the indigenous Arawaks remain
life expectancy 57 (males), 59 (females)
literacy rate 97%
languages English (official), but the Dominican patois reflects earlier periods of French rule
religion Roman Catholic 80%
currency Eastern Caribbean dollar; pound sterling; French franc
GDP (US $) 207 million (1994)
growth rate 1.0% (1994)
exports bananas, coconuts, citrus, lime, bay oil

HISTORY
1493 Visited by the explorer Christopher Columbus, who named the island Dominica ('Sunday Island').
1627 Presented by the English King Charles I to the Earl of Carlisle, but initial European attempts at colonization were fiercely resisted by the indigenous Carib community.
later 18th C Succession of local British and French conflicts over control of the fertile island.
1763 British given possession of the island by the Treaty of Paris (ending the Seven Years' War), but France continued to challenge this militarily until 1805, when there was formal cession in return for the sum of £12,000.
1834 Slaves, who had been brought in from Africa, were emancipated.
1870 Became part of the British Leeward Islands federation.
1940 Transferred to British Windward Islands federation.
1951 Universal adult suffrage established.
1958–62 Part of the West Indies Federation.
1960 Granted separate, semi-independent status, with a legislative council and chief minister.
1961 Edward leBlanc, leader of newly formed DLP, became chief minister.
1974 LeBlanc retired; replaced as chief minister by Patrick John (DLP).
1978 Independence achieved as a republic within the Commonwealth, with John as prime minister.
1980 DFP won convincing victory in general election, and Eugenia Charles became Caribbean's first woman prime minister.
1981 John implicated in plot to overthrow government, but subsequently acquitted.
1983 Small force participated in US-backed invasion of Grenada.
1985 John retried, found guilty, and sentenced to 12 years' imprisonment. Regrouping of left-of-centre parties resulted in new labour Party of Dominica (LPD).
1991 Windward Islands confederation comprising St Lucia, St Vincent, Grenada, and Dominica proposed.
1993 Charles resigned DFP leadership, but continued as prime minister.
1995 DUWP won general election; Edison James appointed prime minister and Eugenia Charles retired from politics.

SEE ALSO Antilles; Caribbean Community and Common Market

The Doppler effect is responsible for the perceived change in pitch of a siren as it approaches and then recedes, and for the ◊red shift of light from distant galaxies. It is named after the Austrian physicist Christian Doppler (1803–1853).

Dorado constellation of the southern hemisphere, represented as a goldfish. It is easy to locate, since the Large ◊Magellanic Cloud marks its southern border. Its brightest star is Alpha Doradus, just under 200 light years from Earth.

Dorchester market town in Dorset, England, on the river Frome, N of Weymouth; population (1991) 15,000. It is the administrative centre for the county. The hill-fort ◊Maiden Castle to the SW was occupied as a settlement from about 2000 BC. The novelist Thomas ◊Hardy was born nearby.

It occupies the site of the Roman town Durnovaria. In the 17th century the Puritans gained control of the town, using the money garnered from the town brewhouse monopoly to pay for poor relief from 1622. In 1642 Dorchester was a centre of Parliamentary revolt, but was captured by the Royalists 1643.

Dordogne river in SW France, rising in Puy-de-Dôme *département* and flowing 490 km/300 mi to join the river Garonne 23 km/14 mi N of Bordeaux. It gives its name to a *département* and is a major source of hydroelectric power.

The valley of the Dordogne is a popular tourist area, and the caves of the wooded valleys of its tributary, the Vézère, have signs of early human occupation. Famous sites include the caves at Lascaux (closed to the public since 1963; an exact replica, Lascaux II, opened 1983), and Les Eyzies.

Doré (Paul) Gustave 1832–1883. French artist. Chiefly known as a prolific illustrator, he was also active as a painter, etcher, and sculptor. He produced closely worked engravings of scenes from, for example, Rabelais, Dante, Cervantes, the Bible, Milton, and Edgar Allan Poe. His views of Victorian London 1869–71, concentrating on desperate poverty and overcrowding in the swollen city, were admired by van Gogh.

Dorian people of ancient Greece. They entered Greece from the N and took most of the Peloponnese from the Achaeans, perhaps destroying the ◊Mycenaean civilization; this invasion appears to have been completed before 1000 BC. Their chief cities were Sparta, Argos, and Corinth.

Doric in Classical architecture, one of the five types of column; see ◊order.

dormancy in botany, a phase of reduced physiological activity exhibited by certain buds, seeds, and spores. Dormancy can help a plant to survive unfavourable conditions, as in annual plants that pass the cold winter season as dormant seeds, and plants that form dormant buds.

For various reasons many seeds exhibit a period of dormancy even when conditions are favourable for growth. Sometimes this dormancy can be broken by artificial methods, such as penetrating the seed coat to facilitate the uptake of water (chitting) or exposing the seed to light. Other seeds require a period of ◊after-ripening.

dormouse small rodent, of the family Gliridae, with a hairy tail. There are about ten species, living in Europe, Asia, and Africa. They are arboreal (live in trees) and nocturnal, hibernating during winter in cold regions. They eat berries, nuts, pollen, and insects.

The dormouse derives its name from French *dormir* 'to sleep' because of its hibernating habit. The common dormouse *Muscardinus avellanarius* lives all over Europe in thickets and forests with undergrowth. It is reddish fawn and 15 cm/6 in long, including the tail. The fat or edible dormouse *Glis glis* lives in continental Europe, and is 30 cm/1 ft long including the tail. It was a delicacy at Roman feasts, and was introduced to SE England by the Romans.

dormouse The 10 species of nocturnal rodents known as dormice resemble small squirrels rather than mice. Dormice feed on seeds, berries, fruits, and nuts during the summer and also store further supplies to sustain them when they wake from hibernation during the winter months. In Victorian England children kept dormice as pets. The edible, or fat, dormouse was considered a delicacy by the Romans and was fattened on walnuts.

dorsal in vertebrates, the surface of the animal closest to the backbone. For most vertebrates and invertebrates this is the upper surface, or the surface furthest from the ground. For bipedal primates such as humans, where the dorsal surface faces backwards, then the word is 'back'.

Dorset county of SW England (*see United Kingdom map*)
towns and cities Dorchester (administrative headquarters), Shaftesbury, Sherborne; resorts: Lyme Regis, Weymouth
features Chesil Bank, a shingle bank along the coast 19 km/11 mi long; Isle of Purbeck, a peninsula where china clay and Purbeck 'marble' are quarried, and which includes Corfe Castle and the holiday resort of Swanage; Dorset Downs; Cranborne Chase; rivers Frome and Stour; Maiden Castle; Tank Museum at Royal Armoured Corps Centre, Bovington, where the cottage of the soldier and writer T E Lawrence is a museum; Canford Heath, the home of some of Britain's rarest breeding birds and reptiles (including the nightjar, Dartford warbler, sand lizard, and smooth snake)
industries Wytch Farm is the largest onshore oilfield in the UK; production at Wareham onshore oilfield started 1991
famous people Anthony Ashley Cooper, Thomas Hardy, Thomas Love Peacock.

Dorset 1st Earl of Dorset. Title of English poet Thomas ◊Sackville.

Dorsey Tommy (Thomas) (1905–1956) and Jimmy (James) (1904–1957) US bandleaders, musicians, and composers during the ◊swing era. They worked together in the Dorsey Brothers Orchestra 1934–35 and 1953–56, but led separate bands in the intervening period. The Jimmy Dorsey band was primarily a dance band; the Tommy Dorsey band was more jazz-oriented and featured the singer Frank Sinatra 1940–42. Both Dorsey bands

DOMINICAN REPUBLIC

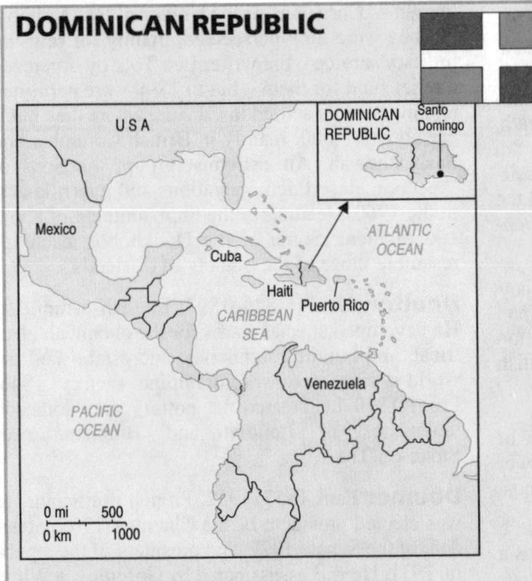

national name *República Dominicana*
area 48,442 sq km/18,700 sq mi
capital Santo Domingo
major towns/cities Santiago de los Caballeros, San Pedro de Macoris
physical features comprises eastern two-thirds of island of Hispaniola; central mountain range with fertile valleys; Pico Duarte 3,174 m/10,417 ft, highest point in Caribbean islands
head of state and government Leoned Fernandez from 1996
political system democratic republic
administrative divisions 30 provinces and the National District
political parties Dominican Revolutionary Party (PRD), moderate, left of centre; Christian Social Reform Party (PRSC), independent socialist; Dominican Liberation Party (PLD), nationalist
population 7,823,000 (1995 est)
population growth rate 1.9% (1990–95); 1.4% (2000–05)
ethnic distribution about 73% of the population are mulattos, of mixed European and African descent; about 16% are European; and 11% African
life expectancy 65 (males), 70 (females)
literacy rate men 85%, women 82%
language Spanish (official)
religion Roman Catholic
currency Dominican Republic peso
GDP (US $) 10.34 billion (1994)
growth rate 4.3% (1994)
exports sugar, gold, silver, tobacco, coffee, nickel, molasses

HISTORY
14th C Settled by Carib Indians, who followed an earlier wave of Arawak Indian immigration.
1492 Visited by Christopher Columbus, who named it Hispaniola ('Little Spain').
1496 At Santo Domingo, the Spanish established the first European settlement in the western hemisphere, which became capital of all Spanish colonies in America.
first half of 16th C One-third of a million Arawaks and Caribs died, as a result of enslavement and exposure to European diseases; black African slaves were consequently brought in to work the island's gold and silver mines, which were swiftly exhausted.
1697 Divided between France, which held the western third (Haiti), and Spain, which held the E (Dominican Republic, or Santo Domingo).
1795 Santo Domingo was ceded to France.
1808 Following a revolt by Spanish Creoles, with British support, Santo Domingo was retaken by Spain.
1821 Became briefly independent after uprising against Spanish rule, and then fell under the control of Haiti.
1844 Separated from Haiti to form Dominican Republic.
1861–65 Under Spanish protection.
1904 The USA took over the near-bankrupt republic's debts.
1916–24 Temporarily occupied by US forces.
1930 Military coup established personal dictatorship of General Rafael Trujillo Molina after overthrow of president Horacio Vázquez.
1937 Army massacred 19,000–20,000 Haitians living in the Dominican provinces adjoining the frontier.
1961 Trujillo assassinated.
1962 First democratic elections resulted in Juan Bosch, founder of the left-wing Dominican Revolutionary Party (PRD), becoming president.
1963 Bosch overthrown in military coup.
1965 30,000 US marines intervened to restore order and protect foreign nationals after Bosch had attempted to seize power.
1966 New constitution adopted. Joaquín Balaguer, protégé of Trujillo and leader of the centre-right Christian Social Reform Party (PRSC), became president.
1978 PRD returned to power, with Silvestre Antonio Guzmán as president.
1982 PRD re-elected, with Jorge Blanco as president.
1985 Blanco forced by International Monetary Fund to adopt austerity measures to save economy.
1986 PRSC returned to power; Balaguer re-elected president.
1990 Balaguer re-elected by a small majority.
1994 Balaguer re-elected; election results disputed by opposition but eventually declared valid on condition that Balaguer serve reduced two-year term.
1996 Leoned Fernandez of the left-wing Dominican Liberation Party (PLD) was elected president.

SEE ALSO Arawak; Carib; Haiti

If the devil doesn't exist, and man has created him, he has created him in his own image and likeness.

FYODOR DOSTOEVSKY *The Brothers Karamazov*

featured in a number of films in the 1940s, and the brothers appeared together in *The Fabulous Dorseys* 1947.

Dortmund city and industrial centre in the ◊Ruhr, in North Rhine–Westphalia, Germany, 58 km/36 mi NE of Düsseldorf; population (1993) 602,400. It is the largest mining town of the Westphalian coalfield and the southern terminus of the Dortmund–Ems Canal. The enlargement of the Wesel–Datteln Canal 1989, connecting Dortmund to the Rhine River, allows barges to travel between Dortmund and Rotterdam in the Netherlands. Industries include iron, steel, construction machinery, engineering, and brewing.

dory marine fish *Zeus faber* found in the Mediterranean and Atlantic. It grows up to 60 cm/2 ft, and has nine or ten long spines at the front of the dorsal fin, and four at the front of the anal fin. It is olive brown or grey, with a conspicuous black spot ringed with yellow on each side. It is considered to be an excellent food fish and is also known as ***John Dory***.

DOS (acronym for ***disc operating system***) computer ◊operating system specifically designed for use with disc storage; also used as an alternative name for a particular operating system, ◊MS-DOS.

Dos Santos José Eduardo 1942– . Angolan left-wing politician, elected president 1979, a member of the People's Movement for the Liberation of Angola (MPLA). By 1989, he had negotiated the withdrawal of South African and Cuban forces, and in 1991 a peace agreement to end the civil war. In 1992 his victory in multiparty elections was disputed by Jonas Savimbi, leader of the rebel group National Union for the Total Independence of Angola (◊UNITA), and fighting resumed, escalating into full-scale civil war 1993. Representatives of the two leaders signed a peace agreement 1994. Dos Santos' offer to make Savimbi vice president in a restructured coalition government was declined by the latter 1996.

Dostoevsky Fyodor Mihailovich 1821–1881. Russian novelist. Remarkable for their profound psychological insight, Dostoevsky's novels have greatly influenced Russian writers, and since the beginning of the 20th century have been increasingly influential abroad. In 1849 he was sentenced to four years' hard labour in Siberia, followed by army service, for printing socialist propaganda. *The House of the Dead* 1861 recalls his prison experiences, followed by his major works *Crime and Punishment* 1866, *The Idiot* 1868–69, and *The Brothers Karamazov* 1879–80.

Born in Moscow, the son of a physician, Dostoevsky was for a short time an army officer. In 1849, during a period of intense tsarist censorship, he was arrested as a member of a free-thinking literary circle and sentenced to death. After a last-minute reprieve he was sent to the penal settlement at Omsk for four years, where the terrible conditions increased his epileptic tendency. Finally pardoned in 1859, he published the humorous *Village of Stepanchikovo*, *The House of the Dead*, and *The Insulted and the Injured* 1862. Meanwhile he had launched two unsuccessful liberal periodicals, in the second of which his *Letters from the Underworld* 1864 appeared. Compelled to work by pressure of debt, he quickly produced *Crime and Punishment* 1866 and *The Gambler* 1867, before fleeing the country to escape from his creditors. He then wrote *The Idiot* (in which the hero is an epileptic like himself), *The Eternal Husband* 1870, and *The Possessed* 1871–72. Returning to Russia 1871, he again entered journalism and issued the personal miscellany *Journal of an Author*, in which he discussed contemporary problems. In 1875 he published *A Raw Youth*, but the great work of his last years is *The Brothers Karamazov*.

dotterel bird *Eudromias morinellus* of the plover family, in order Charadriiformes, nesting on high moors and tundra in Europe and Asia, and migrating south for the winter. About 23 cm/9 in long, its plumage is patterned with black, brown, and white in summer, duller in winter, but always with white eyebrows and breastband. The female is larger than the male, and mates up to five times with different partners, each time laying her eggs and leaving them in the sole care of the male, who incubates and rears the brood.

Douala or ***Duala*** chief port and industrial centre (aluminium, chemicals, textiles, pulp) of Cameroon, on the Wouri River estuary; population (1991) 884,000. Known as Kamerunstadt until 1907, it became a German protectorate 1884 and was capital of German Cameroon 1885–1901.

double bass large bowed four-stringed (sometimes five-stringed) musical instrument, the bass of the violin family. It is descended from the bass viol or violone. Until 1950, after which it was increasingly superseded by the electric bass, it also provided bass support (plucked) for jazz and dance bands. Performers include Domenico Dragonetti, composer of eight concertos, the Russian-born US conductor Serge Koussevitsky (1874–1951), and the US virtuoso Gary Karr. The double bass features in the 'Elephants' solo, No 5 of Saint-Saëns' *Carnival of the Animals* 1897.

double bond two covalent bonds between adjacent atoms, as in the ◊alkenes (–C=C–) and ◊ketones (–C=O–).

double star two stars that appear close together. Many stars that appear single to the naked eye appear double when viewed through a telescope. Some double stars attract each other due to gravity, and orbit each other, forming a genuine ◊binary star, but other double stars are at different distances from Earth, and lie in the same line of sight only by chance. Through a telescope both types look the same.

dough mixture consisting primarily of flour, water, and yeast, which is used in the manufacture of bread. The preparation of dough involves thorough mixing (kneading) and standing in a warm place to 'prove' (increase in volume) so that the ◊enzymes in the dough can break down the starch from the flour into smaller sugar molecules, which are then fermented by the yeast. This releases carbon dioxide, which causes the dough to rise.

Doughty Charles Montagu 1843–1926. English travel writer, author of *Travels in Arabia Deserta* 1888, written after two years in the Middle East searching for biblical relics. He was a role model for English soldier T E ◊Lawrence ('Lawrence of Arabia').

Douglas capital of the Isle of Man in the Irish Sea; population (1991) 22,200. It is a holiday resort and terminus of shipping routes to and from Fleetwood and Liverpool; banking and financial services are important.

Douglas Alfred (Bruce), Lord Douglas 1870–1945. English poet. He became closely associated in London with the Irish writer Oscar ◊Wilde. Their relationship led to Wilde's conviction for homosexual activity, imprisonment, and early death, through the enmity of Douglas's father, the 8th Marquess of ◊Queensberry. Douglas wrote the self-justificatory *Oscar Wilde and Myself* 1914 and the somewhat contradictory *Oscar Wilde, A Summing-Up* 1940.

Douglas Gavin (or Gawain) c. 1475–1522. Scottish poet. His translation into Scots of the Roman poet Virgil's *Aeneid* 1513 was the first translation from the classics into a vernacular of the British Isles. He wrote the allegorical *The Palace of Honour* about 1501.

His language is more archaic than that of some of his predecessors, but Douglas had fire and a power of vivid description and his allegories are ingenious.

Douglas Kirk. Stage name of Issur Danielovitch Demsky 1916– . US film actor. Usually cast as a dynamic though often ill-fated hero, as in *Spartacus* 1960, he was a major star of the 1950s and 1960s in such films as *Ace in the Hole* 1951, *The Bad and the Beautiful* 1953, *Lust for Life* 1956, *The Vikings* 1958, *Seven Days in May* 1964, and *The War Wagon* 1967. He often produced his own films. He is the father of actor Michael Douglas.

Douglas Michael Kirk 1944– . US film actor and producer. His acting range includes both romantic and heroic leads in films such as *Romancing the Stone* 1984 and *Jewel of the Nile* 1985, both of which he produced. He won an Academy Award for his portrayal of a ruthless businessman in *Wall Street* 1987. Among his other films are *Fatal Attraction* 1987, *Basic Instinct* 1991, and *Falling Down* 1993. He is the son of actor Kirk Douglas.

Douglas fir any of some six species of coniferous evergreen tree of the family Pinaceae. The most common is *Pseudotsuga menziesii*, native to western North America and E Asia. It grows 60–90 m/200–300 ft, has long, flat, spirally arranged needles and hanging cones, and produces hard, strong timber. *P. glauca* has shorter, bluish needles and grows to 30 m/100 ft in mountainous areas *P. taxifolia* was introduced to Britain by Scottish botanist David Douglas (1798–1834).

Douglas-Hamilton family name of dukes of Hamilton, seated at Lennoxlove, East Lothian, Scotland.

Douglas-Home Alec (Alexander Frederick) Baron Home of the Hirsel 1903–1995. British Conservative politician. He was foreign secretary 1960–63, and succeeded Harold Macmillan as prime minister 1963. He renounced his peerage (as 14th Earl of Home) and re-entered the Commons after successfully contesting a by-election, but failed to win the 1964 general election, and resigned as party leader 1965. He was again foreign secretary 1970–74, when he received a life peerage. The playwright William Douglas-Home was his brother.

Douglas-Home William 1912–1992. Scottish dramatist. He is noted for his comedies, which include *The Chiltern Hundreds* 1947, *The Secretary Bird* 1968, *Lloyd George Knew My Father* 1972, and *The Kingfisher* 1977. He was the younger brother of the politician Alec Douglas-Home.

As a captain in the Royal Armoured Corps during World War II, he disobeyed orders by refusing to take part in the bombardment of Le Havre because the citizens had not been evacuated. This led to a court martial and a year in prison, an experience upon which his first real success, *Now Barabbas* 1945, was based.

Douglass Frederick. Born Frederick Augustus Washington Bailey 1817–1895. US antislavery campaigner active during the American Civil War 1861–65. He issued a call to blacks to take up arms against the South and helped organize two black regiments. After the Civil War, he held several US government posts, including minister to Haiti 1889–91. He published appeals for full civil rights for blacks and also campaigned for women's suffrage.

Doukhobor member of a Christian sect of Russian origin, now mainly found in Canada, also known as Christians of the Universal Brotherhood.

They were long persecuted, mainly for refusing military service – the writer Leo Tolstoy organized a relief fund for them – but in 1898 were permitted to emigrate and settled in Canada, where they number about 13,000, mainly in British Columbia and Saskatchewan. An extremist group, the Sons of Freedom, staged demonstrations and guerrilla acts in the 1960s, leading to the imprisonment of about 100 of them. Some of the Doukhobor teachings resemble those of the Society of ◊Friends.

Doulton Henry 1820–1897. English ceramicist. He developed special wares for the chemical, electrical, and building industries, and established the world's first stoneware-drainpipe factory 1846. From 1870 he created art pottery and domestic tablewares in London and Burslem, near Stoke-on-Trent.

Doumer Paul 1857–1932. French politician. He was elected president of the Chamber 1905, president of the Senate 1927, and president of the republic 1931. He was assassinated by Gorgulov, a White Russian emigré.

Dounreay former experimental nuclear reactor site on the north coast of Scotland in the Highland region, 12 km/7 mi W of Thurso. It was the site of the world's first fast breeder nuclear reactor 1962–77, when an explosion contaminated beaches. It has since been linked to the high incidence of childhood leukaemia in the area. A second reactor opened 1974 and continued until the site was decommissioned 1994 and replaced with a nuclear reprocessing plant.

Douro (Spanish ***Duero***) river rising in N central Spain and flowing through N Portugal to the Atlantic at Porto; length 800 km/500 mi. Navigation at the river mouth is hindered by sand bars. There are hydroelectric installations. Vineyards (port and Mateus rosé) are irrigated with water from the river.

dove person who takes a moderate, sometimes pacifist, view on political issues. The term originated in the US during the Vietnam War. Its counterpart is a ◊hawk. In more general usage today, a dove is equated with liberal policies, and a hawk with conservative ones.

dove another name for ◊pigeon.

Dover market town and seaport on the southeast coast of Kent, England; population (1991) 34,200. It is Britain's nearest point to mainland Europe, being only 34 km/21 mi from Calais, France. As England's principal port on the English Channel, Dover's development has been chiefly due to the cross-Channel traffic, which includes train, ferry, hovercraft, and other services. It was one of the original ◊Cinque Ports.

Under Roman rule, Dover (*Dubris*) was at the end of ◊Watling Street, and the beacon or 'lighthouse' in the grounds of the Norman castle dates from about 50 AD, making it one of the oldest buildings in Britain.

Dover, Strait of (French ***Pas-de-Calais***) stretch of water separating England from France, and connecting the English Channel with the North Sea. It is about 35 km/22 mi long and 34 km/21 mi wide at its narrowest part. It is one of the world's busiest sea lanes. By 1972 increasing traffic, collisions, and shipwrecks had become so frequent that traffic-routeing schemes were enforced.

dowager the style given to the widow of a British peer or baronet. She may take the style of 'Dowager Countess of Blankshire' (so as not to be confused with the wife of the current holder of the title); alternatively she may take the style of 'Mary, Countess of Blankshire' (although this is the style also used by divorced wives of peers).

Dow Chemical US chemical manufacturing company, one of the largest in the world, founded 1897. Almost half the company's sales are outside the USA and it has large chemical plants in many countries, including the Netherlands, Germany, Brazil, and Japan.

US chemist Herbert Henry Dow (1866–1930) formed the company to extract bromine and chlorine from brine deposits in Michigan to make chlorine bleach. The company soon diversified into other chemicals, including the mustard gas used in World War I. By the end of his life Herbert Dow had developed and patented over 100 chemical processes.

Dowell Anthony James 1943– . English Classical ballet dancer. He is known for his refined, polished style. He was principal dancer with the Royal Ballet 1966–86, and director from 1986.

Dowell joined the Royal Ballet 1961. The choreographer Frederick Ashton chose him to create the role of Oberon in *The Dream* 1964 opposite Antoinette Sibley, the start of an outstanding partnership. His other performances include those in Anthony Tudor's *Shadowplay* 1967, Ashton's *Monotones* 1965, and van Manen's *Four Schumann Pieces* 1975.

Dow Jones average New York Stock Exchange index, the most widely used indicator of US stock-market prices. The average (no longer simply an average but today calculated to take into account changes in the constituent companies) is based on prices of 30 major companies, such as IBM and Walt Disney. It was first compiled 1884 by Charles Henry Dow, cofounder of Dow Jones & Co., publishers of the *Wall Street Journal*.

Dow Jones Index (***Dow Jones Industrial 30 Share Index***) scale for measuring the average share price and percentage change of 30 major US industrial companies. It has been calculated and published since 1897 by the financial news publisher Dow Jones and Co.

Dowland John c. 1563–c. 1626. English composer of lute songs. He introduced daring expressive refinements of harmony and ornamentation to English Renaissance style in the service of an elevated aesthetic of melancholy, as in the masterly *Lachrymae* 1605.

Down county of SE Northern Ireland
area 2,470 sq km/953 sq mi
towns and cities Downpatrick (county town)
features Mourne Mountains; Strangford sea lough
industries agriculture.

Downing Street street in Westminster, London, leading from Whitehall to St James's Park, named after George Downing (died 1684), a diplomat under Cromwell and Charles II. Number 10 is the official residence of the prime minister and number 11 is the residence of the chancellor of the Exchequer. Number 12 is the office of the government whips.

Downs, North and South two lines of chalk hills in SE England. They are much used for sheep pasture. The North Downs run from Salisbury Plain across Hampshire, Surrey, and Kent to the cliffs of South Foreland. They face the South Downs across the Weald of Kent and Sussex. The South Downs run across Sussex to Beachy Head.

Down's syndrome condition caused by a chromosomal abnormality (the presence of an extra copy of chromosome 21), which in humans produces mental retardation; a flattened face; coarse, straight hair; and a fold of skin at the inner edge of the eye (hence the former name 'mongolism'). The condition can be detected by prenatal testing.

Those afflicted are usually born to mothers over 40 (one in 100), and in 1995 French researchers discovered a link between Down's syndrome incidence and paternal age, with men over 40 having an increased likelihood of fathering a Down's syndrome baby.

The syndrome is named after J L H Down (1828–1896), an English physician who studied it. All people with Down's syndrome who live long enough eventually develop early-onset ◊Alzheimer's disease, a form of dementia. This fact led to the discovery in 1991 that some forms of early-onset Alzheimer's disease are caused by a gene defect on chromosome 21.

dowry property or money given by the bride's family to the groom or his family as part of the marriage agreement; the opposite of ◊bridewealth. In 1961 dowries were made illegal in India; however, in 1992 the Indian government reported more than 15,000 murders or suicides between 1988 and 1991 that were a direct result of insufficient dowries.

dowsing ascertaining the presence of water or minerals beneath the ground with a forked twig or pendulum. Unconscious muscular action by the dowser is thought to move the twig, usually held with one fork in each hand, possibly in response to a local change in the pattern of electrical forces. The ability has been known since at least the 16th century and, though not widely recognized by science, it has been used commercially and in archaeology.

Doyle Arthur Conan 1859–1930. Scottish writer. He created the detective Sherlock ◊Holmes and his assistant Dr Watson, who first appeared in *A Study in Scarlet* 1887 and featured in a number of subsequent stories, including *The Hound of the Baskervilles* 1902. Among Doyle's other works is the fantasy adventure *The Lost World* 1912. In his later years he became a spiritualist and wrote a *History of Spiritualism* 1926.

D'Oyly Carte Richard 1844–1901. English producer of the Gilbert and Sullivan operas. They were performed at the Savoy Theatre, London, which he built. The D'Oyly Carte Opera Company, founded 1876, was disbanded 1982 following the ending of its monopoly on the Gilbert and Sullivan operas. The present company, founded 1988, moved to the Alexandra Theatre, Birmingham, 1991.

Drabble Margaret 1939– . English writer. Her novels include *The Millstone* 1965, *The Middle Ground* 1980, *The Radiant Way* 1987, and *The Gates of Ivory* 1991. She portrays contemporary life with toughness and sensitivity, often through the eyes of intelligent modern women.

Draco in astronomy, a large but faint constellation represented as a dragon coiled around the north celestial pole. Due to ◊precession the star Alpha Draconis (Thuban) was the pole star 4,800 years ago. This star seems to have faded, for it is no longer the brightest star in the constellation as it was at the beginning of the 17th century. Gamma Draconis is more than a magnitude brighter. It was extensively observed by James ◊Bradley, who from its apparent changes in position discovered the ◊aberration of starlight and ◊nutation.

Draco lived 7th century BC. Athenian politician, the first to codify the laws of the Athenian city-state. These were notorious for their severity; hence ***draconian***, meaning particularly harsh.

Dracula in the novel *Dracula* 1897 by Bram ◊Stoker, the caped count who, as a ◊vampire, drinks the blood of beautiful women. The original of Dracula is thought to have been Vlad Ţepeş, or Vlad the Impaler, ruler of medieval Wallachia, who used to impale his victims and then mock them. Ţepeş's father took the name *Dracul* from the knightly order of the Dragon. Ţepeş succeeded to the Wallachian throne 1456.

draft compulsory military service; also known as ◊conscription.

drag resistance to motion a body experiences when passing through a fluid – gas or liquid. The aerodynamic drag aircraft experience when travelling through the air represents a great waste of power, so they must be carefully shaped, or streamlined, to reduce drag to a minimum. Cars benefit from ◊streamlining, and aerodynamic drag is used to slow down spacecraft returning from space. Boats travelling through water experience hydrodynamic drag on their hulls, and the fastest vessels are ◊hydrofoils, whose hulls lift out of the water while cruising.

dragon name popularly given to various sorts of lizard. These include the ◊flying dragon *Draco volans* of SE Asia; the komodo dragon *Varanus komodoensis* of Indonesia, at over 3 m/10 ft the largest living lizard; and some Australian lizards with bizarre spines or frills.

dragonfly any of numerous insects of the order Odonata, including the ◊damselfly. They all have long narrow bodies, two pairs of almost equal-sized, glassy wings with a network of veins; short, bristle-like antennae; powerful, 'toothed' mouthparts; and very large compound eyes which may have up to 30,000 facets. They can fly at speeds of up to 64–96 kph/40–60 mph.

Dragonflies hunt other insects by sight, both as adults and as aquatic nymphs. The largest species have a wingspan of 18 cm/7 in, but fossils related to dragonflies have been found with wings of up to 70 cm/28 in across.

dragoon mounted soldier who carried an infantry weapon such as a 'dragon', or short musket, as used by the French army in the 16th century. The name was retained by some later regiments after the original meaning became obsolete.

drag racing motor sport popular in the USA. High-powered single-seater cars with large rear and small front wheels are timed over a 402.2 m/440 yd strip. Speeds of up to 450 kph/280 mph have been attained. *See illustration on following page.*

Drake Francis c. 1540–1596. English buccaneer and explorer. Having enriched himself as a pirate against Spanish interests in the Caribbean 1567–72, he was sponsored by Elizabeth I for an expedition to the Pacific, sailing round the world 1577–80 in the *Golden Hind*, robbing Spanish ships as he went. This was the second circumnavigation of the globe (the first was by the Portuguese explorer Ferdinand Magellan). Drake also helped to defeat the ◊Spanish Armada 1588 as a vice admiral in the *Revenge*.

In 1581 Drake was made mayor of Plymouth, in which capacity he brought fresh water into the city

'Mediocrity knows nothing higher than itself, but talent instantly recognizes genius.'

ARTHUR CONAN DOYLE
The Valley of Fear

'The advantage of time and place in all practical actions is half a victory; which being lost is irrecoverable.'

FRANCIS DRAKE
Letter to Queen Elizabeth I, 1588

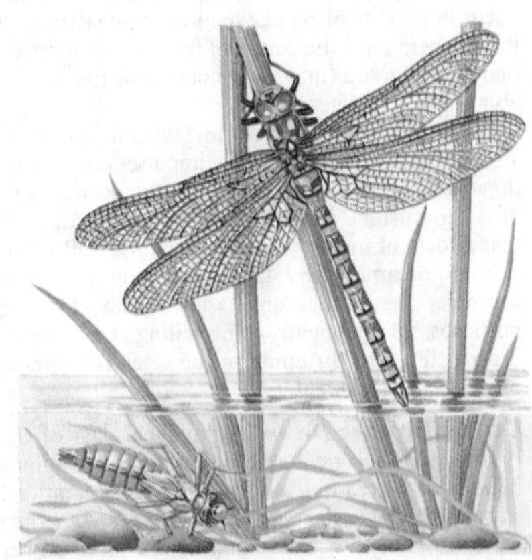

dragonfly Adult dragonflies are long, comparatively slim-bodied insects with two pairs of wings. During the Upper Carboniferous period a giant, dragonflylike insect, *Meganeura*, had a wingspan of up to 70 cm/28 in. After mating, the female dragonfly lays her egg on a submerged plant stem, in mud, or directly into the water. The egg hatches into a nymph that takes about a year to mature; it is a voracious predator that will even attack small fishes.

drag racing A drag racing car. Drag racing is a popular sport in the USA. It is a specialized form of motor racing that was developed in California in the 1930s. *Image Select (UK) Ltd*

by constructing leats from Dartmoor. Drake sailed on his last expedition to the West Indies with Hawkins 1595, capturing Nombre de Dios on the north coast of Panama but failing to seize Panama City. In Jan 1596 he died of dysentery off the town of Puerto Bello (now Portobello), Panama.

drama (Greek 'action') in theatre, any play composed to be performed by actors for an audience. The term is also used collectively to group plays into historical or stylistic periods – for example, Greek drama, Restoration drama – as well as referring to the whole body of work written by a dramatist for performance. Drama is distinct from literature in that it is a performing art open to infinite interpretation, the product not merely of the dramatist but also of the collaboration of director, designer, actors, and technical staff. See also ◊comedy, ◊tragedy, ◊mime, and ◊pantomime.

Drama never changed anybody's mind about anything.

On **DRAMA** David Mamet quoted in *The Times* 15 Sept 1993

draughts board game (known as ***checkers*** in the USA and Canada because of the chequered board of 64 squares) with elements of a simplified form of chess. Each of the two players has 12 men (disc-shaped pieces), and attempts either to capture all the opponent's men or to block their movements.

Dravidian group of non-Indo-European peoples of the Deccan region of India and in N Sri Lanka. The Dravidian language family is large, with about 20 languages spoken in S India; the main ones are Tamil, which has a literary tradition 2,000 years old; Kanarese; Telugu; Malayalam; and Tulu.

Dreadnought class of battleships built for the British navy after 1905 and far superior in speed and armaments to anything then afloat. The first modern battleship to be built, it was the basis of battleship design for more than 50 years. The first Dreadnought was launched 1906, with armaments consisting entirely of big guns.

dream series of events or images perceived through the mind during sleep. Their function is unknown, but Sigmund ◊Freud saw them as wish fulfilment (nightmares being failed dreams prompted by fears of 'repressed' impulses). Dreams occur in periods of rapid eye movement (REM) by the sleeper, when the cortex of the brain is approximately as active as in waking hours. Dreams occupy about a fifth of sleeping time.

If a high level of acetylcholine (chemical responsible for transmission of nerve impulses) is present, dreams occur too early in sleep, causing wakefulness, confusion, and depression, which suggests that a form of memory search is involved. Prevention of dreaming, by taking sleeping pills, for example, has similar unpleasant results. For the purposes of (allegedly) foretelling the future, dreams fell into disrepute in the scientific atmosphere of the 18th century.

Dreamtime or ***Dreaming*** mythical past of the Australian Aborigines, the basis of their religious beliefs and creation stories. In the Dreamtime, spiritual beings shaped the land, the first people were brought into being and set in their proper territories, and laws and rituals were established. Belief in a creative spirit in the form of a huge snake, the Rainbow Serpent, occurs over much of Aboriginal Australia, usually associated with waterholes, rain, and thunder. A common feature of religions across the continent is the Aborigines' bond with the land.

The Dreamtime stories describe how giants and animals sprang from the earth, sea, and sky and crisscrossed the empty continent of Australia before returning into the earth. The places where they travelled or sank back into the land became mountain ranges, rocks, and sites full of sacred meaning. Rituals, which must be re-enacted at certain times of the year in order to maintain the life of the land, are connected with each site. Each Aborigine has a Dreamtime ancestor associated with a particular animal that the person must not kill or injure.

Drees Willem 1886–1988. Dutch socialist politician, prime minister 1948–58. Chair of the Socialist Democratic Workers' Party from 1911 until the German invasion of 1940, he returned to politics in 1947, after being active in the resistance movement. In 1947, as the responsible minister, he introduced a state pension scheme.

Dreiser Theodore Herman Albert 1871–1945. US writer. His works include the naturalist novels *Sister Carrie* 1900 and *An American Tragedy* 1925, based on the real-life crime of a young man who, in his drive to 'make good', drowns a shop assistant he has made pregnant.

Born in Terre Haute, Indiana, Dreiser was a journalist 1889–90 in Chicago and was editor of several magazines. His other novels include *The Financier* 1912, *The Titan* 1914, and *The Genius* 1915. His other works range from autobiographical pieces to poems and short stories. Although his work is criticized for being technically unpolished, it is praised for its powerful realism and sincerity.

Drenthe low-lying northern province of the Netherlands
area 2,660 sq km/1,027 sq mi
capital Assen
cities Emmen, Hoogeveen
physical fenland and moors; well-drained clay and peat soils
industries livestock, arable crops, horticulture, petroleum
population (1995 est) 454,900
history governed in the Middle Ages by provincial nobles and by bishops of Utrecht, Drenthe was eventually acquired by Charles V of Spain 1536. It developed following land drainage initiated in the mid-18th century and was established as a separate province of the Netherlands 1796.

Dresden capital of the *Land* of Saxony, Germany; population (1993) 480,500. Industries include chemicals, machinery, glassware, and musical instruments. It was one of the most beautiful German cities until its devastation by Allied firebombing 1945. Dresden county has an area of 6,740 sq km/2,602 sq mi and a population of 1,772,000. Many old buildings have been rebuilt, or are in the process of rebuilding, including the 18th century Zwinger, the Opera House, and the Taschenberg Palace. The Frauenkirche, destroyed in the 1945 bombing, is to be rebuilt from its rubble in time for the city's 800th anniversary in 2006.
history Under the elector Augustus II the Strong (1694–1733), it became a centre of art and culture. The manufacture of Dresden china, started in Dresden 1709, was transferred to Meissen 1710. The city was bombed by the Allies on the night 13–14 Feb 1945 in a massive air raid, creating the worst firestorm of the war. About 20 sq km/ 8 sq mi of the city were devastated, and deaths were estimated at 35,000–135,000. Following the reunification of Germany 1990 Dresden once again became capital of Saxony.

dressage (French 'preparation') method of training a horse to carry out a predetermined routine of specified movements. Points are awarded for discipline and style.

Dreyer Carl Theodor 1889–1968. Danish film director. His wide range of films include the austere silent classic *La Passion de Jeanne d'Arc/The Passion of Joan of Arc* 1928 and the Expressionist horror film *Vampyr* 1932, after the failure of which Dreyer made no full-length films until *Vredens Dag/Day of Wrath* 1943. His two late masterpieces are *Ordet/The Word* 1955 and *Gertrud* 1964.

Dreyfus Alfred 1859–1935. French army officer, victim of miscarriage of justice, anti-Semitism, and cover-up. Employed in the War Ministry, in 1894 he was accused of betraying military secrets to Germany, court-martialled, and sent to the penal colony on Devil's Island, French Guiana.

He had been a prisoner there for two years when it emerged that the real criminal was a Major Esterhazy; the high command nevertheless attempted to suppress the facts and used forged documents to strengthen their case. After a violent controversy, in which the future prime minister Georges Clemenceau and the novelist Emile Zola championed Dreyfus, he was brought back for a retrial 1899, found guilty with extenuating circumstances, and received a pardon. In 1906 the court of appeal declared him innocent, and he was reinstated in his military rank.

drill large Old World monkey *Mandrillus leucophaeus* similar to a baboon and in the same genus as the ◊mandrill. Drills live in the forests of Cameroon and Nigeria. Brownish-coated, black-faced, and stoutly built, with a very short tail, the male can have a head and body up to 75 cm/2.5 ft long, although females are much smaller.

drilling common woodworking and metal machinery process that involves boring holes with a

Dreyfus The French army officer Alfred Dreyfus. The case of Capt Dreyfus, imprisoned on spurious charges of espionage, was seized on by liberal critics of the French establishment (the army and the Catholic Church in particular), and divided France into *dreyfusards* and *antidreyfusards*. *Topham*

dromedary The dromedary is superbly adapted for life in hot, dry climates. It can go for long periods without drinking, and its body conserves moisture.

drill bit. The commonest kind of drill bit is the fluted drill, which has spiral grooves around it to allow the cut material to escape. In the oil industry, rotary drilling is used to bore oil wells. The drill bit usually consists of a number of toothed cutting wheels, which grind their way through the rock as the drill pipe is turned, and mud is pumped through the pipe to lubricate the bit and flush the ground-up rock to the surface.

In rotary drilling, a drill bit is fixed to the end of a length of drill pipe and rotated by a turning mechanism, the rotary table. More lengths of pipe are added as the hole deepens. The long drill pipes are handled by lifting gear in a steel tower or ◊derrick.

Drinkwater John 1882–1937. English poet and dramatist. He was a prolific writer of lyrical and reflective verse, and also wrote many historical plays, including *Abraham Lincoln* 1918 and *Mary Stuart* 1921. His work had an important influence on the revival of serious drama.

driver in computing, a program that controls a peripheral device. Every device connected to the computer needs a driver program. The driver ensures that communication between the computer and the device is successful.

dromedary variety of Arabian ◊camel. The dromedary or one-humped camel has been domesticated since 400 BC. During a long period without water, it can lose up to one-quarter of its body weight without ill effects.

drug any of a range of substances, natural or synthetic, administered to humans and animals as therapeutic agents: to diagnose, prevent, or treat disease, or to assist recovery from injury. Traditionally many drugs were obtained from plants or animals; some minerals also had medicinal value. Today, increasing numbers of drugs are synthesized in the laboratory. Drugs are administered in various ways, including: orally, by injection, as a lotion or ointment, as a pessary, by inhalation, and by transdermal patch.

drug and alcohol dependence physical or psychological craving for addictive drugs such as alcohol, nicotine, narcotics, tranquillizers, or stimulants (for example, amphetamines). Such substances can alter mood or behaviour. When dependence is established, sudden withdrawal from the drug can cause unpleasant physical and/or psychological reactions, which may be dangerous. See also ◊addiction and ◊alcoholism.

drug misuse illegal use of drugs for nontherapeutic purposes. Under the UK Misuse of Drugs regulations drugs used illegally include: narcotics, such as heroin, morphine, and the synthetic opioids; barbiturates; amphetamines and related substances; ◊benzodiazepine tranquillizers; cocaine, LSD, and cannabis. ***Designer drugs***, for example ecstasy, are usually modifications of the amphetamine molecule, altered in order to evade the law as well as for different effects, and may be many times more powerful and dangerous. Crack, a highly toxic derivative of cocaine, became available to drug users in the 1980s. Some athletes misuse drugs such as ◊ephedrine and ◊anabolic steroids.

Sources of traditional drugs include the 'Golden Triangle' (where Myanmar, Laos, and Thailand meet), Mexico, Colombia, China, and the Middle East.

Druidism religion of the Celtic peoples of the pre-Christian British Isles and Gaul. The word is derived from Greek *drus* 'oak'. The Druids regarded this tree as sacred; one of their chief rites was the cutting of mistletoe from it with a golden sickle. They taught the immortality of the soul and a reincarnation doctrine, and were expert in astronomy. The Druids are thought to have offered human sacrifices.

Druidism was stamped out in Gaul after the Roman conquest. In Britain their stronghold was Anglesey, Wales, until they were driven out by the Roman governor Agricola. They existed in Scotland and Ireland until the coming of the Christian missionaries. What are often termed Druidic monuments – cromlechs and stone circles – are of New Stone Age (Neolithic) origin, though they may later have been used for religious purposes by the Druids. A possible example of a human sacrifice by Druids is Lindow Man, whose body was found in a bog in Cheshire 1984.

drum any of a class of percussion instruments including ***slit drums*** made of wood, ***steel drums*** fabricated from oil drums, and a majority group of ***skin drums*** consisting of a shell or vessel of wood, metal, or earthenware across one or both ends of which is stretched a membrane of hide or plastic.

Drums are struck with the hands or with a stick or pair of sticks; they are among the oldest instruments known. Most drums are of indeterminate low or high pitch and function as rhythm instruments. The exceptions are steel drums, orchestral timpani (kettledrums), and Indian tabla, which are tuned to precise pitches. Double-ended African kalungu ('talking drums') can be varied in pitch by the player squeezing on the tension cords. Frame drums, including the Irish bodhrán and Basque tambour, are smaller and lighter in tone and may incorporate jingles or rattles.

Orchestral drums consist of timpani, tambourine, snare, side, and bass drums, the latter either single-headed (with a single skin) and producing a ringing tone, called a gong drum, or double-headed (with two skins) and producing a dense booming noise of indeterminate pitch. Military bands of foot soldiers employ the snare and side drums, and among cavalry regiments a pair of kettledrums mounted on horseback are played on ceremonial occasions.

Drummond de Andrade Carlos 1902–1987. Brazilian writer. He is generally considered the greatest modern Brazilian poet, and was a prominent member of the Modernist school. His verse, often seemingly casual, continually confounds the reader's expectations of the 'poetical'.

drupe fleshy ◊fruit containing one or more seeds which are surrounded by a hard, protective layer – for example cherry, almond, and plum. The wall of the fruit (◊pericarp) is differentiated into the outer skin (exocarp), the fleshy layer of tissues (mesocarp), and the hard layer surrounding the seed (endocarp).

The coconut is a drupe, but here the pericarp becomes dry and fibrous at maturity. Blackberries are an aggregate fruit composed of a cluster of small drupes.

Druse or ***Druze*** religious sect in the Middle East of some 300,000 people. It began as a branch of Shi'ite Islam, based on a belief in the divinity of the Fatimid caliph al-Hakim (996–1021) and that he will return at the end of time. Their particular doctrines are kept secret, even from the majority of members.

The Druse sect was founded in Egypt in the 11th century, and then fled to Palestine to avoid persecution; today they occupy areas of Syria, Lebanon, and Israel. Their scriptures are drawn from the Bible, the Koran, and Sufi allegories. Druse militia groups formed one of the three main factions involved in the Lebanese civil war (the others were Amal Shi'ite Muslims and Christian Maronites).

dry-cleaning method of cleaning textiles based on the use of volatile solvents, such as trichloroethene (trichloroethylene), that dissolve grease. No water is used. Dry-cleaning was first developed in France 1849.

dryad in Greek mythology, a forest ◊nymph or tree spirit.

drupe The succulent flesh around the 'stone' at the centre of a drupe attracts animals to feed on it. In their turn, the animals then distribute the seed. The ivy *Hedera helix*, shown here, produces drupes. *Premaphotos Wildlife*

Dryden John 1631–1700. English poet and dramatist. He is noted for his satirical verse and for his use of the heroic couplet. His poetry includes the verse satire *Absalom and Achitophel* 1681, *Annus Mirabilis* 1667, and 'A Song for St Cecilia's Day' 1687. Plays include the heroic drama *The Conquest of Granada* 1672, the comedy *Marriage à la Mode* 1673, and *All for Love* 1678, a reworking of Shakespeare's *Antony and Cleopatra*.

dry ice solid carbon dioxide (CO_2), used as a refrigerant. At temperatures above −79°C/ −110.2°F, it sublimes (turns into vapour without passing through a liquid stage) to gaseous carbon dioxide.

'Those book-learned fools who miss the world.'

JOHN DRINKWATER
From Generation to Generation

dry point in printmaking, a technique of engraving on copper, using a hard, sharp tool. The resulting lines tend to be fine and angular, with a strong furry edge created by the metal shavings. Dürer, Rembrandt, and Max Beckmann were outstanding exponents.

dry rot infection of timber in damp conditions by fungi, such as *Merulius lacrymans*, that form a threadlike surface. Whitish at first, the fungus later reddens as reproductive spores are formed. Fungoid tentacles also enter the fabric of the timber, rendering it dry-looking and brittle. Dry rot spreads rapidly through a building.

Drysdale (George) Russell 1912–1981. Australian artist. In 1944 he produced a series of wash drawings for the *Sydney Morning Herald* recording the effects of a severe drought in W New South Wales. The bleakness of life in the Australian outback is a recurring theme in his work, which typically depicts the dried-out, scorched landscape with gaunt figures reflecting fortitude in desolation and poverty.

Dryden A portrait of the English writer John Dryden. He wrote poetry, drama, and critical essays, and turned in later life to translating the classics. *Corbis*

DTP abbreviation for ◊***desktop publishing***.

Dual Entente alliance between France and Russia that lasted from 1893 until the Bolshevik Revolution of 1917.

dualism in philosophy, the belief that reality is essentially dual in nature. The French philosopher René ◊Descartes, for example, referred to thinking and material substance. These entities interact but are fundamentally separate and distinct. Dualism is contrasted with ◊monism, the theory that reality is made up of only one substance.

Duarte José Napoleon 1925–1990. El Salvadorean politician, president 1980–82 and 1984–88. He was mayor of San Salvador 1964–70, and was elected president 1972, but was exiled by the army 1982. On becoming president again 1984, he sought a negotiated settlement with the left-wing guerrillas 1986, but resigned on health grounds.

dub in pop music, a ◊remix, usually instrumental, of a reggae recording, stripped down to the rhythm track. Dub originated in Jamaica with the disc jockeys of mobile sound systems, who would use their playback controls to drop out parts of tracks; later it became common practice to produce a studio dub version as the B-side of a single.

Dubai one of the ◊United Arab Emirates.

Dubček Alexander 1921–1992. Czechoslovak politician, chair of the federal assembly 1989–92. He was a member of the Slovak ◊resistance movement during World War II, and became first secretary of the Communist Party 1967–69. He launched a liberalization campaign (called the ◊Prague Spring) that was opposed by the USSR and led to the Soviet invasion of Czechoslovakia 1968. He was arrested by Soviet troops and expelled from the party 1970. In 1989 he gave speeches at prodemocracy rallies, and after the fall of the hardline regime, he was elected speaker of the National Assembly in Prague, a position to which he was re-elected 1990.

Dublin (Gaelic ***Baile Atha Cliath***) capital and port on the east coast of the Republic of Ireland, at the mouth of the river Liffey, facing the Irish Sea; population (1991) 478,400, Greater Dublin, including Dún Laoghaire (1986 est) 921,000. It is the site of one of the world's largest breweries (Guinness); other industries include textiles, pharmaceuticals, electrical goods, whisky distilling, glass, food processing, and machine tools.

features In the Georgian period many fine squares were laid out, and the Custom House (damaged in the 1921 uprising but later restored) survives. There is a Roman Catholic cathedral, St Mary's (1816); two Protestant cathedrals; and two universities, Trinity College (the University of Dublin) and the National University of Ireland. Trinity College library contains the Book of Kells, a splendidly illuminated 8th-century gospel book produced at the monastery of Kells in County Meath, founded by St Columba. Other buildings are the City Hall (1779), the Four Courts (1796), the National Gallery, Dublin Castle, Dublin Municipal Gallery, National Museum, Leinster House (where the legislature, Dáil Eireann, sits), and the Abbey and Gate theatres.

history The city was founded 840 by the invading Danes, who were finally defeated 1014 at Clontarf, now a northern suburb of the city. Dublin was the centre of English rule from 1171 (exercised from Dublin Castle 1220) until 1922.

Duccio di Buoninsegna *Christ Opening the Eyes of the Blind Man* 1308–11 by Duccio (National Gallery, London). Painted in the bright colours of late Medieval art, this small picture, one of the 34 scenes of the Life from the Passion of Christ on the reverse of his *Maestà*, is a superb example of Duccio's skill in storytelling. *Corbis*

Dublin county in the Republic of Ireland, in Leinster province, facing the Irish Sea; county town Dublin; area 920 sq km/355 sq mi; population (1986) 1,021,000. It is mostly level and low-lying, but rises in the S to 753 m/2,471 ft in Kippure, part of the Wicklow Mountains. The river Liffey enters Dublin Bay. Dublin, the capital of the Republic of Ireland, and Dún Laoghaire are the two major towns.

dubnium synthesized, radioactive, metallic element, symbol Db. It is the first of the ◊transactinide series, atomic number 104, relative atomic mass 262. It is produced by bombarding californium with carbon nuclei and has ten isotopes, the longest-lived of which, Db-262, has a half-life of 70 seconds.

Two institutions claim to be the first to have synthesized it: the Joint Institute for Nuclear Research in Dubna, Russia, in 1964; and the University of California at Berkeley, USA, in 1969.

Dubrovnik (Italian ***Ragusa***) city and port in Croatia on the Adriatic coast; population (1991) 49,700. It manufactures cheese, liqueurs, silk, and leather.

Once a Roman station, Dubrovnik was for a long time an independent republic but passed to Austrian rule 1814–1919.

During the 1991 civil war, Dubrovnik was placed under siege by Yugoslav federal forces (as part of its blockade of the Croatian coast) and subjected to frequent artillery barrages and naval shelling. Medieval buildings and works of art were destroyed.

Dubuffet Jean Philippe Arthur 1901–1985. French artist. He originated ***Art Brut***, 'raw or brutal art', in the 1940s. Inspired by graffiti and children's drawings, he used such varied materials as plaster, steel wool, and straw in his paintings and sculptures to produce highly textured surfaces.

Art Brut emerged 1945 with an exhibition of Dubuffet's own work and of paintings by psychiatric patients and naive, or untrained, artists. His own paintings and sculptural works have a similar quality, primitive and expressive.

Duccio di Buoninsegna c. 1255–c. 1319. Italian painter. As the first major figure in the Sienese school, his influence on the development of painting was profound. His works include his altarpiece for Siena Cathedral, the *Maestà* 1308–11 (Cathedral Museum, Siena). In this the figure of the Virgin is essentially Byzantine in style, with much gold detail, but depicted with a new warmth and tenderness.

Duccio's art is distinct from that of his contemporaries Cimabue and Giotto in being Byzantine in style. However, his work is related less to the stereotyped icons of Greek painters than to the refined products of the Byzantine revival at the imperial court of Constantinople from the 11th century, as exemplified in exquisite manuscript illuminations of the period. The use of gold in the background and detail, an elegant quality of line, and a subtle use of colour are characteristic of his work.

Duce (Italian 'leader') title bestowed on the fascist dictator Benito ◊Mussolini by his followers and later adopted as his official title.

Duchamp Marcel 1887–1968. French-born US artist. He achieved notoriety with his *Nude Descending a Staircase No 2* 1912 (Philadelphia Museum of Art), influenced by Cubism and Futurism. An active exponent of ◊Dada, he invented ◊ready-mades, everyday items (for example, a bicycle wheel mounted on a kitchen stool) which he displayed as works of art.

A major early work that focuses on mechanical objects endowed with mysterious significance is *La Mariée mise à nu par ses célibataires, même/The Bride Stripped Bare by Her Bachelors, Even* 1915–23 (Philadelphia Museum of Art). Duchamp continued to experiment with ◊collage, mechanical imagery, and sculptural assemblages (works constructed of atypical materials) throughout his career. He lived mostly in New York and became a US citizen 1954.

duck any of about 50 species of short-legged waterbirds with webbed feet and flattened bills, of the family Anatidae, order Anseriformes, which also includes the larger geese and swans. Ducks were domesticated for eggs, meat, and feathers by the ancient Chinese and the ancient Maya (see ◊poultry). Most ducks live in fresh water, feeding on worms and insects as well as vegetable matter. They are generally divided into dabbling ducks and diving ducks.

duck The pink-headed duck of India and Nepal, believed to be extinct as no wild specimens have been seen since 1936. All ducks are aquatic with webbed feet and water-repellent plumage to give extra buoyancy.

The three front toes of a duck's foot are webbed and the hind toe is free; the legs are scaly. The broad rounded bill is skin-covered with a horny tip provided with little plates (lamellae) through which the duck is able to strain its food from water and mud. The mallard *Anas platyrhynchos*, 58 cm/1.9 ft, found over most of the northern hemisphere, is the species from which all domesticated ducks originated. The male (drake) has a glossy green head, brown breast, grey body, and yellow bill. The female (duck) is speckled brown, with a duller bill. The male moults and resembles the female for a while just after the breeding season. There are many other species of duck including ◊teal, ◊eider, ◊mandarin duck, ◊merganser, muscovy duck, pintail duck, ◊shelduck, and ◊shoveler. They have different-shaped bills according to their diet and habitat; for example, the shoveler has a wide spade-shaped bill for scooping insects off the surface of water. The main threat to the survival of ducks in the wild is hunting by humans.

duckweed any of a family of tiny plants of the family Lemnaceae, especially of the genus *Lemna*, found floating on the surface of still water throughout most of the world, except the polar regions and tropics. Each plant consists of a flat, circular, leaflike structure 0.4 cm/0.15 in or less across, with a single thin root up to 15 cm/6 in long below.

The plants bud off new individuals and soon cover the surface of the water. Flowers rarely appear, but when they do, they are minute and located in a pocket at the edge of the plant.

ductless gland alternative name for an ◊endocrine gland.

duel fight between two people armed with weapons. A duel is usually fought according to pre-arranged rules with the aim of settling a private quarrel.

In medieval Europe duels were a legal method of settling disputes. By the 16th century the practice had largely ceased but duelling with swords or pistols, often with elaborate ritual, continued unofficially in aristocratic and military circles until the 20th century. In some German universities exclusive duelling clubs continue to this day.

due process of law legal principle, dating from the ◊Magna Carta, the charter of rights granted by King John of England 1215, and now enshrined in the fifth and fourteenth amendments to the US Constitution, that no person shall be deprived of life, liberty, or property without due process of law (a fair legal procedure). In the USA, the provisions have been given a wide interpretation, to include, for example, the right to representation by an attorney.

Dufay Guillaume c. 1400–1474. Flemish composer. He wrote secular songs and sacred music, including 84 songs and eight masses. His work marks a transition from the style of the Middle Ages to the expressive melodies and rich harmonies of the Renaissance.

Dufourspitze second highest of the Alpine peaks, 4,634 m/15,203 ft high. It is the highest peak in the Monte Rosa group of the Pennine Alps on the Swiss-Italian frontier.

Dufy Raoul 1877–1953. French painter and designer. Inspired by Fauvism, he developed a fluent, brightly coloured style in watercolour and oils, painting scenes of gaiety and leisure, such as horse racing, yachting, and life on the beach. He also designed tapestries, textiles, and ceramics.

dugong marine mammal *Dugong dugong* of the order Sirenia (sea cows), found in the Red Sea, the Indian Ocean, and the W Pacific. It can grow to 3.6 m/11 ft long, and has a tapering body with a notched tail and two fore-flippers. It has a very long hind gut (30 m/98 ft in adults) which functions similarly to the rumen in ◊ruminants. Previously it was thought to be the only truly herbivorous marine mammal, feeding mostly on sea grasses and seaweeds, but Australian research 1995 showed that some dugongs eat sea squirts. The dugong is thought to have given rise to the mermaid myth.

duiker (Afrikaans 'diver') any of several antelopes of the family Bovidae, common in Africa. Duikers are shy and nocturnal, and grow to 30–70 cm/12–28 in tall.

Duiker Johannes 1890–1935. Dutch architect of the 1920s and 1930s avant-garde period. A member of the De ◊Stijl group, his works demonstrate great structural vigour. They include the Zonnestraal Sanatorium, Hilversum, 1926–28, co-designed with Bernard Bijvoet (1889–), and the Open Air School 1929–30 and Handelsblad-Cineac News Cinema 1934, both in Amsterdam.

Duisburg river port and industrial city in North Rhine–Westphalia, Germany, at the confluence of the Rhine and Ruhr rivers; population (1993) 538,100. It is the largest inland river port in Europe. Heavy industries include oil refining and the production of steel, copper, zinc, plastics, and machinery.

Dukas Paul Abraham 1865–1935. French composer and teacher. His scrupulous orchestration and chromatically enriched harmonies were admired by Debussy. His small output includes the opera *Ariane et Barbe-Bleue/Ariane and Bluebeard* 1907, the ballet *La Péri/The Peri* 1912, and the animated orchestral scherzo *L'Apprenti sorcier/The Sorcerer's Apprentice* 1897.

duke highest title in the English peerage. It originated in England 1337, when Edward III created his son Edward, Duke of Cornwall.

dulcimer musical instrument, a form of ◊zither, consisting of a shallow open trapezoidal soundbox across which strings are stretched laterally; they are horizontally struck by lightweight hammers or beaters. It produces clearly differentiated pitches of consistent quality and is more agile and wide-ranging in pitch than the harp or lyre. In Hungary the dulcimer, or cimbalon, is in current use.

Of Middle Eastern origin, the dulcimer spread into Europe about 1100 and was introduced to China and Korea about 1800. Examples include the Iraqi *santir*, Chinese *yang shin*, Russian *chang*, Korean *yangum*, and Swiss *hackbrett*.

Dulles John Foster 1888–1959. US politician. Senior US adviser at the founding of the United Nations, he was largely responsible for drafting the Japanese peace treaty of 1951. As secretary of state 1952–59, he was the architect of US Cold War foreign policy, secured US intervention in South Vietnam after the expulsion of the French 1954, and was critical of Britain during the Suez Crisis 1956.

Dulong Pierre Louis 1785–1838. French chemist and physicist. In 1819 he discovered, together with physicist Alexis Petit (1791–1820), the law that now bears their names. ***Dulong and Petit's law*** states that, for many elements solid at room temperature, the product of ◊relative atomic mass and ◊specific heat capacity is approximately constant. He also discovered the explosive nitrogen trichloride 1811.

dulse any of several edible red seaweeds, especially *Rhodymenia palmata*, found on middle and lower shores of the N Atlantic. They may have a single broad blade up to 30 cm/12 in long rising directly from the holdfast which attaches them to the sea floor, or be palmate or fan-shaped. The frond is tough and dark red, sometimes with additional small leaflets at the edge.

Dulwich district of the Greater London borough of Southwark. It contains Dulwich College (founded 1619 by Edward Alleyn, an Elizabethan actor); the Horniman Museum (1901), with a fine ethnological collection; Dulwich Picture Gallery (1814), England's oldest public picture gallery (designed by John Soane, rebuilt 1953 after being bombed during World War II); Dulwich Park; and Dulwich Village.

Duma in Russia, before 1917, an elected assembly that met four times following the short-lived 1905 revolution. With progressive demands the government could not accept, the Duma was largely powerless. After the abdication of Tsar Nicholas II, the Duma directed the formation of a provisional government.

Dumas Alexandre 1824–1895. French author, known as Dumas *fils* (the son of Dumas *père*). He is remembered for the play *La Dame aux camélias/The Lady of the Camellias* 1852, based on his own novel and the source of Verdi's opera *La Traviata*.

Dumas Alexandre 1802–1870. French writer, known as Dumas *père* (the father). His popular historical romances were the reworked output of a 'fiction-factory' of collaborators. They include *Les Trois Mousquetaires/The Three Musketeers* 1844 and its sequels. He is best known for *Le Comte de Monte Cristo/The Count of Monte Cristo*, which appeared in 12 volumes 1845. His play *Henri III et sa cour/Henry III and His Court* 1829 established French romantic historical drama. Dumas *fils* was his son.

Du Maurier Daphne 1907–1989. English novelist. Her romantic fiction includes *Jamaica Inn* 1936, *Rebecca* 1938, and *My Cousin Rachel* 1951, and is set in Cornwall. Her work, though lacking in depth and original insights, is made compelling by her fine story-telling gift. *Jamaica Inn*, *Rebecca*, and her short story *The Birds* were made into films by the English director Alfred Hitchcock. She was the granddaughter of British cartoonist and novelist George Du Maurier.

Du Maurier George (Louis Palmella Busson) 1834–1896. French-born British author and illustrator. He is remembered for the novel *Trilby* 1894, the story of a natural singer able to perform only under the hypnosis of Svengali, her tutor.

Du Maurier was born in Paris. After studying chemistry at University College, London, and art in Paris and Antwerp, he settled in London in 1860. His drawings appeared in journals such as *Once a Week*, the *Cornhill Magazine*, and *Punch*, and he joined the staff of *Punch* 1864. Du Maurier's work covered all aspects of the Victorian social scene in a manner satirical yet at the same time acceptable to his essentially middle-class public. He drew attention particularly to both the Victorian philistine and the devotees of the Aesthetic Movement.

Dumbarton Oaks 18th-century mansion in Washington DC, USA, used for conferences and seminars. It was the scene of a conference held 1944 that led to the foundation of the United Nations.

Dumfries administrative headquarters of Dumfries and Galloway, Scotland; population (1991) 32,100. It is situated on the river Nith. Industries include knitwear, plastics, light engineering, and textiles.

Dumfries and Galloway local authority of Scotland, created 1975, retained in the reorganization of local government 1996 (*see United Kingdom map*)
area 6,500 sq km/2,510 sq mi
towns and cities Dumfries (administrative headquarters)
features Solway Firth; Galloway Hills, setting of John Buchan's *The Thirty-Nine Steps*; Glen Trool National Park; Ruthwell Cross, a runic cross dating from about 800 in Ruthwell Parish Church
industries horses and cattle (for which the Galloway area was renowned), sheep, timber
population (1996 est) 147,900
famous people Robert the Bruce, Robert Burns, Thomas Carlyle.

Dunant Jean Henri 1828–1910. Swiss philanthropist, originator of the international relief agency the Red Cross. At the Battle of Solferino 1859 he helped tend the wounded, and in *Un Souvenir de Solferino* 1862 he proposed the establishment of an international body for the aid of the wounded – an idea that was realized in the Geneva Convention 1864. He shared the 1901 Nobel Peace Prize.

Dunaway (Dorothy) Faye 1941– . US film actress. Her first starring role was in *Bonnie and Clyde* 1967. Her subsequent films, including *Network* 1976 (for which she won an Academy Award)

'A fully equipped duke costs as much to keep up as two Dreadnoughts; and dukes are just as great a terror and they last longer.'

On DUKES
David Lloyd George speech in Newcastle 9 Oct 1909

'All for one, one for all.'

ALEXANDRE DUMAS
The Three Musketeers

duiker The grey duiker *Cephalopus Sylvicapra grimmia* is the commonest species of duiker. It occurs over most of sub-Saharan Africa, surviving in every kind of habitat – except deserts and rainforests – up to an altitude of 4,600 m/15,090 ft. *Premaphotos Wildlife*

❛The only dance masters I could have were Jean-Jacques Rousseau, Walt Whitman and Nietzsche.❜

ISADORA DUNCAN
My Life 1927

and *Mommie Dearest* 1981, received a varying critical reception. She also starred in ◊Polanski's *Chinatown* 1974 and *The Handmaid's Tale* 1990.

Duncan Isadora, originally Angela 1878–1927. US dancer. A pioneer of modern dance, she adopted an emotionally expressive free form, dancing barefoot and wearing a loose tunic, inspired by the ideal of Hellenic beauty. She danced solos accompanied to music by Beethoven and other great composers, believing that the music should fit the grandeur of the dance. Having made her base in Paris 1908, she toured extensively, often returning to Russia after her initial success there 1904.

She died in an accident when her long scarf caught in the wheel of the sportscar in which she was travelling. She was as notorious for her private life as for her work, which was considered scandalous at the time. Her frequent alliances with artists and industrialists, her marriage to the Russian poet Sergei Esenin, and the tragedy of her two children who were drowned in a freak accident, were documented in her autobiography *My Life* 1927.

Dundee city and fishing port, on the north side of the Firth of Tay, Scotland; administrative headquarters (1975–96) of former region of Tayside, and, from 1996, of local authority Dundee City; population (1996 est) 151,000. It is an important shipping and rail centre. Industries include engineering, textiles, electronics, printing, and food processing.

The city developed around the jute industry in the 19th century, and has benefited from the North Sea oil discoveries of the 1970s. There is a university (1967) derived from Queen's College (founded 1881), and other notable buildings include the Albert Institute (1867) and Caird Hall.

Dundee City local authority of Scotland created 1996 (*see United Kingdom map*).

dune mound or ridge of wind-drifted sand common on coasts and in sandy deserts. Loose sand is blown and bounced along by the wind, up the windward side of a dune. The sand particles then fall to rest on the lee side, while more are blown up from the windward side. In this way a dune moves gradually downwind.

In sandy deserts, the typical crescent-shaped dune is called a barchan. ***Seif dunes*** are longitudinal and lie parallel to the wind direction, and ***star-shaped dunes*** are formed by irregular winds.

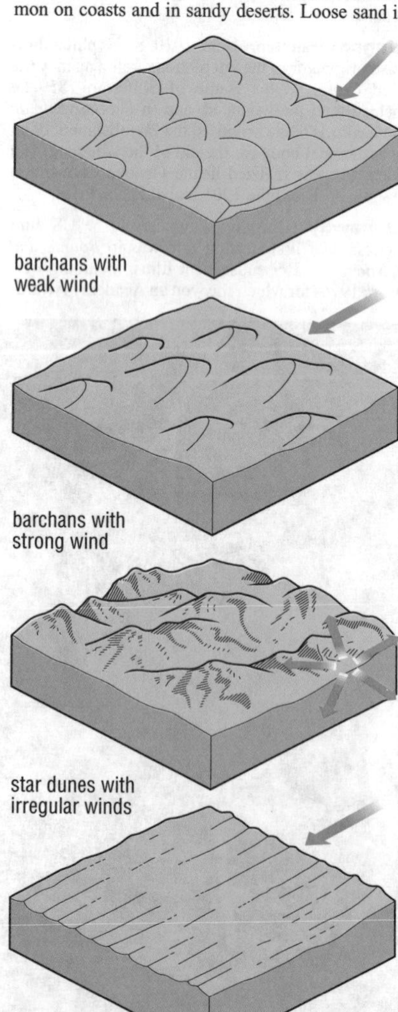

dune The shape of a dune indicates the prevailing wind pattern. Crescent-shaped dunes form in sandy desert with winds from a constant direction. Seif dunes form on bare rocks, parallel to the wind direction. Irregular star dunes are formed by variable winds.

Dunfermline industrial city near the Firth of Forth in Fife region, Scotland; population (1991) 55,100. It is the site of the naval base of Rosyth; industries include engineering, electronics, and textiles. Many Scottish kings, including Robert the Bruce, are buried in Dunfermline Abbey. It is the birthplace of the industrialist Andrew Carnegie.

Dungeness shingle headland on the south coast of Kent, England. It has nuclear power stations, a lighthouse, and a bird sanctuary.

Dunkirk (French ***Dunkerque***) seaport on the north coast of France, in Nord *département*, on the Strait of Dover; population (1990) 71,100. Its harbour is one of the foremost in France, and it has widespread canal links with the rest of France and with Belgium; there is a ferry service to Ramsgate, England. Industries include oil refining, fishing, and the manufacture of textiles, machinery, and soap.

Dunkirk was close to the front line during much of World War I, and in World War II, 337,131 Allied troops (including about 110,000 French) were evacuated from the beaches as German forces approached.

Dunkirk British prisoners on the beaches at Dunkirk in 1940. From 26 May to 4 June 1940 over 850 vessels, many of them small private boats that had sailed over from harbours all along the S coast of England, rescued thousands of British and French troops driven on to the beaches in Dunkirk by the German army. *Library of Congress*

Dún Laoghaire formerly ***Kingstown*** port and suburb of Dublin, Republic of Ireland; population (1986 est) 54,700. It is a terminal for ferries to Britain, and there are fishing industries.

dunlin small gregarious shore bird *Calidris alpina* of the sandpiper family Scolopacidae, order Charadriformes, about 18 cm/7 in long, nesting on moors and marshes in the far northern regions of Eurasia and North America. Chestnut above and black below in summer, it is greyish in winter; the bill and feet are black.

It is the commonest small sandpiper and frequents flat coasts and tidal rivers of Britain.

Dunlop John Boyd 1840–1921. Scottish inventor who founded the rubber company that bears his name. In 1888, to help his child win a tricycle race, he bound an inflated rubber hose to the wheels. The same year he developed commercially practical pneumatic tyres, first patented by Robert William Thomson (1822–1873) 1845 for bicycles and cars.

Thomson's invention had gone practically unnoticed, whereas Dunlop's arrived at a crucial time in the development of transport, and with the rubber industry well established.

dunnock or ***hedge sparrow*** European bird *Prunella modularis* family Prunellidae, similar in size and colouring to the sparrow, but with a slate-grey head and breast, and more slender bill. It is characterized in the field by a hopping gait, with continual twitches of the wings while feeding. It nests in bushes and hedges.

Duns Scotus John c. 1265–c. 1308. Scottish monk, a leading figure in the theological and philosophical system of medieval ◊scholasticism. The church rejected his ideas, and the word 'dunce' is derived from Dunses, a term of ridicule applied to his followers.

He belonged to the Franciscan order, and was known as Doctor Subtilis. In the medieval controversy over universals he advocated ◊nominalism, maintaining that classes of things have no independent reality. On many points he turned against the orthodoxy of Thomas ◊Aquinas; for example, he rejected the idea of a necessary world, favouring a concept of God as absolute freedom capable of spontaneous activity.

Dunstable John c. 1385–1453. English composer of songs and anthems. He is considered one of the founders of Renaissance harmony.

Dunstan, St 924–988. English priest and politician, archbishop of Canterbury from 960. He was abbot of Glastonbury from 945, and made it a centre of learning. Feast day 19 May.

duodecimal system system of arithmetic notation using 12 as a base, at one time considered superior to the decimal number system in that 12 has more factors (2, 3, 4, 6) than 10 (2, 5). It is now superseded by the universally accepted decimal system.

duodenum in vertebrates, a short length of ◊alimentary canal found between the stomach and the small intestine. Its role is in digesting carbohydrates, fats, and proteins. The smaller molecules formed are then absorbed, either by the duodenum or the ileum.

Entry of food to the duodenum is controlled by the pyloric sphincter, a muscular ring at the outlet of the stomach. Once food has passed into the duodenum it is mixed with bile released from the gall bladder and with a range of enzymes secreted from the pancreas, a digestive gland near the top of the intestine. The bile neutralizes the acidity of the gastric juices passing out of the stomach and aids fat digestion.

Du Pré Jacqueline Mary 1945–1987. English cellist. She was celebrated for her proficient technique and powerful interpretations of the classical cello repertory, particularly of Elgar. She had an international concert career while still in her teens and made many recordings.

She married the Israeli pianist and conductor Daniel ◊Barenboim 1967 and worked with him in concerts, as a duo, and in a conductor-soloist relationship until her playing career was ended by multiple sclerosis. Although confined to a wheelchair for the last 14 years of her life, she continued to work as a teacher and to campaign on behalf of other sufferers of the disease.

duralumin lightweight aluminium ◊alloy widely used in aircraft construction, containing copper, magnesium, and manganese.

Duras Marguerite. Assumed name of Marguerite Donnadieu 1914–1996. French writer, dramatist, and filmmaker. Her work includes short stories, plays, and film scripts. She also directed stage productions and film versions of her work. Her novels include *Le Vice-consul/The Vice-Consul* 1966, evoking an existentialist world from the setting of Calcutta; *L'Amant/The Lover* 1984 (Prix Goncourt), which deals with a love affair between a young French woman and a Chinese man; and *Emily L.* 1989. Her autobiographical novel, *La Douleur* 1986, is set in Paris in 1945.

Durban principal port of KwaZulu Natal, South Africa, and second port of the republic; population (urban area, 1991) 1,137,400. It exports coal, maize, and wool; imports heavy machinery and mining equipment; and is also a holiday resort.

Founded 1824 as Port Natal, it was renamed 1835

Dürer *Eve* 1507 by Albrecht Dürer (Prado, Madrid). This nude forms a pair with *Adam*. Inspired by Italian Renaissance art, Dürer developed a system of ideal proportions for the nude. The results, however, particularly with his female figures, show the elegant line and proportions of German Medieval art. *Corbis*

after General Benjamin d'Urban (1777–1849), lieutenant governor of the eastern district of Cape Colony 1834–37. Natal university (1949) is divided between Durban and Pietermaritzburg.

Dürer Albrecht 1471–1528. German artist. He was the leading figure of the northern Renaissance. Highly skilled in drawing and a keen student of nature, he perfected the technique of woodcut and engraving, producing woodcut series such as the *Apocalypse* 1498 and copperplate engravings such as *The Knight, Death, and the Devil* 1513 and *Melancholia* 1514. His paintings include altarpieces and meticulously observed portraits, including many self-portraits.

Dürer was apprenticed first to his father, a goldsmith, then 1486 to Michael Wolgemut (1434–1519), a painter, woodcut artist, and master of a large workshop in Nuremberg. At the age of 13 he drew a portrait of himself from the mirror, the first known self-portrait in the history of European art, and characteristic of his genius. From 1490 he travelled widely, studying Netherlandish and Italian art, and returned to Nuremberg 1495. Other notable journeys were to Venice 1505–07, where he met the painter Giovanni Bellini, and to Antwerp 1520, where he was made court painter to Charles V of Spain and the Netherlands (recorded in detail in his diary).

Durga Hindu goddess; one of the many names for the 'great goddess' ◊***Mahādevī***.

Durham city and administrative headquarters of the county of Durham, England; population (1991) 80,700. Formerly it was a centre for the coal-mining industry (the last pit closed 1993); current industries include textiles, light engineering, carpets, and clothing. It has a Norman cathedral founded 995, with the remains of the theologian and historian Bede; the castle was built 1072 by William I and the university was founded 1832.

Durham county of NE England (*see United Kingdom map*)

towns and cities Durham (administrative headquarters), Peterlee, Newton Aycliffe

features Pennine Hills; rivers Wear and Tees; Beamish open-air industrial museum; site of one of Britain's richest coalfields (pits no longer functioning); Bowes Museum; Barnard Castle

industries sheep and dairy produce; clothing, chemicals. There are also iron and steel processing and light engineering industries

famous people Elizabeth Barrett Browning, Anthony Eden.

Durham John George Lambton, 1st Earl of Durham 1792–1840. British politician. Appointed Lord Privy Seal 1830, he drew up the first Reform Bill 1832, and as governor general of Canada briefly in 1837 he drafted the Durham Report which resulted in the union of Upper and Lower Canada.

Durkheim Emile 1858–1917. French sociologist, one of the founders of modern sociology, who also influenced social anthropology. He worked to establish sociology as a respectable and scientific discipline, capable of diagnosing social ills and recommending possible cures. He examined the bases of social order and the effects of industrialization on traditional social and moral order.

Durkheim was the first lecturer in social science at Bordeaux University 1887–1902, professor of education at the Sorbonne from 1902 and the first professor of sociology there 1913. His four key works are *De la division du travail social/The Division of Labour in Society* 1893, comparing social order in small-scale societies with that in industrial ones; *Les Régles de la méthode/The Rules of Sociological Method* 1895, outlining his own brand of functionalism and proclaiming ◊positivism as the way forward for sociology as a science; *Suicide* 1897, showing social causes of this apparently individual act; and *Les Formes élémentaires de la vie religieuse/The Elementary Forms of Religion* 1912, a study of the beliefs of Australian Aborigines, showing the place of religion in social solidarity.

durra or ***doura*** grass of the genus *Sorghum*, also known as Indian millet, grown as a cereal in parts of Asia and Africa. *Sorghum vulgare* is the chief cereal in many parts of Africa. See also ◊sorghum.

Durrell Gerald Malcolm 1925–1995. English naturalist, writer, and zoo curator. He became director of Jersey Zoological Park 1958, and wrote 37 books, including the humorous memoir *My Family and Other Animals* 1956. He was the brother of the writer Lawrence Durrell.

Durrell Lawrence (George) 1912–1990. British novelist and poet. He lived mainly in the E Mediterranean, the setting of his novels, including the Alexandria Quartet: *Justine*, *Balthazar*, *Mountolive*, and *Clea* 1957–60. He also wrote travel books, including *Bitter Lemons* 1957 about Cyprus. His heady prose and bizarre characters reflect his exotic sources of inspiration. He was the brother of the naturalist Gerald Durrell.

Dürrenmatt Friedrich 1921–1990. Swiss dramatist. He wrote grotesque and ironical tragicomedies, for example *Der Besuch einer alten Dame/The Visit* 1956 and *Die Physiker/The Physicists* 1962. His fascination with the absurd and with black humour can also be seen in his novels, such as *Das Versprechen/The Pledge* 1958.

His work reveals a preoccupation with contemporary spiritual bankruptcy reminiscent of the Danish philosopher Kierkegaard and the Czech writer Kafka.

Durrës chief port of Albania; population (1991) 86,900. It is a commercial and communications centre, with flour mills, soap and cigarette factories, distilleries, and an electronics plant. It was the capital of Albania 1912–21.

Dushanbe formerly (1929–69) ***Stalinabad*** capital of Tajikistan, 160 km/100 mi N of the Afghan frontier; population (1991) 582,000. It is a road, rail, and air centre. Industries include cotton mills, tanneries, meat-packing factories, and printing works. It is the seat of Tajik state university.

In 1990–1991 antigovernment rioting led to a curfew and a state of emergency being imposed; further antigovernment protests followed and Aug 1992 protesters stormed the presidential palace, forcing President Nabiyev's resignation.

Düsseldorf industrial city of Germany, on the right bank of the river Rhine, 26 km/16 mi NW of Cologne, capital of North Rhine–Westphalia; population (1993) 577,600. It is a river port and the commercial and financial centre of the Ruhr area, with food processing, brewing, agricultural machinery, textile, and chemical industries.

dust bowl area in the Great Plains region of North America (Texas to Kansas) that suffered extensive wind erosion as the result of drought and poor farming practice in once fertile soil. Much of the topsoil was blown away in the droughts of the 1930s and the 1980s.

Similar dust bowls are being formed in many areas today, noticeably across Africa, because of overcropping and overgrazing.

Dutch art The full emergence of Dutch art came with the creation of the Dutch Republic in the 17th century. Its sources were the medieval traditions of Flemish, German, and French painting, and later the Renaissance art of Italy. It matured quickly through the works of 17th-century artists such as Hals, Rembrandt, Vermeer, de Hooch, Ruisdael, Cuyp, and Hobbema. As there was no patronage from either court or church, artists had to satisfy the tastes of the prosperous middle classes, for whom they produced scenes of everyday life, landscapes, still lifes, and portraits. There was a marked decline in Dutch art during the 18th and 19th centuries. The two outstanding Dutch artists of modern times are Vincent van Gogh (late 19th century) and Piet Mondrian (first half of the 20th century).

Dutch East India Company trading monopoly of the 17th and 18th centuries; see ◊East India Company (Dutch).

Dutch East Indies former Dutch colony, which in 1945 became independent as ◊Indonesia.

Dutch elm disease disease of elm trees *Ulmus*, principally Dutch, English, and American elm, caused by the fungus *Certocystis ulmi*. The fungus is usually spread from tree to tree by the elm-bark beetle, which lays its eggs beneath the bark. The disease has no cure, and control methods involve injecting insecticide into the trees annually to prevent infection, or the destruction of all elms in a broad band around an infected area, to keep the beetles out.

The disease was first described in the Netherlands and by the early 1930s had spread across Britain and continental Europe, as well as North America. In the 1970s a new epidemic was caused by a much more virulent form of the fungus, probably brought to Britain from Canada.

Dutch Guiana former Dutch colony, which in 1975 became independent as ◊Surinam.

Dutch language member of the Germanic branch of the Indo-European language family, often referred to by scholars as Netherlandic and taken to include the standard language and dialects of the Netherlands (excluding Frisian) as well as Flemish (in Belgium and N France) and, more remotely, its offshoot Afrikaans in South Africa.

Dutch is also spoken in Surinam, South America, and the Netherlands Antilles, South Caribbean. Many people regard Flemish and Dutch as separate languages.

Dutch Reformed Church the main Protestant church in the Netherlands. In theology it follows ◊Calvinism and in government it resembles ◊Presbyterianism. It was first organized during the revolt of the Low Countries against Spanish rule in the 16th century.

The Reformed Church spread wherever the Dutch colonized or emigrated, with major centres in Indonesia, the West Indies, Sri Lanka, and South Africa, where the church gave theological support to apartheid in the 1930s and was expelled from the world community of Dutch Reformed Churches.

'To live outside the law you must be honest.'

Bob Dylan 'Absolutely Sweet Marie' 1966

From the mid-1980s it took steps to distance itself from apartheid and to seek integration between the black and white churches that had been set up.

duty a tax on a good. A customs duty is a tax on goods entering a country (a tax on imports). An excise duty is a type of indirect tax on goods consumed such as petrol, alcohol, or tobacco.

Duvalier François 1907–1971. Right-wing president of Haiti 1957–71. Known as ***Papa Doc***, he ruled as a dictator, organizing the Tontons Macoutes ('bogeymen') as a private security force to intimidate and assassinate opponents of his regime. He rigged the 1961 elections in order to have his term of office extended until 1967, and in 1964 declared himself president for life. He was excommunicated by the Vatican for harassing the Roman Catholic Church, and was succeeded on his death by his son Jean-Claude Duvalier.

Duvalier Jean-Claude 1951– . Right-wing president of Haiti 1971–86. Known as ***Baby Doc***, he succeeded his father François Duvalier, becoming, at the age of 19, the youngest president in the world. He continued to receive support from the USA but was pressured into moderating some elements of his father's regime, yet still tolerated no opposition. In 1986, with Haiti's economy stagnating and with increasing civil disorder, Duvalier fled to France, taking much of the Haitian treasury with him.

Dvořák Antonín Leopold 1841–1904. Czech composer. International recognition came with two sets of *Slavonic Dances* 1878 and 1886. He was director of the National Conservatory, New York, 1892–95. Works such as his *New World Symphony* 1893 reflect his interest in American folk themes, including black and Native American. He wrote nine symphonies; tone poems; operas, including *Rusalka* 1900; large-scale choral works; the *Carnival* 1891–92 and other overtures; violin and cello concertos; chamber music; piano pieces; and songs. His Romantic music extends the Classical tradition of Beethoven and Brahms and displays the influence of Czech folk music.

Dyak or ***Dayak*** several indigenous peoples of Indonesian Borneo (Kalimantan) and Sarawak, including the Bahau of central and E Borneo, the Land Dyak of SW Borneo, and the ◊Iban of Sarawak (sometimes called Sea Dyak). Their languages belong to the Austronesian family. Some anthropologists now call all Dyak peoples Iban. ◊*See feature on pp. 896–897.*

Dyck Anthony van 1599–1641. Flemish painter. He was an assistant to Peter Paul Rubens 1618–20, then worked briefly in England at the court of James I before moving to Italy. In 1627 he returned to his native Antwerp, where he continued to paint religious works and portraits. From 1632 he lived in England and produced numerous portraits of royalty and aristocrats, such as *Charles I on Horseback* about 1638 (National Gallery, London).

The Italian period, 1621–27, is marked by his portraits, which gained in dignity from his Venetian studies, notably those he produced in Genoa (for example the *Marchese Cattaneo*, National Gallery, London); Baroque religious painting also widened his range of style and composition. He returned to Antwerp as the rival of Rubens, having his own flourishing studio, and 1628–32 reached a peak of development.

Again invited to England 1632 by Charles I, he began a record of the royal family and English aristocracy, which, in refinement of style, colour, and composition, left a profound impression on subsequent portraiture in England.

Dvořák The Czech composer Antonín Dvořák in a portrait with his wife. Dvořák successfully blends the two most important factors influencing music in the 19th century: Romanticism, as expressed formally by composers such as Brahms, and nationalism, as embodied in the growing prominence of regional folk song. *Image Select (UK) Ltd*

dye substance that, applied in solution to fabrics, imparts a colour resistant to washing. ***Direct dyes*** combine with the material of the fabric, yielding a coloured compound; ***indirect dyes*** require the presence of another substance (a mordant), with which the fabric must first be treated; ***vat dyes*** are colourless soluble substances that on exposure to air yield an insoluble coloured compound.

Naturally occurring dyes include indigo, madder (alizarin), logwood, and cochineal, but industrial dyes (introduced in the 19th century) are usually synthetic: acid green was developed 1835 and bright purple 1856.

dye-transfer print in photography, a print made by a relatively permanent colour process that uses red, yellow, and blue separation negatives printed together.

Dyfed former county of SW Wales, created 1974, abolished 1996

dyke in earth science, a sheet of ◊igneous rock created by the intrusion of magma (molten rock) across layers of pre-existing rock. (By contrast, a sill is intruded *between* layers of rock.) It may form a ridge when exposed on the surface if it is more resistant than the rock into which it intruded. A dyke is also a human-made embankment built along a coastline (for example, in the Netherlands) to prevent the flooding of lowland coastal regions.

Dylan Bob. Adopted name of Robert Allen Zimmerman 1941– . US singer and songwriter. His lyrics provided catchphrases for a generation and influenced innumerable songwriters. He began in the folk-music tradition. His early songs, as on his albums *The Freewheelin' Bob Dylan* 1963 and *The Times They Are A-Changin'* 1964, were associated with the US civil-rights movement and antiwar protest. From 1965 he worked in an individualistic rock style, as on the albums *Highway 61 Revisited* 1965 and *Blonde on Blonde* 1966. Later albums include *Blood on the Tracks* 1975, *Slow Train Coming* 1979, *Oh, Mercy* 1989, and *Bob Dylan: Unplugged* 1995.

dynamics or ***kinetics*** in mechanics, the mathematical and physical study of the behaviour of bodies under the action of forces that produce changes of motion in them.

dynamite explosive consisting of a mixture of nitroglycerine and diatomaceous earth (diatomite, an absorbent, chalklike material). It was first devised by Alfred Nobel.

dynamo simple generator or machine for transforming mechanical energy into electrical energy. A dynamo in basic form consists of a powerful field magnet between the poles of which a suitable conductor, usually in the form of a coil (armature), is rotated. The mechanical energy of rotation is thus converted into an electric current in the armature.

Present-day dynamos work on the principles described by English physicist Michael Faraday 1830, that an ◊electromotive force is developed in a conductor when it is moved in a magnetic field.

dyne c.g.s. unit (symbol dyn) of force. 10^5 dynes make one newton. The dyne is defined as the force that will accelerate a mass of one gram by one centimetre per second per second.

dyscalculia disability demonstrated by a poor aptitude with figures. A similar disability in reading and writing is called dyslexia.

Dylan US musician and singer–songwriter Bob Dylan, whose folk-based protest anthems of the 1960s earned him the title 'the Voice of a Generation'. Since then his musical repertory has expanded to include rock, country and western, blues, and gospel. However, the early Dylan sound was echoed on his 1992 solo acoustic album *Good As I Been To You*, featuring traditional folk and roots music. *Topham*

dysentery infection of the large intestine causing abdominal cramps and painful ◊diarrhoea with blood. There are two kinds of dysentery: ***amoebic*** (caused by a protozoan), common in the tropics, which may lead to liver damage; and ***bacterial***, the kind most often seen in the temperate zones. Both forms are successfully treated with antibacterials and fluids to prevent dehydration.

dyslexia (Greek 'bad', 'pertaining to words') malfunction in the brain's synthesis and interpretation of written information, popularly known as 'word blindness'.

Dyslexia may be described as specific or developmental to distinguish it from reading or writing difficulties which are acquired. It results in poor ability in reading and writing, though the person may excel in other areas, for example, in mathematics. A similar disability with figures is called dyscalculia. Acquired dyslexia may occur as a result of brain injury or disease.

dysphagia difficulty in swallowing. It may be due to infection, obstruction, spasm in the throat or oesophagus (gullet), or neurological disease or damage.

dysprosium (Greek *dusprositos* 'difficult to get near') silver-white, metallic element of the ◊lanthanide series, symbol Dy, atomic number 66, relative atomic mass 162.50. It is among the most magnetic of all known substances and has a great capacity to absorb neutrons.

It was discovered 1886 by French chemist Paul Lecoq de Boisbaudran (1838–1912).

dystopia imaginary society whose evil qualities are meant to serve as a moral or political warning. The term was coined in 1868 by the English philosopher John Stuart ◊Mill, and is the opposite of a ◊Utopia. George Orwell's *1984* published 1949 and Aldous Huxley's *Brave New World* 1932 are examples of novels about dystopias. Dystopias are common in science fiction.

Dzungarian Gates ancient route in central Asia on the border of Kazakhstan and Xinjiang Uygur region of China, 470 km/290 mi NW of Urumqi. The route was used in the 13th century by the Mongol hordes on their way to Europe.

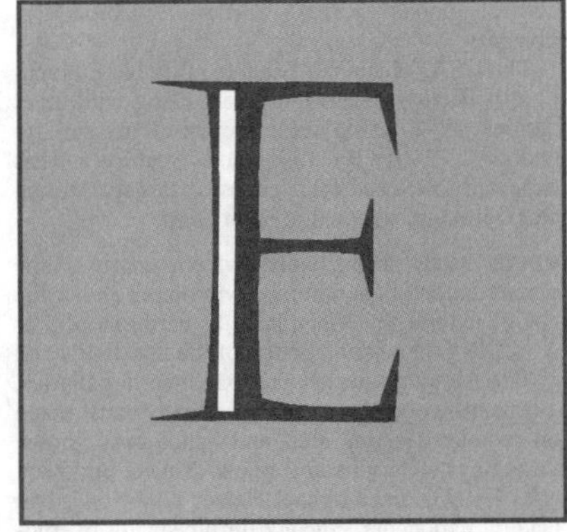

eagle any of several genera of large birds of prey of the family Accipitridae, order Falconiformes, including the golden eagle *Aquila chrysaetos* of Eurasia and North America, which has a 2 m/6 ft wingspan. Eagles occur worldwide, usually building eyries or nests in forests or mountains, and all are fierce and powerful birds of prey. The harpy eagle is the largest eagle. The white-headed bald eagle *Haliaetus leucocephalus* is the symbol of the USA; rendered infertile through the ingestion of agricultural chemicals, it is now rare, except in Alaska.

In Britain the golden eagle is found in the Highlands of Scotland, with a few recolonizing the Lake District. In the 1980s it was facing extinction due to a reduction in numbers and fertility as a result of the livers of its prey being poisoned by insecticides.

Eakins Thomas 1844–1916. US painter, a leading Realist. His most memorable subjects are medical and sporting scenes, characterized by strong contrasts between light and shade, as in his controversial *The Gross Clinic* 1875 (Jefferson Medical College, Philadelphia), a group portrait of a surgeon, his assistants, and students. In his later years he painted distinguished portraits.

Ealing outer borough of W Greater London
features 18th-century Pitshanger Manor; Gunnersbury House and Gunnersbury Park, both Regency-style houses; Ealing Studios (1931), the first British sound-film studios ('Ealing comedies' became a noted genre in British filmmaking); Hoover factory (1932), Art Deco
industries engineering, chemicals
population (1991) 283,600
famous people Spencer Perceval was resident in Ealing 1801–1812.

Ealing Studios British film-producing company headed by Michael ◊Balcon 1937–58. The studio is best remembered for a series of comedies, which had an understated, self-deprecating humour such as *Passport to Pimlico*, *Kind Hearts and Coronets*, *Whisky Galore!* all 1949, *The Man in the White Suit* 1951, and *The Ladykillers* 1955. In 1994 film production began again at Ealing after an interval of nearly 40 years.

Earhart US aviator Amelia Earhart with her navigator Frederick Noonan (left) and Viscount Sibour of Karachi, India, 15 June 1937. She and Noonan were attempting to fly around the world. Just over two weeks after this picture was taken they disappeared over the Pacific. *Corbis*

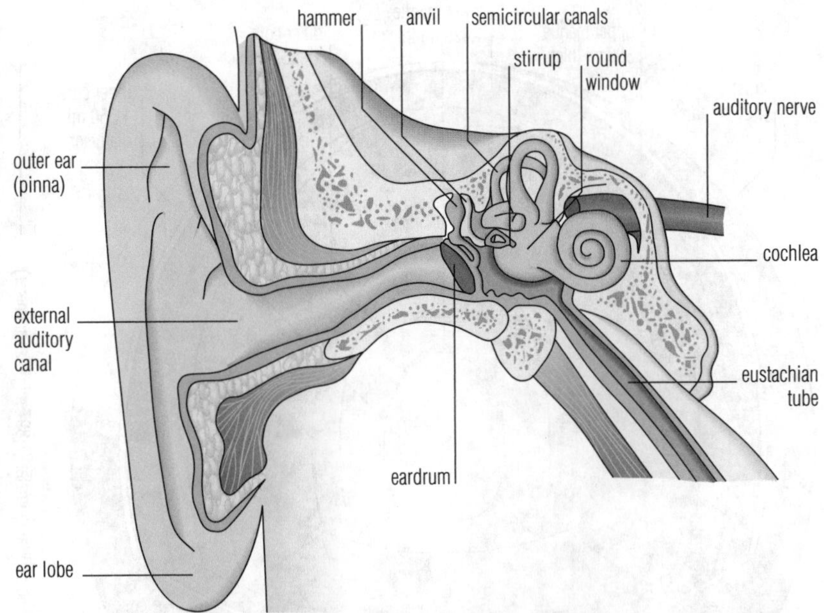

ear The structure of the ear. The three bones of the middle ear – hammer, anvil, and stirrup – vibrate in unison and magnify sounds about 20 times. The spiral-shaped cochlea is the organ of hearing. As sound waves pass down the spiral tube, they vibrate fine hairs lining the tube, which activate the auditory nerve connected to the brain. The semicircular canals are the organs of balance, detecting movements of the head.

Eames Charles (1907–1978) and Ray (born Kaiser, 1916–1988) US designers. A husband-and-wife team, they worked together in California 1941–78. They created some of the most highly acclaimed furniture designs of the 20th century: a moulded plywood chair 1945–46; the Lounge Chair, a black leather-upholstered chair 1956; and a fibreglass armchair 1950–53.

ear organ of hearing in animals. It responds to the vibrations that constitute sound, and these are translated into nerve signals and passed to the brain. A mammal's ear consists of three parts: outer ear, middle ear, and inner ear. The ***outer ear*** is a funnel that collects sound, directing it down a tube to the ***ear drum*** (tympanic membrane), which separates the outer and ***middle ear***s. Sounds vibrate this membrane, the mechanical movement of which is transferred to a smaller membrane leading to the ***inner ear*** by three small bones, the auditory ossicles. Vibrations of the inner ear membrane move fluid contained in the snail-shaped cochlea, which vibrates hair cells that stimulate the auditory nerve connected to the brain. Three fluid-filled canals of the inner ear detect changes of position; this mechanism, with other sensory inputs, is responsible for the sense of balance.

Earhart Amelia 1898–1937. US aviation pioneer and author, who in 1928 became the first woman to fly across the Atlantic. With copilot Frederick Noonan, she attempted a round-the-world flight 1937. Somewhere over the Pacific their plane disappeared.

Born in Atchison, Kansas, Earhart worked as an army nurse and social worker, before discovering that her true calling lay in aviation. In 1928 she became the first woman to fly across the Atlantic as a passenger and in 1932 completed a solo transatlantic flight. During a flight over the Pacific 1937, her plane disappeared without trace, although clues found 1989 on Nikumaroro island, SE of Kiribati's main island group, suggest that she and her copilot might have survived a crash only to die of thirst.

earl in the British peerage, the third title in order of rank, coming between marquess and viscount; it is the oldest of British titles. An earl's wife is a countess.

Earl Marshal in England, one of the Great Officers of State; the office has been hereditary since 1672 in the family of Howard, the dukes of Norfolk. The Earl Marshal is head of the College of Arms, and arranges state processions and ceremonies.

Early English in architecture, the first of the three periods of the English Gothic style, late 12th century to late 13th century. It is characterized by tall, elongated windows (lancets) without mullions (horizontal bars), often grouped in threes, fives, or sevens; the pointed arch; pillars of stone centres surrounded by shafts of black Purbeck marble; and dog-tooth (zig-zag) ornament. Salisbury Cathedral (begun 1220) is almost entirely Early English.

Early English in language, general name for the range of dialects spoken by Germanic settlers in England between the 5th and 11th centuries AD. The literature of the period includes ◊*Beowulf*, an epic in West Saxon dialect, and shorter poems of melancholic dignity such as *The Wanderer* and *The Seafarer*.

'Failure must be but a challenge to others.'

AMELIA EARHART
Last Fight

early warning in war, advance notice of incoming attack, often associated with nuclear attack. There are early-warning radar systems in the UK (◊Fylingdales) , Alaska, and Greenland. ***Airborne early warning*** (AEW) is provided by reconnaissance planes; NATO has such a system.

earth electrical connection between an appliance and the ground. In the event of a fault in an electrical appliance, for example, involving connection between the live part of the circuit and the outer casing, the current flows to earth, causing no harm to the user. In most domestic installations, earthing is achieved by a connection to a metal water-supply pipe.

Earth third planet from the Sun. It is almost spherical, flattened slightly at the poles, and is composed of three concentric layers: the ◊core, the ◊mantle, and the ◊crust. About 70% of the surface (including the north and south polar icecaps) is covered with water. The Earth is surrounded by a life-supporting

eagle The golden eagle is a powerful predator, though carrion forms a large part of its diet. A pair of golden eagles usually has two or three nests, repairing and using a different one each year. Two eggs are usually laid, but the first chick to hatch often kills the second. *Corbis*

Earth **Inside the Earth. The surface of the Earth is a thin crust about 6 km/4 mi thick under the sea and 40 km/25 mi thick under the continents. Under the crust lies the mantle about 2,900 km/ 1,800 mi thick and with a temperature of 1,500–3,000°C/2,700–5,400°F. The inner core is probably solid iron and nickel at about 5,000°C/9,000°F.**

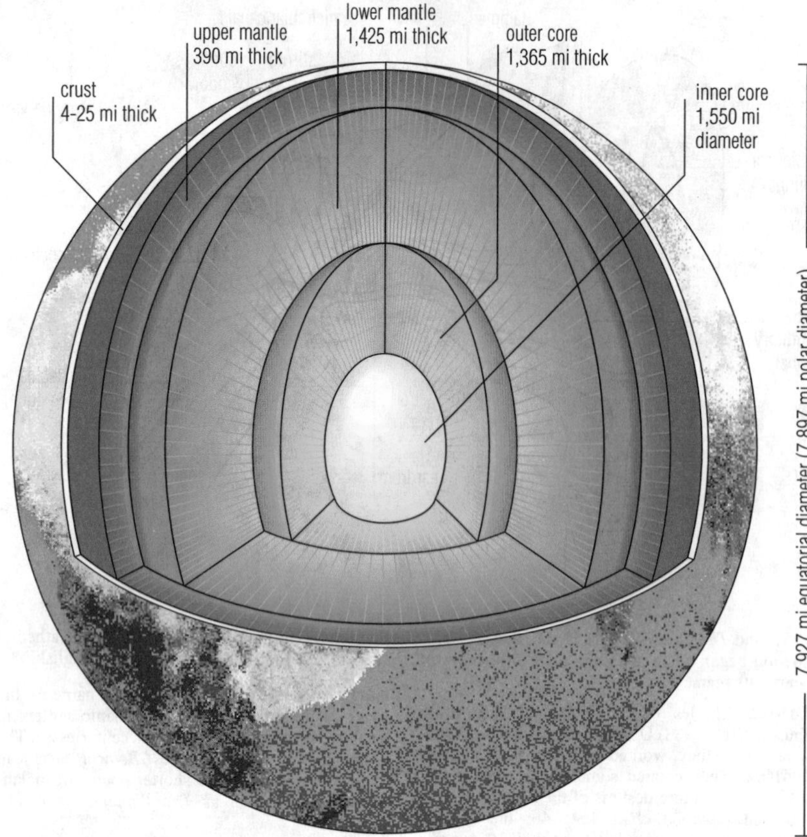

Earth **A satellite shot showing the curvature of the Earth. The Earth has an almost spherical shape, and a diameter of 12,756 km/7,923 mi.** ***Image Select (UK) Ltd***

atmosphere and is the only planet on which life is known to exist.
mean distance from the Sun 149,500,000 km/92,860,000 mi
equatorial diameter 12,756 km/7,923 mi
circumference 40,070 km/24,900 mi
rotation period 23 hr 56 min 4.1 sec
year (complete orbit, or sidereal period) 365 days 5 hr 48 min 46 sec. Earth's average speed around the Sun is 30 kps/18.5 mps; the plane of its orbit is inclined to its equatorial plane at an angle of 23.5°, the reason for the changing seasons
atmosphere nitrogen 78.09%; oxygen 20.95%; argon 0.93%; carbon dioxide 0.03%; and less than 0.0001% neon, helium, krypton, hydrogen, xenon, ozone, radon
surface land surface 150,000,000 sq km/57,500,000 sq mi (greatest height above sea level 8,872 m/29,118 ft Mount Everest); water surface 361,000,000 sq km/139,400,000 sq mi (greatest depth 11,034 m/36,201 ft ◊Mariana Trench in the Pacific). The interior is thought to be an inner core about 2,600 km/1,600 mi in diameter, of solid iron and nickel; an outer core about 2,250 km/1,400 mi thick, of molten iron and nickel; and a mantle of mostly solid rock about 2,900 km/1,800 mi thick, separated by the ◊Mohorovičić discontinuity from the Earth's crust. The crust and the topmost layer of the mantle form about 12 major moving plates, some of which carry the continents. The plates are in constant, slow motion, called tectonic drift.
satellite the ◊Moon
age 4.6 billion years. The Earth was formed with the rest of the ◊Solar System by consolidation of interstellar dust. Life began 3.5–4 billion years ago.

earthenware pottery made of porous clay and fired at relatively low temperatures of up to 1,200°C/2,200°F. It does not vitrify but remains porous, unless glazed. Earthenware may be unglazed (flowerpots, wine-coolers) or glazed (most tableware); the glaze and body characteristically form quite separate layers.

earthquake shaking of the Earth's surface as a result of the sudden release of stresses built up in the Earth's crust. The study of earthquakes is called ◊seismology. Most earthquakes occur along ◊faults (fractures or breaks) in the crust. ◊Plate tectonic movements generate the major proportion: as two plates move past each other they can become jammed and deformed, and a series of shock waves (seismic waves) occur when they spring free. Their force (magnitude) is measured on the ◊Richter scale, and their effect (intensity) on the Mercalli scale. The point at which an earthquake originates is the seismic focus or hypocentre; the point on the Earth's surface directly above this is the epicentre.

In 1987 a California earthquake was successfully predicted by measurement of underground pressure waves; prediction attempts have also involved the study of such phenomena as the change in gases issuing from the ◊crust, the level of water in wells, slight deformation of the rock surface, a sequence of minor tremors, and the behaviour of animals. The possibility of earthquake prevention is remote.

earth science scientific study of the planet Earth as a whole, a synthesis of several traditional subjects such as ◊geology, ◊meteorology, ◊oceanography, ◊geophysics, ◊geochemistry, and ◊palaeontology. It includes the mining and extraction of minerals and gems, the prediction of weather and earthquakes, the pollution of the atmosphere, and the forces that shape the physical world.

Earth Summit (official name ***United Nations Conference on Environment and Development***) international meeting in Rio de Janeiro, Brazil, June 1992, which drew up measures toward world environmental protection. Treaties were made to combat global warming and protect biological diversity.

The USA, which had failed to ratify the Convention of Biological Diversity pact along with other nations 1994, came under renewed pressure to endorse it 1995. By 1996 most wealthy nations expected to exceed their emission targets; Britain and Germany expected to meet them.

earthwork an artwork which involves the manipulation of the natural environment and/or the use of natural materials, such as earth, stones, or wood, largely a phenomenon of the late 1960s and 1970s. Although some were exhibited in galleries, most earthworks were vast and usually constructed on remote, deserted sites and hence only known through photographs and plans. Robert Smithson (1938–1973) and Michael Heizer (1944–), two leading exponents, engaged in physically overpowering works, for example, Heizer's *Complex One, Central Eastern Nevada* (1972, unfinished), an elongated, pyramidal hill of rammed earth supported by steel and concrete.

earthworm ◊annelid worm of the class Oligochaeta. Earthworms are hermaphroditic and deposit their eggs in cocoons. They live by burrowing in the soil, feeding on the organic matter it contains. They are vital to the formation of humus, aerating the soil and levelling it by transferring earth from the deeper levels to the surface as castings.

earwig nocturnal insect of the order Dermaptera. The forewings are short and leathery and serve to protect the hindwings, which are large and are folded like a fan when at rest. Earwigs seldom fly. They have a pincerlike appendage in the rear. The male is distinguished by curved pincers; those of the female are straight. Earwigs are regarded as pests because they feed on flowers and fruit, but they also eat other insects, dead or alive. Eggs are laid beneath the soil, and the female cares for the young even after they have hatched. The male dies before the eggs have hatched.

easement in law, rights that a person may have over the land of another. A common example is a right of way; others are the right to bring water over another's land and the right to a sufficient quantity of light.

east one of the four cardinal points of the compass, indicating that part of the horizon where the Sun rises; when facing north, east is to the right.

East Anglia region of E England, formerly a Saxon kingdom, including Norfolk, Suffolk, and parts of Essex and Cambridgeshire. Norwich is the principal city of East Anglia. The Sainsbury Centre for Visual Arts, opened 1978, at the University of East Anglia, has a collection of ethnographic art and sculpture. East Anglian ports such as Harwich and Felixstowe have greatly developed as trade with the rest of Europe has increased.

East Ayrshire local authority of Scotland created 1996 (*see United Kingdom map*).

East Dunbartonshire local authority of Scotland created 1996 (*see United Kingdom map*).

Easter spring feast of the Christian church, commemorating the Resurrection of Jesus. It is a moveable feast, falling on the first Sunday following the full moon after the vernal equinox (21 March); that is, between 22 March and 25 April. The English name derives from Eostre, Anglo-Saxon goddess of spring, who was honoured in April.

Easter Island or ***Rapa Nui*** Chilean island in the S Pacific Ocean, part of the Polynesian group, about 3,500 km/2,200 mi W of Chile; area about 166 sq km/64 sq mi; population (1985) 2,000. It was first reached by Europeans on Easter Sunday 1722. On it stand over 800 huge carved statues (moai) and the remains of boat-shaped stone houses, the work of Neolithic peoples from Polynesia. The chief centre is Hanga-Roa. ▷ *See feature on pp. 806–807.*

Eastern Cape province of the Republic of South Africa from 1994, formerly part of Cape Province
area 170,616 sq km/65,875 sq mi
capital Bisho
towns and cities East London, Port Elizabeth, Grahamstown
features includes the former independent homelands of the Transkei and the Ciskei; Great Karoo; Drakensberg mountains; Orange River

industries motor manufacturing, textiles, sheep, citrus fruits
population (1995 est) 6,481,300
languages Xhosa 85%, Afrikaans 9%, English 3%.

Eastern Orthodox Church see ◊Orthodox Church.

Easter Rising or ***Easter Rebellion*** in Irish history, a republican insurrection that began on Easter Monday, April 1916, in Dublin. It was inspired by the Irish Republican Brotherhood (IRB) in an unsuccessful attempt to overthrow British rule in Ireland. It was led by Patrick Pearce of the IRB and James Connolly of Sinn Féin.

Arms from Germany intended for the IRB were intercepted but the rising proceeded regardless with the seizure of the Post Office and other buildings in Dublin by 1,500 volunteers. The rebellion was crushed by the British Army within five days, both sides suffering major losses: 220 civilians, 64 rebels, and 134 members of the Crown Forces were killed during the uprising. Pearce, Connolly, and about a dozen rebel leaders were subsequently executed in Kilmainham Jail. Others, including Éamon de Valera, were spared due to US public opinion, to be given amnesty June 1917. ▷*See feature on pp. 550–551.*

East Germany see ◊Germany, East.

East India Company (British) commercial company 1600–1858 chartered by Queen Elizabeth I and given a monopoly of trade between England and the Far East. In the 18th century, the company became, in effect, the ruler of a large part of India, and a form of dual control by the company and a committee responsible to Parliament in London was introduced by Pitt's India Act 1784. The end of the monopoly of China trade came 1834, and after the ◊Indian Mutiny 1857 the crown took complete control of the government of British India; the India Act 1858 abolished the company.

The East India Company set up factories in Masulipatam, near modern Madras, 1611; on the W coast of India in Surat 1612; on the E coast in Madras 1639; and near Calcutta on the Hooghly (one of the mouths of the Ganges) 1640. By 1652 there were 23 English factories in India. Bombay came to the British crown 1662, and was granted to the East India Company for £10 a year. The British victory in the Battle of Plassey 1757 gave the company control of Bengal.

East India Company (Dutch) (*VOC*, or ***Vereenigde Oost-Indische Compagnie***) trading company chartered by the States General (parliament) of the Netherlands, and established in the N Netherlands 1602. It was given a monopoly on Dutch trade in the Indonesian archipelago, and certain sovereign rights such as the creation of an army and a fleet.

In the 17th century some 100 ships were regularly trading between the Netherlands and the East Indies. The company's main base was Batavia in Java (Indonesia); ships sailed there via the Cape of Good Hope, a colony founded by the company 1652 as a staging post. Wars with England and widespread corruption led to a suspension of payments 1781 and a takeover of the company by the Dutch government 1798.

East India Company (French) trading company set up by France 1664 to compete with the British and Dutch East India companies. It established trading ports at Chandernagore in W Bengal and Pondicherry in SE India. The company foundered during the French Revolution, but France retained control over Chandernagore and Pondicherry until 1952 and 1954 respectively.

East Indies the Malay Archipelago; the Philippines are sometimes included. The term is also used to refer more generally to SE Asia.

East Lothian local authority of Scotland created 1996 (*see United Kingdom map*).

Eastman George 1854–1932. US entrepreneur and inventor who founded the Eastman Kodak photographic company 1892. He invented the Kodak box camera 1888. By 1900 his company was selling a pocket camera for as little as one dollar.

East Pakistan former province of ◊Pakistan, now Bangladesh.

EARTH SCIENCE: TIMELINE

1735	English lawyer George Hadley described the circulation of the atmosphere as large-scale convection currents centred on the equator.
1743	Christopher Packe produced the first geological map, of S England.
1744	The first map produced on modern surveying principles was produced by César-François Cassini in France.
1745	In Russia, Mikhail Vasilievich Lomonosov published a catalogue of over 3,000 minerals.
1746	A French expedition to Lapland proved the Earth to be flattened at the poles.
1760	Lomonosov explained the formation of icebergs. John Mitchell proposed that earthquakes are produced when one layer of rock rubs against another.
1766	The fossilized bones of a huge animal (later called *Mosasaurus*) were found in a quarry near the river Meuse, the Netherlands.
1776	James Keir suggested that some rocks, such as those making up the Giant's Causeway in Ireland, may have formed as molten material that cooled and then crystallized.
1779	French naturalist Comte George de Buffon speculated that the Earth may be much older than the 6,000 years suggested by the Bible.
1785	Scottish geologist James Hutton proposed the theory of uniformitarianism: all geological features are the result of processes that are at work today, acting over long periods of time.
1786	German–Swiss Johann von Carpentier described the European ice age.
1793	Jean Baptiste Lamarck argued that fossils are the remains of once-living animals and plants.
1794	William Smith produced the first large-scale geological maps of England.
1795	In France, Georges Cuvier identified the fossil bones discovered in the Netherlands in 1766 as being those of a reptile, now extinct.
1804	French physicists Jean Biot and Joseph Gay-Lussac studied the atmosphere from a hot-air balloon.
1809	The first geological survey of the eastern USA was produced by William Maclure.
1815	In England, William Smith showed how rock strata (layers) can be identified on the basis of the fossils found in them.
1822	Mary Ann Mantell discovered on the English coast the first fossil to be recognized as that of a dinosaur (an iguanodon). In Germany, Friedrich Mohs introduced a scale for specifying mineral hardness.
1825	Cuvier proposed his theory of catastrophes as the cause of the extinction of large groups of animals.
1830	Scottish geologist Charles Lyell published the first volume of *The Principles of Geology*, which described the Earth as being several hundred million years old.
1839	In the USA, Louis Agassiz described the motion and laying down of glaciers, confirming the reality of the ice ages.
1842	English palaeontologist Richard Owen coined the name 'dinosaur' for the reptiles, now extinct, that lived about 175 million years ago.
1846	Irish physicist William Thomson (Lord Kelvin) estimated, using the temperature of the Earth, that the Earth is 100 million years old.
1850	US naval officer Matthew Fontaine Maury mapped the Atlantic Ocean, noting that it is deeper near its edges than at the centre.
1852	Edward Sabine in Ireland showed a link between sunspot activity and changes in the Earth's magnetic field.
1853	James Coffin described the three major wind bands that girdle each hemisphere.
1854	English astronomer George Airy calculated the mass of the Earth by measuring gravity at the top and bottom of a coal mine.
1859	Edwin Drake drilled the world's first oil well at Titusville, Pennsylvania, USA.
1872	The beginning of the world's first major oceanographic expedition, the four-year voyage of the *Challenger*.
1882	Scottish physicist Balfour Stewart postulated the existence of the ionosphere (the ionized layer of the outer atmosphere) to account for differences in the Earth's magnetic field.
1884	German meteorologist Vladimir Köppen introduced a classification of the world's temperature zones.
1890	English geologist Arthur Holmes used radioactivity to date rocks, establishing the Earth to be 4.6 billion years old.
1895	In the USA, Jeanette Picard launched the first balloon to be used for stratospheric research.
1896	Swedish chemist Svante Arrhenius discovered a link between the amount of carbon dioxide in the atmosphere and the global temperature.
1897	Norwegian-US meteorologist Jacob Bjerknes and his father Vilhelm developed the mathematical theory of weather forecasting.
1902	British physicist Oliver Heaviside and US engineer Arthur Edwin Kennelly predicted the existence of an electrified layer in the atmosphere that reflects radio waves. In France, Léon Teisserenc discovered layers of different temperatures in the atmosphere, which he called the troposphere and stratosphere.
1906	Richard Dixon Oldham proved the Earth to have a molten core by studying seismic waves.
1909	Yugoslav physicist Andrija Mohorovičić discovered a discontinuity in the Earth's crust, about 30 km/18 mi below the surface, that forms the boundary between the crust and the mantle.
1912	In Germany, Alfred Wegener proposed the theory of continental drift and the existence of a supercontinent, Pangaea, in the distant past.
1913	French physicist Charles Fabry discovered the ozone layer in the upper atmosphere.
1914	German-US geologist Beno Gutenberg discovered the discontinuity that marks the boundary between the Earth's mantle and the outer core.
1922	British meteorologist Lewis Fry Richardson developed a method of numerical weather forecasting.
1925	A German expedition discovered the Mid-Atlantic Ridge by means of sonar. Edward Appleton discovered a layer of the atmosphere that reflects radio waves; it was later named after him.
1929	By studying the magnetism of rocks, Japanese geologist Motonori Matuyama showed that the Earth's magnetic field reverses direction from time to time.
1935	US seismologist Charles Francis Richter established a scale for measuring the magnitude of earthquakes.
1936	Danish seismologist Inge Lehmann postulated the existence of a solid inner core of the Earth from the study of seismic waves.
1939	In Germany, Walter Maurice Elsasser proposed that eddy currents in the molten iron core cause the Earth's magnetism.
1950	Hungarian-US mathematician John Von Neumann made the first 24-hour weather forecast by computer.
1956	US geologists Bruce Charles Heezen and Maurice Ewing discovered a global network of oceanic ridges and rifts that divide the Earth's surface into plates.
1958	Using rockets, US physicist James Van Allen discovered a belt of radiation (later named after him) around the Earth.
1960	The world's first weather satellite, *TIROS 1*, was launched. US geologist Harry Hammond Hess showed that the sea floor spreads out from ocean ridges and descends back into the mantle at deep-sea trenches.
1963	British geophysicists Fred Vine and Drummond Matthews analysed the magnetism of rocks in the Atlantic Ocean floor and found conclusive proof of seafloor spreading.
1985	A British expedition to the Antarctic discovered a hole in the ozone layer above the South Pole.
1991	A borehole in the Kola Peninsula in Arctic Russia, begun in the 1970s, reached a depth of 12,261 m/40,240 ft (where the temperature was found to be 210°C/410°F).

East Renfrewshire local authority of Scotland created 1996 (*see United Kingdom map*).

East Riding of Yorkshire unitary authority of England created 1996 (*see United Kingdom map*).

East Sussex county of SE England, created 1974, formerly part of Sussex (*see United Kingdom map*)
towns and cities Lewes (administrative headquarters), Newhaven (cross-channel port), Eastbourne, Hastings, Bexhill, Winchelsea, Rye
features Beachy Head, highest headland on the south coast at 180 m/590 ft, the east end of the South Downs; the Weald (including Ashdown Forest); Friston Forest; rivers: Ouse, Cuckmere, East Rother; Romney Marsh; the 'Long Man' chalk hill figure at Wilmington, near Eastbourne; Herstmonceux, with a 15th-century castle and adjacent modern buildings, site of the Greenwich Royal Observatory 1958–90; other castles at Hastings, Lewes, Pevensey, and Bodiam; Battle Abbey and the site of the Battle of Hastings; Michelham Priory; Sheffield Park garden; University of Sussex at Falmer, near Brighton, founded 1961
industries electronics, gypsum, timber; light engineering; agricultural products, including cereals, hops, fruit, and vegetables
famous people former homes of Henry James at Rye, Rudyard Kipling at Burwash, Virginia Woolf at Rodmell.

East Timor disputed territory on the island of ◊Timor in the Malay Archipelago, claimed by Indonesia as the province of Timor Timor; prior to 1975, it was a Portuguese colony for almost 460 years. The people of East Timor are known as Maubere
area 14,874 sq km/5,706 sq mi
capital Dili
industries coffee
population (1990) 747,750
history following Portugal's withdrawal 1975, civil war broke out and the left-wing Revolutionary Front of Independent East Timor (Fretilin) occupied the capital, calling for independence. In opposition, troops from neighbouring Indonesia invaded the territory, declaring East Timor (***Loro Sae***) the 17th province of Indonesia July 1976 – a claim not recognized by the United Nations.

The war and its attendant famine are thought to have caused more than 100,000 deaths, but starvation had been alleviated by the mid-1980s, and the Indonesian government had built schools, roads, and hospitals. Fretilin guerrillas remained active, and in Nov 1991 Indonesian troops fired on pro-independence demonstrators with heavy casualties in the ensuing clashes. More than 1,000 Fretilin guerrillas surrendered Nov 1992 following the capture of their leader, Jose Alexandre Gusmao.

The 1996 Nobel Peace Prize was awarded jointly to Bishop Carlos Belo, a critic of human rights violations by Indonesian soldiers in E Timor, and Jorge Ramas-Horta, an exiled spokesman for the Fretilin Independence Movement.

Eastwood Clint(on) 1930– . US film actor and director. As the 'Man with No Name' in *A Fistful of Dollars* 1964 and *The Good, the Bad, and the Ugly* 1966, he started the vogue for 'spaghetti westerns' (made in Italy or Spain). Later westerns which he both starred in and directed include *High Plains Drifter* 1973, *The Outlaw Josey Wales* 1976, and *Unforgiven* 1992 (two Academy Awards). Other films include *In The Line of Fire* 1993 and *The Bridges of Madison County* 1995. He starred in the TV series *Rawhide* and in the 'Dirty Harry' series of films, and directed *Bird* 1988. He was elected mayor of Carmel, California, 1986.

eau de cologne refreshing toilet water (weaker than perfume), made of alcohol and aromatic oils. Its invention is ascribed to Giovanni Maria Farina (1685–1766), who moved from Italy to Cologne 1709 to manufacture it.

'Nothing gives a fearful man more courage than another's fear.'

UMBERTO ECO
The Name of the Rose
1980

ebony any of a group of hardwood trees of the ebony family Ebenaceae, especially some tropical persimmons of the genus *Diospyros*, native to Africa and Asia. Their very heavy, hard, black timber polishes well and is used in cabinetmaking, inlaying, and for piano keys and knife handles.

Eboracum Roman name for the English city of ◊York. The archbishop of York signs himself 'Ebor'.

EC abbreviation for ***European Community***, former name (to 1993) of the ◊European Union.

Eccles John Carew 1903–1997. Australian physiologist who shared (with Alan Hodgkin (1914–) and Andrew ◊Huxley) the 1963 Nobel Prize for Physiology or Medicine for work on conduction in the central nervous system. In some of his later works, he argued that the mind has an existence independent of the brain.

Ecclesiastes also known as 'The Preacher', a book of the Old Testament, traditionally attributed to ◊Solomon, on the theme of the vanity of human life.

ecclesiastical law church law. In England, the Church of England has special ecclesiastical courts to administer church law. Each diocese has a consistory court with a right of appeal to the Court of Arches (in the archbishop of Canterbury's jurisdiction) or the Chancery Court of York (in the archbishop of York's jurisdiction). They deal with the constitution of the Church of England, church property, the clergy, services, doctrine, and practice. These courts have no influence on churches of other denominations, which are governed by the usual laws of contract and trust.

ECG abbreviation for ◊***electrocardiogram***.

echidna or ***spiny anteater*** toothless, egg-laying, spiny mammal of the order Monotremata, found in Australia and New Guinea. There are two species: *Tachyglossus aculeatus*, the short-nosed echidna, and the rarer *Zaglossus bruijni*, the long-nosed echidna. They feed entirely upon ants and termites, which they dig out with their powerful claws and lick up with their prehensile tongues. When attacked, an echidna rolls itself into a ball, or tries to hide by burrowing in the earth.

echinoderm marine invertebrate of the phylum Echinodermata ('spiny-skinned'), characterized by a five-radial symmetry. Echinoderms have a water-vascular system which transports substances around the body. They include starfishes (or sea stars), brittle-stars, sea lilies, sea urchins, and sea cucumbers.

The skeleton is external, made of a series of limy plates. Echinoderms generally move by using tube-feet, small water-filled sacs that can be protruded or pulled back to the body.

echo repetition of a sound wave, or of a ◊radar or ◊sonar signal, by reflection from a surface. By accurately measuring the time taken for an echo to return to the transmitter, and by knowing the speed of a radar signal (the speed of light) or a sonar signal (the speed of sound in water), it is possible to calculate the range of the object causing the echo (◊echolocation).

A similar technique is used in echo sounders to estimate the depth of water under a ship's keel or the depth of a shoal of fish.

Echo in Greek mythology, a ◊nymph who pined away until only her voice remained, after being rejected by Narcissus.

echolocation or ***biosonar*** method used by certain animals, notably bats, whales, and dolphins, to detect the positions of objects by using sound. The animal emits a stream of high-pitched sounds, generally at ultrasonic frequencies (beyond the range of human hearing), and listens for the returning echoes reflected off objects to determine their exact location.

The location of an object can be established by the time difference between the emitted sound and its differential return as an echo to the two ears. Echolocation is of particular value under conditions when normal vision is poor (at night in the case of bats, in murky water for dolphins). A few species of bird can also echolocate, including cave-dwelling birds such as some species of swiftlets and the South American Oil Bird.

echidna The short-nosed echidna is found throughout Australia. Echidnas are egg-laying mammals (monotremes). They are nocturnal and live almost exclusively on ants and termites.

echo sounder or ***sonar device*** device that detects objects under water by means of ◊sonar – by using reflected sound waves. Most boats are equipped with echo sounders to measure the water depth beneath them. An echo sounder consists of a transmitter, which emits an ultrasonic pulse, and a receiver, which detects the pulse after reflection from the seabed. The time between transmission and receipt of the reflected signal is a measure of the depth of water. Fishing boats use echo sounders to detect shoals of fish and navies use them to find enemy submarines.

Eckhart Johannes, called Meister Eckhart c. 1260–c. 1327. German theologian and leader of a popular mystical movement. In 1326 he was accused of heresy, and in 1329 a number of his doctrines were condemned by the pope as heretical. His theology stressed the absolute transcendence of God, and the internal spiritual development through which union with the divine could be attained.

eclampsia convulsions occurring during pregnancy following ◊pre-eclampsia.

eclecticism in artistic theory, the use of motifs and elements from various styles, periods, and geographical areas. This selection and recombination of features from different sources is a characteristic of Victorian architecture; for example, J F Bentley's design for Westminster Cathedral, London, 1895–1903, in Byzantine style.

eclipse passage of an astronomical body through the shadow of another. The term is usually employed for solar and lunar eclipses, which may be either partial or total, but also, for example, for eclipses by Jupiter of its satellites.

A ***solar eclipse*** occurs when the Moon passes in front of the Sun as seen from Earth, and can happen only at new Moon. During a total eclipse the Sun's ◊corona can be seen. A total solar eclipse can last up to 7.5 minutes. When the Moon is at its farthest from Earth it does not completely cover the face of the Sun, leaving a ring of sunlight visible. This is an ***annular eclipse***. Between two and five solar eclipses occur each year. A ***lunar eclipse*** occurs when the Moon passes into the shadow of the Earth, becoming dim until emerging from the shadow. Lunar eclipses may be partial or total, and they can happen only at full Moon. Total lunar eclipses last for up to 100 minutes; the maximum number each year is three.

eclipsing binary binary (double) star in which the two stars periodically pass in front of each other as seen from Earth. When one star crosses in front of the other the total light received on Earth from the two stars declines. The first eclipsing binary to be noticed was ◊Algol.

ecliptic path, against the background of stars, that the Sun appears to follow each year as the Earth orbits the Sun. It can be thought of as the plane of the Earth's orbit projected on to the ◊celestial sphere (imaginary sphere around the Earth). The ecliptic is tilted at about 23.5° with respect to the celestial equator, a result of the tilt of the Earth's axis relative to the plane of its orbit around the Sun.

Eco Umberto 1932– . Italian writer, semiologist, and literary critic. His works include *The Role of the Reader* 1979, the 'philosophical thriller' *The Name of the Rose* 1983, and *Foucault's Pendulum* 1988.

E. coli abbreviation for ◊*Escherichia coli*.

ecology (Greek *oikos* 'house') study of the relationship among organisms and the environments in which they live, including all living and nonliving components. The chief environmental factors governing the distribution of plants and animals are temperature, humidity, soil, light intensity,

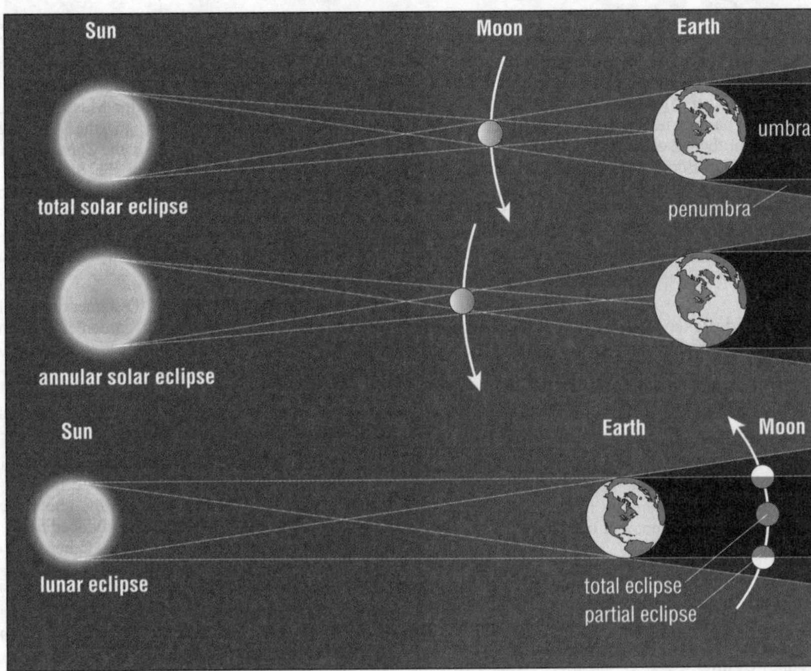

eclipse Three types of eclipse: total solar, annular solar, and lunar.

daylength, food supply, and interaction with other organisms. The term was coined by the biologist Ernst Haeckel 1866.

Ecology may be concerned with individual organisms (for example, behavioural ecology, feeding strategies), with populations (for example, population dynamics), or with entire communities (for example, competition between species for access to resources in an ecosystem, or predator–prey relationships). Applied ecology is concerned with the management and conservation of habitats and the consequences and control of pollution. ▷ *See features on pp. 858–859 and pp. 896–897.*

Economic Community of Central African States (*Communauté Économique des États de l'Afrique Centrale, CEEAC*) organization formed 1983 to foster economic cooperation between member states, which include Burundi, Cameroon, Central African Republic, Chad, Congo, Equatorial Guinea, Gabon, Rwanda, São Tomé and Principe, and Zaire. Angola has observer status.

Economic Community of West African States (ECOWAS, *Communauté Economique des Etats de l'Afrique de l'Ouest*) organization promoting economic cooperation and development, and the prevention of regional conflict established 1975 by the Treaty of Lagos. Its members include Benin, Burkina Faso, Cape Verde, Côte d'Ivoire, Gambia, Ghana, Guinea, Guinea-Bissau, Liberia, Mali, Mauritania, Niger, Nigeria, Senegal, Sierra Leone, and Togo. Its headquarters are in Abuja, Nigeria. Its aim of forming a common market within 15 years has not been achieved, but there has been some trade liberalization. In recent years an ECOWAS peacekeeping force, ECOMOG, has been developed in Liberia.

Economic Cooperation Organization (ECO) Islamic regional grouping formed 1985 by Iran, Pakistan, and Turkey to reduce customs tariffs and promote commerce, with the aim of eventual customs union. In 1992 the newly independent republics of Azerbaijan, Kyrgyzstan, Tajikistan, Turkmenistan, and Uzbekistan were admitted.

economics (Greek 'household management') social science devoted to studying the production, distribution, and consumption of wealth. It consists of the disciplines of microeconomics, the study of individual producers, consumers, or markets, and macroeconomics, the study of whole economies or systems (in particular, areas such as taxation and public spending).

Economics is the study of how, in a given society, choices are made in the allocation of resources to produce goods and services for consumption, and the mechanisms and principles that govern this process. Economics seeks to apply scientific method to construct theories about the processes involved and to test them against what actually happens. Its two central concerns are the efficient allocation of available resources and the problem of reconciling finite resources with a virtually infinite desire for goods and services. Economics analyses the ingredients of economic efficiency in the production process, and the implications for practical policies, and examines conflicting demands for resources and the consequences of whatever choices are made, whether by individuals, enterprises, or governments.

Economics came of age as a separate area of study with the publication of Adam ◊Smith's *The Wealth of Nations* 1776; the economist Alfred Marshall (1842–1924) established the orthodox position of ◊neo-classical economics, which, as modified by John Maynard ◊Keynes, remains the standard today. Major economic thinkers include David ◊Ricardo, Thomas ◊Malthus, J S ◊Mill, Karl ◊Marx, Vilfredo ◊Pareto, and Milton ◊Friedman.

economy of scale in economics, the reduction in costs per item (unit costs) that results from large-scale production. The high capital costs of machinery or a factory are spread across a greater number of units as more are produced. For example, there would sometimes be economies of scale present if a car manufacturer could manufacture cars at £5,000 per car when producing 100,000 cars per year, but at £4,000 per car when producing 200,000 cars per year.

ecosystem in ecology, an integrated unit consisting of the ◊community of living organisms and the nonliving, or physical, environment in a particular area. The relationships among species in an ecosystem are usually complex and finely balanced, and removal of any one species may be disastrous. The removal of a major predator, for example, can result in the destruction of the ecosystem through overgrazing by herbivores.

Ecosystems can be identified at different scales – for example, the global ecosystem consists of all the organisms living on Earth, the Earth itself, and the atmosphere above; a freshwater-pond ecosystem consists of the plants and animals living in the pond, the pond water and all the substances dissolved or suspended in that water, and the rocks, mud, and decaying matter that make up the pond bottom.

Energy and nutrients pass through organisms in an ecosystem in a particular sequence (see ◊food chain): energy is captured through ◊photosynthesis, and nutrients are taken up from the soil or water by plants; both are passed to herbivores that eat the plants and then to carnivores that feed on herbivores. These nutrients are returned to the soil through the ◊decomposition of excrement and dead organisms, thus completing a cycle that is crucial to the stability and survival of the ecosystem. ▷ *See feature on pp. 896–897.*

ECOWAS acronym for ◊***Economic Community of West African States***.

ecstasy or ***MDMA*** (3,4-methylenedioxymethamphetamine) illegal drug in increasing use from the 1980s. It is a modified ◊amphetamine with mild psychedelic effects, and works by depleting serotonin (a neurotransmitter) in the brain. US research 1998 proved it can cause permanent brain damage. Ecstasy was first synthesized 1914 by the Merck pharmaceutical company in Germany, and was one of eight psychedelics tested by the US army 1953.

ECT abbreviation for ◊***electroconvulsive therapy***.

ectopic in medicine, term applied to an anatomical feature that is displaced or found in an abnormal position. An ectopic pregnancy is one occurring outside the womb, usually in a Fallopian tube.

ectoplasm outer layer of a cell's ◊cytoplasm.

ectotherm 'cold-blooded' animal (see ◊poikilothermy), such as a lizard, that relies on external warmth to raise its body temperature so that it can become active. To cool the body, ectotherms seek out a cooler environment.

ECU abbreviation for ***European Currency Unit***, the official monetary unit of the European Union. It is based on the value of the different currencies used in the ◊European Monetary System (EMS).

eclipse Five phases of a lunar eclipse, pictured over the skyline of Toronto on Aug 16 1989. Such a photograph is achieved by repeatedly exposing the same frame over a period of time as the moon moves across the sky. *Corbis*

We used to think that if we knew one, we knew two, because one and one are two. We are finding that we must learn a lot more about 'and'.

ARTHUR EDDINGTON
Quoted in Alan L Mackay *The Harvest of a Quiet Eye*

Ecuador country in South America, bounded N by Colombia, E and S by Peru, and W by the Pacific Ocean. *See country box below.*

ecumenical movement movement for reunification of the various branches of the Christian church. It began in the 19th century with the extension of missionary work to Africa and Asia, where the divisions created in Europe were incomprehensible; the movement gathered momentum from the need for unity in the face of growing secularism in Christian countries and of the challenge posed by such faiths as Islam. The ***World Council of Churches*** was founded 1948.

eczema inflammatory skin condition, a form of dermatitis, marked by dryness, rashes, itching, the formation of blisters, and the exudation of fluid. It may be allergic in origin and is sometimes complicated by infection.

Edam town in the Netherlands on the river IJssel, North Holland province. Founded as a customs post in the 13th century, Edam's prosperity in the 16th and 17th centuries was based upon its cheese trade; it is still famous today for its round cheeses covered in red wax.

Edberg Stefan 1966– . Swedish tennis player. He won the junior Grand Slam 1983 and his first Grand Slam title, the Australian Open, 1985, repeated 1987. Other Grand Slam singles titles include Wimbledon 1988 and 1990 and the US Open 1991 and 1992.

Edda two collections of early Icelandic literature that together constitute our chief source for Old Norse mythology. The term strictly applies to the Younger or Prose Edda, compiled by Snorri Sturluson, a priest, about AD 1230. The Elder or Poetic Edda is the collection of poems discovered around 1643 by Brynjólfr Sveinsson, written by unknown Norwegian poets of the 9th to 12th centuries.

Eddington Arthur Stanley 1882–1944. British astrophysicist. He studied the motions, equilibrium, luminosity, and atomic structure of the stars. In 1919 his observation of stars during a solar eclipse confirmed Albert ◊Einstein's prediction that light is bent when passing near the Sun, in accordance with the general theory of relativity. In *The Expanding Universe* 1933 Eddington expressed the theory that in the spherical universe the outer galaxies or spiral nebulae are receding from one another. In 1924 he showed that the luminosity of a star depends almost exclusively on its mass – a discovery that caused a complete revision of contemporary ideas on stellar evolution.

Eddy Mary Baker 1821–1910. US founder of the Christian Science movement. Her pamphlet *Science of Man* 1869 was followed by *Science and Health with Key to the Scriptures* 1875, which systematically set forth the basis of Christian Science.

eddy current electric current induced, in accordance with ◊Faraday's laws, in a conductor located in a changing magnetic field. Eddy currents can cause much wasted energy in the cores of transformers and other electrical machines.

Edelman Gerald Maurice 1929– . US biochemist who worked out the sequence of 1,330 amino acids that makes up human ◊immunoglobulin, a task completed 1969. For this work he shared the Nobel Prize for Physiology or Medicine 1972 with Rodney ◊Porter.

edelweiss perennial alpine plant *Leontopodium alpinum*, family Compositae, with a white, woolly, star-shaped bloom, found in the high mountains of Eurasia.

Eden (Robert) Anthony, 1st Earl of Avon 1897–1977. British Conservative politician, foreign secretary 1935–38, 1940–45, and 1951–55; prime minister 1955–57, when he resigned after the failure of the Anglo-French military intervention in the ◊Suez Crisis.

Eden resigned as foreign secretary Feb 1938 in protest against Chamberlain's decision to open conversations with the Fascist dictator Mussolini. He was foreign secretary again in the wartime coalition, formed Dec 1940, and in the Conservative government, elected 1951. With the Soviets, he negotiated an interim peace in Vietnam 1954. In April 1955 he succeeded Churchill as prime minister. His use of force in the Suez Crisis led to his resignation Jan 1957, but he continued to maintain that his action was justified.

Eden, Garden of in the Old Testament book of Genesis and in the Koran, the 'garden' in which Adam and Eve lived after their creation, and from which they were expelled for disobedience. Its location has often been identified with the Fertile Crescent in Mesopotamia (now in Iraq) and two of its rivers with the Euphrates and the Tigris.

Edgar David 1940– . English dramatist. After early work as a journalist, Edgar turned to documentary and political theatre. *Destiny*, about the extreme right wing in Britain, was produced by the Royal Shakespeare Company 1976. Other plays include *The Jail Diary of Albie Sachs* 1978; his adaptation from Dickens for the RSC, *The Life and Adventures of Nicholas Nickleby* 1980; *The Shape of the Table* 1990, on the collapse of the Eastern bloc in Europe; and *Pentecost* 1994.

Edgar the Peaceful 944–975. King of all England from 959. He was the younger son of Edmund I, and strove successfully to unite English and Danes as fellow subjects.

Edgehill, Battle of first battle of the English Civil War. It took place 1642, on a ridge in S Warwickshire, between Royalists under Charles I and Parliamentarians under the Earl of Essex. The result was indecisive.

ECUADOR
Republic of

Colombia
Quito
ECUADOR
Peru
PACIFIC OCEAN
ATLANTIC OCEAN
0 mi 500
0 km 1000

national name *República del Ecuador*
area 270,670 sq km/104,479 sq mi
capital Quito
major towns/cities Cuenca
major ports Guayaquil
physical features coastal plain rises sharply to Andes Mountains, which are divided into a series of cultivated valleys; flat, low-lying rainforest in the E; Galápagos Islands; Cotopaxi, the world's highest active volcano. Ecuador is crossed by the equator, from which it derives its name
head of state and government Fabian Alarcon from 1997 (interim)
political system emergent democratic republic
administrative divisions 21 provinces
political parties Social Christian Party (PSC), right-wing; Ecuadorean Roldosista Party (PRE), populist, centre-left; United Republican Party (PUR), right-of-centre coalition; Democratic Left (ID), moderate socialist; Conservative Party (PC), right-wing
population 11,460,000 (1995 est)
population growth rate 2.2% (1990–95); 1.7% (2000–05)
ethnic distribution about 55% mestizo (of Spanish American and American Indian parentage), 25% Indian, 10% Spanish, and 10% African
life expectancy 65 (males), 69 (females)
literacy rate men 88%, women 84%
languages Spanish (official), Quechua, Jivaro, and other Indian languages
religion Roman Catholic
exports bananas, cocoa, coffee, sugar, rice, fruit, balsa wood, fish, petroleum, shrimps, flowers
currency sucre
GDP (US $) 16.55 billion (1994)
growth rate 4.0% (1994)

HISTORY
1450s The area's Amerindian Caras, whose kingdom had its capital at Quito, were conquered by the Incas of Peru.
1531 Spanish conquistador Francisco Pizarro landed on the Ecuadorian coast, en route to Peru, where the Incas were defeated.
1534 Conquered by the Spanish. Quito, which had been destroyed by the Indians, was refounded by Sebastian de Belalcazar; the area became part of the Spanish Viceroyalty of Peru, which covered much of South America, with its capital at Lima (Peru).
later 16th C Spanish established large agrarian estates, owned by Europeans and worked by Amerindian peons.
1739 Became part of the new Spanish Viceroyalty of Nueva Granada, which included Colombia and Venezuela, with its capital in Bogotá (Colombia).
1809 With the Spanish monarchy having been overthrown by Napoleon Bonaparte, the creole middle class began to press for independence.
1822 Spanish Royalists defeated by Field Marshal Antonio José de Sucre, fighting for Simón Bolívar, 'The Liberator', at battle of Pichincha, near Quito; became part of independent Gran Colombia, which also comprised Colombia, Panama, and Venezuela.
1830 Became fully independent state, after leaving Gran Colombia.
1845–60 Political instability, with five presidents holding power, increasing tension between conservative Quito and liberal Guayaquil on the coast, and minor wars with Peru and Colombia.
1860–75 Power held by Gabriel Garcia Moreno, an autocratic theocrat-Conservative who launched education and public works programmes.
1895–1912 Dominated by General Eloy Alfaro, a radical, anti-clerical Liberal from the coastal region, who reduced the power of the church.
1925–48 Great political instability; no president completed his term of office.
1941 Lost territory in Amazonia after defeat in war with Peru.
1948–55 Liberals in power.
1956 Camilo Ponce became first conservative president in 60 years.
1960 Liberals in power, with José María Velasco Ibarra returning as president.
1961 Velasco deposed and replaced by the vice president.
1962 Military junta installed.
1968 Velasco returned as president.
1970s Ecuador emerged as a significant oil producer.
1972 A coup put the military back in power.
1979 New democratic constitution; Liberals in power but opposed by right- and left-wing parties.
1981 Border dispute with Peru flared up again.
1982 Deteriorating economy and austerity measures; strikes, demonstrations, and a state of emergency.
1984–85 No party with a clear majority in the national congress; León Febres Cordero narrowly won the presidency for the Conservatives.
1988 Rodrigo Borja Cevallos elected president for moderate left-wing coalition and introduced unpopular austerity measures.
1992 PUR leader Sixto Duran Ballen elected president; PSC became largest party in congress. Ecuador withdrew from OPEC to enable it to increase its oil exports.
1994 Mounting opposition to Duran's economic liberalization and privatization programme.
1995 Parliament dismissed three key ministers, including the finance minister, for corruption; long-standing border dispute with Peru resolved.
1996 Abdala Bucaram elected president.
1997 President Bucaram dismissed by national congress and replaced by Vice President Rosalia Arteaga, but a national referendum later ratified Fabian Alarcon as interim president.

SEE ALSO Bolívar, Simón; Inca

Edinburgh capital of Scotland and (from 1996) administrative headquarters of City of Edinburgh local authority, near the southern shores of the Firth of Forth; population (1996 est) 447,500. Industries include printing, publishing, banking, insurance, chemical manufactures, distilling, brewing, and some shipbuilding. Edinburgh International Festival of Music and Drama, begun 1947, is the largest in the world. The university was established 1583.
features Edinburgh Castle contains the 12th-century St Margaret's chapel, the oldest building in Edinburgh. The palace of Holyrood House was built in the 15th and 16th centuries on the site of a 12th-century abbey; it is the British sovereign's official Scottish residence. ◊Rizzio, the Italian favourite of Mary Queen of Scots, was murdered here 1566 in her apartments.

The Parliament House, begun 1632, is now the seat of the supreme courts. The Royal Scottish Academy and the National Gallery of Scotland in Classical style are by William Henry Playfair (1789–1857). The episcopal cathedral of St Mary, opened 1879, and St Giles parish church (mostly 15th-century) are the principal churches. The Royal Observatory has been at Blackford Hill since 1896. The principal thoroughfares are Princes Street and the Royal Mile.

The university has a famous medical school; the Heriot-Watt University (established 1885; university status 1966) is mainly a technical institution. The Conference Centre, designed by Terry Farrell, opened 1995; Edinburgh Festival Theatre also opened 1995.
history In Roman times the site was occupied by Celtic peoples and about 617 was captured by Edwin of Northumbria, from whom the city took its name. The early settlement grew up around a castle on Castle Rock, while about a mile to the E another burgh, Canongate, developed around the abbey of Holyrood, founded 1128 by David I. It remained separate from Edinburgh until 1856. Robert the Bruce made Edinburgh a burgh 1329, and established its port at Leith. In 1544 the town was destroyed by the English. After the union with England 1707, Edinburgh lost its political importance but remained culturally pre-eminent.

Edinburgh, City of local authority of Scotland created 1996 (*see United Kingdom map*).

Edinburgh, Duke of title of Prince ◊Philip of the UK.

Edison Thomas Alva 1847–1931. US scientist and inventor, with over 1,000 patents. In Menlo Park, New Jersey, 1876–87, he produced his most important inventions, including the electric light bulb 1879. He constructed a system of electric power distribution for consumers, the telephone transmitter, the megaphone, and the phonograph.

Edison US inventor of the electric light bulb, Thomas Edison. By the end of his life Edison had patented over 1,000 of his famous inventions. *Image Select (UK) Ltd*

Edison's first invention was an automatic repeater for telegraphic messages. Later came the carbon transmitter (used as a microphone in the production of the Bell telephone), the electric filament lamp, a new type of storage battery, and an early cine camera. He also anticipated the Fleming thermionic valve.

Genius is one per cent inspiration and ninety-nine per cent perspiration.

Thomas Edison
Life

Edmonton capital of Alberta, Canada, on the North Saskatchewan River; population (city, 1991) 616,700; (metropolitan area, 1991) 839,900. It is the centre of an oil and mining area to the N and also an agricultural and dairying region. Petroleum pipelines link Edmonton with Superior, Wisconsin, USA, and Vancouver, British Columbia.

Edmund (II) Ironside c. 989–1016. King of England 1016, the son of Ethelred II the Unready. He led the resistance to ◊Canute's invasion 1015, and on Ethelred's death 1016 was chosen king by the citizens of London, whereas the Witan (the king's council) elected Canute. In the struggle for the throne, Edmund was defeated by Canute at Assandun (Ashington), Essex, and they divided the kingdom between them; when Edmund died the same year, Canute ruled the whole kingdom.

Edmund, St c. 840–870. King of East Anglia from 855. In 870 he was defeated and captured by the Danes at Hoxne, Suffolk, and martyred on refusing to renounce Christianity. He was canonized and his shrine at Bury St Edmunds became a place of pilgrimage.

Edo former name for ◊Tokyo until 1868.

education process, beginning at birth, of developing intellectual capacity, manual skill, and social awareness, especially by instruction. In its more restricted sense, the term refers to the process of imparting literacy, numeracy, and a generally accepted body of knowledge.
history of education The earliest known European educational systems were those of ancient Greece. In Sparta the process was devoted mainly to the development of military skills; in Athens, to politics, philosophy, and public speaking, but both were accorded only to the privileged few.

In ancient China, formalized education received impetus from the imperial decree of 165 BC, which established open competitive examinations for the recruitment of members of the civil service, based mainly on a detailed study of literature.

The Romans adopted the Greek system of education and spread it through Western Europe. Following the disintegration of the Roman Empire, widespread education vanished from Europe, although Christian monasteries preserved both learning and Latin. In the Middle Ages, Charlemagne's monastic schools taught the 'seven liberal arts': grammar, logic, rhetoric, arithmetic, geometry, music, and astronomy; elementary schools, generally presided over by a parish priest, instructed children of the poor in reading, writing, and arithmetic. From the monastic schools emerged the theological philosophers of the Scholastic Movement, which in the 11th–13th centuries led to the foundation of the universities of Paris (◊Sorbonne), Bologna, Padua, ◊Oxford, and ◊Cambridge. The capture of Constantinople, capital of the E Roman Empire, by the Turks 1453 propelled its Christian scholars into exile across Europe, and revived European interest in learning.

The Renaissance humanist movement encouraged the free study of all classical writers. It owed much to Arabic scholarly activity, which had continued unabated during the Dark Ages and had reached Europe via Moorish influences in Sicily and Spain. The curriculum of humanist schools, of which Latin was the foundation, was widely adopted, but by the early 18th century organized education was at a low level.

Compulsory attendance at primary schools was first established in the mid-18th century in Prussia, and has since spread almost worldwide. Compulsory schooling in industrialized countries is typically from around age 5 or 6 to around age 15 or 16; public education expenditure is typically around 5% of GNP.
the role of Church and state In England and Wales, prior to the Reformation, the Church was responsible for education. Thereafter, the question of the control of education became a source of bitter sectarian conflict, and it was not until the 19th century that attempts were made to spread literacy throughout society. In Scotland, as early as 1494, freeholders were required by royal statute to send their heirs to school to acquire 'perfect Latin', and from the late 16th century, under the influence of John ◊Knox, churches in every major town had Latin schools attached. The Factory Act of 1802, which applied throughout the UK but was not always observed, required that during the first four years of their apprenticeship children employed by the owners of the newly arising factories were taught reading, writing, and arithmetic.

The British and Foreign Schools Society (1808) and the National Society for Promoting the Education of the Poor in the Principles of the Established Church (1811) set up schools in which basic literacy and numeracy as well as religious knowledge were taught. In 1862, government grants became available for the first time for schools attended by children up to 12. The Elementary Education Act 1870 (Forster's Act) established district school boards all over the country to provide facilities for the elementary education of all children not otherwise receiving it. The school boards were abolished by the Education Act 1902 and their responsibilities transferred to county and borough councils, which became the local education authorities for both higher and elementary education. A further act 1918 raised the school-leaving age to 14.
secondary education, funding and legislation Once the principle of elementary education for all was established, the idea of widely available higher education began to be accepted. The Education Act 1944 introduced a system of secondary education for all, and formed the foundation of much education policy today. This has been revised by two further acts in 1980, which repealed 1976 legislation enforcing ◊comprehensive reorganization, and gave new rights to parents; by the 1981 Education Act which made new provisions for the education of children with special needs; and by legislation in 1986 giving further powers to school governors as part of a move towards increased parental involvement in schools, and in 1987 on the remuneration of teachers. In 1988 a major act introduced a compulsory ◊national curriculum in state schools, compulsory testing of children, financial delegation of budgets to schools, and the possibility of direct funding by government for schools that voted to opt out of local council control.
responsibility for education In the UK, the Department for Education and Employment is responsible for universities throughout Great Britain, and for school education in England. In Wales, primary and secondary education is the responsibility of the Welsh Education Office. There is a Scottish Education Department, under the secretary of state for Scotland. Until direct rule (1972), Northern Ireland had its own Ministry of Education; the responsibility for education is now held by the Education and Library Boards.

Local education authorities (LEAs) are education committees of county and borough councils, responsible for providing educational services locally under the general oversight of the DES, but certain of their powers have been curtailed by the 1988 act. The Inner London Education Authority (ILEA) was abolished by the 1988 act and responsibility for education in London passed to the borough councils.

educational psychology the work of psychologists primarily in schools, including the assessment of children with achievement problems and advising on problem behaviour in the classroom.

Education and Employment, Department for UK government department, established 1944 as Ministry of Education; merged 1995 with the Department of Employment. It is responsible for education, scientific research policies, employment, and training policies. The Secretary of State for Education and Employment has a seat in the Cabinet.

Edward (full name Edward Antony Richard Louis) 1964– . Prince of the UK, third son of Queen Elizabeth II. He is seventh in line to the throne after Charles, Charles's two sons, Andrew, and Andrew's two daughters.

Edward (called ***the Black Prince***) 1330–1376. Prince of Wales, eldest son of Edward III of England. The epithet (probably posthumous) may refer to his black armour. During the Hundred Years' War he fought at the Battle of Crécy 1346 and captured the French king at Poitiers 1356. He ruled Aquitaine 1360–71; during the revolt that eventually ousted him, he caused the massacre of

Education has for its object the formation of character.

Education
Herbert Spencer
Social Statics 2

Limoges 1370. In 1367 he invaded Castile and restored to the throne the deposed king, Pedro the Cruel (1334–69).

Edward I 1239–1307. King of England from 1272, son of Henry III. Edward led the royal forces against Simon de Montfort in the ◊Barons' War 1264–67, and was on a crusade when he succeeded to the throne. He established English rule over all Wales 1282–84, and secured recognition of his overlordship from the Scottish king, although the Scots (under Wallace and Bruce) fiercely resisted actual conquest. In his reign Parliament took its approximate modern form with the ◊Model Parliament 1295. He was succeeded by his son Edward II.

Edward II 1284–1327. King of England from 1307, son of Edward I. Born at Caernarvon Castle, he was created the first Prince of Wales 1301. His invasion of Scotland 1314 to suppress revolt resulted in defeat at ◊Bannockburn. He was deposed 1327 by his wife Isabella (1292–1358), daughter of Philip IV of France, and her lover Roger de ◊Mortimer, and murdered in Berkeley Castle, Gloucestershire. Incompetent and frivolous, and entirely under the influence of his favourites, Edward I struggled throughout his reign with discontented barons. He was succeeded by his son Edward III.

Edward III 1312–1377. King of England from 1327, son of Edward II. He assumed the government 1330 from his mother, through whom in 1337 he laid claim to the French throne and thus began the ◊Hundred Years' War. He was succeeded by his grandson Richard II.

Edward began his reign by attempting to force his rule on Scotland, winning a victory at Halidon Hill 1333. During the first stage of the Hundred Years' War, English victories included the Battle of Crécy 1346 and the capture of Calais 1347. In 1360 Edward surrendered his claim to the French throne, but the war resumed 1369. During his last years his son John of Gaunt acted as head of government.

Edward IV 1442–1483. King of England 1461–70 and from 1471. He was the son of Richard, Duke of York, and succeeded Henry VI in the Wars of the ◊Roses, temporarily losing the throne to Henry when Edward fell out with his adviser ◊Warwick, but regaining it at the Battle of Barnet 1471. He was succeeded by his son Edward V.

Edward was known as Earl of March until his accession. After his father's death he occupied London 1461, and was proclaimed king in place of Henry VI by a council of peers. His position was secured by the defeat of the Lancastrians at Towton 1461 and by the capture of Henry. He quarrelled, however, with Warwick, his strongest supporter, who in 1470–71 temporarily restored Henry, until Edward recovered the throne by his victories at Barnet and Tewkesbury.

Edward V 1470–1483. King of England 1483. Son of Edward IV, he was deposed three months after his accession in favour of his uncle (◊Richard III), and is traditionally believed to have been murdered (with his brother) in the Tower of London on Richard's orders.

Edward VI King Edward VI's coronation medal. The boy-king was a brilliant scholar, deeply interested in theological speculation, and during his short reign the Protestant Reformation in England advanced significantly. *Philip Sauvain*

Edward VI 1537–1553. King of England from 1547, only son of Henry VIII and his third wife, Jane Seymour. The government was entrusted to his uncle the Duke of Somerset (who fell from power 1549), and then to the Earl of Warwick, later created Duke of Northumberland. Edward became a staunch Protestant and during his reign the Reformation progressed. He died from tuberculosis and was succeeded by his sister, Mary I.

Edward VII 1841–1910. King of Great Britain and Ireland from 1901. He was born at Buckingham Palace, the eldest son of Queen Victoria and Prince Albert. As Prince of Wales he was a prominent social figure, but his mother considered him too frivolous to take part in political life.

After his father's death 1861 he undertook many public duties, took a close interest in politics, and was on friendly terms with the party leaders. In 1863 he married Princess Alexandra of Denmark (1844–1925), and they had six children. He toured India 1875–76. He succeeded to the throne 1901 and was crowned 1902. He contributed to the Entente Cordiale 1904 with France and the Anglo-Russian agreement 1907.

Edward VIII 1894–1972. King of Great Britain and Northern Ireland Jan–Dec 1936. The eldest son of George V, he received the title of Prince of Wales 1910 and succeeded to the throne 20 Jan 1936. In Nov 1936 a constitutional crisis arose when Edward wished to marry Wallis Warfield ◊Simpson (see ◊abdication crisis). It was felt that, as a divorcee, she would be unacceptable as queen. On 11 Dec Edward abdicated and left for France, where the couple were married 1937. He was created Duke of Windsor and was governor of the Bahamas 1940–45, subsequently settling in France. He was succeeded by his brother, George VI.

Edwards Blake. Adopted name of William Blake McEdwards 1922– . US film director and writer. He was formerly an actor. Specializing in comedies, he directed the series of *Pink Panther* films 1963–78, starring Peter Sellers. His other work includes *Breakfast at Tiffany's* 1961 and *Blind Date* 1986.

Edwards Jonathan David 1966– . English athlete who won the triple jump title at the 1995 World Championships in Gothenburg with a world record leap of 18.29 metres. He won silver medals at the 1996 Olympic Games and the 1997 World Championships, and a gold at the 1998 European Championships.

Edward the Confessor c. 1003–1066. King of England from 1042, the son of Ethelred II. He lived in Normandy until shortly before his accession. During his reign power was held by Earl ◊Godwin and his son ◊Harold, while the king devoted himself to religion, including the rebuilding of Westminster Abbey (consecrated 1065), where he is buried. His childlessness led ultimately to the Norman Conquest 1066. He was canonized 1161.

Edward the Elder c. 870–924. King of the West Saxons. He succeeded his father ◊Alfred the Great 899. He reconquered SE England and the Midlands from the Danes, uniting Wessex and ◊Mercia with the help of his sister, Athelflad. By the time Edward died, his kingdom was the most powerful in the British Isles. He was succeeded by his son ◊Athelstan.

Edward the Martyr c. 963–978. King of England from 975. Son of King Edgar, he was murdered at Corfe Castle, Dorset, probably at his stepmother Aelfthryth's instigation (she wished to secure the crown for her son, Ethelred). He was canonized 1001.

Edwin c. 585–633. King of Northumbria from 617. He captured and fortified Edinburgh, which was named after him, and was killed in battle with Penda of Mercia 632.

EEC abbreviation for ◊***European Economic Community***.

EEG abbreviation for ◊***electroencephalogram***.

eel any fish of the order Anguilliformes. Eels are snakelike, with elongated dorsal and anal fins. They include the freshwater eels of Europe and North America (which breed in the Atlantic), the marine conger eels, and the morays of tropical coral reefs.

Effelsberg site, near Bonn, Germany, of the world's largest fully steerable radio telescope, the 100-m/328-ft radio dish of the Max Planck Institute for Radio Astronomy, opened 1971.

efficiency in physics, a general term indicating the degree to which a process or device can convert energy from one form to another without loss. It is normally expressed as a fraction or percentage, where 100% indicates conversion with no loss. The efficiency of a machine, for example, is the ratio of the work done by the machine to the energy put into the machine; it is always less than 100% because of frictional heat losses. Certain electrical machines with no moving parts, such as transformers, can approach 100% efficiency.

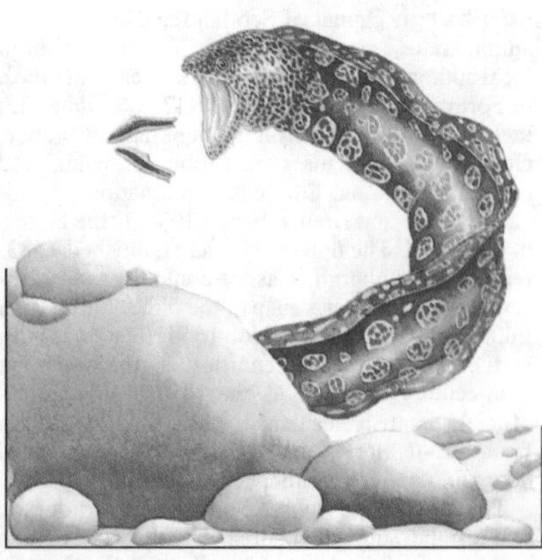

eel There are about 100 kinds of moray found throughout tropical and temperate seas. They generally lurk in rocky crevices from where they can ambush their prey, usually hunting by night. Some morays can reach over 4 m/13 ft in length and, because of their aggression, are considered dangerous to divers.

Since the ◊mechanical advantage, or force ratio, is the ratio of the load (the output force) to the effort (the input force), and the velocity ratio is the distance moved by the effort divided by the distance moved by the load, for certain machines the efficiency can also be defined as the mechanical advantage divided by the velocity ratio.

EFTA acronym for ◊***European Free Trade Association***.

EFTPOS acronym for ***electronic funds transfer at point of sale***, a form of ◊electronic funds transfer.

egalitarianism belief that all citizens in a state should have equal rights and privileges. Interpretations of this can vary, from the notion of equality of opportunity to equality in material welfare and political decision-making. Most states accept the concept of equal opportunities but recognize that people's abilities vary widely. Egalitarianism was one of the principles of the French Revolution.

egg Section through a fertilized bird's egg. Inside a bird's egg is a complex structure of liquids and membranes designed to meet the needs of the growing embryo. The yolk, which is rich in fat, is gradually absorbed by the embryo. The white of the egg provides protein and water. The chalaza is a twisted band of protein which holds the yolk in place and acts as a shock absorber. The airspace allows gases to be exchanged through the shell. The allantois contains many blood vessels which carry gases between the embryo and the outside.

Section through a fertilized egg

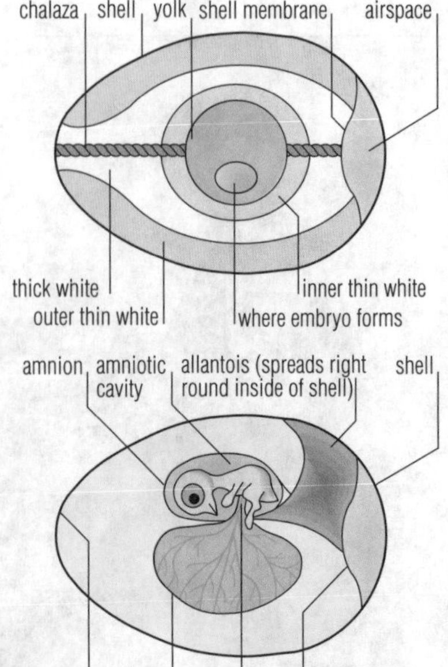

Egbert died 839. King of the West Saxons from 802, the son of Ealhmund, an under-king of Kent. By 829 he had united England for the first time under one king.

egg in animals, the ovum, or female ◊gamete (reproductive cell). After fertilization by a sperm cell, it begins to divide to form an embryo. Eggs may be deposited by the female (◊ovipary) or they may develop within her body (◊vivipary and ◊ovovivipary). In the oviparous reptiles and birds, the egg is protected by a shell, and well supplied with nutrients in the form of yolk.

eggplant another name for ◊aubergine.

Egmont, Mount (Maori ***Taranaki***) symmetrical extinct volcano in North Island, New Zealand, situated S of New Plymouth; it is 2,517 m/8,260 ft high.

ego (Latin 'I') in psychology, the processes concerned with the self and a person's conception of himself or herself, encompassing values and attitudes. In Freudian psychology, the term refers specifically to the element of the human mind that represents the conscious processes concerned with reality, in conflict with the ◊id (the instinctual element) and the ◊superego (the ethically aware element).

egret any of several ◊herons with long tufts of feathers on the head or neck. They belong to the order Ciconiiformes.

Egypt country in NE Africa, bounded N by the Mediterranean Sea, E by the Suez Canal and Red Sea, S by Sudan, and W by Libya. *See country box on p. 346.*

Egypt, ancient ancient civilization, based around the River Nile in Egypt, which emerged 5,000 years ago and reached its peak in the 16th century BC. Ancient Egypt was famed for its great power and wealth, due to the highly fertile lands of the Nile delta, which were rich sources of grain for the whole Mediterranean region. Egyptians were advanced in agriculture, engineering, and applied sciences. Many of their monuments, such as the ◊pyramids and the sphinx, survive today.

Egyptian architecture, ancient the dynastic period spanning the years 4000–30 BC saw the emergence of a distinctive Egyptian architecture, best represented in its tombs and temples, built for pharaohs and priests. Of the tombs, the ◊pyramids are the most striking. These evolved from mastaba – simple tomb structures with sloping sides – through stepped pyramids, such as that at ◊Sakkara about 2650 BC, to the familiar regular pyramids at El Gîza, about 2600–2480 BC. Famous examples are at Karnak, about 1570–1085, and at Luxor, about 1570–1200.

Egyptian art, ancient the art of ancient Egypt falls into three main periods – the Old, Middle, and New Kingdoms – beginning about 3000 BC and spanning 2,000 years overall. During this time, despite some stylistic development, there is remarkable continuity, representing a deeply religious and traditionalist society. Sculpture and painting are highly stylized, following strict conventions and using symbols of a religion centred on the afterlife and idealization of the dead, their servants, families, and possessions. Major collections of Egyptian art are to be found in the National Museum, Cairo, and in the British Museum, London.

The early dynastic period and the Old Kingdom (2920–2134 BC) is exemplified by the monumental statue of the Great Sphinx at El Gîza, about 2530 BC. A gigantic lion figure with a human head, the sphinx is carved from an outcrop of natural rock, 56.4 m/185 ft long and 19.2 m/63 ft high, and guards the path to the pyramid of Khafre. A rich collection of grave goods survive from the period, including clothes, ornaments, jewellery, and weapons, as well as statues in stone and precious metals. The stylistic conventions of painting – such as showing the human figure with head, legs, feet, and face in profile, the upper torso facing forwards, the hips three quarters turned, and the eye enlarged and enhanced – are established. Vivid wall paintings, such as *Geese of Medum* (National Museum, Cairo) about 2530, show a variety of scenes from the life of the time.

Middle Kingdom (2040–1640 BC), a period when Egypt was reunited under one ruler, is typified by tombs hewn from rock, attempts at realism in frescoes, and deepened perception in portrait sculpture, for example the head of Sesostris III (National Museum, Cairo). Typical of the period are sculptures of figures wrapped in mantles, with only head, hands, and feet showing.

New Kingdom (1550–1070 BC) is represented by a softer and more refined style of painting and a new sophistication in jewellery and furnishings. The golden age of the 18th dynasty, 1550–1070 BC, saw the building of the temples of Karnak and Luxor and the maze of tombs in the Valley of the Kings. The pharaohs of the period, Akhenaton and Tutankhamen, inspired an extravagant style exemplified in their carved images, the statues of Akhenaton, the golden coffins of Tutankhamen's mummified body (National Museum, Cairo) about 1361–1352 BC, and the head of Akhenaton's queen, Nefertiti (Museo Archaeologico, Florence) about 1360 BC. The monumental statues of Ramses II in Abu Simbel date from the 13th century BC.

Egyptian religion in the civilization of ancient Egypt, totemic animals, believed to be the ancestors of the clan, were worshipped. Totems later developed into gods, represented as having animal heads. One of the main cults was that of ◊Osiris, the god of the underworld. Immortality, conferred by the magical rite of mummification, was originally the sole prerogative of the king, but was extended under the New Kingdom to all who could afford it; they were buried with the ◊*Book of the Dead.*

The hawk was sacred to Ra and Horus, the ibis to Thoth, the jackal to Anubis. The story of Osiris, who was murdered, mourned by his sister and wife Isis, and then rose again, was enacted in a fertility ritual similar to that of Tammuz.

Under the 18th dynasty a local deity of Thebes, Ammon, came to be regarded as supreme. The pharaoh Akhenaton attempted, without success, to establish Aton as the one national god.

egret *A little egret* Egretta garzetta *fishing in a pool in Gambia, W Africa. Once a rare visitor to the British Isles, in recent years it has become established as a breeding bird. Premaphotos Wildlife*

EGYPT, ANCIENT: TIMELINE

5000 BC	Egyptian culture already well established in the Nile Valley, with Neolithic farming villages.
c. 3050	Menes united Lower Egypt (the delta) with his own kingdom of Upper Egypt.
c. 2630	The architect Imhotep built the step pyramid at Sakkara.
c. 2550	***Old Kingdom*** reached the height of its power and the kings of the 4th dynasty built the pyramids at El Gîza.
c. 2040–1640	***Middle Kingdom***, under which the unity lost towards the end of the Old Kingdom was restored.
c. 1750	Infiltrating Asian Hyksos people established their kingdom in the Nile Delta.
c. 1550	***New Kingdom*** established by the 18th dynasty following the eviction of the Hyksos, with its capital at Thebes. The high point of ancient Egyptian civilization under the pharaohs Thothmes, Hatshepsut, Amenhotep, Akhenaton (who moved the capital to Akhetaton), and Tutankhamen.
c. 1307–1196	19th dynasty: Major building works by Seti I and Ramses II at Thebes, Abydos, and Abu Simbel.
1191	Ramses III defeated the Indo-European Sea Peoples, but after him there was decline, and power within the country passed from the pharaohs to the priests of Amen.
1070–664	***Third Intermediate Period*** during this period Egypt was often divided between two or more dynasties; the nobles became virtually independent.
8th–7th Cs	Brief interlude of rule by kings from Nubia.
666	The Assyrians under Ashurbanipal occupied Thebes.
663–609	Psammetichus I restored Egypt's independence and unity.
525	Egypt was conquered by Cambyses and became a Persian province.
c. 405–340	Period of independence.
332	Conquest by Alexander the Great. On the division of his empire, Egypt went to one of his generals, Ptolemy I, and his descendants, the Macedonian dynasty.
30	Death of Cleopatra, last of the Macedonians, and conquest by the Roman emperor Augustus; Egypt became a province of the Roman Empire.
AD 641	Conquest by the Arabs; the Christianity of later Roman rule was for the most part replaced by Islam.

eider Eider ducks are robustly built sea ducks that dive in shallow waters to feed on shellfish and even crabs. The female plucks the soft downy feathers from her breast and uses them to line the nest. Sitting eiders will allow humans to approach the nest without deserting. The bold markings of the male and the heavy-based bill make this duck easy to identify.

Egyptology the study of ancient Egypt. Interest in the subject was aroused by the Napoleonic expedition's discovery of the ◊Rosetta Stone 1799. Various excavations continued throughout the 19th century and gradually assumed a more scientific character, largely as a result of the work of the British archaeologist Flinders ◊Petrie from 1880 onwards and the formation of the Egyptian Exploration Fund 1882. In 1922 another British archaeologist, Howard Carter, discovered the tomb of Tutankhamen, the only royal tomb with all its treasures intact. Special branches of Egyptology are the study of prehistoric Egypt and the search for papyri (ancient documents) preserved by the dryness of the climate.

Ehrlich Paul 1854–1915. German bacteriologist and immunologist who produced the first cure for ◊syphilis. He developed the arsenic compounds, in particular Salvarsan, that were used in the treatment of syphilis before the discovery of antibiotics. Ehrlich founded ◊chemotherapy. He was also one of the earliest workers on immunology, and through his studies on blood samples the discipline of haematology was recognized. He shared the 1908 Nobel Prize for Physiology or Medicine with Ilya ◊Mechnikov.

Eichmann (Karl) Adolf 1906–1962. Austrian Nazi. As an ◊SS official during Hitler's regime (1933–1945), he was responsible for atrocities against Jews and others, including the implementation of genocide. He managed to escape at the fall of Germany 1945, but was discovered in Argentina 1960, abducted by Israeli agents, tried in Israel 1961 for ◊war crimes, and executed.

eider large marine ◊duck of the genus *Somateria*, family Anatidae, order Anseriformes. They are found on the northern coasts of the Atlantic and Pacific Oceans. The common eider *S. molissima* is highly valued for its soft down, which is used in quilts and cushions for warmth. The adult male has a black cap and belly and a green nape. The rest of the plumage is white with a pink breast and throat, while the female is a mottled brown. The bill is large and flattened and both bill and feet are olive green.

Eid ul-Adha Muslim festival that takes place during the *hajj*, or pilgrimage to Mecca, and commemorates Abraham's willingness to sacrifice his son ◊Ishmael at the command of Allah.

Eid ul-Fitr Muslim festival celebrating the end of Ramadan, the month of fasting.

Eiffel (Alexandre) Gustave 1832–1923. French engineer who constructed the Eiffel Tower for the 1889 Paris Exhibition. The tower, made of iron, is 320 m/1,050 ft high and stands in the Champ de Mars, Paris.

Eiffel set up his own business in Paris 1867 and quickly established his reputation with the construction of a series of ambitious railway bridges, of which the span across the Douro at Oporto, Portugal, was the longest at 160 m/525 ft. In 1881 he provided the iron skeleton for the Statue of Liberty.

Eijkman Christiaan 1858–1930. Dutch bacteriologist. He pioneered the recognition of vitamins as essential to health and identified vitamin B_1 deficiency as the cause of the disease beriberi. He shared the 1929 Nobel Prize for Physiology or Medicine with Frederick Gowland ◊Hopkins.

Eilat alternative spelling of ◊Elat, a port in Israel.

Einstein Albert 1879–1955. German-born US physicist who formulated the theories of ◊relativity, and worked on radiation physics and thermodynamics. In 1905 he published the special theory of relativity, and in 1915 issued his general theory of relativity. He received the Nobel Prize for Physics 1921. His last conception of the basic laws governing the universe was outlined in his ◊unified field theory, made public 1953.

The theories of relativity revolutionized our understanding of matter, space, and time. Einstein also established that light may have a particle nature and deduced 1905 the photoelectric law that governs the production of electricity from light-sensitive metals. He investigated Brownian movement, also 1905, and was able to explain it so that it not only confirmed the existence of atoms but could be used to determine their dimensions. He also proposed the equivalence of mass and energy, which enabled physicists to deepen their understanding of the nature of the atom, and explained radioactivity and other nuclear processes.

EGYPT
Arab Republic of

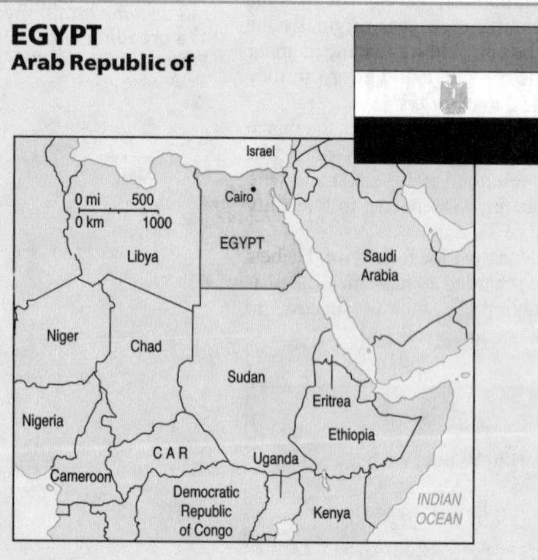

national name *Jumhuriyat Misr al-Arabiya*
area area 1,001,450 sq km/386,990 sq mi
capital Cairo
major towns/cities El Gîza
major ports Alexandria, Port Said, Suez, Damietta, Shubra Al Khayma
physical features mostly desert; hills in E; fertile land along Nile valley and delta; cultivated and settled area is about 35,500 sq km/13,700 sq mi; Aswan High Dam and Lake Nasser; Sinai
head of state Hosni Mubarak from 1981
head of government Kamal Ahmed Ganzouri from 1996
political system democratic republic
administrative divisions 26 governorates
political parties National Democratic Party (NDP), moderate, left of centre; Socialist Labour Party (SLP), right of centre; Liberal Socialist Party, free enterprise; New Wafd Party, nationalist; National Progressive Unionist Party, left-wing
armed forces 436,000 (1995)
conscription 3 years (selective)
defence spend (% GDP) 5.9 (1994)
education spend (% GNP) 5 (1992)
health spend (% GDP) 1 (1990)
death penalty retained and used for ordinary crimes
population 62,931,000 (1995 est)
population growth rate 2.2% (1990–95); 1.7% (2000–05)
age distribution (% of total population) <15 38%, 15–65 57.8%, >65 4.2% (1995)
ethnic distribution 93% native Egyptians
population density (per sq km) 58 (1994)
urban population (% of total) 45 (1995)
labour force 35% of population: 40% agriculture, 22% industry, 38% services (1990)
unemployment 13% (1993)
child mortality rate (under 5, per 1,000 live births) 52 (1994)
life expectancy 60 (men), 63 (women)
education (compulsory years) 5
literacy rate 63% (men), 34% (women)
languages Arabic (official); ancient Egyptian survives to some extent in Coptic; English; French
religions Sunni Muslim 90%, Coptic Christian 7%
TV sets (per 1,000 people) 119 (1992)
currency Egyptian pound
GDP (US $) 42.92 billion (1994)
GDP per capita (PPP) (US $) 3,800 (1993)
growth rate 2.0% (1994)
average annual inflation 16.9% (1985–94); 11.4% (1994)
major trading partners USA, Germany, France, Italy
resources petroleum, natural gas, phosphates, manganese, uranium, coal, iron ore, gold
industries petroleum and petroleum products, food processing, petroleum refinery, textiles, metals, cement, tobacco, sugar crystal and refined sugar, electrical appliances, fertilizers
exports petroleum and petroleum products, textiles, clothing, food, live animals. Principal market: USA 12.9% (1993)
imports wheat, maize, dairy products, machinery and transport equipment, wood and wood products, consumer goods. Principal source: USA 15% (1993)
arable land 2.4% (1993)
agricultural products wheat, cotton, rice, corn, beans

HISTORY
1st C BC–7th C AD Conquered by Augustus AD 30, Egypt passed under rule of Roman, and later Byzantine, governors.
AD 639–42 Arabs conquered Egypt, introducing Islam and Arabic; succession of Arab dynasties followed.
1250 Mamelukes seized power.
1517 Became part of Turkish Ottoman Empire.
1798–1801 Invasion by Napoleon and period of French occupation.
1801 Control regained by Turks.
1869 Opening of Suez Canal made Egypt strategically important.
1881–82 Nationalist revolt resulted in British occupation.
1914 Egypt became a British protectorate.
1922 Achieved nominal independence under King Fuad I.
1936 Full independence achieved from Britain. King Fuad succeeded by his son Farouk.
1946 Withdrawal of British troops except from Suez Canal zone.
1952 Farouk overthrown by army in bloodless coup.
1953 Egypt declared a republic, with General Neguib as president.
1956 Neguib replaced by Col Gamal Nasser. Nasser announced nationalization of Suez Canal; Egypt attacked by Britain, France, and Israel. Cease-fire agreed following US intervention.
1958 Short-lived merger of Egypt and Syria as United Arab Republic (UAR).
1967 Six-Day War with Israel ended in Egypt's defeat and Israeli occupation of Sinai and Gaza Strip.
1970 Nasser died; succeeded by Anwar Sadat.
1973 Attempt to regain territory lost to Israel led to Yom Kippur War; cease-fire arranged by US secretary of state Henry Kissinger.
1978–79 Camp David talks in USA resulted in a peace treaty between Egypt and Israel. Egypt expelled from Arab League.
1981 Sadat assassinated by Muslim fundamentalists, succeeded by Hosni Mubarak.
1983 Improved relations between Egypt and Arab world; only Libya and Syria maintained a trade boycott.
1987 Egypt readmitted to Arab League.
1989 Improved relations with Libya; diplomatic relations with Syria restored.
1991 Joined Gulf War on US-led side. Major force in convening Middle East peace conference in Spain.
1992 Violence between Muslims and Christians.
1994 Government crackdown on Islamic militants.
1995 Abortive attempt to assassinate Mubarak.
1996 Kamal Ahmed Ganzouri appointed prime minister.
1997 Massacre of 58 tourists at Luxor by Islamic extremists.

SEE ALSO Arab–Israeli wars; Camp David Agreements; Egypt, ancient; Suez Canal

Einstein Physicist Albert Einstein in 1944. He developed his theories by using simple 'thought experiments', but the full flowering of his ideas required very complex mathematics. *Topham*

einsteinium synthesized, radioactive, metallic element of the actinide series, symbol Es, atomic number 99, relative atomic mass 254.

It was produced by the first thermonuclear explosion, in 1952, and discovered in fallout debris in the form of the isotope Es-253 (half-life 20 days). Its longest-lived isotope, Es-254, with a half-life of 276 days, allowed the element to be studied at length. It is now synthesized by bombarding lower-numbered ◊transuranic elements in particle accelerators. It was first identified by A Ghiorso and his team who named it in 1955 after Albert Einstein.

Einthoven Willem 1860–1927. Dutch physiologist and inventor of the ◊electrocardiogram. He demonstrated that certain disorders of the heart alter its electrical activity in characteristic ways. He was awarded the 1924 Nobel Prize for Physiology or Medicine.

Eire former name (1937–48) of Southern Ireland, now the Republic of ◊Ireland. In Gaelic the name Eire is also used to refer to the whole of Ireland.

Eisenhower Dwight David ('Ike') 1890–1969. 34th president of the USA 1953–60, a Republican. A general in World War II, he commanded the Allied forces in Italy 1943, then the Allied invasion of Europe, and from Oct 1944 all the Allied armies in the West. As president he promoted business interests at home and conducted the ◊Cold War abroad. His vice president was Richard Nixon.

Eisenhower was born at Denison, Texas, and graduated from West Point military academy in 1915. He became commander in chief of the US and British forces for the invasion of North Africa Nov 1942, commanded the Allied invasion of Sicily July 1943, and announced the surrender of Italy 8 Sept 1943. In Dec he became commander of the Allied Expeditionary Force for the invasion of Europe and was promoted to General of the Army Dec 1944. After the war he served as commander of the US Occupation Forces in Germany, then returned to the USA to become Chief of Staff. He became supreme commander of the Allied Powers in Europe 1950, and organized the defence forces in the North Atlantic Treaty Organization (NATO). He resigned from the army 1952 to campaign for the presidency; he was elected, and re-elected by a wide margin in 1956.

A popular politician, Eisenhower held office during a period of domestic and international tension, although the USA was experiencing an era of postwar prosperity and growth. Major problems during his administration included the ending of the ◊Korean War, the growing civil-rights movement at home, and the ◊Cold War. His proposals on disarmament and the control of nuclear weapons led to the first International Conference on the Peaceful Uses of Atomic Energy, held under the auspices of the United Nations at Geneva 1955.

Eisenman Peter 1932– . US architect. He came to prominence as a member of the New York Five group, along with Richard Meier and Michael Graves. His work draws on mathematics and philosophy, especially ◊Deconstructionism. Early experiments in complexity, such as House X 1978, led to increasingly scrambled designs, for example, Fin d'Ou T Hou S 1983.

Eisenstein Sergei Mikhailovich 1898–1948. Latvian-born Soviet film director. He pioneered film theory and introduced the use of montage (the juxtaposition of shots to create a particular effect) as a means of propaganda, as in *The Battleship Potemkin* 1925. The Soviet dictator Stalin banned the second (and last) part of Eisenstein's projected three-film epic *Ivan the Terrible* 1944–46. His other films include *Strike* 1925, *October* 1928, *Que Viva Mexico!* 1931–32, and *Alexander Nevsky* 1938.

eisteddfod (Welsh 'sitting') traditional Welsh gathering lasting up to a week and dedicated to the encouragement of the bardic arts of music, poetry, and literature. The custom dates from pre-Christian times.

ejector seat device for propelling an aircraft pilot out of the plane to parachute to safety in an emergency, invented by the British engineer James Martin (1893–1981). The first seats of 1945 were powered by a compressed spring; later seats used an explosive charge. By the early 1980s, 35,000 seats had been fitted worldwide, and the lives of 5,000 pilots saved by their use. Seats that can be ejected on takeoff and landing or at low altitude were a major breakthrough of the 1980s.

eland largest species of ◊antelope, *Taurotragus oryx*. Pale fawn in colour, it is about 2 m/6 ft high, and both sexes have spiral horns about 45 cm/18 in long. It is found in central and southern Africa.

elasticity in economics, the measure of response of one variable to changes in another. Such measures are used to test the effects of changes in prices and incomes on demand and supply.

Price elasticity of demand measures the responsiveness of changes in quantity demanded to a change in price of the product.

Income elasticity of demand measures the responsiveness of changes in quantity demanded to a change in income.

elasticity in physics, the ability of a solid to recover its shape once deforming forces (stresses modifying its dimensions or shape) are removed. An elastic material obeys ◊Hooke's law: that is, its deformation is proportional to the applied stress up to a certain point, called the elastic limit, beyond which additional stress will deform it permanently. Elastic materials include metals and rubber; however, all materials have some degree of elasticity.

Elat or ***Eilat*** port at the head of the Gulf of Aqaba, Israel's only outlet to the Red Sea; population (1994) 35,700. Founded 1948, on the site of the Biblical Elath, it is linked by road with Beersheba. There are copper mines and granite quarries nearby, and a major geophysical observatory, opened 1968, is 16 km/10 mi to the N.

Eisenhower US soldier and politician Dwight D Eisenhower. After commanding Allied forces in Europe during World War II, he became the 34th president of the USA 1953. *Sachem*

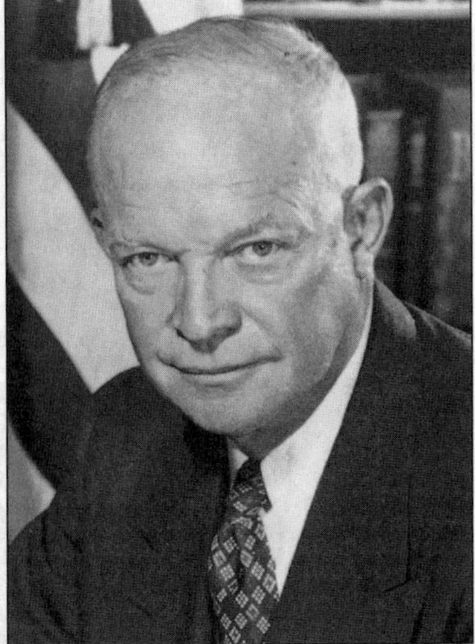

E layer (formerly called the Kennelly–Heaviside layer) the lower regions (90–120 km/56–75 mi) of the ◊ionosphere, which reflect radio waves, allowing their reception around the surface of the Earth. The E layer approaches the Earth by day and recedes from it at night.

Elba island in the Mediterranean Sea, 10 km/6 mi off the west coast of Italy; area 223 sq km/86 sq mi; population (1990 est) 35,000. Iron ore is exported from the island's capital, Portoferraio, to the Italian mainland, and there is a fishing industry. The small uninhabited island of Monte Cristo, 40 km/25 mi to the S, supplied the title of Alexandre Dumas's hero in his historical romance *The Count of Monte Cristo* 1844. Elba was Napoleon's place of exile 1814–15.

Elbe one of the principal rivers of Germany, 1,166 km/725 mi long, rising on the southern slopes of the Riesengebirge, Czech Republic, and flowing NW across the German plain to the North Sea.

Elbruz or ***Elbrus*** highest mountain (5,642 m/18,510 ft) on the continent of Europe, in the Caucasus Mountains, Georgia.

elder in botany, small tree or shrub of the genus *Sambucus*, of the honeysuckle family (Caprifoliaceae), native to North America, Eurasia, and N Africa. Some are grown as ornamentals for their showy yellow or white flower clusters and their colourful black or scarlet berries.

elder in the Presbyterian church, a lay member who assists the minister (or teaching elder) in running the church.

El Dorado fabled city of gold believed by the 16th-century Spanish and other Europeans to exist somewhere in the area of the Orinoco and Amazon rivers.

Eleanor of Aquitaine c. 1122–1204. Queen of France 1137–51 as wife of Louis VII, and of England from 1154 as wife of Henry II. Henry imprisoned her 1174–89 for supporting their sons, the future Richard I and King John, in revolt against him.

She was the daughter of William X, Duke of Aquitaine, and was married 1137–52 to Louis VII of France, but the marriage was annulled. The same year she married Henry of Anjou, who became king of England 1154.

Eleanor of Castile c. 1245–1290. Queen of Edward I of England, the daughter of Ferdinand III of Castile. She married Prince Edward 1254, and accompanied him on his crusade 1270. She died at Harby, Nottinghamshire, and Edward erected stone crosses in towns where her body rested on the funeral journey to London. Several Eleanor Crosses are still standing, for example, at Northampton.

election process of appointing a person to public office or a political party to government by voting. Elections were occasionally held in ancient Greek democracies; Roman tribunes were regularly elected.

In England, elections have been used as a parliamentary process since the 13th century. The secret ballot was adopted 1872 and full equal voting rights won for women 1928. All registered members of the public aged 18 and over may vote in local, parliamentary, and European Parliament elections. The British House of Commons is elected for a maximum of five years; the prime minister can call a general election at any time.

elector (German ***Kurfürst***) any of originally seven (later ten) princes of the Holy Roman Empire who had the prerogative of electing the emperor (in effect, the king of Germany). The electors were the archbishops of Mainz, Trier, and Cologne, the court palatine of the Rhine, the Duke of Saxony, the Margrave of Brandenburg, and the king of Bohemia (in force to 1806). Their constitutional status was formalized 1356 in the document known as the Golden Bull, which granted them extensive powers within their own domains, to act as judges, issue coins, and impose tolls.

electoral college in the US government, the indirect system of voting for the president and vice president. The people of each state officially vote

‘Never do anything against conscience even if the state demands it.’

ALBERT EINSTEIN
Quoted in *Saturday Review* obituary 30 April 1955

not for the presidential candidate, but for a list of electors nominated by each party. The whole electoral-college vote of the state then goes to the winning party (and candidate). A majority is required for election.

The USA has as many electors as it has senators and representatives in Congress, so that the electoral college numbers 538 (535 state electors and three from the District of Columbia), and a majority of 270 electoral votes is needed to win. The system can lead to a presidential candidate being elected with a minority of the total vote over the whole country (as happened when Benjamin Harrison was elected over Grover Cleveland 1888). It has been proposed, for example by President Carter in 1977, to substitute a direct popular vote. A constitutional amendment to this effect failed in 1979, partly because minority groups argued that this would deprive them of their politically influential block vote in key states.

electoral system see ◊vote and ◊proportional representation.

Electra in Greek mythology, daughter of ◊Agamemnon and ◊Clytemnestra, and sister of ◊Orestes and ◊Iphigenia. Her hatred of her mother for murdering her father and her desire for revenge, fulfilled by the return of her brother Orestes, made her the subject of tragedies by the Greek dramatists Aeschylus, Sophocles, and Euripides. In Euripides' tragedy she joins with Orestes in killing Clytemnestra.

electrical relay an electromagnetic switch; see ◊relay.

electric charge property of some bodies that causes them to exert forces on each other. Two bodies both with positive or both with negative charges repel each other, whereas bodies with opposite or 'unlike' charges attract each other, since each is in the ◊electric field of the other. In atoms, ◊electrons possess a negative charge, and ◊protons an equal positive charge. The ◊SI unit of electric charge is the coulomb (symbol C).

A body can be charged by friction, induction, or chemical change and shows itself as an accumulation of electrons (negative charge) or loss of electrons (positive charge) on an atom or body. Atoms have no charge but can sometimes gain electrons to become negative ions or lose them to become positive ions. So-called ◊static electricity, seen in such phenomena as the charging of nylon shirts when they are pulled on or off, or in brushing hair, is in fact the gain or loss of electrons from the surface atoms. A flow of charge (such as electrons through a copper wire) constitutes an electric current; the flow of current is measured in amperes (symbol A).

electric current the flow of electrically charged particles through a conducting circuit due to the presence of a ◊potential difference. The current at any point in a circuit is the amount of charge flowing per second; its SI unit is the ampere (coulomb per second).

Current carries electrical energy from a power supply, such as a battery of electrical cells, to the components of the circuit, where it is converted into other forms of energy, such as heat, light, or motion. It may be either ◊direct current or ◊alternating current.

heating effect When current flows in a component possessing resistance, electrical energy is converted into heat energy. If the resistance of the component is R ohms and the current through it is I amperes, then the heat energy W (in joules) generated in a time t seconds is given by the formula:

$$W = I^2Rt$$

magnetic effect A ◊magnetic field is created around all conductors that carry a current. When a current-bearing conductor is made into a coil it forms an ◊electromagnet with a magnetic field that is similar to that of a bar magnet, but which disappears as soon as the current is switched off. The strength of the magnetic field is directly proportional to the current in the conductor – a property that allows a small electromagnet to be used to produce a pattern of magnetism on recording tape or disc that accurately represents the sound or data to be stored. The direction of the field created around a conducting wire may be predicted by using Maxwell's screw rule, which states that if a right-handed screw is turned so that it moves forwards in the same direction as the current, its direction of rotation will give the direction of the magnetic field.

motor effect A conductor carrying current in a magnetic field experiences a force, and is impelled to move in a direction perpendicular to both the direction of the current and the direction of the magnetic field. The magnitude of the force experienced depends on the length of the conductor and on the strengths of the current and the magnetic field, and is greatest when the conductor is at right angles to the field. A conductor wound into a coil that can rotate between the poles of a magnet forms the basis of an ◊electric motor.

heating effect The conversion of energy from an electrical form into that of heat takes place when current flows through a conductor, the incandescent lamp being a particular example. It is of interest to note that only about 5% of the heat energy appears as light. With direct current and voltage, the power (in watts) dissipated by a circuit is the product of the current in amperes and the applied potential difference in volts. This may be expressed by the equation $W = VI$. The energy, in joules, dissipated by this circuit in t seconds is $VIt = I^2Rt$, since 1 joule = 1 watt second. If no mechanical work is done, all this energy is transformed into heat.

electric field in physics, a region in which a particle possessing electric charge experiences a force owing to the presence of another electric charge. The strength of an electric field, E, is measured in volts per metre ($V\ m^{-1}$). It is a type of ◊electromagnetic field.

electric fish any of several unrelated fishes that have electricity-producing powers, including the South American 'electric eel'. These include *Electrophorus electricus*, which is not a true eel, and in which the lateral tail muscles are modified to form electric organs capable of generating 650 volts; the current passing from tail to head is strong enough to stun another animal. Most electric fishes use weak electric fields to navigate and to detect nearby objects.

electricity all phenomena caused by ◊electric charge, whether static or in motion. Electric charge is caused by an excess or deficit of electrons in the charged substance, and an electric current by the movement of electrons around a circuit. Substances may be electrical conductors, such as metals, which allow the passage of electricity through them, or insulators, such as rubber, which are extremely poor conductors. Substances with relatively poor conductivities that can be improved by the addition of heat or light are known as ◊semiconductors.

Electricity generated on a commercial scale was available from the early 1880s and used for electric motors driving all kinds of machinery, and for lighting, first by carbon arc, but later by incandescent filaments (first of carbon and then of tungsten), enclosed in glass bulbs partially filled with inert gas under vacuum. Light is also produced by passing electricity through a gas or metal vapour or a fluorescent lamp. Other practical applications include telephone, radio, television, X-ray machines, and many other applications in ◊electronics.

The fact that amber has the power, after being rubbed, of attracting light objects, such as bits of straw and feathers, is said to have been known to Thales of Miletus and to the Roman naturalist Pliny. William Gilbert, Queen Elizabeth I's physician, found that many substances possessed this power, and he called it 'electric' after the Greek word meaning 'amber'.

In the early 1700s, it was recognized that there are two types of electricity and that unlike kinds attract each other and like kinds repel. The charge on glass rubbed with silk came to be known as positive electricity, and the charge on amber rubbed with wool as negative electricity. These two charges were found to cancel each other when brought together.

In 1800 Alessandro Volta found that a series of cells containing brine, in which were dipped plates of zinc and copper, gave an electric current, which later in the same year was shown to evolve hydrogen and oxygen when passed through water (◊electrolysis). Humphry Davy, in 1807, decomposed soda and potash (both thought to be elements) and isolated the metals sodium and potassium, a discovery that led the way to ◊electroplating. Other properties of electric currents discovered were the heating effect, now used in lighting and central heating, and the deflection of a magnetic needle, described by Hans Oersted 1820 and elaborated by André Ampère 1825. This work made possible the electric telegraph.

For Michael Faraday, the fact that an electric current passing through a wire caused a magnet to move suggested that moving a wire or coil of wire rapidly between the poles of a magnet would induce an electric current. He demonstrated this 1831, producing the first ◊dynamo, which became the basis of electrical engineering. The characteristics of currents were crystallized about 1827 by Georg Ohm, who showed that the current passing along a wire was equal to the electromotive force (emf) across the wire multiplied by a constant, which was the conductivity of the wire. The unit of resistance (ohm) is named after Ohm, the unit of emf (volt) is named after Volta, and the unit of current (amp) after Ampère.

The work of the late 1800s indicated the wide interconnections of electricity (with magnetism, heat, and light), and about 1855 James Clerk Maxwell formulated a single electromagnetic theory. The universal importance of electricity was decisively proved by the discovery that the atom, until then thought to be the ultimate particle of matter, is composed of a positively charged central core, the nucleus, about which negatively charged electrons rotate in various orbits.

electricity Large coal-fired power stations such as this one at Didcot, S England, require huge amounts of coal to operate – Didcot consumes up to 1,000 truckfuls per day. The electricity produced per tonne of coal may be as high as 2,000 kwh. Concern about acid rain and global warming, however, has made coal-fired power stations controversial. *AEA Technology*

Electricity is the most useful and most convenient form of energy, readily convertible into heat and light and used to power machines. Electricity can be generated in one place and distributed anywhere because it readily flows through wires. It is generated at power stations where a suitable energy source is harnessed to drive ◊turbines that spin electricity generators. Current energy sources are coal, oil, water power (hydroelectricity), natural gas, and ◊nuclear energy. Research is under way to increase the contribution of wind, tidal, solar, and geothermal power. Nuclear fuel has proved a more expensive source of electricity than initially anticipated and worldwide concern over radioactivity may limit its future development.

Electricity is generated at power stations at a voltage of about 25,000 volts, which is not a suitable voltage for long-distance transmission. For minimal power loss, transmission must take place at very high voltage (400,000 volts or more). The generated voltage is therefore increased ('stepped up') by a ◊transformer. The resulting high-voltage electricity is then fed into the main arteries of the ◊grid system, an interconnected network of power stations and distribution centres covering a large area. After transmission to a local substation, the line voltage is reduced by a step-down transformer and distributed to consumers.

Among specialized power units that convert energy directly to electrical energy without the intervention of any moving mechanisms, the most promising are thermionic converters. These use conventional fuels such as propane gas, as in portable military power packs, or, if refuelling is to be avoided, radioactive fuels, as in uncrewed navigational aids and spacecraft.

▷ *See feature on pp. 360–361.*

electric motor a machine that converts electrical energy into mechanical energy. There are various types, including direct-current and induction motors, most of which produce rotary motion. A linear induction motor produces linear (in a straight line) rather than rotary motion.

A simple ***direct-current motor*** consists of a horseshoe-shaped permanent ◊magnet with a wire-wound coil (armature) mounted so that it can rotate between the poles of the magnet. A ◊commutator reverses the current (from a battery) fed to the coil on each half-turn, which rotates because of the mechanical force exerted on a conductor carrying a current in a magnetic field. An ***induction motor*** employs ◊alternating current. It comprises a stationary current-carrying coil (stator) surrounding another coil (rotor), which rotates because of the current induced in it by the magnetic field created by the stator; it thus requires no commutator.

electric power the rate at which an electrical machine uses electrical ◊energy or converts it into other forms of energy – for example, light, heat, mechanical energy. Usually measured in watts (equivalent to joules per second), it is equal to the product of the voltage and the current flowing. An electric lamp that passes a current of 0.4 amps at 250 volts uses 100 watts of electrical power and converts it into light and heat – in ordinary terms it is a 100-watt lamp. An electric motor that requires 6 amps at the same voltage consumes 1,500 watts (1.5 kilowatts), equivalent to delivering about 2 horsepower of mechanical power.

electric ray another name for the ◊torpedo.

electrocardiogram (ECG) graphic recording of the electrical activity of the heart, as detected by electrodes placed on the skin. Electrocardiography is used in the diagnosis of heart disease.

electrochemistry the branch of science that studies chemical reactions involving electricity. The use of electricity to produce chemical effects, ◊electrolysis, is employed in many industrial processes, such as the manufacture of chlorine and the extraction of aluminium. The use of chemical reactions to produce electricity is the basis of electrical ◊cells, such as the dry cell and the Georges Leclanché (1839–1882) cell.

Since all chemical reactions involve changes to the electronic structure of atoms, all reactions are now recognized as electrochemical in nature. Oxidation, for example, was once defined as a process in which oxygen was combined with a substance, or hydrogen was removed from a compound; it is now defined as a process in which electrons are lost.

Electrochemistry is also the basis of new methods of destroying toxic organic pollutants. For example, electrochemical cells have been developed that operate with supercritical water to combust organic waste materials.

electroconvulsive therapy (ECT) or ***electroshock therapy*** treatment mainly for severe ◊depression, given under anaesthesia and with a muscle relaxant. An electric current is passed through one or both sides of the brain to induce alterations in its electrical activity. The treatment can cause distress and loss of concentration and memory, and so there is much controversy about its use and effectiveness.

ECT was first used 1938 but its success in treating depression led to its excessive use for a wide range of mental illnesses against which it was ineffective. Its side effects included broken bones and severe memory loss.

The procedure in use today is much improved, using the minimum shock necessary to produce a seizure, administered under general anaesthetic with muscle relaxants to prevent spasms and fractures. It is the seizure rather than the shock itself that produces improvement. The smaller the shock administered the less damage there is to memory. In 1991 in England and Wales up to 20,000 people received ECT.

electrocution death caused by electric current. It is used as a method of execution in some US states. The condemned person is strapped into a special chair and a shock of 1,800–2,000 volts is administered. See ◊capital punishment.

electrode any terminal by which an electric current passes in or out of a conducting substance; for example, the anode or cathode in a battery or the carbons in an arc lamp. The terminals that emit and collect the flow of electrons in thermionic ◊valves (electron tubes) are also called electrodes: for example, cathodes, plates, and grids.

electrodynamics the branch of physics dealing with electric charges, electric currents and associated forces. ◊Quantum electrodynamics (QED) studies the interaction between charged particles and their emission and absorption of electromagnetic radiation. This field combines quantum theory and relativity theory, making accurate predictions about subatomic processes involving charged particles such as electrons and protons.

electroencephalogram (EEG) graphic record of the electrical discharges of the brain, as detected by electrodes placed on the scalp. The pattern of electrical activity revealed by electroencephalography is helpful in the diagnosis of some brain disorders, in particular epilepsy.

electrolysis in chemistry, the production of chemical changes by passing an electric current through a solution or molten salt (the electrolyte), resulting in the migration of ions to the electrodes: positive ions (cations) to the negative electrode (cathode) and negative ions (anions) to the positive electrode (anode).

During electrolysis, the ions react with the electrode, either receiving or giving up electrons. The resultant atoms may be liberated as a gas, or deposited as a solid on the electrode, in amounts that are proportional to the amount of current passed, as discovered by English chemist Michael Faraday. For instance, when acidified water is electrolysed, hydrogen ions (H^+) at the cathode receive electrons to form hydrogen gas; hydroxide ions (OH^-) at the anode give up electrons to form oxygen gas and water.

One application of electrolysis is electroplating, in which a solution of a salt, such as silver nitrate ($AgNO_3$), is used and the object to be plated acts as the negative electrode, thus attracting silver ions (Ag^+). Electrolysis is used in many industrial processes, such as coating metals for vehicles and ships, and refining bauxite into aluminium; it also forms the basis of a number of electrochemical analytical techniques, such as polarography.

electrolyte solution or molten substance in which an electric current is made to flow by the movement and discharge of ions in accordance with Faraday's laws of ◊electrolysis. The term 'electrolyte' is frequently used to denote a substance that, when dissolved in a specified solvent, usually water, dissociates into ◊ions to produce an electrically conducting medium.

In medicine the term is often used for the ion itself (sodium or potassium, for example). Electrolyte balance may be severely disrupted in illness or injury.

electromagnet coil of wire wound around a soft iron core that acts as a magnet when an electric current flows through the wire. Electromagnets have many uses: in switches, electric bells, solenoids, and metal-lifting cranes.

electromagnetic field in physics, the region in which a particle with an ◊electric charge experiences a force. If it does so only when moving, it is in a pure magnetic field; if it does so when stationary, it is in an electric field. Both can be present simultaneously.

electromagnetic force one of the four fundamental ◊forces of nature, the other three being gravity, the strong nuclear force, and the weak nuclear force. The ◊elementary particle that is the carrier for the electromagnetic (em) force is the photon.

electromagnetic induction in electronics, the production of an ◊electromotive force (emf) in a circuit by a change of magnetic flux through the circuit or by relative motion of the circuit and the magnetic flux. In a closed circuit an ◊induced current will be produced. All dynamos and generators make use of this effect. When magnetic tape is driven past the playback head (a small coil) of a tape-recorder, the moving magnetic field induces an emf in the head, which is then amplified to reproduce the recorded sounds.

If the change of magnetic flux is due to a variation in the current flowing in the same circuit, the phenomenon is known as self-induction; if it is due to a change of current flowing in another circuit it is known as mutual induction.

electromagnetic waves oscillating electric and magnetic fields travelling together through space at a speed of nearly 300,000 km/186,000 mi per second. The (limitless) range of possible wavelengths or ◊frequencies of electromagnetic waves, which can be thought of as making up the electromagnetic spectrum, includes radio waves, infrared radiation, visible light, ultraviolet radiation, X-rays, and gamma rays.

electromotive force (emf) loosely, the voltage produced by an electric battery or generator or, more precisely, the energy supplied by a source of electric power in driving a unit charge around an electrical circuit. The unit is the ◊volt.

electron stable, negatively charged ◊elementary particle; it is a constituent of all atoms, and a member of the class of particles known as ◊leptons. The electrons in each atom surround the nucleus in groupings called shells; in a neutral atom the number of electrons is equal to the number of protons in the nucleus. This electron structure is responsible for the chemical properties of the atom (see ◊atomic structure).

Electrons are the basic particles of electricity. Each carries a charge of 1.602192×10^{-19} coulomb, and all electrical charges are multiples of this quantity. A beam of electrons will undergo ◊diffraction (scattering) and produce interference patterns in the same way as ◊electromagnetic waves such as light; hence they may also be regarded as waves.

electronegativity the ease with which an atom can attract electrons to itself. Electronegative elements attract electrons, so forming negative ions. Linus Pauling devised an electronegativity scale to indicate the relative power of attraction of elements for electrons. Fluorine, the most nonmetallic element, has a value of 4.0 on this scale; oxygen, the next most nonmetallic, has a value of 3.5.

electron gun a part in many electronic devices consisting of a series of ◊electrodes, including a cathode for producing an electron beam. It plays an essential role in ◊cathode-ray tubes (television tubes) and ◊electron microscopes.

electronic funds transfer (EFT) method of transferring funds automatically from one account to another by electronic means, for example ***electronic funds transfer at point of sale*** (EFTPOS), which provides for the automatic transfer of money from buyer to seller at the time of sale. For example, a customer inserts a plastic card into a point-of-sale computer terminal in a supermarket, and telephone lines are used to make an automatic debit from the customer's bank account to settle the bill.

electronic mail The basic structure of an electronic mail system. A message is sent via a telephone line and stored in a central computer. The message remains there until the recipient calls up the central computer and collects the message.

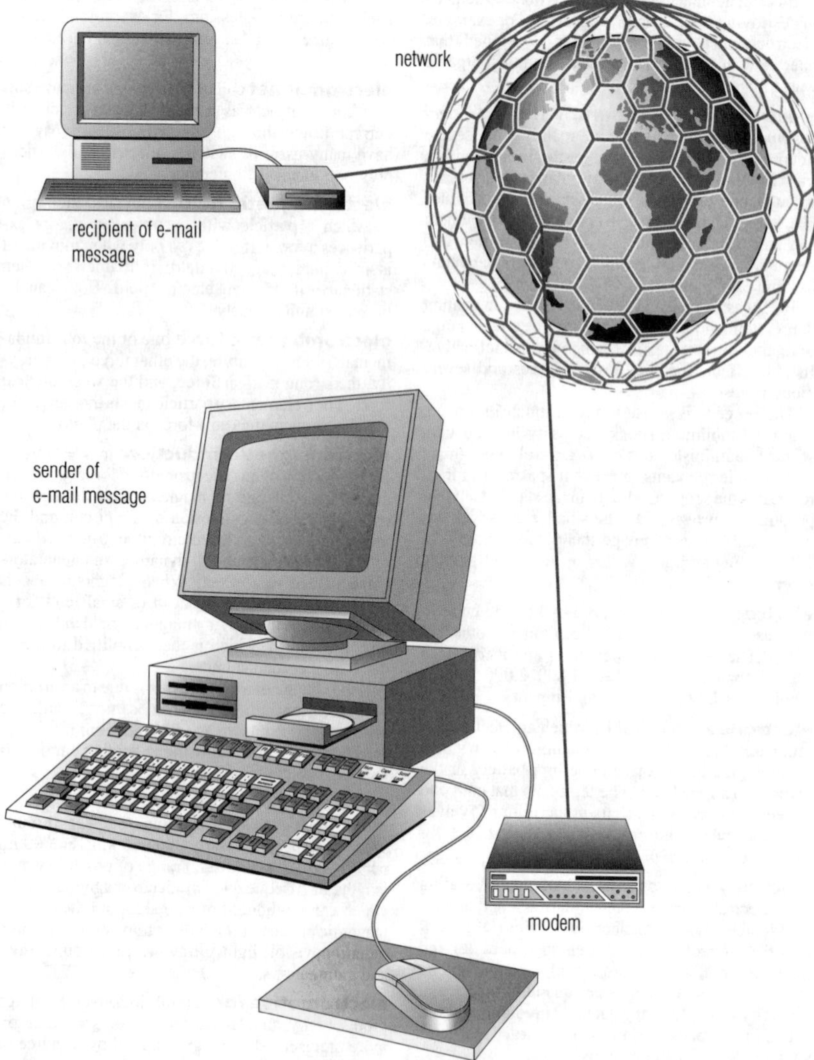

electronic mail or ***e-mail*** private messages sent electronically from computer to computer via network connections such as ◊Ethernet or the Internet, or via telephone lines to a host system. Messages once sent are stored on the network or by the host system until the recipient picks them up.

Subscribers to an electronic mail system type messages in ordinary letter form on a word processor, or microcomputer, and 'drop' the letters into a central computer's memory bank by means of a computer/telephone connector (a ◊modem). The recipient 'collects' the letter by calling up the central computer and feeding a unique password into the system.

electronic music term first applied 1954 to edited tape music composed primarily of electronically generated and modified tones, serially organized to objective scales of differentiation, to distinguish it from the more intuitive methodology of ◊concrete music. The term was subsequently extended to include prerecorded vocal and instrumental sounds organized in a similar way, as in Stockhausen's *Gesang der Jünglinge/Song of the Youths* 1955 and Berio's *Differences* for chamber ensemble and tape 1957. Other pioneers of electronic music are Milton Babbitt and Bruno Maderna. After 1960, with the arrival of the purpose-built synthesizer developed by Robert Moog, Peter Zinovieff, and others, interest switched to computer-aided synthesis, culminating in the 4X system installed at IRCAM, the Institute for Musico-Acoustic Research and Coordination in Paris.

electronic point of sale (EPOS) system used in retailing in which a bar code on a product is scanned at the cash till and the information relayed to the store computer. The computer will then relay back the price of the item to the cash till. The customer can then be given an itemized receipt while the computer removes the item from stock figures. EPOS enables efficient computer stock control and reordering as well as giving a wealth of information about turnover, profitability on different lines, stock ratios, and other important financial indicators.

electronic publishing the distribution of information using computer-based media such as ◊multimedia and ◊hypertext in the creation of electronic 'books'. Critical technologies in the development of electronic publishing were ◊CD-ROM, with its massive yet compact storage capabilities, and the advent of computer networking with its ability to deliver information instantaneously anywhere in the world.

electronics branch of science that deals with the emission of ◊electrons from conductors and ◊semiconductors, with the subsequent manipulation of these electrons, and with the construction of electronic devices. The first electronic device was the thermionic ◊valve, or vacuum tube, in which electrons moved in a vacuum, and led to such inventions as ◊radio, ◊television, ◊radar, and the digital ◊computer. Replacement of valves with the comparatively tiny and reliable transistor from 1948 revolutionized electronic development. Modern electronic devices are based on minute ◊integrated circuits (silicon chips), wafer-thin crystal slices holding tens of thousands of electronic components.

By using solid-state devices such as integrated circuits, extremely complex electronic circuits can be constructed, leading to the development of ◊digital watches, pocket calculators, powerful ◊microcomputers, and word processors.

electronic tagging see ◊tagging, electronic.

electron microscope instrument that produces a magnified image by using a beam of ◊electrons instead of light rays, as in an optical ◊microscope. An electron lens is an arrangement of electromagnetic coils that control and focus the beam. Electrons are not visible to the eye, so instead of an eyepiece there is a fluorescent screen or a photographic plate on which the electrons form an image. The wavelength of the electron beam is much shorter than that of light, so much greater magnification and resolution (ability to distinguish detail) can be achieved. The development of the electron microscope has made possible the observation of very minute organisms, viruses, and even large molecules.

A ◊transmission electron microscope passes the electron beam through a very thin slice of a specimen. A ◊scanning electron microscope looks at the exterior of a specimen. A ◊scanning transmission electron microscope (STEM) can produce a magnification of 90 million times. See also ◊atomic force microscope.

electron spin resonance in archaeology, a nondestructive dating method applicable to teeth, bone, heat-treated flint, ceramics, sediments, and stalagmitic concretions. It enables electrons, displaced by natural radiation and then trapped in the structure, to be measured; their number indicates the age of the specimen.

electron volt unit (symbol eV) for measuring the energy of a charged particle (◊ion or ◊electron) in terms of the energy of motion an electron would gain from a potential difference of one volt. Because it is so small, more usual units are mega-(million) and giga-(billion) electron volts (MeV and GeV).

electrophoresis the ◊diffusion of charged particles through a fluid under the influence of an electric field. It can be used in the biological sciences to separate ◊molecules of different sizes, which diffuse at different rates. In industry, electrophoresis is used in paint-dipping operations to ensure that paint reaches awkward corners.

electroplating deposition of metals upon metallic surfaces by electrolysis for decorative and/or protective purposes. It is used in the preparation of printers' blocks, 'master' audio discs, and in many other processes.

A current is passed through a bath containing a solution of a salt of the plating metal, the object to be plated being the cathode (negative terminal); the anode (positive terminal) is either an inert substance or the plating metal. Among the metals most commonly used for plating are zinc, nickel, chromium, cadmium, copper, silver, and gold.

In electropolishing, the object to be polished is made the anode in an electrolytic solution and by carefully controlling conditions the high spots on the surface are dissolved away, leaving a high-quality stain-free surface. This technique is useful in polishing irregular stainless-steel articles.

electropositivity in chemistry, a measure of the ability of elements (mainly metals) to donate electrons to form positive ions. The greater the metallic character, the more electropositive the element.

electroscope apparatus for detecting ◊electric charge. The simple gold-leaf electroscope consists of a vertical conducting (metal) rod ending in a pair of rectangular pieces of gold foil, mounted inside and insulated from an earthed metal case or glass jar. An electric charge applied to the end of the metal rod makes the gold leaves diverge, because they each receive a similar charge (positive or negative) and so repel each other.

The polarity of the charge can be found by bringing up another charge of known polarity and applying it to the metal rod. A like charge has no effect on the gold leaves, whereas an opposite charge neutralizes the charge on the leaves and causes them to collapse.

electrovalent bond another name for an ◊ionic bond, a chemical bond in which the combining atoms lose or gain electrons to form ions.

elegy ancient Greek verse form, originally combining a hexameter (a verse line of six metrical feet) with a shorter line in a couplet. It was used by the Greeks for ◊epigrams, short narratives, and discursive poems, and adopted by the Roman poets (◊Ovid, ◊Propertius), particularly for erotic verse. In contemporary usage, the term refers to a nostalgic poem or a lament, often a funeral poem. Thomas Gray's 'Elegy Written in a Country Church-Yard' 1751 is one of the best-known elegies in English.

element substance that cannot be split chemically into simpler substances. The atoms of a particular element all have the same number of protons in their nuclei (their ◊atomic number). Elements are classified in the ◊periodic table of the elements. Of the 112 known elements, 92 are known to occur in nature (those with atomic numbers 1–92). Those from 96 to 112 do not occur in nature and are synthesized only, produced in particle accelerators. Eighty-one of the elements are stable; all the others, which include atomic numbers 43, 61, and from 84 up, are radioactive.

Elements are classified as metals, nonmetals, or metalloids (weakly metallic elements) depending on a combination of their physical and chemical properties; about 75% are metallic. Some elements occur abundantly (oxygen, aluminium); others occur moderately or rarely (chromium, neon); some, in particular the radioactive ones, are found in minute (neptunium, plutonium) or very minute (technetium) amounts.

Symbols (devised by Swedish chemist Jöns ◊Berzelius) are used to denote the elements; the symbol is usually the first letter or letters of the English or Latin name (for example, C for carbon, Ca for calcium, Fe for iron, *ferrum*). The symbol represents one atom of the element.

According to current theories, hydrogen and helium were produced in the ◊Big Bang at the beginning of the universe. Of the other elements, those up to atomic number 26 (iron) are made by nuclear fusion within the stars. The more massive elements, such as lead and uranium, are produced when an old star explodes; as its centre collapses, the gravitational energy squashes nuclei together to make new elements.

ELECTRONICS: TIMELINE

1897	The electron was discovered by English physicist John Joseph Thomson.
1904	English physicist Ambrose Fleming invented the diode valve, which allows flow of electricity in one direction only.
1906	The triode electron valve, the first device to control an electric current, was invented by US physicist Lee De Forest.
1947	John Bardeen, William Shockley, and Walter Brattain invented the junction germanium transistor at the Bell Laboratories, New Jersey, USA.
1952	British physicist G W A Dunner proposed the integrated circuit.
1953	Jay Forrester of the Massachusetts Institute of Technology, USA, built a magnetic memory smaller than existing vacuum-tube memories.
1954	The silicon transistor was developed by Gordon Teal of Texas Instruments, USA.
1958	The first integrated circuit, containing five components, was built by US electrical physicist Jack Kilby.
1959	The planar transistor, which is built up in layers, or planes, was designed by Robert Noyce of Fairchild Semiconductor Corporation, USA.
1961	Steven Hofstein designed the field-effect transistor used in integrated circuits.
1971	The first microprocessor, the Intel 4004, was designed by Ted Hoff in the USA; it contained 2,250 components and could add two four-bit numbers in 11-millionths of a second.
1974	The Intel 8080 microprocessor was launched; it contained 4,500 components and could add two eight-bit numbers in 2.5-millionths of a second.
1979	The Motorola 68000 microprocessor was introduced; it contained 70,000 components and could multiply two 16-bit numbers in 3.2-millionths of a second.
1981	The Hewlett-Packard Superchip was introduced; it contained 450,000 components and could multiply two 32-bit numbers in 1.8-millionths of a second.
1985	The Inmos T414 transputer, the first microprocessor designed for use in parallel computers, was launched.
1988	The first optical microprocessor, which uses light instead of electricity, was developed.
1989	Wafer-scale silicon memory chips were introduced: the size of a beer mat, they are able to store 200 million characters.
1990	Memory chips capable of holding 4 million bits of information began to be mass-produced in Japan. The chips can store the equivalent of 520,000 characters, or the contents of a 16-page newspaper. Each chip contains 9 million components packed on a piece of silicon less than 15 mm long by 5 mm wide.
1992	Transistors made from high-temperature superconducting ceramics rather than semiconductors were produced in Japan by Sanyo Electric. The new transistors are ten times faster than semiconductor transistors.
1993	US firm Intel launched the Pentium 64-bit microprocessor. With two separate integer processing units that can run in parallel, it was several times faster than earlier processors.
1996	US researchers created the first all-plastic battery.

elementary particle in physics, a subatomic particle that is not made up of smaller particles, and is thus one of the fundamental units of matter. There are three groups of elementary particles: quarks, leptons, and gauge bosons.

Quarks, of which there are 12 types (up, down, charm, strange, top, and bottom, plus the antiparticles of each), combine in groups of three to produce heavy particles called baryons, and in groups of two to produce intermediate-mass particles called mesons. They and their composite particles are influenced by the strong nuclear force. ***Leptons*** are light particles. Again, there are 12 types: the electron, muon, tau; their neutrinos, the electron neutrino, muon neutrino, and tau neutrino; and the antiparticles of each. These particles are influenced by the weak nuclear force. ***Gauge bosons*** carry forces between other particles. There are four types: the gluons, photon, weakons, and graviton. The gluon carries the strong nuclear force, the photon the electromagnetic force, the weakons the weak nuclear force, and the graviton the force of gravity (see ◊forces, fundamental).

elements, the four earth, air, fire, and water. The Greek philosopher ◊Empedocles believed that these four elements made up the fundamental components of all matter and that they were destroyed and renewed through the action of love and discord.

This belief was shared by ◊Aristotle who also claimed that the elements were mutable and contained specific qualities: cold and dry for earth, hot and wet for air, hot and dry for fire, and cold and wet for water. The theory of the elements prevailed until the 17th century when Robert ◊Boyle redefined an element as a substance 'simple or unmixed, not made of other bodies' and proposed the existence of a greater number than four.

electron microscope The scanning electron microscope. Electrons from the electron gun are focused to a fine point on the specimen surface by the lens systems. The beam is moved across the specimen by the scan coils. Secondary electrons are emitted by the specimen surface and pass through the detector, which produces an electrical signal. The signal is passed to an electronic console, and produces an image on a television-like screen.

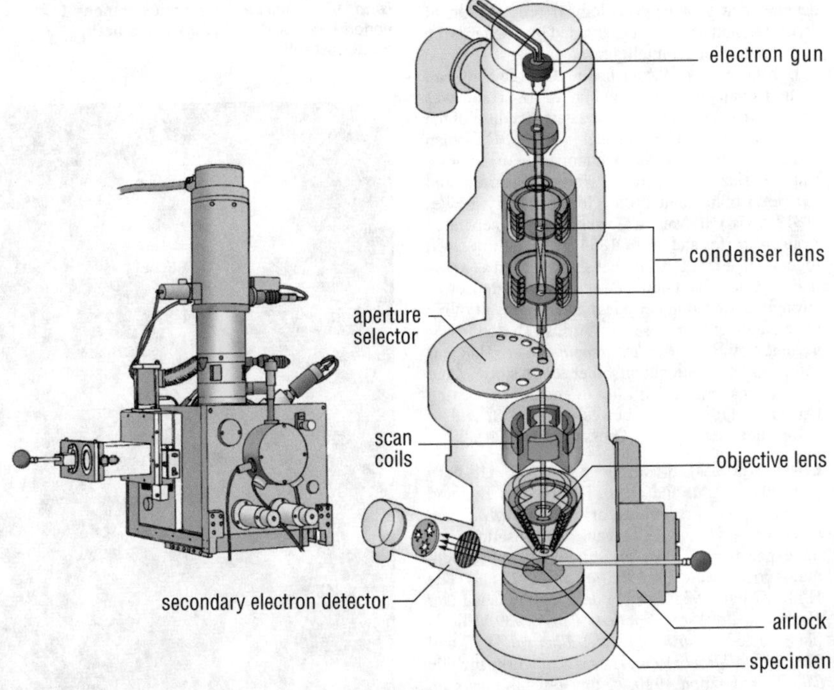

elephant mammal belonging to either of two surviving species of the order Proboscidea: the Asian elephant *Elephas maximus* and the African elephant *Loxodonta africana*. Elephants can grow to 4 m/13 ft and weigh up to 8 tonnes; they have a thick, grey, wrinkled skin, a large head, a long, flexible, prehensile trunk, used to obtain food and water, and upper incisors or tusks, which grow to a considerable length. The African elephant has very large ears and a flattened forehead, and the Asian species has smaller ears and a convex forehead. In India, Myanmar (Burma), and Thailand, Asiatic elephants are widely used for transport and logging.

Elephants are herbivorous, highly intelligent, and extremely social, living in matriarchal herds. The period of gestation is 19–22 months (the longest among mammals), and the lifespan is 60–70 years. Elephants have one of the lowest metabolic rates among placental mammals. Their tusks, which are initially tipped with enamel but later consist entirely of ivory, continue growing throughout life. They are preceded by milk tusks, which are shed at an early age.

Elephants are slaughtered needlessly for the ivory of their tusks, and this, coupled with the fact that they reproduce slowly and do not breed readily in captivity, is leading to their extinction. In Africa, overhunting caused numbers to collapse during the 1980s and the elephant population of E Africa is threatened with extinction. There were 1.3 million African elephants in 1981; fewer than 700,000 in 1988; and about 600,000 in 1990. They were placed on the ◊CITES list of most endangered species in 1989. A world ban on trade in ivory was imposed 1990. The Asian elephant is also listed on the CITES endangered list; its wild population 1996 was only 35,000–54,000. There are around 10,000 working elephants in Asia, most of which are caught from the wild and 'tamed' by starvation and brutality. *See illustration on following page.*

elephantiasis in the human body, a condition of local enlargement and deformity, most often of a leg, though the scrotum, vulva, or breast may also be affected.

The commonest form of elephantiasis is the tropical variety (filariasis) caused by infestation by parasitic roundworms (filaria); the enlargement is due to damage of the lymphatic system and consequent impaired immunity. The swelling reduces dramatically if the affected area is kept rigorously

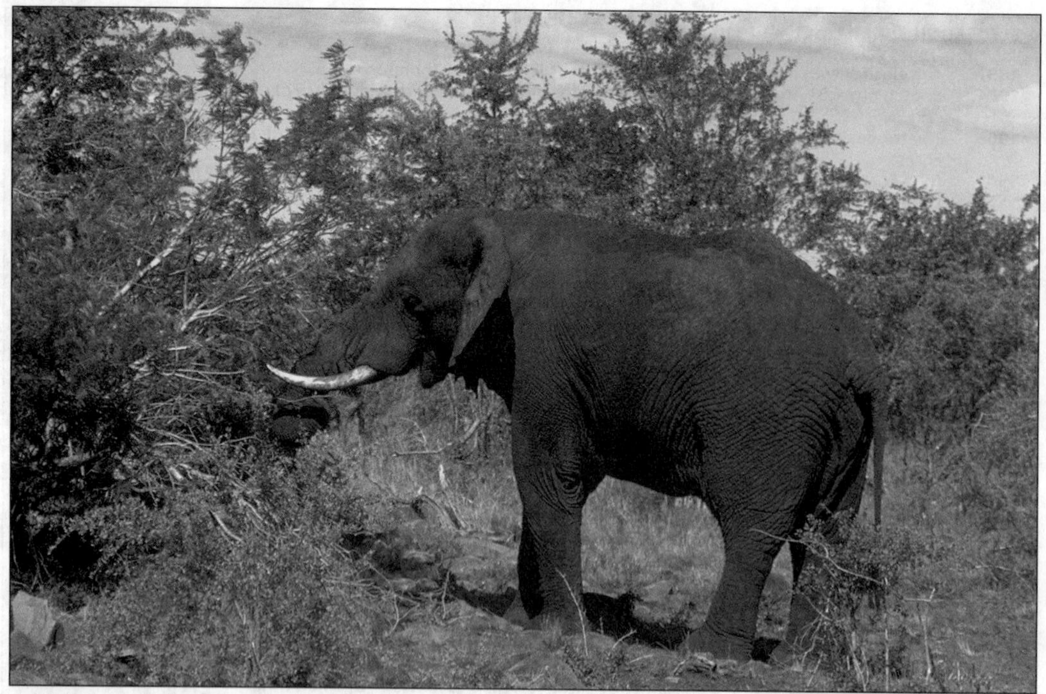

elephant With an enormous bulk to support, African elephants *Loxodonta africana* have to consume large quantities of vegetable matter every day. This elephant is stripping an acacia tree – an example of the damage that can be inflicted on the environment if elephants become too numerous. *Premaphotos Wildlife*

clean and treated with antibiotic cream, combined with rest, after drug treatment has killed all filarial worms.

Eleusinian Mysteries ceremonies in honour of the Greek deities ◊Demeter and ◊Persephone, celebrated in the precincts of the temple of Demeter at Eleusis, in the territory of Athens. Demeter was the Greek goddess of grain.

Eleven Plus examination test designed to select children for grammar school education in the UK, at the time when local authorities provided separate grammar, secondary modern, and occasionally technical schools for children over the age of 11. The examination became defunct on the introduction of ◊comprehensive schools in Scotland, Wales, and most of England during the 1960s and 1970s, although certain education authorities retain the selective system and the Eleven Plus.

Elgar Edward (William) 1857–1934. English composer whose *Enigma Variations* 1899 brought him lasting fame. Although his celebrated oratorio *The Dream of Gerontius* 1900 (based on the written work by theologian John Henry Newman) was initially unpopular in Britain, it was well received in Düsseldorf 1902, leading to a surge of interest in his earlier works, including the *Pomp and Circumstance Marches* 1901.

Among his later works are oratorios, two symphonies, a violin concerto, chamber music, songs, the symphonic poem *Falstaff* 1913, and the poignant cello concerto of 1919.

‘In every parting there is an image of death.’

GEORGE ELIOT
'Amos Barton', *Scenes of Clerical Life*

Elgar The English composer Edward Elgar. His works range from the dignified and publicly oriented *Pomp and Circumstance* marches and the First Symphony to the intimate and emotive *Dream of Gerontius* and the Cello Concerto. *Image Select (UK) Ltd*

Elgin marbles collection of ancient Greek sculptures, including the famous frieze and other sculptures from the Parthenon at Athens, assembled by the 7th Earl of Elgin. Sent to England 1803–1812, and bought for the nation 1816 for £35,000, they are now in the British Museum. Greece has repeatedly asked for them to be returned to Athens.

Elijah lived c. mid-9th century BC. In the Old Testament, a Hebrew prophet during the reigns of the Israelite kings Ahab and Ahaziah. He came from Gilead. He defeated the prophets of ◊Baal, and was said to have been carried up to heaven in a fiery chariot in a whirlwind. In Jewish belief, Elijah will return to Earth to herald the coming of the Messiah.

Eliot George. Pen name of Mary Ann (later Marian) Evans 1819–1880. English novelist. Her works include the pastoral *Adam Bede* 1859; *The Mill on the Floss* 1860, with its autobiographical elements; *Silas Marner* 1861, containing elements of the folk tale; and *Daniel Deronda* 1876. *Middlemarch*, published serially 1871–72, is considered her greatest novel for its confident handling of numerous characters and central social and moral issues. She developed a subtle psychological presentation of character, and her work is pervaded by a penetrating and compassionate intelligence.

Born in Astley, Warwickshire, George Eliot had a strict evangelical upbringing. In 1841 she was converted to ◊free thought. As assistant editor of the *Westminster Review* under John Chapman 1851–53, she made the acquaintance of Thomas Carlyle, Harriet Martineau, Herbert Spencer, and the philosopher and critic George Henry Lewes (1817–1878). Lewes was married but separated from his wife, and from 1854 he and Eliot lived together in a relationship that she regarded as a true marriage and that continued until his death. Lewes strongly believed in her talent and as a result of his encouragement the story 'Amos Barton' was accepted by *Blackwoods Magazine* 1857. This was followed by a number of other short stories, and their success persuaded Eliot to embark on writing her full-length novels. Lewes died 1878, and in 1880 Eliot married John Cross (1840–1924).

Eliot T(homas) S(tearns) 1888–1965. US-born poet, playwright, and critic. He lived in England from 1915. His first volume of poetry, *Prufrock and Other Observations* 1917, caused a sensation with its experimental form and rhythms; subsequent major poems were *The* ◊*Waste Land* 1922 and 'The Hollow Men' 1925. For children he published *Old Possum's Book of Practical Cats* 1939. Eliot's plays include *Murder in the Cathedral* 1935 and *The Cocktail Party* 1950. His critical works include *The Sacred Wood* 1920, setting out his views on poetic tradition. He won the Nobel Prize for Literature 1948.

Eliot was born in St Louis, Missouri, and was educated at Harvard, the Sorbonne, and Oxford. He married and settled in London 1917 and became a British subject 1927, joining the Anglo-Catholic movement within the Church of England the same year. He was for a time a bank clerk, later lecturing and entering publishing at Faber & Faber, where he became a director. As editor of the highly influential literary magazine *Criterion* 1922–39, he was responsible for a critical re-evaluation of metaphysical poetry and Jacobean drama, and wrote perceptively about such European poets as ◊Dante Alighieri, Charles ◊Baudelaire, and Jules ◊Laforgue.

Prufrock and Other Observations expressed the disillusionment of the generation affected by World War I. Eliot's reputation was established by the desolate modernity of *The Waste Land*, and 'The Hollow Men' continued on the same note. *Ash Wednesday* 1930 revealed a change in religious attitude and the *Four Quartets* 1944 confirmed his acceptance of the Christian faith. Among his other works are the dramas *The Confidential Clerk* 1953 and *The Elder Statesman* 1958. His collection *Old Possum's Book of Practical Cats* was used for the popular English composer Andrew Lloyd Webber's musical *Cats* 1981.

Elisha lived mid-9th century BC. In the Old Testament, a Hebrew prophet, successor to Elijah.

elite a small group with power in a society, having privileges and status above others. An elite may be cultural, educational, religious, political (also called 'the establishment' or 'the governing circles'), or social. Sociological interest has centred on how such minorities get, use, and hold on to power, and on what distinguishes elites from the rest of society.

Elizabeth ***the Queen Mother*** 1900– . Wife of King George VI of England. She was born Lady Elizabeth Angela Marguerite Bowes-Lyon, and on 26 April 1923 she married Albert, Duke of York, who became King George VI in 1936. Their children are Queen Elizabeth II and Princess Margaret.

She is the youngest daughter of the 14th Earl of Strathmore and Kinghorne (died 1944), through whom she is descended from Robert Bruce, king of Scotland. When her husband became King George VI she became Queen Consort, and was crowned with him 1937. She adopted the title Queen Elizabeth, the Queen Mother after his death.

Eliot US poet, critic, and dramatist T S Eliot, one of the major figures of 20th-century literature. Born in the USA, Eliot embraced British nationality, culture, and religious traditions. His early and most influential poems, *Prufrock* 1917 and *The Waste Land* 1922, portrayed the disillusionment engendered by World War I in a radically modernist style.

Elizabeth I Queen Elizabeth I of England on her accession to the throne 1558. Her reign was a time of great prosperity and relative tranquillity, despite the ongoing religious strife between Catholics and Protestants. Elizabeth had many suitors, both English and foreign, whose attentions she used to great advantage in both domestic and foreign politics. *Image Select (UK) Ltd*

Elizabeth I 1533–1603. Queen of England 1558–1603, the daughter of Henry VIII and Anne Boleyn. Through her Religious Settlement of 1559 she enforced the Protestant religion by law. The Elizabethan age was expansionist in commerce and geographical exploration, and arts and literature flourished. She was succeeded by James I.

Elizabeth was born at Greenwich, London, 7 Sept 1533. She was well educated in several languages. During the reign of her Roman Catholic half-sister Mary I (1553–58), Elizabeth's Protestant sympathies brought her under suspicion, and she lived in seclusion at Hatfield, Hertfordshire, until on Mary's death she became queen.

Many unsuccessful attempts were made by Parliament to persuade Elizabeth to marry or settle the succession. The rulers of many European states made unsuccessful bids to marry Elizabeth. She found courtship a useful political weapon, and she maintained friendships with, among others, the courtiers ◊Leicester, Sir Walter ◊Raleigh, and ◊Essex. She was known as the Virgin Queen.

The arrival in England 1568 of Mary Queen of Scots and her imprisonment by Elizabeth caused a political crisis, and a rebellion of the feudal nobility of the north followed 1569. Friction between English and Spanish sailors hastened the breach with Spain. When the Dutch rebelled against Spanish tyranny Elizabeth secretly encouraged them; Philip II retaliated by aiding Catholic conspiracies against her. This undeclared war continued for many years, until the landing of an English army in the Netherlands 1585 and Mary's execution 1587, brought it into the open. Philip's Armada (the fleet sent to invade England 1588) met with total disaster.

The war with Spain continued to the end of the reign, while events at home foreshadowed the conflicts of the 17th century. Among the Puritans discontent was developing with Elizabeth's religious settlement, and several were imprisoned or executed. Parliament showed a new independence, and in 1601 forced Elizabeth to retreat on the question of the crown granting manufacturing and trading monopolies. Yet her prestige remained unabated, as shown by the failure of Essex's rebellion 1601.

Elizabeth II (Elizabeth Alexandra Mary) 1926– . Queen of Great Britain and Northern Ireland from 1952, the elder daughter of George VI. She married her third cousin, Philip, the Duke of Edinburgh, 1947. They have four children: Charles, Anne, Andrew, and Edward.

Princess Elizabeth Alexandra Mary was born in London 21 April 1926; she was educated privately, and assumed official duties at 16.

During World War II she served in the Auxiliary Territorial Service, and by an amendment to the Regency Act she became a state counsellor on her 18th birthday. On the death of George VI in 1952 she succeeded to the throne while in Kenya with her husband and was crowned on 2 June 1953.

With an estimated wealth of £5 billion (1994), the Queen is the richest woman in Britain, and probably the world. In April 1993 she voluntarily began paying full rates of income tax and capital gains on her private income, which chiefly consists of the proceeds of a share portfolio and is estimated to be worth around £45 million.

Elizabeth 1709–1762. Empress of Russia from 1741, daughter of Peter the Great. She carried through a palace revolution and supplanted her cousin, the infant Ivan VI (1730–1764), on the throne. She continued the policy of westernization begun by Peter and allied herself with Austria against Prussia.

Elizabethan architecture see ◊English architecture.

Elizabethan literature literature produced during the reign of Elizabeth I of England (1558–1603), characterized by a new energy, richness, and confidence. Renaissance humanism, Protestant zeal, and geographical discovery all contributed to this upsurge of creative power. Drama was the dominant form of the age, and ◊Shakespeare and ◊Marlowe were popular with all levels of society. Other writers of the period include Edmund Spenser, Sir Philip Sidney, Francis Bacon, Thomas Lodge, Robert Greene, and John Lyly.

During this period, the resources of English were increased by the free adoption of words from Latin. There was a balance between the university and courtly elements and the coarse gusto of popular culture. Music was closely related to literature, and competence in singing and musical composition was seen as a normal social skill. Successive editions of the Bible were produced during these years, written with dignity, vividness, and the deliberate intention of reaching a universal audience.

elk large deer *Alces alces* inhabiting N Europe, Asia, Scandinavia, and North America, where it is known as the moose. It is brown in colour, stands about 2 m/6 ft at the shoulders, has very large palmate antlers, a fleshy muzzle, short neck, and long legs. It feeds on leaves and shoots. In North America, the ◊wapiti is called an elk.

Ellesmere second largest island of the Canadian Arctic archipelago, Northwest Territories; area 212,687 sq km/82,097 sq mi. It is for the most part barren or glacier-covered.

Elizabeth II Elizabeth II, Queen of Great Britain and Northern Ireland. As a constitutional monarch, representing the supreme legal and political authority, she summons and dissolves Parliament, gives her official approval to acts of Parliament, sanctions government judicial appointments, and confers honours and awards. She is the head of the Commonwealth, and is queen of Canada, New Zealand, Australia, and several other countries. *Topham*

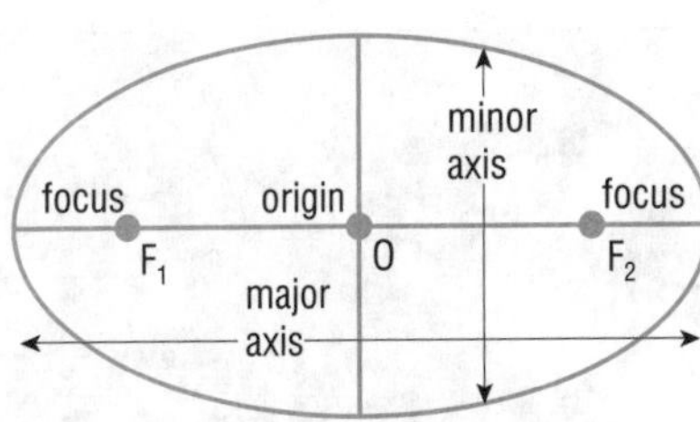

ellipse Technical terms used to describe the ellipse; for all points on the ellipse, the sum of the distances from the two foci, F_1 and F_2, is the same.

Ellice Islands former name of ◊Tuvalu, a group of islands in the W Pacific Ocean.

Ellington Duke (Edward Kennedy) 1899–1974. US pianist. He had an outstanding career as a composer and arranger of jazz. He wrote numerous pieces for his own jazz orchestra, accentuating the strengths of individual virtuoso instrumentalists, and became one of the leading figures in jazz over a 55-year period. Some of his most popular compositions include 'Mood Indigo', 'Sophisticated Lady', 'Solitude', and 'Black and Tan Fantasy'. He was one of the founders of big-band jazz.

'Though God hath raised me high, yet this I count the glory of my crown: that I have reigned with your loves.'

ELIZABETH I
The Golden Speech
1601

ellipse curve joining all points (loci) around two fixed points (foci) such that the sum of the distances from those points is always constant. The diameter passing through the foci is the major axis, and the diameter bisecting this at right angles is the minor axis. An ellipse is one of a series of curves known as ◊conic sections. A slice across a cone that is not made parallel to, and does not pass through, the base will produce an ellipse.

Ellis Island island in New York Harbor, USA; area 11 hectares/27 acres. A former reception centre for steerage-class immigrants during the immigration waves between 1892 and 1943 (12 million people passed through it 1892–1924), it was later used as a detention centre for nonresidents without documentation, or for those who were being deported. It is a National Historic Site (1964) and has the Museum of Immigration (1989). The island was named after a Welshman, Samuel Ellis, who owned it in the late 18th century. *See illustration on following page.*

Ellison Ralph Waldo 1914–1994. US novelist. His *Invisible Man* 1952 portrays with humour and energy the plight of a black man whom postwar American society cannot acknowledge. It is regarded as one of the most impressive novels published in the USA in the 1950s. He also wrote essays collected in *Shadow and Act* 1964. The success of his work encouraged the development of black literature in the 1950s and 1960s.

Ellora archaeological site in Maharashtra State, India, with 35 sculpted and decorated temple caves – ◊Buddhist, ◊Hindu, and ◊Jainist – dating from the late 6th century to the 10th century. They include Visvakarma (a hall about 26 m/86 ft long containing an image of the Buddha), Tin Thal (a three-storeyed Buddhist monastery cave), the Rameswara cave (with beautiful sculptures), and Siva's Paradise, the great temple of Kailasa.

elm any tree of the genus *Ulmus* of the family Ulmaceae, found in temperate regions of the N hemisphere and in mountainous parts of the tropics. All have doubly-toothed leaf margins and bear clusters of small flowers. Most elms reproduce not by seed but by suckering (new shoots arising from the root system). This nonsexual reproduction results in an enormous variety of forms.

The fungus disease *Ceratocystis ulmi*, known as Dutch elm disease because of a severe outbreak in the Netherlands 1924, has reduced the numbers of elm trees in Europe and North America. It is carried from tree to tree by beetles. Elms were widespread throughout Europe to about 4000 BC, when they suddenly disappeared and were not again common until the 12th century. This may have been due to an earlier epidemic of Dutch elm disease.

The common English elm *Ulmus procera* is widely distributed throughout Europe. It reaches 35 m/115 ft, with tufts of small, purplish-brown flowers, which appear before the leaves. *See illustration on following page.*

'The children will not leave unless I do. I shall not leave unless their father does, and the King will not leave the country in any circumstances whatever.'

ELIZABETH THE QUEEN MOTHER
Reply when asked if she would send her children out of England following German bombing of Buckingham Palace

El Niño (Spanish 'the child') warm ocean surge of the ◊Peru Current, so called because it tends to occur at Christmas, recurring every 5–8 years or so

Ellis Island The Immigration Registration room, Ellis Island, New York, 1912. During its 50 years as a reception centre, over 20 million immigrants entered the USA through Ellis Island. A rapidly growing economy and the desire for cheap labour encouraged a relaxed policy of immigration, though the influx of millions of immigrants raised fears about the USA's ability to integrate so many diverse cultures. *Corbis*

in the E Pacific off South America. It involves a change in the direction of ocean currents, which prevents the upwelling of cold, nutrient-rich waters along the coast of Ecuador and Peru. It is an important factor in global weather.

El Niño is believed to be caused by the failure of trade winds and, consequently, of the ocean currents normally driven by these winds. Warm surface waters then flow in from the east. The phenomenon can disrupt the climate of the area, and has played a part in causing famine in Indonesia, drought and bush fires in the Galápagos Islands, rainstorms in California and South America, the destruction of Peru's anchovy harvest and wildlife 1982–1983, algal blooms in Australia's drought-stricken rivers, and an unprecedented number of typhoons in Japan 1991.

El Niño usually lasts for about 18 months, but the 1990 occurrence lasted until June 1995; US climatologists estimated this duration to be the longest in 2,000 years. The last prolonged El Niño 1939–41 caused extensive drought and famine in Bengal.

‘In giving freedom to the slave, we assure freedom to the free, honourable alike in what we give and what we preserve.’

On EMANCIPATION Abraham Lincoln to Congress 1 Dec 1862

elongation in astronomy, the angular distance between the Sun and a planet or other solar-system object as seen from Earth. This angle is 0° at ◊conjunction, 90° at ◊quadrature, and 180° at ◊opposition.

El Paso city in Texas, USA, situated at the base of the Franklin Mountains, on the Rio Grande, opposite the Mexican city of Ciudad Juárez; population (1992) 543,800. It is the centre of an agricultural and cattle-raising area, and there are electronics, food processing, packing, and leather industries, as well as oil refineries and industries based on local iron and copper mines.

El Salvador country in Central America, bounded N and E by Honduras, S and SW by the Pacific Ocean, and NW by Guatemala. *See country box opposite.*

Elton Charles Sutherland 1900–1991. British ecologist, a pioneer of the study of animal and plant forms in their natural environments, and of animal behaviour as part of the complex pattern of life. He defined the concept of ◊food chains and was an early conservationist, instrumental in establishing the Nature Conservancy Council 1949, and much concerned with the impact of introduced species on natural systems.

elm The English elm has the typical elm leaf, oval, toothed, and distinctly lopsided. The seed is surrounded by a yellowish petal-like wing.

Eluard Paul. Pen name of Eugène Grindel 1895–1952. French poet. He expressed the suffering of poverty in his verse, and was a leader of the Surrealists (see ◊Surrealism). He fought in World War I, which inspired his *Poèmes pour la paix/Poems for Peace* 1918, and was a member of the Resistance in World War II. His books include *Poésie et vérité/Poetry and Truth* 1942 and *Au Rendezvous allemand/To the German Rendezvous* 1944.

Elysée Palace ***(Palais de l'Elysée)*** building in Paris erected 1718 for Louis d'Auvergne, Count of Evreux. It was later the home of Mme de Pompadour, Napoleon I, and Napoleon III, and became the official residence of the presidents of France 1870, though President Mitterrand chose not to live there.

Elysium in Greek mythology, originally another name for the Islands of the Blessed, to which favoured heroes were sent by the gods to enjoy a life after death. It was later a region in ◊Hades.

emancipation being liberated, being set free from servitude or subjection of any kind. The changing role of women in social, economic, and particularly in political terms, in the 19th and 20th centuries is sometimes referred to as the 'emancipation of women' (see ◊women's movement).

In the UK, the 1829 Catholic Emancipation Act freed Roman Catholics from the civil disabilities imposed on them by English law. In 1861 the emancipation of Russian serfs was proclaimed. In 1862 President Abraham Lincoln issued an edict freeing all slaves in the Confederate states, known as the Emancipation Proclamation; the Thirteenth Amendment of the Constitution declared the abolition of slavery throughout the USA.

Emancipation Proclamation in US history, President Lincoln's Civil War announcement, 22 Sept 1862, stating that from the beginning of 1863 all black slaves in states still engaged in rebellion against the federal government would be emancipated. Slaves in border states still remaining loyal to the Union were excluded. ▷*See feature on pp. 982–983.*

Emanuel David 1952– . and Elizabeth 1953– . British fashion designers who opened their own salon 1977. They specialized in off-the-shoulder, ornate and opulent evening wear. In 1981 Lady Diana Spencer, now Princess of Wales, commissioned the Emanuels to design her wedding dress. In 1990 Elizabeth Emanuel established her own label in London, continuing to design outfits for singers, actresses, and members of the British royal family.

embargo the legal prohibition by a government of trade with another country, forbidding foreign ships to leave or enter its ports. Trade embargoes may be imposed on a country seen to be violating international laws.

The US Embargo Act 1807 was passed to prevent France and the UK taking measures to stop US ships carrying war weapons to European belligerents. It proved to be a counterproductive move, as did an embargo by Middle Eastern oil producers on oil shipments to W Europe in 1974. A United Nations oil and arms embargo was imposed against the military regime in Haiti 1993–94 and international economic embargoes were imposed against Serbia in 1992–95.

embezzlement in law, theft by an employee of property entrusted to him or her by an employer.

In British law it is no longer a distinct offence from theft.

embolism blockage of a blood vessel by an obstruction called an embolus (usually a blood clot, fat particle, or bubble of air).

embroidery the art of decorating cloth with a needle and thread. It includes broderie anglaise, gros point, and petit point, all of which have been used for the adornment of costumes, gloves, book covers, furnishings, and ecclesiastical vestments.

The earliest embroidery that survives in England is the stole and maniple (a decorative strip of silk worn over the arm), found in the tomb of St Cuthbert in Durham and dating from 905. The ◊Bayeux Tapestry is an embroidery dating from 1067–70.

embryo The development of a bird and a human embryo. In the human, division of the fertilized egg, or ovum, begins within hours of conception. Within a week, a hollow, fluid-containing ball – a blastocyst – with a mass of cells at one end has developed. After the third week, the embryo has changed from a mass of cells into a recognizable shape. At four weeks, the embryo is 3 mm/0.1 in long, with a large bulge for the heart and small pits for the ears. At six weeks, the embryo is 1.5 cm/0.6 in with a pulsating heart and ear flaps. By the eighth week, the embryo (now technically a fetus) is 2.5 cm/1 in long and recognizably human, with eyelids and small fingers and toes.

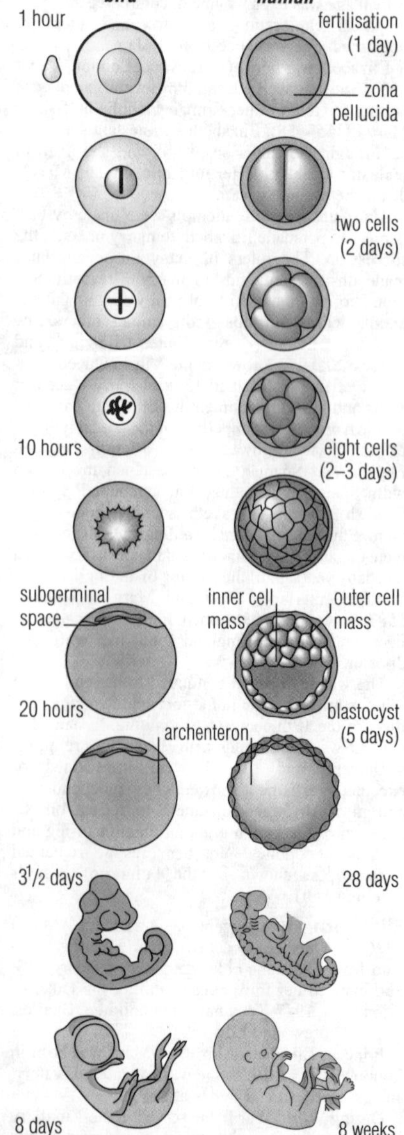

embryo early developmental stage of an animal or a plant following fertilization of an ovum (egg cell), or activation of an ovum by ◊parthenogenesis. In humans, the term embryo describes the fertilized egg during its first seven weeks of existence; from the eighth week onwards it is referred to as a fetus.

In animals the embryo exists either within an egg (where it is nourished by food contained in the yolk), or in mammals, in the ◊uterus of the mother. In mammals (except marsupials) the embryo is fed through the ◊placenta. The plant embryo is found within the seed in higher plants. It sometimes consists of only a few cells, but usually includes a root, a shoot (or primary bud), and one or two ◊cotyledons, which nourish the growing seedling.

embryology study of the changes undergone by an organism from its conception as a fertilized ovum (egg) to its emergence into the world at hatching or birth. It is mainly concerned with the changes in cell organization in the embryo and the way in which these lead to the structures and organs of the adult (the process of ◊differentiation).

Applications of embryology include embryo transplants, both commercial (for example, in building up a prize dairy-cow herd quickly at low cost) and in obstetric medicine (as a method for helping couples with fertility problems to have children).

embryo research the study of human embryos at an early stage, in order to detect hereditary disease and genetic defects, and to investigate the problems of subfertility and infertility. Eggs are fertilized in vitro (see ◊in vitro fertilization) and allowed to grow to the eight-cell stage. One or two cells are then removed for analysis. Diseases that can be tested for include cystic fibrosis, Duchenne's muscular dystrophy, Lesch-Nyhan syndrome, Tay-Sachs disease, and haemophilia A. If the embryo appears healthy it is transferred to the mother.

The Warnock Report 1984 proposed to limit experiment to up to 14 days after fertilization (the point at which it becomes possible to determine whether the embryo will become a single individual or a multiple birth). In 1990 the UK Parliament voted to continue to allow experiments on embryos up to 14 days old, under the control of the Human Fertilization and Embryology Authority.

embryo sac large cell within the ovule of flowering plants that represents the female ◊gametophyte when fully developed. It typically contains eight nuclei. Fertilization occurs when one of these nuclei, the egg nucleus, fuses with a male ◊gamete.

emerald a clear, green gemstone variety of the mineral ◊beryl. It occurs naturally in Colombia, the Ural Mountains, in Russia, Zimbabwe, and Australia.

emeritus (Latin) someone who has retired from an official position but retains their title on an honorary basis: for example, a professor emeritus.

Emerson Ralph Waldo 1803–1882. US philosopher, essayist, and poet. He settled in Concord, Massachusetts, which he made a centre of ◊transcendentalism, and wrote *Nature* 1836, which states the movement's main principles emphasizing the value of self-reliance and the godlike nature of human souls. His two volumes of *Essays* (1841, 1844) made his reputation: 'Self-Reliance' and 'Compensation' in the earlier volume are among the best known.

Born in Boston, Massachusetts, and educated at Harvard, Emerson became a Unitarian minister 1829. In 1832 he resigned and travelled to Europe, meeting the British writers Thomas Carlyle, Samuel Coleridge, and William Wordsworth. On his return to Massachusetts in 1833 he settled in Concord. He worked alongside Margaret Fuller (1810–1850), William Channing (1780–1842), and Henry ◊Thoreau to develop transcendentalism, particularly its

embroidery A piece of Hungarian embroidery with a floral motif. Such decorative needlework has traditionally been a feature of folk costumes and accessories, as well as home furnishings and ecclesiastical vestments. Designs may be abstract or pictorial; texts can also be worked in embroidery. *Corbis*

EL SALVADOR
Republic of

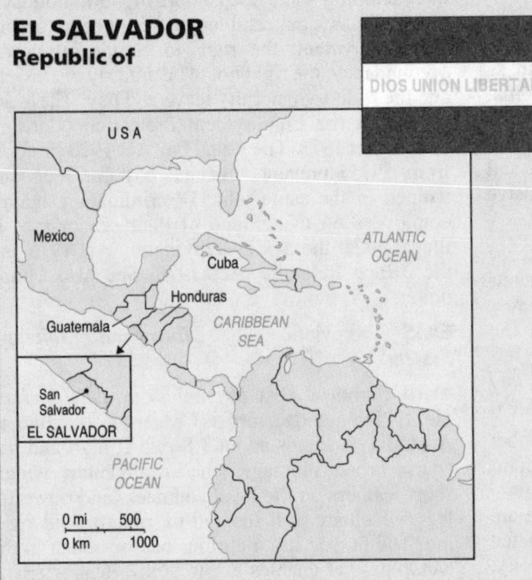

national name *República de El Salvador*
area 21,393 sq km/8,258 sq mi
capital San Salvador
major towns/cities Santa Ana, San Miguel, Nueva San Salvador
physical features narrow coastal plain, rising to mountains in N with central plateau
head of state and government Armando Calderón Sol from 1994
political system emergent democracy
administrative divisions 14 departments
political parties Christian Democrats (PDC), anti-imperialist; Farabundo Martí Liberation Front (FMLN), left-wing; National Republican Alliance (ARENA), extreme right-wing; National Conciliation Party (PCN), right-wing
population 5,768,000 (1995 est)
population growth rate 2.2% (1990–95); 2.0% (2000–05)
ethnic distribution about 92% of the population are mestizos, 6% Indians, and 2% of European origin
life expectancy 64 (males), 69 (females)
literacy rate men 76%, women 70%
languages Spanish, Nahuatl
religions Roman Catholic, Protestant
currency Salvadorean colón
GDP (US $) 8.13 billion (1994)
growth rate 6.0% (1994)
exports coffee, cotton, sugar

HISTORY
11th C Pipils, descendants of the Nahuatl-speaking Toltec and Aztec Indians of Mexico, settled in the country and came to dominate El Salvador until the Spanish conquest.
1524 Conquered by the Spanish adventurer Pedro de Alvarado and made a Spanish colony, with Indian resistance being crushed by 1540.
1821 Independence achieved from Spain; briefly joined with Mexico.
1823 Became part of United Provinces (Federation) of Central America, also embracing Costa Rica, Guatemala, Honduras, and Nicaragua.
1833 Unsuccessful Indian rebellion against Spanish control of land led by Anastasio Aquino.
1841 Became fully independent following dissolution of the Federation.
1859–63 Coffee growing introduced by president Gerardo Barrios.
1932 Peasant uprising, led by Augustín Farabundo Martí, suppressed by military at a cost of the lives of 30,000 Indians and peasants, virtually eliminating native Salvadoreans.
1961 Following a coup, the right-wing National Conciliation Party (PCN) established and in power.
1969 Brief 'Football War' with Honduras, which El Salvador attacked, at the time of a football competition between the two states, following evictions of thousands of Salvadoran illegal immigrants from Honduras.
1977 Allegations of human-rights violations; growth of left-wing Farabundo Martí National Liberation Front (FMLN) guerrilla activities. General Carlos Romero elected president.
1979 A coup replaced Romero with a military-civilian junta.
1980 The archbishop of San Salvador and human rights champion, Oscar Romero, assassinated; country on verge of civil war. José Napoleón Duarte (PDC) became first civilian president since 1931.
1981 Mexico and France recognized the FMLN guerrillas as a legitimate political force, but the USA actively assisted the government in its battle against them; 30,000 were killed 1979–81 by right-wing death squads.
1982 Assembly elections boycotted by left-wing parties. Held amid violence, they were won by far-right National Republican Alliance (ARENA).
1984 Duarte won presidential election.
1986 Duarte sought a negotiated settlement with the guerrillas.
1989 Alfredo Cristiani (ARENA) became president in rigged elections; rebel attacks intensified.
1991 United Nations-sponsored peace accord signed by representatives of the government and the socialist guerrilla group, the FMLN, which now became a political party.
1992 Border dispute with Honduras dating from 1861 finally resolved.
1993 UN-sponsored commission published report on war atrocities; government amnesty cleared those implicated; top military leaders officially retired.
1994 Armando Calderón Sol (ARENA) elected president.
1998 Hurricane Mitch struck 30 Oct, severely affecting agriculture and property.

Emerson US poet and essayist Ralph Waldo Emerson, who became the central figure of New England Transcendentalism – a movement rooted in mystic idealism and reverence for nature. His writings have been influential on American thought; he urged intellectual independence from Europe and was later active in the anti-slavery campaign. *Corbis*

One babe commonly makes four or five out of the adults who prattle and play to it.

RALPH WALDO EMERSON
'Self-Reliance' in *Essays*

theological aspects, as a protest against dogmatic rationalism in religion. In 1840 he helped to launch the literary magazine *The Dial*, which he also edited for a time. He made a second visit to England 1847 and incorporated his impressions in *English Traits* 1856. His poetry, much of which was published in *The Dial*, includes 'The Rhodora', 'Threnody', and 'Brahma'. His later works include *Representative Men* 1850 and *The Conduct of Life* 1870.

emery greyish-black opaque metamorphic rock consisting of ◊corundum and magnetite, together with other minerals such as hematite. It is used as an ◊abrasive.

Emery occurs on the island of Naxos, Greece, and in Turkey.

Emery (Walter) Bryan 1903–1971. British archaeologist, who in 1929–34 in ◊Nubia, N Africa, excavated the barrows at Ballana and Qustol, rich royal tombs of the mysterious X-group people (3rd to 6th centuries AD). He also surveyed the whole region 1963–64 before it was flooded as a result of the building of the Aswan High Dam.

emetic any substance administered to induce vomiting. Emetics are used to empty the stomach in many cases of deliberate or accidental drug overdose. The most frequently used is ipecacuanha.

emf in physics, abbreviation for ◊***electromotive force***.

emu A flightless bird, the emu is found on the open plains and in the forests of Australia. *Australian Overseas Information Office*

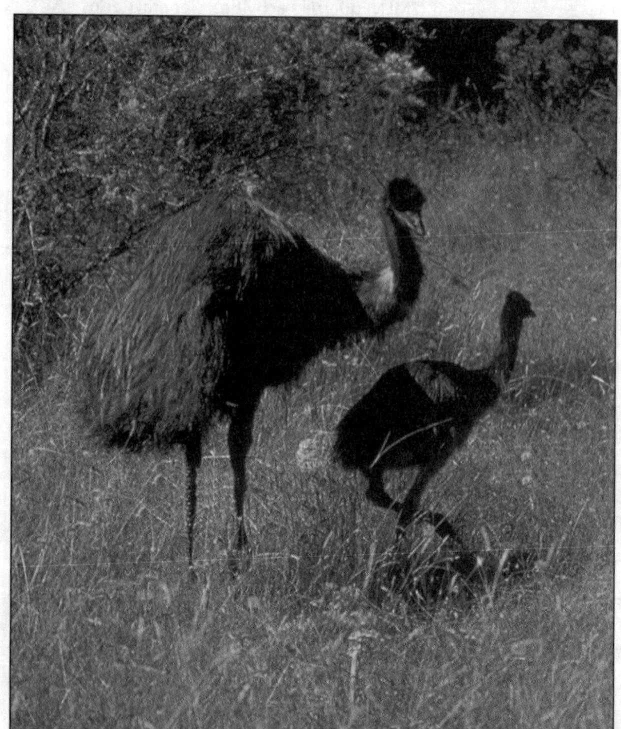

emigration the departure of persons from one country, usually their native land, to settle permanently in another. (See ◊immigration and emigration).

Emilia-Romagna region of N central Italy including much of the Po Valley; area 22,100 sq km/8,531 sq mi; population (1992) 3,920,200. The capital is Bologna; other towns include Reggio, Rimini, Parma, Ferrara, and Ravenna. Agricultural produce includes fruit, wine, sugar beet, beef, and dairy products; oil and natural-gas resources have been developed in the Po Valley.

Emin Pasha Mehmed. Adopted name of Eduard Schnitzer 1840–1892. German explorer, physician, and linguist. Appointed by British general Charles Gordon chief medical officer and then governor of the Equatorial province of S Sudan, he carried out extensive research in anthropology, botany, zoology, and meteorology.

Schnitzer practised medicine in Albania. In 1876 he joined the Egyptian Service, where he was known as Emin Pasha. Isolated by his remote location in Sudan and cut off from the outside world by Arab slave traders, he was 'rescued' by an expedition led by H M Stanley in 1889. He travelled with Stanley as far as Zanzibar but returned to continue his work near Lake Victoria. Three years later he was killed while leading an expedition to the W coast of Africa.

Emmental district in the valley of the Emme River, Berne, Switzerland, where a hard cheese of the same name has been made since the mid-15th century. The main town in Emmental is Langnau.

Emmet Robert 1778–1803. Irish nationalist leader. In 1803 he led an unsuccessful revolt in Dublin against British rule and was captured, tried, and hanged. His youth and courage made him an Irish hero.

emoticon (contraction of ***emotion and icon***) symbol composed of punctuation marks designed to express some form of emotion in the form of a human face. Emoticons were invented by e-mail users to overcome the fact that such communication cannot convey the nonverbal information (body language or vocal intonation) used in ordinary speech. The following examples should be viewed sideways:

:-) smiling :-O shouting :-(glum 8-) wearing glasses and smiling

emotion in psychology, a powerful feeling; a complex state of body and mind involving, in its bodily aspect, changes in the viscera (main internal organs) and in facial expression and posture, and in its mental aspect, heightened perception, excitement and, sometimes, disturbance of thought and judgement. The urge to action is felt and impulsive behaviour may result.

emotivism a philosophical position in the theory of ethics. Emotivists deny that moral judgements can be true or false, maintaining that they merely express an attitude or an emotional response. The concept came to prominence during the 1930s, largely under the influence of *Language, Truth and Logic* 1936 by the English philosopher A J ◊Ayer.

Empedocles c. 493–433 BC. Greek philosopher and scientist who proposed that the universe is composed of four elements – fire, air, earth, and water – which through the action of love and discord are eternally constructed, destroyed, and constructed anew. He lived in Acragas (Agrigentum), Sicily, and according to tradition, he committed suicide by throwing himself into the crater of Mount Etna.

emphysema incurable lung condition characterized by disabling breathlessness. Progressive loss of the thin walls dividing the air spaces (alveoli) in the lungs reduces the area available for the exchange of oxygen and carbon dioxide, causing the lung tissue to expand. The term 'emphysema' can also refer to the presence of air in other body tissues.

Emphysema is most often seen at an advanced stage of chronic ◊bronchitis, although it may develop in other long-standing diseases of the lungs. It destroys lung tissue, leaving behind scar tissue in the form of air blisters called bullae. As the disease progresses, the bullae occupy more and more space in the chest cavity, inflating the lungs and causing severe breathing difficulties. The bullae may be removed surgically, and since early 1994 US trials have achieved measured success using lasers to eliminate them in a procedure called lung-reduction pneumenoplasty (LRP). Lasers are particularly useful where the emphysema is diffuse and bullae are interspersed within healthy tissue. As LRP is a less invasive process, survival rates are improved (90% compared with 75% for conventional surgery) and patients are quicker to recover.

Empire style French decorative arts style prevalent during the rule of the emperor Napoleon Bonaparte (1804–14). A late form of ◊Neo-Classicism, it featured motifs drawn from ancient Egyptian as well as Greek and Roman art. Dark woods and draperies were also frequently used. The influence of the style extended through Europe and North America.

empiricism (Greek *empeiria* 'experience' or 'experiment') in philosophy, the belief that all knowledge is ultimately derived from sense experience. It is suspicious of metaphysical schemes based on a priori propositions, which are claimed to be true irrespective of experience. It is frequently contrasted with ◊rationalism. Empiricism developed in the 17th and early 18th centuries through the work of John ◊Locke, George ◊Berkeley, and David ◊Hume, traditionally known as the British empiricist school.

employment exchange agency for bringing together employers requiring labour and workers seeking employment. Employment exchanges may be organized by central government or by a local authority (known in the UK as Jobcentres), or as private business ventures (employment agencies).

employment law law covering the rights and duties of employers and employees. During the 20th century, statute law rather than common law has increasingly been used to give new rights to employees. Industrial tribunals are statutory bodies that adjudicate in disputes between employers and employees or trade unions and deal with complaints concerning unfair dismissal, sex or race discrimination, and equal pay.

The first major employment legislation in Britain was in the 19th century, regulating conditions in factories. Legislation in this area culminated in the Health and Safety at Work Act 1974, which set up the Health and Safety Commission. Other employees' rights include the right to a formal contract detailing wage rates, hours of work, holidays, injury and sick pay, and length of notice to terminate employment; the right to compensation for ◊redundancy; the right not to be unfairly dismissed; and the right to maternity leave and pay. These are set out in the Employment Protection (Consolidation) Act 1978. The Equal Pay Act 1970 (in force from 1975) prevents unequal pay for men and women in the same jobs. Discrimination against employees on the ground of their sex or race is illegal under the Sex Discrimination Act 1975 and the ◊Race Relations Act 1976. See also ◊trade union.

EMS abbreviation for ◊***European Monetary System***.

emu flightless bird *Dromaius novaehollandiae*, family Dromaiidae, order Casuariidae, native to Australia. It stands about 1.8 m/6 ft high and has coarse brown plumage, small rudimentary wings, short feathers on the head and neck, and powerful legs, which are well adapted for running and kicking. The female has a curious bag or pouch in the windpipe that enables her to emit a characteristic loud booming note. Emus are monogamous, and the male wholly or partially incubates the eggs.

EMU abbreviation for ***economic and monetary union***, the proposed ◊European Union (EU) policy for a single currency and common economic policies. In June 1994 EU finance ministers agreed to postpone the lauch of EMU until 1999, after it emerged that most countries would be unable to meet the economic criteria outlined in the ◊Maastricht Treaty by the original target date of 1997.

emulsifier food ◊additive used to keep oils dispersed and in suspension, in products such as mayonnaise and peanut butter. Egg yolk is a naturally occurring emulsifier, but most of the emulsifiers in commercial use today are synthetic chemicals.

emulsion a stable dispersion of a liquid in another liquid – for example, oil and water in some cosmetic lotions.

enabling act legislative enactment enabling or empowering a person or corporation to take certain actions. Perhaps the best known example of an Enabling Law was that passed in Germany in March 1933 by the Reichstag and Reichsrat. It granted Hitler's cabinet dictatorial powers until April 1937, and effectively terminated parliamentary government in Germany until 1950. The law firmly established the Nazi dictatorship by giving dictatorial powers to the government.

enamel vitrified (glasslike) coating of various colours used for decorative purposes on a metallic or porcelain surface. In ◊cloisonné the various sections of the design are separated by thin metal wires or strips. In champlevé the enamel is poured into engraved cavities in the metal surface.

The ancient art of enamelling is believed to be of Near Eastern origin. Examples of cloisonné enamel have been found in a Mycenaean tomb in Cyprus of the 13th century BC. The champlevé technique was used by Celtic craftsmen of the pre-Christian era (see ◊Celtic art). Enamels were made in the northern provinces of the Roman Empire and reappear in the 6th century AD in Anglo-Saxon England. A great revival of cloisonné enamel began in Constantinople in the 10th century; a great masterpiece of this Byzantine enamel is the Pala d'Oro in St Mark's, Venice. During the Middle Ages the demand for church ornaments, decorated reliquaries, crosses, and so on, encouraged a number of technical developments. The Rhine and Meuse valleys, Limoges in France and N Spain were centres of a new style of champlevé enamel from the 12th century. In the 15th century, in N Italy and at Limoges, *painted enamels* were first made, applied by brush, spatula, or point, over a design scratched in outline on the baseplate. Masters of this form of art were Nardon and Jean Penicaud, Pierre Raymond, and Leonard Limousin. A later development in the 17th century was the minature painted enamel, in which the colours were applied after the enamel was fired and fused, as practised by the Toutin family in Paris. In England, Stubbs produced enamel paintings.

encaustic painting ancient technique of painting, commonly used by the Egyptians, Greeks, and Romans, in which coloured pigments were mixed with molten wax and painted on panels. In the 20th century the technique has been used by the US artist Jasper Johns.

encephalin a naturally occurring chemical produced by nerve cells in the brain that has the same effect as morphine or other derivatives of opium, acting as a natural painkiller. Unlike morphine, encephalins are quickly degraded by the body, so there is no build-up of tolerance to them, and hence no addiction. Encephalins are a variety of ◊peptides, as are ◊endorphins, which have similar effects.

encephalitis inflammation of the brain, nearly always due to viral infection but it may also occur in bacterial and other infections. It varies widely in severity, from shortlived, relatively slight effects of headache, drowsiness, and fever to paralysis, coma, and death.

Encke's comet comet with the shortest known orbital period, 3.3 years. It is named after German mathematician and astronomer Johann Franz Encke (1791–1865), who calculated its orbit in 1819 from earlier sightings.

It was first seen in 1786 by the French astronomer Pierre Méchain (1744–1804). It is the parent body of the Taurid meteor shower and a fragment of it may have hit the Earth in the ◊Tunguska Event 1908. In 1913, it became the first comet to be observed throughout its entire orbit when it was photographed near ◊aphelion (the point in its orbit furthest from the Sun).

enclosure in Britain, appropriation of ◊common land as private property, or the changing of open-field systems to enclosed fields (often used for sheep). This process began in the 14th century and became widespread in the 15th and 16th centuries. It caused poverty, homelessness, and rural depopulation, and resulted in revolts 1536, 1569, and 1607.

Numerous government measures to prevent depopulation were introduced 1489–1640, including the first Enclosure Act 1603, but were sabotaged by landowning magistrates at local level. A new wave of enclosures by Acts of Parliament 1760–1820 reduced the yeoman class of small landowning farmers to agricultural labourers, or forced them to leave the land. The Enclosure Acts applied to 4.5 million acres or a quarter of England. Some 17 million acres were enclosed without any parliamentary act. From 1876 the enclosure of common land in Britain was limited by statutes. Enclosures occurred throughout Europe on a large scale during the 19th century, often at the behest of governments. The last major Enclosure Act was in 1903.

encryption in computing, providing ◊data security by encoding data so that it is meaningless to unauthorized users who do not have the necessary decoding software.

encyclical letter addressed by the pope to Roman Catholic bishops for the benefit of the people. The first was issued by Benedict XIV in 1740, but encyclicals became common only in the 19th century. They may be doctrinal (condemning errors), exhortative (recommending devotional activities), or commemorative. Recent encyclicals include *Pacem in terris* (Pope John XXIII, 1963), *Sacerdotalis celibatus* (on the celibacy of the clergy, Pope Paul VI, 1967), and *Humanae vitae* (Pope Paul VI, 1967, on methods of contraception). Encyclicals are written in Latin.

encyclopedia or ***encyclopaedia*** work of reference covering either all fields of knowledge or one specific subject. Although most encyclopedias are alphabetical, with cross-references, some are organized thematically with indexes, to keep related subjects together.

The earliest extant encyclopedia is the *Historia Naturalis/Natural History* AD 23–79 of ◊Pliny the Elder. The first alphabetical encyclopedia in English was the *Lexicon Technicum/Technical Lexicon* 1704, compiled by John Harris. In 1728 Ephraim Chambers published his *Cyclopaedia*, which coordinated scattered articles by a system of cross-references and was translated into French 1743–45. This translation formed the basis of the *Encyclopédie*, which was edited by Diderot and d'Alembert and published 1751–72. By this time the system of engaging a body of expert compilers and editors was established, and in 1768–71 the *Encyclopaedia Britannica* first appeared. The first encylopedia to be published on CD-ROM was the *Academic American Encyclopedia* 1985.

Other major encyclopedias include the Chinese encyclopedia printed 1726, the German *Conversations-Lexikon/Conversation Lexicon* of Brockhaus, and the French *Grand Dictionnaire Universel du XIXème Siècle/Great Universal Dictionary of the 19th Century* of Pierre Larousse 1866–76.

Encyclopédie encyclopedia in 35 volumes written 1751–77 by a group of French scholars (*Encyclopédistes*) including D'Alembert and Diderot, inspired by the English encyclopedia produced by Ephraim Chambers 1728. Religious scepticism and ◊Enlightenment social and political views were a feature of the work.

The first 28 volumes 1751–72 were edited by Diderot. A further five volumes were produced by other editors 1776–77 and the two-volume index was completed 1780.

endangered species plant or animal species whose numbers are so few that it is at risk of becoming extinct. Officially designated endangered species are listed by the International Union for the Conservation of Nature (◊IUCN).

Endangered species are not a new phenomenon; extinction is an integral part of evolution. The replacement of one species by another usually involves the eradication of the less successful form, and ensures the continuance and diversification of life in all forms. However, this only holds good for natural extinctions; those induced by humans represent an evolutionary dead-end. The great majority of recent extinctions have been directly or indirectly induced by humans; most often by the loss, modification, or pollution of the organism's habitat, but also by over-hunting for 'sport' or commercial purposes.

According to a 1995 report to Congress by the US Fish and Wildlife Service, although seven of the 893 species listed as endangered under the US Endangered Species Act 1968–93 have become extinct, 40% are no longer declining in number. In Feb 1996 a private conservation group, Nature Conservancy, reported around 20,000 native US plant and animal species to be rare or imperilled.

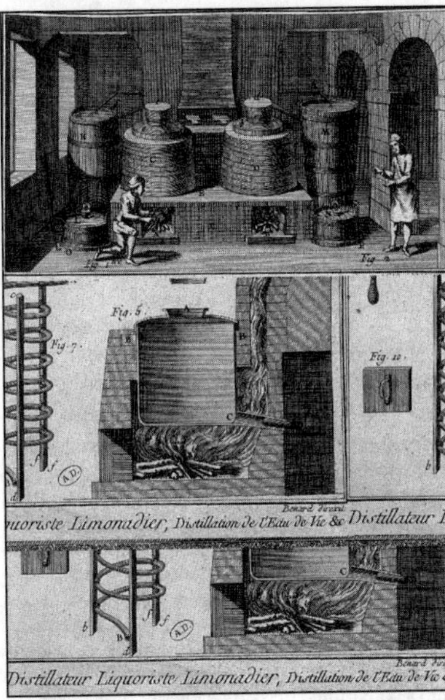

Distillateur Liquoriste Limonadier, Distillation de l'Eau de Vie &

Encyclopédie Illustration and diagram of a distillery from Diderot's *Encyclopédie*, 18th century, Bibliothèque des Arts Décoratifs, Paris, France. The sale of the book was repeatedly prohibited because of its Enlightenment views, and Diderot himself was threatened with imprisonment. *Corbis*

Enders John Franklin 1897–1985. US virologist. With Thomas Weller (1915–) and Frederick Robbins (1916–), he developed a technique for culturing virus material in sufficient quantity for experimental work. This led to the creation of effective vaccines against polio and measles. The three were awarded the Nobel Prize for Physiology or Medicine 1954.

endive cultivated annual plant *Cichorium endivia*, family Compositae, the leaves of which are used in salads and cooking. One variety has narrow, curled leaves; another has wide, smooth leaves. It is related to ◊chicory.

endocrine gland gland that secretes hormones into the bloodstream to regulate body processes. Endocrine glands are most highly developed in vertebrates, but are also found in other animals, notably insects. In humans the main endocrine glands are the pituitary, thyroid, parathyroid, adrenal, pancreas, ovary, and testis.

endolymph fluid found in the inner ◊ear, filling the central passage of the cochlea as well as the

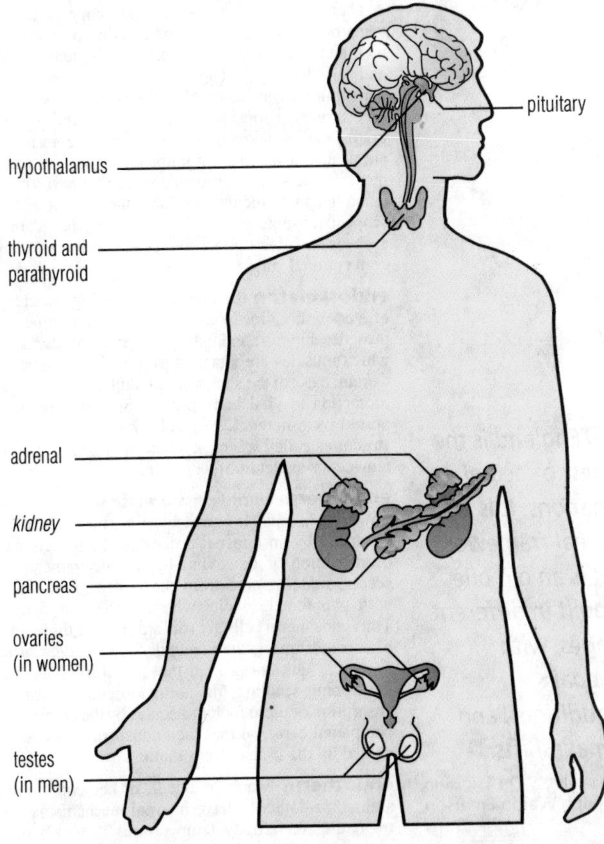

endocrine gland The main human endrocrine glands. These glands produce hormones – chemical messengers – which travel in the bloodstream to stimulate certain cells.

semicircular canals. Sound waves travelling into the ear pass eventually through the three small bones of the middle ear and set up vibrations in the endolymph. These vibrations are detected by receptors in the cochlea, which send nerve impulses to the hearing centres of the brain.

endometriosis common gynaecological complaint in which patches of endometrium (the lining of the womb) are found outside the uterus. This ectopic (abnormally positioned) tissue is present most often in the ovaries. Endometriosis may be treated with analgesics, hormone preparations, or surgery. Between 30 and 40% of women treated for infertility are suffering from the condition.

endoplasm inner, liquid part of a cell's ◊cytoplasm.

endoplasmic reticulum (ER) a membranous system of tubes, channels, and flattened sacs that form compartments within ◊eukaryotic cells. It stores and transports proteins within cells and also carries various enzymes needed for the synthesis of ◊fats. The ◊ribosomes, or the organelles that carry out protein synthesis, are attached to parts of the ER.

Under the electron microscope, ER looks like a series of channels and vesicles, but it is in fact a large, sealed, baglike structure crumpled and folded into a convoluted mass. The interior of the 'bag', the ER lumen, stores various proteins needed elsewhere in the cell, then organizes them into transport vesicles formed by a small piece of ER membrane budding from the main membrane.

endorphin natural substance (a polypeptide) that modifies the action of nerve cells. Endorphins are produced by the pituitary gland and hypothalamus of vertebrates. They lower the perception of pain by reducing the transmission of signals between nerve cells.

Endorphins not only regulate pain and hunger, but are also involved in the release of sex hormones from the pituitary gland. Opiates act in a similar way to endorphins, but are not rapidly degraded by the body, as natural endorphins are, and thus have a long-lasting effect on pain perception and mood. Endorphin release is stimulated by exercise.

endoscopy examination of internal organs or tissues by an instrument allowing direct vision. An endoscope is equipped with an eyepiece, lenses, and its own light source to illuminate the field of vision. The endoscope used to examine the digestive tract is a flexible fibre-optic instrument swallowed by the patient.

There are various types of endoscope in use – some rigid, some flexible – with names prefixed by their site of application (for example, bronchoscope and laryngoscope). The value of endoscopy is in permitting diagnosis without the need for exploratory surgery. Biopsies (tissue samples) and photographs may be taken by way of the endoscope as an aid to diagnosis, or to monitor the effects of treatment. Some surgical procedures can be performed using fine instruments introduced through the endoscope. ◊Keyhole surgery is increasingly popular as a cheaper, safer option for some conditions than conventional surgery.

endoskeleton the internal supporting structure of vertebrates, made up of cartilage or bone. It provides support, and acts as a system of levers to which muscles are attached to provide movement. Certain parts of the skeleton (the skull and ribs) give protection to vital body organs. Sponges are supported by a network of rigid, or semirigid, spiky structures called spicules; a bath sponge is the proteinaceous skeleton of a sponge.

endosperm nutritive tissue in the seeds of most flowering plants. It surrounds the embryo and is produced by an unusual process that parallels the ◊fertilization of the ovum by a male gamete. A second male gamete from the pollen grain fuses with two female nuclei within the ◊embryo sac. Thus endosperm cells are triploid (having three sets of chromosomes); they contain food reserves such as starch, fat, and protein that are utilized by the developing seedling. In 'non-endospermic' seeds, absorption of these food molecules by the embryo is completed early, so that the endosperm has disappeared by the time of germination.

endotherm 'warm-blooded', or homeothermic, animal. Endotherms have internal mechanisms for regulating their body temperatures to levels different from the environmental temperature. See ◊homeothermy.

endowment insurance a type of life insurance that may produce profits. An endowment policy will run for a fixed number of years during which it accumulates a cash value; it can provide a savings plan for a retirement fund.

In Britain, endowment insurance may be used to help with a house purchase, linked to a building society mortgage.

Endymion in Greek mythology, a beautiful young man loved by Selene, the Moon goddess. He was granted eternal sleep in order to remain for ever young. John Keats's poem *Endymion* 1818 is an allegory of searching for perfection.

Energiya most powerful Soviet space rocket, first launched 15 May 1987. Used to launch the Soviet space shuttle, the Energiya ◊booster is capable, with the use of strap-on boosters, of launching payloads of up to 190 tonnes into Earth orbit.

energy capacity for doing ◊work. Potential energy (PE) is energy deriving from position; thus a stretched spring has elastic PE, and an object raised to a height above the Earth's surface, or the water in an elevated reservoir, has gravitational PE. A lump of coal and a tank of petrol, together with the oxygen needed for their combustion, have chemical energy. Other sorts of energy include electrical and nuclear energy, and light and sound. Moving bodies possess kinetic energy (KE). Energy can be converted from one form to another, but the total quantity stays the same (in accordance with the ◊conservation of energy principle).

Although energy is never lost, after a number of conversions it tends to finish up as the kinetic energy of random motion of molecules (of the air, for example) at relatively low temperatures. This is 'degraded' energy that is difficult to convert back to other forms.

$E=mc^2$ ◊Einstein's special theory of ◊relativity 1905 correlates any gain, E, in energy with a gain, m, in mass, by the equation $E = mc^2$, in which c is the speed of light. The conversion of mass into energy in accordance with this equation applies universally, although it is only for nuclear reactions that the percentage change in mass is large enough to detect.

resources So-called energy resources are stores of convertible energy. Nonrenewable resources include the fossil fuels (coal, oil, and gas) and nuclear-fission 'fuels' – for example, uranium-235. Renewable resources, such as wind, tidal, and geothermal power, have so far been less exploited. Hydroelectric projects are well established, and wind turbines and tidal systems are being developed. ▷ *See feature on pp. 360–361.*

energy, alternative energy from sources that are renewable and ecologically safe, as opposed to sources that are nonrenewable with toxic by-products, such as coal, oil, or gas (fossil fuels), and uranium (for nuclear power). The most important alternative energy source is flowing water, harnessed as ◊hydroelectric power. Other sources include the oceans' tides and waves (see ◊tidal power station and ◊wave power), ◊wind power (harnessed by windmills and wind turbines), the Sun (◊solar energy), and the heat trapped in the Earth's crust (◊geothermal energy) (see also ◊cold fusion).

energy conservation methods of reducing energy use through insulation, increasing energy efficiency, and changes in patterns of use. Profligate energy use by industrialized countries contributes greatly to air pollution and the ◊greenhouse effect when it draws on nonrenewable energy sources. Increasing energy efficiency alone could reduce carbon dioxide emissions in several high-income countries by 1–2% a year.

By applying existing conservation methods, UK electricity use could be reduced by 4 gigawatts by the year 2000 – the equivalent of four Sizewell nuclear power stations – according to a study by the Open University. This would also be cheaper than building new generating plants.

energy of reaction energy released or absorbed during a chemical reaction, also called ***enthalpy of reaction*** or ***heat of reaction***. In a chemical reaction, the energy stored in the reacting molecules is rarely the same as that stored in the product molecules. Depending on which is the greater, energy is either released (an exothermic reaction) or absorbed (an endothermic reaction) from the surroundings (see ◊conservation of energy). The amount of energy released or absorbed by the quantities of substances represented by the chemical equation is the energy of reaction.

Enfield outer borough of NE Greater London. It includes the districts of Edmonton and Southgate

features the royal hunting ground of Enfield Chase partly survives in the 'green belt'; early 17th-century Forty Hall; Lea Valley Regional Park, opened 1967

industries engineering (the Royal Small Arms factory, which closed 1989, produced the Enfield rifle), textiles, furniture, cement, electronics, metal, and plastic products

population (1991) 257,400.

Engel (Johann) Carl Ludwig 1778–1840. German architect. From 1815 he worked in Finland. His great Neo-Classical achievement is the Senate Square in Helsinki, which is defined by his Senate House 1818–22 and University Building 1828–32, and crowned by the domed Lutheran cathedral 1830–40.

Engels Friedrich 1820–1895. German social and political philosopher, a friend of, and collaborator with, Karl ◊Marx. His later interpretations of Marxism, and his own philosophical and historical studies such as *Origins of the Family, Private Property, and the State* 1884 (which linked patriarchy with the development of private property), developed such concepts as historical materialism. His use of positivism and Darwinian ideas gave Marxism a scientific and deterministic flavour which was to influence Soviet thinking.

In 1842 Engels's father sent him to work in the cotton factory owned by his family in Manchester, England, where he became involved with ◊Chartism. In 1844 his lifelong friendship with Karl Marx began, and together they worked out the materialist interpretation of history and in 1847–48 wrote the *Communist Manifesto*. Returning to Germany during the 1848–49 revolution, Engels worked with Marx on the *Neue Rheinische Zeitung/New Rhineland Newspaper* and fought on the barricades in Baden. After the defeat of the revolution he returned to Manchester, and for the rest of his life largely supported the Marx family.

Engels's first book was *The Condition of the Working Classes in England* 1845. He summed up the lessons of 1848 in *The Peasants' War in Germany* 1850 and *Revolution and Counter-Revolution in Germany* 1851. After Marx's death Engels was largely responsible for the wider dissemination of his ideas; he edited the second and third volumes of Marx's *Das Kapital* 1885 and 1894.

engine device for converting stored energy into useful work or movement. Most engines use a fuel as their energy store. The fuel is burnt to produce heat energy, which is then converted into movement. Heat engines can be classified according to the fuel they use (◊petrol engine or ◊diesel engine), or according to whether the fuel is burnt inside (◊internal combustion engine) or outside (◊steam engine) the engine, or according to whether they produce a reciprocating or rotary motion (◊turbine or ◊Wankel engine).

engineering the application of science to the design, construction, and maintenance of works, machinery, roads, railways, bridges, harbour installations, engines, ships, aircraft and airports, spacecraft and space stations, and the generation, transmission, and use of electrical power. The main divisions of engineering are aerospace, chemical, civil, electrical, electronic, gas, marine, materials, mechanical, mining, production, radio, and structural.

To practise engineering professionally, university or college training in addition to practical experience is required, but technician engineers usually receive their training through apprenticeships or similar training schemes.

England largest division of the ◊United Kingdom

area 130,357 sq km/50,318 sq mi

capital London

towns and cities Birmingham, Cambridge, Coventry, Leeds, Leicester, Manchester, Newcastle upon Tyne, Nottingham, Oxford, Sheffield, York; ports Bristol, Dover, Felixstowe, Harwich, Liverpool, Portsmouth, Southampton

'England is the best of actual nations. It is no ideal framework, it is an old pile built in different ages, with repairs, additions, and makeshifts.'

On ENGLAND
Ralph Waldo Emerson
English Traits

features variability of climate and diversity of scenery; among European countries, only the Netherlands is more densely populated
exports agricultural (cereals, rape, sugar beet, potatoes); meat and meat products; electronic (software) and telecommunications equipment (main centres Berkshire and Cambridge); scientific instruments; textiles and fashion goods; North Sea oil and gas, petrochemicals, pharmaceuticals, fertilizers; beer; china clay, pottery, porcelain, and glass; film and television programmes, and sound recordings. Tourism is important. There are worldwide banking and insurance interests
currency pound sterling
population (1993 est) 48,500,000
language English, with more than 100 minority languages
religion Christian, with the Church of England as the established church, 31,500,000; and various Protestant groups, of which the largest is the Methodist 1,400,000; Roman Catholic about 5,000,000; Muslim 900,000; Jewish 410,000; Sikh 175,000; Hindu 140,000
government local government changes, which began 1995, created a number of new unitary authorities in England and abolished several counties (*see list of tables on p. 1177 and United Kingdom map*).

For history, see ◊Britain, ancient; ◊United Kingdom.

English the natives and inhabitants of England, part of Britain, as well as their descendants, culture, and language. The English have a mixed cultural heritage combining Celtic, Anglo-Saxon, Norman, and Scandinavian elements.

English architecture the main styles in English architecture are Anglo-Saxon, Norman, Early English (of which Westminster Abbey is an example), Decorated, Perpendicular (15th century), Tudor (a name chiefly applied to domestic buildings of about 1485–1558), Jacobean, Stuart (including the Renaissance and Queen Anne styles), Georgian, the Gothic revival of the 19th century, Modern, and Post-Modern. Notable architects include Christopher Wren, Inigo Jones, John Vanbrugh, Nicholas Hawksmoor, Charles Barry, Edwin Landseer Lutyens, Hugh Casson, Basil Spence, Frederick Gibberd, Denys Lasdun, Richard Rogers, Norman Foster, James Stirling, Terry Farrell, Quinlan Terry, and Zahia Hadid.
Anglo-Saxon (5th–11th century) Much of the architecture of this period, being of timber, has disappeared. The stone church towers that remain, such as at Earls Barton, appear to imitate timber techniques with their 'long and short work' and triangular arches. Brixworth Church, Northamptonshire, is another example of Anglo-Saxon architecture, dating from c. 670.
Norman (11th–12th century) William the Conqueror inaugurated an enormous building programme. He introduced the ***Romanesque style*** of round arches, massive cylindrical columns, and thick walls. At Durham Cathedral 1093–c. 1130, the rib vaults were an invention of European importance in the development of the Gothic style.
Gothic The ***Early English*** (late 12th–late 13th century) began with the French east end of Canterbury Cathedral, designed 1175 by William of Sens (died c. 1180), and is seen in the cathedrals of Wells, Lincoln, and Salisbury. A simple elegant style of lancet windows, deeply carved mouldings, and slender, contrasting shafts of Purbeck marble. ***Decorated*** (late 13th–14th century) is characterized by a growing richness in carving and a fascination with line. The double curves of the ogee arch, elaborate window tracery, and vault ribs woven into star patterns is seen in such buildings as the Lady Chapel at Ely and the Angel Choir at Lincoln. Exeter Cathedral is another example of the Decorated style. The gridded and panelled cages of light of the ***Perpendicular*** (late 14th–mid-16th century) style are a dramatic contrast to the Decorated period; they often convey an impressive sense of unity, space, and power. The chancel of Gloucester Cathedral is early Perpendicular; Kings College Chapel, Cambridge, is late Perpendicular.
Tudor and Elizabethan (1485–1603) This period saw the Perpendicular style interwoven with growing Renaissance influence. Buildings develop a conscious symmetry elaborated with continental Patternbrook details. Hybrid and exotic works result such as Burghley House, Cambridgeshire, 1552–87, and Hardwick Hall, Derbyshire, 1590–97. Longleat House, Wiltshire, 1568–75 is another example.
Jacobean (1603–25) A transition period, with the Renaissance influence becoming more pronounced. Hatfield House 1607–12 in Hertfordshire is Jacobean, so also is Blicking Hall in Norfolk, redesigned around a medieval moated house and completed 1628. Both were designed by the architect Robert Lyminge.
English Renaissance (17th–early 18th century) The provincial scene was revolutionized by Inigo ◊Jones with the Queens House, Greenwich, 1616–35, and the Banqueting House, Whitehall, 1619–22. Strict Palladianism appeared among the half-timber and turrets of Jacobean London. With Christopher ◊Wren a restrained Baroque evolved showing French Renaissance influence, for example St Paul's Cathedral, London, 1675–1710. Nicholas◊Hawksmoor and John ◊Vanbrugh developed a theatrical Baroque style, exemplifed in their design for Blenheim Palace, Oxfordshire, 1705–20.
Georgian (18th–early 19th century) Lord ◊Burlington, reacting against the Baroque, inspired a revival of the pure Palladian style of Inigo Jones, as in Chiswick House 1725–29, London. William ◊Kent, also a Palladian, invented the picturesque garden, as at Rousham, Oxfordshire. Alongside the great country houses, an urban architecture evolved of plain, well-proportioned houses, defining elegant streets and squares; John Wood the Younger's Royal Crescent, Bath, was built 1767–75. The second half of the century mingled Antiquarian and Neo-Classical influences, exquisitely balanced in the work of Robert ◊Adam at Kedleston Hall 1759–70. John ◊Nash carried Neo-Classicism into

cont. on p. 362

ENGLAND: SOVEREIGNS

Reign	Name	Relationship
West Saxon kings		
901–25	Edward the Elder	son of Alfred the Great
925–40	Athelstan	son of Edward I
940–46	Edmund	half-brother of Athelstan
946–55	Edred	brother of Edmund
955–59	Edwy	son of Edmund
959–75	Edgar	brother of Edwy
975–78	Edward the Martyr	son of Edgar
978–1016	Ethelred II	son of Edgar
1016	Edmund Ironside	son of Ethelred
Danish kings		
1016–35	Canute	son of Sweyn I of Denmark, who conquered England 1013
1035–40	Harold I	son of Canute
1040–42	Hardicanute	son of Canute
West Saxon kings (restored)		
1042–66	Edward the Confessor	son of Ethelred II
1066	Harold II	son of Godwin
Norman kings		
1066–87	William I	illegitimate son of Duke Robert the Devil
1087–1100	William II	son of William I
1100–35	Henry I	son of William I
1135–54	Stephen	grandson of William II
House of Plantagenet		
1154–89	Henry II	son of Matilda (daughter of Henry I)
1189–99	Richard I	son of Henry II
1199–1216	John	son of Henry II
1216–72	Henry III	son of John
1272–1307	Edward I	son of Henry III
1307–27	Edward II	son of Edward I
1327–77	Edward III	son of Edward II
1377–99	Richard II	son of the Black Prince
House of Lancaster		
1399–1413	Henry IV	son of John of Gaunt
1413–22	Henry V	son of Henry IV
1422–61, 1470–71	Henry VI	son of Henry V
House of York		
1461–70, 1471–83	Edward IV	son of Richard, Duke of York
1483	Edward V	son of Edward IV
1483–85	Richard III	brother of Edward IV
House of Tudor		
1485–1509	Henry VII	son of Edmund Tudor, Earl of Richmond
1509–47	Henry VIII	son of Henry VII
1547–53	Edward VI	son of Henry VIII
1553–58	Mary I	daughter of Henry VIII
1558–1603	Elizabeth I	daughter of Henry VIII
House of Stuart		
1603–25	James I	great-grandson of Margaret (daughter of Henry VII)
1625–49	Charles I	son of James I
1649–60	*the Commonwealth*	
House of Stuart (restored)		
1660–85	Charles II	son of Charles I
1685–88	James II	son of Charles I
1689–1702	William III and Mary	son of Mary (daughter of Charles I); daughter of James II
1702–14	Anne	daughter of James II
House of Hanover		
1714–27	George I	son of Sophia (granddaughter of James I)
1727–60	George II	son of George I
1760–1820	George III	son of Frederick (son of George II)
1820–30	George IV (regent 1811–20)	son of George III
1830–37	William IV	son of George III
1837–1901	Victoria	daughter of Edward (son of George III)
House of Saxe-Coburg		
1901–10	Edward VII	son of Victoria
House of Windsor		
1910–36	George V	son of Edward VII
1936	Edward VIII	son of George V
1936–52	George VI	son of George V
1952–	Elizabeth II	daughter of George VI

Energy Sources

The streamlined shape of a solar powered car. Streamlining of vehicles reduces air resistance, which cuts down on fuel consumption and increases speed. *Image Select (UK) Ltd*

Humans are using up the world's energy resources in a way no other animal has ever done. We use them to provide light and heating in our homes, to plough the land, to cook our food, to travel, to run our factories, and in countless other ways. Whether we are rural workers in a developing country or urban workers in a wealthy industrial country, we all need energy, although the sources of the energy and the amounts used vary greatly from one society to another.

Sources of energy

There are different forms or types of energy. Fuels such as coal, oil (petroleum), and wood contain chemical energy. When these fuels are burnt, the chemical energy changes to heat and light energy. Electricity is the most important form of energy in the industrialized world, because it can be transported over long distances via cables and transmission lines. It is also a very convenient form of energy, since it can power a wide variety of household appliances and industrial machinery. It is produced by converting the chemical energy from coal, oil, or natural gas in power stations.

Energy resources fall into two broad groups: renewable and nonrenewable. Renewable resources are those which replenish themselves naturally and will either be available always – for example hydroelectric power, solar energy, wind and wave power, tidal energy, and geothermal energy – or will be continue to be available provided supplies are given sufficient time to replenish themselves – for example peat and firewood. Nonrenewable resources are those of which there are limited supplies and which once used are gone forever; these include coal, oil, natural gas, and uranium.

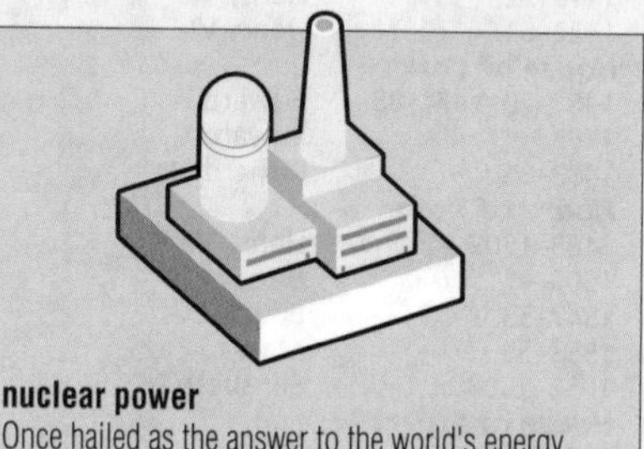

nuclear power
Once hailed as the answer to the world's energy problems, rising costs and loss of public confidence may restrict future growth

Fossil fuels

Coal, oil, and natural gas are called fossil fuels because they are the fossilized remains of plants and animals that lived hundreds of millions of years ago. Burning fossil fuels releases chemicals that cause acid rain, and is gradually increasing the carbon dioxide in the atmosphere, causing global warming.

Fossil fuel resources are not evenly distributed around the world. Over half the world's known oil reserves are in the Middle East; about 40% of the reserves of natural gas are in the Commonwealth of Independent States (CIS), and 25% in the Middle East. About two-thirds of the world's coal is shared between North America, the CIS, and China.

solar
Recent years have seen massive increase in investment in technologies to make use of the Sun's energy

Uranium

Uranium is a radioactive metallic element and a very concentrated source of energy; large reserves are found in Australia, North America, and South Africa. Used to produce electricity in a nuclear power station, a single ton of uranium can produce as much energy as 15,000 tons of coal, or 10,000 tons of oil. Used in the type of nuclear power station now in operation, the world's known uranium supplies have about the same energy content as the known oil reserves. However, these power stations, known as thermal stations or

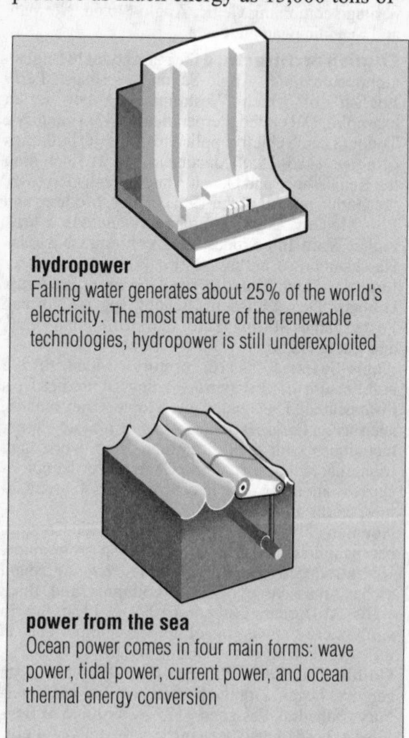

hydropower
Falling water generates about 25% of the world's electricity. The most mature of the renewable technologies, hydropower is still underexploited

power from the sea
Ocean power comes in four main forms: wave power, tidal power, current power, and ocean thermal energy conversion

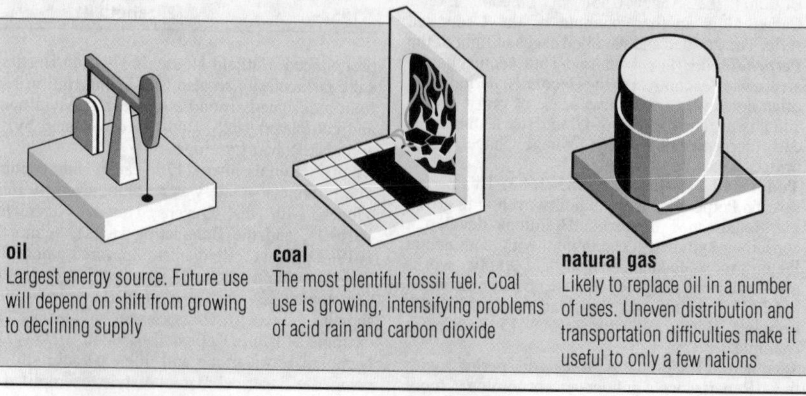

oil
Largest energy source. Future use will depend on shift from growing to declining supply

coal
The most plentiful fossil fuel. Coal use is growing, intensifying problems of acid rain and carbon dioxide

natural gas
Likely to replace oil in a number of uses. Uneven distribution and transportation difficulties make it useful to only a few nations

reactors, use only a small part of the energy available in uranium. The next generation of reactors, known as fast or breeder reactors, release virtually all its energy. These reactors would increase the world's uranium energy reserves by sixty times. However, although nuclear power stations do not produce carbon dioxide or cause acid rain, they do produce radioactive waste which is dangerous and difficult to process or store safely.

Solar energy

Many renewable resources take advantage of the energy in sunlight. The Sun's energy can be tapped directly by photovoltaic cells which convert light into electricity. Other solar energy plants use mirrors to direct sunlight onto pipes containing a liquid. The liquid boils and is used to drive an electricity generator. The Sun's energy also drives the wind and waves, so energy produced by wind farms and wave-driven generators is also derived from the Sun.

Gravitational energy

Hydroelectricity and tidal power stations make use of gravitational forces. The Earth's gravity pulls water downwards through the turbines in a hydroelectric power station. In a tidal power station, the Moon's gravity lifts water as the tides rise, giving the water potential energy (energy due to position) which is released as the water flows through a turbine. Geothermal energy (the heat energy of hot rocks deep beneath the Earth's surface) is due to gravity compressing and heating the rocks when the Earth formed.

The worldwide energy pie

Globally, the largest contributions to current energy resources come from oil (31%), coal (26%), and natural gas (19%). Renewable energy currently supplies about 20% of the world's energy needs, with hydroelectricity supplying 6% of the world's needs and traditional biofuels (firewood, crop wastes, peat, and dung) supplying12%. A small contribution is made by new renewables – for example the conversion of crops such as sugar into alcohol fuel and the burning of waste material.

The contribution solar, wave, tidal, and geothermal power can make to the world's energy resources is currently limited. This is because renewable energy depends on developing ways of capturing and concentrating it. In addition, renewable energy is not always available when needed – rivers can dry up, the wind does not always blow.

It is clear that, in the future, demand for energy will be higher than at present, because of population growth and increased industrialization. Furthermore, the energy available must be at a reasonable cost or economic growth will be held back. This is especially important for developing countries, where lack of money to pay for energy already restricts development.

World energy sources 1996

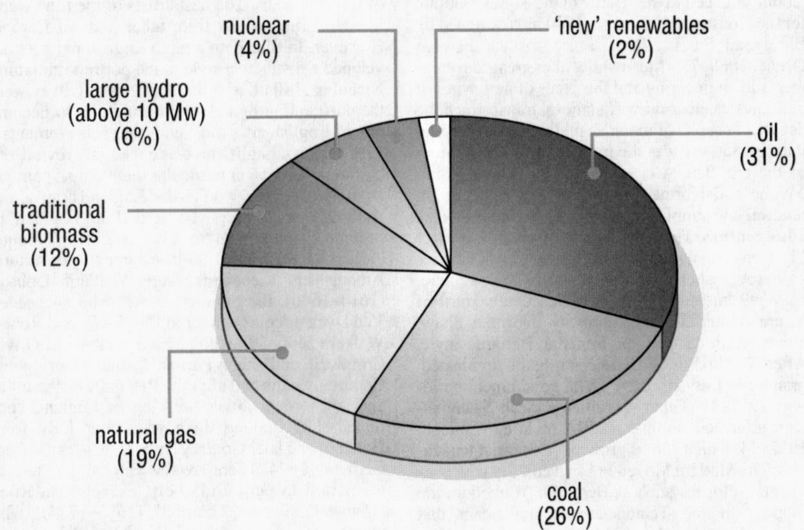

Future solutions

In principle, known resources of nonrenewable energy should be sufficient for several hundred years or more. At the present rate of consumption, oil reserves will last about 40 years; gas reserves will last about 60 years; coal reserves will last about 250 years; and uranium reserves, if used in fast reactors, would last for more than 1,000 years. It is also likely that further fossil-fuel reserves will be discovered as currently known supplies run out. However, in practice, the outlook is uncertain. Increasing concern about pollution might make dirty coal-fired power stations unacceptable in the future.

One alternative is to make greater use of nuclear power, moving to fast reactors and then developing nuclear fusion plants which would mimic the power production process found in the Sun. However, anxiety about safety and waste disposal is already limiting the use of nuclear energy, so it is unlikely to provide the answer in the future.

There is considerable room for development in the use of renewable resources; but with most of the world's energy production based on nonrenewable fuel supplies, the widespread introduction of efficient renewable energy will require a complete restructuring of the ways we produce and use energy.

PETER LAFFERTY

Wind turbines are capable of capturing over half of the wind's energy. However, many thousands of them would be required for wind power to make a significant contribution to our energy needs. *AEA Technology*

SEE ALSO

acid rain; coal; electricity; fast reactor; fossil fuel; fuel cell; natural gas; nuclear energy; petroleum; solar energy; uranium the new century; his designs include Regent Street, London, begun 1811 and the Royal Pavilion, Brighton, 1815–21.

19th century Throughout the century Classic and Gothic engaged in the 'Battle of the Styles': Gothic for the Houses of Parliament 1840–60 (designed by Barra and Pugin), Renaissance for the Foreign Office 1860–75. Meanwhile, the great developments in engineering and the needs of new types of buildings, such as railway stations, transformed the debate. Joseph ◊Paxton's prefabricated Crystal Palace 1850–51 was the most remarkable building of the era. The Arts and Crafts architects Philip ◊Webb and Norman Shaw (1831–1912) brought renewal and simplicity inspired by William Morris.

20th century The early work of Edwin Landseer ◊Lutyens and the white rendered houses of Charles ◊Voysey, such as Broadleys, Windermere, 1898–99, maintained the Arts and Crafts spirit of natural materials and simplicity. Norman Shaw, however, developed an Imperial Baroque style. After World War I Classicism again dominated, grandly in Lutyens' New Delhi government buildings 1912–31. There was often a clean Scandinavian influence, as in the RIBA building, London, 1932–34, which shows growing Modernist tendencies. The Modern Movement arrived fully with continental refugees such as Bertholdt ◊Lubetkin, the founder of the Tecton architectural team that designed London Zoo 1934–38.

The strong social dimension of English 20th-century architecture is best seen in the new town movement. Welwyn Garden City was begun 1919 and developed after World War II. The latest of the new towns, Milton Keynes, was designated 1967. Recently English architects have again achieved international recognition, for example, Norman ◊Foster and Richard ◊Rogers for their High-Tech innovative Lloyds Building, London, 1979–84. James ◊Stirling's work maintained a Modernist technique and planning while absorbing historical and contextual concerns. Recent Post-Modernist architecture includes the Sainsbury Wing of the National Gallery, London, designed by Robert Venturi 1991.

English art painting and sculpture in England from the 10th century. (For English art before the 10th century, see ◊Celtic art and ◊Anglo-Saxon art.) The strong tradition of manuscript illumination was continued from earlier centuries. Portrait painting flourished from the late 15th century (initially led by artists from Germany and the Low Countries) through the 18th (Thomas Gainsborough, Joshua Reynolds) and into the 20th (David Hockney, Lucian Freud). Landscape painting reached its high point in the 19th century with John Constable and J M W Turner. The Pre-Raphaelite Brotherhood produced a Victorian version of medievalism. In the early 20th century the Camden Town Group and the Bloomsbury Group responded to modern influences in painting, and in sculpture the work of Jacob Epstein, Henry Moore, and Barbara Hepworth led progressively towards abstraction. In the 1950s Pop art began in the UK. Artists in the latter part of the 20th century have experimented with mixed and sometimes unusual media such as dead sheep (Damien Hirst) and chocolate (Helen Chadwick, 1953–1996).

medieval: 10th–15th centuries As elsewhere in Europe, the painting and sculpture of this period was religious. Few examples of medieval English painting have survived, though the decoration of churches encouraged wall painting. During the 13th century painting flourished under the patronage of Henry III, but in the 14th it declined as a result of the Wars of the Roses. The 10th-century schools of Winchester and Canterbury produced illuminated manuscripts such as the Benedictional of St Ethelwold, about 960–80 (British Museum, London). Later examples include the Lutterell Psalter about 1340 (British Museum). One of the few named figures of the period was the 13th-century illuminator and chronicler Matthew Paris. The *Wilton Diptych* late 14th century (National Gallery, London), showing Richard II presented to the Virgin and Child, is a rare example of medieval panel painting. What little sculpture has survived the destructions of the Reformation – and, later, the Civil War of the 17th century – is heavily indebted to French works.

Tudor and Elizabethan: 15th–16th centuries The Italian sculptor Torrigiano introduced the Renaissance style in his tomb of Henry VII in Westminster Abbey (1512–18). However, the reign of Henry VIII virtually put an end to church art. Painting survived largely through the influence and example of the German Hans Holbein, who painted portraits of Henry's court. The best artists of the time were, like Holbein, visitors from other parts of Europe. However, in Elizabeth's reign English painters developed a distinctive style in the portrait miniature. Nicholas Hilliard and his pupil Isaac Oliver were the outstanding figures. Portraiture was to become one of English art's most enduring achievements.

17th century English art was once again revitalized by foreign artists, in particular the Flemish painters Peter Paul Rubens, who visited England briefly, and Anthony van Dyck, who settled in England to become court painter to Charles I. His Baroque elegance dominated 17th-century portraiture. Among his successors were William Dobson (1610–1646), the cavalier painter who succeeded Van Dyck as court painter to Charles V, and Robert Walker (1600–59), who painted portraits of Oliver Cromwell and other Puritan leaders. During the Commonwealth and after the Restoration, the influence of foreign artists working in England continued. First among them was Peter Lely from Holland, and later Godfrey Kneller, who came from Germany 1674. There are few English painters of the period to put beside Lely, except John Riley (1646–91), James Thornhill (1676–1734), who worked at Greenwich and Blenheim Palace, and Robert Streater (1624–80), whose mural paintings were notable in an age of portraiture. The Flemish sculptor John Michael Rysbrack carved portraits and monuments, and Grinling Gibbons, a Dutch sculptor, decorated many interiors with woodcarvings, such as panels for St Paul's Cathedral. The English sculptor Nicholas Stone (1587–1647), who was trained in Amsterdam, worked in a Renaissance style.

18th century English art at last became robustly independent, with great achievements in portraiture and landscape. Portraiture was transformed by two outstanding figures, Gainsborough and Reynolds. Both brought a new subtlety and refinement to portraits, their images an expression of the wealth and confidence of English society. The Royal Academy was founded 1768, and as its first president Reynolds was able to promote a Classicism based on art of the Italian High Renaissance. Other important portraitists were Thomas Lawrence, George Romney, and John Hoppner. The German-born Johann Zoffany and England's Arthur Devis (1711–1787) were painters of portraits and 'conversation pieces'. The fashionable portraiture of the 18th century was challenged by William Hogarth, who painted faces and scenes of contemporary life with a vigorous frankness. He was the first English artist to gain an international reputation.

Landscape painting was established in England by the work of foreign artists such as Canaletto. The first British artist to excel at landscape was Richard Wilson, who studied for some years in Rome. Whereas Wilson painted landscape in the 'Italian manner', based on the works of Claude Lorrain, Gainsborough brought to his landscapes a more personal and romantic feeling, his influences being Dutch 17th-century landscapists such as Jacob van Ruisdael and Meindert Hobbema. George Morland was his most successful follower.

The poet and etcher William Blake was a unique figure, fashioning his own highly individual style to express a complex personal mythology. His visionary creations, among the first powerful expressions of Romanticism, briefly inspired Samuel Palmer, who brought a strong note of mysticism to landscape painting. The nightmarish visions of Henry Fuseli reveal a darker strain of Romanticism.

Caricature flourished in the second half of the century, its leading practitioners being James Gillray, Thomas Rowlandson, and Hogarth. Their favourite targets were the Georgian court, the follies and evils of society, and, during the Napoleonic Wars, Napoleon.

At the very end of the century John Flaxman became the leading exponent of Neo-Classical sculpture.

19th century Constable and Turner gave a depth and range to landscape painting that made it one of the most important and popular expressions of English art. Their achievements were complemented by a host of other landscape painters, including Richard Bonington, John Crome, John Sell Cotman, Robert Cozens, Thomas Girtin, and David Cox.

The Pre-Raphaelite movement, established in the 1840s, dominated English art for the rest of the century. Its members – such as Holman Hunt, Dante Gabriel Rossetti, and John Everett Millais – concentrated on religious, literary, and genre subjects, their style colourful and minutely detailed. At first ridiculed, the style of the Pre-Raphaelites produced a host of popular imitators. In the late 19th century the Arts and Crafts movement, dominated by William Morris, promoted a revival of crafts and good design. Book illustration, a revival of which had been inaugurated by Thomas Stothard at the beginning of the century, flourished under the inspiration of both the Pre-Raphaelites and the Arts and Crafts movement, its leading practitioners being Walter Crane, Kate Greenaway, Arthur Rackham, Aubrey Beardsley, Randolph Caldecott, John Tenniel, and William Morris.

Among the most popular artists of the day were George Watts, who made his name with allegories that expressed Victorian pieties; William Etty, who was one of the few artists to concentrate on the nude; Edward Landseer, who specialized in animal pictures; and Lord Leighton and Lawrence Alma-Tadema, both of whom made their reputations with lavish recreations of ancient Greek and Roman life.

By the end of the century English art was being influenced by French artists, in particular Edgar Degas and the Impressionists. The US-born artist James McNeill Whistler was typical, rejecting the concern with storytelling and descriptiveness that characterized so much Victorian art in favour of the aesthetics of form, colour, and tone. English Impressionists founded the New English Arts Club 1886, and French influence, which continued well into the 20th century, can be seen in the work of Wilson Steer, John Singer Sargent (another American working in England), Walter Sickert, and Augustus John.

20th century In 1910 an exhibition arranged by the critic Roger Fry introduced English artists to Post-Impressionism and Fauvism. The Camden Town Group was formed 1911 to encourage artists who were bringing a new sense of form and colour to the depiction of scenes of everyday London life. Walter Sickert, Charles Ginner, and Harold Gilman (1876–1919) were its leading figures. Artists of the Bloomsbury Group, such as Duncan Grant, Dora Carrington, and Vanessa Bell, were more adventurous in their development of the same influences.

Just before World War I Vorticism, the one specifically English art movement, was created by Wyndham Lewis, one of the few artists to be directly influenced by Cubism and Futurism. Paintings by David Bomberg and sculptures by Henri Gaudier-Brzeska and Jacob Epstein are among the movement's main achievements.

Between the world wars, artists soon began to reflect a wide range of styles and intentions. Matthew Smith worked in a Fauvist style; Christopher Wood (1901–1930), Cecil Collins (1908–1989), and L S Lowry developed a childlike naivety. Using a finely detailed realism, Stanley Spencer sought to express a visionary apprehension of everyday life. Ben Nicholson evolved an entirely abstract art; Paul Nash, Ceri Richards (1903–1979), and Graham Sutherland responded to Surrealism. Surrealism was also an influence on the sculptor who dominated English art of this century, Henry Moore. Other important sculptors to emerge at this time were Barbara Hepworth and Ben Nicholson (both abstract), and Jacob Epstein (who soon outgrew Vorticism), Eric Gill, and Frank Dobson (all figurative).

After World War II English art became increasingly pluralistic. A strong figurative tradition was continued, in very different styles, by Francis Bacon (whose nightmarish visions express contemporary spiritual despair), Lucian Freud, Frank Auerbach, John Bratby, Keith Vaughan (1912–1976), Carel Weight (1908–), and (all in varying degrees associated with Pop art) Richard Hamilton, Peter Blake, David Hockney, and R B Kitaj. Abstract painting, which has never had a strong following in England, was practised by Victor Pasmore, Patrick Heron, William Turnbull, and Bridget Riley, the leading figure in Op art. Outstanding among sculptors are Reg Butler, Lynn Chadwick, Kenneth Armitage (1916–), Anthony Caro, Elizabeth Frink, Eduardo Paolozzi, and (more recently) Richard Long, Antony Gormley (1950–), and Damien Hirst. Performance artists include Gilbert and George (who styled themselves 'living sculptures') and Bruce McLean (1944–).

English Channel stretch of water between England and France, leading in the W to the Atlantic Ocean, and in the E via the Strait of Dover to the North Sea; it is also known as ***La Manche*** (French 'the sleeve') from its shape. The ◊Channel Tunnel, opened 1994, runs between Folkestone, Kent, and Sangatte, W of Calais. The English Channel is 450 km/280 mi long W–E; 27 km/17 mi wide at its narrowest (Cap Gris Nez–Dover) and 177 km/110 mi wide at its widest (Ushant–Land's End).

English language member of the Germanic branch of the Indo-European language family. It is traditionally described as having passed through four major stages over about 1,500 years: ***Old English*** or ***Anglo-Saxon*** (c. 500–1050), rooted in the dialects of invading settlers (Jutes, Saxons, Angles, and Frisians); ***Middle English*** (c. 1050–1550), influenced by Norman French after the Conquest 1066 and by ecclesiastical Latin; ***Early Modern English*** (c. 1550–1700), including a standardization of the diverse influences of Middle English; and ***Late Modern English*** (c. 1700 onwards), including in particular the development and spread of current Standard English. Through extensive exploration, colonization, and trade, English spread worldwide from the 17th century onwards and remains the most important international language of trade and technology. It is used in many variations, for example, British, American, Canadian, West Indian, Indian, Singaporean, and Nigerian English, and many pidgins and creoles.

imported dialects and the prominence of Northumbrian The ancestral forms of English were dialects brought from the NW coastlands of Europe to Britain by Angle, Saxon, and Jutish invaders who gained footholds in the SE in the 5th century and over the next 200 years extended their settlements from S England to the middle of Scotland. Scholars distinguish four main early dialects: of the Jutes in Kent (Kentish), the Saxons in the south (West Saxon), the Mercians or S Angles in the Midlands (Mercian), and the Northumbrians or N Angles north of the Humber (Northumbrian). The first dialect of Old English to rise to literary prominence was Northumbrian, and during the early Old English period Northumbrian schools were the most learned in Christendom, producing such scholars as ◊Bede and Alcuin, confidant and adviser of Charlemagne. The Danish invasions of the 9th–11th centuries destroyed Northumbrian culture. A new literature arose in the south, under the guidance of King Alfred, and West Saxon became the standard literary dialect.

Danish and French influence and competition from other languages Until the Danish invasions, Old English was a highly inflected language but appears to have lost many of its grammatical endings in the interaction with Danish. It was further changed by the influence of Norman French after the Conquest 1066. The Middle English period saw a proliferation of regional dialects as earlier forms died out. However, with the rise of London as a metropolis and large-scale immigration from the surrounding area into the city, Midland (roughly corresponding to Mercian of the Old English period) gained predominance and a distinct metropolitan written dialect emerged.

For several centuries English was in competition with other languages: first the various Celtic languages of Britain, then Danish, then French as the language of Plantagenet England and Latin as the language of the Church. In Scotland, English was in competition with Gaelic and Welsh as well as French and Latin (see ◊Scots language).

further influences In 1362 English replaced French as the language of the law courts of England, although the records continued for some time to be kept in Latin. Geoffrey Chaucer was a court poet at this time and strongly influenced the literary style of the London dialect. When William Caxton set up his printing press in London 1477 the new hybrid language (vernacular English mixed with courtly French and scholarly Latin) became increasingly standardized, and by 1611, when the Authorized (King James) Version of the Bible was published, the educated English of the Home Counties and London had become the core of what is now called Standard English. Great dialect variation remained throughout Britain.

By the end of the 16th century, English was firmly established in four countries: England, Scotland, Wales, and Ireland, and with the establishment of the colonies in North America in the early 17th century was spoken in what are now the USA, Canada, and the West Indies. Seafaring, exploration, commerce, and colonial expansion in due course took both the standard language and other varieties throughout the world. By the time of Johnson's dictionary 1755 and the American Declaration of Independence 1776, English was international and recognizable as the language we use today.

current usage The orthography of English was more or less established by 1650, and, in England in particular, a form of standard educated speech spread from the major public (private) schools in the 19th century. This accent was adopted in the early 20th century by the BBC for its announcers and readers, and is variously known as received pronunciation (RP), BBC English, Oxford English, and the King's or Queen's English. It retains prestige as a model for those learning the language. In the UK, however, it is no longer as sought after as it once was.

Generally, Standard English today does not depend on accent but rather on shared educational experience, mainly of the printed language. Present-day English is an immensely varied language, having absorbed material from many other tongues. It is spoken by more than 300 million native speakers, and between 400 and 800 million foreign users. It is the official language of air transport and shipping; the leading language of science, technology, computers, and commerce; and a major medium of education, publishing, and international negotiation. For this reason scholars frequently refer to its latest phase as World English.

English law one of the major European legal systems, ◊Roman law being the other. English law has spread to many other countries, including former English colonies such as the USA, Canada, Australia, and New Zealand.

English law has a continuous history dating from the local customs of the Anglo-Saxons, traces of which survived until 1925. After the Norman Conquest there grew up, side by side with the Saxon shire courts, the feudal courts of the barons and the ecclesiastical courts. From the king's council developed the royal courts, presided over by professional judges, which gradually absorbed the jurisdictions of the baronial and ecclesiastical courts. By 1250 the royal judges had amalgamated the various local customs into the system of ◊common law – that is, law common to the whole country. A second system known as ◊equity developed in the Court of Chancery, in which the Lord Chancellor considered petitions.

In the 17th–18th centuries, common law absorbed the Law Merchant, the international code of mercantile customs. During the 19th century virtually the whole of English law was reformed by legislation; for example, the number of capital offences was greatly reduced.

A unique feature of English law is the doctrine of judicial precedents, whereby the reported decisions of the courts form a binding source of law for future decisions. A judge is bound by decisions of courts of superior jurisdiction but not necessarily by those of inferior courts.

The Judicature Acts 1873–75 abolished a multiplicity of courts, and in their place established the Supreme Court of Judicature, organized in the Court of Appeal and the High Court of Justice; the latter has three divisions – the Queen's Bench, Chancery, and Family Divisions. All High Court judges may apply both common law and equity in deciding cases.

From the Court of Appeal there may be a further appeal to the House of Lords.

English literature for the earliest surviving English literature see ◊Old English literature.

12th–15th century: Middle English period With the arrival of a Norman ruling class at the end of the 11th century, the ascendancy of Norman-French in cultural life began, and it was not until the 13th century that the native literature regained its strength. Prose was concerned chiefly with popular devotional use, but verse emerged typically in the metrical chronicles, such as Layamon's *Brut*, and the numerous romances based on the stories of Charlemagne, the Arthurian legends, and the classical episodes of Troy. First of the great English poets was Geoffrey Chaucer, whose early work reflected the predominant French influence, but later that of Renaissance Italy. Of purely native inspiration was *The Vision of William Concerning Piers the Plowman* of Langland in the old alliterative verse, and the anonymous *Pearl*, *Patience*, and *Gawayne and the Grene Knight*. Chaucer's mastery of versification was not shared by his successors, the most original of whom was John Skelton. More successful were the anonymous authors of songs and carols, and of the ballads, which (for example, those concerned with Robin Hood) often formed a complete cycle. Drama flowered in the form of ◊miracle and ◊morality plays; and prose, although still awkwardly handled by John Wycliffe in his translation of the Bible, rose to a great height with Thomas Malory in the 15th century.

16th century: Elizabethan The Renaissance, which had first touched the English language through Chaucer, came to delayed fruition in the 16th century. Thomas Wyatt and Henry Surrey used the sonnet and blank verse in typically Elizabethan forms and prepared the way for Edmund Spenser, Philip Sidney, Samuel Daniel, Thomas Campion, and others. With Thomas Kyd and Christopher Marlowe, drama emerged into theatrical form; it reached the highest level in the works of Shakespeare and Ben Jonson. Elizabethan prose is represented by Richard Hooker, Thomas North, Roger Ascham, Raphael Holinshed, John Lyly, and others.

17th century English prose achieved full richness in the 17th century, with the Authorized Version of the Bible 1611, Francis Bacon, John Milton, John Bunyan, Jeremy Taylor, Thomas Browne, Izaak Walton, and Samuel Pepys. Most renowned of the 17th-century poets were Milton and John Donne; others include the religious writers George Herbert, Richard Crashaw, Henry Vaughan, and Thomas Traherne, and the Cavalier poets Robert Herrick, Thomas Carew, John Suckling, and Richard Lovelace. In the Restoration period (from 1660) Samuel Butler and John Dryden stand out as poets. Dramatists include Thomas Otway and Nathaniel Lee in tragedy. Comedy flourished with William Congreve, John Vanbrugh, and George Farquhar.

18th century: the Augustan Age Alexander Pope developed the poetic technique of Dryden; in prose Richard Steele and Joseph Addison evolved the polite essay, Jonathan Swift used satire, and Daniel Defoe exploited his journalistic ability. This century saw the development of the ◊novel, through the epistolary style of Samuel Richardson to the robust narrative of Henry Fielding and Tobias Smollett, the comic genius of Laurence Sterne, and the Gothic 'horror' of Horace Walpole. The Neo-Classical standards established by the Augustans were maintained by Samuel Johnson and his circle – Oliver Goldsmith, Edmund Burke, Joshua Reynolds, Richard Sheridan, and others – but the romantic element present in the poetry of James Thomson, Thomas Gray, Edward Young, and William Collins was soon to overturn them.

19th century The *Lyrical Ballads* 1798 of William Wordsworth and Samuel Taylor Coleridge were the manifesto of the new Romantic age. Lord Byron, Percy Bysshe Shelley, and John Keats form a second generation of Romantic poets. In fiction Walter Scott took over the Gothic tradition from Mrs Radcliffe, to create the ◊historical novel, and Jane Austen established the novel of the comedy of manners. Criticism gained new prominence with Coleridge, Charles Lamb, William Hazlitt, and Thomas De Quincey. The novel was further developed by Charles Dickens, William Makepeace Thackeray, the Brontës, George Eliot, Anthony Trollope, and others. The principal poets of the reign of Victoria were Alfred Tennyson, Robert and Elizabeth Browning, Matthew Arnold, the Rossettis, William Morris, and Algernon Swinburne. Among the prose writers of the era were Thomas Macaulay, John Newman, John Stuart Mill, Thomas Carlyle, John Ruskin, and Walter Pater. The transition period at the end of the century saw the poetry and novels of George Meredith and Thomas Hardy; the work of Samuel Butler and George Gissing; and the plays of Arthur Pinero and Oscar Wilde. Gerald Manley Hopkins anticipated the 20th century with the experimentation of his verse forms.

20th century Poets of World War I include Siegfried Sassoon, Rupert Brooke, Wilfred Owen, and Robert Graves. A middle-class realism developed in the novels of H G Wells, Arnold Bennett, E M Forster, and John Galsworthy while the novel's break with traditional narrative and exposition came

'The English have no respect for their language and will not teach their children to speak it ... It is impossible for an Englishman to open his mouth, without making some other Englishman despise him.'

On the ENGLISH LANGUAGE
George Bernard Shaw
preface to *Pygmalion*

'The English may not always be the best writers in the world, but they are incomparably the best dull writers.'

On ENGLISH LITERATURE
Raymond Chandler
The Simple Art of Murder

"That which is not good for the bee hive cannot be good for the bees."

On the ENVIRONMENT
Marcus Aurelius
Meditations

through the Modernists James Joyce, D H Lawrence, Virginia Woolf, Somerset Maugham, Aldous Huxley, Christopher Isherwood, Evelyn Waugh, and Graham Greene. Writers for the stage include George Bernard Shaw, Galsworthy, J B Priestley, Noël Coward, and Terence Rattigan, and the writers of poetic drama, such as T S Eliot, Christopher Fry, W H Auden, Christopher Isherwood, and Dylan Thomas. The 1950s and 1960s produced the 'kitchen sink' dramatists, including John Osborne and Arnold Wesker.

The following decade saw the rise of Harold Pinter, John Arden, Tom Stoppard, Peter Shaffer, Joe Orton, and Alan Ayckbourn. Poets since 1945 include Thom Gunn, Roy Fuller, Philip Larkin, Ted Hughes, and John Betjeman; novelists include William Golding, Iris Murdoch, Angus Wilson, Muriel Spark, Margaret Drabble, Kingsley Amis, Anthony Powell, Alan Sillitoe, Anthony Burgess, John Fowles, Ian McEwan, Martin Amis, Angela Carter, and Doris Lessing.

English Nature agency created 1991 from the division of the ◊Nature Conservancy Council into English, Scottish, and Welsh sections.

engraving art of creating a design by means of inscribing blocks of metal, wood, or some other hard material with a point. With intaglio printing the design is cut into the surface of a plate, usually metal. It is these cuts, often very fine, which hold the ink. In relief printing, by contrast, it is the areas left when the rest has been cut away which are inked for printing. See ◊printmaking.

enhanced radiation weapon another name for the ◊neutron bomb.

enlightenment in Buddhism, the term used to translate the Sanskrit *bodhi*, awakening: perceiving the true nature of the world, the unreality of the self, and becoming liberated from suffering (Sanskrit *duhkha*). By experience of *bodhi* ◊nirvana is attained.

Enlightenment European intellectual movement that reached its high point in the 18th century. Enlightenment thinkers were believers in social progress and in the liberating possibilities of rational and scientific knowledge. They were often critical of existing society and were hostile to religion, which they saw as keeping the human mind chained down by superstition. The American and French revolutions were justified by Enlightenment principles of human natural rights. Leading representatives of the Enlightenment were ◊Voltaire, Gotthold ◊Lessing, and Denis ◊Diderot.

Ennius Quintus c. 239–169 BC. Early Roman poet who wrote tragedies based on the Greek pattern. His epic poem *Annales* (600 lines of which survive) deals with Roman history, and inspired Virgil's *Aeneid*.

enosis (Greek 'union') movement, developed from 1930, for the union of ◊Cyprus with Greece. The campaign (led by ◊EOKA and supported by Archbishop Makarios) intensified from the 1950s. In 1960 independence from Britain, without union, was granted, and increased demands for union led to its proclamation 1974. As a result, Turkey invaded Cyprus, ostensibly to protect the Turkish community, and the island was effectively partitioned.

Ensor James Sidney, Baron Ensor 1860–1949. Belgian painter and printmaker, the most eminent of modern Belgian painters. In a bold style employing vivid colours, he created a surreal and macabre world inhabited by masked figures and skeletons. Such works as his famous *Entry of Christ into Brussels* 1888 (Musée Royale des Beaux-Arts, Brussels) anticipated Expressionism.

Ensor had an English father and a Flemish mother, and was a British subject until 1930, when he became a Belgian. He studied at the academy in Brussels, and first painted dark landscapes and seascapes, but in the 1880s developed a richness of colour and a macabre quality of imagination in which he has been compared with his Flemish forerunners Brueghel and Bosch. He worked quietly at Ostend in a studio over a shop that sold seaside gift oddities, 'happily confined', in his own words, to 'the solitary realm where the mask rules'. 1880–1900 his creative range of subject and style was fully established, appearing in tormented and tragic religious themes and in his grotesque world of masks and animated skeletons. Early works such as his *Christ's Entry into Brussels* were treated with contempt, but 1908 Emile Verhaeren first recognized his gifts, and the exhibition at the Palais des Beaux-Arts in Brussels 1929 may be said to have made the (by then aged) painter's reputation. In addition to paintings he produced a large number of drawings and etchings.

entablature in classical architecture, the upper part of an ◊order, situated above the column and principally composed of the architrave, frieze, and cornice.

entail in law, the settlement of land or other property on a successive line of people, usually succeeding generations of the original owner's family. An entail can be either general, in which case it simply descends to the heirs, or special, when it descends according to a specific arrangement – for example, to children by a named wife. Entails are increasingly rare and the power to make them has often been destroyed by legislation – for example, restrictions in certain states of the USA. In England entails can be easily terminated.

Entebbe city in Uganda, on the northwest shore of Lake Victoria, 20 km/12 mi SW of Kampala, the capital; 1,136 m/3,728 ft above sea level; population (1991) 41,600. Founded 1893, it was the administrative centre of Uganda 1894–1962. In 1976, a French aircraft was hijacked by a Palestinian liberation group. It was flown to Entebbe airport, where the hostages on board were rescued six days later by Israeli troops.

Entente Cordiale (French 'friendly understanding') agreement reached by Britain and France 1904 recognizing British interests in Egypt and French interests in Morocco. It formed the basis for Anglo-French cooperation before the outbreak of World War I 1914.

enterprise zone special zone designated by government to encourage industrial and commercial activity, usually in economically depressed areas. Investment is attracted by means of tax reduction and other financial incentives.

In the UK, enterprise zones were introduced 1980 to encourage regional investment in areas such as the depressed inner cities. Industrial and commercial property are exempt from rates, development land tax and from certain other restrictions such as planning permission. The Isle of Dogs in London's docklands was extensively developed as an enterprise zone 1980–1992. There were four enterprise zones 1994: Inverclyde, N W Kent, Lanarkshire, Sunderland.

enthalpy in chemistry, alternative term for ◊energy of reaction, the heat energy associated with a chemical change.

entomology study of ◊insects.

entrechat (French 'cross-caper') in ballet, criss-crossing of the legs while the dancer is in the air. There are two movements for each beat. Wayne ◊Sleep broke ◊Nijinsky's record of an *entrechat dix* (five beats) with an *entrechat douze* (six beats) 1973.

entrepreneur in business, a person who successfully manages and develops an enterprise through personal skill and initiative. Examples include John D ◊Rockefeller, Henry ◊Ford, Anita ◊Roddick, and Richard ◊Branson.

entropy in ◊thermodynamics, a parameter representing the state of disorder of a system at the atomic, ionic, or molecular level; the greater the disorder, the higher the entropy. Thus the fast-moving disordered molecules of water vapour have higher entropy than those of more ordered liquid water, which in turn have more entropy than the molecules in solid crystalline ice.

In a closed system undergoing change, entropy is a measure of the amount of energy unavailable for useful work. At ◊absolute zero (−273.15°C/−459.67°F/0 K), when all molecular motion ceases and order is assumed to be complete, entropy is zero.

E number code number for additives that have been approved for use by the European Commission (EC). The E written before the number stands for European. E numbers do not have to be displayed on lists of ingredients, and the manufacturer may choose to list ◊additives by their name instead. E numbers cover all categories of additives apart from flavourings.

Additives that are not approved by the European Commission, but are still used in Britain, are represented by a code number without an E.

Enver Pasha 1881–1922. Turkish politician and soldier. He led the military revolt 1908 that resulted in the Young Turks' revolution (see ◊Turkey). He was killed fighting the Bolsheviks in Turkestan.

environment in ecology, the sum of conditions affecting a particular organism, including physical surroundings, climate, and influences of other living organisms. See also ◊biosphere and ◊habitat.

In common usage, 'the environment' often means the total global environment, without reference to any particular organism. In genetics, it is the external influences that affect an organism's development, and thus its ◊phenotype.

environmental archaeology subfield of archaeology aimed at identifying processes, factors, and conditions of past biological and physical environmental systems and how they relate to cultural systems. Archaeologists and natural scientists combine their skills to reconstruct the human uses of plants and animals and how societies adapted to changing environmental conditions.

Environmentally Sensitive Area (ESA) scheme introduced by the UK Ministry of Agriculture 1984, as a result of EC legislation, to protect some of the most beautiful areas of the British countryside from the loss and damage caused by agricultural change. The first areas to be designated ESAs were in the Pennine Dales, the North Peak District, the Norfolk Broads, the Breckland, the Suffolk River Valleys, the Test Valley, the South Downs, the Somerset Levels and Moors, West Penwith, Cornwall, the Shropshire Borders, the Cambrian Mountains, and the Lleyn Peninsula.

The total area designated as ESA's was estimated 1993 at 785,600 hectares. The scheme is voluntary, with farmers being encouraged to adapt their practices so as to enhance or maintain the natural features of the landscape and conserve wildlife habitat. A farmer who joins the scheme agrees to manage the land in this way for at least five years. In return for this agreement, the Ministry of Agriculture pays the farmer a sum that reflects the financial losses incurred as a result of reconciling conservation with commercial farming.

Environmental Protection Agency (EPA) US agency set up 1970 to control water and air quality, industrial and commercial wastes, pesticides, noise, and radiation. In its own words, it aims to protect 'the country from being degraded, and its health threatened, by a multitude of human activities initiated without regard to long-ranging effects upon the life-supporting properties, the economic uses, and the recreational value of air, land, and water'.

environment art large sculptural or spatial works that create environments which the spectator may enter and become absorbed in. Environments frequently incorporate sensory stimuli, such as sound or movement, to capture the observer's attention. The US artists Jim ◊Dine and Claes ◊Oldenburg were early exponents in the 1960s.

Environment, Department of the (DOE) UK government department established 1970, bringing together ministries of Housing and Local Government, Transport, and Building and Works (although Transport returned to an independent status 1975). It is responsible for housing, construction, local government, sport and recreation policies, and preservation of the environment. The current environment secretary is John ◊Gummer.

environment–heredity controversy see ◊nature–nurture controversy.

enzyme biological ◊catalyst produced in cells, and capable of speeding up the chemical reactions necessary for life. They are large, complex ◊proteins, and are highly specific, each chemical reaction requiring its own particular enzyme. The enzyme's specificity arises from its active site, an area with a shape corresponding to part of the molecule with which it reacts (the substrate). The enzyme and the substrate slot together forming an enzyme–substrate complex that allows the reaction to take place, after which the enzyme falls away unaltered.The activity and efficiency of enzymes are influenced by various factors, including temperature and pH conditions.

Digestive enzymes include amylases (which digest starch), lipases (which digest fats), and proteases (which digest protein). Other enzymes play a part in the conversion of food energy into ◊ATP; the manufacture of all the molecular components of the body; the replication of ◊DNA when a cell divides; the production of hormones; and the control of movement of substances into and out of cells.

Enzymes have many medical and industrial uses, from washing powders to drug production, and as research tools in molecular biology. They can be extracted from bacteria and moulds, and ◊genetic engineering now makes it possible to tailor an enzyme for a specific purpose.

Eocene second epoch of the Tertiary period of geological time, 56.5–35.5 million years ago. Originally considered the earliest division of the Tertiary, the name means 'early recent', referring to the early forms of mammals evolving at the time, following the extinction of the dinosaurs.

EOKA acronym for ***Ethnikí Organósis Kipriakóu Agónos*** (National Organization of Cypriot Struggle), an underground organization formed in 1955 by General George Grivas (1898–1974) to fight for the independence of Cyprus from Britain and ultimately its union (*enosis*) with Greece. In 1971, 11 years after the independence of Cyprus, Grivas returned to the island to form EOKA B and to resume the fight for *enosis*, which had not been achieved by the Cypriot government.

Eos in Greek mythology, the goddess of the dawn (Roman Aurora).

ephedrine drug that acts like adrenaline on the sympathetic ◊nervous system (sympathomimetic). Once used to relieve bronchospasm in ◊asthma, it has been superseded by safer, more specific drugs. It is contained in some cold remedies as a decongestant. Side effects include rapid heartbeat, tremor, dry mouth, and anxiety.

Ephedrine is an alkaloid, $C_{10}H_{15}NO_1$, derived from Asian gymnosperms (genus *Ephedra*) or synthesized. It is sometimes misused, and excess leads to mental confusion and increased confidence in one's own capabilities as they actually decline.

Ephesians ◊epistle in the New Testament attributed to ◊Paul but possibly written after his death; the earliest versions are not addressed specifically to the church at Ephesus.

Ephesus ancient Greek seaport in Asia Minor, a centre of the ◊Ionian Greeks, with a temple of Artemis destroyed by the Goths AD 262. Now in Turkey, it is one of the world's largest archaeological sites. St Paul visited the city and addressed a letter (◊epistle) to the Christians there.

Ephesus Among the many fine temples at Ephesus, for centuries a prosperous commercial centre, was the Temple of Artemis, one of the Seven Wonders of the World. Artemis (known by the Romans as Diana), goddess of chastity and childbirth, the Moon, and hunting, was worshipped here. This marble statue of her, found in Ephesus, dates from the 2nd century AD. *Turkish Embassy Information Office*

epic narrative poem or cycle of poems dealing with some great deed – often the founding of a nation or the forging of national unity – and often using religious or cosmological themes. The two main epic poems in the Western tradition are *The Iliad* and *The Odyssey*, attributed to ◊Homer, which were probably chanted in sections at feasts.

Greek and later criticism, which considered the Homeric epic the highest form of poetry, produced the genre of ***secondary epic*** – such as the *Aeneid* of ◊Virgil, Tasso's *Jerusalem Delivered*, and ◊Milton's *Paradise Lost* – which attempted to emulate Homer, often for a patron or a political cause. The term is also applied to narrative poems of other traditions: the Anglo-Saxon *Beowulf* and the Finnish *Kalevala*; in India the *Rāmāyana* and *Mahābhārata* ; and the Babylonian *Gilgamesh*.

epicentre the point on the Earth's surface immediately above the seismic focus of an ◊earthquake. Most damage usually takes place at an earthquake's epicentre. The term sometimes refers to a point directly above or below a nuclear explosion ('at ground zero').

Epictetus c. AD 55–135. Greek Stoic philosopher who encouraged people to refrain from self-interest and to promote the common good of humanity. He believed that people were in the hands of an all-wise providence and that they should endeavour to do their duty in the position to which they were called.

Born at Hierapolis in Phrygia, he lived for many years in Rome as a slave but eventually secured his freedom. He was banished by the emperor ◊Domitian from Rome in AD 89.

Epicureanism system of moral philosophy named after the Greek philosopher Epicurus. He argued that pleasure is the basis of the ethical life, and that the most satisfying form of pleasure is achieved by avoiding pain, mental or physical. This is done by limiting desire as far as possible, and by choosing pleasures of the mind over those of the body.

Epicurus 341–270 BC. Greek philosopher, founder of Epicureanism, who held that all things are made up of atoms. His theory of knowledge stresses the role of sense perception, and in his ethics the most desired condition is a serene detachment based on the avoidance of anxiety and physical pain.

Epicurus taught at Athens from 306 BC, and was influential in both Greek and Roman thinking. For example, his atomic theory was adopted by the Roman Epicurean ◊Lucretius.

epicyclic gear or ***sun-and-planet gear*** gear system that consists of one or more gear wheels moving around another. Epicyclic gears are found in bicycle hub gears and in automatic gearboxes.

epicycloid in geometry, a curve resembling a series of arches traced out by a point on the circumference of a circle that rolls around another circle of a different diameter. If the two circles have the same diameter, the curve is a cardioid.

Epidaurus or ***Epidavros*** ancient Greek city and port on the E coast of Argolis, in the NE Peloponnese. The site contains a well-preserved theatre of the 4th century BC; nearby are the ruins of the temple of Asclepius, the god of healing.

epidemic outbreak of infectious disease affecting large numbers of people at the same time. A widespread epidemic that sweeps across many countries (such as the ◊Black Death in the late Middle Ages) is known as a pandemic.

epidermis outermost layer of ◊cells on an organism's body. In plants and many invertebrates such as insects, it consists of a single layer of cells. In vertebrates, it consists of several layers of cells. The epidermis of plants and invertebrates often has an outer noncellular ◊cuticle that protects the organism from desiccation. In vertebrates, such as reptiles, birds, and mammals, the outermost layer of cells is dead, forming a tough, waterproof layer, known as ◊skin.

epiglottis small flap located behind the root of the tongue in mammals. It closes off the end of the windpipe during swallowing to prevent food from passing into it and causing choking.

The action of the epiglottis is a highly complex reflex process involving two phases. During the first stage a mouthful of chewed food is lifted by the tongue towards the top and back of the mouth. This is accompanied by the cessation of breathing and by the blocking of the nasal areas from the mouth. The second phase involves the epiglottis moving over the larynx while the food passes down into the oesophagus.

epigram short, witty, and pithy saying or short poem. The poem form was common among writers of ancient Rome, including Catullus and Martial. In English, the epigram has been used by Ben Jonson, George Herrick, John Donne, Alexander Pope, Jonathan Swift, W B Yeats, and Ogden Nash. An epigram was originally a religious inscription, such as that on a tomb.

Oscar Wilde and Dorothy Parker produced epigrams in conversation as well as writing. Epigrams are often satirical, as in Wilde's observation: 'Speech was given us to conceal our thoughts.'

'Epigrams succeed where epics fail.'

On EPIGRAMS
Persian proverb

epilepsy medical disorder characterized by a tendency to develop fits, which are convulsions or abnormal feelings caused by abnormal electrical discharges in the cerebral hemispheres of the ◊brain. Epilepsy can be controlled with a number of anticonvulsant drugs.

The term epilepsy covers a range of conditions from mild 'absences', involving momentary loss of awareness, to major convulsions. In some cases the abnormal electrical activity is focal (confined to one area of the brain); in others it is generalized throughout the cerebral cortex. Fits are classified according to their clinical type. They include: the ***grand mal*** seizure with convulsions and loss of consciousness; the fleeting absence of ***petit mal***, almost exclusively a disorder of childhood; ***Jacksonian*** seizures, originating in the motor cortex; and ***temporal-lobe*** fits, which may be associated with visual hallucinations and bizarre disturbances of the sense of smell.

Epilepsy affects 1–3% of the world's population. It may arise spontaneously or may be a consequence of brain surgery, organic brain disease, head injury, metabolic disease, alcoholism or withdrawal from some drugs. Almost a third of patients have a family history of the condition. Most epileptics have infrequent fits that have little impact on their daily lives. Epilepsy does not imply that the sufferer has any impairment of intellect, behaviour, or personality.

epilogue postscript to a book; a short speech or poem at the end of a play, addressed directly to the audience.

Epiphany festival of the Christian church, held 6 Jan, celebrating the coming of the Magi (the three Wise Men) to Bethlehem with gifts for the infant Jesus, and symbolizing the manifestation of Jesus to the world. It is the 12th day after Christmas, and marks the end of the Christmas festivities.

In many countries the night before Epiphany, called Twelfth Night, is marked by the giving of gifts. In the Eastern Orthodox Church, the festival celebrated on this day is known as the theophany and commemorates the baptism of Jesus. Some Orthodox churches use an older calendar and celebrate Epiphany on 18 Jan.

epiphyte any plant that grows on another plant or object above the surface of the ground, and has no roots in the soil. An epiphyte does not parasitize the plant it grows on but merely uses it for support. Its nutrients are obtained from rainwater, organic debris such as leaf litter, or from the air. The greatest diversity of epiphytes is found in tropical areas and includes many orchids. *See illustrations on following page.*

Epirus (Greek ***Ipiros***, 'mainland') region of NW Greece; area 9,200 sq km/3,551 sq mi; population (1991) 339,200. Its capital is Yannina, and it consists of the provinces (nomes) of Arta, Thesprotia, Yannina, and Preveza. There is livestock farming. It was part of an ancient Greek region by the same name: the N part was in Albania, the remainder in NW Greece.

episcopacy in the Christian church, a system of government in which administrative and spiritual power over a district (diocese) is held by a bishop. The Roman Catholic, Eastern Orthodox, Anglican, and Episcopal churches (USA) are episcopalian; episcopacy also exists in some branches of the Lutheran Church; for example, in Scandinavia.

episiotomy incision made in the perineum (the tissue bridging the vagina and rectum) to facilitate

'Nothing is to be had for nothing.'

EPICETUS
Discourses

epiphyte A rainforest tree in Argentina heavily laden with epiphytes, notably orchids and bromeliads, representatives of the two plant families noted for their many epiphytic species. *Premaphotos Wildlife*

childbirth and prevent tearing of the vagina. It may be necessary, mainly for women giving birth for the first time, to widen the birth outlet and prevent perineal tearing. The incision is made in the second stage of labour, as the largest part of the baby's head begins to emerge from the birth canal.

epistemology branch of philosophy that examines the nature of knowledge and attempts to determine the limits of human understanding. Central issues include how knowledge is derived and how it is to be validated and tested.

epistle in the New Testament, any of the 21 letters to individuals or to the members of various churches written by Christian leaders, including the 13 written by St ◊Paul. The term also describes a letter with a suggestion of pomposity and literary affectation, and a letter addressed to someone in the form of a poem, as in the epistles of ◊Horace and Alexander ◊Pope.

The epistolary novel, a story told as a series of (fictitious) letters, was popularized by Samuel ◊Richardson in the 18th century.

epitaph inscription on a tomb, or a short tribute to a dead person.

epithelium in animals, tissue of closely packed cells that forms a surface or lines a cavity or tube. Epithelium may be protective (as in the skin) or secretory (as in the cells lining the wall of the gut).

epoch subdivision of a geological period in the geological time scale. Epochs are sometimes given their own names (such as the Palaeocene, Eocene, Oligocene, Miocene, and Pliocene epochs comprising the Tertiary period), or they are referred to as the late, early, or middle portions of a given period (as the Late Cretaceous or the Middle Triassic epoch).

EPOS acronym for ◊***electronic point of sale***.

epoxy resin synthetic ◊resin used as an ◊adhesive and as an ingredient in paints. Household epoxy resin adhesives come in component form as two separate tubes of chemical, one tube containing resin, the other a curing agent (hardener). The two chemicals are mixed just before application, and the mix soon sets hard.

Epsom town in Surrey, England; population (with Ewell) (1991) 64,400. In the 17th century it was a spa producing Epsom salts. There is a racecourse, where the Derby and the Oaks horse races are held.

The site of Henry VIII's palace of Nonsuch was excavated 1959.

Epsom salts $MgSO_4.7H_2O$ hydrated magnesium sulphate, used as a relaxant and laxative and added to baths to soothe the skin. The name is derived from a bitter saline spring at Epsom, Surrey, England, which contains the salt in solution.

Epstein Jacob 1880–1959. US-born British sculptor. He was influenced by African art and created controversy with several of his works, such as the muscular nude figure *Genesis* 1931 (Whitworth Art Gallery, Manchester). In later years he executed several monumental figures, notably the bronze *St Michael and the Devil* 1959 (Coventry Cathedral) and *Social Consciousness* 1953 (Fairmount Park, Philadelphia).

Epstein's tomb for the dramatist Oscar Wilde 1912 in the Père Lachaise cemetery, Paris (a work strongly influenced by Assyrian art), was at the time condemned as barbaric. His sculpture from 1912 to 1913 was in a harsh, mechanistic style, having affinities with ◊Vorticism and the work of such contemporary artists as Amedeo Modigliani and Constantin ◊Brancusi. The *Rock Drill* 1913 (Tate Gallery, London), which created a sensation when shown at the March 1915 London Group exhibition, originally incorporated a real drill.

equal opportunities the right to be employed or considered for employment without discrimination on the grounds of race, gender, physical or mental disability.

In 1946 a Royal Commission in the UK favoured equal pay for women in Britain. The Equal Pay Act of 1970 guaranteed (in theory) equal pay for equal work. The Sex Discrimination Act 1975 made it illegal to discriminate between men and women in a number of areas (though there were some exceptions). In 1975 the Equal Opportunities Commission was founded, with the power to oversee the operation of both the Equal Pay Act and the Sex Discrimination Act. The Commission was able to examine allegations of discrimination and to take legal action if necessary. ▷*See feature on pp. 1152–1153.*

Equal Opportunities Commission commission established by the UK government 1975 to implement the Sex Discrimination Act 1975. Its aim is to prevent discrimination, particularly on sexual or marital grounds.

equation in chemistry, representation of a chemical reaction by symbols and numbers; see ◊chemical equation.

equation in mathematics, expression that represents the equality of two expressions involving constants and/or variables, and thus usually includes an equals sign (=). For example, the equation $A = \pi r^2$ equates the area A of a circle of radius r to the product πr^2.

The algebraic equation $y = mx + c$ is the general one in coordinate geometry for a straight line.

If a mathematical equation is true for all variables in a given domain, it is sometimes called an identity and denoted by $\equiv$.

Thus $(x + y)^2 \equiv x^2 + 2xy + y^2$ for all $x, y \in R$.

An indeterminate equation is an equation for which there is an infinite set of solutions – for example, $2x = y$. A diophantine equation is an indeterminate equation in which both the solution and the terms must be whole numbers (after Diophantus of Alexandria, c. AD 250).

equator or ***terrestrial equator*** the ◊great circle whose plane is perpendicular to the Earth's axis (the line joining the poles). Its length is 40,092 km/24,901.8 mi, divided into 360 degrees of longitude. The equator encircles the broadest part of the Earth, and represents 0° latitude. It divides the Earth into two halves, called the northern and the southern hemispheres.

The celestial equator is the circle in which the plane of the Earth's equator intersects the ◊celestial sphere.

Equatorial Guinea country in W central Africa, bounded N by Cameroon, E and S by Gabon, and W by the Atlantic Ocean; also five offshore islands including Bioko, off the coast of Cameroon. *See country box opposite.*

equestrianism skill in horse riding, as practised under International Equestrian Federation rules. An Olympic sport, there are three main branches of equestrianism: showjumping, dressage, and three-day eventing.

Showjumping is horse-jumping over a course of fences. The winner is usually the competitor with fewest 'faults' (penalty marks given for knocking down or refusing fences), but in timed competitions it is the competitor completing the course most quickly, additional seconds being added for mistakes. ***Dressage*** tests the horse's obedience skills and the rider's control. Tests consist of a series of movements at walk, trot, and canter, with each movement marked by judges who look for suppleness, balance, and a special harmony between rider and horse. The term is derived from the French 'dresser', which means training. It became an Olympic sport 1960. ***Three-Day Eventing*** tests the all-round abilities of a horse and rider in dressage, cross-country, and showjumping.

The major show-jumping events include the World Championship, the European Championship, and the British Showjumping Derby. In three-day eventing, the main events are the Badminton Horse Trials and the World Championship.

equilateral of a geometrical figure, having all sides of equal length. For example, a square and a rhombus are both equilateral four-sided figures. An equilateral triangle, to which the term is most often applied, has all three sides equal and all three angles equal (at 60°).

equilibrium in physics, an unchanging condition in which an undisturbed system can remain indefinitely in a state of balance. In a static equilibrium, such as an object resting on the floor, there is no motion. In a dynamic equilibrium, in contrast, a steady state is maintained by constant, though opposing, changes. For example, in a sealed bottle half-full of water, the constancy of the water level is a result of molecules evaporating from the surface and condensing on to it at the same rate.

equinox the points in spring and autumn at which the Sun's path, the ◊ecliptic, crosses the celestial equator, so that the day and night are of approximately equal length. The vernal equinox occurs about 21 March and the autumnal equinox, 23 Sept.

equity a company's assets, less its liabilities, which are the property of the owner or shareholders. Popularly, equities are stocks and shares which do not pay interest at fixed rates but pay dividends based on the company's performance. The value of equities tends to rise over the long term, but in the short term they are a risk investment because prices can fall as well as rise. Equity is also used to refer to the paid value of mortgaged real property, most commonly a house.

equity system of law supplementing the ordinary rules of law where the application of these would operate harshly in a particular case; sometimes it is regarded as an attempt to achieve 'natural justice'. So understood, equity appears as an element in most legal systems, and in a number of legal codes judges are instructed to apply both the rules of strict law and the principles of equity in reaching their decisions.

In England equity originated in decisions of the Court of Chancery, on matters that were referred to it because there was no adequate remedy available in the Common Law courts. It developed into a distinct system of law, and until the 19th century, the two systems of common law and equity existed side by side, and were applied in separate law courts. The Judicature Acts 1873–75 established a single High Court of Justice, in which judges could apply both common law and equity to all their decisions. Equitable principles still exist side by side with principles of common law in many branches of the law.

Equity common name for the ***British Actors' Equity Association***, the UK trade union for professional actors in theatre, film, and television, founded 1929. In the USA its full name is the ***American Actors' Equity Association*** and it deals only with performers in the theatre.

era any of the major divisions of geological time, each including several periods, but smaller than an eon. The currently recognized eras all fall within the Phanerozoic eon – or the vast span of time, starting about 570 million years ago, when fossils are found to become abundant. The eras in ascending order are the Palaeozoic, Mesozoic, and Cenozoic. We are living in the Recent epoch of the Quaternary period of the Cenozoic era.

Erasmus Desiderius c. 1466–1536. Dutch scholar and leading humanist of the Renaissance era, who taught and studied all over Europe and was a prolific writer. His pioneer translation of the Greek New Testament (with parallel Latin text) 1516 exposed the Vulgate as a second-hand document. Although opposed to dogmatism and abuse of church power, he remained impartial during Martin ◊Luther's conflict with the pope.

Erasmus was born in Rotterdam, and as a youth he was a monk in an Augustinian monastery near

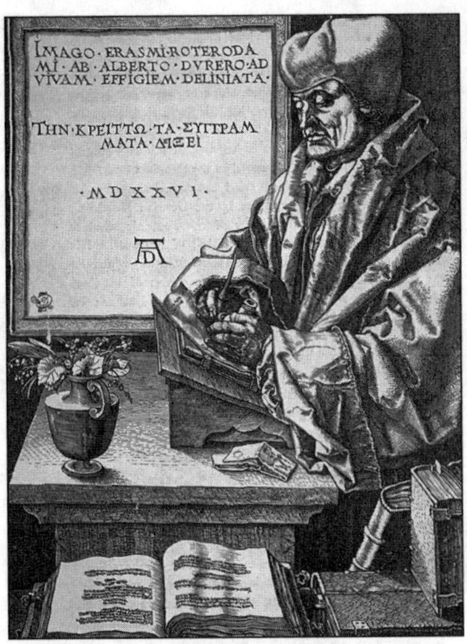

Erasmus The Dutch Renaissance humanist and scholar Desiderius Erasmus. The illegitimate son of Rogerius Gerardus, Erasmus adopted the name Desiderius, which means 'beloved'. *Philip Sauvain*

Gouda. After becoming a priest, he went to study in Paris 1495. He paid the first of a number of visits to England 1499, where he met the physician Thomas Linacre, the politician Thomas More, and the Bible interpreter John Colet, and for a time was professor of divinity and Greek at Cambridge University. He also edited the writings of St Jerome and the early Christian authorities, and published *Encomium Moriae/The Praise of Folly* 1511 (a satire on church and society that quickly became an international bestseller) and *Colloquia* (dialogues on contemporary subjects) 1519. In 1521 he went to Basel, Switzerland, where he edited the writings of the early Christian leaders.

Erastianism belief that the church should be subordinated to the state. The name is derived from Thomas Erastus (1534–1583), a German-Swiss theologian and opponent of Calvinism, who maintained in his writings that the church should not have the power of excluding people as a punishment for sin.

Eratosthenes c. 276–c. 194 BC. Greek geographer and mathematician whose map of the ancient world was the first to contain lines of latitude and longitude, and who calculated the Earth's circumference with an error of about 10%. His mathematical achievements include a method for duplicating the cube, and for finding ◊prime numbers. No work of Eratosthenes survives complete. The most important that remains is on geography – a word that he virtually coined as the title of his three-volume study of the Earth (as much as he knew of it) and its measurement.

erbium soft, lustrous, greyish, metallic element of the ◊lanthanide series, symbol Er, atomic number 68, relative atomic mass 167.26. It occurs with the element yttrium or as a minute part of various minerals. It was discovered 1843 by Carl Mosander (1797–1858), and named after the town of Ytterby, Sweden, near which the lanthanides (rare-earth elements) were first found. Erbium has been used since 1987 to amplify data pulses in optical fibre, enabling faster transmission. Erbium ions in the fibreglass, charged with infrared light, emit energy by amplifying the data pulse as it moves along the fibre.

Erebus in Greek mythology, the god of darkness; also the intermediate region between upper Earth and ◊Hades.

Erebus, Mount the world's southernmost active volcano, 3,794 m/12,452 ft high, on Ross Island, Antarctica. It contains a lake of molten lava, that scientists are investigating in the belief that it can provide a 'window' on to the magma beneath the Earth's crust.

ergo (Latin) therefore; hence.

ergonomics study of the relationship between people and the furniture, tools, and machinery they use at work. The object is to improve work performance by removing sources of muscular stress and general fatigue: for example, by presenting data and control panels in easy-to-view form, making office furniture comfortable, and creating a generally pleasant environment.

ergot certain parasitic fungi (especially of the genus *Claviceps*), whose brown or black grainlike masses replace the kernels of rye or other cereals. *C. purpurea* attacks the rye plant. Ergot poisoning is caused by eating infected bread, resulting in burning pains, gangrene, and convulsions. The large grains of the fungus contain the alkaloid ergotamine.

ergotamine ◊alkaloid $C_{33}H_{35}O_5N_5$ administered to treat migraine. Isolated from ergot, a fungus that colonizes rye, it relieves symptoms by causing the cranial arteries to constrict. Its use is limited by severe side effects, including nausea and abdominal pain.

Erhard Ludwig 1897–1977. West German Christian Democrat politician, chancellor of the Federal Republic 1963–66. The 'economic miracle' of West Germany's recovery after World War II is largely attributed to Erhard's policy of social free enterprise which he initiated during his period as federal economics minister (1949–63).

erica in botany, any plant of the genus *Erica*, family Ericaceae, including the heathers. There are about 500 species, distributed mainly in South Africa with some in Europe.

Ericsson Leif lived c. 970. Norse explorer, son of Eric the Red, who sailed west from Greenland to find a country first sighted by Norsemen 986. He visited Baffin Island then sailed along the Labrador coast to Newfoundland, which was named 'Vinland' (Wine Land), because he discovered grape vines growing there.

The story was confirmed 1961 when a Norwegian expedition, led by Helge Ingstad, discovered the remains of a Viking settlement (dated c. 1000) near the fishing village of L'Anse-aux-Meadows at the northern tip of Newfoundland.

Eric the Red c. 950–1010. Allegedly the first European to find Greenland. According to a 13th-century saga, he was the son of a Norwegian chieftain, and was banished from Iceland about 985 for murder. He then sailed westward and discovered a land that he called Greenland.

Eridanus in astronomy, the sixth largest constellation, which meanders from the celestial equator (see ◊celestial sphere) deep into the southern hemisphere of the sky. Eridanus is represented as a river. Its brightest star is ◊Achernar, a corruption of the Arabic for 'the end of the river'.

Eridu ancient city of Mesopotamia about 5000 BC, according to tradition the cradle of Sumerian civilization. On its site is now the village of Tell Abu Shahrain, Iraq.

Erie city and port on the Pennsylvania bank of Lake Erie, USA; population (1992) 109,300. It has heavy industries and a trade in iron, grain, and freshwater fish. A French fort was built on the site 1753, and a permanent settlement was laid out 1795.

'Man's mind is so formed that it is far more susceptible to falsehood than to truth.'

Desiderius Erasmus
Praise of Folly

EQUATORIAL GUINEA
Republic of

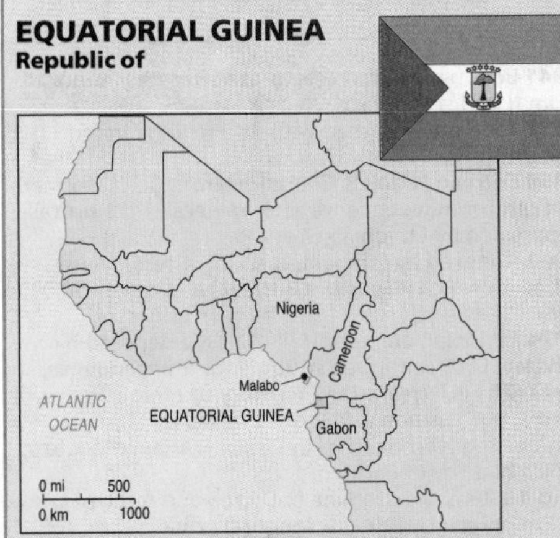

national name *República de Guinea Ecuatorial*
area 28,051 sq km/10,828 sq mi
capital Malabo
major towns/cities Bata
physical features comprises mainland Río Muni, plus the small islands of Corisco, Elobey Grande and Elobey Chico, and Bioko (formerly Fernando Po) together with Annobón (formerly Pagalu); nearly half the land is forested; volcanic mountains on Bioko
head of state Teodoro Obiang Nguema Mbasogo from 1979
head of government Silvestre Siale Bileka from 1993
political system emergent democratic republic
administrative divisions seven provinces
political parties Democratic Party of Equatorial Guinea (PDGE), nationalist, right of centre, militarily controlled; People's Social Democratic Convention (CSDP), left of centre; Democratic Socialist Union of Equatorial Guinea (UDSGE), left of centre
population 400,000 (1995 est)
population growth rate 2.6% (1990–95); 2.4% (2000–05)
ethnic distribution 80–90% of the Fang ethnic group, of Bantu origin; most other groups have been pushed to the coast by Fang expansion
life expectancy 46 (males), 50 (females)
literacy rate 50% (1994)
languages Spanish (official); pidgin English is widely spoken, and on Annobón (whose people were formerly slaves of the Portuguese) a Portuguese patois; Fang and other African patois spoken on Río Muni
religions Roman Catholic, Protestant, animist
currency franc CFA
GDP (US $) 142 million (1994)
growth rate 8.9% (1994)
exports cocoa, coffee, timber

HISTORY
1472 First visited by Portuguese explorers.
1778 Bioko (formerly known as Fernando Po) Island ceded to Spain, which established cocoa plantations there in the late 19th century, importing labour from W Africa.
1885 Mainland territory of Mbini (formerly Rio Muni) came under Spanish rule, the whole colony being known as Spanish Guinea, with the capital at Malabu on Bioko Island.
1920s League of Nations special mission sent to investigate the forced, quasi-slave labour conditions on the Bioko cocoa plantations, then the largest in the world.
1959 Became a Spanish Overseas Province; African population finally granted full citizenship.
early 1960s On the mainland, the Fang people spearheaded a nationalist movement directed against Spanish favouritism towards Bioko Island and its controlling Bubi tribe.
1963 Granted internal autonomy.
1968 Independence achieved from Spain. Macias Nguema, a nationalist Fang, became first president, discriminating against the Bubi community.
1970s Economy collapsed as Spanish settlers and other minorities fled in the face of intimidation by Nguema's brutal, dictatorial regime, which was marked by the murder, torture, and imprisonment of tens of thousands of political opponents and rivals, as well as the closing of churches.
1979 Nguema overthrown, tried and executed. He was replaced by his nephew, Teodoro Obiang Nguema Mbasogo, who established a military regime, but released political prisoners and imposed restrictions on the Catholic Church.
1992 New pluralist constitution approved by referendum.
1993 Obiang's PDGE won first multiparty elections on low turnout.
1996 Obiang re-elected amid claims of fraud by opponents.

SEE ALSO Fang

‘The job of buildings is to improve human relations: architecture must ease them, not make them worse.’

Ralph Erskine
Quoted in *The Times* 16 Sept 1992

Erie, Lake fourth largest of the Great Lakes of North America, connected to Lake Ontario by the Niagara River and bypassed by the Welland Canal; area 9,930 sq mi/25,720 sq km.

It is linked to Lake Huron by Lake St Clair and the St Clair and Detroit rivers and to the Hudson River by the New York State Barge Canal. It is an important component of the St Lawrence Seaway.

Lake Erie ports include Cleveland and Toledo, Ohio; Erie, Pennsylvania; and Buffalo, New York. A US naval victory near the western end of the lake 9 Sept 1813 forced the British to evacuate Detroit. The shallowest of the Great Lakes, Lake Erie has become severely polluted from industrial and municipal waste.

Erigena Johannes Scotus c. 815–c. 877. Medieval philosopher. He was probably Irish and, according to tradition, travelled in Greece and Italy. The French king Charles (II) the Bald invited him to France (before 847), where he became head of the court school. He is said to have visited Oxford, to have taught at Malmesbury, and to have been stabbed to death by his pupils. In his philosophy, he defied church orthodoxy in his writings on cosmology and predestination, and tried to combine Christianity with ◊neo-Platonism.

Erinyes in Greek mythology, another name for the ◊Furies.

Eris in Greek mythology, the personification of Strife, companion of the war-god ◊Ares and a daughter of Night.

Eritrea country in E Africa, bounded N by Sudan, S by Ethiopia, SE by Djibouti, and E by the Red Sea. *See country box below.*

ERM abbreviation for ◊***Exchange Rate Mechanism***.

ermine the ◊stoat during winter, when its coat becomes white. In northern latitudes the coat becomes completely white, except for a black tip on the tail, but in warmer regions the back may remain brownish. The fur is used commercially.

Ernst Max 1891–1976. German artist, a major figure in ◊Dada and then ◊Surrealism. He worked in France 1922–38 and in the USA from 1941. He experimented with collage, photomontage, and surreal images, creating some of the most haunting and distinctive images of 20th-century art. His works include *The Elephant Celebes* 1921 (Tate Gallery, London) and *The Temptation of St Anthony* 1945 (Lehmbruck Museum, Duisburg).

Ernst was born in Brühl, near Cologne, and studied philosophy at Bonn. He first exhibited in Berlin 1916. In 1919 he was a leading figure in Dadaist demonstrations in Cologne, and going to Paris in 1920 he helped André Breton and Paul Eluard in founding the Surrealist movement. He became one of its leading visual exponents, creating fantastical images using 19th-century illustrations, and painting bizarre figures, often half animal, and elaborate, dreamlike landscapes. He invented the technique of frottage (rubbing colour or graphite on paper laid over a textured surface), a technique he saw as akin to Surrealist automatic writing. In his sculpture, he was influenced by primitive art. He worked in a variety of media, producing a ‘collage novel’, *La Femme cent têtes* 1929, working on films with Salvador Dali and Luis Buñuel, and designing sets and costumes for Sergei Diaghilev's Ballets Russes. In 1938 he left the Surrealist group after a disagreement with Breton and in 1941 settled in New York, where he became an important figure in the development of American art. He returned to Paris 1953.

Eros in astronomy, an asteroid, discovered 1898, that can pass 22 million km/14 million mi from the Earth, as observed in 1975. Eros was the first asteroid to be discovered that has an orbit coming within that of Mars. It is elongated, measures about 36 × 12 km/22 × 7 mi, rotates around its shortest axis every 5.3 hours, and orbits the Sun every 1.8 years. The Near Earth Asteroid Rendezvous (NEAR) launched Feb 1996 is estimated to take three years to reach Eros. It will spend a year circling the asteroid in an attempt to determine what it is made of.

Eros in Greek mythology, boy-god of love, traditionally armed with bow and arrows. He was the son of ◊Aphrodite, and fell in love with ◊Psyche. He is identified with the Roman ◊Cupid.

erosion wearing away of the Earth's surface, caused by the breakdown and transportation of particles of rock or soil (by contrast, ◊weathering does not involve transportation). Agents of erosion include the sea, rivers, glaciers, and wind. Water, consisting of sea waves and currents, rivers, and rain; ice, in the form of glaciers; and wind, hurling sand fragments against exposed rocks and moving dunes along, are the most potent forces of erosion. People also contribute to erosion by bad farming practices and the cutting down of forests, which can lead to the formation of dust bowls. There are several processes of erosion including ◊hydraulic action, ◊corrosion, ◊attrition, and ◊solution.

erratic in geology, a displaced rock that has been transported by a glacier or some other natural force to a site of different geological composition. For example, in East Anglia, England, erratics have been found that have been transported from as far away as Scotland and Scandinavia.

error in computing, a fault or mistake, either in the software or on the part of the user, that causes a program to stop running (crash) or produce unexpected results. Program errors, or bugs, are largely eliminated in the course of the programmer's initial testing procedure, but some will remain in most programs. All computer operating systems are designed to produce an error message (on the display screen, or in an error file or printout) whenever an error is detected, reporting that an error has taken place and, wherever possible, diagnosing its cause.

Erse originally a Scottish form of the word *Irish*, a name applied by Lowland Scots to Scottish Gaelic and also sometimes used as a synonym for Irish Gaelic.

Ershad Hussain Muhammad 1930– . Military ruler of Bangladesh 1982–90. He assumed power in a military coup 1982. As president from 1983, Ershad introduced a successful rural-oriented economic programme. He was re-elected 1986 and lifted martial law, but faced continuing political opposition, which forced him to resign. In 1991 he was charged with the illegal possession of arms, and sentenced to ten years' imprisonment; he received a further sentence of three years' imprisonment 1992 after being convicted of corruption. In Jan 1997 he was released on bail to resume leadership of his party.

Erskine Ralph 1914– . English-born architect. He settled in Sweden 1939. He specialized in ◊community architecture before it was named as such. A deep social consciousness and a concern to mould building form in response to climate determine his architecture. His Byker Estate in Newcastle-upon-Tyne 1969–80, where a sheltering wall of dwellings embraces the development, involved a lengthy process of consultation with the residents. A later project is the ‘Ark’, an office building in Hammersmith, London, 1989–91.

Erté Adopted name of Romain de Tirtoff 1892–1990. Russian designer and illustrator. He was active in France and the USA. An exponent of ◊Art Deco, he designed sets and costumes for opera, theatre, and ballet, and his drawings were highly stylized and expressive, featuring elegant, curvilinear women.

Erté (the name was derived from the French pronunciation of his initials) went to Paris 1911 to work as a theatre and ballet set designer. From 1916 to 1926 he produced covers for the US fashion magazine *Harper's Bazaar*, and went to Hollywood 1925 to work as a designer on several films. He continued to design sets and costumes in Europe and the USA for many decades. His illustrations were influenced by 16th-century Persian and Indian miniatures.

ERITREA
State of

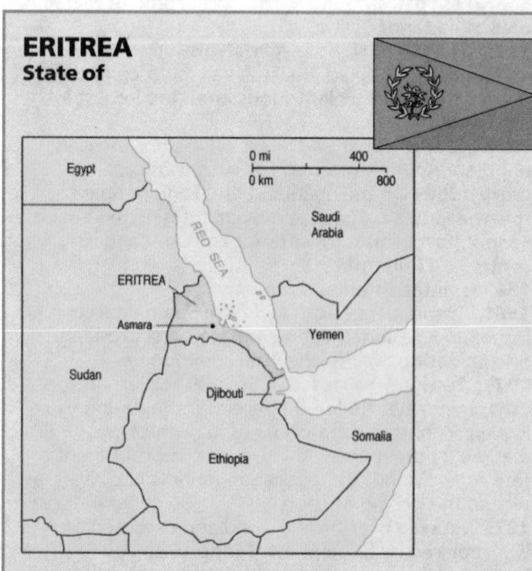

area 125,000 sq km/48,250 sq mi
capital Asmara
major towns/cities Keren, Adigrat
major ports Asab, Massawa
physical features coastline along the Red Sea 1,000 km/620 mi; narrow coastal plain that rises to an inland plateau; Dahlak Islands
head of state and government Issaias Afwerki from 1993
political system emergent democracy
administrative divisions six regions
political parties People's Front for Democracy and Justice (PFDJ) (formerly Eritrean People's Liberation Front: EPLF), left of centre; Eritrean National Pact Alliance (ENPA), moderate, centrist
population 3,531,000 (1995 est)
population growth rate 2.7% (1990–95); 2.5% (2000–05)
ethnic distribution several ethnic groups, including the Amhara and the Tigrais
languages Amharic (official), Tigrinya (official), Arabic, Afar, Bilen, Hidareb, Kunama, Nara, Rashaida, Saho, and Tigre
religions Sunni Muslim, Coptic Christian
currency Ethiopian birr
GDP (US $) 558 million (1994 est)
growth rate 9.4% (1994)
exports salt, gum arabic, hides, cement

HISTORY
4th–7th Cs AD Part of Ethiopian Aksum kingdom.
8th C Islam introduced to coastal areas by Arabs.
12th–16th Cs Under the influence of Ethiopian Abyssinian kingdoms.
mid-16th C Came under the control of the Turkish Ottoman Empire.
1882 Occupied by Italy.
1889 Italian colony of Eritrea created out of Ottoman areas and coastal districts of Ethiopia.
1920s Massawa developed into largest port in E Africa.
1935–36 Used as base for Italy's conquest of Ethiopia and became part of Italian East Africa.
1941 Became British protectorate after Italy removed from N Africa.
1952 Federation formed with Ethiopia by United Nations (UN).
1958 Eritrean People's Liberation Front (EPLF) formed to fight for independence after general strike brutally suppressed by Ethiopian rulers.
1962 Annexed by Ethiopia, sparking a secessionist rebellion which was to last 30 years and claim 150,000 lives.
1974 Ethiopian emperor Haile Selassie deposed by military; EPLF continued struggle for independence.
1977–78 EPLF cleared the territory of Ethiopian forces, but position was soon reversed by Marxist Ethiopian government of Col Haile Mariam Mengistu, which had Soviet backing.
mid-1980s Severe famine in Eritrea and refugee crisis as Ethiopian government sought forcible resettlement.
1990 Strategic port of Massawa captured by Eritrean rebel forces.
1991 Ethiopian president Mengistu overthrown. EPLF secured whole of Eritrea and provisional government formed under Issaias Afwerki.
1993 Independence approved in regional referendum and recognized by Ethiopia. Transitional government established for four-year period, with Afwerki elected president; 500,000 refugees outside Eritrea began to return.
1994 EPLF renamed PFDJ.

SEE ALSO Aksum; Ethiopia; Haile Mariam; Haile Selassie; Mengistu

erythrocyte another name for ◊red blood cell.

erythropoietin (EPO) in biology, a naturally occurring hormone, secreted mainly by the kidneys in adults and the liver in children, that stimulates production of red blood cells, which carry oxygen around the body. It is released in response to a lowered percentage of oxygen in the blood reaching the kidneys, such as in anaemic subjects. Recombinant human erythropoietin is used therapeutically to treat the anaemia associated with chronic kidney failure. A synthetic version is sometimes used illegally by athletes as it increases the oxygen-carrying capacity of the blood.

ESA abbreviation for ◊***European Space Agency***.

Esarhaddon died 669 BC. King of Assyria from 680 BC, when he succeeded his father ◊Sennacherib. He conquered Egypt 674–671 BC.

Esau in the Old Testament, the son of Isaac and Rebekah, and the hirsute elder twin brother of Jacob. Jacob tricked the blind Isaac into giving him the blessing intended for Esau by putting on goatskins for Isaac to feel. Earlier Esau had sold his birthright to Jacob for a 'mess of red pottage'. Esau was the ancestor of the Edomites.

escalator automatic moving staircase that carries people between floors or levels. It consists of treads linked in an endless belt arranged to form strips (steps), powered by an electric motor that moves both steps and handrails at the same speed. Towards the top and bottom the steps flatten out for ease of passage. The first escalator was exhibited in Paris 1900.

escarpment or ***cuesta*** large ridge created by the erosion of dipping sedimentary rocks. It has one steep side (scarp) and one gently sloping side (dip). Escarpments are common features of chalk landscapes, such as the Chiltern Hills and the North Downs in England. Certain features are associated with chalk escarpments, including dry valleys (formed on the dip slope), combes (steep-sided valleys on the scarp slope), and springs.

Escher M(aurits) C(ornelis) 1898–1972. Dutch graphic artist. His prints are often based on mathematical concepts and contain paradoxes and illusions. The lithograph *Ascending and Descending* 1960, with interlocking staircases creating a perspective puzzle, is a typical work.

Escherichia coli rod-shaped Gram-negative bacterium (see ◊bacteria) that lives, usually harmlessly, in the colon of most warm-blooded animals. It is the commonest cause of urinary tract infections in humans. It is sometimes found in water or meat where faecal contamination has occurred and can cause severe gastric problems.

Esenin or ***Yesenin***, Sergey Aleksandrovich 1895–1925. Soviet poet, born in Konstantinovo (renamed Esenino in his honour). He went to Petrograd 1915, attached himself to the Symbolists, welcomed the Russian Revolution, revived peasant traditions and folklore, and initiated the Imaginist group of poets 1919. A selection of his poetry was translated in *Confessions of a Hooligan* 1973. He was married briefly to US dancer Isadora Duncan 1922–23.

esker narrow, steep-walled ridge, often sinuous and sometimes branching, formed beneath a glacier. It is made of sands and gravels, and represents the course of a subglacial river channel. Eskers vary in height from 3–30 m/10–100 ft and can be up to 160 km/100 mi or so in length.

Eskimo Algonquian term for Arctic peoples meaning 'eater of raw meat', now considered offensive. See ◊Inuit.

ESP abbreviation for ◊***extrasensory perception***.

esparto grass *Stipa tenacissima*, native to S Spain, S Portugal, and the Balearics, but now widely grown in dry, sandy locations throughout the world. The plant is just over 1 m/3 ft high, producing greyish-green leaves, which are used for making paper, ropes, baskets, mats, and cables.

Esperanto language devised 1887 by Polish philologist Ludwig L ◊Zamenhof as an international auxiliary language. For its structure and vocabulary it draws on Latin, the Romance languages, English, and German. At its centenary 1987, Esperantists claimed 10–15 million users worldwide.

Esperanto spread from Europe to Japan, Brazil, and especially China. Its structure is completely regular, with consistent endings for nouns and adjectives. The spelling is phonetic, but the accent varies according to the regional background of its users.

espionage the practice of spying; a way to gather ◊intelligence.

Esquivel Adolfo 1932– . Argentinian sculptor and architect. As leader of the Servicio de Paz y Justicia (Peace and Justice Service), a Catholic–Protestant human-rights organization, he was awarded the 1980 Nobel Prize for Peace.

essay short piece of nonfiction, often dealing with a particular subject from a personal point of view. The essay became a recognized genre with French writer Montaigne's 'Essais' 1580 and in English with Francis Bacon's 'Essays' 1597. Today the essay is a part of journalism: articles in the broadsheet newspapers are in the essay tradition.

Abraham Cowley, whose essays appeared 1668, brought a greater ease and freedom to the genre than it had possessed before in England, but it was with the development of periodical literature in the 18th century that the essay became a widely used form. The great names are Joseph Addison and Richard Steele, with their *Tatler* and *Spectator* papers, and later Samuel Johnson and Oliver Goldsmith. In North America the politician and scientist Benjamin Franklin was noted for his style.

A new era was inaugurated by Charles Lamb's 'Essays of Elia' 1820; to the same period belong Leigh Hunt, William Hazlitt, and Thomas De Quincey in England, C A Sainte-Beuve in France, and Ralph Waldo Emerson and Henry Thoreau in the USA. From the 19th century the essay was increasingly used in Europe and the USA as a vehicle for literary criticism. Hazlitt may be regarded as the originator of the critical essay, and his successors include Matthew Arnold and Edmund Gosse. Thomas Macaulay, whose essays began to appear shortly after those of Lamb, presents a strong contrast to Lamb with his vigorous but less personal tone.

There was a revival of the form during the closing years of the 19th and beginning of the 20th centuries, in the work of R L Stevenson, Oliver Wendell Holmes, Anatole France, Théophile Gautier, and Max Beerbohm. The literary journalistic tradition of the essay was continued by James Thurber, Mark Twain, H L Mencken, Edmund Wilson, Desmond MacCarthy, and others, and the critical essay by George Orwell, Cyril Connolly, F R Leavis, T S Eliot, Norman Mailer, John Updike, and others.

Essen city in North Rhine–Westphalia, Germany; population (1993) 624,600. It is the administrative centre of the Ruhr region, situated between the rivers Emscher and Ruhr, and has textile, chemical, and electrical industries. Its 9th–14th-century minster is one of the oldest churches in Germany.

Essene member of an ancient Jewish religious sect located in the area near the Dead Sea c. 200 BC–AD 200, whose members lived a life of denial and asceticism, as they believed that the day of judgement was imminent. The ◊Dead Sea Scrolls, discovered in 1947, are believed by some scholars to be the library of the community. John the Baptist may have been a member of the Essenes.

Essequibo longest river in Guyana, South America, rising in the Guiana Highlands of S Guyana; length 1,014 km/630 mi. Part of the district of Essequibo, which lies to the W of the river, is claimed by Venezuela.

Essex county of SE England
area 3,670 sq km/1,417 sq mi (*see United Kingdom map*)
towns and cities Chelmsford (administrative headquarters), Colchester; ports: Harwich, Tilbury; resorts: Southend-on-Sea, Clacton
features former royal hunting ground of Epping Forest (controlled from 1882 by the City of London); the marshy coastal headland of the Naze; since 1111 at Great Dunmow the Dunmow flitch (side of cured pork) can be claimed every four years by any couple proving to a jury they have not regretted their marriage within the year (winners are few); Stansted, London's third airport; new Roman Catholic cathedral at Brentwood (designed by Quinlan Terry) dedicated 1991
industries dairy products, cereals, fruit, sugar beet, oysters, cars (Ford and Mazda at Dagenham)
population (1991) 1,528,600.
history In 991 the Saxons were defeated by the Vikings at the Battle of the Maldon.
famous people William Harvey.

Essex Robert Devereux, 2nd Earl of Essex 1566–1601. English soldier and politician. He became a favourite with Queen Elizabeth I from 1587, but was executed because of his policies in Ireland. Succeeded to earldom 1576.

Essex fought in the Netherlands 1585–86 and distinguished himself at the Battle of Zutphen. In 1596 he jointly commanded a force that seized and sacked Cádiz. In 1599 he became Lieutenant of Ireland and led an army against Irish rebels under the Earl of Tyrone in Ulster, but was unsuccessful, made an unauthorized truce with Tyrone, and returned without permission to England. He was forbidden to return to court, and when he marched into the City of London at the head of a body of supporters, he was promptly arrested, tried for treason, and beheaded on Tower Green.

Essex Robert Devereux, 3rd Earl of Essex 1591–1646. English soldier. Eldest son of the 2nd earl, he commanded the Parliamentary army at the inconclusive English Civil War battle of Edgehill 1642. Following a disastrous campaign in Cornwall, he resigned his command 1645.

Establishment, the a perceived elite of the professional and governing classes (judges, civil servants, politicians, and so on) who collectively symbolize authority and the status quo.

estate in law, the rights that a person has in relation to any property. Real estate is an interest in any land; personal estate is an interest in any other kind of property.

estate in European history, an order of society that enjoyed a specified share in government. In medieval theory, there were usually three estates – the nobility, the clergy, and the commons – with the functions of, respectively, defending society from foreign aggression and internal disorder, attending to its spiritual needs, and working to produce the base with which to support the other two orders.

When parliaments and representative assemblies developed from the 13th century, their organization reflected this theory, with separate houses for the nobility, the commons (usually burghers and gentry), and the clergy. The fourth estate is the press; the term was coined in the 18th century by the British politician Edmund Burke.

ester organic compound formed by the reaction between an alcohol and an acid, with the elimination of water. Unlike ◊salts, esters are covalent compounds. *See illustration on following page.*

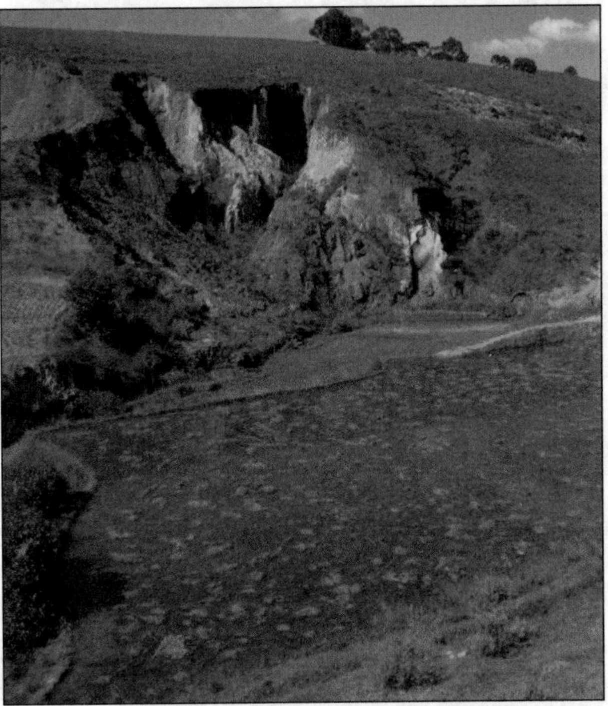

erosion The red scars of erosion are now a common feature of the central plateau of Madagascar. They are the result of relatively recent felling of the natural forests. The impoverished grasslands that have replaced the forests do little to protect the underlying soils, which are washed away during heavy rain, severely damaging rice-growing areas in the valleys.
Premaphotos Wildlife

'The deepest Essex few explore / Where steepest thatch is sunk in flowers / And out of elm and sycamore / Rise flinty fifteenth century towers.'

On **Essex**
John Betjeman 'Essex' in *Collected Poems*

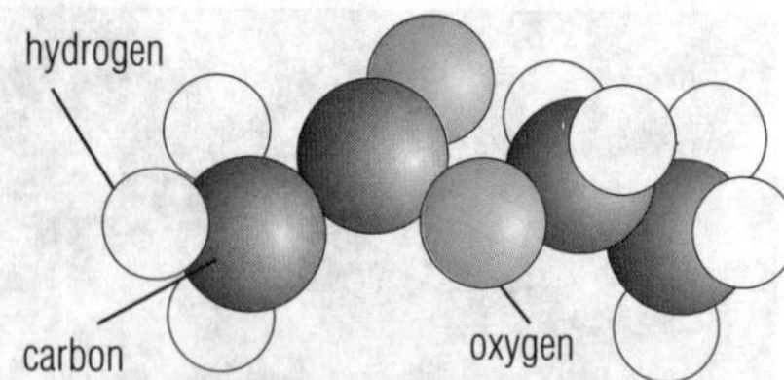

ester Molecular model of the ester ethyl ethanoate (ethyl acetate) $CH_3CH_2CO_2CH_3$.

Estonia country in N Europe, bounded E by Russia, S by Latvia, and N and W by the Baltic Sea. *See country box below.*

Estonian the largest ethnic group in Estonia. There are 1 million speakers of the Estonian language, a member of the Finno-Ugric branch of the Uralic family. Most live in Estonia.

estuary river mouth widening into the sea, where fresh water mixes with salt water and tidal effects are felt.

etching printmaking technique in which a metal plate (usually copper or zinc) is covered with a waxy overlayer (ground) and then drawn on with an etching needle. The exposed areas are then 'etched', or bitten into, by a corrosive agent (acid), so that they will hold ink for printing.

The earliest dated etching is by Urs Graf 1513. Dürer was also a pioneer, with his *The Cannon*, etched on iron. Van Dyck made portrait etchings of his contemporaries (completed in line engraving by assistants 1626–32). Rembrandt in his 300 plates showed himself the greatest of etchers in variety of style, range and depth of expression, in portraits, landscape and subjects taken either from scripture or from daily life. Other notable painter-etchers of the Netherlands were Hercules Seghers, Ostade, Teniers, Paulus Potter and Berchem. Callot, Claude, Watteau, Boucher and Fragonard are among the great French practitioners, and in Italy Tiepolo, with his delicate 'Capricci', Piranesi and Canaletto. Hogarth used etching as well as line-engraving; Rowlandson and Gillray etched in outline, their prints being completed by hand-colouring. Cruikshank's etched illustrations to Dickens's novels are also of note. Crome, Girtin, Cotman and Turner (who etched the outlines for his mezzotinted *Liber Studiorum*) give landscape examples in England, and in France etching was revived by Théodore Rousseau, Daubigny, Corot, Millet and Méryon. Outstanding 20th-century practitioners include Chagall, Derain, Matisse, Picasso, Rouault, and Segonzac.

Eteocles in Greek mythology, son of the incestuous union of ◊Oedipus and Jocasta and brother of Polynices. He denied his brother a share in the kingship of Thebes, thus provoking the expedition of the ◊Seven against Thebes, in which he and his brother died by each other's hands.

ethanal common name ***acetaldehyde*** CH_3CHO one of the chief members of the group of organic compounds known as ◊aldehydes. It is a colourless inflammable liquid boiling at 20.8°C/69.6°F. Ethanal is formed by the oxidation of ethanol or ethene and is used to make many other organic chemical compounds.

ethanal trimer common name ***paraldehyde*** $(CH_3CHO)_3$ colourless liquid formed from ethanal. It is soluble in water.

ethane CH_3CH_3 colourless, odourless gas, the second member of the ◊alkane series of hydrocarbons (paraffins).

ethane-1,2-diol technical name for ◊glycol.

ethanoate common name ***acetate*** $CH_3CO_2h^{2-}$ negative ion derived from ethanoic (acetic) acid; any salt containing this ion. In textiles, acetate rayon is a synthetic fabric made from modified cellulose (wood pulp) treated with ethanoic acid; in photography, acetate film is a non-flammable film made of cellulose ethanoate.

ethanoic acid common name ***acetic acid*** CH_3CO_2H one of the simplest fatty acids (a series of organic acids). In the pure state it is a colourless liquid with an unpleasant pungent odour; it solidifies to an icelike mass of crystals at 16.7°C/62.4°F, and hence is often called glacial ethanoic acid. Vinegar contains 5% or more ethanoic acid, produced by fermentation.

Cellulose (derived from wood or other sources) may be treated with ethanoic acid to produce a cellulose ethanoate (acetate) solution, which can be used to make plastic items by injection moulding or extruded to form synthetic textile fibres.

ethanol common name ***ethyl alcohol*** C_2H_5OH alcohol found in beer, wine, cider, spirits, and other alcoholic drinks. When pure, it is a colourless liquid with a pleasant odour, miscible with water or ether; it burns in air with a pale blue flame. The vapour forms an explosive mixture with air and may be used in high-compression internal combustion engines.

It is produced naturally by the fermentation of carbohydrates by yeast cells. Industrially, it can be made by absorption of ethene and subsequent reaction with water, or by the reduction of ethanal in the presence of a catalyst, and is widely used as a solvent.

Ethanol is used as a raw material in the manufacture of ether, chloral, and iodoform. It can also be added to petrol, where it improves the performance of the engine, or be used as a fuel in its own right (as in Brazil). Crops such as sugar cane may be grown to provide ethanol (by fermentation) for this purpose.

Ethelbert c. 552–616. King of Kent 560–616. He was defeated by the West Saxons 568 but later became ruler of England S of the river Humber. Ethelbert received the Christian missionary Augustine 597 and later converted to become the first Christian ruler of Anglo-Saxon England. He issued the first written code of laws known in England and married a French princess, Bertha.

Ethelred (II) the Unready 968–1016. King of England from 978. The son of King Edgar, Ethelred became king after the murder of his half-brother, Edward the Martyr. He tried to buy off the Danish raiders by paying Danegeld. In 1002, he ordered the massacre of the Danish settlers, provoking an invasion by Sweyn I of Denmark. War with Sweyn and Sweyn's son, Canute, occupied the rest of Ethelred's reign. He was nicknamed the 'Unready' because of his apparent lack of foresight.

ethene common name ***ethylene*** C_2H_4 colourless, flammable gas, the first member of the ◊alkene series of hydrocarbons. It is the most widely used

ESTONIA
Republic of

area 45,000 sq km/17,000 sq mi
capital Tallinn
major towns/cities Tartu, Narva, Kohtla-Järve, Pärnu
physical features lakes and marshes in a partly forested plain; 774 km/481 mi of coastline; mild climate; Lake Peipus and Narva River forming boundary with Russian Federation; Baltic islands, the largest of which is Saaremaa Island
head of state Lennart Meri from 1992
head of government Mart Siimann from 1997
political system emergent democracy
administrative divisions 15 counties or districts
political parties Coalition Party (KMU), ex-communist, left of centre, 'social market'; Isamaa (National Fatherland Party, or Pro Patria), right-wing, nationalist, free market; Estonian Reform Party (ERP), freemarket; Centre Party (CP), moderate nationalist (formerly the Estonian Popular Front (EPF; Rahvarinne); Estonian National Independence Party (ENIP), radical nationalist; Communist Party of Estonia (CPE); Our Home is Estonia; Estonian Social Democratic Party (ESDP) (last three draw much of their support from ethnic Russian community)
population 1,530,000 (1995 est)
population growth rate −0.6% (1990–95); −0.3 (2000–05)
ethnic distribution 62% Finno-Ugric ethnic Estonians, 30% Russian, 3% Ukrainian, 2% Belarussian, and 1% Finnish
life expectancy 66 (men), 75 (women)
literacy rate 99%
languages Estonian (official), allied to Finnish; Russian
religions Lutheran, Russian Orthodox
currency kroon
GDP (US $) 4.57 billion (1994)
growth rate 4.7% (1994)
exports oil and gas (from shale), wood products, flax, dairy and pig products

HISTORY
1st C AD First independent state formed.
9th C Invaded by Vikings.
13th C Tallinn, in the Danish-controlled N, joined Hanseatic League, a N European union of commercial towns; Livonia, comprising S Estonia and Latvia, came under control of German Teutonic Knights and was converted to Christianity.
1561 Sweden took control of N Estonia.
1629 Sweden took control of S Estonia from Poland.
1721 Sweden ceded the country to tsarist Russia.
late 19th C Estonian nationalist movement developed in opposition to Russian political and cultural repression and German economic control.
1914 Occupied by German troops.
1918–19 Estonian nationalists, led by Konstantin Pats, proclaimed and achieved independence, despite efforts by the Russian Red Army to regain control.
1920s Land reforms and cultural advances under democratic regime.
1934 Pats overthrew parliamentary democracy in a quasi-fascist coup at a time of economic depression; Baltic Entente mutual defence pact signed with Latvia and Lithuania.
1940 Estonia incorporated into Soviet Union (USSR); 100,000 Estonians deported to Siberia or killed.
1941–44 German occupation during World War II.
1944 USSR regained control; 'Sovietization' followed, including agricultural collectivization and immigration of ethnic Russians.
late 1980s Beginnings of nationalist dissent, encouraged by *glasnost* initiative of reformist Soviet leader Mikhail Gorbachev.
1988 Popular Front (EPF) established to campaign for democracy. Sovereignty declaration issued by state assembly rejected by USSR as unconstitutional.
1989 Estonian replaced Russian as main language.
1990 CPE monopoly of power abolished; pro-independence candidates secured majority after multiparty elections; coalition government formed with EPF leader Edgar Savisaar as prime minister; Arnold Rüütel became president. Prewar constitution partially restored.
1991 Independence achieved after attempted anti-Gorbachev coup in Moscow; CPE outlawed. Estonia joined United Nations.
1992 Savisaar resigned over food and energy shortages; Isamaa leader Lennart Meri became president and free-marketer Mart Laar prime minister.
1993 Joined Council of Europe; free-trade agreement with Latvia and Lithuania.
1994 Last Russian troops withdrawn. Radical economic-reform programme introduced. Laar resigned.
1995 Former communists won largest number of seats in general election; left-of-centre coalition formed under Tiit Vahi.
1996 President Meri re-elected.
1997 Vahi resigned and was replaced by Mart Siimann.

SEE ALSO Latvia; Lithuania; Russia; Union of Soviet Socialist Republics synthetic organic chemical and is used to produce the plastics polyethene (polyethylene), polychloroethene, and polyvinyl chloride (PVC). It is obtained from natural gas or coal gas, or by the dehydration of ethanol.

Ethene is produced during plant metabolism and is classified as a plant hormone. It is important in the ripening of fruit and in ◊abscission. Small amounts of ethene are often added to the air surrounding fruit to artificially promote ripening. Tomato and marigold plants show distorted growth in concentrations as low as 0.01 parts per million.

ether in chemistry, any of a series of organic chemical compounds having an oxygen atom linking the carbon atoms of two hydrocarbon radical groups (general formula R-O-R′); also the common name for ethoxyethane $C_2H_5OC_2H_5$ (also called diethyl ether).

This is used as an anaesthetic and as an external cleansing agent before surgical operations. It is also used as a solvent, and in the extraction of oils, fats, waxes, resins, and alkaloids.

Ethoxyethane is a colourless, volatile, inflammable liquid, slightly soluble in water, and miscible with ethanol. It is prepared by treatment of ethanol with excess concentrated sulphuric acid at 140°C/284°F.

ether or ***aether*** in the history of science, a hypothetical medium permeating all of space. The concept originated with the Greeks, and has been revived on several occasions to explain the properties and propagation of light. It was supposed that light and other electromagnetic radiation – even in outer space – needed a medium, the ether, in which to travel. The idea was abandoned with the acceptance of ◊relativity.

Etherege George c. 1635–1691. English Restoration dramatist. His play *Love in a Tub* 1664 was the first attempt at the comedy of manners (a genre further developed by Congreve and Sheridan). Later plays include *She Would If She Could* 1668 and *The Man of Mode, or Sir Fopling Flutter* 1676.

Ethernet in computing, a protocol for ◊local area networks. Ethernet was developed principally by the Xerox Corporation, but can now be used on many computers. It allows data transfer at rates up to 10 Mbps.

ethics or ***moral philosophy*** branch of ◊philosophy concerned with the systematic study of human values. It involves the study of theories of conduct and goodness, and of the meanings of moral terms.

In ancient India and China, sages like Buddha and Lao Zi made recommendations about how people should live, as Jesus and Muhammad did in later centuries. However, ethics as a systematic study first appears with the Greek philosopher Socrates in the 5th century BC. Plato thought that objective standards (forms) of justice and goodness existed beyond the everyday world. In his *Nicomachean Ethics*, Aristotle argued that virtue is natural and so leads to happiness, and that moral virtues are acquired by practice, like skills. The Cyrenaics and Epicureans were hedonists who believed in the wise pursuit of pleasure. The Stoics advocated control of the passions and indifference to pleasure and pain.

The 'Christian ethic' is mainly a combination of New Testament moral teaching with ideas drawn from Plato and Aristotle, combining hedonism and rationalism. Medieval ◊scholasticism saw God's will as the ethical standard but tempered it with Aristotelian ethics.

In the 17th century, the Dutch philosopher Spinoza and the English Thomas Hobbes both believed that morals were deducible from prudence, but Spinoza's moral theory is set in a pantheistic metaphysics. In the 18th century, the English cleric Joseph Butler argued that virtue is natural and that benevolence and self-interest tend to coincide. The Scot David Hume, who influenced Jeremy Bentham, argued that moral judgements are based on feelings about pleasant and unpleasant consequences. For the German Immanuel Kant, morality could not have a purpose outside itself, so the good person acts only from duty, not feeling or self-interest, and in accordance with the categorical imperative (the obligation to obey absolute moral law). Utilitarianism, devised by Bentham and refined by J S Mill in the 19th century, has been immensely influential, especially in social policy.

In the 20th century, the British philosopher G E Moore argued in *Principia Ethica* 1903 that the concept of goodness was simple and indefinable. The French Jean-Paul Sartre's existentialist emphasis on choice and responsibility has been influential, too. The English novelist and philosopher Iris Murdoch has explored the relationship between goodness and beauty, whereas Mary Midgley has tried to update Aristotle's view of human nature by reference to studies of animal behaviour.

Ethics is closely linked to anthropology, ethology, political theory, psychology, and sociology. Increasingly, moral philosophers analyse such ethical problems as war, animal rights, abortion, euthanasia, and embryo research; ◊medical ethics has emerged as a specialized branch of ethics.

Ethiopia country in E Africa, bounded N by Eritrea, NE by Djibouti, E and SE by Somalia, S by Kenya, and W and NW by Sudan. *See country box on p. 372.*

ethnic cleansing the forced expulsion of one ethnic group by another to create an homogenous population, for example, of more than 2 million Muslims by Serbs in Bosnia-Herzegovina 1992–95. The term has also been used to describe the killing of Hutus and Tutsis in Rwanda and Burundi 1994, and for earlier mass exiles, as far back as the book of Exodus.

To further their aim of creating a Greater Serbia, Bosnian Serb forces compelled thousands of non-Serbs, Croats, and Muslims to abandon their homes, allowing Serb families from other parts of the former Yugoslavia to occupy them. Wholesale slaughter and other human-rights violations were also allegedly used to implement this policy, which created nearly 700,000 refugees. Croatian troops adopted an ethnic-cleansing policy in Krajina 1995, forcing as many as 150,000 Croatian Serbs to flee their homes after a successful government offensive to retake the region; widespread human-rights violations were reported. (Similar tactics were used by the Nazis against the Jews in World War II.) More peaceful ethnic cleansing continued in 1996 after implementation of the Dayton Peace Accord as separate Muslim Croat and Serb statelets were formed in Bosnia.

ethnicity (from Greek *ethnos* 'a people') people's own sense of cultural identity; a social term that overlaps with such concepts as race, nation, class, and religion. Social scientists use the term ethnic group to refer to groups or societies who feel a common sense of identity, often based on a traditional shared culture, language, religion, and customs. It may or may not include common territory, skin colour, or common descent. The USA, for example, is often described as a multi-ethnic society because many members would describe themselves as members of an ethnic group (Jewish, black, or Irish, for example) as well as their national one (American).

ethnography study of living cultures, using anthropological techniques like participant observation (where the anthropologist lives in the society being studied) and a reliance on informants. Ethnography has provided much data of use to archaeologists as analogies.

ethnology study of contemporary peoples, concentrating on their geography and culture, as distinct from their social systems. Ethnologists make a comparative analysis of data from different cultures to understand how cultures work and why they change, with a view to deriving general principles about human society.

ethnomethodology the study of social order and routines used by people in their daily lives, to explain how everyday reality is created and perceived. Ethnomethodologists tend to use small-scale studies and experiments to examine the details of social life and structure (such as conversations) that people normally take for granted, rather than construct large-scale theories about society.

ethology comparative study of animal behaviour in its natural setting. Ethology is concerned with the causal mechanisms (both the stimuli that elicit behaviour and the physiological mechanisms controlling it), as well as the development of behaviour, its function, and its evolutionary history.

Ethology was pioneered during the 1930s by the Austrians Konrad Lorenz and Karl von Frisch who, with the Dutch zoologist Nikolaas Tinbergen, received the Nobel prize in 1973. Ethologists believe that the significance of an animal's behaviour can be understood only in its natural context, and emphasize the importance of field studies and an evolutionary perspective. A recent development within ethology is ◊sociobiology, the study of the evolutionary function of ◊social behaviour.

Ethiopia The former wealth and importance of Gondar, once the capital of Ethiopia, are suggested by much of its architecture, including this castle built by Emperor Fasilides in the 16th century. From the mid-19th century, when Magdala became the capital, Gondar declined and wars and invasions destroyed many of its fine buildings. The city is now being gradually restored as one of Ethiopia's main tourist attractions. *UNESCO*

ethyl alcohol common name for ◊ethanol.

ethylene common name for ◊ethene.

ethylene glycol alternative name for ◊glycol.

ethyne common name ***acetylene*** CHCH colourless inflammable gas produced by mixing calcium carbide and water. It is the simplest member of the ◊alkyne series of hydrocarbons. It is used in the manufacture of the synthetic rubber neoprene, and in oxyacetylene welding and cutting.

Ethyne was discovered by Edmund Davy 1836 and was used in early gas lamps, where it was produced by the reaction between water and calcium carbide. Its combustion provides more heat, relatively, than almost any other fuel known (its calorific value is five times that of hydrogen). This means that the gas gives an intensely hot flame; hence its use in oxyacetylene torches.

etiolation in botany, a form of growth seen in plants receiving insufficient light. It is characterized by long, weak stems, small leaves, and a pale yellowish colour (chlorosis) owing to a lack of chlorophyll. The rapid increase in height enables a plant that is surrounded by others to quickly reach a source of light, after which a return to normal growth usually occurs.

Etna volcano on the east coast of Sicily, 3,323 m/10,906 ft, the highest in Europe. About 90 eruptions have been recorded since 1800 BC, yet because of the rich soil, the cultivated zone on the lower slopes is densely populated, including the coastal town of Catania. The most recent eruption was in Dec 1985.

Eton College most prestigious of English ◊public schools (that is, private schools) for boys. It provided the UK with 19 prime ministers and more than 20% of all government ministers between 1900 and 1985. Eton was founded 1440 by Henry VI as a grammar school and, after a stormy history which included a rebellion by pupils in 1783, became dominated by the sons of the aristocracy and the wealthy middle classes.

'Alone! – / On this charr'd, blacken'd melancholy waste, / Crown'd by the awful peak, Etna's great mouth.'

On MOUNT ETNA
Matthew Arnold
Empedocles on Etna 1852

Etruscan member of an ancient people inhabiting Etruria, Italy (modern-day Tuscany and part of Umbria) from the 8th to 2nd centuries BC. The Etruscan dynasty of the Tarquins ruled Rome 616–509 BC. At the height of their civilization, in the 6th century BC, the Etruscans achieved great wealth and power from their maritime strength. They were driven out of Rome 509 BC and eventually dominated by the Romans.

Etruscan art the art of the inhabitants of Etruria, central Italy, a civilization which flourished

> "A line is length without breadth."
>
> EUCLID *Elements*

8th–2nd centuries BC. The Etruscans produced sculpture, painting, pottery, metalwork, and jewellery. Etruscan terracotta coffins (*sarcophagi*), carved with reliefs and topped with portraits of the dead reclining on one elbow, were to influence the later Romans and early Christians.

Most examples of Etruscan painting come from excavated tombs, whose frescoes depict scenes of everyday life, mythology, and mortuary rites, typically in bright colours and a vigorous, animated style. Scenes of feasting, dancing, swimming, fishing, and playing evoke a confident people who enjoyed life to the full, and who even in death depicted themselves in a joyous and festive manner. The decline of their civilization, in the shadow of Rome's expansion, is reflected in their later art, which loses its original *joie de vivre* and becomes sombre.

Influences from archaic Greece and the Middle East are evident, as are those from the preceding Iron Age Villanovan culture, but the full flowering of Etruscan art represents a unique synthesis of existing traditions and artistic innovation, which was to have a profound influence on the development of Western art.

étude (French 'study') musical exercise designed to develop technique.

etymology study of the origin and history of words within and across languages. It has two major aspects: the study of the phonetic and written forms of words, and of the semantics or meanings of those words.

Etymological research has been particularly successful in tracing the development of words and word elements within the Indo-European language family. Since languages are always changing and usage differs among cultures, it is important to trace words to their original sources. Standard dictionaries of a language such as English typically contain etymological information within square brackets at the end of each entry.

EU abbreviation for ◊***European Union***.

eucalyptus any tree of the genus *Eucalyptus* of the myrtle family Myrtaceae, native to Australia and Tasmania, where they are commonly known as gum trees. About 90% of Australian timber belongs to the eucalyptus genus, which comprises about 500 species. The trees have dark hardwood timber which is used principally for heavy construction as in railway and bridge building. They are tall, aromatic, evergreen trees with pendant leaves and white, pink, or red flowers.

Eucharist chief Christian sacrament, in which bread is eaten and wine drunk in memory of the death of Jesus. The word comes from the Greek for 'thanksgiving', and refers to the statement in the Gospel narrative that Jesus gave thanks over the bread and the cup. Other names for it are the ***Lord's Supper***, ***Holy Communion***, and (among Roman Catholics, who believe that the bread and wine are transubstantiated, that is, converted to the body and blood of Christ) the ***Mass***. The doctrine of transubstantiation was rejected by Protestant churches during the Reformation.

In Britain, members of the Church of England are required to participate in the Eucharist at least three times a year, with Easter as one.

Euclid c. 330–c. 260 BC. Greek mathematician who wrote the *Stoicheia/Elements* in 13 books, of which nine deal with plane and solid geometry and four with number theory. His great achievement lay in the systematic arrangement of previous discoveries, based on axioms, definitions, and theorems.

Euclid's works, and the style in which they were presented, formed the basis for all mathematical thought and expression for the next 2,000 years. He used two main styles of presentation: the synthetic (in which one proceeds from the known to the unknown via logical steps) and the analytical (in which one posits the unknown and works towards it from the known, again via logical steps).

Eudoxus of Cnidus c. 400–c. 347 BC. Greek mathematician and astronomer. He devised the first system to account for the motions of celestial bodies, believing them to be carried around the Earth on sets of spheres. Work attributed to Eudoxus includes methods to calculate the area of a circle and to derive the volume of a pyramid or a cone.

Probably Eudoxus regarded the celestial spheres as a mathematical device rather than as physically real, but the idea was taken up by ◊Aristotle and became entrenched in astronomical thought until the time of Tycho ◊Brahe.

Eugène Prince of Savoy, (full name François Eugène de Savoie Carignan) 1663–1736. Austrian general who had many victories against the Turkish invaders (whom he expelled from Hungary 1697 in the Battle of Zenta) and against France in the War of the ◊Spanish Succession (battles of Blenheim, Oudenaarde, and Malplaquet).

The son of Prince Eugène Maurice of Savoy-Carignano, he was born in Paris. When Louis XIV refused him a commission he entered the Austrian army, and served against the Turks at the defence of Vienna 1683, and against the French on the Rhine and in Italy ten years later. In the War of the Spanish Succession 1701–14 he shared with the British commander Marlborough in his great victories against the French and won many successes as an independent commander in Italy. He again defeated the Turks 1716–18, and fought a last campaign against the French 1734–35.

eugenics (Greek *eugenes* 'well-born') study of ways in which the physical and mental characteristics of the human race may be improved. The term was coined by the English scientist Francis ◊Galton in 1883. The eugenic principle was abused by the Nazi Party in Germany during the 1930s and early 1940s to justify the attempted extermination of entire social and ethnic groups and the establishment of selective breeding programmes. Modern eugenics is concerned mainly with the elimination of genetic disease.

In 1986 Singapore became the first democratic country to adopt an openly eugenic policy by guaranteeing pay increases to female university

ETHIOPIA

Federal Democratic Republic of (formerly known as *Abyssinia*)

0 mi 500
0 km 1000
Egypt
Saudi Arabia
Sudan
Eritrea
Yemen
Chad
Djibouti
Addis Ababa
ETHIOPIA
CAR
Uganda
Somalia
Democratic Republic of Congo
Kenya
INDIAN OCEAN

national name *Hebretesebawit Ityopia*
area 1,096,900 sq km/423,403 sq mi
capital Addis Ababa
major towns/cities Jimma, Dire Dawa, Harar, Nazret, Dessie, Gondar, Mekele
physical features a high plateau with central mountain range divided by Rift Valley; plains in E; source of Blue Nile River; Danakil and Ogaden deserts
head of state Negasso Ghidada from 1995
head of government Meles Zenawi from 1995
political system transition to democratic federal republic
administrative divisions nine-state federation
political parties Ethiopian People's Revolutionary Democratic Front (EPRDF), nationalist, left of centre; Tigré People's Liberation Front (TPLF); Ethiopian People's Democratic Movement (EPDM); United Oromo Liberation Front, Islamic nationalist
population 55,053,000 (1995 est)
population growth rate 3.0% (1990–95); 2.9% (2000–05)
ethnic distribution over 70 different ethnic groups, the two main ones are the Galla (mainly in the E and S of the central plateau), who comprise about 40% of the population, and the Amhara and Tigrais (largely in the central plateau itself), who constitute about 35%
life expectancy 45 (males), 49 (females)
literacy rate 66%
languages Amharic (official), Tigrinya, Orominga, Arabic
religions Sunni Muslim, Christian (Ethiopian Orthodox Church, which has had its own patriarch since 1976) 40%, animist
currency Ethiopian birr
GDP (US $) 4.68 billion (1994)
growth rate 1.4% (1993)
exports coffee, pulses, oilseeds, hides, skins, butter

HISTORY

1st–7th Cs AD Founded by Semitic immigrants from Saudi Arabia, the kingdom of Aksum and its capital, NW of Aduwa, flourished. It reached its peak in the 4th century when Coptic Christianity was introduced from Egypt.
7th C onwards Islam was spread by Arab conquerors.
11th C Emergence of independent Ethiopian kingdom of Abyssinia, which was to remain dominant for nine centuries.
late 15th C Abyssinia visited by Portuguese explorers.
1889 Abyssinia reunited by Menelik II.
1896 Invasion by Italy defeated by Menelik at Aduwa, who went on to annex Ogaden in the SE and areas to the W.
1916 Haile Selassie became regent.
1930 Haile Selassie became emperor.
1936 Conquered by Italy and incorporated in Italian East Africa.
1941 Return of Emperor Selassie after liberation by the British.
1952 Ethiopia federated with Eritrea.
1962 Eritrea annexed by Selassie; Eritrean People's Liberation front (EPLF) resistance movement began, a rebellion that was to continue for 30 years.
1963 First conference of Selassie-promoted Organization of African Unity (OAU) held at Addis Ababa.
1973–74 Severe famine in N Ethiopia; 200,000 died in Wallo province.
1974 Haile Selassie deposed and replaced by a military government led by General Teferi Benti.
1977 Teferi Benti killed and replaced by Col Mengistu Haile Mariam. Somali forces ejected from the Somali-peopled Ogaden in the SE.
1977–79 'Red Terror' period in which Mengistu's single-party Marxist regime killed thousands of innocent people and promoted collective farming; Tigray People's Liberation Front guerrillas began fighting for regional autonomy in the northern highlands.
1984 Workers' Party of Ethiopia (WPE) declared the only legal political party.
1985 Worst famine in more than a decade; Western aid sent and forcible internal resettlement programmes undertaken in Eritrea and Tigray in the N.
1987 Mengistu Mariam elected president under new constitution. New famine; food aid hindered by guerrillas.
1989 Coup attempt against Mengistu foiled. Peace talks with Eritrean rebels mediated by former US president Jimmy Carter.
1991 Mengistu overthrown; transitional government set up by opposing Ethiopian People's Revolutionary Democratic Front (EPRDF), headed by Meles Zenawi. EPLF took control over Eritrea. Famine gripped the country.
1993 Eritrean independence recognized after referendum; private farming and market sector encouraged by EPRDF government.
1994 New federal constitution adopted.
1995 Ruling EPRDF won majority of seats in first multiparty elections to a interim parliament. Negasso Ghidada chosen as president; Zenawi appointed premier.

SEE ALSO Aksum; Eritrea; Mengistu, Haile Mariam; Haile Selassie; Organization of African Unity

eugenics A French vision of the late 19th century, showing an intellectual family in the 1950s, produced by selective breeding, or eugenics. The English scientist Francis Dalton intoduced the term eugenics in 1883. *Image Select (UK) Ltd*

graduates when they give birth to a child, while offering grants towards house purchases for non-graduate married women on condition that they are sterilized after the first or second child.

Eugénie Marie Ignace Augustine de Montijo 1826–1920. Empress of France, daughter of the Spanish count of Montijo. In 1853 she married Louis Napoleon, who had become emperor as ◊Napoleon III. She encouraged court extravagance and Napoleon III's intervention in Mexico, and urged him to fight the Prussians. After his surrender to the Germans at Sedan, NE France, 1870 she fled to England.

eukaryote in biology, one of the two major groupings into which all organisms are divided. Included are all organisms, except bacteria and cyanobacteria (◊blue-green algae), which belong to the ◊prokaryote grouping. The cells of eukaryotes possess a clearly defined nucleus, bounded by a membrane, within which DNA is formed into distinct chromosomes. Eukaryotic cells also contain mitochondria, chloroplasts, and other structures (organelles) that, together with a defined nucleus, are lacking in the cells of prokaryotes.

Euler Leonhard 1707–1783. Swiss mathematician. He developed the theory of differential equations and the calculus of variations, and worked in astronomy and optics. He also enlarged mathematical notation, developed spherical trigonometry, and demonstrated the significance of the coefficients of trigonometric expansions; Euler's number (e, as it is now called) has various useful theoretical properties and is used in the summation of particular series.

eunuch (Greek *eunoukhos* 'one in charge of a bed') castrated man. Originally eunuchs were bedchamber attendants in harems in the East, but as they were usually castrated to keep them from taking too great an interest in their charges, the term became applied more generally. In China, eunuchs were employed within the imperial harem from some 4,000 years ago and by medieval times wielded considerable political power. Eunuchs often filled high offices of state in India and Persia.

Italian *castrati* were singers castrated as boys to preserve their soprano voices, a practice that ended with the accession of Pope Leo XIII 1878.

euphemism ◊figure of speech whose name in Greek means 'speaking well (of something)'. To speak or write euphemistically is to use a milder, less direct expression rather than one that is considered too vulgar or direct. Thus, 'he passed away' is used in place of 'he died', and 'sleep with someone' substitutes for 'have sex with someone'.

euphonium tenor valved brass band instrument of the bugle type, often mistaken for a tuba, and called a baryton in Germany.

Euphrates (Arabic ***Furat***) river, rising in E Turkey, flowing through Syria and Iraq and joining the river Tigris above Basra to form the river Shatt-al-Arab, at the head of the Persian/Arabian Gulf; 3,600 km/2,240 mi in length. The ancient cities of Babylon, Eridu, and Ur were situated along its course.

Eurasian a person of mixed European and Asian parentage; also, native to or an inhabitant of both Europe and Asia.

Eureka Stockade incident at Ballarat, Australia, when about 150 goldminers, or 'diggers', rebelled against the Victorian state police and military authorities. They took refuge behind a wooden stockade, which was taken in a few minutes by the military on 3 Dec 1854. Some 30 gold diggers were killed, and a few soldiers killed or wounded, but the majority of the rebels were taken prisoner. Among those who escaped was Peter Lalor, their leader. Of the 13 tried for treason, all were acquitted, thus marking the emergence of Australian democracy.

eurhythmics practice of coordinated bodily movement as an aid to musical development. It was founded about 1900 by the Swiss musician Emile ◊Jaques-Dalcroze, professor of harmony at the Geneva conservatoire. He devised a series of 'gesture' songs, to be sung simultaneously with certain bodily actions.

Euripides c. 485–c. 406 BC. Athenian tragic dramatist. He is ranked with Aeschylus and Sophocles as one of the three great tragedians. His plays deal with the emotions and reactions of ordinary people and social issues rather than with deities and the grandiose themes of his contemporaries. He wrote about 90 plays, of which 18 and some long fragments survive. These include *Alcestis* 438 BC, *Medea* 431, *Andromache* about 430, *Hippolytus* 428, the satyr-drama *Cyclops* about 424–423, *Electra* 417, *Trojan Women* 415, *Iphigenia in Tauris* 413, *Iphigenia in Aulis* about 414–412, and *The Bacchae* about 405 (the last two were produced shortly after his death).

Euripides' questioning of contemporary mores and shrewd psychological analyses made him unpopular during his lifetime, and he was cruelly mocked by the contemporary comic playwright Aristophanes, but he had more influence on the development of later drama than either Aeschylus or Sophocles. He has been called the most modern of the three dramatists, and the 'forerunner of Rationalism'. He was essentially a realist whose art reflected the humours and passions of daily life. Plot was almost immaterial to him, and he introduced such innovations as the prologue and the *deus ex machina*, or god who comes on at the end to wind up the plot.

euro monetary unit of the European Union (EU). The currency was officially launched on 1 January 1999. The euro, formerly known as the ECU (European Currency Unit), is based on the value of the different currencies used in the ◊European Monetary System.

Euro Disney or Euro Disneyland theme park at Marne-la-Vallée, 32 km/20 mi E of Paris, France, opened by the American Walt Disney Company April 1992 (see ◊Disney). The park, covering 56 hectares/138 acres, was begun in the 1970s and cost about $3 billion to realize. It is the fourth Disneyland theme park. Although it made a loss of $900 million in its first year, for the six-month period preceding 31 March 1995 the theme park announced a 77% cut in losses, attributable in part to financial restructuring and in part to increased sales.

Largely a reproduction of Disney World in Orlando, Florida, the area is divided into Frontierland, Adventureland, Fantasyland, and Discoveryland, all off Main Street, USA. The original Disneyland in Anaheim, California 1955 was followed by Disney World, Florida 1971 and Tokyo Disneyland, Japan 1983.

Europa in astronomy, the fourth-largest moon of the planet Jupiter, diameter 3,140 km/1,950 mi, orbiting 671,000 km/417,000 mi from the planet every 3.55 days. It is covered by ice and criss-crossed by thousands of thin cracks, each some 50,000 km/30,000 mi long.

Europa in Greek mythology, the daughter of the king of Tyre, carried off by Zeus (in the form of a bull); she personifies the continent of Europe.

Europe the second-smallest continent, occupying 8% of the Earth's surface
area 10,400,000 sq km/4,000,000 sq mi
largest cities (population over 1.5 million) Athens, Barcelona, Berlin, Birmingham, Bucharest, Budapest, Hamburg, Istanbul, Kharkov, Kiev, Lisbon, London, Madrid, Manchester, Milan, Moscow, Paris, Rome, St Petersburg, Vienna, Warsaw
features Mount Elbruz 5,642 m/18,517 ft in the Caucasus Mountains is the highest peak in Europe; Mont Blanc 4,807 m/15,772 ft is the highest peak in the Alps; lakes (over 5,100 sq km/2,000 sq mi) include Ladoga, Onega, Vänern; rivers (over 800 km/500 mi) include the Volga, Danube, Dnieper Ural, Don, Pechora, Dniester, Rhine, Loire, Tagus, Ebro, Oder, Prut, Rhône
physical conventionally occupying that part of Eurasia to the W of the Ural Mountains, N of the Caucasus Mountains, and N of the Sea of Marmara, Europe lies entirely in the northern hemisphere between 36° N and the Arctic Ocean. About two-thirds of the continent is a great plain which covers the whole of European Russia and spreads westwards through Poland to the Low Countries and the Bay of Biscay. To the N lie the Scandinavian highlands, rising to 2,472 m/8,110 ft at Glittertind in the Jotenheim range of Norway. To the S, a series of mountain ranges stretch E–W (Caucasus, Balkans, Carpathians, Apennines, Alps, Pyrenees, and Sierra Nevada). The most westerly point of the mainland is Cape Roca in Portugal; the most southerly location is Tarifa Point in Spain; the most northerly point on the mainland is Nordkynn in Norway.

A line from the Baltic to the Black Sea divides Europe between an eastern continental region and a western region characterized by a series of peninsulas that include Scandinavia (Norway and Sweden), Jutland (mainland Denmark and a small part of Germany), Iberia (Spain and Portugal), and Italy and the Balkans (Greece, Albania, Croatia, Slovenia, Bosnia-Herzegovina, Yugoslavia, Bulgaria, and European Turkey). Because of the large number of bays, inlets, and peninsulas, the coastline is longer in proportion to its size than that of any other continent. The largest islands adjacent to continental Europe are the British Isles, Novaya Zemlya, Sicily, Sardinia, Crete, Corsica, Gotland (in the Baltic Sea), and the Balearic Islands; more distant islands associated with Europe include Iceland, Svalbard, Franz Josef Land, Madeira, the Azores, and the Canary Islands. There are three main groups of lakes: (1) the Alpine lakes with Geneva, Constance, Lucerne, and Neuchatel in Switzerland; Maggiore, Garda, and Como in Italy; Balaton in Hungary; (2) the Scandinavian group with Vänern, Vättern, and Mälaren in Sweden and Mjøsa and Randsfjord in Norway; and (3) the lakes of the central plain, Ladoga, Onega, Peipus, and Ilmen in Russia; Saimaa and others in Finland.
climate the greater part of Europe falls within the northern temperate zone, which is modified by the Gulf Stream in the NW. There are four main climatic zones: the NW region (stretching from N Spain through France to Norway), the Mediterranean zone, central Europe, and E Europe. The NW region has mild winters, cool summers, and cloud and rain all the year round with a maximum in the autumn. The Mediterranean zone has very mild winters, hot, dry summers, and abundant sunshine; most of the rain falls in the spring and autumn. In central Europe winters are cold and the summers warm, with the maximum rainfall in summer. E Europe has extremely cold winters
industries nearly 50% of the world's cars are produced in Europe (Germany, France, Italy, Spain, Russia, Georgia, Ukraine, Latvia, Belarus, UK); the rate of fertilizer consumption on agricultural land is four times greater than that in any other continent; Europe produces 43% of the world's barley (Germany, Spain, France, UK), 41% of its rye (Poland, Germany), 31% of its oats (Poland, Germany, Sweden, France), and 24% of its wheat (France, Germany, UK, Romania); Italy, Spain, and Greece produce more than 70% of the world's olive oil
population (1991 est) 502 million (excluding European Turkey and the former USSR); annual growth rate 0.3%
language mostly Indo-European, with a few exceptions, including Finno-Ugric (Finnish and Hungarian), Basque, and Altaic (Turkish); apart from a

'The day is for honest men, the night for thieves.'

Euripides
Iphigenia in Tauris

'We are asking the nations of Europe between whom rivers of blood have flowed to forget the feuds of a thousand years.'

On **Europe**
Winston Churchill, speech 14 Feb 1948

fringe of Celtic, the NW is Germanic; Letto-Lithuanian languages separate the Germanic from the Slavonic tongues of E Europe; Romance languages spread E–W from Romania through Italy and France to Spain and Portugal
religion Christian (Protestant, Roman Catholic, Eastern Orthodox), Muslim (Turkey, Albania, Bosnia-Herzegovina, Yugoslavia, Bulgaria), Jewish.

European the natives and inhabitants of the continent of Europe and their descendants. Europe is multicultural and, although most of its languages belong to the Indo-European family, there are also speakers of Uralic (such as Hungarian) and Altaic (such as Turkish) languages, as well as Basque.

European Bank for Reconstruction and Development (EBRD) international bank established 1991, with headquarters in London, and an initial capital of 10 billion ECUs, to assist the economic reconstruction of central and E Europe.

European Coal and Steel Community (ECSC) organization established by the Treaty of Paris 1951 (ratified 1952) as a single authority for the coal and steel industries of France, West Germany, Italy, Belgium, Holland, and Luxembourg, eliminating tariffs and other restrictions; in 1967 it became part of the European Community (now the European Union).

The ECSC arose out of the ◊Schuman plan 1950, which proposed a union of the French and German coal and steel industries so as to make future war between the two countries impossible. It was, in effect, a prototype institution for the European Community (EC) itself, under whose authority it came 1967. Subsequent members of the EC automatically became ECSC members also.

European Community (EC) former name (to 1993) of the ◊European Union.

European Court of Human Rights court that hears cases referred from the European Commission of Human Rights, if the Commission has failed to negotiate a friendly settlement in a case where individuals' rights have been violated by a member state, as defined in the 1950 European Convention on Human Rights. The court sits in Strasbourg and comprises one judge for every state that is a party to the 1950 convention. Court rulings have forced the Republic of Ireland to drop its constitutional ban on homosexuality, and Germany to cease to exclude political left- and right-wingers from the civil service.

Britain has never incorporated the Human Rights Convention into its laws, which means that a statute that directly contradicts the convention will always prevail over a Strasbourg decision in a British court. In practice, however, the UK has always passed the necessary legislation to make its laws comply with the court's decisions.

Britain has had the second-worst record of violations of the convention in recent years; by 1991, 191 cases had been brought against the UK, and violations of the convention were found in two-thirds of these. They included illegal telephone tapping, interference with the post, unfair curbs on the press, and unjust restrictions on prisoners' access to lawyers.

European Court of Justice the court of the European Union (EU), which is responsible for interpreting ◊Community law and ruling on breaches of such law. It sits in Luxembourg with judges from the member states.

Most of the court's work reaches it in the form of questions asked by national courts troubled by issues of Community law. The EU Commission can also complain to the court about a member country's failure to perform its obligations under that law. Additionally, member countries, EU institutions, and citizens can ask the court to annul acts of EU bodies. Finally, people can claim compensation from the court for losses suffered as a result of illegal acts of the EU.

When it entered the European Community (now the European Union) in 1973, the United Kingdom agreed to be bound by decisions of the Court of Justice and incorporated the Community treaties into its legal system. Where the court has found UK laws to contravene EU standards, the government has made the necessary changes. Courts in the UK also interpret existing laws to conform, where possible, to EU standards.

European Economic Area (EEA) agreement 1991 between the European Community (now the ◊European Union (EU)) and the ◊European Free Trade Association (EFTA) to create a zone of economic cooperation, extending the EU's four 'single market freedoms' in the movement of capital, goods, services and labour to EFTA, allowing their 380 million citizens to transfer money, shares, and bonds across national borders and to live, study, or work in one another's countries. The pact, which took effect Jan 1994, was seen as a temporary arrangement since most EFTA members hoped, eventually, to join the EU.

European Economic Community (EEC) known as the ***Common Market*** organization established 1957 with the aim of creating a single European market for the products of member states by the abolition of tariffs and other restrictions on trade.

European Free Trade Association (EFTA) organization established 1960 consisting of Iceland, Norway, Switzerland, and (from 1991) Liechtenstein, previously a nonvoting associate member. There are no import duties between members. Of the original EFTA members, Britain and Denmark left (1972) to join the European Community (EC), as did Portugal (1985); Austria, Finland, and Sweden joined the EC's successor, the European Union (EU) 1995.

In 1973 the EC signed agreements with EFTA members, setting up a free-trade area of over 300 million consumers. Trade between the two groups amounted to over half of total EFTA trade. A further pact signed Oct 1991 between the EC and EFTA provided for a ◊European Economic Area (EEA), allowing EFTA greater access to the EC market by ending many of the restrictions. The EEA came into effect Jan 1994.

European Monetary System (EMS) attempt by the European Community (now the European Union) to bring financial cooperation and monetary stability to Europe. It was established 1979 in the wake of the 1974 oil crisis, which brought growing economic disruption to European economies because of floating exchange rates. Central to the EMS is the ◊Exchange Rate Mechanism (ERM), a

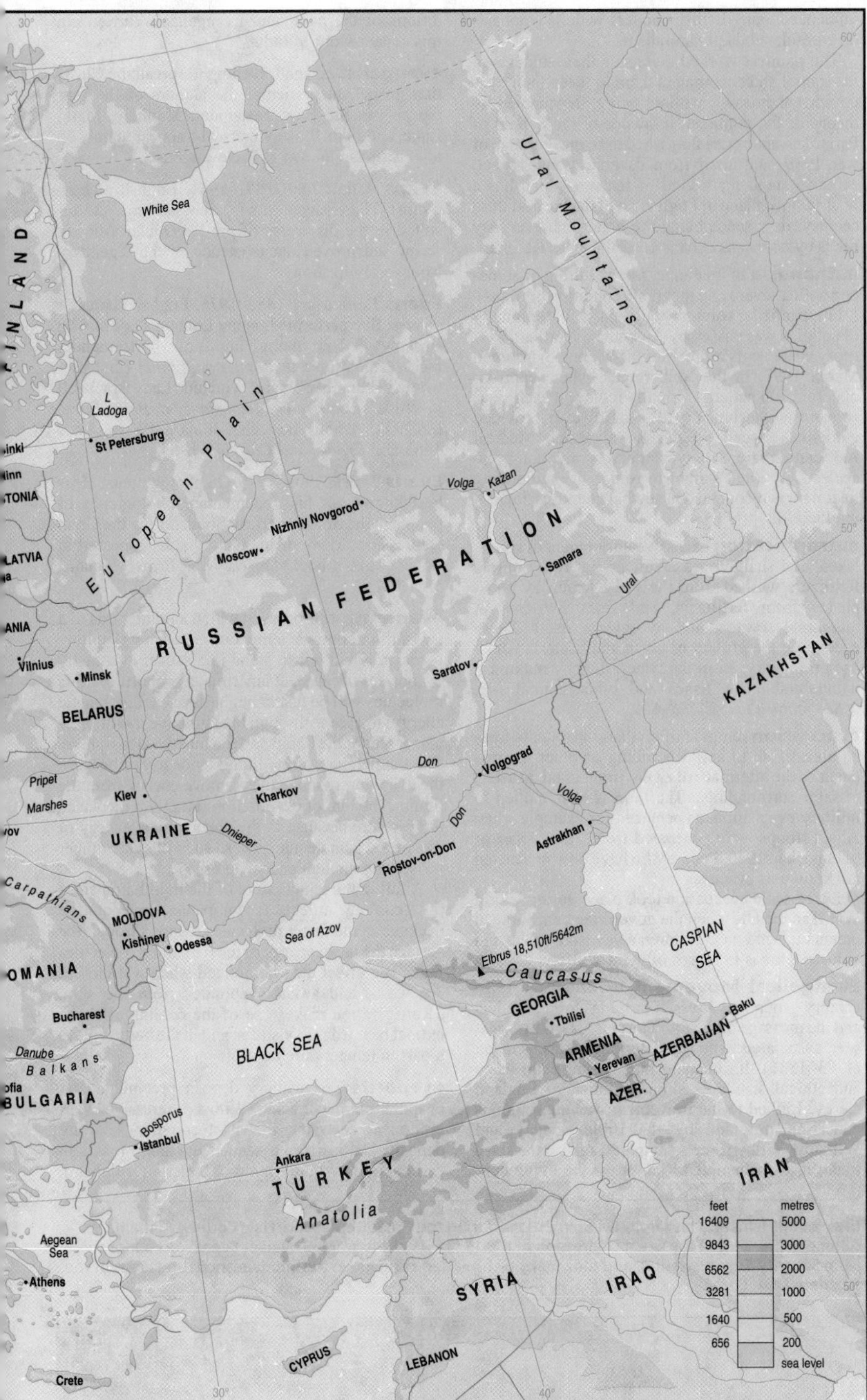

voluntary system of semi-fixed exchange rates based on the European Currency Unit (ECU).

The UK entered the ERM in Oct 1990, but left on 'Black Wednesday', 16 September 1992, when doubts about the prospects for movement towards a single European currency caused speculators to sell the weaker ERM currencies, particularly sterling, so forcing the pound out of its ERM band.

European Monetary Union (EMU) the proposed European Union (EU) policy for a single currency and common economic policies. In 1998 EU leaders formalized the creation of the euro monetary zone, to take effect from 1 Jan 1999.

Three stages are envisaged for EMU. In the first stage, all controls on individual nations' capital flow would be ended, and the European System of Central Banks (ESCB) created. In stage two, the ESCB would begin to regulate money supply. Finally, exchange rates between member states would be fixed, and a single European currency created, and the ESCB would take over the function of all the nations' ◊central banks.

European Parliament the parliament of the ◊European Union, which meets in Strasbourg and Brussels to comment on the legislative proposals of the European Commission. Members are elected for a five-year term. The European Parliament has 626 seats, apportioned on the basis of population, of which Germany has 99; the UK, France, and Italy have 87 each; Spain 64; the Netherlands 31; Belgium, Greece, and Portugal 25 each; Sweden 22; Austria 21; Denmark and Finland 16 each; the Republic of Ireland 15; and Luxembourg 6.

Originally merely consultative, the European Parliament became directly elected 1979, and assumed increased powers. Though still not a true legislative body, it can dismiss the whole Commission and reject the EU budget in its entirety. Full sittings are in Strasbourg; most committees meet in Brussels, and the seat of the secretariat is in Luxembourg. Party groupings since June 1994 are as follows, with number of seats in brackets: ***left of centre*** Group of European Socialist (217), Confederal Group of the Environment: United Left/Nordic Green Left (33); ***centre*** Group of European Liberal Democrats and Reformist Party (52), Non-aligned (31); ***right of centre*** Group of European People's Party (173), Union for Europe Group (54), Group of Euro-Radical Alliance (20), Europe of Nations Group (19).

European Southern Observatory observatory operated jointly by Belgium, Denmark, France, Germany, Italy, the Netherlands, Sweden, and Switzerland with headquarters near Munich. Its telescopes, located at La Silla, Chile, include a 3.6-m/142-in reflector opened 1976 and the 3.58-m/141-in New Technology Telescope opened 1990. By 1988 work began on the Very Large Telescope, consisting of four 8-m/315-in reflectors mounted independently but able to work in combination.

European Space Agency (ESA) organization of European countries (Austria, Belgium, Denmark, Finland, France, Germany, Ireland, Italy, the Netherlands, Norway, Spain, Sweden, Switzerland, and the UK) that engages in space research and technology. Founded 1975; headquarters in Paris.

ESA has developed various scientific and communications satellites, the ◊*Giotto* space probe, and the *Ariane* rockets. ESA built ◊*Spacelab*, and plans to build its own space station, *Columbus*, for attachment to a US space station. The ESA's earth-sensing satellite ERS-2 was launched successfully April 1995. It will work in tandem with ERS-1 launched in 1991, and should improve measurements of global ozone. It will have a laboratory on the International Space Station assembled 1999.

European Union (EU; formerly (to 1993) European Community) political and economic alliance consisting of the ◊European Coal and Steel Community (1952), the ◊European Economic Community (EEC, popularly called the Common-Market, 1957), and the European Atomic Energy Community (Euratom, 1957). The original six members – Belgium, France, West Germany, Italy, Luxembourg, and the Netherlands – were joined by the UK, Denmark, and the Republic of Ireland 1973, Greece 1981, and Spain and Portugal 1986. East Germany was incorporated on German reunification 1990. Austria, Finland, and Sweden joined 1995. There is now a queue of aspiring EU members, most of whose applications to join will eventually be accepted. Cyprus applied 1990; Hungary and Poland 1994; Bulgaria, Estonia, Latvia, Lithuania, Slovakia and Romania 1995; and the Czech Republic 1996. A customs pact with Turkey approved 1995 was seen as the first step towards full membership but the move was criticized by human-rights activists. In 1995 there were more than 360 million people in the EU countries.

A European Charter of Social Rights (see ◊Social Chapter) was approved at the Maastricht summit 1991 by all members except the UK. The same meeting secured agreement on a treaty framework for European union, including political and monetary union, and for a new system of police and military cooperation. After initial rejection by Denmark in a national referendum 1992, the ◊Maastricht Treaty on European union came into effect on 1 Nov 1993 and the new designation European Union was adopted, embracing not only the various bodies of its predecessor, the EC, but also two intergovernmental 'pillars', covering common foreign and security policy (CFSP) and cooperation on justice and home affairs. In 1995 the EU's member nations stated their commitment to the attainment of monetary union by 1999, and in December of the same year they agreed to call the new currency the euro.

The aims of the EU include the expansion of trade, reduction of competition, the abolition of restrictive trading practices, the encouragement of free movement of capital and labour within the alliance, and the establishment of a closer union among European people. A single market with free movement of goods and capital was established Jan 1993 (see ◊Single European Market). The EU reached agreement on closer economic and political cooperation with 12 Middle Eastern and North African countries in the Barcelona Declaration Nov 1995, and an agreement between the USA and the EU to move towards closer economic and political cooperation was signed Dec 1995.

The EU has the following institutions: the European Commission of 20 members pledged to independence of national interests, who initiate Union action (two members each from France, Germany, Italy, Spain, and the UK; and one each from

'I saw Hamlet Prince of Denmark played: but now the old plays begin to disgust this refined age.'

JOHN EVELYN *Diary* 1661

Austria, Belgium, Denmark, Finland, Greece, Ireland, Luxembourg, Netherlands, Portugal, and Sweden); the Council of Ministers of the European Union, which makes decisions on the Commission's proposals; the ◊European Parliament, directly elected from 1979; the Economic and Social Committee, a consultative body; whose 222 members are drawn from social and economic groupings within member states, representing employers, workers and other interest, including consumers; the European Court of Auditors, of 15 members appointed by the Council of Ministers, which audits the Union's affairs; the Committee of the Regions, with 222 members, representing the regions within the Union, serving a four-year term; the Committee of Permanent Representatives (COREPER), consisting of civil servants temporarily seconded by member states to work for the Commission; and the ◊European Court of Justice, to safeguard interpretation of the Rome Treaties (1957) that established the original alliance. A European Investment Bank, based in Luxembourg, has also been established to provide interest-free, long-term financing of approved capital projects.

europium soft, greyish, metallic element of the ◊lanthanide series, symbol Eu, atomic number 63, relative atomic mass 151.96. It is used in lasers and as the red phosphor in colour televisions; its compounds are used to make control rods for nuclear reactors.

Eurydice in Greek mythology, the wife of ◊Orpheus. She was a dryad, or forest nymph, and died from a snake bite. Orpheus attempted unsuccessfully to fetch her back from the realm of the dead.

Euskadi ta Askatasuna (ETA; Basque Nation and Liberty) illegal organization of militant Basque separatists, committed to the separation of the Basque region from the remainder of Spain. Founded 1960, it has political as well as military wings, but its main strategy has been based on violence, with more than 800 deaths attributed to the group over the period 1968–95. Its French counterpart is Iparretarrak ('ETA fighters from the North Side').

Basque claims for autonomy are based on a distinctive language, Euskara, and the fact that a separate republic, Euskadi, existed briefly 1936–37, when its capital Guernica was destroyed by German and Italian bombers supporting General Franco.

A promise of a major devolution of power, through a new constitution, and the creation of a Basque parliament 1980, failed to satisfy ETA leaders, who continued their campaign of violence. A truce called in 1989 broke down and guerrilla activity resumed. In 1995 ETA announced it would stop its campaign of killings if the government agreed to a referendum on Basque independence, but Prime Minister ◊Gonzalez responded by launching a major police offensive against the organization.

eusociality form of social life found in insects such as honey bees and termites, in which the colony is made up of special castes (for example, workers, drones, and reproductives) whose membership is biologically determined. The worker castes do not usually reproduce. Only one mammal, the naked mole rat, has a social organization of this type. A eusocial shrimp was discovered 1996 living in the coral reefs of Belize. *Synalpheus regalis* lives in colonies of up to 300 individuals, all the offspring of a single reproductive female. See also ◊social behaviour.

Eustachian tube small air-filled canal connecting the middle ◊ear with the back of the throat. It is found in all land vertebrates and equalizes the pressure on both sides of the eardrum.

eustatic change worldwide rise or fall in sea level caused by a change in the amount of water in the oceans (by contrast, ◊isostasy involves a rising or sinking of the land). During the last ice age, sea level fell because water became 'locked-up' in the form of ice and snow, and less water reached the oceans.

'Mount Everest is very easy to climb, only just a little too high.'

On MOUNT EVEREST André Roche quoted in the *Observer* 25 Jan 1953

Euston Road School group of English painters associated with the 'School of Drawing and Painting' founded 1937 in Euston Road, London by William Coldstream (b. 1908), Victor Pasmore (b. 1908), Claude Rogers (b. 1907), and Graham Bell (1910–43). Despite its brief existence, the school influenced many British painters with its emphasis on careful, subdued naturalism.

The painters worked alongside their students in the school and encouraged them to 'keep their eyes on what they saw', without being preoccupied by theory or the dominant influence of the School of Paris. The enterprise flourished until the outbreak of war 1939, and apart from its educational aspect, came to stand for a kind of realism which has a well-defined place in English art of the the mid-20th century, its essence being the belief that everyday life is by no means exhausted as the material for art.

euthanasia in medicine, mercy killing of someone with a severe and incurable condition or illness. A bill legalizing voluntary euthanasia for terminally ill patients was passed by Australia's Northern Territory state legislature May 1995 but overturned March 1997. In the Netherlands, where approximately 2,700 patients formally request it each year, euthanasia is technically illegal. However, provided guidelines issued by the Royal Dutch Medical Association are followed, doctors are not prosecuted. A patient's right to refuse life-prolonging treatment is recognized in several countries, including the UK.

eutrophication excessive enrichment of rivers, lakes, and shallow sea areas, primarily by nitrate fertilizers washed from the soil by rain, by phosphates from fertilizers, and from nutrients in municipal sewage, and by sewage itself. These encourage the growth of algae and bacteria which use up the oxygen in the water, thereby making it uninhabitable for fishes and other animal life. ▷ *See feature on pp. 858–859.*

evacuation removal of civilian inhabitants from an area liable to aerial bombing or other hazards (such as the aftermath of an environmental disaster) to safer surroundings. The term is also applied to military evacuation, as occurred for example when Allied troops were evacuated from the beaches of ◊Dunkirk in 1940. People who have been evacuated are known as evacuees.

Large-scale evacuation took place during World War II in the UK when the government encouraged parents to send their children away from urban and industrial areas to places of greater safety.

Evangelical Movement in Britain, a 19th-century group that stressed basic Protestant beliefs and the message of the four Gospels. The movement was associated with the cleric Charles Simeon (1783–1836). It aimed to raise moral enthusiasm and ethical standards among Church of England clergy. Linked to the movement was the religious education provided by the Bible Society and William ◊Wilberforce's campaign against the slave trade; it also attempted to improve the living conditions of the poor, and Evangelicals carried out missionary work in India.

evangelist person travelling to spread the Christian gospel, in particular the authors of the four Gospels in the New Testament: Matthew, Mark, Luke, and John. Proselytizers who appear mainly on television are known as ◊televangelists.

Evans Arthur John 1851–1941. English archaeologist. His excavation of ◊Knossos on Crete resulted in the discovery of pre-Phoenician Minoan script and proved the existence of the legendary Minoan civilization.

Evans Edith Mary 1888–1976. English character actress. She performed on the London stage and on Broadway. Her many imposing performances include the Nurse in *Romeo and Juliet* (first performed 1926); her film roles include Lady Bracknell in Wilde's comedy *The Importance of Being Earnest* 1952. Among her other films are *Tom Jones* 1963 and *Crooks and Coronets* 1969.

Evans Walker 1903–1975. US photographer. He is best known for his documentary photographs of people in the rural American South during the Great Depression. Many of his photographs appeared in James Agee's book *Let Us Now Praise Famous Men* 1941.

evaporation process in which a liquid turns to a vapour without its temperature reaching boiling point. A liquid left to stand in a saucer eventually evaporates because, at any time, a proportion of its molecules will be fast enough (have enough kinetic energy) to escape through the attractive intermolecular forces at the liquid surface into the atmosphere. The temperature of the liquid tends to fall because the evaporating molecules remove energy from the liquid. The rate of evaporation rises with increased temperature because as the mean kinetic energy of the liquid's molecules rises, so will the number possessing enough energy to escape.

A fall in the temperature of the liquid, known as the cooling effect, accompanies evaporation because as the faster molecules escape through the surface the mean energy of the remaining molecules falls. The effect may be noticed when wet clothes are worn, and sweat evaporates from the skin. ◊Refrigeration makes use of the cooling effect to extract heat from foodstuffs, and in the body it plays a part in temperature control.

evaporite sedimentary deposit precipitated on evaporation of salt water. With a progressive evaporation of seawater, the most common salts are deposited in a definite sequence: calcite (calcium carbonate), gypsum (hydrous calcium sulphate),

Evans Bud Fields and his family living in a shack during the Great Depression, Hale County, Alabama, summer 1936. During the Great Depression of the 1930s, US photographer Walker Evans worked for the Farm Security Administration, and took many pictures depicting life in the impoverished rural areas of the southern USA. *Corbis*

halite (sodium chloride), and finally salts of potassium and magnesium.

Calcite precipitates when seawater is reduced to half its original volume, gypsum precipitates when the seawater body is reduced to one-fifth, and halite when the volume is reduced to one-tenth. Thus the natural occurrence of chemically precipitated calcium carbonate is common, of gypsum fairly common, and of halite less common. Because of the concentrations of different dissolved salts in seawater, halite accounts for about 95% of the chlorides precipitated if evaporation is complete. More unusual evaporite minerals include borates (for example borax, hydrous sodium borate) and sulphates (for example glauberite, a combined sulphate of sodium and calcium).

Eve in the Old Testament, the first woman, wife of ◊Adam. She was tempted by Satan (in the form of a snake) to eat the fruit of the Tree of Knowledge of Good and Evil, and then tempted Adam to eat of the fruit as well, thus bringing about their expulsion from the Garden of Eden.

There are two versions of the creation myth in the Bible: in one of them, Eve was created simultaneously with Adam; in the other, she was created from his rib. In the Hebrew writings known as the 'Midrash', ◊Lilith was the first woman (and her children were the wives available to Eve's sons Cain and Abel).

Evelyn John 1620–1706. English diarist and author. He was a friend of the diarist Samuel Pepys, and like him remained in London during the Plague and the Great Fire of London. His fascinating diary, covering the years 1641–1706, and first published 1818, is an important source of information about 17th-century England. He also wrote some 30 books on a wide variety of subjects, including horticulture and the cultivation of trees, history, religion, and the arts. He was one of the founders of the ◊Royal Society.

evening primrose any plant of the genus *Oenothera*, family Onagraceae. Some 50 species are native to North America, several of which now also grow in Europe. Some are cultivated for their oil, which is rich in gamma-linoleic acid (GLA). The body converts GLA into substances which resemble hormones, and evening primrose oil is beneficial in alleviating the symptoms of ◊premenstrual tension. It is also used in treating eczema and chronic fatigue syndrome.

eventing see three-day eventing under ◊equestrianism.

Everage Dame Edna. Character of an Australian 'housewife-superstar', from Moonie Ponds, Victoria, created by Australian Barry ◊Humphries.

Everest, Mount (Chinese ***Qomolungma*** 'goddess mother of the snows/world') (Nepalese ***Sagarmatha*** 'head of the earth') the world's highest mountain above sea level, in the Himalayas, on the China–Nepal frontier; height 8,872 m/29,118 ft (recently measured by satellite to this new height from the former official height of 8,848 m/29,028 ft). It was first climbed by New Zealand mountaineer Edmund ◊Hillary and Sherpa ◊Tenzing Norgay 1953. More than 360 climbers have reached the summit; over 100 have died during the ascent.

The English name comes from George Everest (1790–1866), surveyor general of India. In 1987 a US expedition obtained measurements of ◊K2 that disputed Everest's 'highest mountain' status, but the recent satellite measurements have established Mount Everest as the highest.

Everglades area of swamps, marsh, and lakes in S ◊Florida; area 5,000 sq mi/12,950 sq km. A national park covers the southern tip.

Formed by overflow of Lake Okeechobee after heavy rains, it is one of the wildest areas in the USA, noted for its distinctive plant and animal life. The only human residents are several hundred Seminole, a Native American people. Large drainage programmes have reduced the flow of water from the lake southwards, threatening the region's ecological balance, while pesticide and fertilizer runoff from sugar-cane farms has left the water heavily contaminated. In Feb 1996 the US government announced a $1.5 billion investment plan to rescue the Everglades.

evergreen in botany, a plant such as pine, spruce, or holly, that bears its leaves all year round. Most ◊conifers are evergreen. Plants that shed their leaves in autumn or during a dry season are described as ◊deciduous.

Evert Chris(tine Marie) 1954– . US tennis player. She won her first Wimbledon title 1974, and has since won 21 Grand Slam titles. She became the first woman tennis player to win $1 million in prize money. She has an outstanding two-handed backhand and is a great exponent of baseline technique. From 1974 to 1989 she never failed to reach the quarter-finals at Wimbledon. She married British Davis Cup player John Lloyd 1979 but subsequently divorced him. Evert retired from competitive tennis 1989.

evidence in law, the testimony of witnesses and production of documents and other material in court proceedings, in order to prove or disprove facts at issue in the case. Witnesses must swear or affirm that their evidence is true. In English law, giving false evidence is the crime of ◊perjury.

Documentary evidence has a wide scope including maps, soundtracks, and films, in addition to documents in writing. Objects such as weapons used in crimes may serve as evidence. Evidence obtained illegally, such as a confession under duress, may be excluded from the court.

evolution slow process of change from one form to another, as in the evolution of the universe from its formation in the ◊Big Bang to its present state, or in the evolution of life on Earth. Some Christians and Muslims deny the theory of evolution as conflicting with the belief that God created all things (see ◊creationism). English naturalist Charles ◊Darwin assigned the main role in evolutionary change to ◊natural selection acting on randomly occurring variations (now known to be produced by spontaneous changes or ◊mutations in the genetic material of organisms).

evolution and creationism Organic evolution traces the development of simple unicellular forms to more complex forms, ultimately to the flowering plants and vertebrate animals, including man. The Earth contains an immense diversity of living organisms: about a million different species of animals and half a million species of plants have so far been described. There is overwhelming evidence that this vast array arose by a gradual process of evolutionary divergence and not by individual acts of divine creation as described in the Book of Genesis. There are several lines of evidence: the fossil record, the existence of similarities or homologies between different groups of organisms, embryology, and geographical distribution.

natural selection, sexual selection, and chance The idea of continuous evolution can be traced as far back as ◊Lucretius in the 1st century BC, but it did not gain wide acceptance until the 19th century following the work of Scottish geologist Charles ◊Lyell, French naturalist Jean Baptiste ◊Lamarck, Darwin, and English biologist Thomas Henry ◊Huxley. Natural selection occurs because those individuals better adapted to their particular environments reproduce more effectively, thus contributing their characteristics to future generations. The current theory of evolution, ◊neo-Darwinism, combines Darwin's theory of natural selection with Austrian biologist Gregor ◊Mendel's theories on genetics.

Although neither the general concept of evolution nor the importance of natural selection is doubted by biologists, there remains dispute over other possible processes involved. Besides natural selection and ◊sexual selection, chance may play a large part in deciding which genes become characteristic of a population, a phenomenon called 'genetic drift'. It is now also clear that evolutionary change does not always occur at a constant rate, but that the process can have long periods of relative stability interspersed with periods of rapid change. This has led to new theories, such as the ◊punctuated equilibrium model. See also ◊adaptive radiation.

evolutionary stable strategy (ESS) in ◊sociobiology, an assemblage of behavioural or physical characters (collectively termed a 'strategy') of a population that is resistant to replacement by any forms bearing new traits, because the new traits will not be capable of successful reproduction.

ESS analysis is based on ◊game theory and can be applied both to genetically determined physical characters (such as horn length), and to learned behavioural responses (for example, whether to fight or retreat from an opponent). An ESS may be conditional on the context, as in the rule 'fight if the opponent is smaller, but retreat if the opponent is larger'.

Ewe a group of people inhabiting Ghana and Togo, and numbering about 2.5 million. The Ewe live by fishing and farming, and practise an animist religion. Their language belongs to the Kwa branch of the Niger-Congo family.

ex cathedra (Latin 'from the throne') term describing a statement by the pope, taken to be indisputably true, and which must be accepted by Catholics.

excavation or ***dig*** in archaeology, the systematic recovery of data through the exposure of buried sites and artefacts. Excavation is destructive, and is therefore accompanied by a comprehensive recording of all material found and its three-dimensional locations (its context). As much material and information as possible must be recovered from any dig. A full record of all the techniques employed in the excavation itself must also be made, so that future archaeologists will be able to evaluate the results of the work accurately.

Besides being destructive, excavation is also costly. For both these reasons, it should be used only as a last resort. It can be partial, with only a sample of the site investigated, or total. Samples are chosen either intuitively, in which case excavators investigate those areas they feel will be most productive, or statistically, in which case the sample is drawn using various statistical techniques, so as to ensure that it is representative.

An important goal of excavation is a full understanding of a site's stratigraphy; that is, its vertical layering. These layers or levels can be defined naturally (for example, soil changes), culturally (for example, different occupation levels), or arbitrarily (for example, 10 cm/4 in levels). Excavation can also be done horizontally, to uncover larger areas of a particular layer and reveal the spatial relationships between artefacts and features in that layer. This is known as open-area excavation and is used especially where single-period deposits lie close to the surface, and the time dimension is represented by lateral movement rather than by the placing of one building on top of the preceding one. Most excavators employ a flexible combination of vertical and horizontal digging.

excavator machine designed for digging in the ground, or for earth-moving in general. Diggers with hydraulically powered digging arms are widely used on building sites. They may run on wheels or on ◊caterpillar tracks. The largest excavators are the draglines used in mining to strip away earth covering the coal or mineral deposit.

exchange rate the price at which one currency is bought or sold in terms of other currencies, gold, or accounting units such as the special drawing right (SDR) of the ◊International Monetary Fund. Exchange rates may be fixed by international agreement or by government policy; or they may be wholly or partly allowed to 'float' (that is, find their own level) in world currency markets. Central banks, as large holders of foreign currency, often intervene to buy or sell particular currencies in an effort to maintain some stability in exchange rates.

Is man an ape or an angel? Now I am on the side of the angels.

On EVOLUTION
Benjamin Disraeli, speech in Oxford 25 Nov 1864

evening primrose The evening primrose belongs to a large family of flowering shrubs and plants, many of which bear four-petalled yellow flowers. The evening primrose opens its blooms at night and is pollinated by moths. Oil from the pressed seeds of one species of evening primrose is a source of gamma-linoleic acid which may be used medically for a variety of ailments including the reduction of high cholesterol.

‘Man is nothing else but what he makes of himself. Such is the first principle of existentialism.’

On EXISTENTIALISM
Jean-Paul Sartre

Exchange Rate Mechanism (ERM) voluntary system for controlling exchange rates within the ◊European Monetary System of the European Union (EU) intended to prepare the way for a single currency. The member currencies of the ERM are fixed against each other within a narrow band of fluctuation based on a central European Currency Unit (ECU) rate, but floating against nonmember countries. If a currency deviates significantly from the central ECU rate, the European Monetary Cooperation Fund and the central banks concerned intervene to stabilize the currency.

The ERM was established 1979 with the member countries Belgium, Denmark, France, Germany, Ireland, Italy, Luxembourg, and the Netherlands. Spain joined 1989; the UK joined 1990. In 1991 European leaders planned to complete the final stage of Economic Monetary Union (EMU) by 1998–99, but this appeared unlikely to be achieved and Denmark and the UK were permitted to opt out of EMU. In 1992 Italy and the UK withdrew because they were unable to maintain the levels of their currencies. Those who meet the economic convergence criteria in 1999 are required to move to EMU, irrevocably fixing the conversion rates of their currencies. In 1997 only Luxembourg fulfilled the full convergence criteria. Other member states failed because of high budget balances, levels of public debt, interest rates or rates of inflation.

exchange rate policy policy of government towards the level of the ◊exchange rate of its currency. It may want to influence the exchange rate by using its gold and foreign currency reserves held by its central bank to buy and sell its currency. It can also use interest rates (◊monetary policy) to alter the value of the currency.

A fall in the exchange rate will mean that the price of imports will rise while exporters can choose either to lower prices for their buyers or leave them the same and increase their profit margins. As a result, domestic producers should become more internationally competitive. Import volumes should fall whilst export volumes should rise. Output at home should rise, leading to higher economic growth and a fall in unemployment. There should be an improvement in the current account of the balance of payments too as the gap between export values and import values improves. However, higher import prices will feed through to a rise in inflation in the economy.

excise duty indirect tax levied on certain goods produced within a country, such as petrol, alcohol, and tobacco. It is collected by the government's ◊Customs and Excise department.

exclusion principle in physics, a principle of atomic structure originated by Austrian–US physicist Wolfgang Pauli (1900–1958). It states that no two electrons in a single atom may have the same set of ◊quantum numbers.

Hence, it is impossible to pack together certain elementary particles, such as electrons, beyond a certain critical density, otherwise they would share the same location and quantum number. A white dwarf star is thus prevented from contracting further by the exclusion principle and never collapses.

excommunication in religion, exclusion of an offender from the rights and privileges of the Roman Catholic Church. The English monarchs King John, Henry VIII, and Elizabeth I were all excommunicated.

excretion in biology, the removal of waste products from the cells of living organisms. In plants and simple animals, waste products are removed by diffusion, but in higher animals they are removed by specialized organs. In mammals the kidneys are the principle organs of excretion. Water and metabolic wastes are also excreted in the faeces and, in humans, through the sweat glands; carbon dioxide and water are removed via the lungs.

executor in law, a person appointed in a will to carry out the instructions of the deceased. A person so named has the right to refuse to act. The executor also has a duty to bury the deceased, prove the will, and obtain a grant of probate (that is, establish that the will is genuine and obtain official approval of his or her actions).

Exeter city, administrative headquarters of Devon, England, on the river Exe; population (1991) 98,100. It was founded by the Romans as Isca Dumnoniorum and has medieval, Georgian, and Regency architecture, including a cathedral (1280–1369) and a market centre. Agricultural machinery, pharmaceuticals, textiles, leather goods, and metal products are manufactured here.

existentialism branch of philosophy based on the situation of the individual in an absurd or meaningless universe where humans have free will. Existentialists argue that people are responsible for and the sole judge of their actions as they affect others. The origin of existentialism is usually traced back to the Danish philosopher ◊Kierkegaard; among its proponents were Martin Heidegger in Germany and Jean-Paul ◊Sartre in France.

All self-aware individuals can grasp or intuit their own existence and freedom, and individuals must not allow their choices to be constrained by anything – not even reason or morality. This freedom to choose leads to the notion of nonbeing, or nothingness, which can provoke angst or dread.

Exmoor moorland in Devon and Somerset, England, forming (with the coast from Minehead to Combe Martin) a National Park since 1954. It includes Dunkery Beacon, 520 m/1,707 ft, and the Doone Valley.

exobiology study of life forms that may possibly exist elsewhere in the universe, and of the effects of extraterrestrial environments on Earth organisms. Techniques include space probe experiments designed to detect organic molecules, and the monitoring of radio waves from other star systems.

exocrine gland gland that discharges secretions, usually through a tube or a duct, on to a surface. Examples include sweat glands which release sweat on to the skin, and digestive glands which release digestive juices on to the walls of the intestine. Some animals also have ◊endocrine glands (ductless glands) that release hormones directly into the bloodstream.

Exodus second book of the Old Testament, which relates the departure of the Israelites from slavery in Egypt, under the leadership of ◊Moses, for the Promised Land of Canaan. The journey included the miraculous parting of the Red Sea, with the pharaoh's pursuing forces being drowned as the waters returned. The Exodus is also recorded in the *Hagadda*, which is read at the Seder (during the Jewish festival of Passover) to commemorate the deliverance. During the 40 years of wandering in the wilderness, Moses brought the Ten Commandments down from Mount Sinai.

exorcism rite used in a number of religions for the expulsion of so-called evil spirits. In Christianity it is employed, for example, in the Roman Catholic and Pentecostal churches.

exoskeleton the hardened external skeleton of insects, spiders, crabs, and other arthropods. It provides attachment for muscles and protection for the internal organs, as well as support. To permit growth it is periodically shed in a process called ecdysis.

exosphere the uppermost layer of the ◊atmosphere. It is an ill-defined zone above the thermosphere, beginning at about 700 km/435 mi and fading off into the vacuum of space. The gases are extremely thin, with hydrogen as the main constituent.

expansion in physics, the increase in size of a constant mass of substance caused by, for example, increasing its temperature (◊thermal expansion) or its internal pressure. The expansivity, or coefficient of thermal expansion, of a material is its expansion (per unit volume, area, or length) per degree rise in temperature.

expectorant any substance, often added to cough mixture, to encourage secretion of mucus in the airways to make it easier to cough up. It is debatable whether expectorants have an effect on lung secretions.

experiment in science, a practical test designed with the intention that its results will be relevant to a particular theory or set of theories. Although some experiments may be used merely for gathering more information about a topic that is already well understood, others may be of crucial importance in confirming a new theory or in undermining long-held beliefs.

The manner in which experiments are performed, and the relation between the design of an experiment and its value, are therefore of central importance. In general an experiment is of most value when the factors that might affect the results (variables) are carefully controlled; for this reason most experiments take place in a well-managed environment such as a laboratory or clinic.

experimental archaeology the controlled replication of ancient technologies and behaviour in order to provide hypotheses that can be tested by actual archaeological data. Experiments can range in size from the reproduction of ancient tools in order to learn about their processes of manufacture and use, and their effectiveness, to the construction of whole villages and ancient subsistence practices in long-term experiments.

experimental psychology the application of scientific methods to the study of mental processes and behaviour. This covers a wide range of fields of study, including: human and animal learning, in which learning theories describe how new behaviours are acquired and modified; cognition, the study of a number of functions, such as perception, attention, memory, and language; and physiological psychology, which relates the study of cognition to different regions of the brain. Artificial intelligence refers to the computer simulation of cognitive processes, such as language and problem-solving.

expert system computer program for giving advice (such as diagnosing an illness or interpreting the law) that incorporates knowledge derived from human expertise. It is a kind of ◊knowledge-based system containing rules that can be applied to find the solution to a problem. It is a form of ◊artificial intelligence.

explanation in science, an attempt to make clear the cause of any natural event by reference to physical laws and to observations. The extent to which any explanation can be said to be true is one of the chief concerns of philosophy. Although it may be reasonable to expect that a physical law will hold in the future, that expectation is problematic in that it relies on ◊induction, a much criticized feature of human thought; in fact no explanation can be held to be true for all time.

Explorer series of US scientific satellites. *Explorer 1*, launched Jan 1958, was the first US satellite in orbit and discovered the Van Allen radiation belts around the Earth.

explosive any material capable of a sudden release of energy and the rapid formation of a large volume of gas, leading when compressed to the development of a high-pressure wave (blast).

Combustion and explosion differ essentially only in rate of reaction, and many explosives (called low explosives) are capable of undergoing relatively slow combustion under suitable conditions. High explosives produce uncontrollable blasts. The first low explosive was ◊gunpowder; the first high explosive was ◊nitroglycerine.

exponent or ***index*** in mathematics, a number that indicates the number of times a term is multiplied by itself; for example, $x^2 = x \times x$, $4^3 = 4 \times 4 \times 4$.

Exponents obey certain rules. Terms that contain them are multiplied together by adding the exponents; for example, $x^2 \times x^5 = x^7$. Division of such terms is done by subtracting the exponents; for example, $y^5 \div y^3 = y^2$. Any number with the exponent 0 is equal to 1; for example, $x^0 = 1$ and $99^0 = 1$.

exponential in mathematics, descriptive of a ◊function in which the variable quantity is an exponent (a number indicating the power to which another number or expression is raised). Exponential functions and series involve the constant e = 2.71828.... . Scottish mathematician John Napier devised natural ◊logarithms in 1614 with e as the base.

Exponential functions are basic mathematical functions, written as e^x or exp x. The expression e^x has five definitions, two of which are: (i) e^x is the solution of the differential equation $dx/dt = x$ ($x = 1$ if $t = 0$); (ii) e^x is the limiting sum of the infinite series $1 + x + (x^2/2!) + (x^3/3!) + ... + (x^n/n!)$.

Curves of the form $y = Ae^{-ax}$, where $a > 0$, are known as decay functions; those of the form $y = Be^{bx}$, where $b > 0$, are growth functions. Exponential growth is not constant. It applies, for example, to population growth, where the population doubles in a short time period. A graph of population number against time produces a curve that is characteristically rather flat at first but then shoots almost directly upwards.

export goods or service produced in one country and sold to another. Exports may be visible (goods such as cars physically exported) or invisible (services such as banking and tourism, that are provided in the exporting country but paid for by residents of another country).

The most significant UK ***visible exports*** are oil and manufactured goods (including semi-manufactured goods such as steel as well as finished manufactured goods such as cars). The UK is a net exporter of oil through the exploitation of North Sea reserves. Although manufactured goods contribute about 60% of total exports (including invisibles), the UK is a net importer of manufactured goods because of its small manufacturing base. The UK's ***invisible exports*** are transport, travel, and tourism, and financial services (including banking and insurance). The UK is a net exporter of transport and financial services and a net importer of travel and tourism, because so many British residents take holidays abroad.

exposition in music, the opening statement of a classical sonata, concerto, or symphony first movement, in which the principal themes are clearly outlined.

exposure meter instrument used in photography for indicating the correct exposure – the length of time the camera shutter should be open under given light conditions. Meters use substances such as cadmium sulphide and selenium as light sensors. These materials change electrically when light strikes them, the change being proportional to the intensity of the incident light. Many cameras have a built-in exposure meter that sets the camera controls automatically as the light conditions change.

expressionism in music, use of melodic or harmonic distortion for expressive effect, associated with Schoenberg, Hindemith, Krenek, and others.

Expressionism style of painting, sculpture, and literature that expresses inner emotions; in particular, a movement in early 20th-century art in northern and central Europe. Expressionists tended to distort or exaggerate natural appearance in order to create a reflection of an inner world; the Norwegian painter Edvard Munch's *Skriket/The Scream* 1893 (National Gallery, Oslo) is perhaps the most celebrated example. Expressionist writers include August Strindberg and Frank Wedekind.

Leading Expressionist artists were James Ensor, Oskar Kokoschka, and Chaïm Soutine. The groups *die* ◊*Brücke* and *der* ◊*Blaue Reiter* were associated with this movement, and the Expressionist trend in German art emerged even more strongly after World War I in the work of Max Beckmann and Georg Grosz.

extensive agriculture farming system where the area of the farm is large but there are low inputs (such as labour or fertilizers). Extensive farming generally gives rise to lower yields per hectare than ◊intensive agriculture. For example, in East Anglia, intensive use of land may give wheat yields as high as 53 tonnes per hectare, whereas an extensive wheat farm on the Canadian prairies may produce an average of 8.8 tonnes per hectare.

extensor a muscle that straightens a limb.

extinction in biology, the complete disappearance of a species. In the past, extinctions are believed to have occurred because species were unable to adapt quickly enough to a naturally changing environment. Today, most extinctions are due to human activity. Some species, such as the ◊dodo of Mauritius, the ◊moas of New Zealand, and the passenger ◊pigeon of North America, were exterminated by hunting. Others became extinct when their habitat was destroyed. ◊Endangered species are close to extinction.

Mass extinctions are episodes during which whole groups of species have become extinct, the best known being that of the dinosaurs, other large reptiles, and various marine invertebrates about 65 million years ago. Another mass extinction occurred about 10,000 years ago when many giant species of mammal died out. This is known as the 'Pleistocene overkill' because their disappearance was probably hastened by the hunting activities of prehistoric humans. The greatest mass extinction occurred about 250 million years ago marking the Permian-Triassic boundary (see ◊geological time), when up to 96% of all living species became extinct. It was proposed 1982 that mass extinctions occur periodically, at approximately 26-million-year intervals.

The current mass extinction is largely due to human destruction of habitats, as in the tropical forests and coral reefs; it is far more serious and damaging than mass extinctions of the past because of the speed at which it occurs. Conservative estimates put the rate of extinction due to deforestation alone at 4,000 to 6,000 species a year. Overall, the rate could be as high as one species an hour. Australia has the worst record for extinction: 18 mammals have disappeared since Europeans settled there, and 40 more are threatened.

The last mouse-eared bat *Myotis myotis* in the UK died 1990. This is the first mammal to have become extinct in the UK for 250 years, since the last wolf was exterminated.

▷ *See feature on pp. 896–897.*

extracellular matrix strong material naturally occurring in animals and plants, made up of protein and long-chain sugars (polysaccharides) in which cells are embedded. It is often called a 'biological glue', and forms part of ◊connective tissues such as bone and skin. The cell walls of plants and bacteria, and the ◊exoskeletons of insects and other arthropods, are also formed by types of extracellular matrix.

extradition surrender, by one state or country to another, of a person accused of a criminal offence in the state or country to which that person is extradited. When two nations are involved, extradition is usually governed by a treaty between the two countries concerned. A country usually will not allow extradition for political offences or an offence that it does not treat as a crime, even though it is a crime in the requesting country.

extrasensory perception (ESP) any form of perception beyond and distinct from the known sensory processes. The main forms of ESP are clairvoyance (intuitive perception or vision of events and situations without using the senses); precognition (the ability to foresee events); and telepathy or thought transference (communication between people without using any known visible, tangible, or audible medium). Verification by scientific study has yet to be achieved.

Extremadura autonomous region of W Spain including the provinces of Badajoz and Cáceres; area 41,600 sq km/16,058 sq mi; population (1991) 1,061,900. Irrigated land is used for growing wheat; the remainder is either oak forest or used for pig or sheep grazing.

extroversion or ***extraversion*** personality dimension described by the psychologists Carl ◊Jung and, later, Hans Eysenck. The typical extrovert is sociable, impulsive, and carefree. The opposite of extroversion is ◊introversion.

extrusive rock or ***volcanic rock*** ◊igneous rock formed on the surface of the Earth; for example, basalt. It is usually fine-grained (having cooled quickly), unlike the more coarse-grained intrusive rocks (igneous rocks formed under the surface). The magma (molten rock) that cools to form extrusive rock may reach the surface through a crack, such as the ◊constructive margin at the Mid-Atlantic Ridge, or through the vent of a ◊volcano. Extrusive rock can be either lava (solidified from a flow) or a pyroclastic deposit (hot rocks or ash).

Exxon Corporation the USA's largest oil concern, founded 1888 as the Standard Oil Company (New Jersey), selling petrol under the brand name Esso from 1926 and under the name Exxon in the USA from 1972. The company was responsible for ◊oil spills in Alaska 1989 and New York harbour 1990.

In Sept 1994 a US federal court ruling ordered Exxon to pay $5 billion to the Alaskans affected by the 1989 spill. The settlement collapsed 1991, but a jury concluded 1994 that the disaster had caused $286.8 million in damage to the Alaskan fishing industry.

Eyck Jan van c. 1390–1441. Netherlandish painter, a major figure of European art. One of the first painters to use oil paint effectively, he is noted for his meticulous detail and his brilliance of colour and finish. He painted religious scenes and also portraits, which, though they are among the earliest, are assured and subtle. His works include an altarpiece, *The Adoration of the Lamb* 1432 (St Bavo cathedral, Ghent), and *The Arnolfini Wedding* 1434 (National Gallery, London).

Unlike his presumed elder brother ***Hubert van Eyck*** (died 1426), Jan is a clearly defined historical figure. He worked as a miniaturist 1422–25 in The Hague for John, Duke of Bavaria and Count of Holland (died 1425), and then entered the service of Philip the Good, Duke of Burgundy. He settled in Bruges about 1430, still working for the duke, but employed also by the wealthy burgesses of Bruges. Among his portraits are *Madonna with Chancellor Rolin* 1435/37 (Louvre, Paris), *Madonna with Canon van der Paele* 1436 (Groningen Museum, Bruges), and *Man with a Turban* 1433 (National Gallery, London), thought by some to be a self-portrait. He and his brother may also have illuminated the Turin-Milan Book of Hours (destroyed in the 20th century).

Jan (and perhaps his brother) improved on the already existing technique of oil painting, which allowed subtler effects of tone, colour, and detail than the egg-tempera technique then in common use. However, the brilliance of colour and perfection of enamel-like surface attained by Jan must be attributed also to his superbly skilled and methodical handling of paint, skills acquired as an illuminator.

eye the organ of vision. In the human eye, the light is focused by the combined action of the curved cornea, the internal fluids, and the lens. The insect eye is compound – made up of many separate facets – known as ommatidia, each of which collects light and directs it separately to a receptor to build up an image. Invertebrates have much simpler eyes, with no lenses. Among molluscs, cephalopods have complex eyes similar to those of vertebrates. The mantis shrimp's eyes contain ten colour pigments with which to perceive colour; some flies and fishes have five, while the human eye has only three.

human eye This is a roughly spherical structure contained in a bony socket. Light enters it through the cornea, and passes through the circular opening (pupil) in the iris (the coloured part of the eye). The ciliary muscles act on the lens (the rounded transparent structure behind the iris) to change its shape, so that images of objects at different distances can be focused on the ◊retina. This is at the back of the eye, and is packed with light-sensitive cells (rods and cones), connected to the brain by the optic nerve. *See illustration on following page.*

eyebright any flower of the genus *Euphrasia*, of the figwort family Scrophulariaceae. They are 2–30 cm/1–12 in high, bearing whitish flowers streaked with purple. The name indicates its traditional use as an eye-medicine. It is found in fields throughout Britain.

eye, defects of the abnormalities of the eye that impair vision. Glass or plastic lenses, in the

Eyck *The Madonna with Chancellor Rolin* c. 1435 by Jan van Eyck, Louvre, Paris. The greatest of the early Netherlandish painters, van Eyck was able to combine a startling realism with a rich religious symbolism. The practice of including the donor of the picture in a religious scene (here Chancellor Rolin, clearly confident of his own power and authority) paved the way for the independent portrait. *Corbis*

eye The human eye. The retina of the eye contains about 137 million light-sensitive cells in an area of about 650 sq mm/1 sq in. There are 130 million rod cells for black and white vision and 7 million cone cells for colour vision. The optic nerve contains about 1 million nerve fibres. The focusing muscles of the eye adjust about 100,000 times a day. To exercise the leg muscles to the same extent would need an 80 km/50 mi walk.

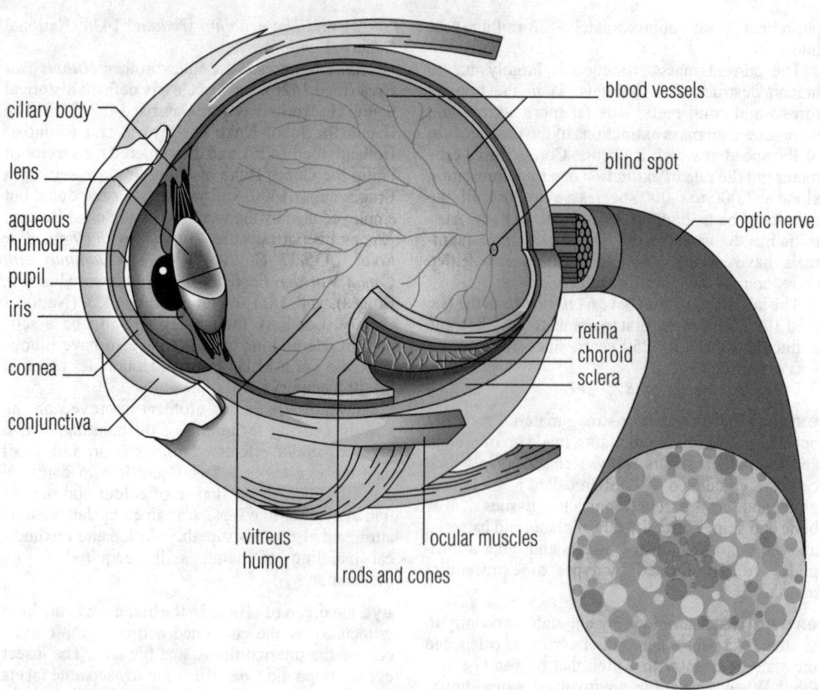

form of spectacles or contact lenses, are the usual means of correction. Common optical defects are ◊short-sightedness or myopia; farsightedness or hypermetropia; lack of ◊accommodation or presbyopia; and ◊astigmatism. Other eye defects include ◊colour blindness.

Eyre Richard (Charles Hastings) 1943– . English stage and film director. He succeeded Peter Hall as artistic director of the National Theatre, London 1988. His stage productions include *Guys and Dolls* 1982, *Bartholomew Fair* 1988, *Richard III* 1990, which he set in 1930s Britain; and *Night of the Iguana* 1992. His films include *The Ploughman's Lunch* 1983, *Laughterhouse* (US *Singleton's Pluck*) 1984, and *Tumbledown* 1988 for television.

Eyre, Lake Australia's largest lake, in central South Australia, which frequently runs dry, becoming a salt marsh in dry seasons; area up to 9,000 sq km/3,500 sq mi. It is the continent's lowest point, 12 m/39 ft below sea level.

Eysenck Hans Jürgen 1916–1997. British psychologist. His work concentrates on personality theory and testing by developing ◊behaviour therapy. He is an outspoken critic of psychoanalysis as a therapeutic method. His theory that intelligence is almost entirely inherited and can be only slightly modified by education aroused controversy.

Ezekiel lived c. 600 BC. In the Old Testament, a Hebrew prophet. Carried into captivity in Babylon by ◊Nebuchadnezzar 597, he preached that Jerusalem's fall was due to the sins of Israel. The book of Ezekiel begins with a description of a vision of supernatural beings.

Ezra in the Old Testament, a Hebrew scribe who was allowed by Artaxerxes, king of Persia (probably Artaxerxes I, 464–423 BC), to lead his people back to Jerusalem from Babylon 458 BC.

He re-established the Mosaic law (laid down by Moses) and forbade intermarriage.

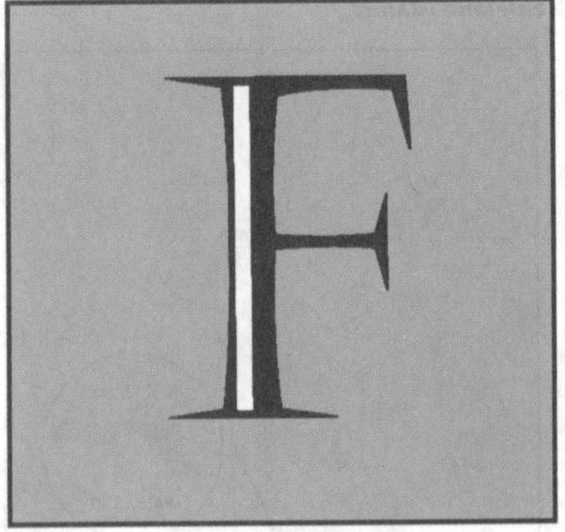

factory act A series of factory acts passed in the 19th century established basic rights for workers, primarily in the textile industry. Many of the great Lancashire cotton mills preferred to employ women and children because of their greater manual dexterity, and the legislation provided the first legal protection for child workers. *Image Select (UK) Ltd*

°F symbol for degrees ◊***Fahrenheit***.

'f/64' group group of US photographers, including Edward ◊Weston, Ansel ◊Adams, and Imogen Cunningham (1883–1976), formed 1932. The sharp focus and clarity of their black and white pictures was achieved by setting the lens aperture to f/64.

FA abbreviation for ***Football Association***.

Fabergé Peter Carl, (born Karl Gustavovich) 1846–1920. Russian goldsmith and jeweller. Among his masterpieces was a series of jewelled Easter eggs, the first of which was commissioned by Alexander III for the tsarina 1884.

His workshops in St Petersburg and Moscow were celebrated for the exquisite delicacy of their products, especially the use of gold in various shades. Fabergé died in exile in Switzerland.

Fabian Society UK socialist organization for research, discussion, and publication, founded in London 1884. Its name is derived from the Roman commander Fabius Maximus, and refers to the evolutionary methods by which it hopes to attain socialism by a succession of gradual reforms. Early members included the playwright George Bernard Shaw and Beatrice and Sidney Webb. The society helped to found the Labour Representation Committee in 1900, which became the Labour Party in 1906.

Fabius Laurent 1946– . French politician, leader of the Socialist Party (PS) 1992–93. As prime minister 1984–86, he introduced a liberal, free-market economic programme, but his career was damaged by the 1985 ◊Greenpeace sabotage scandal. In Jan 1992 he was elected PS first secretary (leader), replacing Pierre Mauroy. He was ousted as leader April 1993, after the Socialists lost more than 200 seats in the March general election.

Fabius Maximus (Quintus Fabius Maximus Verrucosus) c. 260–203 BC. Roman general, known as *Cunctator* or 'Delayer' because of his cautious tactics against Hannibal 217–214 BC, when he continually harassed Hannibal's armies but never risked a set battle.

fable story, in either verse or prose, in which animals or inanimate objects are given the mentality and speech of human beings to point out a moral. Fables are common in folklore and children's literature, and range from the short fables of the ancient Greek writer Aesop to the modern novel *Animal Farm* 1945 by George Orwell.

Fabulists include the Roman Phaedrus, French poet La Fontaine and, in English, Geoffrey Chaucer and Jonathan Swift.

Fabre Jean Henri Casimir 1823–1915. French entomologist whose studies of wasps, bees, and other insects, particularly their anatomy and behaviour, have become classics.

Fabricius Geronimo. Latinized name of Girolamo Fabrizio 1537–1619. Italian anatomist and embryologist. He made a detailed study of the veins and discovered the valves that direct the blood flow towards the heart. He also studied the development of chick embryos.

Fabricius also investigated the mechanics of respiration, the action of muscles, the anatomy of the larynx (about which he was the first to give a full description) and the eye (he was the first to correctly describe the location of the lens and the first to demonstrate that the pupil changes size).

facies in geology, any assemblage of mineral, rock, or fossil features that reflect the environment in which rock was formed.

The set of characters that distinguish one facies from another in a given time stratigraphic unit is used to interpret local changes in simultaneously existing environments. Ancient floods and migrations of the seashore up or down can be traced by changes in facies.

factor a number that divides into another number exactly. For example, the factors of 64 are 1, 2, 4, 8, 16, 32, and 64. In algebra, certain kinds of polynomials (expressions consisting of several or many terms) can be factorized. For example, the factors of $x^2 + 3x + 2$ are $x + 1$ and $x + 2$, since $x^2 + 3x + 2 = (x + 1)(x + 2)$. This is called factorization. See also ◊prime number.

factorial of a positive number, the product of all the whole numbers (integers) inclusive between 1 and the number itself. A factorial is indicated by the symbol '!'. Thus $6! = 1 \times 2 \times 3 \times 4 \times 5 \times 6 = 720$. Factorial zero, 0!, is defined as 1.

factoring lending money to a company on the security of money owed to that company; this is often done on the basis of collecting those debts. The lender is known as the factor. Factoring may also describe acting as a commission agent for the sale of goods.

factory act in Britain, an act of Parliament such as the Health and Safety at Work Act 1974, which governs conditions of work, hours of labour, safety, and sanitary provision in factories and workshops.

In the 19th century legislation was progressively introduced to regulate conditions of work, hours of labour, safety, and sanitary provisions in factories and workshops. The first legislation was the Health and Morals of Apprentices Act 1802.

In 1833 the first factory inspectors were appointed. Legislation was extended to offices, shops, and railway premises 1963. All employees are now covered by the 1974 Act, which is enforced by the Health and Safety Executive.

factory farming intensive rearing of poultry or animals for food, usually on high-protein foodstuffs in confined quarters. Chickens for eggs and meat, and calves for veal are commonly factory farmed. Some countries restrict the use of antibiotics and growth hormones as aids to factory farming, because they can persist in the flesh of the animals after they are slaughtered. The emphasis is on productive yield rather than animal welfare so that conditions for the animals are often very poor. For this reason, many people object to factory farming on moral as well as health grounds.

factory system the basis of manufacturing in the modern world. In the factory system workers are employed at a place where they carry out specific tasks, which together result in a product. This is called the division of labour. Usually these workers will perform their tasks with the aid of machinery. Such ◊mechanization is another feature of the factory system, which leads to mass production. Richard ◊Arkwright pioneered the system in England 1771, when he set up a cotton-spinning factory.

FA Cup abbreviation for ***Football Association Cup***, the major annual soccer knockout competition in England and Wales, open to all member clubs of the British Football Association. First held 1871–72, it is the oldest football knockout competition.

faeces remains of food and other waste material eliminated from the digestive tract of animals by way of the anus. Faeces consist of quantities of fibrous material, bacteria and other microorganisms, rubbed-off lining of the digestive tract, bile fluids, undigested food, minerals, and water.

Faerie Queene, The poem by Edmund ◊Spenser, published 1590–96, dedicated to Elizabeth I. Drawing on the traditions of chivalry and courtly love, the poem was planned as an epic in 12 books, following the adventures of 12 knights, each representing a different chivalric virtue, beginning with the Red Cross Knight of holiness. Only six books were completed. Spenser used a new stanza form, later adopted by Keats, Shelley, and Byron.

Faeroe Islands or ***Faeroes*** alternative spelling of the ◊Faroe Islands, in the N Atlantic.

Fahd (Ibn Abdul Aziz) 1923– . King of Saudi Arabia from 1982, when he succeeded his half-brother Khalid. As head of government, he has been active in trying to bring about a solution to the Middle East conflicts. In Nov 1995 he suffered a stroke, and in Jan 1996 temporarily ceded power to Crown Prince Abdullah, his legal successor.

Fahrenheit Gabriel Daniel 1686–1736. Polish-born Dutch physicist who invented the first accurate thermometer 1724 and devised the Fahrenheit temperature scale. Using his thermometer, Fahrenheit was able to determine the boiling points of liquids and found that they vary with atmospheric pressure.

Fahrenheit scale temperature scale invented 1714 by Gabriel Fahrenheit which was commonly used in English-speaking countries until the 1970s, after which the ◊Celsius scale was generally adopted, in line with the rest of the world. In the Fahrenheit scale, intervals are measured in degrees (°F); $°F = (°C \times 9/5) + 32$.

Fahrenheit took as the zero point the lowest temperature he could achieve anywhere in the laboratory, and, as the other fixed point, body temperature, which he set at 96°F. On this scale, water freezes at 32°F and boils at 212°F. *See list of tables on p. 1177.*

fainting sudden, temporary loss of consciousness caused by reduced blood supply to the brain. It may be due to emotional shock or physical factors, such as pooling of blood in the legs from standing still for long periods.

Fairbanks Douglas, Sr. Stage name of Douglas Elton Ulman 1883–1939. US actor. He played acrobatic swashbuckling heroes in silent films such as *The Mark of Zorro* 1920, *The Three Musketeers* 1921, *Robin Hood* 1922, *The Thief of Bagdad* 1924, and *Don Quixote* 1925. He was married to film star Mary Pickford ('America's Sweetheart') 1920–35. In 1919 he founded ◊United Artists with Charlie Chaplin and D W Griffith.

Fairbanks Douglas Elton, Jr 1909– . US actor. He initially appeared in the same type of swashbuckling film roles as his father, Douglas Fairbanks; for example, in *Catherine the Great* 1934 and *The Prisoner of Zenda* 1937. Later he produced TV films and acted in a variety of productions.

Fairfax Thomas, 3rd Baron Fairfax 1612–1671. English general, commander in chief of the Parliamentary army in the English ◊Civil War. With Oliver ◊Cromwell he formed the ◊New Model Army and defeated Charles I at Naseby. He opposed the king's execution, resigned in protest 1650 against the invasion of Scotland, and participated in the restoration of Charles II after Cromwell's death.

fairy tale magical story, usually a folk tale in origin. Typically in European fairy tales, a poor, brave, and resourceful hero or heroine goes through testing adventures to eventual good fortune.

The Germanic tales collected by the ◊Grimm brothers have been retold in many variants. Charles ◊Perrault's retellings include 'Cinderella' and 'The Sleeping Beauty'. The form may also be adapted for more individual moral and literary purposes, as was done by Danish writer Hans Christian ◊Andersen.

Faisal I 1885–1933. King of Iraq 1921–33. An Arab nationalist leader during World War I, he was instrumental in liberating the Middle East from Ottoman control and was declared king of Syria in 1918 but deposed by the French in 1920. The British then installed him as king in Iraq, where he continued to foster pan-Arabism.

Faisalabad city in Punjab province, Pakistan, 120 km/75 mi W of Lahore; population (1981) 1,092,000. It trades in grain, cotton, and textiles.

Faisal Ibn Abd al-Aziz 1905–1975. King of Saudi Arabia from 1964. He was the younger brother of King Saud, on whose accession 1953 he was declared crown prince. He was prime minister 1953–60 and 1962–75. In 1964 he emerged victorious from a lengthy conflict with his brother and adopted a policy of steady modernization of his country. He was assassinated by his nephew.

fakir originally a Muslim mendicant of some religious order, but in India a general term for an ascetic.

Falange (Spanish 'phalanx') also known as ***Falange Española***. Former Spanish Fascist Party, founded 1933 by José Antonio Primo de Rivera (1903–1936), son of military ruler Miguel ◊Primo de Rivera. It was closely modelled in programme and organization on the Italian Fascists and on the Nazis. In 1937, when ◊Franco assumed leadership, it was declared the only legal party, and altered its name to Traditionalist Spanish Phalanx.

Falasha member of a small community of black Jews originating in Ethiopia. They suffered discrimination there and, after being accorded Jewish status by Israel 1975, began a gradual process of resettlement in Israel. By the early 1980s only about 30,000 Falashim remained in Ethiopia, and the final emigration to Israel took place during the collapse of the Mengistu regime 1991.

The Falashim refer to themselves as *Beta Israel* ('House of Israel').

falcon The dainty Madagascar kestrel *Falco newtoni*, whose main prey is often lizards. It is superficially similar to the common European kestrel, with which it also shares the habit of nesting on buildings and living successfully alongside humans. *Premaphotos Wildlife*

falcon any bird of prey of the genus *Falco*, family Falconidae, order Falconiformes. Falcons are the smallest of the hawks (15–60 cm/6–24 in). They have short curved beaks with one tooth in the upper mandible; the wings are long and pointed, and the toes elongated. They nest in high places and kill their prey on the wing by 'stooping' (swooping down at high speed). They include the peregrine and kestrel.

The peregrine falcon *F. peregrinus*, up to about 50 cm/1.8 ft long, has become re-established in North America and Britain after near extinction (by pesticides, gamekeepers, and egg collectors). When stooping on its intended prey, it is the fastest creature in the world, timed at 240 kph/150 mph.

Other hawks include the hobby *F. subbuteo*, the merlin *F. columbarius* (called pigeon-hawk in North America), and the kestrel *F. tinnunculus*.

Falcón Juan Crisóstomo 1820–1870. Venezuelan marshal and president 1863–68. Falcón's rule saw the beginnings of economic recovery after the chaos of the Federal Wars 1858–63. He travelled around the country putting down uprisings, while his ministers in Caracas built roads, restored the nation's finances, and established foreign trade links. He fell from power because he was unable to tackle splits in the ruling Liberal party.

falconry the use of specially trained falcons and hawks to capture birds or small mammals. Practised since ancient times in the Middle East, falconry was introduced from continental Europe to Britain in Saxon times.

Faldo Nick (Nicholas Alexander) 1957– . English golfer who was the first Briton in 54 years to win three British Open titles, and the only person after Jack ◊Nicklaus to win two successive US Masters titles (1989 and 1990). He is one of only six golfers to win the Masters and British Open in the same year.

Falkirk local authority of Scotland created 1996 (*see United Kingdom map*).

Falkland Islands (Argentine ***Islas Malvinas***) British crown colony in the S Atlantic, 300 miles E of the Straits of Magellan
area 12,173 sq km/4,700 sq mi, made up of two main islands: East Falkland 6,760 sq km/2,610 sq mi, and West Falkland 5,413 sq km/2,090 sq mi
capital Stanley; new port facilities opened 1984, Mount Pleasant airport 1985
features in addition to the two main islands, there are about 200 small islands, all with wild scenery and rich bird life; Mount Usborne (705 m/2,312 ft); moorland
industries wool, alginates (used as dyes and as a food additive) from seaweed beds, fishing (especially squid)
population (1991) 2,120
government a governor (David Tatham from 1992) is advised by an executive council, and a mainly elected legislative council. Administered with the Falklands, but separate dependencies of the UK, are South Georgia and the South Sandwich Islands; see also ◊British Antarctic Territory
history the first European to visit the islands was Englishman John Davis 1592, and at the end of the 17th century they were named after Lord Falkland, treasurer of the British navy. West Falkland was settled by the French 1764. The first British settlers arrived 1765; Spain bought out a French settlement 1766, and the British were ejected 1770–71, but British sovereignty was never ceded, and from 1833, when a few Argentines were expelled, British settlement was continuous.

Argentina asserts its succession to the Spanish claim to the 'Islas Malvinas', but the inhabitants oppose cession. Occupied by Argentina April 1982, the islands were recaptured by British military forces in May–June of the same year. In April 1990 Argentina's congress declared the Falkland Islands and other British-held South Atlantic islands part of the new Argentine province of Tierra del Fuego. In Sept 1995, the UK and Argentina signed an agreement on oil rights in waters surrounding the Falkland Islands.

Falkland Islands, Battle of the in World War I, British naval victory (under Admiral Sir

Falkland Islands

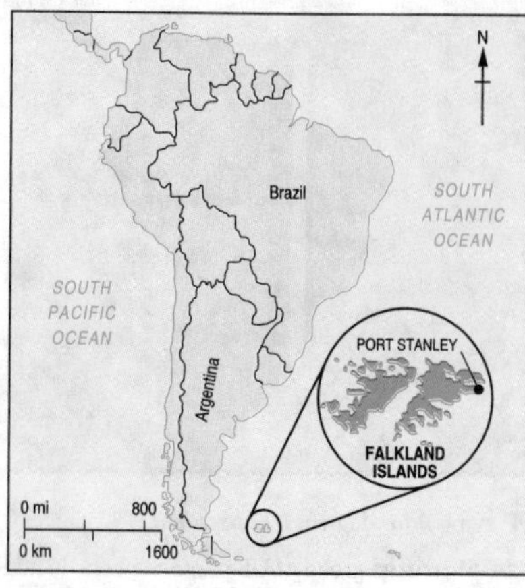

Frederick Sturdee) over German forces under Admiral Maximilian von Spee 8 Dec 1914. Von Spee intended to bombard the Falklands in passing before proceeding around the Cape of Good Hope to arouse the disaffected Boers of South Africa. However, there was already a British force stationed off the Falklands and when von Spee realized he had run into a trap he fled the area. The British gave chase and in the ensuing battle von Spee's squadron was entirely destroyed with a loss of 2,100 crew.

Falklands War war between Argentina and Britain over disputed sovereignty of the Falkland Islands initiated when Argentina invaded and occupied the islands 2 April 1982. On the following day, the United Nations Security Council passed a resolution calling for Argentina to withdraw. A British task force was immediately dispatched and, after a fierce conflict in which more than 1,000 Argentine and British lives were lost, 12,000 Argentine troops surrendered and the islands were returned to British rule 14–15 June 1982. In April 1990 Argentina's congress declared the Falkland Islands and other British-held South Atlantic islands part of the new Argentine province of Tierra del Fuego.

Falla Manuel de (full name Manuel Maria de Falla y Matheu) 1876–1946. Spanish composer. His opera *La vida breve/Brief Life* 1905 (performed 1913) was followed by the ballets *El amor brujo/Love the Magician* 1915 and *El sombrero de tres picos/The Three-Cornered Hat* 1919, and his most ambitious concert work, *Noches en los jardines de España/Nights in the Gardens of Spain* 1916.

Born in Cádiz, he lived in France, where he was influenced by the Impressionist composers Debussy and Ravel. In 1939 he moved to Argentina. The folk idiom of southern Spain is an integral part of his compositions. He also wrote songs and pieces for piano and guitar.

Fall of Man, the myth that explains the existence of evil as the result of some primeval wrongdoing by humanity. It occurs independently in many cultures. The biblical version, recorded in the Old Testament (Genesis 3), provided the inspiration for the epic poem *Paradise Lost* 1667 by John ◊Milton.

The Fall of Man (as narrated in the Bible) occurred in the Garden of Eden when the Serpent tempted Eve to eat the fruit of the Tree of Knowledge. Disobeying God's will, she ate the fruit and gave some to Adam. This caused their expulsion from the Garden and, in Milton's words, 'brought death into the world and all our woe'.

Fallopian tube or ***oviduct*** in mammals, one of two tubes that carry eggs from the ovary to the uterus. An egg is fertilized by sperm in the Fallopian tubes, which are lined with cells whose ◊cilia move the egg towards the uterus.

Fallopius Gabriel. Latinized name of Gabriele Fallopio 1523–1562. Italian anatomist who discovered the ◊Fallopian tubes, which he described as 'trumpets of the uterus', and named the vagina. As well as the reproductive system, he studied the anatomy of the brain and eyes, and gave the first accurate description of the inner ear.

fallout harmful radioactive material released into the atmosphere in the debris of a nuclear explosion (see ◊nuclear warfare) and descending to the surface of the Earth. Such material can enter the food chain, cause ◊radiation sickness, and last for hundreds of thousands of years (see ◊half-life).

fallow land ploughed and tilled, but left unsown for a season to allow it to recuperate. In Europe, it is associated with the medieval three-field system. It is used in some modern ◊crop rotations and in countries that do not have access to fertilizers to maintain soil fertility.

false-colour imagery graphic technique that displays images in false (not true-to-life) colours so as to enhance certain features. It is widely used in displaying electronic images taken by spacecraft; for example, Earth-survey satellites such as *Landsat*. Any colours can be selected by a computer processing the received data.

falsetto in music, a male voice singing in the female (soprano or alto) register.

falsificationism in philosophy of science, the belief that a scientific theory must be under constant scrutiny and that its merit lies only in how well it stands up to rigorous testing. It was first expounded by philosopher Karl ◊Popper in his *Logic of Scientific Discovery* 1934.

Such thinking also implies that a theory can be held to be scientific only if it makes predictions that are clearly testable. Critics of this belief acknowledge the strict logic of this process, but doubt whether the whole of scientific method can be subsumed into so narrow a programme. Philosophers and historians such as Thomas ◊Kuhn and Paul ◊Feyerabend have attempted to use the history of science to show that scientific progress has resulted from a more complicated methodology than Popper suggests.

family in biological classification, a group of related genera (see ◊genus). Family names are not printed in italic (unlike genus and species names), and by convention they all have the ending -idae (animals) or -aceae (plants and fungi). For example, the genera of hummingbirds are grouped in the hummingbird family, Trochilidae. Related families are grouped together in an ◊order.

family group of people related to each other by blood or by marriage. Families are usually described as either 'extended' (a large group of relations living together or in close contact with each other) or 'nuclear' (a family consisting of two parents and their children).

In some societies an extended family consists of a large group of people of different generations closely or distantly related, depending on each other for economic support and security. In other societies the extended family is split into small units, with members living alone or in nuclear families. The 1980s and 90s saw a further decline in the traditional nuclear family.

In 1989–90 42.2% of British families were nuclear. Government figures published in 1996 showed that in the previous ten years the percentage of dependent children living with married parents fell from 83% to 71%. This was paralleled by a rise in the number of children raised by two unmarried parents, and by a single mother, to 1 in 15 and 1 in 12 respectively. In all, more than a quarter of all households consisted of adults living alone, and the resulting fall in the birth rate led to predictions that the population of the UK would start to fall within 20 years.

family planning spacing or preventing the birth of children. Access to family-planning services (see ◊contraceptive) is a significant factor in women's health as well as in limiting population growth. If all those women who wished to avoid further childbirth were able to do so, the number of births would be reduced by 27% in Africa, 33% in Asia, and 35% in Latin America; and the number of women who die during pregnancy or childbirth would be reduced by about 50%.

history English philosopher Jeremy Bentham put forward the idea of birth control 1797, but it was Francis Place, a Radical, who attempted to popularize it in the 19th century, in a treatise entitled *Illustrations and Proofs of the Principle of Population* 1822. A US publication by Charles Knowlton, *The Fruits of Philosophy:* or *The Private Companion of Young Married People* 1832 was reprinted in England in 1834. When a Bristol publisher was prosecuted for selling it 1876, two prominent freethinkers and radicals, Annie ◊Besant and Charles ◊Bradlaugh, had the book published in London in order to provoke a test case in court. A successful outcome, and the resulting publicity, helped to spread information on birth control.

In the UK, family planning and birth control became acceptable partly through the efforts of Marie ◊Stopes who opened a clinic in London in 1921. Other clinics subsequently opened in England were amalgamated to become the Family Planning Association 1930.

In 1912 two articles by Margaret Sanger, 'What every woman should know' and 'What every girl should know', appeared in the New York socialist newspaper *The Call*, advocating birth control as one means of female emancipation. In 1916 she opened a clinic in Brooklyn, and helped to found the American Birth Control League.

In 1965, the United Nations Population Commission recommended the provision of technical assistance on birth control to member nations, and the World Health Organization instigated a programme of research.

famine severe shortage of food affecting a large number of people. Almost 750 million people (equivalent to double the population of Europe) worldwide suffer from hunger and malnutrition. The food availability deficit (FAD) theory explains famines as being caused by insufficient food supplies. This theory was challenged in the 1980s; crop failures do not inevitably lead to famine, nor is it always the case that adequate food supplies are not available nearby. A more recent theory is that famines arise when one group in a society loses its opportunity to exchange its labour or possessions for food.

Fang W African people living in the rainforests of Cameroon, Equatorial Guinea, and NW Gabon, numbering about 2.5 million. The Fang language belongs to the Bantu branch of the Niger-Congo family.

Fang Lizhi 1936– . Chinese political dissident and astrophysicist. He advocated human rights and Western-style pluralism and encouraged his students to campaign for democracy. In 1989, after the Tiananmen Square massacre, he sought refuge in the US embassy in Beijing and, over a year later, received official permission to leave China.

Fanon Frantz Omar 1925–1961. French political writer. His experiences in Algeria during the war for liberation in the 1950s led to the writing of *Les Damnés de la terre/The Wretched of the Earth* 1964, which calls for violent revolution by the peasants of the Third World.

fantasia or *fantasy*, *phantasy*, or *fancy* in music, a free-form instrumental composition for keyboard or chamber ensemble, originating in the late Renaissance, and much favoured by English composers Dowland, Gibbons, and Byrd. It implies the free manipulation of musical figures without regard to models of form. Later composers include Telemann, J S Bach, and Mozart.

fantasy fiction nonrealistic fiction. Much of the world's fictional literature could be classified under this term but, as a commercial and literary genre, fantasy started to thrive after the success of JRR Tolkien's *The Lord of the Rings* 1954–55. Earlier works by such writers as Lord Dunsany, Hope Mirrlees, E R Eddison, and Mervyn Peake, which are not classifiable in fantasy subgenres such as ◊science fiction, ◊horror, or ghost story, could be labelled fantasy.

Much fantasy is pseudomedieval in subject matter and tone. Recent works include Ursula K Le Guin's *Earthsea* series 1968–91, Stephen Donaldson's *Chronicles of Thomas Covenant* 1978–83, and, in the more urban tradition, John Crowley's *Little, Big* 1980, Michael Moorcock's *Gloriana* 1978, and Gene Wolfe's *Free, Live Free* 1985. Such books largely overlap in content with the ◊magic realism of writers such as Gabriel García Márquez, Angela Carter, and Isabel Allende.

Well-known US fantasy authors include Thomas Pynchon (as, for example, in *V*), and Ray Bradbury, whose works are often in the science fiction genre.

Fantin-Latour (Ignace) Henri (Jean Théodore) 1836–1904. French painter. He excelled in delicate still lifes, flower paintings, and portraits. *Homage à Delacroix* 1864 (Musée d'Orsay, Paris) is a portrait group featuring several poets, authors, and painters, including Charles Baudelaire and James McNeill Whistler. At Whistler's suggestion he visited England and perhaps was influenced by the meticulous detail of the Pre-Raphaelites. He produced also some allegorical fancies, often carried out in lithography, but is best known for his still life.

FAO abbreviation for ◊***Food and Agriculture Organization***.

farad SI unit (symbol F) of electrical capacitance (how much electric charge a ◊capacitor can store for a given voltage). One farad is a capacitance of one ◊coulomb per volt. For practical purposes the microfarad (one millionth of a farad, symbol μF) is more commonly used. The farad is named after English scientist Michael Faraday.

faraday unit of electrical charge equal to the charge on one mole of electrons. Its value is 9.648×10^4 coulombs.

Faraday Michael 1791–1867. English chemist and physicist. In 1821 he began experimenting with electromagnetism, and ten years later discovered the induction of electric currents and made the first dynamo. He subsequently found that a magnetic field will rotate the plane of polarization of light (see ◊polarized light). Faraday produced the basic laws of ◊electrolysis 1834.

In 1821 he devised an apparatus that demonstrated the conversion of electrical energy into motive force, for which he is usually credited with the invention of the electric motor.

Faraday's work in chemistry included the isolation of benzene from gas oils 1835. He demonstrated the use of platinum as a catalyst and showed the importance in chemical reactions of surfaces and inhibitors.

Faraday's constant constant (symbol *F*) representing the electric charge carried on one mole of electrons. It is found by multiplying Avogadro's constant by the charge carried on a single electron, and is equal to 9.648×10^4 coulombs per mole.

One faraday is this constant used as a unit. The constant is used to calculate the electric charge needed to discharge a particular quantity of ions during ◊electrolysis.

Faraday's laws three laws of electromagnetic induction, and two laws of electrolysis, all proposed originally by English scientist Michael Faraday:

induction (1) a changing magnetic field induces an electromagnetic force in a conductor; (2) the electromagnetic force is proportional to the rate of change of the field; (3) the direction of the induced electromagnetic force depends on the orientation of the field.

electrolysis (1) the amount of chemical change during electrolysis is proportional to the charge passing through the liquid; (2) the amount of chemical change produced in a substance by a given amount of electricity is proportional to the electrochemical equivalent of that substance.

farce broad popular comedy involving stereotyped characters in complex, often improbable situations

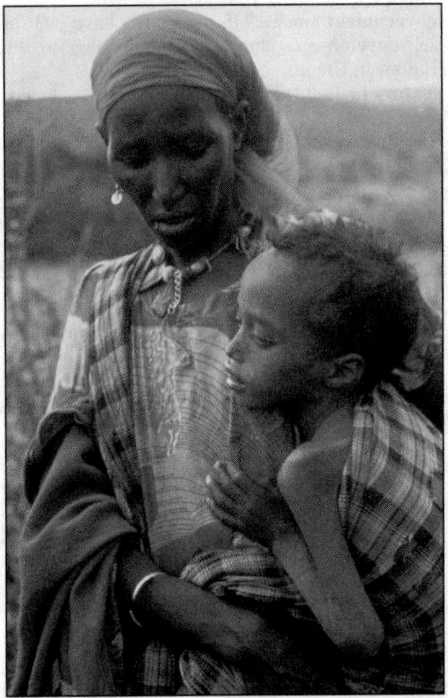

famine Somalian mother with her severely malnourished child. Though the broad causes of famine are overpopulation, drought, and war, the reasons why specific groups are affected – rarely more than 10% of a population – are still unclear. Increasingly governments and aid agencies are searching for solutions to famine by looking at the lives of those who can adapt to dramatic changes in their environment. *Food and Agriculture Organization* frequently revolving around extramarital relationships (hence the term 'bedroom farce').

Originating in the physical knockabout comedy of Greek satyr plays and the broad humour of medieval religious drama, the farce was developed and perfected during the 19th century by Eugène Labiche (1815–1888) and Georges Feydeau (1862–1921) in France and Arthur Pinero in England.

Far East geographical term for all Asia east of the Indian subcontinent.

Fareham town in Hampshire, England, 10 km/6 mi NW of Portsmouth; population (1991) 99,200. Bricks, ceramics, and rope are made and there is engineering and boat building as well as varied light industries, including scientific instruments and horticulture.

Fargo William George 1818–1881. US pioneer of long-distance transport. In 1844 he established with Henry Wells (1805–1878) and Daniel Dunning the first express company to carry freight west of Buffalo. Its success led to his appointment 1850 as secretary of the newly established American Express Company, of which he was president 1868–81. He also established Wells, Fargo & Company 1851, carrying goods express between New York and San Francisco via Panama.

Farmer Frances 1913–1970. US actress. She starred in such films as *Come and Get It* 1936, *The Toast of New York* 1937, and *Son of Fury* 1942, before her career was ended by alcoholism and mental illness.

Farnborough town in Hampshire, England, N of Aldershot; population (1991) 52,500. Experimental work is carried out at the Royal Aircraft Establishment. Aeronautical displays are given at the biennial air show. The mansion of Farnborough Hill was occupied by Napoleon III and the Empress Eugénie, and she, her husband, and her son, are buried in a mausoleum at the Roman Catholic church she built.

Farnese Italian family, originating in upper Lazio, who held the duchy of Parma 1545–1731. Among the family's most notable members were Alessandro Farnese (1468–1549), who became Pope Paul III in 1534 and granted his duchy to his illegitimate son Pier Luigi (1503–1547); and Elizabeth (1692–1766), niece of the last Farnese duke, who married Philip V of Spain and was a force in European politics of the time.

Faroe Islands or ***Faeroe Islands*** or ***Faeroes*** (Danish ***Faerøerne*** 'Sheep Islands') island group (18 out of 22 inhabited) in the N Atlantic, between the Shetland Islands and Iceland, forming an outlying part of ◊Denmark
area 1,399 sq km/540 sq mi; largest islands are Strømø, Østerø, Vagø, Suderø, Sandø, and Bordø
capital Thorshavn on Strømø, population (1992) 14,600
industries fish, crafted goods
currency Danish krone
population (1992 est) 46,800
language Faeroese, Danish
government since 1948 the islands have had full self-government; they do not belong to the European Union
history first settled by Norsemen in the 9th century, the Faroes were a Norwegian province 1380–1709. Their parliament was restored 1852. They withdrew from the European Free Trade Association 1972.

Farouk 1920–1965. King of Egypt 1936–52. He succeeded his father ◊Fuad I. In 1952 a coup headed by General Muhammed Neguib and Colonel Gamal Nasser compelled him to abdicate, and his son Fuad II was temporarily proclaimed in his place.

Farquhar George c. 1677–1707. Irish dramatist. His plays *The Recruiting Officer* 1706 and *The Beaux Stratagem* 1707 are in the tradition of the Restoration comedy of manners, although less robust.

'Spare all I have, and take my life.'
George Farquhar
The Beaux Stratagem

Farrakhan Louis, (born Louis Eugene Walcott) 1933– . African-American religious and political figure. Leader of the ◊Nation of Islam, Farrakhan preaches strict adherence to Muslim values and black separatism. His outspoken views against Jews, homosexuals, and whites have caused outrage. In 1995 he organized the 'Million Men' march of about 400,000 black men in Washington.

Farrell James T(homas) 1904–1979. US novelist and short-story writer. His naturalistic documentary of the Depression, the *Studs Lonigan* trilogy 1932–35 comprising *Young Lonigan, The Young Manhood of Studs Lonigan*, and *Judgment Day*, describes the development of a young Catholic man in Chicago after World War I, and was written from his own experience. *The Face of Time* 1953 is one of his finest works.

Farrell Terry (Terence) 1938– . English architect. He works in a Post-Modern idiom, largely for corporate clients. His Embankment Place scheme 1991 sits theatrically on top of Charing Cross station in Westminster, London. Alban Gate in the City of London 1992 is more towerlike in form.

Farrell's style is robust and eclectic, and he is not afraid to make jokes in architecture, such as the gaily painted giant egg cups that adorn the parapet of his TV AM building in Camden, London, 1981–82. Other works include studios for Limehouse Productions, Henley Royal Regatta HQ, and the Craft Council Galleries.

Farr-Jones Nick (Nicholas) 1962– . Australian rugby union player. He is Australia's most capped scrum half and has captained his country on more than 30 occasions. He was captain of Australia's 1991 World Cup winning team, and plays for Sydney University and New South Wales.

Farrow Mia Villiers 1945– . US film and television actress. Popular since the late 1960s, she was associated with the director Woody ◊Allen, both on and off screen, 1982–92. She starred in his films *Zelig* 1983, *Hannah and Her Sisters* 1986, and *Crimes and Misdemeanors* 1990, as well as in Roman Polanski's *Rosemary's Baby* 1968. In 1992 she split acrimoniously from Allen.

Fars province of SW Iran, comprising fertile valleys among mountain ranges running NW–SE; population (1991) 3,543,800; area 133,300 sq km/51,487 sq mi. The capital is Shiraz, and there are imposing ruins of Cyrus the Great's city of Parargardae and of ◊Persepolis.

Farsi or ***Persian*** language belonging to the Indo-Iranian branch of the Indo-European family, and the official language of Iran (formerly Persia). It is also spoken in Afghanistan, Iraq, and Tajikistan.

Farsi is the language of the province of Fars (Persia proper). It is written in Arabic script, from right to left, and has a large mixture of Arabic religious, philosophical, and technical vocabulary.

fascism political ideology that denies all rights to individuals in their relations with the state; specifically, the totalitarian nationalist movement founded in Italy 1919 by ◊Mussolini and followed by ◊Hitler's Germany 1933.

Fascism was essentially a product of the economic and political crisis of the years after World War I. Units called *fasci di combattimento* (combat groups), from the Latin *fasces*, were originally established to oppose communism. The fascist party, the *Partitio Nazionale Fascista*, controlled Italy 1922–43. Fascism protected the existing social order by forcible suppression of the working-class movement and by providing scapegoats for popular anger such as minority groups: Jews, foreigners, or blacks; it also prepared the citizenry for the economic and psychological mobilization of war.

The term 'fascism' is also applied to similar organizations in other countries, such as the Spanish ◊Falange and the British Union of Fascists under Oswald ◊Mosley.

Neofascist groups still exist in many W European countries, in the USA (the ◊Ku Klux Klan and several small armed vigilante groups), France, Germany, Russia (Pamyat), and elsewhere.Germany experienced an upsurge in neofascist activity in the 1990s, as did the UK with the growth of right-wing racism.

fashion style currently in vogue, primarily applied to clothing. Throughout history, in addition to its mainly functional purpose, clothing has been a social status symbol, conveying information about the class, rank, and wealth of the wearer. Fashions were set by the court and ruling classes until the emergence of the individualistic fashion designer, creating clothes exclusively for wealthy clients, in the 19th century. Mass production and diffusion ranges (less expensive versions of designer ranges) in the 20th century have made the latest designs accessible to a much wider public and fashion has played a much greater role in everyday life.

Fashoda Incident dispute 1898 in the town of Fashoda (now Kodok) situated on the White Nile in SE Sudan, in which a clash between French and British forces nearly led the two countries into war.

Originally a disagreement over local territorial claims, the clash between the French forces under Colonel Marchand and British forces under Lord Kitchener almost precipitated a full-scale war.

Faslane nuclear-submarine (Polaris) base on the river Clyde in Scotland. In the early 1990s there was some internal pressure within the Royal Navy to close it.

Fassbinder Rainer Werner 1946–1982. West German film director. He began as a fringe actor and founded his own 'anti-theatre' before moving into films. His works are mainly stylized indictments of contemporary German society. He made more than 40 films, including *Die bitteren Tränen der Petra von Kant/The Bitter Tears of Petra von Kant* 1972, *Angst essen Seele auf/Fear Eats the Soul* 1974, and *Die Ehe von Maria Braun/The Marriage of Maria Braun* 1979.

Fassett Kaffe 1940– . US knitwear and textile designer. He has been based in the UK from 1964. He co-owns a knitwear company and his textiles appear in important art collections around the world.

fast breeder or ***breeder reactor*** alternative names for ◊fast reactor, a type of nuclear reactor.

fasting the practice of voluntarily going without food. It can be undertaken as a religious observance, a sign of mourning, a political protest (hunger strike), or for slimming purposes.

Fasting or abstinence from certain types of food or beverages occurs in most religious traditions. It is seen as an act of self-discipline that increases spiritual awareness by lessening dependence on the material world. In the Roman Catholic church, fasting is seen as a penitential rite, a means to express repentance for sin. The most commonly observed Christian fasting is in Lent, from Ash Wednesday to Easter Sunday, and recalls the 40 days Christ spent in the wilderness. Roman Catholics and Orthodox usually fast before taking communion and monastic communities observe regular weekly fasts. Devout Muslims go without food or water between sunrise and sunset during the month of Ramadan.

Total abstinence from food for a limited period is prescribed by some ◊naturopaths to eliminate body toxins or make available for recuperative purposes the energy normally used by the digestive system. Prolonged fasting can be dangerous. The liver breaks up its fat stores, releasing harmful by-products called ketones, which results in a condition called ketosis, which develops within three days, an early symptom of which is a smell of pear drops on the breath. Other symptoms include nausea, vomiting, fatigue, dizziness, severe depression, and irritability. Eventually the muscles and other body tissues become wasted, and death results.

fast reactor or ***fast breeder reactor*** ◊nuclear reactor that makes use of fast neutrons to bring about fission. Unlike other reactors used by the nuclear-power industry, it has little or no ◊moderator, to slow down neutrons. The reactor core is surrounded by a 'blanket' of uranium carbide. During operation, some of this uranium is converted into plutonium, which can be extracted and later used as fuel. ◊*See feature on pp. 360–361.*

fat in the broadest sense, a mixture of ◊lipids – chiefly triglycerides (lipids containing three ◊fatty acid molecules linked to a molecule of glycerol). More specifically, the term refers to a lipid mixture that is solid at room temperature (20°C); lipid mixtures that are liquid at room temperature are called ***oils***. The higher the proportion of saturated fatty acids in a mixture, the harder the fat.

Boiling fats in strong alkali forms soaps (saponification). Fats are essential constituents of food for many animals, with a calorific value twice that of carbohydrates; however, eating too much fat, especially fat of animal origin, has been linked with heart disease in humans. In many animals and plants, excess carbohydrates and proteins are converted into fats for storage. Mammals and other vertebrates store fats in specialized connective tissues (◊adipose tissues), which not only act as energy reserves but also insulate the body and cushion its organs. *See illustration on p. 386.*

As a nutrient fat serves five purposes: it is a source of energy (9 kcal/g); makes the diet palatable; provides basic building blocks for cell structure; provides essential fatty acids (linoleic and linolenic); and acts as a carrier for fat-soluble vitamins (A, D, E, and K). Foods rich in fat are butter, lard, margarine, and cooking oils. Products high in monounsaturated or polyunsaturated fats are thought to be less likely to contribute to cardiovascular disease.

Fatah, al- Palestinian nationalist organization, founded 1958 to bring about an independent state of Palestine. It was the first Palestinian resistance group, based 1968–70 in Jordan, then in Lebanon, and from 1982 in Tunisia. Also called the Palestine National Liberation Movement, it is the main component of the ◊Palestine Liberation Organization. Its leader (from 1968) is Yassir ◊Arafat.

Fates in Greek mythology, the three female figures who determined the destiny of human lives. They were envisaged as spinners: Clotho spun the thread of life, Lachesis twisted the thread, and Atropos cut it off. They are analogous to the Roman Parcae and Norse ◊Norns.

fat hen plant *Chenopodium album* widespread in temperate regions, up to 1 m/3 ft tall, with lance- or diamond-shaped leaves, and compact heads of small inconspicuous flowers. Now considered a weed, fat hen was once valued for its fatty seeds and edible leaves.

Father of the Church any of certain teachers and writers of the early Christian church, eminent for their learning and orthodoxy, experience, and sanctity of life. They lived between the end of the 1st and the end of the 7th century, a period divided by the Council of Nicaea 325 into the ante-Nicene and post-Nicene Fathers.

The ante-Nicene Fathers include the Apostolic Fathers: Clement of Rome, Ignatius of Antioch, Polycarp of Smyrna, Barnabas, Justin Martyr, Clement of Alexandria, Origen, Tertullian, and Cyprian. Among the post-Nicene Fathers are Cyril of Alexandria, Athanasius, John Chrysostom, Eusebius of Caesarea, Basil the Great, Ambrose of Milan, Augustine, Pope Leo I, Boethius, Jerome, Gregory of Tours, Pope Gregory the Great, and Bede.

Father's Day day set apart in many countries for honouring fathers, observed on the third Sunday in June in the USA, UK, and Canada. The idea for a father's day originated with Sonora Louise Smart Dodd of Spokane, Washington, USA, in 1909 (after hearing a sermon on Mother's Day), and through her efforts the first Father's Day was celebrated there in 1910.

fathom (Anglo-Saxon *faethm* 'to embrace') in mining, seafaring, and handling timber, a unit of depth measurement (1.83 m/6 ft) used prior to metrication; it approximates to the distance between an adult man's hands when the arms are outstretched.

Fathy Hassan 1900–1989. Egyptian architect. In his work at the village of New Gournia in Upper Egypt 1945–48, he demonstrated the value of indigenous building technology and natural materials in solving contemporary housing problems. This, together with his book *The Architecture of the Poor* 1973, influenced the growth of ◊community architecture enabling people to work directly with architects in building their homes.

Fatimid dynasty of Muslim Shi'ite caliphs founded 909 by Obaidallah, who claimed to be a descendant of Fatima (the prophet Muhammad's

FASHION: TIMELINE

8th C	The spread of Islam and Western contact during the Crusades (11th–12th centuries) influenced European fashion. Near and Middle Eastern traditions of cutting garments to shape adopted by the West.
1515	Early record of styles conveyed by means of fashion dolls. Francis I asked Isabella d'Este in Mantua, Italy, to send a doll dressed in miniature version of her latest fashion, including hairstyle and undergarments, to be copied and presented to women in France.
1678	*Le Nouveau Mercure galante* published in France, the first fashion journal in the modern sense (it lasted only one year).
1759	*The Lady's Magazine* was the first English women's journal to feature fashion plates and articles; fashion coverage gained momentum throughout the 18th century, coinciding with the Industrial Revolution and growth of consumerism.
1789	French Revolution had implications for fashion as extravagant dress became unacceptable in the immediate aftermath of the revolution. French embroidery and lavish decoration were abandoned in favour of simple clothes modelled on English tailored country clothing.
1851	US social reformer Amelia Bloomer visited Britain, promoting her costume of shortened dress and Turkish-style trousers ('bloomers'); the dress reform movement grew, aimed at liberating women from restrictive clothing styles.
1858	English-born Charles Worth established his fashion house in Paris; the birth of *haute couture*.
1860	Crinoline skirts, introduced 1850s, became exceedingly wide (up to 1.8 m/6 ft diameter).
1876	Plimsolls (flat rubber-soled canvas sports shoes) were patented, opening up more active sports for both men and women.
1870s	Some women's magazines included paper patterns for home dressmaking.
***c.* 1880**	Aesthetic dress of subdued colours and understated decoration worn by sophisticated artistic and reforming women in reaction against fussy high Victorian fashion.
1884	International Health Exhibition held in London; exhibitions of 'hygienic' and 'rational' reform dress.
1890s	Leg-of-mutton sleeves entered general fashion, now influenced by avant-garde dress reformers, allowing women more arm movement.
1900–10	Known as *La Belle Epoque* in France; S-bend profile, lace trimmings, and light silks and muslin represented the epitome of feminine elegance.
1910	*Schéhérazade* ballet produced by Diaghilev in Paris sparked off a wave of Orientalism in Western fashion. Women were liberated from tight corseting and narrow waists, but restricted around the knees instead by 'hobble skirts'.
1912	Paul Poiret launched the first designer perfume range.
1920	Coco Chanel designed and popularized the 'little black dress' and casual two- and three-piece classics made from jersey fabric.
1920s	Lucien Lelong, Jean Patou, Jeanne Lanvin, and other Parisian couturiers established ready-to-wear ranges, sold through boutiques. The *garçonne* look: boyish straight-lined dresses, Eton crop or shingled hair, suntan, and cosmetics; bright 'jazz' colours and abstract patterns reflected syncopated Afro-American musical rhythms. Electrification of factories and standardization of garment sizes, pioneered by US assembly-line system of production, made fashion cheaper and more available.
1925	Skirts were worn shorter than ever before.
1928	Italian-born Elsa Schiaparelli launched her fashion career in Paris with *trompe l'oeil* knitted jumpers.
1929	Men's Dress Reform Party founded in Britain, advocating shorts and coloured loose-fitting open-necked shirts; other Western countries followed.
1930s	Bias-cut long-line dresses became fashionable; Madeleine Vionnet was already known for her designs.
1939	Nylon stockings were first exhibited at the New York World Fair.
1941	Clothes rationing was introduced in Britain.
1945	The American GI vest was worn as outerwear, to become known as the T-shirt.
1947	Christian Dior showed his first collection, dubbed the New Look.
1950s	Brigitte Bardot married Sasha Distel; her gingham and broderie anglaise wedding dress was much copied.
1953	The Teddy Boys emerged, wearing long draped jackets, 'slim Jim' ties, and drainpipe trousers.
1955	'Bazaar', Mary Quant's first boutique, opened in King's Road, Chelsea.
***c.* 1956**	Youth movements were by now influencing fashion: Elvis Presley and James Dean were much-imitated idols; the beatnik style of the 'Beat Generation' was also prominent.
1960	The Mods were wearing 'sharp' (clean-cut, close-fitting, neat) Italian suits.
1961	The film *Jules et Jim* set fashion trends; Jeanne Moreau looked up-to-the-minute wearing 1920s dresses designed by Pierre Cardin.
1965	Miniskirts and trouser suits became acceptable.
1968	See-through and plastic mini-dresses by Courrèges; Space Age concept in fashion.
1971	Malcolm McLaren and Vivienne Westwood opened their 'Let It Rock' shop in King's Road, London, selling secondhand Fifties clothes (later renamed 'Sex', selling bondage gear).
early 1970s	Hippie fashions and the 'ethnic look' entered general fashion, incorporating Indian block-printed cottons, cheesecloth, embroidery, velvet, and so on. Nostalgia was reflected in floral-print 'granny' dresses by Laura Ashley. Gloria Vanderbilt jeans were launched, anticipating the 1980s obsession with the designer label.
1970s	Commercialization of pop videos; performers' image and related products (printed T-shirts etc.) were very influential.
1975	Giorgio Armani set up his business and developed the lightweight, unstructured jacket, revolutionizing menswear.
1976	Punk fashions such as spiky hair, black leather, safety pins, and chains were widely featured in the British press; punk group the Sex Pistols dressed by Malcolm McLaren and Vivienne Westwood.
late 1970s	Power dressing; wide shoulders and pinstripes for professional women.
1980	New Romantic look; 'genderbending', mixing and playing with masculine and feminine in dress, exemplified by British singer Boy George and his group Culture Club.
1980s	Japanese designers' loose-fitting monochrome clothes (mostly grey and black); understated, no decoration, often sculptural use of cut and cloth. Best-known designers were Yohji Yamomoto, Issey Miyake, and Rei Kawakubo of Comme des Garçons. French designer Jean-Paul Gaultier, inspired by British punk, featured underwear (especially corsets) as outerwear.
1989	Launch of first 'eco-collections' – fashion which claimed to be environment-friendly, using 'green' methods of manufacture, unbleached cotton etc. T-shirts printed with slogans such as 'Save the Rainforest' entered mainstream fashion in Western Europe and USA.
1992	'Grunge', a deliberately misfitting and dishevelled look mixing new and secondhand clothes (a feature of British street style for the past two decades), represented conscious antifashion and environmental awareness in a period of world recession.

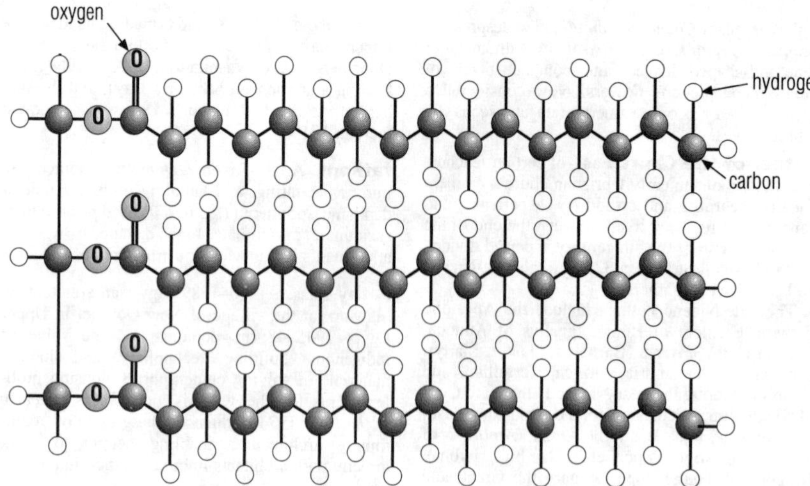

fat The molecular structure of typical fat. The molecule consists of three fatty acid molecules linked to a molecule of glycerol.

If a writer has to rob his mother, he will not hesitate; the Ode on a Grecian Urn is worth any number of old ladies.

WILLIAM FAULKNER *Paris Review* Spring 1956

daughter) and her husband Ali, in N Africa. In 969 the Fatimids conquered Egypt, and the dynasty continued until overthrown by Saladin 1171.

fatty acid or ***carboxylic acid*** organic compound consisting of a hydrocarbon chain, up to 24 carbon atoms long, with a carboxyl group (–COOH) at one end. The covalent bonds between the carbon atoms may be single or double; where a double bond occurs the carbon atoms concerned carry one instead of two hydrogen atoms. Chains with only single bonds have all the hydrogen they can carry, so they are said to be ***saturated*** with hydrogen. Chains with one or more double bonds are said to be ***unsaturated*** (see ◊polyunsaturate). Fatty acids are produced in the small intestine when fat is digested.

Saturated fatty acids include palmitic and stearic acids; unsaturated fatty acids include oleic (one double bond), linoleic (two double bonds), and linolenic (three double bonds). Linoleic acid accounts for more than one third of some margarines. Supermarket brands that say they are high in polyunsaturates may contain as much as 39%. Fatty acids are generally found combined with glycerol in ◊lipids such as tryglycerides.

fatwa in Islamic law, an authoritative legal opinion on a point of doctrine. In 1989 a fatwa calling for the death of British novelist Salman ◊Rushdie was made by the Ayatollah ◊Khomeini of Iran, following publication of Rushdie's controversial and allegedly blasphemous book *The Satanic Verses* 1988.

The artist should love life and show us that it is beautiful; without him, we might doubt it.

GABRIEL FAURÉ Quoted in Mellers *Studies in Contemporary Music* 1947

Faulkner William Cuthbert 1897–1962. US novelist. His works are noted for their difficult narrative styles and epic mapping of a quasi-imaginary Southern region, Yoknapatawpha County. His third and most celebrated novel, *The Sound and the Fury* 1929, deals with the decline of a Southern family, told in four voices, beginning with an especially complex stream-of-consciousness narrative. He was recognized as one of America's greatest writers only after World War II, and was awarded the Nobel Prize for Literature 1949.

Faulkner US novelist William Faulkner, who is remembered for his novels of life in the Deep South. Many of his works deal compassionately with the dissolution of traditional values in the south since the Civil War. He won the Nobel Prize for Literature in 1949. *Corbis*

Faulkner was born in Mississippi, and educated at Mississippi University. He served in the Canadian air force in World War I and was wounded in France; his first novel, *Soldier's Pay* 1929, is about a war veteran. After the war he returned to Oxford, Mississippi, on which he was to model the town of Jefferson in the county of Yoknapatawpha. Later works using highly complex structures include *As I Lay Dying* 1930, *Light in August* 1932, and *Absalom, Absalom!* 1936. These were followed by his less experimental trilogy, *The Hamlet* 1940, *The Town* 1957, and *The Mansion* 1959, covering the rise of the materialistic Snopes family. Other works include *The Unvanquished* 1938, stories of the Civil War, and *The Wild Palms* 1939.

fault in geology, a fracture in the Earth's crust along which the two sides have moved as a result of differing strains in the adjacent rock bodies. Displacement of rock masses horizontally or vertically along a fault may be microscopic, or it may be massive, causing major ◊earthquakes.

If the movement has a major vertical component, the fault is termed a normal fault, where rocks on each side have moved apart, or a reverse fault, where one side has overridden the other (a low angle reverse fault is called a thrust). A lateral fault, or tear fault, occurs where the relative movement is sideways. A particular kind of fault found only in ocean ridges is the transform fault. On a map an ocean ridge has a stepped appearance. The ridge crest is broken into sections, each section offset from the next. Between each section of the ridge crest the newly generated plates are moving past one another, forming a transform fault.

Faults produce lines of weakness that are often exploited by processes of ◊weathering and ◊erosion. Coastal caves and geos (narrow inlets) often form along faults and, on a larger scale, rivers may follow the line of a fault.

Faunus in Roman mythology, the god of fertility and prophecy, with goat's ears, horns, tail and hind legs, identified with the Greek ◊Pan.

Fauré Gabriel (Urbain) 1845–1924. French composer. He wrote songs, chamber music, and a choral *Requiem* 1888. He was a pupil of Saint-Saëns, became professor of composition at the Paris Conservatoire 1896, and was director 1905–20.

Faust legendary magician who sold his soul to the devil. The historical Georg Faust appears to have been a wandering scholar and conjurer in Germany at the start of the 16th century. J W Goethe, Heinrich Heine, Thomas Mann, and Paul Valéry all used the legend, and it inspired musical works by Robert Schumann, Hector Berlioz, C F Gounod, and Ferruccio Busoni.

Earlier figures such as Simon Magus (1st century AD, Middle Eastern practitioner of magic arts) contributed to the Faust legend. In 1587 the first of a series of Faust books appeared. Christopher Marlowe's tragedy *Dr Faustus* was first acted in 1594. In the 18th century the story was a subject for pantomime in England and puppet plays in Germany, and was developed by ◊Goethe into his masterpiece.

Fauvism (French *fauve* 'wild beast') style of painting characterized by a bold use of vivid colours inspired by the work of Vincent van Gogh, Paul Cézanne, and Paul Gauguin. A short-lived but influential art movement, Fauvism originated in Paris 1905. Georges Rouault, Raoul Dufy, Pierre Marquet, André Derain, Maurice de Vlaminck, and Paul Signac were early Fauves.

Fauve artists sought to liberate colour from a merely descriptive function and give it an emotional value of its own. In this they were variously influenced by Cézanne, Gauguin, van Gogh and Seurat, though Seurat was criticized by Matisse for having split up colour in such a way as to lose its value. The group held together loosely for no more than three years, but it had some following in France, Georges Braque and Raoul Dufy being among those who passed through a Fauvist phase, and considerable influence on artists in Germany and Russia, for example Kirchner, Kandinsky, and Jawlensky. ◊Cubism replaced the movement as a centre of interest and dynamic influence by 1909.

Fawcett Millicent, (born Garrett) 1847–1929. English suffragette, younger sister of Elizabeth Garrett ◊Anderson. A non-militant, she rejected the violent acts of some of her contemporaries in the suffrage movement. She joined the first Women's Suffrage Committee 1867 and became president of the Women's Unionist Association 1889.

Fawkes Guy 1570–1606. English conspirator in the ◊Gunpowder Plot to blow up King James I and the members of both Houses of Parliament. Fawkes, a Roman Catholic convert, was arrested in the cellar underneath the House 4 Nov 1605, tortured, and executed. The event is still commemorated in Britain and elsewhere every 5 Nov with bonfires, fireworks, and the burning of the 'guy', an effigy.

fax (common name for ***facsimile transmission*** or ***telefax***) the transmission of images over a ◊telecommunications link, usually the telephone network. When placed on a fax machine, the original image is scanned by a transmitting device and converted into coded signals, which travel via the telephone lines to the receiving fax machine, where an image is created that is a copy of the original. Photographs as well as printed text and drawings can be sent. The standard transmission takes place at 4,800 or 9,600 bits of information per second.

The world's first fax machine, the *pantélégraphe*, was invented by Italian physicist Giovanni Caselli 1866, over a century before the first electronic model came on the market. Standing over 2 m/6.5 ft high, it transmitted by telegraph nearly 5,000 handwritten documents and drawings between Paris and Lyon in its first year.

FBI abbreviation for ◊***Federal Bureau of Investigation***, agency of the US Department of Justice.

fealty in feudalism, the loyalty and duties owed by a vassal to his lord. In the 9th century fealty obliged the vassal not to take part in any action that would endanger the lord or his property, but by the 11th century the specific duties of fealty were established and included financial obligations and military service. Following an oath of fealty, an act of allegiance and respect (homage) was made by the vassal; when a ◊fief was granted by the lord, it was formalized in the process of investiture.

feather rigid outgrowth of the outer layer of the skin of birds, made of the protein keratin. Feathers provide insulation and facilitate flight. There are several types, including long quill feathers on the wings and tail, fluffy down feathers for retaining body heat, and contour feathers covering the body. The colouring of feathers is often important in camouflage or in courtship and other displays. Feathers are normally replaced at least once a year.

Feathers generally consist of two main parts, axis and barbs, the former of which is divided into the quill, which is bare and hollow, and the shaft, which bears the barbs. The quill is embedded in the skin, and has at its base a small hole through which the nourishment passes during the growth of the feather. The barbs which constitute the vane are lath-shaped and taper to a point, and each one supports a series of outgrowths known as barbules, so that each barb is like a tiny feather. Adjacent barbs are linked to each other by hooks on the barbules.

feather star any of an unattached, free-swimming group of sea lilies, order Comatulida. The arms are branched into numerous projections (hence 'feather' star), and grow from a small cup-shaped body. Below the body are appendages that can hold on to a surface, but the feather star is not permanently attached.

February Revolution the first of the two political uprisings of the ◊Russian Revolution in 1917 that led to the overthrow of the tsar and the end of the ◊Romanov dynasty.

The immediate cause of the revolution was the inability of the tsardom to manage World War I. On 8 March (dating by the Western calendar, not adopted at that time in Russia) strikes and bread riots broke out in Petrograd (now St Petersburg), where the troops later mutinied and joined the rioters. A Provisional Government under Prince L'vov was appointed by the ◊Duma (assembly) and Tsar Nicholas II abdicated on 15 March (27 Feb Julian calendar).

The Petrograd Soviet of Workers, Peasants and Soldiers (formed originally during the Russian revolution of 1905) was revived by the Bolsheviks, among other parties, and opposed the Provisional Government, especially when Lenin returned from Switzerland in April. On 16–18 July the Bolsheviks made an unsuccessful attempt to seize power and Lenin was forced into hiding in Finland. The Provisional Government tried to continue the war, but was weakened by serious misunderstandings between the prime minister, Kerensky, and the commander in chief, General Kornilov, who tried unsuccessfully to gain power in Sept 1917. Shortly afterwards the Bolsheviks seized power in the ◊October Revolution.

fecundity the rate at which an organism reproduces, as distinct from its ability to reproduce (◊fertility). In vertebrates, it is usually measured as the number of offspring produced by a female each year.

Federal Bureau of Investigation (FBI) agency of the US Department of Justice that investigates violations of federal law not specifically assigned to other agencies, being particularly concerned with internal security. It was established 1908 and built up a position of powerful autonomy during the autocratic directorship of J Edgar Hoover 1924–72. Louis Joseph Freeh, a former FBI agent and federal prosecutor, became director in 1993.

The FBI reports to the US Attorney General, and investigates espionage, sabotage, kidnapping, bank robbery, civil-rights violations, and fraud against the government, and conducts security clearances. Field divisions are maintained in more than 60 US cities. The FBI's special agents are qualified in law, accounting, or auditing.

Through the Freedom of Information Act it became known that the FBI had kept files on many eminent citizens and that Hoover had abused his power, for example, in investigating the civil rights leader Martin Luther King.

federalism system of government in which two or more separate states unite into a ◊federation under a common central government. The USA is an example of federal government.

federalist in US history, one who advocated the ratification of the US Constitution 1787–88 in place of the Articles of ◊Confederation. The Federalists became in effect the ruling political party during the presidencies of George Washington and John Adams 1789–1801, legislating to strengthen the authority of the newly created federal government.

Federal Reserve System (the 'Fed') US central banking system and note-issuing authority, established 1913 to regulate the country's credit and ◊monetary policy. The Fed consists of the 12 federal reserve banks, their 25 branches and other facilities throughout the country; it is headed by a board of governors in Washington, DC, appointed by the president with Senate approval.

federation political entity made up from a number of smaller units or states where the central government has powers over national issues such as foreign policy and defence, while the individual states retain a high degree of regional and local autonomy. A federation should be distinguished from a confederation, a looser union of states for mutual assistance.

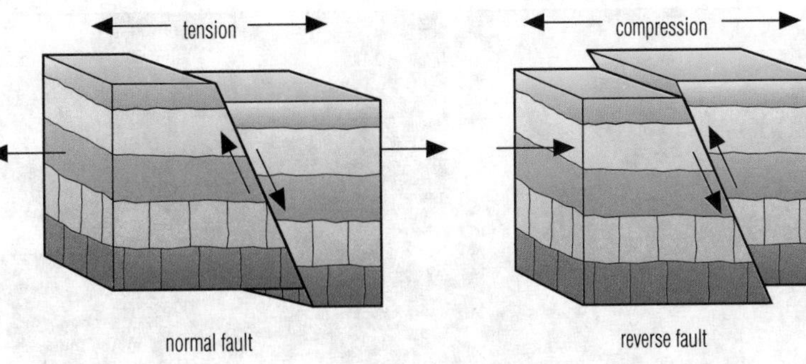

fault Faults are caused by the movement of rock layers, producing such features as block mountains and rift valleys. A normal fault is caused by a tension or stretching force acting in the rock layers. A reverse fault is caused by compression forces. Faults can continue to move for thousands or millions of years.

feedback general principle whereby the results produced in an ongoing reaction become factors in modifying or changing the reaction; it is the principle used in self-regulating control systems, from a simple ◊thermostat and steam-engine ◊governor to automatic computer-controlled machine tools. A fully computerized control system, in which there is no operator intervention, is called a closed-loop feedback system. A system that also responds to control signals from an operator is called an open-loop feedback system.

In self-regulating systems, information about what *is* happening in a system (such as level of temperature, engine speed, or size of workpiece) is fed back to a controlling device, which compares it with what *should* be happening. If the two are different, the device takes suitable action (such as switching on a heater, allowing more steam to the engine, or resetting the tools). The idea that the Earth is a self-regulating system, with feedback operating to keep nature in balance, is a central feature of the ◊Gaia hypothesis.

Feininger Lyonel Charles Adrian 1871–1956. US abstract artist, an early Cubist. He worked at the ◊Bauhaus school of design and architecture in Germany 1919–33, and later helped to found the Bauhaus in Chicago. Inspired by Cubism and *der ◊Blaue Reiter*, he developed a style based on translucent geometric planes arranged in subtle harmonic patterns.

Feininger was born in New York, the son of German immigrants. While in Germany, he formed the ***Blaue Vier*** (Blue Four) 1924 with the painters Alexei von Jawlensky, Wassily Kandinsky, and Paul Klee. He returned to the USA after the rise of the Nazis.

Feldman Morton 1926–1987. US composer. An associate of John Cage and Earle Brown in the 1950s, he devised an indeterminate notation based on high, middle, and low instrumental registers and time cells of fixed duration for his *Projection* series for various ensembles 1950–51, later exploiting the freedoms of classical notation in a succession of reflective studies in vertical tone mixtures including *Madame Press Died Last Week at 90* 1970.

feldspar one of a group of rock-forming minerals, the most abundant group in the Earth's crust. They are the chief constituents of ◊igneous rock and are present in most metamorphic and sedimentary rocks. All feldspars contain silicon, aluminium, and oxygen, linked together to form a framework; spaces within this structure are occupied by sodium, potassium, calcium, or occasionally barium, in various proportions. Feldspars form white, grey, or pink crystals and rank 6 on the ◊Mohs' scale of hardness.

The four extreme compositions of feldspar are orthoclase, $KAlSi_3O_8$; albite, $NaAlSi_3O_8$; anorthite, $CaAl_2Si_2O_8$; and celsian, $BaAl_2Si_2O_8$. These are grouped into plagioclase feldspars, which range from pure sodium feldspar (albite) through pure calcium feldspar (anorthite) with a negligible potassium content; and alkali feldspars (including orthoclase and microcline), which have a high potassium content, less sodium, and little calcium.

felicific calculus or ***hedonic calculus*** in ethics, a technique for establishing the rightness and wrongness of an action. Using the calculus, one can attempt to work out the likely consequences of an action in terms of the pain or pleasure of those affected by the action. The calculus is attributed to English utilitarian philosopher Jeremy Bentham.

Fellini Federico 1920–1993. Italian film director and screenwriter. His work has been a major influence on modern cinema. His films combine dream and fantasy sequences with satire and autobiographical detail. They include *I vitelloni/The Young and the Passionate* 1953, *La strada/The Street* 1954 (Academy Award), *Le notti di Cabiria/Nights of Cabiria* 1956 (Academy Award), *La dolce vita* 1960, *Otto e mezzo/8½* 1963 (Academy Award), *Satyricon* 1969, *Roma/Fellini's Rome* 1972, *Amarcord* 1974 (Academy Award), *La città delle donne/City of Women* 1980, and *Ginger e Fred/Ginger and Fred* 1986. He was presented with a Special Academy Award for his life's work 1993.

His work is intensely personal and vividly original. Peopled with circus, carnival, and music-hall characters and the high society of Rome, his films created iconic images such as that of actress Anita Ekberg in the Trevi Fountain, Rome, in *La dolce vita*. *See illustration on following page.*

felony in ◊criminal law, former term for an offence that is more serious than a ◊misdemeanour; in the USA, a felony is a crime generally punishable by imprisonment for a year or more.

female circumcision or ***female genital mutilation*** operation on women analogous to male ◊circumcision. There are three types: ***Sunna***, which involves cutting off the hood, and sometimes the tip, of the clitoris; ***clitoridectomy***, the excision of the clitoris and removal of parts of the inner and outer labia; ***infibulation*** (most widely practised in Sudan and Somalia), in which the labia are stitched, after excision, leaving a small hole.

Infibulation can lead to problems in later life, especially during menstruation, sexual intercourse, and childbirth. Female circumcision is practised across Muslim Africa between Senegal and Somalia, as well as in the United Arab Emirates, Oman, Yemen, and among Muslims in Malaysia and Indonesia. In 1994 there were at least 90 million women and girls worldwide who had undergone circumcision.

feminism active belief in equal rights and opportunities for women; see ◊women's movement.

Fauvism *Portrait of Henri Matisse* c. 1905 by the French painter André Derain. With its simplified form and its strong, brilliant colours, it is typical of Fauvism. *Corbis*

Fellini Italian film director Federico Fellini. One of the most original filmmakers in the history of cinema, Fellini moved from the comparative realism and astringent satire of *Nights of Cabiria* 1956 and *La dolce vita* 1960 to the Baroque fantasy and autobiography of *8½* 1963 and *The Ship Sails On* 1983. *British Film Institute*

femur the ***thigh-bone***; also the upper bone in the hind limb of a four-limbed vertebrate.

fencing sport of fighting with swords including the foil, derived from the light weapon used in practice duels; the épée, a heavier weapon derived from the duelling sword proper; and the sabre, with a curved handle and narrow V-shaped blade. In sabre fighting, cuts count as well as thrusts. Masks and protective jackets are worn, and hits are registered electronically in competitions. Men's fencing has been part of every Olympic programme since 1896; women's fencing was included from 1924 but only using the foil.

Fender (Clarence) Leo 1909–1991. US guitar-maker. He created the solid-body electric guitar, the Fender Broadcaster 1948 (renamed the Telecaster 1950), and the first electric bass guitar, the Fender Precision, 1951. The Fender Stratocaster guitar dates from 1954. In 1965 he sold the Fender name to CBS, which continues to make the instruments.

Although the guitarist and producer Les Paul (1915–) was also working independently on a solid-body electric guitar, Fender was the first to get his model on the market. The design was totally new, with a one-piece neck bolted on to a wooden body, and could easily be mass-produced.

Fénelon François de Salignac de la Mothe 1651–1715. French writer and ecclesiastic. He entered the priesthood 1675 and in 1689 was appointed tutor to the duke of Burgundy, grandson of Louis XIV. For him he wrote his *Fables* and *Dialogues des morts/Dialogues of the Dead* 1690, *Télémaque/Telemachus* 1699, and *Plans de gouvernement/Plans of Government*.

Fenian movement Irish-American republican secret society, founded 1858 and named after the ancient Irish legendary warrior band of the Fianna. The collapse of the movement began when an attempt to establish an independent Irish republic by an uprising in Ireland 1867 failed, as did raids into Canada 1866 and 1870, and England 1867.

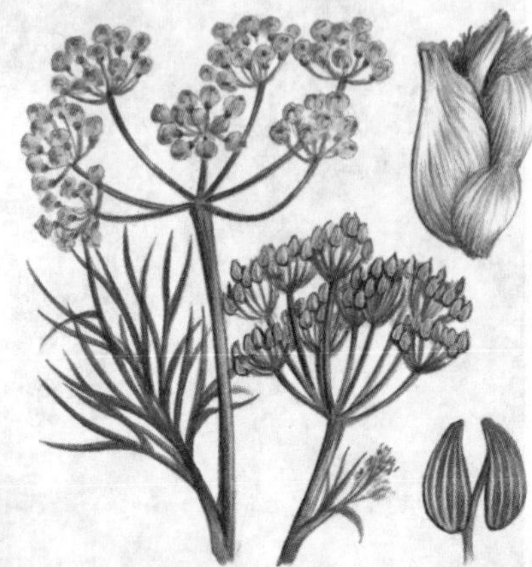

fennel Fennel is a native of the Mediterranean shores. It is one of the largest herbs, growing to a height of 1.5 m/5 ft. The fresh leaves have an aniseed taste, and are chopped and added to sauces and fish dishes.

fennel any of several varieties of a perennial plant *Foeniculum vulgare* with feathery green leaves, of the carrot family Umbelliferae.

Fennels have an aniseed flavour, and the leaves and seeds are used in seasoning. The thickened leafstalks of sweet fennel *F. vulgare dulce* are eaten.

Fenris in Norse mythology, the monstrous wolf of the god Loki. Fenris swallowed the god Odin but was stabbed to death by Odin's son, Vidar.

Fens, the level, low-lying tracts of land in E England, W and S of the Wash, about 115 km/70 mi N–S and 55 km/34 mi E–W. They fall within the counties of Lincolnshire, Cambridgeshire, and Norfolk, consisting of a huge area, formerly a bay of the North Sea, but now crossed by numerous drainage canals and forming some of the most productive agricultural land in Britain. The peat portion of the Fens is known as the Bedford Level.

The first drainage attempts were made by the Romans. After the Norman conquest an earthwork 100 km/60 mi long was constructed as a barrage against the sea. In 1634 the 4th Earl of Bedford brought over the Dutch water-engineer Cornelius Vermuyden (c. 1596–1683) who introduced Dutch methods. Burwell Fen and Wicken Fen, NE of Cambridge, have been preserved undrained as nature reserves.

Fenton Roger 1819–1869. English photographer. He is best known for his comprehensive documentation of the Crimean War 1855. He was a founder member of the Photographic Society (later the Royal Photographic Society) in London 1853 but completely gave up photography 1860.

Ferdinand 1861–1948. King of Bulgaria 1908–18. Son of Prince Augustus of Saxe-Coburg-Gotha, he was elected prince of Bulgaria 1887 and, in 1908, proclaimed Bulgaria's independence from Turkey and assumed the title of tsar. In 1915 he entered World War I as Germany's ally, and in 1918 abdicated.

Ferdinand five kings of Castile, including:

Ferdinand (I) the Great c. 1016–1065. King of Castile from 1035. He began the reconquest of Spain from the Moors and united all NW Spain under his and his brothers' rule.

Ferdinand V 1452–1516. King of Castile from 1474, ***Ferdinand II*** of Aragon from 1479, and ***Ferdinand III*** of Naples from 1504; first king of all Spain. In 1469 he married his cousin ◊Isabella I, who succeeded to the throne of Castile 1474; they were known as 'the Catholic Monarchs' because after 700 years of rule by the ◊Moors, they catholicized Spain. When Ferdinand inherited the throne of Aragon 1479, the two great Spanish kingdoms were brought under a single government for the first time. The conquest of Naples 1500–03 and Navarre 1512, completed the unification of Spain and made it one of the chief powers in Europe.

Ferdinand and Isabella introduced the ◊Inquisition 1480; expelled the Jews, forced the final surrender of the Moors at Granada, and financed Columbus' expedition to the Americas, 1492.

Ferdinand I 1503–1564. Holy Roman emperor who succeeded his brother Charles V 1556; king of Bohemia and Hungary from 1526, king of the Germans from 1531. He reformed the German monetary system and reorganized the judicial Aulic council (*Reichshofrat*). He was the son of Philip the Handsome and grandson of Maximilian I.

Ferdinand II 1578–1637. Holy Roman emperor from 1619, when he succeeded his uncle Matthias; king of Bohemia from 1617 and of Hungary from 1618. A zealous Catholic, he provoked the Bohemian revolt that led to the Thirty Years' War.

Ferdinand III 1608–1657. Holy Roman emperor from 1637 when he succeeded his father Ferdinand II; king of Hungary from 1625. Although anxious to conclude the Thirty Years' War, he did not give religious liberty to Protestants.

Ferdinand 1865–1927. King of Romania from 1914, when he succeeded his uncle Charles I. In 1916 he declared war on Austria. After the Allied victory in World War I, Ferdinand acquired Transylvania and Bukovina from Austria-Hungary, and Bessarabia from Russia. In 1922 he became king of this Greater Romania. His reign saw agrarian reform and the introduction of universal suffrage.

Ferghana city in Uzbekistan, in the fertile Ferghana Valley; population (1990) 183,000. It is the capital of the major cotton- and fruit-growing Ferghana region; nearby are petroleum fields. The Ferghana Valley is divided between the republics of Uzbekistan, Kyrgyzstan, and Tajikistan, causing interethnic violence among Uzbek, Meskhetian, and Kyrgyz communities. An afforestation project is under way in the valley to prevent sand drifts.

Ferguson Alex(ander) 1941– . Scottish football manager. One of British football's most successful managers, he has won nine trophies with Manchester United including four league championship titles.

Fermanagh county of Northern Ireland
area 1,680 sq km/648 sq mi
towns and cities Enniskillen (county town), Lisnaskea, Irvinestown
features in the centre is a broad trough of low-lying land, in which lie Upper and Lower Lough Erne

Fenton English photographer Roger Fenton, whose coverage of the Crimean War made him the first photographer ever to document a war. He took over 350 pictures, travelling in a specially converted 'photographic van' that served as a mobile darkroom. His stark pictures did much to publicize the inadequacies of the British campaign. *Library of Congress*

industries mainly agricultural; livestock, potatoes, tweeds, clothing, cotton thread.

Fermat Pierre de 1601–1665. French mathematician who, with Blaise ◊Pascal, founded the theory of ◊probability and the modern theory of numbers. Fermat also made contributions to analytical geometry. In 1657, Fermat published a series of problems as challenges to other mathematicians, in the form of theorems to be proved.

Fermat's last theorem states that equations of the form $x^n + y^n = z^n$ where x, y, z, and n are all ◊integers have no solutions if $n > 2$. Fermat scribbled the theorem in the margin of a mathematics textbook and noted that he could have shown it to be true had he enough space in which to write the proof. The theorem remained unproven for 300 years (and therefore, strictly speaking, constituted a conjecture rather than a theorem). In 1993, Andrew Wiles of Princeton University, USA, announced a proof; this turned out to be premature, but he put forward a revised proof 1994.

Fermat's principle in physics, the principle that a ray of light, or other radiation, moves between two points along the path that takes the minimum time. It is named after French mathematician Pierre de Fermat, who used it to deduce the laws of ◊reflection and ◊refraction.

fermentation the breakdown of sugars by bacteria and yeasts using a method of respiration without oxygen (◊anaerobic). Fermentation processes have long been utilized in baking bread, making beer and wine, and producing cheese, yoghurt, soy sauce, and many other foodstuffs.

In baking and brewing, yeasts ferment sugars to produce ◊ethanol and carbon dioxide; the latter makes bread rise and puts bubbles into beers and champagne. Many antibiotics are produced by fermentation; it is one of the processes that can cause food spoilage.

Fermi Enrico 1901–1954. Italian-born US physicist who proved the existence of new radioactive elements produced by bombardment with neutrons, and discovered nuclear reactions produced by low-energy neutrons. He took part in the Manhattan Project to construct an atom bomb. His theoretical work included study of the weak nuclear force, one of the fundamental forces of nature. Nobel prize 1938.

Fermi's experimental work on beta-decay in radioactive materials provided further evidence for the existence of the ◊neutrino, as predicted by Austrian physicist Wolfgang Pauli (1900–1958). At the University of Chicago, Fermi built the first nuclear reactor 1942. This was the basis for studies leading to the atomic bomb and nuclear energy.

Fermi Nuclear physicist Enrico Fermi. Among the important contributions he made to nuclear physics were a theory of radioactive decay and the discovery of new radioactive elements. In 1942, at the nuclear research site at Los Alamos in New Mexico, USA, he created the first self-sustaining nuclear chain reaction. *AEA Technology*

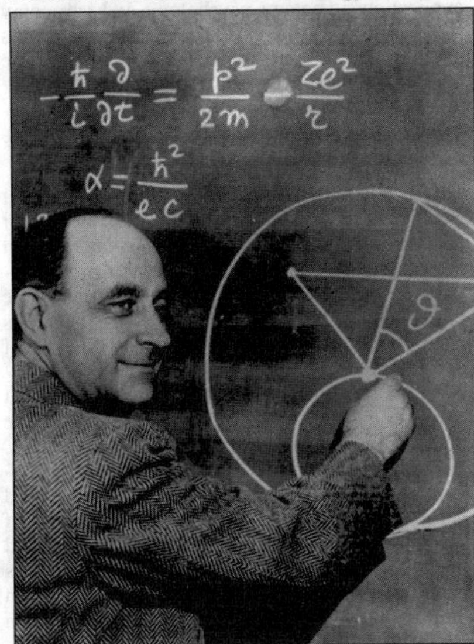

Fermilab (shortened form of ***Fermi National Accelerator Laboratory***) US centre for ◊particle physics at Batavia, Illinois, near Chicago. It is named after Italian–US physicist Enrico Fermi. Fermilab was opened in 1972, and is the home of the Tevatron, the world's most powerful particle ◊accelerator. It is capable of boosting protons and antiprotons to speeds near that of light (to energies of 20 TeV).

fermion in physics, a subatomic particle whose spin can only take values that are half-integers, such as ½ or 3/2. Fermions may be classified as leptons, such as the electron, and baryons, such as the proton and neutron. All elementary particles are either fermions or ◊bosons.

The exclusion principle, formulated by Austrian–US physicist Wolfgang Pauli 1925, asserts that no two fermions in the same system (such as an atom) can possess the same position, energy state, spin, or other quantized property.

fermium synthesized, radioactive, metallic element of the ◊actinide series, symbol Fm, atomic number 100, relative atomic mass 257. Ten isotopes are known, the longest-lived of which, Fm-257, has a half-life of 80 days. Fermium has been produced only in minute quantities in particle accelerators.

It was discovered in 1952 in the debris of the first thermonuclear explosion. The element was named 1955 in honour of US physicist Enrico ◊Fermi.

fern plant of the class Filicales, related to horsetails and clubmosses. Ferns are spore-bearing, not flowering, plants, and most are perennial, spreading by low-growing roots. The leaves, known as fronds, vary widely in size and shape. Some taller types, such as tree-ferns, grow in the tropics. There are over 7,000 species.

Ferns found in Britain include the polypody *Polypodium vulgare*, shield fern *Polystichum*, male fern *Dryopteris filix-mas*, hart's-tongue *Phyllitis scolopendrium*, maidenhair *Adiantum capillus-veneris*, and bracken *Pteridium aquilinum*, an agricultural weed.

Fernández Juan c. 1536–c. 1604. Spanish explorer and navigator. As a pilot on the Pacific coast of South America 1563, he reached the islands off the coast of Chile that now bear his name. Alexander Selkirk (1676–1721) was later marooned on one of these islands, and his life story formed the basis of Daniel Defoe's *Robinson Crusoe*.

Ferrara industrial city and archbishopric in Emilia-Romagna region, N Italy, on a branch of the Po delta 52 km/32 mi W of the Adriatic Sea; population (1992) 137,100. There are chemical industries and textile manufacturers. It became a powerful city state in the 13th century. It has the Gothic castle of its medieval rulers, the House of Este, palaces, museums, and a cathedral, consecrated 1135. The university was founded 1391. Italian religious reformer Girolamo Savonarola was born here, and the poet Torquato Tasso was confined in the asylum 1579–86.

Ferrari Enzo 1898–1988. Italian founder of the Ferrari car-manufacturing company, which specializes in Grand Prix racing cars and high-quality sports cars. He was a racing driver for Alfa Romeo in the 1920s, went on to become one of their designers, and took over their racing division 1929. In 1947 the first 'true' Ferrari was seen. The Ferrari car won more world championship Grand Prix than any other car until very recently, when the McLaren Formula One team equalled their record.

ferret domesticated variety of the Old World ◊polecat. About 35 cm/1.2 ft long, it usually has yellowish-white fur and pink eyes, but may be the dark brown colour of a wild polecat. Ferrets may breed with wild polecats. They have been used since ancient times to hunt rabbits and rats.

Ferrier Kathleen Mary 1912–1953. English contralto. She brought warmth and depth of conviction to English oratorio roles during wartime and subsequently to opera and lieder (songs), including Gluck's *Orfeo ed Euridice*, Mahler's *Das Lied von der Erde/The Song of the Earth*, and the role of Lucretia in Benjamin Britten's *The Rape of Lucretia* 1946.

ferrite ceramic ferrimagnetic material. Ferrites are iron oxides to which small quantities of ◊transition metal oxides (such as cobalt and nickel oxides) have been added. They are used in transformer cores, radio antennae, and, formerly, in computer memories.

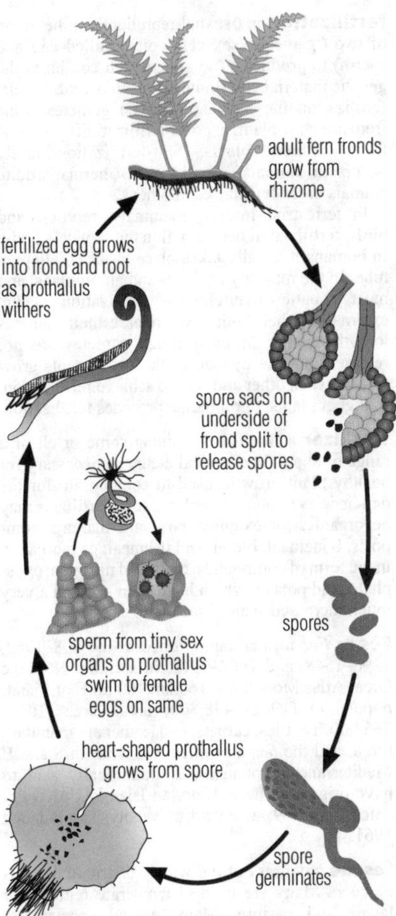
adult fern fronds grow from rhizome
spore sacs on underside of frond split to release spores
spores
spore germinates
heart-shaped prothallus grows from spore
sperm from tiny sex organs on prothallus swim to female eggs on same
fertilized egg grows into frond and root as prothallus withers

fern The life cycle of a fern. Ferns have two distinct forms that alternate during their life cycle. For the main part of its life, a fern consists of a short stem (or rhizome) from which roots and leaves grow. The other part of its life is spent as a small heart-shaped plant called a prothallus.

ferro-alloy alloy of iron with a high proportion of elements such as manganese, silicon, chromium, and molybdenum. Ferro-alloys are used in the manufacture of alloy steels. Each alloy is generally named after the added metal – for example, ferrochromium.

ferroelectric material ceramic dielectric material that, like ferromagnetic materials, has a domain structure that makes it exhibit magnetism and usually the ◊piezoelectric effect. An example is Rochelle salt (potassium sodium tartrate tetrahydrate, $KNaC_4H_4O_6.4H_2O$).

ferromagnetism form of ◊magnetism in which magnetism can be acquired in an external magnetic field and usually retained in its absence, so that ferromagnetic materials are used to make permanent magnets. Examples are iron, cobalt, nickel, and their alloys.

Ferry Jules François Camille 1832–1893. French republican politician, mayor of Paris during the siege of 1870–71. As a member of the republican governments of 1879–85 (prime minister 1880–81 and 1883–85), he was responsible for the 1882 law making primary education free, compulsory, and secular. He directed French colonial expansion in Tunisia 1881 and Indochina (the acquisition of Tonkin in 1885).

fertility an organism's ability to reproduce, as distinct from the rate at which it reproduces (◊fecundity). Individuals become infertile (unable to reproduce) when they cannot generate gametes (eggs or sperm) or when their gametes cannot yield a viable ◊embryo after fertilization.

fertility drug any of a range of drugs taken to increase a female's fertility, developed in Sweden in the mid-1950s. They increase the chances of a multiple birth. The most familiar is gonadotrophin, which is made from hormone extracts taken from the human pituitary gland: follicle-stimulating hormone and lutinizing hormone. It stimulates ovulation in women. As a result of a fertility drug, in 1974 the first sextuplets to survive were born to Susan Rosenkowitz of South Africa.

> *'Whatever Nature has in store for mankind, unpleasant as it may be, man must accept, for ignorance is never better than knowledge.'*
>
> **Enrico Fermi**
> Quoted in Laura Fermi *Atoms in the Family* 1954

❛One does not, by knowing all the physical laws as we know them today, immediately obtain an understanding of anything much.❜

RICHARD PHILLIPS FEYNMAN *The Character of Physical Law*

fertilization in ◊sexual reproduction, the union of two ◊gametes (sex cells, often called egg and sperm) to produce a ◊zygote, which combines the genetic material contributed by each parent. In self-fertilization the male and female gametes come from the same plant; in cross-fertilization they come from different plants. Self-fertilization rarely occurs in animals; usually even ◊hermaphrodite animals cross-fertilize each other.

In terrestrial insects, mammals, reptiles, and birds, fertilization occurs within the female's body. In humans it usually takes place in the ◊Fallopian tube. In the majority of fishes and amphibians, and most aquatic invertebrates, fertilization occurs externally, when both sexes release their gametes into the water. In most fungi, gametes are not released, but the hyphae of the two parents grow towards each other and fuse to achieve fertilization. In higher plants, ◊pollination precedes fertilization.

fertilizer substance containing some or all of a range of about 20 chemical elements necessary for healthy plant growth, used to compensate for the deficiencies of poor or depleted soil. Fertilizers may be organic, for example farmyard manure, composts, bonemeal, blood, and fishmeal; or inorganic, in the form of compounds, mainly of nitrogen, phosphate, and potash, which have been used on a very much increased scale since 1945.

Fès or *Fez* former capital of Morocco 808–1062, 1296–1548, and 1662–1912, in a valley N of the Great Atlas Mountains, 160 km/100 mi E of Rabat; population (1982) 448,800; urban area (1990) 735,000. Textiles, carpets, and leather are manufactured, and the *fez*, a brimless hat worn in S and E Mediterranean countries, is traditionally said to have originated here. Kairwan Islamic University dates from 859; a second university was founded 1961.

fescue any grass of the widely distributed genus *Festuca*. Many are used in temperate regions for lawns and pasture. Many upland species are viviparous. Two common species in W Europe are meadow fescue, up to 80 cm/2.6 ft high, and sheep's fescue, up to 50 cm/1.6 ft high.

fetal therapy diagnosis and treatment of conditions arising in the unborn child. While some anomalies can be diagnosed antenatally, fetal treatments are only appropriate in a few cases – mostly where the development of an organ is affected.

Fetal therapy was first used 1963 with exchange transfusion for haemolytic disease of the newborn, once a serious problem (see also ◊rhesus factor). Today the use of fetal therapy remains limited. Most treatments involve 'needling': introducing fine instruments through the mother's abdominal and uterine walls under ultrasound guidance.

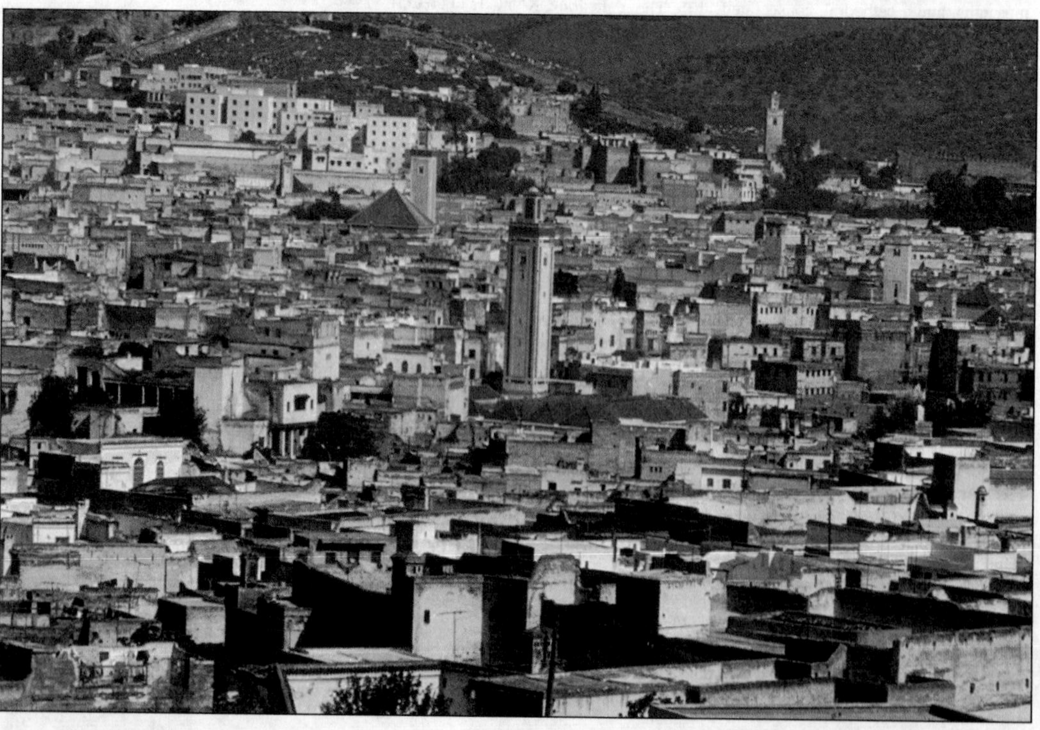

Fès The city of Fès in Morocco, N Africa. Fès was founded at the beginning of the 9th century and by the 14th century had become a major centre for commerce and learning. The Qarawiyin Mosque in Fès is the oldest in Africa and the university was founded 859. The city is famous for its Muslim art and handicraft industries. *UNESCO*

fetishism in anthropology, belief in the supernormal power of some inanimate object that is known as a fetish. Fetishism in some form is common to most cultures, and often has religio-magical significance.

fetishism in psychology, the transfer of erotic interest to an object, such as an item of clothing, whose real or fantasized presence is necessary for sexual gratification. The fetish may also be a part of the body not normally considered erogenous, such as the feet.

fetus or ***foetus*** stage in mammalian ◊embryo development. The human embryo is usually termed a fetus after the eighth week of development, when the limbs and external features of the head are recognizable.

feudalism (Latin *feudem* 'fief', coined 1839) the main form of social organization in medieval Europe. A system based primarily on land, it involved a hierarchy of authority, rights, and power that extended from the monarch downwards. An intricate network of duties and obligations linked royalty, nobility, lesser gentry, free tenants, villeins, and serfs. Feudalism was reinforced by a complex legal system and supported by the Christian church. With the growth of commerce and industry from the 13th century, feudalism gradually gave way to the class system as the dominant form of social ranking.

In return for military service the monarch allowed powerful vassals to hold land, and often also to administer justice and levy taxes. They in turn 'sublet' such rights. At the bottom of the system were the serfs, who worked on their lord's manor lands in return for being allowed to cultivate some for themselves, and so underpinned the system. They could not be sold as if they were slaves, but they could not leave the estate to live or work elsewhere without permission.

The system declined from the 13th century, partly because of the growth of a money economy, with commerce, trade, and industry, and partly because of the many peasants' revolts 1350–1550. Serfdom ended in England in the 16th century, but lasted in France until 1789 and in the rest of Western Europe until the early 19th century. In Russia it continued until 1861.

fever condition of raised body temperature, usually due to infection.

Feydeau Georges Léon Jules Marie 1862–1921. French comic dramatist. He is the author of over 60 farces and light comedies, which have been repeatedly revived in France at the Comédie Française and abroad. These include *La Dame de chez Maxim/The Girl from Maxim's* 1899, *Une Puce à l'oreille/A Flea in her Ear* 1907, *Feu la mère de Madame/My Late Mother-in-Law*, and *Occupe-toi d'Amélie/Look after Lulu*, both 1908.

Feyerabend Paul K 1924–1994. Austrian-born US philosopher of science, who rejected the attempt by certain philosophers (such as Karl ◊Popper) to find a methodology applicable to all scientific research. His works include *Against Method* 1975.

Feyerabend argues that successive theories that apparently concern the same subject (for instance the motion of the planets) cannot in principle be subjected to any comparison that would aim at finding the truer explanation. According to this notion of incommensurability, there is no neutral or objective standpoint, and therefore no rational and objective way in which one particular theory can be chosen over another. Instead, scientific progress is claimed to be the result of a range of sociological factors working to promote politically convenient notions of how nature operates. In the best-selling *Against Method*, he applied an anarchic approach to the study of knowledge and espoused practices, such as the Haitian cult of voodoo, that flew in the face of conventional scientific wisdom.

Feynman Richard P(hillips) 1918–1988. US physicist whose work laid the foundations of quantum electrodynamics. For his work on the theory of radiation he shared the Nobel Prize for Physics 1965 with Julian Schwinger and Sin-Itiro Tomonaga (1906–1979). He also contributed to many aspects of particle physics, including quark theory and the nature of the weak nuclear force.

For his work on quantum electrodynamics, he developed a simple and elegant system of Feynman diagrams to represent interactions between particles and how they moved from one space-time point to another. He had rules for calculating the probability associated with each diagram.

His other major discoveries are the theory of superfluidity (frictionless flow) in liquid helium, developed in the early 1950s; his work on the weak interaction (with US physicist Murray Gell-Mann) and the strong force; and his prediction that the proton and neutron are not elementary particles. Both particles are now known to be composed of quarks.

Fez alternative spelling of ◊Fès, a city in Morocco.

Fianna Fáil (Gaelic 'Soldiers of Destiny') Republic of Ireland political party, founded by the Irish nationalist de Valera 1926, and led since 1994 by Bertie Ahern. It was the governing party in the Republic of Ireland 1932–48, 1951–54, 1957–73, 1977–81, 1982, 1987–94 (from 1993 in coalition with Labour), and from 1997. It aims at the establishment of a united and completely independent all-Ireland republic.

Fibonacci Leonardo, also known as ***Leonardo of Pisa*** c. 1170–c. 1250. Italian mathematician. He published *Liber abaci/The Book of the Calculator* in Pisa 1202, which was instrumental in the introduction of Arabic notation into Europe. From 1960, interest increased in Fibonacci numbers, in their simplest form a sequence in which each number is the sum of its two predecessors (1, 1, 2, 3, 5, 8, 13, ...). They have unusual characteristics with possible applications in botany, psychology, and astronomy (for example, a more exact correspondence than is given by ◊Bode's law to the distances between the planets and the Sun).

In 1220, Fibonacci published *Practica geometriae*, in which he used algebraic methods to solve many arithmetical and geometrical problems.

fibre, dietary or ***roughage*** plant material that cannot be digested by human digestive enzymes; it consists largely of cellulose, a carbohydrate found in plant cell walls. Fibre adds bulk to the gut contents, assisting the muscular contractions that force food along the intestine. A diet low in fibre causes constipation and is believed to increase the risk of developing diverticulitis, diabetes, gall-bladder disease, and cancer of the large bowel – conditions that are rare in nonindustrialized countries, where the diet contains a high proportion of unrefined cereals.

Soluble fibre consists of indigestible plant carbohydrates (such as pectins, hemicelluloses, and gums) that dissolve in water. A high proportion of the fibre in such foods as oat bran, pulses, and vegetables is of this sort. Its presence in the diet has been found to reduce the amount of cholesterol in blood over the short term, although the mechanism for its effect is disputed.

Feynman US physicist Richard Feynman, noted for the major theoretical advances he made in quantum electrodynamics. Feynman began working on the Manhattan Project while at Princeton University and then worked in Los Alamos 1943–46, on the development of the first atomic bomb. *Californian Institute of Technology*

fibreglass glass that has been formed into fine fibres, either as long continuous filaments or as a fluffy, short-fibred glass wool. Fibreglass is heat- and fire-resistant and a good electrical insulator. It has applications in the field of fibre optics and as a strengthener for plastics in ◊GRP (glass-reinforced plastics).

fibre optics branch of physics dealing with the transmission of light and images through glass or plastic fibres known as ◊optical fibres.

fibrin insoluble protein involved in blood clotting. When an injury occurs fibrin is deposited around the wound in the form of a mesh, which dries and hardens, so that bleeding stops. Fibrin is developed in the blood from a soluble protein, fibrinogen.

The conversion of fibrinogen to fibrin is the final stage in blood clotting. Platelets, a type of cell found in blood, release the enzyme thrombin when they come into contact with damaged tissue, and the formation of fibrin then occurs. Calcium, vitamin K, and a variety of enzymes called factors are also necessary for efficient blood clotting.

fibrositis inflammation and overgrowth of fibrous tissue, mainly of the muscle sheaths. It is also known as muscular rheumatism. Symptoms are sudden pain and stiffness, usually relieved by analgesics and rest.

fibula the rear lower bone in the hind leg of a vertebrate. It is paired and often fused with a smaller front bone, the tibia.

Fichte Johann Gottlieb 1762–1814. German philosopher who developed a comprehensive form of subjective idealism, expounded in *The Science of Knowledge* 1794. He was an admirer of Immanuel ◊Kant.

In 1792, Fichte published *Critique of Religious Revelation*, a critical study of Kant's doctrine of the 'thing-in-itself'. For Fichte, the absolute ego posits both the external world (the non-ego) and finite self. Morality consists in the striving of this finite self to rejoin the absolute. In 1799 he was accused of atheism, and was forced to resign his post as professor of philosophy at Jena. He moved to Berlin, where he devoted himself to public affairs and delivered lectures, including *Reden an die deutsche Nation/Addresses to the German People* 1807–08, which influenced contemporary liberal nationalism.

fiction in literature, any work in which the content is completely or largely invented. The term describes imaginative works of narrative prose (such as the novel or the short story), and is distinguished from nonfiction (such as history, biography, or works on practical subjects) and poetry.

This usage reflects the dominance in contemporary Western literature of the novel as a vehicle for imaginative literature: strictly speaking, poems can also be fictional (as opposed to factual). Genres such as the historical novel often combine a fictional plot with real events; biography may also be 'fictionalized' through the use of imagined conversations or events.

Fidei Defensor Latin for the title of 'Defender of the Faith' (still retained by British sovereigns) conferred by Pope Leo X on Henry VIII of England 1521 to reward his writing of a treatise against the Protestant Martin Luther.

fief estate of lands granted to a ◊vassal by his lord after the former had sworn homage, or ◊fealty, promising to serve the lord. As a noble tenure, it carried with it rights of jurisdiction. In the later Middle Ages, it could also refer to a grant of money given in return for service.

field in computing, a specific item of data. A field is usually part of a ***record***, which in turn is part of a ◊file.

field in physics, a region of space in which an object exerts a force on another separate object because of certain properties they both possess. For example, there is a force of attraction between any two objects that have mass when one is in the gravitational field of the other. Other fields of force include ◊electric fields (caused by electric charges) and ◊magnetic fields (caused by circulating electric currents), either of which can involve attractive or repulsive forces.

field enclosed area of land used for farming. Traditionally fields were measured in ◊acres; the current unit of measurement is the hectare (2.47 acres).

In Britain, regular field systems were functioning before the Romans' arrival. The open-field system was in use at the time of the Norman Conquest. Enclosure began in the 14th century and continued into the 19th century.

In the Middle Ages, the farmland of an English rural community was often divided into three large fields (the open-field system). These were worked on a simple rotation basis of one year wheat, one year barley, and one year ◊fallow. The fields were divided into individually owned strips of the width that one plough team with oxen could plough (about 20 m/66 ft). At the end of each strip would be a turning space, either a road or a headland. Through repeated ploughing a ridge-and-furrow pattern became evident. A farmer worked a number of strips in one field.

The open-field communities were subsequently reorganized, the land enclosed, and the farmers' holdings redistributed into individual blocks which were then divided into separate fields. This ◊enclosure process reached its peak during the 18th century. 20th-century developments in agricultural science and technology have encouraged farmers to amalgamate and enlarge their fields, often to as much as 40 hectares/100 acres.

fieldfare gregarious thrush *Turdus pilaris* of the family Muscicapidae, order Passeriformes; it has chestnut upperparts with a pale-grey lower back and neck, and a dark tail. The bird's underparts are a rich ochre colour, spotted with black. It feeds on berries, insects, and other invertebrates. It is a migrant in Britain, breeding in Scandinavia and N Russia.

Fielding Henry 1707–1754. English novelist. His greatest work, *The History of Tom Jones, a Foundling* 1749 (which he described as 'a comic epic poem in prose'), realized for the first time in English the novel's potential for memorable characterization, coherent plotting, and perceptive analysis. The vigour of its comic impetus, descriptions of high and low life in town and country, and its variety of characters made it popular from the very first.

In youth a prolific dramatist, Fielding began writing novels with *An Apology for the Life of Mrs Shamela Andrews* 1741, a merciless parody of Samuel ◊Richardson's *Pamela*.

field marshal the highest rank in many European armies. A British field marshal is equivalent to a US ◊general (of the army).

Field of the Cloth of Gold site between Guînes and Ardres near Calais, France, where a meeting took place between Henry VIII of England and Francis I of France in June 1520, remarkable for the lavish clothes worn and tent pavilions erected. Francis hoped to gain England's support in opposing the Holy Roman emperor, Charles V, but failed.

Fields Gracie. Stage name of Grace Stansfield 1898–1979. English comedian and singer. Much loved by the public, her humorously sentimental films include *Sally in Our Alley* 1931 and *Sing as We Go* 1934.

Fields W C. Stage name of William Claude Dukenfield 1880–1946. US actor and screenwriter. His distinctive speech and professed attitudes such as hatred of children and dogs gained him enormous popularity in such films as *David Copperfield* 1935, *My Little Chickadee* (co-written with Mae West) and *The Bank Dick* both 1940, and *Never Give a Sucker an Even Break* 1941.

Originally a vaudeville performer, he incorporated his former stage routines, such as juggling and pool playing, into his films. He was also a popular radio performer.

Fiennes Ralph Nathaniel 1962– . British film and stage actor. After working with the National Theatre Company and the Royal Shakespeare Company, Fiennes progressed to TV and film work. He performed opposite Juliette Binoche as Heathcliff in *Wuthering Heights* 1992. He appeared in *Schindler's List* 1993, *Quiz Show* 1994, and *Strange Days* 1995. He was nominated for an Academy Award for his leading role in *The English Patient* 1996.

Fiennes Ranulph Twisleton-Wykeham 1944– . British explorer who made the first surface journey around the world's polar circumference between 1979 and 1982. Earlier expeditions included explorations of the White Nile 1969, Jostedalsbre Glacier, Norway, 1970, and the Headless Valley, Canada, 1971. Accounts of his adventures include *A Talent for Trouble* 1970, *Hell on Ice* 1979, and the autobiographical *Living Dangerously* 1987.

fife (German *pfeife*) small transverse ◊flute of similar range to the piccolo. Of Swiss origin, the fife is a popular military band instrument, played with the side drums and associated with historic parades.

Fife local authority of Scotland, created 1975, retained in the reorganization of local government 1996 (*see United Kingdom map*)
area 1,300 sq km/502 sq mi
towns and cities administrative headquarters Glenrothes; Dunfermline, St Andrews, Kirkcaldy, Cupar
features faces the North Sea and Firth of Forth; Lomond Hills in the NW (the only high land); rivers Eden and Leven; Rosyth naval base and dockyard (used for nuclear submarine refits) on northern shore of the Firth of Forth; Tentsmuir, possibly the earliest settled site in Scotland. The ancient palace of the Stuarts was at Falkland, and eight Scottish kings are buried at Dunfermline
industries potatoes, cereals, sugar beet; electronics, petrochemicals (Mossmorran), light engineering, aluminium refining; coal mining
population (1996 est) 351,600.

Fifteen, the ◊Jacobite rebellion of 1715, led by the 'Old Pretender' ◊James Edward Stuart and the Earl of Mar, in order to place the former on the English throne. Mar was checked at Sheriffmuir, Scotland, and the revolt collapsed.

fifth column group within a country secretly aiding an enemy attacking from without. The term originated 1936 during the Spanish Civil War, when General Mola boasted that Franco supporters were attacking Madrid with four columns and that they had a 'fifth column' inside the city.

fig any tree of the genus *Ficus* of the mulberry family Moraceae, including the many cultivated varieties of *F. carica*, originally from W Asia. They produce two or three crops of fruit a year. Eaten fresh or dried, figs have a high sugar content and laxative properties.

In the wild, *F. carica* is dependent on the fig wasp for pollination, and the wasp in turn is parasitic on the flowers. The tropical banyan *F. benghalensis* has less attractive edible fruit, and roots that grow down from its branches. The bo tree under which Buddha became enlightened is the Indian peepul or wild fig *F. religiosa*. *See illustration on following page.*

fighting fish any of a SE Asian genus *Betta* of fishes of the gourami family, especially *B. splendens*, about 6 cm/2 in long and a popular aquarium

'Never trust the man who hath reason to suspect that you know he hath injured you.'

HENRY FIELDING
Jonathan Wild

'Never give a sucker an even break.'

W C FIELDS
Catch phrase

fig Plants of the fig family may range in size from small shrubs to trees reaching 40 m/130 ft or more. They are found throughout the tropics. The edible fig originated in W Asia and has been cultivated for at least 6,000 years. It is now grown mainly in Italy, Turkey, Greece, and California. The fruit may be eaten fresh or preserved and dried. Figs are pollinated by parasitic wasps.

There is a beautiful cave called Fingal's; which proves that nature loves Gothic architecture.

On FINGAL'S CAVE Horace Walpole, letter to the Rev William Cole 28 May 1774

fish. It can breathe air, using an accessory breathing organ above the gill, and can live in poorly oxygenated water. The male has large fins and various colours, including shining greens, reds, and blues. The female is yellowish brown with short fins.

The male builds a nest of bubbles at the water's surface and displays to a female to induce her to lay. Rival males are attacked, and in a confined space, fights may occur. In Thailand, public contests are held.

figure of speech poetic, imaginative, or ornamental expression used for comparison, emphasis, or stylistic effect; usually one of a list of such forms dating from discussions of literary and rhetorical style in Greece in the 5th century BC. These figures include euphemism, hyperbole, metaphor, metonymy, onomatopoeia, oxymoron, personification, pun, simile, synecdoche, and zeugma.

figwort any Old World plant of the genus *Scrophularia* of the figwort family, which also includes foxgloves and snapdragons. Members of the genus have square stems, opposite leaves, and open two-lipped flowers in a cluster at the top of the stem.

The common figwort *Scrophularia nodosa* is found across Europe and N Asia, growing in damp woods and by hedges. It is up to 80 cm/2.6 ft long, with small reddish-brown flowers in late summer, and is pollinated by wasps.

Fiji Islands country comprising 844 islands and islets in the SW Pacific Ocean, about 100 of which are inhabited. *See country box opposite.*

filariasis collective term for several diseases, prevalent in tropical areas, caused by certain roundworm (nematode) parasites. About 80 million people worldwide are infected with filarial worms, mostly in India and Africa.

Symptoms include damaged and swollen lymph vessels leading to grotesque swellings of the legs and genitals (Bancroftian filariasis, ◊elephantiasis), blindness, and dry, scaly skin (◊onchocerciasis). The disease-causing worms are spread mainly by insects, notably mosquitoes and blackflies. Filariasis is treated by drugs to kill the worms, though this does not reverse any swelling.

file in computing, a collection of data or a program stored in a computer's external memory (for example, on ◊disc). It might include anything from information on a company's employees to a program for an adventure game. Serial files hold information as a sequence of characters, so that, to read any particular item of data, the program must read all those that precede it. Random-access files allow the required data to be reached directly.

Fillmore Millard 1800–1874. 13th president of the USA 1850–53, a Whig. Born into a poor farming family in New Cayuga County, New York State, he was Zachary Taylor's vice-president from 1849, and succeeded him on Taylor's death, July 9 1850. Fillmore supported a compromise on slavery 1850 to reconcile North and South which pleased neither side, and he failed to be nominated for another term.

film noir (French 'dark film') term originally used by French critics to describe films characterized by pessimism, cynicism, and a dark, sombre tone.

It has been used to describe black-and-white Hollywood melodramas of the 1940s and 1950s that portrayed the seedy side of life. Typically, the *film noir* is shot with lighting that emphasizes shadow and stark contrasts, abounds in night scenes, and contains a cynical antihero – for example, Philip Marlowe as played by Humphrey Bogart in *The Big Sleep* 1946.

film, photographic strip of transparent material (usually cellulose acetate) coated with a light-sensitive emulsion, used in cameras to take pictures. The emulsion contains a mixture of light-sensitive silver halide salts (for example, bromide or iodide) in gelatin. When the emulsion is exposed to light, the silver salts are invisibly altered, giving a latent image, which is then made visible by the process of ◊developing. Films differ in their sensitivities to light, this being indicated by their speeds. Colour film consists of several layers of emulsion, each of which records a different colour in the light falling on it. When they are viewed, either as a transparency or as a colour print, the colours merge to produce the true colour of the original scene photographed.

film score in contemporary usage, music specially written to accompany a film on the soundtrack. In the early days of cinema a symphonic poem was composed as a loosely-aligned accompaniment to a major silent film, or background music was improvised or assembled by pit musicians with the aid of a Kinothek theme catalogue. With the arrival of optical sound on film came the fully synchronized Hollywood film score. Composers in the European Romantic tradition, including Erich Korngold, Max Steiner, and Franz Waxman, initially tried to adapt the symphonic style to the faster-moving screen action; a more successful transition was made by animated film music specialists, such as Scott Bradley (1914–). After 1950 a younger generation including Alec North and Elmer Bernstein adopted simpler, jazz-oriented idioms.

Composers for silent films include Saint-Saëns, Arthur Honegger, and Edmund Meisel, whose music for Eisenstein's *Battleship Potemkin* 1925 was banned by the authorities. Composers for sound film include Georges Auric, Aaron Copland, Prokofiev, William Walton, Bernard Herrmann, and Ennio Morricone.

filter in chemistry, a porous substance, such as blotting paper, through which a mixture can be passed to separate out its solid constituents.

filter in electronics, a circuit that transmits a signal of some frequencies better than others. A low-pass filter transmits signals of low frequency and direct current; a high-pass filter transmits high-frequency signals; a band-pass filter transmits signals in a band of frequencies.

finch The zebra finch, or spotted-sided finch, is a member of the waxbill family of seed-eating birds found in Australia. While its overall coloration is comparatively uniform, it has bold markings. It has become a popular cagebird and captive breeding of these birds has developed several colour varieties.

filtration technique by which suspended solid particles in a fluid are removed by passing the mixture through a filter, usually porous paper, plastic, or cloth. The particles are retained by the filter to form a residue and the fluid passes through to make up the filtrate. For example, soot may be filtered from air, and suspended solids from water.

final solution (to the Jewish question; German *Endlosung der Judenfrage*) euphemism used by the Nazis to describe the extermination of Jews (and other racial groups and opponents of the regime) before and during World War II in the ◊Holocaust.

The term came from a statement May 1941 by SS commander Heinrich ◊Himmler to Rudolf ◊Hoess, commandant of Auschwitz concentration camp, that Hitler had given orders 'for the final solution of the Jewish question'. Extermination squads (*Einsatzgruppen*) were formed and extermination camps were established in Poland to which Jews were shipped from all parts of German-occupied Europe to be killed by gas or shooting. It is estimated that 6 million Jews, and a further million gypsies, communists, Soviet prisoners, incurable invalids, homosexuals, and other *Untermenschen* ('subhumans') were murdered.

Financial Times Index (FT Index) indicator measuring the daily movement of 30 major industrial share prices on the London Stock Exchange (1935 = 100), issued by the UK *Financial Times* newspaper. Other FT indices cover government securities, fixed-interest securities, gold mine shares, and Stock Exchange activity.

finch any of various songbirds of the family Fringillidae, in the order Passeriformes (perching birds). They are seed-eaters with stout conical beaks. The name may also be applied to members of the Emberizidae (buntings), and Estrildidae (weaver-finches).

Most of the British species may be found in two subfamilies: Fringillinae, with the chaffinch, *Fringilla coelobs*; and Carduelinae, with the greenfinch, *Chloris chloris*, goldfinch, *Carduelis carduelis*, and bullfinch, *Pyrrhula pyrrhula*. Other British finches in the Fringillidae are the hawfinch, *Coccothraustes coccothraustes*, and siskin, *Carduelis spinus*.

fine arts or ***beaux arts*** arts judged predominantly in aesthetic rather than functional terms, for example painting, sculpture, and print making. Architecture is also classified as one of the fine arts, though here the functional element is also important. Music and poetry are also sometimes called fine arts. The fine arts are traditionally contrasted with the applied arts.

Fine Gael (Gaelic 'United Ireland') Republic of Ireland political party founded 1933 by W J ◊Cosgrave and led by John Bruton from 1990. It is socially liberal but fiscally conservative. It formed a coalition government with Labour 1994–97.

fighting fish Siamese fighting fish live in brackish water in ponds and drainage channels in Thailand. The males are extremely aggressive and are bred for their large and brightly coloured fins, which they flare during combat.

Fingal's Cave cave on the island of Staffa, Inner Hebrides, Scotland. It is lined with natural basalt columns, and is 60 m/200 ft long and 20 m/65 ft high. Fingal, based on the Irish hero Finn Mac Cumhaill, was the leading character in Macpherson's Ossianic forgeries. Visited by the German Romantic composer Felix Mendelssohn 1829, the cave was the inspiration of his *Hebrides* overture, otherwise known as *Fingal's Cave*.

fingerprint ridge pattern of the skin on a person's fingertips; this is constant through life and no two are exactly alike. Fingerprinting was first used as a means of identifying crime suspects in India, and was adopted by the English police 1901; it is now widely employed in police and security work. ◊Genetic fingerprinting is a technique that uses DNA to establish an individual's identity.

Finland country in Scandinavia, bounded N by Norway, E by Russia, S and W by the Baltic Sea, and NW by Sweden. *See country box on p. 394.*

Finland, Gulf of eastern arm of the ◊Baltic Sea, separating Finland from Estonia.

Finney Albert 1936– . English stage and film actor. He created the title roles in Keith Waterhouse's stage play *Billy Liar* 1960 and John Osborne's *Luther* 1961, and was associate artistic director of the Royal Court Theatre 1972–75. Later roles for the National Theatre include Tamburlaine in Marlowe's tragedy 1976 and *Macbeth* 1978. His films include *Saturday Night and Sunday Morning* 1960, *Tom Jones* 1963, *Murder on the Orient Express* 1974, and *The Dresser* 1984.

Finney Tom (Thomas) 1922– . English footballer, known as the 'Preston Plumber'. He played for England 76 times, and in every forward position. He was celebrated for his ball control and goal-scoring skills, and was the first person to win the Footballer of the Year award twice.

Finnish language member of the Finno-Ugric language family, the national language of Finland and closely related to neighbouring Estonian, Livonian, Karelian, and Ingrian languages. At the beginning of the 19th century Finnish had no official status, since Swedish was the language of education, government, and literature in Finland. The publication of the *Kalevala*, a national epic poem, in 1835, contributed greatly to the arousal of Finnish national and linguistic feeling.

Finland Lake Hämeenlinna Aulanko, SW Finland. The vast glaciers that covered the area during the Ice Ages created the Finnish landscape of today, typically flat and dotted with thousands of lakes. *A N Suttle Lifefile*

Finn Mac Cumhaill or ***Finn McCool*** legendary Irish hero, identified with a general who organized an Irish regular army in the 3rd century. The Scottish writer James ◊Macpherson featured him (as Fingal) and his followers in the verse of his popular epics 1762–63, which were supposedly written by a 3rd-century bard called ◊Ossian.

Finno-Ugric group or family of more than 20 languages spoken by some 22 million people in scattered communities from Norway in the west to Siberia in the east and to the Carpathian mountains in the south. Members of the family include Finnish, Lapp, and Hungarian.

Fiorucci Elio 1935– . Italian fashion designer and retailer. He established the Fiorucci label in the 1960s, but became best known in the 1970s for bright, casual clothing including slimfit jeans, sold internationally through Fiorucci boutiques.

fir any ◊conifer of the genus *Abies* in the pine family Pinaceae. The true firs include the balsam fir of N North America and the Eurasian silver fir *A. alba*. Douglas firs of the genus *Pseudotsuga* are native to W North America and the Far East.

Firbank (Arthur Annesley) Ronald 1886–1926. English novelist. His work, set in the Edwardian decadent period, has a malicious humour and witty sophistication. It includes *Caprice* 1917, *Valmouth* 1919, and the bizarre fantasy *Concerning the Eccentricities of Cardinal Pirelli* 1926.

Firdausi Abdul Qasim Mansur c. 935–c. 1020. Persian poet. His epic *Shahnama/The Book of Kings* relates the history of Persia in 60,000 verses.

firearm weapon from which projectiles are discharged by the combustion of an explosive. Firearms are generally divided into two main sections:

FIJI ISLANDS
Republic of

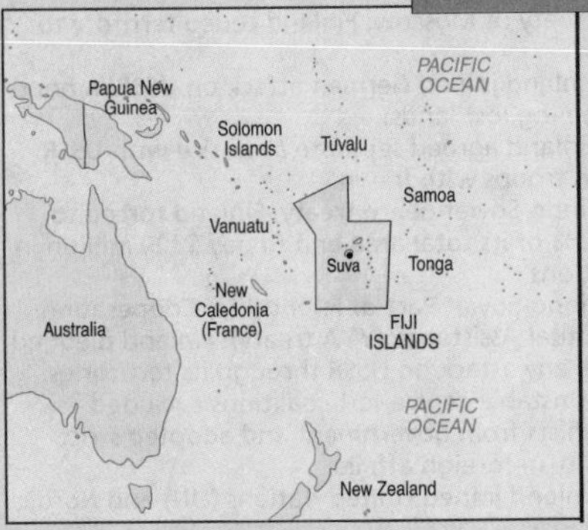

area 18,333 sq km/7,078 sq mi
capital Suva
major ports Lautoka and Levuka
physical features comprises about 844 Melanesian and Polynesian islands and islets (about 100 inhabited), the largest being Viti Levu (10,429 sq km/4,028 sq mi) and Vanua Levu (5,556 sq km/2,146 sq mi); mountainous, volcanic, with tropical rainforest and grasslands; almost all islands surrounded by coral reefs; high volcanic peaks
head of state Ratu Sir Kamisese Mara from 1994
head of government Col Sitiveni Rabuka from 1992
political system democratic republic
administrative divisions four divisions
political parties National Federation Party (NFP), moderate left of centre, Indian; Fijian Labour Party (FLP), left of centre, Indian; United Front, Fijian; Fijian Political Party (FPP), Fijian centrist
population 784,000 (1995 est)
population growth rate 1.5% (1990–95); 1.5% (2000–05)
ethnic distribution 48% Fijians (of Melanesian and Polynesian descent), 51% Asians
life expectancy 64 (males), 68 (females)
literacy rate 87%
languages English (official), Fijian, Hindi
religions Methodist, Hindu, Muslim, Sikh
currency Fiji dollar
GDP (US $) 1.84 billion (1994)
growth rate 5.2% (1994)
exports sugar, coconut oil, ginger, timber, canned fish, gold, molasses, clothing; tourism is important

HISTORY
c. 1500 BC Peopled by Polynesian and, later, Melanesian settlers.
1643 The islands were visited for the first time by a European, the Dutch navigator Abel Tasman.
1830s Arrival of Western Christian missionaries.
1840s–50s Western Fiji came under dominance of a Christian convert prince, Cakobau, ruler of Bau islet, who proclaimed himself Tui Viti (King of Fiji), while the E was controlled by Ma'afu, a Christian prince from Tonga.
1857 British consul appointed, encouraging settlers from Australia and New Zealand to set up cotton farms in Fiji.
1874 Fiji became a British crown colony after deed of cession signed by King Cakobau.
1875–76 A third of the Fijian population wiped out by a measles epidemic; rebellion against British suppressed with the assitance of Fijian chiefs.
1877 Fiji became headquarters of the British Western Pacific High Commission (WPHC), which controlled other British protectorates in the Pacific region.
1879–1916 Indian labourers brought in, on ten-year indentured contracts, to work sugar plantations.
1904 Legislative Council formed, with elected Europeans and nominated Fijians, to advise the British governor.
1963 Legislative Council enlarged; women and Fijians were enfranchised. The predominantly Fijian Alliance Party (AP) formed.
1970 Independence achieved from Britain; Ratu Sir Kamisese Mara of the AP elected as first prime minister.
1973 Ratu Sir George Cakobau, great-grandson of the chief who had sworn allegiance to the British in 1874, became governor-general.
1985 FLP formed by Dr Timoci Bavadra, with trade-union backing.
1987 After general election had brought to power an Indian-dominated coalition led by Dr Bavadra, Lt-Col Sitiveni Rabuka seized power after a military coup, and proclaimed a Fijian-dominated republic outside the Commonwealth.
1990 New constitution, favouring indigenous (Melanese) Fijians, introduced. Civilian rule re-established, with resignations from cabinet of military officers, but Rabuka remained as home affairs minister, with Mara as prime minister.
1992 General election produced coalition government with Rabuka of the FPP as prime minister. Fiji signed the Raratonga Treaty (with Australia, Indonesia, New Zealand, and the USSR), formally declaring the South Pacific a nuclear-free zone.
1993 President Ganilau died and was replaced by Ratu Sir Kamisese Mara.
1994 Rabuka and FPP re-elected.
1997 Fiji re-admitted to the Commonwealth.
1998 Name changed to Fiji Islands

◊artillery (ordnance or cannon), with a bore greater than 2.54 cm/1 in, and ◊small arms, with a bore of less than 2.54 cm/1 in.

Although gunpowder was known in Europe 60 years previously, the invention of guns dates from 1300 to 1325, and is attributed to Berthold Schwartz, a German monk.

fire clay a ◊clay with refractory characteristics (resistant to high temperatures), and hence suitable for lining furnaces (firebrick). Its chemical composition consists of a high percentage of silicon and aluminium oxides, and a low percentage of the oxides of sodium, potassium, iron, and calcium. Fire clays underlie the coal seams in the UK.

fire extinguisher device for putting out a fire. Fire extinguishers work by removing one of the three conditions necessary for fire to continue (heat, oxygen, and fuel), either by cooling the fire or by excluding oxygen. The simplest fire extinguishers contain water, which when propelled onto the fire cools it down. Water extinguishers cannot be used on electrical fires, as there is a danger of electrocution, or on burning oil, as the oil will float on the water and spread the blaze.

Many domestic extinguishers contain liquid carbon dioxide under pressure. When the handle is pressed, carbon dioxide is released as a gas that blankets the burning material and prevents oxygen from reaching it. Dry extinguishers spray powder, which then releases carbon dioxide gas. Wet extinguishers are often of the soda-acid type; when activated, sulphuric acid mixes with sodium bicarbonate, producing carbon dioxide. The gas pressure forces the solution out of a nozzle, and a foaming agent may be added.

Some extinguishers contain halons, which are very effective at smothering fires, but cause damage to the ◊ozone layer, and their use is now restricted.

firefly any winged nocturnal beetle of the family Lampyridae. They all emit light through the process of ◊bioluminescence.

firework a device that produces a display of colour, smoke, noise, or a combination of these three; examples include bangers, catherine wheels, and roman candles. They always generate heat. There are three essential components of a firework; a fuel (since all fireworks are based on combustion), an oxidiser (a substance that readily releases oxygen, to enable the fuel to burn more rapidly and effectively), and a binding agent to hold the first two together. All these materials are compressed in a container, usually cylindrical and made of rolled cardboard. Fireworks were invented in China, and are today common in most countries. Pyrotechnics is the science and art of designing and using fireworks. Fireworks are used for displays and military purposes (including illumination and signalling).

Fuels used in fireworks include charcoal, magnesium, and gunpowder. Commonly used oxidisers include strontium nitrate, potassium chlorate, and potassium perchlorate. Binding agents include poly vinyl chloride, and resorcinol resin.

Specific colours produced include red, by including strontium compounds (which in the flame produce the unstable strontium chloride, giving a red light), blue, from copper compounds, green, from barium compounds, yellow, from the element sodium, and white, from magnesium. Sparks are produced by including metal flakes in the firework, for example titanium or aluminium.

first aid action taken immediately in a medical emergency in order to save a sick or injured person's life, prevent further damage, or facilitate later treatment. See also ◊resuscitation.

First World War another name for ◊World War I, 1914–18.

fiscal policy that part of government policy concerning ◊taxation and other revenues, ◊public spending, and government borrowing (the ◊public sector borrowing requirement).

fiscal year a year as defined by a company or government for financial accounting purposes. A company can choose any 12-month period for its accounting year and in exceptional circumstances may determine a longer or shorter period as its fiscal year. It does not necessarily coincide with the calendar year.

In the UK, the fiscal year runs from 6 April in one year to 5 April in the following year. A company can choose any 12-month period for its accounting year. In the USA, the fiscal year runs from 1 July to 30 June.

Fischer Bobby (Robert James) 1943– . World Chess Champion 1972–5, 1992. In 1958, after proving himself in international competition, he became

FINLAND
Republic of

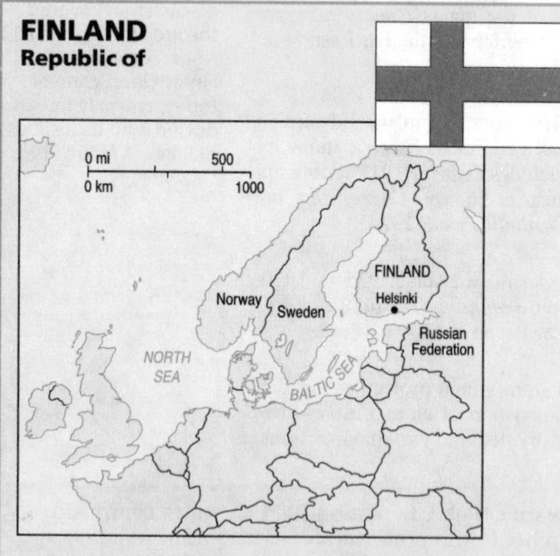

national name *Suomen Tasavalta*
area 338,145 sq km/130,608 sq mi
capital Helsinki (Helsingfors)
major towns/cities Tampere, Espoo, Vantaa
major ports Turku, Oulu
physical features most of the country is forest, with low hills and about 60,000 lakes; one third is within the Arctic Circle; archipelago in S includes Åland Islands; Helsinki is the most northerly national capital on the European continent – at the 70th parallel there is constant daylight for 73 days in summer and 51 days of uninterrupted night in winter
head of state Martti Ahtisaari from 1994
head of government Paavo Lipponen from 1995
political system democratic republic
administrative divisions 12 provinces
political parties Finnish Social Democratic Party (SSDP), moderate left of centre; National Coalition Party (KOK), moderate right of centre; Finnish Centre Party (KESK), radical centrist, rural-oriented; Swedish People's Party (SFP), independent Swedish-oriented; Finnish Rural Party (SMP), farmers and small businesses; Left-Wing Alliance (VL), left-wing
armed forces 31,100 (1995)
conscription up to 11 months, followed by refresher training of 40–100 days (before age 50)
defence spend (% GDP) 2.0 (1994)
education spend (% GNP) 7.3 (1992)
health spend (% GDP) 7.0 (1993)
death penalty abolished 1972
population 5,126,000 (1996 est)
population growth rate 0.5% (1990–95); 0.3% (2000–05)
age distribution (% of total population) <15 19.1%, 15–65 66.8%, >65 14.1% (1995)
ethnic distribution majority descended from Finno-Ugric inhabitants
population density (per sq km) 15.1 (1994)
urban population (% of total) 63 (1995)
labour force 52% of population: 8% agriculture, 31% industry, 61% services (1990)
unemployment 17.1% (1995)
life expectancy 72 (males), 80 (women)
education (compulsory years) 9
literacy rate 99%
languages Finnish 93%, Swedish 6% (both official), small Saami- and Russian-speaking minorities
religions Lutheran 90%, Orthodox 1%
TV sets (per 1,000 people) 505 (1992)
currency markka
GDP (US $) 124.0 billion (1996)
PPP per capita (US $) 17,188 (1995)
growth rate 4.0% (1994)
average annual inflation 3.9% (1985–94); 1.1% (1994)
major trading partners Germany, Sweden, UK, USA, Russia, Denmark, Norway, the Netherlands
resources copper ore, lead ore, gold, zinc ore, silver, peat, hydro-power, forests
industries food processing, paper and paper products, machinery, printing and publishing, wood products, metal products, shipbuilding, chemicals, clothing and footwear
exports metal and engineering products, gold, paper and paper products, machinery, ships, wood and pulp, clothing and footwear, chemicals. Principal market: Germany 13.4% (1994)
imports mineral fuels, machinery and transport equipment, food and live animals, chemical and related products, textiles, iron and steel. Principal source: Germany 14.7% (1994)
arable land 9% (1993)
agricultural products oats, sugar beet, potatoes, barley, hay; forestry and animal husbandry

HISTORY

1st C Occupied by Finnic nomads from Asia who drove out native Saami (Lapps) to the far N.
12th–13th Cs Series of Swedish crusades conquered Finns and converted them to Christianity.
16th–17th Cs Finland was a semi-autonomous Swedish duchy with Swedish landowners ruling Finnish peasants; Finland allowed relative autonomy, becoming a grand duchy 1581.
1634 Finland fully incorporated into Swedish kingdom.
1700–21 Great Northern War between Sweden and Russia; half of Finnish population died in famine and epidemics.
1741–43 and 1788–90 Further Russo-Swedish wars; much of the fighting took place in Finland.
1808 Russia invaded Sweden (with support of Napoleon).
1809 Finland ceded to Russia as grand duchy with Russian tsar as grand duke; Finns retained their own legal system and Lutheran religion and were exempt from Russian military service.
1812 Helsinki became capital of grand duchy.
19th C Growing prosperity was followed by rise of national feeling among new Finnish middle class.
1904–05 Policies promoting Russification of Finland provoked national uprising; Russians imposed military rule.
1917 Finland declared independence.
1918 Bitter civil war between Reds (supported by Russian Bolsheviks) and Whites (supported by Germany); Baron Carl Gustaf Mannerheim led Whites to victory.
1919 Republican constitution adopted with Kaarlo Juho Stahlberg as first president.
1927 Land reform broke up big estates and created many small peasant farms.
1939–40 Winter War: USSR invaded Finland after demand for military bases was refused.
1940 Treaty of Moscow: Finland ceded territory to USSR.
1941 Finland joined German attack on USSR in hope of regaining lost lands.
1944 Finland agreed separate armistice with USSR; German troops withdrawn.
1947 Finno-Soviet peace treaty: Finland forced to cede 12% of its total area and to pay $300 million in reparations.
1948 Finno-Soviet Pact of Friendship, Cooperation, and Mutual Assistance (YYA treaty): Finland pledged to repel any attack on USSR through its territories.
1950s Unstable centre-left coalitions excluded communists from government and adopted strict neutrality in foreign affairs.
1955 Finland joined United Nations (UN) and Nordic Council.
1956 Urho Kekkonen elected president. General strike as a result of unemployment and inflation.
1973 Trade agreements signed with European Economic Community (EEC) and Comecon.
1982 Mauno Koivisto elected president.
1987 New coalition of Social Democrats and conservatives formed.
1991 Big swing to Centre Party in general election.
1994 Martti Ahtisaari (SSDP) elected president.
1995 Finland joined European Union (EU); Social Democrats won general election.

SEE ALSO Åland Islands; Winter War

the youngest grand master in history. He was the author of *Games of Chess* 1959, and was also celebrated for his unorthodox psychological tactics.

Fischer Emil Hermann 1852–1919. German chemist who produced synthetic sugars and, from these, various enzymes. His descriptions of the chemistry of the carbohydrates and peptides laid the foundations for the science of biochemistry. Nobel prize 1902.

About 1882, Fischer began working on a group of compounds that included uric acid and caffeine. He realized that they were all related to a hitherto unknown substance, which he called purine. Over the next few years he synthesized about 130 related compounds, one of which was the first synthetic nucleotide. These studies led to the synthesis of powerful hypnotic drugs derived from barbituric acids (barbiturates).

Fischer Hans 1881–1945. German chemist awarded a Nobel prize 1930 for his work on haemoglobin, the oxygen-carrying, red colouring matter in blood. He determined the molecular structures of three important biological pigments: haemoglobin, chlorophyll, and bilirubin.

Fischl Eric 1948– . US Realist painter. He is known for his narrative, frequently disturbing paintings of suburban Americans at play. His straightforward handling of sexual themes has been considered shocking, as in *Bad Boy* 1981 (Saatchi Collection, London). Fischl's work has affinities with that of Edward ◊Hopper and of ◊Balthus, but unlike the latter's his voyeurism is detached and unerotic. Instead he seeks to reveal the emptiness of instantly gratified, materialistic lives.

fish aquatic vertebrate that uses gills to obtain oxygen from fresh or sea water. There are three main groups: the bony fishes or Osteichthyes (goldfish, cod, tuna); the cartilaginous fishes or Chondrichthyes (sharks, rays); and the jawless fishes or Agnatha (hagfishes, lampreys).

Fishes of some form are found in virtually every body of water in the world except for the very salty water of the Dead Sea and some of the hot larval springs. Of the 30,000 fish species, approximately 2,500 are freshwater.

bony fishes These constitute the majority of living fishes (about 20,000 species). The skeleton is bone, movement is controlled by mobile fins, and the body is usually covered with scales. The gills are covered by a single flap. Many have a ◊swim bladder with which the fish adjusts its buoyancy. Most lay eggs, sometimes in vast numbers, but few of them will survive to become adults. Those species that produce small numbers of eggs very often protect them in nests, or brood them in their mouths. Some fishes are internally fertilized and retain eggs until hatched inside the body, then giving birth to live young. Most bony fishes are ray-finned fishes, but a few, including lungfishes and coelacanths, are fleshy-finned.

cartilaginous fishes These are efficient hunters. There are fewer than 600 known species of sharks and rays. The skeleton is cartilage, the mouth is generally beneath the head, the nose is large and sensitive, and there is a series of open gill slits along the neck region. They have no swimbladder and, in order to remain buoyant, must keep swimming. They may lay eggs ('mermaid's purses') or bear live young. Some types of cartilaginous fishes, such as sharks, retain the shape they had millions of years ago.

jawless fishes Jawless fish have a body plan like that of some of the earliest vertebrates that existed before true fishes with jaws evolved. There is no true backbone but a ◊notochord. The lamprey attaches itself to the fishes on which it feeds by a suckerlike rasping mouth. Hagfishes are entirely marine, very slimy, and feed on carrion and injured fishes.

The world's largest fish is the whale shark *Rhineodon typus*, more than 20 m/66 ft long; the smallest is the dwarf pygmy goby *Pandaka pygmaea*), 7.5–9.9 mm long. The study of fishes is called ichthyology.

fish as food The nutrient composition of fish is similar to that of meat, except that there are no obvious deposits of fat. Examples of fish comparatively high in fat are salmon, mackerel, and herring. White fish such as cod, haddock, and whiting contain only 0.4–4% fat. Fish are good sources of B vitamins and iodine, and the fatty fish livers are good sources of A and D vitamins. Calcium can be obtained from fish with soft skeletons, such as sardines. Roe and caviar have a high protein content (20–25%). *See classification on following page.*

Fisher John, St c. 1469–1535. English cleric, created bishop of Rochester 1504. He was an enthusiastic supporter of the revival in the study of Greek, and a friend of the humanists Thomas More and Desiderius Erasmus. In 1535 he was tried on a charge of denying the royal supremacy of Henry VIII and beheaded. Canonized 1935.

Fisher Ronald Aylmer 1890–1962. English statistician and geneticist. He modernized Charles Darwin's theory of evolution, thus securing the key biological concept of genetic change by natural selection. Fisher developed several new statistical techniques and, applying his methods to genetics, published *The Genetical Theory of Natural Selection* 1930.

fish farming or ***aquaculture*** raising fish (including molluscs and crustaceans) under controlled conditions in tanks and ponds, sometimes in offshore pens. It has been practised for centuries in the Far East, where Japan today produces some 100,000 tonnes of fish a year; the US, Norway, and Canada are also big producers. In the 1980s 10% of the world's consumption of fish was farmed, notably carp, catfish, trout, Atlantic salmon, turbot, eel, mussels, clams, oysters, and shrimp.

fishing and fisheries fisheries can be classified by (1) type of water: freshwater (lake, river, pond); marine (inshore, midwater, deep sea); (2) catch: for example, salmon fishing; (3) fishing method: diving, stunning or poisoning, harpooning, trawling, drifting. The world's total fish catch is about 100 million tonnes a year (1995).

marine fishing Most of the world's catch comes from the oceans, and marine fishing accounts for around 20% of the world's animal-based protein. A wide range of species is included in the landings of the world's marine fishing nations, but the majority belong to the herring and cod groups. The majority of the crustaceans landed are shrimps, and squid and bivalves, such as oysters, are dominant among the molluscs.

Almost all marine fishing takes place on or above the continental shelf, in the photic zone, the relatively thin surface layer (50 m/165 ft) of water that can be penetrated by light, allowing photosynthesis by plant ◊plankton to take place. Pelagic fishing exploits not only large fish such as tuna, which live near the surface in the open sea and are caught in purse-seine nets, with an annual catch of over 30 million tonnes, but also small, shoaling and plankton-feeding fish that live in the main body of the water.

Examples are herring, sardines, anchovies, and mackerel, which are caught with drift nets, purse seines, and pelagic trawls. The fish are often used for fish meal rather than for direct human consumption. Demersal fishes, such as haddock, halibut, plaice, and cod, live primarily on or near the ocean floor, and feed on various invertebrate marine animals.

freshwater fishing Such species as salmon and eels, which migrate to and from fresh and salt water for spawning, may be fished in either system. About a third of the total freshwater catch comes from ◊fish farming methods, which are better developed in freshwater than in marine systems. There is large demand for salmon, trout, carp, eel, bass, pike, perch, and catfish. These are caught in ponds, lakes, rivers, or swamps.

methods The gear and methods used to catch fish are very varied and show much geographical and historical variation. The method chosen for a particular situation will depend on the species being hunted and the nature of the habitat (for example, the speed of the current, the depth of water, and the roughness of the sea bed). It is often useful to divide gear types into active (for example trawls, seines, harpoons, dredges) and passive (drift nets, traps, hooks and lines). Passive gear relies on the fish's own movements to bring them into contact with it, and may involve some method of artificial attraction such as baits or lights. Most fishing gear is operated from boats, ranging from one-person canoes to trawlers about 100 m/330 ft long.

trawling Much of the world's fish catch is caught by trawls. The equipment consists essentially of a tapered bag of netting which is towed through the water. The mouth of the net is kept open in the vertical plane by having floats on the headline and weights on the footrope. The main problem with pelagic trawls is to control the depth of fishing and to relate this to the concentrations of fish. The most effective means of tracking fish for this purpose is by using an ◊echo sounder.

seine nets Seine nets operate by trapping fish within encircling gear. Purse seines, nets that close like a purse, are used to catch pelagic fish such as herring, mackerel, and tuna, which form dense shoals near the surface. Once a shoal has been located, usually by echo sounder, the net is shot around it by one vessel and later hauled in towards another. The nets are large, often as long as 30 nautical miles, and are not usually hauled aboard like trawls. Instead the fish are scooped or pumped out of the net into the ship's hold. They have caused a crisis in the S Pacific where Japan, Taiwan, and South Korea fish illegally in other countries' fishing zones.

gill nets Gill nets passively depend on the fish entangling themselves in the meshes of the net, usually being held fast by their gill covers. An example is the drift net used for pelagic fish, but in many areas it is now superseded by purse seines and pelagic trawls. Drift nets are walls of netting suspended from floats on the surface.

lines and hooks Although a distinct method of catching fish, lines and hooks can be regarded as a special type of trap. Natural or artificial baits are used and the gear may be fished anywhere from the sea bed to the surface. Hooks and lines fished off the sea bed may be towed from moving boats, which is called trolling.

dredges Dredges act like small trawls to collect molluscs and other sluggish organisms; some are hydraulic and use jets of water to dislodge the molluscs from the bottom and wash them into the dredge bag or directly onto the boat via a conveyor belt.

other methods Molluscs may also be gathered by hand, either on foot at low water or by divers below the shoreline. Rakes may be used to dig out cockles from within the sand. Other methods include dip, lift and cast nets, harpoons, and spears.

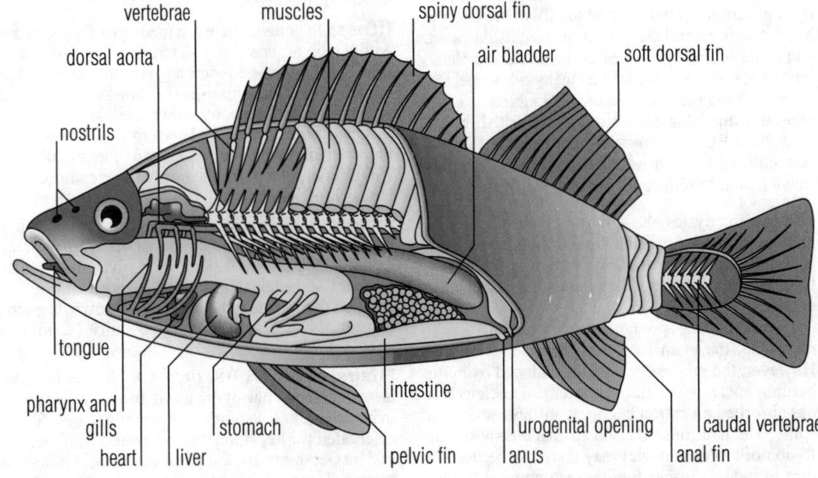

fish The anatomy of a fish. All fishes move through water using their fins for propulsion. The bony fishes, like the specimen shown here, constitute the largest group of fishes with about 20,000 species.

FISH: CLASSIFICATION

Order	Number of species	Examples
***Superclass Agnatha** (jawless fishes)*		
Petromyzoniformes	30	lamprey
Myxiniformes	15	hagfish
***Superclass Gnathostomata** (jawed fishes)*		
***Class Chondrichthyes** (cartilaginous fishes)*		
***Subclass Elasmobranchii** (sharks and rays)*		
Hexanchiformes	6	frilled shark, comb-toothed shark
Heterodontiformes	10	Port Jackson shark
Lamniformes	200	'typical' shark
Rajiformes	300	skate, ray
***Subclass Holocephali** (rabbitfishes)*		
Chimaeriformes	20	chimaera, rabbitfish
***Class Osteichthyes** (bony fishes)*		
***Subclass Sarcopterygii** (fleshy-finned fishes)*		
Coelacanthiformes	1	coelacanth
Ceratodiformes	1	Australian lungfish
Lepidosireniformes	4	South American and African lungfish
***Subclass Actinopterygii** (ray-finned fishes)*		
Superorder Chondrostei		
Polypteriformes	11	bichir, reedfish
Acipensiformes	25	paddlefish, sturgeon
Superorder Holostei		
Amiiformes	8	bowfin, garpike
Superorder Teleostei		
Elopiformes	12	tarpon, tenpounder
Anguilliformes	300	eel
Notacanthiformes	20	spiny eel
Clupeiformes	350	herring, anchovy
Osteoglossiformes	16	arapaima, African butterfly fish
Mormyriformes	150	elephant-trunk fish, featherback
Salmoniformes	500	salmon, trout, smelt, pike
Gonorhynchiformes	15	milkfish
Cypriniformes	350	carp, barb, characin, loache
Siluriformes	200	catfish
Myctophiformes	300	deep-sea lantern fish, Bombay duck
Percopsiformes	10	pirate perch, cave-dwelling amblyopsid
Batrachoidiformes	10	toadfish
Gobiesociformes	100	clingfish, dragonets
Lophiiformes	150	anglerfish
Gadiformes	450	cod, pollack, pearlfish, eelpout
Atheriniformes	600	flying fish, toothcarp, halfbeak
Lampridiformes	50	opah, ribbonfish
Beryciformes	150	squirrelfish
Zeiformes	60	John Dory, boarfish
Gasterosteiformes	150	stickleback, pipefish, seahorse
Channiformes	5	snakeshead
Synbranchiformes	7	cuchia
Scorpaeniformes	700	gurnard, miller's thumb, stonefish
Dactylopteriformes	6	flying gurnard
Pegasiformes	4	sea-moth
Pleuronectiformes	500	flatfish
Tetraodontiformes	250	puffer fish, triggerfish, sunfish
Perciformes	6500	perch, cichlid, damsel fish, gobie, wrass, parrotfish, gourami, marlin, mackerel, tuna, swordfish, spiny eel, mullet, barracuda, sea bream, croaker, ice fish, butterfish

British fisheries In terms of food production, British fisheries are almost entirely marine, and two of the main species that are caught in freshwater (salmon and eel) are ones that spend part of their lives in the sea. Increasing numbers of species are being caught and marketed. In addition to fish there are crustaceans (crabs, lobsters, prawns, and shrimps) and molluscs (whelks, winkles, scallops, oysters, mussels, cockles, and squid). In the UK, the North Sea is overall the most important fishing area, and is the source of most of the haddock and plaice landed at UK ports, as well as many other species.

In 1995 the British government doubled its compensation fund for decommissioned British boats. Under the EU's common fisheries policy, Britain was obliged to open its fishing waters to Spanish trawlers and to reduce its own fishing fleet.

fission in physics, the splitting of a heavy atomic nucleus into two or more major fragments. It is accompanied by the emission of two or three neutrons and the release of large amounts of ◊nuclear energy.

Fission occurs spontaneously in nuclei of uranium-235, the main fuel used in nuclear reactors. However, the process can also be induced by bombarding nuclei with neutrons because a nucleus that has absorbed a neutron becomes unstable and soon splits. The neutrons released spontaneously by the fission of uranium nuclei may therefore be used in turn to induce further fissions, setting up a ◊chain reaction that must be controlled if it is not to result in a nuclear explosion.

❛In a real dark night of the soul it is always three o'clock in the morning, day after day.❜

F Scott Fitzgerald
'The Crack-Up'

fistula in medicine, an abnormal pathway developing between adjoining organs or tissues, or leading to the exterior of the body. A fistula developing between the bowel and the bladder, for instance, may give rise to urinary-tract infection by intestinal organisms.

fitness in genetic theory, a measure of the success with which a genetically determined character can spread in future generations. By convention, the normal character is assigned a fitness of one, and variants (determined by other ◊alleles) are then assigned fitness values relative to this. Those with fitness greater than one will spread more rapidly and will ultimately replace the normal allele; those with fitness less than one will gradually die out.

Fitzgerald Edward 1809–1883. English poet and translator. His poetic version of the *Rubaiyat of Omar Khayyám* 1859 (and often revised), with its resonant and melancholy tone, is more an original creation than a true translation. It is known throughout all the English-speaking countries and has passed through innumerable editions.

Fitzgerald Ella 1918–1996. US jazz singer. She is recognized as one of the finest, most lyrical voices in jazz, both in solo work and with big bands. She is celebrated for her smooth interpretations of George and Ira Gershwin and Cole Porter songs. Her first hit was 'A-Tisket, A-Tasket' 1938.

She excelled at scat singing (jazz singing with nonsense syllables) and was widely imitated in the 1950s and 1960s. Her albums include *Ella Fitzgerald Sings the Rodgers and Hart Songbook* and *Duke Ellington Songbook* in the 1950s, and *Ella and Louis* 1956 with trumpeter Louis Armstrong.

Fitzgerald F(rancis) Scott (Key) 1896–1940. US novelist and short-story writer. His early autobiographical novel *This Side of Paradise* 1920 made him known in the postwar society of the East Coast, and *The Great Gatsby* 1925 epitomizes the Jazz Age.

In 1924 he and his wife Zelda Sayre (1900–1948) moved to the French Riviera, where they became members of a fashionable group of expatriates. His other works include *Tender is the Night* 1934, *The Beautiful and the Damned* 1922, and *The Last Tycoon* (unfinished at his death).

FitzGerald Garret Michael 1926– . Irish politician, leader of the Fine Gael party 1977–87. As Taoiseach (prime minister) 1981–82 and 1982–87, he attempted to solve the Northern Ireland dispute, and participated in the ◊Anglo-Irish Agreement 1985. He tried to remove some of the overtly Catholic features of the constitution to make the Republic more attractive to Northern Protestants.

Fitzpatrick Sean 1963– . New Zealand rugby union player. He is the most-capped All Black of all time, first appearing for his country 1986, and has also made more international appearances than any other hooker in the history of the sport.

Fitzroy Robert 1805–1865. British vice admiral and meteorologist. In 1855 the Admiralty founded the Meteorological Office, which issued weather forecasts and charts, under his charge.

Five Dynasties and Ten Kingdoms chaotic period in Chinese history 907–960 between the ◊Han and ◊Song dynasties, during which regionally based military dictatorships contested for power. The five dynasties, none of which lasted longer than 16 years, were based mainly in N China and the ten kingdoms in the south.

five pillars of Islam the five duties required of every Muslim: repeating the creed, which affirms that Allah is the one God and Muhammad is his prophet; daily prayer or ◊salat; giving alms; fasting during the month of Ramadan; and, if not prevented by ill health or poverty, the hajj, or pilgrimage to Mecca, once in a lifetime.

fjord or ***fiord*** narrow sea inlet enclosed by high cliffs. Fjords are found in Norway, New Zealand, and western parts of Scotland. They are formed when an overdeepened U-shaped glacial valley is drowned by a rise in sea-level. At the mouth of the fjord there is a characteristic lip causing a shallowing of the water. This is due to reduced glacial erosion and the deposition of moraine at this point.

Fitzgerald US jazz singer Ella Fitzgerald with Frank Sinatra in 1969. Discovered at 16 in Harlem, she became famous as a jazz singer with the Chick Webb band in the 1930s before going solo. Her inventive and lucid style made her widely popular for her interpretations of American song standards. *Topham*

Fitzgerald US novelist and short story writer F Scott Fitzgerald with his wife Zelda and family. Their glamorous lives mirrored Fitzgerald's 'Jazz Age' novels, which featured high living, high spending socialites. Zelda ended her life in an asylum and Fitzgerald's alcoholism contributed to his early death from a heart attack. *Corbis*

Fiordland is the deeply indented SW coast of South Island, New Zealand; one of the most beautiful inlets is Milford Sound.

flaccidity in botany, the loss of rigidity (turgor) in plant cells, caused by loss of water from the central vacuole so that the cytoplasm no longer pushes against the cellulose cell wall. If this condition occurs throughout the plant then wilting is seen.

Flaccidity can be induced in the laboratory by immersing the plant cell in a strong saline solution. Water leaves the cell by ◊osmosis causing the vacuole to shrink. In extreme cases the actual cytoplasm pulls away from the cell wall, a phenomenon known as plasmolysis.

flag in botany, another name for ◊iris, especially yellow flag *Iris pseudacorus*, which grows wild in damp places throughout Europe; it is a true water plant but adapts to border conditions. It has a thick rhizome, stiff, bladelike, monocotyledonous leaves, and stems up to 150 cm/5 ft high. The flowers are large and yellow.

flag piece of cloth used as an emblem or symbol for nationalistic, religious, or military displays, or as a means of signalling. Flags have been used since ancient times. Many localities and public bodies, as well as shipping lines, schools, and yacht clubs, have their own distinguishing flags.

symbolism The Stars and Stripes, also called Old Glory, is the flag of the USA; the 50 stars on a field of blue represent the 50 states now in the Union, and the 13 red and white stripes represent the 13 original colonies. Each state also has its own flag. The US presidential standard displays the American eagle, surrounded by 50 stars.

The British national flag, the Union Jack, unites the crosses of St George, St Andrew, and St Patrick, representing England, Scotland, and Ireland. The flags of Australia and New Zealand both incorporate the Union Jack, together with symbols of the Southern Cross constellation.

The Danish *Dannebrog* ('strength of Denmark') is the oldest national flag, used for 700 years. The Swiss flag inspired the Red Cross flag with colours reversed. Muslim states often incorporate in their flags the crescent emblem of Islam and the colour green, also associated with their faith. Similarly Israel uses the Star of David and the colour blue.

The flag of the former USSR placed the crossed hammer and sickle, which represented the workers of town and country, on a red field, the emblem of revolution.

signals A flag is flown upside down to indicate distress; is dipped as a salute; and is flown at half-mast to show mourning. The 'Blue Peter', blue with a white centre, announces that a vessel is about to sail; a flag half red and half white, that a pilot is on board. A yellow flag means 'plague'.

flagellant religious person who uses a whip on him- or herself as a means of penance. Flagellation was practised in many religions from ancient times; notable outbreaks of this type of extremist devotion occurred in Christian Europe in the 11th–16th centuries.

flagellum small hairlike organ on the surface of certain cells. Flagella are the motile organs of certain protozoa and single-celled algae, and of the sperm cells of higher animals. Unlike ◊cilia, flagella usually occur singly or in pairs; they are also longer and have a more complex whiplike action. Each flagellum consists of contractile filaments producing snakelike movements that propel cells through fluids, or fluids past cells. Water movement inside sponges is also produced by flagella.

flag of convenience national flag flown by a ship that has registered in that country in order to avoid legal or tax commitments (also known as offshore registry). Flags of convenience are common in the merchant fleets of Liberia and Panama; ships registered in these countries avoid legislation governing, for example, employment of sailors and minimum rates of pay.

In 1995 75 million gross tonnes of shipping was registered in Panama, making it the world's largest merchant fleet. Ships registered under flags of convenience accounted in 1993 for 34% of the world's fleet but 60% of all maritime accidents.

Less than one-third of British shipping is registered in Britain.

Flaherty Robert Joseph 1884–1951. US film director. He was one of the pioneers of documentary filmmaking. He exerted great influence through his pioneer documentary of Inuit life, *Nanook of the North* 1922, a critical and commercial success.

Later films include *Moana* 1926, a South Seas documentary; *Man of Aran* 1934, *Elephant Boy* 1936, and the Standard Oil-sponsored *Louisiana Story* 1948. Critics subsequently raised questions about the truthfulness of his documentary method.

Flamboyant in French architecture, the Late Gothic style contemporary with the ◊Perpendicular style in England. It is characterized by flamelike decorative work in windows, balustrades, and other projecting features.

flame angry ◊electronic mail message. Users of the ◊Internet use flames to express disapproval of breaches of ◊netiquette or the voicing of an unpopular opinion. An offensive message posted to, for example, a ◊newsgroup, will cause those offended to flame the culprit.

flamenco music and dance of the Andalusian gypsies of S Spain, evolved from Andalusian and Arabic folk music. The *cante* (song) is sometimes performed as a solo but more often accompanied by guitar music and passionate improvised dance. Hand clapping, finger clicking (castanets are a more recent addition), and enthusiastic shouts are all features. Male flamenco dancers excel in powerful, rhythmic footwork while the female dancers place emphasis on the graceful and erotic movements of their hands and bodies.

flame test in chemistry, the use of a flame to identify metal ◊cations present in a solid.

A nichrome or platinum wire is moistened with acid, dipped in a compound of the element, either powdered or in solution, and then held in a hot flame. The colour produced in the flame is characteristic of metals present; for example, sodium burns with an orange-yellow flame, and potassium with a lilac one.

flamingo long-legged and long-necked wading bird, family Phoenicopteridae, of the stork order Ciconiiformes. Largest of the family is the greater or roseate flamingo *Phoenicopterus ruber*, found in Africa, the Caribbean, and South America, with delicate pink plumage and 1.25 m/4 ft tall. They sift the mud for food with their downbent bills, and build colonies of high, conelike mud nests, with a little hollow for the eggs at the top. *See illustration on following page.*

Flaminius Gaius died 217 BC. Roman consul and general. He constructed the Flaminian Way northward from Rome to Rimini 220 BC, and was killed at the battle of Lake Trasimene fighting ◊Hannibal.

Flamsteed John 1646–1719. English astronomer. He began systematic observations of the positions of the stars, Moon, and planets at the Royal Observatory he founded at Greenwich, London, 1676. His observations were published in *Historia Coelestis Britannica* 1725.

As the first Astronomer Royal of England, Flamsteed determined the latitude of Greenwich, the slant of the ecliptic, and the position of the equinox. He also worked out a method of observing the absolute right ascension (a coordinate of the position of a heavenly body) that removed all errors of parallax, refraction, and latitude. Having obtained the positions of 40 reference stars, he then computed positions for the rest of the 3,000 stars in his catalogue.

Flanders region of the Low Countries that in the 8th and 9th centuries extended from Calais to the Scheldt and is now covered by the Belgian provinces of Oost Vlaanderen and West Vlaanderen (East and West Flanders), the French *département* of Nord, and part of the Dutch province of Zeeland. The language is Flemish. East Flanders, capital Ghent, has an area of 3,000 sq km/1,158 sq mi and a population (1995) of 1,349,400. West Flanders, capital Bruges, has an area of 3,100 sq km/1,197 sq mi and a population (1995) of 1,121,100.

history It was settled by Salian Franks as Roman allies 358, and in the 6th century, became a province of the Frankish kingdom. Baldwin I (died 879), the son-in-law of Charles the Bald, became its first count 862. During the following 300 years, the county resisted Norman encroachment, expanded its territory, and became a leading centre of the wool industry. In 1194, Philip II married the niece of Count Philip of Alsace (1143–1191), and so began a period of active French involvement in the county.

There was friction within Flemish society between the pro-French bourgeoisie and nobility and the craftworkers in the towns who supported the English, their major partners in the wool trade. In 1302, the craftworkers seized power in Bruges and Ghent and defeated the French at Courtrai, but the pro-French faction regained control of the county 1328. During the Hundred Years' War, Edward III of England put a trade embargo on Flemish wool, which caused serious economic depression, and led to further popular revolts, which were finally put down at the battle of Roosebeke 1382 by the French. The last count, Louis de Male, died 1384, and the county was inherited by his son-in-law, Philip the Bold of Burgundy (1342–1404), to become part of the Burgundian domains.

Flanders underwent a decline under Austrian rule in the 17th to 19th centuries. Fierce battles were fought here in World War I, such as the Battle of ◊Ypres. In World War II the Battle of Flanders began with the German breakthrough 10 May 1940 and ended with the British amphibious retreat from Dunkirk 27 May–4 June.

flare, solar brilliant eruption on the Sun above a ◊sunspot, thought to be caused by release of magnetic energy. Flares reach maximum brightness within a few minutes, then fade away over about an hour. They eject a burst of atomic particles into space at up to 1,000 kps/600 mps. When these particles reach Earth they can cause radio blackouts, disruptions of the Earth's magnetic field, and ◊aurorae. *See illustration on following page.*

flash flood flood of water in a normally arid area brought on by a sudden downpour of rain. Flash floods are rare and usually occur in mountainous areas. They may travel many kilometres from the site of the rainfall.

Flash Gordon comic strip character created by US cartoonist Alex Raymond 1934. Flash, a Yale graduate and astronaut, starred in outer space adventures with his female companion Dale Arden. He travelled in Dr Zarkov's home-made rocketship to thwart evil warlock Ming the Merciless, emperor of the planet Mongo. His exploits were featured in three Hollywood serials featuring US actor Buster Crabbe, the first of which, *Flash Gordon*, appeared 1936, followed by *Flash Gordon's Trip to Mars* 1938 and *Flash Gordon Conquers the Universe* 1940.

flat in music, a note or a key that is played lower in pitch than the written value, indicated by a flat sign or key signature. It can also refer to inaccurate intonation by a player.

flatfish bony fishes of the order Pleuronectiformes, having a characteristically flat, asymmetrical body with both eyes (in adults) on the upper side.

flamingo A flock of lesser flamingos wading in shallow water in South Africa. Lesser flamingos feed on blue-green algae. A flock may contain as many as one million birds, and can consume over 60 tons of algae in a year. *Corbis*

‘Everything one invents is true, you can be sure of that. Poetry is as exact a science as geometry.’

GUSTAVE FLAUBERT
Letter to Louise Colet 1853

Species include flounders, turbots, halibuts, plaice, and the European soles.

flatworm invertebrate of the phylum Platyhelminthes. Some are free-living, but many are parasitic (for example, tapeworms and flukes). The body is simple and bilaterally symmetrical, with one opening to the intestine. Many are hermaphroditic (with both male and female sex organs) and practise self-fertilization.

Flaubert Gustave 1821–1880. French writer. One of the major novelists of the 19th century, he was the author of *Madame Bovary* 1857, *Salammbô* 1862, *L'Education sentimentale/Sentimental Education* 1869, and *La Tentation de Saint Antoine/The Temptation of St Anthony* 1874. Flaubert also wrote the short stories *Trois Contes/Three Tales* 1877. His dedication to art resulted in a meticulous prose style, realistic detail, and psychological depth, which is often revealed through interior monologue.

Flaubert was born in Rouen. From 1846 until 1854 he was the lover of Louise Colet (c. 1467–1519), but his unrequited love, at the age of 15, for Mme Elisa Schlesinger had more influence on his character.

Madame Bovary, which took many years to prepare, caused a great scandal, and the author and publisher were prosecuted on a charge of violating morals, but were acquitted. In 1858 Flaubert travelled to Carthage and began a serious archaeological and historical study of its surroundings, which he made use of in his second work, *Salammbô*. He became a distinguished member of a small literary set, which included Turgenev, Zola, Daudet, and the Goncourts, and was a personal friend of George Sand.

flare, solar A solar flare is discharged by the Sun. The cloud which billows from the Sun is accompanied by the release of huge amounts of energy including atomic particles. These particles reach Earth hours later dissipating more energy into the high atmosphere than the most destructive hurricanes on record. *Image Select (UK) Ltd*

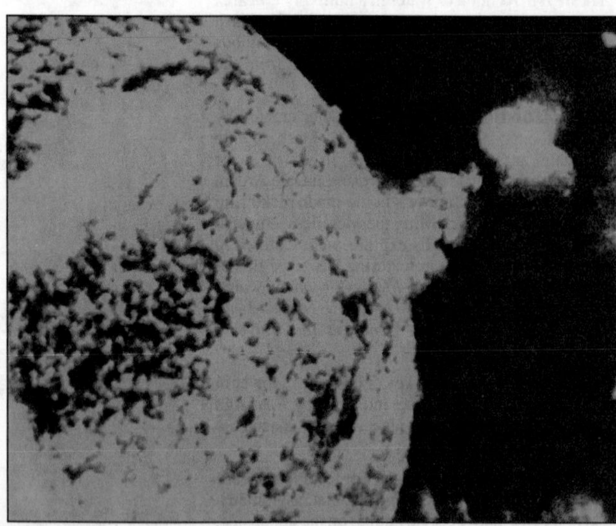

flax any plant of the genus *Linum*, family Linaceae. The species *L. usitatissimum* is the cultivated strain; linen is produced from the fibre in its stems. The seeds yield linseed oil, used in paints and varnishes. The plant, of almost worldwide distribution, has a stem up to 60 cm/24 in high, small leaves, and bright blue flowers.

The residue of the seeds is fed to cattle. The stems are retted (soaked) in water after harvesting, and then dried, rolled, and scutched (pounded), separating the fibre from the central core of woody tissue. The long fibres are spun into linen thread, twice as strong as cotton, yet more delicate, and suitable for lace; shorter fibres are used to make twine or paper.

Russia, Ukraine, Belarus, and Latvia account for half of the total world production of flax. Other producers are Belgium, the Netherlands, and N Ireland.

Flaxman John 1755–1826. English sculptor and illustrator. His Neo-Classical works had a profound effect on English taste. He initially worked for the ◊Wedgwood pottery as a designer, but later turned to illustration and to monumental sculpture. His public works include the monuments to Admiral Nelson and the painter Joshua Reynolds in St Paul's Cathedral, London; and to the Scottish poet Robert Burns in Westminster Abbey.

flea wingless insect of the order Siphonaptera, with blood-sucking mouthparts. Fleas are parasitic on warm-blooded animals. Some fleas can jump 130 times their own height.

Species include the human flea *Pulex irritans*; the rat flea *Xenopsylla cheopsis*, the transmitter of plague and typhus; and (fostered by central heating) the cat and dog fleas *Ctenocephalides felis* and *C. canis*.

fleabane plant of the genera *Erigeron* or *Pulicaria*, family Compositae. Common fleabane *P. dysenterica* has golden-yellow flower heads and grows in wet and marshy places throughout Europe.

Fleischer Max 1889–1972. Austrian-born US cartoonist. With his younger brother, Dave (1894–1972), as director, Fleischer animated and produced cartoon films from 1917. His first major series was *Out of the Inkwell* 1918 starring Koko the Clown. He created the long-running characters Betty Boop and Popeye. His feature films include *Gulliver's Travels* 1939 and *Superman* 1941.

Fleming Alexander 1881–1955. Scottish bacteriologist who discovered the first antibiotic drug, ◊penicillin, in 1928. In 1922 he had discovered lysozyme, an antibacterial enzyme present in saliva, nasal secretions, and tears. While studying this, he found an unusual mould growing on a neglected culture dish, which he isolated and grew into a pure culture; this led to his discovery of penicillin. It came into use in 1941. In 1945 he won the Nobel Prize for Physiology or Medicine with Howard W ◊Florey and Ernst B ◊Chain, whose research had brought widespread realization of the value of penicillin.

Fleming Ian Lancaster 1908–1964. English author. His suspense novels feature the ruthless, laconic James Bond, British Secret Service agent 007. The first novel in the series was *Casino Royale* 1953; others include *From Russia with Love* 1957, *Goldfinger* 1959, and *The Man with the Golden Gun*

Fleming Scottish bacteriologist Alexander Fleming in 1943. Fleming's discovery of penicillin was a classic example of a scientist noting and investigating all observations, even (as here) an unexpected one. Fleming noticed that a mould growing on a culture dish inhibited the growth of bacteria. Isolated and purified, the mould produced penicillin. Commercial production of penicillin was encouraged during World War II. *Topham*

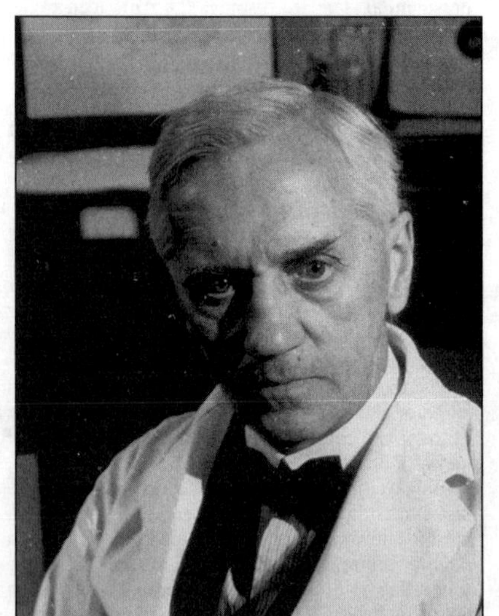

1965. Most of the novels were made into successful films.

Flemish member of the W Germanic branch of the Indo-European language family, spoken in N Belgium and the Nord *département* of France. It is closely related to Dutch.

In opposition to the introduction of French as the official language in the Flemish provinces of Belgium after 1830, a strong Flemish movement arose. Although equality of French and Flemish was not achieved until 1898, it brought about a cultural and political revival of Flemish.

Flemish art painting and sculpture of Flanders (now divided between Belgium, the Netherlands, and France). A distinctive Flemish style emerged in the early 15th century based on manuscript illumination and the art of the Burgundian court. It is distinguished by keen observation, minute attention to detail, bright colours, and superb technique – oil painting was a Flemish invention.

15th century During the 14th century painters in Flanders still worked in the French miniature style. This was transformed into a brilliant school of national art in the 15th century by Hubert and Jan van Eyck, who made Bruges the first centre of Flemish art. The great names of the early period were Robert Campin, Rogier van der Weyden, Dierick Bouts, Petrus Christus, Hugo van der Goes, Hans Memling, and Gerard David. The works of this period were mostly religious, though there were also a few outstanding portraits. A closely observed realism, a fascination with rich materials and fabrics, and an elaborate religious symbolism characterize the period.

16th century Italian influences became strongly felt, and the centre of art production shifted to Antwerp. An important figure is Jan Gossaert, called Mabuse, who changed the whole spirit of Flemish art by Italianizing it under the influence of the work of Leonardo da Vinci and Michelangelo.

Contemporary with Mabuse, however, were painters who defied or ignored the Italian influence. One was the extraordinary painter (who must be classified with the Flemish school, though technically Dutch) Hieronymus Bosch, whose fantasy and strange symbolism are strikingly original. Another was Joachim Patenier, the artist who first painted landscape for its own sake – not merely as a background or irrespective of its inherently exciting or dramatic qualities.

17th century Peter Paul Rubens excelled in every branch of his art, in portraiture, landscape, religious, mythological, and allegorical subjects. For nearly a century the Flemish school of art may be said to have been a reflection of the principles of Rubens. The young Anthony van Dyck worked in Rubens's workshop for two years. At the outset of his career van Dyck's power of conception was greatly superior to his refined taste as a portrait painter. His influence on portraiture would be felt throughout Europe, but especially in England.

David Teniers the Younger and David Teniers the Elder, together with many minor artists, continued the strong tradition of genre painting. Other 17th-century painters are Frans Snyders, painter of animals and of battle-pieces; Casper de Crayer, whose chief works are altarpieces; Adriaen Brouwer, whose humourous genre scenes combined Dutch and Flemish styles; Jakob Jordaens who, after Rubens's death, was the acknowledged leader of the Antwerp school; Gonzales Coques, a pupil of Pieter Brueghel, who excelled in portraiture, taking van Dyck as his model; and Peter Lely, a portrait painter who worked at the English court.

18th–19th centuries Flemish art declined rapidly after the 17th century, and in the 18th century only two painters are noteworthy: Cornelius Huysmans (1648–1727) and Jan van Bloemen, known as 'Orizonte'.

20th century Modern Belgian art at its best has turned to the irrational, with painters deriving their strength from Expressionism and Surrealism. Ensor painted the thronging crowds and masks of dreams, his bitter satires looking back to Bosch. The Surrealists Paul Delvaux and René Magritte, on the other hand, created dream worlds depicted in a cold realism that echoes back to the earliest masters of the Flemish school.

Fletcher Andrew of Saltoun 1655–1716. Scottish patriot, the most outspoken critic of the Union of Scotland with England of 1707. He advocated an independent Scotland, and a republic or limited monarchy, and proposed 'limitations' to the treaty, such as annual Parliaments. After the Treaty of Union he retired to private life.

Fletcher John 1579–1625. English dramatist. He is remarkable for his range, which included tragicomedy and pastoral dramas, in addition to comedy and tragedy. He collaborated with Francis ◊Beaumont in some 12 plays, producing, most notably, the tragicomedies *Philaster* 1610 and *The Maid's Tragedy* about 1611. He is alleged to have collaborated with ◊Shakespeare on *The Two Noble Kinsmen* and *Henry VIII* 1613.

Among some 16 plays credited to Fletcher alone are the pastoral drama *The Faithful Shepherdess* 1610, the tragedy *Bonduca* about 1611–14, *Valentinian* 1618, *Monsieur Thomas*, *The Humorous Lieutenant* both 1619, *The Chances* 1620, *The Pilgrim*, and the comedy *The Wild Goose Chase* both 1621.

'Death hath so many doors to let out life.'

John Fletcher Beaumont and Fletcher *The Customs of the Country*

fleur-de-lis (French 'flower of the lily') heraldic device in the form of a stylized iris flower, borne on coats of arms since the 12th century and adopted by the French royal house of Bourbon.

flexor any muscle that bends a limb. Flexors usually work in opposition to other muscles, the extensors, an arrangement known as antagonistic.

flight or ***aviation*** method of transport in which aircraft carry people and goods through the air. People first took to the air in ◊balloons and began powered flight 1852 in ◊airships, but the history of flying, both for civilian and military use, is dominated by the ◊aeroplane. The earliest planes were designed for ◊gliding; the advent of the petrol engine saw the first powered flight by the ◊Wright brothers 1903 in the USA. This inspired the development of aircraft throughout Europe. Biplanes were succeeded by monoplanes in the 1930s. The first jet plane (see ◊jet propulsion) was produced 1939, and after the end of World War II the development of jetliners brought about a continuous expansion in passenger air travel. In 1969 came the supersonic aircraft ◊Concorde.

history In the 14th century the English philosopher Roger Bacon spoke of constructing an aircraft by means of a hollow globe and liquid fire. He was followed in the 15th century by Albert of Saxony, who also spoke of balloon flight by means of fire in a light sphere.

early ideas Francisco de Lana in 1670 proposed that four hollow balls made of very thin brass should be emptied of air. To them should be attached a small boat and sail, and in that way a balloon would be contrived which could carry a person. The idea was not feasible, since the globes, made of brass only 0.1 mm thick, would have collapsed by reason of their own weight. But although de Lana saw this difficulty, he argued that their shape would prevent that.

balloons It was not until the next century that the real ◊balloon was invented. The beginning of the development of the balloon was the work of two brothers, Joseph and Etienne ◊Montgolfier, who came to the conclusion that a paper bag filled with a 'substance of a cloud-like nature' would float in the atmosphere. Progress was made gradually, and the first person-carrying ascent took place in October 1783, when Pilatre de Rozier went up in a Montgolfier captive balloon. The first woman to ascend was Madame Thible, who went up from Lyons in 1784. In 1859 a flight of over 1,600 km/994 mi was made in the USA.

adding power From 1897 the development of the airship was the special work of Ferdinand ◊Zeppelin. In 1900 he made his first flight with a dirigible balloon carrying five men. It was made of aluminium, supported by gas-bags, and driven by two motors, each of about 12 kW. His third experiment was a great success. This airship carried 11 passengers and attained a speed of about 55 kph/34 mph, travelling about 400 km/248 mi in 11 hours, but was wrecked by a storm in 1908, caught fire, and was completely destroyed.

early gliders In the late 19th century experiments were being made with soaring machines and hang gliders, chiefly by Otto ◊Lilienthal, who, with an arrangement formed on the plan of birds' wings, attempted to imitate their 'soaring flight'. Following up Lilienthal's ideas, the ◊Wright brothers produced their first aeroplane in 1903. In 1908 they went to France where Wilbur Wright created a record by remaining in the air for over an hour while carrying a passenger. He also attained a speed of 60 kph/37 mph.

powered flight In Europe, at the beginning of the 20th century, France led in aeroplane design and Louis ◊Blériot brought aviation much publicity by crossing the Channel 1909, as did the Reims air races of that year. The first powered flight in the UK was made by Samuel Franklin Cody (1862–1913) 1908. In 1912 Sopwith and Bristol both built small biplanes. The first big twin-engined aeroplane was the Handley Page bomber 1917. The stimulus of World War I (1914–18) and rapid development of the petrol engine led to increased power, and speeds rose to 320 kph/200 mph. Streamlining the body of planes became imperative: the body, wings, and exposed parts were reshaped to reduce drag. Eventually the biplane was superseded by the internally braced monoplane structure, for example, the Hawker Hurricane and Supermarine Spitfire fighters and Avro Lancaster and Boeing Flying Fortress bombers of World War II (1939–45).

jet aircraft The German Heinkel 178, built 1939, was the first jet plane; it was driven, not by a ◊propeller as all planes before it, but by a jet of hot gases. The first British jet aircraft, the Gloster E.28/39, flew from Cranwell, Lincolnshire, on 15 May 1941, powered by a jet engine invented by British engineer Frank Whittle. Twin-jet Meteor fighters were in use by the end of the war. The rapid development of the jet plane led to enormous increases in power and speed until air-compressibility effects were felt near the speed of sound, which at first seemed to be a flight speed limit (the sound barrier). To attain ◊supersonic speed, streamlining the aircraft body became insufficient: wings

flight US aviation pioneers Orville (with his back to the camera) and Wilbur Wright shown flying their home-made glider on the sands of Kitty Hawk, North Carolina in 1900. The small extra 'wing' above their heads is the glider's rudder: attached to the front of the aircraft, it gave the glider fore and aft balance. Also included in the design were controls for warping the wings to improve control and stability. *Image Select (UK) Ltd/Exley*

FLIGHT: TIMELINE

1783	First human flight, by Jean F Pilâtre de Rozier and the Marquis d'Arlandes, in Paris, using a hot-air balloon made by Joseph and Etienne Montgolfier; first ascent in a hydrogen-filled balloon by Jacques Charles and M N Robert in Paris.
1785	Jean-Pierre Blanchard and John J Jeffries made the first balloon crossing of the English Channel.
1852	Henri Giffard flew the first steam-powered airship over Paris.
1853	George Cayley flew the first true aeroplane, a model glider 1.5 m/5 ft long.
1891–96	Otto Lilienthal piloted a glider in flight.
1903	First powered and controlled flight of a heavier-than-air craft (aeroplane) by Orville Wright, at Kitty Hawk, North Carolina, USA.
1908	First powered flight in the UK by Samuel Cody.
1909	Louis Blériot flew across the English Channel in 36 minutes.
1914–18	World War I stimulated improvements in speed and power.
1919	First E–W flight across the Atlantic by Albert C Read, using a flying boat; first nonstop flight across the Atlantic E–W by John William Alcock and Arthur Whitten Brown in 16 hours 27 minutes; first complete flight from Britain to Australia by Ross Smith and Keith Smith.
1923	Juan de la Cieva flew the first autogiro with a rotating wing.
1927	Charles Lindbergh made the first W–E solo nonstop flight across the Atlantic.
1928	First transpacific flight, from San Francisco to Brisbane, by Charles Kinsford Smith and C T P Ulm.
1930	Frank Whittle patented the jet engine; Amy Johnson became the first woman to fly solo from England to Australia.
1937	The first fully pressurized aircraft, the Lockheed XC-35, came into service.
1939	Erich Warsitz flew the first Heinkel jet plane, in Germany; Igor Sikorsky designed the first helicopter, with a large main rotor and a smaller tail rotor.
1939–45	World War II – developments included the Hawker Hurricane and Supermarine Spitfire Fighters, and Avro Lancaster and Boeing Flying Fortress bombers.
1947	A rocket-powered plane, the Bell X-1, was the first aircraft to fly faster than the speed of sound.
1949	The de Havilland Comet, the first jet airliner, entered service; James Gallagher made the first nonstop round-the-world flight, in a Boeing Superfortress.
1953	The first vertical takeoff aircraft, the Rolls-Royce 'Flying Bedstead', was tested.
1968	The world's first supersonic airliner, the Russian TU-144, flew for the first time.
1970	The Boeing 747 jumbo jet entered service, carrying 500 passengers.
1976	Anglo-French Concorde, making a transatlantic crossing in under three hours, came into commercial service. A Lockheed SR-17A, piloted by Eldon W Joersz and George T Morgan, set the world air-speed record of 3,529.56 kph/2,193.167 mph over Beale Air Force Base, California, USA.
1978	A US team made the first transatlantic crossing by balloon, in the helium-filled *Double Eagle II*.
1979	First crossing of the English Channel by a human-powered aircraft, *Gossamer Albatross*, piloted by Bryan Allen.
1981	The solar-powered *Solar Challenger* flew across the English Channel, from Paris to Kent, taking 5 hours for the 262 km/162.8 mi journey.
1986	Dick Rutan and Jeana Yeager made the first nonstop flight around the world without refuelling, piloting *Voyager*, which completed the flight in 9 days 3 minutes 44 seconds.
1987	Richard Branson and Per Lindstrand made the first transatlantic crossing by hot-air balloon, in *Virgin Atlantic Challenger*.
1988	*Daedelus*, a human-powered craft piloted by Kanellos Kanellopoulos, flew 118 km/74 mi across the Aegean Sea.
1992	US engineers demonstrated a model radio-controlled ornithopter, the first aircraft to be successfully propelled and manoeuvred by flapping wings.
1993	The US Federal Aviation Authority made the use of an automatic on-board collision avoidance system (TCAS-2) mandatory in US airspace.
1994	The US Boeing 777 airliner makes its first flight. A scale model scramjet (supersonic combustion ramjet) is tested and produces speeds of 9,000 kph/5,590 mph (Mach 8.2).
1998	Swiss balloonist Bertrand Piccard sets a record for the longest non-stop, non-refuelled flight by an aircraft: 9 days, 17 hours and, 55 minutes.

were swept back, engines buried in wings and tail units, and bodies were even eliminated in all-wing delta designs. In the 1950s the first jet airliners, such as the Comet (first introduced 1949), were introduced into service. The late 1960s saw the introduction of the ◊jumbo jet, and in 1976 the Anglo-French Concorde, which makes a transatlantic crossing in under three hours, came into commercial service.

other developments During the 1950s and 1960s research was done on V/STOL (vertical and/or short take-off) aircraft. The British Harrier jet fighter has been the only VTOL aircraft to achieve commercial success, but STOL technology has fed into subsequent generations of aircraft. The 1960s and 1970s also saw the development of variable geometry ('swing-wing') aircraft, the wings of which can be swept back in flight to achieve higher speeds. In the 1980s much progress was made in 'fly-by-wire' aircraft with computer-aided controls. International partnerships have developed both civilian and military aircraft. The Panavia Tornado is a joint project of British, German, and Italian aircraft companies. It is an advanced swing-wing craft of multiple roles – interception, strike, ground support, and reconnaissance. The airbus is a wide-bodied airliner built jointly by companies from France, Germany, the UK, the Netherlands, and Spain.

flight simulator computer-controlled pilot-training device, consisting of an artificial cockpit mounted on hydraulic legs, that simulates the experience of flying a real aircraft. Inside the cockpit, the trainee pilot views a screen showing a computer-controlled projection of the view from a real aircraft, and makes appropriate adjustments to the controls. The computer monitors these adjustments, changes both the alignment of the cockpit on its hydraulic legs, and the projected view seen by the pilot, so a trainee pilot can progress to an advanced stage of training without leaving the ground.

Flinders Matthew 1774–1814. English navigator who explored the Australian coasts 1795–99 and 1801–03. Named after him are Flinders Island, NE of Tasmania, Australia; the Flinders Range in S Australia; and Flinders River in Queensland.

flint compact, hard, brittle mineral (a variety of chert), brown, black, or grey in colour, found in nodules in limestone or shale deposits. It consists of fine-grained silica, SiO_2 (usually ◊quartz), in cryptocrystalline form. Flint implements were widely used in prehistory. When chipped, the flint nodules show a conchoidal (shell-like) fracture and a sharp cutting edge. The earliest flint implements, belonging to Palaeolithic cultures and made by striking one flint against another, are simple, while those of the Neolithic are expertly chipped and formed, and are often ground or polished.

Flintshire unitary authority of Wales created 1996 (*see United Kingdom map*).

Flintstones, the cartoon comedy series appearing on television created by US animators William Hanna and Joseph Barbera 1960. It featured Stone Age caveman Fred Flintstone and his half-wit neighbour Barney Rubble, together with their wives Wilma and Betty leading anachronistic 20th-century lives in the town of Bedrock. Fred's cry of 'Yabba dabba doo!' became his catchphrase.

Flodden, Battle of the defeat of the Scots by the English under the Earl of Surrey 9 Sept 1513 on a site, 5 km/3 mi SE of Coldstream, in Northumberland, England.

Flood, the in the Old Testament, the Koran, and *The Epic of Gilgamesh* (an ancient Sumerian legend), a deluge lasting 40 days and nights, a disaster alleged to have obliterated all humanity except a chosen few (in the Old Testament, the survivors were the family of ◊Noah and the pairs of animals sheltered on his ark).

The story may represent legends of a major local flood; for example, excavations at Ur in Iraq revealed 2.5 m/8 ft of water-laid clay dating from before 4000 BC, over an area of about 645 km/400 mi by 160 km/100 mi.

flooding the inundation of land that is not normally covered with water. Flooding from rivers commonly takes place after heavy rainfall or in the spring after winter snows have melted. The river's discharge (volume of water carried in a given period) becomes too great, and water spills over the banks onto the surrounding flood plain. Small floods may happen once a year – these are called annual floods and are said to have a one-year return period. Much larger floods may occur on average only once every 50 years.

Flooding is least likely to occur in an efficient channel that is semicircular in shape. Flooding can also occur at the coast in stormy conditions or when there is an exceptionally high tide. The Thames Flood Barrier was constructed in 1982 to prevent the flooding of London from the sea.

flood plain area of periodic flooding along the course of river valleys. When river discharge exceeds the capacity of the channel, water rises over the channel banks and floods the adjacent low-lying lands. As water spills out of the channel some alluvium (silty material) will be deposited on the banks to form ◊levees (raised river banks). This water will seep into the flood plain, depositing a new layer of rich fertile alluvium as it does so. Floodplain features include ◊meanders and ◊oxbow lakes.

Many important floodplains, such as the inner Niger delta in Mali, occur in arid areas where their exceptional productivity has great importance for the local economy.

floppy disk in computing, a storage device consisting of a light, flexible disk enclosed in a cardboard or plastic jacket. The disk is placed in a disk drive, where it rotates at high speed. Data are recorded magnetically on one or both surfaces.

Floppy disks were invented by IBM in 1971 as a means of loading programs into the computer. They were originally 8 in/20 cm in diameter and typically held about 240 kilobytes of data. Present-day floppy disks, widely used on ◊microcomputers, are usually either 5.25 in/13.13 cm or 3.5 in/8.8 cm in diameter, and generally hold 0.5–2 ◊megabytes, depending on the disk size, recording method, and whether one or both sides are used.

Flora in Roman mythology, the goddess of flowers, youth, and spring.

Florence (Italian ***Firenze***) capital of ◊Tuscany, N Italy, 88 km/55 mi from the mouth of the river Arno; population (1992) 397,400. It has printing, engineering, and optical industries; many crafts, including leather, gold and silver work, and embroidery; and its art and architecture attract large numbers of tourists. Notable medieval and Renaissance citizens included the writers Dante and Boccaccio, and the

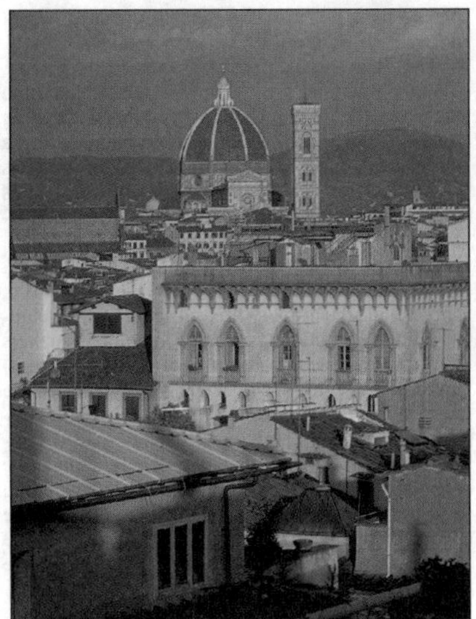

Florence A view over central Florence, Italy, showing the Duomo and campanile. *Image Select (UK) Ltd*

artists Giotto, Leonardo da Vinci, and Michelangelo.
features Florence's architectural treasures include the Ponte Vecchio (1345); the Pitti and Vecchio palaces; the churches of Santa Croce and Santa Maria Novella; the cathedral of Santa Maria del Fiore (1314); and the Uffizi Gallery, which has one of Europe's finest art collections, based on that of the Medicis.
history The Roman town of Florentia was founded in the 1st century BC on the site of the Etruscan town of Faesulae. It was besieged by the Goths AD 405 and visited by Charlemagne 786.

In 1052, Florence passed to Countess Matilda of Tuscany (1046–1115), and from the 11th century onwards gained increasing autonomy. In 1198 it became an independent republic, with new city walls, and governed by a body of 12 citizens. In the 13th–14th centuries, the city was the centre of the struggle between the Guelphs (papal supporters) and Ghibellines (supporters of the Holy Roman emperor). Despite this, Florence became immensely prosperous and went on to reach its cultural peak during the 14th–16th centuries.

From the 15th to the 18th century, the ◊Medici family, originally bankers, were the predominant power, in spite of their having been twice expelled by revolutions. In the first of these, in 1493, a year after Lorenzo de' Medici's death, a republic was proclaimed (with ◊Machiavelli as secretary) that lasted until 1512. From 1494 to 1498, the city was under the control of religious reformer ◊Savonarola. In 1527, the Medicis again proclaimed a republic, which lasted through many years of gradual decline until 1737, when the city passed to Maria Theresa of Austria. The city was ruled by the Habsburg imperial dynasty 1737–1861, and was then the capital of Italy 1865–70. The city was badly damaged in World War II and by floods 1966.

Flores Juan José 1801–1864. Ecuadorian general, president 1830–35 and 1839–45. Born in Venezuela, he joined Simón ◊Bolívar's patriot army in his teens, and soon became one of its most trusted generals. Flores convoked the assembly declaring Ecuador's independence 1830 and was elected its first constitutional president the same year. During his two terms in office Ecuador was an oasis of stability in Spanish America.

floret small flower, usually making up part of a larger, composite flower head. There are often two different types present on one flower head: disc florets in the central area, and ray florets around the edge which usually have a single petal known as the ligule. In the common daisy, for example, the disc florets are yellow, while the ligules are white.

Florey Howard Walter, Baron Florey 1898–1968. Australian pathologist whose research into lysozyme, an antibacterial enzyme discovered by Alexander ◊Fleming, led him to study penicillin (another of Fleming's discoveries), which he and Ernst ◊Chain isolated and prepared for widespread use. With Fleming, they were awarded the Nobel Prize for Physiology or Medicine 1945.

Florida state of the extreme southeastern USA; mainly a peninsula jutting into the Atlantic, which it separates from the Gulf of Mexico; nicknamed Sunshine State
area 152,000 sq km/58,672 sq mi
capital Tallahassee
towns and cities Miami, Tampa, Jacksonville
population (1990) 12,937,900, one of the fastest-growing of the states; including 15% nonwhite; 10% Hispanic, (especially Cuban)
physical 50% forested; lakes (including Okeechobee 1,800 sq km/695 sq mi); Everglades national park (5,000 sq km/1,930 sq mi), with birdlife, mangrove and cypress forests, alligators
features lowlying, mostly less than 30 m/100 ft above sea level; Biscayne national park, a marine park with a living coral reef 320 km/200 mi long; Apalachia, Ocala, and Oscoela national forests; the Florida Keys, 31 islands between the Atlantic Ocean and the Gulf of Mexico, including Key Largo, with Crocodile Lakes national wildlife refuge; Tampa Bay; Fort Lauderdale; St Augustine, the oldest city in the USA; the Spanish fortress, Castillo de San Marcos national monument; Pensacola (1559) with Spanish colonial buildings; Key West, with 19th-century buildings; Tallahassee, with pre-Civil War plantation mansions; Miami, with Art Deco district; John F Kennedy Space Center, Cape Canaveral; Palm Beach island resort; beach resorts on Gulf and on Atlantic; Daytona International Speedway; Walt Disney World, and Epcot (Experimental Prototype Community of Tomorrow) Center; Universal Studios Florida
industries citrus fruits, melons, vegetables, fish, shellfish, phosphates, chemicals, electrical and electronic equipment, aircraft, fabricated metals
famous people Chris Evert, Henry Flagler, James Weldon Johnson, Sidney Poitier, Philip Randolph, Joseph Stilwell
history discovered by Ponce de Leon and under Spanish rule from 1513 until its cession to England 1763; returned to Spain 1783 and purchased by the USA 1819, becoming a state 1845.

Florida Keys series of small coral islands that curve over 240 km/150 mi SW from the southern tip of Florida. The most important are Key Largo and Key West (with a US naval and air station); they depend on fishing and tourism.

florin coin; many European countries have had coins of this name. The first florin was of gold, minted in Florence in 1252. The obverse bore the image of a lily, which led to the coin being called *fiorino* (from Italian *fiore*, flower).

The British florin of two shillings was first struck 1849, initially of silver, and continued in use after decimalization as the equivalent of the ten-pence piece until 1992.

flotation, law of law stating that a floating object displaces its own weight of the fluid in which it floats. See ◊Archimedes principle.

flotation process common method of preparing mineral ores for subsequent processing by making use of the different wetting properties of various components. The ore is finely ground and then mixed with water and a specially selected wetting agent. Air is bubbled through the mixture, forming a froth; the desired ore particles attach themselves to the bubbles and are skimmed off, while unwanted dirt or other ores remain behind.

flotsam, jetsam, and lagan in law, goods cast from ships at sea, due usually to the event or prevention of shipwreck. Flotsam is the debris or cargo found floating; jetsam is what has been thrown overboard to lighten a sinking vessel; lagan is cargo secured, as to a buoy, for future recovery.

flounder small flatfish *Platychthys flesus* of the NE Atlantic and Mediterranean, although it sometimes lives in estuaries. It is dull in colour and grows to 50 cm/1.6 ft.

flour foodstuff made by grinding starchy vegetable materials, usually cereal grains, into a fine powder. Flour may also be made from root vegetables such as potato and cassava, and from pulses such as soya beans and chick peas. The most commonly used cereal flour is wheat flour.

The properties of wheat flour depend on the strain of wheat used. Bread requires strong ('hard') flour, with a high ◊gluten content. Durum flour also has a high gluten content, and is used for pasta. Cakes and biscuits are made from weak ('soft') flour, containing less gluten. Granary flour contains malted flakes of wheat. Wheat flour may contain varying proportions of bran (husk) and wheatgerm (embryo), ranging from 100% wholemeal flour to refined white flour, which has less than 75% of the whole grain. Much of the flour available now is bleached to whiten it; bleaching also destroys some of its vitamin content, so synthetic vitamins are added instead.

Florida

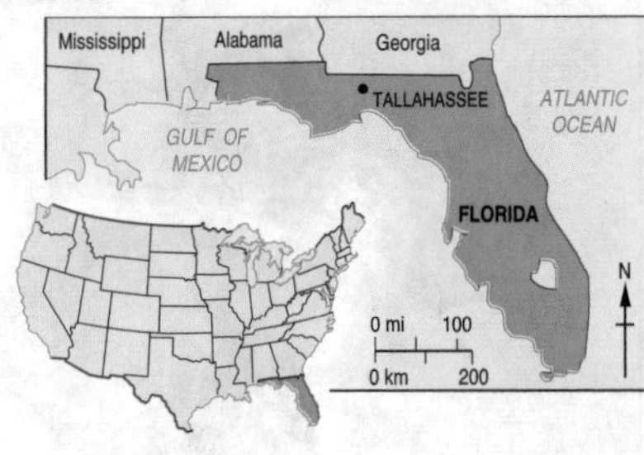

flower the reproductive unit of an ◊angiosperm or flowering ◊plant, typically consisting of four whorls of modified leaves: ◊sepals, ◊petals, ◊stamens, and ◊carpels. These are borne on a central axis or ◊receptacle. The many variations in size, colour, number, and arrangement of parts are closely related to the method of ◊pollination. Flowers adapted for wind pollination typically have reduced or absent petals and sepals and long, feathery ◊stigmas that hang outside the flower to trap airborne pollen. In contrast, the petals of insect-pollinated flowers are usually conspicuous and brightly coloured.

The sepals and petals form the calyx and corolla respectively and together comprise the perianth with the function of protecting the reproductive organs and attracting pollinators.

The stamens lie within the corolla, each having a slender stalk, or filament, bearing the pollen-containing anther at the top. Collectively they are known as the androecium (male organs). The inner whorl of the flower comprises the carpels, each usually consisting of an ◊ovary in which are borne the ◊ovules, and a stigma borne at the top of a slender stalk, or style. Collectively the carpels are known as the gynoecium (female organs).

In size, flowers range from the tiny blooms of duckweeds scarcely visible to the naked eye to the gigantic flowers of the Malaysian *Rafflesia*, which can reach over 1 m/3 ft across. Flowers may either be borne singly or grouped together in ◊inflorescences. The stalk of the whole inflorescence is termed a peduncle, and the stalk of an individual flower is termed a pedicel. A flower is termed hermaphrodite when it contains both male and female reproductive organs. When male and female organs are carried in separate flowers, they are termed monoecious; when male and female flowers are on separate plants, the term dioecious is used.

flowering plant term generally used for ◊angiosperms, which bear flowers with various parts, including sepals, petals, stamens, and carpels.

Sometimes the term is used more broadly, to include both angiosperms and ◊gymnosperms, in which case the ◊cones of conifers and cycads are referred to as 'flowers'. Usually, however, the angiosperms and gymnosperms are referred to collectively as ◊seed plants, or spermatophytes.

In 1996 UK palaeontologists found fossils in S England of what may be the world's oldest flowering plant. *Bevhalstia pebja*, a wetland herb about 25 cm/10 in high, has been dated as early Cretaceous, about 130 million years old.

flugelhorn alto valved brass band instrument of the bugle type. In B flat, it has a similar range to the cornet but is of mellower tone.

fluid mechanics the study of the behaviour of fluids (liquids and gases) at rest and in motion. Fluid mechanics is important in the study of the weather, the design of aircraft and road vehicles, and in industries, such as the chemical industry, which deal with flowing liquids or gases.

fluke any of various parasitic flatworms of the classes Monogenea and Digenea, that as adults live in and destroy the livers of sheep, cattle, horses, dogs, and humans. Monogenetic flukes complete

'In the distant plain lay Florence, pink and gray and brown, with the rusty huge dome of the cathedral dominating its center like a captive balloon ... this is the fairest picture on our planet ... the most satisfying to the eye and the spirit.'

On Florence
Mark Twain
Autobiography

flute The flute was described as 'transverse', as in this period drawing, in order to distinguish it from the recorder, which was also known as 'flute'. The instrument pictured is conical, a feature which persisted until the cylindrical design superseded it in the 19th century. *Antique Instruments*

their life cycle in one host; digenetic flukes require two or more hosts, for example a snail and a human being, to complete their life cycle.

An estimated 40 million people worldwide are infected by food-borne flukes, mostly from undercooked or raw fish or shellfish, according to a WHO report 1994.

fluorescence in scientific usage, very short-lived ◊luminescence (a glow not caused by high temperature). Generally, the term is used for any luminescence regardless of the persistence. ◊Phosphorescence lasts a little longer.

Fluorescence is used in strip and other lighting, and was developed rapidly during World War II because it was a more efficient means of illumination than the incandescent lamp. Recently, small bulb-size fluorescence lamps have reached the market. It is claimed that, if widely used, their greater efficiency could reduce demand for electricity. Other important applications are in fluorescent screens for television and cathode-ray tubes.

fluorescence microscopy technique for examining samples under a ◊microscope without slicing them into thin sections. Instead, fluorescent dyes are introduced into the tissue and used as a light source for imaging purposes. Fluorescent dyes can also be bonded to monoclonal antibodies and used to highlight areas where particular cell proteins occur.

fluoridation addition of small amounts of fluoride salts to drinking water by certain water authorities to help prevent tooth decay. Experiments in Britain, the USA, and elsewhere have indicated that a concentration of fluoride of 1 part per million in tap water retards the decay of children's teeth by more than 50%.

Much concern has been expressed about the risks of medicating the population at large by the addition of fluoride to the water supply, but the medical evidence demonstrates conclusively that there is no risk to the general health from additions of 1 part per million of fluoride to drinking water.

The recommended policy in Britain is to add sodium fluoride to the water to bring it up to the required amount, but implementation is up to each local authority.

fluoride negative ion (F^-) formed when hydrogen fluoride dissolves in water; compound formed between fluorine and another element in which the fluorine is the more electronegative element (see ◊electronegativity).

In parts of India, the natural level of fluoride in water is 10 parts per million. This causes fluorosis, or chronic fluoride poisoning, mottling teeth and deforming bones.

fluorine pale yellow, gaseous, nonmetallic element, symbol F, atomic number 9, relative atomic mass 19. It is the first member of the halogen group of elements, and is pungent, poisonous, and highly reactive, uniting directly with nearly all the elements. It occurs naturally as the minerals fluorite (CaF_2) and cryolite (Na_3AlF_6). Hydrogen fluoride is used in etching glass, and the freons, which all contain fluorine, are widely used as refrigerants.

Fluorine was discovered by the Swedish chemist Karl Scheele in 1771 and isolated by the French chemist Henri Moissan in 1886.

Combined with uranium as UF_6, it is used in the separation of uranium isotopes.

fluorite or ***fluorspar*** a glassy, brittle halide mineral, calcium fluoride CaF_2, forming cubes and octahedra; colourless when pure, otherwise violet, blue, yellow, brown, or green.

Fluorite is used as a flux in iron and steel making; colourless fluorite is used in the manufacture of microscope lenses. It is also used for the glaze on pottery, and as a source of fluorine in the manufacture of hydrofluoric acid.

Deposits of fluorite occur in the N and S Pennines; the blue john from Derbyshire is a banded variety used as a decorative stone.

fluorocarbon compound formed by replacing the hydrogen atoms of a hydrocarbon with fluorine. Fluorocarbons are used as inert coatings, refrigerants, synthetic resins, and as propellants in aerosols. There is concern that the release of fluorocarbons – particularly those containing chlorine (chlorofluorocarbons, CFCs) – depletes the ◊ozone layer, allowing more ultraviolet light from the Sun to penetrate the Earth's atmosphere, and increasing the incidence of skin cancer in humans.

flute or ***transverse flute*** side-blown soprano woodwind instrument of considerable antiquity. The flute is difficult to master but capable of intricate melodies and expressive tonal shading. The player blows across an end hole, the air current being split by the opposite edge which causes pressure waves to form within the tube. The fingers are placed over holes in the tube to create different notes.

The flute has a extensive concert repertoire, including familiar pieces by J S Bach, Mozart, and the pastoral refrain of Debussy's *L'Après-midi d'un faun/Afternoon of a Faun* 1894. Vivaldi wrote a number of concertos for piccolo, and Maderna has composed for alto and bass flutes. Performers include James Galway and the Italian Severino Gazzelloni (1919–).

The instrument originated in Asia about 900 BC. European flutes can be traced back to about 1100, and include the military fife, subsequently developed by the Hotteterre family of instrument-makers into the single-key Baroque flute. Today's orchestral chromatic flutes with extensive keywork derive from further modifications in the 19th century by Theobald Boehm. Now more usually made of silver, gold, or platinum than wood, they include the soprano flute in C4, the higher piccolo in C5, the alto in G3, and the bass flute in C3, a rarity in the orchestra but much in vogue during the avant-garde 1950s as a concert instrument and an evocative accompaniment to films of the *nouvelle vague* era.

fluvioglacial of a process or landform, associated with glacial meltwater. Meltwater, flowing beneath or ahead of a glacier, is capable of transporting rocky material and creating a variety of landscape features, including eskers, kames, and outwash plains.

flux in smelting, a substance that combines with the unwanted components of the ore to produce a fusible slag, which can be separated from the molten metal. For example, the mineral fluorite, CaF_2, is used as a flux in iron smelting; it has a low melting point and will form a fusible mixture with substances of higher melting point such as silicates and oxides.

flux in soldering, a substance that improves the bonding properties of solder by removing contamination from metal surfaces and preventing their oxidation, and by reducing the surface tension of the molten solder alloy. For example, with solder made of lead-tin alloys, the flux may be resin, borax, or zinc chloride.

fly any insect of the order Diptera. A fly has a single pair of wings, antennae, and compound eyes; the hind wings have become modified into knoblike projections (halteres) used to maintain equilibrium in flight. There are over 90,000 species.

The mouthparts project from the head as a proboscis used for sucking fluids, modified in some species, such as mosquitoes, to pierce a victim's skin and suck blood. Discs at the ends of hairs on their feet secrete a fluid enabling them to walk up walls and across ceilings. Flies undergo complete metamorphosis; their larvae (maggots) are without true legs, and the pupae are rarely enclosed in a cocoon. The sexes are similar and coloration is rarely vivid, though some are metallic green or blue.

flying dragon lizard *Draco volans* of the family Agamidae. It lives in SE Asia, and can glide on flaps of skin spread and supported by its ribs. This small (7.5 cm/3 in head and body) arboreal lizard can glide between trees for 6m/20 ft or more.

flying fish any of a family Exocoetidae of marine bony fishes of the order Beloniformes, best represented in tropical waters. They have winglike pectoral fins that can be spread to glide over the water.

flying fox another name for the fruit bat, a fruit-eating ◊bat of the suborder Megachiroptera.

flying squirrel any of 43 known species of squirrel, not closely related to the true squirrels. They are characterized by a membrane along the side of the body from forelimb to hindlimb (in some species running to neck and tail) which allows them to glide through the air. Several genera of flying squirrel are found in the Old World; the New World has the genus *Glaucomys*. Most species are E Asian.

Flynn Errol. Stage name of Leslie Thompson 1909–1959. Australian-born US film actor. He is renowned for his portrayal of swashbuckling heroes in such films as *Captain Blood* 1935, *Robin Hood* 1938, *The Charge of the Light Brigade* 1938, *The Private Lives of Elizabeth and Essex* 1939, *The Sea Hawk* 1940, and *The Master of Ballantrae* 1953. Flynn wrote an autobiography, *My Wicked, Wicked Ways* 1959. He became a US citizen 1942.

flying squirrel Giant flying squirrels can glide over 400 m/440 yd between trees by stretching the broad, fur-covered membranes that extend from the sides of the body to the toes. They live in forested regions of Asia and are active at night.

Flynn Australian-born Hollywood film actor Errol Flynn in *The Adventures of Robin Hood* 1938. Flynn played the swashbuckling hero in many films such as *Captain Blood* 1935 and *The Private Lives of Elizabeth and Essex* 1939. His personal life attracted as much interest as the roles he played, and during the 1940s various scandals led to a decline in his career. *British Film Institute*

flystrike or ***blowfly strike*** or ***sheep strike*** infestation of the flesh of living sheep by blowfly maggots, especially those of the blue blowfly. It is one of the most costly sheep diseases in Australia, affecting all the grazing areas of New South Wales. Control has mainly been by insecticide, but non-chemical means, such as docking of tails and mulesing, are increasingly being encouraged. Mulesing involves an operation to remove the wrinkles of skin which trap moisture and lay the sheep open to infestation.

flywheel heavy wheel in an engine that helps keep it running and smooths its motion. The ◊crankshaft in a petrol engine has a flywheel at one end, which keeps the crankshaft turning in between the intermittent power strokes of the pistons. It also comes into contact with the ◊clutch, serving as the connection between the engine and the car's transmission system.

FM in physics, abbreviation for ◊***frequency modulation***.

f-number or ***f-stop*** measure of the relative aperture of a telescope or camera lens; it indicates the light-gathering power of the lens. In photography, each successive f-number represents a halving of exposure speed.

Fo Dario 1926– . Italian dramatist. His plays are predominantly political satires combining black humour with slapstick. They include *Morte accidentale di un anarchico/Accidental Death of an Anarchist* 1970, and *Non si paga non si paga/Can't Pay? Won't Pay!* 1975/1981. He has also written a one-man show, *Mistero buffo* 1969, based on the medieval mystery plays; and a handbook on the skills of the comic performer, *Tricks of the Trade* 1991.

focal length or ***focal distance*** the distance from the centre of a lens or curved mirror to the focal point. For a concave mirror or convex lens, it is the distance at which parallel rays of light are brought to a focus to form a real image (for a mirror, this is half the radius of curvature). For a convex mirror or concave lens, it is the distance from the centre to the point at which a virtual image (an image produced by diverging rays of light) is formed.

With lenses, the greater the power (measured in dioptres) of the lens, the shorter its focal length. The human eye has a lens of adjustable focal length to allow the light from objects of varying distance to be focused on the retina.

Foch Ferdinand 1851–1929. Marshal of France during World War I. He was largely responsible for the Allied victory at the first battle of the ◊Marne Sept 1914, and commanded on the NW front Oct 1914–Sept 1916. He was appointed commander in chief of the Allied armies in the spring of 1918, and launched the Allied counter-offensive in July that brought about the negotiation of an armistice to end the war.

focus or ***focal point*** in optics, the point at which light rays converge, or from which they appear to diverge, to form a sharp image. Other electromagnetic rays, such as microwaves, and sound waves may also be brought together at a focus. Rays parallel to the principal axis of a lens or mirror are converged at, or appear to diverge from, the ◊principal focus.

fog cloud that collects at the surface of the Earth, composed of water vapour that has condensed on particles of dust in the atmosphere. Cloud and fog are both caused by the air temperature falling below dew point (the temperature at which the air becomes saturated with water vapour). The thickness of fog depends on the number of water particles it contains. Officially, fog refers to a condition when visibility is reduced to 1 km/0.6 mi or less, and mist or haze to that giving a visibility of 1–2 km or about 1 mi.

There are two types of fog. An ***advection fog*** is formed by the meeting of two currents of air, one cooler than the other, or by warm air flowing over a cold surface. Sea fogs commonly occur where warm and cold currents meet and the air above them mixes. A ***radiation fog*** forms on clear, calm nights when the land surface loses heat rapidly (by radiation); the air above is cooled to below its dew point and condensation takes place. A mist is produced by condensed water particles, and a haze by smoke or dust.

In drought areas, for example, Baja California, Canary Islands, Cape Verde Islands, Namib Desert, Peru, and Chile, coastal fogs enable plant and animal life to survive without rain and are a potential source of water for human use (by means of water collectors exploiting the effect of condensation).

Industrial areas uncontrolled by pollution laws have a continual haze of smoke over them, and if the temperature falls suddenly, a dense yellow smog forms.

föhn or ***foehn*** warm dry wind that blows down the leeward slopes of mountains.

The air heats up as it descends because of the increase in pressure, and it is dry because all the moisture was dropped on the windward side of the mountain. In the valleys of Switzerland it is regarded as a health hazard, producing migraine and high blood pressure. A similar wind, chinook, is found on the eastern slopes of the Rocky Mountains in North America.

Fokine Mikhail 1880–1942. Russian choreographer and dancer. He was chief choreographer to the Ballets Russes 1909–14, and with ◊Diaghilev revitalized and reformed the art of ballet, promoting the idea of artistic unity among dramatic, musical, and stylistic elements.

Fokine was born in St Petersburg. His creations for Diaghilev include some of the most famous works in the ballet repertory, such as *Les Sylphides* 1909, *Schéhérazade* and *The Firebird*, both 1910, and *Le Spectre de la rose* and *Petrushka*, both 1911. He also created *The Dying Swan* for Anna Pavlova 1907. As a dancer, he was first soloist with the Maryinsky Theatre (later the Kirov) 1904.

fold in geology, a bend in beds or layers of rock. If the bend is arched in the middle it is called an anticline; if it sags downwards in the middle it is called a syncline. The line along which a bed of rock folds is called its axis. The axial plane is the plane joining the axes of successive beds.

fold mountain mountains formed from large-scale folding of Earth's crust at a destructive margin (where two tectonic plates collide). The Himalayas are an example.

folic acid a ◊vitamin of the B complex. It is found in liver and green leafy vegetables, and is also synthesized by the intestinal bacteria. It is essential for growth, and plays many other roles in the body. Lack of folic acid causes anaemia because it is necessary for the synthesis of nucleic acids and the formation of red blood cells.

Folies-Bergère music hall in Paris, France, built 1869, named after its original proprietor. In the 20th century, it featured lavish productions and striptease acts.

folk dance dance characteristic of a particular people, nation, or region. Many European folk dances are derived from the dances accompanying the customs and ceremonies of pre-Christian times. Some later became ballroom dances (for example, the minuet and waltz). Once an important part of many rituals, folk dance has tended to die out in industrialized countries. Examples of folk dance are Morris dance, farandole, and jota.

The preservation of folk dance in England was promoted by the work of Cecil ◊Sharp.

Folkestone port and holiday resort on the south-east coast of Kent, England, 10 km/6 mi SW of Dover; population (1991) 45,600. It was one of the ◊Cinque Ports. There are ferry and hovercraft services to and from Boulogne and Zeebrugge, and the Channel Tunnel terminal is here. It is the birthplace of the physician William Harvey.

folklore the oral traditions and culture of a people, expressed in legends, riddles, songs, tales, and proverbs. The term was coined 1846 by W J Thoms (1803–1885), but the founder of the systematic study of the subject was Jacob ◊Grimm; see also ◊oral literature.

The approach to folklore has varied greatly: the German scholar Max Müller (1823–1900) interpreted it as evidence of nature myths; James ◊Frazer was the exponent of the comparative study of early and popular folklore as mutually explanatory; Laurence Gomme (1853–1916) adopted a historical analysis; and Bronislaw ◊Malinowski and Alfred Radcliffe-Brown (1881–1955) examined the material as an integral element of a given living culture.

folk music body of traditional music, originally transmitted orally. Many folk songs originated as a rhythmic accompaniment to manual work or to mark a specific ritual. Folk song is usually melodic, not harmonic, and the modes used are distinctive of the country of origin; see ◊world music.

A burgeoning interest in ballad poetry in the later 18th century led to the discovery of a rich body of folk song in Europe. The multi-ethnic background of the USA has conserved a wealth of material derived from European, African, and Latin American sources. A revival of interest in folk music began in the USA in the 1950s led by researcher Alan Lomax (1915–) and the singers Henry Belafonte (1927–), Odetta (1930–), Pete Seeger, Woody Guthrie, Joan Baez, and Bob Dylan, who wrote new material in folk-song style, dealing with contemporary topics such as nuclear weapons and racial prejudice.

In England the late 19th century saw a development in the transcribing and preserving of folk tunes by such people as the Reverend Sabine Baring-Gould and Cecil ◊Sharp. The Folk Song Society was founded 1898 and became the English Folk Dance and Song Society 1911; they censored much of their material. The folk revival of the 1980s was furthered by rock guitarist Richard ◊Thompson and

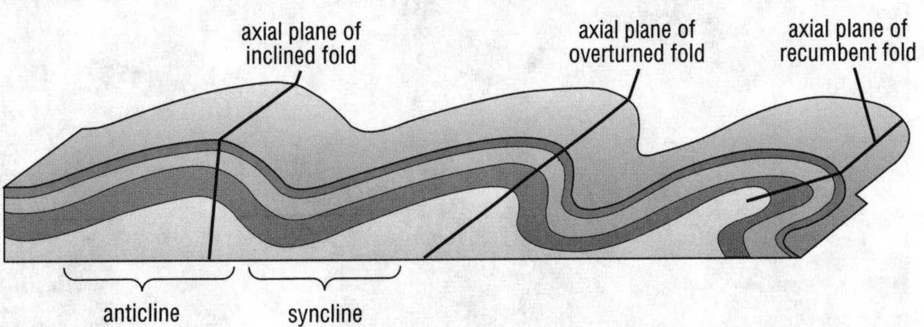

fold The folding of rock strata occurs where compression causes them to buckle. Over time, folding can assume highly complicated forms, as can sometimes be seen in the rock layers of cliff faces or deep cuttings in the rock. Folding contributed to the formation of great mountain chains such as the Himalayas.

such groups as the Pogues (formed 1983), and there was growing interest in roots, or world, music, encompassing traditional as well as modern music from many cultures.

follicle in botany, a dry, usually many-seeded fruit that splits along one side only to release the seeds within. It is derived from a single ◊carpel, examples include the fruits of the larkspurs *Delphinium* and columbine *Aquilegia*. It differs from a pod, which always splits open (dehisces) along both sides.

follicle in zoology, a small group of cells that surround and nourish a structure such as a hair (hair follicle) or a cell such as an egg (Graafian follicle; see ◊menstrual cycle).

follicle-stimulating hormone (FSH) a ◊hormone produced by the pituitary gland. It affects the ovaries in women, stimulating the production of an egg cell.

Luteinizing hormone is needed to complete the process. In men, FSH stimulates the testes to produce sperm. It is used to treat some forms of infertility.

Fomalhaut or ***Alpha Piscis Austrini*** the brightest star in the southern constellation ◊Piscis Austrinus and the 18th brightest star in the night sky. It is 22 light years from Earth, with a true luminosity 13 times that of the Sun.

Fomalhaut is one of a number of stars around which IRAS (the Infra-Red Astronomy Satellite) detected excess infrared radiation, presumably from a region of solid particles around the star. This material may be a planetary system in the process of formation.

Fon a people living mainly in Benin, and also in Nigeria, numbering about 2.5 million. The Fon language belongs to the Kwa branch of the Niger–Congo family. The Fon founded a kingdom which became powerful in the 18th and 19th centuries through the slave trade, and the region became known as the Slave Coast.

Fonda Henry Jaynes 1905–1982. US actor. His engaging style made him ideal in the role of the American pioneer and honourable man. His many films include *The Grapes of Wrath* 1940, *My Darling Clementine* 1946, *12 Angry Men* 1957, and *On Golden Pond* 1981, for which he won the Academy Award for best actor. He was the father of actress Jane ◊Fonda and actor and director Peter Fonda (1939–).

Fonda Jane Seymour 1937– . US actress. Her varied films roles include *Cat Ballou* 1965, *Barefoot in the Park* 1967, *Barbarella* 1968, *They Shoot Horses, Don't They?* 1969, *Julia*, 1977, *The China Syndrome* 1979, *On Golden Pond* 1981 (in which she appeared with her father, Henry Fonda), and *Old Gringo* 1989. She won Academy Awards for *Klute* 1971 and *Coming Home* 1978.

She became active in left-wing politics and in promoting physical fitness.

font or ***fount*** complete set of printed or display characters of the same typeface, size, and style (bold, italic, underlined, and so on). In the UK, font sizes are measured in points, a point being approximately 0.3 mm.

Fonts used in computer setting are of two main types:

Bit-mapped fonts are stored in the computer memory as the exact arrangement of ◊pixels or printed dots required to produce the characters in a particular size on a screen or printer.

Outline fonts are stored in the computer memory as a set of instructions for drawing the circles, straight lines, and curves that make up the outline of each character. They require a powerful computer because each character is separately generated from a set of instructions and this requires considerable computation. Bit-mapped fonts become very ragged in appearance if they are enlarged and so a separate set of bit maps is required for each font size. In contrast, outline fonts can be scaled to any size and still maintain exactly the same appearance.

Fontainebleau town to the SE of Paris, in Seine-et-Marne *département*. The château was built by François I in the 16th century. Mme de Montespan lived here in the reign of Louis XIV, and Mme du Barry in that of Louis XV. Napoleon signed his abdication here 1814. Nearby is the village of Barbizon, the haunt of several 19th-century painters (known as the ◊Barbizon School).

Fontainebleau School French school of Mannerist painting and sculpture. It was established at the court of François I, who brought Italian artists to Fontainebleau, near Paris, to decorate his hunting lodge: Rosso Fiorentino arrived 1530, Francesco Primaticcio came 1532. They evolved a distinctive decorative style using a combination of stucco relief and painting. Their work, with its exuberant ornamental and figurative style, had a lasting impact on French art in the 16th century.

Others associated with the school include Benvenuto Cellini, Niccolò dell'Abbate, Jean Cousin the Elder, and Antoine Caron (c. 1515–c. 1593). Flourishing about 1530–60, this (first) School of Fontainebleau was followed towards the end of the 16th century by a short revival of less note but known as the second school, influenced both by Flemish art and by the School of Bologna. Jacob Bunel (1551–1614), Toussaint Dubreuil (1561–1602) and Martin de Fréminet (1567–1619) are minor artists representative of this phase.

Fontane Theodor 1819–1898. German novelist. His best work, such as the historical novel *Vor den Sturm/Before the Storm* 1878, a critical but sympathetic account of Prussian aristocratic life, and *Effi Briest* 1898, is marked by superb characterization and a concern with the position of women. Among his novels, describing everyday life, are *Irrungen, Wirrungen/Trials and Tribulations* 1888 and *Der Stechlin* 1899. As drama critic of the *Vossische Zeitung* he was one of the first to defend the Norwegian and German playwrights Henrik ◊Ibsen and Gerhardt ◊Hauptmann.

Fonteyn Margot. Stage name of Peggy (Margaret) Hookham 1919–1991. English ballet dancer. She made her debut with the Vic-Wells Ballet in *Nutcracker* 1934 and first appeared as Giselle 1937, eventually becoming prima ballerina of the Royal Ballet, London. Renowned for her perfect physique, clear line, musicality, and interpretive powers, she created many roles in Frederick ◊Ashton's ballets and formed a legendary partnership with Rudolf ◊Nureyev. She retired from dancing 1979.

food anything eaten by human beings and other animals and plants to sustain life and health. The building blocks of food are nutrients, and humans can utilize the following nutrients: ***carbohydrates***, as starches found in bread, potatoes, and pasta; as simple sugars in sucrose and honey; as fibres in cereals, fruit, and vegetables; ***proteins*** as from nuts, fish, meat, eggs, milk, and some vegetables; ***fats*** as found in most animal products (meat, lard, dairy products, fish), also in margarine, nuts and seeds, olives, and edible oils; ***vitamins*** are found in a wide variety of foods, except for vitamin B_{12}, which is mainly found in foods of animal origin; ***minerals*** are found in a wide variety of foods (for example, calcium from milk and broccoli, iodine from seafood, and iron from liver and green vegetables); ***water*** ubiquitous in nature; ***alcohol*** is found in fermented distilled beverages, from 40% in spirits to 0.01% in low-alcohol lagers and beers.

Food and Agriculture Organization (FAO) United Nations agency that coordinates activities to improve food and timber production and levels of nutrition throughout the world. It is also concerned with investment in agriculture and dispersal of emergency food supplies. It has headquarters in Rome and was founded 1945.

food chain in ecology, a sequence showing the feeding relationships between organisms in a particular ◊ecosystem. Each organism depends on the next lowest member of the chain for its food.

Energy in the form of food is shown to be transferred from ◊autotrophs, or producers, which are principally plants and photosynthetic microorganisms, to a series of ◊heterotrophs, or consumers. The heterotrophs comprise the ◊herbivores, which feed on the producers; ◊carnivores, which feed on the herbivores; and ◊decomposers, which break down the dead bodies and waste products of all four groups (including their own), ready for recycling.

In reality, however, organisms have varied diets, relying on different kinds of foods, so that the food chain is an oversimplification. The more complex food web shows a greater variety of relationships, but again emphasizes that energy passes from plants to herbivores to carnivores. *See illustration on p. 406.*

food irradiation the exposure of food to low-level irradiation to kill microorganisms; a technique used in ◊food technology. Irradiation is highly effective, and does not make the food any more radioactive than it is naturally. Irradiated food is used for astronauts and immunocompromised patients in hospitals. Some vitamins are partially destroyed, such as vitamin C, and it would be unwise to eat only irradiated fruit and vegetables.

food poisoning any acute illness characterized by vomiting and diarrhoea and caused by eating food contaminated with harmful bacteria (for example, ◊listeriosis), poisonous food (for example, certain mushrooms, puffer fish), or poisoned food (such as lead or arsenic introduced accidentally during processing). A frequent cause of food poisoning is ◊Salmonella bacteria. Salmonella comes in many forms, and strains are found in cattle, pigs, poultry, and eggs.

Deep freezing of poultry before the birds are properly cooked is a common cause of food poisoning. Attacks of salmonella also come from contaminated eggs that have been eaten raw or cooked only lightly. Pork may carry the roundworm *Trichinella*, and rye the parasitic fungus ergot. The most dangerous food poison is the bacillus that causes ◊botulism. This is rare but leads to muscle paralysis and, often, death. Food irradiation is intended to prevent food poisoning.

food technology the application of science to the commercial processing of foodstuffs. Food is processed to make it more palatable or digestible,

Fonda US film actor Henry Fonda in *The Grapes of Wrath* 1940. Fonda established himself as the upright, self-effacing American hero of many films, such as this one and *12 Angry Men* 1957. Among his finest films are those he made with director John Ford, including *The Grapes of Wrath*, *Young Mr Lincoln* 1939, and *My Darling Clementine* 1946. *British Film Institute*

the traditional methods include boiling, frying, flour-milling, bread-, yoghurt-, and cheese-making, and brewing; or to prevent the growth of bacteria, moulds, yeasts, and other microorganisms; or to preserve it from spoilage caused by the action of ◊enzymes within the food that change its chemical composition, resulting in changes in flavour, odour, colour, and texture of the food.

Preservation enables foods that are seasonally produced to be available all the year. Traditional forms of food preservation include salting, smoking, pickling, drying, bottling, and preserving in sugar. Modern food technology also uses many novel processes and ◊additives, which allow a wider range of foodstuffs to be preserved. All foods undergo some changes in quality and nutritional value when subjected to preservation processes. No preserved food is identical in quality to its fresh counterpart, hence only food of the highest quality should be preserved.

In order to grow, bacteria, yeasts, and moulds need moisture, oxygen, a suitable temperature, and food. The various methods of food preservation aim to destroy the microorganisms within the food, to remove one or more of the conditions essential for their growth, or to make the foods unsuitable for their growth. Adding large amounts of salt or sugar reduces the amount of water available to microorganisms, because the water tied up by these solutes cannot be used for microbial growth. This is the principle in salting meat and fish, and in the manufacture of jams and jellies. These conditions also inhibit the enzyme activity in food. Preservatives may also be developed in the food by the controlled growth of microorganisms to produce fermentation that may make alcohol, or acetic or lactic acid. Examples of food preserved in this way are vinegar, sour milk, yoghurt, sauerkraut, and alcoholic beverages.

Refrigeration below 5°C/41°F (or below 3°C/37°F for cooked foods) slows the processes of spoilage, but is less effective for foods with a high water content. This process cannot kill microorganisms, nor stop their growth completely, and a failure to realize its limitations causes many cases of food poisoning.

Deep freezing (−18°C/−1°F or below) stops almost all spoilage processes, except residual enzyme activity in uncooked vegetables and most fruits, which are blanched (dipped in hot water to destroy the enzymes) before freezing. Preservation by freezing works by rendering the water in foodstuffs unavailable to microorganisms by converting it to ice. Microorganisms cannot grow or divide while frozen, but most remain alive and can resume activity once defrosted. Some foods are damaged by freezing, notably soft fruits and salad vegetables, the cells of which are punctured by ice crystals, leading to loss of crispness. Fatty foods such as cow's milk and cream tend to separate. Freezing has little effect on the nutritive value of foods, though a little vitamin C may be lost in the blanching process for fruit and vegetables.

Pasteurization is used mainly for milk. By holding the milk at 72°C/161.6°F for 15 seconds, all disease-causing bacteria can be destroyed. Less harmful bacteria survive, so the milk will still go sour within a few days.

Ultra-heat treatment is used to produce UHT milk. This process uses higher temperatures than pasteurization, and kills all bacteria present, giving the milk a long shelf life but altering the flavour.

Drying is effective because both microorganisms and enzymes need water to be active. In addition, drying concentrates the soluble ingredients in foods, and this high concentration prevents the growth of bacteria, yeasts, and moulds. Dried food will deteriorate rapidly if allowed to become moist, but provided they are suitably packaged, products will have a long shelf life. Traditionally, foods were dried in the sun and wind, but commercially today, products such as dried milk and instant coffee are made by spraying the liquid into a rising column of dry, heated air; solid foods, such as fruit, are spread in layers on a heated surface.

Freeze-drying is carried out under vacuum. It is less damaging to food than straight dehydration in the sense that foods reconstitute better, and is used for quality instant coffee and dried vegetables. The foods are fast frozen, then dried by converting the ice to vapour under very low pressure. The foods lose much of their weight, but retain the original size and shape. They have a spongelike texture, and rapidly reabsorb liquid when reconstituted. Refrigeration is unnecessary during storage; the shelf life is similar to dried foods, provided the product is not allowed to become moist. The success of the method is dependent on a fast rate of freezing, and rapid conversion of the ice to vapour. Hence, the most acceptable results are obtained with thin pieces of food, and the method is not recommended for pieces thicker than 3 cm/1 in. Fruit, vegetables, meat, and fish have proved satisfactory. This method of preservation is commercially used but the products are most often used as constituents of composite dishes, such as packet meals.

Canning relies on high temperatures to destroy microorganisms and enzymes. The food is sealed in a can to prevent recontamination. The effect of heat processing on the nutritive value of food is variable. For instance, the vitamin C content of green vegetables is much reduced, but, owing to greater acidity, in fruit juices vitamin C is quite well retained. There is also a loss of 25–50% of water-soluble vitamins if the liquor is not used. Vitamin B (thiamine) is easily destroyed by heat treatment, particularly in alkaline conditions. Acid products retain thiamine well, because they require only minimum heat during sterilization. The sterilization process seems to have little effect on retention of vitamins A and B_2. During storage of canned foods, the proportion of vitamins B and C decreases gradually. Drinks may be canned to preserve the carbon dioxide that makes them fizzy.

Pickling utilizes the effect of acetic (ethanoic) acid, found in vinegar, in stopping the growth of moulds. In sauerkraut, lactic acid, produced by bacteria, has the same effect. Similar types of nonharmful, acid-generating bacteria are used to make yoghurt and cheese.

Curing of meat involves soaking in salt (sodium chloride) solution, with saltpetre (sodium nitrate) added to give the meat its pink colour and characteristic taste. Bacteria convert the nitrates in cured meats to nitrites and nitrosamines, which are potentially carcinogenic to humans.

Irradiation is a method of preserving food by subjecting it to low-level radiation (see ◊food irradiation).

Puffing is a method of processing cereal grains. They are subjected to high pressures, then suddenly ejected into a normal atmospheric pressure, causing the grain to expand sharply. This is used to make puffed wheat cereals and puffed rice cakes.

Chemical treatments are widely used, for example in margarine manufacture, in which hydrogen is bubbled through vegetable oils in the presence of a ◊catalyst to produce a more solid, spreadable fat. The catalyst is later removed. Chemicals introduced in processing that remain in the food are known as food additives and include flavourings, preservatives, anti-oxidants, emulsifiers, and colourings.

Food and Agriculture Organization Corn growing in the Shivapuri district in Nepal, part of an integrated plan for agricultural development organized by the FAO. Deforestation had led to severe soil erosion and the pollution of water supplies to the Katmandu Valley. The improvement plan involved planting thousands of trees and, in order to ensure their cooperation in preserving the trees, helping local people to establish businesses such as crop growing and beekeeping. *Food and Agriculture Organization*

foot imperial unit of length (symbol ft), equivalent to 0.3048 m, in use in Britain since Anglo-Saxon times. It originally represented the length of a human foot. One foot contains 12 inches and is one-third of a yard.

foot unit of metrical pattern in poetry; see ◊metre. The five most common types of foot in English poetry are iamb (v–), trochee (– v), dactyl (– vv), spondee (–), and anapaest (vv –); the symbol v stands for an unstressed syllable and – for a stressed one.

Foot Michael Mackintosh 1913– . British Labour politician and writer. A leader of the left-wing Tribune Group, he was secretary of state for employment 1974–76, Lord President of the Council and leader of the House 1976–79, and succeeded James Callaghan as Labour Party leader 1980–83.

foot-and-mouth disease contagious eruptive viral disease of cloven-hoofed mammals, characterized by blisters in the mouth and around the hooves. In cattle it causes deterioration of milk yield and abortions. It is an airborne virus, which makes its eradication extremely difficult. In the UK, affected herds are destroyed; inoculation is practised in Europe, and in the USA, a vaccine was developed in the 1980s.

football, American contact sport similar to the English game of rugby, played between two teams of 11 players, with an inflated oval ball. Players are well padded for protection and wear protective helmets. The Super Bowl, first held in 1967, is now an annual meeting between the winners of the National and American Football Conferences.

The game is played on a field marked out with a series of parallel lines giving a gridiron effect. There is a goalpost at each end of the field, and beyond this an end zone. Games are divided into four quarters of 15 minutes each. Points are scored by running or passing the ball across the goal line (touchdown, 6 points); by kicking it over the goal's crossbar after a touchdown (conversion, 2 points), or from the field during regular play (field goal, 3 points); or by tackling a defending player who has the ball in the end zone, or blocking a defending team's kick so it goes out of bounds from the end zone (safety, 2 points). A team consists of more than 40 players but only 11 are allowed on the field at any one time. *See list of tables on p. 1177.*

football, association or *soccer* form of football originating in the UK, popular in Europe and Latin America. The modern game is played in the UK according to the rules laid down by the home countries' football associations. Slight amendments to the rules take effect in certain competitions and international matches as laid down by the sport's world governing body, Fédération Internationale de Football Association (FIFA, 1904). FIFA organizes

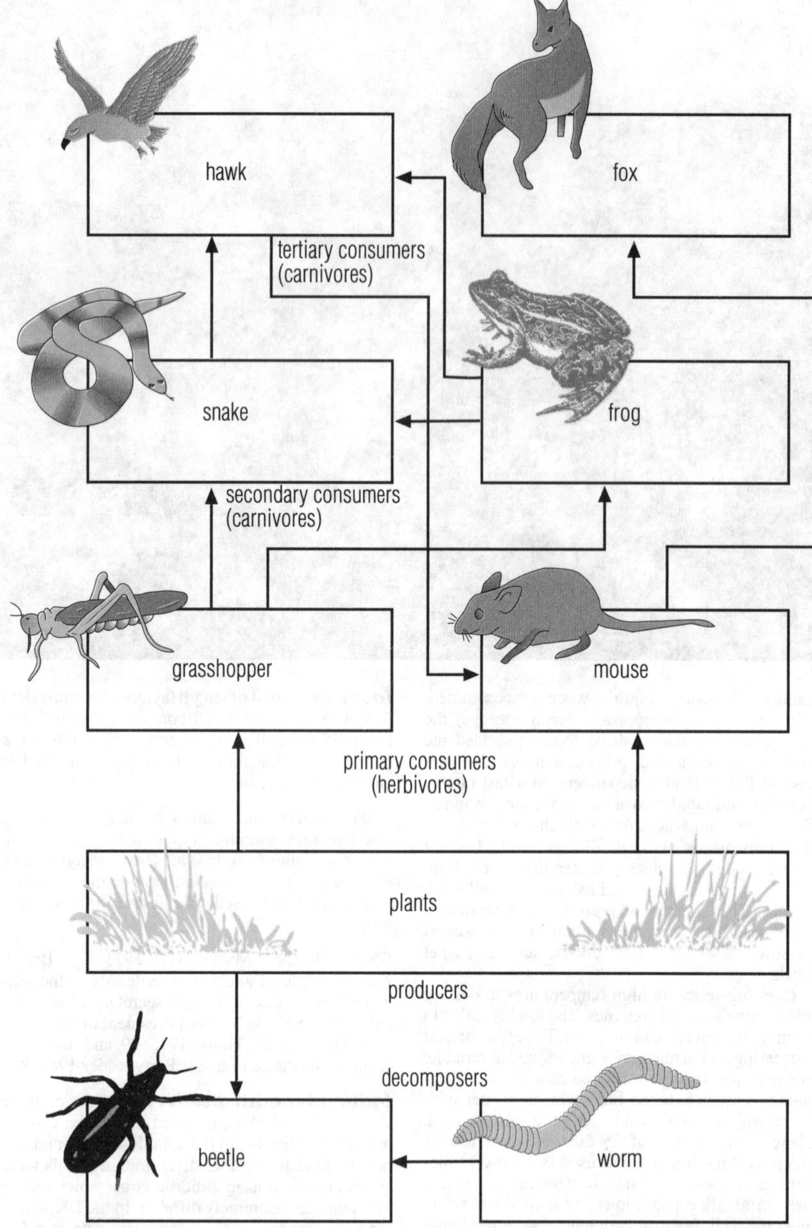

food chain The complex interrelationships between animals and plants in a food chain. Food chains are normally only three or four links long. This is because most of the energy at each link is lost in respiration, and so cannot be passed on to the next link.

the competitions for the World Cup, held every four years since 1930.

The field has a halfway line marked with a centre circle, two penalty areas, and two goal areas. The game is played with an inflated spherical ball. There are two teams each of 11 players, broadly divided into defence (the goalkeeper and defenders), midfield (whose players collect the ball from the defence and distribute it to the attackers), and attack (forwards or strikers). The object of the game is to kick or head the ball into the opponents' goal. When the ball is in play, only the goalkeeper is allowed to touch the ball with the hands and then only in an assigned penalty area. The game is started and restarted after each goal, from the centre spot. It is played for two periods of 45 minutes each, the teams changing ends at half-time. The game is controlled by a referee; two linesmen indicate when the ball is kicked into touch and bring other rule infringements to the referee's attention. Teams committing a foul forfeit possession. For major offences committed within the defenders' penalty area, a penalty kick may be awarded by the referee to the attacking team. *See list of tables on p. 1177.*

Ford US automotive engineer Henry Ford, shown in his first car. Ford's early cars were named alphabetically, albeit in a rather erratic fashion. His first eight models were the A, B, C, F, K, N, R, and S before he finally produced, in 1908, his first mass-produced car, the Model T. When, after 19 years, he ceased production of the Model T, he succeeded it not with the Model U, but another Model A. *Image Select (UK) Ltd*

football, Australian rules game that combines aspects of Gaelic football, rugby, and association football; it is played between two teams of 18 players each, with an inflated oval ball. It is unique to Australia.

The game is played on an oval pitch with a pair of goalposts at each end. On either side of each pair of goalposts is a smaller post. Each team is placed in five lines of three persons each, and three players follow the ball all the time. Points are scored by kicking the ball between the goalposts, without its being touched on the way ('goal', 6 points), or by passing the ball between a goalpost and one of the smaller posts, or causing it to hit a post ('behind', 1 point). There are no scrums, line-outs, or off-side rules. A player must get rid of the ball immediately on starting to run, by kicking, punching, or bouncing it every 10 m/33 ft. No tackling (as in rugby) is allowed.

football, Gaelic kicking and catching game played mainly in Ireland. The two teams have 15 players each. The game is played on a field with an inflated spherical ball. The goalposts have a crossbar and a net across the lower half. Goals are scored by kicking the ball into the net (3 points) or over the crossbar (1 point).

First played 1712, it is now one of the sports under the auspices of the Gaelic Athletic Association. The leading tournament is the All-Ireland Championship (first held 1887); its final is played in Dublin on the third Sunday in September each year, the winners receiving the Sam Maguire Trophy.

forage crop plant that is grown to feed livestock; for example, grass, clover, and kale (a form of cabbage). Forage crops cover a greater area of the world than food crops, and grass, which dominates this group, is the world's most abundant crop, though much of it is still in an unimproved state.

foraminifera any of an order Foraminiferida of marine protozoa with shells of calcium carbonate. Their shells have pores through which filaments project. Some form part of the ◊plankton, others live on the sea bottom.

force any influence that tends to change the state of rest or the uniform motion in a straight line of a body. The action of an unbalanced or resultant force results in the acceleration of a body in the direction of action of the force, or it may, if the body is unable to move freely, result in its deformation (see ◊Hooke's law). Force is a vector quantity, possessing both magnitude and direction; its SI unit is the newton.

According to Newton's second law of motion the magnitude of a resultant force is equal to the rate of change of ◊momentum of the body on which it acts; the force F producing an acceleration a m s^{-2} on a body of mass m kilograms is therefore given by:

$$F = ma$$

See also ◊Newton's laws of motion.

force majeure (French 'superior force') in politics, the use of force rather than the seeking of a political or diplomatic solution to a problem. By this principle, a government could end a strike by sending in troops, instead of attempting to conciliate the strikers.

forces, fundamental in physics, the four fundamental interactions believed to be at work in the physical universe. There are two long-range forces: ***gravity***, which keeps the planets in orbit around the Sun, and acts between all particles that have mass; and the ***electromagnetic force***, which stops solids from falling apart, and acts between all particles with ◊electric charge. There are two very short-range forces which operate only inside the atomic nucleus: the ***weak nuclear force***, responsible for the reactions that fuel the Sun and for the emission of

◊beta particles from certain nuclei; and the ***strong nuclear force***, which binds together the protons and neutrons in the nuclei of atoms. The relative strengths of the four forces are: strong, 1; electromagnetic, 10^{-2}; weak, 10^{-6}; gravitational, 10^{-40}.

By 1971, US physicists Steven Weinberg and Sheldon Glashow, Pakistani physicist Abdus Salam, and others had developed a theory that suggested that the weak and electromagnetic forces were aspects of a single force called the electroweak force; experimental support came from observation at ◊CERN in the 1980s. Physicists are now working on theories to unify all four forces.

Ford Edward Onslow (1852–1901). English sculptor. Among his works are portraits of the politician William Gladstone 1883, the actor Henry Irving (as Hamlet) 1883, General Gordon 1890, and the scientist Thomas Huxley 1900.

Ford Ford Madox. Adopted name of Ford Hermann Hueffer 1873–1939. English author. He wrote more than 80 books, the best known of which are the novels *The Good Soldier* 1915 and *Tietjen's Saga* 1924–28. He edited the *English Review* 1908–10, to which Thomas Hardy, D H Lawrence, Joseph Conrad, Wyndham Lewis, and Ezra Pound contributed. He excelled at a comic mixture of invention and reportage. He was also founder-editor of *The Transatlantic Review* in Paris 1924, which published work by James Joyce and Ernest Hemingway. He was a grandson of the painter Ford Madox Brown.

Ford Gerald R(udolph) 1913– . 38th president of the USA 1974–77, a Republican. He was elected to the House of Representatives 1948, was nominated to the vice-presidency by Richard Nixon 1973 following the resignation of Spiro Agnew (1918–), and became president 1974, when Nixon was forced to resign following the ◊Watergate scandal. He granted Nixon a full pardon Sept 1974. Ford's visit to Vladivostok 1974 resulted in agreement with the USSR on strategic arms limitation. He was defeated by Carter in the 1976 election by a narrow margin.

Ford Harrison 1942– . US film actor. He became internationally known as Han Solo in George Lucas' *Star Wars* 1977, playing the role in the rest of the trilogy, and created the lead role in Steven Spielberg's series of *Indiana Jones* films 1981–89. Other films include *Blade Runner* 1982, *The Mosquito Coast* 1987, *Presumed Innocent* 1990, and *The Fugitive* 1993.

Ford Henry 1863–1947. US automobile manufacturer. He built his first car 1896 and founded the Ford Motor Company 1903. His Model T (1908–27) was the first car to be constructed solely by assembly-line methods and to be mass-marketed; 15 million of these cars were sold.

Ford's innovative policies, such as a $5 daily minimum wage (at the time nearly double the average figure in Detroit) and a five-day working week, revolutionized employment practices, but he opposed the introduction of trade unions. In 1928 he launched the Model A, a stepped-up version of the Model T.

Ford was born in Dearborn, Michigan, and apprenticed to a Detroit machinist 1878. On his father's farm he experimented in the manufacture of a steam tractor. He worked for the Edison Illuminating Company 1891–99 and then for the Detroit Automobile Company before starting his own firm. Victory in a car race at Grosse Point, Michigan, 1901, brought him the publicity he sought, and in 1904 he drove his four-cylindered car '999' to a world record of 39.4 sec for 1 mi/1.6 km over the ice on Lake St Clair. In 1915 Ford turned his attention to the farm tractor; the Fordson tractor was a great commercial success. He also went into the civil aviation business.

Ford was politically active and in 1936 he founded, with his son Edsel Ford (1893–1943), the philanthropic Ford Foundation. He retired in 1945 from the Ford Motor Company, then valued at over $1 billion.

Ford John. Adopted name of Sean Aloysius O'Feeney 1895–1973. US film director. Active from the silent film era, he was one of the key creators of the 'Western', directing *The Iron Horse* 1924; *Stagecoach* 1939 became his masterpiece. He won Academy Awards for *The Informer* 1935, *The Grapes of Wrath* 1940, *How Green Was My Valley* 1941, and *The Quiet Man* 1952.

Ford John c. 1586–c. 1640. English poet and dramatist. His play *'Tis Pity She's a Whore* (performed about 1626, printed 1633) is a study of incestuous passion between brother and sister. His other plays include *The Lover's Melancholy* 1629, *The Broken Heart* 1633, *Love's Sacrifice* 1633, in which Bianca is one of Ford's finest psychological studies of women, and *The Chronicle History of Perkin Warbeck* 1634, one of the best historical dramas since Shakespeare. Dwelling on themes of pathos and frustration, they reflect the transition from a general to an aristocratic audience for drama.

Ford Richard (1944–). US novelist. A leading exponent of 'dirty realism', Ford writes novels and stories that often describe the bleak lives of lonely and damaged people who are constantly on the move; for Ford, a central part of the American psyche.

Fordism mass production characterized by a high degree of job specialization, as typified by the Ford Motor Company's early use of assembly lines. Mass-production techniques were influenced by US management consultant F W Taylor's book *Principles of Scientific Management*.

foreclosure in law, the transfer of title of a mortgaged property from the mortgagor (borrower, usually a home owner) to the mortgagee (loaner, for example a bank) if the mortgagor is in breach of the mortgage agreement, usually by failing to make a number of payments on the mortgage (loan).

Foreign and Commonwealth Office (FCO) UK government department established 1782, as the Foreign Office. It is responsible for conduct of foreign policy, representation of British interests abroad, relations with other members of the ◊Commonwealth, overseas aid policy and administration.

Foreign Legion volunteer corps of foreigners within a country's army. The French ***Légion Etrangère***, founded 1831, is one of a number of such forces. Enlisted volunteers are of any nationality (about half are now French), but the officers are usually French. Headquarters until 1962 was in Sidi Bel Abbés, Algeria; the main base is now Corsica, with reception headquarters at Aubagne, near Marseille, France.

The French foreign legion was founded by Louis-Philippe 'to clear France of foreigners' and since then has always taken cast-offs and undesirables, including those from the French army itself.

Desertion levels are relatively high, around 6%.

foreign relations a country's dealings with other countries. Specialized diplomatic bodies first appeared in Europe during the 18th century. After 1818 diplomatic agents were divided into: ambassadors, papal legates, and nuncios; envoys extraordinary, ministers plenipotentiary, and other ministers accredited to the head of state; ministers resident; and chargés d'affaires, who may deputize for an ambassador or minister, or be themselves the representative accredited to a minor country. Other diplomatic staff may include counsellors and attachés (military, labour, cultural, press). Consuls are state agents with commercial and political responsibilities in foreign towns.

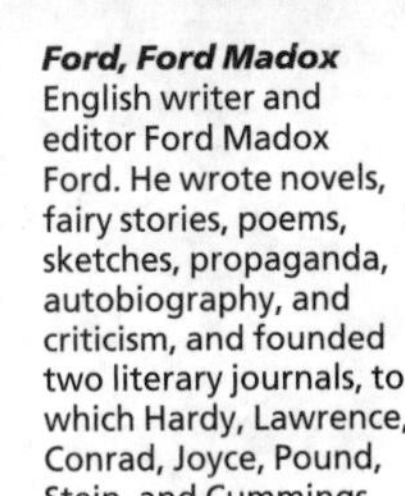

Ford, Ford Madox English writer and editor Ford Madox Ford. He wrote novels, fairy stories, poems, sketches, propaganda, autobiography, and criticism, and founded two literary journals, to which Hardy, Lawrence, Conrad, Joyce, Pound, Stein, and Cummings contributed. *Corbis*

Foreland, North and South chalk headlands projecting from the east coast of Kent, southeast England. ***North Foreland***, with one lighthouse, lies 4 km/2.5 mi east of Margate; ***South Foreland***, with two, lies 5 km/3 mi northeast of Dover. The headlands mark the eastern limit of the North Downs.

Foreman George 1948– . US heavyweight boxer who was the undisputed world heavyweight champion 1973–74. In Nov 1994, at the age of 45, Foreman became the oldest boxer ever to win a championship when he knocked out Michael Moorer to win the International Boxing Federation and World Boxing Association heavyweight title

'People can have the Model T in any colour – so long as it's black.'

HENRY FORD
Quoted in A Nevins *Ford*

Ford US film director John Ford. One of the USA's greatest directors and a pioneer of the Western, he made such classics as *Stagecoach* 1939 (with John Wayne) and *Young Mr Lincoln* 1939, *The Grapes of Wrath* 1940, and *My Darling Clementine* 1946 (all with Henry Fonda). *British Film Institute*

❛I hate the idea of causes, and if I had to choose between betraying my country and betraying my friend, I hope I should have the guts to betray my country.❜

E M FORSTER
Two Cheers for Democracy

belts. Foreman had retired from boxing 1977, but returned to the sport 1987.

forensic medicine branch of medicine used in solving crimes, including determining the cause of death in suspicious circumstances or identifying a criminal from tissue found at the scene of a crime. Forensic psychology involves drawing up a psychological profile of a criminal which often leads to identification.

forensic science the use of scientific techniques to solve criminal cases. A multidisciplinary field embracing chemistry, physics, botany, zoology, and medicine, forensic science includes the identification of human bodies or traces. Ballistics (the study of projectiles, such as bullets), another traditional forensic field, makes use of such tools as the comparison microscope and the electron microscope.

Traditional methods such as ◊fingerprinting are still used, assisted by computers; in addition, blood analysis, forensic dentistry, voice and speech spectrograms, and ◊genetic fingerprinting are increasingly applied. Chemicals, such as poisons and drugs, are analysed by ◊chromatography. ESDA (electrostatic document analysis) is a technique used for revealing indentations on paper, which helps determine if documents have been tampered with.

forest area where trees have grown naturally for centuries, instead of being logged at maturity (about 150–200 years). A natural, or old-growth, forest has a multistorey canopy and includes young and very old trees (this gives the canopy its range of heights). There are also fallen trees contributing to the very complex ecosystem, which may support more than 150 species of mammals and many thousands of species of insects.

The Pacific forest of the west coast of North America is one of the few remaining old-growth forests in the temperate zone. It consists mainly of conifers and is threatened by logging – less than 10% of the original forest remains. ▷ *See feature on pp. 896–897.*

forestry the science of forest management. Recommended forestry practice aims at multipurpose crops, allowing the preservation of varied plant and animal species as well as human uses (lumbering, recreation). Forestry has often been confined to the planting of a single species, such as a rapid-growing conifer providing softwood for paper pulp and construction timber, for which world demand is greatest. In tropical countries, logging contributes to the destruction of ◊rainforests, causing global environmental problems. Small unplanned forests are ◊woodland.

The earliest planned forest dates from 1368 at Nuremberg, Germany; in Britain, planning of forests began in the 16th century. In the UK, Japan, and other countries, forestry practices have been criticized for concentration on softwood conifers to the neglect of native hardwoods.

forgery the making of a false document, painting, or object with deliberate intention to deceive or defraud. The most common forgeries involve financial instruments such as cheques or credit-card transactions or money (counterfeiting). There are also literary forgeries, forged coins, and forged antiques.

Financial gain is not the only motive for forgery. Han van Meegeren probably began painting in the style of Vermeer to make fools of the critics, but found such a ready market for his creations that he became a rich man before he was forced to confess. The archaeological ◊Piltdown Man hoax in England in 1912 also appears to have been a practical joke.

forget-me-not any plant of the genus *Myosotis*, family Boraginaceae, including *M. sylvatica* and *M. scorpioides*, with bright blue flowers.

forging one of the main methods of shaping metals, which involves hammering or a more gradual application of pressure. A blacksmith hammers red-hot metal into shape on an anvil, and the traditional place of work is called a forge. The blacksmith's mechanical equivalent is the drop forge. The metal is shaped by the blows from a falling hammer or ram, which is usually accelerated by steam or air pressure. Hydraulic presses forge by applying pressure gradually in a squeezing action.

formaldehyde common name for ◊methanal.

formalism in art, literature, and music, an emphasis on form and formal structures at the expense of content. Formalism also refers more narrowly to a Russian school of literary theory in the 1920s, which defined literature by its formal, aesthetic qualities, and did not recognize its social content.

Soviet formalism fell into disrepute as an aesthetic self-indulgence and was the focus of the cultural purges of 1948 under Stalin. It was superseded by Socialist Realism.

Formby George 1904–1961. English comedian. He established a stage and screen reputation as an apparently simple Lancashire working lad, and sang such songs as 'Mr Wu' and 'Cleaning Windows', accompanying himself on the ukulele. His father was a music-hall star of the same name.

Formentera smallest inhabited island in the Spanish Balearic Islands, lying S of Ibiza; area 93 sq km/36 sq mi. The chief town is San Francisco Javier and the main port is La Sabina. The main industry is tourism.

formic acid common name for ◊methanoic acid.

formula in chemistry, a representation of a molecule, radical, or ion, in which the component chemical elements are represented by their symbols. An empirical formula indicates the simplest ratio of the elements in a compound, without indicating how many of them there are or how they are combined. A molecular formula gives the number of each type of element present in one molecule. A structural formula shows the relative positions of the atoms and the bonds between them. For example, for ethanoic acid, the empirical formula is CH_2O, the molecular formula is $C_2H_4O_2$, and the structural formula is CH_3COOH.

formula in mathematics, a set of symbols and numbers that expresses a fact or rule. $A = \pi r^2$ is the formula for calculating the area of a circle. Einstein's famous formula relating energy and mass is $E = mc^2$.

Forssmann Werner 1904–1979. German heart surgeon. In 1929 he originated, by experiment on himself, the technique of cardiac catheterization (passing a thin tube from an arm artery up into the heart for diagnostic purposes). He shared the 1956 Nobel Prize for Physiology or Medicine.

Forster E(dward) M(organ) 1879–1970. English novelist, short-story writer, and critic. He was concerned with the interplay of personality and the conflict between convention and instinct. His novels include *A Room with a View* 1908, *Howards End* 1910, and *A Passage to India* 1924. Collections of stories include *The Celestial Omnibus* 1911 and *Collected Short Stories* 1948, and of essays and reviews 'Abinger Harvest' 1936. His most lasting critical work is *Aspects of the Novel* 1927.

Forster published his first novel, *Where Angels Fear to Tread*, 1905. He enhances the superficial situations of his plots with unexpected insights in *The Longest Journey* 1907, *A Room with a View*, and *Howards End*. These three novels explore Forster's preoccupation with the need to find intellectual and spiritual harmony in a world dominated by narrow social conventions. His many years spent in India and as secretary to the Maharajah of Dewas 1921 provided him with the material for his best-known work *A Passage to India*, which explores the relationship between the English and the Indians with insight and wisdom. It is considered to be one of the most influential of modern English novels. *Maurice*, written 1914 and published 1971, has a homosexual theme.

forsythia any temperate E Asian shrub of the genus *Forsythia* of the olive family Oleaceae, which bear yellow bell-shaped flowers in early spring before the leaves appear.

Fort-de-France capital, chief commercial centre, and port of Martinique, West Indies, at the mouth of the Madame River; population (1990) 101,500. It trades in sugar, rum, and cacao.

The Empress Josephine was born at Trois-Ilets on the south side of Fort-de-France Bay.

fortepiano early 18th-century piano invented by Italian maker Bartolommeo Christofori 1709, having small leather-bound hammers and harpsichord strings. Present-day performers include Trevor Pinnock, Gustav Leonhardt, and Jörg Demus.

Forth river in SE Scotland, with its headstreams rising on the northeast slopes of Ben Lomond. It flows approximately 72 km/45 mi to Kincardine where the Firth of Forth begins. The Firth is approximately 80 km/50 mi long, and is 26 km/16 mi wide where it joins the North Sea.

At Queensferry near Edinburgh are the Forth rail (1890) and road (1964) bridges. The Forth and Clyde Canal (1768–90) across the lowlands of Scotland links the Firth with the river Clyde, Grangemouth to Bowling (53 km/33 mi). A coalfield was located beneath the Firth of Forth 1976.

Fort Ticonderoga fort in New York State, USA, near Lake Champlain. It was the site of battles between the British and the French 1758–59, and was captured from the British 10 May 1775 by Benedict ◊Arnold and Ethan Allen (leading the ◊Green Mountain Boys). ▷ *See feature on pp. 32–33.*

FORTRAN (or ***fortran***, acronym for ***formula translation***) high-level computer-programming language suited to mathematical and scientific computations. Developed 1956, it is one of the earliest computer languages still in use. A recent version, Fortran 90, is now being used on advanced parallel computers. ◊BASIC was strongly influenced by FORTRAN and is similar in many ways.

Fortuna in Roman mythology, the goddess of chance and good fortune, identified with the Greek ◊Tyche.

Fortune 500 the 500 largest publicly owned US industrial corporations, a list compiled by the US business magazine *Fortune*. An industrial corporation is defined as one that derives at least 50% of its revenue from manufacturing or mining.

Fort Worth city in NE Texas, USA; population (1992) 454,400. Formerly an important cattle area, it is now a grain, petroleum, aerospace, and railway centre serving the southern USA.

Forty-Five, the ◊Jacobite rebellion 1745, led by Prince ◊Charles Edward Stuart. With his army of Highlanders 'Bonnie Prince Charlie' occupied Edinburgh and advanced into England as far as Derby, but then turned back. The rising was crushed by the Duke of Cumberland at Culloden 1746.

forum (Latin 'market') in an ancient Roman town, the meeting place and market, like the Greek *agora*. In Rome the Forum Romanum contained the Senate House, the public speaking platform, covered halls for trading, temples of Saturn, Concord, and the

forum A view of Trajan's Forum in Rome. The forum (literally 'market-place') was a large, flat, central area found in every Roman town. Rome itself had several, of which Trajan's Forum, begun by the emperor Trajan in AD 113, was the latest and most magnificent. It contains Trajan's Column, a huge monument commemorating his campaigns. *Corbis*

Divine Augustus, and memorial arches. Later constructions included the Forum of ◊Caesar (temple of Venus), the Forum of ◊Augustus (temple of Mars), and the colonnaded Forum of ◊Trajan, containing Trajan's Column.

Fosse Bob (Robert Louis) 1927–1987. US film director. He entered films as a dancer and choreographer from Broadway, making his directorial debut with *Sweet Charity* 1968. He received an Academy Award for his second film as director, *Cabaret* 1972. Other films include *All That Jazz* 1979.

Fossey Dian 1938–1985. US zoologist. From 1975, she studied mountain gorillas in Rwanda and discovered that they committed infanticide and that females were transferred to nearly established groups. Living in close proximity to them, she discovered that they led peaceful family lives. She was murdered by poachers whose snares she had cut.

fossil (Latin *fossilis* 'dug up') a cast, impression, or the actual remains of an animal or plant preserved in rock. Fossils were created during periods of rock formation, caused by the gradual accumulation of sediment over millions of years at the bottom of the sea bed or an inland lake. Fossils may include footprints, an internal cast, or external impression. A few fossils are preserved intact, as with ◊mammoths fossilized in Siberian ice, or insects trapped in tree resin that is today amber. The study of fossils is called ◊palaeontology. Palaeontologists are able to deduce much of the geological history of a region from fossil remains.

About 250,000 fossil species have been discovered – a figure that is believed to represent less than 1 in 20,000 of the species that ever lived. ***Microfossils*** are so small they can only be seen with a microscope. They include the fossils of pollen, bone fragments, bacteria, and the remains of microscopic marine animals and plants, such as foraminifera and diatoms.

fossil fuel fuel, such as coal, oil, and natural gas, formed from the fossilized remains of plants that lived hundreds of millions of years ago. Fossil fuels are a ◊nonrenewable resource and will eventually run out. Extraction of coal and oil causes considerable environmental pollution, and burning coal contributes to problems of ◊acid rain and the ◊greenhouse effect. ▷ *See features on pp. 360–361 and pp. 858–859.*

Foster Greg 1958– . US hurdler. He has won three consecutive World Championship gold medals, the only athlete to achieve this feat.

Foster Jodie. Stage name of Alicia Christian Foster 1962– . US film actress and director. She began acting as a child in a great variety of roles. She starred in *Taxi Driver* and *Bugsy Malone* both 1976, when only 14. Subsequent films include *The Accused* 1988 and *The Silence of the Lambs* 1991 (she won Academy Awards for both), *Sommersby* 1993, and *Nell* 1994. She made her directorial debut with *Little Man Tate* 1991.

Foster Norman Robert 1935– . English architect of the High Tech school. His buildings include the Willis Faber & Dumas insurance offices, Ipswich 1975, the Sainsbury Centre for the Visual Arts, Norwich 1977, the headquarters of the Hong Kong and Shanghai Bank, Hong Kong 1986, and Stansted Airport, Essex, 1991.

He has won numerous international awards for his industrial architecture and design, including RIBA awards for the Stansted project and the Sackler Galleries extension at the Royal Academy of Art, London, 1992, which is a sensitive, yet overtly modern, addition to an existing historic building.

Foucault Jean Bernard Léon 1819–1868. French physicist who used a pendulum to demonstrate the rotation of the Earth on its axis, and invented the ◊gyroscope 1852. In 1862 he made the first accurate determination of the velocity of light.

Foucault investigated heat and light, discovered eddy currents induced in a copper disc moving in a magnetic field, invented a polarizer, and made improvements in the electric arc. In 1860, he invented high-quality regulators for driving machinery at a constant speed; these were used in telescope motors and factory engines.

Foucault Michel Paul 1926–1984. French philosopher who argued that human knowledge and subjectivity are dependent upon specific institutions and practices, and that they change through history. In particular, he was concerned to subvert conventional assumptions about 'social deviants' – the mentally ill, the sick, and the criminal – who, he believed, are oppressed by the approved knowledge of the period in which they live.

Foucault rejected phenomenology and existentialism, and his historicization of the self challenges the ideas of ◊Marxism. He was deeply influenced by the German philosopher Friedrich ◊Nietzsche, and developed an analysis of the operation of power in society using Nietzschean concepts. His publications include *Histoire de la folie/Madness and Civilization* 1961 and *Les Mots et les choses/The Order of Things* 1966.

Foucault French philosopher Michel Foucault, photographed in 1979. He developed the idea that those who have power in society are able to shape the knowledge of their time and to use that knowledge to keep control by labelling as deviant any individual who thinks differently. *Corbis*

Fountains Abbey Cistercian abbey in North Yorkshire, England. It was founded about 1132, and closed 1539 at the Dissolution of the Monasteries. The ruins were incorporated into a Romantic landscaped garden 1720–40 with a lake, formal water garden, temples, and a deer park.

four-colour process colour ◊printing using four printing plates, based on the principle that any colour is made up of differing proportions of the primary colours blue, red, and green. The first stage in preparing a colour picture for printing is to produce separate films, one each for the blue, red, and green respectively in the picture (colour separations). From these separations three printing plates are made, with a fourth plate for black (for shading or outlines and type). Ink colours complementary to those represented on the plates are used for printing – yellow for the blue plate, cyan for the red, and magenta for the green.

Fourdrinier machine papermaking machine patented by the Fourdrinier brothers Henry and Sealy in England 1803. On the machine, liquid pulp flows onto a moving wire-mesh belt, and water drains and is sucked away, leaving a damp paper web. This is passed first through a series of steam-heated rollers, which dry it, and then between heavy calendar rollers, which give it a smooth finish.

Such machines can measure up to 90 m/300 ft in length, and are still in use.

Fourier (François Marie) Charles 1772–1837. French socialist. In *Le Nouveau monde industriel/The New Industrial World* 1829–30, he advocated that society should be organized in self-sufficient cooperative units of about 1,500 people, and marriage should be abandoned.

Fourier Jean Baptiste Joseph 1768–1830. French applied mathematician whose formulation of heat flow 1807 contains the proposal that, with certain constraints, any mathematical function can be represented by trigonometrical series. This principle

'Man is neither the oldest nor the most constant problem that has been posed for human knowledge.'

MICHEL FOUCAULT
The Order of Things

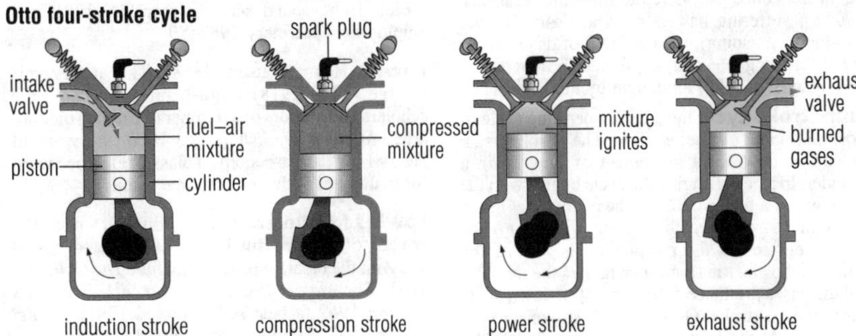

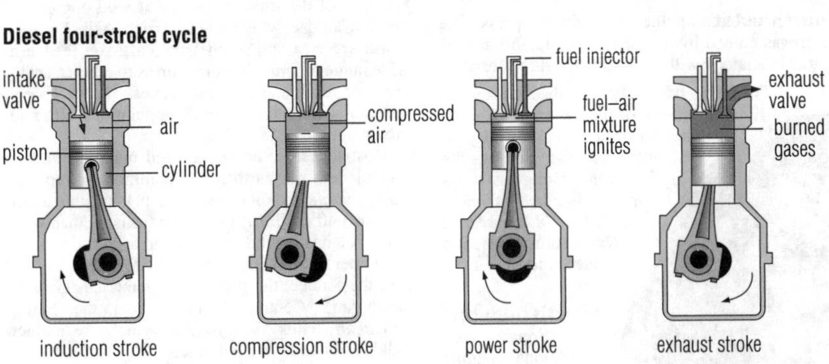

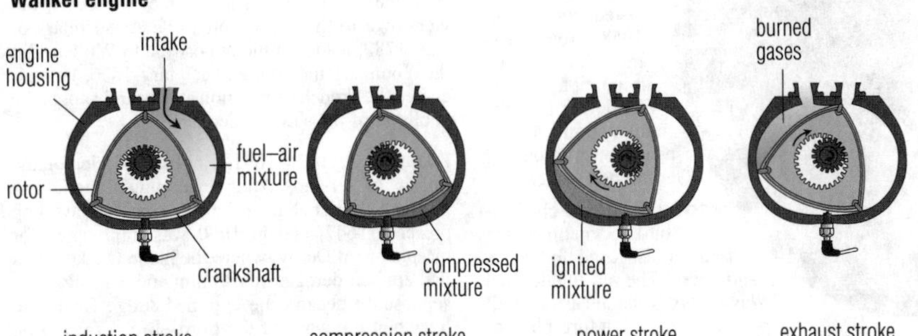

four-stroke cycle The four-stroke cycle of a modern petrol engine. The cycle is also called the Otto cycle, after German engineer Nikolaus Otto who introduced it in 1876. It improved on earlier engine cycles by compressing the fuel mixture before it was ignited.

fox Blanford's fox is found in open country in highland regions of south central Asia and Israel, where it supplements its diet by raiding fruit farms. It has been extensively hunted for its soft grey fur, and is now listed as an endangered species. *Corbis*

Fox Radical English Whig politician Charles Fox. Among the many liberal causes he advocated were the extension of suffrage to 'educated' women and the abolition of slavery. *Image Select (UK) Ltd*

forms the basis of Fourier analysis, used today in many different fields of physics. His idea, not immediately well received, gained currency and is embodied in his *Théorie analytique de la chaleur/The Analytical Theory of Heat* 1822.

Four Noble Truths in Buddhism, a summary of the basic concepts: there is suffering (Sanskrit *duhkha*); suffering has its roots in desire (*tanha*, clinging or grasping); the cessation of desire is the end of suffering, *nirvana*; and this can be reached by the Noble Eightfold Path taught by the Buddha.

four-stroke cycle the engine-operating cycle of most petrol and ◊diesel engines. The 'stroke' is an upward or downward movement of a piston in a cylinder. In a petrol engine the cycle begins with the induction of a fuel mixture as the piston goes down on its first stroke. On the second stroke (up) the piston compresses the mixture in the top of the cylinder. An electric spark then ignites the mixture, and the gases produced force the piston down on its third, power, stroke. On the fourth stroke (up) the piston expels the burned gases from the cylinder into the exhaust. *See illustration on previous page.*

fourth estate another name for the press. The term was coined by the British politician Edmund Burke in analogy with the traditional three ◊estates.

Fourth of July in the USA, the anniversary of the day in 1776 when the ◊Declaration of Independence was adopted by the Continental Congress. It is a public holiday, officially called ***Independence Day***, commemorating independence from Britain.

Fourth Republic the French constitutional regime that was established between 1944 and 1946 and lasted until 4 Oct 1958: from liberation after Nazi occupation during World War II to the introduction of a new constitution by General de Gaulle.

fowl chicken or chicken-like bird. Sometimes the term is also used for ducks and geese. The red jungle fowl *Gallus gallus* is the ancestor of all domestic chickens. It is a forest bird of Asia, without the size or egg-laying ability of many domestic strains. ◊Guinea fowl are of African origin.

Fowler (Peter) Norman 1938–1996. British Conservative politician, chair of the party 1992–94. He was a junior minister in the Heath government, transport secretary in the first Thatcher administration 1979, social services secretary 1981, and employment secretary 1987–89.

Fowler Henry Watson (1858–1933) and Francis George (1870–1918) English brothers who were scholars and authors of a number of English dictionaries. *Modern English Usage* 1926, the work of Henry Fowler, has become a classic reference work for matters of style and disputed usage.

Fowles John Robert 1926– . English writer. His novels, often concerned with illusion and reality and with the creative process, include *The Collector* 1963, *The Magus* 1965, *The French Lieutenant's Woman* 1969 (a best seller, filmed 1981), *Daniel Martin* 1977, *Mantissa* 1982, and *A Maggot* 1985.

fox one of the smaller species of wild dog of the family Canidae, which live in Africa, Asia, Europe, North America, and South America. Foxes feed on a wide range of animals from worms to rabbits, scavenge for food, and also eat berries. They are very adaptable, maintaining high populations close to urban areas.

Most foxes are nocturnal, and make an underground den, or 'earth'. The common or red fox *Vulpes vulpes* is about 60 cm/2 ft long plus a tail ('brush') 40 cm/1.3 ft long. The fur is reddish with black patches behind the ears and a light tip to the tail. Other foxes include the Arctic fox *Alopex lagopus*, the fennec, the grey foxes genus *Urocyon* of North and Central America, and the South American genus *Dusicyon*, to which the extinct Falkland Islands dog belonged.

Fox Charles James 1749–1806. English Whig politician, son of the 1st Baron Holland. He entered Parliament 1769 as a supporter of the court, but went over to the opposition 1774. As secretary of state 1782, leader of the opposition to William Pitt the Younger, and foreign secretary 1806, he welcomed the French Revolution and brought about the abolition of the slave trade.

Fox George 1624–1691. English founder of the Society of ◊Friends. After developing his belief in a mystical 'inner light', he became a travelling preacher 1647, and in 1650 was imprisoned for blasphemy at Derby, where the name Quakers was first applied derogatorily to him and his followers, supposedly because he enjoined Judge Bennet to 'quake at the word of the Lord'. ▷ *See feature on pp. 982–983.*

foxglove any flowering plant of the genus *Digitalis*, family Scrophulariaceae, found in Europe and the Mediterranean region. It bears showy spikes of bell-like flowers, and grows up to 1.5 m/5 ft high.

The wild species *D. purpurea*, native to Britain, produces purple to reddish flowers. Its leaves were the original source of digitalis, a drug used for some heart problems.

foxhound small, keen-nosed hound, up to 60 cm/2 ft tall and black, tan, and white in colour. There are two recognized breeds: the English foxhound, bred for some 300 years to hunt foxes, and the American foxhound, not quite as stocky, used for foxes and other game.

fox-hunting the pursuit of a fox across country on horseback, aided by a pack of foxhounds, specially trained to track the fox's scent.

The aim is to catch and kill the fox. In draghunting, hounds pursue a prepared trail rather than a fox.

Described by the playwright Oscar Wilde as 'the unspeakable in pursuit of the uneatable', fox-hunting has met with increasing opposition. Animal-rights activists condemn it as involving excessive cruelty, and in Britain groups of hunt saboteurs disrupt it. Fox-hunting dates from the late 17th century, when it arose as a practical method of limiting the fox population which endangered poultry farming, but by the early 19th century it was indulged in as a sport by the British aristocracy and gentry who ceremonialized it. In 1998 the Labour government postponed debate on an anti-fox-hunting bill due to lack of parliamentary time, despite widespread support for the bill.

foxtrot ballroom dance originating in the USA about 1914. It is believed to be named after Harry Fox, a US vaudeville comedian who did a distinctive trotting dance to ragtime music.

fractal (from Latin *fractus* 'broken') irregular shape or surface produced by a procedure of repeated subdivision. Generated on a computer screen, fractals are used in creating models of geographical or biological processes (for example, the creation of a coastline by erosion or accretion, or the growth of plants). Sets of curves with such discordant properties were developed in the 19th century in Germany by Georg Cantor and Karl Weierstrass. The name was coined by the French mathematician Benoit Mandelbrod. Fractals are also used for computer art.

fraction in chemistry, a group of similar compounds, the boiling points of which fall within a particular range and which are separated during fractional ◊distillation (fractionation).

fraction (from Latin *fractus* 'broken') in mathematics, a number that indicates one or more equal parts of a whole. Usually, the number of equal parts into which the unit is divided (denominator) is written below a horizontal line, and the number of parts comprising the fraction (numerator) is written above; thus $\frac{2}{3}$ or $\frac{3}{4}$. Such fractions are called ***vulgar*** or ***simple*** fractions. The denominator can never be zero.

A ***proper fraction*** is one in which the numerator is less than the denominator. An ***improper fraction*** has a numerator that is larger than the denominator, for example $\frac{3}{2}$. It can therefore be expressed as a mixed number, for example, $1\frac{1}{2}$. A combination such as $\frac{5}{0}$ is not regarded as a fraction (an object cannot be divided into zero equal parts), and mathematically any number divided by 0 is equal to infinity.

A ***decimal fraction*** has as its denominator a power of 10, and these are omitted by use of the decimal point and notation, for example 0.04, which is $\frac{4}{100}$. The digits to the right of the decimal point indicate the numerators of vulgar fractions whose denominators are 10, 100, 1,000, and so on. Most fractions can be expressed exactly as decimal fractions ($\frac{1}{3}$ = 0.333...). Fractions are also known as the ***rational numbers***; that is, numbers formed by a ratio. Integers may be expressed as fractions with a denominator of 1.

fractionating column device in which many separate ◊distillations can occur so that a liquid mixture can be separated into its components.

Various designs exist but the primary aim is to allow maximum contact between the hot rising vapours and the cooling descending liquid. As the mixture of vapours ascends the column it becomes progressively enriched in the lower-boiling-point components, so these separate out first.

fractionation or ***fractional distillation*** process used to split complex mixtures (such as crude oil) into their components, usually by repeated heating, boiling, and condensation; see ◊distillation.

Fragonard Jean-Honoré 1732–1806. French painter. He was the leading exponent of the Rococo style (along with his teacher François Boucher). His light-hearted subjects, often erotic, include *Les heureux Hazards de l'escarpolette/The Swing* c. 1766 (Wallace Collection, London). His range was extraordinary: he could successfully design a composition in the grand manner, as in *Corrhesus and Callirhoe* 1765 (Louvre), and paint the most exquisite of *fêtes galantes* (aristocratic pastoral fantasy scenes) in *The Swing*, poetic landscapes, and playful yet beautifully executed genre pieces such as *L'Éducation fait tout* c. 1780 (São Paulo, Brazil), in which he showed his appreciation of the charm of childhood. He was a master of every technique – oil, pastel, miniature, gouache, etching, wash, and crayon drawing.

franc French coin, so called from 1360 when it was a gold coin inscribed *Francorum Rex*, 'King of the Franks'. The ***franc CFA*** (*Communauté française d'Afrique*) is the currency of the former French territories in Africa; in France's Pacific territories the ***franc CFP*** (*Communauté française du pacifique*) is used. The currency units of Belgium, Luxembourg, and Switzerland are also called francs.

France country in W Europe, bounded NE by Belgium and Germany, E by Germany, Switzerland, and Italy, S by the Mediterranean Sea, SW by Spain and Andorra, and W by the Atlantic Ocean. *See country box on p. 412 and tables on pp. 413 and 414.*

France Anatole. Pen name of Jacques Anatole François Thibault 1844–1924. French writer. His works are marked by wit, urbanity, and style. His earliest novel was *Le Crime de Sylvestre Bonnard/The Crime of Sylvester Bonnard* 1881; later books include the satiric *L'Ile des pingouins/Penguin Island* 1908. He was a socialist and a supporter of the wrongfully accused officer Alfred ◊Dreyfus. Nobel Prize for Literature 1921.

Francesca Piero della see ◊Piero della Francesca, Italian painter.

Franche-Comté region of E France; area 16,200 sq km/6,253 sq mi; population (1990) 1,097,300. Its capital is Besançon, and it includes the *départements* of Doubs, Jura, Haute Saône, and Territoire de Belfort. In the mountainous Jura, there is farming and forestry, and elsewhere there are engineering and plastics industries.

Once independent and ruled by its own count, it was disputed by France, Burgundy, Austria, and Spain from the 9th century until it became a French province under the Treaty of Nijmegen 1678.

franchise in business, the right given by one company to another to manufacture, distribute, or provide its branded products. It is usual for the franchisor to impose minimum quality conditions on its franchisees to make sure that customers receive a fair deal from the franchisee and ensure that the brand image is maintained.

The franchisor is also often responsible for advertising and product development. It may insist on franchisees buying raw materials from it alone. The franchisee has to pay a levy, usually a percentage of either profit or ◊turnover, to the franchisor.

franchise in politics, the eligibility, right, or privilege to vote at public elections, especially for the members of a legislative body, or parliament. In the UK adult citizens are eligible to vote from the age of 18, with the exclusion of peers, the insane, and criminals.

In the UK it was 1918 before all men had the right to vote, and 1928 before women were enfranchised; in New Zealand women were granted the right as early as 1893.

Francia José Gaspar Rodríguez de 1766–1840. Paraguayan dictator 1814–40, known as ***El Supremo***. A lawyer, he emerged as a strongman after independence was achieved 1811, and was designated dictator by congress 1814. Hostile to the Argentine regime, he sealed off the country and followed an isolationist policy.

***Fragonard** Psyche Showing Her Sisters the Gifts from Cupid* 1753 by Jean-Honoré Fragonard (National Gallery, London). Lavish, sensual, and frivolous, Fragonard's paintings were among the most colourful expressions of the pleasure-loving court of the French king Louis XV. *Corbis*

Francis I 1494–1547. King of France from 1515. He succeeded his cousin Louis XII, and from 1519 European politics turned on the rivalry between him and the Holy Roman emperor Charles V, which led to war 1521–29, 1536–38, and 1542–44. In 1525 Francis was defeated and captured at Pavia and released only after signing a humiliating treaty. At home, he developed absolute monarchy.

Francis II 1544–1560. King of France from 1559 when he succeeded his father, Henri II. He married Mary Queen of Scots 1558. He was completely under the influence of his mother, ◊Catherine de' Medici.

Francis II 1768–1835. Holy Roman emperor 1792–1806. He became Francis I, Emperor of Austria 1804, and abandoned the title of Holy Roman emperor 1806. During his reign Austria was five times involved in war with France, 1792–97, 1798–1801, 1805, 1809, and 1813–14. He succeeded his father, Leopold II.

Franciscan order Catholic order of friars, ***Friars Minor*** or ***Grey Friars***, founded 1209 by Francis of Assisi. Subdivisions were the strict Observants; the Conventuals, who were allowed to own property corporately; and the ◊Capuchins, founded 1529.

The Franciscan order included such scholars as the English scientist Roger Bacon. A female order, the Poor Clares, was founded by St ◊Clare 1215, and lay people who adopt a Franciscan regime without abandoning the world form a third order, Tertiaries.

Francis Ferdinand archduke of Austria, also known as ◊Franz Ferdinand.

Francis Joseph emperor of Austria-Hungary, also known as ◊Franz Joseph.

Francis of Assisi, St (born Giovanni Bernadone) 1182–1226. Italian founder of the Roman Catholic Franciscan order of friars 1209 and, with St Clare, of the Poor Clares 1212. In 1224 he is said to have undergone a mystical experience during which he received the stigmata (five wounds of Jesus). Many stories are told of his ability to charm wild animals, and he is the patron saint of ecologists. His feast day is 4 Oct. Canonized 1228.

Francis of Sales, St 1567–1622. French bishop and theologian. He became bishop of Geneva 1602, and in 1610 founded the order of the Visitation, an order of nuns. He is the patron saint of journalists and other writers. His feast day is 24 Jan. Canonized 1655.

francium radioactive metallic element, symbol Fr, atomic number 87, relative atomic mass 223. It is one of the alkali metals and occurs in nature in small amounts as a decay product of actinium. Its longest-lived isotope has a half-life of only 21 minutes. Francium was discovered and named in 1939 by Marguérite Perey to honour her country.

Franck César Auguste 1822–1890. Belgian composer. His music, mainly religious and Romantic in style, includes the *Symphony in D Minor* 1866–68, *Symphonic Variations* 1885 for piano and orchestra, the *Violin Sonata* 1886, the oratorio *Les Béatitudes/The Beatitudes* 1879, and many organ pieces.

Franco Francisco (Paulino Hermenegildo Teódulo Bahamonde) 1892–1975. Spanish dictator from 1939. As a general, he led the insurgent Nationalists to victory in the Spanish ◊Civil War 1936–39, supported by Fascist Italy and Nazi Germany, and established a dictatorship. In 1942 Franco reinstated a Cortes (Spanish parliament), which in 1947 passed an act by which he became head of state for life.

Franco was born in Galicia, NW Spain. He entered the army 1910, served in Morocco 1920–26, and was appointed Chief of Staff 1935, but demoted to governor of the Canary Islands 1936. Dismissed from this post by the Popular Front (Republican) government, he plotted an uprising with German and Italian assistance, and on the outbreak of the Civil War organized the invasion of Spain by N African troops and foreign legionaries. After the

'The good critic is he who relates the adventures of his soul among masterpieces.'

ANATOLE FRANCE
The Literary Life, dedicatory letter

Franco General Franco in 1938. Leader of the victorious Nationalists in the Spanish Civil War, he established a dictatorship and remained head of state until his death in 1975. *Topham*

death of General Sanjurjo, he took command of the Nationalists, proclaiming himself *caudillo* (leader) of Spain. The defeat of the Republic with the surrender of Madrid 1939 brought all Spain under his government. On the outbreak of World War II, in spite of Spain's official attitude of 'strictest neutrality', his pro-Axis sympathies led him to send aid, later withdrawn, to the German side.

At home, he curbed the growing power of the ◊Falange Española (the fascist party), and in later years slightly liberalized his regime. In 1969 he nominated ◊Juan Carlos as his successor and future king of Spain. He relinquished the premiership 1973, but remained head of state until his death.

Franco-Prussian War 1870–71. The Prussian chancellor Otto von Bismarck put forward a German candidate for the vacant Spanish throne with the deliberate, and successful, intention of provoking the French emperor Napoleon III into declaring war. The Prussians defeated the French at Sedan, then besieged Paris. The Treaty of Frankfurt May 1871 gave Alsace, Lorraine, and a large French indemnity to Prussia. The war established Prussia, at the head of a newly established German empire, as Europe's leading power.

frangipani any tropical American tree of the genus *Plumeria*, especially *P. rubra*, of the dogbane

FRANCE
French Republic

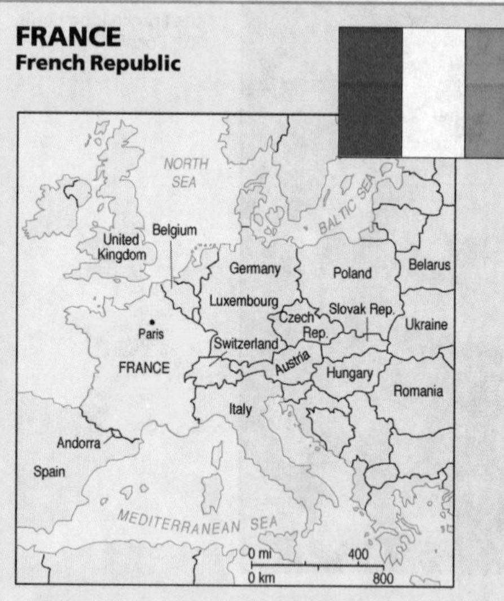

national name *République Française*
area (including Corsica) 543,965 sq km/209,970 sq mi
capital Paris
major towns/cities Lyon, Lille, Bordeaux, Toulouse, Nantes, Strasbourg
major ports Marseille, Nice, Le Havre
physical features rivers Seine, Loire, Garonne, Rhône; mountain ranges Alps, Massif Central, Pyrenees, Jura, Vosges, Cévennes; Auvergne mountain region; Mont Blanc (4,810 m/15,781 ft); Ardennes forest; Riviera; caves of Dordogne with evidence of early humans, including paleolithic cave art at Lascaux; the island of Corsica
territories Guadeloupe, French Guiana, Martinique, Réunion, St Pierre and Miquelon, Southern and Antarctic Territories, New Caledonia, French Polynesia, Wallis and Futuna, Mayotte
head of state Jacques Chirac from 1995
head of government Lionel Jospin from 1997
political system liberal democracy
administrative divisions 22 regions containing 96 departments, four overseas departments, two territorial collectivities, and four overseas territories
political parties Rally for the Republic (RPR), neo-Gaullist conservative; Union for French Democracy (UDF), centre-right; Socialist Party (PS), left of centre; Left Radical Movement (MRG), centre-left; French Communist Party (PCF), Marxist-Leninist; National Front, far-right; Greens, fundamentalist-ecologist; Generation Ecologie, pragmatic ecologist; Movement for France, right-wing, anti-Maastricht
armed forces 409,000; paramilitary gendarmerie 93,400 (June 1995)
conscription none
defence spend (% GDP) 3.3 (1994)
education spend (% GNP) 5.7 (1992)
health spend (% GDP) 7.3 (1993)
death penalty abolished 1981
population 58,333,000 (1996 est)
population growth rate 0.4% (1990–95); 0.2% (2000–05)
age distribution (% of total population) <15 19.6%, 15–65 65.5%, >65 14.9% (1995)
ethnic distribution predominantly French ethnic, of Celtic and Latin descent; Basque minority in the SW; 7% of the population are immigrants – a third of these are from Algeria and Morocco and reside mainly in the Marseilles Midi region and in northern cities, a fifth originate from Portugal, and a tenth each from Italy and Spain
population density (per sq km) 105 (1994)
urban population (% of total) 73 (1995)
labour force 44% of population: 5% agriculture, 29% industry, 66% services (1990)
unemployment 11.7% (1995)
child mortality rate (under 5, per 1,000 live births) 9 (1993)
life expectancy 73 (men), 81 (women)
education (compulsory years) 10
literacy rate 99%
languages French (regional languages include Basque, Breton, Catalan, and Provençal)
religions Roman Catholic; also Muslim, Protestant, and Jewish minorities
TV sets (per 1,000 people) 408 (1992)
currency franc
GDP (US $) 1,540.1 billion (1995)
GDP per capita (PPP) (US $) 19,955 (1995)
growth rate 2.6% (1994/95)
average annual inflation 2.1% (1995)
major trading partners EU (principally Germany, Italy, Benelux, UK); USA
resources coal, petroleum, natural gas, iron ore, copper, zinc, bauxite
industries mining, quarrying, food products, transport equipment, non-electrical machinery, electrical machinery, weapons, metals and metal products, yarn and fabrics, wine, tourism, aircraft, weapons
exports machinery and transport equipment, food and live animals, beverages and tobacco, textile yarn, fabrics and other basic manufactures, clothing and accessories, perfumery and cosmetics. Principal market: Germany 17.1% (1994)
imports food and live animals, mineral fuels, machinery and transport equipment, chemicals and chemical products, basic manufactures. Principal source: Germany 17.8% (1994)
arable land 33.1%
agricultural products wheat, sugar beet, maize, barley, vine fruits, potatoes, fruit, vegetables; livestock and dairy products

HISTORY
5th C BC Celtic peoples invaded the region.
58–51 BC Romans conquered the Celts and formed province of Gaul.
5th C AD Gaul overrun by Franks and other Germanic tribes.
481–511 Frankish chief, Clovis, accepted Christianity and formed a kingdom based at Paris; under his successors, the Merovingian dynasty, the kingdom disintegrated.
751–68 Pepin the Short usurped the Frankish throne, reunified the kingdom, and founded the Carolingian dynasty.
768–814 Charlemagne conquered much of W Europe and created the Holy Roman Empire.
843 Treaty of Verdun divided the Holy Roman Empire into three, with the western portion corresponding to modern France.
9th–10th Cs Weak central government allowed the great nobles to become virtually independent.
987 Frankish crown passed to House of Capet; the Capets ruled the district around Paris, but were surrounded by vassals more powerful than themselves.
1180–1223 Philip II doubled the royal domain and tightened control over the nobles; the power of the Capets gradually extended with support of church and towns.
1328 When Charles IV died without an heir, Philip VI established the House of Valois.
1337 Start of the Hundred Years' War: Edward III of England disputed the Valois succession and claimed the throne. English won victories at Crécy 1346 and Agincourt 1415.
1429 Joan of Arc raised the siege of Orléans; Hundred Years' War ended with Charles VII expelling the English 1453.
16th–17th Cs French kings fought the Habsburgs (of Holy Roman Empire and Spain) for supremacy in W Europe.
1562–98 Civil wars between nobles were fought under religious slogans, Catholic versus Protestant (or Huguenot).
1589–1610 Henry IV, first king of Bourbon dynasty, established peace, religious tolerance, and absolute monarchy.
1634–48 The ministers Richelieu and Mazarin, by intervention in the Thirty Years' War, secured Alsace and made France the leading power in Europe.
1701–14 War of the Spanish Succession: England, Austria, and allies checked expansionism of France under Louis XIV.
1756–63 Seven Years' War: France lost most of its colonies in India and Canada to Britain.
1789 French Revolution abolished absolute monarchy and feudalism; First Republic proclaimed and revolutionary wars began 1792.
1799 Napoleon Bonaparte seized power in coup; crowned himself emperor 1804; France conquered much of Europe.
1814 Defeat of France; restoration of Bourbon monarchy; Napoleon defeated at Waterloo 1815.
1830 Liberal revolution deposed Charles X in favour of his cousin Louis Philippe, the 'Citizen King'.
1848 Revolution established Second Republic; conflict between liberals and socialists; Louis Napoleon, nephew of Napoleon I, elected president.
1852 Louis Napoleon proclaimed Second Empire, taking title Napoleon III.
1870–71 Franco-Prussian War: France lost Alsace-Lorraine; Second Empire abolished; Paris Commune crushed; Third Republic founded.
late 19th C France colonized Indochina, much of N Africa, and the S Pacific.
1914–18 France resisted German invasion in World War I; Alsace-Lorraine recovered 1919.
1936–37 Left-wing 'Popular Front' government of Léon Blum introduced many social reforms.
1939 France entered World War II.
1940 Germany invaded and occupied N France; Marshal Pétain formed right-wing puppet regime at Vichy; resistance maintained by Maquis and Free French; Germans occupied all France 1942.
1944 Allies liberated France; provisional government formed by General Charles de Gaulle, leader of Free French.
1946 Fourth Republic proclaimed.
1949 Became a member of NATO; withdrew from military command structure 1966.
1954 French leave Indochina after eight years of war; guerrilla war against French rule in Algeria.
1957 France was a founder member of the European Economic Community.
1958 Algerian crisis caused collapse of Fourth Republic; De Gaulle took power, becoming president of the Fifth Republic 1959.
1962 Algeria achieved independence.
1968 'May events': revolutionary students rioted in Paris; general strike throughout France.
1981 François Mitterrand elected Fifth Republic's first socialist president.
1986–88 'Cohabitation' of socialist president with conservative prime minister; again 1993–95.
1995 Conservative Jacques Chirac elected president. Widespread condemnation of government's decision to resume nuclear tests in Pacific region.
1996 End to nuclear-testing in S Pacific. Spending cuts agreed to meet European Monetary Union entry criteria. Unemployment at post-war high.
1997 General election called by President Chirac. Unexpected victory for Socialists; Lionel Jospin appointed prime minister. Plans to reduce unemployment. Government accused of policy U-turns.
1998 Protests by unemployed. Law passed to reduce working week to 35 hours, from 2000. Far-right National Front (FN) held balance of power in 19 regions after March elections, and caused divisions within 'mainstream right' on issue of whether or not to accept FN support to form administrations.

SEE ALSO Algeria; De Gaulle, Charles; Franco-Prussian War; French Revolution; Hundred Years' War; Napoleonic Wars

FRANCE: REGIONS AND DÉPARTEMENTS

with official département numbers

Region and département	Capital	Area in sq km/sq mi
Alsace		8,300/3,204
67 Bas-Rhin	Strasbourg	
68 Haut-Rhin	Colmar	
Aquitaine		41,300/15,945
24 Dordogne	Périgueux	
33 Gironde	Bordeaux	
40 Landes	Mont-de-Marsan	
47 Lot-et-Garonne	Agen	
64 Pyrénées-Atlantiques	Pau	
Auvergne		26,000/10,038
03 Allier	Moulins	
15 Cantal	Aurillac	
43 Haute-Loire	Le Puy	
63 Puy-de-Dôme	Clermont-Ferrand	
Basse-Normandie		17,600/6,795
14 Calvados	Caen	
50 Manche	Saint-Lô	
61 Orne	Alençon	
Brittany (Bretagne)		27,200/10,501
22 Côtes-d'Armor	St Brieuc	
29 Finistère	Quimper	
35 Ille-et-Vilaine	Rennes	
56 Morbihan	Vannes	
Burgundy (Bourgogne)		31,600/12,200
21 Côte-d'Or	Dijon	
58 Nièvre	Nevers	
71 Saône-et-Loire	Mâcon	
89 Yonne	Auxerre	
Centre		39,200/15,135
18 Cher	Bourges	
28 Eure-et-Loir	Chartres	
36 Indre	Châteauroux	
37 Indre-et-Loire	Tours	
41 Loir-et-Cher	Blois	
45 Loiret	Orléans	
Champagne-Ardenne		25,600/9,884
08 Ardennes	Charleville-Mézières	
10 Aube	Troyes	
51 Marne	Châlons-sur-Marne	
52 Haute-Marne	Chaumont	
Corsica		8,700/3,359
2B Haute-Corse	Bastia	
2A Corse du Sud	Ajaccio	
Franche-Comté		16,200/6,254
25 Doubs	Besançon	
39 Jura	Lons-le-Saunier	
70 Haute-Saône	Vesoul	
90 Terr. de Belfort	Belfort	
Haute-Normandie		12,300/4,749
27 Eure	Evreux	
76 Seine-Maritime	Rouen	
Ile de France		12,000/4,633
91 Essonne	Evry	
94 Val-de-Marne	Créteil	
95 Val-d'Oise	Cergy-Pontoise	
75 Ville de Paris		
77 Seine-et-Marne	Melun	
92 Hauts-de-Seine	Nanterre	
93 Seine-Saint-Denis	Bobigny	
78 Yvelines	Versailles	
Languedoc-Roussillon		27,400/10,579
11 Aude	Carcassonne	
30 Gard	Nîmes	
34 Hérault	Montpellier	
48 Lozère	Mende	
66 Pyrénées-Orientales	Perpignan	
Limousin		16,900/6,525
19 Corrèze	Tulle	
23 Creuse	Guéret	
87 Haute-Vienne	Limoges	
Lorraine		23,600/9,111
54 Meurthe-et-Moselle	Nancy	
55 Meuse	Bar-le-Duc	
57 Moselle	Metz	
88 Vosges	Épinal	
Midi-Pyrénées		45,300/17,490
09 Ariège	Foix	
12 Aveyron	Rodez	
31 Haute-Garonne	Toulouse	
32 Gers	Auch	
46 Lot	Cahors	
65 Hautes-Pyrénées	Tarbes	
81 Tarn	Albi	
82 Tarn-et-Garonne	Montauban	
Nord-Pas-de-Calais		12,400/4,787
59 Nord	Lille	
62 Pas-de-Calais	Arras	
Pays de la Loire		32,100/12,393
44 Loire-Atlantique	Nantes	
49 Maine-et-Loire	Angers	
53 Mayenne	Laval	
72 Sarthe	Le Mans	
85 Vendée	La Roche-sur-Yon	
Picardie		19,400/7,490
02 Aisne	Laon	
60 Oise	Beauvais	
80 Somme	Amiens	
Poitou-Charentes		25,800/9,961
16 Charente	Angoulême	
17 Charente-Maritime	La Rochelle	
79 Deux-Sèvres	Niort	
86 Vienne	Poitiers	
Provence-Alpes-Côte d'Azur		31,400/12,123
04 Alpes-de-Haute-Provence	Digne	
05 Hautes-Alpes	Gap	
06 Alpes-Maritimes	Nice	
13 Bouches-du-Rhône	Marseille	
83 Var	Draguignan	
84 Vaucluse	Avignon	
Rhône-Alpes		43,700/16,872
01 Ain	Bourg-en-Bresse	
07 Ardèche	Privas	
26 Drôme	Valence	
38 Isère	Grenoble	
42 Loire	St Étienne	
69 Rhône	Lyon	
73 Savoie	Chambéry	
74 Haute-Savoie	Annecy	

family Apocynaceae. Perfume is made from the strongly scented flowers.

Frank member of a group of Germanic peoples prominent in Europe in the 3rd to 9th centuries. Believed to have originated in Pomerania on the Baltic Sea, they had settled on the Rhine by the 3rd century, spread into the Roman Empire by the 4th century, and gradually conquered most of Gaul, Italy, and Germany under the ◊Merovingian and ◊Carolingian dynasties.

The Salian (western) Franks conquered Roman Gaul during the 4th–5th centuries. Their ruler, Clovis, united the Salians with the Ripuarian (eastern) Franks, and they were converted to Christianity. The Merovingians conquered most of western and central Europe, and lasted until the 8th century when the Carolingian dynasty was founded under Charlemagne. The kingdom of the W Franks was fused by the 9th century into a single people with the Gallo-Romans, speaking the modified form of Latin that became modern French.

Frank Anne (Anneliese Marie) 1929–1945. German diarist. She fled to the Netherlands with her family 1933 to escape Nazi anti-Semitism (the ◊Holocaust).

During the German occupation of Amsterdam, they and two other families remained in a sealed-off room, protected by Dutch sympathizers 1942–44, when betrayal resulted in their deportation and Anne's death in Belsen concentration camp. Her diary of her time in hiding was published 1947.

Previously suppressed portions of her diary were published 1989. The house in which the family took refuge is preserved as a museum. Her diary has sold 20 million copies in more than 50 languages and has been made into a play and a film publicizing the fate of millions. *See illustration on following page.*

Frank Robert 1924– . US photographer. He is best known for his informal and unromanticized pictures of American life. These were published, with a foreword by the US novelist Jack Kerouac, as *The Americans* 1959. Since then he has concentrated mainly on filmmaking.

Frankenstein or ***The Modern Prometheus*** Gothic horror story by Mary ◊Shelley, published in England 1818. Frankenstein, a scientist, discovers how to bring inanimate matter to life, and creates a man-monster. When Frankenstein fails to provide a mate to satisfy the creature's human emotions, it seeks revenge by killing Frankenstein's brother and bride. Frankenstein dies in an attempt to destroy his creation.

Frankenthaler Helen 1928– . US Abstract Expressionist painter. She invented the colour-staining technique whereby the unprimed, absorbent canvas is stained or soaked with thinned-out paint, creating deep, soft veils of translucent colour.

Frankfurt-am-Main city in Hessen, Germany, 72 km/45 mi NE of Mannheim; population (1993) 663,600. It is a commercial and banking centre, with electrical and machine industries, and an inland port on the river Main. An international book fair is held here annually.

history Frankfurt was a free imperial city 1372–1806, when it was incorporated into ◊Prussia. It is the birthplace of the poet Goethe. It was the headquarters of the US zone of occupation in World War II and of the Anglo–US zone 1947–49.

Frankfurter Felix 1882–1965. Austrian-born US jurist and Supreme Court justice. As a supporter of liberal causes, Frankfurter was one of the founders of the American Civil Liberties Union 1920. Appointed to the US Supreme Court 1939 by F D Roosevelt, he opposed the use of the judicial veto to advance political ends.

Frankfurt School the members of the ***Institute of Social Research***, set up at Frankfurt University,

Anne op school, ongeveer 11 jaar oud

Frank German-Jewish diarist Anne Frank at her school desk in Amsterdam soon after the outbreak of World War II. Two years later she and her family had to go into hiding to escape persecution. Her diary, which bears poignant witness to the courage and hardship of those in hiding from the Nazis, describes the two years they spent in a closed-off part of an office building in Amsterdam. The family were betrayed and she died in Belsen concentration camp at the age of 16. *Topham*

❛But in this world nothing can be said to be certain, except death and taxes.❜

Benjamin Franklin
Letter to Jean Baptiste Le Roy
13 Nov 1789

Germany, 1923 as the first Marxist research centre. With the rise of Hitler, many of its members went to the USA and set up the institute at Columbia University, New York. In 1969 the institute was dissolved.

In the 1930s, under its second director Max Horkheimer (1895–1973), a group that included Erich Fromm, Herbert Marcuse, and T W Adorno attempted to update Marxism and create a coherent and viable social theory. Drawing on a variety of disciplines as well as the writings of Marx and Freud, they produced works such as *Authority and the Family* 1936 and developed a Marxist perspective known as ***critical theory***. After World War II the institute returned to Frankfurt, although Marcuse and some others remained in the USA. The German and US branches diverged in the 1950s, and the institute was dissolved after Adorno's death, although Jürgen Habermas and others have since attempted to revive its theory and research programme.

frankincense resin of various African and Asian trees of the genus *Boswellia*, family Burseraceae, burned as incense. Costly in ancient times, it is traditionally believed to be one of the three gifts brought by the Magi to the infant Jesus.

Franklin (Stella Marian Sarah) Miles 1879–1954. Australian novelist. Her first novel, *My Brilliant Career* 1901, autobiographical and feminist, drew on her experiences of rural Australian life. *My Career Goes Bung*, written as a sequel, was not published until 1946.

Franklin Aretha 1942– . US soul singer. Her gospel background infuses her four-octave voice with a passionate conviction and authority. Her hits include 'Respect' 1967, 'Chain of Fools' 1968, and the albums *Lady Soul* 1968, *Amazing Grace* 1972, and *Who's Zoomin' Who?* 1985.

Franklin Benjamin 1706–1790. US scientist, statesman, writer, printer, and publisher. He proved that lightning is a form of electricity, distinguished between positive and negative electricity, and invented the lightning conductor. He was the first US ambassador to France 1776–85, and negotiated peace with Britain 1783. As a delegate to the ◊Continental Congress from Pennsylvania 1785–88, he helped to draft the ◊Declaration of Independence and the US Constitution.

A printer, Franklin wrote and published the popular *Poor Richard's Almanac* 1733–58, as well as engaging in scientific experiment and making useful inventions, including bifocal spectacles. A member of the Pennsylvania Assembly 1751–64, he was sent to Britain 1757 to lobby Parliament about tax grievances and achieved the repeal of the ◊Stamp Act; on his return to the USA he was prominent in the deliberations leading up to independence. As ambassador in Paris he enlisted French help for the American Revolution. After independence he became president of Pennsylvania and worked hard to abolish slavery. ▷*See feature on pp. 32–33.*

Franklin John 1786–1847. English naval explorer who took part in expeditions to Australia, the Arctic, and N Canada, and in 1845 commanded an expedition to look for the Northwest Passage from the Atlantic to the Pacific, during which he and his crew perished.

Franklin Rosalind Elsie 1920–1958. English biophysicist whose research on ◊X-ray diffraction of ◊DNA crystals helped Francis ◊Crick and James D ◊Watson to deduce the chemical structure of DNA.

Franz Ferdinand or ***Francis Ferdinand*** 1863–1914. Archduke of Austria. He became heir to Emperor Franz Joseph, his uncle, 1884 but while visiting Sarajevo 28 June 1914, he and his wife were assassinated by a Serbian nationalist. Austria used the episode to make unreasonable demands on Serbia that ultimately precipitated World War I.

Franz Josef Land (Russian ***Zemlya Frantsa Iosifa***) archipelago of over 85 islands in the Arctic Ocean, E of Spitsbergen and NW of Novaya Zemlya, Russia; area 20,720 sq km/8,000 sq mi. There are scientific stations on the islands.

Franz Joseph or ***Francis Joseph*** 1830–1916. Emperor of Austria-Hungary from 1848, when his uncle Ferdinand I abdicated. After the suppression of the 1848 revolution, Franz Joseph tried to establish an absolute monarchy but had to grant Austria a parliamentary constitution 1861 and Hungary equality with Austria 1867. He was defeated in the Italian War 1859 and the Prussian War 1866. In 1914 he made the assassination of his heir and nephew Franz Ferdinand the excuse for attacking Serbia, thus precipitating World War I.

Frasch process process used to extract underground deposits of sulphur. Superheated steam is piped into the sulphur deposit and melts it. Compressed air is then pumped down to force the molten sulphur to the surface. The process was developed in the USA 1891 by German-born Herman Frasch (1851–1914).

Fraser river in British Columbia, Canada. It rises in the Yellowhead Pass of the Rockies and flows NW, then S, then W to the Strait of Georgia. It is 1,370 km/850 mi long and rich in salmon.

Fraser Angus Robert Charles 1965– . English cricketer. A tall right-arm opening bowler renowned for his accuracy, he made his Test debut in 1989 and at the end of the 1998 English season had taken 172 Test wickets in 44 matches at an average of 26.77.

Fraser (John) Malcolm 1930– . Australian Liberal politician, prime minister 1975–83.

In March 1975 he replaced Snedden as Liberal Party leader. In Nov, following the Whitlam government's economic difficulties, he blocked finance bills in the Senate, became prime minister of a caretaker government, and in the consequent general election won a large majority. He lost to Bob ◊Hawke in the 1983 election.

Fraser Antonia 1932– . English author. She has published authoritative biographies, including *Mary Queen of Scots* 1969; historical works, such as *The Weaker Vessel* 1984; and a series of detective novels featuring investigator Jemima Shore.

Fraser Dawn 1937– . Australian swimmer. The only person to win the same swimming event at three consecutive Olympic Games: 100 metres freestyle in 1956, 1960, and 1964. The holder of 27 world records, she was the first woman to break the one-minute barrier for the 100 metres.

FRANCE: RULERS AND HEADS OF STATE

Title	Name	Date of accession	Title	Name	Date of accession
kings	Pepin III/Childerich III	751	*kings*	Louis XIII	1610
	Pepin III	752		Louis XIV	1643
	Charlemagne/Carloman	768		Louis XVI	1774
	Louis I	814		National Convention	1792
	Lothair I	840		Directory (five members)	1795
	Charles II (the Bald)	843	*first consul*	Napoléon Bonaparte	1799
	Louis II	877	*emperor*	Napoléon I	1804
	Louis III	879	*king*	Louis XVIII	1814
	Charles III (the Fat)	882	*emperor*	Napoléon I	1815
	Odo	888	*kings*	Louis XVIII	1815
	Charles III (the Simple)	893		Charles X	1824
	Robert I	922		Louis XIX	1830
	Rudolf	923		Henri V	1830
	Louis IV	936		Louis-Philippe	1830
	Lothair II	954	*heads of state*	Philippe Buchez	1848
	Louis V	986		Louis Cavaignac	1848
	Hugues Capet	987	*president*	Louis Napoléon Bonaparte	1848
	Robert II	996	*emperor*	Napoléon III	1852
	Henri I	1031	*presidents*	Adolphe Thiers	1871
	Philippe I	1060		Patrice MacMahon	1873
	Louis VI	1108		Jules Grevy	1879
	Louis VII	1137		François Sadi-Carnot	1887
	Philippe II	1180		Jean Casimir-Périer	1894
	Louis VIII	1223		François Faure	1895
	Louis IX	1226		Emile Loubet	1899
	Philippe III	1270		Armand Fallières	1913
	Philippe IV	1285		Raymond Poincaré	1913
	Louis X	1314		Paul Deschanel	1920
	Jean I	1316		Alexandre Millerand	1920
	Philippe V	1328		Gaston Doumergue	1924
	Charles IV	1322		Paul Doumer	1931
	Philippe VI	1328		Albert Le Brun	1932
	Jean II	1350		Philippe Pétain (Vichy government)	1940
	Charles V	1356		provisional government	1944
	Charles VI	1380		Vincent Auriol	1947
	Charles VII	1422		René Coty	1954
	Louis XI	1461		Charles de Gaulle	1959
	Charles VIII	1483		Alain Poher	1969
	Louis XII	1498		Georges Pompidou	1969
	François I	1515		Alain Poher	1974
	Henri II	1547		Valéry Giscard d'Estaing	1974
	François II	1559		François Mitterrand	1981
	Charles IX	1560		Jacques Chirac	1995
	Henri III	1574			
	Henri IV	1574			

Fraser Peter 1884–1950. New Zealand Labour politician, born in Scotland. He held various cabinet posts 1935–40, and was prime minister 1940–49.

fraud in law, an act of deception resulting in injury to another. To establish fraud it has to be demonstrated that (1) a false representation (for example, a factually untrue statement) has been made, with the intention that it should be acted upon; (2) the person making the representation knows it is false or does not attempt to find out whether it is true or not; and (3) the person to whom the representation is made acts upon it to his or her detriment.

A contract based on fraud can be declared void, and the injured party can sue for damages.

In 1987 the Serious Fraud Office was set up to investigate and prosecute serious or complex criminal fraud cases.

Fraunhofer Joseph von 1787–1826. German physicist who did important work in optics. The dark lines in the solar spectrum (***Fraunhofer lines***), which reveal the chemical composition of the Sun's atmosphere, were accurately mapped by him.

Fraunhofer determined the dispersion powers and refractive indices of different kinds of optical glass. In the process, he developed the spectroscope, and in 1821 he became the first to use a diffraction grating to produce a spectrum from white light.

Frazer James George 1854–1941. Scottish anthropologist, author of *The Golden Bough* 1890, a pioneer study of the origins of religion and sociology on a comparative basis. It exerted considerable influence on writers such as T S Eliot and D H Lawrence, but by the standards of modern anthropology, many of its methods and findings are unsound.

Frederick V ('the Winter King') 1596–1632. Elector palatine of the Rhine 1610–23 and king of Bohemia 1619–20 (for one winter, hence the name), having been chosen by the Protestant Bohemians as ruler after the deposition of Catholic emperor ◊Ferdinand II. His selection was the cause of the Thirty Years' War. Frederick was defeated at the Battle of the White Mountain, near Prague, in Nov 1620, by the army of the Catholic League and fled to Holland.

Frederick IX 1899–1972. King of Denmark from 1947. He was succeeded by his daughter who became Queen ◊Margrethe II.

Frederick (I) Barbarossa ('red-beard') c. 1123–1190. Holy Roman emperor from 1152. Originally duke of Swabia, he was elected emperor 1152, and was engaged in a struggle with Pope Alexander III 1159–77, which ended in his submission; the Lombard cities, headed by Milan, took advantage of this to establish their independence of imperial control. Frederick joined the Third Crusade, and was drowned while crossing a river in Anatolia.

Frederick II the Great The Prussian king Frederick II the Great is shown in this portrait in his role as patron of the arts, holding his flute and the score of a piece of music he wrote for it. His father had him educated in religious and military affairs, scorning the arts, which he saw as effeminate; but Frederick studied philosophy, mathematics, history, and music by himself, and became a skilled diplomat, soldier, and musician. *Corbis*

Frederick II 1194–1250. Holy Roman emperor from 1212, called 'the Wonder of the World'. He led a crusade 1228–29 that recovered Jerusalem by treaty, without fighting. He quarrelled with the pope, who excommunicated him three times, and a feud began that lasted with intervals until the end of his reign. Frederick, who was a religious sceptic, is often considered the most cultured person of his age. He was the son of Henry VI. ▷ *See feature on pp. 280–281.*

Frederick three kings of Prussia, including:

Frederick (II) the Great 1712–1786. King of Prussia from 1740, when he succeeded his father Frederick William I. In that year he started the War of the ◊Austrian Succession by his attack on Austria. In the peace of 1745 he secured Silesia. The struggle was renewed in the ◊Seven Years' War 1756–63. He acquired West Prussia in the first partition of Poland 1772 and left Prussia as Germany's foremost state. He was an efficient and just ruler in the spirit of the Enlightenment and a patron of the arts.

In his domestic policy he encouraged industry and agriculture, reformed the judicial system, fostered education, and established religious toleration. He corresponded with the French writer Voltaire, and was a talented musician.

In the Seven Years' War, in spite of assistance from Britain, Frederick had a hard task holding his own against the Austrians and their Russian allies; the skill with which he did so proved him to be one of the great soldiers of history.

Frederick III 1831–1888. King of Prussia and emperor of Germany 1888. The son of Wilhelm I, he married the eldest daughter (Victoria) of Queen Victoria of the UK 1858 and, as a liberal, frequently opposed Chancellor Bismarck. He died three months after his accession.

Frederick William 1620–1688. Elector of Brandenburg from 1640, 'the Great Elector'. By successful wars against Sweden and Poland, he prepared the way for Prussian power in the 18th century.

Frederick William I 1688–1740. King of Prussia from 1713, who developed Prussia's military might and commerce.

Frederick William II 1744–1797. King of Prussia from 1786. He was a nephew of Frederick II but had little of his relative's military skill. He was unsuccessful in waging war on the French 1792–95 and lost all Prussia west of the Rhine.

Frederick William III 1770–1840. King of Prussia from 1797. He was defeated by Napoleon 1806, but contributed to his final overthrow 1813–15 and profited by being allotted territory at the Congress of Vienna.

Frederick William IV 1795–1861. King of Prussia from 1840. He upheld the principle of the ◊divine right of kings, but was forced to grant a constitution 1850 after the Prussian revolution 1848. He suffered two strokes 1857 and became mentally debilitated. His brother William (later emperor) took over his duties.

Free Church the Protestant denominations in England and Wales that are not part of the Church of England; for example, the Methodist Church, Baptist Union, and United Reformed Church (Congregational and Presbyterian). These churches joined for common action in the Free Church Federal Council 1940.

Free Church of Scotland the body of Scottish Presbyterians who seceded from the Established Church of Scotland in the Disruption of 1843. In 1900 all but a small section that retains the old name (known as the ***Wee Frees***) combined with the United Presbyterian Church to form the United Free Church of Scotland. Most of this reunited with the Church of Scotland 1929, although there remains a continuing United Free Church of Scotland.

free-enterprise or ***free-market*** economic system where private capital is used in business with profits going to private companies and individuals. The term has much the same meaning as ◊capitalism.

The two largest free-market economies in the world are (1994) the USA and Japan, where the ◊private sector provides about 70% of total output or GDP (◊gross domestic product) and the ◊public sector only 30%. The two other main types of economic system found today are ◊mixed economies and ◊command economies.

free-enterprise economy another term for free-market economy.

free fall the state in which a body is falling freely under the influence of ◊gravity, as in freefall parachuting (◊skydiving). The term weightless is normally used to describe a body in free fall in space.

In orbit, astronauts and spacecraft are still held by gravity and are in fact falling toward the Earth. Because of their speed (orbital velocity), the amount they fall towards the Earth just equals the amount the Earth's surface curves away; in effect they remain at the same height, apparently weightless.

Franz Joseph Austro-Hungarian emperor Franz Joseph. As well as suffering the murders and suicides that befell his family, he reigned over a series of catastrophic events, culminating in an attack on Serbia which hastened the beginning of World War I. *Image Select (UK) Ltd*

Free French in World War II, movement formed by General Charles ◊de Gaulle in the UK June 1940, consisting of French soldiers who continued to fight against the Axis after the Franco-German armistice. They took the name ***Fighting France*** 1942 and served in many campaigns, among them General Leclerc's advance from Chad to Tripolitania 1942, the Syrian campaigns 1941, the campaigns in the Western Desert, the Italian campaign, the liberation of France, and the invasion of Germany. Their emblem was the Cross of Lorraine, a cross with two bars.

freehold in England and Wales, ownership of land for an indefinite period. It is contrasted with a leasehold, which is always for a fixed period. In practical effect, a freehold is absolute ownership.

freeman one who enjoys the freedom of a borough. Since the early Middle Ages, a freeman has been allowed to carry out his craft or trade within the jurisdiction of the borough and to participate in municipal government, but since the development of modern local government, such privileges have become largely honorary.

There have generally been four ways of becoming a freeman: by apprenticeship to an existing freeman; by patrimony, or being the son of a freeman; by redemption, that is, buying the privilege; or, by gift from the borough, the usual method today, when the privilege is granted in recognition of some achievement, benefaction, or special status on the part of the recipient.

freemasonry the beliefs and practices of a group of linked national organizations open to men over the age of 21, united by a common code of morals and certain traditional 'secrets'. Modern freemasonry began in 18th-century Europe. Freemasons do much charitable work, but have been criticized in recent years for their secrecy, their male exclusivity, and their alleged use of influence within and between organizations (for example, the police or local government) to further each other's interests. There are approximately 6 million members.

beliefs Freemasons believe in God, whom they call the 'Great Architect of the Universe'.

history Freemasonry is descended from a medieval guild of itinerant masons, which existed in the 14th century and by the 16th was admitting men unconnected with the building trade. The term 'freemason' may have meant a full member of the guild or one working in freestone, that is, a mason of the highest class. There were some 25 lodges in 17th-century Scotland, of which 16 were in centres of masonic skills such as stonemasonry.

The present order of Free and Accepted Masons originated with the formation in London of the first

Grand Lodge, or governing body, in 1717, and during the 18th century spread from Britain to the USA, continental Europe, and elsewhere. In France and other European countries, freemasonry assumed a political and anticlerical character; it has been condemned by the papacy, and in some countries was suppressed by the state. In Italy the freemasonic lodge P2 was involved in a number of political scandals from the 1980s.

free port port or sometimes a zone within a port, where cargo may be accepted for handling, processing, and reshipment without the imposition of tariffs or taxes. Duties and tax become payable only if the products are for consumption in the country to which the free port belongs.

Free ports are established to take advantage of a location with good trade links. They facilitate the quick entry and departure of ships, unhampered by lengthy customs regulations.

Important free ports include Singapore, Copenhagen, New York, Gdańsk, Macao, San Francisco, and Seattle.

Free Presbyterian Church of Scotland body seceded from the ◊Free Church of Scotland 1893. In 1990 a further split created the Associated Presbyterian Churches of Scotland and Canada.

free radical in chemistry, an atom or molecule that has an unpaired electron and is therefore highly reactive. Most free radicals are very short-lived. They are by-products of normal cell chemistry and rapidly oxidize other molecules they encounter. Free radicals are thought to do considerable damage. They are neutralized by protective enzymes.

Free radicals are often produced by high temperatures and are found in flames and explosions.

The action of ultraviolet radiation from the Sun splits chlorofluorocarbon (CFC) molecules in the upper atmosphere into free radicals, which then break down the ◊ozone layer.

freesia any plant of the South African genus *Freesia* of the iris family Iridaceae, commercially grown for their scented, funnel-shaped flowers.

Free State (formerly Orange Free State) province of the Republic of South Africa
area 127,993 sq km/49,405 sq mi
capital Bloemfontein
towns and cities Springfontein, Kroonstad, Bethlehem, Harrismith, Koffiefontein
features plain of the High Veld; Lesotho forms an enclave on the KwaZulu Natal and Eastern Province border; Orange River; Vaal River
industries grain, wool, cattle, gold, oil from coal, cement, pharmaceuticals
population (1995 est) 2,782,500; 82% ethnic Africans
languages Sotho 57%, Africaans 15%, Xhosa 9%
history original settlements from 1810 were complemented by the ◊Great Trek, and the state was recognized by Britain as independent 1854. Following the South African, or Boer, War 1899–1902, it was annexed by Britain as the Orange River Colony until it entered the union as a province 1910.

free thought post-Reformation movement opposed to Christian dogma. It was represented in Britain in the 17th and 18th century by ◊deism; in the 19th century by the radical thinker Richard Carlile (1790–1843), a pioneer of the free press, and the Liberal politicians Charles Bradlaugh and Lord Morley (1838–1923); and in the 20th century by the philosopher Bertrand Russell.

The tradition is upheld in the UK by the National Secular Society 1866, the *Free Thinker* 1881, the Rationalist Press Association 1899, and the British Humanist Association 1963.

‘I've given offence by saying that I'd as soon write free verse as play tennis with the net down.’

On FREE VERSE
Robert Frost in E Lathem *Interviews with Robert Frost*

Freetown capital of Sierra Leone, W Africa; population (1992) 505,000. It has a naval station and a harbour. Industries include cement, plastics, footwear, and oil refining. Platinum, chromite, diamonds, and gold are traded. It was founded as a settlement for freed slaves in the 1790s.

free trade economic system where governments do not interfere in the movement of goods between countries; there are thus no taxes on imports. In the modern economy, free trade tends to hold within economic groups such as the European Union (EU), but not generally, despite such treaties as the ◊General Agreement on Tariffs and Trade 1948 and subsequent agreements to reduce tariffs. The opposite of free trade is ◊protectionism.

free verse poetry without metrical form. At the beginning of the 20th century, many poets believed that the 19th century had accomplished most of what could be done with regular metre, and rejected it, in much the same spirit as John Milton in the 17th century had rejected rhyme, preferring irregular metres that made it possible to express thought clearly and without distortion.

This was true of T S ◊Eliot and the Imagists; it was also true of poets who, like the Russians Sergey Esenin and Vladimir Mayakovsky, placed emphasis on public performance. The shift to free verse began under the very different influences of US poet Walt Whitman and French poet Stéphane Mallarmé. Poets including Robert Graves and W H Auden have criticized free verse on the ground that it lacks the difficulty of true accomplishment, but their own metrics would have been considered loose by earlier critics. The freeness of free verse is largely relative.

free will the doctrine that human beings are free to control their own actions, and that these actions are not fixed in advance by God or fate. Some Jewish and Christian theologians assert that God gave humanity free will to choose between good and evil; others that God has decided in advance the outcome of all human choices (◊predestination), as in Calvinism.

freeze-drying method of preserving food; see ◊food technology. The product to be dried is frozen and then put in a vacuum chamber that forces out the ice as water vapour, a process known as sublimation.

Many of the substances that give products such as coffee their typical flavour are volatile, and would be lost in a normal drying process because they would evaporate along with the water. In the freeze-drying process these volatile compounds do not pass into the ice that is to be sublimed, and are therefore largely retained.

freeze-thaw form of physical ◊weathering, common in mountains and glacial environments, caused by the expansion of water as it freezes. Water in a crack freezes and expands in volume by 9% as it turns to ice. This expansion exerts great pressure on the rock causing the crack to enlarge. After many cycles of freeze-thaw, rock fragments may break off to form ◊scree slopes.

For freeze-thaw to operate effectively the temperature must fluctuate regularly above and below 0°C/32°F. It is therefore uncommon in areas of extreme and perpetual cold, such as the polar regions.

freezing change from liquid to solid state, as when water becomes ice. For a given substance, freezing occurs at a definite temperature, known as the freezing point, that is invariable under similar conditions of pressure, and the temperature remains at this point until all the liquid is frozen. The amount of heat per unit mass that has to be removed to freeze a substance is a constant for any given substance, and is known as the latent heat of fusion.

freezing point, depression of lowering of a solution's freezing point below that of the pure solvent; it depends on the number of molecules of solute dissolved in it. For a single solvent, such as pure water, all solute substances in the same molar concentration produce the same lowering of freezing point. The depression d produced by the presence of a solute of molar concentration C is given by the equation $d = KC$, where K is a constant (called the cryoscopic constant) for the solvent concerned.

Antifreeze mixtures for car radiators and the use of salt to melt ice on roads are common applications of this principle. Animals in arctic conditions, for example insects or fish, cope with the extreme cold either by manufacturing natural ‘antifreeze’ and staying active, or by allowing themselves to freeze in a controlled fashion, that is, they manufacture proteins to act as nuclei for the formation of ice crystals in areas that will not produce cellular damage, and so enable themselves to thaw back to life again.

Measurement of freezing-point depression is a useful method of determining the molecular weights of solutes. It is also used to detect the illicit addition of water to milk.

Frege (Friedrich Ludwig) Gottlob 1848–1925. German philosopher, the founder of modern mathematical logic. He created symbols for concepts like ‘or’ and ‘if ... then’, which are now in standard use in mathematics. His *Die Grundlagen der Arithmetik/The Foundations of Arithmetic* 1884 influenced Bertrand ◊Russell and Ludwig ◊Wittgenstein. Frege's chief work is *Begriffsschrift/Conceptual Notation* 1879.

Frei Eduardo 1911–1982. Chilean president 1964–70. Elected as the only effective anti-Marxist candidate, he pursued a moderate programme of ‘Chileanization’ of US-owned copper interests. His regime was plagued by inflation and labour unrest, but saw considerable economic development.

Frelimo (acronym for ***Front for the Liberation of Mozambique***) nationalist group aimed at gaining independence for Mozambique from the occupying Portuguese. It began operating from S Tanzania 1962 and continued until victory 1975.

Frémont John Charles 1813–1890. US explorer and politician who travelled extensively throughout the western USA. He surveyed much of the territory between the Mississippi River and the coast of California with the aim of establishing an overland route E–W across the continent. In 1842 he crossed the Rocky Mountains, climbing a peak that is named after him.

French people who are native to or inhabitants of France, as well as their descendents, culture, or primary language, which is one of the Romance languages (see ◊French language). There are also some sociolinguistic minorities within France who speak Catalan, Breton, Flemish, German, Corsican, or Basque.

French Antarctica ***French Southern and Antarctic Territories*** territory created 1955; area 10,100 sq km/3,900 sq mi; population about 200 research scientists. It includes Adélie Land on the Antarctic continent, Kerguelen and Crozet archipelagos, and St Paul and Nouvelle Amsterdam islands in the southern seas. It is administered from Paris.

Port-aux-Français on Kerguelen is the chief centre, with several research stations. There are also research stations on Nouvelle Amsterdam and in Adélie Land and a meteorological station on Possession Island in the Crozet archipelago. St Paul is uninhabited. In 1988 French workers who were illegally building an airstrip, thus violating a United Nations treaty on Antarctica, attacked ◊Greenpeace workers.

French architecture the architecture of France.
early Christian The influence of France's rich collection of Roman buildings (ranging from amphitheatres to temples and aqueducts) can be seen in early Christian church building, which began even before the Romans retreated. The baptistery of St Jean at Poitiers and the crypt of Jouarre near Meaux, both 5th century, use Roman architectural effects to their own ends.
Romanesque Such early Roman-influenced buildings gave way to the first distinctive Romanesque architecture, which reached its zenith in the abbey at Cluny (begun 1088). The style developed and took on regional characteristics, such as tunnel and other types of vaulting, for example, St Philibert at Tournus (11th century).
Gothic The abbey church of St Denis, near Paris, 1132–44, marks the beginning of the Gothic style, characterized by the use of pointed arches and rib vaulting. The cathedral of Notre Dame, Paris, begun 1160, is an example of early Gothic (1130–90). The cathedrals at Chartres, begun 1194, Reims, begun 1211, and Bourges, begun 1209, are examples of lancet Gothic (1190–1240). French Late Gothic, or the Flamboyant style as it was known in France (1350–1520), characterized by flowing tracery, is best represented at Caudebec-en-Caux in Normandy, about 1426, and Moulins in Burgundy.
Renaissance Arriving in France from Italy late in the 15th century, the Renaissance made its greatest impact on the building of châteaux, especially in the Loire Valley, for example, Blois 1515–24 and Chambord 1519–47.
Baroque After a long period of religious warfare, architecture was again given priority. Henry IV's interest in town planning manifested itself in such works as the Place des Vosges, Paris (begun 1605). The Baroque style found expression in Le Vau's work on the château of Vaux-le-Vicomte 1657–61, the gardens of which were designed by Le Notre; the two later worked extensively at Versailles. Under Louis XIV, Hardouin-Mansart enlarged Versailles 1678 and built Les Invalides, Paris, 1680–91.

Neo-Classicism In the 18th century there was a definite move towards Classicism, culminating in the severe works of Boullée and Ledoux. The Classical influence continued in the 19th century, perpetuated to some extent by the revolution of 1789, with works such as the Madeleine, Paris 1804–49, by P A Vignon (1762–1828). By the middle of the century, the grandiose Beaux Arts style was established, most spectacularly in the Opéra, Paris, 1861–74, by Charles Garnier (1825–1898). It was challenged by both the Rationalist approach of Labrouste who was responsible for the Library of Ste Geneviève, Paris, 1843–50, and by the Gothic Revival as detailed in the writings of Viollet-le-Duc.

Art Nouveau Art Nouveau developed towards the end of the 19th century, with centres in Nancy and Paris. Hector Guimard's Paris Metro station entrances, with their flamboyant metal arches, are famous examples of the style.

The Modern Movement In the 1920s the Swiss-born Le Corbusier emerged as the leading exponent of the Modern Movement in France. His masterpieces range from the cubist Villa Savoye at Poissy 1929–31 to the vast, grid-like Unité d'habitation at Marseilles 1947–52. Since the 1950s technological preoccupations have been evident in much modern architecture in France, beginning with the work of Jean Prouvé, for instance his Refreshment Room at Evian 1957, and continuing in more recent projects, such as the Pompidou Centre, Paris, by Renzo Piano and Richard Rogers 1971–77, and the Institut du Monde Arabe, Paris, 1981–87, by Jean Nouvel. In the 1980s, Paris became the site for a number of *Grands Projets* initiated by President Mitterrand, including the cultural complex at Parc de la Villette by Bernard Tschumi (partially opened 1985), the conversion by Gui Aulenti of the Gare d'Orsay into the Musée d'Orsay 1986, I M Pei's glass pyramid for the Louvre 1989, and the Grande Arche at La Défense by Johan Otto von Spreckelsen 1989.

French art painting, sculpture, and decorative arts of France. As the birthplace of the Gothic style, France was a centre for sculpture and manuscript illumination in the Middle Ages, and of tapestry from the 15th century. 17th-century French painting is particularly rich, dominated by the Italianate Classicism of Claude Lorrain and Nicolas Poussin. Subsequent light-hearted Rococo scenes of upper-class leisure gave way with the French Revolution to the Neo-Classicism of Jacques Louis David and Jean Ingres. In the 19th century, Romanticism was superseded first by Realism and then by Impressionism, led by such painters as Claude Monet and Auguste Renoir, which in turn fragmented, via the work of Georges Seurat, Paul Cézanne, and others, into the modern art of the 20th century. Georges Braque (Cubism) and Henri Matisse (Fauvism) were among the pioneers. In sculpture the towering figure was that of Auguste Rodin.

Among the very earliest artistic remains are the cave paintings of Lascaux in S France (18,000 BC). The Celtic period (5th century BC to 1st century AD) left many artefacts and from the Roman occupation (1st century to 5th) there are artefacts and fine buildings. During the Ottonian and Carolingian dynasties, the growing power and wealth of the Christian church helped to sow the seeds of a national culture.

Romanesque: 10th–12th centuries The first distinctively French art was Romanesque. The building of churches, cathedrals, and monasteries gave new impetus to the 'minor arts' – metalwork, textiles, and manuscript illumination. Sculpture was also one of the outstanding achievements of the period, the expressive, highly stylized forms deriving in part from manuscript illumination, as at the cathedral of Autun and the abbeys of Cluny, Moissac, and Souillac. Enamels achieved a new sophistication, with *champlevé* enamelling being produced in Limoges.

Gothic: 12th–14th centuries France played a major role in the development of Gothic. New, soaring cathedrals required large areas of stained glass, some of the finest of which was made for Chartres cathedral. Mural paintings (mostly destroyed) often imitated the colouring of the stained glass. Sculpture acquired a greater elegance and realism, with complex programmes being carved at Chartres, in Paris at Notre Dame, and elsewhere. Portrait sculpture (in the form of sepulchral effigies) began in France in the late 14th century. The carvings produced at the Burgundian court by Claus Sluter during this period are the outstanding examples of late Gothic sculpture. Paris became an international centre for illumination and miniature painting.

15th century Regional schools in painting developed and the first major artists appeared: in Provence, Nicolas Froment; in Burgundy and the north, Simon Marmion (c. 1422–1489); and in the Loire country, Jean Fouquet, Jean Bourdichon (c. 1457–1521), the Maître de Moulins (worked 1480–1500), Jean Perréal (c. 1457–1530). The most important of these is the court portrait painter Jean Fouquet, whose precise realism owes much to Netherlandish painting. His miniatures and those of the Limbourg brothers, creators of the *Très Riches Heures* illuminated prayer books, show remarkable naturalism and flair for ornamentation. Exquisite tapestries were woven, one of the finest being *The Lady with the Unicorn* about 1480 (Musée de Cluny, Paris). With the decline of church commissions, there were few opportunities for sculptors.

Renaissance: 16th century The desire of Francis I to create a centralized art to rival Italy led to his introducing Italian painters (such as Francesco Primaticcio and Niccolò dell'Abbate) into France, and from this followed the development of the School of Fontainebleau. The art of the court portrait and portrait miniature flourished with Corneille de Lyon (c. 1503–1574) and the two leading artists of the period, Jean and François Clouet. Although increasingly influenced by Italian styles, these artists were still indebted to Netherlandish painting. Sculptors, on the other hand – such as Jean Goujon, Jean Cousin (c. 1522–c. 1594), and Germain Pilon (1535–1590) – were more successful in adopting Italian styles. The Renaissance in France also saw brilliant enamelling work, especially by Léonard (c. 1505–c. 1577) and Jean Limousin (c. 1528–c. 1610); the extraordinary ceramics of Bernard Palissy; and fine work by goldsmiths.

Baroque: 17th century Under Louis XIV, Poussin's style became 'official', being promulgated by the Royal Academy (founded 1648). The minister Jean-Baptiste Colbert and the painter Charles Le Brun, painter to the king and director of the academy, controlled all aspects of art production, from state portraits to the furniture and tapestry produced at the Gobelins factory. The painters Georges de La Tour and Louis Le Nain are unusual in that they adopted a realistic style, though they too have a Classical sense of order and poise. A ceremonial form of portraiture was practised by Nicola de Largillière (1656–1746) and Hyacinthe Rigaud. The etcher Jacques Callot provided forceful records of the harsher realities of the period, his works frequently anticipating those of the Spanish artist Francisco Goya.

In the earlier part of the 17th century, French sculpture was mainly sepulchral. Notable sculptors in this line were François Anguier (c. 1604–1669), who modelled the duc de Montmorency's tomb in Moulins, N Auvergne, and Jacques Sarrazin (1588–1660), sculptor of Prince de Condé, Henry II's tomb in Chantilly, N of Paris. A fresh expansion came with the encouragement of a grandiose secular art by Louis XIV. Girardon, whose masterpiece is Cardinal Richelieu's tomb in the Sorbonne church, Paris, was extensively employed on the sculptural decoration of Versailles. Antoine Coysevox carved portraits remarkable for their vitality.

18th century The grandiose decoration of the Louis XIV style gave way to the lightness and charm of Rococo. Jean-Antoine Watteau marks the change of mood, also evident in his followers Jean-Baptiste Pater (1695–1736) and Nicolas Lancret. In Watteau's informal *fêtes galantes*, graceful figures engage in musical and amatory pursuits in theatrical landscape settings which are tinged with melancholy and a sense of the transitory nature of pleasure. A graceful and highly decorative development of this style is found in the work of François Boucher and Jean-Honoré Fragonard, both of whom epitomized the gaiety and frivolity of the court immediately before the Revolution. The style declined sharply in the work of Jean Baptiste Greuze, whose moralizing genre subjects extolling simple virtues became mawkishly sentimental. In contrast with the art of court circles, Jean-Baptiste Chardin painted quiet scenes of domestic bourgeois life. In still life he took up and gave new values to the genre practised by Jean-Baptiste Oudry (1686–1755) and Alexandre-François Desportes (1661–1743) and inspired by Netherlandish models. 18th-century portraiture is represented by the pastellist Maurice Quentin de La Tour and by the elegance of Jean-Marc Nattier (1685–1766), Jean-Baptiste Perroneau (1715–1783), Hubert Drouais (1699–1767) and François-Hubert Drouais (1727–1775), father and son, and Elisabeth Vigée Lebrun. The sculptor Jean Antoine Houdon stands out in the 18th century particularly for his animated and expressive portrait busts.

The end of the 18th century saw a reaction against Rococo and a return to 'the antique' advocated by Joseph Marie Vien (1716–1809). The major exponent of this Neo-Classicism was one of Vien's pupils, David, whose works give dramatic expression to both the Revolution and Napoleon's empire building.

19th century As a return to the past, however, Neo-Classicism had a Romantic element, which appears in the work of Girodet-Trioson (1767–1824), Pierre Prud'hon, and Baron Antoine-Jean Gros (1771–1835). Full-blown Romanticism is strikingly demonstrated in the works of Théodore Géricault and Eugène Delacroix, though Ingres remained a determined upholder of Classicism (the approved style of the Royal Academy throughout the 19th century).

In landscape the beginnings of a new era came with Camille Corot's low-keyed, poetic landscapes, luminous and misty. Although he worked at Barbizon, he is distinct from the Barbizon School, who were 'pure' landscape painters, partly inspired by the Dutch painters Meindert Hobbema and Jacob van Ruisdael. French painters of this group are Jean François Millet, Daubigny (1817–1878), and Theodore Rousseau. By midcentury, Realism had become a challenge to both Neo-Classicism and Romanticism. Gustave Courbet, whose unheroic depictions of everyday life caused a storm of protest, was the main figure of Realism, his art closely linked to his political radicalism. More an attitude than a style, Realism was advanced by Honoré Daumier, a painter and cartoonist noted for his satirical depictions of French life, and the landscape painter Jean François Millet. Edouard Manet may also be regarded as a Realist, his brilliant modern treatment of old-master themes, as in his *Olympia* 1865 (Musée d'Orsay, Paris), causing a scandal.

By focusing on everyday life, Realism prepared the way for the best-known movement of the 19th century, Impressionism. Monet, who began as a member of the group inspired by Manet, is one of Impressionism's central figures. His concentration on the sheer appearance of things, with colours and forms subtly altered by variations of atmosphere and light, was the essence of the movement. Other major Impressionists are Renoir, Camille Pissarro, and Berthe Morisot. Edgar Degas brought to Impressionism a classical sense of structure and form. Although aware of Impressionism, Henri de Toulouse-Lautrec developed his own highly independent style derived from posters, Japanese prints, and Degas.

The Impressionist use of colour suggested various new departures: the Neo-Impressionism (or Pointillismism) of Seurat and Paul Signac; and the forms of Post-Impressionism represented by Cézanne and Paul Gauguin, who both had a profound effect on the development of modern art. Their art is the matrix of a succession of brilliant phases of art from the 1890s, beginning with Symbolism (Odilon Redon, Gustave Moreau, and others) and the group les Nabis.

Rodin infused a Romantic intensity of feeling into the cold formulas of 19th-century sculpture. Notable sculptors include François Rude, who executed the sculptural work on the Arc de Triomphe; Antoine-Louis Barye (1795–1875), known for animal sculptures; Albert Bartholomé (1848–1928), known especially for funerary masks; Henri Laurens (1885–1954), and important sculptor and engraver; Antoine Bourdelle (1861–1929), who combined classic Greek manner with a style of exaggeration conveying heroic energies; and Jean-Baptiste Carpeaux. Degas also produced some innovative sculptures.

20th century Among the most important 20th-century innovators were Georges Braque – who, with the Spanish artist Pablo Picasso, developed and perfected the Cubist style – and Henri Matisse. Matisse, the central figure in Fauvism, produced brilliantly coloured works of a decorative, rhythmic nature. The new ideas of painting successively launched in Paris made that city the centre of an international school, 'l'Ecole de Paris'. Some of its representatives, like Picasso, came originally from outside France, but among the notable French painters are Edouard Vuillard, Pierre Bonnard, Pierre Albert Marquet, Robert Delaunay, Fernand Léger, Georges Rouault, and Raoul Dufy. Aristide Maillol revitalized traditional sculptural forms.

After World War II Paris ceased to be the centre of the artistic world and was succeeded by the USA as the most universal influence on contemporary art. Leading artists of the postwar period include Yves Klein and Jean Dubuffet.

French Community former association consisting of France and those overseas territories joined with it by the constitution of the Fifth Republic, following the 1958 referendum. Many of the constituent states withdrew during the 1960s, and it no longer formally exists, but in practice all former French colonies have close economic and cultural as well as linguistic links with France.

French Equatorial Africa federation of French territories in West Africa. Founded 1910, it consisted of Gabon, Middle Congo, Chad, and Ubangi-Shari (now the Central African Republic), and was ruled from Brazzaville. The federation supported the Free French in World War II and was given representation in the French Fourth Republic 1944–58. In 1958, the states voted for autonomy and the federation was dissolved.

French Guiana (French *Guyane Française*) French overseas *département* from 1946, and administrative region from 1974, on the north coast of South America, bounded W by Surinam and E and S by Brazil
area 83,500 sq km/32,230 sq mi
capital Cayenne
towns and cities St Laurent
features Eurospace rocket launch pad at Kourou; Îles du Salut, which include ◊Devil's Island
industries timber, shrimps, gold
currency franc
population (1990) 114,800
language 90% Creole, French, Native American
famous people Alfred ◊Dreyfus
history first settled by France 1604, the territory became a French possession 1817; penal colonies, including Devil's Island, were established from 1852; by 1945 the shipments of convicts from France ceased.

French Guiana

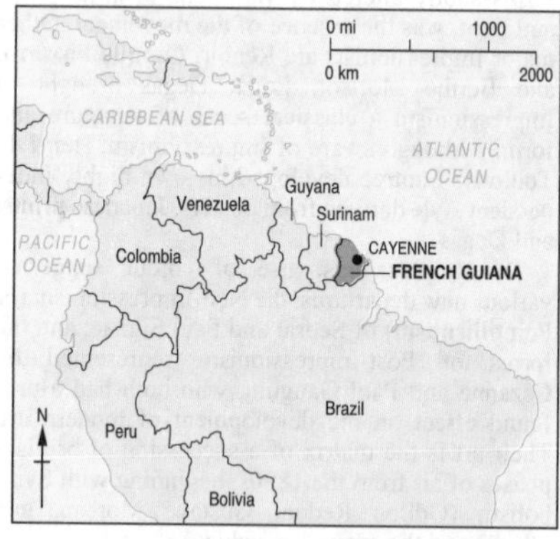

'There was reason to believe that the Revolution, like Saturn, would eventually devour all her children one by one.'

On the French Revolution
Pierre Vergniaud quoted in Alphonse Lamartine *Histoire des Girondins*

French horn musical brass instrument, a descendant of the natural hunting horn, valved and curved into a circular loop, with a funnel-shaped mouthpiece and wide bell.

French India former French possessions in India: Pondicherry, Chandernagore, Karaikal, Mahé, and Yanam (Yanaon). They were all transferred to India by 1954.

French language member of the Romance branch of the Indo-European language family, spoken in France, Belgium, Luxembourg, Monaco, and Switzerland in Europe; also in Canada (principally in the province of Quebec), various Caribbean and Pacific Islands (including overseas territories such as Martinique and French Guiana), and certain N and W African countries (for example, Mali and Senegal).

French developed from Latin as spoken in Gaul and was established as a distinct language by the 9th century. Varieties used north of the river Loire formed the *Langue d'oil* (*oui*) while those to the south formed the *Langue d'oc*, according to their word for 'yes'. By the 13th century the dialect of the Île de France was supreme and became the official medium of the courts and administration of France 1539. Its literary form still serves as the basis of *le bon français* ('correct French'), which is officially protected by the Academie Française (founded 1635 at the behest of Cardinal Richelieu) and by occasional legislation in both France and Quebec. From 1991 a government-approved commission has approved changes to the language, such as the abolition of the circumflex accent in many words, and some simplified spellings.

French literature the literature of France.
The Middle Ages The *Chanson de Roland* (c. 1080) is one of the early *chansons de geste* (epic poems about deeds of chivalry), which were superseded by the Arthurian romances (seen at their finest in the work of Chrétien de Troyes in the 12th century), and by the classical themes of Alexander, Troy, and Thebes. Other aspects of French medieval literature are represented by the anonymous *Aucassin et Nicolette* of the early 13th century; the allegorical *Roman de la Rose/Romance of the Rose*, the first part of which was written by Guillaume de Lorris (c. 1230) and the second by Jean de Meung (c. 1275); and the satiric *Roman de Renart/Story of Renard* of the late 12th century. The period also produced the historians Villehardouin, Joinville, Froissart, and Comines, and the first great French poet, François Villon.
16th century: the Renaissance One of the most celebrated poets of the Renaissance was Ronsard, leader of *La ◊Pléiade* (a group of seven writers); others included Clément Marot (c. 1496–1544) at the beginning of the 16th century and Mathurin Régnier (1573–1613) at its close. In prose the period produced the broad genius of Rabelais and the essayist Montaigne.
17th century The triumph of form came with the great Classical dramatists Corneille, Racine, and Molière, the graceful brilliance of La Fontaine, and the poet and critic Boileau. Masters of prose in the same period include the philosophers Pascal and Descartes; the preacher Bossuet; the critics La Bruyère, Fénelon, and Malebranche; and La Rochefoucauld, Cardinal de Retz, Mme de Sévigné, and Le Sage.
18th century The age of the ◊Enlightenment and an era of prose, with Montesquieu, Voltaire, and Rousseau; the scientist Buffon; the encyclopedist Diderot; the ethical writer Vauvenargues; the novelists Prévost and Marivaux; and the memoir writer Saint-Simon.
19th century Poetry came to the fore again with the Romantics Lamartine, Hugo, Vigny, Musset, Leconte de Lisle, and Gautier; novelists of the same school were George Sand, Stendhal, and Dumas *père*, while criticism is represented by Sainte-Beuve, and history by Thiers, Michelet, and Taine. The realist novelist Balzac was followed by the school of Naturalism, whose representatives were Flaubert, Zola, the Goncourt brothers, Alphonse Daudet, Maupassant, and Huysmans. Nineteenth-century dramatists include Hugo, Musset, and Dumas *fils*. Symbolism, a movement of experimentation and revolt against Classical verse and materialist attitudes, with the philosopher Bergson as one of its main exponents, found its first expression in the work of Gérard de Nerval, followed by Baudelaire, Verlaine, Mallarmé, Rimbaud, Corbière, and the prose writer Villiers de l'Isle Adam; later writers in the same tradition were Henri de Régnier and Laforgue.
20th century Drama and poetry revived with Valéry, Claudel, and Paul Fort, who advocated 'pure poetry'; other writers were the novelists Gide and Proust, and the critics Thibaudet (1874–1936) and later St John Perse, also a poet. The Surrealist movement, which developed from 'pure poetry' through the work of Eluard and Apollinaire, influenced writers as diverse as Giraudoux, Louis Aragon, and Cocteau. The reaction against the Symbolists was seen in the work of Charles Péguy, Rostand, de Noailles, and Romain Rolland. Twentieth-century novelists in the Naturalist tradition were Henri Barbusse, Jules Romains, Julian Green, François Mauriac, Francis Carco, and Georges Duhamel. Other prose writers were Maurois, Malraux, Montherlant, Anatole France, Saint-Exupéry, Alain-Fournier, Pierre Hamp, and J R Bloch, while the theatre flourished with plays by J J Bernard, Anouilh, Beckett, and Ionesco. Distinguished postwar writers include the existentialists Sartre and Camus, 'Vercors' (pen name of Jean Bruller), Simone de Beauvoir, Alain Robbe-Grillet, Romain Gary, Nathalie Sarraute, and Marguerite Duras.

French Revolution A political cartoon in which the forces of the Establishment threaten the newly-formed National Assembly with war, symbolized by the bonfire. In the old States General, the Third Estate (commoners) had consistently been outvoted by the other two (nobility and clergy). So, on 17 June 1789, it withdrew from this body and proclaimed itself as the National Assembly. *Corbis*

French Polynesia French Overseas Territory in the S Pacific, consisting of five archipelagos: Windward Islands, Leeward Islands (the two island groups comprising the ◊Society Islands), ◊Tuamotu Archipelago (including Gambier Islands), ◊Tubuai Islands, and ◊Marquesas Islands
total area 3,940 sq km/1,521 sq mi
capital Papeete on Tahiti
industries cultivated pearls, coconut oil, vanilla; tourism is important
population (1994) 216,600
languages Tahitian (official), French
government the French government is represented by a high commissioner (Paul Roncière). It is administered by a Council of Ministers, with a president elected by the Territorial Assembly from its own members; two deputies are returned to the National Assembly in France and one senator to the Senate
history first visited by Europeans 1595; French protectorate 1843; annexed to France 1880–82; became an Overseas Territory, changing its name from French Oceania 1958; self-governing 1977. Following demands for independence in ◊New Caledonia 1984–85, agitation increased also in Polynesia. ▷ *See feature on pp. 806–807.*

French Revolution the period 1789–1799 that saw the end of the French monarchy. Although the revolution began as an attempt to create a constitutional monarchy, by late 1792 demands for long-overdue reforms resulted in the proclamation of the First Republic. The violence of the revolution, attacks by other nations, and bitter factional struggles, riots, and counter-revolutionary uprisings consumed the republic. This helped bring the extremists to power, and the bloody Reign of Terror followed. French armies then succeeded in holding off their foreign enemies and one of the generals, ◊Napoleon, seized power 1799.

On 5 May 1789, after the monarchy had attempted to increase taxation and control of affairs, the States General (three 'estates' of nobles, clergy, and commons) met at Versailles to try to establish some constitutional controls. Divisions within the States General led to the formation of a national assembly by the third (commons) estate 17 June.

FRENCH REVOLUTION 1789–99

1789 May	Meeting of States General called by Louis XVI to discuss reform of state finances. Nobility opposed reforms.
June	Third (commoners) estate demanded end to system where first (noble) estate and second (church) estate could outvote them; rejected by Louis. Third estate declared themselves a national assembly and 'tennis-court oath' pledged them to draw up new constitution.
July	Rumours of royal plans to break up the assembly led to riots in Paris and the storming of the Bastille. Revolutionaries adopted the tricolour as their flag. Peasant uprisings occurred throughout the country.
1789–91	National-assembly reforms included abolition of noble privileges, dissolution of religious orders, appropriation of church lands, centralization of governments, and limits on the king's power.
1791 June	King Louis attempted to escape from Paris in order to unite opposition to the assembly, but was recaptured.
Sept	The king agreed to a new constitution.
Oct	New legislative assembly met, divided between moderate Girondists and radical Jacobins.
1792 Jan	Girondists formed a new government but their power in Paris was undermined by the Jacobins. Foreign invasion led to the breakdown of law and order. Hatred of the monarchy increased.
Aug	The king was suspended from office and the government dismissed.
Sept	National Convention elected on the basis of universal suffrage; dominated by Jacobins. A republic was proclaimed.
Dec	The king was tried and condemned to death.
1793 Jan	The king was guillotined.
April	The National Convention delegated power to the Committee of Public Safety, dominated by Robespierre. The Reign of Terror began.
1794 July	Robespierre became increasingly unpopular, was deposed and executed.
1795	Moderate Thermidoreans took control of the convention and created a new executive Directory of five members.
1795–99	Directory failed to solve France's internal or external problems and became increasingly unpopular.
1799	Coup d'état overthrew the Directory and a consulate of three was established, including Napoleon as First Consul with special powers.

Repressive measures by ◊Louis XVI led to the storming of the ◊Bastille prison by the Paris mob 14 July 1789. On 20 June 1791 the royal family attempted to escape from the control of the national assembly, but Louis XVI was brought back a prisoner from Varennes and forced to accept a new constitution. War with Austria after 20 April 1792 threatened to undermine the revolution, but on 10 Aug the mob stormed the royal palace, and on 21 Sept the First French Republic was proclaimed. On 21 Jan 1793 Louis XVI was executed.

The moderate ◊Girondins were overthrown 2 June by the ◊Jacobins, and control of the country was passed to the infamous Committee of Public Safety and Maximilien ◊Robespierre. The mass executions of the Reign of Terror (see ◊Terror, Reign of) began 5 Sept, and the excesses led to the overthrow of the committee and Robespierre 27 July 1794. The Directory was established to hold a middle course between royalism and Jacobinism. It ruled until Napoleon seized power 1799 as dictator.

French revolutionary calendar the French Revolution 1789 was initially known as the 1st Year of Liberty. When the monarchy was abolished on 21 Sept 1792, the 4th year became 1st Year of the Republic. This calendar was formally adopted in Oct 1793 but its usage was backdated to 22 Sept 1793, which became 1 Vendémiaire. The calendar was discarded from 1 Jan 1806.

French West Africa group of French colonies administered from Dakar 1895–1958. They are now Senegal, Mauritania, Sudan, Burkina Faso, Guinea, Niger, Côte d'Ivoire, and Benin.

frequency in physics, the number of periodic oscillations, vibrations, or waves occurring per unit of time. The SI unit of frequency is the hertz (Hz), one hertz being equivalent to one cycle per second.

Human beings can hear sounds from objects vibrating in the range 20–15,000 Hz. Ultrasonic frequencies well above 15,000 Hz can be detected by such mammals as bats. Infrasound (low frequency sound) can be detected by some animals and birds. Pigeons can detect sounds as low as 0.1 Hz; elephants communicate using sounds as low as 1 Hz.

One kilohertz (kHz) equals 1,000 hertz; one megahertz (MHz) equals 1,000,000 hertz.

frequency in statistics, the number of times an event occurs. For example, when two dice are thrown repeatedly and the two scores added together, each of the numbers 2 to 12 may have a frequency of occurrence. The set of data including the frequencies is called a frequency distribution, usually presented in a frequency table or shown diagramatically, by a frequency polygon.

frequency modulation (FM) method by which radio waves are altered for the transmission of broadcasting signals. FM is constant in amplitude and varies the frequency of the carrier wave in accordance with the signal being transmitted. Its advantage over AM (◊amplitude modulation) is its better signal-to-noise ratio. It was invented by the US engineer Edwin Armstrong (1890–1954).

Frere John 1740–1807. English antiquary, a pioneering discoverer of Old Stone Age (Palaeolithic) tools in association with large extinct animals at Hoxne, Suffolk, in 1797. He suggested (long before Charles Darwin) that they predated the conventional biblical timescale.

fresco mural painting technique using water-based paint on wet plaster. Some of the earliest frescoes (about 1750–1400 BC) were found in Knossos, Crete (now preserved in the Heraklion Museum). Fresco reached its finest expression in Italy from the 13th to the 17th centuries. Giotto, Masaccio, Michelangelo, and many other artists worked in the medium. In the 20th century the Mexican muralists José Orozco and Diego Rivera used fresco.

When the plasterer has covered the portion of the wall to be painted, the painter superimposes the cartoon and pricks off the outlines with an instrument of wood or bone, or makes an impression of it by pouncing. The cartoon is then removed and the colours are applied, becoming incorporated with the substance of the plaster, and if the process is properly carried out, being as lasting as the plaster itself. Fresco must be executed rapidly before the plaster dries and its effects produced by single touches of the brush.

Frescobaldi Girolamo 1583–1643. Italian composer and virtuoso keyboard player. He was organist at St Peter's, Rome, 1608–28. His fame rests on numerous keyboard toccatas, fugues, ricercares, and capriccios in which he advanced keyboard technique and exploited ingenious and daring modulations of key.

Fresnel Augustin Jean 1788–1827. French physicist who refined the theory of ◊polarized light. Fresnel realized in 1821 that light waves do not vibrate like sound waves longitudinally, in the direction of their motion, but transversely, at right angles to the direction of the propagated wave.

Fresnel first had to confirm the wave theory of light. He demonstrated mathematically that the dimensions of light and dark bands produced by diffraction could be related to the wavelength of the light producing them if light consisted of waves. To explain double refraction, he then arrived at the theory of transverse waves.

Freud Anna 1895–1982. Austrian-born founder of child psychoanalysis in the UK. Her work was influenced by the theories of her father, Sigmund Freud. She held that understanding of the stages of psychological development was essential to the treatment of children, and that this knowledge could only be obtained through observation of the child.

Anna Freud and her father left Nazi-controlled Vienna in 1938 and settled in London. There she began working in a Hampstead nursery. In 1947 she founded the Hampstead Child Therapy Course and Clinic, which specialized in the treatment of children and the training of child therapists.

Freud Lucian 1922– . German-born British painter. He is one of the greatest contemporary figurative artists. He combines meticulous accuracy with a disquieting intensity, emphasizing the physicality of his subjects, whether nudes, still lifes, or interiors. His *Portrait of Francis Bacon* 1952 (Tate Gallery, London) is one of his best-known works. He is a grandson of Sigmund Freud.

Freud Sigmund 1856–1939. Austrian physician who pioneered the study of the ◊unconscious mind. He developed the methods of free association and interpretation of dreams that are basic techniques of ◊psychoanalysis. The influence of unconscious forces on people's thoughts and actions was Freud's discovery, as was his controversial theory of the repression of infantile sexuality as the root of neuroses in the adult. His books include *Die Traumdeutung/The Interpretation of Dreams* 1900, *Jenseits des Lustprinzips/Beyond the Pleasure Principle* 1920, *Das Ich und das Es/The Ego and the Id* 1923, and *Das Unbehagen in der Kultur/Civilization and its Discontents* 1930. His influence has permeated the world to such an extent that it may be discerned today in almost every branch of thought.

From 1886 to 1938 Freud had a private practice in Vienna, and his theories and writings drew largely on case studies of his own patients, who were mainly upper-middle-class, middle-aged women. Much of the terminology of psychoanalysis was coined by Freud, and many terms have passed into popular usage, not without distortion. Nevertheless, Freud's theories have caused disagreement among psychologists and psychiatrists, and his methods of psychoanalysis cannot be applied in every case. *See illustration on following page.*

'Analogies decide nothing, that is true, but they can make one feel more at home.'

SIGMUND FREUD
New Introductory Lectures on Psychoanalysis

Freya in Scandinavian mythology, the goddess of married love and the hearth, wife of Odin and mother of Thor. Freya feasts the souls of half those heroes killed in battle; the others are feasted by Odin. Friday is named after her.

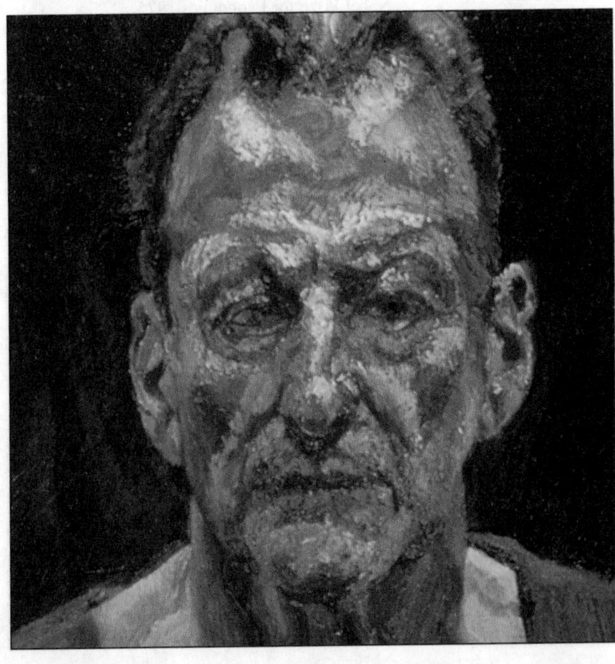

Freud A self-portrait 1990–91 by the English painter Lucian Freud. One of the outstanding figurative artists of his day, Freud combines acute observation with disquieting intensity, emphasizing the physicality of his subjects, which include nudes, still lifes, interiors, and street scenes. *Acquaella Galleries Inc*

Freud The Austrian psychiatrist and pioneer of psychoanalysis, Sigmund Freud. His insights into the human psyche grew in part from his interest in literature, mythology, and comparative religion, and he was a keen collector of archaeological artefacts such as ancient Egyptian statuettes. *Topham*

friar a monk of any order, but originally the title of members of the mendicant (begging) orders, the chief of which were the Franciscans or Minors (Grey Friars), the Dominicans or Preachers (Black Friars), the Carmelites (White Friars), and Augustinians (Austin Friars).

friction in physics, the force that opposes the relative motion of two bodies in contact. The ***coefficient of friction*** is the ratio of the force required to achieve this relative motion to the force pressing the two bodies together.

Friction is greatly reduced by the use of lubricants such as oil, grease, and graphite. Air bearings are now used to minimize friction in high-speed rotational machinery. In other instances friction is deliberately increased by making the surfaces rough – for example, brake linings, driving belts, soles of shoes, and tyres.

Friedan Betty (Elizabeth, born Goldstein) 1921– . US liberal feminist. Her book *The Feminine Mystique* 1963 started the contemporary women's movement in the USA and the UK. She was a founder of the National Organization for Women (NOW) 1966 (and its president 1966–70), the National Women's Political Caucus 1971, and the First Women's Bank 1973. ▷*See feature on pp. 1152–1153.*

❛History suggests that capitalism is a necessary condition for political freedom. Clearly it is not a sufficient condition.❜

MILTON FRIEDMAN *Capitalism and Freedom* 1962

Friedman Milton 1912– . US economist, a pioneer of ◊monetarism. He argued that a country's economy, and hence inflation, can be controlled through its money supply, although most governments lack the 'political will' to cut government spending and thereby increase unemployment. Nobel Prize for Economics 1976.

Friedman believed that inflation is 'always and everywhere a monetary phenomenon'. If the rate of growth of the money supply is limited to the rate of growth of output in the economy (through monetary policy such as changes in interest rates), it should be impossible for increases in costs, such as wages or imports, to be translated into a rise in prices in the economy as a whole.

Friedan Betty Friedan, whose book *The Feminine Mystique* 1963 prompted such a wide response from women who shared her views that in 1966 she helped found the National Organization for Women. She has maintained her moderate reformist position in spite of criticism from more radical feminists, and is regarded as the mother of the women's movement. *Corbis*

Friedrich Caspar David 1774–1840. German Romantic landscape painter. He was active mainly in Dresden. He imbued his subjects – mountain scenes and moonlit seas – with poetic melancholy and was later admired by Symbolist painters.

The Cross in the Mountains 1808 (Gemäldegalerie, Dresden) and *Moonrise over the Sea* 1822 (Nationalgalerie, Berlin) are among his best-known works.

Friel Brian 1929– . Northern Irish dramatist. His work often deals with the social and historical pressures that contribute to the Irish political situation. His first success was with *Philadelphia, Here I Come!* 1964, which dealt with the theme of exile. Later plays include the critically acclaimed *Dancing at Lughnasa* 1990.

In 1980 he founded the Field Day Theatre Company, which produced *Translations* 1981, a study of British cultural colonialism in 19th-century Ireland. Other plays include *The Freedom of the City* 1973, about victims of the Ulster conflict, *Faith Healer* 1980, *Making History* 1988, and *Molly Sweeney* 1994.

Friendly Islands another name for ◊Tonga, a country in the Pacific.

friendly society association that makes provision for the needs of sickness and old age by money payments. There are some 6,500 registered societies in the UK. Among the largest are the National Deposit, Odd Fellows, Foresters, and Hearts of Oak. In the USA similar 'fraternal insurance' bodies are known as benefit societies; they include the Modern Woodmen of America 1883 and the Fraternal Order of Eagles 1898.

In the UK the movement was the successor to the great medieval guilds, but the period of its greatest expansion was in the late 18th and early 19th centuries, after the passing in 1797 of the first legislation providing for the registration of friendly societies.

Friends of the Earth (FoE or FOE) environmental pressure group, established in the UK 1971, that aims to protect the environment and to promote rational and sustainable use of the Earth's resources. It campaigns on such issues as acid rain; air, sea, river, and land pollution; recycling; disposal of toxic wastes; nuclear power and renewable energy; the destruction of rainforests; and pesticides. FoE has branches worldwide.

Friends, Society of or ***Quakers*** Christian Protestant sect founded by George ◊Fox in England in the 17th century. They were persecuted for their nonviolent activism, and many emigrated to form communities elsewhere; for example, in Pennsylvania and New England. They now form a worldwide movement of about 200,000. Their worship stresses meditation and the freedom of all to take an active part in the service (called a meeting, held in a meeting house). They have no priests or ministers.

The name 'Quakers' may originate in Fox's injunction to 'quake at the word of the Lord'. Originally marked out by their sober dress and use of 'thee' and 'thou' to all as a sign of equality, they incurred penalties by their pacifism and refusal to take oaths or pay tithes. In the 19th century many Friends were prominent in social reform, for example, Elizabeth ◊Fry. Quakers have exerted a profound influence on American life through their pacifism and belief in social equality, education, and prison reform. ▷*See feature on pp. 982–983.*

Friesland maritime province of the N Netherlands, which includes the Frisian Islands and land that is still being reclaimed from the former Zuyder Zee; the inhabitants of the province are called ◊Frisians
area 3,400 sq km/1,312 sq mi
capital Leeuwarden
towns and cities Drachten, Harlingen, Sneek, Heerenveen
features sailing is popular; the *Elfstedentocht* (skating race on canals through 11 towns) is held in very cold winters
industries livestock (Friesian cattle originated here; black Friesian horses), dairy products, small boats
population (1995 est) 609,600
history ruled as a county of the Holy Roman Empire during the Middle Ages, Friesland passed to Saxony 1498 and, after a revolt, to Charles V of Spain. In 1579 it subscribed to the Treaty of Utrecht, opposing Spanish rule. In 1748 its stadholder, Prince William IV of Orange, became stadholder of all the United Provinces of the Netherlands.

frigate escort warship smaller than a destroyer. Before 1975 the term referred to a warship larger than a destroyer but smaller than a light cruiser. In the 18th and 19th centuries a frigate was a small, fast sailing warship.

The frigate is the most numerous type of large surface vessel in the British Royal Navy. Britain's type-23 frigate (1988) is armoured, heavily armed (4.5 inch naval gun, 32 Sea Wolf anti-missile and anti-aircraft missiles, and a surface-to-surface missile), and, for locating submarines, has a large helicopter and a hydrophone array towed astern. Engines are diesel-electric up to 17 knots, with gas turbines for spurts of speed up to 28 knots.

Frigga alternative name for the Norse goddess ◊Freya.

fringe benefit in employment, payment in kind over and above wages and salaries. These may include a pension, subsidized lunches, company car, favourable loan facilities, and health insurance. Fringe benefits may, in part, be subject to income tax.

fringe theatre productions that are anti-establishment or experimental. In the UK, the term originated in the 1960s from the activities held on the 'fringe' of the Edinburgh Festival. The US equivalent is off-off-Broadway (off-Broadway is mainstream theatre that is not on Broadway).

Frink Elisabeth 1930–1993. English sculptor. She created rugged, naturalistic bronzes, mainly based on human and animal forms, for example the *Alcock Brown Memorial* for Manchester airport 1962, *In Memoriam* (heads), and *Running Man* 1980.

Frisbee trademark for a platter-shaped, concave disc, used for toss-and-catch games. Thrown with a flick of the wrist, Frisbees spin and sail. They are primarily for recreation or fun, but championships are held in the USA under the auspices of the World Flying Disc Federation. Frisbees were introduced in the USA in the late 1950s.

Frisch Karl von 1886–1982. Austrian zoologist, founder with Konrad ◊Lorenz of ethology, the study of animal behaviour. He specialized in bees, discovering how they communicate the location of sources of nectar by movements called 'dances'. He was awarded the Nobel Prize for Physiology or Medicine 1973 together with Lorenz and Nikolaas ◊Tinbergen.

Frisch Max Rudolf 1911–1991. Swiss dramatist. Inspired by ◊Brecht, his early plays such as *Als der Krieg zu Ende war/When the War Is Over* 1949 are more romantic in tone than his later symbolic dramas, such as *Andorra* 1962, dealing with questions of identity. He also wrote *Biedermann und die Brandstifter/The Fire Raisers* 1958. Some of his plays were originally written for radio. They show a concern with the moral and political problems of the time.

Frisch Ragnar Anton Kittil 1895–1973. Norwegian economist, pioneer of econometrics (the application of mathematical and statistical methods in economics). He shared the first Nobel Prize for Economics in 1969 with Jan ◊Tinbergen.

Frisian or ***Friesian*** member of a Germanic people of NW Europe (Friesland and the Frisian Islands). In Roman times they occupied the coast of Holland and may have taken part in the Anglo-Saxon invasions of Britain. Their language is closely akin to Anglo-Saxon, with which it forms the Anglo-Frisian branch of the West Germanic languages, part of the Indo-European family.

The Frisian language is almost extinct in the German districts of East Friesland, but it has attained some literary importance in the North Frisian Islands and Schleswig and developed a considerable literature in the West Frisian dialect of the Dutch province of Friesland.

Frisian Islands chain of low-lying islands 5–32 km/3–20 mi off the northwest coasts of the Netherlands and Germany, with a northerly extension off the west coast of Denmark. They were formed by

fritillary A Queen of Spain fritillary butterfly *Issoria lathonia* on a knapweed flower. Although common in France and adjacent countries, it is a very rare visitor to the British Isles. *Premaphotos Wildlife*

the sinking of the intervening land. ***Texel*** is the largest and westernmost island, at the southern end of the chain.

fritillary in botany, any plant of the genus *Fritillaria* of the lily family Liliaceae. The snake's head fritillary *F. meleagris* has bell-shaped flowers with purple-chequered markings.

fritillary in zoology, any of a large grouping of butterflies of the family Nymphalidae. Mostly medium-sized, fritillaries are usually orange and reddish with a black criss-cross pattern or spots above and with silvery spots on the underside of the hindwings.

They take their name from the Latin word *fritillus* ('dice box') because of their spotted markings.

Friuli-Venezia Giulia autonomous agricultural and wine-growing region of NE Italy, bordered to the E by Slovenia; area 7,800 sq km/3,011 sq mi; population (1992) 1,195,100. Cities include Udine (the capital), Gorizia, Pordenone, and Trieste.

Formed 1947 from the province of Venetian Friuli and part of Eastern Friuli, to which Trieste was added after its cession to Italy 1954, it was granted autonomy 1963. A Slav minority numbers about 100,000, and in Friuli there is a movement for complete independence.

Frobisher Martin c. 1535–1594. English navigator. He made his first voyage to Guinea, West Africa, 1554. In 1576 he set out in search of the Northwest Passage, and visited Labrador, and Frobisher Bay, Baffin Island. Second and third expeditions sailed 1577 and 1578. He was vice admiral in Drake's West Indian expedition 1585. In 1588, he was knighted for helping to defeat the Armada. He was mortally wounded 1594 fighting against the Spanish off the coast of France.

Froebel Friedrich Wilhelm August 1782–1852. German educationist. He evolved a new system of education using instructive play, described in *Education of Man* 1826 and other works. In 1836 he founded the first kindergarten (German 'garden for children') in Blankenburg, Germany. He was influenced by the Swiss Johann ◊Pestalozzi.

frog any amphibian of the order Anura (Greek 'tailless'). There are about 24 different families of frog, containing more than 3,800 species. There are no clear rules for distinguishing between frogs and toads.

Frogs usually have squat bodies, with hind legs specialized for jumping, and webbed feet for swimming. Most live in or near water, though as adults they are air-breathing. A few live on land or even in trees. Their colour is usually greenish in the genus *Rana*, but other Ranidae are brightly coloured, for instance black and orange or yellow and white. Many use their long, extensible tongues to capture insects. The eyes are large and bulging. Frogs vary in size from the North American little grass frog *Limnaoedus ocularis*, 12 mm/0.5 in long, to the giant aquatic frog *Telmatobius culeus*, 50 cm/20 in long, of Lake Titicaca, South America. Frogs are widespread, inhabiting all continents except Antarctica, and they have adapted to a range of environments including deserts, forests, grasslands, and even high altitudes, with some species in the Andes and Himalayas existing above 5,000 m/19,600 ft.

courtship and reproduction In many species the males attract the females in great gatherings, usually by croaking. In some tropical species, the male's inflated vocal sac may exceed the rest of his body in size. Other courtship 'lures' include thumping on the ground and 'dances'.

Some lay eggs in large masses (spawn) in water. The jelly surrounding the eggs provides support and protection and retains warmth. Some South American frogs build mud-pool 'nests', and African tree frogs make foam nests from secreted mucus. In other species, the eggs may be carried in pockets on the mother's back, brooded by the male in his vocal sac or, as with the Eurasian midwife toad *Alytes obstetricans*, wrapped round the male's hind legs until hatching.

life cycle The tadpoles hatch from the eggs in about a fortnight. At first they are fishlike animals with external gills and a long swimming tail, but no limbs. The first change to take place is the disappearance of the external gills and the development of internal gills, which are still later supplanted by lungs. The hind legs appear before the front legs, and the last change to occur is the diminution and final disappearance of the tail. The tadpole stage lasts about three or four months. At the end of this time the animal leaves the water. Some species, such as the edible frog, are always aquatic. By autumn the frog grows big and sluggish. It stores fat in a special gland in the abdomen; it is this fat that it lives on during hibernation.

species Certain species of frog have powerful skin poisons (alkaloids) to deter predators. 'True frogs' are placed in the worldwide family Ranidae, with 800 species, of which the genus *Rana* is the best known. The North American bullfrog *Rana catesbeiana*, with a croak that carries for miles, is able to jump nine times its own length. The flying frogs, genus *Rhacophorus*, of Malaysia, using webbed fore and hind feet, can achieve a 12 m/40 ft glide. The hairy frog *Astylosternus robustus* is found in W Africa; it has long outgrowths on its flanks, which seem to aid respiration.

froghopper or ***spittlebug*** leaping plant-bug, of the family Cercopidae, in the same order (Homoptera) as leafhoppers and aphids. Froghoppers live by sucking the juice from plants. The pale green larvae protect themselves (from drying out and from predators) by secreting froth ('cuckoo spit') from their anuses.

frogmouth nocturnal bird, related to the nightjar, of which the commonest species, the tawny frogmouth *Podargus strigoides*, is found throughout Australia, including Tasmania. Well camouflaged, it sits and awaits its prey.

Fröhlich Herbert 1905–1991. German-born British physicist who helped lay the foundations for modern theoretical physics in the UK. He revolutionized solid-state theory by importing into it the methods of quantum field theory – the application of quantum theory to particle interactions.

Froissart Jean 1338–1401. French historian and poet. He was secretary to Queen Philippa, wife of Edward III of England. He travelled in Scotland and Brittany, went with Edward the Black Prince to Aquitaine, and in 1368 was in Milan at the same time as the writers Chaucer and Petrarch. He recorded in his *Chroniques/Chronicles* events of 1326–1400, often at first hand.

frog A green tree frog. Tree frogs' toes are well adapted to climbing: the bones are tipped with a disc of cartilage, which increases mobility, and the toes end in adhesive pads, improving grip. Although most tree frogs live and feed in trees, the majority descend to water to breed. *Corbis*

Most of the change we think we see in life / Is due to truths being in or out of favour.

Robert Frost
'The Black Cottage'

Fromm Erich 1900–1980. German psychoanalyst who moved to the USA 1933 to escape the Nazis. He believed that human beings experience a separation from nature and from other people which gives them the freedom to decide on the course their lives should take. This gives their lives meaning but also causes anxiety.

Fromm was influenced by Karl Marx and existentialism as much as by psychoanalysis. He stressed the role of culture in the formation of personality, a view that distinguished him from traditional psychoanalysts. He also described the authoritarian personality (the servile, obedient type of person who wants to accept authority), particularly to explain the success of Nazism.

Fromm's basic ideas are set out in *The Fear of Freedom* 1941 and *The Sane Society* 1955. He urged people to give up the materialistic way of life for one based on meaningful love in *The Art of Loving* 1956 and *To Have or to Be* 1976.

frond large leaf or leaflike structure; in ferns it is often pinnately divided. The term is also applied to the leaves of palms and less commonly to the plant bodies of certain seaweeds, liverworts, and lichens.

Fronde French revolts 1648–53 against the administration of the chief minister ◊Mazarin during Louis XIV's minority. In 1648–49 the Paris parlement attempted to limit the royal power, its leaders were arrested, Paris revolted, and the rising was suppressed by the royal army under Louis II Condé. In 1650 Condé led a new revolt of the nobility, but this was suppressed by 1653. The defeat of the Fronde enabled Louis to establish an absolutist monarchy in the later 17th century.

I travel light; as light, / That is, as a man can travel who will / Still carry his body around because / Of its sentimental value.

Christopher Fry
The Lady's Not for Burning

front in meteorology, the boundary between two air masses of different temperature or humidity. A ***cold front*** marks the line of advance of a cold air mass from below, as it displaces a warm air mass; a ***warm front*** marks the advance of a warm air mass as it rises up over a cold one. Frontal systems define the weather of the mid-latitudes, where warm tropical air is constantly meeting cold air from the poles. An ***occluded front*** is a composite form, where a cold front meets a warm front and merges with it.

frontal lobotomy operation on the brain. See ◊leucotomy.

frost condition of the weather that occurs when the air temperature is below freezing, 0°C/32°F. Water in the atmosphere is deposited as ice crystals on the ground or exposed objects. As cold air is heavier than warm, ground frost is more common than hoar frost, which is formed by the condensation of water particles in the same way that ◊dew collects.

Frost Robert Lee 1874–1963. US poet. His accessible, colloquial blank verse, often flavoured with New England speech patterns, is written with an individual voice and penetrating vision. His poems include 'Mending Wall' ('Something there is that does not love a wall'), 'The Road Not Taken', and 'Stopping by Woods on a Snowy Evening' and are collected in *Complete Poems* 1951.

frostbite the freezing of skin or flesh, with formation of ice crystals leading to tissue damage. The treatment is slow warming of the affected area; for example, by skin-to-skin contact or with lukewarm water. Frostbitten parts are extremely vulnerable to infection, with the risk of gangrene.

Frost US poet Robert Frost. At a time when US poets such as T S Eliot and Ezra Pound were turning to European culture for inspiration, Robert Frost, keen to develop a home-grown American poetic idiom, turned to the everyday rural life of New England, his rhythms and vocabulary those of American speech. *Corbis*

frost hollow depression or steep-sided valley in which cold air collects on calm, clear nights. Under clear skies, heat is lost rapidly from ground surfaces, causing the air above to cool and flow downhill (as katabatic wind) to collect in valley bottoms. Fog may form under these conditions and, in winter, temperatures may be low enough to cause frost.

frost shattering alternative name for ◊freeze-thaw.

Froude James Anthony 1818–1894. English historian whose *History of England from the Fall of Wolsey to the Defeat of the Spanish Armada* in 12 volumes 1856–70 was a classic Victorian work.

FRS abbreviation for ***Fellow of the ◊Royal Society***.

fructose $C_6H_{12}O_6$ a sugar that occurs naturally in honey, the nectar of flowers, and many sweet fruits; it is commercially prepared from glucose.

It is a monosaccharide, whereas the more familiar cane or beet sugar is a disaccharide, made up of two monosaccharide units: fructose and glucose. It is sweeter than cane sugar and can be used to sweeten foods for people with diabetes.

fruit (from Latin *frui* 'to enjoy') in botany, the ripened ovary in flowering plants that develops from one or more seeds or carpels and encloses one or more seeds. Its function is to protect the seeds during their development and to aid in their dispersal. Fruits are often edible, sweet, juicy, and colourful. When eaten they provide vitamins, minerals, and enzymes, but little protein. Most fruits are borne by perennial plants.

Fruits are divided into three agricultural categories on the basis of the climate in which they grow. ***Temperate fruits*** require a cold season for satisfactory growth; the principal temperate fruits are apples, pears, plums, peaches, apricots, cherries, and soft fruits, such as strawberries. ***Subtropical fruits*** require warm conditions but can survive light frosts; they include oranges and other citrus fruits, dates, pomegranates, and avocados. ***Tropical fruits*** cannot tolerate temperatures that drop close to freezing point; they include bananas, mangoes, pineapples, papayas, and litchis. Fruits can also be divided botanically into ***dry*** (such as the capsule, ◊follicle, ◊schizocarp, ◊nut, caryopsis, pod or legume, lomentum, and ◊achene) and those that become ***fleshy*** (such as the ◊drupe and the ◊berry).

The fruit structure consists of the ◊pericarp or fruit wall, which is usually divided into a number of distinct layers. Sometimes parts other than the ovary are incorporated into the fruit structure, resulting in a false fruit or ◊pseudocarp, such as the apple and strawberry. True fruits include the tomato, orange, melon, and banana. Fruits may be dehiscent, which open to shed their seeds, or indehiscent, which remain unopened and are dispersed as a single unit. Simple fruits (for example, peaches) are derived from a single ovary, whereas compositae or multiple fruits (for example, blackberries) are formed from the ovaries of a number of flowers. In ordinary usage, 'fruit' includes only sweet, fleshy items; it excludes many botanical fruits such as acorns, bean pods, thistledown, and cucumbers (see ◊vegetable).

methods of seed dispersal Efficient seed dispersal is essential to avoid overcrowding and enable plants to colonize new areas; the natural function of a fruit is to aid in the dissemination of the seeds which it contains. A great variety of dispersal mechanisms exist: winged fruits are commonly formed by trees, such as ash and elm, where they are in an ideal position to be carried away by the wind; some wind-dispersed fruits, such as clematis and cotton, have plumes of hairs; others are extremely light, like the poppy, in which the capsule acts like a pepperpot and shakes out the seeds as it is blown about by the wind. Some fruits float on water; the coconut can be dispersed across oceans by means of its buoyant fruit. Geraniums, gorse, and squirting cucumbers have explosive mechanisms, by which seeds are forcibly shot out at dehiscence. Animals often act as dispersal agents either by carrying hooked or sticky fruits (burs) attached to their bodies, or by eating succulent fruits, the seeds passing through the alimentary canal unharmed.

frustum (from Latin for 'a piece cut off') in geometry, a 'slice' taken out of a solid figure by a pair of parallel planes. A conical frustum, for example, resembles a cone with the top cut off. The volume and area of a frustum are calculated by subtracting the volume or area of the 'missing' piece from those of the whole figure.

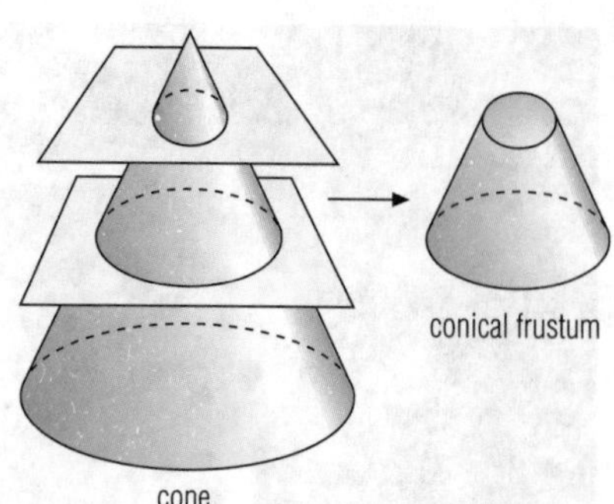

frustum The frustum, a slice taken out of a cone.

Fry (Edwin) Maxwell 1899–1987. English architect. He was a pioneer of the ◊Modern Movement in Britain. Representative is his Sun House, Hampstead, London, 1935, with its horizontally banded windows and white stucco finish. Fry worked in partnership with Walter ◊Gropius 1934–36, and with Denys ◊Lasdun (among others) 1951–58. He was ◊Le Corbusier's senior architect at Chandigarh, India, 1951–54.

Fry Christopher Harris 1907– . English dramatist. He was a leader of the revival of verse drama after World War II with *The Lady's Not for Burning* 1948, *Venus Observed* 1950, and *A Sleep of Prisoners* 1951.

Fry Elizabeth, (born Gurney) 1780–1845. English Quaker philanthropist. She formed an association for the improvement of conditions for female prisoners 1817, and worked with her brother, Joseph Gurney (1788–1847), on an 1819 report on prison reform.

Fry Roger (Eliot) 1866–1934. English artist and art critic. An admirer of the French painter Paul Cézanne, he championed Post-Impressionism in Britain. He was a member of the Bloomsbury Group and founded the ◊Omega Workshops to improve design and to encourage young artists. His critical essays, which were very influential in the 1920s and 1930s, are contained in *Vision and Design* 1920.

Frye (Herman) Northrop 1912– . Canadian literary critic. He is concerned especially with the role and practice of criticism and the relationship between literature and society. His *Anatomy of Criticism* 1957 was very influential.

FT Index abbreviation for ***◊Financial Times Index***, a list of leading share prices.

Fuad I 1868–1936. King of Egypt from 1922. Son of the Khedive Ismail, he succeeded his elder brother Hussein Kiamil as sultan of Egypt 1917; when Egypt was declared independent 1922 he assumed the title of king.

Fuad II 1952– . King of Egypt 1952–53, between the abdication of his father ◊Farouk and the establishment of the republic. He was a grandson of Fuad I.

Fuchs (Emil Julius) Klaus 1911–1988. German spy who worked on atom bomb research in the USA in World War II, and subsequently in the UK. He was imprisoned 1950–59 for passing information to the USSR and resettled in eastern Germany.

fuchsia any shrub or herbaceous plant of the genus *Fuchsia* of the evening-primrose family Onagraceae. Species are native to South and Central America and New Zealand, and bear red, purple, or pink bell-shaped flowers that hang downward.

The genus was named in 1703 after German botanist Leonhard Fuchs (1501–1566).

fuel any source of heat or energy, embracing the entire range of materials that burn in air (combustibles). A ***nuclear fuel*** is any material that produces energy by nuclear fission in a nuclear reactor.

fuel-air explosive warhead containing a highly flammable petroleum and oxygen mixture; when released over a target, this mixes with the oxygen in the atmosphere and produces a vapour which, when ignited, causes a blast approximately five times more powerful than conventional high explosives.

Fuel-air explosives were used by the US Air Force in the 1991 Gulf War against Iraqi defensive positions.

fuel cell cell converting chemical energy directly to electrical energy.

It works on the same principle as a battery but is continually fed with fuel, usually hydrogen. Fuel cells are silent and reliable (no moving parts) but expensive to produce.

Hydrogen is passed over an ◊electrode (usually nickel or platinum) containing a ◊catalyst, which strips electrons off the atoms. These pass through an external circuit while hydrogen ions (charged atoms) pass through an ◊electrolyte to another electrode, over which oxygen is passed. Water is formed at this electrode (as a by-product) in a chemical reaction involving electrons, hydrogen ions, and oxygen atoms. If the spare heat also produced is used for hot water and space heating, 80% efficiency in fuel is achieved.

fuel injection injecting fuel directly into the cylinders of an internal combustion engine, instead of by way of a carburettor. It is the standard method used in ◊diesel engines, and is now becoming standard for petrol engines. In the diesel engine, oil is injected into the hot compressed air at the top of the second piston stroke and explodes to drive the piston down on its power stroke. In the petrol engine, fuel is injected into the cylinder at the start of the first induction stroke of the ◊four-stroke cycle.

Fuentes Carlos 1928– . Mexican novelist, lawyer, and diplomat. His first novel *La región más transparente/Where the Air Is Clear* 1958 encompasses the history of the country from the Aztecs to the present day.

More than other Mexican novelists, he presents the frustrated social philosophy of the failed Mexican revolution. He received international attention for *The Death of Artemio Cruz* 1962, *Terra nostra* 1975, and *El gringo veijo/The Old Gringo* 1985. *The Campaign* 1991 is set during the revolutionary wars leading to independence in Latin America.

Fugard Athol Harold Lanigan 1932– . South African dramatist, director, and actor. His plays often deal with the effects of apartheid. His first successful play was *The Blood Knot* 1961, which was produced in London and New York. This was followed by *Hello and Goodbye* 1965 and *Boesman and Lena* 1969. Other plays include *Statements After an Arrest under the Immorality Act* 1973, *A Lesson from Aloes* 1980, *Master Harold and the Boys* 1982, *A Place with the Pigs* 1987, *My Children! My Africa!* 1989, and *The Township Plays* 1993. His film roles include General Smuts in *Gandhi* 1982.

fugue (Latin 'flight') in music, a contrapuntal form with two or more subjects (principal melodies) for a number of parts, which enter in succession in direct imitation of each other or transposed to a higher or lower key, and may be combined in augmented form (larger note values). It represents the highest form of contrapuntal ingenuity in works such as J S Bach's *Das musikalische Opfer/The Musical Offering* 1747, on a theme of Frederick II of Prussia, and *Die Kunst der Fuge/The Art of the Fugue* published 1751, and Beethoven's *Grosse Fuge/Great Fugue* for string quartet 1825–26.

Fujian or ***Fukien*** province of SE China, bordering Taiwan Strait, opposite Taiwan. There has been rapid economic development since 1980 when it was designated one of China's Special Economic Zones in order to attract foreign investment
area 123,100 sq km/47,517 sq mi
capital Fuzhou
physical dramatic mountainous coastline
features being developed for tourists; designated as a pace-setting province for modernization
industries sugar, rice, special aromatic teas, tobacco, timber, fruit
population (1990) 30,610,000.

Fujimori Alberto 1939– . Peruvian politician, president from 1990. As leader of the newly formed Cambio 90 (Change 90) he campaigned on a pro-market reformist ticket and defeated his more experienced Democratic Front opponent. Lacking an assembly majority and faced with increasing opposition to his policies, he imposed military rule early 1992. In 1993 a plebiscite narrowly approved his constitutional reform proposals, allowing him to seek, and achieve, re-election 1995.

In Aug 1994 Fujimori dismissed his wife as first lady, claiming that she was 'disloyal' and opposed him politically. She denied the charges, and challenged his leadership; in Nov 1995 they divorced.

Fujisankei Japanese communications group, the world's fourth largest media conglomerate, with nearly 100 companies. It owns Japan's (and the world's) largest radio network, a national newspaper and the country's most successful television chain, plus record and video concerns.

Fujitsu Japanese electronics combine, the world's second biggest computer manufacturer (behind IBM) after its purchase of the UK firm ICL in 1990. Fujitsu's turnover in the year ending March 1990 was £9,816 million, of which only 4% was from Europe.

Fujiwara in Japanese history, the ruling clan 858–1185. During that period (the latter part of the ◊Heian), the office of emperor became merely ceremonial, with power exercised by chancellors and regents, who were all Fujiwara and whose daughters in every generation married into the imperial family. There was a Fujiwara in Japanese government as recently as during World War II.

Fujiyama or ***Mount Fuji*** Japanese volcano and highest peak, on Honshu Island, near Tokyo; height 3,778 m/12,400 ft. Extinct since 1707, it has a ◊Shinto shrine and a weather station on its summit. Fuji has long been revered for its picturesque cone-shaped crater peak, and figures prominently in Japanese art, literature, and religion.

Fukien alternative transcription of ◊Fujian, a province of SE China.

Fulani people of W African culture from the southern Sahara and Sahel. Traditionally nomadic pastoralists and traders, Fulani groups are found in Senegal, Guinea, Mali, Burkina Faso, Niger, Nigeria, Chad, and Cameroon. The Fulani language is divided into four dialects and belongs to the W Atlantic branch of the Niger-Congo family; it has more than 10 million speakers.

Fulbright (James) William 1905–1995. US Democratic politician. A US senator 1945–75, he was responsible for the Fulbright Act 1946, which provided grants for thousands of Americans to study abroad and for overseas students to study in the USA. Fulbright chaired the Senate Foreign Relations Committee 1959–74, and was a strong internationalist and supporter of the United Nations. He was an advocate of military and economic aid to Western nations but a powerful critic of US involvement in the Vietnam War.

Fuller (Richard) Buckminster 1895–1983. US architect, engineer, and social philosopher. He embarked on an unorthodox career in an attempt to maximize energy resources through improved technology. In 1947 he invented the lightweight geodesic dome, a hemispherical ◊space-frame of triangular components linked by rods, independent of buttress or vault and capable of covering large-span areas. Within 30 years over 50,000 had been built.

He also invented a Dymaxion (a combination of the words 'dynamics' and 'maximum') house 1928 and car 1933 that were inexpensive and conformed to his concept of using the least amount of energy output to gain maximum interior space and efficiency, respectively.

Among his books are *Ideas and Integrities* 1963, *Utopia or Oblivion* 1969, and *Critical Path* 1981.

Fuller Peter 1947–1990. English art critic. From the mid-1970s, he attacked the complacency of the art establishment and emphasized tradition over fashion. From 1988 these views, and an increased interest in the spiritual power of art, were voiced in his own magazine *Modern Painters*.

Fuller Roy (Broadbent) 1912–1991. English poet and novelist. His early verse, including the collections *Poems* 1940 and *The Middle of a War* 1944, was concerned with social problems. Later work includes *Brutus's Orchard* 1957 and *The Reign of Sparrows* 1980. *New and Collected Poems 1934–1984* was published 1985. Novels include *Image of a Society* 1956, *My Child, My Sister* 1965, and *The Carnal Island* 1970. *The Strange and the Good: Collected Memoirs* was published 1989.

fullerene form of carbon, discovered 1985, based on closed cages of carbon atoms. The molecules of the most symmetrical of the fullerenes are called ◊buckminsterfullerenes (or buckyballs). They are perfect spheres made up of 60 carbon atoms linked together in 12 pentagons and 20 hexagons fitted together like those of a spherical football. Other fullerenes, with 28, 32, 50, 70, and 76 carbon atoms, have also been identified.

Fullerenes can be made by arcing electricity between carbon rods. They may also occur in candle flames and in clouds of interstellar gas. Fullerene chemistry may turn out to be as important as organic chemistry based on the benzene ring. Already, new molecules based on the buckyball enclosing a metal atom, and 'buckytubes' (cylinders of carbon atoms arranged in hexagons), have been made. Applications envisaged include using the new molecules as lubricants, semiconductors, and superconductors, and as the starting point for making new drugs.

fuller's earth soft, greenish-grey rock resembling clay, but without clay's plasticity. It is formed largely of clay minerals, rich in montmorillonite, but a great deal of silica is also present. Its absorbent

fuller's earth The Bentonite Hills in Capitol Reef National Park, Utah, USA, have a landscape quite unlike any other within the park. The well-drained fuller's earth soils are capable of supporting only a few hardy examples of the resident fauna and flora in an area where aridity is already extreme. *Premaphotos Wildlife* properties make it suitable for removing oil and grease, and it was formerly used for cleaning fleeces ('fulling'). It is still used in the textile industry, but its chief application is in the purification of oils. Beds of fuller's earth are found in the southern USA, Germany, Japan, and the UK.

full score in music, a complete transcript of a composition showing all parts individually, as opposed to a short score or piano score that is condensed into fewer lines of music.

fulmar any of several species of petrels of the family Procellariidae, which are similar in size and colour to herring gulls. The northern fulmar *Fulmarus glacialis* is found in the N Atlantic and visits land only to nest, laying a single egg.

fulminate any salt of fulminic (cyanic) acid (HOCN), the chief ones being silver and mercury. The fulminates detonate (are exploded by a blow); see ◊detonator.

fumitory any plant of the genus *Fumeria*, family Fumariaceae, native to Europe and Asia. The common fumitory *F. officinalis* grows to 50 cm/20 in tall, and produces pink flowers tipped with blackish red; it has been used in medicine for stomach and liver complaints.

Funchal capital and chief port of the Portuguese island of Madeira, on the S coast; population (1987) 44,100. Tourism and Madeira wine are the main industries.

Founded 1421 by the Portuguese navigator João Gonçalves Zarco, it was under Spanish rule 1580–1640 and under Britain 1801 and 1807–14.

function in mathematics, a function f is a non-empty set of ordered pairs $(x, f(x))$ of which no two can have the same first element. Hence, if

$$f(x) = x^2$$

two ordered pairs are (−2,4) and (2,4). The set of all first elements in a function's ordered pairs is called the ***domain***; the set of all second elements is the ***range***. In the algebraic expression $y = 4x^3 + 2$, the dependent variable y is a function of the independent variable x, generally written as $f(x)$.

Functions are used in all branches of mathematics, physics, and science generally; for example, the formula

$$t = 2\pi\sqrt{(l/g)}$$

shows that for a simple pendulum the time of swing t is a function of its length l and of no other variable quantity (π and g, the acceleration due to gravity, are ◊constants).

functional group in chemistry, a small number of atoms in an arrangement that determines the chemical properties of the group and of the molecule to which it is attached (for example, the carboxyl group COOH, or the amine group NH_2). Organic compounds can be considered as structural skeletons, with a high carbon content, with functional groups attached.

functionalism in the social sciences, the view of society as a system made up of a number of interrelated parts, all interacting on the basis of a common value system or consensus about basic values and common goals. Every social custom and institution is seen as having a function in ensuring that society works efficiently; deviance and crime are seen as forms of social sickness.

Functionalists often describe society as an organism with a life of its own, above and beyond the sum of its members. The French sociologists Auguste Comte and Emile ◊Durkheim and the American Talcott ◊Parsons assumed functionalist approaches for their studies.

Functionalism in architecture and design, the principle of excluding everything that serves no practical purpose. Central to 20th-century ◊Modernism, the Functionalist ethic developed as a reaction against the 19th-century practice of imitating and combining earlier styles. Its finest achievements are in the realms of ◊industrial architecture and office furnishings.

Leading exponents of Functionalism were the German ◊Bauhaus school, the Dutch group De ◊Stijl, and the Scandinavians, especially the Swedish and Finnish designers. Prominent architects in the field were ◊Le Corbusier and Walter ◊Gropius.

fundamental in musical acoustics, the lowest ◊harmonic of a musical tone, corresponding to the audible pitch.

FUNDAMENTAL CONSTANTS

Constant	Symbol	Value in SI units
acceleration of free fall	g	$9.80665\ m\ s^{-2}$
Avogadro's constant	NA	$6.02252 \times 10^{23}\ mol^{-1}$
Boltzmann's constant	k = R/NA	$1.380622 \times 10^{-23}\ J\ K^{-1}$
electronic charge	e	$1.602192 \times 10^{-19}\ C$
electronic rest mass	me	$9.109558 \times 10^{-31}\ kg$
Faraday's constant	F	$9.648670 \times 10^{4}\ C\ mol^{-1}$
gas constant	R	$8.31434\ J\ K^{-1}\ mol^{-1}$
gravitational constant	G	$6.664 \times 10^{-11}\ N\ m^2\ kg^{-2}$
Loschmidt's number	NL	$2.68719 \times 10^{25}\ m^{-3}$
neutron rest mass	mn	$1.67492 \times 10^{-27}\ kg$
Planck's constant	h	$6.626196 \times 10^{-34}\ J\ s$
proton rest mass	mp	$1.672614 \times 10^{-27}\ kg$
speed of light	c	$2.99792458 \times 10^{8}\ m\ s^{-1}$
standard atmospheric pressure	P	$1.01325 \times 10^{5}\ Pa$
Stefan–Boltzmann constant	σ	$5.6697 \times 10^{-8}\ W\ m^{-2}\ K^{-4}$

fundamental constant physical quantity that is constant in all circumstances throughout the whole universe. Examples are the electric charge of an electron, the speed of light, Planck's constant, and the gravitational constant.

fundamental forces see ◊forces, fundamental.

fundamentalism in religion, an emphasis on basic principles or articles of faith. Christian fundamentalism emerged in the USA just after World War I (as a reaction to theological modernism and the historical criticism of the Bible) and insisted on belief in the literal truth of everything in the Bible. Islamic fundamentalism insists on strict observance of Muslim Shari'a law.

fundamental particle another term for ◊***elementary particle***.

funerary practice ritual or act surrounding the disposal of a dead body, by burial, cremation, or other means (such as exposure). Solemn acts such as the preparation of the body, song (laments), offering of gifts, the funeral procession, provision of a memorial, and mourning are subject to codes of procedure in most cultures.

There is evidence for ritualized burial as early as the Neanderthals, and further evidence from the upper Palaeolithic for the burial of skulls alone. By the 3rd millennium BC graves began to be used for successive burials, and the monumental pyramids were constructed as tombs in Egypt. The Egyptian ◊*Book of the Dead* (c. 1600 BC) preserves magic formulas to be used in approaching the underworld. Cremation was practised by Indo-European groups (Greeks and Teutons), but because of Christian concern for the resurrection it was suppressed in Europe until the modern era; in Egypt, as in some other cultures, bodies were preserved by a process of embalming. Pyramids, beehive tombs in Mycenean Greece, neolithic barrows and bronze age tumuli, mausoleums, caves, catacombs, and ship burials (for example, ◊Sutton Hoo) testify to the variety of burial, while decorated vases (from sub-Mycenean Greece) and plain urns have been used to contain the ashes of the cremated dead. In India, bodies may be set afloat into the sacred river Ganges; some Native American peoples practised ritual exposure.

fungicide any chemical ◊pesticide used to prevent fungus diseases in plants and animals. Inorganic and organic compounds containing sulphur are widely used.

fungus (plural ***fungi***) any of a group of organisms in the kingdom Fungi. Fungi are not considered plants. They lack leaves and roots, they contain no chlorophyll, and they reproduce by spores. Moulds, yeasts, rusts, smuts, mildews, mushrooms, and toadstools are all types of fungi.

Because fungi have no chlorophyll, they must get food from organic substances. They are either ◊parasites, existing on living plants or animals, or ◊saprotrophs, living on dead matter. Many of the most serious plant diseases are caused by fungi, and several fungi attack humans and animals. Athlete's foot, ◊thrush, and ◊ringworm are fungal diseases.

Some 50,000 different species have been identified. Some are edible, but many are highly poisonous. Before the classification Fungi came into use, they were included within the division Thallophyta, along with algae and bacteria. Two familiar fungi are bread mould, which illustrates the typical many-branched body of the organism, called the mycelium, made up of threadlike hyphae; and mushrooms, which are the sexually reproductive fruiting bodies of an underground mycelium.

The mycelium of a true fungus is made up of many hyphae woven and intertwined. When the organism is ready to reproduce, the hyphae become closely packed into a solid mass called the fruiting body, which in most instances is small and inconspicuous but may be very large; mushrooms, toadstools, and bracket fungi are all examples of large fruiting bodies. These carry and distribute the spores. Most species of fungi reproduce both asexually and sexually.

In 1992 an individual honey fungus *Armallaria ostoyae* was identified as the world's largest living thing, having an underground network of hyphae covering 600 hectares/1,480 acres. It was found in Washington State, USA, and estimated to be between 500 and 1,000 years old.

funicular railway railway with two cars connected by a wire cable wound around a drum at the top of a steep incline. Funicular railways of up to 1.5 km/1 mi exist in Switzerland.

Funj Islamic dynasty that ruled the Sudan from 1505 to the 1820s, when the territory was taken over by the Turkish government of Egypt. During the 16th and 17th centuries the Funj extended their territories westwards and in the 18th century fought a series of wars against Ethiopia. From the late 1600s there were severe internal conflicts, with the warrior aristocracy challenging and eventually supplanting the ruling family.

funk dance music of black US origin, relying on heavy percussion in polyrhythmic patterns. Leading exponents include James ◊Brown and George Clinton (1940–).

Initially used for a hard-bop jazz style and as a loose term of approbation in rhythm and blues, funk became a defined category in the 1970s as ◊disco music geared to a black audience, less slick and mechanical than mainstream disco.

Funk Casimir 1884–1967. Polish-born US biochemist who pioneered research into vitamins. He was the first to isolate niacin (nicotinic acid, one of the vitamins of the B complex).

Funk proposed that certain diseases are caused by dietary deficiencies. In 1911 he demonstrated that rice extracts cure beriberi in pigeons. As the extract contains an ◊amine, he mistakenly concluded that he had discovered a class of 'vital amines', a phrase soon reduced to 'vitamins'.

fur the ◊hair of certain animals. Fur is an excellent insulating material and so has been used as clothing, although this is vociferously criticized by many groups on humane grounds. The methods of breeding or trapping animals are often cruel. Mink, chinchilla, and sable are among the most valuable, the wild furs being finer than the farmed. Fur such as mink is made up of a soft, thick, insulating layer called underfur and a top layer of longer, lustrous guard hairs.

Furs have been worn since prehistoric times and have long been associated with status and luxury (ermine traditionally worn by royalty, for example), except by certain ethnic groups like the Inuit. The fur trade had its origin in North America, exploited by the Hudson's Bay Company from the late 17th century. The chief centres of the fur trade are New York, London, St Petersburg, and Kastoria in Greece. It is illegal to import furs or skins of endangered species listed by ◊CITES; for example, the leopard. Many synthetic fibres are widely used as substitutes.

Furies in Greek mythology, the Erinyes, appeasingly called the Eumenides ('kindly ones'). They were the daughters of Earth or of Night, represented as winged maidens with serpents twisted in their hair. They punished such crimes as filial disobedience, murder, inhospitality, and oath-breaking, but were also associated with fertility.

furlong unit of measurement, originating in Anglo-Saxon England, equivalent to 220 yd (201.168 m).

A furlong consists of 40 rods, poles, or perches; 8 furlongs equal one statute ◊mile. Its literal meaning is 'furrow-long', and refers to the length of a furrow in the common field characteristic of medieval farming.

furnace structure in which fuel such as coal, coke, gas, or oil is burned to produce heat for various purposes. Furnaces are used in conjunction with ◊boilers for heating, to produce hot water, or steam for driving turbines – in ships for propulsion and in power stations for generating electricity. The largest furnaces are those used for smelting and refining metals, such as the ◊blast furnace, electric furnace, and ◊open-hearth furnace.

furniture movable functional items such as tables, chairs, and beds needed to make a room or a home more comfortable and easier to live and work in. Furniture may be made from a wide variety of materials, including wood, stone, metal, plastic, papier-mâché, glass, cane, and textiles. Styles vary from plain utilitarian to richly ornate, and decoration may be added in the form of carving, inlay, veneer, paint, gilding, or upholstery.

Furniture reflects evolving technology and fashion, and has often been valued more as a status symbol than for actual use. The quantity and variety of furniture, as well as its comfort, have increased in the West, especially in the last 300 years.

the ancient Mediterranean Wood is the most commonly used material for making furniture, but because it decays quite quickly, very little ancient furniture survives. The ancient Egyptians had wooden beds, chairs, tables, and stools, decorated with carving, gilding, or veneer. Egyptian woodworkers are thought to have invented the mortice and tenon joint, which strengthened and stabilized frames of seats and items such as chests.

In Classical Greece and Rome only the wealthiest people owned furniture; much of this was made of bronze and stone, some of it carved to look like wood. The feet of chairs and tables in the ancient world were often shaped like animals' paws or hoofs. Couches were an important feature of wealthy Greek and Roman households, since people both reclined on them during meals and slept on them at night. Tables were usually low enough to be stored under couches when not in use. A common style of chair in ancient Greece was the *klismos*, which had curved legs. The Romans adopted many Greek furniture designs, adapting them to suit their own tastes; they liked upholstered chairs and stools, and introduced large tables made from a single slab of marble, supported at either end by carved upright slabs.

Oriental furniture In ancient times furniture was a sign of social rank, and only the very wealthy owned the expertly crafted furniture that was first produced in China during the 3rd century BC. Styles in China later divided into the simple forms found in people's homes, and the ornate items made for emperors and their officials. All furniture, however, was skilfully made, with precisely cut joints which eliminated the need for nails or dowels. Japanese furniture was made of wood, often lacquered and inlaid with shells. It was both sparse and lightweight, consisting mainly of storage cabinets and low tables, since people traditionally both sat and slept on mats on the floor. Furniture in ancient India was more luxurious; a wealthy home might have canopied beds and divans, tables, storage chests for clothes, benches, and chairs, all lavishly draped and upholstered with spreads, curtains, and pillows.

medieval Europe Most of the furniture made before 1300 in Europe was crudely built of painted or gilded wood. Landowners and important clergy travelled a great deal, frequently taking their entire households and furniture along with them. Thus, although furniture was heavy and solid, much of it could be dismantled for carrying from place to place. Folding X-frame chairs with fabric seats were popular, and chests were important pieces of furniture, since they were portable, and could be used for seating as well as storage. Hinges were often made of leather, which was cheap and easily obtained; more valuable chests had decorative iron hinges and locks.

the Renaissance From about 1300, fashionable Italian furnituremakers produced work for their wealthy clients that showed the influence of ancient Greece and Rome, and their ideas soon spread to the rest of Europe. They used finer wood than their predecessors, and decorated their work with intricate carvings, gilding, and paintings. Chests were still important, but were more grandly decorated than anything made earlier. The addition of legs to chests led to the development of cupboards and cabinets containing small drawers. Cabinets were built in two parts, with a top section resting on a larger base. Elaborately carved four-poster beds were hung with expensive curtains, often embroidered with flowers, birds, or scenes from Classical mythology.

17th-century Europe Classical designs were still very much in evidence, but with far more decoration added than before. World exploration brought new and exotic materials to European furnituremakers, who inlaid furniture with tropical woods, semiprecious stones, and shells. Walnut replaced oak as the fashionable wood to use, and rich upholstery became a desirable status symbol. Chests of drawers on legs, tall cupboards, and long sideboards developed from Renaissance cabinets and cupboards. Furniture became more luxurious, especially under the influence of the French king Louis XIV, whose new furniture for his palace at Versailles featured the new technique of veneering, as well as carving, lacquer, and precious metals, especially silver.

early 18th-century Europe After the grand and heavy Louis XIV style, fashions entered the Rococo period, becoming lighter and more frivolous. Following Louis XIV's death, power passed to a regent, the Duke of Orléans, who preferred more graceful designs known as the Régence style. Under the next king, Louis XV, gentle curves replaced straight lines; legs of furniture were carved into S-curves, the fronts of cupboards and chests of drawers were curved and had decorative, asymmetrical bronze and ormolu mounts swirling across them in the form of plants and animals. A low chest of drawers on legs, the commode, was popular in most of Europe. The Chinese-inspired style known as chinoiserie produced such features as wooden furniture carved to look like bamboo and then lacquered. British furniture design was more subdued: the Palladian style continued to use Classical elements and the Queen Anne style was very simple and restrained.

Neo-Classicism In the second half of the 18th century European furniture design turned away from flowing Rococo curves and back to straight lines, symmetry, and Classical motifs; this became known as the Neo-Classical period. In Britain this style was typified by the elegant designs of Robert Adam, which were decorated with urns, columns, and mouldings based on those of ancient Rome. Mahogany was the fashionable wood of the period. Pale colours were popular, some furniture was painted white and decorated with gilding.

North America Around the end of the 18th century the North American colonies, which until now had followed English fashions, began to develop styles of their own. One notable style was ◊Shaker furniture. Based on traditional English wooden furniture, it is elegant and functional, without any decoration.

early 19th century The Neo-Classical period in France gave way to the Empire style, developed under Napoleonic rule. It was drawn from ancient Roman, Greek, and Egyptian architecture, and was heavy and imposing. Curved legs on furniture were fashionable, as well as elaborately carved sphinxes and characters from Classical mythology. Beds were draped with silk or velvet hung from above to give the impression of a tent. Following Napoleon's exile, the grand Empire style which had been associated with him gradually lost its appeal. In Britain and the USA another variation on the Neo-Classical style was the Regency style. This was similar to the French Empire style, but lighter and more graceful, and instead of carved decoration, brass inlay became the fashion, along with Oriental-style lacquer.

mid-19th century Much of this period was taken up with revivals of earlier styles. Gothic details were added to Regency furniture; Rococo and Renaissance revivals followed, with decoration and upholstery applied liberally. Mahogany remained popular, but now it was used to make heavy, ornate furniture, often with mirrored doors. In contrast with earlier periods, rooms now tended to be crowded with furniture, resulting in a jumbled profusion of styles, decoration, and ornament.

late 19th century The Arts and Crafts movement was a reaction against mass-produced furniture and textiles. It tried to promote high standards of design in handmade furniture, with subtler decoration that depended more on the skill involved than on ostentation. Furniture was more likely to be made of oak than the earlier mahogany. Art Nouveau developed, also as a reaction to the heavy revival styles. The fashion now was for flowing, natural shapes, with an extreme tendency towards asymmetry. Metalwork and carved wood lent themselves well to Art Nouveau designs. Both the Arts and Crafts movement and Art Nouveau became unfashionable after World War I.

20th century The availability of new materials such as plastic, plywood, steel, aluminium, and fibreglass, combined with methods of mass production have led to a profusion of rapidly changing styles. There has been a demand for lightweight, inexpensive furniture that is easy to maintain. The ◊Bauhaus school, founded 1919, pioneered the use of tubular steel frames for furniture. Art Deco, between the two world wars, developed out of the non-naturalistic elements of Art Nouveau, using designs that could be mass-produced. It was unusual among modern styles in that it used nonfunctional ornament, such as zigzags, circles, triangles, and suns, to decorate furniture.

further education college college in the UK for students over school-leaving age that provides courses for skills towards an occupation or trade, and general education at a level below that of a degree course. Further education colleges were removed from local authority control in 1993.

Furtwängler (Gustav Heinrich Ernst Martin) Wilhelm 1886–1954. German conductor. He was leader of the Berlin Philharmonic Orchestra 1924–54. His interpretations of Wagner, Bruckner, and Beethoven were valued expressions of monumental national grandeur, but he also gave first performances of Bartök, Schoenberg's *Variations for Orchestra* 1928, and Hindemith's opera *Mathis der Maler/Mathis the Painter* 1934, a work implicitly critical of the Nazi regime. He ascended rapidly from theatre to opera orchestras in Mannheim 1915–20 and Vienna 1919–24, then to major appointments in Leipzig and Vienna.

fuse in electricity, a wire or strip of metal designed to melt when excessive current passes through. It is a safety device to stop at that point in the circuit when surges of current would otherwise damage equipment and cause fires. In explosives, a fuse is a cord impregnated with chemicals so that it burns slowly at a predetermined rate. It is used to set off a main explosive charge, sufficient length of fuse being left to allow the person lighting it to get away to safety.

Fuseli (John) Henry, (born Johann Heinrich Füssli) 1741–1825. Swiss-born British Romantic artist. He painted macabre and dreamlike images, such as *The Nightmare* 1781 (Institute of Arts, Detroit), which come close in feelings of horror and the unnatural to the English Gothic novels of his day. His subjects include scenes from Milton and Shakespeare.

The son of a Swiss portrait painter, he emigrated to England 1764, and was encouraged by Reynolds to become a painter and study in Italy. The period spent there, 1770–78, made him a devotee of Michelangelo, though his own work depends for its interest on so different an element as the Romantic love of horror and fantasy. *The Nightmare* made him immediately famous, and the contributions to Boydell's 'Shakespeare Gallery' that followed gave further scope to his imagination. The sensation produced by the subject, rather than beauty of paint, was his main concern.

fusel oil liquid with a characteristic unpleasant smell, obtained as a by-product of the distillation of the product of any alcoholic fermentation, and used

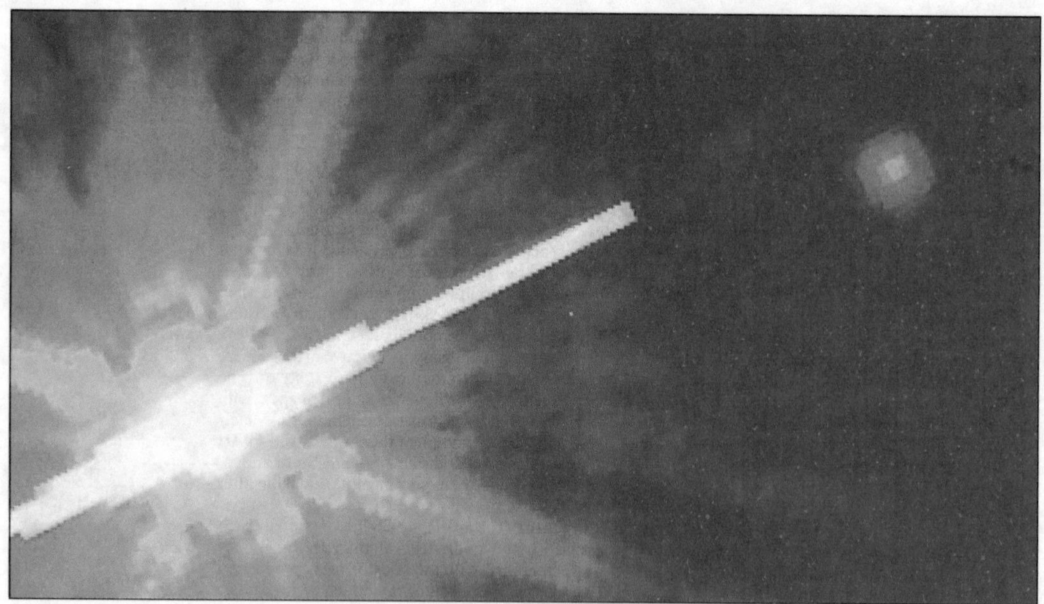

fusion The dwarf star Gliese 105A and its much smaller companion, Gliese 105C, seen from the Hubble Space Telescope. The object to the upper right, GL 105C, is one of the dimmest and least massive stars ever seen; scientists from Mount Palomar Observatory believe its mass to be about 8–9% of that of our Sun, which is thought to be the minimum mass needed for a star to achieve hydrogen fusion. The bright white spikes in the picture are caused by the Hubble Telescope's CCD camera, and appear whenever there is a relatively bright object in the field of view. *Corbis*

in paints, varnishes, essential oils, and plastics. It is a mixture of fatty acids, alcohols, and esters.

fusion in music, a combination of styles; the term usually refers to jazz-rock fusion. Jazz trumpeter Miles Davis began to draw on rock music in the late 1960s, and jazz-rock fusion flourished in the 1970s with bands like Weather Report (formed 1970 in the USA) and musicians like English guitarist John McLaughlin (1942–).

fusion in physics, the fusing of the nuclei of light elements, such as hydrogen, into those of a heavier element, such as helium. The resultant loss in their combined mass is converted into energy. Stars and thermonuclear weapons work on the principle of nuclear fusion.

Very high temperatures and pressures are thought to be required in order for fusion to take place. Under these conditions the atomic nuclei can approach each other at high speeds and overcome the mutual repulsion of their positive charges. At very close range another force, the strong nuclear force, comes into play, fusing the particles together to form a larger nucleus. In 1991 in an experiment that lasted 2 seconds, a 1.7 megawatt pulse of power was produced by the Joint European Torus (JET) at Culham, Oxfordshire, UK. This was the first time that a substantial amount of fusion power had been produced in a controlled experiment, as opposed to a bomb. Attempts at creating ◊cold fusion have not had confirmed success.

future in business, a contract to buy or sell a specific quantity of a particular commodity or currency (or even a purely notional sum, such as the value of a particular stock index) at a particular date in the future. There is usually no physical exchange between buyer and seller. It is only the difference between the ground value and the market value that changes. Such transactions are a function of the futures market.

futures trading buying and selling commodities (usually cereals and metals) at an agreed price for delivery several months ahead. The notional value of the futures contracts traded annually worldwide is $140,000 bn (1994).

Futurism literary and artistic movement 1909–14, originating in Paris.

The Italian poet Filippo ◊Marinetti published the *Futurist Manifesto* 1909 urging Italian artists to join him in Futurism. In their works the Futurists eulogized the modern world and the 'beauty of speed and energy'. Combining the shifting geometric planes of Cubism with vibrant colours, they aimed to capture the dynamism of a speeding car or train by the simultaneous repetition of forms. As a movement Futurism died out during World War I, but the Futurists' exultation in war and violence was seen as an early manifestation of ◊fascism.

Gino Severini painted a topsy-turvy landscape as if seen from the window of a moving train, in *Suburban Train Arriving in Paris* 1915 (Tate Gallery, London), and Giacomo Balla attempted to represent speed in such pictures as *Abstract Speedwake of a Speeding Car* 1919 (Tate Gallery, London).

Umberto Boccioni, a sculptor, froze his figures as if they were several frames of a film moving at once. ◊Vorticism was a similar movement in Britain 1912–15, glorifying modern technology, energy, and violence.

Fuzhou or ***Foochow*** industrial port and capital of Fujian province, on Min River in SE China; population (1993) 1,290,000. The main industries that have developed since the area was declared a Special Economic Zone in 1979 include steel rolling and the manufacture of television sets and tape recorders; rice, sugar, tea, and fruit pass through the port. There are joint foreign and Chinese factories.

The Mazu (Matsu) island group, occupied by the Nationalist Chinese, is offshore.

fuzzy logic in mathematics and computing, a form of knowledge representation suitable for notions (such as 'hot' or 'loud') that cannot be defined precisely but depend on their context. For example, a jug of water may be described as too hot or too cold, depending on whether it is to be used to wash one's face or to make tea.

The central idea of fuzzy logic is probability of set membership. For instance, referring to someone 175 cm/5 ft 9 in tall, the statement 'this person is tall' (or 'this person is a member of the set of tall people') might be about 70% true if that person is a man, and about 85% true if that person is a woman.

Fylingdales site in the North Yorkshire Moors National Park, England, of an early-warning radar station, linked with similar stations in Greenland and Alaska, to give a four-minute warning of nuclear attack.

Fyn (German ***Fünen***) island forming part of Denmark and lying between the mainland and Zealand; capital Odense; area 2,976 sq km/1,149 sq mi; population (1995) 467,700.

fyrd Anglo-Saxon local militia in Britain. All freemen were obliged to defend their shire but, by the 11th century, a distinction was drawn between the ***great fyrd***, for local defence, and the ***select fyrd***, drawn from better-equipped and experienced warriors who could serve farther afield.

g symbol for ◊*gram*.

gabbro mafic (consisting primarily of dark-coloured crystals) igneous rock formed deep in the Earth's crust. It contains pyroxene and calcium-rich feldspar, and may contain small amounts of olivine and amphibole. Its coarse crystals of dull minerals give it a speckled appearance.

Gable (William) Clark 1901–1960. US actor. A star for more than 30 years in 90 films, he played romantic roles such as Rhett Butler in *Gone With the Wind* 1939. His other films include *The Painted Desert* 1931 (his first), *It Happened One Night* 1934 (Academy Award), *Mutiny on the Bounty* 1935, and *The Misfits* 1961. He was nicknamed the 'King of Hollywood'.

Gabo Naum. Adopted name of Naum Neemia Pevsner 1890–1977. Russian-born US abstract sculptor. One of the leading exponents of Constructivism, he was one of the first artists to make ◊kinetic sculpture. In later works he often used transparent plastics in works that attempt to define space rather than occupy it, as in *Linear Construction* 1942 (Tate Gallery, London).

Gabo and his brother Antoine Pevsner (1886–1962) published their ideas in the *Realist Manifesto* 1920. From this period date many of Gabo's most important works, including geometric constructions in metal and transparent plastic and the *Vibrating Rod* 1920 (Tate Gallery, London), one of the earliest sculptures employing real motion. In the 1920s he taught at the ◊Bauhaus school of design in Germany.

Gabon country in central Africa, bounded N by Cameroon, E and S by the Congo, W by the Atlantic Ocean, and NW by Equatorial Guinea. *See country box below.*

Gabor Dennis 1900–1979. Hungarian-born British physicist. In 1947 he invented the holographic method of three-dimensional photography (see ◊holography). He was awarded a Nobel prize 1971.

Gaborone capital of Botswana, mainly an administrative and government-service centre; population (1991) 133,500. The University of Botswana and Swaziland (1976) is here. The city developed after it replaced Mafeking as the country's capital 1965. Light industries include textiles, brewing, printing and publishing, and construction.

Gabriel in the New Testament, the archangel who foretold the birth of John the Baptist to Zacharias and of Jesus to the Virgin Mary. He is also mentioned in the Old Testament in the book of Daniel. In Muslim belief, Gabriel revealed the Koran to Muhammad and escorted him on his ◊Night Journey.

Gabrieli Giovanni c. 1555–1612. Italian composer. He succeeded his uncle Andrea Gabrieli (c. 1533–1585) as organist of St Mark's, Venice. His sacred and secular works include numerous madrigals, motets, and the antiphonal *Sacrae Symphoniae* 1597, sacred canzonas and sonatas for brass choirs, strings, and organ, in spatial counterpoint.

Gaddafi alternative form of ◊Khaddhafi, Libyan leader.

Gaddi Italian family of artists. ***Gaddo*** (c. 1260–1332) was a painter and mosaic worker, a friend of Cimabue, whose influence has been perceived in the *Coronation of the Virgin with Saints and Angels*, a mosaic in the cathedral at Florence attributed to Gaddo. Other works attributed to him are the mosaics in Sta Maria Maggiore and those of the choir of the old St Peter's, Rome. His son, ***Taddeo*** (c. 1300–1366) was a pupil of Giotto and is considered one of his most important followers. His paintings include the frescoes *Virgin and Child between Four Prophets* and other scenes from the life of the Virgin in the Baroncelli Chapel in Santa Croce, Florence, 1332, as well as works at Pisa, Pistoia and in various galleries. The son of Taddeo, ***Agnolo*** (died 1396), worked in the Vatican 1369, probably with his brother Giovanni. Frescoes in Santa Croce depicting the legend of the Cross, and in the cathedral of Prato, 1392–95, representing the legends of the Virgin and the Sacred Girdle, are attributed to him.

gadolinium silvery-white metallic element of the lanthanide series, symbol Gd, atomic number 64, relative atomic mass 157.25. It is found in the products of nuclear fission and used in electronic components, alloys, and products needing to withstand high temperatures.

Gadsden Purchase in US history, the purchase of approximately 77,700 sq km/30,000 sq mi in what is now New Mexico and Arizona by the USA 1853. The land was bought from Mexico for $10 million in a treaty, negotiated by James Gadsden (1788–1858) of South Carolina, to construct a transcontinental railroad route, the Southern Pacific, completed in the 1880s.

Gaelic language member of the Celtic branch of the Indo-European language family, spoken in Ireland, Scotland, and (until 1974) the Isle of Man. Gaelic has been in decline for several centuries, discouraged until recently within the British state. There is a small Gaelic-speaking community in Nova Scotia, Canada.

It is, along with English, one of the national languages of the Republic of Ireland, with over half a million speakers, and is known there as both Irish and Irish Gaelic. In Scotland, speakers of Gaelic number around 90,000 and are concentrated in the Western Isles, in parts of the NW coast and in the city of Glasgow.

Gagarin Yuri (Alexeyevich) 1934–1968. Soviet cosmonaut who in 1961 became the first human in space aboard the spacecraft *Vostok 1*. He became a pilot 1957, and on 12 April 1961 completed one orbit of the Earth, taking 108 minutes from launch to landing. He died in a plane crash while training for the *Soyuz 3* mission.

Gagauz or ***Gagauze*** ethnic minority of Christian Orthodox Turks, of whom 153,000 (90%) live in S Moldova. In Oct 1990, Gagauz separatists unilaterally declared a breakaway republic, fearing a resurgence of ethnic Romanian nationalism as Moldova moved toward independence. A state of emergency was declared later the same month after the separatists held unauthorized elections to an independent parliament.

Gaia or ***Ge*** in Greek mythology, the goddess of the Earth. She sprang from primordial Chaos and herself produced Uranus, by whom she was the mother of the Cyclopes and ◊Titans.

'Till now man has been up against Nature, from now on he will be up against his own nature.'

DENNIS GABOR
Inventing the Future

GABON
Gabonese Republic

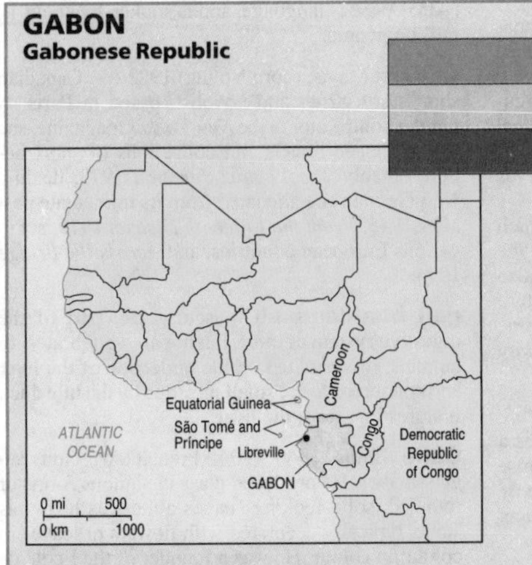

national name *République Gabonaise*
area 267,667 sq km/103,319 sq mi
capital Libreville
major towns/cities Masuku (Franceville)
major ports Port-Gentil and Owendo
physical features virtually the whole country is tropical rainforest; narrow coastal plain rising to hilly interior with savanna in E and S; Ogooué River flows N–W
head of state Omar Bongo from 1964
head of government Paulin Obame-Nguema from 1994
political system emergent democracy
administrative divisions nine provinces, subdivided into 37 departments
political parties Gabonese Democratic Party (PDG), nationalist; Gabone Progress Party (PGP), left of centre; National Rally of Woodcutters (RNB), left of centre
population 1,320,000 (1995 est)
population growth rate 2.8% (1990–95); 2.5% (2000–05)
ethnic distribution 40 Bantu peoples in four main groupings: the Fang, Eshira, Mbede, and Okande; there are also Pygmies and about 10% Europeans (mainly French)
life expectancy 52 (males), 55 (females)
literacy rate 61%
languages French (official), Bantu
religions Roman Catholic, also Muslim, animist
currency franc CFA
GDP (US $) 3.94 billion (1994)
growth rate 1.3% (1994)
exports petroleum, manganese, uranium, timber and wood products, including okoume

HISTORY
12th C Immigration of Bantu speakers into an area previously peopled by Pygmies.
1472 Gabon Estuary first visited by Portuguese navigators, who named it Gabao ('hooded cloak'), after the shape of the coastal area.
17th–18th Cs Fang, from Cameroon in N, and Omiene peoples colonized the area, attracted by presence in coastal areas of European traders, who developed the ivory and slave trades, which lasted until the mid-19th century.
1839–42 Mpongwe coastal chiefs agreed to transfer sovereignty to French; Catholic and Protestant missionaries attracted to the area.
1849 Libreville ('Free Town') formed by slaves from a slave ship liberated by the French.
1889 Became part of French Congo, with Congo.
1910 Became part of French Equatorial Africa, which also comprised Congo, Chad, and the Central African Republic.
1890s–1920s Human and natural resources exploited by private concessionary companies.
1940–44 Supported the 'Free French' anti-Nazi cause during World War II.
1946 Became overseas territory within the French Community, with its own assembly.
1960 Independence achieved; Léon M'ba, a Fang of the pro-French Gabonese Democratic Block (BDG) became the first president.
1964 Attempted military coup by supporters of rival party foiled with French help.
1967 M'ba died and was succeeded by protégé, Albert Bernard Bongo, from the Teke community.
1968 One-party state established, with BDG dissolved and replaced by Gabonese Democratic Party (PDG).
1973 Bongo converted to Islam and changed his first name to Omar, but continued to follow pro-Western policy course and exploit rich mineral resources to increase prosperity.
1989 Coup attempt against Bongo defeated as economy deteriorated.
1990 PDG won first multiparty elections since 1964 amid allegations of ballot-rigging. French troops sent in to maintain order following antigovernment riots.
1993 National unity government formed, including some opposition members.
1998 Bongo re-elected for seven years.
1999 Jean-François Ntoutoume-Emane becomes prime minister.

SEE ALSO Fang; Free French; Pygmy

I do not feel obliged to believe that the same God who has endowed us with sense, reason, and intellect has intended us to forgo their use.

GALILEO
Attributed remark

Gaia hypothesis theory that the Earth's living and nonliving systems form an inseparable whole that is regulated and kept adapted for life by living organisms themselves. The planet therefore functions as a single organism, or a giant cell. The hypothesis was elaborated by British scientist James Lovelock (1919–) and first published 1968.

gain in electronics, the ratio of the amplitude of the output signal produced by an amplifier to that of the input signal.

Gainsborough Thomas 1727–1788. English landscape and portrait painter, one of the major figures of English art. His success was based on his society portraits, which at their best combine the elegance of the period with subtle characterization. In landscape painting he was one of the first British artists to follow the Dutch example in painting realistic scenes rather than imaginative Italianate scenery. *Mr and Mrs Andrews* about 1750 (National Gallery, London) illustrates both these points.

Gainsborough was largely self-taught. In 1760 he settled in Bath and painted society portraits. In 1774 he went to London, where he became one of the original members of the Royal Academy and the principal rival of Joshua Reynolds in portraiture. The portrait of his wife (Courtauld Institute, London) and *The Morning Walk* (National Gallery, London) show his sense of character and the elegance of his mature work. A constant tendency to experiment produced the 'fancy pictures' or imaginative compositions of his late years, the *Diana and Actaeon* (Royal Collection), unfinished when he died, being an example. Hundreds of drawings, often in a mixture of media, show his continued pursuit of landscape for its own sake.

His sitters included the royal family, the actors David Garrick and Sarah Siddons, the writer Samuel Johnson, the politician Edmund Burke, and the dramatist Richard Sheridan.

Gaitskell Hugh (Todd Naylor) 1906–1963. British Labour politician. In 1950 he became minister of economic affairs, and then chancellor of the Exchequer until Oct 1951. In 1955 he defeated Aneurin Bevan for the succession to Attlee as party leader, and tried to reconcile internal differences on nationalization and disarmament. He was re-elected leader in 1960.

gal symbol for ◊***gallon***, ◊***galileo***.

Galahad in Arthurian legend, one of the knights of the Round Table. Galahad succeeded in the quest for the ◊Holy Grail because of his virtue. He was the son of ◊Lancelot of the Lake.

Gainsborough *Portrait of Muilman, Crockatt and Keeble* 1753–55 by Thomas Gainsborough. Painted when he was in his early twenties, this portrait is more informal and direct than many of his later society pictures. It is typical, however, of his distinctive skill in balancing the two strongest elements of English painting, portraiture and landscape painting. *Sotheby's*

Galápagos Islands (official name ***Archipiélago de Colón***) group of 12 large and several hundred smaller islands in the Pacific about 800 km/500 mi from the mainland, belonging to Ecuador; area 7,800 sq km/3,000 sq mi; population (1990) 9,800. The capital is San Cristóbal. The islands are a nature reserve; their unique fauna (including giant tortoises, iguanas, penguins, flightless cormorants, and Darwin's finches, which inspired Charles ◊Darwin to formulate the principle of evolution by natural selection) is under threat from introduced species. The main industry is tuna and lobster fishing.

Galatia ancient province of Asia Minor. It was occupied in the 3rd century BC by the ◊Gauls, and became a Roman province 25 BC.

galaxy congregation of millions or billions of stars, held together by gravity. ***Spiral galaxies***, such as the ◊Milky Way, are flattened in shape, with a central bulge of old stars surrounded by a disc of younger stars, arranged in spiral arms like a Catherine wheel. ***Barred spirals*** are spiral galaxies that have a straight bar of stars across their centre, from the ends of which the spiral arms emerge. The arms of spiral galaxies contain gas and dust from which new stars are still forming. ***Elliptical galaxies*** contain old stars and very little gas. They include the most massive galaxies known, containing a trillion stars. At least some elliptical galaxies are thought to be formed by mergers between spiral galaxies. There are also irregular galaxies. Most galaxies occur in clusters, containing anything from a few to thousands of members.

Our own Galaxy, the Milky Way, is about 100,000 light years in diameter, and contains at least 100 billion stars. It is a member of a small cluster, the ◊Local Group. The Sun lies in one of its spiral arms, about 25,000 light years from the centre. ▷ *See feature on pp. 70–71.*

Galbraith John Kenneth 1908– . Canadian-born US economist who criticized the neoclassical view that in the economy market forces were in a state approximating perfect competition. He suggested that the 'affluent society' develops an economic imbalance, devoting too many resources to the production of consumer goods and not enough to public services and infrastructure. His commitment to the development of the public sector was in sympathy with ◊Keynesian economics. In his book *The Affluent Society* 1958, he documents the tendency of free-market capitalism to create private splendour and public squalor.

Galen c.129–c.200. Greek physician and anatomist whose ideas dominated Western medicine for almost 1,500 years. Central to his thinking were the theories of ◊humours and the threefold circulation of the blood. He remained the highest medical authority until Andreas ◊Vesalius and William ◊Harvey exposed the fundamental errors of his system.

Galen postulated a circulation system in which the liver produced the natural spirit, the heart the vital spirit, and the brain the animal spirit. He also wrote about philosophy and believed that Nature expressed a divine purpose, a belief that became increasingly popular with the rise of Christianity (Galen himself was not a Christian).

galena mineral consisting of lead sulphide, PbS, the chief ore of lead. It is lead-grey in colour, has a high metallic lustre and breaks into cubes because of its perfect cubic cleavage. Galena occurs mainly among limestone deposits in Australia, Mexico, Russia, Kazakhstan, the UK, and the USA.

Galicia region of central Europe, extending from the northern slopes of the Carpathian Mountains to the Romanian border. Once part of the Austrian Empire, it was included in Poland after World War I and divided 1945 between Poland and the USSR.

Galicia mountainous but fertile autonomous region of NW Spain, formerly an independent kingdom; area 29,400 sq km/11,348 sq mi; population (1991) 2,731,700. It includes La Coruña, Lugo, Orense, and Pontevedra. Industries include the mining of tungsten and tin, and fishing; Galicia has the largest fishing fleet in the European Union. The language is similar to Portuguese.

Galilee region of N Israel (once a Roman province in Palestine) which includes Nazareth and Tiberias, frequently mentioned in the Gospels of the New Testament.

Galilee, Sea of alternative name for Lake ◊Tiberias in N Israel.

galileo unit (symbol gal) of acceleration, used in geological surveying. One galileo is 10^{-2} metres per second per second. The Earth's gravitational field often differs by several milligals (thousandths of gals) in different places, because of the varying densities of the rocks beneath the surface.

Galileo properly Galileo Galilei 1564–1642. Italian mathematician, astronomer, and physicist. He developed the astronomical telescope and was the first to see sunspots, the four main satellites of Jupiter, and the appearance of Venus going through phases, thus proving it was orbiting the Sun. Galileo discovered that freely falling bodies, heavy or light, have the same, constant acceleration and that a body moving on a perfectly smooth horizontal surface would neither speed up nor slow down.

Galileo's work founded the modern scientific method of deducing laws to explain the results of observation and experiment. His observations were an unwelcome refutation of the ideas of the Greek philosopher ◊Aristotle taught at the church-run universities, largely because they made plausible for the first time the Sun-centred theory of Polish astronomer Nicolaus ◊Copernicus. Galileo's persuasive *Dialogo sopra i due massimi sistemi del mondo/Dialogues on the Two Chief Systems of the World* 1632 was banned by the church authorities in Rome and he was made to recant by the Inquisition. ▷ *See feature on pp. 70–71.*

Galileo spacecraft launched from the space shuttle *Atlantis* Oct 1989, on a six-year journey to Jupiter. *Galileo*'s probe entered the atmosphere of Jupiter Dec 1995. It radioed information back to the orbiter for 57 minutes before it was destroyed by atmospheric pressure. The orbiter continued circling Jupiter until 1997. Despite technical problems data and pictures were successfully relayed to Earth.

gall abnormal outgrowth on a plant that develops as a result of attack by insects or, less commonly, by bacteria, fungi, mites, or nematodes. The attack causes an increase in the number of cells or an enlargement of existing cells in the plant. Gall-forming insects generally pass the early stages of their life inside the gall.

Galla or ***Oromo*** nomadic pastoralists inhabiting S Ethiopia and NW Kenya. Galla is a Hamito-Semitic (Afro-Asiatic) language, and is spoken by about 12 million people.

Gallant Mavis, (born Young) 1922– . Canadian short-story writer and novelist, based in Paris. A regular contributor to the *New Yorker* magazine, she has published novels and collections of short fiction, notably *The Pegnitz Junction* 1973, dealing with German life alienated from its immediate past after 1945, *From the Fifteenth District* 1979, set in various European countries, and *Across the Bridge* 1994.

gall bladder small muscular sac, part of the digestive system of most, but not all, vertebrates. In humans, it is situated on the underside of the liver and connected to the small intestine by the bile duct. It stores bile from the liver.

Gallé Emile 1846–1904. French Art Nouveau glassmaker. He produced glass in sinuous forms or rounded, solid-looking shapes almost as heavy as stone, typically decorated with flowers or leaves in colour on colour. He was a founder of the Ecole de Nancy, a group of French Art Nouveau artists who drew inspiration from his 1890s work and adopted his style of decoration and techniques.

Galle Johann Gottfried 1812–1910. German astronomer. He located the planet Neptune 1846, close to the position predicted by French mathematician Urbain ◊Leverrier and the English astronomer J C ◊Adams.

galley ship powered by oars, and usually also equipped with sails. Galleys typically had a crew of hundreds of rowers arranged in banks. They were used in warfare in the Mediterranean from antiquity until the 18th century. France maintained a fleet of some 40 galleys, crewed by over 10,000 convicts, until 1748.

Galliano John 1960– . English fashion designer. His elegant and innovative designs are often inspired by historical motifs (for example, 'Dickensian' clothing), the elements of which he redesigns to create progressive collections. In 1990 he designed the costumes for a production of Ashley Page's ballet *Corrulao*, performed by the Ballet Rambert.

Gallic Wars series of military campaigns 58–51 BC in which Julius Caesar, as proconsul of Gaul, annexed Transalpine Gaul (the territory that formed the geographical basis of modern-day France). His final victory over the Gauls led by Vercingetorix 52 BC left him in control of the land area from the Rhine to the Pyrenees and from the Alps to the Atlantic. The final organization of the provinces followed under Augustus.

Gallipoli port in European Turkey, giving its name to the peninsula (ancient name ***Chersonesus***) on which it stands. In World War I, at the instigation of Winston Churchill, an unsuccessful attempt was made Feb 1915–Jan 1916 by Allied troops to force their way through the Dardanelles and link up with Russia. The campaign was fought mainly by Australian and New Zealand (◊ANZAC) forces, who suffered heavy losses. An estimated 36,000 Commonwealth troops died during the nine-month campaign.

gallium grey metallic element, symbol Ga, atomic number 31, relative atomic mass 69.75. It is liquid at room temperature. Gallium arsenide (GaAs) crystals are used in microelectronics, since electrons travel a thousand times faster through them than through silicon.

gallium arsenide GaAs compound of gallium and arsenic, used in lasers, photocells, and microwave generators. Its semiconducting properties make it a possible rival to ◊silicon for use in microprocessors. Chips made from gallium arsenide require less electric power and process data faster than those made from silicon.

Gallo Robert Charles 1937– . US scientist credited with identifying the virus responsible for ◊AIDS. Gallo discovered the virus, now known as human immunodeficiency virus (HIV), in 1984; the French scientist Luc Montagnier (1932–) of the Pasteur Institute, Paris, discovered the virus, independently, in 1983.

gallon imperial liquid or dry measure, equal to 4.546 litres, and subdivided into four quarts or eight pints. The US gallon is equivalent to 3.785 litres.

Galloway ancient area of SW Scotland, now part of the region of ◊Dumfries and Galloway.

gallstone pebblelike, insoluble accretion formed in the human gall bladder or bile ducts from cholesterol or calcium salts present in bile. Gallstones may cause pain, indigestion, or jaundice. They can be dissolved with medication or removed, either by means of an endoscope or, along with the gall bladder, in an operation known as cholecystectomy.

Gallup George Horace 1901–1984. US journalist and statistician, who founded in 1935 the American Institute of Public Opinion and devised the Gallup Poll, in which public opinion is sampled by questioning a number of representative individuals (see ◊opinion poll).

Galsworthy John 1867–1933. English novelist and dramatist. His work examines the social issues of the Victorian period. He wrote *The Forsyte Saga* 1906–1922 and its sequel, the novels collectively entitled *A Modern Comedy* 1929. Soames Forsyte, the central character of the *Forsyte Saga* series, is the embodiment of Victorian values and feeling for property, and the wife whom he also 'owns' – Irene – was based on Galsworthy's wife. His plays include *The Silver Box* 1906. Nobel Prize for Literature 1932.

Galtieri Leopoldo Fortunato 1926– . Argentine general, president 1981–82. A leading member from 1979 of the ruling right-wing military junta and commander of the army, Galtieri became president in 1981. Under his leadership the junta ordered the seizure 1982 of the Falkland Islands (Malvinas), a British colony in the SW Atlantic claimed by Argentina. After the surrender of his forces he resigned as army commander and was replaced as president. He and his fellow junta members were tried for abuse of human rights and court-martialled for their conduct of the war; he was sentenced to 12 years in prison in 1986.

Galton Francis 1822–1911. English scientist, inventor, and explorer who studied the inheritance of physical and mental attributes with the aim of improving the human species. He was the first to use twins to try to assess the influence of environment on development, and is considered the founder of ◊eugenics (a term he coined). Knighted 1909.

Galvani Luigi 1737–1798. Italian physiologist who discovered galvanic, or voltaic, electricity in 1762, when investigating the contractions produced in the muscles of dead frogs by contact with pairs of different metals. His work led quickly to Alessandro ◊Volta's invention of the electrical ◊cell, and later to an understanding of how nerves control muscles.

galvanizing process for rendering iron rustproof, by plunging it into molten zinc (the dipping method), or by electroplating it with zinc.

galvanometer instrument for detecting small electric currents by their magnetic effect.

Galway county on the W coast of the Republic of Ireland, in the province of Connacht; county town Galway; area 5,940 sq km/2,293 sq mi; population (1991) 180,300. Towns include Ballinasloe, Tuam, Clifden, and Loughrea (near which deposits of lead, zinc, and copper were found 1959). The east is low-lying. In the south are the Slieve Aughty Mountains and Galway Bay, with the Aran Islands. To the W of Lough Corrib is Connemara, a wild area of moors, hills, lakes, and bogs. The Shannon is the principal river.

Galway fishing port and county town of County Galway, Republic of Ireland; population (1991) 50,800. It produces textiles and chemicals, and there is salmon and eel fishing. University College is part of the national university, and Galway Theatre stages Irish Gaelic plays.

Galway James 1939– . Irish flautist. He played with the London Symphony Orchestra 1966, Royal Philharmonic Orchestra 1967–69, and was principal flautist with the Berlin Philharmonic Orchestra 1969–75 before taking up a solo career.

Gama Vasco da c. 1469–1524. Portuguese navigator. He commanded an expedition in 1497 to discover the route to India around the Cape of Good Hope in modern South Africa. On Christmas Day 1497 he reached land, which he named Natal. He then crossed the Indian Ocean, arriving at Calicut (now Kozhikode in Kerala) May 1498, and returned to Portugal Sept 1499.

Da Gama was born in Sines, SW Portugal, and was chosen by King Manoel I for his 1497 expedition. In 1502 he founded a Portuguese colony in Mozambique. In the same year he attacked and plundered Calicut in revenge for the murder of some Portuguese sailors. After 20 years of retirement, he was dispatched to India again as Portuguese viceroy in 1524, but died two months after his arrival in Goa.

Gambetta Léon Michel 1838–1882. French politician, organizer of resistance during the Franco-Prussian War, and founder in 1871 of the Third Republic. In 1881–82 he was prime minister for a few weeks.

Gambia river in W Africa, 1,000 km/620 mi long, which gives its name to The Gambia. It rises in Guinea and flows west along the country to the Atlantic Ocean.

Gambia, The country in W Africa, bounded north, east, and south by Senegal and west by the Atlantic Ocean. *See country box on p. 430.*

gambling or ***gaming*** staking of money or anything else of value on the outcome of a competition. Forms of gambling include betting on sports results, casino games like blackjack and roulette, card games like poker, brag, and cribbage, fruit machines, and lotteries. Association football (via football pools) and horse racing attract gambling through either off- or on-course betting.

In the UK commercial gambling is restricted to premises licensed and registered under statute. These include gaming clubs and casinos, amusement arcades, and pubs. To run controlled premises an applicant must first obtain a certificate of consent from the Gaming Board of Great Britain. A gaming licence must then be obtained from a betting licensing committee of magistrates. Lotteries are controlled by the Lotteries and Amusements Act 1976. Generally lotteries that raise money for charity are legal and those carried out for profit are not. The UK launched its first national lottery 1994. Premium Bonds are also a form of lottery.

Gambling is a multibillion-dollar operation worldwide and can be addictive. Gamblers Anonymous was set up in the UK 1964 to help compulsive gamblers overcome their addiction. Gam-anon provides support for relatives of gamblers.

gamelan Indonesian orchestra employing tuned gongs, xylophones, metallophones (with bars of metal), cymbals, drums, flutes, and fiddles, the music of which has inspired such Western composers as Claude Debussy, Colin McPhee, John Cage, Benjamin Britten, and Philip Glass. Originally court music with Hindustan influences, it withdrew under Dutch colonial administration to rural communities, and was played as an accompaniment to ceremonial occasions, dancing, and puppet theatre. The music is improvised and based on interlocking tonal and rhythmic patterns.

gamete cell that functions in sexual reproduction by merging with another gamete to form a ◊zygote. Examples of gametes include sperm and egg cells. In most organisms, the gametes are haploid (they contain half the number of chromosomes of the parent), owing to reduction division or ◊meiosis.

Galileo Engraving from the original title page of Galileo's *De Systemate Mundi*, depicting Aristotle, Ptolemy, and Copernicus. His work attracted great interest and praise from students and patrons, but Galileo repeatedly fell foul of the Catholic Church for his adherence to the theories of Copernicus. *Corbis*

Galileo The *Galileo* spacecraft about to be detached from the Earth-orbiting space shuttle *Atlantis* at the beginning of its six-year journey to Jupiter. *National Aeronautical Space Agency*

GAMBIA
Republic of The

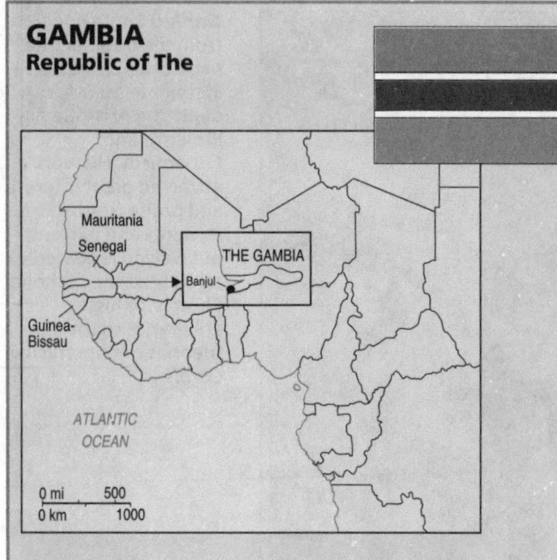

area 10,402 sq km/4,018 sq mi
capital Banjul
major towns/cities Serekunda, Bakau, Georgetown
physical features consists of narrow strip of land along the river Gambia; river flanked by low hills
head of state and government (interim) Yahya Jameh from 1994
political system transitional
administrative divisions elected council in the capital; part-elected, part-appointed in some areas, in others authority rests with chiefs of ethnic groups
political parties Progressive People's Party (PPP), moderate centrist; National Convention Party (NCP), left of centre
population 1,118,000 (1995 est)
population growth rate 3.8% (1990–95); 2.4% (2000–05)
ethnic distribution wide mix of ethnic groups, the largest is the Mandingo (about 40%); other main groups are the Fula, Wolof, Jola, and Serahuli
life expectancy 43 (males), 47 (females)
literacy rate men 39%, women 16%
languages English (official), Mandinka, Fula and other native tongues
religions Muslim 90%, with animist and Christian minorities
currency dalasi
GDP (US $) 373 million (1994)
growth rate 6.2% (1994)
exports groundnut oil, groundnut cake, cotton, hides and skins, cotton lint. Tourism is important

HISTORY
13th C Wolof, Malinke (Mandingo), and Fulani tribes settled in the region from E and N.
14th C Part of the great Muslim Mali Empire, which, centred to NE, also extended across Senegal, Mali, and S Mauritania.
late 15th C–1591 Part of the Songhai Empire, which superseded the Mali Empire.
1455 Gambia river first sighted by the Portuguese.
17th C British and French established small settlements on the river at Fort James and Albreda.
1843 The Gambia became a British crown colony, administered with Sierra Leone until 1888.
1965 Independence achieved as a constitutional monarchy within the Commonwealth, with Dawda K Jawara of the People's Progressive Party (PPP) as prime minister at the head of a multiparty democracy.
1970 Became a republic, with Jawara as president.
1981 Attempted coup foiled with the help of Senegal.
1982 Formed with Senegal the Confederation of Senegambia, which involved integration of military forces, economic and monetary union, and coordinated foreign policy.
1994 Jawara ousted in military coup, and fled to Senegal; Yahya Jameh named acting head of state.
1995 Counter-coup attempt failed.
1996 Civilian constitution adopted.

SEE ALSO Fulani; Mali Empire

game theory group of mathematical theories, developed in 1944 by Oscar Morgenstern (1902–1977) and John ◊Von Neumann, that seeks to abstract from invented game-playing scenarios and their outcome the essence of situations of conflict and/or cooperation in the real political, business, and social world.

gametophyte the ◊haploid generation in the life cycle of a plant that produces gametes; see ◊alternation of generations.

gamma radiation very high-frequency electromagnetic radiation, similar in nature to X-rays but of shorter wavelength, emitted by the nuclei of radioactive substances during decay or by the interactions of high-energy electrons with matter. Cosmic gamma rays have been identified as coming from pulsars, radio galaxies, and quasars, although they cannot penetrate the Earth's atmosphere.

Gamma rays are stopped only by direct collision with an atom and are therefore very penetrating; they can, however, be stopped by about 4 cm/1.5 in of lead or by a very thick concrete shield. They are less ionizing in their effect than alpha and beta particles, but are dangerous nevertheless because they can penetrate deeply into body tissues such as bone marrow. They are not deflected by either magnetic or electric fields.

Gamma radiation is used to kill bacteria and other microorganisms, sterilize medical devices, and change the molecular structure of plastics to modify their properties (for example, to improve their resistance to heat and abrasion).

gamma-ray astronomy the study of gamma rays from space. Much of the radiation detected comes from collisions between hydrogen gas and cosmic rays in our Galaxy. Some sources have been identified, including the Crab nebula and the Vela pulsar (the most powerful gamma-ray source detected).

Gamma rays are difficult to detect and are generally studied by use of balloon-borne detectors and artificial satellites. The first gamma-ray satellites were *SAS II* (1972) and *COS B* (1975), although gamma-ray detectors were carried on the *Apollo 15* and *16* missions. *SAS II* failed after only a few months, but *COS B* continued working until 1982, carrying out a complete survey of the galactic disc. The Compton Gamma Ray Observatory was launched by US space shuttle *Atlantis* in 1991 to study the gamma-ray sky for five years.

Gamow George (Georgi Antonovich) 1904–1968. Russian-born US cosmologist, nuclear physicist, and popularizer of science. His work in astrophysics included a study of the structure and evolution of stars and the creation of the elements. He explained how the collision of nuclei in the solar interior could produce the nuclear reactions that power the Sun. With the 'hot ◊Big Bang' theory, he indicated the origin of the universe.

Gamsakhurdia Zviad 1939–1993. Georgian politician, president 1990–92. He was a fervent nationalist and an active anticommunist. His increasingly dictatorial style of government and his attitude to non-ethnic Georgians led to his forced removal and flight to neighbouring Armenia 1992. He returned to W Georgia 1993 to lead a rebellion against Edvard ◊Shevardnadze's presidency, but Shevardnadze, with Russian help, destroyed his ill-equipped supporters, and the deposed president was later reported dead.

Gance Abel 1889–1981. French film director. His films were grandiose melodramas. *Napoléon* 1927 was one of the most ambitious silent epic films. It features colour tinting and triple-screen sequences, as well as multiple-exposure shots, and purported to suggest that Napoleon was the fulfilment of the French Revolution.

Ganda people of the Baganda, the majority ethnic group in Uganda; the Baganda also live in Kenya. Until the 19th century they formed an independent kingdom, the largest in E Africa. It was a British protectorate 1894–1962, and the monarchy was officially overthrown in 1966. Their language, Luganda, belongs to the Niger-Congo language family and has about 3 million speakers.

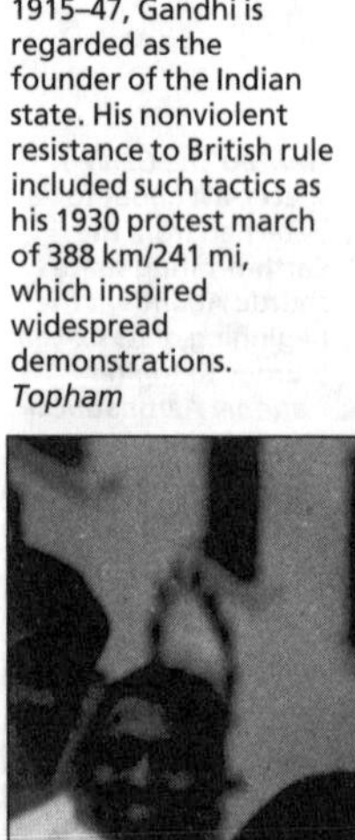

Gandhi Indian political leader Mahatma Gandhi with his granddaughters. Leader of the nationalist movement 1915–47, Gandhi is regarded as the founder of the Indian state. His nonviolent resistance to British rule included such tactics as his 1930 protest march of 388 km/241 mi, which inspired widespread demonstrations. *Topham*

Gandhi Indira Priyadarshani, (born Nehru) 1917–1984. Indian politician, prime minister of India 1966–77 and 1980–84, and leader of the ◊Congress Party 1966–77 and subsequently of the Congress (I) party. She was assassinated 1984 by members of her Sikh bodyguard, resentful of her use of troops to clear malcontents from the Sikh temple at ◊Amritsar.

Her father, Jawaharlal Nehru, was India's first prime minister. She married Feroze Gandhi in 1942 (died 1960, not related to Mahatma Gandhi) and had two sons, Sanjay Gandhi (1946–1980), who died in an aeroplane crash, and Rajiv ◊Gandhi, who was assassinated 1991. In 1975 the validity of her reelection to parliament was questioned, and she declared a state of emergency. During this time Sanjay Gandhi implemented a social and economic programme (including an unpopular family-planning policy) which led to his mother's defeat 1977.

Gandhi Mahatma (Sanskrit 'Great Soul'). Honorific name of Mohandas Karamchand Gandhi 1869–1948. Indian nationalist leader. A pacifist, he led the struggle for Indian independence from the UK by advocating nonviolent noncooperation (*satyagraha*, defence of and by truth) from 1915. He was imprisoned several times by the British authorities and was influential in the nationalist ◊Congress Party and in the independence negotiations 1947. He was assassinated by a Hindu nationalist in the violence that followed the partition of British India into India and Pakistan.

Gandhi was born in Porbandar, Gujarat, and studied law in London, later practising as a barrister. He settled in South Africa where until 1914 he led the Indian community in opposition to racial discrimination. Returning to India, he emerged as leader of the Indian National Congress. He organized hunger strikes and events of civil disobedience, and campaigned for social reform, including religious tolerance and an end to discrimination against the so-called untouchable ◊caste. ▷*See feature on pp. 432–433.*

Gandhi Rajiv 1944–1991. Indian politician, prime minister from 1984 (following his mother Indira Gandhi's assassination) to Nov 1989. As prime minister, he faced growing discontent with his party's elitism and lack of concern for social issues. He was assassinated at an election rally.

Elder son of Indira Gandhi and grandson of Nehru, Rajiv Gandhi initially displayed little interest in politics and became a pilot with Indian Airlines. But after the death in a plane crash of his brother Sanjay (1946–1980), he was elected to his brother's Amethi parliamentary seat 1981. In the Dec 1984 parliamentary elections he won a record majority. His reputation was tarnished by a scandal concerning alleged kickbacks to senior officials from an arms deal with the Swedish munitions firm Bofors and, following his party's defeat in the general election of Nov 1989, Gandhi was forced to resign as premier. He was killed by a bomb 21 May in the middle of the 1991 election campaign.

Ganesh Hindu god, son of Siva and Parvati; he is represented as elephant-headed and is worshipped as a remover of obstacles.

Ganges (Hindi ***Ganga***) major river of India and Bangladesh; length 2,510 km/1,560 mi. It is the most sacred river for Hindus. Its chief tributary is the Jumna (Yamuna, length 1,385 km/860 mi), which joins the Ganges near Allahabad, where there is a sacred bathing place. The Ganges is joined in its delta in Bangladesh by the river ◊Brahmaputra, and the river's most commercially important and westernmost channel to the Bay of Bengal is the Hooghly.

ganglion (plural ***ganglia***) solid cluster of nervous tissue containing many cell bodies and ◊synapses, usually enclosed in a tissue sheath; found in invertebrates and vertebrates. In many invertebrates, the central nervous system consists mainly of ganglia connected by nerve cords. The ganglia in the head (cerebral ganglia) are usually well developed and are analogous to the brain in vertebrates. In vertebrates, most ganglia occur outside the central nervous system.

Gang of Four in Chinese history, the chief members of the radical faction that played a key role in directing the ◊Cultural Revolution. It included communist leader Mao Zedong's widow ◊Jiang Qing; the other members were three young Shanghai politicians: Zhang Chunqiao, Wang Hongwen, and Yao Wenyuan. The gang tried to seize power after the death of Mao Zedong 1976, staging militia coups in Shanghai and Beijing (Peking). Their quest failed and the Gang of Four were arrested. Publicly tried 1980, all, with the exception of Yao Wenyuan, were found guilty of treason. Yao Wenyuan was sentenced to 20 years' imprisonment and released 1996. The other three members died 1991–92; Jiang Qing committed suicide.

gangrene death and decay of body tissue (often of a limb) due to loss of blood supply to the area and subsequent bacterial action; the affected part gradually turns black and causes blood poisoning. Treatment is by surgical removal of the tissue or the affected part (amputation).

gangsterism organized crime, particularly in the USA as a result of the 18th Amendment (◊Prohibition) in 1919. Bootlegging activities (importing or making illegal liquor) and speakeasies (where alcohol could be illegally purchased) gave rise to rivalry that resulted in hired gangs of criminals (gangsters) and gun battles. One of the most notorious gangsters was Al ◊Capone.

gannet The Cape gannet *Morus capensis*. It forms dense breeding colonies around the coasts of S Africa, incubating its single egg with its feet. Gannets are accomplished 'plunge divers' and make a spectacular sight when fishing. *Premaphotos Wildlife*

gannet three species of N Atlantic seabirds, family Sulidae, order Pelecaniformaes. The largest is *Sula bassana*. When fully grown, it is white with a buff tinge on the head and neck; the bill is long and thick and compressed at the point; the wings are black-tipped with a span of 1.7 m/5.6 ft. It breeds on cliffs in nests made of grass and seaweed, where only one (white) egg is laid. Gannets feed on fish that swim near the surface, such as herrings and pilchards.

Gansu or ***Kansu*** province of NW China
area 530,000 sq km/204,580 sq mi
capital Lanzhou
features subject to earthquakes; the 'Silk Road' (now a motor road) passed through it in the Middle Ages, carrying trade to central Asia
industries coal, oil, hydroelectric power from the Huang He (Yellow) River
population (1990) 22,930,000, including many Muslims.

Ganymede in astronomy, the largest moon of the planet Jupiter, and the largest moon in the Solar System, 5,260 km/3,270 mi in diameter (larger than the planet Mercury). It orbits Jupiter every 7.2 days at a distance of 1.1 million km/700,000 mi. Its surface is a mixture of cratered and grooved terrain. Molecular oxygen was identified on Ganymede's surface 1994. The space probe *Galileo* detected a magnetic field around Ganymede 1996; this suggests it may have a molten core.

Ganymede in Greek mythology, a youth so beautiful he was chosen as cupbearer to Zeus.

Garbo Greta. Stage name of Greta Lovisa Gustafsson 1905–1990. Swedish-born US film actress. She went to the USA 1925, and her captivating beauty and leading role in *Flesh and the Devil* 1927 made her one of Hollywood's greatest stars. Her later films include *Mata Hari* 1931, *Grand Hotel* 1932, *Queen Christina* 1933, *Anna Karenina* 1935, *Camille* 1936, and *Ninotchka* 1939. Her ethereal qualities and romantic mystery on the screen intermingled with her seclusion in private life. She retired 1941.

Garbus Martin 1930– . US lawyer specializing in civil-liberty cases. His clients have included Soviet dissident Andrei Sacharov, Nelson Mandela, and Vaclav Havel, for whom he drafted the section on civil liberties in the Czech constitution. He has also represented the comedian Lenny Bruce, the advocate of psychedelics Timothy Leary, Viking Penguin in the Salman Rushdie case, and black people in Mississippi wanting to exercise their right to vote. His books include *Ready for the Defence* 1987 and *Traitors and Heroes*.

García Lorca Federico. Spanish poet. See ◊Lorca, Federico García.

García Márquez Gabriel (Gabo) 1928– . Colombian novelist. His sweeping novel *Cien años de soledad/One Hundred Years of Solitude* 1967 (which tells the story of a family over a period of six generations) is an example of magic realism, a technique used to heighten the intensity of realistic portrayal of social and political issues by introducing grotesque or fanciful material. His other books include *El amor en los tiempos del cólera/Love in the Time of Cholera* 1985 and *The General in His Labyrinth* 1991, which describes the last four months of Simón Bolívar's life. Nobel Prize for Literature 1982.

García Perez Alan 1949– . Peruvian politician, leader of the moderate, left-wing America Popular Revolutionary Alliance (APRA) party; president 1985–90. He inherited an ailing economy and was forced to trim his socialist programme, losing to political novice Alberto Fujimori in the 1990 presidential elections.

Garda, Lake largest lake in Italy; situated on the border between the regions of Lombardia and Veneto; area 370 sq km/143 sq mi.

garden plot of land, usually belonging to a householder. It can be cultivated to produce food or to create pleasant surroundings. Pleasure gardens were common in all ancient civilizations. In medieval Europe gardens were devoted to growing medicinal plants and herbs but in the 16th century formal recreational gardens became a feature of larger town and country houses. The taste for formality continued into the 19th century, when a more natural look became fashionable. Most 18th-century rural workers had vegetable gardens and the practice was continued wherever possible in the new industrial towns. The miniature landscaped garden with lawns and flowerbeds became a feature of 20th-century housing estates in Europe and the USA.

Garbo Swedish film actress Greta Garbo in *Queen Christina* 1933. Garbo went to Hollywood in the mid-1920s and created a legend as the mysterious and often tragic heroine in historical dramas such as *Queen Christina* and *Anna Karenina* 1935, though she also appeared in comedies such as *Ninotchka* 1939. *British Film Institute*

'I never said, "I want to be alone." I only said, "I want to be left alone." There is all the difference.'

Greta Garbo

garden city in the UK, a town built in a rural area and designed to combine town and country advantages, with its own industries, controlled developments, private and public gardens, and cultural centre. The idea was proposed by Ebenezer ◊Howard, who in 1899 founded the Garden City Association, which established the first garden city: Letchworth in Hertfordshire. A second, Welwyn, 35 km/22 mi from London, was started 1919. The New Towns Act 1946 provided the machinery for developing ◊new towns on some of the principles advocated by Howard (for example Stevenage, begun 1947).

Garfield James A(bram) 1831–1881. 20th president of the USA 1881, a Republican. A compromise candidate for the presidency, he held office for only four months before being assassinated in a Washington DC railway station by a disappointed office-seeker. His short tenure was marked primarily by struggles within the Republican party over influence and cabinet posts.

'One single minute of reconciliation is worth more than an entire lifetime of friendship.'

Gabriel García Márquez
One Hundred Years of Solitude

gargoyle spout projecting from the roof gutter of a building with the purpose of directing water away from the wall. The term is usually applied to the ornamental forms found in Gothic architecture; these were carved in stone in the form of fantastic animals, angels, or human heads. Gargoyles are often found on churches and cathedrals.

Garibaldi Giuseppe 1807–1882. Italian soldier who played a central role in the unification of Italy

cont. on p. 434

Garibaldi Italian hero of the Risorgimento, Giuseppe Garibaldi. His enthusiastic leadership and colourful exploits fired the hearts of Italians. He never wavered from his single purpose, the unification of Italy under Italian rule, and he perhaps did more than any other person to bring it about. *Image Select UK Ltd*

Gandhi and Indian Independence

Jawaharlal Nehru (left) and Mahatma Gandhi during a break on the opening day of the All-India Congress Committee in Bombay on 6 July 1936, when Nehru had just taken office as its leader. *Popper*

The history of India's struggle to free itself from British rule is dominated by the figure of Mohandas Karamchand Gandhi, known popularly as Mahatma ('great soul'). A philosopher and social campaigner as well as a charismatic politician, Gandhi led the Indian nationalist movement from 1915. Through skilful use of symbolic imagery from India's past and Hindu culture, he succeeded in widening the appeal of what had previously been an upper-class, city-based campaign to create a popular mass movement that drew support from India's huge rural population. He was assassinated in 1948, less than six months after India had achieved independence from Britain as a partitioned state.

The Indian nationalist movement before Gandhi

Some historians have seen the Indian Great Rebellion or Mutiny of 1857 as the first stirring of nationalist sentiment in India. However, this localized armed uprising, which was triggered by a mutiny of Indian troops, was not so much an independence movement as a final attempt to regain power by the traditional landed ruling elite of northern India, whose influence had decreased greatly since British rule was established in the late 18th and early 19th centuries.

It was not until the 1870s – with the spread of English education, an upsurge in newspaper and book publication, and improvements in communications (notably the railway and telegraph) – that a modern Indian nationalist movement could develop. In 1885, in Bombay, the Indian National Congress was formed, to hold annual debates and campaign for more rapid Indianization of the civil service. Its nominal leader was a liberal British former civil servant, A O Hume; he was supported by younger Western-educated Indian professionals.

During this period Congress was predominantly a moderate body, dominated by politicians from the Western-influenced ports of Bombay, Calcutta, and Madras. Its leaders, such as the liberal Gopal Krishna Gokhale, believed the British government would listen to their reasoned arguments and would gradually give greater roles in local and regional government to Indians. It avoided religious issues, although in 1906 a new party, the All India Muslim League, was founded to promote the interests of the country's Muslim minority.

The era of Gandhi's dominance: 1920–33

Nationalist politics in India were radicalized by the experience of World War I, when Indian troops fought for the Imperial cause in Europe and the Middle East. Economic sacrifices imposed by the war led to trade-union unrest. As a partial reward, the British government passed the 1919 Government of India Act, which gave Indians more political power in provincial government; and the secretary of state, Edwin Montagu, announced that the goal of British rule was 'responsible' Indian self-government within the Empire. However, these concessions failed to satisfy Congress and the Muslim League, who from 1916 were jointly committed to achieving home rule.

Opposition to British rule was fuelled in April 1919 by the massacre of at least 379 Indian protesters in Amritsar, Punjab, northern India, under the orders of Brigadier-General Reginald Edward Dyer. A campaign of civil disobedience, known as satyagraha ('grasping the truth'), involving non-cooperation with the British Raj, was launched under the leadership of Mahatma Gandhi. He had used the technique of passive resistance in campaigns in defence of the rights of Indians in South Africa before 1915, and now called on educated Indians in crucial positions to withdraw their labour and to refuse to buy foreign cloth and alcohol. The aim was for the Raj to grind to a halt, forcing the British to concede self-rule quickly.

Unfortunately, the campaign moved beyond Gandhi's control and became violent in 1922, culminating in the slaughter of 22 policemen in a north Indian village. Gandhi was arrested and imprisoned for two years. On his release, he avoided active politics, concentrating instead on the promotion of hand production of textiles as a means of strengthening traditional Indian village life. His return to the political stage was prompted by Congress's demand for immediate independence at its annual meeting in Lahore 1929. In support of this, in March 1930 Gandhi

Mahatma Gandhi with some of his followers on the Salt March in 1930. Gandhi was a pioneer of non-violent protest, encouraging the Indian people to refuse to cooperate with the British government. The Salt March was a protest against the government's tax on salt and the ban forbidding Indians to produce their own. *Corbis*

led a second mass movement, with the 385-km/240-mi Salt March across western India to collect salt from the sea at Dandi; this was in defiance of the British government, which not only imposed a tax on salt but also made it illegal for people to produce it themselves. The salt protest was followed by a three-year campaign of civil disobedience which, like that of 1920–22, became increasingly radicalized, culminating in peasant tax protests at a time of economic depression.

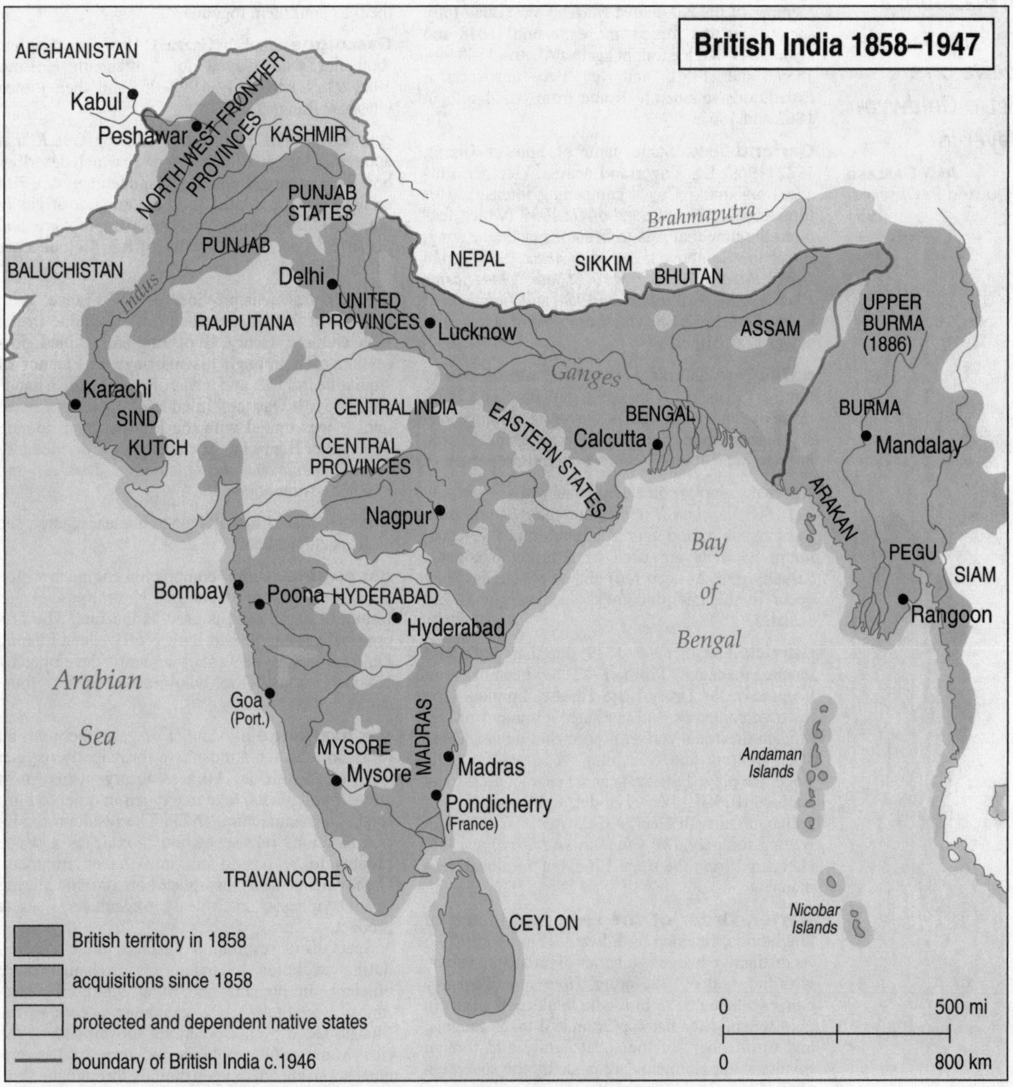

Towards partition: 1933–47

In 1933 Gandhi switched his attention to social reform, and campaigned – engaging in two major fasts – against the Hindu caste system and its discrimination against the 'untouchables', at the bottom rung of Indian society. From the 1930s political leadership of the nationalist movement moved increasingly into the hands of the professional politicians: Jawaharlal Nehru, the Cambridge University-educated, moderate socialist leader of the Indian National Congress from 1936, and the London-trained barrister Muhammad Ali Jinnah, leader of the Muslim League from 1934. In 1935, under a new Government of India Act, elected Indian politicians were given substantial control over the provincial governments. These soon became dominated by Congress, led by Nehru. He believed in strong central government, economic planning, and, unlike Gandhi, investment in industrial development. He was also a secularist who, like Gandhi, favoured achieving independence as a united state.

In 1942, as Japan invaded southeast Asia and British forces were tied up defending Myanmar (Burma), Congress launched a wave of strikes. Gandhi called this the 'Quit India' movement; it was designed to make the country ungovernable and force a British pull-out. The British responded by imprisoning the leaders of Congress and using troops to restore order: during 1943 there were more than 90,000 arrests and 1,000 deaths. After World War II, with a Labour government in power in Britain and following a naval mutiny in India (1946), it was finally decided to concede full independence to India, and Louis Mountbatten was sent out as Governor-General (Viceroy) to negotiate a swift departure.

Amid mounting Hindu and Muslim communal tensions across northern India, the Muslim League, led by the terminally ill Jinnah, remained unyielding in its demand (adopted in the Lahore Resolution of 1940) for the creation of a separate Muslim state of Pakistan. This state was to consist of the Muslim-dominated areas of East Bengal (now Bangladesh) and the Indus valley region of the northwest. Nehru, unwilling to press for the alternative of a loose federation of autonomous provinces, reluctantly conceded to this demand, and independence and partition occurred on 15 Aug 1947.

British India 1858–1947

British territory in 1858
acquisitions since 1858
protected and dependent native states
boundary of British India c.1946

Muslims waiting for protected transport from India to the newly created state of Pakistan. India was partitioned into separate Hindu and Muslim states in Aug 1947, and by the time this photograph was taken, a month later, thousands of people were on the move from one country to the other. Half a million people died in the violence that accompanied the upheaval. *Popper*

Independence and its aftermath

Partition was accompanied by bloody communal riots, in which more than half a million people died. Almost 7 million Muslim, Hindu, and Sikh refugees left their homes, migrating in opposing directions across the new borders. It led subsequently to border disputes and wars, the most serious in 1971, when East Pakistan seceded from West Pakistan to become Bangladesh. Gandhi did his utmost to encourage calm and tolerance, notably in the divided city of Calcutta, but to little avail. In Jan 1948 he was assassinated by a Hindu fanatic.

Although Gandhi's vision for India was only partly realized, his inspiring example as a pacifist, environmentalist, and campaigner for the oppressed has been widely influential. His campaign for the uplift of the untouchables has resulted in their being redesignated Harijans, 'children of god'; they now have affirmative-action education and reserved quotas in public-service employment to improve their prospects. The Green movement has been clearly influenced by his ideas on sustainable development; and his methods of non-violent protest and hunger strikes have been adopted by pro-democracy activists in China, and by Aung San Suu Kyi in Myanmar.

Ian Derbyshire

SEE ALSO
Amritsar Massacre; caste; Congress Party; Gandhi, Mahatma; India, history; Jinnah, Muhammad Ali; Muslim League; Nehru, Jawaharlal; Pakistan

'I was born at the age of twelve on a Metro-Goldwyn-Mayer lot.'

JUDY GARLAND
Quoted in *Observer* 1951

by conquering Sicily and Naples 1860. From 1834 a member of the nationalist Mazzini's ◊Young Italy society, he was forced into exile until 1848 and again 1849–54. He fought against Austria 1848–49, 1859, and 1866, and led two unsuccessful expeditions to liberate Rome from papal rule in 1862 and 1867.

Garland Judy. Stage name of Frances Gumm 1922–1969. US singer and actress. Her performances are marked by a compelling intensity. Her films include *The Wizard of Oz* 1939 (which featured the tune that was to become her theme song, 'Over the Rainbow'), *Babes in Arms* 1939, *Strike Up the Band* 1940, *Meet Me in St Louis* 1944, *Easter Parade* 1948, *A Star is Born* 1954, and *Judgment at Nuremberg* 1961. She was the mother of actress and singer Liza Minnelli.

garlic perennial plant *Allium sativum* of the lily family Liliaceae, with white flowers. The bulb, made of small segments, or cloves, is used in cookery. Garlic has been used effectively as a fungicide in ◊sorghum. It also has antibacterial properties.

garnet group of silicate minerals with the formula $X_3Y_2(SiO_4)_3$, when X is calcium, magnesium, iron, or manganese, and Y is iron, aluminium, or chromium. Garnets are used as semiprecious gems (usually pink to deep red) and as abrasives. They occur in metamorphic rocks such as gneiss and schist.

Garrick David 1717–1779. English actor and theatre manager. From 1747 he became joint licensee of the Drury Lane Theatre, London, with his own company, and instituted a number of significant theatrical conventions including concealed stage lighting and banishing spectators from the stage. He played Shakespearean characters such as Richard III, King Lear, Hamlet, and Benedick, and collaborated with George Colman (1732–1794) in writing the play *The Clandestine Marriage* 1766. He retired from the stage 1766, but continued as a manager.

Garter, Order of the senior British order of knighthood, founded by Edward III in about 1347. Its distinctive badge is a garter of dark blue velvet, with the motto of the order, *Honi soit qui mal y pense* ('Shame be to him who thinks evil of it') in gold letters. Membership is limited to 25 knights, and to members of the royal family and foreign royalties; appointments are made by the sovereign alone. St George's Chapel, Windsor, is the chapel of the order.

Garvey Marcus Moziah 1887–1940. Jamaican political thinker and activist, an early advocate of black nationalism. He led a Back to Africa movement for black Americans to establish a black-governed country in Africa. The Jamaican cult of ◊Rastafarianism is based largely on his ideas.

Garvey founded the UNIA (Universal Negro Improvement Association) in 1914 and established branches in New York and other US cities. Aiming to achieve human rights and dignity for black people through black pride and economic self-sufficiency, he was considered one of the first militant black nationalists.

gas in physics, a form of matter, such as air, in which the molecules move randomly in otherwise empty space, filling any size or shape of container into which the gas is put. A sugar-lump sized cube of air at room temperature contains 30 trillion molecules moving at an average speed of 500 metres per second (1,800 kph/1,200 mph). Gases can be liquefied by cooling, which lowers the speed of the molecules and enables attractive forces between them to bind them together.

garlic Garlic is a perennial bulb of the onion family. It grows about 30 cm/12 in high, and has pale spherical flowers. It has been used since ancient Egyptian times as a herb. In the Middle Ages, it was thought to keep away vampires, no doubt because of the unpleasant smell imparted to the breath of regular users.

Gascoigne Paul, ('Gazza') 1967– . English footballer who played for Tottenham Hotspur 1988–91, Lazio, Italy 1992–95, and then joined Glasgow Rangers.

gas constant in physics, the constant R that appears in the equation $PV = nRT$, which describes how the pressure P, volume V, and temperature T of an ideal gas are related (n is the amount of gas in moles). This equation combines ◊Boyle's law and ◊Charles's law. R has a value of 8.3145 joules per kelvin per mole.

Gascony ancient province of SW France. With Guienne it formed the duchy of Aquitaine in the 12th century; Henry II of England gained possession of it through his marriage to Eleanor of Aquitaine in 1152, and it was often in English hands until 1451. It was then ruled by the king of France until it was united with the French royal domain 1607 under Henry IV. The area is now divided into several *départements*, including Landes and Pyrénées-Atlantiques.

gas-cooled reactor type of nuclear reactor; see ◊advanced gas-cooled reactor.

gas engine internal-combustion engine in which a gas (coal gas, producer gas, natural gas, or gas from a blast furnace) is used as the fuel. The first practical gas engine was built 1860 by Jean Etienne Lenoir, and the type was subsequently developed by Nikolaus August Otto, who introduced the ◊four-stroke cycle.

gas exchange movement of gases between an organism and the atmosphere, principally oxygen and carbon dioxide. All aerobic organisms (most animals and plants) take in oxygen in order to burn food and manufacture ◊ATP. The resultant oxidation reactions release carbon dioxide as a waste product to be passed out into the environment. Green plants also absorb carbon dioxide during ◊photosynthesis, and release oxygen as a waste product.

Specialized respiratory surfaces have evolved during evolution to make gas exchange more efficient. In humans and other tetrapods (four-limbed vertebrates), gas exchange occurs in the ◊lungs, aided by the breathing movements of the ribs. Many adult amphibia and terrestrial invertebrates can absorb oxygen directly through the skin. The bodies of insects and some spiders contain a system of air-filled tubes known as ◊tracheae. Fish have ◊gills as their main respiratory surface. In plants, gas exchange generally takes place via the ◊stomata and the air-filled spaces between the cells in the interior of the leaf.

Gaskell Elizabeth (Cleghorn, born Stevenson) 1810–1865. English novelist. Her most popular book, *Cranford* 1853, is the study of a small, close-knit circle in a small town, modelled on Knutsford, Cheshire, where she was brought up. Her other books, which often deal with social concerns, include *Mary Barton* 1848, *North and South* 1855, *Sylvia's Lovers* 1863–64, and the unfinished *Wives and Daughters* 1866. She wrote a frank and sympathetic biography of her friend Charlotte ◊Brontë 1857.

gas laws physical laws concerning the behaviour of gases. They include ◊Boyle's law and ◊Charles's law, which are concerned with the relationships between the pressure, temperature, and volume of an ideal (hypothetical) gas. These two laws can be combined to give the general or universal gas law, which may be expressed as:

$$(\text{pressure} \times \text{volume})/\text{temperature} = \text{constant}$$

Van der Waals' law includes corrections for the nonideal behaviour of real gases.

gasohol motor fuel that is 90% petrol and 10% ethanol (alcohol). The ethanol is usually obtained by fermentation, followed by distillation, using maize, wheat, potatoes, or sugar cane. It was used in early cars before petrol became economical, and its use was revived during the 1940s war shortage and the energy shortage of the 1970s, for example in Brazil.

gastroenteritis inflammation of the stomach and intestines, giving rise to abdominal pain, vomiting, and diarrhoea. It may be caused by food or other poisoning, allergy, or infection. Dehydration may be severe and it is a particular risk in infants.

Gaskell English novelist Elizabeth Gaskell. The wife of a Unitarian minister, Gaskell lived in Manchester. Set in the slums of the industrial towns of the region, her novels were among the first to portray the moral and social evils of industrialization. *Corbis*

gastroenterology medical speciality concerned with disorders of the digestive tract and associated organs such as the liver, gall bladder and pancreas.

gastrolith stone that was once part of the digestive system of a dinosaur or other extinct animal. Rock fragments were swallowed to assist in the grinding process in the dinosaur digestive tract. Once the animal has decayed, smooth round stones remain – often the only clue to their past use is the fact that they are geologically different from their surrounding strata.

gastropod any member of a very large class (Gastropoda) of ◊molluscs. Gastropods are single-shelled (in a spiral or modified spiral form), have eyes on stalks, and move on a flattened, muscular foot. They have well-developed heads and rough, scraping tongues called radulae. Some are marine, some freshwater, and others land creatures, but all tend to inhabit damp places. Gastropods include snails, slugs, limpets, and periwinkles.

gas turbine engine in which burning fuel supplies hot gas to spin a ◊turbine. The most widespread application of gas turbines has been in aviation. All jet engines (see under ◊jet propulsion) are modified gas turbines, and some locomotives and ships also use gas turbines as a power source. They are also used in industry for generating and pumping purposes.

gas warfare military use of gas to produce a toxic effect on the human body. See ◊chemical warfare.

Gates Bill (William) Henry, III 1955– . US businessman and computer scientist. He co-founded ◊Microsoft Corporation 1975 and was responsible for supplying MS-DOS, the operating system that ◊IBM chose to use in the IBM PC. In 1997 Gates controlled a $39.8 billion shareholding in Microsoft, making him the world's richest individual. When the IBM deal was struck, Microsoft did not actually have an operating system, but Gates bought one from another company, renamed it MS-DOS, and modified it to suit IBM's new computer. Microsoft also retained the right to sell MS-DOS to other computer manufacturers, and because the IBM PC was not only successful but easily copied by other manufacturers, MS-DOS found its way onto the vast majority of PCs. The revenue from MS-DOS allowed Microsoft to expand into other areas of software.

Gateshead port in Tyne and Wear, NE England; population (1994 est) 202,400. It is situated on the south bank of the river Tyne, opposite Newcastle upon Tyne. Formerly a port for the Tyne coalfields and a railway workshop centre, present-day industries include engineering, chemicals, glass, paint, plastics, clothing, printing, and rubber. Metroland, in the Metro Centre Shopping Complex, is the top tourist attraction in the NE.

Gatling Richard Jordan 1818–1903. US inventor of a rapid-fire gun. Patented in 1862, the Gatling gun had ten barrels arranged as a cylinder rotated by a hand crank. Cartridges from an overhead hopper or drum dropped into the breech mechanism, which loaded, fired, and extracted them at a rate of 320 rounds per minute. The Gatling gun was superseded by the ◊machine gun invented by Hiram Maxim (1840–1916) in 1889.

GATT acronym for ◊***General Agreement on Tariffs and Trade***.

Gatwick site of Gatwick Airport, West Sussex, England, constructed 1956–58. One of London's three international airports, it is situated 42 km/26 mi south from London's city centre.

Gaudí Antonio 1852–1926. Spanish architect. He is distinguished for his flamboyant ◊Art Nouveau style. Gaudí worked mainly in Barcelona, designing both domestic and industrial buildings. He introduced colour, unusual materials, and audacious technical innovations. His spectacular Church of the Holy Family, Barcelona, begun 1883, is still under construction.

His design for Casa Milá, a blocks of flats in Barcelona (begun 1905), is wildly imaginative, with an undulating façade, vertically thrusting wrought-iron balconies, and a series of sculpted shapes that protrude from the roof. The central feature of his Parque Güell in Barcelona is a snakelike seat faced with a mosaic of broken tiles and cutlery.

Gaudier-Brzeska Henri, (born Henri Gaudier) 1891–1915. French sculptor, active in London from 1911. He is regarded as one of the outstanding sculptors of his generation. He became a member of the English Vorticist movement, which sought to reflect the energy of the industrial age through an angular, semi-abstract style. His works include the portrait *Horace Brodsky* 1913 (Tate Gallery, London) and *Birds Erect* 1914 (Museum of Modern Art, New York).

gauge any scientific measuring instrument – for example, a wire gauge or a pressure gauge. The term is also applied to the width of a railway or tramway track.

gauge boson or ***field particle*** any of the particles that carry the four fundamental forces of nature (see ◊forces, fundamental). Gauge bosons are ◊elementary particles that cannot be subdivided, and include the photon, the graviton, the gluons, and the weakons.

Gauguin (Eugène Henri) Paul 1848–1903. French Post-Impressionist painter. Going beyond the Impressionists' concern with ever-changing appearances, he developed a heavily symbolic and decorative style characterized by his sensuous use of pure colours. In his search for a more direct and intense experience of life, he moved to islands in the South Pacific, where he created many of his finest works.

Born in Paris, Gauguin spent his childhood in Peru. He took up full-time painting 1883 and became a regular contributor to the Impressionists' last four group exhibitions 1880–86. In the period 1886–91 he spent much of his time in the village of Pont Aven in Brittany, where he concentrated on his new style, Synthetism, based on the use of powerful, expressive colours and boldly outlined areas of flat tone. Influenced by Symbolism, he chose subjects reflecting his interest in the beliefs of other cultures. He made brief visits to Martinique and Panama 1887–88, and 1888 spent two troubled months with Vincent van Gogh in Arles, Provence. He lived in Tahiti 1891–93 and 1895–1901, and from 1901 in the Marquesas Islands, where he died. It was in Tahiti that he painted one of his best-known works, *Where Do We Come From? What Are We? Where Are We Going?* 1897 (Museum of Fine Art, Boston).

Gaul the Celtic-speaking peoples who inhabited France and Belgium in Roman times; also their territory. Certain Gauls invaded Italy around 400 BC, sacked Rome 387 BC, and settled between the Alps and the Apennines; this district, known as Cisalpine Gaul, was conquered by Rome in about 225 BC.

The Romans annexed S Gaul, from the Alps to the Rhone valley in about 120 BC. This became Gallia Narbonensis. The remaining area, from the Atlantic to the Rhine, was invaded and subjugated by Julius ◊Caesar in the ◊Gallic Wars of 58–51 BC. This was later organized into the three imperial provinces: Aquitania in the W, Belgica in the N, and Lugdunensis in the centre and NW of what is now France.

Gaulle Charles de. French politician, see Charles ◊de Gaulle.

gaullism political philosophy deriving from the views of Charles ◊de Gaulle but not necessarily confined to Gaullist parties, or even to France. Its basic tenets are the creation and preservation of a strongly centralized state and an unwillingness to enter into international obligations at the expense of national interests. The Rally for the Republic is an influential neo-Gaullist party in contemporary France.

Gaultier Jean-Paul 1952– . French fashion designer. He launched his first collection 1978, designing clothes that went against fashion trends, inspired by London's street style. His clothes are among the most influential in the French ready-to-wear market, and he has also become a popular media figure.

gauss c.g.s. unit (symbol Gs) of magnetic induction or magnetic flux density, replaced by the SI unit, the ◊tesla, but still commonly used. It is equal to one line of magnetic flux per square centimetre. The Earth's magnetic field is about 0.5 Gs, and changes to it over time are measured in gammas (one gamma equals 10^{-5} gauss).

Gauss Carl Friedrich 1777–1855. German mathematician who worked on the theory of numbers, non-Euclidean geometry, and the mathematical development of electric and magnetic theory. A method of neutralizing a magnetic field, used to protect ships from magnetic mines, is called 'degaussing'. In statistics, the normal distribution curve, which he studied, is sometimes known as the Gaussian distribution. Between 1800 and 1810 Gauss concentrated on astronomy. He developed a quick method for calculating an asteroid's orbit from only three observations and published this work – a classic in astronomy – 1809.

Gautama family name of the historical ◊Buddha.

Gauteng (Sotho for 'Place of Gold') province of the Republic of South Africa from 1994, known as Pretoria-Witwatersrand-Vereeniging before 1995
area 18,760 sq km/7,243 sq mi
capital Johannesburg
towns and cities Pretoria, Vereeniging, Krugersdorp, Benoni, Germiston
features Vaal River
industries gold mining, coal, iron and steel, uranium, chemicals, railway workshops, tobacco, maize
population (1995 est) 7,048,300
languages Afrikaans 20%, Zulu 18%, English 15%.

Gautier Théophile 1811–1872. French Romantic poet. His later works emphasized the perfection of form and the polished beauty of language and imagery (for example, *Emaux et camées/Enamels and Cameos* 1852). He was also a novelist (*Mademoiselle de Maupin* 1835) and later turned to journalism. His belief in the supreme importance of form in art, at the cost both of sentiment and ideas, inspired the poets who were later known as *Les ◊Parnassiens*.

Gavaskar Sunil Manohar 1949– . Indian cricketer. Between 1971 and 1987 he scored a record 10,122 test runs in a record 125 matches (including 106 consecutive tests) until overtaken by Allan Border in 1993.

gavial large reptile *Gavialis gangeticus* related to the crocodile. It grows to about 7 m/23 ft long, and has a very long snout with about 100 teeth in its jaws. Gavials live in rivers in N India, where they feed on fish and frogs. They have been extensively hunted for their skins, and are now extremely rare.

Gaviria (Trujillo) Cesar 1947– . Colombian Liberal Party politician, president 1990–94. He was finance minister 1986–87 and minister of government 1987–89. He supported the extradition of drug traffickers wanted in the USA and sought more US aid in return for stepping up the drug war.

Gauguin Self-portrait of Paul Gauguin, painted 1893–94. Gauguin's distinctive Post-Impressionistic style developed from a desire to revitalize his painting, inspired by the people and colours of Tahiti where he lived 1891–93 and 1895–1901. *Topham*

Gawain in Arthurian legend, one of the knights of the Round Table who participated in the quest for the ◊Holy Grail. He is the hero of the 14th-century epic poem *Sir Gawayne and the Greene Knight*.

Gay John 1685–1732. English poet and dramatist. He wrote *Trivia* 1716, a verse picture of 18th-century London. His *The Beggar's Opera* 1728, a 'Newgate pastoral' using traditional songs and telling of the love of Polly for highwayman Captain Macheath, was an extraordinarily popular success. Its satiric political touches led to the banning of *Polly*, a sequel.

Gaye Marvin 1939–1984. US pop singer and songwriter. His hits, including 'Stubborn Kinda Fellow' 1962, 'I Heard It Through the Grapevine' 1968, and 'What's Goin' On' 1971, exemplified the Detroit ◊Motown sound.

Gay-Lussac Joseph Louis 1778–1850. French physicist and chemist who investigated the physical properties of gases, and discovered new methods of producing sulphuric and oxalic acids. In 1802 he discovered the approximate rule for the expansion of gases now known as ◊Charles's law; see also ◊gas laws.

gay politics political activity by homosexuals in pursuit of equal rights and an end to discrimination. A gay political movement first emerged in the late 1960s in New York with the founding of the Gay

> *Art is either plagiarism or revolution.*
>
> PAUL GAUGUIN
> Quoted in Huneker *Pathos of Distance*

Gauss German mathematician, astronomer, and physicist Karl Gauss was born in 1777 in Brunswick to poor parents. His prodigious talent for mathematics was noticed at the age of 14 by the Duke of Brunswick, who subsequently financed the remainder of his academic schooling. Gauss went on to make discoveries in virtually every field of physics and mathematics, many of which were not discovered until after his death. *Image Select (UK) Ltd*

gazelle The Thomson's gazelle from the open plains of Sudan, Kenya, and N Tanzania has a distinctive dark stripe along its sides. There are 15 races of Thomson's gazelle, varying only slightly in colour and horn size.

Liberation Front. It aimed to counter negative and critical attitudes to homosexuality and encouraged pride and solidarity among homosexuals.

The appearance of the AIDS virus in the early 1980s produced a new wave of hostility towards homosexuals but also put them in the forefront of formulating an effective response to the epidemic and raising the public's awareness of its dangers.

Gaza Strip strip of land on the Mediterranean sea, occupied by Israel 1967–94 when responsibility for its administration was transferred to the ◊Palestine Liberation Organization; capital Gaza; area 363 sq km/140 sq mi; population (1994) 724,500, mainly Palestinians, plus about 2,500 Israeli settlers. Agriculture is the main activity, producing citrus fruits, wheat, and olives.

Part of the British mandate of Palestine until 1948, it was then occupied by Egypt. It was invaded by Israel 1956, reoccupied 1967, and retained 1973. Clashes between the Israeli authorities and the Arab Palestinian inhabitants escalated to ◊Intifada (uprising) 1988. In 1992 the UN Security Council issued a statement condemning Israel for allowing 'the continued deterioration of the situation in the Gaza Strip', after clashes between Israeli troops and Palestinian demonstrators left five Palestinians dead and more than 60 wounded. Under the terms of a historic Israeli-PLO accord, signed 1993, the area was transferred to Palestinian control 1994, although Israel remained responsible for its foreign policy and defence until a final overall agreement for all the formerly occupied territories was implemented. Israel closed the border from Jan 1995, causing economic crisis.

'I don't think that the possible death of 120 million people is a matter for charity. It is a matter of moral imperative.'

Bob Geldof
To Margaret Thatcher on the threatened famine in Africa 1985

gazelle any of a number of species of lightly built, fast-running antelopes found on the open plains of Africa and S Asia, especially those of the genus *Gazella*.

GCC abbreviation for ◊***Gulf Cooperation Council***

GCE abbreviation for ***General Certificate of Education***, in the UK, the public examination formerly taken at the age of 16 at Ordinary level (O level) and still taken at 18 at Advanced level (A level). The GCE O-level examination was superseded 1988 by the General Certificate of Secondary Education (◊GCSE).

GCHQ (abbreviation for ***Government Communications Headquarters***) the centre of the British government's electronic surveillance operations, in Cheltenham, Gloucestershire. It monitors broadcasts of various kinds from all over the world. It was established in World War I, and was successful in breaking the German Enigma code in 1940.

In addition there are six listening stations: at Bude, Cornwall; Culm Head, Somerset; Brora and Hawklaw, Scotland; Irton Moor, N Yorkshire; and Cheadle, Greater Manchester. There is an outpost in Cyprus.

gecko The tokay gecko is one of the largest and most common geckos – 28 cm/11 in long. It is found in Asia and Indonesia and is thought to bring good luck to the houses in which it lives. It feeds on insects such as cockroaches, and on small lizards, mice, and even small birds.

GCSE (***General Certificate of Secondary Education***) in the UK, from 1988, examination for 16-year-old pupils, superseding both GCE O-level and CSE, and offering qualifications for up to 60% of school leavers in any particular subject.

Gdańsk (German ***Danzig***) Polish port; population (1993) 466,500. Oil is refined, and textiles, televisions, and fertilizers are produced. The annexation of the city by Germany marked the beginning of World War II. It reverted to Poland 1945. In the 1980s there were repeated antigovernment strikes at the Lenin shipyards, the birthplace of Solidarity, the Polish resistance movement to pro-Soviet communism; many were closed 1996.

GDP abbreviation for ◊***gross domestic product***.

gear toothed wheel that transmits the turning movement of one shaft to another shaft. Gear wheels may be used in pairs, or in threes if both shafts are to turn in the same direction. The gear ratio – the ratio of the number of teeth on the two wheels – determines the torque ratio, the turning force on the output shaft compared with the turning force on the input shaft. The ratio of the angular velocities of the shafts is the inverse of the gear ratio.

Geber Latinized form of Jabir ibn Hayyan c. 721–c. 776. Arabian alchemist. His influence lasted for more than 600 years, and in the late 1300s his name was adopted by a Spanish alchemist whose writings spread the knowledge and practice of alchemy throughout Europe.

Gebrselassie Haile 1973– . Ethiopian long-distance runner who won the men's 10,000 metres gold medal at the 1996 Olympics and has also won three consecutive 10,000 metres world titles, 1993–97. In 1998 he regained the 5,000 and 10,000 metres world records he had previously won but had lost to Kenyans Daniel Komen and Paul Tergat.

gecko any of a group of lizards (family Gekkonidae). Geckos are common worldwide in warm climates, and have large heads and short, stout bodies. Many have no eyelids. Their sticky toe pads enable them to climb vertically and walk upside down on smooth surfaces in their search for flies, spiders, and other prey. There are about 850 known species of gecko.

Geddes Patrick 1854–1932. Scottish town planner. He established the importance of surveys, research work, and properly planned 'diagnoses before treatment'. His major work is *City Development* 1904.

Gehenna another name for ◊hell; in the Old Testament, a valley S of Jerusalem where children were sacrificed to the Phoenician god Moloch and fires burned constantly.

Gehrig Lou (Henry Louis) 1903–1941. US baseball player. Nicknamed 'the Iron Horse' for his incomparable stamina and strength, he was signed by the New York Yankees 1923. Voted the American League's most valuable player 1927, 1931, 1934, and 1936, he achieved a remarkable lifetime 493 home runs, a .340 lifetime batting average, and a record 2,130 consecutive games played. He was elected to the Baseball Hall of Fame 1939.

Gehry Frank Owen 1929– . US architect, based in Los Angeles. His architecture approaches abstract art in its use of collage and montage techniques. His own experimental house in Santa Monica 1977, Edgemar Shopping Center and Museum, Santa Monica, 1988, and the Vitra Furniture Museum, Weil am Rhein, Switzerland, 1989 – his first building in Europe – demonstrate his vitality.

Geiger Hans (Wilhelm) 1882–1945. German physicist who produced the ◊Geiger counter. He spent the period 1906–12 in Manchester, England, working with Ernest ◊Rutherford on ◊radioactivity. In 1908 they designed an instrument to detect and count alpha particles, positively charged ionizing particles produced by radioactive decay. In 1928 Geiger and Walther Müller produced a more sensitive version of the counter, which could detect all kinds of ionizing radiation.

Geiger counter any of a number of devices used for detecting nuclear radiation and/or measuring its intensity by counting the number of ionizing particles produced (see ◊radioactivity). It detects the momentary current that passes between ◊electrodes in a suitable gas when a nuclear particle or a radiation pulse causes the ionization of that gas. The electrodes are connected to electronic devices that enable the number of particles passing to be measured. The increased frequency of measured particles indicates the intensity of radiation.

Geingob Hage Gottfried 1941– . Namibian politician, prime minister from 1990. He played a major role in the South West Africa's People's Organization (SWAPO), acting as a petitioner to the United Nations (UN) 1964–71, to obtain international recognition for SWAPO. Geingob was appointed founding director of the UN Institute for Namibia in Lusaka, 1975. He became the first prime minister of an independent Namibia.

geisha female entertainer (music, singing, dancing, and conversation) in Japanese teahouses and at private parties. Geishas survive mainly as a tourist attraction. They are apprenticed from childhood and highly skilled in traditional Japanese arts and graces.

gel solid produced by the formation of a three-dimensional cage structure, commonly of linked large-molecular-mass polymers, in which a liquid is trapped. It is a form of ◊colloid. A gel may be a jellylike mass (pectin, gelatin) or have a more rigid structure (silica gel).

Gelderland (English ***Guelders***) province of the E Netherlands
area 5,020 sq km/1,938 sq mi
capital Arnhem
towns and cities Apeldoorn, Nijmegen, Ede
industries livestock, textiles, electrical goods
population (1995 est) 1,864,700
history in the Middle Ages Gelderland was divided into Upper Gelderland (Roermond in N Limburg) and Lower Gelderland (Nijmegen, Arnhem, Zutphen). These territories were inherited by Charles V of Spain, but when the revolt against Spanish rule reached a climax 1579, Lower Gelderland joined the United Provinces of the Netherlands.

Geldof Bob 1954– . Irish rock singer. He was the leader of the group the Boomtown Rats 1975–86. In the mid-1980s he instigated the charity Band Aid, which raised about £60 million for famine relief, primarily for Ethiopia.

In partnership with musician Midge Ure (1953–), Geldof gathered together many pop celebrities of the day to record Geldof's song 'Do They Know It's Christmas?' 1984, donating all proceeds to charity. He followed it up with two simultaneous celebrity concerts 1985 under the name Live Aid, which were broadcast live worldwide.

geisha A woodcut of a geisha, a Japanese professional entertainer and companion, with her *shamisen* (an instrument resembling a guitar). Although the geishas acquired a reputation as prostitutes, they were highly accomplished in traditional Japanese arts and rarely offered sexual favours. *Corbis*

Geldof Irish rock musician Bob Geldof achieved success as leader of the new wave group The Boomtown Rats in the late 1970s. He has received a variety of international awards for his role in such pop charity events as Band Aid and Live Aid. *Topham*

gelignite type of ◊dynamite.

Gelon c. 540–478 BC. Tyrant of Syracuse. Gelon took power in Gela, then capital of Sicily 491, and then transferred the capital to Syracuse. He refused to help the mainland Greeks against ◊Xerxes 480 BC, but later the same year defeated the Carthaginians under Hamilcar Barca at Himera, on the north coast of Sicily, leaving Syracuse as the leading city in the western Greek world.

gem mineral valuable by virtue of its durability (hardness), rarity, and beauty, cut and polished for ornamental use, or engraved. Of 120 minerals known to have been used as gemstones, only about 25 are in common use in jewellery today; of these, the diamond, emerald, ruby, and sapphire are classified as precious, and all the others semiprecious; for example, the topaz, amethyst, opal, and aquamarine.

Among the synthetic precious stones to have been successfully produced are rubies, sapphires, emeralds, and diamonds (first produced by General Electric in the USA 1955).

Gemayel Amin 1942– . Lebanese politician, a Maronite Christian; president 1982–88. He succeeded his brother, president-elect ***Bechir Gemayel*** (1947–1982), on his assassination on 14 Sept 1982. The Lebanese parliament was unable to agree on a successor when his term expired, so separate governments were formed under rival Christian and Muslim leaders.

Gemeinschaft and ***Gesellschaft*** German terms (roughly, 'community' and 'association') coined by Ferdinand ◊Tönnies 1887 to contrast social relationships in traditional rural societies with those in modern industrial societies. He saw *Gemeinschaft* (traditional) as intimate and positive, and *Gesellschaft* (modern) as impersonal and negative.

Gemini prominent zodiacal constellation in the northern hemisphere represented as the twins Castor and Pollux. Its brightest star is ◊Pollux; ◊Castor is a system of six stars. The Sun passes through Gemini from late June to late July. Each Dec, the Geminid meteors radiate from Gemini. In astrology, the dates for Gemini are between about 21 May and 21 June (see ◊precession).

Gemini project US space programme (1965–66) in which astronauts practised rendezvous and docking of spacecraft, and working outside their spacecraft, in preparation for the ◊Apollo Moon landings. Gemini spacecraft carried two astronauts and were launched by Titan rockets.

gender in grammar, one of the categories into which nouns are divided in many languages, such as masculine, feminine, and neuter (as in Latin, German, and Russian), masculine and feminine (as in French, Italian, and Spanish), or animate and inanimate (as in some Native American languages). Grammatical gender may or may not correspond with sex: in French, *la soeur* ('the sister') is feminine, but so is *la plume* ('the pen'). In German, *das Mädchen* ('the girl') is neuter.

gene unit of inherited material, encoded by a strand of ◊DNA and transcribed by ◊RNA. In higher organisms, genes are located on the ◊chromosomes. A gene consistently affects a particular character in an individual – for example, the gene for eye colour. Also termed a Mendelian gene, after Austrian biologist Gregor ◊Mendel, it occurs at a particular point, or locus, on a particular chromosome and may have several variants, or ◊alleles, each specifying a particular form of that character – for example, the alleles for blue or brown eyes. Some alleles show ◊dominance. These mask the effect of other alleles, known as ◊recessive.

In the 1940s, it was established that a gene could be identified with a particular length of DNA, which coded for a complete protein molecule, leading to the 'one gene, one enzyme' principle. Later it was realized that proteins can be made up of several ◊polypeptide chains, each with a separate gene, so this principle was modified to 'one gene, one polypeptide'. However, the fundamental idea remains the same, that genes produce their visible effects simply by coding for proteins; they control the structure of those proteins via the genetic code, as well as the amounts produced and the timing of production.

In modern genetics, the gene is identified either with the cistron (a set of ◊codons that determines a complete polypeptide) or with the unit of selection (a Mendelian gene that determines a particular character in the organism on which ◊natural selection can act). Genes undergo ◊mutation and ◊recombination to produce the variation on which natural selection operates. See also ◊Human Genome Project.

genealogy the study and tracing of family histories. In the UK, the Society of Genealogists in London (established 1911) with its library containing thousands of family papers, marriage index (6 million names of persons married before 1837), and collection of parish register copies, undertakes and assists research.

gene amplification technique by which selected DNA from a single cell can be duplicated indefinitely until there is a sufficient amount to analyse by conventional genetic techniques. The technique has been used to analyse DNA from a man who died in 1959, showing the presence of sequences from the HIV virus in his cells. It can also be used to test for genetic defects in a single cell taken from an embryo, before the embryo is reimplanted in ◊in vitro fertilization.

gene bank collection of seeds or other forms of genetic material, such as tubers, spores, bacterial or yeast cultures, live animals and plants, frozen sperm and eggs, or frozen embryos. These are stored for possible future use in agriculture, plant and animal breeding, or in medicine, genetic engineering, or the restocking of wild habitats where species have become extinct. Gene banks will be increasingly used as the rate of extinction increases, depleting the Earth's genetic variety (biodiversity).

gene pool total sum of ◊alleles (variants of ◊genes) possessed by all the members of a given population or species alive at a particular time.

general senior military rank, the ascending grades being major general, lieutenant general, and general.

General Agreement on Tariffs and Trade (GATT) organization within the United Nations founded 1948 with the aim of encouraging ◊free trade between nations by reducing tariffs, subsidies, quotas, and regulations that discriminate against imported products. GATT was effectively replaced by the ◊World Trade Organization Jan 1995.

General Assembly highest governing body of the Presbyterian Church and the supreme court of the Church of ◊Scotland. In the General Assemblies of the established Church of Scotland sit representatives from each presbytery. This assembly meets every year in May. It has judicial and legislative power; cases brought from lower courts are settled in this one.

General Motors the USA's largest company, a vehicle manufacturer founded 1908 in Flint, Michigan, from a number of small carmakers; it went on to acquire many more companies, including those that produced the Oldsmobile, Pontiac, Cadillac, and Chevrolet. It has headquarters in Detroit, Michigan; and New York.

general strike refusal to work by employees in several key industries, with the intention of paralysing the economic life of a country. In British history, the General Strike was a nationwide strike called by the Trade Union Congress (TUC) on 3 May 1926 in support of the miners' union. Elsewhere, the general strike was used as a political weapon by anarchists and others (see ◊syndicalism), especially in Spain and Italy. See also ◊strike.

The immediate cause of the 1926 General Strike was the report of a royal commission on the coal-mining industry (*Samuel Report* 1926) which, among other things, recommended a cut in wages. The mine-owners wanted longer hours as well as lower wages. The miners' union, under the leadership of A J Cook, resisted with the slogan 'Not a penny off the pay, not a minute on the day'. A coal strike started in early May 1926 and the miners asked the TUC to bring all major industries out on strike in support of the action; eventually it included more than 2 million workers. The Conservative government under Stanley Baldwin used troops, volunteers, and special constables to maintain food supplies and essential services, and had a monopoly on the information services, including BBC radio. After nine days the TUC ended the general strike, leaving the miners – who felt betrayed by the TUC – to remain on strike, unsuccessfully, until Nov 1926. The Trades Disputes Act of 1927 made general strikes illegal.

generate in mathematics to produce a sequence of numbers from either the relationship between one number and the next or the relationship between a member of the sequence and its position. For example, $u_{n+1} = 2u_n$ generates the sequence 1, 2, 4, 8, ... ; $a_n = n(n+1)$ generates the sequence of numbers 2, 6, 12, 20, ...

generator machine that produces electrical energy from mechanical energy, as opposed to an ◊electric motor, which does the opposite. A simple generator (dynamo) consists of a wire-wound coil (armature) that is rotated between the poles of a permanent magnet. The movement of the wire in the magnetic field induces a current in the coil by ◊electromagnetic induction, which can be fed by means of a ◊commutator as a continuous direct current into an external circuit. Slip rings instead of a commutator produce an alternating current, when the generator is called an alternator.

Genesis first book of the Old Testament, which includes the stories of the creation of the world, Adam and Eve, the Flood, and the history of the Jewish patriarchs Abraham, Isaac, Jacob, and Joseph (who brought his people to Egypt).

gene-splicing see ◊genetic engineering.

Genet Jean 1910–1986. French dramatist, novelist, and poet. His turbulent life and early years spent in prison are reflected in his drama, characterized by ritual, role-play, and illusion, in which his characters act out their bizarre and violent fantasies. His plays include *Les Bonnes/The Maids* 1947, *Le Balcon/The Balcony* 1957, and two plays dealing with the Algerian situation: *Les Nègres/The Blacks* 1959 and *Les Paravents/The Screens* 1961. His best-known novels include *Notre Dame des fleurs/Our Lady of the Flowers* 1944 and *Miracle de la rose/Miracle of the Rose* 1946.

gene therapy proposed medical technique for curing or alleviating inherited diseases or defects; certain infections, and several kinds of cancer in which affected cells from a sufferer would be removed from the body, the ◊DNA repaired in the laboratory (◊genetic engineering), and the functioning cells reintroduced. In 1990 a genetically engineered gene was used for the first time to treat a patient.

Gene therapy is not the final answer to inherited disease; it may cure the patient but it cannot prevent him or her from passing on the genetic defect to any children. However, it does hold out the promise of a

‘And they were both naked, the man and his wife, and were not ashamed.’

GENESIS
Old Testament, 2:25

cure for various other conditions, including heart disease and some cancers.

genetic code the way in which instructions for building proteins, the basic structural molecules of living matter, are 'written' in the genetic material ◊DNA. This relationship between the sequence of bases (the subunits in a DNA molecule) and the sequence of ◊amino acids (the subunits of a protein molecule) is the basis of heredity. The code employs ◊codons of three bases each; it is the same in almost all organisms. A genetic map of the worm *Caenorhabditis elegans* was created 1998, the first complete map of a multi-celled living creature.

genetic disease any disorder caused at least partly by defective genes or chromosomes. In humans there are some 3,000 genetic diseases, including cystic fibrosis, Down's syndrome, haemophilia, Huntington's chorea, some forms of anaemia, spina bifida, and Tay-Sachs disease.

genetic engineering deliberate manipulation of genetic material by biochemical techniques. It is often achieved by the introduction of new ◊DNA, usually by means of a virus or ◊plasmid. This can be for pure research, ◊gene therapy, or to breed functionally specific plants, animals, or bacteria. These organisms with a foreign gene added are said to be transgenic.

practical uses In genetic engineering, the splicing and reconciliation of genes is used to increase knowledge of cell function and reproduction, but it can also achieve practical ends. For example, plants grown for food could be given the ability to fix nitrogen, found in some bacteria, and so reduce the need for expensive fertilizers, or simple bacteria may be modified to produce rare drugs. A foreign gene can be inserted into laboratory cultures of bacteria to generate commercial biological products, such as synthetic insulin, hepatitis-B vaccine, and interferon. Gene splicing was invented 1973 by the US scientists Stanley Cohen and Herbert Boyer, and patented in the USA 1984.

new developments Developments in genetic engineering have led to the production of growth hormone, and a number of other bone-marrow stimulating hormones. New strains of animals have also been produced; a new strain of mouse was patented in the USA 1989 (the application was rejected in the European Patent Office). A vaccine against a sheep parasite (a larval tapeworm) was developed by genetic engineering, and the first genetically engineered food went on sale 1994. See also ◊clone.

During the late 1990s a substantial number of groups formed to protest against genetic engineering within food and agriculture.

genetic fingerprinting or ***genetic profiling*** technique used for determining the pattern of certain parts of the genetic material ◊DNA that is unique to each individual. Like conventional fingerprinting, it can accurately distinguish humans from one another, with the exception of identical siblings from multiple births. It can be applied to as little material as a single cell.

Genetic fingerprinting involves isolating DNA from cells, then comparing and contrasting the sequences of component chemicals between individuals. The DNA pattern can be ascertained from a sample of skin, hair, or semen. Although differences are minimal (only 0.1% between unrelated people), certain regions of DNA are unique to individuals.

Genetic fingerprinting was developed in the UK by Professor Alec Jeffreys (1950–), and is now allowed as a means of legal identification. It is used in paternity testing, forensic medicine, and inbreeding studies.

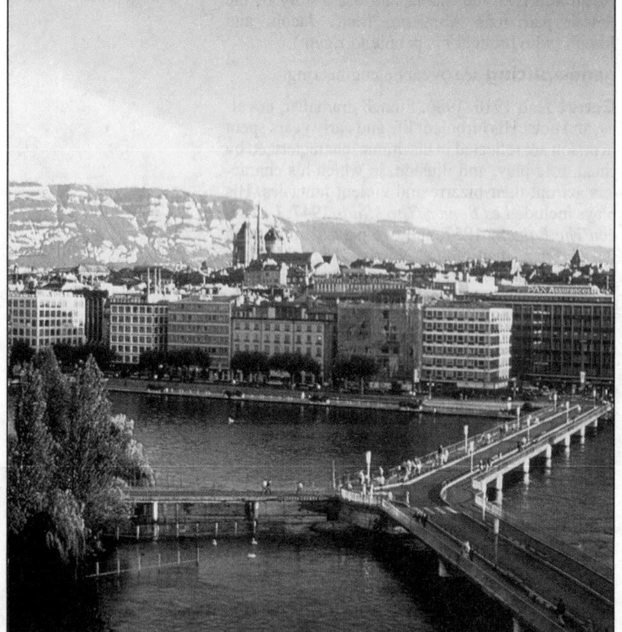

Geneva *A view of Geneva across the river Rhône, which flows from Lake Geneva. St Peter's Cathedral (12th–14th centuries) is in the distance, and beyond it Mount Salève.* ***Swiss National Tourist Office***

genetics the science of ◊heredity that attempts to explain how characteristics are passed on from one generation to the next. The founder of genetics was Austrian biologist Gregor ◊Mendel, whose experiments with peas showed that inheritance of characteristics takes place by means of discrete 'particles', later called ◊genes. Since Mendel, genetics has advanced greatly, first through ◊breeding experiments and light-microscope observations (classical genetics), later by means of biochemical and electron-microscope studies (molecular genetics).

genetic screening the identification of the genetic make-up of an individual to determine if he or she is at risk of developing a hereditary disease later in life, or is a carrier for a particular ◊genetic disease which might be passed on to offspring.

Geneva (French ***Genève***) Swiss city, capital of Geneva canton, on the shore of Lake Geneva; population (1994) city 174,400; canton 391,100. It is a point of convergence of natural routes and is a cultural and commercial centre. Industries include the manufacture of watches, scientific and optical instruments, foodstuffs, jewellery, and musical boxes. CERN, the particle physics research organization, is here.

The site on which Geneva stands was the chief settlement of the Allobroges, a central European tribe who were annexed to Rome 121 BC; Julius Caesar built an entrenched camp here. Under the Protestant theologian John ◊Calvin, it became a centre of the Reformation 1536–64. Geneva was annexed by France 1798; it was freed 1814 and entered the Swiss Confederation 1815. In 1864 the International Red Cross Society was established in Geneva.

Geneva Convention international agreement 1864 regulating the treatment of those wounded in war, and later extended to cover the types of weapons allowed, the treatment of prisoners and the sick, and the protection of civilians in wartime. The rules were revised at conventions held 1906, 1929, and 1949, and by the 1977 Additional Protocols.

Geneva, Lake (French ***Lac Léman***) largest of the central European lakes, between Switzerland and France; area 580 sq km/225 sq mi.

Geneva Protocol international agreement 1925 designed to prohibit the use of poisonous gases, chemical weapons, and bacteriological methods of warfare. It came into force 1928 but was not ratified by the USA until 1974.

Genghis Khan c. 1167–1227. Mongol conqueror, ruler of all Mongol peoples from 1206. He began the conquest of N China 1213, overran the empire of the shah of Khiva 1219–25, and invaded N India, while his lieutenants advanced as far as the Crimea. When he died, his empire ranged from the Yellow Sea to the Black Sea; it continued to expand after his death to extend from Hungary to Korea. Genghis Khan controlled probably a larger area than any other individual in history. He was not only a great military leader, but the creator of a stable political system.

genitalia reproductive organs of sexually reproducing animals, particularly the external/visible organs of mammals: in males, the penis and the scrotum, which contains the testes, and in females, the clitoris and vulva.

Genji alternative name for ◊Minamoto, an ancient Japanese clan. Prince Genji, 'the shining prince', is the hero of one of Japan's best-known literary works, *Genji Monogatari/The Tale of Genji*, whose author is known as ◊Murasaki.

Genoa (Italian ***Genova***) historic city in NW Italy, capital of Liguria; population (1992) 667,600. It is Italy's largest port; industries include oil-refining, chemicals, engineering, and textiles.

history Decline followed its conquest by the Lombards 640, but from the 10th century it established a commercial empire in the W Mediterranean. At its peak about 1300, the city had a virtual monopoly of European trade with the East. Strife between lower-class Genoese and the ruling mercantile-aristocratic oligarchy led to weakness and domination by a succession of foreign powers, including Pope John XXII (1249–1334), Robert of Anjou, King of Naples (1318–43), and Charles VI of France (1368–1422). During the 15th century, most of its trade and colonies were taken over by Venice or the Ottomans. Rebuilt after World War II, it became the busiest port on the Mediterranean, and the first to build modern container facilities.

genocide deliberate and systematic destruction of a national, racial, religious, or ethnic group defined by the exterminators as undesirable. The term is commonly applied to the policies of the Nazis during World War II (what they called the 'final solution' – the extermination of all 'undesirables' in occupied Europe, particularly the Jews). See ◊Holocaust.

genome the full complement of ◊genes carried by a single (haploid) set of ◊chromosomes. The term may be applied to the genetic information carried by an individual or to the range of genes found in a given species. The human genome is made up of 75,000 genes. See also ◊Human Genome Project.

genotype the particular set of ◊alleles (variants of genes) possessed by a given organism. The term is usually used in conjunction with ◊phenotype, which is the product of the genotype and all environmental effects. See also ◊nature–nurture controversy.

genre a particular kind of work within an art form, differentiated by its structure, content, or style. For instance, the novel is a literary genre and the historical novel is a genre of the novel. The Western is a genre of film, and the symphonic poem is a musical genre. It is also a term specifically applied to paintings which depict familiar scenes of everyday life.

Genscher Hans-Dietrich 1927– . German politician, chair of the West German Free Democratic Party (FDP) 1974–85, foreign minister 1974–92. As FDP leader, he masterminded the party's switch of allegiance from the Social Democratic Party to the Christian Democratic Union, which resulted in the downfall of the Helmut ◊Schmidt government 1982.

Gentile (Latin 'nations') any person who is not Jewish (the term 'non-Jew' is usually preferred now). In the Hebrew Bible the Gentiles are included in the future promised for Israel, which is seen as leading all nations to God, but the word was sometimes used to indicate 'heathen', and the ◊Talmud contains warnings and restrictions on dealings with Gentiles.

Gentile da Fabriano, (born Niccolo di Giovanni di Massio) c. 1370–c. 1427. Italian painter of frescoes and altarpieces. He was one of the most important exponents of the International Gothic style. Gentile was active in Venice, Florence, Siena, Orvieto, and Rome and collaborated with the artists Pisanello and Jacopo Bellini. His *Adoration of the Magi* 1423 (Uffizi, Florence) is rich in detail and colour.

He worked in Venice 1408–14 on frescoes for the Doge's Palace and was the master of Jacopo Bellini. Other notable works are the altarpiece of the Quaratesi family 1425, of which the centre panel, *Madonna and Child*, is in the British Royal Collection and the wings and other panels in the Uffizi and Vatican galleries; and a *Madonna with Saints* (Berlin).

Gentile Giovanni 1875–1944. Italian philosopher and politician, whose writings formed the basis of the Italian fascist state under Mussolini. As minister of education from 1924, he reformed both the school and university systems. He edited the *Encyclopedia Italiana* and wrote the entry in it for 'fascism'. He was assassinated by partisans.

Gentili Alberico 1552–1608. Italian jurist. He practised law in Italy but having adopted Protestantism was compelled to flee to England, where he lectured on Roman law in Oxford. His publications, such as *De Jure Belli libri tres/On the Law of War, Book Three* 1598, made him the first true international law writer and scholar.

genus (plural ***genera***) group of ◊species with many characteristics in common. Thus all doglike species (including dogs, wolves, and jackals) belong to the genus *Canis* (Latin 'dog'). Species of the same genus are thought to be descended from a common ancestor species. Related genera are grouped into ◊families.

geochemistry science of chemistry as it applies to geology. It deals with the relative and absolute abundances of the chemical elements and their ◊isotopes in the Earth, and also with the chemical changes that accompany geological processes.

geochronology the branch of geology that deals with the dating of the Earth by studying its rocks and contained fossils. The ◊geological time chart is a result of these studies.

geode in geology, a subspherical cavity into which crystals have grown from the outer wall into the centre. Geodes often contain very well-formed crystals of quartz (including amethyst), calcite, or other minerals.

geodesic dome hemispherical dome, a type of ◊space-frame, whose surface is formed out of short rods arranged in triangles. The rods lie on geodesics (the shortest lines joining two points on a curved surface). This type of dome allows large spaces to be enclosed using the minimum of materials, and was patented by US engineer Buckminster Fuller 1954.

geodesy methods of surveying the Earth for making maps and correlating geological, gravitational, and magnetic measurements. Geodesic surveys, formerly carried out by means of various measuring techniques on the surface, are now commonly made by using radio signals and laser beams from orbiting satellites.

Geoffrey of Monmouth c. 1100–1154. Welsh writer and chronicler. While a canon at Oxford, he wrote *Historia Regum Britanniae/History of the Kings of Britain* c. 1139, which included accounts of the semilegendary kings Lear, Cymbeline, and Arthur, and *Vita Merlini*, a life of the legendary wizard. He was bishop-elect of St Asaph, N Wales, 1151 and ordained a priest 1152.

geographical information system (GIS) computer software that makes possible the visualization and manipulation of spatial data, and links such data with other information such as customer records.

geography the study of the Earth's surface; its topography, climate, and physical conditions, and how these factors affect people and society. It is usually divided into ***physical geography***, dealing with landforms and climates, and ***human geography***, dealing with the distribution and activities of peoples on Earth.

history Early preclassical geographers concentrated on map-making, surveying, and exploring. In classical Greece theoretical ideas first became a characteristic of geography. ◊Aristotle and ◊Pythagoras believed the Earth to be a sphere, ◊Eratosthenes was the first to calculate the circumference of the world, and ◊Herodotus investigated the origin of the Nile floods and the relationship between climate and human behaviour.

During the medieval period the study of geography progressed little in Europe, but the Muslim world retained much of the Greek tradition, embellishing the 2nd-century maps of ◊Ptolemy. During the early Renaissance the role of the geographer as an explorer and surveyor became important.

The foundation of modern geography as an academic subject stems from the writings of Friedrich ◊Humboldt and Johann Ritter, in the late 18th and early 19th centuries, who for the first time defined geography as a major branch of scientific inquiry.

geological time time scale embracing the history of the Earth from its physical origin to the present day. Geological time is traditionally divided into eons (Phanerozoic, Proterozoic, and Archaeozoic), which in turn are divided into eras, periods, epochs, ages, and finally chrons.

geology science of the Earth, its origin, composition, structure, and history. It is divided into several branches: ***mineralogy*** (the minerals of Earth), ***petrology*** (rocks), ***stratigraphy*** (the deposition of successive beds of sedimentary rocks), ***palaeontology*** (fossils), and ***tectonics*** (the deformation and movement of the Earth's crust).

Geology is regarded as part of earth science, a more widely embracing subject that brings in meteorology, oceanography, geophysics, and geochemistry.

geomagnetic reversal another term for ◊polar reversal.

geometric mean in mathematics, the *n*th root of the product of *n* positive numbers. The geometric mean *m* of two numbers *p* and *q* is such that $m = \sqrt{(p \times q)}$. For example, the mean of 2 and 8 is $\sqrt{(2 \times 8)} = \sqrt{16} = 4$.

geometric progression or ***geometric sequence*** in mathematics, a sequence of terms (progression) in which each term is a constant multiple (called the common ratio) of the one preceding it. For example, 3, 12, 48, 192, 768, ... is a geometric progression with a common ratio 4, since each term is equal to the previous term multiplied by 4. Compare ◊arithmetic progression.

The sum of *n* terms of a geometric series

$$1 + r + r^2 + r^3 + ... + rn - 1$$

is given by the formula

$$S_n = (1 - r^n)/(1 - r)$$

for all $r \neq 1$. For $r = 1$, the geometric series can be summed to infinity:

$$S_{\$az} = 1/(1 - r).$$

In nature, many single-celled organisms reproduce by splitting in two so that one cell gives rise to 2, then 4, then 8 cells, and so on, forming a geometric sequence 1, 2, 4, 8, 16, 32, ..., in which the common ratio is 2.

geometry branch of mathematics concerned with the properties of space, usually in terms of plane (two-dimensional) and solid (three-dimensional) figures. The subject is usually divided into ***pure geometry***, which embraces roughly the plane and solid geometry dealt with in ◊Euclid's *Elements*, and ***analytical*** or ◊***coordinate geometry***, in which problems are solved using algebraic methods. A third, quite distinct, type includes the non-Euclidean geometries.

Geometry probably originated in ancient Egypt, in land measurements necessitated by the periodic inundations of the river Nile, and was soon extended into surveying and navigation. Early geometers were the Greek mathematicians Thales, Pythagoras, and Euclid. Analytical methods were introduced and developed by the French philosopher René ◊Descartes in the 17th century. From the 19th century, various non-Euclidean geometries were devised by Carl Friedrich Gauss, János Bolyai, and Nikolai Lobachevsky. These were later generalized by Bernhard ◊Riemann and found to have applications in the theory of relativity.

geophysics branch of earth science using physics to study the Earth's surface, interior, and atmosphere. Studies also include winds, weather, tides, earthquakes, volcanoes, and their effects.

George I 1660–1727. King of Great Britain and Ireland from 1714. He was the son of the first elector of Hanover, Ernest Augustus (1629–1698), and his wife Sophia (1630–1714), and a great-grandson of James I. He succeeded to the electorate 1698, and became king on the death of Queen Anne. He attached himself to the Whigs, and spent most of his reign in Hanover, never having learned English.

George's children were George II and Sophia Dorothea (1687–1757), who married Frederick William (later king of Prussia) 1706 and was the mother of Frederick the Great.

George II 1683–1760. King of Great Britain and Ireland from 1727, when he succeeded his father, George I. His victory at Dettingen 1743, in the War of the Austrian Succession, was the last battle commanded by a British king. He married Caroline

George III Caricature by James Gillray depicting George III as the king of Brobdignag scrutinizing Napoleon as Gulliver, based on a scene in Swift's *Gulliver's Travels*. This is an unusually favourable portrayal of the king. *Philip Sauvain*

of Anspach 1705. He was succeeded by his grandson George III.

George III 1738–1820. King of Great Britain and Ireland from 1760, when he succeeded his grandfather George II. His rule was marked by intransigence resulting in the loss of the American colonies, for which he shared the blame with his chief minister Lord North, and the emancipation of Catholics in England. Possibly suffering from porphyria, he had repeated attacks of insanity, permanent from 1811. He was succeeded by his son George IV. He married Princess ◊Charlotte Sophia of Mecklenburg-Strelitz 1761.

George IV 1762–1830. King of Great Britain and Ireland from 1820, when he succeeded his father George III, for whom he had been regent during the king's period of insanity 1811–20. In 1785 he secretly married a Catholic widow, Maria Fitzherbert (1756–1837), but in 1795 also married Princess ◊Caroline of Brunswick, in return for payment of his debts. He was a patron of the arts. His prestige was undermined by his treatment of Caroline (they separated 1796), his dissipation, and his extravagance. He was succeeded by his brother, the duke of Clarence, who became William IV.

George V 1865–1936. King of Great Britain from 1910, when he succeeded his father Edward VII. He was the second son, and became heir 1892 on the death of his elder brother Albert, Duke of Clarence. In 1893, he married Princess Victoria Mary of Teck (Queen Mary), formerly engaged to his brother. During World War I he made several visits to the front. In 1917, he abandoned all German titles for himself and his family. The name of the royal house was changed from Saxe-Coburg-Gotha (popularly known as Brunswick or Hanover) to Windsor.

George VI 1895–1952. King of Great Britain from 1936, when he succeeded after the abdication of his brother Edward VIII, who had succeeded their father George V. Created Duke of York 1920, he married in 1923 Lady Elizabeth Bowes-Lyon (1900–), and their children are Elizabeth II and Princess Margaret. *See illustration on following page.*

George I 1845–1913. King of Greece 1863–1913. The son of Christian IX of Denmark, he was nominated to the Greek throne and, in spite of early unpopularity, became a highly successful constitutional monarch. He was assassinated by a Greek in Salonika.

George II 1890–1947. King of Greece 1922–23 and 1935–47. He became king on the expulsion of his father Constantine I 1922 but was himself overthrown 1923. Restored by the military 1935, he set up a dictatorship under Joannis ◊Metaxas, and went into exile during the German occupation 1941–45.

George, Edward Alan John (Eddie) 1938– . British banker, governer of the Bank of England from 1993. When he became governor he showed himself to be a hard-line advocate of low inflation. Response to his efforts came with the Bank of England Act of 1998, which strengthened the Bank's governance and accountability, as well as formalizing its responsibility for the conduct of monetary policy.

'George the First was always reckoned / Vile, but viler George the Second; / And what mortal ever heard / Any good of George the Third? / When from earth the Fourth descended / God be praised, the Georges ended!'

On the GEORGES of Great Britain, Walter Savage Landor 'Epigram'

George VI George VI announcing the outbreak of World War II from Buckingham Palace Sept 1939. After his unexpected accession to the throne following his brother Edward VIII's abdication 1936, he overcame his natural shyness and a severe stammer to become a popular wartime leader. *Image Select (UK) Ltd*

George, St patron saint of England. The story of St George rescuing a woman by slaying a dragon, evidently derived from the ◊Perseus legend, first appears in the 6th century. The cult of St George was introduced into W Europe by the Crusaders. His feast day is 23 April.

He is said to have been martyred at Lydda in Palestine 303, probably under the Roman emperor Diocletian.

Georgetown capital and port of Guyana, situated at the mouth of the Demerara River on the Caribbean coast; population (1992) 200,000. There is food processing and shrimp fishing.
history Founded in 1781 by the British from a Dutch settlement captured in Demerara. It was held by the Dutch, who renamed it Stabroek, from 1784, and ceded to Britain in 1814. In 1831 it was renamed Georgetown and became the capital of British Guiana.
features Old wooden buildings built on brick stilts; St George's Cathedral (1892) is one of the world's tallest wooden buildings, 43.5 m/143 ft high.

Georgetown or ***Penang*** chief port of the Federation of Malaysia, and capital of Penang, on the island of Penang; population (1991) 219,000. It produces textiles and toys.

Georgia state in SE USA; nicknamed Empire State of the South/Peach State
area 152,600 sq km/58,904 sq mi
capital Atlanta
towns and cities Columbus, Savannah, Macon
features Okefenokee Swamp national wildlife refuge (1,700 sq km/656 sq mi); Golden Isles, including Cumberland Island national seashore, St Simon's Island (with Fort Frederica national monument), Sea Island, and Jekyll Island; Chattahoochee national forest; Savannah (founded 1733), with a 4-sq km/2.5-sq mi historic district with town squares and over 1,000 restored houses, site of the Siege of Savannah (1779); Atlanta, site of the 1996 Olympic Games, with Martin Luther King Jr national historic district; Fort Jackson on Salter's Island, the oldest colonial fort in the state
population (1990) 6,478,200.

Georgia country in the Caucasus of SE Europe, bounded N by Russia, E by Azerbaijan, S by Armenia, and W by the Black Sea. *See country box opposite.*

Georgia

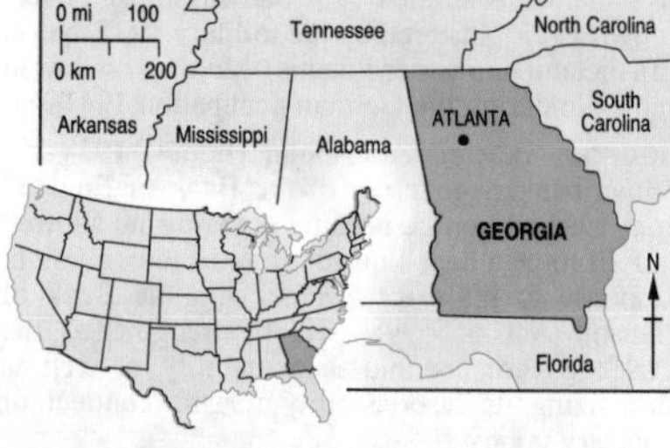

Georgian or ***Grazinian*** the people of a number of related groups which make up the largest ethnic group in Georgia and the surrounding area. There are 3–4 million speakers of Georgian, a member of the Caucasian language family. 'Georgian' is a distortion of *Gurji*, the name by which these people were known to the Turks.

Georgian period of English architecture, furniture making, and decorative art between 1714 and 1830. The architecture is mainly Classical in style, although external details and interiors were often rich in Rococo carving. Furniture was frequently made of mahogany and satinwood, and mass production became increasingly common; designers included Thomas Chippendale, George Hepplewhite, and Thomas Sheraton. The silver of this period is particularly fine, and ranges from the earlier, simple forms to the ornate, and from the Neo-Classical style of Robert Adam to the later, more decorated pre-Victorian taste. See also ◊English architecture.

geostationary orbit circular path 35,900 km/22,300 mi above the Earth's equator on which a ◊satellite takes 24 hours, moving from west to east, to complete an orbit, thus appearing to hang stationary over one place on the Earth's surface. Geostationary orbits are used particularly for communications satellites and weather satellites.

geothermal energy energy extracted for heating and electricity generation from natural steam, hot water, or hot dry rocks in the Earth's crust. Water is pumped down through an injection well where it passes through joints in the hot rocks. It rises to the surface through a recovery well and may be converted to steam or run through a heat exchanger. Dry steam may be directed through turbines to produce electricity. It is an important source of energy in volcanically active areas such as Iceland and New Zealand.

Gerald of Wales English name of ◊Giraldus Cambrensis, medieval Welsh bishop and historian.

gerbil any of numerous small rodents of the family Cricetidae with elongated back legs and good hopping or jumping ability. They have furry tails. Many of the 13 genera live in dry, sandy, or sparsely vegetated areas of Africa and Asia. The Mongolian jird or gerbil *Meriones unguiculatus* is a popular pet.

geriatrics medical speciality concerned with diseases and problems of the elderly.

Géricault (Jean Louis André) Théodore 1791–1824. French painter and graphic artist. One of the main figures of the Romantic movement, he brought a new energy and emotional intensity to painting. His subjects included spirited horses, Napoleonic cavalry officers, and portraits, including remarkable studies of the insane, such as *A Kleptomaniac* 1822–23 (Musée des Beaux Arts, Ghent). His *The Raft of the Medusa* 1819 (Louvre, Paris), a vast history piece, was notorious in its day for its grim depiction of a recent scandal in which shipwrecked sailors had turned to murder and cannibalism in order to survive.

In *The Raft of the Medusa*, the Classical nude of Jacques Louis David, realism of subject, and a Romantic force of feeling were characteristically blended. A visit to England followed 1820–22, and marked a change of direction. The sporting print and English genre picture both attracted Géricault, *The Derby at Epsom* 1821 (Louvre, Paris) being a striking result, and he made several lithographs of London life and character and in addition an equestrian portrait of the Prince Regent (Wallace Collection, London).

germ colloquial term for a microorganism that causes disease, such as certain ◊bacteria and ◊viruses. Formerly, it was also used to mean something capable of developing into a complete organism (such as a fertilized egg, or the ◊embryo of a seed).

German the native people or inhabitants of Germany, or a person of German descent. In eastern Germany the Sorbs (or Wends) comprise a minority population who speak a Slavic language. The Austrians and Swiss Germans speak German, although they are ethnically distinct. German-speaking minorities are found in France (Alsace-Lorraine), Romania (Transylvania), Czech Republic, Siberian Russia, Central Asia, Poland, and Italy (Tyrol).

German architecture the architecture of Germany which, in its early history and development, takes in that of Austria and the former Czechoslovakia. Little evidence remains of Roman occupation. The earliest buildings of note date from the reign of Charlemagne (742–814); for example, the chapel in Aachen 805.
Romanesque The abbey church of St Riquier at Centual 799 provided a model from which the German Romanesque style developed, reaching its peak in the cathedrals of Mainz 1081 and Worms about 1175, and in the many Romanesque churches (with distinctive trefoil-shaped east ends) that existed in Cologne until the devastation of World War II.
Gothic The German Gothic style was derived from northern French Gothic, but evolved its own distinctive character, incorporating elements of the hall churches of Westphalia and Bavaria, which had side aisles equal in height to the nave, as well as elements of the brick town halls of NE Germany, such as the late-14th-century example at Torun (now in Poland). Examples range from St Elizabeth at Marburg 1237, a hall church with trefoil-shaped east end and northern French Gothic features, to the pure High Gothic east end of Cologne Cathedral 1248.
Renaissance The Renaissance was influential only spasmodically in Germany, its flow being interrupted by the Thirty Years' War 1618–48. However, the works of Elias Holl (1573–1646), especially his town hall in Augsburg 1615–20, are significant.
Baroque and Rococo Around 1700 Italian Baroque made itself felt in southern Germany, culminating in the works of Fischer von Erlach and Hildebrandt in Vienna and in the Zwinger pavilion in Dresden 1709 by Matthaeus Pöppelmann (1662–1736). In church building the brothers Cosmas (1686–1739) and Eqid (1692–1750) Asam created a masterpiece of German Baroque in the tiny St John Nepomuk in Munich 1733–46. Balthasar Neumann outstepped his Baroque predecessors, creating such Rococo masterpieces as the palace at Würzburg 1720–44.
Neo-Classicism In northern Germany Neo-Classicism developed in reaction to the excesses of the Rococo style, manifesting itself first in the designs of Friedrich Gilly (1772–1800) and later in the work of Karl Friedrich Schinkel, active mostly in Berlin, and Leo von Klenze (1784–1864) in Munich. Klenze's Alte Pinakothek 1826–36 is one of the seminal works of museum building. Klenze also worked in styles other than the Neo-Classical and his architecture marks the beginning of an eclectic approach in German building that was to last until the end of the century.
20th-century trends At the start of the 20th century many of the ideas at the heart of modern architecture

found expression in Germany. The machine aesthetic of Peter Behrens gave rise to the Bauhaus school and the early works of Walter Gropius and Mies van der Rohe, later classed as hallmarks of the International Style. Expressionism in architecture was also influenced by Behrens and developed by Erich Mendelsohn and Hans Pöelzig (1869–1936). Most of these architects were to flee Germany in the years immediately preceding World War II, leaving the way clear for the totalitarian Neo-Classicism of the Nazi architect Albert Speer.

In the years of reconstruction following the war many towns and cities were rebuilt in an orthodox Modernist style, the historic centre of Dresden being one exception. Distinctive voices did emerge, however, among them that of the Expressionist Hans Scharoun. The Berlin Philharmonic 1956–83 is his masterpiece. Through the 1970s and 1980s the works of Oswald Mathias Ungers (1929–) and Joseph Paul Kleihues (1933–) were notable for creating a form of lyrical rationalism. The German Architecture Museum, Frankfurt 1979–84, by Ungers is a good example.

German art painting and sculpture in the Germanic north of Europe from the 8th century AD to the present. This includes Germany, Austria, and Switzerland. The Gothic style is represented by a wealth of woodcarvings and paintings for churches. Influences came from first the Low Countries and then Renaissance Italy, shown in the work of such painters as Albrecht Dürer and Hans Holbein. The Baroque and Neo-Classical periods, though important in Germany, had no individual artists of that stature; the Romantic movement produced the nature mysticism of Caspar David Friedrich. In the 20th century, Expressionism began as an almost entirely German movement; Dada was founded in Switzerland; and the Bauhaus school of art and design was influential worldwide. Recent German art includes the multimedia work of Joseph Beuys, dealing with wartime experiences.

Ottonian: about 950–1050 Many prehistoric artefacts have been found in Germanic areas, and a wealth of Celtic works remain, but it was not until the Ottonian era that a distinctively national style emerged. This drew on earlier Carolingian and Byzantine art, but developed a vigorous character of its own. Manuscript illumination flourished in Trier and in Reichenau, where the *Gospel of Otto III* about 1000 (Bayerische Staatsbibliotek, Munich) was produced. Works of sculpture include the wooden *Gero Crucifix* about 970 (Cologne cathedral) and the bronze doors and column of Hildesheim, near Hanover, 1015.

Middle Ages: 12th–15th centuries The 12th century was a period of little artistic activity, though the rock carving of *The Deposition* at the Externsteine, near Detmold, 1215, is an extraordinary achievement. At the beginning of the 13th century, the Gothic style reached Germany from France. The most important surviving monuments of this style are the series of figures (dating from between 1230 and 1250) decorating the cathedrals of Freiburg, Bamberg, Naumburg, Strasbourg, Paderborn, and Münster. The *Bamberg Rider* late 13th century, in Bamberg cathedral, a free-standing equestrian carving, is one of the most original sculptures of the period. Painting flourished during the 14th century, the style being that of International Gothic. An elegant, courtly style, International Gothic was common to most of Europe, though by the early 15th century distinctive regional variations had been developed by German artists such as Bertram von Minden (c. 1345–c. 1415) and Konrad von Soest (c. 1378–c. 1415) in Westphalia, Stephan Lochner in Cologne, and Meister Franke in Hamburg. A second generation of 15th-century painters, drawing increasingly on Flemish, Burgundian, and Renaissance influences, includes Hans Pleydenwurff (c. 1420–1472) and Michael Wolgemut (1434–1519) in Nuremberg, Lucas Moser (fl. 1430s), and Holbein the Elder in Swabia, Hans Multscher (c. 1400–1467) in Ulm, Michael Pacher (c. 1435–1498) in Bavaria, Konrad Laib (active 1440–1460) in Austria, Konrad Witz in Switzerland, and Martin Schongauer in Alsace.

Renaissance: 16th century The first 30 years of the 16th century, during which deeply rooted German medieval traditions struggled to come to terms with ideas from Renaissance Italy, saw some of the finest achievements in German art. The leading sculptors were Veit Stoss and Peter Vischer the Elder (c. 1460–1529), both of Nuremberg, and Tilman Riemenschneider of Würzburg, all of whom combine a mannered angular development of Gothic drapery with considerably increased freedom of movement and naturalism of expression. Vischer made the bronze statues on the tomb of Emperor Maximilian in Innsbruck 1513.

Among painters, Matthias Grünewald was an artist of great emotional force, his essentially medieval vision almost entirely untouched by the Renaissance. However, the greatest figure of the period, Albrecht Dürer of Nuremberg, was strongly influenced by Renaissance art and sought to merge German and Italian styles. He excelled at portrait painting, engraving, and drawing, where he combined clarity of design with rich and exquisite detail. Important contemporaries were Hans Holbein, Hans Baldung Grien, and Albrecht Altdorfer, one of the first true landscape painters. Lucas Cranach the Elder, a painter of portraits and mythological scenes, carried to the middle of the century something of the spirit of its opening years. From the 1530s onwards the Reformation brought about a sharp decline in artistic activity.

17th century At the very beginning of the century there was the solitary figure of Adam Elsheimer, who made an important contribution to the development of landscape painting. But the Thirty Years' War (1618–48) checked almost all artistic activity

GEORGIA
Republic of

Russian Federation
GEORGIA
Tbilisi
BLACK SEA
CASPIAN SEA
Armenia
Azerbaijan
Iran
0 mi 500
0 km 1000

area 69,700 sq km/26,911 sq mi
capital Tbilisi
major towns/cities Kutaisi, Rustavi, Batumi, Sukhumi
physical features largely mountainous with a variety of landscape from the subtropical Black Sea shores to the ice and snow of the crest line of the Caucasus; chief rivers are Kura and Rioni
head of state Eduard Shevardnadze from 1992
head of government Otar Patsatsia from 1993
political system transitional
administrative divisions two autonomous republics, Abkhazia and Adzharia; one autonomous region, South Ossetia
political parties Citizens' Union of Georgia (CUG), nationalist, pro-Shevardnadze; National Democratic Party of Georgia (NDPG), nationalist; Round Table/Free Georgia Bloc, nationalist; Georgian Popular Front (GPF), moderate nationalist, prodemocratization; Georgian Communist Party (GCP); National Independence Party (NIP), ultranationalist
population 5,442,000 (1996 est)
population growth rate 0.1% (1990–95); 0.4% (2000–05)
ethnic distribution 70% ethnic Georgian, 8% Armenian, 7% ethnic Russian, 5% Azeri, 3% Ossetian, 2% Abkhazian, and 2% Greek
life expectancy 69 (men), 76 (women)
literacy rate 99%
language Georgian
religions Georgian Orthodox, also Islam
currency lari
GDP (US $) 2 billion (1996)
growth rate −35.0% (1994)
exports tea, citrus and orchard fruits, tung oil, tobacco, vine fruits, silk, hydroelectricity

HISTORY
4th C BC Georgian kingdom founded.
1st C BC Part of the Roman Empire.
AD 337 Christianity adopted.
458 Tbilisi founded by King Vakhtang Gorgasal.
mid-7th C Tbilisi brought under Arab rule.
1121 Tbilisi liberated by King David II the Builder, of the Gagrationi dynasty, which traced its ancestry to King David. An empire was established across the Caucasus region, remaining powerful until Mongol onslaughts in the 13th and 14th centuries.
1555 W Georgia fell to Turkey and E Georgia to Persia (Iran).
1783 Treaty of Georgievsk established Russian dominance over Georgia.
1804–13 First Russo-Iranian war.
late 19th C Abolition of serfdom and beginnings of industrialization; Georgian Church suppressed.
1918 Independence established after Russian Revolution.
1921 Invaded by Red Army and Soviet republic established.
1922–36 Linked with Armenia and Azerbaijan as the Transcaucasian Federation.
1930s Rapid industrial development, but resistance to agricultural collectivization and violent political purges of Georgian Soviet dictator Joseph Stalin.
1936 Became separate republic within the USSR.
early 1940s 200,000 Meskhetians deported from S Georgia to Central Asia under Stalin's orders.
1972 Drive against endemic corruption by Georgian Communist Party (GCP) leader Eduard Shevardnadze.
1977 Initiative Group for the Defence of Human Rights formed by Zviad Gamsakhurdia, a nationalist intellectual.
1978 Violent demonstrations by nationalists in Tbilisi.
1981–88 Increasing demands for autonomy encouraged from 1986 by the *glasnost* initiative of the reformist Soviet leader Mikhail Gorbachev.
1989 Formation of nationalist Georgian Popular Front led the minority Abkhazian and Ossetian communities in the NW and central N Georgia to demand secession, provoking interethnic clashes. State of emergency imposed in Abkhazia; 20 pro-independence demonstrators massacred in Tbilisi by Soviet troops; Georgian sovereignty declared by parliament.
1990 Nationalist coalition triumphed in elections and Gamsakhurdia became president. GCP seceded from Communist Party of USSR.
1991 Independence declared. GCP outlawed and all relations with USSR severed. Demonstrations against increasingly dictatorial Gamsakhurdia; state of emergency declared. Georgia failed to join new Commonwealth of Independent States (CIS) as civil war raged.
1992 Gamsakhurdia fled to Armenia; Shevardnadze, with military backing, appointed interim president. Admitted into United Nations (UN). Clashes continued in South Ossetia and Abkhazia, where independence had been declared.
1993 Conflict with Abkhazi separatists intensified, forcing Shevardnadze to seek Russian military help. Pro-Gamsakhurdia revolt was put down by government forces and Gamsakhurdia died.
1994 Georgia joined CIS. Military cooperation pact signed with Russia. Cease-fire agreed with Abkhazi separatists; 2,500 Russian peacekeeping troops deployed in region and paramilitary groups disarmed. Inflation exceeded 5,000% per annum.
1995 Shevardnadze survived an assassination attempt and was re-elected; mass privatization programme launched.
1996 Cooperation pact with European Union signed as economic growth resumed and the monthly inflation fell to below 3%.
1997 New opposition party formed, Front for the Reinstatement of Legitimate Power in Georgia. Talks between government and breakaway Abkhazi government.
1998 Shevardnadze survived another assassination attempt. Outbreak of fighting in Abkhazia.

SEE ALSO Abkhazia; Ossetia; Russian Federation; Union of Soviet Socialist Republics

Everybody should know that Germany will not go it alone: there will be no restless Reich.

On **Germany**
Helmut Kohl
quoted in the
International Herald Tribune 3 Oct 1990

and the art of the second half of the 17th century is mainly a court art, based on imported Baroque models and with little connection to anything that had gone before. It was not until the end of the century that Germany produced an architect and sculptor of note in Andreas Schluter (1662–1714), who built part of the *Schloss* (palace) in Berlin and made the equestrian statue of the 'Great Elector', Frederick William of Brandenburg.

Baroque: 18th century During the first half of the 18th century a development of the Baroque style took place in S Germany in which architecture, sculpture, and painting were combined to produce the most striking theatrical effects. Although the origins of this style are to be found in Italy, it represents an important and original German contribution to the Baroque movement. The 18th century produced little notable native painting. The most important painter working in Germany during the first half of the century, Anthoine Pesne (1683–1757), was French, and the great Venetian Giovanni Tiepolo worked some years in Würzburg in the middle of the century.

The end of the century, however, saw the development of Neo-Classicism, a style that was enthusiastically adopted in Germany and retained its popularity until the middle of the 19th century. Anton Raphael Mengs, its leading painter, spent many years in Italy and based his style on the Italian painters of the High Renaissance. The theoretician of Neo-Classicism was the art historian Johann Winckelmann, its leading sculptor Gottfried Schadow (1764–1850).

19th century Running parallel with the Neo-Classical style was the Romantic movement in painting, its clarity of form showing Neo-Classical influence. At the beginning of this movement stand the Nazarenes, a group of painters, active in Rome, who in their aims and methods anticipated the English Pre-Raphaelite Brotherhood. Their leader was Friedrich Overbeck (1789–1869). Philip Otto Runge followed a similar line. More frankly Romantic was the work of the landscape painter Caspar David Friedrich, whose work is gloomy and full of religious sentiment. The Romantic style was carried on in the next generation by Ludwig Richter (1803–1884), Moritz von Schwind (1804–1871), Alfred Rethel (1816–1859), and, later in the century, the Swiss artist Arnold Böcklin.

Realism was adopted by Adolf von Menzel (1815–1905) and Wilhelm Leibl (1844–1900), and Impressionism by Max Liebermann (1847–1935) and Lovis Corinth (1858–1925); Paula Modersohn-Becker (1876–1907) was inspired by Post-Impressionism, her style making her a precursor of Expressionism.

20th century The early 20th century was dominated by Expressionism, practised by two major groups. *Die Brücke*, formed in Dresden 1905, included Ernst Kirchner, Emil Nolde, Karl Schmidt-Rottluff, and Erich Heckel. The more lyrical *die Blaue Reiter*, formed in Munich 1911, included August Macke, Gabriele Münter, and the Russians Alexei von Jawlensky and Wassily Kandinsky, perhaps the first totally abstract painter. Other Expressionists were the sculptor Ernst Barlach, the graphic artist Käthe Kollwitz, the Austrian painter Oskar Kokoschka, and the Swiss painter and graphic artist Paul Klee.

The Dada movement, formed in Zürich 1916, was a reaction to World War I, its anarchic iconoclasm appealing to George Grosz, Kurt Schwitters, and Max Ernst. Also a reaction to the horrors of the war was the Neue Sachlichkeit/New Objectivity movement, which expressed the bitter social criticism of George Grosz, Max Beckmann, and Otto Dix. On the other hand the social and constructive possibilities of modern art were developed in the Bauhaus art school.

When the Nazis condemned all these movements as 'degenerate art', there was a wholesale dispersal of German artists in Europe and America. After World War II many German artists sought an art that tried to come to terms with the traumas of the country's recent history. The first to win an international reputation was Joseph Beuys, who was increasingly drawn to performance art. Another artist to gain prominence was Anselm Kiefer. Jorg Immendorf (1945–) and Georg Baselitz (1938–) brought about a revival of figurative painting known as Neo-Expressionism, a style that combined the dynamic colours, forms, and brushwork of the Expressionists of *die Brücke* with a keen irony typical of the postwar world.

Germanic languages branch of the Indo-European language family, divided into ***East Germanic*** (Gothic, now extinct), ***North Germanic*** (Danish, Faroese, Icelandic, Norwegian, Swedish), and ***West Germanic*** (Afrikaans, Dutch, English, Flemish, Frisian, German, Yiddish).

The Germanic languages differ from the other Indo-European languages most prominently in the consonant shift known as Grimm's law: the sounds *p, t, k* became either (as in English) *f, th, h* or (as in Old High German) *f, d, h*. Thus, the typical Indo-European of the Latin *pater* is *father* in English and *Fater* in Old High German. In addition, the Indo-European *b, d, g* moved to become *p, t, k* (in English) or (in Old High German) *f, ts, kh*; compare Latin *duo*, English *two*, and German *zwei* (pronounced tsvai).

Germanicus Caesar 15 BC–AD 19. Roman general. He was the adopted son of the emperor ◊Tiberius and married the emperor ◊Augustus' granddaughter Agrippina. Although he refused the suggestion of his troops that he claim the throne on the death of Augustus, his military victories in Germany made Tiberius jealous. Sent to the Middle East, he died near Antioch, possibly murdered at the instigation of Tiberius. He was the father of ◊Caligula and Agrippina, mother of ◊Nero.

germanium brittle, grey-white, weakly metallic (◊metalloid) element, symbol Ge, atomic number 32, relative atomic mass 72.6. It belongs to the silicon group, and has chemical and physical properties between those of silicon and tin. Germanium is a semiconductor material and is used in the manufacture of transistors and integrated circuits. The oxide is transparent to infrared radiation, and is used in military applications.

German language member of the Germanic group of the Indo-European language family, the national language of Germany and Austria, and an official language of Switzerland. There are many spoken varieties of German, including High German (*Hochdeutsch*) and Low German (*Plattdeutsch*).

'High' and 'Low' refer to dialects spoken in the highlands or the lowlands rather than to social status. *Hochdeutsch* originated in the central and southern highlands of Germany, Austria, and Switzerland; *Plattdeutsch* from the lowlands of N Germany. Standard and literary German is based on High German, in particular on the Middle German dialect used by Martin Luther for his translation of the Bible in the 16th century. Low German is closer to English in its sound system, the verb 'to make' being *machen* in High German but *maken* in Low German.

German literature the literature of Germany.

Old High German The most substantial extant work of the period is the fragmentary alliterative poem the *Hildebrandslied* (about 800).

Middle High German There was a flowering of the vernacular, which had been forced into subservience to Latin after the early attempts at encouragement by Charlemagne. The court epics of Hartmann von Aue (c. 1170–1215), Gottfried von Strassburg (flourished 1200), and Wolfram von Eschenbach (flourished early 13th century) were modelled on French style and material, but the folk epic, the *Nibelungenlied*, revived the spirit of the old heroic Germanic sagas. Adopted from France and Provence, the *Minnesang* (love lyric) reached its height in the poetry of Walther von der Vogelweide (c. 1170–c. 1230).

Early Modern This period begins in the 16th century with the standard of language set by Martin Luther's Bible. Also in this century came the climax of popular drama in the *Fastnachtsspiel* as handled by the songwriter Hans Sachs. In the later 16th and early 17th centuries French influence was renewed and English influence, by troupes of players, was introduced. Martin Opitz's *Buch von der deutschen Poeterey* 1624, in which he advocates the imitation of foreign models, epitomizes the German Renaissance, which was followed by the Thirty Years' War, vividly described in H J C Grimmelshausen's *Simplicissimus* 1669.

18th century French Classicism predominated, but Romanticism was anticipated by the Germanic *Messias* of Klopstock. Both the playwright G E Lessing and the critic J G Herder were admirers of Shakespeare, and Herder's enthusiasm inaugurated the *Sturm und Drang* phase which emphasized individual inspiration. His collection of folk songs was symptomatic of the feeling that inspired Gottfried Bürger's ballad *Lenore*. The greatest representatives of the Classical period at the end of the century were Wolfgang von Goethe and Friedrich Schiller.

19th century In the early years of the century the Romantic school flourished, its theories based on the work of J L Teck and the brothers August and Friedrich von Schlegel. Major Romantics included Novalis, Achim von Arnim, Clemens Brentano, J F von Eichendorff, Adelbert von Chamisso, J L Uhland, and E T A Hoffmann. With the playwrights Heinrich von Kleist and Franz Grillparzer in the early 19th century, stress on the poetic element in drama ended, and the psychological aspect soon received greater emphasis. Emerging around 1830 was the 'Young German' movement, with Heinrich Heine among its leaders, which the authorities tried to suppress. Other 19th-century writers include Jeremias Gotthelf (1797–1854), who recounted stories of peasant life; the psychological novelist Friedrich Spielhagen (1829–1911); poets and novella writers Gottfried Keller and Theodor Storm (1817–1888); and the realist novelists Wilhelm Raabe (1831–1910) and Theodor Fontane (1819–1898). Influential in literature, as in politics and economics, were Karl Marx and Friedrich Nietzsche.

20th century Outstanding writers included the lyric poets Stefan George and Rainer Maria Rilke; the poet and dramatist Hugo von Hofmannsthal (1874–1929); and the novelists Thomas and Heinrich Mann, E M Remarque, and Hermann Hesse. Just before World War I Expressionism emerged in the poetry of Georg Trakl (1887–1914). It dominated the novels of Franz Kafka and the plays of Ernst Toller (1893–1939), Franz Werfel, and Georg Kaiser, and was later to influence Bertolt Brecht. Under Nazism many good writers left the country, while others were silenced or ignored. After World War II came the Swiss dramatists Max Frisch and Friedrich Dürrenmatt, the novelists Heinrich Böll, Christa Wolf (1929–), and Siegfried Lenz (1926–), the poet Paul Celan (1920–1970), and the poet and novelist Günter ◊Grass.

German measles or ***rubella*** mild, communicable virus disease, usually caught by children. It is marked by a sore throat, pinkish rash, and slight fever, and has an incubation period of two to three weeks. If a woman contracts it in the first three months of pregnancy, it may cause serious damage to the unborn child.

German shepherd breed of dog also known as the Alsatian. It is about 63 cm/25 in tall and has a wolflike appearance, a thick coat with many varieties of colouring, and a distinctive gait. German Shepherds are used as police dogs because of their courage and high intelligence.

German silver or ***nickel silver*** silvery alloy of nickel, copper, and zinc. It is widely used for cheap jewellery and the base metal for silver plating. The letters EPNS on silverware stand for ***e***lectro***p***lated ***n***ickel ***s***ilver.

German spring offensive Germany's final offensive on the Western Front during World War I. By early 1918, German forces outnumbered the Allies on the Western Front. Germany staged three separate offensives, which culminated in the Second ◊Battle of the Marne, fought between 15 July and 6 Aug. It marked the turning point of World War I. After winning the battle the Allies advanced steadily, and by Sept Germany had lost all the territory it had gained during the spring.

Germany Federal Republic of; country in central Europe, bounded N by the North and Baltic Seas and Denmark, E by Poland and the Czech Republic, S by Austria and Switzerland, and W by France, Luxembourg, Belgium, and the Netherlands. *See country box opposite and table on p. 444.*

Germany, East (German Democratic Republic, GDR) country 1949–90, formed from the Soviet zone of occupation in the partition of Germany following World War II. East Germany became a sovereign state 1954, and was reunified with West Germany Oct 1990. See ◊Germany, Federal Republic of.

Germany, West (Federal Republic of Germany, FRG) country 1949–90, formed from the British,

GERMANY
Federal Republic of

national name *Bundesrepublik Deutschland*
area 357,041 sq km/137,853 sq mi
capital Berlin (government offices moving in phases from Bonn back to Berlin)
major towns/cities Cologne, Munich, Essen, Frankfurt-am-Main, Dortmund, Stuttgart, Düsseldorf, Leipzig, Dresden, Bremen, Duisberg, Hanover
major ports Hamburg, Kiel, Bremerhaven, Rostock
physical features flat in N, mountainous in S with Alps; rivers Rhine, Weser, Elbe flow N, Danube flows SE, Oder, Neisse flow N along Polish frontier; many lakes, including Müritz ; Black Forest, Harz Mountains, Erzgebirge (Ore Mountains), Bavarian Alps, Fichtelgebirge, Thüringer Forest
head of state Roman Herzog from 1994
head of government Gerhard Schroeder from 1998
political system liberal democratic federal republic
administrative divisions 16 states
political parties Christian Democratic Union (CDU), right of centre, 'social market'; Christian Social Union (CSU), right of centre; Social Democratic Party (SPD), left of centre; Free Democratic Party (FDP), liberal; Greens, environmentalist; Party of Democratic Socialism (PDS), reform-socialist (formerly Socialist Unity Party: SED)
armed forces 337,900 (June 1995)
conscription 10 months
defence spend (% GDP) 2.0 (1994)
education spend (% GNP) 5.4 (1991)
health spend (% GDP) 6.0 (1993)
death penalty abolished in the Federal Republic of Germany 1949 and in the German Democratic Republic 1987
population 81,992,000 (1996 est)
population growth rate 0.6% (1990–95); −0.1% (2000–05)
age distribution (% of total population) <15 16.1%, 15–65 68.7%, >65 15.2% (1995)
ethnic distribution predominantly Germanic; notable Danish and Slavonic ethnic minorities in the N; significant population of foreigners, including 1.9 million officially recognized *Gastarbeiter* ('guest workers'), predominantly Turks, Greeks, Italians, and Yugoslavs; by 1993 the FRG had received more than 200,000 refugees fleeing the Yugoslav civil war
population density (per sq km) 228 (1994)
urban population (% of total) 87 (1995)
labour force 50% of population: 4% agriculture, 38% industry, 58% services (1990)
unemployment 8.2% (1995)
child mortality rate (under 5, per 1,000 live births) 7 (1993)
life expectancy 72 (men), 78 (women)
education (compulsory years) 12
literacy rate 99%
language German
religions Protestant (mainly Lutheran) 43%, Roman Catholic 36%
TV sets (per 1,000 people) 558 (1992)
currency Deutschmark
GDP (US $) 2,353.2 billion (1996)
GDP per capita (PPP) (US $) 20,370 (1995)
growth rate 1.9% (1994/95)
average annual inflation 2.2% (1995)
major trading partners EU (particularly France, Ireland, and the Netherlands), USA, Japan, Switzerland
resources lignite, hard coal, potash salts, crude oil, natural gas, iron ore, copper, timber, nickel, uranium
industries mining, road vehicles, chemical products, transport equipment, non-electrical machinery, metals and metal products, electrical machinery, electronic goods, cement, food and beverages
exports road vehicles, electrical machinery, metals and metal products, textiles, chemicals. Principal market: France 13% (1994)
imports road vehicles, electrical machinery, food and live animals, clothing and accessories, crude petroleum and petroleum products. Principal source: France 11.1% (1994)
arable land 32.7% (1993)
agricultural products potatoes, sugar beet, barley, wheat, maize, rapeseed, vine fruits; livestock (cattle, pigs, and poultry) and fishing

HISTORY

c. 1000 BC Germanic tribes from Scandinavia began to settle the region between the rivers Rhine, Elbe, and Danube.
AD 9 Romans tried and failed to conquer Germanic tribes.
5th C Germanic tribes plundered Rome, overran W Europe, and divided it into tribal kingdoms.
496 Clovis, King of the Franks, conquered the Alemanni tribe of western Germany.
772–804 After series of fierce wars, Charlemagne extended Frankish authority over Germany, subjugated the Saxons and imposed Christianity, and took title of Holy Roman emperor.
843 Treaty of Verdun divided the Holy Roman Empire into three, with E portion corresponding to modern Germany; local princes became virtually independent.
919 Henry the Fowler restored central authority and founded Saxon dynasty.
962 Otto the Great enlarged the kingdom and revived title of Holy Roman emperor.
1024–1254 Emperors of Salian and Hohenstaufen dynasties came into conflict with popes; frequent civil wars allowed German princes to regain independence.
12th C German expansion eastwards into lands between rivers Elbe and Oder.
13th–14th Cs Hanseatic League of Allied German cities became a great commercial and naval power.
1438 Title of Holy Roman emperor became virtually hereditary in the Habsburg family of Austria.
1517 Martin Luther began the Reformation; Emperor Charles V tried to suppress Protestantism; civil war.
1555 Peace of Augsburg.
1618–48 Thirty Years' War: bitter conflict, partly religious, between certain German princes and emperor, with foreign intervention; the war wrecked the German economy and reduced the Holy Roman Empire to a name.
1701 Frederick I, Elector of Brandenburg, promoted to King of Prussia.
1740 Frederick the Great of Prussia seized Silesia from Austria and retained it through war of Austrian Succession (1740–48) and Seven Years' War (1756–63).
1772–95 Prussia joined Russia and Austria in the partition of Poland.
1792 Start of French revolutionary wars, involving many German states.
1806 Holy Roman Empire abolished; France formed puppet Confederation of the Rhine in western Germany and defeated Prussia at Battle of Jena.
1813–15 Defeat of Napoleon at Battles of Leipzig and Waterloo.
1814–15 Congress of Vienna rewarded Prussia with Rhineland, Westphalia, and much of Saxony; loose German Confederation formed by 39 independent states.
1848–49 Liberal revolutions in many German states; Frankfurt Assembly sought German unity; revolutions suppressed.
1862 Otto von Bismarck became prime minister of Prussia.
1866 Seven Weeks' War: Prussia defeated Austria, dissolved German Confederation, and established North German Confederation under Prussian leadership.
1870–71 Franco-Prussian War; S German states agreed to German unification; German Empire proclaimed, with King of Prussia as emperor and Bismarck as chancellor.
1890 Wilhelm II dismissed Bismarck and sought to make Germany a leading power in world politics.
1914 Germany encouraged Austrian attack on Serbia that started World War I; Germany invaded Belgium and France.
1918 Germany defeated; revolution overthrew monarchy.
1919 Treaty of Versailles: Germany lost land to France, Denmark, and Poland; demilitarization and reparations imposed; Weimar Republic proclaimed.
1922–23 Hyperinflation: in 1922, one dollar was worth 50 marks; in 1923, one dollar was worth 2.5 trillion marks.
1929 Start of economic slump caused mass unemployment and brought Germany close to revolution.
1933 Adolf Hitler, leader of Nazi Party, became chancellor.
1934 Hitler took title of *Führer* (leader), murdered rivals, and created one-party state with militaristic and racist ideology; rearmament reduced unemployment.
1938 Germany annexed Austria and Sudetenland; occupied remainder of Czechoslovakia 1939.
1939 German invasion of Poland started World War II; Germany defeated France 1940, attacked USSR 1941, and pursued extermination of Jews.
1945 Germany defeated and deprived of its conquests; eastern lands transferred to Poland; USA, USSR, UK, and France established zones of occupation.
1948–49 Disputes between Western allies and USSR led to Soviet blockade of West Berlin.
1949 Partition of Germany: US, French, and British zones in W Germany became Federal Republic of Germany with Konrad Adenauer as chancellor; Soviet zone in E Germany became communist German Democratic Republic led by Walter Ulbricht.
1953 Uprising in East Berlin suppressed by Soviet troops.
1955 West Germany became a member of NATO; East Germany joined the Warsaw Pact.
1957 West Germany was a founder-member of the European Economic Community.
1960s 'Economic miracle': West Germany achieved rapid growth and great prosperity.
1961 East Germany constructed Berlin Wall to prevent emigration to West Berlin.
1969 Willy Brandt, Social Democratic Party chancellor of West Germany, sought better relations with USSR and East Germany.
1971 Erich Honecker succeeded Ulbricht as leader of communist party, and became head of state 1976.
1972 Basic Treaty established relations between West Germany and East Germany as between foreign states.
1982 Helmut Kohl (Christian Democratic Union) became West German chancellor.
1989 Mass exodus of East Germans to West Germany via Hungary; Honecker replaced; East Germany opened frontiers, including Berlin Wall.
1990 Collapse of communist regime in East Germany; reunification of Germany with Kohl as chancellor.
1991 Maastricht Treaty: Germany took the lead in pressing for closer European integration.
1995 Unemployment reached postwar high of 3.8 million.
1996 Public sector labour dispute over welfare reform plans and the worsening economy. Spending cuts agreed to meet European Monetary Union entry criteria.
1997 Unemployment reached record levels. Former East German leader, Egon Krenz, and two colleagues convicted of manslaughter.
1998 Unemployment reached postwar high of 12.6% in January. Opposition SPD chose charismatic moderate, Gerhard Schröder, as candidate for chancellor in September elections, after his re-election in March as minister-president of Lower Saxony. Far-right German People's Union (GVU) won 13% of vote in Saxony-Anhalt, in eastern Germany. CDU-CSU-FDP coalition defeated in Sept general election and a 'Red-Green' coalition government was formed by the SPD and the Greens, with Gerhard Schröder as chancellor. Kohl replaced as leader by Wolfgang Schäuble.

SEE ALSO Prussia; Reformation; World War I; World War II

GERMANY: STATES

State	Capital	Area in sq km/sq mi
Baden-Württemberg	Stuttgart	35,800/13,822
Bavaria	Munich	70,600/27,258
Berlin	Berlin	880/339
Brandenburg	Potsdam	25,900/10,000
Bremen	Bremen	400/154
Hamburg	Hamburg	760/293
Hessen	Wiesbaden	21,100/8,146
Lower Saxony	Hanover	47,400/18,301
Mecklenburg-West Pomerania	Schwerin	22,900/8,841
North Rhine-Westphalia	Düsseldorf	34,100/13,166
Rhineland-Palatinate	Mainz	19,800/7,644
Saarland	Saarbrücken	2,570/992
Saxony	Dresden	17,050/6,583
Saxony-Anhalt	Magdeburg	25,900/10,000
Schleswig-Holstein	Kiel	15,700/6,061
Thuringia	Erfurt	15,500/5,984

US, and French occupation zones in the partition of Germany following World War II; reunified with East Germany Oct 1990. See ◊Germany, Federal Republic of.

germination in botany, the initial stages of growth in a seed, spore, or pollen grain. Seeds germinate when they are exposed to favourable external conditions of moisture, light, and temperature, and when any factors causing dormancy have been removed.

Geronimo (Spanish name for *Goyahkla*) 1829–1909. Chief of the Chiricahua Apache Indians and war leader. From 1875 to 1885, he fought US federal troops, as well as settlers encroaching on tribal reservations in the Southwest, especially in SE Arizona and New Mexico. After surrendering to General George Crook March 1886, and agreeing to go to Florida where their families were being held, Geronimo and his followers escaped. Captured again Aug 1886, they were taken to Florida, then to Alabama, and finally to Fort Sill, Oklahoma, where Geronimo became a farmer.

‘Fourscore and seven years ago our fathers brought forth upon this continent a new nation, conceived in liberty, and dedicated to the proposition that all men are created equal.’

Abraham Lincoln
GETTYSBURG ADDRESS
19 Nov 1863

Gershwin George (born Jacob) 1898–1937. US composer. He wrote concert works including the tone poems *Rhapsody in Blue* 1924 and *An American in Paris* 1928, and popular musicals and songs, many with lyrics by his brother ***Ira Gershwin*** (1896–1983), including ‘I Got Rhythm’, ‘'S Wonderful’, and ‘Embraceable You’. His opera *Porgy and Bess* 1935 incorporated jazz rhythms and popular song styles in an operatic format.

Gertler Mark 1891–1939. English painter. He was a pacifist and a noncombatant during World War I, and his best-known work, *Merry-Go-Round* 1916 (Tate Gallery, London), is often seen as an expressive symbol of anti-militarism. He suffered from depression and committed suicide.

Gestalt (German ‘form’) concept of a unified whole that is greater than, or different from, the sum of its parts; that is, a complete structure whose nature is not explained simply by analysing its constituent elements. A chair, for example, will generally be recognized as a chair despite great variations between individual chairs in such attributes as size, shape, and colour.

Gestalt psychology regards all mental phenomena as being arranged in organized, structured wholes, as opposed to being composed of simple sensations. Gestalt psychologists' experiments show that the brain is not a passive receiver of information, but that it structures all its input in order to make sense of it, a belief that is now generally accepted; however, other principles of Gestalt psychology have received considerable criticism.

Gestapo (contraction of ***Geheime Staatspolizei***) Nazi Germany's secret police, formed 1933, and under the direction of Heinrich ◊Himmler from 1934. There was no appeal against Gestapo authority and it had sweeping powers to deal with acts or individuals it considered against the national interest. It was one of the most feared and brutal elements of the Nazi regime, using torture and terrorism to stamp out anti-Nazi resistance. It was declared a criminal organization at the Nuremberg Trials 1946.

gestation in all mammals except the ◊monotremes (platypus and spiny anteaters), the period from the time of implantation of the embryo in the uterus to birth. This period varies among species; in humans it is about 266 days, in elephants 18–22 months, in cats about 60 days, and in some species of marsupial (such as opossum) as short as 12 days.

Gethsemane site of the garden where Judas Iscariot, according to the New Testament, betrayed Jesus. It is on the Mount of Olives, E of Jerusalem. When Jerusalem was divided between Israel and Jordan 1948, Gethsemane fell within Jordanian territory.

Getty J(ean) Paul 1892–1976. US oil billionaire, president of the Getty Oil Company from 1947, and founder of the Getty Museum (housing the world's highest-funded art collections) in Malibu, California. In 1985 his son ***John Paul Getty Jr*** (1932–) established an endowment fund of £50 million for the National Gallery, London.

Gettysburg site of one of the decisive battles of the American ◊Civil War: a Confederate defeat by Union forces 1–3 July 1863, at Gettysburg, Pennsylvania, 80 km/50 mi northwest of Baltimore. The South's heavy losses at Gettysburg came in the same week as their defeat at Vicksburg, and the Confederacy remained on the defensive for the rest of the war. The battle ended Robert E ◊Lee's invasion of the North.

The site is now a national cemetery, at the dedication of which President Lincoln delivered the ***Gettysburg Address*** 19 Nov 1863, a speech in which he reiterated the principles of freedom, equality, and democracy embodied in the US Constitution. The address begins with ‘Fourscore and seven years ago’, and ends with an assertion of ‘government of the people, by the people, and for the people’.

Getz Stan(ley), (born Gayetzby) 1927–1991. US saxophonist. He was one of the foremost tenor-sax players of his generation. In the 1950s he was a leading exponent of the cool jazz school, as on the album *West Coast Jazz* 1955. In the 1960s he turned to the Latin American bossa nova sound, which gave him a hit single, ‘The Girl from Ipanema’ 1964. Later he experimented with jazz-rock fusion.

Getz became a professional musician at 15, working with the big-band leaders of the era: Tommy Dorsey, Stan Kenton, Benny Goodman, and Woody Herman. Technically brilliant but never showy, he was influenced by Lester Young, and became a cult hero in the cool-jazz movement with

Geronimo Apache Indian chief Geronimo, who led his people against white settlers in Arizona for over ten years, shown here after his surrender 1886. He subsequently became a prosperous Christian farmer in Oklahoma and a national celebrity. *Sachem*

its tendency towards subtlety and restraint. In the early 1960s *Jazz Samba*, *Big Band Bossa Nova*, and other albums brought jazz to a wider public.

geyser natural spring that intermittently discharges an explosive column of steam and hot water into the air due to the build-up of steam in underground chambers. One of the most remarkable geysers is Old Faithful, in Yellowstone National Park, Wyoming, USA. Geysers also occur in New Zealand and Iceland.

g-force force that pilots and astronauts experience when their craft accelerate or decelerate rapidly. One *g* is the ordinary pull of gravity. Early astronauts were subjected to launch and reentry forces of up to six *g* or more; in the space shuttle, more than three *g* is experienced on liftoff. Pilots and astronauts wear *g*-suits that prevent their blood pooling too much under severe *g*-forces, which can lead to unconsciousness.

Ghana country in W Africa, bounded N by Burkina Faso, E by Togo, S by the Gulf of Guinea, and W by Côte d'Ivoire. *See country box opposite.*

Ghana, ancient trading empire that flourished in NW Africa between the 5th and 13th centuries. Founded by the Soninke people, the Ghana Empire was based, like the Mali Empire that superseded it, on the Saharan gold trade. Trade consisted mainly of the exchange of gold from inland deposits for salt from the coast. At its peak in the 11th century, it occupied an area that includes parts of present-day Mali, Senegal, and Mauritania. Wars with the Berber tribes of the Sahara led to its fragmentation and collapse in the 13th century, when much of its territory was absorbed into Mali.

ghat in Hinduism, broad steps leading down to one of the sacred rivers. Some of these, known as ‘burning ghats’, are used for cremation.

Ghats, Eastern and Western twin mountain ranges in S India, E and W of the central plateau; a few peaks reach about 3,000 m/9,800 ft. They are connected by the Nilgiri Hills.

Ghent (Flemish ***Gent***, French ***Gand***) city and port in East Flanders, NW Belgium; population (1995) 227,000. Industries include textiles, chemicals, electronics, metallurgy, and motor-vehicle manufacturing. The cathedral of St Bavon (12th–14th centuries) has paintings by van Eyck and Rubens.

ghetto (Old Venetian *gèto* ‘foundry’) any deprived area occupied by a minority group, whether voluntarily or not. Originally a ghetto was the area of a town where Jews were compelled to live, decreed by a law enforced by papal bull 1555. The term came into use 1516 when the Jews of Venice were expelled to an island within the city which contained an iron foundry. Ghettos were

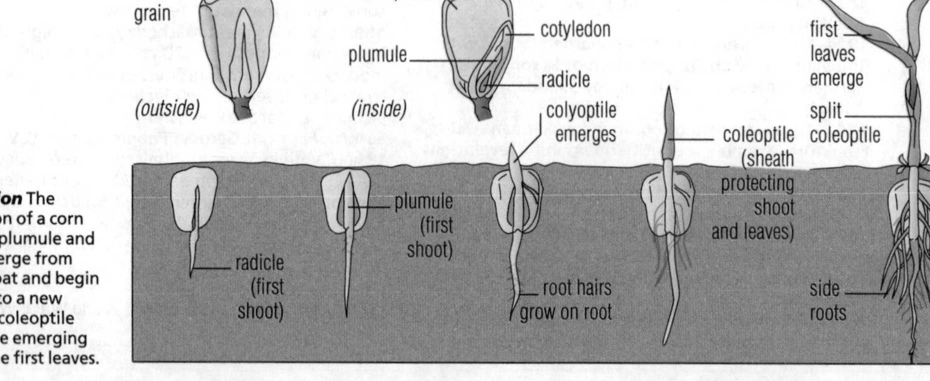

germination The germination of a corn grain. The plumule and radicle emerge from the seed coat and begin to grow into a new plant. The coleoptile protects the emerging bud and the first leaves.

Gershwin US composer George Gershwin with his elder brother Ira, who wrote the lyrics for many of his songs. Among the works on which they collaborated was the opera *Porgy and Bess* 1935, which features such classic songs as 'Summertime' and 'It ain't necessarily so'. *Corbis*

abolished, except in E Europe, in the 19th century, but the concept and practice were revived by the Germans and Italians 1940–45.

Ghibelline in medieval Germany and Italy, a supporter of the emperor and member of a rival party to the Guelphs (see ◊Guelph and Ghibelline).

Ghiberti Lorenzo 1378–1455. Italian sculptor and goldsmith. In 1402 he won the commission for a pair of gilded bronze doors for the baptistry of Florence cathedral. The North Doors, on which he worked for over 20 years, consist of 28 panels of gilded bronze representing New Testament scenes. While showing an awareness of Renaissance innovation, these scenes retain a strong element of International Gothic. He produced a second pair 1425–52, the East Doors, or *Gates of Paradise*, one of the masterpieces of the early Italian Renaissance. Also of gilded bronze, they consist of 10 much larger panels of Old Testament scenes. In these panels Renaissance features are much stronger. Around 1450 he wrote *Commentarii/Commentaries*, the earliest surviving autobiography of an artist and an important source of information on the art of his time.

Ghirlandaio Domenico, (adopted name of Domenico di Tommaso Bigordi) c. 1449–1494. Italian fresco painter. One of the greatest Italian masters of fresco and a principal representative of the narrative art of the late 15th century, he was the head of a large and prosperous workshop in Florence and the master of Michelangelo. His first major work was the *Life of St Fina* in the Cappella Fina, 1475, and his frescoes in Florence include those for the Sassetti Chapel in Santa Trinità, 1485, and for the choir of Sta Maria Novella (the *Life of St Francis*, 1485, and the scenes from the life of St John the Baptist and the Virgin, his masterpiece, 1486–90). Of the two frescoes he contributed to the Sistine Chapel to the order of Sixtus IV, 1481, the *Calling of St Andrew and St Peter* remains. Ghirlandaio produced not only frescoes and mosaics but many religious subjects on panel and portraits. He also worked in Pisa, Rome, and San Gimignano, and painted many portraits.

GI abbreviation for ***government issue***, hence (in the USA) a common soldier.

Giacometti Alberto 1901–1966. Swiss sculptor and painter. In the 1940s, he developed a highly original style, creating thin, rough-textured single figures in bronze. These emaciated figures have often been seen as an expression of the acute sense of alienation of people in the modern world. *Man Pointing* 1947 is one of many examples in the Tate Gallery, London.

His first works show the strong influence of Surrealism, as in *The Palace at 4 am* 1932 (Museum of Modern Art, New York), a fantastic cage reminiscent of a stage set. After 1945 he worked mainly on his attenuated single figures and busts, works which express the way in which an object is transformed by perception. This obsession with the ever-changing nature of perception is also evident in his drawings and paintings, in which haunting, disembodied images emerge from a dense network of fine, tentative marks.

Giambologna (Giovanni da Bologna or Jean de Boulogne) 1529–1608. Flemish-born sculptor. He was active mainly in Florence and Bologna. In 1583 he completed his public commission for the Loggia dei Lanzi in Florence, *The Rape of the Sabine Women*, a dynamic group of muscular, contorted figures and a prime example of Mannerist sculpture. He also produced the *Neptune Fountain* 1563–67 in Bologna and the equestrian statues of the Medici grand dukes Cosimo and Ferdinando.

giant in many mythologies and folklore, a person of extraordinary size, often characterized as stupid and aggressive. In Greek mythology the giants grew from the spilled blood of Uranus and rebelled against the gods. During the Middle Ages, wicker effigies of giants were carried in midsummer processions in many parts of Europe and sometimes burned.

Giant's Causeway stretch of basalt columns forming a headland on the north coast of Antrim, Northern Ireland. It was formed by an outflow of lava in Tertiary times that has solidified in polygonal columns.

Gibberd Frederick Ernest 1908–1984. English architect and town planner. He was a pioneer of the ◊Modern Movement in England. His works include the new towns of Harlow, England, and Santa Teresa, Venezuela; the Catholic Cathedral, Liverpool 1960; and the Central London Mosque, Regent's Park 1969.

gibbon any of several small S Asian apes of the genus *Hylobates*, including the subgenus *Symphalangus*. The common or lar gibbon *H. lar* is about 60 cm/2 ft tall, with a body that is hairy except for the buttocks, which distinguishes it from other types of apes. Gibbons have long arms and no tail. They are arboreal in habit, and very agile when swinging from branch to branch. On the ground they walk upright. *See illustration on following page.*

Gibbon Edward 1737–1794. English historian. He wrote one major work, arranged in three parts,

'My early and invincible love of reading, which I would not exchange for the treasures of India.'

Edward Gibbon
Memoirs of My Life

GHANA

Republic of (formerly the *Gold Coast*)

area 238,305 sq km/91,986 sq mi
capital Accra
major towns/cities Kumasi
major ports Sekondi-Takoradi, Tema
physical features mostly tropical lowland plains; bisected by river Volta
head of state and government Jerry Rawlings from 1981
political system emergent democracy
administrative divisions nine regions, subdivided into 58 districts
political parties National Democratic Congress (NDC), centrist, progovernment; New Patriotic Party (NPP), left of centre
population 17,453,000 (1995 est)
population growth rate 3.0% (1990–95); 2.8% (2000–05)
ethnic distribution over 75 ethnic groups; most significant are the Akan in the S and W (44%), the Mole-Dagbani in the N, the Ewe in the S, the Ga in the region of the capital city, and the Fanti in the coastal area
life expectancy 54 (males), 58 (females)
literacy rate men 70%, women 51%
languages English (official) and African languages
religions Christian 62%, Muslim 16%, animist
currency cedi
GDP (US $) 5.32 billion (1994)
growth rate 3.8% (1994)
exports cocoa, coffee, timber, gold, diamonds, manganese, bauxite

HISTORY

5th–early 13th Cs Ghana Empire (from which present-day country's name derives) flourished, with its centre 500 mi/805 km to the NW, in Mali.
13th C In coastal and forest areas Akan peoples founded first states.
15th C Gold-seeking Mande traders entered N Ghana from the NE, founding Dagomba and Mamprussi states; Portuguese navigators visited coastal region, naming it the 'Gold Coast', building a fort at Elmina, and slave trading began.
17th C Gonja kingdom founded in N by Mande speakers; Ga and Ewe states founded in the SE by immigrants from Nigeria; in central Ghana, controlling gold reserves around Kumasi, the Ashanti, a branch of the Akans, founded what became the most powerful state in pre-colonial Ghana.
1618 British trading settlement established on Gold Coast.
18th–19th Cs Centralized Ashanti kingdom at its height, dominating between Komoe river in the W and Togo mountains in the E and active in slave trade; Fante state powerful along coast in the S.
1874 Britain, after ousting the Danes and Dutch and defeating the Ashanti, made the Gold Coast (the southern provinces) a Crown Colony.
1898–1901 After three further military campaigns, Britain finally subdued and established protectorates over Ashanti and the northern territories.
early 20th C The colony developed into a major cocoa-exporting region.
1917 West Togoland, formerly German-ruled, was administered with the Gold Coast as British Togoland.
1949 Campaign for independence launched by Kwame Nkrumah, who formed Convention People's Party (CPP) and became prime minister in 1952.
1957 Independence achieved, within the Commonwealth, as Ghana, which included British Togoland; Nkrumah became prime minister. Policy of 'African socialism' and non-alignment pursued.
1960 Became a republic, with Nkrumah as president.
1964 Ghana became a one-party state, dominated by the CCP, and developed links with communist bloc.
1966 Nkrumah deposed in military coup and replaced by General Joseph Ankrah; political prisoners released.
1969 Ankrah replaced by General Akwasi Afrifa, who initiated a return to civilian government.
1970 Edward Akufo-Addo elected president.
1972 Another coup placed Col Ignatius Acheampong at the head of a military government as economy deteriorated.
1978 Acheampong deposed in a bloodless coup led by Frederick Akuffo; another coup put Flight-Lt Jerry Rawlings, a populist soldier who launched a drive against corruption, in power.
1979 Return to civilian rule under Hilla Limann.
1981 Rawlings seized power again. All political parties banned.
1992 Pluralist constitution approved in referendum, lifting the ban on political parties. Rawlings won presidential elections.
1996 Rawlings re-elected.

SEE ALSO Ashanti; Ghana, ancient; Gold Coast

gibbon There are nine species of these lesser, tail-less apes found in SE Asian rainforests and monsoon forests. They eat mainly fruit and move with great agility through the trees by swinging from branch to branch suspended by their long arms – this is known as brachiation. On stronger branches, gibbons will also walk in an upright posture. The largest gibbon, the siamang, may reach lengths of 90 cm/3 ft.

The History of the Decline and Fall of the Roman Empire 1776–88, a continuous narrative from the 2nd century AD to the fall of Constantinople 1453.

He began work on it while in Rome 1764. Although immediately successful, he was compelled to reply to attacks on his account of the early development of Christianity by a 'Vindication' 1779. His *Autobiography*, pieced together from fragments, appeared 1796. From 1783 Gibbon lived in Lausanne, Switzerland, but he returned to England and died in London.

Gibbons Grinling 1648–1720. Dutch woodcarver who settled in England c. 1667. He produced carved wooden panels (largely of birds, flowers, and fruit) for St Paul's Cathedral, London, and for many large English country houses including Petworth House, Sussex, and Hampton Court, Surrey. He was carpenter to English monarchs from Charles II to George I. Features of his style include acanthus whorls in oak, and trophies of musical instruments in oak and limewood.

'Sadness is almost never anything but a form of fatigue.'

ANDRÉ GIDE
Journal

Gibbons Orlando 1583–1625. English composer. He wrote sacred anthems, instrumental fantasias, and madrigals including *The Silver Swan* for five voices 1612, and became organist at Westminster Abbey, London, 1623.

Gibbs James 1682–1754. Scottish Neo-Classical architect. He studied under the late-Baroque architect Carlo Fontana (1638–1714) in Rome and was a close friend and follower of Christopher ◊Wren. His buildings include the churches of St Mary-le-Strand, 1714–17, and St Martin-in-the-Fields, London, 1722–26, and the circular Radcliffe Camera, Oxford, 1737–49, which shows the influence of Italian Mannerism.

Gibbs Josiah Willard 1839–1903. US theoretical physicist and chemist who developed a mathematical approach to thermodynamics and established vector methods in physics. He devised the phase rule and formulated the Gibbs adsorption isotherm.

Gibraltar British dependency, situated on a narrow rocky promontory in S Spain, the ***Rock of Gibraltar***
area 6.5 sq km/2.5 sq mi
features strategic naval and air base, with NATO underground headquarters and communications centre; colony of Barbary apes; the frontier zone is adjoined by the Spanish port of La Línea
exports mainly a trading centre for the import and re-export of goods
population (1993) 29,000
history captured from Spain 1704 by English admiral George Rooke (1650–1709), it was ceded to Britain under the Treaty of Utrecht 1713. A referendum 1967 confirmed the wish of the people to remain in association with the UK, but Spain continues to claim sovereignty and closed the border 1969–85. In 1989, the UK government announced it would reduce the military garrison by half. Ground troops were withdrawn 1991, but navy and airforce units remained.
currency Gibraltar government notes and UK coinage
language English
religion mainly Roman Catholic
government the governor has executive authority, with the advice of the Gibraltar council, and there is an elected house of assembly (chief minister Joe Bossano from 1988).

'Gibraltar is not merely a post of pride; it is a post of power, of connection, and of commerce; one which makes us invaluable to our friends and dreadful to our enemies.'

On GIBRALTAR
Edmund Burke, speech in House of Commons
12 Dec 1782

Gibraltar

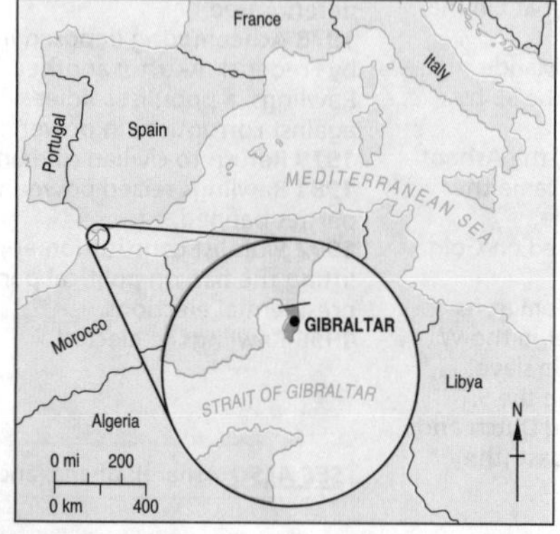

Gibraltar, Strait of strait between N Africa and Spain, with the Rock of Gibraltar to the north side and Jebel Musa to the south, the so-called Pillars of Hercules.

Gibson Guy Penrose 1918–1944. British bomber pilot of World War II. He became famous as leader of the 'dambuster raids' 16–17 May 1943; he formed 617 squadron specifically to bomb the ◊Ruhr Dams, and as wing commander led the raid personally, dropping the first bomb on the Mohne Dam. He was awarded the Victoria Cross for his leadership in this action.

Gibson Mel 1956– . Australian actor. He became an international star following lead roles in *Mad Max* 1979 and *Mad Max II* 1982 which was released in the USA as *Road Warrior*. His other films include *The Year of Living Dangerously* 1982, *Mutiny on the Bounty* 1984 as Fletcher Christian, and the *Lethal Weapon* series. He directed and starred in *Braveheart* 1995, which received five Academy Awards, including Best Picture and Best Director.

Gibson William 1948– . US writer. His debut novel *Neuromancer* 1984 established the 'cyberpunk' genre of computer-talk fantasy adventure and won both the Hugo and Nebula awards for science fiction. Gibson is credited with inventing the concept of virtual reality in *Neuromancer*. It was followed by *Count Zero* 1986 and *Mona Lisa Overdrive* 1988. Other works include *The Difference Engine* 1990, co-written with Bruce Sterling (1954–), about Babbage's original 19th-century computer.

Gibson Desert desert in central Western Australia, between the Great Sandy Desert to the N and the Great Victoria Desert in the S; area 220,000 sq km/85,000 sq mi.

Gide André (Paul Guillaume) 1869–1951. French novelist, dramatist, and critic. His work is largely autobiographical and concerned with the conflict between desire and conventional morality. It includes *Les Nourritures terrestres/Fruits of the Earth* 1897, *L'Immoraliste/The Immoralist* 1902, *La Porte étroite/Strait is the Gate* 1909, *Les Caves du Vatican/The Vatican Cellars* 1914, and *Les Faux-monnayeurs/The Counterfeiters* 1926.

He was a cofounder of the influential literary periodical *Nouvelle Revue française* 1908, and kept an almost lifelong *Journal*. Nobel Prize for Literature 1947.

Gielgud (Arthur) John 1904– . English actor and director. He is one of the greatest Shakespearean actors of his time. He made his debut at the Old Vic 1921 and played Hamlet 1929. His stage appearances ranged from roles in works by Anton Chekhov and Richard Sheridan to those of Alan Bennett, Harold Pinter, and David Storey. He won an Academy Award for his role as a butler in the film *Arthur* 1981. Other film credits include *Richard III* 1955, *Becket* 1964, *Oh! What a Lovely War* 1969, *Providence* 1977, *Chariots of Fire* 1980, and *Prospero's Books* 1991.

Gierek Edward 1913– . Polish communist politician. He entered the Politburo of the ruling Polish United Workers' Party (PUWP) in 1956 and was party leader 1970–80. His industrialization programme plunged the country heavily into debt and sparked a series of ◊Solidarity-led strikes.

Giffard Henri 1825–1882. French inventor of the first passenger-carrying powered and steerable airship, called a dirigible, built 1852. The hydrogen-filled airship was 43 m/144 ft long, had a 2,200-W/3-hp steam engine that drove a three-bladed propeller, and was steered using a sail like rudder. It flew at an average speed of 5 kph/3 mph.

giga- prefix signifying multiplication by 10^9 (1,000,000,000 or 1 billion), as in gigahertz, a unit of frequency equivalent to 1 billion hertz.

gigabyte in computing, a measure of ◊memory capacity, equal to 1,024 ◊megabytes. It is also used, less precisely, to mean 1,000 billion ◊bytes.

Gigli Beniamino 1890–1957. Italian lyric tenor. His radiant tone and affectionate characterizations brought a natural realism to roles in Puccini, Gounod, and Massenet.

Gilbert Cass 1859–1934. US architect. He was a major developer of the ◊skyscraper. He designed the Woolworth Building, New York, 1913, the highest building in America (265 m/868 ft) when built and famous for its use of Gothic decorative detail.

Gilbert Humphrey c. 1539–1583. English soldier and navigator who claimed Newfoundland (landing at St John's) for Elizabeth I in 1583. He died when his ship sank on the return voyage.

Gilbert W(illiam) S(chwenk) 1836–1911. English humorist and dramatist. He collaborated with composer Arthur ◊Sullivan, providing the libretti for their series of light comic operas from 1871 performed by the ◊D'Oyly Carte Opera Company; they include *HMS Pinafore* 1878, *The Pirates of Penzance* 1879, and *The Mikado* 1885. He published a collection of his humorous verse and drawings, *Bab Ballads*, 1869, followed by a second volume 1873.

Gilbert Walter 1932– . US molecular biologist who studied genetic control, seeking the mechanisms that switch genes on and off. By 1966 he had established the existence of the lac repressor, a molecule that suppresses lactose production. Further work on the sequencing of ◊DNA nucleotides won him a share of the 1980 Nobel Prize for Chemistry, with Frederick ◊Sanger and Paul ◊Berg.

Gilbert William 1540–1603. English scientist who studied magnetism and static electricity, deducing that the Earth's magnetic field behaves as if a bar magnet joined the North and South poles. His book on magnets, published 1600, is the first printed scientific book based wholly on experimentation and observation.

Gilbert and Ellice Islands former British colony in the Pacific, known since independence 1978 as the countries of ◊Tuvalu and ◊Kiribati.

Gide André Gide grew up in a strict Protestant family, but died an agnostic. Throughout his life, he encountered conflicting extremes, as when, impressed by the ideals of Communism, he joined the Communist Party 1934, only to renounce it two years later after a visit to the Soviet Union. *Corbis*

Gilbert and George Gilbert Proesch (1943–) and George Passmore (1942–) English painters and performance artists. They became known in the 1960s for their presentations of themselves as works of art, or 'living sculptures'. They also produce large emblematic photoworks. Their use of both erotic and ambiguous political material has been controversial. They received the Turner Prize 1986.

gilding application of gilt (gold or a substance that looks like it) to a surface. From the 19th century, gilt was often applied to ceramics and to the relief surfaces of woodwork or plasterwork to highlight a design.

Gilgamesh hero of Sumerian, Hittite, Akkadian, and Assyrian legend, and lord of the Sumerian city of Uruk. The 12 verse books of the *Epic of Gilgamesh* were recorded in a standard version on 12 cuneiform tablets by the Assyrian king Ashurbanipal's scholars in the 7th century BC, and the epic itself is older than Homer's *Iliad* by at least 1,500 years. The epic's incident of the Flood is similar to the Old Testament account.

gill in biology, the main respiratory organ of most fishes and immature amphibians, and of many aquatic invertebrates. In all types, water passes over the gills, and oxygen diffuses across the gill membranes into the circulatory system, while carbon dioxide passes from the system out into the water.

gill imperial unit of volume for liquid measure, equal to one-quarter of a pint or 5 fluid ounces (0.142 litre). It is used in selling alcoholic drinks.

Gill (Arthur) Eric (Rowton) 1882–1940. English sculptor, graphic designer, engraver, and writer. He designed the typefaces Perpetua 1925 and Gill Sans (without serifs) 1927, and created monumental stone sculptures with clean, simplified outlines, such as *Prospero and Ariel* 1929–31 on Broadcasting House, London.

He studied lettering at the Central School of Art in London, and began his career carving inscriptions on tombstones. A keen advocate of craft skill in an age of mass production, Gill was a leader in the revival of interest in lettering and book design. His views on art combine Catholicism, socialism, and the Arts and Crafts tradition. His books include *An Essay on Typography* 1931, *Work and Leisure* 1934, *Art in a Changing Civilisation* 1934, *Necessity of Belief* 1937, *Sacred and Secular* 1940, and *Autobiography* 1940.

Gillespie Dizzy (John Birks) 1917–1993. US jazz trumpeter. With Charlie ◊Parker, he was the chief creator and exponent of the ◊bebop style (*Groovin' High* is a CD re-issue of their seminal 78-rpm recordings). Gillespie influenced many modern jazz trumpeters, including Miles Davis.

Gill English sculptor and engraver Eric Gill at work, photographed around 1930. Gill began studying to be an architect, but gave it up to learn stonemasonry. He revived the art of working directly in stone, without making preliminary models of clay. *Corbis*

Although associated mainly with small combos, Gillespie formed his first big band 1945 and toured with a big band in the late 1980s, as well as in the intervening decades; a big band can be heard on *Dizzy Gillespie at Newport* 1957.

Gillray James 1757–1815. English caricaturist. His fierce, sometimes gross caricatures were satirical and topical. Before the French Revolution his main targets were George III, the Prince of Wales, and various political figures. Later his ferocity was patriotically aimed against the French and Napoleon.

Gilman Charlotte Anna, (born Perkins) 1860–1935. US feminist socialist poet, novelist, and historian, author of *Women and Economics* 1898, proposing the ending of the division between 'men's work' and 'women's work' by abolishing housework. From 1909 to 1916 she wrote and published a magazine called *The Forerunner*, in which her feminist Utopian novel *Herland* 1915 was serialized.

gin (Dutch *jenever* 'juniper') alcoholic drink made by distilling a mash of maize, malt, or rye, with juniper flavouring. It was first produced in the Netherlands. In Britain, the low price of corn led to a mania for gin during the 18th century, resulting in the Gin Acts of 1736 and 1751 which reduced gin consumption to a quarter of its previous level.

ginger SE Asian reedlike perennial *Zingiber officinale*, family Zingiberaceae; the hot-tasting underground root is used as a condiment and in preserves.

Gingrich Newt (Newton Leroy) 1943– . US Republican politician, speaker (leader) of the ◊House of Representatives 1995–98. A radical-right admirer of Reagan, he was the driving force behind his party's victory in the 1994 congressional elections, when it gained a House majority for the first time since 1954. On taking office, he sought to implement a conservative, populist manifesto, 'Contract with America', designed to reduce federal powers, balance the budget, tackle crime, and limit congressional terms.

Ginsberg (Irwin) Allen 1926–1997. US poet and political activist. His reputation as a visionary, overtly political poet was established by *Howl* 1956, which expressed and shaped the spirit of the ◊Beat Generation and criticized the materialism of contemporary US society. His other major poem, *Kaddish* 1961, deals with the breakdown and death of his schizophrenic mother. *Collected Poems 1947–1980* was published 1985. His work draws heavily on Oriental philosophies.

ginseng plant *Panax ginseng*, family Araliaceae, with a thick, forked aromatic root used in alternative medicine as a tonic.

Giorgione da Castelfranco, (Giorgio Barbarelli) c. 1475–1510. Italian Renaissance painter. Active in Venice, he created the Renaissance poetic landscape, with its rich colours, soft forms, and gentle sense of intimacy. An example is his *Sleeping Venus* about 1510 (Gemäldegalerie, Dresden), a work that was probably completed by ◊Titian. A poetical and enigmatic beauty seems personal to him, and is clearly apparent in *The Tempest* 1508, a dreamlike painting in which impassive figures are set against the background of an approaching electric storm – its significance lies more in its mood that its subject.

Apart from the *Sleeping Venus*, only four other pictures are generally accepted as unquestionably his: the *Castelfranco Altarpiece* (sometimes known as the *Madonna and Child Enthroned with Two Saints*), in the cathedral of Castelfranco; *The Three Philosophers*, the *Portrait of a Lady* (both Kunsthistorisches Museum, Vienna); and *The Tempest* (or *Storm*) (Accademia, Venice). Though he produced very few works, he greatly influenced Titian and other Venetian painters.

Giotto space probe built by the European Space Agency to study ◊Halley's comet. Launched by an Ariane rocket in July 1985, *Giotto* passed within 600 km/375 mi of the comet's nucleus on 13 March 1986.

Giotto di Bondone c. 1267–1337. Italian painter and architect. Widely considered the founder of modern painting, he had a profound influence on the development of European art. He broke away from the conventions of the Byzantine style and introduced a new naturalism, painting saints as real people, solid, lifelike, and expressive. His style gave a greater narrative coherence, dramatic power, and dignity to the depiction of biblical incidents. His main works are cycles of frescoes in churches in Florence and Padua.

Giotto was probably taught by Giovanni Cimabue. He was given commissions in Tuscany, Rome, and Naples, most of which have been lost, but the series of frescoes that decorates the walls of the Arena chapel, Padua, is enough to establish him as one of the major figures of Western art. Painted in 1303–06, these frescoes illustrate the life of Christ and the life of the Virgin Mary in 38 scenes. The figures display an unprecedented majesty and sense of form, and convey great dramatic power.

His sole surviving work as an architect is the bell tower (campanile) of Florence cathedral, begun 1334, when he was made director of public works in Florence. It was unfinished at his death, and the design was later altered.

giraffe world's tallest mammal, *Giraffa camelopardalis*, belonging to the ruminant family Giraffidae. It stands over 5.5 m/18 ft tall, the neck accounting for nearly half this amount. The giraffe has two to four small, skin-covered, hornlike

gin A scene from Hogarth's *Gin Lane* 1751 showing how the availability of cheap spirits led to such social ills as maternal neglect, suicide, and starvation. The Gin Act of the same year prohibited the retail sale of gin by distillers. *Image Select (UK) Ltd*

'What if someone gave a war & Nobody came?'

ALLEN GINSBERG 'Graffiti'

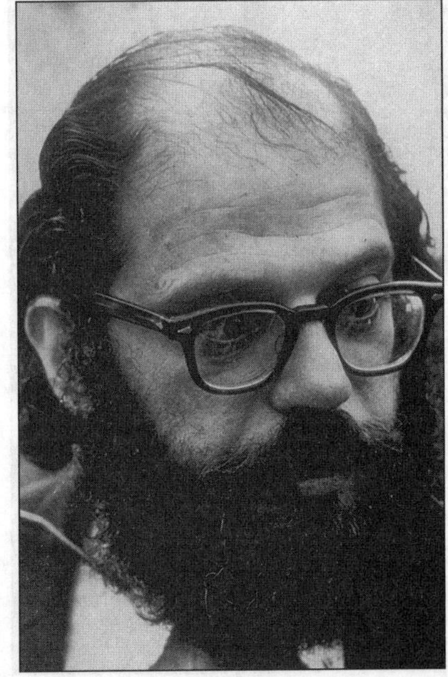

Ginsberg US poet Allen Ginsberg, one of the outspoken leaders of the Beat Generation. His spontaneous, loosely structured verse draws heavily on personal experience and freely expresses his outrage at the spiritual emptiness of modern life. His imagery is stark and sometimes shocking. *Penguin Books Ltd*

structures on its head and a long, tufted tail. The skin has a mottled appearance and is reddish brown and cream. Giraffes are found only in Africa, south of the Sahara Desert.

Giraldus Cambrensis (Welsh ***Gerallt Gymro***) c. 1146–c. 1220. Welsh historian, born in Pembrokeshire. He studied in Paris, took holy orders about 1172, and soon afterwards became archdeacon of Brecknock. In 1184 he accompanied Prince John to Ireland. He was elected bishop of St Davids 1198, but failed to gain possession of his see. He wrote a history of the conquest of Ireland by Henry II, *Itinerarium Cambriae/Journey through Wales* 1191, and an autobiography.

Giraudoux (Hippolyte) Jean 1882–1944. French dramatist and novelist. He wrote the plays *Amphitryon 38* 1929, *La Guerre de Troie n'aura pas lieu/Tiger at the Gates* 1935, and *La Folle de Chaillot/The Madwoman of Chaillot* 1945. His novels include *Suzanne et la Pacifique/Suzanne and the Pacific* 1921, *Eglantine* 1927, and *Les Aventures de Jérôme Bardini* 1930.

Giraudoux's plays reflect his range of interests and his technical proficiency in a variety of genres, including fairy-tale fantasies, historical and legendary plays, poetic drama, and light comedy. Although he often dealt with weighty and urgent themes, the most striking quality of his work is a graceful and witty sense of the fantastic.

Girl Guide female member of the ◊Scout organization founded 1910 in the UK by Robert Baden-Powell and his sister Agnes. There are three branches: Rainbows (age 5–7); Brownie Guides (age 7–10); Guides (10–15). The World Association of Girl Guides and Girl Scouts (as they are known in the USA) has over 6.5 million members.

Gironde navigable estuary 80 km/50 mi long, formed by the mouths of the Garonne and Dordogne rivers in SW France. The Lot, length 480 km/300 mi, is a tributary of the Garonne.

Girondin member of the right-wing republican party in the French Revolution, so called because a number of their leaders came from the Gironde region. They were driven from power by the ◊Jacobins 1793.

Giscard d'Estaing Valéry 1926– . French conservative politician, president 1974–81. He was finance minister to Charles de Gaulle 1962–66 and Georges Pompidou 1969–74. As founder and president of the Union pour la Démocratie Française (UDF) 1978–96, Giscard sought to project himself as leader of a 'new centre'.

Giscard was active in the wartime Resistance. After a distinguished academic career, he worked in the Ministry of Finance and entered the National Assembly for Puy de Dôme in 1956 as an Independent Republican. After Pompidou's death he was narrowly elected president in 1974, in difficult economic circumstances; he was defeated by the socialist Mitterrand in 1981. He returned to the National Assembly in 1984. In 1989 he resigned from the National Assembly to play a leading role in the European Parliament. In 1996 he stood down as UDF president, returned to the National Assembly, taking the chair of the Foreign Affairs Committee.

Gish Lillian (Diana). Stage name of Lillian de Guiche 1899–1993. US film and stage actress. She worked with the director D W Griffith, playing virtuous heroines in *Way Down East* and *Orphans of the Storm* both 1920. Deceptively fragile, she made a notable Hester in Victor Sjöström's *The Scarlet Letter* 1926 (based on the novel by Nathaniel Hawthorne). Her career continued well into the 1980s with films such as *The Whales of August* 1987. Gish appeared in over 100 films. She was the sister of the actress ***Dorothy Gish*** (1898–1968).

Gissing George Robert 1857–1903. English writer. His work deals with social issues and has a tone of gloomy pessimism. Among his books are *The Nether World* 1889, about the London poor; *New Grub Street* 1891, about a writer whose marriage breaks up; *The Odd Woman* 1893, about early feminists; and the semi-autobiographical *Private Papers of Henry Ryecroft* 1903. He also wrote studies of the novelist Charles Dickens and other critical works.

Giulio Romano adopted name of Giulio Pippi de Giannuzzi c. 1499–1546. Italian painter and architect. As assistant to Raphael, he developed a Mannerist style, creating effects of exaggerated movement and using rich colours, as in the frescoes in the Palazzo del Tè, Mantua.

Having studied under Raphael, he became his chief assistant on the *Sala del Incendio* frescoes in the Vatican. He succeeded Raphael as head of his Rome workshop, together with Giovanni Francesco Penni (c. 1488–c. 1528), completing the *Sala di Costantino* frescoes and other works, including the *Transfiguration* (Vatican). In 1524 he entered the service of Federico Gonzaga, Duke of Mantua, and in 1526 he rebuilt the Palazzo del Tè, a Mannerist building of capricious design decorated with Giulio's frescoes inside, which range from the extremes of illusionism in the *Sala di Psyche/Psyche's Room* to the grotesque in the *Sala dei Giganti/Room of the Giants*. Later he designed the façade of the church of S Petronio in Bologna.

Givenchy Hubert James Marcel Taffin de 1927– . French fashion designer. His simple, reasonably priced mix-and-match blouses, skirts, and slacks earned him instant acclaim when he opened his couture house in Paris 1952. He was noted for his embroidered and printed fabrics and his imaginative use of accessories. In the 1960s he designed both screen and personal wardrobes for Audrey Hepburn, creating for her the princess dress of the 1961 film *Breakfast at Tiffany's*.

Gîza, El or ***al-Jizah*** site of the Great Pyramids and Sphinx; a suburb of ◊Cairo, Egypt; population (1992) 2,144,000. It has textile and film industries.

gizzard muscular grinding organ of the digestive tract, below the ◊crop of birds, earthworms, and some insects, and forming part of the ◊stomach. The gizzard of birds is lined with a hardened horny layer of the protein keratin. Most birds swallow sharp grit which aids maceration of food in the gizzard.

glacial deposition the laying-down of rocky material once carried by a glacier. When ice melts, it deposits the material that it has been carrying. The material dumped on the valley floor forms a deposit called till or boulder clay, which comprises angular particles of all sizes from boulders to clay. Till can be moulded by ice to form drumlins, egg-shaped hills. At the snout of the glacier, material piles up to form a ridge called a terminal moraine.

Meltwater flowing away from a glacier will carry some of the till many kilometres away. Several landforms owe their existence to meltwater – these are called fluvioglacial landforms and include the long ridges called eskers. Meltwater may fill depressions eroded by the ice to form ribbon lakes.

glacial erosion the wearing-down and removal of rocks and soil by a glacier. Glacial erosion forms impressive landscape features, including the glacial trough (valley), arêtes (steep ridges), corries (enlarged hollows), and pyramidal peaks (high mountain peaks with concave faces).

glacial trough or ***U-shaped valley*** steep-sided, flat-bottomed valley formed by a glacier. Features characteristic of glacial deposition, such as drumlins (egg-shaped hills) and eskers (long ridges), are commonly found on the floor of the trough, together with linear lakes called ribbon lakes.

glacier tongue of ice, originating in mountains in snowfields above the snowline, which moves slowly downhill and is constantly replenished from its source. The scenery produced by the erosive action of glaciers is characteristic and includes ◊glacial troughs (U-shaped valleys), ◊corries, and ◊arêtes. In lowlands, the laying down of ◊moraine (rocky debris once carried by glaciers) produces a variety of landscape features.

Glaciers form where annual snowfall exceeds annual melting and drainage. The snow compacts to ice under the weight of the layers above. Under pressure the ice moves plastically (changing its shape permanently). When a glacier moves over an uneven surface, deep crevasses are formed in rigid upper layers of the ice mass; if it reaches the sea or a lake, it breaks up to form icebergs. A glacier that is formed by one or several valley glaciers at the base of a mountain is called a piedmont glacier. A body of ice that covers a large land surface or continent, for example Greenland or Antarctica, and flows outward in all directions is called an ice sheet.

gladiator in ancient Rome, a trained fighter, recruited mainly from slaves, criminals, and prisoners of war, who fought to the death in arenas for the entertainment of spectators. The custom was introduced into Rome from Etruria in 264 BC and continued until the 5th century AD.

gladiolus any plant of the genus *Gladiolus* of S European and African cultivated perennials of the iris family Iridaceae, with brightly coloured, funnel-shaped flowers, borne in a spike; the swordlike leaves spring from a corm.

Gladstone William Ewart 1809–1898. British Liberal politician, four times prime minister. He entered Parliament as a Tory in 1833 and held ministerial office, but left the party 1846 and after 1859 identified himself with the Liberals. He was chancellor of the Exchequer 1852–55 and 1859–66, and prime minister 1868–74, 1880–85, 1886, and 1892–94. He introduced elementary education 1870 and vote by secret ballot 1872 and many reforms in Ireland, although he failed in his efforts to get a Home Rule Bill passed.

glacier Glaciar Piedras Blancas, a valley glacier in the Parque Nacional los Glaciares, Argentina. Here the glacier forms icebergs when it reaches water. Around three-quarters of the world's fresh water is found in the form of glaciers. *Sally Jenkins*

Gladstone British Liberal politician William Gladstone, who was prime minister four times. Queen Victoria disliked Gladstone, an extremely serious man, preferring the more charming and flamboyant Disraeli. *Image Select (UK) Ltd*

Gladstone was born in Liverpool. In Robert Peel's government he was president of the Board of Trade 1843–45 and colonial secretary 1845–46. He left the Tory Party with the Peelite group in 1846. He was chancellor of the Exchequer in Aberdeen's government 1852–55 and in the Liberal governments of Palmerston and John Russell 1859–66. In his first term as prime minister he carried through a series of reforms, including the disestablishment of the Church of Ireland, the Irish Land Act, and the abolition of the purchase of army commissions and of religious tests in the universities. His second government carried the second Irish Land Act and the Reform Act 1884 but was confronted with problems in Ireland, Egypt, and South Africa, and lost prestige through its failure to relieve General ◊Gordon in Sudan. Returning to office in 1886, Gladstone introduced his first Home Rule Bill, which was defeated by the secession of the Liberal Unionists, and he thereupon resigned. After six years' opposition he formed his last government; his second Home Rule Bill was rejected by the Lords, and in 1894 he resigned. ▷ *See feature on pp. 550–551.*

Glamorgan (Welsh ***Morgannwg***) three former counties of S Wales – Mid Glamorgan, South Glamorgan, and West Glamorgan – created 1974 from the former county of Glamorganshire and abolished in the reorganization of local authorities 1996.

glam rock or ***glitter rock*** pop music in a conventional rock style performed by elaborately made-up and overdressed musicians. English singers Marc Bolan (1947–1977) and David ◊Bowie and the band Roxy Music (1970–83) pioneered glam rock in the early 1970s.

gland specialized organ of the body that manufactures and secretes enzymes, hormones, or other chemicals. In animals, glands vary in size from small (for example, tear glands) to large (for example, the pancreas), but in plants they are always small, and may consist of a single cell. Some glands discharge their products internally, ◊endocrine glands, and others, ◊exocrine glands, externally.

glandular fever or ***infectious mononucleosis*** viral disease characterized at onset by fever and painfully swollen lymph nodes; there may also be digestive upset, sore throat, and skin rashes. Lassitude persists for months or even years, and recovery can be slow. It is caused by the Epstein–Barr virus.

Glasgow city and administrative headquarters of former region of Strathclyde, Scotland (1975–96), and, from 1996, of local authority Glasgow City
population (1996 est) 618,400
industries engineering; chemicals; printing; whisky distilling and blending; brewing; electronics; textiles; shipbuilding
features buildings include the 12th-century cathedral of St Mungo; the Cross Steeple (part of the historic Tolbooth); the universities of Glasgow, established 1451 (present buildings constructed 1868–70) and Strathclyde, established 1964; the Royal Exchange; the Stock Exchange; Kelvingrove Art Gallery (Impressionist collection); the Glasgow School of Art, designed by C R ◊Mackintosh; the Burrell Collection at Pollock Park, bequeathed by shipping magnate William Burrell (1861–1958); Mitchell Library; 19th-century Greek Revival buildings designed by Alexander Thomson.

Glasgow City local authority of Scotland created 1996 (*see United Kingdom map*).

glasnost (Russian 'openness') Soviet leader Mikhail ◊Gorbachev's policy of liberalizing various aspects of Soviet life, such as introducing greater freedom of expression and information and opening up relations with Western countries. *Glasnost* was introduced and adopted by the Soviet government 1986. ▷ *See feature on pp. 1090–1091.*

glass transparent or translucent substance that is physically neither a solid nor a liquid. Although glass is easily shattered, it is one of the strongest substances known. It is made by fusing certain types of sand (silica); this fusion occurs naturally in volcanic glass (see ◊obsidian).

In the industrial production of common types of glass, the type of sand used, the particular chemicals added to it (for example, lead, potassium, barium), and refinements of technique determine the type of glass produced. Types of glass include: soda glass; flint glass, used in cut-crystal ware; optical glass; stained glass; heat-resistant glass; and glasses that exclude certain ranges of the light spectrum. Blown glass is either blown individually from molten glass (using a tube up to 1.5 m/4.5 ft long), as in the making of expensive crafted glass, or blown automatically into a mould – for example, in the manufacture of light bulbs and bottles; pressed glass is simply pressed into moulds, for jam jars, cheap vases, and light fittings; while sheet glass, for windows, is made by putting the molten glass through rollers to form a 'ribbon', or by floating molten glass on molten tin in the 'float glass' process; ◊fibreglass is made from fine glass fibres. Metallic glass is produced by treating alloys so that they take on the properties of glass while retaining the malleability and conductivity characteristic of metals.

Glass Philip 1937– . US composer. As a student of Nadia Boulanger, he was strongly influenced by Indian music; his work is characterized by repeated rhythmic figures that are continually expanded and modified. His compositions include the operas *Einstein on the Beach* 1976, *Akhnaten* 1984, *The Making of the Representative for Planet 8* 1988, and the *'Low' Symphony* 1992 on themes from David Bowie's *Low* album.

glass-reinforced plastic (GRP) a plastic material strengthened by glass fibres, sometimes erroneously called ◊fibreglass. Glass-reinforced plastic is a favoured material for boat hulls and for the bodies and some structural components of performance cars; it is also used in the manufacture of passenger cars.

Glastonbury market town in Somerset, England, on the river Brue; population (1991) 7,750. There is light industry and tourism. Nearby are two excavated lake villages thought to have been occupied for about 150 years before the Romans came to Britain. Glastonbury Tor, a hill with a ruined church tower, rises to 159 m/522 ft.

The first church on the site was traditionally founded in the 1st century by Joseph of Arimathea. Legend has it that he brought the Holy Grail to Glastonbury. The ruins of the Benedictine abbey built in the 10th and 11th centuries by Dunstan and his followers were excavated 1963 and the site of the grave of King Arthur and Queen Guinevere was thought to have been identified. One of Europe's largest pop festivals is held outside Glastonbury most years in June.

Glauber Johann Rudolf 1604–1670. German chemist who about 1625 discovered the salt known variously as Glauber's salt and '*sal mirabile*' (sodium sulphate). He made his living selling patent medicines and used the salt to treat almost any complaint.

Glauber's salt crystalline sodium sulphate decahydrate $Na_2SO_4.10H_2O$, produced by the action of sulphuric acid on common salt. It melts at 87.8°F/31°C; the latent heat stored as it solidifies makes it a convenient thermal energy store. It is used in medicine as a laxative.

glaucoma condition in which pressure inside the eye (intraocular pressure) is raised abnormally as excess fluid accumulates. It occurs when the normal outflow of fluid within the chamber of the eye (aqueous humour) is interrupted. As pressure rises, the optic nerve suffers irreversible damage, leading to a reduction in the field of vision and, ultimately, loss of eyesight.

The most common type, ***chronic glaucoma***, cannot be cured, but, in many cases, it is controlled by drug therapy. Laser treatment often improves drainage for a time; surgery to create an artificial channel for fluid to leave the eye offers more long-term relief. ***Acute glaucoma*** is a medical emergency and treatment is required urgently since damage to the optic nerve begins within hours of onset.

glaze transparent vitreous coating for pottery and porcelain, which gives the object a shiny, protective finish and helps to keep it from leaking and chipping. Glaze is applied by dipping a formed ceramic body into it or by painting onto the surface. It is fixed by firing in a kiln. Different mineral glazes will combine chemically with different bodies (according to the minerals present in the clay). Glazed pottery is first known from the mid-to late-Neolithic in Egypt, where glass was first made.

Gleiwicz (now ***Gliwice***, Poland) small German town on the border with Poland about 130 km/80 mi NW of Kraków; site of a 'provocation' engineered by Germany Aug 1939 to provide an excuse for the invasion of Poland.

Glencoe glen in southern Scotland (modern ◊Strathclyde Region), where members of the Macdonald clan were massacred on 13 Feb 1692. John Campbell, Earl of Breadalbane, was the chief instigator. It is now a winter sports area.

Glendower Owen c. 1359–c. 1416. (Welsh ***Owain Glyndwr***) Welsh nationalist leader of a successful revolt against the English in N Wales, who defeated Henry IV in three campaigns 1400–02, although Wales was reconquered 1405–13.

Gleneagles glen in Tayside, Scotland, famous for its golf course and for the Gleneagles Agreement, formulated 1977 at the Gleneagles Hotel by Commonwealth heads of government, that 'every practical step (should be taken) to discourage contact or competition by their nationals' with South Africa, in opposition to apartheid.

Glenn John Herschel, Jr 1921– . US astronaut and politician. On 20 February 1962, he became the first American to orbit the Earth, doing so three times in the Mercury spacecraft *Friendship 7*, in a flight lasting 4hr 55min. After retiring from ◊NASA, he was elected to the US Senate as a Democrat from Ohio 1974; re-elected 1980 and 1986. In 1998 he became the oldest man in space at 77, on a short flight aboard the space shuttle *Discovery*.

gliding the art of using air currents to fly unpowered aircraft. Technically, gliding involves the gradual loss of altitude; gliders designed for soaring flight (utilizing air rising up a cliff face or hill, warm air rising as a thermal above sun-heated ground, and so on) are known as sailplanes.
soaring There are three main methods of gaining height after launch: air currents, thermals, and thunderstorms. Air currents follow the contours of the land below them, and though in relation to the air itself the sailplane is losing height, the wind blowing up the side of a hill may enable it to gain more height than it is losing. By circling in a thermal, the glider can soar upwards for many hundreds of metres. By using the ascending currents in or near thunderstorms even greater heights can be attained.
long cross-country flights These are usually accomplished by the use of thermals. The glider first gains height in a thermal, then glides, gradually losing height, to the next thermal, where the process is repeated. By this method, which requires great skill and judgement of weather conditions, sailplanes may fly several hundred kilometres.
launching Launching may be by rubber catapult from a hilltop, or by aircraft tow (the towing cable is released by the glider pilot when sufficient height has been gained). Once in the air, speed is maintained by depressing the nose and thus losing height in relation to the surrounding air.
history Gliding played an important part in the development of ◊flight. Pioneers include George Cayley (1773–1857), Otto ◊Lilienthal, Octave Chanute (1832–1910), and the ◊Wright brothers, the last-named perfecting gliding technique in 1902.

Glinka Mikhail Ivanovich 1804–1857. Russian composer. He broke away from the prevailing Italian influence and turned to Russian folk music as the inspiration for his opera *A Life for the Tsar* (originally *Ivan Susanin*) 1836. His later works include the opera *Ruslan and Lyudmila* 1842 and the instrumental fantasia *Kamarinskaya* 1848.

global positioning system (GPS) US satellite-based navigation system, a network of satellites in six orbits, each circling the Earth once every 24 hours. Each satellite sends out a continuous time signal, plus an identifying signal. To fix position, a user needs to be within range of four satellites, one to provide a reference signal and three to provide directional bearings. The user's receiver can then calculate the position from the difference in time between receiving the signals from each satellite.

global warming imminent climate change that is attributed to the ◊greenhouse effect. Greenhouse gases are warming the Earth's atmosphere and disastrous effects are predicted. These include a rise in global sea level, and resulting flooding of low-lying areas; fluctuations in temperature and precipitation, with droughts, heat waves, fires, and flooding; and the melting of mountain glaciers.

A 1995 United Nations summit in Berlin agreed to take action to reduce gas emissions. Delegates at the summit, from more than 120 countries, approved a two-year negotiating process aimed at

'All the world over, I will back the masses against the classes.'

William Gladstone
Speech in Liverpool
28 June 1886

Globe Theatre The galleries of the new Globe Theatre, London, which opened in 1997. It was built as a replica of the 17th-century theatre where many of Shakespeare's plays were originally performed. *Corbis*

setting specific targets for reducing greenhouse gases after the year 2000. A 1997 UN conference held in Kyoto, Japan, agreed that emissions should be cut by 5.2% of 1990 levels by 2012. ▷*See feature on pp. 858–859.*

Globe Theatre 17th-century London theatre, octagonal and open to the sky, near Bankside, Southwark, where many of Shakespeare's plays were performed by Richard Burbage and his company. Built 1599 by Cuthbert Burbage, it was burned down 1613 after a cannon, fired during a performance of *Henry VIII*, set light to the thatch. It was rebuilt in 1614 but pulled down in 1644. The site was rediscovered Oct 1989 near the remains of the contemporaneous Rose Theatre.

In August 1996 the reconstructed Globe Theatre was opened to the public, with a performance of Shakespeare's *The Two Gentlemen of Verona*, the first stage production to be held on the site of the Elizabethan theatre in more than 380 years.

globular cluster spherical or near-spherical ◊star cluster containing from approximately 10,000 to millions of stars. More than a hundred globular clusters are distributed in a spherical halo around our Galaxy. They consist of old stars, formed early in the Galaxy's history. Globular clusters are also found around other galaxies.

glockenspiel percussion instrument of light metal keys mounted on a carrying frame for use in military bands or on a standing frame for use in an orchestra (in which form it resembles a small xylophone or celesta).

glomerulus in the kidney, the cluster of blood capillaries at the threshold of the renal tubule, or nephron, responsible for filtering out the fluid that passes down the tubules and ultimately becomes urine. In the human kidney there are approximately one million tubules, each possessing its own glomerulus.

Glomma river in Norway, 570 km/350 mi long. The largest river in Scandinavia, it flows into the Skagerrak (an arm of the North Sea) at Fredrikstad.

Glorious Revolution in British history, the events surrounding the removal of James II from the throne and his replacement by Mary, his daughter, and William of Orange as joint sovereigns in 1689. James had become increasingly unpopular on account of his unconstitutional behaviour and Catholicism. Various elements in England, including seven prominent politicians, plotted to invite the Protestant William to invade. Arriving at Torbay on 5 Nov 1688, William rapidly gained support and James was allowed to flee to France after the army deserted him. William and Mary then accepted a new constitutional settlement, the Bill of Rights 1689, which assured the ascendency of parliamentary power over sovereign rule.

'In this I have striven to be more painter and poet than musician.'

Christoph Willibald Gluck
On *Armide*, quoted in Neumann *History of Music* 1886

Glossinidae insect family containing the ◊tsetse fly. **classification** Glossinidae is in order Diptera, class Insecta, phylum Arthropoda.

glossolalia the gift of speaking in tongues, usually claimed to be unknown by the speaker and interpreted by someone else. It is referred to in the New Testament, Acts 2:4, and is believed to be a gift of the Holy Spirit. It is a distinct feature of many revivals, especially the ◊Pentecostal movement and the ◊charismatic movement in the 20th century.

glottis in medicine, narrow opening at the upper end of the larynx that contains the vocal cords.

Gloucester city, port, and administrative headquarters of Gloucestershire, England; population (1991) 101,600. Industries include the manufacture of aircraft components, agricultural machinery, and match-making. There was a Roman colony (Glevum) here at the end of the 1st century AD. The 11th–14th-century cathedral has a Norman nucleus and additions in every style of Gothic. The Museum of Advertising and Packaging was established 1984 by Robert Opie.

Gloucestershire county of SW England
area 2,640 sq km/1,019 sq mi (*see United Kingdom map*)
towns and cities Gloucester (administrative headquarters), Stroud, Cheltenham, Tewkesbury, Cirencester
features Cotswold Hills; river Severn and tributaries; Berkeley Castle, where Edward II was murdered; Prinknash Abbey, where pottery is made; Cotswold Farm Park, near Stow-on-the-Wold, which has rare and ancient breeds of farm animals; Tewkesbury Abbey
industries cereals, fruit, dairy products; engineering, coal in the Forest of Dean; timber
population (1991) 528,400
famous people Edward Jenner, John Keble, Gustav Holst.

glow-worm wingless female of some luminous beetles (fireflies) in the family Lampyridae. The luminous organs situated under the abdomen serve to attract winged males for mating. There are about 2,000 species, distributed worldwide.

Gluck Christoph Willibald von 1714–1787. German composer. He settled in Vienna as kapellmeister to Maria Theresa 1754. In 1762 his *Orfeo ed Euridice/Orpheus and Eurydice* revolutionized the 18th-century conception of opera by giving free scope to dramatic effect. *Orfeo* was followed by *Alceste/Alcestis* 1767 and *Paride ed Elena/Paris and Helen* 1770.

In 1762 his *Iphigénie en Aulide/Iphigenia in Aulis* 1774, produced in Paris, brought to a head the fierce debate over the future of opera in which Gluck's French style had the support of Marie Antoinette while his Italian rival Nicolò Piccinni (1728–1800) had the support of Madame Du Barry. With *Armide* 1777 and *Iphigénie en Tauride/Iphigenia in Tauris* 1779 Gluck won a complete victory over Piccinni.

glucose or ***dextrose*** or ***grape sugar*** $C_6H_{12}O_6$ monosaccharide sugar present in the blood and manufactured by green plants during ◊photosynthesis. The ◊respiration reactions inside cells involves the oxidation of glucose to produce ◊ATP, the 'energy molecule' used to drive many of the body's biochemical reactions. In humans and other vertebrates optimum blood glucose levels are maintained by the hormone ◊insulin.

glue type of ◊adhesive.

glue ear or ***secretory otitis media*** condition commonly affecting small children, in which the Eustachian tube, which normally drains and ventilates the middle ◊ear, becomes blocked with mucus. The resulting accumulation of mucus in the middle ear muffles hearing. It is the leading cause of deafness (usually transient) in children.

glue-sniffing or ***solvent misuse*** inhalation of the fumes from organic solvents of the type found in paints, lighter fuel, and glue, for their hallucinatory effects. As well as being addictive, solvents are dangerous for their effects on the user's liver, heart, and lungs. It is believed that solvents produce hallucinations by dissolving the cell membrane of brain cells, thus altering the way the cells conduct electrical impulses.

gluon in physics, a ◊gauge boson that carries the ◊strong nuclear force, responsible for binding quarks together to form the strongly interacting subatomic particles known as ◊hadrons. There are eight kinds of gluon. Gluons are believed to exist in balls ('glueballs') that behave as single particles.

gluten protein found in cereal grains, especially wheat and rye. Gluten enables dough to expand during rising. Sensitivity to gliadin, a type of gluten, gives rise to ◊coeliac disease.

glyceride ◊ester formed between one or more acids and glycerol (propan-1,2,3-triol). A glyceride is termed a mono-, di-, or triglyceride, depending on the number of hydroxyl groups from the glycerol that have reacted with the acids. Glycerides, chiefly

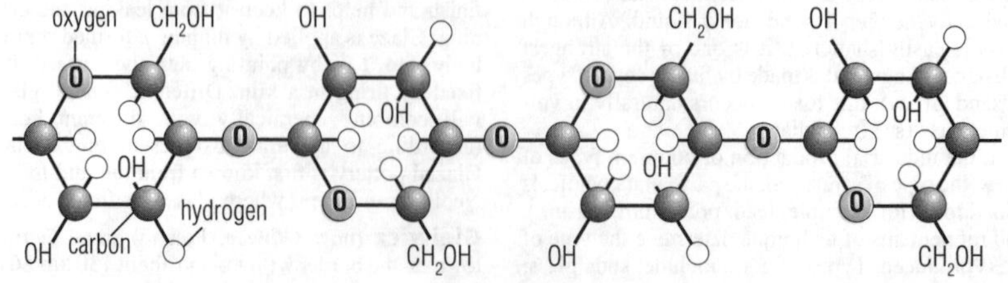

glycogen A typical polysaccharide molecule, glycogen (animal starch), is formed from linked glucose ($C_6H_{12}O_6$) molecules. A glycogen molecule has 100–1,000 linked glucose units.

triglycerides, occur naturally as esters of ◊fatty acids in plant oils and animal fats.

glycerol or ***glycerine*** or ***propan-1,2,3-triol*** $HOCH_2CH(OH)CH_2OH$ thick, colourless, odourless, sweetish liquid. It is obtained from vegetable and animal oils and fats (by treatment with acid, alkali, superheated steam, or an enzyme), or by fermentation of glucose, and is used in the manufacture of high explosives, in antifreeze solutions, to maintain moist conditions in fruits and tobacco, and in cosmetics.

glycine $CH_2(NH_2)COOH$ the simplest amino acid, and one of the main components of proteins. When purified, it is a sweet, colourless crystalline compound. Glycine was found 1994 in the star-forming region Sagittarius B2. The discovery is important because of its bearing on the origins of life on Earth.

glycogen polymer (a polysaccharide) of the sugar ◊glucose made and retained in the liver as a carbohydrate store, for which reason it is sometimes called animal starch. It is a source of energy when needed by muscles, where it is converted back into glucose by the hormone ◊insulin and metabolized.

glycol or ***ethylene glycol*** or ***ethane-1,2-diol*** $(CH_2OH)_2$ thick, colourless, odourless, sweetish liquid. It is used in antifreeze solutions, in the preparation of ethers and esters (used for explosives), as a solvent, and as a substitute for glycerol.

Glyndebourne site of an opera house in East Sussex, England, established 1934 by John Christie (1882–1962). Operas are staged at an annual summer festival and a touring company is also based there.

GMT abbreviation for ◊***Greenwich Mean Time***.

gnat small fly of the family Culicidae, the mosquitoes. The eggs are laid in water, where they hatch into wormlike larvae, which pass through a pupal stage to emerge as adult insects. Species include *Culex pipiens*, abundant in England; the carrier of malaria *Anopheles maculipennis*; and the banded mosquito *Aedes aegypti*, which transmits yellow fever.

gneiss coarse-grained ◊metamorphic rock, formed under conditions of increasing temperature and pressure, and often occurring in association with schists and granites. It has a foliated, laminated structure, consisting of thin bands of micas and/or amphiboles alternating with granular bands of quartz and feldspar. Gneisses are formed during regional metamorphism; ***paragneisses*** are derived from sedimentary rocks and ***orthogneisses*** from igneous rocks.

gnome in fairy tales, a small, mischievous spirit of the earth. The males are bearded, wear tunics and hoods, and often guard an underground treasure. The garden gnome, an ornamental representation of these spirits, was first brought from Germany to England 1850 by Charles Isham for his mansion Lamport Hall, Northamptonshire.

Gnosticism esoteric cult of divine knowledge (a synthesis of Christianity, Greek philosophy, Hinduism, Buddhism, and the mystery cults of the Mediterranean), which flourished during the 2nd and 3rd centuries and was a rival to, and influence on, early Christianity. The medieval French ◊Cathar heresy and the modern Mandean sect (in S Iraq) descend from Gnosticism.

Gnostic 4th-century codices discovered in Egypt in the 1940s include the Gospel of St Thomas (unconnected with the disciple) and the Gospel of Mary, probably originating about AD 135. Gnosticism envisaged the world as a series of emanations from the highest of several gods. The lowest emanation was an evil god (the demiurge) who created the material world as a prison for the divine sparks that dwell in human bodies. The Gnostics identified this evil creator with the God of the Old Testament, and saw the Adam and Eve story and the ministry of Jesus as attempts to liberate humanity from his dominion, by imparting divine secret wisdom.

GNP abbreviation for ◊***gross national product***.

gnu or ***wildebeest*** either of two species of African ◊antelope, genus *Connochaetes*, with a cowlike face, a beard and mane, and heavy curved horns in both sexes. The body is up to 1.3 m/4.2 ft at the shoulder and slopes away to the hindquarters. Vast herds move together on migration. ▷ *See feature on pp. 704–705.*

gnu The brindled gnu or blue wildebeest *Connochaetes taurinus* is known for the huge migratory herds which can be observed each year in the Serengeti–Masai Mara plains in E Africa. It is a close grazer, so relies heavily on the renewal of the long grasses through regular burning. *Premaphotos Wildlife*

go board game originating in China 3,000 years ago, and now the national game of Japan. It is played by placing small counters on a large grid. The object is to win territory and eventual superiority. It is far more complex and subtle than chess, the mathematical possibilities being 10 to the power of 720.

Goa state of India
area 3,700 sq km/1,428 sq mi
capital Panaji
population (1991) 1,169,800
features Portuguese colonial architecture; church with remains of St Francis Xavier
industries rice, pulses, cashew nuts, coconuts, ragi (a cereal), iron ore, tourism
history captured by the Portuguese 1510; the inland area was added in the 18th century. Goa was incorporated into India as a union territory with ◊Daman and Diu 1961 and became a state 1987

goat ruminant mammal of the genus *Capra* in the family Bovidae, closely related to the sheep. Both males and females have horns and beards. They are sure-footed animals, and feed on shoots and leaves more than on grass. Domestic varieties are descended from the scimitar-horned wild goat *C. aegagrus* and have been kept for over 9,000 years in S Europe and Asia. They are kept for milk or for mohair (the angora and cashmere). Wild species include the ibex *C. ibex* of the Alps, and markhor *C. falconeri* of the Himalayas, 1 m/3 ft high and with long twisted horns. The Rocky Mountain goat *Oreamnos americanus* is a 'goat antelope' and is not closely related to true goats.

Gobbi Tito 1913–1984. Italian baritone singer. His vibrant *bel canto* was allied to a resourceful talent for *verismo* characterization in Italian opera, notably Verdi and Puccini, and as Figaro in *Le Nozze di Figaro/The Marriage of Figaro*.

Gobelins French tapestry factory, originally founded as a dyeworks in Paris by Gilles and Jean Gobelin about 1450. The firm began to produce tapestries in the 16th century, and in 1662 the establishment was bought for Louis XIV by his minister Colbert. With the support of the French government, it continues to make tapestries.

Gobi Desert vast desert region of Central Asia in the independent state of Mongolia, and Inner Mongolia, China. It covers an area of 1,280,000 sq km/500,000 sq mi (800 km/500 mi north–south and 1,600 km/1,000 mi east–west) and lies on a high plateau 900–1,500 m/2,950–4,920 ft above sea level. It is mainly rocky, with shifting sands, and salt marshes at lower levels. ▷ *See feature on pp. 308–309.*

Gobind Singh 1666–1708. Indian religious leader, the tenth and last guru (teacher) of Sikhism, 1675–1708, and founder of the Sikh brotherhood known as the Khalsa. On his death, the Sikh holy book, the *Guru Granth Sahib*, replaced the line of human gurus as the teacher and guide of the Sikh community.

During a period of Sikh persecution, Gobind Singh asked those who were willing to die for their faith to join him. The first five willing to risk their lives were named the *panj pyares* 'faithful ones' by him and proclaimed the first members of the Khalsa. He also introduced the names Singh (lion) for male Sikhs, and Kaur (princess) for female Sikhs.

God the concept of a supreme being, a unique creative entity, basic to several monotheistic religions (for example Judaism, Christianity, Islam); in many polytheistic cultures (for example Norse, Roman, Greek), the term 'god' refers to a supernatural being who personifies the force behind an aspect of life (for example Neptune, Roman god of the sea). Since the 17th century, advances in science and the belief that the only valid statements were those verifiable by the senses have had a complex influence on the belief in God. (See also ◊monotheism, ◊polytheism, ◊deism, ◊theism, and ◊pantheism.)

Godard Jean-Luc 1930– . French film director. He was one of the leaders of ◊New Wave cinema. His works are often characterized by experimental editing techniques and an unconventional dramatic form. His films include *A bout de souffle/Breathless* 1959, *Vivre sa Vie/It's My Life* 1962, *Pierrot le fou* 1965, *Weekend* 1968, *Sauve qui peut (la vie)/Slow Motion* 1980, and *Je vous salue, Marie/Hail Mary* 1985.

Goddard Robert Hutchings 1882–1945. US rocket pioneer. His first liquid-fuelled rocket was launched at Auburn, Massachusetts, in 1926. By 1935 his rockets had gyroscopic control and carried cameras to record instrument readings. Two years later a Goddard rocket gained the world altitude record with an ascent of 3 km/1.9 mi.

Goddard Space Flight Center NASA installation at Greenbelt, Maryland, USA, responsible for the operation of NASA's unmanned scientific satellites, including the ◊Hubble Space Telescope. It is also home of the National Space Science Data centre, a repository of data collected by satellites.

'If God did not exist, it would be necessary to invent him.'

On God
Voltaire, letter 10 Nov 1770

Godiva or *Godgifu*, Lady c. 1040–1080. Wife of Leofric, Earl of Mercia (died 1057). Legend has it that her husband promised to reduce the heavy taxes on the people of Coventry if she rode naked through the streets at noon. The grateful citizens remained indoors as she did so, but 'Peeping Tom' bored a hole in his shutters and was struck blind.

He who seizes the right moment, / Is the right man.

Johann Wolfgang von Goethe
Faust

'God Save the King/Queen' British national anthem. The melody resembles a composition by John ◊Bull and similar words are found from the 16th century. In its present form it dates from the 1745 Jacobite Rebellion, when it was used as an anti-Jacobite Party song.

Godthaab (Greenlandic ***Nuuk***) capital and largest town of Greenland; population (1993) 12,200. It is a storage centre for oil and gas, and the chief industry is fish processing.

Godunov Boris Fyodorovich 1552–1605. Tsar of Russia from 1598, elected after the death of Fyodor I, son of Ivan the Terrible. Godunov's rule was marked by a strengthening of the Russian church. It was also the beginning of the Time of Troubles, a period of instability. He was assassinated by a pretender to the throne who professed to be Dmitri, a brother of Fyodor and the rightful heir. The legend that has grown up around this forms the basis of Pushkin's play *Boris Godunov* 1831 and Mussorgsky's opera of the same name 1874.

Godwin Earl of Wessex from 1020. He secured the succession to the throne in 1042 of ◊Edward the Confessor, to whom he married his daughter Edith, and whose chief minister he became. King Harold II was his son.

Godwin William 1756–1836. English philosopher, novelist, and father of the writer Mary Shelley. His *Enquiry Concerning Political Justice* 1793 advocated an anarchic society based on a faith in people's essential rationality. At first a Nonconformist minister, he later became an atheist. His first wife was Mary ◊Wollstonecraft.

Goebbels (Paul) Joseph 1897–1945. German Nazi leader. As minister of propaganda from 1933, he brought all cultural and educational activities under Nazi control and built up sympathetic movements abroad to carry on the 'war of nerves' against Hitler's intended victims. He was appointed special plenipotentiary for total war Aug 1944 and was granted powers to draft any able-bodied person in the Reich into war work. On the capture of Berlin by the Allies, he committed suicide.

Goering Hermann Wilhelm 1893–1946. Nazi leader, German field marshal from 1938. He was part of Hitler's inner circle, and with Hitler's rise to power was appointed commissioner for aviation from 1933 and built up the Luftwaffe (airforce). He built a vast economic empire in occupied Europe, but later lost favour and was expelled from the party in 1945. Tried at Nuremberg for war crimes, he poisoned himself before he could be executed.

Goering was appointed minister of the interior for Prussia 1933, which gave him full control of the police and security forces; he organized the Gestapo and had the first concentration camps built, then handed control to the SS to enable him to concentrate on developing the Luftwaffe. He supervised the four-year economic plan to ready the country for war 1935–39. The Luftwaffe's failure to break the British air defences was a serious blow to his reputation from which he never really recovered.

Goes Hugo van der c. 1440–1482. Flemish painter. Chiefly active in Ghent, he was one of the major figures of early Flemish art. His works were highly praised by Italian Renaissance artists, particularly his *Portinari Altarpiece* about 1475 (Uffizi, Florence), typically rich both in symbolism and naturalistic detail.

He began with small panels warmly coloured and detailed in the van ◊Eyck fashion, but from about 1474 he worked on a larger scale, using cool and translucent colour and often expressing great emotional intensity. The *Portinari Altarpiece* was executed for the agent of the Medici at Bruges, Tommaso Portinari. It made a great impression on the Florentines, and Goes was favourably mentioned by the historian Giorgio ◊Vasari. Other works are the *Adoration of the Magi* (Staatliche Museen, Berlin), *Death of the Virgin*, about 1480 (Musée Communale des Beaux Arts, Bruges), and *Monk Meditating* (Metropolitan Museum, New York).

A good picture is equivalent to a good deed.

Vincent van Gogh
Letter 1890

Goethe Johann Wolfgang von 1749–1832. German poet, novelist, dramatist, and scholar. He is generally considered the founder of modern German literature, and was the leader of the Romantic ◊*Sturm und Drang* movement. His masterpiece is the poetic play *Faust* 1808 and 1832. His other works include the partly autobiographical *Die Leiden des Jungen Werthers/The Sorrows of the Young Werther* 1774; the classical dramas *Iphigenie auf Tauris/Iphigenia in Tauris* 1787, *Egmont* 1788, and *Torquato Tasso* 1790; the *Wilhelm Meister* novels 1795–1829; the short novel *Die Wahlverwandschaften/Elective Affinities* 1809; and scientific treatises including *Farbenlehre/Treatise on Colour* 1810.

Gogh A self-portrait of Vincent van Gogh, titled *Portrait of the Artist. Image Select (UK) Ltd*

Goethe was born in Frankfurt-am-Main, and studied law. Inspired by Shakespeare, to whose work he was introduced by the critic J G von ◊Herder, he wrote the play *Götz von Berlichingen* 1773, heralding the *Sturm und Drang* movement. The inspiration for *Die Leiden des Jungen Werthers* came from an unhappy love affair. He took part in public life at the court of Duke Charles Augustus in Weimar 1775–86, and pursued his interests in scientific research. A year and a half spent in Italy 1786–88 was a period of great development for Goethe, when he outgrew the *Sturm und Drang* movement and worked towards the Greek ideal of calm and harmony.

The publication of *Wilhelm Meisters Lehrjahre/Wilhelm Meister's Apprenticeship* 1795–96 established Goethe's enduring fame throughout Europe. *Faust*, written in the intervals between other work, over a period of more than 50 years, reflects the evolution of Goethe's own thinking and character, from youth to age.

Gog and Magog in Old Testament prophecy, an enemy ruler and his followers who will do battle with Israel. The names appear in the New Testament in the prophecies of the end of time contained in the book of Revelation, 20:8–10, as two nations under the control of Satan. In later literature the names have been used as conventional representations of those who oppose the people of God.

Gogh Vincent (Willem) van 1853–1890. Dutch Post-Impressionist painter. He began painting in the 1880s, his early works often being sombre depictions of peasant life, such as *The Potato Eaters* 1885 (Van Gogh Museum, Amsterdam). Influenced by the Impressionists and by Japanese prints, he developed a freer style characterized by intense colour and expressive brushwork, as seen in his *Sunflowers* series 1888. His influence on modern art, particularly on Expressionism, has been immense.

His numerous works (over 800 paintings and 700 drawings) include still lifes, portraits (many self-portraits), and landscapes, such as *The Starry Night* 1889 (Museum of Modern Art, New York) and *Crows over Wheatfield* 1890 (Van Gogh Museum, Amsterdam). His most creative time was 1888 in Arles, Provence, in the company of the painter Paul Gauguin, when he produced views of the town and such pictures as *Orchard in Blossom* and *The Chair and Pipe*.

Gogol Nicolai Vasilyevich 1809–1852. Russian writer. His first success was a collection of stories, *Evenings on a Farm near Dikanka* 1831–32, followed by *Mirgorod* 1835. Later works include *Arabesques* 1835, the comedy play *The Inspector General* 1836, and the picaresque novel *Dead Souls* 1842, which satirizes Russian provincial society. He also wrote the short stories 'The Overcoat' and 'The Nose'.

Goh Chok Tong 1941– . Singapore politician, prime minister from 1990. A trained economist, Goh became a member of Parliament for the ruling People's Action Party 1976. Rising steadily through the party ranks, he was appointed deputy prime minister 1985, and subsequently chosen by the cabinet as Lee Kuan Yew's successor, first as prime minister and from 1992 also as party leader.

goitre enlargement of the thyroid gland seen as a swelling on the neck. It is most pronounced in simple goitre, which is caused by iodine deficiency. More common is toxic goitre or ◊hyperthyroidism, caused by overactivity of the thyroid gland.

Golan Heights (Arabic ***Jawlan***) plateau on the Syrian border with Israel, bitterly contested in the ◊Arab–Israeli Wars and annexed by Israel 14 Dec 1981. In the 1996 peace talks Syria insisted that Israel withdraw from the Golan Heights, following its capture 1967.

gold heavy, precious, yellow, metallic element; symbol Au, atomic number 79, relative atomic mass 197.0. It is unaffected by temperature changes and is highly resistant to acids. For manufacture, gold is alloyed with another strengthening metal (such as copper or silver), its purity being measured in ◊carats on a scale of 24.

Gold occurs naturally in veins, but following erosion it can be transported and redeposited. It has long been valued for its durability, malleability, and ductility, and its uses include dentistry and jewellery. As it will not corrode, it is also used in the manufacture of electric contacts for computers and other electrical devices.

Gold Coast former name for ◊Ghana, but historically the west coast of Africa from Cape Three Points to the Volta River, where alluvial gold is washed down. Portuguese and French navigators visited this coast in the 14th century, and a British trading settlement developed into the colony of the Gold Coast 1618. With its dependencies of Ashanti and Northern Territories plus the trusteeship territory of Togoland, it became Ghana 1957. The name is also used for many coastal resort areas – for example, in Florida, USA.

goldcrest smallest European bird, *Regulus regulus*, family Muscicapidae, order Passeriformes, about 9 cm/3.5 in long and weighing 5 g/0.011 lb. It is olive green, with a bright yellow streak across the crown, and is found throughout Europe.

Golden Age in classical mythology, the earliest period of human life, when human beings lived without labour and sorrow. This was followed by silver and bronze ages, the age of heroes, and the iron age of labour and strife. The term has since been applied to great periods of literature in national cultures: the late Republican and Augustan ages in Rome and the 17th century in France and Spain.

Golden Ass, The or *Metamorphoses* ◊picaresque adventure by the Roman writer Lucius Apuleius, written in Latin about AD 160, sometimes described as the world's first novel. Lucius,

goldcrest The smallest British bird, the goldcrest, weighs about 6 g (less than ¼ oz). It is widespread in Europe and Asia and builds its nest high up in trees.

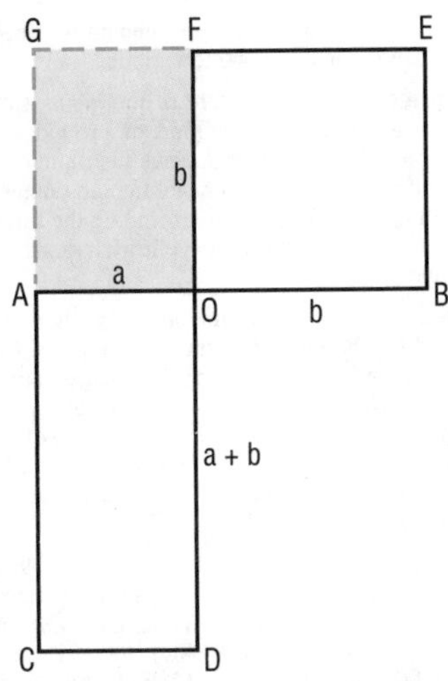

golden section The golden section is the ratio a:b, equal to 8:13. A golden rectangle is one, like that shaded in the picture, that has its length and breadth in this ratio. These rectangles are said to be pleasant to look at and have been used instinctively by artists in their pictures.

transformed into an ass, describes his exploits with a band of robbers, weaving into the narrative several ancient legends, including that of Cupid and Psyche.

Golden Fleece in Greek legend, the fleece of the winged ram Chrysomallus, which hung on an oak tree at Colchis and was guarded by a dragon. It was stolen by ◊Jason and the Argonauts.

Golden Horde the invading Mongol-Tatar army that first terrorized Europe from 1237 under the leadership of Batu Khan, a grandson of Genghis Khan. ◊Tamerlane broke their power 1395, and ◊Ivan III ended Russia's payment of tribute to them 1480.

golden section visually satisfying ratio, first constructed by the Greek mathematician ◊Euclid and used in art and architecture. It is found by dividing a line AB at a point O such that the rectangle produced by the whole line and one of the segments is equal to the square drawn on the other segment. The ratio of the two segments is about 8:13 or 1:1.618, and a rectangle whose sides are in this ratio is called a golden rectangle. The ratio of consecutive ◊Fibonacci numbers tends to the golden ratio.

goldfinch songbird *Carduelis carduelis*, family Fringillidae, order Passeriformes, found in Eurasia, N Africa, and North America. It is about 12 cm/4.5 in long and black, white, and red about the head, with gold and black wings.

goldfish fish *Carassius auratus* of the ◊carp family, found in E Asia. Greenish-brown in its natural state, it has for centuries been bred by the Chinese, taking on highly coloured and sometimes freakishly shaped forms. Goldfish can see a greater range of colours than any other animal tested.

Golding William (Gerald) 1911–1993. English novelist. His work is often principally concerned with the fundamental corruption and evil inherent in human nature. His first book, *Lord of the Flies* 1954, concerns the degeneration into savagery of a group of English schoolboys marooned on a Pacific island after an atomic war; it is a chilling allegory about the savagery lurking beneath the thin veneer of modern 'civilized' life. *Pincher Martin* 1956 is a study of greed and self-delusion. Later novels include *The Spire* 1964 and *Darkness Visible* 1979.

The Sea Trilogy, *Rites of Passage* 1980 (Booker Prize), *Close Quarters* 1987, and *Fire Down Below* 1989, tells the story of a voyage to Australia in Napoleonic times through the eyes of a callow young aristocrat. Nobel Prize for Literature 1983.

Goldoni Carlo 1707–1793. Italian dramatist. He wrote popular comedies for the Sant'Angelo theatre, which drew on the traditions of the ◊commedia dell'arte, *Il servitore di due padroni/The Servant of Two Masters* 1743, *Il bugiardo/The Liar* 1750, and *La locandiera/Mine Hostess* 1753. In 1761 he moved to Paris, where he directed the Italian theatre and wrote more plays, including *L'Eventail/The Fan* 1763.

gold rush large influx of gold prospectors to an area where gold deposits have recently been discovered. Cities such as Johannesburg, Melbourne, and San Francisco either originated or were considerably enlarged by gold rushes. Melbourne's population trebled from 77,000 to some 200,000 between 1851 and 1853.

Goldsmith Oliver 1728–1774. Irish writer. His works include the novel *The Vicar of Wakefield* 1766; the poem 'The Deserted Village' 1770; and the play *She Stoops to Conquer* 1773. In 1761 Goldsmith met Samuel ◊Johnson, and became a member of his circle. Johnson found a publisher for *The Vicar of Wakefield* to save Goldsmith from imprisonment for debt at the instigation of his landlady.

gold standard system under which a country's currency is exchangeable for a fixed weight of gold on demand at the central bank. It was almost universally applied 1870–1914, but by 1937 no single country was on the full gold standard. Britain abandoned the gold standard 1931; the USA abandoned it 1971. Holdings of gold are still retained because it is an internationally recognized commodity, which cannot be legislated upon or manipulated by interested countries.

Goldwyn Samuel. Adopted name of Schmuel Gelbfisz (Samuel Goldfish) 1882–1974. US film producer. Born in Poland, he emigrated to the USA 1896. He founded the Goldwyn Pictures Corporation 1917, which eventually merged into Metro-Goldwyn-Mayer (MGM) 1924, although he was not part of the deal. He remained an independent producer for many years, making classics such as *Wuthering Heights* 1939, *The Little Foxes* 1941, *The Best Years of Our Lives* 1946, and *Guys and Dolls* 1955. He was famed for his illogical aphorisms known as 'goldwynisms', for example 'Include me out'.

golf outdoor game in which a small rubber-cored ball is hit with a wooden- or iron-faced club into a series of holes using the least number of shots. On the first shot for each hole, the ball is hit from a tee, which elevates the ball slightly off the ground; subsequent strokes are played off the ground. Most courses have 18 holes and are approximately 5,500 m/6,000 yd in length. Golf developed in Scotland in the 15th century.

the hole Each hole is made up of distinct areas: the tee, from where players start at each hole; the green, a finely manicured area where the hole is located; the fairway, the grassed area between the tee and the green, not cut as finely as the green; and the rough, the perimeter of the fairway, which is left to grow naturally. Natural hazards such as trees, bushes, and streams make play more difficult, and there are additional hazards in the form of sand-filled bunkers and artificial lakes.

clubs Clubs consist of woods and irons, and are numbered according to the angle at which the face of the club is set (the higher the number, the more acute the angle; clubs with a straight face send the ball the furthest). Most players also carry a wedge, a faced iron set at a sharp acute angle with a deep flange, this being ideal for bunker play. All carry a putter for holing out on the greens; this is the only club that has a wide variety of shapes to suit individual styles.

stroke and match play Golf is played in two principal forms: stroke play (also known as medal play) and match play. In stroke play the lowest aggregate score for a round determines the winner. Play may be more than one round, in which case the aggregate score for all rounds counts. In match play, the object is to win holes by scoring less than one's opponent(s).

handicaps Golf's handicap system allows for golfers of all levels to compete on equal terms. Players are handicapped according to the number of strokes they take for a round; for example, a player who took 83 shots to go round a course with a par (standard score) of 71 would be given a handicap of 12. Handicapping enables players of different standards to compete on even terms by conceding or receiving strokes. In all championships and in all major tournaments, however, competitors play level.

competitions The major golfing events are the British Open (first held 1860), US Open (first held 1895), US Masters (first held 1934), and US Professional Golfers Association (PGA) (first held 1916). Other events include the World Match-Play Championship, and the British PGA. *See list of tables on p. 1177.*

Golding English novelist William Golding. He came to sudden fame 1954 with *The Lord of the Flies*, which describes the descent into savagery of a group of schoolboys marooned on an island. Though essentially religious, Golding's works are sombre allegories on the human capacity for self-deception and evil. *Topham*

Goldwyn US film producer Sam Goldwyn became one of the most powerful figures in Hollywood during its golden age. Many stars, including Rudolf Valentino, Ronald Colman, Gary Cooper, Danny Kaye, and David Niven, began their screen careers in Goldwyn's studios. *Sachem*

Golgi Camillo 1843–1926. Italian cell biologist who produced the first detailed knowledge of the fine structure of the nervous system. His use of silver salts in staining cells proved so effective in showing up the components and fine processes of nerve cells that even the synapses – tiny gaps between the cells – were visible. The Golgi apparatus was first described by him 1898. He shared the 1906 Nobel Prize for Physiology or Medicine with Santiago Ramón y Cajal, who followed up Golgi's work.

Golgi apparatus or ***Golgi body*** stack of flattened membranous sacs found in the cells of ◊eukaryotes. Many molecules travel through the Golgi apparatus on their way to other organelles or to the endoplasmic reticulum. Some are modified or assembled inside the sacs.

Goliath in the Old Testament, a champion of the ◊Philistines, who was said to have been slain by a stone from a sling by the young ◊David in single combat in front of their opposing armies.

'The man recover'd of the bite, / The dog it was that died.'

OLIVER GOLDSMITH
'Elegy on the Death of a Mad Dog'

‘There is really no such thing as Art. There are only artists.’

E H Gombrich
The Story of Art, introduction 1950

Gombrich Ernst (Hans Joseph) 1909– . Austrian-born British art historian. One of his abiding concerns is the problems of content and symbolism in painting. His studies are deeply analytical and make connections with other fields, such as the psychology of perception. Among his works are *The Story of Art* 1950 (revised 1995), written for a popular audience, and *Art and Illusion* 1959. He was director of the University of London Warburg Institute 1959–76.

Gómez Juan Vicente 1864–1935. Venezuelan dictator 1908–35. The discovery of oil during his rule attracted US, British, and Dutch oil interests and made Venezuela one of the wealthiest countries in Latin America. Gómez amassed a considerable personal fortune and used his well-equipped army to dominate the civilian population.

Gomułka Władysław 1905–1982. Polish communist politician, party leader 1943–48 and 1956–70. He introduced moderate reforms, including private farming and tolerance for Roman Catholicism. He was forced to resign the party leadership 1970 after sudden food-price rises induced a wave of strikes and riots.

gonad the part of an animal's body that produces the sperm or egg cells (ova) required for sexual reproduction. The sperm-producing gonad is called a ◊testis, and the egg-producing gonad is called an ◊ovary.

gonadotrophin any hormone that supports and stimulates the function of the gonads (sex glands); some gonadotrophins are used as ◊fertility drugs.

Goncharov Ivan Alexandrovitch 1812–1891. Russian novelist. His first novel, *A Common Story* 1847, was followed 1858 by his humorous masterpiece *Oblomov*, which satirized the indolent Russian landed gentry.

Goncourt, de Edmond (1822–1896) and Jules (1830–1870) French writers. The brothers collaborated in producing a compendium, *L'Art du XVIIIème siècle/18th-Century Art* 1859–75, historical studies, and a *Journal* published 1887–96 that depicts French literary life of their day. Edmond de Goncourt founded the Académie Goncourt, opened 1903, which awards an annual prize, the Prix Goncourt, to the author of the best French novel of the year. Equivalent to the Commonwealth Booker Prize in prestige, it has a monetary value of only 50 francs.

Gond a heterogenous people of central India, about half of whom speak unwritten languages belonging to the Dravidian family. The rest speak Indo-European languages. There are over 4 million Gonds, most of whom live in Madhya Pradesh, E Maharashtra, and N Andra Pradesh, although some live in Orissa. Traditionally, many Gonds practised shifting cultivation; agriculture and livestock remain the basis of the economy. Gond beliefs embrace Hinduism as well as a range of more ancient gods and spirits.

Gondwanaland or ***Gondwana*** southern landmass formed 200 million years ago by the splitting of the single world continent ◊Pangaea. (The northern landmass was ◊Laurasia.) It later fragmented into the continents of South America, Africa, Australia, and Antarctica, which then drifted slowly to their present positions. The baobab tree found in both Africa and Australia is a relic of this ancient land mass.

gonorrhoea common sexually transmitted disease arising from infection with the bacterium *Neisseria gonorrhoeae*, which causes inflammation of the genito-urinary tract. Infected men experience pain while urinating and a discharge from the penis; infected women often have no external symptoms. Untreated gonorrhoea carries the threat of sterility to both sexes; there is also the risk of blindness in a baby born to an infected mother. The condition is treated with antibiotics.

‘This man has a nice smile, but he has got iron teeth.’

On Mikhail Gorbachev
Andrei Gromyko, speech 1985

González Julio 1876–1942. Spanish sculptor and painter. He established the use of wrought and welded iron as an expressive sculptural medium. Influenced by the Cubism of his close friend Pablo Picasso, and also by Russian Constructivism and Surrealism, he created open, linear designs using rods and bands of iron, as in *Woman with a Mirror* about 1936–37 (IVAM, Centre Julio González, Valencia). From the mid-1930s he produced moulded, fragmented torsos from sheet iron and naturalistic, commemorative sculptures of Spanish peasant women in revolt, for example *Montserrat* 1936–37 (Stedelijk Museum, Amsterdam).

González Márquez Felipe 1942– . Spanish socialist politician, leader of the Socialist Workers' Party (PSOE), prime minister 1982–96. His party was re-elected 1989 and 1993, but his popularity suffered as a result of economic upheaval and revelations of corruption within his administration. During 1995 he was himself briefly under investigation for alleged involvement with antiterrorist death squads in the 1980s, and in 1996 he and his party were narrowly defeated in the general elections.

Gooch Graham Alan 1953– . English cricketer. Gooch played for Essex, and became England's leading run-scorer in Test cricket when he overtook David Gower's record at the Oval 1993. He made his first-class debut 1973 and his England debut 1975. Banned for three years for captaining an unofficial England side to South Africa 1982, he went on to captain England on 34 occasions. He scored a world record match total of 456 runs against India 1990. In 1993 he joined the select band of cricketers to reach the milestone of 100 centuries. He retired from Test cricket 1995 having played in 118 Test matches.

Good Friday in the Christian church, the Friday before Easter, which is observed in memory of the Crucifixion (the death of Jesus on the cross).

Goodman Benny (Benjamin David) 1909–1986. US clarinetist. He was nicknamed the ‘King of Swing’ for the new jazz idiom he introduced with arranger Fletcher Henderson (1897–1952). In 1934 he founded his own 12-piece band, which combined the expressive improvisatory style of black jazz with disciplined precision ensemble playing. He is associated with such numbers as ‘Blue Skies’ and ‘Let's Dance’.

Goodman Paul 1911–1972. US writer and social critic whose many works (novels, plays, essays) express his anarchist, anti-authoritarian ideas. He studied young offenders in *Growing up Absurd* 1960.

Goodwood racecourse NE of Chichester, West Sussex, England. Its races include the Goodwood Cup and Sussex Stakes, held July/Aug. There was a motor-racing track there 1948–66, and in 1982 the road races of the world cycling championships were staged there.

Goodyear Charles 1800–1860. US inventor who developed rubber coating 1837 and vulcanized rubber 1839, a method of curing raw rubber to make it strong and elastic.

goose aquatic bird of several genera (especially *Anser*) in the family Anatidae, which also includes ducks and swans, order Anseriformes. There are about 12 species, which occur in the Nearctic and Palaearctic regions. Both genders are similar in appearance: they have short, webbed feet, placed nearer the front of the body than in other members of the order Anatidae, and the beak is slightly hooked. They feed entirely on grass and plants, build nests of grass and twigs on the ground, and lay 5–9 eggs, white or cream-coloured, according to species.

The ***barnacle goose*** *Branta leucopsis* is about 60 cm/2 ft long, and weighs about 2 kg/4.5 lb. It is black and white, marbled with blue and grey, and the beak is black. The ***bean goose*** *A. fabalis* is a grey species of European wild goose with an orange or yellow and black bill. It breeds in northern Europe and Siberia. The ***Brent goose*** *Branta bernicla* is a small goose, black or brown, white, and grey in colour. It is almost completely herbivorous, feeding on eel grass (Zostera) and algae. The ***greylag goose*** *Anser anser* is the ancestor of domesticated geese. Other species include the ***Canada goose*** *Branta canadensis* (common to North America and introduced into Europe in the 18th century), the ***pink-footed goose*** *A. brachyrhynchus*, the ***white-fronted goose*** *A. albifrons*, and the ***ne-ne*** or ***Hawaiian goose*** *Branta sandvicensis*.

gooseberry edible fruit of *Ribes uva-crispa*, a low-growing bush related to the currant. It is straggling in its growth, bearing straight sharp spines in groups of three, and rounded, lobed leaves. The flowers are green, and hang on short stalks. The fruits are globular, hairy, and generally green, but there are reddish and white varieties.

gopher burrowing rodent of the genus *Citellus*, family Sciuridae. It is a kind of ground squirrel represented by some 20 species distributed across W North America and Eurasia. Length ranges from 15 cm/6 in to 90 cm/16 in, excluding the furry tail; colouring ranges from plain yellowish to striped and spotted species.

Gopher (derived from ***go for***; alternatively, named for the mascot of the University of Minnesota, where it was invented) menu-based server on the ◊Internet that indexes resources and retrieves them according to user choice via any one of several built-in methods such as FTP (File Transfer Protocol) or Telnet. Gopher servers can also be accessed via the ◊World Wide Web.

Gorbachev Mikhail Sergeyevich 1931– . Soviet president, in power 1985–91. He was a member of the Politburo from 1980. As general secretary of the Communist Party (CPSU) 1985–91 and president of the Supreme Soviet 1988–91, he introduced liberal reforms at home (◊*perestroika* and ◊*glasnost*), proposed the introduction of multiparty democracy, and attempted to halt the arms race abroad. He became head of state 1989. He was awarded the Nobel Peace Prize 1990.

Gorbachev radically changed the style of Soviet leadership, encountering opposition to the pace of change from both conservatives and radicals, but failed both to realize the depth of hostility this aroused against him in the CPSU and to distance himself from the Party. His international reputation suffered in the light of harsh state repression of nationalist demonstrations in the Baltic states. Following an abortive coup attempt by hardliners Aug 1991, international acceptance of independence for the Baltic states, and accelerated moves towards independence in other republics, Gorbachev's power base as Soviet president was weakened and in Dec 1991 he resigned. He contested the 1996 Russian presidential elections, but attracted only 0.5% of the vote. ▷ *See feature on pp. 1090–1091.*

Gordian knot in Greek mythology, the knot tied by King Gordius of Phrygia that – so an oracle revealed – could be unravelled only by the future conqueror of Asia. According to tradition, Alexander the Great, unable to untie it, cut it with his sword 334 BC.

Gordimer Nadine 1923– . South African novelist, an opponent of apartheid and censorship. Her finest writing is characterized by beautiful evocations of the rural Transvaal, effective renderings of sexuality, and interacting characters from different racial backgrounds. Her first novel, *The Lying Days*, appeared 1953; her other works include *The Conservationist* 1974, the volume of short stories *A Soldier's Embrace* 1980, *July's People* 1981, and *Why Haven't You Written?* 1992. Nobel Prize for Literature 1991.

Gordon Charles George 1833–1885. British general sent to Khartoum in the Sudan 1884 to rescue English garrisons that were under attack by the ◊Mahdi, Muhammad Ahmed; he was himself besieged for ten months by the Mahdi's army. A relief expedition arrived 28 Jan 1885 to find that Khartoum had been captured and Gordon killed two days before.

Gore Al(bert) 1948– . US politician, vice president from 1993. A Democrat, he became a member of the House of Representatives 1977–79, and was senator for Tennessee 1985–92. He is on the conservative wing of the party, but holds liberal views on such matters as women's rights, environmental issues, and abortion.

gorge narrow steep-sided valley (or canyon) that may or may not have a river at the bottom. A gorge may be formed as a ◊waterfall retreats upstream, eroding away the rock at the base of a river valley; or it may be caused by rejuvenation, when a river begins to cut downwards into its channel once again (for example, in response to a fall in sea level). Gorges are common in limestone country.

Gorgon in Greek mythology, any of three sisters, Stheno, Euryale, and Medusa, who had wings, claws, enormous teeth, and snakes for hair. Medusa, the only one who was mortal, was killed by ◊Perseus, but even in death her head was still so frightful that it turned the onlooker to stone.

gorilla largest of the apes, *Gorilla gorilla*, found in the dense forests of West Africa and mountains of central Africa. The male stands about 1.8 m/6 ft and weighs about 200 kg/450 lbs. Females are about half the size. The body is covered with blackish hair, silvered on the back in older males. Gorillas live in family groups; they are vegetarian, highly intelligent, and will attack only in self-defence. They are dwindling in numbers, being shot for food by some local people, or by poachers taking young for zoos, but protective measures are having some effect.

Gorillas construct stoutly built nests in trees for overnight use. The breast-beating movement, once thought to indicate rage, actually signifies only nervous excitement. There are three races – western lowland, eastern lowland, and mountain gorillas.

Göring Hermann. German spelling of ◊Goering, Nazi leader.

Gorky (Russian *Gor'kiy*) name 1932–90 of ◊Nizhni-Novgorod, a city in central Russia.

Gorky Arshile. Adopted name of Vosdanig Manoūg Adoian 1904–1948. Armenian-born US painter. He painted in several Modernist styles before developing a semi-abstract surreal style, using organic shapes and vigorous brushwork. His works, such as *The Liver Is the Cock's Comb* 1944 (Albright-Knox Art Gallery, Buffalo), are noted for their sense of fantasy. Among Gorky's major influences were Picasso, Kandinsky, Miró, and Cézanne, and he in turn influenced the emerging Abstract Expressionists. He lived in the USA from 1920.

Gorky Maxim. Pen name of Alexei Maximovich Peshkov 1868–1936. Russian writer. Born in Nizhni-Novgorod (named Gorky 1932–90 in his honour), he was exiled 1906–13 for his revolutionary principles. His works, which include the play *The Lower Depths* 1902 and the memoir *My Childhood* 1913–14, combine realism with optimistic faith in the potential of the industrial proletariat.

gorse or ***furze*** or ***whin*** Eurasian genus of plants *Ulex*, family Leguminosae, consisting of thorny shrubs with spine-shaped leaves densely clustered along the stems, and bright-yellow, coconut-scented flowers. The gorse bush *U. europaeus* is an evergreen and grows on heaths and sandy areas throughout W Europe.

goshawk or ***northern goshawk*** woodland hawk *Accipiter gentilis*, order Falconiformes, similar in appearance to the peregrine falcon, but with shorter wings and legs. It is used in falconry. The male is much smaller than the female. It is ash grey on the upper part of the body and white underneath. The tail has dark bands across it.

Gospel (Middle English 'good news') in the New Testament generally, the message of Christian salvation; in particular the four written accounts of the life of Jesus by Matthew, Mark, Luke, and John. Although the first three give approximately the same account or synopsis (thus giving rise to the name 'Synoptic Gospels'), their differences from John have raised problems for theologians.

The so-called fifth Gospel, or Gospel of St Thomas (not connected with the disciple Thomas), is a 2nd-century collection of 114 sayings of Jesus. It was found in a Coptic translation contained in a group of 13 papyrus codices, discovered in Upper Egypt 1945, which may have formed the library of a Gnostic community (see ◊Gnosticism).

Gorky The Russian writer Maxim Gorky. He worked to support himself from the age of eight, and was self-educated. After a period of exile he returned to the Soviet Union 1928 as an ardent supporter of the government, and became the first president of the Union of Soviet Writers 1934. *Corbis*

gospel music vocal music developed in the 1920s in the black Baptist churches of the US South from spirituals. Outstanding among the early gospel singers was Mahalia Jackson, but from the 1930s to the mid-1950s male harmony groups predominated, among them the Dixie Hummingbirds, the Swan Silvertones, and the Five Blind Boys of Mississippi. Many of those classic gospel groups continued to perform into the 1990s, though with altered line-ups. The Edwin Hawkins Singers (formed 1967) had a pop hit 1969 with the hymn 'Oh Happy Day'.

The founder of gospel music is Thomas A Dorsey (1899–1993) from Georgia, who from 1932 wrote hundreds of gospel compositions, including 'Peace in the Valley' 1937 and 'Take My Hand, Precious Lord'. White gospel, or country gospel, includes religious ballads popular in bluegrass.

Gossaert Jan. Flemish painter, known as ◊Mabuse.

Göteborg (German ***Gothenburg***) port and industrial city (ships, vehicles, chemicals) on the west coast of Sweden, at the mouth of the Göta River; population (1994 est) 444,600. It is Sweden's second largest city and is linked with Stockholm by the Göta Canal (built 1832). The city was founded 1619 by King Gustavus Adolphus. There is a cathedral (1633) and a technical university (1829).

Goth E Germanic people who settled near the Black Sea around AD 2nd century. There are two branches, the eastern Ostrogoths and the western Visigoths. The ***Ostrogoths*** were conquered by the Huns 372. They regained their independence 454 and under ◊Theodoric the Great conquered Italy 488–93; they disappeared as a nation after the Byzantine emperor ◊Justinian I reconquered Italy 535–55.

The ***Visigoths*** migrated to Thrace. Under ◊Alaric they raided Greece and Italy 395–410, sacked Rome, and established a kingdom in S France. Expelled from there by the Franks, they established a Spanish kingdom which lasted until the Moorish conquest of 711.

Gothic architecture style of architecture that flourished in Europe from the mid-12th century to the end of the 15th century. It is characterized by the vertical lines of tall pillars and spires, greater height in interior spaces, the pointed arch, rib vaulting, and the flying buttress.

Gothic architecture originated in Normandy and Burgundy in the 12th century. Essentially the style of the Catholic countries of Europe, including Hungary and Poland, it attained its highest excellence in France and England. It developed forms on a regional basis, often of great complexity and beauty, and was used for all secular buildings as well as for cathedrals, churches, and monasteries. The style prevailed in W Europe until the 16th century when Classic architecture was revived.

France In France, Gothic architecture may be divided into four periods. Early Gothic (1130–90) saw the introduction of ogival (pointed) vaults, for example Notre Dame, Paris (begun 1160). In lancet Gothic (1190–1240) pointed arches were tall and narrow, as in Chartres Cathedral (begun 1194), and Bourges Cathedral (begun 1209). Rayonnant Gothic (1240–1350) takes its name from the series of chapels that radiate from the cathedral apse, as in Sainte Chapelle, Paris, 1226–30. Late Gothic or the Flamboyant style (1350–1520) is exemplified in St Gervais, Paris.

Italy In Italy Gothic had a classical basis, characterized by vast spans with simple arches on a basilican plan. A notable example of Italian Gothic is Milan Cathedral.

Germany In Germany, the Gothic style until the end of the 13th century was at first heavily influenced by that of France; for example Cologne Cathedral, the largest in N Europe, was built after the model of Amiens. Many churches were built of brick, not of stone.

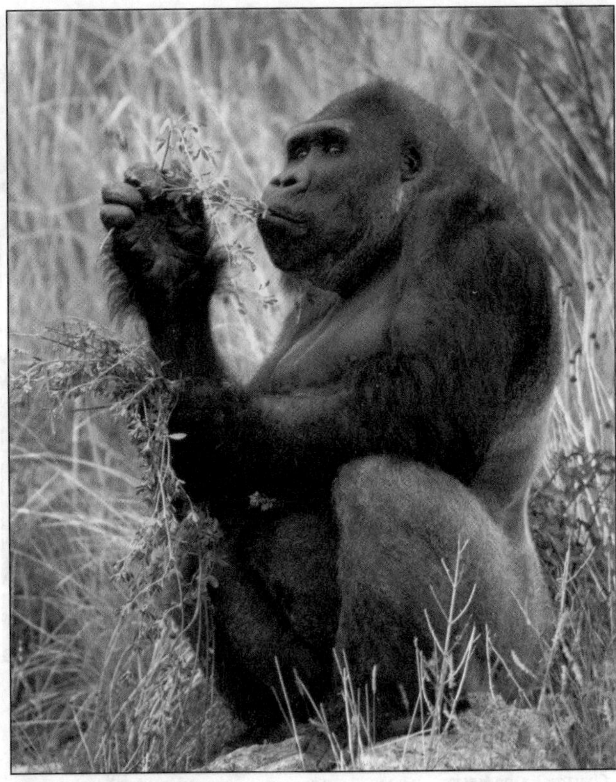

gorilla A male western lowland gorilla feeding. Gorillas move around in family groups, feeding on a variety of plant material as they go, within the group's home range of 10–40 sq km/4–15.5 sq mi. At night each member of the group builds its own nest of twigs and branches; very young gorillas sleep with their mothers. *Corbis*

England In England the Gothic style is divided into Early English (1200–75), for example, Salisbury Cathedral; Decorated (1300–75), for example, York Minster; and Perpendicular (1400–1575), for example, Winchester Cathedral.

pointed arch and window designs The real basis of Gothic architecture, and that which differentiates it from the heavier Romanesque style, is its elaborate and highly scientific system of vaulting and buttressing, made possible by the presence of the pointed arch. One result of the improved system was an increase of window area in the walls between buttresses – the walls no longer had to carry the main weight of the roof and could therefore be thinner and pierced with impunity. Lancet windows (windows topped by pointed arches) were grouped in twos or threes under an enclosing arch, the remaining contained space being pierced with small circular openings. Later the stonework between the various windows and openings ('lights') was reduced to slender stone bars ('mullions'), and the whole enclosed group of 'lights' became a single window. The upper portion of the window within the arch was filled with tracery, consisting at first of geometrical patterns, then later of flowing patterns, and finally of quasi-rectangular openings in the form of a grid (an effect achieved largely by the introduction of horizontal transoms in the larger windows).

These phases of window design, rather than any vital principle of construction, led to the formal division of English Gothic architecture into its three main stages. *See illustration on following page.*

Gothic art style of painting and sculpture that dominated European art from the late 12th century until the early Renaissance. Manuscripts were lavishly decorated, and the façades of the great Gothic churches held hundreds of sculpted figures and profuse ornamentation. Altarpieces were a central feature and colour was freely used in interiors, with stained glass replacing mural painting to some extent in N European churches. In Italy, fresco painting flourished. See also ◊medieval art, ◊International Gothic.

Gothic novel literary genre established by Horace Walpole's *The Castle of Otranto* 1765 and marked by mystery, violence, and horror; other exponents were the English writers Anne Radcliffe, Matthew 'Monk' Lewis, Mary Shelley, the Irish writer Bram Stoker, and Edgar Allan Poe in the USA.

Gothic Revival the resurgence of interest in Gothic architecture, as displayed in the late 18th and

> *'Better a ball in the brain than to flicker out unheeded.'*
>
> George Gordon of Khartoum, *Diary* Nov 1884

Gothic architecture A view looking east along the nave of Amiens cathedral, France, built 1220–70. Although Chartres Cathedral is considered the most complete Gothic church because of its superb sculpture and stained glass, many critics think that in purely architectural terms Amiens marks the summit of the Gothic style. Its sense of soaring height is breathtaking. *Corbis*

19th centuries, notably in Britain and the USA. Gothic Revival buildings include Sir Charles Barry and Augustus Pugin's Houses of Parliament, London, 1836–65, and the St Pancras Station Hotel, London, 1868–74, by Gilbert Scott; the Town Hall, Vienna, 1872–83, by Friedrich von Schmidt (1825–1891); and Trinity Church, New York, 1846, by Richard Upjohn (1802–1878).

The growth of Romanticism led some writers, artists, and antiquaries to embrace a fascination with Gothic forms that emphasized the supposedly bizarre and grotesque aspects of the Middle Ages. During the Victorian period, however, a far better understanding of Gothic forms was achieved, and this resulted in some impressive Neo-Gothic architecture, as well as some desecration of genuine Gothic churches in the name of 'restoration'.

gouache or ***body colour*** painting medium in which watercolour is mixed with white pigment. Applied in the same way as watercolour, gouache gives a chalky finish similar to that of ◊tempera painting. It has long been popular in continental Europe, where Dürer and Boucher were both masters of the technique. Poster paints are usually a form of gouache.

Gough Darren 1970– . English cricketer. A right-arm fast bowler and hard-hitting late order batsman, he made his England Test debut in 1994, and by the end of the 1998 English season had taken 104 wickets in 27 matches at an average of 27.79. He made his first-class debut for Yorkshire in 1989.

Gould Elliott. Stage name of Elliot Goldstein 1938– . US film actor. A successful child actor, his film debut *The Night They Raided Minsky's* 1968 led to starring roles in such films as *M.A.S.H.* 1970, *The Long Goodbye* 1972, and *Capricorn One* 1978.

Gould Jay (Jason) 1836–1892. US financier, born in New York. He is said to have caused the financial panic on 'Black Friday', 24 Sept 1869, through his efforts to corner the gold market.

Gould Stephen Jay 1941– . US palaeontologist and writer. In 1972 he proposed the theory of punctuated equilibrium, suggesting that the evolution of species did not occur at a steady rate but could suddenly accelerate, with rapid change occurring over a few hundred thousand years. His books include *Ever Since Darwin* 1977, *The Panda's Thumb* 1980, *The Flamingo's Smile* 1985, and *Wonderful Life* 1990.

'Science is all those things which are confirmed to such a degree that it would be unreasonable to withhold one's provisional consent.'

STEPHEN JAY GOULD
Lecture on evolution

Gounod Charles François 1818–1893. French composer and organist. His operas, notably *Faust* 1859 and *Roméo et Juliette* 1867, and church music, including *Messe solennelle/Solemn Mass* 1849, combine graceful melody and elegant harmonization. His *Méditation sur le prélude de Bach/Meditation on Bach's 'Prelude'* 1889 for soprano and instruments, based on Prelude No 1 of Bach's *Well-Tempered Clavier*, achieved popularity as 'Gounod's *Ave Maria*'.

gourd any of various members of the family Cucurbitaceae, including melons and pumpkins. In a narrower sense, the name applies only to the genus *Lagenaria*, of which the bottle gourd or calabash *Lagenaria siceraria* is best known.

gout hereditary form of ◊arthritis, marked by an excess of uric acid crystals in the tissues, causing pain and inflammation in one or more joints (usually of the feet or hands). Acute attacks are treated with ◊anti-inflammatories.

government any system whereby political authority is exercised. Modern systems of government distinguish between liberal democracies, totalitarian (one-party) states, and autocracies (authoritarian, relying on force rather than ideology). The Greek philosopher Aristotle was the first to attempt a systematic classification of governments. His main distinctions were between government by one person, by few, and by many (monarchy, oligarchy, and democracy), although the characteristics of each may vary between states and each may degenerate into tyranny (rule by an oppressive elite in the case of oligarchy or by the mob in the case of democracy).

The French philosopher Montesquieu distinguished between constitutional governments – whether monarchies or republics – which operated under various legal and other constraints, and despotism, which was not constrained in this way. Many of the words used (dictatorship, tyranny, totalitarian, democratic) have acquired negative or positive connotations that make it difficult to use them objectively.

The term ***liberal democracy*** was coined to distinguish Western types of democracy from the many other political systems that claimed to be democratic. Its principal characteristics are the existence of more than one political party, relatively open processes of government and political debate, and a separation of powers. ***Totalitarian*** has been applied to both fascist and communist states and denotes a system where all power is centralized in the state, which in turn is controlled by a single party that derives its legitimacy from an exclusive ideology. ***Autocracy*** describes a form of government that has emerged in a number of Third World countries, where state power is in the hands either of an individual or of the army; normally ideology is not a central factor, individual freedoms tend to be suppressed where they may constitute a challenge to the authority of the ruling group, and there is a reliance upon force. Other useful distinctions are between ***federal*** governments (where powers are dispersed among various regions which in certain respects are self-governing) and ***unitary*** governments (where powers are concentrated in a central authority); and between ***presidential*** (where the head of state is also the directly elected head of government, not part of the legislature) and ***parliamentary*** systems (where the government is drawn from an elected legislature that can dismiss it).

Government Communications Headquarters centre of the British government's electronic surveillance operations, popularly known as ◊GCHQ.

government expenditure another name for ◊public spending.

governor in engineering, any device that controls the speed of a machine or engine, usually by regulating the intake of fuel or steam. Scottish inventor James ◊Watt invented the steam-engine governor in 1788. It works by means of heavy balls, which rotate on the end of linkages and move in or out because of ◊centrifugal force according to the speed of rotation. The movement of the balls closes or opens the steam valve to the engine. When the engine speed increases too much, the balls fly out, and cause the steam valve to close, so the engine slows down. The opposite happens when the engine speed drops too much.

Gowda H D Deve 1933– . Indian political leader, prime minister 1996–97. Chosen as prime minister May 1996, he led a 13-party United Front coalition government, but was forced to step down April 1997 when the Congress Party withdrew support. He was succeeded as prime minister by Inder Kumar Gujral (1920–); the new government included almost all members of the preceding Gowda cabinet.

Gower David Ivon 1957– . English left-handed cricketer who played for Leicestershire 1975–89 and for Hampshire 1990–93. He was England's record run scorer in Test cricket from 1992, when he surpassed Geoffrey Boycott's record, until 1993, when his total was overtaken by Graham Gooch. He retired in 1993.

Gowon Yakubu 1934– . Nigerian politician, head of state 1966–75. He became chief of staff, and in the military coup of 1966 seized power. After the Biafran civil war 1967–70, he reunited the country with his policy of 'no victor, no vanquished'. He was overthrown by a military coup.

Goya Francisco José de Goya y Lucientes 1746–1828. Spanish painter and engraver. One of the major figures of European art, Goya depicted all aspects of Spanish life – portraits, including those of the royal family, religious works, scenes of war and of everyday life. Towards the end of his life, he created strange, nightmarish works, the 'Black Paintings', with such horrific images as *Saturn Devouring One of His Sons* about 1822 (Prado, Madrid). His series of etchings include *The Disasters of War* 1810–14, depicting the horrors of the French invasion of Spain.

In 1789 he was appointed court painter to Charles IV. The eroticism of his *Naked Maja* and *Clothed Maja* about 1800–05 (Prado, Madrid) caused such outrage that he was questioned by the Inquisition. Technically, Goya attained brilliant effects by thin painting over a red earth ground. Much influenced by Rembrandt ('Rembrandt, Velázquez, and Nature' were, he said, his guides), he turned in later years to a dusky near-monochrome. His skill, however, seemed to increase with age, and the *Milkmaid of Bordeaux*, one of his last paintings, shows him using colour with great freedom.

Gozzoli Benozzo c. 1421–1497. Florentine painter. He was a late exponent of the ◊International Gothic style. He is known for his fresco *The Procession of the Magi* 1459–61 in the chapel of the Palazzo Medici-Riccardi, Florence, where the walls are crowded with figures, many of them portraits of the Medici family.

Graaf Regnier de 1641–1673. Dutch physician and anatomist who discovered the ovarian follicles, which were later named Graafian follicles. He named the ovaries and gave exact descriptions of the testicles. He was also the first to isolate and collect the secretions of the pancreas and gall bladder.

Graafian follicle fluid-filled capsule that surrounds and protects the developing egg cell inside the ovary during the ◊menstrual cycle. After the egg cell has been released, the follicle remains and is known as a corpus luteum.

Grable Betty (Elizabeth Ruth) 1916–1973. US actress, singer, and dancer. She who starred in *Moon over Miami* 1941, *I Wake Up Screaming* 1941, and *How to Marry a Millionaire* 1953. As a publicity stunt, her legs were insured for a million dollars. Her popularity peaked during World War II when US soldiers voted her their number-one pin-up girl.

Gracchus Tiberius Sempronius c. 163–133 BC and Gaius Sempronius c. 153–121 BC in ancient Rome, two brothers who worked for agrarian reform. As ◊tribune (magistrate) 133 BC, Tiberius tried to redistribute land away from the large slave-labour farms in order to benefit the poor as well as increase the number of those eligible for military service by providing them with the miniumum property requirement. He was murdered by a mob of senators. Gaius, tribune 123–122 BC, revived his brother's legislation, and introduced other reforms, but was outlawed by the Senate and killed in a riot.

Grace W(illiam) G(ilbert) 1848–1915. English cricketer. By profession a doctor, he became the best batsman in England. He began playing first-class cricket at the age of 16, scored 152 runs in his first Test match, and scored the first triple century 1876. Throughout his career, which lasted nearly 45 years, he scored more than 54,000 runs. He scored 2,739 runs in 1871, the first time any batsman had scored 2,000 runs in a season. An all-rounder, he took nearly 3,000 first-class wickets. Grace played in 22 Test matches.

Graces in Greek mythology, three goddesses (Aglaia, Euphrosyne, Thalia), daughters of Zeus

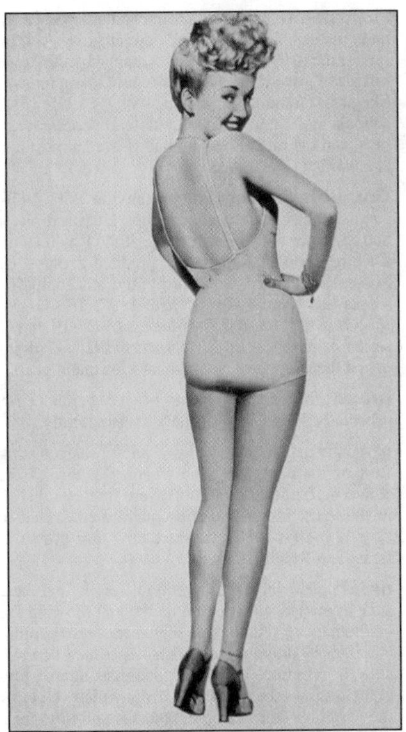

Grable US film actress Betty Grable. Also a singer and dancer, she appeared in the musicals *Follow the Fleet* 1936 and *Pin-Up Girl* 1944, and the comedy *The Beautiful Blond from Bashful Bend* 1949. *Topham*

and Hera, personifications of pleasure, charm, and beauty; the inspirers of the arts and the sciences.

gradient on a graph, the slope of a straight or curved line. The slope of a curve at any given point is represented by the slope of the ◊tangent at that point.

Graf Steffi 1969– . German lawn-tennis player who brought Martina ◊Navratilova's long reign as the world's number-one female player to an end. Graf reached the semifinal of the US Open 1985 at the age of 16, and won five consecutive Grand Slam singles titles 1988–89. She was Wimbledon ladies' single champion 1988, 1989, 1991, 1992, 1993, 1995, and 1996.

graffiti (Italian 'scratched drawings') inscriptions or drawings carved, scratched, or drawn on public surfaces, such as walls, fences, or public-transport vehicles. Tagging is the act of writing an individual logo on surfaces with spray paint or large felt-tip pens.

grafting in medicine, the operation by which an organ or other living tissue is removed from one organism and transplanted into the same or a different organism.

In horticulture, it is a technique widely used for propagating plants, especially woody species. A bud or shoot on one plant, termed the scion, is inserted into another, the stock, so that they continue growing together, the tissues combining at the point of union. In this way some of the advantages of both plants are obtained. Grafting is usually only successful between species that are closely related and is most commonly practised on roses and fruit trees. See also ◊transplant.

Graham Billy (William Franklin) 1918– . US Protestant evangelist, known for the dramatic staging and charismatic eloquence of his preaching. Graham has preached to millions during worldwide crusades and on television, bringing many thousands to conversion to, or renewal of, Christian faith.

Graham Martha 1894–1991. US dancer, choreographer, teacher, and director. The greatest exponent of modern dance in the USA, she developed a distinctive vocabulary of movement, the Graham Technique, now taught worldwide. Her pioneering technique, designed to express inner emotion and intention through dance forms, represented the first real alternative to classical ballet.

Graham founded her own dance school 1927 and started a company with students from the school 1929. She created over 170 works, including *Appalachian Spring* 1944 (score by Aaron Copland), *Clytemnestra* 1958, the first full-length modern dance work, and *Lucifer* 1975. She danced in most of the pieces she choreographed until her retirement from performance in the 1960s. Graham had a major influence on such choreographers in the contemporary dance movement as Robert Cohan, Glen Tetley, Merce Cunningham, Norman Morrice, Paul Taylor, and Robert North.

Graham Thomas 1805–1869. Scottish chemist who laid the foundations of physical chemistry (the branch of chemistry concerned with changes in energy during a chemical transformation) by his work on the diffusion of gases and liquids. Graham's law 1829 states that the diffusion rate of a gas is inversely proportional to the square root of its density.

His work on ◊colloids (which have larger particles than true solutions) was equally fundamental; he discovered the principle of dialysis, that colloids can be separated from solutions containing smaller molecules by the differing rates at which they pass through a semipermeable membrane.

Grahame Kenneth 1859–1932. Scottish-born writer. The early volumes of sketches of childhood, *The Golden Age* 1895 and *Dream Days* 1898, were followed by his masterpiece *The Wind in the Willows* 1908. It was dramatized by A A Milne as *Toad of Toad Hall* 1929.

grain the smallest unit of mass in the three English systems (avoirdupois, troy, and apothecaries' weights) used in the UK and USA, equal to 0.0648 g. It was reputedly the weight of a grain of wheat. One pound avoirdupois equals 7,000 grains; one pound troy or apothecaries' weight equals 5,760 grains.

gram metric unit of mass; one-thousandth of a kilogram.

grammar (Greek *grammatike tekhne* 'art of letters') the rules for combining words into phrases, clauses, sentences, and paragraphs. The standardizing impact of print has meant that spoken or colloquial language is often perceived as less grammatical than written language, but all forms of a language, standard or otherwise, have their own grammatical systems. People often acquire several overlapping grammatical systems within one language; for example, a formal system for writing and standard communication and a less formal system for everyday and peer-group communication. See also ◊parts of speech and ◊transformational grammar.

grammar school in the UK, a secondary school catering for children of high academic ability, usually measured by the eleven-plus examination. Most grammar schools have now been replaced by ◊comprehensive schools.

Grammy award any of several prizes given annually by the US National Academy of Recording Arts and Sciences since 1958. The categories include Album of the Year, Record of the Year (single), Best New Artist of the Year, and Best Performance subdivided by sex and genre.

Grampian former region of Scotland, created 1975, abolished 1996.

Grampian Mountains range that separates the Highlands from the Lowlands of Scotland, running NE from Strathclyde. It takes in the S Highland region (which includes Ben Nevis, the highest mountain in the British Isles at 1,340 m/4,406 ft), northern Tayside, and the southern border of Grampian Region itself (the Cairngorm Mountains, which include Ben Macdhui 1,309 m/4,296 ft). The region includes Aviemore, a winter holiday and sports centre.

grampus common name for Risso's dolphin *Grampus griseus*, a slate-grey dolphin found in tropical and temperate seas. These dolphins live in large schools and can reach 4 m/13 ft in length. The name grampus is sometimes also used for the killer ◊whale.

Gramsci Antonio 1891–1937. Italian Marxist who attempted to unify social theory and political practice. He helped to found the Italian Communist Party 1921 and was elected to parliament 1924, but was imprisoned by the Fascist leader Mussolini from 1926; his *Quaderni di carcere/Prison Notebooks* were published posthumously 1947.

Goya Carnival Scene (The Burial of the Sardine) (detail) c. 1815, Academia de San Fernando, Madrid, Spain. Goya delighted in the colour and energy of Spain's many carnivals and processions. But even in this picture of a Corpus Christi festival there are hints, in the masks and fancy dress, of the sinister elements that emerge so powerfully in many of his later works. *Spanish Tourist Office*

Granada city in the Sierra Nevada in Andalusia, S Spain; population (1994) 271,000. It produces textiles, soap, and paper. The *Alhambra*, a fortified hilltop palace, was built in the 13th and 14th centuries by the Moorish kings.

history Founded by the Moors in the 8th century, it became the capital of an independent kingdom 1236–1492, when it was the last Moorish stronghold to surrender to the Spaniards. Ferdinand and Isabella, the first sovereigns of a united Spain, are buried in the cathedral (built 1529–1703).

Grand Canal (Chinese ***Da Yune***) the world's longest canal. It is 1,600 km/1,000 mi long and runs N from Hangzhou to Tianjin, China; it is 30–61 m/100–200 ft wide, and reaches depths of over 1.5 km/1 mi. The earliest section was completed 486 BC; the central section linking the Chiang Jiang (Yangtse-Kiang) and Huang He (Yellow) rivers was built AD 605–610; and the northern section was built AD 1282–92, during the reign of Kublai Khan.

Grand Canyon gorge of multicoloured rock strata cut by and containing the Colorado River, N

Graham US ballet dancer and choreographer Martha Graham, who has exerted a great influence on modern dance. She set up her own dance academy in 1927 and developed a technique of dance based on the principles of contraction and release, in which the spine is flexible and movement comes from the solar plexus. Graham has favoured three-dimensional sets which fuse dance and design and has explored Japanese mime and Absurd themes in *Lucifer* (1975) and *Phaedra's Dream* (1983). *Corbis*

Grand Canyon The Grand Canyon, Arizona, USA. This gorge, which was cut through the rock by the Colorado River, is in the Grand Canyon National Park. It is a major tourist attraction. *Image Select (UK) Ltd*

Arizona, USA. It is 350 km/217 mi long, 6–29 km/4–18 mi wide, and reaches depths of over 1.7 km/1.1 mi. It was made a national park 1919. Millions of tourists visit the canyon each year.

Grand Guignol genre of short horror play originally produced at the Grand Guignol theatre in Montmartre, Paris (named after the bloodthirsty character Guignol in late 18th-century marionette plays).

Grand National in horse-racing, any of several steeplechases, such as the one run at Aintree, England, during the Liverpool meeting in March or April over 7,242 m/4.5 mi, with 30 formidable jumps. The highest jump is the Chair at 156 cm/5 ft 2 in. It was first run 1839. There is a growing movement to ban the races on grounds of cruelty to the horses.

grand opera type of opera without any spoken dialogue (unlike the *opéra-comique*), as performed at the Paris Opéra in the 1820s to 1880s. Grand operas were extremely long (five acts), and included incidental music and a ballet. Composers of grand opera include D F E Auber, Giacomo Meyerbeer, and Ludovic Halévy; examples include Verdi's *Don Carlos* 1867 and Meyerbeer's *Les Huguenots* 1836.

Grand Remonstrance petition passed by the English Parliament in Nov 1641 that listed all the alleged misdeeds of Charles I and demanded parliamentary approval for the king's ministers and the reform of the church. Charles refused to accept the Grand Remonstrance and countered by trying to arrest five leading members of the House of Commons (Pym, Hampden, Holles, Hesilrige, and Strode). The worsening of relations between king and Parliament led to the outbreak of the English Civil War in 1642.

grand slam in tennis, the winning of four major tournaments in one season: the Australian Open, the French Open, Wimbledon, and the US Open. In golf, it is also winning the four major tournaments in one season: the US Open, the British Open, the Masters, and the PGA (Professional Golfers Association). In baseball, a grand slam is a home run with runners on all the bases. A grand slam in bridge is when all 13 tricks are won by one team.

‘I know no method to secure the repeal of bad or obnoxious laws so effective as their stringent execution.’

ULYSSES GRANT
Inaugural address
4 March 1869

grand unified theory in physics, a sought-for theory that would combine the theory of the strong nuclear force (called ◊quantum chromodynamics) with the theory of the weak nuclear and electromagnetic forces. The search for the grand unified theory is part of a larger programme seeking a ◊unified field theory, which would combine all the forces of nature (including gravity) within one framework.

Granger (James Lablache) Stewart 1913–1993. English film actor. After several leading roles in British romantic melodramas during World War II (such as *The Man in Grey* 1940) he moved to Hollywood 1950 and subsequently appeared in such films as *Scaramouche* 1952, *The Prisoner of Zenda* 1952, *Beau Brummel* 1954, and *Moonfleet* 1955.

granite coarse-grained intrusive ◊igneous rock, typically consisting of the minerals quartz, feldspar, and mica. It may be pink or grey, depending on the composition of the feldspar. Granites are chiefly used as building materials. Granites often form large intrusions in the core of mountain ranges, and they are usually surrounded by zones of ◊metamorphic rock (rock that has been altered by heat or pressure). Granite areas have characteristic moorland scenery. In exposed areas the bedrock may be weathered along joints and cracks to produce a tor, consisting of rounded blocks that appear to have been stacked upon one another.

Grant Cary. Stage name of Archibald Alexander Leach 1904–1986. British-born actor, a US citizen from 1942. His witty, debonair personality made him a screen favourite for more than three decades. He was directed by Alfred ◊Hitchcock in *Suspicion* 1941, *Notorious* 1946, *To Catch a Thief* 1955, and *North by Northwest* 1959. His other films include *She Done Him Wrong* 1933, *Bringing Up Baby* 1937, and *The Philadelphia Story* 1940. He received a 1970 Academy Award for general excellence.

Grant Duncan (James Corrowr) 1885–1978. Scottish painter and designer. He was a member of the ◊Bloomsbury Group and a pioneer of Post-Impressionism in the UK. He lived with the painter Vanessa Bell (1879–1961) from about 1914 and worked with her on decorative projects, such as those at the ◊Omega Workshops. Later works, such as *Snow Scene* 1921, show great fluency and a subtle use of colour. One of his finest portraits is *Vanessa Bell* 1942 (Tate Gallery, London).

Grant Ulysses S(impson), (born Hiram Ulysses Grant) 1822–1885. US Civil War general in chief for the Union and 18th president of the USA 1869–77. As a Republican president, he carried through a liberal ◊Reconstruction policy in the South. He failed to suppress extensive political corruption within his own party and cabinet, which tarnished the reputation of his second term.

On the outbreak of the Civil War, Grant received a commission on the Mississippi front. He took command there in 1862, and by his capture of Vicksburg in 1863 brought the whole Mississippi front under Northern control. In 1864 he was made commander in chief. He slowly wore down the Confederate general Lee's resistance, and in 1865 received his surrender at Appomattox. He was elected president 1868 and re-elected 1872. As president, he reformed the civil service and ratified the Treaty of Washington with the UK 1871.

grant-maintained school in the UK, a state school that has voluntarily withdrawn itself from local authority support (an action called opting out), and instead is maintained directly by central government. The schools are managed by their own boards of governors. The first school to opt out was Skegness Grammar School in 1989. By 1995, 1,040 schools had opted out, well below government targets, and the rate of opt-out had slowed almost to a standstill.

Granville-Barker Harley Granville 1877–1946. English theatre director and author. He was director and manager with J E Vedrenne at the Royal Court Theatre, London, 1904–18, producing plays by Shaw, Yeats, Ibsen, Galsworthy, and Masefield. His works include the plays *Waste* 1907, *The Voysey Inheritance* 1905, and *The Madras House* 1910. His series of *Prefaces to Shakespeare* 1927–47 influenced the staging of Shakespeare for many years.

grape fruit of any vine of the genus *Vitis*, especially *V. vinifera*, of the Vitaceae family.

grapefruit round, yellow, juicy, sharp-tasting fruit of the evergreen tree *Citrus paradisi* of the Rutaceae family. Grapefruits were first established in the West Indies and subsequently cultivated in Florida by the 1880s; they are now also grown in Israel and South Africa.

graph pictorial representation of numerical data, such as statistical data, or a method of showing the mathematical relationship between two or more variables by drawing a diagram. There are often two axes, or reference lines, at right angles intersecting at the origin – the zero point, from which values of the variables (for example, distance and time for a moving object) are assigned along the axes. Pairs of simultaneous values (the distance moved after a particular time) are plotted as points in the area between the axes, and the points then joined by a smooth curve to produce a graph.

graphical user interface (GUI) or ***WIMP*** (windows, icons, menus, pointing device) in computing, a type of ◊user interface in which programs and files appear as icons (small pictures), user options are selected from pull-down menus, and data are displayed in windows (rectangular areas),

Grant General Ulysses S Grant at City Point, near Hopewell, Virginia, June 1864. Respected as a war hero, Grant was nominated as the Republican Party's presidential candidate in 1868. He was elected and served two terms, marred by poor administration, financial scandals, and official corruption. *Sachem*

which the operator can manipulate in various ways. The operator uses a pointing device, typically a ◊mouse, to make selections and initiate actions. The concept of the graphical user interface was developed by the Xerox Corporation in the 1970s, was popularized with the Apple Macintosh computers in the 1980s, and is now available on many types of computer – most notably as Windows, an operating system for IBM PC-compatible microcomputers developed by the software company Microsoft.

graphic equalizer control used in hi-fi systems that allows the distortions introduced by unequal amplification of different frequencies to be corrected.

graphics card in computing, a peripheral device that processes and displays graphics.

graphite blackish-grey, laminar, crystalline form of ◊carbon. It is used as a lubricant and as the active component of pencil lead. Graphite has a very high melting point (3,500°C/6,332°F), and is a good conductor of heat and electricity. It absorbs neutrons and is therefore used to moderate the chain reaction in nuclear reactors.

graph notation in music, an invented sign language representing unorthodox sounds objectively in pitch and time, or alternatively representing sounds of orthodox music in a visually unorthodox manner. A form of graph notation for speech patterns used in phonetics was adopted by Stockhausen in *Carré/Squared* 1959–60.

Graphic representation of sounds begins with medieval plainchant, which originally aimed at recording the real inflection of a singing voice. Its reappearance in modern times dates from 1856, with the invention by León Scott of the phonautograph for recording visual traces of speech sounds.

graphology the study of the writing system of a language, including the number and formation of letters, spelling patterns, accents, and punctuation. In the 19th century it was believed that analysis of a person's handwriting could give an indication of their personality, a belief still held in a more limited fashion today.

Grappelli Stephane 1908–1997. French jazz violinist. He played in the Quintette du Hot Club de France 1934–39, in partnership with the guitarist Django ◊Reinhardt. Romantic improvisation was a hallmark of his style.

Grappelli spent World War II in the UK and returned several times to record there, including a number of jazz albums with the classical violinist Yehudi Menuhin in the 1970s. Of his other collaborations, an LP with the mandolinist David Grisman (1945–) reached the US pop chart 1981. He continued to give live performances in the mid 1990s.

grass plant of the large family Gramineae of monocotyledons, with about 9,000 species distributed worldwide except in the Arctic regions. The majority are perennial, with long, narrow leaves and jointed, hollow stems; hermaphroditic flowers are borne in spikelets; the fruits are grainlike. Included are bluegrass, wheat, rye, maize, sugarcane, and bamboo.

Grass Günter (Wilhelm) 1927– . German writer. The grotesque humour and socialist feeling of his novels *Die Blechtrommel/The Tin Drum* 1959 and *Der Butt/The Flounder* 1977 are also characteristic of many of his poems. Other works include *Katz und Maus/Cat and Mouse* 1961, *Hundejahre/Dog Years* 1963, and *Ortlich betäubt/Local Anaesthetic* 1969. Deeply committed politically, Grass's works contain a mixture of scurrility, humour, tragedy, satire, and marvellously inventive imagery.

grasshopper insect of the order Orthoptera, usually with strongly developed hind legs, enabling it to leap. The femur of each hind leg in the male usually has a row of protruding joints that produce the characteristic chirping when rubbed against the hard wing veins. Members of the order include ◊locusts, ◊crickets, and katydids. All members of the family feed voraciously on vegetation.

Grateful Dead, the US psychedelic rock group formed 1965. Their shows featured long improvisations and subtle ensemble playing, seldom fully captured in recording; albums include *Live Dead* 1969, *Workingman's Dead* 1970, and *Built to Last* 1989. They continued to tour until the death of Jerry Garcia 1995.

Formed at the heart of the San Francisco ◊hippie scene, the Dead represented an alternative life style to a core of fans (Deadheads) who followed the constantly touring band around the world. Out of their vast repertoire of original and nonoriginal material, they are especially identified with the song 'Truckin'' (from *American Beauty* 1970).

Grattan Henry 1746–1820. Irish politician. He entered the Irish parliament in 1775, led the patriot opposition, and obtained free trade and legislative independence for Ireland 1782. He failed to prevent the Act of Union of Ireland and England in 1805, sat in the British Parliament from that year, and pressed for Catholic emancipation.

Graubünden (French ***Grisons***) Swiss canton, the largest in Switzerland; area 7,106 sq km/2,743 sq mi; population (1990) 170,400. The main sources of the river Rhine rise here. It also includes the resort of Davos and, in the Upper Engadine, St Moritz. The capital is Chur. Romansch is still widely spoken. Graubünden entered the Swiss Confederation 1803.

gravel coarse ◊sediment consisting of pebbles or small fragments of rock, originating in the beds of lakes and streams or on beaches. Gravel is quarried for use in road building, railway ballast, and for an aggregate in concrete. It is obtained from quarries known as gravel pits, where it is often found mixed with sand or clay.

Graves Robert (Ranke) 1895–1985. English poet and writer. He was severely wounded on the Somme in World War I, and his frank autobiography *Goodbye to All That* 1929 contains outstanding descriptions of the war. *Collected Poems* 1975 contained those verses he wanted preserved, some of which were influenced by the American poet Laura Riding, with whom he lived for some years. His fiction includes the two novels of ancient Rome, *I Claudius* and *Claudius the God*, both 1934. His most significant critical work is *The White Goddess: A Historical Grammar of Poetic Myth* 1948, revised edition 1966.

Graves first achieved notice for his war poetry, but he largely rejected his early poetry and developed much further in his later verse. The poems of his maturity, 1926–39, are technically confident, rhetorically simple, and are among the finest of modern love poems. After World War II, he became increasingly interested in Sufism and Eastern religious philosophy and mythology, the subject of many of his later poems. His works include *Collected Poems* 1965, *Poems 1965–68* 1968, *Poems 1968–1970* 1970, and *Poems 1970–72* 1972.

Gravesend town on the river Thames, Kent, SE England, linked by ferry with Tilbury opposite; population (1991) 51,400. Industries include electrical goods, engineering, printing, and papermaking.

gravimetric analysis in chemistry, a technique for determining, by weighing, the amount of a particular substance present in a sample. It usually involves the conversion of the test substance into a compound of known molecular weight that can be easily isolated and purified.

gravimetry study of the Earth's gravitational field. Small variations in the gravitational field (gravimetric anomalies) can be caused by varying densities of rocks and structure beneath the surface. Such variations are measured by a device called a gravimeter, which consists of a weighted spring that is pulled further downwards where the gravity is stronger (at a Bouguer anomaly, an increase in the Earth's gravity observed near a mountain or dense rock mass). Gravimetry is used by geologists to map the subsurface features of the Earth's crust, such as underground masses of heavy rock like granite, or light rock like salt. *See illustration on following page.*

gravitational field the region around a body in which other bodies experience a force due to its gravitational attraction. The gravitational field of a massive object such as the Earth is very strong and easily recognized as the force of gravity, whereas that of an object of much smaller mass is very weak and difficult to detect. Gravitational fields produce only attractive forces.

gravitational field strength (symbol *g*) the strength of the Earth's gravitational field at a particular point. It is defined as the the gravitational force in newtons that acts on a mass of one kilogram. The value of *g* on the Earth's surface is taken to be 9.806 N kg^{-1}.

The symbol *g* is also used to represent the acceleration of a freely falling object in the Earth's gravitational field.

Near the Earth's surface and in the absence of friction due to the air, all objects fall with an acceleration of 9.806 m s^{-2}.

gravitational lensing bending of light by a gravitational field, predicted by Einstein's general theory of relativity. The effect was first detected 1917 when the light from stars was found to be bent as it passed the totally eclipsed Sun. More remarkable is the splitting of light from distant quasars into two or more images by intervening galaxies. In 1979 the first double image of a quasar produced by gravitational lensing was discovered and a quadruple image of another quasar was later found.

graviton in physics, the ◊gauge boson that is the postulated carrier of the gravitational force.

gravity force of attraction that arises between objects by virtue of their masses. On Earth, gravity

grasshopper This striking *Eumastax* grasshopper was unknown to science when it was photographed in a Peruvian rainforest. It belongs to the exclusively tropical family Eumastacidae, often called monkey hoppers, in which the antennae are very short. Adult grasshoppers may be fully winged or may lack wings altogether, a characteristic of many mountain-dwelling and rainforest species. *Premaphotos Wildlife*

'Love is a universal migraine / A bright stain on the vision / Blotting out reason.'

Robert Graves
'Symptoms of Love'

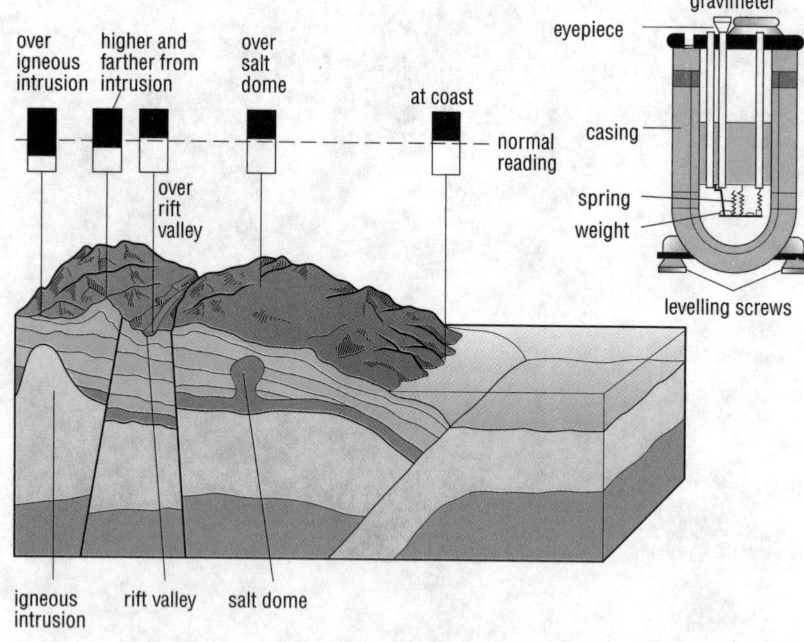

gravimetry The gravimeter is an instrument for measuring the force of gravity at a particular location. Variations in the force of gravity acting on a weight suspended by a spring cause the spring to stretch. The gravimeter is used in aerial surveys. Geological features such as intrusions and salt domes are revealed by the stretching of the spring.

'The curfew tolls the knell of parting day, / The lowing herd winds slowly o'er the lea, / The ploughman homeward plods his weary way, / And leaves the world to darkness and to me.'

Thomas Gray
'Elegy Written in a Country Churchyard'

is the force of attraction between any object in the Earth's gravitational field and the Earth itself. It is regarded as one of the four fundamental ◊forces of nature, the other three being the ◊electromagnetic force, the ◊strong nuclear force, and the ◊weak nuclear force. The gravitational force is the weakest of the four forces, but it acts over great distances. The particle that is postulated as the carrier of the gravitational force is the ◊graviton.

measuring forces of attraction An experiment for determining the force of attraction between two masses was first planned in the mid-18th century by the Reverend J Mitchell, who did not live to work on the apparatus he had designed and completed. After Mitchell's death the apparatus came into the hands of Henry ◊Cavendish, who largely reconstructed it but kept to Mitchell's original plan. The attracted masses consisted of two small balls, connected by a stiff wooden beam suspended at its middle point by a long, fine wire. The whole of this part of the apparatus was enclosed in a case, carefully coated with tinfoil to secure, as far as possible, a uniform temperature within the case. Irregular distribution of temperature would have resulted in convection currents of air which would have had a serious disturbing effect on the suspended system. To the beam was attached a small mirror with its plane vertical. A small glazed window in the case allowed any motion of the mirror to be observed by the consequent deviations of a ray of light reflected from it. The attracting masses consisted of two equal, massive lead spheres. Using this apparatus, Cavendish, in 1797, obtained for the gravitational constant G the value 6.6×10^{-11} N m^2 kg^{-2}. The apparatus was refined by Charles Vernon Boys (1855–1944) and he obtained the improved value 6.6576×10^{-11} N m^2 kg^{-2}. The value generally used today is 6.6720×10^{-11} N m^2 kg^{-2}.

gravure one of the three main ◊printing methods, in which printing is done from a plate etched with a pattern of recessed cells in which the ink is held. The greater the depth of a cell, the greater the strength of the printed ink. Gravure plates are expensive to make, but the process is economical for high-volume printing and reproduces illustrations well.

gray SI unit (symbol Gy) of absorbed radiation dose. It replaces the rad (1 Gy equals 100 rad), and is defined as the dose absorbed when one kilogram of matter absorbs one joule of ionizing radiation. Different types of radiation cause different amounts of damage for the same absorbed dose; the SI unit of ***dose equivalent*** is the ◊sievert.

Gray (Kathleen) Eileen (Moray) 1879–1976. Irish-born architect and furniture designer. Her Art Deco furniture explored the use of tubular metal, glass, and new materials such as aluminium.

Gray Thomas 1716–1771. English poet. His *Elegy Written in a Country Churchyard* 1751, a dignified contemplation of death, is one of the most quoted poems in the English language. Other poems include *Ode on a Distant Prospect of Eton College* 1747, *The Progress of Poesy*, and *The Bard* both 1757. He is now seen as a precursor of Romanticism.

grayling freshwater fish *Thymallus thymallus* of the family Salmonidae. It has a long multirayed dorsal fin, and a coloration shading from silver to purple. It is found in northern parts of Europe, Asia, and North America.

grayling The grayling is found in lakes and rivers throughout much of central and N Europe. It resembles a small salmon and is indeed related to salmon and trout. The scientific name of this freshwater fish is *Thymallus thymallus* and it is said that a freshly caught fish has a scent similar to the herb thyme.

Graz capital of Styria province, and second-largest city in Austria; population (1991) 237,800. Industries include engineering, chemicals, iron, steel, and automobile manufacturing. It has a 15th-century cathedral and a university founded 1573. Lippizaner horses are bred near here.

Graziano Rocky (Thomas Rocco Barbella) 1922–1990. US middleweight boxing champion who fought in the 1940s and 1950s. Although he was not noted for his boxing skills or finesse, his colourful, brawling style made him popular. He compiled a record of 67 wins, 10 losses and 6 draws between 1942 and 1952. Three of his bouts, with Tony Zale 1946, 1947, and 1948, were considered classics.

Great Artesian Basin the largest area of artesian water in the world. It underlies much of Queensland, New South Wales, and South Australia, and in prehistoric times formed a sea. It has an area of 1,750,000 sq km/676,250 sq mi.

Great Australian Bight broad bay of the Indian Ocean in S Australia, notorious for storms. It was discovered by a Dutch navigator, Captain Thyssen, 1627. The coast was charted by the English explorer Captain Matthew Flinders 1802.

Great Barrier Reef chain of coral reefs and islands about 2,000 km/1,250 mi long, off the E coast of Queensland, Australia, at a distance of 15–45 km/10–30 mi. It is made up of 3,000 individual reefs, and is believed to be the world's largest living organism. The formation of the reef is now thought to be a recent geological event.

Great Bear popular name for the constellation ◊Ursa Major.

Great Britain official name for ◊England, ◊Scotland, and ◊Wales, and the adjacent islands (except the Channel Islands and the Isle of Man) from 1603, when the English and Scottish crowns were united under James I of England (James VI of Scotland). With Northern ◊Ireland it forms the ◊United Kingdom.

great circle circle drawn on a sphere such that the diameter of the circle is a diameter of the sphere. On the Earth, all meridians of longitude are half great circles; among the parallels of latitude, only the equator is a great circle.

Great Dane breed of large, short-haired dog, often fawn or brindle in colour, standing up to 76 cm/30 in tall, and weighing up to 70 kg/154 lb. It has a large head and muzzle, and small, erect ears. It was used in Europe for hunting boar and stags.

Great Dividing Range E Australian mountain range, extending 3,700 km/2,300 mi N–S from Cape York Peninsula, Queensland, to Victoria. It includes the Carnarvon Range, Queensland, which has many Aboriginal cave paintings, the Blue Mountains in New South Wales, and the Australian Alps.

Greater London Council (GLC) in the UK, local authority that governed London 1965–86. When the GLC was abolished (see ◊local government), its powers either devolved back to the borough councils or were transferred to certain non-elected bodies.

Great Exhibition world fair held in Hyde Park, London, UK, in 1851, proclaimed by its originator Prince Albert as 'the Great Exhibition of the Industries of All Nations'. In practice, it glorified British manufacture: over half the 100,000 exhibits were from Britain or the British Empire. Over 6 million people attended the exhibition. The exhibition hall, popularly known as the Crystal Palace, was constructed of glass with a cast-iron frame, and designed by Joseph ◊Paxton.

Great Lakes series of five freshwater lakes along the US–Canadian border: Lakes Superior, Michigan, Huron, Erie, and Ontario; total area 245,000 sq km/94,600 sq mi. Interconnecting canals make them navigable by large ships, and they are drained by the ◊St Lawrence River. The whole forms the St Lawrence Seaway.

Great Lakes

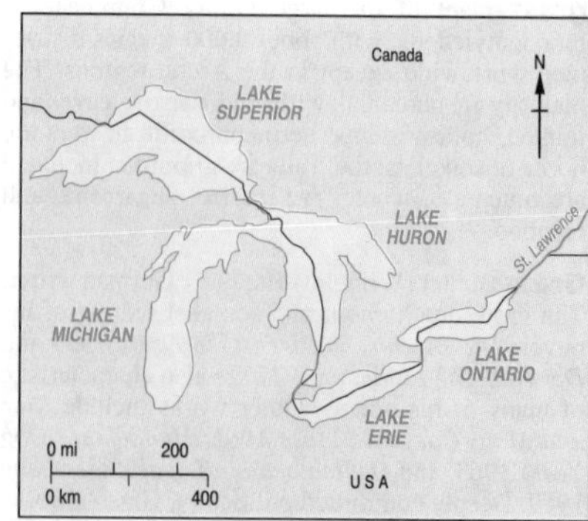

Great Leap Forward change in the economic policy of the People's Republic of China introduced by ◊Mao Zedong under the second five-year plan of 1958–62. The aim was to achieve rapid and simultaneous agricultural and industrial growth through the creation of large new agro-industrial communes. The inefficient and poorly planned allocation of state resources led to the collapse of the strategy by 1960 and the launch of a 'reactionary programme', involving the use of rural markets and private subsidiary plots. More than 20 million people died in the Great Leap famines of 1959–61.

Great Patriotic War (1941–45) war between the USSR and Germany during ◊World War II. When Germany invaded the USSR in June 1941,

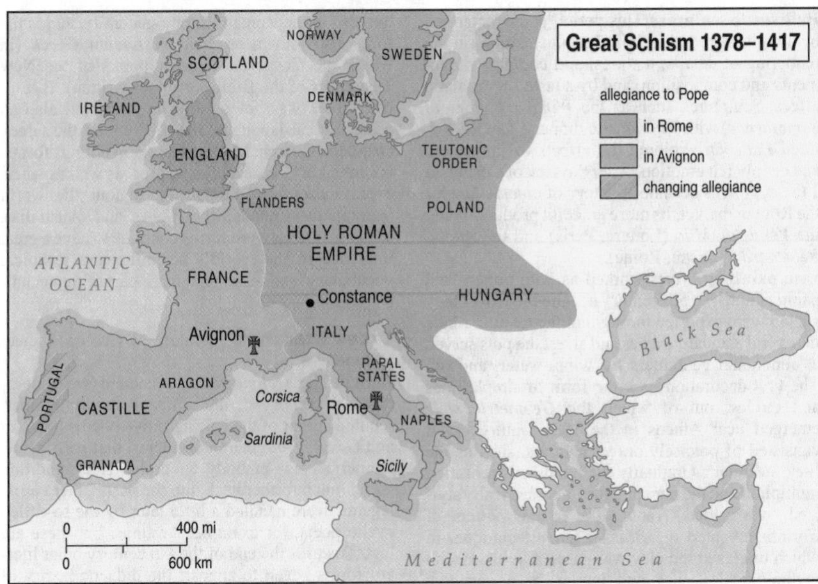

the Soviet troops retreated, carrying out a scorched earth policy of burning and destroying everything that might be of use to the invading army, and relocating strategic industries beyond the Ural Mountains. Stalin remained in Moscow and the Soviet forces, inspired to fight on by his patriotic speeches, launched a counter-offensive. The Allies tried to provide the USSR with vital supplies through Murmansk and Archangel despite German attempts to blockade the ports. In 1942 the Germans failed to take Leningrad and Moscow, and launched an attack towards the river Volga and to capture oil wells at Baku. In Aug 1942 the Germans attacked Stalingrad but it was held by the Russians. A substantial German force was forced to surrender at Stalingrad in Jan 1943. The Red Army, under the command of Marshal Zhukov, gradually forced the Germans back and by Feb 1945 the Russians had reached the German border. In April 1945 the Russians, who had made tremendous sacrifices (20 million dead and millions more wounded) entered Berlin. In May 1945 the war ended.

Great Plains semi-arid region to the E of the Rocky Mountains, USA, stretching as far as the 100th meridian of longitude through Oklahoma, Kansas, Nebraska, and the Dakotas. The plains, which cover one-fifth of the USA, extend from Texas in the S over 2,400 km/1,500 mi N to Canada. Ranching and wheat farming have resulted in overuse of water resources to such an extent that available farmland has been reduced by erosion.

Great Power any of the major European powers of the 19th century: Russia, Austria (Austria-Hungary), France, Britain, and Prussia.

Great Red Spot prominent oval feature, 14,000 km/8,500 mi wide and some 30,000 km/20,000 mi long, in the atmosphere of the planet ◊Jupiter, S of the equator. Space probes show it to be an anticlockwise vortex of cold clouds, coloured possibly by phosphorus.

Great Rift Valley longest 'split' in the Earth's surface; see ◊Rift Valley, Great.

Great Sandy Desert desert in N Western Australia; 415,000 sq km/160,000 sq mi. It is also the name of an arid region in S Oregon, USA.

Great Schism in European history, the period 1378–1417 in which rival popes had seats in Rome and in Avignon; it was ended by the election of Martin V during the Council of Constance 1414–17.

Great Trek in South African history, the movement of 12,000–14,000 Boer (Dutch) settlers from Cape Colony 1835 and 1845 to escape British rule. They established republics in Natal and the Transvaal. It is seen by many white South Africans as the main event in the founding of the present republic and was cited as a justification for whites-only rule.

Great Wall of China continuous defensive wall stretching from W Gansu to the Gulf of Liaodong (2,250 km/1,450 mi). It was built under the Qin dynasty from 214 BC to prevent incursions by the Turkish and Mongol peoples and extended westwards by the Han dynasty. Some 8 m/25 ft high, it consists of a brick-faced wall of earth and stone, has a series of square watchtowers, and has been carefully restored. It is so large that it can be seen from space.

Great War another name for ◊World War I.

grebe any of 19 species of water birds belonging to the family Podicipedidae, order Podicipediformes. The great crested grebe *Podiceps cristatus* is the largest of the Old World grebes. It feeds on fish, and lives in ponds and marshes in Eurasia, Africa, and Australia.

grebe The great crested grebe is easily recognized by its long slender neck and daggerlike bill. It has a wide range: Europe, Asia, Africa south of the Sahara, Australia, and New Zealand. Its diet consists largely of fish, caught by diving beneath the surface of the lakes, ponds, rivers, and coastal waters where it lives.

Greco, El (Doménikos Theotokopoulos) 1541–1614. Spanish painter called 'the Greek' because he was born in Crete. He settled in Toledo and painted elegant portraits and intensely emotional religious scenes with increasingly distorted figures and unearthly light, such as *The Burial of Count Orgaz* 1586 (church of S Tomé, Toledo).

His passionate insistence on rhythm and movement and vehement desire for intensity of expression were conveyed by the elongation and distortion of figures, and unusual and disturbing colour schemes with calculated clashes of crimson, lemon yellow, green and blue, and livid flesh tones. Perspective and normal effects of lighting were disregarded, and the young El Greco is recorded as having said that the daylight blinded him to the inner light. In a modern and 'expressionist' fashion he was projecting a vision conceived in the mind and emotions. The characteristic El Greco can be seen in the *Martyrdom of St Maurice* 1581–84 (Madrid, Escorial). The huge *Burial of Count Orgaz* combined austere Spanish dignity with rapturous sublimity. Later compositions include *The Agony in the Garden* (National Gallery, London, and other versions) and the soaring vertical ascent of *Pentecost*, *Resurrection*, and *Adoration of the Shepherds* (Prado, Madrid). *See illustration on following page.*

Greece country in SE Europe, comprising the S Balkan peninsula, bounded N by the Former Yugoslav Republic of Macedonia and Bulgaria, NW by Albania, NE by Turkey, E by the Aegean Sea, S by the Mediterranean Sea, and W by the Ionian Sea. *See country box on p. 463.*

Greece, ancient ancient civilization that flourished 2,500 years ago on the shores of the Ionian and Aegean Seas (modern Greece and the western coast of Turkey). Although its population never exceeded 2 million, ancient Greece made great innovations in philosophy, politics, science, architecture, and the arts, and Greek culture forms the basis of Western civilization to this day. *See map on following page and timeline on p. 464.*

Greek architecture the architecture of ancient Greece is the base for virtually all architectural developments in Europe. The Greeks invented the ◊entablature, which allowed roofs to be hipped (inverted V-shape), and perfected the design of arcades with support columns. There were three styles, or orders, of columns: Doric (with no base), Ionic (with scrolled capitals), and Corinthian (with acanthus-leafed capitals).

Of the Greek orders, the Doric is the oldest; it is said to have evolved from a former timber prototype. The finest example of a Doric temple is the Parthenon in Athens (447–438 BC). The origin of the Ionic is uncertain. The earliest building in which the Ionic capital appears is the temple of Artemis (Diana) at Ephesus (530 BC). The gateway to the Acropolis in Athens (known as the Propylaea) has internal columns of the Ionic order. The most perfect example is the Erechtheum (421–406 BC) in Athens.

The Corinthian order belongs to a later period of Greek art. A leading example is the temple of Zeus (Jupiter) Olympius in Athens (174 BC), completed under Roman influence AD 129. The monumental and sumptuously ornamental Mausoleum in Halicarnassus (353 BC) was one of the ◊Seven Wonders of the World.

Greek art the sculpture, painting (almost entirely vase decoration), mosaic, and crafts of ancient Greece. It is usually divided into three periods:

'Of all man's work on earth, it alone could be seen from Mars.'

On the GREAT WALL OF CHINA
John Gunther
Inside Asia

Great Wall of China The Great Wall stretches away to the horizon at Mutianyu, 90 km/55 mi NE of Beijing. The wall is a Ming dynasty (1368–1644) rebuilding of the much older walls of the Qin and Han dynasties, which were begun in 214 BC. *Corbis*

Greco, El A detail from *The Virgin with Saints Ines and Tecla* 1597–99 by El Greco (National Gallery of Scotland). Illuminated by an unearthly light, El Greco's pale, slender, and ethereal figures inhabit a spiritual rather than physical world. *Corbis*

Archaic (late 8th century–480 BC), showing Egyptian influence; ***Classical*** (480–323 BC), characterized by dignified and eloquent realism; and ***Hellenistic*** (323–27 BC), more exuberant or dramatic. Sculptures of human figures dominate all periods, and vase painting was a focus for artistic development for many centuries.

Archaic sculpture Nearly all Greek sculptures were for use on or in temples. And just as the temple column evolved from the tree trunk that supported the primitive temple or dwelling, so the statue evolved from a rough-shaped trunk, probably representing a deity. Several examples of this block type of wooden image existed in classical times. One was revered in the Parthenon as being the most ancient image of the goddess Athena. Surviving works are stone statues of naked standing men (*kouroi*) and draped women (*korai*) show an Egyptian influence in their rigid frontality. By about 500 BC figures are allowed to relax their weight on to one leg, and they gradually become more lifelike. Subjects were usually depicted smiling.

Classical sculpture Expressions assumed a dignified serenity. New poses and a greater sense of movement were allowed by the use of bronze (hollow-cast by the lost-wax method), but relatively few bronze sculptures survive, and many are known only through Roman copies in marble. A good example is Myron's bronze *Diskobolus/The Discus Thrower* 460–450 BC. Other outstanding bronzes are the elegant *Charioteer of Delphi* about 480 BC (Delphi Museum) and the powerful *Zeus or Poseidon* about 460 BC (National Museum, Athens). This greater freedom can be seen in the carved Parthenon reliefs of riders and horses, supervised by Phidias. The sculptures of the Parthenon are widely seen as the finest expression of the balance between harmony and energy that characterizes this period. Polykleitos' sculpture *Doryphoros/The Spear Carrier* 450–440 BC was of such harmony and poise that it set a standard for beautiful proportions. Praxiteles introduced the female nude into the sculptural repertory with the graceful *Aphrodite of Cnidus* about 350 BC. Two other important sculptors were Lysippus and Scopas.

Hellenistic sculpture This period is characterized by a high degree of technical sophistication (in the rendering of details, textures, and complex movements and composition) and by a taste for dramatic effect. Sculptures such as the *Winged Victory of Samothrace*, with its dramatic drapery, and the tortured *Laocoön* explored the effects of movement and deeply felt emotion. After the sack of Corinth in 146 BC, Athens became a factory of *objets d'art* for the Roman market, its more graceful products being the *Venus de Milo* (Louvre, Paris) and the *Apollo Belvedere* (Vatican, Rome).

vase painting Artists worked as both potters and painters until the 5th century BC, and the works they signed were exported throughout the empire. Made in several standard shapes and sizes, the pots served as functional containers for wine, water, and oil. The first decoration took the form of simple lines and circles, out of which the ***Geometric style*** emerged near Athens in the 10th century BC. It consisted of precisely drawn patterns, such as the 'key meander'. Gradually the bands of decoration multiplied and the human figure, geometrically stylized, was added. About 700 BC the potters of Corinth invented the ***Black Figure*** technique, in which unglazed red clay was painted in black with mythological scenes and battles in a narrative frieze. About 530 BC Athenian potters reversed the process and developed the more sophisticated ***Red Figure*** pottery, which allowed for more detailed and elaborate painting of the figures in red against a black background. Their style grew increasingly naturalistic, showing lively scenes from daily life. The finest examples date from the mid-6th to the mid-5th century BC in Athens. Later painters tried to follow art trends and represent spatial depth, dissipating the unique quality of their fine linear technique.

crafts The ancient Greeks excelled in gems, cameos, coins, and fine metalwork, particularly jewellery, their skills often acquired from Egypt and Mesopotamia. They also invented the pictorial mosaic, fine examples being found in Obyathos, Olympia, Alexandria, and Macedonia. From the 5th century BC onwards, floors were paved with coloured pebbles depicting mythological subjects. Later, specially cut cubes of stone and glass called *tesserae* were used, and Greek artisans working for the Romans reproduced paintings, such as *Alexander at the Battle of Issus* from Pompeii, the originals of which are lost.

Greek language

Greek language member of the Indo-European language family, which has passed through at least five distinct phases since the 2nd millennium BC: ***Ancient Greek*** 14th–12th centuries BC; ***Archaic Greek***, including Homeric epic language, until 800 BC; ***Classical Greek*** until 400 BC; ***Hellenistic Greek***, the common language of Greece, Asia Minor, W Asia, and Egypt to the 4th century AD, and ***Byzantine Greek***, used until the 15th century and still the ecclesiastical language of the Greek Orthodox Church. ***Modern Greek*** is principally divided into the general vernacular (***Demotic Greek***) and the language of education and literature (***Katharevousa***).

In its earlier phases Greek was spoken mainly in Greece, the Aegean islands, the west coast of Asia Minor, and in colonies in Sicily, the Italian mainland, S Spain, and S France. Hellenistic Greek was an important language not only in the Middle East but also in the Roman Empire generally, and is the form also known as ***New Testament Greek*** (in which the Gospels and other books of the New Testament of the Bible were first written). Byzantine Greek was not only an imperial but also an ecclesiastical language, the medium of the Greek Orthodox Church. Modern Greek, in both its forms, is spoken in Greece and in Cyprus, as well as wherever Greeks have settled throughout the world (principally Canada, the USA, and Australia). Classical Greek word forms continue to have a great influence in the world's scientific and technical vocabulary, and make up a large part of the technical vocabulary of English.

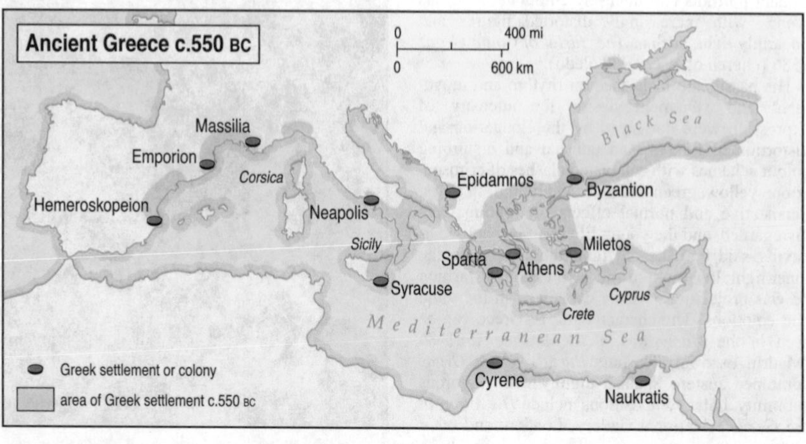

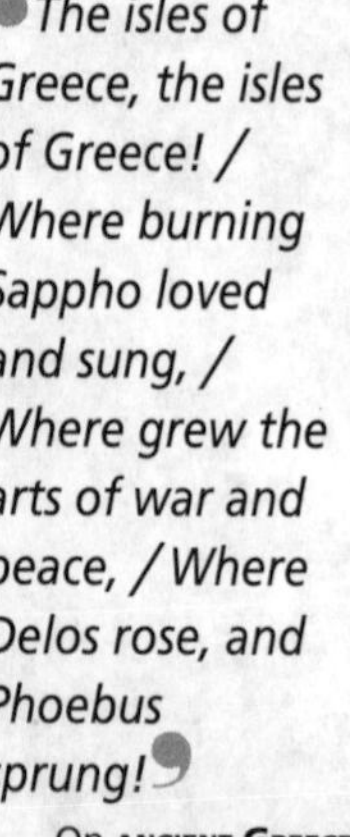

The isles of Greece, the isles of Greece! / Where burning Sappho loved and sung, / Where grew the arts of war and peace, / Where Delos rose, and Phoebus sprung!

On ANCIENT GREECE
George Byron
Don Juan 1819–29

Greek literature

Greek literature literature of Greece, ancient and modern.

ancient The ***Archaic period*** of ancient Greek literature (8th century–c. 480 BC) begins with ◊Homer, reputed author of the epic narrative poems the *Iliad* and *Odyssey*, but there is evidence that parts of the Homeric epics embody an oral literary tradition going much further back into the past. Other heroic legends were handled a little later by the so-called cyclic poets, for example, Arctinus, but these are lost. Towards the end of the 8th century other literary forms began to appear: the didactic poetry of Hesiod, whose *Works and Days* deals with morals as they pertain to agricultural life, and the various kinds of lyric which flourished for two centuries, particularly in Ionia and the Aegean islands. Besides choral lyric (Alcman, Stesichorus), there were elegiac and iambic (Archilochus, Mimnermus, Semonides of Amorgos, Solon, Theognis, Tyrtaeus); epigram (Simonides of Ceos); table-songs (Terpander); and political lyrics (Alcaeus). This kind of poetry served also as a vehicle of moral ideas for Solon, Theognis, and Tyrtaeus, of invective for Archilochus, of ardent passion for Sappho, or of the merely elegant and affected as in Anacreon. At the very end of the Archaic period stands the first Greek historian, Hecataeus of Miletus, who wrote in prose.

During the ***Classical period*** (c. 480–323 BC) lyric poetry reached its perfection with Pindar and Bacchylides. New literary genres appeared, especially in Athens, which for 150 years after the Persian Wars was the intellectual and artistic capital of the Greek world. Drama reached unsurpassed heights: tragedy with Aeschylus, Sophocles, and Euripides, and comedy with Eupolis, Cratinus, and Aristophanes. In the second half of the 5th and most of the 4th centuries BC prose flowered in several forms, including history, philosophy, and speeches (Herodotus, Thucydides, Xenophon, Plato, Aristotle, Isocrates, and Demosthenes).

During the ***Hellenistic period*** (323–27 BC), after the death of Alexander the Great, Athens lost its preponderance, but its philosophical schools continued to flourish with such teachers as Epicurus, Zeno of Citium, and Theophrastus, as also did comedy (Menander). The principal centres of Greek culture now were Antioch, Pergamum, Pella and, above all, the Ptolemaic court at Alexandria with its library which attracted poets and scientists alike. Alexandrian poetry revived some forms that had fallen into disuse: epic (Apollonius of Rhodes), didactic (Aratus), epigram and hymn (Callimachus). Herodas reintroduced mime, which had been first given literary form in the 5th century by Sophron. In this period also bucolic (pastoral) poetry begins with Theocritus. It was, moreover, an age of erudition, notably in the field of philology and textual criticism, exemplified in the work of Aristophanes of Byzantium and Callimachus, and in that of mathematics and geography (Eratosthenes, Euclid). Most of the great names of the Hellenistic period belong to the 3rd century. From 150 BC the influence of Rome became progressively stronger, and the Greek narrative of its ascendancy is that of Polybius. The 1st century BC also saw the first Greek anthology of epigrams, compiled by Meleager, and the work of the Jewish writers Philo Judaeus and Josephus, and the New Testament writers.

In the ***Roman period*** (c. 27 BC–c. AD 330) the city of Rome became the capital of the civilized world, and Latin the literary language *par excellence*. However, Greek continued to be spoken throughout the Mediterranean basin, and the following writers were outstanding: Flavius Arrianus, Dion Cassius, and Dionysius of Halicarnassus on history; Epictetus, Plutarch, and Marcus Aurelius on ethics and related subjects; Strabo and Pausanias on geography; Ptolemy on astronomy; Galen on medicine; Dionysius of Halicarnassus, Apollonius Dyscolus, Demetrius (author of *On Style*), and Longinus on grammar and literary criticism; Plotinus on neo-Platonism; and the theologians Clement and Origen on Christianity. The Roman period was also an age of compilers (Aelianus, Athenaeus, Diodorus Siculus). Rhetoric was represented by Aelius Aristides and moral satire by Lucian, while the novel appeared with Heliodorus (*Theagenes and Charicleia*).

modern After the fall of Constantinople, the Byzantine tradition was perpetuated in the Classical Greek writing of, for example, the 15th-century chronicles of Cyprus, various historical works in the 16th and 17th centuries, and educational and theological works in the 18th century. The 17th and 18th centuries saw much controversy over whether to write in the Greek vernacular (Demotic), the classical language (*Katharevousa*), or the language of the Eastern Orthodox Church. Adamantios Korais (1748–1833), the first great modern writer, produced a compromise language; he was followed by the prose and drama writer and poet Aleksandros Rhangavis ('Rangabe') (1810–1892), and others.

The 10th-century epic of *Digenis Akritas* is usually considered to mark the beginnings of modern Greek vernacular literature, and the Demotic was kept alive in the flourishing Cretan literature of the 16th and 17th centuries, in numerous popular songs, and in the Klephtic ballads of the 18th century. With independence in the 19th century the popular movement became prominent with the Ionian poet Dionysios Solomos (1798–1857), Andreas Kalvos (1796–1869), and others, and later with Iannis Psichari (1854–1929), short-story writer and dramatist, and the prose writer Alexandros Papadiamandis (1851–1911), who influenced many younger writers, for example Konstantinos Hatzopoulos (1868–1921), poet and essayist. After the 1920s, the novel began to emerge with Stratis Myrivilis (1892–1969) and Nikos Kazantzakis (1885–1957), author of *Zorba the Greek* 1946 and also a poet. There were also the Nobel-prize-winning poets George Seferis (1900–1971) and Odysseus Elytis (1911–1996).

Greek Orthodox Church see ◊Orthodox Church.

Greenaway Kate (Catherine) 1846–1901. English illustrator. She specialized in drawings of children. In 1877 she first exhibited at the Royal Academy, London, and began her collaboration with the colour printer Edmund Evans (1826–1905), with whom she produced a number of children's books, including *Mother Goose*. *See illustration on following page.*

Greenaway Peter 1942– . Welsh film director. His films are highly stylized and cerebral, richly visual, and often controversial. His feeling for perspective and lighting reveal his early training as a painter. *The Draughtsman's Contract* 1983, a tale of 18th-century country-house intrigue, is dazzling in its visual and narrative complexity. Other films include *A Zed and Two Noughts* 1985, *Drowning by Numbers* 1988, *The Cook, the Thief, His Wife and*

GREECE
Hellenic Republic

national name *Elliniki Dimokratia*
area 131,957 sq km/50,935 sq mi
capital Athens
major ports Piraeus, Thessaloníki, Patras, Iráklion
physical features mountainous (Mount Olympus); a large number of islands, notably Crete, Corfu, and Rhodes, and Cyclades and Ionian Islands
head of state Costis Stephanopoulos from 1995
head of government Costas Simitis from 1996
political system democratic republic
administrative divisions 13 regions divided into 51 departments
political parties Panhellenic Socialist Movement (PASOK), nationalist, democratic socialist; New Democracy Party (ND), centre-right; Democratic Renewal (DIANA), centrist; Communist Party (KJKE), left-wing; Political Spring, moderate, left of centre
armed forces 171,300; gendarmerie 26,500; National Guard 35,000 (June 1995)
conscription 19–24 months
defence spend (% GDP) 5.7 (1994)
education spend (% GNP) 3.1 (1992)
health spend (% GDP) 4.3 (1993)
death penalty abolished 1993
population 10,490,000 (1996 est)
population growth rate 0.4% (1990–95); 0.0% (2000–05)
age distribution (% of total population) <15 16.7%, 15–65 67.4%, >65 15.9% (1995)
ethnic distribution predominantly Greek; main minorities are Turks, Slavs, and Albanians
population density (per sq km) 79 (1994)
urban population (% of total) 65 (1995)
labour force 42% of population: 23% agriculture, 27% industry, 50% services (1990)
unemployment 8.8% (1995)
child mortality rate (under 5, per 1,000 live births) 10 (1993)
life expectancy 74 (men), 79 (women)
education (compulsory years) 9
literacy rate 98% (men), 89% (women)
languages Greek (official), Macedonian (100,000–200,000 est)
religions Greek Orthodox; also Roman Catholic
TV sets (per 1,000 people) 201 (1992)
currency drachma
GDP (US $) 122.8 billion (1996)
GDP per capita (PPP) (US $) 11,650 (1995)
growth rate 2.0% (1994/95)
average annual inflation 9.7% (1995)
major trading partners Germany, Italy, France, the Netherlands, USA, UK
resources bauxite, nickel, iron pyrites, magnetite, asbestos, marble, salt, chromite, lignite
industries food products, metals and metal products, textiles, petroleum refineries, machinery and transport equipment, tourism, wine
exports fruit and vegetables, clothing, mineral fuels and lubricants, textiles, iron and steel, aluminium and aluminium alloys. Principal market: Germany 23.7% (1993)
imports petroleum and petroleum products, machinery and transport equipment, food and live animals, chemicals and chemical products. Principal source: Germany 16.9% (1993)
arable land 18.3% (1993)
agricultural products fruit and vegetables, cereals, sugar beet, tobacco, olives; livestock and dairy products

HISTORY
c. 2000–1200 BC Mycenaean civilization flourished.
c. 1500–1100 BC Central Greece and Peloponnese invaded by tribes of Achaeans, Aeolians, Ionians, and Dorians.
c. 1000–500 BC Rise of the Greek city states; Greek colonies established around the shores of the Mediterranean.
c. 490–404 BC Ancient Greek culture reached its zenith in the democratic city state of Athens.
357–338 BC Philip II of Macedon won supremacy over Greece; cities fought to regain and preserve independence.
146 BC Roman Empire defeated Macedon and annexed Greece.
476 AD Western Roman Empire ended; Eastern Empire continued as Byzantine Empire, based at Constantinople, with essentially Greek culture.
1204 Crusaders partitioned Byzantine Empire; Athens, Achaea, and Thessaloniki came under Frankish rulers.
late 14th C–1461 Ottoman Turks conquered mainland Greece and captured Constantinople 1453; Greek language and culture preserved by Orthodox Church.
1685 Venetians captured Peloponnese; regained by Turks 1715.
late 18th C Beginnings of Greek nationalism among émigrés and merchant class.
1814 *Philike Hetairia* ('Friendly Society') formed by revolutionary Greek nationalists in Odessa.
1821 *Philike Hetairia* raised Peloponnese brigands in revolt against Turks; War of Independence ensued.
1827 Battle of Navarino: Britain, France, and Russia intervened to destroy Turkish fleet; Count Ioannis Kapodistrias elected president of Greece.
1829 Treaty of Adrianople: under Russian pressure, Turkey recognized independence of small Greek state.
1832 Great Powers elected Otto of Bavaria as king of Greece.
1843 Coup forced King Otto to grant a constitution.
1862 Mutiny and rebellion led King Otto to abdicate.
1863 George of Denmark became king of the Hellenes.
1864 Britain transferred Ionian islands to Greece.
1881 Following Treaty of Berlin (1878), Greece was allowed to annex Thessaly and part of Epirus.
late 19th C Politics dominated by Kharilaos Trikoupis, who emphasized economic development, and Theodoros Deliyiannis, who emphasized territorial expansion.
1897 Greco-Turkish War ended in Greek defeat.
1908 Cretan Assembly led by Eleutherios Venizelos proclaimed union with Greece.
1910 Venizelos became prime minister and introduced financial, military, and constitutional reforms.
1912–13 Balkan Wars: Greece annexed a large area of Epirus and Macedonia.
1916 'National Schism': Venizelos formed rebel pro-Allied government while royalists remained neutral.
1917–18 Greek forces fought on Allied side in World War I.
1919–22 Greek invasion of Asia Minor; after Turkish victory, a million refugees came to Greece.
1924 Republic declared amid great political instability.
1935 Greek monarchy restored with George II.
1936 General Ioannia Metaxas established right-wing dictatorship.
1940 Greece successfully repelled Italian invasion.
1941–44 German occupation of Greece; rival monarchist and communist resistance groups operated from 1942.
1946–49 Civil war: communists defeated by monarchists with military aid from Britain and USA.
1952 Became a member of NATO.
1967 'Greek Colonels' seized power under George Papadopoulos; political activity banned; King Constantine II exiled.
1973 Republic proclaimed with Papadopoulos as president.
1974 Cyprus crisis caused downfall of military regime; Constantine Karamanlis returned from exile to form Government of National Salvation and restore democracy.
1981 Andreas Papandreou elected Greece's first socialist prime minister; Greece entered the European Community.
1989–93 Election defeat of Panhellenic Socialist Movement (PASOK) followed by unstable coalition governments.
1993 PASOK returned to power.
1996 Costas Simitis succeeded Papandreou as prime minister. PASOK retained its majority in the general election.
1997 Direct talks with Turkey resulted in agreement to settle all future disputes peacefully.

SEE ALSO Athens; Byzantine Empire; Mycenaean civilization; Roman Empire

In human relations, kindness and lies are worth a thousand truths.

GRAHAM GREENE
The Heart of the Matter

GREECE, ANCIENT: TIMELINE

c. 1550–1100 BC	The first Greek civilization, based around the city of Mycenae; it owed much to the Minoan civilization of Crete and may have been produced by the intermarriage of Greek-speaking invaders with the original inhabitants.
c. 1300	A new wave of invasions began. The Achaeans overran Greece and Crete, destroying the Minoan and Mycenaean civilizations and penetrating Asia Minor.
1000	Aeolians, Ionians, and Dorians had settled in the area that is now Greece. Many independent city states, such as Sparta and Athens, had developed.
c. 800–500	During the Archaic Period, Ionian Greeks led the development of philosophy, science, and lyric poetry. The Greeks became great sea traders, and founded colonies around the coasts of the Mediterranean and the Black Sea, from Asia Minor in the east to Spain in the west.
776	The first Olympic games held.
594	The laws of Solon took the first step towards a more democratic society.
c. 560–510	The so-called 'tyranny' of the Pisistratids in Athens was typical of a pre-democratic stage that many Greek cities passed through after overturning aristocratic rule.
545	From this date the Ionian cities in Asia Minor fell under the dominion of the Persian Empire.
507	Cleisthenes, ruler of Athens, is credited with the establishment of democracy. Other cities followed this lead, but Sparta remained unique, a state in which a ruling race, organized on military lines, dominated the surrounding population.
499–494	The Ionian cities, aided by Athens, revolted unsuccessfully against the Persians.
490	Darius of Persia invaded Greece only to be defeated by the Athenians at Marathon and forced to withdraw.
480	Another invasion by the Persian emperor Xerxes, after being delayed by the heroic defence of Thermopylae by 300 Spartans, was defeated at sea off Salamis.
480–323	The Classical Period in ancient Greece.
479	The Persians defeated on land at Plataea.
478	The Ionian cities, now liberated, formed a naval alliance with Athens, the Delian League.
455–429	Under Pericles, the democratic leader of Athens, drama, sculpture, and architecture were at their peak.
433	The Parthenon in Athens was completed.
431–404	The Peloponnesian War destroyed the political power of Athens, but Athenian thought and culture remained influential. Sparta became the leading Greek power.
370	The philosopher Plato opened his Academy in Athens.
338	Philip II of Macedon (359–336 BC) took advantage of the wars between the city states and conquered Greece.
336–323	Rule of Philip's son, Alexander the Great. Alexander overthrew the Persian Empire, conquered Syria and Egypt, and invaded the Punjab. After his death, his empire was divided among his generals, but his conquests had spread Greek culture across the known world.
280	Achaean League of 12 Greek city states formed in an attempt to maintain their independence against Macedon, Egypt, and Rome.
146	Destruction of Corinth. Greece became part of the Roman Empire. Under Roman rule Greece remained a cultural centre and Hellenistic culture remained influential.

Greenaway *Afternoon Tea*, by the English illustrator Kate Greenaway. *Image Select (UK) Ltd*

Her Lover 1989, *Prospero's Books* 1991, and *The Pillow Book* 1995.

green belt area surrounding a large city, officially designated not to be built on but preserved where possible as open space (for agricultural and recreational use). In the UK the first green belts were established from 1938 around conurbations such as London in order to prevent urban sprawl. New towns were set up to take the overspill population.

Greene (Henry) Graham 1904–1991. English writer. His novels of guilt, despair, and penitence are set in a world of urban seediness or political corruption in many parts of the world. They include *Brighton Rock* 1938, *The Power and the Glory* 1940, *The Heart of the Matter* 1948, *The Third Man* 1949, *The Honorary Consul* 1973, and *Monsignor Quixote* 1982.

Stamboul Train 1932 proved the success of a format used by Greene with equal skill in other works, which he preferred to describe as 'entertainments'. They include *A Gun for Sale* 1936, *The Confidential Agent* 1939, *The Ministry of Fear* 1943, and *The Third Man* (written as a film script). Greene also wrote lighter, comic novels, including *Our Man in Havana* 1958 and *Travels with My Aunt* 1969.

greenfinch olive-green songbird *Carduelis chloris*, family Fringillidae, order Passeriformes, common in Europe and N Africa. It has bright-yellow markings on the outer tail feathers and wings.

greenfly plant-sucking insect, a type of ◊aphid.

Greenham Common site of a continuous peace demonstration 1981–90 on public land near Newbury, Berkshire, UK, outside a US airbase. The women-only camp was established 1981 in protest against the siting of US cruise missiles in the UK. The demonstrations ended with the closure of the base. Greenham Common reverted to standby status, and the last US cruise missiles were withdrawn 1991.

greenhouse effect phenomenon of the Earth's atmosphere by which solar radiation, trapped by the Earth and re-emitted from the surface, is prevented from escaping by various gases in the air. The result is a rise in the Earth's temperature (◊global warming). The main greenhouse gases are carbon dioxide, methane, and ◊chlorofluorocarbons (CFCs). Fossil-fuel consumption and forest fires are the main causes of carbon dioxide build-up; methane is a byproduct of agriculture (rice, cattle, sheep). Water vapour is another greenhouse gas.

The United Nations Environment Programme estimates that by 2025, average world temperatures will have risen by 1.5°C with a consequent rise of 20 cm in sea level. Low-lying areas and entire countries would be threatened by flooding and crops would be affected by the change in climate. However, predictions about global warming and its possible climatic effects are tentative and often conflicting .

At the 1992 Earth Summit it was agreed that by 2000 countries would stabilize carbon dioxide emissions at 1990 levels, but to halt global warming, emissions would probably need to be cut by 60%. Any increases in carbon dioxide emissions are expected to come from transport. The Berlin Mandate, agreed unanimously at the climate conference in Berlin 1995, committed industrial nations to the continuing reduction of greenhouse gas emissions after 2000, when the existing pact to stabilize emissions runs out. ▷ *See features on pp. 360–361 and pp. 858–859.*

Greenland (Greenlandic ***Kalaalit Nunaat***) world's largest island, lying between the North Atlantic and Arctic Oceans east of North America
area 2,175,600 sq km/840,000 sq mi
capital Godthåb (Greenlandic *Nuuk*) on the W coast
features the whole of the interior is covered by a vast ice sheet (the remnant of the last glaciation); the island has an important role strategically and in civil aviation, and shares military responsibilities with the USA; there are lead and cryolite deposits, and offshore oil is being explored
economy fishing and fish-processing
population (1993) 55,100; Inuit, Danish, and other European
language Greenlandic (Ammassalik Eskimoan)

Greenland

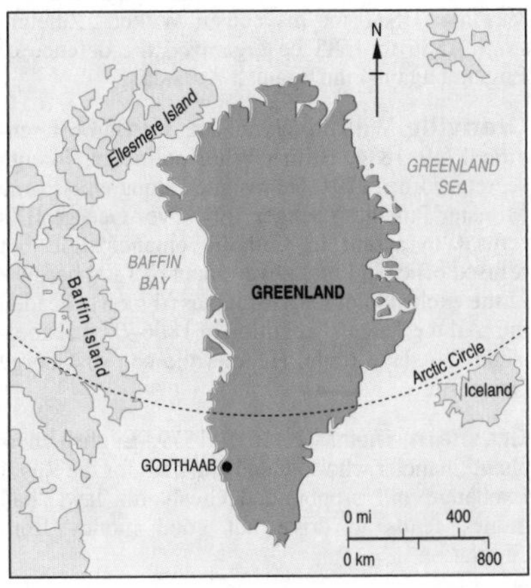

history Greenland was discovered about 982 by Eric the Red, who founded colonies on the W coast soon after Inuit from the North American Arctic had made their way to Greenland. Christianity was introduced to the Vikings about 1000. In 1261 the Viking colonies accepted Norwegian sovereignty, but early in the 15th century all communication with Europe ceased, and by the 16th century the colonies had died out, but the Inuit had moved on to the east coast. It became a Danish colony in the 18th century, and following a referendum 1979 was granted full internal self-government 1981.

Greenland Sea area of the ◊Arctic Ocean between Spitsbergen and Greenland, and N of the Norwegian Sea.

Green Man or ***Jack-in-the-Green*** in English folklore, a figure dressed and covered in foliage, associated with festivities celebrating the arrival of spring. His face is represented in a variety of English church carvings, in wood or stone, often with a protruding tongue. Similar figures also occur in French and German folklore.

Green Mountain Boys in US history, Revolutionary irregular troops who fought to protect the Vermont part of what was then New Hampshire colony from land claims made by neighbouring New York. In the American Revolution they captured ◊Fort Ticonderoga from the British. Their leader was Ethan Allen (1738–1789), who was later captured by the British. Vermont declared itself an independent republic, refusing to join the Union until 1791.

green movement collective term for the individuals and organizations involved in efforts to protect the environment. The movement encompasses political parties such as the ◊Green Party and organizations like ◊Friends of the Earth and ◊Greenpeace.

Greenock port on the S shore of the Firth of Clyde, Strathclyde, Scotland; population (1991) 50,000. Industries include shipbuilding, engineering, electronics, chemicals, and sugar refining.

Green Paper publication issued by a British government department setting out various aspects of a matter on which legislation is contemplated, and inviting public discussion and suggestions. In due course it may be followed by a ◊White Paper, giving details of proposed legislation.

Green Party political party aiming to 'preserve the planet and its people', based on the premise that incessant economic growth is unsustainable. The leaderless party structure reflects a general commitment to decentralization. Green parties sprang up in W Europe in the 1970s and in E Europe from 1988. Parties in different countries are linked to one another but unaffiliated with any pressure group.

A show of concern for the environment has increasingly been adopted by mainstream politics in Europe and the USA, rendering the Greens a less effective separate force. In Germany, the Green Party is the country's third largest force and has been represented in the *Bundestag* since 1983.

The British Green Party was founded 1973 as the Ecology Party (initially solely environmental). In the 1989 European elections, the British Green Party polled over 2 million votes but received no seats in Parliament, because Britain was the only country in Europe not to have some form of proportional representation. Internal disagreements from 1990 reduced its effectiveness and popular appeal and its membership contracted.

GREEN MOVEMENT: TIMELINE

1681	The last dodo, a long-standing symbol of the need for species conservation, died on the island of Mauritius.
1798	Thomas Malthus's *Essay on the Principle of Population* published, setting out the idea that humans are also bound by ecological constraints.
1824	Society for the Prevention of Cruelty to Animals founded in England.
1835–39	Droughts and famine in India resulted in the first connections being made between environmental damage (deforestation) and climate change.
1864	George Marsh's 'Man and Nature' was the first comprehensive study of humans' impact on the environment.
1865	Commons Preservation Society founded in England, raising the issue of public access to the countryside, taken further by the mass trespasses of the 1930s.
1868	First laws passed in the UK to protect birds.
1872	Yellowstone National Park created in the USA; a full system of national parks was established 40 years later.
1893	National Trust founded in the UK to buy land in order to preserve places of natural beauty and cultural landmarks.
1913	British Ecological Society founded.
1915	Ecological Society of America founded.
1930	Chlorofluorocarbons (CFCs) invented; they were hailed as a boon for humanity as they were not only cheap and nonflammable but were also thought not to be harmful to the environment.
1934	Russian ecologist G F Gause first stated the principles of competitive exclusion, related to a species' niche.
1935	British ecologist Arthur Tansley first coined the term 'ecosystem'.
1940	Population biologist Charles Elton developed the idea of trophic levels in a community of organisms.
1948	United Nations created special environmental agency, the International Union for the Conservation of Nature (IUCN).
1952	Air pollution caused massive smog in London, killing some 4,000 people and leading to clean-air legislation.
1962	Rachel Carson wrote *Silent Spring*, which attacked the use of chemical pesticides and inspired the creation of the environmental movement.
1967	US biologists MacArthur and Wilson proposed their 'Theory of Island Biogeography' which related population and community size to island size. The theory is still widely used in the design of nature reserves today.
1968	Garret Hardin's essay 'The Tragedy of the Commons' challenged individuals to recognize their personal reponsibility for environmental degradation as a result of lifestyle choices.
1969	Friends of the Earth launched in USA as a breakaway group from increasingly conservative Sierra Club.
1970	The Man and the Biosphere Programme was initiated by UNESCO, providing for an international network of biosphere reserves.
1971	The Convention on Wetlands of International Importance (especially concerned with wildfowl habitat) signed in Ramsar, Iran and started a List of Wetlands of International Importance.
1972	The UN Conference on the Human Environment held in Sweden led to the creation of the UN Environment Programme (UNEP).
	Blueprint for Survival, a detailed analysis of the human race's ecological predicament and proposed solutions, published in UK by Teddy Goldsmith and others from the *Ecologist* magazine.
1973	The Convention on International Trade in Endangered Species of Wild Fauna and Flora (CITES) signed in Washington DC.
1974	First scientific warning of serious depletion of protective ozone layer in upper atmosphere by CFCs.
1979	English naturalist James Lovelock proposed his Gaia hypothesis, viewing the planet as a single organism.
1980	The World Conservation Strategy launched by the IUCN, with the WWF and UNEP, showed how conservation contributes to development.
	US president Jimmy Carter commissioned *Global 2000* report, reflecting entry of environmental concerns into mainstream of political issues.
1983	German Greens (Die Grünen) won 5% of vote, giving them 27 seats in the Bundestag.
1985	Greenpeace boat *Rainbow Warrior* sunk by French intelligence agents in a New Zealand harbour during a protest against French nuclear testing in the S Pacific. One crew member was killed.
1986	The first 'Red List' of endangered animals compiled by IUCN.
1988	NASA scientist James Hansen warned US Congress of serious danger of global warming: 'The greenhouse effect is here'.
1989	European elections put green issues firmly on political agenda as Green parties across Europe attracted unprecedented support; especially in the UK, where the Greens received some 15% of votes cast (though not of seats).
	The Green Consumer Guide published in the UK, one of many such books worldwide advocating 'green consumerism'.
	International trade in ivory banned under CITES legislation in an effort to protect the African elephant from poachers.
1991	The Gulf War had massive environmental consequences, primarily as a result of the huge quantity of oil discharged into the Persian Gulf from Kuwait's oilfields. Many felt this was just the start of a grim future of wars over ever-decreasing resources.
1992	The UN convened the 'Earth Summit' in Rio de Janeiro, Brazil, to discuss global planning for a sustainable future. The Convention on Biological Diversity and the Convention on Climate Change were opened for signing.
1993	The Convention on Biological Diversity came into force.
1994	Protests against roadbuilding in many parts of the UK; for example, in 'Battle of Wanstonia', green activists occupied buildings and trees in E London in attempt to halt construction of M11 motorway.
1995	Animal-rights activists campaigned against the export of live animals. In May 1995 Greenpeace's London headquarters were raided by the Ministry of Defence and files and computer discs were confiscated.
1996	A new political force, Real World, was formed in the UK from a coalition of 32 campaigning charities and pressure groups.
1998	German Greens in coalition government, with representatives in top ministerial posts.

‘Human beings have an inalienable right to invent themselves; when that right is pre-empted it is called brain-washing.’

GERMAINE GREER
The Times 1 Feb 1986

Greenpeace international environmental pressure group, founded 1971, with a policy of nonviolent direct action backed by scientific research. During a protest against French atmospheric nuclear testing in the S Pacific 1985, its ship *Rainbow Warrior* was sunk by French intelligence agents, killing a crew member. In 1995 it played a prominent role in opposing the disposal of waste from an oil rig in the North Sea, and again attempted to disrupt French nuclear tests in the Pacific.

green pound exchange rate used by the European Union (EU) for the conversion of EU agricultural prices to sterling. The prices for all EU members are set in European Currency Units (ECUs) and are then converted into green currencies for each national currency.

green revolution in agriculture, the change in methods of arable farming instigated in the 1940s and 1950s in Third World countries. The intent was to provide more and better food for their populations, albeit with a heavy reliance on chemicals and machinery. In practice, it tended to benefit primarily those land-owners who could afford the investment necessary for such intensive agriculture. Much of the food produced was exported as ◊cash crops, so that local diet has not always improved. It was abandoned by some countries in the 1980s and ◊intermediate technologies have been adopted instead.

Greenwich Outer London borough of SE Greater London. It includes the districts of ◊Woolwich and Eltham.
features the Queen's House 1637, designed by Inigo Jones, the first Palladian-style building in England, since 1937 housing the National Maritime Museum; the Royal Naval College, designed by Christopher Wren 1694 as a naval hospital to replace a palace previously on this site (the birthplace of Henry VIII, Mary, Elizabeth I), and used as a college since 1873; the Royal Observatory (founded here 1675). The source of Greenwich Mean Time was moved to Herstmonceux, East Sussex 1958, and then to Cambridge 1990, but the Greenwich meridian (0°) remains unchanged. Part of the buildings have been taken over by the National Maritime Museum, and named Flamsteed House after the first ◊Astronomer Royal. The *Cutty Sark*, one of the great tea clippers, is preserved as a museum of sail and Francis Chichester's *Gipsy Moth IV* is also here
population (1991) 207,650.

Greenwich Mean Time (GMT) local time on the zero line of longitude (the ***Greenwich meridian***), which passes through the Old Royal Observatory at Greenwich, London. It was replaced 1986 by coordinated universal time (UTC), but continued to be used to measure longitudes and the world's standard time zones; see ◊time.

Greer Germaine 1939– . Australian academic and feminist, author of *The Female Eunuch* 1970. The book is a polemical study of how patriarchy – through the nuclear family and capitalism – subordinates women by forcing them to conform to feminine stereotypes that effectively ‘castrate’ them. It has been criticized by other feminists for placing too much emphasis on sexual liberation as the way forward. In *Sex and Destiny: The Politics of Human Fertility* 1984, a critique of the politics of fertility and contraception, Greer seemed to reverse this position. *The Change* 1991 is a positive view of the menopause.

Greer *The Australian feminist Germaine Greer came to prominence in the 1970s with her polemical study The Female Eunuch, which argues that women have to determine their own social and sexual identities. Some feminists criticized her later works, such as Sex and Destiny 1984, in which she argued that sexual liberation was often to women's detriment. Greer has also written on Shakespeare and on the nature of ageing. Penguin Books Ltd*

Gregorian chant any of a body of plainsong choral chants associated with Pope Gregory the Great (540–604), which became standard in the Roman Catholic Church.

Gregory name of 16 popes, including:

Gregory (I) the Great (St Gregory) c. 540–604. Pope from 590 who asserted Rome's supremacy and exercised almost imperial powers. In 596 he sent St ◊Augustine to England. He introduced the choral Gregorian chant into the liturgy. Feast day 12 March.

Gregory VII (monastic name ***Hildebrand***) c. 1023–1085. Chief minister to several popes before his election to the papacy 1073. He claimed power to depose kings, denied lay rights to make clerical appointments, and attempted to suppress simony (the buying and selling of church preferments) and to enforce clerical celibacy, making enemies of both rulers and the church. He was driven from Rome and died in exile. His feast day is 25 May. Canonized 1606.

Gregory XIII 1502–1585. Pope from 1572 who introduced the reformed ***Gregorian calendar***, still in use, in which a century year is not a leap year unless it is divisible by 400.

Gregory of Tours, St c. 538–594. French Christian bishop of Tours from 573, author of a *History of the Franks*. His feast day is 17 Nov.

Grenada island country in the Caribbean, the southernmost of the Windward Islands. *See country box opposite.*

grenade small missile, containing an explosive or other charge, usually thrown (hand grenade) but sometimes fired from a rifle. Hand grenades are generally fitted with a time fuse of about four seconds: a sufficient amount of time for the grenade to reach the target but not enough for the enemy to pick it up and throw it back.

Grenades were known in the 15th century, but were obsolete by the 19th, only being revived in the Russo-Japanese War 1905. They were revived once more when trench warfare began in World War I, first as locally-manufactured missiles – empty cans filled with gunpowder and stones, with a primitive fuse – and then as an official, properly-designed weapon. Rifle grenades were also developed in World War I, to achieve a greater range than was possible with the hand grenade.

The three standard patterns which survived World War I were the British Mills bomb and the French ‘pineapple’ grenade, both ball-like objects easily thrown, and the German stick grenade which carried the metal canister of explosive on the end of a wooden handle.

Grenadines chain of about 600 small islands in the Caribbean Sea, part of the group known as the Windward Islands. They are divided between ◊St Vincent and ◊Grenada.

Grenoble Alpine city in the Isère *département*, Rhône-Alpes region, SE France; population (1990) 154,000. Industries include engineering, nuclear research, hydroelectric power, computers, technology, chemicals, plastics, and gloves. There is a 12th–13th-century cathedral, a university (1339), and the Institut Laue-Langevin for nuclear research. It is the site of the ESRF (European Synchrotron Radiation Facility), the brightest X-ray machine in the world, inaugurated 1994. The 1968 Winter Olympics were held here.

Grenville George 1712–1770. British Whig politician, prime minister, and chancellor of the Exchequer, whose introduction of the ◊Stamp Act 1765 to raise revenue from the colonies was one of the causes of the American Revolution. His government was also responsible for prosecuting the radical John ◊Wilkes.

Grenville Richard c. 1541–1591. English naval commander and adventurer who died heroically aboard his ship *The Revenge* when attacked by Spanish warships. Grenville fought in Hungary and Ireland 1566–69, and was knighted about 1577. In 1585 he commanded the expedition that founded Virginia, USA, for his cousin Walter ◊Raleigh. From 1586 to 1588 he organized the defence of England against the Spanish Armada.

Grenville William Wyndham, 1st Baron Grenville 1759–1834. British Whig politician, foreign secretary from 1791. He resigned along with Prime Minister Pitt the Younger 1801 over George III's refusal to assent to Catholic emancipation but refused office in Pitt's government of 1804 because of the exclusion of Charles James ◊Fox. He headed the ‘All the Talents’ coalition of 1806–07 that abolished the slave trade. He was the son of George Grenville.

Gresham Thomas c. 1519–1579. English merchant financier who founded and paid for the Royal Exchange and propounded Gresham's law: ‘bad money tends to drive out good money from circulation’.

Gretna Green village in Dumfries and Galloway region, Scotland, where runaway marriages were legal after they were banned in England 1754; all that was necessary was the couple's declaration, before witnesses, of their willingness to marry. From 1856 Scottish law required at least one of the parties to be resident in Scotland for a minimum of 21 days before the marriage, and marriage by declaration was abolished 1940.

Gretzky Wayne 1961– . Canadian ice-hockey player, probably the best in the history of the National Hockey League (NHL). Gretzky played with the Edmonton Oilers 1979–88 and with the Los Angeles Kings from 1988. He took just 11 years to break the NHL scoring record of 1,850 goals (accumulated by Gordie Howe over 26 years) and won the Hart Memorial Trophy as the NHL's most valuable player of the season a record nine times (1980–87, 1989).

grievous bodily harm (GBH) in English law, very serious physical damage suffered by the victim of a crime. The courts have said that judges should not try to define grievous bodily harm but leave it to the jury to decide.

Grey Beryl 1927– . English dancer. Prima ballerina with the Sadler's Wells Company 1942–57, she then danced internationally, and was artistic director of the London Festival Ballet 1968–79.

Grey Charles, 2nd Earl Grey 1764–1845. British Whig politician. He entered Parliament 1786, and in 1806 became First Lord of the Admiralty, and foreign secretary soon afterwards. As prime minister 1830–34, he carried the Great Reform Bill that reshaped the parliamentary representative system 1832 and the act abolishing slavery throughout the British Empire 1833.

Grey Edward, 1st Viscount Grey of Fallodon 1862–1933. British Liberal politician, nephew of Charles Grey. As foreign secretary 1905–16 he negotiated an entente with Russia 1907, and backed France against Germany in the ◊Agadir Incident of 1911. In 1914 he said: ‘The lamps are going out all over Europe; we shall not see them lit again in our lifetime.’

Grey George 1812–1898. British colonial administrator in Australia and New Zealand. He was appointed governor of South Australia 1840 and managed to bring the colony out of bankruptcy by 1844. He was lieutenant governor of New Zealand 1845–53, governor of Cape Colony, S Africa, 1854–61, and governor of New Zealand 1861–68. He then entered the New Zealand parliament and was premier 1877–79.

Grey Lady Jane 1537–1554. Queen of England for nine days, 10–19 July 1553, the great-granddaughter of Henry VII. She was married 1553 to Lord Guildford Dudley (died 1554), son of the Duke of ◊Northumberland. Edward VI was persuaded by Northumberland to set aside the claims to the throne of his sisters Mary and Elizabeth. When Edward died on 6 July 1553, Jane reluctantly accepted the crown and was proclaimed queen four days later. Mary, although a Roman Catholic, had the support of the populace, and the Lord Mayor of London announced that she was queen 19 July. Grey was executed on Tower Green.

Grey (Pearl) Zane 1872–1939. US author of Westerns. He wrote more than 80 books, including *Riders of the Purple Sage* 1912, and was primarily responsible for the creation of the Western as a literary genre.

greyhound ancient breed of dog, with a long narrow head, slight build, and long legs. It stands up to 75 cm/30 in tall. It is renowned for its swiftness, and can exceed 60 kph/40 mph. Greyhounds were bred to hunt by sight, their main quarry being hares. Hunting hares with greyhounds is the basis of the ancient sport of ◊coursing.

greyhound racing spectator sport, invented in the USA 1919, that has a number of greyhounds pursuing a mechanical hare around a circular or oval track. It is popular in Great Britain and Australia, attracting much on- and off-course betting. The leading race in the UK is the Greyhound Derby, first held 1927, now run at Wimbledon, London. There are approximately 87 race tracks in the UK.

grid network by which electricity is generated and distributed over a region or country. It contains many power stations and switching centres and allows, for example, high demand in one area to be met by surplus power generated in another.

The term is also used for any grating system, as in a cattle grid and a conductor in a storage battery or electron gun.

grid reference on a map, numbers that are used to show location. The numbers at the bottom of the map (eastings) are given before those at the side (northings). On British Ordnance Survey maps, a four-figure grid reference indicates a specific square, whereas a six-figure grid reference indicates a point within a square.

Grieg Edvard (Hagerup) 1843–1907. Norwegian nationalist composer. Much of his music is small-scale, particularly his songs, dances, sonatas, and piano works, strongly identifying with Norwegian folk music. Among his orchestral works are the *Piano Concerto in A Minor* 1869 and the incidental music for Henrik Ibsen's drama *Peer Gynt* 1876, commissioned by Ibsen and the Norwegian government.

Grieg studied in Germany at the Leipzig Conservatoire and in Copenhagen. He was a director of the Christiania (Oslo) Philharmonic Society 1866 and played a part in the formation of the Norwegian Academy of Music.

Grierson John 1898–1972. Scottish film producer, director, and theoretician. He pioneered the documentary film in Britain in the 1930s when he produced a series of information and publicity shorts for the General Post Office (GPO). The best known is *Night Mail* 1936, an account of the journey of the London–Glasgow mail train, directed by Basil Wright (1907–1987) and Harry Watt (1906–1987), with a score by Benjamin Britten and a commentary written by poet W H Auden.

grievance cause of complaint. Sexual harassment or unfair promotion policies may be a source of grievance for workers. They may take this up through their company's grievance procedure, which will often have been negotiated with a trade union. If they are sacked as a result, they may go to an industrial tribunal.

griffin mythical monster, the supposed guardian of hidden treasure, with the body, tail, and hind legs of a lion, and the head, forelegs, and wings of an eagle.

Griffith D(avid) W(ark) 1875–1948. US film director. He was an influential figure in the development of cinema as an art. He made hundreds of 'one-reelers' 1908–13, in which he pioneered the techniques of masking, fade-out, flashback, cross-cut, close-up, and long shot. After much experimentation with photography and new techniques he directed *The Birth of a Nation* 1915, about the aftermath of the Civil War, later criticized as degrading to blacks. His other films include the epic *Intolerance* 1916, *Broken Blossoms* 1919, *Way Down East* 1920, *Orphans of the Storm* 1921, and *The Struggle* 1931. He was a cofounder of United Artists 1919. He made two unsuccessful sound films.

griffon small breed of dog originating in Belgium. Red, black, or black and tan in colour and weighing up to 5 kg/11 lb, griffons are square-bodied and round-headed. There are rough- and smooth-coated varieties. The name is also applied to several larger breeds of hunting dogs with rough coats.

griffon vulture Old World vulture *Gyps fulvus* of the family Accipitridae, found in S Europe, W and Central Asia, and parts of Africa. It has a bald head with a neck ruff, and is 1.1 m/3.5 ft long with a wingspan of up to 2.7 m/9 ft.

Grignard (François Auguste) Victor 1871–1935. French chemist. In 1900 he discovered a series of organic compounds, the Grignard reagents, that found applications as some of the most versatile reagents in organic synthesis. Members of the class contain a hydrocarbon radical, magnesium, and a halogen such as chlorine. He shared the 1912 Nobel Prize for Chemistry.

Grillparzer Franz 1791–1872. Austrian poet and dramatist. His plays include the tragedy *Die Ahnfrau/The Ancestress* 1817, the classical *Sappho* 1818, and the trilogy *Das goldene Vliess/The Golden Fleece* 1821. His two greatest dramas are *Des Meeres und der Liebe Wellen/The Waves of Sea and Love* 1831 and *Der Traum, ein Leben/A Dream is Life* 1834.

Grimaldi Joseph 1779–1837. English clown. Born in London, he was the son of an Italian actor. He appeared on the stage at two years old. He gave his name 'Joey' to all later clowns, and excelled as 'Mother Goose' performed at Covent Garden 1806.

Grimm brothers Jakob (Ludwig Karl) (1785–1863) and Wilhelm (1786–1859), philologists and collectors of German fairy tales such as 'Hansel and Gretel' and 'Rumpelstiltskin'. Joint compilers of an exhaustive dictionary of German, they saw the study of language and the collecting of folk tales as strands in a single enterprise. Encouraged by a spirit of Romantic nationalism, the brothers collected stories from friends, relatives, and villagers. *Kinder und Hausmärchen/Nursery and Household Tales* were published as successive volumes 1812, 1815, and 1822. Jakob was professor of philology at Göttingen and formulator of ◊Grimm's law. His *Deutsche Grammatick/German Grammar* 1819 was the first historical treatment of the ◊Germanic languages.

Grimm's law in linguistics, the rule (formulated 1822 by Jakob Grimm) by which certain prehistoric sound changes have occurred in the consonants of Indo-European languages: for example Latin *p* became English and German *f* sound, as in *pater – father, Vater*.

Grimond Jo(seph), Baron Grimond 1913–1993. British Liberal politician. As leader of the Liberal Party 1956–67, he aimed at making it 'a new radical party to take the place of the Socialist Party as an alternative to Conservatism'. An old-style Whig and a man of culture and personal charm, he had a considerable influence on postwar British politics, although he never held a major public position. During his term of office, the number of Liberal seats in Parliament doubled.

'I moved the whole world onto a twenty-foot screen. I was a greater discover than Columbus. I condensed history into three hours and made them live it.'

D W Griffith
Quoted in A Rogers St Johns *The Honeycomb*

GRENADA

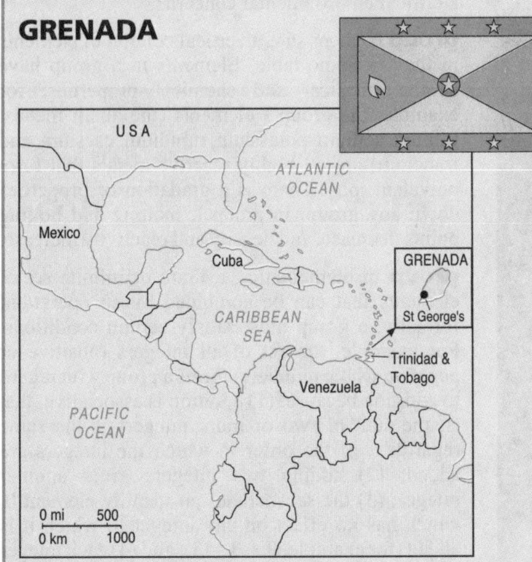

area (including the Grenadines, notably Carriacou) 344 sq km/133 sq mi
capital St George's
major towns/cities Grenville, Hillsborough (Carriacou)
physical features southernmost of the Windward Islands; mountainous; Grand-Anse beach; Annandale Falls; the Great Pool volcanic crater
head of state Elizabeth II from 1974, represented by governor general Reginald Palmer from 1992
head of government Keith Mitchell from 1995
political system emergent democracy
administrative divisions six parishes
political parties Grenada United Labour Party (GULP), nationalist, left of centre; National Democratic Congress (NDC), centrist; National Party (TNP), centrist
population 96,000 (1995 est)
population growth rate 0.3% (1990–95)
ethnic distribution majority is of black African descent
life expectancy 69
literacy rate 96%
languages English (official); some French-African patois spoken
religions Roman Catholic 53%, Anglican, Seventh Day Adventist, Pentecostal
currency Eastern Caribbean dollar
GDP (US $) 172 million (1994)
growth rate 0.9% (1994)
exports cocoa, nutmeg, bananas, mace, textiles

HISTORY
1498 Sighted by the explorer Christopher Columbus; Spanish named it Grenada since its hills were reminiscent of the famous Andalusian city.
1650 Colonized by French settlers from Martinique, who faced resistance from the local Carib Indian community armed with poison arrows, before the defeated Caribs performed a mass suicide.
1783 Ceded to Britain as a colony by the Treaty of Versailles; black African slaves imported to work cotton, sugar, and tobacco plantations.
1795 Abortive rebellion against British rule led by Julien Fedon, a black planter inspired by the ideas of the French Revolution.
1834 Slavery abolished.
1950 Left-wing Grenada United Labour Party (GULP) founded by trade union leader Eric Gairy.
1951 Universal adult suffrage granted and GULP elected to power in a nonautonomous local assembly.
1958–62 Part of the Federation of the West Indies.
1967 Internal self-government achieved.
1974 Independence achieved within the Commonwealth, with Gairy as prime minister.
1979 Autocratic Gairy removed in bloodless coup led by left-wing Maurice Bishop of the New Jewel Movement; constitution suspended and a People's Revolutionary Government established.
1982 Relations with the USA and Britain deteriorated as ties with Cuba and the Soviet Union strengthened.
1983 After attempts to improve relations with the USA, Bishop was overthrown by left-wing opponents, precipitating military coup by Gen Hudson Austin. Bishop and three colleagues executed. USA invaded, accompanied by troops from other E Caribbean countries; there were 250 fatalities. Austin arrested and 1974 constitution reinstated.
1984 Newly formed centre-left New National Party (NNP) won general election and its leader, Herbert Blaize, became prime minister.
1989 Blaize replaced as leader of NNP, but remained as head of government; on his death, he was succeeded by Ben Jones.
1991 Inconclusive general election; Nicholas Braithwaite of the centrist National Democratic Congress (NDC) became prime minister. Windward Islands confederation proposed.
1995 Brathwaite retired and was succeeded as prime minister by the new NDC leader, George Brizan. General election won by NNP, led by Keith Mitchell. A plague of pink mealy bugs caused damage to crops estimated at $60 million, depriving 15,000 farmers of an income.

SEE ALSO Carib; West Indies, Federation of

The human mind is like an umbrella – it functions best when open.

Walter Adolf Gropius Quoted in the *Observer* 1965

Not to know something is a great part of wisdom.

Hugo Grotius *Docta Ignorantia*

Grimsby fishing port and administrative headquarters of North East Lincolnshire, England; population (1991) 90,500. It declined in the 1970s when Icelandic waters were closed to British fishing fleets.

Grimshaw Nicholas Thomas 1939– . English architect. His work has developed along distinctly High Tech lines, diverging sharply from that of his former partner, Terry ◊Farrell. His *Financial Times* printing works, London 1988, is an uncompromising industrial building, exposing machinery to view through a glass outer wall. The British Pavilion for Expo'92 in Seville, created in similar vein, addressed problems of climatic control, incorporating a huge wall of water in its façade and sail-like mechanisms on the roof.

Gris Juan. Adopted name of José Victoriano Gonzalez 1887–1927. Spanish painter, one of the earliest Cubists. He developed a distinctive geometrical style, often strongly coloured. He experimented with paper collage and made designs for Serge Diaghilev's Ballets Russes 1922–23.

Gris went to Paris 1906, meeting Picasso, whose disciple he became, and began to paint about 1910. He had a precise and scientific outlook and delighted in variations of geometric form effectively combined with an imitative rendering of substance; for example, the grain of wood and the use of *papiers collés* – abstract collage. In addition to oil paintings he produced some etchings and lithographs as book illustrations.

Gromyko Andrei Andreyevich 1909–1989. President of the USSR 1985–88. As ambassador to the USA from 1943, he took part in the Tehran, Yalta, and Potsdam conferences; as United Nations representative 1946–49, he exercised the Soviet veto 26 times. He was foreign minister 1957–85. It was Gromyko who formally nominated Mikhail Gorbachev as Communist Party leader 1985.

Groningen most northerly province of the Netherlands, on the Ems estuary and including the innermost W Friesian Islands; area 2,350 sq km/907 sq mi; population (1995 est) 558,000; capital Groningen. Other towns and cities are Hoogezand-Sappemeer, Stadskanaal, Veendam, Delfzijl, and Winschoten. Industries include natural gas, arable farming, dairy produce, sheep, and horses.

history Under the power of the bishops of Utrecht from 1040, Groningen became a member of the Hanseatic League 1284. Taken by Spain 1580, it was recaptured by Maurice of Nassau 1594.

grooming in biology, the use by an animal of teeth, tongue, feet, or beak to clean fur or feathers. Grooming also helps to spread essential oils for waterproofing. In many social species, notably monkeys and apes, grooming of other individuals is used to reinforce social relationships.

grooming Bonnet macaques *Macaca radiata* from S India usually spend the hottest part of the day grooming each other. This helps not only to keep their skins free of parasites but also to strengthen social relationships. *Premaphotos Wildlife*

Gropius Walter Adolf 1883–1969. German architect, in the USA from 1937. He was an early exponent of the ◊International Style, defined by glass curtain walls, cubic blocks, and unsupported corners – the model factory and office building at the 1914 Cologne Werkbund exhibition, designed with Adolph Meyer, was an early example. A founder director of the ◊Bauhaus school in Weimar 1919–28, he advocated teamwork in design and artistic standards in industrial production. He was responsible for the new Bauhaus premises in Dessau 1925–26. From 1937 he was professor of architecture at Harvard. His other works include the Fagus Works (a shoe factory in Prussia) 1911 and the Harvard Graduate Centre 1949–50.

Gropius German-born US architect and designer Walter Gropius. He was one of the outstanding architects of his time and also a teacher of unsurpassed importance – he founded the Bauhaus, the most influential art school of the 20th century. *Corbis*

gross domestic product (GDP) value of the output of all goods and services produced within a nation's borders, normally given as a total for the year. It thus includes the production of foreign-owned firms within the country, but excludes the income from domestically owned firms located abroad. In the UK, the percentage increase in GDP from one year to the next is the standard measure of economic growth. See also ◊gross national product.

Grossglockner highest mountain in Austria, rising to 3,797 m/12,457 ft in the Hohe Tauern range of the Tirol Alps.

gross national product (GNP) the most commonly used measurement of the wealth of a country. GNP is defined as the total value of all goods and services produced by firms owned by the country concerned. It is measured as the ◊gross domestic product plus income from abroad, minus income earned during the same period by foreign investors within the country; see also ◊national income.

Grosz George 1893–1959. German-born US Expressionist painter and graphic artist. He was a founder of the Berlin Dada group 1918, and excelled in savage satirical drawings criticizing the government and the military establishment. After numerous prosecutions, he fled his native Berlin 1932 and went to the USA.

His brilliant drawings make him a leader in the school of German Expressionism, but from 1933 he and his work disappeared into oblivion so far as the majority of Germans were concerned, since his paintings were among those condemned in the Nazi dictator Hitler's exhibition ◊Degenerate Art. Even in the late 1920s, long before Hitler had come to power, Grosz's *Ecce Homo*, showing Christ on the Cross wearing a gas mask and army boots, brought him to court on a charge of blasphemy. He is also associated with the *Neue Sachlichkeit* (New Objectivity) movement.

Grotius Hugo, or ***Huig de Groot*** 1583–1645. Dutch jurist and politician. His book *De Jure Belli et Pacis/On the Law of War and Peace* 1625 is the foundation of international law.

Grotowski Jerzy 1933–1999. Polish theatre director. His ascetic theory of performance in *Towards a Poor Theatre* 1968 has had a great influence on experimental theatre in the USA and Europe. His most famous productions were *Akropolis* 1962, *The Constant Prince* 1965, and *Apocalypsis cum Figuris* 1969, which he toured widely. His company, originally the Theatre of the Thirteen Rows, was renamed the Laboratory Theatre 1962.

ground water water collected underground in porous rock strata and soils; it emerges at the surface as springs and streams. The groundwater's upper level is called the water table. Sandy or other kinds of beds that are filled with groundwater are called aquifers. Recent estimates are that usable ground water amounts to more than 90% of all the fresh water on Earth; however, keeping such supplies free of pollutants entering the recharge areas is a critical environmental concern.

group in chemistry, a vertical column of elements in the ◊periodic table. Elements in a group have similar physical and chemical properties; for example, the group I elements (the alkali metals: lithium, sodium, potassium, rubidium, caesium, and francium) are all highly reactive metals that form univalent ions. There is a gradation of properties down any group: in group I, melting and boiling points decrease, and density and reactivity increase.

group in mathematics, a finite or infinite set of elements that can be combined by an operation; formally, a group must satisfy certain conditions. For example, the set of all integers (positive or negative whole numbers) forms a group with regard to addition because: (1) addition is associative, that is, the sum of two or more integers is the same regardless of the order in which the integers are added; (2) adding two integers gives another integer; (3) the set includes an identity element 0, which has no effect on any integer to which it is added (for example, $0 + 3 = 3$); and (4) each integer has an inverse (for instance, 7 has the inverse -7), such that the sum of an integer and its inverse is 0.

grouper any of several species of large sea perch (Serranidae), found in warm waters. Some species grow to 2 m/6.5 ft long, and can weight 300 kg/660 lbs. Formerly game fish, they are now commercially exploited as food.

Group of Seven (G7) the seven leading industrial nations of the world: the USA, Japan, Germany, France, the UK, Italy, and Canada, which account for more than three-fifths of global GDP. Since 1975 their heads of government have met once a year to discuss economic and, increasingly, political matters; annuals summits are also attended by the president of the European Commission and, from 1991, Russia.

grouse fowl-like game bird of the subfamily Tetraonidae, order Galliformes, in the pheasant family Phasianidae. Grouse are native to North America and N Europe. They are mostly ground-living. During the mating season the males undertake elaborate courtship displays in small individual territories (◊leks). Among the most familiar are the ***red grouse*** *Lagopus scoticus*, a native of Britain; the ◊***ptarmigan***; the ***ruffed grouse*** *Bonasa umbellus*, common in North American woods; and the ***capercaillie*** *Tetrao urogallus* and ***blackcock*** *Tetrao tetrix*, both known in Britain. The grouse-shooting season is 12 Aug to 10 Dec.

growth hormone (GH) or **somatotrophin**, hormone from the anterior ◊pituitary gland that promotes growth of long bones and increases protein synthesis. If it is lacking in childhood, dwarfism results; excess GH causes gigantism. Growth hormone releasing hormone (GHRH) and the peptide somatostatin, both produced in the hypothalamus, control its release.

growth ring another name for ◊annual ring.

groyne wooden or concrete barrier built at right angles to a beach in order to block the movement of material along the beach by longshore drift.

Grozny capital of Chechnya and of the former Russian republic of Checheno-Ingush; population (1992) 388,000. Situated on the Sunzha River, it was founded 1818 as a Cossack fortress. Large-scale oil production began 1893 and it became a major oil centre with pipelines to the Caspian Sea at Makhachkala and the Black Sea at Tuapse. Half its residential areas were damaged beyond repair and its infrastructure destroyed by Russian bombing 1994–95.

GRP abbreviation for ◊***glass-reinforced plastic***.

Grünewald Matthias, or Mathis Gothardt-Neithardt c. 1475–1528. German painter, architect, and engineer. Untouched by the spirit of the Renaissance, he created works that, though medieval in spirit, had a wholly new intensity of feeling. His altarpiece at Isenheim, southern Alsace, 1515 (Unterlinden Museum, Colmar, France), with its grotesquely tortured figure of Jesus and its radiant *Resurrection*, is his most important work.

grunge rock-music style of the early 1990s, characterized by a thick, abrasive, distorted sound. Grunge evolved from ◊punk in the Seattle, Washington, area of the USA and came to prominence with the chart success of the band ◊Nirvana 1991.

g-scale scale for measuring force by comparing it with the force due to ◊gravity (*g*), often called ◊g-force.

Guadalajara industrial city (textiles, glass, soap, pottery), capital of Jalisco state, W Mexico; population (1990) 2,847,000. It is a key communications centre. It has a 16th–17th-century cathedral, the Governor's Palace, and an orphanage with murals by the Mexican painter José Orozco (1883–1949).

Guadalcanal largest of the ◊Solomon Islands; area 6,500 sq km/2,510 sq mi; population (1991) 60,700. Gold, copra, and rubber are produced.

Guadeloupe island group in the Leeward Islands, West Indies, an overseas *département* of France. The main islands are Basse-Terre and Grande-Terre
area 1,705 sq km/658 sq mi
chief town The chief town and seat of government is Basse-Terre (on the island of the same name), population (1988) 14,000.
population (1990) 387,000 (77% mulatto, 10% black, and 10% mestizo). The people of St Barthélemy and Les Saintes are mainly descended from 17th century Norman and Breton settlers
languages French (official); Creole (the main language)
industries sugar refining and rum distilling
history Columbus reached here 1493, and the indigenous Caribs fought against Spanish colonization. A French colony was established 1635.

Guam largest of the ◊Mariana Islands in the W Pacific, an unincorporated territory of the USA
area 540 sq km/208 sq mi
capital Agaña
towns and cities Apra (port), Tamuning
features major US air and naval base, much used in the Vietnam War; tropical, with much rain
industries sweet potatoes, fish; tourism is important
currency US dollar
population (1992) 140,200
language English, Chamorro (basically Malay-Polynesian)
religion 96% Roman Catholic
government popularly elected governor (Joseph F Ada from 1991) and single-chamber legislature
history claimed by Magellan for Spain 1521. The indigenous population dwindled from 80,000 in 1668 to 1,500 in 1783, partly as a result of infectious disease, partly as a result of Spanish brutality. Guam was ceded by Spain to the USA 1898; occupied by Japan as an air and naval base 1941–44; achieved full US citizenship and self-government from 1950. It became the headquarters of the US Pacific Strategic Air Command 1954 and is also central command for all US naval operations in the W Pacific. A referendum 1982 favoured the status of a commonwealth, in association with the USA. ▷ *See feature on pp. 806–807.*

guanaco hoofed ruminant *Lama guanacoe* of the camel family, found in South America on pampas and mountain plateaux. It grows to 1.2 m/4 ft at the shoulder, with head and body about 1.5 m/5 ft long. It is sandy brown in colour, with a blackish face, and has fine wool. It lives in small herds and is the ancestor of the domestic ◊llama and ◊alpaca.

Guangdong or ***Kwantung*** province of S China
area 231,400 sq km/89,320 sq mi
capital Guangzhou
features tropical climate; Hainan, Leizhou peninsula, Hong Kong, and the foreign enclave of Macao in the Pearl River delta
industries rice, sugar, tobacco, minerals, fish
population (1990) 63,210,000.

Guangxi or ***Kwangsi Chuang*** autonomous region in S China
area 220,400 sq km/85,074 sq mi
capital Nanning
industries rice, sugar, fruit
population (1990) 42,246,000, including the Zhuang people, allied to the Thai, who form China's largest ethnic minority.

Guangzhou or ***Kwangchow*** or ***Canton*** capital of Guangdong province, S China; population (1993) 3,560,000. Industries include shipbuilding, engineering, chemicals, and textiles. It was the first Chinese port opened to foreign trade.

guano dried excrement of fish-eating birds that builds up under nesting sites. It is a rich source of nitrogen and phosphorous, and is widely collected for use as fertilizer. Some 80% comes from the sea cliffs of Peru.

Grünewald *Crucifixion* c. 1519 by Grünewald (National Gallery of Art, Washington). Unlike his great contemporary, Dürer, Grünewald was untouched by the elegance and harmony of Italian Renaissance art. His dark, harrowing pictures are among the most vivid expressions of an intense religious art that has a long history in German culture. *Corbis*

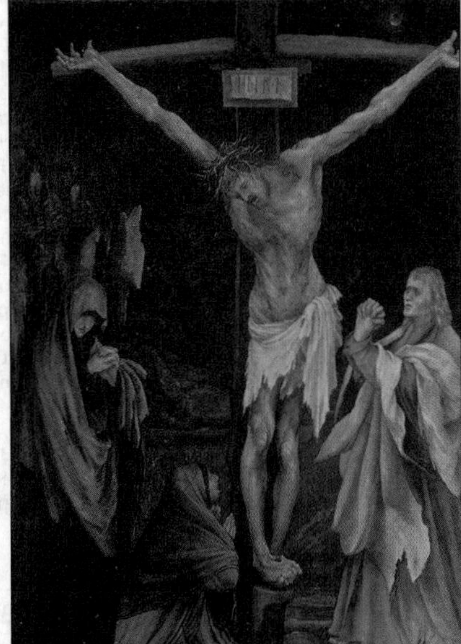

Guanyin in Chinese Buddhism, the goddess of mercy. In Japan she is ***Kannon*** or Kwannon, an attendant of the Amida Buddha (Amitābha). Her origins are Indian from the male bodhisattva Avalokiteśvara.

guarana Brazilian woody climbing plant *Paullinia cupana*, family Sapindaceae. A drink made from its roasted seeds has a high caffeine content, and it is the source of the drug known as zoom in the USA. Starch, gum, and several oils are extracted from it for commercial use.

Guaraní member of a Native American people who formerly inhabited the area that is now Paraguay, S Brazil, and Bolivia; they now live mainly in reserves. About 1 million speak Guaraní, a member of the Tupian language group.

guard cell in plants, a specialized cell on the undersurface of leaves for controlling gas exchange and water loss. Guard cells occur in pairs and are shaped so that a pore, or ◊stomata, exists between them. They can change shape with the result that the pore disappears. During warm weather, when a plant is in danger of losing excessive water, the guard cells close, cutting down evaporation from the interior of the leaf.

Guardi Francesco 1712–1793. Italian painter. He produced souvenir views of his native Venice that were commercially less successful than Canaletto's but are now considered more atmospheric, with subtler use of reflected light. His output was large and he seems to have been assisted by his son Giacomo (1764–1835), who produced *gouache* views in a style of his own. As well as famous buildings and splendid occasions, Guardi painted insular byways and architectural caprices with ruins, with a sparkling touch and a sense of atmosphere that might be called impressionist. *See illustration on following page.*

Guarneri family of stringed-instrument makers of Cremona, Italy. Giuseppe 'del Gesù' Guarneri (1698–1744) produced the finest models.

Guatemala country in Central America, bounded N and NW by Mexico, E by Belize and the Caribbean Sea, SE by Honduras and El Salvador, and SW by the Pacific Ocean. *See country box on p. 470.*

Guatemala City capital of Guatemala; population (1990 est) 1,675,600. It produces textiles, tyres, footwear, and cement. It was founded 1776 when its predecessor (Antigua) was destroyed in an earthquake. It was severely damaged by another earthquake 1976.

guava tropical American tree *Psidium guajava* of the myrtle family Myrtaceae; the astringent yellow pear-shaped fruit has a high vitamin-C content.

Guayaquil largest city and chief port of Ecuador near the mouth of the Guayas River; population (1990) 1,508,000. The economic centre of Ecuador and the capital of Guayas province, Guayaquil manufactures machinery and consumer goods, processes food, and refines petroleum. It was founded 1537 by the Spanish explorer Francisco de Orellana. The port exports bananas, cacao, and coffee.

Gucci Italian–US company manufacturing and retailing leather luggage and accessories from the 1960s, and designing clothes for men and women from 1969. The Gucci family firm was founded in Italy in the 15th century. In 1905 Guccio Gucci moved from millinery to saddlery, and the business was expanded by his three sons, principally Aldo Gucci (1905–1990), who was responsible for the company's growth in the USA.

gudgeon any of an Old World genus *Gobio* of freshwater fishes of the carp family, especially *G. gobio* found in Europe and N Asia on the gravel bottoms of streams. It is olive-brown, spotted with black, and up to 20 cm/8 in long, with a distinctive barbel (a sensory fleshy filament) at each side of the mouth.

Guelph and Ghibelline rival parties in medieval Germany and Italy, which supported the papal party and the Holy Roman emperors respectively. They originated in the 12th century as partisans of rival German houses, that of Welf (hence Guelph or

***Guardi** Venice: Punta della Dogana with Santa Maria della Salute* by Guardi (National Gallery, London). Views of Venice were extremely popular during the 18th century, Guardi's being valued for capturing both the city's vitality and also its subtle effects of light and atmosphere. *Corbis*

Guelf) of the dukes of Bavaria, and that of the lords of ◊Hohenstaufen (whose castle at Waiblingen gave the Ghibellines their name). The Hohenstaufens supplied five Roman emperors: Conrad II (1138–52); Conrad's nephew Frederick Barbarossa (1152–89); Frederick's son, Henry VI 'The Severe' (1190–97); and Frederick's grandson and great-grandson Frederick II (1212–50) and Conrad IV (1250–54); but the dynasty died out 1268. The Guelphs early became associated with the papacy because of their mutual Hohenstaufen enemy. In Italy, the terms were introduced about 1242 in Florence; the names seem to have been grafted on to pre-existing papal and imperial factions within the city-republics.

Guérin Camille 1872–1961. French bacteriologist who, with Albert ◊Calmette, developed the ◊BCG vaccine for tuberculosis 1921.

Guernica large oil painting (3.5 m × 7.8 m/11 ft 5 in × 25 ft 6 in) by Pablo Picasso as a mural for the Spanish pavilion at the Paris Exposition Universelle 1937 (now in the Prado, Madrid), inspired by the bombing of Guernica, the seat of the Basque parliament during the Spanish Civil War. The painting, executed entirely in black, white, and grey, has become a symbol of the senseless destruction of war.

Guernsey second largest of the ◊Channel Islands; area 63 sq km/24.3 sq mi; population (1991) 58,900. The capital is St Peter Port. Products include electronics, tomatoes, flowers, and butterflies; from 1975 it has been a major financial centre. Guernsey cattle, which are a distinctive pale fawn colour and give rich, creamy milk, originated here. Guernsey has belonged to the English crown since 1066, but was occupied by German forces 1940–45. The island has no jury system; instead, it has a Royal Court with 12 jurats (full-time unpaid jurors appointed by an electoral college) with no legal training. This system dates from Norman times. Jurats cannot be challenged or replaced.

guerrilla (Spanish 'little war') irregular soldier fighting in a small, unofficial unit, typically against an established or occupying power, and engaging in sabotage, ambush, and the like, rather than pitched battles against an opposing army. Guerrilla tactics have been used both by resistance armies in wartime (for example, the Vietnam War) and in peacetime by national liberation groups and militant political extremists (for example, the Tamil Tigers).

The term was first applied to the Spanish and Portuguese resistance to French occupation during the Peninsular War 1808–14. Guerrilla techniques were widely used in World War II – for example, in Greece and the Balkans. Political activists who resort to violence, particularly urban guerrillas, tend to be called 'freedom fighters' by those who support their cause, 'terrorists' by those who oppose it. Efforts by governments to put a stop to their activities have had only sporadic success. In the UK, the Prevention of Terrorism Act 1984 was aimed particularly at the Irish Republican Army.

Guevara Che (Ernesto) 1928–1967. Latin American revolutionary. He was born in Argentina and trained there as a doctor, but left his homeland 1953 because of his opposition to the right-wing president Juan Perón. In effecting the Cuban revolution of 1959, he was second only to Castro and Castro's brother Raúl. In 1965 he went to the Congo to fight against white mercenaries, and then to Bolivia, where he was killed in an unsuccessful attempt

GUATEMALA
Republic of

national name *República de Guatemala*
area 108,889 sq km/42,031 sq mi
capital Guatemala City
major towns/cities Quezaltenango, Puerto Barrios (naval base)
physical features mountainous; narrow coastal plains; limestone tropical plateau in N; frequent earthquakes
head of state and government Alvaro Arzú from 1996
political system democratic republic
administrative divisions 22 departments
political parties Guatemalan Christian Democratic Party (PDCG), Christian, centre-left; Centre Party (UCN), centrist; Revolutionary Party (PR), radical; Movement of National Liberation (MLN), extreme right-wing; Democratic Institutional Party (PID), moderate conservative; Solidarity and Action Movement (MAS), right of centre; Guatemalan Republican Front (FRG), right-wing; National Advancement Party (PAN), right of centre; Social Democratic Party (PSD), right of centre
population 10,621,000 (1995 est)
population growth rate 2.9% (1990–95); 2.7% (2000–05)
ethnic distribution two main ethnic groups: Indians and ladinos (non-Indians, including Europeans, black Africans, and mestizos). Indians are descended from the highland Mayas
life expectancy 62 (males), 67 (females)
literacy rate men 63%, women 47%
languages Spanish (official); 45% speak Mayan languages
religions Roman Catholic 70%, Protestant 30%
currency quetzal
GDP (US $) 13.3 billion (1994)
growth rate 4.0% (1994)
exports coffee, bananas, cotton, sugar, beef, chicle gum, essential oils, cardamoms

HISTORY
c. AD 250–900 Part of Maya civilization.
1524 Conquered by the Spanish adventurer Pedro de Alvarado and became a Spanish colony.
1821 Independence achieved from Spain, joining Mexico initially.
1823 Became part of United Provinces (Federation) of Central America, also embracing Costa Rica, El Salvador, Honduras, and Nicaragua.
1839 Achieved full independence.
1844–65 Rafael Carrera held power as president.
1873–85 The country was modernized on Liberal lines by President Justo Rufino Barrios, the army was built up, and coffee growing introduced.
1944 Juan José Arevalo became president, ending a period of rule by dictators. Socialist programme of reform instituted by Arevalo and his successor, from 1951, Col Jacobo Arbenz Guzman; social security system introduced and land redistributed.
1954 Col Carlos Castillo Armas became president in US-backed coup, after United Front Company plantations had been nationalized by Arbenz. Land reform halted.
1963 Castillo assassinated and military coup made Col Enrique Peralta president.
1966 Cesar Méndez elected president as civilian rule restored.
1970s More than 50,000 died in a spate of political violence as the military regime sought to liquidate left-wing dissidents.
1970 Carlos Araña elected president, with military back in power.
1976 An earthquake killed 27,000 and left more than 1 million homeless.
1981 Growth of antigovernment guerrilla movement. Death squads and soldiers killed an estimated 11,000 civilians during the year.
1982 Right-wing army coup installed General Ríos Montt as head of junta and then as president, determined to fight corruption and end violence.
1983 Montt removed in coup led by General Mejía Victores, who declared amnesty for the guerrillas.
1985 New constitution adopted; PDCG won congressional elections; Marco Vinicio Cerezo Arevalo became civilian president.
1989 Coup attempt against Cerezo foiled. Over 100,000 people killed and 40,000 reported missing since 1980.
1991 Jorge Serrano Elías of MAS elected president. Diplomatic relations established with Belize, which Guatemala had long claimed.
1993 President Serrano deposed after attempting to impose authoritarian regime; Ramiro de Leon Carpio, a human-rights ombudsman, elected president by assembly.
1994 Peace talks held with Guatemalan Revolutionary National Unity (URNG) rebels. Right-wing parties secured a majority in congress after elections.
1995 Government criticized by USA and United Nations for widespread human-rights abuses. First cease-fire by rebels in 30 years.
1996 Alvaro Arzú elected president. Peace agreement with URNG ended 36-year war.
1998 Hurricane Mitch struck 1 Nov, causing widespread damage to crops and property.

SEE ALSO Maya

to lead a peasant rising. He was an orthodox Marxist and renowned for his guerrilla techniques.

Guiana NE part of South America that includes ◊French Guiana, ◊Guyana, and ◊Surinam.

Guienne ancient province of SW France which formed the duchy of Aquitaine with Gascony in the 12th century. Its capital was Bordeaux. It became English 1154 and passed to France 1453.

guild or *gild* medieval association, particularly of artisans or merchants, formed for mutual aid and protection and the pursuit of a common purpose, religious or economic. Guilds became politically powerful in Europe but after the 16th century their position was undermined by the growth of capitalism.

The earliest form of economic guild, the guild merchant, arose during the 11th and 12th centuries; this was an organization of the traders of a town, who had been granted a practical monopoly of its trade by charter. As the merchants often strove to exclude craftworkers from the guild, and to monopolize control of local government, the craft guilds came into existence in the 12th and 13th centuries. These, which included journeymen (day workers) and apprentices as well as employers, regulated prices, wages, working conditions, and apprenticeship, prevented unfair practices, and maintained high standards of craft; they also fulfilled many social, religious, and charitable functions. By the 14th century they had taken control of local government, ousting the guild merchant.

Guildford city in Surrey, S England, on the river Wey; population (1991) 66,000. It has a ruined Norman castle, a cathedral (founded 1936 and completed 1961), and the University of Surrey (1966). There is a cattle market, and industries include flour-milling, plastics, engineering, vehicles, and pharmaceuticals. The Yvonne Arnaud Theatre opened 1965.

Guildford Four four Irish victims of miscarriage of justice who spent 14 years in prison convicted of terrorist bombings of pubs in Guildford and Woolwich 1974. They were released 1989 when an investigation concluded that the arresting Surrey police had given misleading evidence and, in consequence, their convictions were subsequently quashed.

guild socialism early 20th-century movement in Britain whose aim was to organize and control the industrial life of the country through self-governing democratic guilds of workers. Inspired by Catholicism, it was anti-materialist and attempted to arrest what it saw as a spiritual decline in modern civilization. The National Guilds League was founded 1915, and at its height there were over 20 guilds, but the league was dissolved 1925.

Guilin or ***Kweilin*** principal tourist city of S China, on the Li River, Guangxi province; population (1990) 364,000. The dramatic limestone mountains are a tourist attraction.

guillemot diving seabird of the auk family Alcidae, order Charadriiformes, that breeds in large numbers on rocky N Atlantic and Pacific coasts. The ***common guillemot*** *Uria aalge* has a long straight bill and short tail and wings; the plumage is sooty brown and white. The ***black guillemot*** *Cepphus grylle* is mostly black, with orange legs when breeding.

guillotine beheading device consisting of a metal blade that descends between two posts. It was common in the Middle Ages and was introduced 1791 in an improved design by physician Joseph Ignace Guillotin (1738–1814) in France. It was subsequently used for executions during the French Revolution. It is still in use in some countries.

guillotine in politics, a device used by UK governments in which the time allowed for debating a bill in the House of Commons is restricted so as to ensure its speedy passage to receiving the royal assent (that is, to becoming law).

Guimard Hector Germain 1867–1942. French architect. He was a leading exponent of the ◊Art Nouveau style in France. His flamboyant designs of glazed canopies for a number of Paris Métro station exteriors are one of Art Nouveau's most enduring images. In another of his projects, the Castel Béranger apartment block, Paris, 1894–98, he emphasized the importance of detail by designing each apartment to a different plan. Within the building, the Art Nouveau style is apparent on everything from stonework to door handles.

guinea English gold coin, notionally worth 21 shillings (£1.05). It has not been minted since 1817, when it was superseded by the gold sovereign, but was used until 1971 in billing professional fees.

Guinea country in W Africa, bounded N by Senegal, NE by Mali, SE by Côte d'Ivoire, S by Liberia and Sierra Leone, W by the Atlantic Ocean, and NW by Guinea-Bissau. *See country box below.*

Guinea-Bissau country in W Africa, bounded N by Senegal, E and SE by Guinea, and SW by the Atlantic Ocean. *See country box on p. 472.*

guinea fowl chicken-like African bird of the family Numididae, order Galliformes. The group includes the ***helmet guinea fowl*** *Numida meleagris*, which has a horny growth on the head, white-spotted feathers, and fleshy cheek wattles. It is the ancestor of the domestic guinea fowl.

guinea pig species of ◊cavy, a type of rodent.

Guinevere Welsh ***Gwenhwyfar*** in British legend, the wife of King ◊Arthur. Her adulterous love affair with the knight ◊Lancelot of the Lake led ultimately to Arthur's death.

Guinness Irish brewing family who produced the dark, creamy stout of the same name. In 1752 Arthur Guinness (1725–1803) inherited £100 and used it to set up a brewery in Leixlip, County Kildare, which was moved to Dublin 1759. The business grew under his son Arthur (1767–1855) and under Arthur's son Benjamin (1798–1868), who developed an export market in the USA and Europe. In the 1980s, the family interest in the business declined to no more than 5% as the company expanded by taking over large and established firms such as Bells in 1985 and Distillers in 1986 (the takeover of the latter led to a trial 1990; see ◊Guinness affair).

Guinness Alec 1914– . English actor of stage and screen. He joined the Old Vic 1936. His films include *Great Expectations* 1946, *Kind Hearts and Coronets* 1949 (in which he played eight parts), *The Bridge on the River Kwai* 1957 (Academy Award), and *Star Wars* 1977. A subtle character actor, he played the enigmatic spymaster in TV adaptations of John Le Carré's *Tinker, Tailor, Soldier, Spy* 1979 and *Smiley's People* 1981.

Guinness affair in British law, a case of financial fraud during the takeover of Distillers by the brewing company Guinness 1986. Those accused of acting illegally to sustain Guinness share prices included Ernest Saunders, the former chief executive. The trial, which lasted Feb–Aug 1990, was widely seen as the first major test of the government's legislation aimed at increasing control of financial dealings on London's Stock Exchange. Ernest Saunders, Gerald Ronson, and Sir Jack Lyons were found guilty on a variety of theft and false-accounting charges.

guitar six-stringed, or twelve-stringed, flat-bodied musical instrument, plucked or strummed with the fingers. The ***Hawaiian guitar***, laid across the lap, uses a metal bar to produce a distinctive gliding tone; the solid-bodied ***electric guitar***, developed in the 1950s by Les Paul and Leo Fender, mixes and amplifies vibrations from electromagnetic pickups at different points to produce a range of tone qualities.

Derived from a Moorish original, the guitar spread throughout Europe in medieval times, becoming firmly established in Italy, Spain, and the

'The conventional army loses if it does not win. The guerrilla wins if he does not lose.'

On GUERRILLAS
Henry Kissinger
Foreign Affairs

GUINEA
Republic of

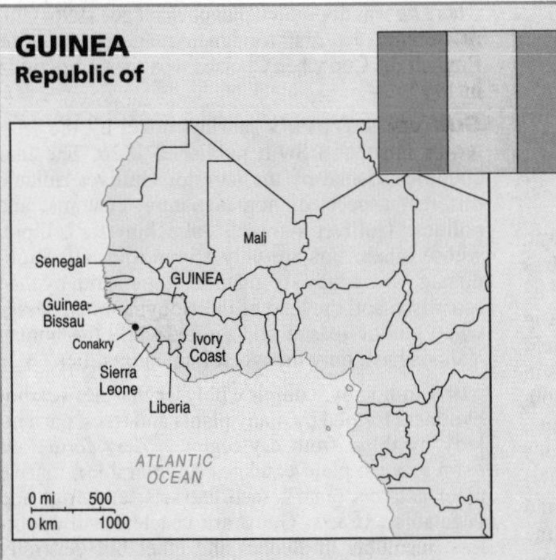

national name *République de Guinée*
area 245,857 sq km/94,901 sq mi
capital Conakry
major towns/cities Labé, Nzérékoré, Kankan, Kindia
physical features flat coastal plain with mountainous interior; sources of rivers Niger, Gambia, and Senegal; forest in SE; Fouta Djallon, area of sandstone plateaus, cut by deep valleys
head of state and government Lansana Conté from 1984
political system emergent democratic republic
administrative divisions eight provinces
political parties Party of Unity and Progress (PUP), centrist; Rally of the Guinean People (RPG), left of centre; Union of the New Republic (UNR), left of centre; Party for Renewal and Progress (PRP), left of centre
population 6,700,000 (1995 est)
population growth rate 3.0% (1990–95); 2.9% (2000–05)
ethnic distribution 24 ethnic groups, including the Malinke, Peul, and Soussou
life expectancy 44 (men), 45 (women)
literacy rate men 35%, women 13%
languages French (official), African languages (of which eight are official)
religions Muslim 95%, Christian
currency Guinean franc
GDP (US $) 3.4 billion (1994)
growth rate 4.0% (1994)
exports coffee, rice, palm kernels, alumina, bauxite, diamonds

HISTORY
c. AD 900 The Susi people, a community related to the Malinke, immigrated from NE, pushing the indigenous Baga towards the Atlantic coast.
13th C Susi kingdoms established, extending their influence to the coast; NE Guinea was part of Muslim Mali Empire, centred to NE.
mid-15th C Portuguese traders visited the coast and later developed trades in slaves and ivory.
1849 French protectorate established over coastal region around Nunez river, which was administered with Senegal.
1890 Separate Rivieres du Sud colony formed.
1895 Renamed as French Guinea, the colony became part of French West Africa.
1946 French Guinea became an overseas territory of France.
1958 Full independence achieved from France as Guinea after referendum rejected remaining within French Community; Sékou Touré of the Democratic Party of Guinea (PDG) elected president.
1960s and 1970s Touré established socialist one-party state, leading to deterioration in economy as 200,000 fled abroad.
1979 Strong opposition to Touré's rigid Marxist policies forced him to accept return to mixed economy and legalise private enterprise.
1984 Touré died. Bloodless military coup brought Col Lansana Conté to power; PDG outlawed, political prisoners released; market-centred economic reforms.
1985 Attempted coup against Conté while he was out of the country was foiled by loyal troops.
1991 Antigovernment general strike and mass protests.
1992 Constitution amended to allow for multiparty politics.
1993 Conté narrowly re-elected in first direct presidential election.
1995 Assembly elections won by Conté's supporters.
1996 Attempted military coup thwarted.

SEE ALSO French Community; Mali Empire

GUINEA-BISSAU
Republic of (formerly *Portuguese Guinea*)

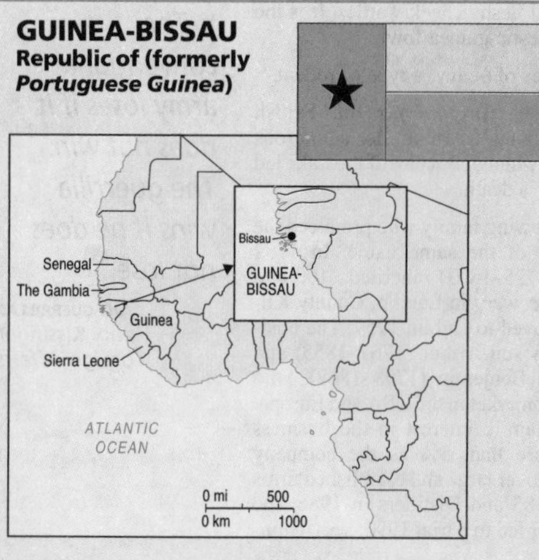

national name *República da Guiné-Bissau*
area 36,125 sq km/13,944 sq mi
capital Bissau (main port)
major towns/cities Mansôa, São Domingos
physical features flat coastal plain rising to savanna in E
head of state João Bernardo Vieira from 1980
head of government Carlos Correia from 1997
political system emergent democracy
administrative divisions eight regions and one autonomous section
political parties African Party for the Independence of Portuguese Guinea and Cape Verde (PAIGC), nationalist socialist; Party for Social Renovation (PRS), left of centre; Guinea-Bissau Resistance–Bafata Movement (PRGB-MB), centrist
population 1,073,000 (1995 est)
population growth rate 2.1% (1990–95); 2.1% (2000–05)
ethnic distribution majority originate from Africa, and comprise five main ethnic groups: the Balante in the central region, the Fulani in the N, the Malinke in the northern central area, and the Mandyako and Pepel near the coast
life expectancy 42 (men), 45 (women)
literacy rate men 50%, women 24%
languages Portuguese (official), Crioulo (Cape Verdean dialect of Portuguese), African languages
religions animist 65%, Muslim 38%, Christian 5% (mainly Roman Catholic)
currency Guinean peso
GDP (US $) 248 million (1994 est)
growth rate 6.9% (1994)
exports rice, coconuts, peanuts, fish, timber, cashew nuts, cotton, palm kernels

HISTORY
10th C Known as Gabu, became a tributary kingdom of the Mali Empire to NE.
1446 Portuguese arrived, establishing nominal control over coastal areas and capturing slaves to send to Cape Verde.
1546 Gabu kingdom became independent of Mali and survived until 1867.
1879 Portugal, which had formerly administered the area with Cape Verde islands, created the separate colony of Portuguese Guinea.
by 1915 The interior had been subjugated by the Portuguese.
1956 African Party for the Independence of Portuguese Guinea and Cape Verde (PAIGC) formed to campaign for independence from Portugal.
1961 The PAIGC began to wage a guerrilla campaign against Portuguese rule.
1973 Independence was declared in the two- thirds of the country that had fallen under the control of the PAIGC; heavy losses sustained by Portuguese troops who had tried to put down the uprising.
1974 Independence separately from Cape Verde accepted by Portugal, with Luiz Cabral (PAIGC) president.
1980 Cabral deposed, and João Vieira became chair of a council of revolution.
1981 PAIGC confirmed as the only legal party, with Vieira as its secretary general; Cape Verde decided not to form a union.
1984 New constitution made Vieira head of both government and state.
1991 Other parties legalized in response to public pressure.
1994 PAIGC secured a clear assembly majority and Vieira narrowly won first multiparty presidential elections.
1997 Carlos Correia appointed prime minister.

Spanish American colonies. Its 20th-century revival owes much to Andrés Segovia, Julian Bream, and John Williams. The guitar's prominence in popular music can be traced from the traditions of the US Midwest.

Guiyang or ***Kweiyang*** capital and industrial city of Guizhou province, S China; population (1993) 1,070,000. Industries include metals and machinery.

Guizhou or ***Kweichow*** province of S China
area 174,000 sq km/67,164 sq mi
capital Guiyang
industries rice, maize, nonferrous minerals
population (1990) 32,730,000.

Gujarat or ***Gujerat*** state of W India, formed from N and W Bombay State 1960
area 196,000 sq km/75,656 sq mi
capital Gandhinagar
features heavily industrialized; includes most of the Rann of Kutch; the Gir Forest (the last home of the wild Asian lion); Karjan Dam
industries cotton, petrochemicals, oil, gas, rice, textiles, fishing, coal, limestone
language Gujarati (Gujerati), Hindi
population (1994 est) 44,235,000.

Gujarati inhabitants of Gujarat on the NW coast of India. The Gujaratis number approximately 30 million and speak their own Indo-European language, Gujarati. They are predominantly Hindu (90%), with Muslim (8%) and Jain (2%) minorities.

gull The sharp, heavy beak typical of gulls can be clearly seen on this lesser black-backed gull. *Premaphotos Wildlife*

gulag Russian term for the system of prisons and labour camps used to silence dissidents and opponents of the Soviet regime. In the Stalin era (1920s–1930s), thousands of prisoners died from the harsh conditions of these remote camps.

Gulf Cooperation Council (GCC) Arab organization for promoting peace in the Persian Gulf area, established 1981. Its declared purpose is 'to bring about integration, coordination, and cooperation in economic, social, defence, and political affairs among Arab Gulf states'. Its members include Bahrain, Kuwait, Oman, Qatar, Saudi Arabia, and the United Arab Emirates; its headquarters are in Riyadh, Saudi Arabia.

Gulf States oil-rich countries sharing the coastline of the ◊Persian Gulf (Bahrain, Iran, Iraq, Kuwait, Oman, Qatar, Saudi Arabia, and the United Arab Emirates). In the USA, the term refers to those states bordering the Gulf of Mexico (Alabama, Florida, Louisiana, Mississippi, and Texas).

Gulf Stream warm ocean ◊current that flows north from the warm waters of the Gulf of Mexico. Part of the current is diverted east across the Atlantic, where it is known as the North Atlantic Drift, and warms what would otherwise be a colder climate in the British Isles and NW Europe.

Gulf War war 16 Jan–28 Feb 1991 between Iraq and a coalition of 28 nations led by the USA. (It is also another name for the ◊Iran–Iraq War.) The invasion and annexation of Kuwait by Iraq on 2 Aug 1990, provoked by a dispute over a shared oilfield and the price of oil, led to a build-up of US troops in Saudi Arabia, eventually totalling over 500,000. The UK subsequently deployed 42,000 troops, France 15,000, Egypt 20,000, and other nations smaller contingents. The United Nations (UN) Security Council authorized the use of force if Iraq did not withdraw before 15 Jan 1991. The deadline was ignored, and US and allied forces launched an air offensive lasting six weeks, in which 'smart' weapons came of age, destroyed about one-third of Iraqi equipment and inflicted massive casualties. A 100-hour ground war followed, which effectively destroyed the remnants of the 500,000-strong Iraqi army in or near Kuwait.

The cost to the USA of the war was $61.1 billion, including $43.1 billion contributed by the allies. Estimates of Iraqi casualties are in the range of 80,000–150,000 troops and 100,000–200,000 civilians. The war created 2–3 million refugees. Severe environmental damage, including the world's worst ◊oil spills, affected a large area.

gull seabird of the subfamily Larinae, family Laridae, order Charadriiformes, especially the genus *Larus*. Gulls are usually 25–75 cm/10–30 in long, white with grey or black on the back and wings, and have large bills. Juvenile birds are mainly of brown, mottled appearance. They are highly gregarious, breeding in colonies.

The ***common black-headed gull*** *L. ridibundus*, common on both sides of the Atlantic, is grey and white with (in summer) a dark-brown head and a red beak. The ***herring gull*** *L. argentatus*, common in the northern hemisphere, has white and pearl-grey plumage and a yellow beak. The ***oceanic great black-backed gull*** *L. marinus*, found in the Atlantic, is over 75cm/2.5 ft long.

Gullit Ruud 1962– . Dutch international footballer who was captain when the Netherlands won the European Championship 1988. After playing in the Netherlands with Haarlem, Feyenoord, and PSV Eindhoven, he transferred to AC Milan 1987. In 1995 he transferred from Sampdoria to Chelsea, where he was appointed player/manager 1996. Gullit became the first foreign manager to win the English FA Cup when Chelsea won the competition in 1997.

Gulliver's Travels satirical novel by the Irish writer Jonathan ◊Swift published 1726. The four countries visited by the narrator Gulliver ridicule different aspects of human nature, customs, and politics. Gulliver's travels take him to Lilliput, whose inhabitants are only 15 cm/6 in tall; Brobdignag, where they are gigantic; Laputa, run by mad scientists; and the land of the Houyhnhnms, horses who embody reason and virtue, while the human Yahoos have only the worst human qualities.

gum in botany, complex polysaccharides (carbohydrates) formed by many plants and trees, particularly by those from dry regions. They form four main groups: plant exudates (gum arabic); marine plant extracts (agar); seed extracts; and fruit and vegetable extracts. Gums are tasteless and odourless, insoluble in alcohol and ether but generally soluble in water. They are used for adhesives, fabric sizing, in confectionery, medicine, and calico printing.

Gummer John Selwyn 1939– . British Conservative politician, secretary of state for the environment 1993–97. He was minister of state for employment 1983–84, paymaster general 1984–85, minister for agriculture 1985–89, secretary of state for agriculture 1989–93, and chair of the party 1983–85.

gumtree common name for the ◊eucalyptus tree.

gun any kind of firearm or any instrument consisting of a metal tube from which a projectile is

Gunpowder Plot The main conspirators of the Gunpowder Plot 1605. Rob Catesby was the leader of the plot, while Guy Fawkes was the explosives expert. Their disaffection with James I arose from his failure to implement tolerance measures for Catholics as had been widely anticipated. *Philip Sauvain*

discharged; see also ◊artillery, ◊machine gun, ◊pistol, and ◊small arms.

gun metal type of ◊bronze, an alloy high in copper (88%), also containing tin and zinc, so-called because it was once used to cast cannons. It is tough, hard-wearing, and resists corrosion.

Gunnell Sally 1966– . British hurdler. She won the 1986 Commonwealth 100-metre hurdles gold medal before moving on to 400-metre hurdles. In 1994 she became the first woman athlete to complete the athletics Grand Slam, winning gold medals over 400-metre hurdles at the 1992 Olympics, 1993 World Championships (breaking the world record), 1990 and 1994 Commonwealth Games, and 1994 European Championships.

gunpowder or ***black powder*** the oldest known ◊explosive, a mixture of 75% potassium nitrate (saltpetre), 15% charcoal, and 10% sulphur. Sulphur ignites at a low temperature, charcoal burns readily, and the potassium nitrate provides oxygen for the explosion. As gunpowder produces lots of smoke and burns quite slowly, it has progressively been replaced since the late 19th century by high explosives, although it is still widely used for quarry blasting, fuses, and fireworks.

Gutenberg A page from Gutenberg's Bible, c. 1456. Johann Gutenberg was a pioneer of printing. He introduced the methods of movable type to Europe based on processes used by the Chinese since the 11th century. *Image Select (UK) Ltd*

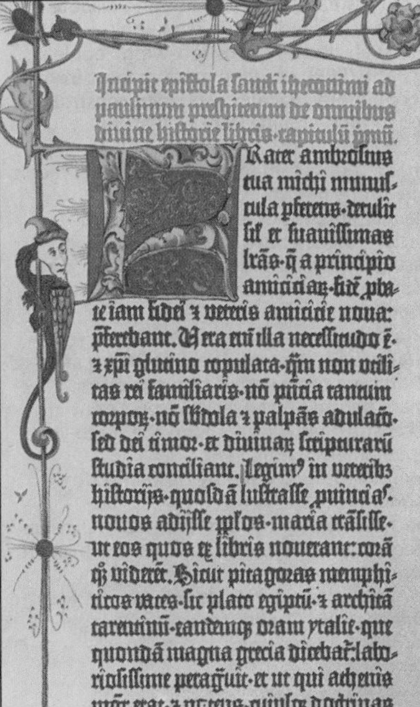

Incipit epistola sancti iheronimi ad
paulinum presbiterum de omnibus
divine historie libris. capitulum primum.
Frater ambrosius
tua michi munus-
cula perferens detulit
sil et suavissimas
lrãs. q̃ a principio
amicicias. fide pba-
te iam fidei et veteris amicicie nova:
pferebant. Vera enĩ illa necessitudo ẽ.
et xpi glutino copulata. q̃m non utili-
tas rei familiaris. nõ pñcia tantum
corporum. nõ subdola et palpãs adulacio.
sed dei timor. et divinarum scripturarũ
studia conciliant. Legim⁹ in veteribus
historiis. quosdã lustrasse provincias.
novos adiisse populos. maria transisse.
ut eos quos ex libris noverant: corã
quoque viderent. Sicut pitagoras memphi-
ticos vates. sic plato egiptum. et architam
tarentinum. eandemque oram ytalie. que
quondã magna grecia dicebatur: labo-
riosissime peragravit. et ut qui athenis
magister erat. et potens. cuiusque doctrinas

Gunpowder is believed to have been invented in China in the 10th century, but may also have been independently discovered by the Arabs. Certainly the Arabs produced the first known working gun 1304. Gunpowder was used in warfare from the 14th century but it was not generally adapted to civil purposes until the 17th century, when it began to be used in mining.

Gunpowder Plot in British history, the Catholic conspiracy to blow up James I and his parliament on 5 Nov 1605. It was discovered through an anonymous letter. Guy ◊Fawkes was found in the cellar beneath the Palace of Westminster, ready to fire a store of explosives. Several of the conspirators were killed, and Fawkes and seven others were executed. The event is commemorated annually in England on 5 Nov by fireworks and burning 'guys' (effigies) on bonfires.

Guomindang Chinese National People's Party, founded 1894 by ◊Sun Yat-sen, which overthrew the Manchu Empire 1912. From 1927 the right wing, led by ◊Chiang Kai-shek, was in conflict with the left, led by Mao Zedong until the communist victory 1949 (except for the period of the Japanese invasion 1937–45). It survives as the dominant political party of Taiwan, where it is still spelled ***Kuomintang***. However, in recent years there have been splits between mainland-born hardliners and moderates, led by the president of Taiwan and Kuomintang leader Lee Teng-hui.

Gupta dynasty Indian hereditary rulers who reunified and ruled over much of northern and central India 320–550. The dynasty's stronghold lay in the Magadha region of the middle Ganges valley, with the capital ◊Pataliputra. Gupta influence was extended through military conquest E, W, and S by Chandragupta I, Chandragupta II, and Samudragupta. Hun raids in the NW from the 6th century undermined the Guptas' decentralized administrative structure. At the empire's height, the Hindu and Buddhist religions, commerce, and the arts flourished in what is seen as a golden or classical age of Indian civilization.

Gurdjieff George Ivanovitch 1877–1949. Russian occultist and mystic who influenced the modern human-potential movement. His famous text is *Meetings with Remarkable Men* (English translation 1963). The mystic ◊Ouspensky was a disciple who expanded his ideas.

After years of wandering in central Asia, in 1912 Gurdjieff founded in Moscow the Institute for the Harmonious Development of Man, based on a system of raising consciousness (involving learning, group movement, manual labour, dance, and a minimum of sleep) known as the Fourth Way. After the 1917 Revolution he established similar schools in parts of Europe.

gurdwara Sikh place of worship and meeting. As well as a room housing the *Guru Granth Sahib*, the holy book, the gurdwara contains a kitchen and eating area for the *langar*, or communal meal.

Gurkha a people living in the mountains of Nepal, whose young men have been recruited since 1815 for the British and Indian armies. They are predominantly Tibeto-Mongolians, but their language is Khas, a dialect of a northern Indic language.

guru Hindi *gurū* Hindu or Sikh leader, or religious teacher.

Guru Granth Sahib the holy book of Sikhism, a collection of nearly 6,000 hymns by the first five and the ninth Sikh gurus, but also including the writings of some Hindus and Muslims. It is regarded as a living guru and treated with the respect that this implies. Guru Gobind Singh instructed Sikhs to look upon it as their guide, a symbolic representation of all the gurus. The original copy of the *Guru Granth Sahib* is kept in the Golden Temple in Amritsar, which was built especially to house it. When the *Guru Granth Sahib* is moved, it must be accompanied by five Khalsa Sikhs who correspond to the attendants who would accompany an honoured person. The *Guru Granth Sahib* is taken into a separate room at night; it must always be approached with respect, and with clean hands.

The *Guru Granth Sahib* teaches that there is one God and that all people are equal. It accepts the concepts of ◊reincarnation and the laws of ◊karma. It prohibits the use of intoxicants and rejects both idol worship and formal priesthood. It promotes the idea of *sewa*, or service to others – Sikhs should give their money or, more importantly, their time and effort, to those in need.

Guscott Jeremy Clayton 1965– . English rugby union player for Bath, England and the British Lions. A fast, elusive centre player, he was a key member of the England side which won three Grand Slams between 1991 and 1995. He has played on three consecutive British Lions tours since 1989, most memorably in the second Test on the 1997 tour of South Africa when he sealed the series for the Lions with a late drop goal.

Gush Emunim (Hebrew 'bloc of the faithful') Israeli fundamentalist group, founded 1973, which claims divine right to settlement of the West Bank, Gaza Strip, and Golan Heights as part of Israel. The claim is sometimes extended to the Euphrates.

Gustavus or ***Gustaf*** six kings of Sweden, including:

Gustavus V or ***Gustaf V*** 1858–1950. King of Sweden from 1907, when he succeeded his father Oscar II. He married Princess Victoria, daughter of the Grand Duke of Baden 1881, thus uniting the reigning Bernadotte dynasty with the former royal house of Vasa.

Gustavus VI or ***Gustaf VI*** 1882–1973. King of Sweden from 1950, when he succeeded his father Gustavus V. He was an archaeologist and expert on Chinese art. He was succeeded by his grandson ◊Carl XVI Gustavus. His first wife was Princess Margaret of Connacht (1882–1920), and in 1923 he married Lady Louise Mountbatten (1889–1965), sister of the Earl of Mountbatten of Burma.

Gustavus Adolphus (Gustavus II or Gustaf II) 1594–1632. King of Sweden from 1611, when he succeeded his father Charles IX. He waged successful wars with Denmark, Russia, and Poland, and in the ◊Thirty Years' War became a champion of the

Guthrie, Woody Woody Guthrie wrote more than 1,000 songs, of which 'This Land is Your Land' is probably the best known. His work deals mainly with social and political themes; he also wrote songs for children and recorded a number of 'Dust Bowl Ballads' in the 1930s for the American Library of Congress Folk Song Archive. *Corbis*

Protestant cause. Landing in Germany 1630, he defeated the German general Wallenstein at Lützen, SW of Leipzig 6 Nov 1632, but was killed in the battle. He was known as the 'Lion of the North'.

Gustavus Vasa (Gustavus I or Gustaf I) 1496–1560. King of Sweden from 1523, when he was elected after leading the Swedish revolt against Danish rule. He united and pacified the country and established Lutheranism as the state religion.

gut or ***alimentary canal*** in the ◊digestive system, the part of an animal responsible for processing food and preparing it for entry into the blood. The gut consists of a tube divided into segments specialized to perform different functions. The front end (the mouth) is adapted for food intake and for the first stages of digestion. The stomach is a storage area, although digestion of protein by the enzyme pepsin starts here; in many herbivorous mammals this is also the site of cellulose digestion. The small intestine follows the stomach and is specialized for digestion and for absorption. The large intestine, consisting of the colon, caecum, and rectum, has a variety of functions, including cellulose digestion, water absorption, and storage of faeces. From the gut nutrients are carried to the liver via the hepatic portal vein, ready for assimilation by the cells.

Gutenberg Johannes (Gensfleisch) c. 1398–1468. German printer, the inventor of printing from movable metal type, based on the Chinese wood-block-type method (although Laurens Janszoon Coster (c. 1370–1440) has a rival claim). Gutenberg began work on the process in the 1440s and in 1450 set up a printing business in Mainz. By 1456 he had produced the first printed Bible (known as the Gutenberg Bible). *See illustration on previous page.*

Guthrie (William) Tyrone 1900–1971. English theatre director, notable for his innovative approach. Administrator of the Old Vic and Sadler's Wells theatres 1939–45, he helped found the Ontario (Stratford) Shakespeare Festival 1953 and the Minneapolis theatre now named after him. He pioneered the modern concept of open-stage productions for medieval and Renaissance plays.

Guthrie Woody (Woodrow Wilson) 1912–1967. US folk singer and songwriter. His left-wing protest songs, 'dustbowl ballads', and 'talking blues' influenced, among others, Bob Dylan; they include 'Deportees', 'Hard Travelin'', and 'This Land Is Your Land'. *See illustration on previous page.*

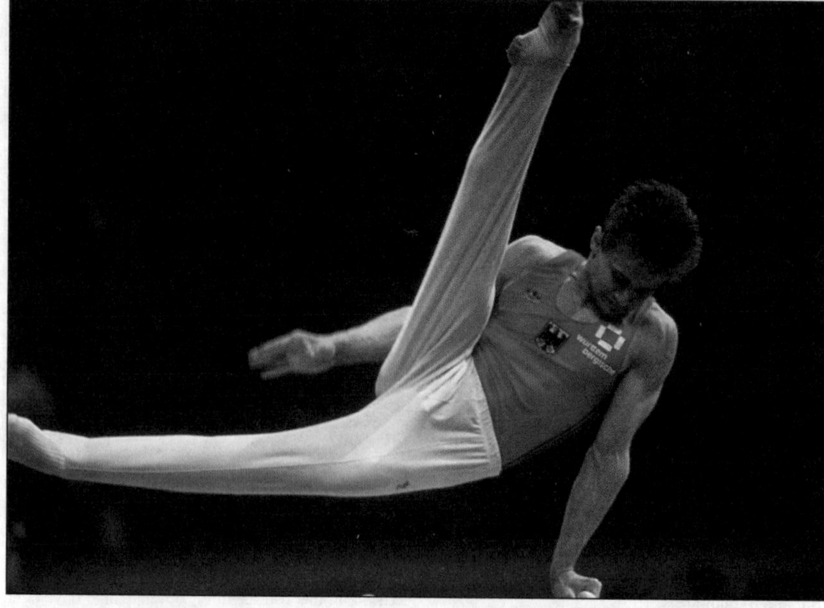

gymnastics A gymnast performing at the World Gymnastics Championships 1992. Originally a form of physical training used in ancient Greece, gymnastics was revived in Germany in the 19th century and is now a popular sport. *Image Select (UK) Ltd*

guttation secretion of water on to the surface of leaves through specialized pores, or ◊hydathodes. The process occurs most frequently during conditions of high humidity when the rate of transpiration is low. Drops of water found on grass in early morning are often the result of guttation, rather than dew.

Guyana country in South America, bounded N by the Atlantic Ocean, E by Surinam, S and SW by Brazil, and NW by Venezuela. *See country box on page below.*

Guzmán Blanco Antonio 1829–1899. Venezuelan dictator and military leader who seized power 1870 and remained absolute ruler until 1889. He modernized Caracas to become the political capital; committed resources to education, communications, and agriculture; and encouraged foreign trade.

Gwent former county of S Wales, created 1974, abolished 1996.

Gwyn or ***Gwynn*** Nell (Eleanor) 1650–1687. English comedy actress from 1665. She was formerly an orange-seller at Drury Lane Theatre, London. The poet Dryden wrote parts for her, and from 1669 she was the mistress of Charles II.

Gwynedd unitary authority of Wales, created 1974; in the reorganization of local government 1996, the Ise of ◊Anglesey, formerly part of Gwynedd, became a separate authority (*see United Kingdom map*).

gymnastics physical exercises, originally for health and training (so called from the way in which men of ancient Greece trained: *gymnos* 'naked'). The *gymnasia* were schools for training competitors for public games. Men's gymnastics includes high bar, parallel bars, horse vault, rings, pommel horse, and floor exercises. Women's gymnastics includes asymmetrical bars, side horse vault, balance beam, and floor exercises. Also popular are sports

GUYANA
Cooperative Republic of

USA
Mexico
ATLANTIC OCEAN
Cuba
CARIBBEAN SEA
GUYANA
Venezuela
Georgetown
PACIFIC OCEAN
Surinam
Brazil
0 mi 500
0 km 1000

area 214,969 sq km/82,978 sq mi
capital (and port) Georgetown
major towns/cities Linden, Rose Hall, Corriverton
major ports New Amsterdam
physical features coastal plain rises into rolling highlands with savanna in S; mostly tropical rainforest; Mount Roraima; Kaietur National Park, including Kaietur Fall on the Potaro (tributary of Essequibo) 250 m/821 ft
head of state Janet Jagan from 1997
head of government Samuel Hinds from 1992
political system democratic republic
administrative divisions ten regions
political parties People's National Congress (PNC), Afro-Guyanan, nationalist socialist; People's Progressive Party (PPP), Indian-based, left-wing
population 835,000 (1995 est)
population growth rate 0.9% (1990–95); 1.1% (2000–05)
ethnic distribution about 51% East Indians descended from settlers from the subcontinent of India; about 43% Afro-Indian; small minorities of American-Indians, Chinese, and Europeans
life expectancy 62 (men), 68 (women)
literacy rate men 98%, women 95%
languages English (official), Hindi, Native American
religions Hindu 54%, Christian 27%, Sunni Muslim 15%
currency Guyana dollar
GDP (US $) 540 million (1994 est)
growth rate 8.5% (1994)
exports sugar, rice, rum, timber, diamonds, bauxite, shrimps, molasses

HISTORY
1498 The explorer Christopher Columbus sighted Guyana, whose name, 'land of many waters', was derived from a local Amerindian word.
c. 1620 Settled by Dutch West India Company, who established armed bases and brought in slaves from Africa.
1814 After period of French rule, Britain occupied Guyana during the Napoleonic Wars and purchased Demerara, Berbice, and Essequibo.
1831 Became British colony under name of British Guiana.
1834 Slavery was abolished, resulting in an influx of indentured labourers from India and China to work on sugar plantations.
1860 Settlement of the Rupununi Savanna commenced.
1860s Gold was discovered.
1899 International arbitration tribunal found in favour of British Guiana in a long-running dispute with Venezuela over lands W of Essequibo river.
1953 Assembly elections won by left-wing People's Progressive Party (PPP), drawing most support from the Indian community; Britain suspended constitution and installed interim administration, fearing communist takeover.
1961 Internal self-government granted; Cheddi Jagan (PPP) became prime minister.
1964 PNC leader Forbes Burnham led PPP–PNC coalition; racial violence between the Asian- and African-descended communities.
1966 Independence achieved from Britain as Guyana, with Burnham as prime minister.
1970 Guyana became a republic within the Commonwealth, with Raymond Arthur Chung as president; Burnham remained as prime minister.
1980 Burnham became first executive president under new constitution, which ended the three-year boycott of parliament by the PPP.
1985 Burnham died; succeeded by Desmond Hoyte (PNC), as economy deteriorated.
1992 PPP had decisive victory in first completely free assembly elections for 20 years; Cheddi Jagan became president; privatization programme launched.
1997 Prime minister Samuel Hinds became president, following the death of Cheddi Jagan. Janet Jagan elected president in December.

acrobatics, performed by gymnasts in pairs, trios, or fours to music, where the emphasis is on dance, balance, and timing, and rhythmic gymnastics, choreographed to music and performed by individuals or six-girl teams, with small hand apparatus such as a ribbon, ball, or hoop.

Gymnastics was first revived in 19th-century Germany as an aid to military strength, and was also taken up by educationists including Friedrich ◊Froebel and Johann ◊Pestalozzi, becoming a recognized part of the school curriculum. Today it is a popular spectator sport.

gymnosperm (Greek 'naked seed') in botany, any plant whose seeds are exposed, as opposed to the structurally more advanced ◊angiosperms, where they are inside an ovary. The group includes conifers and related plants such as cycads and ginkgos, whose seeds develop in ◊cones.

gynaecology medical speciality concerned with disorders of the female reproductive system.

gynoecium or ***gynaecium*** collective term for the female reproductive organs of a flower, consisting of one or more ◊carpels, either free or fused together.

gypsum common sulphate ◊mineral, composed of hydrous calcium sulphate, $CaSO_4.2H_2O$. It ranks 2 on the Mohs' scale of hardness. Gypsum is used for making casts and moulds, and for blackboard chalk.

Gypsy English name for a member of the ◊Romany people.

gyre circular surface rotation of ocean water in each major sea (a type of ◊current). Their movements are dictated by the prevailing winds and the ◊Coriolis effect. Gyres move clockwise in the northern hemisphere and anticlockwise in the southern hemisphere.

gyroscope mechanical instrument, used as a stabilizing device and consisting, in its simplest form, of a heavy wheel mounted on an axis fixed in a ring that can be rotated about another axis, which is also fixed in a ring capable of rotation about a third axis. Applications of the gyroscope principle include the gyrocompass, the gyropilot for automatic steering, and gyro-directed torpedoes.

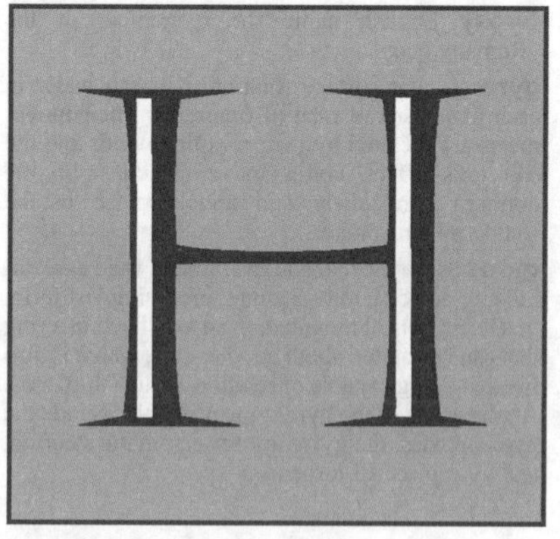

Haakon seven kings of Norway, including:

Haakon IV 1204–1263. King of Norway from 1217, the son of Haakon III. Under his rule, Norway flourished both militarily and culturally; he took control of the Faroe Islands, Greenland 1261, and Iceland 1262–64. His court was famed throughout N Europe.

Haakon VII 1872–1957. King of Norway from 1905. Born Prince Charles, the second son of Frederick VIII of Denmark, he was elected king of Norway on separation from Sweden, and in 1906 he took the name Haakon. In World War II he carried on the resistance from Britain during the Nazi occupation of his country. He returned 1945.

Haarlem industrial city and capital of the province of North Holland, the Netherlands, 20 km/12 mi W of Amsterdam; population (1994) 150,200. At Velsea to the N a road-rail tunnel runs under the North Sea Canal, linking North and South Holland. Industries include chemicals, pharmaceuticals, textiles, and printing. Haarlem is in an area of flowering bulbs and has a 15th–16th-century cathedral and a Frans Hals museum.

habeas corpus (Latin 'you may have the body') in law, a writ directed to someone who has custody of a person, ordering him or her to bring the person before the court issuing the writ and to justify why the person is detained in custody. Traditional rights to habeas corpus were embodied in the English Habeas Corpus Act 1679.

Haber Fritz 1868–1934. German chemist whose conversion of atmospheric nitrogen to ammonia opened the way for the synthetic fertilizer industry. His study of the combustion of hydrocarbons led to the commercial 'cracking' or fractional distillation of natural oil (petroleum) into its components (for example, diesel, petrol, and paraffin). In electrochemistry, he was the first to demonstrate that oxidation and reduction take place at the electrodes; from this he developed a general electrochemical theory.

At the outbreak of World War I in 1914, Haber was asked to devise a method of producing nitric acid for making high explosives. Later he became one of the principals in the German chemical-warfare effort, devising weapons and gas masks, which led to protests against his Nobel prize 1918.

Haber process or ***Haber–Bosch process*** industrial process by which ammonia is manufactured by direct combination of its elements, nitrogen and hydrogen. The reaction is carried out at 400–500°C/752–932°F and at 200 atmospheres pressure. The two gases, in the proportions of 1:3 by volume, are passed over a ◊catalyst of finely divided iron.

Around 10% of the reactants combine, and the unused gases are recycled. The ammonia is separated either by being dissolved in water or by being cooled to liquid form.

$$N_2 + 3H_2 \rightleftharpoons 2NH_3$$

habitat localized ◊environment in which an organism lives, and which provides for all (or almost all) of its needs. The diversity of habitats found within the Earth's ecosystem is enormous, and they are changing all the time. Many can be considered inorganic or physical; for example, the Arctic ice cap, a cave, or a cliff face. Others are more complex; for instance, a woodland or a forest floor. Some habitats are so precise that they are called microhabitats, such as the area under a stone where a particular type of insect lives. Most habitats provide a home for many species.

Habsburg or ***Hapsburg*** European royal family, former imperial house of Austria–Hungary. A Habsburg, Rudolf I, became king of Germany 1273 and began the family's control of Austria and Styria. They acquired a series of lands and titles, including that of Holy Roman emperor which they held 1273–91, 1298–1308, 1438–1740, and 1745–1806. The Habsburgs reached the zenith of their power under the emperor Charles V (1519–1556) who divided his lands, creating an Austrian Habsburg line (which ruled until 1918) and a Spanish line (which ruled to 1700).

hacking unauthorized access to a computer, either for fun or for malicious or fraudulent purposes. Hackers generally use microcomputers and telephone lines to obtain access. In computing, the term is used in a wider sense to mean using software for enjoyment or self-education, not necessarily involving unauthorized access. The most destructive form of hacking is the introduction of a computer ◊virus.

Hacking can be divided into four main areas: ◊viruses, phreaking (accessing the telephone network illegally to make free long-distance phone calls), software piracy (stripping away the protective coding that should prevent the software being copied), and accessing operating systems. In the UK, hacking is illegal under the Computer Misuse Act 1990. A survey 1993–96 of 10,000 organizations in the UK showed that only 3% had been troubled by hackers. A 1996 US survey co-sponsored by the FBI showed 41% of academic, corporate, and government organizations interviewed had had their computer systems hacked into during 1995.

Hackman Gene 1931– . US actor. He became a star as 'Popeye' Doyle in *The French Connection* 1971 and continued to play a variety of often combative roles in such films as *The Conversation* 1974, *The French Connection II* 1975, *Mississippi Burning* 1988, *Unforgiven* 1992, and *The Quick and the Dead* 1995.

Hackney inner borough of N central Greater London. It includes the districts of Shoreditch, Hoxton, and Stoke Newington
features Hackney Downs and Hackney Marsh, formerly the haunt of highwaymen, now a leisure area; The Theatre, Shoreditch, site of England's first theatre 1576; the Geffrye Museum of the domestic arts; early 16th-century Sutton House, housing the Early Music Centre; Spitalfields market, moved here 1991. The hackney carriage, a carriage for hire that was originally horse-drawn, is so named because horses were bred here in the 14th century
population (1991) 181,200
famous people Richard Burbage, Daniel Defoe, Kate Greenaway.

hadal zone the deepest level of the ocean, below the abyssal zone, at depths of greater than 6,000 m/19,500 ft. The ocean trenches are in the hadal zone. There is no light in this zone and pressure is over 600 times greater than atmospheric pressure.

haddock marine fish *Melanogrammus aeglefinus* of the cod family found off the N Atlantic coast. It is brown with silvery underparts and black markings above the pectoral fins. It can grow to a length of 1 m/3 ft.

Hades in Greek mythology, the underworld where spirits went after death, usually depicted as a cavern or pit underneath the Earth, the entrance of which was guarded by the three-headed dog Cerberus. It was presided over by the god Pluto or Hades (Roman Dis). Pluto was the brother of Zeus and married ◊Persephone, daughter of Demeter and Zeus.

Hadith collection of the teachings of ◊Muhammad and stories about his life, regarded by Muslims as a guide to living second only to the ◊Koran.

The teachings were at first transmitted orally, but this led to a large number of Hadiths whose origin was in doubt; later, scholars such as Muhammad al-Bukhari (810–870) collected together those believed to be authentic, and these collections form the Hadith accepted by Muslims today.

Hadlee Richard John 1951– . New Zealand cricketer who broke Ian Botham's world record of 373 test wickets and improved the total to 431, a figure then beaten by Kapil Dev 1994. He played for Canterbury (NZ) and Nottinghamshire (England). In 1990 he retired from test cricket.

Hadrian (Publius Aelius Hadrianus) AD 76–138. Roman emperor from 117. He was adopted by his relative, the emperor ◊Trajan, whom he succeeded. He abandoned Trajan's conquests in Mesopotamia and adopted a defensive policy aimed at fixing the boundaries of the empire, which included the building of ◊Hadrian's Wall in Britain. He travelled more widely than any other emperor, and consolidated both the army and Roman administration.

Hadrian introduced administrative, financial, and legal reforms. Some of his largest building projects were at Rome (including the Pantheon, his own mausoleum, and his villa at Tivoli) and Athens, where his new town and appointment as archon of Athens 112 reveals his fondness for Greek culture. He was also a cultivated poet and patron of the arts.

Hadrian's Wall Roman frontier system built AD 122–126 to mark England's northern boundary and abandoned about 383; its ruins run 185 km/115 mi from Wallsend on the river Tyne to Maryport, W Cumbria. In some parts, the wall was covered with a glistening, white coat of mortar. The fort at South Shields, Arbeia, built to defend the eastern end, is being reconstructed.

hadron in physics, a subatomic particle that experiences the strong nuclear force. Each is made up of two or three indivisible particles called ◊quarks. The hadrons are grouped into the ◊baryons (protons, neutrons, and hyperons) and the ◊mesons (particles with masses between those of electrons and protons).

Haeckel Ernst Heinrich Philipp August 1834–1919. German zoologist and philosopher. His theory of 'recapitulation', expressed as 'ontogeny repeats phylogeny' (or that embryonic stages represent past stages in the organism's evolution), has been superseded, but it stimulated research in embryology.

haematology medical speciality concerned with disorders of the blood.

haemoglobin protein used by all vertebrates and some invertebrates for oxygen transport because the two substances combine reversibly. In vertebrates it occurs in red blood cells (erythrocytes), giving them their colour.

In the lungs or gills where the concentration of oxygen is high, oxygen attaches to haemoglobin to form oxyhaemoglobin. This process effectively increases the amount of oxygen that can be carried in the bloodstream. The oxygen is later released in the body tissues where it is at a low concentration, and the deoxygenated blood returned to the lungs or gills. Haemoglobin will combine also with carbon monoxide to form carboxyhaemoglobin, but in this case the reaction is irreversible.

haemophilia any of several inherited diseases in which normal blood clotting is impaired. The sufferer experiences prolonged bleeding from the slightest wound, as well as painful internal bleeding without apparent cause.

Haemophilias are nearly always sex-linked, transmitted through the female line only to male infants; they have afflicted a number of European royal households. Males affected by the most common form are unable to synthesize Factor VIII, a protein involved in the clotting of blood. Treatment is primarily with Factor VIII (now mass-produced by recombinant techniques), but the haemophiliac remains at risk from the slightest incident of bleeding. The disease is a painful one that causes deformities of joints.

haemorrhage loss of blood from the circulatory system. It is 'manifest' when the blood can be seen, as when it flows from a wound, and 'occult' when the bleeding is internal, as from an ulcer or internal injury.

Rapid, profuse haemorrhage causes ◊shock and may prove fatal if the circulating volume cannot be replaced in time. Slow, sustained bleeding may lead to ◊anaemia. Arterial bleeding is potentially more serious than blood lost from a vein. It may be stemmed by applying pressure directly to the wound.

haemorrhagic fever any of several virus diseases of the tropics in which high temperatures over several days end in haemorrhage from nose, throat, and intestines, with up to 90% mortality.

Haemorrhagic fever viruses belong to a number of different families including flaviviruses (yellow fever and dengue), arenaviruses (Lassa fever), bunyaviruses (Rift Valley fever and Crimean–Congo fever), hantaviruses (haemorrhagic fever with renal syndrome), and filoviruses (Ebola virus disease and Marburg disease).

The causative organism of W African ◊Lassa fever lives in rats (which betray no symptoms), but in ◊Marburg disease and Ebola virus disease the host animal is the green monkey. See also ◊dengue fever.

Hâfiz Shams al-Din Muhammad c. 1326–c. 1390. Persian lyric poet. He was born in Shiraz and taught in a Dervish college there. His *Diwan*, a collection of short odes, extols the pleasures of life and satirizes his fellow Dervishes.

hafnium (Latin *Hafnia* 'Copenhagen') silvery, metallic element, symbol Hf, atomic number 72, relative atomic mass 178.49. It occurs in nature in ores of zirconium, the properties of which it resembles. Hafnium absorbs neutrons better than most metals, so it is used in the control rods of nuclear reactors; it is also used for light-bulb filaments.

Haganah Zionist military organization in Palestine. It originated under the Turkish rule of the Ottoman Empire before World War I to protect Jewish settlements, and many of its members served in the British forces in both world wars. After World War II it condemned guerrilla activity. It formed the basis of the Israeli army after Israel was established 1948.

Hagen Walter Charles 1892–1969. US golfer, a flamboyant character. He won 11 major championships 1914–29. An exponent of the match-play game, he won the US PGA Championship five times, four in succession.

Haggard H(enry) Rider 1856–1925. English novelist. He used his experience in the South African colonial service in his romantic adventure tales, including *King Solomon's Mines* 1885 and *She* 1887. He also published *Rural England* 1902.

haggis Scottish dish made from a sheep's or calf's heart, liver, and lungs, minced with onion, oatmeal, suet, spices, and salt, mixed with stock, and traditionally boiled in the animal's stomach for several hours.

Haggis is traditionally served at Hogmanay (New Year's Eve) and on Burns' Night (25 Jan).

Hagia Sophia (Greek 'holy wisdom') Byzantine building in Istanbul, Turkey, built 532–37 as a Christian cathedral, replacing earlier churches. From 1453 to 1934 it was an Islamic mosque; in 1934 it became a museum.

Haganah Haganah volunteers training at Belsen in 1948. The Hebrew word *haganah* means 'defence', and the group was founded to defend Jewish settlements in Palestine. In 1948 it became the national army of Israel. *Corbis*

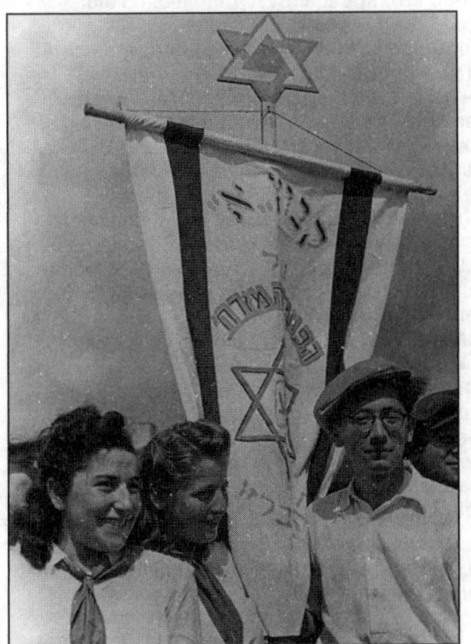

Hagler Marvin 1954– . US boxer who was the undisputed world middleweight champion from 1980 to 1987. He won 13 of his 15 World Title fights, losing only to Sugar Ray Leonard. Subsequently, he became a movie actor.

Hague, The (Dutch ***'s-Gravenhage*** or ***Den Haag***) capital of the province of South Holland and seat of the Netherlands government, linked by canal with Rotterdam and Amsterdam; population (1994) 445,300.

features The Gothic Hall of Knights (1280) in the Binnenhof, where the annual opening of parliament takes place; the 16th-century town hall; and the Peace Palace (1913), which houses the United Nations International Court of Justice; the 17th-century Mauritshuis (Royal Picture Gallery). The seaside resort of ***Scheveningen*** (patronized by Wilhelm II and Winston Churchill), with its Kurhaus, is virtually incorporated.

history The city grew up around a hunting lodge after a castle was built nearby 1248. The States-General (parliament) established itself here 1585, and from the 17th century the city was a centre of European diplomacy.

Hague William Jefferson 1961– . British politician, leader of the Conservative Party from 1997. He came to public attention in 1977 when, at the age of 16, he addressed his party's annual conference. He entered the House of Commons in 1989 and joined John Major's cabinet as Secretary of State for Wales in 1995. Hague was elected leader following the resignation of John Major after his defeat in the May 1997 general election.

hahnium name proposed by US scientists for the element also known as ◊unnilpentium (atomic number 105), in honour of German nuclear physicist Otto Hahn. The symbol is Ha.

Haifa port in NE Israel, at the foot of Mount Carmel; population (1994) 246,700. Industries include oil refining and chemicals. It is the capital of a district of the same name.

history Haifa was taken by the crusaders 1100, Napoleon 1799, and Egypt 1839. It was surrendered by Egypt to Turkey 1840. Occupied by the British 1918, it became part of mandated Palestine 1922. The Arabs surrendered to Israeli rule during the Arab–Israeli War 1948–49.

Haig Alexander Meigs 1924– . US general and Republican politician. He became President Nixon's White House chief of staff at the height of the ◊Watergate scandal, was NATO commander 1974–79, and secretary of state to President Reagan 1981–82.

Haig Douglas, 1st Earl Haig 1861–1928. British army officer, commander in chief in World War I. His Somme offensive in France in the summer of 1916 made considerable advances only at enormous cost to human life, and his Passchendaele offensive in Belgium from July to Nov 1917 achieved little at a similar loss. He was created field marshal 1917 and, after retiring, became first president of the ◊British Legion 1921.

haiku seventeen-syllable Japanese verse form, usually divided into three lines of five, seven, and five syllables. ◊Bashō popularized the form in the 17th century. It evolved from the 31-syllable *tanka* form dominant from the 8th century.

hail precipitation in the form of pellets of ice (hailstones). It is caused by the circulation of moisture in strong convection currents, usually within cumulonimbus ◊clouds.

Water droplets freeze as they are carried upwards. As the circulation continues, layers of ice are deposited around the droplets until they become too heavy to be supported by the currents and they fall as a hailstorm.

Haile Selassie Ras (Prince) Tafari, ('the Lion of Judah') 1892–1975. Emperor of Ethiopia 1930–74. He pleaded unsuccessfully to the League of Nations against the Italian conquest of his country 1935–36, and was then deposed and fled to the UK. He went to Egypt 1940 and raised an army which he led into Ethiopia Jan 1941 alongside British forces and was restored to the throne 5 May. He was deposed by a military coup 1974 and died in captivity the following year. Followers of the Rastafarian religion (see ◊Rastafarianism) believe that he was the Messiah, the incarnation of God (Jah).

Hailsham Quintin McGarel Hogg, Baron Hailsham of St Marylebone 1907– . British lawyer and Conservative politician. Having succeeded as 2nd Viscount Hailsham 1950, he renounced the title 1963 to re-enter the House of Commons, and was then able to contest the Conservative Party leadership elections, but took a life peerage 1970 on his appointment as Lord Chancellor 1970–74. He was Lord Chancellor again 1979–87.

Hailwood Mike (Stanley Michael Bailey) 1940–1981. English motorcyclist. Between 1961 and 1967 he won nine world titles and a record 14 titles at the Isle of Man TT races between 1961 and 1979.

Hainan island in the South China Sea; area 34,000 sq km/13,124 sq mi; population (1990) 6,557,000. The capital is Haikou. In 1987 Hainan was designated a Special Economic Zone; in 1988 it was separated from Guangdong and made a new province. It is China's second-largest island.

Hainaut industrial province of SW Belgium; capital Mons; area 3,800 sq km/1,467 sq mi; population (1995) 1,286,600. It produces coal, iron, and steel.

hair fine filament growing from mammalian skin. Each hair grows from a pit-shaped follicle embedded in the second layer of the skin, the dermis. It consists of dead cells impregnated with the protein keratin.

The average number of hairs on a human head varies from 98,000 (red-heads) to 120,000 (blondes). Each grows at the rate of 5–10 mm/0.2–0.4 in per month, lengthening for about three years before being replaced by a new one. A coat of hair helps to insulate land mammals by trapping air next to the body. The thickness of this layer can be varied at will by raising or flattening the coat. In some mammals a really heavy coat may be so effective that it must be shed in summer and a thinner one grown. Hair also aids camouflage, as in the zebra and the white winter coats of Arctic animals; and protection, as in the porcupine and hedgehog; bluffing enemies by apparently increasing the size, as in the cat; sexual display, as in humans and the male lion; and its colouring or erection may be used for communication. In 1990 scientists succeeded for the first time in growing human hair in vitro.

hairstreak any of a group of butterflies, belonging to the family Lycaenidae, to which blues and coppers also belong. Hairstreaks live in both temperate and tropical regions. Most of them are brownish or greyish-blue with hairlike tips at the end of their hind wings. *See illustration on following page.*

Haiti country in the Caribbean, occupying the W part of the island of Hispaniola; to the E is the Dominican Republic. *See country box on p. 478.*

Haitink Bernard 1929– . Dutch conductor. He has been associated with the Concertgebouw Orchestra, Amsterdam, from 1958, and the London Philharmonic Orchestra from 1967; musical director at Glyndebourne 1977–87 and at the Royal Opera House, Covent Garden, London, from 1987. A noted interpreter of Mahler and Shostakovitch, he also conducted Mozart's music for the film *Amadeus*.

hajj pilgrimage to Mecca that should be undertaken by every Muslim at least once in a lifetime, unless he or she is prevented by financial or health difficulties. A Muslim who has been on hajj may take the additional name Hajji. Many of the pilgrims on hajj also visit Medina, where the prophet Muhammad is buried.

hake any of various marine fishes of the cod family, found in N European, African, and American waters. They have silvery, elongated bodies and attain a length of 1 m/3 ft. They have two dorsal fins and one long anal fin. The silver hake *Merluccius bilinearis* is an important food fish.

Hakluyt Richard c. 1552–1616. English geographer whose chief work is *The Principal Navigations, Voyages and Discoveries of the English Nation* 1598–1600. He was assisted by Sir Walter Raleigh.

halal (Arabic 'lawful') conforming to the rules laid down by Islam. The term can be applied to all aspects of life, but usually refers to food permissible under Muslim dietary laws, including meat from

'D. is a very weak-minded fellow I am afraid, and, like the feather pillow, bears the marks of the last person who has sat on him!'

Douglas Haig
Of the 17th Earl of Derby, in letter 14 Jan 1918

hairstreak Hairstreak butterflies are found in both the Old and New World. This purple hairstreak *Quercusia quercus* is typical of lowland oakwoods in the British Isles. It spends most of its time perched up on the canopy of woods and forests and seldom comes down to ground level. *Premaphotos Wildlife*

animals that have been slaughtered in the correct ritual fashion.

Haldane J(ohn) B(urdon) S(anderson) 1892–1964. British physiologist, geneticist, and author of popular science books. In 1936 he showed the genetic link between haemophilia and colour blindness.

Hale George Ellery 1868–1938. US astronomer. He made pioneer studies of the Sun and founded three major observatories. In 1889 he invented the spectroheliograph, a device for photographing the Sun at particular wavelengths. In 1917 he established on Mount Wilson, California, a 2.5-m/100-in reflector, the world's largest telescope until superseded 1948 by the 5-m/200-in reflector on Mount Palomar, planned by Hale just before he died.

He, more than any other, was responsible for the development of observational astrophysics in the USA. He also founded the Yerkes Observatory in Wisconsin 1897.

Hale-Bopp, Comet *see table p.247.*

Hales Stephen 1677–1761. English scientist who studied the role of water and air in the maintenance of life. He gave accurate accounts of water movement in plants. He demonstrated that plants absorb air, and that some part of that air is involved in their nutrition. His work laid emphasis on measurement and experimentation.

Hales's work on air revealed the dangers of breathing 'spent' air in enclosed places, and he invented a ventilator which improved survival rates when introduced on ships, in hospitals, and in prisons.

Haley Bill 1927–1981. US pioneer of rock and roll. He was originally a western-swing musician. His songs 'Rock Around the Clock' 1954 and 'Shake, Rattle and Roll' 1955 were big hits of the early rock-and-roll era.

half-life during ◊radioactive decay, the time in which the strength of a radioactive source decays to half its original value. In theory, the decay process is never complete and there is always some residual radioactivity. For this reason, the half-life of a radioactive isotope is measured, rather than the total decay time. It may vary from millionths of a second to billions of years.

Radioactive substances decay exponentially; thus the time taken for the first 50% of the isotope to decay will be the same as the time taken by the next 25%, and by the 12.5% after that, and so on.

halibut any of several large flatfishes of the genus *Hippoglossus*, in the family Pleuronectidae, found in the Atlantic and Pacific oceans. The largest of the flatfishes, they may grow to 2 m/6 ft and weigh 90–135 kg/200–300 lb. They are very dark mottled brown or green above and pure white beneath.

Halicarnassus ancient city in Asia Minor (now Bodrum in Turkey), where the tomb of Mausolus, built about 350 BC by widowed Queen Artemisia, was one of the Seven Wonders of the World. The Greek historian Herodotus was born there.

Halifax capital of Nova Scotia, E Canada's main port; population (1986) 296,000. Industries include oil refining and food processing. There are six military bases and it is a major centre of oceanography. It was founded by British settlers 1749.

HAITI
Republic of

national name *République d'Haïti*
area 27,750 sq km/10,712 sq mi
capital Port-au-Prince
major towns/cities Cap-Haïtien, Gonaïves, Les Cayes, Port-de-Paix, Jérémie
physical features mainly mountainous and tropical; occupies western third of Hispaniola Island in Caribbean Sea
head of state René Preval from 1995
head of government Herve Denis from 1997
political system transitional
administrative divisions nine departments
political parties National Front for Change and Democracy (FNCD), left of centre; Lavalas Political Organization, populist
population 7,259,000 (1996 est)
population growth rate 2.0% (1990–95); 2.1% (2000–05)
ethnic distribution about 95% black African descent, the remainer are mulattos or Europeans
life expectancy 55 (men), 58 (women)
literacy rate men 59%, women 47%
languages French (official, spoken by literate 10% minority), Creole (official)
religions Christian 95% (of which 80% are Roman Catholic), voodoo 4%
currency gourde
GDP (US $) 1.62 billion (1994)
growth rate −13.2% (1994)
exports coffee, sugar, sisal, cotton, cocoa, bauxite

HISTORY
14th C Settled by Carib Indians, who followed an earlier wave of Arawak Indian immigration.
1492 The first landing place of the explorer Christopher Columbus in the New World, who named the island Hispaniola ('Little Spain').
1496 At Santo Domingo, now in the Dominican Republic to the E, the Spanish established the first European settlement in the Western hemisphere, which became capital of all Spanish colonies in America.
first half of 16th C A third of a million Arawaks and Caribs died, as a result of enslavement and exposure to European diseases; black African slaves were consequently brought in to work the island's gold and silver mines, which were swiftly exhausted.
1697 Spain ceded western third of Hispaniola to France, which became known as Haiti, but kept the E, which was known as Santo Domingo (the Dominican Republic).
1804 Independence achieved after uprising against French colonial rule led by the former slave, Toussaint l'Ouverture, who died in prison 1803, and Jean-Jacques Dessalines.
1818–43 Ruled by Jean-Pierre Boyer, who excluded the blacks from power.
1821 Santo Domingo fell under the control of Haiti until 1844.
1847–59 Blacks reasserted themselves under President Faustin Soulouque.
1915 Haiti invaded by USA as a result of political instability caused by black-mulatto friction; remained under US control until 1934.
1956 Dr François Duvalier (Papa Doc), a voodoo physician, seized power in military coup and was elected president one year later.
1964 Duvalier pronounced himself president for life, establishing a dictatorship based around a personal militia, the Tonton Macoutes.
1971 Duvalier died, succeeded by his son, Jean-Claude (Baby Doc); thousands murdered during Duvalier era.
1986 Duvalier deposed and fled the country; replaced by Lt-Gen Henri Namphy as head of a governing council.
1988 Leslie Manigat became president, but was ousted in military coup by Brig-Gen Prosper Avril, who installed a civilian government under military control.
1989 Coup attempt against Avril foiled; US aid resumed.
1990 Left-wing Catholic priest Jean-Bertrand Aristide elected president.
1991 Aristide overthrown in military coup led by Brig-Gen Raoul Cedras. Sanctions imposed by Organization of American States (OAS) and USA.
1993 United Nations (UN) embargo imposed. Aristide's return blocked by military.
1994 Threat of US invasion led to regime recognizing Aristide as president, under agreement brokered by former US president Jimmy Carter. US troops landed peacefully; Cedras relinquished power and withdrew to Panama; Aristide returned.
1995 UN peacekeepers drafted in to replace US troops. Assembly elections won by Aristide's supporters. Claudette Werleigh appointed prime minister. René Preval elected to replace Aristide as president.
1996 Peaceful handover of power to Preval.
1997 Caretaker prime minister Rosny Smarth resigned and replaced by Herve Denis.

SEE ALSO Arawak; Aristide, Jean-Bertrand; Dominican Republic; Duvalier, François

Halifax woollen textile town in West Yorkshire, England, on the river Calder; population (1991) 91,100. The cloth trade dates from the 15th century. Present-day industries include textiles, carpets, clothing, and engineering.

Halifax Edward Frederick Lindley Wood, 1st Earl of Halifax (2nd creation) 1881–1959. British Conservative politician, viceroy of India 1926–31. As foreign secretary 1938–40 he was associated with Chamberlain's 'appeasement' policy.

Halifax George Savile, 1st Marquess of Halifax 1633–1695. English politician. He entered Parliament 1660, and was raised to the peerage by Charles II, by whom he was also later dismissed. He strove to steer a middle course between extremists, and became known as 'the Trimmer'. He played a prominent part in the revolution of 1688.

Hall Peter (Reginald Frederick) 1930– . English theatre, opera, and film director. He was director of the Royal Shakespeare Theatre in Stratford-upon-Avon 1960–68 and developed the Royal Shakespeare Company 1968–73 until appointed director of the National Theatre 1973–88. He founded the Peter Hall Company 1988, and established a new repertory company based at the Old Vic Theatre, London, in 1996.

Hall's stage productions include Samuel Beckett's *Waiting for Godot* 1955, *The Wars of the Roses* 1963, Harold Pinter's *The Homecoming* stage 1967 and film 1973. He has directed operas at Covent Garden, London; Bayreuth, Germany; and New York, and in 1984 was appointed artistic director of opera at Glyndebourne, East Sussex, with productions of *Carmen* 1985 and *Albert Herring* 1985–86.

Hall Radclyffe. Pen name of Marguerite Radclyffe-Hall 1880–1943. English novelist. *The Well of Loneliness* 1928 brought her notoriety because of its lesbian theme. Her other works include the novel *Adam's Breed* 1926 (Femina Vie Heureuse and Tait Black Memorial prizes) and five early volumes of poetry.

Hall effect production of a voltage across a conductor or semiconductor carrying a current at a right angle to a surrounding magnetic field. It was discovered 1897 by the US physicist Edwin Hall (1855–1938). It is used in the ***Hall probe*** for measuring the strengths of magnetic fields and in magnetic switches.

Haller Albrecht von 1708–1777. Swiss physician and scientist, founder of neurology. He studied the muscles and nerves, and concluded that nerves provide the stimulus that triggers muscle contraction. He also showed that it is the nerves, not muscle or skin, that receive sensation.

Halley Edmond 1656–1742. English astronomer. He not only identified 1705 the comet that was later to be known by his name, but also compiled a star catalogue, detected the ◊proper motion of stars, using historical records, and began a line of research that, after his death, resulted in a reasonably accurate calculation of the astronomical unit.

Halley calculated that the comet sightings reported 1456, 1531, 1607, and 1682 all represented reappearances of the same comet. He reasoned that the comet would follow a parabolic path and announced 1705 in his *Synopsis Astronomia Cometicae* that it would reappear 1758.

He made many other notable contributions to astronomy, including the discovery of the proper motions of ◊Aldebaran, ◊Arcturus, and ◊Sirius, and working out a method of obtaining the solar parallax by observations made during a transit of Venus. He was Astronomer Royal from 1720.

Halley's comet comet that orbits the Sun about every 76 years, named after Edmond Halley who calculated its orbit. It is the brightest and most conspicuous of the periodic comets. Recorded sightings go back over 2,000 years. It travels around the Sun in the opposite direction to the planets. Its orbit is inclined at almost 20° to the main plane of the Solar System and ranges between the orbits of Venus and Neptune. It will next reappear 2061.

The comet was studied by space probes at its last appearance 1986. The European probe *Giotto* showed that the nucleus of Halley's comet is a tiny and irregularly shaped chunk of ice, measuring some 15 km/10 m long by 8 km/5 m wide, coated by a layer of very dark material, thought to be composed of carbon-rich compounds. This surface coating has a very low ◊albedo, reflecting just 4% of the light it receives from the Sun. Although the comet is one of the darkest objects known, it has a glowing head and tail produced by jets of gas from fissures in the outer dust layer. These vents cover 10% of the total surface area and become active only when exposed to the Sun. The force of these jets affects the speed of the comet's travel in its orbit.

Halliwell Geraldine Estelle (Geri) 1972– . English pop singer, formerly 'Ginger Spice' of the ◊Spice Girls. She left the group in May 1998, and became a United Nations (UN) goodwill ambassador in October, focusing on breast cancer and birth control awareness. Also in October, she sang at Prince Charles's 50th birthday party and signed a £2,000,000 record deal with Chrysalis Records for three solo albums. She was born in Watford, near London, England.

hallmark official mark stamped on British gold, silver, and (from 1913) platinum, instituted 1327 (royal charter of London Goldsmiths) in order to prevent fraud. After 1363, personal marks of identification were added. Now tests of metal content are carried out at authorized assay offices in London, Birmingham, Sheffield, and Edinburgh; each assay office has its distinguishing mark, to which is added a maker's mark, date letter, and mark guaranteeing standard.

Hallowe'en evening of 31 Oct, immediately preceding the Christian feast of Hallowmas or All Saints' Day. Customs associated with Hallowe'en in the USA and the UK include children wearing masks or costumes, and 'trick or treating' – going from house to house collecting sweets, fruit, or money.

Hallowe'en is associated with the ancient Celtic festival of ***Samhain***, which marked the end of the year and the beginning of winter. It was believed that on the evening of Samhain supernatural creatures were abroad and the souls of the dead were allowed to revisit their former homes.

Hallstatt archaeological site in Upper Austria, SW of Salzburg. The salt workings date from prehistoric times. In 1846 over 3,000 graves were discovered belonging to a 9th–5th century BC Celtic civilization transitional between the Bronze and Iron ages.

hallucinogen any substance that acts on the ◊central nervous system to produce changes in perception and mood and often hallucinations. Hallucinogens include ◊LSD, ◊peyote, and ◊mescaline. Their effects are unpredictable and they are illegal in most countries. They work by chemical interference with the normal action of neurotransmitters in the brain.

halogen any of a group of five nonmetallic elements with similar chemical bonding properties: fluorine, chlorine, bromine, iodine, and astatine. They form a linked group in the ◊periodic table of the elements, descending from fluorine, the most reactive, to astatine, the least reactive. They combine directly with most metals to form salts, such as common salt (NaCl). Each halogen has seven electrons in its valence shell, which accounts for the chemical similarities displayed by the group.

halon organic chemical compound containing one or two carbon atoms, together with ◊bromine and other ◊halogens. The most commonly used are halon 1211 (bromochlorodifluoromethane) and halon 1301 (bromotrifluoromethane). The halons are gases and are widely used in fire extinguishers. As destroyers of the ◊ozone layer, they are up to ten times more effective than ◊chlorofluorocarbons (CFCs), to which they are chemically related. Levels in the atmosphere are rising by about 25% each year, mainly through the testing of fire-fighting equipment. The use of halons in fire extinguishers was banned Jan 1994. ▷ *See feature on pp. 858–859.*

Hals Frans c. 1581–1666. Flemish-born painter. The pioneer in the Dutch school of free, broad brushwork, he painted directly on to the canvas to create portraits that are spontaneous and full of life. His work includes the famous *Laughing Cavalier* 1624 (Wallace Collection, London), and group portraits of military companies, governors of charities, and others.

Almost nothing of his early career is known, but one of his earliest works, *The Banquet of the Officers of the St George Militia Company* 1616 (Frans Hals Museum, Haarlem) is strikingly original. In its naturalness and vivacity it completely outmoded the conventional group portraits, with their stiff figures in dull poses. During his last years he painted perhaps his most important works, the two deeply moving group portraits of the administrators of the almshouses of Haarlem 1664 (Frans Hals Museum, Haarlem).

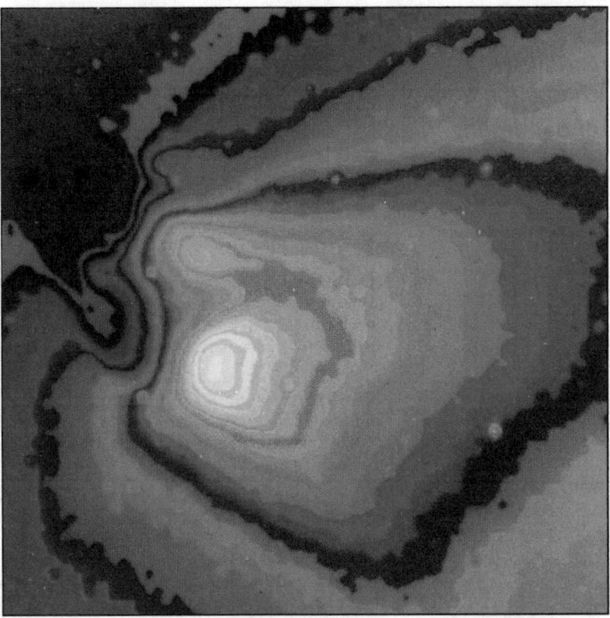

Halley's comet Halley's comet photographed from Skylab 1986 in the visible wavelengths. The comet, a dark mass in the upper left of the photograph, is seen trailing jets of gas behind it. *Image Select (UK) Ltd*

Hamburg largest inland port of Europe, in Germany, on the river Elbe; population (1993) 1,701,600. Industries include oil, chemicals, electronics, and cosmetics.

It is capital of the *Land* of Hamburg, and an archbishopric from 834. In alliance with Lübeck, it founded the ◊Hanseatic League.

Hamburg administrative region (German *Land*) of Germany
area 760 sq km/293 sq mi
capital Hamburg
features comprises the city and surrounding districts; there is a university, established 1919, and the Hamburg Schauspielhaus is one of Germany's leading theatres
industries refined oil, chemicals, electrical goods, ships, processed food
population (1994 est) 1,703,000
religion 74% Protestant, 8% Roman Catholic
history in 1510 the emperor Maximilian I made

Hals *The Bohemian* by Dutch artist Frans Hals. Painting directly on to the canvas with broad, confident brushstrokes, Hals was able to create portraits of remarkable spontaneity and naturalness. *Corbis*

‘We are not permitted to choose the frame of our destiny. But what we put into it is ours.’

DAG HAMMARSKJÖLD
Markings 1963

Hamburg a free imperial city, and in 1871 it became a state of the German Empire.

Hamilcar Barca c. 270–228 BC. Carthaginian general, father of ◊Hannibal. From 247 to 241 BC in the First ◊Punic War he harassed the Romans in Sicily and Italy and then led an expedition to Spain, where he died in battle.

Hamilton capital (since 1815) of Bermuda, on Bermuda Island; population about (1980) 1,617. It has a deep-sea harbour. Hamilton was founded 1612.

Hamilton port in Ontario, Canada; population (1986) 557,000. Linked with Lake Ontario by the Burlington Canal, it has a hydroelectric plant and steel, heavy machinery, electrical, chemical, and textile industries.

Hamilton town in South Lanarkshire, Scotland, and its administrative headquarters; population (1991) 50,000. Industries include textiles, electronics, and engineering.

Hamilton Alexander 1757–1804. US politician who influenced the adoption of a constitution with a strong central government and was the first secretary of the Treasury 1789–95. He led the Federalist Party, and incurred the bitter hatred of Aaron ◊Burr when he voted against Burr and in favour of Thomas Jefferson for the presidency 1801. Challenged to a duel by Burr, Hamilton was wounded and died the next day.

Hamilton Emma, Lady, (born Amy Lyon) c. 1761–1815. English courtesan. In 1782 she became the mistress of Charles Greville (1794–1865) and in 1786 of his uncle Sir William Hamilton (1730–1803), the British envoy to the court of Naples, who married her 1791. After Admiral ◊Nelson's return from the Nile 1798 during the Napoleonic Wars, she became his mistress and their daughter, Horatia, was born 1801.

Hamilton Iain Ellis 1922– . Scottish composer. His intensely emotional and harmonically rich works include striking viola and cello sonatas; the ballet *Clerk Saunders* 1951; the operas *Pharsalia* 1968 and *The Royal Hunt of the Sun* 1967–69, which renounced melody for inventive chordal formations; and symphonies.

Hamilton James, 3rd Marquis and 1st Duke of Hamilton 1606–1649. Scottish adviser to Charles I. He led an army against the ◊Covenanters (supporters of the National Covenant 1638 to establish Presbyterianism) 1639 and subsequently took part in the negotiations between Charles and the Scots. In the second English Civil War he led the Scottish invasion of England, but was captured at Preston and executed.

Handel The composer Georg Friedrich Handel, German by birth and later naturalized British, was almost an exact contemporary of J S Bach. Although both composers wrote many vocal works, Handel wrote for the theatre as well as for the church; his compositions also admit a greater range of influences. *Image Select (UK) Ltd*

Hamilton Richard 1922– . English artist, a pioneer of Pop art. His collage *Just What Is It That Makes Today's Homes So Different, So Appealing?* 1956 (Kunsthalle, Tübingen, Germany) is often cited as the first Pop art work: its 1950s interior, inhabited by the bodybuilder Charles Atlas and a pin-up, is typically humorous, concerned with popular culture and contemporary kitsch.

He was particularly concerned with the photographic image, which he skilfully combined with oil paint in his *Portrait of Gaitskell as a Monster of Filmland* 1963 (Arts Council of Great Britain). In other works he has taken images from various sources, usually commercial, to create a composition as in *Interior II* 1964 (Tate Gallery, London), while his *Cosmetic Studies* 1969 consist of collages in which fragments of fashion photographs are combined to make a single face. His series *Swingeing London 67* 1967 comments on the prosecution for drugs of his art dealer Robert Fraser and the singer Mick Jagger.

Hammarskjöld Dag (Hjalmar Agne Carl) 1905–1961. Swedish secretary general of the United Nations 1953–61. He opposed Britain over the ◊Suez Crisis 1956. His attempts to solve the problem of the Congo (now Zaire), where he was killed in a plane crash, were criticized by the USSR. He was awarded the Nobel Peace Prize 1961.

hammer throwing event in track and field athletics. The hammer is a spherical weight attached to a wire with a handle. The competitors spin the hammer over their heads to gain momentum, within the confines of a circle, and throw it as far as they can. The senior men's hammer weighs 7.26 kg/16 lb and may originally have been a blacksmith's hammer. Women and junior men throw lighter implements.

hammerhead any of several species of shark of the genus *Sphyrna*, found in tropical seas, characterized by having eyes at the ends of flattened extensions of the skull. Hammerheads can grow to 4 m/13 ft.

Hammersmith and Fulham inner borough of W central Greater London, N of the Thames
features Hammersmith Terrace, 18th-century houses on riverside; Parish Church of St Paul (1631); Lyric Theatre (1890); Fulham Palace, residence of the bishops of London from the 12th century until 1973, it is one of the best medieval domestic sites in London, with buildings dating from the 15th century; Riverside studios; Olympia exhibition centre (1884); 18th-century Hurlingham Club; White City Stadium
population (1991) 136,500
famous people Leigh Hunt; Ouida and Henri Gaudier-Brzeska were residents.

Hammerstein Oscar, II 1895–1960. US lyricist and librettist. He collaborated with Richard ◊Rodgers over a period of 16 years on some of the best-known American musicals, including *Oklahoma!* 1943 (Pulitzer prize), *Carousel* 1945, *South Pacific* 1949 (Pulitzer prize), *The King and I* 1951, and *The Sound of Music* 1959.

He was a grandson of opera impresario Oscar Hammerstein. He earned his first successes with *Rose Marie* 1924, music by Rudolf Friml (1879–1972); *Desert Song* 1926, music by Sigmund Romberg (1887–1951); and *Show Boat* 1927, music by Jerome Kern. *Show Boat* represented a major step forward in integration of plot and character. After a period of moderate success in film music, he joined Rodgers and began a 16-year collaboration.

Hammett (Samuel) Dashiell 1894–1961. US crime novelist. He introduced the ‘hard-boiled’ detective character into fiction and attracted a host of imitators, with works including *The Maltese Falcon* 1930 (filmed 1941), *The Glass Key* 1931 (filmed 1942), and his most successful novel, the light-hearted *The Thin Man* 1932 (filmed 1934). His Marxist politics were best expressed in *Red Harvest* 1929, which depicts the corruption of capitalism in ‘Poisonville’.

Hammett was a former Pinkerton detective agent. In 1951 he was imprisoned for contempt of court for refusing to testify during the McCarthy era of anti-communist witch hunts. He lived with the dramatist Lillian ◊Hellman for the latter half of his life.

Hammond organ electric organ invented in the USA by Laurens Hammond 1934 and widely used in gospel music. Hammond applied valve technology to miniaturize Thaddeus Cahill's original ‘tone-wheel’ concept, introduced draw-slide registration to vary timbre, and incorporated a distinctive tremulant using rotating speakers. The Hammond organ was a precursor of the synthesizer.

Hammurabi died c. 1750 BC. king of Babylon from c. 1792 BC. He united his country and took it to the height of its power. He authorized a legal code, of which a copy was found in 1902.

Hamnett Katharine 1948– . English fashion designer. She is particularly popular in the UK and Italy. Her oversized T-shirts promoting peace and environmental campaigns attracted attention 1983–84. She produces well-cut, inexpensive designs for men and women, predominantly in natural fabrics. In 1989 she began showing her collections in Paris, and in 1993 launched hand-knitwear and leather collections.

Hampden John 1594–1643. English politician. His refusal in 1636 to pay ◊ship money, a compulsory tax levied to support the navy, made him a national figure. In the Short and Long Parliaments he proved himself a skilful debater and parliamentary strategist.

King Charles's attempt to arrest him and four other leading MPs made the Civil War inevitable. He raised his own regiment on the outbreak of hostilities, and on 18 June 1643 was mortally wounded at the skirmish of Chalgrove Field in Oxfordshire.

Hampden Park Scottish football ground, opened 1903, home of the Queen's Park club and the national Scottish team. It plays host to the Scottish FA Cup and League Cup final each year, as well as semifinals and other matches.

Hampshire county of S England (*see United Kingdom map*)
towns and cities Winchester (administrative headquarters), Gosport
features New Forest, area 373 sq km/144 sq mi, a Saxon royal hunting ground; the river Test, which has trout fishing; the river Itchen; Hampshire Basin, where Britain has onshore and offshore oil; Danebury, 2,500-year-old Celtic hillfort; Beaulieu (including National Motor Museum); Broadlands (home of Lord Mountbatten); Highclere castle (home of the Earl of Carnarvon, with gardens by Capability Brown); Hambledon, where the first cricket club was founded 1750; site of the Roman town of Silchester, the only one in Britain known in such detail; Jane Austen's cottage 1809–17 is a museum; naval base at Gosport; Twyford Down section of the M3 motorway was completed 1994 despite protests
industries agricultural including watercress growing; oil from refineries at Fawley; chemicals, pharmaceuticals, electronics, shipbuilding
famous people Gilbert White, Jane Austen, Charles Dickens.

Hampton Lionel 1909– . US jazz musician. He was a top bandleader of the 1940s and 1950s. Originally a drummer, Hampton introduced the vibraphone, an electronically vibrated percussion instrument, to jazz music. With the Benny ◊Goodman band from 1936, he fronted his own big band 1941–65 and subsequently led small groups.

Hampton Court Palace former royal residence near Richmond, London, built 1515 by Cardinal ◊Wolsey and presented by him to Henry VIII 1525. Henry subsequently enlarged and improved it. In the 17th century William and Mary made it their main residence outside London, and the palace was further enlarged by Christopher Wren, although only part of his intended scheme was completed. Part of the building was extensively damaged by fire 1986.

The last monarch to live at Hampton Court was George II, who died 1760. During his life many of the Tudor apartments were pulled down and replaced. The palace was opened to the public, free of charge, by Queen Victoria 1838.

hamster rodent of the family Cricetidae with a thickset body, short tail, and cheek pouches to carry food. Several genera are found across Asia and in

SE Europe. The golden hamster *Mesocricetus auratus* lives in W Asia and SE Europe. All golden hamsters now kept as pets originated from one female and 12 young captured in Syria 1930.

Hamsun Knut. Pseudonym of Knut Pedersen 1859–1952. Norwegian novelist. His first novel *Sult/Hunger* 1890 was largely autobiographical. Other works include *Pan* 1894 and *Markens grøde/The Growth of the Soil* 1917. He attacked the established 'realistic' writers such as Ibsen and Bjørnson, maintaining that a subjective, irrational approach revealed more of the true nature of an individual. He was the first of many European and American writers to attempt to capture 'the unconscious life of the soul'. Nobel prize 1920. His hatred of capitalism made him sympathize with Nazism and he was fined 1946 for collaboration, but his reputation was subsequently restored.

Han the majority ethnic group in China, numbering about 990 million. The Hans speak a wide variety of dialects of the same monosyllabic language, a member of the Sino-Tibetan family. Their religion combines Buddhism, Taoism, Confucianism, and ancestor worship.

Hancock John 1737–1793. US politician and a leader of the American Revolution. As president of the Continental Congress 1775–77, he was the first to sign the Declaration of Independence 1776. Because he signed it in a large, bold hand (in popular belief, so that it would be big enough for George III to see), his name became a colloquial term for a signature in the USA. He coveted command of the Continental Army, deeply resenting the selection of George ◊Washington. He was governor of Massachusetts 1780–85 and 1787–93.

Hancock Tony (Anthony John) 1924–1968. English lugubrious radio and television comedian. *Hancock's Half Hour* from 1954 showed him famously at odds with everyday life. He also appeared in films, including *The Rebel* 1960 and *The Wrong Box* 1966.

handball game resembling football but played with the hands instead of the feet. It was popularized in Germany in the late 19th century. The indoor game has 7 players in a team; the outdoor version (field handball) has 11. Indoor handball was introduced as an Olympic event in 1972 for men, and in 1976 for women.

Handel Georg Friedrich, (originally Händel) 1685–1759. German composer, a British subject from 1726. His first opera, *Almira*, was performed in Hamburg 1705. In 1710 he was appointed kapellmeister to the elector of Hanover (the future George I of England). In 1712 he settled in England, where he established his popularity with such works as the *Water Music* 1717 (written for George I). His great choral works include the *Messiah* 1742 and the later oratorios *Samson* 1743, *Belshazzar* 1745, *Judas Maccabaeus* 1747, and *Jephtha* 1752.

Visits to Italy 1706–10 inspired a number of operas and oratorios, and in 1711 his opera *Rinaldo* was performed in London. *Saul* and *Israel in Egypt* (both 1739) were unsuccessful, but his masterpiece the *Messiah* was acclaimed on its first performance in Dublin 1742. Other works include the pastoral *Acis and Galatea* 1718 and a set of variations for harpsichord that were later nicknamed 'The Harmonious Blacksmith'.

Handley Tommy (Thomas Reginald) 1892–1949. English radio comedian. His popular programme *ITMA (It's That Man Again)* ran from 1939 until his death.

Han dynasty Chinese ruling family 206 BC–AD 220 established by Liu Bang (256–195 BC) after he overthrew the ◊Qin dynasty, and named after the Han River. There was territorial expansion to the W, SW, and N, including the conquest of Korea by emperor Wudi (Wu-ti, ruled 141–87 BC) and the suppression of the ◊Xiongnu invaders. Under the Han, a Confucianist-educated civil service was established and Buddhism introduced.

Divided into the eras of the Western Han 206 BC–AD 8 and the Eastern Han AD 25–220, it was a time of internal peace, except AD 8–25. The building of new canals allowed long-distance trading, while the arts and technologies (including the invention of paper) flourished. The dynasty collapsed under the weight of court intrigues, rebellions, and renewed threat from the Xiongnu, and was replaced by the ◊Three Kingdoms.

hang-gliding technique of unpowered flying using air currents, perfected by US engineer Francis Rogallo in the 1970s. The aeronaut is strapped into a carrier, attached to a sail wing of nylon stretched on an aluminium frame like a paper dart, and jumps into the air from a high place, where updraughts of warm air allow soaring on the thermals. See ◊gliding.

hanging execution by suspension, usually with a drop of 0.6–2 m/2–6 ft, so that the powerful jerk of the tightened rope breaks the neck. This was once a common form of ◊capital punishment in Europe and is still practised in some states in the USA. It was abolished in the UK 1965.

Hanging Gardens of Babylon in antiquity, gardens at Babylon, the capital of Mesopotamia, considered one of the ◊Seven Wonders of the World. According to legend, King Nebuchadnezzar constructed the gardens in the 6th century BC for one of his wives, who was homesick for her birthplace in the Iranian mountains. Archaeological excavations at the site of Babylon, 88 km/55 mi S of Baghdad in modern Iraq, have uncovered a huge substructure that may have supported irrigated gardens on terraces.

hanging valley valley that joins a larger glacial trough at a higher level than the trough floor. During glaciation the ice in the smaller valley was unable to erode as deeply as the ice in the trough, and so the valley was left perched high on the side of the trough when the ice retreated. A river or stream flowing along the hanging valley often forms a waterfall as it enters the trough.

Hangzhou or ***Hangchow*** port and capital of Zhejiang province, China; population (1993) 1,740,000. It has jute, steel, chemical, tea, and silk industries. Hangzhou has fine landscaped gardens and was the capital of China 1127–1278 under the Sung dynasty.

Hanks Tom 1956– . US actor. His amiable features and mainstream appeal, often seen to best advantage in romantic comedies such as *Sleepless in Seattle* 1993, made his casting as the AIDS-afflicted lawyer in *Philadelphia* 1993 (Academy Award) all the more controversial. His other notable roles include the drunken baseball coach in *A League of their Own* 1992, and the title role in *Forrest Gump* 1994 (Academy Award).

He featured in a number of lightweight comedy dramas during the 1980s, most notably in *Splash* 1984, and *Big* 1988, in which he played a boy transformed into a grown man. His other films include *Dragnet* 1987 and *Turner and Hooch* 1989.

Hanley Ellery 1965– . English rugby league player, a regular member of the Great Britain team since 1984 and the inspiration behind Wigan's domination of the sport in the 1980s. He joined Leeds 1991.

Hanley started his career in 1981 with Bradford Northern before his transfer to Wigan 1985 for a then world record £85,000. He has since won all the top honours of the game in Britain as well as earning a reputation in Australia, the world's top rugby league nation.

Hannibal 247–c. 182 BC. Carthaginian general from 221 BC, son of Hamilcar Barca. His siege of Saguntum (now Sagunto, near Valencia) precipitated the Second ◊Punic War with Rome. Following a campaign in Italy (after crossing the Alps in 218), Hannibal was the victor at Trasimene in 217 and Cannae in 216, but he failed to take Rome. In 203 he returned to Carthage to meet a Roman invasion but was defeated at Zama in 202 and exiled in 196 at Rome's insistence.

Hanoi capital of Vietnam, on the Red River; population (1989) 1,088,900. Central Hanoi has one of the highest population densities in the world: 1,300 people per hectare/3,250 per acre. Industries include textiles, paper, and engineering.

Captured by the French 1873, it was the capital of French Indochina 1887–1946. It was the capital of North Vietnam 1954–76.

Hanover industrial city, capital of Lower Saxony, Germany; population (1993) 525,300. Industries include machinery, vehicles, electrical goods, rubber, textiles, and oil refining.

From 1386, it was a member of the ◊Hanseatic League, and from 1692 capital of the electorate of Hanover (created a kingdom 1815). ◊George I of England was also Elector of Hanover, and the two countries shared the same monarch until the accession of Victoria 1837. Since ◊Salic law meant a woman could not rule in Hanover, the throne passed to her uncle Ernest, Duke of Cumberland. His son was forced by the Prussian prime minister ◊Bismarck to abdicate 1866, and Hanover became a Prussian province. In 1946, Hanover was merged with Brunswick and Oldenburg to form the *Land* of Lower Saxony.

Hanover German royal dynasty that ruled Great Britain and Ireland 1714–1901. Under the Act of ◊Settlement 1701, the succession passed to the ruling family of Hanover, Germany, on the death of Queen Anne. On the death of Queen Victoria, the crown passed to Edward VII of the house of Saxe-Coburg.

Hansard official report of the proceedings of the British Houses of Parliament, named after Luke Hansard (1752–1828), printer of the House of Commons *Journal* from 1774. It is published by Her Majesty's Stationery Office. The name *Hansard* was officially adopted 1943.

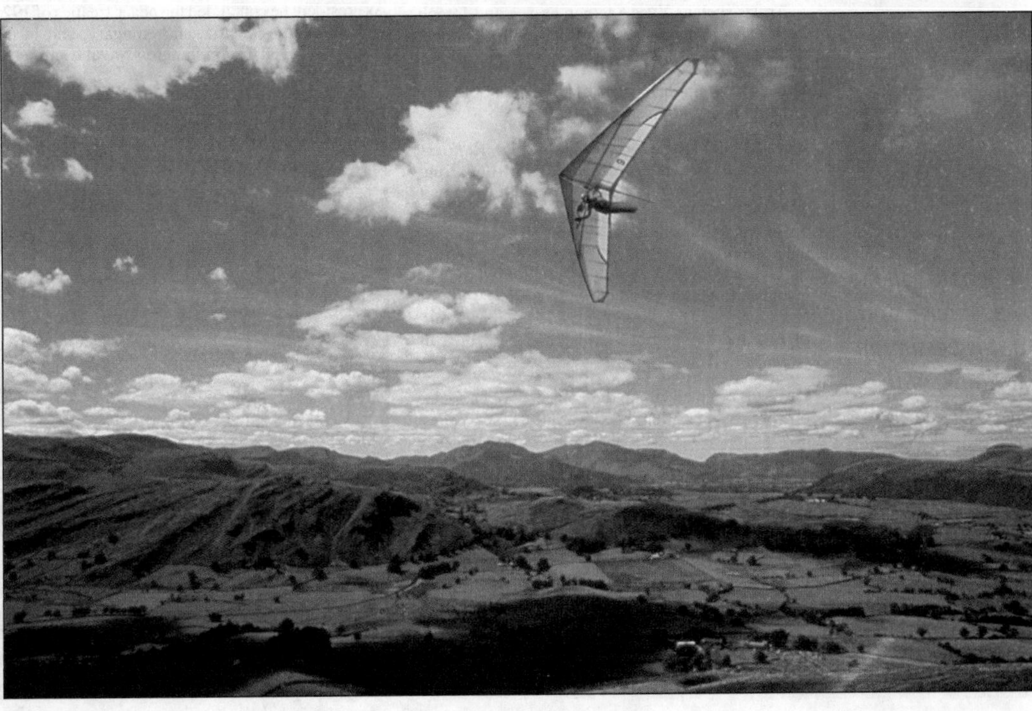

hang-gliding This sport involves hanging in a harness from a cloth wing stretched on an aluminium frame, and jumping from a high point. It is a dangerous sport, which became popular in the 1960s. *Image Select (UK) Ltd*

America's present need is not heroics, but healing; not nostrums but normalcy; not revolution, but restoration.

WARREN G HARDING
Speech in Boston
14 May 1920

The first official reports were published from 1803 by the political journalist William Cobbett who, during his imprisonment 1810–12, sold the business to his printer Thomas Curson Hansard, son of Luke Hansard. The publication of the debates remained in the hands of the family until 1889.

Hanseatic League (German *Hanse* 'group, society') confederation of N European trading cities from the 12th century to 1669. At its height in the late 14th century the Hanseatic League included over 160 cities and towns, among them Lübeck, Hamburg, Cologne, Breslau, and Kraków.

The basis of the league's power was its monopoly of the Baltic trade and its relations with Flanders and England. The decline of the Hanseatic League from the 15th century was caused by the closing and moving of trade routes and the development of nation states.

Hansom Joseph Aloysius 1803–1882. English architect and inventor. His works include the Birmingham town hall 1831, but he is remembered as the designer of the hansom cab 1834, a two-wheel carriage with a seat for the driver on the outside.

Hanukkah or ***Hanukah*** or ***Chanukkah*** in Judaism, an eight-day festival of lights that takes place at the beginning of Dec. It celebrates the recapture and rededication of the Temple in Jerusalem by Judas Maccabaeus 164 BC.

During Hanukkah, candles are lit each night and placed in an eight-branched candlestick, or menorah: this commemorates the Temple lamp that stayed miraculously lit for eight days on one day's supply of oil until a new supply could be made.

Hanuman in the Sanskrit epic *Rāmāyana*, the Hindu monkey god and king of Hindustan (N India). He helped Rama (an incarnation of the god Vishnu) to retrieve his wife Sita, abducted by Ravana of Lanka (now Sri Lanka).

haploid having a single set of ◊chromosomes in each cell. Most higher organisms are ◊diploid – that is, they have two sets – but their gametes (sex cells) are haploid. Some plants, such as mosses, liverworts, and many seaweeds, are haploid, and male honey bees are haploid because they develop from eggs that have not been fertilized. See also ◊meiosis.

happening an event which combines the visual arts and improvised theatre. Happenings became popular in the USA in the 1960s, influenced by the composer John Cage's theories concerning the role of chance in art, and closely related to ◊performance art and ◊environment art. They were associated particularly with the US painter Allen Kaprow (1927–), who first used the term 1959, as well as with the pop artists Jim Dine, Roy Lichtenstein, Claes Oldenburg, and Robert Rauschenberg.

Artists such as Yves Klein in France and Joseph Beuys in Germany have developed the political potential of happenings.

Hapsburg English form of ◊Habsburg, former imperial house of Austria–Hungary.

Harald (III) Hardrada or ***Harald the Ruthless*** (Norwegian ***Harald Hardraòde***) 1015–1066. King of Norway 1045–66, ruling jointly with Magnus I 1045–47.

He engaged in an unsuccessful attempt to conquer Denmark 1045–62; extended Norwegian rule in Orkney, Shetland, and the Hebrides; and tried to conquer England together with Tostig, Earl of Northumbria. They were defeated by King Harold of England at Stamford Bridge and both died in battle.

People call me a pessimist; and if it is pessimism to think, with Sophocles, that 'not to have been born is best', then I do not reject the designation.

THOMAS HARDY
Quoted in William Archer *Real Conversations*

Harappa ruined city in the Punjab, NW Pakistan, of a prehistoric culture known as the ◊Indus Valley civilization, which flourished from 2500 to 1600 BC. It is one of two such great cities excavated; the other is ◊Mohenjo Daro.

Harare capital of Zimbabwe, on the Mashonaland plateau, about 1,525 m/5,000 ft above sea level; population (1992) 1,184,200. It is the centre of a rich farming area (tobacco and maize), with metallurgical and food processing industries.

The British occupied the site 1890 and named it Fort Salisbury in honour of Lord Salisbury, then prime minister of the UK. It was capital of the Federation of Rhodesia and Nyasaland 1953–63.

Harbin or ***Haerhpin*** or ***Pinkiang*** port on the Songhua River, NE China, capital of Heilongjiang province; population (1993) 3,100,000. Industries include metallurgy, machinery, paper, food processing, and sugar refining, and it is a major rail junction. Harbin was developed by Russian settlers after Russia was granted trading rights here 1896, and more Russians arrived as refugees after the October Revolution 1917. In World War II, it was the key objective of the Soviet invasion of Manchuria Aug 1945.

hardcore in pop music, of any style, the more extreme and generally less commercial end of the spectrum: hardcore ◊techno is a minimalist electronic dance music; hardcore ◊rap is aggressive or offensive; hardcore punk jettisons form and melody for speed and ◊noise.

There are several main tendencies within hardcore punk. The very similar styles known as thrash, speed metal, and grindcore, are played on guitars and drums as fast as possible with loud, angry shouting; exponents include Napalm Death (formed in England 1982). The most influential US hardcore band has been Black Flag (formed 1977). Other bands seek to explore the 'hard core of reality' in lyrics that deal with depravity and degradation; the US Swans (formed 1980) are an example.

The term 'artcore' is sometimes used for bands like Sonic Youth that employ noise with a more nuanced effect.

hard disk in computing, a storage device consisting of a rigid metal disk coated with a magnetic material. Data are read from and written to the disk by means of a unit called a disk drive. The hard disk may be permanently fixed into the drive or in the form of a disk pack that can be removed and exchanged with a different pack. Hard disks vary from large units with capacities of over 3,000 megabytes, intended for use with mainframe computers, to small units with capacities as low as 20 megabytes, intended for use with microcomputers.

Hardicanute c. 1019–1042. King of Denmark from 1028, and of England from 1040; son of Canute. In England he was considered a harsh ruler.

Hardie (James) Keir 1856–1915. Scottish socialist, member of Parliament 1892–95 and 1900–15. He worked in the mines as a boy and in 1886 became secretary of the Scottish Miners' Federation. In 1888 he was the first Labour candidate to stand for Parliament; he entered Parliament independently as a Labour member 1892 and was a chief founder of the ◊Independent Labour Party 1893. A pacifist, he strongly opposed the Boer War, and his idealism in his work for socialism and the unemployed made him a popular hero.

Harding Warren G(amaliel) 1865–1923. 29th president of the USA 1921–23, a Republican. He opposed US membership of the League of Nations. As president he concluded the peace treaties of 1921 with Germany, Austria, and Hungary, and in the same year called the Washington Naval Conference to resolve conflicting British, Japanese, and US ambitions in the Pacific.

hardness physical property of materials that governs their use. Methods of heat treatment can increase the hardness of metals. A scale of hardness was devised by German–Austrian mineralogist Friedrich ◊Mohs in the 1800s, based upon the hardness of certain minerals from soft talc (Mohs' hardness 1) to diamond (10), the hardest of all materials.

Hardouin-Mansart Jules 1646–1708. French architect to Louis XIV from 1675. He designed the lavish Baroque extensions to the palace of Versailles (from 1678) and the Grand Trianon. Other works include the Invalides Chapel (1680–91), the Place de Vendôme (from 1698), and the Place des Victoires, all in Paris.

Hardwar city in Uttar Pradesh, India, on the right bank of the river Ganges; population (1991) 147,300. The name means 'door of Hari' (or Vishnu). It is one of the holy places of the Hindu religion and a pilgrimage centre. The *Kumbhmela* festival, held every 12th year in honour of the god Siva, attracts about 1 million pilgrims.

hardware the mechanical, electrical, and electronic components of a computer system, as opposed to the various programs, which constitute ◊software. Hardware associated with a microcomputer might include the power supply and housing of its processor unit, its circuit boards, VDU (screen), disk drive, keyboard, and printer.

hard water water that does not lather easily with soap, and produces a deposit or 'scale' in kettles. It is caused by the presence of certain salts of calcium and magnesium.

Temporary hardness is caused by the presence of dissolved hydrogencarbonates (bicarbonates); when the water is boiled, they are converted to insoluble carbonates that precipitate as 'scale'. ***Permanent hardness*** is caused by sulphates and silicates, which are not affected by boiling. Water can be softened by ◊distillation, ◊ion exchange (the principle underlying commercial water softeners), addition of sodium carbonate or of large amounts of soap, or boiling (to remove temporary hardness).

Hardy Oliver, (born Norvell) 1892–1957. US film comedian, member of the duo ◊Laurel and Hardy.

Hardy Thomas 1840–1928. English novelist and poet. His novels, set in rural 'Wessex' (his native West Country), portray intense human relationships played out in a harshly indifferent natural world.

His first completed novel, *Desperate Remedies* 1871, was a murder story published at his own expense. It was followed by *Under the Greenwood Tree* 1872, *A Pair of Blue Eyes* 1872–73, and his first successful work, *Far From the Madding Crowd*. *The Return of the Native* marks a major step forward in Hardy's development, being a highly charged novel in which the vast brooding expanse of Egdon Heath is said to be the real hero. *The Trumpet Major* 1880 and *A Laodicean* 1881 are

Hardie Keir Hardie addressing an antiwar rally in London 1914. Hardie played an important part in the establishment of the early Labour Party, and was an ardent pacifist who campaigned against Britain's involvement in World War I. *Image Select (UK) Ltd*

harebell The harebell, also known as witches' thimble, is a plant of northern temperate regions and usually grows in dry, grassy locations. It has blue, bell-shaped flowers that appear from July to Sept. *Premaphotos Wildlife*

unremarkable, but *The Mayor of Casterbridge* is shaped round a penetrating study of the character of Michael Henchard. *The Woodlanders* gives a sensitive picture of the rhythmic life of a tree-cutting, fence-making community and was followed by *Tess of the d'Urbervilles*, subtitled 'A Pure Woman'. This novel outraged public opinion by portraying as its heroine a woman who had been seduced. An even greater outcry followed *Jude the Obscure*, a grim study of the downward path of an intelligent and sensitive young man, ending in a tragedy that spreads far beyond Jude himself. The reception of this work reinforced Hardy's decision to confine himself to verse in his later years. His poetry includes the *Wessex Poems* 1898, the blank-verse epic of the Napoleonic Wars *The Dynasts* 1903–08, and several volumes of lyrics.

hare mammal of the genus *Lepus* of the family Leporidae (which also includes rabbits) in the order Lagomorpha. Hares are larger than rabbits, with very long, black-tipped ears, long hind legs, and short, upturned tails.

Throughout the long breeding season June–Aug, there are chases and 'boxing matches' among males and females; the expression 'mad as a March hare' arises from this behaviour.

Hare David 1947– . British dramatist and screenwriter, who co-founded the theatre company Joint Stock 1974. His plays satirize the decadence of post-war Britain, and include *Slag* 1970, *Teeth 'n' Smiles* 1975, *Fanshen* 1975 on revolutionary Chinese communism, *Plenty* 1978, and *Pravda* 1985 (with Howard ◊Brenton) on Fleet Street journalism. A recent trilogy of plays looks critically at three aspects of the establishment in Britain: *Racing Demon* 1990 at the Church of England, *Murmuring Judges* 1991 at the legal system, and *The Absence of War* 1994. His screenplays include *Wetherby* and *Plenty* both 1985, *Paris by Night* 1988, and *The Absence of War* 1994. He has also published an autobiography *Writing Left-Handed* 1991.

harebell perennial plant *Campanula rotundifolia* of the ◊bellflower family, with bell-shaped blue flowers, found on dry grassland and heaths. It is known in Scotland as the bluebell.

Hare Krishna popular name for a member of the ◊International Society for Krishna Consciousness, derived from their chant.

harelip congenital facial deformity, a cleft in the upper lip and jaw, which may extend back into the palate (cleft palate). It can be remedied by surgery.

Hargreaves James c. 1720–1778. English inventor who co-invented a carding machine for combing wool 1760. About 1764 he invented his 'spinning jenny' (patented 1770), which enabled a number of threads to be spun simultaneously by one person.

Harijan (Hindi 'children of god') member of the Indian ◊caste of untouchables. The term was introduced by Mahatma Gandhi during the independence movement. ▷ *See feature on pp. 432–433.*

Haringey inner borough of N Greater London. It includes the suburbs of Wood Green, Tottenham, Hornsey, and Harringey
features Bruce Castle, Tottenham, an Elizabethan manor house (said to stand on the site of an earlier castle built by Robert the Bruce's father); Alexandra Palace (1873), with park; Finsbury Park (1869), one of the earliest municipal parks
population (1991) 202,200
famous people Rowland Hill.

Harlech town in Gwynedd, N Wales; population (1991) 1,230. The castle, now in ruins, was built by the English king Edward I 1283–89. It was captured by the Welsh chieftain Owen Glendower 1404–08 and by the Yorkists in the Wars of the ◊Roses 1468.

Harlem Globetrotters US touring basketball team that plays exhibition matches worldwide. Comedy routines as well as their great skills are features of the games. They were founded 1927 by Abraham Saperstein (1903–1966).

Harlem Renaissance movement in US literature in the 1920s that used Afro-American life and black culture as its subject matter; it was an early manifestation of black pride in the USA. The centre of the movement was the Harlem section of New York City.

Harlow Jean. Stage name of Harlean Carpentier 1911–1937. US film actress. She was the original 'platinum blonde' and the wisecracking sex symbol of the 1930s. Her films include *Hell's Angels* 1930, *Red Dust* 1932, *Platinum Blonde* 1932, *Dinner at Eight* 1933, *China Seas* 1935, and *Saratoga* 1937, during the filming of which she died (her part was completed by a double).

harmattan in meteorology, a dry and dusty NE wind that blows over W Africa.

harmonica pocket-sized reed organ blown directly from the mouth, invented by Charles Wheatstone 1829; see ◊mouth organ.

harmonics in music, a series of partial vibrations that combine to form a musical tone. The number and relative prominence of harmonics produced determines an instrument's tone colour (timbre). An oboe is rich in harmonics, the flute has few. Harmonics conform to successive divisions of the sounding air column or string: their pitches are harmonious.

harmonium keyboard reed organ of the 19th century, powered by foot-operated bellows and incorporating lever-action knee swells to influence dynamics. It was invented by Alexandre Debain in Paris about 1842.

Widely adopted in the USA as a home and church instrument, in France and Germany the harmonium flourished as a concert solo and orchestral instrument, being written for by Sigfrid Karg-Elert, Arnold Schoenberg (*Herzgewächse/Heart's Bloom* 1907), and Karlheinz Stockhausen (*Der Jahreslauf/The Course of the Years* 1977).

harmony in music, any simultaneous combination of sounds, as opposed to melody, which is a succession of sounds. Although the term suggests a pleasant or agreeable sound, it is applied to any combination of notes, whether consonant or dissonant. The theory of harmony deals with the formation of chords and their interrelation and logical progression.

The founder of harmonic theory was Jean-Philippe ◊Rameau. In his *Traité de l'harmonie/Treatise on Harmony* 1722, he established a system of chord classification on which subsequent methods of harmony have been based.

harness racing form of horse racing, also known as trotting or pacing, in which the horses are harnessed, pull a light vehicle (sulky) and compete at either a trotting or pacing gait. If a horse breaks the pace and gallops, the driver must start it again.

Harold I 1016–1040. King of England from 1035. The illegitimate son of Canute, known as ***Harefoot***, he claimed the throne 1035 when the legitimate heir Hardicanute was in Denmark. He was elected king 1037.

Harold II c. 1020–1066. King of England from Jan 1066. He succeeded his father Earl Godwin 1053 as earl of Wessex. In 1063 William of Normandy (◊William the Conqueror) tricked him into swearing to support his claim to the English throne, and when the Witan (a council of high-ranking religious and secular men) elected Harold to succeed Edward the Confessor, William prepared to invade. Meanwhile, Harold's treacherous brother Tostig (died 1066) joined the king of Norway, Harald Hardrada (1015–1066), in invading Northumbria. Harold routed and killed them at Stamford Bridge 25 Sept. Three days later William landed at Pevensey, Sussex, and Harold was killed at the Battle of Hastings 14 Oct 1066.

harp plucked musical string instrument, with the strings stretched vertically within a wood and brass soundbox of triangular shape. The orchestral harp is the largest instrument of its type. It has up to 47 diatonically tuned strings, in the range B0–C7 (seven octaves), and seven double-action pedals to alter pitch. Composers for the harp include Mozart, Maurice Ravel, Carlos Salzedo, and Heinz Holliger. The harp has also been used in folk music, as both a solo and accompanying instrument, and is associated with Wales and Ireland.

Harper's Ferry village in W Virginia, USA, where the Potomac and Shenandoah rivers meet. In 1859 antislavery leader John ◊Brown seized the federal government's arsenal here, an action that helped precipitate the Civil War.

harpsichord the largest and grandest of 18th-century keyboard string instruments, used in orchestras and as a solo instrument. The strings are plucked by 'jacks' made of leather or quill, and multiple keyboards offering variation in tone are common. The revival of the harpsichord repertoire in the 20th century owes much to Wanda Landowska and Ralph Kirkpatrick (1911–1984).

Harpy in early Greek mythology, a wind spirit; in later legend the Harpies have horrific women's faces and the bodies of vultures.

Harrier the only truly successful vertical takeoff and landing fixed-wing aircraft, often called the *jump jet*. It was built in Britain and made its first flight 1966. It has a single jet engine and a set of swivelling nozzles. These deflect the jet exhaust vertically downwards for takeoff and landing, and to the rear for normal flight. Designed to fly from confined spaces with minimal ground support, it refuels in midair.

harrier bird of prey of the genus *Circus*, family Accipitridae, order Falconiformes. Harriers have long wings and legs, a short beak, an owl-like frill of thickset feathers around the face, and soft plumage. They eat frogs, birds, snakes, and small mammals, and chiefly frequent marshy districts. They are found throughout the world. *See illustration on following page.*

harrier The eight races of the marsh harrier, a long-winged hawk, are found among fens, swamps, marshes, and reed beds throughout Europe, North Africa, and the islands of the Indian Ocean and the Pacific. They feed on reptiles, amphibians, eggs, small mammals, and even carrion which they seek by quartering the ground in low flight and then dropping down.

harrier breed of hound, similar to a ◊foxhound but smaller, used in packs for hare-hunting.

❛Bred en bawn in a brier-patch!❜

JOEL CHANDLER HARRIS
Uncle Remus. Legends of the Old Plantation

Harris southern part of ◊Lewis with Harris, in the Outer ◊Hebrides Islands off Scotland; area 500 sq km/193 sq mi; population (1971) 2,900. It is joined to Lewis by a narrow isthmus. Harris tweeds are produced here.

Harris Arthur Travers 1892–1984. British marshal of the Royal Air Force in World War II. Known as 'Bomber Harris', he was commander in chief of Bomber Command 1942–45.

Harris Joel Chandler 1848–1908. US author. He wrote tales narrated by the former slave 'Uncle Remus', based on black folklore and involving the characters Brer Rabbit, Brer Fox, Brer Wolf, and Brer Bear.

Harrison Benjamin 1833–1901. 23rd president of the USA 1889–93, a Republican. He called the first Pan-American Conference, which led to the establishment of the Pan-American Union, to improve inter-American cooperation and develop commercial ties. In 1948 this became the ◊Organization of American States.

Harrison Rex (Reginald Carey) 1908–1990. English film and theatre actor. He appeared in over 40 films and numerous plays, often portraying sophisticated and somewhat eccentric characters, such as the waspish Professor Higgins in *My Fair Lady* 1964 (Academy Award), the musical version of *Pygmalion*. His other films include *Blithe Spirit* 1945, *The Ghost and Mrs Muir* 1947, and *Dr Doolittle* 1967.

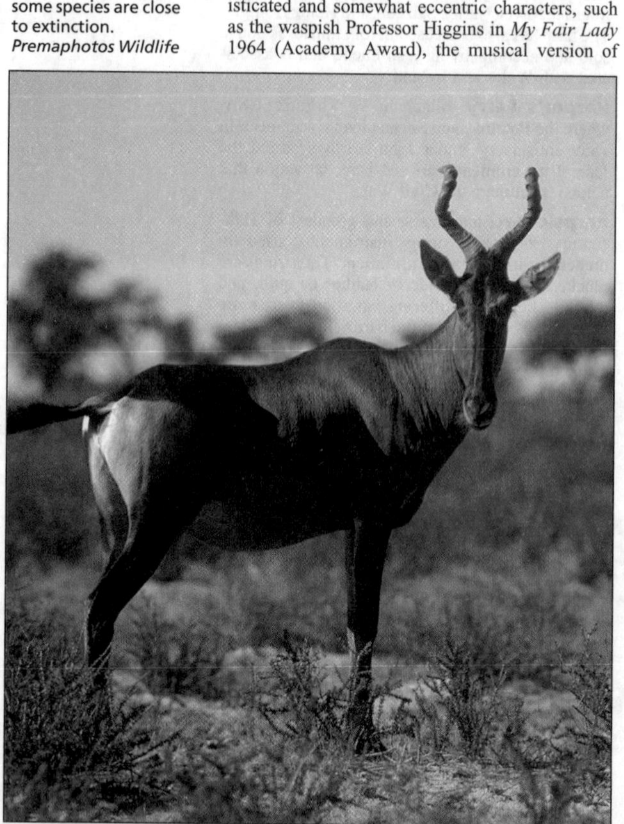

hartebeest With its long face and lyre-shaped horns, the hartebeest is one of Africa's most distinctive antelopes. It lives in small herds, often with other herd animals such as zebra and gnu. Numbers are now greatly reduced and some species are close to extinction.
Premaphotos Wildlife

Harrison Tony 1937– . English poet, translator, and dramatist. He caused controversy with his poem *V* 1987, dealing with the desecration of his parents' grave by Liverpool football supporters, and the play *The Blasphemers' Banquet* 1989, which attacked (in the name of Molière, Voltaire, Byron, and Omar Khayyam) the death sentence on Salman Rushdie. He has also translated and adapted Molière. *Black Daisies for the Bride* (poems) appeared 1993.

Harrison William Henry 1773–1841. 9th president of the US 1841. Elected 1840 as a Whig, he died one month after taking office. His political career was based largely on his reputation as an Indian fighter, and his campaign was constructed to give the impression that he was a man of the people with simple tastes and that the New Yorker, Martin ◊Van Buren, his opponent, was a 'foppish' sophisticate.

Harrogate resort and spa in North Yorkshire, England; population (1991) 66,200. There is a US communications station at Menwith Hill.

harrow agricultural implement used to break up the furrows left by the ◊plough and reduce the soil to a fine consistency or tilth, and to cover the seeds after sowing. The traditional harrow consists of spikes set in a frame; modern harrows use sets of discs.

Harrow Outer London borough of NW Greater London
features Harrow School (1571)
population (1991) 200,100
famous people R B Sheridan, Charles Kingsley, Robert Ballantyne, Matthew Arnold, Anthony Trollope.

Harsha-Vardhana c. 590–c. 647. Supreme ruler (*sakala-Uttarapathanatha*) of N India from 606. Through a succession of military victories, he established a large pan-regional empire in N and central India, extending to Kashmir in the NW. It was connected by loose feudalistic tributary ties.

Originally chief of the Pushyabhutis, based in Thanesar near Delhi, he united his throne through a marriage alliance with the Maukharis, whose headquarters at Kanauj, in the upper Ganges valley, became his capital. A devout Buddhist, he was an enlightened and cultured ruler.

hartebeest large African antelope *Alcelaphus buselaphus* with lyre-shaped horns set close on top of the head in both sexes. It may grow to 1.5 m/5 ft at the rather humped shoulders and up to 2 m/6 ft long. Although they are clumsy-looking runners, hartebeest can reach 65 kph/40 mph.

Hartington Spencer Compton Cavendish, Marquess of Hartington and 8th Duke of Devonshire 1833–1908. British politician, first leader of the Liberal Unionists 1886–1903. As war minister he opposed devolution for Ireland in cabinet and later led the revolt of the Liberal Unionists that defeated Gladstone's Irish Home Rule bill 1886. Hartington refused the premiership three times, 1880, 1886, and 1887, and led the opposition to the Irish Home Rule bill in the House of Lords 1893. ▷ *See feature on pp. 550–551.*

Hartlepool unitary authority of England created 1996 *(see United Kingdom map)*.

Hartley L(eslie) P(oles) 1895–1972. English novelist and short-story writer. His early works explored the sinister. His chief works are the trilogy *The Shrimp and the Anemone* 1944, *The Sixth Heaven* 1946, and *Eustace and Hilda* 1947 (Tait Black Memorial Prize), on the intertwined lives of a brother and sister. Later works include *The Go-Between* 1953 (filmed 1971) and *The Hireling* 1957, which explore sexual relationships between the classes.

Hartnell Norman Bishop 1901–1979. English fashion designer. He was known for his ornate evening gowns and tailored suits and coats. He worked for the designer Lucille 1923 before founding his own studio. Appointed dressmaker to the British royal family 1938, he created Queen Elizabeth II's wedding dress, when she was Princess Elizabeth, 1947, and her coronation gown 1953. The Hartnell fashion house closed 1992.

hart's-tongue fern *Phyllitis scolopendrium* whose straplike undivided fronds, up to 60 cm/24 in long, have prominent brown spore-bearing organs on the undersides. The plant is native to Eurasia and E North America, and is found on walls, in shady rocky places, and in woods.

Hartz Mountains range running N–S in Tasmania, Australia, with two remarkable peaks: Hartz Mountain (1,254 m/4,113 ft) and Adamsons Peak (1,224 m/4,017 ft).

Harvard University the oldest educational institution in the USA, founded 1636 at New Towne (later Cambridge), Massachusetts, and named after John Harvard (1607–1638), who bequeathed half his estate and his library to it. Women were first admitted 1969; the women's college of the university is Radcliffe College.

harvestman arachnid of the order Opiliones, with very long, thin legs and a small body. Harvestmen are distinguished from true spiders by the absence of a waist or constriction in the oval body. They feed on small insects and spiders, and lay their eggs in autumn, to hatch the following spring or early summer. They are found from the Arctic to the tropics.

harvest mite another name for the ◊chigger, a parasitic mite.

Harvey William 1578–1657. English physician who discovered the circulation of blood. In 1628 he published his book *De motu cordis/On the Motion of the Heart and the Blood in Animals*. He also explored the development of chick and deer embryos.

Haryana state of NW India, formed 1966
area 44,200 sq km/17,061 sq mi
capital Chandigarh
features part of the Ganges plain; a centre of Hinduism
industries sugar, cotton, oilseed, textiles, cement, iron ore, rice, pulses
population (1994) 17,925,000
language Hindi.

Hasdrubal Barca Carthaginian general, son of Hamilcar Barca and younger brother of Hannibal. He remained in command in Spain when Hannibal invaded Italy during the Second Punic War and, after fighting there against Scipio until 208, marched to Hannibal's relief. He was defeated and killed in the Metaurus valley, NE Italy.

Hašek Jaroslav 1883–1923. Czech writer. His masterpiece is an anti-authoritarian comic satire on military life under Austro-Hungarian rule, *The Good Soldier Švejk* 1921–23. During World War I he deserted to Russia, and eventually joined the Bolsheviks.

hashish drug made from the resin contained in the female flowering tops of hemp (◊cannabis).

Hasid or ***Hassid, Chasid*** (plural ***Hasidim, Hassidim, Chasidim***) member of a sect of Orthodox Jews, originating in 18th-century Poland under the leadership of Israel Ba'al Shem Tov (c. 1700–1760). Hasidic teachings encourage prayer, piety, and 'serving the Lord with joy'. Many of their ideas are based on the ◊kabbala.

Hasidism spread against strong opposition throughout E Europe during the 18th and 19th centuries, led by charismatic leaders, the *zaddikim*. The sect emphasized ecstatic prayer, while denouncing the intellectual approach of talmudic academies. Hasidic men dress in the black suits and broad-brimmed hats of 18th-century European society, a tradition which they conservatively maintain. A resistance to modernization had led some Hasids to oppose Zionism, though others are active supporters of Israel.

Hasina Wazed Sheika 1947– . Bangladeshi political leader, prime minister and defence minister from 1996. She led the centrist Awami League (AL) back to power 1996 after an interval of 21 years. The daughter of Sheik Mujibur Rahman, the country's first president who was assassinated 1975, Hasina escaped death when her father and other family members were murdered. She returned from exile abroad 1981 and assumed the leadership of the AL a year later. She led campaigns which ousted the military dictatorship of General Ershad 1990 and the Bangladesh National Party (BNP) government of Begum Khaleda Zia 1996.

Hassan II 1929– . King of Morocco from 1961 and a moderating influence in the Middle East in recent years. Following riots in Casablanca 1965, he established a royal dictatorship, but returned to constitutional government, with a civilian prime minister leading a government of national unity 1984. From 1976 he undertook the occupation of the part of Western Sahara ceded by Spain.

Hastert J Dennis (Denny) 1942– . US Republican politician, speaker of the House of Representatives from 1999. He was appointed as the House Republican representative on the White House Healthcare Reform Task Force 1993, chaired by Hillary Clinton, and chaired the Speaker's Steering Committee on Health and the Resource Group on Health. He was appointed Chief Deputy Whip for the Republicans in 1995, and was a member of the Commerce Committee and the Committee of Government Reform and Oversight. Hastert promised, in his first speech as speaker, a bipartisan spirit, emphasizing the need to end the partisan combat that characterized Congress during 1998.

Hastings resort in East Sussex, England, on the English Channel; population (1991) 80,800. William the Conqueror landed at Pevensey and defeated Harold at the Battle of ◊Hastings 1066. The chief of the ◊Cinque Ports, it has ruins of a Norman castle.

Hastings Warren 1732–1818. British colonial administrator. A protégé of Lord Clive, who established British rule in India, Hastings carried out major reforms, and became governor general of Bengal 1774. Impeached for corruption on his return to England 1785, he was acquitted 1795.

Hastings, Battle of battle 14 Oct 1066 at which William, Duke of Normandy ('the Conqueror') defeated Harold, King of England, and himself took the throne. The site is 10 km/6 mi inland from Hastings, at Senlac, Sussex; it is marked by Battle Abbey.

Having defeated an attempt by King Harald Hardrada of Norway at Stamford Bridge, Harold moved south with an army of 9,000 to counter the landing of the duke of Normandy, who had laid a claim to the English throne, at Pevensey Bay, Kent.

The Normans dominated the battle with archers supported by cavalry, breaking through ranks of infantry. Both sides suffered heavy losses but the decimation of the English army and Harold's death left England open to Norman rule.

Hatfield town in Hertfordshire, England, 8 km/5 mi E of St Albans; population (1991) 31,100. Designated a new town 1948, it has light engineering industries. It was the site of the 12th-century palace of the bishops of Ely, which was seized by Henry VIII and inhabited by Edward VI and Elizabeth I before their accession. James I gave the palace in part exchange to Robert ◊Cecil, 1st Earl of Salisbury, who replaced it 1611 with the existing Jacobean mansion, Hatfield House.

Hathor (temenos (dwelling) of Horus) in ancient Egyptian mythology, the sky goddess, the wife or mother of Horus, also goddess of dance, music, and love, corresponding to the Greek Aphrodite. She is depicted as a cow, since texts describe her as the great celestial cow who created all the world; or she is depicted as a human with a helmet in the shape of a sun-disc with cow's horns. She was popular with women, as their protector, and was later associated with ◊Isis.

Hatshepsut c. 1473–c. 1458 BC. Queen (pharaoh) of ancient Egypt during the 18th dynasty. She was the daughter of Thothmes I, and the wife and half-sister of Thothmes II. Throughout his reign real power lay with Hatshepsut, and she continued to rule after his death, as regent for her nephew Thothmes III. Her reign was a peaceful and prosperous time.

Hatshepsut reigned as a man, and is shown dressed as a pharaoh, with a beard. When she died or was forced to abdicate, Thothmes III defaced her monuments. The ruins of her temple at Deir el-Bahri survive.

Hattersley Roy Sydney George 1932– . British Labour politician and author. On the right wing of the Labour Party, he was prices secretary 1976–79, and deputy leader of the party 1983–1992. In 1994 he announced his retirement from active politics, and later expressed disagreement with some policies of the new party leadership.

Haughey Charles James 1925– . Irish politician, leader of Fianna Fáil 1979–92. He was Taoiseach (prime minister) 1979–81, March–Nov 1982, and 1987–92, when he was replaced by Albert Reynolds. Previously he had been justice, agriculture, and finance minister.

Hauptmann Gerhart Johann Robert 1862–1946. German dramatist. A strong proponent of an uncompromising naturalism in the theatre, Hauptmann's work has been widely produced. *Die Weber/The Weavers* 1892, his finest play, is an account of a revolt of Silesian weavers in 1844. His other plays include *Vor Sonnenaufgang/Before Dawn* 1889, the comedy *Der Biberpelz/The Beaver Coat* 1893, and a tragicomedy of the Berlin underworld *Die Ratten/The Rats* 1910. Nobel Prize for Literature 1912.

Haussmann Georges Eugène. Baron Haussmann 1809–1891. French administrator. He replanned medieval Paris 1853–70 to achieve the current city plan, with long wide boulevards and parks. The cost of his scheme and his authoritarianism caused opposition, and he was made to resign from his post.

haustorium (plural ***haustoria***) specialized organ produced by a parasitic plant or fungus that penetrates the cells of its host to absorb nutrients. It may be either an outgrowth of hyphae (see ◊hypha), as in the case of parasitic fungi, or of the stems of flowering parasitic plants, as in dodders (*Cuscuta*).

haute couture (French 'high dressmaking') from *couture*, 'sewing' or 'needlework', high-quality made-to-measure clothing designed by a couturier (a fashion designer who produces couture clothing). It is an expensive line of clothing which relies heavily upon the work of specialists to execute a couturier's design. Many couture houses have closed since the mass production of ready-to-wear clothing was introduced in the 1950s.

The production of *haute couture* is regulated by the Chambre Syndicale de la Haute Couture Parisienne, the union of dress designers founded in Paris 1868. A system similar to that of the Paris couture houses was operated by British court dressmakers, and also by fashion houses designing and making for royalty.

Haute-Normandie or *Upper Normandy* coastal region of NW France lying between Basse-Normandie and Picardy and bisected by the river Seine; area 12,300 sq km/4,757 sq mi; population (1990) 1,737,200. It comprises the *départements* of Eure and Seine-Maritime; its capital is Rouen. Ports include Dieppe and Fécamp. The area has many beech forests.

Havana capital and port of Cuba, on the northwest coast of the island; population (1990) 2,096,100. Products include cigars and tobacco, sugar, coffee, and fruit. The palace of the Spanish governors and the stronghold of La Fuerza (1583) survive.
history founded on the south coast as ***San Cristobál de la Habana*** by Spanish explorer Diego Velásquez 1515, it was moved to its present site on a natural harbour 1519. It became the capital of Cuba in the late 16th century. Taken by Anglo-American forces 1762, it was returned to Spain 1763 until independence 1898. The blowing up of the US battleship *Maine* in the harbour that year began the ◊Spanish-American War.

Havel Václav 1936– . Czech dramatist and politician, president of Czechoslovakia 1989–92 and of the Czech Republic from 1993. His plays include *The Garden Party* 1963 and *Largo Desolato* 1985, about a dissident intellectual. Havel became widely known as a human-rights activist. He was imprisoned 1979–83 and again 1989 for support of Charter 77, a human-rights manifesto. As president of Czechoslovakia he sought to preserve a united republic, but resigned in recognition of the breakup of the federation 1992. In 1993 he became president of the newly independent Czech Republic.

Havering outer London borough of NE Greater London. It includes the districts of Hornchurch and Romford
features 15th-century Church House, Romford; St Andrew's church, the only church in England to have a bull's head and horns instead of a cross at the east end; site of a small medieval palace, known as The Bower, at Havering atte Bower; this was the official residence of queens of England until 1620, after which time it fell into decay and was sold during the Commonwealth; the present Bower House was built 1729; some of the grounds of the medieval palace survive as Havering Country Park
population (1991) 229,500.

Hawaii Pacific state of the USA; nicknamed Aloha State
area 16,800 sq km/6,485 sq mi
capital Honolulu on Oahu
towns and cities Hilo
physical Hawaii consists of a chain of some 20 volcanic islands, of which the chief are:

(1) ***Hawaii***, noted for Mauna Kea (4,201 m/13,788 ft), the world's highest island mountain; Mauna Loa (4,170 m/13,686 ft), the world's largest active volcanic crater; and Kilauea, the world's most active volcano;

(2) ***Maui***, the second largest of the islands;

(3) ***Oahu***, the third largest, with Waikiki beach and the Pearl Harbor naval base;

(4) ***Kauai***; and (5) ***Molokai***, site of a historic leper colony

features (1) Hawaii (or Big Island), with Hawaii Volcanoes national park, including Mauna Kea (with telescopes that make Hawaii a world centre for astronomy); Kau Desert; the Waipio Valley with waterfalls; Honokaa (where the first macadamia trees were planted 1881); Puukohola national historic site (temples built 1791); Hulihea Palace (the king's summer residence, 1880s); (2) Maui, with Haleakala national park; the Alexander and Baldwin Sugar Museum; Wailuku historical district; Lahaina (with a banyan tree planted 1873); (3) Oahu, the most populated of the islands, and the most popular with tourists, including Honolulu, with Waikiki beach, the Mission House Museum (home of the first US missionaries, dating from the 1820s), Kawaiahao Church (1842), Iolani Palace (1882, the only royal palace in the USA), Aliiolani Hale (the old judiciary building), Honolulu Hale (1929, the City Hall), the Honolulu Academy of Arts, and Pearl Harbor naval base, including the USS *Arizona* Pearl Harbor Memorial; (4) Kauai, a former plantation town, with Waimea Canyon (1,097 m/3,600 ft deep, 3.2 km/2 mi wide, and 16 km/10 mi long), and Waioli Mission (founded 1837 at Hanalei); (5) Molokai, a leper colony until 1888, with the Meyer Sugar Mill (1878), and the Kalaupapa national historic park. Surfing originated in ancient Hawaii.
industries sugar, coffee, pineapples, flowers, women's clothing; tourism is the chief source of income
population (1991) 1,135,000 (34% European, 25% Japanese, 14% Filipino, 12% Hawaiian, 6% Chinese)
language English
religion Christianity; Buddhist minority
history a Polynesian kingdom from the 6th century, the islands were united as one kingdom in the late 18th century. Because of US, British, and French rivalry over the islands, Kamehameha III placed Hawaii under US protection 1851. Under the Reciprocity Treaty imposed 1887, in exchange for duty-free sugar transport, Pearl Harbor was ceded to the USA, who established a naval base there. Republican forces overthrew the monarchy 1893 (for which the USA officially apologized 1993), and the republican government agreed to annexation by the USA 1898. It became a US territory 1900, and the 50th state of the Union 1959. Japan's air attack on Pearl Harbor 7 Dec 1941 crippled the US Pacific fleet and

Hawaii

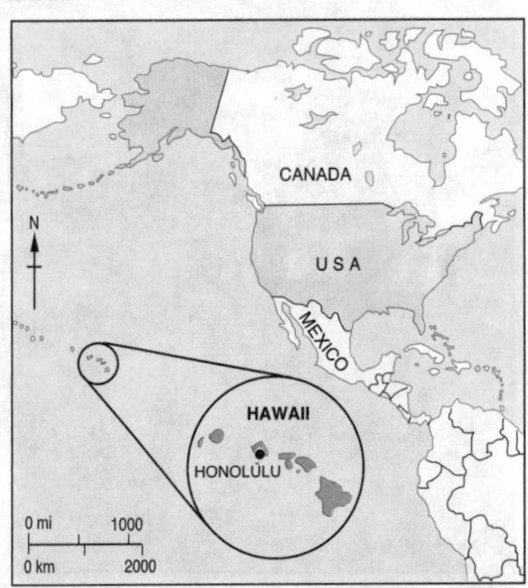

An event has happened, upon which it is difficult to speak, and impossible to be silent.

Edmund Burke, on the impeachment of WARREN HASTINGS 1789

Everywhere in Havana there hangs the perfume of cigar smoke. Cuba is lucky in this, her characteristic smell, it is agreeable and sophisticated.

On HAVANA
Dane Chandos *Isles to Windward*

❛What other dungeon is so dark as one's own heart! What jailer so inexorable as one's self!❜

Nathaniel Hawthorne
The House of the Seven Gables

turned the territory into an armed camp, under martial law, for the remainder of the war.

Capt James Cook, who called Hawaii the Sandwich Islands, was the first known European visitor 1778. By 1842, the indigenous population had fallen by 90% since Cook's arrival. This was mainly because of the introduction of new diseases, to which the population had no natural immunity, in particular smallpox, measles, tuberculosis, leprosy, and syphilis. Another factor, especially in the earlier part of the 19th century, was the exodus of young men who enlisted as sailors on foreign ships. ▷ *See feature on pp. 806–807.*

hawfinch European finch *Coccothraustes coccothraustes*, family Fringillidae, order Passeriformes, about 18 cm/7 in long. It feeds on berries and seeds, and can crack cherry stones with its large and powerful bill. The male has brown plumage, a black throat, black wing quills, a white wing bar, white tip of the tail, and the neck is crossed at the back by a broad band of ash colour.

The nest is built of twigs and mosses in lichen-covered trees, 2–10 m/6.5–33 ft above ground. Its food consists of the fruit of the pine, hornbeam, plum, cherry, hawthorn, laurel, and holly. It is abundant in southern Europe and is distributed in the temperate parts of Asia.

hawk person who believes in the use of military action rather than mediation as a means of solving a political dispute. The term first entered the political language of the USA during the 1960s, when it was applied metaphorically to those advocating continuation and escalation of the Vietnam War. Those with moderate, or even pacifist, views were known as ◊doves.

hawk any of a group of small to medium-sized birds of prey of the family Accipitridae, other than eagles, kites, ospreys, and vultures. The name is used especially to describe the genera *Accipiter* and *Buteo*. Hawks have short, rounded wings compared with falcons, and keen eyesight; the sparrow hawk and goshawk are examples.

❛I'm a Christian socialist who happens to be an atheist.❜

Bill Hayden
Age

Hawke Bob (Robert James Lee) 1929– . Australian Labor politician, prime minister 1983–91, on the right wing of the party. He was president of the Australian Council of Trade Unions 1970–80. He announced his retirement from politics 1992.

Hawking Stephen (William) 1942– . English physicist whose work in general ◊relativity – particularly gravitational field theory – led to a search for a quantum theory of gravity to explain ◊black holes and the ◊Big Bang, singularities that classical relativity theory does not adequately explain. His book *A Brief History of Time* 1988 gives a popular account of cosmology and became an international bestseller.

Hawking's objective of producing an overall synthesis of quantum mechanics and relativity theory began around the time of the publication in 1973 of his seminal book *The Large Scale Structure of Space–Time*, written with G F R Ellis. His most remarkable result, published in 1974, was that black holes could in fact emit particles in the form of thermal radiation – the so-called Hawking radiation.

Hawking English physicist Stephen Hawking, photographed in 1982. He developed motor neurone disease, a rare form of degenerative paralysis, while still a college student, and uses a wheelchair and communication equipment. *Corbis*

Hawkins Coleman (Randolph) 1904–1969. US virtuoso tenor saxophonist. He was, until 1934, a soloist in the swing band led by Fletcher Henderson (1898–1952), and was an influential figure in bringing the jazz saxophone to prominence as a solo instrument.

Hawks Howard (Winchester) 1896–1977. US director, screenwriter, and producer. He made a wide range of classic films in virtually every American genre. Swift-moving and immensely accomplished, his films include the gangster movie *Scarface* 1932, the screwball comedy *Bringing Up Baby* 1938, the ◊*film noir The Big Sleep* 1946, and the musical comedy *Gentlemen Prefer Blondes* 1953.

Hawksmoor Nicholas 1661–1736. English architect. He was assistant to Christopher ◊Wren in designing various London churches and St Paul's Cathedral and joint architect with John ◊Vanbrugh of Castle Howard and Blenheim Palace. His genius is displayed in a quirky and uncompromising style incorporating elements from both Gothic and Classical sources.

Haworth (Walter) Norman 1883–1950. English organic chemist who was the first to synthesize a vitamin (ascorbic acid, vitamin C) 1933, for which he shared a Nobel prize 1937. He made significant advances in determining the structures of many carbohydrates, particularly sugars.

Haworth Parsonage home of the English novelists Charlotte, Emily, and Anne ◊Brontë. Their father, Patrick Brontë, was vicar of Haworth, a hillside village on the edge of the Yorkshire moors, from 1820 until his death 1861. *Wuthering Heights*, *Jane Eyre*, and *Agnes Grey* were written here 1847. The house was given to the Brontë Society 1928 and is now a Brontë museum. Haworth is now part of the town of ◊Keighley.

hawthorn shrub or tree of the genus *Crataegus* of the rose family Rosaceae. Species are most abundant in E North America, but there are also many in Eurasia. All have alternate, toothed leaves and bear clusters of showy white, pink, or red flowers. Small applelike fruits can be red, orange, blue, or black. Hawthorns are popular as ornamentals.

Hawthorne Nathaniel 1804–1864. US writer. He was the author of American literature's first great classic novel, *The Scarlet Letter* 1850. Set in 17th-century Puritan Boston, it tells the powerful allegorical story of a 'fallen woman' and her daughter who are judged guilty according to men's, not nature's laws. He wrote three other novels, including *The House of the Seven Gables* 1851, and many short stories, a form he was instrumental in developing, including *Tanglewood Tales* 1853, classic Greek legends retold for children.

hay preserved grass used for winter livestock feed. The grass is cut and allowed to dry in the field before being removed for storage in a barn.

The optimum period for cutting is when the grass has just come into flower and contains most feed value. During the natural drying process, the moisture content is reduced from 70–80% down to a safe level of 20%. In normal weather conditions, this takes from two to five days, during which time the hay is turned by machine to ensure even drying.

Hayden Bill (William George) 1933– . Australian Labor politician. He was leader of the Australian Labor Party and of the opposition 1977–83, minister of foreign affairs 1983, and governor general 1989–96.

Haydn (Franz) Joseph 1732–1809. Austrian composer. He was a major exponent of the classical sonata form in his numerous chamber and orchestral works (he wrote more than 100 symphonies). He also composed choral music, including the oratorios *The Creation* 1798 and *The Seasons* 1801. He was the first great master of the string quartet, and was a teacher of Mozart and Beethoven.

Haydn, born in Lower Austria, was *kapellmeister* 1761–90 to Prince Esterházy. His work also includes operas, church music, and songs, and the 'Emperor's Hymn', adopted as the Austrian, and later the German, national anthem.

Hayek Friedrich August von 1899–1992. Austrian economist who taught at the London School of Economics 1931–50. His *The Road to Serfdom* 1944 was a critical study of socialist trends in

Haydn The Austrian composer Franz Joseph Haydn in an engraving of c. 1792 by Luigi Schiavotti. One of the great composers who defined the universal style of Viennese Classical music, Haydn spent most of his creative life, however, in isolation at the estate of the Esterházy family in Hungary. *Image Select (UK) Ltd*

Britain. He won the 1974 Nobel Prize for Economics with Gunnar Myrdal.

Hayes Rutherford (Birchard) 1822–1893. 19th president of the USA 1877–81, a Republican. Born in Ohio, he was a major general on the Union side in the Civil War. During his presidency federal troops were withdrawn from the Southern states (after the ◊Reconstruction) and the Civil Service reformed.

hay fever allergic reaction to pollen, causing sneezing, with inflammation of the nasal membranes and conjunctiva of the eyes. Symptoms are due to the release of ◊histamine. Treatment is by antihistamine drugs.

Scientists prefer to call it ***seasonal rhinitis*** since it is not caused only by grass pollen but by that of flowers and trees as well; some people also react to airborne spores and moulds which are prevalent in autumn.

Hay-on-Wye (Welsh ***Y Gelli***) town in Powys, Wales, on the south bank of the river Wye, known as the 'town of books' because of the huge secondhand bookshop started there 1961 by Richard Booth; it was followed by others.

Hays Office film regulation body in the USA 1922–45. Officially known as the Motion Picture Producers and Distributors of America, it was created by the major film companies to improve the industry's image and provide internal regulation, including a strict moral code.

The office was headed by Will H Hays (1879–1954). A Production Code, listing all the subjects forbidden to films, was begun 1930 and lasted until 1966, when it was replaced by a ratings system.

Hayworth Rita. Stage name of Margarita Carmen Cansino 1918–1987. US dancer and film actress. She gave vivacious performances in 1940s musicals and played erotic roles in *Gilda* 1946 and *Affair in Trinidad* 1952. She was known as Hollywood's 'goddess' during the height of her career. She was married to Orson Welles 1943–48 and appeared in his film *The Lady from Shanghai* 1948. She gave assured performances in *Pal Joey* 1957 and *Separate Tables* 1958.

hazardous waste waste substance, usually generated by industry, which represents a hazard to the environment or to people living or working nearby. Examples include radioactive wastes, acidic resins, arsenic residues, residual hardening salts, lead from car exhausts, mercury, nonferrous sludges, organic solvents, asbestos, chlorinated solvents, and pesticides. The cumulative effects of toxic waste can take some time to become apparent (anything from a few hours to many years), and pose a serious threat to the ecological stability of the planet; its economic disposal or recycling is the subject of research. ▷ *See feature on pp. 858–859.*

Hayworth With her flame-red hair which became her trademark, US actress Rita Hayworth brought to her varied roles an erotic and alluring screen image. Frequently associated with tempestuous *femme fatale* roles, she was also the dancing star of 1940s musicals. She was seen to best advantage in the title role of the film *Gilda* 1946.

hazel shrub or tree of the genus *Corylus*, family Corylaceae, including the European common hazel or cob *C. avellana*, of which the filbert is the cultivated variety. North American species include the American hazel *C. americana*.

Hazlitt William 1778–1830. English essayist and critic. His work is characterized by invective, scathing irony, an intuitive critical sense, and a gift for epigram. His essays include 'Characters of Shakespeare's Plays' 1817, 'Lectures on the English Poets' 1818–19, 'English Comic Writers' 1819, and 'Dramatic Literature of the Age of Elizabeth' 1820.

Other works are *Table Talk* 1821–22; *The Spirit of the Age* 1825, literary studies in which he argues that the personality of the writer is germane to a criticism of what they write; and *Liber Amoris* 1823, in which he revealed aspects of his love life.

H-bomb abbreviation for ◊***hydrogen bomb***.

Headingley Leeds sports centre, home of the Yorkshire County Cricket Club and Leeds Rugby League Club. The two venues are separated by a large stand.

The cricket ground has been a centre for test matches since 1899 and the crowd of 158,000 for the five-day England–Australia test match 1948 is an English record. Britain's first official test match against New Zealand was at Headingley 1908. The rugby ground is one of the best in the country. It was the first club to install undersoil heating.

Healey Denis Winston, Baron Healey 1917– . British Labour politician. While minister of defence 1964–70 he was in charge of the reduction of British forces east of Suez. He was chancellor of the Exchequer 1974–79. In 1976 he contested the party leadership, losing to James Callaghan, and again in 1980, losing to Michael Foot, to whom he was deputy leader 1980–83. In 1987 he resigned from the shadow cabinet.

Health Education Authority (HEA) UK authority established 1987 to provide information and advice about health directly to the public; promote the development of health education in England and AIDS health education in the UK; and support and advise government departments, health authorities, local authorities, voluntary organizations, and other bodies or individuals concerned with health education. The HEA is also responsible for carrying out national campaigns and promoting research.

From 1 April 1996, the HEA was funded on a contract basis, seeking contracts from the Department of Health and other organizations to deliver health promotion programmes and projects for the supply of health promotion material, research, and expertise.

health, world the health of people worldwide is monitored by the ◊World Health Organization (WHO). Outside the industrialized world in particular, poverty and degraded environmental conditions mean that easily preventable diseases are widespread: WHO estimated 1990 that 1 billion people, or 20% of the world's population, were diseased, in poor health, or malnourished. In North Africa and the Middle East, 25% of the population were ill.
vaccine-preventable diseases Every year, 46 million infants are not fully immunized; 2.8 million children die and 3 million are disabled due to vaccine-preventable diseases (polio, tetanus, diphtheria, whooping cough, tuberculosis, and measles).
diarrhoea Every year, there are 750 million cases in children, causing 4 million deaths. Oral rehydration therapy can correct dehydration and prevent 65% of deaths due to diarrhoeal disease. The basis of therapy is prepackaged sugar and salt. Treatment to cure the disease costs less than 20 cents, but fewer than one-third of children are treated in this way.
tuberculosis 1.6 billion people carry the bacteria, and there are 3 million deaths every year. Some 95% of all patients could be cured within six months using a specific antibiotic therapy which costs less than $30 per person.
prevention and cure Increasing health spending in industrialized countries by only $2 per head would enable immunization of all children to be performed, polio to be eradicated, and drugs provided to cure all cases of diarrhoeal disease, acute respiratory infection, tuberculosis, malaria, schistosomiasis, and most sexually transmitted diseases.

Heaney Seamus (Justin) 1939– . Irish poet and critic. He has written powerful verse about the political situation in Northern Ireland and reflections on Ireland's cultural heritage. Collections include *Death of a Naturalist* 1966, *Field Work* 1979, *The Haw Lantern* 1987, and *New and Selected Poems 1966–1987* 1990. He was professor of poetry at Oxford 1989–94. Nobel Prize for Literature 1995.

Heard Island and McDonald Islands group of islands forming an Australian external territory in the S Indian Ocean, about 4,000 km/2,500 mi SW of Fremantle; area 410 sq km/158 sq mi. They were discovered 1833, annexed by Britain 1910, and transferred to Australia 1947. They are unpopulated. ***Heard Island***, 42 km/26 mi by 19 km/12 mi, is glacier-covered, although the volcanic mountain Big Ben (2,742 m/9,000 ft) is still active. A weather station was built 1947. ***Shag Island*** is 8 km/5 mi to the N and the craggy McDonalds are 42 km/26 mi to the W.

hearing aid any device to improve the hearing of partially deaf people. Hearing aids usually consist of a battery-powered transistorized microphone/amplifier unit and earpiece. Some miniaturized aids are compact enough to fit in the ear or be concealed in the frame of eyeglasses.

Hearns Thomas 1958– . US boxer who in 1988 became the first man to win world titles at five different weight classes in five separate fights.

hearsay evidence evidence given by a witness based on information passed to that person by others rather than evidence experienced at first hand by the witness. It is usually not admissible as evidence in criminal proceedings.

Hearst William Randolph 1863–1951. US newspaper publisher, celebrated for his introduction of banner headlines, lavish illustration, and the sensationalist approach known as 'yellow journalism'. A campaigner in numerous controversies, and a strong isolationist, he was said to be the model for Citizen Kane in the 1941 film of that name by Orson Welles.

heart muscular organ that rhythmically contracts to force blood around the body of an animal with a circulatory system. Annelid worms and some other invertebrates have simple hearts consisting of thickened sections of main blood vessels that pulse regularly. An earthworm has ten such hearts. Vertebrates have one heart. A fish heart has two chambers – the thin-walled atrium (once called the auricle) that expands to receive blood, and the thick-walled ventricle that pumps it out. Amphibians and most reptiles have two atria and one ventricle; birds and mammals have two atria and two ventricles. The beating of the heart is controlled by the autonomic nervous system and an internal control centre or pacemaker, the sinoatrial node.
the cardiac cycle The cardiac cycle is the sequence of events during one complete cycle of a heart beat. This consists of the simultaneous contraction of the two atria, a short pause, then the simultaneous contraction of the two ventricles, followed by a longer pause while the entire heart relaxes. The contraction phase is called 'systole' and the relaxation phase which follows is called 'diastole'. The whole cycle is repeated 70–80 times a minute under resting conditions.

heart attack or ***myocardial infarction*** sudden onset of gripping central chest pain, often accompanied by sweating and vomiting, caused by death of a portion of the heart muscle following obstruction of a coronary artery by thrombosis (formation of a blood clot). Half of all heart attacks result in death within the first two hours, but in the remainder survival has improved following the widespread use of thrombolytic (clot-buster) drugs.

The love of liberty is the love of others; the love of power is the love of ourselves.

WILLIAM HAZLITT 'The Times Newspaper', *Political Essays*

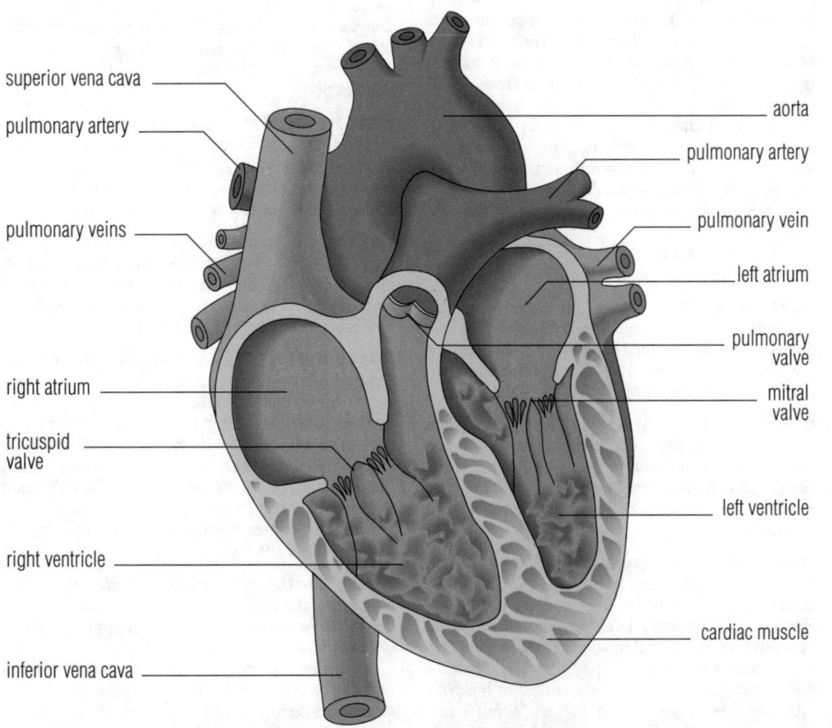

heart The structure of the human heart. During an average lifetime, the human heart beats more than 2,000 million times and pumps 500 million l/110 million gal of blood. The average pulse rate is 70–72 beats per minute at rest for adult males, and 78–82 beats per minute for adult females.

After a heart attack, most people remain in hospital for seven to ten days, and may make a gradual return to normal activity over the following months.

heartbeat the regular contraction and relaxation of the heart, and the accompanying sounds. As blood passes through the heart a double beat is heard. The first is produced by the sudden closure of the valves between the atria and the ventricles. The second, slightly delayed sound, is caused by the closure of the valves found at the entrance to the major arteries leaving the heart. Diseased valves may make unusual sounds, known as heart murmurs.

heartburn burning sensation behind the breastbone (sternum). It results from irritation of the lower oesophagus (gullet) by excessively acid stomach contents, as sometimes happens during pregnancy and in cases of duodenal ulcer or obesity. It is often due to a weak valve at the entrance to the stomach that allows its contents to well up into the oesophagus.

heart disease disorder affecting the heart; for example, ◊ischaemic heart disease, in which the blood supply through the coronary arteries is reduced by ◊atherosclerosis; ◊valvular heart disease, in which a heart valve is damaged; and cardiomyophathy, where the heart muscle itself is diseased.

heart–lung machine apparatus used during heart surgery to take over the functions of the heart and the lungs temporarily. It has a pump to circulate the blood around the body and is able to add oxygen to the blood and remove carbon dioxide from it. A heart–lung machine was first used for open-heart surgery in the USA 1953.

heat form of energy possessed by a substance by virtue of the vibrating movement (kinetic energy) of its molecules or atoms. Heat energy is transferred by conduction, convection, and radiation. It always flows from a region of higher ◊temperature (heat intensity) to one of lower temperature. Its effect on a substance may be simply to raise its temperature, or to cause it to expand, melt (if a solid), vaporize (if a liquid), or increase its pressure (if a confined gas).
measurement Quantities of heat are usually measured in units of energy, such as joules (J) or calories (cal). The ***specific heat*** of a substance is the ratio of the quantity of heat required to raise the temperature of a given mass of the substance through a given range of temperature to the heat required to raise the temperature of an equal mass of water through the same range. It is measured by a ◊calorimeter.
conduction, convection, and radiation Conduction is the passing of heat along a medium to neighbouring parts with no visible motion accompanying the transfer of heat – for example, when the whole length of a metal rod is heated when one end is held in a fire. Convection is the transmission of heat through a fluid (liquid or gas) in currents – for example, when the air in a room is warmed by a fire or radiator. Radiation is heat transfer by infrared rays. It can pass through a vacuum, travels at the same speed as light, can be reflected and refracted, and does not affect the medium through which it passes. For example, heat reaches the Earth from the Sun by radiation.

For the transformation of heat, see ◊thermodynamics.

heat capacity in physics, the quantity of heat required to raise the temperature of an object by one degree. The ***specific heat capacity*** of a substance is the heat capacity per unit of mass, measured in joules per kilogram per kelvin (J kg^{-1} K^{-1}).

heath in botany, any woody, mostly evergreen shrub of the family Ericaceae, native to Europe, Africa, and North America. Many heaths have bell-shaped pendant flowers. In the Old World the genera *Erica* and *Calluna* are the most common heaths, and include ◊heather.

'It is the unpleasant and unacceptable face of capitalism.'
EDWARD HEATH
On the Lonrho scandal *Hansard* 15 May 1973

Heath Edward (Richard George) 1916– . British Conservative politician, party leader 1965–75. As prime minister 1970–74 he took the UK into the European Community but was brought down by economic and industrial relations crises at home. He was replaced as party leader by Margaret Thatcher 1975, and became increasingly critical of her policies and her opposition to the UK's full participation in the EC. During John Major's administration, he continued his attacks on 'Eurosceptics' within the party.

In 1990 he undertook a mission to Iraq in an attempt to secure the release of British hostages. He returned 1993 to negotiate the release of three Britons held prisoner by Iraq.

heather low-growing evergreen shrub of the heath family, common on sandy or acid soil. The common heather *Calluna vulgaris* is a carpet-forming shrub, growing up to 60 cm/24 in high and bearing pale pink-purple flowers. It is found over much of Europe and has been introduced to North America.

Heathrow major international airport to the W of London in the Greater London borough of Hounslow, approximately 24 km/14 mi from the city centre. Opened 1946, it is one of the world's busiest airports, with four terminals. It was linked with the London underground system 1977. It was the target of three mortar attacks by the Irish Republican Army (IRA) March 1994, all of which failed to detonate.

heat of reaction alternative term for ◊energy of reaction.

heat pump machine, run by electricity or another power source, that cools the interior of a building by removing heat from interior air and pumping it out or, conversely, heats the inside by extracting energy from the atmosphere or from a hot-water source and pumping it in.

heat shield any heat-protecting coating or system, especially the coating (for example, tiles) used in spacecraft to protect the astronauts and equipment inside from the heat of re-entry when returning to Earth. Air friction can generate temperatures of up to 1,500°C/2,700°F on re-entry into the atmosphere.

heat storage any means of storing heat for release later. It is usually achieved by using materials that undergo phase changes, for example, Glauber's salt and sodium pyrophosphate, which melts at 70°C/158°F. The latter is used to store off-peak heat in the home: the salt is liquefied by cheap heat during the night and then freezes to give off heat during the day.

Other developments include the use of plastic crystals, which change their structure rather than melting when they are heated. They could be incorporated in curtains or clothing.

heatstroke or ***sunstroke*** rise in body temperature caused by excessive exposure to heat. Mild heatstroke is experienced as feverish lassitude, sometimes with simple fainting; recovery is prompt following rest and replenishment of salt lost in sweat. Severe heatstroke causes collapse akin to that seen in acute ◊shock, and is potentially lethal without prompt treatment, including cooling the body carefully and giving fluids to relieve dehydration.

heat treatment in industry, the subjection of metals and alloys to controlled heating and cooling after fabrication to relieve internal stresses and improve their physical properties. Methods include ◊annealing, ◊quenching, and ◊tempering.

heaven in Christianity and some other religions, the abode of God and the destination of the virtuous after death. In Islam, heaven is seen as a paradise of material delights, though such delights are generally accepted as being allegorical.

heavy metal in music, a style of rock characterized by histrionic guitar solos and a macho swagger. Heavy metal developed out of the hard rock of the late 1960s and early 1970s, was performed by such groups as Led Zeppelin and Deep Purple, and enjoyed a resurgence in the late 1980s. Bands include Van Halen (formed 1974), Def Leppard (formed 1977), and Guns n' Roses (formed 1987).

The term comes from *The Naked Lunch* by US author William Burroughs.

heavy water or ***deuterium oxide*** D_2O water containing the isotope deuterium instead of hydrogen (relative molecular mass 20 as opposed to 18 for ordinary water).

Its chemical properties are identical with those of ordinary water, but its physical properties differ slightly. It occurs in ordinary water in the ratio of about one part by mass of deuterium to 5,000 parts by mass of hydrogen, and can be concentrated by electrolysis, the ordinary water being more readily decomposed by this means than the heavy water. It has been used in the nuclear industry because it can slow down fast neutrons, thereby controlling the chain reaction.

Hebe in Greek mythology, the goddess of youth, daughter of Zeus and Hera.

Hebei or ***Hopei*** or ***Hupei*** province of N China
area 202,700 sq km/78,242 sq mi
capital Shijiazhuang
features includes special municipalities of Beijing and Tianjin
industries cereals, textiles, iron, steel
population (1990) 60,280,000.

Hebrew member of the Semitic people who lived in Palestine at the time of the Old Testament and who traced their ancestry to ◊Abraham of Ur, a city of Sumer.

Hebrew Bible the sacred writings of Judaism (some dating from as early as 1200 BC), called by Christians the ◊Old Testament. It includes the Torah (the first five books, ascribed to Moses), historical and prophetic books, and psalms, originally written in Hebrew and later translated into Greek (◊Septuagint) and other languages.

Hebrew language member of the ◊Afro-Asiatic language family spoken in SW Asia by the ancient Hebrews, sustained for many centuries in the ◊Diaspora as the liturgical language of Judaism, and revived by the late-19th-century Haskalah intellectual movement, which spread modern European culture among Jews. The language developed in the 20th century as Israeli Hebrew, the national language of the state of Israel. It is the original language of the Old Testament of the Bible.

Such English words as *cherub*, *chutzpah*, *Jehovah/Yahweh*, *kosher*, *rabbi*, *sabbath*, *seraph*, and *shibboleth* are borrowings from Hebrew. The Hebrew alphabet (called the *aleph-beth*) is written from right to left.

Hebrides group of more than 500 islands (fewer than 100 inhabited) off W Scotland; total area 2,900 sq km/1,120 sq mi. The Hebrides were settled by Scandinavians during the 6th to 9th centuries and passed under Norwegian rule from about 890 to 1266.

The ***Inner Hebrides*** include ◊Skye, ◊Mull, ◊Jura, ◊Islay, ◊Iona, ◊Rum, Raasay, Coll, Tiree, Colonsay, Muck, and uninhabited Staffa.

The ***Outer Hebrides*** form the islands area of the ◊Western Isles administrative area, separated from the Inner Hebrides by the Little Minch. They include ◊Lewis with Harris, North Uist, South Uist, ◊Barra, and St Kilda.

Hebron (Arabic ***El Khalil***) town on the West Bank of the Jordan, occupied by Israel in 1967, and due to be returned to Palestinian control as part of the Israeli–Palestinian peace process in 1996; population (1996) 120,500. It was in a front-line position in the confrontation between Israelis and Arabs in the ◊Intifada; in 1994 39 Palestinians were killed while at prayer at the Hebron mosque by an Israeli settler. In 1995 Israel and the PLO agreed that Israeli troops would hand over Hebron to Palestinian authority the following year, while retaining an Israeli military presence to protect the Jewish residents of the town.

The mosque of Hebron is the traditional site of the tombs of Abraham, Isaac, and Jacob.

Hecate in Greek mythology, a goddess of the underworld and magic, sometimes identified with ◊Artemis and the Moon.

Hecht Ben 1893–1964. US dramatist, screenwriter and film director. He was formerly a journalist. His play *The Front Page* 1928 was adapted several times for the cinema by other writers. His own screenplays included *Twentieth Century* 1934, *Gunga Din* and *Wuthering Heights* both 1939, *Spellbound* 1945, and *Actors and Sin* 1952. His directorial credits include *Crime without Passion* 1934. His autobiography, *Child of the Century*, was published 1954.

hectare metric unit of area equal to 100 ares or 10,000 square metres (2.47 acres), symbol ha. Trafalgar Square, London's only metric square, was laid out as one hectare.

Hector in Greek mythology, a Trojan prince, son of King Priam and husband of Andromache, who, in the siege of ◊Troy, was the foremost warrior on the Trojan side until he was killed by ◊Achilles.

hedge or ***hedgerow*** row of closely planted shrubs or low trees, generally acting as a land division and windbreak. Hedges also serve as a source of food and as a refuge for wildlife, and provide a ◊habitat not unlike the understorey of a natural forest.
decline Between 1945 and 1990, nearly 25% of Britain's hedgerows were destroyed. In 1996, the government estimated that more than 10,000 mi/16,000 km of hedgerows were disappearing each year because of neglect and grubbing out. A further threat is posed by spray drift of pesticides.
rescue plans In all, more than 600 plant species, 1,500 insects, 65 birds, and 20 mammals have been found to use Britain's 280,000 miles of hedgerows. Among this diverse flora and fauna are 13 species which are either in very rapid decline or endangered globally. Ancient and species-rich hedgerows were among the 14 key wildlife habitats found in Britain on which the government and leading wildlife charities had agreed rescue plans, as a follow-up to the 1992 Rio Earth Summit.

hedgehog nocturnal, insectivorous mammal of the genus *Erinaceus*, order Insectivora, family Erinaceidae, native to Europe, Asia, and Africa. The body, including the tail, is 30 cm/1 ft long. It is greyish brown in colour, has a piglike snout, and is covered with sharp spines. When alarmed it can roll itself into a ball. Hedgehogs feed on insects, slugs, mice, frogs, young birds, and carrion which they hunt by scent and sound. The young are born in the late spring or early summer, and are blind, helpless, and covered with soft spines. After about a month of feeding on their mother's milk, she teaches them to find their own food. In the autumn, hedgehogs usually hibernate until spring.

hedge sparrow another name for ◊***dunnock***, a small European bird.

hedonism ethical theory that pleasure or happiness is, or should be, the main goal in life. Hedonist sects in ancient Greece were the ◊Cyrenaics, who held that the pleasure of the moment is the only human good, and the ◊Epicureans, who advocated the pursuit of pleasure under the direction of reason. Modern hedonistic philosophies, such as those of the British philosophers Jeremy Bentham and J S Mill, regard the happiness of society, rather than that of the individual, as the aim.

Hegel Georg Wilhelm Friedrich 1770–1831. German philosopher who conceived of mind and nature as two abstractions of one indivisible whole, Spirit. His system, which is a type of ◊idealism, traces the emergence of Spirit in the logical study of concepts and the process of world history.

Hegel's works include *The Phenomenology of Spirit* 1807, *Encyclopaedia of the Philosophical Sciences* 1817, and *Philosophy of Right* 1821.

hegemony (Greek *hegemonia* 'authority') political dominance of one power over others in a group in which all are supposedly equal. The term was first used for the dominance of Athens over the other Greek city states, later applied to Prussia within Germany, and, in more recent times, to the USA and the USSR with regard to the rest of the world.

Hegira flight of the prophet Muhammad; see ◊Hijrah.

Heian in Japanese history, the period 794–1185, from the foundation of Kyoto as the new capital to the seizure of power by the Minamoto clan. The cutoff date may also be given as 1186, 1192, or 1200. The Heian period was the golden age of Japanese literature and of a highly refined culture at court; see also ◊Japanese art.

Heidegger Martin 1889–1976. German philosopher, often classed as an existentialist. He believed that Western philosophy had 'forgotten' the fundamental question of the 'meaning of Being', and his work concerns the investigation of what he thought were the different types of being appropriate to people and to things in general.

Heidelberg city on the south bank of the river Neckar, 19 km/12 mi SE of Mannheim, in Baden-Württemberg, Germany; population (1993) 139,900. Heidelberg University, the oldest in Germany, was established 1386. The city is overlooked by the ruins of its 13th–17th-century castle, 100 m/330 ft above the river.

Heidegger German philosopher Martin Heidegger. Though he insisted he was not an existentialist, Heidegger's analysis of the human predicament in terms of such categories as angst and authenticity is regarded as one of the most significant contributions to the broad stream of existentialist thought. His standing suffered both because of his connection with the Nazi Party during the 1930s, and because of the increasingly mystical and oracular tone of his later works. *Topham*

Heidelberg School group of Australian Impressionist artists (including Tom Roberts, Arthur Streeton, and Charles Conder) working near the village of Heidelberg in Melbourne in the 1880s–90s. The school had its most famous exhibition 1889, called the '9 by 5', from the size of the cigar-box lids used.

Heifetz Jascha 1901–1987. Russian-born US violinist. He was one of the great virtuosos of the 20th century. He first performed at the age of five, and before he was 17 had played in most European capitals, and in the USA, where he settled 1917. He popularized a clear, unemotional delivery suited to radio and recordings.

Heilongjiang or ***Heilungkiang*** province of NE China, in ◊Manchuria
area 463,600 sq km/178,950 sq mi
capital Harbin
features China's largest oilfield, near Anda
industries cereals, gold, coal, copper, zinc, lead, cobalt
population (1990) 34,770,000.

Heine Heinrich (Christian Johann) 1797–1856. German Romantic poet and journalist. He wrote *Reisebilder* 1826–31, blending travel writing and satire, and *Das Buch der Lieder/The Book of Songs* 1827. Disillusioned by undercurrents of anti-Semitism and antiliberal censorship, he severed his ties with Germany and from 1831 lived mainly in Paris. Franz Schubert and Robert Schumann set many of his lyrics to music.

Heinlein Robert A(nson) 1907– . US science-fiction writer. Associated with the pulp magazines of the 1940s, he wrote the militaristic novel *Starship Troopers* 1959 and the utopian cult novel *Stranger in a Strange Land* 1961. His work helped to increase the legitimacy of science fiction as a literary genre.

Heisenberg Werner (Karl) 1901–1976. German physicist who developed ◊quantum theory and formulated the ◊uncertainty principle, which concerns matter, radiation, and their reactions, and places absolute limits on the achievable accuracy of measurement. He was awarded a Nobel prize 1932 for work he carried out when only 24.

During World War II Heisenberg worked for the Nazis on nuclear fission, but his team were many months behind the Allied atom-bomb project. After the war he worked on superconductivity.

Hejaz province of Saudi Arabia, on the Red Sea. A former independent kingdom, it merged 1932 with Nejd to form ◊Saudi Arabia; population (1985 est) 3,043,200. The capital is Mecca.

Hekmatyar Gulbuddin 1949– . Afghani Islamic fundamentalist guerrilla leader, prime minister 1993–94 and 1996. Hekmatyar became a Mujaheddin guerrilla in the 1980s, leading the fundamentalist faction of the Hezb-i-Islami (Islamic Party), dedicated to the overthrow of the Soviet-backed communist regime in Kabul. Under a peace agreement with President Burhanuddin Rabbani 1993, he became prime minister, but in Jan 1994 he renewed attacks on the Rabbani administration. He was subsequently dismissed from the premiership, but again struck up an alliance with Rabbani and returned to Kabul June 1996, when he became combined prime minister, defence minister, and finance minister. However, in Sept he was driven out of Kabul (along with Rabbani) by the ◊Talibaan (fundamentalist student army) who had seized control of much of Afghanistan.

Hel or ***Hela*** in Norse mythology, the goddess of the underworld.

Helen in Greek mythology, the daughter of Zeus and Leda, and the most beautiful of women. She married ◊Menelaus, King of Sparta, but during his absence, was abducted by Paris, Prince of Troy. This precipitated the Trojan War. Afterwards she returned to Sparta with her husband.

Helena, St c. 248–c. 328. Roman empress, mother of Constantine the Great, and a convert to Christianity. According to legend, she discovered the true cross of Jesus in Jerusalem.

Helicobacter pylori spiral-shaped swimming bacterium that causes gastritis and stomach ◊ulcers when it colonizes the stomach lining. Without antibiotic treatment, infection can be permanent. *H. pylori* may also contribute towards stomach cancer.

A link was established between infection with *H. pylori* and migraine by Italian researchers in 1998. Migraine incidence was vastly reduced after the bacterium had been eradicated by antibiotics.

Helicon mountain in central Greece, on which was situated a spring and a sanctuary sacred to the ◊Muses.

helicopter powered aircraft that achieves both lift and propulsion by means of a rotary wing, or rotor, on top of the fuselage. It can take off and land vertically, move in any direction, or remain stationary in the air. It can be powered by piston or jet engine. The ◊autogiro was a precursor.

The rotor of a helicopter has two or more blades of aerofoil cross-section like an aeroplane's wings. Lift and propulsion are achieved by angling the blades as they rotate. Experiments using the concept of helicopter flight date from the early 1900s, with the first successful lift-off and short flight 1907. Ukrainian–US engineer Igor ◊Sikorsky built the first practical single-rotor craft in the USA 1939.

A single-rotor helicopter must also have a small tail rotor to counter the torque, or tendency of the body to spin in the opposite direction to the main rotor. Twin-rotor helicopters, like the Boeing Chinook, have their rotors turning in opposite directions to prevent the body from spinning. Helicopters are now widely used in passenger service, rescue missions on land and sea, police pursuits and traffic control, firefighting, and agriculture. In war they carry troops and equipment into difficult terrain, make aerial reconnaissance and attacks, and carry the wounded to aid stations. *See illustration on following page.*

Heliopolis ancient Egyptian centre (the biblical ***On***) of the worship of the sun god Ra, NE of Cairo and near the village of Matariah. Heliopolis was also the Greek name for ◊Baalbek.

Helios in Greek mythology, the sun god – thought to make his daily journey across the sky in a chariot – and father of ◊Phaethon.

heliosphere region of space through which the ◊solar wind flows outwards from the Sun. The ***heliopause*** is the boundary of this region, believed to lie about 100 astronomical units from the Sun, where the flow of the solar wind merges with the interstellar gas.

heliotrope decorative plant of the genus *Heliotropium* of the borage family Boraginaceae, with distinctive spikes of blue, lilac, or white flowers, including the Peruvian or cherry pie heliotrope *H. peruvianum*.

'What experience and history teach us, however, is this, that peoples and governments have never learned anything from history.'
GEORG HEGEL
Lectures on the Philosophy of History

'An expert is someone who knows some of the worst mistakes that can be made in his subject and how to avoid them.'
WERNER CARL HEISENBERG
The Part and the Whole

helicopter The helicopter is controlled by varying the rotor pitch (the angle of the rotor blade as it moves through the air). For backwards flight, the blades in front of the machine have greater pitch than those behind the craft. This means that the front blades produce more lift and a backwards thrust. For forwards flight, the situation is reversed. In level flight, the blades have unchanging pitch.

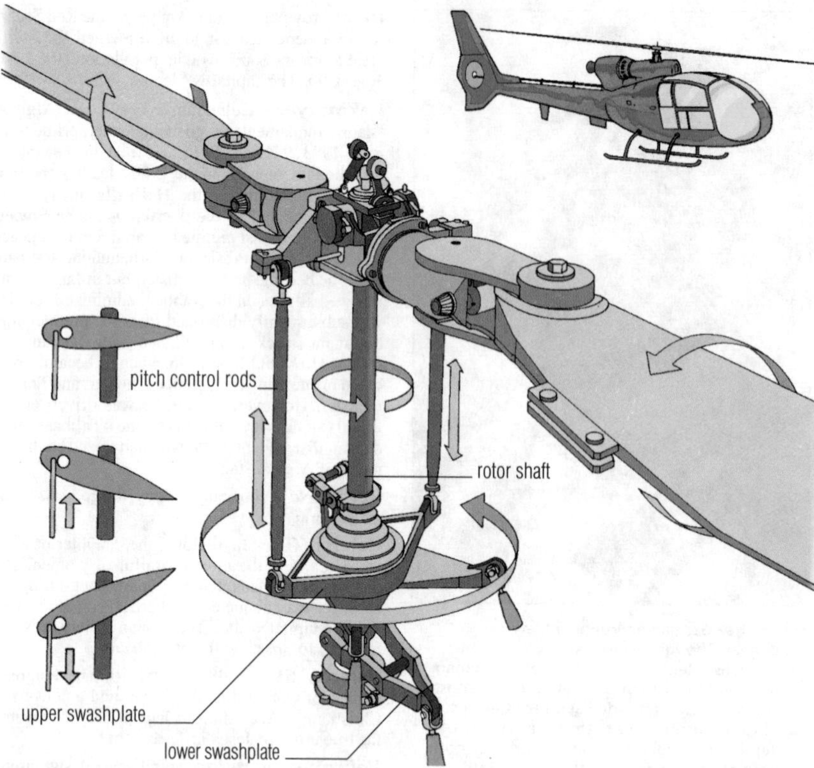

The infliction of cruelty with a good conscience is a delight to moralists. That is why they invented Hell.

On HELL
Bertrand Russell
'On the Value of Scepticism'

helium (Greek *helios* 'Sun') colourless, odourless, gaseous, nonmetallic element, symbol He, atomic number 2, relative atomic mass 4.0026. It is grouped with the ◊inert gases, is nonreactive, and forms no compounds. It is the second-most abundant element (after hydrogen) in the universe, and has the lowest boiling (−268.9°C/−452°F) and melting points (−272.2°C/−458°F) of all the elements. It is present in small quantities in the Earth's atmosphere from gases issuing from radioactive elements (from ◊alpha decay) in the Earth's crust; after hydrogen it is the second-lightest element.

Helium is a component of most stars, including the Sun, where the nuclear-fusion process converts hydrogen into helium with the production of heat and light. It is obtained by compression and fractionation of naturally occurring gases. It is used for inflating balloons and as a dilutant for oxygen in deep-sea breathing systems. Liquid helium is used extensively in low-temperature physics (cryogenics).

helix in mathematics, a three-dimensional curve resembling a spring, corkscrew, or screw thread. It is generated by a line that encircles a cylinder or cone at a constant angle.

hell in various religions, a place of posthumous punishment. In Hinduism, Buddhism, and Jainism, hell is a transitory state of the transmigrating person, but in Christianity and Islam it is eternal (◊purgatory is transitory). Judaism does not postulate such punishment.

In the Bible, the word 'hell' is used to translate Hebrew and Greek words all meaning 'the place of departed spirits, the abode of the dead' (see ◊Hades). In medieval Christian theology, hell is the place where unrepentant sinners suffer the torments of the damned, but the 20th-century tendency has been to regard hell as a state of damnation (that is, everlasting banishment from the sight of God) rather than a place.

hellebore poisonous European herbaceous plant of the genus *Helleborus* of the buttercup family Ranunculaceae. The stinking hellebore *H. foetidus* has greenish flowers early in the spring.

helleborine temperate Old World orchid of the genera *Epipactis* and *Cephalanthera*, including the marsh helleborine *E. palustris* and the hellebore orchid *E. helleborine* introduced to North America.

Cynicism is an unpleasant way of saying the truth.

LILLIAN HELLMAN
The Little Foxes

Hellene (Greek *Hellas* 'Greece') alternative name for a Greek.

Hellenic period (from *Hellas*, Greek name for Greece) classical period of ancient Greek civilization, from the first Olympic Games 776 BC until the death of Alexander the Great 323 BC.

Hellenistic period period in Greek civilization from the death of Alexander 323 BC until the accession of the Roman emperor Augustus 27 BC. Alexandria in Egypt was the centre of culture and commerce during this period, and Greek culture spread throughout the Mediterranean region and the near East.

Heller Joseph 1923– . US novelist. He drew on his experiences in the US air force in World War II to write his best-selling ◊*Catch-22* 1961, satirizing war, the conspiracy of bureaucratic control, and the absurdism of history. A film based on the book appeared 1970.

His other works include the novels *Something Happened* 1974, *Good As Gold* 1979, and *Closing Time* 1994; and the plays *We Bombed in New Haven* 1968 and *Clevinger's Trial* 1974.

Hellman Lillian Florence 1907–1984. US dramatist. Her work is concerned with contemporary political and social issues. *The Children's Hour* 1934 on accusations of lesbianism, *The Little Foxes* 1939 on industrialists, and *Toys in the Attic* 1960 are all examples of a social critique cast in the form of the 'well-made play'. In the 1950s she was summoned to appear before the House Committee on Un-American Activities.

She lived 31 years with the writer Dashiell Hammett, and in her will set up a fund to promote Marxist doctrine. Since her death there has been dispute over the accuracy of her memoirs, for example *Pentimento* 1973.

Helmand longest river in Afghanistan. Rising in the Hindu Kush, W of Kabul, it flows SW for 1,125 km/703 mi before entering the marshland surrounding Lake Saberi on the Iranian frontier.

Helmont Jean Baptiste van 1579–1644. Belgian doctor who was the first to realize that there are gases other than air, and claimed to have coined the word 'gas' (from Greek *cháos*).

Helmont identified four gases: carbon dioxide, carbon monoxide, nitrous oxide, and methane. He was the first to take the melting point of ice and the boiling point of water as standards for temperature and the first to use the term 'saturation' to signify the combination of an acid and a base. In medicine, Helmont used remedies that specifically considered the type of disease, the organ affected and the causative agent. He demonstrated acid as the digestive agent in the stomach.

Héloïse 1101–1164. Abbess of Paraclete in Champagne, France, correspondent and lover of ◊Abelard. She became deeply interested in intellectual study in her youth and was impressed by the brilliance of Abelard, her teacher, whom she secretly married.

After her affair with Abelard, and the birth of a son, Astrolabe, she became a nun 1129, and with Abelard's assistance, founded a nunnery at Paraclete. Her letters show her strong and pious character and her devotion to Abelard.

helot member of a class of serfs in ancient Messenia and Sparta who were probably the indigenous inhabitants. Their cruel treatment by the Spartans became proverbial.

Helpmann Robert Murray 1909–1986. Australian dancer, choreographer, and actor. The leading male dancer with the Sadler's Wells Ballet, London 1933–50, he partnered Margot ◊Fonteyn in the 1940s.

His forte was characterization rather than virtuosity, best displayed in his memorable role as the comic Ugly Sister in Frederick Ashton's *Cinderella*, for which he used his gift for mime and other theatrical effects. His other comic roles include Doctor Coppelius in *Coppélia* and the bridegroom in Ashton's *A Wedding Bouquet*, but he was equally at home in dramatic roles, such as the Red King in de Valois' *Checkmate*. His film appearances include *The Red Shoes* 1948, *The Tales of Hoffman* 1951, *Chitty Chitty Bang Bang* 1968, and the title role in Nureyev's *Don Quixote* 1973.

Helsinki (Swedish ***Helsingfors***) capital and port of Finland; population (1994) 516,000. Industries include shipbuilding, engineering, and textiles. The port is kept open by icebreakers in winter.

Helsinki was founded 1550 by King Gustavus Vasa of Sweden, N of its present location. After Finland was ceded to Russia 1809, Helsinki became capital of the grand duchy 1812 and remained the capital after independence 1917. The city contains the parliament house, an 18th-century cathedral, many buildings by the German-born architect Carl Ludwig Engel of the early 19th century, and many in national Romantic style from around 1900, including the railway station by Eliel Saarinen.

Helsinki Conference international meeting 1975 at which 35 countries, including the USSR and the USA, attempted to reach agreement on cooperation in security, economics, science, technology,

hell Religions vary in their conception of hell as a permanent and unalterable state or as a temporary stage in the progress of the soul. In medieval Christianity it was taken literally as a place of everlasting torment, as depicted in this German woodcut, dating from around 1400. *Corbis*

and human rights. This established the ◊Conference on Security and Cooperation in Europe.

Helvetius Claude Adrien 1715–1771. French philosopher. In *De l'Esprit* 1758 he argued, following David ◊Hume, that self-interest, however disguised, is the mainspring of all human action and that, since conceptions of good and evil vary according to period and locality, there is no absolute good or evil. He also believed that intellectual differences are only a matter of education.

hematite principal ore of iron, consisting mainly of iron(III) oxide, Fe_2O_3. It occurs as ***specular hematite*** (dark, metallic lustre), ***kidney ore*** (reddish radiating fibres terminating in smooth, rounded surfaces), and a red earthy deposit.

Hemel Hempstead town in Hertfordshire, England, designated a new town 1946; population (1991) 79,200. Industries include manufacture of paper, electrical goods, and office equipment.

Hemingway Ernest (Miller) 1899–1961. US writer. War, bullfighting, and fishing are used symbolically in his work to represent honour, dignity, and primitivism – prominent themes in his short stories and novels, which include *A Farewell to Arms* 1929, *For Whom the Bell Tolls* 1941, and *The Old Man and the Sea* 1952 (Pulitzer prize). His deceptively simple writing style attracted many imitators. Nobel Prize for Literature 1954.

He became a journalist and was wounded while serving on a volunteer ambulance crew in Italy in World War I. In 1921 he settled in Paris, where he met the writers Gertrude ◊Stein and Ezra ◊Pound. His style was influenced by Stein, who also introduced him to bullfighting, a theme in his first novel, *Fiesta (The Sun Also Rises)* 1927, and the memoir *Death in the Afternoon* 1932. *A Farewell to Arms* deals with wartime experiences on the Italian front, and *For Whom the Bell Tolls* has a Spanish Civil War setting. He served as war correspondent both in that conflict and in Europe during World War II. His last years were spent mainly in Cuba. He committed suicide.

hemlock plant *Conium maculatum* of the carrot family Umbelliferae, native to Europe, W Asia, and N Africa. Reaching up to 2 m/6 ft high, it bears umbels of small white flowers. The whole plant, especially the root and fruit, is poisonous, causing paralysis of the nervous system. The name 'hemlock' is also applied to members of the genus *Tsuga* of North American and Asiatic conifers of the pine family.

hemp annual plant *Cannabis sativa*, family Cannabaceae. Originally from Asia, it is cultivated in most temperate countries for its fibres, produced in the outer layer of the stem, and used in ropes, twines, and, occasionally, in a type of linen or lace. ◊Cannabis is obtained from certain varieties of hemp.

The name 'hemp' is extended to similar types of fibre: ***sisal hemp*** and ***henequen*** obtained from the leaves of *Agave* species native to Yucatán and cultivated in many tropical countries, and ***manila hemp*** obtained from *Musa textilis*, a plant native to the Philippines and the Maluku.

Henan or ***Honan*** province of E central China
area 167,000 sq km/64,462 sq mi
capital Zhengzhou
features river plains of the Huang He (Yellow River); ruins of Xibo, the 16th-century BC capital of the Shang dynasty, were discovered here in the 1980s
industries cereals, cotton
population (1990) 86,140,000.

henbane poisonous plant *Hyoscyamus niger* of the nightshade family Solanaceae, found on waste ground throughout most of Europe and W Asia. A branching plant, up to 80 cm/31 in high, it has hairy leaves and a nauseous smell. The yellow flowers are bell-shaped. Henbane is used in medicine as a source of hyoscyamine and scopolamine.

Hendrix Jimi (James Marshall) 1942–1970. US rock guitarist, songwriter, and singer. He was legendary for his virtuoso experimental technique and flamboyance. *Are You Experienced?* 1967 was his first album. His performance at the 1969 Woodstock festival included a memorable version of *The Star-Spangled Banner* and is recorded in the film *Woodstock* 1970. He greatly expanded the vocabulary of the electric guitar and influenced both rock and jazz musicians.

Hengist died c. 488. Legendary leader, with his brother ***Horsa***, of the Jutes, who originated in Jutland and settled in Kent about 450, the first Anglo-Saxon settlers in Britain.

Henley Royal Regatta UK ◊rowing festival on the river Thames, inaugurated 1839. It is as much a social as a sporting occasion. The principal events are the solo *Diamond Challenge Sculls* and the *Grand Challenge Cup*, the leading event for eight-oared shells. The regatta is held in July.

Henman Tim(othy) 1974– . British tennis player. In 1996 he became the first Briton for 23 years to reach the quarter-finals of the men's singles at Wimbledon. In the same year he won a silver medal in the men's doubles at the Atlanta Olympic Games. In Jan 1997 he achieved his first win on the ATP Tour and with good performances in other tournaments, including the Australian Open, he made it into the top 15 of the world rankings for the first time.

henna small shrub *Lawsonia inermis* of the loosestrife family Lythraceae, found in Iran, India, Egypt, and N Africa. The leaves and young twigs are ground to a powder, mixed to a paste with hot water, and applied to fingernails and hair, giving an orange-red hue. The colour may then be changed to black by applying a preparation of indigo.

Henna may also be used to dye both natural and synthetic textiles.

Hendrix US rock guitarist Jimi Hendrix (centre) with fellow members of The Jimi Hendrix Experience, Noel Redding (bass guitar) and Mitch Mitchell (drums). Left-handed Hendrix taught himself to play a right-handed guitar upside down, a style that became his trademark. His extravagant stage antics and showmanship were cultivated in Britain, after he was discovered and promoted by Chas Chandler, formerly of The Animals. *Corbis*

Henrietta Maria 1609–1669. Queen of England 1625–49. The daughter of Henry IV of France, she married Charles I of England 1625. By encouraging him to aid Roman Catholics and make himself an absolute ruler, she became highly unpopular and was exiled 1644–60. She returned to England at the Restoration but retired to France 1665.

henry SI unit (symbol H) of ◊inductance (the reaction of an electric current against the magnetic field that surrounds it). One henry is the inductance of a circuit that produces an opposing voltage of one volt when the current changes at one ampere per second. It is named after the US physicist Joseph Henry.

Henry (Charles Albert David), known as ***Harry*** 1984– . Prince of the UK; second child of the Prince and Princess of Wales.

Henry Joseph 1797–1878. US physicist, inventor of the electromagnetic motor 1829 and of a telegraphic apparatus. He also discovered the principle of electromagnetic induction, roughly at the same time as Michael ◊Faraday, and the phenomenon of self-induction. The unit of inductance, the ***henry***, is named after him.

Henry William 1774–1836. English chemist and physician. In 1803 he formulated ***Henry's law***, which states that when a gas is dissolved in a liquid at a given temperature, the mass that dissolves is in direct proportion to the pressure of the gas.

Henry I 1068–1135. King of England from 1100. Youngest son of William the Conqueror, he succeeded his brother William II. He won the support of the Saxons by granting them a charter and marrying a Saxon princess. An able administrator, he established a professional bureaucracy and a system of travelling judges. He was succeeded by Stephen.

Henry II 1133–1189. King of England from 1154, when he succeeded ◊Stephen. He was the son of ◊Matilda and Geoffrey of Anjou (1113–1151). He curbed the power of the barons, but his attempt to bring the church courts under control had to be abandoned after the murder of Thomas à ◊Becket. During his reign the English conquest of Ireland began. He was succeeded by his son Richard I.

He was lord of Scotland, Ireland, and Wales, and count of Anjou, Brittany, Poitou, Normandy, Maine, Gascony, and Aquitaine. He was married to Eleanor of Aquitaine.

> *'In dogs and birds he was most expert, and exceeding fond of hunting. He passed nights without sleep and was untiring in his activities.'*
>
> On **King Henry II**
> Walter Map *De Nugis Curialum* 1181–92

henbane Golden henbane *Hyoscyamus aureus*, a native of SW Asia, growing in Israel. Often evil smelling, henbanes are extremely poisonous although an alkaloid extracted from them, hyoscyamine, has important medicinal uses. *Premaphotos Wildlife*

His deeds exceeded all his speech; / He ne'er lift up his hand but conquered.

On **Henry V**
William Shakespeare
Henry VI Part I
1589–92

Henry III 1207–1272. King of England from 1216, when he succeeded John, but he did not rule until 1227. His financial commitments to the papacy and his foreign favourites led to de ◊Montfort's revolt 1264. Henry was defeated at Lewes, Sussex, and imprisoned. He was restored to the throne after the royalist victory at Evesham 1265. He was succeeded by his son Edward I.

The royal powers were exercised by a regency until 1232 and by two French nobles, Peter des Roches and Peter des Rivaux, until the barons forced their expulsion 1234, marking the start of Henry's personal rule. While he was in prison, de Montfort ruled in his name. On his release Henry was weak and senile and his eldest son, Edward, took charge of the government.

Henry IV (Bolingbroke) 1367–1413. King of England from 1399, the son of ◊John of Gaunt. In 1398 he was banished by ◊Richard II for political activity but returned 1399 to head a revolt and be accepted as king by Parliament. He was succeeded by his son Henry V.

He had difficulty in keeping the support of Parliament and the clergy, and had to deal with baronial unrest and Owen ◊Glendower's rising in Wales. In order to win support he had to conciliate the church by a law for the burning of heretics, and to make many concessions to Parliament.

Henry V 1387–1422. King of England from 1413, son of Henry IV. Invading Normandy 1415 (during the Hundred Years' War), he captured Harfleur and defeated the French at ◊Agincourt. He invaded again 1417–19, capturing Rouen. His military victory forced the French into the Treaty of Troyes 1420, which gave Henry control of the French government. He married ◊Catherine of Valois 1420 and gained recognition as heir to the French throne by his father-in-law Charles VI, but died before him. He was succeeded by his son Henry VI.

Henry VI 1421–1471. King of England from 1422, son of Henry V. He assumed royal power 1442 and sided with the party opposed to the continuation of the Hundred Years' War with France. After his marriage 1445, he was dominated by his wife, ◊Margaret of Anjou. The unpopularity of the government, especially after the loss of the English conquests in France, encouraged Richard, Duke of York, to claim the throne, and though York was killed 1460, his son Edward IV proclaimed himself king 1461 (see Wars of the ◊Roses). Henry was captured 1465, temporarily restored 1470, but again imprisoned 1471 and then murdered.

Henry VII 1457–1509. King of England from 1485, son of Edmund Tudor, Earl of Richmond (c. 1430–1456), and a descendant of ◊John of Gaunt.

He spent his early life in Brittany until 1485, when he landed in Britain to lead the rebellion against Richard III which ended with Richard's defeat and death at ◊Bosworth. By his marriage to Elizabeth of York 1486, he united the houses of York and Lancaster. Yorkist revolts continued until 1497, but Henry restored order after the Wars of the ◊Roses by the ◊Star Chamber and achieved independence from Parliament by amassing a private fortune through confiscations. He was succeeded by his son Henry VIII.

Henry VIII *King Henry VIII, an oil painting by Hans Holbein.* Henry VIII dominated the transition of England from a medieval to a Renaissance state. His patronage of the arts and his diplomatic and military adventures ended a long period of relative English insignificance in European culture and politics after the Hundred Years' War. Above all, his seizure of control of the English church brought Reformation politics and social changes to Britain. *Image Select (UK) Ltd*

Henry VIII 1491–1547. King of England from 1509, when he succeeded his father Henry VII and married Catherine of Aragon, the widow of his brother.

During the period 1513–29 Henry pursued an active foreign policy, largely under the guidance of his Lord Chancellor, Cardinal Wolsey, who shared Henry's desire to make England stronger. Wolsey was replaced by Thomas More 1529 for failing to persuade the pope to grant Henry a divorce. After 1532 Henry broke with papal authority, proclaimed himself head of the church in England, dissolved the monasteries, and divorced Catherine. His subsequent wives were Anne Boleyn, Jane Seymour, Anne of Cleves, Catherine Howard, and Catherine Parr.

He was succeeded by his son Edward VI.

Henry I c. 1008–1060. King of France from 1031. He spent much of his reign in conflict with ◊William the Conqueror, then duke of Normandy.

Henry II 1519–1559. King of France from 1547. He captured the fortresses of Metz and Verdun from the Holy Roman emperor Charles V and Calais from the English. He was killed in a tournament.

In 1526 he was sent with his brother to Spain as a hostage, being returned when there was peace 1530. He married Catherine de' Medici 1533, and from then on was dominated by her, Diane de Poitiers, and Duke Montmorency. Three of his sons, Francis II, Charles IX, and Henry III, became kings of France.

Henry III 1551–1589. King of France from 1574. He fought both the ◊Huguenots (headed by his successor, Henry of Navarre) and the Catholic League (headed by the third Duke of Guise). Guise expelled Henry from Paris 1588 but was assassinated. Henry allied with the Huguenots under Henry of Navarre to besiege the city, but was assassinated by a monk.

Henry IV 1553–1610. King of France from 1589. Son of Antoine de Bourbon and Jeanne, Queen of Navarre, he was brought up as a Protestant and from 1576 led the ◊Huguenots. On his accession he settled the religious question by adopting Catholicism while tolerating Protestantism. He restored peace and strong government to France and brought back prosperity by measures for the promotion of industry and agriculture and the improvement of communications. He was assassinated by a Catholic extremist.

Henry (I) the Fowler c. 876–936. King of Germany from 919, and duke of Saxony from 912. He secured the frontiers of Saxony, ruled in harmony with its nobles, and extended German influence over the Danes, the Hungarians, and the Slavonic tribes. He was about to claim the imperial crown when he died.

Henry (II) the Saint 973–1024. King of Germany from 1002, Holy Roman emperor from 1014, when he recognized Benedict VIII as pope. He was canonized 1146.

Henry (III) the Black 1017–1056. King of Germany from 1028, Holy Roman emperor from 1039 (crowned 1046). He raised the empire to the height of its power, and extended its authority over Poland, Bohemia, and Hungary.

Henry IV 1050–1106. Holy Roman emperor from 1056. He was involved from 1075 in a struggle with the papacy. Excommunicated twice (1076 and 1080), Henry deposed ◊Gregory VII and set up the antipope Clement III (died 1191) by whom he was crowned Holy Roman emperor 1084.

Henry V 1086–1125. Holy Roman emperor from 1106. He continued the struggle with the church until the settlement of the ◊investiture contest 1122.

Henry VI 1165–1197. Holy Roman emperor from 1190. As part of his plan for making the empire universal, he captured and imprisoned Richard I of England and compelled him to do homage.

Henry VII c. 1269–1313. Holy Roman emperor from 1308. He attempted unsuccessfully to revive the imperial supremacy in Italy.

Henry, O Pen name of William Sydney Porter 1862–1910. US short-story writer. His collections include *Cabbages and Kings* 1904 and *The Four Million* 1906. His stories are written in a colloquial style and employ skilled construction with surprise endings.

Henry the Lion 1129–1195. Duke of Bavaria 1156–80, duke of Saxony 1142–80, and duke of Lüneburg 1180–85. He was granted the Duchy of Bavaria by the Emperor Frederick Barbarossa. He founded Lübeck and Munich. In 1162 he married Matilda, daughter of Henry II of England. His refusal in 1176 to accompany Frederick Barbarossa to Italy led in 1180 to his being deprived of the duchies of Bavaria and Saxony. Henry led several military expeditions to conquer territory in the East.

Henry the Navigator 1394–1460. Portuguese prince, the fourth son of John I. He set up a school for navigators 1419 and under his patronage Portuguese sailors explored and colonized Madeira, the Cape Verde Islands, and the Azores; they sailed down the African coast almost to Sierra Leone.

Henson Jim (James Maury) 1936–1990. US puppeteer who created the television Muppet characters, including Kermit the Frog, Miss Piggy, and Fozzie Bear. The Muppets became popular on the children's educational TV series *Sesame Street*, which first appeared in 1969 and soon became regular viewing in over 80 countries. In 1976 Henson created *The Muppet Show*, which ran for five years and became one of the world's most widely seen TV programmes, reaching 235 million viewers in 100 countries. Several Muppet movies followed.

Henze Hans Werner 1926– . German composer. His immense and stylistically restless output is marked by a keen literary sensibility and seductive use of orchestral coloration, as in the opera *Elegy for Young Lovers* 1959–61 and the cantata *Being Beauteous* 1963. Among recent works are the opera *Das Verratene Meer/The Sea Betrayed* 1992.

Following the student unrest of 1968 he suddenly renounced the wealthy musical establishment in favour of a militantly socialist stance in works such as the abrasive *El Cimarrón* 1969–70 and *Voices* 1973, austere settings of 22 revolutionary texts in often magical sonorities.

heparin anticoagulant substance produced by cells of the liver, lungs, and intestines. It normally inhibits the clotting of blood by interfering with the production of thrombin, which is necessary for clot formation. Heparin obtained from animals is administered after surgery to limit the risk of ◊thrombosis, or following pulmonary ◊embolism to ensure that no further clots form, and during haemodialysis.

hepatic of or pertaining to the liver.

hepatitis any inflammatory disease of the liver, usually caused by a virus. Other causes include alcohol, drugs, gallstones, ◊lupus erythematous, and amoebic ◊dysentery. Symptoms include weakness, nausea, and jaundice.

Five different hepatitis viruses have been identified; A, B, C, D, and E. The hepatitis A virus (HAV) is the commonest cause of viral hepatitis, responsible for up to 40% of cases worldwide. It is spread by contaminated food. Hepatitis B, or serum hepatitis, is a highly contagious disease spread by blood products or in body fluids. It often culminates in liver failure, and is also associated with liver cancer, although only 5% of those infected suffer chronic liver damage. During 1995, 1.1 million people died of hepatitis B. Around 300 million people are carriers. Vaccines are available against hepatitis A and B.

Hepatitis C is mostly seen in people needing frequent transfusions. Hepatitis D, which only occurs in association with hepatitis B, is common in the Mediterranean region. Hepatitis E is endemic in India and South America.

Hepburn Audrey, (born Hepburn-Ruston) 1929–1993. British actress of Anglo-Dutch descent. She often played innocent, childlike characters. Slender and doe-eyed, she set a different style from the more ample women stars of the 1950s. After playing minor parts in British films in the early 1950s, she became a Hollywood star in *Roman Holiday* 1951, for which she won an Academy Award, and later starred in such films as *Funny Face* 1957 and *My Fair Lady* 1964.

Hepburn Katharine 1909– . US actress. She appeared in such films as *Morning Glory* 1933 (Academy Award), *Little Women* 1933, *Bringing Up Baby* 1938, *The Philadelphia Story* 1940, *The African Queen* 1951, *Pat and Mike* 1952, *Guess Who's Coming to Dinner* 1967 (Academy Award), *Lion in Winter* 1968 (Academy Award), and *On Golden Pond* 1981 (Academy Award).

Woman of the Year 1942 was her first film with her frequent partner Spencer Tracy. She also had a distinguished stage career, and made feisty self-assurance her trademark.

Hephaestus in Greek mythology, the god of fire and metalcraft (Roman Vulcan), son of Zeus and Hera, and husband of Aphrodite. He was lame.

Hepplewhite George died 1786. English furnituremaker. His name is associated with Neo-Classicism. His reputation rests upon his book of designs *The Cabinetmaker and Upholsterer's Guide*, published posthumously 1788, which contains over 300 designs, characterized by simple elegance and utility. No piece of furniture has been identified as being made by him.

heptathlon multi-event athletics discipline for women consisting of seven events over two days: 100 metres hurdles, high jump, shot put, 200 metres (day one); long jump, javelin, 800 metres (day two). Points are awarded for performances in each event in the same way as the ◊decathlon. It replaced the pentathlon (five events) in international competition 1981.

Hepworth (Jocelyn) Barbara 1903–1975. English sculptor. She developed an abstract style, characteristic works (carved in wood or stone) being slender, upright forms reminiscent of standing stones or totems; and round, hollowed forms with spaces bridged by wires or strings, as in *Pelagos* 1946 (Tate Gallery, London). Her public commissions include *Winged Figure* 1962 (John Lewis Building, London) and *Single Form* 1962–63 (United Nations, New York).

Hera in Greek mythology, the goddess of women and marriage (Roman Juno), sister and consort of Zeus, mother of Hephaestus, Hebe, and Ares.

Heracles in Greek mythology, a hero (Roman Hercules), son of Zeus and Alcmene, famed for strength. While serving Eurystheus, king of Argos, he performed 12 labours, including the cleansing of the ◊Augean stables. Driven mad by the goddess Hera, he murdered his first wife Megara and their children, and was himself poisoned by mistake by his second wife Deianira.

Heraclitus c. 544–c. 483 BC. Greek philosopher who believed that the cosmos is in a ceaseless state of flux and motion, fire being the fundamental material that accounts for all change and motion in the world. Nothing in the world ever stays the same, hence the dictum, 'one cannot step in the same river twice'.

Heraclius c. 575–641. Byzantine emperor from 610. His reign marked a turning point in the empire's fortunes. Of Armenian descent, he recaptured Armenia 622, and other provinces 622–28 from the Persians, but lost them to the Muslims 629–41.

heraldry insignia and symbols representing a person, family, or dynasty; the science of armorial bearings. Heraldry originated with simple symbols used on shields and banners for recognition in battle. By the 14th century, it had become a complex pictorial language with its own regulatory bodies (courts of chivalry), used by noble families, corporate bodies, cities, and realms. The world's oldest heraldic court is the English College of Arms founded by Henry V; it was granted its first charter 1484 by Richard III.

In a coat of arms, the charges (heraldic symbols) are placed on the shield or escutcheon. The surface of the shield is termed the field, and coats of arms are distinguished not only by their charges, but also by the colouring, or tincture, of this field, which is engraved to represent a metal, a colour, or a fur. Above the shield is set a helmet. This in turn is draped with a cloth, often one with scalloped edges, which is known as the mantling or lambrequin. Its lining is the colour of the principal metal of the shield, its outside the principal colour. Above the helmet is the crest, which originated in a fan or plume of feathers, but in the 15th and 16th centuries developed into a weighty device moulded out of leather or wood for use in tournaments. At the joint between the mantling and the crest is a twisted skein of silk of the principal colour and metal of the arms, termed the wreath, or torse.

an achievement Peers, knights grand cross, and, in Scotland, chiefs of clans and a few others, are entitled to have their shield and helmet supported by two creatures (usually human beings or animals). Many important corporations also have supporters. A shield with its helmet, mantling, crest, and supporters forms a group known as an achievement. The most familiar supporters are probably the lion and unicorn in the English royal achievement.

marshalling and quartering The practice of combining two or more independent coats of arms on one shield, used chiefly to denote marriage, or to represent other families through heiresses, is termed marshalling. Quartering, a subdivision of marshalling, became common in the 14th century. An early example of quartered arms are those of Isabella, wife of Edward II, who bore in the four quarters the arms of England, France, Navarre, and Champagne.

Herat capital of Herat province, and the largest city in W Afghanistan, on the N banks of the Hari Rud River; population (1988) 177,000. A principal road junction, it was a great city in ancient and medieval times.

herb any plant (usually a flowering plant) tasting sweet, bitter, aromatic, or pungent, used in cooking, medicine, or perfumery; technically, a herb is any plant in which the aerial parts do not remain above ground at the end of the growing season.

herbaceous plant plant with very little or no wood, dying back at the end of every summer. The herbaceous perennials survive winters as underground storage organs such as bulbs and tubers.

herbalism in alternative medicine, the prescription and use of plants and their derivatives for medication. Herbal products are favoured by alternative practitioners as 'natural medicine', as opposed to modern synthesized medicines and drugs, which are regarded with suspicion because of the dangers of side effects and dependence.

Many herbal remedies are of proven efficacy both in preventing and curing illness. Medical herbalists claim to be able to prescribe for virtually any condition, except those so advanced that surgery is the only option.

herbarium collection of dried, pressed plants used as an aid to identification of unknown plants and by taxonomists in the ◊classification of plants. The plant specimens are accompanied by information, such as the date and place of collection, by whom collected, details of habitat, flower colour, and local names.

Herbaria range from small collections containing plants of a limited region, to the large university and national herbaria (some at ◊botanical gardens) containing millions of specimens from all parts of the world.

Herbert George 1593–1633. English poet. His volume of religious poems, *The Temple*, appeared 1633, shortly before his death. His intense though quiet poems embody his religious struggles ('The Temper', 'The Collar') or poignantly contrast mortality and eternal truth ('Vertue', 'Life') in a deceptively simple language.

The high regard in which he was held in the 17th century waned early in the 18th, and for a century or more his poetry was considered uncouth. The Romantic poet Coleridge did much to restore it to favour. It is noted for its colloquial phraseology, pliable verse forms, and quiet music; its apparent simplicity is its greatest strength.

'Sweet spring, full of sweet days and roses, A box where sweets compacted lie.'

GEORGE HERBERT 'Virtue'

herbicide any chemical used to destroy plants or check their growth; see ◊weedkiller.

herbivore animal that feeds on green plants (or photosynthetic single-celled organisms) or their products, including seeds, fruit, and nectar. The most numerous type of herbivore is thought to be the zooplankton, tiny invertebrates in the surface waters of the oceans that feed on small photosynthetic algae. Herbivores are more numerous than other animals because their food is the most abundant. They form a vital link in the food chain between plants and carnivores.

herb Robert wild geranium *Geranium robertianum* found throughout Europe and central Asia and naturalized in North America. About 30 cm/12 in high, it bears hairy leaves and small pinkish to purplish flowers.

Herculaneum ancient city of Italy between Naples and Pompeii. Along with Pompeii, it was buried when Vesuvius erupted AD 79. It was excavated from the 18th century onwards.

Hercules in astronomy, the fifth-largest constellation, lying in the northern hemisphere. Despite its size it contains no prominent stars. Its most important feature is the best example in the northern hemisphere of a ◊globular cluster of stars 22,500 light years from Earth, which lies between Eta and Zeta Herculis.

Hercules Roman form of ◊Heracles.

Herder Johann Gottfried von 1744–1803. German poet, critic, and philosopher. Herder's critical writings indicated his intuitive rather than reasoning trend of thought. He collected folk songs of all

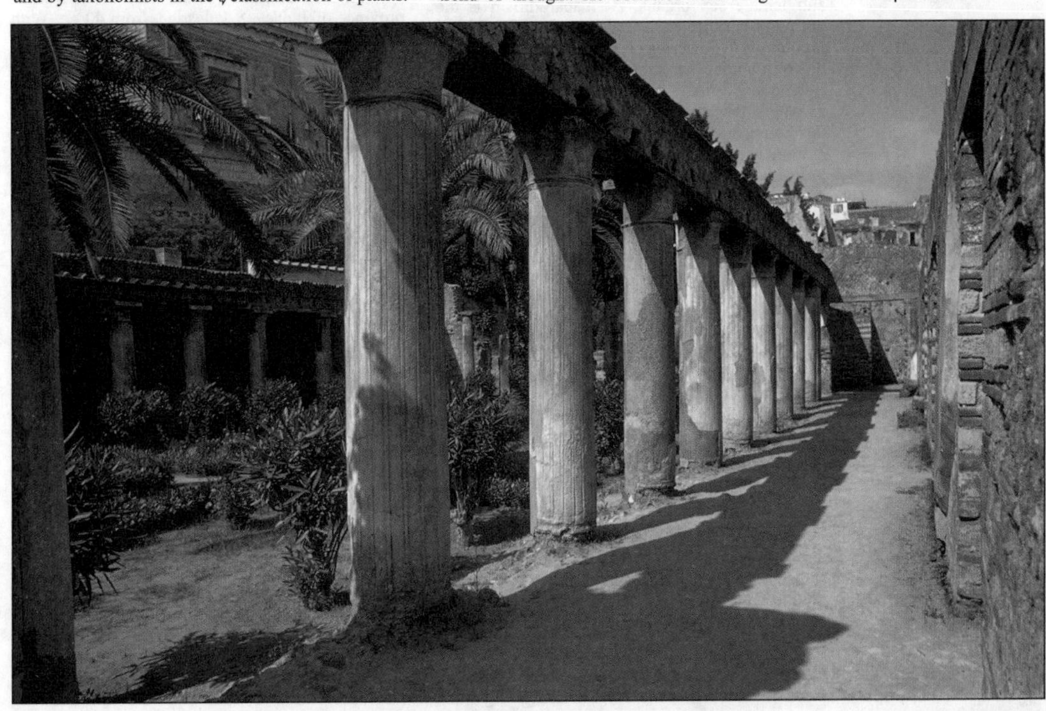

Herculaneum A colonnaded courtyard in the ruins of the Roman town of Herculaneum. Like nearby Pompeii, Herculaneum was destroyed by the eruption of the volcano Vesuvius AD 79. Whereas Pompeii was buried under a rain of volcanic ash and the inhabitants had to flee or die, Herculaneum was more slowly engulfed by lava and there was little loss of life. Herculaneum was much smaller than Pompeii, but it was prosperous and its houses were often smarter than comparable ones in Pompeii. *Corbis*

nations in *Stimmen der Völker in Liedern* 1778–79, and in the *Ideen zur Philosophie der Geschichte der Menschheit/Outlines of a Philosophy of the History of Man* 1784–91 he outlined the stages of human cultural development. Herder gave considerable impetus to the *Sturm und Drang* Romantic movement in German literature.

heredity in biology, the transmission of traits from parent to offspring. See also ◊genetics.

Hereford town in the county of Hereford and Worcester, on the river Wye, England; population (1991) 50,200. Products include cider, beer, cattle, leather goods, metal goods, and chemicals. The cathedral, which was begun 1079, contains a *Mappa Mundi* ('map of the world' about 1314), a medieval map of the world. An appeal was launched 1988 and the money was raised to restore and preserve the map. It has the largest chained library in the world.

Hereford and Worcester county of W central England, created 1974 from the counties of Herefordshire and Worcestershire
area 3,930 sq km/1,517 sq mi *(see United Kingdom map)*
towns and cities Worcester (administrative headquarters), Hereford, Kidderminster, Evesham, Ross-on-Wye, Ledbury
features rivers: Wye, Severn; Malvern Hills (high point Worcester Beacon, 425 m/1,395 ft) and Black Mountains; fertile Vale of Evesham; Droitwich, once a Victorian spa, reopened its baths 1985 (the town lies over a subterranean brine reservoir)
industries mainly agricultural: apples, pears, cider, hops, vegetables, Hereford cattle; carpets; porcelain; some chemicals; salt; food processing; engineering
population (1991) 676,700
famous people William Langland, Edward Elgar, A E Housman, John Masefield.

heresy (Greek *hairesis* 'parties' of believers) any doctrine opposed to orthodox belief, especially in religion. Those holding ideas considered heretical by the Christian church have included Gnostics, Arians, Pelagians, Montanists, Albigenses, Waldenses, Lollards, and Anabaptists.

Hereward the Wake lived 11th century. English leader of a revolt against the Normans 1070. His stronghold in the Isle of Ely was captured by William the Conqueror 1071. Hereward escaped, but his fate is unknown.

Herman Woody (Woodrow Charles) 1913–1987. US jazz bandleader and clarinetist. A child prodigy, he was leader of his own orchestra at 23, and after 1945 formed his Thundering Herd band. Soloists in this or later versions of the band included Lester ◊Young and Stan ◊Getz.

hermaphrodite organism that has both male and female sex organs. Hermaphroditism is the norm in such species as earthworms and snails, and is common in flowering plants. Cross-fertilization is the rule among hermaphrodites, with the parents functioning as male and female simultaneously, or as one or the other sex at different stages in their development. Human hermaphrodites are extremely rare.

Pseudohermaphrodites have the internal sex organs of one sex, but the external appearance of the other. The true sex of the latter becomes apparent at adolescence when the normal hormone activity appropriate to the internal organs begins to function.

hermeneutics philosophical tradition concerned with the nature of understanding and interpretation of human behaviour and social traditions. From its origins in problems of biblical interpretation, hermeneutics has expanded to cover many fields of enquiry, including aesthetics, literary theory, and science. The German philosophers Wilhelm ◊Dilthey, Martin ◊Heidegger, and Hans-Georg Gadamer (1900–) were influential contributors to this tradition.

'Youth (I confess) hath me mis-led; / But Age hath brought me right to Bed.'

ROBERT HERRICK
'His Own Epitaph'

Hermes in Greek mythology, a god, son of Zeus and ◊Maia; messenger of the gods. He wore winged sandals, a wide-brimmed hat, and carried a staff around which serpents coiled. Identified with the Roman Mercury and ancient Egyptian Thoth, he protected thieves, travellers, and merchants.

Hermes Trismegistus Greek 'the Thrice Great Hermes', another name for the ancient Egyptian god Thoth, supposed author of the *Hermetica* (2nd–3rd centuries AD), a body of writings expounding a Hellenistic mystical philosophy (Hermetism) in which the Sun is regarded as the visible manifestation of God.

hermit crab kind of ◊crab.

hernia or ***rupture*** protrusion of part of an internal organ through a weakness in the surrounding muscular wall, usually in the groin. The appearance is that of a rounded soft lump or swelling.

Hero and Leander in Greek mythology, a pair of lovers. Hero was a priestess of Aphrodite at Sestos on the Hellespont, in love with Leander on the opposite shore at Abydos. When he was drowned while swimming across during a storm, she threw herself into the sea.

Herod Agrippa I 10 BC–AD 44. Ruler of Palestine from AD 41. His real name was Marcus Julius Agrippa, erroneously called 'Herod' in the Bible. Grandson of Herod the Great, he was made tetrarch (governor) of Palestine by the Roman emperor Caligula and king by Emperor Claudius AD 41. He put the apostle James to death and imprisoned the apostle Peter. His son was Herod Agrippa II.

Herod Agrippa II c. 40–c. 93 AD. King of Chalcis (now S Lebanon), son of Herod Agrippa I. He was appointed by the Roman emperor Claudius about AD 50, and in AD 60 tried the apostle Paul. He helped the Roman commander Titus (subsequently emperor) take and sack Jerusalem AD 70, then went to Rome, where he died.

Herod Antipas 21 BC–AD 39. Tetrarch (governor) of the Roman province of Galilee, N Palestine, 4 BC–AD 39, son of Herod the Great. He divorced his wife to marry his niece Herodias, and was responsible for the death of John the Baptist. Jesus was brought before him on Pontius Pilate's discovery that he was a Galilean and hence of Herod's jurisdiction, but Herod returned him without giving any verdict. In AD 38 Herod Antipas went to Rome to try to persuade Emperor Caligula to give him the title of king, but was instead banished.

Remains of one of his royal palaces were excavated at Masada 1963–64. There were important finds of ancient texts, mosaic floors, decorated walls of the royal palace, and reservoirs.

Herodotus c. 484–c. 424 BC. Greek historian. He wrote a nine-book history of the Greek–Persian struggle that culminated in the defeat of the Persian invasion attempts 490 and 480 BC. Herodotus was the first historian to apply critical evaluation to his material, while also recording divergent opinions.

After four years in Athens, he travelled widely in Egypt, Asia, and the Black Sea region of E Europe, before settling at Thurii in S Italy 443 BC.

Herod the Great 74–4 BC. King of the Roman province of Judaea, S Palestine, from 40 BC. With the aid of Mark Antony, he established his government in Jerusalem 37 BC. He rebuilt the Temple in Jerusalem, but his Hellenizing tendencies made him suspect to orthodox Jewry. His last years were a reign of terror, and in the New Testament Matthew alleges that he ordered the slaughter of all the infants in Bethlehem to ensure the death of Jesus, whom he foresaw as a rival. He was the father of Herod Antipas.

heroin or ***diamorphine*** powerful ◊opiate analgesic, an acetyl derivative of ◊morphine. It is more addictive than morphine but causes less nausea. It has an important place in the control of severe pain in terminal illness, severe injuries, and heart attacks, but is widely used illegally.

The major regions of opium production, for conversion to heroin, are the 'Golden Crescent' of Afghanistan, Iran, and Pakistan, and the 'Golden Triangle' across parts of Myanmar (Burma), Laos, and Thailand. Heroin was discovered in Germany 1898.

heron large to medium-sized wading bird of the family Ardeidae, order Ciconiiformes, which also includes bitterns, egrets, night herons, and boatbills. Herons have sharp bills, broad wings, long legs, slender bodies, and soft plumage. They are found mostly in tropical and subtropical regions, but also in temperate zones, on lakes, fens, and mudflats, where they wade searching for prey.

They capture small animals, such as fish, molluscs, and worms, by spearing them with their long bills. Herons nest on trees, bushes, ivy-covered rocks, or reeds, making a loose fabric of sticks lined with grass or leaves; they lay greenish or drab-coloured eggs, varying in number from two to seven with the different species.

herpes any of several infectious diseases caused by viruses of the herpes group. ***Herpes simplex I*** is the causative agent of a common inflammation, the cold sore. ***Herpes simplex II*** is responsible for genital herpes, a highly contagious, sexually transmitted disease characterized by painful blisters in the genital area. It can be transmitted in the birth canal from mother to newborn. ***Herpes zoster*** causes ◊shingles; another herpes virus causes chickenpox.

A number of antiviral drugs are used to treat these infections, which are particularly troublesome in patients whose immune systems are suppressed. The drug acyclovir, originally introduced for the treatment of genital herpes, has now been shown to modify the course of chickenpox and the related condition shingles, by reducing the duration of the illness.

The Epstein–Barr virus of ◊glandular fever also belongs to this group.

Herr Michael 1940– . US writer. *Dispatches* 1977, his book of Vietnam reportage, became an international best seller, praised for its bold and savage depiction of war. He was co-author of several screenplays, including *Apocalypse Now* 1979 and *Full Metal Jacket* 1987.

Herrick Robert 1591–1674. English poet and cleric. He published *Hesperides: or the Works both Humane and Divine of Robert Herrick* 1648, a collection of verse admired for its lyric quality, including the well-known poems 'Gather ye rosebuds' and 'Cherry ripe'.

The 'divine' poems are, on the whole, unremarkable, but the 'humane' works are rich and varied, owing much to Roman models such as ◊Catullus and ◊Martial and to native influences such as Ben ◊Jonson and popular ballads. They range in scale from couplets to Horatian odes and verse epistles, and cover such subjects as religion, politics, love, erotic fantasy, the value of poetry, and the changing cycles of life in the countryside.

herring any of various marine fishes of the herring family (Clupeidae), but especially the important food fish *Clupea harengus*. A silvered greenish blue, it swims close to the surface, and may be 25–40 cm/10–16 in long. Herring travel in schools several kilometres long and wide. They are found in large quantities off the E coast of North America,

heron The grey heron *Ardea cinerea* can be seen in this typical fishing pose from W Europe through Asia to Japan and down into much of Africa and Madagascar. It builds an untidy stick nest, usually high up in trees, forming colonies known as heronries. *Premaphotos Wildlife*

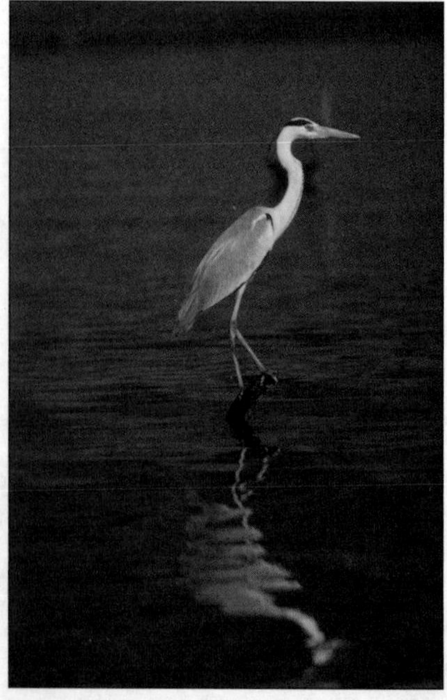

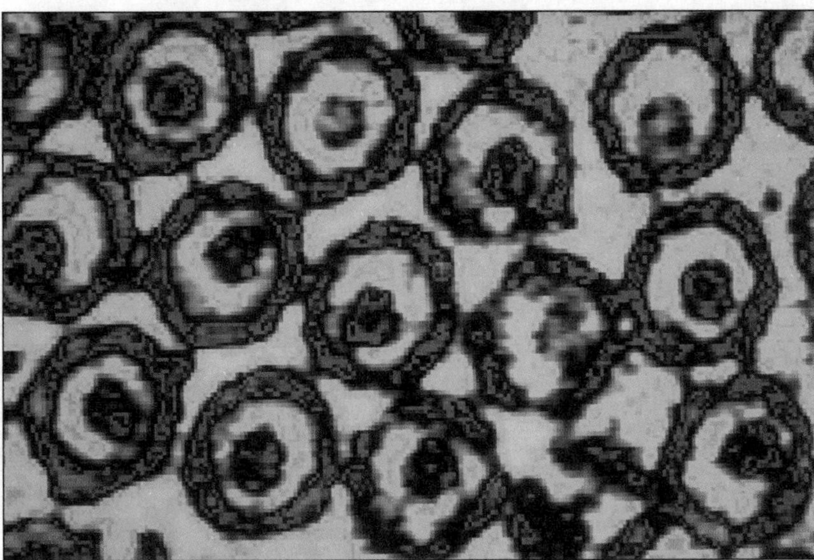

herpes A false-colour micrograph of the *Herpes simplex* or cold sore virus. Herpes is the name given to any of several infectious diseases – including cold sores, genital herpes, shingles, chickenpox, and glandular fever – caused by the viruses in the herpes group. *SmithKline Beecham plc.*

and the shores of NE Europe. Overfishing and pollution have reduced their numbers.

Herriot Edouard 1872–1957. French Radical socialist politician. An opponent of Poincaré, who as prime minister carried out the French occupation of the Ruhr, Germany, he was briefly prime minister 1924–25, 1926, and 1932. As president of the chamber of deputies 1940, he opposed the policies of the right-wing Vichy government and was arrested and later taken to Germany; he was released 1945 by the Soviets.

Herriot James. Pen name of James Alfred Wight 1916–1995. English writer. A practising veterinary surgeon, he wrote of his experiences in a series of humorous books which described the life of a young vet working in a Yorkshire village in the late 1930s. His first three books were published as a compilation under the title *All Creatures Great and Small* 1972.

Herschel Caroline (Lucretia) 1750–1848. German-born English astronomer, sister of William ◊Herschel, and from 1772 his assistant in Bath, England. She discovered eight comets and worked on her brother's catalogue of star clusters and nebulae.

Herschel John Frederick William 1792–1871. English scientist, astronomer, and photographer who discovered thousands of close double stars, clusters, and nebulae. He coined the terms 'photography', 'negative', and 'positive', discovered sodium thiosulphite as a fixer of silver halides, and invented the cyanotype process; his inventions also include astronomical instruments.

Herschel (Frederick) William 1738–1822. German-born English astronomer. He was a skilled telescopemaker, and pioneered the study of binary stars and nebulae. He discovered the planet Uranus 1781 and infrared solar rays 1801. He catalogued over 800 double stars, and found over 2,500 nebulae, catalogued by his sister Caroline Herschel; this work was continued by his son John Herschel. By studying the distribution of stars, William established the basic form of our Galaxy, the Milky Way.

Herschel discovered the motion of binary stars around one another, and recorded it in his *Motion of the Solar System in Space* 1783. In 1789 he built, in Slough, Berkshire, a 1.2-m/4-ft telescope of 12 m/40 ft focal length (the largest in the world at the time), but he made most use of a more satisfactory 46-cm/18-in instrument. He discovered two satellites of Uranus and two of Saturn.

Hertfordshire county of SE England
area 1,630 sq km/629 sq mi *(see United Kingdom map)*
towns and cities Hertford (administrative headquarters), St Albans, Watford, Hatfield, Hemel Hempstead, Bishop's Stortford, Letchworth (the first ◊garden city, followed by Welwyn 1919 and Stevenage 1947)
features rivers: Lea, Stort, Colne; part of the Chiltern Hills; Hatfield House; Knebworth House (home of Lord Lytton); Brocket Hall (home of Palmerston and Melbourne); home of G B ◊Shaw at Ayot St Lawrence; Berkhamsted Castle (Norman); Rothamsted agricultural experimental station
industries engineering, aircraft, electrical goods, paper and printing; general agricultural goods; barley for brewing industry, dairy farming, market gardening, horticulture, tanning
population (1991) 975,800
famous people Henry Bessemer, Cecil Rhodes, Graham Greene.

What that man ever invented, under the name of pleasure-grounds can equal these fields in Hertfordshire?

On Hertfordshire
William Cobbett
Rural Rides
24 June 1822

hertz SI unit (symbol Hz) of frequency (the number of repetitions of a regular occurrence in one second). Radio waves are often measured in megahertz (MHz), millions of hertz, and the clock rate of a computer (the frequency of its internal electronic clock) is usually measured in megahertz. The unit is named after Heinrich Hertz.

Hertz Heinrich Rudolf 1857–1894. German physicist who studied electromagnetic waves, showing that their behaviour resembles that of light and heat waves.

Hertz confirmed James Clerk ◊Maxwell's theory of electromagnetic waves. In 1888, he realized that electric waves could be produced and would travel through air, and he confirmed this experimentally. He went on to determine the velocity of these waves (which were later called radio waves) and, on showing that it was the same as that of light, devised experiments to show that the waves could be reflected, refracted, and diffracted.

Hertzog James Barry Munnik 1866–1942. South African politician, prime minister 1924–39, founder of the Nationalist Party 1913 (the United South African National Party from 1933). He opposed South Africa's entry into both world wars.

Hertzsprung–Russell diagram in astronomy, a graph on which the surface temperatures of stars are plotted against their luminosities. Most stars, including the Sun, fall into a narrow band called the ◊main sequence. When a star grows old it moves from the main sequence to the upper right part of the graph, into the area of the giants and supergiants. At the end of its life, as the star shrinks to become a white dwarf, it moves again, to the bottom left area. It is named after the Dane Ejnar Hertzsprung (1873–1967) and the American Henry Norris Russell (1877–1957), who independently devised it in the years 1911–13.

Herzegovina or ***Hercegovina*** part of ◊Bosnia-Herzegovina (which was formerly, until 1991, a republic of Yugoslavia).

Herzl Theodor 1860–1904. Austrian founder of the Zionist movement. The ◊Dreyfus case convinced him that the only solution to the problem of anti-Semitism was the resettlement of the Jews in a state of their own. His book *Jewish State* 1896 launched political ◊Zionism, and he became the first president of the World Zionist Organization 1897.

Herzog Werner. Adopted name of Werner Stipetic 1942– . German film director. He often takes his camera to exotic and impractical locations. His original and visually splendid films include *Aguirre*

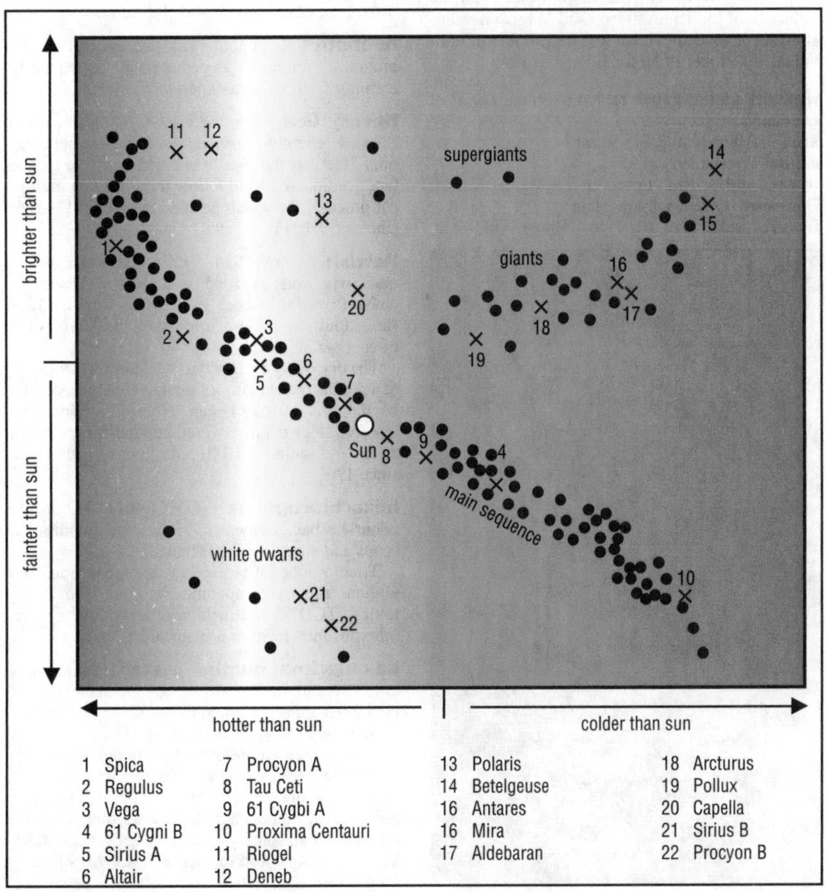

Hertzsprung–Russell diagram The Hertzsprung–Russell diagram relates the brightness (or luminosity) of a star to its temperature. Most stars fall within a narrow diagonal band called the main sequence. A star moves off the main sequence when it grows old. The Hertzsprung–Russell diagram is one of the most important diagrams in astrophysics.

If we hate a person, we hate something in our image of him that lies within ourselves. What is not within ourselves doesn't upset us.

HERMANN HESSE
Demian

der Zorn Gottes/Aguirre Wrath of God 1972, *Nosferatu Phantom der Nacht/Nosferatu Phantom of the Night* 1979, and *Fitzcarraldo* 1982.

Heseltine Michael (Ray Dibdin) 1933– . English Conservative politician, deputy prime minister 1995–97. A member of Parliament from 1966, he was secretary of state for the environment 1990–92 and for trade and industry 1992–95.

Heseltine was minister of the environment 1979–83, when he succeeded John Nott. As minister of defence from 1983, he resigned Jan 1986 over allegations of malpractice in the Westland affair and was then seen as a major rival to Margaret Thatcher. In Nov 1990, Heseltine's challenge to Thatcher's leadership of the Conservative Party brought about her resignation.

Hesiod lived 8th century BC. Greek poet. The earliest of the Greek didactic poets, he is often contrasted with ◊Homer as the other main representative of the early epic. He is the author of *Works and Days*, a moralizing and didactic poem of rural life, and *Theogony*, an account of the origin of the world and of the gods. Both poems include the myth of ◊Pandora.

Hesperides in Greek mythology, the Greek maidens who guarded a tree bearing golden apples in the Islands of the Blessed (also known as the Hesperides). The apples were taken by the hero ◊Heracles in one of his labours.

Hess (Walter Richard) Rudolf 1894–1987. German Nazi leader. Imprisoned with Adolf Hitler 1924–25, he became his private secretary, taking down *Mein Kampf* from his dictation. In 1933 he was appointed deputy *Führer* to Hitler, a post he held until replaced by Goering Sept 1939. On 10 May 1941 he landed by air in the UK with his own compromise peace proposals and was held a prisoner of war until 1945, when he was tried at Nuremberg as a war criminal and sentenced to life imprisonment. He died in Spandau prison, Berlin.

Hesse Hermann 1877–1962. German writer, a Swiss citizen from 1923. A conscientious objector in World War I and a pacifist opponent of Hitler, he published short stories, poetry, and novels, including *Peter Camenzind* 1904, *Siddhartha* 1922, and *Steppenwolf* 1927. Later works, such as *Das Glasperlenspiel/The Glass Bead Game* 1943, show the influence of Indian mysticism and Jungian psychoanalysis. Above all, Hesse was the prophet of individualism. Nobel Prize for Literature 1946.

Hessen administrative region (German *Land*) of Germany
area 21,100 sq km/8,145 sq mi
capital Wiesbaden
towns and cities Frankfurt-am-Main, Kassel, Darmstadt, Offenbach-am-Main
features valleys of the rivers Rhine and Main; Taunus Mountains, rich in mineral springs, as at Homburg and Wiesbaden; see also ◊Swabia
industries wine, timber, chemicals, cars, electrical engineering, optical instruments
population (1994 est) 5,967,000
religion Protestant 61%, Roman Catholic 33%
history until 1945, Hessen was divided in two by a strip of Prussian territory, the southern portion consisting of the valleys of the rivers Rhine and the Main, the northern being dominated by the Vogelsberg Mountains (744 m/2,442 ft). Its capital was Darmstadt.

Hess German Nazi leader Rudolf Hess. He joined the Nazi Party 1920, was imprisoned with Hitler 1923–25, and became deputy leader 1933. He landed in Britain 1941 with compromise peace proposals, but was taken into captivity as a prisoner of war. Sentenced to life imprisonment at Nuremberg, he spent the last 42 years of his life in Spandau Prison, Berlin. *Topham*

Hestia in Greek mythology, the goddess of the hearth (Roman Vesta), daughter of ◊Kronos and Rhea.

Heston Charlton. Stage name of John Charles Carter 1924– . US film actor. He often starred in biblical and historical epics, for example, as Moses in *The Ten Commandments* 1956, and in the title role in *Ben Hur* 1959 (Academy Award). His other film appearances include *Major Dundee* 1965 and *Earthquake* 1974.

heterogeneous reaction in chemistry, a reaction where there is an interface between the different components or reactants. Examples of heterogeneous reactions are those between a gas and a solid, a gas and a liquid, two immiscible liquids, or two different solids.

heterosexuality sexual preference for, or attraction mainly to, persons of the opposite sex.

heterostyly in botany, having ◊styles of different lengths.

Certain flowers, such as primroses (*Primula vulgaris*), have different-sized ◊anthers and styles to ensure cross-fertilization (through ◊pollination) by visiting insects.

heterotroph any living organism that obtains its energy from organic substances produced by other organisms. All animals and fungi are heterotrophs, and they include herbivores, carnivores, and saprotrophs (those that feed on dead animal and plant material).

heterozygous in a living organism, having two different ◊alleles for a given trait. In ◊homozygous organisms, by contrast, both chromosomes carry the same allele. In an outbreeding population an individual organism will generally be heterozygous for some genes but homozygous for others.

heuristics in computing, a process by which a program attempts to improve its performance by learning from its own experience.

Hevesy Georg von 1885–1966. Hungarian-born Swedish chemist, discoverer of the element hafnium. He was the first to use a radioactive isotope (see ◊radioactivity) to follow the steps of a biological process, for which he won the Nobel Prize for Chemistry 1943.

Hewish Antony 1924– . English radio astronomer who was awarded, with Martin ◊Ryle, the Nobel Prize for Physics 1974 for his work on ◊pulsars, rapidly rotating neutron stars that emit pulses of energy.

The discovery by Jocelyn Bell Burnell (1943–) of a regularly fluctuating signal, which turned out to be the first pulsar, began a period of intensive research. Hewish discovered another three straight away, and more than 170 pulsars have been found since 1967.

hexachlorophene $(C_6HCl_3OH)_2CH_2$ white, odourless bactericide, used in minute quantities in soaps and surgical disinfectants.

Trichlorophenol is used in its preparation, and, without precise temperature control, the highly toxic TCDD (tetrachlorodibenzodioxin; see ◊dioxin) may form as a by-product.

hexadecimal number system or ***hex*** number system to the base 16. In hex the decimal numbers 0–15 are represented by the characters 0, 1, 2, 3, 4, 5, 6, 7, 8, 9, A, B, C, D, E, F. Hexadecimal numbers are often preferred by computer programmers because they are more easily converted to the computer's internal ◊binary (base-two) code than are decimal numbers, and, because they are more compact than binary numbers are more easily keyed, checked, and memorized. *See list of tables on p. 1177.*

Heydrich Reinhard Tristan Eugen 1904–1942. German Nazi, head of the *Sicherheitsdienst* (SD), the party's security service, and Heinrich ◊Himmler's deputy. He was instrumental in organizing the ◊final solution, the policy of genocide used against Jews and others. 'Protector' of Bohemia and Moravia from 1941, he was ambushed and killed the following year by three members of the Czechoslovak forces in Britain, who had landed by parachute. Reprisals followed, including several hundred executions and the massacre in ◊Lidice.

Heyerdahl Thor 1914– . Norwegian ethnologist. He sailed on the ancient-Peruvian-style raft *Kon-Tiki* from Peru to the Tuamotu Archipelago along the Humboldt Current 1947, and in 1969–70 used ancient-Egyptian-style papyrus-reed boats to cross the Atlantic. His expeditions were intended to establish that ancient civilizations could have travelled the oceans in similar fashion, but his theories are largely discounted by anthropologists. His voyages are described in *Kon-Tiki* and *The Ra Expeditions*. He also crossed the Persian Gulf 1977, written about in *The Tigris Expedition*.

Heywood Thomas c. 1570–c. 1650. English actor and dramatist. He wrote or adapted over 220 plays, including the domestic tragedy *A Woman Kilde with Kindnesse* 1602–03. He also wrote an *Apology for Actors* 1612, in answer to attacks on the morality of the theatre.

Hezbollah or ***Hizbollah*** (Party of God) extremist Muslim organization founded by the Iranian Revolutionary Guards who were sent to Lebanon after the 1979 Iranian revolution. Its aim is to spread the Islamic revolution of Iran among the Shi'ite population of Lebanon. Hezbollah is believed to be the umbrella movement of the groups that held many of the Western hostages taken from 1984.

In 1996 Hezbollah guerrillas, opposed to the Middle East peace process, engaged in renewed hostilities with Israeli forces stationed in southern Lebanon.

Hezekiah in the Old Testament, king of Judah from 719 BC. Against the advice of the prophet Isaiah he rebelled against Assyrian suzerainty in alliance with Egypt, but was defeated by ◊Sennacherib and had to pay out large amounts in indemnities. He carried out religious reforms.

HF in physics, abbreviation for ***high*** ◊***frequency***. HF radio waves have frequencies in the range 3–30 MHz.

Hiawatha 16th-century Native American teacher and Onondaga chieftain. He is said to have welded the Five Nations (later joined by a sixth) of the ◊Iroquois into the league of the Long House, as the confederacy was known in what is now upper New York State. Hiawatha is the hero of H W Longfellow's epic poem *The Song of Hiawatha*.

hibernation state of dormancy in which certain animals spend the winter. It is associated with a dramatic reduction in all metabolic processes, including body temperature, breathing, and heart rate. It is a fallacy that animals sleep throughout the winter.

The body temperature of the Arctic ground squirrel falls to below 0°C/32°F during hibernation. Hibernating bats may breathe only once every 45 minutes, and can go for up to 2 hours without taking a breath.

hibiscus any plant of the genus *Hibiscus* of the mallow family. Hibiscuses range from large herbaceous plants to trees. Popular as ornamental plants because of their brilliantly coloured, red to white, bell-shaped flowers, they include *H. syriacus* and *H. rosa-sinensis* of Asia and the rose mallow *H. palustris* of North America.

Hickok 'Wild Bill', (James Butler) 1837–1876. US pioneer and law enforcer, a legendary figure in the West. In the Civil War he was a sharpshooter and scout for the Union army. He then served as marshal in Kansas, killing as many as 27 people. He was a prodigious gambler and was fatally shot from behind while playing poker in Deadwood, South Dakota.

hickory tree of the genus *Carya* of the walnut family, native to North America and Asia. It provides a valuable timber, and all species produce nuts, although some are inedible. The pecan

hibiscus *The Hibiscus rosa-sinensis flowering in cultivation in Israel. With their large, showy flowers, several hibiscus species are widely cultivated as ornamentals, but others are grown for their fibre and their edible pods (okra) and fruit. Premaphotos Wildlife*

C. illinoensis is widely cultivated in the southern USA, and the shagbark *C. ovata* in the northern USA.

hieroglyphic (Greek 'sacred carved writing') Egyptian writing system of the mid-4th millennium BC–3rd century AD, which combines picture signs with those indicating letters. The direction of writing is normally from right to left, the signs facing the beginning of the line. It was deciphered 1822 by the French Egyptologist J F Champollion (1790–1832) with the aid of the ◊***Rosetta Stone***, which has the same inscription carved in hieroglyphic, demotic, and Greek. Hieroglyphics were replaced for everyday use by cursive writing from about 700 BC onwards.

hi-fi (abbreviation for ***high-fidelity***) faithful reproduction of sound from a machine that plays recorded music or speech. A typical hi-fi system includes a turntable for playing vinyl records, a cassette tape deck to play magnetic tape recordings, a tuner to pick up radio broadcasts, an amplifier to serve all the equipment, possibly a compact-disc player, and two or more loudspeakers.

Advances in mechanical equipment and electronics, such as digital recording techniques and compact discs, have made it possible to eliminate many distortions in sound-reproduction processes.

Higgs boson or ***Higgs particle*** postulated ◊elementary particle whose existence would explain why particles have mass. The current theory of elementary particles, called the standard model, cannot explain how mass arises. To overcome this difficulty, Peter Higgs (1929–) of the University of Edinburgh and Thomas Kibble (1932–) of Imperial College, London proposed in 1964 a new particle that binds to other particles and gives them their mass. The Higgs boson has not yet been detected experimentally.

High Church group in the ◊Church of England that emphasizes aspects of Christianity usually associated with Catholics, such as ceremony and hierarchy. The term was first used in 1703 to describe those who opposed Dissenters, and later for groups such as the 19th-century ◊Oxford Movement.

high commissioner representative of one independent Commonwealth country in the capital of another, ranking with ambassador.

high-definition television (HDTV) ◊television system offering a significantly greater number of scanning lines, and therefore a clearer picture, than that provided by conventional systems.

Higher in Scottish education, a public examination taken at the age of 17, one year after the Scottish O grade. Highers are usually taken in four or five subjects and qualify students for entry to higher education.

high jump field event in athletics in which competitors leap over a horizontal crossbar held between rigid uprights at least 3.66 m/12 ft apart. The bar is placed at increasingly higher levels. Elimination occurs after three consecutive failures to clear the bar.

Highland local authority of Scotland, created 1973, retained in the reorganization of local authorities 1996 *(see United Kingdom map)*
area 26,100 sq km/10,077 sq mi
towns and cities Inverness (administrative headquarters), Thurso, Wick
features comprises almost half the country; Grampian Mountains; Ben Nevis (highest peak in the UK); Loch Ness, Caledonian Canal; Inner Hebrides; the Queen Mother's castle of Mey at Caithness; John O'Groats' House; Dounreay (site of Atomic Energy Authority's first experimental fast-breeder reactor and a nuclear processing plant, decommissioned 1994, and replaced by nuclear-waste reprocessing plant)
industries oil services, winter sports, timber, livestock, grouse and deer hunting, salmon fishing, sheep farming, aluminium smelting, pulp and paper production, distilling
population (1991) 204,000
famous people Alexander Mackenzie, William Smith
language English; 7.5% Gaelic-speaking.

Highland Clearances forced removal of tenants from large estates in Scotland during the early 19th century, as landowners 'improved' their estates by switching from arable to sheep farming. It led ultimately to widespread emigration to North America.

Highland Games traditional Scottish outdoor gathering that includes tossing the caber, putting the shot, running, dancing, and bagpipe playing.

Highlands one of the three geographical divisions of Scotland, lying to the N of a geological fault line that stretches from Stonehaven in the North Sea to Dumbarton on the Clyde. It is a mountainous region of hard rocks, shallow infertile soils, and high rainfall.

High Tech (abbreviation for ***high technology***) in architecture, an approach to design, originating in the UK in the 1970s, which concentrates on technical innovation, often using exposed structure and services as a means of creating exciting forms and spaces. The Hong Kong and Shanghai Bank, Hong Kong, 1986, designed by Norman ◊Foster, is a masterpiece of High Tech architecture.

highwayman in English history, a thief on horseback who robbed travellers on the highway (those who did so on foot were known as footpads). Highwaymen continued to flourish well into the 19th century. With the development of regular coach services in the 17th and 18th centuries, the highwaymen's activities became notorious, and the Bow Street runners (see ◊police) were organized to suppress them.

Among the best-known highwaymen were Jonathan Wild (c. 1682–1725), Claude Duval (1643–1670), John Nevison (1639–1684), the original hero of the 'ride to York', Dick ◊Turpin and his partner Tom King, and Jerry Abershaw (c. 1773–1795). Favourite haunts were Hounslow and Bagshot heaths and Epping Forest, around London.

High Wycombe market town in Buckinghamshire, on the river Wye, England; population (1991) 71,700. Hughenden Manor, home of Benjamin Disraeli is here. RAF Strike Command has its underground headquarters (built 1984) beneath the Chiltern Hills nearby, a four-storey office block used as Joint Headquarters in the Gulf War 1991. Products include furniture, paper, precision instruments, clothing.

hijacking illegal seizure or taking control of a vehicle and/or its passengers or goods. The term dates from 1923 and originally referred to the robbing of freight lorries. Subsequently it (and its derivative 'skyjacking') has been applied to the seizure of aircraft, usually in flight, by an individual or group, often with some political aim. International treaties (Tokyo 1963, The Hague 1970, and Montreal 1971) encourage cooperation against hijackers and make severe penalties compulsory.

Hijrah (Arabic 'flight') or ***Hegira*** the flight from Mecca to Medina of the prophet Muhammad, which took place AD 622 as a result of the persecution of the prophet and his followers. The Muslim calendar dates from this event, and the day of the Hijrah is celebrated as the Muslim New Year.

Hilbert David 1862–1943. German mathematician, philosopher, and physicist whose work was fundamental to 20th-century mathematics. He founded the formalist school with *Grundlagen der Geometrie/Foundations of Geometry* 1899, which was based on his idea of postulates. In 1900 Hilbert proposed a set of 23 problems for future mathematicians to solve, and gave 20 axioms to provide a logical basis for Euclidean geometry.

Hildebrand Benedictine monk who became Pope ◊Gregory VII.

Hildebrandt Johann Lucas von 1668–1745. Italian-born Austrian architect. He trained under Carlo Fontana (1638–1714), the leading Baroque architect in late 17th-century Rome, and was successor to Viennese court architect Johann Fischer von Erlach (1656–1723). His Baroque masterpiece is the Belvedere, Vienna, 1693–1724, which comprises the Upper and Lower Palaces, divided by magnificent gardens.

Hill Damon 1960– . English racing driver. The son of Graham Hill, he began his Formula One racing career with Brabham in 1992 before joining Williams. He won his first Grand Prix in Hungary in 1993. In 1996 he won the Formula One World Drivers' Championship.

Hill (Norman) Graham 1929–1975. English motor-racing driver. He won the Dutch Grand Prix 1962,

Hill British reformer Rowland Hill, who introduced the prepaid postal service known as the penny post. He was secretary to the Post Office 1854–64. He had begun his career as a teacher, introducing the system of self-government at his school in Birmingham and arguing that moral influence provided the best form of discipline. *Corbis*

progressing to the world driver's title 1962 and 1968. In 1972 he became the first Formula One World Champion to win the Le Mans Grand Prix d'Endurance (Le Mans 24-Hour Race). He was also the only driver to win the Formula One World Championship, Le Mans 24-Hour Race, and the Indianapolis 500 Race in his career as a driver. He was killed in an air crash.

Hill Octavia 1838–1912. English campaigner for housing reform and public open spaces. She cofounded the ◊National Trust 1894.

Hill Rowland 1795–1879. British Post Office official who invented adhesive stamps and prompted the introduction of the penny prepaid post in 1840 (previously the addressee paid, according to distance, on receipt). *See illustration on previous page.*

Hilliard Portrait of an unknown woman 1585 by Nicholas Hilliard, the finest miniaturist of the Elizabethan and Jacobean courts. In his book on miniature painting, *The Arte of Limning* c. 1600, he wrote of trying to catch 'these lovely graces, witty smilings, and these stolen glances which suddenly, like lightning, pass'. *D.S. Lavender*

Hill and Adamson David Octavius Hill (1802–1870) and Robert R Adamson (1821–1848) Scottish photographers who worked together 1843–48. They made extensive use of the ◊calotype process in their portraits of leading members of the Free Church of Scotland and their views of Edinburgh and the Scottish fishing village of Newhaven. They produced some 2,500 calotypes. Their work was rediscovered around 1900.

Hillary Edmund (Percival) 1919– . New Zealand mountaineer. In 1953, with Nepalese Sherpa mountaineer Tenzing Norgay, he reached the summit of Mount Everest, the first to climb the world's highest peak. As a member of the Commonwealth Transantarctic Expedition 1957–58, he was the first person since R F Scott to reach the South Pole overland, on 3 Jan 1958.

Hillel c. 60 BC–000. Hebrew scholar, lawyer, and teacher; member of the Pharisaic movement (see ◊Pharisee). His work was accepted by later rabbinic Judaism and is noted for its tolerance.

hill figure in Britain, any of a number of ancient figures, usually of animals, cut from downland turf to show the underlying chalk. Examples include the ◊White Horses, the Long Man of Wilmington, East Sussex, and the Cerne Abbas Giant, Dorset. Their origins are variously attributed to Celts, Romans, Saxons, Druids, or Benedictine monks.

hillfort European Iron Age site with massive banks and ditches for defence, used as both a military camp and a permanent settlement. An example is Maiden Castle, Dorset, England.

Hilliard Nicholas c. 1547–1619. English miniaturist and goldsmith. Court artist to Elizabeth I and James I, he painted many leading figures of Tudor and Stuart society, including Francis Drake, Walter Raleigh, and Mary Queen of Scots. Outstanding among his works are several portraits of Elizabeth I and *An Unknown Young Man Amid Roses* about 1590 (Victoria and Albert Museum, London).

He based his style on that of Hans Holbein, who had worked at the court of Henry VIII, though he also learned from contemporary French artists (he is known to have visited France in the 1570s). He wrote *The Arte of Limninge*, a book on painting in miniature, 1593. After 1600 he was gradually superseded by his pupil Isaac Oliver. His son ***Lawrence Hilliard*** (1582–after 1640) was also a miniaturist.

Hillingdon outer borough of W Greater London. It includes the district of Uxbridge
features Cedar House (about 1850); Hillingdon parish workhouse (1747); Swakeleys, Jacobean mansion at Ickenham; Grand Union Canal; Heathrow airport (1946), built on the site of a Neolithic settlement
population (1991) 231,600.

Himachal Pradesh state of NW India
area 55,700 sq km/21,500 sq mi
capital Shimla
features mainly agricultural state, one-third forested, with softwood timber industry
industries timber, grain, rice, fruit, seed potatoes
population (1994 est) 5,530,000; mainly Hindu
language Pahari, Hindi
history created as a union territory 1948, it became a full state 1971.

Certain hill areas were transferred to Himachal Pradesh from the Punjab 1966.

Himalayas vast mountain system of central Asia, extending from the Indian states of Kashmir in the W to Assam in the E, covering the S part of Tibet, Nepal, Sikkim, and Bhutan. It is the highest mountain range in the world. The two highest peaks are Mount ◊Everest and ◊K2. Other peaks include ◊Kangchenjunga, Makalu, Annapurna, and Nanga Parbat, all over 8,000 m/26,000 ft.

Himera Greek city on the north coast of Sicily, founded about 649 BC by exiles from Syracuse. In 483 BC Theron of Acragas expelled the ruling tyrant, Terillus, who then looked for support from Carthage. In the Battle of Himera 480 BC, Theron and his son-in-law ◊Gelon of Syracuse defeated Terillus and the Carthaginian army. Himera was finally destroyed 409 BC by the Carthaginians.

Himalayas Mount Machhapuchhre (6,993 m/ 22,943 ft) in Nepal, one of the few mountains in the Himalayas never to have been climbed. An expedition came close to the summit in 1957, but turned back at the insistence of the sherpas, who believed the mountain to be sacred. Climbing the 'fish-tail' mountain is now forbidden. *Sally Jenkins*

Himmler Heinrich 1900–1945. German Nazi leader, head of the ◊SS elite corps from 1929, the police and the ◊Gestapo secret police from 1936, and supervisor of the extermination of the Jews in E Europe. During World War II he replaced Hermann Goering as Hitler's second-in-command. He was captured May 1945 and committed suicide.

Born in Munich, he joined the Nazi Party in 1925 and became chief of the Bavarian police 1933. His accumulation of offices meant he had command of all German police forces by 1936, which made him one of the most powerful people in Germany. He was appointed minister of the interior 1943 in an attempt to stamp out defeatism and following the ◊July Plot 1944 became commander in chief of the home forces. In April 1945 he made a proposal to the Allies that Germany should surrender to the USA and Britain but not to the USSR, which was rejected.

Hinault Bernard 1954– . French cyclist, one of four men to have won the ◊Tour de France five times (1978–85); the others being Jacques Anquetil (1934–1988), Eddie ◊Merckx, and Miguel ◊Indurain.

Hīnayāna (Sanskrit 'lesser vehicle') Mahāyāna Buddhist name for ◊Theravāda Buddhism.

Hindemith Paul 1895–1963. German composer and teacher. His operas *Cardillac* 1926, revised 1952, and *Mathis der Maler/Mathis the Painter* 1933–35, are theatrically astute and politically aware; as a teacher in Berlin 1927–33 he encouraged the development of a functional modern repertoire ('Gebrauchsmusik'/'utility music') for home and school.

In 1939 he emigrated to the USA, where he taught at Yale University and was influential in promoting a measured Neo-Classical idiom of self-evident contrapuntal mastery but matter-of-fact tone, exemplified in *Ludus Tonalis* for piano 1942 and the *Symphonic Metamorphoses on Themes of Carl Maria von Weber* 1944. In later life he revised many of his earlier compositions to conform with a personal theory of tonality.

Hindenburg Paul Ludwig Hans Anton von Beneckendorf und Hindenburg 1847–1934. German field marshal and right-wing politician. During World War I he was supreme commander and, with Erich von Ludendorff, practically directed Germany's policy until the end of the war. He was president of Germany 1925–33.

Born in Posen of a Prussian Junker (aristocratic landowner) family, he was commissioned 1866, served in the Austro-Prussian and Franco-German wars, and retired 1911. Given the command in East Prussia Aug 1914, he received the credit for the defeat of the Russians at ◊Tannenberg and was promoted to supreme commander and field marshal. Re-elected president 1932, he was compelled to invite Adolf Hitler to assume the chancellorship Jan 1933.

Hindi language member of the Indo-Iranian branch of the Indo-European language family, the official language of the Republic of India, although resisted as such by the Dravidian-speaking states of the south. Hindi proper is used by some 30% of Indians, in such northern states as Uttar Pradesh and Madhya Pradesh.

Hindi has close historical and cultural links with Sanskrit, the classical language of Hinduism, and is written (from left to right) in Devanagari script. Bihari, Punjabi, and Rajasthani, the dominant language varieties in the states of Bihar, Punjab, and Rajasthan, are claimed by some to be varieties of Hindi (dialects), by others to be distinct languages.

Hindley, Myra 1942– . British murderer who, with Ian Brady, was found guilty of the murder of two children and a 17-year-old youth between 1963 and 1965. They were known as 'the Moors Murderers' because they buried most of their victims on Saddleworth Moor in the Pennines, England. They abducted and sexually abused the children before killing them.

Hinduism (Hindu *sanatana dharma* 'eternal tradition') religion originating in N India about 4,000 years ago, which is superficially and in some of its forms polytheistic, but has a concept of the supreme spirit, ◊Brahman, above the many divine manifestations. These include the triad of chief gods (the Trimurti): Brahma, Vishnu, and Siva (creator, preserver, and destroyer). Central to Hinduism are the beliefs in reincarnation and ◊karma; the oldest scriptures are the ◊*Vedas*. Temple worship is almost universally observed and there are many festivals.

Hinduism Sculpted dancing figure from the 13th-century Kesava Temple, Somnathpur, in the SW Indian state of Karnataka. In Hinduism, dancing is a potent symbol of the cosmic life cycle of creation, conservation, destruction, incarnation, and liberation. The creator god Siva is often portrayed dancing. *Sally Jenkins*

There are over 805 million Hindus worldwide. Women are not regarded as the equals of men but should be treated with kindness and respect. Muslim influence in N India led to the veiling of women and the restriction of their movements from about the end of the 12th century.

roots Hindu beliefs originated in the Indus Valley civilization about 4,500 years ago. Much of the tradition that is now associated with Hinduism stems from the ritual and religion of the Aryans who invaded N India about 3,000 years ago.

scriptures The *Veda* collection of hymns, compiled by the Aryans, was followed by the philosophical ◊*Upanishads*, centring on the doctrine of Brahman, and the epics *Rāmāyana* and *Mahābhārata* (which includes the *Bhagavad-Gītā*), all from before the Christian era.

beliefs Hindu belief and ritual can vary greatly even between villages. Some deities achieve widespread popularity such as Krishna, Hanuman, Lakshmi, and Durga; others, more localized and specialized, are referred to particularly in times of sickness or need. Some deities manifest themselves in different incarnations or avatars such as Rama or Krishna, both avatars of the god Vishnu.

Underlying this multifaceted worship is the creative strength of Brahman, the supreme being. Hindus believe that all living things are part of Brahman: they are sparks of atman or divine life that transmute from one body to another, sometimes descending into the form of a plant or an insect, sometimes the body of a human. This is all according to its karma or past actions which are the cause of its sufferings or joy as it rises and falls in samsara (the endless cycle of birth and death). Humans have the opportunity, through knowledge and devotion, to break the karmic chain and achieve final liberation, or moksha. The atman is then free to return to Brahman.

The creative force of the universe is recognized in the god Brahma. Once he has brought the cosmos into being, it is sustained by Vishnu and then annihilated by the god Siva, only to be created once more by Brahma. Vishnu and Siva are, respectively, the forces of light and darkness, preservation and destruction, with Brahma as the balancing force that enables the existence and interaction of life. The cosmos is seen as both real and an illusion (*maya*), since its reality is not lasting; the cosmos is itself personified as the goddess Maya.

practice Hinduism has a complex of rites and ceremonies performed within the framework of the *jati*, or caste system, under the supervision of the Brahman priests and teachers. In India, caste is traditionally derived from the four classes of early Hindu society: brahmans (priests), kshatriyas (nobles and warriors), vaisyas (traders and cultivators), and sudras (servants). A fifth class, the untouchables, regarded as polluting in its origins, remained (and still largely remains) on the edge of Hindu society. The Indian Constituent Assembly 1947 made discrimination against the Scheduled Castes or Depressed Classes illegal, but strong prejudice continues.

Western influence The International Society for Krishna Consciousness (ISKON), the Western organization of the Hare Krishna movement, was introduced to the West by Swami Prabhupada (1896–1977). Members are expected to lead ascetic lives. It is based on devotion to Krishna which includes study of the *Bhagavad-Gītā*, temple and home ritual, and the chanting of the name Hare (saviour) Krishna.

Hindu Kush mountain range in central Asia, length 800 km/500 mi, greatest height Tirich Mir, 7,690 m/25,239 ft, in Pakistan. The narrow Khyber Pass (53 km/33 mi long) connects Pakistan with Afghanistan and was used by ◊Babur and other invaders of India. The present road was built by the British in the Afghan Wars.

Hindustan ('land of the Hindus') the whole of India, but more specifically the plain of the Ganges and Jumna rivers, or that part of India N of the Deccan.

Hindustani member of the Indo-Iranian branch of the Indo-European language family, closely related to Hindi and Urdu and originating in the bazaars of Delhi. It is a ◊lingua franca in many parts of the Republic of India.

Hine Lewis Wickes 1874–1940. US sociologist and photographer. His dramatic photographs of child labour conditions in US factories at the beginning of the 20th century led to changes in state and local labour laws.

Hingis Martina 1980– . Czech-born Swiss tennis player. In 1996 she became the youngest ever winner of a Grand Slam title when she won the Wimbledon women's doubles title at the age of 15 years 282 days. In Jan 1997, at 16 years 92 days, she won the women's singles at the Australian Open. Three months later she became the youngest player to be ranked as number one in the world since the women's official rankings began.

hip-hop popular music originating in New York in the early 1980s, created with scratching (a percussive effect obtained by manually rotating a vinyl record) and heavily accented electronic drums behind a ◊rap vocal. Within a decade, ◊digital sampling had largely superseded scratching. The term 'hip-hop' also comprises break dancing and graffiti.

Hipparchus c. 190–c. 120 BC. Greek astronomer and mathematician. He invented trigonometry and calculated the lengths of the solar year and the lunar month, discovered the precession of the equinoxes, made a catalogue of 850 fixed stars, and advanced Eratosthenes' method of determining the situation of places on the Earth's surface by lines of latitude and longitude.

Hipparcos (acronym for ***high precision parallax collecting satellite***) satellite launched by the European Space Agency Aug 1989. Named after the Greek astronomer Hipparchus, it is the world's first ◊astrometry satellite and is providing precise positions, distances, colours, brightnesses, and apparent motions for over 100,000 stars.

hippie member of a youth movement of the late 1960s, also known as flower power, which originated in San Francisco, California, and was characterized by nonviolent anarchy, concern for the environment, and rejection of Western materialism. The hippies formed a politically outspoken, antiwar, artistically prolific counterculture in North America and Europe. Their colourful psychedelic style, inspired by drugs such as ◊LSD, emerged in fashion, graphic art, and music by bands such as Love (1965–71), the ◊Grateful Dead, Jefferson Airplane (1965–74), and ◊Pink Floyd.

Hippocrates c. 460–c. 377 BC. Greek physician, often called the founder of medicine. Important Hippocratic ideas include cleanliness (for patients and physicians), moderation in eating and drinking, letting nature take its course, and living where the air is good. He believed that health was the result of the 'humours' of the body being in balance; imbalance caused disease. These ideas were later adopted by ◊Galen. He wrote the ***Hippocratic Oath***, which embodies the essence of medical ethics.

'Life is short, science is so long to learn, opportunity is elusive, experience is dangerous, judgement is difficult.'

HIPPOCRATES *Aphorisms* 1

Hippolytus in Greek mythology, the son of Theseus. When he rejected the love of his stepmother, Phaedra, she falsely accused him of making advances to her and turned Theseus against him. Killed by Poseidon at Theseus' request, he was in some accounts of the legend restored to life when his innocence was proven.

hippopotamus (Greek 'river horse') large herbivorous, even-toed hoofed mammal of the family Hippopotamidae. The common hippopotamus *Hippopotamus amphibius* is found in Africa. It weighs up to 3,200 kg/7,040 lb, stands about 1.6 m/5.25 ft tall, and has a brown or slate-grey skin. It is an endangered species.

Hippos are social and gregarious animals. Because they dehydrate rapidly (at least twice as quickly as humans), they must stay close to water. When underwater, adults need to breath every 2–5 min and calves every 30 sec. When out of water, their skin exudes an oily red fluid that protects against the Sun's ultraviolet rays. The hippopotamus spends the day wallowing in rivers or waterholes, only emerging at night to graze. It can eat up to 25–40 kg/55–88 lb of grass each night.

There are an estimated 157,000 hippos in Africa (1993), but they are under threat from hunters because of the value of their meat, hides, and large canine teeth (up to 0.5 m/1.6 ft long), which are used as a substitute for ivory.

hire purchase (HP) form of credit under which the buyer pays a deposit and makes instalment payments at fixed intervals over a certain period for a particular item. The buyer has immediate possession, but does not own the item until the final instalment has been paid.

Hirohito (regnal era name ***Shōwa***) 1901–1989. Emperor of Japan from 1926, when he succeeded his father Taishō (Yoshihito). After the defeat of Japan in World War II 1945, he was made a figurehead monarch by the US-backed 1946 constitution. He is believed to have played a reluctant role in General ◊Tōjō's prewar expansion plans. He was succeeded by his son ◊Akihito.

As the war turned against Japan from June 1942 he belatedly began to exert more influence over his government but was too late to act before the atomic bombs were dropped on Hiroshima and Nagasaki. His speech on Japanese radio 15 Aug 1945 announcing the previous day's surrender was the first time a Japanese emperor had directly addressed his people.

Hiroshige Andō 1797–1858. Japanese artist. He was one of the leading exponents of ◊ukiyo-e prints, an art form whose flat, decorative style and choice of everyday subjects influenced such artists as James Whistler and Vincent van Gogh. His landscape prints, often employing snow or rain to create atmosphere, include *Tōkaidō gojūsan tsugi/53 Stations on the Tōkaidō Highway* 1833.

Hirohito Hirohito, Emperor of Japan 1926–89. Hirohito was the titular leader of Japan during World War II and survived as monarch after the Japanese surrender, providing stability and continuity within the country until his death 1989. *Topham*

At first it was a giant column that soon took the shape of a supramundane mushroom.

On the explosion of the first atomic bomb over HIROSHIMA
William L Laurence in the *New York Times* 1945

Hiroshige was born in Edo (now Tokyo), and most of his subjects were taken from the vicinity of Edo or were scenes on the old Tokaido highway between Edo and Kyoto. His last series, *Meishō Edo hyakkei/100 Famous Views of Edo* 1856–58, was incomplete at his death. He is thought to have made over 5,000 different prints.

Hiroshima industrial city and port on the south coast of Honshu Island, Japan, destroyed by the first wartime use of an atomic bomb 6 Aug 1945. The city has largely been rebuilt since the war; population (1994) 1,077,000.

Towards the end of World War II the city was utterly devastated by the first US atomic bomb dropped by the *Enola Gay*; the strike on ◊Nagasaki followed three days later. More than 10 sq km/4 sq mi were obliterated, with very heavy damage outside that area. Casualties totalled at least 137,000 out of a population of 343,000: 78,150 were found dead, others died later. By 1995 the death toll, which included individuals who had died from radiation-related diseases in recent years, had climbed to 192,000.

Hispaniola (Spanish 'little Spain') West Indian island, first landing place of Columbus in the New World, 6 Dec 1492; it is now divided into ◊Haiti and the ◊Dominican Republic.

Hiss Alger 1904–1996. US diplomat and civil servant. A former State Department official, he was accused of spying for the USSR and was imprisoned 1950 for perjury when he denied the charge. The official Soviet commission on KGB archives reported in 1992 that Hiss had never been a spy, although other historical evidence suggests a still inconclusive verdict.

Hiss was president of the Carnegie Endowment for International Peace when he was accused in 1948 by a former Soviet agent, Whittaker Chambers (1901–1961), of having passed information to the USSR during the period 1926–37. He was convicted of perjury for swearing before the House Un-American Activities Committee that he had not spied for the USSR. The case was decisive in shaping the anticommunist witch-hunts of Senator Joseph ◊McCarthy.

That men do not learn very much from the lessons of history is the most important of all the lessons that history has to teach.

On HISTORY
Aldous Huxley 'Case of Voluntary Ignorance' *Collected Essays*

histamine inflammatory substance normally released in damaged tissues, which also accounts for many of the symptoms of ◊allergy. It is an amine, $C_5H_9N_3$. Substances that neutralize its activity are known as ◊antihistamines. Histamine was first described 1911 by British physiologist Henry Dale (1875–1968).

histology study of plant and animal tissue by visual examination, usually with a ◊microscope. Stains are often used to highlight structural characteristics such as the presence of starch or distribution of fats.

histology in medicine, the laboratory study of cells and tissues.

historical materialism the application of the principles of ◊dialectical materialism to history and sociology. This decrees that the social, political, and cultural superstructure of a society is determined by its economic base and that developments are therefore governed by laws with no room for the influence of individuals. In this theory, change occurs through the meeting of opposing forces (thesis and antithesis) which leads to the production of a higher force (synthesis).

historical novel fictional prose narrative set in the past. Literature set in the historic rather than the immediate past has always abounded, but in the West, Walter Scott began the modern tradition by setting imaginative romances of love, impersonation, and betrayal in a past based on known fact; his use of historical detail, and subsequent imitations of this technique by European writers, gave rise to the genre.

Television has brought back murder into the home – where it belongs.

ALFRED HITCHCOCK
Quoted in the *Observer* 19 Dec 1965

Some historical novels of the 19th century were overtly nationalistic, but most were merely novels set in the past to heighten melodrama while providing an informative framework; the genre was used by Alessandro Manzoni, Victor Hugo, Charles Dickens, and James Fenimore Cooper, among many others. In the 20th century the historical novel also became concerned with exploring psychological states and the question of differences in outlook and mentality in past periods. Examples of this are Robert Graves' novels about the Roman emperor *I, Claudius* and *Claudius the God*, and Margaret Yourcenar's *Memoirs of Hadrian*.

historicism in architecture and the visual arts, the copying of styles from the past, for example the Gothic and Classical revivals of the 19th century. It implies a detailed imitation, rather than the ironic reference that is common in ◊Post-Modernism or the selection of existing styles to combine with an artist's own work as in ◊eclecticism.

history record of the events of human societies. The earliest surviving historical records are inscriptions concerning the achievements of Egyptian and Babylonian kings. As a literary form in the Western world, historical writing, or historiography, began in the 5th century BC with the Greek Herodotus, who was first to pass beyond the limits of a purely national outlook. Contemporary historians make extensive use of statistics, population figures, and primary records to justify historical arguments.

A generation after Herodotus, Thucydides brought to history a strong sense of the political and military ambitions of his native Athens. His close account of the ◊Peloponnesian War was continued by ◊Xenophon. Later Greek history and Roman history tended towards rhetoric; Sallust tried to recreate the style of Thucydides, but Livy wrote an Augustan history of his city and its conquests, while Tacitus expressed his cynicism about the imperial dynasty.

Medieval history was dominated by a religious philosophy sustained by the Christian church. English chroniclers of this period are Bede, William of Malmesbury, and Matthew Paris. France produced great chroniclers of contemporary events in Jean Froissart and Philippe Comines. The Renaissance revived historical writing and the study of history both by restoring classical models and by creating the science of textual criticism. A product of the new secular spirit was Machiavelli's *History of Florence* 1520–23.

This critical approach continued into the 17th century but the 18th century ◊Enlightenment disposed of the attempt to explain history in theological terms, and an interpretive masterpiece was produced by Edward Gibbon, *The Decline and Fall of the Roman Empire* 1776–88. An attempt to formulate a historical method and a philosophy of history, that of the Italian Giovanni Vico, remained almost unknown until the 19th century. Romanticism left its mark on 19th-century historical writing in the tendency to exalt the contribution of the individual 'hero', and in the introduction of a more colourful and dramatic style and treatment, variously illustrated in the works of the French historian Jules Michelet and the British writers Thomas Carlyle and Thomas Macaulay.

During the 20th century the study of history has been revolutionized, partly through the contributions of other disciplines, such as the sciences and anthropology. The deciphering of the Egyptian and Babylonian inscriptions was of great importance. Researchers and archaeologists have traced developments in prehistory, and have revealed forgotten civilizations such as that of Crete. Anthropological studies of primitive society and religion, which began with James Frazer's *Golden Bough* 1890, have attempted to analyse the bases of later forms of social organization and belief. The changes brought about by the Industrial Revolution and the accompanying perception of economics as a science forced historians to turn their attention to economic questions. Karl Marx's attempt to find in economic development the most significant, although not the only, determining factor in social change, has influenced many historians. History from the point of view of ordinary people is now recognized as an important element in historical study. Associated with this is the collection of spoken records known as ***oral history***.

history of ideas discipline that studies the history and development of ideas and theories in terms of their origins and influences. The historian of ideas seeks to understand their significance in their original contexts.

Hitchcock Suspense, melodrama, and fleeting personal appearances are the hallmarks of Alfred Hitchcock's films. A meticulous director, a supreme technician and visual artist, Hitchcock contributed significantly to the growth of cinema as an art form.

Hitler German Nazi dictator Adolf Hitler with Italian leader Benito Mussolini in Berlin. In the late 1930s Hitler was rapidly expanding German power and influence, and an alliance with Mussolini meant further influence in the Mediterranean and an ally for Hitler's policy of annexing Austria and the Sudetenland. *Topham*

Hitachi Japanese electrical and electronic company, one of the world's largest and most diversified manufacturers of industrial machinery. It has offices in 39 countries and over 100 factories, which manufacture 40,000 different products, ranging from electrical home appliances and stereo and high-tech telecommunications equipment (for which it is best known) to heavy industrial machinery, such as hydroelectric turbines and nuclear generators. As one of Japan's largest private employers, it had net sales 1990–91 of over £31 billion.

Hitchcock Alfred (Joseph) 1899–1980. English film director, a US citizen from 1955. A master of the suspense thriller, he was noted for his meticulously drawn storyboards that determined his camera angles and for his cameo walk-ons in his own films. His *Blackmail* 1929 was the first successful British talking film; *The Thirty-Nine Steps* 1935 and *The Lady Vanishes* 1939 are British suspense classics. He went to Hollywood 1940, and his work there included *Rebecca* 1940, *Notorious* 1946, *Strangers on a Train* 1951, *Rear Window* 1954, *Vertigo* 1958, *Psycho* 1960, and *The Birds* 1963.

Hitler Adolf 1889–1945. German Nazi dictator, born in Austria. He was *Führer* (leader) of the Nazi Party from 1921 and wrote *Mein Kampf/My Struggle* 1925–27. As chancellor of Germany from 1933 and head of state from 1934, he created a dictatorship by playing party and state institutions against each other and continually creating new offices and appointments. His position was not seriously challenged until the failed ◊July Plot 1944 to assassinate him. In foreign affairs, he reoccupied the Rhineland and formed an alliance with the Italian Fascist Benito ◊Mussolini 1936, annexed Austria 1938, and occupied the Sudetenland under the ◊Munich Agreement. The rest of Czechoslovakia was annexed March 1939. The ◊Ribbentrop–Molotov pact was followed in Sept by the invasion of Poland and the declaration of war by Britain and France (see ◊World War II). He committed suicide as Berlin fell.

Leader of the German Workers' Party (Nazi Party) from 1921, Hitler instituted a programme that mixed nationalism with ◊anti-Semitism. He wrote his political testament, *Mein Kampf* while in prison following an unsuccessful uprising Munich 1932.

Hittite member of any of a succession of peoples who inhabited Anatolia and N Syria from the 3rd millennium to the 1st millennium BC. The city of Hattusas (now Boğazköy in central Turkey) became the capital of a strong kingdom which overthrew the Babylonian Empire. After a period of eclipse the Hittite New Empire became a great power (about 1400–1200 BC), which successfully waged war with Egypt. The Hittite language is an Indo-European language.

The original Hittites inhabited a number of city-states in E Anatolia, one of which, Hatti, gained supremacy over the others. An Indo-European people invaded the country about 2000 BC, made themselves the ruling class, and intermarried with the original inhabitants. The Hittites developed advanced military, political, and legal systems. The New Empire concluded a peace treaty with Egypt 1269 BC, but was eventually overthrown by the Sea Peoples. Small Hittite states then arose in N Syria, the most important of which was ◊Carchemish; these were conquered by the Assyrians in the 8th century BC. Carchemish was conquered 717.

The Hittites used a cuneiform script, modelled on the Babylonian, for ordinary purposes, and a hieroglyphic script for inscriptions on monuments. The Hittite royal archives were discovered at Hattusas 1906–07 and deciphered 1915.

Hittite A relief sculpture adorning a chamber wall at the holy Hittite site of Yazilikaya, in central Anatolia, Turkey. The figures are armed with sicklelike objects. The grotto of Yazilikaya is situated 2 km/1.2 mi north-east of the citadel of Hattusas, capital of the Hittite kingdom. The walls of the grotto contain carved images of gods and goddesses. *Corbis*

Hoban Perhaps James Hoban's most famous building, the White House in Washington DC, USA. It is based on the design of Leinster Hall near Dublin and was designed in 1792. *Corel*

HIV abbreviation for ***human immunodeficiency virus*** the infectious agent that is believed to cause ◊AIDS. It was first discovered in 1983 by Luc Montagnier of the Pasteur Institute in Paris, who called it lymphocyte-associated virus (LAV). Independently, US scientist Robert Gallo of the National Cancer Institute in Bethesda, Maryland, claimed its discovery in 1984 and named it human T-lymphocytotrophic virus 3 (HTLV-III).

transmission Worldwide, heterosexual activity accounts for three-quarters of all HIV infections. In addition to heterosexual men and women, high-risk groups are homosexual and bisexual men, prostitutes, intravenous drug-users sharing needles, and haemophiliacs and other patients treated with contaminated blood products. The virus has a short life outside the body, which makes transmission of the infection by methods other than sexual contact, blood transfusion, and shared syringes extremely unlikely.

the development of HIV Many people who have HIV in their blood are not ill; in fact, it was initially thought that during the delay between infection with HIV and the development of AIDS, the virus lay dormant. However, US researchers estimated in 1995 that HIV reproduces at a rate of a billion viruses a day, even in individuals with no symptoms, but is held at bay by the immune system producing enough white blood cells (CD4 cells) to destroy them. Gradually, the virus mutates so much that the immune system is unable to continue to counteract; people with advanced AIDS have virtually no CD4 cells remaining. These results indicate the importance of treating HIV-positive individuals before symptoms develop, rather than delaying treatment until the onset of AIDS.

HIV statistics In 1997 there were an estimated just under 30 million (1% of the world's adult population) HIV infections in the world, with around 1,000 infected babies born every day. In Sub-Saharan Africa there were an estimated 20 million HIV sufferers, in South and Southeast Asia 6 million, in South America 1.3 million, in North America 860,000, and Western Europe 150,000 (figures released by the United Nations AIDS programme, UNAIDS).

vaccine Trials of an HIV vaccine began in the USA in June 1998 with 5,000 high-risk volunteers (gay men and those with HIV-infected partners) receiving the vaccine or a placebo. Significant results will take several years to become apparent.

Hmong a SE Asian highland people. They are predominantly hill farmers, rearing pigs and cultivating rice and grain, and many are involved in growing the opium poppy. Estimates of the size of the Hmong population vary between 1.5 million and 5 million, the greatest number being in China. Although traditional beliefs remain important, many have adopted Christianity. Their language belongs to the Sino-Tibetan family. The names Meo or Miao, sometimes used to refer to the Hmong, are considered derogatory.

hoatzin tropical bird *Opisthocomus hoatzin* found only in the Amazon, resembling a small pheasant in size and appearance. The bill is thick and the facial skin blue. Adults are olive with white markings

hoatzin The hoatzin lives in riverside forests in northern South America. Young hoatzin are unusual in that they leave their nests in the trees soon after hatching and clamber about using two hooked claws at the bend of each wing.

Hobbema *The Avenue, Middleharnis* 1689 by Meindert Hobbema (National Gallery, London). One of the best-known images of Dutch landscape painting, *The Avenue* is based on a carefully-balanced contrast between the vast, windswept sky and the neat, well-husbanded landscape. *Corbis*

above and red-brown below. It is the only bird belonging to the family Opisthocomidae, order Galliformes.

Hoban James C 1762–1831. Irish-born architect. He emigrated to the USA where he designed the White House, Washington, DC; he also worked on the Capitol and other public buildings.

Hobart capital and port of Tasmania, Australia; population (1994) 194,200. Products include zinc, textiles, and paper. Founded 1804 as a penal colony, it was named after Lord Hobart, then secretary of state for the colonies.

The University of Tasmania, established 1890, is at Hobart.

Hobbema Meindert Lubbertszoon 1638–1709. Dutch landscape painter. A pupil of Ruisdael, his early work is derivative, but later works are characteristically realistic and unsentimental. His best-known work is *The Avenue, Middelharnis* 1689 (National Gallery, London).

He was the outstanding interpreter of the Dutch rural picturesque in the second half of the 17th century, painting woods, water mills, winding tracks, streams and cottages with delightful sympathy. There is much that is obscure about his career and the chronology of his work. He obtained a post in the excise at 30, and it has been assumed that he then gave up painting, with the exception of his masterpiece, *The Avenue, Middelharnis*. He died in poverty and was buried in the pauper section of an Amsterdam cemetery. His works are now widely distributed in the world's galleries.

Hobbes Thomas 1588–1679. English political philosopher and the first thinker since Aristotle to attempt to develop a comprehensive theory of nature, including human behaviour. In *Leviathan* 1651, he advocates absolutist government as the only means of ensuring order and security; he saw this as deriving from the ◊social contract.

Hobbes analysed everything, including human behaviour, in terms of matter and motion. He is now best remembered for his political philosophy, in which he defended absolute sovereignty as the only way to prevent life from being 'nasty, brutish, and short', as he alleged it was in a state of nature. He based this absolute sovereignty on a social contract among individuals, but the sovereign has duties only to God.

Hobitt, The or ***There and Back Again*** fantasy for children by J R R Tolkien, published in the UK 1937. It describes the adventures of Bilbo Baggins, a 'hobbit' (small humanoid) in an ancient world, Middle-Earth, populated by dragons, dwarves, elves, and other mythical creatures, including the wizard Gandalf. *The Hobbit*, together with Tolkien's later trilogy *The Lord of the Rings* 1954–55, achieved cult status in the 1960s. By 1991, 35 million copies had been sold worldwide, more than any other work of fiction.

Hobbs Jack (John Berry) 1882–1963. English cricketer who represented his country 61 times. In all first-class cricket he scored a world record 61,237 runs, including a record 197 centuries in a career that lasted nearly 30 years.

hobby small falcon *Falco subbuteo* found across Europe and N Asia. It is about 30 cm/1 ft long, with a grey back, streaked front, and chestnut thighs. It is found in open woods and heaths, and feeds on insects and small birds. It nests in southern Britain, migrating south of the Sahara in winter. It uses abandoned nests, often of crows, instead of building its own.

Ho Chi Minh adopted name of Nguyen Tat Thanh 1890–1969. North Vietnamese communist politician, premier and president 1954–69. Having trained in Moscow shortly after the Russian Revolution, he headed the communist ◊Vietminh from 1941 and fought against the French during the ◊Indochina War 1946–54, becoming president and prime minister of the republic at the armistice. Aided by the communist bloc, he did much to develop industrial potential. He relinquished the premiership 1955, but continued as president. In the years before his death, Ho successfully led his country's fight against US-aided South Vietnam in the ◊Vietnam War 1954–75.

Ho Chi Minh City (until 1976 ***Saigon***) chief port and industrial city of S Vietnam; population (1989) 3,169,100. Industries include shipbuilding, textiles, rubber, and food products. Saigon was the capital of the Republic of Vietnam (South Vietnam) from 1954 to 1976, when it was renamed.

Ho Chi Minh Trails North Vietnamese troop and supply routes to South Vietnam via Laos during the ◊Vietnam War 1954–75. In an unsuccessful attempt to disrupt the trail between 1964 and 1973, the USA dropped 2 million tonnes of bombs in Laos, a country with which it was not at war.

Hochschüle für Gestaltung German educational institution for design 1951–68, established in Ulm to carry on the work of the prewar ◊Bauhaus which had been closed by the Nazis. The school was notable for its rigorous commitment to a systematic design methodology and for the severe Minimalism of the designs which emerged from it.

The first director was Max Bill (1908–). He was followed by Tomas Maldonado (1922–), an Argentinian theoretician. The majority of Germany's most influential industrial designers of the postwar years, Hans Gugelot (1920–1965) among them, graduated from the Hochschüle.

hockey game played with hooked sticks and a ball, the object being to hit a small solid ball into the goal. It is played between two teams, each of not more than 11 players. Hockey has been an Olympic sport since 1908 for men and since 1980 for women. In North America it is known as 'field hockey', to distinguish it from ◊ice hockey.

The ground is 91.5 m/100 yd long and 54.9 m/60 yd wide. Goals, 2.13 m/7 ft high and 3.65 m/4 yd wide, are placed within a striking circle of a 14.64 m/16 yd radius, from which all shots at goal must be made. The white ball weighs about 155 grams/5.5 oz, circumference about 228 mm/9 in. Most sticks are about 91 cm/3 ft long and they must not exceed 50 mm/2 in diameter. The game is started by a 'push-back' (or 'bully-off'). The ball may be stopped with the hand, but not held, picked up, thrown or kicked, except by the goalkeeper in his or her own striking circle. If the ball is sent into touch, it is returned to play by a 'push-in'. The game is divided into two 35-minute periods; it is controlled by two umpires, one for each half of the field. A game using hooked sticks, not unlike the contemporary ones, was played by the ancient Greeks, and under the names of 'hurley' and 'shinty' a primitive form of the game was played in Ireland and Scotland.

The rules of the game are established by the International Hockey Rules Board, a committee set up by the International Hockey Federation. They are common to both the men's and women's games. The women's game is governed by the All England Women's Hockey Association, founded 1895. Indoor hockey is becoming popular in the UK and Europe.

Hockney David 1937– . English painter and graphic artist, resident in California. He has experimented prolifically with technique, and has produced drawings, etchings (*Six Fairy Tales from the Brothers Grimm* 1970), photo collages, and sets for opera. A characteristic work is his portrait *Mr and Mrs Clark and Percy* 1971 (Tate Gallery, London).

Born in Yorkshire, he studied at Bradford School of Art and then at the Royal College of Art, London, 1959–1962. One of the best-known figures in British Pop art, he exhibited at the Young Contemporaries Show 1961 and held his first solo exhibition 1963, showing paintings that exploited pictorial ambiguities in a witty, self-consciously naive manner.

In 1964 he went to California and many of his later paintings are concerned with Los Angeles life. The swimming pool became one of his favourite subjects, illustrating a preoccupation with surface pattern and effects of light.

Hockney English artist David Hockney in 1975 with his sets for Stravinsky's opera *The Rake's Progress*. One of the leading figures of Pop art, Hockney developed a colourful, graphic style that lent itself to bold and innovative stage designs. *Corbis*

Hodgkin British crystallographer Dorothy Hodgkin, who determined the structure of penicillin and vitamin B_{12} using crystallographic methods. Hodgkin became the third woman to win a Nobel prize 1964 (for chemistry) and was awarded the Order of Merit 1965 – the first woman to receive the award since Florence Nightingale. *Image Select (UK) Ltd*

As well as illustrations to Grimm, he has produced a series of etchings updating Hogarth's *The Rake's Progress* 1963. In 1975 he designed the sets and costumes for the Glyndebourne Festival Theatre production of Igor Stravinsky's opera *The Rake's Progress*. He has also designed sets at La Scala, Milan, and the Metropolitan Opera House, New York.

Hoddle Glen 1957– . English footballer. In 1996, at the age of 38, Hoddle became the manager of the England team.

An elegant midfield player with brilliant passing skills, he played 484 games for Tottenham Hotspur (1975–87), scoring 106 goals. In 1979 he won the first of 53 full England caps, but despite his abundant talent was never guaranteed a regular place in the side. He enjoyed a season with Monaco in the French League (1987–88) before a knee injury appeared to have ended his career. In 1991, be became player-manager of Swindon Town, moving to Chelsea in 1993. In 1996, just one year after retiring as a player, he was appointed England manager in succession to Terry Venables. However in February 1999 he was dismissed from this post following his comment that disabled people are being punished for sins in a former life.

Hodgkin Dorothy Mary Crowfoot 1910–1994. English biochemist who analysed the structure of penicillin, insulin, and vitamin B_{12}. Hodgkin was the first to use a computer to analyse the molecular structure of complex chemicals, and this enabled her to produce three-dimensional models. Nobel Prize for Chemistry 1964.

Hodgkin studied the structures of calciferol (vitamin D_2), lumisterol, and cholesterol iodide, the first complex organic molecule to be determined completely by the pioneering technique of X-ray crystallography, a physical analysis technique devised by Lawrence Bragg (1890–1971), and at the time used only to confirm formulas predicted by organic chemical techniques. She also used this technique to determine the structure of penicillin, insulin, and vitamin B_{12}.

Hodgkin Howard 1932– . English painter. Influenced by Italian miniatures, his small pictures are full of movement and colour, the paint frequently spreading over the frame. Though they have a specific subject – often an encounter between friends – they are abstract, the artist slowly reducing an incident or scene to a few broad brush strokes and patterned dabs. An example is *Dinner at Smith Square* 1975–79 (Tate Gallery, London).

Hodgkin Thomas 1798–1866. English physician who first recognized Hodgkin's disease. He pioneered the use of the stethoscope in the UK. He was also the first person to stress the importance of postmortem examinations.

Hodgkin's disease or ***lymphadenoma*** rare form of cancer mainly affecting the lymph nodes and spleen. It undermines the immune system, leaving the sufferer susceptible to infection.

However, it responds well to radiotherapy and ◊cytotoxic drugs, and long-term survival is usual.

Hoess Rudolf Franz 1900–1947. German commandant of ◊Auschwitz concentration camp 1940–43. Under his control, more than 2.5 million people were exterminated. Arrested by Allied military police in 1946, he was handed over to the Polish authorities, who tried and executed him in 1947.

Hoffa Jimmy (James Riddle) 1913–c. 1975. US labour leader, president of the International Brotherhood of Teamsters (transport workers) from 1957. He was jailed 1967–71 for attempted bribery of a federal court jury after he was charged with corruption. He was released by President Nixon with the stipulation that he did not engage in union activities, but was evidently attempting to reassert influence when he disappeared. He is generally believed to have been murdered.

Hoffman Dustin 1937– . US actor. He became popular in the 1960s with his unconventional looks, short stature, and versatility. He won Academy Awards for his performances in *Kramer vs Kramer* 1979 and *Rain Man* 1988. His other films include *The Graduate* 1967, *Midnight Cowboy* 1969, *Little Big Man* 1970, *All the President's Men* 1976, *Tootsie* 1982, *Hook* 1991, and *Outbreak* 1995. He appeared on Broadway in the 1984 revival of *Death of a Salesman*, also filmed for television 1985.

Hoffmann Josef 1870–1956. Austrian architect. Influenced by Art Nouveau, he was one of the founders of the Wiener Werkstätte/Vienna Workshops (a modern design cooperative of early 20th-century Vienna), and a pupil of Otto ◊Wagner. One of his best-known works is the Purkersdorf Sanatorium 1903–05.

Hoffman's voltameter in chemistry, an apparatus for collecting gases produced by the ◊electrolysis of a liquid.

It consists of a vertical E-shaped glass tube with taps at the upper ends of the outer limbs and a reservoir at the top of the central limb. Platinum electrodes fused into the lower ends of the outer limbs are connected to a source of direct current. At the beginning of an experiment, the outer limbs are completely filled with electrolyte by opening the taps. The taps are then closed and the current switched on. Gases evolved at the electrodes bubble up the outer limbs and collect at the top, where they can be measured.

Hofmeister Wilhelm Friedrich Benedikt 1824–1877. German botanist. He studied plant development and determined how a plant embryo, lying within a seed, is itself formed out of a single fertilized egg (ovule). He also discovered that mosses and ferns display an alternation of generations, in which the plant has two forms, spore-forming and gamete-forming.

hog member of the ◊pig family. The river hog *Potamochoerus porcus* lives in Africa, south of the Sahara. Reddish or black, up to 1.3 m/4.2 ft long plus tail, and 90 cm/3 ft at the shoulder, this gregarious animal roots for food in many types of habitat. The giant forest hog *Hylochoerus meinerzthageni* lives in thick forests of central Africa and grows up to 1.9 m/6 ft long.

Hogan Paul 1940– . Australian TV comic, film actor, and producer. The box-office hit *Crocodile Dundee* (considered the most profitable film in Australian history) 1986 and *Crocodile Dundee II* 1988 brought him international fame.

Hogarth William 1697–1764. English painter and engraver. He produced portraits and moralizing genre scenes, such as the series of prints *A Rake's Progress* 1735 (Soane Museum, London). His portraits are remarkably direct and full of character, for example *Heads of Six of Hogarth's Servants* about 1750–55 (Tate Gallery, London).

He published *A Harlot's Progress*, a series of six engravings, 1732. Other series followed, including *Marriage à la Mode* 1745, *Industry and Idleness* 1749, and *The Four Stages of Cruelty* 1751. In his book *The Analysis of Beauty* 1753 he attacked uncritical appreciation of the arts and proposed a double curved line as a key to visual beauty.

Hogg Quintin, British politician; see Lord ◊Hailsham.

hogweed genus of plants *Heracleum*, family Umbelliferae; the giant hogweed *H. mantegazzianum* grows over 3 m/9 ft high.

Hohenstaufen German family of princes, several members of which were Holy Roman emperors 1138–1208 and 1214–54. They were the first German emperors to make use of associations with Roman law and tradition to aggrandize their office, and included Conrad III; Frederick I (Barbarossa), the first to use the title Holy Roman emperor (previously the title Roman emperor was used); Henry VI; and Frederick II.

The last of the line, Conradin, was executed 1268 with the approval of Pope Clement IV while

An ego is just imagination. And if a man doesn't have imagination he'll be working for someone else for the rest of his life.

Jimmy Hoffa
Esquire

Hogarth, William *Shortly After the Marriage* by William Hogarth (National Gallery, London). This is the second scene from his six-picture series *Marriage à la Mode*, a satire tracing the downfall of a fashionable young couple. *Corbis*

'In Hollywood now when people die they don't say 'Did he leave a will?' but 'Did he leave a diary?''

On HOLLYWOOD
Liza Minnelli quoted in the *Observer Magazine* 13 Aug 1989

attempting to gain his Sicilian inheritance. They were supported by the Ghibellines (see ◊Guelph and Ghibelline), who took their name from the family's castle of Waiblingen.

Hohenzollern German family, originating in Württemberg, the main branch of which held the titles of ◊elector of Brandenburg from 1415, king of Prussia from 1701, and German emperor from 1871. The last emperor, Wilhelm II, was dethroned 1918 after the disastrous course of World War I. Another branch of the family were kings of Romania 1881–1947.

Hōjō family family that were regents (*shikken*) and effective rulers of Japan 1203–1333, during most of the Kamakura (◊Minamoto) shogunate. Among its members were Hōjō Yasutoki (regent 1224–42), Hōjō Tokiyori (regent 1245–56), and Hōjō Shigetoki (1198–1261), a high official whose writings on politics were influential.

Hokkaido formerly (until 1868) ***Yezo*** or ***Ezo*** northernmost of the four main islands of Japan, separated from Honshu to the S by Tsugaru Strait and from Sakhalin to the N by Soya Strait; area 83,500 sq km/32,231 sq mi; population (1995) 5,692,000, including 16,000 ◊Ainus. The capital is Sapporo. Natural resources include coal, mercury, manganese, oil and natural gas, timber, and fisheries. Coal mining and agriculture are the main industries.

Snow-covered for half the year, Hokkaido was little developed until the Meiji Restoration 1868 when disbanded samurai were settled here. Intensive exploitation followed World War II, including heavy and chemical industrial plants, development of electric power, and dairy farming. An artificial harbour has been constructed at Tomakomai, and an undersea rail tunnel links the old port of Hakodate with Aomori on Honshu, but remains as yet closed to public transport.

Hokusai Katsushika 1760–1849. Japanese artist. He was the leading printmaker of his time and a major exponent of ◊ukiyo-e. He published *Fugaku sanjū-rokkei/36 Views of Mount Fuji* about 1823–29, and produced outstanding pictures of almost every kind of subject – birds, flowers, courtesans, and scenes from legend and everyday life. *Under the Wave at Kanagawa* (British Museum, London) is typical.

Hokusai was born in Edo (now Tokyo) and studied wood engraving and then (under Katsukawa Shunshō, 1726–1792) painting and colour block printing. He devoted himself for the most part to the illustration of books. His many works include *Manga/Ten Thousand Sketches* 1814, a pictorial encyclopaedia of all aspects of Japanese life in 15 volumes; and his monochrome *One Hundred Views of Mount Fuji* 1835 in 3 volumes. His colour prints, *36 Views of Mount Fuji*, prove him a master of colour, his combination of greens, blues and yellows being a striking innovation. His knowledge of Western art is shown through his experiments with perspective.

Holbein Hans, ***the Elder*** c. 1464–1524. German painter. Painting mainly religious works, he belonged to the school of Rogier van der ◊Weyden and Hans Memling in his early paintings but showing Renaissance influence in such a work as the *Basilica of St Paul* 1502 (Staatsgalerie, Augsburg). His principal work is the altarpiece *St Sebastian* 1515–17 (Alte Pinakothek, Munich). He was the father of Hans Holbein the Younger.

Holbein A drawing of a scholar 1535 by Hans Holbein the Younger, J Paul Getty Museum, Malibu, California, USA. One of the finest portraitists of his day, with a subtle, minutely detailed style, Holbein left an invaluable record of the personalities of the 16th century. He died of plague in London. *Royal Academy of Arts*

Holbein Hans, ***the Younger*** 1497–1543. German painter and woodcut artist, a major figure of German Renaissance art. He is best known for his portraits, in particular those of the court of Henry VIII of England. One of the finest graphic artists of his age, he executed a woodcut series *Dance of Death* about 1525, and designed title pages for Luther's New Testament and Thomas More's *Utopia*.

He was born in Augsburg. In 1515 he went to Basel, where he became friendly with the scholar and humanist Erasmus and illustrated his *Praise of Folly*. He painted three portraits of Erasmus 1523.

He travelled widely in Europe and while in England as painter to Henry VIII he created a remarkable evocation of the English court in a series of graphic, perceptive portraits. Among his sitters were Henry VIII and Thomas More. During his time at the English court, he also painted miniature portraits, inspiring Nicholas Hilliard. One of his pictures of this period is *The (French) Ambassadors* 1533 (National Gallery, London).

Holden William. Stage name of William Franklin Beedle 1918–1981. US film actor. He was a star in the late 1940s and 1950s. He played a wide variety of leading roles in such films as *Sunset Boulevard* 1950, *Stalag 17* 1953, *Bridge on the River Kwai* 1957, *The Wild Bunch* 1969, and *Network* 1976.

Hölderlin (Johann Christian) Friedrich 1770–1843. German lyric poet. His poetry attempted to reconcile Christianity and the religious spirit of ancient Greece and to naturalize the forms of Greek verse in German. His work includes *Hyperion* 1797–99, an epistolary novel; translations of Sophocles 1804; and visionary poems such as the elegy 'Menons Klagen um Diotima/Menon's Lament for Diotima' and the brilliantly apocalyptic 'Patmos' 1806.

Although he upheld the ideals of classical Greece as a model for contemporary society, Hölderlin showed an awareness of the prevalent materialism and commercialism, which he condemned in many of his works. His translations of Sophocles' *Antigone* and *Oedipus* may have influenced his style, which is often based on Greek prosody. His poetry was not appreciated during his lifetime; Goethe and Schiller did not understand his aims, and only when he was rediscovered by Rainer Maria Rilke and Stefan George did Hölderlin become recognized as one of Germany's major poets.

holding company company with a controlling shareholding in one or more subsidiaries. In the UK, there are many large holding companies with varying degrees of control over their subsidiaries. They frequently provide cost-saving services such as marketing or financial expertise.

Holiday Billie. Stage name of Eleanora Gough McKay 1915–1959. US jazz singer, also known as 'Lady Day'. She made her debut in clubs in Harlem, New York, and became known for her emotionally charged delivery and idiosyncratic phrasing; she brought a blues feel to performances with swing bands. Songs she made her own include 'Stormy Weather', 'Strange Fruit', and 'I Cover the Waterfront'.

Holinshed Raphael, or ***Hollingshead*** c. 1520–c. 1580. English historian. He published two volumes of the *Chronicles of England, Scotland, and Ireland* 1578, which are a mixture of fact and legend. The *Chronicles* were used as a principal source by Elizabethan dramatists for their plots. Nearly all Shakespeare's historical plays (other than the Roman histories), as well as *Macbeth*, *King Lear*, and *Cymbeline*, are based on Holinshed's work.

holism in philosophy, the concept that the whole is greater than the sum of its parts.

holistic medicine umbrella term for an approach that virtually all alternative therapies profess, which considers the overall health and lifestyle profile of a patient, and treats specific ailments not primarily as conditions to be alleviated but rather as symptoms of more fundamental disease.

Holland popular name for the ◊Netherlands; also two provinces of the Netherlands, see ◊North Holland and ◊South Holland.

Holland John Philip 1840–1914. Irish engineer who developed some of the first submarines. He began work in Ireland in the late 1860s and emigrated to the USA 1873. His first successful boat was launched 1881 and, after several failures, he built the *Holland* 1893, which was bought by the US Navy two years later.

The first submarine, the *Fenian Ram* 1881, was built with financial support from the Irish Fenian society, who hoped to use it against England. Holland continued after 1895 to build submarines for various navies but died in poverty after his company became embroiled in litigation with backers.

Hollerith Herman 1860–1929. US inventor of a mechanical tabulating machine, the first device for data processing. Hollerith's tabulator was widely publicized after being successfully used in the 1890 census. The firm he established, the Tabulating Machine Company, was later one of the founding companies of ◊IBM.

holly tree or shrub of the genus *Ilex*, family Aquifoliaceae, including the English Christmas holly *I. aquifolium*, an evergreen with spiny, glossy leaves, small white flowers, and poisonous scarlet berries on the female tree. Leaves of the Brazilian holly *I. paraguayensis* are used to make the tea ***yerba maté***.

Holly Buddy. Stage name of Charles Hardin Holley 1936–1959. US rock-and-roll singer, guitarist, and songwriter. He had a distinctive, hiccuping vocal style and was an early experimenter with recording techniques. Many of his hits with his band, the Crickets, such as 'That'll Be the Day' 1957, 'Peggy Sue' 1957, and 'Maybe Baby' 1958, have become classics. He died in a plane crash.

hollyhock plant of the genus *Althaea* of the mallow family Malvaceae. *A. rosea*, originally a native of Asia, produces spikes of large white, yellow, or red flowers, 3 m/10 ft high when cultivated as a biennial.

Hollywood district in the city of Los Angeles, California; the centre of the US film industry from 1911. It is the home of film studios such as 20th Century Fox, MGM, Paramount, Columbia Pictures, United Artists, Disney, and Warner Brothers. Many film stars' homes are situated nearby in Beverly Hills and other communities adjacent to Hollywood.

Holmes Larry 1949– . US boxer. He was world heavyweight champion 1978–85. He made 20 successful title defences, stopping 15 of his opponents. In 1996, at the age of 46, he announced the end of his career.

Holmes, Sherlock fictitious private detective, created by the English writer Arthur Conan ◊Doyle in *A Study in Scarlet* 1887 and recurring in novels and stories until 1927. Holmes' ability to make inferences from slight clues always astonishes the narrator, Dr Watson.

The criminal mastermind against whom Holmes repeatedly pits his wits is Professor James Moriarty. Holmes is regularly portrayed at his home, 221b Baker Street, London, where he plays the violin and has bouts of determined action interspersed by lethargy and drug-taking. His characteristic pipe and deerstalker hat were the addition of an illustrator.

holmium (Latin *Holmia* 'Stockholm') silvery, metallic element of the ◊lanthanide series, symbol Ho, atomic number 67, relative atomic mass 164.93. It occurs in combination with other rare-earth metals and in various minerals such as gadolinite. Its compounds are highly magnetic.

The element was discovered in 1878, spectroscopically, by the Swiss chemists L Soret and Delafontaine, and independently in 1879 by Swedish chemist Per Cleve (1840–1905), who named it after Stockholm, near which it was found.

Holocaust, the the annihilation of an estimated 16 million people by the ◊Hitler regime 1933–45, principally in the numerous extermination and ◊concentration camps, most notably Auschwitz, Sobibor, Treblinka, and Maidanek in Poland, and Belsen, Buchenwald, and Dachau in Germany. Of the victims around 6 million were Jews (over 67% of European Jews); around 10 million Ukrainian,

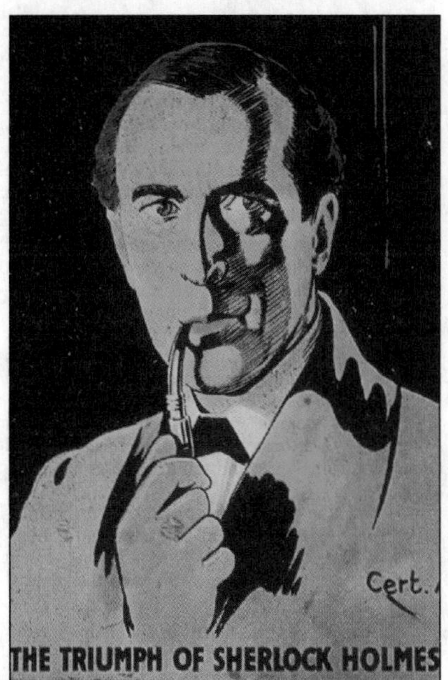

Holmes A cinema poster featuring Arthur Wontner as Sherlock Holmes, Arthur Conan Doyle's celebrated private detective. Holmes's pipe and deerstalker hat were the inventions of illustrator Sidney Paget. *Image Select (UK) Ltd*

Polish, and Russian civilians and prisoners of war, Romanies, socialists, homosexuals, and others (labelled 'defectives') were also imprisoned and/or exterminated. Victims were variously starved, tortured, experimented on, and worked to death. Millions were executed in gas chambers, shot, or hanged. It was euphemistically termed the ◊final solution (of the Jewish question). The precise death toll will never be known. Holocaust museums and memorial sites have been established in Israel and in other countries.

Holocene epoch of geological time that began 10,000 years ago, the second and current epoch of the Quaternary period. During this epoch the glaciers retreated, the climate became warmer, and humans developed significantly.

hologram three-dimensional image produced by ◊holography. Small, inexpensive holograms appear on credit cards and software licences to guarantee their authenticity.

holography method of producing three-dimensional (3-D) images by means of ◊laser light. Holography uses a photographic technique (involving the splitting of a laser beam into two beams) to produce a picture, or hologram, that contains 3-D information about the object photographed. Some holograms show meaningless patterns in ordinary light and produce a 3-D image only when laser light is projected through them, but reflection holograms produce images when ordinary light is reflected from them (as found on credit cards).

Although the possibility of holography was suggested as early as 1947, it could not be demonstrated until a pure coherent light source, the laser, became available 1963. The technique of holography is also applicable to sound, and bats may navigate by ultrasonic holography. Holographic techniques also have applications in storing dental records, detecting stresses and strains in construction and in retail goods, detecting forged paintings and documents, and producing three-dimensional body scans. The technique of detecting strains is of widespread application. It involves making two different holograms of an object on one plate, the object being stressed between exposures. If the object has distorted during stressing, the hologram will be greatly changed, and the distortion readily apparent.

Using holography, digital data can be recorded page by page in a crystal. In 1993 10,000 pages (100 megabytes) of digital data were stored in an iron-doped lithium nobate crystal measuring 1 cm^3.

Holst Gustav(us Theodore von) 1874–1934. English composer of distant Swedish descent. He wrote operas, including *Sávîtri* 1908 and *At the Boar's Head* 1924; ballets; choral works, including *Hymns from the Rig Veda* 1908–12 and *The Hymn of Jesus* 1917; orchestral suites, including *The Planets* 1914–16; and songs. He was a lifelong friend of Ralph ◊Vaughan Williams, with whom he shared an enthusiasm for English folk music. His musical style, although tonal and drawing on folk song, tends to be severe. He was the father of Imogen Holst (1907–), musicologist and his biographer.

Holy Alliance 'Christian Union of Charity, Peace, and Love' initiated by Alexander I of Russia 1815 and signed by every crowned head in Europe. The alliance became associated with Russian attempts to preserve autocratic monarchies at any price, and served as an excuse to meddle in the internal affairs of other states. Ideas of an international army acting in the name of the alliance were rejected by Britain and Austria 1818 and 1820.

Holy Communion another name for the ◊Eucharist, a Christian sacrament.

Holy Grail in medieval Christian legend, the dish or cup used by Jesus at the Last Supper, supposed to have supernatural powers. Together with the spear with which he was wounded at the Crucifixion, it was an object of quest by King Arthur's knights in certain stories incorporated in the Arthurian legend.

According to one story, the blood of Jesus was collected in the Holy Grail by ◊Joseph of Arimathaea at the Crucifixion, and he brought it to Britain where he allegedly built the first church, at Glastonbury. At least three churches in Europe possess vessels claimed to be the Holy Grail.

Holy Land Christian term for ◊Israel, because of its association with Jesus and the Old Testament.

Holy Loch western inlet of the Firth of Clyde, W Scotland, with a US nuclear submarine base.

Holyoake Keith Jacka 1904–1983. New Zealand National Party politician, prime minister 1957 (for two months) and 1960–72, during which time he was also foreign minister. He favoured a property-owning democracy.

holy orders Christian priesthood, as conferred by the laying on of hands by a bishop. It is held by the Roman Catholic, Eastern Orthodox, and Anglican churches to have originated in Jesus' choosing of the apostles.

The Anglican church has three orders (bishop, priest, and deacon); the Roman Catholic Church includes also subdeacon, acolyte, exorcist, reader, and door-keepers, and, outside the priesthood, ◊tertiary.

Holy Roman Empire empire of ◊Charlemagne and his successors, and the German Empire 962–1806, both being regarded as the Christian (hence 'holy') revival of the Roman Empire. At its height it comprised much of western and central Europe. See ◊Habsburg.

Holyrood House royal residence in Edinburgh, Scotland. The palace was built 1498–1503 on the site of a 12th-century abbey by James IV. It has associations with Mary, Queen of Scots, and Charles Edward, the Young Pretender.

Holy See the diocese of the ◊pope.

Holy Spirit third person of the Christian ◊Trinity, also known as the Holy Ghost or the Paraclete, usually depicted as a white dove.

Holy Week in the Christian church, the last week of ◊Lent, when Christians commemorate the events that led up to the crucifixion of Jesus. Holy Week begins on Palm Sunday and includes Maundy Thursday, which commemorates the Last Supper.

Home Counties the counties in close proximity to London, England: Hertfordshire, Essex, Kent, Surrey, Buckinghamshire, Berkshire, and formerly Middlesex.

home front the organized sectors of domestic activity in wartime, mainly associated with World Wars I and II. Features of the UK home front in World War II included the organization of the black-out, evacuation, air-raid shelters, the Home Guard, rationing, and distribution of gas masks. With many men on active military service, women were called upon to carry out jobs previously undertaken only by men.

Home Guard unpaid force formed in Britain May 1940 to repel the expected German invasion, and known until July 1940 as the Local Defence Volunteers. It consisted of men aged 17–65 who had not been called up, formed part of the armed forces of the crown, and was subject to military law. Over 2 million strong in 1944, it was disbanded 31 Dec 1945, but revived 1951, then placed on a reserve basis 1955, and ceased activities 1957.

Homelands Policy South Africa's apartheid policy which set aside ◊Black National States for black Africans.

Home Office British government department established 1782 to deal with all the internal affairs

holography Recording a transmission hologram. Light from a laser is divided into two beams. One beam goes directly to the photographic plate. The other beam reflects off the object before hitting the photographic plate. The two beams combine to produce a pattern on the plate which contains information about the 3-D shape of the object. If the exposed and developed plate is illuminated by laser light, the pattern can be seen as a 3-D picture of the object.

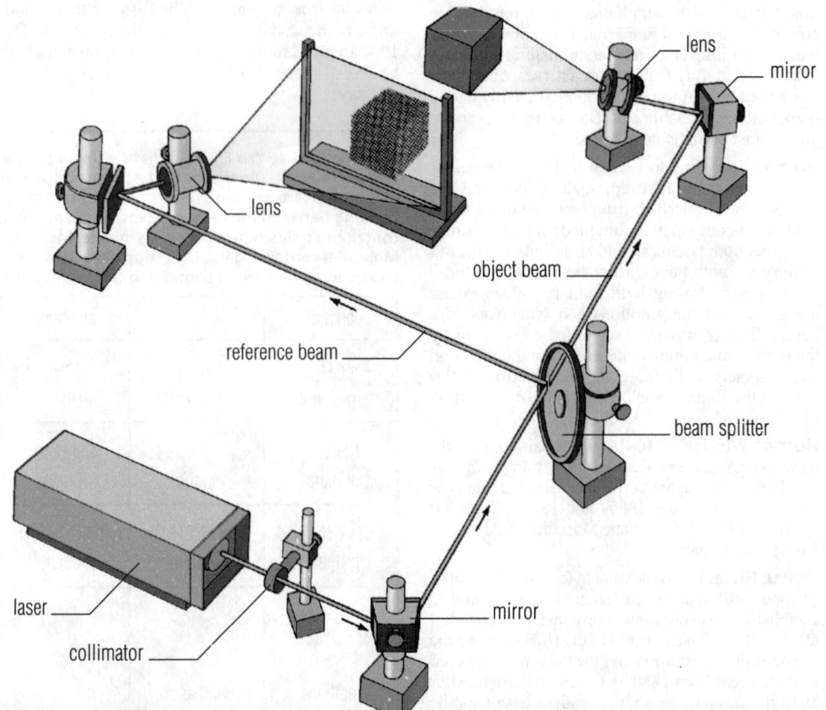

It has long been an axiom of mine that the little things are infinitely the most important.

SHERLOCK HOLMES
Arthur Conan Doyle
The Adventures of Sherlock Holmes 1892

This body, which was called and still calls itself the Holy Roman Empire, was by no means Holy, nor Roman, nor an Empire.

On the HOLY ROMAN EMPIRE
Voltaire *Essai sur les moeurs et l'esprit des nations*

Homer *Returning Fishing Boats* by US artist Winslow Homer (Mayer Collection). A leading US realist, who often turned to outdoor subjects, Homer was particularly successful at catching the subtle colours and tones of the sea. *Corbis*

of England except those specifically assigned to other departments. Responsibilities include the police, the prison service, immigration, race relations, and broadcasting. The home secretary, the head of the department, holds cabinet rank. There is a separate secretary of state for Scotland and another for Wales. The home secretary has certain duties in respect of the Channel Islands and the Isle of Man.

homeopathy alternative spelling of ◊***homoeopathy***.

homeostasis maintenance of a constant internal state in an organism, particularly with regard to pH, salt concentration, temperature, and blood sugar levels. Stable conditions are important for the efficient functioning of the ◊enzyme reactions within the cells, which affect the performance of the entire organism.

homeothermy maintenance of a constant body temperature in endothermic (warm-blooded) animals, by the use of chemical processes to compensate for heat loss or gain when external temperatures change. Such processes include generation of heat by the breakdown of food and the contraction of muscles, and loss of heat by sweating, panting, and other means.

Mammals and birds are homeotherms, whereas invertebrates, fish, amphibians, and reptiles are cold-blooded or poikilotherms. Homeotherms generally have a layer of insulating material to retain heat, such as fur, feathers, or fat (see ◊blubber). Their metabolism functions more efficiently due to homeothermy, enabling them to remain active under most climatic conditions.

Homer according to ancient tradition, the author of the Greek narrative epics, the ◊*Iliad* and the ◊*Odyssey* (both derived from oral tradition). Little is known about the man, but modern research suggests that both poems should be assigned to the 8th century BC, with the *Odyssey* the later of the two.

The epics, dealing with military values, social hierarchy, and the emotions and objectives of a heroic class of warriors, supported or opposed by the gods, had an immediate and profound effect on Greek society and culture and were a strong influence on the Roman poet ◊Virgil in the composition of his *Aeneid*.

'True friendship's laws are by this rule express'd, / Welcome the coming, speed the parting guest.'

HOMER
Odyssey translated by Alexander Pope

Homer Winslow 1836–1910. US painter and lithographer. A leading Realist, he is known for his vivid seascapes, in both oil and watercolour, most of which date from the 1880s and 1890s. *The Gulf Stream* 1899 (Metropolitan Museum of Art, New York) is an example.

Home Rule, Irish movement to repeal the Act of ◊Union 1801 that joined Ireland to Britain and to establish an Irish parliament responsible for internal affairs. In 1870 Isaac Butt (1813–1879) formed the Home Rule Association and the movement was led in Parliament from 1880 by Charles ◊Parnell. After 1918 the demand for an independent Irish republic replaced that for home rule.

Gladstone's Home Rule bills 1886 and 1893 were both defeated. A third bill was introduced by the Liberals in 1912, which aroused opposition in Ireland where the Protestant minority in Ulster feared domination by the Catholic majority. Ireland appeared on the brink of civil war but the outbreak of World War I rendered further consideration of Home Rule inopportune. In 1920 the Government of Ireland Act introduced separate parliaments in the North and South and led to the treaty 1921 that established the Irish Free State. ▷*See feature on pp. 550–551.*

Home Rule League organization demanding home rule for India, established Sept 1916. The Indian demand for home rule was inspired by the unsuccessful ◊Easter Rising in Ireland the previous April. It was launched by theosophist and educationalist Annie ◊Besant, who received support from the leading Indian nationalist Bal Gangadhar Tilak (1856–1920). She was briefly interned in Madras 1917. The organization faded after the introduction of the India Act 1919 and the initiation of Mahatma ◊Gandhi's non-cooperation campaign.

Homestead Act in US history, an act of Congress 1862 to encourage settlement of land in the west by offering 65-hectare/160-acre plots cheaply or even free to those willing to cultivate and improve the land for a stipulated amount of time. By 1900 about 32 million hectares/80 million acres had been distributed. Homestead lands are available to this day.

homicide in law, the killing of a human being. This may be unlawful, lawful, or excusable, depending on the circumstances. Unlawful homicides include ◊murder, ◊manslaughter, ◊infanticide, and causing death by dangerous driving. Lawful homicide occurs where, for example, a police officer is justified in killing a criminal in the course of apprehension or when a person is killed in self-defence or defence of others.

homoeopathy or ***homeopathy*** system of alternative medicine based on the principle that symptoms of disease are part of the body's self-healing processes, and on the practice of administering extremely diluted doses of natural substances found to produce in a healthy person the symptoms manifest in the illness being treated. Developed by German physician Samuel Hahnemann (1755–1843), the system is widely practised today as an alternative to allopathic (orthodox) medicine, and many controlled tests and achieved cures testify its efficacy.

In 1992, the German health authority, the *Bundesgesundheitsamt*, banned 50 herbal and homeopathic remedies containing ◊alkaloids because they are toxic, and set dose limits on 550 other natural remedies.

homogeneous reaction in chemistry, a reaction where there is no interface between the components. The term applies to all reactions where only gases are involved or where all the components are in solution.

homologous in biology, a term describing an organ or structure possessed by members of different taxonomic groups (for example, species, genera, families, orders) that originally derived from the same structure in a common ancestor. The wing of a bat, the arm of a monkey, and the flipper of a seal are homologous because they all derive from the forelimb of an ancestral mammal.

homologous series any of a number of series of organic chemicals with similar chemical properties in which members differ by a constant relative molecular mass.

Alkanes (paraffins), alkenes (olefins), and alkynes (acetylenes) form such series in which members differ in mass by 14, 12, and 10 atomic mass units respectively. For example, the alkane homologous series begins with methane (CH_4), ethane (C_2H_6), propane (C_3H_8), butane (C_4H_{10}), and pentane (C_5H_{12}), each member differing from the previous one by a CH_2 group (or 14 atomic mass units).

homophony music comprising a melody lead and accompanying harmony, in contrast to ***heterophony*** and ***polyphony*** in which different melody lines of equal importance are combined.

homosexuality sexual preference for, or attraction to, persons of one's own sex; in women it is referred to as ◊lesbianism.

Both sexes use the term 'gay'. Men and women who are attracted to both sexes are referred to as bisexual. The extent to which homosexual behaviour is caused by biological or psychological factors is an area of disagreement among experts.

homologous series The systematic naming of simple straight-chain organic molecules depends on two-part names. The first part of a name indicates the number of carbon atoms in the chain: one carbon, meth-; two carbons, eth-; three carbons, prop-; etc. The second part of each name indicates the kind of bonding between the carbon atoms, or the atomic group attached to the chain. The name of a molecule containing only single bonds ends in -ane. Molecules with double bonds have names ending with -ene. Molecules containing the OH group have names ending in -anol; those containing CO groups have names ending in -anone; those containing the carboxyl group -COOH- have names ending in -anoic acid.

alkane	alcohol	aldehyde	ketone	carboxylic acid	alkene
CH_4 methane	CH_3OH methanol	HCHO methanal	—	HCOOH methanoic acid	—
CH_3CH_3 ethane	CH_3CH_2OH ethanol	CH_3CHO ethanal	—	CH_3COOH ethanoic acid	CH_2CH_2 ethene
$CH_3CH_2CH_3$ propane	$CH_3CH_2CH_2OH$ propanol	CH_3CH_2CHO propanal	CH_3COCH_3 propanone	CH_3CH_2COOH propanoic acid	CH_2CHCH_3 propene
methane	methanol	methanal	propanone	methanoic acid	ethene

Although some ancient civilizations (notably ancient Greece and Confucian China) accepted homosexuality, other societies have punished homosexual acts. In 12th-century Europe sodomy was punishable by burning and since then homosexuals have suffered varying degrees of prejudice and prosecution. In the latter half of the 20th century discrimination against homosexuals has decreased as a result of pressure from campaigners (see ◊gay politics).

Laws relating to homosexuality and the age of consent differ from country to country. In some countries homosexual acts are illegal. In EU countries (except the Isle of Man) homosexuality between consenting adults is legal. Male homosexuals fear further discrimination as a result of the discovery of the AIDS virus.

In 1991 the Isle of Man rejected the decriminalization of male homosexual acts and is the only part of the European Union to treat homosexuality as criminal. In Denmark from 1989, gay men in a registered partnership have all the legal rights of married couples except for adoption. In Britain homosexuality ceased to be illegal over the age of 21 in 1967, and the age of consent was lowered to 18 in 1994.

homozygous in a living organism, having two identical ◊alleles for a given trait. Individuals homozygous for a trait always breed true; that is, they produce offspring that resemble them in appearance when bred with a genetically similar individual; inbred varieties or species are homozygous for almost all traits.

◊Recessive alleles are only expressed in the homozygous condition. See also ◊heterozygous.

Homs or ***Hums*** city, capital of Homs district, W Syria, near the Orontes River; population (1993) 537,000. Silk, cereals, and fruit are produced in the area, and industries include silk textiles, oil refining, and jewellery. ◊Zenobia, Queen of Palmyra, was defeated at Homs by the Roman emperor ◊Aurelian 272.

Honan alternative name of ◊***Henan***, a province of China.

Honda Japanese vehicle manufacturer, founded 1948. By the late 1980s the company was producing more than 1.5 million cars and 3 million motorcycles annually.

Founded by a mechanic, Soichirō Honda (1906–1991), the company originally produced only motorcycles; Honda cars were introduced 1964. The racing motorcycles were first seen in Europe at the 1959 Isle of Man TT races. Honda entered Formula One Grand Prix car racing 1964. They ceased car racing 1968 but in the early 1980s provided engines for Formula Two and Formula Three cars before supplying engines to Formula One teams 1983.

Honduras country in Central America, bounded N by the Caribbean Sea, SE by Nicaragua, S by the Pacific Ocean, SW by El Salvador, and W and NW by Guatemala. *See country box below.*

Honecker Erich 1912–1994. German communist politician, in power in East Germany 1973–89, elected chair of the council of state (head of state) 1976. He governed in an outwardly austere and efficient manner and, while favouring East–West détente, was a loyal ally of the USSR. In 1989, following a wave of prodemocracy demonstrations, he was replaced as leader of the Socialist Unity Party (SED) and head of state by Egon ◊Krenz, and expelled from the Communist Party. He died in exile in Chile.

Honegger Arthur 1892–1955. Swiss composer. He was one of the group of composers known as *Les Six*. His work was varied in form, for example, the opera *Antigone* 1927, the ballet *Skating Rink* 1922, the oratorio *Le Roi David/King David* 1921, programme music (*Pacific 231* 1923), and the *Symphonie liturgique/Liturgical Symphony* 1946. He also composed incidental music for Abel Gance's silent movie classics *La Roue/The Wheel* 1923 and *Napoléon* 1927.

Hōnen 1133–1212. Japanese Buddhist monk who founded the ◊Pure Land school of Buddhism.

honey sweet syrup produced by honey ◊bees from the nectar of flowers. It is stored in honeycombs and made in excess of their needs as food for the winter. Honey comprises various sugars, mainly laevulose and dextrose, with enzymes, colouring matter, acids, and pollen grains. It has antibacterial properties and was widely used in ancient Egypt, Greece, and Rome as a wound salve. It is still popular for sore throats, in hot drinks or in lozenges.

honeyeater The Kauaioo was thought to be extinct, like the other three species of Hawaiian honeyeaters, but was rediscovered in 1960. It was saved by its relatively plain feathers; the other, more colourful, Hawaiian honeyeaters were hunted to extinction.

honeyeater or ***honey-sucker*** small, brightly coloured bird of the family Meliphagidae, with a long, curved beak and long tail. They have a long protrusible tongue divided into four at the end to form a brush for collecting nectar from flowers. They are native to Australia.

Honeyeaters from Australasia colonized Hawaii, where four species evolved of which only one, the *Kauaioo*, survives; thought to be extinct, it was rediscovered 1960. Larger honeyeaters, such as the blue-faced honeyeater *Entomyza cyanotis* of northeastern Australia, which is 30 cm/12 in long, also eat insects and fruit.

honey guide in botany, line or spot on the petals of a flower that indicate to pollinating insects the position of the nectaries (see ◊nectar) within the flower. The orange dot on the lower lip of the toadflax flower (*Linaria vulgaris*) is an example. Sometimes the markings reflect only ultraviolet light, which can be seen by many insects although it is not visible to the human eye.

honeysuckle vine or shrub of the genus *Lonicera*, family Caprifoliaceae. The common honeysuckle or woodbine *L. periclymenum* of Europe is a

'There is no doubt that the first requirement for a composer is to be dead.'

Arthur Honegger
I Am a Composer
1951

HONDURAS
Republic of

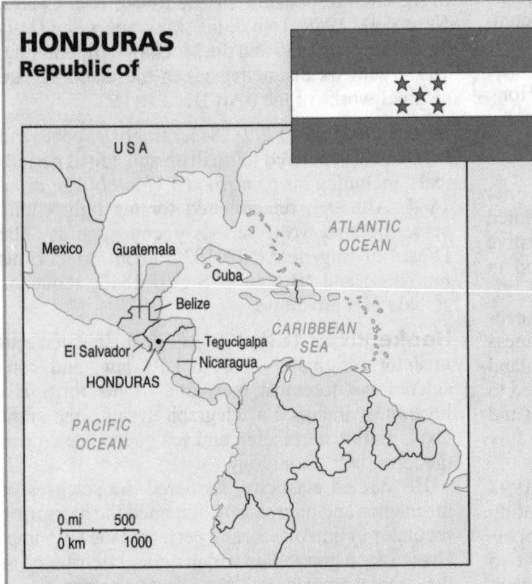

national name *República de Honduras*
area 112,100 sq km/43,282 sq mi
capital Tegucigalpa
major towns/cities San Pedro Sula, El Progreso, Choluteca
major ports La Ceiba, Puerto Cortés
physical features narrow tropical coastal plain with mountainous interior, Bay Islands, Caribbean reefs
head of state and government Carlos Flores from 1997
political system democratic republic
administrative divisions 18 departments
political parties Liberal Party of Honduras (PLH), centre-left; National Party of Honduras (PNH), right-wing
population 5,816,000 (1996 est)
population growth rate 3.0% (1990–95); 2.5% (2000–05)
ethnic distribution about 90% of mixed Indian and Spanish descent (known as ladinos or mestizos); there are also Salvadorean, Guatemalan, American, and European minorities
life expectancy 64 (men), 68 (women)
literacy rate men 76%, women 71%
languages Spanish (official), English, Indian languages
religion Roman Catholic
currency lempira
GDP (US $) 3.3 billion (1994)
growth rate −1.4% (1994)
exports coffee, bananas, meat, sugar, timber (including mahogany, rosewood), shrimps, lobsters

HISTORY
c. AD 250–900 Part of culturally advanced Maya civilization.
1502 Visited by Christopher Columbus, who named the country Honduras ('depths') after the deep waters off the N coast.
1525 Colonized by Spain, who founded the town of Trujillo, but met with fierce resistance from the native Indian population.
17th C onwards The northern 'Mosquito Coast' fell under the control of British buccaneers, as the Spanish concentrated on the inland area, with a British protectorate being established over the coast until 1860.
1821 Achieved independence from Spain and became part of Mexico.
1823 Became part of United Provinces (Federation) of Central America, also embracing Costa Rica, El Salvador, Guatemala, and Nicaragua, with the Honduran liberal, Gen Francisco Morazan, president of the Federation from 1830.
1838 Achieved full independence when the federation dissolved.
1880 Capital transferred from Comayagua to Tegucigalpa.
later 19th–early 20th Cs The USA's economic involvement significant, with banana production, which provided two-thirds of exports in 1913, being controlled by the United Fruit Company; political instability, with frequent changes of constitution and military coups.
1925 Brief civil war.
1932–49 Under a right-wing National Party (PNH) dictatorship, led by Gen Tiburcio Carias Andino.
1963–74 Following a series of military coups, Gen Oswaldo López Arelano held power, before resigning after allegedly accepting bribes from a US company.
1969 Brief 'Football War' with El Salvador, which attacked Honduras at the time of a football competition between the two states, following evictions of thousands of Salvadoran illegal immigrants from Honduras.
1980 First civilian government in more than a century elected, with Dr Roberto Suazo of the centrist Liberal Party (PLH) as president, but the commander in chief of the army, Gen Gustavo Alvárez, retained considerable power.
1983 Close involvement with the USA in providing naval and air bases and allowing Nicaraguan counter-revolutionaries ('Contras') to operate from Honduras.
1984 Alvarez ousted in coup led by junior officers led by General Walter López Reyes, resulting in policy review towards USA and Nicaragua.
1986 José Azcona del Hoyo (PLH) elected president after electoral law changed, making Suazo ineligible for presidency, and despite receiving fewer votes than his opponent.
1989 Government and opposition declared support for Central American peace plan to demobilize Nicaraguan Contras (thought to number 55,000 with their dependents) based in Honduras. PNH won assembly elections; its leader, Rafael Leonardo Callejas Romero, elected president.
1992 Border dispute with El Salvador dating from 1861 finally resolved.
1993 PLH, under Carlos Roberto Reina Idiaquez, won assembly and presidential elections; economy began to improve, but unemployment rate 40%.
1997 Carlos Flores (PLH) elected pesident.
1998 Hurricane Mitch struck end Oct, killing over 5,600. Estimated cost of damage $5 billion.

SEE ALSO Contra; Maya; Mosquito Coast

Hong Kong

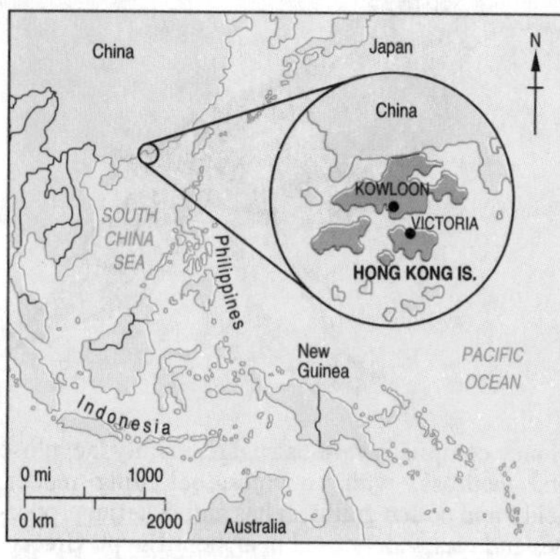

climbing plant with sweet-scented flowers, reddish and yellow-tinted outside the creamy white inside; it now grows in the NE USA.

‘Mr Hooke, who is the most, and promises the least, of any man in the world that I ever saw’

On Robert Hooke
Samuel Pepys *Diary*
15 Feb 1664

Hong Kong special administrative region in the SE of China, comprising Hong Kong Island; the Kowloon Peninsula; many other islands, of which the largest is Lantau; and the mainland New Territories. A former British crown colony, it reverted to Chinese control July 1997
area 1,070 sq km/413 sq mi
capital Victoria (Hong Kong City)
towns and cities Kowloon, Tsuen Wan (in the New Territories)
features an enclave of Kwantung province, China, it has one of the world's finest natural harbours; Hong Kong Island is connected with Kowloon by undersea railway and ferries; a world financial centre, its stock market has four exchanges
environment world's most densely populated city; surrounding waters heavily polluted
exports textiles, clothing, electronic goods, clocks, watches, cameras, plastic products; a large proportion of the exports and imports of S China are transshipped here; tourism is important
population (1995 est) 6,189,800; 57% Hong Kong Chinese, most of the remainder refugees from the mainland
language English, Chinese
religion Confucianist, Buddhist, Taoist, with Muslim and Christian minorities
government Hong Kong is a special administrative region within China, with a chief executive, Tung Chee-hwa, from 1997. There is an executive council, which comprises a mixture of business and political figures, and an appointed legislative council. Until reversion to Chinese control July 1997 Hong Kong was a British dependency administered by a crown-appointed governor who presided over an unelected executive council.
history formerly part of China, Hong Kong Island was occupied by Britain 1841, during the first of the ◊Opium Wars, and ceded by China under the 1842 Treaty of Nanking. The Kowloon Peninsula was acquired under the 1860 Beijing (Peking) Convention and the New Territories secured on a 99-year lease from 1898. The colony, which developed into a major centre for Sino-British trade during the late 19th and early 20th centuries, was occupied by Japan 1941–45. The restored British administration promised, after 1946, to increase self-government. These plans were shelved, however, after the 1949 communist revolution in China. During the 1950s almost 1 million Chinese (predominantly Cantonese) refugees fled to Hong Kong. Immigration continued during the 1960s and 1970s, raising the colony's population from 1 million in 1946 to 5 million in 1980, leading to the imposition of strict border controls during the 1980s. From 1975, 160,000 Vietnamese ◊boat people fled to Hong Kong; in 1991 some 61,000 remained. The UK government began forced repatriation 1989. Hong Kong's economy expanded rapidly during the corresponding period and the colony became one of Asia's major commercial, financial, and industrial centres, boasting the world's busiest container port from 1987. As the date (1997) for the termination of the New Territories' lease approached, negotiations on Hong Kong's future were opened between Britain and China 1982. These culminated 1984 in an agreement that Britain would transfer full sovereignty of the islands and New Territories to China 1997 in return for Chinese assurance that Hong Kong's social and economic freedom and capitalist lifestyle would be preserved for at least 50 years.

Under the ‘one country, two systems’ agreement, in 1997 Hong Kong would become a special administrative region within China, with its own laws, currency, budget, and tax system, and would retain its free-port status and authority to negotiate separate international trade agreements. A 150-member committee responsible for overseeing Hong Kong's reversion to Chinese sovereignty was appointed by the Chinese government Dec 1995. The committee, consisting of 94 citizens from Hong Kong and 56 from China, was formed to choose an election committee, which in turn would select a chief executive to succeed the British governor of Hong Kong. The committee would also decide which of Hong Kong's laws were to be amended or repealed mid-1997, and who would serve in the provisional government.

Tung Chee-hwa was elected to become the first chief executive (replacing the British-appointed governor) of the Hong Kong Special Administrative Region (HKSAR) when Hong Kong reverted to Chinese sovereignty in July 1997.

In Jan 1997 Tung announced that the new Executive Council would comprise a mixture of business and political figures with strong links with mainland China. In Feb 1997 the Chinese parliament voted to substantially dilute Hong Kong's bill of rights and freedoms of association and assembly after the July 1997 handover.

Hong Kong's incoming government April 1997 confirmed its critics' worst fears by clearly stating that draconian curbs would be imposed on operations of political organizations and the right to protest after the handover of the colony to China at the end of June. The office of Tung Chee-Hwa, Chief Executive of the incoming government, issued a document setting out a programme for reviving some of the most restrictive curbs on the rights to dissent which were scrapped by the outgoing colonial administration and introducing measures clearly targetted at weakening Hong Kong's large pro-democracy organizations.

Honiara port and capital of the Solomon Islands, on the northwest coast of Guadalcanal Island, on the river Mataniko; population (1989) 33,750.

honi soit qui mal y pense (French ‘shame on him or her who thinks evil of it’) the motto of England's Order of the Garter.

Honolulu (Hawaiian ‘sheltered bay’) capital city and port of Hawaii, on the south coast of Oahu; population (1992) 371,000. It is a holiday resort, noted for its beauty and tropical vegetation, with some industry.

Hooch *Woman and Her Maid in a Courtyard* by Pieter de Hooch (National Gallery, London). De Hooch's finest works were realistic depictions of the lives of the people who bought his pictures – the neat, hard-working Dutch middle classes. *Corbis*

honours list military and civil awards approved by the sovereign of the UK and published on New Year's Day and on her official birthday in June. Many Commonwealth countries, for example, Australia and Canada, also have their own honours list.

The Political Honours Scrutiny Committee is a group of privy councillors established after Lloyd George's extravagant abuse of the honours system to reward party benefactors. Names are considered for honours in four ways: (1) from senior government officials; (2) nominated personally by the Queen; (3) directly from the major political parties, through the chief whip; and (4) through the prime minister who can add to or subtract from all the above lists.

Honshu principal island of Japan. It lies between Hokkaido to the NE and Kyushu to the SW; area 231,100 sq km/89,205 sq mi, including 382 smaller islands; population (1995) 100,995,000. A chain of volcanic mountains runs along the island, which is subject to frequent earthquakes. The main cities are Tokyo, Yokohama, Osaka, Kobe, Nagoya, and Hiroshima.

Honthorst Gerrit van 1590–1656. Dutch painter. He painted biblical, mythological, and genre pictures, using a contrast of extremes of light and shade. He studied in Rome 1610–20, where he was greatly influenced by Caravaggio and painted artificially lit night scenes; a fine example is his *Christ before Caiaphas* (National Gallery, London).

Hooch Pieter de 1629–1684. Dutch painter. He painted harmonious domestic interiors and courtyards. *The Courtyard of a House in Delft* 1658 (National Gallery, London) is a typical work.

Hooch was born near Rotterdam and was a pupil of Berchem. He worked mainly in Delft, where he first came under the strong influence of Vermeer. It was during this Delft period that he painted his interiors, and courtyard and garden scenes, all characterized by a sensitive rendering of space, light and atmosphere, and a clarity and precision that gives them an untroubled stillness and order.

Hood Raymond Mathewson 1881–1934. US architect. He designed several New York skyscrapers of the 1920s and 1930s, and was a member of the team responsible for the Rockefeller Center, New York, 1929. Two of his skyscrapers, the *Daily News* building 1930 and the McGraw-Hill building, 1931, with its distinctive green-tile cladding, are seminal works of the ◊Art Deco style.

Hood Thomas 1799–1845. English poet and humorist. He entered journalism and edited periodicals, including his own *Hood's Monthly Magazine* 1844. Although remembered for his light comic verse, he also wrote serious poems such as ‘The Dream of Eugene Aram’ 1839, about a notorious murderer; and ‘Bridge of Sighs’ 1843, about the suicide of a prostitute.

Hooke Robert 1635–1703. English scientist and inventor, originator of ◊Hooke's law, and considered the foremost mechanic of his time. His inventions included a telegraph system, the spirit level, marine barometer, and sea gauge. He coined the term ‘cell’ in biology.

He studied elasticity, furthered the sciences of mechanics and microscopy, invented the hairspring regulator in timepieces, and perfected the air pump. His work on gravitation and in optics contributed to the achievements of his contemporary Isaac ◊Newton.

Hooker John Lee 1917– . US blues guitarist, singer, and songwriter. He was one of the foremost blues musicians. His first record, ‘Boogie Chillen’ 1948, was a blues hit and his percussive guitar style made him popular with a rock audience from the 1950s. His albums include *Urban Blues* 1968 and *Boom Boom* 1992 (also the title of his 1962 song).

Hooker Joseph Dalton 1817–1911. English botanist who travelled to the Antarctic and India, and made many botanical discoveries. His works include *Flora Antarctica* 1844–47, *Genera plantarum* 1862–83, and *Flora of British India* 1875–97.

Hooke's law law stating that the deformation of a body is proportional to the magnitude of the deforming force, provided that the body's elastic limit (see ◊elasticity) is not exceeded. If the elastic limit is not reached, the body will return to its original size once the force is removed. The law was discovered by Robert Hooke 1676.

hoopoe The hoopoe is the sole member of its family, the Upupidae. With its orange-pink body plumage, boldly striped wings and tail, and huge, erectile crest, it is an unmistakable bird. It feeds mainly on the ground on worms, insects, and other invertebrates. Hoopoes are found throughout much of Europe, N Africa, and central and S Asia.

Hook of Holland (Dutch ***Hoek van Holland*** 'corner of Holland') small peninsula and village in South Holland, the Netherlands; the terminus for ferry services with Harwich (Parkeston Quay), England.

hookworm parasitic roundworm (see ◊worm) of the genus *Necator*, with hooks around the mouth. It lives mainly in tropic and subtropic regions, but also in humid areas in temperate climates. The eggs are hatched in damp soil, and the larvae bore into the host's skin, usually through the soles of the feet. They make their way to the small intestine, where they live by sucking blood. The eggs are expelled with faeces, and the cycle starts again. The human hookworm causes anaemia, weakness, and abdominal pain. It is common in areas where defecation occurs outdoors.

hoopoe bird *Upupa epops* in the order Coraciiformes, slightly larger than a thrush, with a long, thin bill and a bright, buff-coloured crest tipped with black that expands into a fan shape. The wings are banded with black and white, and the rest of the plumage is black, white, and buff. It ranges over southern Eurasia down to southern Africa, India, Malaya.

Hoover Herbert (Clark) 1874–1964. 31st president of the USA 1929–33, a Republican. He was secretary of commerce 1921–28. Hoover lost public confidence after the stock-market crash of 1929, when he opposed direct government aid for the unemployed in the Depression that followed.

As a mining engineer, Hoover travelled widely before World War I. After the war he organized relief work in occupied Europe; a talented administrator, he was subsequently associated with numerous international relief organizations, and became food administrator for the USA 1917–19. He defeated the Democratic candidate for the presidency, Al Smith (1873–1944), by a wide margin. The shantytowns, or ***Hoovervilles***, of the homeless that sprang up around large cities after the stock-market crash were evidence of his failure to cope with the effects of the Depression.

Hoover US Republican politician Herbert Hoover, whose term as president coincided with the financial collapse of 1929 and the ensuing Depression. Hoover, who believed in ultimate recovery through private enterprise, was criticized for the ineffectiveness of the measures he initiated. *Library of Congress*

Hoover J(ohn) Edgar 1895–1972. US director of the Federal Bureau of Investigation (FBI) from 1924 until his death. He built up a powerful network for the detection of organized crime. His drive against alleged communist activities after World War II, and his opposition to the Kennedy administration and others, brought much criticism for abuse of power.

He served under eight presidents, none of whom would dismiss him, since he kept files on them and their associates. Hoover waged a personal campaign of harassment against leaders of the civil-rights movement, notably Martin Luther ◊King, Jr.

Hoover Dam highest concrete dam in the USA, 221 m/726 ft, on the Colorado River at the Arizona–Nevada border. It was begun built 1931–36. Known as ***Boulder Dam*** 1933–47, its name was restored by President Truman as the reputation of the former president, Herbert Hoover, was revived. It impounds Lake Mead, and has a hydroelectric power capacity of 1,300 megawatts.

Hope Bob. Stage name of Leslie Townes Hope 1903– . British-born US comedian. He is best remembered for seven films he made with Bing ◊Crosby and Dorothy Lamour between 1940 and 1962, whose titles all began *The Road to* (*Singapore*, *Zanzibar*, *Morocco*, *Utopia*, *Rio*, *Bali*, and *Hong Kong*). Other films include *The Cat and the Canary* 1939 and *The Facts of Life* 1960.

He was taken to the USA 1907, and became a Broadway and radio star in the 1930s. He has received several special Academy Awards.

Hopei alternative transcription of ◊***Hebei***, a province of China.

Hopewell Native American agricultural culture of the central USA, dated about AD 200. The Hopewell built burial mounds up to 12 m/40 ft high and structures such as Serpent Mound in Ohio; see also ◊Moundbuilder.

Hopi Native American people, numbering approximately 9,000, who live mainly in mountain villages in the SW USA, especially NE Arizona. They farm and herd sheep and live in houses of stone or adobe (mud brick), forming small towns on rocky plateaus. Their language belongs to the Uto-Aztecan family.

Hopkins Anthony (Philip) 1937– . Welsh actor. Among his stage appearances are *Equus*, *Macbeth*, *Pravda*, and the title role in *King Lear*. His films include *The Lion in Winter* 1968, *The Silence of the Lambs* (Academy Award) 1991, *Howards End* 1992, and *Shadowlands* and *The Remains of the Day*, both 1993.

Hopkins Frederick Gowland 1861–1947. English biochemist whose research into diets revealed the necessity of certain trace substances, now known as vitamins, for the maintenance of health. Hopkins shared the 1929 Nobel Prize for Physiology or Medicine with Christiaan ◊Eijkman, who had arrived at similar conclusions.

Hopkins also established that there are certain ◊amino acids that the body cannot produce itself. Another discovery he took part in was that contracting muscle accumulates lactic acid.

Hopkins Gerard Manley 1844–1889. English poet and Jesuit priest. His works are marked by originality of diction and rhythm and include 'The Wreck of the Deutschland' (1876), and 'The Windhover' and 'Pied Beauty' (both 1877). His poetry is profoundly religious and records his struggle to gain faith and peace, but also shows freshness of feeling and delight in nature. His employment of 'sprung rhythm' (the combination of traditional regularity of stresses with varying numbers of syllables in each line) greatly influenced later 20th-century poetry.

hoplite in ancient Greece, a heavily armed infantry soldier.

Hopper Dennis 1936– . US film actor and director. He caused a sensation with the anti-establishment *Easy Rider* 1969, but his *The Last Movie* 1971 was poorly received by the critics. He made a comeback in the 1980s directing such films as *Colors* 1988. His work as an actor includes *Rebel Without a Cause* 1955, *The American Friend/Der amerikanische Freund* 1977, *Apocalypse Now* 1979, *Blue Velvet* 1986, and *Speed* 1994.

Hopper Edward 1882–1967. US painter and etcher, one of the foremost American Realists. His views of life in New England and New York in the 1930s and 1940s, painted in rich, dark colours, convey a brooding sense of emptiness and solitude, as in *Nighthawks* 1942 (Art Institute, Chicago).

Born in Nyack, New York, he studied at the Commercial Art School, New York, and then at the New York School of Art, where his teacher Robert Henri (1865–1929), associated with the ◊Ashcan School, was an important influence.

He visited Europe several times between 1906 and 1910, though he remained uninfluenced by avant-garde development, preferring to devote himself to painting the urban background of American life. An example is his street scene *Early Sunday Morning* 1930 (Whitney Museum of American Art, New York).

hops female fruit heads of the hop plant *Humulus lupulus*, family Cannabiaceae; these are dried and used as a tonic and in flavouring beer. In designated areas in Europe, no male hops may be grown, since seedless hops produced by the unpollinated female plant contain a greater proportion of the alpha acid that gives beer its bitter taste.

Horace (full name Quintus Horatius Flaccus) 65–8 BC. Roman lyric poet and satirist. He became a leading poet under the patronage of Emperor Augustus. His works include *Satires* 35–30 BC; the four books of *Odes*, about 25–24 BC; *Epistles*, a series of verse letters; and an influential critical work, *Ars poetica*. They are distinguished by their style, wit, discretion, and patriotism.

Horace was born at Venusia, S Italy. He fought under ◊Brutus at Philippi, lost his estate, and was reduced to poverty. In about 38 Virgil introduced him to his patron Maecenas, who gave him a farm in the Sabine hills and recommended him to the patronage of Augustus.

Horae in Greek mythology, the goddesses of the seasons, daughters of Zeus and ◊Themis, three or four in number, sometimes personified.

Hordern Michael Murray 1911–1995. English character actor. He has appeared in stage roles such as Shakespeare's Lear and Prospero, and in plays by Tom Stoppard and Harold Pinter. His films include *The Man Who Never Was* 1956, *The Spy Who Came in From the Cold* 1965, *The Bed Sitting Room* 1969, and *Joseph Andrews* 1976.

Hore-Belisha (Isaac) Leslie, 1st Baron Hore-Belisha 1893–1957. British politician. A National Liberal, he was minister of transport 1934–37, introducing ***Belisha beacons*** to mark pedestrian crossings. As war minister from 1937, until removed by Chamberlain 1940 on grounds of temperament, he introduced peacetime conscription 1939.

horehound any plant of the genus *Marrubium* of the mint family Labiatae. The white horehound *M. vulgare*, found in Europe, N Africa, and W Asia and naturalized in North America, has a thick, hairy stem and clusters of dull white flowers; it has medicinal uses.

horizon the limit to which one can see across the surface of the sea or a level plain, that is, about 5 km/3 mi at 1.5 m/5 ft above sea level, and about 65 km/40 mi at 300 m/1,000 ft.

hormone (Greek 'arousing') secretion of the ◊endocrine glands, concerned with control of body functions. The major glands are the thyroid, parathyroid, pituitary, adrenal, pancreas, ovary, and testis. Hormones bring about changes in the functions of various organs according to the body's requirements. The ◊hypothalamus, which adjoins the

'The American system of rugged individualism.'

HERBERT HOOVER
Campaign speech 1928

'The world is charged with the grandeur of God.'

GERARD MANLEY HOPKINS
'God's Grandeur'

'My aim in painting has always been the most exact transcription possible of my most intimate impressions of nature.'

EDWARD HOPPER

pituitary gland, at the base of the brain, is a control centre for overall coordination of hormone secretion; the thyroid hormones determine the rate of general body chemistry; the adrenal hormones prepare the organism during stress for 'fight or flight'; and the sexual hormones such as oestrogen govern reproductive functions.

There are also hormone-secreting cells in the kidney, liver, gastrointestinal tract, thymus (in the neck), pineal (in the brain), and placenta. Many diseases due to hormone deficiency can be relieved with hormone preparations.

hormone-replacement therapy (HRT) use of ◊oestrogen and progesterone to help limit the unpleasant effects of the menopause in women. The treatment was first used in the 1970s.

At the menopause, the ovaries cease to secrete natural oestrogen. This results in a number of symptoms, including hot flushes, anxiety, and a change in the pattern of menstrual bleeding. It is also associated with osteoporosis, or a thinning of bone, leading to an increased incidence of fractures, frequently of the hip, in older women. Oestrogen preparations, taken to replace the decline in natural hormone levels, combined with regular exercise can help to maintain bone strength in women. In order to improve bone density, however, HRT must be taken for five years, during which time the woman will continue to menstruate. Many women do not find this acceptable.

Hormuz or ***Ormuz*** small island, area 41 sq km/16 sq mi, in the Strait of Hormuz, belonging to Iran. It is strategically important because oil tankers leaving the Persian Gulf for Japan and the West have to pass through the strait to reach the Arabian Sea.

horn member of a family of lip-reed wind instruments used for signalling and ritual, and sharing features of a generally conical bore (although the orchestral horn is of part conical and part straight bore) and curved shape, producing a pitch of rising or variable inflection. The modern valve horn is a 19th-century hybrid B flat/F instrument; the name ***French horn*** strictly applies to the earlier *cor à pistons* which uses lever-action rotary valves and produces a lighter tone. The ***Wagner tuba*** is a horn variant in tenor and bass versions devised by Wagner to provide a fuller horn tone in the lower range. Composers for horn include Mozart, Haydn, Richard Strauss (*Till Eulenspiegel* 1895), Ravel, and Benjamin Britten (*Serenade for Tenor, Horn, and Strings* 1943). Many horns are based on animal horns, for example the shofar of Hebrew ritual and the medieval oliphant and gemshorn, and shells, for example the conch shell of Pacific island peoples.

Horns in metal originated in South America and also Central Asia (Tibet, India, Nepal), and reached Europe along with the technology of metalwork in the Bronze Age. The familiar hunting horn, unchanged for many centuries, was adapted and enlarged in the 18th century to become an orchestral instrument, its limited range of natural harmonics extended by a combination of lip technique and hand stopping within the bell and the use of extension crooks for changes of key.

Horn Gyula 1932– . Hungarian economist and politician, president of the Hungarian Socialist Party (HSP) from 1990 and prime minister from 1994. Under his leadership the ex-communist HSP enjoyed a resurgence, capturing an absolute majority in the July 1994 assembly elections. Despite opposition to the ongoing economic restructuring programme, Horn, as a trained economist, recognized the need to press on with reforms and formed a coalition with the centrist Free Democrats.

hornbeam any tree of the genus *Carpinus* of the birch family Betulaceae. They have oval, serrated leaves and bear pendant clusters of flowers, each with a nutlike seed attached to the base. The trunk is usually twisted, with smooth grey bark.

hornbill omnivorous bird of the family Bucerotidae, order Coraciiformes, found in Africa, India, and Malaysia. It is about 1 m/3 ft long, and has a powerful down-curved bill, usually surmounted by a bony growth or casque. During the breeding season, the female walls herself into a hole in a tree and does not emerge until the young are hatched. There are about 45 species.

Hornbills feed chiefly on the ground, their food consisting of insects, small mammals, and reptiles. The ***great hornbill*** *Buceros bicornis* of SE Asia can reach up to 1.3 m/4.3 ft in length.

The ***southern ground hornbill*** lives in groups of about three to five birds (though sometimes as many as 10) with only one breeding pair, and the rest acting as helpers. On average, only one chick is reared successfully every nine years. Lifespan can be 40 years or more.

hornblende green or black rock-forming mineral, one of the ◊amphiboles; it is a hydrous silicate of calcium, iron, magnesium, and aluminium. Hornblende is found in both igneous and metamorphic rocks.

hornet kind of ◊wasp.

hornfels ◊metamorphic rock formed by rocks heated by contact with a hot igneous body. It is fine-grained and brittle, without foliation.

Hornfels may contain minerals only formed under conditions of great heat, such as andalusite, Al_2SiO_5, and cordierite, $(Mg,Fe)_2Al_4Si_5O_{18}$. This rock, originating from sedimentary rock strata, is found in contact with large igneous ◊intrusions where it represents the heat-altered equivalent of the surrounding clays. Its hardness makes it suitable for road building and railway ballast.

hornbill Though quite remarkable, the beak of the yellow-billed hornbill *Tockus flavirostris* lacks the prominent casque found in some of the larger members of the family. Hornbills occur in Old World tropical regions. This species is common in dry bush country from Ethiopia to South Africa. *Premaphotos Wildlife*

Horowitz Vladimir Horowitz enjoyed world acclaim as a virtuoso pianist, particularly with his interpretations of the Romantic repertoire. As a boy he expected to become a composer, but to earn a living he became a pianist. Apart from some bravura transcriptions, none of his own compositions have yet been made public. *Sony Classical*

hornwort nonvascular plant of the class Anthocerotae; it is related to the ◊liverworts and ◊mosses, with which it forms the order Bryophyta. Hornworts are found in warm climates, growing on moist shaded soil. The name is also given to an aquatic flowering plant of the family Ceratophyllaceae. Found in slow-moving water, it has whorls of finely divided leaves and may grow up to 2 m/7 ft long.

Like the other bryophytes, hornworts exist in two alternating reproductive phases (see ◊alternation of generations) – a leafy gametophyte, which produces gametes, or sex cells, and a small horned sporophyte, which produces spores and grows upwards from the gametophyte. Unlike the sporophytes of mosses and liverworts, the hornwort sporophyte survives the death of the gametophyte.

horoscope in Western astrology, a chart of the position of the Sun, Moon, and planets relative to the ◊zodiac at the moment of birth.

In casting a horoscope, the astrologer draws a circular diagram divided into 12 sections, or houses, showing the 12 signs of the zodiac around the perimeter and the Sun, Moon, and planets as they were at the subject's time and place of birth. These heavenly bodies are supposed to represent different character traits and influences, and by observing their positions and interrelations the astrologer may gain insight into the subject's personality and foretell the main outlines of his or her career.

Horowitz Vladimir 1904–1989. Russian-born US pianist. He made his US debut 1928 with the New York Philharmonic Orchestra. A leading interpreter of Liszt, Schumann, and Rachmaninov, he toured worldwide until the early 1950s, when he retired to devote more time to recording. His rare concert appearances 1965–86 displayed undiminished brilliance.

horror genre of fiction and film, devoted primarily to scaring the reader or audience, but often also aiming to be cathartic through their exaggeration of the bizarre and grotesque.

Dominant figures in the horror tradition are Mary Shelley (◊*Frankenstein* 1818), Edgar Allan Poe, Bram Stoker, H P Lovecraft and, among contemporary writers, Stephen King and Clive Barker.

Horror is derived from the Gothic novel, which dealt in shock effects, as well as from folk tales and ghost stories throughout the ages. Horror writing tends to use motifs such as vampirism, the eruption of ancient evil, and monstrous transformation, which often derive from folk traditions, as well as more recent concerns such as psychopathology.

horse hoofed, odd-toed, grazing mammal *Equus caballus* of the family Equidae, which also includes zebras and asses. The many breeds of domestic horse of Euro-Asian origin range in colour from white to grey, brown, and black. The yellow-brown Mongolian wild horse, or Przewalski's horse *E. przewalskii*, named after its Polish 'discoverer' about 1880, is the only surviving species of wild horse.

Przewalski's horse has become extinct in the wild because of hunting and competition with domestic animals for food; about 800 survive in captivity, and there are plans to reintroduce them to Mongolia.

There are basically three types of domestic horse: the light riding horse, the heavy horse or draught horse, and the pony.

light horse Breeds of light horse are descended from the ***Arab***, small, agile, highly spirited, and intelligent; and ***Thoroughbred***, derived from the Arab via English mares, used in horse racing for its speed (the present stock is descended from three Arab horses introduced to Britain in the 18th century, especially the Darley Arabian; they are therefore closely related and so have only a limited range of genetic characteristics to improve with breeding).

heavy horse Among breeds of heavy horse are the ***shire***, the largest draught horse in the world at 17 hands (1 hand = 10.2 cm/4 in), descended from the medieval war horses which carried knights in armour, and marked by long hair or 'feathering' round its fetlocks (ankles); the ***Clydesdale***, smaller than the shire but possessing great strength and endurance; and the ***Suffolk punch***, a sturdy all-round working horse.

pony The pony, with a smaller build (under 14.2 hands, or 1.47 m/58 in), combines the qualities of various of the larger breeds of horse. Pony breeds include the ***Highland***, the largest and strongest of native British breeds, unequalled for hardiness and staying power; the ***Welsh cob***, similar to the Highland but faster; the smaller ***New Forest***; and, smaller again, the ***Exmoor*** and ***Dartmoor***. The smallest breed of pony is the hardy ***Shetland***, about 70 cm/27 in high. The ***Dales*** and ***Fell*** ponies of Cumbria were formerly used by farmers as working horses. The ***Connemara*** is a large Irish breed, frequently used as a polo pony.

The ***mule*** is the usually sterile offspring of a female horse and a male ass, and a hardy pack animal; the ***hinny*** is a similarly sterile offspring of a male horse and a female ass, but less useful as a beast of burden.

horse chestnut any tree of the genus *Aesculus* of the family Hippocastanaceae, especially *A. hippocastanum*, originally from SE Europe but widely planted elsewhere. Horse chestnuts have large, showy spikes of bell-shaped flowers and bear large, shiny, inedible seeds in capsules (conkers). The horse chestnut is not related to the true chestnut. In North America it is called buckeye.

horsefly any of over 2,500 species of fly, belonging to the family Tabanidae. The females suck blood from horses, cattle, and humans; males live on plants and suck nectar. The larvae are carnivorous.

Horse Guards in the UK, the Household Cavalry, or Royal Horse Guards, formed 1661. Their headquarters, in Whitehall, London, England, were erected in 1753 by John Vardy (1718–65) from a design by William ◊Kent, on the site of the Tilt Yard of Whitehall Palace.

horsepower imperial unit (abbreviation hp) of power, now replaced by the ◊watt. It was first used by the engineer James ◊Watt, who employed it to compare the power of steam engines with that of horses. Watt found a horse to be capable of 366 foot-pounds of work per second but, in order to enable him to use the term 'horsepower' to cover the additional work done by the more efficient steam engine, he exaggerated the pulling power of the horse by 50%. Hence, one horsepower is equal to 550 foot-pounds per second/745.7 watts, which is more than any real horse could produce. The metric horsepower is 735.5 watts; the standard US horsepower is 746 watts.

horse racing sport of racing mounted or driven horses. Two forms in Britain are ***flat racing***, for Thoroughbred horses over a flat course, and ***National Hunt racing***, in which the horses have to clear obstacles.

In Britain, racing took place in Stuart times and with its royal connections became known as the 'sport of kings'. Early racecourses include Chester, Ascot, and Newmarket. The English classics were introduced 1776 with the St Leger (run at Doncaster), followed by the Oaks 1779 and Derby 1780 (both run at Epsom), and 2,000 Guineas 1809 and 1,000 Guineas 1814 (both run at Newmarket). The governing body for the sport is the Jockey Club, founded about 1750. The National Hunt Committee was established 1866. Elsewhere, races include the Australian Melbourne Cup 1861 (at Flemington Park, Victoria) and the US Triple Crown: the Belmont Stakes 1867 (at New York), the Preakness Stakes 1873 (at Pimlico, Baltimore), and the Kentucky Derby 1875 (at Churchill Downs, Louisville). Another major race in the USA is the end-of-season Breeders' Cup 1984, with $10 million in prize money at stake.

Steeplechasing is a development of foxhunting, of which ***point-to-point*** is the amateur version, and ***hurdling*** a version with less severe, and movable, fences. Outstanding steeplechases are the Grand National 1839 (at Aintree, Liverpool) and Cheltenham Gold Cup 1924 (at Cheltenham). The leading hurdling race is the Champion Hurdle 1927 (at Cheltenham). ***Harness racing*** is popular in North America. It is for standard-bred horses pulling a two-wheeled sulky on which the driver sits. Leading races include the Hambletonian and Little Brown Jug. *See list of tables on p. 1177.*

horseradish hardy perennial *Armoracia rusticana*, native to SE Europe but naturalized elsewhere, family Cruciferae. The thick, cream-coloured root is strong-tasting and is often made into a condiment.

horseradish The horseradish is a hairy perennial with wavy, indented leaves and small white flowers. The plant grows to a height of 60–90 cm/2–3 ft and has a thick taproot. It originated on the borders of Europe and Asia.

horsetail plant of the genus *Equisetum*, related to ferns and club mosses; some species are also called ***scouring rush***. There are about 35 living species, bearing their spores on cones at the stem tip. The upright stems are ribbed and often have spaced whorls of branches. Today they are of modest size, but hundreds of millions of years ago giant treelike forms existed.

Horta Victor, Baron Horta 1861–1947. Belgian ◊Art Nouveau architect. He was responsible for a series of apartment buildings in Brussels, the first of which, Hôtel Tassel 1892, is striking in its use of sinuous forms and decorative ironwork in the interior, particularly the staircase. His sumptuous Hôtel Solvay 1895–1900 and Maison du Peuple 1896–99 are more complete, interior and exterior being unified in a stylistic whole.

Horthy Miklos de Nagybánya 1868–1957. Hungarian politician and admiral. Leader of the counter-revolutionary White government, he became regent 1920 on the overthrow of the communist Bela Kun regime by Romanian and Czechoslovak intervention. He represented the conservative and military class, and retained power until World War II, trying (although allied to Hitler) to retain independence of action. In 1944 he tried to negotiate a surrender to the USSR but Hungary was taken over by the Nazis and he was deported to Germany. He was released from German captivity the same year by the Western Allies and allowed to go to Portugal, where he died.

horticulture art and science of growing flowers, fruit, and vegetables. Horticulture is practised in gardens and orchards, along with millions of acres of land devoted to vegetable farming. Some areas, like California, have specialized in horticulture because they have the mild climate and light fertile soil most suited to these crops.

Horus in ancient Egyptian mythology, the hawk-headed sun god, son of Isis and Osiris, of whom the pharaohs were declared to be the incarnation.

Hosking Eric (John) 1909–1990. English wildlife photographer. He is known for his documentation of British birds, especially owls. Beginning at the age of eight and still photographing in Africa at 80, he covered all aspects of birdlife and illustrated a large number of books, published between 1940 and 1990.

Hoskins Bob (Robert William) 1942– . English character actor. He progressed to fame from a series of supporting roles. Films include *The Long Good Friday* 1980, *The Cotton Club* 1984, *Mona Lisa* 1985, *A Prayer for the Dying* 1987, and *Who Framed Roger Rabbit?* 1988.

hospice residential facility specializing in palliative care for terminally ill patients and their relatives.

hospital facility for the care of the sick, injured, and incapacitated.

In ancient times, temples of deities such as ◊Aesculapius offered facilities for treatment and by the 4th century, the Christian church had founded hospitals for lepers, cripples, the blind, the sick, and the poor. The oldest surviving hospital in Europe is the 7th-century Hôtel Dieu, Paris; in Britain, the most ancient are St Bartholomew's 1123 and St Thomas's 1200 in London; and in the Americas the Hospital of Jesus of Nazareth, Mexico, 1524.

Medical knowledge advanced during the Renaissance, and hospitals became increasingly secularized after the Reformation. In the 19th century, further progress was made in hospital design, administration, and staffing (Florence ◊Nightingale played a significant role in this). In the 20th century there has been an increasing trend towards specialization.

host in biology, an organism that is parasitized by another. In ◊commensalism, the partner that does not benefit may also be called the host. *See illustration on following page.*

hostage person taken prisoner as a means of exerting pressure on a third party, usually with threats of death or injury. Sept–Nov 1991 saw the release of the longest-held British hostages in Lebanon, Terry ◊Waite and John McCarthy (captured 20 Jan 1987 and 17 April 1986 respectively); other hostages released included Jackie Mann (captured 12 May 1989) and Jesse Turner (captured 24 Jan 1987).

'Hostage is a crucifying aloneness . . . A man hanging by his fingernails over the edge of chaos.'

On the HOSTAGE Brian Keenan Quoted in *Independent* 31 Aug 1990

Hottentot ('stammerer') South African term for a variety of different African peoples; it is nonscientific and considered derogatory by many. The name ◊Khoikhoi is preferred.

Houdini Harry. Stage name of Erich Weiss 1874–1926. US escapologist and conjurer. He was renowned for his escapes from ropes and handcuffs, from straitjackets and prison cells.

Born in Budapest, he was the son of a rabbi. He wrote books and articles on magic and was deeply interested in spiritualism, and campaigned against fraudulent mindreaders and mediums.

Hounsfield Godfrey Newbold 1919– . English engineer, a pioneer of ◊tomography, the application of computer techniques to X-raying the human body. He shared the Nobel Prize for Physiology or Medicine 1979.

Hounslow outer borough of W Greater London. It includes the districts of Heston, Brentford, and Isleworth

host An orb web spider *Nephila clavipes* in Argentina acting as host to the larva of a parasitic wasp. The larva feeds on the host's tissues through a hole which it has cut in the abdominal wall. *Premaphotos Wildlife*

features reputed site of Caesar's crossing of the Thames 54 BC at Brentford; Hounslow Heath, formerly the haunt of highwaymen; 16th-century Osterley Park, reconstructed by Robert Adam in the 1760s; 16th-century Syon House, seat of duke of Northumberland, where Lady Jane Grey was offered the crown 1553; the artist William Hogarth's House, Chiswick; Boston Manor House (1662); Chiswick House, Palladian villa designed by Richard ◊Burlington 1725–29; site of London's first civil airport (1919)
population (1991) 204,400
famous people Thomas Gresham.

Houphouët-Boigny Félix 1905–1993. Côte d'Ivoire right-wing politician, president 1960–93. He held posts in French ministries, and became president of the Republic of Côte d'Ivoire on independence 1960, maintaining close links with France, which helped to boost an already thriving economy and encourage political stability. Pro-Western and opposed to communist intervention in Africa, Houphouët-Boigny was strongly criticized for maintaining diplomatic relations with South Africa. He was re-elected for a seventh term 1990 in multiparty elections, amid allegations of ballot rigging and political pressure.

hour period of time comprising 60 minutes; 24 hours make one calendar day.

Hours, Book of in medieval Europe, a collection of liturgical prayers for the use of the faithful.

Books of Hours appeared in England in the 13th century, and contained short prayers and illustrations, with each prayer suitable for a different hour of the day, in honour of the Virgin Mary. The enormous demand for Books of Hours was a stimulus for the development of Gothic illumination. A notable example is the *Très Riches Heures du Duc de Berry*, illustrated in the early 15th century by the ◊Limbourg brothers.

housefly fly of the genus *Musca*, found in and around dwellings, especially *M. domestica*, a common worldwide species. Houseflies are grey and have mouthparts adapted for drinking liquids and sucking moisture from food and manure.

Houseman John. Adopted name of Jacques Haussman 1902–1988. US theatre, film, and television producer and character actor.

He co-founded the Mercury Theater with Orson Welles, and collaborated with such directors as Max Ophuls, Vicente Minelli, and Nicholas Ray. He won an Academy Award for his acting debut in *The Paper Chase* 1973, and recreated his role in the subsequent TV series.

Among the films he produced are *The Bad and the Beautiful* 1952 and *Lust for Life* 1956.

house music dance music of the 1980s originating in the inner-city clubs of Chicago, USA, combining funk with European high-tech pop, and using dub, digital sampling, and cross-fading. ***Acid house*** has minimal vocals and melody, instead surrounding the mechanically emphasized 4/4 beat with stripped-down synthesizer riffs and a wandering bass line. Other variants include ***hip house***, with rap elements, and ***handbag*** (mainstream).

House of Commons lower chamber of the UK ◊Parliament.

House of Lords upper chamber of the UK ◊Parliament.

Its members are unelected and comprise the ***temporal peers***: all hereditary peers of England created to 1707, all hereditary peers of Great Britain created 1707–1800, and all hereditary peers of the UK from 1801 onwards; all hereditary Scottish peers (under the Peerage Act 1963); all peeresses in their own right (under the same act); all life peers (both the ◊law lords and those created under the Life Peerages Act 1958); and the ***spiritual peers***: the two archbishops and 24 of the bishops (London, Durham, and Winchester by right, and the rest by seniority). Since the Parliament Act 1911 the powers of the Lords have been restricted in that they may delay a bill passed by the Commons but not reject it. The Lords are presided over by the lord chancellor. In 1998 the Labour government announced its intention to remove the right of hereditary peers to sit and vote in the House of Lords.

House of Representatives lower house of the US ◊Congress, with 435 members elected at regular two-year intervals, every even year, in Nov.

All spending bills must, in accordance with Section 7 of Article 1 of the constitution, originate in the House, thus making its financial committees particularly influential bodies. The House also has sole powers of instigating impeachment proceedings. Members of the House must reside in the roughly equal-sized constituencies they represent, making their outlooks particularly parochial.

House Un-American Activities Committee (HUAC) Congressional committee, established 1938 as the Special Committee to Investigate Un-American Activities under the leadership of Martin Dies (1900–1972). Noted for its public investigation of alleged subversion, particularly of communists, it was renamed the House Internal Security Committee 1945. It achieved its greatest notoriety during the 1950s through its hearings on communism in the movie industry. Known from 1969 as the House Internal Security Committee, it was abolished 1975.

housing provision of residential accommodation. All countries have found some degree of state housing provision or subsidy essential, even in free-enterprise economies such as the USA. In the UK, flats and houses to rent (intended for people with low incomes) are built by local authorities under the direction of the secretary of state for environment.

Housing legislation in Britain began with the Artisans' Dwellings Act of 1875, which gave powers to local councils to condemn properties and clear slums within their boundaries. The Housing of the Working Classes Act 1890 strengthened earlier acts and encouraged local councils to undertake housing improvement schemes. Under an act of 1919, the government offered a subsidy for houses built by a local council for rent. Individuals who provided housing include George Peabody, who set up the Peabody Trust to build homes for the poor in the Spitalfields district of London, and Octavia Hill, whose housing scheme enabled the lease of homes to poor people in Marylebone. Factory owners also built homes for their workers, such as Titus Salt (the model town of Saltaire), William Hesketh Lever (the garden village of Port Sunlight), and George Cadbury (the garden village of Bournville).

Housman A(lfred) E(dward) 1859–1936. English poet and classical scholar. His *A Shropshire Lad* 1896, a series of deceptively simple, nostalgic, balladlike poems, has been popular since World War I. This was followed by *Last Poems* 1922, *More Poems* 1936, and *Collected Poems* 1939.

As a scholar his great work was his edition of the Roman poet Manilius, which is a model of textual criticism and marks him as one of the greatest English Latinists; he also edited the works of ◊Juvenal and ◊Lucan.

Houston port in Texas, USA; linked by the Houston Ship Canal to the Gulf of Mexico, in the Gulf Coastal Plain; population (1992) 1,690,200; metropolitan area (1992) 3,962,000. A major centre of finance and commerce, Houston is also one of the busiest US ports. Industrial products include refined petroleum, oil-field equipment, and petrochemicals, chief of which are synthetic rubber, plastics, insecticides, and fertilizers. Other products include iron and steel, electrical and electronic machinery, paper products, and milled rice.
history Houston was first settled 1826, and was originally called Harrisburg. It was destroyed 1836 by the Mexican army while in pursuit of the Texas army. It became a major cotton port and, following the discovery of oil 1907 and the completion of the ship canal 1914, its importance grew rapidly, and it became a leading oil centre, with natural gas pipelines.
features The Museum of Fine Arts houses the Bayou Bend Collection of American decorative arts. Other art centres include the Menil Collection 1987, and the Rothko Chapel, which contains 14 paintings by Mark Rothko. The Grand Opera House dates from 1894, and the Houston Symphony Orchestra performs at the Jesse H Jones Hall for the Performing Arts 1966. Rice University 1912 and the Texas Medical Center 1945, including the M D Anderson Cancer Center, are here. The Lyndon B Johnson Space Center 1961 is the command post for flights by US astronauts. The Astrodome is the world's first all-purpose, air-conditioned domed stadium.

Houston Sam (Samuel) 1793–1863. US general who won independence for Texas from Mexico 1836 and was president of the Republic of Texas 1836–45. Houston, Texas, is named after him.

Houston was governor of the state of Tennessee and later US senator for and governor of the state of Texas. He took Indian citizenship when he married a Cherokee.

Houston Whitney 1963– . US soul ballad singer. She has had a string of consecutive number-one hits in the USA and Britain. They include 'Saving All My Love for You' 1985, 'I Wanna Dance With Somebody (Who Loves Me)' 1987, 'Where Do Broken Hearts Go' 1988, and 'I Will Always Love You' 1992. She made her acting debut in the film *The Bodyguard* 1992.

Hove residential town and seaside resort in East Sussex, England, adjoining Brighton to the W; population (1991) 67,600. It was one of the world's pioneering film-making centres at the turn of the century.

The Brighton School of British film-makers was working in the area at the turn of the century, led by James Williamson (1855–1933) and George Albert Smith (1864–1959), who pioneered the use of

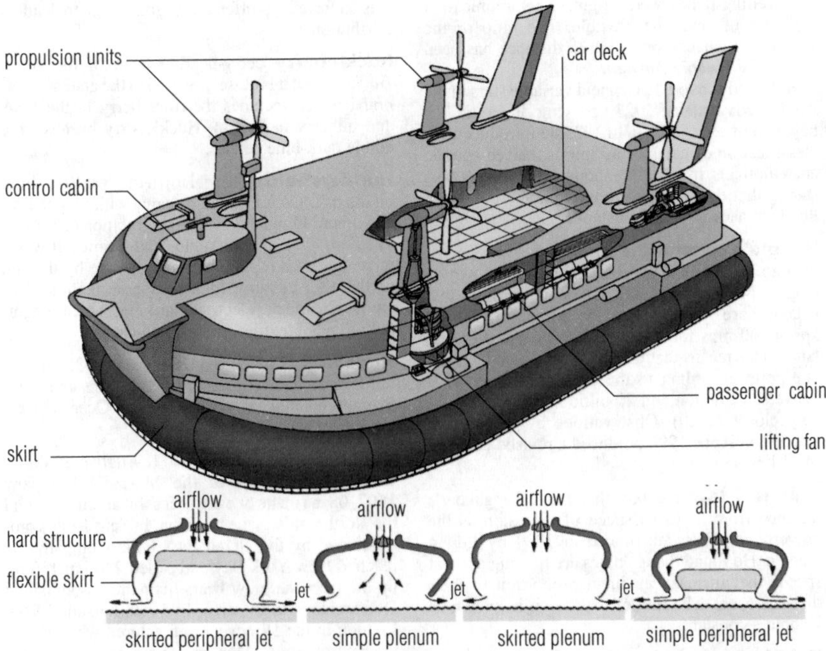

hovercraft There are several alternative ways of containing the cushion of air beneath the hull of a hovercraft. The passenger-carrying hovercraft that sails across the English Channel has a flexible skirt; other systems are the open plenum and the peripheral jet.

close-ups and, together with Charles Urban, invented the first commercially viable cinematographic colour process used in motion pictures, Kinemacolor, 1906. It was the home of English novelist Ivy Compton-Burnett 1892–1916.

hovercraft vehicle that rides on a cushion of high-pressure air, free from all contact with the surface beneath, invented by British engineer Christopher Cockerell 1959. Hovercraft need a smooth terrain when operating overland and are best adapted to use on waterways. They are useful in places where harbours have not been established.

Large hovercraft (SR-N4) operate a swift car-ferry service across the English Channel, taking only about 35 minutes between Dover and Calais. They are fitted with a flexible 'skirt' that helps maintain the air cushion.

A military version made of fibreglass, the M-10, is tough, manoeuvrable, and less noisy.

Howard Catherine c. 1520–1542. Queen consort of ◊Henry VIII of England from 1540. In 1541 the archbishop of Canterbury, Thomas Cranmer, accused her of being unchaste before marriage to Henry and she was beheaded 1542 after Cranmer made further charges of adultery.

Howard Charles, 2nd Baron Howard of Effingham and 1st Earl of Nottingham 1536–1624. English admiral, a cousin of Queen Elizabeth I. He commanded the fleet against the Spanish Armada while Lord High Admiral 1585–1618.

Howard Ebenezer 1850–1928. English town planner. He pioneered the ideal of the ◊garden city through his book *Tomorrow* 1898 (republished as *Garden Cities of Tomorrow* 1902).

Howard John Winston 1939– . Australian politician, prime minister from 1996. Firmly on the conservative wing of the Liberal party, after entering the federal parliament in 1974, Howard served in the governments of Malcolm Fraser 1975–83, and then held senior opposition posts. He has the unusual distinction of being leader of his party on two separate occasions.

Howard Leslie. Stage name of Leslie Howard Stainer 1893–1943. English actor. His films include *The Scarlet Pimpernel* 1935, *The Petrified Forest* 1936, *Pygmalion* 1938, and *Gone With the Wind* 1939.

Howard Trevor Wallace 1913–1988. English actor. His films include *Brief Encounter* 1945, *Sons and Lovers* 1960, *Mutiny on the Bounty* 1962, *Ryan's Daughter* 1970, and *Conduct Unbecoming* 1975.

Howe (Richard Edward) Geoffrey, Baron Howe of Aberavon 1926– . British Conservative politician, member of Parliament for Surrey East. As chancellor of the Exchequer 1979–83 under Margaret Thatcher, he put into practice the monetarist policy which reduced inflation at the cost of a rise in unemployment. In 1983 he became foreign secretary, and in 1989 deputy prime minister and leader of the House of Commons. On 1 Nov 1990 he resigned in protest at Thatcher's continued opposition to Britain's greater integration in Europe.

Howe Gordie (Gordon) 1926– . Canadian ice-hockey player who played for the Detroit Red Wings (National Hockey League) 1946–71 and then the New England Whalers (World Hockey Association). In the NHL, he scored more goals (801), assists (1,049), and points (1,850) than any other player in ice-hockey history until beaten by Wayne Gretsky. Howe played professional hockey until he was over 50.

Howe Richard, 1st Earl Howe 1726–1799. British admiral. He cooperated with his brother William against the colonists during the American Revolution and in the French Revolutionary Wars commanded the Channel fleets 1792–96.

Howe William, 5th Viscount Howe 1729–1814. British general. During the American Revolution he won the Battle of Bunker Hill 1775, and as commander in chief in America 1776–78 captured New York and defeated Washington at Brandywine and Germantown. He resigned in protest at lack of home government support.

Howells William Dean 1837–1920. US novelist and editor. The 'dean' of US letters in the post-Civil War era, and editor of *The Atlantic Monthly*, he championed the realist movement in fiction and encouraged many younger authors. He wrote 35 novels, 35 plays, and many books of poetry, essays, and commentary.

His novels, filled with vivid social detail, include *A Modern Instance* 1882 and *The Rise of Silas Lapham* 1885, about the social fall and moral rise of a New England paint manufacturer, a central fable of the 'Gilded Age'.

howitzer cannon, in use since the 16th century, with a particularly steep angle of fire. It was much developed in World War I for demolishing the fortresses of the trench system. The multinational NATO FH70 field howitzer is mobile and fires, under computer control, three 43 kg/95 lb shells at 32 km/20 mi range in 15 seconds.

Howlin' Wolf stage name of Chester Arthur Burnett 1910–1976. US blues singer, songwriter, harmonica player, and guitarist. His most influential recordings, made in Chicago, feature the electric guitarist Hubert Sumlin (1931–) and include 'Smokestack Lightnin'' 1956, 'Little Red Rooster' 1961, and 'Killin' Floor' 1965.

Born in rural Mississippi, Wolf moved to Memphis, Tennessee, 1948. He got his nickname from a habitual falsetto vocal call. He had a large, charismatic presence and his music is rough-edged and uncompromising. Most of his material was written by himself ('Sitting On Top of the World' 1957, 'Wang Dang Doodle' 1960) or Willie Dixon (1915–1992) ('Spoonful'), or both ('Back Door Man').

Howrah or ***Haora*** city of West Bengal, India, on the right bank of the river Hooghly, opposite Calcutta; population (1981) 742,298. The capital of Howrah district, it has jute and cotton factories; rice, flour, and saw mills; chemical factories; and engineering works. Howrah suspension bridge, opened 1943, spans the river.

Hoxha Enver 1908–1985. Albanian communist politician, the country's leader from 1954. He founded the Albanian Communist Party 1941, and headed the liberation movement 1939–44. He was prime minister 1944–54, also handling foreign affairs 1946–53, and from 1954 was first secretary of the Albanian Party of Labour. In policy he was a Stalinist and independent of both Chinese and Soviet communism.

Hoyle Fred(erick) 1915– . English astronomer, cosmologist, and writer. His astronomical research has dealt mainly with the internal structure and evolution of the stars.In 1948 he developed with

'Space isn't remote at all. It's only an hour's drive away if your car could go straight upwards.'

FRED HOYLE
Quoted in the *Observer* Sept 1979

howitzer A 240 mm/9.4 in howitzer being used by the US army in Italy 1944. Historically, a howitzer fired shells with a high, arching trajectory, but in this century many designs have fired high-speed shells with a low trajectory.
Library of Congress

Hermann ◊Bondi and Thomas Gold (1920–) the ◊steady-state theory of the universe. In 1957, with William Fowler (1911–1995), he showed that chemical elements heavier than hydrogen and helium may be built up by nuclear reactions inside stars.

Fowler and Hoyle proposed that all the elements may be synthesized from hydrogen by successive fusions. When the gas cloud reaches extremely high temperatures, the hydrogen has turned to helium and neon, whose nuclei interact, releasing particles that unite to build up nuclei of new elements.

In 1964 Hoyle proposed a new theory of gravitation. According to this theory, matter is not evenly distributed throughout space, but forms self-gravitating systems. These may range in diameter from a few kilometres to a million light years. Formed from clouds of hydrogen gas, they vary greatly in density.

He has also suggested that life originated in bacteria and viruses contained in the gas clouds of space and was then delivered to the Earth by passing comets.

Hrabal Bohumil 1914–1997. Czechoslovak writer. He began writing after 1962. His novels depict ordinary people caught up in events they do not control or comprehend, including *Ostre sledované vlaky/Closely Observed Trains* 1965 (filmed 1967).

Hsuan Tung name adopted by Henry ◊P'u-i on becoming emperor of China 1908.

HTML (*H*yper*T*ext *M*arkup *L*anguage) standard for structuring and describing a document on the ◊World-Wide Web. The HTML standard provides labels for constituent parts of a document (eg. headings and paragraphs) and permits the inclusion of images, sounds, and 'hyperlinks' to other documents. A ◊browser program is then used to convert this information into a graphical document on-screen. HTML is a specific example of ◊SGML (the international standard for text encoding). As such it is not a rigid standard but is constantly being improved to incorporate new features and allow greater freedom of design. In 1995 the specifications for HTML version 3.0 were put forward.

Hua Guofeng or ***Hua Kuofeng*** 1920– . Chinese politician, leader of the Chinese Communist Party (CCP) 1976–81, premier 1976–80. He dominated Chinese politics 1976–77, seeking economic modernization without major structural reform. From 1978 he was gradually eclipsed by Deng Xiaoping. Hua was ousted from the Politburo Sept 1982 but remained a member of the CCP Central Committee.

Huai-Hai, Battle of decisive campaign 1948–49 in the Chinese Civil War (1946–49). The name is derived from the two main defensive positions held by the nationalist ◊Guomindang force: the Huang (Huai) River in Shandong and Jiangsu provinces, and the Lung Hai railway. Communist forces from the E and W captured Suzhou (Soochow), a key railway junction, on 1 Dec 1948. On 6 Jan 1949 they secured a crushing victory at Yungchung to the SW, facilitating an advance on Shanghai, which fell in the spring of 1949.

Huang He or ***Hwang Ho*** river in China; length 5,464 km/3,395 mi. It takes its name (meaning 'yellow river') from its muddy waters. Formerly known as 'China's sorrow' because of disastrous floods, it is now largely controlled through hydroelectric works and flood barriers. The flood barriers, however, are ceasing to work because the silt is continually raising the river bed.

Huáscar c. 1495–1532. King of the Incas. He shared the throne with his half-brother Atahualpa from 1525, but the latter overthrew and murdered him during the Spanish conquest.

Hubbard L(afayette) Ron(ald) 1911–1986. US science-fiction and fantasy writer, founder in 1954 of ◊Scientology.

Hubble Edwin (Powell) 1889–1953. US astronomer. He discovered the existence of ◊galaxies outside our own, and classified them according to their shape. His theory that the universe is expanding is now generally accepted.

His data on the speed at which galaxies were receding (based on their ◊red shifts) were used to determine the portion of the universe that we can ever come to know, the radius of which is called the ***Hubble radius***. Beyond this limit, any matter will be travelling at the speed of light, so communication with it will never be possible. The ratio of the velocity of galactic recession to distance has been named the ***Hubble constant***.

Hubble discovered ◊Cepheid variable stars in the Andromeda galaxy 1923, proving it to lie far beyond our own Galaxy. In 1925 he introduced the classification of galaxies as spirals, barred spirals, and ellipticals. In 1929 he announced ***Hubble's law***, stating that the galaxies are moving apart at a rate that increases with their distance.

Hubble's constant in astronomy, a measure of the rate at which the universe is expanding, named after Edwin Hubble. Observations suggest that galaxies are moving apart at a rate of 50–100 kps/30–60 mps for every million ◊parsecs of distance. This means that the universe, which began at one point according to the ◊Big Bang theory, is between 10 billion and 20 billion years old (probably closer to 20). Observations by the Hubble Space Telescope 1996 produced a revised constant of 73 kps/45 mps.

Hubble's law the law that relates a galaxy's distance from us to its speed of recession as the universe expands, announced in 1929 by Edwin Hubble. He found that galaxies are moving apart at speeds that increase in direct proportion to their distance apart. The rate of expansion is known as Hubble's constant.

Hubble Space Telescope (HST) space-based astronomical observing facility, orbiting the Earth at an altitude of 610 km/380 mi. It consists of a 2.4 m/94 in telescope and four complimentary scientific instruments, is roughly cylindrical, 13 m/43 ft long, and 4 m/13 ft in diameter, with two large solar panels. HST produces a wealth of scientific data, and allows astronomers to observe the birth of stars, find planets around neighbouring stars, follow the expanding remnants of exploding stars, and search for black holes in the centre of galaxies. HST is a cooperative programme between the European Space Agency (ESA) and the US agency NASA, and is the first spacecraft specifically designed to be serviced in orbit as a permanent space-based observatory. It was launched 1990.

By having a large telescope above Earth's atmosphere, astronomers are able to look at the universe with unprecedented clarity. Celestial observations by HST are unhampered by clouds and other atmospheric phenomena that distort and attenuate starlight. In particular, the apparent twinkling of starlight caused by density fluctuations in the atmosphere limits the clarity of ground-based telescopes. HST performs at least ten times better than such telescopes and can see almost back to the edge of the universe and to the beginning of time (see ◊Big Bang).

Before HST could reach its full potential, a flaw in the shape of its main mirror, discovered two months after the launch, had to be corrected. In Dec 1993, as part of a planned servicing and instrument upgrade mission, NASA astronauts aboard the space shuttle *Endeavour* installed a set of corrective lenses to compensate for the error in the mirror figure. HST is also being used to detail the distribution of dust and stars in nearby galaxies, watch the collisions of galaxies in detail, infer the evolution of galaxies, and measure the age of the universe.

In Dec 1995 HST was trained on an 'empty' area of sky near the Plough, now termed the Hubble Deep Field. Around 1,500 galaxies, mostly new discoveries, were photographed. A servicing mission in Feb 1997 replaced two instruments with new ones designed to record spectra from several objects at once, and to take spectra in the infrared. ▷ *See feature on pp. 70–71.*

Hubei or ***Hupei*** province of central China, through which flow the river Chang Jiang and its tributary the Han Shui

area 187,500 sq km/72,375 sq mi

capital Wuhan

features high land in the W, the river Chang breaking through from Sichuan in gorges; elsewhere low-lying, fertile land; many lakes

industries beans, cereals, cotton, rice, vegetables, copper, gypsum, iron ore, phosphorus, salt

population (1990) 54,760,000.

hubris in Greek thought, an act of transgression or overweening pride. In ancient Greek tragedy, hubris was believed to offend the gods, and to lead to retribution.

huckleberry berry-bearing bush of the genus *Gaylussacia*; it is closely related to the genus *Vaccinium*, which includes the ◊blueberry in the USA and bilberry in Britain. Huckleberry bushes have edible dark-blue berries.

Huddersfield industrial town in West Yorkshire, on the river Colne, linked by canal with Manchester and other N England centres; population (1988 est) 121,800. A village in Anglo-Saxon times, it was a thriving centre of woollen manufacture by the end of the 18th century; industries now include dyestuffs, chemicals, electrical and mechanical engineering, wool textiles, prams, and carpets.

Hudson river of the NE USA; length 485 km/300 mi. It rises in the Adirondack Mountains and flows S, emptying into a bay of the Atlantic Ocean at New York City.

Hudson Henry c. 1565–1611. English explorer. Under the auspices of the Muscovy Company 1607–08, he made two unsuccessful attempts to find the Northeast Passage to China. In Sept 1609, commissioned by the Dutch East India Company, he reached New York Bay and sailed 240 km/150 mi up the river that now bears his name, establishing Dutch claims to the area. In 1610, he sailed from London in the *Discovery* and entered what is now the Hudson Strait. After an icebound winter, he was turned adrift by a mutinous crew in what is now Hudson Bay.

Hudson Rock. Stage name of Roy Scherer Jr 1925–1985. US film actor. He was a star from the mid-1950s to the mid-1960s, and appeared in several melodramas directed by Douglas Sirk and in three comedies co-starring Doris Day (including *Pillow Talk* 1959). He went on to have a successful TV career in the 1970s.

Hudson Bay inland sea of NE Canada, linked with the Atlantic Ocean by ***Hudson Strait*** and with the Arctic Ocean by Foxe Channel; area 1,233,000 sq km/476,000 sq mi. It is named after Henry Hudson, who reached it 1610.

Hudson River School group of US landscape painters of the early 19th century. They painted the dramatic scenery of the Hudson River Valley and the Catskill Mountains in New York State, their style influenced by the Romantic landscapes of J M W Turner and John Martin. The best-known members of the school was Thomas Cole, who set up his studio at Catskill 1826, and Albery Bierstadt.

Hudson's Bay Company chartered company founded by Prince ◊Rupert 1670 to trade in furs with North American Indians. In 1783 the rival

Hudson US film actor Rock Hudson whose good looks made him one of Hollywood's leading stars. A former truck driver, Hudson had no acting experience when he was given his first chance in films, and later had to undergo intensive coaching and grooming. His death from AIDS 1985 shocked film-goers around the world. *Topham*

North West Company was formed, but in 1851 this became amalgamated with the Hudson's Bay Company. It is still Canada's biggest fur company, but today also sells general merchandise through department stores and has oil and natural gas interests.

Huelva port and capital of Huelva province, Andalusia, SW Spain, near the mouth of the river Odiel; population (1994) 145,000. Industries include shipbuilding, oil refining, fisheries, and trade in ores from Río Tinto. Columbus began and ended his voyage to America at nearby Palos de la Frontera.

Huesca capital of Huesca province in Aragon, N Spain; population (1991) 50,000. Industries include engineering and food processing. Among its buildings are a fine 13th-century cathedral and the former palace of the kings of Aragon.

Hughes (James Mercer) Langston 1902–1967. US poet and novelist. Known as 'the poet laureate of Harlem', he became one of the foremost black American literary figures, writing such collections of poems as *The Weary Blues* 1926. In addition to his poetry he wrote a series of novels, short stories, and essays. His autobiography *The Big Sea* appeared 1940.

Hughes Howard (Robard) 1905–1976. US tycoon. Inheriting wealth from his father, who had patented a successful oil-drilling bit, he created a legendary financial empire. A skilled pilot, he manufactured and designed aircraft. He formed a film company in Hollywood and made the classic film *Hell's Angels* 1930 about aviators of World War I; later successes included *Scarface* 1932 and *The Outlaw* 1944. From his middle years he was a recluse.

Hughes Richard (Arthur Warren) 1900–1976. English writer. His study of childhood, *A High Wind in Jamaica*, was published 1929; his story of a ship's adventures in a hurricane, *In Hazard*, 1938; and the historical novel *The Fox in the Attic* 1961. He also wrote some poetry and plays (his *Collected Plays* appeared 1928), and short stories.

Hughes Ted (Edward James) 1930–1998. English poet, poet laureate 1984–98. His work is characterized by its harsh portrayal of the crueller aspects of nature, by its reflection of the agonies of personal experience, and by the employment of myths of creation and being, as in *Crow* 1970 and *Gaudete* 1977. Collections include *The Hawk in the Rain* 1957, *Lupercal* 1960 and *Wodwo* 1967. He received the Whitbread Literary Award for *Tales from Ovid* 1997 and *Birthday Letters* 1998. In 1956 he married the US poet Sylvia ◊Plath.

Hughes Thomas 1822–1896. English writer. He was the author of *Tom Brown's School Days* 1857, a simple story of Rugby School under Thomas ◊Arnold, with an underlying religious sense. It had a sequel, *Tom Brown at Oxford* 1861.

Hughes William Morris 1862–1952. Australian politician, prime minister 1915–23; originally Labor, he headed a national cabinet. After resigning as prime minister 1923, he held many other cabinet posts 1934–41.

Hugo Victor (Marie) 1802–1885. French novelist, poet, and dramatist. The verse play *Hernani* 1830 firmly established Hugo as the leader of French Romanticism. This was the first of a series of dramas produced in the 1830s and early 1840s, including *Le Roi s'amuse* 1832 and *Ruy Blas* 1838. His melodramatic novels include *Notre-Dame de Paris* 1831, and *Les Misérables* 1862.

Hugo's position in French literature is important: he gave French Romanticism a peculiarly decorative character and kept the Romantic spirit alive in France for some 30 years after its apparent demise. His writing is notable for its vitality, wide scope, graceful lyrical power, rhetorical magnificence, the ability to express pathos, awe, and indignation; and the variety of style and skill displayed in his handling of metre and language.

Huguenot French Protestant in the 16th century; the term referred mainly to Calvinists. Severely persecuted under Francis I and Henry II, the Huguenots survived both an attempt to exterminate them (the Massacre of ◊St Bartholomew 24 Aug 1572) and the religious wars of the next 30 years. In 1598 Henry IV (himself formerly a Huguenot) granted them toleration under the Edict of ◊Nantes. Louis XIV revoked the edict 1685, attempting their forcible conversion, and 400,000 emigrated.

Some of the nobles adopted Protestantism for political reasons, causing the civil wars 1592–98. The Huguenots lost military power after the revolt at La Rochelle 1627–29, but were still tolerated by the chief ministers Richelieu and Mazarin. Provoked by Louis XIV they left, taking their industrial skills with them; 40,000 settled in Britain, where their descendants include the actor David Garrick and the textile manufacturer Samuel Courtauld. Many settled in North America, founding new towns. Only in 1802 was the Huguenot church again legalized in France.

Hui one of the largest minority ethnic groups in China, numbering about 8,612,000. Members of the Hui live all over China, but are concentrated in the northern central region. They have been Muslims since the 10th century, for which they have suffered persecution both before and since the communist revolution.

Hukbalahap movement left-wing Filipino peasant resistance campaign 1942–54. Formed to challenge the Japanese wartime occupation of the Philippines 1942–45, it carried out guerrilla attacks against the Japanese from its base in central Luzon. After World War II, it opposed the Filipino landed elite and its American allies and established an alternative government in Luzon. During the Korean War, a government military campaign 1950–54 defeated the 'Huks'.

Hull officially ***Kingston upon Hull*** city and port on the north bank of the Humber estuary, England, where the river Hull flows into it, Humberside, England; population (1991) 254,100. It is linked with the south bank of the estuary by the Humber Bridge, the world's longest single-span suspension bridge. Industries include fish processing, vegetable oils, flour milling, electrical goods, textiles, paint, pharmaceuticals, chemicals, caravans, aircraft, and sawmilling.

Hull Cordell 1871–1955. US Democratic politician. As F D Roosevelt's secretary of state 1933–44, he opposed German and Japanese aggression. He was identified with the Good Neighbour policy of nonintervention in Latin America. In his last months of office he paved the way for a system of collective security, for which he was called 'father' of the United Nations. Nobel Peace Prize 1945.

He was born in Tennessee. He was a member of Congress 1907–33. After Dec 1941 foreign policy was handled more directly by Roosevelt, but Hull was active in reaching agreements with ◊Vichy France, though these were largely cancelled by the rising influence of General Charles ◊de Gaulle.

Hulme Keri 1947– . New Zealand poet and novelist. She won the Commonwealth Booker Prize with her first novel *The Bone People* 1985. This centres on an autistic child and those close to him. Acutely responsive to maritime landscape, it lyrically incorporates the more mystical aspects of Maori experience. Other works include the novella *Lost Possessions* 1985, *The Windeater/Te Kaihau* 1986, a collection of short stories, and *Strands* 1990, a book of poetry.

human body the physical structure of the human being. It develops from the single cell of the fertilized ovum, is born at 40 weeks, and usually reaches sexual maturity between 11 and 18 years of age. The bony framework (skeleton) consists of more than 200 bones, over half of which are in the hands and feet. Bones are held together by joints, some of which allow movement. The circulatory system supplies muscles and organs with blood, which provides oxygen and food and removes carbon dioxide

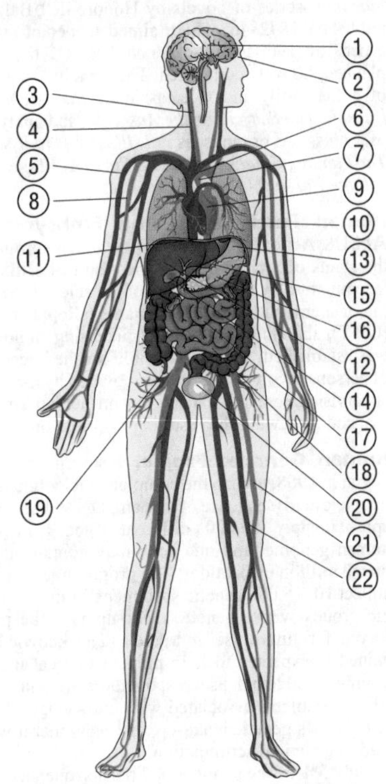

Key
1. brain
2. eye
3. cartoid artery
4. jugular vein
5. subclavian vein
6. superior vena cava
7. aorta
8. subclavian artery
9. heart
10. lungs
11. diaphragm
12. liver
13. stomach
14. gall bladder
15. kidney
16. pancreas
17. small intestine
18. large intestine
19. appendix
20. bladder
21. femoral artery
22. femoral vein

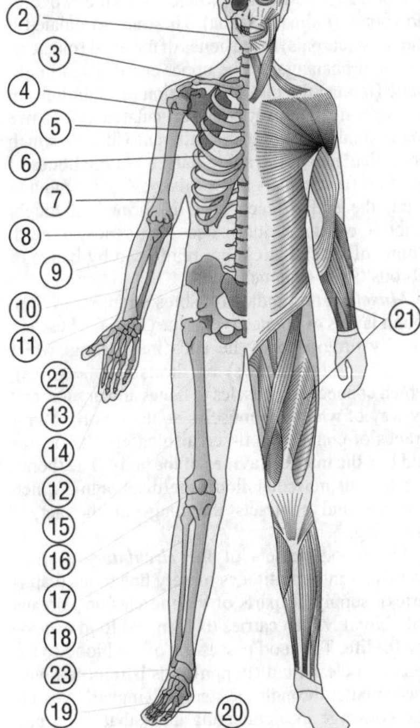

Key
1. cranium (skull)
2. mandible
3. clavicle
4. scapular
5. sternum
6. rib cage
7. humerus
8. vertabra
9. ulna
10. radius
11. pelvis
12. coccyx
13. metacarpals
14. phalanges
15. femur
16. patella
17. fibula
18. tibia
19. metatarsals
20. phalanges
21. superfical (upper) layer of muscles
22. carpals
23. tarsals

human body The adult human body has approximately 650 muscles, 100 joints, 97,000 km/ 60,000 mi of blood vessels and 13,000 nerve cells. There are 206 bones in the adult body, nearly half of them in the hands and feet.

HUMAN BODY: COMPOSITION	
Chemical element or substance	**Body weight (%)**
Pure elements	
oxygen	65
carbon	18
hydrogen	10
nitrogen	3
calcium	2
phosphorus	1.1
potassium	0.35
sulphur	0.25
sodium	0.15
chlorine	0.15
magnesium, iron, manganese, copper, iodine, cobalt, zinc	traces
Water and solid matter	
water	60–80
total solid material	20–40
Organic molecules	
protein	15–20
lipid	3–20
carbohydrate	1–15
small organic	0–1

and other waste products. Body functions are controlled by the nervous system and hormones.

skeleton The skull is mounted on the spinal column, or spine, a chain of 24 vertebrae. The ribs, 12 on each side, are articulated to the spinal column behind, and the upper seven meet the breastbone (sternum) in front. The lower end of the spine rests on the pelvic girdle, composed of the triangular sacrum, to which are attached the hipbones (ilia), which are fused in front. Below the sacrum is the tailbone (coccyx). The shoulder blades (scapulae) are held in place behind the upper ribs by muscles, and connected in front to the breastbone by the two collarbones (clavicles).

Each shoulder blade carries a cup (glenoid cavity) into which fits the upper end of the armbone (humerus). This articulates below with the two forearm bones (radius and ulna). These are articulated at the wrist (carpals) to the bones of the hand (metacarpals and phalanges). The upper end of each thighbone (femur) fits into a depression (acetabulum) in the hipbone; its lower end is articulated at the knee to the shinbone (tibia) and calf bone (fibula), which are articulated at the ankle (tarsals) to the bones of the foot (metatarsals and phalanges). At a moving joint, the end of each bone is formed of tough, smooth cartilage, lubricated by ◊synovial fluid. Points of special stress are reinforced by bands of fibrous tissue (ligaments).

Muscles are bundles of fibres wrapped in thin, tough layers of connective tissue (fascia); these are usually prolonged at the ends into strong, white cords (tendons, sinews) or sheets (aponeuroses), which connect the muscles to bones and organs, and by way of which the muscles do their work. Membranes of connective tissue also enfold the organs and line the interior cavities of the body. The thorax has a stout muscular floor, the diaphragm, which expands and contracts the lungs in the act of breathing.

The blood vessels of the ***circulatory system***, branching into multitudes of very fine tubes (capillaries), supply all parts of the muscles and organs with blood, which carries oxygen and food necessary for life. The food passes out of the blood to the cells in a clear fluid (lymph); this is returned with waste matter through a system of lymphatic vessels that converge into collecting ducts that drain into large veins in the region of the lower neck. Capillaries join together to form veins which return blood, depleted of oxygen, to the heart.

A finely branching ***nervous system*** regulates the function of the muscles and organs, and makes their needs known to the controlling centres in the central nervous system, which consists of the brain and spinal cord. The inner spaces of the brain and the cord contain cerebrospinal fluid. The body processes are regulated both by the nervous system and by hormones secreted by the endocrine glands. Cavities of the body that open onto the surface are coated with mucous membranes, which secrete a lubricating fluid (mucus).

The exterior surface of the body is covered with ***skin***. Within the skin are the sebaceous glands, which secrete sebum, an oily fluid that makes the skin soft and pliable, and the sweat glands, which secrete water and various salts. From the skin grow hairs, chiefly on the head, in the armpits, and around the sexual organs; and nails shielding the tips of the fingers and toes; both hair and nails are modifications of skin tissue. The skin also contains nerve receptors for sensations of touch, pain, heat, and cold.

The human ***digestive system*** is nonspecialized and can break down a wide variety of foodstuffs. Food is mixed with saliva in the mouth by chewing and is swallowed. It enters the stomach, where it is gently churned for some time and mixed with acidic gastric juice. It then passes into the small intestine. In the first part of this, the duodenum, it is broken down further by the juice of the pancreas and duodenal glands, and mixed with bile from the liver, which splits up the fat. The jejunum and ileum continue the work of digestion and absorb most of the nutritive substances from the food. The large intestine completes the process, reabsorbing water into the body, and ejecting the useless residue as faeces.

The body, to be healthy, must maintain water and various salts in the right proportions; the process is called ***osmoregulation***. The blood is filtered in the two kidneys, which remove excess water, salts, and metabolic wastes. Together these form urine, which has a yellow pigment derived from bile, and passes down through two fine tubes (ureters) into the bladder, a reservoir from which the urine is emptied at intervals (micturition) through the urethra. Heat is constantly generated by the combustion of food in the muscles and glands, and by the activity of nerve cells and fibres. It is dissipated through the skin by conduction and evaporation of sweat, through the lungs in the expired air, and in other excreted substances. Average body temperature is about 38°C/100°F (37°C/98.4°F in the mouth).

Human Comedy, The (French *La Comédie humaine*) series of novels by Honoré de ◊Balzac, published 1842–46, which aimed to depict every aspect of 19th-century French life. Of the 143 planned, 80 were completed. These include studies of human folly and vice, as in *Le Recherche de l'absolu/The Search for the Absolute*, and analyses of professions or ranks, as in *L'Illustre Gaudissart/The Famous Gaudissart* and *Le Curé de village/The Village Parson*.

Human Fertilization and Embryology Act UK Act of Parliament 1990 which determined the status of a child born as the result of artificial insemination by donor (AID), of the scientific mixing of sperm and eggs in a woman's fallopian tubes (GIFT), and embryo transfer. A licensing authority was established, and is reponsible for the licensing of persons involved in activities covered by the Bill, supervising research carried out on human embyros, and reviewing the resulting information.

Human Genome Project research scheme, begun in 1988, to map the complete nucleotide (see ◊nucleic acid) sequence of human ◊DNA. There are approximately 80,000 different ◊genes in the human genome, and one gene may contain more than 2 million nucleotides. The programme aims to collect 10–15,000 genetic specimens from 722 ethnic groups whose genetic make-up is to be preserved for future use and study. The knowledge gained is expected to help prevent or treat many crippling and lethal diseases, but there are potential ethical problems associated with knowledge of an individual's genetic make-up, and fears that it will lead to genetic discrimination.

Only 3% of the genome had been sequenced by mid 1998. The deadline for the complete sequencing of the human genome was brought forward two years to 2003, in September 1998, with the additional aim of completing 90% by 2001.

The Human Genome Organization (HUGO) coordinating the project expects to spend $1 billion over the first five years, making this the largest research project ever undertaken in the life sciences. Work is being carried out in more than 20 centres around the world.

Concerns – such as that, for example, knowledge of an individual's genes may make that person an unacceptable insurance risk – have led to planned legislation on genome privacy in the USA, and 3% of HUGO's funds have been set aside for research-ing and reporting on the ethical implications of the project.

Sequencing Each strand of DNA carries a sequence of chemical building blocks, the nucleotides. There are only four different types of nucleotide, but the number of possible combinations is immense. The different combinations of nucleotides produce different proteins in the cell, and thus determine the structure of the body and its individual variations. To establish the nucleotide sequence, DNA strands are broken into fragments, which are duplicated (by being introduced into cells of yeast or the bacterium *Escherichia coli*) and distributed to the research centres.

Genes account for only a small amount of DNA sequence. Over 90% of DNA appears not to have any function, although it is perfectly replicated each time the cell divides, and handed on to the next generation. Many higher organisms have large amounts of redundant DNA and it may be that this is an advantage, in that there is a pool of DNA available to form new genes if an old one is lost by mutation.

humanism belief in the high potential of human nature rather than in religious or transcendental values. Humanism culminated as a cultural and literary force in 16th-century Renaissance Europe in line with the period's enthusiasm for classical literature and art, growing individualism, and the ideal of the all-round male who should be statesman and poet, scholar and warrior. ◊Erasmus is a great exemplar of Renaissance humanism.

human rights civil and political rights of the individual in relation to the state; see also ◊civil rights.

Human Rights Act UK act of Parliament 1998 which gave further provision to rights and freedoms guaranteed under the European Convention on Human Rights. The enactment of a UK Code of Rights incorporated the European Convention into domestic law, enabling people to secure decisions on their human rights from British courts and not only from the European Court of Human Rights in Strasbourg. Prior to 1998, Britain had been virtually alone among the major Western European nations in having no direct means for its citizens to assert European Convention rights through the national courts.

Human Rights, Universal Declaration of charter of civil and political rights drawn up by the United Nations 1948. They include the right to life, liberty, education, and equality before the law; to freedom of movement, religion, association, and information; and to a nationality.

Under the European Convention of Human Rights 1950, the Council of Europe established the European Commission of Human Rights, which investigates complaints by states or individuals. Its findings are examined by the European Court of Human Rights (established 1959), whose compulsory jurisdiction has been recognized by a number of states, including the UK.

Human Rights Watch US nonpartisan pressure group that monitors and publicizes human-rights abuses by governments, especially attacks on those who defend human rights in their own countries. It comprises Africa Watch, Americas Watch, Asia Watch, Middle East Watch, and Helsinki Watch; the last-named monitors compliance with the 1975 Helsinki accords by the 35 signatory countries.

The first Watch committee was established 1978. By 1990 the organization was sending more than 100 investigative missions to some 60 countries around the world. Human Rights Watch does not accept financial support from governments or government-funded organizations.

human species, origins of evolution of humans from ancestral ◊primates. The African apes (gorilla and chimpanzee) are shown by anatomical and molecular comparisons to be the closest living relatives of humans. Humans are distinguished from apes by the size of their brain and jaw, their bipedalism, and their elaborate culture. Molecular studies put the date of the split between the human and African ape lines at 5–7 million years ago. There are only fragmentary remains of ape and ***hominid*** (of the human group) fossils from this period. Bones of the earliest known human ancestor, a hominid named *Australopithecus ramidus* 1994, were found in Ethiopia and dated as 4.4 million years old. ▷ *See feature on pp. 518–519.*

Humayun also known as ***Nasir ud-Din Muhammad*** 1508–1556. Second Mogul emperor of N India 1530–40 and 1554–56. The son of ◊Babur, he inherited an unsettled empire and faced constant challenges from his three brothers. Following defeat by the Afghan Sher Shad Suri (died 1545), he fled into exile in Persia 1540. Returning to India, he reoccupied Delhi and Agra 1555 but died within a year. He was succeeded by his son ◊Akbar.

Humber estuary in NE England formed by the Ouse and Trent rivers, which meet E of Goole and flow 60 km/38 mi to enter the North Sea below Spurn Head. The main ports are Hull on the north side, and Grimsby on the south side.

Humberside former county of NE England, formed 1974 out of N Lincolnshire and parts of the East and West Ridings of Yorkshire, and reorganized 1996 as part of local government changes, which split Humberside into the unitary authorities of East Riding of Yorkshire, Kingston upon Hull, North East Lincolnshire, and North Lincolnshire.

Humboldt (Friedrich Wilhelm Heinrich) Alexander. Baron von Humboldt 1769–1859. German geophysicist, botanist, geologist, and writer who, with French botanist Aimé Bonpland (1773–1858), explored the regions of the Orinoco and Amazon rivers in South America 1800–04, and gathered 60,000 plant specimens. He was a founder of ecology.

Humboldt aimed to erect a new science, a 'physics of the globe', analysing the deep physical interconnectedness of all terrestrial phenomena. He believed that geological phenomena were to be understood in terms of basic physical causes (for example, terrestrial magnetism or rotation).

One of the first popularizers of science, he gave a series of lectures later published as *Kosmos/Cosmos* 1845–62, an account of the relations between physical environment and flora and fauna.

Humboldt Current former name of the ◊Peru Current.

Hume (George) Basil 1923– . English Roman Catholic cardinal from 1976. A Benedictine monk, he was abbot of Ampleforth in Yorkshire 1963–76, and in 1976 became archbishop of Westminster, the first monk to hold the office.

Hume David 1711–1776. Scottish philosopher whose *Treatise of Human Nature* 1739–40 is a central text of British ◊empiricism. Examining meticulously our modes of thinking, he concluded that they are more habitual than rational. Consequently, he not only held that speculative metaphysics was impossible, but also arrived at generally sceptical positions about reason, causation, necessity, identity, and the self.

Hume John 1937– . Northern Ireland Catholic politician, leader of the Social Democratic Labour Party (SDLP) from 1979. Hume was a founder member of the Credit Union Party, which later became the SDLP.

In 1993 he held talks with Sinn Féin leader, Gerry Adams, prompting a joint Anglo–Irish peace initiative, which in turn led to a general cease-fire 1994–96. Despite the collapse of the cease-fire, Hume continued in his efforts to broker a settlement. He was awarded the Nobel Peace Prize 1998, jointly with David ◊Trimble.

hum, environmental disturbing sound of frequency about 40 Hz, heard by individuals sensitive to this range, but inaudible to the rest of the population. It may be caused by industrial noise pollution or have a more exotic origin, such as the jet stream, a fast-flowing high-altitude (about 15,000 m/50,000 ft) mass of air.

humerus the upper bone of the forelimb of tetrapods. In humans, the humerus is the bone above the elbow.

humidity the quantity of water vapour in a given volume of the atmosphere (absolute humidity), or the ratio of the amount of water vapour in the atmosphere to the saturation value at the same temperature (relative humidity). At dew point (the temperature at which the air becomes saturated with water vapour) the relative humidity is 100%. Condensation (the conversion of vapour to liquid) may then occur. Relative humidity is measured by various types of ◊hygrometer.

hummingbird any of various brilliantly coloured birds of the family Trochilidae, order Apodiformes, found in the Americas. The name is derived from the sound produced by the rapid vibration of their wings. Hummingbirds have long, needlelike bills and tongues to obtain nectar from flowers and capture insects. They are the only birds able to fly backwards. There are over 300 species.

hummingbird With their often vivid coloration and spectacular flying ability, hummingbirds are among the most exciting birds of the Americas. Feeding mainly on nectar and insects, hummingbirds are able to fly forwards, downwards, upwards, and even backwards.

humours, theory of theory prevalent in the West in classical and medieval times that the human body was composed of four kinds of fluid: phlegm, blood, choler or yellow bile, and melancholy or black bile. Physical and mental characteristics were explained by different proportions of humours in individuals.

An excess of phlegm produced a 'phlegmatic', or calm, temperament; of blood a 'sanguine', or passionate, one; of yellow bile a 'choleric', or irascible, temperament; and of black bile a 'melancholy', or depressive, one. The Greek physician Galen connected the theory to that of the four elements (see ◊elements, the four): the phlegmatic was associated with water, the sanguine with air, the choleric with fire, and the melancholic with earth. An imbalance of the humours could supposedly be treated by diet.

Humperdinck Engelbert 1854–1921. German composer. He studied in Cologne and Munich and assisted Richard Wagner in the preparation of *Parsifal* 1879 at Bayreuth. He wrote the musical fairy operas *Hänsel und Gretel* 1893, and *Königskinder/King's Children* 1910.

Humphrey Doris 1895–1958. US choreographer, dancer, and teacher. She was one of the pioneers of modern dance. Her movement technique was based on the shifting imbalance of weight, either falling towards or recovering from two absolute positions – the upright or horizontal. Her works include *The Shakers* 1930, *With My Red Fires* 1936, and *Day on Earth* 1947. Her book *The Art of Making Dances* 1959 is still a highly regarded study on choreography.

Humphries (John) Barry 1934– . Australian actor and author. He is best known for his satirical one-person shows and especially for the creation of the character of Mrs (later Dame) Edna Everage. His comic strip 'The Adventures of Barry Mackenzie', published in the British weekly *Private Eye* 1963–74, was the basis for two films, *The Adventures of Barry Mackenzie* 1972 and *Barry Mackenzie Holds His Own* 1974, in which Humphries also acted.

humus component of ◊soil consisting of decomposed or partly decomposed organic matter, dark in colour and usually richer towards the surface. It has a higher carbon content than the original material and a lower nitrogen content, and is an important source of minerals in soil fertility.

Hun member of any of a number of nomad Mongol peoples who were first recorded historically in the 2nd century BC, raiding across the Great Wall into China. They entered Europe about AD 372, settled in the area that is now Hungary, and imposed their supremacy on the Ostrogoths and other Germanic peoples. Under the leadership of Attila they attacked the Byzantine Empire, invaded Gaul, and threatened Rome. After Attila's death in 453 their power was broken by a revolt of their subject peoples. The ***White Huns***, or Ephthalites, a kindred people, raided Persia and N India in the 5th and 6th centuries.

Hunan province of S central China
area 210,500 sq km/81,253 sq mi
capital Changsha
features Dongting Lake; farmhouse in Shaoshan village where Mao Zedong was born
industries rice, tea, tobacco, cotton; nonferrous minerals
population (1990) 60,660,000.

hundred subdivision of a shire in England, Ireland, and parts of the USA. The term was originally used by Germanic peoples to denote a group of 100 warriors, also the area occupied by 100 families or equalling 100 hides (one hide being the amount of land necessary to support a peasant family). When the Germanic peoples settled in England, the hundred remained the basic military and administrative division of England until its abolition 1867.

hundred days in European history, the period 20 March–28 June 1815, marking the French emperor Napoleon's escape from imprisonment on Elba to his departure from Paris after losing the battle of Waterloo 18 June.

The phrase also describes other periods of new administration. In 1898 Emperor Te Tsung of China attempted 100 days of reform (11 June–16 Sept), under the guidance of K'ang Yu-wei. In 1931 Benito Mussolini and G Forzano wrote *The 100 Days*. It is also applied to the reform period in the administration of US president F D Roosevelt from his inauguration on 4 March 1933 when much of the legislation for his New Deal programme was initiated. English prime minister Harold Wilson used the phrase in *Purpose and Power* 1966.

Hundred Flowers campaign in Chinese history, a movement 1956–57 of open political and intellectual debate, encouraged by ◊Mao Zedong.

The campaign was begun in May 1956, soon after Soviet leader Nikita Khrushchev's 'secret speech' attacking the excesses of Stalinism, and was brought to a close May 1957, with 200,000 intelligentsia critics being exiled to remote rural areas in what became known as the anti-rightist campaign. The name was derived from a slogan from Chinese classical history: 'Let a hundred flowers bloom and a hundred schools of thought contend.'

hundredweight imperial unit (abbreviation cwt) of mass, equal to 112 lb (50.8 kg). It is sometimes called the long hundredweight, to distinguish it from the short hundredweight or ***cental***, equal to 100 lb (45.4 kg).

Hundred Years' War series of conflicts between England and France 1337–1453. Its origins lay with the English kings' possession of Gascony (SW France), which the French kings claimed as

cont. on p. 520

'Never literary attempt was more unfortunate than my Treatise of Human Nature. It fell dead-born from the press.'

David Hume
My Own Life

HUNDRED YEARS' WAR: TIMELINE

1340	The English were victorious at the naval battle of Sluys.
1346	Battle of Crécy, a victory for the English.
1347	The English took Calais.
1356	Battle of Poitiers, where Edward the Black Prince defeated the French. King John of France was captured.
late 1350s–early 1360s	France had civil wars, brigandage, and the popular uprising of the Jacquerie.
1360	Treaty of Brétigny-Calais. France accepted English possession of Calais and of a greatly enlarged duchy of Gascony. John was ransomed for £500,000.
1369–1414	The tide turned in favour of the French, and when there was another truce in 1388, only Calais, Bordeaux, and Bayonne were in English hands. A state of half-war continued for many years.
1415	Henry V invaded France and won a victory at Agincourt, followed by conquest of Normandy.
1420	In the Treaty of Troyes, Charles VI of France was forced to disinherit his son, the Dauphin, in favour of Henry V, who was to marry Catherine, Charles's daughter. Most of N France was in English hands.
1422–28	After the death of Henry V his brother Bedford was generally successful.
1429	Joan of Arc raised the siege of Orléans, and the Dauphin was crowned Charles VII at Rheims.
1430–53	Even after Joan's capture and death the French continued their successful counteroffensive, and in 1453 only Calais was left in English hands.

The Search for Human Origins

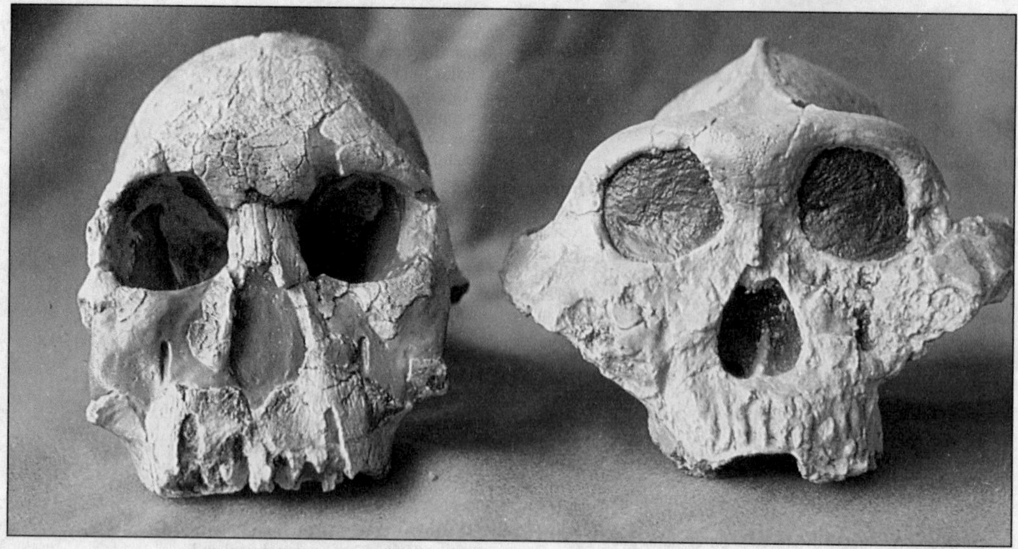

Skulls and other fossil remains provide vital clues in the search for human origins. The skull on the right is of the 'robust' group of australopithecines called *Paranthropus*. The australopithecines lived in southern and eastern Africa between 4 million and about 1 million years ago and are the earliest human-like apes. They shared features with living apes but were distinguished from them by their upright posture and their human-like teeth. *Homo habilis* (skull on left) lived about 2.5–1.6 million years ago, and may represent a transitional species between the australopithecines and the later hominines. Archaeological evidence suggests that *H. habilis* was the first human-like being to use stone tools. *Chris Stringer, Natural History Museum*

The most distant origins of the human species lie in Africa, some 4–5 million years ago, when apelike creatures developed the habit of walking upright. But how, and when, did these ancestors of ours develop into the modern human, *Homo sapiens*? Here scientists disagree, offering varying theories which call on evidence from fossil finds and, increasingly, from development in DNA research.

Ardipithecus and australopithecines

One candidate for the earliest human ancestor is a 4.4-million-year-old creature called *Ardipithecus ramidus*, whose fossil teeth and jaw and bone fragments were found in Ethiopia in 1994. Until these remains have been studied in detail, however, it will remain unclear whether *Ardipithecus* lies on the human evolutionary line, or whether it represents a fossil ape. If it is an ape, then the earliest members of the human line are represented by the somewhat later australopithecines ('southern apes').

Australopithecine fossils have been discovered in eastern and southern Africa. They are subdivided into two groups: *Australopithecus* and *Paranthropus*. *Australopithecus*, the gracile, or lightly built, australopithecines, are known from sites in northern Kenya dating from 2–4 million years ago; *Paranthropus*, the robust australopithecines, date from 1–2.5 million years ago.

All the australopithecines were apparently bipeds (they regularly walked upright on two legs). In details of their teeth, jaws, and brain size, however, they differ sufficiently among themselves to warrant division into at least three species of *Australopithecus*: *A. anamensis*, *A. afarensis*, and *A. africanus*; and three species of *Paranthropus*: *P. aethiopicus*, *P. robustus*, and *P. boisei*. It is possible that the earlier *A. anamensis* gave rise to the later species of *Australopithecus*, while *P. aethiopicus* was the ancestor of the later species of *Paranthropus*. In 1974 most of the skeleton of an *A. afarensis* female was discovered and nicknamed Lucy; her age was estimated at 3.1 million years. Study of these, and other, australopithecine remains, suggests that although they were bipeds, they still had apelike brain sizes, body proportions, and other characteristics.

By about 2.5 million years ago, the fossil evidence shows the presence of at least two, and perhaps as many as four, separate species of hominines (humans and our close relatives). A split seems to have occurred in the hominine line, with one segment evolving towards the genus *Homo*, and modern humans, and the others developing into species of *Paranthropus* that became extinct about 1 million years ago. The large chewing teeth, jaws, and jaw muscles of robust australopithecines seem to represent a specialised adaptation for eating hard food such as seeds and nuts.

Homo habilis *and* Homo erectus

Although experts do not all agree, some believe that, after the evolutionary split that led to the robust australopithecines, *Australopithecus africanus* evolved into the genus *Homo*. Others believe we may have briefly shared an ancestry with the early robust australopithecine line. The transition to true humans occurred 2.7–2.3 million years ago. Early *Homo* fossils dating from this period display a mixture of traits: some have relatively big brains, but large, australopithecine-sized teeth, while others have small, *Homo*-sized teeth and small, australopithecine-sized brains.

A number of fossil skulls and jaws from this period, found in Tanzania, Kenya, Malawi, and Ethiopia, have been placed in the category *H. habilis*, 'Handy Man', because some of the fossils were found with early stone tools. *H. habilis* possessed traits that link it both with the earlier australopithecines and with later members of the genus *Homo*. However, some experts believe the variation in *habilis* fossils is so great that at least two separate species are represented: the smaller one called *H. habilis*, and the larger one *H. rudolfensis* (after Lake Rudolf, an old name for Lake Turkana in northern Kenya). The earliest stone tools come from sites in Africa dated at about 2.5 million years ago; they may have been made by members of the line leading to *Homo*, or by robust australopithecines. These tools and bone debris suggest that hominines were supplementing plant foods by eating some meat, through scavenging or hunting.

Fossils of a larger-brained, smaller-toothed form, known earliest from northern Kenya at 1.8–1.9 million years ago, have been placed in the species *H. erectus*, or a more primitive ancestral form *H. ergaster*, 'Work Man'. Initially, *H. ergaster/erectus* was apparently limited to Africa; but soon after this, *H. erectus* is known from tropical areas of the Old World, and later from temperate Asia and Europe. Stone tools, butchered bones, and hearths suggest that hominine behaviour was becoming more complex, although it is not clear whether *erectus* was a scavenger or a hunter.

A POSSIBLE ANCESTOR
Fossil footbones found in Sterkfontein Caves and studied in 1994 show a unique combination of an ape-like foot and a human-like ankle bone of a possible ancestor that lived at least 3 million years ago
AFRICA
Rift Valley
Sterkfontein Caves
foot of great ape
"Little Foot" fossil
modern human foot
human-like ankle bone
ape-like toe bone
The bones indicate a foot that would be adept at clasping branches and well adapted for standing and walking on two legs
Walking upright gave the humans greater mobility for hunting and foraging for food
REUTER

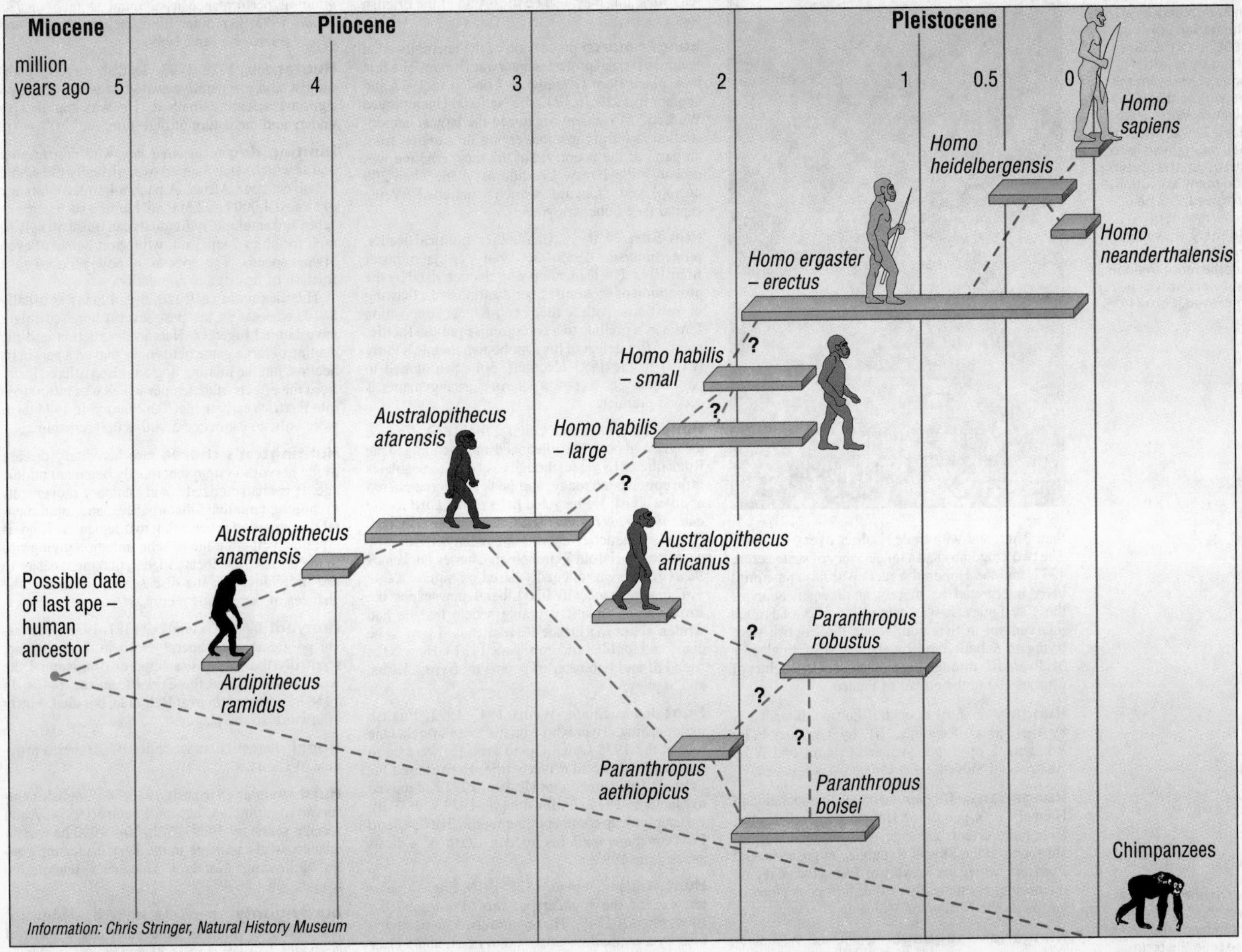

The possible ancestry of the modern human.

Homo sapiens – *the Multiregional Model*

There are two diametrically opposed views on how *H. sapiens* evolved, with many intermediate views between them. Supportersof the Multiregional Model say that *H. erectus* gave rise to *H. sapiens* across its whole range, which, about 700,000 years ago, included Africa, China, Java (Indonesia), and probably Europe. They claim that the regional differences which underlie modern racial variation began to develop when *H. erectus* dispersed around the Old World over 1 million years ago.

Recent proponents of multiregional evolution emphasise the importance of gene flow between the regional lines. In fact, they regard the continuity in time and space between the various forms of *H. erectus* and their regional descendants to be so complete that they should all be regarded as representing only one species, *H. sapiens*.

The Out of Africa Model

The opposing view is that *H. sapiens* had a restricted origin in time and space. Modern supporters of this idea focus on Africa as the most important region. Some of them argue that the later stages of human evolution, like the earlier ones, were characterized by splits and the coexistence of separate species. They recognize an intermediate species between *H. erectus* and *H. sapiens*, called *H. heidelbergensis*.

According to them, by about 600,000 years ago, some *erectus* populations in Africa and Europe had changed sufficiently in skull form to be recognized as a new species, *H. heidelbergensis*, named after a 500,000-year-old jawbone found near Heidelberg, Germany. Members of this species had less projecting faces, more prominent noses, and larger braincases than *erectus* fossils. *H. heidelbergensis* is known from Africa, Europe, and possibly China, about 300,000–600,000 years ago. After this, it apparently gave rise to two species: *H. sapiens* in Africa, and *H. neanderthalensis* (the Neanderthals) in Europe and W Asia.

The consequent Out of Africa Model says that *H. sapiens* evolved in Africa more than 130,000 years ago. Part of the stock of early modern humans then spread from Africa into adjoining regions and eventually reached Australia, Europe, and the Americas (probably by 60,000, 40,000, and 15,000 years ago respectively). Regional (racial) variation only developed during and after the dispersal, so that there is no continuity of regional features between *H. erectus* and the present inhabitants of the same regions. In line with this theory, and contrary to the Multiregional Model, studies of fossil material of the last 50,000 years also seem to indicate that many racial features in the human skeleton have developed only over the last 30,000 years.

Like the Multiregional Model, this view accepts that *H. erectus* evolved into new species in inhabited regions outside Africa, but argues that these became extinct without evolving into modern humans. Some, such as the Neanderthals, were displaced and then replaced as modern humans spread into their regions.

... and an African Eve?

In 1987, research on living humans on the genetic material called mitochondrial DNA (mtDNA, which is passed on only by the mother) led to the reconstruction of a hypothetical female ancestor for all modern humans. This 'Eve' was believed to have lived in Africa about 200,000 years ago, though re-examination of the research suggested that these conclusions may have been premature. However, further support for a recent African origin has come from many more genetic studies of both mtDNA and nuclear DNA. Nevertheless, much more genetic and fossil evidence will be needed before we can complete the first chapters of the human story.

CHRIS STRINGER

SEE ALSO
evolution; Leakey, Louis; Leakey, Mary; Neanderthal

Hungary Soviet tanks in Budapest during the Hungarian uprising 1956. In Oct 1956 Hungary revolted against its communist government and Soviet alliance. Within two days, 2,500 Soviet tanks had been called in to put down the uprising, and many executions followed. The new government of Hungary, however, soon granted the people more freedom, and standards of living improved. *Corbis*

their ◊fief, and with trade rivalries over ◊Flanders. The two kingdoms had a long history of strife before 1337, and the Hundred Years' War has sometimes been interpreted as merely an intensification of these struggles. It was caused by fears of French intervention in Scotland, which the English were trying to subdue, and by the claim of England's ◊Edward III (through his mother Isabel, daughter of Charles IV) to the crown of France.

Hungary country in central Europe, bounded N by the Slovak Republic, NE by Ukraine, E by Romania, S by Yugoslavia and Croatia, and W by Austria and Slovenia. *See country box opposite.*

Hungarian or ***Magyar*** the majority population of Hungary or a people of Hungarian descent; also, their culture and language. Hungarian minorities are found in the Slovak Republic, Yugoslavia, and Romania, where the Székely of Transylvania regard themselves as ethnically distinct but speak Hungarian, as do the Csángó of Moldavia.

Hungarian language member of the Finno-Ugric language group, spoken principally in Hungary but also in parts of the Slovak Republic, Romania, and Yugoslavia. Hungarian is known as Magyar among its speakers. It is written in a form of the Roman alphabet in which *s* corresponds to English *sh*, and *sz* to *s*.

Like the Turks, the Magyars originated in NE Asia; the term 'Hungarian' appears to derive from the Turkish *on ogur* ('ten arrows'), describing their ten tribes; this may also be the origin of the English 'ogre'.

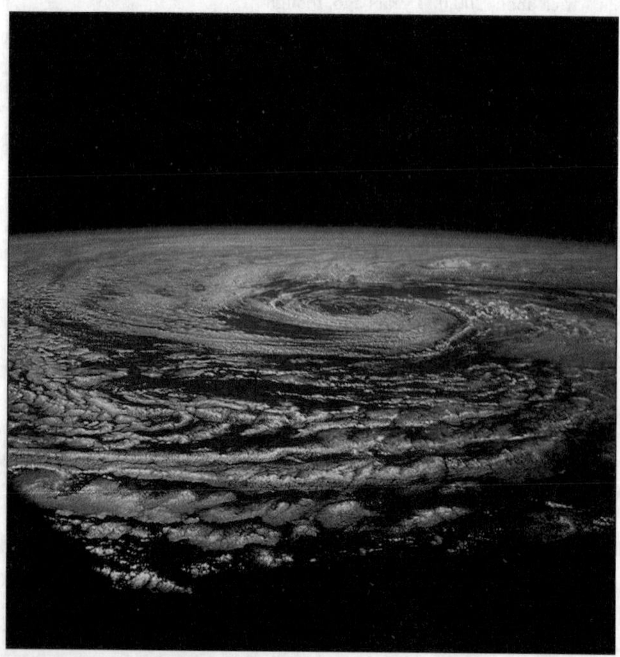

hurricane A hurricane over the Caribbean taken from above. At one time the term hurricane was only used to describe violent revolving tropical storms that occurred in the West Indies, but the term is now used to describe such a storm anywhere in the world. *Image Select (UK) Ltd*

hunger march procession of the unemployed, a feature of social protest in interwar Britain. The first took place from Glasgow to London in 1922 and another in 1929. In 1932 the National Unemployed Workers' Movement organized the largest demonstration, with groups converging on London from all parts of the country, but the most emotive was probably the Jarrow Crusade of 1936, when 200 unemployed shipyard workers marched to the capital (see ◊unemployment).

Hun Sen 1950– . Cambodian political leader, prime minister 1985–93, deputy prime minister from 1993. His leadership was characterized by the promotion of economic liberalization and a thawing in relations with exiled non-Khmer opposition forces as a prelude to a compromise political settlement. After defeat of his Cambodian People's Party (CCP) in the 1993 elections, Hun Sen agreed to participate in a power-sharing arrangement as second premier.

Hunt (James Henry) Leigh 1784–1859. English essayist and poet. He influenced and encouraged the Romantics. His verse, though easy and agreeable, is little appreciated today, and he is best remembered as an essayist. He recycled parts of his *Lord Byron and some of his Friends* 1828, in which he criticized Byron's character, as *Autobiography* 1850. The character of Harold Skimpole in Charles Dickens's *Bleak House* was allegedly based on him.

The appearance in his Liberal newspaper the *Examiner* of an unfavourable article that he had written about the Prince Regent caused him to be convicted for libel and imprisoned 1813. He was the friend of and publisher of poems by Byron, Keats, and Shelley.

Hunt James Simon Wallis 1947–1993. English motor-racing driver who won his first Formula One race at the 1975 Dutch Grand Prix. He went on to win the 1976 world driver's title. Hunt started his Formula One career with Hesketh 1973 and moved to Maclaren 1976–79, finishing in 1979 with Wolf. He later took up commentating for the BBC's Grand Prix coverage until his sudden death of a heart attack June 1993.

Hunt William Holman 1827–1910. English painter, one of the founders of the ◊Pre-Raphaelite Brotherhood 1848. His paintings, characterized both by a meticulous attention to detail and a clear moral and religious symbolism, include *The Awakening Conscience* 1853 (Tate Gallery, London) and *The Light of the World* 1854 (Keble College, Oxford).

Hunt's works are both intensely realistic and symbolic. *The Shadow of Death*, for example, a minutely detailed depiction of a biblical carpenter's workshop, shows a shadow of the Crucifixion cast on the workshop wall by the stretched arms of Jesus. Because of his insistence on exact historical and archaeological detail, particularly for his religious works, Hunt visited Palestine and Syria 1854 and produced *The Scapegoat* 1856, with a meticulous study of the scenery around the Dead Sea, and *The Finding of Our Saviour in the Temple* 1860 (Birmingham City Art Gallery).

He also painted scenes of contemporary life, including *A Hireling Shepherd* 1852, *Strayed Sheep* 1852. Throughout his career he remained the most fervent adherent to the Pre-Raphaelite conception of 'truth to nature'.

Hunt was born in London. He joined the Royal Academy schools 1844 and first exhibited at the Academy 1846. He met John Millais and Dante Gabriel Rossetti 1848, and all three quickly became involved in founding the Pre-Raphaelite Brotherhood. At this period he was strongly influenced by John Ruskin's book *Modern Painters*. His earlier pictures – many of them scenes from literature – include *Rienzi* 1848, *Valentine and Sylvia* 1851 (greatly praised by Ruskin), and *Claudio and Isabella* 1853. His style changed little during his career, though he turned more and more to religious scenes.

His book *Pre-Raphaelitism and the Pre-Raphaelite Brotherhood* 1907 gives a clear account of his ideals and of the history of the movement.

Hunter Holly 1958– . US actress. She first came to prominence with *Broadcast News* and *Raising Arizona* both 1987. She gave an Academy Award-winning performance as a mute woman in *The Piano* 1993; her other films include *Always* and *Miss Firecracker* both 1989.

Hunter John 1728–1793. Scottish surgeon, pathologist, and comparative anatomist who insisted on rigorous scientific method. He was the first to understand the nature of digestion.

hunting dog or ***painted dog*** wild dog *Lycaon pictus* which once roamed over virtually the whole of sub-Saharan Africa. A pack might have a range of almost 4,000 km/2,500 mi, hunting such game as zebra and antelope. Individuals can run at 50 kph/30 mph for up to 5 km/3 mi, with short bursts of even higher speeds. The species is now reduced to a fraction of its original population.

The maximum pack size found today is usually 8–10, whereas in the past several hundred might have hunted together. Habitat destruction and the decline of large game herds have played a part in its decline, but the hunting dog has also suffered badly from the effects of distemper which was introduced into E Africa early in the 20th century. In 1994 there were only an estimated 5,000–6,000 remaining.

Huntington's chorea rare hereditary disease of the nervous system that mostly begins in middle age. It is characterized by involuntary movements (◊chorea), emotional disturbances, and rapid mental degeneration progressing to ◊dementia. There is no known cure but the genetic mutation giving rise to the disease was located 1993, making it easier to test individuals for the disease and increasing the chances of developing a cure.

Hunyadi János Corvinus c. 1387–1456. Hungarian politician and general. Born in Transylvania, reputedly the son of the emperor ◊Sigismund, he won battles against the Turks from the 1440s. In 1456 he defeated them at Belgrade, but died shortly afterwards of the plague.

Hupei alternative transcription of ◊Hebei, a province of China.

Hurd Douglas (Richard) 1930– . English Conservative politician, home secretary 1985–89 and foreign secretary 1989–95. In Nov 1990 he was an unsuccessful candidate in the Tory leadership contest following Margaret Thatcher's unexpected resignation.

hurdy-gurdy musical stringed instrument resembling a violin in tone but using a form of keyboard to play a melody and drone strings to provide a continuous harmony. An inbuilt wheel, turned by a handle, acts as a bow.

hurling or ***hurley*** stick-and-ball game played between two teams of 15 players each, popular in Ireland. Its object is to hit the ball, by means of a curved stick, into the opposing team's goal. If the ball passes under the goal's crossbar three points are scored; if it passes above the crossbar one point is scored. First played over 3,000 years ago, the game was at one time outlawed. The rules were standardized 1884, and are now under the control of the Gaelic Athletic Association. The premier competition, the All-Ireland Championship, was first held 1887.

Huron second largest of the Great Lakes of North America, on the US–Canadian border; area 23,160 sq mi/60,000 sq km. It includes Georgian Bay, Saginaw Bay, and Manitoulin Island.

It receives Lake Superior's waters through the Sault Ste Marie River, and Lake Michigan's through the Straits of Mackinac. It drains south into Lake Erie through the St Clair River–Lake St Clair–Detroit River system. There are a number of small Michigan and Ontario ports on its shores. Jesuit missionaries established the first European settlement, on Georgian Bay, 1638.

Huron (French *hure* 'rough hair of the head') nickname for a member of a confederation of five Iroquoian Native American peoples living in North America near lakes Huron, Erie, and Ontario in the 16th and 17th centuries. They were almost wiped out by the Iroquois. In the 17th century, surviving Hurons formed a group called Wyandot, some of whose descendants now live in Quebec and Oklahoma.

hurricane revolving storm in tropical regions, called ***typhoon*** in the N Pacific. It originates at latitudes between 5° and 20° N or S of the equator, when the surface temperature of the ocean is above 27°C/80°F. A central calm area, called the eye, is surrounded by inwardly spiralling winds (anticlockwise in the northern hemisphere) of up to 320 kph/200 mph. A hurricane is accompanied by lightning and torrential rain, and can cause extensive damage. In meteorology, a hurricane is a wind of force 12 or more on the ◊Beaufort scale.

During 1995 the Atlantic Ocean region suffered 19 tropical storms, 11 of them hurricanes. This was the third-worst season since 1871, causing 137 deaths. The most intense hurricane recorded in the Caribbean/Atlantic sector was Hurricane Gilbert 1988, with sustained winds of 280 kph/175 mph and gusts of over 320 kph/200 mph.

Hurston Zora Neale 1901–1960. US writer. She was associated with the ◊Harlem Renaissance. She collected traditional Afro-American folk tales in *Mules and Men* 1935 and *Tell My Horse* 1938. Among her many other works are the novel *Their Eyes Were Watching God* 1937 and her autobiography *Dust Tracks on a Road* 1942.

Although her conservative philosophy of her later years alienated many of her contemporaries, she was a key figure for following generations of black women writers, including Alice Walker, who edited a collection of her writings, *I Love Myself When I Am Laughing* 1979.

Hurt William 1950– . US actor. His films include *Altered States* 1980, *The Big Chill* 1983, *Kiss of the Spider Woman* 1985 (Academy Award), *Broadcast News* 1987, and *The Accidental Tourist* 1988.

Husák Gustáv 1913–1991. Leader of the Communist Party of Czechoslovakia (CCP) 1969–87 and president 1975–89. After the 1968 Prague Spring of liberalization, his task was to restore control, purge the CCP, and oversee the implementation of a new, federalist constitution. He was deposed in the popular uprising of Nov–Dec 1989 and expelled from the CCP Feb 1990.

Husák, a lawyer, was active in the Resistance movement during World War II, and afterwards in the Slovak Communist Party (SCP), and was imprisoned on political grounds 1951–60. Rehabilitated, he was appointed first secretary of the SCP 1968 and CCP leader 1969–87. As titular state president he pursued a policy of cautious reform. He stepped down as party leader 1987, and was replaced as state president by Václav ◊Havel Dec 1989 following the 'velvet revolution'.

husky any of several breeds of sledge dog used in Arctic regions, growing to 70 cm/27.5 in high, and weighing about 50 kg/110 lbs, with pricked ears, thick fur, and a bushy tail. The Siberian husky is the best known.

Huss John, (Czech *Jan*) c. 1373–1415. Bohemian Christian church reformer, rector of Prague University from 1402, who was excommunicated for attacks on ecclesiastical abuses. He was summoned

HUNGARY
Republic of

national name *Magyar Köztársaság*
area 93,032 sq km/35,910 sq mi
capital Budapest
major towns/cities Miskolc, Debrecen, Szeged, Pécs
physical features Great Hungarian Plain covers E half of country; Bakony Forest, Lake Balaton, and Transdanubian Highlands in the W; rivers Danube, Tisza, and Raba; more than 500 thermal springs
head of state Arpád Göncz from 1990
head of government Viktor Orban from 1998
political system emergent democratic republic
administrative divisions 19 counties and the capital city (with 22 districts)
political parties over 50, including Hungarian Socialist Party (HSP), reform-socialist; Alliance of Free Democrats (AFD), centrist, radical free market; Hungarian Democratic Forum (MDF), nationalist, centre-right; Independent Smallholders Party (ISP), right of centre, agrarian; Christian Democratic People's Party (KDNP), right of centre; Federation of Young Democrats, liberal, anticommunist
armed forces 70,500 (1995)
conscription 12 months (men aged 18–23)
defence spend (% GDP) 1.6 (1994)
education spend (% GNP) 7.0 (1992); 6.7 (1993)
health spend (% GDP)
death penalty abolished 1990
population 10,049,000 (1996 est)
population growth rate −0.5% (1990–95); −0.3% (2000–05)
age distribution (% of total population) <15 18.1%, 15–65 67.9%, >65 14% (1995)
ethnic distribution 93% native Hungarian, or Magyar; there is a large Gypsy community of around 600,000; other ethnic minorities include Germans, Croats, Romanians, Slovaks, Serbs, and Slovenes
population density (per sq km) 110.5 (1994)
urban population (% of total) 65 (1995)
labour force 46% of population: 15% agriculture, 38% industry, 55% services (1990)
unemployment 10.9% (1994)
child mortality rate (under 5, per 1,000 live births) 15 (1993)
life expectancy 68 (men), 75 (women)
education (compulsory years) 10
literacy rate 99%
languages Hungarian (or Magyar), one of the few languages of Europe with non-Indo-European origins; it is grouped with Finnish, Estonian, and others in the Finno-Ugric family
religions Roman Catholic 67%, Calvinist 20%, other Christian denominations, Judaism
TV sets (per 1,000 people) 414 (1992)
currency forint
GDP (US $) 41.37 billion (1994)
GDP per capita (PPP) (US $) 6,060 (1993)
growth rate 2.9% (1994)
average annual inflation 18.8% (1994); 19.0% (1985–94)
major trading partners Germany, CIS countries, Italy, Austria, USA
resources lignite, brown coal, natural gas, petroleum, bauxite, hard coal
industries food and beverages, tobacco, steel, chemicals, petroleum and plastics, engineering, transport equipment, pharmaceuticals, textiles, cement
exports raw materials, semi-finished products, industrial consumer goods, food and agricultural products, transport equipment. Principal market: Germany 26.6% (1993)
imports mineral fuels, raw materials, semi-finished products, transport equipment, food products, consumer goods. Principal source: Germany 21.6% (1993)
arable land 54% (1993)
agricultural products wheat, maize, sugar beet, barley, potatoes, sunflowers, grapes; livestock and dairy products

HISTORY
1st C AD Region formed part of the Roman Empire.
4th C Germanic tribes overran central Europe.
c. 445 Attila the Hun established a short-lived empire, including Hungarian nomads living far to the E.
c. 680 Hungarians settled between the Don and Dniepr rivers under Khazar rule.
9th C Hungarians invaded central Europe; ten tribes united under Árpád, chief of the Magyar tribe, who conquered the area corresponding to modern Hungary 896.
10th C Hungarians colonized Transylvania and raided their neighbours for plunder and slaves.
955 Battle of Lech: Germans led by Otto the Great defeated Hungarians.
1001 St Stephen founded Hungarian kingdom to replace tribal organization and converted Hungarians to Christianity.
12th C Hungary became a major power when King Béla III won temporary supremacy over the Balkans.
1308–86 Angevin dynasty ruled after Arpádian line died out.
1456 Battle of Belgrade: János Hunyadi defeated Ottoman Turks and saved Hungary from invasion.
1458–90 Under Mátyás I Corvinus, Hungary enjoyed military success and cultural renaissance.
1526 Battle of Mohács: Turks under Suleiman the Magnificent decisively defeated Hungarians.
16th C Partition of Hungary between Turkey, Austria, and semi-autonomous Transylvania.
1699 Treaty of Karlowitz: Austrians expelled the Turks from Hungary, which was re-unified under Habsburg rule.
1707 Prince Ferenc Rákóczi II led uprising against Austrians, who promised to respect Hungarian constitution 1711.
1780–90 Joseph II's attempts to impose uniform administration throughout Austrian Empire provoked nationalist reaction among Hungarian nobility.
early 19th C 'National Revival' movement led by Count Stephen Széchenyi and Lajos Kossuth.
1848 Hungarian Revolution: nationalists proclaimed self-government; Croat minority resisted Hungarian rule.
1849 Kossuth repudiated Habsburg monarchy; Austrians crushed revolution with Russian support.
1867 Austria conceded equality to Hungary within the dual monarchy of Austria-Hungary.
1918 Austria-Hungary collapsed in military defeat; Count Mihály Károlyi proclaimed Hungarian Republic.
1919 Communists took power under Béla Kun; Romanians invaded; Admiral Miklós Horthy overthrew Béla Kun.
1920 Treaty of Trianon: Hungary lost 72% of its territory to Czechoslovakia, Romania, and Yugoslavia; Horthy restored Kingdom of Hungary with himself as regent.
1921 Count István Bethlen became prime minister of authoritarian aristocratic regime.
1938–41 Diplomatic collaboration with Germany allowed Hungary to regain territories lost 1920; Hungary declared war on USSR in alliance with Germany 1941.
1944 Germany occupied Hungary and installed Nazi regime.
1945 USSR 'liberated' Hungary; Smallholder's Party won free elections, but communists led by Mátyás Rákosi took over by stages 1946–49.
1947 Peace treaty restored 1920 frontiers.
1949 Hungary became a Soviet-style dictatorship; Rákosi pursued Stalinist policies of collectivization and police terror.
1956 Hungarian uprising: anti-Soviet demonstrations led prime minister Imre Nagy to propose democratic reforms and neutrality; USSR invaded, and installed János Kádár as communist leader.
1961 Kádár began to introduce pragmatic liberal reforms of a limited kind.
1988 Károly Grosz replaced Kádár and accelerated reform; Hungarian Democratic Forum formed by opposition groups.
1989 Communist dictatorship dismantled; transitional constitution restored multiparty democracy; opening of border with Austria destroyed the 'Iron Curtain'.
1990 Elections won by centre-right coalition led by József Antall, who pursued radical free-market reforms.
1991 Withdrawal of Soviet forces completed.
1994 Gyula Horn, the leader of the ex-communist Hungarian Socialist Party, became prime minister, pledging to continue reform policies.
1996 Friendship treaty with Slovak Republic signed. Cooperation treaty with Romania.
1997 Hungary invited to join NATO and to begin negotiations for membership of the European Union. Referendum gave clear vote in favour of joining NATO.
1998 Viktor Orban, leader of right-of-centre Fidesz, became prime minister after May general election.

SEE ALSO Austro-Hungarian Empire; Warsaw Pact

Hussein Iraqi leader Saddam Hussein at an emergency Arab summit meeting in 1987. He has held on to his position as president despite unpopularity brought about by a costly defeat by the Western allies in the 1991 Gulf War and his persecution of religious and ethnic minorities in his own country. *Corbis*

before the Council of Constance 1414, defended the English reformer John Wycliffe, rejected the pope's authority, and was burned at the stake. His followers were called Hussites.

There is no substitute for talent. Industry and all the virtues are of no avail.

ALDOUS HUXLEY
Point Counter Point

Hussein Saddam 1937– . Iraqi politician, in power from 1968, president from 1979. He presided over the Iran-Iraq war 1980–88, and harshly repressed Kurdish rebels in N Iraq. He annexed Kuwait 1990 but was driven out by a US-dominated coalition army Feb 1991. Defeat in the ◊Gulf War led to unrest, and both the Kurds in the N and Shi'ites in the S rebelled. His savage repression of both revolts led to charges of genocide. In 1995, to counter evidence of rifts among his closest supporters, he called a presidential election, in which he was elected (unopposed) with 99.6% of the vote. In Sept 1996 his involvement in Kurdish faction fighting in N Iraq provoked air retaliation by US forces. His lack of cooperation with United Nations weapons inspectors in 1998 caused further military tension, culminating in air strikes by the USA and UK.

Hussein ibn Ali c. 1854–1931. Leader of the Arab revolt 1916–18 against the Turks. He proclaimed himself king of the Hejaz 1916, accepted the caliphate 1924, but was unable to retain it due to internal fighting. He was deposed 1924 by Ibn Saud.

Hussein ibn Talal 1935–1999. King of Jordan 1952–99. By 1967 he had lost all his kingdom west of the river Jordan in the ◊Arab-Israeli Wars, and in 1970 suppressed the ◊Palestine Liberation Organization acting as a guerrilla force against his rule on the remaining East Bank territories. Subsequently, he became a moderating force in Middle Eastern politics, and in 1994 signed a peace agreement with Israel, ending a 46-year-old 'state of war' between the two countries.

Great-grandson of Hussein ibn Ali, he became king following the mental incapacitation of his father, Talal. After Iraq's annexation of Kuwait 1990 he attempted to mediate between the opposing sides, at the risk of damaging his relations with both sides. In 1993 he publicly distanced himself from Iraqi leader Saddam Hussein.

Husserl Edmund Gustav Albrecht 1859–1938. German philosopher, regarded as the founder of ◊phenomenology, the study of mental states as consciously experienced. His early phenomenology resembles linguistic philosophy because he examined the meaning and our understanding of words.

He hoped phenomenology would become the science of all sciences. He influenced Martin ◊Heidegger and affected sociology through the work of Alfred Schütz (1899–1959). Husserl's main works are *Logical Investigations* 1900, *Phenomenological Philosophy* 1913, and *The Crisis of the European Sciences* 1936.

Operationally, God is beginning to resemble not a ruler but the last fading smile of a cosmic Cheshire cat.

JULIAN HUXLEY
Religion without Revelation

Hussey Obed 1792–1860. US inventor who developed one of the first successful reaping machines 1833 and various other agricultural machinery. His reaping machine used the principle of a reciprocating knife cutting against stationary guards or figures. The cutter was attached to a crank activated by gearing, connected to one of the wheels. The contraption was pulled by horses walking alongside the standing grain. During the harvest of 1834, he demonstrated the reaper to farmers and began to sell the machines; in 1851 he went to Britain and demonstrated the reaper at Hull and Barnardscastle. He was invited to show it to Prince Albert, who bought two.

Hussite follower of John ◊Huss. Opposed to both German and papal influence in Bohemia, the Hussites waged successful war against the Holy Roman Empire from 1419, but Roman Catholicism was finally re-established 1620.

Huston John (Marcellus) 1906–1987. US film director, screenwriter, and actor. An impulsive and individualistic filmmaker, he often dealt with the themes of greed, treachery in human relationships, and the loner. His works as a director include *The Maltese Falcon* 1941 (his debut), *The Treasure of the Sierra Madre* 1948 (in which his father Walter Huston starred and for which both won Academy Awards), *The African Queen* 1951, and his last, *The Dead* 1987.

His other films include *Key Largo* 1948, *Moby Dick* 1956, *The Misfits* 1961, *Fat City* 1972, and *Prizzi's Honor* 1984.

Hutchinson Anne Marbury 1591–1643. American colonial religious leader. In 1634, she and her family followed the Puritan clergyman John Cotton (1584–1652) from England to Massachusetts Bay Colony. Preaching a unique theology which emphasized the role of faith, she gained a wide following. The colony's leaders, including Cotton, felt threatened by Hutchinson and in 1637 she was banished and excommunicated. Settling in Long Island, she and her family were killed by Indians.

Hutterian Brethren Christian sect closely related to the ◊Mennonites.

Hutton James 1726–1797. Scottish geologist, known as the 'founder of geology', who formulated the concept of ◊uniformitarianism. In 1785 he developed a theory of the igneous origin of many rocks.

His *Theory of the Earth* 1788 proposed that the Earth was incalculably old. Uniformitarianism suggests that past events could be explained in terms of processes that work today. For example, the kind of river current that produces a certain settling pattern in a bed of sand today must have been operating many millions of years ago, if that same pattern is visible in ancient sandstones.

Hutton Len (Leonard) 1916–1990. English cricketer, born in Pudsey, West Yorkshire. He captained England in 23 test matches 1952–56 and was England's first professional captain. In 1938 at the Oval he scored 364 against Australia, a world record test score until beaten by Gary ◊Sobers 1958.

Hutu member of the majority ethnic group of Burundi and Rwanda, numbering around 9,500,000. The Hutu tend to live as peasant farmers. Traditionally they have been dominated by the Tutsi minority; there is a long history of violent conflict between the two groups. The Hutu language belongs to the Bantu branch of the Niger-Congo family.

Huxley Aldous (Leonard) 1894–1963. English writer of novels, essays, and verse. From the disillusionment and satirical eloquence of *Crome Yellow* 1921, *Antic Hay* 1923, and *Point Counter Point* 1928, Huxley developed towards the Utopianism exemplified by *Island* 1962. The science fiction novel *Brave New World* 1932 shows human beings mass-produced in laboratories and rendered incapable of freedom by indoctrination and drugs.

Huxley's later devotion to mysticism led to his experiments with the hallucinogenic drug mescalin, recorded in *The Doors of Perception* 1954. His other works include the philosophical novel *Eyeless in Gaza* 1936, *After Many a Summer* 1939 (Tait Black Memorial Prize), the biography of Père Joseph (1577–1638) *Grey Eminence* 1941, and *The Devils of Loudun* 1952. He was the grandson of Thomas Henry Huxley and brother of Julian Huxley.

Huxley English writer Aldous Huxley. He began by writing social satires such as *Antic Hay* 1923 and then moved on to novels of ideas, the best known of which, *Brave New World* 1932, is a futuristic novel about a world made inhuman by science. His later writings are concerned increasingly with mysticism and include accounts of his experiences with hallucinogenic drugs. *Topham*

Huxley Andrew Fielding 1917– . English physiologist, awarded the Nobel prize 1963 with Alan Hodgkin (1914–) for work on nerve impulses, discovering how ionic mechanisms are used in nerves to transmit impulses.

Huxley Hugh Esmor 1924– . English physiologist who, using the electron microscope and thin slicing techniques, established the detailed structural basis of muscle contraction. Muscle fibres contain a large number of longitudinally arranged myofibrils, which, Huxley demonstrated, are composed of thick and thin filaments of the proteins myosin and actin. He showed how the filaments are attached to one another in a woven pattern, and suggested that muscle contraction is brought about by sliding movements of two sets of filaments.

By coincidence, Andrew Huxley (no relation), working separately, came to the same conclusions at about the same time in the 1950s, although they disagree on the exact details.

Huxley Julian Sorell 1887–1975. English biologist, first director general of UNESCO, and a founder of the World Wildlife Fund (now the World Wide Fund for Nature). He wrote popular science books, including *Essays of a Biologist* 1923.

Huxley Thomas Henry 1825–1895. English scientist and humanist. Following the publication of Charles Darwin's *On the Origin of Species* 1859, he became known as 'Darwin's bulldog', and for many years was a prominent champion of evolution. In 1869, he coined the word 'agnostic' to express his own religious attitude, and is considered the founder of scientific humanism.

From 1846 to 1850 Huxley was the assistant ship's surgeon on HMS *Rattlesnake* on its voyage around the South Seas. The observations he made on the voyage, especially of invertebrates, were published and made his name in the UK.

Hu Yaobang 1915–1989. Chinese politician, Communist Party (CCP) chair 1981–87. A protégé of the communist leader Deng Xiaoping, Hu presided over a radical overhaul of the party structure and personnel 1982–86. His death ignited the prodemocracy movement, which was eventually crushed in ◊Tiananmen Square June 1989.

Hu, born into a peasant family in Hunan province, was a political commissar during the 1934–35 ◊Long March. In 1941 he served under Deng and later worked under him in provincial and central government. Hu was purged as a 'capitalist roader' during the 1966–69 ◊Cultural Revolution, rehabilitated 1975, but disgraced again when Deng fell from prominence 1976. In 1978, with Deng in power, Hu became head of the revived secretariat 1980 and CCP chair 1981. He was dismissed Jan 1987 for his relaxed handling of a wave of student unrest Dec 1986.

Huygens Christiaan, or Huyghens 1629–1695. Dutch mathematical physicist and astronomer. He proposed the wave theory of light, developed the pendulum clock 1657, discovered polarization, and observed Saturn's rings. He made important advances in pure mathematics, applied mathematics, and mechanics, which he virtually founded.

Huygens's study of probability, including game theory, originated the modern concept of the expectation of a variable. He also improved the telescope.

Huysmans J(oris) K(arl). Adopted name of Charles Marie Georges Huysmans 1848–1907. French novelist. His novel *A rebours/Against Nature* 1884, with its self-absorbed aestheticism, symbolized the decadent movement (see ◊decadence). The writing of *Là-bas/Down There* 1891, the life of a Satanist, prompted Huysmans to turn to Catholicism and *En route* 1895 describes his religious journey.

His novel *Marthe* 1876, the story of a courtesan, was followed by other novels, all of which feature solitary protagonists. Other works include the realistic *En ménage* 1881. *La Cathédrale/The Cathedral* 1898 is among the finest pieces of mystic literature, while *L'Oblat/The Lay Brother* 1903 and *Les Foules de Lourdes/The Crowds of Lourdes* 1906 are his chief later works.

hyacinth any bulb-producing plant of the genus *Hyacinthus* of the lily family Liliaceae, native to the E Mediterranean and Africa. The cultivated hyacinth *H. orientalis* has large, scented, cylindrical heads of pink, white, or blue flowers. The ◊water hyacinth, genus *Eichhornia*, is unrelated, a floating plant from South America.

hyaline membrane disease former name for ◊respiratory distress syndrome.

hybrid offspring from a cross between individuals of two different species, or two inbred lines within a species. In most cases, hybrids between species are infertile and unable to reproduce sexually. In plants, however, doubling of the chromosomes (see ◊polyploid) can restore the fertility of such hybrids.

hydathode specialized pore, or less commonly, a hair, through which water is secreted by hydrostatic pressure from the interior of a plant leaf onto the surface. Hydathodes are found on many different plants and are usually situated around the leaf margin at vein endings. Each pore is surrounded by two crescent-shaped cells and resembles an open ◊stoma, but the size of the opening cannot be varied as in a stoma. The process of water secretion through hydathodes is known as ◊guttation.

Hyde Douglas 1860–1949. Irish scholar and politician. Founder president of the Gaelic League 1893–1915 (aiming to promote a cultural, rather than political, nationalism), he was the first president of Eire 1938–45. His first book 1889 was written in Irish. *Beside the Fire* 1890 is regarded as the first scholarly work on Irish Gaelic folk-tales; he also wrote the first literary history of Ireland 1899.

Hyderabad capital city of the S central Indian state of ◊Andhra Pradesh, on the river Musi; population (1991) 4,280,000. Products include carpets, silks, and metal inlay work. It was formerly the capital of the state of Hyderabad. Buildings include the Jama Masjid mosque and Golconda fort.

The princely state of Hyderabad, which occupied the greater part of the region known as the Deccan, was by far the largest of India's princely states. In 1956 the state of Hyderabad was divided between Maharashtra, Mysore, and Andhra Pradesh.

Hyderabad city in Sind province, SE Pakistan; population (1981) 795,000. It produces gold, pottery, glass, and furniture. The third-largest city of Pakistan, it was founded 1768.

Hyder Ali or ***Haidar Ali*** c. 1722–1782. Indian general, sultan of Mysore in SW India from 1759. In command of the army in Mysore from 1749, he became the ruler of the state 1761, and rivalled British power in the area until his triple defeat by Sir Eyre ◊Coote 1781 during the Anglo-French wars. He was the father of Tipu Sultan.

Hydra in astronomy, the largest constellation, winding across more than a quarter of the sky between ◊Cancer and ◊Libra in the southern hemisphere. Hydra is named after the multiheaded monster slain by Hercules. Despite its size, it is not prominent; its brightest star is second-magnitude Alphard.

Hydra in Greek mythology, a huge monster with nine heads. If one were cut off, two would grow in its place. One of the 12 labours of ◊Heracles was to kill it.

hydra in zoology, any member of the family Hydridae, or freshwater polyps, of the phylum Cnidaria (coelenterates). The body is a double-layered tube (with six to ten hollow tentacles around the mouth), 1.25 cm/0.5 in long when extended, but capable of contracting to a small knob. Usually fixed to waterweed, hydras feed on minute animals that are caught and paralysed by stinging cells on the tentacles.

Hydras reproduce asexually in the summer and sexually in the winter. They have no specialized organs except those of reproduction.

hydrangea any flowering shrub of the genus *Hydrangea* of the saxifrage family Hydrangeaceae, native to Japan. Cultivated varieties of *H. macrophylla* normally produce round heads of pink flowers, but these may be blue if certain chemicals, such as alum or iron, are in the soil. The name is from the Greek for 'water vessel', after the cuplike seed capsules.

hydrate chemical compound that has discrete water molecules combined with it. The water is known as water of crystallization and the number of water molecules associated with one molecule of the compound is denoted in both its name and chemical formula: for example, $CuSO_4.5H_2O$ is copper(II) sulphate pentahydrate.

hydration in earth science, a form of chemical weathering caused by the expansion of certain minerals as they absorb water. The expansion weakens the parent rock and may cause it to break up.

hydraulic action in earth science, the erosive force exerted by water (as distinct from the forces exerted by rocky particles carried by water). It can wear away the banks of a river, particularly at the outer curve of a meander (bend in the river), where the current flows most strongly.

Hydraulic action occurs as a river tumbles over a waterfall to crash onto the rocks below. It will lead to the formation of a plunge pool below the waterfall.

hydraulic radius measure of a river's channel efficiency (its ability to discharge water), used by water engineers to assess the likelihood of flooding. The hydraulic radius of a channel is defined as the ratio of its cross-sectional area to its wetted perimeter (the part of the cross-section that is in contact with the water).

The greater the hydraulic radius, the greater the efficiency of the channel and the less likely the river is to flood. The highest values occur when channels are deep, narrow, and semi-circular in shape.

hydraulics field of study concerned with utilizing the properties of water and other liquids, in particular the way they flow and transmit pressure, and with the application of these properties in engineering. It applies the principles of ◊hydrostatics and hydrodynamics. The oldest type of hydraulic machine is the hydraulic press, invented by Joseph Bramah (1748–1814) in England 1795. The hydraulic principle of pressurized liquid increasing mechanical efficiency is commonly used on vehicle braking systems, the forging press, and the hydraulic systems of aircraft and excavators.

A hydraulic press consists of two liquid-connected pistons in cylinders, one of narrow bore, one of large bore. A force applied to the narrow piston applies a certain pressure (force per unit area) to the liquid, which is transmitted to the larger piston. Because the area of this piston is larger, the force exerted on it is larger. Thus the original force has been magnified, although the smaller piston must move a great distance to move the larger piston only a little, hence mechanical efficiency is gained in force but lost in movement.

hydride chemical compound containing hydrogen and one other element, and in which the hydrogen is the more electronegative element (see ◊electronegativity).

Hydrides of the more reactive metals may be ionic compounds containing a hydride anion (H^-).

hydrocarbon any of a class of chemical compounds containing only hydrogen and carbon (for example, the alkanes and alkenes). Hydrocarbons are obtained industrially principally from petroleum and coal tar.

hydrocephalus potentially serious increase in the volume of cerebrospinal fluid (CSF) within the ventricles of the brain. In infants, since their skull plates have not fused, it causes enlargement of the head, and there is a risk of brain damage from CSF pressure on the developing brain.

Hydrocephalus may be due to mechanical obstruction of the outflow of CSF from the ventricles or to faulty reabsorption. Treatment usually involves surgical placement of a shunt system to

'Irrationally held truths may be more harmful than reasoned errors.'

THOMAS HENRY HUXLEY 'The Coming of Age of the Origin of Species' *Science and Culture*

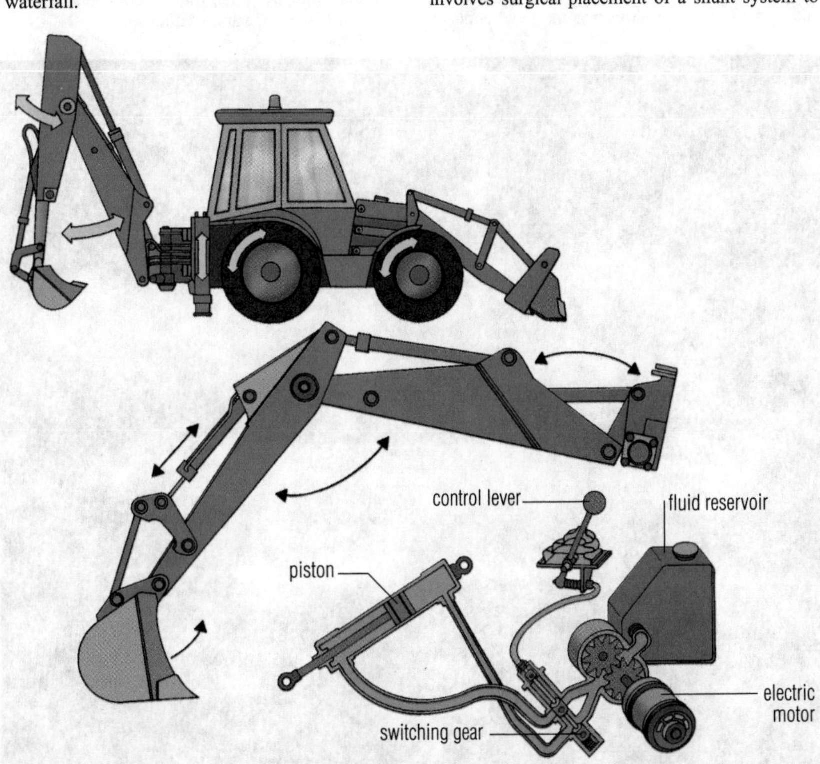

hydraulics The mechanical excavator utilizes hydraulic rams. The ram consists of a piston in a cylinder connected by pipes to a fluid reservoir. The lever opens a valve that admits high-pressure fluid to one side of the piston, forcing it and the digger arm which is connected to it to move.

drain the fluid into the abdominal cavity. In infants, the condition is often seen in association with ◊spina bifida. Hydrocephalus may occur as a consequence of brain injury or disease.

hydrochloric acid HCl solution of hydrogen chloride (a colourless, acidic gas) in water. The concentrated acid is about 35% hydrogen chloride and is corrosive. The acid is a typical strong, monobasic acid forming only one series of salts, the chlorides. It has many industrial uses, including recovery of zinc from galvanized scrap iron and the production of chlorine. It is also produced in the stomachs of animals for the purposes of digestion.

hydrocyanic acid or ***prussic acid*** solution of hydrogen cyanide gas (HCN) in water. It is a colourless, highly poisonous, volatile liquid, smelling of bitter almonds.

hydrodynamics branch of physics dealing with fluids (liquids and gases) in motion.

hydroelectric power electricity generated by moving water. In a typical scheme, water stored in a reservoir, often created by damming a river, is piped into water ◊turbines, coupled to electricity generators. In ◊pumped storage plants, water flowing through the turbines is recycled. A ◊tidal power station exploits the rise and fall of the tides. About one-fifth of the world's electricity comes from hydroelectric power.

Hydroelectric plants have prodigious generating capacities. The Grand Coulee plant in Washington State, USA, has a power output of around 10,000 megawatts. The Itaipu power station on the Paraná River (Brazil/Paraguay) has a potential capacity of 12,000 megawatts. Work on the world's largest hydroelectric project, the Three Gorges Dam on the Chang Jiang, was officially inaugurated Dec 1994. By 1996, around 600,000 sq km/231,660 sq mi of land had been flooded worldwide for hydroelectric reservoirs. ▷ *See feature on pp. 360–361.*

hydrofoil wing that develops lift in the water in much the same way that an aeroplane wing develops lift in the air. A hydrofoil boat is one whose hull rises out of the water owing to the lift, and the boat skims along on the hydrofoils. The first hydrofoil was fitted to a boat 1906. The first commercial hydrofoil went into operation 1956. One of the most advanced hydrofoil boats is the Boeing ◊jetfoil. Hydrofoils are now widely used for fast island ferries in calm seas.

hydrogen (Greek *hydro* + *gen* 'water generator') colourless, odourless, gaseous, nonmetallic element, symbol H, atomic number 1, relative atomic mass 1.00797. It is the lightest of all the elements and occurs on Earth chiefly in combination with oxygen as water. Hydrogen is the most abundant element in the universe, where it accounts for 93% of the total number of atoms and 76% of the total mass. It is a component of most stars, including the Sun, whose heat and light are produced through the nuclear-fusion process that converts hydrogen into helium. When subjected to a pressure 500,000 times greater than that of the Earth's atmosphere, hydrogen becomes a solid with metallic properties, as in one of the inner zones of Jupiter. Hydrogen's common and industrial uses include the hardening of oils and fats by hydrogenation, the creation of high-temperature flames for welding, and as rocket fuel. It has been proposed as a fuel for road vehicles.

Its isotopes ◊deuterium and ◊tritium (half-life 12.5 years) are used in nuclear weapons, and deuterons (deuterium nuclei) are used in synthesizing elements. The element's name refers to the generation of water by the combustion of hydrogen, and was coined in 1787 by French chemist Louis Guyton de Morveau (1737–1816).

hydrogenation addition of hydrogen to an unsaturated organic molecule (one that contains ◊double bonds or ◊triple bonds). It is widely used in the manufacture of margarine and low-fat spreads by the addition of hydrogen to vegetable oils. Vegetable oils contain double carbon-to-carbon bonds and are therefore examples of unsaturated compounds. When hydrogen is added to these double bonds, the oils become saturated and more solid in consistency.

hydrogen bomb bomb that works on the principle of nuclear ◊fusion. Large-scale explosion results from the thermonuclear release of energy when hydrogen nuclei are fused to form helium nuclei. The first hydrogen bomb was exploded at Eniwetok Atoll in the Pacific Ocean by the USA 1952.

hydrogen carbonate or ***bicarbonate*** compound containing the ion HCO_3^-, an acid salt of carbonic acid (solution of carbon dioxide in water). When heated or treated with dilute acids, it gives off carbon dioxide. The most important compounds are ◊sodium hydrogen carbonate (bicarbonate of soda), and calcium hydrogen carbonate.

hydrogen sulphide H_2S poisonous gas with the smell of rotten eggs. It is found in certain types of crude oil where it is formed by decomposition of sulphur compounds. It is removed from the oil at the refinery and converted to elemental sulphur.

hydrography study and charting of Earth's surface waters in seas, lakes, and rivers.

hydrological cycle alternative name for the ◊water cycle, by which water is circulated between the Earth's surface and its atmosphere.

hydrogen bomb The mushroom cloud associated with atomic explosions. This cloud followed the testing of a 18–22 megaton American hydrogen bomb on 1 March 1954 in the Marshall Islands. This is the largest bomb ever tested by the USA. *Image Select (UK) Ltd*

hydrology study of the location and movement of inland water, both frozen and liquid, above and below ground. It is applied to major civil engineering projects such as irrigation schemes, dams, and hydroelectric power, and in planning water supply.

hydrolysis chemical reaction in which the action of water or its ions breaks down a substance into smaller molecules. Hydrolysis occurs in certain inorganic salts in solution, in nearly all nonmetallic chlorides, in esters, and in other organic substances. It is one of the mechanisms for the breakdown of food by the body, as in the conversion of starch to glucose.

hydrolysis in earth science, a form of chemical weathering caused by the chemical alteration of certain minerals as they react with water. For example, the mineral feldspar in granite reacts with water to from a white clay called ◊china clay.

hydrophilic (Greek 'water-loving') in chemistry, a term describing ◊functional groups with a strong affinity for water, such as the carboxyl group (–COOH).

If a molecule contains both a hydrophilic and a ◊hydrophobic group (a group that repels water), it may have an affinity for both aqueous and nonaqueous molecules. Such compounds are used to stabilize ◊emulsions or as ◊detergents.

hydrophobia another name for the disease ◊rabies.

hydrophobic (Greek 'water-hating') in chemistry, a term describing ◊functional groups that repel water (the opposite of ◊hydrophilic).

hydrophone underwater ◊microphone and ancillary equipment capable of picking up waterborne sounds. It was originally developed to detect enemy submarines but is now also used, for example, for listening to the sounds made by whales.

hydrophyte plant adapted to live in water, or in waterlogged soil.

Hydrophytes may have leaves with a very reduced or absent ◊cuticle and no ◊stomata (since there is no need to conserve water), a reduced root and water-conducting system, and less supporting tissue since water buoys plants up. There are often numerous spaces between the cells in their stems and roots to make ◊gas exchange with all parts of the plant body possible. Many have highly divided leaves, which lessens resistance to flowing water; an example is spiked water milfoil *Myriophyllum spicatum*.

hydroplane on a submarine, a movable horizontal fin angled downwards or upwards when the vessel is descending or ascending. It is also a highly manoeuvrable motorboat with its bottom rising in steps to the stern, or a ◊hydrofoil boat that skims over the surface of the water when driven at high speed.

hydroponics cultivation of plants without soil, using specially prepared solutions of mineral salts. Beginning in the 1930s, large crops were grown by hydroponic methods, at first in California but since then in many other parts of the world.

Julius von Sachs (1832–1897) 1860 and W Knop 1865 developed a system of plant culture in water whereby the relation of mineral salts to plant growth could be determined, but it was not until about 1930 that large crops could be grown. The term was first coined by US scientist W F Gericke.

hydrosphere the water component of the Earth, usually encompassing the oceans, seas, rivers, streams, swamps, lakes, groundwater, and atmospheric water vapour.

hydrostatics in physics, the branch of statics dealing with fluids in equilibrium – that is, in a static condition. Practical applications include shipbuilding and dam design.

hydrothermal in geology, pertaining to a fluid whose principal component is hot water, or to a mineral deposit believed to be precipitated from such a fluid.

hydrothermal vein crack in rock filled with minerals precipitated through the action of circulating high-temperature fluids. Igneous activity often gives rise to the circulation of heated fluids that migrate outwards and move through the surrounding rock. When such solutions carry metallic ions, ore-mineral deposition occurs in the new surroundings on cooling.

hydrothermal vent hot fissure in the ocean floor, also known as a smoker, associated with an ◊ocean ridge. Hot, mineral-rich ground water erupts through the vent into the sea, forming thick clouds of suspended material. The clouds may be dark or light, depending on the mineral content, thus producing 'white smokers' or 'black smokers'. Sea water percolating through the sediments and crust is heated in the active area beneath and dissolves minerals from the hot rocks.

As the charged water is returned to the ocean, the sudden cooling causes these minerals to precipitate from solution, so forming the suspension. The chemical-rich water around a smoker gives rise to colonies of bacteria, and these form the basis of food chains that can be sustained without sunlight and photosynthesis. Strange animals that live in such regions include huge tube worms 2 m/6 ft long, giant clams, and species of crab, anemone, and shrimp found nowhere else.

hydroxide any inorganic chemical compound containing one or more hydroxyl (OH) groups and generally combined with a metal. Hydroxides include sodium hydroxide (caustic soda, NaOH), potassium hydroxide (caustic potash, KOH), and calcium hydroxide (slaked lime, $Ca(OH)_2$).

hydroxyl group an atom of hydrogen and an atom of oxygen bonded together and covalently bonded to an organic molecule. Common compounds containing hydroxyl groups are alcohols and phenols. In chemical reactions, the hydroxyl group (–OH) frequently behaves as a single entity.

hydroxypropanoic acid technical name for ◊lactic acid.

hyena any of three species of carnivorous mammals in the family Hyaenidae, living in Africa and Asia. Hyenas have extremely powerful jaws. They are scavengers, although they will also attack and kill live prey.

The species are: the striped hyena *Hyaena hyaena* found from Asia Minor to India; the brown hyena *H. brunnea*, found in S Africa; and the spotted hyena *Crocuta crocuta*, common south of the Sahara. The ◊aardwolf also belongs to the hyena family.

Hygieia in Greek mythology, the goddess of health (Roman Salus), daughter of Asclepius.

hygrometer in physics, any instrument for measuring the humidity, or water vapour content, of a gas (usually air). A wet and dry bulb hygrometer consists of two vertical thermometers, with one of the bulbs covered in absorbent cloth dipped into water. As the water evaporates, the bulb cools, producing a temperature difference between the two thermometers. The amount of evaporation, and hence cooling of the wet bulb, depends on the relative humidity of the air.

Other hygrometers work on the basis of a length of natural fibre, such as hair or a fine strand of gut, changing with variations in humidity. In a dew-point hygrometer, a polished metal mirror gradually cools until a fine mist of water (dew) forms on it. This gives a measure of the dew point (the temperature at which the air becomes saturated with water vapour), from which the air's relative humidity can be calculated.

Hyksos ('rulers of foreign lands') nomadic, probably Semitic people who came to prominence in Egypt in the 18th century BC, and established their own dynasty in the Nile delta, which lasted until 1550 BC. They introduced bronze metallurgy and the use of the horse-drawn chariot.

Hymen in Greek mythology, a god of the marriage ceremony. In painting, he is represented as a youth carrying a bridal torch.

hymn song in praise of a deity. Examples include Akhenaton's hymn to the Aton in ancient Egypt, the ancient Greek Orphic hymns, Old Testament psalms, extracts from the New Testament (such as the 'Ave Maria'), and hymns by the British writers John Bunyan ('Who would true valour see') and Charles Wesley ('Hark! the herald angels sing'). The earliest sources of modern hymn melodies can be traced to the 11th and 12th centuries, and the earliest polyphonic settings date from the late 14th century. ◊Gospel music and carols are forms of Christian hymn singing.

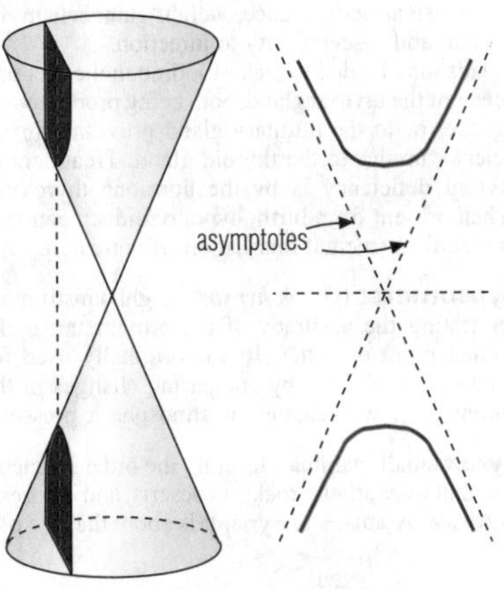

hyperbola The hyperbola is produced when a cone is cut by a plane. It is one of a family of curves called conic sections: the circle, ellipse, and parabola. These curves are produced when the plane cuts the cone at different angles and positions.

Hypatia c. 370–c. 415. Greek philosopher, born in Alexandria. She studied Neo-Platonism in Athens, and succeeded her father Theon as professor of philosophy at Alexandria. She was murdered, it is thought by Christian fanatics.

hyperactivity condition of excessive activity in young children, combined with restlessness, inability to concentrate, and difficulty in learning. There are various causes, ranging from temperamental predisposition to brain disease. In some cases food ◊additives have come under suspicion; in such instances modification of the diet may help. Mostly there is improvement at puberty, but symptoms may persist in the small proportion diagnosed as having ◊attention-deficit hyperactivity disorder.

hyperbola in geometry, a curve formed by cutting a right circular cone with a plane so that the angle between the plane and the base is greater than the angle between the base and the side of the cone. All hyperbolae are bounded by two asymptotes (straight lines which the hyperbola moves closer and closer to but never reaches). A hyperbola is a member of the family of curves known as ◊conic sections.

A hyperbola can also be defined as a path traced by a point that moves such that the ratio of its distance from a fixed point (focus) and a fixed straight line (directrix) is a constant and greater than 1; that is, it has an eccentricity greater than 1.

hyperbole ◊figure of speech; the Greek name suggests 'going over the top'. When people use hyperbole, they exaggerate, usually to emphasize a point ('If I've told you once I've told you a thousand times not to do that').

hypercharge in physics, a property of certain ◊elementary particles, analogous to electric charge, that accounts for the absence of some expected behaviour (such as decay) in terms of the short-range strong nuclear force, which holds atomic nuclei together.

hypertension abnormally high ◊blood pressure due to a variety of causes, leading to excessive contraction of the smooth muscle cells of the walls of the arteries. It increases the risk of kidney disease, stroke, and heart attack.

Hypertension is one of the major public health problems of the developed world, affecting 15–20% of adults in industrialized countries (1996). It may be of unknown cause (***essential hypertension***), or it may occur in association with some other condition, such as kidney disease (***secondary*** or ***symptomatic hypertension***). It is controlled with a low-salt diet and drugs.

hypertext system for viewing information (both text and pictures) on a computer screen in such a way that related items of information can easily be reached. For example, the program might display a map of a country; if the user clicks (with a ◊mouse) on a particular city, the program will display information about that city.

hyperthyroidism or ***thyrotoxicosis*** overactivity of the thyroid gland due to enlargement or tumour. Symptoms include accelerated heart rate, sweating, anxiety, tremor, and weight loss. Treatment is by drugs or surgery.

hypertrophy abnormal increase in size of a body organ or tissue.

hypha (plural ***hyphae***) delicate, usually branching filament, many of which collectively form the mycelium and fruiting bodies of a ◊fungus. Food molecules and other substances are transported along hyphae by the movement of the cytoplasm, known as 'cytoplasmic streaming'.

Typically hyphae grow by increasing in length from the tips and by the formation of side branches. Hyphae of the higher fungi (the ascomycetes and basidiomycetes) are divided by cross walls or septa at intervals, whereas those of lower fungi (for example, bread mould) are undivided. However, even the higher fungi are not truly cellular, as each septum is pierced by a central pore, through which cytoplasm, and even nuclei, can flow. The hyphal walls contain ◊chitin, a polysaccharide.

hypnosis artificially induced state of relaxation or altered attention characterized by heightened suggestibility. There is evidence that, with susceptible persons, the sense of pain may be diminished, memory of past events enhanced, and illusions or hallucinations experienced. Posthypnotic amnesia (forgetting what happened during hypnosis) and posthypnotic suggestion (performing an action after hypnosis that had been suggested during it) have also been demonstrated.

Hypnosis has a number of uses in medicine. Hypnotically induced sleep, for example, may assist the healing process, and hypnotic suggestion (◊hypnotherapy) may help in dealing with the symptoms of emotional and psychosomatic disorders. The Austrian physician Friedrich Anton ◊Mesmer is said to be the discoverer of hypnosis, but he called it 'animal magnetism', believing it to be a physical force or fluid. The term 'hypnosis' was coined by James Braid (1795–1860), a British physician and surgeon who was the first to regard it as a psychological phenomenon.

hypnotherapy use of hypnotic trance and post-hypnotic suggestions to relieve stress-related conditions such as insomnia and hypertension, or to break health-damaging habits or addictions. Though it is an effective method of modifying behaviour, its effects are of short duration unless it is used as an adjunct to ◊psychotherapy.

hypnotic any substance (such as ◊barbiturate, ◊benzodiazepine, alcohol) that depresses brain function, inducing sleep. Prolonged use may lead to physical or psychological addiction.

hypocaust floor raised on tile piers, heated by hot air circulating beneath it. It was first used by the Romans for baths about 100 BC.

Hypocausts were a common feature of stone houses in the colder parts of the Roman Empire, but could not be used in timber-framed buildings. Typically the house of a wealthy person would have one furnace heating several rooms. During the 1st century AD channels were built into walls and roofs in order to distribute heat more evenly around the building.

hypocycloid in geometry, a cusped curve traced by a point on the circumference of a circle that rolls around the inside of another larger circle. (Compare ◊epicycloid.)

hypogeal term used to describe seed germination in which the ◊cotyledons remain below ground. It can refer to fruits that develop underground, such as peanuts *Arachis hypogea*.

hypoglycaemia condition of abnormally low level of sugar (glucose) in the blood (below 60 g/100 ml), which starves the brain. It causes weakness, sweating, and mental confusion, sometimes fainting.

Hypoglycaemia is most often seen in ◊diabetes. Low blood sugar occurs when the diabetic has taken too much insulin. It is treated by administering glucose.

hypotenuse the longest side of a right-angled triangle, opposite the right angle. It is of particular application in Pythagoras' theorem (the square of the hypotenuse equals the sum of the squares of the other two sides), and in trigonometry where the ratios sine and ◊cosine are defined as the ratios opposite/hypotenuse and adjacent/hypotenuse respectively.

hypothalamus region of the brain below the ◊cerebrum which regulates rhythmic activity and physiological stability within the body, including water balance and temperature. It regulates the production of the pituitary gland's hormones and controls that part of the ◊nervous system governing the involuntary muscles.

hypothermia condition in which the deep (core) temperature of the body falls below 35°C. If it is not discovered, coma and death ensue. Most at risk are the aged and babies (particularly if premature).

hypothyroidism or ***myxoedema*** deficient functioning of the thyroid gland, causing slowed mental and physical performance, weight gain, sensitivity to cold, and susceptibility to infection.

This may be due to lack of iodine in the diet or a defect of the thyroid gland, both being productive of ◊goitre; or to the pituitary gland providing insufficient stimulus to the thyroid gland. Treatment of thyroid deficiency is by the hormone thyroxine. When present from birth, hypothyroidism can lead to cretinism (mental retardation) if untreated.

hypsometer (Greek *hypsos* 'height') instrument for testing the accuracy of a thermometer at the boiling point of water. It was originally used for determining altitude by comparing changes in the boiling point with changes in atmospheric pressure.

hyrax small mammal, forming the order Hyracoidea, that lives among rocks, in deserts, and in forests in Africa, Arabia, and Syria. It is about the size of a rabbit, with a plump body, short legs, short ears, brownish fur, and long, curved front teeth.

There are four toes on the front limbs, and three on the hind, each of which has a tiny hoof. There are nine species.

hyssop aromatic herb *Hyssopus officinalis* of the mint family Labiatae, found in Asia, S Europe, and around the Mediterranean. It has blue flowers, oblong leaves, and stems that are woody near the ground but herbaceous above.

hysterectomy surgical removal of all or part of the uterus (womb). The operation is performed to treat fibroids (benign tumours growing in the uterus) or cancer; also to relieve heavy menstrual bleeding. A woman who has had a hysterectomy will no longer menstruate and cannot bear children.

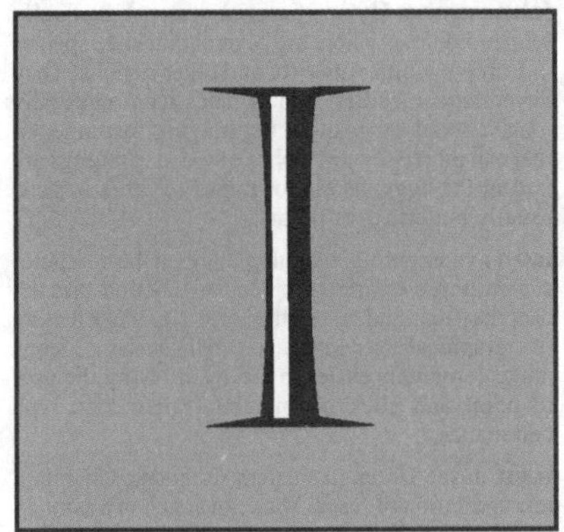

Iapetus Ocean or ***Proto-Atlantic*** sea that existed in early ◊Palaeozoic times between the continent that was to become Europe and that which was to become North America. The continents moved together in the late Palaeozoic, obliterating the ocean. When they moved apart once more, they formed the Atlantic.

Iaşi (German ***Jassy***) city in NE Romania; population (1993) 328,000. It has chemical, machinery, electronic, and textile industries. It was the capital of the principality of Moldavia 1568–1889.

iatrogenic caused by medical treatment; the term 'iatrogenic disease' may be applied to any pathological condition or complication that is caused by the treatment, the facilities, or the staff.

Ibadan city in SW Nigeria and capital of Oyo state; population (1992 est) 1,295,000. Industries include chemicals, electronics, plastics, and vehicles.

Iban or ***Sea Dyak*** the ◊Dyak people of central Borneo. Approximately 250,000 Iban live in the interior uplands of Sarawak, while another 10,000 live in the border area of W Kalimantan. Traditionally the Iban live in long houses divided into separate family units, and practise shifting cultivation. Their languages belong to the Austronesian family.

Ibáñez Vicente Blasco 1867–1928. Spanish novelist and politician. His novels include *La barraca/The Cabin* 1898, the most successful of his regional works; *Sangre y arena/Blood and Sand* 1908, the story of a famous bullfighter; and *Los cuatro jinetes del Apocalipsis/The Four Horsemen of the Apocalypse* 1916, a product of the effects of World War I. He was actively involved in revolutionary politics.

Ibarruri Dolores, known as ***La Pasionaria*** ('the passion flower') 1895–1989. Spanish Basque politician, journalist, and orator; she was first elected to the Cortes in 1936. She helped to establish the Popular Front government and was a Loyalist leader in the Civil War. When Franco came to power in 1939 she left Spain for the USSR, where she was active in the Communist Party. She returned to Spain in 1977 after Franco's death and was re-elected to the Cortes at the age of 81.

Iberia name given by ancient Greek navigators to the Spanish peninsula, derived from the river Iberus (Ebro). Anthropologists have given the name '***Iberian***' to a Neolithic people, traces of whom are found in the Spanish peninsula, southern France, the Canary Isles, Corsica, and part of North Africa.

ibex any of various wild goats found in mountainous areas of Europe, NE Africa, and Central Asia. They grow to 100 cm/3.5 ft, and have brown or grey coats and heavy horns. They are herbivorous and live in small groups.

ibis any of various wading birds, about 60 cm/2 ft tall, in the same family, Threskiornidae, order Ciconiiformes, as spoonbills. Ibises have long legs and necks, and long, curved bills, rather blunt at the end, with the upper mandible grooved. Their plumage is generally black and white. Various species occur in the warmer regions of the world.

The ***scarlet ibis***, *Guara ruber*, a South American species, is brilliant scarlet with a few black patches. The scarlet colour is derived from accumulated pigment from the aquatic invertebrates that form its food.

The ***glossy ibis*** *Plegadis falcinellus* is found in all continents except South America. The ***Japanese ibis*** is in danger of extinction because of the loss of its habitat; fewer than 25 birds remain. The ***sacred ibis*** *Threskiornis aethiopica* of ancient Egypt is still found in the Nile basin.

Ibiza one of the ◊Balearic Islands, a popular tourist resort; area 596 sq km/230 sq mi; population (1990 est) 71,000. The capital and port, also called Ibiza, has a cathedral.

IBM (abbreviation for ***International Business Machines***) multinational company, the largest manufacturer of computers in the world. The company is a descendant of the Tabulating Machine Company, formed 1896 by US inventor Herman ◊Hollerith to exploit his punched-card machines. It adopted its present name 1924. By 1991 it had an annual turnover of $64.8 billion and employed about 345,000 people, but in 1992 and 1993 it made considerable losses. The company acquired Lotus Development Corporation 1995. By 1996 IBM had, under new management, recovered financially, with an annual turnover of more than $70 billion.

Ibn Battuta 1304–1368. Arab traveller born in Tangier. In 1325, he went on an extraordinary 120,675-km/75,000-mi journey via Mecca to Egypt, E Africa, India, and China, returning some 30 years later. During this journey he also visited Spain and crossed the Sahara to Timbuktu. The narrative of his travels, *The Adventures of Ibn Battuta*, was written with an assistant, Ibn Juzayy.

Ibn Saud Abdul Aziz 1880–1953. First king of Saudi Arabia from 1932. His father was the son of the sultan of Nejd, at whose capital, Riyadh, Ibn Saud was born. In 1891 a rival group seized Riyadh, and Ibn Saud went into exile with his father, who resigned his claim to the throne in his son's favour. In 1902 Ibn Saud recaptured Riyadh and recovered the kingdom, and by 1921 he had brought all central Arabia under his rule. In 1924 he invaded the Hejaz, of which he was proclaimed king in 1926. Nejd and the Hejaz were united 1932 in the kingdom of Saudi Arabia.

Ibn Sina Arabic name of ◊Avicenna, scholar, and translator.

Ibo or ***Igbo*** member of a people of the W African Ibo culture occupying SE Nigeria and numbering about 18 million. Primarily cultivators, they inhabit the richly forested tableland bounded by the river Niger to the west and the river Cross to the east. They are divided into five main groups, and their languages belong to the Kwa branch of the Niger-Congo family.

Ibsen Henrik (Johan) 1828–1906. Norwegian dramatist and poet. His realistic and often controversial plays revolutionized European theatre. Driven into voluntary exile 1864–91 by opposition to the satirical *Kjærlighedens komedie/Love's Comedy* 1862, he wrote the symbolic verse dramas *Brand* 1866 and *Peer Gynt* 1867, followed by realistic plays dealing with social issues, including *Samfundets støtter/Pillars of Society* 1877, *Et dukkehjem/A Doll's House* 1879, *Gengangere/Ghosts* 1881, *En folkefiende/An Enemy of the People* 1882, and *Hedda Gabler* 1890. By the time he returned to Norway, he was recognized as the country's greatest living writer.

In his 'social problem' plays, Ibsen returned persistently to themes that had preoccupied him in *Brand* and *Peer Gynt*: the gulf between the ideal and the actual; the struggle to achieve personal integrity and fulfil one's vocation; the influence of the past and its 'inheritance of sin' on individuals and society generally. After his return to Norway 1891, he made a more overt use of symbolism to dramatize the confrontation of tortured and aspiring souls with their ultimate destinies, in the plays *Bygmester Solness/The Master Builder* 1892, *Lille Eyolf/Little Eyolf* 1894, *John Gabriel Borkman* 1896, and *Naar vi døde vaagner/When We Dead Awaken* 1899.

Icarus in astronomy, an ◊Apollo asteroid 1.5 km/1 mi in diameter, discovered 1949. It orbits the Sun every 409 days at a distance of 28–300 million km/18–186 million mi (0.19–2.0 astronomical units). It was the first asteroid known to approach the Sun closer than does the planet Mercury. In 1968 it passed 6 million km/4 million mi from the Earth.

ibis A white ibis holds its long beak close to the water while hunting for fish and small molluscs near a shoreline in Florida, USA. *Corbis*

Icarus in Greek mythology, the son of ◊Daedalus, who with his father escaped from the labyrinth in Crete by making wings of feathers fastened with wax. Icarus plunged to his death when he flew too near the Sun and the wax melted.

ICBM abbreviation for ***intercontinental ballistic missile***; see ◊nuclear warfare.

ice solid formed by water when it freezes. It is colourless and its crystals are hexagonal. The water molecules are held together by hydrogen bonds.

The freezing point of ice, used as a standard for measuring temperature, is 0° for the Celsius and Réaumur scales and 32° for the Fahrenheit. Ice expands in the act of freezing (hence burst pipes), becoming less dense than water (0.9175 at 5°C/41°F).

'It is better to die on your feet than to live on your knees.'

Dolores Ibarruri
Speech in Paris
3 Sept 1936

ice age any period of glaciation occurring in the Earth's history, but particularly that in the Pleistocene epoch, immediately preceding historic times. On the North American continent, ◊glaciers reached as far south as the Great Lakes, and an ice sheet spread over N Europe, leaving its remains as far south as Switzerland.

There were several glacial advances separated by interglacial stages during which the ice melted and temperatures were higher than today.

Formerly there were thought to have been only three or four glacial advances, but recent research has shown about 20 major incidences. There were four in the Precambrian era, one in the Ordovician, and one at the end of the Carboniferous and beginning of the Permian. The occurrence of an ice age is governed by a combination of factors: (1) the Earth's change of attitude in relation to the Sun, that is, the way it tilts in a 41,000-year cycle and at the same time wobbles on its axis in a 22,000-year cycle, making the time of its closest approach to the Sun come at different seasons; and (2) the 92,000-year cycle of eccentricity in its orbit round the Sun, changing it from an elliptical to a near circular orbit, the severest period of an ice age coinciding with the approach to circularity. There is a possibility that the Pleistocene ice age is not yet over. It may reach another maximum in another 60,000 years.

ICE AGE: MAJOR ICE AGES

Name	Date (years ago)
Pleistocene	1.64 million–10,000
Permo-Carboniferous	330–250 million
Ordovician	440–430 million
Verangian	615–570 million
Sturtian	820–770 million
Gnejso	940–880 million
Huronian	2,700–1,800 million

Ice Age, Little period of particularly severe winters that gripped N Europe between the 13th and 17th centuries. Contemporary writings and paintings show that Alpine glaciers were much more extensive than at present, and rivers such as the Thames, which do not ice over today, were so frozen that festivals could be held on them.

iceberg floating mass of ice, about 80% of which is submerged, rising sometimes to 100 m/300 ft

'One should never put on one's best trousers to go out to battle for freedom and truth.'

Henrik Ibsen
An Enemy of the People

ice hockey The Maple Leaf ice hockey team of Toronto. Developed in Canada, ice hockey is now widely played in the USA, the former Soviet republics, the Czech and Slovak republics, Sweden, Germany, and Finland. In this vigorous and fast-moving game, the puck sometimes travels at speeds of over 160 km/100 mi per hour. *Canadian Tourist Office*

above sea level. Glaciers that reach the coast become extended into a broad foot; as this enters the sea, masses break off and drift towards temperate latitudes.

ice cream rich, creamy, frozen confectionery, made commercially from the early 20th century from various milk products, sugar, and fruit and nut flavourings, usually with additives to improve keeping qualities and ease of serving.
history Ice cream originated as a means of preserving milk, and was originally made by mixing ice with milk and sugar. Ice cream was made in China before 1000 BC and probably introduced to Europe by Marco Polo; water ices were known in ancient Greece and Persia. The first synthetic ice cream was made in Australia in 1855, although it was only in the 20th century that the cost of ice cream fell sufficiently for it to become a mass-market food. Italy and Russia were renowned for ice cream even before it became a mechanized industry, first in the USA and in the 1920s in Britain. Technical developments from the 1950s made possible the mass distribution of a 'soft' ice cream resembling the original type in appearance.
the science of ice cream Ice cream is a foam, a mixture of small crystals of ice surrounding pockets of air, trapped and held in place by globular clusters of fat proteins (cream and eggs). The long protein molecules begin to unwind as the ingredients are heated to form a custard. The air gives ice cream its light taste, and reduces the sensation of cold when eating.

ice hockey game played on ice between two teams of six, developed in Canada from hockey or bandy. A rubber disc (puck) is used in place of a ball. Players wear skates and protective clothing.

The governing body is the International Ice Hockey Federation (IIHF) founded 1908. Ice hockey has been included in the Olympics since 1920 when it was part of the Summer Games programme. Since 1924 it has been part of the Winter Olympics. The Stanley Cup is the game's leading play-off tournament, contested after the season-long National Hockey League, and was first held 1916.

Iceland island country in the N Atlantic Ocean, situated S of the Arctic Circle, between Greenland and Norway. *See country box opposite.*

Icelandic language member of the N Germanic branch of the Indo-European language family, spoken only in Iceland and the most conservative in form of the Scandinavian languages. Despite seven centuries of Danish rule, Icelandic has remained virtually unchanged since the 12th century.

Since independence in 1918, Icelandic has experienced a revival, as well as governmental protection against such outside linguistic influences as English-language broadcasting. Early Icelandic literature is largely anonymous and seems to have originated in Norse colonies in the British Isles (around 9th–10th centuries). The two Eddas and several Sagas date from this period. Halldor Laxness (1902–), writing about Icelandic life in the style of the Sagas, was awarded a Nobel prize 1955.

Iceland spar form of ◊calcite, $CaCO_3$, originally found in Iceland. In its pure form Iceland spar is transparent and exhibits the peculiar phenomenon of producing two images of anything seen through it. It is used in optical instruments. The crystals cleave into perfect rhombohedra.

iceman nickname given to the preserved body of a prehistoric man discovered in a glacier on the Austrian–Italian border 1991. On the basis of the clothing and associated artefacts, the body was at first believed to be 4,000 years old, from the Bronze Age. Carbon dating established its age at about 5,300 years. The discovery led to a reappraisal of the boundary between the Bronze and the Stone Age.

Iceni ancient people of E England, who revolted against occupying Romans under ◊Boudicca.

ice-skating see ◊skating.

I Ching or ***Book of Changes*** ancient Chinese book of divination based on 64 hexagrams, or patterns of six lines. The lines may be 'broken' or 'whole' (yin or yang) and are generated by tossing yarrow stalks or coins. The enquirer formulates a question before throwing, and the book gives interpretations of the meaning of the hexagrams.

The *I Ching* is thought to have originated in the 2nd millennium BC, with commentaries added by Confucius and later philosophers. It is not used for determining the future but for making the enquirer aware of inherent possibilities and unconscious tendencies.

ichneumon fly The female of the ichneumon fly (or wasp) *Rhyssa persuasoria*. She is using her long ovipositor to insert an egg into a larva of the wood wasp *Sirex gigas*, which lives in a tunnel burrowed into a pine trunk. *Premaphotos Wildlife*

ichneumon fly any parasitic wasp of the family Ichneumonidae. There are several thousand species in Europe, North America, and other regions. They have slender bodies, and females have unusually long, curved ovipositors (egg-laying instruments) that can pierce several inches of wood. The eggs are laid in the eggs, larvae, or pupae of other insects, usually butterflies or moths.

icon in computing, a small picture on the computer screen, representing an object or function that the user may manipulate or otherwise use. It is a feature of ◊graphical user interface (GUI) systems. Icons make computers easier to use by allowing the user to point and click on pictures, rather than type commands.

icon in the Greek or Eastern Orthodox Church, a representation of Jesus, Mary, an angel, or a saint, in painting, low relief, or mosaic. The painted icons were traditionally done on wood. After the 17th century and mainly in Russia, a *riza*, or gold and silver covering that leaves only the face and hands visible (and may be adorned with jewels presented by the faithful in thanksgiving), was often added as protection.

Icon painting originated in the Byzantine Empire; many examples were destroyed by the ◊iconoclasts in the 8th and 9th centuries. The Byzantine style of painting predominated in the Mediterranean region and in Russia until the 12th century, when Russian, Greek, and other schools developed. Notable among them was the Russian ◊Novgorod School, inspired by the work of the Byzantine refugee Theophanes the Greek (c. 1330–1405). Andrei ◊Rublev is the outstanding Russian icon painter.

iconoclast (Greek 'image-breaker') literally, a person who attacks religious images, originally in obedience to the injunction of the Second Commandment not to worship 'graven images'. Under the influence of Islam and Judaism, an iconoclastic movement calling for the destruction of religious images developed in the Byzantine Empire, and was endorsed by the Emperor Leo III in 726. Fierce persecution of those who made and venerated icons followed, until iconoclasm was declared a heresy in the 9th century. The same name was applied to those opposing the use of images at the Reformation, when there was much destruction in churches.

iconography in art history, significance attached to symbols that can help to identify subject matter (for example, a saint holding keys usually represents St Peter) and place a work of art in its historical context. The pioneer of this approach was the German art historian Erwin Panofsky (1892–1968).

icosahedron (plural ***icosahedra***) regular solid with 20 equilateral (equal-sided) triangular faces. It is one of the five regular ◊polyhedra, or Platonic solids.

id in Freudian psychology, the mass of motivational and instinctual elements of the human mind, whose activity is largely governed by the arousal of specific needs. It is regarded as the ◊unconscious element of the human psyche, and is said to be in conflict with the ◊ego and the ◊superego.

Idaho state of northwestern USA; nickname Gem State
area 216,500 sq km/83,569 sq mi
capital Boise
towns and cities Pocatello, Idaho Falls
features Rocky Mountains; Sawtooth Mountains, with peaks up to 11,800 feet; Snake River, which runs through Hell's Canyon (2,330 m/7,647 ft), the deepest gorge in North America, and has the National Reactor Testing Station on the plains of its upper reaches; Shoshone Falls; Salmon River; Craters of the Moon national monument; Lava Hot Springs; Coeur d'Alene Lake, with a large population of ospreys; Nez Percé national historic park; Old Mission at Cataldo (1850), the oldest building in the state; Coeur d'Alene Native American reservation; EBR-1, the first nuclear reactor in the USA to generate usable amounts of electricity, now a national historic landmark; Soda Springs, with the only artificial geyser in the world; Sun Valley, the first ski resort in the USA (1935) and site of the world's first chair lifts
industries potatoes, wheat, livestock, timber, silver, lead, zinc, antimony
population (1991) 1,039,000.

Idaho

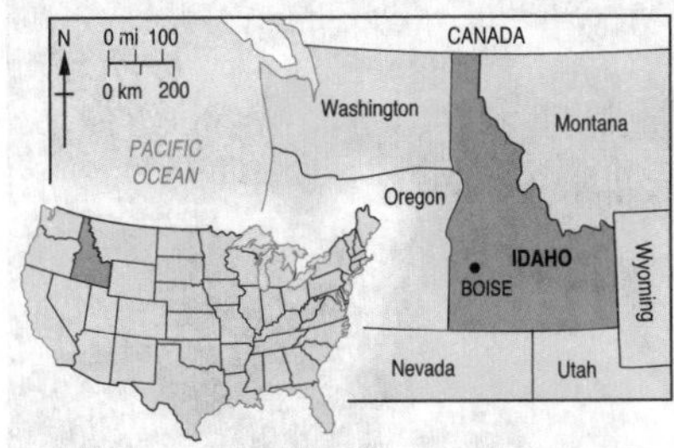

idealism in philosophy, the theory that states that the external world is fundamentally immaterial and a dimension of the mind. Objects in the world exist but, according to this theory, they lack substance.

identikit a set of drawings of different parts of the face used to compose a likeness of a person for identification. It was evolved by Hugh C McDonald (1913–) in the USA. It has largely been replaced by photofit, based on photographs, which produces a more realistic likeness. Identikit was first used by the police in Britain 1961.

Ides in the Roman calendar, the 15th day of March, May, July, and Oct, and the 13th day of all other months (the word originally indicated the full moon); Julius Caesar was assassinated on the Ides of March 44 BC.

idiot savant (French 'knowledgeable idiot') person who has a specific mental skill that has developed at the expense of general intelligence. An idiot savant is educationally slow but may be able to calculate the day of the week for any date, or memorize a large quantity of text. Most idiots savants are male.

Ife town in W Nigeria, traditionally the oldest of the Yoruba kingdoms in the region. Ife was established in the 6th century and became an important Iron-Age town. It was the cultural and religious, though not political, centre of the region, and reached its peak about 1300. Many sculptures in bronze, brass, clay, and ivory have been excavated in and around the town.

Ifugao an indigenous people of N Luzon in the Philippines, numbering approximately 70,000. In addition to practising shifting cultivation on highland slopes, they build elaborate terraced rice fields. Their language belongs to the Austronesian family.

Ignatius Loyola, St (born Iñigo López de Recalde) 1491–1556. Spanish noble who founded the ◊Jesuit order 1534, also called the Society of Jesus. Canonized 1622.

His deep interest in the religious life began in 1521, when reading the life of Jesus while recuperating from a war wound. He visited the Holy Land in 1523, studied in Spain and Paris, where he took vows with St Francis Xavier, and was ordained 1537. He then moved to Rome and with the approval of Pope Paul III began the Society of Jesus, sending missionaries to Brazil, India, and Japan, and founding Jesuit schools. Feast day 31 July.

Ignatius of Antioch, St died c. 110. Christian martyr. Traditionally a disciple of St John, he was bishop of Antioch, and was thrown to the wild beasts in Rome. He wrote seven epistles, important documents of the early Christian church. Feast day 1 Feb.

igneous rock rock formed from cooling magma or lava, and solidifying from a molten state. Igneous rocks are largely composed of silica (SiO_2) and they are classified according to their crystal size, texture, method of formation, or chemical composition, for example by the proportions of light and dark minerals.

Igneous rocks that crystallize below the Earth's surface are called plutonic or intrusive, depending on the depth of formation. They have large crystals produced by slow cooling; examples include dolerite and granite. Those extruded at the surface are called extrusive or volcanic. Rapid cooling results in small crystals; basalt is an example.

ignis fatuus another name for ◊will-o'-the-wisp.

ignition coil ◊transformer that is an essential part of a petrol engine's ignition system. It consists of two wire coils wound around an iron core. The primary coil, which is connected to the car battery, has only a few turns. The secondary coil, connected via the ◊distributor to the ◊spark plugs, has many turns. The coil takes in a low voltage (usually 12 volts) from the battery and transforms it to a high voltage (about 20,000 volts) to ignite the engine.

When the engine is running, the battery current is periodically interrupted by means of the contact breaker in the distributor. The collapsing current in the primary coil induces a current in the secondary coil, a phenomenon known as ◊electromagnetic induction. The induced current in the secondary coil is at very high voltage, typically about 15,000–20,000 volts. This passes to the spark plugs to create sparks.

ignition temperature or ***fire point*** minimum temperature to which a substance must be heated before it will spontaneously burn independently of the source of heat; for example, ethanol has an ignition temperature of 425°C/798°F and a flash point (the point at which it will ignite on the application of a small flame) of 12°C/54°F.

Iguaçú Falls or ***Iguassú Falls*** waterfall in South America, on the border between Brazil and Argentina. The falls lie 19 km/12 mi above the junction of the river Iguaçú with the Paraná. The falls are divided by forested rocky islands and form a spectacular tourist attraction. The water plunges in 275 falls, many of which have separate names. They have a height of 82 m/269 ft and a width of about 4 km/2.5 mi. *See illustration on following page.*

'Alone in Iceland you are alone indeed, and the homeless, undisturbed wilderness gives something of its awful calm to the spirit.'

On **Iceland**
Miss Oswald *By Fell and Fjord* 1882

ICELAND
Republic of

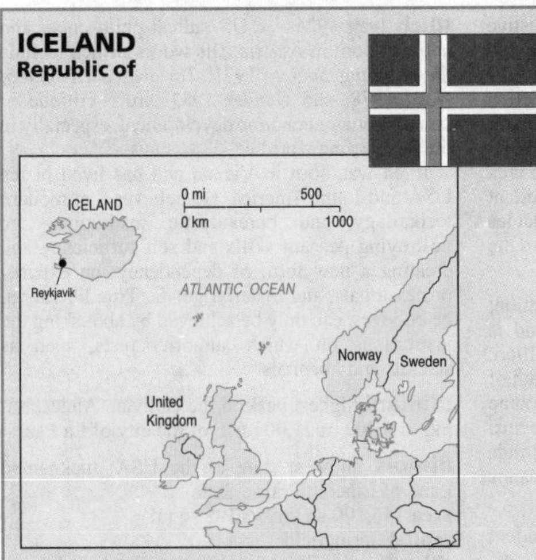

national name *Lýðveldið Ísland*
area 103,000 sq km/39,758 sq mi
capital Reykjavík
major towns/cities Akureyri, Akranes
physical features warmed by the Gulf Stream; glaciers and lava fields cover 75% of the country; active volcanoes, geysers, hot springs, and new islands created offshore (Surtsey in 1963); subterranean hot water heats 85% of Iceland's homes; Sidujokull glacier moves at 100 metres a day
head of state Vigdís Finnbogadóttir from 1980
head of government David Oddsson from 1991
political system democratic republic
administrative divisions 23 counties within eight districts
political parties Independence Party (IP), right of centre; Progressive Party (PP), radical socialist; People's Alliance (PA), socialist; Social Democratic Party (SDP), moderate, left of centre; Citizens' Party, centrist; Women's Alliance, women- and family-oriented
armed forces no defence forces of its own; US forces under NATO are stationed there: 2,500 military personnel and a 130-strong coastguard (1995)
conscription n/a
defence spend (% GDP) n/a
education spend (% GNP) 5.8 (1992)
health spend (% GDP) 6.9 (1993)
death penalty abolished 1928
population 269,000 (1995 est)
population growth rate 1.1% (1990–95); 0.9% (2000–05)
age distribution (% of total population) <15 24.5%, 15–65 64.3%, >65 11.2% (1995)
ethnic distribution most of the population is descended from Norwegians and Celts
population density (per sq km) 3 (1994)
urban population (% of total) 92 (1995)
labour force 56% of population: 11% agriculture, 27% industry, 62% services (1990)
unemployment 5% (1995)
child mortality rate (under 5, per 1,000 live births) 6 (1993)
life expectancy 75 (men), 81 (women)
education (compulsory years) 9
literacy rate 99%
languages Icelandic, the most archaic Scandinavian language
religion Evangelical Lutheran
TV sets (per 1,000 people) 319 (1992)
currency krona
GDP (US $) 7.1 billion (1995)
GDP per capita (PPP) (US $) 20,000 (1995)
growth rate 2.0% (1994/95)
average annual inflation 2.9% (1993); 12.8% (1985–94)
major trading partners EU (principally Germany, Denmark, and UK), Norway, USA, Japan
resources aluminium, diatomite, hydroelectric and thermal power, fish
industries mining, fish processing, processed aluminium, fertilizer, construction, cement
exports fish products, aluminium, ferrosilicon, diatomite, fertilizer, animal products. Principal market: UK 20.5% (1994)
imports machinery and transport equipment, motor vehicles, petroleum and petroleum products, foodstuffs, textiles. Principal source: Norway 14.3% (1994)
arable land 0.1% (1993)
agricultural products hay, potatoes, turnips; fishing industry, dairy products and livestock (chiefly lamb)

HISTORY
7th C Iceland discovered by Irish seafarers.
874 First Norse settler, Ingólfr Arnarson, founded a small colony at Rekyavík.
c. 900 Norse settlers came in larger numbers, mainly from Norway.
930 Settlers established an annual parliament, the Althing, to make laws and resolve disputes.
985 Eric the Red left Iceland to found a settlement in Greenland.
1000 Icelanders adopted Christianity.
1263 Icelanders recognized authority of the King of Norway after brief civil war.
1397 Norway and Iceland united with Denmark and Sweden under a single monarch.
15th C Norway and Iceland were increasingly treated as appendages of Denmark, especially after Sweden seceded in 1449.
1602 Denmark introduced a monopoly on Icelandic trade.
1783 Poisonous volcanic eruption caused great loss of life.
1814 Norway passed to the Swedish crown; Iceland remained under Danish rule.
1845 Althing re-established in modernized form.
1854 Danish monopoly on trade abolished.
1874 New constitution gave Iceland limited autonomy.
1918 Iceland was granted full self-government under the Danish crown.
1940 British forces occupied Iceland after Germany invaded Denmark; US troops took over 1941.
1944 Iceland became an independent republic under President Sveinn Björnsson.
1949 Became a member of NATO.
1953 Joined the Nordic Council.
1958 Introduction of exclusive 19-km/12-mi fishing limit led to first 'Cod War', when Icelandic patrol boats clashed with British fishing boats.
1972–73 Iceland extended its fishing limit 80 km/50 mi; renewed confrontation with Britain.
1975–76 Further extension of fishing limit to 341 km/200 mi caused third 'Cod War' with the UK.
1980 Vigdis Finnbogadóttir became the first woman president of Iceland.
1985 Iceland declared itself a nuclear-free zone.
1992 Iceland defied world ban to resume whaling industry.

Iguaçú Falls Iguaçú Falls, South America (formerly Victoria Falls), the most voluminous waterfall in the world. Over half of its 275 cataracts fall into a single chasm known as The Devil's Throat. Iguaçú is a Guaraní Indian word meaning 'great waters'. *Sally Jenkins*

'In a consumer society there are inevitably two kinds of slaves: the prisoners of addiction and the prisoners of envy.'

IVAN ILLICH
Tools for Conviviality

iguana any lizard, especially the genus *Iguana*, of the family Iguanidae, which includes about 700 species and is chiefly confined to the Americas. The common iguana *I. iguana* of Central and South America is a vegetarian and may reach 2 m/6 ft in length.

iguanodon plant-eating ◊dinosaur of the order *Ornithiscia*, whose remains are found in deposits of the Lower Cretaceous age, together with the remains of other ornithiscians such as stegosaurus and triceratops. It was 5–10 m/16–32 ft long and, when standing upright, 4 m/13 ft tall. It walked on its hind legs, using its long tail to balance its body.

Ijsselmeer lake in the Netherlands, area 1,217 sq km/470 sq mi. It was formed 1932 after the Zuider Zee was cut off from the North Sea by a dyke 32 km/20 mi long (the *Afsluitdijk*); it has been freshwater since 1944. The rivers Vecht, IJssel, and Zwatewater empty into the lake.

Four polders have been reclaimed, primarily for agriculture: Wieringermeer Polder 193 sq km/75 sq mi (1930); Northeast Polder 469 sq km/181 sq mi (1942); East Flevoland Polder 528 sq km/204 sq mi (1957); and South Flevoland Polder 430 sq km/166 sq mi (1968).

Ikhnaton another name for ◊Akhenaton, pharaoh of Egypt.

Ile-de-France region of N France; area 12,000 sq km/4,632 sq mi; population (1990) 10,660,600. It includes the French capital, Paris, and the towns of Versailles, Sèvres, and St-Cloud and comprises the *départements* of Essonne, Val-de-Marne, Val d'Oise, Ville de Paris, Seine-et-Marne, Hauts-de-Seine, Seine-Saint-Denis, and Yvelines. From here the early French kings extended their authority over the whole country.

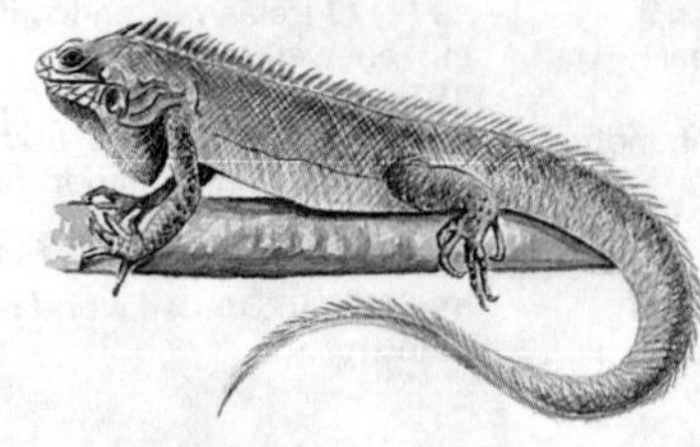

iguana The common iguana lives mainly in trees but is an excellent swimmer. It has a characteristic crest of comblike spines running down the length of its back. Young animals are bright green, becoming darker with age.

ileum part of the small intestine of the ◊digestive system, between the duodenum and the colon, that absorbs digested food.

Its wall is muscular so that waves of contraction (peristalsis) can mix the food and push it forward. Numerous fingerlike projections, or villi, point inwards from the wall, increasing the surface area available for absorption. The ileum has an excellent blood supply, which receives the food molecules passing through the wall and transports them to the liver.

Iliad Greek epic poem, product of an oral tradition; it was possibly written down by 700 BC and is attributed to ◊Homer. The title is derived from Ilion, the Greek name for Troy. Its subject is the wrath of the Greek hero Achilles at the loss of his concubine Briseis, and at the death of his friend Patroclus, during the Greek siege of Troy. The poems ends with the death of the Trojan hero Hector at the hands of Achilles.

Iliescu Ion 1930– . Romanian president 1990–96. A former member of the Romanian Communist Party (PCR) and of Nicolae Ceaușescu's government, Iliescu swept into power on Ceaușescu's fall as head of the National Salvation Front.

Iliescu was elected a member of the PCR central committee 1968, becoming its propaganda secretary 1971. At the outbreak of the 'Christmas revolution' 1989, Iliescu was one of the first leaders to emerge, becoming president of the Provisional Council of National Unity Feb 1990. He won an overwhelming victory in the presidential elections May 1990, despite earlier controversy over his hard line. He was defeated in the second ballot run-off race for the presidency Nov 1996.

Ilium in classical mythology, an alternative name for the city of ◊Troy, taken from its founder Ilus.

illegitimacy in law, the status of a child born to a mother who is not legally married; a child may be legitimized by subsequent marriage of the parents. The nationality of the child is usually that of the mother.

In England and Wales, more than one-third of children were born out of wedlock 1995, compared to under one-fifth in 1985. Recent acts have progressively removed many of the historic disadvantages of illegitimacy, culminating in the Family Law Reform Act 1987 under which ◊custody and ◊maintenance provisions are now the same as for legitimate children.

Illich Ivan 1926– . US radical philosopher and activist, born in Austria. His works, which include *Deschooling Society* 1971, *Towards a History of Need* 1978, and *Gender* 1983, are a critique of contemporary economic development, especially in the developing world.

Illich was born in Vienna and has lived in the USA and Latin America. He believes that modern technology and bureaucratic institutions are destroying peasant skills and self-sufficiency and creating a new form of dependency: on experts, professionals, and material goods. True liberation, he believes, can only be achieved by abolishing the institutions on which authority rests, such as schools and hospitals.

Illimani highest peak in the Bolivian Andes, rising to 6,402 m/21,004 ft E of the city of La Paz.

Illinois midwest state of the USA; nicknamed Land of Lincoln/Prairie State
area 146,100 sq km/56,395 sq mi
capital Springfield
cities Chicago, Rockford, Peoria, Decatur, Aurora
features Lake Michigan; the Mississippi, Illinois, Ohio, and Rock rivers; Cahokia Mounds, the largest group of prehistoric earthworks in the USA; prairies; Shawnee national forest; Nauvoo, founded 1839 by the Mormons, and their point of departure 1846 on the trek that led them to Utah; Abraham Lincoln's home in Springfield; Galena, a lead-mining town dating from the 1820s, with pre-Civil War buildings; Chicago, with the Art Institute of Chicago, the Museum of Science and Industry, the Sears Tower, and the Rookery (1886) with a lobby designed by Frank Lloyd Wright 1905; Frank Lloyd Wright's home and studio, Oak Park; Ernest

Illinois

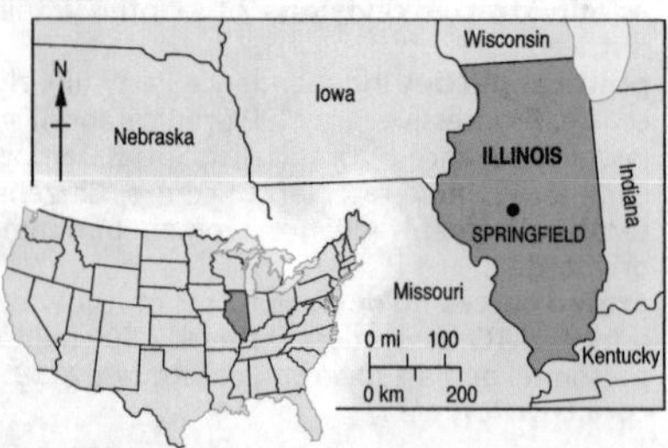

Hemingway's boyhood home, Oak Park; the Dana Thomas House, Springfield, designed by Frank Lloyd Wright 1903; gambling casinos on replicas of 19th-century Mississippi paddle boats
industries soya beans, cereals, meat and dairy products, machinery, electrical and electronic equipment
population (1991) 11,543,000
famous people Jane Addams, Saul Bellow, Frances Cabrini, Clarence Darrow, Enrico Fermi, Ernest Hemingway, Jesse Jackson, Abraham Lincoln, Edgar Lee Masters, Ronald Reagan, Louis Sullivan, Frank Lloyd Wright.

illumination or *illuminance* the brightness or intensity of light falling on a surface. It depends upon the brightness, distance, and angle of any nearby light sources. The SI unit is the ◊lux.

Illyria ancient name for the eastern coastal region of the Adriatic, N of the Gulf of Corinth, conquered by Philip of Macedon. Julius Caesar was governor of the province of Illyricum 59 BC. The Albanians are the survivors of its ancient peoples.

Illyrian works of art include the figurative 'Situla art' of the 6th century BC, depicting feasting and games. The Roman province of Illyricum was the birthplace of St Jerome, the scholar.

ilmenite oxide of iron and titanium, iron titanate ($FeTiO_3$); an ore of titanium. The mineral is black, with a metallic lustre. It is found as an accessory mineral in mafic igneous rocks and in sands.

image compression in computing, one of a number of methods used to reduce the amount of information required to represent an image, so that it takes up less computer memory and can be transmitted more rapidly and economically via telecommunications systems. It is used in fax transmission and in videophone and multimedia systems.

imaginary number term often used to describe the non-real element of a ◊complex number. For the complex number $(a + ib)$, ib is the imaginary number where $i = \sqrt{-1}$, and b any real number.

Imagism movement in Anglo-American poetry that flourished 1912–14 and affected much US and British poetry and critical thinking thereafter. A central figure was Ezra Pound, who asserted the principles of free verse, complex imagery, and poetic impersonality.

Pound encouraged Hilda Doolittle to sign her verse H D Imagiste and in 1914 edited the *Des Imagistes* anthology. Poets subsequently influenced by this movement include T S Eliot, William Carlos Williams, Wallace Stevens, and Marianne Moore. Imagism established modernism in English-language verse.

imago sexually mature stage of an ◊insect.

imam (Arabic 'leader') in a mosque, the leader of congregational prayer, but generally any notable Islamic leader.

IMF abbreviation for ◊***International Monetary Fund***.

Imhotep c. 2630 BC– . Egyptian physician and architect, adviser to King Zoser (3rd dynasty). He is thought to have designed the step pyramid at Sakkara, and his tomb (believed to be in the N Sakkara cemetery) became a centre of healing. He was deified as the son of ◊Ptah and was identified with Aesculapius, the Greek god of medicine.

Immaculate Conception in the Roman Catholic Church, the belief that the Virgin Mary was, by a special act of grace, preserved free from ◊original sin from the moment she was conceived. This article of the Catholic faith was for centuries the subject of heated controversy, opposed by St Thomas Aquinas and other theologians, but generally accepted from about the 16th century. It became a dogma in 1854 under Pope Pius IX.

immigration and emigration movement of people from one country to another. Immigration is movement to a country; emigration is movement from a country. Immigration or emigration on a large scale is often for economic reasons or because of religious, political, or social persecution (which may create ◊refugees), and often prompts restrictive legislation by individual countries.

The USA has received immigrants on a larger scale than any other country, more than 50 million during its history.

In the UK, Commonwealth Immigration Acts were passed 1962 and 1968, and replaced by a single system of control under the Immigration Act of 1971. The British Nationality Act 1981 further restricted immigration by ruling that only a British citizen has the right to live in the United Kingdom; see ◊citizenship.

immunity the protection that organisms have against foreign microorganisms, such as bacteria and viruses, and against cancerous cells (see ◊cancer). White blood cells, or leucocytes, are produced by the body in response to infection. They include neutrophils and ◊macrophages, which can engulf invading organisms and other unwanted material, and natural killer cells that destroy cells infected by viruses and cancerous cells. Some of the most important immune cells are the ◊B cells and ◊T cells. Immune cells coordinate their activities by means of chemical messengers or lymphokines, including the antiviral messenger ◊interferon. The lymph nodes play a major role in organizing the immune response.

Immunity is also provided by a range of physical barriers such as the skin, tear fluid, acid in the stomach, and mucus in the airways. ◊AIDS is one of many viral diseases in which the immune system is affected.

immunization conferring immunity to infectious disease by artificial methods. The most widely used technique is ◊vaccination.

Immunization is an important public health measure. If most of the population has been immunized against a particular disease, it is impossible for an epidemic to take hold.

Vaccination against smallpox was developed by Edward ◊Jenner in 1796. In the late 19th century Louis ◊Pasteur developed vaccines against cholera, typhoid, typhus, plague, and yellow fever. In 1991, the WHO and UNICEF announced that four out of five children around the world are now immunized against six killer diseases: measles, tetanus, polio, diphtheria, whooping cough, and tuberculosis. Ten years ago this figure was only one in five children.

immunocompromised lacking a fully effective immune system. The term is most often used in connection with infections such as ◊AIDS where the virus interferes with the immune response (see ◊immunity).

Other factors that can impair the immune response are pregnancy, diabetes, old age, malnutrition and extreme stress, making someone susceptible to infections by microorganisms (such as listeria) that do not affect normal, healthy people. Some people are immunodeficient; others could be on ◊immunosuppressive drugs.

immunodeficient lacking one or more elements of a working immune system. Immune deficiency is the term generally used for patients who are born with such a defect, while those who acquire such a deficiency later in life are referred to as ◊immunocompromised or immunosuppressed.

A serious impairment of the immune system is sometimes known as SCID, or Severe Combined Immune Deficiency. At one time children born with this condition would have died in infancy. They can now be kept alive in a germ-free environment, then treated with a bone-marrow transplant from a relative, to replace the missing immune cells. At present, the success rate for this type of treatment is still fairly low. See also ◊gene therapy.

immunoglobulin human globulin ◊protein that can be separated from blood and administered to confer immediate immunity on the recipient. It participates in the immune reaction as the antibody for a specific ◊antigen (disease-causing agent).

Normal immunoglobulin (gamma globulin) is the fraction of the blood serum that, in general, contains the most antibodies, and is obtained from plasma pooled from about a thousand donors. It is given for short-term (two to three months) protection when a person is at risk, mainly from hepatitis A (infectious hepatitis), or when a pregnant woman, not immunized against ◊German measles, is exposed to the rubella virus.

Specific immunoglobulins are injected when a susceptible (nonimmunized) person is at risk of infection from a potentially fatal disease, such as hepatitis B (serum hepatitis), rabies, or tetanus. These immunoglobulins are prepared from blood pooled from donors convalescing from the disease.

immunosuppressive any drug that suppresses the body's normal immune responses to infection or foreign tissue. It is used in the treatment of autoimmune disease (see ◊autoimmunity); as part of chemotherapy for leukaemias, lymphomas, and other cancers; and to help prevent rejection following organ transplantation.

Immunosuppressed patients are at greatly increased risk of infection.

impala African antelope *Aepyceros melampus* found from Kenya to South Africa in savannas and open woodland. The body is sandy brown. Males have lyre-shaped horns up to 75 cm/2.5 ft long. Impalas grow up to 1.5 m/5 ft long and 90 cm/3 ft tall. They live in herds and spring high in the air when alarmed.

impeachment judicial procedure by which government officials are accused of wrongdoing and brought to trial before a legislative body. In the USA the House of Representatives may impeach offenders to be tried before the Senate, as in the case of President Andrew Johnson 1868. Richard

impala This male impala in the Kruger National Park, South Africa, is part of a bachelor herd. A pursued impala can reach speeds of 60 kph/37 mph and clear obstacles 3 m/10 ft high in a single leap. *Premaphotos Wildlife*

The conquest of the earth, which mostly means the taking it away from those who have a different complexion or slightly flatter noses than ourselves, is not a pretty thing when you look into it.

On IMPERIALISM
Joseph Conrad
Heart of Darkness
1902

◊Nixon resigned the US presidency 1974 when threatened by impeachment. President Bill ◊Clinton's impeachment trial took place 1999.

impedance the total opposition of a circuit to the passage of alternating electric current. It has the symbol *Z*. For an ◊alternating current (AC) it includes the resistance *R* and the reactance *X* (caused by capacitance (the property of a capacitor that determines how much charge can be stored in it for a given potential difference between its terminals) or ◊inductance); the impedance can then be found using the equation $Z^2 = R^2 + X^2$.

imperialism policy of extending the power and rule of a government beyond its own boundaries. A country may attempt to dominate others by direct rule or by less obvious means such as control of markets for goods or raw materials. The latter is often called ◊neocolonialism.

In the 19th century, imperialism was synonymous with the establishment of colonies, and was overtly and often flamboyantly practised. Britain, for example, revelled in its expansionist policies, and its colonies and dominions all bore evidence of rule by the 'mother country'. Place names such as Victoria in Australia and Canada, Victoria Falls in Rhodesia (the falls now form the border between Zambia and Zimbabwe), and Victoria Peak in Hong Kong are examples of this boastful display of empire. After World War II the British Empire was progressively dismembered and, while traditional imperialism was continued by the USSR until 1991, other leading nations adopted more subtle forms of economic imperialism, or neocolonialism.

imperial system traditional system of units developed in the UK, based largely on the foot, pound, and second (f.p.s.) system. In 1991 it was announced that the acre, pint, troy ounce, mile, yard, foot, and inch would remain in use indefinitely for beer, cider, and milk measures, and in road-traffic signs and land registration. Other units, including the fathom and therm, were to be phased out by 1994. *See list of tables on p. 1177.*

Imperial War Museum British military museum, founded 1917. It includes records of all operations fought by British forces since 1914. Its present building (formerly the Royal Bethlehem, or Bedlam, Hospital) in Lambeth Road, London, was opened 1936. It was rebuilt and enlarged 1989.

impetigo skin infection with either streptococcus or staphylococcus bacteria, characterized by encrusted yellow sores on the skin. Particularly common in infants and small children, it is highly contagious but curable with antibiotics.

Imphal capital of Manipur state on the Manipur River, India; population (1991) 201,000; a communications and trade centre (tobacco, sugar, fruit). It was besieged March–June 1944, when Japan invaded Assam, but held out with the help of supplies dropped by air.

implantation in mammals, the process by which the developing ◊embryo attaches itself to the wall of the mother's uterus and stimulates the development of the ◊placenta. In humans it occurs 6–8 days after ovulation.

In some species, such as seals and bats, implantation is delayed for several months, during which time the embryo does not grow; thus the interval between mating and birth may be longer than the ◊gestation period.

impotence in medicine, a physical inability to perform sexual intercourse (the term is not usually applied to women). Impotent men fail to achieve an erection, and this may be due to illness, the effects of certain drugs, or psychological factors.

The US Food and Drug Administration (FDA) approved the drug Viagra for prescription to people who suffer from impotence in March 1998. Viagra works by dilating the blood vessels of the penis. Side effects include headaches and fainting (due to dilation of blood vessels elsewhere), and blue tinted vision.

Impressionism movement in painting that originated in France in the 1860s and dominated European and North American painting in the late 19th century. The Impressionists wanted to depict real life, to paint straight from nature, and to capture the changing effects of light. The term was first used abusively to describe Claude Monet's painting *Impression: Sunrise* 1872. Other Impressionists were Auguste Renoir and Alfred Sisley, and the style was adopted for periods by Paul Cézanne, Edouard Manet, and Edgar Degas.

The starting point of Impressionism was the 'Salon des Refusés', an exhibition 1873 of work rejected by the official Salon. This was followed by the Impressionists' own exhibitions 1874–86, where their work aroused fierce opposition. Their styles were diverse, but all experimented with effects of light and movement created with distinct brushstrokes and fragments of colour juxtaposed on the canvas rather than mixed on the palette. By the 1880s, the movement's central impulse had dispersed, and a number of new styles emerged, later described as ◊Post-Impressionism.

British Impressionism The British 'Impressionists' comprised a loose group of minor artists less concerned with the effects of light than with creating an impression of sentiment. The most notable British Impressionist painter was Philip Wilson Steer; others include Henry Tonks (1862–1937), Harold Knight (1874–1961), and Walter Sickert.

Impressionism Auguste Renoir *The Swing* 1876, Musée d'Orsay, Paris, France. Renoir's preoccupation with light and shade is typical of the Impressionists. He painted directly from life, and tried to capture the movement of shadows as in this painting, with its dappled shade cast by overhanging trees. *Corbis*

imprinting in ◊ethology, the process whereby a young animal learns to recognize both specific individuals (for example, its mother) and its own species.

Imprinting is characteristically an automatic response to specific stimuli at a time when the animal is especially sensitive to those stimuli (known as the sensitive period). Thus, goslings learn to recognize their mother by following the first moving object they see after hatching; as a result, they can easily become imprinted on other species.

inbreeding in ◊genetics, the mating of closely related individuals. It is considered undesirable because it increases the risk that offspring will inherit copies of rare deleterious ◊recessive alleles (genes) from both parents and so suffer from disabilities.

Inca member of an ancient Peruvian civilization of Quechua-speaking Indians that began in the Andean highlands about 1200; by the time of the Spanish Conquest in the 1530s, the Inca ruled from Ecuador in the north to Chile in the south.

The Inca empire dominated the Andean region militarily. Conquered peoples were transplanted into new homelands near the capital, Cuzco, until they had assimilated Inca culture; they were then resettled. The empire was an agriculturally based theocracy, with priest-rulers at the top of the hierarchy, and with 'the Inca', believed to be a descendant of the Sun, as emperor. An extensive road system united the highland and coastal cities but made them vulnerable to the Spanish, who, after conquest, enslaved the people in mining and food-producing ventures. Today's Quechua-speaking Indians are descendants of the Inca civilization; many still live in the farming villages of the highlands of Peru.

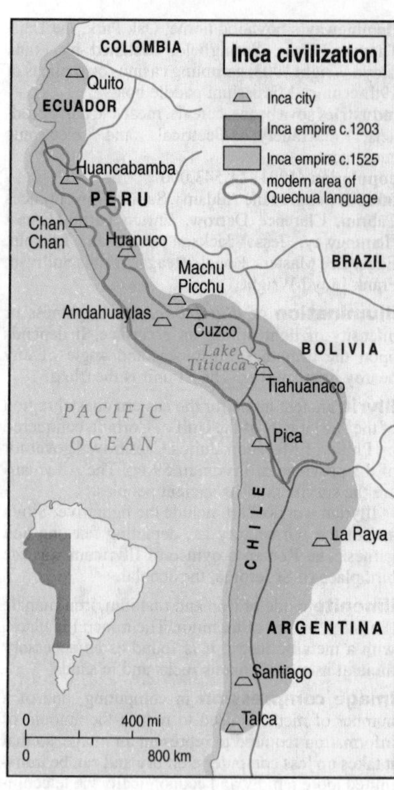

The Inca priesthood allotted labour for irrigation, and built temples and fortresses (made of stone blocks, fitted together without mortar), according to family groups. Produce was collected and similarly distributed; numerical records of stores were kept by means of knotted cords, or 'quipus', writing being unknown. Medicine and advanced surgery were practised and the dead were mummified. The Inca ruin of Machu Picchu, a mountain sanctuary built about 1500, is near Cuzco. In 1987 a chronicle describing the Inca empire by the Spanish writer Juan de Betanzos was rediscovered after 400 years.

Incan art see ◊pre-Columbian art.

incandescence emission of light from a substance in consequence of its high temperature. The colour of the emitted light from liquids or solids depends on their temperature, and for solids generally the higher the temperature the whiter the light. Gases may become incandescent through ionizing radiation (radiation that knocks electrons from atoms during its passage, thereby leaving ions in its path), as in the glowing vacuum ◊discharge tube.

incarnation assumption of living form (plant, animal, human) by a deity; for example, the gods of Greece and Rome, Hinduism, and Christianity (Jesus as the second person of the Trinity).

incendiary bomb bomb containing inflammable matter. Usually dropped by aircraft, incendiary bombs were used in World War I and incendiary shells were used against Zeppelin aircraft. Incendiary bombs were a major weapon in attacks on cities in World War II, causing widespread destruction. To hinder firefighters, delayed-action high-explosive bombs were usually dropped with them. In the Vietnam War, US forces used ◊napalm in incendiary bombs.

incest sexual intercourse between persons thought to be too closely related to marry; the exact relationships that fall under the incest taboo vary widely from society to society. A biological explanation for the incest taboo is based on the necessity to avoid ◊inbreeding.

inch imperial unit of linear measure, a twelfth of a foot, equal to 2.54 centimetres. It was defined in

Inca The Inca fortress of Pisac, Peru, which was perched on a mountain top. Despite having neither wheeled transport nor a developed system of writing, the Incas sustained an empire that endured for 300 years and eventually stretched for about 3,000 km/1,860 mi along the Andes, until the arrival of the Spaniards in the 1530s. *Corbis*

statute by Edward II of England as the length of three barley grains laid end to end.

Inchon formerly ***Chemulpo*** chief port of Seoul, South Korea; population (1990) 1,818,300. It produces steel and textiles.

incisor sharp tooth at the front of the mammalian mouth. Incisors are used for biting or nibbling, as when a rabbit or a sheep eats grass. Rodents, such as rats and squirrels, have large continually-growing incisors, adapted for gnawing. The elephant tusk is a greatly enlarged incisor. In humans, the incisors are the four teeth at the front centre of each jaw.

inclination angle between the ◊ecliptic and the plane of the orbit of a planet, asteroid, or comet. In the case of satellites orbiting a planet, it is the angle between the plane of orbit of the satellite and the equator of the planet.

income earnings of an individual or business organization over a period of time. Gross earnings are earnings before tax and other deductions, while net earnings are earnings after tax. Earned income is income received from working, while unearned income is income such as interest and dividends from financial and other wealth. The income of a whole economy is often measured by ◊gross national product or ◊gross domestic product.

income support in the UK, ◊social security benefit payable to people who are unemployed or who work for less than 24 hours per week and whose financial resources fall below a certain level. It replaced supplementary benefit 1988.

The number of people living on income support virtually doubled between 1979 (4.4 million) and 1992 (8.7 million).

income tax direct tax levied on personal income, mainly wages and salaries, but which may include the value of receipts other than in cash. It is one of the main instruments for achieving a government's income redistribution objectives. In contrast, indirect taxes are duties payable whenever a specific product is purchased; examples include VAT and customs duties.

Most countries impose income taxes on company (corporation) profits and on individuals (personal), although the rates and systems differ widely from country to country. Personal income taxes are usually progressive so that the poorest members of society pay little or no tax, while the rich make much larger contributions.

In the UK the rates of tax and allowances are set out yearly in the annual Finance Act, which implements the recommendations agreed to by the House of Commons in the budget presented by the chancellor of the Exchequer. William Pitt introduced an income tax 1799–1801 to finance the wars with revolutionary France; it was re-imposed 1803–16 for the same purpose, and was so unpopular that all records of it were destroyed when it was abolished. Peel reintroduced the tax in 1842 and it has been levied ever since, forming an important part of government finance. At its lowest, 1874–76, it was 0.83%; at its highest, 1941–46, the standard rate was 50%.

A major change in the UK system of taxation was introduced April 1996, the ***self-assessment*** system, requiring the taxpayer to deliver a completed tax return and also calculate the amount of income tax due. The change affected mainly those who are self-employed; employees whose tax is deducted under the ◊PAYE system were not affected by the new system.

incontinence failure or inability to control evacuation of the bladder or bowel (or both in the case of double incontinence). It may arise as a result of injury, childbirth, disease, or senility.

incubus in the popular belief of the Middle Ages in Europe, a male demon who had sexual intercourse with women in their sleep. Supposedly the women then gave birth to witches and demons. Succubus is the female equivalent.

indemnity in law, an undertaking to compensate another for damage, loss, trouble, or expenses, or the money paid by way of such compensation – for example, under fire-insurance agreements.

indenture in law, a ◊deed between two or more people. Historically, an indenture was a contract between a master and apprentice. The term derives from the practice of writing the agreement twice on paper or parchment and then cutting it with a jagged edge so that both pieces fit together, proving the authenticity of each half.

indentured labour work under a restrictive contract of employment for a fixed period in a foreign country in exchange for payment of passage, accommodation, and food. Indentured labour was the means by which many British people emigrated to North America during the colonial era, and in the 19th–early 20th centuries it was used to recruit Asian workers for employment elsewhere in European colonial empires.

Independence Day public holiday in the USA, commemorating the adoption of the ◊Declaration of Independence 4 July 1776.

Independent Labour Party (ILP) British socialist party, founded in Bradford 1893 by the Scottish member of Parliament Keir Hardie. In 1900 it joined with trades unions and Fabians in founding the Labour Representation Committee, the nucleus of the ◊Labour Party. Many members left the ILP to join the Communist Party 1921, and in 1932 all connections with the Labour Party were severed. After World War II the ILP dwindled, eventually becoming extinct. James Maxton (1885–1946) was its chair 1926–46.

independent school in the UK, a school run privately without direct assistance from the state. A group of old-established and prestigious independent schools are known as ◊public schools.

The sector includes most boarding education in the UK. Although most independent secondary schools operate a highly selective admissions policy for entrants at the age of 11 or 13, some specialize in the teaching of slow learners or difficult children and a few follow particular philosophies of progressive education.

index in economics, an indicator of a general movement in wages and prices over a specified period.

For example, the retail price index (RPI) records changes in the ◊cost of living. The *Financial Times* Industrial Ordinary Share Index (FT) indicates the general movement of the London Stock Exchange market in the UK; the US equivalent is the Dow Jones Index.

index (Latin 'sign, indicator') (plural ***indices***) in mathematics, another term for ◊exponent, the number that indicates the power to which a term should be raised.

Index Librorum Prohibitorum (Latin 'Index of Prohibited Books') the list of books formerly officially forbidden to members of the Roman Catholic Church. The process of condemning books and bringing the Index up to date was carried out by a congregation of cardinals, consultors, and examiners from the 16th century until its abolition 1966.

India country in S Asia, bounded N by China, Nepal, and Bhutan; E by Myanmar and Bangladesh; NW by Pakistan and Afghanistan; and SE, S, and SW by the Indian Ocean. *See country box on p. 534 and tables on p. 537.*

India Acts legislation passed 1858, 1919, and 1939 which formed the basis of British rule in India until independence 1947. The 1858 Act abolished the administrative functions of the British ◊East India Company, replacing them with direct rule from London. The 1919 Act increased Indian participation at local and provincial levels but did not meet nationalist demands for complete internal self-government. The 1939 Act outlined a federal structure but was never implemented.

Indiana state of the midwest USA; nicknamed Hoosier State
area 93,700 sq km/36,168 sq mi
capital Indianapolis
cities Fort Wayne, Gary, Evansville, South Bend
features Ohio and Wabash rivers; Wyandotte Cavern; Indiana Dunes national lakeshore, on Lake Michigan; Vincennes, the oldest community in the state; Indianapolis, the scene of the Indianapolis 500 car race, with the Indianapolis Motor Speedway Hall of Fame Museum; Lincoln boyhood national memorial; New Harmony, Robert Owen's utopian community; Amish country; the inhabitants of the state are known as Hoosiers.
industries maize, pigs, soya beans, limestone, machinery, electrical goods, coal, steel, iron, chemicals
population (1991) 5,610,000
famous people Hoagy Carmichael, Eugene V Debs, Theodore Dreiser, Michael Jackson, Cole Porter, J Dan Quayle, Wilbur Wright

Indiana

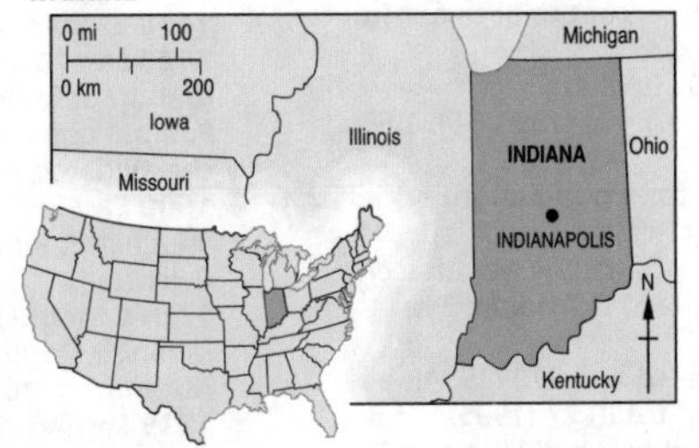

Indianapolis capital and largest city of Indiana, on the White River; population (1992) 746,500; metropolitan area (1992) 1,424,000. It is an industrial centre and venue of the Indianapolis 500 car race.

Indian architecture architecture of the Indian subcontinent. Essentially, there are four periods or

'The country of a hundred nations and a hundred tongues, of a thousand religions and two million gods ... mother of history, grandmother of legend, great-grandmother of Tradition.'

On India
Mark Twain *More Tramps Abroad*

styles in Indian architecture: Buddhist, Hindu, Muslim, and Western. In function, design, and decoration, Indian architecture was for many centuries essentially religious. The Buddhist style of temple-building emerged during the 4th century BC and formed the classical architecture of India. The Hindu styles did not begin to fully develop until about the 6th century AD, and Muslim styles were brought by the Mogul invasions beginning AD 1000 (e.g., the Taj Mahal). Finally, European styles were introduced during the British colonial period. *See illustration on p. 536.*

Buddhist The classical architecture of India emerged during the Buddhist dynasties, which began in the 4th century BC. Cave temples appeared in the 3rd century BC, imitating the structure and decoration of the wooden architecture of the period (now entirely lost). From small rock-cut shrines and sanctuaries, they evolved into large complex temples and monasteries, their walls richly decorated with reliefs, statues, or paintings. They include the temple at Karli (1st century AD) and the Ajanta Buddhist cave temples. The earliest surviving ◊stupas, reliquary mounds, date from the 2nd century BC. They too became larger and more complex, culminating in such monuments as the Great Stupa of Sanchi (3rd century BC–1st century AD), a huge dome surrounded by railings and elaborately carved gateways. Secular buildings from the Buddhist period include the palace of Emperor Aśoka (273–232 BC) at Patna, modelled on a palace in Persepolis, Persia.

Hindu Although examples of Hindu architecture can be dated to the later centuries BC, a characteristic style began to flourish in the 6th century AD with the growth of Hindu dynasties. Hindu temples initially

INDIA
Republic of

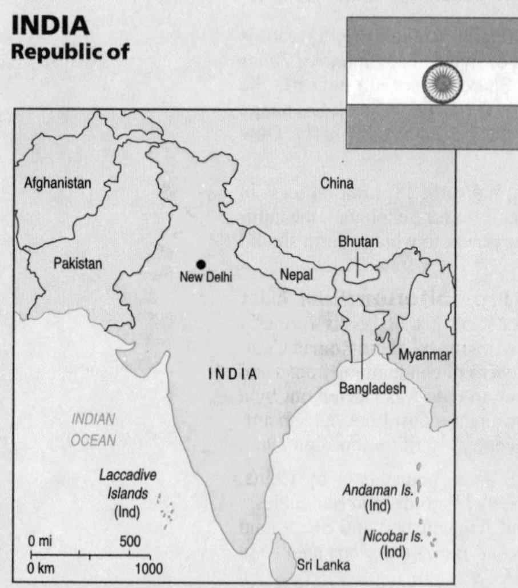

national name Hindi *Bharat*
area 3,166,829 sq km/1,222,396 sq mi
capital New Delhi
major towns/cities Bangalore, Hyderabad, Ahmedabad, Kanpur, Pune, Nagpur, Bhopal, Jaipur, Lucknow, Surat
major ports Calcutta, Bombay, Chennai (Madras)
physical features Himalaya mountains on N border; plains around rivers Ganges, Indus, Brahmaputra; Deccan peninsula S of the Narmada River forms plateau between Western and Eastern Ghats mountain ranges; desert in W; Andaman and Nicobar Islands, Lakshadweep (Laccadive Islands)
head of state Kocheril Raman Narayanan from 1997
head of government Atal Behari Vajpayee from 1998
political system liberal democratic federal republic
administrative divisions 25 states and seven centrally administered Union Territories
political parties All India Congress Committee, or Congress, cross-caste and cross-religion coalition, left of centre; Janata Dal (People's Party), secular, left of centre; Bharatiya Janata Party (BJP), radical right-wing, Hindu-chauvinist; Communist Party of India (CPI), Marxist-Leninist; Communist Party of India–Marxist (CPI–M), West Bengal-based moderate socialist
armed forces 11,450,000 (June 1995)
conscription none, although all citizens are constitutionally obliged to perform national service when called upon
defence spend (% GDP) 2.8 (1994)
education spend (% GNP) 3.7 (1992)
health spend (% GDP) 6.0 (1990)
death penalty limited to exceptional circumstances, such as political assassinations.
population 984,004,000 (1998 est)
population growth rate 1.9% (1990–95); 1.6% (2000–05)
age distribution (% of total population) <15 35.2%, 15–65 60.2%, >65 4.6% (1995)
ethnic distribution 72% of Indo-Aryan descent; 25% (predominantly in the S) Dravidian; 3% Mongoloid
population density (per sq km) 279 (1994)
urban population (% of total) 27 (1995)
labour force 43% of population: 64% agriculture, 16% industry, 20% services (1990)
unemployment 9.1%
child mortality rate (under 5, per 1,000 live births) 122 (1994)
life expectancy 60 (men), 61 (women)
education (compulsory years) 8
literacy rate 62% (men), 34% (women)
languages Hindi, English, and 17 other official languages: Assamese, Bengali, Gujarati, Kannada, Kashmiri, Konkani, Malayalam, Manipur, Marathi, Nepali, Oriya, Punjabi, Sanskrit, Sindhi, Tamil, Telugu, Urdu; more than 1,650 dialects
religions Hindu 83%, Sunni Muslim 11%, Christian 2.5%, Sikh 2%
TV sets (per 1,000 people) 64 (1996)
currency rupee
GDP (US $) 378.6 billion (1997)
GDP per capita (PPP) (US $) 1,240 (1993)
growth rate 5.1% (1983–93)
average annual inflation 10.2% (1994)
major trading partners USA, CIS, UK, Germany
resources coal, iron ore, copper ore, bauxite, chromite, gold, manganese ore, zinc, lead, limestone, crude oil, natural gas, diamonds
industries mining (including coal, iron and manganese ores, diamonds, and gold), manufacturing (iron and steel, mineral oils, shipbuilding, chemical products, road transport, cotton cloth, sugar, petroleum refinery products)
exports tea (world's largest producer), coffee, fish, iron and steel, leather, textiles, clothing, polished diamonds, handmade carpets, engineering goods, chemicals. Principal market: USA 18% (1993/94)
imports non-electrical machinery, mineral fuels and lubricants, pearls, precious and semiprecious stones, chemicals, transport equipment. Principal source: USA 11.7% (1993/94)
arable land 50.5% (1993)
agricultural products cotton, tea, wheat, rice, coffee, cashew nuts, jute, spices, sugar cane, oil seeds

HISTORY

c. 2500–1500 BC The earliest Indian civilization evolved in the Indus Valley with the city states of Harappa and Mohenjo Daro.
c. 1500–1200 BC Aryan peoples from the NW overran N India and the Deccan; Brahmanism (a form of Hinduism) developed.
321 BC Chandragupta, founder of the Mauryan dynasty, began to unite N India in a Hindu Empire.
268–232 BC Mauryan Empire reached its height under Aśoka.
c. 180 BC Shunga dynasty replaced the Mauryans; Hindu Empire began to break up into smaller kingdoms.
AD 320–480 Gupta dynasty reunified N India.
c. 500 Raiding Huns from Central Asia destroyed the Gupta dynasty; India reverted to many warring kingdoms.
11th–12th Cs Rajput princes of N India faced repeated Muslim invasions by Arabs, Turks, and Afghans, and in 1206 the first Muslim dynasty was established at Delhi.
14th–16th Cs Muslim rule extended over N India and the Deccan; S remained independent under the Hindu Vijayanagar dynasty.
1498 Explorer Vasco da Gama reached India.
1526 Last Muslim invasion: Zahir ud-din Muhammad (Babur) defeated the Sultan of Delhi at Battle of Panipat and established the Mogul Empire, which was consolidated by Akbar the Great (1556–1605).
1600 East India Company founded by English merchants, who settled in Madras, Bombay, and Calcutta.
17th C Mogul Empire reached its zenith under Jahangir (1605–27), Shah Jehan (1628–58), and Aurangzeb (1658–1707).
1739 Persian king Nadir Shah invaded India and destroyed Mogul prestige; British and French supported rival princes in subsequent internal wars.
1757 Battle of Plassey: Robert Clive defeated Siraj al-Daulah, nawab of Bengal, which came under control of British East India Company.
1772–85 Warren Hastings, British governor general of Bengal, raised native army and pursued expansionist policies.
early 19th C British took control (directly or indirectly) throughout India by defeating powerful Indian states in a series of regional wars.
1858 'Indian Mutiny': mutiny in Bengal army erupted into widespread anti-British revolt; rebels sought to restore powers of Mogul emperor.
1858 British defeated the rebels; East India Company dissolved; India came under the British crown.
1885 Indian National Congress founded in Bombay as focus for nationalism.
1909 Morley–Minto Reforms: Indians received right to elect members of Legislative Councils; Hindus and Muslims formed separate electorates.
1919 British forces killed 379 Indian demonstrators at Amritsar; India Act (Montagu–Chelmsford Reforms) conceded a measure of provincial self-government.
1920–22 Mohandas Gandhi won control of the Indian National Congress; campaign of civil disobedience in support of demand for complete self-rule.
1935 India Act provided for Indian control of federal legislature, with defence and external affairs remaining the viceroy's responsibility.
1940 Muslim League called for India to be partitioned along religious lines.
1947 British India partitioned into two independent dominions of India (mainly Hindu) and Pakistan (mainly Muslim) amid bloody riots; Jawaharlal Nehru of Congress Party became prime minister.
1950 India became a republic within the Commonwealth.
1962 India lost brief border war with China; retained Kashmir in war with Pakistan 1965.
1966 Indira Gandhi, daughter of Nehru, became prime minister.
1971 India defeated Pakistan in war and helped East Pakistan become independent as Bangladesh.
1975 Found guilty of electoral corruption, Mrs Gandhi declared state of emergency and arrested opponents.
1977–79 Janata Party formed government under Morarji Desai.
1980 Mrs Gandhi, heading Congress Party splinter group, Congress (I) ('I' for Indira), returned to power.
1984 Troops cleared Sikh separatists from the Golden Temple, Amritsar; Mrs Gandhi assassinated by Sikh bodyguards; her son, Rajiv Gandhi, became prime minister.
1989 After financial scandals, Congress ('I' was removed after Mrs Gandhi's assassination) lost elections; V P Singh formed Janata Dal minority government.
1990 Direct rule imposed on Jammu and Kashmir after upsurge in Muslim separatist violence; rising interethnic and religious conflict.
1991 Rajiv Gandhi assassinated; P V Narasimha Rao formed minority Congress government.
1992 Destruction of mosque at Ayodhya, N India, by Hindu extremists resulted in widespread violence.
1996 H D Deve Gowda became prime minister of a coalition government. Madras renamed Chennai. Rao resigned as Congress party president.
1997 Gowda government fell; new United Front government formed, led by Inder Kumar Gujral. Sikh Akali Dal party and BNP successful in state elections. Kocheril Raman Narayanan became first 'untouchable' to be elected president. Disagreement within government about economic policies. Discussions began to normalize relations with Pakistan. Gujral resigned, but stayed on as caretaker prime minister.
1998 Atal Behari Vajpayee, leader of Bharatiya Janata party, elected prime minister. Sonia Gandhi became leader of Congress Party. Nuclear tests provoked international condemnation and Pakistan's first-ever nuclear tests.

SEE ALSO Buddhism; Congress Party; East India Company; Gandhi; Hinduism; Kashmir drew heavily on Buddhist styles, though their plans were based on mandalas, schematic diagrams of the creation of the universe. The Temple of Vishnu at Deogarh (6th century) is the earliest extant stone-built temple. The Elephanta cave temples, richly decorated with carvings, date from the 8th–9th centuries. Many Hindu temples were sculpted out of rock (rather than cut into rock, as cave temples were), for example, the Temple of Kailasa at Ellora (8th century AD) which is the world's largest monolithic temple. Whether rock-cut or stone-built, Hindu temples became highly ornate, and characterized by a high tower covering the main shrine. The Visvanatha Temple, Khajurāho, is typical. In the north, Hindu architecture began to decline following the Mogul invasions which began AD 1000. In the south, where it continued to develop, vast compounds grew up around temples, the gates of the perimeter walls becoming large, highly carved pyramids.

Muslim During the early period of Muslim architecture, a Persian style was imported directly, for example, the Great Mosque in Delhi, the Qutb-ul-Islam 1193. During the second period, beginning 1526 with the founding of the Mogul dynasty, the evolution of Indian architecture was influenced by local architects and craftsmen. This era gave rise to such monuments as the Tomb of Humayun, Delhi, 1569, the now abandoned city of Fatehpur-Sikri 1568–75, and the Taj Mahal at Agra (1632–49), one of the most familiar architectural images of India.

Western The architecture of the colonial period and independence has carried on in the complex tradition ranging from Sir Edwin ◊Lutyens and Sir Herbert Baker's plan for New Delhi to ◊Le Corbusier's plan and buildings for Chandigarh 1950–56.

Indian art the arts of the Indian subcontinent (present-day India, Pakistan, and Bangladesh). Indian art dates back to the ancient Indus Valley civilization, about 3000–1500 BC, centred on the cities of ◊Harappa and ◊Mohenjo Daro. Surviving artefacts reflect the influence of ◊Mesopotamian art. Beginning about 1800 BC, the Aryan invasions gave rise to the Hindu religion and arts celebrating its gods, heroes, and scenes from the two great epics, the *Mahābhārata* and the *Rāmāyana*. From the 5th century BC, Buddhist art developed, following the life and enlightenment of the Buddha Sakyamuni. A third strand was added in the 16th–17th centuries when the Mogul Empire introduced ◊Islamic art to the subcontinent.

Buddhist art Early Buddhist art developed in relation to the architecture of the stupa (temple shrines to the Buddha and his disciples), typically using symbols to represent the Buddha. The first appearance of the Buddha in human form was in the sculptures of the Mathura tradition (2nd century BC) and those of Gandhara (2nd–6th centuries BC) – possibly the greatest school of Buddhist sculpture. The Gandhara sculptures show Greek influence and, along with the Buddhist religion, were exported to China, Korea, and Japan. The profound depth of relief of the Mathura work was followed by the gentler sculptures of Gupta (about 5th century AD). The Ajanta caves near Bombay, first begun about 200 BC, contain the finest example of Gupta art – mural paintings from the 5th–7th centuries which, though religious in intent, reflect a sophisticated, courtly society.

Hindu art From the 4th century AD, influenced by Buddhist art, Hindu artists created huge temple complexes; for example, at Orissa, Konarak, and Khajurāho. They also built cave sanctuaries, the most famous being at Elephanta, near Bombay, with a monumental depiction of the three forces of creation, preservation, and destruction, portrayed as Shiva with three heads. The caves at Ellora feature an ensemble of religious art (Buddhist, Hindu, and Jain) dating from the 6th and 7th centuries. At Khajurāho, celestial dancing girls, the Asparas, adorn the temple façades. Later Hindu art includes the jewel-like depictions from the lives of Krishna and Rama in palm-leaf manuscripts, known as Rajput paintings.

Mogul art From the 11th century, Muslim invaders destroyed Buddhist and Hindu temple art and introduced the mosque and, with it, Islamic art styles. By the 16th century, the Moguls had established an extensive empire. Persian painters were imported and Hindu artists trained in their workshops, a fusion that formed part of the liberal emperor ◊Akbar's cultural plan and resulted in the exquisite

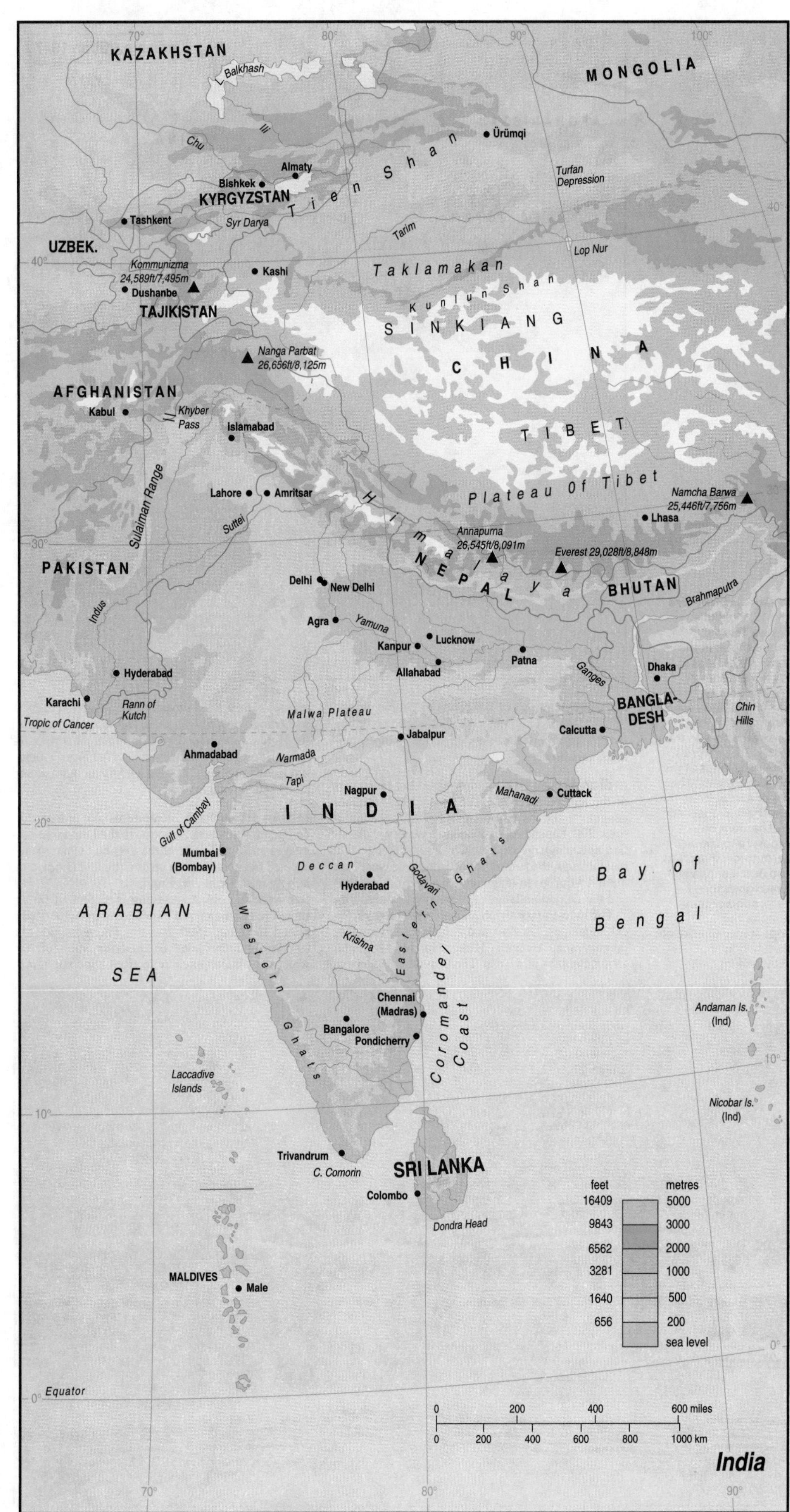

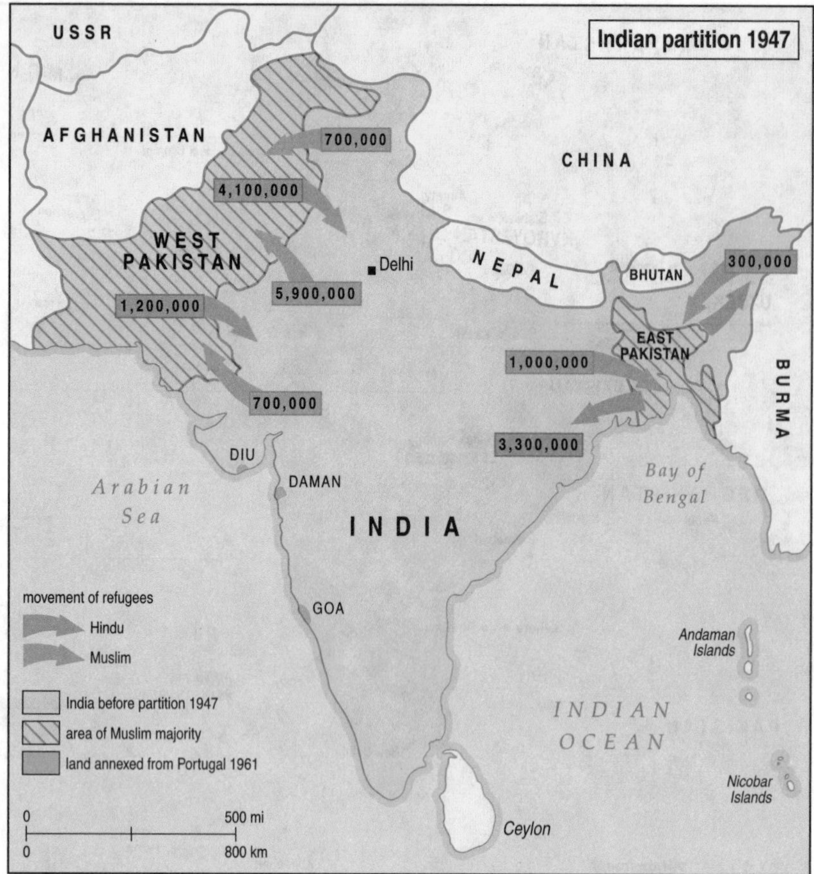

Indian partition 1947

miniature paintings of the courts of ◊Jahangir and ◊Shah Jahan. The subjects of miniature painting ranged from portraiture and histories to birds, animals, and flowers.

Indian languages traditionally, the languages of the subcontinent of India; since 1947, the languages of the Republic of India. These number some 200, depending on whether a variety is classified as a language or a dialect. They fall into five main groups, the two most widespread of which are the Indo-European languages (mainly in the north) and the Dravidian languages (mainly in the south).

The Indo-European languages include two classical languages, Sanskrit and Pali, and such modern languages as Bengali, Hindi, Gujarati, Marathi, Oriya, Punjabi, and Urdu. The Dravidian languages include Kannada, Malayalam, Tamil, and Telugu. A wide range of scripts is used, including Devanagari for Hindi, Arabic for Urdu, and distinct scripts for the various Dravidian languages. The Sino-Tibetan group of languages is used widely in Assam and along the Himalayas.

Indian literature literature of the Indian subcontinent, written in Sanskrit, in the Dravidian languages such as Tamil, in the vernacular languages derived from Sanskrit, such as Urdu and Hindi, and, largely in this century, English.

Sanskrit The oldest surviving examples of Indian literature are the sacred Hindu texts from the Vedic period of about 1500–200 BC. These include the ◊*Vedas* and the later *Upanishads* 800–200 BC, which are philosophical reflections upon the *Vedas*. Of the same period are the *Sutras* 500–200 BC, collections of aphorisms and doctrinal summaries, including the *Kamasutra* on erotic love. During the epic period (400 BC–AD 400) two major epics were written down: the ◊*Mahābhārata* (which contains the ◊*Bhagavad-Gītā*) and the shorter *Rāmāyana*, both about 300 BC.

By the classical period (from AD 400), lyric poetry, romances, and drama had developed, the leading poet and dramatist of the period being ◊Kālidāsa. The *Panchatantra*, a collection of Hindu myths, were written down in the 4th century AD.

Dravidian The Dravidian languages of the south, which are unrelated to Sanskrit, had their own strong and ancient literary traditions, though gradually they were influenced by the literatures of the north. The two major works of Tamil are the verse anthologies the *Pattuppattu* and the *Ettutogaiad*, both 1st century AD.

vernacular By AD 1000 extensive vernacular literatures had developed – largely through popularizations of Sanskrit classics – in those languages derived from Sanskrit, such as Urdu, Hindi, and Gujarati. From the 17th century, Urdu poetry flourished at the Mogul court, where it was strongly influenced by classical Persian literature. The poets Asadullah Ghalib (1797–1869) and Muhammad Iqbāl wrote in Urdu and Persian. Bengali literature in particular was encouraged by the wide use of printing presses in the 19th century. Bengali writers include Bankim Chandra Chatterji, Romesh Chunder Dutt (1848–1909), and Rabindranath Tagore who was awarded the Nobel Prize for Literature 1913. The spiritual and political leader Mahatma Gandhi wrote in Gujarati.

Indian music classical musical culture represented in North India, Pakistan, Nepal, and Bangladesh by the Hindustani tradition, and in South India and Sri Lanka by the Karnatic tradition. An oral culture of great antiquity, allied to Muslim traditions of the Middle East and Central Asia, it resembles the medieval European troubadour tradition of composer-performer, being an art of skilful extemporization in a given mood (rasa), selecting from a range of melody prototypes (ragas) and rhythmic formulae (talas), understood in the same way as in the West 'blues' defines a mood, a scale, and a form, and 'boogie-woogie' an associated rhythm.

Indian music is geared to the time of day, and a composition/performance is not fixed in duration. An ensemble consists of a melody section, featuring voice, sitar, sarod, surbahar, violins, shrill reed woodwinds, or harmonium, solo or in combination; a drone section featuring the vina or tambura, providing a resonant harmonic ground; and a rhythm section of high and low tuned hand drums. The music has a natural buoyancy, the melody effortlessly rising, in contrast to the tonal gravitational pull exerted in European tonal music. The sounds of Indian music are rich in high frequencies, giving an impression of luminous radiance. Popular awareness of Indian music in the West increased after world tours since the 1950s by virtuosos Ravi Shankar (sitar) and Ali Akhbar Khan (sarod). In Britain, a tradition of popular music thrives among expatriate communities and in schools.

Indian Mutiny or ***Sepoy Rebellion*** or ***Mutiny*** revolt 1857–58 of Indian soldiers (Sepoys) against the British in India. The uprising was confined to the north, from Bengal to the Punjab, and central India. It led to the end of rule by the British ◊East India Company and its replacement by direct British crown administration.

The majority of support for the mutiny came from the army and recently dethroned princes, but in some areas it developed into a peasant uprising and general revolt. It included the seizure of Delhi by the rebels, its siege and recapture by the British, and the defence of Lucknow by a British garrison. One of the rebel leaders was ◊Nana Sahib.

Indian National Congress (INC) official name for the ◊Congress Party of India.

Indian Ocean ocean between Africa and Australia, with India to the N, and the southern boundary being an arbitrary line from Cape Agulhas to S Tasmania; area 73,500,000 sq km/28,371,000 sq mi; average depth 3,872 m/12,708 ft. The greatest depth is the Java Trench 7,725 m/25,353 ft.

India of the Princes the 562 Indian states ruled by princes during the period of British control. They

Indian architecture The 13th-century Kesava Temple, Somnathpur, in the state of Karnataka, SW India. Temple architecture in Karnataka developed a distinctive, highly decorated style in the 12th–13th centuries under the kings of the Hoysala dynasty. The use of a local stone that is soft when quarried and hardens on exposure to the air permitted a sharpness and detail of carving which gives the decoration of these temples the appearance of intricate metalwork. *Sally Jenkins*

INDIA: EMPERORS

Reign	Name
Mauryan emperors	
325–297 BC	Chandragupta Maurya
297–272 BC	Bindusara
272–268 BC	interregnum
268–232 BC	Aśoka
232–224 BC	Dasaratha
224–215 BC	Samprati
215–202 BC	Salisuka
202–195 BC	Devavarman
195–187 BC	Satadhanvan
187–185 BC	Brihadratha
Gupta emperors	
AD 320–50	Chandragupta I
350–76	Samudragupta
376–415	Chandragupta II
415–55	Kumaragupta I
455–70	Skandagupta
470–75	Kumaragupta II
475–500	Budhagupta
500–15	Vainyagupta
515–30	Narasimhagupta
530–40	Kumaragupta III
540–50	Vishnugupta
Mogul emperors	
Great Moguls	
1526–30	Babur (Zahiruddin Muhammad)
1530–56	Humayun (Nasiruddin Muhammad)*
1556–1605	Akbar (Jalaluddin Muhammad)
1605–27	Jahangir (Nuruddin)
1627–28	Dewar Baksh
1628–58	Shah Jahan (Shihabuddin; dethroned)
1658–1707	Aurangzeb (Muhiyuddin)
Lesser Moguls	
1707–07	Azam Shah
1707–12	Shah Alam I (Muhammad Mu'azzam)
1712–12	Azim-ush Shan
1712–13	Jahandar Shah (Muhammad Muizzuddin)
1713–19	Farrukh Siyar (Jalaluddin Muhammad)
1719–19	Rafi ud-Darayat (Shamsuddin)
1719–19	Rafi ud-Daula Shah Jahan II
1719–19	Nikusiyar
1719–48	Muhammad Shah (Nasiruddin)
1748–54	Ahmad Shah Bahadur (Abu al-Nasir Muhammad)
1754–60	Alamgir II (Muhammad Azizuddin)
1760–60	Shah Jahan III
1760–1806	Shah Alam II (Jalaluddin Ali Jauhar; deposed briefly in 1788)
1806–37	Akbar Shah II (Muhiyuddin)
1837–58	Bahadur Shah II (Abul al-Zafar Muhammad Sirajuddin; banished)

*Humayun was defeated 1540 and expelled from India until 1555, leaving N India under the control of Sher Shah Suri (died 1545), Islam Shah, and Sikander Shah.

occupied an area of 1,854,347 sq km/715,964 sq mi (45% of the total area of pre-partition India) and had a population of over 93 million. At the partition of British India in 1947 the princes were given independence by the British government but were advised to adhere to either India or Pakistan. Between 1947 and 1950 all except ◊Kashmir were incorporated in either country.

indicator in chemistry, a compound that changes its structure and colour in response to its environment. The commonest chemical indicators detect changes in ◊pH (for example, ◊litmus), or in the oxidation state of a system (redox indicators).

indicator species plant or animal whose presence or absence in an area indicates certain environmental conditions, such as soil type, high levels of pollution, or, in rivers, low levels of dissolved oxygen. Many plants show a preference for either alkaline or acid soil conditions, while certain trees require aluminium, and are found only in soils where it is present. Some lichens are sensitive to sulphur dioxide in the air, and absence of these species indicates atmospheric pollution.

indie (short for ***independent***) in music, a record label that is neither owned nor distributed by one of the large conglomerates ('majors') that dominate the industry. Without a corporate bureaucratic structure, the independent labels are often quicker to respond to new trends and more idealistic in their aims. What has become loosely known as indie music therefore tends to be experimental, amateurish, or at the cutting edge of street fashion. The term became current in the UK with the small labels created to disseminate punk rock in the 1970s.

indigenous the people, animals, or plants that are native to a country, but especially a people whose territory has been colonized by others (particularly Europeans). Examples of indigenous peoples include Australian Aborigines and Native Americans. A World Council of Indigenous Peoples is based in Canada.

indigo violet-blue vegetable dye obtained from plants of the genus *Indigofera*, family Leguminosae, but now replaced by a synthetic product. It was once a major export crop of India.

indium (Latin *indicum* 'indigo') soft, ductile, silver-white, metallic element, symbol In, atomic number 49, relative atomic mass 114.82. It occurs in nature in some zinc ores, is resistant to abrasion, and is used as a coating on metal parts. It was discovered 1863 by German metallurgists Ferdinand Reich (1799–1882) and Hieronymus Richter (1824–1898), who named it after the two indigo lines of its spectrum.

individualism in politics, a view in which the individual takes precedence over the collective: the opposite of ◊collectivism. The term possessive individualism has been applied to the writings of John ◊Locke and Jeremy ◊Bentham, describing society as comprising individuals interacting through market relations.

Indo-Aryan languages another name for the ◊Indo-European languages.

Indochina French name given by the French to their colonies in SE Asia: ◊Cambodia, ◊Laos, and ◊Vietnam, which became independent after World War II.

Indochina War war of independence 1946–54 between the nationalist forces of what was to become Vietnam and France, the occupying colonial power.

In 1945 Vietnamese nationalist communist leader ◊Ho Chi Minh proclaimed an independent Vietnamese republic, which soon began an armed struggle against French forces. France in turn set up a noncommunist state four years later. In 1954, after the siege of ◊Dien Bien Phu, a cease-fire was agreed between France and China that resulted in the establishment of two separate states, North and South Vietnam, divided by the 17th parallel.

Attempts at reunification of the country led subsequently to the ◊Vietnam War.

INDIA: STATES AND UNION TERRITORIES

State	Capital	Area in sq km/sq mi
Andhra Pradesh	Hyderabad	275,100/106,216
Arunachal Pradesh	Itanagar	83,700/32,316
Assam	Dispur	78,400/30,270
Bihar	Patna	173,900/67,142
Delhi	Delhi	1,500/579
Goa	Panaji	3,700/1,428
Gujarat	Gandhinagar	196,000/75,675
Haryana	Chandigarh	44,200/17,065
Himachal Pradesh	Shimla	55,700/21,505
Jammu and Kashmir	Srinagar	222,200/85,791
Karnataka	Bangalore	191,800/74,053
Kerala	Thiruvananthapuram	38,900/15,019
Madhya Pradesh	Bhopal	443,400/171,196
Maharashtra	Bombay	307,700/118,802
Manipur	Imphal	22,300/8,610
Meghalaya	Shillong	22,400/8,648
Mizoram	Aizawl	21,100/8,146
Nagaland	Kohima	16,600/6,409
Orissa	Bhubaneswar	155,700/60,115
Punjab	Chandigarh	50,400/19,459
Rajasthan	Jaipur	342,200/132,123
Sikkim	Gangtok	7,100/2,741
Tamil Nadu	Chennai*	130,100/50,231
Tripura	Agartala	10,500/4,054
Uttar Pradesh	Lucknow	294,400/113,667
West Bengal	Calcutta	88,700/34,247
Union territory	**Capital**	**Area in sq km/sq mi**
Andaman and Nicobar Islands	Port Blair	8,200/3,166
Chandigarh	Chandigarh	114/44
Dadra and Nagar Haveli	Silvassa	490/189
Daman and Diu	Daman	112/43
Lakshadweep	Kavaratti	32/12
Pondicherry	Pondicherry	492/189

* formerly Madras, to 1996

Indo-European languages family of languages that includes some of the world's major classical languages (Sanskrit and Pali in India, Zend Avestan in Iran, Greek and Latin in Europe), as well as several of the most widely spoken languages (English worldwide; Spanish in Iberia, Latin

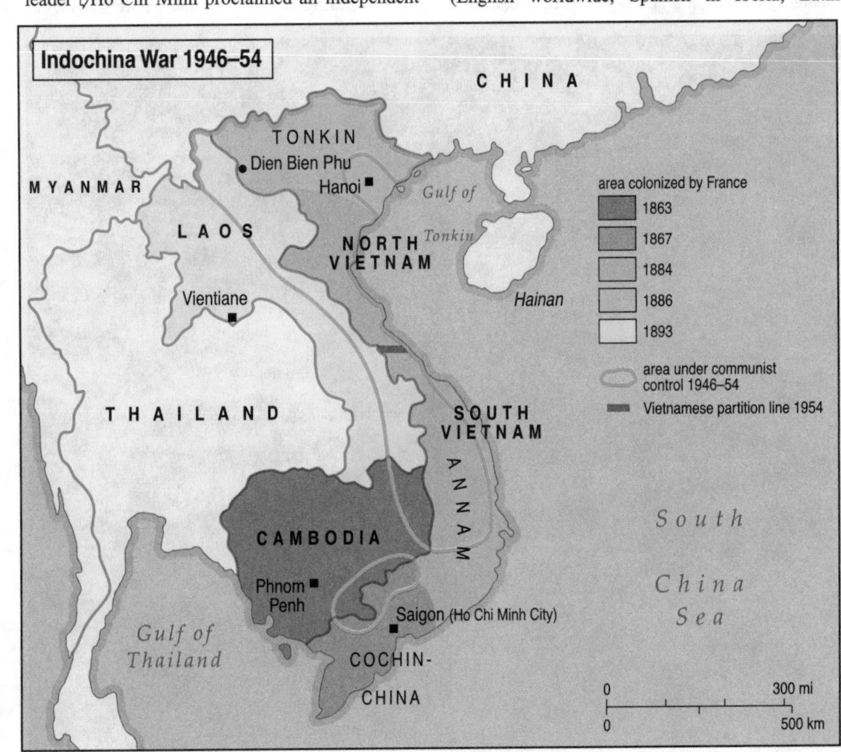

Indochina War 1946–54

America, and elsewhere; and the Hindi group of languages in N India). Indo-European languages were once located only along a geographical band from India through Iran into NW Asia, E Europe, the northern Mediterranean lands, N and W Europe and the British Isles.

When first discussed and described in the 19th century, this family was known as the Aryan and then the Indo-Germanic language family. Because of unwelcome associations with the Nazi idea of 'Aryan' racial purity and superiority, both titles have been abandoned by scholars in favour of the neutral 'Indo-European'.

In general terms, many Indo-European languages (such as English, French, and Hindi) have tended to evolve from the highly inflected to a more open or analytic grammatical style that does not greatly depend on complex grammatical endings to nouns, verbs, and adjectives. Eastern Indo-European languages are often called the *satem* group (Zend 'a hundred') while western Indo-European languages are the *centum* group (Latin 'a hundred'); this illustrates a split that occurred over 3,000 years ago, between those that had an *s*-sound in certain words and those that had a *k*-sound. Scholars have reconstructed a Proto-Indo-European ancestral language by comparing the sound systems and historical changes within the family, but continue to dispute the original homeland of this ancient form, some arguing for N Europe, others for Russia north of the Black Sea.

Indo-Germanic languages former name for the ◊Indo-European languages.

Indonesia country in SE Asia, made up of 13,677 islands situated on or near the equator, between the Indian and Pacific oceans. It is the world's fourth most populous country, surpassed only by China, India, and the USA. *See country box opposite.*

Indra Hindu god of the sky, shown as a four-armed man on a white elephant, carrying a thunderbolt. The intoxicating drink soma, used in religious ritual as a sacrifice to the gods, is associated with him.

indri largest living lemur *Indri indri* of Madagascar. Black and white, almost tailless, it has long arms and legs. It grows to 70 cm/2.3 ft long. It is diurnal and arboreal. Its howl is doglike or human in tone.

induced current electric current that appears in a closed circuit when there is relative movement of its conductor in a magnetic field. The effect is known as the ***dynamo effect***, and is used in all ◊dynamos and generators to produce electricity. See ◊electromagnetic induction.

inductance in physics, the phenomenon where a changing current in a circuit builds up a magnetic field which induces an ◊electromotive force either in the same circuit and opposing the current (self-inductance) or in another circuit (mutual inductance). The SI unit of inductance is the henry (symbol H).

A component designed to introduce inductance into a circuit is called an inductor (sometimes inductance) and is usually in the form of a coil of wire. The energy stored in the magnetic field of the coil is proportional to its inductance and the current flowing through it. See ◊electromagnetic induction.

induction in obstetrics, deliberate intervention to initiate labour before it starts naturally; then it usually proceeds normally.

Induction involves rupture of the fetal membranes (amniotomy) and the use of the hormone oxytocin to stimulate contractions of the womb. In biology, induction is a term used for various processes, including the production of an ◊enzyme in response to a particular chemical in the cell, and the ◊differentiation of cells in an ◊embryo in response to the presence of neighbouring tissues.

induction in philosophy, the process of observing particular instances of things in order to derive general statements and laws of nature. It is the opposite of ◊deduction, which moves from general statements and principles to the particular.

Induction was criticized by the Scottish philosopher David ◊Hume because it relied upon belief rather than valid reasoning. In the philosophy of science, the 'problem of induction' is a crucial area of debate: however much evidence there is for a proposition, there is the possibility of a future counter-instance that will invalidate the explanation. Therefore, it is argued, no scientific statement can be said to be true.

induction in physics, an alteration in the physical properties of a body that is brought about by the influence of a field. See ◊electromagnetic induction and ◊magnetic induction.

induction coil type of electrical transformer, similar to an ◊ignition coil, that produces an intermittent high-voltage alternating current from a low-voltage direct current supply.

It has a primary coil consisting of a few turns of thick wire wound around an iron core and passing a low voltage (usually from a battery). Wound on top of this is a secondary coil made up of many turns of thin wire. An iron armature and make-and-break mechanism (similar to that in an electric bell) repeatedly interrupts the current to the primary coil, producing a high, rapidly alternating current in the secondary circuit.

indulgence in the Roman Catholic Church, the total or partial remission of temporal punishment for sins that remain to be expiated after penitence and confession have secured exemption from eternal punishment. The doctrine of indulgence began as the commutation of church penances in exchange for suitable works of charity or money gifts to the church, and became a great source of church revenue. This trade in indulgences roused Martin Luther to initiate the Reformation 1517. The Council of Trent 1563 recommended moderate retention of indulgences, and they continue, notably in 'Holy Years'.

Indurain Miguel Larraya 1964– . Spanish cyclist. He was the first rider to win the Tour de France in five consecutive years (1991–1995). In 1992 he became only the sixth rider to win the Tour de France and the Giro d'Italia in the same year, a feat he repeated in 1993. In 1994 he set a new one hour world record of 53.04 kms/32.96 mi. In 1996 he won the Individual Time-Trial gold medal at the Atlanta Olympics.

Indus river in Asia, rising in Tibet and flowing 3,180 km/1,975 mi to the Arabian Sea. In 1960 the use of its waters, including those of its five tributaries, was divided between India (rivers Ravi, Beas, Sutlej) and Pakistan (rivers Indus, Jhelum, Chenab).

Industrial architecture any type of building that has emerged as a direct result of the ◊Industrial Revolution, for example factories, warehouses, stations, office buildings, department stores, and certain types of bridge. Typically, industrial structures employ standardized, mass-produced components, commonly associated with engineering. More importantly, they are unadorned, even anti-decorative. Although principally utilitarian, this style of building has influenced the development of the ◊Modern Movement and many parallels can be drawn between Industrial architecture and the ◊High Tech approach.

Landmark structures in the UK include the iron lattice-work bridge at Coalbrookdale 1777–79; Kings Cross Station, London 1851–52, by Lewis Cubitt (1799–1883); and the Boatstore, Sheerness Royal Naval Dockyard 1858–60. In the USA the development of Industrial architecture is closely linked to the ◊Chicago School, while in continental Europe it is associated with a tradition of engineering, as in the AEG turbine factory, Berlin, 1909, by Peter ◊Behrens, and the airship hangers at Orly, France, 1916–24, by Eugène Freysinnet (1879–1962). Other more recent examples feature in the work of Pier Luigi ◊Nervi and Santiago Calatrava (1951–), notably the latter's spectacular suspension bridges in Seville, Spain.

industrial design branch of artistic activity that came into being as a result of the need to design machine-made products, introduced by the Industrial Revolution in the 18th century. The purpose of industrial design is to ensure that goods satisfy the demands of fashion, style, function, materials, and cost.

Industrial design became a fully fledged professional activity in the early 20th century through the efforts of the pioneering US industrial designers who worked with the large-scale manufacturers of the new mass-produced technological goods – Eastman Kodak, Gestetner, General Electric, and others. From the USA the profession moved across the Atlantic in the years after 1945. Germany and Italy made special contributions to its evolution after that date and by the 1980s all the main industrialized countries had their own industrial design professions.

industrial dispute disagreement between an employer and its employees, usually represented by a trade union, over some aspect of the terms or conditions of employment. A dispute is often followed by industrial action, in the form of a ◊strike or a work to rule, whereby employees work strictly according to the legal terms of their contract of employment.

industrialization process by which an increasing proportion of a country's economic activity is involved in industry. It is essential for economic development and largely responsible for the growth of cities (◊urbanization).

It is usually associated with the modernization of developing countries, beginning with the manufacture of simple goods that can replace imports.

industrial law or ***labour law*** the body of law relating to relationships between employers (and

Indonesia Rice terraces are characteristic of Indonesia, where rice is the most important crop. Production is concentrated on the fertile island of Java, providing 70% of income for people in rural areas. In the late 1980s Indonesia, once the world's largest importer of rice, had become totally self-sufficient. *United Nations*

their representatives), employees (and their representatives), and government.

industrial relations relationship between employers and employees, and their dealings with each other. The aim of good industrial relations is to achieve a motivated, capable workforce that sees its work as creative and fulfilling. A breakdown in industrial relations can lead to an industrial dispute where one party takes industrial action. When agreement cannot be reached by free collective bargaining, outside arbitration is often sought (in Britain the Advisory Conciliation and Arbitration Service, ACAS, was set up 1975).

Industrial Revolution the sudden acceleration of technical and economic development that began in Britain in the second half of the 18th century. The traditional agrarian economy was replaced by one dominated by machinery and manufacturing, made possible through technical advances such as the steam engine. This transferred the balance of political power from the landowner to the industrial capitalist and created an urban working class. From 1830 to the early 20th century, the Industrial Revolution spread throughout Europe and the USA and to Japan and the various colonial empires. *See timeline on following page.*

industrial sector any of the different groups into which industries may be divided: primary, secondary, tertiary, and quaternary. Primary industries extract or use raw materials; for example, mining and agriculture. Secondary industries are manufacturing industries, where raw materials are processed or components are assembled. Tertiary industries supply services such as retailing. The quaternary sector of industry is concerned with the professions and those services that require a high level of skill, expertise, and specialization. It includes education, research and development, administration, and financial services such as accountancy.

industrial tribunal independent panel that rules on disputes between employers and employees or trade unions relating to statutory terms and conditions of employment. Employment issues brought before it include unfair dismissal, redundancy, equal opportunities, and discrimination at work. The panel is made up of a lawyer, a union representative, and a management representative.

INDONESIA
Republic of

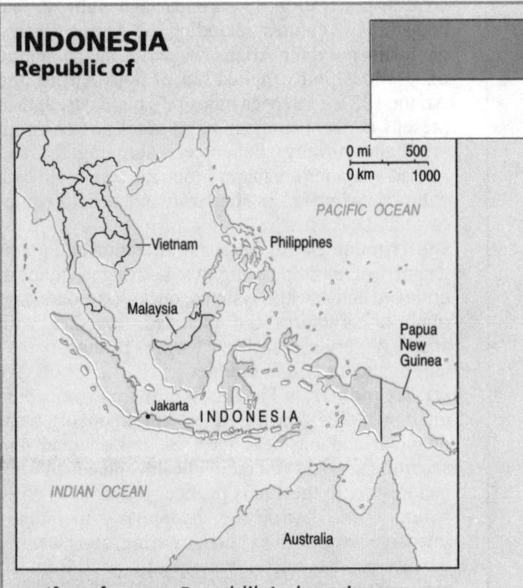

national name *Republik Indonesia*
area 1,904,569 sq km/735,164 sq mi
capital Jakarta
major towns/cities Bandung, Yogyakarta (Java), Medan, Banda Aceh, Palembang (Sumatra), Denpasar (Bali), Kupang (Timor)
major ports Tanjung Priok, Surabaya, Semarang (Java), Ujung Pandang (Sulawesi)
physical features comprises 13,677 tropical islands (over 6,000 of them are inhabited): the Greater Sundas (including Java, Madura, Sumatra, Sulawesi, and Kalimantan [part of Borneo]), the Lesser Sundas/ Nusa Tenggara (including Bali, Lombok, Sumbawa, Flores, Sumba, Alor, Lomblen, Timor, Roti, and Savu), Maluku/Moluccas (over 1,000 islands including Ambon, Ternate, Tidore, Tanimbar, and Halmahera), and Irian Jaya (part of New Guinea); over half the country is tropical rainfores; it has the largest expanse of peatlands in the tropics (17–27 million hectares). A million hectares of pristine swamp forest is to be drained in Central Kalimantan; President Suharto endorsed the project 1996 without environmental assessment
head of state and government B J Habibie from 1998
political system authoritarian nationalist republic
administrative divisions 27 provinces
political parties Sekber Golkar, ruling military-bureaucrat-farmers' party; United Development Party (PPP), moderate Islamic; Indonesian Democratic Party (PDI), nationalist Christian
armed forces 274,500; paramilitary and part-time auxiliary forces 1.67 million (1995)
conscription 2 years (selective)
defence spend (% GDP) 1.4 (1994)
education spend (% GNP) 2.2 (1992)
health spend (% GDP) 0.7 (1990)
death penalty retained and used for ordinary crimes
population 200,453,000 (1996 est)
population growth rate 1.6% (1990–95); 1.3% (2000–05)
age distribution (% of total population) <15 33.0%, 15–65 62.7%, >65 4.3% (1995)
ethnic distribution comprises more than 300 ethnic groups, the majority of which are of Malay descent; important Malay communities include Javanese (about one-third of the population), Sundanese (7%), and Madurese (3%); the largest non-Malay community is the Chinese (2%); substantial numbers of Indians, Melanesians, Micronesians, and Arabs
population density (per sq km) 102.1 (1995)
urban population (% of total) 35% (1995)
labour force 44% of population: 55% agriculture, 14% industry, 31% services (1990)
unemployment 2.8% (1993)
child mortality rate (under 5, per 1,000 live births) 111 (1994)
life expectancy 61 (men), 65 (women)
education (compulsory years) 6
literacy rate 84% (men), 68% (women)
languages Bahasa Indonesia (official), closely related to Malay; there are 583 regional languages and dialects; Javanese is the most widely spoken local language. Dutch is also spoken
religions Muslim 88%, Christian 10%, Buddhist and Hindu 2% (the continued spread of Christianity, together with an Islamic revival, have led to greater religious tensions)
TV sets (per 1,000 people) 60 (1992)
currency rupiah
GDP (US $) 174.6 billion (1994)
GDP per capita (PPP) (US $) 3,270 (1993)
growth rate 7.3% (1994)
average annual inflation 9.6% (1994); 8.0% (1985–94)
major trading partners Singapore, Japan, USA, Hong Kong, Australia, Germany, the Netherlands
resources petroleum (principal producer of petroleum in the Far East), natural gas, bauxite, nickel (world's third-largest producer), copper, tin (world's second-largest producer), gold, coal, forests
industries petroleum refinery, food processing, textiles, wood products, tobacco, chemicals, fertilizers, rubber, cement
exports petroleum and petroleum products, natural and manufactured gas, textiles, rubber, palm oil, wood and wood products, electrical and electronic products, coffee, fishery products, coal, copper, tin, pepper, tea. Principal market: Japan 27.9% (1994)
imports machinery, transport and electrical equipment, manufactured goods, chemical and mineral products. Principal source: Singapore 40% (1994)
arable land 9.9% (1993)
agricultural products rice, cassava, maize, coffee, spices, tea, cocoa, tobacco, sugar cane, sweet potatoes, palm, rubber, coconuts, nutmeg; fishing

HISTORY
3000–500 BC Immigrants from S China displaced original Melanesian population.
6th C AD Start of Indian cultural influence; small Hindu and Buddhist kingdoms developed.
8th C Buddhist maritime empire of Srivijaya expanded to include all Sumatra and Malay peninsula.
13th C Islam introduced to Sumatra by Arab merchants.
14th C Eastern Javanese kingdom of Majapahit destroyed Srivijaya and dominated the region.
c. 1520 Empire of Majapahit disintegrated; Javanese nobles fled to Bali.
16th C Portuguese merchants broke Muslim monopoly of spice trade.
1602 Dutch East India Company founded; it displaced the Portuguese and monopolized trade.
17th C Dutch introduced coffee plants and established informal control over central Java.
1799 Netherlands took over interests of bankrupt Dutch East India Company.
1808 French forces occupied Java; British expelled them 1811 and returned Java to the Netherlands 1816.
1824 Anglo-Dutch Treaty: Britain recognized entire Indonesian archipelago as Dutch sphere of influence.
1825–30 Java War: Prince Dipo Negoro led unsuccessful revolt against Dutch rule; further revolt 1894–96.
19th C Dutch formalized control over Java and conquered other islands; cultivation of coffee and sugar under tight official control made the Netherlands Indies one of the richest colonies in the world.
1901 Dutch introduced 'Ethical Policy' supposed to advance native interests.
1908 Dutch completed conquest of Bali.
1927 Communist revolts suppressed; Achmed Sukarno founded Indonesian Nationalist Party (PNI) to unite diverse anti-Dutch elements.
1929 Dutch imprisoned Sukarno and tried to suppress PNI.
1942–45 Japanese occupation; PNI installed as anti-Western puppet government.
1945 When Japan surrendered, President Sukarno declared an independent republic, but Dutch set about restoring colonial rule by force.
1947 Dutch 'police action': all-out attack on Java and Sumatra conquered two-thirds of the republic.
1949 Under US pressure, Dutch agreed to transfer sovereignty of the Netherlands Indies (except Dutch New Guinea or Irian Jaya) to the Republic of the United States of Indonesia.
1950 President Sukarno abolished federalism and proclaimed unitary Republic of Indonesia dominated by Java; revolts in Sumatra and South Moluccas.
1959 To combat severe political instability, Sukarno imposed authoritarian 'guided democracy'.
1963 The Netherlands ceded Irian Jaya to Indonesia.
1963–66 Indonesia tried to break up Malaysia by means of blockade and guerrilla attacks.
1965–66 Clashes between communists and army; General Raden Suharto imposed emergency administration and massacred up to 700,000 alleged communists.
1968 Suharto formally replaced Sukarno as president and proclaimed 'New Order' under strict military rule.
1970s Rising oil exports brought significant agricultural and industrial growth.
1975 Indonesia invaded East Timor when Portuguese rule collapsed; 200,000 died in ensuing war.
1986 After suppressing revolt on Irian Jaya, Suharto introduced a transmigration programme to settle 65,000 Javanese there and on outer islands.
1991 Democracy Forum launched to promote political dialogue.
1993 President Suharto re-elected for sixth consecutive term.
1994 Sukarno's daughter, Megawati Sukarnoputri, elected head of opposition party PDI.
1996 Megawati ousted by rival faction within PDI (aided by Suharto); government crackdown on opponents, including PDI supporters. Hundreds killed in ethnic riots in West Kalimantam province.
1997 Golkar party won landslide victory in assembly elections. Singapore and Malaysia pledged financial support. Drought and famine in Irian Jaya.
1998 Currency fell sharply in value and economy contracted, provoking urban riots. Suharto re-elected president despite student campaigns against him; security forces killed 12 students at Trisakti University. Over 500 killed in violent clashes in May; Suharto resigned as president, handing over power to B J Habibie. 'Reform cabinet' formed and early elections promised.
1999 The government consented to consider further the possibility of autonomy for East Timor.

SEE ALSO Dutch East India Company; Java; Sumatra

INDUSTRIAL REVOLUTION: TIMELINE

1709	Abraham Darby introduced coke smelting to his ironworks at Coalbrookdale in Shropshire.
1712	The first workable steam-powered engine was developed by Thomas Newcomen.
1730	The seed drill was invented by Jethro Tull. This was a critical point of the agricultural revolution which freed labour from the fields and lowered crop prices.
1740	Crucible steelmaking was discovered by Benjamin Huntsman, a clockmaker of Doncaster.
1759	The first Canal Act was passed by the British Parliament; this led to the construction of a national network of inland waterways for transport and industrial supplies. By 1830 there were 6,500 km/4,000 mi of canals in Britain.
1763	The spinning jenny, which greatly accelerated cotton spinning, was invented by James Hargreaves in Blackburn.
1764	Pierre Trosanquet, a French engineer, developed a new method of road building. Similar techniques were used by Thomas Telford in Britain to build modern roads from 1803.
1765	James Watt produced a more reliable and efficient version of the Newcomen engine.
1779	The spinning mule, which made the production of fine yarns by machine possible, was developed in Bolton by Samuel Crompton.
1785	The power loom marked the start of the mechanised textile industry.
1785–99	Techniques of mass production of interchangeable parts were developed by the arms industry in the USA, led by Eli Whitney.
1793	The problem of supplying cotton fast enough for the textile industry was solved by Eli Whitney's cotton gin.
1797	The first true industrial lathe was invented, virtually simultaneously, by Henry Maudslay in England and David Wilkinson in the USA.
1802	The first electric battery capable of mass production was designed by William Cruickshank in England.
1811–16	Textile workers known as Luddites staged widespread protests against low pay and unemployment in Nottinghamshire, which involved destroying new machines.
c. 1812	The population of Manchester passed 100,000.
c. 1813	Industrial employment overtook agricultural employment in England for the first time.
1825	The first regular railway services started between Stockton and Darlington in northeast England.
1826	The Journeymen Steam Engine Fitters, the first substantial industrial trade union, was established in Manchester.
1829	With his steam locomotive *Rocket*, English engineer George Stephenson won a contest to design locomotives for the new Manchester–Liverpool railway.
1831–52	British industrial production doubled.
1832	Hippolyte Pixii of France produced a prototype electricity generator using magnets.
1832	The Reform Act concerning elections to the British Parliament gave representation to the industrial cities.
1833	The first effective Factory Act was passed in Britain regulating child labour in cotton mills.
c. 1840	The USA became the world leader for railroads, with over 5,000 km/3,000 mi laid. By 1860 this would rise to 50,000 km/30,000 mi.
1840s	Cornelius Vanderbilt and John Jacob Astor became the most prominent millionaires of the industrial age.
1842	Cotton-industry workers in England staged a widespread strike.
1846	Repeal of the Corn Law in Britain reduced agricultural prices, thereby helping industry.
1851	Britain celebrated its industrial achievements in the Great Exhibition.
1852–80	British industrial production doubled again.
1858	The 'great stink' of London dramatized the increasing pollution in the cities.
c. 1860	New York City became the first US city with over 1 million inhabitants.

Industrial Workers of the World (IWW) labour movement founded in Chicago, USA 1905, and in Australia 1907, the members of which were popularly known as the Wobblies. The IWW was dedicated to the overthrow of capitalism and the creation of a single union for workers, but divided on tactics.

industry the extraction and conversion of raw materials, the manufacture of goods, and the provision of services. Industry can be either low technology, unspecialized, and labour-intensive, as in countries with a large unskilled labour force, or highly automated, mechanized, and specialized, using advanced technology, as in the industrialized countries. Major recent trends in industrial activity have been the growth of electronic, robotic, and microelectronic technologies, the expansion of the offshore oil industry, and the prominence of Japan and other Pacific-region countries in manufacturing and distributing electronics, computers, and motor vehicles.

British industry The prominent trends in industrial activity in Britain from the 1970s onwards have been the growth of the offshore oil and gas industries, the rapid growth of electronic and microelectronic technologies, and a continuous rise in the share of total employment of service industries. At the same time there has been a decline in traditional industries such as steel-making, ship-building, and coal mining. Recessions 1974–75 and 1980–81, due in part to fluctuating energy costs, have been offset by increased productivity, but the increased output was achieved with fewer workers, and unemployment has been a persistent feature of the period.

Electronics and automated controls are now applied extensively throughout industry, particularly in steel mills, oil refineries, coal mines, and chemical plants. The UK is the sixth largest user of industrial robots in the world. Another area of technological strength is ◊biotechnology, using fermentation techniques for food, beverage, and antibiotic production. The main areas of research and development expenditure are electronics, chemicals and pharmaceuticals, aerospace, mechanical engineering, and motor vehicles. The highest growth in manufacturing in the past decade has been in the chemical, electrical, and instrument engineering sectors. In 1988, the number of people employed in the manufacturing industry dropped below 5 million for the first time since the 19th century.

mineral products The British Steel Corporation accounts for 82–85% of Britain's steel output by volume, and is the world's fourth largest steel company. The sector is strong in the manufacture of special steels, alloys, and finished products for the engineering industries. Manipulation of materials by smelting, casting, rolling, extruding, and drawing is also carried out.

chemicals Accounting for about 10% of manufacturing net output, this industry produces a complete range of products including fertilizers, plastics, pharmaceuticals, soap, toiletries, and explosives.

mechanical engineering Machine tools, industrial engines, mechanical handling equipment, construction equipment, and industrial plant are all significant products in this area. Britain is the Western world's largest producer of agricultural tractors.

motor vehicles Recent years have seen a large increase in the volume of imports in this sector, notably from Europe and Japan, but more foreign makes are being assembled in the UK. British manufacturers still provide a major export.

aerospace In order to compete with the USA in this area, Britain resorted to European and multinational cooperative ventures, including the Airbus passenger airliner and the Ariane rocket for the launching of satellites, but it pulled out of both Airbus and Ariane 1987. The space industry's major strength at present is the manufacture of satellites. Aircraft (civil and military), helicopters, aero-engines, and guided weapons are major products, supported by a comprehensive range of aircraft and airfield equipment and systems.

construction Building, repair, alteration and maintenance of buildings, highways, bridges, tunnels, drainage and sewage systems, docks, harbours, and offshore structures are included, together with ancillary services such as wiring, heating, ventilation, and air conditioning.

service industries The fastest growing sectors during the 1970s (measured by employment) were financial and business services, professional and scientific services (including health and education), and leisure. In the 1980s finance continued to grow strongly, and franchising, particularly in labour-intensive areas such as hotel, catering, and cleaning businesses, became a widespread new form of organization.

world industry On the global scale, the period after World War II has been marked by the development of traditional industry such as shipbuilding and motor manufacture in then low-cost countries, such as Japan, Korea, and others in the Pacific region. This has been followed by moves into new industrial products, such as electronics and computers, in which these countries have dominated the world. In the West, the USA has been most successful partly because of the great size of its home market, while the states of the former USSR, and to a lesser extent Europe, resorted to protectionist tariff and quota barriers, and attempts to implement economic planning as a tool for economic growth.

Indus Valley civilization one of the four earliest ancient civilizations of the Old World (the other three being the ◊Sumerian civilization 3500 BC; ◊Egypt 3000 BC; and ◊China 2200 BC), developing in the NW of the Indian subcontinent about 2500 BC.

◊Mohenjo Daro and ◊Harappa were the two main city complexes, but many more existed along the Indus Valley, now in Pakistan. Remains include grid-planned streets with municipal drainage, public and private buildings, baths, temples, and a standardized system of weights and measures – all of which testify to centralized political control. Evidence exists for trade with Sumer and Akkad. The ◊Aryan invasion of about 1500 BC probably led to its downfall.

inert gas or ***noble gas*** any of a group of six elements (helium, neon, argon, krypton, xenon, and radon), so named because they were originally thought not to enter into any chemical reactions. This is now known to be incorrect: in 1962, xenon was made to combine with fluorine, and since then, compounds of argon, krypton, and radon with fluorine and/or oxygen have been described.

The extreme unreactivity of the inert gases is due to the stability of their electronic structure. All the electron shells of inert gas atoms are full and, except for helium, they all have eight electrons in their outermost (◊valency) shell. The apparent stability of this electronic arrangement led to the formulation of the ◊octet rule to explain the different types of chemical bond found in simple compounds.

inertia in physics, the tendency of an object to remain in a state of rest or uniform motion until an external force is applied, as stated by Isaac Newton's first law of motion (see ◊Newton's laws of motion).

infante and ***infanta*** title given in Spain and Portugal to the sons (other than the heir apparent) and daughters, respectively, of the sovereign. The heir apparent in Spain bears the title of prince of Asturias.

infanticide in law, the killing of a child under 12 months old by its mother. More generally, any killing of a newborn child, usually as a method of population control and most frequently of girls (especially in India and China), although boys are killed in countries where bride prices are high.

Worldwide, for every 100 men there are 105 women; in India the average has fallen to 93 women for every 100 men, but in some regions there are fewer than 85 women per 100 men. Research carried out at a Bombay hospital revealed 1995 that for every aborted male, there were 1,000 aborted females.

In some areas of rural China there are 28 single men (between the ages of 25 and 44) for every single woman.

infantile paralysis former term for poliomyelitis. See ◊polio.

infant mortality rate measure of the number of infants dying under one year of age, usually expressed as the number of deaths per 1,000 live births. Improved sanitation, nutrition, and medical care have considerably lowered figures throughout much of the world; for example in the 18th century in the USA and UK infant mortality was about 500 per thousand, compared with under 10 per thousand in 1989. The lowest infant mortality rate is in Japan, at 4.5 per 1,000 live births. In much of the developing world, however, the infant mortality rate remains high.

infarct or ***infarction*** death and scarring of a portion of the tissue in an organ, as a result of congestion or blockage of a blood vessel serving it.

Myocardial infarction is the technical term for a heart attack.

infection invasion of the body by disease-causing organisms (pathogens or germs) that become established, multiply, and produce symptoms. Bacteria and viruses cause most diseases, but diseases are also caused by other microorganisms, protozoans, and other parasites.

Most pathogens enter and leave the body through the digestive or respiratory tracts. Polio, dysentery, and typhoid are examples of diseases contracted by ingestion of contaminated foods or fluids. Organisms present in the saliva or nasal mucus are spread by airborne or droplet infection; fine droplets or dried particles are inhaled by others when the affected individual talks, coughs, or sneezes. Diseases such as measles, mumps, and tuberculosis are passed on in this way.

A less common route of entry is through the skin, either by contamination of an open wound (as in tetanus) or by penetration of the intact skin surface, as in a bite from a malaria-carrying mosquito. Relatively few diseases are transmissible by skin-to-skin contact. Glandular fever and herpes simplex (cold sore) may be passed on by kissing, and the group now officially bracketed as sexually transmitted diseases (◊STDs) are mostly spread by intimate contact.

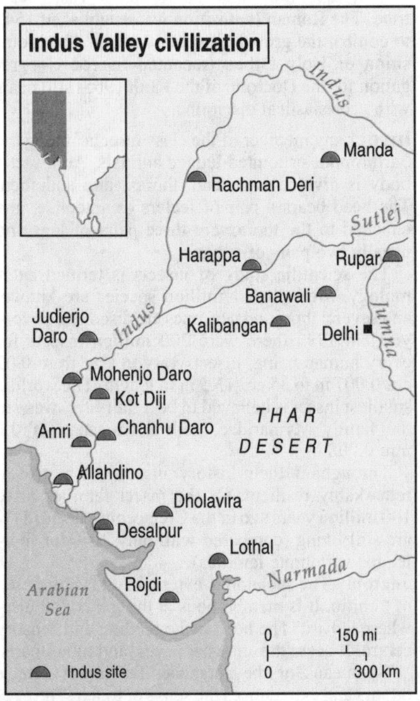

Indus Valley civilization

Indus
Manda
Rachman Deri
Sutlej
Harappa
Rupar
Banawali
Jumna
Judierjo Daro
Indus
Kalibangan
Delhi
Mohenjo Daro
Kot Diji
Amri
Chanhu Daro
THAR DESERT
Allahdino
Dholavira
Desalpur
Lothal
Narmada
Arabian Sea
Rojdi
0 150 mi
0 300 km
Indus site

inferiority complex in psychology, a ◊complex or cluster of repressed fears, described by Alfred ◊Adler, based on physical inferiority. The term is popularly used to describe general feelings of inferiority and the overcompensation that often ensues.

infinite series in mathematics, a series of numbers consisting of a denumerably infinite sequence of terms. The sequence $n, n^2, n^3, \ldots$ gives the series $n + n^2 + n^3 + \ldots$. For example, $1 + 2 + 3 + \ldots$ is a divergent infinite arithmetic series, and $8 + 4 + 2 + 1 + \frac{1}{2} + \ldots$ is a convergent infinite geometric series that has a sum to infinity of 16.

infinity mathematical quantity that is larger than any fixed assignable quantity; symbol ∞. By convention, the result of dividing any number by zero is regarded as infinity.

inflammation defensive reaction of the body tissues to disease or damage, including redness, swelling, and heat. Denoted by the suffix *-itis* (as in appendicitis), it may be acute or chronic, and may be accompanied by the formation of pus. This is an essential part of the healing process.

Inflammation occurs when damaged cells release a substance (◊histamine) that causes blood vessels to widen and leak into the surrounding tissues. This phenomenon accounts for the redness, swelling, and heat. Pain is due partly to the pressure of swelling and also to irritation of nerve endings. Defensive white blood cells congregate within an area of inflammation to engulf and remove foreign matter and dead tissue.

inflation in economics, a rise in the general level of prices. The many causes include cost-push inflation, which results from rising production costs. ***Demand-pull inflation*** occurs when overall demand exceeds supply. ***Suppressed inflation*** occurs in controlled economies and is reflected in rationing, shortages, and black-market prices. ***Hyperinflation*** is inflation of more than 50% in one month. ***Deflation***, a fall in the general level of prices, is the reverse of inflation.

inflection or ***inflexion*** in grammatical analysis, an ending or other element in a word that indicates its grammatical function (whether plural or singular, masculine or feminine, subject or object, and so on).

In a highly inflected language like Latin, nouns, verbs, and adjectives have many inflectional endings (for example, in the word *amabunt* the base *am* means 'love' and the complex *abunt* indicates the kind of verb, the future tense, indicative mood, active voice, third person, and plurality). English has few inflections: for example, the *s* for plural forms (as in *the books*) and for the third person singular of verbs (as in *He runs*).

inflorescence in plants, a branch, or system of branches, bearing two or more individual flowers. Inflorescences can be divided into two main types: cymose (or definite) and racemose (or indefinite). In a ***cymose inflorescence***, the tip of the main axis produces a single flower and subsequent flowers arise on lower side branches, as in forget-me-not *Myosotis* and chickweed *Stellaria*; the oldest flowers are, therefore, found at the tip. A ***racemose inflorescence*** has an active growing region at the tip of its main axis, and bears flowers along its length, as in hyacinth *Hyacinthus*; the oldest flowers are found near the base or, in cases where the inflorescence is flattened, towards the outside.

The stalk of the inflorescence is called a peduncle; the stalk of each individual flower is called a pedicel.

influenza any of various viral infections primarily affecting the air passages, accompanied by systemic effects (effects relating to the body as a whole) such as fever, chills, headache, joint and muscle pains, and lassitude. Treatment is with bed rest and analgesic drugs such as aspirin or paracetamol.

inflorescence Inflorescence (arrangement of flowers on a stalk) of the dragonmouth *Horminium pyrenaicum*. Here a flower spike consists of whorls of flowers (verticillasters) with gaps between them. *Premaphotos Wildlife*

Depending on the virus strain, influenza varies in virulence and duration, and there is always the risk of secondary (bacterial) infection of the lungs (pneumonia). Vaccines are effective against known strains but will not give protection against newly evolving viruses. The 1918–19 influenza pandemic (see ◊epidemic) killed about 20 million people worldwide.

information superhighway popular collective name for the ◊Internet and other related large scale computer networks. The term was first used 1993 by US vice president Al Gore in a speech outlining plans to build a high-speed national data communications network.

information technology (IT) collective term for the various technologies involved in processing and transmitting information. They include computing, telecommunications, and microelectronics.

Word processing, databases, and spreadsheets are just some of the computing ◊software packages that have revolutionized work in the office environment. Not only can work be done more quickly than before, but IT has given decisionmakers the opportunity to consider far more data when making decisions.

infrared astronomy study of infrared radiation produced by relatively cool gas and dust in space, as in the areas around forming stars. In 1983, the Infra-Red Astronomy Satellite (IRAS) surveyed the entire sky at infrared wavelengths. It found five new comets, thousands of galaxies undergoing bursts of star formation, and the possibility of planetary systems forming around several dozen stars.

Planets and gas clouds emit their light in the far and mid-infrared region of the spectrum. The Infra-red Space Observatory (ISO), launched Nov 1995, observes a broad wavelength (3–200 micrometres) in this region. It is 10,000 times more sensitive than IRAS, and will search for ◊brown dwarfs (cool masses of gas smaller than the Sun). ▷ *See feature on pp. 70–71.*

infrared radiation invisible electromagnetic radiation of wavelength between about 0.75 micrometres and 1 millimetre – that is, between the limit of the red end of the visible spectrum and the shortest microwaves. All bodies above the ◊absolute zero of temperature absorb and radiate infrared radiation. Infrared radiation is used in medical photography and treatment, and in industry, astronomy, and criminology. *See illustration on following page.*

infrastructure relatively permanent facilities that serve an industrial economy. Infrastructure usually includes roads, railways, other communication networks, energy and water supply, and

infrared radiation Image of a building made using infrared radiation. The building is warmer than its surroundings and therefore emits more radiation in this range of the spectrum, resulting in a visible representation in the longer wavelengths. *Image Select (UK) Ltd*

education and training facilities. Some definitions also include sociocultural installations such as health-care and leisure facilities.

Ingres Jean-Auguste-Dominique 1780–1867. French painter. A leading Neo-Classicist, he was a student of Jacques Louis ◊David. He studied and worked in Rome about 1807–20, where he began the *Odalisque* series of sensuous female nudes, then went to Florence, and returned to France 1824. His portraits painted in the 1840s–50s are meticulously detailed and highly polished.

A master draughtsman, he considered drawing 'the probity of art', and developed his style – based on the study of ◊Raphael and marked by clarity of line and a cool formality – in fierce opposition to the Romanticism of Eugène ◊Delacroix. His major works, which exercised a profound influence on 19th-century French Academic art, include *Roger and Angelica* 1819 (Louvre, Paris), *La Grande Baigneuse* 1808 (Louvre, Paris), and *La Grande Odalisque* 1814 (Louvre, Paris), and the portraits *Madame Moitessier* 1856 (National Gallery, London) and *François Marius* 1807 (Musée Granet, Aix-en-Provence).

Ingushetia Russian autonomous republic on the northern slopes of the Caucasus mountains
area 2,000 sq km/770 sq mi
capital Nazran
population (1994 est) 250,000 (Ingush 85%)
industries farming and cattle-raising; petroleum drilling
religion Islam
history The Ingush people became Russian subjects 1810 and did not resist Russian occupation of the Caucasus in the mid-19th century. In 1924 Ingushetia became an autonomous republic of the USSR, and in 1936 was merged with Chechnya to form the Autonomous Republic of Checheno-Ingush. The republic was dissolved 1944 and a large part of the population deported for alleged wartime collaboration. Khrushchev reconstituted the republic 1957 and 232,000 Chechens and Ingush returned from exile. In 1992, following border clashes with the Chechens, Ingushetia was made an autonomous republic in its own right.

inheritance tax in the UK, a tax charged on the value of an individual's estate on his/her death, including gifts made within the previous seven years. It replaced capital transfer tax 1986 (which in turn replaced estate duty 1974).

initiative in politics, a device whereby constitutional voters may play a direct part in making laws. A proposed law may be drawn up and signed by petitioners, and submitted to the legislature. A ◊referendum may be taken on a law that has been passed by the legislature but that will not become operative unless the voters assent to it. Switzerland was the first country to make use of the device.

injunction court order that forbids a person from doing something, or orders him or her to take certain action. Breach of an injunction is ◊contempt of court.

ink coloured liquid used for writing, drawing, and printing. Traditional ink (blue, but later a permanent black) was produced from gallic acid and tannic acid, but inks are now based on synthetic dyes.

Inkatha Freedom Party (IFP) (from the grass coil worn by Zulu women for carrying head loads; its many strands give it strength) South African political party, representing the nationalist aspirations of the country's largest ethnic group, the Zulus. It was founded as a paramilitary organization 1975 by its present leader, Chief Gatsha ◊Buthelezi, with the avowed aim of creating a nonracial democratic political situation. The party entered South Africa's first multiracial elections April 1994, after an initial violent boycott, and emerged with 10% of the popular vote.

Inkatha initially tried to work with the white regime and, as a result, Buthelezi was widely regarded as a collaborator. Revelations, in 1991 and 1994, that Inkatha had received covert financial aid from the South African government and support from the security services increased the ◊African National Congress (ANC) distrust of its motives, while Inkatha resented the dominant role played by the ANC in constitutional negotiations.

INLA abbreviation for ◊***Irish National Liberation Army***.

Innocent thirteen popes including:

Innocent III c. 1161–1216. Pope from 1198. He asserted papal power over secular princes, in particular over the succession of Holy Roman emperors. He also made King ◊John of England his vassal, compelling him to accept Stephen ◊Langton as archbishop of Canterbury. He promoted the fourth Crusade and crusades against the non-Christian Livonians and Letts, and the Albigensian heretics of S France.

Innocents' Day or ***Childermas*** festival of the Roman Catholic Church, celebrated 28 Dec in memory of the ***Massacre of the Innocents***, the children of Bethlehem who were allegedly slaughtered by King ◊Herod after the birth of Jesus.

Innsbruck capital of Tirol state, W Austria; population (1991) 118,100. It is a tourist and winter sports centre and a route junction for the Brenner Pass. The 1964 and 1976 Winter Olympics were held here.

Inns of Court four private legal societies in London, England: Lincoln's Inn, Gray's Inn, Inner Temple, and Middle Temple. All barristers (advocates in the English legal system) must belong to one of the Inns of Court. The main function of each Inn is the education, government, and protection of its members. Each is under the administration of a body of Benchers (judges and senior barristers).

innuendo indirect, unpleasant comment; a sly hint. 'I am sure you have brought up your child well – to the best of your ability.' 'I wouldn't take any books when you go to stay with Alan, if I were you. They have a habit of disappearing there.' The essence of an innuendo is that it must be capable of an innocent explanation. The speaker must be able to charge the listener with misinterpretation or oversensitivity, if the innuendo is challenged.

inoculation injection into the body of dead or weakened disease-carrying organisms or their toxins (◊vaccine) to produce immunity by inducing a mild form of a disease.

inorganic chemistry branch of chemistry dealing with the chemical properties of the elements and their compounds, excluding the more complex covalent compounds of carbon, which are considered in ◊organic chemistry.

The origins of inorganic chemistry lay in observing the characteristics and experimenting with the uses of the substances (compounds and elements) that could be extracted from mineral ores. These could be classified according to their chemical properties: elements could be classified as metals or nonmetals; compounds as acids or bases, oxidizing or reducing agents, ionic compounds (such as salts), or covalent compounds (such as gases). The arrangement of elements into groups possessing similar properties led to Mendeleyev's ◊periodic table of the elements, which prompted chemists to predict the properties of undiscovered elements that might occupy gaps in the table. This, in turn, led to the discovery of new elements, including a number of highly radioactive elements that do not occur naturally.

inorganic compound compound found in organisms that are not typically biological.

Water, sodium chloride, and potassium are inorganic compounds because they are widely found outside living cells. The term is also applied to those compounds that do not contain carbon and that are not manufactured by organisms. However, carbon dioxide is considered inorganic, contains carbon, and is manufactured by organisms during respiration. See ◊organic compound.

inquest inquiry held by a ◊coroner into an unexplained death. At an inquest, a coroner is assisted by a jury of between 7 and 11 people. Evidence is on oath, and medical and other witnesses may be summoned.

Inquisition tribunal of the Roman Catholic Church established 1233 to suppress heresy (dissenting views), originally by excommunication. Sentence was pronounced during a religious ceremony, the ◊auto-da-fé. The Inquisition operated in France, Italy, Spain, and the Holy Roman Empire, and was especially active after the ◊Reformation; it was later extended to the Americas. Its trials were conducted in secret, under torture, and penalties ranged from fines, through flogging and imprisonment, to death by burning.

During the course of the Spanish Inquisition, until its abolition 1834, some 60,000 cases were tried. The Roman Inquisition was established 1542 to combat the growth of Protestantism. The Inquisition or Holy Office (renamed Sacred Congregation for the Doctrine of the Faith 1965) still deals with ecclesiastical discipline.

insect any member of the class Insecta among the ◊arthropods or jointed-legged animals. An insect's body is divided into head, thorax, and abdomen. The head bears a pair of feelers or antennae, and attached to the thorax are three pairs of legs and usually two pairs of wings.

The scientific study of insects is termed entomology. More than 1 million species are known, and several thousand new ones are discovered every year; in 1995 there were 200 million insects for every human being. Insects vary in size from 0.02 cm/0.007 in to 35 cm/13.5 in in length. The world's smallest insect is believed to be a 'fairy fly' wasp in the family Mymaridae, with a wingspan of 0.2 mm/0.008 in.

Throughout their history insects have proved remarkably resilient. Of the insect families alive 100 million years ago in the Cretaceous period, 84% are still living (compared with only 20% for four-legged vertebrate families).

anatomy The skeleton is external and is composed of ◊chitin. It is membranous at the joints, but elsewhere is hard. The head is the feeding and sensory centre. It bears the antennae, eyes, and mouthparts.

By means of the antennae, the insect detects odours and experiences the sense of touch. The eyes include compound eyes and simple eyes (ocelli). Compound eyes are formed of a large number of individual facets or lenses; there are about 4,000 lenses to each compound eye in the housefly. The mouthparts include a labrum, or upper lip; a pair of principal jaws, or mandibles; a pair of accessory jaws, or maxillae; and a labium, or lower lip. These mouthparts are modified in the various insect groups, depending on the diet. The thorax is the locomotory centre, and is made up of three segments: the pro-, meso-, and metathorax. Each bears a pair of legs, and, in flying insects, the second and third of these segments also each bear a pair of wings.

Wings are composed of an upper and a lower membrane, and between these two layers they are strengthened by a framework of chitinous tubes known as veins. The abdomen is the metabolic and reproductive centre, where digestion, excretion, and the sexual functions take place. In the female, there is very commonly an egg-laying instrument, or ovipositor, and many insects have a pair of tail feelers, or cerci. Most insects breathe by means of fine airtubes called tracheae, which open to the exterior by a pair of breathing pores, or spiracles. Reproduction is by diverse means. In most insects, mating occurs once only, and death soon follows.

growth and metamorphosis When ready to hatch from the egg, the young insect forces its way through the chorion, or eggshell, and growth takes place in cycles that are interrupted by successive moults. After moulting, the new cuticle is soft and pliable, and is able to adapt itself to increase in size and change of form.

Most of the lower orders of insects pass through a direct or incomplete ◊metamorphosis. The young closely resemble the parents and are known as nymphs.

The higher groups of insects undergo indirect or complete metamorphosis. They hatch at an earlier stage of growth than nymphs and are termed ◊larvae. The life of the insect is interrupted by a resting pupal stage when no food is taken. During this stage, the larval organs and tissues are transformed into those of the imago, or adult. Before pupating, the insect protects itself by selecting a suitable hiding place, or making a cocoon of some material which will merge in with its surroundings. When an insect is about to emerge from the ◊pupa, or protective sheath, it undergoes its final moult, which consists of shedding the pupal cuticle. The classification of insects is largely based upon characters of the mouthparts, wings, and metamorphosis. Insects are divided into two subclasses: Apterygota (wingless insects), with 4 orders; and Pterygota (winged insects), with 24 orders divided into two groups according to their method of development.

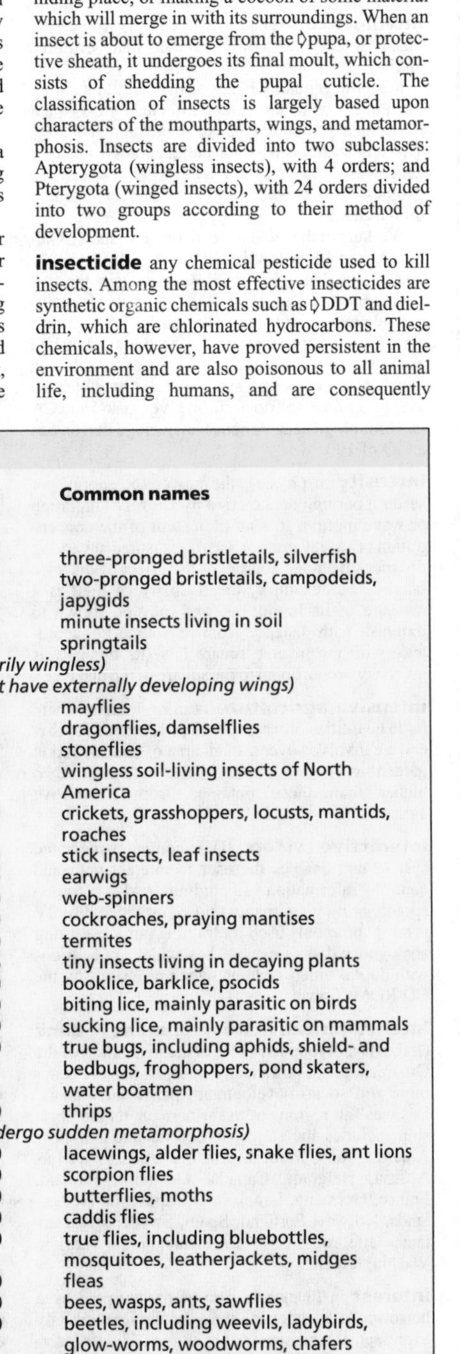

insect Body plan of an insect. The general features of the insect body include a segmented body divided into head, thorax, and abdomen, jointed legs, feelers or antennae, and usually two pairs of wings. Insects often have compound eyes with a large field of vision.

insecticide any chemical pesticide used to kill insects. Among the most effective insecticides are synthetic organic chemicals such as ◊DDT and dieldrin, which are chlorinated hydrocarbons. These chemicals, however, have proved persistent in the environment and are also poisonous to all animal life, including humans, and are consequently banned in many countries. Other synthetic insecticides include organic phosphorus compounds such as malathion. Insecticides prepared from plants, such as derris and pyrethrum, are safer to use but need to be applied frequently and carefully.

INSECTS: CLASSIFICATION

Subclass/Order	Number of species	Common names
Apterygota *(wingless insects)*		
Thysanura	350	three-pronged bristletails, silverfish
Diplura	400	two-pronged bristletails, campodeids, japygids
Protura	50	minute insects living in soil
Collembola	1500	springtails
Pterygota *(winged insects or forms secondarily wingless)*		
Exopterygota *(young resemble adults but have externally developing wings)*		
Ephemeroptera	1,000	mayflies
Odonata	5,000	dragonflies, damselflies
Plecoptera	3,000	stoneflies
Grylloblattodea	12	wingless soil-living insects of North America
Orthoptera	20,000	crickets, grasshoppers, locusts, mantids, roaches
Phasmida	2,000	stick insects, leaf insects
Dermaptera	1,000	earwigs
Embioptera	150	web-spinners
Dictyoptera	5,000	cockroaches, praying mantises
Isoptera	2,000	termites
Zoraptera	16	tiny insects living in decaying plants
Psocoptera	1,600	booklice, barklice, psocids
Mallophaga	2,500	biting lice, mainly parasitic on birds
Anoplura	250	sucking lice, mainly parasitic on mammals
Hemiptera	55,000	true bugs, including aphids, shield- and bedbugs, froghoppers, pond skaters, water boatmen
Thysanoptera	5,000	thrips
Endopterygota *(young unlike adults, undergo sudden metamorphosis)*		
Neuroptera	4,500	lacewings, alder flies, snake flies, ant lions
Mecoptera	300	scorpion flies
Lepidoptera	165,000	butterflies, moths
Trichoptera	3,000	caddis flies
Diptera	70,000	true flies, including bluebottles, mosquitoes, leatherjackets, midges
Siphonaptera	1,400	fleas
Hymenoptera	100,000	bees, wasps, ants, sawflies
Coloeoptera	350,000	beetles, including weevils, ladybirds, glow-worms, woodworms, chafers

insectivore any animal whose diet is made up largely or exclusively of insects. In particular, the name is applied to mammals of the order Insectivora, which includes the shrews, hedgehogs, moles, and tenrecs.

insectivorous plant plant that can capture and digest live prey (normally insects), to obtain nitrogen compounds that are lacking in its usual marshy habitat. Some are passive traps, for example, the pitcher plants *Nepenthes* and *Sarracenia*. One pitcher-plant species has container-traps holding 1.6 l/3.5 pt of the liquid that 'digests' its food, mostly insects but occasionally even rodents. Others, for example, sundews *Drosera*, butterworts *Pinguicula*, and Venus flytraps *Dionaea muscipula*, have an active trapping mechanism. Insectivorous plants have adapted to grow in poor soil conditions where the number of microorganisms recycling nitrogen compounds is very much reduced. In these circumstances other plants cannot gain enough nitrates to grow. See also ◊leaf.

inselberg (German 'island mountain') or ***kopje*** prominent steep-sided hill of resistant solid rock, such as granite, rising out of a plain, usually in a tropical area. Its rounded appearance is caused by so-called onion-skin ◊weathering, in which the surface is eroded in successive layers.

The Sugar Loaf in Rio de Janeiro harbour in Brazil, and Ayers Rock in Northern Territory, Australia, are famous examples.

insemination, artificial see ◊artificial insemination.

instinct in ◊ethology, behaviour found in all equivalent members of a given species (for example, all the males, or all the females with young) that is presumed to be genetically determined.

Examples include a male robin's tendency to attack other male robins intruding on its territory and the tendency of many mammals to care for their offspring. Instincts from ◊reflexes in that they differ involve very much more complex actions, and learning often plays an important part in their development.

insectivorous plant The insect traps of North American pitcher plants are modified leaves. Insects are lured into the pitchers by sweet secretions and then tumble into the fluid at the base, where they drown and are slowly digested.

❛Intelligence is quickness to apprehend as distinct from ability, which is capacity to act wisely on the thing apprehended.❜

On INTELLIGENCE
Alfred North Whitehead *Dialogues* 15 Dec 1939

instrument landing system (ILS) landing aid for aircraft that uses ◊radio beacons on the ground and instruments on the flight deck. One beacon (localizer) sends out a vertical radio beam along the centre line of the runway. Another beacon (glide slope) transmits a beam in the plane at right angles to the localizer beam at the ideal approach-path angle. The pilot can tell from the instruments how to manoeuvre to attain the correct approach path.

insulator any poor ◊conductor of heat, sound, or electricity. Most substances lacking free (mobile) ◊electrons, such as non-metals, are electrical or thermal insulators. Usually, devices of glass or porcelain, called insulators, are used for insulating and supporting overhead wires.

insulin protein ◊hormone, produced by specialized cells in the islets of Langerhans in the pancreas, that regulates the metabolism (rate of activity) of glucose, fats, and proteins. Insulin was discovered by Canadian physician Frederick ◊Banting, who pioneered its use in treating ◊diabetes.

Normally, insulin is secreted in response to rising blood sugar levels (after a meal, for example), stimulating the body's cells to store the excess. Failure of this regulatory mechanism in diabetes mellitus requires treatment with insulin injections or capsules taken by mouth. Types vary from pig and beef insulins to synthetic and bioengineered ones. They may be combined with other substances to make them longer-or shorter-acting. Implanted, battery-powered insulin pumps deliver the hormone at a preset rate, to eliminate the unnatural rises and falls that result from conventional, subcutaneous (under the skin) delivery. Human insulin has now been produced from bacteria by ◊genetic engineering techniques, but may increase the chance of sudden, unpredictable ◊hypoglycaemia, or low blood sugar. In 1990 the Medical College of Ohio developed gelatin capsules and an aspirinlike drug which helps the insulin pass into the bloodstream.

insurance contract guaranteeing compensation to the payer of a premium against loss by fire, death, accident, and so on, which is known as assurance in the case of a fixed sum and insurance where the payment is proportionate to the loss.

intaglio design cut into the surface of gems or seals by etching or engraving; an ◊engraving technique.

integer any whole number. Integers may be positive or negative; 0 is an integer, and is often considered positive. Formally, integers are members of the set $Z = \{... -3, -2, -1, 0, 1, 2, 3, ...\}$. Fractions, such as ½ and 0.35, are known as non-integral numbers ('not integers').

integral calculus branch of mathematics concerned with finding volumes and areas and summing infinitesimally small quantities.

An example of a definite integral can be thought of as finding the area under a curve (as represented by an algebraic expression or function) between particular values of the function's variable. In practice, integral calculus provides scientists with a powerful tool for doing calculations that involve a continually varying quantity (such as determining the position at any given instant of a space rocket that is accelerating away from Earth). Its basic principles were discovered in the late 1660s independently by the German philosopher ◊Leibniz and the British scientist ◊Newton.

integrated circuit (IC), popularly called ***silicon chip***, a miniaturized electronic circuit produced on a single crystal, or chip, of a semiconducting material – usually silicon. It may contain many thousands of components and yet measure only 5 mm/0.2 in square and 1 mm/0.04 in thick. The IC is encapsulated within a plastic or ceramic case, and linked via gold wires to metal pins with which it is connected to a ◊printed circuit board and the other components that make up such electronic devices as computers and calculators.

Integrated Services Digital Network (ISDN) internationally developed telecommunications system for sending signals in ◊digital format along optical fibres and coaxial cable. It involves converting the 'local loop' – the link between the user's telephone and the digital telephone exchange – from an ◊analogue system into a digital system, thereby greatly increasing the amount of information that can be carried. The first large-scale use of ISDN began in Japan 1988.

intelligence in military and political affairs, information, often secretly or illegally obtained, about other countries. ***Counter-intelligence*** is information on the activities of hostile agents. Much intelligence is gained by technical means, such as satellites and the electronic interception of data.

The British intelligence services consist of M(ilitary) I(ntelligence) 6, the secret intelligence service, which operates mainly under Foreign Office control; the counter-intelligence service, M(ilitary) I(ntelligence) 5, which is responsible directly to the prime minister for internal security and has Scotland Yard's ◊Special Branch as its executive arm; and Government Communications Headquarters, which carries out electronic surveillance for the other two branches. The overall head of intelligence in the UK is the chair of the Joint Intelligence Committee.

US equivalents of MI6 include the Central Intelligence Agency (CIA) and the National Security Agency; the Federal Bureau of Investigation (FBI) is responsible for US counter-intelligence.

intelligence in psychology, a general concept that summarizes the abilities of an individual in reasoning and problem solving, particularly in novel situations. These consist of a wide range of verbal and nonverbal skills and therefore some psychologists dispute a unitary concept of intelligence.

intelligence test test that attempts to measure innate intellectual ability, rather than acquired ability.

It is now generally believed that a child's ability in an intelligence test can be affected by his or her environment, cultural background, and teaching. There is scepticism about the accuracy of intelligence tests, but they are still widely used as a diagnostic tool when children display learning difficulties.

Workers in this field have included Francis ◊Galton, Alfred Binet (1857–1911), Cyril Burt (1883–1971), and Hans ◊Eysenck. Binet devised the first intelligence test in 1905. The concept of intelligence quotient (IQ) was adopted by US psychologist Lewis Terman in 1915. The IQ is calculated according to the formula: IQ = MA/CA x 100 in which MA is 'mental age' (the age at which an average child is able to perform given tasks) and CA is 'chronological age', hence an average person has an IQ of 100.

intensity in physics, the power (or energy per second) per unit area carried by a form of radiation or wave motion. It is an indication of the concentration of energy present and, if measured at varying distances from the source, of the effect of distance on this. For example, the intensity of light is a measure of its brightness, and may be shown to diminish with distance from its source in accordance with the inverse square law (its intensity is inversely proportional to the square of the distance).

intensive agriculture farming system where large quantities of inputs, such as labour or fertilizers, are involved over a small area of land. ◊Market gardening is an example. Yields are often much higher than those obtained from ◊extensive agriculture.

interactive video (IV) computer-mediated system that enables the user to interact with and control information (including text, recorded speech, or moving images) stored on video disc. IV is most commonly used for training purposes, using analogue video discs, but has wider applications with digital video systems which are based on the CD-ROM format.

Inter-American Development Bank (IADB) bank founded 1959, at the instigation of the Organization of American States, to finance economic and social development, particularly in the less wealthy regions of the Americas. Its membership includes the states of Central and Southern America, the Caribbean, and the USA, as well as Austria, Belgium, Canada, Denmark, Finland, France, Germany, Israel, Italy, Japan, the Netherlands, Norway, Portugal, Spain, Sweden, Switzerland, and the UK. Its headquarters are in Washington DC.

interest in finance, a sum of money paid by a borrower to a lender in return for the loan, usually expressed as a percentage per annum. ***Simple interest*** is interest calculated as a straight percentage of the amount loaned or invested. In ***compound interest***, the interest earned over a period of time (for example, per annum) is added to the investment, so that at the end of the next period interest is paid on that total.

interface in computing, the point of contact between two programs or pieces of equipment. The term is most often used for the physical connection between the computer and a peripheral device, which is used to compensate for differences in such operating characteristics as speed, data coding, voltage, and power consumption.

interference in physics, the phenomenon of two or more wave motions interacting and combining to produce a resultant wave of larger or smaller amplitude (depending on whether the combining waves are in or out of ◊phase with each other).

Interference of white light (multiwavelength) results in spectral coloured fringes; for example, the iridescent colours of oil films seen on water or soap bubbles (demonstrated by ◊Newton's rings). Interference of sound waves of similar frequency produces the phenomenon of beats, often used by musicians when tuning an instrument. With monochromatic light (of a single wavelength), interference produces patterns of light and dark bands. This is the basis of ◊holography, for example. Interferometry can also be applied to radio waves, and is a powerful tool in modern astronomy.

interferometer in physics, a device that splits a beam of light into two parts, the parts being recombined after travelling different paths to form an interference pattern of light and dark bands. Interferometers are used in many branches of science and industry where accurate measurements of distances and angles are needed.

interferon naturally occurring cellular protein that makes up part of the body's defences against viral disease. Three types (alpha, beta, and gamma) are produced by infected cells and enter the bloodstream and uninfected cells, making them immune to virus attack.

Interferon was discovered 1957 by Scottish virologist Alick Isaacs. Interferons are cytokines, small molecules that carry signals from one cell to another. They can be divided into two main types: ***type I*** (alpha, beta, tau, and omega) interferons are more effective at bolstering cells' ability to resist infection; ***type II*** (gamma) interferon is more important to the normal functioning of the immune system. Alpha interferon may be used to treat some cancers; interferon beta 1b has been found useful in the treatment of ◊multiple sclerosis.

Intermediate Nuclear Forces Treaty agreement signed Dec 1987 between the USA and the USSR to eliminate all ground-based nuclear missiles in Europe that were capable of hitting only European targets (including European Russia). It reduced the countries' nuclear arsenals by some 2,000 (4% of the total). The treaty included provisions for each country to inspect the other's bases.

intermediate technology application of mechanics, electrical engineering, and other technologies, based on inventions and designs developed in scientifically sophisticated cultures, but utilizing materials, assembly, and maintenance methods found in technologically less advanced regions (known as the developing world).

Intermediate technologies aim to allow developing countries to benefit from new techniques and inventions of the industrialized world, without the burdens of costly maintenance and supply of fuels and spare parts that in the developing world would represent an enormous and probably uneconomic overhead.

intermezzo in music, a one-act comic opera, such as Pergolesi's *La Serva Padrona/The Maid as Mistress* 1732; also a short orchestral interlude played between the acts of an opera to denote the passage of time. By extension, an intermezzo can also be a short piece to be played between other more substantial works, such as Brahms' *Three Intermezzos for Piano* 1892.

intermolecular force or ***van der Waals' force*** force of attraction between molecules. Intermolecular forces are relatively weak; hence simple molecular compounds are gases, liquids, or low-melting-point solids.

windpump

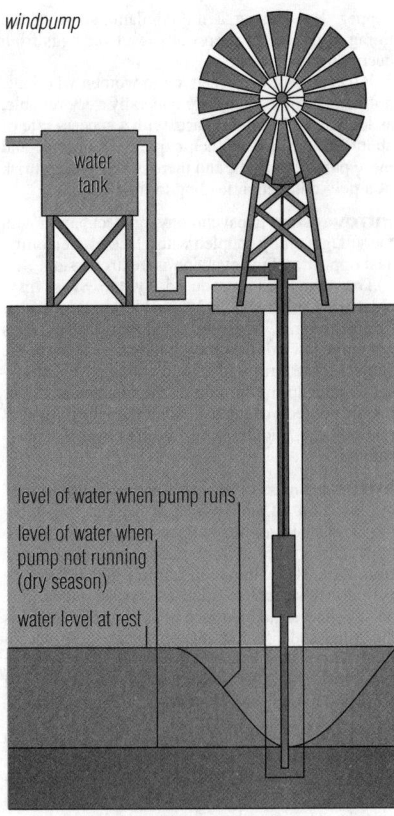

intermediate technology The simple windmill is an example of intermediate technology if it utilizes local materials and traditional design. In this way, there is no need for complex maintenance and repair, nor expensive spare parts.

internal-combustion engine heat engine in which fuel is burned inside the engine, contrasting with an external-combustion engine (such as the steam engine) in which fuel is burned in a separate unit. The ◊diesel engine and ◊petrol engine are both internal-combustion engines. Gas ◊turbines and ◊jet and ◊rocket engines are sometimes also considered to be internal-combustion engines because they burn their fuel inside their combustion chambers.

International, the coordinating body established by various labour and socialist organizations throughout the world, including:

First International or ***International Working Men's Association*** 1864–72, formed in London under Karl ◊Marx.

Second International 1889–1940, founded in Paris.

Third (Socialist) International or ***Comintern*** 1919–43, formed in Moscow by the Soviet leader Lenin, advocating from 1933 a popular front (communist, socialist, liberal) against the German dictator Hitler.

Fourth International or ***Trotskyist International*** 1938, somewhat indeterminate, anti-Stalinist.

Revived Socialist International 1951, formed in Frankfurt, Germany, a largely anticommunist association of social democrats.

International Atomic Energy Agency (IAEA), agency of the United Nations established in 1957 to advise and assist member countries in the development and peaceful application of nuclear power, and to guard against its misuse. It has its headquarters in Vienna, and is responsible for research centres in Austria and Monaco, and the International Centre for Theoretical Physics, Trieste, Italy, established in 1964. It conducts inspections of nuclear installations in countries suspected of developing nuclear weapons, for example Iraq and North Korea.

International Bank for Reconstruction and Development specialized agency of the United Nations. Its popular name is the ◊World Bank.

International Brigade international volunteer force on the Republican side in the Spanish ◊Civil War 1936–39.

International Court of Justice main judicial organ of the ◊United Nations, in The Hague, the Netherlands. It hears international law disputes as well as playing an advisory role to UN organs. It was set up by the UN charter 1945 and superseded the World Court. There are 15 judges, each from a different member state.

International Date Line (IDL) imaginary line that approximately follows the 180° line of longitude. The date is put forward a day when crossing the line going west, and back a day when going east. The IDL was chosen at the International Meridian Conference 1884.

International Development Department (IDD), UK official body (until 1997 the Overseas Development Administration) that deals with development assistance to overseas countries, including financial aid on concessionary terms and technical assistance, usually in the form of sending specialists to other countries and giving training in the UK.

International Gothic late Gothic style of painting and sculpture flourishing in Europe in the late 14th and 15th centuries. It is characterized by bright colours, a courtly elegance, and a naturalistic rendering of detail. Originally evolving in the court art of France and Burgundy, it spread to many parts of Europe, its leading exponents including the Italian Simone Martini (c. 1284–1344) and the Franco-Flemish ◊Limbourg brothers.

It had its origin in the illuminated manuscript, transferring to the panel picture the brilliant colour, the fine detail and rich sense of pattern, and the individual characterization of the painters of miniatures in manuscripts. The style was practised notably by the Franco-Flemish school of painter-illuminators, including the three Limbourg brothers, whose masterpiece was *Les Très Riches Heures du Duc de Berry*; Jean Malouel, who worked in Paris and Dijon; Henri Belle-chose, who followed Malouel in Dijon; and Melchoir Broederlam of Ypres, who became painter to Philip the Bold, Duke of Burgundy.

International Labour Organization (ILO) agency of the United Nations, established 1919, which formulates standards for labour and social conditions. Its headquarters are in Geneva. It was awarded the Nobel Peace Prize 1969.

international law body of rules generally accepted as governing the relations between countries, pioneered by Hugo ◊Grotius, especially in matters of human rights, territory, and war.

The scope of the law is now extended to space – for example, the 1967 treaty that (among other things) banned nuclear weapons from space.

International Monetary Fund (IMF) specialized agency of the United Nations, headquarters Washington DC, established under the 1944 ◊Bretton Woods agreement and operational since 1947. It seeks to promote international monetary cooperation and the growth of world trade, and to smooth multilateral payment arrangements among member states. IMF standby loans are available to members in balance-of-payments difficulties (the amount being governed by the member's quota), usually on the basis that the country must agree to take certain corrective measures.

The IMF also operates other drawing facilities, including several designed to provide preferential credit to developing countries with liquidity problems. Having previously operated in US dollars linked to gold, since 1972 the IMF has used the ◊special drawing right (SDR) as its standard unit of account, valued in terms of a weighted 'basket' of currencies. Since 1971, IMF rules have been progressively adapted to floating exchange rates.

International Organization for Standardization (ISO) international organization founded 1947 to standardize technical terms, specifications, units, and so on. Its headquarters are in Geneva.

International Society for Krishna Consciousness (ISKCON) or ***Gaudiya Vaisnavism*** Hindu sect based on the demonstration of intense love for Krishna (an incarnation of the god Vishnu), especially by chanting the mantra 'Hare Krishna'. Members wear distinctive yellow robes, and men often have their heads partly shaven. Their holy books are the Hindu scriptures and particularly the *Bhagavad-Gītā*, which they study daily.

The sect was introduced to the West by Swami Prabhupada (real name A C Bhaktivedanta, 1896–1977), a Sanskrit scholar from Calcutta; he established a group in New York 1965. Members believe that by chanting the mantra and meditating on it, they may achieve enlightenment and so remove themselves from the cycle of reincarnation. They are expected to live ascetic lives, avoiding meat, eggs, alcohol, tea, coffee, and other drugs; sexual relationships should only take place within marriage and solely for procreation.

In the UK, the centre of worship is Bhakti-Vedanta Manor in Letchmore Heath, Hertfordshire.

International Style or ***International Modern*** architectural style, an early and influential phase of the ◊Modern Movement, originating in Western Europe in the 1920s but finding its fullest expression in the 1930s, notably in the USA. It is characterized by a dominance of geometric, especially rectilinear, forms; emphasis on asymmetrical composition; large expanses of glazing; and white rendered walls. Examples are Walter ◊Gropius's Bauhaus building, Dessau, Germany, 1925–26; ◊Le Corbusier's Villa Savoye, Poissy, France, 1927–31; Alvar ◊Aalto's Viipuri Library, Finland (now in Russia), 1927–35; and ◊Mies van der Rohe's Barcelona Pavilion 1929.

International Union for the Conservation of Nature organization established by the ◊United Nations to promote the conservation of wildlife and habitats as part of the national policies of member states.

It has formulated guidelines and established research programmes (for example, International Biological Programme, IBP) and set up advisory bodies (such as Survival Commissions, SSC). In 1980, it launched the World Conservation Strategy to highlight particular problems, designating a small number of areas as World Heritage Sites to ensure their survival as unspoiled habitats (for example, Yosemite National Park in the USA, and the Simen Mountains in Ethiopia). It also compiles the Red Data List of Threatened Animals, classifying species according to their vulnerability to extinction.

Internet global computer network connecting governments, companies, universities, and many other networks and users. ◊Electronic mail, conferencing, and chat services are all supported across the network, as are the ability to access remote computers and send and retrieve files.

The technical underpinnings of the Internet were developed as a project funded by the Advanced Research Project Agency (ARPA) to research how to build a network that would withstand bomb damage. The Internet itself began 1984 with funding from the US National Science Foundation as a means to allow US universities to share the resources of five regional supercomputing centres. The number of users grew quickly, and in the early 1990s access became cheap enough for domestic users to have their own links on home personal computers. As the amount of information available via the Internet grew, indexing and search services such as Gopher, Archie, Veronica, and WAIS were created by Internet users to help both themselves and others. The newer ◊World-Wide Web allows seamless browsing across the Internet via ◊hypertext. *See illustration on following page.*

Internet Service Provider (ISP) in computing, any company that sells dial-up access to the Internet. Several types of company provide Internet access, including on-line information services such as ◊CompuServe and ◊America Online (AOL), electronic conferencing systems, and local bulletin board systems (BBSs).

internment detention of suspected criminals without trial. Foreign citizens are often interned during times of war or civil unrest.

Internment was introduced for the detention of people suspected of terrorist acts in Northern Ireland by the UK government 1971. It has now been discontinued.

interplanetary matter gas and dust thinly spread through the Solar System. The gas flows outwards from the Sun as the ◊solar wind.

Fine dust lies in the plane of the Solar System, scattering sunlight to cause the ◊zodiacal light. Swarms of dust shed by comets enter the Earth's atmosphere to cause ◊meteor showers.

Interpol (acronym for ***International Criminal Police Organization***) agency founded following the

Internet The Internet is accessed by users via a modem to the service provider's hub, which handles all connection requests. Once connected, the user can access a whole range of information from many different sources, including the World-Wide Web.

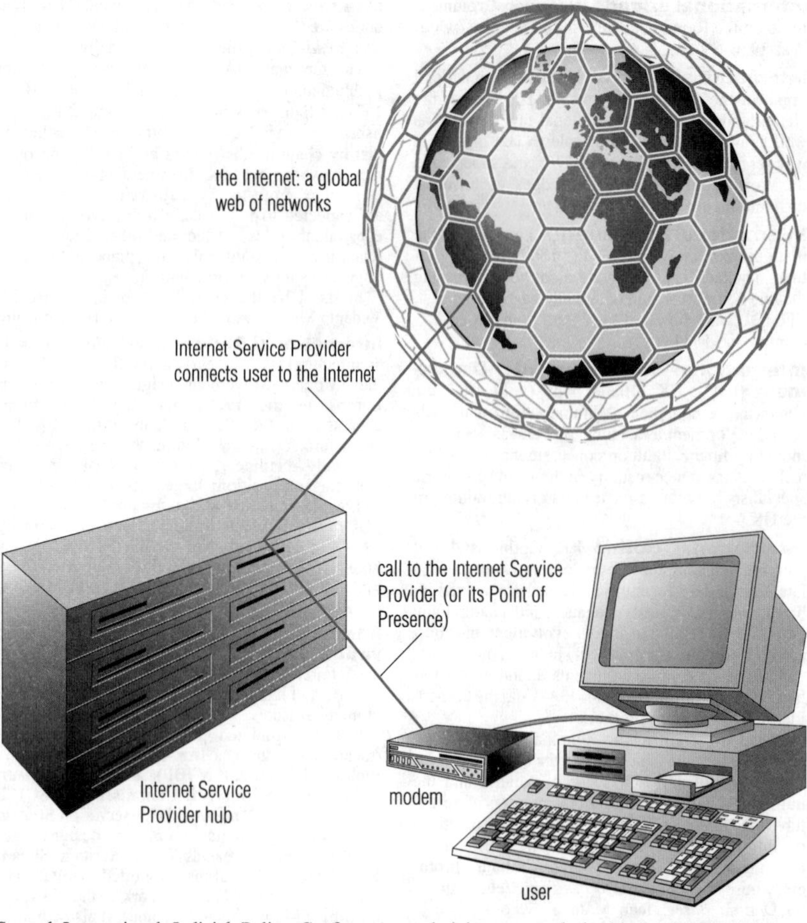

Second International Judicial Police Conference 1923 with its headquarters in Vienna, and reconstituted after World War II with its headquarters in Paris. It has an international criminal register, fingerprint file, and methods index.

intersex individual that is intermediate between a normal male and a normal female in its appearance (for example, a genetic male that lacks external genitalia and so resembles a female).

Intersexes are usually the result of an abnormal hormone balance during development (especially during ◊gestation) or of a failure of the ◊genes controlling sex determination. The term ◊hermaphrodite is sometimes used for intersexes, but should be confined to animals that normally have both male and female organs.

interval in music, the pitch difference between two notes, expressed in terms of the diatonic scale, for example a fifth, or as a harmonic ratio, 3:2.

intestacy absence of a will at a person's death. Special legal rules apply on intestacy for appointing administrators to deal with the deceased person's affairs, and for disposing of the deceased person's property in accordance with statutory provisions.

Intifada Palestinian women protest, holding stones, the main weapon of the Intifada, in the West Bank town of Bet Sachour. Strong anti-Israeli feeling among Palestinians in Israeli-occupied territories has repeatedly erupted into violence, with casualties and fatalities on both sides. *Corbis*

intestine in vertebrates, the digestive tract from the stomach outlet to the anus. The human small intestine is 6 m/20 ft long, 4 cm/1.5 in in diameter, and consists of the duodenum, jejunum, and ileum; the large intestine is 1.5 m/5 ft long, 6 cm/2.5 in in diameter, and includes the caecum, colon, and rectum. Both are muscular tubes comprising an inner lining that secretes alkaline digestive juice, a submucous coat containing fine blood vessels and nerves, a muscular coat, and a serous coat covering all, supported by a strong peritoneum, which carries the blood and lymph vessels, and the nerves. The contents are passed along slowly by ◊peristalsis (waves of involuntary muscular action). The term intestine is also applied to the lower digestive tract of invertebrates.

Intifada (Arabic 'resurgence' or 'throwing off') Palestinian uprising; also the title of the involved Liberation Army of Palestine, a loosely organized group of adult and teenage Palestinians active 1987–93 in attacks on armed Israeli troops in the occupied territories of Palestine. The 1993 peace accord between Israel and the Palestine Liberation Organization effectively liberated the occupied territories of Gaza and Jericho. However, extremist groups that had participated in the Intifada, notably the militant wing of the Hamas Islamic fundamentalist group, opposed the accord and continued a campaign of violence within Israel. Tensions around Jerusalem and the West Bank town of Hebron Oct 1996 threatened to provoke a renewal of the Intifada.

intranet in computing, the use of software and other technology developed for the Internet on internal company ◊networks. Many company networks use the same ◊protocols as the Internet, namely TCP/IP. Therefore the same technology that enables the World-Wide Web can be used on an internal network to build an organization-wide web of internal documents that is familiar, easy to use, and comparatively inexpensive.

intrauterine device (IUD) or ***coil***, a contraceptive device that is inserted into the womb (uterus). It is a tiny plastic object, sometimes containing copper. By causing a mild inflammation of the lining of the uterus it prevents fertilized eggs from becoming implanted.

IUDs are not usually given to women who have not had children. They are generally very reliable, as long as they stay in place, with a success rate of about 98%. Some women experience heavier and more painful periods, and there is a very slight risk of a pelvic infection leading to infertility.

introversion in psychology, preoccupation with the self, generally coupled with a lack of sociability. The opposite of introversion is ◊extroversion.

The term was introduced by the Swiss psychiatrist Carl Jung 1924 in his description of ◊schizophrenia, where he noted that 'interest does not move towards the object but recedes towards the subject'. The term is also used within psychoanalysis to refer to the turning of the instinctual drives towards objects of fantasy rather than the pursuit of real objects. Another term for this sense is fantasy cathexis.

intrusion mass of ◊igneous rock that has formed by 'injection' of molten rock, or magma, into existing cracks beneath the surface of the Earth, as distinct from a volcanic rock mass which has erupted from the surface. Intrusion features include vertical cylindrical structures such as stocks, pipes, and necks; sheet structures such as dykes that cut across the strata and sills that push between them; laccoliths, which are blisters that push up the overlying rock; and batholiths, which represent chambers of solidified magma and contain vast volumes of rock.

Inuit people inhabiting the Arctic coasts of North America, the eastern islands of the Canadian Arctic, and the ice-free coasts of Greenland. The total number of Inuit (1993 est) is 125,000 (the singular form is Inuk). There are three languages, all of the same family: Yupik, spoken in Siberia and SW Alaska; Aleut, spoken in SW Alaska; and Inupiaq spoken from N Alaska to Greenland. The traditional way of life was as semi-nomadic hunters of marine animals.

In 1989 the Canadian government agreed to transfer to the 17,000 Inuit of the E Arctic an area in Northwest Territories about half the size of France (see ◊Nunavut), including rights to hunt and fish; their right to levy royalties from the exploitation of mineral resources was restricted to a limited area. A cash payment was also agreed in compensation for the Inuit's renunciation of other areas where they formerly lived. Creation of the homeland was approved in a regional plebiscite 1992. A final land claims agreement, signed May 1993 on Baffin Island (proposed capital of Nunavut), gave the Inuit outright ownership of 353,610 sq km/136,493 sq mi of the land, and mineral rights to 36,257 sq km/13,995 sq mi.

An Inuit Circumpolar Conference was formed 1977 to promote Inuit interests throughout the Arctic. It was granted nongovernmental-organization status at the United Nations 1983.

Inverclyde local authority of Scotland created 1996 (*see United Kingdom map*).

Inverness town and administrative headquarters of Highland local authority (previously Highland Region, 1975–1996), Scotland, at the head of the Moray Firth, lying in a sheltered site at the mouth of the river Ness; population (1991) 41,200. It is a tourist centre with tweed, tanning, engineering, distilling, iron-founding, boat-building, and electronics industries.

invertebrate animal without a backbone. The invertebrates comprise over 95% of the million or so existing animal species and include sponges, coelenterates, flatworms, nematodes, annelid worms, arthropods, molluscs, echinoderms, and primitive aquatic chordates, such as sea squirts and lancelets.

investiture contest conflict between the papacy and the Holy Roman Empire 1075–1122, which centred on the right of lay rulers to appoint prelates (investiture).

It began with the decree of 1075 in which Pope Gregory VII forbade lay investiture and with Henry IV's excommunication the following year after he refused to accept the ruling. There was a lull in the conflict after Henry's death 1106, but in 1111, Henry V captured Paschal II (c.1050–1118), and forced him to concede that only lay rulers could

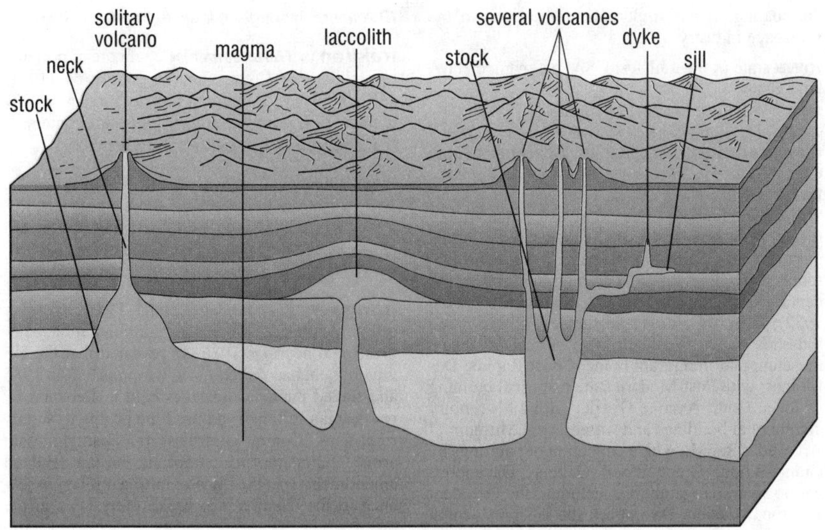

intrusion Igneous intrusions can be a variety of shapes and sizes. Laccoliths are domed circular shapes, and can be many miles across. Sills are intrusions that flow between rock layers. Pipes or necks connect the underlying magma chamber to surface volcanoes.

endow prelates with their temporalities (lands and other possessions). When this was overturned by the Lateran Council of 1112, the church split between propapal and pro-imperial factions, and fighting broke out in Germany and Italy. Settlement was reached 1122 at the Diet of Worms, when it was agreed that lay rulers could not appoint prelates but could continue to invest them with their temporalities.

invisible in economics, term describing a service on the ◊balance of payments account. Invisible exports is exports of services and invisible imports are imports of services.

in vitro fertilization (IVF; 'fertilization in glass') allowing eggs and sperm to unite in a laboratory to form embryos. The embryos (properly called pre-embryos in their two- to eight-celled state) are stored by cooling to the temperature of liquid air (cryopreservation) until they are implanted into the womb of the otherwise infertile mother (an extension of ◊artificial insemination). The first baby to be produced by this method was born 1978 in the UK. In cases where the Fallopian tubes are blocked, fertilization may be carried out by intra-vaginal culture, in which egg and sperm are incubated (in a plastic tube) in the mother's vagina, then transferred surgically into the uterus.

Recent extensions of the in vitro technique have included the birth of a baby from a frozen embryo (Australia 1984) and from a frozen egg (Australia 1986). Pioneers in the field have been the British doctors Robert Edwards (1925–) and Patrick Steptoe (1913–1988). As yet the success rate is relatively low; only 15–20% of in vitro fertilizations result in live births.

Io in astronomy, the third-largest moon of the planet Jupiter, 3,630 km/2,260 mi in diameter, orbiting in 1.77 days at a distance of 422,000 km/262,000 mi. It is the most volcanically active body in the Solar System, covered by hundreds of vents that erupt not lava but sulphur, giving Io an orange-coloured surface.

In July 1995 the Hubble Space Telescope revealed the appearance of a 320-km/200-mi yellow spot on the surface of Io, located on the volcano Ra Patera. Though clearly volcanic in origin, astronomers are unclear as to the exact cause of the new spot.

Using data gathered by the spacecraft *Galileo*, US astronomers concluded 1996 that Io has a large metallic core.

iodine (Greek *iodes* 'violet') greyish-black nonmetallic element, symbol I, atomic number 53, relative atomic mass 126.9044. It is a member of the ◊halogen group. Its crystals give off, when heated, a violet vapour with an irritating odour resembling that of chlorine. It only occurs in combination with other elements. Its salts are known as iodides, which are found in sea water. As a mineral nutrient it is vital to the proper functioning of the thyroid gland, where it occurs in trace amounts as part of the hormone thyroxine. Absence of iodine from the diet leads to ◊goitre. Iodine is used in photography, in medicine as an antiseptic, and in making dyes.

Its radioactive isotope ^{131}I (half-life of eight days) is a dangerous fission product from nuclear explosions and from the nuclear reactors in power plants, since, if ingested, it can be taken up by the thyroid and damage it. It was discovered 1811 by French chemist B Courtois (1777–1838).

iodoform (chemical name ***triiodomethane***) CHI_3, an antiseptic that crystallizes into yellow hexagonal plates. It is soluble in ether, alcohol, and chloroform, but not in water.

ion atom, or group of atoms, that is either positively charged (◊cation) or negatively charged (◊anion), as a result of the loss or gain of electrons during chemical reactions or exposure to certain forms of radiation.

Iona island in the Inner Hebrides; area 850 hectares/2,100 acres. A centre of early Christianity, it is the site of a monastery founded 563 by St ◊Columba. It later became a burial ground for Irish, Scottish, and Norwegian kings. It has a 13th-century abbey.

ion engine rocket engine that uses ◊ions (charged particles) rather than hot gas for propulsion. Ion engines have been successfully tested in space, where they will eventually be used for gradual rather than sudden velocity changes. In an ion engine, atoms of mercury, for example, are ionized (given an electric charge by an electric field) and then accelerated at high speed by a more powerful electric field.

Ionesco Eugène 1912–1994. Romanian-born French dramatist. He was a leading exponent of the Theatre of the ◊Absurd. Most of his plays are in one act and concern the futility of language as a means of communication. These include *La Cantatrice chauve/The Bald Prima Donna* 1950 and *La Leçon/The Lesson* 1951. Later full-length plays include *Le Rhinocéros* 1958 and *Le Roi se meurt/Exit the King* 1961.

The comic word-play of *La Cantatrice chauve* was inspired by the artificial sentences of a teach-yourself English book, and parodies both everyday conversation and the theatre. It has played in Paris virtually without a break since its first performance 1950.

ion exchange process whereby an ion in one compound is replaced by a different ion, of the same charge, from another compound. It is the basis of a type of ◊chromatography in which the components of a mixture of ions in solution are separated according to the ease with which they will replace the ions on the polymer matrix through which they flow. The exchange of positively charged ions is called cation exchange; that of negatively charged ions is called anion exchange.

Ion-exchange is used in commercial water softeners to exchange the dissolved ions responsible for the water's hardness with others that do not have this effect. For example, when hard water is passed over an ion-exchange resin, the dissolved calcium and magnesium ions are replaced by either sodium or hydrogen ions, so the hardness is removed.

Ionia in Classical times the E coast of the Aegean Sea and the offshore islands, settled about 1000 BC by the Ionians; it included the cities of Ephesus, Miletus, and later Smyrna, and the islands of Chios and Samos.

Ionian member of a Hellenic people from beyond the Black Sea who crossed the Balkans around 1980 BC and invaded Asia Minor. Driven back by the ◊Hittites, they settled all over mainland Greece, later being supplanted by the Achaeans.

Ionian Islands (Greek ***Ionioi Nisoi***) island group off the west coast of Greece; area 860 sq km/332 sq mi; population (1991) 191,000. A British protectorate from 1815 until their cession to Greece 1864, they include Cephalonia (Greek *Kefallínia*); Corfu (*Kérkyra*), a Venetian possession 1386–1797; Cythera (*Kithira*); Ithaca (*Itháki*), the traditional home of ◊Odysseus; Leukas (*Levkás*); Paxos (*Paxoí*); and Zante (*Zákynthos*).

Ionian Sea part of the Mediterranean Sea that lies between Italy and Greece, to the S of the Adriatic Sea, and containing the Ionian Islands.

Ionic in Classical architecture, one of the five types of column; see ◊order. *See illustration on following page.*

ionic bond or ***electrovalent bond*** bond produced when atoms of one element donate electrons to

Ionesco The French dramatist Eugène Ionesco. His work, along with that of other writers such as Jean Genet, Harold Pinter, and Samuel Beckett, is known as the Theatre of the Absurd, in which human existence is seen as meaningless and communication breaks down into irrational speech or silence. *Corbis*

Ionic The capital of an elegant Ionic column at the Erectheum, Athens, built 421–406 BC. This temple is named after Erectheus, a mythical king of Athens. The Ionic column is named after Ionia in Asia Minor, where it is said to have originated and was initially used more than in mainland Greece. In the 5th century BC it was taken up in Athens, its delicacy being found particularly appropriate for smaller temples such as the Erectheum. *Corbis*

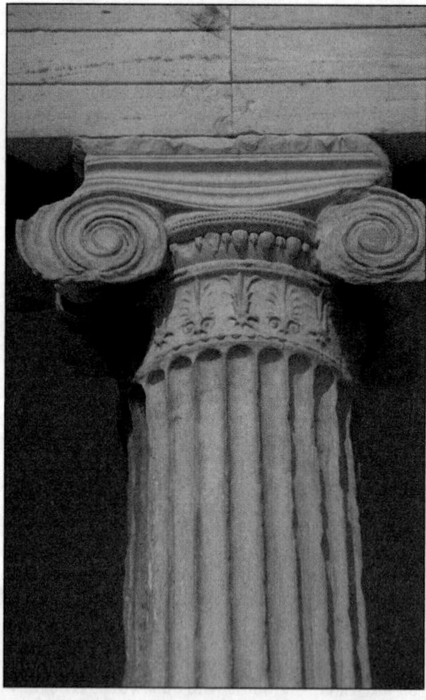

atoms of another element, forming positively and negatively charged ◊ions respectively. The attraction between the oppositely charged ions constitutes the bond. Sodium chloride (Na^+Cl^-) is a typical ionic compound.

Each ion has the electronic structure of an inert gas (see ◊noble gas structure). The maximum number of electrons that can be gained is usually two.

ionic compound substance composed of oppositely charged ions. All salts, most bases, and some acids are examples of ionic compounds. They possess the following general properties: they are crystalline solids with a high melting point; are soluble in water and insoluble in organic solvents; and always conduct electricity when molten or in aqueous solution. A typical ionic compound is sodium chloride (Na^+Cl^-).

ionization process of ion formation. It can be achieved in two ways. The first way is by the loss or gain of electrons by atoms to form positive or negative ions.

$$Na - e^- \rightarrow Na^+$$
$$\tfrac{1}{2}Cl_2 + e^- \rightarrow Cl^-$$

In the second mechanism, ions are formed when a covalent bond breaks, as when hydrogen chloride gas is dissolved in water. One portion of the molecule retains both electrons, forming a negative ion, and the other portion becomes positively charged. This bond-fission process is sometimes called disassociation.

$$HCl_{(g)} + aq \rightleftharpoons H^+_{(aq)} + Cl^-_{(aq)}$$

ionization chamber device for measuring ionizing radiation (radiation that knocks electrons from atoms during its passage, thereby leaving ions in its path). The radiation ionizes the gas in the chamber and the ions formed are collected and measured as an electric charge. Ionization chambers are used for determining the intensity of X-rays or the disintegration rate of radioactive materials.

ionization potential measure of the energy required to remove an ◊electron from an ◊atom. Elements with a low ionization potential readily lose electrons to form ◊cations.

ionosphere ionized layer of Earth's outer ◊atmosphere (60–1,000 km/38–620 mi) that contains sufficient free electrons to modify the way in which radio waves are propagated, for instance by reflecting them back to Earth. The ionosphere is thought to be produced by absorption of the Sun's ultraviolet radiation.

ion plating method of applying corrosion-resistant metal coatings. The article is placed in argon gas, together with some coating metal, which vaporizes on heating and becomes ionized (acquires charged atoms) as it diffuses through the gas to form the coating. It has important applications in the aerospace industry.

"I never knew what desert was till I came here; it is a very wonderful thing to see; and suddenly in the middle of it all, out of nothing, out of a little cold water, springs up a garden. Such a garden!"

On IRAN
Gertrude Bell, letter to Horace Marshall
18 June 1892

Iowa state of the midwest USA; nicknamed Hawkeye State
area 145,800 sq km/56,279 sq mi
capital Des Moines
towns and cities Cedar Rapids, Davenport, Sioux City
features Mississippi River; prairies; Iowa Lakes; 90% of land farmed; Effigy Mounds national monument, with prehistoric Native American burial ground; the Amana colonies, seven villages founded by German-Swiss immigrants in the 19th century as a utopian religious community (ended 1932); Herbert Hoover birthplace, library, and museum near West Branch; Czech Village, museum, and immigrant home, Cedar Rapids; Des Moines, with Post-Modern state historical building of Iowa, Court Avenue District with 19th-century commercial buildings and warehouses; Museum of Art, Cedar Rapids, with a collection of paintings by Grant Wood; Grant Wood Gallery, Davenport; casino riverboat gambling, including the President Riverboat Casino, Davenport; the US presidential race starts at Des Moines with the Iowa Caucuses
industries cereals, soya beans, pigs and cattle, chemicals, farm machinery, electrical goods, hardwood lumber, minerals
population (1991) 2,795,000
famous people 'Bix' Beiderbecke, Buffalo Bill, Herbert Hoover, Glenn Miller, Lillian Russell, Grant Wood
history part of the ◊Louisiana Purchase 1803, Iowa remains an area of small farms. It became a state 1846.

Iowa

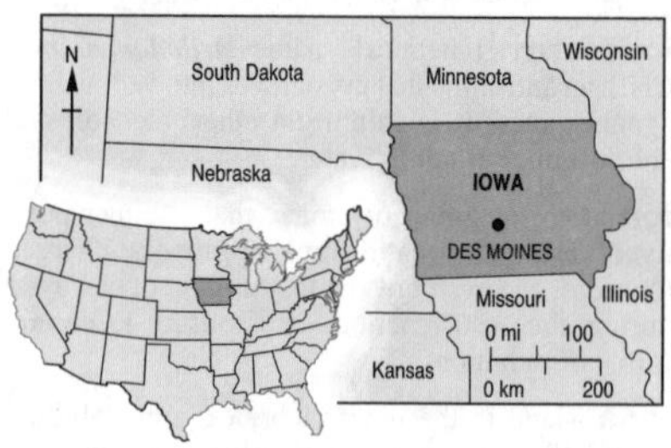

ipecacuanha or *ipecac* South American plant *Psychotria ipecacuanha* of the madder family Rubiaceae, the dried roots of which are used as an emetic and in treating amoebic dysentery.

Iphigenia in Greek mythology, a daughter of Agamemnon and Clytemnestra. She was sacrificed by her father at Aulis to secure favourable winds for the Greek fleet in the expedition against Troy, on instructions from the prophet Calchas. According to some accounts, she was saved by the goddess ◊Artemis, and made her priestess.

Ipoh capital of Perak state, Peninsular Malaysia; population (1991) 383,000. The economy is based on tin mining.

Ipswich river port on the Orwell estuary, administrative headquarters of Suffolk, England; population (1991) 117,000. Industries include engineering, printing, brewing, flour-milling, and the manufacture of textiles, plastics, electrical goods, fertilizers, and tobacco; British Telecom laboratories are here. Ipswich was an important wool port in the 16th century. It was the birthplace of Cardinal Wolsey and home of the painter Thomas Gainsborough.

IQ (abbreviation for ***intelligence quotient***) the ratio between a subject's 'mental' and chronological ages, multiplied by 100. A score of 100 ± 10 in an ◊intelligence test is considered average.

Iqbāl Muhammad 1876–1938. Islamic poet and thinker. His literary works, in Urdu and Persian, were mostly verse in the classical style, suitable for public recitation. He sought through his writings to arouse Muslims to take their place in the modern world.

His most celebrated work, the Persian *Asrā-e khūdī/Secrets of the Self* 1915, put forward a theory of the self that was opposite to the traditional abnegation found in Islam. He was an influence on the movement that led to the creation of Pakistan.

IRA abbreviation for ◊***Irish Republican Army***.

Iráklion or ***Heraklion*** chief commercial port and capital city of Crete, Greece; population (1991) 117,200. There is a ferry link to Piraeus on the mainland. The archaeological museum contains a fine collection of antiquities from the island.

Iran country in SW Asia, bounded N by Armenia, Azerbaijan, the Caspian Sea, and Turkmenistan; E by Afghanistan and Pakistan; S and SW by the Gulf of Oman and the Persian Gulf; W by Iraq; and NW by Turkey. *See country box opposite.*

Irangate US political scandal 1987 involving senior members of the Reagan administration. Congressional hearings 1986–87 revealed that the US government had secretly sold weapons to Iran 1985 and traded them for hostages held in Lebanon by pro-Iranian militias, and used the profits to supply right-wing Contra guerrillas in Nicaragua with arms. The attempt to get around the law (Boland amendment) specifically prohibiting military assistance to the Contras also broke other laws in the process.

Arms, including Hawk missiles, were sold to Iran via Israel violating the law prohibiting the sale of US weapons for resale to a third country listed as a 'terrorist nation', as well as the law requiring sales above $14 million to be reported to Congress. The negotiator in the field was Lt Col Oliver North, a military aide to the National Security Council. North and his associates were also channelling donations to the Contras from individuals and from other countries, including $2 million from Taiwan, $10 million from the sultan of Brunei, and $32 million from Saudi Arabia. Reagan persistently claimed to have no recall of events, and some evidence was withheld on grounds of 'national security'. North was tried and convicted May 1989 on charges of obstructing Congress and unlawfully destroying government documents. National Security Adviser, Poindexter, was found guilty on all counts 1990. In Dec 1993 the independent prosecutor Lawrence Walsh published his final report. It asserted that Reagan and Bush were fully aware of attempts to free US hostages in Lebanon 1985–86 by means of unsanctioned arms sales to Iran.

Iranian language the main language of Iran, more commonly known as Persian or ◊Farsi.

Iran–Iraq War war between Iran and Iraq 1980–88, claimed by the former to have begun with the Iraqi offensive 21 Sept 1980, and by the latter with the Iranian shelling of border posts 4 Sept 1980. Occasioned by a boundary dispute over the ◊Shatt-al-Arab waterway, it fundamentally arose because of Saddam Hussein's fear of a weakening of his absolute power base in Iraq by Iran's encouragement of the Shi'ite majority in Iraq to rise against the Sunni government. An estimated 1 million people died in the war.

The war's course was marked by offensive and counter-offensive, interspersed with extended periods of stalemate. Chemical weapons were used,

IRAN

Islamic Republic of (formerly *Persia*)

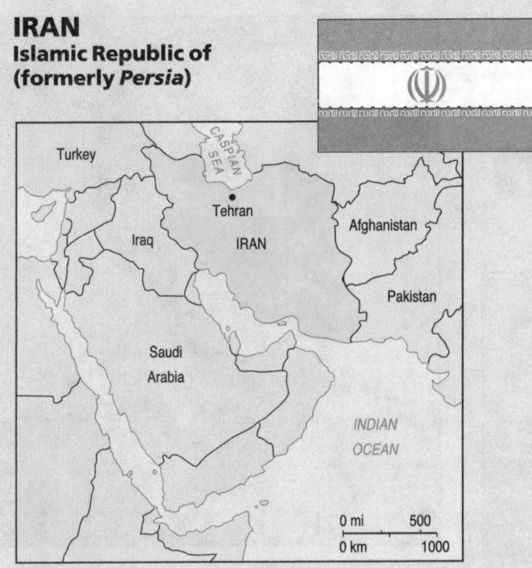

national name *Jomhori-e-Islami-e-Irân*
area 1,648,000 sq km/636,128 sq mi
capital Tehran
major towns/cities Isfahan, Mashhad, Tabriz, Shiraz, Ahvaz, Bakhtaran, Qom
major ports Abadan
physical features plateau surrounded by mountains, including Elburz and Zagros; Lake Rezayeh; Dasht-Ekavir Desert; occupies islands of Abu Musa, Greater Tunb and Lesser Tunb in the Gulf
Leader of the Islamic Revolution Seyed Ali Khamenei from 1989
head of state and government Seyyed Mohammad Khatami from 1997
political system authoritarian Islamic republic
administrative divisions 24 provinces, 472 counties, and 499 municipalities
political parties none officially recognized
population 67,283,000 (1995 est)
population growth rate 2.7% (1990–95); 2.5% (2000–05)
ethnic distribution about 63% of Persian origin, 18% Turkic, 13% other Iranian, 3% Kurdish, and 3% Arabic
life expectancy 67 (men), 68 (women)
literacy rate men 65%, women 43%
languages Farsi (official), Kurdish, Turkish, Arabic, English, French
religions Shi'ite Muslim (official) 94%, Sunni Muslim, Zoroastrian, Christian, Jewish, and Baha'i
currency rial
GDP (US $) 69.8 billion (1994 est)
growth rate −1.0% (1994)
exports carpets, cotton textiles, metalwork, leather goods, oil, petrochemicals, fruit

HISTORY
***c.* 2000 BC** Migration from southern Russia of Aryans, from whom the Persians claim descent.
612 BC The Medes, a people from NW Iran, destroyed the Iraq-based Assyrian Empire to the W and established their own empire which extended into central Anatolia (Turkey-in-Asia).
550 BC Cyrus the Great overthrew the Medes Empire and founded the First Persian Empire, the Achaemenid, conquering much of Asia Minor, including Babylonia (Palestine and Syria) in 539 BC. Expansion continued, into Afghanistan, under Darius I, who ruled 521–486 BC.
499–449 BC The Persian Wars with Greece ended Persian domination of the ancient world.
330 BC Collapse of Achaemenid Empire following defeat by Alexander the Great of Macedon.
AD 224 Sassanian Persian Empire founded by Ardashir, with its capital at Ctesiphon, in the NE.
637 Sassanian Empire destroyed by Muslim Arabs at battle of Qadisiya; Islam replaced Zoroastrianism.
750–1258 Dominated by the Persianized Abbasid dynasty, who reigned as caliphs (Islamic civil and religious leaders), with a capital in Baghdad (Iraq).
1380s Conquered by the Mongol leader, Tamerlane.
1501 Emergence of Safavids; the arts and architecture flourished, particularly under Abbas I, 'the Great', who ruled 1588–1629.
1736 The Safavids were deposed by the warrior Nadir Shah Afshar, who ruled until 1747.
1790 Rise of the Qajars, who transferred the capital from Isfahan in central Iran to Tehran, further N.
19th C Increasing influence in the N of Tsarist Russia, who took Georgia and much of Armenia 1801–28 and, in the S and E, Britain, with whom Iran fought 1856–57 over claims to Herat (W Afghanistan).
1906 Parliamentary constitution adopted after a brief revolution.
1925 Weak and corrupt Qajar Dynasty overthrown, with some British official help, in a coup by Col Reza Khan, a nationalist Iranian Cossack military officer, who was crowned shah ('king of kings'), with the title Reza Shah Pahlavi.
1920s onwards Economic modernization, Westernization, and secularization programme launched, which proved unpoular with traditionalist elements.
1935 Name changed from Persia to Iran.
1941 Due to his pro-German sentiments, Pahlavi Shah was forced to abdicate during World War II by Allied occupation forces and was succeeded by his son, Mohammad Reza Pahlavi, who continued the modernization programme.
1946 British, US, and Soviet occupation forces left Iran.
1951 Oilfields nationalized by radical Prime Minister Muhammad Mossadeq as anti-British and US sentiment increased.
1953 Mossadeq deposed, the nationalization plan changed, and the US-backed shah, Muhammad Reza Shah Pahlavi, took full control of the government.
1963 Hundreds of protesters, who demanded the release of the arrested fundamentalist Shi'ite Muslim leader, Ayatollah Ruhollah Khomeini, were killed by troops.
1970s Rapid economic expansion, as world oil prices spiralled.
1975 The shah introduced single-party system.
1977 Mysterious death in Najaf of Mustafa, the eldest son of the exiled Ayatollah Ruhollah Khomeini, sparked demonstrations by theology students, which were suppressed with the loss of six lives.
1978 Opposition to the shah organized from France by Ayatollah Ruhollah Khomeini, who demanded a return to the principles of Islam. Hundreds of demonstrators were killed by troops in Jaleh Square, Tehran.
1979 Amid mounting demonstrations by students and clerics, the shah left the country; Khomeini returned to create a non-party theocratic Islamic state. Revolutionaries seized 66 US hostages at embassy in Tehran; US economic boycott.
1980 Iraq invaded Iran, provoking a bitter war; death of exiled shah.
1981 US hostages released.
1985–87 Fighting intensified in Iran–Iraq War, with heavy loss of life.
1988 Cease-fire in the war; talks with Iraq began.
1989 Khomeini issued a fatwa (public order) for the death of British writer Salman Rushdie for blasphemy against Islam. On Khomeini's death, Ayatollah Ali Khamenei was elected interim Leader of the Revolution; the pragmatic speaker of Iranian parliament Hashemi Rafsanjani was elected president.
1990 Generous peace terms with Iraq accepted to close the Iran–Iraq war.
1991 Nearly one million Kurds arrived from NW Iraq, fleeing persecution by Saddam Hussein after the Gulf War between Iraq and UN forces.
1993 President Rafsanjani re-elected; free-market economic reforms introduced.
1996 Rafsanjani supporters won assembly elections.
1997 Moderate politician Seyyed Mohammad Khatami elected president.

SEE ALSO Iran-Iraq War; Islam; Khomeini, Ayatollah; Kurd; Persia, ancient

cities and the important oil installations of the area were the target for bombing raids and rocket attacks, and international shipping came under fire in the Persian Gulf (including in 1987 the US frigate *Stark*, which was attacked by the Iraqi airforce). Among Arab states, Iran was supported by Libya and Syria, the remainder supporting Iraq. Iran also benefited from secret US arms shipments, the disclosure of which in 1986 led to considerable scandal in the USA, ◊Irangate. The intervention of the USA 1987, ostensibly to keep the sea lanes open, but seen by Iran as support for Iraq, heightened, rather than reduced, tension in the Gulf, and United Nations attempts to obtain a cease-fire failed. The war ended in Aug 1988 after cease-fire talks in Geneva.

Iraq country in SW Asia, bounded N by Turkey, E by Iran, SE by the Persian Gulf and Kuwait, S by Saudi Arabia, and W by Jordan and Syria. *See country box on p. 552.*

Ireland one of the British Isles, lying to the west of Great Britain, from which it is separated by the Irish Sea. It comprises the provinces of Ulster, Leinster, Munster, and Connacht, and is divided into the Republic of ◊Ireland (which occupies the south, centre, and northwest of the island) and Northern ◊Ireland (which occupies the northeast corner and forms part of the United Kingdom).

The centre of Ireland is a lowland, about 60–120 m/200–400 ft above sea level; hills are mainly around the coasts, although there are a few peaks over 1,000 m/3,000 ft high, the highest being Carrantuohill ('the inverted reaping hook'), 1,040 m/3,415 ft, in Macgillicuddy's Reeks, County Kerry. The entire western coastline is an intricate alternation of bays and estuaries. Several of the rivers flow in sluggish courses through the central lowland and then cut through fjordlike valleys to the sea. The ◊Shannon in particular falls 30 m/100 ft in its last 26 km/16 mi above Limerick, and is used to produce hydroelectric power.

The lowland bogs that cover parts of central Ireland are intermingled with fertile limestone country where dairy farming is the chief occupation. The bogs are an important source of fuel in the form of ◊peat, Ireland being poorly supplied with coal.

The climate is mild, moist, and changeable. The annual rainfall on the lowlands varies from 76 cm/30 in in the east to 203 cm/80 in in some western districts, but much higher falls are recorded in the hills.

Ireland: history in prehistoric times Ireland underwent a number of invasions from Europe, the most important of which was that of the Gaels in the 3rd century BC. Gaelic Ireland was divided into kingdoms, nominally subject to an *Ardri* or High King; the chiefs were elected under the tribal or Brehon law, and were usually at war with one another. Ireland was known to the Romans as Hibernia, but no invasion was ever attempted. Christianity was introduced by St ◊Patrick about 432, and during the 5th and 6th centuries Ireland became the home of a civilization which sent out missionaries to Britain and Europe. From about 800 the Danes began to raid Ireland, and later founded Dublin and other coastal towns, until they were defeated by High King Brian Boru at Clontarf 1014. Anglo-Norman adventurers invaded Ireland 1167, but by the end of the medieval period English rule was still confined to the Pale, the territory around Dublin. The Tudors adopted a policy of conquest, confiscation of Irish land, and plantation by English settlers, and further imposed the ◊Reformation and English law on Ireland. The most important of the plantations was that of Ulster, carried out under James I 1610. In 1641 the Irish took advantage of the developing struggle in England between king and Parliament to begin a revolt which was crushed by Oliver ◊Cromwell 1649, the estates of all 'rebels' being confiscated. Another revolt 1689–91 was also defeated, and the Roman Catholic majority held down by penal laws. In 1739–41 a famine killed one-third of the population of 1.5 million.

The subordination of the Irish parliament to that of England, and of Irish economic interests to English, led to the rise of a Protestant patriot party, which in 1782 forced the British government to remove many commercial restrictions and grant the Irish parliament its independence. This did not satisfy the population, who in 1798, influenced by French revolutionary ideas, rose in rebellion, but were again defeated; and in 1800 William ◊Pitt induced the Irish parliament to vote itself out of existence by the Act of ◊Union, effective 1 Jan 1801, which brought Ireland under the aegis of the British crown. During another famine 1846–51, 1.5 million people emigrated, mostly to the USA.

By the 1880s there was a strong movement for home rule for Ireland; Gladstone supported it but was defeated by the British Parliament. By 1914,

cont. on p. 552

Ireland and the Home Rule Campaign

Irish politician, member of Parliament, and president of the Land League Charles Stewart Parnell, who made Home Rule for Ireland a live issue. In spite of his great ability, his relationship with Katharine O'Shea (whom he later married) led to his political downfall. *Michael Nicholson*

Irish peasants being evicted from their cottage at the height of the potato famine. The British government offered minimal relief to the starving, not wishing to interfere in the 'operation of natural causes' *Image Select (UK) Ltd*

Ireland in the 19th century was beset by political, economic, and religious discontents. The 1801 Act of Union between Great Britain and Ireland failed to incorporate Ireland into the British political system. Despite the achievement of Catholic emancipation in 1829, Catholics remained economically disadvantaged. Ireland had not industrialized (except in the north-east around Belfast); its land system was seen as inefficient and unjust; and after the Great Famine of 1845–49 its population went into long-term decline.

Such circumstances encouraged the formation of nationalist movements, mainly supported by Catholics. Some movements, such as the Irish Republican Brotherhood (IRB) founded in 1858, sought self-government by the use of force. Others sought limited self-government through peaceful agitation; the most influential of these was the Home Rule party.

Home Rule and the rise of Parnell

In 1868 Liberal prime minister William Gladstone, determined to 'pacify Ireland', disestablished the (Protestant) Church of Ireland and gave certain rights to tenant farmers, but this failed to meet Irish expectations. In 1870 the Home Rule League, which campaigned for a devolved Irish parliament, was founded by the Protestant Isaac Butt. The Home Rule party won 61 of 103 seats in the 1874 general election, but found itself isolated in the Westminster Parliament. From 1877 Butt was challenged by a group of MPs who systematically obstructed British legislation in protest at the neglect of Irish affairs. The most prominent of these was the Protestant landowner Charles Stewart Parnell. By 1880 he had taken the leadership of the Irish party and become president of a new tenants' rights association, the Land League.

In some places land agitation was accompanied by violence. Gladstone responded with new concessions in the 1881 Land Act, but suppressed the Land League and imprisoned its leaders, including Parnell. Parnell was released on the understanding that he would help to pacify Ireland. The Chief Secretary for Ireland resigned in protest at this 'Kilmainham Treaty', and his successor, Lord Frederick Cavendish, was assassinated in Phoenix Park by a fringe nationalist group, the Invincibles. The assassination temporarily dashed Parnell's hopes of further cooperation with Gladstone on Home Rule. However, in the 1885 election the Irish Party won 86 seats, giving them the balance of power between Liberals and Conservatives.

Gladstone, who had become sympathetic to Home Rule, now endorsed it. He took office with Irish support in 1886 and introduced a Home Rule Bill, but it was defeated by the Conservatives and a defecting group of Liberal Unionists. At the subsequent election the Conservatives and Liberal Unionists won a comfortable majority.

The fall of Parnell and the eclipse of Home Rule

In 1890 Parnell's political aspirations were shattered when his affair with Mrs O'Shea became public knowledge. Catholic Ireland and many of Gladstone's English Protestant supporters were scandalized. Gladstone announced that he would resign if Parnell remained as Irish Party leader. A majority of the Irish Party voted to depose Parnell. Parnell refused to accept this and the Home Rule movement split into Parnellite and anti-Parnellite factions. Parnell died, worn out, in October 1891.

Gladstone returned to power in 1892 and passed the second Home Rule Bill through the House of Commons, but it was thrown out by the House of Lords. The Unionists returned to power in 1895. The Irish Party reunited under John Redmond in 1900, but was still weakened by

Eamon de Valera addressing crowds in 1922. De Valera's ideal was a united Ireland, and he refused to accept its partition into north and south, though as prime minister of Eire he later rejected Winston Churchill's offer of a united Ireland in exchange for Irish participation in World War II. *Corbis*

On the morning of Easter Monday, 1916 **a group of about 150 Irish nationalists took over the General Post Office in Sackville Street, Dublin, and declared Ireland a republic. The rebels were driven out when the building caught fire and received little public sympathy until the British began executing the leaders of the rising.** *Image Select (UK) Ltd*

personal rivalries. In 1906 the Liberals returned to power, but made only limited concessions to Nationalists.

The Parnell split encouraged interest in new forms of nationalism. In 1893 the Gaelic League, aimed at reviving the Irish language, was founded. More significantly, from around 1900, separatism revived. In 1905 Arthur Griffith founded Sinn Féin, which advocated a fully independent Irish Parliament with the British monarch as head of state, as a compromise between Home Rule and separatism. Some Sinn Féiners advocated a fully independent republic.

The Third Home Rule Bill and the Ulster Crisis

The 1910 new elections gave Redmond the balance of power. In 1912, after constitutional changes had curbed the power of the House of Lords, Asquith's Liberal government introduced a third Home Rule Bill, scheduled to come into force by 1914. Ulster Unionists threatened to resist it by force, and from 1912 organized a private army, the Ulster Volunteer Force (UVF). Negotiations took place to discuss the option of the Protestant north-east seceding from a future Irish state, but broke down over the extent of the area be excluded.

In 1913, nationalists set up the Irish Volunteers as a counterweight to the UVF. Sectarian tensions mounted, fed on the nationalist side by a perception that the government was lukewarm on Home Rule. Civil war in Ireland seemed inevitable.

War and revolution

When World War I broke out Redmond pledged Irish support for the British war effort in return for the passage of Home Rule into law, suspended for the duration of the war. This split the Irish Volunteers; the majority, calling themselves 'National Volunteers', went with Redmond, leaving a minority of 'Irish Volunteers' who argued that Britain rather than Germany was the main threat to Irish liberties.

At Easter 1916 a section of the Irish Volunteers and the left-wing Citizen Army staged a rebellion in Dublin. The suppression of this 'Easter Rising' and the execution of 16 of its leaders led to a reaction in favour of separatism. From 1917 the Irish Party lost support to a reorganized Sinn Féin under Eamon de Valera, a suvivor of the 1916 rising. In the December 1918 general election the Home Rule party was virtually wiped out, taking 6 seats to Sinn Féin's 73 and the Unionists' 26.

The Sinn Féin deputies set up their own parliament, Dail Eireann. The Volunteers, now calling themselves the 'Irish Republican Army' (IRA), intimidated government sympathizers and launched guerrilla attacks on crown forces and government agents. The government responded with indiscriminate repression often carried out by militarized police recruits from Britain (the 'Black-and-Tans').

The most prominent IRA leader was the dynamic IRB president and minister for finance, Michael Collins. Unlike de Valera, Collins accepted the compromise that the Anglo-Irish Treaty offered, and signed the treaty that made Ireland a British Dominion. *Corbis*

The Anglo-Irish Treaty

In 1920 the government passed the Government of Ireland Act, which set up two Home Rule parliaments: one in Belfast (for the six northeastern counties) and one in Dublin. The Dublin parliament was stillborn as only Sinn Féiners contested the election, but the Northern one was opened in May 1921. Soon afterwards a truce was called and negotiations began between the British government and Sinn Féin. In December 1921 the Irish negotiators, led by Griffith and the dynamic IRB president Michael Collins, signed a treaty that gave Ireland Dominion status under the Crown.

The Anglo-Irish Treaty divided Sinn Féin. Collins, Griffith, and their supporters saw the Treaty as the best deal possible under the circumstances; others, led by de Valera (who had not attended the Treaty negotiations), saw partition and Dominion status as a betrayal of the ideal of a fully independent 32-county republic. A majority of the inhabitants of the new state endorsed the Treaty in an election in 1922, but this was followed by a year-long civil war, eventually won by the pro-Treaty side, which embittered Irish life for a generation. During the war Griffith died of exhaustion and Collins was shot. Remaining supporters of the old Home Rule party were absorbed into the pro-Treaty party, now led by William Cosgrave, first prime minister of the Irish Free State.

PATRICK MAUME

SEE ALSO
Collins, Michael; de Valera, Eamon; Easter Rising; Ireland: history; Kilmainham Treaty; Parnell, Charles Stewart; Redmond, John; Sinn Féin

IRAQ
Republic of

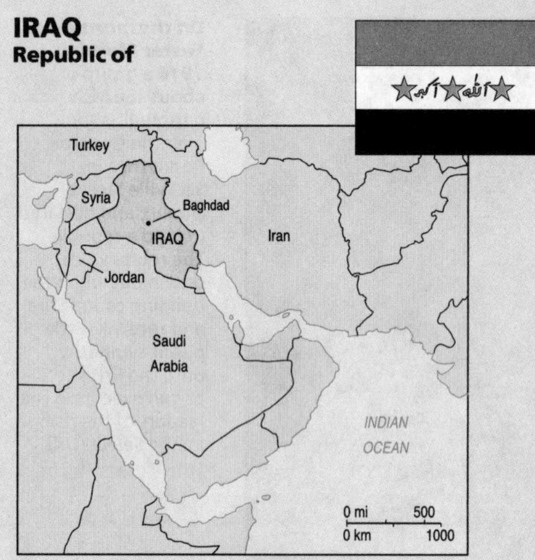

national name *al Jumhouriya al 'Iraqia*
area 434,924 sq km/167,881 sq mi
capital Baghdad
major towns/cities Mosul, Basra, Kirkuk
major ports Basra and Um Qass closed from 1980
physical features mountains in N, desert in W; wide valley of rivers Tigris and Euphrates running NW–SE; canal linking Baghdad and Persian Gulf opened 1992
head of state and government Saddam Hussein al-Tikriti from 1979
political system one-party socialist republic
administrative divisions 15 provinces
political party Arab Ba'ath Socialist Party, nationalist socialist
population 20,607,000 (1996 est)
population growth rate 2.5% (1990–95); 2.8% (2000–05)
ethnic distribution about 79% Arab, 16% Kurdish (mainly in the NE), 3% Persian, and 2% Turkish
life expectancy 65 (men), 67 (women)
literacy rate men 70%, women 49%
languages Arabic (official); Kurdish, Assyrian, Armenian
religions Shi'ite Muslim 60%, Sunni Muslim 37%, Christian 3%
currency Iraqi dinar
GDP (US $) 57.7 billion (1994 est)
growth rate 0.0% (1994)
exports crude oil, wool, cotton, dates (80% of world supply)

HISTORY
c. 3400 BC The world's oldest civilization, the Sumerian, arose in the land between the rivers Euphrates and Tigris, known as lower Mesopotamia, which lies in the heart of modern Iraq. Its cities included Lagash, Eridu, Uruk, Kish, and Ur.
c. 2350 BC The confederation of Sumerian city-states was forged into an empire by the Akkadian leader Sargon.
7th C BC The Assyrian Empire covered much of the Middle East.
612 BC The Assyrian capital of Nineveh was destroyed by Babylon and Mede (in NW Iran).
c. 550 BC Mesopotamia came under Persian control.
AD 114 Conquered by the Romans.
266 Came under the rule of the Sassanians.
637 Sassanian Empire destroyed by Muslim Arabs at battle of Qadisiya, in southern Iraq; Islam spread.
750–1258 Dominated by Abbasid dynasty, who reigned as caliphs in Baghdad.
1258 Baghdad invaded and burned by Tatars.
1401 Baghdad was destroyed by Mongol ruler Tamerlane.
1533 Annexed by Suleiman the Magnificent, becoming part of the Ottoman Empire.
1916 Occupied by Britain during World War I.
1920 Iraq became a British League of Nations protectorate.
1921 Hashemite dynasty established, with Faisal I installed by Britain as king.
1932 Independence achieved from British protectorate status.
1941–45 Occupied by Britain during World War II.
1955 Signed the Baghdad Pact collective security treaty with the UK, Iran, Pakistan, and Turkey.
1958 Monarchy overthrown in military-led revolution, in which King Faisal was assassinated; Iraq became a republic; joined Jordan in an Arab Federation; withdrew from Baghdad Pact as left-wing military regime assumed power.
1963 Joint socialist-nationalist Ba'athist-military coup headed by Col Salem Aref and backed by US CIA; reign of terror launched against the left.
1968 Ba'athist military coup put Maj-Gen Ahmed Hassan al-Bakr in power.
1979 Al-Bakr replaced by Saddam Hussein of the Arab Ba'ath Socialist Party.
1980 War between Iraq and Iran broke out.
1985–87 Fighting intensified, with heavy loss of life.
1988 Cease-fire; talks began with Iran. Iraq used chemical weapons against Kurdish rebels seeking greater autonomy in the NW.
1989 Unsuccessful coup against President Hussein; Iraq launched ballistic missile in successful test.
1990 Peace treaty favouring Iran agreed. Iraq invaded and annexed Kuwait in Aug. US forces massed in Saudi Arabia at request of King Fahd. UN ordered Iraqi withdrawal and imposed total trade ban; further UN resolution sanctioned force. All foreign hostages released.
1991 US-led Allied forces launched aerial assault on Iraq and destroyed country's infrastructure; land–sea–air offensive to free Kuwait successful. Uprisings of Kurds and Shi'ites brutally suppressed by surviving Iraqi troops. Allied troops established 'safe havens' for Kurds in the N prior to withdrawal, and left rapid-reaction force near Turkish border.
1992 UN imposed 'no-fly zone' over S Iraq to protect Shi'ites.
1993 Iraqi incursions into 'no-fly zone' prompted US-led alliance aircraft to bomb 'strategic' targets in Iraq. Continued persecution of Shi'ites in the S.
1994 Iraq renounced claim to Kuwait, but failed to fulfill other conditions required for lifting of UN sanctions.
1995 UN sanctions extended. Defection to Jordan of two of Saddam Hussein's top military aides and sons-in-law. Hussein elected (uncontested) in closely monitored presidential election.
1996 Iraqi-backed attacks on northern Kurds prompted US retaliation; air strikes destroyed Iraqi military bases in S. Agreement with UN to allow 'oil-for-food' deal.
1997 Iraq continued to resist US and Allied pressure to allow UN weapons inspections.
1998 Potential military confrontation with Western powers over weapons inspections averted by UN secretary general. However a spate of non-cooperation by Iraq with UN inspectors led to a further military build-up by West, Dec, which culminated in Operation Desert Fox, a series of air strikes over four days.
1999 US–UK forces clashed with Iraqi forces over a 'no-fly zone' in southern Iraq.

SEE ALSO Gulf War; Hussein, Saddam; Iran-Iraq War; Ottoman Empire; Sumerian civilization

home rule was conceded but World War I delayed implementation.

The Easter Rising took place April 1916, when nationalists seized the Dublin general post office and proclaimed a republic. After a week of fighting, the revolt was suppressed by the British army and most of its leaders executed. From 1918 to 1921 there was guerrilla warfare against the British army, especially by the Irish Republican Army (◊IRA), formed by Michael Collins 1919. This led to a split in the rebel forces, but in 1921 the Anglo-Irish Treaty resulted in partition and the creation of the Irish Free State in S Ireland. For history since that date, see ◊Ireland, Republic of; ◊Ireland, Northern. ▷ *See feature on pp. 550–551 and table on p. 555.*

Ireland, Northern constituent part of the United Kingdom
area 13,460 sq km/5,196 sq mi
capital Belfast
towns and cities Londonderry, Enniskillen, Omagh, Newry, Armagh, Coleraine
features Mourne Mountains, Belfast Lough and Lough Neagh; Giant's Causeway; comprises the six counties (Antrim, Armagh, Down, Fermanagh, Londonderry, and Tyrone) that form part of Ireland's northernmost province of Ulster
exports engineering, shipbuilding, textile machinery, aircraft components; linen and synthetic textiles; processed foods, especially dairy and poultry products; rubber products, chemicals
currency pound sterling
population (1993 est) 1,632,000
language English; 5.3% Irish-speaking
religion Protestant 51%, Roman Catholic 38%
famous people Viscount Montgomery, Lord Alanbrooke
government direct rule from the UK since 1972. Northern Ireland is entitled to send 17 members to the Westminster Parliament. The province costs the UK government £3 billion annually
history for history pre-1921, see ◊Ireland: history.

The creation of Northern Ireland dates from 1921 when the Irish Free State (subsequently the Republic of Ireland) was established separately from the mainly Protestant counties of Ulster (six out of nine), which were given limited self-government but continued to send members to the House of Commons. Spasmodic outbreaks of violence by the ◊Irish Republican Army (IRA) occurred, but only in 1968–69 were there serious disturbances arising from Protestant political dominance and discrimination against the Roman Catholic minority in employment and housing. British troops were sent 1969 to restore peace and protect Catholics, but disturbances continued and in 1972 the parliament at Stormont was prorogued and superseded by direct rule from Westminster.

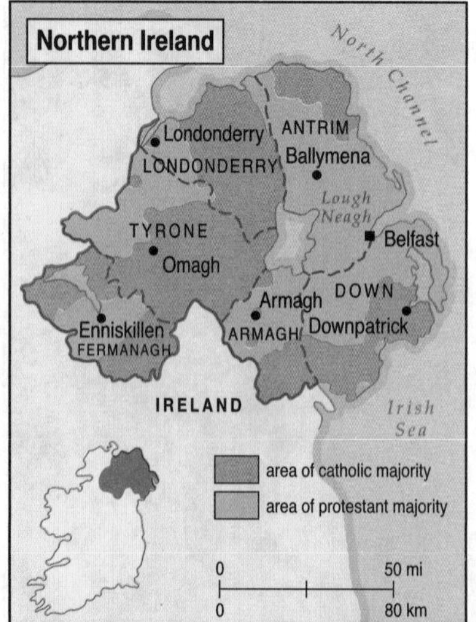

Under the ◊Anglo-Irish Agreement 1985, the Republic of Ireland was given a consultative role (via an Anglo-Irish conference) in the government of Northern Ireland, but agreed that there should be no change in its status except by majority consent. The agreement was approved by Parliament, but all 12 Ulster members gave up their seats, so that by-elections could be fought as a form of 'referendum' on the views of the province itself. A similar boycotting of the Northern Ireland Assembly led to its dissolution 1986 by the UK government.

The question of Northern Ireland's political future was debated in talks held in Belfast April–Sept 1991. Follow-up talks between the British government and the main Northern Ireland parties Sept–Nov 1992 made little progress. In Sept 1993 it emerged that the Catholic nationalist Social Democratic Labour Party (SDLP) and Sinn Féin (political wing of the outlawed IRA) had held talks aimed at achieving a political settlement. In Dec 1993 London and Dublin issued a joint peace proposal, the Downing Street Declaration, for consideration by all parties.

IRA cease-fires In Aug 1994 the Provisional IRA announced a unilateral cease-fire. A framework document, a basis for peace negotiations, was issued by the London and Dublin governments in Feb 1995. Its proposal for an Ulster-Ireland legislative body with limited powers was countered by the Irish government rescinding its constitutional claim to Ulster and the UK government giving its support to a separate Northern Ireland assembly.

In May 1995 Sinn Féin engaged in the first public talks with British government officials since 1973.

However, Sinn Féin continued to refuse the original British government-Unionist demand that talks could not proceed until the IRA had begun decommissioning arms. Amid the deadlock, the IRA broke the cease-fire with a renewed campaign of violence. In May 1997 the IRA announced a renewal of its cease-fire with effect from 20 July 1997 but during the second half of Dec 1997 violence in Northern Ireland appeared to be spreading.

multi-party talks The political process was saved following a visit to convicted loyalist terrorists in Maze prison by Mo Mowlam, secretary of state for Northern Ireland. At the end of the meeting, the prisoners dropped their opposition to the talks. On 13 Jan 1998, at the talks at Stormont Castle, Belfast, all parties involved – including Sinn Féin – agreed on the Northern Ireland Political Talks Document, jointly proposed by the British and Irish governments as a basis for negotiation. The document outlined a scheme with institutions to link not only Belfast, Dublin, and London but Glasgow and Cardiff. A referendum on the settlement process was held on 22 May in Northern Ireland and the Republic.

Among the principal elements of the agreement reached on Good Friday were the devolution of a wide range of executive and legislative powers to a Northern Ireland Assembly, in which executive posts would be shared on a proportional basis; the establishment of a North/South Ministerial Council, accountable to the Assembly and the Irish Parliament; and a British–Irish Council to bring together the two governments and representatives of devolved administrations in Northern Ireland, Scotland, and Wales. There would also be a new British-Irish Agreement to replace the Anglo-Irish Agreement signed in 1985.

On 10 May Sinn Féin decided to support the 'Yes' vote in the referendum. Sinn Féin's constitution was changed in order to enable party members take seats in the new Belfast assembly envisaged in the Good Friday agreement. Ian Paisley's Democratic Unionist Party and the Orange Order strongly opposed the deal. The Ulster Unionist Council voted on 18 April to endorse the settlement. The IRA remained opposed to the decommissioning of weapons. On 22 May 1998 the Good Friday agreement was endorsed.

The elections to the new power-sharing Northern Ireland Assembly took place on 25 June 1998 and resulted in the return of a large pro-agreement majority. David Trimble, leader of the Ulster Unionist Party, was elected by the Assembly as Northern Ireland's First Minister, with Seamus Mallon of the nationalist SDLP as his deputy. He enjoyed the support of the Popular Unionist Party, which was linked to loyalist paramilitaries.

In Sept Sinn Féin appointed Martin McGuinness its main negotiator with the international committee overseeing the decommissioning of arms; a historic meeting between David Trimble and Gerry Adams took place; and the first group of terrorist prisoners, both republicans and royalists, was released from the Maze prison. Nevertheless, the peace process met with further difficulties. Punishment beatings and shootings by republicans and loyalists rose to a rate of almost one a day during Jan 1999.

Ireland, Republic of country occupying the main part of the island of Ireland, NW Europe. It is bounded E by the Irish Sea, S and W by the Atlantic Ocean, and NE by Northern Ireland. *See country box below.*

Irian Jaya western portion of the island of New Guinea, province of Indonesia
area 420,000 sq km/162,000 sq mi

IRELAND, Republic of

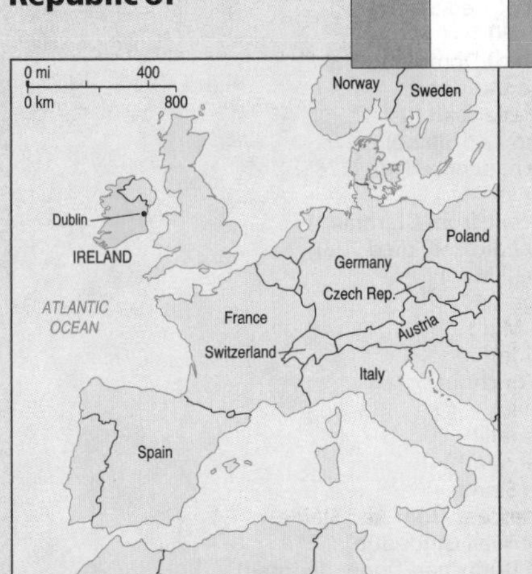

national name *Eire*
area 70,282 sq km/27,146 sq mi
capital Dublin
major ports Cork, Dun Laoghaire, Limerick, Waterford, Galway
physical features central plateau surrounded by hills; rivers Shannon, Liffey, Boyne; Bog of Allen, source of domestic and national power; Macgillicuddy's Reeks, Wicklow Mountains; Lough Corrib, lakes of Killarney; Galway Bay and Aran Islands
head of state Mary McAleese from 1997
head of government Bertie Ahern from 1997
political system democratic republic
administrative divisions 26 counties within four provinces
political parties Fianna Fáil (Soldiers of Destiny), moderate centre-right; Fine Gael (Irish Tribe or United Ireland Party), moderate centre-left; Labour Party, moderate left of centre; Progressive Democrats, radical free-enterprise
armed forces 12,900 (1995)
conscription none
defence spend (% GDP) 1.2 (1994)
education spend (% GNP) 6.2 (1992)
health spend (% GDP) 5.1 (1993)
death penalty abolished 1990
population 3,553,000 (1995 est)
population growth rate 0.4% (2000–05)
age distribution (% of total population) <15 24.4%, 15–65 64.3%, >65 11.2% (1995)
ethnic distribution most of the population has Celtic origins
population density (per sq km) 50 (1994)
urban population (% of total) 58 (1995)
labour force 37% of population: 14% agriculture, 29% industry, 57% services (1990)
unemployment 12.9% (1995)
child mortality rate (under 5, per 1,000 live births) 7 (1993)
life expectancy 73 (men), 78 (women)
education (compulsory years) 9
literacy rate 99%
languages Irish Gaelic and English (both official)
religions Roman Catholic 95%, Church of Ireland, other Protestant denominations
TV sets (per 1,000 people) 304 (1992)
currency Irish pound (punt Eireannach)
GDP (US $) 60.8 billion (1995)
GDP per capita (PPP) (US $) 16,431 (1995)
growth rate 7.7% (1994/95)
average annual inflation 2.2% (1995)
major trading partners UK, USA, Germany, France
resources lead, zinc, peat, limestone, gypsum, petroleum, natural gas, copper, silver
industries textiles, machinery, chemicals, electronics, motor vehicle manufacture, food processing, beer
exports beef and dairy products, live animals, machinery and transport equipment, electronic goods, chemicals. Principal market: UK 27.8% (1994)
imports petroleum products, machinery and transport, chemicals, foodstuffs, animal feed, textiles and clothing. Principal source: UK 36.4% (1994)
arable land 13.1% (1993)
agricultural products barley, potatoes, sugar beet, wheat, oats; livestock and dairy products

HISTORY

3rd C BC The Gaels, a Celtic people, invaded Ireland and formed about 150 small kingdoms.
c. AD 432 St Patrick introduced Christianity.
5th–9th Cs Irish Church remained a centre of culture and scholarship throughout the Dark Ages.
9th–11th Cs The Vikings raided Ireland until defeated by High King Brian Boru at Clontarf 1014.
12th–13th Cs Anglo-Norman adventurers conquered much of Ireland, but no central government was formed and many became assimilated.
14th–15th Cs Irish chieftains recovered their lands, restricting English rule to the Pale around Dublin.
1536 Henry VIII of England made ineffectual efforts to impose the Protestant Reformation on Ireland.
1541 Irish Parliament recognized Henry VIII as king of Ireland; Henry gave peerages to Irish chieftains.
1579 English suppressed Desmond rebellion, confiscated rebel lands, and tried to 'plant' them with English settlers.
1610 James I established plantation of Ulster with Protestant settlers from England and Scotland.
1641 Catholic Irish rebelled against English rule; Oliver Cromwell brutally reasserted English control 1649–50; Irish landowners evicted and replaced with English landowners.
1689–91 Williamite War: following the 'Glorious Revolution', the Catholic Irish unsuccessfully supported James II against Protestant William III in civil war; penal laws barred Catholics from obtaining wealth and power 1695.
1720 Act passed declaring British Parliament's right to legislate for Ireland.
1739–41 Famine killed one third of population.
1782 Protestant landlords led by Henry Grattan secured end of restrictions on Irish trade and parliament.
1798 British suppressed revolt by Society of United Irishmen (with French support) led by Wolfe Tone.
1800 Act of Union abolished Irish parliament and created United Kingdom of Great Britain and Ireland, effective 1801.
1829 Daniel O'Connell secured Catholic Emancipation Act, which permitted Catholics to enter parliament.
1846–51 Potato famine reduced population by 20% through starvation and emigration.
1870 Land Act increased security for tenants but failed to halt agrarian disorder; Isaac Butt formed political party to campaign for Irish Home Rule (devolution).
1885 Home Rulers, led by Charles Stewart Parnell, held balance of power in parliament; first Home Rule Bill rejected 1886; second defeated 1893.
1905 Arthur Griffith founded the nationalist movement Sinn Féin ('Ourselves Alone').
1914 Ireland came close to civil war as Ulster prepared to resist implementation of Home Rule Act (postponed because of World War I).
1916 Easter Rising: nationalists proclaimed a republic in Dublin; British crushed revolt and executed 15 leaders.
1919 Sinn Féin MPs formed an Irish parliament in Dublin in defiance of the British government.
1919–21 Irish Republican Army (IRA) waged guerrilla war against British forces.
1921 Anglo-Irish Treaty partitioned Ireland; N Ireland (Ulster) remained part of the United Kingdom; S Ireland won full internal self-government with dominion status.
1922 Irish Free State proclaimed; IRA split over Anglo-Irish Treaty led to civil war 1922–23.
1932 Anti-Treaty party, Fianna Fáil, came to power under Éamonn de Valéra.
1937 New constitution established Eire (Gaelic name for Ireland) as a sovereign state and refused to acknowledge partition.
1949 After remaining neutral in World War II, Eire left the Commonwealth and became the Republic of Ireland.
1973 Ireland joined European Economic Community.
1985 Anglo-Irish Agreement gave the Republic of Ireland a consultative role, but no powers, in the government of Northern Ireland.
1990 Mary Robinson became the first woman president of Ireland.
1993 Downing Street Declaration: joint Anglo-Irish peace proposal for Northern Ireland issued.
1994 Cease-fires announced by Catholic and Protestant paramilitaries in Northern Ireland.
1995 Ulster framework peace document issued.
1997 Fianna Fáil leader Bertie Ahern became prime minister; Mary MacAleese elected president.
1998 Historic, multiparty agreement (the Good Friday Agreement) was reached on the future of Northern Ireland. Referendum showed large majority in favour of dropping Ireland's claim to the North.

SEE ALSO Anglo-Irish Agreement; Easter Rising; Fianna Fáil; Home Rule, Irish; Irish Republican Army

capital Jayapura
industries copper
population (1990) 1,648,700
history part of the Dutch East Indies 1828 as Western New Guinea; retained by the Netherlands after Indonesian independence 1949 but ceded to Indonesia 1963 by the United Nations and remained part of Indonesia by an 'Act of Free Choice' 1969. In the 1980s, 283,500 hectares/700,000 acres were given over to Indonesia's controversial transmigration programme for the resettlement of farming families from overcrowded Java, causing destruction of rainforests and displacing indigenous people. In 1989 Indonesia began construction of a space launching pad on the island of Biak, near the equator.

iridium (Latin *iridis* 'rainbow') hard, brittle, silver-white, metallic element, symbol Ir, atomic number 77, relative atomic mass 192.2. It is twice as heavy as lead and is resistant to tarnish and corrosion. It is one of the so-called platinum group of metals; it occurs in platinum ores and as a free metal (◊native metal) with osmium in osmiridium, a natural alloy that includes platinum, ruthenium, and rhodium.

It is alloyed with platinum for jewellery and used for watch bearings and in scientific instruments. It was named 1804 by English chemist Smithson Tennant (1761–1815) for its iridescence in solution.

iridology diagnostic technique based on correspondences between specific areas of the iris and bodily functions and organs.

It was discovered in the 19th century independently by a Hungarian and a Swedish physician, and later refined and developed in the USA by Bernard Jensen. Iridology is of proven effectiveness in monitoring general wellbeing and indicating the presence of organic disorders, but cannot be as specific about the nature and extent of these as orthodox diagnostic techniques.

iris in anatomy, the coloured muscular diaphragm that controls the size of the pupil in the vertebrate eye. It contains radial muscle that increases the pupil diameter and circular muscle that constricts the pupil diameter. Both types of muscle respond involuntarily to light intensity.

iris in botany, perennial northern temperate flowering plant of the genus *Iris*, family Iridaceae. The leaves are usually sword-shaped; the purple, white, or yellow flowers have three upright inner petals and three outward- and downward-curving sepals. The wild yellow iris is called flag.

Many cultivated varieties derive from *I. germanica*. Orris root, used in perfumery, is the violet-scented underground stem of the S European iris *I. florentina*. The ◊crocus also belongs to this family.

Irish people of Irish culture from Ireland or those of Irish descent. The Irish mainly speak English, though there are approximately 30,000–100,000 speakers of Irish Gaelic (see ◊Gaelic language), a Celtic language belonging to the Indo-European family.

IRELAND: KINGS AND QUEENS

445–452	Niall of the Nine Hostages (king of Tara; traditional ancestor of claimants to the high kingship)
452–463	Lóegaire (son)
463–482	Ailill Molt (grandnephew of Niall)
482–507	Lugaid (son of Lóegaire)
507–534	Muirchertach I (great-grandson of Niall)
534–544	Tuathal Máelgarb (great-grandson of Niall)
544–565	Diarmait I (great-grandson of Niall)
565–566	Domnall Ilchelgach (brother; co-regent)
566–569	Ainmire (fourth in descent from Niall)
569–572	Bétán I (son of Muirchertach I)
569–572	Eochaid (son of Domnall Ilchelgach; co-regent)
572–586	Báetán II (fourth in descent from Niall)
586–598	Áed (son of Ainmire)
598–604	Áed Sláine (son of Diarmait I)
598–604	Colmán Rímid (son of Báetán I; co-regent)
604–612	Áed Uaridnach (son of Domnall Ilchelgach)
612–615	Máel Cobo (son of Áed)
615–628	Suibne Menn (grandnephew of Muirchertach I)
628–642	Domnall (son of Áed)
642–654	Conall Cáel (son of Máel Cobo)
642–658	Cellach (brother; co-regent)
658–665	Diarmait II (son of Áed Sláine)
658–665	Blathmac (brother; co-regent)
665–671	Sechnussach (son)
671–675	Cennfáelad (brother)
675–695	Fínsnechta Fledach (grandson of Áed Sláine)
695–704	Loingsech (grandson of Domnall)
704–710	Congal Cennmagair (grandson of Domnall)
710–722	Fergal (great-grandson of Áed Uaridnach)
722–724	Fogartach (great-grandson of Diarmait II)
724–728	Cináed (fourth in descent from Áed Sláine)
728–734	Flaithbertach (son of Loingsech; deposed, died 765)
734–743	Áed allán (son of Fergal)
743–763	Domnall Midi (seventh in descent from Diarmait I)
763–770	Niall Frossach (son of Fergal; abdicated, died 778)
770–797	Donnchad Midi (son of Domnall Midi)
797–819	Áed Oirdnide (son of Niall Frossach)
819–833	Conchobar (son of Donnchad Midi)
833–846	Niall Caille (son of Áed Oirdnide)
846–862	Máel Sechnaill I (nephew of Conchobar)
862–879	Áed Findliath (son of Niall Caille)
879–916	Flann Sinna (son of Máel SechnailII)
916–919	Niall Glúundub (son of Áed Findliath)
919–944	Donnchad Donn (son of Flann Sinna)
944–956	Congalach Cnogba (tenth in descent from Áed Sláine)
956–980	Domnall ua Néill (grandson of Niall Glúundub)
980–1002	Máel Sechnaill II (grandson of Donnchad Donn; deposed)
1002–1014	Brian Boru (Dál Cais; king of Munster)
1014–1022	Máel Sechnaill II (restored; interregnum 1022–72)
1072–1086	Tairrdelbach I (grandson of Brian Bóruma; king of Munster)
1086–1119	Muirchertach II (son)
1119–1121	Domnall ua Lochlainn (fourth in descent from Domnall ua Néill?; king of Ailech)
1121–1156	Tairrdelbach II (Ua Conchobair; king of Connacht)
1156–1166	Muirchertach III (grandson of Domnall ua Lochlainn)
1166–1186	Ruaidrí (son of Tairrdelbach II; deposed, died 1198; regional kingships under English domination)

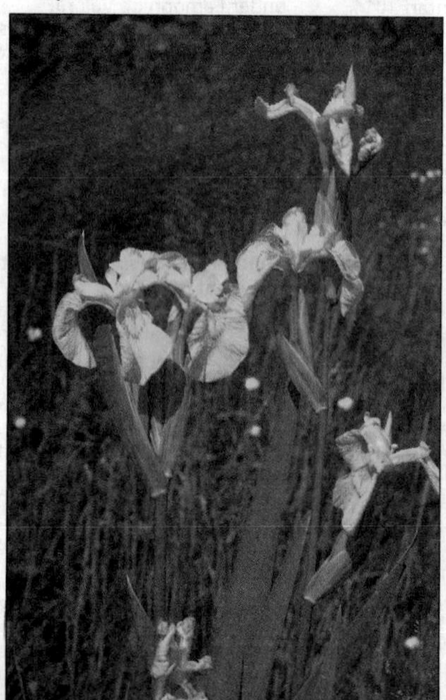

iris The flowers of the yellow flag *Iris pseudacorus* are pollinated by several large species of bumble bees. The plump pods later split to release large, cookielike brown seeds. *Premaphotos Wildlife*

Celtic tribes, the ancestors of the Irish, migrated to Ireland about 300 BC. Later known as Gaels (Irishmen), they settled on the Isle of Man and SW Scotland, and established colonies in W Wales, Devon, and Cornwall.

Irish Gaelic first official language of the Irish Republic, but much less widely used than the second official language, English. See ◊Gaelic language.

Irish literature early Irish literature, in Gaelic, consists of the sagas, which are mainly in prose, and a considerable body of verse. The chief cycles are that of Ulster, which deals with the mythological ◊Conchobar and his followers, and the Ossianic, which has influenced European literature through ◊Macpherson's version.

Early Irish poetry has a unique lyric quality and consists mainly of religious verse and nature poetry, for example, St Patrick's hymn and Ultán's hymn to St Brigit. Much pseudo-historical verse is also extant, ascribed to such poets as Mael Mura (9th century), Mac Liac (10th century), and Flann Mainistrech (11th century). Religious literature in prose includes sermons, saints' lives (for example, those in the *Book of Lismore* and in the writings ofMichael O'Clery), and visions. History is represented by annals and by isolated texts like the *Cogad Gaedel re Gallaib*, an account of the Viking invasions by an eye-witness. The 'official' or 'court' verse of the 13th to 17th centuries was produced by a succession of professional poets, notably Tadhg Dall O' Huiginn (died c. 1617), Donnchadh Mór O'Dálaigh (died 1244), and Geoffrey Keating (died 1646), who wrote in both verse and prose. The bardic schools ceased to exist by the end of the 17th century. Metre became accentual, rather than syllabic. The greatest exponents of the new school were Egan O'Rahilly (early 18th century) and the religious poet Tadhg Gaelach O'Súilleabháin. The late 19th century onwards saw a resurgence of Irish literature written in English. Oscar ◊Wilde, G B ◊Shaw, and James ◊Joyce represent those who chose to live outside Ireland. More culturally nationalistic were the writers including W B ◊Yeats who supported the Gaelic League (aiming to revivify the Irish language) and founded the Abbey Theatre Company in Dublin: this provided a milieu for the realism and fantasy of J M ◊Synge and the intensity and compassion of Sean ◊O'Casey. Since World War II, Ireland has produced the Nobel prize-winning dramatist Samuel ◊Beckett, novelists of the calibre of Brian ◊Moore and Edna O'Brien (1936–), and Nobel prize-winning poet Seamus ◊Heaney.

Irish National Liberation Army (INLA) guerrilla organization committed to the end of British rule in Northern Ireland and the incorporation of Ulster into the Irish Republic. The INLA

IRELAND, NORTHERN: TIMELINE 1967–

1967	Northern Ireland Civil Rights Association set up to press for equal treatment for Catholics in the provinces.
1968	Series of civil-rights marches sparked off rioting and violence, especially in Londonderry.
1969	Election results weakened Terence O'Neil's Unionist government. Further rioting led to call-up of (Protestant-based) B-Specials to Royal Ulster Constabulary. Chichester-Clark replaced O'Neil. Irish Republican Army (IRA) split into 'official' and more radical 'provisional' wings. Resumption of IRA activities: urban guerrilla warfare in the north and kidnap and murder in the south. RUC disarmed and B-Specials replaced by nonsectarian Ulster Defence Regiment (UDR). British Army deployed in Belfast and Londonderry.
1971	First British soldier killed. Brian Faulkner replaced Chichester-Clark. IRA stepped up bombing campaign. Internment of people suspected of IRA membership introduced.
1972	'Bloody Sunday' in Londonderry when British troops fired on demonstrators: 13 killed. Direct rule from Westminster introduced. Constitution suspended. IRA extended bombing campaign to mainland England. Seven soldiers killed in bomb attack in Aldershot.
1973	Sunningdale Agreement, to establish Council of Ireland with representatives from north and south.
1974	'Power sharing' between Protestant and Catholic groups tried but failed. Bombs in Guildford and Birmingham caused a substantial number of fatalities.
1976	British Ambassador in Dublin, Christopher Ewart Biggs, assassinated. Ulster Peace Movement founded by Betty Williams and Mairead Corrigan, later awarded Nobel Prize for Peace.
1979	British MP Airey Neave assassinated by Irish National Liberation Army (INLA) at the House of Commons. Earl Mountbatten and three others killed by IRA bomb.
1980	Meeting of British prime minister Margaret Thatcher and Irish premier Charles Haughey on a peaceful settlement to the Irish question. Hunger strikes and 'dirty protests' started by Republican prisoners in pursuit of political status.
1981	Hunger strikes by detainees of Maze Prison led to deaths of Bobby Sands and nine other hunger strikers; Anglo-Irish Intergovernmental Council formed.
1982	Northern Ireland Assembly created to devolve legislative and executive powers back to the province. Social Democratic Labour Party (19%) and Sinn Féin (10%) boycotted the assembly.
1983	Six killed in IRA bomb attack outside Harrods, London.
1984	Series of reports from various groups on the future of the province. IRA bomb at Conservative Party conference in Brighton killed five people. Second Anglo-Irish Intergovernmental Council summit meeting agreed to oppose violence and cooperate on security; Britain rejected ideas of confederation or joint sovereignty.
1985	Meeting of Margaret Thatcher and Irish premier Garrett Fitzgerald at Hillsborough produced Anglo-Irish agreement on the future of Ulster; regarded as a sell-out by Unionists.
1986	Unionist opposition to Anglo-Irish agreement included protests and strikes. Loyalist violence against police. Unionist MPs boycotted Westminster.
1987	IRA bombed British Army base in West Germany. Unionist boycott of Westminster ended. Extradition clauses of Anglo-Irish Agreement approved in Eire. IRA bombed Remembrance Day service at Enniskillen, killing 11 people – later admitted it to be a 'mistake'.
1988	Three IRA bombers killed by security forces on Gibraltar.
1989	After serving fourteen years in prison, the 'Guildford Four' were released when their convictions were ruled unsound by the Court of Appeal.
1990	Anglo-Irish Agreement threatened when Eire refused extraditions. Convictions of 'Birmingham Six' also called into question and sent to the Court of Appeal. Murder of Ian Gow, MP.
1991	IRA renewed bombing campaign on British mainland, targetting a meeting of the cabinet in Downing Street and railway stations. Formal talks on political future of Northern Ireland initiated by Peter Brooke, Secretary of State for Northern Ireland.
1992	Leaders of four main political parties as well as British and Irish government ministers held round-table talks for first time in 70 years; ended without agreement. UDA officially proscribed as an illegal organization. The 3,000th death since 1969 as a result of terrorist activity in Northern Ireland occurred.
1993	British government had secret talks with Sinn Féin and IRA on a possible end to conflict. Talks began between SDLP leader John Hulme and Sinn Féin president Gerry Adams. John Major and Irish prime minister Albert Reynolds issued joint peace proposal, the Downing Street Declaration.
1994	Total number of casualties to date was 3,169, and 38,680 injured. There were 18,000 troops in Northern Ireland.
1995	Framework document forming a basis for peace negotiations issued. Sinn Féin engaged in the first public talks with British government officials since 1973.
1996	Deadlock on all-party talks continued over decommissioning of arms by the IRA. Sinn Féin and SDLP opposed British government–Unionist proposals for electing representatives to talks. IRA bombings broke cease-fire and disrupted peace process.
1997	July: second IRA cease-fire announced; UK Labour government resumes contact with Sinn Féin.
1998	January: multi-party talks resume at Stormont Castle, Belfast. April: the Northern Ireland Political Talks Document (also known as the Good Friday agreement) is released. May: the Good Friday agreement is accepted in parallel referenda by the people of Northern Ireland and the Republic of Ireland.

was a 1974 offshoot of the Irish Republican Army (IRA). Among the INLA's activities was the killing of British politician Airey Neave 1979. The INLA refused to participate in the Aug 1994 cease-fire declared by Sinn Féin, the political wing of the Irish Republican Army, but in April 1995 announced that it was renouncing the use of violence.

The group's leader, Gino Gallagher, was shot and killed in Belfast Jan 1996, allegedly by feuding INLA members.

Irish Republican Army (IRA) militant Irish nationalist organization formed 1919, the paramilitary wing of the nationalist party ◊Sinn Féin (led by Gerry Adams). Its aim is to create a united Irish socialist republic including Ulster. To this end, the IRA habitually carries out bombings and shootings. Despite its close association with Sinn Féin, it is not certain that the politicians have direct control of the military, the IRA usually speaking as a separate, independent organization. The chief common factor shared by Sinn Féin and the IRA is the aim of a united Ireland.

In 1969 the IRA split into two wings, one 'official' and the other 'provisional'. The official wing sought reunification by political means, while the ***Provisional IRA***, or Provos as they became known, carried on with terrorist activities, their objective being the expulsion of the British from Northern Ireland. It is this wing, of younger, strongly sectarian Ulster Catholics, who are now generally regarded and spoken of as the IRA.

The IRA announced a cessation of its military activities Aug 1994, in response to a UK–Irish peace initiative. However, the insistence by the government in London that Sinn Féin could enter into all-party negotiations about the future of Ireland only after the IRA had decommissioned its weaponry was seen as unacceptable by the more militant members of the organization, who broke the cease-fire Feb 1996. Subsequent bombing cast doubt over the whole peace process and raised the question of how much influence Sinn Féin has over its military allies, and how much control the leadership of the IRA has over its active members. UK–Unionist plans for elections to select representatives to the talks also met with opposition from Sinn Féin. ▷ *See feature on pp. 550–551.*

iron hard, malleable and ductile, silver-grey, metallic element, symbol Fe (from Latin *ferrum*), atomic number 26, relative atomic mass 55.847. It is the fourth most abundant element (the second most abundant metal, after aluminium) in the Earth's crust. Iron occurs in concentrated deposits as the ores hematite (Fe_2O_3), spathic ore ($FeCO_3$), and magnetite (Fe_3O_4). It sometimes occurs as a free metal, occasionally as fragments of iron or iron–nickel meteorites.

Iron is the most common and most useful of all metals; it is strongly magnetic and is the basis for ◊steel, an alloy with carbon and other elements (see also ◊cast iron). In electrical equipment it is used in all permanent magnets and electromagnets, and forms the cores of transformers and magnetic amplifiers. In the human body, iron is an essential component of haemoglobin, the molecule in red blood cells that transports oxygen to all parts of the body. A deficiency in the diet causes a form of anaemia.

Iron Age developmental stage of human technology when weapons and tools were made from iron. Iron was produced in Thailand by about 1600 BC but was considered inferior in strength to bronze until about 1000 when metallurgical techniques improved and the alloy steel was produced by adding carbon during the smelting process.

Iron Age cultures include Hallstatt (named after a site in Austria), La Tène (from a site in Switzerland), and Marnian (from the Marne region, France). ▷ *See feature on pp. 200–201.*

ironclad wooden warship covered with armour plate. The first to be constructed was the French *Gloire* 1858, but the first to be launched was the British HMS *Warrior* 1859. The first battle between ironclads took place during the American Civil War, when the Union *Monitor* fought the Confederate *Virginia* (formerly the *Merrimack*) 9 March 1862. The design was replaced by battleships of all-metal construction in the 1890s.

Iron Cross medal awarded for valour in the German armed forces. Instituted in Prussia 1813, it consists of a Maltese iron cross, edged with silver.

Iron Curtain in Europe after World War II, the symbolic boundary between capitalist West and communist East during the ◊Cold War. The term was popularized by the UK prime minister Winston Churchill from 1945.

An English traveller to Bolshevik Russia, Ethel Snowden (1881–1951), used the term with reference to the Soviet border 1920. The Nazi minister Goebbels used it a few months before Churchill 1945 to describe the divide between Soviet-dominated and other nations that would follow German capitulation.

Iron Guard profascist group controlling Romania in the 1930s. To counter its influence, King Carol II established a dictatorship 1938 but the Iron Guard forced him to abdicate 1940.

iron ore any mineral from which iron is extracted. The chief iron ores are ◊magnetite, a black oxide; ◊hematite, or kidney ore, a reddish oxide; ◊limonite, brown, impure oxyhydroxides of iron; and siderite, a brownish carbonate.

'From Stettin in the Baltic to Trieste in the Adriatic, an iron curtain has descended across the Continent.'

On the IRON CURTAIN
Winston Churchill, speech
5 March 1946

I am always at a loss to know how much to believe of my own stories.

Washington Irving *Tales of a Traveller*

Iron ores are found in a number of different forms, including distinct layers in igneous intrusions, as components of contact metamorphic rocks, and as sedimentary beds. Much of the world's iron is extracted in Russia, Kazakhstan, and the Ukraine. Other important producers are the USA, Australia, France, Brazil, and Canada; over 40 countries produce significant quantities of ore.

iron pyrites or ***pyrite*** FeS_2 common iron ore. Brassy yellow, and occurring in cubic crystals, it is often called 'fool's gold', since only those who have never seen gold would mistake it.

Irons Jeremy 1948– . English actor. His aristocratic bearing, immaculate grooming, and precise diction have led to frequent casting as a repressed, upper-class character. A hint of ambiguity under this surface sheen has made him perfect for such film roles as Claus von Bulow in *Reversal of Fortune* 1990 (Academy Award) and the twin brothers in *Dead Ringers* 1988. Other key films include *The French Lieutenant's Woman* 1981, *The Mission* 1986, and *Damage* 1992.

irony literary technique that uses words to convey a meaning opposite to their literal sense, through the use of humour or sarcasm. It can be traced through all periods of literature, from classical Greek and Roman epics and dramas to the subtle irony of ◊Chaucer and the 20th-century writer's method for dealing with despair, as in Samuel ◊Beckett's *Waiting for Godot*.

Iroquois a confederation of NE Native Americans, the Six Nations (Cayuga, Mohawk, Oneida, Onondaga, and Seneca, with the Tuscarora after 1723), traditionally formed by Hiawatha (actually a priestly title) 1570.

irrationalism feature of many philosophies rather than a philosophical movement. Irrationalists deny that the world can be comprehended by conceptual thought, and often see the human mind as determined by unconscious forces.

irrational number a number that cannot be expressed as an exact ◊fraction. Irrational numbers include some square roots (for example, $\sqrt{2}$, $\sqrt{3}$, and $\sqrt{5}$ are irrational) and numbers such as π (the ratio of the circumference of a circle to its diameter, which is approximately equal to 3.14159) and e (the base of ◊natural logarithms, approximately 2.71828).

Irrawaddy (Myanmar ***Ayeryarwady***) chief river of Myanmar (Burma), flowing roughly north–south for 2,090 km/1,300 mi across the centre of the country into the Bay of Bengal. Its sources are the Mali and N'mai rivers; its chief tributaries are the Chindwin and Shweli.

irredentist (Latin *redemptus*, bought back) person who wishes to reclaim the lost territories of a state. The term derives from an Italian political party founded about 1878 intending to incorporate Italian-speaking areas into the newly formed state.

irrigation artificial water supply for dry agricultural areas by means of dams and channels. Drawbacks are that it tends to concentrate salts at the surface, ultimately causing soil infertility, and that rich river silt is retained at dams, to the impoverishment of the land and fisheries below them.

Irvine Andrew Robertson 1951– . British rugby union player who held the world record for the most points scored in senior international rugby with 301 (273 for Scotland, 28 for the British Lions) between 1972 and 1982.

Irving Henry. Stage name of John Henry Brodribb 1838–1905. English actor. He established his reputation from 1871, chiefly at the Lyceum Theatre in London, where he became manager 1878. He staged a series of successful Shakespearean productions, including *Romeo and Juliet* 1882, with himself and Ellen ◊Terry playing the leading roles. He was the first actor to be knighted, 1895.

Irving Washington 1783–1859. US essayist and short-story writer. He published a mock-heroic *History of New York* 1809, supposedly written by the Dutchman 'Diedrich Knickerbocker'. In 1815 he went to England where he published *The Sketch Book of Geoffrey Crayon, Gent.* 1820, which contained such stories as 'Rip Van Winkle' and 'The Legend of Sleepy Hollow'.

His other works include *The Alhambra* 1832, sketches about Spanish subjects, and *Tour of the Prairies* 1835, about the American West. His essays and tales remain popular.

The whole of Isfahan gives the feeling of a great deal of labour and loveliness and thought spent on the light, airy, evanescent side of things.

On **Isfahan** Freya Stark, letter 28 April 1943

Isaac in the Old Testament, a Hebrew patriarch, son of ◊Abraham and Sarah, and father of Esau and Jacob.

Isabella (I) the Catholic 1451–1504. Queen of Castile from 1474, after the death of her brother Henry IV. By her marriage with ◊Ferdinand of Aragon 1469, the crowns of two of the Christian states in the Moorish-held Spanish peninsula were united. Her youngest daughter was Catherine of Aragon, first wife of Henry VIII of England.

She introduced the ◊Inquisition into Castile, expelled the Jews and the Moors, and gave financial encouragement to ◊Columbus. The Catholic church proposed to beatify Isabella in 1992, an announcement which aroused the indignation of Jewish groups.

Isabella II 1830–1904. Queen of Spain from 1833, when she succeeded her father Ferdinand VII (1784–1833). The Salic Law banning a female sovereign had been repealed by the Cortes (parliament), but her succession was disputed by her uncle Don Carlos de Bourbon (1788–1855). After seven years of civil war, the ◊Carlists were defeated. She abdicated in favour of her son Alfonso XII in 1868.

Isabella of France 1292–1358. Daughter of King Philip IV of France, she married King Edward II of England 1308, but he slighted and neglected her for his favourites, first Piers Gaveston (died 1312) and later the Despenser family. Supported by her lover, Roger de Mortimer, Isabella conspired to have Edward deposed and murdered.

Isaiah lived 8th century BC. in the Old Testament, the first major Hebrew prophet. The Book of Isaiah in the Old Testament was traditionally believed to be written by him, but it is now thought that large parts of it are the work of at least two other writers.

Isaiah was the son of Amos, probably of high rank, and lived largely in Jerusalem.

Isaurian 8th-century Byzantine imperial dynasty, originating in Asia Minor.

Members of the family had been employed as military leaders by the Byzantines, and they gained great influence and prestige as a result. Leo III acceded in 717 as the first Isaurian emperor, and was followed by Constantine V (718–75), Leo IV (750–80), and Leo's widow Irene, who acted as regent for their son before deposing him 797 and assuming the title of emperor herself. She was deposed 802. The Isaurian rulers maintained the integrity of the empire's borders. With the exception of Irene, they attempted to suppress the use of religious icons.

ISBN (abbreviation for ***International Standard Book Number***) code number used for ordering or classifying book titles. Every book printed now has a number on its back cover or jacket, preceded by the letters ISBN. It is a code to the country of origin and the publisher. The number is unique to the book, and will identify it anywhere in the world.

ischaemic heart disease (IHD) disorder caused by reduced perfusion of the coronary arteries due to ◊atherosclerosis. It is the commonest cause of death in the Western world, leading to more than a million deaths each year in the USA and about 160,000 in the UK. See also ◊coronary artery disease.

Early symptoms of IHD include ◊angina or palpitations, but sometimes a heart attack is the first indication that a person is affected.

ISDN abbreviation for ◊***Integrated Services Digital Network***, a telecommunications system.

Isfahan or ***Esfahan*** industrial city (steel, textiles, carpets) in central Iran; population (1991) 1,127,000. It was the ancient capital (1598–1722) of ◊Abbas I, and its features include the Great Square, Grand Mosque, and Hall of Forty Pillars.

Isherwood Christopher William Bradshaw 1904–1986. English novelist. He lived in Germany 1929–33 just before Hitler's rise to power, a period that inspired *Mr Norris Changes Trains* 1935 and *Goodbye to Berlin* 1939, creating the character of Sally Bowles (the basis of the musical *Cabaret* 1968). Returning to England, he collaborated with W H ◊Auden in three verse plays.

Ishiguro Kazuo 1954– . Japanese-born British novelist. His novel *An Artist of the Floating World* won the 1986 Whitbread Prize, and *The Remains of the Day* won the 1989 Booker Prize. His work is characterized by a sensitive style and subtle structure.

Ishiguro's first novel, *A Pale View of Hills* 1982, takes place mainly in his native Nagasaki, dealing obliquely with the aftermath of the atom bomb. *An Artist of the Floating World* is set entirely in Japan but thematically linked to *The Remains of the Day* (filmed 1993), which is about an English butler coming to realize the extent of his self-sacrifice and self-deception. All three have in common a melancholy reassessment of the past. A recent work is *The Unconsoled* 1995.

Ishmael in the Old Testament, the son of ◊Abraham and his wife Sarah's Egyptian maid Hagar; traditional ancestor of Muhammad and the Arab people. He and his mother were driven away by Sarah's jealousy. Muslims believe that it was Ishmael, not Isaac, whom God commanded Abraham to sacrifice, and that Ishmael helped Abraham build the ◊Kaaba in Mecca.

Ishtar Mesopotamian goddess of love and war, worshipped by the Babylonians and Assyrians, and personified as the legendary queen Semiramis.

Isidore of Seville c. 560–636. Writer and missionary. His *Ethymologiae* was the model for later medieval encyclopedias and helped to preserve classical thought during the Middle Ages; his *Chronica Maiora* remains an important source for the history of Visigothic Spain. As bishop of Seville from 600, he strengthened the church in Spain and converted many Jews and Aryan Visigoths.

Isis the principal goddess of ancient Egypt. She was the daughter of Geb and Nut (Earth and Sky), and as the sister-wife of Osiris searched for his body after his death at the hands of his brother, Set. Her son Horus then defeated and captured Set, but cut off his mother's head because she would not allow Set to be killed. She was later identified with ◊Hathor. The cult of Isis ultimately spread to Greece and Rome.

Islam (Arabic 'submission', that is, to the will of Allah) religion founded in the Arabian peninsula in the early 7th century AD. It emphasizes the oneness of God, his omnipotence, beneficence, and inscrutability. The sacred book is the Koran, which Muslims believe was divinely revealed to ◊Muhammad, the prophet or messenger of Allah. There are two main Muslim sects: ◊Sunni and ◊Shi'ite. Other trends include Sufism, a mystical movement originating in the 8th century.

beliefs The fundamental beliefs of Islam are contained in the *Shahada*: 'I bear witness that there is no God but Allah and Muhammad is the Prophet of Allah', which is a constituent part of the *adhan*. Other beliefs central to Islam are the Creation, Fall of Adam, angels and jins, heaven and hell, Day of Judgement, God's predestination of good and evil, and the succession of scriptures revealed to the prophets, including Moses and Jesus. The perfect, final form of the scriptures is the Koran or Quran, divided into 114 *suras* or chapters, with each chapter being divided into a number of *ayat* (verses).

Islamic law Islam embodies a secular law (the *Shari'a* or 'Main Path'), which is clarified for Shi'ites by reference to their own version of the *sunna*, 'practice' of the prophet as transmitted by his companions and embodied in the Hadith; the Sunni sect also take into account *ijma'*, expert, universal consent of practices and beliefs among the faithful. For the Sufi, the *Shari'a* is the starting point on the 'Sufi Path' to self-enlightenment. A *mufti* is a legal expert who guides the courts in their interpretation. (In Turkey, until the establishment of the republic 1924, the mufti had supreme spiritual authority.)

organization There is no organized church or priesthood, although Muhammad's descendants (the Hashim family) and popularly recognized holy men, mullahs, and ayatollahs are accorded respect.

observances The Shari'a includes the observances known as the 'Five Pillars of the Faith' which are binding to all adult believers. The observances include: *shahada* or profession of the faith; *salat* or worship five times a day facing the holy city of ◊Mecca (the call to prayer is given by a muezzin, usually from the minaret or tower of a mosque); *zakat* or obligatory almsgiving; *saum* or fasting sunrise to sunset through Ramadan (ninth month of the year, which varies with the calendar); and the *hajj* or pilgrimage to Mecca at least once in a lifetime.

divisions On the prophet's death 632, the question of the immediate succession to the leadership gave rise to political splits which were later formalized as doctrinal differences. Muhammad was followed as leader by a succession of 'rightly guided caliphs' – Abu Bakr, Umar, Uthman, and Ali, the last-named being the prophet's son-in-law. The Shi'a tradition began as the party within the Islamic community that supported the candidacy of Ali; it later developed a theology based on Ali's mystical role as Muhammad's true successor. The Sunni sect recognize all the four caliphs as lawful rulers, whereas the Shi'ites, who see legitimacy vested in the lineage of the prophet, regard the first three as only rulers, not caliphs.

history Islam was founded as a universal missionary religion, and between 711 and 1492 spread east into India, west over N Africa, then north across Gibraltar into the Iberian peninsula. During the Middle Ages, Islamic scholars preserved and developed ancient Greco-Roman learning, while the Dark Ages prevailed in Christian Europe. Islam was seen as an enemy of Christianity by European countries during the Crusades, and Christian states united against a Muslim nation as late as the Battle of Lepanto 1571.

Driven from Europe, Islam remained established in N Africa and the Middle East. In recent years Islamic regimes have been established in Iran, Afghanistan, and Sudan. Elsewhere, militant Islamic neo-fundamentalist groups have sprung up, which base their theological ideas on the textual foundation of Islam represented by the Koran. Such groups are opposed to secular governments which they see as promoting Western values.

modern trends and 'fundamentalism' These modern trends, often referred to as fundamentalism, are considered by many to be socio-political phenomena inspired by Muhammad Abd al-Wahab (1703–1792), who called upon Muslims to return to the fundamentals of Islam. The ideological strands that reflect his views throughout the Muslim world have been shaped by a variety of local factors.

The Muslim Brotherhood (founded in Egypt by Hassan al-Banna in 1928) was the chief influence, ideologically and operationally, that spurred the growth of many contemporary movements. By the late 1950s the Muslim world had been subject to enormous cultural and economic influences from the Western industrialized world, which had a disruptive impact on the traditional Islamic value system. This gave the Muslim Brotherhood the impetus to develop their ideas, which had a similar impact on Muslims as did the earlier Wahabi movement. Both movements called for a return to puritanism in Islam; both were at the forefront of the opposition to governments which they viewed as corrupt. Although the Muslim Brotherhood did not proclaim total rejection of Western industrial culture, it sought to replace the 'ethical vacuum' with Islamic values. The organization came into conflict with Egyptian president Gamal Abdel Nasser in 1956 and with Syrian president Hafez al-Assad in 1980; in both cases, the result of the confrontation was the outlawing of the group by the governments, which saw the Brotherhood's growing popularity as a threat to the political establishment.

The call for Islamic revivalism has also been used by groups seeking power in the Islamic world, often leading to an inaccurate interpretation of Islam. An example is the Afghan ◊Talibaan, who deny women's basic rights despite the equal relationship between the sexes prescribed by the Koran. The misrepresentation of Islam results in widening further the gulf between itself and the West.

Today, the term fundamentalism is used generically to refer to many Muslim activist groups and parties. The religious extremism often implied by the term is similar to the concept of *ghulat*. In Islamic history, this term was used for individuals accused of fanaticism. Although the term was more often used to refer to extreme Shiite groups, it serves to illustrate that the Islamic faith has suffered the same tendency towards extremism and violence as have other world religions.

Islam is a major force throughout the Arab world and a focus for nationalism among the peoples of the Central Asian Republics. It is also a significant factor in Pakistan, Indonesia, and Malaysia. Islam is the second largest religion in the UK. *See timeline on following page.*

Islamabad capital of Pakistan from 1967, in the Potwar district, at the foot of the Margala Hills and immediately NW of Rawalpindi; population (1988) 201,000. The city was designed by Constantinos Doxiadis in the 1960s. The Federal Capital Territory of Islamabad has an area of 907 sq km/350 sq mi and a population (1985) of 379,000.

Islamic architecture the architecture of the Muslim world, highly diverse but unified by climate, culture, and a love of geometric and arabesque ornament, as well as by the mobility of ideas, artisans, and architects throughout the region. The central public buildings are ◊mosques, often with a dome and minaret (slender turret or tower); domestic houses face an inner courtyard and are grouped together, with vaulted streets linking the blocks.

The mosque is the centre of religious life throughout the Islamic world, the *masjid* or 'place of prostration'. The major mosque in a city is the *masjid al-jum'a*, the Friday mosque. The mosque form originated in Muhammad's house in Medina (where he fled from Mecca 622). It was a mud-walled courtyard enclosure with a shaded perimeter. The elements of the mosque are essentially functional rather than symbolic. There is no division between the sacred and secular. A *mihrab* niche indicates the orientation to Mecca. To the right of the *mihrab* stands the *minbar*, the pulpit. A minaret signifies the presence of the mosque and provides a platform from which the muezzin calls the faithful to prayer. A courtyard *sahn* is a place of gathering for the community.

The Arab-type mosque plan of columned halls surrounding a courtyard is found throughout N Africa, Arabia, Syria, and Mesopotamia; an example is the mosque of Ahmad ibn Tulun, Cairo, Egypt, 876–79. The other great mosque type is the four-*eyvan* mosque originating in Iran. Here the courtyard has a high *eyvan*, or arched recess, in the centre of each side. This plan comes from the Persian house and is seen at its noblest in the Masjid-i-Jum'a in Isfahan, Iran, 8th–18th centuries. A very flexible plan form, it is found from Cairo to central Asia in mosques, theological colleges, caravanserais, and hospitals.

In the Ottoman Empire, the stimulus of the ◊Hagia Sophia (532–37), Istanbul, the great church of Justinian, inspired the development of the imperial Turkish mosque in which the open courtyard of the Arab and Iranian mosques is translated into a great space enclosed by a large central dome; an example is the Suleymaniye, Istanbul, 1550–57, by Sinan.

The minaret was originally square, following the towers of Christian churches. Spiral minarets are found but most commonly they take the form of a tapering cylindrical tower.

The Islamic city is a highly organic entity. The basic cellular unit is the courtyard house, representing the desire for privacy and familial obligations of Muslim life. The houses are grouped into quarters, often of a tribal or ethnic character. Each quarter has its own mosques and facilities. At the centre of the city stands the focus of the community, the congregational mosque, the *masjid al-jum'a*. The arteries of this intricate organism are the vaulted streets of the souk, or bazaar, which thread outwards from the *masjid al-jum'a* towards the great gates of the enclosing fortified walls. The key monuments and facilities of the city are found along the souk – the religious colleges, baths, hospitals, and fountains. Examples of these are found in Fez, Morocco; Aleppo, Syria; and Isfahan, Iran.

Islamic private houses are invariably inward-looking courtyard houses. A bent corridor (for privacy) leads from the gated entry from the public lane into a courtyard paved with tiles, often planted with shade trees and with a pool at the centre. Surrounding the courtyard are the principal rooms of the house. Different sides of the courtyard may provide separate accommodation for sections of the extended family.

decoration and colour In Islam there is a general dislike of figurative representation. As a consequence, architectural decoration relies on calligraphic script and abstract ornament, often combined with a passion for colour, intensified by the desert environment. The domes and courts of such buildings as the 17th-century Masjid-i-Sháh, Isfahan, Iran, are entirely clothed in faience tiles. Arabic script is used extensively in the earliest surviving Islamic building, the Dome of the Rock, Jerusalem, AD 691, and thereafter the word of God plays a significant role in architectural decoration.

Islamic gardens In a largely arid region, the Islamic garden represents an image of paradise. The basic plan is a rectangular enclosure walled against the dust of the desert and divided into at least four sections by water channels. Pavilions are placed at focal points within the gardens. An example is Chehel Sutun, Isfahan, 17th century.

Islamic art art and design of the Muslim world, dating from the foundation of the Islamic faith in the 7th century AD. The traditions laid down by Islam created devout, painstaking craftsmen whose creative purpose was the glory of God. Elements and motifs were borrowed from ◊Byzantine, ◊Coptic, and ◊Persian Sassanian (AD 224–642) traditions and fused into a distinctive decorative style, based on arabic calligraphy. Sculpture was prohibited and carvers turned instead to exquisite inlay and fretwork, notably on doors and screens, in Islamic monuments such as the Alhambra Palace, Granada, Spain, and the Taj Mahal, India. Today, Islamic art is to be found predominately in Egypt, Iran, Iraq, Turkey, the Indian subcontinent, and the Central Asian Republics.

calligraphy Regarded as the highest of all arts due to its role in transcribing the Koran, calligraphy was used to decorate pottery, textiles, metalwork, and architecture. Scripts ranged in style from the cursive Naskh with its extended flourishes to the angular Kufic. Interlacing patterns based on geometry and stylized plant motifs (including the swirling ◊arabesque) typically framed and enhanced the lettering.

ceramics Drawing on Chinese techniques and styles, Muslim potters developed their own distinc-

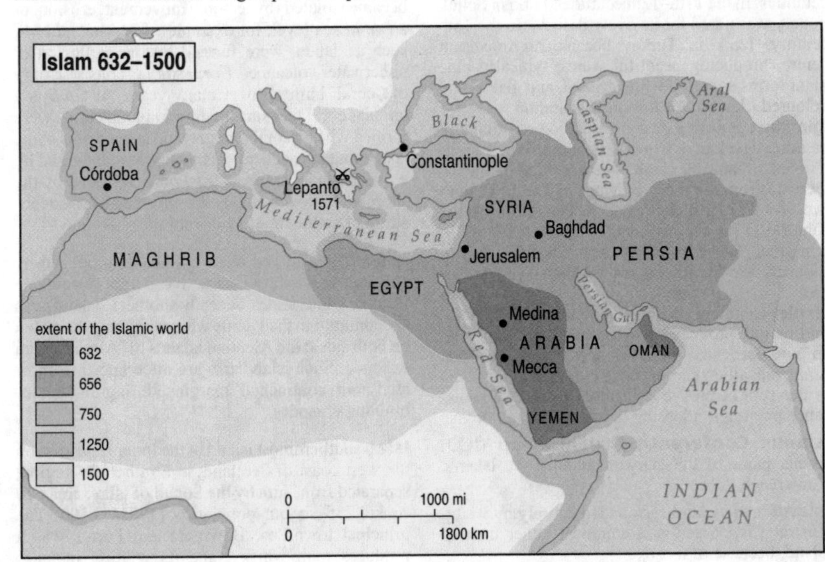

ISLAM: TIMELINE

3rd–6th Cs	The eastern Roman Empire and the Persian Sassanians were in continuous conflict for the domination of Syria, Egypt, and Asia Minor.
571	Birth of Muhammad, the prophet of Islam, in Mecca.
6th–7th Cs	Islam began in Arabia, calling for a new way of life based on submission to God. An Islamic state was established that developed further during the formative period of the four Orthodox caliphs or successors to the prophet, Abu Bakr, Umar, Uthman, and Ali. During this period the Persians were defeated (637) and their capital Cteisphon was captured.
8th C	Islam expanded under the Umayyad and Abbasid dynasties to Spain and Sind; southern France was invaded; Southern Italy was occupied. The early schools of Islamic law continued to develop during this period and the legal doctrine became integrated into the legal practices of the courts.
9th C	Turkish slave Mamelukes rose to power in Baghdad and a dictatorship was established in Egypt that occupied Syria, in a move towards the fragmentation of the main Islamic state.
10th C	The Fatimid Shiite Isma'ili sect conquered Cairo in 969. Al-Azhar University was founded in 972. With the insanity of the Fatimid caliph (who believed himself God) and his death in 1018, a new religion appeared in the form of the Druze Shia subsect, comprised of those adherents who believed in his divinity.
11th C	The Abbasid and Fatimid dynasties and the Byzantine empire declined. The central Asian Turkish nomads known as the Seljuks emerged. Islamic law became stagnant. The first Crusade captured Jerusalem in 1099.
12th C	Muslims were reunited in a jihad or holy war, and recaptured Jerusalem under the leadership of Saladin. The Mongols emerged as a new force, seizing Persia and part of Syria.
13th C	The Mongols continued their march, sacking Baghdad. With the fall of the city 1258 and the death of the caliph Mustasim, the Abbasid caliphate ended. Only two years later the Mongols were defeated by Qutuz at the decisive Battle of Ayn Jalut on the way to Damascus, ending their expansion towards the heartland of the Muslim world. Thirty years later the Mongol khan converted to Islam. This was followed by the emergence of the first Ottomans in Turkey.
14th C	Ottoman Turks invaded Bulgarian territory up to the Balkans.
15th C	In the Second Battle of Kossova in 1446 Serbia was annexed to Turkey, with Bosnia as its vassal. Muhammad al-Fath conquered Constantinople in 1453. Albania was annexed to the Ottoman Turkish empire. Granada, the last Muslim state in Spain, fell to Ferdinand and Isabella. The Safavid dynasty was founded in Persia.
16th–17th Cs	Ottoman power reached its height during the reign of the Ottoman Sulayman the Magnificent 1520–56. The first unsuccessful Ottoman siege of Vienna was in 1529, and the second in 1683. With the defeat of the Ottomans in the naval battle of Lepanto, their dominance of the Mediterranean ended. The forcible conversion of Muslims to Catholicism began in Spain.
18th C	In Arabia, Muhammad ibn-Abd-al-Wahab (1703–1787) preached a return to fundamental Muslim values.
19th C	Muhammad Ali was appointed pasha of Egypt by the Turks in 1805, after subduing the Mamelukes. He occupied Mecca and Taif in 1813 and continued across Arabia, expelling the Saudis from their capital Dariyya in 1818. European powers took control of many territories that had previously come under Muslim rule. In 1876 Britain purchased shares in the Suez Canal and became involved in Egypt, with military occupation following in 1882. In 1878 Turkey handed Cyprus to Britain and a year later, after the Treaty of Berlin, Turkey lost 80% of its European territory.
20th C	European expansion continued in the Middle East. During World War I, the Arabs revolted against Ottoman Turkish rule. In 1921, the British made kings of two sons of the Sharif of Mecca, Abdullah ibn Hussein of Transjordan and Faisal of Iraq. Mustafa Kemal abolished the Turkish sultanate in 1922 and became the first president of Turkey. Reza Shah seized the government in Persia in 1925. Abdul Aziz Ibn Saud captured Riyadh and Mecca, assuming the title of king in 1926. Hasan al-Banna founded the Muslim Brotherhood in Egypt in 1928. Egyptian president Gamal Abdel Nasser nationalized the Suez Canal in 1956 and executed Sayyid Qutb, the leader of the Muslim Brotherhood. The secular Pahlavi dynasty ended in 1979 with the exile of his son following the return from exile of Ayatollah Khomeini, who declared Iran an Islamic Republic. The Iraq–Iran War was followed by Saddam Hussein's invasion of Kuwait (1990) and the Gulf War. Revivalist movements arose, calling for a return to fundamental Islamic values; Islamic regimes were established in Iran, Afghanistan, and Sudan.

tive, often coloured, lustres and glazes, which were later influential in the development of European ceramics. In the 11th–12th centuries Turkish Seljuk pottery was noted for its lively designs. In the 16th century, Iznik in Turkey became an important centre, producing beautiful wares, typically blue plant forms against a white ground, and glazed and coloured tilework for mosque decoration.

miniature painting A court tradition of miniature painting developed, which was primarily representational, featuring both humans and animals. Derived from the ivory carvings of Fatimid Egypt (AD 969–1171), it flourished in Persia during the Timurid (15th century) and Safavid (1502–1736) dynasties. The Tabriz school was transplanted to India by the Mogul emperor Akbar (see ◊Indian art).

textiles Islamic weavers, notably those of the Fatimid period, produced silk brocades and carpets of an unprecedented fineness and beauty. Turkish *ushak* medallion carpets were exported to the West in the 16th century and featured in many Renaissance paintings, adorning floors, walls, and desks.

Islamic Conference Organization (ICO) former name of the ◊Organization of the Islamic Conference (OIC).

island area of land surrounded entirely by water. Australia is classed as a continent rather than an island, because of its size.

Islands can be formed in many ways. ***Continental islands*** were once part of the mainland, but became isolated (by tectonic movement, erosion, or a rise in sea level, for example). ***Volcanic islands***, such as Japan, were formed by the explosion of underwater volcanoes. ***Coral islands*** consist mainly of ◊coral, built up over many years. An ***atoll*** is a circular coral reef surrounding a lagoon; atolls were formed when a coral reef grew up around a volcanic island that subsequently sank or was submerged by a rise in sea level. ***Barrier islands*** are found by the shore in shallow water, and are formed by the deposition of sediment eroded from the shoreline.

island arc curved chain of islands produced by volcanic activity at a destructive margin (where one tectonic plate slides beneath another). Island arcs are common in the Pacific where they ring the ocean on both sides; the Aleutian Islands off Alaska are an example. Such island arcs are often later incorporated into continental margins during mountain-building episodes.

Islay southernmost island of the Inner Hebrides, on the west coast of Scotland, in Strathclyde Region, separated from Jura by the Sound of Islay; area 610 sq km/235 sq mi; population (1991) 3,500. The principal towns are Bowmore and Port Ellen. It produces malt whisky, and its wildlife includes eagles and rare wintering geese. A wave-power electricity-generating station opened 1991 near Portnahaven on the Rinns of Islay.

Isle of Ely former county of England, in East Anglia. It was merged with Cambridgeshire 1965.

Isle of Man see ◊Man, Isle of.

Isle of Wight see ◊Wight, Isle of.

islets of Langerhans groups of cells within the pancreas responsible for the secretion of the hormone insulin. They are sensitive to the blood sugar, producing more hormone when glucose levels rise.

Islington inner borough of N Greater London. It includes the suburbs of Finsbury, Barnsbury, and Holloway

features Sadler's Wells music hall, built 1638 when Clerkenwell springs were exploited and Islington Spa became famous; present Sadler's Wells theatre (1927–31), where opera and ballet companies were established under direction of Lilian ◊Baylis; 17th-century houses at Newington Green; 18th- and 19th-century squares and terraces in Canonbury, Highbury, and Barnsbury; Wesley's Chapel (1777, restored 1978), with museum of Methodism and John Wesley's house; Regents canal, with tunnel 886 m/2,910 ft long; Tower Theatre (1952) in early 16th-century Canonbury Tower; Kings Head, pioneer of public-house theatres in the late 1960s; Almeida Theatre; Packington estate; Business Design Centre; Chapel Market; Pentonville and Holloway prisons

famous people Duncan Grant, Vanessa Bell, George Weedon Grossmith, Basil Spence, and Yehudi Menuhin all lived here

population (1991) 164,700.

Ismail 1830–1895. Khedive (governor) of Egypt 1866–79. A grandson of Mehmet Ali, he became viceroy of Egypt 1863 and in 1866 received the title of khedive from the Ottoman sultan. He amassed huge foreign debts and in 1875 Britain, at Prime Minister Disraeli's suggestion, bought the khedive's Suez Canal shares for nearly £4 million, establishing Anglo-French control of Egypt's finances. In 1879 the UK and France persuaded the sultan to appoint Tewfik, his son, khedive in his place.

Ismail I 1486–1524. Shah of Persia from 1501. He was the founder of the Safavi dynasty, and established the first national government since the Arab conquest and Shi'ite Islam as the national religion.

ISO in photography, a numbering system for rating the speed of films, devised by the International Standards Organization.

isobar line drawn on maps and weather charts linking all places with the same atmospheric pressure (usually measured in millibars). When used in weather forecasting, the distance between the isobars is an indication of the barometric gradient (the rate of change in pressure). Where the isobars are close together, cyclonic weather is indicated, bringing strong winds and a depression, and where far apart anticyclonic, bringing calmer, settled conditions.

Isocrates 436–338 BC. Greek rhetorician and one of the ten Attic Orators. His fame principally rests upon a political pamphlet, the 'Panegyric', in which he advocates Greek unity and supremacy. He was a professional speechwriter and teacher of rhetoric, but because of his weak voice and extreme shyness he never spoke in the courts or addressed a public meeting. Other published works include the manifesto 'Against the Sophists'.

isolationism in politics, concentration on internal rather than foreign affairs; a foreign policy having no interest in international affairs that do not affect the country's own interests.

Isolde or *Iseult* in Celtic and medieval legend, the wife of King Mark of Cornwall who was brought from Ireland by his nephew ◊Tristan. She and Tristan accidentally drank the aphrodisiac given to her by her mother for her marriage, were separated as lovers, and finally died together.

isomer chemical compound having the same molecular composition and mass as another, but with different physical or chemical properties owing to the different structural arrangement of its constituent atoms. For example, the organic compounds butane ($CH_3(CH_2)_2CH_3$) and methyl propane ($CH_3CH(CH_3)CH_3$) are isomers, each possessing four carbon atoms and ten hydrogen atoms but differing in the way that these are arranged with respect to each other.

Structural isomers have obviously different constructions, but ***geometrical*** and ***optical isomers*** must be drawn or modelled in order to appreciate the difference in their three-dimensional arrangement. Geometrical isomers have a plane of symmetry and arise because of the restricted rotation of atoms around a bond; optical isomers are mirror images of each other. For instance, 1,1-dichloroethene ($CH_2{=}CCl_2$) and 1,2-dichloroethene ($CHCl{=}CHCl$) are structural isomers, but there are two possible geometric isomers of the latter (depending on whether the chlorine atoms are on the same side or on opposite sides of the plane of the carbon–carbon double bond).

isometrics system of muscular exercises without apparatus – for example, by contracting particular sets of muscles. These exercises, some of which can be performed without visible movement, have been recommended to sedentary workers as a way of getting fit, but can be damaging when practised by the unskilled.

isomorphism the existence of substances of different chemical composition but with similar crystalline form.

isoprene $CH_2CHC(CH_3)CH_2$ (technical name ***methylbutadiene***) colourless, volatile fluid obtained from petroleum and coal, used to make synthetic rubber.

isorhythm in music, a form in which a given rhythm cyclically repeats, although the corresponding melody notes may change. It was used in European medieval music, and is still practised in classical Indian music. The composers Berg, Cage, and Messiaen used isorhythmic procedures.

isostasy the theoretical balance in buoyancy of all parts of the Earth's ◊crust, as though they were floating on a denser layer beneath. There are two theories of the mechanism of isostasy, the Airy hypothesis and the Pratt hypothesis, both of which have validity. In the Airy hypothesis crustal blocks have the same density but different depths: like ice cubes floating in water, higher mountains have deeper roots. In the Pratt hypothesis, crustal blocks have different densities allowing the depth of crustal material to be the same.

isotope one of two or more atoms that have the same atomic number (same number of protons), but which contain a different number of neutrons, thus differing in their atomic masses. They may be stable or radioactive, naturally occurring or synthesized. The term was coined by English chemist Frederick Soddy, pioneer researcher in atomic disintegration.

Isozaki Arata 1931– . Japanese architect. One of Kenzo ◊Tange's team 1954–63, he has tried to blend Western Post-Modernist with elements of traditional Japanese architecture. His works include Ochanomizu Square, Tokyo (retaining the existing façades), the Museum of Contemporary Art, Los Angeles (begun 1984), and buildings for the 1992 Barcelona Olympics.

Israel country in SW Asia, bounded N by Lebanon, E by Syria and Jordan, S by the Gulf of Aqaba and W by Egypt and the Mediterranean Sea. *See country box on p. 560.*

Israel ancient kingdom of N ◊Palestine, formed after the death of Solomon by Jewish peoples seceding from the rule of his son Rehoboam and electing Jeroboam as their leader.

It is named after the descendants of the Old Testament patriarch Jacob, whose name was changed to Israel. Jews believe that the land of Israel was given to them for ever by God when he brought them out of Egypt under Moses' guidance. The name is therefore sometimes used to refer to the Jews themselves, as in 'the people of Israel' or, in the context of biblical times, 'Israelites'.

Israëls Jozef 1824–1911. Dutch painter. In 1870 he settled in The Hague and became a leader of the Hague School of landscape painters, who shared some of the ideals of the ◊Barbizon School in France. His low-keyed and sentimental scenes of peasant life recall the work of ◊Millet.

Issigonis Alec (Alexander Arnold Constantine) 1906–1988. Turkish-born British engineer who designed the Morris Minor 1948 and the Mini-Minor 1959 cars, comfortable yet cheaper to run than their predecessors. He is credited with adding the word 'mini' to the English language.

Issus, Battle of battle 333 BC in which Alexander the Great defeated the Persian king Darius III at the ancient port of Issus in Cilicia, about 80 km/50 mi west of present-day Adana, Turkey. Darius' family were captured during the battle which secured Alexander's supply route in preparation for his invasion of the Persian Empire.

Istanbul city and chief seaport of Turkey; population (1990) urban area 6,407,200; city 6,293,400. It produces textiles, tobacco, cement, glass, and leather. Founded as Byzantium about 660 BC, it was renamed Constantinople AD 330 and was the capital of the ◊Byzantine Empire until captured by the Turks 1453. As Istamboul it was capital of the Ottoman Empire until 1922.
features the harbour of the Golden Horn; Hagia Sophia (Emperor Justinian's church of the Holy Wisdom, 537, now a mosque); Sultan Ahmet Mosque, known as the Blue Mosque, from its tiles; Topkapi Palace of the Sultans, with a harem of 400 rooms (now a museum). The Selimye Barracks in the suburb of Usküdar (Scutari) was used as a hospital in the Crimean War; the rooms used by Florence Nightingale, with her personal possessions, are preserved as a museum.

IT abbreviation for ◊***information technology***.

Itagaki Taisuke 1837–1919. Japanese military and political leader. He was the founder of Japan's first political party, the Jiyūtō (Liberal Party) 1875–81. Involved in the overthrow of the ◊Tokugawa shogunate and the ◊Meiji restoration 1866–68, Itagaki became a champion of democratic principles while continuing to serve in the government for short periods.

After ennoblement 1887 he retained the leadership of the party and cooperated with ◊Itō Hirobumi in the establishment of parliamentary government in the 1890s.

Itaipu world's largest hydroelectric plant, situated on the Paraná River, SW Brazil. A joint Brazilian-Paraguayan venture, it came into operation 1984; it supplies hydroelectricity to a wide area.

Italian architecture architecture of the Italian peninsula after the fall of the Roman Empire. In the earliest styles – Byzantine, Romanesque, and Gothic – the surviving buildings are mostly churches. From the Renaissance and Baroque periods there are also palaces, town halls, and so on.
Byzantine (5th–11th centuries) Italy is rich in examples of this style of architecture, which is a mixture of oriental and classical elements; examples are the monuments of Justinian in Ravenna and the basilica of San Marco, Venice, about 1063.

ISLAND: MAJOR ISLANDS

Name (location)	Area in sq km/sq mi
Greenland (North Atlantic)	2,175,600/840,000
New Guinea (SW Pacific)	800,000/309,000
Borneo (SW Pacific)	744,100/287,300
Madagascar (Indian Ocean)	587,000/227,000
Baffin (Canadian Arctic)	507,258/195,928
Sumatra (Indian Ocean)	473,600/182,860
Honshu (NW Pacific)	230,966/89,176
Great Britain (N Atlantic)	229,978/88,795
Victoria (Canadian Arctic)	217,206/83,896
Ellesmere (Canadian Arctic)	196,160/75,767
Sulawesi (Indian Ocean)	189,216/73,057
South Island, New Zealand (SW Pacific)	149,883/57,870
Java (Indian Ocean)	126,602/48,900
North Island, New Zealand (SW Pacific)	114,669/44,274
Cuba (Caribbean Sea)	110,800/44,800
Newfoundland (NW Atlantic)	108,860/42,030
Luzon (W Pacific)	104,688/40,420
Iceland (N Atlantic)	103,000/39,800
Mindanao (W Pacific)	94,630/36,537
Ireland – N and the Republic (N Atlantic)	84,400/32,600
Hokkaido (NW Pacific)	83,515/32,245
Sakhalin (NW Pacific)	76,400/29,500
Hispaniola – Dominican Republic and Haiti (Caribbean Sea)	76,000/29,300
Banks (Canadian Arctic)	70,000/27,038
Tasmania (SW Pacific)	67,800/26,200
Sri Lanka (Indian Ocean)	64,600/24,900
Devon (Canadian Arctic)	55,247/21,331

Romanesque (10th–13th centuries) In N Italy buildings in this style are often striped in dark and light marble; Sicily has Romanesque churches.
Gothic (13th–15th centuries) Italian Gothic differs a great deal from that of N Europe. Façades were elaborately decorated: mosaics and coloured marble were used, and sculpture placed around windows and doors. The enormous cathedral of Milan, 15th century, was built in the N European style.
Renaissance (15th–16th centuries) The style was developed by the Florentine Brunelleschi and his contemporaries, inspired by Classical models. The sculptor Michelangelo is associated with the basilica of St Peter's, Rome. In Venice the villas of Palladio continued the purity of the High Renaissance. Other outstanding architects of the Renaissance include Bramante, Giulio Romano, Sangallo, Vignola, and Sansovino.
Baroque (17th century) The Baroque style flourished with the oval spaces of Bernini (for example, the church of S Andrea al Quirinale, Rome) and Boromini, Cortona, and the fantasies of Guarini in Turin (such as the church of S Lorenzo).
Neo-Classicism (18th–19th centuries) In the 18th century Italian architecture was less significant, and a dry Classical revival prevailed. In the 19th century Neo-Classicism was the norm, as in much of Europe.
20th century The Futurist visions of Sant'Elia opened the century. Between World Wars I and II pure Modernism was explored (under the influence of Fascism) together with a stripped Classicism, as

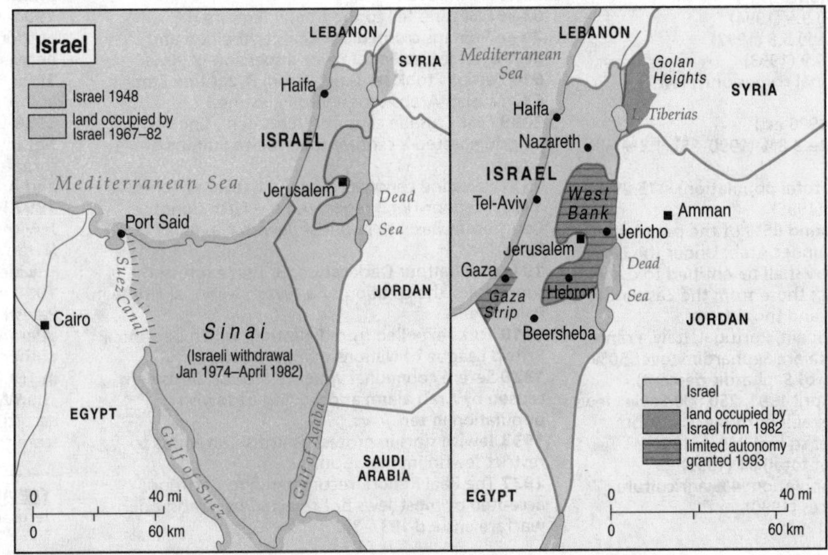

in the Rationalism of Terragni. Nervi's work showed the expressive potential of reinforced concrete. Terragni and Gio Ponti pioneered the Modern Movement. Since the 1970s, Neo-Rationalism and a related concern with the study of the traditional types of European cities have exerted great influence, led by the work of Aldo Rossi. High Tech architecture is represented by Renzo Piano.

Italian art distinctively Italian art began to emerge during the 13th century, drawing on medieval, Byzantine, and Classical art. The works of Giotto were the first major achievement of Italian painting. Throughout the 14th century the courtly ◊International Style flourished. From 1400 to 1600 Italy was the home of the Renaissance, and its painting and sculpture closely reflected the profound social, religious, political, and intellectual changes of the era. Increasingly prosperous and powerful cities such as Florence, Siena, Venice, Rome, Mantua, and Ferrara produced a host of major artists, including Masaccio, Mantegna, Piero della Francesca, Botticelli, Leonardo da Vinci, Raphael, Michelangelo, and Titian. During this period the influence of Italian art began to spread throughout Europe. ◊Mannerism flourished briefly during the second half of the 16th century. The beginning of the 17th century saw the birth of the last great Italian art movement, the ◊Baroque. During the 18th and 19th centuries there were few Italian artists of international stature; Canaletto was one of the few. The early 20th century saw the emergence of ◊Futurism and, in the works of artists such as de Chirico, ◊Metaphysical Painting. After World War II, Italian artists largely reflected international trends; leading figures included Sandro Chia and Francesco Clemente. ▷ *See feature on p. 626–627.*

ISRAEL
State of

national name *Medinat Israel*
area 20,800 sq km/8,029 sq mi (as at 1949 armistice)
capital Jerusalem (not recognized by the United Nations)
major towns/cities Bat-Yam, Holon, Ramat Gan, Petach Tikva, Beersheba
major ports Tel Aviv/Jaffa, Haifa, 'Akko (formerly Acre), Eilat
physical features coastal plain of Sharon between Haifa and Tel Aviv noted since ancient times for fertility; central mountains of Galilee, Samaria, and Judea; Dead Sea, Lake Tiberias, and river Jordan Rift Valley along the E are below sea level; Negev Desert in the S; Israel occupies Golan Heights, West Bank, E Jerusalem, and Gaza Strip (the last was awarded limited autonomy, with West Bank town of Jericho, 1993)
head of state Ezer Weizman from 1993
head of government Binyamin Netanyahu from 1996
political system democratic republic
administrative divisions six districts
political parties Israel Labour Party, moderate, left of centre; Consolidation Party (Likud), right of centre; Meretz (Vitality), left-of-centre alliance
armed forces 172,000; reserves of 602,000 (1995)
conscription voluntary for Christians, Circassians, and Muslims; compulsory for Jews and Druzes (men 36 months, women 21 months)
defence spend (% GDP) 9.5 (1994)
education spend (% GNP) 5.8 (1992)
health spend (% GDP) 1.9 (1993)
death penalty exceptional crimes only; last execution 1962
population 5,664,000 (1996 est)
population growth rate 3.8% (1990–95); 1.3% (2000–05)
age distribution (% of total population) <15 29.1%, 15–65 61.4%, >65 9.5% (1995)
ethnic distribution around 85% of the population is Jewish, most of the remainder Arab. Under the Law of Return 1950, 'every Jew shall be entitled to come to Israel as an immigrant'; those from the East and E Europe are Ashkenazim, and those from Mediterranean Europe (Spain, Portugal, Italy, France, Greece) and Arab N Africa are Sephardim (over 50% of the population is now of Sephardic descent). Between Jan 1990 and April 1991, 250,000 Soviet Jews emigrated to Israel. An Israeli-born Jew is a Sabra
population density (per sq km) 249.4 (1994)
urban population (% of total) 91 (1995)
labour force 39% of population: 4% agriculture, 29% industry, 67% services (1990)
unemployment 7.2% (1994)
child mortality rate (under 5, per 1,000 live births) 9 (1993)
life expectancy 74 (men), 78 (women)
education (compulsory years) 11
literacy rate 96%
languages Hebrew and Arabic (official); English, Yiddish, European, and W Asian languages
religions Israel is a secular state, but the predominant faith is Judaism 85%; also Sunni Muslim, Christian, and Druse
TV sets (per 1,000 people) 271 (1992)
currency shekel
GDP (US $) 77.77 billion (1994)
GDP per capita (PPP) (US $) 15,130 (1993)
growth rate 4.1% (1980–93)
average annual inflation 14% (1994)
major trading partners USA, UK, Germany, Belgium, Italy, Japan, Switzerland
resources potash, bromides, magnesium, sulphur, copper ore, gold, salt, petroleum, natural gas
industries food processing, beverages, tobacco, electrical machinery, chemicals, petroleum and coal products, metal products, diamond polishing, transport equipment, tourism
exports citrus fruits, worked diamonds, machinery and parts, military hardware, food products, chemical products, textiles and clothing. Principal market: USA 30.1% (1993)
imports machinery and parts, rough diamonds, chemicals and related products, crude petroleum and petroleum products, motor vehicles. Principal source: USA 17.2% (1993)
arable land 17% (1993)
agricultural products citrus fruits, vegetables, potatoes, wheat, melons, pumpkins, avocados; livestock (poultry) and fish production

HISTORY
c. 2000 BC Abraham, father of the Jewish race, is believed to have come to Palestine from Mesopotamia.
c. 1225 BC Moses led the Jews out of slavery in Egypt towards the promised land of Palestine.
11th C BC Saul established a Jewish kingdom in Palestine; developed by kings David and Solomon.
586 BC Jews defeated by Babylon and deported; many returned to Palestine 539 BC.
333 BC Alexander the Great of Macedonia conquered the entire region.
142 BC Jewish independence restored after Maccabean revolt.
63 BC Palestine fell to the Roman Empire.
70 AD Romans crushed the Zealot rebellion and destroyed Jerusalem; start of dispersion of Jews.
614 Persians took Jerusalem from Byzantine Empire.
637 Muslim Arabs conquered Palestine.
1099 First Crusade captured Jerusalem; Christian kingdom lasted a century then fell to Sultans of Egypt.
1517 Palestine conquered by the Ottoman Turks.
1897 Theodor Herzl organized the First Zionist Congress at Basel to publicise Jewish claims to Palestine.
1917 The Balfour Declaration: Britain expressed support for the creation of a Jewish National Home in Palestine.
1918 Turks expelled from Palestine, which became a British League of Nations mandate 1920.
1929 Severe communal violence around Jerusalem caused by Arab alarm at doubling of Jewish population in ten years.
1933 Jewish riots in protest at British attempts to restrict Jewish immigration.
1937 The Peel Report, recommending partition, accepted by most Jews but rejected by Arabs; open warfare ensued 1937–38.
1939 Britain postponed independence plans and increased military presence.
1946 Resumption of terrorist violence; Jewish extremists blew up British headquarters in Jerusalem.
1947 United Nations (UN) voted for partition of Palestine.
1948 Britain withdrew; Independent State of Israel proclaimed with David Ben-Gurion as prime minister; Israel repulsed invasion by Arab nations; many Palestinian Arabs settled in refugee camps in the Gaza Strip and West Bank.
1952 Col Gamal Nasser of Egypt stepped up blockade of Israeli ports and support of Arab guerrillas in Gaza.
1956 War between Israel and Egypt; Israeli invasion of Gaza and Sinai followed by withdrawal 1957.
1963 Levi Eshkol succeeded Ben-Gurion as prime minister.
1964 Palestine Liberation Organization (PLO) founded to unite Palestinian Arabs with the aim of overthrowing the state of Israel.
1967 Israel defeated Egypt, Syria, and Jordan in the Six-Day War; Gaza, West Bank, E Jerusalem, Sinai, and Golan Heights captured.
1969 Golda Meir (Labour) elected prime minister; Yassir Arafat became president of the PLO; escalation of terrorism and border raids.
1973 Yom Kippur War: Israel repulsed surprise attack by Egypt and Syria.
1974 Golda Meir succeeded by Yitzhak Rabin.
1977 Right-wing Likud bloc took office under Menachem Begin; President Anwar Sadat of Egypt began peace initiative.
1979 Camp David talks ended with signing of peace treaty between Israel and Egypt; Israel withdrew from Sinai.
1980 United Jerusalem declared capital of Israel.
1982 Israeli forces invaded S Lebanon to drive out PLO guerrillas; occupation continued until 1985.
1985 Labour and Likud formed coalition government led by Shimon Peres 1985–86 and Yitzhak Shamir 1986–90.
1988 International criticism of Israeli handling of Palestinian uprising (Intifada) in occupied territories.
1990 Shamir headed Likud government following the breakup of the coalition; PLO formally recognized the state of Israel.
1991 Iraq launched missile attacks on Israel in Gulf War; Middle East peace talks began in Madrid.
1992 Labour government elected under Yitzhak Rabin.
1993 Rabin and Arafat signed peace accord; Israel granted limited autonomy to Gaza Strip and Jericho.
1994 Arafat became head of autonomous Palestinian authority in Gaza and Jericho; peace agreement between Israel and Jordan.
1995 Rabin assassinated by Jewish opponent of peace accord; Peres became prime minister.
1996 Likud government elected under Binyamin Netanyahu, critic of peace accord; peace process threatened in spite of meeting between Netanyahu and Arafat.
1997 Israeli schoolgirls killed by Jordanian soldier. Jewish settlement in E Jerusalem widely condemned. Netanyahu's government investigated for corruption. Suicide bombs by Hamas in Jerusalem.
1998 Violence flared on West Bank between Palestinians and Israeli troops. Netanyahu demanded guarantees about security from the Palestinian authorities; the peace process stalled. Bomb explosion in Tel Aviv. Ariel Sharon appointed foreign minister. The Wye River Memorandum, an American-brokered accord, paved the way for some Israeli withdrawal from the West Bank.

SEE ALSO Arab-Israeli Wars; Camp David Agreements; Jerusalem; Palestine; Zionism

Italian language member of the Romance branch of the Indo-European language family, the most direct descendant of Latin. Broadcasting and films have standardized the Italian national tongue, but most Italians speak a regional dialect as well as standard Italian.

The standard language originates in the Tuscan dialect of the Middle Ages, particularly as used for literary purposes by ◊Dante Alighieri. Its development parallels the integration of the Italian peninsula and the plains south of the Alps into a cultural and national unity. With a strong infusion of Latin for religious, academic, and educational purposes, written standard Italian has tended to be highly formal and divorced from the many regional dialects, which are often mutually unintelligible. Italian has provided English with much of the vocabulary of music, such as *adagio, arpeggio, cello, crescendo, and pianoforte*; Italian cuisine (*lasagne, macaroni, pasta, pizza, ravioli, spaghetti, tagliatelle*); and an assortment of social comment (*extravaganza, graffiti, imbroglio, mafia, seraglio*).

Italian literature the literature of Italy originated in the 13th century with the Sicilian school, which imitated Provençal poetry.

medieval The works of St Francis of Assisi and Jacopone da Todi reflect the religious faith of that time. Guido Guinicelli (1230–c. 1275) and Guido Cavalcanti developed the spiritual conception of love and influenced Dante Alighieri, whose *Divina commedia/Divine Comedy* 1307–21 is generally recognized as the greatest work of Italian literature. Petrarch was a humanist and a poet, celebrated for his sonnets, while Boccaccio is principally known for his tales.

Renaissance The *Divina commedia* marked the beginning of the Renaissance. Boiardo dealt with the Carolingian epics in his *Orlando innamorato/Roland in Love* 1487, which was completed and transformed by Lodovico Ariosto as *Orlando furioso/The Frenzy of Roland* 1516. Their contemporaries Niccolò Machiavelli and Francesco Guicciardini (1483–1540) are historians of note. Torquato Tasso wrote his epic *Gerusalemme liberata/Jerusalem Delivered* 1574 in the spirit of the Counter-Reformation.

17th century This period was characterized by the exaggeration of the poets Giovanni Battista Marini (1569–1625) and Gabriello Chiabrera (1552–1638). In 1690 the 'Academy of Arcadia' was formed, including among its members Innocenzo

> *'The Tuscan's siren tongue, / That music in itself, whose sounds are song, / The poetry of speech.'*
>
> On the ITALIAN LANGUAGE
> George Byron *Childe Harold's Pilgrimage* 1812–18

ITALY
Republic of

national name *Repubblica Italiana*
area 301,300 sq km/116,332 sq mi
capital Rome
major towns/cities Milan, Turin, Bologna
major ports Naples, Genoa, Palermo, Bari, Catania, Trieste
physical features mountainous (Maritime Alps, Dolomites, Apennines) with narrow coastal lowlands; continental Europe's only active volcanoes: Vesuvius, Etna, Stromboli; rivers Po, Adige, Arno, Tiber, Rubicon; islands of Sicily, Sardinia, Elba, Capri, Ischia, Lipari, Pantelleria; lakes Como, Maggiore, Garda
head of state Oscar Luigi Scalfaro from 1992
head of government Romano Prodi from 1996
political system democratic republic
administrative divisions 94 provinces within 20 regions (of which five have a greater degree of autonomy)
political parties Forza Italia (Go Italy!), free market, right of centre; Northern League (LN), Milan-based, federalist, right of centre; National Alliance (AN), neofascist; Italian Popular Party (PPI), Catholic, centrist; Italian Renewal Party, centrist; Democratic Party of the Left (PDS), pro-European, moderate left-wing (ex-communist); Italian Socialist Party (PSI), moderate socialist; Italian Republican Party (PRI), social democratic, left of centre; Democratic Alliance (AD), moderate left of centre; Christian Democratic Centre (CCD), Christian, centrist; Olive Tree alliance, centre-left; Panella List, radical liberal; Union of the Democratic Centre (UDC), right of centre; Pact for Italy, reformist; Communist Refoundation (RC), Marxist; Verdi, environmentalist; La Rete (the Network), anti-Mafia
armed forces 286,800 (1995)
conscription 12 months
defence spend (% GDP) 2.1 (1994)
education spend (% GNP) 5.4 (1992)
health spend (% GDP) 6.2 (1993)
death penalty abolished 1994
population 57,226,000 (1996 est)
population growth rate 0.1% (1990–95); −0.2% (2000–05)
age distribution (% of total population) <15 15.1%, 15–65 68.9%, >65 16% (1995)
ethnic distribution mainly Italian; some minorities of German origin
population density (per sq km) 190 (1994)
urban population (% of total) 67% (1995)
labour force 43% of the population: 9% agriculture, 31% industry, 60% services (1990)
unemployment 12% (1995)
child mortality rate (under 5, per 1,000 live births) 9 (1993)
life expectancy 73 (men), 80 (women)
education (compulsory years) 8
literacy 98% (men), 96% (women)
languages Italian; German, French, Slovene, and Albanian minorities
religion Roman Catholic 100% (state religion)
TV sets (per 1,000 people) 421 (1992)
currency lira
GDP (US $) 1,207.7 billion (1996)
GDP per capita (PPP) (US $) 19,536 (1995)
growth rate 3.0% (1994/95)
average annual inflation 4.2% (1995)
major trading partners EU (principally Germany, France, and UK), USA
resources lignite, lead, zinc, mercury, potash, sulphur, fluorspar, bauxite, marble, petroleum, natural gas, fish
industries machinery and machine tools, textiles, leather, footwear, food and beverages, steel, motor vehicles, chemical products, wine, tourism
exports machinery and transport equipment, textiles, clothing, footwear, wine (leading producer and exporter), metals and metal products, chemicals, wood, paper and rubber goods. Principal market: Germany 19.4% (1993)
imports mineral fuels and lubricants, machinery and transport equipment, chemical products, foodstuffs, metal products. Principal source: Germany 19.5% (1993)
arable land 30% (1993)
agricultural products sugar beet, grapes, wheat, maize, tomatoes, olives, citrus fruits, vegetables; fishing

HISTORY
4th and 3rd Cs BC Italian peninsula united under Roman rule.
AD 476 End of Western Roman Empire.
568 Invaded by Lombards.
756 Papal States created in central Italy.
800 Charlemagne united Italy and Germany in Holy Roman Empire.
12th and 13th Cs Papacy and Holy Roman Empire contended for political supremacy; papal power reached its peak under Innocent III (1198–1216).
1183 Cities of Lombard League (founded 1164) became independent.
14th C Beginnings of Renaissance in N Italy.
15th C Most of Italy ruled by five rival states: the city-states of Milan, Florence, and Venice; the Papal States; and the Kingdom of Naples.
1494 Charles VIII of France invaded Italy.
1529–59 Spanish Habsburgs dominate.
17th C Italy effectively part of Spanish Empire; economic and cultural decline.
1713 Treaty of Utrecht gave political control of most of Italy to Austrian Habsburgs.
1796–1814 France conquered Italy, setting up satellite states.
1815 Old regimes largely restored; Italy divided between Austria, Papal States, Naples, Sardinia, and four duchies.
1831 Giuseppe Mazzini founded 'Young Italy' movement with aim of creating unified republic.
1848–49 Liberal revolutions occurred throughout Italy; reversed everywhere except Sardinia, which became centre of nationalism under leadership of Count Camillo di Cavour.
1859 France and Sardinia forcibly expelled Austrians from Lombardy.
1860 Sardinia annexed duchies and Papal States (except Rome); Giuseppe Garibaldi overthrew Neapolitan monarchy.
1861 Victor Emmanuel II of Sardinia proclaimed King of Italy at Turin.
1866 Italy gained Venetia after defeat of Austria by Prussia.
1870 Italian forces occupied Rome in defiance of Pope, completing unification of Italy.
1882 Italy joined Germany and Austria-Hungary in Triple Alliance.
1896 Attempt to conquer Ethiopia defeated at Battle of Adowa.
1900 King Umberto I assassinated by an anarchist.
1912 Annexation of Libya and Dodecanese after Italo-Turkish War.
1915 Italy entered World War I on side of Allies.
1919 Peace treaties awarded Trentino, South Tyrol, and Trieste to Italy.
1922 Mussolini established fascist dictatorship following period of strikes and agrarian revolts.
1935–36 Conquest of Ethiopia.
1939 Invasion of Albania.
1940 Italy entered World War II as ally of Germany.
1943 Allies invaded southern Italy; Mussolini removed from power; Germans occupied northern and central Italy.
1945 Allies completed liberation.
1946 Monarchy replaced by republic.
1947 Peace treaty stripped Italy of its colonies.
1948 New constitution adopted; Christian Democrats emerged as main party of government in political system marked by ministerial instability.
1957 Italy became a founder member of European Economic Community (EEC).
1963 Creation of first of long series of fragile centre-left coalition governments.
1976 Communists attempt to join coalition, the 'historic compromise', rejected by Christian Democrats.
1978 Christian Democrat Aldo Moro, architect of historic compromise, murdered by Red Brigade guerrillas infiltrated by Western intelligence agents.
1983–87 Bettino Craxi, Italy's first Socialist prime minister, led coalition; economy improved.
1993 Major political crisis triggered by exposure of government corruption and Mafia links; governing parties discredited; new electoral system replaced proportional representation with 75% majority voting.
1994 Media tycoon Silvio Berlusconi created new party, Forza Italia, and formed right-wing coalition.
1995 Lamberto Dini headed non-party government of 'experts'.
1996 Olive Tree Alliance won general election; Romano Prodi became prime minister.
1997 Prodi survived parliamentary vote of censure; later resigned, 'grand coalition' sought; Prodi continues, with Communist support; Prodi cleared of corruption charges.

SEE ALSO Renaissance; Rome, ancient; Vatican City State

ITALY: REGIONS

Region	Capital	Area in sq km/sq mi
Abruzzi	Aquila	10,800/4,169
Basilicata	Potenza	10,000/3,861
Calabria	Catanzaro	15,100/5,830
Campania	Naples	13,600/5,250
Emilia-Romagna	Bologna	22,100/8,532
Friuli-Venezia Giulia*	Udine	7,800/3,011
Lazio	Rome	17,200/6,640
Liguria	Genoa	5,400/2,084
Lombardy	Milan	23,900/9,227
Marche	Ancona	9,700/3,745
Molise	Campobasso	4,400/1,698
Piedmont	Turin	25,400/9,806
Puglia	Bari	19,300/7,451
Sardinia*	Cagliari	24,100/9,305
Sicily*	Palermo	25,700/9,922
Trentino-Alto Adige*	Trento**	13,600/5,250
Tuscany	Florence	23,000/8,880
Umbria	Perugia	8,500/3,281
Valle d'Aosta*	Aosta	3,300/1,274
Veneto	Venice	18,400/7,104
	total	301,300/116,320

* special autonomous regions
** also Bolzano-Bozen

Frugoni (1692–1768) and Metastasio. Other writers include Salvator Rosa, the satirist.

18th century Giuseppe Parini (1729–1799) ridiculed the abuses of his day, while Vittorio Alfieri attacked tyranny in his dramas. Carlo Goldoni wrote comedies.

19th century Ugo Foscolo is chiefly remembered for his patriotic verse. Giacomo Leopardi is not only the greatest lyrical poet since Dante but also a master of Italian prose. The Romantic Alessandro Manzoni is best known as a novelist, and influenced among others the novelist Antonio Fogazzaro. A later outstanding literary figure, Giosuè Carducci, was followed by the verbose Gabriele d'Annunzio, writing of sensuality and violence, and Benedetto Croce, historian and philosopher, who between them dominated Italian literature at the turn of the century.

20th century Writers include the realist novelists Giovanni Verga and Grazia Deledda, winner of the Nobel prize 1926, the dramatist Luigi Pirandello, and the novelists Ignazio Silone and Italo Svevo. Poets of the period include Dino Campana and Giuseppe Ungaretti; and among the modern school are Nobel prizewinners Eugenio Montale and Salvatore Quasimodo. Novelists of the post-Fascist period include Alberto Moravia, Carlo Levi, Cesare Pavese, Vasco Pratolini (1913–), Elsa Morante (1916–), Natalia Ginsburg (1916–), Giuseppe Tomasi, Prince of Lampedusa, and the writers Italo Calvino, Leonardo Sciascia, and Primo Levi.

Italian Somaliland former Italian trust territory on the Somali coast of Africa extending to 502,300 sq km/194,999 sq mi. Established 1892, it was extended 1925 with the acquisition of Jubaland from Kenya; administered from Mogadishu; under British rule 1941–50. Thereafter it reverted to Italian authority before uniting with British Somaliland 1960 to form the independent state of Somalia.

italic style of printing in which the letters slope to the right *like this*, introduced by the printer Aldus Manutius of Venice in 1501. It is usually used side by side with the erect Roman type to distinguish titles of books, films, and so on, and for purposes of emphasis and (mainly in the USA) citation. The term 'italic' is also used for the handwriting style developed for popular use in 1522 by Vatican chancery scribe Ludovico degli Arrighi.

Italy country in S Europe, bounded N by Switzerland and Austria, E by Slovenia, Croatia, and the Adriatic Sea, S by the Ionian and Mediterranean seas, and W by the Tyrrhenian and Ligurian seas and France. It includes the Mediterranean islands of Sardinia and Sicily. *See country box on p. 561.*

iteroparity in biology, the repeated production of offspring at intervals throughout the life cycle. It is usually contrasted with ◊semelparity, where each individual reproduces only once during its life.

Ithaca (Greek *Itháki*) Greek island in the Ionian Sea, area 93 sq km/36 sq mi. Important in pre-Classical Greece, Ithaca was (in Homer's poem) the birthplace of ◊Odysseus, though this is sometimes identified with the island of Leukas (some archaeologists have equated ancient Ithaca with Leukas rather than modern Ithaca).

Itō Hirobumi. Prince 1841–1909. Japanese politician, prime minister 1887, 1892–96, 1898, 1900–01. He was a key figure in the modernization of Japan and was involved in the ◊Meiji restoration 1866–68 and in official missions to study forms of government in the USA and Europe in the 1870s and 1880s. As minister for home affairs, he helped draft the Meiji constitution of 1889.

Iturbide Agustín de 1783–1824. Mexican military leader (*caudillo*) who led the conservative faction in the nation's struggle for independence from Spain. In 1822 he crowned himself Emperor Agustín I. His extravagance and failure to restore order led all other parties to turn against him, and he reigned for less than a year (see ◊Mexican Empire).

IUCN abbreviation for ◊***International Union for the Conservation of Nature***.

Ivan six rulers of Russia, including:

Ivan (III) the Great 1440–1505. Grand duke of Muscovy from 1462. He revolted against Tatar overlordship by refusing tribute to Grand Khan Ahmed 1480. He claimed the title of tsar, and used the double-headed eagle as the Russian state emblem.

Ivan (IV) the Terrible 1530–1584. Grand duke of Muscovy from 1533. He assumed power 1544 and was crowned as first tsar of Russia 1547. He conquered Kazan 1552, Astrakhan 1556, and Siberia 1581. He reformed the legal code and local administration 1555 and established trade relations with England. In his last years he alternated between debauchery and religious austerities, executing thousands and, in rage, his own son.

Ivan attempted to centralize his rule in Muscovy. He campaigned against the Tatars of Kazan, Astrakhan, and elsewhere, but his policy of forming Russia into an empire led to the fruitless 24-year Livonian war. His regime was marked by brutality, evidenced by the destruction (sacking) of Novgorod.

Ives Charles Edward 1874–1954. US composer. He experimented with ◊atonality, quarter tones, clashing time signatures, and quotations from popular music of the time. He wrote five symphonies, including *Dvorakian Symphony No 1* 1895–98 and *Holidays Symphony* 1904–13; chamber music, including the *Concord Sonata*; and the orchestral works *Three Places in New England* 1903–14 and *The Unanswered Question* 1908.

IVF abbreviation for ◊***in vitro fertilization***.

ivory hard white substance of which the teeth and tusks of certain mammals are composed. Among the most valuable are elephants' tusks, which are of unusual hardness and density. Ivory is used in carving and other decorative work, and is so valuable that poachers continue to illegally destroy the remaining wild elephant herds in Africa to obtain it.

Poaching for ivory has led to the decline of the African elephant population from 2 million to approximately 600,000, with the species virtually extinct in some countries. Trade in ivory was halted by Kenya 1989, but Zimbabwe continued its policy of controlled culling to enable the elephant population to thrive and to release ivory for export. China and Hong Kong have refused to obey an international ban on ivory trading.

Vegetable ivory is used for buttons, toys, and cheap ivory goods. It consists of the hard albumen of the seeds of a tropical palm *Phytelephas macrocarpa*, and is imported from Colombia.

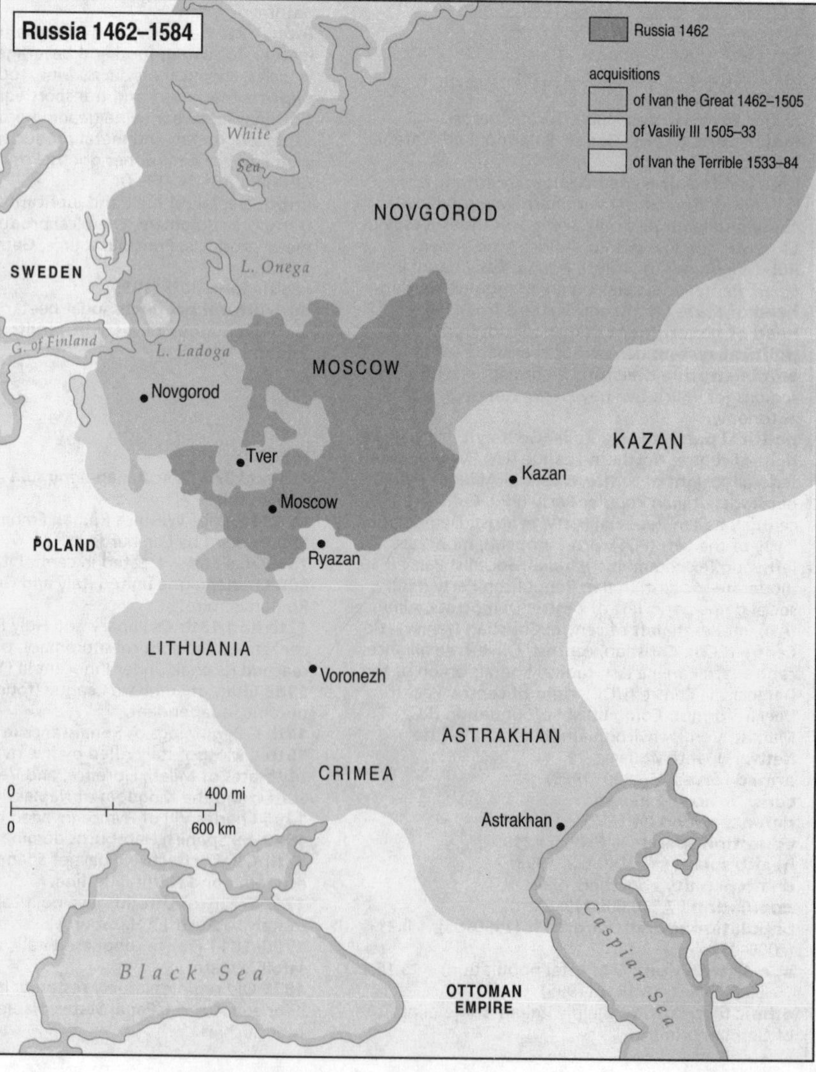

Iwo Jima, Battle of The Battle of Iwo Jima, one of the bloodiest confrontations between US and Japanese forces in World War II. US troops invaded the island Feb 1945 and are shown here raising the flag while still under enemy fire. Casualties were high; about 6,000 US marines were killed and Japanese losses are estimated at around 20,000. *Corbis*

Ivory Coast See ◊Côte d'Ivoire.

Ivory James Francis 1928– . US film director. He established his reputation with the Indian-made *Shakespeare Wallah* 1965, which began collaborations with Ishmail ◊Merchant and writer Ruth Prawer ◊Jhabvala. Ivory subsequently directed films in various genres in India, the USA and Europe, but became associated with adaptations of classic literature, including *The Bostonians* 1984, *A Room with a View* 1987, *Maurice* 1987, and *Howards End* 1992. He directed *The Remains of the Day* 1993, and *Jefferson in Paris* 1995.

ivy any tree or shrub of the genus *Hedera* of the ginseng family Araliaceae. English or European ivy *H. helix* has shiny, evergreen, triangular or oval-shaped leaves, and clusters of small, yellowish-green flowers, followed by black berries. It climbs by means of rootlike suckers put out from its stem, and is injurious to trees.

Ground ivy *Glechoma hederacea* is a small, originally European creeping plant of the mint family Labiatae; the North American poison ivy *Rhus radicans* belongs to the cashew family Anacardiaceae.

Ivy League eight long-established colleges and universities in the USA with prestigious academic and social reputations: Brown, Columbia, Cornell, Dartmouth, Harvard, Pennsylvania, Princeton, and Yale.

Iwo Jima largest of the Japanese Volcano Islands in the W Pacific Ocean, 1,222 km/760 mi S of Tokyo; area 21 sq km/8 sq mi. Annexed by Japan 1891, it was captured by the USA 1945 after fierce fighting. It was returned to Japan 1968.

Iwo Jima, Battle of intense fighting between Japanese and US forces 19 Feb–17 March 1945 during World War II. In Feb 1945, US marines landed on the island of Iwo Jima, a Japanese air base, intending to use it to prepare for a planned final assault on mainland Japan. The 22,000 Japanese troops put up a fanatical resistance but the island was finally secured 16 March. US casualties came to 6,891 killed and 18,700 wounded, while only 212 of the Japanese garrison survived.

Izetbegović Alija 1925– . Bosnia-Herzegovinan politician, president from 1990. A lifelong opponent of communism, he founded the Party of Democratic Action (PDA) 1990, ousting the communists in multiparty elections that year. Adopting a moderate stance during the civil war in Bosnia-Herzegovina, he sought an honourable peace for his country in the face of ambitious demands from Serb and Croat political leaders, and signed the Dayton peace accord 1995. He was re-elected president of a three-member collective presidency 1996 (with Serb nationalist Momcil Krajisnik and Croat Kresimir Zubak).

Izmir formerly ***Smyrna*** port and naval base in Turkey; population (1990) 1,757,400. Products include steel, electronics, and plastics. The largest annual trade fair in the Middle East is held here. It is the headquarters of ◊North Atlantic Treaty Organization SE Command.

history Originally Greek (founded about 1000 BC), it was of considerable importance in ancient times, vying with Ephesus and Pergamum as the first city of Asia. It was destroyed by ◊Tamerlane 1402 and became Turkish 1424. It was developed in the 16th century as an international trading centre, much of its trade gained at the expense of Venice. It was occupied by the Greeks 1919 but retaken by the Turks 1922; in the same year it was largely destroyed by fire.

Iznik modern name of ancient ◊Nicaea, a town in Turkey noted for the richly decorated pottery and tiles produced there in the 15th and 16th centuries.

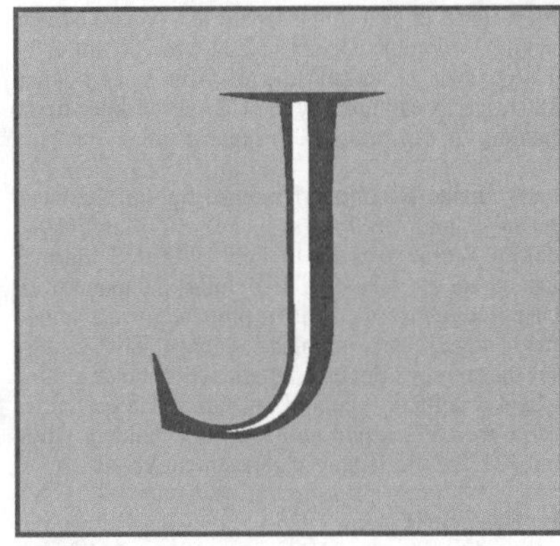

jabiru stork *Jabiru mycteria*, family Ciconiidae, order Ciconiiformes, found in Central and South America. It is 1.5 m/5 ft tall with white plumage. The head is black and red with a massive, slightly upturned bill. The neck is bare of feathers and can be puffed out, a manoeuvre which is probably used in social rituals.

jacamar insect-eating bird of the family Galbulidae, in the same order (Piciformes) as woodpeckers, found in dense tropical forest in Central and South America. It has a long, straight, sharply-pointed bill, a long tail, and paired toes. The plumage is golden bronze with a steely lustre. Jacamars are usually seen sitting motionless on trees from which they fly out to catch insects on the wing, then return to crack them on a branch before eating them. The largest species is *Jacamerops aurea*, which is nearly 30 cm/12 in long.

'The burden of being black is that you have to be superior just to be equal. But the glory of it is that, once you achieve, you have achieved, indeed.'

Jesse Jackson
Quoted in the *Christian Science Monitor* 26 Sept 1979

jacana or ***lily trotter*** wading bird, family Jacanidae, order Charadriiformes, with very long toes and claws enabling it to walk on the flat leaves of river plants. There are seven species. Jacanas are found in Mexico, Central America, South America, Africa, S Asia, and Australia. The female ***pheasant-tailed jacana*** *Hydrophasianus chirurgus* of Asia has a 'harem' of two to four males.

jacaranda any tropical American tree of the genus *Jacaranda* of the bignonia family Bignoniaceae, with fragrant wood and showy blue or violet flowers, commonly cultivated in the southern USA.

jack tool or machine for lifting, hoisting, or moving heavy weights, such as motor vehicles. A ***screw jack*** uses the principle of the screw to magnify an applied effort; in a car jack, for example, turning the handle many times causes the lifting screw to rise slightly, and the effort is magnified to lift heavy weights. A ***hydraulic jack*** uses a succession of piston strokes to increase pressure in a liquid and force up a lifting ram.

jackal any of several wild dogs of the genus *Canis*, found in S Asia, S Europe, and N Africa. Jackals can grow to 80 cm/2.7 ft long, and have greyish-brown fur and a bushy tail.

jacana The American jacana, or lily trotter, is a common waterbird of lagoons and marshes in Mexico and Central America. Jacanas have extremely long toes and claws for walking on floating vegetation.

The ***golden jackal*** *C. aureus* of S Asia, S Europe, and N Africa is 45 cm/1.5 ft high and 60 cm/2 ft long. It is greyish-yellow, darker on the back. Nocturnal, it preys on smaller mammals and poultry, although packs will attack larger animals. It will also scavenge. The ***side-striped jackal*** *C. adustus* is found over much of Africa; the ***black-backed jackal*** *C. mesomelas* occurs only in the south of Africa.

jackdaw Eurasian bird *Corvus monedula* of the crow family Corvidae, order Passeriformes. It is mainly black, but greyish on the sides and back of the head, and about 33 cm/1.1 ft long. It nests in tree holes or on buildings. Usually it lays five bluish-white eggs, mottled with tiny dark brown spots. Jackdaws feed on a wide range of insects, molluscs, spiders, worms, birds' eggs, fruit, and berries.

Jackson largest city and capital of Mississippi, on the Pearl River; population (1992) 196,200. It produces furniture, cottonseed oil, and iron and steel castings, and owes its prosperity to the discovery of gas fields to the S in the 1930s. Named after Andrew Jackson, later president, it dates from 1821 and was virtually destroyed by Union troops 1863, during the American Civil War.

Jackson 'Stonewall' (Thomas Jonathan) 1824–1863. US Confederate general in the American Civil War. He acquired his nickname and his reputation at the first Battle of Bull Run, from the firmness with which his brigade resisted the Northern attack. In 1862 he organized the Shenandoah Valley campaign and assisted Robert E ◊Lee's invasion of Maryland. He helped to defeat General Joseph E Hooker's Union army at the battle of Chancellorsville, Virginia, but was fatally wounded by one of his own soldiers in the confusion of battle.

Jackson Andrew 1767–1845. 7th president of the USA 1829–37, a Democrat. A major general in the War of 1812, he defeated a British force at New Orleans 1815 (after the official end of the war 1814) and was involved in the war that led to the purchase of Florida 1819. The political organization he built as president, with Martin Van Buren (1782–1862), was the basis for the modern ◊Democratic Party.

Jackson Colin Ray 1967– . Welsh athlete who won the 110 metres hurdles gold medal at the 1993 World Championships at Stuttgart in a world record time of 12.91 sec. He gained a silver medal at the 1988 Olympic Games, and won three consecutive European titles 1990–98 and two consecutive Commonwealth titles, 1990–94. He also excelled indoors, and in 1994 set an indoor world 60 metres hurdles record of 7.30 sec.

Jackson Glenda 1936– . English actress and politician; Labour member of Parliament 1992 and parliamentary under-secretary for transport from 1997. Her many stage appearances for the Royal Shakespeare Company include *Marat/Sade* 1966, Hedda in *Hedda Gabler* 1975, and Cleopatra in *Antony and Cleopatra* 1978. Among her films are the Oscar-winning *Women in Love* 1969, *Sunday Bloody Sunday* 1971, and *A Touch of Class* 1973.

Jackson Jesse Louis 1941– . US Democratic politician, a cleric and campaigner for minority rights. He contested his party's 1984 and 1988 presidential nominations in an effort to increase voter registration and to put black issues on the national agenda. He is an eloquent public speaker.

Born in North Carolina and educated in Chicago, Jackson emerged as a powerful Baptist preacher and black activist politician, working first with the civil-rights leader Martin Luther King, Jr, then on building the political machine that gave Chicago a black mayor 1983. Jackson sought to construct what he called a rainbow coalition of ethnic-minority and socially deprived groups.

Jackson Michael Joseph 1958– . US rock singer and songwriter. He turned professional 1969 as the youngest member of the Jackson Five, whose first hit single was 'I Want You Back'. His first solo hit was 'Got to Be There' 1971; his worldwide popularity peaked with the albums *Thriller* 1982, *Bad* 1987, and *Dangerous* 1991. Jackson's career faltered after allegations of child abuse, but he returned with the album *History* 1995. His videos and live performances are meticulously choreographed.

Jacksonville port, resort, and commercial centre in NE Florida, USA; population (1992) 661,200. The port has naval installations and ship-repair yards. To the north the Cross-Florida Barge Canal links the Atlantic with the Gulf of Mexico. Manufactured goods include wood and paper products, chemicals, and processed food.

Jackson US rock singer and songwriter Michael Jackson. His success reached its peak with the albums *Thriller* 1982 and *Bad* 1987, but suffered a decline in the early 1990s after an allegation of sexual abuse was settled out of court. *Topham*

Jack the Ripper popular name for the unidentified mutilator and murderer of at least five women prostitutes in the Whitechapel area of London 1888.

The murders understandably provoked public outrage; the police were heavily criticized, which later led to a reassessment of police procedures. Jack the Ripper's identity has never been discovered, although several suspects have been proposed, including members of the royal household.

Jacob in the Old Testament, Hebrew patriarch, son of Isaac and Rebecca, who obtained the rights of seniority from his twin brother Esau by trickery. He married his cousins Leah and Rachel, serving their father Laban seven years for each, and at the time of famine in Canaan joined his son Joseph in Egypt. His 12 sons were the traditional ancestors of the 12 tribes of Israel.

Jacob François 1920– . French biochemist who, with Jacques ◊Monod and André Lwoff (1902–), pioneered research into molecular genetics and showed how the production of proteins from ◊DNA is controlled. They shared the Nobel Prize for Physiology or Medicine 1965.

Jacobean style in the arts, particularly in architecture and furniture, during the reign of James I (1603–25) in England. Following the general lines of Elizabethan design, but using classical features more widely, it adopted many motifs from Italian ◊Renaissance design.

Jacobi Derek George 1938– . English actor. His powerful and sensitive talent has ensured a succession of leading roles in Shakespearean and other mainly serious drama on stage, television, and film. In the theatre he has several times played the title role in *Hamlet*, notably in 1979 in the newly reformed Old Vic production in London. Other stage work includes *Cyrano de Bergerac* 1983, *Becket* 1991, and *Macbeth* 1993–94. Films include *Day of the Jackal* 1973, *Little Dorrit* 1987, *Henry V* 1989, and *Dead Again* 1991. Television appearances include the acclaimed title role in *I, Claudius* 1976 (BAFTA award).

Jacobin member of an extremist republican club of the French Revolution founded in Versailles 1789. Helped by ◊Danton's speeches, they proclaimed the French republic, had the king executed, and overthrew the moderate ◊Girondins 1792–93. Through the Committee of Public Safety, they began the Reign of Terror, led by ◊Robespierre. After his execution 1794, the club was abandoned and the name 'Jacobin' passed into general use for any left-wing extremist.

Jacobite in Britain, a supporter of the royal house of Stuart after the deposition of James II 1688. They include the Scottish Highlanders, who rose unsuccessfully under ◊Claverhouse 1689; and those who rose in Scotland and N England under the leadership of ◊James Edward Stuart, the Old Pretender, 1715, and followed his son ◊Charles Edward Stuart in an invasion of England that reached Derby 1745–46. After the defeat at ◊Culloden, Jacobitism disappeared as a political force.

Jacquard Joseph Marie 1752–1834. French textile manufacturer. He invented a punched-card system for programming designs on a carpetmaking loom. In 1801 he constructed looms that used a series of punched cards to control the pattern of longitudinal warp threads depressed before each sideways passage of the shuttle. On later machines the punched cards were joined to form an endless loop that represented the 'program' for the repeating pattern of a carpet.

Jacquard-style punched cards were used in the early computers of the 1940s–1960s.

Jacquerie French peasant uprising 1358, caused by the ravages of the English army and French nobility during the Hundred Years' War, which reduced the rural population to destitution. The word derives from the nickname for French peasants, Jacques Bonhomme.

Jacuzzi Candido 1903–1986. Italian-born US engineer who invented the Jacuzzi, a pump that produces a whirlpool effect in a bathtub. The Jacuzzi was commercially launched as a health and recreational product in the mid-1950s.

jade semiprecious stone consisting of either jadeite, $NaAlSi_2O_6$ (a pyroxene), or nephrite, $Ca_2(Mg,Fe)_5Si_8O_{22}(OH,F)_2$ (an amphibole), ranging from colourless through shades of green to black according to the iron content. Jade ranks 5.5–6.5 on the Mohs' scale of hardness.

The early Chinese civilization discovered jade, bringing it from E Turkestan, and carried the art of jade-carving to its peak. The Olmecs, Aztecs, Maya, and the Maori have also used jade for ornaments, ceremony, and utensils.

Jade Emperor or ***Yu Huang*** in Chinese religion, the supreme god of pantheistic Taoism, who watches over human actions and is the ruler of life and death.

Jaffa (biblical name ***Joppa***) port in W Israel, part of ◊Tel Aviv from 1950. It was captured during the ◊Crusades in the 12th century, by the French emperor Napoleon 1799, and by the British field marshal Allenby 1917.

Jaffna capital of Jaffna district, Northern Province, Sri Lanka; population (1990) 129,000. It was the focal point of Hindu Tamil nationalism and the scene of recurring riots during the 1980s.

Thirty thousand Tamils have been killed in a 12-year war between the government and Tamil Tigers fighting for the establishment of an independent homeland, Eelam, on the northern tip of Sri Lanka. Peace negotiations broke down April 1995 and Jaffna fell to government forces Dec 1995.

Jagan Cheddi Berrat 1918–1997. Guyanese left-wing politician, president from 1992. He led the People's Progressive Party (PPA) from 1950, and was the first prime minister of British Guyana 1961–64. As candidate for president 1992, he opposed privatization as leading to 'recolonization'. The PPA won a decisive victory, and Jagan replaced Desmond Hoyte. He died in office and was succeeded by Samuel Hinds.

jaguar largest species of ◊cat *Panthera onca* in the Americas, formerly ranging from the southwestern USA to southern South America, but now extinct in most of North America. It can grow up to 2.5 m/8 ft long including the tail.

The background colour of the fur varies from creamy white to brown or black, and is covered with black spots. The jaguar is usually solitary. *See illustration on following page.*

jaguarundi wild cat *Felis yaguoaroundi* found in forests in Central and South America. Up to 1.1 m/3.5 ft long, it is very slim with rather short legs and short rounded ears. It is uniformly coloured dark brown or chestnut. A good climber, it feeds on birds and small mammals and, unusually for a cat, has been reported to eat fruit.

jackal The black-backed jackal *Canis mesomelas* is a common sight on the savannas of S Africa. It hunts singly for small animals and in packs for larger prey, often scavenging on carcasses left by larger predators such as lions.
Premaphotos Wildlife

Jahangir ('Holder of the World') adopted name of Salim 1569–1627. 3rd Mogul emperor of India 1605–27, succeeding his father ◊Akbar the Great. The first part of his reign was marked by peace, prosperity, and a flowering of the arts, but the latter half by rebellion and succession conflicts.

In 1622 he lost Kandahar province in Afghanistan to Persia. His rule was marked by the influence of his Persian wife Nur Jahan and her conflict with Prince Khurran (later ◊Shah Jahan). Jahangir designed the Shalimar Gardens in Kashmir and buildings and gardens in Lahore.

Jainism (Hindi *jaina* 'person who overcomes') ancient Indian religion, sometimes regarded as an offshoot of Hinduism. Jains emphasize the importance of not injuring living beings, and their code of ethics is based on sympathy and compassion for all forms of life. They also believe in ◊karma but not in any deity. It is a monastic, ascetic religion. There are two main sects: the Digambaras and the Swetambaras. Jainism practises the most extreme form of nonviolence (*ahimsā*) of all Indian sects, and influenced the philosophy of Mahatma Gandhi. Jains number approximately 6 million; the majority live in India.

Jainism's sacred books record the teachings of Mahavira (c. 599–527 BC), the last in a line of 24 great masters called Tirthankaras (or *jainas*). Mahavira was born in Vessali (now Bihar), E India. He became an ascetic at the age of 30, achieved enlightenment at 42, and preached for 30 years.

During the 3rd century BC two divisions arose regarding the extent of austerities. The Digambaras ('sky-clad') believe that enlightenment can only occur when all possessions have been given up, including clothes, and that it can only be achieved when a soul is born into a human male body. Monks of this sect go naked on the final stages of their spiritual path. The Swetambaras ('white-clad') believe that both human sexes can achieve enlightenment and that nakedness is not a prerequisite.

Jaipur capital of Rajasthan, India; population (1991) 1,458,000. It was formerly the capital of the state of Jaipur, which was merged with Rajasthan 1949. Products include textiles and metal products.

Features include the Jantar Mantar observatory, built by Maharajah Jai Singh II 1728; it contains the world's largest sundial. The five-storey Hawa Mahal or Palace of the Winds (1799) is a notable landmark. The city was painted pink, the traditional colour of welcome, in honour of the visit of Prince Albert, consort of Queen Victoria, 1883. It is also noted for its blue pottery.

Jakarta or ***Djakarta***(formerly until 1949 ***Batavia***) capital of Indonesia on the northwest coast of Java; population (1993) 9,000,000. Industries include textiles, chemicals, and plastics; a canal links it with its port of Tanjung Priok where rubber, oil, tin, coffee, tea, and palm oil are among its exports; also a tourist centre. Jakarta was founded by Dutch traders 1619.

Jalalabad capital of Nangarhar province, E Afghanistan, on the road from Kabul to Peshawar in Pakistan; population (1988 est) 55,000 (numbers swelled to over 1 million during the civil war). The city was besieged by Mujaheddin rebels after the withdrawal of Soviet troops from Afghanistan 1989.

Jamaica island in the Caribbean Sea, S of Cuba and W of Haiti. *See country box on p. 566.*

James Henry 1843–1916. US novelist. He lived in Europe from 1875 and became a naturalized British subject 1915. His novels deal with the social, moral, and aesthetic issues arising from the complex relationship of European to American culture. Initially a master of psychological realism, noted for the complex subtlety of his prose style, James became increasingly experimental, writing some of

Jahangir Third of the emperors of the Mogul dynasty, Jahangir. Son of Akbar who was considered to be the greatest of the Moguls, Jahangir's reign was marred by an addiction to alcohol and opium.
Philip Sauvain

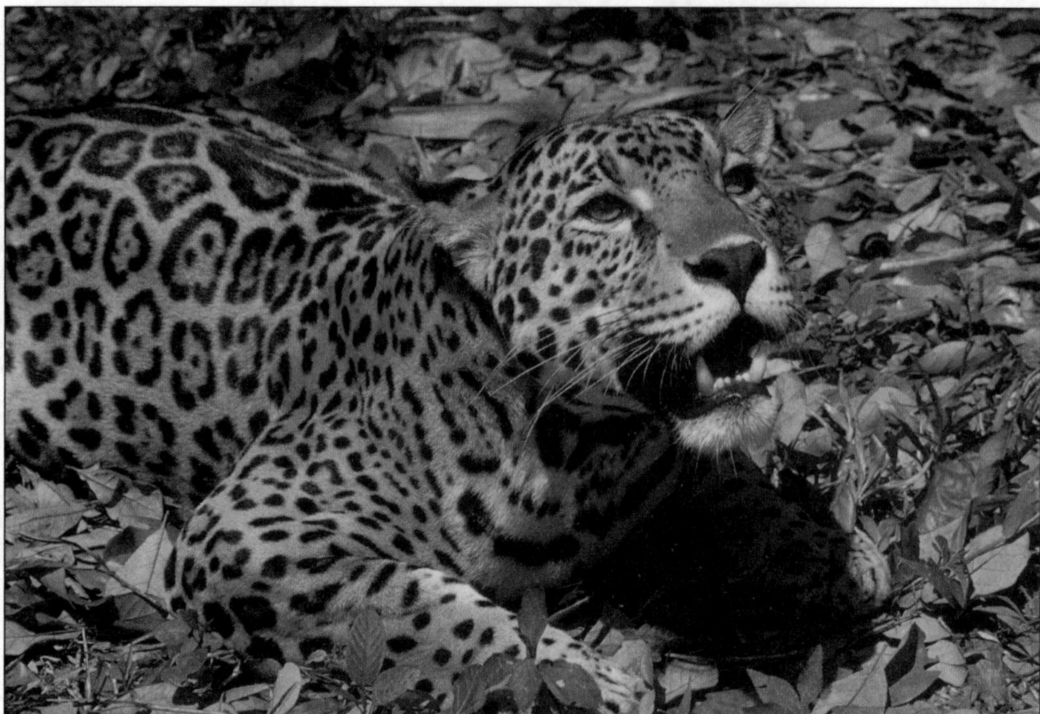

jaguar A jaguar in Central America. Camouflage and stalking are more important than speed for jaguars to catch their prey, which includes deer, wild pigs, capybaras, caimans, and turtles. Jaguars are usually solitary, with males and females remaining together for only a few weeks during mating. *Corbis*

the essential works of early Modernism. His major novels include *The Portrait of a Lady* 1881, *The Bostonians* 1886, *What Maisie Knew* 1887, *The Ambassadors* 1903, and *The Golden Bowl* 1904. He also wrote more than a hundred shorter works of fiction, notably the novella *The Aspern Papers* 1888 and the supernatural/psychological riddle *The Turn of the Screw* 1898.

Other major novels include *Roderick Hudson* 1876, *The American* 1877, *Washington Square* 1881, *The Tragic Muse* 1890, *The Spoils of Poynton* 1897, *The Awkward Age* 1899, and *The Wings of the Dove* 1902. Collections of short stories include *Terminations* 1895 and *The Altar of the Dead* 1909. He also wrote travel sketches, including *The American Scene* 1906, which records his impressions on returning to the USA after 20 years' absence, and literary criticism, including *Notes on Novelists* 1914. Two works, *The Ivory Tower* and *The Sense of the Past*, unfinished at the time of his death, were published 1917.

James Jesse Woodson 1847–1882. US bank and train robber. He was a leader, with his brother Frank (1843–1915), of the Quantrill raiders, a Confederate guerrilla band in the Civil War. Jesse was killed by Bob Ford, an accomplice; Frank remained unconvicted and became a farmer.

James P(hyllis) D(orothy), Baroness James of Holland Park 1920– . English detective novelist. She created the characters Superintendent Adam Dalgliesh and private investigator Cordelia Gray. She was a tax official, hospital administrator, and civil servant before turning to writing. Her books include *Death of an Expert Witness* 1977, *The Skull Beneath the Skin* 1982, *A Taste for Death* 1986, and *Original Sin* 1994.

James William 1842–1910. US psychologist and philosopher. He was among the first to take an approach emphasizing the ends or purposes of behaviour and to advocate a scientific, experimental psychology. His *Varieties of Religious Experience* 1902 is one of the most important works on the psychology of religion.

In his classic *Principles of Psychology* 1890, James introduced the notion of the 'stream of consciousness' (thought, consciousness, or subjective life regarded as a flow rather than as separate bits), and propounded the theory of ◊emotions now known as the James–Lange theory. James wrote extensively on abnormal psychology and had much to contribute to the study of the paranormal.

James (I) the Conqueror 1208–1276. King of Aragon from 1213, when he succeeded his father. He conquered the Balearic Islands and took Valencia from the ◊Moors, dividing it with Alfonso X of Castile by a treaty of 1244. Both these exploits are recorded in his autobiography *Libre dels feyts/Chronicle*. He largely established Aragon as the dominant power in the Mediterranean.

James I 1566–1625. King of England from 1603 and Scotland (as ***James VI***) from 1567. The son of Mary Queen of Scots and Lord Darnley, he succeeded on his mother's abdication from the Scottish throne, assumed power 1583, established a strong centralized authority, and in 1589 married Anne of Denmark (1574–1619).

As successor to Elizabeth I in England, he alienated the Puritans by his High Church views and Parliament by his assertion of ◊divine right, and was generally unpopular because of his favourites, such as ◊Buckingham, and his schemes for an alliance with Spain. He was succeeded by his son Charles I.

James II 1633–1701. King of England and Scotland (as ***James VII***) from 1685, second son of Charles I. He succeeded Charles II. James married Anne Hyde 1660 (1637–1671, mother of Mary II and Anne) and ◊Mary of Modena 1673 (mother of James Edward Stuart). He became a Catholic 1671, which led first to attempts to exclude him from the succession, then to the rebellions of ◊Monmouth and Argyll (1530–1573), and finally to the Whig and Tory leaders' invitation to William of Orange to take the throne 1688. James fled to France, then led an uprising in Ireland 1689, but after defeat at the Battle of the ◊Boyne 1690 remained in exile in France.

James I 1394–1437. King of Scotland 1406–37, who assumed power 1424. He was a cultured and strong monarch whose improvements in the administration of justice brought him popularity among the common people. He was assassinated by a group of conspirators led by the Earl of Atholl.

JAMAICA

area 10,957 sq km/4,230 sq mi
capital Kingston
major towns/cities Montego Bay, Spanish Town, St Andrew, Portmore
physical features mountainous tropical island; Blue Mountains (so called because of the haze over them)
head of state Elizabeth II from 1962, represented by governor general Howard Felix Hanlan Cooke from 1991
head of government Percival Patterson from 1992
political system constitutional monarchy
administrative divisions 14 parishes
political parties Jamaica Labour Party (JLP), moderate, centrist; People's National Party (PNP), left of centre; National Democratic Union (NDM), centrist
population 2,447,000 (1995 est)
population growth rate 0.7% (1990–95); 1.0% (2000–05)
ethnic distribution nearly 80% of African descent; about 15% of mixed African-European origin. There are also Chinese, Indian, and European minorities
life expectancy 71 (men), 76 (women)
literacy rate men 98%, women 99%
language English, Jamaican creole
religions Protestant 70%, Rastafarian
currency Jamaican dollar
GDP (US $) 3.91 billion (1994)
growth rate 0.8% (1994)
exports sugar, bananas, bauxite, rum, cocoa, coconuts, liqueurs, cigars, citrus, alumina, gypsum. Tourism is important

HISTORY

c. AD 900 Settled by Arawak Indians, who gave the island the name Jamaica ('well watered').
1494 The explorer Christopher Columbus reached Jamaica.
1509 Occupied by Spanish; much of the Arawak community died from exposure to European diseases; black African slaves were brought in to work the sugar plantations.
1655 Captured by Britain and became its most valuable Caribbean colony.
1838 Slavery abolished.
1870 Banana plantations established as sugar-cane industry declined in face of competition from European beet sugar.
1938 Serious riots during the economic depression and, as a sign of growing political awareness, the People's National Party (PNP) was formed by Norman Manley.
1944 First constitution adopted.
1958–62 Part of West Indies Federation.
1959 Internal self-government granted.
1962 Independence achieved within the Commonwealth, with Alexander Bustamante of the centre-right Jamaica Labour Party (JLP) as prime minister.
1967 JLP re-elected under Hugh Shearer.
1972 Michael Manley of the PNP became prime minister and pursued a policy of economic self-reliance.
1980 JLP elected, with Edward Seaga as prime minister, following violent election campaign.
1981 Diplomatic links with Cuba severed; free-market economic programme pursued.
1983 JLP won all 60 seats in the general election.
1988 Island badly damaged by Hurricane Gilbert.
1989 PNP won a landslide victory with a newly-moderate Manley returning as prime minister.
1992 Manley retired; succeeded by Percival Patterson.
1993 PNP increased its majority in general election.

SEE ALSO Arawak; West Indies, Federation of the

James US writer and master of the psychological novel, Henry James, who later became a naturalized British subject. His early and later novels are concerned with the interaction of American and European culture. Mid-career, he tackled political aspiration and social reform in novels such as *The Bostonians* 1886. *Corbis*

James II 1430–1460. King of Scotland from 1437, who assumed power 1449. The only surviving son of James I, he was supported by most of the nobles and parliament. He sympathized with the Lancastrians during the Wars of the ◊Roses, and attacked English possessions in S Scotland. He was killed while besieging Roxburgh Castle.

James III 1451–1488. King of Scotland from 1460, who assumed power 1469. His reign was marked by rebellions by the nobles, including his brother Alexander, Duke of Albany. He was murdered during a rebellion supported by his son, who then ascended the throne as James IV.

James IV 1473–1513. King of Scotland from 1488, who married Margaret (1489–1541, daughter of Henry VII) 1503. He came to the throne after his followers murdered his father, James III, at Sauchieburn. His reign was internally peaceful, but he allied himself with France against England, invaded 1513, and was defeated and killed at the Battle of ◊Flodden. James IV was a patron of poets and architects as well as a military leader.

James V 1512–1542. King of Scotland from 1513, who assumed power 1528. During the long period of his minority, he was caught in a struggle between pro-French and pro-English factions. When he assumed power, he allied himself with France and upheld Catholicism against the Protestants. Following an attack on Scottish territory by Henry VIII's forces, he was defeated near the border at Solway Moss 1542.

James VI of Scotland. See ◊James I of England.

James VII of Scotland. See ◊James II of England.

James Francis Edward Stuart 1688–1766. British prince, known as the ***Old Pretender*** (for the ◊Jacobites, he was James III). Son of James II, he was born at St James's Palace and after the revolution of 1688 was taken to France. He landed in Scotland 1715 to head a Jacobite rebellion but withdrew through lack of support. In his later years he settled in Rome.

Jameson Leander Starr 1853–1917. British colonial administrator. In South Africa, early in 1896, he led the Jameson Raid from Mafeking into Transvaal to support the non-Boer colonists there, in an attempt to overthrow the government (for which he served some months in prison). Returning to South Africa, he succeeded Cecil ◊Rhodes as leader of the Progressive Party of Cape Colony, where he was prime minister 1904–08.

James, St several Christian saints, including:

James, St (called ***the Great***) lived 1st century AD. New Testament apostle, originally a Galilean fisher. He was the son of Zebedee and brother of the apostle John. He was put to death by ◊Herod Agrippa. James is the patron saint of Spain. Feast day 25 July.

James, St (called ***the Just***) lived 1st century AD. The New Testament brother of Jesus, to whom Jesus appeared after the Resurrection. Leader of the Christian church in Jerusalem, he was the author of the biblical Epistle of James.

James, St (called ***the Little***) lived 1st century AD. In the New Testament, a disciple of Christ, son of Alphaeus. Feast day 3 May.

Jamestown first permanent British settlement in North America, established by Captain John Smith 1607. It was capital of Virginia 1624–99. In the nearby Jamestown Festival Park there is a replica of the original Fort James, and models of the ships (*Discovery*, *Godspeed*, and *Constant*) that carried the 105 pioneers.

Jammu winter capital of the state of Jammu and Kashmir, India; population (1991) 206,000. It stands on the river Tavi and was linked to India's rail system 1972.

Jammu and Kashmir state of N India
area 222,200 sq km/85,791 sq mi
capital Jammu (winter); Srinagar (summer)
towns and cities Leh
industries timber, grain, rice, fruit, silk, carpets
population (1994) 8,435,000 (Indian-occupied territory)
history part of the Mogul Empire from 1586, Jammu came under the control of Gulab Singh 1820. In 1947 Jammu was attacked by Pakistan and chose to become part of the new state of India. Dispute over the area (see ◊Kashmir) caused further hostilities 1971 between India and Pakistan (ended by the Simla agreement 1972). Since then, separatist agitation has developed, complicating the territorial dispute between India and Pakistan. In 1996 the National Congress Party, which aims to retain the state within India, won the first local elections to be held since the separatist violence broke out 1990.

James I James I of England was already king of Scotland, as James VI, when he acceded to the English throne 1603. Although a physically weak man, he was extremely learned and wrote two books advocating the 'divine right of kings'. *Philip Sauvain*

Janáček Leoš 1854–1928. Czech composer. He became director of the Conservatoire at Brno 1919 and professor at the Prague Conservatoire 1920. His music, highly original and influenced by Moravian folk music, includes arrangements of folk songs, operas (*Jenůfa* 1904, *The Cunning Little Vixen* 1924), and the choral *Glagolitic Mass* 1926.

Janata alliance of political parties in India formed 1971 to oppose Indira Gandhi's ◊Congress Party. Victory in the election brought Morarji ◊Desai to power as prime minister but he was unable to control the various groups within the alliance and resigned 1979. His successors fared little better, and the elections of 1980 overwhelmingly returned Indira Gandhi to office.

Janata Dal (People's Party) Indian centre-left coalition, formed Oct 1988 under the leadership of V P ◊Singh and comprising the Janata, Lok Dal (B), Congress (S), and Jan Morcha parties. In a loose alliance with the Hindu fundamentalist Bharatiya Janata Party and the Communist Party of India, the Janata Dal was victorious in the Nov 1989 general election, taking power out of the hands of the Congress (I) Party. Following internal splits, its minority government fell Nov 1990. Since 1992, several breakaway Janata Dal factions have been formed. The party has drawn particularly strong support from Hindu lower castes and, with its secular outlook, recently from Muslims. It formed the core of the new governments of H D Deve Gowda June 1996 and Inder Kumar Gujral April 1997.

janissary (Turkish *yeniçeri* 'new force') bodyguard of the Ottoman sultan, the Turkish standing army from the late 14th century until 1826. Until the 16th century janissaries were Christian boys forcibly converted to Islam; after this time they were allowed to marry and recruit their own children. The bodyguard ceased to exist when it revolted against the decision of the sultan in 1826 to raise a regular force. The remaining janissaries were killed in battle or executed after being taken prisoner.

Jansen Cornelius Otto 1585–1638. Dutch Roman Catholic theologian, founder of Jansenism with his book *Augustinus* 1640. He became professor at Louvain, Belgium, 1630, and bishop of Ypres, Belgium, 1636.

Jansenism Christian teaching of Cornelius Jansen, which divided the Roman Catholic Church in France in the mid-17th century. Emphasizing the more predestinatory approach of St Augustine of Hippo's teaching, Jansenism was supported by the philosopher Pascal and Antoine Arnauld (a theologian linked with the Cistercian abbey of Port Royal). Jansenists were excommunicated 1719.

Jansenists held that people are saved by God's grace, not by their own willpower, because all spiritual initiatives are God's. The Jesuits disagreed with this because they believed their spiritual exercises trained the will to turn towards God.

jansky unit of radiation received from outer space, used in radio astronomy. It is equal to 10^{-26} watts per square metre per hertz, and is named after US engineer Karl Jansky.

Jansky Karl Guthe 1905–1950. US radio engineer who in 1932 discovered that the Milky Way galaxy emanates radio waves; he did not follow up his discovery, but it marked the birth of radioastronomy. *See illustration on following page.*

Janus in Roman mythology, the god of doorways and passageways, patron of the beginning of the day, month, and year, after whom January is named; he is represented as having two faces, one looking forwards and one back. In Roman ritual, the doors of Janus in the Forum were closed when peace was established.

Japan country in NE Asia, occupying a group of islands of which the four main ones are Hokkaido,

'I am not a Monsieur who can shift his religion as easily as he can shift his shirt when he comes in from tennis.'

JAMES I OF ENGLAND
Attributed remark

'Japan offers as much novelty perhaps as an excursion to another planet.'

On JAPAN
Isabella Bird
Unbeaten Tracks in Japan 1880

Jansky The US radio engineer Karl Guthe Jansky. In the course of his research on interference to radio reception, Jansky discovered that the Milky Way galaxy gave off radio waves. This was the beginning of the science of radioastronomy. *Image Select (UK) Ltd*

Honshu, Kyushu, and Shikoku. Japan is situated between the Sea of Japan (to the W) and the N Pacific (to the E), E of North and South Korea. *See country box opposite.*

Japan Current or ***Kuroshio*** warm ocean ◊current flowing from Japan to North America.

Japanese inhabitants of Japan; people of Japanese culture or descent. Japan is an unusually homogeneous society, which has always been adept at assimilating influences from other cultures but has not readily received immigrants; discrimination against foreigners is legal in Japan. The ◊Japanese language is the only one spoken, though English is considered fashionable and is much used in advertising. Religion is syncretic and it is common for Japanese to take part in both Buddhist and Shinto rituals while professing belief in neither.

Although Japan has a highly distinctive culture, Korean and Chinese influences were absorbed during the early centuries AD, including Confucian philosophy and Buddhism (from China). Chinese influence in Japan waned during the decline of the Tang Dynasty (AD 618–907). The 12th century saw the rise of the code of warriors, the ◊samurai. During the late 19th century the feudal society was abolished, compulsory education extended to all, and Japan began to develop its Westernized industrial base.

Japanese architecture the buildings of Japan, notably domestic housing, temples and shrines, castles, and modern high-rises. Traditional Japanese buildings were made of wood with sliding doors, screens, and paper windows; they had projecting eaves and harmonious proportions. Temples and town planning derived from 6th-century Chinese sources, with Chinese influence especially evident in the may-storeyed ◊pagodas and the hipped and gabled, tiled roofs. Western styles were introduced from the mid-19th century.

traditional The best-known module is the tatami straw mat, the universal floor covering from the 17th century, which is also used to measure room size; however, the size of a tatami mat, around 1 × 2 m/3 × 6 ft, varies somewhat in different parts of the country. Sliding room dividers (*fusuma*) make the interior space adaptable, and wall panels and paper windows (*shōji*) can be slid back in hot weather. A narrow veranda encircles the house under the eaves; the steep roofs are thatched, tiled, or covered with cypress bark. The emphasis is on simple, geometric design, uncluttered space, and functional use of natural materials. A town house would have a small enclosed garden; a house with grounds would be oriented to the maximum appreciation of the surrounding nature. The imperial Katsura Palace 1620–58 epitomizes the restrained elegance of the traditional style, in this period also called tea-house style.

‘The necessary things are done by bringing out and polishing the beauty of the simple materials they used in making the building.’

On Japanese Architecture
Frank Lloyd Wright
An Autobiography

modern architecture The Japanese emulation of foreign models after the country's isolation ended in the mid-19th century included the erection of Western-style buildings, some designed by foreign architects, such as the American Frank Lloyd ◊Wright's Imperial Hotel, Tokyo, 1916, others by Japanese, such as the huge Versailles-style Akasaka Palace, Tokyo, 1909, by Tōkuma Katayama (1853–1917) and the Bank of Tokyo 1890–96 by Kingo Tatsuno (1854–1919). Notable Japanese architects of the late 20th century are Kenzō ◊Tange, Arata ◊Isozaki, and Tadao Ando (1941–). Traditional aesthetics and sensitive adaptation to the site still characterize the best Japanese architecture.

Japanese art the painting, sculpture, printmaking, and design of Japan. Early Japanese art was influenced by China. Painting later developed a distinct Japanese character, bolder and more angular, with the spread of Zen Buddhism in the 12th century. Ink painting and calligraphy flourished, followed by book illustration and decorative screens. Japanese prints developed in the 17th century, with multicolour prints invented around 1765. Buddhist sculpture proliferated from 580, and Japanese sculptors excelled at portraits. Japanese pottery stresses simplicity.

Japanese art *Lovers in a Plum Blossom Garden*, an illustration from the book *Nise Murasaki inaka Genji* published during the period of economic austerity of the 1830s and 1840s. A dandy imitating the hero of Murasaki's *The Tale of Genji* stands in a plum orchard with a lover. Both wear gorgeous brocade robes. *Corbis*

Jōmon period (10,000–300 BC) This was characterized by cord-marked pottery.

Yayoi period (300 BC–AD 300) Elegant pottery with geometric designs and *dōtaku*, bronze bells decorated with engravings, were produced.

Kofun period (300–552) Burial mounds held *haniwa*, clay figures, some of which show Chinese influence.

Asuka period (552–646) Buddhist art, introduced from Korea 552, flourished in sculpture, metalwork, and embroidered silk banners. Painters' guilds were formed.

Nara period (646–794) Religious and portrait sculptures were made of bronze, clay, or lacquer. A few painted scrolls, screens, and murals survive. Textiles were decorated with batik, tie-dye, stencils, embroidery, and brocade.

Heian period (794–1185) Buddhist statues became formalized and were usually made of wood. Shinto images emerged. A native style of secular painting, yamato-e, developed, especially in scroll painting, with a strong emphasis on surface design. Lacquerware was also decoratively stylized.

Kamakura period (1185–1392) Sculpture and painting became vigorously realistic. Portraits were important, as were landscapes and religious, narrative, and humorous picture scrolls.

Ashikaga or Muromachi period (1392–1568) The rapid ink sketch in line and wash introduced by Zen priests from China became popular and the Kano School of painting was established. Pottery gained in importance from the spread of the tea ceremony (*cha-no-yu*). Masks and costumes were made for Nō theatre.

Momoyama period (1568–1615) Artists produced beautiful screens to decorate palaces and castles. The arrival of Korean potters inspired new styles.

Tokugawa or Edo period (1615–1867) The ukiyo-e print, depicting everyday life, originated in genre paintings of 16th- and 17th-century kabuki actors and teahouse women. It developed into the woodcut and after 1740 the true colour print, while its range of subject matter expanded. Ukiyo-e artists include Utamaro, Hiroshige, and Hokusai. Lacquer and textiles became more sumptuous. Tiny carved figures (*netsuke*) were mostly made from ivory or wood.

Meiji period (1868–1912) Painting was influenced by styles of Western art, for example Impressionism.

Shōwa period (1926–89) Attempts were made to revive the traditional Japanese painting style and to combine traditional and foreign styles.

Japanese language language of E Asia, spoken almost exclusively in the islands of Japan. Traditionally isolated, but possibly related to Korean, Japanese was influenced by Mandarin Chinese especially in the 6th–9th centuries and is written in Chinese-derived ideograms supplemented by two syllabic systems.

Japanese has a well-defined structure of syllables; words end with a vowel or *n* (*futon, jūdō, ninja, kimono, shōgun, sumō, tōfu*). The distinction between long and short vowels affects meaning (long ones are usually, as in this volume, indicated by a macron, or line over the letter). Japanese is written in a triple system: its *kanji* ideograms are close to their Chinese originals; *hiragana* is a syllabary for the general language; and *katakana* is a syllabary for foreign names and borrowings. In print, the three systems blend on the page much as when italic type is used together with roman.

Japanese literature earliest surviving works include the 8th-century *Man'yōshū/Collection of a Myriad Leaves*, with poems by Hitomaro and Akahito (the principal form being the tanka, a five-line stanza of 5, 7, 5, 7, 7 syllables), and the prose *Kojiki/Record of Ancient Matters*. The late 10th and early 11th centuries produced such writers as ◊Murasaki Shikibu, whose *The Tale of Genji* is one of the finest works of Japanese literature.

During the 14th century the ◊Nō drama developed from ceremonial religious dances, combined with monologues and dialogues. *Heike monogatari* was written in the 14th century. In the early 15th century Zeami (1363–1443) wrote manuals on drama. The 17th century saw the beginnings of ◊kabuki, the popular drama of Japan; of ◊haiku; and of the modern novel. During the late 19th and early 20th centuries the influences of Western and Russian literature produced Realist writers,

JAPAN

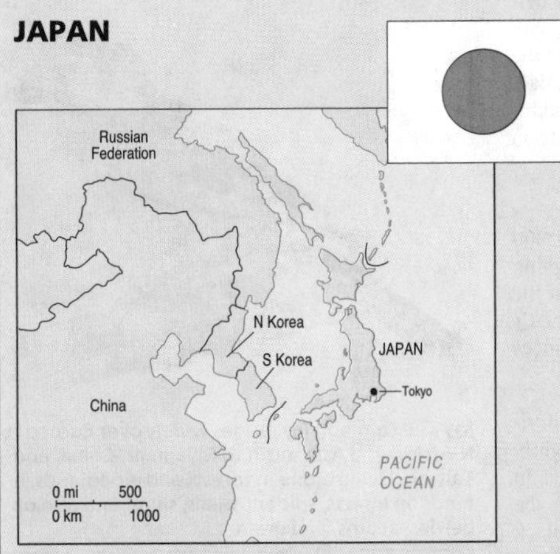

national name *Nippon*
area 377,535 sq km/145,822 sq mi
capital Tokyo
major towns/cities Fukuoka, Kitakyushu, Kyoto, Sapporo
major ports Osaka, Nagoya, Yokohama, Kobe, Kawasaki
physical features mountainous, volcanic (Mount Fuji, volcanic Mount Aso, Japan Alps); comprises over 1,000 islands, the largest of which are Hokkaido, Honshu, Kyushu, and Shikoku
head of state (figurehead) Emperor Akihito (Heisei) from 1989
head of government Ryutaro Hashimoto from 1996
political system liberal democracy
administrative divisions 47 prefectures
political parties Liberal Democratic Party (LDP), right of centre; Shinshinto (New Frontier Party) opposition coalition, centrist reformist; Social Democratic Party of Japan (SDPJ, former Socialist Party), left of centre but moving towards centre; Shinto Sakigake (New Party Harbinger), right of centre; Japanese Communist Party (JCP), socialist; Democratic Party of Japan (DPJ), Sakigate and SDPJ dissidents
armed forces self-defence forces: 239,500; US forces stationed there: 44,800 (1995)
conscription none
defence spend (% GDP) 1.0 (1994)
education spend (% GNP) 4.7 (1992)
health spend (% GDP) 5.2 (1993)
death penalty retained and used for ordinary crimes
population 125,932,000 (1998 est)
population growth rate 0.3% (1990–95); 0.1% (2000–05)
age distribution (% of total population) <15 16.2%, 15–65 69.6%, >65 14.1% (1995)
ethnic distribution more than 99% of Japanese descent; Ainu (aboriginal people of Japan) in N Japan (Hokkaido, Kuril Islands)
population density (per sq km) 330 (1994)
urban population (% of total) 78 (1995)
labour force 52% of population: 7% agriculture, 34% industry, 59% services (1990)
unemployment 3.1% (1995)
child mortality rate (under 5, per 1,000 live births) 6 (1993)
life expectancy 76.6 (men), 83 (females; highest life expectancy in the world)
education (compulsory years) 9
literacy rate 99%
languages Japanese; also Ainu
religions Shinto, Buddhist (often combined), Christian
TV sets (per 1,000 people) 614 (1992)
currency yen
GDP (US $) 4,599.7 billion (1996)
GDP per capita (PPP) (US $) 21,117 (1995)
growth rate 0.9% (1994/95)
average annual inflation 0.7% (1994)
trading partners USA, China, Australia, Republic of Korea, Indonesia, Germany, Taiwan, Hong Kong
resources coal, iron, zinc, copper, natural gas, fish
industries motor vehicles, steel, machinery, electrical and electronic equipment, chemicals, textiles
exports motor vehicles, electronic goods and components, chemicals, iron and steel products, scientific and optical equipment. Principal market: USA 29.7% (1994)
imports mineral fuels, foodstuffs, live animals, bauxite, iron ore, copper ore, coking coal, chemicals, textiles, wood. Principal source: USA 22.8% (1994)
arable land 10.7% (1993)
agricultural products rice, potatoes, cabbages, sugar cane, sugar beet, citrus fruit; one of the world's leading fishing nations (8.1 million tons in 1993)

HISTORY

660 BC According to legend, Jimmu Tenno, descendent of the sun goddess, became the first emperor of Japan.
c. 400 AD The Yamato, one of many warring clans, unified central Japan; Yamato chiefs are the likely ancestors of the Imperial family.
5th–6th Cs Writing, Confucianism, and Buddhism spread to Japan from China and Korea.
646 Start of the Taika Reform: Emperor Kotoku organized central government on the Chinese model.
794 Heian became Imperial capital; later called Kyoto.
858 Imperial court fell under control of the Fujiwara clan, who reduced the emperor to a figurehead.
11th C Central government grew ineffectual; real power exercised by great landowners (daimyo) with private armies of samurai.
1185 Minamoto clan seized power under Yoritomo, who established military rule.
1192 Emperor gave Yoritomo the title of shogun (general); the shogun ruled in the name of the emperor.
1274 Mongol conqueror Kublai Khan attempted to invade Japan, making a second attempt 1281; each time Japan was saved by a typhoon.
1336 Warlord Takauji Ashikaga overthrew the Minamoto shogunate; emperor recognized Ashikaga shogunate 1338.
16th C Power of Ashikagas declined; constant civil war.
1543 Portuguese sailors became the first Europeans to reach Japan; followed by Spanish, Dutch, and English traders.
1630s Japan adopted policy of isolation: all travel forbidden and all foreigners expelled except small colony of Dutch traders on Deshima island.
1853 USA sent warships to Edo with demand that Japan open diplomatic and trade relations; Japan conceded 1854.
1867 Revolt by isolationist nobles overthrew the Tokugawa shogunate.
1868 Emperor Mutsuhito assumed full powers, adopted the title *Meiji* ('enlightened rule'), moved Imperial capital from Kyoto to Edo (renamed Tokyo), and launched policy of swift Westernization.
1894–95 Sino-Japanese War: Japan expelled Chinese from Korea.
1902 Japan entered a defensive alliance with Britain; ended 1921.
1904–05 Russo-Japanese War: Japan drove Russians from Manchuria and Korea; Korea annexed 1910.
1914 Japan entered World War I and occupied German possessions in Far East.
1923 Earthquake destroyed much of Tokyo and Yokohama.
1931 Japan invaded Chinese province of Manchuria and created puppet state of Manchukuo; Japanese government came under control of military and extreme nationalists.
1937 Japan resumed invasion of China.
1940 After Germany defeated France, Japan occupied French Indo-China.
1941 Japan attacked US fleet at Pearl Harbor; USA and Britain declared war on Japan.
1942 Japanese conquered Thailand, Burma, Malaya, Dutch East Indies, Philippines, and northern New Guinea.
1945 USA dropped atomic bombs on Hiroshima and Nagasaki; Japan surrendered; US general Douglas MacArthur headed Allied occupation administration.
1947 MacArthur supervised introduction of democratic 'Peace Constitution', accompanied by demilitarization and land reform; occupation ended 1952.
1955 Liberal Democratic Party (LDP) founded with support of leading businessmen.
1956 Japan admitted to United Nations.
1950s–70s Japan experienced rapid economic development; growth of manufacturing exports led to great prosperity.
1993 Economic recession and financial scandals brought downfall of LDP government in general election. Coalition government formed.
1995 Earthquake devastated Kobe.
1996 General election produced inconclusive result; minority LDP government subsequently formed.
1997 Strong growth in economy. Major political party realignments. Financial crash after bank failures.
1998 Finance ministry resigned following officials' implication in corruption. Government approved $124-billion economic stimulus package as unemployment reached record 3.6%.

SEE ALSO Hiroshima; Russo-Japanese War; Shinto; shogun; Sino-Japanese Wars

followed by the Naturalist and 'Idealistic' novelists, whose romantic preoccupation with self-expression gave rise to the still popular 'I-novels' of, for example, ◊Dazai Osamu. A reaction against the autobiographical school came from ◊Tanizaki Jun-ichirō; later novelists include Kawabata Yasunari (Nobel Prize 1968). After World War II cultural dislocation and problems of identity were addressed by a new generation of writers such as Abe Kōbō (1924–1993).

Jaques-Dalcroze Emile 1865–1950. Swiss composer and teacher. He is remembered for his system of physical training by rhythmical movement to music (◊eurhythmics), and founded the Institut Jaques-Dalcroze in Geneva 1915.

jarrah type of ◊eucalyptus tree of W Australia, with durable timber.

Jarrett Keith 1945– . US jazz pianist and composer. An eccentric innovator, he performs both alone and with small groups. Jarrett was a member of the rock-influenced Charles Lloyd Quartet 1966–67, and played with Miles Davis 1970–71. *The Köln Concert* 1975 is a characteristic solo live recording.

Jarrow town in Tyne and Wear, NE England, on the south bank of the Tyne, 10 km/6 mi E of Newcastle and connected with the north bank by the Tyne Tunnel (1967); population (1991) 29,300. The Venerable Bede lived in a monastery here in the early 8th century. Industries include chemicals, oil, iron and steel.

Jarrow Crusade march in 1936 from Jarrow to London, protesting at the high level of unemployment following the closure of Palmer's shipyard in the town. The march was led by Labour MP Ellen Wilkinson, and it proved a landmark event of the 1930s Depression. In 1986, on the fiftieth anniversary of the event, a similar march was held to protest at the high levels of unemployment in the 1980s.

Jarry Alfred 1873–1907. French satiric dramatist. His grossly farcical *Ubu Roi* 1896 foreshadowed the Theatre of the ◊Absurd and the French Surrealist movement in its freedom of staging and subversive humour.

Jaruzelski Wojciech Witold 1923– . Polish general, communist leader from 1981, president 1985–90. He imposed martial law for the first year of his rule, suppressed the opposition, and banned trade-union activity, but later released many political prisoners. In 1989, elections in favour of the free trade union Solidarity forced Jaruzelski to speed up democratic reforms, overseeing a transition to a new form of 'socialist pluralist' democracy and stepping down as president 1990.

jasmine any subtropical plant of the genus *Jasminum* of the olive family Oleaceae, with white or yellow flowers. The common jasmine *J. officinale* has fragrant pure white flowers yielding jasmine oil, used in perfumes; the Chinese winter jasmine *J. nudiflorum* has bright yellow flowers that appear before the leaves.

Jason in Greek mythology, the leader of the Argonauts who sailed in the *Argo* to Colchis in search of the ◊Golden Fleece. He eloped with ◊Medea, daughter of the king of Colchis, who had helped him achieve his goal, but later deserted her.

A little rebellion now and then is a good thing.
THOMAS JEFFERSON
Letter to James Madison 30 Jan 1787

jasper hard, compact variety of ◊chalcedony SiO_2, usually coloured red, brown, or yellow. Jasper can be used as a gem.

Jat an ethnic group living in Pakistan and N India, and numbering about 11 million; they are the largest group in N India. The Jat are predominantly farmers. They speak Punjabi, a language belonging to the Iranian branch of the Indo-European family.

Jataka collections of Buddhist legends compiled at various dates in several countries; the oldest and most complete has 547 stories. They were collected before AD 400. They give an account of previous incarnations of the Buddha, and the verse sections of the text form part of the Buddhist canon. The Jataka stories were one of the sources of inspiration for the fables of Aesop.

jaundice yellow discoloration of the skin and whites of the eyes caused by an excess of bile pigment in the bloodstream. Approximately 60% of newborn babies exhibit some degree of jaundice, which is treated by bathing in white, blue, or green light that converts the bile pigment bilirubin into a water-soluble compound that can be excreted in urine. A serious form of jaundice occurs in rhesus disease (see ◊rhesus factor).

Bile pigment is normally produced by the liver from the breakdown of red blood cells, then excreted into the intestines. A build-up in the blood is due to abnormal destruction of red cells (as in some cases of ◊anaemia), impaired liver function (as in ◊hepatitis), or blockage in the excretory channels (as in gallstones or ◊cirrhosis). The jaundice gradually recedes following treatment of the underlying cause.

Jaurès (Auguste Marie Joseph) Jean (Léon) 1859–1914. French socialist politician and advocate of international peace. He was a lecturer in philosophy at Toulouse until his election 1885 as a deputy (member of parliament). In 1893 he joined the Socialist Party, established a united party, and in 1904 founded the newspaper *L'Humanité*, becoming its editor until his assassination.

Java or ***Jawa*** most important island of Indonesia, situated between Sumatra and Bali
area (with the island of Madura) 132,000 sq km/51,000 sq mi
capital Jakarta (also capital of Indonesia)
towns ports include Surabaya and Semarang; Bandung
physical about half the island is under cultivation, the rest being thickly forested. Mountains and sea breezes keep temperatures down, but humidity is high, with heavy rainfall from Dec to March
features a chain of mountains, some of which are volcanic, runs along the centre, rising to 2,750 m/9,000 ft. The highest mountain, Semeru (3,676 m/12,060 ft), is in the east
industries rice, coffee, cocoa, tea, sugar, rubber, quinine, teak, petroleum
population (with Madura; 1990) 107,581,300, including people of Javanese, Sundanese, and Madurese origin, with differing languages
religion predominantly Muslim
history fossilized early human remains (*Homo erectus*) were discovered 1891–92. In central Java there are ruins of magnificent Buddhist monuments and of the Sivaite temple in Prambanan. The island's last Hindu kingdom, Majapahit, was destroyed about 1520 and followed by a number of short-lived Javanese kingdoms. The Dutch East India company founded a factory 1610. Britain took over during the Napoleonic period, 1811–16, and Java then reverted to Dutch control. Occupied by Japan 1942–45, Java then became part of the republic of ◊Indonesia.

Life exists in the universe only because the carbon atom possesses certain exceptional qualities.
JAMES JEANS
Mysterious Universe

Javanese the largest ethnic group in the Republic of Indonesia. There are more than 50 million speakers of Javanese, which belongs to the western branch of the Austronesian family. Although the Javanese have a Hindu-Buddhist heritage, they are today predominantly Muslim, practising a branch of Islam known as *Islam Jawa*, which contains many Sufi features.

The Javanese are known for their performing arts, especially their shadow theatre and gamelan orchestras, their high-quality metalwork, and batik resist-dyed cloth. Although the majority of Javanese depend on the cultivation of rice in irrigated fields, there are many large urban centres with developing industries. To relieve the pressure on the land, farmers have been moved under Indonesia's controversial transmigration scheme to less populated islands such as Sulawesi (Celebes) and Irian Jaya (W New Guinea).

javelin spear used in athletics events. The men's javelin is about 260 cm/8.5 ft long, weighing 800 g/28 oz; the women's 230 cm/7.5 ft long, weighing 600 g/21 oz. It is thrown from a scratch line at the end of a run-up. The centre of gravity on the men's javelin was altered 1986 to reduce the vast distances (90 m/100 yd) that were being thrown.

jay any of several birds of the crow family Corvidae, order Passeriformes, generally brightly coloured and native to Eurasia and the Americas. In the Eurasian common jay *Garrulus glandarius*, the body is fawn with patches of white, blue, and black on the wings and tail. Jays are shy and retiring in their habits, and have a screeching cry with the power to vary it by mimicking other birds.

jay The common jay ranges widely over Europe to N Africa, and Asia south to Myanmar, China, and Taiwan. Living alone in forests and woodlands, it feeds on insects, spiders, snails, slugs, and also on berries, acorns, and grain.

Jay Margaret Ann 1939– . Baroness of Paddington. British Labour minister for women and deputy leader of the House of Lords from 1997. Jay, created a life peer in 1992, was principal opposition spokesperson on health in the House of Lords 1995–97 and Minister of State for Health during part of 1997. She was appointed minister for women in the cabinet reshuffle in 1997. As leader of the House of Lords, she had the task in late 1998 of steering through a reluctant chamber the government's plans to scrap the right of hereditary peers to sit and vote in the House of Lords.

Jayawardene Junius Richard 1906–1996. Sri Lankan politician. Leader of the United Nationalist Party from 1973, he became prime minister 1977 and the country's first president 1978–88. Jayawardene embarked on a free-market economic strategy, but was confronted with increasing Tamil-Sinhalese ethnic unrest, forcing the imposition of a state of emergency 1983.

jazz polyphonic syncopated music, characterized by solo virtuosic improvisation, which developed in the USA at the turn of the 20th century. Initially music for dancing, often with a vocalist, it had its roots in black American and other popular music. Developing from ◊blues and spirituals (religious folk songs) in the southern states, it first came to prominence in the early 20th century in New Orleans, St Louis, and Chicago, with a distinctive flavour in each city.

Traits common to all types of jazz are the modified rhythms of West Africa; the emphasis on improvisation; Western European harmony emphasizing the dominant seventh and the clash of major and minor thirds; characteristic textures and ◊timbres, first exemplified by a singer and rhythm section (consisting of a piano, bass, drums, and guitar or a combination of these instruments), and later by the addition of other instruments such as the saxophone and various brass instruments, and later still by the adoption of electrically amplified instruments.

jazz dance dance based on African techniques and rhythms, developed by black Americans around 1917. It entered mainstream dance in the 1920s, mainly in show business, and from the 1960s the teachers and choreographers Matt Mattox (1921–) and Luigi (1925–) expanded it.

J-curve in economics, a graphic illustration of the likely effect of a currency devaluation on the balance of payments. Initially, there will be a deterioration as import prices increase and export prices decline, followed by a decline in import volume and upsurge of export volume.

Jeans James Hopwood 1877–1946. British mathematician and scientist. In physics he worked on the kinetic theory of gases and on forms of energy radiation; in astronomy, his work focused on giant and dwarf stars, the nature of spiral nebulae, and the origin of the cosmos. In 1928 he stated his belief that matter was continuously being created in the universe (a forerunner of the steady-state theory).

Jedda alternative spelling for the Saudi Arabian port ◊Jiddah.

Jefferson Thomas 1743–1826. 3rd president of the USA 1801–09, founder of the Democratic Republican Party. He published *A Summary View of the Rights of America* 1774 and as a member of the Continental Congresses of 1775–76 was largely responsible for the drafting of the ◊Declaration of Independence. He was governor of Virginia 1779–81, ambassador to Paris 1785–89, secretary of state 1789–93, and vice president 1797–1801. His political philosophy of 'agrarian democracy'

JAZZ: TIMELINE

1880–1900	Jazz originated chiefly in New Orleans from ragtime, which was popularized at the turn of the century by Scott Joplin and others.
***c.* 1912**	Dixieland jazz appeared in New Orleans, a blend of ragtime and blues with improvisation (Louis Armstrong, Sidney Bechet, Jelly Roll Morton, Earl Hines).
1920s	During Prohibition, the centre of jazz moved to Chicago (Louis Armstrong, Bix Beiderbecke) and St Louis. By the end of the decade the focus had shifted to New York City (Art Tatum, Fletcher Henderson), to radio and recordings.
1930s	The swing bands used call-and-response arrangements with improvised solos of voice and instruments (Paul Whiteman, Benny Goodman).
1940s	Swing grew into the big-band era with jazz composed as well as arranged (Glenn Miller, Duke Ellington); rise of West Coast jazz (Stan Kenton) and rhythmically complex, fast, and highly improvised bebop (Charlie Parker, Dizzy Gillespie, Thelonius Monk).
1950s	Jazz had ceased to be dance music; cool jazz (Stan Getz, Miles Davis, Lionel Hampton, Modern Jazz Quartet) developed in reaction to the insistent, 'hot' bebop and hard bop.
1960s	Free-form or free jazz (Ornette Coleman, John Coltrane). Jazz rock pioneered by Miles Davis and others.
1970s	Jazz rock or fusion (US group Weather Report, formed 1970; British guitarist John McLaughlin, 1942–); jazz funk (US saxophonist Grover Washington Jr, 1943–); more eclectic free jazz (US pianist Keith Jarrett).
1980s	Resurgence of tradition (US trumpeter Wynton Marsalis; British saxophonist Courtney Pine, 1965–) and avant-garde (US chamber-music Kronos Quartet, formed 1978; anarchic British group Loose Tubes, 1983–89).
1990s	No single style predominated, as jazz reached a post-modernist stage of development, in which music of every style was considered valid.

Jefferson An original portrait of the third US president Thomas Jefferson, by the American artist Rembrandt Peale. Jefferson sat for the portrait in 1800, and so admired it that he asked Peale to make a copy for him in 1801. *Corbis*

placed responsibility for upholding a virtuous American republic mainly upon a citizenry of independent yeoman farmers. His many interests included architecture and he designed the Capitol at Richmond, Virginia. ▷ *See feature on pp. 32–33.*

Jeffreys Alec John 1950– . British geneticist who discovered the DNA probes necessary for accurate ◊genetic fingerprinting so that a murderer or rapist could be identified by, for example, traces of blood, tissue, or semen.

Jeffreys of Wem George, 1st Baron Jeffreys of Wem 1644–1689. Welsh judge, popularly known as 'the hanging judge'. He became Chief Justice of the King's Bench 1683, and presided over many political trials, notably those of Philip Sidney, Titus Oates, and Richard Baxter, becoming notorious for his brutality. In 1685 he was made a peer and Lord Chancellor and, after ◊Monmouth's rebellion, conducted the 'bloody assizes' during which 320 rebels were executed and hundreds more flogged, imprisoned, or transported. He was captured when attempting to flee the country after the revolution of 1688, and died in the Tower of London.

Jehosophat 4th king of Judah c. 873–c. 849 BC; he allied himself with Ahab, king of Israel, in the war against Syria.

Jehovah also *Jahweh* in the Old Testament, the name of God, revealed to Moses; in Hebrew texts of the Old Testament the name was represented by the letters YHVH (without the vowels 'a o a') because it was regarded as too sacred to be pronounced.

The terms *Adonai* ('Lord') and *Hashem* ('the Name') were also used in order to avoid directly mentioning God.

Jehovah's Witness member of a religious organization originating in the USA 1872 under Charles Taze Russell (1852–1916). Jehovah's Witnesses attach great importance to Christ's second coming, which Russell predicted would occur 1914, and which Witnesses still believe is imminent. All Witnesses are expected to take part in house-to-house preaching; there are no clergy.

Witnesses believe that after the second coming the ensuing Armageddon and Last Judgement, which entail the destruction of all except the faithful, are to give way to the Theocratic Kingdom. Earth will continue to exist as the home of humanity, apart from 144,000 chosen believers who will reign with Christ in heaven.

Witnesses believe that they should not become involved in the affairs of this world, and their tenets, involving rejection of obligations such as military service, have often brought them into conflict with authority.

Jehu c. 842–815 BC. King of Israel. He led a successful rebellion against the family of ◊Ahab and was responsible for the death of Jezebel.

Jekyll Gertrude 1843–1932. English landscape gardener and writer. She created over 200 gardens, many in collaboration with the architect Edwin ◊Lutyens. In her books, she advocated natural gardens of the cottage type, with plentiful herbaceous borders.

Originally a painter and embroiderer, she took up gardening at the age of 48 because of worsening eyesight. Her home at Munstead Wood, Surrey, was designed for her by Lutyens.

Jekyll and Hyde two conflicting sides of a personality, as in the novel by the Scottish writer R L Stevenson, *The Strange Case of Dr Jekyll and Mr Hyde* 1886, where the good Jekyll by means of a potion periodically transforms himself into the evil Hyde.

Jellicoe Geoffrey Alan 1900–1996. English architect, landscape architect, and historian. His contribution to 20th-century thinking on landscapes and gardens was mainly through his writings, notably *Landscape of Man* 1975. However, he also made an impact as a designer, working in a contemplative and poetic vein and frequently incorporating water and sculptures. Representative of his work are the Kennedy Memorial at Runnymede, Berkshire, 1965 (a granite path winds uphill to the memorial stone, which stands beside an American Scarlet oak), and the gardens at Sutton Place, Sussex, 1980–84.

Jellicoe studied at the Architectural Association in London and as early as 1925 co-authored an extensively researched publication *Italian Gardens of the Renaissance*. His designs show the influence of modern artists, such as Paul ◊Klee and Ben ◊Nicholson, while his information centre and restaurant at Cheddar Gorge, Somerset 1934, reflects the work of German architect Erich Mendelsohn (1887–1953). Other examples of his work are at St Pauls Walden Bury, Hertfordshire (1936–89), Schute House garden, Wiltshire (1970–89), the Atlanta Historical Gardens, Atlanta, Georgia (1992–93), and the Moody Gardens, Galveston, Texas (1995–).

jellyfish marine invertebrate of the phylum Cnidaria (coelenterates) with an umbrella-shaped body composed of a semi-transparent gelatinous substance, with a fringe of stinging tentacles. Most adult jellyfishes move freely, but during parts of their life cycle many are polyplike and attached. They feed on small animals that are paralysed by stinging cells in the jellyfishes' tentacles.

Jenkins Roy Harris, Baron Jenkins of Hillhead. Lord Jenkins 1920– . British politician. He became a Labour minister 1964, was home secretary 1965–67 and 1974–76, and chancellor of the Exchequer 1967–70. He was president of the European Commission 1977–81. In 1981 he became one of the founders of the Social Democratic Party and was elected 1982, but lost his seat 1987. In the same year, he was elected chancellor of Oxford University and made a life peer.

jellyfish After fertilization, the gametes of a jellyfish may be released into the water as larvae (middle right) or retained in a brood pouch. After settling, the larvae change into a sedentary polyp stage (bottom right) similar to that of a coral. More polyps (bottom left) are produced by simple budding. These polyps may divide again to form the so-called ephyra larvae (middle left). These larvae eventually grow into the free-swimming medusa more familiarly known as a jellyfish (top).

Jenkins's Ear, War of war 1739 between Britain and Spain, arising from Britain's illicit trade in Spanish America; it merged into the War of the ◊Austrian Succession 1740–48. The name derives from the claim of Robert Jenkins, a merchant captain, that his ear had been cut off by Spanish coastguards near Jamaica. The incident was seized on by opponents of Robert ◊Walpole who wanted to embarrass his government's antiwar policy and force war with Spain.

Jenner Edward 1749–1823. English physician who pioneered vaccination. In Jenner's day, smallpox was a major killer. His discovery 1796 that inoculation with cowpox gives immunity to smallpox was a great medical breakthrough. Jenner observed that people who worked with cattle and contracted cowpox from them never subsequently caught smallpox. In 1798 he published his findings that a child inoculated with cowpox, then two

jellyfish A moon jellyfish swimming in the Pacific. Jellyfish propel themselves through the water by alternately contracting and relaxing their bodies. The mouth is in the centre of the underside, and is surrounded by long lobes that trap the small creatures on which it feeds. *Corbis*

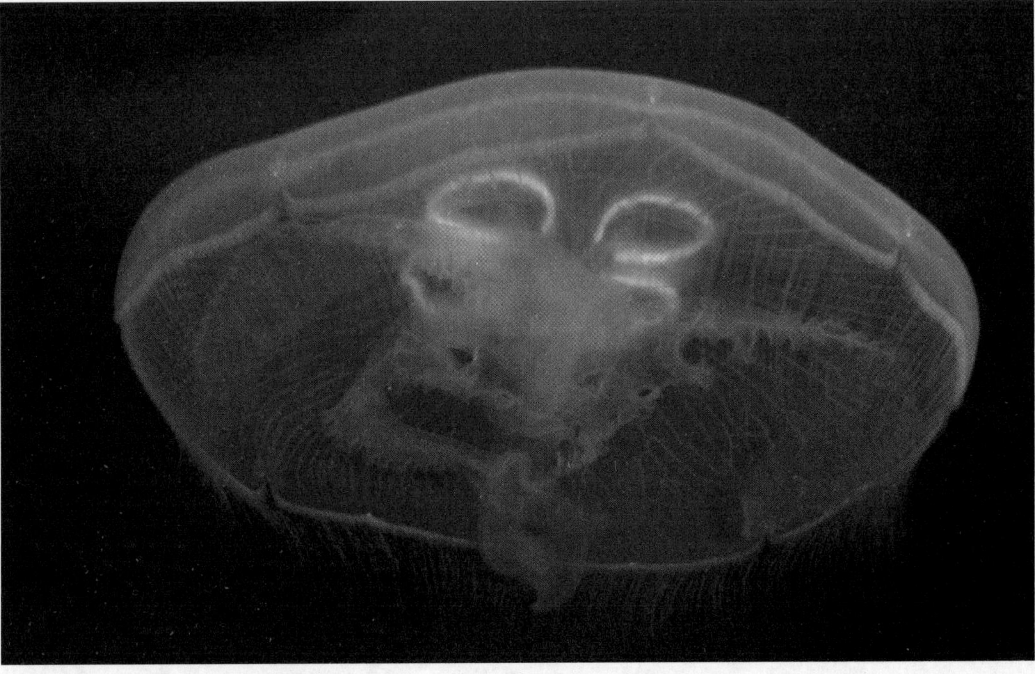

It is always the best policy to speak the truth – unless, of course, you are an exceptionally good liar.

JEROME K JEROME *The Idler* Feb 1892

months later with smallpox, did not get smallpox. He coined the word 'vaccination' from the Latin word for cowpox, *vaccinia*.

Jennings Pat (Patrick) 1945– . Irish footballer. In his 21-year career he was an outstanding goalkeeper. He won a British record 119 international caps for Northern Ireland 1964–86 (now surpassed by Peter Shilton (1949–)), and played League football for Watford, Tottenham Hotspur, and Arsenal.

Jentink's duiker small and shy antelope *Cephalophus jentinki* that plunges into bushes when startled. It is acutely threatened by deforestation in its remaining habitat in W Africa where it is also hunted. One captive breeding colony exists in Texas and there are hopes of establishing others as the immediate future for this species in the wild appears to be bleak.

jerboa small, nocturnal, leaping rodent belonging to the family Dipodidae. There are about 25 species of jerboa, native to N Africa and SW Asia. Typical is the common N African jerboa *Jaculus orientalis* with a body about 15 cm/6 in long and a 25 cm/10 in tail with a tuft at the tip. At speed it moves in a series of long jumps with its forefeet held close to its body.

Jeremiah lived 7th–6th century BC. Old Testament Hebrew prophet, whose ministry continued 626–586 BC. He was imprisoned during ◊Nebuchadnezzar's siege of Jerusalem on suspicion of intending to desert to the enemy. On the city's fall, he retired to Egypt.

Jericho town in Jordan, N of the Dead Sea, occupied by Israel 1967–94 when responsibility for its administration was transferred to the ◊Palestine Liberation Organization (PLO). Jericho was settled by 8000 BC, and by 6000 BC had become a walled city with 2,000 inhabitants. In the Old Testament it was the first Canaanite stronghold captured by the Israelites, and its walls, according to the Book of ◊Joshua, fell to the blast of Joshua's trumpets. Successive archaeological excavations since 1907 show that the walls of the city were destroyed many times.

Jeroboam lived 10th century BC. First king of Israel c. 922–901 BC after it split away from the kingdom of Judah.

Jerome Jerome K(lapka) 1859–1927. English journalist and writer. His works include the humorous essays 'Idle Thoughts of an Idle Fellow' 1889; the novel *Three Men in a Boat* 1889, a humorous account of a trip on the Thames from Kingston to Oxford; and the play *The Passing of the Third Floor Back* (story 1908, dramatized version 1910).

Jerome, St c. 340–420. One of the early Christian leaders and scholars known as the Fathers of the Church. His Latin versions of the Old and New Testaments form the basis of the Roman Catholic Vulgate. He is usually depicted with a lion. Feast day 30 Sept.

Jersey largest of the ◊Channel Islands; capital St Helier; area 117 sq km/45 sq mi; population (1991) 85,200. It is governed by a lieutenant governor representing the English crown and an assembly. Jersey cattle were originally bred here. The island was occupied 1940–45 by German forces. Jersey zoo (founded 1959 by Gerald Durrell) is engaged in breeding some of the world's endangered species.

Jersey City city of NE New Jersey, USA; population (1992) 228,600. It faces Manhattan Island, to which it is connected by tunnels. A former port, it is now an industrial centre.

The associations of history and belief, deep-rooted in the first memories of childhood, dissolve before the actual apparition.

On JERUSALEM Robert Byron *The Road to Oxiana*

Jerusalem ancient city of Palestine, divided 1948 between Jordan and the new republic of Israel; area (pre-1967) 37.5 sq km/14.5 sq mi, (post-1967) 108 sq km/42 sq mi, including areas of the West Bank; population (1994) 578,800 (70% Israelis, 30% Palestinians). In 1950 the western New City was proclaimed as the Israeli capital, and, having captured from Jordan the eastern Old City 1967, Israel affirmed 1980 that the united city was the country's capital; the United Nations does not recognize East Jerusalem as part of Israel, and regards Tel Aviv as the capital.

features Seven gates into the Old City through the walls built by Selim I (1467–1520); buildings: the Church of the Holy Sepulchre (built by Emperor Constantine 335) and the mosque of the Dome of the Rock. The latter stands on the site of the ◊Temple built by King Solomon in the 10th century BC, and the Western ('wailing') Wall, held sacred by Jews, is part of the walled platform on which the Temple once stood. The Hebrew University of Jerusalem opened 1925.

religions Christianity, Judaism, and Muslim, with Roman Catholic, Anglican, Eastern Orthodox, and Coptic bishoprics. In 1967 Israel guaranteed freedom of access of all faiths to their holy places.

history

1400 BC Jerusalem was ruled by a king subject to Egypt.

c. 1000 BC David made it the capital of a united Jewish kingdom.

586 BC The city was destroyed by Nebuchadnezzar, King of Babylonia, who deported its inhabitants.

539–529 BC Under Cyrus the Great of Persia the exiled Jews were allowed to return to Jerusalem and a new settlement was made.

c. 445 BC The city walls were rebuilt.

333 BC Conquered by Alexander the Great.

63 BC Conquered by the Roman general Pompey.

AD 29 or 30 Under the Roman governor Pontius Pilate, Jesus was executed here.

70 A Jewish revolt led to the complete destruction of the city by the Roman emperor Titus.

135 On its site the emperor Hadrian founded the Roman city of Aelia Capitolina.

614 The city was pillaged by the Persian Chosroës II while under Byzantine rule.

637 It was first conquered by Islam.

1099 Jerusalem was captured by the Crusaders and became the Kingdom of Jerusalem under Godfrey of Bouillon.

1187 Recaptured by Saladin, Sultan of Egypt.

1229 Holy Roman Emperor Frederick II Hohenstaufen won back Jerusalem.

1244 It was taken by Khwarismian Turks, ending Frankish rule of Jerusalem.

1517 Became part of the Ottoman Empire.

1917 Britain captured Jerusalem from the Turks and occupied Palestine.

1922–1948 Jerusalem was the capital of the British mandate.

▷ *See feature on pp. 280–281.*

Jerusalem artichoke a variety of ◊artichoke.

Jesuit member of the largest and most influential Roman Catholic religious order (also known as the ***Society of Jesus***) founded by ◊Ignatius Loyola 1534, with the aims of protecting Catholicism against the Reformation and carrying out missionary work. During the 16th and 17th centuries Jesuits were missionaries in Japan, China, Paraguay, and among the North American Indians. The order had (1991) about 29,000 members (15,000 priests plus students and lay members). There are Jesuit schools and universities.

history The Society of Jesus received papal approval 1540. Its main objects were defined as educational work, the suppression of heresy, and missionary work among nonbelievers (its members were not confined to monasteries). Loyola infused into the order a spirit of military discipline, with long and arduous training. Their political influence resulted in their expulsion during 1759–68 from Portugal, France, and Spain, and suppression by Pope Clement XIV 1773.

The order was revived by Pius VII 1814, but has since been expelled from many of the countries of Europe and the Americas, and John Paul II criticized the Jesuits 1981 for supporting revolution in South America. Their head (general) is known as the 'Black Pope' from the colour of his cassock; Pieter-Hans Kolvenbach was elected general 1983.

Jesus c. 4 BC–AD 29 or 30. Hebrew preacher on whose teachings ◊Christianity was founded. According to the accounts of his life in the four Gospels, he was born in Bethlehem, Palestine, son of God and the Virgin Mary, and brought up by Mary and her husband Joseph as a carpenter in Nazareth. After adult baptism, he gathered 12 disciples, but his preaching antagonized the Roman authorities and he was executed by crucifixion. Three days later there came reports of his ◊resurrection and, later, his ascension to heaven.

Through his legal father Joseph, Jesus belonged to the tribe of Judah and the family of David, the second king of Israel, a heritage needed by the Messiah for whom the Hebrew people were waiting. In AD 26 or 27 his cousin John the Baptist proclaimed the coming of the promised Messiah and baptized Jesus, who then made two missionary journeys through the district of Galilee. His teaching, summarized in the Sermon on the Mount, aroused both religious opposition from the ◊Pharisees and secular opposition from the party supporting the Roman governor ◊Herod Antipas. When Jesus returned to Jerusalem (probably AD 29), a week before the Passover festival, he was greeted by the people as the Messiah, and the Hebrew authorities (aided by the apostle Judas) had him arrested and condemned to death, after a hurried trial by the Sanhedrin (supreme Jewish court). The Roman procurator, Pontius Pilate, confirmed the sentence, stressing the threat posed to imperial authority by Jesus' teaching.

jet hard, black variety of lignite, a type of coal. It is cut and polished for use in jewellery and ornaments. Articles made of jet have been found in Bronze Age tombs.

In Britain, jet occurs in quantity near Whitby and along the Yorkshire coast. It became popular as mourning jewellery after the death of Prince Albert in 1861.

JET (abbreviation for ***Joint European Torus***) research facility in England that conducts experiments on nuclear fusion. It is the focus of the European effort to produce a safe and environmentally sound fusion-power reactor. On 9 November 1991, the JET ◊tokamak, operating with a mixture of deuterium and iritium, produced a 1.7 megawatt pulse of power in an experiment that lasted two seconds. This was the first time that a substantial amount of energy has been produced by nuclear power in a controlled experiment.

jetfoil advanced type of ◊hydrofoil boat built by Boeing, propelled by water jets. It features horizontal, fully submerged hydrofoils fore and aft and has a sophisticated computerized control system to maintain its stability in all waters

Jetfoils have been in service worldwide since 1975. A jetfoil service operates across the English Channel between Dover and Ostend, Belgium, with a passage time of about 1.5 hours. Cruising speed of the jetfoil is about 80 kph/50 mph.

jet lag the effect of a sudden switch of time zones in air travel, resulting in tiredness and feeling 'out of step' with day and night. In 1989 it was suggested that use of the hormone melatonin helped to lessen the effect of jet lag by resetting the body clock. See also ◊circadian rhythm.

jet propulsion method of propulsion in which an object is propelled in one direction by a jet, or stream of gases, moving in the other. This follows from Isaac ◊Newton's third law of motion: 'To every action, there is an equal and opposite reaction.' The most widespread application of the jet principle is in the jet engine, the most common kind of aircraft engine. The jet engine is a kind of ◊gas turbine.

jet stream narrow band of very fast wind (velocities of over 150 kph/95 mph) found at altitudes of 10–16 km/6–10 mi in the upper troposphere or lower stratosphere. Jet streams usually occur about the latitudes of the Westerlies (35°–60°)

Jew follower of ◊Judaism, the Jewish religion. The term is also used to refer to those who claim descent from the ancient Hebrews, a Semitic people of the Middle East. Today, some may recognize their ethnic heritage but not practise the religious or cultural traditions. The term came into use in medieval Europe, based on the Latin name for Judeans, the people of Judah. Prejudice against Jews is termed ◊anti-Semitism.

Jew's harp musical instrument consisting of a two-pronged metal frame inserted between the teeth, and a springlike tongue plucked with the finger. The resulting drone excites resonances in the mouth that can be varied in pitch to produce a melody.

Jezebel in the Old Testament, daughter of the king of Sidon. She married King Ahab of Israel, and was brought into conflict with the prophet Elijah by her introduction of the worship of Baal.

Jhabvala Ruth Prawer 1927– . Adoptively Indian novelist. Born in Cologne of Polish parents and educated in England, she went to live in India when she married 1951. Her novels explore the idiosyncratic blend of East and West in the Indian middle class, as in *Esmond in India* 1957. She has also written successful film scripts, including a treatment of her own novel *Heat and Dust*, awarded the Booker Prize 1975. Her film scripts for *A Room with a View* 1987 and *Howards End* 1992 both received Academy awards.

Jiang Jie Shi alternate transcription of ◊Chiang Kai-shek.

Jiang Qing or ***Chiang Ching*** 1914–1991. Chinese communist politician, third wife of the party leader Mao Zedong. In 1960 she became minister for culture, and played a key role in the 1966–69 Cultural Revolution as the leading member of the Shanghai-based ◊Gang of Four, who attempted to seize power 1976. She was sentenced to life imprisonment 1981.

Jiangsu or ***Kiangsu*** province on the coast of E China
area 102,200 sq km/39,449 sq mi
capital Nanjing
features the swampy mouth of the river Chang Jiang; the special municipality of Shanghai
industries cereals, rice, tea, cotton, soya beans, fish, silk, ceramics, textiles, coal, iron, copper, cement
population (1990) 68,170,000
history Jiangsu was originally part of the Wu kingdom, and Wu is still a traditional local name for the province. Jiangsu's capture by Japan 1937 was an important step in that country's attempt to conquer China.

Jiangxi or ***Kiangsi*** province of SE China
area 164,800 sq km/63,613 sq mi
capital Nanchang
industries rice, tea, cotton, tobacco, porcelain, coal, tungsten, uranium
population (1990) 38,280,000
history the province was Mao Zedong's original base in the first phase of the Communist struggle against the Nationalists.

Jiang Zemin 1926– . Chinese political leader, state president from 1993. He succeeded ◊Zhao Ziyang as Communist Party leader after the Tiananmen Square massacre of 1989. Jiang is a cautious proponent of economic reform who has held with unswerving adherence to the party's 'political line'.

The son-in-law of ◊Li Xiannian, Jiang joined the Chinese Communist Party's politburo 1967 after serving in the Moscow embassy and as mayor of Shanghai. He subsequently succeeded ◊Deng Xiaoping as head of the influential central military commission and replaced Yang Shangkun as state president March 1993.

Jicarilla member of a Native American people who originally inhabited parts of New Mexico and Arizona, and now live on a reservation in New Mexico. Their language belongs to the Athabascan family.

Jiddah or ***Jedda*** port in Hejaz, Saudi Arabia, on the eastern shore of the Red Sea; population (1991 est) 1,500,000. Industries include cement, steel, and oil refining. Pilgrims pass through here on their way to Mecca.

jig a dance popular in the British Isles during the 16th century, which is thought to have developed into the gigue, later commonly used as the last movement of a Baroque suite.

jihad (Arabic 'conflict') holy war undertaken by Muslims against nonbelievers. In the Mecca Declaration 1981, the Islamic powers pledged a jihad against Israel, though not necessarily military attack.

Jilin or ***Kirin*** province of NE China in central ◊Manchuria
area 187,000 sq km/72,182 sq mi
capital Changchun
population (1990) 25,150,000.

Jim Crow the systematic practice of segregating black Americans, which was common in the southern USA until the 1960s. Jim Crow laws are laws designed to deny civil rights to blacks or to enforce the policy of segregation, which existed until Supreme Court decisions and civil-rights legislation of the 1950s and 1960s (Civil Rights Act 1964, Voting Rights Act 1965) denied their legality. See also ◊black.

Jinan or ***Tsinan*** city and capital of Shandong province, China; population (1993) 2,050,000. It has food-processing and textile industries.

Jin dynasty or ***Chin dynasty*** hereditary rulers of N China, including Manchuria and part of Mongolia, 1122–1234, during the closing part of the ◊Song era (960–1279). The dynasty was founded by Juchen (Jurchen) nomad hunters, who sacked the northern Song capital Kaifeng 1126, forcing the Song to retreat south to Hangzhou. The Jin eventually ruled N China as far south as the Huai River. Over time, the Juchen became Sinicized, but from 1214 lost much of their territory to the ◊Mongols led by Genghis Khan.

Jerusalem The Wailing Wall, the remaining part of the Temple of Jerusalem, the holiest place of pilgrimage and prayer for Jews. It is also known as the Western Wall. The first temple on the site was built by King Solomon in 950 BC. Since AD 692 the Dome of the Rock, the Muslim temple, has stood on the same site. *Corbis*

jet propulsion Two forms of jet engine. In the turbojet, air passing into the air intake is compressed by the compressor and fed into the combustion chamber where fuel burns. The hot gases formed are expelled at high speed from the rear of the engine, driving the engine forwards and turning a turbine which drives the compressor. In the turbofan, some air flows around the combustion chamber and mixes with the exhaust gases. This arrangement is more efficient and quieter than the turbojet.

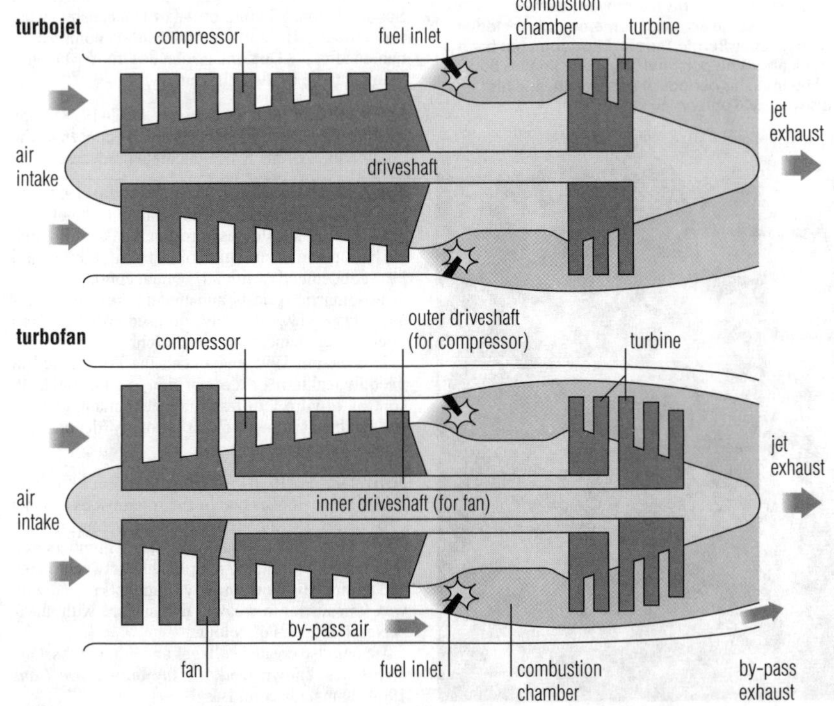

Jinnah Muhammad Ali 1876–1948. Indian politician, Pakistan's first governor general from 1947. He was president of the ◊Muslim League 1916, 1934–48, and by 1940 was advocating the need for a separate state of Pakistan; at the 1946 conferences in London he insisted on the partition of British India into Hindu and Muslim states. ▷ *See feature on pp. 432–433.*

jinni (plural ***jinn***) in Muslim mythology, a member of a class of spirits able to assume human or animal shape.

Jinsha Jiang river that rises in SW China and forms the ◊Chang Jiang (Yangtze Kiang) at Yibin.

Jivaro a Native American people of the tropical forests of SE Ecuador and NE Peru. They live by farming, hunting, fishing, and weaving; the Jivaro language belongs to the Andean-Equatorial family. They were formerly notorious for preserving the hair and shrunken skin of the heads of their enemies as battle trophies.

jive energetic American dance that evolved from the jitterbug, popular in the 1940s and 1950s; a forerunner of rock and roll.

Joachim of Fiore c. 1132–1202. Italian mystic, born in Calabria. In his mystical writings he interpreted history as a sequence of three ages, that of the Father, Son, and Holy Spirit, the last of which, the age of perfect spirituality, was to begin 1260. His messianic views were taken up enthusiastically by many followers.

Joachim Joseph 1831–1907. Austro-Hungarian violinist and composer. He studied under Mendelssohn and founded the Joachim Quartet (1869–1907). Joachim played and conducted the music of his friend Brahms. His own compositions include pieces for violin and orchestra, chamber, and orchestral works.

Joan mythical Englishwoman supposed to have become pope 855, as John VIII, and to have given birth to a child during a papal procession. The myth was exposed in the 17th century.

Joan of Arc, St (French Jeanne d'Arc) c. 1412–1431. French military leader. In 1429 she persuaded the future Charles VII that she had a divine mission to expel the occupying English from N France (see ◊Hundred Years' War) and secure his coronation. She raised the siege of Orléans, defeated the English at Patay, north of Orléans, and Charles was crowned in Reims. However, she failed to take Paris and was captured May 1430 by the Burgundians, who sold her to the English, and she was executed.

Man is born unto trouble, as the sparks fly upward.

JOB
New Testament, 5:7

Job lived c. 5th century BC. In the Old Testament, Hebrew leader who in the Book of Job questioned God's infliction of suffering on the righteous while enduring great sufferings himself. Although Job comes to no final conclusion, his book is one of the first attempts to explain the problem of human suffering in a world believed to be created and governed by a God who is all-powerful and all-good.

Jobcentre in the UK, a state-run ◊employment exchange

Jockey Club governing body of English ◊horse racing. It was founded about 1750 at the Star and Garter, Pall Mall, London.

Jodhpur city in Rajasthan, India, formerly capital of Jodhpur princely state, founded 1459 by Rao Jodha; population (1991) 668,000. It is a market centre and has the training college of the Indian air force, an 18th-century Mogul palace, and a red sandstone fort. A style of riding breeches is named after it.

Jodrell Bank site in Cheshire, England, of the Nuffield Radio Astronomy Laboratories of the University of Manchester. Its largest instrument is the 76 m/250 ft radio dish (the Lovell Telescope), completed 1957 and modified 1970. A 38 × 25 m/125 × 82 ft elliptical radio dish was introduced 1964, capable of working at shorter wave lengths.

Joel prophet of Judah in the Old Testament, who predicts punishments for Judah's sins, to be followed by a restoration of God's grace and the nation's triumph over its enemies.

Joffre Joseph Jacques Césaire 1852–1931. Marshal of France during World War I. He was chief of general staff 1911. The German invasion of Belgium 1914 took him by surprise, but his stand at the Battle of the ◊Marne resulted in his appointment as supreme commander of all the French armies 1915. His failure to make adequate preparations at Verdun 1916 and the military disasters on the ◊Somme led to his replacement by Nivelle Dec 1916.

Johannesburg largest city of South Africa, situated on the Witwatersrand River in Gauteng Province; population (urban area, 1991) 1,916,100. It is the centre of a large gold-mining industry; other industries include engineering works, meat-chilling plants, and clothing factories.

Notable buildings include the law courts, Escom House (Electricity Supply Commission), the South African Railways Administration Building, the City Hall, Chamber of Mines and Stock Exchange, the Witwatersrand (1921) and Rand Afrikaans (1966) universities, and the Union Observatory. Johannesburg was founded after the discovery of gold 1886 and was probably named after Jan (Johannes) Meyer, the first mining commissioner.

John Augustus Edwin 1878–1961. Welsh painter. He is known for his vivacious portraits, including *The Smiling Woman* 1910 (Tate Gallery, London) of his second wife, Dorelia McNeill. His sitters included such literary figures as Thomas Hardy, Dylan Thomas, W B Yeats, T E Lawrence, and James Joyce. His portraits are outstanding in their combined certainty of drawing and temperamental handling of paint. His sense of colour and a modified Post-Impressionism appear in their most assured in his landscapes of the south of France and his flower pieces. He was the brother of Gwen ◊John, who was also a distinguished painter, particularly of serene interiors.

John Elton. Stage name of Reginald Kenneth Dwight 1947– . English pop singer, pianist, and composer. His best-known album, *Goodbye Yellow Brick Road* 1973, includes the hit 'Bennie and the Jets'. Among his many other highly successful songs are 'Rocket Man', 'Crocodile Rock', and 'Daniel' all 1972, 'Candle in the Wind' 1973, 'Pinball Wizard' 1975, 'Blue Eyes' 1982, 'Nikita' 1985, and 'Sacrifice' 1989, the latter from his album *Sleeping with the Past.*

John Gwen(dolen Mary) 1876–1939. Welsh painter. She lived in France for most of her life. Many of her paintings depict young women or nuns (she converted to Catholicism 1913), but she also painted calm, muted interiors. Her style was characterized by a sensitive use of colour and tone.

'Even in his achievements there was something missing. ... He had the mental abilities of a great king but the inclinations of a petty tyrant.'

On King John
W C Warren
King John

John (I) Lackland 1167–1216. King of England from 1199 and acting king from 1189 during his brother Richard the Lion-Heart's absence on the third Crusade.

He lost Normandy and almost all the other English possessions in France to Philip II of France by 1205. His repressive policies and excessive taxation brought him into conflict with his barons, and he was forced to seal the ◊Magna Carta 1215. Later repudiation of it led to the first Barons' War 1215–17, during which he died.

John's bad reputation was only partially deserved. It resulted from his intrigues against his brother Richard I, his complicity in the death of his nephew Prince Arthur of Brittany, a rival for the English throne, and the effectiveness of his ruthless taxation policy, as well as his provoking Pope Innocent III to excommunicate England 1208–13. John's attempt to limit the papacy's right of interference in episcopal elections, which traditionally were the preserve of English kings, was resented by monastic sources, and these provided much of the evidence upon which his reign was later judged.

John two kings of France, including:

John II 1319–1364. King of France from 1350. He was defeated and captured by the Black Prince at Poitiers 1356 and imprisoned in England. Released 1360, he failed to raise the money for his ransom and returned to England 1364, where he died.

John name of 23 popes, including:

John XXII (born Jacques Dues) 1249–1334. Pope 1316–34. He spent his papacy in Avignon, France, engaged in a long conflict with the Holy Roman emperor, Louis of Bavaria, and the Spiritual Franciscans, a monastic order who preached the absolute poverty of the clergy.

John XXIII (Angelo Giuseppe Roncalli) 1881–1963. Pope from 1958. He improved relations with the USSR in line with his encyclical *Pacem in Terris/Peace on Earth* 1963, established Roman Catholic hierarchies in newly emergent states, and summoned the Second Vatican Council, which reformed church liturgy and backed the ecumenical movement.

'John XXIII' (Baldassare Costa) c. 1370–1419. Anti-pope 1410–15. In an attempt to end the ◊Great Schism he was elected pope by a council of cardinals in Bologna, but was deposed by the Council of Constance 1415, together with the popes of Avignon and Rome. His papacy is not recognized by the church.

John three kings of Poland, including:

John III Sobieski 1624–1696. King of Poland from 1674. He became commander in chief of the army 1668 after victories over the Cossacks and Tatars. A victory over the Turks 1673 helped to get him elected to the Polish throne, and he saved Vienna from the besieging Turks 1683.

John English pop singer Elton John in 1991. One of the most successful stars of the 1970s and 1980s, he was distinctive for his flamboyant clothes, energetic stage act, and his memorable melodies with lyrics by Bernie Taupin. Elton John has been frank about his personal life, discussing his bouts of bulimia, his periods of depression, and his bisexuality. *Topham*

John six kings of Portugal, including:

John I 1357–1433. King of Portugal from 1385. An illegitimate son of Pedro I, he was elected by the Cortes (parliament). His claim was supported by an English army against the rival king of Castile, thus establishing the Anglo-Portuguese Alliance 1386. He married Philippa of Lancaster, daughter of ◊John of Gaunt.

John IV 1604–1656. King of Portugal from 1640. Originally duke of Braganza, he was elected king when the Portuguese rebelled against Spanish rule. His reign was marked by a long war against Spain, which did not end until 1668.

John VI 1769–1826. King of Portugal and regent for his insane mother ***Maria I*** from 1799 until her death 1816. He fled to Brazil when the French invaded Portugal 1807 and did not return until 1822. On his return Brazil declared its independence, with John's elder son Pedro as emperor.

John Bull imaginary figure who is a personification of England, similar to the American Uncle Sam. He is represented in cartoons and caricatures as a prosperous farmer of the 18th century.

John of Damascus, St c. 676–c. 754. Eastern Orthodox theologian and hymn writer, a defender of image worship against the iconoclasts (image-breakers). Contained in his *The Fountain of Knowledge* is 'An Accurate Exposition of the Orthodox Faith', an important chronicle of theology from the 4th to 7th centuries. He was born in Damascus, Syria. Feast day 4 Dec.

John of Gaunt 1340–1399. English nobleman and politician, born in Ghent, Belgium, fourth son of Edward III, Duke of Lancaster from 1362. He distinguished himself during the Hundred Years' War. During Edward's last years, and the years before Richard II attained the age of majority, he acted as head of government, and Parliament protested against his corrupt rule.

John of Salisbury c. 1115–1180. English philosopher and historian. His *Policraticus* portrayed the church as the guarantee of liberty against the unjust claims of secular authority.

He studied in France 1130–1153, in Paris with ◊Abelard and at Chartres. He became secretary to Thomas à Becket and supported him against Henry II, and fled to France after Becket's murder, becoming bishop of Chartres 1176.

John of the Cross, St 1542–1591. Spanish Roman Catholic Carmelite friar from 1564, who was imprisoned several times for attempting to impose the reforms laid down by St Teresa. His verse describes spiritual ecstasy. Feast day 24 Nov.

John o' Groats village in NE Highland Region, Scotland, about 3 km/2 mi W of Duncansby Head, proverbially Britain's northernmost point. It is named after the Dutchman John de Groot, who built a house there in the 16th century.

John Paul I (Albino Luciani) 1912–1978. Pope 26 Aug–28 Sept 1978. His name was chosen as the combination of his two immediate predecessors.

John Paul II (Karol Jozef Wojtyla) 1920– . Pope from 1978, the first non-Italian to be elected pope since 1522. He was born near Kraków, Poland. He has upheld the tradition of papal infallibility and has condemned artificial contraception, women priests, married priests, and modern dress for monks and nuns – views that have aroused criticism from liberalizing elements in the church.

In a March 1995 encyclical, the Pope stated in unequivocal terms his opposition to abortion, birth control, in vitro fertilization, genetic manipulation, and euthanasia, as well as strongly denouncing capital punishment.

Johns Jasper 1930– . US painter, sculptor, and printmaker. He was one of the foremost exponents of ◊Pop art. He rejected abstract art, favouring such mundane subjects as flags, maps, and numbers as a means of exploring the relationship between image and reality. His work employs pigments mixed with wax (encaustic) to create a rich surface with unexpected delicacies of colour.

He has also created collages and lithographs. One of his best-known works is the bronze *Ale Cans* 1960 (Kunstmuseum, Basel).

John Paul II Pope John Paul II, the first non-Italian to become pope since 1522. He combines a colourful and more accessible image of the papacy with sternly conservative attitudes to issues such as abortion, contraception, and homosexuality. *Topham*

Johns W(illiam) E(arl), 'Captain' 1893–1968. English author. From 1932 he wrote popular novels about World War I flying ace 'Biggles', now sometimes criticized for chauvinism, racism, and sexism. Johns was a flying officer in the RAF (there is no rank of captain) until his retirement 1930.

John, St lived 1st century AD. New Testament apostle. Traditionally, he wrote the fourth Gospel and the Johannine Epistles (when he was bishop of Ephesus), and the Book of Revelation (while exiled to the Greek island of Patmos). His emblem is an eagle; his feast day 27 Dec.

Johnson Amy 1903–1941. English aviator. She made a solo flight from England to Australia 1930, in 9½ days, and in 1932 made the fastest ever solo flight from England to Cape Town, South Africa. Her plane disappeared over the English Channel in World War II while she was serving with the Air Transport Auxiliary.

Johnson Andrew 1808–1875. 17th president of the USA 1865–69, a Democrat. He was a congressman from Tennessee 1843–53, governor of Tennessee 1853–57, senator 1857–62, and vice president 1865. He succeeded to the presidency on Lincoln's assassination (15 April 1865). His conciliatory policy to the defeated South after the Civil War involved him in a feud with the Radical Republicans, culminating in his impeachment 1868 before the Senate, which failed to convict him by one vote. Among his achievements was the purchase of Alaska from Russia 1867.

Johnson Celia 1908–1982. English actress. She was perceived as quintessentially English. She starred with Trevor Howard in the romantic film *Brief Encounter* 1946; later films include *The Captain's Paradise* 1953 and *The Prime of Miss Jean Brodie* 1968.

Johnson Jack (John Arthur) 1878–1946. US heavyweight boxer. He overcame severe racial prejudice to become the first black heavyweight champion of the world 1908 when he travelled to Australia to challenge Tommy Burns. The US authorities wanted Johnson 'dethroned' because of his colour but could not find suitable challengers until 1915, when he lost the title in a dubious fight decision to the giant Jess Willard.

Johnson Lyndon Baines 1908–1973. 36th president of the USA 1963–69, a Democrat. He was elected to Congress 1937–49 and the Senate 1949–60. Born in Texas, he brought critical Southern support as J F Kennedy's vice-presidential running mate 1960, and became president on Kennedy's assassination.

Following Kennedy's assassination, Johnson successfully won congressional support for many of Kennedy's New Frontier social reform proposals, most conspicuously in the area of civil rights. He moved beyond the New Frontier to declare 'war on poverty' supported by Great Society legislation (civil rights, education, alleviation of poverty). His foreign policy met with considerably less success. After the ◊Tonkin Gulf Incident, which escalated US involvement in the ◊Vietnam War, support won by Johnson's domestic reforms dissipated, and he declined to run for re-election 1968.

Johnson Michael 1967– . US track and field athlete. At Atlanta in 1996 Johnson became the first man in Olympic history to win gold medals at both 200 and 400 metres. In the 200 metres final he set a new world record of 19.32 seconds and finished .36 seconds ahead of the second placed athlete, a margin of victory only bettered by Jesse ◊Owens at the 1936 Olympics.

Johnson Philip Cortelyou 1906– . US architect. He coined the term 'International Style' 1932. Originally designing in the style of ◊Mies van der Rohe, he later became an exponent of ◊Post-Modernism. He designed the giant AT&T building in New York 1978, a pink skyscraper with a Chippendale-style cabinet top.

Johnson Samuel, (Dr Johnson) 1709–1784. English lexicographer, author, and critic. He was also a brilliant conversationalist and the dominant figure in 18th-century London literary society. His *Dictionary*, published 1755, remained authoritative for over a century, and is still remarkable for the vigour of its definitions. In 1764 he founded the Literary Club, whose members included the painter Joshua Reynolds, the political philosopher Edmund Burke, the dramatist Oliver Goldsmith, the actor David Garrick, and James ◊Boswell, Johnson's biographer.

Johnson's first meeting with Boswell was 1763. A visit with Boswell to Scotland and the Hebrides 1773 was recorded in *A Journey to the Western Isles of Scotland* 1775. Other works include a satire imitating Juvenal, *The Vanity of Human Wishes* 1749, the philosophical romance *Rasselas* 1759, an edition of Shakespeare 1765, and the classic *Lives of the English Poets* 1779–81.

John the Baptist, St c. 12 BC–c. AD 27. In the New Testament, an itinerant preacher. After preparation in the wilderness, he proclaimed the coming of the Messiah and baptized Jesus in the river Jordan. He was later executed by ◊Herod Antipas at the request of Salome, who demanded that his head be brought to her on a platter.

Johnson Lyndon B Johnson became president of the USA 1963 after the assassination of John F Kennedy. He introduced a broad range of social reforms, including major advances in black civil rights, but his extension of Kennedy's policy of US involvement in Vietnam led to riots on university campuses and made his administration deeply unpopular. *United Nations*

John was the son of Zacharias and Elizabeth (a cousin of Jesus' mother), and born in Nazareth, Galilee. He and Jesus are often shown together as children.

joint in any animal with a skeleton, a point of movement or articulation. In vertebrates, it is the point where two bones meet. Some joints allow no motion (the sutures of the skull), others allow a very small motion (the sacroiliac joints in the lower back), but most allow a relatively free motion. Of these, some allow a gliding motion (one vertebra of the spine on another), some have a hinge action (elbow and knee), and others allow motion in all directions (hip and shoulder joints) by means of a ball-and-socket arrangement. The ends of the bones at a moving joint are covered with cartilage for greater elasticity and smoothness, and enclosed in an envelope (capsule) of tough white fibrous tissue lined with a membrane which secretes a lubricating and cushioning ◊synovial fluid. The joint is further strengthened by ligaments. In invertebrates with an ◊exoskeleton, the joints are places where the exoskeleton is replaced by a more flexible outer covering, the arthrodial membrane, which allows the limb (or other body part) to bend at that point.

Joint European Torus experimental nuclear-fusion machine, known as ◊JET.

Joinville Jean, Sire de Joinville c. 1224–c. 1317. French historian, born in Champagne. He accompanied Louis IX on the crusade of 1248–54, which he described in his *History of St Louis*.

Joliot-Curie Frédéric (Jean) Joliot (1900–1958) and Irène (born Curie) (1897–1956). French physicists. They made the discovery of artificial ◊radioactivity, for which they were jointly awarded the 1935 Nobel Prize for Chemistry.

Irène was the daughter of Marie and Pierre ◊Curie and began work at her mother's Radium Institute 1921. In 1926 she married Frédéric, a pupil of her mother's, and they began a long and fruitful collaboration. In 1934 they found that certain elements exposed to radiation themselves become radioactive.

Jolson Al. Stage name of Asa Yoelson 1886–1950. Russian-born US singer and entertainer. Popular in Broadway theatre and vaudeville, he was chosen to star in the first talking picture, *The Jazz Singer* 1927.

Jonah lived 7th century BC. Hebrew prophet whose name is given to a book in the Old Testament. According to this, he fled by ship to evade his mission to prophesy the destruction of Nineveh. The crew threw him overboard in a storm, as a bringer of ill fortune, and he spent three days and nights in the belly of a whale before coming to land.

Jonathan Chief (Joseph) Leabua 1914–1987. Lesotho politician. A leader in the drive for independence, Jonathan became prime minister of Lesotho 1965. As prime minister, Jonathan played a pragmatic role, allying himself in turn with the South African government and the Organization of African Unity. His rule was ended by a coup 1986.

Jones Allen 1937– . English painter, sculptor, and printmaker. He was a leading exponent of ◊Pop art. His colourful paintings are executed in the style of commercial advertising, and unabashedly celebrate the female form, for example, *Perfect Match* 1966–67 (Wallraf-Richartz Museum, Cologne). His witty, abbreviated imagery of women clad in bustiers, garter-belts, stocking tops, and stiletto-heeled shoes is intended as a comment on male fantasies and sexual fetishes.

Jones Bobby (Robert Tyre) 1902–1971. US golfer. He was the game's greatest amateur player, who never turned professional but won 13 major amateur and professional tournaments, including the Grand Slam of the amateur and professional opens of both the USA and Britain 1930.

Jones Inigo 1573–1652. English Classical architect. He introduced the Palladian style to England. Born in London, he studied in Italy where he encountered the works of Palladio. He was employed by James I to design scenery for Ben Jonson's masques and appointed Surveyor of the King's Works 1615–42. He designed the Queen's House, Greenwich, 1616–35, and his English Renaissance masterpiece, the Banqueting House in Whitehall, London, 1619–22. His work was to

'Architecture is the art of how to waste space.'

Philip Johnson
Quoted in the *New York Times* 27 Dec 1964

'Sir, I look upon every day to be lost, in which I do not make a new acquaintance.'

Samuel Johnson
Quoted in James Boswell's *Life of Johnson* 1791

Jones *Commemorative engraving of Inigo Jones, from a portrait by van Dyck, c. 1640, Library of Congress, Washington DC, USA. Jones was a great innovator, both in introducing the Palladian style of architecture to England from Venice, and in being the first English stage designer to use the proscenium arch and moveable scenery. Corbis*

provide the inspiration for the Palladian Revival a century later.

jonquil species of small daffodil *Narcissus jonquilla*, family Amaryllidaceae, with yellow flowers. Native to Spain and Portugal, it is cultivated elsewhere.

> *'Talking and eloquence are not the same: to speak, and to speak well, are two things.'*
>
> BEN JONSON
> *Discoveries made upon Men and Matter*

Jonson Ben(jamin) 1572–1637. English dramatist, poet, and critic. *Every Man in his Humour* 1598 established the English 'comedy of humours', in which each character embodies a 'humour', or vice, such as greed, lust, or avarice. This was followed by *Cynthia's Revels* 1600 and *The Poetaster* 1601. His first extant tragedy is *Sejanus* 1603, with Burbage and Shakespeare as members of the original cast. His great comedies are *Volpone, or The Fox* 1606, *The Alchemist* 1610, and *Bartholomew Fair* 1614. He wrote extensively for court entertainment in the form of ◊masques produced with scenic designer Inigo ◊Jones.

Jonson had a unique comic vision and technical mastery of form. His work has had a profound influence on English drama and literature for example, on the Restoration dramatists and on novelists such as Henry ◊Fielding and Tobias ◊Smollett.

Joplin Janis 1943–1970. US blues and rock singer. She was lead singer with the San Francisco group Big Brother and the Holding Company 1966–68. Her biggest hit, Kris Kristofferson's 'Me and Bobby McGee', was released on the posthumous *Pearl* album 1971.

Joplin Scott 1868–1917. US ◊ragtime pianist and composer. He was active in Chicago. His 'Maple Leaf Rag' 1899 was the first instrumental sheet music to sell a million copies, and 'The Entertainer', as the theme tune of the film *The Sting* 1973, revived his popularity. He was an influence on Jelly Roll Morton and other early jazz musicians.

Jonson *A portrait of the English writer and critic Ben Jonson. He was born in London, and was a bricklayer and a soldier before becoming involved in theatre as an actor and a playwright. His eventful life also included killing a man in a duel and narrowly escaping hanging, and being imprisoned for writing seditious material. Corbis*

Jordaens Jacob 1593–1678. Flemish painter. His style follows Rubens, whom he assisted in various commissions. Much of his work is exuberant and on a large scale, including scenes of peasant life and mythological subjects, as well as altarpieces and portraits.

He was the pupil of Adam van Noort, whose daughter he married, and his development is parallel with that of Rubens, in whose studio he worked. He painted with immense gusto and might be called a coarser Rubens. After the latter's death he was the leading figure of Flemish Baroque painting.

Jordan country in SW Asia, bounded N by Syria, NE by Iraq, E, SE and S by Saudi Arabia, S by the Gulf of Aqaba, and W by Israel. *See country box opposite.*

Jordan river rising on Mount Hermon, Syria, at 550 m/1,800 ft above sea level and flowing S for about 320 km/200 mi via the Sea of Galilee to the Dead Sea, 390 m/1,290 ft below sea level. It occupies the northern part of the Great Rift Valley; its upper course forms the boundary of Israel with Syria and the kingdom of Jordan; its lower course runs through Jordan; the West Bank has been occupied by Israel since 1967.

Jordan Michael Jeffrey 1963– . US basketball player. He played for the Chicago Bulls from 1984, and led them to National Basketball Association (NBA) championship wins 1991, 1992, 1993, and 1996. As a rookie he led the NBA in points scored (2,313). During the 1986–87 season he scored 3,000 points, only the second player in NBA history to do so. He retired from professional basketball Oct 1993, but returned to the game March 1995. He announced his retirement again in 1999.

Joseph in the New Testament, the husband of the Virgin Mary, a descendant of King David of the Tribe of Judah, and a carpenter by trade. Although Jesus was not the son of Joseph, Joseph was his legal father. According to Roman Catholic tradition, he had a family by a previous wife, and was an elderly man when he married Mary.

Joseph in the Old Testament, the 11th and favourite son of ◊Jacob, sold into Egypt by his jealous half-brothers. After he had risen to power there, they and his father joined him to escape from famine in Canaan.

Joseph Keith Sinjohn, Baron Joseph 1918–1994. British Conservative politician. A barrister, he entered Parliament 1956. He held ministerial posts 1962–64, 1970–74, 1979–81, and was secretary of state for education and science 1981–86.

He served in the governments of Harold Macmillan, Alec Douglas-Home, and Edward Heath during the 1960s and 1970s, but it was not until Margaret Thatcher came to office 1979 that he found a prime minister truly receptive to his views and willing to translate them into policies. With her, he founded the right-wing Centre for Policy Studies, which sought to discover and apply the secrets of the successful market economies of West Germany and Japan.

Joseph I 1678–1711. Holy Roman emperor from 1705 and king of Austria, of the house of Habsburg. He spent most of his reign involved in fighting the War of the ◊Spanish Succession.

Joseph II 1741–1790. Holy Roman emperor from 1765, son of Francis I (1708–1765). The reforms he carried out after the death of his mother, ◊Maria Theresa, 1780, provoked revolts from those who lost privileges.

Josephine Marie Josèphe Rose Tascher de la Pagerie 1763–1814. As wife of ◊Napoleon Bonaparte, she was empress of France 1804–1809. Born on the island of Martinique, she married in 1779 Alexandre de ◊Beauharnais, and in 1796 Napoleon, who divorced her 1809 because she had not produced children.

Joseph of Arimathaea, St lived 1st century AD. In the New Testament, a wealthy Hebrew, member of the Sanhedrin (supreme court), and secret supporter of Jesus. On the evening of the Crucifixion he asked the Roman procurator Pilate for Jesus' body and buried it in his own tomb. According to tradition, Joseph brought the Holy Grail to England about AD 63 and built the first Christian church in Britain, at Glastonbury. Feast day 17 March.

Joplin *US blues and rock singer of the 1960s, Janis Joplin. With her rasping 'black' blues voice and intense manner, Joplin rapidly became a favourite with rock concert audiences, for whom she was a symbol of the rebellious youth culture of the 1960s. She died of a drugs overdose at the age of 27. Topham*

Josephson Brian David 1940– . Welsh physicist, a leading authority on ◊superconductivity. In 1973 he shared a Nobel prize for his theoretical predictions of the properties of a supercurrent through a tunnel barrier (the Josephson effect), which led to the development of the Josephson junction.

Josephson junction device used in 'superchips' (large and complex integrated circuits) to speed the passage of signals by a phenomenon called 'electron tunnelling'. Although these superchips respond a thousand times faster than the ◊silicon chip, they have the disadvantage that the components of the Josephson junctions operate only at temperatures close to ◊absolute zero. They are named after Welsh theoretical physicist Brian Josephson.

Josephus Flavius AD 37–c. 100. Jewish historian and general, born in Jerusalem. He became a Pharisee and commanded the Jewish forces in Galilee in their revolt against Rome from AD 66 (which ended with the mass suicide at Masada). He wrote *Antiquities of the Jews*, an early history to AD 66; *The Jewish War*; and an autobiography.

Joshua lived 13th century BC. In the Old Testament, successor of Moses, who led the Jews in their return to and conquest of the land of Canaan. The city of Jericho was the first to fall – according to the Book of Joshua, the walls crumbled to the blast of his trumpets.

Josiah c. 647–609 BC. King of Judah. Grandson of Manasseh and son of Amon, he succeeded to the throne at the age of eight. The discovery of a Book of Instruction (probably Deuteronomy, a book of the Old Testament) during repairs of the Temple 621 BC stimulated thorough reform, which included the removal of all sanctuaries except that of Jerusalem. He was killed in a clash at ◊Megiddo with Pharaoh-nechoh, king of Egypt.

Jospin Lionel 1937– . French politician, prime minister from 1997. Leader of the centre-left Socialist Party (PS) 1981–88 and since 1995. A loyal supporter of President Francois Mitterrand between 1981–95, he was education minister 1988–92. After being only narrowly defeated by Jacques Chirac in the May 1995 presidential election, he led the PS to victory in the June 1997 National Assembly elections.

Josquin Desprez or *des Prés* 1440–1521. Franco-Flemish composer. His synthesis of Flemish structural counterpoint and Italian harmonic expression, acquired in the service of the Rome papal chapel 1484–1503, marks a peak in Renaissance vocal music. In addition to masses on secular as well as sacred themes, including the *Missa*

JORDAN
Hashemite Kingdom of

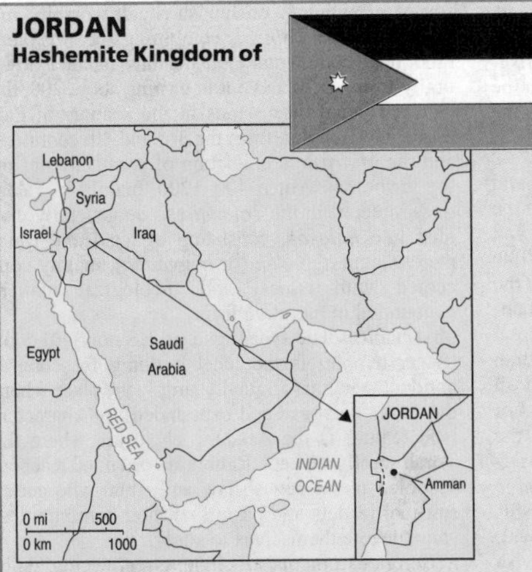

national name *Al Mamlaka al Urduniya al Hashemiyah*
area 89,206 sq km/34,434 sq mi (West Bank 5,879 sq km/2,269 sq mi)
capital Amman
major towns/cities Zarqa, Irbid
major ports Aqaba
physical features desert plateau in E; rift valley separates E and W banks of the river Jordan
head of state King Abdullah ibn Hussein from 1999
head of government Abdul-Karim Kabariti from 1996
political system constitutional monarchy
administrative divisions eight governorates
political parties independent groups loyal to the king predominate; of the 21 parties registered since 1992, the most significant is the Islamic Action Front (IAF), Islamic fundamentalist
population 5,335,000 (1998 est)
population growth rate 4.9% (1990–95); 3.0% (2000–05)
ethnic distribution majority of Arab descent; minor Circassian, Armenians, and Kurdish minorities
life expectancy 66 (men), 70 (women)
literacy rate men 89%, women 70%
languages Arabic (official), English
religions Sunni Muslim 80%, Christian 8%
currency Jordanian dinar
GDP (US $) 7.9 billion (1997)
growth rate 5.7% (1994)
exports potash, phosphates, citrus, vegetables, fertilizers, pharmaceuticals, textiles, cement, detergent, soap, plastics

HISTORY
13th C BC Oldest known 'states' of Jordan, including Gideon, Ammon, Moab, and Edom, established.
c. 1000 BC East Jordan was part of kingdom of Israel, under David and Solomon.
4th C BC SE Jordan occupied by the independent Arabic-speaking Nabataeans.
64 BC Conquered by Romans and became part of province of Arabia.
AD 636 Became largely Muslim after the Byzantine forces of Emperor Heraclius were defeated by Arab armies at battle of Yarmuk, in N Jordan.
1099–1187 Part of the Latin Kingdom established by the Crusaders in Jerusalem.
from early 16th C Part of Turkish Ottoman Empire, administered from Damascus.
1920 Trans-jordan (the area E of the river Jordan) and Palestine (which includes the West Bank) were placed under British administration by a League of Nations mandate.
1923 Trans-jordan separated from Palestine and was recognized by Britain as a substantially independent state under the rule of Emir Abdullah ibn Hussein, a member of the Hashemite dynasty of Arabia.
1946 Trans-jordan achieved independence achieved from Britain, with Abd Allah as king; name changed to Jordan.
1948 British mandate for Palestine expired, leading to fighting between Arabs and Jews, who each claimed the area.
1950 Jordan annexed West Bank; 400,000 Palestinian refugees flooded into Jordan, putting pressure on the economy.
1951 King Abdullah was assassinated in Jerusalem; he was succeeded by his son, King Talal.
1952 Partially democratic constitution introduced.
1953 Hussein ibn Tal Abdulla el Hashim officially became king of Jordan, after his father, King Talal, stepped down owing to mental illness.
1958 Jordan and Iraq formed Arab Federation that ended when the Iraqi monarchy was deposed.
1967 Israel defeated Egypt, Syria, and Jordan in the Arab–Israeli Six-Day War, and captured and occupied the West Bank, including Arab Jerusalem. Martial law imposed.
1970–71 Jordanians moved against the increasingly radicalized Palestine Liberation Organization (PLO), which had launched guerrilla raids on Israel from Jordanian territory, resulting in bloody civil war, before PLO leadership fled abroad.
1976 Lower house dissolved, political parties banned, elections postponed until further notice.
1980 Jordan emerged as important ally of Iraq in its war against Iran, an ally of Syria, with whom Jordan's relations were tense.
1982 Hussein tried to mediate in Arab-Israeli conflict, following the Israeli invasion of Lebanon.
1984 Women voted for the first time; parliament recalled.
1985 Hussein and PLO leader Yassir Arafat put forward framework for Middle East peace settlement. Secret meeting between Hussein and Israeli prime minister.
1988 Hussein announced willingness to cease administering the West Bank as part of Jordan, passing responsibility to the PLO, and the suspension of parliament.
1989 Prime Minister Zaid al-Rifai resigned; Hussein promised new parliamentary elections. Riots over price increases of up to 50% following fall in oil revenues. First parliamentary elections for 22 years; Muslim Brotherhood won 25 of 80 seats but exiled from government; martial law lifted.
1990 Hussein unsuccessfully tried to mediate after Iraq's invasion of Kuwait. Massive refugee problems as thousands fled to Jordan from Kuwait and Iraq.
1991 24 years of martial law ended; ban on political parties lifted; remained neutral during the Gulf War involving Saddam Hussein's Iraq.
1993 Candidates loyal to Hussein won majority in parliamentary elections; several leading Islamic fundamentalists lost their seats.
1994 Economic cooperation pact singed with PLO. Peace treaty signed with Israel, ending 46-year-old 'state of war'.
1996 Abdul-Karim Kabariti appointed prime minister.
1999 King Hussein died after a long fight against cancer. He had earlier appointed his eldest son Abdullah as his successor.

SEE ALSO Hussein, ibn Talal; Israel; Ottoman Empire; Palestine

'L'Homme armé'/Mass on 'The Armed Man' 1504, he also wrote secular chansons such as 'El Grillo'/ 'The Cricket' employing imitative vocal effects.

Joubert Piet (Petrus Jacobus) 1831–1900. Boer general in South Africa. He opposed British annexation of the Transvaal 1877, proclaimed its independence 1880, led the Boer forces in the First ◊South African War against the British 1880–81, defeated ◊Jameson 1896, and fought in the Second South African War.

joule SI unit (symbol J) of work and energy, replacing the ◊calorie (one joule equals 4.2 calories)

It is defined as the work done (energy transferred) by a force of one newton acting over one metre. It can also be expressed as the work done in one second by a current of one ampere at a potential difference of one volt. One watt is equal to one joule per second.

Joule James Prescott 1818–1889. English physicist. His work on the relations between electrical, mechanical, and chemical effects led to the discovery of the first law of ◊thermodynamics.

He determined the mechanical equivalent of heat (Joule's equivalent) 1843, and the SI unit of energy, the ◊joule, is named after him. He also discovered Joule's law, which defines the relation between heat and electricity; and with Irish physicist Lord ◊Kelvin in 1852 the Joule–Kelvin (or Joule–Thomson) effect.

journalism profession of reporting, photographing, or editing news events for the mass media – ◊newspapers, magazines, radio, television, documentary films, and newsreels – and for news agencies. In 1992, at least 61 journalists were killed in the line of duty worldwide and 123 were in jail on 1 Jan 1993.

Professional bodies include the NUJ (National Union of Journalists) in the UK and the ANG (American Newspaper Guild) in the USA. In the UK the NCTJ (National Council for the Training of Journalists) sets standards and awards proficiency certificates. Standards are also set by awards, such as those founded by J ◊Pulitzer.

journeyman a man who served his apprenticeship in a trade and worked as a fully qualified employee. The term originated in the regulations of the medieval trade ◊guilds; it derives from the French *journée* ('a day') because journeymen were paid daily

Each guild normally recognized three grades of worker – apprentices, journeymen, and masters. As a qualified tradesman, a journeyman might have become a master with his own business but most remained employees.

Jovian (Flavius Claudius Jovianus) c. 331–364. Roman emperor from 363. Captain of the imperial bodyguard, he was chosen as emperor by the troops after ◊Julian's death. He concluded an unpopular peace with the ◊Sassanian Empire and restored Christianity as the state religion.

Joyce James Augustine Aloysius 1882–1941. Irish writer. His originality lies in evolving a literary form to express the complexity of the human mind, and he revolutionized the form of the English novel with his 'stream of consciousness' technique. His works include *Dubliners* 1914 (short stories), *A Portrait of the Artist as a Young Man* 1916, ◊*Ulysses* 1922, and *Finnegans Wake* 1939.

Ulysses, which records the events of a single Dublin day, experiments with language and combines direct narrative with the unspoken and unconscious reactions of the characters. Banned at first for obscenity in the USA and the UK, it made a great impact and is generally regarded as Joyce's masterpiece. It was first published in Paris, where Joyce settled after World War I. *Finnegans Wake*, a story about a Dublin publican and his family, continued Joyce's experiments with language. In this work the word-coining which had been a feature of *Ulysses* was pushed to its limits and punning language and allegory are used to explore various levels of meaning, while attempting a synthesis of all existence.

'Journalism – an ability to meet the challenge of filling the space.'
On JOURNALISM
Rebecca West *New York Herald Tribune* 22 April 1956

Joyce William 1906–1946. Traitor to Britain. Born in New York, son of a naturalized Irish-born American, he perpetuated fascist activity in the UK as a 'British subject'. During World War II he made

Joyce Irish writer James Joyce. Though he was a voluntary exile from his homeland for most of his life, his fiction is a vivid, detailed, and affectionate recreation of the Dublin of the 1900s; his characters, from every walk of Irish life, re-enact ancient Greek and Celtic myths. *Corbis*

propaganda broadcasts from Germany to the UK, his upper-class accent earning him the nickname Lord Haw Haw. He was hanged for treason.

Juan Carlos 1938– . King of Spain. The son of Don Juan, pretender to the Spanish throne, he married Princess Sofia, eldest daughter of King Paul of Greece, 1962. In 1969 he was nominated by ◊Franco to succeed on the restoration of the monarchy intended to follow Franco's death; his father was excluded because of his known liberal views. Juan Carlos became king 1975.

Juárez Benito Pablo 1806–1872. Mexican politician, president 1861–65 and 1867–72. In 1861 he suspended repayments of Mexico's foreign debts, which prompted a joint French, British, and Spanish expedition to exert pressure. French forces invaded and created an empire for ◊Maximilian, brother of the Austrian emperor. After their withdrawal in 1867, Maximilian was executed, and Juárez returned to the presidency.

Judah or ***Judaea*** district of S Palestine. After the death of King Solomon 922 BC, Judah adhered to his son Rehoboam and the Davidic line, whereas the rest of Israel elected Jeroboam as ruler of the northern kingdom. In New Testament times, Judah was the Roman province of Judaea, and in current Israeli usage it refers to the southern area of the West Bank.

Judah Ha-Nasi 'the Prince' c. AD 135–c. 220. Jewish scholar who with a number of colleagues edited the collection of writings known as the *Mishnah*, which formed the basis of the ◊*Talmud*, in the 2nd century AD. He was a rabbi and president of the Sanhedrin (supreme religious court).

Judaism the religion of the ancient Hebrews and their descendants the Jews, based, according to the Old Testament, on a covenant between God and Abraham about 2000 BC, and the renewal of the covenant with Moses about 1200 BC. Judaism is the oldest monotheistic faith, the forebear of Christianity and Islam. It rests on the concept of one eternal invisible God, whose will is revealed in the Torah and who has a special relationship with the Jewish people. The Torah comprises the first five books of the Bible (the Pentateuch), which contains the history, laws, and guide to life for correct behaviour. Besides those living in Israel, there are large Jewish populations in the USA, the former USSR (mostly Russia, Ukraine, Belarus, and Moldova), the UK and Commonwealth nations, and in Jewish communities throughout the world. There are approximately 18 million Jews, with about 9 million in the Americas, 5 million in Europe, and 4 million in Asia, Africa, and the Pacific.

scriptures As well as the Torah, the Hebrew Bible contains histories, writings of the prophets, and writings such as the Psalms and Proverbs. A further source of authority on Jewish ritual, worship, and practice is the *Talmud*, combining the *Mishnah*, rabbinical commentary on the law handed down orally from AD 70 and put in writing about 200; the *Gemara*, legal discussions in the schools of Palestine and Babylon from the 3rd and 4th centuries; and the *Midrash*, a collection of commentaries on the scriptures written 400–1200, mainly in Palestine. Material in the *Talmud* can be generally divided into *halakah*, consisting of legal and ritual matters, and *aggadah* (or *haggadah*), mainly concerned with ethical and theological matters expounded in narrative form.

observances The synagogue (in US non-Orthodox usage, temple) is the local building for congregational worship (originally simply the place where the Torah was read and expounded); its characteristic feature is the Ark, the enclosure where the Torah scrolls are kept. Rabbis are ordained teachers schooled in the Jewish law and ritual who act as spiritual leaders and pastors of their communities; some devote themselves to study.

Religious practices include: circumcision, daily services in Hebrew, observance of the Sabbath (sunset on Friday to sunset Saturday) as a day of rest, and, among Orthodox Jews, strict dietary laws (see ◊kosher). High holy days include Rosh Hashanah marking the Jewish New Year (first new moon after the autumn equinox) and, a week later, the religious fast Yom Kippur (Day of Atonement). Other holidays are celebrated throughout the year to commemorate various events of biblical history.

divisions In the late Middle Ages, when Europe and W Asia were divided into Christian and Islamic countries, the Jewish people also found itself divided into two main groups. Jews in central and eastern Europe, namely in Germany and Poland, were called Ashkenazi. Sephardic Jews can trace their tradition back to the Mediterranean countries, particularly Spain and Portugal under Muslim rule. When they were expelled 1492 they settled in N Africa, the E Mediterranean, the Far East, and N Europe. The two traditions differ in a number of ritual and cultural ways but their theology and basic Jewish practice is the same. The Hasidic sects of eastern Europe and some N African and Oriental countries also differ from other groups in their rites but they, too, maintain the concept of divine authority.

In the 19th and early 20th centuries there was a move by some Jewish groups away from traditional or orthodox observances. This trend gave rise to a number of groups within Judaism. ***Orthodox Jews***, who form the majority, assert the supreme authority of the Torah and adhere to all the traditions of Judaism, including the strict dietary laws (see ◊kosher) and the segregation of women in the synagogue. ***Reform Judaism*** rejects the idea that Jews are the chosen people, has a liberal interpretation of the dietary laws, and takes a critical attitude towards the Torah. ***Conservative Judaism*** is a compromise between Orthodox and Reform in its acceptance of the traditional law, making some allowances for modern conditions, although its services and ceremonies are closer to Orthodox than to Reform. ***Liberal Judaism***, or ***Reconstructionism***, goes further than Reform in attempting to adapt Judaism to the needs of the modern world and to interpret the Torah in the light of current scholarship. In all the groups except Orthodox, women are not segregated in the synagogue, and there are female rabbis in both Reform and Liberal Judaism.

JUDAISM: TIMELINE

c. 2000 BC	Led by Abraham, the ancient Hebrews emigrated from Mesopotamia to Canaan.
18th C–1580	Some settled on the borders of Egypt and were put to forced labour.
13th C	They were rescued by Moses, who aimed at their establishment in Palestine. Moses received the Ten Commandments from God and brought them to the people. The main invasion of Canaan was led by Joshua about 1274.
12th–11th Cs	During the period of Judges, ascendancy was established over the Canaanites.
c. 1000	Complete conquest of Palestine and the union of all Judea was achieved under David, and Jerusalem became the capital.
10th C	Solomon succeeded David and enjoyed a reputation for great wealth and wisdom, but his lack of a constructive policy led, after his death, to the secession of the north of Judea (Israel) under Jeroboam, with only the tribe of Judah remaining under the house of David as the southern kingdom of Judah.
9th–8th Cs	Assyria became the dominant power in the Middle East. Israel purchased safety by tribute, but the basis of the society was corrupt, and prophets such as Amos, Isaiah, and Micah predicted destruction. At the hands of Tiglathpileser and his successor Shalmaneser IV, the northern kingdom (Israel) was made into Assyrian provinces after the fall of Samaria 721, although the southern kingdom of Judah was spared as an ally.
586–458	Nebuchadnezzar took Jerusalem and carried off the major part of the population to Babylon. Judaism was retained during exile, and was reconstituted by Ezra on the return to Jerusalem.
520	The Temple, originally built by Solomon, was restored.
c. 444	Ezra promulgated the legal code that was to govern the future of the Jewish people.
4th–3rd Cs	After the conquest of the Persian Empire by Alexander the Great, the Syrian Seleucid rulers and the Egyptian Ptolemaic dynasty struggled for Palestine, which came under the government of Egypt, although with a large measure of freedom.
2nd C	With the advance of Syrian power, Antiochus IV attempted intervention in the internal quarrels of the Hebrews, even desecrating the Temple, and a revolt broke out 165 led by the Maccabee family.
63	Judea's near-independence ended when internal dissension caused the Roman general Pompey to intervene, and Roman suzerainty was established.
1st C AD	A revolt led to the destruction of the Temple 66–70 by the Roman emperor Titus. Judean national sentiment was encouraged by the work of Rabbi Johanan ben Zakkai (c. 20–90), and, following him, the president of the Sanhedrin (supreme court) was recognized as the patriarch of Palestinian Jewry.
2nd–3rd Cs	Greatest of the Sanhedrin presidents was Rabbi Judah Ha-Nasi, who codified the traditional law in the *Mishnah*. The Palestinian *Talmud* (c. 375) added the *Gemara* to the *Mishnah*.
4th–5th Cs	The intellectual leadership of Judaism passed to the descendants of the 6th-century exiles in Babylonia, who compiled the Babylonian *Talmud*.
8th–13th Cs	Judaism enjoyed a golden era, producing the philosopher Saadiah, the poet Jehudah Ha-levi (c. 1075–1141), the codifier Moses Maimonides, and others.
14th–17th Cs	Where Christianity became the dominant or state religion, the Jews were increasingly segregated from mainstream life and trade by the Inquisition, anti-Semitic legislation, or by expulsion. The Protestant and Islamic states and their colonies allowed for refuge. Persecution led to messianic hopes, strengthened by the 16th-century revival of Kabbalism, culminating in the messianic movement of Shabbatai Sevi in the 17th century.
18th–19th Cs	Outbreaks of persecution increased with the rise of European nationalism. Reform Judaism, a rejection of religious orthodoxy and an attempt to interpret it for modern times, began in Germany 1810 and soon was established in England and the USA. In the late 19th century, large numbers of Jews fleeing persecution (pogrom) in Russia and E Europe emigrated to the USA, leading to the development of large Orthodox, Conservative, and Reform communities there. Many became Americanized and lost interest in religion.
20th C	Zionism, a nationalist movement dedicated to achieving a secure homeland where the Jewish people would be free from persecution, was founded 1896; this led to the establishment of the state of Israel 1948. Liberal Judaism (more radical than Reform) developed in the USA. In 1911 the first synagogue in the UK was founded. The Nazi German regime 1933–45 exterminated 6 million European Jews. Hundreds of thousands of survivors took refuge in preexisting Jewish settlements in what eventually became the new state of Israel. Although most Israeli and American Jews were not affiliated with synagogues after the 1950s, they continued to affirm their Jewish heritage. Both Orthodox and Hasidic Judaism, however, flourished in their new homes and grew rapidly in the 1970s and 1980s.

Judas Iscariot lived 1st century AD. In the New Testament, the disciple who betrayed Jesus Christ. Judas was the treasurer of the group. At the last Passover supper, he arranged, for 30 pieces of silver, to point out Jesus to the chief priests so that they could arrest him. Afterward Judas was overcome with remorse and committed suicide.

Jude, St lived 1st century AD. Supposed half-brother of Jesus and writer of the Epistle of Jude in the New Testament; patron saint of lost causes. Feast day 28 Oct.

judge person invested with power to hear and determine legal disputes. In the UK, judges are chosen from barristers of long standing, but solicitors can be appointed circuit judges. Judges of the High Court, the crown courts, and the county courts are appointed at the advice of the Lord Chancellor, and those of the Court of Appeal and the House of Lords at the advice of the prime minister, although all judges are appointed by the crown. The independence of the higher judiciary is ensured by the principle that they hold their office during good behaviour and not at the pleasure of the crown. They can be removed from office only by a resolution of both houses of Parliament.

Judges book of the Old Testament, describing the history of the Israelites from the death of Joshua to the reign of Saul, under the command of several leaders known as Judges (who deliver the people from repeated oppression).

judicial review in English law, action in the High Court to review the decisions of lower courts, tribunals, and administrative bodies. Various court orders can be made: certiorari (which quashes the decision); mandamus (which commands a duty to be performed); prohibition (which commands that an action should not be performed because it is unauthorized); a declaration (which sets out the legal rights or obligations); or an ◊injunction.

judicial separation action in a court by either husband or wife, in which it is not necessary to prove an irreconcilable breakdown of a marriage, but in which the grounds are otherwise the same as for divorce. It does not end a marriage, but a declaration may be obtained that the complainant need no longer cohabit with the defendant. The court can make similar orders to a divorce court in relation to custody and support of children and maintenance.

judiciary in constitutional terms, the system of courts and body of judges in a country. The independence of the judiciary from other branches of the central authority is generally considered to be an essential feature of a democratic political system. This independence is often written into a nation's constitution and protected from abuse by politicians.

Judith in the Old Testament, a Jewish widow who saved her community from a Babylonian siege by pretending to seduce and then beheading the enemy general Holofernes. Her story is much represented in Western art.

judo (Japanese *jū do*, 'gentle way') form of wrestling of Japanese origin. The two combatants wear loose-fitting, belted jackets and trousers to facilitate holds, and falls are broken by a square mat; when one has established a painful hold that the other cannot break, the latter signifies surrender by slapping the ground with a free hand. Degrees of proficiency are indicated by the colour of the belt: for novices, white, then yellow, orange (2 degrees), green (2 degrees), blue (2 degrees), brown (2 degrees), then black (Dan grades; 10 degrees, of which 1st to 5th Dan wear black belts, 6th to 9th wear red and white, and 10th wears solid red).

Judo is a synthesis of methods from the many forms of jujitsu, the traditional Japanese skill of self-defence and offence without weapons, which was originally practised as a secret art by the feudal samurai. Today, judo has been adopted throughout the world in the armed forces, the police, and in many schools. It became an Olympic sport 1964. The world championship was first held 1956 for men, 1980 for women; it is now contested biennially.

Juggernaut or ***Jagannath*** a name for Vishnu, the Hindu god, meaning 'Lord of the World'. His temple is in Puri, Orissa, India. A statue of the god, dating from about 318, is annually carried in procession on a large vehicle (hence the word 'juggernaut'). Devotees formerly threw themselves beneath its wheels.

jugular vein one of two veins in the necks of vertebrates; they return blood from the head to the superior (or anterior) ◊vena cava and thence to the heart.

jujitsu or ***jujutsu*** traditional Japanese form of self-defence; the modern form is ◊judo.

jujube tree of the genus *Zizyphus* of the buckthorn family Thamnaceae, with berrylike fruits.

The common jujube *Z. jujuba* of Asia, Africa, and Australia, cultivated in S Europe and California, has fruit the size of small plums, known as Chinese dates when preserved in syrup.

Juliana 1909– . Queen of the Netherlands 1948–80. The daughter of Queen Wilhelmina (1880–1962), she married Prince Bernhard of Lippe-Biesterfeld in 1937. She abdicated 1980 and was succeeded by her daughter ◊Beatrix.

Julian of Norwich c. 1342–after 1413. English mystic. She lived as a recluse, and recorded her visions in *The Revelation of Divine Love* 1403, which shows the influence of neo-Platonism.

Julian the Apostate 332–363. Roman emperor. Born in Constantinople, the nephew of Constantine the Great, he was brought up as a Christian but early in life became a convert to paganism. Sent by Constantius to govern Gaul 355, he was proclaimed emperor by his troops 360, and in 361 was marching on Constantinople when Constantius' death allowed a peaceful succession. He revived pagan worship and refused to persecute heretics. He was killed in battle against the Persians of the ◊Sassanian Empire.

Julius II. (born Giuliano della Rovere) 1443–1513. Pope 1503–13. A politician who wanted to make the Papal States the leading power in Italy, he formed international alliances first against Venice and then against France. He began the building of St Peter's Church in Rome 1506 and was a patron of the artists Michelangelo and Raphael.

July Plot or ***July Conspiracy*** in German history, an unsuccessful attempt to assassinate the dictator Adolf Hitler and overthrow the Nazi regime 20 July 1944. Colonel von Stauffenberg planted a bomb under the conference table at Hitler's headquarters at Rastenburg, East Prussia. Believing that Hitler had been killed, Stauffenberg flew to Berlin to join Field Marshal von Witzleben and General von Beck to proclaim a government headed by resistance leader and former lord mayor of Leipzig Carl Goerdeler. However, in his absence someone moved the briefcase, so Hitler was only slightly injured, though five senior officers were killed. Telephone communications remained intact, counter measures were taken in Berlin by Major Ernst Remer, and the conspirators fumbled their coup attempt. Reprisals were savage: the conspirators and their sympathizers were given the choice of committing suicide or being hanged. At least 250 officers died this way, including Field Marshal Rommel, and some 10,000 people were sent to concentration camps.

July Revolution revolution 27–29 July 1830 in France that overthrew the restored Bourbon monarchy of Charles X and substituted the constitutional monarchy of Louis Philippe, whose rule (1830–48) is sometimes referred to as the July Monarchy.

jumbo jet popular name for a generation of huge wide-bodied airliners including the Boeing 747, which is 71 m/232 ft long, has a wingspan of 60 m/196 ft, a maximum takeoff weight of nearly 400 tonnes, and can carry more than 400 passengers.

jumping hare or ***springhare*** either of two African species of long-eared rodents of the only genus (*Pedetes*) in the family Pedetidae. The springhare *P. capensis* is about 40 cm/16 in long and resembles a small kangaroo with a bushy tail. It inhabits dry sandy country in E central Africa.

Juneau ice-free port and state capital of Alaska, USA, on Gastineau Channel in the S Alaska panhandle; population (1992) 28,400. Juneau is the commercial and distribution centre for the fur-trading and mining of the Panhandle region; also important are salmon fishing, fish processing, and lumbering.

Jung Carl Gustav 1875–1961. Swiss psychiatrist. He collaborated with Sigmund ◊Freud from 1907 until their disagreement 1914 over the importance of sexuality in causing psychological problems. Jung studied myth, religion, and dream symbolism, saw the unconscious as a source of spiritual insight, and distinguished between introversion and extroversion.

Jung devised the word-association test in the early 1900s as a technique for penetrating a subject's unconscious mind. He also developed his theory concerning emotional, partly repressed ideas which he termed 'complexes'. In place of Freud's emphasis on infantile sexuality, Jung introduced the idea of a 'collective unconscious' which is made up of many archetypes or 'congenital conditions of intuition'.

jungle popular name for ◊rainforest.

Jung Swiss psychiatrist Carl Gustav Jung. Jung was a contemporary of Sigmund Freud and they both believed that the unconscious mind plays an important role in determining the psychological health of an individual. Jung disagreed with Freud's theory that sexuality was heavily involved in this. *Image Select (UK) Ltd*

juniper aromatic evergreen tree or shrub of the genus *Juniperus* of the cypress family Cupressaceae, found throughout temperate regions. Its berries are used to flavour gin. Some junipers are erroneously called ◊cedars.

junk bond derogatory term for a security officially rated as 'below investment grade'. It is issued in order to raise capital quickly, typically to finance a takeover to be paid for by the sale of assets once the company is acquired. Junk bonds have a high yield, but are a high-risk investment.

Junker member of the landed aristocracy in Prussia; favoured by Frederick the Great and ◊Bismarck, they controlled land, industry, trade, and the army, and exhibited privilege and arrogance. From the 15th century until the 1930s they were the source of most of the Prussian civil service and officer corps.

Juno in Roman mythology, the principal goddess, identified with the Greek ◊Hera. The wife of Jupiter and queen of heaven, she was concerned with all aspects of women's lives.

junta (Spanish 'council') the military rulers of a country, especially after an army takeover, as in Turkey 1980. Other examples include Argentina, under Juan Perón and his successors; Chile, under Augusto Pinochet; Paraguay, under Alfredo Stroessner; Peru, under Manuel Odría; Uruguay, under Juan Bordaberry, and Myanmar since 1988. Juntas rarely remain collective bodies, eventually becoming dominated by one member.

Jupiter or ***Jove*** in Roman mythology, the chief god, identified with the Greek ◊Zeus. He was god of the sky, associated with lightning and thunderbolts; protector in battle; and bestower of victory. The son of Saturn, he married his sister Juno, and reigned on Mount Olympus as lord of heaven. His most famous temple was on the Capitoline Hill in Rome.

Jupiter the fifth planet from the Sun, and the largest in the Solar System, with a mass equal to 70% of all the other planets combined, 318 times that of Earth's. It is largely composed of hydrogen and helium, liquefied by pressure in its interior, and probably with a rocky core larger than Earth. Its main feature is the Great Red Spot, a cloud of rising gases, 14,000 km/8,500 mi wide and 30,000 km/20,000 mi long, revolving anticlockwise; its colour is thought to be due to red phosphorous.
mean distance from the Sun 778 million km/484 million mi
equatorial diameter 142,800 km/88,700 mi
rotation period 9 hr 51 min
year (complete orbit) 11.86 Earth years
atmosphere consists of clouds of white ammonia crystals, drawn out into belts by the planet's high speed of rotation (the fastest of any planet). Darker

'As far as we can discern, the sole purpose of human existence is to kindle a light in the darkness of mere being.'

CARL GUSTAV JUNG
Memories, Dreams, Reflections

Jupiter Jupiter with four of its satellites: Callisto, bottom right; Ganymede, lower left; Europa, centre; and Io, upper left. All these moons were discovered by Galileo in the 17th century. They are known as the Galilean satellites. *Image Select (UK) Ltd*

orange and brown clouds at lower levels may contain sulphur, as well as simple organic compounds. Further down still, temperatures are warm, a result of heat left over from Jupiter's formation, and it is this heat that drives the turbulent weather patterns of the planet. In 1995, the *Galileo* probe revealed Jupiter's atmosphere to consist of 0.2% water, less than previously estimated.

surface although largely composed of hydrogen and helium, Jupiter probably has a rocky core larger than Earth.

satellites Jupiter has 16 moons. The four largest moons, Io, Europa (which is the size of our Moon), Ganymede, and Callisto, are the Galilean satellites, discovered 1610 by Galileo (Ganymede, which is about the size of Mercury, is the largest moon in the Solar System).

Juppé Alain Marie 1945– . French neo-Gaullist politician, foreign minister 1993–95 and prime minister 1995–97. In 1976, as a close lieutenant of Jacques Chirac, he helped to found the right-of-centre Rally for the Republic (RPR) party, of which he later became secretary-general, then president. He was appointed premier by newly-elected president Chirac May 1995 but, within months, found his position under threat as a result of a housing scandal. Opposition to his government's economic programme, particularly welfare cuts, provoked a general strike Nov 1995. In the 1997 general election his party was defeated.

Jura island of the Inner Hebrides; area 380 sq km/147 sq mi; population (1991) 196. It is separated from Scotland by the Sound of Jura. The whirlpool Corryvreckan (Gaelic 'Brecan's cauldron') is off the north coast.

Jura Mountains series of parallel mountain ranges running SW–NE along the French-Swiss frontier between the rivers Rhône and Rhine, a distance of 250 km/156 mi. The highest peak is Crête de la Neige, 1,723 m/5,650 ft.

The mountains give their name to a *département* of France, and in 1979 a Jura canton was established in Switzerland, formed from the French-speaking areas of Berne.

'But who will guard the guards themselves?'

JUVENAL
Satires VI

Jurassic period of geological time 208–146 million years ago; the middle period of the Mesozoic era. Climates worldwide were equable, creating forests of conifers and ferns; dinosaurs were abundant, birds evolved, and limestones and iron ores were deposited.

The name comes from the Jura Mountains in France and Switzerland, where the rocks formed during this period were first studied.

jurisprudence the science of law in the abstract – that is, not the study of any particular laws or legal system, but of the principles upon which legal systems are founded.

jury body of lay people (usually 12) sworn to decide the facts of a case and reach a verdict in a court of law. Juries, used mainly in English-speaking countries, are implemented primarily in criminal cases, but also sometimes in civil cases; for example, inquests and libel trials.

The British jury derived from Germanic custom. It was introduced into England by the Normans. Originally it was a body of neighbours who gave their opinion on the basis of being familiar with the protagonists and background of a case. Eventually it developed into an impartial panel, giving a verdict based solely on evidence heard in court. The jury's duty is to decide the facts of a case: the judge directs them on matters of law.

The basic principles of the British system have been adopted in the USA, most Commonwealth countries, and some European countries (for example, France). Grand juries are still used in the USA at both state and federal levels to decide whether there is a case to be referred for trial.

justice of the peace (JP) in England, an unpaid ◊magistrate. In the USA, where JPs receive fees and are usually elected, their courts are the lowest in the states, and deal only with minor offences, such as traffic violations; they may also conduct marriages.

justiciar the chief justice minister of Norman and early Angevin kings, second in power only to the king. By 1265, the government had been divided into various departments, such as the Exchequer and Chancery, which meant that it was no longer desirable to have one official in charge of all.

Justinian I c. 483–565. Byzantine emperor from 527. He recovered N Africa from the Vandals, SE Spain from the Visigoths, and Italy from the Ostrogoths, largely owing to his great general Belisarius. He ordered the codification of Roman law, which has influenced European jurisprudence; he built the church of Hagia Sophia in Constantinople, and closed the university in Athens 529.

Justin, St c. 100–c. 163. One of the early Christian leaders and writers known as the Fathers of the Church. Born in Palestine of a Greek family, he was converted to Christianity and wrote two *Apologies* in its defence. He spent the rest of his life as an itinerant missionary, and was martyred in Rome. Feast day 1 June.

just-in-time (JIT) production management practice requiring that incoming supplies arrive at the time when they are needed by the customer, most typically in a manufacturer's assembly operations. JIT requires considerable cooperation between supplier and customer, but can reduce expenses and improve efficiency, for example by reducing stock levels and by increasing the quality of goods supplied.

jute fibre obtained from two plants of the genus *Corchorus* of the linden family: *C. capsularis* and *C. olitorius*. Jute is used for sacks and sacking, upholstery, webbing, twine, and stage canvas.

In the fabrication of bulk packaging and tufted carpet backing, it is now often replaced by synthetic polypropylene. The world's largest producer of jute is Bangladesh.

Jute member of a Germanic people who originated in Jutland but later settled in Frankish territory. They occupied Kent, SE England, about 450, according to tradition under Hengist and Horsa, and conquered the Isle of Wight and the opposite coast of Hampshire in the early 6th century.

Jutland peninsula of N Europe; area 29,500 sq km/11,400 sq mi. It is separated from Norway by the Skagerrak and from Sweden by the Kattegat, with the North Sea to the west. The larger northern part belongs to Denmark, the southern part to Germany.

Jutland, Battle of World War I naval battle between British and German forces 31 May 1916, off the west coast of Jutland. Its outcome was indecisive, but the German fleet remained in port for the rest of the war.

Juvenal (Decimus Junius Juvenalis) c. AD 60–140. Roman satirical poet. His 16 surviving *Satires* give an explicit and sometimes brutal picture of the corrupt Roman society of his time. Very little is known of his life, but his native place, if not his birthplace, was Aquinum (now Aquino, S Italy). Juvenal is twice mentioned by ◊Martial, and he may be the author of a well-known dedication (probably to an altar to Ceres) by one Juvenal who held military rank and some civil offices at Aquinum. This reference to military service agrees with the story of Sidonius Apollinaris (5th century) that Juvenal quarrelled with Paris, a famous ballet dancer in the reign of Domitian, and was sent to the Egyptian frontier as an officer of a local garrison.

juvenile delinquency offences against the law that are committed by young people.

juvenile offender young person who commits a criminal offence. In UK law, young people under the age of 17 are commonly referred to as juveniles, although for some purposes a distinction is made between 'children' (under the age of 14) and 'young persons' (14–16). A juvenile under the age of ten may not be found guilty of an offence.

Most legal proceedings in respect of juveniles are brought in specially constituted magistrates' courts known as juvenile courts, where the procedure is simpler and less formal than in an adult magistrates' court. Members of the public are not admitted and the name of the juvenile may not be disclosed in any report of the proceedings. Juvenile offenders cannot be sentenced to imprisonment; instead they may be committed to a young offender institution.

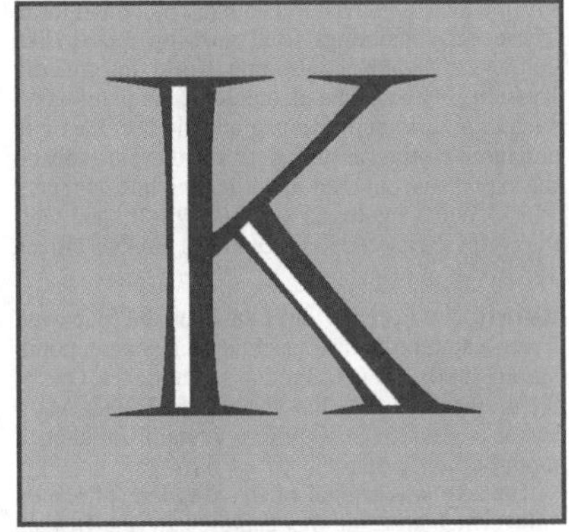

K2 or ***Chogori*** second-highest mountain above sea level, 8,611 m/28,261 ft, in the Karakoram range, in a disputed region of Pakistan. It was first climbed 1954 by an Italian expedition.

The peak was designated 'K2' by Lt-Col Henry Godwin-Austen in his surveying log since it was the second peak in the Karakorams to be surveyed and mapped. It was later unofficially called Mount Godwin-Austen in his honour, although this alternative name has largely gone out of use.

Kaaba (Arabic 'chamber') in Mecca, Saudi Arabia, an oblong building in the quadrangle of the Great Mosque, into the NE corner of which is built the Black Stone declared by the prophet Muhammad to have been given to Abraham by the archangel Gabriel, and revered by Muslims. All Muslims face towards the Ka'aba when they pray, and it is the focus of the hajj (pilgrimage).

Kabardin-Balkar autonomous republic of SW Russian Federation
area 12,500 sq km/4,825 sq mi
capital Nalchik
physical N Caucasus Mountains
industries ore mining, timber, engineering, coal, food processing, timer, grain, livestock breeding, dairy farming, vine growing
population (1992) 784,000 (58% Kabardinians and Balkars)
history under Russian control from 1557; annexed 1827. An autonomous republic from 1936. The Balkars were deported to Soviet Central Asia 1943 for alleged collaboration with the Germans, and returned 1956. Many of the Russian population are of Cossack descent.

kabbala (Hebrew 'tradition') or ***cabbala*** ancient esoteric Jewish mystical tradition of philosophy containing strong elements of pantheism, yet akin to neo-Platonism. Kabbalistic writing reached its peak between the 13th and 16th centuries. It is largely rejected by current Judaic thought as medieval superstition, but is basic to the Hasid sect. Among its earliest documents are the *Sefir Jezirah/The Book of Creation*, attributed to Rabbi Akiba (died 120). The *Zohar/Book of Light* was written in Aramaic in about the 13th century.

Kabila Laurent-Desiré 1939– . Congolese soldier and politician, president of the Democratic Republic of Congo (formerly Zaire) from 1997. His opposition to the oppressive regime of President Mobutu was encouraged by the presidents of neighbouring Angola, Rwanda, and Uganda, who supported his Tutsi-led uprising which became, in Nov 1996, the focus of opposition to Mobutu as the Alliance of Democratic Forces for the Liberation of Congo (ADFL). By March 1997, ADFL forces, led by Kabila, had made rapid advances westwards from the Great Lake region and in May were at the outskirts of the capital, Kinshasa. President Mandela of South Africa tried unsuccessfully to broker a political agreement and, when this failed, Mobutu fled the country, and Kabila declared himself president.

Kabinda part of Angola; see ◊Cabinda.

kabuki (Japanese 'music, dance, skill') drama originating in late 16th-century Japan, drawing on ◊Nō, puppet plays, and folk dance. Its colourful, lively spectacle became popular in the 17th and 18th centuries. Many kabuki actors specialize in particular types of character, female impersonators (*onnagata*) being the biggest stars.

Kabul capital of Afghanistan, 2,100 m/6,900 ft above sea level, on the river Kabul; population (1993 est) 700,000. Products include textiles, plastics, leather, and glass. It commands the strategic routes to Pakistan via the ◊Khyber Pass. There is a university (1931), the tomb of Zahir (Babur), founder of the Mogul empire, and the Dar ol-Aman palace, which houses the parliament and government departments.

Kabul has been in existence for over 3,000 years. It became the capital 1776, was captured by the British 1839 and 1879, and was under Soviet control 1979–89. In 1992 the city saw fierce fighting during the Mujaheddin takeover and ousting of the Soviet-backed Najibullah regime. In 1995 government forces succeeded in expelling the Mujaheddin from the city. However, in 1996 Kabul fell to the Talibaan (Islamic students' army).

Kádár János 1912–1989. Hungarian communist leader, in power 1956–88, after suppressing the national uprising. As leader of the Hungarian Socialist Workers' Party (HSWP) and prime minister 1956–58 and 1961–65, Kádár introduced a series of market-socialist economic reforms, while retaining cordial political relations with the USSR.

Kafka Franz 1883–1924. Austrian novelist. He wrote in German. His three unfinished allegorical novels *Der Prozess/The Trial* 1925, *Das Schloss/The Castle* 1926, and *Amerika/America* 1927 were posthumously published despite his instructions that they should be destroyed. His short stories include 'Die Verwandlung/The Metamorphosis' 1915, in which a man turns into a huge insect. His vision of lonely individuals trapped in bureaucratic or legal labyrinths can be seen as a powerful metaphor for modern experience. Kafka's work has considerably influenced other modern writers, including Samuel ◊Beckett and Albert ◊Camus.

Kafue river in central Zambia, a tributary of the Zambezi, 965 km/600 mi long. The upper reaches of the river form part of the Kafue national park (1951). Kafue town, 44 km/27 mi S of Lusaka, population (1980) 35,000, is the centre of Zambia's heavy industry. A hydroelectric power station opened 1972 on the lower Kafue river at Kafue Gorge; its 600,000-kW generating facility was expanded to 900,000 in the late 1970s by the construction of a storage dam upstream.

kagu crested bird *Rhynochetos jubatus*, the only member of its family that is placed in the crane order (Gruiformes). It is found in New Caledonia in the S Pacific. About 50 cm/1.6 ft long, it is virtually flightless and nests on the ground. The introduction of cats and dogs has endangered its survival.

Kahlo Frida 1907–1954. Mexican painter. Combining the folk arts of South America with Classical and Modern styles, she concentrated on surreal self-portraits in which she explored both her own physical disabilities (she was crippled in an accident when 15) and broader political and social issues. Her work became popular during the 1980s. She was the wife of the painter Diego Rivera.

Kaieteur waterfall on the river Potaro, a tributary of the Essequibo, Guyana. At 250 m/822 ft, it is five times as high as Niagara Falls.

Kaifeng former capital of China, 907–1127, and of Honan province; population (1990) 508,000. It has lost its importance because of the silting-up of the nearby Huang He River.

Kairouan Muslim holy city in Tunisia, N Africa, S of Tunis; population (1994) 102,600. It is a centre of carpet production. The city, said to have been founded AD 617, ranks after Mecca and Medina as a place of pilgrimage.

Kaiser title formerly used by the Holy Roman Emperors, Austrian emperors 1806–1918, and German emperors 1871–1918. The word, like the Russian 'tsar', is derived from the Latin *Caesar*.

kakapo nocturnal, flightless parrot *Strigops habroptilus*, order Psittaciformes, that lives in burrows in New Zealand. It is green, yellow, and brown with a disc of feathers round its eyes. It weighs up to 3.5 kg/7.5 lb. When in danger, its main defence is to keep quite still. Because of the introduction of predators such as dogs, cats, rats, and ferrets, it is in danger of extinction, there being only about 40 birds left. *See illustration on following page.*

Kalahari Desert semi-desert area forming most of Botswana and extending into Namibia, Zimbabwe, and South Africa; area about 900,000 sq km/347,400 sq mi. The only permanent river, the Okavango, flows into a delta in the northwest forming marshes rich in wildlife. Its inhabitants are the nomadic Kung ▷ *See feature on pp. 308–309.*

kabuki An actor playing the part of a samurai in kabuki theatre. Behind him is a backdrop depicting Mount Fuji. *Corbis*

kale type of ◊cabbage.

Kalevala ('land of Kaleva') Finnish national epic poem compiled from legends and ballads by Elias Lönnrot 1835–49; its hero is Väinämöinen, god of music and poetry. It inspired the poet Longfellow, who borrowed its metre and some of its incidents for his *Hiawatha*, and the composer Sibelius.

Kali in Hindu mythology, the goddess of destruction and death. She is the wife of ◊Siva.

Kālidāsa lived 5th century AD. Indian epic poet and dramatist. His works, in Sanskrit, include the classic drama *Sakuntalā*, the love story of King Dushyanta and the nymph Sakuntala.

Kalimantan province of the republic of Indonesia occupying part of the island of Borneo; area 543,900 sq km/210,000 sq mi; population (1990) 9,099,900. The land is mostly low-lying, with mountains in the north. Towns and cities include Banjermasin and Balikpapan. Industries include petroleum, rubber, coffee, copra, pepper, and timber.

Kalinin Mikhail Ivanovich 1875–1946. Soviet politician, founder of the newspaper *Pravda*. He

'It's often better to be in chains than to be free.'

FRANZ KAFKA
The Trial

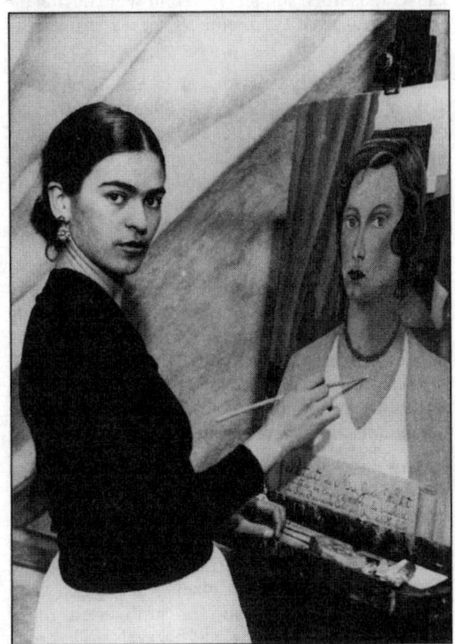

Kahlo Mexican painter Frida Kahlo photographed in San Francisco, USA 1931. The injuries she suffered in a road accident at the age of 15 caused her to abandon her ambition to study medicine. She became a painter, and continued to paint until her death, despite eventually being confined to bed with painful spinal problems. *Corbis*

kakapo The kakapo is a nocturnal ground-living parrot of New Zealand. It is the only flightless parrot. Due to introduced ground predators such as stoats and rats, its numbers have been reduced to only two breeding populations on small, offshore islands.

was prominent in the 1917 October Revolution, and in 1919 became head of state (president of the Central Executive Committee of the Soviet government until 1937, then president of the Presidium of the Supreme Soviet until 1946).

Kaliningrad formerly ***Königsberg*** Baltic naval base in W Russia; population (1994) 415,000. Industries include engineering and paper. It was the capital of East Prussia until the latter was divided between the USSR and Poland 1945 under the Potsdam Agreement, when it was renamed in honour of President Kalinin.

Kali-Yuga in Hinduism, the last of the four yugas (ages) that make up one cycle of creation. The Kali-Yuga, in which Hindus believe we are now living, is characterized by wickedness and disaster, and leads up to the destruction of this world in preparation for a new creation and a new cycle of yugas.

Kalki in Hinduism, the last avatar (manifestation) of Vishnu, who will appear at the end of the Kali-Yuga, or final age of the world, to destroy it in readiness for a new creation.

Kalmyk or ***Kalmuck*** autonomous republic of central Russian Federation
area 75,900 sq km/29,300 sq mi
capital Elista
physical on Caspian Sea
industries mainly agricultural, including cattle breeding and the production of fodder crops, fishing, canning
population (1992) 327,000 (45% Kalmyk)
history settled by Chinese migrants in the 17th century; established as an autonomous region 1920; an autonomous republic from 1935, but abolished 1943 because of alleged collaboration with the Germans during the siege of Stalingrad, and restored 1958.

Kaltenbrunner Ernst 1903–1946. Austrian Nazi leader. After the annexation of Austria 1938 he joined police chief Himmler's staff, and as head of the Security Police (SD) from 1943 was responsible for the murder of millions of Jews (see the ◊Holocaust) and Allied soldiers in World War II. After the war, he was tried at Nuremberg for war crimes and hanged Oct 1946.

Kamakura city on Honshu Island, Japan, near Tokyo; population (1990) 174,300. It was the seat of the first shogunate 1192–1333, which established the rule of the samurai class, and the Hachimangu Shrine is dedicated to the gods of war; the 13th-century statue of Buddha (Daibutsu) is 13 m/43 ft high. From the 19th century, artists and writers (for example, the novelist Kawabata) settled here.

Kamchatka mountainous peninsula separating the Bering Sea and Sea of Okhotsk, forming (together with the Chukchi and Koryak national districts) a region of the Russian Federation, in E Siberia. Its capital, Petropavlovsk, is the only town; agriculture is possible only in the south. Most of the inhabitants are fishers and hunters.

kame geological feature, usually in the form of a mound or ridge, formed by the deposition of rocky material carried by a stream of glacial meltwater. Kames are commonly laid down in front of or at the edge of a glacier (kame terrace), and are associated with the disintegration of glaciers at the end of an ice age. They are made of well-sorted rocky material, usually sands and gravels. The rock particles tend to be rounded (by attrition) because they have been transported by water.

Kamenev Lev Borisovich, (born Rosenfeld) 1883–1936. Russian leader of the Bolshevik movement after 1917 who, with Stalin and Zinoviev, formed a ruling triumvirate in the USSR after Lenin's death 1924. His alignment with the Trotskyists led to his dismissal from office and from the Communist Party by Stalin 1926. Arrested 1934 after Kirov's assassination, Kamenev was secretly tried and sentenced, then retried, condemned, and shot 1936 for allegedly plotting to murder Stalin.

kamikaze (Japanese 'wind of the gods') special force of suicide pilots established 1944 as part of the Japanese air force, whose objective was to crash-dive planes, loaded with bombs, onto US and British ships during World War II.

Initially many different types of aircraft were used but later the *Okha*, a specifically designed piloted flying bomb, was developed. Kamikaze squads sank or severely damaged at least six major vessels Nov 1944– Jan 1945, causing major problems for Allied shipping until their base in the Philippines was destroyed by Allied air strikes.

Kampala capital of Uganda, on Lake Victoria; population (1991) 773,000. It is linked by rail with Mombasa. Products include tea, coffee, textiles, fruit, and vegetables. Built on six hills at an altitude of about 1,220 m/4,000 ft, it was the capital of the kingdom of Buganda in the 19th century, became the headquarters of the Imperial British East Africa Company 1890, and was made capital of Uganda 1962.

Kampuchea former name (1975–89) of ◊Cambodia.

Kandahar city in Afghanistan, 450 km/280 mi SW of Kabul, capital of Kandahar province and a trading centre, with wool and cotton factories; population (1988) 225,500. It is surrounded by a mud wall 8 m/25 ft high. When Afghanistan became independent 1747, Kandahar was its first capital.

Kandinsky Vasily 1866–1944. Russian-born painter. He was a pioneer of abstract art. Between 1910 and 1914 he produced the series *Improvisations* and *Compositions*, the first known examples of purely abstract work in 20th-century art. He was an originator of the Expressionist ◊*Blaue Reiter* movement 1911–12, and taught at the ◊Bauhaus school of design in Germany 1921–33.

Born in Moscow, he studied in Munich and in 1902 joined the Berlin ◊Sezession. He travelled widely 1903–08, finally settling in Murnau with the painter Gabriele Münter. By this stage his original experiments with Post-Impressionist styles had given way to a Fauvist freedom of colour and form. These early paintings used glowing mosaic-like colours to evoke a fairy-tale world inspired by Russian folklore. The elements of his paintings – such as a horse and rider – gradually became more and more abstract as he concentrated exclusively on the expressive qualities of colour and line. He spent World War I in Russia and finally left Nazi Germany for Paris 1933, becoming a French citizen 1939.

Kandy city in central Sri Lanka, on the Mahaweli River; capital of a district of the same name; population (1990) 104,000. Products include tea. One of the most sacred Buddhist shrines, the Dalada Maligawa, is situated in Kandy; it contains an alleged tooth of the Buddha.

The city was capital of the kingdom of Kandy 1480–1815, when it was captured by the British. The chief campus of the University of Sri Lanka (1942) is at Peradenia, 5 km/3 mi away.

kangaroo any marsupial of the family Macropodidae found in Australia, Tasmania, and New Guinea. Kangaroos are plant-eaters and most live in groups. They are adapted to hopping, the vast majority of species having very large back legs and feet compared with the small forelimbs. The larger types can jump 9 m/30 ft in a single bound. Most are nocturnal. Species vary from small rat kangaroos, only 30 cm/1 ft long, through the medium-sized wallabies, to the large red and great grey kangaroos (*Macropus rufus* and *M. giganteus*), which are the largest living marsupials. These may be 1.8 m/5.9 ft long with 1.1 m/3.5 ft tails.

The kangaroo produces a small, single young or 'joey' (often only 2cm/1 in long), after a very short gestation, usually in early summer. Immediately after it is born, the young kangaroo climbs into its mother's pouch and attaches itself to a nipple which squirts milk into its mouth at intervals. It stays in the pouch, with excursions as it matures, for about 280 days.

Kangchenjunga Himalayan mountain on the Nepal–Sikkim border, 8,586 m/28,170 ft high, 120 km/75 mi SE of Mount Everest. The name means 'five treasure houses of the great snows'. Kangchenjunga was first climbed by a British expedition 1955.

Ka Ngwane former black homeland in Mpumalanga Province, South Africa.

Kannada or ***Kanarese*** language spoken in S India, the official state language of Karnataka; also spoken in Tamil Nadu and Maharashtra. There are over 20 million speakers of Kannada, which belongs to the Dravidian family. Written records in Kannada date from the 5th century AD.

kamikaze USS *Bunker Hill*, hit by two Japanese kamikaze planes 11 May 1945. The attack killed 372 and injured 264 men. A product of Japan's desperation during the final stages of the war in the Pacific during World War II, the kamikaze missions could be devastatingly effective. *Library of Congress*

Kano capital of Kano state in N Nigeria, trade centre of an irrigated area; population (1992 est) 699,900. Products include bicycles, glass, furniture, textiles, and chemicals. Founded about 1000 BC, Kano is a walled city, with New Kano extending beyond the walls.

Kanpur formerly *Cawnpore* capital of Kanpur district, Uttar Pradesh, India, SW of Lucknow, on the river Ganges; a commercial and industrial centre (cotton, wool, jute, chemicals, plastics, iron, steel); population (1991) 2,029,900.

Kansas state in central USA; nicknamed Sunflower State
area 213,200 sq km/82,296 sq mi
capital Topeka
cities Kansas City, Wichita, Overland Park
features Great Plains; Cimarron national grassland; Kansas and Arkansas rivers; Dodge City, once 'cowboy capital of the world', with the capitol (1866), and historic Ward-Meade Park; the Eisenhower Center, with his boyhood home, at Abilene; Pony Express station, Hanover; Wichita Cowtown, a frontier-era reproduction; Kansas Cosmosphere and Space Center
industries wheat, cattle, coal, petroleum, natural gas, aircraft, minerals
population (1991) 2,495,000
famous people Amelia Earhart; Dwight D Eisenhower; William Inge; Buster Keaton; Carry Nation; Charlie Parker
history explored by Francisco de Coronado for Spain 1541 and La Salle for France 1682; ceded to the USA 1803 as part of the Louisiana Purchase. Kansas was the first state to prohibit alcohol (1880), and prohibition was not lifted until 1948.

Kansas

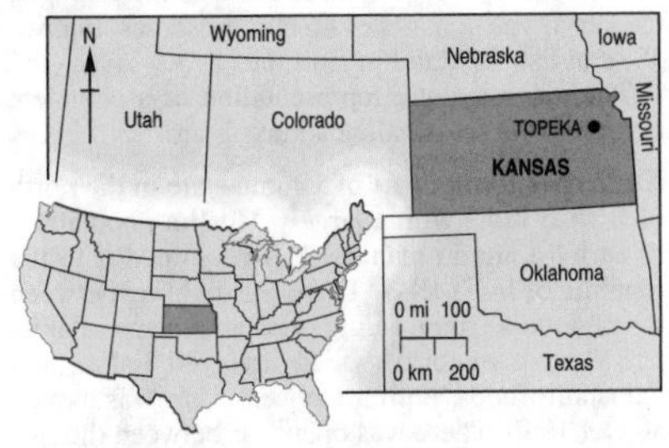

Kansas City twin city in the USA at the confluence of the Missouri and Kansas rivers, partly in Kansas and partly in Missouri; population (1992) of Kansas City (Kansas) 146,500, Kansas City (Missouri) 431,550. It is a market and agricultural distribution centre and one of the chief livestock centres of the USA. Kansas City, Missouri, has car-assembly plants and Kansas City, Kansas, has the majority of offices.
history The city was founded as a trading post by French fur trappers about 1826. In the 1920s and 1930s Kansas City was run by boss Tom Pendergast, of the Ready-Mix Concrete Company, and in the nightclubs on Twelfth Street under his 'protection' jazz musicians such as Lester Young, Count Basie, and Charlie Parker performed.

Kansu alternative spelling for the Chinese province ◊Gansu.

Kant Immanuel 1724–1804. German philosopher. He believed that knowledge is not merely an aggregate of sense impressions but is dependent on the conceptual apparatus of the human understanding, which is itself not derived from experience. In ethics, Kant argued that right action cannot be based on feelings or inclinations but conforms to a law given by reason, the categorical imperative.

It was in his *Kritik der reinen Vernunft/Critique of Pure Reason* 1781 that Kant inaugurated a revolution in philosophy by turning attention to the mind's role in constructing our knowledge of the objective world. He also argued that God's existence could not be proved theoretically. His other main works are *Kritik der praktischen Vernunft/Critique of Practical Reason* 1788 and *Kritik der Urteilskraft/Critique of Judgement* 1790. *See illustration on following page.*

Kanto flat, densely populated region of E Honshu Island, Japan; area 32,377 sq km/12,505 sq mi; population (1995) 1,423,800. The chief city is Tokyo.

kangaroo The red kangaroo *Macropus rufus* is one of the largest of the kangaroos. Although the males are red, the females are usually a bluish grey. Like the grey kangaroo, the red kangaroo lives in small herds, sheltering by rocky outcrops during the heat of the day and emerging at dusk to spend the night grazing. *Australian Overseas Information Office*

KANU (acronym for ***Kenya African National Union***) political party founded 1944 and led by Jomo ◊Kenyatta from 1947, when it was the Kenya African Union (KAU); it became KANU on independence 1964. The party formed Kenyatta's political power base in 1963 when he became prime minister; in 1964 he became the first president of Kenya (retaining office until his death 1978). KANU was the sole political party 1982–91. It secured an overwhelming majority in multiparty elections 1993, but opposition parties disputed the results and their claims of malpractices were partly supported by independent Commonwealth observers.

Kaohsiung city and port on the west coast of Taiwan; population (1992) 1,396,400. Industries include aluminium ware, fertilizers, cement, oil refineries, iron and steel works, shipyards, and food processing. Kaohsiung began to develop as a commercial port after 1858; its industrial development came about while it was occupied by Japan 1895–1945.

kaoliang variety of ◊sorghum.

kaolin group of clay minerals, such as kaolinite, $Al_2Si_2O_5(OH)_4$, derived from the alteration of aluminium silicate minerals, such as ◊feldspars and ◊mica. It is used in medicine to treat digestive upsets, and in poultices.

Kaolinite is economically important in the ceramic and paper industries. It is mined in the UK, the USA, France, and the Czech Republic.

kapok silky hairs that surround the seeds of certain trees, particularly the kapok tree *Bombax ceiba* of India and Malaysia, and the silk-cotton tree *Ceiba pentandra*, a native of tropical America. Kapok is used for stuffing cushions and mattresses and for sound insulation; oil obtained from the seeds is used in food and soap preparation.

Karachai-Cherkessia autonomous republic of SW Russian Federation, part of Stavropol territory.
area 14,100 sq km/5,442 sq mi
capital Cherkessk
physical in the Caucasus Mountains; densely forested
industries ore mining, chemical and woodworking industries, livestock breeding, grain; tourism is important
population (1992) 431,000
history autonomous region 1922; divided into two 1926. Karachai region abolished 1943 when the Karachai people were exiled to Central Asia for alleged collaboration with the Germans. They returned 1957, and Karachai–Cherkess autonomous region was formed. An autonomous republic from 1990.

Karachi largest city and chief seaport of Pakistan, and capital of Sind province, NW of the Indus delta; population (1994) 9,500,000. Industries include engineering, chemicals, plastics, and textiles. It was the capital of Pakistan 1947–59.

Karadžić Radovan 1945– . Montenegrin-born leader of the Bosnian Serbs, leader of the community's unofficial government 1992–96. He cofounded the Serbian Democratic Party of Bosnia-Herzegovina (SDS-BH) 1990 and launched the siege of Sarajevo 1992, plunging the country into a prolonged and bloody civil war. A succession of peace initiatives for the region failed due to his ambitious demands for Serbian territory.

In the autumn of 1995, Karadžić agreed to enter peace negotiations; in Nov he signed the US-sponsored Dayton peace accord, under the terms of which he was forced to step down as the Bosnian Serb prime minister, though he remained a dominant backstage force. He was charged with genocide and crimes against humanity at the Yugoslav War Crimes Tribunal in The Hague, Netherlands, Nov 1995. He stepped down as party leader July 1996.

Karaganda industrial city (coal, copper, tungsten, manganese) in Kazakhstan, linked by canal with the Irtysh River; capital of Karaganda region; population (1991) 1,339,900.

Karajan Herbert von 1908–1989. Austrian conductor. He dominated European classical music performance after 1947. He was principal conductor of the Berlin Philharmonic Orchestra 1955–89, artistic director of the Vienna State Opera 1957–64, and of the Salzburg Festival 1956–60. A perfectionist, he cultivated an orchestral sound of notable smoothness and transparency; he also staged operas and directed his own video recordings. He recorded the complete Beethoven symphonies three times, and had a special affinity with Mozart and Bruckner, although his repertoire extended from Bach to Schoenberg.

Kara-Kalpak autonomous republic of Uzbekistan
area 158,000 sq km/61,000 sq mi
capital Nukus
towns and cities Munyak
industries cotton, rice, wheat, fish, wine, leather goods
population (1990) 1,244,700 (Kara-kalpaks, Uzbeks, Kazakhs)
history named after the Kara-Kalpak ('black hood') people who live S of the Sea of Aral and were conquered by Russia 1867. An autonomous Kara-Kalpak region was formed 1926 within Kazakhstan, transferred to the Soviet republic 1930, made a republic 1932, and attached to Uzbekistan 1936.

'Two things fill the mind with ever-increasing wonder and awe … the starry heavens above me and the moral law within me.'

IMMANUEL KANT
Critique of Practical Reason

Kant German philosopher Immanuel Kant. He revolutionized philosophy by asserting that actions are motivated by rational rather than emotional considerations. *Image Select (UK) Ltd*

Karakoram mountain range in central Asia, divided among China, Pakistan, and India. Peaks include K2, Masharbrum, Gasharbrum, and Mustagh Tower. Ladakh subsidiary range is in NE Kashmir on the Tibetan border.

Kara-Kum sandy desert occupying most of Turkmenistan; area about 310,800 sq km/120,000 sq mi. It is crossed by the Caspian railway.

Karamanlis Konstantinos 1907–1998. Greek politician of the New Democracy Party. A lawyer and an anticommunist, he was prime minister Oct 1955–March 1958, May 1958–Sept 1961, and Nov 1961–June 1963 (when he went into self-imposed exile because of a military coup). He was recalled as prime minister on the fall of the regime of the 'colonels' July 1974, and was president 1980–85.

Kara Sea (Russian ***Kavaskoye More***) part of the Arctic Ocean off the north coast of the Russian Federation, bounded to the NW by the island of Novaya Zemlya and to the NE by Severnaya Zemlya. Novy Port on the Gulf of Ob is the chief port, and the Yenisei River also flows into it.

karate (Japanese 'empty hand') one of the ◊martial arts. Karate is a type of unarmed combat derived from *kempo*, a form of the Chinese Shaolin boxing. It became popular in the West in the 1930s.

Karelia autonomous republic of NW Russian Federation
area 172,400 sq km/66,550 sq mi
capital Petrozavodsk
physical mainly forested
industries fishing, timber, chemicals, coal
population (1992) 800,000
history Karelia was annexed to Russia by Peter the Great 1721 as part of the grand duchy of Finland. In 1917 part of Karelia was retained by Finland when it gained its independence from Russia. The remainder became an autonomous region 1920 and an autonomous republic 1923 of the USSR. Following the wars of 1939–40 and 1941–44, Finland ceded 46,000 sq km/18,000 sq mi of Karelia to the USSR. Part of this territory was incorporated in the Russian Soviet Republic and part in the Karelian autonomous republic 1956. A movement for the reunification of Russian and Finnish Karelia emerged in the late 1980s.

Karen group of SE Asian peoples, numbering 1.9 million. They live in E Myanmar (formerly Burma), Thailand, and the Irrawaddy delta. Their language belongs to the Thai division of the Sino-Tibetan family. In 1984 the Burmese government began a large-scale military campaign against the Karen National Liberation Army (KNLA), the armed wing of the Karen National Union (KNU).

Kariba Dam concrete dam on the Zambezi River, on the Zambia–Zimbabwe border, about 386 km/240 mi downstream from the Victoria Falls, constructed 1955–60 to supply power to both countries. The dam crosses Kariba Gorge, and the reservoir, Lake Kariba, has important fisheries.

Karloff Boris. Stage name of William Henry Pratt 1887–1969. English-born US actor. He is best known for his work in the USA. He achieved Hollywood stardom with his role as the monster in the film *Frankenstein* 1931. Several popular sequels followed as well as starring appearances in other films including *Scarface* 1932, *The Lost Patrol* 1934, and *The Body Snatcher* 1945. In 1941 Karloff gained acclaim on Broadway in *Arsenic and Old Lace*. He continued in television and films until *Targets* 1967.

karma (Sanskrit 'action') in Hinduism, the sum of a human being's actions, carried forward from one life to the next, resulting in an improved or worsened fate. Buddhism has a similar belief, except that no permanent personality is envisaged, the karma relating only to volitional tendencies carried on from birth to birth, unless the power holding them together is dispersed in the attainment of nirvana.

Karmal Babrak 1929–1996. Afghani communist politician, president 1979–86. In 1965 he formed what became the banned People's Democratic Party of Afghanistan (PDPA) 1977. As president, with Soviet backing, he sought to broaden the appeal of the PDPA but encountered wide resistance from the ◊Mujaheddin (Muslim guerrillas). He was persuaded to step down as president and PDPA leader May 1986 as the USSR sought a compromise with opposition groupings. In July 1991, he returned to Afghanistan from exile in Moscow.

Karnak village in modern Egypt, on the east bank of the river Nile, that gives its name to the temple of Ammon (mainly constructed by pharaohs of the 18th and 19th dynasties, including Seti I and Ramses II) around which the major part of the ancient city of ◊Thebes was built. An avenue of rams leads to ◊Luxor.

Karroo The Karroo National Park near Beaufort West in South Africa. Though much of the Karroo is very dry, some areas, made fertile by seasonal rains, are used for sheep rearing and crop growing. *Premaphotos Wildlife*

Karnataka formerly (until 1973) ***Mysore*** state in SW India
area 191,800 sq km/74,035 sq mi
capital Bangalore
industries mainly agricultural; minerals include manganese, chromite, India's only sources of gold and silver, sandalwood processing
population (1994) 48,150,000
language Kannada
famous people Hyder Ali, Tipu Sultan.

Karpov Anatoly Yevgenyevich 1951– . Russian chess player. He succeeded Bobby Fischer of the USA as world champion 1975, and held the title until losing to Gary Kasparov 1985. He lost to Kasparov again 1990.

Karroo two areas of semi-desert in Eastern Cape Province, South Africa, divided into the Great Karroo and Little Karroo by the Swartberg Mountains. The two Karroos together have an area of about 260,000 sq km/100,000 sq mi.

karst landscape characterized by remarkable surface and underground forms, created as a result of the action of water on permeable limestone, which is soluble in the weak acid of rainwater. Erosion takes place most swiftly along cracks and joints in the limestone and these open up into gullies called grikes. The rounded blocks left upstanding between them are called clints.

The feature takes its name from the Karst region on the Adriatic coast of Slovenia and Italy, but the name is applied to landscapes throughout the world, the most dramatic of which is found near the city of Guilin in the Guangxi province of China.

karyotype in biology, the set of ◊chromosomes characteristic of a given species. It is described as the number, shape, and size of the chromosomes in a single cell of an organism. In humans for example, the karyotype consists of 46 chromosomes, in mice 40, crayfish 200, and in fruit flies 8.

The diagrammatic representation of a complete chromosome set is called a karyogram.

Kashmir former part of Jammu state in the north of British India with a largely Muslim population, ruled by a Hindu maharajah, who joined it to the republic of India 1947. There was fighting between the pro-India Hindu ruling class and the pro-Pakistan Muslim majority which involved Indian and Pakistani troops, until a UN cease-fire was agreed 30 Oct 1948. There was open war between the two countries 1965–66 and 1971. It is today divided under the terms of the 1972 Simla Agreement between the Pakistani area of Kashmir and the Indian state of ◊Jammu and Kashmir.

Since 1990 it has been riven by Muslim separatist violence, with more than 150,000 Indian troops deployed in Kashmir 1993. These were criticized by human-rights groups for torture, rape, and killing. Estimates of casualties 1990–93 range from 8,000 to 20,000. Separatist violence escalated during 1995 and several Westerners were taken hostage, with one casualty. The main political party in Jammu and Kashmir, the separatist Jammu and Kashmir Liberation Front (JKLF), is divided into Indian- and Pakistan-based factions. In Oct 1996 the National Conference Party, which aims to retain the area within India, won the first local elections to be held since the separatist violence broke out 1990.

Kashmir had been under the sway of Hindu India for many centuries when Muslim rule was established by the 14th century. Mogul rule began in the 16th century but was brought to a halt by the Afghan invasion of 1753. This was followed by a period of Sikh overlordship from 1819. During the Sikh wars of the mid-19th century, a new Hindu-ruled state of Jammu and Kashmir was put together by Maharaja Gulab Singh, a Dogra Rajput, with a home base in Jammu.

Kashmir Pakistan-occupied area, 30,445 sq mi/78,900 sq km, in the northwest of the former state of Kashmir (now ◊Jammu and Kashmir). Azad ('free') Kashmir in the west has its own legislative assembly based in Muzaffarabad while Gilgit and Baltistan regions to the north and east are governed directly by Pakistan. The Northern Areas are claimed by India and Pakistan
population (1995) 2,800,000
towns and cities Gilgit, Skardu
features W Himalayan peak Nanga Parbat 8,126 m/26,660 ft, Karakoram Pass, Indus River, Baltoro Glacier.

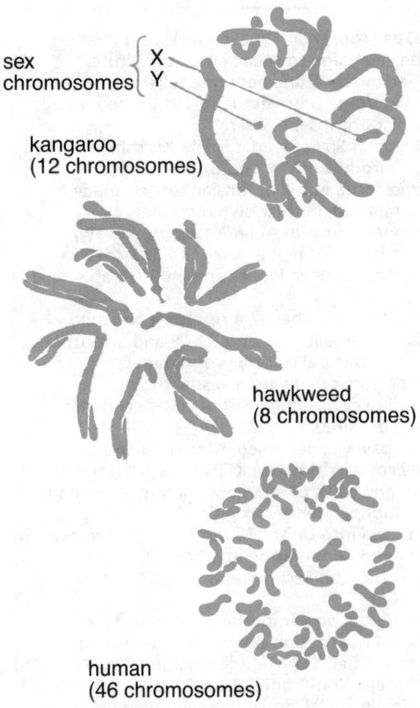

karyotype The characteristics, or karyotype, of the chromosomes vary according to species. The kangaroo has 12 chromosomes, the hawkweed has 8, and a human being has 46.

Kashmiri inhabitants of or natives to the state of Jammu and Kashmir, a disputed territory divided between India and Pakistan. There are approximately 6 million Kashmiris, 4 million of whom live on the Indian side of the cease-fire line.

Kashmiri is also an Indo-European language that the orthodox write using a Sarada script. Although Kashmir's ruling families are Hindu, the majority of the population is Muslim. Among them live Hindu Brahmins, called pandit, who perform religious services and are involved in teaching and administration. The workers, or karkum, are often wealthier than the priestly class. In the Vale of Kashmir, the majority of Muslims are farmers, cultivating rice, wheat, and other crops. There is also a Punjabi-speaking Sikh minority, while on the borders of the Vale there are Muslim Gujars, who have an affinity with the Hindu Dogra people. In Ladakh to the north, there are Buddhist peoples who have much in common with Tibetans.

Kasparov Gary Kimovich, (born Garri Weinstein) 1963– . Azerbaijan-born chess player. When he beat his (then Soviet) compatriot Anatoly Karpov to win the world title 1985, he was the youngest-ever champion at 22 years 210 days. In Oct 1995, he beat Viswanathan Anand in the Professional Chess Association championship.

Kathak one of the four main Indian dance styles (others are ◊Bharat Natyam, Kathakali, and ◊Manipuri). It is primarily concerned with music and rhythm with the story subsumed to secondary importance and is danced on the floor (not on a raised stage) amid a seated audience. The feet of the dancers, adorned by ankle bells, are used as percussion instruments.

Kathakali one of the four main Indian dance styles (others are ◊Bharat Natyam, Kathak, and ◊Manipuri). It is an integration of drama, singing, and instrumental music, characterized by a range of highly stylized gestures. It originated in the extreme south of India and reached its artistic peak during the 17th century. The stories are derived from Hindu mythology and each individual character is represented by a different coloured mask or make-up. It is performed in a temple or public square after dusk, with performances sometimes lasting the entire night.

Kathmandu or ***Katmandu*** capital of Nepal; population (1991) 419,100. Founded in the 8th century on an ancient pilgrim and trade route from India to Tibet and China, it has a royal palace, Buddhist temples, monasteries, and a tourist centre.

Katsura Tarō 1847–1913. Prince of Japan, army officer, politician, and prime minister (1901–06, 1908–11, 1912–13). He was responsible for the Anglo-Japanese treaty of 1902 (an alliance against Russia), the successful prosecution of the Russo-Japanese war 1904–05, and the annexation of Korea 1910.

Kattegat sea passage between Denmark and Sweden. It is about 240 km/150 mi long and 135 km/85 mi wide at its broadest point.

Katyn Forest forest near Smolensk, SW of Moscow, Russia, where 4,500 Polish officer prisoners of war (captured in the German-Soviet partition of Poland 1940) were shot; 10,000 others were killed elsewhere. In 1989 the USSR accepted responsibility for the massacre.

Katz Bernard 1911– . British biophysicist. He shared the 1970 Nobel Prize for Physiology or Medicine for work on the biochemistry of the transmission and control of signals in the nervous system, vital in the search for remedies for nervous and mental disorders.

Kaunas formerly (until 1917) ***Kovno*** industrial river port (textiles, chemicals, agricultural machinery) in Lithuania, on the Niemen River; population (1995) 415,000. It was the capital of Lithuania 1910–40.

Kaunda Kenneth David 1924– . Zambian politician, president 1964–91. Imprisoned 1958–60 as founder of the Zambia African National Congress, in 1964 he became the first prime minister of Northern Rhodesia, then the first president of independent Zambia. In 1973 he introduced one-party rule. He supported the nationalist movement in Southern Rhodesia, now Zimbabwe, and survived a coup attempt 1980 thought to have been promoted by South Africa. He was elected chair of the Organization of African Unity 1970 and 1987. He lost the first multiparty election to Frederick Chiluba 1991. In 1995 he was elected president of the United National Independence Party (UNIP) and announced his return to active politics. In 1996 the Zambian constitution was controversially amended, making it impossible for non-second-generation Zambians to stand for the presidency, thereby effectively debarring Kaunda from future contests. In Jan 1998, while under house arrest, he was charged with backing an abortive coup in Oct 1997.

kauri pine New Zealand timber conifer *Agathis australis*, family Araucariaceae. Its fossilized gum deposits are valued in varnishes; the wood is used for carving and handicrafts.

Kawabata Yasunari 1899–1972. Japanese novelist. He translated Lady ◊Murasaki, and was the author of *Snow Country* 1947 and *A Thousand Cranes* 1952. His novels are characterized by melancholy and loneliness. He was the first Japanese to win the Nobel Prize for Literature, 1968.

Kawasaki industrial city (iron, steel, shipbuilding, chemicals, textiles) on Honshu Island, Japan; population (1994) 1,171,000.

kayak long, narrow, sealskin-covered boat with a small opening in the middle for the paddler, used by Inuit fishers and sealers, and now adapted for recreational use.

Kaye Danny. Stage name of David Daniel Kaminski 1913–1987. US actor, comedian, and singer. He appeared in many films, including *Wonder Man* 1944, *The Secret Life of Walter Mitty* 1946, and *Hans Christian Andersen* 1952. He achieved success on Broadway in *Lady in the Dark* 1940. He also starred on television, had his own show 1963–67, toured for UNICEF, and guest-conducted major symphony orchestras in later years.

kayser unit of wave number (number of waves in a unit length), used in spectroscopy. It is expressed as waves per centimetre, and is the reciprocal of the wavelength. A wavelength of 0.1 cm has a wave number of 10 kaysers.

Kayseri (ancient name ***Caesarea Mazaca***) capital of Kayseri province, central Turkey; population (1990) 421,400. It produces textiles, carpets, and tiles. In Roman times it was capital of the province of Cappadocia.

Kazakh or ***Kazak*** a pastoral Kyrgyz people of Kazakhstan. Kazakhs also live in China (Xinjiang, Gansu, and Qinghai), Mongolia, and Afghanistan. There are 5–7 million speakers of Kazakh, a Turkic language belonging to the Altaic family. They are predominantly Sunni Muslim, although pre-Islamic customs have survived. Kazakhs herd horses and make use of camels; they also keep cattle. Traditionally the Kazakhs lived in tents and embarked on seasonal migrations in search of fresh pastures. Collectivized herds were established in the 1920s and 1930s.

Kazakhstan country in central Asia, bounded N by Russia, W by the Caspian Sea, E by China, and S by Turkmenistan, Uzbekistan, and Kyrgyzstan. *See country box on p. 586.*

Kazan capital of Tatarstan, central Russian Federation, on the river Volga; population (1994) 1,092,000. It is a transport, commercial, and industrial centre (engineering, oil refining, petrochemicals, textiles, large fur trade). Formerly the capital of a Tatar khanate, Kazan was captured by Ivan IV 'the Terrible' 1552.

Kazan Elia, (born Kazanjoglous) 1909– . US stage and film director. He was a founder of the theatre workshop known as the Actors Studio 1947. Plays he directed include *The Skin of Our Teeth* 1942, *A Streetcar Named Desire* 1947 (filmed 1951), *Death of a Salesman* 1949, and *Cat on a Hot Tin Roof* 1955; films include *Gentleman's Agreement* 1947 (Academy Award), *On the Waterfront* 1954, *East of Eden* 1955, and *The Visitors* 1972.

Kazantzakis Nikos 1885–1957. Greek writer. His works include the poem *I Odysseia/The Odyssey* 1938 (which continues Homer's *Odyssey*), and the novels *Zorba the Greek* 1946, *Christ Recrucified* 1948, *The Greek Passion*, and *The Last Temptation of Christ*, both 1951. *Zorba the Greek* was filmed 1964 and *The Last Temptation of Christ* (controversially) 1988.

kazoo simple wind instrument adding a buzzing quality to the singing voice on the principle of 'comb and paper' music.

kea hawklike greenish parrot *Nestor notabilis*, family Psittacidae, order Psittaciformes, found in New Zealand. It eats insects, fruits, and discarded sheep offal. The Maori name imitates its cry.

Kean Edmund 1787–1833. English tragic actor. He was noted for his portrayal of villainy in the Shakespearean roles of Shylock, Richard III, and Iago. He died on stage, playing Othello opposite his son as Iago.

Keating Paul John 1944– . Australian politician, Labor Party (ALP) leader and prime minister 1991–96. He was treasurer and deputy leader of the ALP 1983–91. In 1993 he announced plans for Australia to become a federal republic by the year 2001, which incited a mixed reaction among Australians. He and his party lost the 1996 general election to John ◊Howard, leader of the Liberal Party.

Keating was active in ALP politics from the age of 15. He held several posts in Labor's shadow ministry 1976–83. As finance minister 1983–91 under Bob ◊Hawke, Keating was unpopular with the public for his harsh economic policies. He successfully challenged Hawke for the ALP party leadership 1991 and his premiership was confirmed by the 1993 general election victory of the ALP, for an unprecedented fifth term of office.

Keaton Buster (Joseph Francis) 1896–1966. US comedian, actor, and film director. After being a star in vaudeville, he became one of the great comedians of the silent film era, with an inimitable deadpan expression (the 'Great Stone Face') masking a sophisticated acting ability. His films include *One Week* 1920, *The Navigator* 1924, *The General* 1927, and *The Cameraman* 1928.

He rivalled Charlie Chaplin in popularity until studio problems ended his creative career. He then made only shorts and guest appearances, as in Chaplin's *Limelight* 1952 and *A Funny Thing Happened on the Way to the Forum* 1966. *See illustration on following page.*

Keats John 1795–1821. English Romantic poet. He produced work of the highest quality and promise before dying at the age of 25. *Poems* 1817, *Endymion* 1818, the great odes (particularly 'Ode to a Nightingale' and 'Ode on a Grecian Urn' written

'The inability of those in power to still the voices of their own consciences is the great force leading to change.'

Kenneth Kaunda
Quoted in the *Observer* July 1965

''Beauty is truth, truth beauty,' – that is all / Ye know on earth, and all ye need to know.'

John Keats
'Ode on a Grecian Urn'

KAZAKHSTAN
Republic of

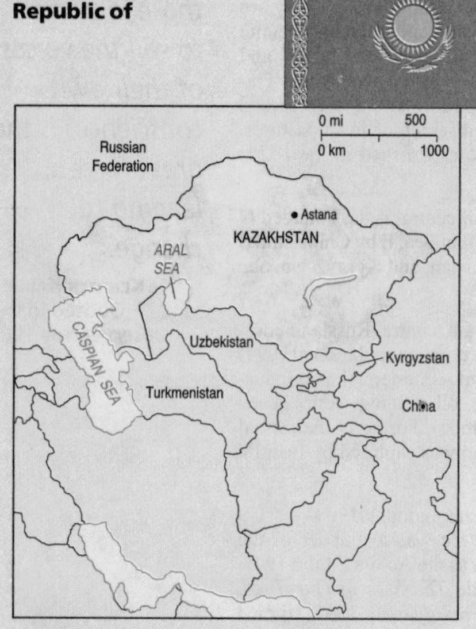

national name *Kazak Respublikasy*
area 2,717,300 sq km/1,049,150 sq mi
capital Almaty (until 2000; then Akmola)
major towns/cities Karaganda, Semipalatinsk, Petropavlovsk, Chimkent
physical features Caspian and Aral seas, Lake Balkhash; Steppe region; natural gas and oil deposits in the Caspian Sea
head of state Nursultan Nazarbayev from 1990
head of government Nurlan Balgimbayev from 1997
political system authoritarian nationalist
administrative divisions 19 provinces
political parties Congress of People's Unity of Kazakhstan, moderate, centrist; People's Congress of Kazakhstan, moderate, ethnic; Socialist Party of Kazakhstan (SPK), left-wing; Republican Party, right-of-centre coalition
population 16,820,000 (1996 est)
population growth rate 0.5% (1990–95); 0.8% (2000–05)
life expectancy 67 (men), 75 (women) (1995–2000)
literacy rate 97.5%
languages Kazakh (official), related to Turkish; Russian
religion Sunni Muslim
currency tenge
GDP (US $) 18 billion (1994)
growth rate −8.9% (1995)
exports ferrous and non-ferrous metals, mineral products (including petroleum and petroleum products), chemicals. Principal market: Russia 42.1% (1995)

HISTORY
early Christian era Settled by Mongol and Turkic tribes.
8th C Spread of Islam.
10th C Southward migration into E Kazakhstan of Kazakh tribes, displaced from Mongolia by the Mongols.
13th–14th Cs Part of the Mongol Empire.
late 15th C Kazakhs emerged as a distinct ethnic group from the Kazakh Orda tribal confederation.
early 17th C The nomadic, cattle-breeding Kazakhs split into smaller groups, united in the three Large, Middle, and Lesser Hordes (federations), led by khans (chiefs).
1731–42 Faced by attacks from the E by Oirot Mongols, protection was sought from the Russian tsars, and Russian control was gradually established.
1822–48 Conquest by tsarist Russia completed, with the deposition of the khans; followed by large-scale Russian and Ukrainian peasant settlement of the steppes after the abolition of serfdom in Russia in 1861.
1887 Almaty, established 1854 as a fortified trading centre and captured by the Russians 1865, destroyed by an earthquake.
1916 150,000 killed in anti-Russian rebellion.
1917 Bolshevik coup in Russia followed by outbreak of civil war in Kazakhstan.
1920 Autonomous republic in USSR.
early 1930s More than 1 million died of starvation during the campaign to collectivize agriculture.
1936 Joined the USSR and became a full union republic.
early 1940s Volga Germans deported to the republic by Soviet dictator Joseph Stalin.
1954–56 Part of Soviet leader Nikita Khrushchev's ambitious 'Virgin Lands' agricultural extension programme; large influx of Russian settlers made Kazakhs a minority in their own republic.
1986 Nationalist riots in Alma-Alta (now Almaty) after reformist Soviet leader Mikhail Gorbachev ousted local communist leader and installed an ethnic Russian.
1989 Nursultan Nazarbayev, a reformist and mild nationalist, became leader of the KCP and instituted economic and cultural reform programmes, encouraging foreign inward investment.
1990 Nazarbayev became head of state; economic sovereignty declared.
1991 Nazarbayev condemned attempted anti-Gorbachev coup in Moscow; KCP abolished. Joined new Commonwealth of Independent States, formed at Almaty; independence recognized by USA.
1992 Admitted into United Nations and Conference on Security and Cooperation in Europe (CSCE; now the Organization on Security and Cooperation in Europe, OSCE).
1993 Presidential power increased by new constitution. Privatization programme launched; Kazakhstan ratified START-1 (disarmament treaty) and the Nuclear Non-Proliferation Treaty.
1994 Economic, social, and military union with Kyrgyzstan and Uzbekistan.
1995 Economic and military cooperation pact with Russia. Achieved nuclear-free status. Nazarbayev's popular mandate re-ratified in national referendum.
1996 Agreement signed with Kyrgyzstan and Uzbekistan to form single economic market.
1997 Nurlan Balgimbayev appointed prime minister. Major oil agreements with China. Astana (formerly known as Akmola) designated as new capital.
1998 Opposition unite to form People's Front.

SEE ALSO Kazakh; Russian Federation; Union of Soviet Socialist Republics

1819, published 1820), and the narratives 'Isabella; or the Pot of Basil' 1818, 'Lamia' 1819, and 'The Eve of St Agnes' 1820, show his lyrical richness and talent for drawing on both classical mythology and medieval lore.

Born in London, Keats studied at Guy's Hospital 1815–17, but then abandoned medicine for poetry. *Endymion* was harshly reviewed by the Tory *Blackwood's Magazine* and *Quarterly Review*, largely because of Keats's friendship with the radical writer Leigh Hunt (1784–1859). In 1819 he fell in love with Fanny Brawne (1802–1865). Suffering from tuberculosis, he sailed to Italy 1820 in an attempt to regain his health, but died in Rome. Valuable insight into Keats's poetic development is provided by his *Letters*, published 1848.

Keats's poetry often deals with the relationship between love and death, beauty and decay. The odes reflect his feelings about the death of his brother and human mortality. 'Ode to a Nightingale' is a symbol of beauty's power to surmount death, a theme which reappears in 'Ode on a Grecian Urn', where the figures on the vase are seen to epitomize an enduring truth, while 'Ode to Autumn' asserts the fulfilment of complete fruition and ripeness.

Keble John 1792–1866. Anglican priest and religious poet. His sermon on the decline of religious faith in Britain, preached 1833, heralded the start of the ◊Oxford Movement, a Catholic revival in the Church of England. He wrote four of the *Tracts for the Times* (theological treatises in support of the movement), and was professor of poetry at Oxford 1831–41. His book of poems, *The Christian Year* 1827, was very popular in the 19th century. Keble College, Oxford, was founded 1870 in his memory.

Keaton US comedy star Buster Keaton in a scene from *The General* 1927, a film set in the American Civil War. He became one of the stars of silent films and, because of his distinctive deadpan expression, was nicknamed the 'Great Stone Face'.

Keck Telescope world's largest optical telescope, situated on Mauna Kea, Hawaii. It has a primary mirror 10 m/33 ft in diameter, unique in that it consists of 36 hexagonal sections, each controlled and adjusted by a computer to generate single images of the objects observed.

Kedah state in NW Peninsular Malaysia; capital Alor Setar; area 9,400 sq km/3,628 sq mi; population (1993) 1,412,000. Products include rice, rubber, tapioca, tin, and tungsten. Kedah was transferred by Thailand to Britain 1909, and was one of the Unfederated Malay States until 1948.

Keegan Kevin 1951– . Manager of England football team. During his playing career was European Footballer of the Year in 1978 and 1979.

Keighley industrial town on the river Aire, NW of Bradford in West Yorkshire, England; population (1991) 49,600. Haworth, home of the Brontë family of writers, is now part of Keighley. Industries include woollens and worsteds, textile machinery, and machine tools.

Keillor Garrison Edward 1942– . US writer and humorist. His hometown Anoka, Minnesota, in the American Midwest, inspired his popular, richly comic stories about Lake Wobegon.

Keïta Salif 1949– . Malian singer and songwriter. His combination of traditional rhythms and vocals with electronic instruments made him popular in the West in the 1980s; in Mali he worked 1973–83 with the band Les Ambassadeurs and became a star throughout W Africa, moving to

France 1984. His albums include *Soro* 1987 and *Amen* 1991.

Keitel Wilhelm 1882–1946. German field marshal in World War II, chief of the supreme command from 1938 and Hitler's chief military adviser. He dictated the terms of the French armistice 1940 and was a member of the court which sentenced many officers to death for their part in the ◊July Plot 1944. He signed Germany's unconditional surrender in Berlin 8 May 1945. Tried at Nuremberg for war crimes, he was hanged.

Kekulé von Stradonitz Friedrich August 1829–1896. German chemist whose theory 1858 of molecular structure revolutionized organic chemistry. He proposed two resonant forms of the ◊benzene ring.

In 1865 Kekulé announced his theory of the structure of benzene, which he envisaged as a hexagonal ring of six carbon atoms connected by alternate single and double bonds. In 1867 he proposed the tetrahedral carbon atom, which was to become the cornerstone of modern structural organic chemistry.

Kelantan state in NE Peninsular Malaysia; capital Kota Baharu; area 14,900 sq km/5,751 sq mi; population (1993) 1,221,700. It produces rice, rubber, copra, tin, manganese, and gold. Kelantan was transferred by Siam to Britain 1909 and until 1948 was one of the Unfederated Malay States.

Keller Helen Adams 1880–1968. US author and campaigner for the blind. She became blind and deaf after an illness when she was only 19 months old, but the teaching of Anne Sullivan, her lifelong companion, enabled her to learn the names of objects and eventually to speak. Keller graduated with honours from Radcliffe College 1904; published several books, including *The Story of My Life* 1902; and toured the world, lecturing to raise money for the blind.

Kellogg–Briand Pact agreement negotiated 1927 between the USA and France to renounce war and seek settlement of disputes by peaceful means. It took its name from the US secretary of state Frank B Kellogg (1856–1937) and the French foreign minister Aristide Briand. Most other nations subsequently signed. Some successes were achieved in settling South American disputes, but the pact made no provision for measures against aggressors and became ineffective in the 1930s, with Japan in Manchuria, Italy in Ethiopia, and Hitler in central Europe.

Kells, Book of 8th-century illuminated manuscript of the Gospels produced at the monastery of Kells in County Meath, Ireland. It is now in Trinity College library, Dublin. ▷ *See feature on pp. 200–201.*

Kelly Gene (Eugene Curran) 1912–1996. US film actor, dancer, choreographer, and director. He was a major star of the 1940s and 1950s in a series of MGM musicals, including *On the Town* 1949, *Singin' in the Rain* 1952 (both of which he codirected), and *An American in Paris* 1951. He also directed *Hello Dolly* 1969.

Kelly Grace Patricia 1929–1982. US film actress. She starred in *High Noon* 1952, *The Country Girl* 1954, for which she received an Academy Award, and *High Society* 1955. She also starred in three Hitchcock films – *Dial M for Murder* 1954, *Rear Window* 1954, and *To Catch a Thief* 1955. She retired from acting after marrying Prince Rainier III of Monaco 1956.

Kelly Petra 1947–1992. German politician and activist. She was a vigorous campaigner against nuclear power and other environmental issues and founded the German Green Party 1972. She was a member of the Bundestag (parliament) 1983–90, but then fell out with her party.

Kelman James 1946– . Scottish novelist and short-story writer. His works are angry, compassionate, and ironic, and make effective use of the trenchant speech patterns of his native Glasgow. These include the novels *The Busconductor Hines* 1984, *A Disaffection* 1989, and *How Late It Was, How Late* 1994 (Booker Prize); the short-story collections *Greyhound for Breakfast* 1987 and *The Burn* 1991; and the play *The Busker* 1985.

Keller Left deaf and blind by an illness in infancy, Helen Keller nevertheless achieved a high standard of education through the instruction of her lifelong companion and teacher Anne Sullivan, who was herself partially sighted. Keller is pictured here in her graduation gown. *Corbis*

keloid in medicine, overgrowth of fibrous tissue, usually produced at the site of a scar. Surgical removal is often unsuccessful, because the keloid returns.

kelp collective name for large brown seaweeds, such as those of the Fucaceae and Laminariaceae families. Kelp is also a term for the powdery ash of burned seaweeds, a source of iodine.

The brown kelp *Macrocystis pyrifera*, abundant in Antarctic and sub-Antarctic waters, is one of the fastest-growing organisms known, reaching 100 m/320 ft. It is farmed for the alginate industry, its rapid surface growth allowing cropping several times a year, but it is an alien pest in N Atlantic waters.

Kelvin William Thomson, 1st Baron Kelvin 1824–1907. Irish physicist who introduced the kelvin scale, the absolute scale of temperature. His work on the conservation of energy 1851 led to the second law of ◊thermodynamics.

Kelvin's knowledge of electrical theory was largely responsible for the first successful transatlantic telegraph cable. In 1847 he concluded that electrical and magnetic fields are distributed in a manner analogous to the transfer of energy through an elastic solid. From 1849 to 1859, Kelvin also developed the work of English scientist Michael ◊Faraday into a full theory of magnetism, arriving at an expression for the total energy of a system of magnets.

kelvin scale temperature scale used by scientists. It begins at ◊absolute zero (−273.15°C) and increases by the same degree intervals as the Celsius scale; that is, 0°C is the same as 273.15 K and 100°C is 373.15 K.

Kemal Atatürk Mustafa. Turkish politician; see ◊Atatürk.

Kemble (John) Philip 1757–1823. English actor and theatre manager. He excelled in tragedy, including the Shakespearean roles of Hamlet and Coriolanus. As manager of Drury Lane 1788–1803 and Covent Garden 1803–17 in London, he introduced many innovations in theatrical management, costume, and scenery.

He was the son of the strolling player Roger Kemble (1721–1802), whose children included the actors Charles Kemble and Mrs ◊Siddons.

Kemp Will died 1603. English clown. A member of several Elizabethan theatre companies, he joined the Chamberlain's Men 1594, acting in the roles of Dogberry in Shakespeare's *Much Ado About Nothing* and Peter in *Romeo and Juliet*. He published *Kempe's Nine Days' Wonder* 1600, an account of his nine-day dance to Norwich from London.

Kempe Margerie, (born Brunham) c. 1373–c. 1439. English Christian mystic. She converted to religious life after a period of mental derangement, and travelled widely as a pilgrim. Her *Boke of Margery Kempe* about 1420 describes her life and experiences, both religious and worldly. It has been called the first autobiography in English.

Kempe Rudolf 1910–1976. German conductor. Renowned for the clarity and fidelity of his interpretations of the works of Richard Strauss and Wagner's *Ring* cycle, he conducted Britain's Royal Philharmonic Orchestra 1961–75 and was musical director of the Munich Philharmonic from 1967.

Kempis Thomas à. Medieval German monk and religious writer; see ◊Thomas à Kempis.

Kendall Edward Calvin 1886–1972. US biochemist. In 1914 he isolated the hormone thyroxine, the active compound of the thyroid gland. He went on to work on secretions from the adrenal gland, among which he discovered the steroid cortisone. For this Kendall shared the 1950 Nobel Prize for Physiology or Medicine with Philip Hench (1896–1965) and Tadeus ◊Reichstein.

kendo (Japanese *kendō* 'the way of the sword') Japanese armed ◊martial art in which combatants fence with bamboo replicas of samurai swords. Masks and padding are worn for protection. The earliest recorded reference to kendo is from AD 789.

Keneally Thomas Michael 1935– . Australian novelist. He won the Booker Prize with *Schindler's Ark* 1982, a novel based on the true account of Polish Jews saved from the gas chambers in World War II by a German industrialist.

Among his other books are *The Chant of Jimmie Blacksmith* 1972 (filmed 1978), based on the life of the Aboriginal bushranger Jimmy Governor, *Confederates* 1980, *A Family Madness* 1986 and *A River Town* 1995.

Kennedy Edward Moore ('Ted') 1932– . US Democratic politician. He aided his brothers John and Robert Kennedy in their presidential campaigns of 1960 and 1968 respectively, and entered politics as a senator for Massachusetts 1962. He failed to gain the presidential nomination 1980, largely because of questions about his delay in reporting a car crash at Chappaquiddick Island, near Cape Cod, Massachusetts, 1969, in which his passenger, Mary Jo Kopechne, was drowned.

Kennedy John F(itzgerald) ('Jack') 1917–1963. 35th president of the USA 1961–63, a Democrat; the first Roman Catholic and the youngest person to be elected president. In foreign policy he carried through the unsuccessful ◊Bay of Pigs invasion of Cuba, and secured the withdrawal of Soviet missiles from the island 1962. His programme for reforms at home, called the New Frontier, was posthumously carried out by Lyndon Johnson. Kennedy was assassinated while on a visit to Dallas, Texas, on 22 Nov 1963. Lee Harvey Oswald (1939–1963), who was within a few days shot dead by Jack Ruby (1911–1967), was named as the assassin.

Son of financier Joseph Kennedy, John was born in Brookline, Massachusetts, educated at Harvard and briefly at the London School of Economics, and served in the navy in the Pacific during World War II. In 1953 he married socialite Jacqueline Lee Bouvier (1929–1995).

Kennedy The 35th president of the USA, John F Kennedy, the youngest person to be elected to the office. He was assassinated after less than three years in power. *Sachem*

'Science may have found a cure for most evils; but it has found no remedy for the worst of them all – the apathy of human beings.'

HELEN KELLER
My Religion

'And so, my fellow Americans: ask not what your country can do for you – ask what you can do for your country.'

JOHN F KENNEDY
Inaugural address
20 Jan 1962

When the going gets tough, the tough get going.

Joseph Kennedy
Quoted in J H Cutler
Honey Fitz

It was in foreign affairs that Kennedy's presidency was most notable. Early in 1961 came the fiasco of the Bay of Pigs, which, though partially carried over from the previous administration, was undoubtedly Kennedy's responsibility. This was redeemed by his masterly handling of the ◊Cuban missile crisis 1962, where his calm and firm approach had a prolonged effect on US–Soviet relations. The Nuclear ◊Test Ban Treaty 1963 achieved a further lessening of tension. Kennedy's internationalism won him a popular European reputation not attained by any of his predecessors. He visited W Europe 1961 and 1963, and was tumultuously received on each occasion. The US involvement in the Vietnam War began during Kennedy's administration.

Kennedy Joseph Patrick 1888–1969. US industrialist and diplomat; ambassador to the UK 1937–40. A self-made millionaire, he ventured into the film industry, then set up the Securities and Exchange Commission (SEC) for F D Roosevelt. He groomed each of his sons – Joseph Patrick Kennedy, Jr (1915–1944), John F Kennedy, Robert Kennedy, and Edward Kennedy – for a career in politics.

Kennedy Nigel Paul 1956– . English violinist. He is credited with expanding the audience for classical music. His 1986 recording of Vivaldi's *Four Seasons* sold more than 1 million copies.

Kennedy Robert Francis ('Bobby') 1925–1968. US Democratic politician and lawyer. He was presidential campaign manager for his brother John F ◊Kennedy 1960, and as attorney general 1961–64 pursued a racket-busting policy and promoted the Civil Rights Act of 1964. He was also a key aide to his brother. When John Kennedy's successor, Lyndon Johnson, preferred Hubert H Humphrey for the 1964 vice-presidential nomination, Kennedy resigned and was elected senator for New York. In 1968 he campaigned for the Democratic Party's presidential nomination, but during a campaign stop in California was assassinated by Sirhan Bissara Sirhan (1944–), a Jordanian.

Kennedy Space Center ◊NASA launch site on Merritt Island, near Cape Canaveral, Florida, used for *Apollo* and space-shuttle launches. The first flight to land on the Moon (1969) and *Skylab*, the first orbiting laboratory (1973), were launched here.

The Center is dominated by the Vehicle Assembly Building, 160 m/525 ft tall, used for assembly of ◊*Saturn* rockets and space shuttles.

Kenneth I (called ***MacAlpin***) died 860. King of Scotland from about 844. Traditionally, he is regarded as the founder of the Scottish kingdom (Alba) by virtue of his final defeat of the Picts about 844. He invaded Northumbria six times, and drove the Angles and the Britons over the river Tweed.

Kenneth II died 995. King of Scotland from 971, son of Malcolm I. He invaded Northumbria several times, and his chiefs were in constant conflict with Sigurd the Norwegian over the area of Scotland north of the river Spey. He is believed to have been murdered by his subjects.

Kensington and Chelsea inner borough of central Greater London
features Holland House (about 1606) and Holland Park; Camden House (about 1612); Kensington Palace, Jacobean house redesigned by Christopher ◊Wren for William and Mary 1689; Kensington Gardens, with statue of Peter Pan; Leighton House (1866); Imperial College of Science and Technology (1907); Kensington and Chelsea Town Hall (1976) designed by Basil ◊Spence; museums – Victoria and Albert, Natural History, Science, and Geology; Royal College of Music; Royal College of Art; Notting Hill Carnival, held each August, is the largest street carnival in Europe
population (1991) 138,400
famous people William Wilberforce lived here.

Kent county of SE England, known as the 'garden of England'
area 3,730 sq km/1,440 sq mi (*see United Kingdom map*)
towns and cities Maidstone (administrative headquarters), Canterbury, Dover, Chatham, Rochester, Sheerness, Tunbridge Wells; resorts: Folkestone, Margate, Ramsgate
features the North Downs; rivers: Thames, Darent, Medway, Stour; New Ash Green, a new town; Romney Marsh; the Isles of Grain, Sheppey, and Thanet; Weald (agricultural area); Leeds Castle (converted to a palace by Henry VIII); Hever Castle (where Henry VIII courted Anne Boleyn); Chartwell (Churchill's country home); Sissinghurst Castle and gardens; the Brogdale Experimental Horticulture Station at Faversham, with the world's finest collection of apple and other fruit trees; the former RAF Manston became Kent International Airport 1989
industries hops, apples, soft fruit, cement, paper, oil refining, shipbuilding. The East Kent coalfield ceased production 1989
population (1991) 1,508,900
famous people Christopher Marlowe, Edward Heath.

Kent Edward George Nicholas Paul Patrick, 2nd Duke of Kent 1935– . British prince, grandson of George V. His father, ***George*** (1902–1942), was created Duke of Kent just before his marriage in 1934 to Princess Marina of Greece and Denmark (1906–1968). The second duke succeeded when his father (George Edward Alexander Edmund) was killed in an air crash on active service with the RAF.

He was educated at Eton public school and Sandhurst military academy, and then commissioned in the Royal Scots Greys. In 1961 he married Katharine Worsley (1933–) and his heir is ***George*** (1962–), Earl of St Andrews. His brother, ***Prince Michael*** (1942–), became an officer with the Hussars in 1962. His sister, ***Princess Alexandra*** (1936–), married in 1963 Angus Ogilvy (1928–), younger son of the 12th Earl of Airlie; they have two children, James (1964–) and Marina (1966–).

Kent William 1684–1748. English architect, landscape gardener, and interior designer. Working closely with Richard ◊Burlington, he was foremost in introducing the Palladian style to Britain from Italy, excelling in richly carved, sumptuous interiors and furnishings, as at Holkham Hall, Norfolk (begun 1734). Immensely versatile, he also worked in a Neo-Gothic style, and was a pioneer in Romantic landscape gardening, for example, the grounds of Stowe House in Buckinghamshire.

Kentigern, St (also called ***Mungo***) c. 518–603. First bishop of Glasgow, born at Culross, Scotland. Anti-Christian factions forced him to flee to Wales, where he founded the monastery of St Asaph. In 573 he returned to Glasgow and founded the cathedral there. Feast day 14 Jan.

Kentucky state in S central USA; nicknamed Bluegrass State
area 104,700 sq km/40,414 sq mi
capital Frankfort
towns and cities Louisville, Lexington, Owensboro, Covington, Bowling Green
features Ohio and Kentucky rivers; Cumberland Gap national park; Daniel Boone national forest; Red River Gorge; Abraham Lincoln's birthplace at Hodgenville; Fort Knox, the US gold bullion depository
industries tobacco, cereals, textiles, coal, whisky, horses, transport vehicles
population (1991) 3,713,000
famous people Muhammad Ali, Daniel Boone, Louis D Brandeis, Kit Carson, Henry Clay, D W Griffith, Thomas Hunt Morgan, Harland 'Colonel' Sanders, Robert Penn Warren
history Kentucky was the first region west of the Alleghenies settled by American pioneers. James Harrod founded Harrodsburg 1774; in 1775 Daniel Boone, who blazed his Wilderness Trail 1767, founded Boonesboro. Originally part of Virginia, Kentucky became a state 1792. Badly divided over the slavery question, the state was racked by guerrilla warfare and partisan feuds during the Civil War.

Kentucky

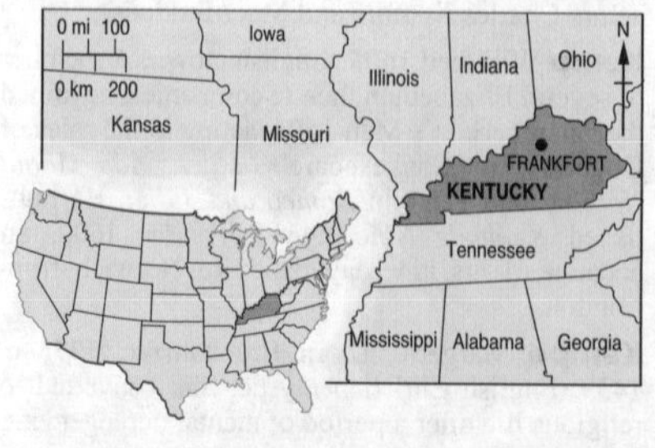

Kenya country in E Africa, bounded N by Sudan and Ethiopia, E by Somalia, SE by the Indian Ocean, SW by Tanzania, and W by Uganda. *See country box opposite.*

Kenya, Mount or ***Kirinyaga*** extinct volcano from which Kenya takes its name, 5,199 m/17,057 ft; the first European to climb it was Halford Mackinder 1899.

Kenyatta Jomo. Assumed name of Kamau Ngengi c. 1894–1978. Kenyan nationalist politician, prime minister from 1963, as well as the first president of Kenya from 1964 until his death. He led the Kenya African Union from 1947 (KANU from 1963) and was active in liberating Kenya from British rule.

A member of the Kikuyu ethnic group, Kenyatta was born near Fort Hall, son of a farmer. Brought up at a Church of Scotland mission, he joined the Kikuyu Central Association (KCA), devoted to recovery of Kikuyu lands from white settlers, and became its president. He spent some years in Britain, returning to Kenya 1946. He became president of the Kenya African Union (successor to the banned KCA 1947). In 1953 he was sentenced to seven years' imprisonment for his management of the guerrilla organization ◊Mau Mau, though some doubt has been cast on his complicity. Released to exile in N Kenya 1959, he was allowed to return to Kikuyuland 1961 to negotiate Kenya's independence, and became prime minister 1963 (also president from 1964) of independent Kenya. His slogans were *'Uhuru na moja'* (Freedom and unity) and *'Harambee'* (Let's get going).

Kenyatta Kenyan politician Jomo Kenyatta celebrating Kenya's independence 1963. He was the first president of independent Kenya 1964–78. *Corbis*

Kepler Johannes 1571–1630. German mathematician and astronomer. He formulated what are now called Kepler's laws of planetary motion: (1) the orbit of each planet is an ellipse with the Sun at one of the foci; (2) the radius vector of each planet sweeps out equal areas in equal times; (3) the squares of the periods of the planets are proportional to the cubes of their mean distances from the Sun.

Kepler was one of the first advocates of Sun-centred cosmology, as put forward by ◊Copernicus. Kepler's laws are the basis of our understanding of the Solar System, and such scientists as Isaac ◊Newton built on his ideas. His *Rudolphine Tables*, the first modern astronomical tables, based on Tycho ◊Brahe's observations, was published 1627.
▷ *See feature on pp. 70–71.*

Kerala state of SW India, formed 1956 from the former princely states of Travancore and Cochin
area 38,900 sq km/15,015 sq mi
capital Thiruvananthapuram
features most densely populated, and most literate (60%), state of India; strong religious and caste divisions make it politically unstable
industries tea, coffee, rice, oilseed, rubber, textiles, chemicals, electrical goods, fish
population (1994 est) 30,555,000
language Kannada, Malayalam, Tamil

keratin fibrous protein found in the ◊skin of vertebrates and also in hair, nails, claws, hooves, feathers, and the outer coating of horns. If pressure is put on some parts of the skin, more keratin is produced, forming thick calluses that protect the layers of skin beneath.

kerb crawling accosting women in the street from a motor vehicle for the purposes of ◊prostitution. In the UK, this is an offence under the Sexual Offences Act 1985. This legislation, recommended by the Criminal Law Revision Committee, aims to prevent women being annoyed in the street and to mitigate the nuisance caused to residents in neighbourhoods where prostitutes and their clients gather. The act also prohibits persistently soliciting women even when the man is not in a vehicle. It is not an offence to solicit men by kerb crawling.

Kerbela or ***Karbala*** holy city of the Shi'ite Muslims, 96 km/60 mi SW of Baghdad, Iraq; population (1987) 296,700. Kerbela is built on the site of the battlefield where Husein, son of ◊Ali and Fatima, was killed 680 while defending his succession to the khalifate; his tomb in the city is visited every year by many pilgrims.

Kerekou Mathieu Ahmed 1933– . Benin socialist politician and soldier, president 1980–91 and from 1996. In 1972, when deputy head of the Dahomey army, he led a coup to oust the ruling president and establish his own military government. He embarked on a programme of 'scientific socialism', changing his country's name to Benin to mark this change of direction. In 1987 he resigned from the army and confirmed a civilian administration. He was re-elected president 1989, but lost to Nicéphore Soglo in the 1991 presidential elections. He surprisingly won the1996 presidential elections despite claims of fraud.

Kerensky Alexandr Feodorovich 1881–1970. Russian revolutionary politician, prime minister of the second provisional government before its collapse Nov 1917, during the ◊Russian Revolution. He was overthrown by the Bolshevik revolution and fled to France 1918 and to the USA 1940.

Kerguelen Islands or ***Desolation Islands*** volcanic archipelago in the Indian Ocean, part of the French Southern and Antarctic Territories; area 7,215 km/2,787 sq mi. It was discovered 1772 by the Breton navigator Yves de Kerguelen and annexed by France 1949. Uninhabited except for scientists (centre for joint study of geomagnetism with Russia), the islands support a unique wild cabbage containing a pungent oil.

Kern Jerome David 1885–1945. US composer. Many of Kern's songs have become classics, notably 'Smoke Gets in Your Eyes' from his musical *Roberta* 1933. He wrote the operetta *Show Boat* 1927, which includes the song 'Ol' Man River'.

kerosene thin oil obtained from the distillation of petroleum; a highly refined form is used in jet aircraft fuel. Kerosene is a mixture of hydrocarbons of the ◊paraffin series.

Kerouac Jack (Jean Louis) 1922–1969. US novelist. He named and epitomized the ◊Beat Generation of the 1950s. The first of his autobiographical, myth-making books, *The Town and the City* 1950, was followed by the rhapsodic ◊*On the Road* 1957. Other works written with similar free-wheeling energy and inspired by his interests in jazz and Buddhism include *The Dharma Bums* 1958, *Doctor Sax* 1959, and *Desolation Angels* 1965. His major contribution to poetry was *Mexico City Blues* 1959.

Kerouac became a legendary symbol of youthful rebellion from the late 1950s, but before his early death from alcoholism he had become a semi-recluse, unable to cope with his fame.

> *'I had nothing to offer anybody except my own confusion.'*
>
> Jack Kerouac, *On the Road*

Kerry county of the Republic of Ireland, W of Cork, in the province of Munster; county town Tralee; area 4,700 sq km/1,814 sq mi; population (1991) 121,700. Low lying in the north, to the south are the highest mountains in Ireland, including Carrantuohill (part of ◊Macgillycuddy's Reeks), the highest peak in Ireland at 1,041 m/3,417 ft. The western coastline is deeply indented and there are many rivers and lakes, notably the Lakes of Killarney. Industries include engineering, woollens, shoes, cutlery, fishing, farming; tourism is important.

Kesselring Albert 1885–1960. German field marshal in World War II, commander of the Luftwaffe (air force) 1939–40, during the invasions of

KENYA
Republic of

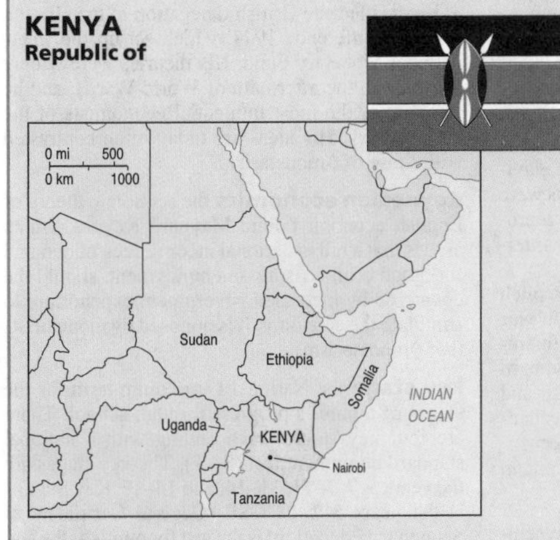

national name *Jamhuri ya Kenya*
area 582,600 sq km/224,884 sq mi
capital Nairobi
major towns/cities Kisumu
major ports Mombasa
physical features mountains and highlands in W and centre; coastal plain in S; arid interior and tropical coast; semi-desert in N; Great Rift Valley, Mount Kenya, Lake Nakuru (salt lake with world's largest colony of flamingos), Lake Turkana (Rudolf)
head of state Daniel arap Moi from 1978
head of government Daniel arap Moi from 1978
political system authoritarian nationalist
administrative divisions seven provinces and the Nairobi municipality
political parties Kenya African National Union (KANU), nationalist, centrist; Forum for the Restoration of Democracy–Kenya (FORD–Kenya), left of centre; Forum for the Restoration of Democracy–Asili (FORD–Asili), left of centre; Democratic Party (DP), centrist; Safina, centrist
armed forces 24,200; paramilitary force 5,000 (1994)
conscription none
defence spend (% GDP) 2.2 (1994)
education spend (% GNP) 5.4 (1992)
health spend (% GDP) 2.7 (1990)
death penalty retained and used for ordinary crimes
population 28,337,000 (1998 est)
population growth rate 3.6% (1990–95); 3.0% (2000–05)
age distribution (% of total population) <15 47.7%, 15–65 49.4%, >65 2.9% (1995)
ethnic distribution main ethnic groups are the Kikuyu (about 21%), the Luhya (14%), the Luo (13%), the Kalenjin (11%), the Kamba (11%), the Kisii (6%), and the Meru (5%); there are also Asian, Arab, and European minorities
population density (per sq km) 47 (1994)
urban population (% of total) 28 (1995)
labour force 48% of population: 80% agriculture, 7% industry, 13% services (1990)
unemployment 16% (1992 est)
child mortality rate (under 5, per 1,000 live births) 101 (1997)
life expectancy 57 (men), 61 (women)
education (years) 8 (not compulsory, but free)
literacy rate 80% (men), 59% (women)
languages Kiswahili (official), English; there are many local dialects
religions Roman Catholic, Protestant, Muslim, traditional tribal religions
TV sets (per 1,000 people) 10 (1992)
currency Kenya shilling
GDP (US $) 6.86 billion (1994)
GDP per capita (PPP) (US $) 1,400 (1993)
growth rate 3.0% (1994)
average annual inflation 28.8% (1994); 17.8% (1985–93)
trading partners UK, Germany, Japan, United Arab Emirates
resources soda ash, fluorspar, salt, limestone, rubies, gold, vermiculite, diatonite, garnets
industries food processing, petroleum refinery and petroleum products, textiles and clothing, leather products, chemicals, cement, paper and paper products, beverages, tobacco, ceramics, rubber and metal products, vehicle assembly, tourism
exports coffee, tea, petroleum products, soda ash, horticultural products. Principal market: UK 16.4% (1993)
imports crude petroleum, motor vehicles, industrial machinery, iron and steel, chemicals, basic manufactures. Principal source: UK 16.3% (1993)
arable land 6.9% (1993)
agricultural products coffee, tea, maize, wheat, sisal, sugar cane, pineapples, cotton, horticulture; dairy products

HISTORY
8th C Arab traders began to settle along coast of E Africa.
16th C Portuguese defeated coastal states and exerted spasmodic control over them.
18th C Sultan of Oman reasserted Arab overlordship of E African coast, making it subordinate to Zanzibar.
19th C Europeans, closely followed by Christian missionaries, began to explore inland.
1887 British East African Company leased area of coastal territory from sultan of Zanzibar.
1895 Britain claimed large inland region as East African Protectorate.
1903 Railway from Mombasa to Uganda built using Indian labourers, many of whom settled in the area; British and South African settlers began to farm highlands.
1920 East African Protectorate became crown colony of Kenya, with legislative council elected by white settlers (and by Indians and Arabs soon afterwards).
1923 Britain rejected demand for internal self-government by white settlers.
1944 First African appointment to legislative council; Kenyan African Union (KAU) founded to campaign for African rights.
1947 Jomo Kenyatta became leader of KAU, which was dominated by Kikuyu tribe.
1952 Mau Mau (Kikuyu secret society) began terrorist campaign to drive white settlers from tribal lands; Mau Mau largely suppressed by 1954 but state of emergency lasted for eight years.
1953 Kenyatta charged with management of Mau Mau activities and imprisoned by the British.
1956 Africans allowed to elect members of legislative council on restricted franchise.
1959 Kenyatta released from prison, but exiled to N Kenya.
1960 Britain announced plans to prepare Kenya for majority African rule.
1961 Kenyatta allowed to return to help negotiate Kenya's independence.
1963 Kenya achieved independence with Kenyatta as prime minister.
1964 Kenya became a republic with Kenyatta as president.
1967 East African Community (EAC) formed by Kenya, Tanzania, and Uganda to retain customs union inherited from colonial period.
1969 Kenya became one-party state under Kenyan African National Union (KANU).
1977 Political and economic disputes led to collapse of EAC.
1978 Death of President Kenyatta; succeeded by Daniel arap Moi.
1984 Violent clashes between government troops and ethnic Somali population at Wajir.
1989 Moi announced release of political prisoners.
1991 Multiparty system conceded after Oginga Odinga launched opposition group.
1992 Moi re-elected in multiparty elections amid allegations of fraud.
1995 New Centrist party, Safina, formed by palaeoanthropologist Richard Leakey.
1997 Demonstrations calling for democratic reform. Constitutional reforms adopted.
1998 Electoral commission ratified President Moi's re-election. KANU won slim majority in general election.

SEE ALSO Kenyatta, Jomo; Mau Mau

❛But this long run *is a misleading guide to current affairs.* In the long run *we are all dead.*❜

John Maynard Keynes
A Tract on Monetary Reform

❛So sits enthroned in vegetable pride / Imperial Kew by Thames's glittering side.❜

On **Kew Gardens**
Erasmus Darwin 'The Economy of Vegetation' *The Botanic Garden*

Poland and the Low Countries and the early stages of the Battle of Britain. He later served under Field Marshal Rommel in N Africa, took command in Italy 1943, and was commander in chief on the western front March 1945. His death sentence for war crimes at the Nuremberg trials 1947 was commuted to life imprisonment, but he was released 1952.

kestrel or ***windhover*** hawk *Falco tinnunculus* of the family Falconidae, order Falconiformes, which breeds in Europe, Asia, and Africa, migrating southwards in winter. About 30 cm/1 ft long, the male has a head and tail of bluish grey, and its back is a light chestnut brown with black spots. The female is slightly larger and reddish brown above, with bars. The kestrel hunts mainly by hovering in midair while searching for prey. It feeds on small mammals, insects, frogs, and worms. It rarely builds its own nest, but uses those of other birds, such as crows and magpies, or scrapes a hole on some cliff-ledge.

ketone member of the group of organic compounds containing the carbonyl group (C=O) bonded to two atoms of carbon (instead of one carbon and one hydrogen as in ◊aldehydes). Ketones are liquids or low-melting-point solids, slightly soluble in water. An example is propanone (acetone, CH_3COCH_3), used as a solvent.

kettle hole pit or depression formed when a block of ice from a receding glacier becomes isolated and buried in glacial debris (till). As the block melts the till collapses to form a hollow, which may become filled with water to form a kettle lake or pond. Kettle holes range from 5 m/15 ft to 13 km/8 mi in diameter, and may exceed 33 m/100 ft in depth.

Kew Gardens popular name for the Royal Botanic Gardens, Kew, Surrey, England. They were founded 1759 by Augusta of Saxe-Coburg (1719–1772), the mother of King George III, as a small garden and passed to the nation by Queen Victoria 1840. By then they had expanded to almost their present size of 149 hectares/368 acres and since 1841 have been open daily to the public. They contain a collection of over 25,000 living plant species and many fine buildings. The gardens are also a centre for botanical research.

The ◊herbarium is the biggest in the world, with over 5 million dried plant specimens. Kew also has a vast botanical library, the Jodrell Laboratory, and three museums. The buildings include the majestic Palm House 1848, the Temperate House 1862, both designed by Decimus Burton, and the Chinese Pagoda, some 50 m/165 ft tall, designed by William Chambers 1761. More recently, two additions have been made to the glasshouses: the Alpine House 1981 and the Princess of Wales Conservatory, a futuristic building for plants from ten different climatic zones, 1987. Much of the collection of trees at Kew was destroyed by a gale 1987.

key in music, the ◊diatonic scale around which a piece of music is written; for example, a passage in the key of C major will mainly use the notes of the C major scale. The term is also used for the lever activated by a ◊keyboard player, such as a piano key, or the finger control on a woodwind instrument.

kestrel The kestrel is a small falcon that feeds mainly on invertebrates and tiny mammals. It catches them on the ground and may often be seen hanging in the air beside motorways. The kestrel is sometimes referred to as the 'windhover'.

keyboard in music, a set of 'keys' (levers worked by the fingers or feet) arranged in order, forming part of various keyboard instruments and enabling the performer to play a much larger number of strings or reeds than could otherwise be controlled. The keyboard is a major innovation of Western music, introduced to medieval instruments of the organ type (including the portative organ and the reed organ), and subsequently transferred to Renaissance stringed instruments such as the clavichord and hurdy-gurdy. Keyboard instruments were designed to enable precise and objective reproduction of musical intervals, without the intervention of musical expression.

Keyboards introduced consistent scaling to pitch space at the time that the Mercator projection was revolutionizing geographical mapmaking. Instrument-makers seized on the user-friendly keyboard mechanism to create new markets for amateur and domestic use, creating in the clavichord a mechanized plectrum guitar, in the harpsichord a mechanized lute, in the hurdy-gurdy a keyboard viol, and in the fortepiano a mechanized dulcimer.

keyboard in computing, an input device resembling a typewriter keyboard, used to enter instructions and data. There are many variations on the layout and labelling of keys. Extra numeric keys may be added, as may special-purpose function keys, whose effects can be defined by programs in the computer.

keyhole surgery or ***minimally invasive surgery*** term used to describe operations that do not involve cutting into the body in the traditional way. These procedures are performed either by means of ◊endoscopy or by passing fine instruments through catheters inserted into the body by way of large blood vessels.

Probably the best-known example is percutaneous transluminal coronary angioplasty (PTCA) to treat coronary artery disease. It involves passing a balloon-tipped catheter into a large artery in the groin and advancing it until the tip comes to rest in a narrowed coronary vessel; the balloon is then inflated to widen the diseased vessel. PTCA is performed in selected cases as an alternative to the conventional procedure of coronary artery bypass grafting (CABG).

Advocates of keyhole surgery claim it is safer and cheaper than conventional surgery, requiring a shorter hospital stay and less disruption to the patient's life. However, one or two such procedures have been called into question, either because they do not yield the long-term result of open surgery or because they are performed by people inexperienced in the technique. In roughly a third of cases treated by PTCA, for instance, the artery becomes blocked again within six months, requiring further surgery. ▷*See feature on pp. 1024–1025.*

Keynes John Maynard, 1st Baron Keynes 1883–1946. English economist. His *General Theory of Employment, Interest, and Money* 1936 proposed the prevention of financial crises and unemployment by adjusting demand through government control of credit and currency. He is responsible for that part of economics now known as macroeconomics.

Keynes led the British delegation at the Bretton Woods Conference 1944, which set up the International Monetary Fund. His theories were widely accepted in the aftermath of World War II, and he was one of the most influential economists of the 20th century. His ideas are today often contrasted with those of ◊monetarism.

Keynesian economics the economic theory of English economist John Maynard Keynes, which argues that a fall in national income, lack of demand for goods, and rising unemployment should be countered by increased government expenditure to stimulate the economy. It is opposed by monetarists (see ◊monetarism).

key stage the National Curriculum term for the stages of a pupil's progress through school. There are four key stages, each ending with a national standard attainment test (SAT). The key stages are the years 5–7, 7–11, 11–14, and 14–17. Key Stage 1 is the years 5–7. ◊GCSE (General Certificate of Secondary Education) is the test for pupils at the end of Key Stage 4.

KGB secret police of the USSR, the ***Komitet Gosudarstvennoy Bezopasnosti*** (Committee of State Security), which was in control of frontier and general security and the forced-labour system. KGB officers held key appointments in all fields of daily life, reporting to administration offices in every major town. On the demise of the Soviet Union

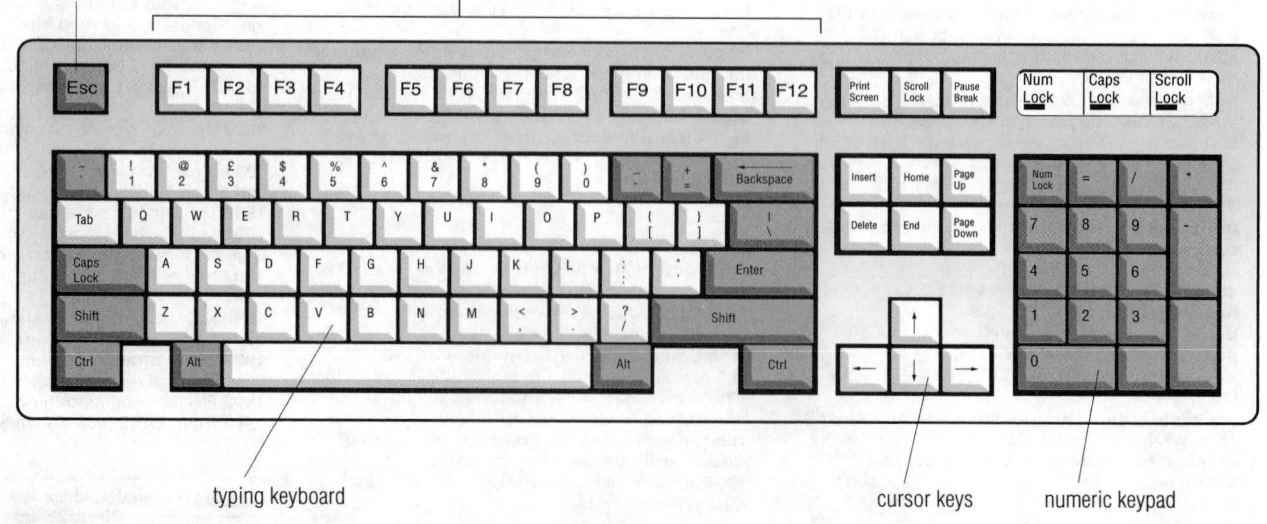

keyboard A standard 102-key keyboard. As well as providing a QWERTY typing keyboard, the function keys (labelled F1–F12) may be assigned tasks specific to a particular system.

1991, the KGB was superseded by the Federal Counterintelligence Service, which was renamed the Federal Security Service (FSB) 1995, when its powers were expanded to enable it to combat corruption and organized crime, and to undertake foreign-intelligence gathering.

The KGB had at least 220,000 border guards, with reinforcements of 80,000 volunteer militia members. Many KGB officers were also said to hold diplomatic posts in embassies abroad. Headed by General Vladimir Kryuchkov 1988–91, the KGB coordinated the military crackdown on Azerbaijan 1990 and on the Baltic states 1991.

After the attempted anti-Gorbachev coup of 1991, reforms intended to curb the political activities of the KGB were introduced: its leadership was removed and KGB troops were placed under the control of the Defence Ministry; the presidential guard was removed from KGB authority; and government communications were transferred to the aegis of a state committee.

Khabarovsk territory of the Russian Federation, in SE Siberia, bordering the Sea of Okhotsk and drained by the Amur River; area 824,600 sq km/318,501 sq mi; population (1985) 1,728,000. The capital is Khabarovsk. Mineral resources include gold, coal, and iron ore.

Khachaturian Aram Il'yich 1903–1978. Armenian composer. His use of folk themes is shown in the ballets *Gayaneh* 1942, which includes the 'Sabre Dance', and *Spartacus* 1956.

Khaddhafi Moamer al, or ***Gaddafi*** or ***Qaddafi*** 1942– . Libyan revolutionary leader. Overthrowing King Idris 1969, he became virtual president of a republic, although he nominally gave up all except an ideological role 1974. He favours territorial expansion in N Africa reaching as far as the Democratic Republic of Congo, has supported rebels in Chad, and has proposed mergers with a number of countries. During the ◊Gulf War, however, he advocated diplomacy rather than war. His theories, based on those of the Chinese communist leader Mao Zedong, are contained in a *Green Book*.

Khaddhafi's alleged complicity in international terrorism led to his country's diplomatic isolation during the 1980s and in 1992 United Nations sanctions were imposed against Libya after his refusal to allow extradiction of two suspects in the Lockerbie and Union de Transports Aériens bombings. In 1995 Khaddhafi faced an escalating campaign of violence by Islamic militants, the strongest challenge to his regime to date.

Khakass autonomous republic of central Russian Federation, in Krasnoyarsk territory
area 61,900 sq km/23,855 sq mi
capital Abakan
physical includes the Minusinsk River basin
industries coal and ore mining, timber, woodworking, sheep and goat farming
population (1992) 581,000
history an autonomous republic from 1991.

Khalistan projected independent Sikh state. See ◊Sikhism.

Khama Seretse 1921–1980. Botswanan politician, prime minister of Bechuanaland 1965, and first president of Botswana from 1966 until his death.

Son of the Bamangwato chief Sekoma II (died 1925), Khama studied law in Britain and married an Englishwoman, Ruth Williams. This marriage was strongly condemned by his uncle Tshekedi Khama, who had been regent during his minority, as contrary to tribal custom, and Seretse Khama was banished 1950. He returned 1956 on his renunciation of any claim to the chieftaincy.

khamsin hot southeasterly wind that blows from the Sahara desert over Egypt and parts of the Middle East from late March to May or June. It is called *sharav* in Israel.

Khan Imran Niazi 1952– . Pakistani cricketer. An all-rounder, he played cricket in England for Worcestershire and Sussex and made his test debut 1971. He played 88 test matches for Pakistan, of which 48 were as captain. In 1992 he captained his country to victory in the World Cup. He scored 17,771 first-class runs at an average of 36.87, and took 1,287 wickets at an average of 22.32. He retired 1992.

Khan Jahangir 1963– . Pakistani squash player. He won the world open championship a record six times 1981–85 and 1988, and was World Amateur champion 1979, 1983, and 1985. He announced his retirement 1993.

Khan was ten times British Open champion 1982–91. After losing to Geoff Hunt (Australia) in the final of the 1981 British Open, he did not lose again until Nov 1986 when he lost to Ross Norman (New Zealand) in the World Open final.

Khan, Aga Islamic leader, see ◊Aga Khan.

Khardung Pass road linking the Indian town of Leh with the high-altitude military outpost on the Siachen Glacier at an altitude of 5,401 m/17,730 ft in the Karakoram range, Kashmir. It is thought to be the highest road in the world.

Kharkov capital of the Kharkov region, E Ukraine, 400 km/250 mi E of Kiev; population (1992) 1,622,000. It is a railway junction and industrial city (engineering, tractors), close to the Donets Basin coalfield and Krivoy Rog iron mines. Kharkov was founded 1654 as a fortress town.

Khartoum capital and trading centre of Sudan, at the junction of the Blue and White Nile; population (1983) 561,000, and of Khartoum North, across the Blue Nile, 341,000. ◊Omdurman is also a suburb of Khartoum, giving the urban area a population of over 1.3 million.

Khartoum was founded 1830 by ◊Mehmet Ali. General ◊Gordon was killed at Khartoum by the Mahdist rebels 1885. A new city was built after the site was recaptured by British troops under Kitchener 1898.

Khazar member of a people of Turkish origin from the lower Volga basin of Central Asia, who formed a commercial link and a buffer state in the 7th–12th centuries between the Arabs and the Byzantine Empire, and later between the Byzantine Empire and the Baltic. Their ruler adopted Judaism as the state religion in the 8th century. In the 11th century, Slavonic and nomadic Turks invaded, and by the 13th century the Khazar empire had been absorbed by its neighbours. It has been suggested that the Khazars were the ancestors of some of the Jews living in E European countries and now throughout the world.

khedive title granted by the Turkish sultan to his Egyptian viceroy 1867, retained by succeeding rulers until 1914.

Khe Sanh in the Vietnam War, US Marine outpost near the Laotian border and just south of the demilitarized zone between North and South Vietnam. Garrisoned by 4,000 Marines, it was attacked unsuccessfully by 20,000 North Vietnamese troops 21 Jan–7 April 1968.

Khmer or ***Kmer*** the largest ethnic group in Cambodia, numbering about 7 million. Khmer minorities also live in E Thailand and S Vietnam. Living mainly in agricultural and fishing villages under a chief, Khmers practise Theravāda Buddhism and trace descent through both male and female lines. Traditionally, Khmer society was divided into six groups: the royal family, the Brahmans (who officiated at royal festivals), Buddhist monks, officials, commoners, and slaves. The Khmer language belongs to the Mon-Khmer family of Austro-Asiatic languages.

The Khmer empire, an early SE Asian civilization, was founded AD 616 and came under Indian cultural influence as part of the SE Asian kingdom of Funan. The earliest inscriptions in the Khmer language date from the 7th century AD. The Khmer empire reached its zenith in the 9th-13th centuries, with the building of the capital city and temple complex at Angkor. The Khmers were eventually pushed back by the Thais into the territory they occupy today. The anti-French nationalists of Cambodia adopted the name Khmer Republic 1971–75, and the name continues in use by the communist movement called the ◊Khmer Rouge.

Khmer Republic former name (1970–76) of ◊Cambodia.

Khmer Rouge communist movement in Cambodia (Kampuchea) formed in the 1960s. Controlling the country 1974–78, it was responsible for mass deportations and executions under the leadership of ◊Pol Pot. Since then it has conducted guerrilla warfare.

The Khmer Rouge formed the largest opposition group to the US-backed regime led by Lon Nol 1970–75. By 1974 they controlled the countryside, and in 1975 captured the capital, Phnom Penh. Initially former prime minister Prince ◊Sihanouk was installed as head of state, but internal disagreements led to the creation of the Pol Pot government 1976. From 1978, when Vietnam invaded the country, the Khmer Rouge conducted a guerrilla campaign against the Vietnamese forces. Pol Pot retired as military leader 1985 and was succeeded by the more moderate Khieu Samphan. After the withdrawal of Vietnamese forces 1989, the Khmer Rouge continued its warfare against the Vietnamese-backed government. A UN-brokered peace treaty 1991 between Cambodia's four warring factions gave the Khmer Rouge its share of representation in the ruling Supreme National Council, but failed to win a renunciation of the guerrillas' goal of regaining domination of Cambodia.

Khoikhoi (formerly ***Hottentot***) a people living in Namibia and the Cape Province of South Africa, and numbering about 30,000. Their language is related to San (spoken by the Kung) and belongs to the Khoisan family. Like the Kung, the Khoikhoi once inhabited a wider area, but were driven into the Kalahari Desert by invading Bantu peoples and Dutch colonists in the 18th century. They live as nomadic hunter-gatherers, in family groups, and have animist beliefs.

Khoisan the smallest group of languages in Africa. It includes fewer than 50 languages, spoken mainly by the people of the Kalahari Desert (including the Khoikhoi and Kung). Two languages from this group are spoken in Tanzania. The Khoisan languages are known for their click consonants (clicking sounds made with the tongue, which function as consonants).

Khomeini Ayatollah Ruhollah 1900–1989. Iranian Shi'ite Muslim leader. Exiled for opposition to Shah Pahlavi from 1964, he returned when the shah left the country 1979, and established a fundamentalist Islamic republic. His rule was marked by a protracted war with Iraq, and suppression of opposition within Iran, executing thousands of opponents.

Khorana Har Gobind 1922– . Indian-born US biochemist who in 1976 led the team that first synthesized a biologically active ◊gene. In 1968 he shared the Nobel Prize for Physiology or Medicine for research on the chemistry of the genetic code and its function in protein synthesis. Khorana's work provides much of the basis for gene therapy and biotechnology.

Khrushchev Nikita Sergeyevich 1894–1971. Soviet politician, secretary general of the Communist Party 1953–64, premier 1958–64. He emerged as leader from the power struggle following Stalin's death and was the first official to denounce Stalin, 1956. His de-Stalinization programme gave rise to revolts in Poland and Hungary 1956. Because of problems with the economy and foreign affairs,

'Whether you like it or not, history is on our side. We will bury you.'

NIKITA KHRUSHCHEV
Speech to Western diplomats in Moscow 18 Nov 1956

Khomeini Shi'ite Muslims in Tehran reach out to their leader Ayatollah Khomeini on his return from exile in Feb 1979. He had been out of Iran for 15 years, exiled for denouncing the Shah's westernization of the country. Now, with the Shah himself in exile, Khomeini was able to establish a fundamentalist Islamic republic. *Corbis*

After a dreary journey over the wild plains of the Ukraine, it breaks upon the traveller with all the glittering and gorgeous splendour of an Asiatic city.

On Kiev
J L Stephens *Incidents of Travel in the Russian and Turkish Empires*

including conflict with the USA in the ◊Cuban missile crisis 1962) and the personal feud with Mao Zedong that led to the Sino-Soviet split, he was ousted by Leonid Brezhnev and Alexei Kosygin. However, by 1965 his reputation was to some extent officially restored. In April 1989 his Feb 1956 'secret speech' against Stalin was officially published for the first time.

Born near Kursk, the son of a miner, Khrushchev fought in the post-Revolutionary civil war 1917–20, and in World War II organized the guerrilla defence of his native Ukraine.

Khufu lived c. 2550 BC. Egyptian king of Memphis, who built the largest of the pyramids, known to the Greeks as the pyramid of Cheops (the Greek form of Khufu).

Khulna capital of Khulna region, SW Bangladesh, situated close to the Ganges delta; population (1991) 545,800. Industry includes shipbuilding and textiles; it trades in jute, rice, salt, sugar, and oilseed.

Khuzestan province of SW Iran, which includes the chief Iranian oil resources; population (1991) 3,175,900. Cities include Ahvaz (capital) and the ports of Abadan and Khuninshahr. There have been calls for Sunni Muslim autonomy, under the name Arabistan.

Khwārizmī, al- Muhammad ibn-Mūsā c. 780–c. 850. Persian mathematician. The word 'algebra' comes from part of the title of his book (*al-jabr*), in which he introduced to the West the Hindu–Arabic decimal number system. He compiled astronomical tables and was responsible for introducing the concept of zero into Arab mathematics.

Khyber Pass pass 53 km/33 mi long through the mountain range that separates Pakistan from Afghanistan. The Khyber Pass was used by invaders of India. The present road was constructed by the British during the Afghan Wars.

Kiangsi alternative spelling of ◊Jiangxi, a province of China.

Kiangsu alternative spelling of ◊Jiangsu, a province of China.

kibbutz Israeli communal collective settlement with collective ownership of all property and earnings, collective organization of work and decision-making, and communal housing for children. A modified version, the *Moshav Shitufi*, is similar to the ◊collective farms that were typical of the USSR. Other Israeli cooperative rural settlements include the *Moshav Ovdim*, which has equal opportunity, and the similar but less strict *Moshav* settlement.

Kidd 'Captain' William c. 1645–1701. Scottish pirate. He spent his youth privateering for the British against the French off the North American coast, and in 1695 was given a royal commission to suppress piracy in the Indian Ocean. Instead, he joined a group of pirates in Madagascar. On his way to Boston, Massachusetts, he was arrested 1699, taken to England, and hanged. His execution marked the end of some 200 years of semi-official condoning of piracy by the British government.

Kidderminster market town in the West Midlands of England, on the river Stour; population (1991) 54,600. It has a carpet industry dating from about 1735. Other industries include woollen and worsted yarn, textile machinery, sugar beet, tinplating, and chemicals.

kidney in vertebrates, one of a pair of organs responsible for fluid regulation, excretion of waste products, and maintaining the ionic composition of the blood. The kidneys are situated on the rear wall of the abdomen. Each one consists of a number of long tubules; the outer parts filter the aqueous components of blood, and the inner parts selectively reabsorb vital salts, leaving waste products in the remaining fluid (urine), which is passed through the ureter to the bladder.

The action of the kidneys is vital, although if one is removed, the other enlarges to take over its function. A patient with two defective kidneys may continue near-normal life with the aid of a kidney machine or continuous ambulatory peritoneal ◊dialysis (CAPD); or a kidney transplant may be recommended.

kidney machine medical equipment used in ◊dialysis.

In all Africa there can scarcely be a lusher, greener spot than the slopes of this enormous mountain.

On Kilimanjaro
Elspeth Huxley *The Sorcerer's Apprentice*

Kiel Baltic port (fishing, shipbuilding, electronics, engineering) in Germany; capital of Schleswig-Holstein; population (1993) 249,100. Kiel Week in June is a yachting meeting.

Kiel Canal formerly ***Kaiser Wilhelm Canal*** waterway 98.7 km/61 mi long that connects the Baltic with the North Sea. Built by Germany in the years before World War I, the canal allowed the German navy to move from Baltic bases to the open sea without travelling through international waters, although it was also of value to commercial traffic. It was declared an international waterway by the Versailles Treaty 1919.

Kierkegaard Søren Aabye 1813–1855. Danish philosopher and theologian, often considered to be the founder of ◊existentialism. He argued that no system of thought could explain the unique experience of the individual. He defended Christianity, suggesting that God cannot be known through reason, but only through a 'leap of faith'. His chief works are *Enten-Eller/Either-Or* 1843 and *Begrebet Angest/Concept of Dread* 1844.

Kiev capital of Ukraine, industrial centre (chemicals, clothing, leatherwork), on the confluence of the Desna and Dnieper rivers; population (1992) 2,643,000. It was the capital of Russia in the Middle Ages.

features St Sophia cathedral (11th century) and Kiev-Pechersky Monastery (both now museums) survive, and also remains of the Golden Gate, an arched entrance to the old walled city, built 1037. The gate is surmounted by the small Church of the Annunciation. The Kiev ballet and opera are renowned.

history Kiev was founded in the 5th century by ◊Vikings. The Slav domination of Russia began with the rise of Kiev, the 'mother of Russian cities'; Kiev replaced ◊Novgorod as the capital of Russia 882 and was the original centre of the Orthodox Christian faith 988. It declined in importance in the 12th century and the capital was moved to Vladimir 1169. During World War II, Kiev was the third-largest city of the USSR and was occupied by Germany 1941–43.

Kigali capital of Rwanda, central Africa, 80 km/50 mi E of Lake Kivu; population (1993) 234,500. Products include coffee, hides, shoes, paints, and varnishes; there is tin mining. The city was under German colonial administration from 1895, and under Belgium 1919–62, when it became capital of independent Rwanda.

Kikuyu the dominant ethnic group in Kenya, numbering about 3 million. The Kikuyu are primarily cultivators, although many are highly educated and have entered the professions. Their language belongs to the Bantu branch of the Niger-Congo family.

Up to 2,000 were killed and 50,000 made homeless 1991–94 in attacks by Masai and Kalenjin peoples attempting to oust them from the Rift Valley.

Kildare county of the Republic of Ireland, in the province of Leinster; county town Naas; area 1,690 sq km/652 sq mi; population (1991) 122,516. It is wet and boggy in the north and includes part of the Bog of Allen; the village of Maynooth, with a training college for Roman Catholic priests; and the Curragh, a plain that is the site of the national stud and headquarters of Irish horse racing at Tully. Products include oats, barley, potatoes, and cattle.

Kilimanjaro volcano in Tanzania, the highest mountain in Africa, 5,900 m/19,364 ft.

Kilkenny county of the Republic of Ireland, in the province of Leinster; county town Kilkenny; area 2,060 sq km/795 sq mi; population (1991) 73,600. It has the rivers Nore, Suir, and Barrow. Industries include coal mining, clothing, footwear, brewing, and agricultural activities such as cattle rearing and dairy farming.

killer whale or ***orca*** toothed whale *Orcinus orca* of the dolphin family, found in all seas of the world. It is black on top, white below, and grows up to 9 m/30 ft long. It is the only whale that has been observed to prey on other whales, as well as on seals and seabirds.

Killiecrankie, Battle of in British history, during the first ◊Jacobite uprising, defeat on 7 May 1689 of General Mackay (for William of Orange) by John Graham of ◊Claverhouse, a supporter of James II, at Killiecrankie, Scotland. Despite the victory, Claverhouse was killed and the revolt soon petered out; the remaining forces were routed on 21 Aug.

Killy Jean-Claude 1943– . French skier. He won all three gold medals (slalom, giant slalom, and downhill) at the 1968 Winter Olympics in Grenoble. The first World Cup winner 1967, he retained the title 1968 and also won three world titles.

Kilmainham Treaty in Irish history, an informal secret agreement in April 1882 that secured the release of the nationalist Charles ◊Parnell from Kilmainham jail, Dublin, where he had been imprisoned for six months for supporting Irish tenant farmers who had joined the Land League's campaign for agricultural reform.

The British government realized that Parnell could quell violence more easily out of prison than in it. In return for his release, he agreed to accept the Land Act of 1861. The Kilmainham Treaty marked a change in British policy in Ireland from confrontation to cooperation, with the government attempting to conciliate landowners and their tenants, who were refusing to pay rent. This strategy was subsequently threatened by the ◊Phoenix Park Murders. ▷ *See feature on pp. 550–551.*

Kilmarnock town and administrative headquarters of East Ayrshire, Scotland, 32 km/20 mi SW of Glasgow; population (1991) 44,300. Industries include carpets, agricultural machinery, woollens, lace, footwear, earthenware, and whisky; Robert Burns's first book of poems was published here 1786.

kiln high-temperature furnace used commercially for drying timber, roasting metal ores, or for making cement, bricks, and pottery. Oil- or gas-fired kilns are used to bake ceramics at up to 1,760°C/3,200°F; electric kilns do not generally reach such high temperatures.

kilobyte (K or KB) in computing, a unit of memory equal to 1,024 ◊bytes. It is sometimes used, less precisely, to mean 1,000 bytes. In the metric system, the prefix 'kilo-' denotes multiplication by 1,000 (as in kilometre, a unit equal to 1,000 metres). However, computer memory size is based on the ◊binary number system, and the most convenient binary equivalent of 1,000 is 2^{10}, or 1,024.

kilogram SI unit (symbol kg) of mass equal to 1,000 grams (2.24 lb). It is defined as a mass equal to that of the international prototype, a platinum-iridium cylinder held at the International Bureau of Weights and Measures in Sèvres, France.

kilometre unit of length (symbol km) equal to 1,000 metres, equivalent to 3,280.89 ft or 0.6214 (about ⅝) of a mile.

kilowatt unit (symbol kW) of power equal to 1,000 watts or about 1.34 horsepower.

kilowatt-hour commercial unit of electrical energy (symbol kWh), defined as the work done by a power of 1,000 watts in one hour and equal to 3,600 joules. It is used to calculate the cost of electrical energy taken from the domestic supply.

Kimberley diamond-mining capital city of Northern Cape Province, South Africa, 153 km/95 mi NW of Bloemfontein; population (1991) 167,100. Its mines have been controlled by De Beers Consolidated Mines since 1887.

kimberlite an igneous rock that is ultramafic (containing very little silica); a type of alkaline ◊peridotite with a porphyritic texture (larger crystals in a fine-grained matrix), containing mica in addition to olivine and other minerals. Kimberlite represents the world's principal source of diamonds.

Kimberlite is found in carrot-shaped pipelike ◊intrusions called diatremes, where mobile material from very deep in the Earth's crust has forced itself upwards, expanding in its ascent. The material, brought upwards from near the boundary between crust and mantle, often altered and fragmented, includes diamonds. Diatremes are found principally near Kimberley, South Africa, from which the name of the rock is derived, and in the Yakut area of Siberia, Russia.

Kim Il Sung 1912–1994. North Korean communist politician and marshal. He became prime minister 1948 and led North Korea in the ◊Korean War 1950–53. He became president 1972, retaining the presidency of the Communist Workers' party. He liked to be known as the 'Great Leader' and campaigned constantly for the reunification of Korea. His son Kim Jong Il, known as the 'Dear Leader', succeeded him.

Kim Jong Il 1942– . North Korean communist politician, national leader from 1994, when he succeeded his father, ◊Kim Il Sung. Despite his official designation 'Dear Leader', he lacked his father's charisma and did not automatically inherit the public adulation accorded to him.

Kim Jong Il held a succession of senior party posts from the early 1960s. He was a member of the politburo from 1974 and its controlling inner presidium from 1980 and, although he had received no military training, was made commander in chief of the armed forces in 1991. The belief that he masterminded terrorist activities in the 1970s and 1980s made the West apprehensive about the succession.

kimono traditional Japanese costume. Worn in the Heian period (more than 1,000 years ago), it is still used by women for formal wear and informally by men.

For the finest kimonos a rectangular piece of silk (about 11 m/36 ft × 0.5 m/1.5 ft) is cut into seven pieces for tailoring. The design (which must match perfectly over the seams and for which flowers are the usual motif) is then painted by hand, using various processes, and may be enhanced by embroidery or gilding. The accompanying ***obi***, or sash, about 4 m/13 ft × 10 cm/4 in for men and wider for women, is also embroidered.

Kim Young Sam 1927– . South Korean democratic politician, president from 1993. A member of the National Assembly from 1954 and president of the New Democratic Party (NDP) from 1974, he lost his seat and was later placed under house arrest because of his opposition to President Park Chung Hee. In 1983 he led a prodemocracy hunger strike but in 1987 failed to defeat Roh Tae-woo in the presidential election. In 1990 he merged the NDP with the ruling party to form the Democratic Liberal Party (DLP), now known as the New Korean Party. He won the 1992 presidential election, assuming office Feb 1993. As president, he encouraged greater political openness, some deregulation of the economy, and a globalization (*segyehwa*) initiative.

kinesis (plural ***kineses***) in biology, a nondirectional movement in response to a stimulus; for example, woodlice move faster in drier surroundings. Taxis is a similar pattern of behaviour, but there the response is directional.

kinetic art in the visual arts, a work of art (usually sculpture) incorporating real or apparent movement. The term, coined in the 1920s by Naum ◊Gabo and Antoine Pevsner (1886–1962), encompasses Alexander ◊Calder's celebrated 1930s mobiles as well as the mechanical kinetic works of Swiss sculptor Jean Tinguely (1925–), which were programmed to destroy themselves (thus also pertaining to ◊performance art).

kinetic energy the energy of a body resulting from motion. It is contrasted with ◊potential energy.

kinetics the branch of chemistry that investigates the rates of chemical reactions.

kinetics branch of ◊dynamics dealing with the action of forces producing or changing the motion of a body; kinematics deals with motion without reference to force or mass.

kinetic theory theory describing the physical properties of matter in terms of the behaviour – principally movement – of its component atoms or molecules. The temperature of a substance is dependent on the velocity of movement of its constituent particles, increased temperature being accompanied by increased movement. A gas consists of rapidly moving atoms or molecules and, according to kinetic theory, it is their continual impact on the walls of the containing vessel that accounts for the pressure of the gas. The slowing of molecular motion as temperature falls, according to kinetic theory, accounts for the physical properties of liquids and solids, culminating in the concept of no molecular motion at ◊absolute zero (0K/−273°C).

By making various assumptions about the nature of gas molecules, it is possible to derive from the kinetic theory the various gas laws (such as ◊Avogadro's hypothesis, ◊Boyle's law, and ◊Charles's law).

King US blues singer and guitarist B B King performing at Alexandra Palace, London, in 1979. In the early part of his career he was admired mainly in blues circles, but from the 1960s he became known to a much wider audience. He first toured Europe in 1968. *Corbis*

King B B (Riley) 1925– . US blues guitarist, singer, and songwriter. One of the most influential electric-guitar players, he became an international star in the 1960s. His albums include *Blues Is King* 1967, *Lucille Talks Back* 1975, and *Blues 'n' Jazz* 1983.

King Billie Jean, (born Moffitt) 1943– . US tennis player. She won a record 20 Wimbledon titles 1961–79 and 39 Grand Slam titles. She won the Wimbledon singles title six times, the US Open singles title four times, the French Open once, and the Australian Open once.

King Martin Luther Jr 1929–1968. US civil-rights campaigner, black leader, and Baptist minister. He first came to national attention as leader of the ◊Montgomery, Alabama, bus boycott 1955, and was one of the organizers of the march of 200,000 people on Washington DC 1963 to demand racial equality. An advocate of nonviolence, he was awarded the Nobel Peace Prize 1964. He was assassinated in Memphis, Tennessee; James Earl Ray (1928–) was convicted of the murder, but there is little evidence to suggest that he committed the crime.

Born in Atlanta, Georgia, son of a Baptist minister, King founded the Southern Christian Leadership Conference 1957. A brilliant and moving speaker, he was the symbol of, and leading figure in, the campaign for integration and equal rights in the late 1950s and early 1960s. In the mid-1960s his moderate approach was criticized by black militants. He was the target of intensive investigation by the federal authorities, chiefly the FBI under J Edgar ◊Hoover. His personal life was scrutinized and criticized by those opposed to his policies.

'Injustice anywhere is a threat to justice everywhere.'

Martin Luther King
Letter from Birmingham jail, Alabama, 16 April 1963

King W(illiam) L(yon) Mackenzie 1874–1950. Canadian Liberal prime minister 1921–26, 1926–30, and 1935–48. He maintained the unity of the English- and French-speaking populations, and was instrumental in establishing equal status for Canada with Britain.

king crab or ***horseshoe crab*** marine arthropod, class Arachnida, subclass Xiphosura, which lives on the Atlantic coast of North America, and the coasts of Asia. The upper side of the body is entirely covered with a rounded shell, and it has a long spinelike tail. It is up to 60 cm/2 ft long. It is unable to swim, and lays its eggs in the sand at the high-water mark.

kingdom the primary division in biological ◊classification. At one time, only two kingdoms were recognized: animals and plants. Today most biologists prefer a five-kingdom system, even though it still involves grouping together organisms that are probably unrelated. One widely accepted scheme is as follows: Kingdom Animalia (all multicellular animals); Kingdom Plantae (all plants, including seaweeds and other algae, except blue-green); Kingdom Fungi (all fungi, including the unicellular yeasts, but not slime moulds); Kingdom Protista or Protoctista (protozoa, diatoms, dinoflagellates, slime moulds, and various other lower organisms with eukaryotic cells); and Kingdom Monera (all prokaryotes – the bacteria and cyanobacteria, or ◊blue-green algae). The first four of these kingdoms make up the eukaryotes.

When only two kingdoms were recognized, any organism with a rigid cell wall was a plant, and so bacteria and fungi were considered plants, despite their many differences. Other organisms, such as the photosynthetic flagellates (euglenoids), were claimed by both kingdoms. The unsatisfactory nature of the two-kingdom system became evident during the 19th century, and the biologist Ernst ◊Haeckel was among the first to try to reform it. High-power microscopes have revealed more about the structure of cells; it has become clear that there is a fundamental difference between cells without a nucleus (◊prokaryotes) and those with a nucleus (◊eukaryotes). However, these differences are larger than those between animals and higher plants, and are unsuitable for use as kingdoms. At present there is no agreement on how many kingdoms there are in the natural world.

kingfisher heavy-billed bird of the worldwide family Alcedinidae, order Coraciiformes, found near streams, ponds, and coastal areas. The head is exceptionally large, and the long angular beak is keeled; the tail and wings are relatively short, and the legs very short, with short toes. Kingfishers plunge-dive for fish and aquatic insects. The nest is usually a burrow in a riverbank.There are 88 species, the largest being the Australian ◊kookaburra. The Alcedinidae are sometimes divided into the subfamilies Daceloninae, Alcedininae, and Cerylinae.

The common European kingfisher *Alcedo atthis* has greenish-blue plumage, with a bright blue head and tail, and white patches at the side of the neck; the bill is black with an orange-tinted base, and it is a bright chestnut colour below with red legs. It is generally found by rivers, canals, and streams, sitting on a branch overhanging the water, waiting to dive onto fish, which form its principal diet; having sighted the prey it dives perpendicularly, with folded wings, and returning with the morsel, dashes it against a stone or tree-branch before swallowing it. Kingfishers feed also on insects, and on small crustaceans. Their eggs are usually deposited in a chamber at the end of a tunnel that the breeding pair excavate in a suitable bank by a stream.

Kingsley Ben (Krishna Banji) 1943– . British film actor of Indian descent. He usually plays character parts. He played the title role of *Gandhi* 1982, for which he won an Academy Award, and appeared in *Betrayal* 1982, *Testimony* 1987, and *Pascali's Island* 1988.

Kingsley Charles 1819–1875. English author. A rector, he was known as the 'Chartist clergyman' because of such social novels as *Yeast* 1848 and *Alton Locke* 1850. His historical novels include

kingfisher The kingfisher, with its brilliantly coloured plumage and daggerlike beak, is unmistakeable. It is found in Europe, N Africa to Asia, New Guinea, and the Solomon Islands. When hunting, it perches on a branch overhanging a stream or lake, watching for prey, or it flies low over the water, perhaps hovering for a few seconds before diving.

If Margaret Thatcher wins on Thursday, I warn you not to be ordinary, I warn you not to be young, I warn you not to fall ill, and I warn you not to grow old.

NEIL KINNOCK
Speech at Bridgend, Wales, 7 June 1983

Westward Ho! 1855 and *Hereward the Wake* 1866. He also wrote, for children, *The Water Babies* 1863. He was deeply interested in social questions, and threw himself wholeheartedly into the schemes of social relief which were supported under the name of Christian Socialism, writing many tracts and articles as 'Parson Lot'.

King's Lynn port and market town at the mouth of the Great Ouse River, Norfolk, E England; population (1991) 41,300. A thriving port in medieval times, it was called Lynn until its name was changed by Henry VIII. Industries include food canning, sugar-beet refining, brewing, fishing, and engineering.

Kingston capital and principal port of Jamaica, West Indies, the cultural and commercial centre of the island; population (1991) 587,800 (metropolitan area). Founded 1693, Kingston became the capital of Jamaica 1872.

Kingston upon Hull official name of ◊Hull, a city and, from 1996, a unitary authority of England, (*see United Kingdom map*).

Kingston upon Thames outer borough of SW Greater London; administrative headquarters of Surrey

features seven Saxon kings, from Edward the Elder in 900 to Ethelred the Unready in 979, were crowned at Kingston, their coronation stone is preserved here, set with seven silver pennies; oldest of the three Royal Boroughs of England, with ancient right to elect own High Steward and Recorder; Kingston Grammar School, founded by Elizabeth I 1561

industries aviation, chemicals, engineering, plastics, printing, refrigeration

population (1991) 133,000.

Kingstown capital and principal port of St Vincent and the Grenadines, West Indies, in the SW of the island of St Vincent; population (1991) 26,200.

kinkajou Central and South American carnivore *Potos flavus* of the raccoon family. Yellowish-brown, with a rounded face and slim body, the kinkajou grows to 55 cm/1.8 ft with a 50 cm/1.6 ft tail, and has short legs with sharp claws. It spends its time in trees and has a prehensile tail. It feeds largely on fruit.

Kinnock Neil Gordon 1942– . British Labour politician, party leader 1983–92. Born and educated in Wales, he was elected to represent a Welsh constituency in Parliament 1970 (Islwyn from 1983). He was further left than prime ministers Wilson and Callaghan, but as party leader (in succession to Michael Foot) adopted a moderate position, initiating a major policy review 1988–89. He resigned as party leader after Labour's defeat in the 1992 general election. In 1994 he left parliament to become a European commissioner and was given the transport portfolio.

kin selection in biology, the idea that ◊altruism shown to genetic relatives can be worthwhile, because those relatives share some genes with the individual that is behaving altruistically, and may continue to reproduce. Alarm-calling in response to predators is an example of a behaviour that may have evolved through kin selection: relatives that are warned of danger can escape and continue to breed, even if the alarm caller is caught.

Kinshasa formerly ***Léopoldville*** capital of the Democratic Republic of Congo on the River Congo/Zaïre, 400 km/250 mi inland from the port of Matadi; population (1991 est) 3,804,000. Industries include chemicals, textiles, engineering, food processing, and furniture. It was founded by the explorer Henry Stanley 1887.

kinship in anthropology, human relationship based on blood or marriage, and sanctified by law and custom. Kinship forms the basis for such social groupings as the family, clan, or tribe.

Most human societies have evolved strict social rules, customs, and taboos regarding kinship and sexual behaviour (such as the prohibition of incest), marriage, and inheritance.

The great greygreen, greasy Limpopo River, all set about with fever trees.

RUDYARD KIPLING
'The Elephant's Child', *Just-So Stories*

Kipling (Joseph) Rudyard 1865–1936. English writer, born in India. *Plain Tales from the Hills* 1888, about Anglo-Indian society, contains the earliest of his masterly short stories. His books for children, including *The Jungle Book* 1894–95, *Just So Stories* 1902, *Puck of Pook's Hill* 1906, and the picaresque novel *Kim* 1901, reveal his imaginative identification with the exotic. Poems such as 'Danny Deever', 'Gunga Din', and 'If–' express an empathy with common experience, which contributed to his great popularity, together with a vivid sense of 'Englishness' (sometimes denigrated as a kind of jingoist imperialism). His work is increasingly valued for its complex characterization and subtle moral viewpoints. Nobel Prize for Literature 1907.

Kipling Starting his career at the age of 17, as a reporter on the *Civil and Military Gazette* in Lahore, India, Rudyard Kipling became a master of many literary forms. Although his poems are nowadays criticized for their somewhat jingoistic tone, his short stories remain popular as masterpieces of the genre. *Corbis*

Born in Bombay, Kipling was educated at the United Services College at Westward Ho!, Devon, England, which provided the background for *Stalky and Co* 1899. At the age of 17 he returned to India as sub-editor of the *Lahore Civil and Military Gazette*, being promoted to *The Pioneer of Allahabad* 1887; during these years he wrote the stories which appeared in *Plain Tales from the Hills*, *Soldiers Three* 1890, and *Wee Willie Winkie* 1890. Returning to London 1889 he published the novel *The Light that Failed* 1890 and *Barrack-Room Ballads* 1892. He lived largely in the USA 1892–99, where he produced the two *Jungle Books* and *Captains Courageous* 1897. Settling in Sussex, SE England, he published *Kim*, usually regarded as his greatest work of fiction; the *Just So Stories*; *Puck of Pook's Hill*; and *Rewards and Fairies* 1910.

Kirchhoff Gustav Robert 1824–1887. German physicist who with R W von ◊Bunsen developed spectroscopic analysis in the 1850s and showed that all elements, heated to incandescence, have their individual spectra.

Kirchhoff's laws two laws governing electric circuits devised by the German physicist Gustav Kirchhoff. Kirchhoff's first law states that the total current entering any junction in a circuit is the same as the total current leaving it. This is an expression of the conservation of electric charge. Kirchhoff's second law states that the sum of the potential drops across each resistance in any closed loop in a circuit is equal to the total electromotive force acting in that loop. The laws are equally applicable to DC and AC circuits.

Kirchner Ernst Ludwig 1880–1938. German artist. He was a leading member of the Expressionist *die ◊Brücke* group in Dresden from 1905 and in Berlin from 1911. In Berlin he painted city scenes and portraits, using lurid colours and bold diagonal paint strokes recalling woodcut technique; his *Self-Portrait with Model* 1909 (Kunsthalle, Hamburg) is characteristic of his earlier style. In time his colours became more subdued, his works, particularly his landscapes, more sedate.

Kirghiz a pastoral people numbering approximately 1.5 million. They inhabit the central Asian region bounded by the Hindu Kush, the Himalayas, and the Tian Shan mountains. The Kirghiz are Sunni Muslims, and their Turkic language belongs to the Altaic family.

The Kirghiz live in Tajikistan, Uzbekistan, Kyrgyzstan, China (Xinjiang), and Afghanistan (Wakhan corridor). The most isolated group, because of its geographical situation and its international border problems, is found in Afghanistan. The highest political authority is traditionally entitled khan. During the winter the Kirghiz live in individual family yurts (tents made of felt). In summer they come together in larger settlements of up to 20 yurts. They herd sheep, goats, and yaks, and use Bactrian camels for transporting their possessions.

Kirghizia alternative form of ◊Kyrgyzstan, a country in central Asia.

Kiribati republic in the W central Pacific Ocean, comprising three groups of coral atolls: the 16 Gilbert Islands, 8 uninhabited Phoenix Islands, 8 of the 11 Line Islands, and the volcanic island of Banaba. *See country box opposite.*

Kirkwall administrative headquarters and port of the Orkney Islands, Scotland, on the north coast of the largest island, Mainland; population (1991) 6,700. The Norse cathedral of St Magnus dates from 1137.

Kirov Sergei Mironovich 1886–1934. Russian Bolshevik leader who joined the party 1904 and played a prominent part in the 1918–20 civil war. As one of ◊Stalin's closest associates, he became first secretary of the Leningrad Communist Party. His assassination, possibly engineered by Stalin, led to the political trials held during the next four years as part of the ◊purge.

Kirov Ballet Russian ballet company based in St Petersburg, founded 1738. Originally called the Imperial Ballet, it was renamed 1935 (after an assassinated Communist Party leader). The Kirov dancers are renowned for their cool purity of line, lyrical mobility, and gravity-defying jumps; the corps de ballet is famed for its precision and musicality. The classical ballets of Marius ◊Petipa make up the backbone of the company's repertory and many of the world's most acclaimed classical dancers, such as Anna ◊Pavlova, Rudolf ◊Nureyev, and Mikhail ◊Baryshnikov, are graduates of the company. Oleg Vinogradov (1937–) has been its artistic director since 1972.

Kissinger Henry Alfred 1923– . German-born US diplomat. After a brilliant academic career at Harvard University, he was appointed national security adviser 1969 by President Nixon, and was secretary of state 1973–77. His missions to the USSR and China improved US relations with both countries.

In 1973 he shared the Nobel Peace Prize with Le Duc Tho, the North Vietnamese Politburo member, for his role in the Vietnamese peace negotiations, and he took part in Arab-Israeli peace negotiations 1973–75. In 1983, President Reagan appointed him to head a bipartisan commission on Central America. He was widely regarded as the most powerful member of Nixon's administration.

kiss of life (artificial ventilation) in first aid, another name for ◊artificial respiration.

Kiswahili another name for the ◊Swahili language.

Kitaj R(onald) B(rooks) 1932– . US painter and graphic artist, active in Britain. His work is mainly figurative, and employs a wide range of allusions to art, history, and literature. *The Autumn of Central Paris (After Walter Benjamin)* 1972–74 is a typical work. His distinctive use of colour was in part inspired by studies of the Impressionist painter Degas.

Kitakyushu industrial port city (coal, steel, chemicals, cotton thread, plate glass, alcohol) in Japan, on the Hibiki Sea, N Kyushu Island, formed 1963 by the amalgamation of Moji, Kokura, Tobata, Yawata, and Wakamatsu; population (1994) 1,015,000. A tunnel (1942) links it with Honshu.

Kitasato Shibasaburō 1852–1931. Japanese bacteriologist who discovered the plague bacillus while investigating an outbreak of plague in Hong Kong.

Kitchener British commander of forces and imperialist governor Lord Kitchener. As war minister during World War I, he was a source of inspiration to British soldiers, driving a successful recruitment campaign with the slogan 'Your country needs YOU'. *Image Select (UK) Ltd*

He was the first to grow the tetanus bacillus in pure culture. He and German bacteriologist Emil von ◊Behring discovered that increasing nonlethal doses of tetanus toxin give immunity to the disease.

Kitchener city in SW Ontario, Canada; population (1986) 151,000, metropolitan area (with Waterloo) 311,000. Manufacturing includes agricultural machinery and tyres. Settled by Germans from Pennsylvania in the 1800s, it was known as Berlin until 1916.

Kitchener Horatio Herbert, 1st Earl Kitchener of Khartoum 1850–1916. British soldier and administrator. He defeated the Sudanese dervishes at Omdurman 1898 and reoccupied Khartoum. In South Africa, he was Chief of Staff 1900–02 during the Boer War, and commanded the forces in India 1902–09. He was appointed war minister on the outbreak of World War I, and drowned when his ship was sunk on the way to Russia.

Kitchener was born in County Kerry, Ireland. He was commissioned 1871, and transferred to the Egyptian army 1882. Promoted to commander in chief 1892, he forced a French expedition to withdraw in the ◊Fashoda Incident. During the South African War he acted as Lord Roberts's Chief of Staff. He conducted war by scorched-earth policy and created the earliest concentration camps for civilians. Subsequently he commanded the forces in India and acted as British agent in Egypt, and in 1914 received an earldom. As British secretary of state for war from 1914, he modernized the British forces. He was one of the first to appreciate that the war would not be 'over by Christmas' and planned for a three-year war for which he began raising new armies. He bears some responsibility for the failure of the ◊Gallipoli campaign, having initially refused any troops for the venture, and from then on his influence declined.

kitchen-sink painters loose-knit group of British painters, active in the late 1940s and early 1950s. They depicted drab, everyday scenes with an aggressive technique and often brilliant, 'crude' colour. The best known artists of the group were John Bratby (1928–1992), Derrick Greaves (1927–), Edward Middleditch (1923–1987), and Jack Smith (1928–). The group disbanded after a few years but interest in them revived in the 1990s.

kite one of about 20 birds of prey in the family Accipitridae, order Falconiformes, found in all parts of the world. Kites have long, pointed wings and, usually, a forked tail.

The red kite *Milvus milvus*, found in Europe, has a forked tail and narrow wings, and is about 60 cm/2 ft long. Its general colour is reddish-brown, with tail feathers of a light red, barred with brown; the bill is black and strongly curved. The kite feeds on small birds, fishes, small mammals, carrion, and sometimes insects. Its nest, which is formed largely of rags and twigs, is generally placed in the cleft of a tree. The darker and slightly smaller black kite *M. migrans* is found over most of the Old World. It is a scavenger as well as a hunter.

kitsch (German 'trash') in the arts, anything that claims to have an aesthetic purpose but is tawdry and tasteless. It usually applies to cheap sentimental works produced for the mass market, such as those found in souvenir shops and chain stores, but it is also used for any art that is considered in bad taste.

In the 1960s Pop art began to explore the potential of kitsch, and since the 1970s pop culture and various strands of Post-Modernism have drawn heavily on it. The US artist Jeff Koons (1955–) employs kitsch extensively.

Kitt Peak National Observatory observatory in the Quinlan Mountains near Tucson, Arizona, USA, operated by AURA (Association of Universities for Research into Astronomy). Its main telescopes are the 4-m/158-in Mayall reflector, opened 1973, and the McMath Solar Telescope, opened 1962, the world's largest of its type.

kiwi The little spotted kiwi is one of three species of kiwi found in New Zealand. Kiwis have a good sense of smell – rare among birds – which is used to locate worms for food. The nostrils are at the tip of the pointed bill.

Kitwe commercial centre for the Zambian copperbelt; population (1990) 338,000. To the S are Zambia's emerald mines.

kiwi flightless bird *Apteryx australis*, family Apterygidae, the only family in the order Apterygiformes, found only in New Zealand. It has long, hairlike brown plumage, minute wings and tail, and a very long beak with nostrils at the tip. It is nocturnal and insectivorous. It lays two white eggs, each weighing up to 450 g/15.75 oz.

All kiwi species have declined since European settlement of New Zealand, and the little spotted kiwi is most at risk. It survives only on one small island reservation, which was stocked with birds from the mainland.

kiwi fruit or ***Chinese gooseberry*** fruit of a vine-like plant *Actinidithia chinensis*, family Actinidiaceae, commercially grown on a large scale in New Zealand. Kiwi fruits are egg-sized, oval, and of similar flavour to a gooseberry, with a fuzzy brown skin.

Klaipeda formerly ***Memel*** port in Lithuania, on the Baltic coast at the mouth of the river Dange; population (1995) 203,000. Industries include shipbuilding and iron foundries; it trades in timber, grain, and fish. It was founded on the site of a local fortress 1252 as the castle of Memelburg by the Teutonic Knights, joined the ◊Hanseatic League soon after, and has changed hands among Sweden, Russia, and Germany. Lithuania annexed Klaipeda 1923, and after German occupation 1939–45 it was restored to Soviet Lithuania 1945–91.

Klammer Franz 1953– . Austrian skier. He won a record 35 World Cup downhill races between 1974 and 1985. Olympic gold medallist 1976. He was the combined world champion 1974, and the World Cup downhill champion 1975–78 and 1983.

KIRIBATI

Republic of (formerly part of the Gilbert and Ellice Islands)

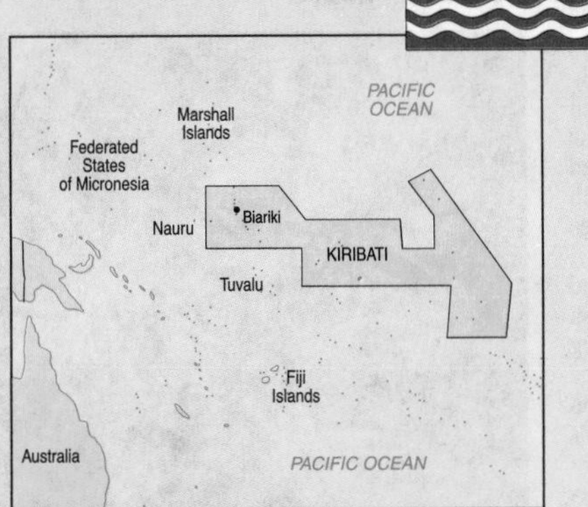

national name *Ribaberikin Kiribati*
area 717 sq km/277 sq mi
capital (and port) Bairiki (on Tarawa Atoll)
major ports Betio (on Tarawa)
physical features comprises 33 Pacific coral islands: the Kiribati (Gilbert), Rawaki (Phoenix), Banaba (Ocean Island), and three of the Line Islands including Kiritimati (Christmas Island); island groups crossed by equator and International Date Line
head of state and government Teburoro Tito from 1994
political system liberal democracy
administrative divisions seven districts
political parties Maneaban Te Mauri (MTM), dominant faction; National Progressive Party (NPP), former governing faction 1979–94
population 80,000 (1996 est)
population growth rate 1.7% (1990–95)
ethnic distribution predominantly Micronesian, with a Polynesian minority; also European and Chinese minorities
literacy rate 90% (1985)
language English (official), Gilbertese
religions Roman Catholic, Protestant (Congregationalist)
currency Australian dollar
GDP (US $) 68 million (1995)
growth rate 2.5% (1992)
exports copra, fish

HISTORY
1st millenium BC Settled by Austronesian-speaking peoples.
1606 Visited by Spanish explorers.
late 18th C Visited by British naval officers.
1857 Christian mission established.
1892 Gilbert (Kiribati) and Ellice (Tuvalu) Islands proclaimed a British protectorate.
1916–39 Uninhabited Phoenix Islands, Christmas Island, Ocean Island, and Line Island (Banaba) added to colony.
1942–43 Occupied by Japanese, it was the scene of fierce fighting with US troops.
later 1950s UK tested nuclear weapons on Christmas Island (Kiritimati).
1958 Christmas Island transferred to Australia.
1963 Legislative council established.
1974 Legislative council was replaced by an elected House of Assembly.
1975 The mainly Melanesian-populated Ellice Islands separated to become Tuvalu.
1977 The predominantly Micronesian-populated Gilbert Islands granted internal self-government.
1979 Independence achieved within the Commonwealth, as the Republic of Kiribati, with Ieremia Tabai as president.
1985 Kiribati's first political party, the opposition Christian Democrats, formed.
1991 Tabai re-elected but not allowed under constitution to serve further term; Teatao Teannaki won run-off presidential election.
1994 Government resigned, after losing vote of confidence. Ruling National Progressive Party (NPP) defeated in general election. Teburoro Tito elected president.

SEE ALSO Australasia–Oceania; Tuvalu

'Art does not reproduce the visible; rather, it makes visible.'

PAUL KLEE
Creative Credo 1918

Klaproth Martin Heinrich 1743–1817. German chemist who first identified the elements uranium and zirconium, in 1789, and was the second person to isolate titanium, chromium, and cerium. He was a pioneer of analytical chemistry.

Klaus Václav 1941– . Czech politician and economist, prime minister of the Czech Republic from 1993. Prior to the break-up of Czechoslovakia, he served in the government of Václav Havel and was chair of Civic Forum from 1990, breaking away to form the right-of-centre Civic Democratic Party (CDP) 1991. When the new independent republic was created, Jan 1993, Klaus became its first prime minister.

Klee Paul 1879–1940. Swiss painter and graphic artist. He was one of the most original and prolific artists of the 20th century. Endlessly inventive and playful, and suggesting a childlike innocence, his works are an exploration of the potential of line, plane, and colour. *Twittering Machine* 1922 (Museum of Modern Art, New York) is typical.

Klee studied in Munich and absorbed a variety of influences from painters old and modern (Blake, Goya, Hans von Marées, and Cézanne among them) before setting out – in his own words – to work 'as one new-born'. With Kandinsky, Marc, and Macke, he took part in founding the ◊*Blaue Reiter* group 1912, and taught at the Bauhaus 1921–31, though the style he developed – influenced as much by the art of children and the insane as it was by any school or movement – was unique and makes him difficult to classify neatly.

Klein Calvin (Richard) 1942– . US fashion designer. His collections are characterized by the smooth and understated, often in natural fabrics such as mohair, wool, and suede, in subtle colours. He set up his own business 1968, specializing in designing coats and suits, and expanded into sportswear in the mid-1970s. His designer jeans became a status symbol during the same period.

Klein Melanie, (born Reizes) 1882–1960. Austrian child psychoanalyst. She pioneered child psychoanalysis and play studies, and was influenced by Sigmund ◊Freud's theories. She published *The Psychoanalysis of Children* 1960.

Klein intended to follow a medical career. She gave this up when she married, but after the birth of her three children became interested in psychoanalysis. In 1919 she published her first paper on the psychoanalysis of young children. She moved to London 1926, where the main part of her work was done. In 1934 Klein extended her study to adult patients, and her conclusions, based on her observations of infant and childhood anxiety, were published in her book *Envy and Gratitude* 1957.

Klemperer Otto 1885–1973. German conductor. He was celebrated for his interpretation of contemporary and Classical music (especially Beethoven and Brahms). He conducted the Los Angeles Orchestra 1933–39 and the Philharmonia Orchestra, London, from 1959.

kleptomania (Greek *kleptēs* 'thief') behavioural disorder characterized by an overpowering desire to possess articles for which one has no need. In kleptomania, as opposed to ordinary theft, there is no obvious need or use for what is stolen and sometimes the sufferer has no memory of the theft.

Klimt Gustav 1862–1918. Austrian painter. He was influenced by *Jugendstil* (Art Nouveau) and was a founding member of the Vienna ◊Sezession group 1897. His paintings, often sensual and erotic, have a jewelled effect similar to mosaics, for example *The Kiss* 1909 (Musée des Beaux-Arts, Strasbourg). His many portraits include *Judith I* 1901 (Österreichische Galerie, Vienna).

Klimt's paintings and other decorative works (for example, the mosaics for the Palais Stoclet, Brussels) are characterized by academic forms that are obscured by massed repetitive decorative elements. His use of decorative fragments and gold backgrounds is derived from Byzantine mosaics, but his depiction of women – as seductive and dangerous – is typical of *fin-de-siècle* ◊decadence. Examples are the *Jurisprudence* panel 1903–07 (destroyed 1945) and his ideal woman as *Pallas Athene*.

Klondike gold-mining area in ◊Yukon, Canada, named after the river valley where gold was found 1896. About 30,000 people moved to the area during the following few months.

Klimt *Portrait of Margaret Stonborough-Wittgenstein* 1905 by Gustav Klimt (Neue Pinakothek, Munich). Sensual and richly decorative, Klimt's paintings are among the finest expressions of Art Nouveau. Even in portraits, as here, the sitters seem secondary to the overall decorative effect. *Corbis*

Klopstock Friedrich Gottlieb 1724–1803. German poet. His religious epic *Der Messias/The Messiah* 1748–73 and *Oden/Odes* 1771 anticipated Romanticism. Written in hexameters, *Der Messias* is a very uneven poem, some parts of it being imbued with deep feeling and fervour, while others are flat and trivial.

km symbol for ◊***kilometre***.

knapweed any of several weedy plants of the genus *Centaurea*, family Compositae. In the common knapweed *C. nigra*, also known as hardhead, the hard bract-covered buds break into purple composite heads. It is native to Europe and has been introduced to North America.

Kneller Godfrey, (born Gottfried Kniller) 1646–1723. German-born portrait painter who lived in England from 1674. Successful and prolific (he painted nearly 6,000 portraits), he dominated English portraiture of the late 17th and early 18th centuries. He was court painter to Charles II, James II, William III, and George I.

Acting as an artistic link between Stuart and Georgian society, Kneller helped to prepare English art for the major achievements in portraiture during the first half of 18th century. Among his paintings are the series *Hampton Court Beauties* (Hampton Court, Richmond, Surrey, a sequel to Peter Lely's *Windsor Beauties*), and 48 portraits of the members of the Whig Kit Cat Club 1702–17 (National Portrait Gallery, London).

Knesset the Israeli parliament, consisting of a single chamber of 120 deputies elected for a period of four years.

knifefish any fish of the genus *Gymnotus* and allied genera of fishes, family Gymnotidae, in which the body is deep at the front, drawn to a narrow or pointed tail at the rear, the main fin being the well-developed long ventral that completes the knife-like shape. The ventral fin is rippled for forward or backward locomotion. Knifefishes produce electrical fields, which they use for navigation.

knighthood, order of fraternity carrying with it the rank of knight, admission to which is granted as a mark of royal favour or as a reward for public services. During the Middle Ages in Europe such fraternities fell into two classes, religious and secular. The first class, including the ◊Templars and the Knights of ◊St John, consisted of knights who had taken religious vows and devoted themselves to military service against the Saracens (Arabs) or other non-Christians. The secular orders probably arose from bands of knights engaged in the service of a prince or great noble.

The Order of the Garter, founded about 1347, is the oldest now in existence; there are eight other British orders: the Thistle founded 1687, the Bath 1725, the St Patrick 1788, the St Michael and St George 1818, the Star of India 1861, the Indian Empire 1878, the Royal Victorian Order 1896, and the Order of the British Empire (OBE) 1917. The Order of Merit (OM), founded 1902, comprises the sovereign and no more than 24 prominent individuals. A knight bachelor belongs to the lowest stage of knighthood, not being a member of any specially named order.

Knock village in County Mayo, W Ireland, known for its church shrine (the Basilica of Our Lady, Queen of Ireland), one of three national places of pilgrimage (with Lough Derg and Croagh Patrick). On 21 Aug 1879 it was the scene of an alleged apparition of the Virgin Mary, St Joseph, and St John to a group of about 14 people.

knocking in a spark-ignition petrol engine, a phenomenon that occurs when unburned fuel-air mixture explodes in the combustion chamber before being ignited by the spark. The resulting shock waves produce a metallic knocking sound. Loss of power occurs, which can be prevented by reducing the compression ratio, re-designing the geometry of the combustion chamber, or increasing the octane number of the petrol (usually by the use of tetraethyl lead anti-knock additives, or increasingly by MTBE – methyl tertiary butyl ether in unleaded petrol).

Knossos chief city of ◊Minoan Crete, near present-day Iráklion, 6 km/4 mi SE of Candia. The archaeological site, excavated by Arthur ◊Evans 1899–1935, dates from about 2000–1400 BC, and includes the palace throne room, the remains of frescoes, and construction on more than one level.

Excavation of the palace of the legendary King Minos showed that the story of Theseus' encounter with the Minotaur in a labyrinth was possibly derived from the ritual 'bull-leaping' by young

knapweed Brown knapweed *Centaurea nemoralis*, which is found in Asia, Europe, and N Africa, favours lowland chalky soils. Its purple-red, thistlelike flowers are a favourite source of nectar for bumblebees and butterflies. *Premaphotos Wildlife*

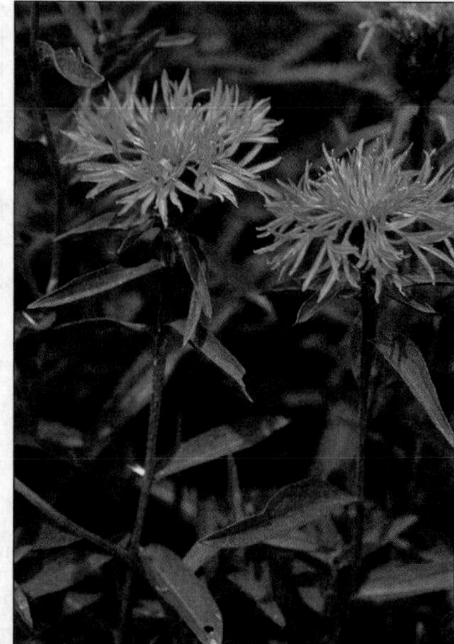

people depicted in the palace frescoes and from the mazelike layout of the palace.

knot wading bird *Calidris canutus* of the sandpiper family Scolopacidae, order Charadriiformes. It is about 25 cm/10 in long, with a short bill, neck, and legs. In the winter, it is grey above and white below, but in the breeding season, it is brick-red on the head and chest and black on the wings and back. It feeds on insects and molluscs.

Breeding in North American and Eurasian arctic regions, knots travel widely in winter, to be found as far south as South Africa, Australasia, and southern parts of South America.

knot in navigation, unit by which a ship's speed is measured, equivalent to one ◊nautical mile per hour (one knot equals about 1.15 miles per hour). It is also sometimes used in aviation.

knotgrass annual plant *Polygonum aviculare* of the dock family. The small lance-shaped leaves have bases that sheathe the slender stems, giving a superficial resemblance to grass. Small pinkish flowers are followed by seeds that are a delicacy for birds. It grows on bare ground including seashores, and is found worldwide except in the polar regions. Often low-growing, it may have stems up to 2 m/6 ft long.

knowledge-based system (KBS) computer program that uses an encoding of human knowledge to help solve problems. It was discovered during research into ◊artificial intelligence that adding heuristics (rules of thumb) enabled programs to tackle problems that were otherwise difficult to solve by the usual techniques of computer science.

Chess-playing programs have been strengthened by including knowledge of what makes a good position, or of overall strategies, rather than relying solely on the computer's ability to calculate variations.

Knox John c. 1505–1572. Scottish Protestant reformer, founder of the Church of Scotland. He spent several years in exile for his beliefs, including a period in Geneva where he met John ◊Calvin.

Originally a Roman Catholic priest, Knox is thought to have been converted by the reformer George Wishart. When Wishart was burned for heresy, Knox went into hiding, but later preached the reformed doctrines. Captured by French troops in Scotland 1547, he was imprisoned in France, sentenced to the galleys, and released only by the intercession of the British government 1549. In England he assisted in compiling the Prayer Book, as a royal chaplain from 1551. On Mary's accession 1553 he fled the country and in 1557 was, in his absence, condemned to be burned. In 1559 he returned to Scotland. He was tried for treason but acquitted 1563. He returned to Scotland 1559 to promote Presbyterianism. His books include *First Blast of the Trumpet Against the Monstrous Regiment of Women* 1558 and *History of the Reformation in Scotland* 1586.

Knox John Knox, the 16th-century Scottish Protestant reformer and founder of Presbyterianism. Originally a Roman Catholic, Knox spent some years in exile after the accession of Mary Queen of Scots and met with Calvin in Geneva. Knox was an outspoken and zealous preacher, and his influence on the Scottish Reformation was seminal. *Corbis*

koala marsupial *Phascolarctos cinereus* of the family Phalangeridae, found only in E Australia. It feeds almost entirely on eucalyptus shoots. It is about 60 cm/2 ft long, and resembles a bear. The popularity of its greyish fur led to its almost complete extermination by hunters. The koala has been under protection since 1936; however, in the period 1985–95 numbers have fallen from 400,000 to between 40,000 and 80,000.

kōan in Zen Buddhism, a superficially nonsensical question or riddle used by a Zen master to help a pupil achieve satori (◊enlightenment). A *kōan* supposedly cannot be understood through the processes of logic; its solution requires attainment of a higher level of insight. An often repeated example is 'What is the sound of one hand clapping?'

Kobe deep-water port in S Honshu, Japan; population (1994) 1,479,000. It originated as a ◊treaty port 1868–99 (for foreigners exempt from Japanese law). Port Island, an artificial island of 5 sq km/2 sq mi in Kobe harbour, was created 1960–68 from the rock of nearby mountains. It was one of the world's largest construction projects, and is now a residential and recreation area with a luxury hotel, amusement park, and conference centres. It is linked to the city by a driverless, computerized monorail.

An earthquake registering 7.2 on the Richter scale hit Kobe Jan 1995, causing widespread devastation and leaving more than 5,370 people dead, nearly 27,000 injured, and over 45,000 homes destroyed.

Koch (Heinrich Hermann) Robert 1843–1910. German bacteriologist. Koch and his assistants devised the techniques for culturing bacteria outside the body, and formulated the rules for showing whether or not a bacterium is the cause of a disease. Nobel Prize for Physiology or Medicine 1905.

His techniques enabled him to identify the bacteria responsible for tuberculosis 1882 and cholera 1883. He investigated anthrax bacteria in the 1870s and showed that they form spores which spread the infection.

Kodály Zoltán 1882–1967. Hungarian composer and educationist. With Béla Bartók, he recorded and transcribed Magyar folk music, the scales and rhythm of which he incorporated in a deliberately nationalist style. His works include the cantata *Psalmus Hungaricus* 1923, a comic opera *Háry János* 1925–27, and orchestral dances and variations. His 'Kodály method' of school music education is widely practised.

Koestler Arthur 1905–1983. Hungarian-born British writer. Imprisoned by the Nazis in France 1940, he escaped to England. His novel *Darkness at Noon* 1940, regarded as his masterpiece, is a fictional account of the Stalinist purges, and draws on his experiences as a prisoner under sentence of death during the Spanish Civil War. He also wrote extensively about creativity, science, parapsychology, politics, and culture.

Koestler's other novels include *Thieves in the Night* 1946, *The Lotus and the Robot* 1960, and *The Call Girls* 1972. His nonfiction work includes *The Act of Creation* 1964 and *The Thirteenth Tribe* 1976. Autobiographical works include *Arrow in the Blue* 1952 and *The Invisible Writing* 1954. He was a member of the Voluntary Euthanasia Society and committed suicide with his wife after suffering for a long time from Parkinson's disease.

kohl (Arabic) powdered antimony sulphide, used in Asia and the Middle East to darken the area around the eyes. Commonly used eyeliners also contain carbon (bone black, lamp black, carbon black) or black iron oxide.

Kohl Helmut 1930– . German conservative politician, leader of the Christian Democratic Union (CDU) from 1976, West German chancellor (prime minister) 1982–90, and German chancellor 1990–98. He oversaw the reunification of East and West Germany 1989–90 and in 1990 won a resounding victory to become the first chancellor of reunited Germany. He achieved a historic fourth electoral victory 1994; in Nov 1996 he entered his 15th year as chancellor, overtaking the record previously held by Konrad Adenauer, Kohl's political mentor.

kohlrabi variety of kale *Brassica oleracea*. The leaves of kohlrabi shoot from a globular swelling on the main stem; it is used for food and resembles a turnip.

Koivisto Mauno Henrik 1923– . Finnish politician, prime minister 1968–70 and 1979–82, and president 1982–94. He was finance minister 1966–67 and led a Social Democratic Party coalition as prime minister 1968–70. He became interim president 1981 after the resignation of Urho Kekkonen, and was elected president the following year. As president he shared power with Centre Party prime minister Esko Aho in Finland's unusual 'dual executive'.

Kok Wim 1938– . Dutch trade unionist and politician, leader of the Labour Party (PvdA) and prime minister from 1994. After an inconclusive general election May 1994, Kok eventually succeeded in forming a broad-based three-party coalition of the PvdA with the People's Party of Freedom and Democracy (VVD) and Democrats 66, both centrist parties.

Kokoschka Oskar 1886–1980. Austrian Expressionist painter. Initially influenced by the Vienna ◊Sezession painters, he painted vivid landscapes, and highly charged allegories and portraits, for example his self-portrait with Alma Mahler, *The Bride of the Wind (The Tempest)* 1914 (Kunstmuseum, Basel).

His early works, such as *The Dreaming Youths* 1908, show the influence of Klimt, but this soon gave way to an angular and distorted graphic style. Sombre and intense, the 'psychological portraits' of this period are among his most important works: *Hans Tietze and Erica Tietze-Conrat* 1909 (Museum of Modern Art, New York) is a good example.

He taught in Dresden 1919–24, where he came into closer contact with the artists of *die Brücke*. His colours became brighter and he turned increasingly to landscapes, which often share the restlessness and urgency of his portraits. He moved to Vienna 1931 and to Prague 1934. In 1938, when the Nazis condemned his work as ◊Degenerate Art, he settled in England, taking British citizenship 1947. Though some of his later work was increasingly decorative, paintings such as *Time, Gentlemen Please* 1971–72, his last self-portrait, remain vivid and dramatic.

kola alternative spelling of ◊cola, a genus of tropical tree.

Kola Peninsula (Russian ***Kol'skiy Poluostrov***) peninsula in the N Russian Federation, bounded S and E by the White Sea and N by the Barents Sea; area 129,500 sq km/50,000 sq mi; population 1.3 million (of whom 2,000 are Saami). Kola is coterminous with Murmansk region. Apatite and other minerals are exported. Heavy pollution from nickel smelting has damaged a large area of forest.

Kolchak Alexander Vasilievich 1874–1920. Russian admiral, commander of the White forces in Siberia after the Russian Revolution. He proclaimed himself Supreme Ruler of Russia 1918, but was later handed over to the Bolsheviks by his own men and shot.

Koller Carl 1857–1944. Austrian ophthalmologist who introduced local anaesthesia 1884, using cocaine. When psychoanalyst Sigmund ◊Freud discovered the painkilling properties of cocaine, Koller recognized its potential as a local anaesthetic. He carried out early experiments on animals and on himself, and the technique quickly became standard in ophthalmology, dentistry, and other areas in cases where general anaesthesia exposes the patient to needless risk.

Kollontai Alexandra Mikhailovna, (born Domontovich) 1872–1952. Russian revolutionary, politician, and writer. In 1905 she published *On the Question of the Class Struggle*, and, as commissar for public welfare, was the only female member of the first Bolshevik government. She campaigned for domestic reforms such as acceptance of free love, simplification of divorce laws, and collective child care.

In 1896, while on a tour of a large textile factory, she saw the appalling conditions of factory workers in Russia, and devoted herself to improving conditions for working women. She was harassed by the police for her views and went into exile in Germany 1914. On her return to the USSR 1917 she joined the Bolsheviks. She was sent abroad by Stalin, first as trade minister, then as ambassador to Sweden 1943.

Kollontai took part in the armistice negotiations ending the Soviet-Finnish War 1944. She toured the USA to argue against its involvement in World War I and organized the first all-Russian Congress of Working and Peasant Women 1918. In 1923 she published 'The Love of Worker Bees', a collection of short stories.

Kollwitz Käthe, (born Schmidt) 1867–1945. German graphic artist and sculptor, born in Königsberg, East Prussia (now Kaliningrad, in Russia). One of the leading Expressionists, she is noted for the harrowing drawings, woodcuts, etchings, and lithographs on the themes of social injustice and human suffering.

Among her principal works are the *Peasants' War* series, 1902–08, the poster *Bread, Children Starving* 1924, the woodcut cycle *Never Again War!* 1924, and the lithographs *Death* completed 1936.

Komi a Finnish people living mainly in the tundra and coniferous forests of the autonomous republic of Komi in the NW Urals, Russia. They raise livestock, grow timber, and mine coal and oil. Their language, Zyryan, belongs to the Finno-Ugric branch of the Uralic family.

Komi autonomous republic of N central Russian Federation
area 415,900 sq km/160,580 sq mi
capital Syktyvkar; population (1992) 235,000
physical in basin of the Pechora River
industries livestock breeding, coal, oil, timber, gas, asphalt, building materials
population (1992) 1,225,000
history annexed by the princes of Moscow in the 14th century. An autonomous region for the Komi people 1921; an autonomous republic from 1936. An oil spill from a pipeline 1994 covered over 67 sq km/26 sq mi of Arctic tundra, polluting rivers and endangering wildlife.

Kommunizma, Pik or ***Communism Peak*** highest mountain in the ◊Pamirs, a mountain range in Tajikistan; 7,495 m/24,599 ft. As part of the former USSR, it was known as Mount Garmo until 1933 and Mount Stalin 1933–62.

Kongo African kingdom flourishing in the lower Congo region in the 14th–18th centuries. Although it possessed a sophisticated system of government, its power began to decline early in the 17th century under the impact of intensified slave trading and the interventions of Portuguese merchants and missionaries. In the late 19th century the kingdom was incorporated in the Portuguese colony of Angola. The Kongo people rebelled against colonial rule 1913–17.

Kongur Shan mountain peak in China, 7,719 m/25,325 ft high, part of the Pamir range (see ◊Pamirs). The 1981 expedition that first reached the summit was led by British climber Chris Bonington.

Koniev Ivan Stepanovich 1898–1973. Soviet marshal who in World War II liberated Ukraine from the invading German forces 1943–44 and then 1945 advanced from the south on Berlin to link up with the British-US forces. He commanded all Warsaw Pact forces 1955–60.

Konoe Fumimaro, Prince 1891–1946. Japanese politician and prime minister 1937–39 and 1940–41. Entering politics in the 1920s, Konoe was active in trying to curb the power of the army in government and preventing an escalation of the war with China. He helped to engineer the fall of the ◊Tōjō government 1944 but committed suicide after being suspected of war crimes.

Kon-Tiki legendary creator god of Peru and sun king who ruled the country later occupied by the ◊Incas and was supposed to have migrated out into the Pacific. The name was used by explorer Thor ◊Heyerdahl 1947 for his raft.

Konya (Roman ***Iconium***) city in SW central Turkey; population (1990) 513,300. Carpets and silks are made here, and the city contains the monastery of the dancing ◊dervishes.

kookaburra or ***laughing jackass*** largest of the world's ◊kingfishers *Dacelo novaeguineae*, family Alcedinidae, order Coraciiformes, found in Australia, with an extraordinary laughing call. It feeds on insects and other small creatures. The body and tail measure 45 cm/18 in, the head is greyish with a dark eye stripe, and the back and wings are flecked brown with grey underparts. It nests in shady forest regions, but will also frequent the vicinity of houses, and its cry is one of the most familiar sounds of the bush in eastern Australia.

kookaburra Because of its loud laughing call, this bird is often called the laughing kookaburra or even laughing jackass. It is the largest member of the kingfisher family and is found in the lightly wooded or open country of Australia where it feeds largely on insects and other small creatures including rodents and reptiles.

kora 21-string instrument of W African origin made from gourds, with a harplike sound, traditionally played by griots (hereditary troubadours) of the old Mali empire to accompany praise songs and historical ballads.

Koran (alternatively transliterated as ***Quran***) the sacred book of ◊Islam, written in Arabic. It is said to have been divinely revealed through the angel Gabriel, or Jibra'el, to the prophet Muhammad between about AD 610 and 632. The Koran is the prime source of all Islamic ethical and legal doctrines.

The Koran is divided into 114 suras (chapters), some very long, others consisting of only a few words. It includes many events also described in the Hebrew Bible but narrated from a different viewpoint. Other issues are also discussed, giving injunctions relevant to situations that needed alteration or clarification and addressing problems that the Muslims faced at the time it was written.

Korda Alexander Laszlo 1893–1956. Hungarian-born British film producer and director. He was a dominant figure in the British film industry during the 1930s and 1940s. His films include *The Private Life of Henry VIII* 1933, *The Third Man* 1949, and *Richard III* 1956.

Kordofan former province of central Sudan, known as the 'White Land'; area 146,990 sq km/56,752 sq mi; population (1983) 3,093,300. It was divided 1994 into three new federal states: North, South, and West Kordofan (or Kurdofan). The area is mainly undulating plain, with acacia scrub producing gum arabic, marketed in the chief town El Obeid. Formerly a rich agricultural region, it has been overtaken by desertification.

Korea peninsula in E Asia, divided into north and south; see ◊Korea, North, and ◊Korea, South.

Korean person who is native to or an inhabitant of Korea; also the language and culture. There are approximately 33 million Koreans in South Korea, 15 million in North Korea, and 3 million elsewhere, principally in Japan, China (Manchuria), Russia, Kazakhstan, Uzbekistan, and the USA.

Korean language language of Korea, written from the 5th century AD in Chinese characters until the invention of an alphabet by King Sejong 1443. The linguistic affiliations of Korean are unclear, but it may be distantly related to Japanese.

Korea, North country in E Asia, bounded NE by Russia, N and NW by China, E by the Sea of Japan, S by South Korea, and W by the Yellow Sea. *See country box opposite.*

Korea, South country in E Asia, bounded N by North Korea, E by the Sea of Japan, S by the Korea Strait, and W by the Yellow Sea. *See country box on p. 600.*

Korean War war 1950–53 between North Korea (supported by China) and South Korea, aided by the United Nations (UN); the troops were mainly US. North Korean forces invaded South Korea 25 June 1950, and the UN Security Council, owing to a walk-out by the USSR, voted to oppose them. The North Koreans held most of the South, with the UN forces holding a small area, the Pusan perimeter, in the southeast, when US reinforcements arrived Sept 1950 and forced their way through to the North Korean border with China. The course of the war changed after the surprise landing of US troops later the same month at Inchon on South Korea's NW coast. The troops, led by General Douglas ◊MacArthur, fought their way through North Korea to the Chinese border in little over a month. On 25 Oct 1950 Chinese troops attacked across the Yalu River, driving the UN forces below the original boundary of the ◊38th parallel. Truce negotiations began 1951, but the war did not end until 1953, with the restoration of the original boundary. The armistice was signed with North Korea; South Korea did not participate.

Kornberg Arthur 1918– . US biochemist. In 1956 he discovered the enzyme DNA-polymerase, which enabled molecules of the genetic material ◊DNA to be synthesized for the first time. For this work he shared the 1959 Nobel Prize for Physiology or Medicine. By 1967 he had synthesized a biologically active artificial viral DNA.

Korolev Sergei Pavlovich 1906–1966. Russian designer of the first Soviet intercontinental missile, used to launch the first ◊*Sputnik* satellite 1957 and the ◊*Vostok* spacecraft, also designed by Korolev, in which Yuri ◊Gagarin made the world's first space flight 1961.

Korolev and his research team built the first Soviet liquid-fuel rocket, launched 1933. His innovations in rocket and space technology include ballistic missiles, rockets for geophysical research, launch vehicles, and crewed spacecraft. Korolev was also responsible for the *Voskhod* spaceship, from which the first space walks were made.

Kos or ***Cos*** fertile Greek island, one of the Dodecanese, in the Aegean Sea; area 287 sq km/111 sq mi. It gives its name to the Cos lettuce.

Kościusko highest mountain in Australia (2,229 m/7,316 ft), in New South Wales. The mineralogist Paul Strzelecki, who was born in Prussian Poland, climbed the mountain 1840. He thought one of the summit tops resembled the grave of the Polish revolutionary hero Tadeusz Kościuszko, and named it after him.

Kościuszko Tadeusz Andrzej 1746–1817. Polish general and nationalist. He served with George Washington in the American Revolution (1776–83). He returned to Poland 1784, fought against the Russian invasion that ended in the partition of Poland, and withdrew to Saxony. He returned 1794 to lead the revolt against the occupation, but was defeated by combined Russian and Prussian forces and imprisoned until 1796.

kosher (Hebrew 'appropriate') conforming to religious law with regard to the preparation and consumption of food; in Judaism, conforming to the Mosaic law of the Book of Deuteronomy. For example, only animals that chew the cud and have cloven hooves (cows and sheep, but not pigs) may be eaten. There are rules governing their humane slaughter and their preparation (such as complete draining of blood) which also apply to fowl. Only fish with scales and fins may be eaten; not shellfish. Milk products may not be cooked or eaten with meat or poultry, or until four hours after eating them. Utensils for meat must be kept separate from those for milk. There have been various explanations for the origins of these laws, particularly hygiene: pork and shellfish spoil quickly in a hot climate. Many Reform Jews no longer feel obliged to observe these laws.

Kosovo or ***Kossovo*** autonomous region 1945–1990 of S Serbia; capital Priština; area 10,900 sq km/4,207 sq mi; population (1991) 2,012,500, consisting of about 210,000 Serbs and about 1.8 million Albanians. Products include wine, nickel, lead, and zinc. Since it is largely inhabited by Albanians and bordering on Albania, there have been demands for unification with that country, while in the late 1980s Serbians agitated for Kosovo to be merged with the rest of Serbia. A state of emergency was declared Feb 1990 after fighting broke out between ethnic Albanians, police, and Kosovo Serbs. The parliament and government were dissolved July 1990 and the Serbian parliament formally annexed Kosovo Sept 1990.

The Serbian invasion brought Kosovo to the brink of civil war. Albanian institutions and media were suppressed, and 'emergency legislation' was used to rid industry of Albanian employees at all levels. In 1991 the Kosovo assembly, though still technically dissolved, organized a referendum on sovereignty which received 99% support. It elected a provisional government, headed by Bujar Bukoshi, which was recognized by Albania Oct 1991. In May 1992 the Albanian majority held unsanctioned elections, choosing Ibrahim Rugova as president and selecting a 130-member parliament. Serbia regarded the elections as illegal but allowed them to proceed.

Negotiations over Kosovo took place in February 1999 at Rambouillet near Paris, France. The two sides – the Kosovo Liberation Army and Serbia – accepted ten fundamental principles, including that Kosovo had to be granted greater autonomy.

At the end of March 1999 NATO forces launched air strikes against Yugoslavia in an attempt to force Serbia to halt its repression of ethnic Albanians in Kosovo. This led to the expulsion by Serb military forces of many thousands of Kosovo Albanians into Albania and Macedonia. Widespread killings of ethnic Albanians by Serb forces were reported.

Kossuth Lajos 1802–1894. Hungarian nationalist and leader of the revolution of 1848. He proclaimed Hungary's independence of Habsburg rule, became governor of a Hungarian republic 1849, and, when it was defeated by Austria and Russia, fled first to Turkey and then to exile in Britain and Italy.

Kosygin Alexei Nikolaievich 1904–1980. Soviet politician, prime minister 1964–80. He was elected to the Supreme Soviet 1938, became a member of the Politburo 1946, deputy prime minister 1960, and succeeded Khrushchev as premier (while Brezhnev succeeded him as party secretary). In the late 1960s Kosygin's influence declined.

Kourou river and second-largest town of French Guiana, NW of Cayenne, site of the Guiana Space Centre of the European Space Agency; population (1990) 11,200. Situated near the equator, it is an ideal site for launches of satellites into ◊geostationary orbit.

Kovac Michal 1930– . Slovak politician, president from 1993, when Czechoslovakia split in two to become the Czech and Slovak republics. He was known to favour some confederal arrangement with the Czech Republic and, in consequence, his election was welcomed by the Czech government.

After a career as an academic economist and banker, he served as Slovak minister of finance in the post-communist administration between 1989 and 1991. He was the speaker of Czechoslovakia's federal assembly from 1992 and became the Slovak Republic's first president.

Kowloon peninsula on the Chinese coast forming part of the former British crown colony of Hong Kong; the city of Kowloon is a residential area and one of the most densely populated places in the world. It is connected by rail to Canton. Kowloon Peninsula was ceded to the British 1860.

Krajina region on the frontier between Croatia and Bosnia-Herzegovina; the chief town is Knin. Dominated by Serbs, the region proclaimed itself an autonomous Serbian province after Croatia declared its independence from Yugoslavia 1991. Krajina was the scene of intense inter-ethnic fighting during the civil war in Croatia 1991–92 and, following the cease-fire Jan 1992, 10,000 UN troops were deployed here and in E and W Slavonia. Croatian forces recaptured the region in a major offensive Aug 1995, forcing an estimated 150,000 Serbs to flee their homes.

Krakatoa (Indonesian ***Krakatau***) volcanic island in Sunda strait, Indonesia, that erupted 1883, causing 36,000 deaths on Java and Sumatra by the tidal waves that followed. The island is now uninhabited.

Kraków or ***Cracow*** city in Poland, on the river Vistula; population (1993) 751,300. It is an industrial centre producing railway wagons, paper, chemicals, and tobacco. It was capital of Poland about 1300–1595.

Its university, at which the astronomer ◊Copernicus was a student, was founded about 1400, making it one of the oldest in central Europe. There is a 14th-century Gothic cathedral.

Krasnodar territory of the SW Russian Federation, in the N Caucasus Mountains, adjacent to the Black Sea; area 83,600 sq km/32,290 sq mi; population (1991 est) 5,174,800. The capital is Krasnodar. In addition to stock rearing and the production of grain, rice, fruit, and tobacco, oil is refined.

Krasnoyarsk industrial city (locomotives, paper, timber, cement, gold refining, and a large hydroelectric works) on the Yenisei River in central Siberia, Russian Federation; population (1994) 914,000. There is an early-warning and space-tracking radar phased array at nearby Abalakova.

Krasnoyarsk territory of the Russian Federation in central Siberia stretching north to the Arctic Ocean; area 2,401,600 sq km/927,617 sq mi; population (1985) 3,430,000. The capital is Krasnoyarsk. It is drained by the Yenisei River. Mineral resources include gold, graphite, coal, iron ore, and uranium.

Kravchuk Leonid 1934– . Ukrainian politician, president 1990–94. Formerly a member of the Ukrainian Communist Party (UCP), he became its ideology chief in the 1980s. After the suspension of the UCP 1991, Kravchuk became an advocate of independence and market-centred economic reform. Faced with a rapidly deteriorating economic situation 1993, he assumed direct control of government, eliminating the post of prime minister. He was, however, defeated by former prime minister Leonid ◊Kuchma in the 1994 presidential elections.

Krebs Hans Adolf 1900–1981. German-born British biochemist. He discovered the citric acid cycle, also known as the ◊Krebs cycle, the final pathway by which food molecules are converted into energy in living tissues. For this work he shared the 1953 Nobel Prize for Physiology or Medicine.

Krebs first became interested in the process by which the body degrades amino acids. He discovered that nitrogen atoms are the first to be removed (deamination) and are then excreted as

KOREA, NORTH

People's Democratic Republic of

national name *Chosun Minchu-chui Inmin Konghwa-guk*
area 120,538 sq km/46,528 sq mi
capital Pyongyang
major towns/cities Chongjin, Nampo, Wonsan, Sinuiji
physical features wide coastal plain in W rising to mountains cut by deep valleys in interior
head of state Kim Jong Il from 1994
head of government Hong Song Nam from 1997
political system communism
administrative divisions nine provinces, two cities
political parties Korean Workers' Party (KWP), Marxist-Leninist (leads Democratic Front for the Reunification of the Fatherland, including Korean Social Democratic Party and Chondoist Chongu Party)
population 22,466,000 (1996 est)
population growth rate 1.9% (1990–95); 1.3% (2000–05)
ethnic distribution entirely Korean, with the exception of a 50,000 Chinese minority
life expectancy 68 (men), 74 (women)
literacy rate 99%
language Korean
religions Chondoist, Buddhist, Christian, traditional beliefs
currency won
GDP (US $) 21.5 billion (1995 est)
growth rate −5.0% (1992)
exports coal, iron, copper, textiles, chemicals

HISTORY

2333 BC Legendary founding of Korean state by Tangun dynasty.
1122 BC–4th C AD Period of Chinese Kija dynasty.
668–1000 Peninsula unified by Buddhist Shilla kingdom, with capital at Kyongju.
1392–1910 Period of Chosun, or Yi, dynasty, during which Korea became a vassal of China and Confucianism became dominant intellectual force.
1910 Korea formally annexed by Japan.
1920s and 1930s Heavy industries developed in the coal-rich N, with Koreans forcibly conscripted as low-paid labourers; suppression of Korean culture led to development of resistance movement.
1945 Russian and US troops entered Korea at the end of World War II, forced surrender of Japanese, and divided the country in two at the 38th parallel.
1946 Soviet-backed provisional government installed, dominated by Moscow-trained Korean communists, including Kim Il Sung; radical programme of land reform and nationalization launched.
1948 Democratic People's Republic of Korea declared after pro-USA Republic of Korea founded in the S; Soviet troops withdrew.
1950 North Korea invaded South Korea to unite the nation, beginning the Korean War.
1953 Armistice agreed to end Korean War, which had involved US participation on the side of South Korea, and Chinese on that of North Korea. The war ended in stalemate, at a cost of 2 million lives.
1961 Friendship treaty signed with China.
1972 New constitution, with executive president, adopted. Talks with South Korea about possible reunification.
1983 Four South Korean cabinet ministers assassinated in Rangoon, Burma (Myanmar), by North Korean army officers.
1985 Improved relations with the Soviet Union.
1990 Diplomatic contacts with South Korea and Japan suggested a thaw in North Korea's relations with rest of world.
1991 Became a member of the United Nations. Signed nonaggression agreement with South Korea.
1992 Signed Nuclear Safeguards Agreement, allowing international inspection of nuclear facilities. Also signed pact with South Korea for mutual inspection of nuclear facilities.
1994 Kim Il Sung died; succeeded by his son, Kim Jong Il. Agreement to halt nuclear-development programme in return for US aid, resulting in easing of 44-year-old US trade embargo.
1996 US aid in the face of severe famine; rice imported from South Korea.
1997 Hong Song Nam became prime minister. Grave food shortages worsened.
1998 UN food-aid operation instituted in effort to avert widespread famine. First direct talks with South Korea since 1994 ended in stalemate.

SEE ALSO Korean War; Korea, South

urea in the urine. He then investigated the processes involved in the production of urea from the removed nitrogen atoms, and by 1932 he had worked out the basic steps in the urea cycle.

Krebs cycle or ***citric acid cycle*** or ***tricarboxylic acid cycle*** final part of the chain of biochemical reactions by which organisms break down food using oxygen to release energy (respiration). It takes place within structures called ◊mitochondria in the body's cells, and breaks down food molecules in a series of small steps, producing energy-rich molecules of ◊ATP.

Kreisler Fritz 1875–1962. Austrian violinist and composer. He was a US citizen from 1943. His prolific output of recordings in the early 20th century introduced a wider public to classical music from old masters such as J S Bach and Couperin to moderns such as de Falla and Rachmaninov. He also composed and recorded romantic pieces in the style of the classics, often under a pseudonym. He gave the first performance of Elgar's *Violin Concerto* 1910, dedicated to him by the composer.

kremlin citadel or fortress of Russian cities. The Moscow kremlin dates from the 12th century, and the name 'the Kremlin' was once synonymous with the Soviet government.

Krenz Egon 1937– . East German communist politician. A member of the East German Socialist Unity Party (SED) from 1955, he joined its politburo 1983 and was a hardline protégé of Erich ◊Honecker, succeeding him as party leader and head of state 1989 after widespread prodemocracy demonstrations. He resigned Dec 1989 after only a few weeks in office; in 1997 he was convicted of manslaughter in connection with the deaths of East Germans who had attempted to flee to the West during the period of communist rule.

krill any of several Antarctic crustaceans of the order Euphausiacea, the most common species being *Euphausia superba*. Shrimplike, it is up to 5 cm/2 in long, with two antennae, five pairs of legs, seven pairs of light organs along the body, and is coloured orange above and green beneath. It is the most abundant animal, numbering perhaps 600 trillion (million million).

Moving in enormous swarms, krill constitute the chief food of the baleen whales, and have been used to produce a protein concentrate for human consumption, and meal for animal feed.

Krishna incarnation of the Hindu god ◊Vishnu. The devotion of the ◊bhakti movement is usually directed towards Krishna; an example of this is the ◊International Society for Krishna Consciousness. Many stories are told of Krishna's mischievous youth, and he is the charioteer of Arjuna in the *Bhagavad-Gītā*.

Krishna Menon Vengalil Krishnan 1897–1974. Indian politician who was a leading light in the Indian nationalist movement. He represented India at the United Nations 1952–62, and was defence minister 1957–62, when he was dismissed by Nehru following China's invasion of N India.

He was barrister of the Middle Temple in London, and Labour member of St Pancras Borough Council 1934–47. He was secretary of the India League in the UK from 1929, and in 1947 was appointed Indian high commissioner in London. He became a member of the Indian parliament 1953,

KOREA, SOUTH
Republic of Korea

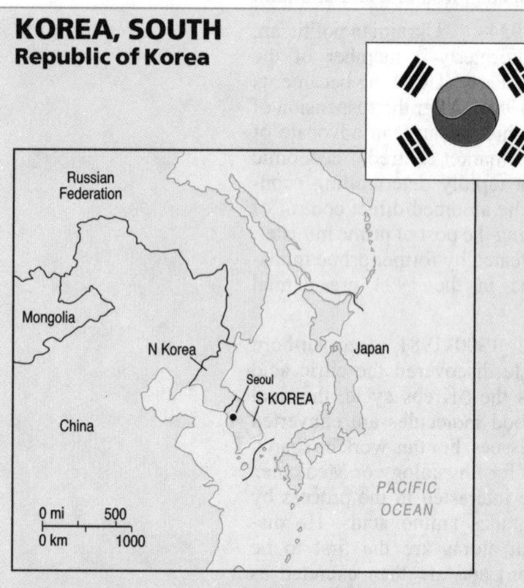

national name *Daehan Min-kuk*
area 98,799 sq km/38,161 sq mi
capital Seoul
major towns/cities Taegu, Kwangchu, Taejon
major ports Pusan, Inchon
physical features southern end of a mountainous peninsula separating the Sea of Japan from the Yellow Sea
head of state Kim Dae Jung from 1998
head of government Kim Jong Pil from 1998
political system emergent democracy
administrative divisions nine provinces and six cities with provincial status
political parties New Korea Party (NKP, formerly Democratic Liberal Party (DLP)), right of centre; National Congress for New Politics (NCNP), centre-left; Democratic Party (DP), left of centre; New Democratic Party (NDP), centrist, pro-private enterprise; United Liberal Democratic Party (ULD), ultra-conservative, pro-private enterprise
armed forces 633,000 (1995)
conscription 26 months (army); 30 months (navy and air force)
defence spend (% GDP) 3.6 (1994)
education spend (% GNP) 4.2 (1992)
health spend (% GDP) 2.7 (1990)
death penalty retained and used for ordinary crimes
population 45,314,000 (1996 est)
population growth rate 1.0% (1990–95); 0.8% (2000–05)
age distribution (% of total population) <15 37.1%, 15–65 57.1%, >65 5.8% (1995)
ethnic distribution with the exception of a small Nationalist Chinese minority, the population is almost entirely of Korean descent
population density (per sq km) 450 (1994)
urban population (% of total) 81 (1995)
labour force 46% of population: 18% agriculture, 35% industry, 47% services (1990)
unemployment 2.8% (1994)
child mortality rate (under 5, per 1,000 live births) 9 (1994)
life expectancy 68 (men), 74 (women)
education (compulsory years) 9
literacy rate 99% (men), 94% (women)
language Korean
religions Shamanist, Buddhist, Confucian, Protestant, Roman Catholic
TV sets (per 1,000 people) 211 (1992)
currency won
GDP (US $) 376.5 billion (1994)
GDP per capita (PPP) (US $) 9,710 (1993)
growth rate 8.4% (1994)
average annual inflation 6.2% (1994); 5.9% (1985–93)
trading partners Japan, USA, Germany, Saudi Arabia, Australia, Hong Kong, Singapore, China
resources coal, iron ore, tungsten, gold, molybdenum, graphite, fluorite, natural gas, hydroelectric power, fish
industries electrical machinery, transport equipment (principally motor vehicles and shipbuilding), chemical products, textiles and clothing, iron and steel, electronics equipment, food processing, tourism
exports electrical machinery, textiles, clothing, footwear, telecommunications and sound equipment, chemical products, ships ('invisible export' – overseas construction work). Principal market: USA 21.4% (1994)
imports machinery and transport equipment (especially electrical machinery), petroleum and petroleum products, grain and foodstuffs, steel, chemical products, basic manufactures. Principal source: Japan 24.8% (1994)
arable land 19% (1993)
agricultural products rice, maize, barley, potatoes, sweet potatoes, fruit; livestock (chiefly pigs and cattle)

HISTORY
2333 BC Traditional date of founding of Korean state by Tangun (mythical son from union of bear-woman and god).
1122 BC Ancient texts record founding of kingdom in Korea by Chinese nobleman Kija.
194 BC NW Korea united under warlord, Wiman.
108 BC Korea conquered by Chinese.
1st–7th Cs AD Three Korean kingdoms – Koguryo, Paekche, and Silla – competed for supremacy.
668 Korean peninsula unified by Buddhist Silla kingdom.
1258 Korea accepted overlordship of Mongol Yüan Empire.
1392 Yi dynasty founded by General Yi Song-gye, vassal of Chinese Ming Empire; Confucianism replaced Buddhism as official creed.
1592 and 1597 Japanese invasions repulsed by Korea.
1636 Manchu invasion forced Korea to sever ties with Ming dynasty.
18th–19th Cs Korea resisted change in political and economic life and rejected contact with Europeans.
1864 Attempts to reform government and strengthen army by Taewongun (who ruled in name of his son, King Kojong); converts to Christianity persecuted.
1873 Taewongun forced to cede power to Queen Min; reforms reversed; government authority collapsed.
1882 Chinese occupied Seoul and installed governor.
1894–95 Sino-Japanese War: Japan forced China to recognize independence of Korea; Korea fell to Japanese influence.
1896 Fearing for his life, King Kojong sought protection of Russian legation.
1904–05 Russo-Japanese War: Japan ended Russian influence in Korea.
1910 Korea formally annexed by Japan; Japanese settlers introduced modern industry and agriculture; Korean language banned.
1919 'Samil' nationalist movement suppressed by Japanese.
1945 After defeat of Japan in World War II, Russia occupied regions of Korea N of 38th parallel (demarcation line agreed at Yalta Conference) and US occupied regions S of it.
1948 USSR refused to permit United Nations (UN) supervision of elections in N zone; S zone became independent as Republic of Korea, with Syngman Rhee as president.
1950 North Korea invaded South Korea; UN forces (mainly from USA) intervened to defend South Korea; China intervened in support of North Korea.
1953 Korean War ended with armistice which restored 38th parallel; no peace treaty agreed and US troops remained in South Korea.
1960 President Syngman Rhee forced to resign by student-led protests against corruption and fraudulent elections.
1961 Military coup placed General Park Chung Hee in power; major programme of industrial development began.
1972 Martial law imposed; presidential powers increased.
1979 President Park assassinated; interim government of President Choi Kyu-Hah introduced liberalizing reforms.
1979 General Chun Doo Hwan assumed power after anti-government riots; Korea emerged as leading shipbuilding nation and exporter of electronic goods.
1987 Constitution made more democratic as a result of Liberal pressure; ruling Democratic Justice Party (DJP) candidate Roh Tae Woo elected president amid allegations of fraud.
1988 Olympic Games held in Seoul.
1991 Large-scale anti-government protests forcibly suppressed; South Korea joined UN.
1992 South Korea established diplomatic relations with China; Kim Young Sam elected president.
1994 US military presence stepped up in response to perceived threat from North Korea.
1996 Roh Tae Woo and Chun Doo Hwan charged with treason for alleged role in massacre of demonstrators 1980 and sentenced to lengthy prison sentences.
1997 South Korea admitted to OECD. Koh Kun appointed prime minister. Severe economic crisis affects the country.
1998 Kim Dae Jung sworn in as president, with Kim Jong Pil as prime minister. Financial system opened up. More than 2,000 prisoners released, including 74 political prisoners.

SEE ALSO Korea, North; Korean War; Russo-Japanese War

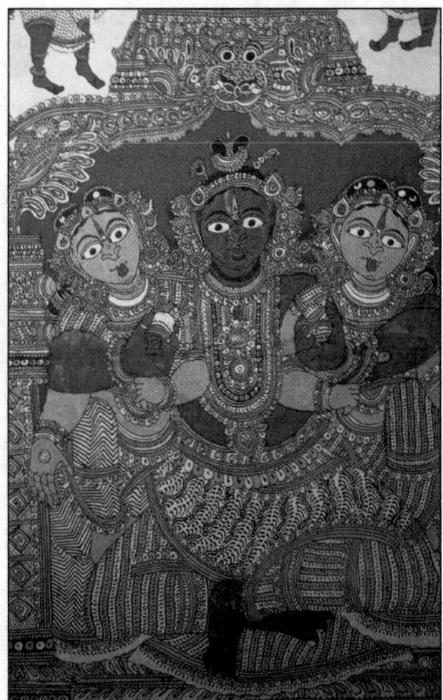

Krishna A batik depicting Krishna as the incarnation of Vishnu at Benares, India. In Hindu belief, an incarnation of Vishnu appears whenever the world is in need of protection. Krishna was the incarnation before Buddha, and Kalkin, the incarnation to follow him, has not yet come. *Corbis*

and minister without portfolio 1956. He was dismissed by Nehru 1962 when China invaded India after Menon's assurances to the contrary.

Kristallnacht 'night of (broken) glass' 9–10 Nov 1938 when the Nazi militia in Germany and Austria mounted a concerted attack on Jews, their synagogues, homes, and shops. More than 200,000 were arrested and sent to concentration camps, and 91 Jews were killed during the Kristallnacht. Part of the ◊Holocaust, Kristallnacht took place following the assassination of a German embassy official in Paris by a Polish-Jewish youth.

Kristiansen Ingrid 1956– . Norwegian athlete, an outstanding long-distance runner of 5,000 metres, 10,000 metres, marathon, and cross-country races. She has won all the world's leading marathons. In 1986 she knocked 45.68 seconds off the world 10,000 metres record. She was the world cross-country champion 1988 and won the London marathon 1984–85 and 1987–88.

Krivoi Rog (Russian 'crooked horn') (or ***Kryvyy Rih***) city in central Ukraine, 130 km/80 mi SW of Dnepropetrovsk; population (1992) 729,000. The surrounding district is rich in iron ore, and there is a metallurgical industry.

Kronos or ***Cronus*** in Greek mythology, the ruler of the world and one of the ◊Titans. He was the father of Zeus, who overthrew him.

Kropotkin Peter Alexeivich, Prince Kropotkin 1842–1921. Russian anarchist. Imprisoned for revolutionary activities 1874, he escaped to the UK 1876 and later moved to Switzerland. Expelled from Switzerland 1881, he went to France, where he was imprisoned 1883–86. He lived in Britain until 1917, when he returned to Moscow. Among his works are *Memoirs of a Revolutionist* 1899, *Mutual Aid* 1902, and *Modern Science and Anarchism* 1903.

Kruger (Stephanus Johannes) Paul(us) 1825–1904. President of the Transvaal 1883–1900. He refused to remedy the grievances of the uitlanders (English and other non-Boer white residents) and so precipitated the Second ◊South African War.

Kruger National Park game reserve in Mpumalanga Province, South Africa, between the Limpopo and Crocodile rivers; it is the largest in the world (about 20,720 sq km/8,000 sq mi). The Sabie Game Reserve was established 1898 by President Kruger, and the park declared 1926.

Krupp German steelmaking armaments firm, founded 1811 by Friedrich Krupp (1787–1826) and developed by his son Alfred Krupp by pioneering the Bessemer steelmaking process. The company developed the long-distance artillery used in World War I, and supported Hitler's regime in preparation for World War II, after which the head of the firm, Alfred Krupp (1907–1967), was imprisoned.

krypton (Greek *kryptos* 'hidden') colourless, odourless, gaseous, nonmetallic element, symbol Kr, atomic number 36, relative atomic mass 83.80. It is grouped with the inert gases and was long believed not to enter into reactions, but it is now known to combine with fluorine under certain conditions; it remains inert to all other reagents. It is present in very small quantities in the air (about 114 parts per million). It is used chiefly in fluorescent lamps, lasers, and gas-filled electronic valves.

Krypton was discovered 1898 in the residue from liquid air by British chemists William Ramsay and Morris Travers; the name refers to their difficulty in isolating it.

K-T boundary geologists' shorthand for the boundary between the rocks of the ◊Cretaceous and the ◊Tertiary periods 65 million years ago. It marks the extinction of the dinosaurs and in many places reveals a layer of iridium, possibly deposited by the meteorite that crashed into the Yucatán Peninsula, which may have caused the extinction by its impact. In 1996 US geologists discovered a small iridium-containing pebble believed to be a fragment of the meteorite.

Kuala Lumpur capital of the Federation of Malaysia; area 240 sq km/93 sq mi; population (1991) 1,145,000. The city developed after 1873 with the expansion of tin and rubber trading; these are now its main industries. Formerly within the state of Selangor, of which it was also the capital, it was created a federal territory 1974.

Kubitschek Juscelino 1902–1976. Brazilian president 1956–61. His term as president saw political peace, civil liberty, and rapid economic growth at the cost of high inflation and corruption. He had a strong commitment to public works and the construction of Brasília as the nation's capital.

Kublai Khan c. 1216–1294. Mongol emperor of China from 1259. He completed his grandfather ◊Genghis Khan's conquest of N China from 1240, and on his brother Mungo's death 1259 established himself as emperor of China. He moved the capital to Beijing and founded the Yuan dynasty, successfully expanding his empire into Indochina, but was defeated in an attempt to conquer Japan 1281.

Kubrick Stanley 1928–1999. US film director, producer, and screenwriter. His films include *Paths of Glory* 1957, *Lolita* 1962, *Dr Strangelove* 1964, *2001: A Space Odyssey* 1968, *A Clockwork Orange* 1971, *The Shining* 1979, *Full Metal Jacket* 1987, and *Eyes Wide Shut* 1999. More than any of his American contemporaries, Kubrick achieved complete artistic control over his films, which are ambitious in both scale and technique.

Kuchma Leonid 1938– . Ukrainian politician, prime minister 1992–93 and president from 1994. A traditional Soviet technocrat, he worked his way up the hierarchy of the Communist Party (CPSU) and, when the USSR was dissolved and Ukraine gained independence 1991, was well placed to assume senior positions within the Ukrainian administration. As prime minister, Kuchma established himself as a moderate reformer and in July 1994 became president, defeating the incumbent Leonid Kravchuk. Once in power, his programme for reform proved more pro-Western than originally pledged.

Kristallnacht Clearing up the wreckage of a Jewish shop in Germany after a night of attack by the Nazis. Following the assassination of a member of the German embassy in Paris by a Jew, the Nazis launched an organized attack on Jewish shops and homes. The night of 9–10 Nov 1938 came to be known as Kristallnacht – the night of (broken) glass. *Corbis*

kudu either of two species of African antelope of the genus *Tragelaphus*. The greater kudu *T. strepsiceros* is fawn-coloured with thin white vertical stripes, and stands 1.3 m/4.2 ft at the shoulder, with head and body 2.4 m/8 ft long. Males have long spiral horns. The greater kudu is found in bush country from Angola to Ethiopia. The similar lesser kudu *T. imberbis* lives in E Africa and is 1 m/3 ft at the shoulder.

kudzu Japanese creeper *Pueraria lobata*, family Leguminosae, which helps fix nitrogen (see ◊nitrogen cycle) and can be used as fodder, but became a pest in the southern USA when introduced to check soil erosion.

Kuhn Thomas Samuel 1922–1996. US historian and philosopher of science, who showed that social and cultural conditions affect the directions of science. *The Structure of Scientific Revolutions* 1962 argued that even scientific knowledge is relative, dependent on the ◊paradigm (theoretical framework) that dominates a scientific field at the time. Such paradigms (for example, Darwinism and Newtonian theory) are so dominant that they are uncritically accepted as true, until a 'scientific revolution' creates a new orthodoxy. Kuhn's ideas have also influenced ideas in the social sciences.

Kuiper Gerard Peter 1905–1973. Dutch-born US astronomer who made extensive studies of the Solar System. His discoveries included the atmosphere of the planet Mars and that of Titan, the largest moon of the planet Saturn. He was adviser to many NASA exploratory missions, and pioneered the use of telescopes on high-flying aircraft. The Kuiper Airborne Observatory, one such telescope, is named after him; it was permanently grounded Oct 1995.

Kuiper belt ring of small, icy bodies orbiting the Sun beyond the outermost planet. The Kuiper belt, named after US astronomer Gerard Kuiper who proposed its existence in 1951, is thought to be the source of comets that orbit the Sun with periods of

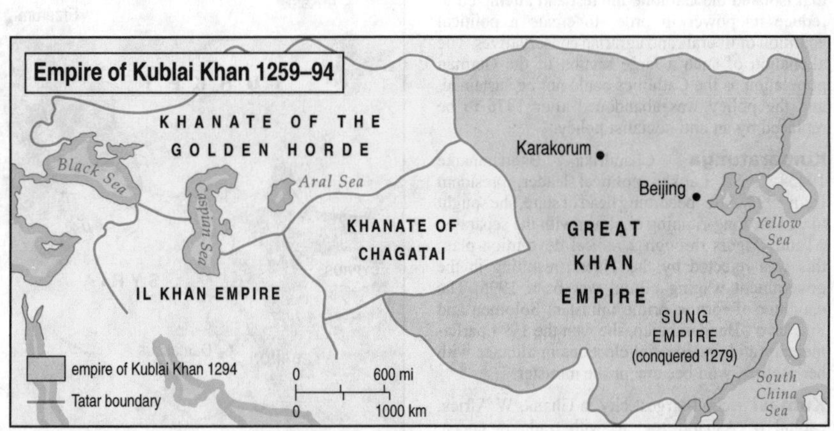

Ku Klux Klan The Ku Klux Klan attempted, at times successfully, to become an accepted part of mainstream politics – here they are seen parading through Washington. However, internal rivalries, a series of scandals, and a greater public awareness of their racism and violence meant that they achieved only local influence. *Library of Congress*

less than 200 years. The first member of the Kuiper belt was seen 1992.

In 1995 the first comet-sized objects were discovered; previously the only objects found had diameters of at least 100 km/63 mi (comets generally have diameters of less than 10 km/6.3 mi).

Ku Klux Klan US secret society dedicated to white supremacy, founded 1866 in the southern states of the USA to oppose ◊Reconstruction after the American ◊Civil War and to deny political rights to the black population. Members wore hooded white robes to hide their identity, and burned crosses at their night-time meetings. Today the Klan has evolved into a paramilitary extremist group and has forged loose ties with other white supremacist groups.

It was originally headed by former Confederate general Nathan Bedford Forrest (1821–1877) and was disbanded 1869 under pressure from members who opposed violence. Scattered groups continued a campaign of lynching and flogging, prompting the government to pass the restrictive Ku Klux Klan Acts of 1871. The society re-emerged 1915 in Atlanta, Georgia, and increased in strength during the 1920s as a racist, anti-Semitic, anti-Catholic, and anticommunist organization, with membership reaching more than 4 million. It was publicized in the 1960s for terrorizing civil-rights activists and organizing racist demonstrations. In the 1990s it began actively recruiting and organizing in the UK, with membership coming primarily from existing extreme-right groupings.

kulak Russian term for a peasant who could afford to hire labour and often acted as village usurer. The kulaks resisted the Soviet government's policy of collectivization, and in 1930 they were 'liquidated as a class', with up to 5 million being either killed or deported to Siberia.

Kulturkampf German word for a policy introduced by Chancellor Bismarck in Germany 1873 that isolated the Catholic interest and attempted to reduce its power in order to create a political coalition of liberals and agrarian conservatives. The alienation of such a large section of the German population as the Catholics could not be sustained, and the policy was abandoned after 1876 to be replaced by an anti-socialist policy.

Kumaratunga Chandrika Bandaranaike 1945– . Sri Lankan political leader, president from 1994. After becoming head of state, she sought to end the long-running civil war with the separatist ◊Tamil Tigers through a radical devolution plan; this was rejected by the Tigers, resulting in the government waging all-out war from 1995. The daughter of former prime ministers Solomon and Sirimavo ◊Bandaranaike, she won the 1994 parliamentary and presidential elections in alliance with her mother, who became prime minister.

Kumasi second-largest city in Ghana, W Africa, capital of Ashanti region, with trade in cocoa, rubber, and cattle; its market is one of the largest in W Africa; population (1988 est) 385,200. From the late 17th century until 1901, when it was absorbed into the British Gold Coast Colony, Kumasi was capital of the Ashanti confederation.

kumquat small orange-yellow fruit of any of several evergreen trees of the genus *Fortunella*, family Rutaceae. Native to E Asia, kumquats are cultivated throughout the tropics. The tree grows 2.4–3.6 m/8–12 ft high and has dark green shiny leaves and white scented flowers. The fruit is eaten fresh (the skin is edible), preserved, or candied. The oval or Nagami kumquat is the most common variety.

Kun Béla 1886–1937. Hungarian politician. He created a Soviet republic in Hungary March 1919, which was overthrown Aug 1919 by a Western blockade and Romanian military actions. The succeeding regime under Admiral Horthy effectively liquidated both socialism and liberalism in Hungary.

Kundera Milan 1929– . Czech writer. His first novel, *The Joke* 1967, brought him into official disfavour in Prague, and, unable to publish further works, he moved to France. Other novels include *The Book of Laughter and Forgetting* 1979 and *The Unbearable Lightness of Being* 1984 (filmed 1988).

Kung (formerly ***Bushman***) member of a small group of hunter-gatherer peoples of the NE Kalahari, southern Africa, still living to some extent nomadically. Their language belongs to the ◊Khoisan family.

kung fu (Mandarin *ch'üan fa*) Chinese art of unarmed combat, one of the ◊martial arts. It is practised in many forms, the most popular being *wing chun*, 'beautiful springtime'. The basic principle is to use attack as a form of defence. Kung fu dates from the 6th century, and was popularized in the West by the film actor Bruce Lee in the 1970s.

Kunming formerly ***Yunnan*** capital of Yunnan province, China, on Lake Dian Chi, about 2,000 m/6,500 ft above sea level; population (1993) 1,450,000. Industries include chemicals, textiles, and copper smelted with nearby hydroelectric power.

Kuomintang original spelling of the Chinese nationalist party, now known (outside Taiwan) as ◊Guomindang.

Kurd people of Kurdish culture, living mostly in the Taurus and Sagros mountains of E Turkey, W Iran, and N Iraq in the region called ◊Kurdistan. About 1 million Kurds were made homeless and 25,000 killed as a result of chemical-weapon attacks by Iraq 1984–89, and in 1991 more than 1 million were forced to flee their homes in N Iraq. They are predominantly Sunni Muslims, although there are some Shi'ites in Iran.

There are approximately 12 million Kurds in Turkey, 5 million in Iran, 4 million in Iraq, 500,000 in Syria, and 500,000 in Azerbaijan, Armenia, and Georgia. Several million live elsewhere in Europe. Although divided among several states, they have nationalist aspirations, and the growth of a pan-Kurdish movement has been helped by the recent move to towns (undertaken in search of work and to escape repression). A Kurdish parliament in exile was established in The Hague, the Netherlands, 1995 by Kurdish exiles from Turkey, Iran, and Iraq, where the Kurds have suffered discriminatory legislation, as well as repression in several other countries, most brutally in Iraq.

Kurdish language language belonging to the Indo-Iranian branch of the Indo-European family, closely related to Farsi (Persian). It is spoken by the Kurds, a geographically divided ethnic group. Its numerous dialects fall into two main groups: northern Kurmanji and southern Kurmanji (also known as Sorani). Around 60% of Kurds speak one of the northern Kurmanji dialects. Related languages include Zaza and Gurani. Three different alphabets are used – Arabic, Latin, and Cyrillic.

Kurdish is the second official language in Iraq and the official language of the Kurdish autonomous region in the north of the country. Use of Kurdish is suppressed in Syria and Turkey, but is tolerated in Iran.

Kurdistan or ***Kordestan*** hilly region in SW Asia near Mount Ararat, where the borders of Iran, Iraq,

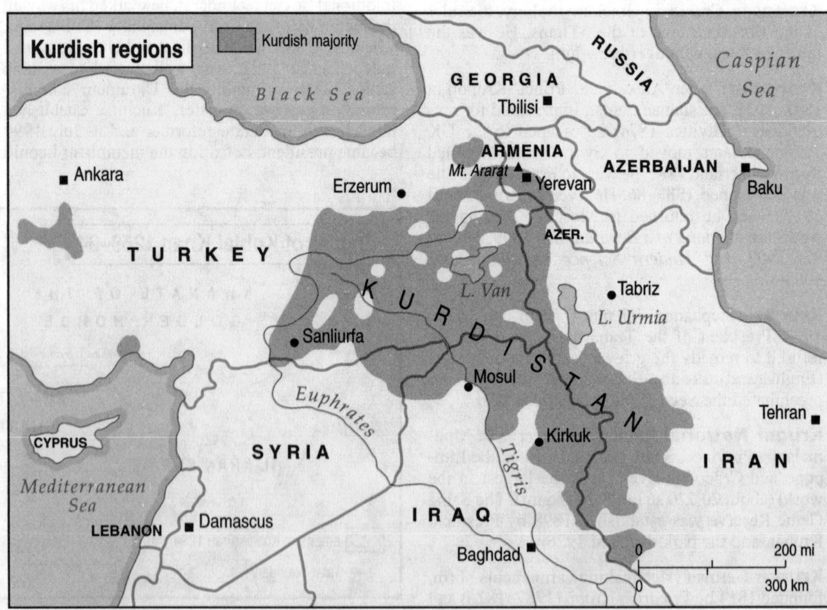

Syria, Turkey, Armenia, and Azerbaijan meet; area 193,000 sq km/74,600 sq mi; total population around 18 million. It is the home of the Kurds and is the area over which Kurdish nationalists have traditionally fought to win sovereignty. It is also the name of a NW Iranian province, covering 25,000 sq km/9,650 sq mi, population (1991) 1,233,500.

Situated on the ancient Silk Road, on the northern edge of the Fertile Crescent, Kurdistan grew to be a prosperous area during the Middle Ages. Its steady decline began in the 16th century when sea traffic replaced the Silk Road. Today, despite being one of the poorest areas in the Middle East in terms of income per head, it holds rich oil reserves and is the source of much of the water that flows into Syria, Iraq, and W Iran.

Kureishi Hanif 1954– . English dramatist, filmmaker, and novelist. His work concentrates on the lives of Asians living in Britain. His early plays *Outskirts* 1981 and *Birds of Passage* 1983 were followed by the screenplays for the films *My Beautiful Laundrette* 1984 and *Sammy and Rosie Get Laid* 1987, both directed by Stephen Frears. He wrote and directed the film *London Kills Me* 1991. *The Buddha of Suburbia* 1990 was followed by another novel, *The Black Album* 1995.

Kuril Islands or ***Kuriles*** chain of about 50 small islands stretching from the NE of Hokkaido, Japan, to the S of Kamchatka, Russia; area 14,765 sq km/5,700 sq mi; population (1990) 25,000. Some of them are of volcanic origin. Two of the Kurils (Etorofu and Kunashiri) are claimed by Japan and Russia; they are of strategic importance and also have mineral deposits.

The Kurils were discovered 1634 by a Russian navigator and were settled by Russians. Japan seized them 1875 and held them until they were taken by Soviet forces Aug 1945. Japan still claims the southernmost two (Etorofu and Kunashiri) and also the nearby small islands of Habomai and Shikotan (not part of the Kurils). The question of the S Kurils prevents signature of a Japan–Russia peace treaty to formally end World War II.

Kurosawa Akira 1910–1998. Japanese director. His film *Rashōmon* 1950 introduced Western audiences to Japanese cinema. Epics such as *Shichinin no samurai/Seven Samurai* 1954 combine spectacle with intimate human drama. Kurosawa's films with a contemporary setting include *Drunken Angel* 1948 and *Ikiru/Living* 1952, both using illness as metaphor. *Yōjimbō* 1961, *Kagemusha* 1981, and *Ran* 1985 (loosely based on Shakespeare's *King Lear*) are historical films with an increasingly bleak outlook.

Kurosawa Japanese film director Akira Kurosawa, the first Japanese filmmaker to win international acclaim. His films, many of them epics based on Japanese history or literature, are noted for their striking imagery and compelling characterization. They include *Rashōmon* 1950, *Ikiru* 1952, *The Seven Samurai* 1954, and *Ran* 1985, a Japanese version of *King Lear*. *Topham*

Kuroshio or ***Japan Current*** warm ocean ◊current flowing from Japan to North America.

Kursk capital city of Kursk region of W Russian Federation; population (1994) 439,000. Industries include chemicals, machinery, alcohol, and tobacco. It dates from the 9th century.

In World War II, Kursk was the site of the Battle of Kursk July 1943 between German and Soviet forces; the greatest tank battle in history and a turning point in the Eastern Front campaign.

Kursk, Battle of in World War II, unsuccessful German offensive against a Soviet salient July 1943. Kursk was the greatest tank battle in history and proved to be a turning point in the Eastern Front campaign. With nearly 6,000 tanks and 2 million troops involved the battle was hard fought, reaching its climax with the pitched battle 12 July between 700 German and 850 Soviet tanks.

Kusana dynasty or ***Yueh-chih dynasty*** N Indian family ruling between the 1st and 2nd centuries AD. The greatest Kusana king was Kaniska (ruled c. 78–102). A devout Buddhist and liberal patron of the arts, he extended the empire across central and E India. In decline by 176, the dynasty was overthrown by the ◊Sassanians about 240.

Kutuzov Mikhail Illarionovich. Prince of Smolensk 1745–1813. Commander of the Russian forces in the Napoleonic Wars. He commanded an army corps at ◊Austerlitz and the army in its retreat 1812. After the burning of Moscow that year, he harried the French throughout their retreat and later took command of the united Prussian armies.

Kuwait country in SW Asia, bounded N and NW by Iraq, E by the Persian Gulf, and S and SW by Saudi Arabia. *See country box below.*

Kuwait City (Arabic ***Al Kuwayt***) formerly ***Qurein*** chief port and capital of the state of Kuwait, on the southern shore of Kuwait Bay; population (1993) 31,200. Kuwait is a banking and investment centre. It was heavily damaged during the Gulf War.

kW symbol for ◊***kilowatt***.

Kwa Ndebele former black homeland in former Transvaal Province, South Africa; now partly in Mpumalanga and partly in Gauteng.

To be an artist means never to look away.

AKIRA KUROSAWA
Quoted in the *Guardian* 1980

KUWAIT
State of

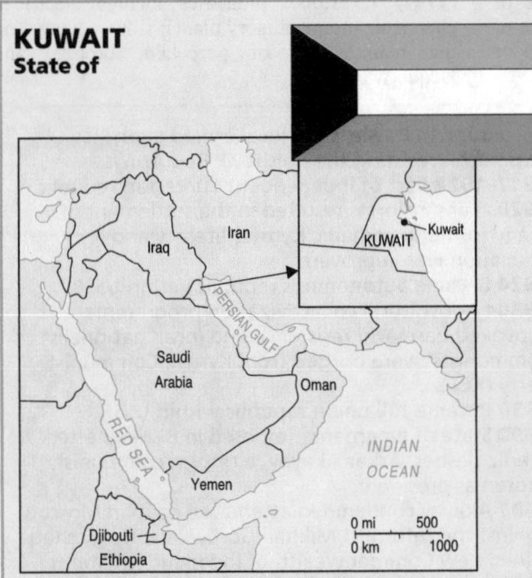

national name *Dowlat al Kuwait*
area 17,819 sq km/6,878 sq mi
capital Kuwait (also chief port)
major towns/cities Jahra, Ahmadi, Fahaheel
physical features hot desert; islands of Failaka, Bubiyan, and Warba at NE corner of Arabian Peninsula
head of state Sheikh Jabir al-Ahmad al-Jabir as-Sabah from 1977
head of government Crown Prince Sheikh Saad al-Abdullah as-Salinas as-Sabah from 1978
political system absolute monarchy
administrative divisions four districts
political parties none
population 1,687,000 (1996 est)
population growth rate −6.5% (1990–95); 2.5% (2000–05)
ethnic distribution about 42% Kuwaiti, 40% non-Kuwaiti Arab, 5% Indian and Pakistani, and 4% Iranian
life expectancy 72 (men), 77 (women)
literacy rate men 77%, women 67%
languages Arabic (official) 78%, Kurdish 10%, Farsi 4%, English
religions Sunni Muslim, Shi'ite Muslim, Christian
currency Kuwaiti dinar
GDP (US $) 24.19 billion (1994)
growth rate −4.0% (1994)
exports oil, chemical fertilizers, shrimps, metal pipes, building materials

HISTORY
c. 3000 BC Archaeological evidence suggests that coastal parts of Kuwait may have been part of a commercial civilization contemporary with the Sumerian, based in Mesopotamia (the Tigris and Euphrates valley area of Iraq).
c. 323 BC Visited by Greek colonists at time of Alexander the Great.
7th C AD Islam introduced.
late 16th C Fell under the nominal control of the Turkish Ottoman Empire.
1710 Control was assumed by the Utab, a member of the Anaza tribal confederation in N Arabia, and Kuwait city was founded, soon developing from a fishing village into an important port.
1756 Autonomous sheikdom of Kuwait founded by Abd Rahman of the al-Sabah family, a branch of the Utab.
1776 British East India Company set up a base in the Gulf.
1899 Concerned at the potential threat of growing Ottoman and German influence, Britain signed a treaty with Kuwait, establishing a self-governing protectorate in which the Emir received an annual subsidy from Britain in return for agreeing not to alienate any territory to a foreign power.
1914 Britain recognized Kuwait as an 'independent government under British protection'.
1922–33 Agreement on frontiers with Iraq, to the N, and Najd (later Saudi Arabia) to the SW.
1938 Oil discovered; large-scale exploitation after World War II transformed the economy.
1961 Full independence achieved from Britain, with Sheik Abdullah al-Salem al-Sabah as emir. Attempted Iraqi invasion discouraged by dispatch of British troops to the Gulf.
1962 Constitution introduced, with franchise restricted to 10% of the population.
1965 Sheik Abdullah died; succeeded by his brother, Sheik Sabah al-Salem al-Sabah.
1977 Sheik Sabah died; succeeded by Crown Prince Jabir. National Assembly dissolved.
1981 National Assembly was reconstituted.
1983 Shi'ite guerrillas bombed targets in Kuwait; 17 arrested.
1986 National assembly dissolved.
1987 Kuwaiti oil tankers reflagged, received US Navy protection; missile attacks by Iran.
1988 Aircraft hijacked by pro-Iranian Shi'ites demanding release of convicted guerrillas; Kuwait refused.
1989 Two of the convicted guerrillas released.
1990 Prodemocracy demonstrations suppressed. Kuwait annexed by Iraq in Aug, causing extensive damage to property and environment. Emir set up government in exile in Saudi Arabia.
1991 Kuwait liberated by US-led coalition forces. New government omitted any opposition representatives.
1992 Reconstituted national assembly elected, with opposition nominees, including Islamic candidates, winning majority of seats.
1993 Incursions by Iraq into Kuwait repelled by US-led air strikes on Iraqi military sites.
1994 Massing of Iraqi troops on Kuwait border prompted US-led response. Iraqi president Saddam Hussein publicly renounced claim to Kuwait.
1996 Pro-government candidates secured most of the seats in elections.
1997 Secular National Democratic Rally (NDR) established May. Illegal immigrants ordered to leave the country, Nov.
1998 US forces deployed from Kuwait during four-day air strikes on Iraq.

SEE ALSO Iran–Iraq War; Gulf War

Kyoto The Kiyomizudea temple in the hills above Kyoto. One of Japan's major religious centres, Kyoto abounds in shrines and temples, both Buddhist and Shinto. The capital of Japan for a thousand years, and one of the few Japanese cities not to be bombed during World War II, Kyoto retains a strong sense of Japanese heritage. *Japan National Tourist Organization*

Kwangchu or ***Kwangju*** capital of South Cholla province, SW South Korea; population (1990) 1,144,700. It is at the centre of a rice-growing region. A museum in the city houses a large collection of Chinese porcelain dredged up 1976 after lying for over 600 years on the ocean floor.

Kwannon or ***Kannon*** in Japanese Buddhism, a form, often regarded as female (and known to the West as 'goddess of mercy'), of the bodhisattva ◊Avalokiteśvara. Kwannon is sometimes depicted with many arms extending compassion.

kwashiorkor severe protein deficiency in children under five years, resulting in retarded growth, lethargy, ◊oedema, diarrhoea, and a swollen abdomen. It is common in Third World countries with a high incidence of malnutrition.

KwaZulu former black homeland in former Natal Province, South Africa. In 1994 it became part of ◊KwaZulu Natal Province. It achieved self-governing status 1971. In 1994 it was placed under a state of emergency in the run-up to the first multiracial elections, after mounting violence by the Zulu-based ◊Inkatha party threatened to destabilize the election process. Homelands were to progressively disappear under the 1993 nonracial constitution, but Inkatha's leader (and the homeland's chief minister), Mangosuthu Buthelezi, won substantial concessions for KwaZulu prior to agreeing to participate in the elections.

KwaZulu Natal province of the Republic of South Africa, formed from the former province of Natal and the former independent homeland of KwaZulu
area 91,481 sq km/35,321 sq mi
capital Pietmaritzburg
towns and cities Durban, Richards Bay
features Ndumu Game Reserve; Kosi Bay Nature Reserve; Sodwana Bay National Park; Maple Lane Nature Reserve; St Lucia National Park, which extends from coral reefs of the Indian Ocean north of Umfolozi River (whales, dolphins, turtles, crayfish), over forested sandhills to inland grasslands and swamps of Lake St Lucia, 324 sq km/125 sq mi (reedbuck, buffalo, crocodiles, hippopotami, black rhinos, cheetahs, pelicans, flamingos, storks); it is under threat from titanium mining
industries oil refining, coal, iron and steel, sugar, maize, fruit, black wattle, maize, tobacco, vegetables
population (1995 est) 8,713,100; 75% Zulu
languages Zulu 80%, English 15%, Afrikaans 2%
history The South African government agreed June 1995 to establish a commission to investigate the worsening situation in the province, where politically motivated violence was rife. The conflict lay between followers of Mangosuthu ◊Buthelezi, the leader of ◊Inkatha, who wants federal states for Kwazulu Natal, and those of the Zulu king, Goodwill Zwerethini.

kyanite aluminium silicate, Al_2SiO_5, a pale-blue mineral occurring as blade-shaped crystals. It is an indicator of high-pressure conditions in metamorphic rocks formed from clay sediments. Andalusite, kyanite, and sillimanite are all polymorphs.

Kyd Thomas c. 1557–1595. English dramatist. He was the author of a bloody revenge tragedy, *The Spanish Tragedy* printed about 1590, which anticipated elements present in Shakespeare's *Hamlet*.

His *Pompey the Great* 1594 is a translation from the French. He probably wrote *Solyman and Perseda* 1592, and perhaps had a part in *Arden of Feversham* 1592, the first of many domestic tragedies. Kyd's work is characterized by technical skill and a vigorous sense of theatricality.

Kyoto former capital of Japan 794–1868 (when the capital was changed to Tokyo) on Honshu Island, linked by canal with Biwa Lake; population (1994) 1,391,000. Industries include electrical, chemical, and machinery plants; silk weaving; and the manufacture of porcelain, bronze, and lacquerware.

KYRGYZSTAN
Republic of

0 mi 500
0 km 1000
Kazakhstan
Bishkek
China
Uzbekistan
KYRGYZSTAN
Tajikistan
Turkmenistan

national name *Kyrgyz Respublikasy*
area 198,500 sq km/76,641 sq mi
capital Bishkek (formerly Frunze)
major towns/cities Osh, Przhevalsk, Kyzyl-Kiya, Tokmak, Djalal-Abad
physical features mountainous, an extension of the Tian Shan range
head of state Askar Akayev from 1990
head of government Kubanychbek Djumaliev from 1998
political system emergent democracy
administrative divisions six regions
political parties Party of Communists of Kyrgyzstan (banned 1991–92); Ata Meken, Kyrgyz-nationalist; Erkin Kyrgyzstan, Kyrgyz-nationalist; Social Democratic Party, nationalist, pro-Akayev; Democratic Movement of Kyrgyzstan, nationalist reformist
population 4,469,000 (1996 est)
population growth rate 1.7% (1990–95); 1.5% (2000–05)
ethnic distribution 53% ethnic Kyrgyz, 22% Russian, 13% Uzbek, 3% Ukrainian, and 2% German
life expectancy 65 (men), 73 (women)
literacy rate 97%
language Kyrgyz, a Turkic language
religion Sunni Muslim
currency som
GDP (US $) 2.66 billion (1994)
growth rate −26.2% (1994)
exports cereals, sugar, cotton, coal, oil, sheep, yaks, horses

HISTORY
8th C Spread of Islam.
10th C onwards Southward migration of the Kyrgyz people from the upper Yenisei River region to the Tian-Shan region; accelerated following the rise of the Mongol Empire in the 13th century.
13th–14th Cs Part of the Mongol Empire.
1685 Came under the control of the Mongol Oirots following centuries of Turkic rule.
1758 Kyrgyz people became nominal subjects of the Chinese Empire, following the Oirots' defeat by the Chinese rulers, the Manchus.
early 19th C Came under the suzerainty of the Khanate (chieftaincy) of Kokand, to the W.
1864–76 Incorporated into the tsarist Russian Empire.
1916–17 Many Kyrgyz migrated to China after Russian suppression of rebellion in Central Asia and the outbreak of civil war following the 1917 October Revolution in Russia, with local armed guerrillas (*basmachi*) resisting the Bolshevik Red Army.
1917–1924 Part of independent Turkestan republic.
1920s Land reforms resulted in the settlement of many formerly nomadic Kyrgyz; literacy and education was improved.
1924 Became autonomous republic within USSR.
1930s Agricultural collectivization programme provoked basmachi resistance and local 'nationalist communists' were purged from Kyrgyz Communist Party (KCP).
1936 Became full union republic within USSR.
1990 State of emergency imposed in Bishkek after ethnic clashes. Askar Akayev, a reform communist, chosen as president.
1991 Akayev condemned attempted coup in Moscow against the reformist Mikhail Gorbachev; Kyrgyzstan joined new Commonwealth of Independent States (CIS); independence recognized by USA.
1992 Joined the United Nations and Conference on Security and Cooperation in Europe (CSCE; now the OSCE). Market-centred economic reform programme instituted.
1994 National referenda overwhelmingly supported Akayev's presidency. Joined Central Asian Union, with Kazakhstan and Uzbekistan.
1995 Pro-Akayev independents successful in elections to a new bicameral legislature.
1996 Constitutional amendment increased powers of president. Agreement with Kazakhstan and Uzbekistan to create single economic market.
1997 Private ownership of land legalized but privatization programme suspended. Agreement on border controls with Russia.
1998 Apas Jumagulov resigned as prime minister and replaced by Kubanychbek Djumaliev.

SEE ALSO Manchu; Russian Federation; Turkestan; Union of Soviet Socialist Republics

features The city has more than 2,000 temples and shrines, including Tō-ji (1380), Kiyomizu-dera (1633), Ryōan-ji with its 15th-century Zen rock and sand garden, Sanjusangendo (1266), and the former Ashikaga shoguns' villas Kinkaku-ji and Ginkaku-ji (the 'gold and silver pavilions'). Other features are the Gion teahouse district with traditional geishas, the silk-weavers' district of Nishijin, 17th-century sake warehouses in Fushimi, Momoyama castle, and Japan's oldest theatre, the Minamiza kabuki theatre (early 17th century).
history Like previous Japanese capitals, Kyoto was originally laid out in a grid pattern derived from China. Civil wars, especially that between the Taira and Minamoto clans in the 12th century and the Ōnin war 1467–77, caused great destruction in the capital, and it has been periodically ravaged by fire, most recently 1864, when almost 80% of the city was laid waste. Although the shogunate was at times based elsewhere, Kyoto remained the seat of the imperial court until the Meiji restoration 1868, and is still a cultural centre.

Kyprianou Spyros 1932– . Cypriot politician, president 1977–88. Foreign minister 1961–72, he founded the federalist, centre-left Democratic Front 1976. He became secretary to Archbishop Makarios in London 1952 and returned with him to Cyprus 1959. On the death of Makarios 1977 he became acting president and was then elected.

Kyrgyzstan or ***Kirghizia*** country in central Asia, bounded N by Kazakhstan, E by China, W by Uzbekistan, and S by Tajikistan. *See country box opposite.*

Kyrie eleison (Greek 'Lord have mercy') the words spoken or sung at the beginning of the mass in the Catholic, Orthodox, and Anglican churches. Following the Introit, it has three parts of text: Kyrie Eleison, Christe Eleison, Kyrie Eleison, each of which is repeated three times, reflecting the Holy Trinity.

Kyushu southernmost of the main islands of Japan, separated from Shikoku and Honshu islands by Bungo Channel and Suo Bay, but connected to Honshu by bridge and rail tunnel
area 42,150 sq km/16,270 sq mi, including about 370 small islands
capital Nagasaki
cities Fukuoka, Kumamoto, Kagoshima
physical mountainous, volcanic, with subtropical climate
features the active volcano Aso-take (1,592 m/5,225 ft), with the world's largest crater
industries coal, gold, silver, iron, tin, rice, tea, timber
population (1995) 13,424,000.

'Oh eyes, no eyes, but fountains fraught with tears; / Oh life, no life, but lively form of death; / Oh world, no world, but mass of public wrongs.'

Thomas Kyd
The Spanish Tragedy

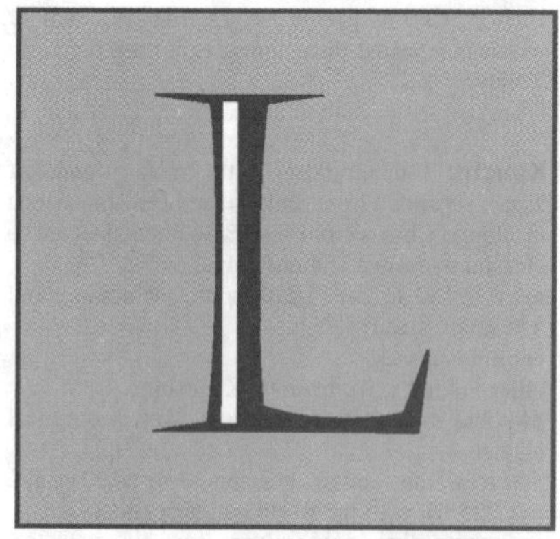

Laban Rudolf von 1879–1958. Hungarian dance theoretician. He is known as the leader of modern dance theory. He invented Labanotation 1928, an accurate, detailed system of recording steps and movements, commonly used as a means of copyright protection for choreographers. It uses a set of graphic symbols arranged on a vertical staff that represents the human body, and the varying length of the symbols indicates the timing of the movements. He researched the connection between psychology and motion in his theoretical work.

labelled compound or ***tagged compound*** chemical compound in which a radioactive isotope is substituted for a stable one. The path taken by such a compound through a system can be followed, for example by measuring the radiation emitted. This powerful and sensitive technique is used in medicine, chemistry, biochemistry, and industry.

labelling in sociology, defining or describing a person in terms of his or her behaviour; for example, describing someone who has broken a law as a criminal. Labelling theory deals with human interaction, behaviour, and control, particularly in the field of deviance.

labellum lower petal of an orchid flower; it is a different shape from the two lateral petals and gives the orchid its characteristic appearance. The labellum is more elaborate and usually larger than the other petals. It often has distinctive patterning to encourage ◊pollination by insects; sometimes it is extended backwards to form a hollow spur containing nectar.

Labor Party in Australia, a political party based on socialist principles. It was founded 1891 and first held office 1904. It formed governments 1929–31 and 1939–49, but in the intervening periods internal discord provoked splits, and reduced its effectiveness. It returned to power under Gough Whitlam 1972–75, and again under Bob Hawke 1983, he was succeeded as party leader and prime minister by Paul Keating 1991, who subsequently lost the 1996 general election.

Labour Day legal holiday in honour of workers. In Canada and the USA, ***Labor Day*** is celebrated on the first Monday in September. In many countries it coincides with ◊May Day, the first day of May.

Labour Party UK political party based on socialist principles, originally formed to represent workers. It was founded 1900 as the ◊Labour Representation Committee and first held office 1924. The first majority Labour government 1945–51 introduced ◊nationalization and the National Health Service, and expanded ◊social security. Labour was again in power 1964–70 and 1974–79. The party leader (Tony Blair from 1994) is elected by an electoral college, with a weighted representation of the Parliamentary Labour Party (30%), constituency parties (30%), and trade unions (40%). The Labour Party, the Trades Union Congress, and the cooperative movement together form the National Council of Labour, whose aims are to coordinate political activities and take joint action on specific issues.

In opposition from 1979, the party adopted a policy of unilateral nuclear disarmament 1986, a major factor in its defeat in the 1987 general election. Under Blair's leadership, Labour launched a campaign to revise the party's constitution by scrapping Clause 4, concerning common ownership of the means of production, and ending trade union direct sponsorship of members of Parliament; a new charter was approved 1995. Using the title 'New Labour', Blair sought to move the party nearer to the 'middle ground' of politics to secure the 'middle England' vote. The party returned to power after a landslide victory in the 1997 general election, with its highest share of the national vote since 1966.

‘A pious man is one who would be an atheist under an atheist king.’

JEAN DE LA BRUYÈRE
The Characters

Labour Representation Committee in British politics, a forerunner 1900–1906 of the Labour Party. The committee was founded in Feb 1900 after a resolution drafted by Ramsay ◊MacDonald and moved by the Amalgamated Society of Railway Workers (now the National Union of Railwaymen) was carried at the 1899 Trades Union Congress (TUC). The resolution called for a special congress of the TUC parliamentary committee to campaign for more Labour members of Parliament. Ramsay MacDonald became its secretary. Following his efforts, 29 Labour members of Parliament were elected in the 1906 general election, and the Labour Representation Committee was renamed the Labour Party.

Labrador area of NE Canada, part of the province of Newfoundland, lying between Ungava Bay on the NW, the Atlantic Ocean on the E, and the Strait of Belle Isle on the SE; area 266,060 sq km/102,699 sq mi; population (1986) 28,741. It consists primarily of a gently sloping plateau with an irregular coastline of numerous bays, fjords, inlets, and cliffs (60–120 m/200–400 ft high). Industries include fisheries, timber and pulp, and many minerals. Hydroelectric resources include Churchill Falls on Churchill River, where one of the world's largest underground power houses is situated. There is a Canadian air force base at Goose Bay.

La Bruyère Jean de 1645–1696. French writer and moralist. He was born in Paris, studied law, took a post in the revenue office, and in 1684 entered the service of the French commander the Prince of ◊Condé as tutor to his grandson. His 'Caractères/The Characters' 1688, a penetrating study of human behaviour in the form of satirical pen-portraits of his contemporaries, made him many enemies. The work is remarkable also for its highly critical account of French society in the last years of the 17th century. La Bruyère's style is notable for its rich vocabulary and infinite variety of phrase.

laburnum any flowering tree or shrub of the genus *Laburnum* of the pea family Leguminosae. The seeds are poisonous. *L. anagyroides*, native to the mountainous parts of central Europe, is often grown as an ornamental tree. The flowers, in long drooping clusters, are usually bright yellow and appear in early spring.

Labyrinth in Greek legend, the maze designed by the Athenian artisan Daedalus at Knossos in Crete for King Minos, as a home for the Minotaur – a monster, half man and half bull. After killing the Minotaur, Theseus, the prince of Athens, was guided out of the Labyrinth by a thread given to him by the king's daughter Ariadne.

labyrinthitis inflammation of the part of the inner ear responsible for the sense of balance (the labyrinth). It results in dizziness, which may then cause nausea and vomiting. It is usually caused by a viral infection of the ear (◊otitis), which resolves in a few weeks. The nausea and vomiting may respond to anti-emetic drugs.

lac resinous incrustation exuded by the female of the lac insect *Laccifer lacca*, which eventually covers the twigs of trees in India and the Far East. The gathered twigs are known as stick lac, and yield a useful crimson dye; shellac, which is used in varnishes, polishes, and leather dressings, is manufactured commercially by melting the separated resin and spreading it into thin layers or flakes.

laccolith intruded mass of igneous rock that forces apart two strata and forms a round lens-shaped mass many times wider than thick. The overlying layers are often pushed upward to form a dome. A classic development of laccoliths is illustrated in the Henry, La Sal, and Abajo mountains of SE Utah, USA, found on the Colorado plateau.

lace delicate, decorative, openwork textile fabric. Lace is a European craft with centres in Belgium, Italy, France, Germany, and England.

Needlepoint or ***point lace*** (a development of embroidery) originated in Italy in the late 15th or early 16th centuries. Lace was first made from linen thread and sometimes also with gold, silver, or silk; cotton, wool, and synthetic fibres have been used more recently.

Bobbin or ***pillow*** ('true') ***lace*** is made by twisting threads together in pairs or groups, according to a pattern marked out by pins set in a cushion. It is said to have been invented by Barbara Uttmann (born 1514) of Saxony; elaborate patterns may require over a thousand bobbins.

Machine lace was first produced 1809 by John Heathcote using a bobbin net machine; the principles of this system are kept today in machines making plain net. The earliest machine for making true lace, reproducing the movements of the workers' fingers, was invented in England by John Leavers 1813. It had a wooden frame with mostly wooden moving parts, but worked on the same principle as the modern machines in Nottingham, England, the centre of machine-made lace.

lacewing insect of the families Hemerobiidae (the brown lacewings) and Chrysopidae (the green lacewings) of the order Neuroptera. Found throughout the world, lacewings are so called because of the intricate veining of their two pairs of semi-transparent wings. They have narrow bodies and long

lace Lacemaker at work, Bruges, Belgium. The delicate, open fabric of lace is traditionally worked into intricate designs by twisting threaded bobbins around pins stuck into a cushion to mark out the pattern. The time-consuming and eye-straining work of the traditional lacemakers has largely been replaced by machine lace, though the old craft survives in several European centres. *Corbis*

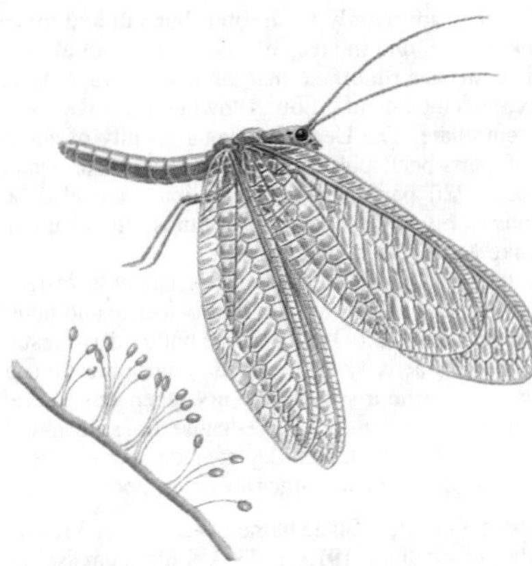

lacewing Lacewing adults are slender-bodied flies with two pairs of wings covered with a network of veins – hence the name. They are often green in colour and have long antennae. Both adults and larvae feed voraciously on greenfly and other aphids so they are valuable to gardeners.

thin antennae. The larvae (called aphid lions) are predators, especially on aphids.

laches in law, neglect and unreasonable delay in enforcing an equitable right. If the court is satisfied that a plaintiff has taken an unnecessarily long time in pursuing a case, the action may be struck out.

Laclos Pierre-Ambroise-François Choderlos de 1741–1803. French author. An army officer, he wrote a single novel in letter form, *Les Liaisons dangereuses/Dangerous Liaisons* 1782, an analysis of moral corruption. A cynical and unscrupulous libertine, the Vicomte de Valmont, encouraged by the Marquise de Merteuil, seduces and destroys two innocent women. A moral twist is given at the end of the book when Valmont is killed in a duel and the Marquise de Merteuil is hideously disfigured by smallpox. The work was adapted as a play 1985 by Christopher Hampton (1946–) and as a film 1988, directed by Stephen Frears (1941–).

lacquer waterproof resinous varnish obtained from oriental trees *Toxicodendron verniciflua*, and used for decorating furniture and art objects. It can be applied to wood, fabric, leather, or other materials, with or without added colours. The technique of making and carving small lacquerwork objects was developed in China, probably as early as the 4th century BC, and was later adopted in Japan.

lacrosse Canadian ball game, adopted from the North American Indians, and named after a fancied resemblance of the lacrosse stick (crosse) to a bishop's crosier. Thongs across the curved end of the crosse form a pocket to carry the small rubber ball. The field is approximately 100 m/110 yd long and a minimum of 55 m/60 yd wide in the men's game, which is played with 10 players per side; the women's field is larger, and there are 12 players per side. The goals are just under 2 m/6 ft square, with loose nets. The world championship was first held 1967 for men, and 1969 for women.

lactation secretion of milk in mammals, from the mammary glands. In late pregnancy, the cells lining the lobules inside the mammary glands begin extracting substances from the blood to produce milk. The supply of milk starts shortly after birth with the production of colostrum, a clear fluid consisting largely of water, protein, antibodies, and vitamins. The production of milk continues practically as long as the baby continues to suckle.

lactic acid or ***2-hydroxypropanoic acid*** $CH_3CHOHCOOH$ organic acid, a colourless, almost odourless liquid, produced by certain bacteria during fermentation and by active muscle cells when they are exercised hard and are experiencing ◊oxygen debt. An accumulation of lactic acid in the muscles may cause cramp. It occurs in yoghurt, buttermilk, sour cream, poor wine, and certain plant extracts, and is used in food preservation and in the preparation of pharmaceuticals.

lactose white sugar, found in solution in milk; it forms 5% of cow's milk. It is commercially prepared from the whey obtained in cheese-making. Like table sugar (sucrose), it is a disaccharide, consisting of two basic sugar units (monosaccharides), in this case, glucose and galactose. Unlike sucrose, it is tasteless.

Ladakh subsidiary range of the ◊Karakoram Mountains and district of NE Kashmir, India, on the border of Tibet; chief town Leh. After China occupied Tibet 1951, it made claims on the area.

Ladd Alan 1913–1964. US actor. His first leading role, as the professional killer in *This Gun for Hire* 1942, made him a star. His most famous role was as the gunslinging stranger in *Shane* 1953, but his career declined after the mid-1950s. His last role was in *The Carpetbaggers* 1964.

Ladoga (Russian ***Ladozhskoye***) largest lake on the continent of Europe, in the Russian Federation, just NE of St Petersburg; area 18,400 sq km/7,100 sq mi. It receives the waters of several rivers, including the Svir, which drains Lake Onega and runs to the Gulf of Finland by the river Neva.

Lady in the UK, the formal title of the daughter of an earl, marquis, or duke; and of any woman whose husband is above the rank of baronet or knight, as well as (by courtesy only) the wives of these latter ranks.

ladybird or ***ladybug*** beetle of the family Coccinellidae, generally red or yellow in colour, with black spots. There are more than 5,200 species, 42 of which are found in Britain. As larvae and adults, they feed on aphids and scale-insect pests. Ladybirds have been used as a form of ◊biological control since the 19th century.

Lady Day British name for the Christian festival (25 March) of the Annunciation of the Virgin Mary; until 1752 it was the beginning of the legal year in England, and it is still a quarter day (date for the payment of quarterly rates or dues).

Laënnec René Théophile Hyacinthe 1781–1826. French physician, inventor of the ◊stethoscope 1816. He advanced the diagnostic technique of auscultation (listening to the internal organs) with his book *Traité de l'auscultation médiaté* 1819, which quickly became a medical classic.

Lafayette Marie Joseph Paul Yves Roch Gilbert de Motier. Marquis de Lafayette 1757–1834. French soldier and politician. He fought against Britain in the American Revolution 1777–79 and 1780–82. During the French Revolution he sat in the National Assembly as a constitutional royalist and in 1789 presented the Declaration of the Rights of Man. After the storming of the ◊Bastille, he was given command of the National Guard. In 1792 he fled the country after attempting to restore the monarchy and was imprisoned by the Austrians until 1797. He supported Napoleon Bonaparte 1815, sat in the chamber of deputies as a Liberal from 1818, and played a leading part in the revolution of 1830.

He was a popular hero in the USA, and the cities of Lafayette in Louisiana and Indiana are named after him, as was the Lafayette Escadrille – American aviators flying for France during World War I, before the USA entered the war 1917.

ladybird Ladybirds are small beetles usually with brightly coloured carapaces. The red coloration with black spots is a warning to potential predators, such as birds, that they are distasteful. When attacked by ants, ladybirds secrete a sticky fluid which entangles their antennae long enough to allow the beetle to escape. Ladybirds feed mainly on aphids.

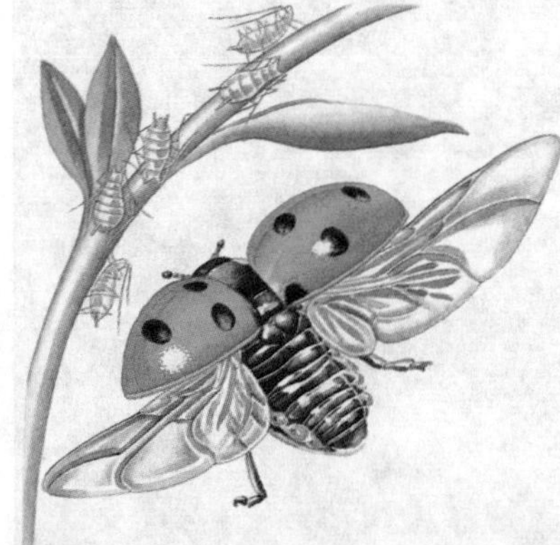

Lafayette Marie-Madeleine. Comtesse de Lafayette 1634–1693. French author. Her *Mémoires* of the French court are keenly observed, and *La Princesse de Clèves* 1678 is the first French psychological novel and *roman à clef* ('novel with a key'), in that real-life characters (including the writer François de ◊La Rochefoucauld, for many years her lover) are presented under fictitious names.

La Fontaine Jean de 1621–1695. French poet. He was born at Château-Thierry, Champagne, and from 1656 lived largely in Paris, the friend of the playwrights Molière and Racine, and the poet Boileau. His works include *Contes et nouvelles en vers* 1665–74, a series of witty and bawdy tales in verse, and *Fables choisies mises en vers* 1668–94, his universally known verse fables. He also wrote *Les Amours de Psyché et de Cupidon/The Loves of Cupid and Psyche* 1669.

Laforgue Jules 1860–1887. French poet. He experimented with new kinds of verse forms, rhythms, and vocabulary, and pioneered ◊free verse. His work, which was also influenced by the Symbolists, is often marked by a lyrical irony. It made a considerable impact on 20th-century poets, including Ezra Pound and T S Eliot. His books of verse include *Les Complaintes* 1885 and *Imitation de Notre-Dame la lune* 1886, while his best-known prose work is the collection of short stories *Moralités légendaires* 1887.

Lagash Sumerian city N of Shatra, Iraq, under independent and semi-independent rulers from about 3000–2700 BC. Besides objects of high artistic value, it has provided about 30,000 clay tablets giving detailed information on temple administration. Lagash was discovered 1877 and excavated by Ernest de Sarzec, then French consul in Basra.

Lagerfeld Karl Otto 1938– . German-born fashion designer. He has been a leading figure on the fashion scene from the early 1970s. As design director at Chanel for both the couture and ready-to-wear collections from 1983, he updated the Chanel look. He showed his first collection under his own label 1984.

Lagerkvist Pär Fabian 1891–1974. Swedish writer. His work includes lyric poetry, dramas, and novels. At first influenced by expressionism, notably in his poems *Aòngest/Angst* 1916 and *Kaos/Chaos* 1918, he later matured towards a critical humanism, already evident in his play *Han som fick leva om sitt liv/The Man Who Lived his Life Over* 1928. He bitterly opposed the evils of Germany's Nazi regime in the play *Bödeln/The Hangman* 1935 and the historical novel *Dvärgen/The Dwarf* 1944. For his novel *Barabbas* 1950 he received the Nobel Prize for Literature 1951.

Lagerlöf Selma Ottiliana Lovisa 1858–1940. Swedish novelist. Her first work was the romantic historical novel *Gösta Berling's saga/The Story of Göst Berling* 1891. The children's fantasy *Nils Holgerssons underbara resa/The Wonderful Voyage of Nils Holgersson* 1906–07 grew from her background as a schoolteacher. She was the first woman to receive a Nobel prize, 1909.

lagoon coastal body of shallow salt water, usually with limited access to the sea. The term is normally used to describe the shallow sea area cut off by a ◊coral reef or barrier islands.

Lagos chief port and former capital of Nigeria, located at the western end of an island in a lagoon and linked by bridges with the mainland via Iddo Island; population (1992 est) 1,347,000; metropolitan area (1995) 10.3 million. It is the world's most densely populated city. Industries include chemicals, metal products, and fish. Its surrounding waters are heavily polluted.

One of the most important slaving ports, Lagos was bombarded and occupied by the British 1851, becoming the colony of Lagos 1862. Abuja was designated the new capital 1982 (officially recognized as such 1992).

Lagrange Joseph Louis 1736–1813. Italian-born French mathematician. His *Mécanique analytique* 1788 applied mathematical analysis, using principles established by Isaac ◊Newton, to such problems as the movements of planets when affected by

‘We are effectively destroying ourselves by violence masquerading as love.’

R D Laing
The Politics of Experience

each other's gravitational force. He presided over the commission that introduced the metric system in 1793.

Lagrangian points five locations in space where the centrifugal and gravitational forces of two bodies neutralize each other; a third, less massive body located at any one of these points will be held in equilibrium with respect to the other two. Three of the points, L1–L3, lie on a line joining the two large bodies. The other two points, L4 and L5, which are the most stable, lie on either side of this line. Their existence was predicted in 1772 by French mathematician Joseph Louis Lagrange.

La Guardia Fiorello Henry 1882–1947. US Republican politician; congressman 1917, 1919, 1923–33; mayor of New York 1933–45. Elected against the opposition of the powerful Tammany Hall Democratic Party organization, he improved the administration, suppressed racketeering, and organized unemployment relief, slum-clearance schemes, and social services. Although nominally a Republican, he supported the Democratic president F D Roosevelt's ◊New Deal. La Guardia Airport, in New York City, is named after him.

lahar mudflow formed of a fluid mixture of water and volcanic ash. During a volcanic eruption, melting ice may combine with ash to form a powerful flow capable of causing great destruction. The lahars created by the eruption of Nevado del Ruiz in Colombia, South America, in 1985 buried 22,000 people in 8 m/26 ft of mud.

Lahnda language spoken by 15–20 million people in Pakistan and N India. It is closely related to Punjabi and Romany, and belongs to the Indo-Iranian branch of the Indo-European language family.

Lahore capital of the province of Punjab and second city of Pakistan; population (1981) 2,920,000. Industries include engineering, textiles, carpets, and chemicals. It is associated with the Mogul rulers Akbar, Jahangir, and Aurangzeb, whose capital it was in the 16th and 17th centuries.

Laibach German name of ◊Ljubljana, a city in Slovenia.

Lailat ul-Barah the *Night of Forgiveness* Muslim festival which takes place two weeks before the beginning of the fast of Ramadan (the ninth month of the Islamic year) and is a time for asking and granting forgiveness.

Lailat ul-Isra Wal Mi'raj Muslim festival that celebrates the prophet Muhammad's ◊Night Journey.

Lailat ul-Qadr the *Night of Power* Muslim festival which celebrates the giving of the Koran to Muhammad. It usually falls at the end of Ramadan.

Laing R(onald) D(avid) 1927–1989. Scottish psychoanalyst. He was the originator of the social theory of mental illness; for example, that schizophrenia is promoted by family pressure for its members to conform to standards alien to themselves. His books include *The Divided Self* 1960 and *The Politics of the Family* 1971.

Influenced by existentialist philosophy, Laing inspired the antipsychiatry movement, which questions the usefulness of the concept of mental illness and of psychiatric treatment. In *The Divided Self* he criticized the psychiatrist's role as one that, with its objective scientific outlook, depersonalized the patient. By investigating the personal interactions within the families of diagnosed schizophrenics, he found that the seemingly bizarre behaviour normally regarded as indicating the illness began to make sense.

laissez faire (French ‘let alone’) theory that the state should not intervene in economic affairs, except to break up a monopoly. The phrase originated with the Physiocrats, 18th-century French economists whose maxim was *laissez faire et laissez passer* (literally, ‘let go and let pass’ – that is, leave the individual alone and let commodities circulate freely). The degree to which intervention should take place is still one of the chief problems of economics. The Scottish economist Adam ◊Smith justified the theory in *The Wealth of Nations* 1776.

The 20th century has seen an increasing degree of state intervention to promote social benefits, which after World War II in Europe was extended into the field of nationalization of leading industries and services. However, from the 1970s, *laissez-faire* policies were again pursued in the UK and the USA. In the 1990s the Conservative UK government opposed European Union efforts to incorporate social benefits in monetary-union legislation.

lake body of still water lying in depressed ground without direct communication with the sea. Lakes are common in formerly glaciated regions, along the courses of slow rivers, and in low land near the sea. The main classifications are by origin: ***glacial lakes***, formed by glacial scouring; ***barrier lakes***, formed by landslides and glacial moraines; ***crater lakes***, found in volcanoes; and ***tectonic lakes***, occurring in natural fissures.

Crater lakes form in the ◊calderas of extinct volcanoes, for example Crater Lake, Oregon. Subsidence of the roofs of limestone caves in ◊karst landscape exposes the subterranean stream network and provides a cavity in which a lake can develop. Tectonic lakes form during tectonic movement, as when a rift valley is formed. Lake Tanganyika was created in conjunction with the East African Great Rift Valley. Glaciers produce several distinct types of lake, such as the lochs of Scotland and the Great Lakes of North America.

Lakes are mainly freshwater, but salt and bitter lakes are found in areas of low annual rainfall and little surface runoff, so that the rate of evaporation exceeds the rate of inflow, allowing mineral salts to accumulate. The Dead Sea has a salinity of about 250 parts per 1,000 and the Great Salt Lake, Utah, about 220 parts per 1,000. Salinity can also be caused by volcanic gases or fluids, for example Lake Natron, Tanzania.

In the 20th century large artificial lakes have been created in connection with hydroelectric and other works. Some lakes have become polluted as a result of human activity. Sometimes ◊eutrophication (a state of overnourishment) occurs, when agricultural fertilizers leaching into lakes cause an explosion of aquatic life, which then depletes the lake's oxygen supply until it is no longer able to support life.

lake A lake near Morondava in Madagascar. The water lilies are *Nymphaea stellata* and the trees in the distance, growing on dry land, are baobabs *Adansonia grandidieri*. Most lakes are the focal point of an ecosystem, drawing together a broad range of animal and plant life. *Premaphotos Wildlife*

Lake Veronica. Stage name of Constance Frances Marie Ockelman 1919–1973. US film actress. She was almost as celebrated for her much imitated ‘peekaboo’ hairstyle as for her acting. She co-starred with Alan Ladd in several films during the 1940s, including *This Gun for Hire* and *The Glass Key* both 1942, and *The Blue Dahlia* 1946. She also appeared in *Sullivan's Travels* 1942 and *I Married a Witch* 1942.

Lake District region in Cumbria, England; area 1,800 sq km/700 sq mi. It contains the principal English lakes, which are separated by wild uplands rising to many peaks, including Scafell Pike (978 m/3,210 ft), the highest peak in England. It was made a national park 1951.

The Lake District has associations with the writers Wordsworth, Coleridge, Southey, De Quincey, Ruskin, and Beatrix Potter, and was made a national park 1951.

lake dwelling prehistoric village built on piles driven into the bottom of a lake or at the lake-edge. Such villages are found throughout Europe, in W Africa, South America, Borneo, and New Guinea. British examples include a lake village of the 1st centuries BC and AD excavated near Glastonbury, Somerset.

Lakshadweep group of 36 coral islands, 10 inhabited, in the Indian Ocean, 320 km/200 mi off the Malabar coast, forming a Union Territory of the Republic of India; area 32 sq km/12 sq mi; population (1994 est) 56,000. The administrative headquarters are on Kavaratti Island. Products include coir, copra, and fish. The religion is Islam. The first Western visitor was Vasco da Gama 1499. The islands were British from 1877 until Indian independence and were created a Union Territory 1956. Formerly known as the Laccadive, Minicoy, and Amindivi Islands, they were renamed Lakshadweep 1973.

Lakshmi Hindu goddess of wealth and beauty, consort of Vishnu; her festival is ◊Diwali.

Lalique René 1860–1945. French designer and manufacturer of ◊Art Nouveau glass, jewellery, and house interiors. The Lalique factory continues in production at Wingen-sur-Moder, Alsace, under his son Marc and granddaughter Marie-Claude.

Lallans variant of ‘lowlands’ and a name for Lowland Scots, whether conceived as a language in its own right or as a northern dialect of English. Because of its rustic associations, Lallans has been known since the 18th century as ‘the Doric’, in contrast with the ‘Attic’ usage of Edinburgh (‘the Athens of the North’). See ◊Scots language.

Lamaism Buddhism of Tibet and Mongolia, a form of Mahāyāna Buddhism. Buddhism was introduced into Tibet AD 640, but the real founder of Tibetan Buddhism was the Indian missionary Padma Sambhava, who was active about 750. Tibetan Buddhism developed several orders, based on lineages of teachings transmitted by reincarnated lamas (teachers). In the 14th–15th centuries Tongkha-pa founded the sect of Geluk-pa (‘virtuous’), which became the most powerful order in the country. Its head is the ◊Dalai Lama, who is considered an incarnation of the Bodhisattva Avalokiteśvara. Residing at the palace of Potala in Lhasa, the Dalai Lama exercised both spiritual and temporal authority as head of the Tibetan state, aided by the ◊Panchen Lama. However, in 1959, following an unsuccessful uprising against the Chinese occupation of Tibet, the 14th Dalai Lama fled the country.

Before Chinese communist rule, it was estimated that one in four of Tibet's male population was a Lamaist monk, but now their numbers are greatly reduced. ▷ *See feature on pp. 162–163.*

Lamarck Jean Baptiste de 1744–1829. French naturalist. His theory of evolution, known as Lamarckism, was based on the idea that acquired characteristics (changes acquired in an individual's lifetime) are inherited by the offspring, and that organisms have an intrinsic urge to evolve into better-adapted forms. *Philosophie zoologique/Zoological Philosophy* 1809 outlined his 'transformist' (evolutionary) ideas. In this work he tried to show that various parts of the body developed because they were necessary, or disappeared because of disuse when variations in the environment caused a change in habit. If these body changes were inherited over many generations, new species would eventually be produced. His theory is now discredited. Lamarck was the first to distinguish vertebrate from invertebrate animals by the presence of a bony spinal column. He was also the first to establish the crustaceans, arachnids, and annelids among the invertebrates. It was Lamarck who coined the word 'biology'.

Lamartine Alphonse Marie Louis de 1790–1869. French poet. He wrote romantic poems, including *Méditations poétiques/Poetical Meditations* 1820, followed by *Nouvelles méditations/New Meditations* 1823, and *Harmonies poétiques et religieuses/Poetical and Religious Harmonies* 1830. His *Histoire des Girondins/History of the Girondins* 1847 helped to inspire the revolution of 1848. Lamartine was the first to sound a more personal note in his poetry and to establish a direct bond between himself and his public.

Lamb Charles 1775–1834. English essayist and critic. He collaborated with his sister ***Mary Lamb*** (1764–1847) on *Tales from Shakespeare* 1807, and his *Specimens of English Dramatic Poets Contemporary with Shakespeare, with Notes* 1808 revealed him as a penetrating critic and helped to revive interest in Elizabethan plays. As 'Elia' he contributed essays to the *London Magazine* from 1820 (collected 1823 and 1833). His charming, witty essays are still widely read and admired; they include 'A Dissertation on Roast Pig', 'Mrs Battle's Opinions on Whist', 'Dream Children', and 'The Supernatural Man'. He had great personal charm and included among his friends and correspondents Wordsworth, Southey, Coleridge, William Hazlitt, and Leigh Hunt.

lambert unit of luminance (the light shining from a surface), equal to one ◊lumen per square centimetre. In scientific work the ◊candela per square metre is preferred.

Lambert John 1619–1684. English general, a cavalry commander in the Civil War under Cromwell (at the battles of Marston Moor, Preston, Dunbar, and Worcester). Lambert broke with Cromwell over the proposal to award him the royal title. After the Restoration he was imprisoned for life.

Lambeth inner borough of S central Greater London. It includes the districts of Waterloo, Kennington, Clapham, Stockwell, and Brixton
features Lambeth Palace, chief residence of the archbishop of Canterbury since 1200, with brick Tudor gatehouse (1495); Tradescant museum of gardening history; the South Bank, including Royal Festival Hall, Hayward Gallery, National Theatre, the Art Deco Oxo Wharf Tower (1928) now converted into mixed-use development; the Oval (headquarters of Surrey County Cricket Club from 1846) at Kennington, where the first England–Australia test match was played 1880; Old Vic theatre (1816–18); Brixton Prison; Anti-Slavery Archive in Brixton
population (1991) 244,800

Lambeth Conference meeting of bishops of the Anglican Communion every ten years, presided over by the archbishop of Canterbury; its decisions on doctrinal matters are not binding.

lamina in flowering plants (◊angiosperms), the blade of the ◊leaf on either side of the midrib. The lamina is generally thin and flattened, and is usually the primary organ of ◊photosynthesis. It has a network of veins through which water and nutrients are conducted. More generally, a lamina is any thin, flat plant structure, such as the ◊thallus of many seaweeds.

Lammas ('loaf-mass') medieval festival of harvest, celebrated 1 Aug. At one time it was an English quarter day (date for payment of quarterly rates or dues), and is still a quarter day in Scotland.

lammergeier Old World vulture *Gypaetus barbatus*, also known as the bearded vulture, with a wingspan of 2.7 m/9 ft. It ranges over S Europe, N Africa, and Asia, in wild mountainous areas. It feeds on offal and carrion and drops bones onto rocks to break them and so get at the marrow.

Lamont Norman Stewart Hughson 1942– . UK Conservative politician, chief secretary of the Treasury 1989–90, chancellor of the Exchequer 1990–93. In Sept 1992, despite earlier assurances to the contrary, he was forced to suspend Britain's membership of the European Community (now the European Union) ◊Exchange Rate Mechanism (ERM). He was replaced as chancellor by Kenneth Clarke May 1993 and defeated in the 1997 general election.

Lampedusa Giuseppe Tomasi di 1896–1957. Italian aristocrat. He was the author of *Il gattopardo/The Leopard* 1958 (translated into English 1960), a novel set in his native Sicily during the period following its annexation by Garibaldi 1860. It chronicles the reactions of an aristocratic family to social and political upheavals.

lamp, electric device designed to convert electrical energy into light energy. In a ***filament lamp*** such as a light bulb an electric current causes heating of a long thin coil of fine high-resistance wire enclosed at low pressure inside a glass bulb. In order to give out a good light the wire must glow white-hot and therefore must be made of a metal, such as tungsten, that has a high melting point. The efficiency of filament lamps is low because most of the electrical energy is converted to heat.

A ***fluorescent lamp*** uses an electrical discharge or spark inside a gas-filled tube to produce light. The inner surface of the tube is coated with a fluorescent material that converts the ultraviolet light generated by the discharge into visible light. Although a high voltage is needed to start the discharge, these lamps are far more efficient than filament lamps at producing light.

lamprey any of various eel-shaped jawless fishes belonging to the family Petromyzontidae. A lamprey feeds on other fish by fixing itself by its round mouth to its host and boring into the flesh with its toothed tongue. Lampreys breed in fresh water, and the young live as larvae for about five years before migrating to the sea. Henry I of England is said to have died from eating too many, hence the phrase 'a surfeit of lampreys'.

Lanark former county town of Lanarkshire, Scotland; now capital of Clydesdale district, Strathclyde Region; population (1991) 8,900. William Wallace once lived here, and later returned to burn the town and kill the English sheriff. New Lanark to the S was founded as a cotton-spinning centre and 'model community' by Robert Owen and Richard Arkwright at the end of the 18th century, with the aim of providing decent conditions for workers and their families.

Lancashire county of NW England
area 3,040 sq km/1,173 sq mi (*see United Kingdom map*)
towns and cities Preston (administrative headquarters), which forms part of Central Lancashire New Town from 1970 (together with Fulwood, Bamber Bridge, Leyland, and Chorley); Lancaster, Accrington, Blackburn, Burnley; ports Fleetwood and Heysham; seaside resorts Blackpool, Morecambe, and Southport
features the river Ribble; the Pennines; the Forest of Bowland (moors and farming valleys); Pendle Hill
industries formerly a world centre of cotton manufacture, now replaced with high-technology aerospace and electronics industries. There is dairy farming and market gardening
population (1991) 1,384,000
famous people Kathleen Ferrier, Gracie Fields, George Formby, Rex Harrison.

Lancaster, Chancellor of the Duchy of public office created 1351 and attached to the crown since 1399. The office of Chancellor of the Duchy is a sinecure without any responsibilities, usually held by a member of the cabinet with a special role outside that of the regular ministries; for example, Harold Lever as financial adviser to the Wilson–Callaghan governments from 1974.

LAKE: MAJOR LAKES

Name and location	Area in sq km/sq mi
Caspian Sea (Azerbaijan/Russia/Kazakhstan/Turkmenistan/Iran)	370,990/143,240
Superior (USA/Canada)	82,071/31,700
Victoria (Tanzania/Kenya/Uganda)	69,463/26,820
Aral Sea (Kazakhstan/Uzbekistan)	64,500/24,904
Huron (USA/Canada)	59,547/23,000
Michigan (USA)	57,735/22,300
Tanganyika (Malawi/Zaire/Zambia/Burundi)	32,880/12,700
Baikal (Russia)	31,456/12,150
Great Bear (Canada)	31,316/12,096
Malawi (Tanzania/Malawi/Mozambique)	28,867/11,150
Great Slave (Canada)	28,560/11,031
Erie (USA/Canada)	25,657/9,910
Winnipeg (Canada)	25,380/9,417
Ontario (USA/Canada)	19,547/7,550
Balkhash (Kazakhstan)	18,421/7,115
Ladoga (Russia)	17,695/6,835
Chad (Chad/Niger/Nigeria)	16,310/6,300
Maracaibo (Venezuela)	13,507/5,217

Lancaster British heavy bomber of World War II made by the Avro company. It was first flown June 1941 and developed into the RAF's best heavy bomber of the war. Lancaster bombers were responsible for the sinking of the German battleship the *Tirpitz* and the 'dambuster' raids 1944.

Lancaster city in Lancashire, England, on the river Lune; population (1991) 125,600. It was the former county town of Lancashire (now Preston). Industries include paper, furniture, plastics, chemicals, textiles, and floor coverings. A castle here, which incorporates Roman work, was captured by Cromwell during the Civil War. The Ruskin Library (1996) at the University of Lancaster houses a collection of works by John Ruskin.

Lancaster Burt (Burton Stephen) 1913–1994. US film actor, formerly a circus acrobat. A star from his first film, *The Killers* 1946, he proved himself adept both at action roles and more complex character parts as in such films as *From Here to Eternity* 1953, *Elmer Gantry* 1960 (Academy Award), *The Leopard/Il Gattopardo* 1963, *The Swimmer* 1968, and *Atlantic City* 1980.

Following his successful screen debut and several further underworld films, he switched to swashbuckling in *The Flame and the Arrow* 1950 and *The Crimson Pirate* 1952, taking pride in performing his own stunts. In a different vein, he took on the role of a down-at-heel ex-alcoholic in *Come Back Little Sheba* 1953. He continued to alternate heroic roles with offbeat characterizations like the odious gossip columnist of *Sweet Smell of Success* 1957. In 1948 he became one of the first Hollywood stars to form his own production company, Hecht-Hill-Lancaster.

Lancaster Osbert 1908–1986. English cartoonist and writer. In 1939 he began producing daily 'pocket cartoons' for the *Daily Express*, in which he satirized current social mores through such characters as Maudie Littlehampton. In the 1930s and 1940s he produced several tongue-in-cheek guides to architectural fashion (such as *Homes, Sweet Homes* 1939 and *Drayneflete Revisited* 1949), from which a number of descriptive terms, such as Pont Street Dutch and Stockbroker Tudor, have entered the language.

Lancaster, House of English royal house, a branch of the Plantagenets. It originated 1267 when Edmund (died 1296), the younger son of Henry III, was granted the earldom of Lancaster. Converted to a duchy for Henry of Grosmont (died 1361), it passed to John of Gaunt 1362 by his marriage to Blanche, Henry's daughter. John's son, Henry IV, established the royal dynasty of Lancaster 1399, and he was followed by two more Lancastrian kings, Henry V and Henry VI.

lancelet any one of a variety of marine animals of subphylum cephalocordates (see ◊chordate), genus

'The greatest pleasure I know, is to do a good action by stealth, and to have it found out by accident.'

CHARLES LAMB
'Table Talk by the late Elia'

If only people knew as much about painting as I do, they would never buy my pictures.

EDWIN LANDSEER
Quoted in Campbell Lennie *Landseer the Victorian Paragon*

Amphioxus, about 2.5 cm/1 in long. It has no skull, brain, eyes, heart, vertebral column, centralized brain, or paired limbs, but there is a notochord (a supportive rod which may be regarded as the precursor of the backbone) running from end to end of the body, a tail, and a number of gill slits. Found in all seas, it burrows in the sand but when disturbed swims freely.

Lancelot of the Lake in British legend, one of King Arthur's knights, the lover of Queen Guinevere. Originally a folk hero, he first appeared in the Arthurian cycle of tales in the 12th century.

Land (plural *Länder*) federal state of Germany or Austria.

Land Edwin Herbert 1909–1991. US inventor of the ◊Polaroid Land camera 1947. The camera developed the film in one minute inside the camera and produced an 'instant' photograph.

Land League Irish peasant-rights organization, formed 1879 by Michael ◊Davitt and Charles ◊Parnell to fight against tenant evictions. Through its skilful use of the boycott against anyone who took a farm from which another had been evicted, it forced Gladstone's government to introduce a law 1881 restricting rents and granting tenants security of tenure.

landlord and tenant in law, the relationship that exists between an owner of land or buildings (the landlord) and a person granted the right to occupy them (the tenant). The landlord grants a lease or tenancy, which may be for a year, a term of years, a week, or any other definite, limited period.

In the UK there was traditionally freedom of contract between landlord and tenant, but wartime shortage of rented accommodation for lower-income groups led to abuse by unscrupulous landlords and from 1914 acts were passed affording protection for tenants against eviction and rent increases. The shortage was aggravated by World War II and from 1939 Rent Acts were passed greatly increasing the range of dwellings so protected. Extensive decontrol under the 1957 Rent Act led to hardship, and further legislation followed, notably the Rent Act of 1974, under which tenants of furnished and unfurnished premises were given equal security of tenure. The Housing Act of 1980 attempted to make it more attractive to landlords to let property, while still safeguarding the tenant, notably by creating a new category of tenure – the protected shorthold.

Legislation aimed at stimulating additional investment in the provision of residential property for letting came into force in 1989. In that year the private sector held 8% of the total housing market. The Housing Act 1988 brought about the most significant changes in housing law for over 30 years. The act incorporates deregulation in the private sector and a reduction in the role of local authorities in providing housing. Tenancies created after 1989 are no longer subject to the 'fair rent' provisions introduced in 1965. 'Assured tenancies' are lettings at market value with less opportunity or security of tenure than under previous housing acts.

Landor Walter Savage 1775–1864. English poet and essayist. He lived much of his life abroad, dying in Florence, where he had fled to avoid a libel suit 1858. His works include the epic poem *Gebir* 1798, the tragedy *Count Julian* 1812, and *Imaginary Conversations of Literary Men and Statesmen* 1824–29. Landor has a high place among prose writers for his restrained and finished style; his shorter poems have the same classic simplicity.

Land Registry, HM official body set up 1925 to register legal rights to land in England and Wales. There has been a gradual introduction, since 1925, of compulsory registration of land in different areas of the country. This requires the purchaser of land to register details of his or her title and all other rights (such as mortgages and ◊easements) relating to the land. Once registered, the title to the land is guaranteed by the Land Registry, subject to those interests that cannot be registered; this makes the buying and selling of land easier and cheaper. The records are open to public inspection (since Dec 1990).

Landsat series of satellites used for monitoring the Earth's resources. The first was launched in 1972.

Landsbergis Vytautas 1932– . President of Lithuania 1990–93. He became active in nationalist politics in the 1980s, founding and eventually chairing the anticommunist Sajudis independence movement 1988. When Sajudis swept to victory in the republic's elections 1990, Landsbergis chaired the Supreme Council of Lithuania, becoming, in effect, president. He immediately drafted the republic's declaration of independence from the USSR which, after initial Soviet resistance, was recognized 1991. He formed the right-of-centre Homeland Union 1993 which won the general election 1996, Landsbergis taking the chair of the new parliament.

landscape architecture designing landscapes, composed of both natural and artificial elements. Frederick Law Olmsted (1822–1903), who was responsible for the layout of Central Park, New York, 1857, is considered one of its earliest exponents. Today, the work of landscape architects frequently involves the creation of national parks, the reclamation of industrial sites, and the creation of 'new towns'.

landscape painting comparatively late product of art in the West, though the contemplation of mountain and water and their rendering in pictures were cultivated in China in the early centuries AD. In Western art it first appears as a background and as such became an element in the illuminated manuscripts and paintings of the Middle Ages. The Flemish painter Patenier is usually credited with having first made landscape a primary feature of interest. Impressionism was the last great phase of landscape objectively treated, though it was not the end of its development. Cézanne made landscape into a study of essential structure underlying all natural forms; Vincent van Gogh made it a vehicle for expressing personal emotion.

Landseer Edwin Henry 1802–1873. English painter, sculptor, and engraver of animal studies. Much of his work reflects the Victorian taste for sentimental and moralistic pictures, for example *Dignity and Impudence* 1839 (Tate Gallery, London). His works show close knowledge of animal forms and he established a vogue for Highland animal and sporting scenes, much encouraged by Queen Victoria's patronage. Among his best-known works are *The Old Shepherd's Chief Mourner* 1837, *Monarch of the Glen* 1851, and *The Stag at Bay* 1846. His works were popularized in enormous numbers of engravings. His sculptures include the lions at the base of Nelson's Column in Trafalgar Square, London, 1857–67.

Land's End promontory of W Cornwall, 15 km/9 mi WSW of Penzance, the westernmost point of England. A group of dangerous rocks, the Longships, extend a mile out beyond Land's End; they are marked by a lighthouse.

landslide sudden downward movement of a mass of soil or rocks from a cliff or steep slope. Landslides happen when a slope becomes unstable, usually because the base has been undercut or because materials within the mass have become wet and slippery. Earthquakes may precipitate landslides.

Landsteiner Karl 1868–1943. Austrian-born US immunologist. He discovered the ABO ◊blood group system 1900–02, and aided in the discovery of the Rhesus blood factors 1940. He also discovered the polio virus. Nobel prize 1930.

Lanfranc c. 1010–1089. Italian archbishop of Canterbury from 1070; he rebuilt the cathedral, replaced English clergy by Normans, enforced clerical celibacy, and separated the ecclesiastical from the secular courts. His skill in theological controversy did much to secure the church's adoption of the doctrine of transubstantiation.

Lang Andrew 1844–1912. Scottish historian and folklore scholar. His writings include historical works; anthropological studies, such as *Myth, Ritual and Religion* 1887 and *The Making of Religion* 1898; novels; and the series of children's books which he inspired and edited, beginning with *The Blue Fairy Book* 1889.

Lang Fritz 1890–1976. Austrian film director. His films are characterized by a strong sense of fatalism and alienation. His German films include *Metropolis* 1927, the sensational *M* 1931, in which Peter Lorre starred as a child-killer, and the series of Dr Mabuse films, after which he fled from the Nazis to Hollywood 1935. His US films include *Fury* 1936, *You Only Live Once* 1937, *Scarlet Street* 1945, *Rancho Notorious* 1952, and *The Big Heat* 1953. He returned to Germany and directed a third picture in the Dr Mabuse series 1960.

lang k(athryn) d(awn) 1961– . Canadian singer. Her mellifluous voice and androgynous image have gained her a wide following beyond the country-music field where she first established herself. Her albums include *Angel With a Lariat* 1987,

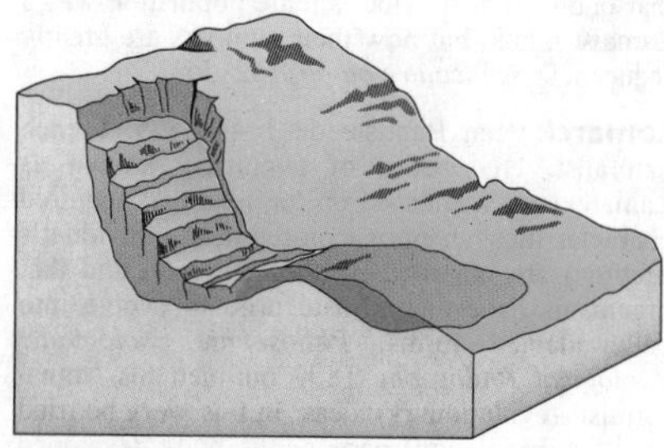

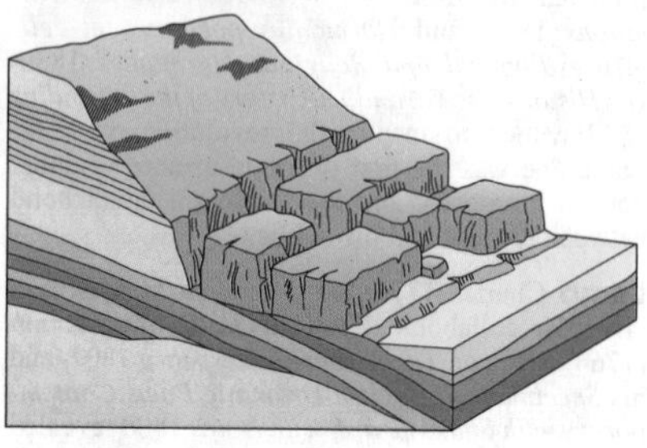

landslide Types of landslide. A mudflow is a tongue of mud that slides downhill. A slump is a fall of a large mass that stays together after the fall. A landslip occurs when beds of rock move along a lower bed.

Lang A still from the classic silent film *Metropolis* 1927 by Austrian director Fritz Lang, one of the major figures in the development of cinema. Leaving Germany when the Nazis came to power, he made most of his films in Hollywood.

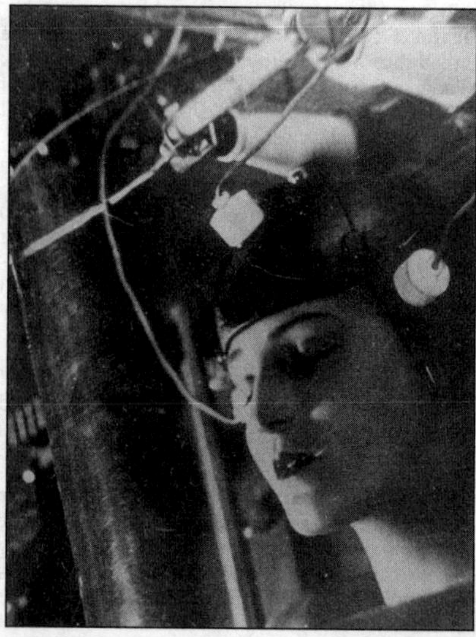

The wildest most impressive place I ever saw on the coasts of Britain.

On LAND'S END
Thomas Carlyle
Reminiscences of My Irish Journey in 1849

***Lange** A family of Mexican migrant field workers, California c. 1937* by US photographer Dorothea Lange, Library of Congress. Lange's stark photographs of farm workers of the 1930s helped to win support for relief programs during the Depression and had a profound influence on US photojournalism. *Library of Congress*

Shadowland 1988, *Absolute Torch and Twang* 1989, the mainstream *Ingénue* 1992, *Even Cowgirls get the Blues* 1993, and *All You Can Eat* 1995. In 1992 she starred in the film *Salmonberries* by Percy Adlon.

Lange David Russell 1942– . New Zealand Labour politician, prime minister 1983–89. He was elected to the House of Representatives 1977. Labour had a decisive win in the 1984 general election on a non-nuclear military policy, which Lange immediately put into effect, despite criticism from the USA. He introduced a free-market economic policy and was re-elected 1987. He resigned 1989 over a disagreement with his finance minister.

Lange Dorothea, (born Nutzhorn) 1895–1965. US photographer. She was hired 1935 by the federal Farm Security Administration to document the westward migration of farm families from the Dust Bowl of the southern central USA. Her photographs, characterized by a gritty realism, were widely exhibited and subsequently published as *An American Exodus: A Record of Human Erosion* 1939.

Langland William c. 1332–c. 1400. English poet. His alliterative *The Vision of William Concerning Piers the Plowman* was written in three (or possibly four) versions between about 1367 and 1386. The poem forms a series of allegorical visions, in which Piers develops from the typical poor peasant to a symbol of Jesus, and condemns the social and moral evils of 14th-century England.

Langton Stephen c. 1150–1228. English priest who was mainly responsible for drafting the charter of rights, the ◊Magna Carta. When in 1207 Pope Innocent III secured Langton's election as archbishop of Canterbury, King John refused to recognize him, and he was not allowed to enter Canterbury until 1213. He supported the barons in their struggle against John and worked for revisions to both church and state policies.

Langtry Lillie. Stage name of Emilie Charlotte le Breton 1853–1929. English actress, the mistress of the future Edward VII. She first appeared professionally in London 1881, and had her greatest success as Rosalind in Shakespeare's *As You Like It*. She was known as the 'Jersey Lily' from her birthplace in the Channel Islands and considered to be one of the most beautiful women of her time.

language human communication through speech, writing, or both. Different nationalities or ethnic groups typically have different languages or variations on particular languages; for example, Armenians speaking the Armenian language and British and Americans speaking distinctive varieties of the English language. One language may have various ◊dialects, which may be seen by those who use them as languages in their own right. There are about 6,000 languages spoken worldwide, but 90% of these are in some danger of falling into disuse. More than half the world's population speaks one of just five languages – Chinese, English, Hindi, Russian, and Spanish.

The term language is also used for systems of communication with languagelike qualities, such as animal language (the way animals communicate), body language (gestures and expressions used to communicate ideas), sign language (gestures for the deaf or for use as a ◊lingua franca, as among Native Americans), and computer languages (such as BASIC and COBOL).

language media Natural human language has a neurological basis centred on the left hemisphere of the brain and is expressed through two distinct media in most present-day societies: mouth and ear (the medium of sound, or phonic medium), and hand and eye (the medium of writing, or graphic medium).

languages and dialects When forms of language are as distinct as Dutch and Arabic, it is obvious that they are different languages. When, however, they are mutually intelligible, as are Dutch and Flemish, a categorical distinction is harder to make. Rather than say that Dutch and Flemish are dialects of a common Netherlandic language, as some scholars put it, Dutch and Flemish speakers may, for traditional reasons that include ethnic pride and political distinctness, prefer to talk about two distinct languages. To strengthen the differences among similar languages, groups may emphasize those differences (for example, the historical distancing of Portuguese from Castilian Spanish) or adopt different scripts (Urdu is written in Arabic script, its relative Hindi in Devanagari script). From outside, Italian appears to be a single language; inside Italy, it is a standard variety resting on a base of many very distinct dialects. The terms 'language' and 'dialect' are not therefore easily defined and distinguished. English is today the most widespread world language, but it has so many varieties (often mutually unintelligible) that scholars now talk about 'Englishes' and even 'the English languages' – all, however, are united for international purposes by Standard English.

language families When scholars decide that languages are cognate (that is, have a common origin), they group them into a language family. Membership of a family is established through a range of correspondences, such as *f* and *p* in certain English and Latin words (as in *father/pater* and *fish/piscis*). By such means, English and Latin are shown to have long ago shared a common 'ancestor'. Some languages, such as French, Spanish, and Italian, fall easily into family groups, while others, such as Japanese, are not easy to classify, and others still, such as Basque, appear to have no linguistic kin anywhere (and are known as ***isolates***). The families into which the languages of the world are grouped include the ◊Indo-European (the largest, with subfamilies or branches from northern India to Ireland), the Hamito-Semitic or Afro-Asiatic (with a Hamitic branch in N Africa and a Semitic branch in W Asia and Africa, and containing Arabic, Hebrew, and Berber), the Finno-Ugric (including Finnish and Hungarian), the Sino-Tibetan (including Chinese and Tibetan), the Malayo-Polynesian or Austronesian (including Malay and Maori), and the Uto-Aztecan (one of many Native American families, including Ute and Aztec or Nahuatl).

Linguists estimate that there are about 6,000 distinct languages in the world. The number is uncertain because: (1) it is not always easy to establish whether a speech form is a distinct language or a dialect of another language; (2) some parts of the world remain incompletely explored (such as New Guinea); and (3) the rate of language death is often unknown (for example, in Amazonia, where many undescribed Native American languages have died out). It is also difficult to estimate the precise number of speakers of many languages, especially where communities mix elements from several languages elsewhere used separately (as in parts of India). The Indo-European language family is considered to have about 2 billion speakers worldwide, Sino-Tibetan about 1,040 million, Hamito-Semitic about 230 million, and Malayo-Polynesian about 200 million. Chinese (which may or may not be a single language) is spoken by around 1 billion people, English by about 350 million native speakers and at least the same number of non-natives, Spanish by 250 million, Hindi 200 million, Arabic 150 million, Russian 150 million, Portuguese 135 million, Japanese 120 million, German 100 million, French 70 million, Italian 60 million, Korean 60 million, Tamil 55 million, and Vietnamese 50 million.

❛The limits of my language mean the limits of my world.❜

On LANGUAGE
Ludwig Wittgenstein
Tractatus Logico-Philosophicus

Languedoc former province of S France, bounded by the river Rhône, the Mediterranean Sea, and the regions of Guienne and Gascony. It took its name from the Romance ◊Provençal language widely spoken in S France in the Middle Ages and known as *langue d'oc* (*oc* meaning 'yes'). The French spoken north of the Loire, with which it was in competition, was known as *langue d'oïl* (*oïl* meaning 'yes').

Languedoc-Roussillon region of S France, comprising the *départements* of Aude, Gard, Hérault, Lozère, and Pyrénées-Orientales; area 27,400 sq km/10,576 sq mi; population (1990) 2,115,000. Its capital is Montpellier, and products include fruit, vegetables, wine, and cheese.

langur any of various leaf-eating Old World monkeys of several genera, especially the genus *Presbytis*, that live in trees in S Asia. There are about 20 species.

lanolin sticky, purified wax obtained from sheep's wool and used in cosmetics, soap, and leather preparation.

langur A grey langur *Presbytis entellus* exhibiting the leaf-eating habits of its kind. This animal is highly adapted to its diet and can digest leaves which are avoided by most other herbivorous mammals. Widespread in India and Sri Lanka, it is often found around human habitations as well as in forests. *Premaphotos Wildlife*

A journey of a thousand miles must begin with a single step.

LAO ZI
Tao Tê Ching

lanthanide any of a series of 15 metallic elements (also known as rare earths) with atomic numbers 57 (lanthanum) to 71 (lutetium). One of its members, promethium, is radioactive. All occur in nature. Lanthanides are grouped because of their chemical similarities (most are trivalent, but some can be divalent or tetravalent), their properties differing only slightly with atomic number.

lanthanum (Greek *lanthanein* 'to be hidden') soft, silvery, ductile and malleable, metallic element, symbol La, atomic number 57, relative atomic mass 138.91, the first of the lanthanide series. It is used in making alloys.

Lanvin Jeanne 1867–1946. French fashion designer. She is known for her mother-and-daughter ensembles, which she began making in the early 1900s. The influence of Oriental patterns 1910 led her to create Eastern-style evening wear in velvet and satin, and she became well known for her chemise-style designs just before World War I. Her work was characterized by fine craft and embroidery and her label became a prosperous couture business.

Lanzarote most easterly of the Spanish Canary Islands; area 795 sq km/307 sq mi; capital Arrecife. The desertlike volcanic landscape is dominated by the Montañas de Fuego ('Mountains of Fire') with more than 300 volcanic cones.

Lanzhou or *Lanchow* capital of Gansu province, China, on the river Huang He, 190 km/120 mi S of the Great Wall; population (1993) 1,320,000. Industries include oil refining, chemicals, fertilizers, and synthetic rubber.

Lao people who live along the Mekong river system in Laos (2 million) and N Thailand (9 million). The Lao language is a member of the Sino-Tibetan family. The majority of Lao live in rural villages. During the wet season, May–Oct, they grow rice in irrigated fields, though some shifting or swidden cultivation is practised on hillsides. Vegetables and other crops are grown during drier weather. The Lao are predominantly Buddhist though a belief in spirits, *phi*, is included in Lao devotions.

Laocoön in classical mythology, a Trojan priest of Apollo and a visionary, brother of Anchises. He and his sons were killed by serpents when he foresaw disaster for Troy in the ◊Trojan horse left by the Greeks. The scene of their death is the subject of a classical marble group, rediscovered in the Renaissance, and forms an episode in Virgil's *Aeneid*.

Laois or ***Laoighis*** county of the Republic of Ireland, in the province of Leinster; county town Port Laoise; area 1,720 sq km/664 sq mi; population (1991) 52,300. It was formerly known as Queen's County. It is flat, except for the Slieve Bloom Mountains in the northwest, and there are many bogs. Industries include sugar beet, dairy products, woollens, and agricultural machinery.

Laos landlocked country in SE Asia, bounded N by China, E by Vietnam, S by Cambodia, W by Thailand, and NW by Myanmar. *See country box below.*

Lao Zi or ***Lao Tzu*** c. 604–531 BC. Chinese philosopher. He is commonly regarded as the founder of ◊Taoism, with its emphasis on the Tao, the inevitable and harmonious way of the universe. The *Tao Tê Ching*, the Taoist scripture, is attributed to him but apparently dates from the 3rd century BC.

La Paz capital city of Bolivia, in Murillo province, 3,800 m/12,400 ft above sea level; population (1992) 711,000 (metropolitan area 1,126,000). It is in a canyon formed by the La Paz river, and is the world's highest capital city. Products include textiles and copper. Founded 1548 by the Spaniard Alonso de Mendoza on the site of an Inca village, it has been the seat of government since 1898, but Sucre is the legal capital and seat of the judiciary.

lapis lazuli rock containing the blue mineral lazurite in a matrix of white calcite with small amounts of other minerals. It occurs in silica-poor igneous of other minerals. It occurs in silica-poor igneous

Lao Zi Ancient Chinese philosopher Lao Zi. Scholars now believe that the bible of Taoism, the *Tao Tê Ching*, was written anonymously but attributed to Lao-Zi following an old Chinese custom of ascribing such works to respected men of wisdom. *Image Select (UK) Ltd*

rocks and metamorphic limestones found in Afghanistan, Siberia, Iran, and Chile. Lapis lazuli was a valuable pigment of the Middle Ages, also used as a gemstone and in inlaying and ornamental work.

Laplace Pierre Simon. Marquis de Laplace 1749–1827. French astronomer and mathematician. In 1796 he theorized that the Solar System originated from a cloud of gas (the nebular hypothesis). He studied the motion of the Moon and planets, and

LAOS

Lao People's Democratic Republic

national name *Saathiaranagroat Prachhathippatay Prachhachhon Lao*
area 236,790 sq km/91,400 sq mi
capital Vientiane
major towns/cities Luang Prabang (the former royal capital), Pakse, Savannakhet
physical features landlocked state with high mountains in E; Mekong River in W; rainforest covers nearly 60% of land
head of state Khamtay Siphandon from 1998
head of government Sisavath Keobounphanh from 1998
political system communist, one-party state
administrative divisions 17 provinces
political party Lao People's Revolutionary Party (LPRP, the only legal party)
population 5,035,000 (1996 est)
population growth rate 3.0% (1990–95); 2.6% (2000–05)
ethnic distribution 60% Laotian, predominantly Lao Lum, 35% hill dwellers, and 5% Vietnamese and Chinese
life expectancy 50 (men), 53 (women)
literacy rate 84%
languages Lao (official), French, English
religions Theravāda Buddhist 85%, animist beliefs among mountain dwellers
currency new kip
GDP (US $) 1.5 billion (1994)
growth rate 8.4% (1994)
exports hydroelectric power from the Mekong is exported to Thailand, timber, teak, coffee, electricity, gypsum, tin

HISTORY
c. 2000–500 BC Early Bronze Age civilizations in central Mekong River and Plain of Jars regions.
5th–8th Cs Occupied by immigrants from S China.
8th C onwards Theravāda Buddhism spread by Mon monks.
9th–13th Cs Part of the sophisticated Khmer Empire, centred on Angkor in Cambodia.
12th C Small independent principalities, notably Luang Prabang, established by Lao invaders from Thailand and Yunnan, S China; they adopted Buddhism.
14th C United by King Fa Ngum; the first independent Laotian state, Lan Xang, formed. It was to dominate for four centuries, broken only by a period of Burmese rule 1574–1637.
17th C First visited by Europeans.
1713 The Lan Xang kingdom split into three separate kingdoms, Luang Prabang, Vientiane, and Champassac, which became tributaries of Siam (Thailand) from the late 18th century.
1893–1945 Laos was a French protectorate, comprising the three principalities of Luang Prabang, Vientiane, and Champassac.
1945 Temporarily occupied by Japan.
1946 Retaken by France, despite opposition by the Chinese-backed Lao Issara (Free Laos) nationalist movement.
1950 Granted semi-autonomy in French Union, as an associated state under the constitutional monarchy of the king of Luang Prabang.
1954 Independence achieved from France under the Geneva Agreements, but civil war broke out between a moderate royalist faction of the Lao Issara, led by Prince Souvanna Phouma, and the communist, Chinese-backed Pathet Lao (Land of the Lao) led by Prince Souphanouvong (Souvanna's half-brother).
1957 Coalition government, headed by Souvanna Phouma, established by Vientiane Agreement.
1959 Savang Vatthana became king.
1960 Right-wing pro-Western government seized power, headed by Prince Boun Gum.
1962 Geneva Agreement established new coalition government, led by Souvanna Phouma, but civil war continued, the Pathet Lao receiving backing from the North Vietnamese, and Souvanna Phouma from the USA.
1973 Vientiane cease-fire agreement divided the country between the communists and the Souvanna Phouma regime and brought the withdrawal of US, Thai, and North Vietnamese forces.
1975 Communists seized power; republic proclaimed, with Prince Souphanouvong as head of state and the Communist Party leader Kaysone Phomvihane as the controlling prime minister.
1979 Food shortages and the flight of 250,000 refugees to Thailand led to an easing of the drive towards nationalization and agricultural collectivization.
1985 Greater economic liberalization received encouragement from the Soviet Union's reformist leader Mikhail Gorbachev.
1989 First assembly elections since communist takeover; Vietnamese troops withdrawn.
1991 Kaysone Phomvihane was elected president and the army commander General Khamtay Siphandon became prime minister. Security and cooperation pact signed with Thailand, and agreement reached on phased repatriation of Laotian refugees.
1992 Phomvihane died; replaced as president by Nouhak Phoumsavan.
1995 The US lifted its 20-year aid embargo.
1996 Military tightened its grip on political affairs; but inward investment and private enterprise encouraged, fuelling economic expansion.
1997 Membership of Association of South East Asian Nations (ASEAN) announced.
1998 Khamtay Siphandon became president and was replaced as prime minister by Sisavath Keobounphanh.

published a five-volume survey of ◊celestial mechanics, *Traité de méchanique céleste* 1799–1825. This work contained the law of universal attraction – the law of gravity as applied to the Earth – and explanations of such phenomena as the ebb and flow of tides and the precession of the equinoxes. Among his mathematical achievements was the development of probability theory.

Lapland region of Europe within the Arctic Circle in Norway, Sweden, Finland, and the Kola Peninsula of NW Russia, without political definition. Its chief resources are chromium, copper, iron, timber, hydroelectric power, and tourism. The indigenous population are the ◊Saami (formerly known as Lapps), 10% of whom are nomadic, the remainder living mostly in coastal settlements. Lapland has low temperatures, with three months' continuous daylight in summer and three months' continuous darkness in winter. There is summer agriculture.

La Plata capital of Buenos Aires province, Argentina; population (1991) 542,600; metropolitan area (1992 est) 676,100. Industries include meat packing and petroleum refining. It was founded 1882.

laptop computer portable microcomputer, small enough to be used on the operator's lap. It consists of a single unit, incorporating a keyboard, floppy disc and hard disc drives, and a screen. The screen often forms a lid that folds back in use. It uses a liquid-crystal or gas-plasma display, rather than the bulkier and heavier cathode-ray tubes found in most display terminals.

lapwing Eurasian bird *Vanellus vanellus* of the plover family, also known as the ***green plover*** and, from its call, as the ***peewit***. Bottle-green above and white below, with a long thin crest and rounded wings, it is about 30 cm/1 ft long. It inhabits moorland in Europe and Asia.

Lara Brian 1969– . Trinidadian cricket player. A left-handed batsman, he plays first-class cricket for Trinidad and Tobago. In 1994 he broke the world individual test batting record with an innings of 375 against England, and later the same year he broke the world record for an individual innings in first-class cricket with an unbeaten 501 for Warwickshire against Durham.

larch any tree of the genus *Larix*, of the family Pinaceae. The common larch *L. decidua* grows to 40 m/130 ft. It is one of the few ◊conifers to shed its leaves annually. The small needlelike leaves are replaced every year by new bright-green foliage, which later darkens.

larch A native of the mountains of central Europe, the larch is now widely cultivated for timber and is often used to shelter hardwood saplings. The larch is one of the few conifers to shed its leaves. *Premaphotos Wildlife*

lard clarified edible pig fat. It is used in cooking and in the manufacture of margarine, soaps, and ointments.

Lardner Ring(old Wilmer) 1885–1933. US short-story writer. A sports reporter, he based his characters on the people he met professionally. His collected volumes of short stories include *You Know Me, Al* 1916, *Round Up* 1929, and *Ring Lardner's Best Short Stories* 1938, all written in colloquial language.

lares and penates in Roman mythology, spirits of the farm and of the store cupboard, often identified with the family ancestors, whose shrine was the centre of worship in Roman homes.

Large Electron Positron Collider (LEP) the world's largest particle ◊accelerator, in operation from 1989 at the CERN laboratories near Geneva in Switzerland. It occupies a tunnel 3.8 m/12.5 ft wide and 27 km/16.7 mi long, which is buried 180 m/590 ft underground and forms a ring consisting of eight curved and eight straight sections. Electrons and positrons enter the ring after passing through the Super Proton Synchrotron accelerator. They travel in opposite directions around the ring, guided by 3,328 bending magnets and kept within tight beams by 1,272 focusing magnets. As they pass through the straight sections, the particles are accelerated by a pulse of radio energy. Once sufficient energy is accumulated, the beams are allowed to collide. Four giant detectors are used to study the resulting shower of particles.

In 1996, LEP resumed operation after a £210 million upgrade. The upgraded machine is called LEP2, and can generate collision energy of 161 gigaelectron volts.

La Rioja region of N Spain; area 5,000 sq km/1,930 sq mi; population (1991) 263,400. The river Ebro passes through the region, but it is a tributary of the Río Oja, which gives its name to the region. The capital is Logroño. La Rioja is known for its red and white oaked wines.

lark songbird of the family Alaudidae, order Passeriformes, found mainly in the Old World, but also in North America. Larks are brownish-tan in colour and usually about 18 cm/7 in long; they nest on the ground in the open. The skylark *Alauda arvensis* sings as it rises almost vertically in the air. It is light brown, and 18 cm/7 in long.

Larkin Philip Arthur 1922–1985. English poet. His perfectionist, pessimistic verse appeared in *The Less Deceived* 1955, *The Whitsun Weddings* 1964, and *High Windows* 1974. He edited *The Oxford Book of 20th-Century English Verse* 1973. After his death, his letters and other writings, which he had instructed should be destroyed, revealed an intolerance and misanthropy not found in his published material. *Collected Poems* was published 1988.

Larne seaport of County Antrim, Northern Ireland, on Lough Larne, terminus of sea routes to Stranraer, Liverpool, Dublin, and other places; population (1991) 17,500.

La Rochefoucauld François, Duc de 1613–1680. French writer. His *Réflexions, ou sentences et maximes morales/Reflections, or Moral Maxims*, published anonymously 1665, is a collection of brief, epigrammatic, and cynical observations on life and society, with the epigraph 'Our virtues are mostly our vices in disguise'. The work is remarkable for its literary excellence and its bitter realism in the dissection of basic human motives, making La Rochefoucauld a forerunner of modern 'psychological' writers.

La Rochelle fishing port in W France; population (1990) 73,700. It is the capital of Charente-Maritime *département*. Industries include shipbuilding, chemicals, and motor vehicles. A Huguenot stronghold, it was taken by Cardinal Richelieu in the siege of 1627–28.

Larousse Pierre Athenase 1817–1875. French grammarian and lexicographer. His encyclopedic dictionary, the *Grand Dictionnaire universel du XIXème siècle/Great Universal 19th-Century Dictionary* 1865–76, continues to be published in revised form.

Lartigue Jacques-Henri Charles Auguste 1894–1986. French photographer. He began taking photographs of his family at the age of seven, and went on to make ◊autochrome colour prints of women. During his lifetime he took over 40,000 photographs, documenting everyday people and situations.

lapwing The red-wattled lapwing *Vanellus indicus* is common throughout the Indian subcontinent and, like the European lapwing, prefers open habitats. Lapwings perform an elaborate courtship dance. When danger threatens their ground-built nest they try to draw attention away from it by feigning a broken wing. *Premaphotos Wildlife*

larva stage between hatching and adulthood in those species in which the young have a different appearance and way of life from the adults. Examples include tadpoles (frogs) and caterpillars (butterflies and moths). Larvae are typical of the invertebrates, some of which (for example, shrimps) have two or more distinct larval stages. Among vertebrates, it is only the amphibians and some fishes that have a larval stage. *See illustration on following page.*

laryngitis inflammation of the larynx, causing soreness of the throat, a dry cough, and hoarseness. The acute form is due to a virus or other infection, excessive use of the voice, or inhalation of irritating smoke, and may cause the voice to be completely lost. With rest, the inflammation usually subsides in a few days.

larynx in mammals, a cavity at the upper end of the trachea (windpipe) containing the vocal cords. It is stiffened with cartilage and lined with mucous membrane. Amphibians and reptiles have much simpler larynxes, with no vocal cords. Birds have a similar cavity, called the ***syrinx***, found lower down the trachea, where it branches to form the bronchi. It is very complex, with well-developed vocal cords.

'Deprivation is for me what daffodils were for Wordsworth.'

PHILIP LARKIN
Quoted in the *Observer* 1979

la Salle René Robert Cavelier, Sieur de 1643–1687. French explorer. He made an epic voyage through North America, exploring the Mississippi River down to its mouth, and in 1682 founded Louisiana. When he returned with colonists, he failed to find the river mouth again, and was eventually murdered by his mutinous men.

Las Casas Bartolomé de 1474–1566. Spanish missionary, historian, and colonial reformer, known as '***the Apostle of the Indies***'. He was one of the first Europeans to call for the abolition of Indian slavery in Latin America. He took part in the conquest of Cuba in 1513, but subsequently worked for Native American freedom in the Spanish colonies. In 1530, shortly before the conquest of Peru, he persuaded the Spanish government to forbid slavery there. *Apologetica historia de las Indias* (first published 1875–76) is his account of Indian traditions and his witnessing of Spanish oppression of the Indians.

Lascaux cave system in SW France with prehistoric wall paintings. It is richly decorated with realistic and symbolic paintings of aurochs (wild cattle), horses, and red deer of the Upper Palaeolithic period, about 15,000 BC. The cave, near Montignac in the Dordogne, was discovered 1940. Similar paintings are found in ◊Altamira, Spain. The opening of the Lascaux cave to tourists led to deterioration of the paintings; the cave was closed 1963 and a facsimile opened 1983.

'Lascaux is the Parthenon of prehistory.'

On LASCAUX
Cyril Connolly
'Dordogne', *Ideas and Places*

Lasdun Denys Louis 1914– . English Modernist architect. Many of his designs emphasize the horizontal layering of a building, creating the effect of

larva The larva of the monarch butterfly *Danaus plexippus* on its food plant. The great advantage of having a larval stage in the life cycle is that the larvae and the adults do not eat the same food and so there is no competition between parent and offspring. *Premaphotos Wildlife*

geological strata extending into the surrounding city or landscape. This effect can be seen in his designs for the University of East Anglia, Norwich, 1962–68, and the National Theatre on London's South Bank 1967–76.

Lasdun worked in partnership with Wells Coates (1895–1958) 1935–37 and from 1938 was a member of Berthold Lubetkin's Tecton Group until its dissolution 1948. His first significant work, Hallfield Housing Estate, Paddington, London 1951–59, shows Tecton influence. Other works of note include Keeling House council flats, Bethnal Green, London, 1952–55 and the Royal College of Physicians in Regent's Park, London, 1960–64.

laser (acronym for ***light amplification by stimulated emission of radiation***) device for producing a narrow beam of light, capable of travelling over vast distances without dispersion, and of being focused to give enormous power densities (10^8 watts per cm^2 for high-energy lasers). The laser operates on a principle similar to that of the ◊maser (a high-frequency microwave amplifier or oscillator). The uses of lasers include communications (a laser beam can carry much more information than can radio waves), cutting, drilling, welding, satellite tracking, medical and biological research, and surgery. Lasers are also used as entertainment in theatres, concerts, and light shows.

laser material Any substance the majority of whose atoms or molecules can be put into an excited energy state can be used as laser material. Many solid, liquid, and gaseous substances have been used, including synthetic ruby crystal (used for the first extraction of laser light 1960, and giving a high-power pulsed output) and a helium–neon gas mixture, capable of continuous operation, but at a lower power.

applications A blue shortwave laser was developed in Japan 1988. Its expected application is in random access memory (◊RAM) and ◊compact disc recording, where its shorter wavelength will allow a greater concentration of digital information to be stored and read. A gallium arsenide chip, produced by IBM 1989, contains the world's smallest lasers in the form of cylinders of ◊semiconductor roughly one-tenth of the thickness of a human hair; a million lasers can fit on a chip 1 cm/2.5 in square.

laser printer computer ◊printer in which the image to be printed is formed by the action of a laser on a light-sensitive drum, then transferred to paper by means of an electrostatic charge. Laser printers are page printers, printing a complete page at a time. The printed image, which can take the form of text or pictures, is made up of tiny dots, or ink particles. The quality of the image generated depends on the fineness of these dots. Because they produce very high-quality print and are virtually silent, small laser printers (along with ink-jet printers, which spray fine jets of quick-drying ink onto paper) have replaced dot-matrix and daisywheel printers as the most popular type of microcomputer printer.

laser surgery use of intense light sources to cut, coagulate, or vaporize tissue. Less invasive than normal surgery, it destroys diseased tissue gently and allows quicker, more natural healing. It can be used by way of a flexible endoscope to enable the surgeon to view the diseased area at which the laser needs to be aimed. ▷ *See feature on pp. 1024–1025.*

Las Palmas or ***Las Palmas de Gran Canaria*** tourist resort on the NE coast of Gran Canaria, Canary Islands; population (1994) 372,000. Products include sugar and bananas.

La Spezia port in NW Italy, chief Italian naval base; population (1992) 100,500. Industries include shipbuilding, engineering, electrical goods, and textiles.

Lassa fever acute disease caused by a virus, first detected 1969, and spread by a species of rat found only in W Africa. It is classified as a ◊haemorrhagic fever and characterized by high fever, headache, muscle pain, and internal bleeding. There is no known cure.

Las Vegas city in Nevada, USA, known for its nightclubs and gambling casinos; population (1992) 295,500. Las Vegas entertains millions of visitors each year and is an important convention centre. Founded 1855 in a ranching area, the modern community developed with the coming of the railroad 1905. The first casino-hotel opened 1947.

La Tène prehistoric settlement at the east end of Lake Neuchâtel, Switzerland, which has given its name to a culture of the Iron Age. The culture lasted from the 5th century BC to the Roman conquest. ▷ *See feature on pp. 200–201.*

latent heat in physics, the heat absorbed or released by a substance as it changes state (for example, from solid to liquid) at constant temperature and pressure.

lateral moraine linear ridge of rocky debris deposited near the edge of a ◊glacier. Much of the debris is material that has fallen from the valley side onto the glacier's edge, having been weathered by ◊freeze-thaw (the alternate freezing and thawing of ice in cracks); it will, therefore, tend to be angular in nature. Where two glaciers merge, two lateral moraines may join together to form a ***medial moraine*** running along the centre of the merged glacier.

Lateran Treaties series of agreements that marked the reconciliation of the Italian state with the papacy in 1929. They were hailed as a propaganda victory for the Fascist regime. The treaties involved recognition of the sovereignty of the ◊Vatican City State, the payment of an indemnity for papal possessions lost during unification in 1870, and agreement on the role of the Catholic church within the Italian state in the form of a concordat between Pope Pius XI and the dictator Mussolini.

laterite red residual soil characteristic of tropical rainforests. It is formed by the weathering of basalts, granites, and shales and contains a high percentage of aluminium and iron hydroxides. It may form an impermeable and infertile layer that hinders plant growth.

latex (Latin 'liquid') fluid of some plants (such as the rubber tree and poppy), an emulsion of resins, proteins, and other organic substances. It is used as the basis for making rubber. The name is also applied to a suspension in water of natural or synthetic rubber (or plastic) particles used in rubber goods, paints, and adhesives.

lathe machine tool, used for turning. The workpiece to be machined, usually wood or metal, is held and rotated while cutting tools are moved against it. Modern lathes are driven by electric motors.

latifundium (Latin for 'broad' and 'farm') in ancient Rome, a large agricultural estate designed to make maximum use of cheap labour, whether free workers or slaves. In present-day Italy, Spain, and South America, the term *latifondo* refers to a large agricultural estate worked by low-paid casual or semiservile labour in the interests of absentee landlords.

Latimer Hugh c. 1485–1555. English Christian church reformer and bishop. After his conversion to Protestantism in 1524 he was imprisoned several times but was protected by Cardinal Wolsey and Henry VIII.

Latimer was appointed bishop of Worcester in 1535, but resigned in 1539. Under Edward VI his sermons denouncing social injustice won him great influence, but he was arrested for heresy in 1553 after the accession of the Catholic Mary, and two years later he was burned at the stake in Oxford.

Latin Indo-European language of ancient Italy. Latin has passed through four influential phases: as the language of (1) republican Rome, (2) the Roman Empire, (3) the Roman Catholic Church, and (4) W

laser printer A laser printer works by transferring tiny ink particles contained in a toner cartridge to paper via a rubber belt. The image is produced by laser on a light-sensitive drum within the printer.

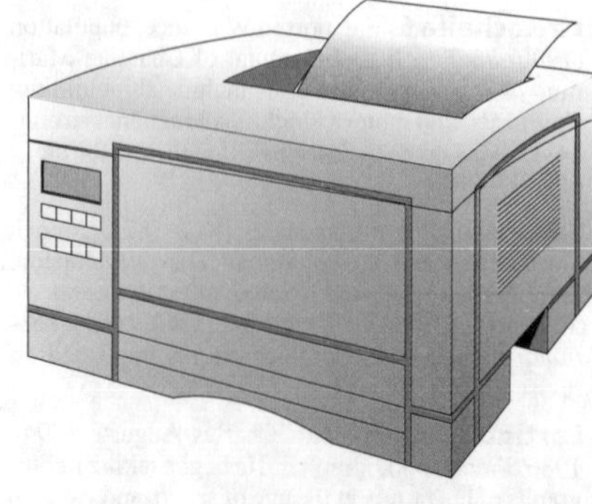

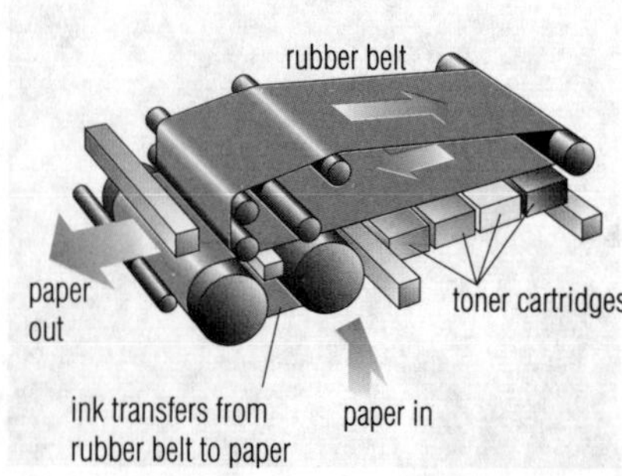

European culture, science, philosophy, and law during the Middle Ages and the Renaissance. During the third and fourth phases, much Latin vocabulary entered the English language. It is the parent form of the ◊Romance languages, noted for its highly inflected grammar and conciseness of expression.

The direct influence of Latin in Europe has decreased since Renaissance times but is still considerable, and indirectly both the language and its classical literature still affect many modern languages and literatures. The insistence of Renaissance scholars upon an exact classical purity, together with the rise of the European nation-states, contributed to the decline of Latin as an international cultural medium.

Latin America large territory in the Western hemisphere south of the USA, consisting of Mexico, Central America, South America, and the West Indies. The main languages spoken are Spanish, Portuguese, and French.

Latin American Integration Association (*Asociación Latino-Americana de Integración* (ALADI)) organization aiming to create a common market in Latin America; to promote trade it applies tariff reductions preferentially on the basis of the different stages of economic development that individual member countries have reached. Formed in 1990 to replace the Latin American Free Trade Association, it has 11 members: Argentina, Bolivia, Brazil, Chile, Colombia, Ecuador, Mexico, Paraguay, Peru, Uruguay, and Venezuela. Its headquarters are in Bogotá, Colombia.

Latin literature literature written in the Latin language.
early literature Only a few hymns and inscriptions survive from the earliest period of Latin literature before the 3rd century BC. Greek influence began with the work of Livius Andronicus (c. 284–204 BC), who translated the *Odyssey* and Greek plays into Latin. Naevius and Ennius both attempted epics on patriotic themes; the former used the native 'Saturnian' metre, but the latter introduced the Greek hexameter. Plautus and Terence successfully adapted Greek comedy to the Roman stage. Accius and Pacuvius produced tragic verse. Lucilius (190–103 BC) founded Latin verse satire, while the writings of Cato the Elder were the first important works in Latin prose.
Golden Age (70 BC–AD 18) In the *De Rerum natura* of Lucretius, and the passionate lyrics of Catullus, Latin verse reached maturity. Cicero set a standard for Latin prose, in his orations, philosophical essays, and letters. To the same period of the Roman republic belong the commentaries of Caesar on his own campaigns. Other prose writers of this period include Cornelius Nepos, Sallust, and Marcus Terentius Varro.
Augustan Age (43 BC–AD 18) Within the Golden Age, this is usually regarded as the finest period of Latin literature. There is strong patriotic feeling in the work of the poets Virgil and Horace and the historian Livy, who belonged to the emperor Augustus' court circle. Virgil produced the one great Latin epic, the *Aeneid*, while Horace brought charm and polish to both lyric and satire. Younger poets of the period were Ovid, who wrote ironically about love and mythology, and the elegiac and erotic poets Tibullus and Propertius. Tragedy was again in vogue, and was attempted by Asinius Pollio (76 BC–AD 5), Varius Rufus (74–14 BC), and Augustus himself.
Silver Age (AD 18–c. 130) The second major period of imperial literature begins with the writers of Nero's reign: the Stoic philosopher Seneca; Lucan, author of the epic *Pharsalia*; the satirist Persius; and the novelist Petronius. Around the end of the 1st century and at the beginning of the 2nd came the historian and annalist Tacitus and the satirical poet Juvenal; other writers of this period were the epigrammatist Martial, the scientific encyclopedist Pliny the Elder, the letter-writer Pliny the Younger, the critic Quintilian, the historian Suetonius, and the epic poet Statius.
2nd–5th centuries There was only one pagan writer of importance, the romancer Apuleius, but there were some able Christian writers, such as Tertullian and Cyprian, who were followed by Arnobius (died 327) and Lactantius (died 325). In the 4th century there was a poetic revival, with Ausonius, Claudian, and the Christian poets Prudentius and St Ambrose.

The Classical period ends, and the Middle Ages begin, with St Augustine's *City of God* and St Jerome's translation of the Bible.
Middle Ages Throughout the Middle Ages, Latin remained the language of the church and was normally employed for theology, philosophy, histories, and other learned works. Latin verse, adapted to rhyme and non-classical metres, was used both for hymns and for the secular songs of scholars, as in the ◊*Carmina Burana*. Medieval Latin vernacular gradually evolved into the regional and national ◊Romance languages, including French, Italian, and Spanish. Even after the Reformation, Latin retained its prestige as the international language of scholars and was used as such by the English writers Thomas More, Francis Bacon, John Milton, and many others.

latitude and longitude Locating a point on a globe using latitude and longitude. Longitude is the angle between the terrestrial meridian through a place and the standard meridian 0° passing through Greenwich, England. Latitude is the angular distance of a place from the equator.

Point X lies on longitude 60°W

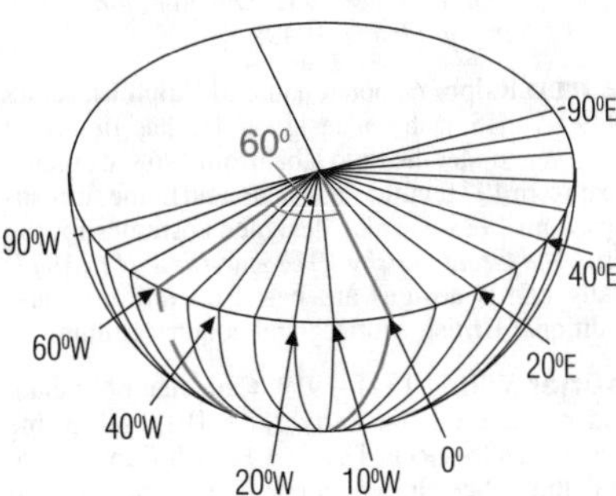

Point X lies on latitude 20°S

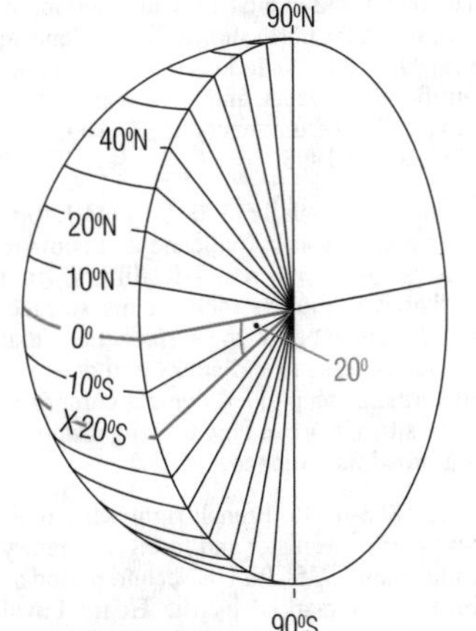

latitude and longitude imaginary lines used to locate position on the globe. Lines of latitude are drawn parallel to the equator, with 0° at the equator and 90° at the north and south poles. Lines of longitude are drawn at right angles to these, with 0° (the Prime Meridian) passing through Greenwich, England.

Latium Latin name for ◊Lazio, a region of W central Italy surrounding Rome.

La Tour Georges de 1593–1652. French painter. Many of his pictures – which range from religious paintings to domestic genre scenes – are illuminated by a single source of light, with deep contrasts of light and shade, as in *Joseph the Carpenter* about 1645 (Louvre, Paris). His style suggests a connection with the Dutch 'candle light' painters ◊Honthorst and Terbrugghen (1588–1629), who were followers of ◊Caravaggio. La Tour transformed the style of these painters into a grave and simplified beauty, *The New-born Child* (Musée de Rennes) being a well-known example. Other works are *The Hurdy-Gurdy Player* (Museum of Fine Art, Nantes), an early work, and *St Sebastian Tended by St Irene* (Staatliche Museen, Berlin).

Latter-day Saint member of the Christian sect known as the ◊Mormons.

Laughton One of the finest character actors of the 1930s, Charles Laughton played the leading roles in the films *The Private Life of Henry VIII* 1933, *Mutiny on the Bounty* 1935, and *The Hunchback of Notre Dame* 1939. *British Film Institute*

Latvia country in N Europe, bounded E by Russia, N by Estonia, N and NW by the Baltic Sea, S by Lithuania, and SE by Belarus. *See country box on p. 616.*

Latvian language or *Lettish* language of Latvia; with Lithuanian it is one of the two surviving members of the Balto-Slavic branch of the Indo-European language family.

Latynina Larissa Semyonovna 1935– . Soviet gymnast. She has won more Olympic medals than any person in any sport. She won 18 between 1956 and 1964, including nine gold medals. She won a total of 12 individual Olympic and world championship gold medals.

Laud William 1573–1645. English priest; archbishop of Canterbury from 1633. Laud's High Church policy, support for Charles I's unparliamentary rule, censorship of the press, and persecution of the Puritans all aroused bitter opposition, while his strict enforcement of the statutes against enclosures and of laws regulating wages and prices alienated the propertied classes. His attempt to impose the use of the Prayer Book on the Scots precipitated the English ◊Civil War. Impeached by Parliament 1640, he was imprisoned in the Tower of London and beheaded.

Lauda Niki (Nikolas Andreas) 1949– . Austrian motor-racing driver who won the Formula One World Championship 1975, 1977, and 1984. He was also runner-up 1976.

Lauda was Formula Two champion 1972, and drove for March, BRM, Ferrari, and Brabham before his retirement 1978. He returned to the sport 1984 and won his third world title in a McLaren before eventually retiring 1985 to concentrate on his airline business, Lauda-Air.

laudanum alcoholic solution (tincture) of the drug ◊opium. Used formerly as a narcotic and painkiller, it was available in the 19th century from pharmacists on demand in most of Europe and the USA.

Lauderdale John Maitland, 1st Duke of Lauderdale 1616–1682. Scottish politician. Formerly a zealous ◊Covenanter, he joined the Royalists 1647, and as high commissioner for Scotland 1667–79 persecuted the Covenanters. He was created duke of Lauderdale 1672, and was a member of the ◊Cabal ministry 1667–73.

laughing gas popular name for ◊nitrous oxide, an anaesthetic.

Laughton Charles 1899–1962. English actor who became a US citizen 1950. Initially a classical stage actor, he joined the Old Vic 1933. His film appearances include such roles as the king in *The Private Life of Henry VIII* 1933 (Academy Award), Captain Bligh in *Mutiny on the Bounty* 1935, and Quasimodo in *The Hunchback of Notre Dame* 1939. In 1955 he directed *Night of the Hunter* and in 1962 appeared in *Advise and Consent*.

Laurasia northern landmass formed 200 million years ago by the splitting of the single world continent ◊Pangaea. (The southern landmass was

LATVIA
Republic of

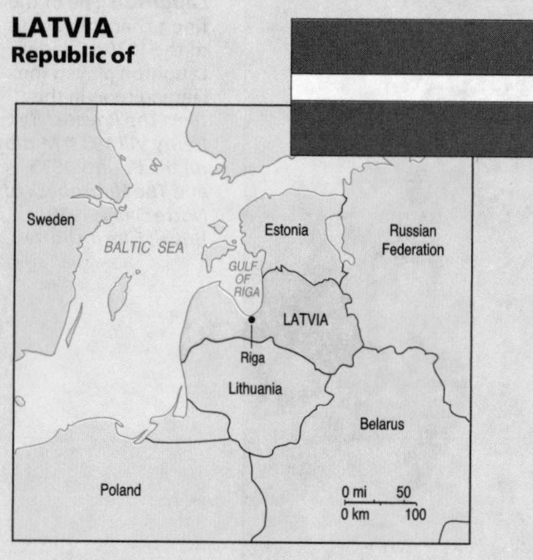

national name *Latvijas Republika*
area 63,700 sq km/24,595 sq mi
capital Riga
major towns/cities Daugavpils, Jurmala, Jelgava
major ports Ventspils and Leipāja
physical features wooded lowland (highest point 312 m/1,024 ft), marshes, lakes; 472 km/293 mi of coastline; mild climate
head of state Guntis Ulmanis from 1993
head of government Gunter Krasts from 1997
political system emergent democratic republic
administrative divisions 26 districts, 56 towns, and 37 urban settlements
political parties Latvian Way, right of centre; Latvian National and Conservative Party (LNNK), right-wing, nationalist; Economic-Political Union (formerly known as Harmony for Latvia and Rebirth of the National Economy), centrist; Ravnopravie (Equal Rights), centrist; For the Fatherland and Freedom (FFF), extreme nationalist; Latvian Peasants' Union (LZS), rural-based, centre-left; Union of Christian Democrats, centre-right; Democratic Centre Party, centrist; Movement for Latvia, pro-Russian, populist; Master in Your Own Home (Saimnieks), ex-communist, populist
population 2,557,000 (1995 est)
population growth rate −0.9% (1990–95); −0.5% (2000–05)
ethnic distribution 53% of Latvian ethnic descent, 34% ethnic Russian, 4% Belarussian, 3% Ukrainian, 2% Polish, and 1% Lithuanian
life expectancy 64 (men), 75 (women)
literacy rate 99%
language Latvian
religions Lutheran, Roman Catholic, Russian Orthodox
currency lat
GDP (US $) 5.8 billion (1994)
growth rate 2.0% (1994)
exports electronic and communications equipment including long-distance telephone exchanges, electric railway carriages, motorcycles, consumer durables, sawn timber, paper and woollen goods, meat and dairy products

HISTORY
9th–10th Cs Invaded by Vikings and Russians.
13th C Conquered by crusading German Teutonic Knights, who named the area Livonia and converted population to Christianity; Riga joined Hanseatic League, a N European union of commercial towns.
1520s Lutheranism established as a result of the Reformation.
16th–17th Cs Successively under Polish, Lithuanian, and Swedish rule.
1721 Tsarist Russia took control.
1819 Serfdom abolished.
1900s Emergence of independence movement.
1914–18 Under partial German occupation during World War I.
1918–19 Independence proclaimed and achieved after Russian Red Army troops expelled by German, Polish, and Latvian forces.
1920s Land reforms introduced by Farmers' Union government of Karlis Ulmanis.
1934 Democracy overthrown and, at time of economic depression, Ulmanis established autocratic regime; Baltic Entente mutual defence pact with Estonia and Lithuania.
1940 Incorporated into Soviet Union (USSR) as constituent republic, following secret German–Soviet agreement.
1941–44 Occupied by Germany.
1944 USSR regained control; mass deportations of Latvians to Central Asia, followed by immigration of ethnic Russians; agricultural collectivization.
1960s and 1970s Extreme repression of Latvian cultural and literary life.
1980s Nationalist dissent began to grow, influenced by the Polish Solidarity movement and Mikhail Gorbachev's glasnost ('openness') initiative in USSR.
1988 Latvian Popular Front established to campaign for independence. Prewar flag readopted; official status given to Latvian language.
1989 Latvian parliament passed a sovereignty declaration.
1990 Popular Front secured majority in local elections and its leader, Ivan Godmanir, became prime minister. Latvian CP split into pro-independence and pro-Moscow wings. Entered 'transitional period of independence'; the Baltic Council reformed.
1991 Soviet troops briefly seized key installations in Riga. Overwhelming vote for independence in referendum. Full independence achieved following failure of anti-Gorbachev coup attempt in Moscow; CP outlawed. Joined United Nations (UN); market-centred economic reform programme instituted.
1992 Curbing of rights of noncitizens prompted Russia to request minority protection by UN.
1993 Right-of-centre Latvian Way won most seats in general election, and Valdis Birkavs became premier; free-trade agreement with Estonia and Lithuania.
1994 Last Russian troops departed. Birkavs replaced by Maris Gailis; economic growth resumed.
1995 Trade and cooperation agreement signed with European Union (EU). General election produced a 'hung parliament', in which extremist parties received most support. Latvia applied officially for EU membership. Independent Andris Skele became prime minister.
1996 Guntis Ulmanis re-elected president. Finance minister and deputy prime minister resigned from eight-party coalition.
1997 New political party formed, Latvian National Party of Reforms. Prime Minister Skele replaced by Guntar Krasts.

SEE ALSO Russian Federation; Union of Soviet Socialist Republics

◊Gondwanaland.) It consisted of what was to become North America, Greenland, Europe, and Asia, and is believed to have broken up about 100 million years ago with the separation of North America from Europe.

laurel any evergreen tree of the European genus *Laurus*, family Lauraceae, with glossy, aromatic leaves, yellowish flowers, and black berries. The leaves of sweet bay or poet's laurel *L. nobilis* are used in cooking. Several species are cultivated worldwide. In classical times *L. nobilis* was used to make wreaths for victorious athletes.

Laurel and Hardy Stan Laurel (stage name of Arthur Stanley Jefferson) (1890–1965) and Oliver Hardy (1892–1957) US film comedians. They were one of the most successful comedy teams in film history (Stan was slim, Oliver rotund). Their partnership began 1927, survived the transition from silent films to sound, and resulted in more than 200 short and feature-length films. Among these are *Pack Up Your Troubles* 1932, *Our Relations* 1936, and *A Chump at Oxford* 1940.

Laurel and Hardy
Popular comic duo Laurel (left) and Hardy, one of the most successful comedy teams in cinema history. Between 1927 and 1952 they made a huge number of short films as well as feature-length films such as *Way Out West* 1937.
British Film Institute

Lauren Ralph. Adopted name of Ralph Lipschitz 1939– . US fashion designer. He has produced menswear under the Polo label from 1968, women's wear from 1971, children's wear, and home furnishings from 1983. He also designed costumes for the films *The Great Gatsby* 1973 and *Annie Hall* 1977. Many of his designs are based on uniforms and traditional British sporting and country clothing.

Laurier Wilfrid 1841–1919. Canadian politician, leader of the Liberal Party 1887–1919 and prime minister 1896–1911. The first French-Canadian to hold the office, he encouraged immigration into Canada from Europe and the USA, established a separate Canadian navy, and sent troops to help Britain in the Boer War.

Lausanne resort and capital of Vaud canton, W Switzerland, above the north shore of Lake Geneva; population (1990) 123,200. Industries include chocolate, scientific instruments, and publishing. There is a cathedral 1275 and university 1537. An Olympic Museum opened 1993.

lava molten rock (usually 800–1,100°C/1,500–2,000°F) that erupts from a ◊volcano and cools to form extrusive ◊igneous rock. It differs from magma in that it is molten rock on the surface; magma is molten rock below the surface. Lava that is high in silica is viscous and sticky and does not flow far; it forms a steep-sided conical composite volcano. Low-silica lava can flow for long distances and forms a broad flat volcano.

Laval Pierre 1883–1945. French right-wing politician. He was prime minister and foreign secretary 1931–32, and again 1935–36. His second period as prime minister was marked by the Hoare–Laval Pact for concessions to Italy in Abyssinia (now

Ethiopia). In World War II he joined Pétain's ◊Vichy government as vice premier June 1940; dismissed Dec 1940, he was reinstated by Hitler's orders as head of the government and foreign minister 1942. His part in the deportation of French labour to Germany during the war made him universally hated and he was tried for treason and executed.

lavender sweet-smelling herb, genus *Lavandula*, of the mint family Labiatae, native to W Mediterranean countries. The bushy low-growing *L. angustifolia* has long, narrow, erect leaves of a silver-green colour. The flowers, borne on a terminal spike, vary in colour from lilac to deep purple and are covered with small fragrant oil glands. The oil is extensively used in pharmacy and the manufacture of perfumes.

laver any of several edible red seaweeds, including *Porphyra umbicalis*. Growing on the shore and below, attached to rocks and stones, laver forms thin, irregularly rounded sheets of tissue up to 20 cm/8 in across. It becomes almost black when dry. In Wales it is made into laver bread, a national delicacy, fried with bacon and eaten at breakfast.

Laver Rod(ney George) 1938– . Australian lawn-tennis player. He was one of the greatest left-handed players, and the only player to win the Grand Slam twice (1962 and 1969). He won four Wimbledon singles titles, the Australian title three times, the US Open twice, and the French Open twice. He turned professional after winning Wimbledon in 1962 but returned when the championships were opened to professionals in 1968.

Lavoisier Antoine Laurent 1743–1794. French chemist. He proved that combustion needs only a part of the air, which he called oxygen, thereby destroying the theory of phlogiston (an imaginary 'fire element' released during combustion). With astronomer and mathematician Pierre de ◊Laplace, he showed 1783 that water is a compound of oxygen and hydrogen. In this way he established the basic rules of chemical combination.

Lavoisier established that organic compounds contain carbon, hydrogen, and oxygen. From quantitative measurements of the changes during breathing, he showed that carbon dioxide and water are normal products of respiration.

law body of rules and principles under which justice is administered or order enforced in a state or nation. In western Europe there are two main systems: Roman law and English law. US law is a modified form of English law.

Roman law is the legal system of ancient Rome. It is now the basis of civil law, one of the main European legal systems. It originated under the republic, was developed under the empire, and continued in use in the Byzantine Empire until 1453. First codified 450 BC and finalized under Justinian AD 528–534, it advanced to a system of international law (*jus gentium*), applied in disputes between Romans and foreigners or provincials, or between provincials of different states. Church influence led to the adoption of Roman law throughout western continental Europe, and it was spread to E Europe and parts of Asia by the French *Code Napoléon* in the 19th century. Scotland and Quebec (because of their French links) and South Africa (because of its link with Holland) also have it as the basis of their legal systems.

English law derives from Anglo-Saxon customs, which were too entrenched to be broken by the Norman Conquest and still form the basis of the ◊common law, which by 1250 had been systematized by the royal judges. Unique to English law is the doctrine of *stare decisis* (Latin 'to stand by things decided'), which requires that courts abide by former precedents (or decisions) when the same points arise again in litigation.

Law Andrew Bonar 1858–1923. British Conservative politician. Elected leader of the opposition 1911, he became colonial secretary in Asquith's coalition government 1915–16, chancellor of the Exchequer 1916–19, and Lord Privy Seal 1919–21 in Lloyd George's coalition. He formed a Conservative Cabinet 1922, but resigned on health grounds.

Law Commission in the UK, either of two statutory bodies established 1965 (one for England and Wales and one for Scotland) which consider proposals for law reform and publish their findings. They also keep British law under constant review, systematically developing and reforming it by, for example, the repeal of obsolete and unnecessary enactments.

law courts bodies that adjudicate in legal disputes. Civil and criminal cases are usually dealt with by separate courts. In many countries there is a hierarchy of courts that provide an appeal system.

In England and Wales the court system was reorganized under the Courts Act 1971. The higher courts are: the ***House of Lords*** (the highest court for the whole of Britain), which deals with both civil and criminal appeals; the ***Court of Appeal***, which is divided between criminal and civil appeal courts; the ***High Court of Justice*** dealing with important civil cases; ***crown courts***, which handle criminal cases; and ***county courts***, which deal with civil matters. ***Magistrates' courts*** deal with minor criminal cases and are served by ◊justices of the peace or stipendiary (paid) magistrates; and ***juvenile courts*** are presided over by specially qualified justices. There are also special courts, such as the Restrictive Practices Court and the Employment Appeal Tribunal.

The courts are organized in six circuits. The towns of each circuit are first-tier (High Court and circuit judges dealing with both criminal and civil cases), second-tier (High Court and circuit judges dealing with criminal cases only), or third-tier (circuit judges dealing with criminal cases only). Cases are allotted according to gravity among High Court and circuit judges and recorders (part-time judges with the same jurisdiction as circuit judges). In Scotland, the supreme civil court is the ***Court of Session***, with appeal to the House of Lords; the highest criminal court is the ***High Court of Justiciary***, with no appeal to the House of Lords.

law lords in England, the ten Lords of Appeal in Ordinary who, together with the Lord Chancellor and other peers, make up the House of Lords in its judicial capacity. The House of Lords is the final court of appeal in both criminal and civil cases. Law lords rank as life peers.

Lawrence D(avid) H(erbert) 1885–1930. English writer. His work expresses his belief in emotion and the sexual impulse as creative and true to human nature. His writing first received attention after the publication of the semi-autobiographical *The White Peacock* 1911 and *Sons and Lovers* 1913. Other novels include *The Rainbow* 1915, *Women in Love* 1921, and *Lady Chatterley's Lover*, printed privately in Italy 1928. He also wrote short stories (for example, 'The Woman Who Rode Away', written in Mexico 1922–25) and poetry (*Collected Poems* 1928). His interest in sex as a life force and bond was often censured: *The Rainbow* was suppressed for obscenity, and *Lady Chatterley's Lover* could only be published in an expurgated form in the UK 1932. Not until 1961, when the obscenity law was successfully challenged, was it published in the original text.

Law British Conservative politician Andrew Bonar Law. He made his fortune in the iron business in Glasgow before entering politics. He was one of the British representatives in the negotiations over the terms of settlement at the end of World War I and was a signatory to the Treaty of Versailles. *Image Select (UK) Ltd*

Lausanne A view of Lausanne, Switzerland, showing the 13th-century Gothic cathedral of Notre-Dame. It became Protestant in the 16th century when Lausanne was one of the principal intellectual centres of the Reformation. Having the largest port on Lake Geneva, Lausanne is the commercial and financial centre of a rich agricultural area. It also attracts many international conferences. *Swiss National Tourist Office*

Lawrence T(homas) E(dward), known as ***Lawrence of Arabia*** 1888–1935. British soldier, scholar, and translator. Appointed to the military intelligence department in Cairo, Egypt, during World War I, he took part in negotiations for an Arab revolt against the Ottoman Turks, and in 1916 attached himself to the emir Faisal. He became a guerrilla leader of genius, combining raids on Turkish communications with the organization of a joint Arab revolt, described in *The Seven Pillars of Wisdom* 1926.

Lawrence Thomas 1769–1830. English painter, the leading portraitist of his day. He became painter to George III 1792 and president of the Royal Academy 1820–30. Queen Charlotte 1789 (National Gallery, London) is one of his finest portraits. After the Napoleonic wars he was commissioned by the Prince Regent to paint the allied sovereigns and dignitaries, travelling in state for this purpose to Aix-la-Chapelle, Vienna and Rome; the portraits are now in the Waterloo Room, Windsor, and include some of his most brilliant works, for example the *Pope Pius VII*.

lawrencium synthesized, radioactive, metallic element, the last of the actinide series, symbol Lr, atomic number 103, relative atomic mass 262. Its only known isotope, Lr-257, has a half-life of 4.3 seconds and was originally synthesized at the University of California at Berkeley 1961 by bombarding californium with boron nuclei.

Lawson Nigel, Baron Lawson of Blaby 1932– . British Conservative politician. A former financial journalist, he was financial secretary to the Treasury 1979–81, secretary of state for energy 1981–83, and chancellor of the Exchequer 1983–89. He resigned after criticism by government adviser Alan Walters over his policy of British membership of the ◊European Monetary System.

laxative substance used to relieve constipation (infrequent bowel movement). Regular exercise and a diet high in vegetable fibre are believed to be the best means of preventing and treating constipation.

Layamon English poet. He was the author of the *Brut*, a chronicle of about 16,000 alliterative lines on the history of Britain from the legendary Roman senator and general ◊Brutus to ◊Cadwalader, which gives the earliest version of the Arthurian legend in English. It is based on the French rendering by Robert Wace (c. 1100–c. 1175) of the Latin *Historia Regum Britanniae* by ◊Geoffrey of Monmouth, with additions from Celtic legend.

Lazarus in the New Testament, the brother of Martha, a friend of Jesus, raised by him from the

'Ignorance of the law excuses no man; not that all men know the law, but because 'tis an excuse every man will plead, and no man can tell how to confute him.'

On LAW
John Selden 'Law', *Table Talk* 1689

''Be a good animal, true to your instincts,' was his motto.'

D H LAWRENCE
The White Peacock

leaf Leaf shapes and arrangements on the stem are many and varied; in cross-section, a leaf is a complex arrangement of cells surrounded by the epidermis. This is pierced by the stomata through which gases enter and leave.

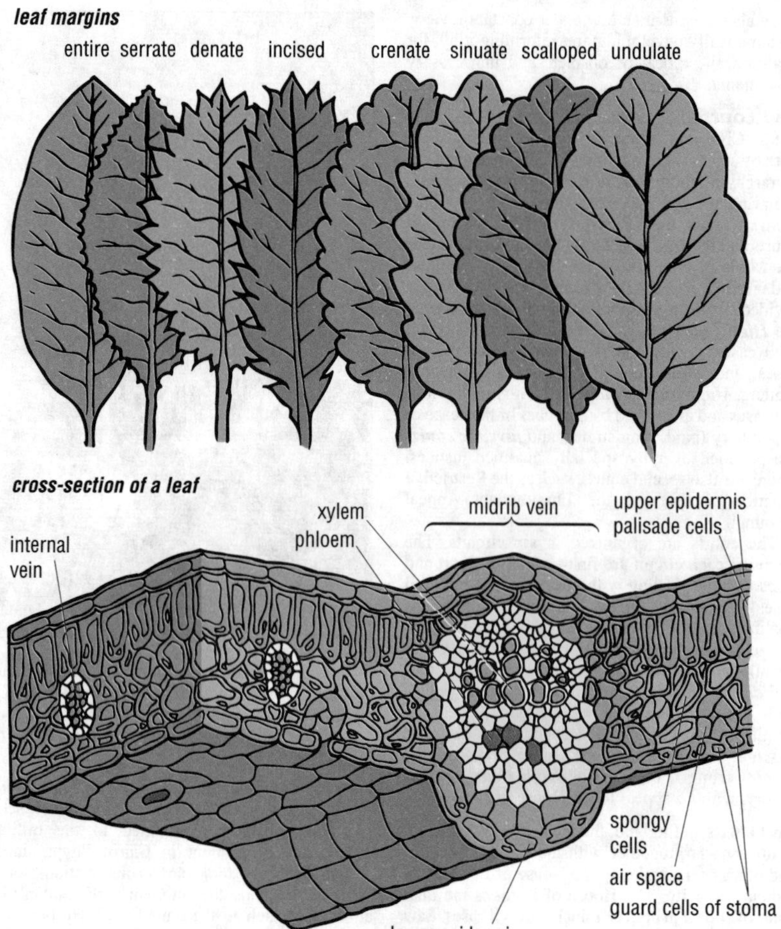

dead. Lazarus is also the name of a beggar in a parable told by Jesus (Luke 16).

Lazio (Roman ***Latium***) region of W central Italy; area 17,200 sq km/6,639 sq mi; capital Rome; population (1992 est) 5,162,100. Products include olives, wine, chemicals, pharmaceuticals, and textiles. Home of the Latins from the 10th century BC, it was dominated by the Romans from the 4th century BC.

LCD abbreviation for ◊***liquid-crystal display***.

L-dopa chemical, normally produced by the body, which is converted by an enzyme to dopamine in the brain. It is essential for integrated movement of individual muscle groups. L-dopa is a left-handed isomer of an amino acid $C_9H_{11}NO_2$. As a treatment, it relieves the rigidity of ◊Parkinson's disease, but may have significant side effects such as extreme mood changes, hallucinations, and uncontrolled writhing movements. It is often given in combination with other drugs to improve its effectiveness at lower doses.

Lea river that rises N of Luton, Bedfordshire, England, and joins the river Thames at Blackwall; length 74 km/46 mi. It is the source of much of London's water supply.

LEA in the UK, abbreviation for ***local education authority***.

Leach Bernard Howell 1887–1979. English potter. His simple designs, inspired by a period of study in Japan, pioneered a revival of the art. He established the Leach Pottery at St Ives, Cornwall, 1920.

leaching process by which substances are washed through or out of the soil. Fertilizers leached out of the soil drain into rivers, lakes, and ponds and cause water pollution. In tropical areas, leaching of the soil after the destruction of forests removes scarce nutrients and can lead to a dramatic loss of soil fertility.

Leacock Stephen Butler 1869–1944. Canadian political scientist, historian, and humorist. His humour has survived his often rather conservative political writings. His butts include the urban plutocracy and (in the parodies of *Frenzied Fictions* 1918) popular fiction, as well as human folly generally. His other humorous works include *Literary Lapses* 1910 and the controversial because recognizable *Sunshine Sketches of a Little Town* 1912.

'Lord Ronald ... flung himself from the room, flung himself upon his horse and rode madly off in all directions.'

STEPHEN LEACOCK
'Gertrude the Governess'

lead heavy, soft, malleable, grey, metallic element, symbol Pb (from Latin *plumbum*), atomic number 82, relative atomic mass 207.19. Usually found as an ore (most often in galena), it occasionally occurs as a free metal (◊native metal), and is the final stable product of the decay of uranium.

Lead is the softest and weakest of the commonly used metals, with a low melting point; it is a poor conductor of electricity and resists acid corrosion. As a cumulative poison, lead enters the body from lead water pipes, lead-based paints, and leaded petrol. (In humans, exposure to lead shortly after birth is associated with impaired mental health between the ages of two and four.) The metal is an effective shield against radiation and is used in batteries, glass, ceramics, and alloys such as pewter and solder.

lead–acid cell type of ◊accumulator (storage battery).

Leadbelly Stage name of Huddie William Ledbetter c. 1889–1949. US blues and folk singer, songwriter, and guitarist. He was a source of inspiration for the urban folk movement of the 1950s. He was 'discovered' in prison by folklorists John Lomax (1875–1948) and Alan Lomax (1915–), who helped him begin a professional concert and recording career 1934. His songs include 'Rock Island Line' and 'Good Night, Irene'.

leaded petrol petrol that contains ◊antiknock, a mixture of the chemicals tetraethyl lead and dibromoethane. The lead from the exhaust fumes enters the atmosphere, mostly as simple lead compounds, which are poisonous to the developing nervous systems of children.

lead ore any of several minerals from which lead is extracted. The primary ore is galena or lead sulphite PbS. This is unstable, and on prolonged exposure to the atmosphere it oxidizes into the minerals cerussite $PbCO_3$ and anglesite $PbSO_4$. Lead ores are usually associated with other metals, particularly silver – which can be mined at the same time – and zinc, which can cause problems during smelting. Most commercial deposits of lead ore are in the form of veins, where hot fluids have leached the ore from cooling ◊igneous masses and deposited it in cracks in the surrounding country rock, and in thermal ◊metamorphic zones, where the heat of igneous intrusions has altered the minerals of surrounding rocks.

Lead is mined in over 40 countries, but half of the world's output comes from the USA, Canada, Russia, Kazakhstan, Uzbekistan, Canada, and Australia.

leaf lateral outgrowth on the stem of a plant, and in most species the primary organ of ◊photosynthesis. The chief leaf types are cotyledons (seed leaves), scale leaves (on underground stems), foliage leaves, and bracts (in the axil of which a flower is produced).

Typically leaves are composed of three parts: the sheath or leaf base, the petiole or stalk, and the lamina or blade. The lamina has a network of veins through which water and nutrients are conducted. Structurally the leaf is made up of ◊mesophyll cells surrounded by the epidermis and usually, in addition, a waxy layer, termed the cuticle, which prevents excessive evaporation of water from the leaf tissues by transpiration. The epidermis is interrupted by small pores, or stomata, through which gas exchange between the plant and the atmosphere occurs.

A simple leaf is undivided, as in the beech or oak. A compound leaf is composed of several leaflets, as in the blackberry, horse-chestnut, or ash tree (the latter being a ◊pinnate leaf). Leaves that are shed in the autumn are termed deciduous, while evergreen leaves are termed persistent.

leaf-hopper any of numerous species of plant-sucking insects (order Homoptera) of the family Cicadellidae. They feed on the sap of leaves.

leaf insect insect of the order Phasmida, about 10 cm/4 in long, with a green, flattened body, remarkable for closely resembling the foliage on which it lives. It is most common in SE Asia. Leaf insects are related to stick insects and ◊mantises.

League of Arab States (Arab League) organization of Arab states established in Cairo 1945 to promote Arab unity, primarily in opposition to Israel. The original members were Egypt, Syria, Iraq, Lebanon, Transjordan (Jordan 1949), Saudi Arabia, and Yemen. They were later joined by Algeria, Bahrain, Comoros, Djibouti, Kuwait, Libya, Mauritania, Morocco, Oman, Palestine, the PLO, Qatar, Somalia, Sudan, Tunisia, and the United Arab Emirates. In 1979 Egypt was suspended and the league's headquarters transferred to Tunis in protest against the Egypt–Israeli peace, but Egypt was readmitted as a full member 1989, and in 1990 its headquarters returned to Cairo.

League of Nations international organization formed after World War I to solve international disputes by arbitration. Established in Geneva, Switzerland, 1920, the League included representatives from states throughout the world, but was severely weakened by the US decision not to become a member, and had no power to enforce its decisions. It was dissolved 1946. Its subsidiaries included the International Labour Organization and the Permanent Court of International Justice in The Hague, the Netherlands, both now under the auspices of the ◊United Nations (UN).

The League of Nations was suggested in US president Woodrow Wilson's Fourteen Points 1917 as part of the peace settlement for World War I. The League covenant was drawn up by the Paris peace conference 1919 and incorporated into the Versailles and other peace treaties. The member states undertook to preserve the territorial integrity of all, and to submit international disputes to the League.

Leakey Louis Seymour Bazett 1903–1972. Kenyan archaeologist, anthropologist, and palaeontologist. With his wife Mary Leakey, he discovered fossils of extinct animals in the ◊Olduvai Gorge in Tanzania, as well as many remains of an early human type. Leakey's conviction that human origins lie in Africa was opposed to contemporary opinion.

leaf insect This adult female *Phyllium* leaf insect, a newly discovered species in New Guinea, is mimicking a dead brown leaf. Other species are green and mimic living leaves. *Premaphotos Wildlife*

Leakey Mary Douglas, (born Nicol) 1913–1996. English paleolithic archaeologist and discoverer of East African fossil hominids. In 1948 she discovered, on Rusinga Island, Lake Victoria, E Africa, the prehistoric ape skull known as *Proconsul*, about 20 million years old; and human footprints at Laetoli, to the south, about 3.75 million years old. ▷ *See feature on pp. 518–519.*

Leakey Richard Erskine Frere 1944– . Kenyan palaeoanthropologist. In 1972 he discovered at Lake Turkana, Kenya, an apelike skull estimated to be about 2.9 million years old; it had some human characteristics and a brain capacity of 800 cu cm/49 cu in. In 1984 his team found an almost complete skeleton of *Homo erectus* some 1.6 million years old. He is the son of Louis and Mary Leakey.

He was appointed director of the Kenyan Wildlife Service 1988, waging a successful war against poachers and the ivory trade, but was forced to resign 1994 in the face of political interference. In 1995 he co-founded the Kenyan political party Safina (Swahili for Noah's Ark).

Leamington officially ***Royal Leamington Spa*** town and health resort in the West Midlands, England, on the river Leam, adjoining Warwick; population (1991) 55,400. The Royal Pump Room offers spa treatment. The first tennis club started here 1872.

Lean David 1908–1991. English film director. His films, noted for their painstaking craftsmanship, include early work codirected with playwright Noël Coward. *Brief Encounter* 1946 established Lean as a leading talent. Among his later films are such accomplished epics as *The Bridge on the River Kwai* 1957 (Academy Award), *Lawrence of Arabia* 1962 (Academy Award), and *Dr Zhivago* 1965. The unfavourable reaction to *Ryan's Daughter* 1970 caused him to withdraw from filmmaking for over a decade, but *A Passage to India* 1984 represented a return to form.

Lear Edward 1812–1888. English artist and humorist. His *Book of Nonsense* 1846 popularized the ◊limerick (a five-line humorous verse). He first attracted attention by his paintings of birds, and later turned to landscapes. He travelled to Italy, Greece, Egypt, and India, publishing books on his travels with his own illustrations, and spent most of his later life in Italy.

learning theory in psychology, any theory or body of theories about how behaviour in animals and human beings is acquired or modified by experience. Two main theories are classical and operant ◊conditioning.

leasehold in law, land or property held by a tenant (lessee) for a specified period (unlike ◊freehold, outright ownership), usually at a rent from the landlord (lessor).

Under English law, houses and flats are often held on a lease for a period, such as 99 years, for which a lump sum is paid, plus an annual 'ground rent': the entire property reverts to the original owner at the end of the period.

leasing form of renting, like ◊hire purchase, typically used by businesses to finance the acquisition of land, buildings, machinery, and other industrial equipment. It differs from hire purchase in that responsibility for maintenance lies with the company which leases out the land or equipment.

least action, principle of in physics, an alternative expression of Newton's laws of motion that states that a particle moving between two points under the influence of a force will follow the path along which its total action is least. Action is a quantity related to the average difference between the kinetic energy and the potential energy of the particle along its path. The principle is only true where no energy is lost from the system; for example an object moving in free fall in a gravitational field. It is closely related to ◊Fermat's principle of least time which governs the path taken by a ray of light.

leather material prepared from the hides and skins of animals, by tanning with vegetable tannins and chromium salts. Leather is a durable and water-resistant material, and is used for bags, shoes, clothing, and upholstery. There are three main stages in the process of converting animal skin into leather: cleaning, tanning, and dressing. Tanning is often a highly polluting process.

Leatherhead town in Surrey, England, SW of London, on the river Mole at the foot of the North Downs; population (1991) 42,900. It has industrial research stations, the Thorndike Theatre (1968), and the Royal School for the Blind (1799). Industries include engineering and electrical goods.

leatherjacket larva of the ◊crane fly.

Leavis F(rank) R(aymond) 1895–1978. English literary critic. With his wife Q(ueenie) D(orothy) Leavis (1906–1981), he cofounded and edited the influential literary review *Scrutiny* 1932–53. He championed the work of D H Lawrence and James Joyce and in 1962 attacked C P Snow's theory of 'the two cultures' (the natural alienation of the arts and sciences in intellectual life). His critical works, introducing a new seriousness to the study of literature, include *New Bearings in English Poetry* 1932, which placed T S ◊Eliot centrally in the modern poetic tradition, *The Great Tradition* 1948, and *The Common Pursuit* 1952.

Leavitt Henrietta Swan 1868–1921. US astronomer who in 1912 discovered the period–luminosity law, which links the brightness of a ◊Cepheid variable star to its period of variation. This law allows astronomers to use Cepheid variables as 'standard candles' for measuring distances in space.

Lebanon country in W Asia, bounded N and E by Syria, S by Israel, and W by the Mediterranean Sea. *See country box on p. 621.*

Lebed Aleksandr Ivanovich 1950– . Russian soldier and politician. He was briefly national security adviser 1996 and successfully negotiated a peace settlement which ended the 1994–96 civil war in Chechnya. Sacked by President Boris Yeltsin 1996, he later formed the National Republican Party.

Lebensraum (German 'living space') theory developed by Adolf Hitler for the expansion of Germany into E Europe, and in the 1930s used by the Nazis to justify their annexation of neighbouring states on the grounds that Germany was overpopulated.

Leblanc Nicolas 1742–1806. French chemist who in the 1780s developed a process for making soda ash (sodium carbonate, Na_2CO_3) from common salt (sodium chloride, NaCl). Soda ash was widely used industrially in making glass, paper, soap, and various chemicals. In the Leblanc process, salt was first converted into sodium sulphate by the action of sulphuric acid, which was then roasted with chalk or limestone (calcium carbonate) and coal to produce a mixture of sodium carbonate and sulphide. The carbonate was leached out with water and the solution crystallized.

Lebowa former black homeland in Northern Transvaal Province, South Africa. It achieved self-governing status 1972.

Le Brun Charles 1619–1690. French Baroque artist. Court painter to Louis XIV from 1662, he became director of the French Academy and of the Gobelins factory, which produced art, tapestries, and furnishings for the new palace of Versailles. As director of the Academy, and with the patronage of the powerful minister Colbert, he became the virtual dictator of art in France, ensuring through commissions and training that the arts and crafts served to glorify the reign of Louis XIV, the 'Sun King'. He worked on large decorative schemes, including the *Galerie des Glaces* (Hall of Mirrors) at Versailles 1679–84, and painted official portraits.

Le Carré John. Pen name of David John Moore Cornwell 1931– . English writer of thrillers. His low-key realistic accounts of complex espionage include *The Spy Who Came in from the Cold* 1963, *Tinker Tailor Soldier Spy* 1974, *Smiley's People* 1980, *The Russia House* 1989, *The Night Manager* 1993, and *Our Game* 1995. He was a member of the Foreign Service 1960–64.

lecithin lipid (fat), containing nitrogen and phosphorus, that forms a vital part of the cell membranes of plant and animal cells.

Leconte de Lisle Charles Marie René 1818–1894. French poet. He played an important part in formulating the aims of the anti-Romantic group *Les* ◊*Parnassiens* and became their acknowledged leader. His work, characterized by classic regularity and faultlessness of form, drew inspiration from the ancient world; it includes *Poèmes antiques/Antique Poems* 1852, *Poèmes barbares/Barbaric Poems* 1862, and *Poèmes tragiques/Tragic Poems* 1884.

Le Corbusier assumed name of Charles-Edouard Jeanneret 1887–1965. Swiss-born French architect. He was an early and influential exponent of the ◊Modern Movement and one of the most innovative of 20th-century architects. His distinct brand of Functionalism first appears in his town-planning proposals of the early 1920s, which advocate 'vertical garden cities' with zoning of living and working areas and traffic separation as solutions to urban growth and chaos. From the 1940s several of his designs for multistorey villas were realized, notably his Unité d'habitation, Marseilles, 1947–52 (now demolished), using his Modulor system of standard-sized units mathematically calculated according to the proportions of the human figure (see ◊Fibonacci, ◊golden section).

His white-stuccoed, Cubist-style villas of the 1920s were designed as 'machines for living in', making the most of space and light through open-plan interiors, use of *pilotis* (stilts carrying the building), and roof gardens. He moved on to a more expressive mode (anticipating ◊Brutalism) with rough, unfinished exteriors, as in the Ministry of Education, Rio de Janeiro, 1936–45, designed with Lucio Costa (1902–) and Oscar ◊Niemeyer. In

'Far and few, far and few, / Are the lands where the Jumblies live; / Their heads are green, and their hands are blue, / And they went to sea in a Sieve.'

Edward Lear
'The Jumblies',
Nonsense Songs

'It was man who ended the Cold War ... It wasn't weaponry, or technology, or armies or campaigns. It was just man.'

John Le Carré
The Secret Pilgrim
1990

Le Corbusier The Pilgrimage Church of Notre Dame de Haut at Ronchamp, France, built by Le Corbusier. This highly acclaimed design combines artistic simplicity with functionality; it was planned with meticulous attention to detail and constructed from rough-cast concrete. It is typical of the style of Le Corbusier, one of the most influential modernist architects of the 20th century. *Corbis*

the reconstruction period after World War II, Le Corbusier's urbanization theories were highly influential, disseminated through the work of the urban planning body CIAM, although only in the gridlike layout of the new city of Chandigarh, India, 1951–56, was he able to see his visions of urban zoning fully realized. His sculptural design for the church of Notre-Dame du Haut du Ronchamp 1950–54 is a supreme example of aesthetic Functionalism. His books *Vers une Architecture/ Towards a New Architecture* 1923 and *Le Modulor* 1948 have had worldwide significance for town planning and building design.

LED abbreviation for ◊***light-emitting diode***.

Leda in Greek mythology, the wife of Tyndareus and mother of ◊Clytemnestra. Zeus, who came to her as a swan, was the father of her other children: ◊Helen of Troy and the twins ◊Castor and Pollux.

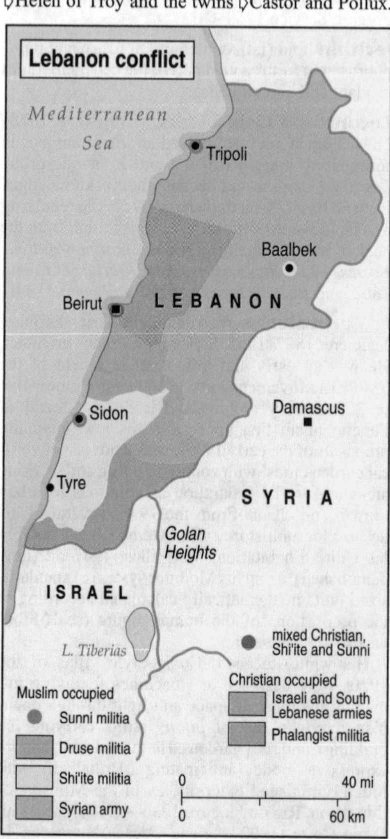

Lederberg Joshua 1925– . US geneticist who showed that bacteria can reproduce sexually, combining genetic material so that offspring possess characteristics of both parent organisms. In 1958 he shared the Nobel Prize for Physiology or Medicine with George Beadle (1903–1989) and Edward Tatum (1909–1975).

Lederberg is a pioneer of genetic engineering, a science that relies on the possibility of artificially shuffling genes from cell to cell. He realized 1952 that bacteriophages (viruses which invade bacteria) can transfer genes from one bacterium to another, a discovery that led to the deliberate insertion by scientists of foreign genes into bacterial cells.

Ledoux Claude-Nicolas 1736–1806. French Neo-Classical architect. He is stylistically comparable to E L Boullée (1728–1799) in his use of austere, geometric forms, exemplified in his series of 44 toll houses surrounding Paris (of which only four remain), notably the Barrière de la Villette in the Place de Stalingrad, Paris, 1785–89.

Le Duc Anh 1920– . Vietnamese soldier and communist politician, president from 1992. A member of the politburo's military faction, he is regarded as a conservative, anxious to maintain tight party control over domestic policies.

Le Duc Tho 1911–1990. North Vietnamese diplomat who was joint winner (with US secretary of state Kissinger) of the 1973 Nobel Peace Prize for his part in the negotiations to end the Vietnam War. He indefinitely postponed receiving the award.

Led Zeppelin UK rock group 1969–80, founders of the ◊heavy metal genre. Their overblown style, with long solos, was based on rhythm and blues; songs like 'Stairway to Heaven' have become classics.

Lee Bruce. Stage name of Lee Yuen Kam 1941–1973. US 'Chinese Western' film actor. He was an expert in ◊kung fu, who popularized the oriental martial arts in the West with pictures such as *Fists of Fury* 1972 (made in Hong Kong) and *Enter the Dragon* 1973.

Lee Christopher Frank Carandini 1922– . English film actor. His gaunt figure was memorable in the title role of *Dracula* 1958 and several of its sequels. His numerous other films include *Hamlet* 1948, *The Mummy* 1959, *Julius Caesar* 1970, and *The Man with the Golden Gun* 1974.

Lee Gypsy Rose (born Rose Louise Hovick) 1914–1970. US entertainer. An 'elegant lady' in striptease routines, she was also a published author. She wrote two mystery novels, *The G-String Murders* 1941 and *Mother Finds a Body* 1942. Her autobiography *Gypsy: A Memoir* 1957 was adapted for stage 1959 and film 1962.

Lee Jennie (Janet). Baroness Lee of Asheridge 1904–1988. British socialist politician. She became a member of Parliament for the Independent Labour Party at the age of 24 and in 1934 married Aneurin ◊Bevan. On the left wing of the Labour Party, she was on its National Executive Committee 1958–70 and was minister of education 1967–70, during which time she was responsible for founding the Open University in 1969.

Lee Laurie 1914–1997. English writer. His works include the autobiographical novel *Cider with Rosie* 1959, a classic evocation of childhood; nature poetry such as *The Bloom of Candles* 1947; and travel writing including *A Rose for Winter* 1955.

Lee Robert E(dward) 1807–1870. US military strategist and Confederate general in the ◊American Civil War. As military adviser to Jefferson Davis (1808–1889), president of the Confederacy, and as commander of the army of N Virginia, he made several raids into Northern territory, but was defeated at ◊Gettysburg and surrendered 1865.

Lee was commissioned 1829 and served in the Mexican War. In 1859 he suppressed John ◊Brown's raid on Harper's Ferry. On the outbreak of the Civil War 1861 he joined the Confederate army of the Southern States, and in 1862 received the command of the army of N Virginia and won the Seven Days' Battle defending Richmond, Virginia, the Confederate capital, against General McClellan's Union forces. In 1863 Lee won victories at Fredericksburg and Chancellorsville, and in 1864 at Cold Harbor, but was besieged in Petersburg, June 1864–April 1865. He surrendered to General Grant 9 April 1865 at ◊Appomattox Court House.

Lee Spike (Shelton Jackson) 1957– . US film director, actor, and writer. His work presents the bitter realities of contemporary African-American life, often in an aggressive or controversial manner. His films, in which he sometimes appears, include *She's Gotta Have It* 1986, *Do The Right Thing* 1989, *Malcolm X* 1992, *Crooklyn* 1994, *Clockers* and *Girl 6* (both 1995).

leech annelid worm forming the class Hirudinea. Leeches inhabit fresh water, and in tropical countries infest damp forests. As bloodsucking animals they are injurious to people and animals, to whom they attach themselves by means of a strong mouth adapted to sucking. Formerly, the medicinal leech *Hirudo medicinalis* was used extensively for 'bleeding' for a variety of ills. It is still cultivated as the source of the anticoagulant hirudin.

Leeds industrial city in West Yorkshire, England, on the river Aire; population (1991 est) 680,700. Industries include engineering, printing, chemicals,

Lee US Confederate general Robert E Lee. In the American Civil War, Lee was commander of the army of N Virginia, and military adviser to Jefferson Davis, president of the Confederacy. He surrendered 1865. *Image Select (UK) Ltd*

LEBANON
Republic of

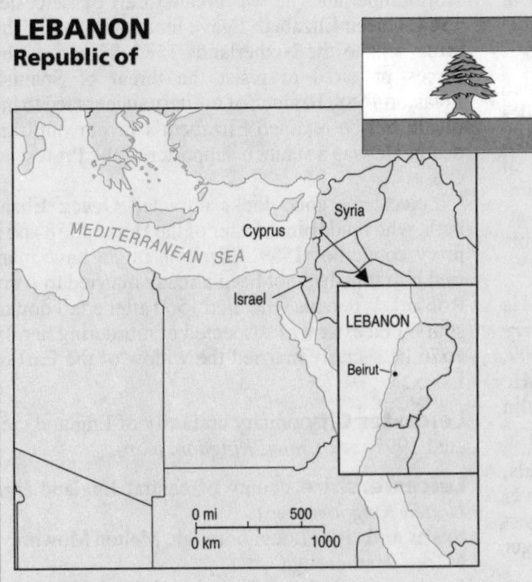

national name *Jumhouria al-Lubnaniya*
area 10,452 sq km/4,034 sq mi
capital (and port) Beirut
major towns/cities Zahlé
major ports Tripoli, Tyre, Sidon, Jounieh
physical features narrow coastal plain; fertile Bekka valley running N–S between Lebanon and Anti-Lebanon mountain ranges
head of state Elias Hrawi from 1989
head of government Rafik al-Hariri from 1992
political system emergent democratic republic
administrative divisions five regional units
political parties Phalangist Party, Christian, radical, nationalist; Progressive Socialist Party (PSP), Druse, moderate, socialist; National Liberal Party (NLP), Maronite, centre-left; National Bloc, Maronite, moderate; Lebanese Communist Party (PCL), nationalist, communist; Parliamentary Democratic Front, Sunni Muslim, centrist
population 3,009,000 (1995 est)
population growth rate 3.3% (1990–95); 1.5% (2000–05)
ethnic distribution about 90% Arab, with Armenian, Assyrian, Jewish, Turkish, and Greek minorities
life expectancy 65 (men), 69 (women)
literacy rate men 88%, women 73%
languages Arabic (official), French, Armenian, English
religions Muslim 58% (Shiite 35%, Sunni 23%), Christian 27% (mainly Maronite), Druse 3%; other Christian denominations including Orthodox, Armenian, and Roman Catholic
currency Lebanese pound
GDP (US $) 7.3 billion (1993)
growth rate 7.1% (1993)
exports citrus and other fruit, vegetables; industrial products to Arab neighbours

HISTORY
5th C BC–1st C AD Part of the E Mediterranean Phoenician Empire.
1st C Came under Roman rule and Christianity introduced.
635 Islam introduced by Arab tribes, who settled in S Lebanon.
11th C Druse faith developed by local Muslims.
1516 Became part of the Turkish Ottoman Empire.
1860 Massacre of thousands of Christian Maronites by the Muslim Druse led to French intervention.
1920–41 Administered by French under a League of Nations mandate.
1943 Independence achieved as a republic, with constitution that enshrined Christian and Muslim power-sharing.
1945 Joined Arab League.
1948–49 Lebanon joined first Arab war against Israel; Palestinian refugees settled in the S.
1958 Revolt by radical Muslims opposed to pro-Western policies of the Christian president, Camille Chamoun.
1964 Palestine Liberation Organization (PLO) founded in Beirut.
1967 More Palestinian refugees settled in Lebanon following the Arab–Israeli war.
1971 PLO expelled from Jordan; established headquarters in Lebanon.
1975 Outbreak of civil war between conservative Christians and leftist Muslims backed by PLO.
1976 Cease-fire agreed; Syrian-dominated Arab deterrent force formed to keep the peace, but considered by Christians as an occupying force.
1978 Israel launched limited invasion of S Lebanon in search of PLO guerrillas. International United Nations peacekeeping force unable to prevent further fighting.
1979 Part of S Lebanon declared an 'independent free Lebanon' by right-wing army officer.
1982 Bachir Gemayel, a Maronite Christian, elected president but assassinated; he was succeeded by his brother Amin Gemayel. Israel again invaded Lebanon. Palestinians withdrew from Beirut under supervision of international peacekeeping force; PLO moved its headquarters to Tunis.
1983 Agreement reached for the withdrawal of Syrian and Israeli troops but abrogated under Syrian pressure; intense fighting between Christian Phalangists and Muslim Druse militias.
1984 Most of international peacekeeping force withdrawn. Radical Muslim militia took control of W Beirut.
1985 Lebanon in chaos; many foreigners taken hostage and Israeli troops withdrawn.
1987 Syrian troops sent into Beirut.
1988 Agreement on Christian successor to Gemayel failed and General Michel Aoun appointed to head caretaker military government; Premier Selim el-Hoss set up rival government; threat of partition hung over country.
1989 General Aoun declared 'war of liberation' against Syrian occupation; Arab League-sponsored talks resulted in a cease-fire and a revised constitution recognizing Muslim majority; René Mouhawad assassinated after 17 days as president; Maronite Christian Elias Hrawi named as successor; Aoun occupied presidential palace, rejecting constitution.
1990 Release of Western hostages began. General Aoun, crushed by Syrians, surrendered and legitimate government was restored.
1991 Government extended control to the whole country. Treaty of cooperation with Syria signed.
1992 Remaining Western hostages released. Pro-Syrian administration re-elected with Rafik al-Hariri as prime minister after many Christians boycotted general election.
1993 Israel launched attacks against Shia fundamentalist Hezbollah strongholds in S Lebanon before the USA and Syria brokered agreement to avoid use of force.
1996 Israel attacked S Lebanon, launching a rocket attack on Beirut in response to Hezbollah activity, effectively ending the 1993 agreement. USA, Israel, Syria, and Lebanon attempted to broker a new cease-fire.

SEE ALSO Druse; Hezbollah; Palestine Liberation Organization; Shi'ite

glass, woollens, clothing, plastics, paper, metal goods, and leather goods. Notable buildings include the Town Hall designed by Cuthbert Brodrick, Leeds University (1904), the Art Gallery (1844), Temple Newsam museum (early 16th century, altered about 1630), and the Cistercian Abbey of Kirkstall (1147). It is a centre of communications where road, rail, and canal (to Liverpool and Goole) meet. Opera North is based here, and the Leeds International Pianoforte Competition is held here every three years. A new museum shares the Royal Armouries collection, exchanging items with the Tower of London.

leek onionlike plant of the genus *Allium* of the lily family Liliaceae. The cultivated leek is a variety of the wild *A. ampeloprasum* of the Mediterranean area and Atlantic islands. The lower leaf parts form the bulb, which is eaten as a vegetable. It is the national emblem of Wales.

Lee Kuan Yew 1923– . Singapore politician, prime minister 1959–90. Lee founded the anticommunist Socialist People's Action Party 1954 and entered the Singapore legislative assembly 1955. He was elected the country's first prime minister 1959, and took Singapore out of the Malaysian federation 1965. He was succeeded by Goh Chok Tong 1990, but held on to the party leadership until 1992.

Lee Teng-hui 1923– . Taiwanese right-wing politician, vice president 1984–88, president and Kuomintang (see ◊Guomindang) party leader from 1988. Lee, the country's first island-born leader, is viewed as a reforming technocrat. He was directly elected president 1996, defying Chinese opposition to the democratic contest. He has significantly accelerated the pace of liberalization and Taiwanization.

Leeuwenhoek Anton van 1632–1723. Dutch pioneer of microscopic research. He ground his own lenses, some of which magnified up to 300 times. With these he was able to see individual red blood cells, sperm, and bacteria, achievements not repeated for more than a century.

Leeuwenhoek A plate published around 1795 showing microscopic animals, spermatozoa, and plants. The diagrams were originally prepared by Anton van Leeuwenhoek, using the simple microscopes that he designed and made. *Image Select (UK) Ltd*

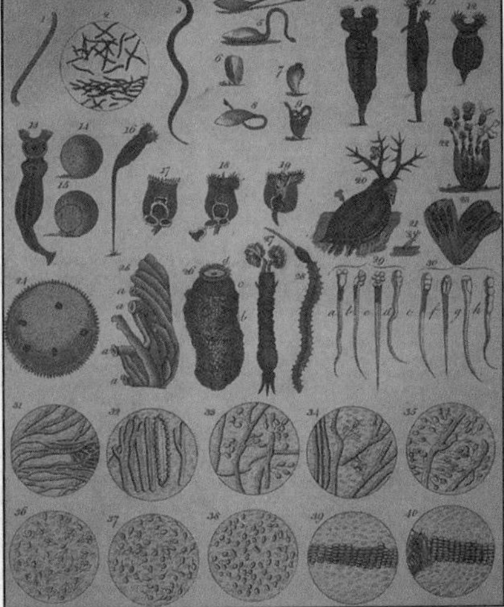

Leeward Islands (1) group of islands, part of the ◊Society Islands, in ◊French Polynesia, S Pacific; (2) general term for the northern half of the Lesser ◊Antilles in the West Indies; (3) former British colony in the West Indies (1871–1956) comprising Antigua, Montserrat, St Christopher (St Kitts)–Nevis, Anguilla, and the Virgin Islands.

left wing in politics, the socialist parties. The term originated in the French national assembly of 1789, where the nobles sat in the place of honour to the right of the president, and the commons sat to the left. This arrangement has become customary in European parliaments, where the progressives sit on the left and the conservatives on the right.

legacy in law, a gift of personal property made by a testator in a will and transferred on the testator's death to the legatee. ***Specific legacies*** are definite named objects; a ***general legacy*** is a sum of money or item not specially identified; a ***residuary legacy*** is all the remainder of the deceased's personal estate after debts have been paid and the other legacies have been distributed.

legal aid public assistance with legal costs. In Britain it is given only to those below certain thresholds of income and unable to meet the costs. There are separate provisions for civil and criminal cases. Since 1989 legal aid is administered by the Legal Aid Board.

legend (Latin *legere* 'to read') traditional or undocumented story about famous people, commonly religious in character and frequently posing problems of authenticity. Legends are typically narrative, in the form of verse or prose novella, although more complex forms such as drama or ballad are possible. It is typical for legends to avoid a strict documentary account in favour of a more poetic and religious interpretation of reality. The term was originally applied to the books of readings designed for use in Christian religious service, and was extended to the stories of saints' lives read in monasteries.

Léger Fernand 1881–1955. French painter and designer. He was associated with ◊Cubism. From around 1909 he evolved a characteristic style of simplified forms, clear block outlines, and bold colours. Mechanical forms are constant themes in his work, which includes designs for the Swedish Ballet 1921–22, murals, and the abstract film *Ballet mécanique/Mechanical Ballet* 1924. He was in the USA 1940–45, but returned to Paris 1945. In addition to paintings he produced a number of lithographs and book illustrations, and designs for wall decoration, mosaic, and stained glass.

legion Roman army unit. In the later republic and the empire a legion comprised 5,000–6,000 men, mainly foot soldiers, organized in centuries (units of 60–100). Legions were designated by numbers and honorary titles, and served as garrisons or armies in the field. Under the empire there were 25–30 legions, with soldiers serving about 25 years before their discharge with a pension.

legionnaires' disease pneumonia-like disease, so called because it was first identified when it broke out at a convention of the American Legion in Philadelphia in 1976. Legionnaires' disease is caused by the bacterium *Legionella pneumophila*, which breeds in warm water (for example, in the cooling towers of air-conditioning systems). It is spread in minute water droplets, which may be inhaled. The disease can be treated successfully with antibiotics, though mortality can be high in elderly patients.

legislature lawmaking body or bodies in a political system. Some legislatures are unicameral (having one chamber), and some bicameral (with two). In most democratic countries with bicameral legislatures the 'lower', or popular, chamber is the more powerful but there are exceptions, the most notable being in the USA, where the upper chamber, the ◊Senate, is constitutionally more powerful than the lower, the House of Representatives. Most lower or single chambers are popularly elected and upper chambers are filled by appointees or a mixture of appointed and elected members. In the USA, both chambers are elected, whereas in the UK, the lower chamber, the ◊House of Commons, is elected and the upper chamber, the ◊House of Lords, is filled by hereditary members or appointees.

Legnano, Battle of defeat of Holy Roman emperor Frederick Barbarossa by members of the Lombard League in 1176 at Legnano, northwest of Milan. It was a major setback to the emperor's plans for imperial domination over Italy and showed for the first time the power of infantry against feudal cavalry.

legume plant of the family Leguminosae, which has a pod containing dry seeds. The family includes peas, beans, lentils, clover, and alfalfa (lucerne). Legumes are important in agriculture because of their specialized roots, which have nodules containing bacteria capable of fixing nitrogen from the air and increasing the fertility of the soil. The edible seeds of legumes are called pulses.

Lehár Franz 1870–1948. Hungarian composer. He wrote many operettas, among them *The Merry Widow* 1905, *The Count of Luxembourg* 1909, *Gypsy Love* 1910, and *The Land of Smiles* 1929. He also composed songs, marches, and a violin concerto.

Le Havre industrial port (engineering, chemicals, oil refining) in Normandy, NW France, on the river Seine; population (1990) 197,200. It is the largest port in Europe, and has transatlantic passenger links.

Leibniz Gottfried Wilhelm 1646–1716. German mathematician, philosopher, and diplomat. Independently of, but concurrently with, English scientist Isaac ◊Newton, he developed the branch of mathematics known as ◊calculus. In his metaphysical works, such as *The Monadology* 1714, he argued that everything consisted of innumerable units, ***monads***, the individual properties of which determined each thing's past, present, and future.

Monads, although independent of each other, interacted predictably; this meant that Christian faith and scientific reason need not be in conflict and that 'this is the best of all possible worlds'. Leibniz's optimism is satirized in French philosopher Voltaire's novel *Candide*.

Leibovitz Annie 1950– . US photographer. Her elaborately staged portraits of American celebrities appeared first in *Rolling Stone* magazine and later in *Vanity Fair*. The odd poses in which her sitters allow themselves to be placed suggest an element of self-mockery.

Leicester industrial city on the river Soar and administrative headquarters of Leicestershire, England, and Leicester City unitary authority; population (1991) 270,500. Industries include food processing, hosiery, footwear, knitwear, engineering, electronics, printing, and plastics. Founded AD 50 as the Roman *Ratae Coritanorum*, Leicester is one of the oldest cities in England. The guildhall dates from the 14th century and ruined Bradgate House was the home of Lady Jane Grey.

Leicester Robert Dudley, Earl of Leicester c. 1532–1588. English courtier. Son of the Duke of Northumberland, he was created Earl of Leicester 1564. Queen Elizabeth I gave him command of the army sent to the Netherlands 1585–87 and of the forces prepared to resist the threat of Spanish invasion 1588. His lack of military success led to his recall, but he retained Elizabeth's favour until his death. He was a staunch supporter of the Protestant cause.

Leicester's good looks attracted Queen Elizabeth, who made him Master of the Horse 1558 and a privy councillor 1559. Elizabeth might have married him if he had not been already married to Amy Robsart. When his wife died 1560 after a fall downstairs, Leicester was suspected of murdering her. In 1576 he secretly married the widow of the Earl of Essex.

Leicester City unitary authority of England created 1997 (*see United Kingdom map*).

Leicestershire county of central England (*see United Kingdom map*)
towns and cities Loughborough, Melton Mowbray, Market Harborough
features river Soar; Charnwood Forest; Vale of Belvoir (under which are large coal deposits)
industries horses, cattle, sheep, dairy products, coal, Stilton cheese, hosiery, footwear, bell founding
famous people Titus Oates, Thomas Babington Macaulay, C P Snow.

Leiden or ***Leyden*** city in South Holland province, the Netherlands; population (1994) 114,900. Industries include textiles and cigars. It has been a printing centre since 1580, with a university established 1575. It is linked by canal to Haarlem, Amsterdam, and Rotterdam.

Leigh Mike 1943– . English dramatist and filmmaker, noted for his sharp, carefully improvised social satires. His work for television includes *Nuts in May* 1976 and *Abigail's Party* 1977; his films include *High Hopes* 1989, *Life Is Sweet* 1991, *Naked* 1993, and *Secrets and Lies* 1996.

Leigh Vivien. Stage name of Vivien Mary Hartley 1913–1967. Indian-born English actress. She appeared on the stage in London and New York, and won Academy Awards for her performances as Scarlett O'Hara in *Gone With the Wind* 1939 and as Blanche du Bois in *A Streetcar Named Desire* 1951. She was married to Laurence Olivier 1940–60, and starred with him in the play *Antony and Cleopatra* 1951. Her other films include *Lady Hamilton* 1941, *Anna Karenina* 1948, and *Ship of Fools* 1965.

Leinster southeastern province of the Republic of Ireland, comprising the counties of Carlow, Dublin, Kildare, Kilkenny, Laois, Longford, Louth, Meath, Offaly, Westmeath, Wexford, and Wicklow; area 19,630 sq km/7,577 sq mi; capital Dublin; population (1991) 1,860,000.

Leipzig city in W Saxony, Germany, 145 km/90 mi SW of Berlin; population (1993) 494,200. Products include furs, leather goods, cloth, glass, cars, and musical instruments.

leishmaniasis any of several parasitic diseases caused by microscopic protozoans of the genus *Leishmania*, identified by William Leishman (1865–1926), and transmitted by sandflies. It occurs in two main forms: ***visceral*** (also called kala-azar), in which various internal organs are affected, and ***cutaneous***, where the disease is apparent mainly in the skin. Leishmaniasis occurs in the Mediterranean region, Africa, Asia, and Central and South America. There are 12 million cases of leishmaniasis annually.

leitmotif (German 'leading motive') in music, a recurring theme or motive used to illustrate a character or idea. Wagner frequently used this technique in his operas, and it was later adopted in music for film.

Leitrim county of the Republic of Ireland, in the province of Connacht, bounded NW by Donegal Bay; county town Carrick-on-Shannon; area 1,530 sq km/591 sq mi; population (1991) 25,300. The rivers Shannon, Bonet, Drowes, and Duff run through it. Industries include potatoes, cattle, linen, woollens, pottery, coal, iron, lead, sheep, and oats.

lek in biology, a closely spaced set of very small ◊territories each occupied by a single male during the mating season. Leks are found in the mating

lek Males of the small European bee *Lasioglossum calceatum* form leks on vegetation. Lekking behaviour is now known to be quite common in insects; it is found in butterflies, moths, flies, and wasps, as well as in many kinds of bees.
Premaphotos Wildlife

lemon The lemon tree and fruit. The juice of the lemon fruit contains about four times as much citric acid as is found in the orange. It is a major commercial source of citric acid.

systems of several ground-dwelling birds (such as grouse) and a few antelopes.

The lek is a traditional site where both males and females congregate during the breeding season. The males display to passing females in the hope of attracting them to mate. Once mated, the females go elsewhere to lay their eggs or to complete gestation.

Lely Peter. Adopted name of Pieter van der Faes 1618–1680. Dutch painter. He was active in England from 1641, painting fashionable portraits in the style of van Dyck. His subjects included Charles I, Cromwell, and Charles II. He painted a series of admirals, *Flagmen* (National Maritime Museum, London), and one of *The Windsor Beauties* (Hampton Court, Richmond), fashionable women of Charles II's court.

Lemaître Georges Edouard 1894–1966. Belgian cosmologist. He proposed the ◊Big Bang theory of the origin of the universe 1933. US astronomer Edwin ◊Hubble had shown that the universe was expanding, but it was Lemaître who suggested that the expansion had been started by an initial explosion, the Big Bang, a theory that is now generally accepted.

Le Mans industrial city in Sarthe *département*, W France; population (1990) 148,500, conurbation 191,000. It has a motor-racing circuit where the annual endurance 24-hour race (established 1923) for sports cars and their prototypes is held.

lemming small rodent of the family Cricetidae, especially the genus *Lemmus*, comprising four species worldwide in northern latitudes. It is about 12 cm/5 in long, with thick brownish fur, a small head, and a short tail. Periodically, when their population exceeds the available food supply, lemmings undertake mass migrations.

Lemmon Jack (John Uhler III) 1925– . US character actor. He has often been cast as the lead in comedy films, such as *Some Like It Hot* 1959, but is equally skilled in serious roles, as in *The China Syndrome* 1979, *Save the Tiger* 1973 (Academy Award), and *Missing* 1982. His other films include *That's Life* 1986, *JFK* 1991, *The Player* 1993, *Short Cuts* 1994, and *A Weekend in the Country* 1995.

Lemnos (Greek ***Límnos***) Greek island in the north of the Aegean Sea
area 476 sq km/184 sq mi
towns Kastron, Mudros
physical of volcanic origin, rising to 430 m/1,411 ft
industries mulberries and other fruit, tobacco, sheep
population (1992) 16,400.

lemon sour fruit of the small, evergreen, semitropical lemon tree *Citrus limon*. It may have originated in NW India, and was introduced into Europe by the Spanish Moors in the 12th or 13th century. It is now grown in Italy, Spain, California, Florida, South Africa, and Australia.

lemur prosimian ◊primate of the family Lemuridae, inhabiting Madagascar and the Comoros Islands. There are about 16 species, ranging from mouse-sized to dog-sized animals; the pygmy mouse lemur, *Microcebus myoxinus*, weighing 30g/1 oz, is the smallest primate. Lemurs are arboreal, and some species are nocturnal. They have long, bushy tails, and feed on fruit, insects, and small animals. Many are threatened with extinction owing to loss of their forest habitat and, in some cases, from hunting.

Lena longest river in Asiatic Russia, 4,400 km/2,730 mi, with numerous tributaries. Its source is near Lake Baikal, and it empties into the Arctic Ocean through a delta 400 km/240 mi wide. It is ice-covered for half the year.

Lendl Ivan 1960– . Czech-born US lawn-tennis player. He won eight Grand Slam singles titles, including the US and French titles three times each, taking more than $15 million in prize money. He retired 1994, citing a degenerative spinal condition.

lend-lease in US history, an act of Congress passed in March 1941 that gave the president power to order 'any defense article for the government of any country whose defense the president deemed vital to the defense of the USA'. During World War II, the USA negotiated many lend-lease agreements, notably with Britain and the Soviet Union. The aim of such agreements was to ignore trade balances among the participating countries during the war effort and to aid the Allied war effort without fanning isolationist sentiments.

Lend-lease was officially stopped in Aug 1945, by which time goods and services to the value of $42 billion had been supplied in this way, of which the British Empire had received 65% and the Soviet Union 23%.

Lenglen Suzanne 1899–1938. French tennis player, Wimbledon singles and doubles champion 1919–23 and 1925, and Olympic champion 1921. She became professional in 1926. She also popularized sports clothes designed by Jean ◊Patou.

Lenin Vladimir Ilyich. Adopted name of Vladimir Ilyich Ulyanov 1870–1924. Russian revolutionary, first leader of the USSR, and communist theoretician. Active in the 1905 Revolution, Lenin had to leave Russia when it failed, settling in Switzerland 1914. He returned to Russia after the February revolution of 1917 (see ◊Russian Revolution). He led the Bolshevik revolution Nov 1917 and became leader of a Soviet government, concluded peace with Germany, and organized a successful resistance to White Russian (protsarist) uprisings and foreign intervention 1918–20. His modification of traditional Marxist doctrine to fit conditions prevailing in Russia became known as ***Marxism-Leninism***, the basis of communist ideology.

Lenin was born on 22 April 1870 in Simbirsk (now renamed Ulyanovsk), on the river Volga, and became a lawyer in St Petersburg. A Marxist from 1889, he was sent to Siberia for spreading revolutionary propaganda 1895–1900. He then edited the political paper *Iskra* ('The Spark') from abroad, and visited London several times. In *What is to be Done?* 1902, he advocated that a professional core of Social Democratic Party activists should spearhead the revolution in Russia, a suggestion accepted by the majority (*bolsheviki*) at the London party congress 1903. From Switzerland he attacked socialist support for World War I as aiding an 'imperialist' struggle, and wrote *Imperialism* 1917.

After the renewed outbreak of revolution Feb/March 1917, he was smuggled back into Russia by the Germans so that he could take up his revolutionary activities and remove Russia from the war, allowing Germany to concentrate the war effort on the Western Front. On arriving in Russia, Lenin established himself at the head of the Bolsheviks, against the provisional government of Kerensky; a complicated power struggle ensued, but eventually Lenin triumphed 8 Nov 1917; a Bolshevik government was formed, and peace negotiations with Germany were begun leading to the signing of the Treaty of Brest Litovsk 3 March 1918.

From the overthrow of the provisional government Nov 1917 until his death, Lenin effectively controlled the Soviet Union, although an assassination attempt 1918 injured his health. He founded the Third (Communist) ◊International 1919. With communism proving inadequate to put the country on its feet, he introduced the private-enterprise ◊New Economic Policy 1921. *See illustration on following page.*

Leningrad former name (1924–91) of the Russian city ◊St Petersburg.

Leningrad, Siege of in World War II, German siege of the Soviet city of Leningrad (now St Petersburg, Russia) 1 Sept 1941–27 Jan 1944. Some 1 million inhabitants of the city are reckoned to have died during the 900 days of the siege, either from disease, starvation, or enemy action.

Leninism modification of ◊Marxism by ◊Lenin which argues that in a revolutionary situation the industrial proletariat is unable to develop a truly revolutionary consciousness without strong leadership. The responsibility for this is taken on by the Communist Party, which acts as the 'vanguard of the proletariat' in leading it to revolution, before then assuming political control in a dictatorship of the proletariat. Only when the proletariat achieves a full socialist awareness will the power of the party, and ultimately the state itself, wither away.

lemur The fork-marked lemur is tree-dwelling, with large eyes that look forwards over a small, pointed nose. The long, bushy tail is used for balance and, when held in different positions, as a signal to other lemurs.

'It is true that liberty is precious – so precious that it must be rationed.'

VLADIMIR ILYICH LENIN
Quoted in S and B Webb *Soviet Communism* 1933

lend-lease US bombers and fighters being handed over to Soviet officers as part of the lend-lease programme during World War II. As the survival of Russia was vital to the war effort, the USA provided it with goods and services worth over $10 billion. *Corbis*

Lenin Vladimir Ilyich Lenin addressing a crowd in St Petersburg April 1917, shortly after his return from exile. The figure to Lenin's left is Leon Trotsky. By Oct of the same year the last remnants of the tsarist state had been swept away and Lenin, as leader of the Bolsheviks, had become virtual dictator of Russia.

Lennon John Winston 1940–1980. UK rock singer, songwriter, and guitarist; a founder member of the ◊Beatles. He lived in the USA from 1971. Both before the band's break-up 1970 and in his solo career, he collaborated intermittently with his wife Yoko Ono (1933–). 'Give Peace a Chance', a hit 1969, became an anthem of the peace movement. His solo work alternated between the confessional and the political, as on the album *Imagine* 1971. He was shot dead by a fan in New York.

'Will the people in the cheaper seats clap your hands? All the rest of you, if you'll just rattle your jewellery.'

JOHN LENNON
Royal Variety Performance
4 Nov 1963

Le Nôtre André 1613–1700. French landscape gardener. He created the gardens at Versailles 1662–90 and les Tuileries, Paris. His grandiose scheme for Versailles complemented Le Vau's original design for the palace façade, extending its formal symmetry into the surrounding countryside with vast *parterres* (gardens having beds and paths arranged to form a pattern), radiating avenues, and unbroken vistas.

lens in optics, a piece of a transparent material, such as glass, with two polished surfaces – one concave or convex, and the other plane, concave, or convex – that modifies rays of light. A convex lens brings rays of light together; a concave lens makes the rays diverge. Lenses are essential to spectacles, microscopes, telescopes, cameras, and almost all optical instruments.

The image formed by a single lens suffers from several defects or ◊aberrations, notably spherical aberration in which an image becomes blurred, and chromatic aberration in which an image in white light tends to have coloured edges. Aberrations are corrected by the use of compound lenses, which are built up from two or more lenses of different refractive index.

lensing, gravitational see ◊gravitational lensing.

Lent in the Christian church, the 40-day period of fasting that precedes Easter, beginning on Ash Wednesday, but omitting Sundays.

lenticel small pore on the stems of woody plants or the trunks of trees. Lenticels are a means of gas exchange between the stem interior and the atmosphere. They consist of loosely packed cells with many air spaces in between.

lentil annual Old World plant *Lens culinaris* of the pea family Leguminosae. The plant, which resembles vetch, grows 15–45 cm/6–18 in high and has white, blue, or purplish flowers. The seeds, contained in pods about 1.6 cm/0.6 in long, are widely used as food. Common varieties are the greyish French lentil and the red Egyptian lentil.

Lenya Lotte. Adopted name of Karoline Wilhelmine Blamauer 1898–1981. Austrian actress and singer. She was married five times, twice to the composer Kurt Weill, first in 1926, with whom she emigrated to the USA 1935. She appeared in several of the Brecht–Weill operas, notably *Die Dreigroschenoper/The Threepenny Opera* 1928. Her plain looks and untrained singing voice brought added realism to her stage roles.

Lenz's law in physics, a law stating that the direction of an electromagnetically induced current (generated by moving a magnet near a wire or a wire in a magnetic field) will be such as to oppose the motion producing it. It is named after German physicist Heinrich Friedrich Lenz (1804–1865), who announced it in 1833.

Leo zodiacal constellation in the northern hemisphere, represented as a lion. The Sun passes through Leo from mid-Aug to mid-Sept. Its brightest star is first-magnitude ◊Regulus at the base of a pattern of stars called the Sickle. In astrology, the dates for Leo are between about 23 July and 22 Aug (see ◊precession).

Leo (III) the Isaurian c. 680–741. Byzantine emperor and soldier. He seized the throne in 717, successfully defended Constantinople against the Saracens 717–18, and attempted to suppress the use of images in church worship (see ◊iconoclast).

Leo thirteen popes, including:

Leo (I) the Great (St Leo) c. 390–461. Pope from 440. He helped to establish the Christian liturgy. Leo summoned the Chalcedon Council where his Dogmatical Letter was accepted as the voice of St Peter. Acting as ambassador for the emperor Valentinian III (425–455), Leo saved Rome from devastation by the Huns by buying off their king, Attila.

Leo III c. 750–816. Pope from 795. After the withdrawal of the Byzantine emperors, the popes had become the real rulers of Rome. Leo III was forced to flee because of a conspiracy in Rome and took refuge at the court of the Frankish king Charlemagne. He returned to Rome 799 and crowned Charlemagne emperor on Christmas Day 800, establishing the secular sovereignty of the pope over Rome under the suzerainty of the emperor (who became the Holy Roman emperor).

Leo X Giovanni de' Medici 1475–1521. Pope from 1513. The son of Lorenzo the Magnificent of Florence, he was created a cardinal at 13. He bestowed on Henry VIII of England the title of Defender of the Faith. A patron of the arts, he sponsored the rebuilding of St Peter's Church, Rome. He raised funds for this by selling indulgences (remissions of punishment for sin), a sale that led the religious reformer Martin Luther to rebel against papal authority. Leo X condemned Luther in the bull *Exsurge domine* 1520 and excommunicated him 1521.

León city in Castilla-León, Spain; population (1994) 147,000. It was the capital of the kingdom of León from the 10th century until 1230, when it was merged with Castile.

Leonard Sugar Ray (Ray Charles) 1956– . US boxer. In 1988 he became the first man to have won world titles at five officially recognized weights. In 1976 he was Olympic light-welterweight champion; he won his first professional title in 1979 when he beat Wilfred Benitez for the World Boxing Council (WBC) welterweight title. He later won titles at junior middleweight (World Boxing Association; WBA version) 1981, middleweight (WBC) 1987, light-heavyweight (WBC) 1988, and super-middleweight (WBC) 1988. In 1989 he drew with Thomas Hearns. He retired 1992.

Leonardo da Vinci 1452–1519. Italian painter, sculptor, architect, engineer, and scientist. One of the greatest figures of the Italian Renaissance, he was active in Florence, Milan, and, from 1516, France. In painting he developed the use of both chiaroscuro (the contrast of light and shadow) and also *sfumato* (the subtle graduation of colours and tones), both techniques helping to extend the emotional depth and complexity of painting. His notebooks and drawings show an immensely inventive and enquiring mind, studying aspects of the natural and scientific world from anatomy and botany to aerodynamics and hydraulics. ▷*See feature on pp. 626–627.*

Leoncavallo Ruggero 1858–1919. Italian operatic composer. He played in restaurants, composing in his spare time, until the success of *I Pagliacci/The Strolling Players* 1892. His other operas include *La Bohème/Bohemian Life* 1897 (contemporary with Puccini's version) and *Zaza* 1900.

Leone Sergio 1921–1989. Italian film director, responsible for popularizing 'spaghetti' Westerns (Westerns made in Italy and Spain, usually with a US leading actor and a European supporting cast and crew) and making a world star of Clint Eastwood. His films include *Per un pugno di dollari/A Fistful of Dollars* 1964, *C'era una volta il West/Once Upon a Time in the West* 1968, and *C'era una volta il America/Once Upon a Time in America* 1984.

Leonidas King of Sparta. He was killed 480 BC while defending the pass of ◊Thermopylae with 300 Spartans, 700 Thespians, and 400 Thebans against a huge Persian army.

leopard or ***panther*** cat *Panthera pardus*, found in Africa and Asia. The background colour of the coat is golden, and the black spots form rosettes that differ according to the variety; black panthers are simply a colour variation and retain the patterning as a 'watered-silk' effect. The leopard is 1.5–2.5 m/5–8 ft long, including the tail, which may measure 1 m/3 ft.

The ***snow leopard*** or ***ounce*** *P. uncia*, which has irregular rosettes of much larger black spots on a light cream or grey background, is a native of mountains in central Asia. The ***clouded leopard*** *Neofelis nebulosa* is rather smaller, about 1.75 m/5.8 ft overall, with large blotchy markings rather than rosettes, and is found in SE Asia. There are seven subspecies, of which six are in danger of extinction, including the ***Amur leopard*** and the ***South Arabian leopard***.

Leopardi Giacomo, Count Leopardi 1798–1837. Italian romantic poet. The first collection of his uniquely pessimistic poems, *I Versi/Verses*, appeared 1824 and was followed by his philosophical *Operette morali/Minor Moral Works* 1827, in prose, and *I Canti/Lyrics* 1831.

Leopold I 1790–1865. King of the Belgians from 1831. He was elected to the throne on the creation of an independent Belgium. Through his marriage, when prince of Saxe-Coburg, to Princess Charlotte Augusta, he was the uncle of Queen Victoria of Great Britain and had considerable influence over her.

Leopold II 1835–1909. King of the Belgians from 1865, son of Leopold I. He financed the US journalist Henry Stanley's explorations in Africa, which resulted in the foundation of the Congo Free State (now Zaire), from which he extracted a huge fortune by ruthless exploitation.

Leopold III 1901–1983. King of the Belgians 1934–51. He surrendered to the German army in World War II 1940. Postwar charges against his conduct led to a regency by his brother Charles and his eventual abdication 1951 in favour of his son Baudouin.

Leopold I 1640–1705. Holy Roman emperor from 1658, in succession to his father Ferdinand III. He warred against Louis XIV of France and the Ottoman Empire.

Leopold II 1747–1792. Holy Roman emperor in succession to his brother Joseph II. He was the son of Empress Maria Theresa of Austria. His hostility to the French Revolution led to the outbreak of war a few weeks after his death.

Lepanto, Battle of sea battle 7 Oct 1571, between the Ottoman Empire and 'Holy League' forces from Spain, Venice, Genoa, and the Papal States, jointly commanded by the Spanish soldier Don John of Austria. The combined western fleets broke Muslim sea power. The battle fought in the Mediterranean Gulf of Corinth off Lepanto (Italian name of the Greek port of Naupaktos), then in Turkish possession, was the last major naval engagement to be fought by galleys.

Le Pen Jean-Marie 1928– . French extreme right-wing politician. In 1972 he formed the French National Front, supporting immigrant repatriation and capital punishment; the party gained 14% of the national vote in the 1986 election. Le Pen was elected to the European Parliament 1984.

Lepenski Vir site of one of Europe's oldest farming settlements (6th millennium BC), now submerged by an artificial lake on the river Danube in Yugoslavia on the Romanian border. It was preceded by a camp of hunter-fishers, with large limestone sculptures of strange fishlike beings.

lepidoptera order of insects, including ◊butterflies and ◊moths, which have overlapping scales on their wings; the order consists of about 165,000 species.

leprechaun (Old Irish 'small body') in Irish folklore, a fairy in the shape of an old man, sometimes conceived as a cobbler, with a hidden store of gold.

leprosy or ***Hansen's disease*** chronic, progressive disease caused by a bacterium *Mycobacterium leprae* closely related to that of tuberculosis. The infection attacks the skin and nerves. Once common in many countries, leprosy is now confined almost entirely to the tropics. It is controlled with drugs.

There are two principal manifestations. ***Lepromatous leprosy*** is a contagious, progressive form distinguished by the appearance of raised blotches and lumps on the skin and thickening of the skin and nerves, with numbness, weakness, paralysis, and ultimately deformity of the affected parts. In ***tuberculoid leprosy***, sensation is lost in some areas of the skin; sometimes there is loss of pigmentation and hair. The visible effects of long-standing leprosy (joint damage, paralysis, loss of fingers or toes) are due to nerve damage and injuries of which the sufferer may be unaware.

Leptis Magna ruined city in Libya, 120 km/75 mi E of Tripoli. It was founded by the Phoenicians, then came under Carthage, and in 47 BC under Rome. Excavation in the 20th century revealed remains of fine Roman buildings.

lepton any of a class of light ◊elementary particles that are not affected by the strong nuclear force; they do not interact strongly with other particles or nuclei. The leptons are comprised of the ◊electron, ◊muon, and ◊tau, and their ◊neutrinos (the electron neutrino, muon neutrino, and tau neutrino), plus their six ◊antiparticles.

Lérida (Catalan ***Lleida***) capital of Lérida province, N Spain, on the river Segre; 132 km/82 mi W of Barcelona; population (1994) 114,000. Industries include leather, paper, glass, and cloth. It has a palace of the kings of Aragon.

Lermontov Mikhail Yurevich 1814–1841. Russian Romantic poet and novelist. In 1837 he was sent into active military service in the Caucasus for writing a revolutionary poem on the death of Pushkin, which criticized court values, and for participating in a duel. Among his works are the psychological novel *A Hero of Our Time* 1840 and a volume of poems *October* 1840.

Lerner Alan Jay 1918–1986. US lyricist. He collaborated with Frederick Loewe on musicals including *Brigadoon* 1947, *Paint Your Wagon* 1951, *My Fair Lady* 1956, *Gigi* 1958, and *Camelot* 1960.

Lerwick port in Shetland, Scotland; population (1991) 7,300. It is the administrative headquarters of the Shetland Islands. Main occupations include fishing and oil supply services. Hand-knitted shawls are a speciality. A Viking tradition survives in the Jan festival of Up-Helly-Aa when a replica of a longship is burned.

Le Sage Alain-René 1668–1747. French novelist and dramatist. His novels include *Le Diable boiteux/The Devil upon Two Sticks* 1707 and his picaresque masterpiece *Gil Blas de Santillane* 1715–35, which is much indebted to Spanish originals. He also published over 100 plays.

lesbianism homosexuality (sexual attraction to one's own sex) between women, so called from the Greek island of Lesbos (now Lesvos), the home of ◊Sappho the poet and her followers to whom the behaviour was attributed.

Lesbos alternative spelling of ◊Lesvos, an island in the Aegean Sea.

lesion any change in a body tissue that is a manifestation of disease or injury.

Lesotho landlocked country in southern Africa, an enclave within South Africa. *See country box below.*

less developed country (LDC) any country late in developing an industrial base, and dependent on cash crops and unprocessed minerals. The terms 'less developed' and 'developing' imply that industrial development is desirable or inevitable; many people prefer to use 'Third World'.

Lesseps Ferdinand Marie, Vicomte de Lesseps 1805–1894. French engineer. He designed and built the ◊Suez Canal 1859–69. He began work on the Panama Canal 1881, but withdrew after failing to construct it without locks.

Lessing Doris May, (born Tayler) 1919– . English novelist, brought up in Rhodesia. Concerned with social and political themes, particularly the place of women in society, her work includes *The Grass is Singing* 1950, the five-novel series *Children of Violence* 1952–69, *The Golden Notebook* 1962, *The Good Terrorist* 1985, *The Fifth Child* 1988, *Under My Skin* 1994, and *Love, Again* 1996. She has also written an 'inner space fiction' series *Canopus in Argus: Archives* 1979–83, and, under the pen name 'Jane Somers', *The Diary of a Good Neighbour* 1981.

Lessing Gotthold Ephraim 1729–1781. German dramatist and critic. His plays include *Miss Sara Sampson* 1755, *Minna von Barnhelm* 1767, *Emilia Galotti* 1772, and the verse play *Nathan der Weise* 1779. His works of criticism *Laokoon* 1766 and *Hamburgische Dramaturgie* 1767–68 influenced German literature: the former analysed the functions of poetry and the plastic arts, and the latter attacked restrictive French classical drama in favour of the freer approach of Shakespeare. He also produced many theological and philosophical writings.

Lesvos Greek island in the Aegean Sea, near the coast of Turkey
area 2,154 sq km/831 sq mi
capital Mytilene
industries olives, wine, grain
population (1991) 103,700

It is terrible to destroy a person's picture of himself in the interests of truth or some other abstraction.

DORIS LESSING
The Grass is Singing

cont. on p. 628

LESOTHO
Kingdom of

area 30,355 sq km/11,717 sq mi
capital Maseru
major towns/cities Teyateyaneng, Mafeteng, Roma, Quthing
physical features mountainous with plateaus, forming part of South Africa's chief watershed
political system constitutional monarchy
head of state King Letsie III from 1996
head of government Ntsu Mokhehle from 1993
administrative divisions ten districts
political parties Basotho National Party (BNP), traditionalist, nationalist, right of centre; Basutoland Congress Party (BCP), left of centre
population 2,050,000 (1995 est)
population growth rate 2.7% (1990–95); 2.6% (2000–05)
ethnic distribution almost entirely Bantus (of Southern Sotho) or Basotho
life expectancy 54 (men), 63 (women)
literacy rate 60%
languages Sesotho, English (official), Zulu, Xhosa
religions Protestant 42%, Roman Catholic 38%
currency loti
GDP (US $) 886 million (1994)
growth rate 2.4% (1993)
exports wool, mohair, diamonds, cattle, wheat, vegetables

HISTORY
18th C Formerly inhabited by nomadic hunter-gatherer San, Zulu-speaking Ngunis, and Sotho-speaking peoples settled in the region.
1820s Under the name of Basutoland, the Sotho nation was founded by Moshoeshoe I, who united the people to repulse Zulu attacks from the S.
1843 Moshoeshoe I negotiated British protection as tension with the South African Boers increased.
1868 Became a British territory, administered by Cape Colony (in South Africa) from 1871.
1884 Became a British Crown Colony, after a revolt against Cape Colony control; Basuto chiefs were allowed to govern according to custom and tradition, but rich agricultural land W of the Caledon river was lost to South Africa.
1900s Served as a migrant labour reserve for South Africa's mines and farms.
1952 Left-of-centre Basutoland African Congress, later Congress Party (BCP), founded by Ntsu Mokhehle to campaign for self rule.
1966 Independence achieved within the Commonwealth, as the Kingdom of Lesotho, with Moshoeshoe II as king and Chief Leabua Jonathan of the conservative Basotho National Party (BNP) as prime minister.
1970 State of emergency declared; the king briefly forced into exile after attempting to increase his authority.
1973 State of emergency lifted; BNP won majority of seats in general election.
1975 Members of the ruling party attacked by South African-backed guerrillas, who opposed African National Congress (ANC) guerrillas using Lesotho as a base.
1986 South Africa imposed border blockade, forcing deportation of 60 ANC members. General Lekhanya ousted Chief Jonathan in a coup.
1990 Lekhanya replaced in coup by Col Elias Ramaema and Moshoeshoe II dethroned and replaced by son, as King Letsie III.
1993 Free multiparty elections ended military rule; Ntsu Mokhehle (BCP) became prime minister.
1994 Fighting between rival army factions ended by peace deal, brokered by Organization of African Unity.
1995 Letsie abdicated to restore King Moshoeshoe II to the throne.
1996 King Moshoeshoe II killed in car accident; King Letsie III restored to throne.

Leonardo da Vinci

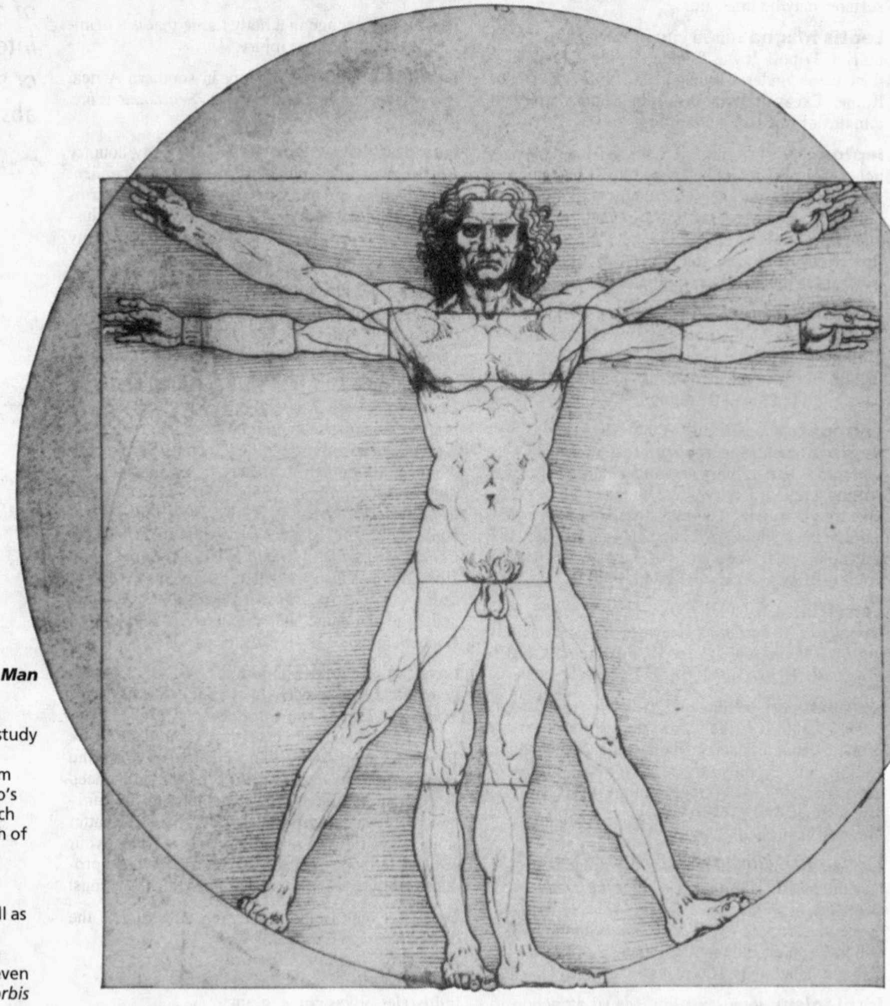

The Vetruvian Man c. 1490, Galleria dell'Accademia, Venice, Italy. A study of anatomical proportions from one of Leonardo's notebooks, which contain a wealth of observations on topics such as perspective and anatomy, as well as designs for weapons, flying machines, and even a diving-suit. *Corbis*

Early life

The Renaissance artist and scientist Leonardo da Vinci was born on 15 April 1452, in a small village near the town of Vinci, in Tuscany, central Italy. He was the illegitimate son of Piero da Vinci, a lawyer, and Caterina, a peasant girl. He was raised by his father and step-mother, and seems to have developed an early fascination with the natural world.

At the age of 15 or 16 he entered one of the finest studios in Florence, that of the painter and sculptor Andrea del Verrocchio, where he would have met young artists such as Botticelli, Lorenzo di Credi, and Perugino. The earliest example of his work is an angel he painted for Verrocchio's *Baptism of Christ* (Uffizi Gallery, Florence). The figure's delicacy marked him out as a pupil of exceptional talent.

Early career: Florence

Surprisingly, Leonardo's early years in Florence were unremarkable. He had all the qualities that should have made for a outstanding career in 15th-century Florence – contemporaries noted his intelligence, charm, good looks, and talent. But he received only a few, comparatively modest commissions, among them his *Annunciation* about 1473 (Uffizi), and his delicate portrait *Ginevra dei Benci* about 1474 (National Gallery, Washington).

When he was 29, however, he began work on his remarkable *Adoration of the Magi* (Uffizi), which in its complexity of structure and emotional intensity strikes a completely new note in Renaissance painting. Yet less than a year later, in 1482, he left his first major work unfinished and moved to Milan to work for Duke Lodovico Sforza.

Maturity: Milan

It is not clear why Leonardo was so eager to leave Florence. The most likely explanation is that he found the city intellectually and artistically inhibiting. Florence was, certainly, at the heart of the Italian Renaissance. But its achievement was based on a deep respect for classical culture, first Roman and then (by Leonardo's day) Greek. Leonardo was not a scholar. He knew little Latin and no Greek and in his notebooks he scorned mere 'book learning' as second-hand knowledge. He wanted to approach the world directly, utterly sure of his own abilities to observe, deduce, and understand. His attitude – confident, forward looking and impatient with tradition – marks a profound change in the character of the Renaissance. Increasingly the focus of the Renaissance was not the recovery of lost glories but the discovery of new worlds.

In Milan, where he spent the next 17 years under the patronage of Duke Lodovico, Leonardo seems to have found the conditions he needed. He painted some of his finest works, including *Lady with an Ermine* about 1485, a portrait of Lodovico's mistress (Czartorsky Collection, Kraków); two versions of the *Virgin and Child* (the Louvre, Paris, and the National Gallery, London); and his famous *Last Supper* 1495–98, which is a fresco in the monastery of Santa Maria delle Grazie.

He also began work on a huge equestrian statue in memory of Lodovico's father, though the massive amounts of bronze required to cast it had to be used to make cannons – Lodovico's hold on power was precarious. He invented an array of weapons and fortifications, wrote music, and designed costumes and stage machinery for pageants and plays. Following the devastating plagues of 1484 and 1485 he took a keen interest in town planning.

Scientific researches

In Milan Leonardo also had the time to pursue his own diverse studies with greater concentration, tirelessly filling thousands of pages with small, intricate drawings of plants, animals, people and places; with sketches for paintings and sculptures; and with observations, theories and fantasies, the text written backwards so that it has to be read in a mirror. (As he was left-handed this mirror-writing may have been a convenience rather than an attempt to keep his ideas secret, as is generally believed.)

He devised dozens of astonishing inventions, including flying machines, submarines and automatons, and wrote a treatise on painting. He dissected corpses, at a time when the practice was regarded with the deepest suspicion, making detailed notes and drawings that show an understanding of anatomy and human biology far in advance of his time. He made drawings to illustrate mathematical principles, including the famous 'man in a circle' about 1492, a graphic expression of his belief that 'man is the measure of all things'.

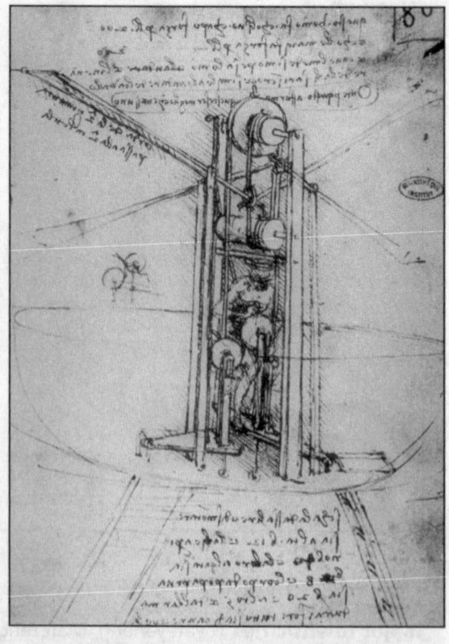

Design for a flying machine c. 1486–90 by Leonardo da Vinci, Institut de France, Paris. Often drawn away from his painting by his scientific interests, da Vinci filled many notebooks with observations and inventions. This man-powered flying machine attempts to imitate the flapping of a bird's wings. *Topham Picture Source*

This self-portrait, drawn during Leonardo's stay in Milan, when he was almost 60 years old, is the only image of him known to survive. *Corbis*

Though he kept his notes unsystematically, his mind passing quickly from one subject to another, he saw them forming the basis of an encyclopedia of all human knowledge – the new knowledge of keen observation. Many of his notes have been lost, though as recently as 1965 more material, including a 14-year diary, was discovered in a library in Spain.

Return to Florence

In 1499 the French invaded Milan and Lodovico fell from power. Leonardo left quickly, travelling to Mantua and Venice before returning to Florence, where for a few years he concentrated on his scientific researches. But he was soon restless and spent 10 months (1502–03) in the service of Cesare Borgia, the ruthlessly ambitious commander of the papal army, for whom he worked as a mapmaker and engineer, designing canals, harbours and other projects.

It was during this second period in Florence that he produced two of his most important works. The first was his *Mona Lisa* 1503–05 (Louvre), perhaps the best-known painting in the world. A portrait of the wife of a wealthy Florence merchant, it is one of the finest examples of Leonardo's style, the forms softly modelled, the sitter's smile gentle and enigmatic, the background mysterious and otherworldly.

The second major work of this period, begun in 1505, was a mural depicting the battle of Anghiari, a famous victory for Florence. Michelangelo was commissioned to paint a companion piece, the battle of Cascina. The men disliked one another and the commissions became a battle for artistic supremacy that was followed with keen interest in Florence and beyond, not least by the young Raphael, who watched the artists at work. Both murals have been lost, though preparatory drawings and copies show that they were intensely dramatic works that had a profound effect on the development of late Renaissance art.

Ginevra de'Benci (c. 1474), National Museum of Art, Washington, USA. Though one of Leonardo da Vinci's earliest independent works, this portrait already exhibits his characteristic fascination with an air of mystery and dreaminess. The influence of Flemish painting is seen in his use of an outdoor setting. *Topham Picture Source*

Later years: Milan and Rome

In 1506 Leonardo returned to Milan, this time at the request of the city's French ruler, Charles d'Amboise. As usual he divided his time between practical projects (he was the city's engineer and architect), his scientific research, and his paintings, the finest of which is his *Virgin and Child with St Anne* about 1508 (Louvre). He also designed a second equestrian monument (never completed), and drew a famous self-portrait (Royal Library, Turin), the only known image of him to survive.

Still searching for challenges, in 1513, at the age of 61, he moved to Rome to seek the patronage of the new pope, Leo X, who was attempting to return the mother-city of the Church to its former glory. The move was not a success, however, for Leonardo's commissions amounted to little more than a few unrealized architectural projects. It was probably during this period, however, that he began painting his last and in many ways his most enigmatic work, *St John the Baptist* about 1515 (Louvre).

Last years: France

Even in old age Leonardo was restless, and in 1516, though famous throughout Italy, he accepted the invitation of Francis I to work in France as his 'premier painter, architect and engineer'. He lived in the chateau of Cloux, near the royal palace at Amboise in the Loire valley, central France. It was there that he tried to bring some order to his wide-ranging researches, and even found time to carry out his official functions, including designing a palace (not built), designing court festivals, and devising a system for controlling the powerful river Loire (never realized). It was there, on 2 May 1519, that he died, at the age of 67.

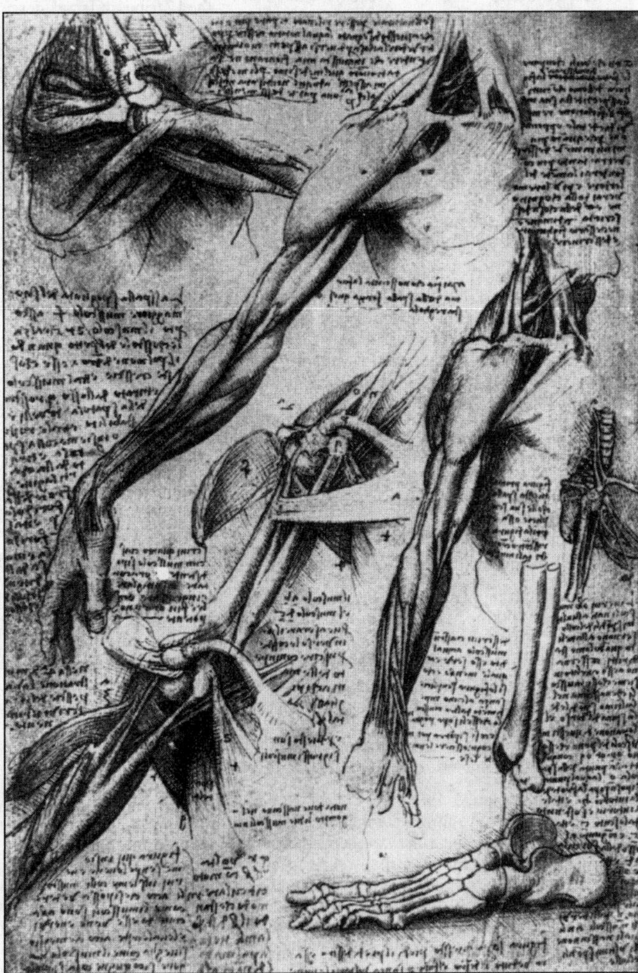

Study of a hand placed palm downwards c. 1490, Galleria dell'Accademia, Venice, Italy. An example of the minutely detailed anatomical studies contained in Leonardo's notebooks. The notebooks were all written in a backwards script, and were not known to his contemporaries. *Corbis*

CHRIS MURRAY

The wise man is not the man who gives the right answers; he is the one who asks the right questions.

CLAUDE LÉVI-STRAUSS
The Raw and the Cooked

history ancient name Lesbos; an Aeolian settlement, the home of the poets Alcaeus and Sappho; conquered by the Turks from Genoa 1462; annexed to Greece 1913.

Lethe in Greek mythology, a river of the underworld whose waters, when drunk, brought forgetfulness of the past.

Letsie III 1964– . King of Lesotho 1990–95 and from 1996. He succeeded his father, King Moshoeshoe II, as Crown Prince David Mohato Bereng Seeiso 1990 when Moshoeshoe was deposed by the army. Letsie voluntarily abdicated 1995 when his father was reinstated to the throne. Moshoeshoe was killed in a car accident 1996 and Crown Prince David was chosen as his successor, ascending the throne for a second time.

letter written or printed message, chiefly a personal communication. Letters are valuable as reflections of social conditions and of literary and political life. Legally, ownership of a letter (as a document) passes to the recipient, but the copyright remains with the writer.

letterpress method of printing from raised type, pioneered by Johann ◊Gutenberg in Europe in the 1450s.

lettuce annual edible plant *Lactuca sativa*, family Compositae, believed to have been derived from the wild species *L. serriola*. There are many varieties, including the cabbage lettuce, with round or loose heads, and the Cos lettuce, with long, upright heads.

leucocyte another name for a ◊white blood cell.

leucotomy or ***lobotomy*** a brain operation to sever the connections between the frontal lobe and underlying structures. It was widely used in the 1940s and 1950s to treat severe psychotic or depressive illness. Though it achieved some success, it left patients dull and apathetic; there was also a considerable risk of epilepsy. It was largely replaced by the use of psychotropic drugs from the late 1950s.

leukaemia any one of a group of cancers of the blood cells, with widespread involvement of the bone marrow and other blood-forming tissue. The central feature of leukaemia is runaway production of white blood cells that are immature or in some way abnormal. These rogue cells, which lack the defensive capacity of healthy white cells, overwhelm the normal ones, leaving the victim vulnerable to infection. Treatment is with radiotherapy and ◊cytotoxic drugs to suppress replication of abnormal cells, or by bone-marrow transplantation.

Abnormal functioning of the bone marrow also suppresses production of red blood cells and blood ◊platelets, resulting in ◊anaemia and a failure of the blood to clot.

Levant former name for the E Mediterranean region, or more specifically, the Mediterranean coastal regions of Turkey, Syria, Lebanon, and Israel.

Le Vau Louis 1612–1670. French architect. He was a leading exponent of the Baroque style. His design for the château of Vaux-le-Viscomte outside Paris (begun 1657) provided the inspiration for the remodelling of Versailles, on which he worked from 1669. Many of Le Vau's additions to the palace, notably the elegantly symmetrical garden façade, were altered by later enlargements under ◊Hardouin-Mansart. Le Vau also contributed to the east front of the Louvre 1667 and designed les Tuileries, Paris.

levee naturally formed raised bank along the side of a river channel. When a river overflows its banks, the rate of flow is less than that in the channel, and silt is deposited on the banks. With each successive flood the levee increases in size so that eventually the river may be above the surface of the surrounding flood plain.

It is the duty of righteous men to make war on all undeserved privilege, but one must not forget that this is a war without end.

PRIMO LEVI
'The Grey Zone', *The Drowned and the Saved* 2

Levellers democratic party in the English Civil War. The Levellers found wide support among Cromwell's New Model Army and the yeoman farmers, artisans, and small traders, and proved a powerful political force 1647–49. Their programme included the establishment of a republic, government by a parliament of one house elected by male suffrage, religious toleration, and sweeping social reforms. Cromwell's refusal to implement this programme led to mutinies by Levellers in the army, which, when suppressed by Cromwell 1649, ended the movement. They were led by John ◊Lilburne.

True Levellers (also known as ◊Diggers) were denounced by the Levellers because of their more radical methods.

Leven, Loch lake in Tayside Region, Scotland; area 16 sq km/6 sq mi. It is drained by the river Leven, and has seven islands; Mary Queen of Scots was imprisoned 1567–68 on Castle Island. It has been a national nature reserve since 1964. Leven is also the name of a sea loch in Strathclyde, Scotland.

lever simple machine consisting of a rigid rod pivoted at a fixed point called the fulcrum, used for shifting or raising a heavy load or applying force in a similar way. Levers are classified into orders according to where the effort is applied, and the load-moving force developed, in relation to the position of the fulcrum.

A ***first-order*** lever has the load and the effort on opposite sides of the fulcrum – for example, a seesaw or pair of scissors. A ***second-order*** lever has the load and the effort on the same side of the fulcrum, with the load nearer the fulcrum – for example, nutcrackers or a wheelbarrow. A ***third-order*** lever has the effort nearer the fulcrum than the load, with both on the same side of it – for example, a pair of tweezers or tongs. The mechanical advantage of a lever is the ratio of load to effort, equal to the perpendicular distance of the effort's line of action from the fulcrum divided by the distance to the load's line of action.

Leverrier Urbain Jean Joseph 1811–1877. French astronomer. He predicted the existence and position of the planet ◊Neptune from its influence on the orbit of the planet ◊Uranus. It was discovered 1846. The possibility that another planet might exist beyond Uranus, influencing its orbit, had already been suggested. Leverrier calculated the orbit and apparent diameter of the hypothetical planet, and wrote to a number of observatories, asking them to test his prediction of its position. Johann ◊Galle at the Berlin Observatory found it immediately, within 1° of Leverrier's coordinates.

Lévesque René 1922–1987. French-Canadian politician. In 1968 he founded the Parti Québecois, with the aim of an independent Quebec, but a referendum rejected the proposal in 1980. He was premier of Quebec 1976–85.

Levi Primo 1919–1987. Italian novelist. He joined the anti-Fascist resistance during World War II, was captured, and sent to the concentration camp at Auschwitz. He wrote of these experiences in *Se questo è un uomo/If This Is a Man* 1947. His other books, all based on his experience of the war, include *The Periodic Table* 1975 and *Moments of Reprieve* 1981.

leviathan in the Old Testament, a sea monster (thought to be the whale), later associated in Christian literature with Satan. The term was also used to describe the monstrous qualities of wealth or power invested in one person, as in the political treatise *Leviathan* by the English philosopher Thomas ◊Hobbes.

Levi-Montalcini Rita 1909– . Italian neurologist who discovered nerve-growth factor, a substance that controls how many cells make up the adult nervous system. She shared the 1986 Nobel Prize for Physiology or Medicine with her coworker, US biochemist Stanley Cohen (1922–).

Levinson Barry 1932– . US film director and screenwriter. Working in Hollywood's mainstream, he has been responsible for some of the best adult comedy films of the 1980s and 1990s. Winning cult status for the offbeat realism of *Diner* 1982, Levinson went on to make such large-budget movies as *Good Morning Vietnam* 1987, *Tin Men* 1987, *Rain Man* 1988 (Academy Awards for best picture and best director), *Bugsy* 1991, and *Toys* 1992.

Lévi-Strauss Claude 1908– . French anthropologist who helped to formulate the principles of ◊structuralism by stressing the interdependence of cultural systems and the way they relate to each other. In his analyses of kinship, myth, and symbolism, Lévi-Strauss argued that, though the superficial appearance of these factors might vary between societies, their underlying structures were universal and could best be understood in terms of binary oppositions: left and right, male and female, nature and culture, the raw and the cooked, and so on. His works include *Tristes Tropiques* 1955 – an intellectual autobiography – and *Mythologiques/Mythologies* 1964–71.

Lewis, Carl US athlete Carl Lewis touches down at 8.38 m/27 ft 6 in to win the gold medal in the long jump competition at the Goodwill Games in Seattle, 1990. Lewis has also competed in 100-m, 200-m, and relay events. He has won nine Olympic gold medals. *Corbis*

levitation counteraction of gravitational forces on a body. As claimed by medieval mystics, spiritualist mediums, and practitioners of transcendental meditation, it is unproven. In the laboratory it can be produced scientifically; for example, electrostatic force and acoustical waves have been used to suspend water drops for microscopic study. It is also used in technology; for example, in magnetic levitation as in ◊maglev trains.

Levite in the Old Testament, a member of one of the 12 tribes of Israel, descended from Levi, a son of ◊Jacob. The Levites performed the lesser services of the Temple; the high priesthood was confined to the descendants of Aaron, the brother of Moses.

Lewes, Battle of battle in 1264 caused by the baronial opposition to the English king Henry III, led by Simon de Montfort, Earl of Leicester (1208–65). The king was defeated and captured at the battle.

The barons objected to Henry's patronage of French nobles in the English court, his weak foreign policy, and his support for the papacy against the Holy Roman Empire. In 1258, they forced him to issue the Provisions of Oxford, providing for the establishment of a baronial council to run the government, carry out reforms, and keep a check on royal power, and when he later refused to implement them, they revolted. They defeated and captured the king at Lewes in Sussex. Their revolt was broken by de Montfort's death and defeat at Evesham in 1265.

Lewis (Harry) Sinclair 1885–1951. US novelist. He made a reputation with satirical, but sentimental, social documentary novels, principally *Main Street* 1920, depicting American small-town life; and *Babbitt* 1922, the story of a real-estate dealer of the Midwest caught in the conventions of his milieu. These were followed by *Arrowsmith* 1925, a study of the pettiness in medical science; *Elmer Gantry* 1927, a satiric portrayal of evangelical religion; and *Dodsworth* 1929, about a US industrialist. He was the first American to be awarded the Nobel Prize for Literature, 1930.

Lewis Jerry Lee 1935– . US rock-and-roll and country singer and pianist. His trademark was the boogie-woogie-derived 'pumping piano' style in hits such as 'Whole Lotta Shakin' Going On' and 'Great Balls of Fire' 1957; later recordings include 'What Made Milwaukee Famous' 1968.

Lewis Lennox 1966– . British-born boxer who won the world heavyweight title 1992, becoming the first British boxer to do so in the 20th century. He was awarded the title when the reigning champion, Riddick Bowe, refused to fight him. After defending the title successfully for nearly two years, he lost to Oliver McCall 1994. He turned professional 1989, won the European title 1990, and the British title 1991.

Lewis (William) Arthur 1915– . British economist born on St Lucia, West Indies. He specialized in the economic problems of developing countries and created a model relating the terms of trade between less developed and more developed nations to their respective levels of labour productivity in agriculture. He shared the Nobel Prize for Economics with an American, Theodore Schultz, 1979. He wrote many books, including the *Theory of Economic Growth* 1955.

Lewis Carl (Frederick Carlton) 1961– . US track and field athlete. He won nine gold medals and one silver in four successive Olympic Games. At the 1984 Olympic Games he equalled the performance of Jesse ◊Owens, winning gold medals in the 100 and 200 metres, 400-metre relay, and long jump. In the 1988 Olympics he repeated his golds in the 100 metres and long jump, and won a silver in the 200 metres. In the 1992 Olympics he repeated his success in the long jump and anchored the USA's record-breaking 400-metre relay team. He won the long jump gold medal at the Atlanta Olympics 1996.

Lewis C Day. Irish poet; see Cecil ◊Day-Lewis.

Lewis C(live) S(taples) 1898–1963. English academic and writer, born in Belfast. His books include the medieval study *The Allegory of Love* 1936 and the space fiction *Out of the Silent Planet* 1938. He became a committed Christian 1931 and wrote essays in popular theology such as *The Screwtape Letters* 1942 and *Mere Christianity* 1952, the autobiographical *Surprised by Joy* 1955, and a series of seven novels of Christian allegory for children, set in the magic land of Narnia, beginning with *The Lion, the Witch, and the Wardrobe* 1950.

Lewis (Percy) Wyndham 1882–1957. English writer and artist. He pioneered ◊Vorticism, a variant of Cubist and Futurist ideas, which with its feeling of movement sought to reflect the age of industry. He had a hard and aggressive style in both his writing and his painting. His literary works include the novels *Tarr* 1918, *The Childermass* 1928, and *The Apes of God* 1930; the essay 'Time and Western Man' 1927; and an autobiography, *Blasting and Bombadiering* 1937. He also edited the literary and artistic magazine *Blast* 1914–15. In addition to works of a semi-abstract kind he painted a number of portraits, including those of the poets Edith Sitwell, Ezra Pound and T S Eliot.

Lewis and Clark Meriwether Lewis (1774–1809) and William Clark (1770–1838) US explorers. Lewis was commissioned 1803 by President Thomas Jefferson to find a land route to the Pacific, and chose Clark to accompany him. They followed the Missouri River to its source, crossed the Rocky Mountains (aided by an Indian woman, Sacajawea) and followed the Columbia River to the Pacific, then returned overland to St Louis 1804–06.

Lewisham inner borough of SE Greater London. It includes the suburbs of ◊Blackheath, Sydenham, Catford, and ◊Deptford
features Deptford shipbuilding yard (1512–1869); Armoury Mill produced steel for armour in the 16th century, musket barrels in the Napoleonic Wars, and gold and silver thread for Victorian uniforms
population (1991) 215,300
famous people birthplace of James Elroy Fletcher; home of Samuel Smiles, Arthur Sullivan, W G Grace, Ernest Dowson, Ernest Shackleton.

Lewis with Harris largest island in the Outer Hebrides; area 2,220 sq km/857 sq mi; population (1991) 21,700. Its main town is Stornoway. It is separated from NW Scotland by the Minch. There are many lakes and peat moors. Harris is famous for its tweeds.

Lexington and Concord, Battle of first battle of the ◊American Revolution 19 April 1775 at Lexington, Massachusetts, USA. The first shots were fired when British troops, sent to seize illegal military stores and arrest rebel leaders John Hancock and Samuel Adams, were attacked by the local militia (minutemen). Although a somewhat inconclusive action in itself, it sparked wider rebellion and so precipitated the revolution.

Leyden alternative form of ◊Leiden, a city in the Netherlands.

Leyden Lucas van see ◊Lucas van Leyden, Dutch painter.

Lhasa ('the Forbidden City') capital of the autonomous region of ◊Tibet, China, at an altitude of 5,000 m/16,400 ft; population (1992) 124,000. Products include handicrafts and light industry. The holy city of ◊Lamaism, Lhasa was closed to Westerners until 1904, when members of a British expedition led by Col Francis E Younghusband visited the city. It was annexed with the rest of Tibet 1950–51 by China, and the spiritual and temporal head of state, the Dalai Lama, fled 1959 after a popular uprising against Chinese rule. Monasteries have been destroyed and monks killed, and an influx of Chinese settlers has generated resentment.

liana woody, perennial climbing plant with very long stems, which grows around trees up to the canopy, where there is more sunlight. Lianas are common in tropical rainforests, where individual stems may grow up to 78 m/255 ft long.

Liao river in NE China, frozen Dec–March; the main headstream rises in the mountains of Inner Mongolia and flows east, then south to the Gulf of Liaodong; length 1,450 km/900 mi.

Liao dynasty family that ruled part of NE China and Manchuria 945–1125 during the ◊Song era. It was founded by cavalry-based Qidan (Khidan) people, Mongolian-speakers who gradually became Sinicized. They were later defeated by the nomadic Juchen (Jurchen) who founded the ◊Jin dynasty.

Liaoning province of NE China
area 151,000 sq km/58,300 sq mi
capital Shenyang
towns Anshan, Fushun, Liaoyang
features one of China's most heavily industrialized areas
industries cereals, coal, iron, salt, oil
population (1990) 39,980,000
history developed by Japan 1905–45, including the Liaodong Peninsula, whose ports had been captured from the Russians.

Liaquat Ali Khan Nawabzada 1895–1951. Indian politician, deputy leader of the ◊Muslim League 1940–47, first prime minister of Pakistan from 1947. He was assassinated by objectors to his peace policy with India.

libel in law, defamation published in a permanent form, such as in a newspaper, book, or broadcast. In English law a statement is defamatory if it lowers the plaintiff in the estimation of right-thinking people generally. Defences to libel are: to show that the statement was true, or fair comment; or to show that it was privileged (this applies, for example, to the reporting of statements made in Parliament or in a court); or, in certain circumstances, making a formal apology. The stringency of English libel law has been widely criticized as limiting the freedom of the press.

Libel actions are tried by a judge with a jury, and the jury decides the amount of the damages. However, in 1990 the Court of Appeal was given new powers to reduce or increase damages awards by juries, irrespective of whether the parties to the appeal agree or not.

liana *Lianas reaching to the tops of giant forest trees in the Montagne d'Ambre rainforest in Madagascar. Flowers and fruits usually grow directly from the woody stems.*
Premaphotos Wildlife

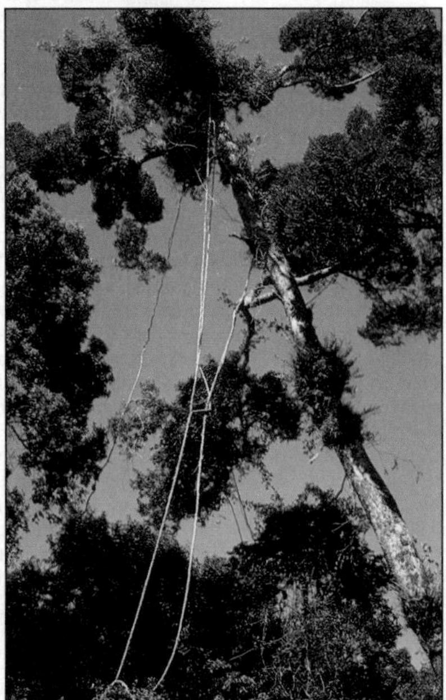

liberal arts or ***the arts*** collective term for the visual arts, music, and literature together with certain subjects of study, such as philosophy, history, languages, and sociology. The concept dates back to the classical idea of the pursuits worthy of a free man (which were seen as intellectual rather than manual).

Liberal Democrats in UK politics, common name for the ◊Social and Liberal Democrats.

liberalism political and social theory that favours representative government, freedom of the press, speech, and worship, the abolition of class privileges, the use of state resources to protect the welfare of the individual, and international ◊free trade. It is historically associated with the Liberal Party in the UK and the Democratic Party in the USA.

Liberalism developed during the 17th–19th centuries as the distinctive theory of the industrial and commercial classes in their struggle against the power of the monarchy, the church, and the feudal landowners. Economically it was associated with ◊*laissez faire*, or nonintervention. In the late 19th and early 20th centuries its ideas were modified by the acceptance of universal suffrage and a certain amount of state intervention in economic affairs, in order to ensure a minimum standard of living and to remove extremes of poverty and wealth. The classical statement of liberal principles is found in *On Liberty* and other works of the British philosopher J S Mill.

Liberal Party British political party, the successor to the ◊Whig Party, with an ideology of liberalism. In the 19th century, it represented the interests of commerce and industry. Its outstanding leaders were Palmerston, Gladstone, and Lloyd George. From 1914 it declined, and the rise of the Labour Party pushed the Liberals into the middle ground. After World War II they were reduced to a handful of members of Parliament. A revival began under the leadership 1956–67 of Jo Grimond and continued under Jeremy Thorpe, David Steel, and Paddy Ashdown.

The Liberals joined forces with the Social Democratic Party (SDP) as the Alliance for the 1983 and 1987 elections. In 1988 a majority of the SDP voted to merge with the Liberals to form the ◊Social and Liberal Democrats.

Liberal Party, Australian political party established 1944 by Robert Menzies, after a Labor landslide, and derived from the former United Australia Party. After the voters rejected Labor's extensive nationalization plans, the Liberals were in power 1949–72 and 1975–83 and were led in succession by Harold Holt, John Gorton, William McMahon, Billy Snedden, Malcolm Fraser, John Hewson, Alexander Downer, and John ◊Howard. The Liberal Party returned to power 1996 in a coalition with the National Party.

liberation theology Christian theory of Jesus' primary importance as the 'Liberator', personifying the poor and devoted to freeing them from oppression. Enthusiastically (and sometimes violently) adopted in Latin America, it embodies a Marxist interpretation of the class struggle, especially by Third World nations. It has been criticized by some Roman Catholic authorities, including Pope John Paul II.

The concept of Jesus is based on Matthew 19:21, 25:35, 40. The movement was initiated by the Peruvian priest Gustavo Gutierrez in his book *The Theology of Liberation* 1969.

Liberia country in W Africa, bounded N by Guinea, E by Côte d'Ivoire, S and SW by the Atlantic Ocean, and NW by Sierra Leone. *See country box on p. 630.*

libido in Freudian psychology, the energy of the sex instinct, which is to be found even in a newborn child. The libido develops through a number of

'She's the sort of woman who lives for others – you can always tell the others by their hunted expression.'
C S LEWIS
Screwtape Letters

LIBERIA
Republic of

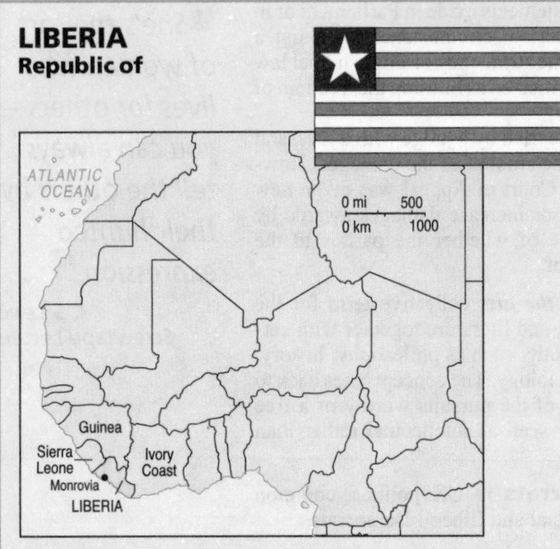

area 111,370 sq km/42,989 sq mi
capital and port Monrovia
major ports Buchanan, Greenville
physical features forested highlands; swampy tropical coast where six rivers enter the sea
head of state and government Ruth Perry from 1996
political system emergent democratic republic
administrative divisions nine counties, six territories, and the capital district
political parties National Democratic Party of Liberia (NDPL), nationalist, left of centre; National Patriotic Front of Liberia (NPFL), left of centre; United Democratic Movement of Liberia for Democracy (Ulimo), left of centre
population 3,039,000 (1995 est)
population growth rate 3.3% (1990–95); 3.1% (2000–05)
ethnic distribution 95% indigenous peoples, including the Kpelle, Bassa, Gio, Kru, Grebo, Mano, Krahn, Gola, Ghandi, Loma, Kissi, Vai, and Bella; 5% descended from US repatriated slaves
life expectancy 54 (men), 57 (women)
literacy rate men 50%, women 29%
languages English (official), over 20 Niger-Congo languages
religions animist, Sunni Muslim, Christian
currency Liberian dollar
GDP (US $) 973 million (1992)
growth rate −14.6% (1992)
exports iron ore, rubber (Africa's largest producer), timber, diamonds, coffee, cocoa, palm oil, oil

HISTORY
1821 Purchased by the philanthropic American Colonization Society and turned into a settlement for liberated black slaves from the southern USA.
1847 Recognized as an independent republic.
1869 The True Whig Party founded, which was to dominate politics for more than a century, providing all presidents.
1926 Large concession sold to Firestone Rubber Company as foreign indebtedness increased.
1944 William Tubman, a descendant of US slaves, elected president.
1971 Tubman died; succeeded by William Tolbert.
1980 Tolbert assassinated in military coup led by Sgt Samuel Doe, who banned political parties and launched a drive against corruption.
1984 New constitution approved in referendum. National Democratic Party (NDPL) founded by Doe as political parties relegalized.
1985 Doe and the NDPL won decisive victories in allegedly rigged elections.
1990 Doe killed as a bloody civil war broke out, involving Charles Taylor and General Hezekiah Bowen, who led rival rebel armies, the National Patriotic Front (NPFL) and the Armed Forces of Liberia (AFL), and which claimed 150,000 lives and left 2 million homeless. West African peacekeeping force drafted in. Amos Sawyer, with NPFL backing, became interim head of government.
1992 Monrovia under siege by Taylor's rebel forces as fighting continued.
1993 Peace agreement signed under OAU–UN auspices, but soon collapsed.
1995 Ghanaian-backed peace proposals accepted by rebel factions; interim Council of State established, comprising leaders of three main rebel factions and chaired by Wilton Sankawulo.
1996 Renewed fighting in capital; USA began evacuation of foreigners. Peace plan reached in talks convened by the Economic Community of West African States (ECOWAS); Ruth Perry became Liberia's first female head of state.

SEE ALSO Doe, Samuel

phases, described by Sigmund Freud in his theory of infantile sexuality. The source of the libido is the ◊id. The phases of the libido are identified by Freud as the oral stage, when a child tests everything by mouth, the anal stage, when the child gets satisfaction from control of its body, and the genital stage, when the libido becomes concentrated in the sex organs.

Libra faint zodiacal constellation on the celestial equator (see ◊celestial sphere) adjoining Scorpius, and represented as the scales of justice. The Sun passes through Libra during Nov. The constellation was once considered to be a part of Scorpius, seen as the scorpion's claws. In astrology, the dates for Libra are between about 23 Sept and 23 Oct (see ◊precession).

library collection of information (usually in the form of books) held for common use. The earliest was in Nineveh in Babylonian times. The first public library was opened in Athens 330 BC. All ancient libraries were reference libraries: books could be consulted but not borrowed. Lending or circulating libraries did not become popular until the 18th century; they became widespread in the 19th century with the rapid development of public libraries. Free public libraries probably began in the 15th century. In the UK, the first documented free public library was established in Manchester 1852, after the 1850 Public Library Act.
classification Books have, as a rule, been grouped according to contemporary scholastic disciplines. The first catalogue of the Bodleian Library, Oxford, published 1605, shows that the library was arranged according to the four faculties into which studies at the University of Oxford were then divided: theology, medicine, law, and arts. As subjects of study have diversified and multiplied, classification has been extended to take in new subjects and divisions and combinations of existing subjects.

Books are now usually classified by one of two major systems: Dewey Decimal Classification (now known as Universal Decimal Classification), invented in the USA by Melvil Dewey, and the Library of Congress system. Library cataloguing systems range from cards to microfiche to computer databases with on-line terminals. These frequently make use of ◊ISBN numbers (International Standard Book Numbers) and, for magazines and journals, ISSN numbers.
cataloguing Catalogues originally listed books after they had been placed on the library shelves, hence early catalogues were nearly always in some classified sequence. From the 17th century onwards a catalogue arranged in alphabetical order of authors' names came to be regarded as the library's main catalogue. The author catalogue is generally supplemented by a full or partial subject catalogue, arranged in either classified or alphabetical order of subjects. A typical catalogue entry gives the author's name, the book's title, edition, and imprint, and possibly also a note on its subject matter or its publishing history, and indicates where the book is to be found in the library.

Public libraries did not usually permit open access to their shelves until the early years of the 20th century; many national and university libraries, on account of the size and value of their collections, still restrict access. It was therefore, and sometimes still is, necessary to consult the catalogue before obtaining a publication. It may also be necessary to consult the catalogue in order to find one's way round a large library, even when access to the shelves is direct. Most libraries display guides to the use of their catalogues and refer to the supplementary bibliographies and indexes which are provided for readers' use.

The form of the catalogue has varied according to its purpose and the materials and techniques available for its compilation. Parchment being scarce and costly in the Middle Ages, catalogues were often written in odd blank spaces or on a spare page of some manuscript kept in the library. Only the librarian would need to use such a list to check the books in his care. After printing had become common and the use of libraries had become more general, library catalogues were issued as printed volumes. Printed catalogues had two advantages: they could be consulted outside the library, and, if they described a great or specialized collection of books, they formed valuable bibliographies.

The accelerated growth of library collections and the mounting cost of printing led to the replacement or supplementation of the printed catalogue by either a catalogue on paper slips kept in binders, a sheaf catalogue, or a catalogue on cards kept in a cabinet of drawers. This was easy to consult and to keep up to date with insertions, withdrawals, and replacements of worn cards, but its maintenance was costly and its size could be cumbersome. Developments in photography made it possible to reproduce card catalogues in printed book form. Electronic ◊data processing used in conjunction with microphotography has made it possible to issue updated catalogues in the form of loose-leaf books, or to store a library's complete, updated catalogue on microfilm for display on screens (readers). It has also made the exchange of catalogue information much easier, so that work done by a single organization may be used directly by others without waiting for printed cards or published lists.

libretto (Italian 'little book') the text of an opera or other dramatic vocal work, or the scenario of a ballet.

Libreville (French 'free town') capital of Gabon, on the estuary of the river Gabon; population (1992) 352,000. Products include timber, oil, and minerals. It was founded 1849 as a refuge for slaves freed by the French, and was capital of French Equatorial Guinea 1888–1904. Since the 1970s the city has developed rapidly due to the oil trade. There is a cathedral, the Sainte-Exupéry French Cultural Centre, and a university (1976).

Libya country in N Africa, bounded N by the Mediterranean Sea, E by Egypt, SE by Sudan, S by Chad and Niger, and W by Algeria and Tunisia. *See country box opposite.*

licence document issued by a government or other recognized authority conveying permission to the holder to do something otherwise prohibited, and designed to facilitate accurate records, the maintenance of order, and collection of revenue. Examples are licences required for marriage, driving, keeping a gun, and for sale of alcohol. The term also refers to permission (in writing or not) granted by a person; for example, allowing use of his or her land for an agreed purpose. An example of a contractual licence is attendance on the property of another for the purpose of public entertainment.

licensing practice by which fashion designers allow manufacturers to use their names on cosmetics, perfume bottles, jewellery, and other fashion and household accessories. It was pioneered by Pierre ◊Cardin.

licensing laws laws governing the sale of alcoholic drinks. Most countries have some restrictions on the sale of alcoholic drinks, if not an outright ban, as in the case of Islamic countries.

In Britain, sales can only be made by pubs, restaurants, shops, and clubs which hold licences obtained from licensing justices. The hours during which alcoholic drinks can be sold are restricted, but they have been extended in England and Wales in line with Scotland. Since 1988, licensed premises can sell alcohol between 11 am and 11 pm Monday to Saturday, and 12 noon to 3 pm and 7 pm to 10.30 pm on Sundays. These hours may be extended for special occasions, by application to the licensing justices.

lichen any organism of the group Lichenes, which consists of a specific fungus and a specific alga existing in a mutually beneficial relationship. Found as coloured patches or spongelike masses adhering to trees, rocks, and other substrates, lichens flourish

LIBYA

Great Socialist People's Libyan Arab Republic

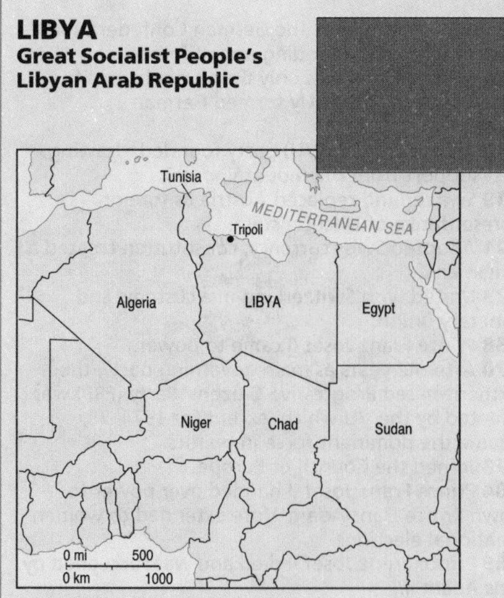

national name *Jamahiriya al-Arabiya al-Libya al-Shabiya al-Ishtirakiya al-Uzma*
area 1,759,540 sq km/679,182 sq mi
capital Tripoli
major ports Benghazi, Misurata, Tobruk
physical features flat to undulating plains with plateaus and depressions stretch S from the Mediterranean coast to an extremely dry desert interior
head of state and government Moamer al-Khaddhafi from 1969
political system one-party socialist state
administrative divisions 13 provinces
political party Arab Socialist Union (ASU), radical, left-wing
population 5,407,000 (1995 est)
population growth rate 3.5% (1990–95); 3.2% (2000–05)
ethnic distribution majority are of Berber and Arab origin, with a small number of Tebou amd Touareg nomads and semi-nomads, mainly in the S
life expectancy 62 (men), 65 (women)
literacy rate men 75%, women 50%
language Arabic
religion Sunni Muslim
currency Libyan dinar
GDP (US $) 32.8 billion (1994 est)
growth rate −4.5% (1994)
exports oil, natural gas

HISTORY
7th C BC Tripolitania, in western Libya, was settled by Phoenicians, who founded Tripoli, and became eastern province of Carthaginian kingdom, which was centred on Tunis to the W.
4th C BC Cyrenaica, in eastern Libya, colonized by Greeks, who called it Libya.
74 BC Became a Roman province, with Tripolitania part of Africa Nova province and Cyrenaica combined with Crete as a province.
19 BC The desert region of Fezzan (Phazzania), inhabited by Garmante people, was conquered by Rome.
6th C AD Came under control of Byzantine Empire.
7th C Conquered by Arabs, who spread Islam: Egypt ruled Cyrenaica and Morrocan Berber Almohads controlled Tripolitania.
mid-16th C Became part of Turkish Ottoman Empire, who combined the three ancient regions into one regency in Tripoli.
1711 Karamanli (Qaramanli) dynasty established virtual independence from Ottomans.
1835 Ottoman control reasserted.
1911–12 Conquered by Italy.
1920s Resistance to Italian rule by the Sanusi order and Umar al-Mukhtar.
1934 Colony named Libya.
1942 Italians ousted, and area divided into three provinces: Fezzan (under French control), Cyrenaica, and Tripolitania (under British control).
1951 Achieved independence as the United Kingdom of Libya, under King Idris, the former Amir of Cyrenaica and leader of the Sanusi order.
1959 Oil discovered, transforming the economy, but also leading to unsettling social changes.
1969 King deposed in a military coup led by Col Moamer al-Khaddhafi. Revolution Command Council set up and the Arab Socialist Union (ASU) proclaimed the only legal party in a new puritanical Islamic-socialist republic which sought Pan-Arab unity.
1970s Economic activity collectivized, oil industry nationalized, opposition suppressed by Khaddhafi's revolutionary regime.
1972 Proposed federation of Libya, Syria, and Egypt abandoned.
1980 Proposed merger with Syria abandoned. Libyan troops began fighting in northern Chad.
1986 US bombing of Khaddhafi's headquarters, following allegations of his complicity in terrorist activities.
1988 Diplomatic relations with Chad restored; political prisoners freed; economy liberalised.
1989 US navy shot down two Libyan planes; reconciliation with Egypt.
1992 Khaddhafi under international pressure to extradite suspected Lockerbie and UTA (Union de Transports Aériens) bombers for trial outside Libya. United Nations (UN) sanctions imposed; several countries severed diplomatic and air links with Libya.
1995 Antigovernment campaign of violence by Islamicists. Hundreds of Palestinians and thousands of foreign workers expelled.

SEE ALSO Khaddafi, Moamer al

under adverse conditions. Some lichens have food value, for example, reindeer moss and Iceland moss; others give dyes, such as litmus, or are used in medicine. They are sensitive to atmospheric pollution (see ◊indicator species).

Lichtenstein Roy 1923–1997. US Pop artist. He was best known for using advertising imagery and comic-strip techniques, often focusing on popular ideals of romance and heroism, as in *Whaam!* 1963 (Tate Gallery, London). He also produced sculptures in brass, plastic, and enamelled metal.

Liddell Hart Basil Henry 1895–1970. British military strategist. He was an exponent of mechanized warfare, and his ideas were adopted in Germany in 1935 in creating the 1st Panzer Division, combining motorized infantry and tanks. From 1937 he advised the UK War Office on army reorganization.

Lidice Czechoslovak mining village, replacing one destroyed by the Nazis on 10 June 1942 as a reprisal for the assassination of Reinhard ◊Heydrich. The men were shot, the women sent to concentration camps, and the children taken to Germany.

Liebig Justus, Baron von 1803–1873. German chemist, a major contributor to agricultural chemistry. He introduced the theory of compound ◊radicals and discovered chloroform and chloral.

Many new methods of organic analysis were introduced by Liebig, and he devised ways of determining hydrogen, carbon, and halogens in organic compounds. He demonstrated that plants absorb minerals (and water) from the soil and postulated that the carbon used by plants comes from carbon dioxide in the air rather than from the soil.

Liechtenstein landlocked country in W central Europe, bounded E by Austria and W by Switzerland. *See country box on p. 632.*

lied (German 'song', plural ***lieder***) musical dramatization of a poem, usually for solo voice and piano; referring to Romantic songs of Schubert, Schumann, Brahms, and Hugo Wolf.

lie detector instrument that records graphically certain body activities, such as thoracic and abdominal respiration, blood pressure, pulse rate, and galvanic skin response (changes in electrical resistance of the skin). Marked changes in these activities when a person answers a question may indicate that the person is lying.

Liège (Flemish ***Luik***) industrial city (weapons, textiles, paper, chemicals), capital of Liège province in Belgium, SE of Brussels, on the river Meuse; population (1995) 192,000. The province of Liège has an area of 3,900 sq km/1,505 sq mi and a population (1995) of 1,015,000.

Lifar Serge 1905–1986. Ukrainian dancer and choreographer. He studied under ◊Nijinsky, joined the Diaghilev company 1923, and was artistic director and principal dancer of the Paris Opéra 1929–44 and 1947–59. He completely revitalized the company and in so doing, reversed the diminished fortunes of French ballet. A great experimenter, he produced his first ballet without music, *Icare* 1935. He developed the role of the male dancer in his *Prometheus* 1929 and *Romeo and Juliet* (music by Prokofiev) 1955.

life the ability to grow, reproduce, and respond to such stimuli as light, heat, and sound. It is thought that life on Earth began about 4 billion years ago. Over time, life has evolved from primitive single-celled organisms to complex multicellular ones. The earliest fossil evidence of life is threadlike chains of cells discovered 1980 in deposits in NW Australia that have been dated as 3.5 billion years old.

Life originated in the primitive oceans. The original atmosphere, 4,000 million years ago, consisted of carbon dioxide, nitrogen, and water. It has been shown in the laboratory that more complex organic molecules, such as ◊amino acids and ◊nucleotides, can be produced from these ingredients by passing electric sparks through a mixture. It has been suggested that lightning was extremely common in the early atmosphere, and that this combination of conditions could have resulted in the oceans becoming rich in organic molecules, the so-called 'primeval soup'. These molecules may then have organized into clusters capable of reproducing and of developing eventually into simple cells.

Once the atmosphere changed to its present composition, life could only be created by living organisms (a process called ◊biogenesis).

life cycle in biology, the sequence of developmental stages through which members of a given species pass. Most vertebrates have a simple life cycle consisting of ◊fertilization of sex cells or ◊gametes, a period of development as an ◊embryo, a period of juvenile growth after hatching or birth, an adulthood including ◊sexual reproduction, and finally death. Invertebrate life cycles are generally more complex and may involve major reconstitution of the individual's appearance (◊metamorphosis) and completely different styles of life. Plants have a special type of life cycle with two distinct phases, known as ◊alternation of generations. Many insects such as cicadas, dragonflies, and mayflies have a long larval or pupal phase and a short adult phase. Dragonflies live an aquatic life as larvae and an aerial life during the adult phase. In

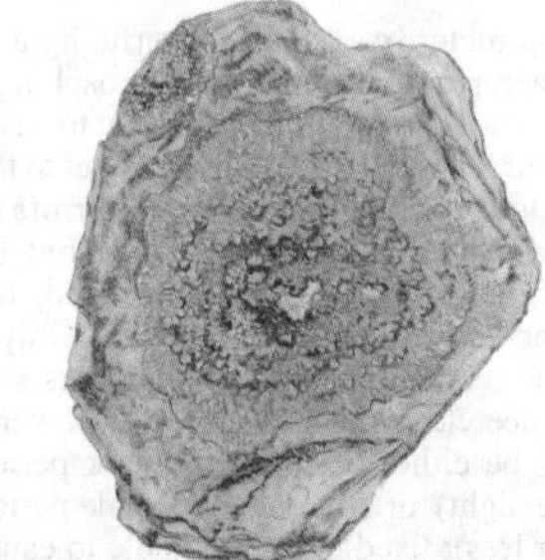

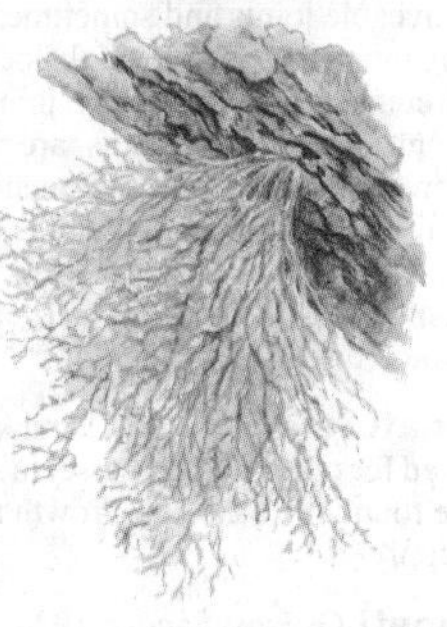

lichen A lichen is a symbiotic association between an alga and a fungus – in other words, each lichen is not one organism but two. Lichens grow very slowly, usually as encrustations on rocks, walls, or wood. They are found throughout the world but are unable to survive where the atmosphere is polluted, so they are good indicators of clean air.

LIECHTENSTEIN
Principality of

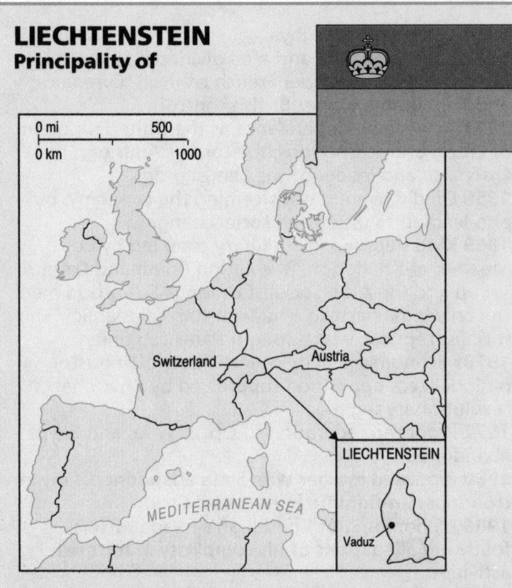

national name *Fürstentum Liechtenstein*
area 160 sq km/62 sq mi
capital Vaduz
major towns/cities Balzers, Schaan, Ruggell
physical features landlocked Alpine; includes part of Rhine Valley in W
head of state Prince Hans Adam II from 1989
head of government Mario Frick from 1993
political system constitutional monarchy
administrative divisions two districts comprising 11 communes
political parties Patriotic Union (VU), conservative; Progressive Citizens' Party (FBP), conservative
population 30,629 (1994 est)
population growth rate 1.4% (1990–95)
ethnic distribution indigenous population of Alemannic origin; one-third of the population are foreign-born resident workers
life expectancy 78 (men), 83 (women)
literacy rate 99%
languages German (official); an Alemannic dialect is also spoken
religions Roman Catholic (87%), Protestant
currency Swiss franc
GDP (US $) 1.52 billion (1994)
growth rate −0.1% (1994)
exports microchips, dental products, small machinery, processed foods, postage stamps

HISTORY
c. AD 500 Settled by the Germanic-speaking Alemanni tribe.
1342 Became a sovereign state.
1434 Present boundaries established.
1719 Former independent lordships of Schellenberg and Vaduz were united by the Princes of Liechtenstein to form the present state.
1815–66 A member of the German Confederation.
1868 Abolished its standing armed forces.
1871 Liechtenstein was only German principality to stay outside the newly formed German Empire.
1918 Patriotic Union (VU) party founded, drawing most support from the mountainous S.
1919 Switzerland replaced Austria as foreign representative of Liechtenstein.
1921 Adopted Swiss currency; constitution created a parliament.
1923 United with Switzerland in a customs and monetary union.
1938 Prince Franz Josef II came to power.
1970 After 42 years as main governing party, the northern-based Progressive Citizens' Party (FBP) was defeated by the VU which, except for 1974–78, became the dominant force in politics.
1978 Joined the Council of Europe.
1984 Prince Franz Josef II handed over power to Crown Prince Hans Adam. Vote extended to women in national elections.
1989 Prince Franz Josef II died and was succeeded by Hans Adam II.
1990 Became a member of the United Nations.
1991 Became seventh member of European Free Trade Association.
1993 Mario Frick of the VU became Europe's youngest head of government, aged 28, after two general elections.

many invertebrates and protozoa there is a sequence of stages in the life cycle, and in parasites different stages often occur in different host organisms.

life expectancy average lifespan that can be presumed of a person at birth. It depends on nutrition, disease control, environmental contaminants, war, stress, and living standards in general. There is a marked difference between industrialized countries, which generally have an ageing population, and the poorest countries, such as Bangladesh and Ethiopia, where life expectancy is much shorter.

life sciences scientific study of the living world as a whole, a new synthesis of several traditional scientific disciplines including ◊biology, ◊zoology, and ◊botany, and newer, more specialized areas of study such as ◊biophysics and ◊sociobiology. This approach has led to many new ideas and discoveries as well as to an emphasis on ◊ecology, the study of living organisms in their natural environments.

LIFFE (acronym for ***London International Financial Futures Exchange***) one of the exchanges in London where ◊futures contracts are traded. It opened 1982. It provides a worldwide exchange for futures dealers and investors, and began options trading in 1985. It was a forerunner of the ◊Big Bang in bringing US-style 'open-house' dealing (as opposed to telephone dealing) to the UK.

Liffey river in the eastern Republic of Ireland, flowing from the Wicklow Mountains to Dublin Bay; length 80 km/50 mi.

lift (US ***elevator***) device for lifting passengers and goods vertically between the floors of a building. US inventor Elisha Graves ◊Otis developed the first passenger lift, installed in 1857. The invention of the lift allowed the development of the skyscraper from the 1880s.

ligament strong, flexible connective tissue, made of the protein ◊collagen, which joins bone to bone at moveable joints and sometimes encloses the joints. Ligaments prevent bone dislocation (under normal circumstances) but allow joint flexion. The ligaments around the joints are composed of white fibrous tissue. Other ligaments are composed of yellow elastic tissue, which is adapted to support a continuous but varying stress, as in the ligament connecting the various cartilages of the ◊larynx (voice box).

ligature any surgical device (nylon, gut, wire) used for tying a blood vessel to stop it bleeding, or to tie round the base of a growth to constrict its blood supply.

Ligeti György Sándor 1923– . Hungarian-born Austrian composer. He developed a dense, highly chromatic, polyphonic style in which melody and rhythm are sometimes lost in shifting blocks of sound. He achieved international prominence with *Atmosphères* 1961 and *Requiem* 1965, which achieved widespread fame as background music for Stanley Kubrick's film epic *2001: A Space Odyssey* 1968. Other works include an opera *Le Grand Macabre* 1978, and *Poème symphonique* 1962, for 100 metronomes.

light electromagnetic waves in the visible range, having a wavelength from about 400 nanometres in the extreme violet to about 770 nanometres in the extreme red. Light is considered to exhibit particle and wave properties, and the fundamental particle, or quantum, of light is called the photon. The speed of light (and of all electromagnetic radiation) in a vacuum is approximately 300,000 km/186,000 mi per second, and is a universal constant denoted by *c*.

Isaac ◊Newton was the first to discover, 1666, that sunlight is composed of a mixture of light of different colours in certain proportions and that it could be separated into its components by dispersion. Before his time it was supposed that dispersion of light produced colour instead of separating already existing colours. The speed of light was first measured accurately in 1676 by Danish astronomer Ole Römer (1644–1710).

light bulb incandescent filament lamp, first demonstrated by Joseph Swan in the UK 1878 and Thomas Edison in the USA 1879. The present-day light bulb is a thin glass bulb filled with an inert mixture of nitrogen and argon gas. It contains a filament made of fine tungsten wire. When electricity is passed through the wire, it glows white hot, producing light.

light-emitting diode (LED) means of displaying symbols in electronic instruments and devices. An LED is made of ◊semiconductor material, such as gallium arsenide phosphide, that glows when electricity is passed through it. The first digital watches and calculators had LED displays, but many later models use ◊liquid-crystal displays.

lighthouse structure carrying a powerful light to warn ships or aeroplanes that they are approaching a place (usually land) dangerous or important to navigation. The light is magnified and directed out to the horizon or up to the zenith by a series of mirrors or prisms. Increasingly lighthouses are powered by electricity and automated rather than staffed; the more recent models also emit radio signals. Only a minority of the remaining staffed lighthouses still use dissolved acetylene gas as a source of power.

Lights may be either flashing (the dark period exceeding the light) or rotating (the dark period being equal or less); fixed lights are liable to cause confusion. The pattern of lighting is individually varied so that ships or aircraft can identify the lighthouse. Among early lighthouses were the Pharos of Alexandria (about 280 BC) and those built by the Romans at Ostia, Ravenna, Boulogne, and Dover. In England beacons burning in church towers served as lighthouses until the 17th century, and in the earliest lighthouses, such as the Eddystone, first built 1698, open fires or candles were used. Where reefs or sandbanks made erection of a lighthouse impossible, lightships were often installed; increasingly these are being replaced by fixed, small, automated lighthouses. Where it is impossible to install a fixed structure, unattended lightbuoys equipped for up to a year's service may be used. In the UK, these are gradually being converted from acetylene gas in cylinders to solar power. In fog, sound signals are made (horns, sirens, explosives), and in the case of lightbuoys, fog bells and whistles are operated by the movement of the waves.

In the UK there are three lighthouse authorities: Trinity House, the Northern Lighthouse Board, and Commissioners of Irish Lights.

lightning high-voltage electrical discharge between two charged rainclouds or between a cloud and the Earth, caused by the build-up of electrical charges. Air in the path of lightning ionizes (becomes conducting), and expands; the accompanying noise is heard as thunder. Currents of 20,000 amperes and temperatures of 30,000°C/54,000°F are common.

lightning conductor device that protects a tall building from lightning strike by providing an easier path for current to flow to earth than through the building. It consists of a thick copper strip of very low resistance connected to the ground below. A good connection to the ground is essential and is made by burying a large metal plate deep in the damp earth.

light pen in computing, a device resembling an ordinary pen, used to indicate locations on a computer screen. With certain computer-aided design (◊CAD) programs, the light pen can be used to instruct the computer to change the shape, size, position, and colours of sections of a screen image.

The pen has a photoreceptor at its tip that emits signals when light from the screen passes beneath it. From the timing of this signal and a gridlike representation of the screen in the computer memory, a computer program can calculate the position of the light pen.

light second unit of length, equal to the distance travelled by light in one second. It is equal to 2.997925×10^8 m/9.835592×10^8 ft. See ◊light year.

light watt unit of radiant power (brightness of light). One light watt is the power required to produce a perceived brightness equal to that of light at a wavelength of 550 nanometres and 680 lumens.

light year in astronomy, the distance travelled by a beam of light in a vacuum in one year, approximately 9.46 trillion (million million) km/5.88 trillion miles.

lignin naturally occurring substance produced by plants to strengthen their tissues. It is difficult for ◊enzymes to attack lignin, so living organisms cannot digest wood, with the exception of a few specialized fungi and bacteria. Lignin is the essential ingredient of all wood.

lignite type of ◊coal that is brown and fibrous, with a relatively low carbon content. As a fuel it is less efficient because more of it must be burned to produce the same amount of energy generated by bituminous coal. Lignite also has a high sulphur content and is more polluting. It is burned to generate power in Scandinavia and some former eastern bloc countries because it is the only fuel resource available without importing.

Liguria coastal region of NW Italy, which includes the resorts of the Italian Riviera, lying between the western Alps and the Mediterranean Gulf of Genoa. The region comprises the provinces of Genova, La Spezia, Imperia, and Savona, with a population (1992 est) of 1,668,900 and an area of 5,418 sq km/2,093 sq mi. Genoa is the chief city and port.

Li Hongzhang or ***Li Hung-chang*** 1823–1901. Chinese politician, promulgator of Western ideas and modernization. He was governor general of Zhili (or Chihli) and high commissioner of the Northern Ports 1870–95, responsible for foreign affairs. He established a modern navy, the Beiyang fleet, 1888, which was humiliatingly destroyed in the ◊Sino-Japanese War.

Likud alliance of right-wing Israeli political parties that defeated the Labour Party coalition in the 1977 election and brought Menachem Begin to power. In 1987 Likud became part of an uneasy national coalition with Labour, formed to solve Israel's economic crisis. In 1989 another coalition was formed under Yitzhak Shamir. Likud was defeated by the Labour Party in the 1992 general election. After 1993, under the leadership of Binyamin Netanyahu, it adopted a much harder line in the Middle East peace process. In 1996 Netanyahu became Israel's first directly-elected prime minister, forming a Likud-led government.

lilac any flowering Old World shrub of the genus *Syringa* (such as *S. vulgaris*) of the olive family Oleaceae, bearing panicles (clusters) of small, sweetly scented, white or purplish flowers.

Lilburne John c. 1614–1657. English republican agitator. He was imprisoned 1638–40 for circulating Puritan pamphlets, fought in the Parliamentary army in the Civil War, and by his advocacy of a democratic republic won the leadership of the Levellers, the democratic party in the English Revolution.

Lilienthal Otto 1848–1896. German aviation pioneer who inspired US aviators Orville and Wilbur ◊Wright. From 1891 he made and successfully flew many gliders, including two biplanes, before he was killed in a glider crash.

Lilienthal demonstrated the superiority of cambered wings over flat wings – the principle of the aerofoil. In his planes the pilot was suspended by the arms, as in a modern hang-glider. He achieved glides of more than 300 m/1,000 ft.

Lilith in the Old Testament, an Assyrian female demon of the night. According to Jewish tradition in the ◊Talmud, she was the wife of Adam before Eve's creation.

Lille (Flemish ***Ryssel***) industrial city (textiles, chemicals, engineering, distilling), capital of Nord-Pas-de-Calais, France, on the river Deûle; population (1990) 178,300, metropolitan area 936,000. The world's first entirely automatic underground system was opened here 1982. The Eurostar train stops here, at the new Lille Europe station.

During the Middle Ages, Lille was the capital of Flanders. Claimed by Louis XIV 1667, it was captured by the Duke of Marlborough 1708, and ceded to France by the Treaty of Utrecht 1713. It was occupied by the Germans in World War I.

lightning Thunderstorm over Chicago, USA. The heat generated by a lightning flash causes oxygen and nitrogen in the atmosphere to combine, forming nitrates that are carried down to the Earth by the rain. This helps to replenish nutrients in the soil. *Corbis*

Lillee Dennis Keith 1949– . Australian cricketer. He is regarded as the best fast bowler of his generation. He made his Test debut in the 1970–71 season and subsequently played for his country 70 times. Lillee was the first to take 300 wickets in Test cricket. He played Sheffield Shield cricket for Western Australia and at the end of his career made a comeback with Tasmania.

Lilongwe capital of Malawi since 1975, on the Lilongwe River; population (1993) 268,000. Products include tobacco and textiles. Capital Hill, 5 km/3 mi from the old city, is the site of government buildings and offices.

lily plant of the genus *Lilium*, family Liliaceae, of which there are some 80 species, most with showy, trumpet-shaped flowers growing from bulbs. The lily family includes hyacinths, tulips, asparagus, and plants of the onion genus. The term 'lily' is also applied to many lilylike plants of allied genera and families.

lily The martagon, or turk's cap, lily *Lilium martagon* in flower in the Swiss Alps. Native to mainland Europe and Asia, the martagon has become naturalized in woods at scattered locations around the British Isles. *Premaphotos Wildlife*

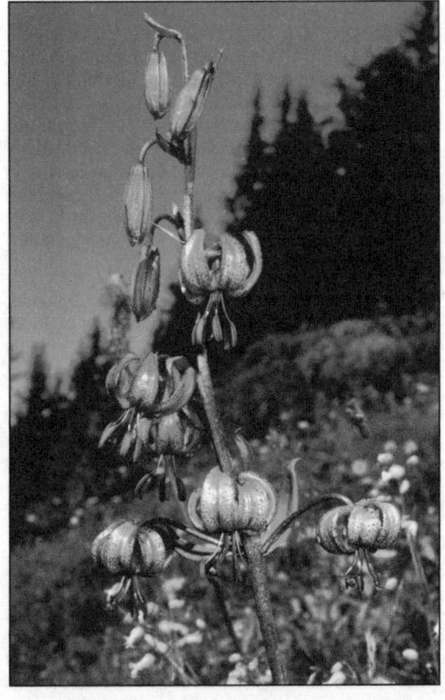

lily of the valley plant *Convallaria majalis* of the lily family Liliaceae, growing in woods in Europe, N Asia, and North America. The small, pendant, white flowers are strongly scented. The plant is often cultivated.

Lima capital of Peru, an industrial city (textiles, chemicals, glass, cement) on the Rimac River, with its port at Callao; population (1993) 5,706,100. It was founded by the Spaniard Francisco Pizarro 1535, and rebuilt after it was destroyed by an earthquake 1746. Surviving structures of the Spanish colonial period include the National University of San Marcos, founded 1551, the cathedral, the government palace (the rebuilt palace of the viceroys), and the Senate House, originally the headquarters of the Inquisition. A third of the population live in shantytowns on the outskirts of the city.

limbo in Christian theology, a region for the souls of those who were not admitted to the divine vision. *Limbus infantum* was a place where unbaptized infants enjoyed inferior blessedness, and *limbus patrum* was where the prophets of the Old Testament dwelt. The word was first used in this sense in the 13th century by Thomas Aquinas.

Limbourg province of N Belgium, bounded N and E by the Netherlands; capital Hasselt; area 2,422 sq km/935 sq mi; population (1995) 771,600. Industries include sugar refining and food processing; towns include Genk and Tongeren. It has the river Demer, the Kempen heathland in the N, rich coalfields, and agriculture in the S. The province was formerly part of the feudal duchy of Limburg (which was divided 1839 into today's Belgian and Dutch provinces).

Limbourg brothers Franco-Flemish painters, Paul (Pol), Herman, and Jan (Hennequin, Janneken), active in the late 14th and early 15th centuries, first in Paris, then at the ducal court of Burgundy. Patronized by Jean de Berry, Duke of Burgundy, from about 1404, they illustrated two Books of ◊Hours that are masterpieces of the ◊International Gothic style, the *Belles Heures* about 1408 (Metropolitan Museum of Art, New York), and *Les Très Riches Heures du Duc de Berry* about 1413–15 (Musée Condé, Chantilly). Their miniature paintings include a series of scenes representing the months, presenting an almost fairytale world of pinnacled castles with lords and ladies, full of detail and brilliant decorative effects. All three brothers were dead by 1416.

Limburg southernmost province of the Netherlands, on the river Maas (Meuse); capital Maastricht; area 2,170 sq km/838 sq mi; population (1995 est) 1,130,050. Industries include chemicals, cement, fertilizer; mixed arable farming and horticulture are also important. The former coal industry is still remembered at Kerkrade, alleged site of the first European coal mine. A monument marks the *Drielandenpunt*, where the Dutch, German, and Belgian borders meet. The province was formerly part of the duchy of Limburg (which was divided 1839 into today's Dutch and Belgian provinces).

lime or ***quicklime*** CaO (technical name ***calcium oxide***) white powdery substance used in making mortar and cement. It is made commercially by heating calcium carbonate ($CaCO_3$), obtained from limestone or chalk, in a lime kiln. Quicklime readily absorbs water to become calcium hydroxide ($Ca(OH)_2$), known as slaked lime, which is used to reduce soil acidity.

lime small thorny bush *Citrus aurantifolia* of the rue family Rutaceae, native to India. The white flowers are succeeded by light green or yellow fruits, limes, which resemble lemons but are more globular in shape.

lime or ***linden*** deciduous tree, genus *Tilia*, of the family Tiliaceae native to the northern hemisphere. The leaves are heart-shaped and coarsely toothed, and the flowers are cream-coloured and fragrant. The ***common lime*** *T. vulgaris* bears greenish-yellow fragrant flowers in clusters on a winged stalk, succeeded by small round fruits. It was a common tree in lowland regions of prehistoric England. The ***small-leaved lime*** *T. cordata* is found in areas of ancient woodland in SE England.

limerick five-line humorous verse, often nonsensical, which first appeared in England about 1820 and was popularized by Edward ◊Lear. An example is: 'There was a young lady of Riga, Who rode with a smile on a tiger; They returned from the ride With the lady inside, And the smile on the face of the tiger.'

Limerick county of the Republic of Ireland, in the province of Munster; county town Limerick; area 2,690 sq km/1,038 sq mi; population (1991) 161,900. The land is fertile, with hills in the south. Industries include dairy products, lace, and hydroelectric power.

Limerick county town of Limerick, Republic of Ireland, the main port of W Ireland, on the Shannon estuary; population (1991) 52,000. It was founded in the 12th century. Industries include flour milling, tanning, and brewing.

limestone sedimentary rock composed chiefly of calcium carbonate $CaCO_3$, either derived from the shells of marine organisms or precipitated from solution, mostly in the ocean. Caves commonly occur in limestone. ◊Karst is a type of limestone landscape. Various types of limestone are used as building stone. ◊Marble is metamorphosed limestone. Certain so-called marbles are not in fact marbles but fine-grained fossiliferous limestones that take an attractive polish.

limestone pavement bare rock surface resembling a block of chocolate, found on limestone plateaus. It is formed by the weathering of limestone into individual upstanding blocks, called clints, separated from each other by joints, called grykes. The weathering process is thought to entail a combination of freeze-thaw (the alternate freezing and thawing of ice in cracks) and carbonation (the dissolving of minerals in the limestone by weakly acidic rainwater). Malham Tarn in North Yorkshire is an example of a limestone pavement.

limewater common name for a dilute solution of slaked lime (calcium hydroxide, $Ca(OH)_2$). In chemistry, it is used to detect the presence of carbon dioxide. If a gas containing carbon dioxide is bubbled through limewater, the solution turns milky owing to the formation of calcium carbonate ($CaCO_3$).

Limitation, Statutes of in English law, acts of Parliament limiting the time within which legal action must be inaugurated. Actions for breach of contract and most other civil wrongs must be started within six years. Personal injury claims must usually be brought within three years. In actions in respect of land and of contracts under seal, the period is 12 years.

‘No man is good enough to govern another man without that other's consent.’

ABRAHAM LINCOLN
Speech, 16 Oct 1854

limited company company for whose debts the members are liable only to a limited extent. The capital of a limited company is divided into small units, and profits are distributed according to shareholding. It is the usual type of company formation in the UK and has its origins in the trading companies that began to proliferate in the 16th century.

limited liability legal safeguard that allows shareholders to be liable for their company's debts only up to and including the value of their shareholding. For example, if a limited liability company goes bankrupt with debts of £1 million, the shareholders are not liable for any of that debt, although the value of their shares in the company would be worthless. Private and public limited companies, cooperatives, and public corporations have limited liability in the UK, but sole proprietorships and most partnerships do not.

limiting factor in biology, any factor affecting the rate of a metabolic reaction. Levels of light or of carbon dioxide are limiting factors in ◊photosynthesis because both are necessary for the production of carbohydrates. In experiments, photosynthesis is observed to slow down and eventually stop as the levels of light decrease.

limits, territorial and fishing the limits of sea area to which an adjoining coastal state can claim territorial or fishing rights under ◊maritime law.

Limoges city and capital of Limousin, France; population (1990) 136,400. Fine enamels were made here in the medieval period, and it is the centre of the modern French porcelain industry. Other industries include textiles, electrical equipment, and metal goods. The city was sacked by the Black Prince, the eldest son of Edward III of England, 1370.

limonite iron ore, mostly poorly crystalline iron oxyhydroxide, but usually mixed with ◊hematite and other iron oxides. Also known as brown iron ore, it is often found in bog deposits.

Limousin former province and modern region of central France; area 16,900 sq km/6,544 sq mi; population (1990) 722,900. It consists of the *départements* of Corrèze, Creuse, and Haute-Vienne. The chief town is Limoges. A thinly populated and largely infertile region, it is crossed by the mountains of the Massif Central. Fruit and vegetables are produced in the more fertile lowlands. Kaolin is mined.

limpet any of various marine ◊snails belonging to several families and genera, especially *Acmaea* and *Patella*. A limpet has a conical shell and adheres firmly to rocks by its disclike foot. Limpets leave their fixed positions only to graze on seaweeds, always returning to the same spot. They are found in the Atlantic and Pacific.

Limpopo river in SE Africa, rising in the Transvaal and reaching the Indian Ocean in Mozambique; length 1,600 km/1,000 mi.

Lin Biao or ***Lin Piao*** 1908–1971. Chinese politician and general. He joined the communists 1927, became a commander of ◊Mao Zedong's Red Army, and led the Northeast People's Liberation Army in the civil war after 1945. He became defence minister 1959, and as vice chair of the party 1969 he was expected to be Mao's successor. In 1972 the government announced that Lin had been killed in an aeroplane crash in Mongolia on 17 Sept 1971 while fleeing to the USSR following an abortive coup attempt.

Lincoln industrial city in Lincolnshire, England; population (1991) 82,000. Manufacturing includes excavators, cranes, gas turbines, radios, vehicle components, cattle feed, pharmaceuticals, power units for oil platforms, and cosmetics.

Under the Romans it was the flourishing colony of Lindum, and in the Middle Ages it was a centre for the wool trade. Paulinus built a church here in the 7th century, and the 11th–15th-century cathedral has the earliest Gothic work in Britain. The 12th-century High Bridge is the oldest in Britain still to have buildings on it.

Lincoln industrial city and capital of Nebraska, USA; population (1992) 197,500. Industries include engineering, pharmaceuticals, electronic and electrical equipment, and food processing. It was known as Lancaster until 1867, when it was renamed after Abraham Lincoln and designated the state capital.

Lincoln Abraham 1809–1865. 16th president of the USA 1861–65, a Republican. In the American ◊Civil War, his chief concern was the preservation of the Union from which the Confederate (Southern) slave states had seceded on his election. In 1863 he announced the freedom of the slaves with the Emancipation Proclamation. He was re-elected 1864 with victory for the North in sight, but was assassinated at the end of the war.

early career Lincoln was born in a log cabin in Kentucky. Self-educated, he practised law from 1837 in Springfield, Illinois. He was a member of the state legislature 1832–42, during which period he was known as Honest Abe, and in 1846 sat in Congress, although his law practice remained his priority. The repeal of the Missouri Compromise 1854 and the reopening of the debate on the extension of slavery in the new territories of the USA drew him back into politics. He joined the new Republican Party 1856 and two years later was chosen as their candidate for senator in Illinois, opposing the incumbent Stephen Douglas, who had been largely responsible for repeal of the Compromise. In the ensuing debate, Lincoln revealed his power as an orator, but failed to wrest the post from Douglas. However, he had established a national reputation and in 1860 was chosen by the Republicans, now pledged to oppose the extension of slavery, as their presidential candidate. He was elected on a minority vote, defeating Douglas and another Democratic Party candidate.

presidency Prior to Lincoln's inauguration, seven Southern states proclaimed their formal secession from the Union. Lincoln's inaugural address March 1861 was conciliatory: he declared he had no intention of interfering with slavery where it already existed, but pronounced the Union indissoluble, declaring that no state had the right to secede from it. His refusal to concede to Confederate demands for the evacuation of the federal garrison at Fort Sumter, Charleston, South Carolina the following month precipitated the first hostilities of the Civil War.

In 1862, following an important Union victory at Antietam, Lincoln proclaimed the emancipation of all slaves in states engaged in rebellion, thereby surpassing the limits of the constitution he had gone to war to maintain. In the Gettysburg Address 1863 he declared the aims of preserving a 'nation conceived in liberty, and dedicated to the proposition that all men are created equal'. With the war turning in favour of the North, he was re-elected 1864 with a large majority on a National Union ticket, having advocated a reconciliatory policy towards the South 'with malice towards none, with charity for all'.

Lincoln US president Abraham Lincoln. Lincoln, a Republican, was the 16th president of the USA. He was assassinated 1865, five days after the surrender of the Confederate forces in the American Civil War. *Image Select (UK) Ltd*

Five days after General Lee's surrender, Lincoln was shot in a theatre audience by an actor and Confederate sympathizer, John Wilkes ◊Booth.

Lincolnshire county of E England
area 5,890 sq km/2,274 sq mi (*see United Kingdom map*)
towns and cities Lincoln (administrative headquarters), Skegness
features Lincoln Wolds; marshy coastline; the Fens in the SE; rivers: Witham, Welland; 16th-century Burghley House; Belton House, a Restoration mansion; Gibralter Point National Nature Reserve
industries cattle, sheep, horses, cereals, flower bulbs, oil, vegetables
population (1991) 584,500
famous people Isaac Newton, John Wesley, Alfred Tennyson, Margaret Thatcher.

Lind Jenny (Johanna Maria) 1820–1887. Swedish soprano. She had a remarkable range, and was nicknamed the 'Swedish nightingale'. She toured the USA 1850–52 under the management of circus promoter P T Barnum.

Lindbergh Charles A(ugustus) 1902–1974. US aviator. He made the first solo nonstop flight in 33.5 hours across the Atlantic (Roosevelt Field, Long Island, New York, to Le Bourget airport, Paris) 1927 in the *Spirit of St Louis*, a Ryan monoplane designed by him.

Lindbergh attended the US Army School in Texas 1924 and became an officer in the Army Air Service Reserve 1925. Learning that Raymond B Orteig had offered a prize of £25,000 for the person who first made a nonstop air flight between New York and Paris, he appealed to some St Louis businessmen, who agreed to finance him.

linden another name for the ◊lime tree.

Lindisfarne or ***Holy Island*** island in the North Sea, area 10 sq km/4 sq mi, 3 km/2 mi off Northumberland, England, with which it is connected by a causeway. St ◊Aidan founded a monastery here 635.

Lindow Man remains of an Iron Age man discovered in a peat bog at Lindow Marsh, Cheshire, UK, in 1984. The chemicals in the bog had kept the body in an excellent state of preservation. 'Pete Marsh', as the archaeologists nicknamed him, had been knocked unconscious, strangled, and then had his throat cut before being thrown into the bog. He may have been a sacrificial victim, as Celtic peoples often threw offerings to the gods into rivers and marshes. His stomach contained part of an unleavened barley 'bannock' that might have been given as a sacrificial offering. His well-cared-for nails indicate that he might have been a Druid prince who became a willing sacrifice.

linear accelerator or ***linac*** in physics, a type of particle ◊accelerator in which the particles move along a straight tube. Particles pass through a linear accelerator only once – unlike those in a cyclotron (a ring-shaped accelerator), which make many revolutions, gaining energy each time. The world's longest linac is the Stanford Linear Collider, in the USA, in which electrons and positrons are accelerated along a straight track 3.2 km/2 mi long and then steered into a head-on collision with other particles.

linear equation in mathematics, a relationship between two variables that, when plotted on Cartesian axes produces a straight-line graph; the equation has the general form $y = mx + c$, where m is the slope of the line represented by the equation and c is the y-intercept, or the value of y where the line crosses the y-axis in the ◊Cartesian coordinate system. Sets of linear equations can be used to describe the behaviour of buildings, bridges, trusses, and other static structures.

linear motor type of electric motor, an induction motor in which the fixed stator and moving armature are straight and parallel to each other (rather than being circular and one inside the other as in an ordinary induction motor). Linear motors are used, for example, to power sliding doors. There is a magnetic force between the stator and armature; this force has been used to support a vehicle, as in the experimental ◊maglev linear motor train.

Lineker Gary 1960– . English footballer. He scored over 250 goals in 550 games for Leicester, Everton, Barcelona, and Tottenham. With 48 goals in 80 internationals he failed by one goal to equal Bobby Charlton's record of 49 goals for England. Lineker was elected Footballer of the Year 1986 and 1992, and was leading scorer at the 1986 World Cup finals. In 1993 he moved to Japan to play for Nagoya Grampus Eight.

linen yarn spun and the textile woven from the fibres of the stem of the ◊flax plant. Used by the ancient Egyptians, linen was introduced by the Romans to northern Europe, where production became widespread. Religious refugees from the Low Countries in the 16th century helped to establish the linen industry in England, but here and elsewhere it began to decline in competition with cotton in the 18th century.

To get the longest possible fibres, flax is pulled, rather than cut by hand or machine, just as the seed bolls are beginning to set. After preliminary drying, it is steeped in water so that the fibre can be more easily separated from the wood of the stem, then hackled (combed), classified, drawn into continuous fibres, and spun. Bleaching, weaving, and finishing processes vary according to the final product, which can be sailcloth, canvas, sacking, cambric, or lawn. Because of the length of its fibre, linen yarn has twice the strength of cotton, and yet is superior in delicacy, so that it is suitable for lace making. It mixes well with synthetics.

line printer computer ◊printer that prints a complete line of characters at a time. Line printers can achieve very high printing speeds of up to 2,500 lines a minute, but can print in only one typeface, cannot print graphics, and are very noisy. Today, most users prefer ◊laser printers.

ling any of several deepwater long-bodied fishes of the cod family found in the N Atlantic. The species *Molva molva* is found off NW Europe. It reaches 2 m/6 ft long and is 20 kg/45 lb in weight.

ling another name for common ◊heather.

lingam in Hinduism, the phallic emblem of the god ◊Siva, the yoni being the female equivalent.

lingua franca any language that is used as a means of communication by groups who do not themselves normally speak that language; for example, English is a lingua franca used by Japanese doing business in Finland, or by Swedes in Saudi Arabia. Many of the world's lingua francas are ◊pidgin or trade languages.

linguistics scientific study of language. Linguistics has many branches, such as origins (historical linguistics), the changing way language is pronounced (phonetics), derivation of words through various languages (etymology), development of meanings (semantics), and the arrangement and modifications of words to convey a message (grammar). Applied linguistics is the use of lingustics to aid understanding in other areas of language-based study, such as dictionary compilation and foreign-language teaching.

linkage in genetics, the association between two or more genes that tend to be inherited together because they are on the same chromosome. The closer together they are on the chromosome, the less likely they are to be separated by crossing over (one of the processes of ◊recombination) and they are then described as being 'tightly linked'.

Linlithgow tourist centre in Lothian Region, Scotland; population (1991) 11,900. Linlithgow Palace, now in ruins, was once a royal residence, and Mary Queen of Scots was born there.

Linnaeus (Latinized form of Carl von Linné) Carolus 1707–1778. Swedish naturalist and physician. His botanical work *Systema naturae* 1735 contained his system for classifying plants into groups depending on shared characteristics (such as the number of stamens in flowers), providing a much-needed framework for identification. He also devised the concise and precise system for naming plants and animals, using one Latin (or Latinized) word to represent the genus and a second to distinguish the species. For example, in the Latin name of the daisy, *Bellis perennis*, *Bellis* is the name of the genus to which the plant belongs, and *perennis* distinguishes the species from others of the same genus.

linnet small seed-eating bird *Acanthis cannabina*, of the finch family Fringillidae, order Passeriformes, which is very abundant in Europe, Asia, and NW Africa. The male has a chestnut back with a pink breast and grey head, the female is mainly a dull brown.

linoleum (Latin *lini oleum* 'linseed oil') floor covering made from linseed oil, tall oil, rosin, cork, woodflour, chalk, clay, and pigments, pressed into sheets with a jute backing. Oxidation of the oil is accelerated by heating, so that the oil mixture solidifies into a tough, resilient material. Linoleum was invented in England in 1860 by Frederick Walton. Synthetic floor coverings are now popular and the use of linoleum has declined.

Linotype trademark for a typesetting machine once universally used for newspaper work, which sets complete lines (slugs) of hot-metal type as operators type the copy at a keyboard. It was invented in the USA in 1884 by German-born Ottmar Mergenthaler. It has been replaced by phototypesetting.

Lin Piao alternative transliteration of ◊Lin Biao.

linseed seeds of the flax plant *Linum usitatissimum*, from which linseed oil is expressed, the residue being used as cattle feed. The oil is used in paint, wood treatments and varnishes, and in the manufacture of linoleum.

Linz capital of Upper Austria and industrial port (iron, steel, metalworking) on the river Danube in N Austria; population (1991) 203,000.

lion cat *Panthera leo*, now found only in Africa and NW India. The coat is tawny, the young having darker spot markings that usually disappear in the adult. The male has a heavy mane and a tuft at the end of the tail. Head and body measure about 2 m/6 ft, plus 1 m/3 ft of tail, the lioness being slightly smaller. Lions produce litters of two to six cubs, and often live in prides of several adult males and females with several young.

Capable of short bursts of speed, lions skilfully collaborate in stalking herbivorous animals. Females remain with the pride while males remain only for a couple of years or so, before being supplanted by a competing coalition of males. Males tend to cannibalize the young; about a third of all young are eaten. *See illustration on following page.*

Lipari Islands or ***Aeolian Islands*** volcanic group of seven islands off NE Sicily, including ***Lipari*** (on which is the capital of the same name), ***Stromboli*** (active volcano 926 m/3,038 ft high), and ***Vulcano*** (also with an active volcano); area 114 sq km/44 sq mi.

lipase enzyme responsible for breaking down fats into fatty acids and glycerol. It is produced by the ◊pancreas and requires a slightly alkaline environment. The products of fat digestion are absorbed by the intestinal wall.

Lipchitz Jacques 1891–1973. Lithuanian-born sculptor. He was active in Paris from 1909 and emigrated to the USA 1941. He was one of the first Cubist sculptors, his best-known piece being *Man with a Guitar* 1916 (Museum of Modern Art, New York). In the 1920s he experimented with small open forms he called 'transparents'. His later works, often political allegories, were characterized by heavy, contorted forms.

Li Peng 1928– . Chinese communist politician, a member of the Politburo from 1985, head of government 1987–98 and chairman of the National People's Congress from 1998. He sought improved relations with the USSR before its demise, and has favoured maintaining firm central and party control over the economy.

Li was adopted by the communist leader Zhou Enlai. He studied at the communist headquarters of Yan'an 1941–47 and trained as a hydroelectric engineer at the Moscow Power Institute from 1948. He was appointed minister of the electric power industry 1981, a vice premier 1983, and prime minister 1987.

In 1989 he launched the crackdown on demonstrators in Beijing that led to the massacre in ◊Tiananmen Square.

lipid any of a large number of esters of fatty acids, commonly formed by the reaction of a fatty acid with glycerol (see ◊glyceride). They are soluble in alcohol but not in water. Lipids are the chief constituents of plant and animal waxes, fats, and oils.

Li Po c. 705–762. Chinese poet. He used traditional literary forms, but his exuberance, the boldness of his imagination, and the intensity of his feeling have won him recognition as perhaps the greatest of all

'Nature does not make jumps.'

CAROLUS LINNAEUS
Philosophia Botanica

lion Lions can sleep for over 18 hours a day, particularly after a large kill. Unlike other cats, lions live and hunt in groups (prides). Usually they kill only once or twice a week, hunting ruminants such as gazelles, zebra, and wildebeest. *Premaphotos Wildlife*

Chinese poets. Although he was mostly concerned with higher themes, he is also remembered for his celebratory verses on drinking.

Lippershey Hans c. 1570–c. 1619. Dutch lens-maker, credited with inventing the telescope in 1608.

Lippi Filippino c. 1457–1504. Italian painter. He was trained by his father Filippo ◊Lippi and ◊Botticelli. His most important works are frescoes in the Strozzi Chapel of Sta Maria Novella in Florence, painted in a graceful but also dramatic and at times bizarre style that anticipated later developments of ◊Mannerism.

He painted many altarpieces and frescoes, most of which show the grace and delicacy he derived from Botticelli, especially in the depiction of figures and the treatment of light, fluttering draperies. His earlier works include the *Vision of St Bernard*, an altarpiece in the chapel of the Badia, Florence; the *Madonna and Child with Sts Victor, John the Baptist, Bernard, and Zenobius* 1485 (Uffizi, Florence); and the *Virgin and Child with Sts Jerome and Dominic*, 1485 (National Gallery, London).

Lippi Fra Filippo c. 1406–1469. Italian painter. His most important works include frescoes depicting the lives of St Stephen and St John the Baptist 1452–66 (Prato Cathedral), which in their use of perspective and grouping of figures show the influence of ◊Masaccio. He also painted many altarpieces featuring the Madonna.

Lippi *Portrait of a Youth* c. 1485 by Filippino Lippi, National Museum of Art, Washington, USA. One of Lippi's earliest works, this portrait of a youth shows the influence of Lippi's teacher, Botticelli. Confident, frank, and elegant, it is typical of 15th-century Florentine painting. *Corbis*

Lippi was born in Florence and patronized by the Medici family. The painter and biographer Giorgio ◊Vasari gave a colourful account of his life including how, as a monk, he was tried in the 1450s for abducting a nun (the mother of his son Filippino Lippi).

liquefaction the process of converting a gas to a liquid, normally associated with low temperatures and high pressures (see ◊condensation).

liquefied petroleum gas (LPG) liquid form of butane, propane, or pentane, produced by the distillation of petroleum during oil refining. At room temperature these substances are gases, although they can be easily liquefied and stored under pressure in metal containers. They are used for heating and cooking where other fuels are not available.

liqueur alcoholic beverage made by infusing flavouring substances (fruits, herbs, spices) in alcohol. Specific recipes are closely guarded commercial secrets. Originally liqueurs were used as medicines and are still thought of as digestives.

liquid state of matter between a ◊solid and a ◊gas. A liquid forms a level surface and assumes the shape of its container. Its atoms do not occupy fixed positions as in a crystalline solid, nor do they have freedom of movement as in a gas. Unlike a gas, a liquid is difficult to compress since pressure applied at one point is equally transmitted throughout (Pascal's principle). ◊Hydraulics makes use of this property.

liquid air air that has been cooled so much that it has liquefied. This happens at temperatures below about −196°C/−321°F. The various constituent gases, including nitrogen, oxygen, argon, and neon, can be separated from liquid air by the technique of ◊fractionation.

liquidation in economics, the winding up of a company by converting all its assets into money to pay off its liabilities.

liquid-crystal display (LCD) display of numbers (for example, in a calculator) or pictures (such as on a pocket television screen) produced by molecules of a substance in a semiliquid state with some crystalline properties, so that clusters of molecules align in parallel formations. The display is a blank until the application of an electric field, which 'twists' the molecules so that they reflect or transmit light falling on them.

liquidity in economics, the state of possessing sufficient money and/or assets to be able to pay off all liabilities. Liquid assets are those such as shares that may be converted quickly into cash, as opposed to property.

liquorice perennial European herb *Glycyrrhiza glabra*, family Leguminosae. The long, sweet root yields an extract which is made into a hard black paste and used in confectionery and medicines.

Lisbon (Portuguese ***Lisboa***) city and capital of Portugal, in the SW of the country, on the tidal lake and estuary formed by the river Tagus; population (1987) 830,500. Industries include steel, textiles, chemicals, pottery, shipbuilding, and fishing. It has been the capital since 1260 and reached its peak of prosperity in the period of Portugal's empire during the 16th century. In 1755 an earthquake killed 60,000 people and destroyed much of the city.

Lisburn cathedral city and market town in Antrim, Northern Ireland, on the river Lagan; population (1991) 42,100. It produces linen and furniture.

listed building in Britain, a building officially recognized as having historical or architectural interest and therefore legally protected from alteration or demolition. In England the listing is drawn up by the secretary of state for the environment under the advice of the English Heritage organization, which provides various resources for architectural conservation.

There are about 500,000 listed buildings in England and around 1 million in Britain as a whole, the largest number in Western Europe. In England they are divided into categories I, II*, and II and in Scotland A, B, and C. Grade I buildings, which are defined as being of 'exceptional interest', constitute less than 2% of entries on the list. Grade II* buildings constitute about 4% of entries. The listing system incorporates all pre-1700 buildings that have not been substantially altered, and almost all those built between 1700 and 1840.

Lister Joseph, 1st Baron Lister 1827–1912. English surgeon. He was the founder of antiseptic surgery, influenced by Louis ◊Pasteur's work on bacteria. He introduced dressings soaked in carbolic acid and strict rules of hygiene to combat wound sepsis in hospitals. ▷ *See feature on pp. 1024–1025.*

liquid-crystal display A liquid-crystal display consists of a liquid crystal sandwiched between polarizing filters similar to polaroid sunglasses. When a segment of the seven-segment display is electrified, the liquid crystal twists the polarized light from the front filter, allowing the light to bounce off the rear reflector and illuminate the segment.

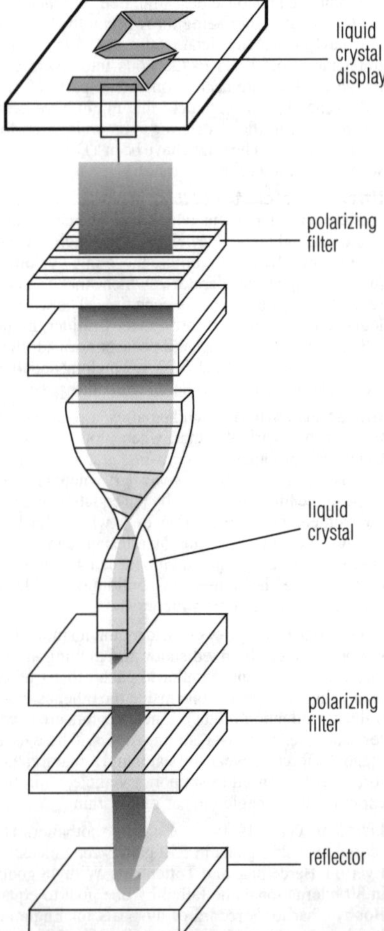

listeriosis disease of animals that may occasionally infect humans, caused by the bacterium *Listeria monocytogenes*. The bacteria multiply at temperatures close to 0°C/32°F, which means they may flourish in precooked frozen meals if the cooking has not been thorough. Listeriosis causes flulike symptoms and inflammation of the brain and its surrounding membranes. It can be treated with penicillin.

Liszt Franz 1811–1886. Hungarian pianist and composer. An outstanding virtuoso of the piano, he was an established concert artist by the age of 12. His expressive, romantic, and frequently chromatic works include piano music (*Transcendental Studies* 1851), masses and oratorios, songs, organ music, and a symphony. Much of his music is programmatic; he also originated the symphonic poem. Liszt travelled widely in Europe, producing an operetta *Don Sanche* in Paris at the age of 14. As musical director and conductor at Weimar 1848–59, he championed the music of Berlioz and Wagner.

Retiring to Rome, he turned again to his early love of religion, and in 1865 became a secular priest (adopting the title Abbé), while continuing to teach and give concert tours for which he also made virtuoso piano arrangements of orchestral works by Beethoven, Schubert, and Wagner.

litany in the Christian church, a form of prayer or supplication led by a priest with set responses by the congregation. It was introduced in the 4th century.

litchi or ***lychee*** evergreen tree *Litchi chinensis* of the soapberry family Sapindaceae. The delicately flavoured ovate fruit is encased in a brownish rough outer skin and has a hard seed. The litchi is native to S China, where it has been cultivated for 2,000 years.

literacy ability to read and write. The level at which functional literacy is set rises as society becomes more complex, and it becomes increasingly difficult for an illiterate person to find work and cope with the other demands of everyday life. Over 1 billion adults in the world, most of them women, are unable to read or write. Africa and Asia have the world's highest illiteracy rates. Surveys in the USA, the UK, and France in the 1980s found far greater levels of functional illiteracy than official figures suggest, as well as revealing a lack of basic general knowledge, but no standard of measurement has been agreed.

literary criticism establishment of principles governing literary composition, and the assessment and interpretation of literary works. Contemporary criticism offers analyses of literary works from structuralist, semiological, feminist, Marxist, and psychoanalytical perspectives, whereas earlier criticism tended to deal with moral or political ideas, or with a literary work as a formal object independent of its creator.

The earliest systematic literary criticism was the *Poetics* of Aristotle; a later Greek critic was the author of the treatise *On the Sublime*, usually attributed to Longinus. Horace and Quintilian were influential Latin critics. The Italian Renaissance introduced humanist criticism, and the revival of classical scholarship exalted the authority of Aristotle and Horace. Like literature itself, European criticism then applied Neo-Classical, Romantic, and modern approaches.

literature words set apart in some way from ordinary everyday communication. In the ancient oral traditions, before stories and poems were written down, literature had a mainly public function – mythic and religious. As literary works came to be preserved in writing, and, eventually, printed, their role became more private, serving as a vehicle for the exploration and expression of emotion and the human situation.

poetry and prose In the development of literature, aesthetic criteria have come increasingly to the fore, although these have been challenged on ideological grounds by some recent cultural critics. The English poet and critic Coleridge defined prose as words in their best order, and poetry as the 'best' words in the best order. The distinction between poetry and prose is not always clear-cut, but in practice poetry tends to be metrically formal (making it easier to memorize), whereas prose corresponds more closely to the patterns of ordinary speech. Poetry therefore had an early advantage over prose in the days before printing, which it did not relinquish until comparatively recently.

Over the centuries poetry has taken on a wide range of forms, from the lengthy narrative such as the ◊epic, to the lyric, expressing personal emotion in songlike form; from the ◊ballad and the 14-line ◊sonnet, to the extreme conciseness of the 17-syllable Japanese ◊haiku.

Prose came into its own in the West as a vehicle for imaginative literature with the rise of the novel in the 18th century, and ◊fiction has since been divided into various genres such as the historical novel, detective fiction, fantasy, and science fiction. See also the literature of particular countries, under ◊English literature, ◊French literature, ◊United States literature, and so on.

lithium (Greek *lithos* 'stone') soft, ductile, silver-white, metallic element, symbol Li, atomic number 3, relative atomic mass 6.941. It is one of the ◊alkali metals, has a very low density (far less than most woods), and floats on water (specific gravity 0.57); it is the lightest of all metals. Lithium is used to harden alloys, and in batteries; its compounds are used in medicine to treat manic depression.

lithography printmaking technique invented 1798 by Aloys Senefelder, based on the mutual repulsion of grease and water. A drawing is made with greasy crayon on an absorbent stone, which is then wetted. The wet stone repels ink (which is greasy) applied to the surface and the crayon absorbs it, so that the drawing can be printed. Lithographic printing is used in book production, posters, and prints.

lithosphere topmost layer of the Earth's structure, forming the jigsaw of plates that take part in the movements of ◊plate tectonics. The lithosphere comprises the ◊crust and a portion of the upper ◊mantle. It is regarded as being rigid and moves about on the semi-molten ◊asthenosphere. The lithosphere is about 75 km/47 mi thick.

Lithuania country in N Europe, bounded N by Latvia, E by Belarus, S by Poland and the Kaliningrad area of Russia, and W by the Baltic Sea. *See country box on p. 640.*

Lithuanian the majority ethnic group living in Lithuania, comprising 80% of the population.

Lithuanian language Indo-European language spoken by the people of Lithuania, which through its geographical isolation has retained many ancient features of the Indo-European language family. It acquired a written form in the 16th century, using the Latin alphabet, and is currently spoken by some 3–4 million people.

litmus dye obtained from various lichens and used in chemistry as an indicator to test the acidic or alkaline nature of aqueous solutions; it turns red in the presence of acid, and blue in the presence of alkali.

litre metric unit of volume (symbol l), equal to one cubic decimetre (1.76 imperial pints/2.11 US pints).

Little Bighorn river in Montana, USA, a tributary of the Bighorn. It was the site of Lt-Col George ◊Custer's defeat by the ◊Sioux Indians 25 June 1876 under their chiefs Crazy Horse and Sitting Bull, known as Custer's last stand.

Little Dipper another name for the most distinctive part of the constellation ◊Ursa Minor, the Little Bear.

Little Richard Stage name of Richard Wayne Penniman 1932– . US rock singer and pianist. He was one of the creators of rock and roll with his wildly uninhibited renditions of 'Tutti Frutti' 1956, 'Long Tall Sally' 1956, and 'Good Golly Miss Molly' 1957. His subsequent career in soul and rhythm and blues was interrupted by periods as a Seventh-Day Adventist cleric.

Little Rock largest city and capital of Arkansas, USA; population (1992) 176,900. Products include metal goods, oil-field and electronic equipment, chemicals, clothing, and processed food.

Littlewood Joan Maud 1914– . English theatre director. She established the Theatre Workshop 1945 and was responsible for many vigorous productions at the Theatre Royal, Stratford, London, 1953–75, such as *A Taste of Honey* 1959, Brendan Behan's *The Hostage* 1959–60, and *Oh, What a Lovely War* 1963.

liturgy in the Christian church, any written, authorized version of a service for public worship, especially the Roman Catholic ◊Mass.

Litvinov Maxim. Adopted name of Meir Walach 1876–1951. Soviet politician, commissioner for foreign affairs under Stalin from Jan 1931 until his removal from office in May 1939. Litvinov believed in cooperation with the West and obtained US recognition of the USSR in 1934. In the League of Nations he advocated action against the ◊Axis (the alliance of Nazi Germany and Fascist Italy); he was therefore dismissed just before the signing of the Hitler–Stalin nonaggression pact 1939. After the German invasion of the USSR, he was ambassador to the USA 1941–43.

Liu Shaoqi or ***Liu Shao-chi*** 1898–1969. Chinese communist politician, in effective control of government 1960–65. A Moscow-trained labour organizer, he was a firm proponent of the Soviet style of government based around disciplined one-party control, the use of incentive gradings, and priority for industry over agriculture. This was opposed by ◊Mao Zedong, but began to be implemented by Liu while he was state president 1960–65.

liver large organ of vertebrates, which has many regulatory and storage functions. The human liver is situated in the upper abdomen, and weighs about 2 kg/4.5 lb. It is divided into four lobes. The liver receives the products of digestion, converts glucose to glycogen (a long-chain carbohydrate used for storage), and breaks down fats. It removes excess amino acids from the blood, converting them to urea, which is excreted by the kidneys. The liver also synthesizes vitamins, produces bile and blood-clotting factors, and removes damaged red cells and toxins such as alcohol from the blood.

Liverpool city and seaport in Merseyside, NW England; population (1991 est) 448,300. Liverpool is the UK's chief Atlantic port with miles of specialized, mechanized quays on the river Mersey. Imports include crude oil, grain, ores, edible oils, timber, and containers. There are ferries to Ireland and the Isle of Man. Traditional industries, such as ship-repairing, have declined. Present-day industries include flour milling, sugar refining, electrical engineering, food processing, chemicals, soap, margarine, tanning, and motor vehicles. The Mersey Tunnel (1886), rail tunnel, and Queensway Tunnel (1934) link Liverpool and Birkenhead. Kingsway Tunnel (1971) links Liverpool and Wallasey.

features Bluecoat Chambers (1717); Town Hall (1754); St George's Hall (1838–54), a fine example of Classical architecture; Anglican Cathedral, designed by George Gilbert Scott (begun 1904, completed 1980); Roman Catholic Metropolitan Cathedral of Christ the King, designed by Frederick ◊Gibberd, consecrated 1967; the Tate Gallery in the north in former Albert Dock, opened 1987; the

Liszt Hungarian composer and piano virtuoso Franz von Liszt, photographed in about 1880. Although he was born in Hungary, he never spoke Hungarian; he died in France, having lived in France, Switzerland, Italy, and Germany and travelled widely throughout Europe. *Corbis.*

'Let such teach others who themselves excel, / And censure freely who have written well.'

On LITERARY CRITICISM
Alexander Pope
Essay on Criticism
1711

'Any work that aspires, however humbly, to the condition of art should carry its justification in every line.'

On LITERATURE
Joseph Conrad *The Nigger of the Narcissus* 1897, author's note

'Peace is indivisible.'

MAXIM LITVINOV
Speech to League of Nations July 1936

Walker Art Gallery (1877); and the Liverpool Philharmonic Orchestra, founded 1840 (became Royal LPO 1957). Britain's first International Garden Festival was held here 1984. The ◊Beatles were born here; the Liverpool Institute for the Performing Arts, the world's first university of pop music, opened 1995.

history Liverpool grew in importance during the 18th century as a centre of the slave trade, and until the early 20th century through the export of the textiles of Lancashire and Yorkshire.

Liverpool Robert Banks Jenkinson, 2nd Earl Liverpool 1770–1828. British Tory politician. He entered Parliament 1790 and was foreign secretary 1801–03, home secretary 1804–06 and 1807–09, war minister 1809–12, and prime minister 1812–27. His government conducted the Napoleonic Wars to a successful conclusion, but its ruthless suppression of freedom of speech and of the press aroused such opposition that during 1815–20 revolution frequently seemed imminent.

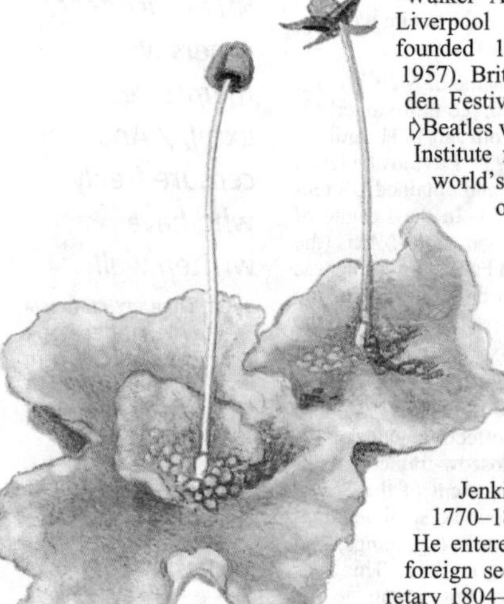

liverwort Liverworts belong to a group of plants, called the Bryophyta, that also includes the mosses. Neither mosses nor liverworts possess true roots and both require water to enable the male gametes to swim to the female sex organs to fertilize the eggs. Unlike mosses most liverworts have no, or only very frail, leaves.

liverwort plant of the class Hepaticae, of the bryophyte division of nonvascular plants, related to mosses, found growing in damp places. The main sexual generation consists of a ◊thallus, which may be flat, green, and lobed, like a small leaf, or leafy and mosslike. The spore-bearing generation is smaller, typically parasitic on the thallus, and throws up a capsule from which spores are spread.

Livingstone David 1813–1873. Scottish missionary explorer. In 1841 he went to Africa, reached Lake Ngami 1849, followed the Zambezi to its mouth, saw the Victoria Falls 1855, and went to East and Central Africa 1858–64, reaching Lakes Shirwa and Malawi. From 1866, he tried to find the source of the river Nile, and reached Ujiji in Tanganyika in Nov 1871. British explorer Henry Stanley joined him in Ujiji. Livingstone not only mapped a great deal of the African continent but also helped to end the Arab slave trade.

Livingstone Ken(neth) 1945– . British left-wing Labour politician. He was leader of the Greater London Council (GLC) 1981–86 and a member of Parliament from 1987. He stood as a candidate for the Labour Party leadership elections 1992.

Livonia former region in Europe on the E coast of the Baltic Sea, comprising most of present-day Latvia and Estonia. Conquered and converted to Christianity in the early 13th century by the Livonian Knights, a crusading order, Livonia was independent until 1583, when it was divided between Poland and Sweden. In 1710 it was occupied by Russia, and in 1721 was ceded to Peter the Great, Tsar of Russia.

Livorno (English ***Leghorn***) industrial port in W Italy; population (1992) 166,400. Industries include shipbuilding, distilling, and motor vehicles. A fortress town since the 12th century, it was developed by the Medici family. It has a naval academy and is also a resort.

lizard The frilled lizard of N Australia and New Guinea has a rufflike collar of skin – up to 25 cm/10 in across – around its neck. The collar normally lies flat but, if alarmed, the lizard raises the brightly coloured collar and opens its mouth to intimidate an enemy.

Livy (Titus Livius) 59 BC–AD 17. Roman historian. He was the author of a *History of Rome* from the city's foundation to 9 BC, based partly on legend. It was composed of 142 books, of which 35 survive, covering the periods from Aeneas' arrival in Italy to 293 BC and from 218 to 167 BC.

Li Xiannian 1909–1992. Chinese politician, member of the Chinese Communist Party (CCP) Politburo from 1956. He fell from favour during the 1966–69 Cultural Revolution, but was rehabilitated as finance minister 1973, supporting cautious economic reform. He was state president 1983–88.

lizard reptile of the suborder Lacertilia, which together with snakes constitutes the order Squamata. Lizards are generally distinguishable from snakes by having four legs, moveable eyelids, eardrums, and a fleshy tongue, but some lizards are legless and snakelike in appearance. There are over 3,000 species of lizard worldwide.

Like other reptiles, lizards are abundant in the tropics, although some species live as far north as the Arctic circle. There are about 20 families of lizards, including geckos, chameleons, skinks, monitors, agamas, and iguanas. The common or viviparous lizard *Lacerta vivipara*, about 15 cm/6 in long, is found throughout Europe; in the far north, it hibernates through the long winter. Like many other species, it can shed its tail as a defence, later regrowing it.

Lizard Point southernmost point of England in Cornwall. The coast is broken into small bays overlooked by two cliff lighthouses. The heathland is notable for Cornish heath and other plants similar to those found in SW Europe.

Ljubljana (German ***Laibach***) capital and industrial city (textiles, chemicals, paper, leather goods) of Slovenia, near the confluence of the rivers Ljubljanica and Sava; population (1991) 276,100. It has a nuclear research centre and is linked with S Austria by the Karawanken road tunnel under the Alps (1979–83).

history Founded by Augustus 34 BC, it was taken by the French 1809 and made the governmental seat of the Illyrian Provinces (part of Napoleon's empire) until 1813. It then came under Austrian rule and was ceded to Yugoslavia 1918; Slovenia gained its independence 1992.

llama South American even-toed hoofed mammal *Lama glama* of the camel family, about 1.2 m/4 ft high at the shoulder. Llamas can be white, brown, or dark, sometimes with spots or patches. They are very hardy, and require little food or water. They spit profusely when annoyed. Llamas are used in Peru as beasts of burden, and also for their wool, milk, and meat.

Llanelli formerly ***Llanelly*** industrial port in Dyfed, Wales; population (1991) 45,000. Industries include tin plate, copper smelting, chemicals, bricks, and lenses.

Llanfair P G village in Anglesey, Wales; full name ***Llanfairpwllgwyngyllgogerychwyrndrobwl-llantysiliogogogoch*** (St Mary's church in the hollow of the white hazel near the rapid whirlpool of St Tysillio's church, by the red cave), the longest place name in the UK.

Llewelyn I 1173–1240. Prince of Wales from 1194. He extended his rule to all Wales not in Norman hands, driving the English from N Wales 1212, and taking Shrewsbury 1215. During the early part of Henry III's reign, he was several times attacked by English armies. He was married to Joanna, illegitimate daughter of King John.

Llewelyn II ap Gruffydd c. 1225–1282. Prince of Wales from 1246, grandson of Llewelyn I. In 1277 Edward I of England compelled Llewelyn to acknowledge him as overlord and to surrender S Wales. His death while leading a national uprising ended Welsh independence.

Lloyd Marie. Stage name of Matilda Alice Victoria Wood 1870–1922. English music-hall artist. Her Cockney songs embodied the music-hall traditions of 1890s comedy.

Lloyd Selwyn. See ◊Selwyn Lloyd, British Conservative politician.

Lloyd George David, 1st Earl Lloyd-George of Dwyfor 1863–1945. Welsh Liberal politician, prime minister of Britain 1916–22. A pioneer of social reform, as chancellor of the Exchequer 1908–15 he introduced old-age pensions 1908 and health and unemployment insurance 1911. High unemployment, intervention in the Russian Civil War, and use of the military police force, the ◊Black and Tans, in Ireland eroded his support as prime minister, and the creation of the Irish Free State 1921 and his pro-Greek policy against the Turks caused the collapse of his coalition government.

Lloyd George was born in Manchester, became a solicitor, and was member of Parliament for Caernarvon Boroughs from 1890. During the Boer War, he was prominent as a pro-Boer. His 1909 budget (with graduated direct taxes and taxing land values) provoked the Lords to reject it, and resulted in the Act of 1911 limiting their powers. He held ministerial posts during World War I until 1916 when there was an open breach between him and Prime Minister ◊Asquith, and he became prime minister of a coalition government. Securing a unified Allied command, he enabled the Allies to withstand the last German offensive and achieve victory. After World War I he had a major role in the Versailles peace treaty. In the 1918 elections, he achieved a huge majority over Labour and Asquith's followers. He had become largely distrusted within his own party by 1922, and never regained power.

Lloyd's Register of Shipping international society for the survey and classification of merchant shipping, which provides rules for the construction and maintenance of ships and their machinery. It was founded in 1760. Lloyd's is governed by a large committee representing ship-owners, ship-builders, marine engineers, and underwriters. The register book, published annually, contains particulars of all known sea-going ships of 100 tonnes/98 tons gross and over.

Lloyd Webber Andrew 1948– . English composer. His early musicals, with lyrics by Tim Rice, include *Joseph and the Amazing Technicolor Dreamcoat* 1968, *Jesus Christ Superstar* 1971, and *Evita* 1978, based on the life of the Argentine leader Eva Perón. He also wrote *Cats* 1981, based on T S Eliot's *Old Possum's Book of Practical Cats*, *Starlight Express* 1984, *The Phantom of the Opera* 1986, and *Aspects of Love* 1989. Other works include *Variations for Cello* 1978, written for his brother Julian Lloyd Webber (1951–) who is a solo cellist, and a *Requiem Mass* 1985.

Llull Ramon c. 1232–1316. Catalan scholar and mystic. He produced treatises on theology, mysticism, and chivalry in Catalan, Latin, and Arabic. His *Ars magna* was a mechanical device, a kind of prototype computer, by which all problems could be solved by manipulating fundamental Aristotelian categories. He also wrote the prose romance *Blanquerna* in his native Catalan, the first novel written in a Romance language.

loa spirit in ◊voodoo. Loas may be male or female, and include Maman Brigitte, the loa of death and cemeteries, and Aida-Wedo, the rainbow snake. Believers may be under the protection of one particular loa.

loach carplike freshwater fish, family Cobitidae, with a long narrow body, and no teeth in the small, downward-pointing mouth, which is surrounded by barbels. Loaches are native to Asian and European waters.

loam type of fertile soil, a mixture of sand, silt, clay, and organic material. It is porous, which allows for good air circulation and retention of moisture.

Lobachevsky Nikolai Ivanovich 1792–1856. Russian mathematician who founded non-Euclidean geometry, concurrently with, but independently of, Karl ◊Gauss in Germany and János Bolyai (1802–1860) in Hungary. Lobachevsky published the first account of the subject in 1829, but his work went unrecognized until Georg ◊Riemann's system was published.

In Euclid's system, two parallel lines will remain equidistant from each other, whereas in Lobachevskian geometry, the two lines will approach zero in one direction and infinity in the other. In Euclidean geometry the sum of the angles of a triangle is always equal to the sum of two right angles; in

Lobachevskian geometry, the sum of the angles is always less than the sum of two right angles. In Lobachevskian space, also, two geometric figures cannot have the same shape but different sizes.

lobby individual or pressure group that sets out to influence government action. The lobby is prevalent in the USA, where the term originated in the 1830s from the practice of those wishing to influence state policy waiting for elected representatives in the lobby of the Capitol. Under the UK lobby system, certain parliamentary journalists are given unofficial access to confidential news.

Lobengula 1836–1894. King of Matabeleland (now part of Zimbabwe) 1870–93. After accepting British protection from internal and external threats to his leadership 1888, Lobengula came under increasing pressure from British mining interests to allow exploitation of goldfields near Bulawayo. He was overthrown 1893 by a military expedition organized by Cecil ◊Rhodes's South African Company.

lobotomy another name for the former brain operation, ◊leucotomy.

lobster large marine crustacean of the order Decapoda. Lobsters are grouped with freshwater ◊crayfish in the suborder Reptantia ('walking'), although both lobsters and crayfish can also swim, using their fanlike tails. Lobsters have eyes on stalks and long antennae, and are mainly nocturnal. They scavenge and eat dead or dying fish. True lobsters, family Homaridae, are distinguished by having very large 'claws' or pincers on their first pair of legs, and smaller ones on their second and third pairs. Spiny lobsters, family Palinuridae, have no large pincers.

Species include the common lobster *Homarus gammarus* found off Britain, which is bluish-black, the closely related American lobster *H. americanus*, the spiny lobster *Palinurus vulgaris* found off Britain, and the Norwegian lobster *Nephrops norvegicus*, a small orange species.

local area network (LAN) in computing, a ◊network restricted to a single room or building. Local area networks enable around 500 devices to be connected together.

local government that part of government dealing mainly with matters concerning the inhabitants of a particular area or town, usually financed at least in part by local taxes. In the UK and USA, local government has comparatively large powers and responsibilities.

Historically, in European countries such as France, Germany, and the USSR, local government tended to be more centrally controlled than in Britain, although German cities have a tradition of independent action, as exemplified in Berlin, and France from 1969 moved towards regional decentralization. In the USA the system shows evidence of the early type of settlement (for example, in New England the town is the unit of local government, in the South the county, and in the northern central states the combined county and township). In Australia, although an integrated system similar to the British was planned, the scattered nature of settlement, apart from the major towns, has prevented implementation of any uniform tiered arrangement.

In the UK, following a review of local government structure (completed 1994), the administrative divisions of England, Scotland, and Wales were reorganized, and the changes implemented in several phases from 1995. (*See list of tables on p. 1177 for new unitary authorities and see United Kingdom map.*)

Local Group in astronomy, a cluster of about 30 galaxies that includes our own, the Milky Way. Like other groups of galaxies, the Local Group is held together by the gravitational attraction among its members, and does not expand with the expanding universe. Its two largest galaxies are the Milky Way and the Andromeda galaxy; most of the others are small and faint.

Locarno, Pact of series of diplomatic documents initialled in Locarno, Switzerland, 16 Oct 1925 and formally signed in London 1 Dec 1925. The pact settled the question of French security, and the signatories – Britain, France, Belgium, Italy, and Germany – guaranteed Germany's existing frontiers with France and Belgium. Following the signing of the pact, Germany was admitted to the League of Nations.

loc. cit. abbreviation for ***loco citato*** (Latin 'at the place cited'), used in reference citation.

Lochaber wild mountainous district of Highland Region, Scotland, including Ben Nevis, the highest mountain in the British Isles. Fort William is the chief town of the area. It is the site of large hydroelectric installations.

Lochner Stephan c. 1400–1451. German painter. Active in Cologne from 1442, he was a master of the ◊International Gothic style. Most of his work is still in Cologne, notably the *Virgin in the Rose Garden* about 1440 (Wallraf-Richartz Museum) and *Adoration of the Magi* 1448 (Cologne Cathedral). His work combines the delicacy of the International Gothic style with the naturalism of Flemish painting.

Loch Ness Scottish lake; see ◊Ness, Loch.

lock construction installed in waterways to allow boats or ships to travel from one level to another. The earliest form, the flash lock, was first seen in the East in 1st-century-AD China and in the West in 11th-century Holland. By this method barriers temporarily dammed a river and when removed allowed the flash flood to propel the waiting boat through any obstacle. This was followed in 12th-century China and 14th-century Holland by the pound lock. In this system the lock has a gate at each end. Boats enter through one gate when the levels are the same both outside and inside. Water is then allowed in (or out of) the lock until the level rises (or falls) to the new level outside the other gate.

Locks are important to shipping where canals link oceans of differing levels, such as the Panama Canal, or where falls or rapids are replaced by these adjustable water 'steps'.

lock and key devices that provide security, usually fitted to a door of some kind. In 1778 English locksmith Robert Barron made the forerunner of the mortise lock, which contains levers that the key must raise to an exact height before the bolt can be moved. The Yale lock, a pin-tumbler cylinder design, was invented by US locksmith Linus Yale, Jr, in 1865. More secure locks include combination locks, with a dial mechanism that must be turned certain distances backwards and forwards to open, and time locks, which are set to be opened only at specific times.

llama On the Chilean altiplano llamas are penned before being sheared for their wool. Llamas are highly valued because they cause far less damage to this fragile habitat than sheep or cattle. They provide meat, milk, and wool, and their dung is used as a fuel. *Premaphotos Wildlife*

Locke John 1632–1704. English philosopher. His *Essay concerning Human Understanding* 1690 maintained that experience was the only source of knowledge (empiricism), and that 'we can have knowledge no farther than we have ideas' prompted by such experience. *Two Treatises on Government* 1690 helped to form contemporary ideas of liberal democracy. For Locke, the physical universe was a mechanical system of material bodies, composed of corpuscules, or 'invisible particles'. He believed

All men are liable to error; and most men are, in many points, by passion or interest, under temptation to it.

JOHN LOCKE
Essay concerning Human Understanding

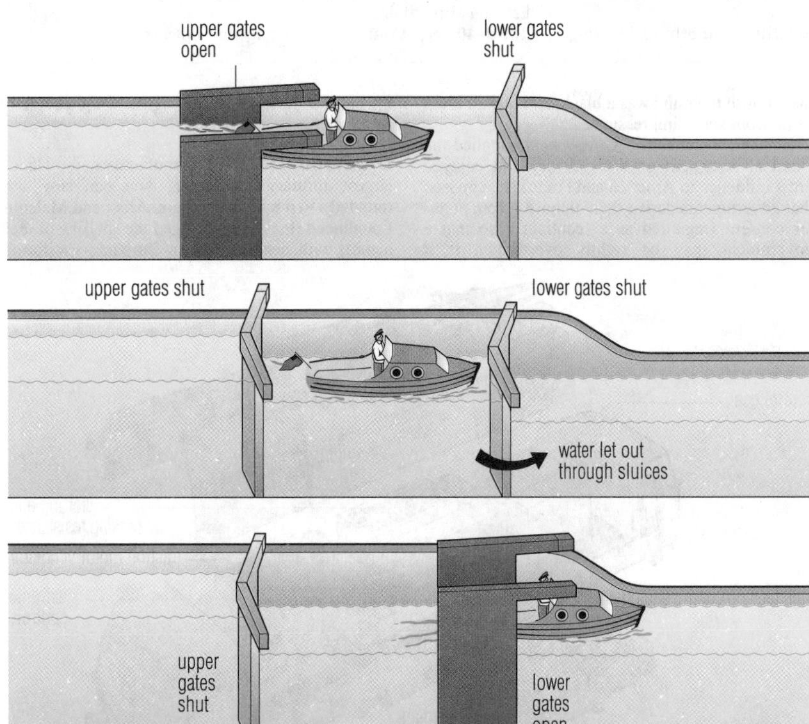

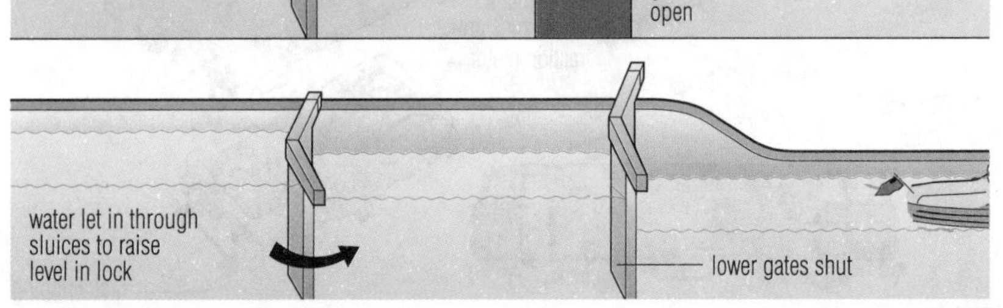

lock Travelling downstream, a boat enters the lock with the lower gates closed. The upper gates are then shut and the water level lowered by draining through sluices. When the water level in the lock reaches the downstream level, the lower gates are opened.

LITHUANIA
Republic of

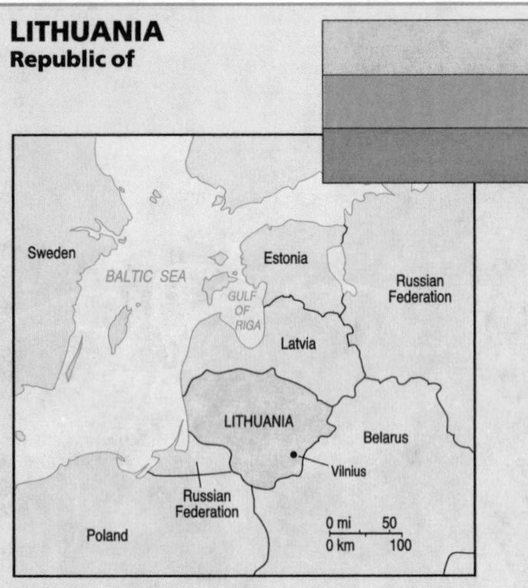

national name *Lietuvos Respublika*
area 65,200 sq km/25,174 sq mi
capital Vilnius
major towns/cities Kaunas, Klaipeda, Siauliai, Panevezys
physical features central lowlands with gentle hills in W and higher terrain in SE; 25% forested; some 3,000 small lakes, marshes, and complex sandy coastline; river Nemen
head of state Valdas Adamkus from 1998
head of government Gediminas Vagnorius from 1996
political system emergent democracy
administrative divisions 44 districts, 92 towns, and 22 urban settlements
political parties Lithuanian Democratic Labour Party (LDLP), reform-socialist (ex-communist); Homeland Union–Lithuanian Conservatives (Tevynes Santara), right of centre, nationalist; Christian Democratic Party of Lithuania, centre-right; Lithuanian Social Democratic Party, left of centre
population 3,728,000 (1996 est)
population growth rate −0.1% (1990–95); 0.1% (2000–05)
ethnic distribution 80% Lithuanian ethnic descent, 9% ethnic Russian, 7% Polish, 2% Belarussian, and 1% Ukrainian
life expectancy 67 (men), 76 (women)
literacy rate 98%
language Lithuanian (official)
religions predominantly Roman Catholic; Lithuanian Lutheran Church
currency litas
GDP (US $) 5.22 billion (1994)
growth rate 0.6% (1994)
exports heavy engineering, electrical goods, shipbuilding, cement, food processing, bacon, dairy products, cereals, potatoes

HISTORY
late 12th C Became a separate nation.
1230 Mindaugas united the Lithuanian tribes to resist attempted invasions by German and Livonian Teutonic Knights, and adopted Christianity.
14th C Strong Grand Duchy formed by Gediminas, founder of Vilnius and Jogaila dynasty, and his son, Algirdas; absorbing Ruthenian territories to E and S, it stretched from the Baltic to the Black Sea and E, nearly reaching Moscow.
1410 Led by Duke Vytautas, and in alliance with Poland, the Teutonic Knights were defeated decisively at Battle of Tannenberg.
1569 Joined Poland in a confederation, under the Union of Lublin, in which Poland had the upper hand and the Lithuanian upper classes were Polonized.
1795 Came under the control of Tsarist Russia, following the partition of Poland; 'Lithuania Minor' (Kaliningrad) fell to Germany.
1831 and 1863 Failed revolts for independence.
1880s Development of an organized nationalist movement.
1914–18 Occupied by German troops in World War I.
1918–19 Independence declared and, after uprising against attempted imposition of Soviet Union (USSR) control, was achieved as a democratic republic.
1920–39 Province and city of Vilnius occupied by Poles.
1926 Democracy overthrown in an authoritarian coup by Antanas Smetona, who became president.
1934 Baltic Entente mutual-defence pact signed with Estonia and Latvia.
1939–40 Secret German-Soviet agreement brought most of Lithuania under Soviet influence as a constituent republic.
1941 Lithuania revolted, creating own government, but during World War II Germany again occupied the country and 210,000, mainly Jews, were killed.
1944 USSR resumed rule.
1944–52 Lithuanian guerrillas fought USSR, which persecuted the Catholic Church, collectivized agriculture, and deported half a million Balts to Siberia.
1972 Demonstrations against Soviet government.
1980s Growth in nationalist dissent, influenced by Polish Solidarity movement and glasnost ('openness') initiative of Soviet leader Mikhail Gorbachev.
1988 Popular Front formed, the Sajudis, to campaign for increased autonomy; parliament declared Lithuanian the state language and readopted the flag of interwar republic.
1989 Communist Party (CP) split into pro-Moscow and nationalist wings, and lost local monopoly of power; over 1 million took part in nationalist demonstrations.
1990 Nationalist Sajudis won elections and their leader, Vytautas Landsbergis, became president; unilateral declaration of independence rejected by USSR, who imposed an economic blockade.
1991 Soviet paratroopers briefly occupied key buildings in Vilnius, killing 13; CP outlawed; independence recognized by USSR and Western nations and admitted into United Nations.
1992 Ex-communist Democratic Labour Party (LDLP) won majority in parliamentary elections as economic restructuring caused contraction in GDP.
1993 LDLP leader Algirdas Brazauskas elected president, and Adolfas Slezevicius became prime minister. Free-trade agreement with other Baltic states. Last Russian troops departed.
1994 Friendship and cooperation treaty with Poland.
1994 Trade and cooperation agreement with European Union.
1996 Slezevicius resigned over banking scandal and was replaced by Laurynas Stankevicius. Homeland Union won parliamentary elections; Gediminas Vagnorius became prime minister.
1997 Border treaty signed with Russia.
1998 Valdas Adamkus became president.

SEE ALSO Landsbergis, Vytautas; Union of Soviet Socialist Republics

that at birth the mind was a blank, and that all ideas came from sense impressions.

His *Two Treatises on Government* supplied the classical statement of Whig theory and enjoyed great influence in America and France. It supposed that governments derive their authority from popular consent (regarded as a 'contract'), so that a government may be rightly overthrown if it infringes such fundamental rights of the people as religious freedom.

Lockheed US aircraft manufacturer, the USA's largest military contractor. The company was founded 1916 by two brothers, Allan and Malcolm Loughheed (they later changed the spelling of their name), with headquarters in Burbank, California. Lockheed built the Vega plane in 1926 (later used by Amelia ◊Earhart in her solo transatlantic flight), the first fully pressurized aircraft, the XC-35, 1937, the P-38 Lightning fighter of World War II, and the TriStar passenger plane of the 1960s. After a merger the company became Lockheed Martin Aeronautical Systems.

lockjaw former name for ◊tetanus, a type of bacterial infection.

lock-out industrial action taken by employers whereby they prevent workers coming to work.

Lockwood Margaret Mary 1916–1990. English actress. Between 1937 and 1949 she acted exclusively in the cinema, appearing in Alfred Hitchcock's *The Lady Vanishes* 1938 and in *The Wicked Lady* 1945. After 1955 she made only one film, *The Slipper and the Rose* 1976, although she periodically appeared on stage and on television until her retirement 1980.

locomotive engine for hauling railway trains. In 1804 Richard Trevithick built the first steam engine to run on rails. Locomotive design did not radically improve until British engineer George Stephenson built the *Rocket* 1829, which featured a multitube boiler and blastpipe, standard in all following steam locomotives. Today most locomotives are diesel or electric: diesel locomotives have a powerful diesel engine, and electric locomotives draw their power from either an overhead cable or a third rail alongside the ordinary track.

In a steam locomotive, fuel (usually coal, sometimes wood) is burned in a furnace. The hot gases and flames produced are drawn through tubes running through a huge water-filled boiler and heat up the water to steam. The steam is then fed to the cylinders, where it forces the pistons back and forth. Movement of the pistons is conveyed to the wheels by cranks and connecting rods. Diesel locomotives have a powerful diesel engine, burning oil.

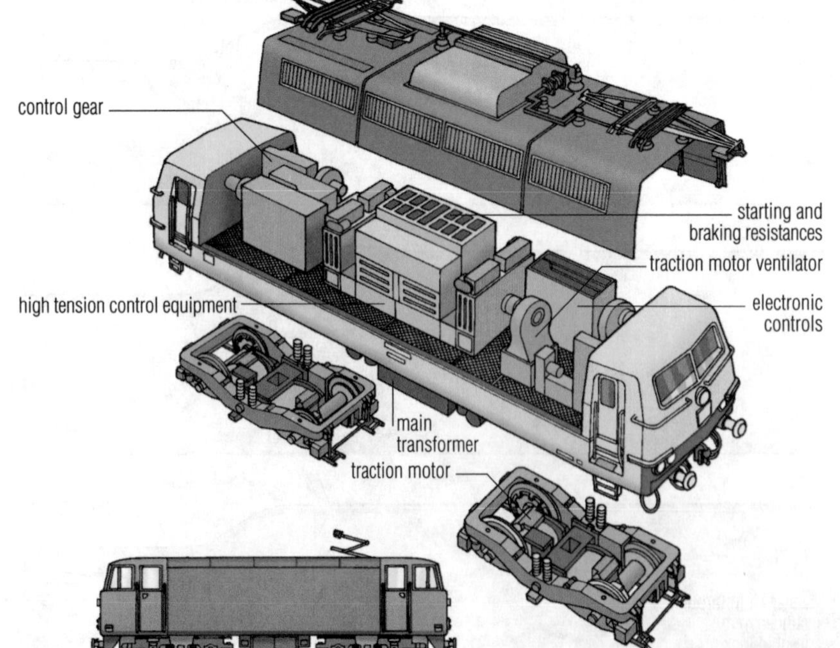

locomotive The drive of an electric locomotive is provided by powerful electric motors (traction motors) in the bogies beneath the body of the locomotive. The motors are controlled by equipment inside the locomotive. Both AC and DC power supplies are used, although most modern systems use a 2500 V supply.

The engine may drive a generator to produce electricity to power electric motors that turn the wheels, or the engine drives the wheels mechanically or through a hydraulic link. A number of gas-turbine locomotives are in use, in which a turbine spun by hot gases provides the power to drive the wheels.

locus (Latin 'place') in mathematics, traditionally the path traced out by a moving point, but now defined as the set of all points on a curve satisfying given conditions. For example, the locus of a point that moves so that it is always at the same distance from another fixed point is a circle.

locust swarming grasshopper, with short antennae and auditory organs on the abdomen, in the family Acrididae. As winged adults, flying in swarms, locusts may be carried by the wind hundreds of miles from their breeding grounds; on landing they devour all vegetation. Locusts occur in nearly every continent.

The migratory locust *Locusta migratoria* ranges from Europe to China, and even small swarms may cover several square kilometres and weigh thousands of tonnes. Control by spreading poisoned food among the bands is very effective, but it is cheapest to spray concentrated insecticide solutions from aircraft over the insects or the vegetation on which they feed. They eat the equivalent of their own weight in a day, and, flying at night with the wind, may cover some 500 km/300 mi. The largest known swarm covered 1,036 sq km/400 sq mi, comprising approximately 40 billion insects.

lode geological deposit rich in certain minerals, generally consisting of a large vein or set of veins containing ore minerals. A system of veins that can be mined directly forms a lode, for example the mother lode of the California gold rush.

lodestar or ***loadstar*** a star used in navigation or astronomy, often ◊Polaris, the Pole Star.

Lodge David John 1935– . English novelist, short-story writer, dramatist, and critic. Much of his fiction concerns the role of Catholicism in mid-20th-century England, explored both through broad comedy and parody, as in *The British Museum is Falling Down* 1967, and realistically, as in *How Far Can You Go?* 1980. Other works include *Changing Places* 1975 and its sequel *Small World* 1984, *Nice Work* 1988, the play *The Writing Game* 1990, *Paradise News* 1991, and *Therapy* 1995.

Łódź industrial city (textiles, machinery, dyes) in central Poland, 120 km/75 mi SW of Warsaw; population (1993) 844,900.

loess yellow loam, derived from glacial meltwater deposits and accumulated by wind in periglacial regions during the ◊ice ages. Loess usually attains considerable depths, and the soil derived from it is very fertile. There are large deposits in central Europe (Hungary), China, and North America.

Loewe Frederick 1904–1988. US composer of musicals. In 1942 he joined forces with the lyricist Alan Jay Lerner, and their joint successes include *Brigadoon* 1947, *Paint Your Wagon* 1951, *My Fair Lady* 1956, *Gigi* 1958, and *Camelot* 1960.

log in mathematics, abbreviation for ◊***logarithm***.

log any apparatus for measuring the speed of a ship; also the daily record of events on board a ship or aircraft. The log originally consisted of a piece of weighted wood attached to a line with knots at equal intervals that was cast from the rear of a ship. The vessel's speed was estimated by timing the passage of the knots with a sandglass (like an egg timer). Today logs use electromagnetism and sonar.

loganberry hybrid between a ◊blackberry and a ◊raspberry with large, tart, dull-red fruit. It was developed by US judge James H Logan 1881.

logarithm or ***log*** the ◊exponent or index of a number to a specified base – usually 10. For example, the logarithm to the base 10 of 1,000 is 3 because $10^3 = 1{,}000$; the logarithm of 2 is 0.3010 because $2 = 10^{0.3010}$. Before the advent of cheap electronic calculators, multiplication and division could be simplified by being replaced with the addition and subtraction of logarithms.

For any two numbers x and y (where $x = b^a$ and $y = b^c$) $x \times y = b^a \times b^c = b^{a+c}$; hence we would add the logarithms of x and y, and look up this answer in antilogarithm tables.

Tables of logarithms and antilogarithms are available that show conversions of numbers into logarithms, and vice versa. For example, to multiply 6,560 by 980, one looks up their logarithms (3.8169 and 2.9912), adds them together (6.8081), then looks up the antilogarithm of this to get the answer (6,428,800). Natural or Napierian logarithms are to the base e, an ◊irrational number equal to approximately 2.7183.

logic branch of philosophy that studies valid reasoning and argument. It is also the way in which one thing may be said to follow from, or be a consequence of, another (deductive logic). Logic is generally divided into the traditional formal logic of Aristotle and the symbolic logic derived from Friedrich Frege and Bertrand Russell.

Aristotle's *Organon* is the founding work on logic, and Aristotelian methods, as revived in the medieval Christian church by the French scholar Peter Abelard in the 12th century, were used in the synthesis of ideas aimed at in scholasticism. As befitted the spirit of the Renaissance, the English philosopher Francis Bacon considered many of the general principles used as premises by the scholastics to be groundless; he envisaged that in natural philosophy principles worthy of investigation would emerge by 'inductive' logic, which works backwards from the accumulated facts to the principle that accounts for them.

logical positivism doctrine that the only meaningful propositions are those that can be verified empirically. Metaphysics, religion, and aesthetics are therefore meaningless. However, the doctrine itself cannot be verified empirically and so is self-refuting. Logical positivism was characteristic of the Vienna Circle in the 1920s and 1930s, and was influenced by Friedrich Frege, Bertrand Russell, and Ludwig Wittgenstein.

logic gate or ***logic circuit*** in electronics, one of the basic components used in building ◊integrated circuits. The five basic types of gate make logical decisions based on the functions NOT, AND, OR, NAND (NOT AND), and NOR (NOT OR). With the exception of the NOT gate, each has two or more inputs. The properties of a logic gate, or of a combination of gates, may be defined and presented in the form of a diagram called a truth table, which lists the output that will be triggered by each of the possible combinations of input signals. The process has close parallels in computer programming, where it forms the basis of binary logic.

LOGO (Greek *logos* 'word') high-level computer programming language designed to teach mathematical concepts. Developed about 1970, it became popular in schools and with home computer users because of its 'turtle graphics' feature. This allows the user to write programs that create line drawings on a computer screen, or drive a small mobile robot (a 'turtle' or 'buggy') around the floor.

locust The migratory locust *Locusta migratoria*. When these locusts swarm, sometimes in their billions, the damage they cause to crops and natural vegetation is phenomenal. Each locust devours its own body weight every day. *Premaphotos Wildlife*

logos (Greek 'word') term in Greek, Hebrew, and Christian philosophy and theology. It was used by Greek philosophers as the embodiment of 'reason' in the universe. Under Greek influence the Jews came to conceive of 'wisdom' as an aspect of God's activity. The Jewish philosopher Philo (1st century AD) attempted to reconcile Platonic, Stoic, and Hebrew philosophy by identifying the logos with the Jewish idea of 'wisdom'. Several of the New Testament writers took over Philo's conception of the logos, which they identified with Christ and hence with the second person of the Trinity.

Lohengrin in late 13th-century Germanic legend, a heroic knight, son of ◊Parsifal. Summoned by the ◊Holy Grail to vindicate Elsa of Brabant, Lohengrin is conveyed to the place of combat by a swan-drawn boat, but though he saves Elsa and marries her, he must leave again when she breaks the condition of not asking his name.

Loire longest river in France, rising in the Cévennes Mountains, at 1,350 m/4,430 ft and flowing for 1,050 km/650 mi first north then west until it reaches the Bay of Biscay at St Nazaire, passing Nevers, Orléans, Tours, and Nantes. It gives its name to the *départements* of Loire, Haute-Loire, Loire-Atlantique, Indre-et-Loire, Maine-et-Loire, and Saône-et-Loire. There are many châteaux and vineyards along its banks.

Loki in Norse mythology, one of the Aesir (the principal gods), but the cause of dissension among the gods, and the slayer of ◊Balder. His children are the Midgard serpent Jörmungander, which girdles the Earth; the wolf Fenris; and Hela, goddess of death.

Lollard follower of the English religious reformer John ◊Wycliffe in the 14th century. The Lollards condemned the doctrine of the transubstantiation of the bread and wine of the Eucharist, advocated the diversion of ecclesiastical property to charitable uses, and denounced war and capital punishment. They were active from about 1377; after the passing of the statute *De heretico comburendo* ('The Necessity of Burning Heretics') 1401 many Lollards were burned, and in 1414 they raised an unsuccessful revolt in London, known as Oldcastle's rebellion. Lollardy lingered on in London and East Anglia, and in the 16th century became absorbed into the Protestant movement.

Lombard or ***Langobard*** member of a Germanic people who invaded Italy 568 and occupied Lombardy (named after them) and central Italy. Their capital was Monza. They were conquered by the Frankish ruler Charlemagne 774.

Lombard league association of N Italian towns and cities (not all of which were in Lombardy) established 1164 to maintain their independence against the Holy Roman emperors' claims of sovereignty. Venice, Padua, Brescia, Milan, and Mantua were among the founders. Supported by Milan and Pope Alexander III (1105–1181), the league defeated Frederick Barbarossa at Legnano in N Italy

'One of the most wonderful rivers in the world, mirroring from sea to source a hundred cities and five hundred towers.'

On the LOIRE
Oscar Wilde, letter Nov 1880

"There is in the aspect of London a certain magnificence; the magnificence of weight, solidity, energy, imperturbability, and an unconquered continuance."

On LONDON
Arthur Symons
London 1918

1179 and effectively resisted Otto IV (1175–1218) and Frederick II, becoming the most powerful champion of the ◊Guelph cause. Internal rivalries led to its dissolution 1250.

Lombardy (Italian ***Lombardia***) region of N Italy, including Lake Como; capital Milan; area 23,900 sq km/9,225 sq mi; population (1992 est) 8,882,400. It is the country's chief industrial area (chemicals, pharmaceuticals, engineering, textiles).

Lombardy League, The Italian regional political party, committed to federalism, which models itself on the 12th–15th-century Lombard League. In 1993 it became the core of a new conservative-populist political grouping, the Northern League, led by Umberto Bossi. The Northern League eventually entered into a coalition government led by Prime Minister Silvio Berlusconi, but later left. Having founded a 'parliament of the north' in Mantua in 1995, in 1996 it contested the general election on a separatist platform, calling for the creation of an economically dominant Nordnazione, embracing Tuscany, Piedmont and Lombardy. In Sept 1996, on behalf of the Northern League, Bossi declared an independent state of Padania.

Lomé capital and port of Togo; population (1990) 450,000. It is a centre for gold, silver, and marble crafts; industries include steel production and oil refining.

Lomé Convention convention in 1975 that established economic cooperation between the European Community (now the European Union) and African, Caribbean, and Pacific (ACP) developing countries. It was renewed 1979, 1985, and 1989. At the end of 1996 70 ACP states were parties to the Convention. Grants are given to the ACP developing countries chiefly via the European Development Fund (EDF).

Lomond, Loch largest freshwater Scottish lake, 37 km/21 mi long, area 70 sq km/27 sq mi, divided between Strathclyde and Central regions. It is overlooked by the mountain Ben Lomond (973 m/3,192 ft) and is linked to the Clyde estuary.

London city in SW Ontario, Canada, on the river Thames, 160 km/100 mi SW of Toronto; population (1986) 342,000. It has tanneries, breweries, and factories making hosiery, radio and electrical equipment, leather, and shoes. It dates from 1826 and is the seat of the University of Western Ontario.

London capital of England and the United Kingdom, on the river Thames; its metropolitan area, ***Greater London***, has an area of 1,580 sq km/610 sq mi and population (1994 est) of 6,967,000 (larger metropolitan area about 9 million). The ***City of London***, known as the 'square mile', area 274 hectares/677 acres, is the financial and commercial centre of the UK. Greater London (see ◊London, Greater) from 1965 comprises the City of London and 32 boroughs. London is the only major European capital without a strategic authority covering the whole area.
history Roman Londinium was established soon after the Roman invasion AD 43; in the 2nd century London became a walled city; by the 11th century, it was the main city of England and gradually extended beyond the walls to link with the originally separate Westminster. 19th century London was the largest city in the world (in population).
features The Tower of London, built by William the Conqueror on a Roman site, houses the crown jewels and the royal armouries; 15th-century Guildhall; the Monument (a column designed by Christopher Wren) marks the site in Pudding Lane where the Great Fire of 1666 began; Mansion House (residence of the lord mayor); Barbican arts and conference centre; Central Criminal Court (Old Bailey) and the Inner and Middle Temples; Covent Garden, once a vegetable market, is now a tourist shopping and entertainment area.
architecture London contains buildings in all styles of English architecture since the 11th century. Norman: the White Tower, Tower of London; St Bartholomew's, Smithfield; the Temple Church. Gothic: Westminster Abbey; Westminster Hall; Lambeth Palace; Southwark Cathedral. Tudor: St James's Palace; Staple Inn. 17th century: Banqueting Hall, Whitehall (Inigo Jones); St Paul's; Kensington Palace; many City churches (all by Wren). 18th century: Somerset House (Chambers); St Martin-in-the-Fields; Buckingham Palace. 19th century: British Museum (Neo-Classical); Houses of Parliament; Law Courts (Neo-Gothic); Westminster Cathedral (Byzantine style). 20th century: Lloyd's of London.
government Since 1986 there has been no central authority for Greater London; responsibility is divided between individual boroughs and central government.

The City of London has been governed by a corporation from the 12th century. Its structure and the electoral procedures for its common councillors and aldermen are medievally complex, and it is headed by the lord mayor (who is, broadly speaking, nominated by the former and elected annually by the latter). After being sworn in at the Guildhall, he or she is presented the next day to the lord chief justice at the Royal Courts of Justice in Westminster, and the Lord Mayor's Show is a ceremonial procession there in Nov.
commerce and industry From Saxon times the Port of London dominated the Thames from Tower Bridge to Tilbury; its activity is now centred outside the metropolitan area, and downstream Tilbury has been extended to cope with container traffic. The prime economic importance of modern London is as a financial centre. There are various industries, mainly on the outskirts. There are also recording, broadcasting, television, and film studios; publishing companies; and the works and offices of the national press. Tourism is important.

Some of the docks in the East End of London, once the busiest in the world, have been sold to the Docklands Development Corporation, which has built offices, houses, factories, and a railway. The world's largest office development project is at ◊Canary Wharf.
education and entertainment Museums: British, Victoria and Albert, Natural History, Science museums; galleries: National Gallery, National Portrait Gallery, Tate Gallery, Hayward Gallery, Wallace Collection, Courtauld Institute Galleries. London University is the largest in Britain, while the Inns of Court have been the training school for lawyers since the 13th century. London has been the centre of English drama since its first theatre was built by James Burbage 1576.
boroughs The inner London boroughs of Greater London are: Camden, Hackney, Hammersmith and Fulham, Haringey, Islington, Kensington and Chelsea, Lambeth, Lewisham, Newham, Southwark, Tower Hamlets, Wandsworth, and the City of Westminster. The outer London boroughs of Greater London are: Barking and Dagenham, Barnet, Bexley, Brent, Bromley, Croydon, Ealing, Enfield, Greenwich, Harrow, Havering, Hillingdon, Hounslow, Kingston upon Thames, Merton, Redbridge, Richmond-upon-Thames, Sutton, and Waltham Forest.

London Jack (John Griffith Chaney) 1876–1916. US novelist. His works, which are often based on his own life, typically concern the human struggle for survival against extreme natural forces, as dramatized in such novels as *The Call of the Wild* 1903, *The Sea Wolf* 1904, and *White Fang* 1906.

London Contemporary Dance Theatre British modern dance company formed by entrepreneur Robin Howard 1967. Its aim was to introduce modern dance based on the principles of Martha ◊Graham to Britain. Its first artistic director was Robert Cohan. Several important choreographers have emerged from the company and its school, such as Richard Alston (1948–) and Siobhan Davies (1950–).

Londonderry or ***Derry*** historic city and port on the river Foyle, County Londonderry, Northern Ireland; population (1991) 21,500. Industries include textiles, chemicals, shirt manufacturing, and acetylene from naphtha.
features the Protestant cathedral of St Columba (1633); the Guildhall (rebuilt 1912), containing stained glass windows presented by livery companies of the City of London.
history Londonderry dates from the foundation of a monastery by St Columba AD 546. James I of England granted the borough and surrounding land to the citizens of London. The Irish Society was formed to build and administer the city and a large colony of English Protestants was established. The city was besieged by the armies of James II in the Siege of Londonderry 1688–89.

Londonderry or ***Derry*** county of Northern Ireland, divided into four districts: Coleraine, Derry, Limavady, Magherafelt
area 2,070 sq km/799 sq mi
towns and cities Londonderry (county town), Coleraine, Portstewart
features rivers Foyle, Bann, and Roe; borders Lough Neagh
industries mainly agricultural, but farming is hindered by heavy rainfall; flax, cattle, sheep, food processing, textiles, light engineering
famous people Joyce Cary, Seamus Heaney.

London, Greater metropolitan area of ◊London, England, comprising the City of London, which forms a self-governing enclave, and 32 surrounding boroughs; area 1,580 sq km/610 sq mi; population (1991) 6,679,700. The population of Inner London is 2,504,500 and that of Outer London 4,175,200. Certain powers were exercised over this whole area by the Greater London Council (GLC) 1974–86.

London, Treaty of secret treaty signed 26 April 1915 between Britain, France, Russia, and Italy. It promised Italy territorial gains (at the expense of Austria-Hungary) on condition that it entered World War I on the side of the Triple Entente (Britain, France, and Russia). Italy's intervention did not achieve the rapid victories expected. Britain and France refused to honour the treaty and, in the postwar peace treaties, Italy received far less territory than promised.

London University university originated in 1826 with the founding of University College, to provide higher education free from religious tests. In 1836 a charter set up an examining body with power to grant degrees. London University opened all its degrees to women in 1878, the first British university to do so. Its complex substructure of smaller colleges had by 1991 been rationalized to 24 colleges, medical schools, and major institutes, plus 19 affiliated centres.

lone pair in chemistry, a pair of electrons in the outermost shell of an atom that are not used in bonding. In certain circumstances, they will allow the atom to bond with atoms, ions, or molecules (such as boron trifluoride, BF_3) that are deficient in electrons, forming coordinate covalent (dative) bonds in which they provide both of the bonding electrons.

Long Richard 1945– . English Conceptual artist. In the vanguard of 1960s young artists wishing to break away from studio-created art, he has worked both outdoors and on the spot in galleries. He has used natural materials such as stone, slate, wood, and mud to represent the ritualized traces of early peoples, notably in *River Avon Driftwood* 1977 (Museum of Contemporary Art, Ghent). Only photographic records remain of much of his work.

Long Beach city in SW California, USA; population (1992) 438,800. A port and industrial city, it also has oil wells and a naval shipyard. Manufactured goods include aircraft, ships, petroleum products, chemicals, fabricated metals, electronic equipment, and processed food. It is also a convention centre. Long Beach forms part of Greater Los Angeles.

Longfellow Henry Wadsworth 1807–1882. US poet. He is remembered for his ballads ('Excelsior', 'The Village Blacksmith', 'The Wreck of the Hesperus') and the mythic narrative epics *Evangeline* 1847, *The Song of Hiawatha* 1855, and *The Courtship of Miles Standish* 1858.

Longfellow was born in Portland, Maine. He graduated from Bowdoin College and taught modern languages there and at Harvard University 1835–54, after which he travelled widely. The most popular US poet of the 19th century, Longfellow was also an adept translator. His other works include six sonnets on Dante, a translation of Dante's *Divine Comedy*, and *Tales of a Wayside Inn* 1863, which includes the popular poem 'Paul Revere's Ride'.

"Thy fate is the common fate of all / Into each life some rain must fall."

HENRY WADSWORTH LONGFELLOW
'The Rainy Day'

Longford county of the Republic of Ireland, in the province of Leinster; county town Longford; area 1,040 sq km/401 sq mi; population (1991) 30,300. It is low-lying with bogs and has the rivers Camlin, Inny, and Shannon (which forms its western boundary), and several lakes. Agricultural activities include stock rearing and the production of oats and potatoes.

Longinus Dionysius Cassius AD 213–273. Greek philosopher and rhetorician. He came from Emesa, Syria, and taught in Athens for many years. As adviser to ◊Zenobia of Palmyra, he instigated her revolt against Rome and was put to death when she was captured.

Long Island island E of Manhattan and SE of Connecticut, USA, separated from the mainland by Long Island Sound and the East River; 193 km/120 mi long by about 48 km/30 mi wide; area 3,627 sq km/1,400 sq mi; population (1984) 6,818,480. It includes two boroughs of New York City (Queens and Brooklyn), John F Kennedy airport, suburbs, and resorts. It also has Brookhaven National Laboratory for atomic research, the world's largest automotive museum, the New York Aquarium, and a whaling museum. The popular resort of Coney Island is actually a peninsula in the southwest.

longitude see ◊latitude and longitude.

longitudinal wave ◊wave in which the displacement of the medium's particles is in line with or parallel to the direction of travel of the wave motion.

long jump field event in athletics in which competitors sprint up to and leap from a take-off board into a sandpit measuring 9 metres in length. The take-off board is 1 metre from the landing area. Each competitor usually has six attempts, and the winner is the one with the longest jump.

Long March in Chinese history, the 10,000 km/6,000 mi trek undertaken 1934–35 by ◊Mao Zedong and his communist forces from SE to NW China, under harassment from the Guomindang (nationalist) army. Some 100,000 communists left Mao's first headquarters in Jiangxi province Oct 1934, and only 8,000 lasted the journey to arrive about a year later in Shanxi, which became their new base. The march cemented Mao Zedong's control of the movement.

Long Parliament English Parliament 1640–53 and 1659–60, which continued through the Civil War. After the Royalists withdrew 1642 and the Presbyterian right was excluded 1648, the remaining ◊Rump ruled England until expelled by Oliver Cromwell 1653. Reassembled 1659–60, the Long Parliament initiated the negotiations for the restoration of the monarchy.

Longshan or ***Lung-shan*** site of a sophisticated late Neolithic culture 2500–1700 BC in N China now situated in the province of Shandong in the lower Huang He (Yellow River) valley. The culture was the immediate precursor of the bronze-using ◊Shang civilization. Its distinctive burnished black ceramics were kiln-fired and were the first in the Far East to be made on the fast wheel.

long-sightedness or ***hypermetropia*** defect of vision in which a person is able to focus on objects in the distance, but not on close objects. It is caused by the failure of the lens to return to its normal rounded shape, or by the eyeball being too short, with the result that the image is focused on a point behind the retina. Long-sightedness is corrected by wearing spectacles fitted with ◊converging lenses, each of which acts like a magnifying glass.

loquat The loquat is a small, evergreen tree or shrub belonging to the Rosaceae family. It is native to China and Japan and is also known as the Japanese medlar. It is widely cultivated both as a decorative tree and for its edible, plumlike, yellowish fruits. The fruit is especially good for preserving.

loom any machine for weaving yarn or thread into cloth. The first looms were used to weave sheep's wool about 5000 BC. A loom is a frame on which a set of lengthwise threads (warp) is strung. A second set of threads (weft), carried in a shuttle, is inserted at right angles over and under the warp.

In most looms the warp threads are separated by a device called a treddle to create a gap, or shed, through which the shuttle can be passed in a straight line. A kind of comb called a reed presses each new line of weave tight against the previous ones. All looms have similar features, but on the power loom, weaving takes place automatically at great speed. Mechanization of weaving began 1733 when British inventor John Kay invented the flying shuttle. In 1785 British inventor Edmund Cartwright introduced a steam-powered loom. Among recent developments are shuttleless looms, which work at very high speed, passing the weft through the warp by means of 'rapiers', and jets of air or water.

Loos Adolf 1870–1933. Austrian architect. His buildings include private houses on Lake Geneva 1904 and the Steiner House in Vienna 1910. In his article 'Ornament and Crime' 1908 he rejected the ornamentation and curved lines of the Viennese *Jugendstil* movement (see ◊Art Nouveau).

Loos Anita 1893–1981. US writer. She was the author of the humorous fictitious diary *Gentlemen Prefer Blondes* 1925. She became a screenwriter 1912 and worked on more than 60 films, including D W Griffith's *Intolerance* 1916.

loosestrife any of several plants of the family Primulaceae, including the yellow loosestrife *Lysimachia vulgaris*, with spikes of yellow flowers, and the low-growing creeping jenny *Lysimachia nummularia*. The striking purple loosestrife *Lythrum saclicaria* belongs to the family Lythraceae.

loquat evergreen tree *Eriobotrya japonica* of the family Rosaceae, native to China and Japan and also known as the ***Japan medlar***. The golden pear-shaped fruit has a delicate sweet-sour taste.

Lope de Vega (Carpio) Felix. Spanish poet and dramatist; see ◊Vega, Lope de.

Lorca Federico García 1898–1936. Spanish poet and playwright. His plays include *Bodas de sangre/Blood Wedding* 1933, *Yerma* 1934, and *La casa de Bernarda Alba/The House of Bernarda Alba* 1936. His poems include the collection *Romancero gitano/Gypsy Ballad-book* 1928 and the 'Lament' written for the bullfighter Ignacio Sánchez Mejías. Lorca was shot by the Falangists during the Spanish Civil War.

Early collections of poetry were *Libros de poemas/Books of Poems* 1921 and *Canciones/Gypsy Songs* 1927. He established himself with the *Romancero gitano*, a collection of mysterious and beautiful ballads of gypsy life and Andalusian folklore. In 1929–30 he visited New York, and his experiences there are reflected in *Poeta en Nuevo York/Poet in New York* 1940. Returning to Spain, he founded a touring theatrical company and began to write plays.

Lord in the UK, prefix used informally as alternative to the full title of a marquess, earl, or viscount; normally also in speaking of a baron, and as a courtesy title before the forename and surname of younger sons of dukes and marquesses.

Lord Advocate chief law officer of the crown in Scotland who has ultimate responsibility for criminal prosecutions in Scotland.

Lord Chancellor UK state official; see ◊Chancellor, Lord.

Lord Lieutenant in the UK, the sovereign's representative in a county, who recommends magistrates for appointment. It is an unpaid position and the retirement age is 75.

Lord's one of England's test-match grounds and the headquarters of cricket's governing body, the Marylebone Cricket Club (MCC), since 1788. The ground is named after Yorkshireman Thomas Lord (1757–1832) who developed the first site at Dorset Square in 1787. He moved the ground to a field at North Bank, Regent's Park, in 1811, and in 1814 developed the ground at its present site at St John's Wood. Lord's is also the home of the Middlesex Cricket Club.

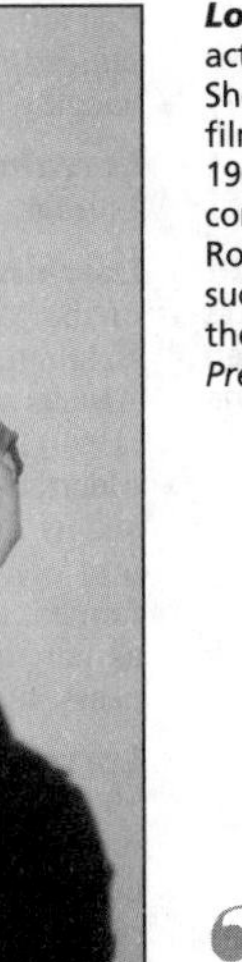

Loren The Italian actress Sophia Loren. She starred in several films in the 1950s and 1960s, and made a comeback in 1994 in Robert Altman's successful portrait of the fashion industry *Prêt-à-Porter*. *Corbis*

Lords, House of upper house of the UK ◊Parliament.

Lord's Prayer in the New Testament, the prayer taught by Jesus to his disciples. It is sometimes called 'Our Father' or 'Paternoster' from the opening words in English and Latin respectively.

Lord's Supper in the Christian church, another name for the ◊Eucharist.

Lorelei in Germanic folklore, a river ◊nymph of the Rhine who lures sailors onto the rock where she sits combing her hair. The Lurlei rock S of Koblenz is 130 m/430 ft high.

Loren Sophia. Stage name of Sofia Scicolone 1934– . Italian film actress. Her boldly sensual appeal was promoted by her husband, producer Carlo Ponti. Her work includes *Aida* 1953, *The Key* 1958, *La Ciociara/Two Women* 1960, *Judith* 1965, and *Firepower* 1979.

Lorenz Konrad Zacharias 1903–1989. Austrian ethologist. He studied the relationship between instinct and behaviour, particularly in birds, and described the phenomenon of ◊imprinting 1935. His books include *King Solomon's Ring* 1952 (on animal behaviour) and *On Aggression* 1966 (on human behaviour). In 1973 he shared the Nobel Prize for Physiology or Medicine with Nikolaas ◊Tinbergen and Karl von ◊Frisch.

lorikeet any of various small, brightly coloured parrots, found in SE Asia and Australasia.

Lorimer Robert Stodart 1864–1929. Scottish architect. The most prolific architect representative of the Scottish Arts and Crafts movement, Lorimer drew particularly from Scottish vernacular buildings of the 16th and 17th centuries to create a series of mansions and houses, practically planned with picturesque, turreted exteriors. Examples of his work include Ardkinglas House, Argyll, 1906, and Ruwallan House, Ayrshire, 1902.

loris any of various small prosimian primates of the family Lorisidae. Lorises are slow-moving, arboreal, and nocturnal. They have very large eyes;

‘So this gentleman said a girl with brains ought to do something with them besides think.’

ANITA LOOS
Gentlemen Prefer Blondes

‘It is a good morning exercise for a research scientist to discard a pet hypothesis every day before breakfast. It keeps him young.’

KONRAD LORENZ
The So-Called Evil

loris The two species of loris are primitive primates related to bush babies and pottos. The slow loris lives among the trees of the rainforests in S and SE Asia where it feeds at night mainly on insects and plant material although it will take small birds and their eggs. It gets its name because of its slow, deliberate movements.

Nineteen suburbs in search of a metropolis.

On **Los Angeles**
H L Mencken
Americana

true lorises have no tails. They climb without leaping, gripping branches tightly and moving on or hanging below them.

Lorrain Claude. French painter; see ◊Claude Lorrain.

Lorraine region of NE France in the upper reaches of the Meuse and Moselle rivers; bounded N by Belgium, Luxembourg, and Germany and E by Alsace; area 23,600 sq km/9,095 sq mi; population (1990) 2,305,700. It comprises the *départements* of Meurthe-et-Moselle, Meuse, Moselle, and Vosges, and its capital is Nancy. There are deposits of coal, iron ore, and salt; grain, fruit, and livestock are farmed. In 1871 the region was ceded to Germany as part of Alsace-Lorraine. The whole area saw heavy fighting in World War I.

Lorre Peter. Stage name of Lazlo Löwenstein 1904–1964. Hungarian character actor. He made his international reputation as the whistling child murderer in Fritz Lang's thriller *M* 1930. Becoming one of Hollywood's best-loved lowlifes, he played opposite Humphrey Bogart in *The Maltese Falcon* 1941, *Casablanca* 1942, and *Beat the Devil* 1954, and in several films with the portly British actor Sydney Greenstreet. Lorre twice worked with the English thriller director Alfred Hitchcock: on *The Man Who Knew Too Much* 1934 and *Secret Agent* 1936. He then played the Japanese detective Mr Moto in a series of eight B-movies, and also starred in Frank Capra's *Arsenic and Old Lace* 1944.

lory bird of the subfamily Loriinae, of the ◊parrot order Psittaciformes. Lories are very brightly coloured and characterized by a tongue with a brushlike tip adapted for feeding on pollen and nectar from flowers. They are widely distributed in Australasia.

Los Angeles city and port in SW California, USA; population (1994) 3,700,000; greater metropolitan area of Los Angeles–Long Beach (1992) 15,048,000. Industries include aerospace, electronics, motor vehicles, chemicals, clothing, printing, and food processing.

features Hollywood, centre of the film industry since 1911; the Hollywood Bowl concert arena; observatories at Mount Wilson and Mount Palomar; Disneyland; the Huntingdon Art Gallery and Library; and the John Paul Getty museum of art (a re-creation of a Roman villa in ◊Herculaneum) housing the Classical collection, the rest of its exhibits being housed in the enlarged John Paul Getty Centre across the town in Brentwood.

history Los Angeles was established as a Spanish settlement 1781, but it was a farming region with orange groves until the early 20th century, when it annexed neighbouring communities and acquired distant water supplies, a deep-water port, and the film industry. In the 1920s large petroleum deposits were found in the area. The aircraft industry developed here soon after and grew rapidly during World War II. There were serious race riots in 1965 and 1992. In 1994 an earthquake (6.6 on the Richter scale) struck the city, killing 61 people and displacing an estimated 25,000.

Greater Los Angeles comprises 86 towns, including Long Beach, Redondo Beach, Venice, Santa Monica, Burbank, Compton, Beverly Hills, Glendale, Pasadena, and Pomona. It covers 10,000 sq km/4,000 sq mi.

Losey Joseph Walton 1909–1984. US film director. Blacklisted as a former communist in the ◊McCarthy era, he settled in England, where his films included *The Servant* 1963, *Accident* 1967, and *The Go-Between* 1971.

lost-wax technique method of making sculptures; see ◊*cire perdue*.

Lot in the Old Testament, Abraham's nephew, who escaped the destruction of Sodom. Lot's wife disobeyed the condition of not looking back at Sodom and was punished by being turned into a pillar of salt.

He can run, but he can't hide.

Joe Louis
Of his opponent
Billy Conn,
9 June 1946

Lothair 825–869. King of Lotharingia from 855, when he inherited the region from his father, the Holy Roman emperor Lothair I.

Lothair I 795–855. Holy Roman emperor from 817 in association with his father Louis I. On Louis's death 840, the empire was divided between Lothair and his brothers; Lothair took N Italy and the valleys of the rivers Rhône and Rhine.

Lothair II c. 1070–1137. Holy Roman emperor from 1133 and German king from 1125. His election as emperor, opposed by the ◊Hohenstaufen family of princes, was the start of the feud between the ◊Guelph and Ghibelline factions, who supported the papal party and the Hohenstaufens' claim to the imperial throne respectively.

Lotharingia medieval region W of the Rhine, between the Jura Mountains and the North Sea; the northern portion of the lands assigned to Lothair I when the Carolingian empire was divided. It was called after his son King Lothair, and later corrupted to Lorraine; it is now part of Alsace-Lorraine, France.

Lothian former region of Scotland, created 1975, abolished 1996.

lottery game of chance in which tickets sold may win a prize. State-sponsored lotteries are an effective means of raising revenue, often used for education and other public needs.

types of lottery In the UK lotteries are subject to strict government regulation. There are four main types of lawful lottery: amusements with prizes; small lotteries conducted as part of the entertainment offered at fêtes and sporting events; private lotteries, with ticket restrictions, for example, sold to people working on the same premises; and society lotteries conducted for charitable, sporting, or other purposes. Unlike many other European countries, the UK places strict limits on the value of the prize offered by society lotteries, which may not exceed £4,000. Where the value of the tickets exceeds £10,000 the lottery must be registered with the Gaming Board.

In the UK the largest lottery is the national lottery, launched 1994, which offers prizes often in excess of £10 million per week.

Lotto Lorenzo c. 1480–1556. Italian painter. He was active in Bergamo, Treviso, Venice, Ancona, and Rome. His early works were influenced by Giovanni Bellini; his mature style belongs to the High Renaissance. He painted religious works but is best known for his portraits, which often convey a sense of unease or an air of melancholy.

He evolved a rich and imaginative style, and in portraiture approached greatness, as in the *Prothonotary Apostolic, Giuliano* (National Gallery). His most celebrated altarpieces are in the churches of the Carmine and SS Giovanni e Paolo, Venice, the cathedral at Asola, and at Monte San Giusto near Ancona, where the church contains a *Crucifixion* with 23 life-size figures.

lotus any of several different plants, especially the water lily *Nymphaea lotus*, frequent in Egyptian art, and *Nelumbo nucifera*, the pink Asiatic lotus, a sacred symbol in Hinduism and Buddhism, whose flower head floats erect above the water.

Others are those of the genus *Lotus*, family Leguminosae, including the bird's foot trefoil *Lotus corniculatus*; the ◊jujube shrub *Zizyphus lotus*, known to the ancient Greeks, who used its fruit to make a type of bread and also a wine supposed to induce happy oblivion; and the American lotus *Nelumbo lutea*, a pale yellow water lily of the southern USA.

Lotus motorcar company founded 1952 by Colin Chapman (1928–1982), who built his first racing car 1948, and also developed high-powered production saloon and innovative sports cars, such as the Lotus-Cortina and Lotus Elan. Lotus was one of the leading Grand Prix manufacturers from 1960, when it entered Formula One. In 1995 the company withdrew from racing car production.

Lotus 1-2-3 ◊spreadsheet computer program, produced by Lotus Development Corporation. It first appeared 1982 and its combination of spreadsheet, graphics display, and data management contributed to the rapid acceptance of the IBM Personal Computer in businesses.

Lotus-Eaters in Homer's *Odyssey*, a mythical people living on the lotus plant, which induced travellers to forget their journey home.

Lotus Sūtra scripture of Mahāyāna Buddhism. The original is in Sanskrit (*Saddharmapundarīka Sūtra*) and is thought to date from some time after 100 BC. It says that the Buddha teaches different things to beings according to their capacity, and illustrates the principle with numerous parables.

loudspeaker electromechanical device that converts electrical signals into sound waves, which are radiated into the air. The most common type of loudspeaker is the moving-coil speaker. Electrical signals from, for example, a radio are fed to a coil of fine wire wound around the top of a cone. The coil is surrounded by a magnet. When signals pass through it, the coil becomes an electromagnet, which by moving causes the cone to vibrate, setting up sound waves.

Loughborough industrial town in Leicestershire, England; population (1991) 46,900. Occupations include engineering, bell-founding, electrical goods, knitwear, footwear, hosiery, and pharmaceuticals.

Louis Joe. Assumed name of Joseph Louis Barrow 1914–1981. US boxer, nicknamed 'the Brown Bomber'. He was world heavyweight champion 1937–49 and made a record 25 successful defences (a record for any weight). He made a comeback and lost to Ezzard Charles in a world title fight 1950.

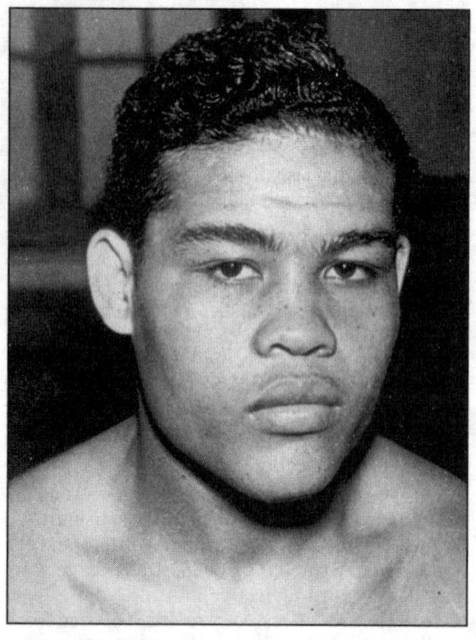

Louis US boxer and world heavyweight champion Joe Louis. He is seen here just before his defence of the championship against Tommy Farr, a British challenger. Farr was one of the record number of 25 unsuccessful challengers during the 12 years that Louis remained champion. *Topham*

Louis eighteen kings of France, including:

Louis (I) the Pious 788–840. Holy Roman emperor from 814, when he succeeded his father Charlemagne.

Louis III c. 863–882. King of N France from 879, while his brother Carloman (866–884) ruled S France. He was the son of Louis II. Louis countered a revolt of the nobility at the beginning of his reign, and his resistance to the Normans made him a hero of epic poems.

Louis IV (d'Outremer) c. 921–954. King of France from 936. His reign was marked by the rebellion of nobles who refused to recognize his authority. As a result of his liberality they were able to build powerful feudal lordships. He was raised in England after his father Charles III the Simple, had been overthrown in 922 by Robert I. After the death of Raoul, Robert's brother-in-law and successor, Louis was chosen by the nobles to be king. He had difficulties with his vassal Hugh the Great, and skirmishes with the Hungarians, who had invaded S France.

Louis (VI) the Fat 1081–1137. King of France from 1108. He led his army against feudal brigands, the English (under Henry I), and the Holy Roman Empire, temporarily consolidating his realm and extending it into Flanders. He was a benefactor to the church, and his advisers included Abbot Suger (c. 1081–1151).

Louis VII c. 1120–1180. King of France from 1137, who led the Second ◊Crusade. He annulled his marriage to Eleanor of Aquitaine 1152, whereupon Eleanor married Henry of Anjou, later ◊Henry II of England. Louis was involved in a bitter struggle with Henry 1152–74.

Louis VIII 1187–1226. King of France from 1223, who was invited to become king of England in place of ◊John by the English barons, and unsuccessfully invaded England 1215–17.

Louis IX St 1214–1270. King of France from 1226, leader of the 7th and 8th ◊Crusades. He was defeated in the former by the Muslims, spending four years in captivity. He died in Tunis. He was canonized 1297. ▷ *See feature on pp. 280–281.*

Louis (X) the Stubborn 1289–1316. King of France who succeeded his father Philip IV in 1314. His reign saw widespread discontent among the nobles, which he countered by granting charters guaranteeing seigneurial rights, although some historians claim that by using evasive tactics, he gave up nothing.

Louis XI 1423–1483. King of France from 1461. He broke the power of the nobility (headed by ◊Charles the Bold) by intrigue and military power.

Louis XII 1462–1515. King of France from 1498. He was duke of Orléans until he succeeded his cousin Charles VIII to the throne. His reign was devoted to Italian wars.

Louis XIII 1601–1643. King of France from 1610 (in succession to his father Henry IV), he assumed royal power in 1617. He was under the political control of Cardinal ◊Richelieu 1624–42.

Louis XIV (called ***the Sun King***) 1638–1715. King of France from 1643, when he succeeded his father Louis XIII; his mother was Anne of Austria. Until 1661 France was ruled by the chief minister, Jules Mazarin, but later Louis took absolute power, summed up in his saying *L'Etat c'est moi* ('I am the state'). Throughout his reign he was engaged in unsuccessful expansionist wars – 1667–68, 1672–78, 1688–97, and 1701–13 (the War of the ◊Spanish Succession) – against various European alliances, always including Britain and the Netherlands. He was a patron of the arts.

foreign policy Following the death of his father-in-law, Philip II of Spain, Louis claimed the Spanish Netherlands and attempted 1667–68 to annex the territory, but was frustrated by an alliance of the Netherlands, Britain, and Sweden. Having detached Britain from the alliance, he invaded the Netherlands 1672, but the Dutch stood firm (led by ◊William of Orange) and despite the European alliance formed against France, achieved territorial gains at the Peace of Nijmegen 1678.

Hostilities were renewed in the war of the League of Augsburg 1688–97 between Louis and the Grand Alliance (including Britain), formed by William of Orange. The French were victorious on land, but the French fleet was almost destroyed at the Battle of La Hogue 1692 and the Treaty of Ryswick forced Louis to give up all his conquests since 1678. The acceptance by Louis of the Spanish throne in 1700 (for his grandson) precipitated the War of the Spanish Succession, with England encouraged to join against the French by Louis' recognition of the Old Pretender as James III. Although the Treaty of Utrecht 1713 gave Spain to Louis' grandson, the war effectively ended French supremacy in Europe, and left France virtually bankrupt.

In 1660 Louis married the Infanta Maria Theresa of Spain, but he was greatly influenced by his mistresses, including Louise de La Vallière, Madame de Montespan, and Madame de Maintenon.

Louis XV 1710–1774. King of France from 1715, with the Duke of Orléans as regent until 1723. He was the great-grandson of Louis XIV. Indolent and frivolous, Louis left government in the hands of his ministers, the Duke of Bourbon and Cardinal Fleury (1653–1743). On the latter's death he attempted to rule alone but became entirely dominated by his mistresses, Madame de Pompadour and Madame Du Barry. His foreign policy led to French possessions in Canada and India being lost to England.

Louis XVI 1754–1793. King of France from 1774, grandson of Louis XV, and son of Louis the Dauphin. He was dominated by his queen, ◊Marie Antoinette, and French finances fell into such confusion that in 1789 the States General (parliament) had to be summoned, and the ◊French Revolution began. Louis lost his personal popularity in June 1791 when he attempted to flee the country, and in Aug 1792 the Parisians stormed the Tuileries palace and took the royal family prisoner. Deposed in 1792, Louis was sentenced for treason in 1793 and guillotined.

Louis XVI Louis XVI of France. As a result of his wife Marie Antoinette's behaviour and his own opposition to economic and social reforms, the French monarchy declined in popularity during his rule, and this culminated in the French Revolution. The couple were tried for treason and guillotined in 1793. *Corbis*

Louis XVII 1785–1795. Nominal king of France, the son of Louis XVI. During the French Revolution he was imprisoned with his parents in 1792 and probably died in prison.

Louis XVIII 1755–1824. King of France 1814–24, the younger brother of Louis XVI. He assumed the title of king in 1795, having fled into exile in 1791 during the French Revolution, but became king only on the fall of Napoleon I in April 1814. Expelled during Napoleon's brief return (the 'hundred days') in 1815, he resumed power after Napoleon's final defeat at Waterloo, pursuing a policy of calculated liberalism until ultra-royalist pressure became dominant after 1820.

Louisiana state in S USA; nickname Pelican State

area 135,900 sq km/52,457 sq mi

capital Baton Rouge

towns and cities New Orleans, Shreveport, Lafayette, Lake Charles

features Mississippi River; Cajun country (Acadiana) including St Martinville and Lafayette (40% of the population speak Cajun French); Poverty Point State Commemorative Area, with prehistoric Native American sites dating from 1800–500 BC; Natchitoches, the oldest permanent European settlement of the Louisiana Purchase; plantation mansions; New Orleans, the birthplace of Dixieland jazz, with Mardi Gras celebrations, the French Quarter (*Vieux Carre*) around Jackson Square, and St Louis Cathedral (1794); the old state capitol, Baton Rouge (1849)

industries rice, cotton, sugar, oil, natural gas, chemicals, sulphur, fish and shellfish, salt, processed foods, petroleum products, timber, paper

population (1991) 4,252,000; including Cajuns, descendants of 18th-century religious exiles from Canada, who speak a French dialect

famous people Louis Armstrong, P G T Beauregard, Huey Long

history explored by the Spanish Piñeda 1519, Cabeza de Vaca 1528, and De Soto 1541 and by the French explorer La Salle 1862, who named it after Louis XIV and claimed it for France. It became Spanish 1762–1800, then French, then passed to the USA 1803 under the ◊Louisiana Purchase; admitted to the Union as a state 1812. The Civil War destroyed the plantation economy. Recovery was slow, but in the 1930s Louisiana became one of the world's major centres of petrochemical manufacturing, based on oil wells in the Gulf of Mexico.

Louisiana

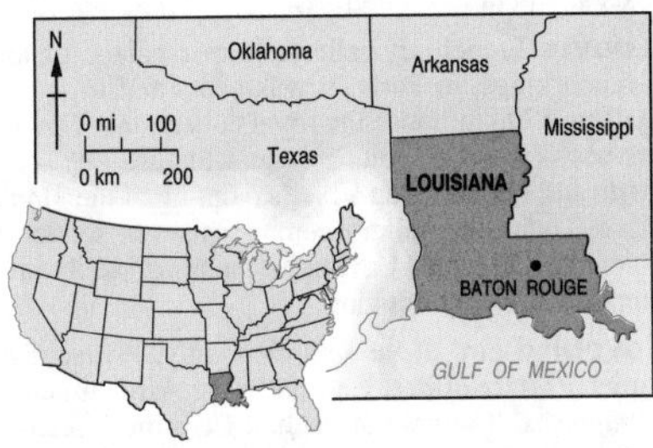

Louisiana Purchase purchase by the USA from France 1803 of an area covering about 2,144,000 sq km/828,000 sq mi, including the present-day states of Louisiana, Missouri, Arkansas, Iowa, Nebraska, North Dakota, South Dakota, and Oklahoma. The purchase, which doubled the size of the USA, marked the end of Napoleon's plans for a colonial empire and ensured free navigation on the Mississippi River for the USA.

Louis Philippe 1773–1850. King of France 1830–48. Son of Louis Philippe Joseph, Duke of Orléans 1747–93; both were known as ***Philippe Egalité*** from their support of the 1792 Revolution. Louis Philippe fled into exile 1793–1814, but became king after the 1830 revolution with the backing of the rich bourgeoisie. Corruption discredited his regime, and after his overthrow, he escaped to the UK and died there.

Louis XIV style French decorative arts style prevalent during the reign of the 'Sun King' (1643–1715), characterized by both ornate Baroque features and classical themes. It was used especially for the sumptuous formal furniture made for the royal palaces. The interior designer Charles Le Brun designed all the furniture, tapestries, and carpets for Versailles and the Louvre in Louis XIV style.

The Louis XV style (1715–74) was the French Rococo, a lighter style than Louis XIV, characterized by the use of chinoiserie, asymmetry, and the scroll motif. The Louis XVI style (1774–92) represented early ◊Neo-Classicism.

Lourdes town in Midi-Pyrénées region, SW France, on the Gave de Pau River; population (1982) 18,000. Its Christian shrine to St ◊Bernadette has a reputation for miraculous cures and Lourdes is an important Catholic pilgrimage centre.

louse parasitic insect of the order Anoplura, which lives on mammals. It has a flat, segmented body without wings, and a tube attached to the head, used for sucking blood from its host. Some lice occur on humans, including the head louse *Pediculus capitis* and the body louse *Pediculus corporis*, a typhus carrier.

Louth smallest county of the Republic of Ireland, in the province of Leinster; county town Dundalk; area 820 sq km/317 sq mi; population (1991)

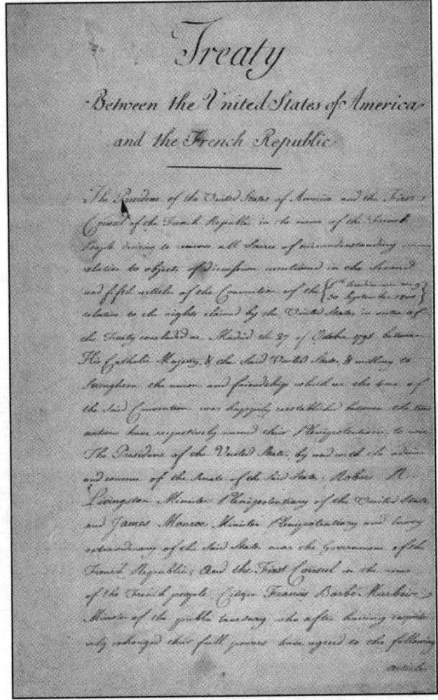

Treaty

Between the United States of America and the French Republic

The President of the United States of America and the First Consul of the French Republic in the name of the French People desiring to remove all Source of misunderstanding relative to objects of discussion mentioned in the Second and fifth articles of the Convention of the {8th Vendémiaire an 9 / 30 September 1800} relative to the rights claimed by the United States in virtue of the Treaty concluded at Madrid the 27 of October 1795, between His Catholic Majesty & the Said United States, & willing to Strengthen the union and friendship which at the time of the Said Convention was happily reestablished between the two nations have respectively named their Plenipotentiaries to wit The President of the United States, by and with the advice and consent of the Senate of the Said States; Robert R. Livingston Minister Plenipotentiary of the United States and James Monroe Minister Plenipotentiary and Envoy extraordinary of the Said States near the Government of the French Republic; And the First Consul in the name of the French people, Citizen Francis Barbé Marbois Minister of the public treasury who after having respectively exchanged their full powers have agreed to the following articles

Louisiana Purchase The first page of the Louisiana Purchase document of 1803, by which the French Republic sold Louisiana to the USA. Desperate for funds to finance Napoleon's military ambitions, the French government sold Louisiana for $15 million. *Corbis*

90,700. It is low-lying. There is cattle-rearing, and oats and potatoes are grown.

Louvre French art gallery, former palace of the French kings, in Paris. It was converted to an art gallery 1793 to house the royal collections. Two of its best-known exhibits are the sculpture *Venus de Milo* and Leonardo da Vinci's painting of the *Mona Lisa*. Today the gallery comprises seven sections: ancient, Oriental, Egyptian, painting, sculpture, applied arts, and drawing.

lovebird bird of the ◊parrot family, Psittacidae, order Psittaciformes, especially the African genus *Agapornis*. They are so named from the affection the male displays towards the female. They are generally just larger than sparrows (about 16 cm/6 in) and coloured green with reds, yellows, and black as head patterns.

Lovecraft H(oward) P(hillips) 1890–1937. US writer of horror fiction. His stories of hostile, supernatural forces have lent names and material to many other writers in the genre. Much of his work on this theme was collected in *The Outsider and Others* 1939.

Lovelace Richard 1618–1658. English poet. Imprisoned 1642 for petitioning for the restoration of royal rule, he wrote 'To Althea, from Prison', and during a second term in jail 1648 arranged the publication of his collection *Lucasta* 1649. His poetry is varied in style and content, some in the 'metaphysical' style of conceits, some more courtly and graceful.

Stone walls do not a prison make / Nor iron bars a cage.

RICHARD LOVELACE 'To Althea, from Prison'

Lovell (Alfred Charles) Bernard 1913– . English radio astronomer, director 1951–81 of ◊Jodrell Bank Experimental Station (now Nuffield Radio Astronomy Laboratories). During World War II Lovell worked on developing a radar system to improve the aim of bombers in night raids. After the war he showed that radar could be a useful tool in astronomy, and lobbied for a radio-astronomy station to be set up. Jodrell Bank was built near Manchester 1951–57. Several large radio telescopes were constructed, including a 76-m/250-ft instrument. Although its high cost was criticized, its public success after tracking the Soviet satellite *Sputnik I* 1957 assured its future.

Low Countries region of Europe that consists of ◊Belgium and the ◊Netherlands, and usually includes ◊Luxembourg.

Lowe John 1947– . English darts player. He has won most of the major titles including the world championships in 1979 and 1987. In 1986 he achieved the first televised nine-dart finish at the MFI Championship at Reading.

Lowell Amy Lawrence 1874–1925. US poet. She began her career by publishing the conventional *A Dome of Many-Colored Glass* 1912 but eventually succeeded Ezra Pound as leader of the Imagists (see ◊Imagism). Her works, in free verse, include *Sword Blades and Poppy Seed* 1916.

Lowell Percival 1855–1916. US astronomer who predicted the existence of a planet beyond Neptune, starting the search that led to the discovery of Pluto 1930. In 1894 he founded the Lowell Observatory in Flagstaff, Arizona.

Lowell Robert Traill Spence, Jr 1917–1977. US poet. His brutal yet tender verse stressed the importance of individualism, especially during times of war. His works include *Lord Weary's Castle* 1946 (Pulitzer prize), *Life Studies* 1959, and *For the Union Dead* 1964. Much of his poetry is confessional.

Lowell Observatory US astronomical observatory founded by Percival Lowell at Flagstaff, Arizona, with a 61-cm/24-in refractor opened 1896. The observatory now operates other telescopes at a nearby site on Anderson Mesa including the 1.83-m/72-in Perkins reflector of Ohio State and Ohio Wesleyan universities.

Lower Austria (German *Niederösterreich*) largest federal state of Austria; drained by the river Danube; area 19,200 sq km/7,411 sq mi; population (1994) 1,511,600. Its capital is St Pölten. In addition to wine, sugar beet, and grain, there are reserves of oil. Manufactured products include textiles, chemicals, and metal goods.

May the force be with you.

GEORGE LUCAS *Star Wars*

Lower Saxony (German *Niedersachsen*) administrative region (German *Land*) of N Germany
area 47,400 sq km/18,296 sq mi
capital Hanover
towns and cities Brunswick, Osnabrück, Oldenburg, Göttingen, Wolfsburg, Salzgitter, Hildesheim
features Lüneburg Heath
industries cereals, cars, machinery, electrical engineering
population (1994 est) 7,648,000
religion 75% Protestant, 20% Roman Catholic
history formed 1946 from Hanover, Oldenburg, Brunswick, and Schaumburg-Lippe.

Lowestoft resort town and most easterly port in Britain, in Suffolk, England, 62 km/38 mi NE of Ipswich; population (1990 est) 58,000. There is fishing and fish processing, and radar and electrical equipment is produced.

low-level language in computing, a programming language designed for a particular computer and reflecting its internal ◊machine code; low-level languages are therefore often described as machine-oriented languages. They cannot easily be converted to run on a computer with a different central processing unit, and they are relatively difficult to learn because a detailed knowledge of the internal working of the computer is required. Since they must be translated into machine code by an assembler program, low-level languages are also called ◊assembly languages.

Lowry L(aurence) S(tephen) 1887–1976. English painter. His works depict life in the industrial towns of the north of England, painted with a calculated naivety of style. Typically they feature gaunt, simplified factories and terraced houses, painted in an almost monochrome palette, and sticklike figures, often in animated groups. *The Pond* 1950 (Tate Gallery, London) is an example.

Born in Manchester, he spent the rest of his life in nearby Salford, earning his living as a rent collector. Uninfluenced by current trends, he had developed his own distinctive style by the 1920s. He concentrated on the life around him, his paintings sometimes inspired by a humorous anecdote, as in *The Arrest* 1927 (Castle Museum, Nottingham). He also painted remote seascapes, lonely hill landscapes and some striking portraits, for example *A Manchester Man* 1936.

Loy Myrna. Stage name of Myrna Williams 1905–1993. US film actress, a Hollywood star of the 1930s. A self-confident, independent woman as well as a glamorous comedienne, she brought a new kind of personality to US cinema. She played Nora Charles in the *Thin Man* series 1934–47 co-starring William Powell. Her other films include *The Mask of Fu Manchu* 1932 and *The Rains Came* 1939.

Loyalist member of approximately 30% of the US population remaining loyal to Britain in the ◊American Revolution. The term also refers to people in Northern Ireland who wish to remain part of the United Kingdom rather than unifying with the Republic of Ireland.

Loyola founder of the Jesuits. See ◊Ignatius Loyola.

LSD (abbreviation for ***lysergic acid diethylamide***) psychedelic drug, a ◊hallucinogen. Colourless, odourless, and easily synthesized, it is nonaddictive and nontoxic, but its effects are unpredictable. Its use is illegal in most countries.

The use of LSD as a means to increased awareness and enhanced perception was popularized in the 1960s by US psychologist Timothy Leary (1920–1996), novelist Ken Kesey, and chemist Augustus Owsley Stanley III. A series of laws to ban LSD were passed in the USA from 1965 and in the UK in 1966; other countries followed suit. The drug had great influence on the ◊hippie movement.

Luanda formerly ***Loanda*** capital and industrial port (cotton, sugar, tobacco, timber, textiles, paper, oil) of Angola; population (1995) 2,250,000. Founded 1575, it became a Portuguese colonial administrative centre as well as an outlet for slaves transported to Brazil.

Luang Prabang or ***Louangphrabang*** Buddhist religious centre in Laos, on the Mekong River at the head of river navigation; population (1985) 68,400. It was the capital of the kingdom of Luang Prabang, incorporated in Laos 1946, and the royal capital of Laos 1946–75.

Lubbers Rudolph Franz Marie (Ruud) 1939– . Dutch politician, prime minister of the Netherlands 1982–94. Leader of the right-of-centre Christian Democratic Appeal (CDA), he became minister for economic affairs 1973. In 1995 he was widely tipped to succeed Willy Claes as secretary-general of NATO, but his candidature was blocked by the USA.

Lübeck seaport of Schleswig-Holstein, Germany, on the Baltic Sea, 60 km/37 mi NE of Hamburg; population (1993) 217,100. Industries include machinery, aeronautical and space equipment, steel, ironwork, shipbuilding and servicing, fish canning; Lübeck is known for its wine trade and its marzipan.

Founded 1143, it has five Gothic churches and a cathedral dating from 1173. The Holstentor (1477) with its twin towers is the emblem of the city. Once head of the powerful ◊Hanseatic League, it later lost much of its trade to Hamburg and Bremen, but improved canal and port facilities helped it to retain its position as a centre of Baltic trade. Lübeck was a free state of both the empire and the Weimar Republic.

Lubetkin Berthold Romanovich 1901–1990. Russian-born architect. He settled in the UK 1930 and formed, with six young architects, a group called Tecton. His pioneering designs include Highpoint I, a block of flats in Highgate, London, 1933–35, and the curved lines of the Penguin Pool 1933 at London Zoo, which employ ◊reinforced concrete to sculptural effect.

During the 1930s, Tecton was responsible for many buildings erected in England in the ◊International Style then flourishing elsewhere in Europe, including the Gorilla House 1937 at the London Zoo and a health centre for the London borough of Finsbury 1938. The group was also a training ground for the avant-garde architects of the next generation, such as Denys Lasdun.

Lubitsch Ernst 1892–1947. German film director. He worked in the USA from 1921. Known for his stylish comedies, his sound films include *Trouble in Paradise* 1932, *Design for Living* 1933, *Ninotchka* 1939, and *To Be or Not to Be* 1942.

Lublin city in Poland, on the Bystrzyca River, 150 km/95 mi SE of Warsaw; population (1993) 352,500. Industries include textiles, engineering, aircraft, and electrical goods. A trading centre from the 10th century, it has an ancient citadel, a 16th-century cathedral, and a university (1918). A council of workers and peasants proclaimed Poland's independence at Lublin 1918, and a Russian-sponsored committee of national liberation, which proclaimed itself the provincial government of Poland at Lublin 31 Dec 1944, was recognized by Russia five days later.

lubricant substance used between moving surfaces to reduce friction. Carbon-based (organic) lubricants, commonly called grease and oil, are recovered from petroleum distillation.

Lucan (Marcus Annaeus Lucanus) AD 39–65. Latin poet. He was a nephew of the writer Seneca and favourite of Nero until the emperor became jealous of his verse. Lucan then joined a republican conspiracy and committed suicide on its failure. His epic poem *Pharsalia* deals with the civil wars of Caesar and Pompey 49–48 BC, and was influential in the Middle Ages and Renaissance.

Lucas George 1944– . US film director and producer. His imagination was fired by the comic books in his father's store. He wrote and directed *Star Wars* 1977 and wrote and produced *The Empire Strikes Back* 1980 and *Return of the Jedi* 1983. His other films as director are *THX 1138* 1971 and *American Graffiti* 1973. Later works as a producer include *Raiders of the Lost Ark* 1981, *Indiana Jones and the Temple of Doom* 1984, *Willow* 1988, and *Indiana Jones and the Last Crusade* 1989.

Lucas van Leyden 1494–1533. Dutch painter and engraver. Active in Leiden and Antwerp, he was a pioneer of Netherlandish genre scenes, for example *The Chess Players* c. 1510 (Staatliche Museen, Berlin). His woodcuts and engravings, often more highly regarded than his paintings, were inspired by Albrecht ◊Dürer, but they also possess a distinctive charm and inventiveness of their own which is characteristic in all his work. His paintings show an Italian influence, his unusual colour and pictorial imagination being exemplified in *Lot and his Daughters* (Louvre, Paris). His work was a major influence on ◊Rembrandt.

Lucca city in NW Italy; population (1990) 91,100. It was an independent republic from 1160 until its absorption into Tuscany 1847.

Luce (Ann) Clare Boothe 1903–1987. US journalist, playwright, and politician. She was managing editor of *Vanity Fair* magazine 1933–34, and wrote several successful plays, including *The Women* 1936 and *Margin for Error* 1940, both of which were made into films. She served as a Republican member of Congress 1943–47 and as ambassador to Italy 1953–57.

Luce Henry Robinson 1898–1967. US publisher, founder of Time, Inc, which publishes the weekly news magazine *Time* 1923, the business magazine *Fortune* 1930, the pictorial magazine *Life* 1936, and the sports magazine *Sports Illustrated* 1954. He married Clare Boothe Luce in 1935.

Lucerne (German ***Luzern***) capital and tourist centre of Lucerne canton, Switzerland, on the river Reuss where it flows out of Lake Lucerne; population (1994) city 61,700, canton 337,700. It developed around a Benedictine monastery, established about 750, and owes its prosperity to its position on the St Gotthard road and railway.

lucerne another name for the plant ◊alfalfa.

Lucerne, Lake (German ***Vierwaldstättersee***) scenic lake in central Switzerland; area 114 sq km/44 sq mi.

Lucian c. 125–c. 190. Greek writer. In his satirical dialogues, he pours scorn on religions and mocks human pretensions. His 65 genuine works also include rhetorical declamations, literary criticism, biography, and romance. Among the most interesting of his works are *Dialogues of the Gods*, *Dialogues of the Dead*, *Zeus Confounded*, and *Zeus Tragedian*. His *True History* inspired ◊Rabelais's *Voyage of Pantagruel*, Swift's ◊*Gulliver's Travels*, and ◊Cyrano de Bergerac's *Journey to the Moon*.

Lucifer (Latin 'bearer of light') in Christian theology, another name for the ◊devil, the leader of the angels who rebelled against God. Lucifer is also another name for the morning star (the planet ◊Venus).

Lucknow capital and industrial city (engineering, chemicals, textiles, many handicrafts) of the state of Uttar Pradesh, India; population (1991) 1,669,200.

Lucknow, Siege of during the Indian Mutiny, siege of the British Residency at Lucknow, India, 2 July–16 Nov 1857. Over 500 British troops and civilians with 700 loyal Indian troops were besieged in the residency building for four months until a relief column finally broke through the mutineers' blockade. The city was not recaptured until March 1858.

Lucretia Roman woman, the wife of Collatinus, said to have committed suicide after being raped by Sextus, son of Tarquinius Superbus, the last king of Rome. According to tradition, this incident led to the dethronement of Tarquinius and the establishment of the Roman Republic in 509 BC.

Lucretius (Titus Lucretius Carus) c. 99–55 BC. Roman poet and ◊Epicurean philosopher. His *De Rerum natura/On the Nature of The Universe*, a didactic poem in six books, envisaged the whole universe as a combination of atoms, and had some concept of evolutionary theory.

Lucullus Lucius Licinius c. 110–c. 56 BC. Roman general and consul. As commander against ◊Mithridates of Pontus 74–66 he proved to be one of Rome's ablest generals and administrators, until superseded by Pompey.

Lüda or ***Lü-ta*** or ***Hüta*** industrial port (engineering, chemicals, textiles, oil refining, shipbuilding, food processing) in Liaoning, China, on Liaodong Peninsula, facing the Yellow Sea; population (1986) 4,500,000. It comprises the naval base of Lüshun (known under 19th-century Russian occupation as Port Arthur) and the commercial port of Dalien (formerly Talien/Dairen). Both were leased to Russia 1898, but were ceded to Japan after the ◊Russo-Japanese War; Lüshun was under Japanese siege 1904–05. After World War II, Lüshun was occupied by Russian airborne troops (it was returned to China 1955) and Russia was granted shared facilities at Dalien until 1955.

Luddite one of a group of people involved in machine-wrecking riots in N England 1811–16. The movement was primarily a revolt against the unemployment caused by the introduction of machines in the Industrial Revolution. The organizer of the Luddites was referred to as General Ludd, but may not have existed. Many Luddites were hanged or transported to penal colonies, such as Australia.

Lucas van Leyden *Potiphar's Wife* by Dutch artist Lucas van Leyden. Though he painted mainly religious works, van Leyden's attention to the details and manners of contemporary life make him an important figure in the development of genre painting, which focuses on everyday scenes. *Corbis*

Ludendorff Erich von 1865–1937. German general, chief of staff to ◊Hindenburg in World War I, and responsible for the eastern-front victory at the Battle of ◊Tannenberg 1914. After Hindenburg's appointment as chief of general staff and Ludendorff's as quartermaster-general 1916, he was also politically influential and the two were largely responsible for the conduct of the war from then on. He took part in the Nazi rising in Munich 1923 and sat in the Reichstag (parliament) as a right-wing Nationalist.

Ludwig Carl Friedrich Wilhelm 1816–1895. German physiologist who invented graphic methods of recording events within the body, including the kymograph 1847, a rotating drum on which a stylus charts a continuous record of blood pressure and temperature. He demonstrated that the circulation of the blood is purely mechanical in nature and involves no occult vital forces.

Ludwig I 1786–1868. King of Bavaria 1825–48, succeeding his father Maximilian Joseph I. He made Munich an international cultural centre, but his association with the dancer Lola Montez, who dictated his policies for a year, led to his abdication.

Ludwig II 1845–1886. King of Bavaria from 1864, when he succeeded his father Maximilian II. He supported Austria during the Austro-Prussian War 1866, but brought Bavaria into the Franco-Prussian War as Prussia's ally and in 1871 offered the German crown to the king of Prussia. He was the composer Richard Wagner's patron and built the Bayreuth theatre for him. Declared insane 1886, he drowned himself soon after.

Ludwig III 1845–1921. King of Bavaria 1913–18, when he abdicated upon the formation of a republic.

Luening Otto 1900– . US composer. He was appointed to Columbia University 1949, and in 1951 began a series of pioneering compositions for instruments and tape, some in partnership with Vladimir Ussachevsky (1911–) (*Incantation* 1952, *A Poem in Cycles and Bells* 1954). In 1959 he became codirector, with Milton Babbitt and Ussachevsky, of the Columbia-Princeton Electronic Music Center.

Luftwaffe German air force used both in World War I and (as reorganized by the Nazi leader Hermann Goering in 1933) in World War II. The Luftwaffe also covered anti-aircraft defence and the launching of the flying bombs ◊V1 and V2.

Germany was not supposed to have an air force under the terms of the Treaty of Versailles 1918, so the Luftwaffe was covertly trained and organized using Lufthansa, the national airline, as a cover; its existence was officially announced 1935. It was an entirely tactical force under the command of Hermann ◊Goering but headed by Field Marshal Milch from 1936, subordinated to the General Staff as a direct support arm for the army, and was one of the vital components of the *Blitzkrieg* tactics.

Lugano, Lake lake partly in Italy, between lakes Maggiore and Como, and partly in Switzerland; area 49 sq km/19 sq mi.

luge type of ◊toboggan.

Lugosi Bela. Stage name of Bela Ferenc Denzso Blasko 1884–1956. Hungarian-born US film actor. Acclaimed for his performance in *Dracula* on Broadway 1927, Lugosi began acting in feature films 1930. His appearance in the film version of *Dracula* 1931 marked the start of Lugosi's long career in horror films – among them, *Murders in the Rue Morgue* 1932, *The Raven* 1935, and *The Wolf Man* 1941.

lugworm any of a genus *Arenicola* of marine annelid worms that grow up to 10 in/25 cm long. They are common burrowers between tidemarks and are useful for their cleansing and powdering of the beach sand.

Lu Hsün alternative transliteration of Chinese writer ◊Lu Xun.

Lukács Georg 1885–1971. Hungarian philosopher and literary critic, one of the founders of 'Western' or 'Hegelian' Marxism, a philosophy opposed to the Marxism of the official communist movement. He also wrote on aesthetics and the sociology of literature. In *History and Class Consciousness* 1923, he discussed the process of reification (an alleged social process whereby relations between human beings are transformed into impersonal relations between things), and argued that bourgeois thought was 'false consciousness'. Rejected by official socialist literati, he was also an outsider to the dominant literary movements of the West. He repudiated the view held by both, according to him, that 'literature and art really can be manipulated according to the needs of the day'. He argued for realism in literature and opposed modernism. *See illustration on following page.*

'Nothing can be created out of nothing.'

LUCRETIUS
De Rerum Natura

Luke, St lived 1st century AD. Traditionally the compiler of the third Gospel and of the Acts of the Apostles in the New Testament. He is the patron

Lukács Controversial Marxist philosopher and literary theoretician Georg Lukács, photographed around 1950. He believed that the evils of the Stalinist era were a necessary stage in the restructuring of society under Communism – 'the greatest sacrifice revolution asked from us'. *Corbis*

saint of painters; his emblem is a winged ox, and his feast day 18 Oct. Luke is supposed to have been a Greek physician born in Antioch (Antakiyah, Turkey) and to have accompanied Paul after the ascension of Jesus.

Lully Jean-Baptiste. Adopted name of Giovanni Battista Lulli 1632–1687. French composer of Italian origin. He was court composer to Louis XIV. He composed music for the ballet and for Molière's plays, and established French opera with such works as *Alceste* 1674 and *Armide et Rénaud* 1686. He was also a ballet dancer.

lumbago pain in the lower region of the back, usually due to strain or faulty posture. If it occurs with ◊sciatica, it may be due to pressure on spinal nerves by a slipped disc (a protrusion of the soft inner substance of an intervertebral disc through the outer covering). Treatment includes rest, application of heat, and skilled manipulation. Surgery may be needed in rare cases.

lumbar puncture or ***spinal tap*** insertion of a hollow needle between two lumbar (lower back) vertebrae to withdraw a sample of cerebrospinal fluid (CSF) for testing. Normally clear and colourless, the CSF acts as a fluid buffer around the brain and spinal cord. Changes in its quantity, colour, or composition may indicate neurological damage or disease.

Lumbini birthplace of ◊Buddha in the foothills of the Himalayas near the Nepalese-Indian frontier. A sacred garden and shrine were established here in 1970 by the Nepalese government.

lumen SI unit (symbol lm) of luminous flux (the amount of light passing through an area per second). The lumen is defined in terms of the light falling on a unit area at a unit distance from a light source of luminous intensity of one ◊candela. One lumen at a wavelength of 5,550 angstroms equals 0.0014706 watts.

Lumet Sidney 1924– . US film director. His prolific and eclectic body of work covers such powerful, intimate dramas as *12 Angry Men* 1957, or intense, urban dramas such as *Serpico* 1973, and *Dog Day Afternoon* 1975. Among his other films are *Fail Safe* 1964, *Equus* 1977, and *Running on Empty* 1988.

Lumière Auguste Marie Louis Nicolas (1862–1954) and Louis Jean (1864–1948) French brothers who pioneered cinematography. In 1895 they patented their cinematograph, a combined camera and projector operating at 16 frames per second, and opened the world's first cinema in Paris. Their first films were short static shots of everyday events such as *La Sortie des usines Lumière* 1895 about workers leaving a factory and *L'Arroseur arrosé* 1895, the world's first fiction film. Production was abandoned in 1900.

luminescence emission of light from a body when its atoms are excited by means other than raising its temperature. Short-lived luminescence is called fluorescence; longer-lived luminescence is called phosphorescence. Certain living organisms produce ◊bioluminescence.

luminosity or ***brightness*** in astronomy, the amount of light emitted by a star, measured in ◊magnitudes. The apparent brightness of an object decreases in proportion to the square of its distance from the observer. The luminosity of a star or other body can be expressed in relation to that of the Sun.

Lumumba Patrice Emergy 1925–1961. Congolese politician, prime minister of Zaire 1960. Imprisoned by the Belgians, but released in time to attend the conference giving the Congo independence in 1960, he led the National Congolese Movement to victory in the subsequent general election. He was deposed in a coup and murdered some months later.

Lundy Island rocky island at the entrance to the Bristol Channel; 19 km/12 mi NW of Hartland Point, Devon, England; area 9.6 sq km/3.7 sq mi. Formerly used by pirates and privateers as a lair, it is now a National Trust bird sanctuary and the first British marine nature reserve (1987).

lung large cavity of the body, used for ◊gas exchange. It is essentially a sheet of thin, moist membrane that is folded so as to occupy less space. Most tetrapod (four-limbed) vertebrates have a pair of lungs occupying the thorax. The lung tissue, consisting of multitudes of air sacs and blood vessels, is very light and spongy, and functions by bringing inhaled air into close contact with the blood so that oxygen can pass into the organism and waste carbon dioxide can be passed out. The efficiency of lungs is enhanced by breathing movements, by the thinness and moistness of their surfaces, and by a constant supply of circulating blood.

lungfish three genera of fleshy-finned bony fishes of the subclass Dipnoi, found in Africa, South America, and Australia. They have elongated bodies, and grow to about 2 m/6 ft, and in addition to gills have 'lungs' with which they can breathe air during periods of drought conditions.

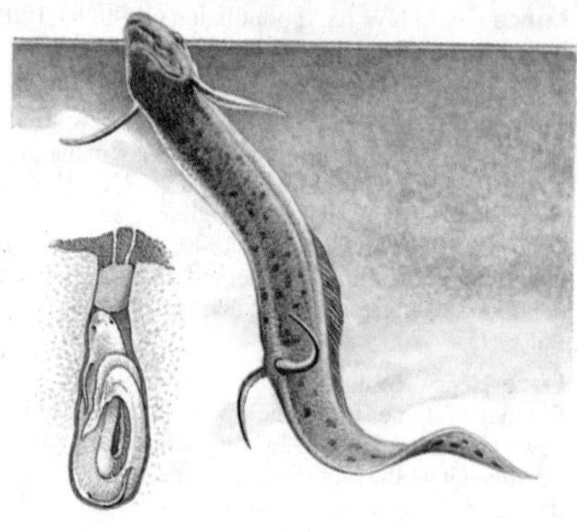

lungfish The lungfish resembles a short-bodied eel. It has a pair of lungs and can breathe air in water that is poor in oxygen. The various species of lungfishes are found in the lakes and rivers of South America and central Africa but, when the water courses evaporate during the dry season, the fishes survive by burrowing into the mud.

Luo the second-largest ethnic group of Kenya, living in the Lake Victoria region and in 1987 numbering some 2,650,000. The Luo traditionally live by farming livestock. The Luo language is of the Nilo-Saharan family.

Luoyang or ***Loyang*** industrial city (machinery and tractors) in Henan province, China, south of the river Huang He; population (1986) 1,190,000. It was formerly the capital of China and an important Buddhist centre in the 5th and 6th centuries.

lung Human lungs contain 300,000 million tiny blood vessels that would stretch for 2,400 km/1,500 mi if laid end to end. A healthy adult at rest breathes 12 times a minute; a baby breathes at twice this rate. Each breath brings 350 millilitres of fresh air into the lungs, and expels 150 millilitres of stale air from the nose and throat.

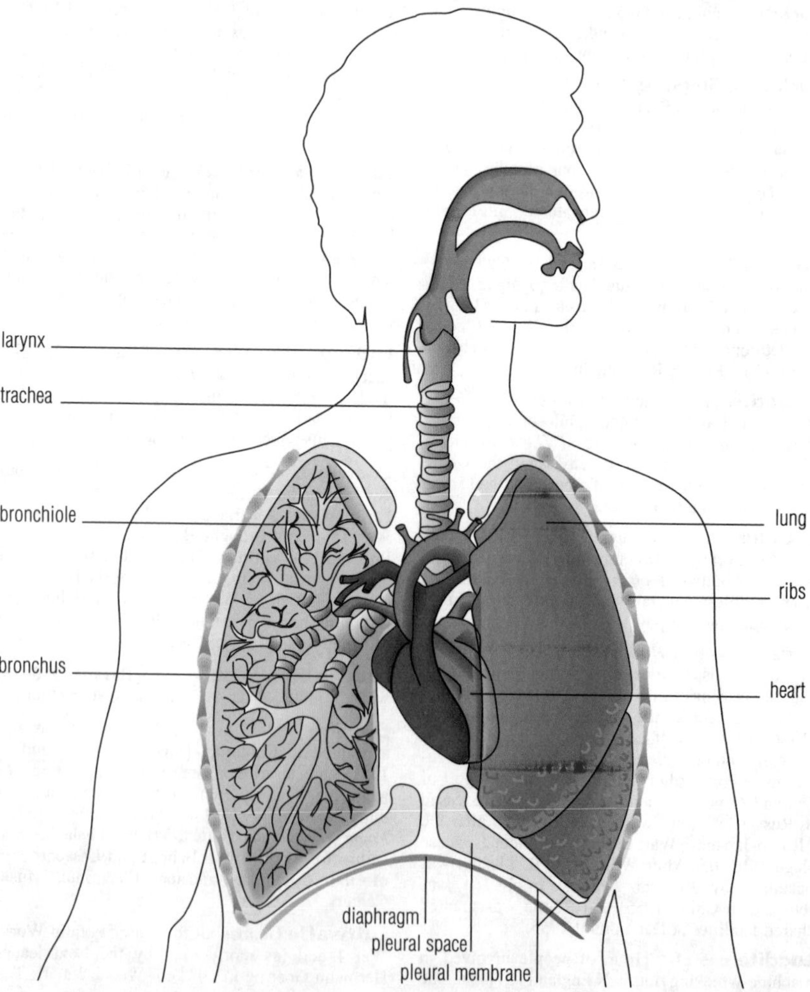

Lupercalia Roman festival celebrated 15 Feb. Goats were sacrificed at the Lupercal, the cave where Romulus and Remus, the twin founders of Rome, were supposedly suckled by a wolf (*lupus*). Youths then ran around the boundaries of the city carrying whips made from the hides of the sacrificed goats, blows from which were believed to cure sterility in women.

lupin any plant of the genus *Lupinus*, which comprises about 300 species, family Leguminosae. Lupins are native to Mediterranean regions and parts of North and South America, and some species are naturalized in Britain. Their spikes of pealike flowers may be white, yellow, blue, or pink. *L. albus* is cultivated in some places for cattle fodder and for green manuring.

lupus in medicine, any of various diseases characterized by lesions of the skin. One form (lupus vulgaris) is caused by the tubercle bacillus (see ◊tuberculosis). The organism produces ulcers that spread and eat away the underlying tissues. Treatment is primarily with standard antituberculous drugs, but ultraviolet light may also be used.

Luria Salvador Edward 1912–1991. Italian-born US physician who was a pioneer in molecular biology, especially the genetic structure of viruses. Luria was a pacifist and was identified with efforts to keep science humanistic. He shared the Nobel Prize for Physiology or Medicine 1969.

Lurie Alison 1926– . US novelist and critic. Her subtly written and satirical novels include *Imaginary Friends* 1967; *The War Between the Tates* 1974; *Foreign Affairs* 1985, a tale of transatlantic relations that won a Pulitzer prize; *The Truth About Lorin Jones* 1988; and *Women and Children* 1994.

Lusaka capital of Zambia from 1964 (of Northern Rhodesia 1935–64), 370 km/230 mi NE of Livingstone; it is a commercial and agricultural centre (flour mills, tobacco factories, vehicle assembly, plastics, printing); population (1990) 982,000.

Lusitania ancient area of the Iberian peninsula, roughly equivalent to Portugal. Conquered by Rome 139 BC, the province of Lusitania rebelled periodically until it was finally conquered by Pompey 73–72 BC.

lute member of a family of stringed musical instruments of the 14th–18th centuries, including the mandore, theorbo, and chitarrone. Lutes are pear-shaped with up to seven courses of strings (single or double), plucked with the fingers. Music for lutes is written in special notation called tablature (an old form of notation indicating finger positions on a graph representing the fingerboard and strings) and chords are played simultaneously, not arpeggiated as for guitar. Modern lutenists include Julian Bream and Anthony Rooley (1944–).

luteinizing hormone hormone produced by the pituitary gland. In males, it stimulates the testes to produce androgens (male sex hormones). In females, it works together with follicle-stimulating hormone to initiate production of egg cells by the ovary. If fertilization occurs, it plays a part in maintaining the pregnancy by controlling the levels of the hormones oestrogen and progesterone in the body.

lutetium (Latin *Lutetia* 'Paris') silver-white, metallic element, the last of the ◊lanthanide series, symbol Lu, atomic number 71, relative atomic mass 174.97. It is used in the 'cracking', or breakdown, of petroleum and in other chemical processes.

Luther Martin 1483–1546. German Christian church reformer, a founder of Protestantism. While he was a priest at the University of Wittenberg, he wrote an attack on the sale of indulgences (remissions of punishment for sin). The Holy Roman emperor Charles V summoned him to the Diet (meeting of dignitaries of the Holy Roman Empire) of Worms in Germany, in 1521, where he refused to retract his objections. Originally intending reform, his protest led to schism, with the emergence, following the ◊Augsburg Confession 1530 (a statement of the Protestant faith), of a new Protestant church. Luther is regarded as the instigator of the Protestant revolution, and Lutheranism is now the predominant religion of many N European countries, including Germany, Sweden, and Denmark.

Luther was born in Eisleben, the son of a miner; he studied at the University of Erfurt, spent three years as a monk in the Augustinian convent there, and in 1507 was ordained priest. Shortly afterwards he attracted attention as a teacher and preacher at the University of Wittenberg; and in 1517, after returning from a visit to Rome, he attained nationwide celebrity for his denunciation of the Dominican monk Johann Tetzel (1455–1519), one of those sent out by the pope to sell indulgences as a means of raising funds for the rebuilding of St Peter's Basilica in Rome.

Luther Lucas Cranach's 1521 painting of Martin Luther, the leader of the Protestant Reformation. The painting is on display at the Uffizi Gallery, Florence. *Corbis*

On 31 Oct 1517, Luther nailed on the church door in Wittenberg a statement of 95 theses concerning indulgences, and the following year he was summoned to Rome to defend his action. His reply was to attack the papal system even more strongly, and in 1520 he publicly burned in Wittenberg the papal bull (edict) that had been launched against him. On his way home from the imperial Diet of Worms he was taken into 'protective custody' by the elector of Saxony in the castle of Wartburg. Later he became estranged from the Dutch theologian Erasmus, who had formerly supported him in his attacks on papal authority, and engaged in violent controversies with political and religious opponents. After the Augsburg Confession 1530, Luther gradually retired from the Protestant leadership. His translation of the scriptures marks the emergence of modern German.

> *My conscience is taken captive by God's word, I cannot and will not recant anything. ... Here I stand. I can do no other. God help me. Amen.*
>
> **Martin Luther**
> Speech at the Diet of Worms 18 April 1521

Lutheranism form of Protestant Christianity derived from the life and teaching of Martin Luther; it is sometimes called Evangelical to distinguish it from the other main branch of European Protestantism, the Reformed. The most generally accepted statement of Lutheranism is that of the Confession of ◊Augsburg 1530 but Luther's Shorter Catechism also carries great weight. It is the largest Protestant body, including some 80 million persons, of whom 40 million are in Germany, 19 million in Scandinavia, 8.5 million in the USA and Canada, with most of the remainder in central Europe.

Luthuli Albert John, or ***Lutuli*** c. 1898–1967. South African politician, president of the African National Congress 1952–67. Luthuli, a Zulu tribal chief, preached nonviolence and multiracialism. Arrested in 1956, he suffered certain restrictions from 1959. He was under suspended sentence for burning his pass (an identity document required of non-white South Africans) when awarded the 1960 Nobel Peace Prize.

Luton industrial city and the administrative headquarters of Luton unitary authority, England, 53 km/33 mi SW of Cambridge; population (1991) 171,700. Luton airport is a secondary airport for London. Manufacturing includes cars, chemicals, engineering components, electrical goods, ballbearings, as well as, traditionally, hats. Luton Hoo, a Robert Adam mansion, was built 1762. The park was laid out by 'Capability' Brown.

Luton unitary authority of England created 1997 (*see United Kingdom map*).

Lutosławski Witold 1913–1994. Polish composer and conductor. His output includes three symphonies, *Paroles tissées/Teased Words* 1965 for tenor and chamber orchestra, dedicated to Peter Pears, and *Chain I* for orchestra 1981. For 30 years he conducted most of the world's leading orchestras in his own compositions, and was greatly influential both within and beyond his native land.

His early major compositions, such as *Variations on a Theme of Paganini* 1941 for two pianos and *First Symphony* 1947, drew some criticism from the communist government. After 1956, under a more liberal regime, he adopted avant-garde techniques, including improvisatory and ◊aleatoric forms, in *Venetian Games* 1961.

Lutyens (Agnes) Elizabeth 1906–1983. English composer. Her works, using the twelve-tone system, are expressive and tightly organized, and include chamber music, stage, and orchestral works. Her choral and vocal works include a setting of the Austrian philosopher Ludwig Wittgenstein's *Tractatus* and a cantata *The Tears of Night*. She also composed much film and incidental music. She was the daughter of architect Sir Edwin Lutyens.

Lutyens Edwin Landseer 1869–1944. English architect. His designs ranged from the picturesque, such as Castle Drogo, Devon, 1910–30, to Renaissance-style country houses, and ultimately evolved into a Classical style as seen in the Cenotaph, London, 1919, and the Viceroy's House, New Delhi, India, 1912–31. His complex use of space, interest in tradition, and distorted Classical language have proved of great interest to a number of Post-Modern architects, especially Robert Venturi.

lux SI unit (symbol lx) of illuminance or illumination (the light falling on an object). It is equivalent to one ◊lumen per square metre or to the illuminance of a surface one metre distant from a point source of one ◊candela. The lux replaces the foot-candle (one foot-candle equals 10.76 lux).

Luxembourg capital of the country of Luxembourg, on the Alzette and Petrusse rivers; population (1995) 76,000. The 16th-century Grand Ducal Palace, European Court of Justice, and European Parliament secretariat are situated here, but plenary sessions of the parliament are now held only in Strasbourg, France. Industries include steel, chemicals, textiles, and processed food.

A Roman fortress was built on the rocky plateau to control movement between France and Germany. The old town, including the 17th-century cathedral and town hall (1830–38), stands on the plateau; more recent development has spread across lower areas linked by bridges.

Luxembourg landlocked country in W Europe, bounded N and W by Belgium, E by Germany, and S by France. *See country box on p. 650.*

Luxembourg province of SE Belgium
area 4,400 sq km/1,698 sq mi
capital Arlon
towns and cities Bastogne, St Hubert, Bouillon
industries dairy products, iron and steel, tobacco
physical situated in the SE Ardennes and widely forested; rivers Ourthe, Semois, and Lesse
population (1995) 240,300
history formerly part of the Grand Duchy of Luxembourg, it became a Belgian province 1831.

Luxembourg Accord French-initiated agreement 1966 that a decision of the Council of Ministers of the European Community (now the European Union) may be vetoed by a member whose national interests are at stake.

Luxembourg, Palais de palace in Paris, France, in which the Senate sits. It was built 1615 for the Queen Marie de' Medici by Salomon de Brosse (about 1571–1626).

Luxemburg Rosa 1870–1919. Polish-born German communist. She helped found the Polish Social Democratic Party in the 1890s (which later became the Polish Communist Party). She was a leader of the left wing of the German Social Democratic Party from 1898 and collaborator with Karl Liebknecht in founding the communist Spartacus League 1918 (see ◊Spartacist). She was murdered with him by army officers during the Jan 1919 Berlin workers' revolt.

> *Freedom is always and exclusively freedom for the one who thinks differently.*
>
> **Rosa Luxemburg**
> *The Russian Revolution*

Luxor (Arabic *al-Uqsur*) small town in Egypt on the east bank of the river Nile; population (1992) 146,000. As the ancient city of Thebes it was the

'Night hath a thousand eyes.'

JOHN LYLY
Maides Metamorphose

capital for several centuries, reaching the height of its wealth and splendour during the reigns of Thothmes III and his successors; his great-grandson, Amenhotep III (c. 1411–1375 BC) built the Temple of Luxor. The Theban necropolis, on the W bank, includes the tombs of the pharaohs in the Valley of the Kings.

Lu Xun pen name of Chon Shu-jêu 1881–1936. Chinese short-story writer. His three volumes of satirically realistic stories, *Call to Arms*, *Wandering*, and *Old Tales Retold*, reveal the influence of the Russian writer Nicolai Gogol. He was also an important polemical essayist and literary critic.

Luzon largest island of the ◊Philippines; area 108,130 sq km/41,750 sq mi; capital Quezon City; population (1970) 18,001,270. The chief city is Manila, capital of the Philippines. Industries include rice, timber, and minerals. It has US military bases. In 1991 the volcanic Mount Pinatubo, 88 km/55 mi N of Manila, erupted after lying dormant for 600 years. Volcanic ash covered an area of 2,600 sq km/1,000 sq mi and brought economic catastrophe.

Lviv (Russian ***Lvov***) capital and industrial city of Lviv region, Ukraine; population (1992) 807,000. Industries include textiles, metals, and engineering. The university was founded 1661. Lviv was formerly a trade centre on the Black Sea–Baltic route. Founded in the 13th century, it was Polish 1340–1772, Austrian 1772–1919, Polish 1919–39, and annexed by the USSR 1945. It was the site of violent nationalist demonstrations Oct 1989, prior to Ukraine gaining independence 1991.

lycanthropy in folk belief, the transformation of a human being into a wolf; or, in psychology, a delusion involving this belief.

Lyceum ancient Athenian gymnasium and garden, with covered walks, where the philosopher Aristotle taught. It was SE of the city and named after the nearby temple of Apollo Lyceus. Its remains were discovered beneath a car park Jan 1997.

lychee alternative spelling of ◊litchi, a fruit-bearing tree.

Lycra synthetic fibre composed mainly of elastomer and other stretch fibres. It was introduced as a fabric for underwear, such as girdles, bras, and support stockings, but it became a popular material for sports and casual wear such as stretch leggings in the 1980s–90s.

Lycurgus Spartan lawgiver. He was believed to have been a member of the royal house of the ancient Greek city-state of Sparta, who, while acting as regent, gave the Spartans their constitution and system of education. Many modern scholars believe him to be purely mythical.

Lydgate John c. 1370–c. 1450. English poet. He was a Benedictine monk and later prior. His numerous works, including poems, moral tales, legends of the saints, and histories, were often translations or adaptations. His chief works are *Troy Book*, written 1412–21 at the request of Henry V when Prince of Wales, *The Siege of Thebes* 1420–22, and *The Fall of Princes* 1431–38.

Lydia ancient kingdom in Anatolia (7th–6th centuries BC), with its capital at Sardis. The Lydians were the first Western people to use standard coinage. Their last king, Croesus, was defeated by the Persians in 546 BC.

Lyell Charles 1797–1875. Scottish geologist. In his *Principles of Geology* 1830–33, he opposed the French anatomist Georges ◊Cuvier's theory that the features of the Earth were formed by a series of catastrophes, and expounded the Scottish geologist James ◊Hutton's view, known as ◊uniformitarianism, that past events were brought about by the same processes that occur today – a view that influenced Charles ◊Darwin's theory of ◊evolution.

Lyell suggested that the Earth was as much as 240 million years old (in contrast to the 6,000 years of prevalent contemporary theory), and provided the first detailed description of the ◊Tertiary period, dividing it into the Eocene, Miocene, and older and younger Pliocene periods. Darwin simply applied Lyell's geological method – explaining the past through what is observable in the present – to biology.

Lyly John c. 1553–1606. English dramatist and author. His romance *Euphues, or the Anatomy of Wit* 1578, with its elaborate stylistic devices, gave rise to the word 'euphuism' for a mannered rhetorical style. It was followed by a second part, *Euphues and his England*, 1580.

Lyme disease disease transmitted by tick bites that affects all the systems of the body. It has a 10% mortality rate. First described in 1975 following an outbreak in children living around Lyme, Connecticut, USA, it is caused by the microorganism *Borrelia burgdorferi*, isolated by Burgdorfer and Barbour in the USA in 1982. Untreated, the disease attacks the joints, nervous system, heart, liver, kidneys, and eyes, but responds to penicillin or tetracycline. In the UK the sheep tick is the main carrier.

lymph fluid found in the lymphatic system of vertebrates, similar in composition to blood plasma. Lymph carries some nutrients, and white blood cells to the tissues, and waste matter away from them.

Lymph is drained from the tissues by lymph capillaries, which empty into larger lymph vessels (lymphatics). These lead to lymph nodes (small, round bodies chiefly situated in the neck, armpit, groin, thorax, and abdomen), which process the

LUXEMBOURG
Grand Duchy of

national name *Grand-Duché de Luxembourg*
area 2,586 sq km/998 sq mi
capital Luxembourg
major towns/cities Esch-Alzette, Dudelange, Petange
physical features on the river Moselle; part of the Ardennes (Oesling) forest in N
head of state Grand Duke Jean from 1964
head of government Jean-Claude Juncker from 1995
political system liberal democracy
administrative divisions 12 cantons
political parties Christian Social Party (PCS), moderate, left of centre; Luxembourg Socialist Workers' Party (POSL), moderate, socialist; Democratic Party (PD), centre-left; Communist Party of Luxembourg, pro-European left-wing
armed forces 800 (1995); gendarmerie 560
conscription none
defence spend (% GDP) 1.2 (1994)
education spend (% GNP) 4.1 (1992)
health spend (% GDP) 6.3 (1993)
death penalty abolished 1979
population 401,000 (1994 est)
population growth rate 1.3% (1990–95)
age distribution (% of total population) <15 17%, 15–65 69%, >65 14% (1994)
ethnic distribution majority descended from the Moselle Franks
population density (per sq km) 155 (1994)
urban population (% of total) 88 (1993)
labour force 43% of population: 4% agriculture, 27% industry, 69% services (1990)
unemployment 3.6% (1995)
child mortality rate (under 5, per 1,000 live births) 8.5 (1992)
life expectancy 72 (men), 79 (women)
education (compulsory years) 9
literacy rate 100%
languages French, German, local Letzeburgesch (all official)
religion Roman Catholic
TV sets (per 1,000 people) 267 (1992)
currency Luxembourg franc
GDP (US $) 17.0 billion (1995)
GDP per capita (PPP) (US $) 30,596 (1995)
growth rate 3.7% (1994/95)
average annual inflation 3.0% (1995)
major trading partners EU (principally Belgium, Germany, and France)
resources iron ore
industries steel and rolled steel products, chemicals, rubber and plastic products, metal and machinery products, paper and printing products, food products, financial services
exports base metals and manufactures, mechanical and electrical equipment, rubber and related products, plastics, textiles and clothing. Principal market: Germany 28.2% (1993)
imports machinery and electrical apparatus, transport equipment, mineral products. Principal source: Belgium 38.1% (1993)
arable land 27%
agricultural products maize, roots and tubers, wheat, forage crops, grapes; livestock rearing and dairy farming

HISTORY

963 Luxembourg became autonomous within the Holy Roman Empire under Siegfried, Count of Ardennes.
1060 Conrad, descendent of Siegfried, took the title Count of Luxembourg.
1354 Emperor Charles IV promoted Luxembourg to status of duchy.
1441 Luxembourg ceded to dukes of Burgundy.
1482 Luxembourg came under Habsburg control.
1555 Luxembourg became part of Spanish Netherlands on division of Habsburg domains.
1684–97 Much of Luxembourg occupied by France.
1713 Treaty of Utrecht transferred Spanish Netherlands to Austria.
1797 Conquered by revolutionary France.
1815 Congress of Vienna made Luxembourg a grand duchy, under King William of the Netherlands.
1830 Most of Luxembourg supported Belgian revolt against the Netherlands.
1839 Western part of Luxembourg assigned to Belgium.
1842 Luxembourg entered the Zollverein (German customs union).
1867 Treaty of London confirmed independence and neutrality of Luxembourg to allay French fears about possible inclusion in a unified Germany.
1870s Development of iron and steel industry.
1890 Link with Dutch crown ended on accession of Queen Wilhelmina, since Luxembourg's law of succession did not permit a woman to rule; Adolphe of Nassau-Weilburg became grand duke.
1912 Revised law of succession allowed Marie-Adelaide to become grand duchess.
1914–18 Occupied by Germany.
1919 Plebiscite overwhelmingly favoured continued independence; Marie-Adelaide abdicated after allegations of collaboration with Germany; succeeded by Grand Duchess Charlotte.
1921 Entered into close economic links with Belgium.
1940 Invaded by Germany.
1942–44 Annexed by Germany.
1948 Luxembourg formed Benelux customs union with Belgium and the Netherlands.
1949 Luxembourg became a founding member of North Atlantic Treaty Organization (NATO).
1958 Luxembourg became a founding member of European Economic Community (EEC).
1964 Grand Duchess Charlotte abdicated in favour of her son Jean.
1974–79 Christian Social Party outside governing coalition for first time since 1919.
1994 Former premier Jacques Santer became president of European Commission (EC).
1995 Jean-Claude Juncker became prime minister.

SEE ALSO Belgium; Netherlands

◊lymphocytes produced by the bone marrow, and filter out harmful substances and bacteria. From the lymph nodes, vessels carry the lymph to the thoracic duct and the right lymphatic duct, which drain into the large veins in the neck.

lymph nodes small masses of lymphatic tissue in the body that occur at various points along the major lymphatic vessels. Tonsils and adenoids are large lymph nodes. As the lymph passes through them it is filtered, and bacteria and other micro-organisms are engulfed by cells known as macrophages. Lymph nodes are sometimes mistakenly called lymph 'glands', and the term 'swollen glands' refers to swelling of the lymph nodes caused by infection.

lymphocyte type of white blood cell with a large nucleus, produced in the bone marrow. Most occur in the ◊lymph and blood, and around sites of infection. B lymphocytes or ◊B cells are responsible for producing ◊antibodies. T lymphocytes or ◊T cells have several roles in the mechanism of ◊immunity.

Lynch Jack (John Mary) 1917– . Irish politician, prime minister 1966–73 and 1977–79. A Gaelic footballer and a barrister, in 1948 he entered the parliament of the republic as a Fianna Fáil member.

lynching killing of an alleged offender by an individual or group having no legal authority. In the USA it originated in 1780 with creation of a 'committee of vigilance' in Virginia; it is named after a member of that committee, Captain William Lynch, to whom is attributed 'Lynch's law'. Later examples occurred mostly in the Southern states after the Civil War, and were racially motivated.

Lynn Vera Margaret Lewis 1917– . English singer. Known during World War II as the 'Forces' Sweetheart', she became famous with such songs as 'We'll Meet Again', 'White Cliffs of Dover', and in 1952 'Auf Wiederseh'n, Sweetheart'.

lynx cat *Felis lynx* found in rocky and forested regions of North America and Europe. About 1 m/3 ft in length, it has a short tail and tufted ears, and the long, silky fur is reddish brown or grey with dark spots. The North American bobcat or bay lynx *Felix rufus* looks similar but is smaller.

Lyon (English *Lyons*) industrial city (textiles, chemicals, machinery, printing) and capital of Rhône *département*, Rhône-Alpes region, at the confluence of the rivers Rhône and Saône, 275 km/170 mi NNW of Marseille; population (1990) 422,400, conurbation 1,221,000. It is the third-largest city of France. Formerly a chief fortress of France, it was the ancient Lugdunum, taken by the Romans 43 BC.

Lyons Joseph Aloysius 1879–1939. Australian politician, founder of the United Australia Party 1931, prime minister 1931–39. Lyons followed the economic orthodoxy of the time, drastically cutting federal spending. His wife ***Enid Muriel Lyons*** (1897–1981) was the first woman member of the House of Representatives and of the federal cabinet.

Lyons Joseph Nathaniel 1848–1917. British entrepreneur, founder of the catering firm of J Lyons in 1894. He popularized teashops, and the 'Corner Houses' incorporating several restaurants of varying types were long a feature of London life.

lyophilization technical term for the ◊freeze-drying process used for foods and drugs and in the preservation of organic archaeological remains.

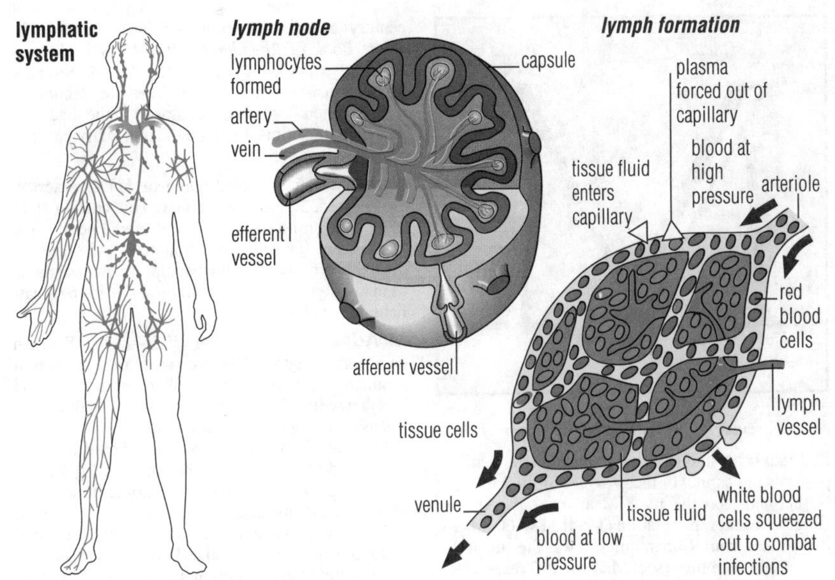

lymph Lymph is the fluid that carries nutrients and white blood cells to the tissues. Lymph enters the tissue from the capillaries (right) and is drained from the tissues by lymph vessels. The lymph vessels form a network (left) called the lymphatic system. At various points in the lymphatic system, lymph nodes (centre) filter and clean the lymph.

Lyra small but prominent constellation of the northern hemisphere, represented as the lyre of Orpheus. Its brightest star is ◊Vega. Epsilon Lyrae is a system of four gravitationally linked stars. Beta Lyrae is an eclipsing binary. The Ring nebula, M57, is a ◊planetary nebula.

lyre stringed instrument of great antiquity. It consists of a soundbox with two curved arms extended upwards to a crosspiece to which four to ten strings are attached. It is played with a plectrum or the fingers. It originated in Asia, and was widespread in ancient Greece and Egypt.

lyrebird any bird of the family Menuridae, order Passeriformes. There are two species, both in the genus *Menura*, both found in SE Australia. They are large birds with very stout beaks and short, rounded wings; the tail has 16 feathers, and in the males the exterior pair of feathers are curved in the shape of a lyre; the tail of the female is long, broad and normal in shape.

lyretail African fish *Aphyosemion australe* 6 cm/2.4 in long, whose tail has two outward-curving fin supports for a central fin area which looks like the strings of a lyre. The male is bright blue with red markings; the less brightly coloured female has plainer fins.

lyricism in the arts, the expressive or sensual qualities of a work. For instance, lyric poetry expresses the writer's thoughts and feelings. In painting, lyrical abstraction (*abstraction lyrique*) refers to a French style of abstract art of the 1940s and 1950s that was more spontaneous and expressive than geometrical abstraction (see ◊Tachisme).

lyric poem any short, personal, and passionate form of verse. Lyric poetry is a genre; it does not imply a particular rhyme scheme or technique. Sonnets, odes, and elegies are lyric poems, for example, since they express strong feeling or ideas. Originally, a lyric was a song sung to a lyre, and song texts are still called lyrics.

Lysander died 395 BC. Spartan general, politician, and admiral. He brought the ◊Peloponnesian War between Athens and Sparta to a successful conclusion by capturing the Athenian fleet at Aegospotami 405 BC, and by starving Athens into surrender in the following year. He set up puppet governments in Athens and its former allies, and tried to secure for himself the Spartan kingship, but was killed in battle with the Thebans 395 BC.

Lysenko Trofim Denisovich 1898–1976. Soviet biologist who believed in the inheritance of ◊acquired characteristics (changes acquired in an individual's lifetime) and used his position under Joseph Stalin officially to exclude Gregor ◊Mendel's theory of inheritance. He was removed from office after the fall of Nikita Khrushchev 1964.

Lysippus or ***Lysippos*** lived 4th century BC. Greek sculptor. He made a series of portraits of Alexander the Great (Roman copies survive, including examples in the British Museum and the Louvre) and also sculpted the *Apoxyomenos*, an athlete (copy in the Vatican), and a colossal *Hercules* (lost).

lysis in biology, any process that destroys a cell by rupturing its membrane or cell wall (see ◊lysosome).

lysosome membrane-enclosed structure, or organelle, inside a ◊cell, principally found in animal cells. Lysosomes contain enzymes that can break down proteins and other biological substances. They play a part in digestion, and in the white blood cells known as phagocytes, the lysosome enzymes attack ingested bacteria.

Lytham St Annes resort in Lancashire, England, on the river Ribble; 10 km/6 mi SE of Blackpool; population (1991) 40,900. It has a championship golf course.

Lytton Edward George Earle Lytton Bulwer, 1st Baron Lytton 1803–1873. English writer. His novels successfully followed every turn of the public taste of his day and include the Byronic *Pelham* 1828, *The Last Days of Pompeii* 1834, and *Zanoni* 1842. His plays include *Richelieu* 1838.

MA abbreviation for the degree of *Master of Arts*.

Maastricht industrial city (metallurgy, textiles, pottery) and capital of the province of Limburg, the Netherlands, on the river Maas, near the Dutch-Belgian frontier; population (1994) 118,100. Maastricht dates from Roman times. It was the site of the Maastricht summit (see Maastricht Treaty) Dec 1991.

Maastricht Treaty treaty on European union which took effect 1 Nov 1993, from which date the European Community (EC) became known as the ◊European Union (EU). Issues covered by the treaty included the EU's decision-making process and the establishment of closer links on foreign and military policy. A European Charter of Social Rights (see ◊Social Chapter) was approved by all member states except the UK.

The treaty was signed 10 Dec 1991 by leaders of EC nations in Maastricht, the Netherlands. Ratification by the parliaments of member states was preceded by a national referendum in France, Spain, Ireland, and twice in Denmark.

Among the aims of the treaty were the strengthening and convergence of the economies of member states so as to establish an economic and monetary union, including a single and stable currency; common citizenship for nationals of member states; a common foreign and security policy, including the eventual framing of a common defence policy; free movement of persons, while ensuring their safety and security; and a closer union among the peoples of Europe in accordance with the principle of subsidiarity (the devolution of decision-making to the lowest level possible).

'We know no spectacle so ridiculous as the British public in one of its periodical fits of morality.'

Thomas Macaulay
'Moore's "Life of Lord Byron"', *Literary Essays*

Maazel Lorin Varencove 1930– . US conductor and violinist. He became musical director of the Pittsburgh Symphony Orchestra 1986. A wide-ranging repertoire includes opera, from posts held at Berlin, Vienna, Bayreuth, and Milan, in addition to the symphonic repertoire, in particular Sibelius and Tchaikovsky. His orchestral preparation is noted for its inner precision and dynamic range. He recorded the *Requiem Mass* 1985 and *Variations for Cello and Six-Piece Rock Bank* 1978, orchestrated 1986 (after Paganini) by Andrew Lloyd Webber.

Mabinogion, The (Welsh *mabinogi* 'instruction for young poets') collection of medieval Welsh myths and folk tales put together in the mid-19th century and drawn from two manuscripts: *The White Book of Rhydderch* 1300–25 and *The Red Book of Hergest* 1375–1425. *The Mabinogion* proper consists of four tales, three of which concern a hero named Pryderi. Other stories in the medieval source manuscripts touch on the legendary court of King ◊Arthur.

McAdam Scottish civil engineer John McAdam. McAdam developed a procedure for the construction of roads, the principles of which are still used today. Roads are raised above the countryside and are prepared by compacting small gravel on top of larger stones to allow easy drainage. *Image Select (UK) Ltd*

Mabuse Jan. Adopted name of Jan Gossaert c. 1478–c. 1533. Flemish painter. His visit to Italy 1508 with Philip of Burgundy started a new vogue in Flanders for Italianate ornament and Classical detail in painting, including sculptural nude figures, as in his *Neptune and Amphitrite* about 1516 (Staatliche Museen, Berlin).

McAdam John Loudon 1756–1836. Scottish engineer, inventor of the ***macadam*** road surface. It originally consisted of broken granite bound together with slag or gravel, raised for drainage. Today, it is bound with tar or asphalt.

McAdam introduced a method of road building that raised the road above the surrounding terrain, compounding a surface of small stones bound with gravel on a firm base of large stones. A camber, making the road slightly convex in section, ensured that rainwater rapidly drained off the road and did not penetrate the foundation. By the end of the 19th century, most of the main roads in Europe were built in this way.

macadamia edible nut from the tree *Macadamia ternifolia*, family Proteaceae, native to Australia and cultivated in Hawaii, South Africa, Zimbabwe, and Malawi.

McAleese Mary Patricia 1951– . Irish lawyer and academic. President from 1997. She was nominated by the ruling Fianna Fáil and Progressive Democrats and secured a clear victory in the election for president. She held academic posts at Trinity College, Dublin, 1975–87, and was Pro-Vice-Chancellor at Queen's University, Belfast 1994–97. She has connections in both Catholic and Protestant communities.

Macao Portuguese possession on the S coast of China, about 65 km/40 mi W of Hong Kong, from which it is separated by the estuary of the Pearl River; it consists of a peninsula and the islands of Taipa and Colôane
area 17 sq km/7 sq mi
capital Macao, on the peninsula
features the peninsula is linked to Taipa by a bridge and to Colôane by a causeway
currency pataca
population (1994 est) 395,300
language Cantonese; Portuguese (official)
religion Buddhist, with 6% Catholic minority
government under the constitution ('organic statute') of 1990, Macao enjoys political autonomy. Executive power is held by the governor. The governor works with a cabinet of five appointed secretaries and confers with a 10-member consultative council and a 23-member legislative council, comprising seven government appointees, eight indirectly elected by business associations, and eight directly elected by universal suffrage. The legislative council frames internal legislation, but any bills passed by less than a two-thirds majority can be vetoed by the governor. A number of 'civic associations' and interest groups function, sending representatives to the legislative council
history Macao was first established as a Portuguese trading and missionary post in the Far East 1537, and was leased from China 1557. It was annexed 1849 and recognized as a Portuguese colony by the Chinese government in a treaty 1887. The port declined in prosperity during the late 19th and early 20th centuries, as its harbour silted up and international trade was diverted to Hong Kong and the new treaty ports. The colony thus concentrated instead on local 'country trade' and became a centre for gambling and, later, tourism

In 1951 Macao became an overseas province of Portugal, sending an elected representative to the Lisbon parliament. After the Portuguese revolution 1974, it became a 'special territory' and was granted considerable autonomy under a governor appointed by the Portuguese president

In 1986 negotiations opened between the Portuguese and the Chinese governments over the question of the return of Macao's sovereignty under 'one country, two systems' terms similar to those agreed by China and the UK for ◊Hong Kong. These negotiations were concluded 1987 by the signing of the Macao Pact, under which Portugal agreed to hand over sovereignty to the People's Republic 1999, and China agreed in return to guarantee to maintain the port's capitalist economic and social system for at least 50 years

In 1990 administrative, economic, and financial autonomy was secured from Portugal; this followed the approval of a new 'organic statute' for the territory by both Portugal's parliament and Macao's legislative assembly.

Macao

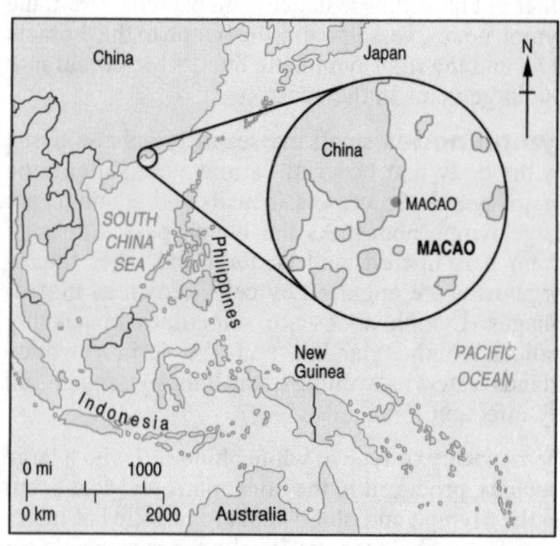

macaque Old World monkey of the genus *Macaca*. Various species of these medium-sized monkeys live in forests from the Far East to N Africa. The ◊rhesus and the ◊Barbary ape are part of this group.

MacArthur Douglas 1880–1964. US general in World War II, commander of US forces in the Far East and, from March 1942, of the Allied forces in the SW Pacific. After the surrender of Japan he commanded the Allied occupation forces there. During 1950 he commanded the UN forces in Korea, but in April 1951, after expressing views contrary to US and UN policy, he was relieved of all his commands by President Truman.

Macaulay (Emilie) Rose 1881–1958. English novelist. The serious vein of her early novels changed to light satire in *Potterism* 1920 and *Keeping up Appearances* 1928. Her later books include *The World My Wilderness* 1950 and *The Towers of Trebizond* 1956 (Tait Black Memorial Prize). Her work reflects the contemporary scene with wit and a shrewd understanding.

Macaulay Thomas Babington, 1st Baron Macaulay 1800–1859. English historian, essayist, poet, and politician, secretary of war 1839–41. His *History of England* in five volumes 1849–61 celebrates the Glorious Revolution of 1688 as the crowning achievement of the Whig party.

McAuley Dave 1961– . Irish boxer who won the International Boxing Federation (IBF) flyweight championship in 1989, and has made more

MacArthur US general Douglas MacArthur in 1945. He had been Allied supreme commander in the SW Pacific area since 1942 and helped plan the defeat of Japan in World War II. *Sachem*

successful defences of a world title than any other boxer. He won the British title in 1986.

macaw any of various large, brilliantly coloured, long-tailed tropical American ◊parrots of three genera: *Ara*, such as the blue and yellow macaw, *A. ararauna*; *Aratinga*; and *Anodorhynchus*. They can be recognized by the massive bill and extremely long tail.

Macbeth died 1057. King of Scotland from 1040. The son of Findlaech, hereditary ruler of Moray, he was commander of the forces of Duncan I, King of Scotia, whom he killed in battle 1040. His reign was prosperous until Duncan's son Malcolm III led an invasion and killed him at Lumphanan.

McBride Willie John (William James) 1940– . Irish Rugby Union player. He was capped 63 times by Ireland, and won a record 17 British Lions caps. He played on five Lions tours, 1962, 1966, 1968, 1971, and in 1974 as captain when they returned from South Africa undefeated.

McCabe John 1939– . English pianist and composer. His works include three symphonies, two violin concertos, an opera *The Play of Mother Courage* 1974, and orchestral works including *The Chagall Windows* 1974 and *Concerto for Orchestra* 1982. He was director of the London College of Music 1983–90.

Maccabee or ***Hasmonaean***, member of an ancient Hebrew family founded by the priest Mattathias (died 166 BC) who, with his sons, led the struggle for independence against the Syrians in the 2nd century BC. Judas (died 161) reconquered Jerusalem 164 BC, and Simon (died 135) established its independence 142 BC. The revolt of the Maccabees lasted until the capture of Jerusalem by the Romans 63 BC. The story is told in four books of the ◊Apocrypha.

McCarthy Joe (Joseph Raymond) 1908–1957. US right-wing Republican politician. His unsubstantiated claim 1950 that the State Department and US army had been infiltrated by communists started a wave of anticommunist hysteria, wild accusations, and blacklists, which continued until he was discredited 1954. He was censured by the US Senate for misconduct. ***McCarthyism*** came to represent the practice of using innuendo and unsubstantiated accusations against political adversaries.

McCarthy Mary Therese 1912–1989. US novelist and critic. Much of her work looks probingly at US society, for example, the novel *The Groves of Academe* 1952, which describes the anti-Communist witch-hunts of the time (see Joe ◊McCarthy), and *The Group* 1963 (filmed 1966), which follows the post-college careers of eight women.

McCartney (James) Paul 1942– . UK rock singer, songwriter, and bass guitarist. He was a member of the ◊Beatles, and leader of the pop group Wings 1971–81. His subsequent solo hits have included collaborations with Michael Jackson and Elvis Costello. Together with composer Carl Davis, McCartney wrote the *Liverpool Oratorio* 1991, his first work of classical music.

Macclesfield industrial town in Cheshire, NW England, on the edge of the Pennines; population (1990 est) 69,000. Formerly the centre of the silk industry, present-day industries include textiles, light engineering, paper, and plastics.

McClintock Barbara 1902–1992. US geneticist who discovered jumping ◊genes (genes that can change their position on a chromosome from generation to generation). This would explain how originally identical cells take on specialized functions as skin, muscle, bone, and nerve, and also how evolution could give rise to the multiplicity of species. Nobel Prize for Physiology or Medicine 1983.

McClure Robert John le Mesurier 1807–1873. Irish-born British admiral and explorer. While on an expedition 1850–54 searching for John ◊Franklin, he was the first to pass through the Northwest Passage.

McColgan Elizabeth 1964– . Scottish long-distance runner who became the 1992 world 10,000 metres champion. She won consecutive gold medals at the Commonwealth games in 1986 and 1990 at the same distance, and won the 1996 London Marathon.

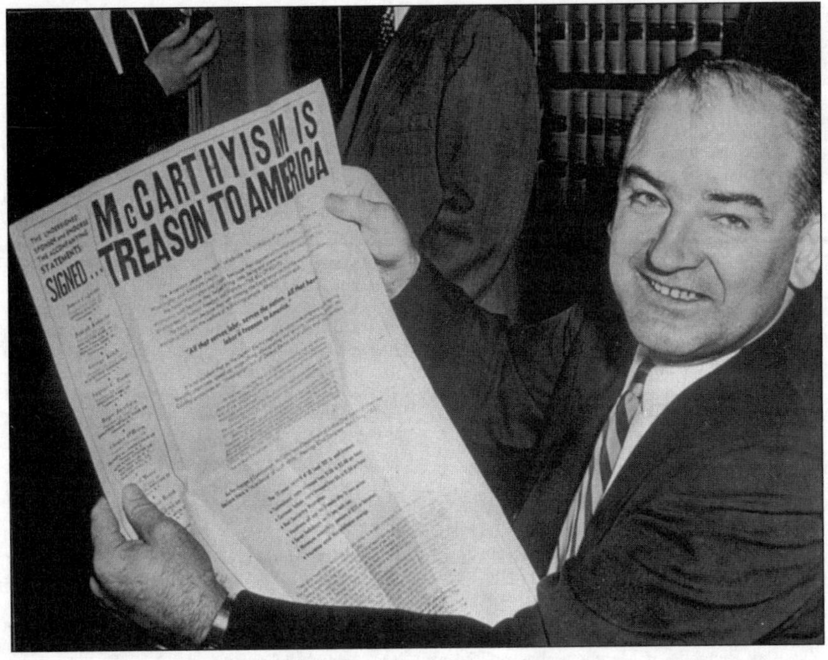

McCarthy US senator Joe McCarthy in 1954. He was described by President Truman as 'a pathological character assassin'. When Eisenhower became president, McCarthy was appointed chair of the Permanent Subcommittee on Investigations, and in this capacity he conducted campaigns of vilification against many prominent Americans he believed were communists. *Topham*

MacCormac Richard Cornelius 1938– . English architect. His work shows a clear geometric basis with a concern for the well-made object reminiscent of the ◊Arts and Crafts tradition. The residential building at Worcester College, Oxford, 1983 epitomizes his approach: the student rooms are intricately related in a complex geometric plan and stepped section. He became president of the Royal Institute of British Architects 1991. His other works include Coffee Hall flat, Milton Keynes, 1974; housing in Duffryn, Wales 1974; and Fitzwilliam College, Cambridge, 1986.

McCrea Joel 1905–1991. US film actor. He played in several major 1930s and 1940s productions, such as *Dead End* 1937 and *Sullivan's Travels* 1941. In later decades he was associated almost exclusively with the Western genre, notably *Ride the High Country* 1962, now recognized as a classic Western film.

McCullers (Lula) Carson, (born Smith) 1917–1967. US novelist. Most of her writing, including the novels *The Heart is a Lonely Hunter* 1940 and *Reflections in a Golden Eye* 1941, is set in her native South. Her work has been characterized as 'Southern Gothic' for its images of the grotesque, using physical abnormalities to project the spiritual and psychological distortions of Southern experience. Other works include her novel, *The Member of the Wedding* 1946, which was also a stage success, and the novella *The Ballad of the Sad Café* 1951.

McCullin Don(ald) 1935– . English war photographer. He started out as a freelance photojournalist for the Sunday newspapers. His coverage of hostilities in the Congo 1967, Vietnam 1968, Biafra 1968 and 1970, and Cambodia 1970 are notable for their pessimistic vision. He has published several books of his work, among them *Destruction Business*.

MacDiarmid Hugh. Pen name of Christopher Murray Grieve 1892–1978. Scottish poet. A nationalist and Marxist, he was one of the founders 1928 of the National Party of Scotland. His works include *A Drunk Man looks at the Thistle* 1926 and the collections *First Hymn to Lenin* 1931 and *Second Hymn to Lenin* 1935, in which poetry is made relevant to politics. He developed a form of modern poetic Scots, based on an amalgam of Middle and Modern Scots, and was the leader of the Scottish literary renaissance of the 1920s and 1930s.

Macdonald Flora 1722–1790. Scottish heroine who rescued Prince Charles Edward Stuart, the Young Pretender, after his defeat at Culloden 1746. Disguising him as her maid, she escorted him from her home in the Hebrides to France. She was arrested, but released 1747.

Macdonald John Alexander 1815–1891. Canadian Conservative politician, prime minister 1867–73 and 1878–91. In 1857 he became prime minister of Upper Canada. He took the leading part in the movement for federation, and in 1867 became the first prime minister of Canada. He was defeated 1873 but returned to office 1878 and retained it until his death.

MacDonald (James) Ramsay 1866–1937. British politician, first Labour prime minister Jan–Oct 1924 and 1929–31. Failing to deal with worsening economic conditions, he left the party to form a coalition government 1931, which was increasingly dominated by Conservatives, until he was replaced by Stanley Baldwin 1935.

MacDonald joined the ◊Independent Labour Party 1894, and became first secretary of the new Labour Party 1900. In Parliament he led the party 1906–14 and 1922–31 and was prime minister of the first two Labour governments.

MacDonald was born in Scotland, the son of a labourer. He was elected to Parliament 1906, and led the party until 1914, when his opposition to World War I lost him the leadership. This he recovered 1922, and in Jan 1924 he formed a government dependent on the support of the Liberal Party. When this was withdrawn in Oct the same year, he was forced to resign. He returned to office 1929, again as leader of a minority government, which collapsed 1931 as a result of the economic crisis. MacDonald left the Labour Party to form a national government with backing from both Liberal and Conservative parties. He resigned the premiership 1935.

McDonald's US fast-food chain, the largest in the world, specializing in hamburgers. In the West

MacDonald British politician Ramsay MacDonald. He became the first Labour prime minister 1924 and 1929–31, and then led a coalition government 1931–35. As a Labour prime minister he was hampered by the lack of an overall majority and the worsening economic conditions, and by subsequently working in a coalition with the Liberals and Conservatives, he lost the support of many of his Labour colleagues. *Topham*

'Men never do anything good except out of necessity.'

NICCOLÒ MACHIAVELLI
Discourse

the company has been criticized by environmentalists for uneconomic grazing land use (see ◊meat) and for contributing to litter and the greenhouse effect by its packaging.

Macdonnell Ranges mountain range in central Australia, Northern Territory, with the town of Alice Springs; highest peak Mount Zeil 1,510 m/4,955 ft.

Macedonia ancient region of Greece, forming parts of modern Greece, Bulgaria, and the Former Yugoslav Republic of Macedonia. Macedonia gained control of Greece after Philip II's victory at Chaeronea 338 BC. His son, ◊Alexander the Great, conquered a vast empire. Macedonia became a Roman province 146 BC.

Macedonia landlocked country in SE Europe, bounded N by Serbia, W by Albania, S by Greece, and E by Bulgaria. *See country box below.*

Macedonia (Greek ***Makedhonia***) mountainous region of N Greece, part of the ancient country of Macedonia which was divided between Serbia, Bulgaria, and Greece after the Balkan Wars of 1912–13. Greek Macedonia is bounded W and N by Albania and the Former Yugoslav Republic of Macedonia; area 34,177 sq km/13,200 sq mi; population (1991) 2,263,000. There are two regions, Macedonia Central, and Macedonia East and Thrace. The chief city is Thessaloniki. The Former Yugoslav Republic of Macedonia has refused to give up claims to the present Greek province of Macedonia, and has placed the star of Macedonia, symbol of the ancient Greek Kings of Macedonia, on its flag. Fertile valleys produce grain, olives, grapes, tobacco, and livestock. Mount Olympus rises to 2,918 m/9,570 ft on the border with Thessaly.

Macedonian people of Macedonian culture from the Former Yugoslav Republic of Macedonia and the surrounding area, especially Greece, Albania, and Bulgaria. Macedonian, a Slavic language belonging to the Indo-European family, has 1–1.5 million speakers. The Macedonians are predominantly members of the Greek Orthodox Church and write with a Cyrillic script. They are known for their folk arts.

The Macedonian language and ethnic identification have been subject to repression, especially in Bulgaria and Greece.

McEnroe John Patrick 1959– . US tennis player whose brash behaviour and fiery temper on court dominated the men's game in the early 1980s. He was three times winner of Wimbledon 1981 and 1983–84. He also won three successive US Open titles 1979–81 and again in 1984. A fine doubles player, McEnroe also won ten Grand Slam titles, seven in partnership with Peter Flemming.

McEwan Ian Russell 1948– . English novelist and short-story writer. His works often have sinister or macabre undertones and contain elements of violence and bizarre sexuality, as in the short stories in *First Love, Last Rites* 1975. His novels include *The Comfort of Strangers* 1981, *The Child in Time* 1987, *Black Dogs* 1992, *The Daydreamer* 1994, and *Amsterdam* 1998, for which he won the Booker Prize.

Macgillycuddy's Reeks range of mountains in SW Ireland lying W of Killarney, in County Kerry; Carrauntoohill 1,041 m/3,414 ft is the highest peak in Ireland.

McGwire Mark 1963– . US baseball player, a first baseman for the St Louis Cardinals who in 1998 set a new major league record of 70 home runs in a season, breaking the previous record of 61 set by Roger Maris of the New York Yankees in 1961. Also in 1998 he became the first player in major league history to hit 50 home runs or more in three consecutive seasons. Born in California, he made his major league debut for the Oakland As in 1986. He was transferred to St Louis during the 1997 season.

Mach Ernst 1838–1916. Austrian philosopher and physicist. He was an empiricist, believing that science is a record of facts perceived by the senses, and that acceptance of a scientific law depends solely on its standing the practical test of use; he opposed concepts such as Isaac ◊Newton's 'absolute motion'. ◊***Mach numbers*** are named after him.

Machado Antonio 1875–1939. Spanish poet and dramatist. He was inspired by the Castilian countryside in his lyric verse, collected in *Soledades/Solitudes* 1902 – enlarged as *Soledades, galerías y otros poemas/Solitudes, Galleries and Other Poems* 1907 – and *Campos de Castilla/Countryside of Castile* 1912, which contains some of his finest work. His verse is nostalgic and full of anguish at the sense of time passing, yet also expresses hope for the future.

Machado de Assis Joaquim Maria 1839–1908. Brazilian writer and poet. He is generally regarded as the greatest Brazilian novelist. His sceptical, ironic wit is well displayed in his 30 volumes of novels and short stories, including *Epitaph for a Small Winner* 1880 and *Dom Casmurro* 1900.

Machel Samora Moises 1933–1986. Mozambique nationalist leader, president 1975–86. Machel was active in the liberation front ◊Frelimo from its conception 1962, fighting for independence from Portugal. He became Frelimo leader 1966, and Mozambique's first president from independence 1975 until his death in a plane crash.

Machiavelli Niccolò 1469–1527. Italian politician and author. His name is synonymous with cunning and cynical statecraft. In his chief political writings, *Il principe/The Prince* 1513 and *Discorsi/Discourses* 1531, he discussed ways in which rulers can advance the interests of their states (and themselves) through an often amoral and opportunistic manipulation of other people.

Machiavelli was born in Florence and was second chancellor to the republic 1498–1512. On the accession to power of the ◊Medici family 1512, he was arrested and imprisoned on a charge of conspiracy, but in 1513 was released to exile in the country.

machine device that allows a small force (the effort) to overcome a larger one (the load). There are three basic machines: the inclined plane (ramp), the lever, and the wheel and axle. All other machines are combinations of these three basic types. Simple machines derived from the inclined plane include the wedge, the gear, and the screw; the spanner is derived from the lever; the pulley from the wheel.

The principal features of a machine are its ◊mechanical advantage (the ratio of load to effort), its velocity ratio (the ratio of the distance moved by an effort force to the distance moved by the machine's load in the same time), and its ◊efficiency (the work done by the load divided by the work done by the effort); the latter is expressed

MACEDONIA

Former Yugoslav Republic of (official international name); **Republic of Macedon** (official internal name)

national name *Republika Makedonija*
area 25,700 sq km/9,920 sq mi
capital Skopje
major towns/cities Bitolj, Prilep, Kumanovo, Tetovo
physical features mountainous; rivers: Struma, Vardar; lakes: Ohrid, Prespa, Scutari; partly Mediterranean climate with hot summers
head of state (acting) Stojan Andov from 1995
head of government Branko Crvenkovski from 1992
political system emergent democracy
administrative divisions by local commune or township
political parties Socialist Party (SP); Social Democratic Alliance of Macedonia (SM) bloc, left of centre; Party for Democratic Prosperity (PDP), ethnic Albanian, left of centre; Internal Macedonian Revolutionary Organisation–Democratic Party for Macedonian National Unity (VMRO–DPMNE), radical nationalist; Democratic Party of Macedonia (DPM), nationalist, free market
population 2,174,000 (1996 est)
population growth rate 1.1% (1990–95); 0.7% (2000–05)
ethnic distribution 66% Macedonian ethnic descent, 22% ethnic Albanian, 5% Turkish, 3% Romanian, 2% Serb, and 2% Muslim, comprising Macedonian Slavs who converted to Islam during the Ottoman era, and known as Pomaks. This ethnic breakdown is disputed by Macedonia's ethnic Albanian population, who claim that they form 40% of the population, and seek autonomy. It is also contested by ethnic Serbs, who claim that they number 250,000
life expectancy 68 (men), 72 (women)
literacy rate 90%
language Macedonian, closely allied to Bulgarian and written in Cyrillic
religions Christian, mainly Orthodox; Muslim 2.5%
currency Macedonian denar
GDP (US $) 2 billion (1994)
growth rate −40.0% (1989–93)

HISTORY
4th C BC Part of the ancient great kingdom of Macedonia, which included N Greece and SW Bulgaria and, under Alexander the Great, conquered a vast empire; Thessaloniki founded.
146 BC Macedonia became a province of the Roman Empire.
395 AD On the division of the Roman Empire, came under the control of Byzantine Empire, with its capital at Constantinople.
6th C Settled by Slavs, who later converted to Christianity.
9th–14th Cs Under successive rule by Bulgars, Byzantium, and Serbia.
1371 Became part of the Islamic Ottoman Empire.
late 19th C The 'Internal Macedonian Revolutionary Organization', through terrorism, sought to provoke Great Power intervention against the Turks.
1912–13 After First Balkan War, partitioned between Bulgaria, Greece, and the area that constitutes the current republic of Serbia.
1918 Serbian part included in what was to become Yugoslavia; Serbian imposed as official language.
1941–44 Occupied by Bulgaria.
1945 Created a republic within Yugoslav Socialist Federation.
1967 The Orthodox Macedonian archbishopric of Skopje, forcibly abolished 200 years earlier by the Turks, was restored.
1980 Rise of nationalism after death of Yugoslav leader Tito.
1991 Kiro Gligorov, a pragmatic former communist, became president. Referendum supported independence.
1992 Independence declared, and accepted by Serbia/Yugoslavia, but international recognition withheld because of objections to name by Greece.
1993 Sovereignty recognized by UK and Albania; won United Nations membership under provisional name of Former Yugoslav Republic of Macedonia; Greece blocked full European Union (EU) recognition.
1994 Independence recognized by USA; trade embargo imposed by Greece.
1995 Independence recognized by Greece; trade embargo lifted. President Gligorov survived assassination attempt.
1997 Plans to reduce strength of UN Preventive Deployment Force (UNPREDEP) were abandoned. Government announced compensation for public's losses in failed investment schemes.
1998 UN extended mandate of UNPREDEP.

SEE ALSO Alexander the Great; Byzantine Empire; Balkan Wars; Ottoman Empire; Yugoslavia as a percentage. In a perfect machine, with no friction, the efficiency would be 100%. All practical machines have efficiencies of less than 100%, otherwise perpetual motion would be possible.

machine code in computing, a set of instructions that a computer's central processing unit (CPU) can understand and obey directly, without any translation. Each type of CPU has its own machine code. Because machine-code programs consist entirely of binary digits (bits), most programmers write their programs in an easy-to-use high-level language. A high-level program must be translated into machine code – by means of a compiler or interpreter program – before it can be executed by a computer.

machine gun rapid-firing automatic gun. The Maxim (named after its inventor, US-born British engineer H S Maxim (1840–1916)) of 1884 was recoil-operated, but some later types have been gas-operated (Bren) or recoil assisted by gas (some versions of the Browning).

The forerunner of the modern machine gun was the Gatling (named after its US inventor R J Gatling), perfected in the USA in 1860 and used in the Civil War. It had a number of barrels arranged about a central axis, and the breech containing the reloading, ejection, and firing mechanism was rotated by hand, shots being fired through each barrel in turn. The ***sub-machine-gun***, exploited by Chicago gangsters in the 1920s, was widely used in World War II; for instance, the Thompson, often called the Tommy gun. See ◊small arms.

machine tool automatic or semi-automatic power-driven machine for cutting and shaping metals. The most common machine tool is the ◊lathe, which shapes shafts and similar objects. A milling machine cuts metal with a rotary toothed cutting wheel. Other machine tools cut, plane, grind, drill, and polish. The use of precision machine tools in mass-production assembly methods ensures that all duplicate parts produced are virtually identical.

Mach number ratio of the speed of a body to the speed of sound in the undisturbed medium through which the body travels. Mach 1 is reached when a body (such as an aircraft) has a velocity greater than that of sound ('passes the sound barrier'), namely 331 m/1,087 ft per second at sea level. It is named after Austrian physicist Ernst ◊Mach.

Machu Picchu ruined Inca city in Peru, built about AD 1500, NW of Cuzco, discovered 1911 by Hiram Bingham. It stands at the top of cliffs 300 m/1,000 ft high and contains the well-preserved remains of houses and temples.

Macintosh range of microcomputers originally produced by Apple Computers. The Apple Macintosh, introduced 1984, was the first popular microcomputer with a ◊graphical user interface. The success of the Macintosh prompted other manufacturers and software companies to create their own graphical user interfaces. Most notable of these are Microsoft Windows, which runs on IBM PC-compatible microcomputers, and OSF/Motif, from the Open Software Foundation, which is used with many Unix systems.

In 1994 Apple licensed the Macintosh for the first time, thus enabling other manufacturers to make cheaper machines, the first appearing 1996.

Macintosh Charles 1766–1843. Scottish manufacturing chemist who invented a waterproof fabric, lined with rubber, that was used for raincoats – hence ***mackintosh***. Other waterproofing processes have now largely superseded this method.

McKay Heather Pamela, (born Blundell) 1941– . Australian squash player. She won 14 consecutive Australian titles 1960–1973 and was twice World Open champion (inaugurated 1976). She won the British Open title an unprecedented 16 years in succession 1962–1977. Between 1962 and 1980 she was unbeaten.

Macke August 1887–1914. German Expressionist painter. He was a founding member of the ◊*Blaue Reiter* group in Munich. With Franz ◊Marc he developed a semi-abstract style, and became noted for his simple, brightly coloured paintings of park and street scenes. He first met Marc and Kandinsky 1909, and in 1912 he and Marc went to Paris, where they encountered the abstract style of Robert Delaunay (Orphism). In 1914 Macke visited Tunis with Paul ◊Klee, and was inspired to paint a series of brightly coloured watercolours largely composed of geometrical shapes but still representational. He was killed in World War I.

McKellen Ian Murray 1939– . English actor. Acclaimed as the leading Shakespearean player of his generation, his stage roles include Richard II 1968, Macbeth 1977, Max in Martin Sherman's *Bent* 1979, Platonov in Chekhov's *Wild Honey* 1986, Iago in *Othello* 1989, and Richard III 1990. His films include *Priest of Love* 1982 and *Plenty* 1985.

Mackendrick Alexander 1912–1993. US-born Scottish film director and teacher. He was responsible for some of ◊Ealing Studios' finest films, including *Whisky Galore!* 1949, *The Man in the White Suit* 1951, and *Mandy* 1952. *The Ladykillers* 1955, which proved to be Ealing's last major film, possesses a macabre eccentricity that places it in the front rank of British comedy. Mackendrick went to Hollywood to direct *Sweet Smell of Success* 1957.

Mackenzie (Edward Montague) Compton 1883–1972. Scottish author. He published his first novel *The Passionate Elopement* 1911. Later works were *Carnival* 1912, *Sinister Street* 1913–14 (an autobiographical novel), and the comic *Whisky Galore* 1947.

Mackenzie River river in the Northwest Territories, Canada, flowing NW from Great Slave Lake to the Arctic Ocean; about 1,800 km/1,120 mi long. It is the main channel of the Finlay-Peace-Mackenzie system, 4,241 km/2,635 mi long. It was named after the British explorer Alexander Mackenzie (1764–1820), who saw it 1789.

mackerel any of various fishes of the mackerel family Scombroidia, especially the common mackerel *Scomber scombrus* found in the N Atlantic and Mediterranean. It weighs about 0.7 kg/1.5 lb, and is blue with irregular black bands down its sides, the latter and the under surface showing a metallic sheen. It has a deeply forked tail, and a sleek, streamlined body form.

McKern (Reginald) Leo 1920– . Australian character actor. Active in the UK, he is probably best known for his portrayal of the barrister Rumpole in the television series *Rumpole of the Bailey*. His films include *Moll Flanders* 1965, *A Man for All Seasons* 1966, and *Ryan's Daughter* 1970.

Mackerras (Alan) Charles (MacLaurin) 1925– . Australian conductor. He has helped to make the music of the Czech composer Leoš Janáček more widely known. He was conductor of the English National Opera 1970–78.

McKinley William 1843–1901. 25th president of the USA 1897–1901, a republican. His term as president was marked by the USA's adoption of an imperialist policy, as exemplified by the Spanish-American War 1898 and the annexation of the Philippines. He was first elected to Congress 1876. He was assassinated.

McKinley, Mount or ***Denali*** peak in Alaska, USA, the highest in North America, 6,194 m/20,320 ft.

Mackintosh Charles Rennie 1868–1928. Scottish architect, designer, and painter. He worked initially in the ◊Art Nouveau idiom but later developed a unique style, both rational and expressive. Influenced by the ◊Arts and Crafts movement, he

'The setting is enough, is almost too much in itself. It is nearly too good to be believed that there should be something to see here.'

On Machu Picchu
Sacheverell Sitwell
Golden Wall and Mirador

Machu Picchu The ruins of the Incan stronghold Machu Picchu stand on a terraced ridge in the Andes, northwest of Cuzco, Peru. Government buildings were erected under a system of labour taxation that required citizens to serve on building projects, on state-owned farms, and in the army. *Corbis*

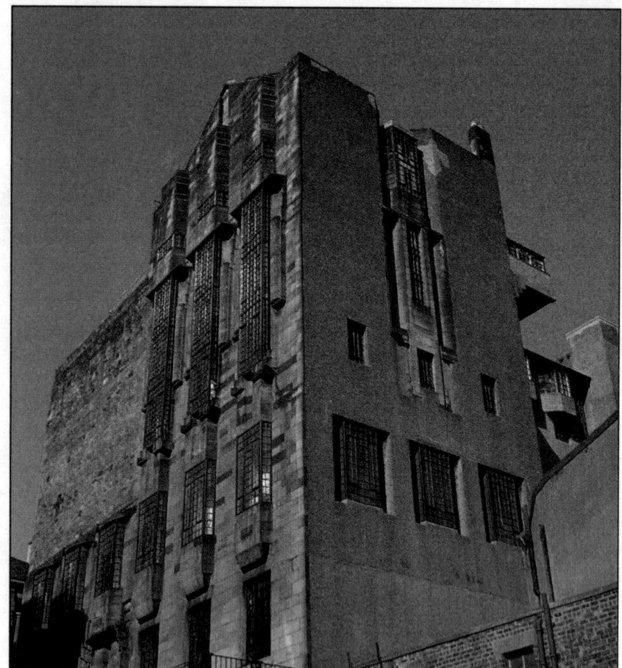

Mackintosh Charles Rennie Mackintosh's most famous building, the Glasgow School of Art. Mackintosh was a leading Art Nouveau designer, and was also influenced by the Arts and Crafts movement, though he rejected their medieval revival. *Corbis*

designed furniture and fittings, cutlery, and lighting to go with his interiors. Although initially influential, particularly on Austrian architects such as J M Olbrich and Josef Hoffman, Mackintosh was not successful in his lifetime and has only recently come to be regarded as a pioneer of modern design. His chief works include the Glasgow School of Art 1896, various Glasgow tea rooms 1897–1911, and Hill House, Helensburgh, 1902–03.

Mackmurdo Arthur Heygate 1851–1942. English designer and architect. He founded the Century Guild 1882, a group of architects, artists, and designers inspired by William ◊Morris and John ◊Ruskin. His textile designs are forerunners of ◊Art Nouveau.

MacLaine Shirley. Stage name of Shirley MacLean Beatty 1934– . US actress. A versatile performer, her films include Alfred Hitchcock's *The Trouble with Harry* 1955 (her debut), *The Apartment* 1960, and *Terms of Endearment* 1983, for which she won an Academy Award. Her many offscreen interests (politics, writing) have limited her film appearances. She is the sister of Warren Beatty.

McLaren racing-car company, makers of the successful Formula One Grand Prix car of the 1980s. The team was founded 1966 by New Zealand driver Bruce McLaren, and by 1993 had equalled Ferrari's all-time record of 104 Grand Prix wins.

Bruce McLaren was killed in an accident 1970, but the company continued and was re-formed 1980 as McLaren International under John Barnard and Ron Dennis. The company diversified 1995 to produce a very successful sports GT car, the F1, with a top speed of over 368 kph/230 mph and a price of around £450,000. McLaren world champions have included Emerson Fittipaldi 1974, James Hunt 1976, Niki Lauda 1984, Alain Prost 1985, 1986, 1989, and Ayrton Senna 1988, 1990, 1991.

Maclean Alistair 1922–1987. Scottish adventure novelist. His first novel, *HMS Ulysses* 1955, was based on wartime experience. It was followed by *The Guns of Navarone* 1957 and other adventure novels. Many of his books were made into films.

Maclean Donald Duart 1913–1983. British spy who worked for the USSR while in the UK civil service. He defected to the USSR 1951 together with Guy ◊Burgess.

Maclean was recruited by the Soviet ◊KGB in Cambridge. He worked for the UK Foreign Office in Washington 1944 and then Cairo 1948 before returning to London, becoming head of the American Department at the Foreign Office 1950.

‘As usual the Liberals offer a mixture of sound and original ideas. Unfortunately none of the sound ideas is original and none of the original ideas is sound.’

HAROLD MACMILLAN
Speech to London Conservatives
7 March 1962

MacLeish Archibald 1892–1982. US poet. He made his name with the long narrative poem *Conquistador* 1932, which describes Cortés' march to the Aztec capital, but his later plays in verse, *Panic* 1935 and *Air Raid* 1938, deal with contemporary problems. He was Boylston Professor of Rhetoric at Harvard 1949–62, and his essays in *Poetry and Opinion* 1950 reflect his feeling that a poet should be 'committed', expressing his outlook in his verse.

MacLennan Robert (Adam Ross) 1936– . Scottish centrist politician; member of Parliament for Caithness and Sutherland from 1966. He left the Labour Party for the Social Democrats (SDP) 1981, and was SDP leader 1988 during merger negotiations with the Liberals. He then became a member of the new Social and Liberal Democrats.

McLuhan (Herbert) Marshall 1911–1980. Canadian theorist of communication who emphasized the effects of technology on modern society. He coined the phrase 'the medium is the message', meaning that the form rather than the content of information has become crucial. His works include *The Gutenberg Galaxy* 1962 (in which he coined the phrase 'the global village' for the worldwide electronic society then emerging), *Understanding Media* 1964, and *The Medium Is the Massage* (sic) 1967.

MacMahon Marie Edmé Patrice Maurice, Comte de MacMahon 1808–1893. Marshal of France. Captured at Sedan 1870 during the Franco-Prussian War, he suppressed the ◊Paris Commune after his release, and as president of the republic 1873–79 worked for a royalist restoration until forced to resign.

Macmillan (Maurice) Harold, 1st Earl of Stockton 1894–1986. British Conservative politician, prime minister 1957–63; foreign secretary 1955 and chancellor of the Exchequer 1955–57. In 1963 he attempted to negotiate British entry into the European Economic Community, but was blocked by French president de Gaulle. Much of his career as prime minister was spent defending the retention of a UK nuclear weapon, and he was responsible for the purchase of US Polaris missiles 1962.

Macmillan was MP for Stockton 1924–29 and 1931–45, and for Bromley 1945–64. As minister of housing 1951–54 he achieved the construction of 300,000 new houses a year. He became prime minister on the resignation of Anthony ◊Eden after the Suez crisis, and led the Conservative Party to victory in the 1959 elections on the slogan 'You've never had it so good'. Internationally, his realization of the 'wind of change' in Africa advanced the independence of former colonies.

MacMillan Kenneth 1929–1992. Scottish choreographer. He was director of the Royal Ballet 1970–77 and then principal choreographer 1977–92. He was also director of Berlin's German Opera ballet company 1966–69. A daring stylist, he often took risks with his choreography, expanding the ballet's vocabulary with his frequent use of historical sources, religious music, and occasional use of dialogue. His works include *Romeo and Juliet* 1965 (filmed 1966) for Margot Fonteyn and Rudolf Nureyev.

He is also renowned for his work with the Canadian dancer Lynn Seymour, including *Le Baiser de la fée* 1960 and *The Invitation* 1960. In *Anastasia* 1967 MacMillan contrasted different eras, musical styles, and incorporated newsreel footage. Other works include *The Song of the Earth* 1965, *Elite Syncopations* 1974, *Mayerling* 1978, *Orpheus* 1982, and *The Prince of the Pagodas* 1989.

MacMillan Kirkpatrick 1813–1878. Scottish blacksmith who invented the bicycle 1839. His invention consisted of a 'hobby-horse' that was fitted with treadles and propelled by pedalling.

MacNeice (Frederick) Louis 1907–1963. British poet, born in Belfast. He made his debut with *Blind Fireworks* 1929 and developed a polished ease of expression, reflecting his classical training, as in the autobiographical and topical *Autumn Journal* 1939. He is noted for his low-key, socially committed but politically uncommitted verse; and his ability to reflect the spirit of his times in his own emotional experience earned him an appreciative public.

Later works include the play *The Dark Tower* 1947, written for radio (he was employed by the BBC features department 1941–61); a verse translation of Goethe's *Faust* 1949; and the collections *Springboard* 1944 and *Solstices* 1961. *Collected Poems* 1966 was revised 1979 and *Selected Plays* appeared 1993.

Mâcon capital of the French *département* of Saône-et-Loire, on the river Saône, 72 km/45 mi N of Lyon; population (1990) 38,500. It produces wine. Mâcon dates from ancient Gaul, when it was known as ***Matisco***.

McPartland Jimmy (James Duigald) 1907–1991. US cornet player. He was one of the founders of the Chicago school of jazz in the 1920s. He was influenced by Louis Armstrong and Bix Beiderbecke, whom he replaced in a group called the Wolverines 1924. He also recorded with guitarist Eddie Condon, and from the late 1940s often worked with his wife, British pianist ***Marian McPartland*** (1920–).

Macpherson James 1736–1796. Scottish writer and literary forger. He was the author of *Fragments of Ancient Poetry collected in the Highlands of Scotland* 1760, followed by the epics *Fingal* 1761 and *Temora* 1763, which he claimed as the work of the 3rd-century bard ◊Ossian. After his death they were shown to be forgeries, but nevertheless influenced the development of the Romantic movement in Britain and in Europe.

Macquarie Lachlan 1762–1824. Scottish administrator in Australia. He succeeded Admiral ◊Bligh as governor of New South Wales 1809, raised the demoralized settlement to prosperity, and did much to rehabilitate ex-convicts. In 1821 he returned to Britain in poor health, exhausted by struggles with his opponents. Lachlan River and Macquarie River and Island are named after him.

Macquarie Island outlying Australian territorial possession, a Tasmanian dependency, some 1,370 km/850 mi SE of Hobart; area 170 sq km/65 sq mi; it is uninhabited except for an Australian government research station.

McQueen Steve (Terrence Steven) 1930–1980. US film actor. He was admired for his portrayals of the strong, silent loner, and noted for performing his own stunt work. After television success in the 1950s, he became a film star with *The Magnificent Seven* 1960. His films include *The Great Escape* 1963, *Bullitt* 1968, *Papillon* 1973, and *The Hunter* 1980.

macramé art of making decorative fringes and lacework with knotted threads. The name comes from the Arabic word for 'striped cloth', which is often decorated in this way.

Macready William Charles 1793–1873. English actor. Noted for his roles as Shakespeare's tragic heroes (Macbeth, Lear, and Hamlet), he was partly responsible for persuading the theatre to return to the original texts of Shakespeare and abandon the earlier, bowdlerized versions. He was manager of Drury Lane Theatre, London, 1841–43.

macro in computer programming, a new command created by combining a number of existing ones. For example, a word processing macro might create a letterhead or fax cover sheet, inserting words, fonts, and logos with a single keystroke or mouse click. Macros are also useful to automate computer communications – for example, users can write a macro to ask their computer to dial an Internet service provider, retrieve e-mail, and then disconnect. A macro key on the keyboard combines the effects of pressing several individual keys.

macrobiotics dietary system of organically grown foods. It originates in Zen Buddhism, and attempts to balance the principles of ◊yin and yang, thought to be present in foods in different proportions.

macrophage type of ◊white blood cell, or leucocyte, found in all vertebrate animals. Macrophages specialize in the removal of bacteria and other microorganisms, or of cell debris after injury. Like phagocytes, they engulf foreign matter, but they are larger than phagocytes and have a longer life span. They are found throughout the body, but mainly in the lymph and connective tissues, and especially the lungs, where they ingest dust, fibres, and other inhaled particles.

MAD abbreviation for ***mutual assured destruction***, the basis of the theory of ◊deterrence by possession of nuclear weapons.

Madagascar island country in the Indian Ocean, off the coast of E Africa, about 400 km/280 mi from Mozambique. *See country box opposite.*

mad cow disease common name for ◊bovine spongiform encephalopathy, an incurable brain condition in cattle.

MADAGASCAR
Democratic Republic of

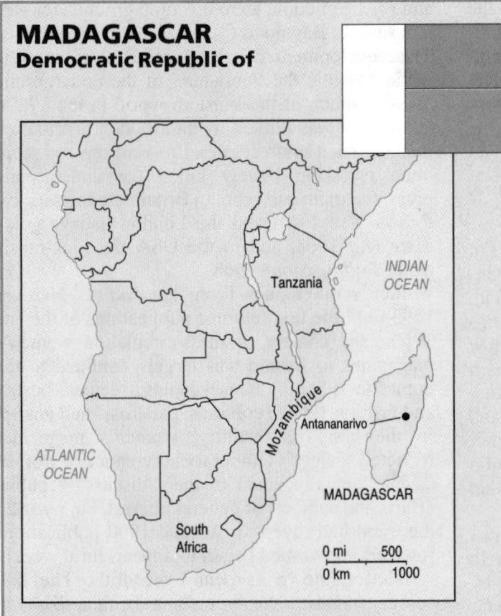

national name *Repoblika Demokratika n'i Madagaskar*
area 587,041 sq km/226,598 sq mi
capital Antananarivo
major towns/cities Fianarantsoa
major ports Toamasina, Antsiranana, Toliary, Mahajanga
physical features temperate central highlands; humid valleys and tropical coastal plains; arid in S
head of state Didier Ratsiraka from 1997
head of government Pascal Rakotomavuo from 1997
political system emergent democratic republic
administrative divisions six provinces
political parties National Front for the Defence of the Malagasy Socialist Revolution (FNDR), left-of-centre coalition; Comité des Forces Vives, pro-Zafy, left-of-centre coalition
population 14,763,000 (1995 est)
population growth rate 3.2% (1990–95); 3.1% (2000–05)
ethnic distribution 18 main Malagasy tribes of Malaysian-Polynesian origin; also French, Chinese, Indians, Pakistanis, and Comorans
life expectancy 54 (men), 57 (women)
literacy rate men 88%, women 73%
languages Malagasy (official), French, English
religions traditional beliefs, Roman Catholic, Protestant
currency Malagasy franc
GDP (US $) 3.36 billion (1993)
growth rate 2.7% (1993)
exports coffee, cloves, vanilla, sugar, chromite, shrimps

HISTORY
c. 6th–10th Cs AD Settled by migrant Indonesians.
1500 First visited by European navigators.
17th C Development of Merina and Sakalava kingdoms in the central highlands and W coast.
1642–74 France established a coastal settlement at Fort-Dauphin, which they abandoned after a massacre by local inhabitants.
late 18th–early 19th C Merinas, united by their ruler Andrianampoinimerina, became dominant kingdom and court converted to Christianity.
1861 Ban on Christianity (imposed in 1828) and entry of Europeans lifted by the Merina king, Radama II.
1885 Became a French protectorate.
1895 Merina army defeated by French and became a colony; slavery abolished.
1942–43 British troops invaded to overthrow a French administration allied to the pro-Nazi Germany Vichy regime and install an anti-Nazi Free French government.
1947–48 Nationalist uprising brutally suppressed by French.
1960 Independence achieved from France, with Philibert Tsiranana, the leader of the Social Democratic Party (PSD), as president.
1972 Merina-dominated army overthrew the government of Tsiranana, dominated by the cotier (coastal tribes), as economy deteriorated.
1975 Martial law imposed; new one-party state Marxist constitution adopted, with Lt-Commander Didier Ratsiraka as president.
1978 More than 1,000 people killed in race riots in Majunga city in NW.
1980 Ratsiraka abandoned Marxist experiment, which had involved nationalization and severing ties with France.
1983 Ratsiraka re-elected, despite strong opposition from radical socialist movement under Monja Jaona.
1990 Political opposition legalized; 36 new parties created.
1991 Antigovernment demonstrations. Ratsiraka formed new unity government, which included opposition members.
1992 Constitutional reform approved by referendum.
1993 Albert Zafy elected president and pro-Zafy left-of-centre coalition won majority in multiparty assembly elections.
1995 Referendum backed appointment of prime minister by president, rather than assembly.
1997 Pascal Rakotomavuo became prime minister and Didier Ratsiraka president.

Madeira group of islands forming an autonomous region of Portugal off the NW coast of Africa, about 420 km/260 mi N of the Canary Islands. Madeira, the largest, and Porto Santo are the only inhabited islands. The Desertas and Selvagens are uninhabited islets. Their mild climate makes them a year-round resort
area 796 sq km/308 sq mi
capital Funchal, on Madeira
physical Pico Ruivo, on Madeira, is the highest mountain at 1,861 m/6,106 ft
industries Madeira (a fortified wine), sugar cane, fruit, fish, handicrafts
population (1994 est) 256,000
history Portuguese from the 15th century; occupied by Britain 1801 and 1807–14. In 1956 Madeira gained partial autonomy but remains a Portuguese overseas territory.

Madeira

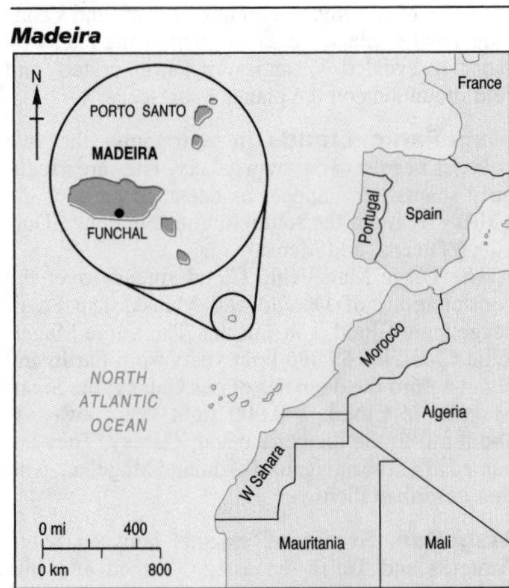

Madeira River river of W Brazil; length 3,250 km/2,020 mi. It is formed by the rivers Beni and Mamoré, and flows NE to join the Amazon.

Madhya Bharat state of India 1950–56. It was a union of 24 states of which Gwalior and Indore were the most important. In 1956 Madhya Bharat was absorbed in ◊Madhya Pradesh.

Madhya Pradesh state of central India; the largest of the Indian states
area 443,400 sq km/171,196 sq mi
capital Bhopal
towns and cities Indore, Jabalpur, Gwalior, Durg-Bhilainagar, Raipur, Ujjain
industries cotton, oilseed, sugar, textiles, engineering, paper, aluminium, limestone, diamonds, steel
population (1994 est) 71,950,000
language Hindi
history formed 1950 from the former British province of Central Provinces and Berar and the princely states of Makrai and Chattisgarh; lost some south-western districts 1956, including ◊Nagpur, and absorbed Bhopal, Madhya Bharat, and Vindhya Pradesh. In 1984 some 2,600 people died in ◊Bhopal from an escape of poisonous gas.

Madison capital of Wisconsin, USA, 193 km/120 mi NW of Chicago, between lakes Mendota and Monona; population (1992) 195,200. Industries include agricultural machinery and medical equipment.

Madison James 1751–1836. 4th president of the USA 1809–17. In 1787 he became a member of the Philadelphia Constitutional Convention and took a leading part in drawing up the US Constitution and the Bill of Rights. He allied himself firmly with Thomas ◊Jefferson against Alexander ◊Hamilton in the struggle between the more democratic views of Jefferson and the aristocratic, upper-class sentiments of Hamilton. As secretary of state in Jefferson's government 1801–09, Madison completed the ◊Louisiana Purchase negotiated by James Monroe.

Madison Square Garden venue in New York, built as a boxing arena and also used for concerts. The current 'Garden' is the fourth to bear the name and staged its first boxing match 1968. It is situated over Pennsylvania Station on 7th Avenue, New York City, and has a capacity of 20,000.

Madonna Italian name for the Virgin ◊Mary, meaning 'my lady'.

Madonna stage name of Madonna Louise Veronica Ciccone 1958– , US pop singer and actress. Her first hit was 'Like a Virgin' 1984; others include 'Material Girl' 1985 and 'Like a Prayer' 1989. Her films include *Desperately Seeking Susan* 1985, *Dick Tracy* 1990, *A League of Their Own* 1992, and *Evita* 1996.

In the early years of her career she frequently employed Catholic trappings in her dress and stage show. Her book *Sex* was published 1992, coinciding with the release of the dance album *Erotica*. *See illustration on following page.*

Madras former name, to 1996, of Chennai, an industrial port and capital of the state of Tamil Nadu, India.

Madras former name of ◊Tamil Nadu, a state of India.

Madrid industrial city (leather, chemicals, furniture, tobacco, paper) and capital of Spain and of Madrid province; population (1994) 3,041,000. Built on an elevated plateau in the centre of the country, at 655 m/2,183 ft it is the highest capital city in Europe and has excesses of heat and cold. Madrid province has an area of 8,000 sq km/3,088 sq mi and a population of 4,855,000.
features The Real Academia de Bellas Artes (1752); the Prado museum (1785); the royal palace (1764), built for Philip V; the 15th century Retiro Park; the Plaza Mayor (1617–20); the Akalá Arch; and the basilica of San Francisco el Grande (1761–84).

Madison 4th US president James Madison, whose proposals at the Constitutional Convention 1787 earned him the title of 'father of the US Constitution'. His second term was marked by the war with Britain 1812–14, known as 'Madison's War', in which Washington was captured and the White House burned. *Library of Congress*

Madonna US singer and actress Madonna, one of the most successful and controversial pop icons of the 1980s and 1990s. For some, the frank eroticism of her songs and stage acts is a spirited refusal to pander to the prevalent submissive image of female sexuality. For others, it is a cynical manipulation of sexual stereotypes. *Warner Bros Records Inc.*

history Madrid began as the Moorish city of Magerit. It was captured 1083 by King Alfonso VI of Castile. It remained a small provincial town until Philip II made it his capital 1561 because of its position at the centre of the Iberian peninsula. In 1808 there was an uprising against the occupation by Napoleon's troops. During the Spanish Civil War it was the centre of opposition to Franco, and was besieged by the Nationalists 1936–39.

madrigal form of secular song in four or five parts, usually sung without instrumental accompaniment. It originated in 14th-century Italy. Madrigal composers include Andrea Gabrieli, Monteverdi, Thomas Morley, and Orlando Gibbons.

'We possess only the happiness we are able to understand.'

MAURICE MAETERLINCK *Wisdom and Destiny*

Maecenas Gaius Cilnius c. 69–8 BC. Roman patron of the arts, and close friend and diplomatic agent of ◊Augustus. He was influential in providing encouragement and material support for the Augustan poets Horace and Virgil.

maenad in Greek mythology, one of the women participants in the orgiastic rites of ◊Dionysus; maenads were also known as ***Bacchae***.

Maeterlinck Maurice Polydore Marie Bernard, Count Maeterlinck 1862–1949. Belgian poet and dramatist. His plays include *Pelléas et Mélisande* 1892 (on which Debussy based his opera), *L'Oiseau bleu/The Blue Bird* 1908, and *Le Bourgmestre de Stilmonde/The Burgomaster of Stilemonde* 1918. This last celebrates Belgian resistance in World War I, a subject that led to his exile in the USA 1940. His philosophical essays include 'Le Trésor des humbles/The Treasure of the Humble' 1896 and 'La vie des abeilles/The Life of the Bee' 1901. Nobel Prize for Literature 1911.

Maeterlinck Belgian Symbolist writer Maurice Maeterlinck studied law at Ghent, but gave it up for literature. His preoccupation with the mystery of life and death led him to write studies of nature.

Mafeking, Siege of Boer siege during the South African War of British-held town (now Mafikeng) 12 Oct 1899–17 May 1900. The British commander Col Robert Baden-Powell held the Boers off and kept morale high until a relief column arrived and relieved the town. The raising of the siege was a great boost to morale in Britain.

MAFF abbreviation for ***Ministry of Agriculture, Fisheries and Food.***

Mafia (Italian 'swank') secret society reputed to control organized crime such as gambling, loansharking, drug traffic, prostitution, and protection; connected with the ◊Camorra of Naples. It originated in Sicily in the late Middle Ages and now operates chiefly there and in countries to which Italians have emigrated, such as the USA and Australia. During the early 1990s many centre and right-wing Italian politicians, such as the former Christian Democrat prime minister Giulio Andreotti, became discredited when it emerged that they had had dealings with the Mafia.

It began as a society that avenged wrongs against Sicilian peasants by means of terror and vendetta. In 19th-century Sicily the Mafia was employed by absentee landlords to manage their *latifundia* (landed estates), and through intimidation it soon became the unofficial ruling group. Despite the expropriation and division of the *latifundia* after World War II, the Mafia remains powerful in Sicily. The Italian government has waged periodic campaigns of suppression, notably 1927, when the Fascist leader Mussolini appointed Cesare Mori as prefect of Palermo. Mori's methods were, however, as suspect as those of the people he was arresting, and he was fired 1929. A further campaign was waged 1963–64. The Calabrian mafia (known as the 'Ndrangeta) and the Camorra allegedly worked together in attempting to assassinate lawyers investigating the Mafia 1993–94. It was calculated 1992 that the Mafia was Italy's biggest business, earning one out of every eight lire and accounting for 12% of national product.

mafic rock plutonic rock composed chiefly of dark-coloured minerals containing abundant magnesium and iron, such as olivine and pyroxene. It is derived from ***magnesium*** and ***ferric*** (iron). The term mafic also applies to dark-coloured minerals rich in iron and magnesium as a group.

Magadha kingdom of ancient NE India, roughly corresponding to the middle and southern parts of modern ◊Bihar. It was the scene of many incidents in the life of the Buddha and was the seat of the ◊Mauryan dynasty founded in the 3rd century BC. Its capital Pataliputra was a great cultural and political centre.

magazine publication brought out periodically, typically containing articles, essays, short stories, reviews, and illustrations.

The earliest illustrations were wood engravings; the half-tone process was invented 1882 and photogravure was used commercially from 1895. ◊Printing and paper-manufacturing techniques progressed during the 19th century, making larger print runs possible. Advertising began to appear in magazines around 1800; it was a significant factor by 1850 and crucial to most magazines' finances by 1880. Specialist magazines for different interests and hobbies, and ◊comic books, appeared in the 20th century.

In the UK, distribution and sale of magazines is largely through newsagents' shops; in the USA, postal subscriptions account for a large percentage of sales. Publications that give details of television schedules regularly achieve the highest sales.

history Among the first magazines in Britain were the *Compleat Library* 1691 and the *Gentleman's Journal* 1692, which contained articles and book reviews. Notable successors, mainly with a mixture of political and literary comment, included Richard ◊Steele's *Tatler* 1709, Joseph ◊Addison's *Spectator* 1711, the *Gentleman's Magazine* 1731 (the first to use the word 'magazine' in this sense) by Edward Cave (1691–1754), the Radical John ◊Wilkes's *North Briton* 1762, the *Edinburgh Review* 1802, *Quarterly Review* 1806, *Blackwood's Magazine* 1817, and *Contemporary Review* 1866.

The 1930s saw the rise of the photojournalism magazines such as *Life* in the USA and the introduction of colour printing. The US pulp magazines of the 1930s and 1940s, specializing in crime fiction and science fiction, were breeding grounds for writers such as Raymond Chandler and Isaac Asimov. The development of cheap offset litho printing made possible the flourishing of the underground press in much of the Western world in the 1960s, although it was limited by unorthodox distribution methods such as street sales. Prosecutions and economic recession largely killed the underground press; the main survivors in Britain are the satirical *Private Eye* 1961, and the London listings guide *Time Out* 1968, and in the USA the rock-music paper *Rolling Stone* 1968.

women's magazines From the *Ladies' Mercury* 1693 until the first feminist publications of the late 1960s, the content of mass-circulation women's magazines in Britain was largely confined to the domestic sphere – housekeeping, recipes, beauty and fashion, advice columns, patterns – and gossip. In the late 18th century, women's magazines reflected society's temporary acceptance of women as intellectually equal to men, discussing public affairs and subjects of general interest, but by 1825 the trend had reversed. Around 1900 publications for working women began to appear, lurid weekly novelettes known as penny dreadfuls. The first colour magazine for women in Britain, *Woman*, appeared 1937.

Magdalenian final cultural phase of the Palaeolithic (Old Stone Age) in W Europe, best known for its art, and lasting from c. 16,000–10,000 BC. It was named after the rock-shelter of La Madeleine in SW France.

Magdeburg industrial city (vehicles, paper, textiles, machinery) and capital of Saxony-Anhalt, Germany, on the river Elbe; population (1993) 272,400. A former capital of Saxony, Magdeburg became capital of Saxony-Anhalt on German reunification 1990. There is a 13th-century Gothic cathedral. In 1938 the city was linked by canal with the Rhine and Ruhr rivers. Magdeburg county has an area of 11,530 sq km/4,451 sq mi, and a population of 1,250,000.

Magellan Ferdinand c. 1480–1521. Portuguese navigator. In 1519 he set sail in the *Victoria* from Seville with the intention of reaching the East Indies by a westerly route. He sailed through the ◊Strait of Magellan at the tip of South America, crossed an ocean he named the Pacific, and in 1521 reached the Philippines, where he was killed in a battle with the islanders. His companions returned to Seville 1522, completing the voyage under del ◊Cano.

Magellan was brought up at court and entered the royal service, but later transferred his services to Spain. He and his Malay slave, Enrique de Malacca, are considered the first circumnavigators of the globe, since they had once sailed from the Philippines to Europe.

Magellan NASA space probe to ◊Venus, launched May 1989; it went into orbit around Venus Aug 1990 to make a detailed map of the planet by radar. It revealed volcanoes, meteorite craters, and fold mountains on the planet's surface.

Magellanic Clouds in astronomy, the two galaxies nearest to our own galaxy. They are irregularly shaped, and appear as detached parts of the ◊Milky Way, in the southern constellations ◊Dorado, ◊Tucana, and Mensa.

The Large Magellanic Cloud spreads over the constellations of Dorado and Mensa. The Small Magellanic Cloud is in Tucana. The Large Magellanic Cloud is 169,000 light years from Earth, and about a third the diameter of our Galaxy; the Small Magellanic Cloud, 180,000 light years away, is about a fifth the diameter of our Galaxy. They are named after the navigator Ferdinand Magellan, who first described them.

Magellan, Strait of channel between South America and Tierra del Fuego, named after the Portuguese navigator Ferdinand Magellan. It is 595 km/370 mi long, and joins the Atlantic and Pacific oceans.

Maggiore, Lago lake partly in Italy, partly in the Swiss canton of Ticino, with Locarno on its northern shore, 63 km/39 mi long and up to 9 km/5.5 mi wide (area 212 sq km/82 sq mi), with fine scenery.

maggot soft, plump, limbless larva of flies, a typical example being the larva of the blowfly which is deposited as an egg on flesh.

Maghreb name for NW Africa (Arabic 'far west', 'sunset'). The Maghreb powers – Algeria, Libya, Morocco, Tunisia, and Western Sahara – agreed on economic coordination 1964–65, with Mauritania cooperating from 1970. In 1989 these countries formed an economic union known as the Arab Maghreb Union. Chad and Mali are sometimes included. Compare ◊Mashraq, the Arab countries of the E Mediterranean.

magi (singular ***magus***) priests of the Zoroastrian religion of ancient Persia, noted for their knowledge of astrology. The term is used in the New Testament of the Latin Vulgate Bible where the Authorized Version gives 'wise men'. The magi who came to visit the infant Jesus with gifts of gold, frankincense, and myrrh (the Adoration of the Magi) were in later tradition described as 'the three kings' – Caspar, Melchior, and Balthazar.

magic art of controlling the forces of nature by supernatural means such as charms and ritual. The central ideas are that like produces like (***sympathetic magic***) and that influence carries by contagion or association; for example, by the former principle an enemy could be destroyed through an effigy, by the latter principle through personal items such as hair or nail clippings. See also ◊witchcraft.

Most early religious practices and much early art were rooted in beliefs in magical processes. There are similarities between magic and the use of symbolism in religious ritual. Under Christianity existing magical rites were either suppressed (although they survived in modified form in folk custom and superstition) or replaced by those of the church itself. Those still practising the ancient rites were persecuted as witches.

magic bullet term sometimes used for a drug that is specifically targeted on certain cells or tissues in the body, such as a small collection of cancerous cells (see ◊cancer) or cells that have been invaded by a virus. ◊Monoclonal antibodies are increasingly being used to direct the drug to a specific target.

magic realism in 20th-century literature, a fantastic situation realistically treated, as in the works of many Latin American writers such as Isabel ◊Allende, Jorge Luis ◊Borges, and Gabriel ◊García Márquez. The technique of magic realism was pioneered in Europe by E T A Hoffman and Hermann ◊Hesse. The term was coined in the 1920s to describe German paintings. In the UK it has been practised by, among others, Angela ◊Carter.

magic square in mathematics, a square array of different numbers in which the rows, columns, and diagonals add up to the same total. A simple example employing the numbers 1 to 9, with a total of 15, has a first row of 6, 7, 2; a second row of 1, 5, 9; and a third row of 8, 3, 4.

Maginot Line French fortification system along the German frontier from Switzerland to Luxembourg built 1929–36 under the direction of the war minister, André Maginot. It consisted of semi-underground forts joined by underground passages, and was protected by antitank defences; lighter fortifications continued the line to the sea. In 1940 German forces pierced the Belgian frontier line and outflanked the Maginot Line.

magistrate in English law, a person who presides in a magistrates' court: either a justice of the peace (with no legal qualifications, and unpaid) or a stipendiary magistrate. Stipendiary magistrates are paid, qualified lawyers working mainly in London and major cities.

magistrates' court in England and Wales, a local law court that mainly deals with minor criminal cases. A magistrates' court consists of between two and seven lay justices of the peace (who are advised on the law by a clerk to the justices), or a single paid lawyer called a stipendiary magistrate. It deals with some civil matters, too, such as licensing certain domestic and matrimonial proceedings, and may include a juvenile court.

maglev (acronym for ***magnetic levitation***) high-speed surface transport using the repellent force of superconductive magnets (see ◊superconductivity) to propel and support, for example, a train above a track. Technical trials on a maglev train track began in Japan in the 1970s, and a speed of 500 kph/310 mph has been reached, with a cruising altitude of 10 cm/4 in. The train is levitated by electromagnets and forward thrust is provided by linear motors aboard the cars, propelling the train along a reaction plate.

A small low-power maglev monorail system is in use at Birmingham Airport, England. A subway line using maglev carriages began operating in Osaka, Japan, 1990.

magma molten rock material beneath the Earth's surface from which ◊igneous rocks are formed. ◊Lava is magma that has reached the surface and solidified, losing some of its components on the way.

Magna Carta (Latin 'great charter') in English history, the charter granted by King John 1215, traditionally seen as guaranteeing human rights against the excessive use of royal power. As a reply to the king's demands for excessive feudal dues and attacks on the privileges of the church, Archbishop Langton proposed to the barons the drawing-up of a binding document 1213. John was forced to accept this at Runnymede (now in Surrey) 15 June 1215.

Magna Carta begins by reaffirming the rights of the church. Certain clauses guard against infringements of feudal custom: for example, the king was prevented from making excessive demands for money from his barons without their consent. Others are designed to check extortions by officials or maladministration of justice: for example, no freeman to be arrested, imprisoned, or punished except by the judgement of his peers or the law of the land. The privileges of London and the cities were also guaranteed.

As feudalism declined Magna Carta lost its significance, and under the Tudors was almost forgotten. During the 17th century it was rediscovered and reinterpreted by the Parliamentary party as a democratic document. Four original copies exist, one each in Salisbury and Lincoln cathedrals and two in the British Library.

magnesia common name for ◊magnesium oxide.

magnesium lightweight, very ductile and malleable, silver-white, metallic element, symbol Mg, atomic number 12, relative atomic mass 24.305. It is one of the ◊alkaline-earth metals, and the lightest of the commonly used metals. Magnesium silicate, carbonate, and chloride are widely distributed in nature. The metal is used in alloys and flash photography. It is a necessary trace element in the human diet, and green plants cannot grow without it since it is an essential constituent of the photosynthetic pigment ◊chlorophyll ($C_{55}H_{72}MgN_4O_5$).

magnesium oxide or ***magnesia*** MgO, white powder or colourless crystals, formed when magnesium is burned in air or oxygen; a typical basic oxide. It is used to treat acidity of the stomach, and in some industrial processes; for example, as a lining brick in furnaces, because it is very stable when heated.

magnet any object that forms a magnetic field (displays ◊magnetism), either permanently or temporarily through induction, causing it to attract materials such as iron, cobalt, nickel, and alloys of these. It always has two ◊magnetic poles, called north and south.

magnetic compass device for determining the direction of the horizontal component of the Earth's magnetic field. It consists of a magnetized needle with its north-seeking pole clearly indicated, pivoted so that it can turn freely in a plane parallel to the surface of the Earth (in a horizontal circle). The needle will turn so that its north-seeking pole points towards the Earth's magnetic north pole. See also ◊compass.

Walkers, sailors, and other travellers use a magnetic compass to find their direction. The direction of the geographic, or true, North Pole is, however, slightly different from that of the magnetic north pole, and so the readings obtained from a compass of this sort must be adjusted using tables of magnetic corrections or information marked on local maps.

magnetic declination see ◊angle of declination.

magnetic dip see ◊dip, magnetic and ◊angle of dip.

magnetic dipole the pair of north and south magnetic poles, separated by a short distance, that makes up all magnets. Individual magnets are often called 'magnetic dipoles'. Single magnetic poles, or monopoles, have never been observed despite being searched for.

magnetic field region around a permanent magnet, or around a conductor carrying an electric current, in which a force acts on a moving charge or on a magnet placed in the field. The field can be represented by lines of force, which by convention link north and south poles and are parallel to the directions of a small compass needle placed on them. A magnetic field's magnitude and direction are given by the ◊magnetic flux density, expressed in ◊teslas. See also ◊polar reversal. *See illustration on following page.*

magnetic flux measurement of the strength of the magnetic field around electric currents and magnets. Its SI unit is the ◊weber; one weber per square metre is equal to one tesla. The amount of magnetic flux through an area equals the product of the area and the magnetic field strength at a point within that area. It is a measure of the number of magnetic field lines passing through the area.

magnetic induction the production of magnetic properties in unmagnetized iron or other ferromagnetic material when it is brought close to a magnet. The material is influenced by the magnet's magnetic field and the two are attracted. The

'To no one will we sell, to no one will we deny, or delay, right or justice.'

MAGNA CARTA

Magna Carta The Magna Carta of 1215. The name was given to distinguish the charter from smaller-sized reissues, not for political reasons. *Image Select (UK) Ltd*

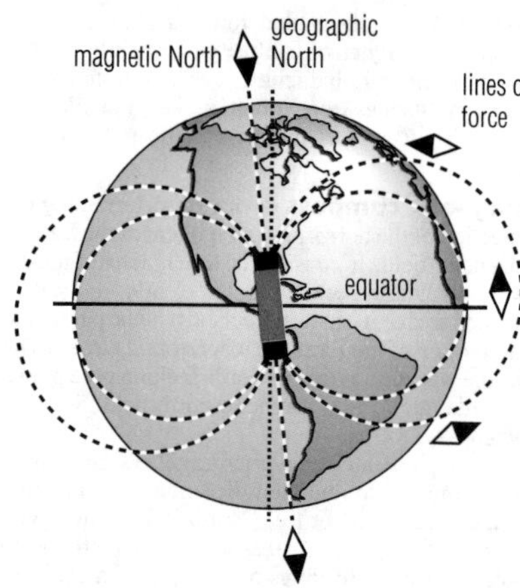

magnetic field The Earth's magnetic field is similar to that of a bar magnet with poles near, but not exactly at, the geographic poles. Compass needles align themselves with the magnetic field, which is horizontal near the equator and vertical at the magnetic poles.

induced magnetism may be temporary, disappearing as soon as the magnet is removed, or permanent depending on the nature of the iron and the strength of the magnet.

magnetic-ink character recognition (MICR) in computing, a technique that enables special characters printed in magnetic ink to be read and input rapidly to a computer. MICR is used extensively in banking because magnetic-ink characters are difficult to forge and are therefore ideal for marking and identifying cheques.

magnetic material one of a number of substances that are strongly attracted by magnets and can be magnetized. These include iron, nickel, and cobalt, and all those ◊alloys that contain a proportion of these metals.

Soft magnetic materials can be magnetized very easily, but the magnetism induced in them (see ◊magnetic induction) is only temporary. They include Stalloy, an alloy of iron with 4% silicon used to make the cores of electromagnets and transformers, and the materials used to make 'iron' nails and paper clips.

Hard magnetic materials can be permanently magnetized by a strong magnetic field. Steel and special alloys such as Alcomax, Alnico, and Ticonal, which contain various amounts of aluminium, nickel, cobalt, and copper, are used to make permanent magnets. The strongest permanent magnets are ceramic, made under high pressure and at high temperature from powders of various metal oxides.

magnetic pole region of a magnet in which its magnetic properties are strongest. Every magnet has two poles, called north and south. The north (or north-seeking) pole is so named because a freely suspended magnet will turn so that this pole points towards the Earth's magnetic north pole. The north pole of one magnet will be attracted to the south pole of another, but will be repelled by its north pole. Unlike poles may therefore be said to attract, like poles to repel.

magnetic resonance imaging (MRI) diagnostic scanning system based on the principles of nuclear magnetic resonance. MRI yields finely detailed three-dimensional images of structures within the body without exposing the patient to harmful radiation. The technique is invaluable for imaging the soft tissues of the body, in particular the brain and the spinal cord.

Claimed as the biggest breakthrough in diagnostic imaging since the discovery of X-rays, MRI is a noninvasive technique based on a magnet which is many thousands of times stronger than the Earth's magnetic field. It causes nuclei within the atoms of the body to align themselves in one direction. When a brief radio pulse is beamed at the body the nuclei spin, emitting weak radio signals as they realign themselves to the magnet. These signals, which are characteristic for each type of tissue, are converted electronically into images on a viewing screen.

Also developed around magnetic technology, ***magnetic resonance spectroscopy (MRS)*** is a technique for investigating conditions in which there is a disturbance of the body's energy metabolism, including ischaemia (the reduction of blood supply to any part of the body) and toxic damage due to drugs or other chemicals. MRS is also of value in diagnosing some cancers.

magnetic storm in meteorology, a sudden disturbance affecting the Earth's magnetic field, causing anomalies in radio transmissions and magnetic compasses. It is probably caused by ◊sunspot activity.

magnetic strip or ***magnetic stripe***, thin strip of magnetic material attached to a plastic card (such as a credit card) and used for recording data.

magnetic tape narrow plastic ribbon coated with an easily magnetizable material on which data can be recorded. It is used in sound recording, audiovisual systems (videotape), and computing. For mass storage on commercial mainframe computers, large reel-to-reel tapes are still used, but cartridges are coming in. Various types of cartridge are now standard on minis and PCs, while audio cassettes are sometimes used with home computers.

magnetism phenomena associated with ◊magnetic fields. Magnetic fields are produced by moving charged particles: in electromagnets, electrons flow through a coil of wire connected to a battery; in permanent magnets, spinning electrons within the atoms generate the field.

susceptibility Substances differ in the extent to which they can be magnetized by an external field (susceptibility). Materials that can be strongly magnetized, such as iron, cobalt, and nickel, are said to be ***ferromagnetic***; this is due to the formation of areas called domains in which atoms, weakly magnetic because of their spinning electrons, align to form areas of strong magnetism. Magnetic materials lose their magnetism if heated to the Curie temperature. Most other materials are ***paramagnetic***, being only weakly pulled towards a strong magnet. This is because their atoms have a low level of magnetism and do not form domains. ***Diamagnetic*** materials are weakly repelled by a magnet since electrons within their atoms act as electromagnets and oppose the applied magnetic force. ***Antiferromagnetic*** materials have a very low susceptibility that increases with temperature; a similar phenomenon in materials such as ferrites is called ***ferrimagnetism***.

application Apart from its universal application in dynamos, electric motors, and switch gears, magnetism is of considerable importance in advanced technology – for example, in particle ◊accelerators for nuclear research, memory stores for computers, tape recorders, and ◊cryogenics.

magnetite black, strongly magnetic opaque mineral, Fe_3O_4, of the spinel group, an important ore of iron. Widely distributed, magnetite is found in nearly all igneous and metamorphic rocks. Some deposits, called lodestone, are permanently magnetized. Lodestone has been used as a compass since the first millennium BC. Today the orientations of magnetite grains in rocks are used in the study of the Earth's magnetic field (see ◊palaeomagnetism).

magneto simple electric generator, often used to provide the electricity for the ignition system of motorcycles and used in early cars. It consists of a rotating magnet that sets up an electric current in a coil, providing the spark.

magnetohydrodynamics (MHD) field of science concerned with the behaviour of ionized gases or liquid in a magnetic field. Systems have been developed that use MHD to generate electrical power.

magnetometer device for measuring the intensity and orientation of the magnetic field of a particular rock or of a certain region. In archaeology, distortions of the magnetic field occur when structures, such as kilns or hearths, are present. A magnetometer allows such features to be located without disturbing the ground, and excavation to be concentrated in the most likely area.

magnetosphere volume of space, surrounding a planet, controlled by the planet's magnetic field, and acting as a magnetic 'shell'. The Earth's magnetosphere extends 64,000 km/40,000 mi towards the Sun, but many times this distance on the side away from the Sun.

magnetron thermionic ◊valve (electron tube) for generating very high-frequency oscillations, used in radar and to produce microwaves in a microwave oven. The flow of electrons from the tube's cathode to one or more anodes is controlled by an applied magnetic field.

magnet therapy in alternative medicine, use of applied magnetic fields to regulate potentially pathogenic disorders in the electrical charges of body cells and structures. Practitioners apply it as a stimulant of the body's self-healing processes, to enhance tissue repair and the healing of bone fractures, as an adjunct of structural therapies such as chiropractic, and as an alternative to needling in acupuncture.

Magnificat in the New Testament, the song of praise sung by Mary, the mother of Jesus, on her visit to her cousin Elizabeth shortly after the Annunciation. It is used in the liturgy of some Christian churches in the form of a canticle (a hymn or song of praise based on scripture) based on text from Luke's Gospel 1:46–55 ('My soul doth magnify the Lord ...'). It is sung at Roman Catholic vespers and Anglican evensong.

magnification measure of the enlargement or reduction of an object in an imaging optical system. ***Linear magnification*** is the ratio of the size (height) of the image to that of the object. ***Angular magnification*** is the ratio of the angle subtended at the observer's eye by the image to the angle subtended by the object when viewed directly.

magnitude in astronomy, measure of the brightness of a star or other celestial object. The larger the number denoting the magnitude, the fainter the object. Zero or first magnitude indicates some of the brightest stars. Still brighter are those of negative magnitude, such as Sirius, whose magnitude is

magnetism A bar magnet surrounded by iron filings. The majority of the iron filings are attracted to the ends of the magnet where the magnetic forces are concentrated. Between the poles, the filings are attracted to the electromagnetic waves of the magnet's field. *Image Select (UK) Ltd*

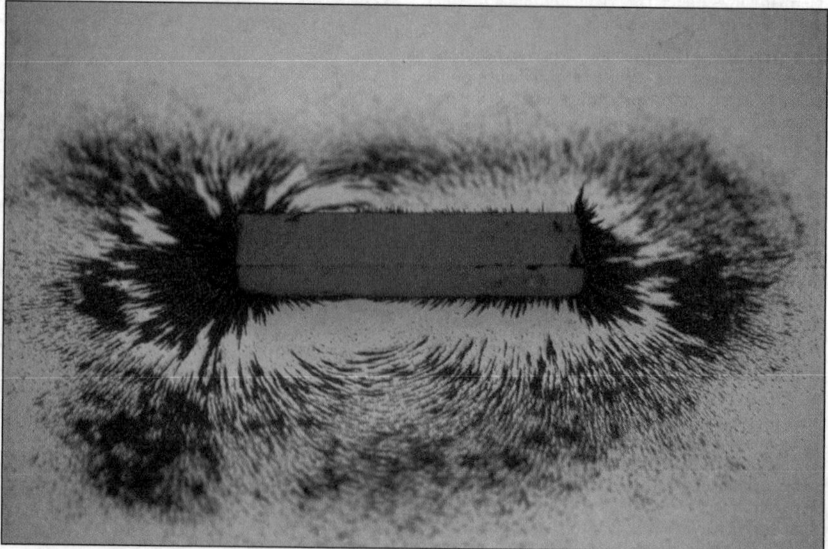

−1.46. ***Apparent magnitude*** is the brightness of an object as seen from Earth; ***absolute magnitude*** is the brightness at a standard distance of 10 parsecs (32.6 light years).

Each magnitude step is equal to a brightness difference of 2.512 times. Thus a star of magnitude 1 is $(2.512)^5$ or 100 times brighter than a sixth-magnitude star just visible to the naked eye. The apparent magnitude of the Sun is −26.8, its absolute magnitude +4.8.

magnolia tree or shrub of the genus *Magnolia*, family Magnoliaceae, native to North America and E Asia. Magnolias vary in height from 60 cm/2 ft to 30 m/150 ft. The large, fragrant single flowers are white, rose, or purple.

magnum opus (Latin) a great work of art or literature.

magpie any bird of a genus *Pica* in the crow family Corvidae, order Passeriformes. It feeds on insects, snails, young birds, and carrion, and is found in Europe, Asia, N Africa, and W North America. The common magpie *P. pica* is about 45 cm/18 in long, and has black and white plumage, the long tail having a metallic gloss.

Magritte René François Ghislain 1898–1967. Belgian painter, one of the major figures in Surrealism. His work focuses on visual paradoxes and everyday objects taken out of context. Recurring motifs include bowler hats, apples, and windows, for example *Golconda* 1953 (private collection), in which men in bowler hats are falling from the sky to a street below.

Influenced by de ◊Chirico, Magritte joined the other Surrealists in Paris 1927, returning to Brussels 1930. His most influential works are those that question the relationship between image and reality, as in *The Treason of Images* 1928–29 (Los Angeles County Museum of Art), in which a picture of a smoker's pipe appears with the words 'Ceci n'est pas une pipe' (This is not a pipe).

Maguire Seven seven Irish victims of a miscarriage of justice. In 1976 Annie Maguire, five members of her family, and a family friend were imprisoned in London for possessing explosives. All seven of the convictions were overturned June 1991.

Magyar the largest ethnic group in Hungary, comprising 92% of the population. Magyars are of mixed Ugric and Turkic origin, and they arrived in Hungary towards the end of the 9th century. The Magyar language (see ◊Hungarian language) belongs to the Uralic group.

Mahābhārata (Sanskrit 'great poem of the Bharatas') Sanskrit Hindu epic consisting of 18 books and 90,000 stanzas, probably composed in its present form about 300 BC. It forms with the *Rāmāyana* the two great epics of the Hindus. It contains the ◊*Bhagavad-Gītā*, or *Song of the Blessed*, an episode in the sixth book. The poem, set on the plain of the Upper Ganges, deals with the fortunes of the rival families of the Kauravas and the Pandavas and reveals the ethical values of ancient Indian society and individual responsibility in particular.

Mahādeva (Sanskrit 'great god') title given to the Hindu god ◊Siva.

Mahādevī (Sanskrit 'great goddess') title given to Sakti, the consort of the Hindu god Siva. She is worshipped in many forms, including her more active manifestations as Kali or Durga and her peaceful form as Parvati.

Maharashtra state in W central India
area 307,700 sq km/118,802 sq mi
capital Bombay
towns and cities Pune, Nagpur, Ulhasnagar, Sholapur, Nasik, Thana, Kolhapur, Aurangabad, Sangli, Amravati
features cave temples of Ajanta, containing Buddhist murals and sculptures dating from 200 BC–7th century AD; Ellora cave temples 6th–9th century with Buddhist, Hindu, and Jain sculptures
industries cotton, rice, groundnuts, sugar, minerals
population (1994 est) 85,600
language Marathi 50%
religion Hindu 80%, Parsee, Jain, and Sikh minorities
history formed 1960 from the southern part of the former Bombay state.

maharishi (Sanskrit *mahā* 'great', *rishi* 'sage') Hindu guru (teacher), or spiritual leader.

Mahathir bin Mohamed 1925– . Prime minister of Malaysia from 1981. Leader of the New United Malays' National Organization (UMNO Baru), his 'look east' economic policy, which emulates Japanese industrialization, has met with considerable success.

mahatma (Sanskrit 'great soul') title conferred on Mohandas ◊Gandhi by his followers as the first great national Indian leader.

Mahāyāna (Sanskrit 'greater vehicle') one of the two major forms of ◊Buddhism, found in China, Korea, Japan, and Tibet. Veneration of bodhisattvas (those who achieve enlightenment but remain on the human plane in order to help other living beings) is a fundamental belief in Mahāyāna, as is the idea that everyone has within them the seeds of Buddhahood.

The *Lotus Sūtra* describes the historical Buddha as only one manifestation of the eternal Buddha, the ultimate law (*dharma*) of the cosmos and the omnipresent and compassionate saviour. The *Perfection of Wisdom Sūtra* teaches that all phenomena are empty of permanent existence, and advocates the bodhisattua path to Buddhahood. ▷ *See feature on pp. 162–163.*

Mahdi (Arabic 'he who is guided aright') in Islam, the title of a coming messiah who will establish a reign of justice on Earth. The title has been assumed by many Muslim leaders, notably the Sudanese sheik Muhammad Ahmed (1848–1885), who headed a revolt 1881 against Egypt and 1885 captured Khartoum.

Mahfouz Naguib 1911– . Egyptian novelist and playwright. His novels, which deal with the urban working class, include the semi-autobiographical *Khan al-Kasrain/The Cairo Trilogy* 1956–57. His *Children of Gebelawi* 1959 was banned in Egypt because of its treatment of religious themes. He won the Nobel Prize for Literature 1988. He was seriously wounded in a knife attack by Islamic militants outside his home in Cairo in Oct 1994.

mah-jong (Chinese 'sparrows') or ***mah-jongg*** originally an ancient Chinese card game, dating from the Song dynasty 960–1279. It is now usually played by four people with 144 small ivory tiles, divided into six suits.

Mahler Alma (born Schindler) 1879–1964. Austrian pianist and composer of *lieder* (songs). She was the daughter of the artist Anton Schindler and abandoned composing when she married the composer Gustav Mahler 1902. After Mahler's death she lived with the architect Walter Gropius; their daughter Manon's death inspired Berg's Violin Concerto. She later married the writer Franz Werfel.

Mahler Gustav 1860–1911. Austrian composer and conductor. His epic symphonies express a world-weary Romanticism in visionary tableaux incorporating folk music and pastoral imagery. He composed nine large-scale symphonies, many with voices, including Symphony No 2 *Resurrection* 1884–86, revised 1893–96, and left a tenth unfinished. He also composed orchestral *lieder* (songs) including *Das Lied von der Erde/The Song of the Earth* 1909 and *Kindertotenlieder/Dead Children's Songs* 1901–04.

Mahler was born in Bohemia (now the Czech Republic); he studied at the Vienna Conservatoire, and conducted in Prague, Leipzig, Budapest, and Hamburg 1891–97. He was director of the Vienna Court Opera from 1897 and conducted the New York Philharmonic from 1910. The *Adagietto* slow movement from Symphony No 5 provided a perfect foil for Luchino Visconti's film *Death in Venice* 1971.

Mahmud I 1696–1754. Ottoman sultan from 1730. After restoring order to the empire in Istanbul 1730, he suppressed the ◊janissary rebellion 1731 and waged war against Persia 1731–46. He led successful wars against Austria and Russia, concluded by the Treaty of Belgrade 1739. He was a patron of the arts and also carried out reform of the army.

Mahmud II 1785–1839. Ottoman sultan from 1808 who attempted to westernize the declining empire, carrying out a series of far-reaching reforms in the civil service and army. The pressure for Greek independence after 1821 led to conflict with Britain, France, and Russia, and he was forced to recognize Greek independence 1830.

mahogany timber from any of several genera of trees found in the Americas and Africa. Mahogany is a tropical hardwood obtained chiefly by rainforest logging. It has a warm red colour and takes a high polish. True mahogany comes from trees of the genus *Swietenia*, but other types come from the Spanish and Australian cedars, the Indian redwood, and other trees of the mahogany family Meliaceae, native to Africa and the E Indies.

Mahomed Ismail 1931– . South African lawyer, appointed the country's first non-white judge 1991. As legal adviser to ◊SWAPO, he was the author of Namibia's constitution, which abolished capital punishment. He has defended many anti-apartheid activists in political trials.

Mahón or ***Port Mahon*** capital and port of the Spanish island of Minorca; population (1981) 21,900. Probably founded by the Carthaginians, it was under British occupation 1708–56 and 1762–82.

Mahratta rivals of the Mogul emperors in the 17th and 18th centuries; see ◊Maratha.

Maia in Greek mythology, daughter of ◊Atlas and mother of ◊Hermes.

Maidanek German ◊concentration camp near Lublin, Poland. Originally established as a labour camp 1939 it was converted to an extermination centre early 1942. It was responsible for the deaths of about 1,380,000 Jews before being closed in the face of the advancing Soviets 1944.

Maiden Castle prehistoric hillfort and later earthworks near Dorchester, Dorset, England. The site was inhabited from Neolithic times (about 2000 BC) and was stormed by the Romans AD 43.

Maidenhead town in Berkshire, S England, 40 km/25 mi W of London, on the river Thames; population (1991) 59,600. Industries include computer software, plastics, pharmaceuticals, and printing. It is a boating centre.

Maidstone town in Kent, SE England, on the river Medway, administrative headquarters of the county; population (1991) 90,900. Industries include agricultural machinery and paper. Maidstone has the ruins of All Saints' College 1260. The Elizabethan Chillington Manor is an art gallery and museum.

Maikop capital of Adgeya, Autonomous Republic of the Russian Federation, on the river Bielaia, with timber mills, distilleries, tanneries, and tobacco and furniture factories; population (1992) 149,000.

Mailer Norman Kingsley 1923– . US writer and journalist. One of the most prominent figures of postwar American literature, he gained wide attention with his first, bestselling book *The Naked and the Dead* 1948, a naturalistic war novel. His later works show his personal engagement with history, politics, and psychology. Always a pugnacious and

Mailer US novelist and journalist Norman Mailer. Mailer's first success was *The Naked and the Dead* 1948, a novel based on his experiences in the US army and one of the most important books to come out of World War II. A pugnacious social commentator, Mailer channelled much of his energy into journalism, combining factual analysis with frank autobiographical commentary. *The Prisoner of Sex* 1971 was his response to feminism, and *Marilyn* 1973 was a controversial biography of Marilyn Monroe. *Topham*

People with vision usually do more harm than good.

John Major
Quoted in *The Economist* 1993

controversial writer, his polemics on the theory and practice of violence-as-sex brought him into direct conflict with feminist Kate Millet in a series of celebrated debates during the 1970s.

His essay 'White Negro' in *Advertisements for Myself* 1959 was a seminal statement of the artistic need to rebel against cultural conformity. His other books include *An American Dream* 1965, *The Armies of the Night* 1968 (Pulitzer prize), *The Executioner's Song* 1979 (Pulitzer prize), *Ancient Evenings* 1983, *Harlot's Ghost* 1991, *Pablo and Fernande* 1994, and *Potrait of Picasso as a Young Man* 1995. A combative public figure, Mailer cofounded the magazine *Village Voice* in the 1950s, edited *Dissent*, and in 1969 ran for mayor of New York City.

mail merge in computing, a feature offered by some word-processing packages that enables a list of personal details, such as names and addresses, to be combined with a general document outline to produce individualized documents.

Maimonides Moses (Moses Ben Maimon) 1135–1204. Spanish-born Jewish rabbi and philosopher, one of the greatest Hebrew scholars. He attempted to reconcile faith and reason. His codification of Jewish law is known as the *Mishneh Torah/Torah Reviewed* 1180; he also formulated the Thirteen Principles, which summarize the basic beliefs of Judaism. His philosophical classic *More nevukhim/The Guide to the Perplexed* 1176–91 helped to introduce Aristotelian thought into medieval philosophy.

Maine northeasternmost state of the USA, largest of the New England states; nicknamed Pine Tree State
area 86,200 sq km/33,273 sq mi
capital Augusta
towns and cities Portland, Lewiston, Bangor
physical Appalachian Mountains; 80% of the state is forested
features Kennebec and Penobscot rivers; 5,600 km/3,500 mi of coastline; Acadia national park, the first national park in eastern USA; Baxter state park, with Mount Katahdin (1,605 m/5,267 ft), the highest peak in the state; Moosehead Lake (190 sq km/120 sq mi), New England's largest lake; Portland Museum of Art, housing a collection of American art
industries dairy and market garden produce, paper, pulp, timber, footwear, textiles, fish, lobster; tourism is important
population (1991) 1,235,000
famous people Henry Wadsworth Longfellow, Kate Douglas Wiggin, Edward Arlington Robinson, Edna St Vincent Millay
history permanently settled by the British from 1623; absorbed by Massachusetts 1691; became a state 1820.

Maine

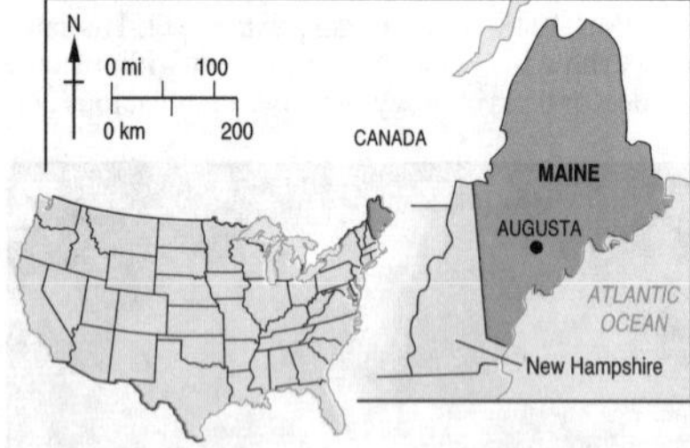

mainframe large computer used for commercial data processing and other large-scale operations. Because of the general increase in computing power, the differences between the mainframe, ◊supercomputer, ◊minicomputer, and ◊microcomputer (personal computer) are becoming less marked. Mainframe manufacturers include IBM, Amdahl, Fujitsu, and Hitachi. Typical mainframes have from 32 to 256 MB of memory and tens of gigabytes of disc storage.

main sequence in astronomy, the part of the ◊Hertzsprung–Russell diagram that contains most of the stars, including the Sun. It runs diagonally from the top left of the diagram to the lower right. The most massive (and hence brightest) stars are at the top left, with the least massive (coolest) stars at the bottom right.

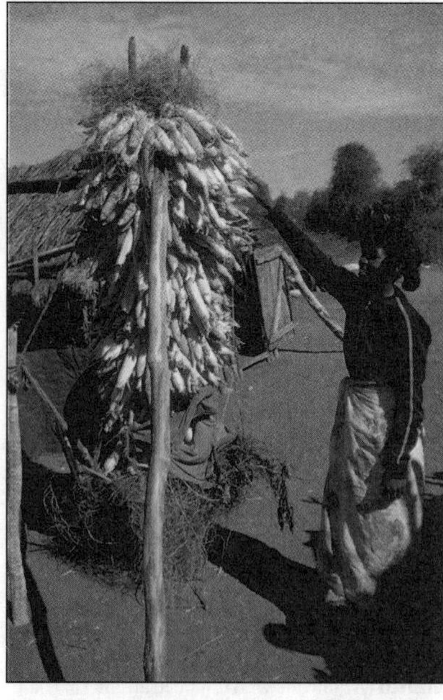

maize In the impoverished semi-desert country of S Madagascar maize is an important crop. It is seen here being dried in the traditional fashion, on a post set up in front of the farmer's house. *Premaphotos Wildlife*

maintenance in law, payments to support children or a spouse, under the terms of an agreement, or by a court order. In Britain, financial provision orders are made on divorce, but a court action can also be brought for maintenance without divorce proceedings. Applications for maintenance of illegitimate children are now treated in the same way as for legitimate children. Under the Child Support Act 1991 the Department of Social Security can assess suitable levels of maintenance and enforce payment.

Maintenon Françoise d'Aubigné, Marquise de 1635–1719. Second wife of Louis XIV of France from 1684, and widow of the writer Paul Scarron (1610–1660). She was governess to the children of Mme de Montespan by Louis, and his mistress from 1667. She secretly married the king after the death of Queen Marie Thérèse 1683. Her political influence was considerable and, as a Catholic convert from Protestantism, her religious opinions were zealous.

Mainz (French ***Mayence***) capital of Rhineland-Palatinate, Germany, on the Rhine, 37 km/23 mi WSW of Frankfurt-am-Main; population (1993) 185,200. In Roman times it was a fortified camp and became the capital of Germania Superior.

maize (North American ***corn***) plant *Zea mays* of the grass family. Grown extensively in all subtropical and warm temperate regions, its range has been extended to colder zones by hardy varieties developed in the 1960s. It is widely used as animal feed. Sweetcorn is a variety of maize.

majolica or ***maiolica*** tin-glazed ◊earthenware and the richly decorated enamel pottery produced in Italy in the 15th to 18th centuries. The name derives from the Italian form of Majorca, the island from where Moorish lustreware made in Spain was shipped to Italy. During the 19th century the word was used to describe moulded earthenware with relief patterns decorated in coloured glazes.

Major John 1943– . British Conservative politician, prime minister 1990–97. He was foreign secretary 1989 and chancellor of the Exchequer 1989–90. In Nov 1990 he became prime minister on winning the Conservative Party leadership election after the resignation of Margaret Thatcher.

His initial positive approach to European Community matters was hindered from 1991 by divisions within the Conservative Party. He was returned to power in the 1992 general election. In 1993 he won backing for his launch of a joint UK-Irish peace initiative on Northern Ireland 1993, which led to a general cease-fire 1994. In June 1995, following local and European election defeats and continuing divisions within the Conservative Party, he resigned as party leader in a bid for party unity, and was narrowly re-elected. After a decisive defeat in the 1997 general election, he announced his resignation from the party leadership.

Majorca (Spanish ***Mallorca***) largest of the ◊Balearic Islands, belonging to Spain, in the W Mediterranean
area 3,640 sq km/1,405 sq mi
capital Palma
features the highest mountain is Puig Mayor, 1,445 m/4,741 ft
industries olives, figs, oranges, wine, brandy, timber, sheep; tourism is the mainstay of the economy
population (1990 est) 582,000
history captured 797 by the Moors, it became the kingdom of Majorca 1276, and was united with Aragon 1343.

Makarios III (born Mikhail Christodoulou Mouskos) 1913–1977. Cypriot politician, Greek Orthodox archbishop 1950–77. A leader of the Greek-Cypriot resistance organization ◊EOKA, he was exiled by the British to the Seychelles 1956–57 for supporting armed action to achieve union with Greece (*enosis*). He was president of the republic of Cyprus 1960–77 (briefly deposed by a Greek military coup July–Dec 1974).

Makarova Natalia Romanovna 1940– . Russian ballerina. She danced with the Kirov Ballet 1959–70, then sought political asylum in the West, becoming one of the greatest international dancers of the ballet boom of the 1960s and 1970s. A dancer of exceptional musicality and heightened dramatic sense, her roles include the title role in *Giselle* and Aurora in *The Sleeping Beauty*. She has also danced modern works including Jerome Robbins' *Other Dances* 1976, which he created for her.

She has also produced ballets, such as *La Bayadère* 1974, for the American Ballet Theater, and *Swan Lake* 1988, for the London Festival Ballet.

Makeba Miriam Zenzile 1932– . South African singer. In political exile 1960–90, she was one of the first world-music performers to make a name in the West, and is particularly associated with 'The Click Song', which features the glottal clicking sound of her Xhosa language. She was a vocal opponent to apartheid, and South Africa banned her records.

Makhachkala formerly (until 1922) ***Port Petrovsk*** capital of Dagestan, Autonomous Republic of the Russian Federation, on the Caspian Sea, SE of Grozny, from which pipelines bring petroleum to Makhachkala's refineries; other

Makarova Russian ballerina Natalia Makarova. She was esteemed for her technical skill, emotional spontaneity, and intuitive response to dance. She danced with the Kirov Ballet from 1959 until 1970 when she sought political asylum in the West. Following *perestroika*, she was able once again to dance with the Kirov Ballet in London and visited Leningrad in 1989. *Corbis*

industries include shipbuilding, meat packing, chemicals, matches, and cotton textiles; population (1994) 327,000.

Makua a people living to the north of the Zambezi River in Mozambique. With the Lomwe people, they make up the country's largest ethnic group. The Makua are mainly farmers, living in villages ruled by chiefs. The Makua language belongs to the Niger-Congo family, and has about 5 million speakers.

Malabo port and capital of Equatorial Guinea, on the island of Bioko; population (1992) 35,000. It was founded in the 1820s by the British as ***Port Clarence***. Under Spanish rule it was known as ***Santa Isabel*** (until 1973).

Malacca or ***Melaka*** state of W Peninsular Malaysia; capital Malacca; area 1,700 sq km/656 sq mi; population (1993) 583,400 (about 70% Chinese). Products include rubber, tin, and wire. The town originated in the 13th century as a fishing village and later developed into a trading port. Portuguese from 1511, then Dutch from 1641, it was ceded to Britain 1824, becoming part of the Straits Settlements.

Malacca, Strait of channel between Sumatra and the Malay Peninsula; length 965 km/600 mi; it narrows to less than 38 km/24 mi wide. It carries all shipping between the Indian Ocean and the South China Sea.

malachite common ◊copper ore, basic copper carbonate, $Cu_2CO_3(OH)_2$. It is a source of green pigment and is used as an antifungal agent in fish farming, as well as being polished for use in jewellery, ornaments, and art objects.

Málaga industrial seaport (sugar refining, distilling, brewing, olive-oil pressing, shipbuilding) and holiday resort in Andalusia, Spain; capital of Málaga province on the Mediterranean; population (1994) 531,000. Founded by the Phoenicians and taken by the Moors 711, Málaga was capital of the Moorish kingdom of Malaga from the 13th century until captured 1487 by the Catholic monarchs Ferdinand and Isabella.

Malagasy inhabitants of or natives to Madagascar. It seems likely that the earliest settlers came by sea, some 1,500 years ago, from Indonesia. The Malagasy language has about 9 million speakers; it belongs to the Austronesian family.

Malamud Bernard 1914–1986. US novelist and short-story writer. He first attracted attention with *The Natural* 1952, a mythic story about a baseball hero. It established Malamud's central concern of moral redemption and transcendence, which was more typically dealt with in books set in Jewish immigrant communities. These drew on the magical elements and mores of the European Yiddish tradition and include such novels as *The Assistant* 1957, *The Fixer* 1966, *Dubin's Lives* 1979, and *God's Grace* 1982. Short story collections include *The Magic Barrel* 1958, *Rembrandt's Hat* 1973, and *The Stories of Bernard Malamud* 1983.

malapropism amusing slip of the tongue, arising from the confusion of similar-sounding words; for example, 'the pineapple (pinnacle) of politeness'. The term derives from the French *mal à propos* (inappropriate); historically, it is associated with Mrs Malaprop, a character in Richard Sheridan's play *The Rivals* 1775.

malaria infectious parasitic disease of the tropics transmitted by mosquitoes, marked by periodic fever and an enlarged spleen. When a female mosquito of the *Anopheles* genus bites a human who has malaria, it takes in with the human blood one of four malaria protozoa of the genus *Plasmodium*. This matures within the insect and is then transferred when the mosquito bites a new victim. Malaria affects about 267 million people in 103 countries. In sub-Saharan Africa alone between 1.5 and 2 million children die from malaria and its consequences each year.

infection Inside the human body the parasite settles first in the liver, then multiplies to attack the red blood cells. Within the red blood cells the parasites multiply, eventually causing the cells to rupture and other cells to become infected. The cell rupture tends to be synchronized, occurring every 2–3 days, when the symptoms of malaria become evident.

treatment ◊Quinine, the first drug used against malaria, has now been replaced by synthetics, such as chloroquine, used to prevent or treat the disease. However, chloroquine-resistant strains of the main malaria parasite, *Plasmodium fulciparum*, are spreading rapidly in many parts of the world. The controversial drug mefloquine (Lariam) is widely prescribed for use in areas where chloroquine-resistant malaria prevails, but it has been linked to unpleasant side effects. Another drug, artemether, was found in 1996 trials to be as effective as quinine in the treatment of cerebral malaria.

The last recorded outbreak of malaria in the UK occurred in Kent in the early 1950s. However, 2,500 cases are reported each year in people who have contracted the disease elsewhere.

Malawi country in SE Africa, bounded N and NE by Tanzania; E, S, and W by Mozambique; and W by Zambia. *See country box below.*

Malawi, Lake or ***Lake Nyasa*** African lake, bordered by Malawi, Tanzania, and Mozambique, formed in a section of the Great ◊Rift Valley. It is about 500 m/1,650 ft above sea level and 560 km/350 mi long, with an area of 28,749 sq km/11,100 sq mi and a depth of 700 m, making it the 9th biggest lake in the world.

Malay a large group of peoples, comprising the majority population of the Malay Peninsula and Archipelago, and also found in S Thailand and coastal Sumatra and Borneo. Their language belongs to the western branch of the Austronesian family.

Malayalam southern Indian language, the official language of the state of Kerala. Malayalam is closely related to Tamil, also a member of the Dravidian language family; it is spoken by about 20 million people.

Malayan Emergency civil conflict in British-ruled Malaya, officially lasting from 1948 to 1960. The Communist Party of Malaya (CPM) launched an insurrection, calling for immediate Malayan independence. Britain responded by mounting a large-scale military and political counter-insurgency operation, while agreeing to eventual independence. In 1957 Malaya became independent and the state of emergency was ended 1960, although some CPM guerrillas continue to operate.

Malay language member of the Western or Indonesian branch of the Malayo-Polynesian language family, used in the Malay peninsula and many of the islands of Malaysia and Indonesia. The Malay language can be written in either Arabic or Roman scripts. The dialect of the S Malay peninsula is the basis of both Bahasa Malaysia and Bahasa Indonesia, the official languages of Malaysia and Indonesia. Bazaar Malay is a widespread pidgin variety used for trading and shopping.

> *The past exudes legend: one can't make pure clay of time's mud.*
>
> **Bernard Malamud** *Dubin's Lives*

MALAWI
Republic of (formerly *Nyasaland*)

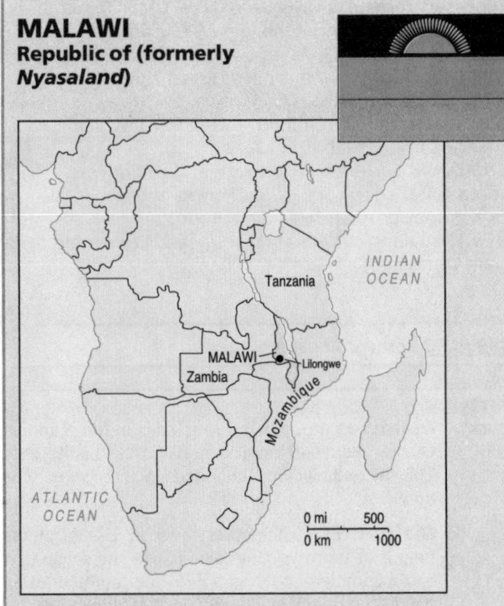

national name *Malawi*
area 118,000 sq km/45,560 sq mi
capital Lilongwe
major towns/cities Blantyre, Mzuzu, Zomba
physical features landlocked narrow plateau with rolling plains; mountainous W of Lake Malawi
head of state and government Bakili Muluzi from 1994
political system emergent democratic republic
administrative divisions three regions, subdivided into 24 districts
political parties Malawi Congress Party (MCP), multiracial, right-wing; United Democratic Front (UDF), left of centre; Alliance for Democracy (AFORD), left of centre
population 11,129,000 (1995 est)
population growth rate 3.5% (1990–95); 2.0% (2000–05)
ethnic distribution almost all indigenous Africans, divided into numerous ethnic groups, such as the Chewa, Nyanja, Tumbuka, Yao, Lomwe, Sena, Tonga, and Ngoni. There are also Asian and European minorities
life expectancy 48 (men), 50 (women)
literacy rate 22%
languages English, Chichewa (both official)
religions Christian 75%, Muslim 20%
currency Malawi kwacha
GDP (US $) 1.29 billion (1994)
growth rate −12.0% (1994)
exports tea, tobacco, cotton, peanuts, sugar

HISTORY
1st–4th Cs AD Immigration by Bantu-speaking peoples.
1480 Foundation of Maravi (Malawi) Confederacy, which covered much of central and southern Malawi and lasted into the 17th century.
1530 First visited by the Portuguese.
1600 Ngonde kingdom founded in northern Malawi by immigrants from Tanzania.
18th C Chikulamayembe state founded by immigrants from E of Lake Nyasa; slave trade flourished and Islam introduced in some areas.
mid-19th C Swahili-speaking Ngoni peoples, from South Africa, and Yao entered the region, dominating settled agriculturalists; Christianity introduced by missionaries, such as David Livingstone.
1891 Became the British protectorate of Nyasaland; cash crops, particularly coffee, introduced.
1915 Violent uprising, led by Rev John Chilembwe, against white settlers who had moved into the fertile S, taking land from the local population.
1953 Became part of white-dominated Central African Federation, which included South Rhodesia (Zimbabwe) and North Rhodesia (Zambia).
1958 Dr Hastings Kamuzu Banda returned to the country after working abroad for 40 years and became head of the conservative-nationalist Nyasaland/Malawi Congress Party (MCP), which spearheaded the campaign for independence.
1963 Central African Federation dissolved.
1964 Independence achieved, within the Commonwealth, as Malawi, with Banda as prime minister.
1966 Became a one-party republic, with Banda as president.
1967 Banda became the pariah of Black Africa by recognizing the racist, white-only republic of South Africa.
1971 Banda made president for life.
1970s Reports of human-rights violations and murder of Banda's opponents.
1980s Economy began to deteriorate after nearly two decades of expansion.
1986–89 Influx of nearly a million refugees from Mozambique.
1992 Calls for multiparty politics. Countrywide industrial riots caused many fatalities. Western aid suspended over human-rights violations.
1993 Referendum overwhelmingly supported ending of one-party rule.
1994 New multiparty constitution adopted. Bakili Muluzi, of the United Democratic Front (UDF), elected president in first free elections for 30 years. Inconclusive assembly elections.
1995 Banda and former minister of state John Tembo charged with conspiring to murder four political opponents 1983, but were cleared.

MALAYSIA
Federation of

national name *Persekutuan Tanah Malaysia*
area 329,759 sq km/127,287 sq mi
capital Kuala Lumpur
major towns/cities Johor Baharu, Ipoh, Georgetown (Penang), Kuala Trengganu, Kuala Baharu, Petalong Jaya, Kuching in Sarawak, Kota Kinabalu in Sabah
major ports Port Kelang
physical features comprises peninsular Malaysia (the nine Malay states – Johore, Kedah, Kelantan, Negri Sembilan, Pahang, Perak, Perlis, Selangor, Trengganu – plus Malacca and Penang); the states of Sabah and Sarawak and the federal territory of Kuala Lumpur; 75% tropical jungle; central mountain range (Mount Kinabalu, the highest peak in SE Asia); swamps in E; Niah caves (Sarawak)
head of state Jaafar bin Abd al-Rahman from 1994
head of government Mahathir bin Mohamed from 1981
political system liberal democracy
administrative divisions 13 states
political parties New United Malays' National Organization (UMNO Baru), Malay-oriented nationalist; Malaysian Chinese Association (MCA), Chinese-oriented, conservative; Gerakan Party, Chinese-oriented, socialist; Malaysian Indian Congress (MIC), Indian-oriented; Democratic Action Party (DAP), multiracial but Chinese-dominated, left of centre; Pan-Malayan Islamic Party (PAS), Islamic; Semangat '46 (Spirit of 1946), moderate, multiracial
armed forces 114,500; reserve force 58,300; paramilitary force 186,000 (1994)
conscription none
defence spend (% GDP) 3.9 (1994)
education spend (% GNP) 5.5 (1992)
health spend (% GDP) 1.3 (1990)
death penalty retained and used for ordinary crimes
population 20,140,000 (1995 est)
population growth rate 2.4% (1990–95); 1.7% (2000–05)
age distribution (% of total population) <15 38.0%, 15–65 58.1%, >65 3.9% (1995)
ethnic distribution 58% of the population is Malay, four-fifths of whom live in rural areas; 32% is Chinese, four-fifths of whom are in towns; 9% is Indian, mainly Tamil
population density (per sq km) 60 (1994)
urban population (% of total) 54 (1995)
labour force 39% of population: 27% agriculture, 23% industry, 50% services (1990)
unemployment 2.9% (1994)
child mortality rate (under 5, per 1,000 live births) 15 (1994)
life expectancy 69 (men), 73 (women)
education (compulsory years) 11
literacy rate 87% (men), 70% (women)
languages Malay (official), English, Chinese, Tamil, Iban
religions Muslim (official), Buddhist, Hindu, local beliefs
TV sets (per 1,000 people) 150 (1992)
currency ringgit
GDP (US $) 70.62 billion (1994)
GDP per capita (PPP) (US $) 8,360 (1993)
growth rate 9.2% (1994)
average annual inflation 3.7% (1994); 2.7% (1985–93)
major trading partners Japan, USA, Singapore, Taiwan, UK and other EU countries
resources tin, bauxite, copper, iron ore, petroleum, natural gas, forests
industries electrical and electronic appliances (particularly radio and TV receivers), food processing, rubber products, industrial chemicals, wood products, petroleum refinery, motor vehicles, tourism
exports palm oil, rubber, crude petroleum, machinery and transport equipment, timber, tin, textiles, electronic goods. Principal market: Singapore 21.7% (1993)
imports machinery and transport equipment, chemicals, foodstuffs, crude petroleum, consumer goods. Principal source: Japan 27.4% (1993)
arable land 3.2% (1993)
agricultural products rice, cocoa, palm, rubber, pepper, coconuts, tea, pineapples

HISTORY
1st C AD Peoples of Malay peninsula influenced by Indian culture and Buddhism.
8th–13th Cs Malay peninsula formed part of Buddhist Srivijaya Empire based in Sumatra.
14th C Siam (Thailand) expanded to included most of Malay peninsula.
1403 Muslim traders founded port of Malacca.
1511 Portuguese attacked and captured Malacca.
1641 Portuguese ousted from Malacca by Dutch after seven-year blockade.
1786 British East India Company established a trading post on island of Penang.
1795–1815 Britain occupied Dutch colonies after France conquered the Netherlands.
1819 Stamford Raffles of East India Company obtained Singapore from Sultan of Johore.
1824 Anglo-Dutch Treaty ceded Malacca to Britain in return for territory in Sumatra.
1826 British possessions of Singapore, Penang, and Malacca formed Straits Settlements, ruled by governor of Bengal; ports prospered and expanded.
1840 Sultan of Brunei gave Sarawak to James Brooke, whose family ruled until 1946.
1851 Responsibility for Straits Settlements assumed by governor general of India.
1858 British government, through India Office, took over administration of Straits Settlements.
1867 Straits Settlements became crown colony of British Empire.
1874 British protectorates established over four Malay states of Perak, Salangor, Pahang, and Negri Sembilan, which federated 1896.
1888 Britain declared protectorate over N Borneo (Sabah).
late 19th C Millions of Chinese and thousands of Indians migrated to Malaya.
1909–14 Britain assumed indirect rule over five northern Malay states after agreement with Siam.
1941–45 Japanese occupation.
1946 United Malay National Organization (UMNO) founded to oppose British plans for centralized Union of Malaya.
1948 Britain federated nine Malay states with Penang and Malacca to form single colony of Federation of Malaya.
1948–60 Malayan emergency: British forces suppressed insurrection by communist guerrillas.
1957 Federation of Malaya became independent with Prince Abdul Rahman (leader of UMNO) as prime minister.
1963 Federation of Malaya combined with Singapore, Sarawak, and Sabah to form Federation of Malaysia.
1963–66 'The Confrontation' – guerrillas supported by Indonesia opposed federation.
1965 Singapore withdrew from Federation of Malaysia.
1968 Philippines claimed sovereignty over Sabah.
1969 Malay resentment of Chinese economic dominance resulted in race riots in Kuala Lumpur.
1971 *Bumiputra* policies which favoured ethnic Malays in education and employment introduced by Tun Abul Razak of UMNO.
1981 Mahathir bin Muhammad (UMNO) became prime minister; government increasingly dominated by Muslim Malays.
1987 Malay-Chinese relations deteriorated; over 100 opposition activists arrested.
1988 UMNO split over Mahathir's leadership style; his supporters formed UMNO Baru (New UMNO); his critics formed Semangat '46, a new multiracial party 1989.
1991 Launch of economic development policy aimed at 7% annual growth.
1996 Semangat '46 rejoined UMNO Baru, which remained under Mahathir's leadership.
1998 Deputy prime minister Anwar Ibrahim was sacked for alleged corruption. He led anti-government protests in Kuala Lumpur.
1999 The jailing of Anwar Ibrahim leads to rioting in Kuala Lumpur.

SEE ALSO Borneo; Singapore

'I believe in the brotherhood of all men, but I don't believe in wasting brotherhood on anyone who doesn't want to practise it with me.'

MALCOLM X
Speech at Harvard Law School 1964

Malayo-Polynesian family of languages spoken in Malaysia, better known as ◊***Austronesian***.

Malay Peninsula southern projection of the continent of Asia, lying between the Strait of Malacca, which divides it from Sumatra, and the China Sea. The northern portion is partly in Myanmar (formerly Burma), partly in Thailand; the south forms part of Malaysia. The island of Singapore lies off its southern extremity.

Malaysia country in SE Asia, comprising the Malay Peninsula, bounded N by Thailand, and surrounded E and S by the South China Sea and W by the Strait of Malacca; and the states of Sabah and Sarawak in the N part of the island of Borneo (S Borneo is part of Indonesia). *See country box above.*

Malcolm four kings of Scotland, including:

Malcolm III called ***Canmore*** c. 1031–1093. King of Scotland from 1058, the son of Duncan I (murdered by ◊Macbeth 1040). He fled to England when the throne was usurped by Macbeth, but recovered S Scotland and killed Macbeth in battle 1057. He was killed at Alnwick while invading Northumberland, England.

Malcolm X adopted name of Malcolm Little 1926–1965. US black nationalist leader. While serving a prison sentence for burglary 1946–53, he joined the ◊Black Muslims sect. On his release he campaigned for black separatism, condoning violence in self-defence, but 1964 modified his views to found the Islamic, socialist Organization of Afro-American Unity, preaching racial solidarity.

He grew up in foster homes in Michigan, Massachusetts, and New York. Convicted of robbery 1946, he spent seven years in prison, becoming a follower of Black Muslim leader Elijah Muhammad and converting to Islam. In 1952 he officially changed his name to Malcolm X to signify his rootlessness in a racist society. Having become an influential national and international leader, Malcolm X publicly broke with the Black Muslims 1964. A year later he was assassinated by ◊Nation of Islam opponents while addressing a rally in Harlem, New York City.

Maldives group of 1,196 islands in the N Indian Ocean, about 640 km/400 mi SW of Sri Lanka, only 203 of which are inhabited. *See country box opposite.*

Maldon English market town in Essex, at the mouth of the river Chelmer. It was the scene of a battle commemorated in a 325-line fragment of an Anglo-Saxon poem *The Battle of Maldon*, describing the defeat and death of Ealdorman Byrhtnoth by the Vikings in 991.

Malé capital and chief atoll of the Maldives in the Indian Ocean; population (1990) 55,100. It trades in copra, breadfruit, fish, and palm products; it is also a growing tourist centre.

Malebranche Nicolas 1638–1715. French philosopher. His *De la Recherche de la vérité/Search after Truth* 1674–78 was inspired by René ◊Descartes; he maintained that exact ideas of external objects are obtainable only through God.

Malenkov Georgi Maximilianovich 1902–1988. Soviet prime minister 1953–55, Stalin's designated successor but abruptly ousted as Communist Party

MALDIVES
Republic of the

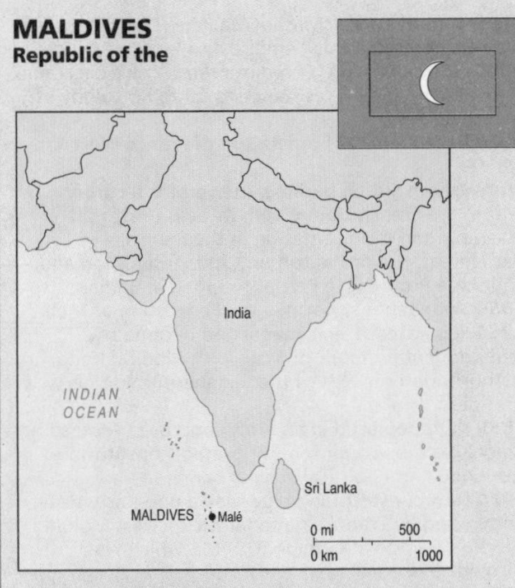

national name *Divehi Raajjeyge Jumhooriyaa*
area 298 sq km/115 sq mi
capital Malé
major towns/cities Seenu
physical features comprises 1,196 coral islands, grouped into 12 clusters of atolls, largely flat, none bigger than 13 sq km/5 sq mi, average elevation 1.8 m/6 ft; 203 are inhabited
head of state and government Maumoon Abd al-Gayoom from 1978
political system authoritarian nationalist
administrative divisions 20 districts
political parties none; candidates elected on basis of personal influence and clan loyalties
population 238,363 (1993 est)
population growth rate 3.3% (1990–95)
ethnic distribution four 'ethnic strains' of the indigenous population: Dravidian in the northern islands, Arab in the middle islands, Sinhalese in the southern islands, and Negro or Ravare
life expectancy 60 (men), 63 (women)
literacy rate 92%
languages Divehi (Sinhalese dialect), English
religion Sunni Muslim
currency rufiya
GDP (US $) 157.9 million (1992)
growth rate 6.6% (1994)
exports coconuts, copra, bonito (fish related to tuna), garments

HISTORY
12th C AD Islam introduced by seafaring Arabs, who displaced the indigenous Dravidian population.
14th C Ad-Din sultanate established.
1558–73 Under Portuguese rule.
1645 Became a dependency of Ceylon (Sri Lanka), which was ruled by the Dutch until 1796 and then by the British, with Sinhalese and Indian colonies being established.
1887 Became an internally self-governing British protectorate, which remained a dependency of Sri Lanka until 1948.
1932 Formerly hereditary, the sultanate became an elected position when the Maldives' first constitution was introduced.
1953 The Maldive Islands became a republic within the Commonwealth, as the ad-Din sultanate was abolished.
1954 Sultan restored.
1959–60 Secessionist rebellion in Suvadiva (Huvadu) and Addu southern atolls.
1965 Achieved full independence outside the Commonwealth.
1968 Sultan deposed after referendum; republic reinstated with Ibrahim Nasir as president.
1975 Britain closed an airforce staging post on the southern island of Gan, leading to a substantial loss in income.
1978 The autocratic Nasir retired; replaced by Maumoon Abd al-Gayoom.
1980s Economic growth boosted by rapid development of tourist industry.
1982 Rejoined the Commonwealth.
1985 Became a founder member of the South Asian Association for Regional Cooperation.
1986 The High Court sentenced the exiled Nasir in absentia to 25 years' banishment on charges of embezzlement of public funds, but a pardon was granted two years later.
1988 Coup attempt by Sri Lankan mercenaries, thought to have the backing of former president Nasir, was foiled by Indian paratroops.

secretary within two weeks of Stalin's death by ◊Khrushchev, and forced out as prime minister 1955 by ◊Bulganin.

Malevich Kasimir Severinovich 1878–1935. Russian abstract painter. In 1912 he visited Paris where he was influenced by Cubism, and in 1913 launched his own abstract style, ◊Suprematism. He reached his most abstract in *White on White* about 1918 (Museum of Modern Art, New York), a white square painted on a white background, but later returned to figurative themes treated in a semi-abstract style.

Mali landlocked country in NW Africa, bounded to the NE by Algeria, E by Niger, SE by Burkina Faso, S by Côte d'Ivoire, SW by Senegal and Guinea, and W and N by Mauritania. *See country box on p. 666.*

malic acid COOHCH$_2$CH(OH)COOH organic crystalline acid that can be extracted from apples, plums, cherries, grapes, and other fruits, but occurs in all living cells in smaller amounts, being one of the intermediates of the ◊Krebs cycle.

Malcolm X US black militant leader Malcolm X. Once a leading member of the Black Muslim organization, he broke away to form a rival group, the militant Organization of Afro-American Unity. The hostility between the two groups increased and he was assassinated 1965. *Topham*

Mali Empire Muslim state in NW Africa during the 7th–15th centuries. Thriving on its trade in gold, it reached its peak in the 14th century under Mansa Musa (reigned 1312–37), when it occupied an area covering present-day Senegal, Gambia, Mali, and S Mauritania. Mali's territory was similar to (though larger than) that of the Ghana Empire (see ◊Ghana, ancient), and gave way in turn to the ◊Songhai Empire.

Malinowski Bronislaw Kasper 1884–1942. Polish-born British anthropologist, one of the founders of the theory of ◊functionalism in the social sciences. During expeditions to the Trobriand Islands (now part of Papua New Guinea) 1914–16 and 1917–18, his detailed studies of the islanders led him to see customs and practices in terms of their function in creating and maintaining social order. His fieldwork involved a revolutionary system of 'participant observation' whereby the researcher became completely involved in the life of the people he studied.

mallard common wild duck *Anas platyrhynchos*, of the subfamily Anatinae order Anseriformes, from which domestic ducks were bred. It is found almost worldwide. The male, which can grow to a length of 60 cm/2 ft, usually has a glossy green head, white collar, and chestnut brown breast, while the female is mottled brown.

Mallarmé Stéphane 1842–1898. French poet. A leader of the Symbolist school, he became known as a poet's poet for his condensed, hermetic verse and unorthodox syntax, reaching for the ideal world of the intellect. His belief that poetry should be evocative and suggestive was reflected in *L'Après-midi d'un faune/Afternoon of a Faun* 1876 (illustrated by Manet), which inspired the composer Debussy. Later works are *Poésies complètes/Complete Poems* 1887, *Vers et prose/Verse and Prose* 1893, and the prose *Divagations/Digressions* 1897.

Malle Louis 1932–1995. French film director. After a period as assistant to director Robert Bresson, he directed *Les Amants/The Lovers* 1958, audacious for its time in its explicitness. His subsequent films, made in France and the USA, include *Zazie dans le métro* 1961, *Viva Maria* 1965, *Pretty Baby* 1978, *Atlantic City* 1980, *Au Revoir les Enfants* 1988, *Milou en mai* 1989, and *Damage* 1993.

mallee small trees and shrubs of the genus *Eucalyptus* with many small stems and thick underground roots that retain water. Before irrigation farming began, dense thickets of mallee characterized most of NW Victoria, Australia, known as the mallee region.

Mallorca Spanish form of ◊Majorca, an island in the Mediterranean.

mallow any flowering plant of the family Malvaceae, especially of the genus *Malva*, including the European common mallow *M. sylvestris*; the tree mallow *Lavatera arborea*; and the marsh mallow *Althaea officinalis*. Most mallows have pink or purple flowers.

Malmö industrial port (shipbuilding, engineering, textiles) in SW Sweden, situated across the Öresund from Copenhagen, Denmark; population (1994 est) 242,700. Founded in the 12th century, Malmö is Sweden's third-largest city.

malnutrition condition resulting from a defective diet where certain important food nutrients (such as protein, vitamins, or carbohydrates) are absent. It can lead to deficiency diseases. A related problem is ◊undernourishment. The World Health Organization estimated 1995 that one-third of the world's children are undernourished.

According to UNICEF, in 1996 around 86 million children under the age of five (50% of all under-fives) in South Asia were malnourished, compared to 32 million (25%) in sub-Saharan Africa.

Malory Thomas c. 1410–1471. English author. He is known for the prose romance *Le Morte D'Arthur* written about 1470, printed 1485. It deals with the exploits of King ◊Arthur's knights of the Round Table and the quest for the ◊Holy Grail.

Malory is thought to have been the Warwickshire landowner of that name who was member of Parliament for Warwick 1445 and was subsequently charged with rape, theft, and attempted murder.

Malouf David George Joseph 1934– . Australian poet, novelist, and short-story writer. He is of Lebanese and English extraction. His poetry collections include *Neighbours in a Thicket* 1974, which won several awards, *Wild Lemons* 1980, and *First Things Last* 1980. Malouf's first novel *Johnno* 1975 deals with his boyhood in Brisbane. It was followed by *An Imaginary Life* 1978 and other novels, including *Fly Away Peter* 1982, *The Great World* 1990, and *Remembering Babylon* 1993. He has also written opera librettos for *Voss* 1986, from the novel of Patrick White (1853–1906), and *La Mer de Glace* 1991.

Malplaquet, Battle of during the War of the ◊Spanish Succession, victory of the British, Dutch, and Austrian forces over the French forces 11 Sept 1709 at Malplaquet, in Nord *département*, France. The joint Imperial force lost over 20,000 troops and the French 12,000, both having begun with about 90,000.

‘For love that time was not as love is nowadays.’
THOMAS MALORY
Le Morte d'Arthur

MALI
Republic of

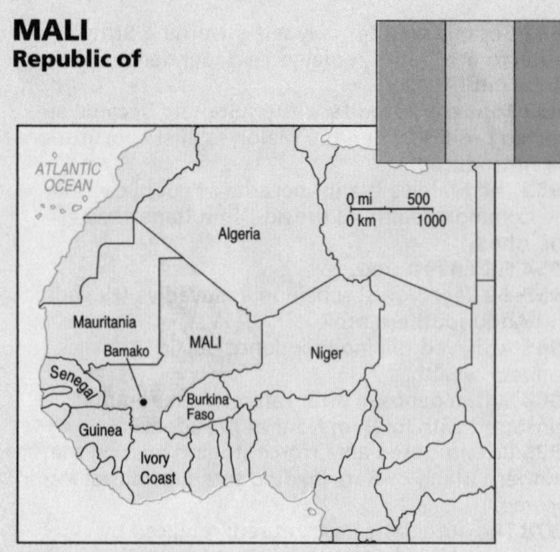

national name *République du Mali*
area 1,240,142 sq km/478,695 sq mi
capital Bamako
major towns/cities Mopti, Kayes, Ségou, Timbuktu, Sikasso
physical features landlocked state with river Niger and savanna in S; part of the Sahara in N; hills in NE; Senegal River and its branches irrigate the SW
head of state Alpha Oumar Konare from 1992
head of government Ibrahim Boubaker Keita from 1994
political system emergent democratic republic
administrative divisions six regions and 42 counties
political parties Alliance for Democracy in Mali (ADEMA), left of centre; National Committee for Democratic Initiative (CNID), centre-left; Assembly for Democracy and Progress (RDP), left of centre; Civic Society and the Democracy and Progress Party (PDP), left of centre; Malian People's Democratic Union (UDPM), nationalist socialist
population 10,759,000 (1995 est)
population growth rate 3.2% (1990–95); 2.9% (2000–05)
ethnic distribution around 50% belong to the Mande group, including the Bambara, Malinke, and Sarakole; other significant groups include the Fulani, Minianka, Senutu, Songhai, and the nomadic Tuareg in the N
life expectancy 44 (men), 48 (women)
literacy rate men 41%, women 24%
languages French (official), Bambara
religions Sunni Muslim 90%, animist, Christian
currency franc CFA
GDP (US $) 1.9 billion (1994)
growth rate 2.4% (1994)
exports cotton, peanuts, livestock, fish, gold

HISTORY
5th–13th Cs Ghana Empire founded by the agriculturist Soninke people, based on the Saharan gold trade, for which Timbuktu became an important centre. With its capital at Kumbi, 125 mi/200 km N of Bamako, in SE Mauritania, at its height in the 11th century it covered much of the western Sahel, comprising parts of present-day Mali, Senegal, and Mauritania. Wars with Muslim Berber tribes from the N led to its downfall.
13th–15th Cs Ghana Empire was superseded by the Muslim Mali Empire of the Malinke (Mandingo) people of the SW, and from which the country derives its name. At its peak, under Mansa Musa in the 14th century, it covered parts of Mali, Senegal, Gambia, and S Mauritania.
15th–16th Cs The Muslim Songhai Empire, centred around Timbuktu and Gao, superseded the Mali Empire. Under Sonni Ali Ber, who ruled 1464–92, it covered Mali, Senegal, Gambia, and parts of Mauritania, Niger, and Nigeria and included a professional army and civil service.
1591 Songhai Empire destroyed by Moroccan Berbers, under Ahmad al-Mansur, who launched an invasion to take over western Sudanese gold trade and took control over Timbuktu.
18th–19th Cs Niger valley region was divided between the Tuareg, around Gao in the NE and the Fulani and Bambara kingdoms, around Macina and Bambara in the centre and SW.
late 18th C Western Mali visited by the Scots explorer Mungo Park.
mid-19th C The Islamic Tukolor, as part of a jihad (holy war) conquered much of western Mali, including the Fulani and Bambara kingdoms, while in the S, Samori Ture, a Muslim Malinke (Mandingo) warrior, created a small empire.
1880–95 Region conquered by French, who overcame Tukolor and Samori resistance to establish colony of French Sudan.
1904 Became part of federation of French West Africa.
1946 French Sudan became an overseas territory within the French Union, with its own territorial assembly and representation in the French parliament; the pro-autonomy Sudanese Union and Sudanese Progressive Parties founded in Bamako.
1959 With Senegal, formed the Federation of Mali.
1960 Separated from Senegal and became the independent Republic of Mali, with Modibo Keita, an authoritarian socialist of the Sudanese Union party, as president.
1968 Keita replaced in an army coup by Lt Moussa Traoré, as the economy deteriorated: constitution suspended and political activity banned.
1974 New constitution made Mali a one-party state, dominated by Traoré's nationalistic socialist Malian People's Democratic Union (UDPM), which was formed 1976.
1979 More than a dozen killed after a student strike was crushed.
1985 Five-day conflict with Burkina Faso over long-standing border dispute; mediated by International Court of Justice.
late 1980s Closer ties developed with the West and free-market economic policies pursued, including privatization, as Soviet influence waned.
1991 Violent demonstrations and strikes against one-party rule led to 150 deaths; Traoré ousted in a coup led by Lt-Col Amadou Toumani Toure.
1992 Referendum endorsed new democratic constitution. The opposition Alliance for Democracy in Mali (ADEMA) won multiparty elections; Alpha Oumar Konare elected president. Coalition government formed. Peace pact signed with Tuareg rebels fighting in N Mali for greater autonomy.
1993–94 Student unrest forced two changes of prime minister. Ex-president Traoré sentenced to death for his role in suppressing the 1991 riots.

SEE ALSO Ghana, ancient; Mali Empire

malpractice in law, ◊negligence by a professional person, usually a doctor, that may lead to an action for damages by the client.

Malraux André Georges 1901–1976. French writer, art critic, and politician. An active anti-fascist, he gained international renown for his novel *La Condition humaine/Man's Estate* 1933, set during the Nationalist/Communist Revolution in China in the 1920s. *L'Espoir/Days of Hope* 1937 is set in Civil War Spain, where he was a bomber pilot in the International Brigade. In his revolutionary novels he frequently depicts individuals in situations where they are forced to examine the meaning of their own life. He also made an outstanding contribution to aesthetics with *La Psychologie de l'art* 1947–49, revised as *Les Voix du silence/The Voices of Silence* 1951.

Malraux rejected communism and supported the Gaullist resistance during World War II, becoming minister of information in de Gaulle's government 1945–46 and minister of cultural affairs 1960–69.

malt in brewing, grain (barley, oats, or wheat) artificially germinated and then dried in a kiln. Malts are fermented to make beers or lagers, or fermented and then distilled to produce spirits such as whisky.

Malta island in the Mediterranean Sea, S of Sicily, E of Tunisia, and N of Libya. *See country box opposite.*

Malta, Knights of another name for members of the military-religious order of the Hospital of ◊St John of Jerusalem.

maltase enzyme found in plants and animals that breaks down the disaccharide maltose into glucose.

Malthus Thomas Robert 1766–1834. English economist. His *Essay on the Principle of Population* 1798 (revised 1803) argued for population control, since populations increase in geometric ratio and food supply only in arithmetic ratio, and influenced Charles ◊Darwin's thinking on natural selection as the driving force of evolution.

Malthus saw war, famine, and disease as necessary checks on population growth. Later editions of his work suggested that 'moral restraint' (delaying marriage, with sexual abstinence before it) could also keep numbers from increasing too quickly, a statement seized on by later birth-control pioneers (the 'neo-Malthusians').

maltose $C_{12}H_{22}O_{11}$ a ◊disaccharide sugar in which both monosaccharide units are glucose. It is produced by the enzymic hydrolysis of starch and is a major constituent of malt, produced in the early stages of beer and whisky manufacture.

Maluku or ***Moluccas*** group of Indonesian islands; area 74,500 sq km/28,764 sq mi; population (1990) 1,857,800. The capital is Ambon, on Amboina. As the Spice Islands, they were formerly part of the Netherlands East Indies; the S Moluccas attempted secession from the newly created Indonesian republic from 1949; exiles continued agitation in the Netherlands.

Maluku

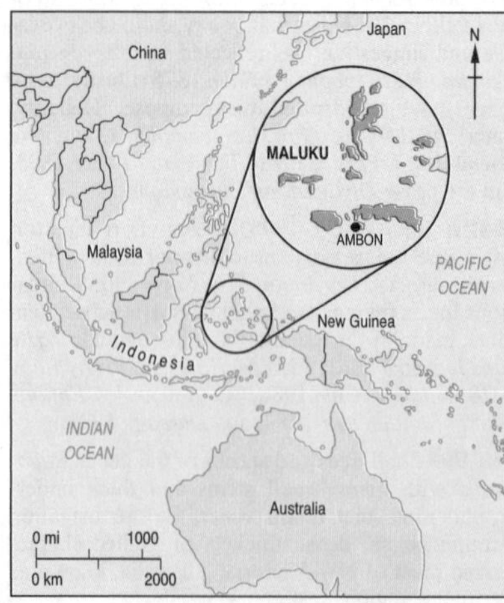

Malvern English spa town in Hereford and Worcester, on the east side of the Malvern Hills, which extend for about 16 km/10 mi and have their high point in Worcester Beacon 425 m/1,395 ft; population (1991) 31,500. The Malvern Festival 1929–39, associated with the playwright G B Shaw and the composer Edward Elgar, was revived 1977. Malvern College 1863 and the Royal Radar Establishment are here.

mamba one of two venomous snakes, genus *Dendroaspis*, of the cobra family Elapidae, found in Africa S of the Sahara. Unlike cobras, they are not hooded. The ***green mamba*** *D. angusticeps* is 1.5 m/5 ft long or more and lives in trees. The ***black mamba*** *D. polylepis* is the largest venomous snake in Africa, occasionally as long as 3.4 m/11 ft, and spends more time on the ground.

Mameluke member of a powerful political class that dominated Egypt from the 13th century until their massacre 1811 by Mehmet Ali. The Mamelukes were originally descended from freed Turkish slaves. They formed the royal bodyguard in the 13th century, and in 1250 placed one of their own number on the throne. Mameluke sultans ruled Egypt until the Turkish conquest of 1517, and they remained the ruling class until 1811.

Mamet David Alan 1947– . US dramatist, film screenwriter, and director. His plays, with their vivid, freewheeling language and urban settings, are often compared with those of Harold Pinter. His *American Buffalo* 1975, about a gang of hopeless robbers, was his first major success. It was followed by *Sexual Perversity in Chicago* 1978 and *Glengarry Glen Ross* 1983, a dark depiction of American business ethics. Later works included the plays *Speed the Plow* 1988, *Oleanna* 1992, about a sexual harassment case, and *Cryptogram* 1994, about childhood uncertainty. His screenplays have included *The Postman Always Rings Twice 1981*, *The Verdict* 1982, *The Untouchables* 1987, and *Things Change* 1987, which he also directed.

mammal animal characterized by having mammary glands in the female; these are used for suckling the young. Other features of mammals are ◊hair (very reduced in some species, such as whales); a middle ear formed of three small bones (ossicles); a lower jaw consisting of two bones only; seven vertebrae in the neck; and no nucleus in the red blood cells.

Mammals are divided into three groups:

placental mammals, where the young develop inside the ◊uterus, receiving nourishment from the blood of the mother via the ◊placenta;

marsupials, where the young are born at an early stage of development and develop further in a pouch on the mother's body;

monotremes, where the young hatch from an egg outside the mother's body and are then nourished with milk.

The monotremes are the least evolved and have been largely displaced by more sophisticated ◊marsupials and placentals, so that there are only a few types surviving (platypus and echidna). Placentals have spread to all parts of the globe, and where placentals have competed with marsupials, the placentals have in general displaced marsupial types. However, marsupials occupy many specialized niches in South America and, especially, Australasia.

There are over 4,000 species of mammals, adapted to almost every way of life. The smallest shrew weighs only 2 g/0.07 oz, the largest whale up to 140 tonnes.

mammary gland in female mammals, a milk-producing gland derived from epithelial cells underlying the skin, active only after the production of young. In all but monotremes (egg-laying mammals), the mammary glands terminate in teats which aid infant suckling. The number of glands and their position vary between species.

mammography X-ray procedure used to screen for breast cancer. It can detect abnormal growths at an early stage, before they can be seen or felt.

Mammon evil personification of wealth and greed; originally a Syrian god of riches, cited in the New Testament as opposed to the Christian god.

mammoth extinct elephant of the genus *Mammuthus*, whose remains are found worldwide. Some were 50% taller than modern elephants. The woolly mammoth *Elephas primigenius* of northern zones, the size of an Indian elephant, had long fur and large inward-curving tusks. Various species of mammoth were abundant in both the Old World and the New World in Pleistocene times, and were hunted by humans for food.

Managua capital and chief industrial city of Nicaragua, on the lake of the same name; population (1991 est) 615,000. It has twice been destroyed by earthquake and rebuilt, 1931 and 1972; it was also badly damaged during the civil war in the late 1970s.

manakin any bird of the order Passeriformes, family Pipridae, found in South and Central America, about 15 cm/6 in long and often brightly coloured. The males of the genus *Manacus* clear a patch of the forest floor with a small tree as a display perch.

Manama (Arabic ***Al Manamah***) capital and free trade port of Bahrain, on Bahrain Island; population (1991) 137,000. It handles oil and entrepôt trade.

manatee any plant-eating aquatic mammal of the genus *Trichechus* constituting the family Trichechidae in the order Sirenia (sea cows). Manatees occur in marine bays and sluggish rivers, usually in turbid water. Their forelimbs are flippers; their hindlimbs are absent, but they have a short, rounded and flattened tail that is used for propulsion. The marine manatee grows up to about 4.5 m/15 ft long and weighs up to 600 kg/1,323 lb.

There are three species of manatee, the ***Amazonian manatee*** *T. Inunguis*, ***African manatee*** *T. Senegalensis*, and ***West Indian manatee*** *T. manatus*. All are in danger of becoming extinct as a result of pollution and because they are hunted for food. *See illustration on following page.*

Manaus capital of Amazonas, Brazil, on the Rio Negro, near its confluence with the Amazon; population (1991) 996,700. It can be reached by seagoing vessels, although it is 1,600 km/1,000 mi from the Atlantic. Formerly a centre of the rubber trade, it developed as a tourist centre in the 1970s.

MAMMALS: CLASSIFICATION

Order	Typical species
Monotremata	echidna, platypus
Marsupiala	kangaroo, koala, opossum
Insectivora	shrew, hedgehog, mole
Chiroptera	bat
Primates	lemur, monkey, ape, human
Edentata	anteater, armadillo, sloth
Pholidota	pangolin
Dermoptera	flying lemur
Rodentia	rat, mouse, squirrel, porcupine
Lagomorpha	rabbit, hare, pika
Cetacea	whale, dolphin
Carnivora	cat, dog, weasel, bear
Pinnipedia	seal, walrus
Artiodactyla	pig, deer, cattle, camel, giraffe
Perissodactyla	horse, rhinoceros, tapir
Sirenia	dugong, manatee
Tubulidentata	aardvark
Hyracoidea	hyrax
Proboscidea	elephant

Manchester city in NW England, on the river Irwell, 50 km/31 mi E of Liverpool. It is a manufacturing (textile machinery, chemicals, rubber, engineering, electrical equipment, paper, printing, processed foods) and financial centre; population (1991) 404,900. It is linked by the Manchester Ship Canal, opened 1894, to the river Mersey and the sea.

features It is the home of the Hallé Orchestra, the Royal Northern College of Music, Chetham's School of Music, Manchester Grammar School (1515), the Royal Exchange (built 1869, now a theatre), town hall designed by Alfred ◊Waterhouse, the Free Trade Hall (1843), Liverpool Road station (the world's oldest surviving passenger station), the Whitworth Art Gallery, and the Cotton Exchange (now a leisure centre). The Castlefield Urban Heritage Park includes the Granada television studios, including the set of the soap opera *Coronation Street*, open to visitors, and also the Greater Manchester Museum of Science and Industry.

history Originally a Roman camp (*Mancunium*), Manchester is mentioned in the Domesday Book, and by the 13th century was already a centre for the wool trade. Its damp climate made it ideal for cotton, introduced in the 16th century, and from the

MALTA
Republic of

national name *Repubblika Ta'Malta*
area 320 sq km/124 sq mi
capital and port Valletta
major towns/cities Rabat
major ports Marsaxlokk
physical features includes islands of Gozo 67 sq km/26 sq mi and Comino 3 sq km/1 sq mi
head of state Mifsud Bonnici from 1994
head of government Edward Fenech Adami from 1987
political system liberal democracy
administrative divisions none; administered from the capital
political parties Malta Labour Party (MLP), moderate, left of centre; Nationalist Party (PN), Christian, centrist, pro-European
population 370,402 (1995 est)
population growth rate 0.7% (1990–95)
ethnic distribution essentially European, supposedly originated from ancient N African kingdom of Carthage
life expectancy 72 (men), 76 (women)
literacy rate 84%
languages Maltese, English (both official)
religion Roman Catholic 98%
currency Maltese lira
GDP (US $) 2.6 billion (1994)
growth rate 5.1% (1994)
exports vegetables, knitwear, handmade lace, plastics, electronic equipment. Tourism is important

HISTORY
7th C BC Invaded and subjugated by the Carthaginians from North Africa.
218 BC Came under Roman control.
AD 60 Converted to Christianity by the apostle Paul, who was shipwrecked.
395 On the division of the Roman Empire, became part of the Eastern (Byzantine) portion, dominated by Constantinople.
870 Came under Arab rule.
1091 Arabs defeated by the Norman count Roger I of Sicily, and the Roman Catholic Church was re-established.
1530 Handed over by Holy Roman Emperor Charles V to a religious military order, the Hospitallers (Knights of St John of Jerusalem).
1798–1802 Briefly occupied by the French.
1814 Annexed to Britain by the Treaty of Paris on condition that the Roman Catholic Church was maintained and the Maltese Declaration of Rights honoured.
later 19th C–early 20th C Became a vital British naval base, with a famous dockyard that developed as the economic mainstay of the islands.
1942 Awarded the George Cross for its valour in resisting severe Italian aerial attacks during World War II.
1947 Achieved self-government.
1955 Dom Mintoff of the left-of-centre Malta Labour Party (MLP) became prime minister.
1956 Referendum approved MLP's proposal for integration with the UK. Plebiscite opposed and boycotted by the right-of-centre Nationalist Party (PN).
1958 MLP rejected the final British integration proposal.
1962 PN elected, with Dr Giorgio Borg Olivier as prime minister.
1964 Independence achieved from Britain, within the Commonwealth. Ten-year defence and economic-aid treaty with UK signed.
1971 Mintoff adopted policy of nonalignment and declared 1964 treaty invalid; negotiations began for leasing the NATO base in Malta.
1972 Seven-year NATO agreement signed.
1974 Became a republic.
1979 British military base closed; closer links established with communist and Arab states, including Libya.
1984 Mintoff retired and was replaced by Karmenu Mifsud Bonnici as prime minister and MLP leader.
1987 Edward Fenech Adami (PN) narrowly elected prime minister and adopted a more pro-European and pro-American policy stance than the preceding administration.
1990 Formal application made for European Community membership.
1994 Mifsud Bonnici elected president.

manatee Manatees, dugongs, and sea-cows are plant-eating, aquatic mammals that belong to the order Sirenia. It has been suggested that mis-sightings of these animals gave rise to the tales of mermaids. There are three species of manatee; two inhabit the estuaries and coastal waters of the Americas while the other is found off the W African coast.

mid-18th century onwards the Manchester area was a world centre of manufacture, using cotton imported from North America and India. Unrest after the Napoleonic Wars led to the Peterloo Massacre 1819 when troops charged a political meeting at St Peter's Fields. After 1945 there was a sharp decline, and many disused mills were refurbished to provide alternative industrial uses.

It was the focus for the Manchester school of political economists, including John Bright and Richard Cobden, who campaigned for the repeal of the Corn Laws in the first half of the 19th century, and the original home of the *Guardian* newspaper (founded as the *Manchester Guardian* 1821). Its pop-music scene flourished in the 1980s.

Manchester, Greater metropolitan county of NW England, created 1974; in 1986, most of the functions of the former county council were transferred to metropolitan district councils
area 1,290 sq km/498 sq mi
towns and cities Manchester, Bolton, Oldham, Rochdale, Salford, Stockport, and Wigan
features Manchester Ship Canal links it with the river Mersey and the sea; Old Trafford cricket ground at Stretford, and the football ground of Manchester United; a second terminal opened at Manchester Airport 1993
industries engineering, textiles, textile machinery, chemicals, plastics, electrical goods, electronic equipment, paper, printing, rubber, and asbestos
population (1991) 2,499,400

Manchu or ***Qing*** last ruling dynasty in China, from 1644 until its overthrow 1912; its last emperor was the infant ◊P'u-i. Originally a nomadic people from Manchuria, they established power through a series of successful invasions from the north, then granted trading rights to the USA and Europeans, which eventually brought strife and the ◊Boxer Rebellion.

Manchukuo former Japanese puppet state in Manchuria and Jehol 1932–45, ruled by the former Chinese emperor Henry ◊P'u-i.

Manchuria European name for the NE region of China, comprising the provinces of Heilongjiang, Jilin, and Liaoning. It was united with China by the Manchu dynasty 1644, but as the Chinese Empire declined, Japan and Russia were rivals for its control. The Russians were expelled after the ◊Russo-Japanese War 1904–05, and in 1932 Japan consolidated its position by creating a puppet state, ***Manchukuo***, nominally led by the Chinese pretender to the throne Henry P'u-i. At the end of World War II the Soviets occupied Manchuria in a two-week operation Aug 1945. Japanese settlers were expelled when the region was returned to Chinese control.

'The sun shall never set on so glorious a human achievement.'

Nelson Mandela
On the end of apartheid in South Africa, quoted in *Independent on Sunday* 14 May 1994

Mandaean member of the only surviving Gnostic sect of Christianity (see ◊Gnosticism). The Mandaeans live near the Euphrates, S Iraq, and their sacred book is the *Ginza*. The sect claims descent from John the Baptist, but its incorporation of Christian, Hebrew, and indigenous Persian traditions keeps its origins in dispute.

Mandalay chief city of the Mandalay division of Myanmar (formerly Burma), on the river Irrawaddy, about 495 km/370 mi N of Yangon (Rangoon); population (1983) 533,000. Founded by King Mindon Min 1857, it was capital of Burma 1857–85, and has many pagodas, temples, and monasteries.

Mandarin (Sanskrit *mantrin* 'counsellor') standard form of the ◊Chinese language. Historically it derives from the language spoken by mandarins, Chinese imperial officials, from the 7th century onwards. It is used by 70% of the population and taught in schools of the People's Republic of China.

mandarin duck kind of ◊duck, genus *Aix galericulata*, 40 cm/16 in long. The drake's head has a long, erectile crest, green, purple and chestnut in colour, and one of the wing-feathers is expanded to form an orange 'sail'. They were introduced to Britain from the Far East, and have established feral breeding populations in Surrey.

mandate in history, a territory whose administration was entrusted to Allied states by the League of Nations under the Treaty of Versailles after World War I. Mandated territories were former German and Turkish possessions (including Iraq, Syria, Lebanon, and Palestine). When the United Nations replaced the League of Nations 1945, mandates that had not achieved independence became known as ◊trust territories.

In general, mandate means any official command; in politics also the right (given by the electors) of an elected government to carry out its programme of policies.

Mandela Nelson (Rolihlahla) 1918– . South African politician and lawyer, president from 1994. President of the ◊African National Congress (ANC) 1991–97. Imprisoned from 1964, as organizer of the then banned ANC, he became a symbol of unity for the worldwide anti-◊apartheid movement. In 1990 he was released, the ban on the ANC having been lifted, and entered into negotiations with the government about a multiracial future for South Africa. In 1994 he was sworn in as South Africa's first post-apartheid president after the ANC won 62.65% of the vote in universal-suffrage elections. He shared the Nobel Peace Prize 1993 with South African president F W de Klerk.

Mandela was born near Umbata, S of Lesotho, the son of a local chief. In a trial of several ANC leaders, he was acquitted of treason 1961, but was once more arrested 1964 and given a life sentence on charges of sabotage and plotting to overthrow the government. In Feb 1990 he was released from prison on the orders of state president F W de Klerk and in July 1991 was elected, unopposed, to the presidency of the ANC. In Dec 1991 the ANC began constitutional negotiations with the government and in Feb 1993 Mandela and President de Klerk agreed to the formation of a government of national unity after free, nonracial elections (that took place in 1994). Relations between Mandela and de Klerk deteriorated when former members of de Klerk's security forces were prosecuted 1996.

Mandela married the South African civil-rights activist Winnie Mandela 1955. They separated 1992 and were divorced 1996. His autobiography, *Long Walk to Freedom* 1994 was widely acclaimed, and his state visit to Britain July 1996 was a resounding success.

Mandela South African politician and lawyer Nelson Mandela in July 1990, shortly after his release from prison. A powerful symbol of the black struggle against apartheid, Nelson Mandela was imprisoned for 27 years on a charge of conspiring to overthrow the South African government. On his release he was named head of the African National Congress and played a leading role in organizing the first multiracial elections April 1994 in which he was chosen as the first president of a free and democratically ruled South Africa. *Topham*

Mandela Winnie (Nomzamo) 1934– . Civil-rights activist in South Africa, former wife of Nelson Mandela. A leading spokesperson for the African National Congress (ANC) during Nelson Mandela's imprisonment 1964–90, in 1991 she received a six-year prison sentence for her role in the kidnapping and assault of four youths. Her sentence was later waived and in 1994, following the ANC's victory in the country's first universal suffrage elections, she was given a deputy ministerial post in the new government. In 1995 she was dismissed from her cabinet post, following allegations of dereliction of duty.

Mandelbrot Benoit B 1924– . Polish-born French mathematician who coined the term fractal to describe geometrical figures in which an identical motif repeats itself on an ever-diminishing scale. The concept is associated with ◊chaos theory.

Mandelstam Osip Emilevich 1891–1938. Russian poet. He was a leader of the Acmeist movement, which developed a neoclassical emphasis on clear words about demystified realities. The son of a Jewish merchant, he was sent to a concentration camp by the communist authorities in the 1930s, and died there. His posthumously published work, with its classic brevity, established his reputation as one of the greatest 20th-century Russian poets.

mandolin plucked string instrument with four to six pairs of strings (courses), tuned like a violin, which flourished 1600–1800. It takes its name from its almond-shaped body (Italian *mandorla* 'almond'). The ***Neapolitan mandolin***, a different instrument which appeared about 1750, is played with a plectrum and has metal strings.

mandragora or ***mandrake*** plant of the Old World genus *Mandragora* of almost stemless plants with narcotic properties, of the nightshade family Solanaceae. They have large leaves, pale blue or violet flowers, and globose berries known as devil's apples. The humanoid shape of the root of *M. officinarum* gave rise to the superstition that it shrieks when pulled from the ground.

mandrill large W African forest-living baboon *Mandrillus sphinx*, most active on the ground. It has large canine teeth, a bright red nose, and cheeks striped with blue. There are red callosities on the buttocks; the fur is brown, apart from a yellow beard.

Manes in ancient Rome, the spirits of the dead, worshipped as divine and sometimes identified with the gods of the underworld (Dis and Proserpine).

Manet Edouard 1832–1883. French painter. One of the foremost French artists of the 19th century, he is often regarded as the father of modern painting. Rebelling against the academic tradition, he developed a clear and unaffected realist style that was one of the founding forces of ◊Impressionism. His subjects were mainly contemporary, such as *A Bar at the Folies-Bergère* 1882 (Courtauld Art Gallery, London).

Manet received a very traditional academic art education under a history painter; his real influences were Goya, Velázquez, and Courbet. His *Déjeuner sur l'herbe/Picnic on the Grass* 1863 and *Olympia* 1865 (both Musée d'Orsay, Paris), though both based on Renaissance masterpieces, offended conservative tastes in their matter-of-fact treatment of the nude body. Though he never exhibited with the Impressionists – he had a classical sense of order and composition – many of them were were strongly influenced by his pioneering works, and he in turn, from the early 1870s, was influenced by figures such as Berthe ◊Morisot, his works becoming lighter in both touch and colour.

mangabey any of the Old World monkeys of the tropical African genus *Cercocebus*. The four species have long tails that can be used for support, although they are not fully prehensile.

manganese hard, brittle, grey-white metallic element, symbol Mn, atomic number 25, relative atomic mass 54.9380. It resembles iron (and rusts), but it is not magnetic and is softer. It is used chiefly in making steel alloys, also alloys with aluminium and copper, and is also used in fertilizers, paints, and industrial chemicals. It is a necessary trace element in human nutrition.

manganese ore any mineral from which manganese is produced. The main ores are the oxides, such as ***pyrolusite***, MnO_2; ***hausmannite***, Mn_3O_4; and ***manganite***, MnO(OH). Manganese ores may accumulate in metamorphic rocks or as sedimentary deposits, frequently forming nodules on the sea floor. The world's main producers are Georgia, Ukraine, South Africa, Brazil, Gabon, and India.

manganese (IV) oxide or ***manganese dioxide*** MnO_2 brown solid that acts as a depolarizer in dry batteries by oxidizing the hydrogen gas produced to water.

mangelwurzel or ***mangold*** variety of the common beet *Beta vulgaris* used chiefly as feed for cattle and sheep.

mango evergreen tree *Mangifera indica* of the cashew family Anacardiaceae, native to India but now widely cultivated for its oval fruits in other tropical and subtropical areas, such as the West Indies.

mangrove any of several shrubs and trees, especially of the mangrove family Rhizophoraceae, found in the muddy swamps of tropical and subtropical coasts and estuaries. By sending down aerial roots from their branches, they rapidly form close-growing mangrove thickets. Their timber is impervious to water and resists marine worms. Mangrove swamps are rich breeding grounds for fish and shellfish.

Manhattan island 20 km/12.5 mi long and 4 km/2.5 mi wide, lying between the Hudson and East rivers and forming a borough of the city of ◊New York, USA. It includes the Wall Street business centre, Broadway and its theatres, Carnegie Hall (1891), the World Trade Center (1973), the Empire State Building (1931), the United Nations headquarters (1952), Madison Square Garden, and Central Park. First settled by the Dutch who bought the island from Algonquin Indians 1626, it was ceded to the British 1674.

Manhattan Project code name for the development of the ◊atom bomb in the USA in World War II, to which the physicists Enrico Fermi and J Robert Oppenheimer contributed.

manic depression or ***bipolar disorder*** mental disorder characterized by recurring periods of either ◊depression or mania (inappropriate elation, agitation, and rapid thought and speech) or both. Sufferers may be genetically predisposed to the condition. Some cases have been improved by taking prescribed doses of ◊lithium.

Manichaeism religion founded by the prophet Mani (Latinized as Manichaeus, c. 216–276). Despite persecution, Manichaeism spread and flourished until about the 10th century. Based on the concept of dualism, it held that the material world is evil, an invasion of the spiritual realm of light by the powers of darkness; particles of divine light imprisoned in evil matter were to be rescued by messengers such as Jesus, and finally by Mani himself.

Mani proclaimed his creed in 241 at the Persian court. Returning from missions to China and India, he was put to death at the instigation of the Zoroastrian priesthood.

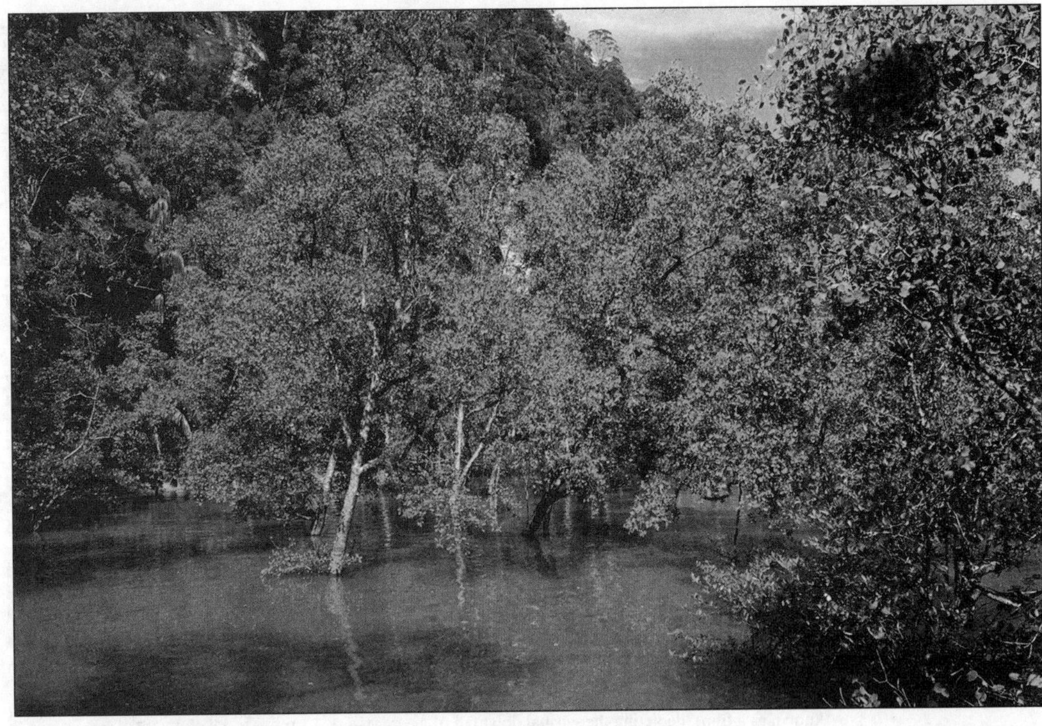

mangrove Trees of the Sonneratiaceae family such as these *Sonnerata alba* from Borneo are also known as mangroves, and often grow intermixed with the more familiar *Rhizophora* mangroves. The extensive root system in a mangrove swamp helps to trap mud and silt, preventing it from being washed out to sea. The trees are adapted to cope with the salt water that engulfs the roots at each high tide. *Premaphotos Wildlife*

manifesto in politics, the published prospectus of a party, setting out the policies that the party will pursue if elected to govern. When elected to power a party will often claim that the contents of its manifesto constitute a ◊mandate to introduce legislation to bring these policies into effect. In an unprecedented move, in 1996 the UK Labour Party put its manifesto to a pre-election ballot of its membership.

In art, a manifesto is a document setting out the aims and aspirations of an artistic movement. For example, the Futurists and the Surrealists published manifestoes.

Manila industrial port (textiles, tobacco, distilling, chemicals, shipbuilding) and capital of the Philippines, on the island of Luzon; population of the metropolitan area (including ◊Quezon City) 9,000,000 (1994); city (1990) 1,601,000.
history Manila was founded by Spain 1571, captured by the USA 1898; during World War II it was occupied by the Japanese 1942–45 and the old city to the south of the river Pasig was reduced to rubble in fighting between US and Japanese troops 1945. It was replaced as capital by Quezon City 1948–76.

manioc another name for the plant ◊cassava.

Manipur state of NE India
area 22,300 sq km/8,610 sq mi
capital Imphal
features Loktak Lake; original Indian home of polo
industries grain, fruit, vegetables, sugar, textiles, cement, handloom weaving
population (1994 est) 2,010,000 (30% are hill tribes)
language Manipuri, English
religion Hindu 70%
history administered from the state of Assam until 1947 when it became a Union Territory. It became a state 1972.

Manipuri one of the four main Indian dance styles (others are ◊Bharat Natyam, ◊Kathak, and ◊Kathakali). Originating in the northeast of India, it has its roots in folklore sources. Danced with a light, lyrical grace and uncomplicated technique by many dancers, its dramas are supported by dialogue and song.

Man, Isle of island in the Irish Sea, a dependency of the British crown, but not part of the UK
area 570 sq km/220 sq mi
capital Douglas
towns and cities Ramsey, Peel, Castletown
features Snaefell 620 m/2,035 ft; annual TT (Tourist Trophy) motorcycle races, gambling casinos, Britain's first free port, tax haven; tailless Manx cat
industries light engineering products; tourism, banking, and insurance are important
currency the island produces its own coins and notes in UK currency denominations
population (1991) 69,800
language English (Manx, nearer to Scottish than Irish Gaelic, has been almost extinct since the 1970s)
government crown-appointed lieutenant-governor, a legislative council, and the representative House of Keys, which together make up the Court of Tynwald, passing laws subject to the royal assent. Laws passed at Westminster only affect the island if specifically so provided
history Norwegian until 1266, when the island was ceded to Scotland; it came under UK administration 1765.

Man, Isle of

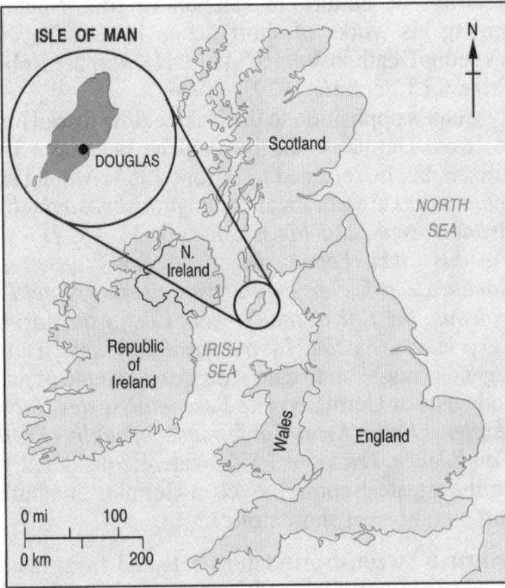

Manitoba prairie province of Canada
area 650,000 sq km/250,900 sq mi
capital Winnipeg
features lakes Winnipeg, Winnipegosis, and Manitoba (area 4,700 sq km/1,814 sq mi); 50% forested
exports grain, manufactured foods, beverages, machinery, furs, fish, nickel, zinc, copper, and the world's largest caesium deposits
population (1991) 1,092,600
history trading posts and forts were built here by fur traders in the 18th century. The first settlers were dispossessed Scottish Highlanders 1812. Known as the Red River settlement, it was administered by the Hudson's Bay Company until purchased by the new dominion of Canada 1869. This prompted the Riel Rebellion 1869–70. It was given the name

Manitoba

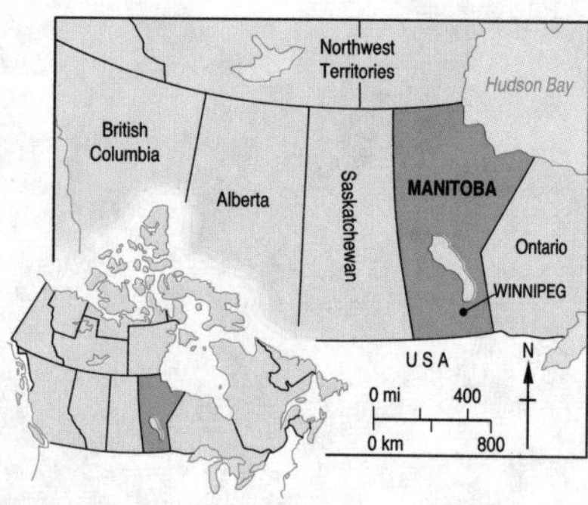

Manitoba when it became a province 1870. The area of the province was extended 1881 and 1912.

Manley Michael (Norman) 1924–1997. Jamaican politician, leader of the socialist People's National Party from 1969, and prime minister 1972–80 and 1989–92.

His father, ***Norman Manley*** (1893–1969), was the founder of the People's National Party and prime minister 1959–62.

Mann Heinrich 1871–1950. German novelist. He left Nazi Germany 1937 with his brother Thomas ◊Mann and went to the USA. His books include *Im Schlaraffenland/In the Land of Cockaigne* 1901; *Professor Unrat/The Blue Angel* 1904 (widely known as a film), depicting the sensual downfall of a schoolmaster; a scathing trilogy dealing with Kaiser Wilhelm II's Germany *Das Kaiserreich/The Empire* 1918–25; and two volumes on the career of Henry IV of France 1935–38. His novels show Germany in its new, vulgar prosperity from the end of the 19th century to the period just before World War I, and his best works were suppressed for a time.

Mann Thomas 1875–1955. German novelist and critic. A largely subjective artist, he drew his themes from his own experiences and inner thoughts. He was constantly preoccupied with the idea of death in the midst of life and with the position of the artist in relation to society. His first novel was *Buddenbrooks* 1901, a saga of a merchant family which traces through four generations the gradual growth of decay as culture slowly saps virility. *Der Zauberberg/The Magic Mountain* 1924, a vast symbolic work on the subject of disease in sick minds and bodies, and also the sickness of Europe, probes the question of culture in relation to life. Notable among his works of short fiction is 'Der Tod in Venedig/Death in Venice' 1913. He won the Nobel Prize for Literature 1929.

Mann's opposition to the Nazi regime forced him to leave Germany and in 1940 he became a US citizen, but he returned to Europe 1954. Among his other works are a biblical tetralogy *Joseph und seine Brüde/Joseph and his Brothers* 1933–43; *Doktor Faustus, das Leben des deutschen Tonsetzers Adrian Leverkuehn, erzählt von einem Freund/Dr Faustus: the Life of the German Composer Adrian Leverkuehn, as told by a Friend* 1947, the Faust legend brought up to date with a background of pre- and postwar Germany; *Die Bekenntnisse des Hochstaplers Felix Krull/Confessions of Felix Krull, Condidence Trickster* 1954, widely considered to be the greatest comic novel in German literature; and a number of short stories.

'Mannheim is a splendid town, both from its admirable buildings and the glossy neatness of the houses. They are too fine to live in, and seem only made to be looked at.'

On **Mannheim**
William Hazlitt *Notes of a Journey through France and Italy* 1826

manna sweetish exudation obtained from many trees such as the ash and larch, and used in medicine. The Old Testament (Exodus 16) relates that God provided manna for the Israelites in the desert when there was no other food. The manna of the Bible is thought to have been from the tamarisk tree, or a form of lichen.

Mannerheim Carl Gustav Emil von 1867–1951. Finnish general and politician, leader of the conservative forces in the civil war 1917–18 and regent 1918–19. He commanded the Finnish army in the fight against Soviet invasion 1939–40 and 1941–44, negotiated the peace settlement with the USSR, and was president of Finland 1944–46.

Mannerism in a general sense some idiosyncrasy, extravagance or affectation of style or manner in art, though it has more specific reference to Italian painting in the 16th century and represents a distinct phase between the art of the High Renaissance and the rise of Baroque. It was largely based on an admiration for Michelangelo and a consequent exaggeration of the emphasis of his composition and the expressive distortion of his figures.

Mannerist characteristics are an excessive muscularity or elongation of the figure; violent or strained gesture; crowded composition, often showing many discrepancies of proportion and scale; and a corresponding violence of colour. These tendencies developed in Florence, Rome, and Bologna, and the unrest they show may be partly related to the disturbing effect of the Reformation and also to the sack of Rome 1527, which upset the routine of many painters.

Mannheim Karl 1893–1947. Hungarian sociologist who settled in the UK 1933. In *Ideology and Utopia* 1929 he argued that all knowledge, except in mathematics and physics, is ideological, a reflection of class interests and values; that there is therefore no such thing as objective knowledge or absolute truth. He distinguished between ruling-class ideologies and those of utopian or revolutionary groups, arguing that knowledge is created by a continual power struggle between rival groups and ideas. Later works such as *Man and Society* 1940 analysed contemporary mass society in terms of its fragmentation and susceptibility to extremist ideas and totalitarian governments.

Manning Henry Edward 1808–1892. English priest, one of the leaders of the Oxford Movement. In 1851 he was converted from the Church of England to Roman Catholicism, and in 1865 became archbishop of Westminster. He was created a cardinal 1875.

Manoel I 1469–1521. King of Portugal from 1495, when he succeeded his uncle John II (1455–1495). He was known as 'the Fortunate', because his reign was distinguished by the discoveries made by Portuguese navigators and the expansion of the Portuguese empire.

manometer instrument for measuring the pressure of liquids (including human blood pressure) or gases. In its basic form, it is a U-tube partly filled with coloured liquid. Greater pressure on the liquid surface in one arm will force the level of the liquid in the other arm to rise. A difference between the pressures in the spaces in the two arms is therefore registered as a difference in the heights of the liquid in the arms.

manometer The manometer indicates gas pressure by the rise of liquid in the tube.

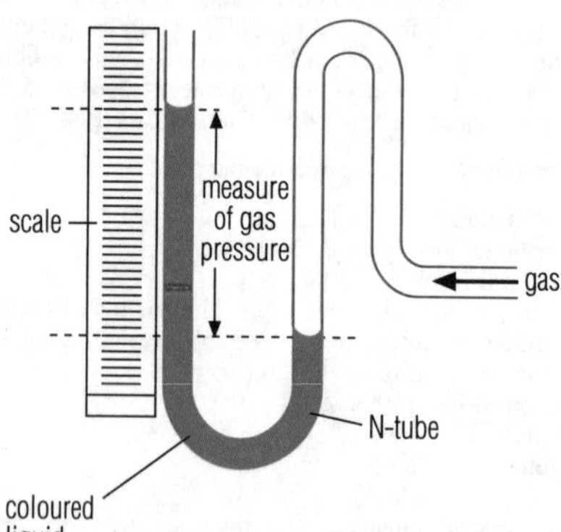

manor basic economic unit in ◊feudalism in Europe, established in England under the Norman conquest. It consisted of the lord's house and cultivated land, land rented by free tenants, land held by villagers, common land, woodland, and waste land.

Man Ray see Man ◊Ray.

Mansart Jules Hardouin-. See ◊Hardouin-Mansart, Jules.

Mansell Nigel 1954– . English motor-racing driver. He started his Formula One career with Lotus 1980. Runner-up in the world championship on two occasions, he became world champion 1992 and in the same year announced his retirement from Formula One racing, having won a British record of 30 Grand Prix races. He returned to Formula One racing 1994.

He joined the Newman–Haas team 1993 to compete in the PPG IndyCar championship series and won the championship in his debut season. He returned to Formula One racing in selected races 1994, and signed for Mercedes-McLaren 1995. However, after experiencing problems with Mercedes-McLaren cars during the 1995 season, he parted company with the team.

Mansfield industrial town (textiles, shoes, machinery, chemicals, coal) in Nottinghamshire, England, on the river Maun, 22 km/14 mi N of Nottingham; population (1991) 71,900.

Mansfield Katherine. Pen name of Kathleen Beauchamp 1888–1923. New Zealand writer. She lived most of her life in England. Her delicate artistry emerges not only in her volumes of short stories – such as *In a German Pension* 1911, *Bliss* 1920, and *The Garden Party* 1923 – but also in her 'Letters' and *Journal*. She married the critic John Middleton Murry 1913.

manslaughter in English law, the unlawful killing of a human being in circumstances less culpable than ◊murder – for example, when the killer suffers extreme provocation, is in some way mentally ill (diminished responsibility), did not intend to kill but did so accidentally in the course of another crime or by behaving with criminal recklessness, or is the survivor of a genuine suicide pact that involved killing the other person.

Mans, Le see ◊Le Mans.

Mansur lived c. 1700. Mogul painter. He started work at the court of ◊Akbar, contributing several miniatures to the *Akbar-nama* (a book of miniatures painted for the Mogul emperor), and later painted court scenes and portraits at the court of ◊Jahangir. He is best known for his animal paintings, which combine close observation and highly decorative stylization.

manta another name for ◊devil ray, a large fish.

Mantegna Andrea c. 1431–1506. Italian painter and engraver, one of the major figures of the early Renaissance. He painted religious and mythological subjects, his works noted for his frequent use of elements taken from Roman antique architecture and sculpture, for their hard, linear style, and for his innovative use of perspective and composition. *The Agony in the Garden* about 1455 (National Gallery, London) is among his best-known works.

Mantegna was born in Vicenza. He was brought up and trained by Francesco Squarcione at Padua, his master entering him in the guild of painters before he was 11. Like Squarcione, and indeed most N Italian artists, he was influenced by the scuptures of ◊Donatello at Padua, and he was later impressed by the paintings of the Florentines, ◊Uccello and Filippo ◊Lippi. The spirit of Florence is joined with that of Venice in Mantegna, for he was also influenced in style by Jacopo Bellini, whose daughter Lodovisia he married 1453.

Becoming the Gonzaga family's court painter in 1460, he painted the frescoes of the Camera degli Sposi (Bridal Chamber) in the Castello, which portrayed the Gonzaga family on the walls, and the first Renaissance illusionistic ceiling painting above. His Vatican frescoes of 1488 were later destroyed, but the series of tempera paintings of the *Triumphs of Caesar* 1490 for the Gonzagas survives at Hampton Court, London.

mantis any insect of the family Mantidae, related to cockroaches. Some species can reach a length of 20 cm/8 in. There are about 2,000 species of mantis, mainly tropical. Mantises are often called 'praying mantises' because of the way they hold their front legs, adapted for grasping prey, when at rest.

mantissa in mathematics, the decimal part of a ◊logarithm. For example, the logarithm of 347.6 is 2.5411; in this case, the 0.5411 is the mantissa, and the integral (whole number) part of the logarithm, the 2, is the ◊characteristic.

mantle intermediate zone of the Earth between the ◊crust and the ◊core, accounting for 82% of Earth's volume.

The boundary between the mantle and the crust above is the ◊Mohorovičić discontinuity, located at an average depth of 32 km/20 mi. The lower boundary with the core is the Gutenburg discontinuity at an average depth of 2,900 km/1813 mi.

The mantle is subdivided into ***upper mantle***, ***transition zone***, and ***lower mantle***, based upon the different velocities with which seismic waves travel through these regions. Seismic velocities in the upper mantle are overall less than those in the transition zone and those of the transition zone are in turn less than those of the lower mantle. Faster propagation of seismic waves in the lower mantle implies that the lower mantle is more dense than the upper mantle.

The mantle is composed primarily of magnesium, silicon, and oxygen in the form of ◊silicate minerals. In the upper mantle, the silicon in silicate minerals, such as olivine, is surrounded by four oxygen atoms. Deeper in the transition zone greater pressures promote denser packing of oxygen such that some silicon is surrounded by six oxygen atoms, resulting in magnesium silicates with garnet and pyroxene structures. Deeper still, all silicon is surrounded by six oxygen atoms so that the new mineral $MgSiO_3$-perovskite predominates.

Mantle Mickey Charles 1931–1995. US baseball player. Signed by the New York Yankees, he broke into the major leagues 1951. A powerful switch-hitter (able to bat with either hand), he also excelled as a centre-fielder. In 1956 he won baseball's Triple Crown, leading the American League in batting average, home runs, and runs batted in. He retired 1969 after 18 years with the Yankees and seven World Series championships.

mantra in Hindu or Buddhist belief, one or more symbolic sounds repeatedly intoned to assist concentration and develop spiritual power; for example, *om*, which in Hinduism represents the names of Brahma, Vishnu, and Siva. Followers of a guru may receive their own individual mantra.

Mantua (Italian ***Mantova***) capital of Mantua province, Lombardy, Italy, on an island of a lagoon of the river Mincio, SW of Verona; industry (chemicals, brewing, printing); population (1981) 60,866. The poet Virgil was born near Mantua, which dates from Roman times; it has Gothic palaces and a cathedral founded in the 12th century.

Manu in Hindu mythology, the founder of the human race, who was saved by ◊Brahma from a deluge.

Manuel II 1889–1932. King of Portugal 1908–10. He ascended the throne on the assassination of his father, Carlos I, but was driven out by a revolution 1910, and lived in England.

manufacturing base share of the total output in a country's economy contributed by the manufacturing sector. This sector has greater potential for productivity growth than the service sector, which is labour-intensive; in manufacturing, productivity can be increased by replacing workers with technically advanced capital equipment. It is also significant because of its contribution to exports.

Manutius or ***Manuzio*** Aldus 1449–1515. Italian printer, established in Venice (which he made the publishing centre of Europe) from 1490; he introduced ◊italic type and was the first to print books in Greek.

Manx Gaelic ◊Gaelic language of the Isle of Man.

Manzoni Alessandro, Count Manzoni 1785–1873. Italian poet and novelist. He was the author of the historical romance *I promessi sposi/The Betrothed* 1825–27, revised 1842, set in Spanish-occupied Milan during the 17th century. He also wrote the widely admired *Inni sacri/Sacred Hymns* 1812–22 and an ode to Napoleon, *Il cinque maggio/The Fifth of May* 1822. He is regarded as the greatest Italian novelist although later writers have often avoided his extreme romanticism. Verdi's *Requiem* commemorates him.

Maoism form of communism based on the ideas and teachings of the Chinese communist leader ◊Mao Zedong. It involves an adaptation of ◊Marxism to suit conditions in China and apportions a much greater role to agriculture and the peasantry in the building of socialism, thus effectively bypassing the capitalist (industrial) stage envisaged by Marx. In addition, Maoism stresses ideological, as well as economic, transformation, based on regular contact between party members and the general population.

Maori the Polynesian people of pre-European New Zealand, who numbered 294,200 in 1986, about 10% of the total population. Their language, Maori, belongs to the eastern branch of the Austronesian family.

The Maori colonized New Zealand from about AD 850, establishing a flourishing civilization throughout the country. First contact with Europeans came at the end of the 18th century. Until about 1860, relations between Maori and European settlers were generally good, though based on mutual economic exploitation rather than any great understanding. Though earlier treaties had confirmed Maori sovereignty, the Treaty of Waitangi 1840 and subsequent influx of settlers from Britain effectively ended Maori political autonomy. Recent years have seen a significant increase in Maori consciousness, demands for a comprehensive review of the Treaty, and Maori claims to some 70% of the country's land.

Mao Tse-tung alternative transcription of ◊Mao Zedong.

Mao Zedong or ***Mao Tse-tung*** 1893–1976. Chinese political leader and Marxist theoretician. A founder of the Chinese Communist Party (CCP) 1921, Mao soon emerged as its leader. He organized the ◊Long March 1934–35 and the war of liberation 1937–49, following which he established a People's Republic and communist rule in China; he headed the CCP and government until his death. His influence diminished with the failure of his 1958–60 ◊Great Leap Forward, but he emerged dominant again during the 1966–69 ◊Cultural Revolution. Mao adapted communism to Chinese conditions, as set out in his *Little Red Book*.

Mao, son of a peasant farmer in Hunan province, was once library assistant at Beijing University and a headteacher in Changsha. He became chief of CCP propaganda under the Guomindang (nationalist) leader Sun Yat-sen (Sun Zhong Shan) until dismissed by Sun's successor Chiang Kai-shek (Jiang Jie Shi). In 1931–34 Mao set up a communist republic in Jiangxi and, together with Zhu De, marshalled the Red Army in the Long March to Shaanxi to evade Guomindang suppressive tactics. In Yan'an 1936–47, he built up a people's republic and married his third wife ◊Jiang Qing 1939. CCP head from 1935, Mao set up an alliance with the nationalist forces 1936–45 aimed at repelling the Japanese invaders. Civil war with the Guomindang was renewed from 1946 to 1949, when Mao defeated them at Nanjing and established the People's Republic and CCP rule under his leadership. During the civil war, he successfully employed mobile, rural-based guerrilla tactics. Mao served as party head until his death Sept 1976 and as state president until 1959. After the damages of the Cultural Revolution, the Great Helmsman, as he was called, worked with his prime minister ◊Zhou Enlai to oversee reconstruction.

Mao's writings and thoughts dominated the functioning of the People's Republic 1949–76. He wrote some 2,300 publications, comprising 3 million words; 740 million copies of his *Quotations* have been printed. Adapting communism to Chinese conditions, he stressed the need for rural rather than urban-based revolutions in Asia, for reducing rural–urban differences, and for perpetual revolution to prevent the emergence of new elites. Mao helped precipitate the Sino-Soviet split 1960 and was a firm advocate of a nonaligned Third World strategy. After 1978, the leadership of Deng Xiaoping reinterpreted Maoism and criticized its policy excesses, but many of Mao's ideas remain valued.

Mao Zedong Mao Zedong was one of the founders of the Chinese Communist Party and the leader of the People's Republic of China 1949–76. *Image Select (UK) Ltd*

Mantegna *Samson and Delilah* by Mantegna (National Gallery, London). This is one of Mantegna's late works, one in a series of biblical subjects. Strikingly original, it is painted in monochrome (grisaille) to create the impression of sculpture. *Corbis*

map diagrammatic representation of an area – for example, part of the Earth's surface or the distribution of the stars. Modern maps of the Earth are made using satellites in low orbit to take a series of overlapping stereoscopic photographs from which a three-dimensional image can be prepared. The earliest accurate large-scale maps appeared about 1580.

Conventional aerial photography, laser beams, microwaves, and infrared equipment are also used for land surveying. Many different kinds of ◊map projection (the means by which a three-dimensional body is shown in two dimensions) are used in map-making. Detailed maps requiring constant updating are kept in digital form on computer so that minor revisions can be made without redrafting.

The ◊Ordnance Survey is the official body responsible for the mapping of Britain; it produces maps in a variety of scales, such as the Landranger series (scale 1:50,000). Large-scale maps – for example, 1:25,000 – show greater detail at a local level than small-scale maps; for example, 1:100,000.

'Letting a hundred flowers blossom and a hundred schools of thought contend is the policy for promoting progress in the arts and the sciences and a flourishing socialist culture in our land.'

MAO ZEDONG
Speech in Beijing, 27 Feb 1957

Mapai (Miphlegeth Poale Israel) Israeli Workers' Party or Labour Party, founded 1930. Its leading figure until 1965 was David Ben-Gurion. In 1968, the party allied with two other democratic socialist parties to form the Israeli Labour Party, led initially by Levi Eshkol and later by Golda Meir.

maple deciduous tree of the genus *Acer*, family Aceraceae, with lobed leaves and green flowers, followed by two-winged fruits, or samaras. There are over 200 species, chiefly in northern temperate regions. The ◊sycamore *A. pseudoplatanus* is native to Europe. The sugar maple *A. saccharum*, a North American species, is the source of maple syrup. *See illustration on following page.*

Mappa Mundi 13th-century symbolic map of the world. It is circular and shows Asia at the top, with Europe and Africa below and Jerusalem at the

maple Maples are typically deciduous with lobed leaves and winged fruit, or keys. They grow throughout the north temperate regions of the world. The leaves are often strikingly coloured in the autumn.

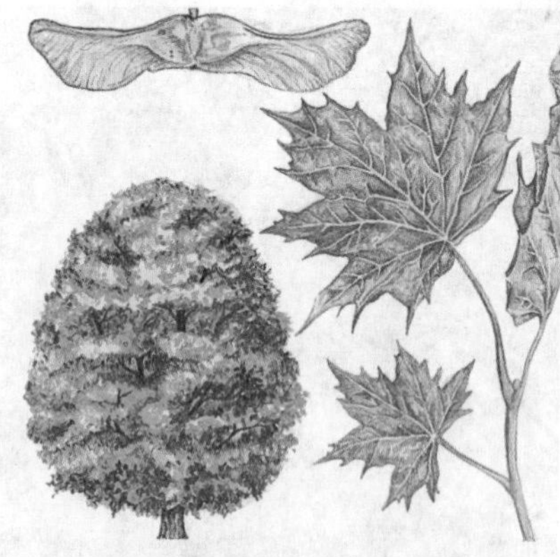

centre (reflecting Christian religious rather than geographical belief). It was drawn by David de Bello, a canon at Hereford Cathedral, England, who left the map to the cathedral, where it was used as an altarpiece.

Mapplethorpe Robert 1946–1989. US art photographer. He was known for his use of racial and homo-erotic imagery in chiefly fine platinum prints. He developed a style of polished elegance in his gallery art works, whose often culturally forbidden subject matter caused controversy.

map projection ways of depicting the spherical surface of the Earth on a flat piece of paper. Traditional projections include the ***conic***, ***azimuthal***, and ***cylindrical***. The most famous cylindrical projection is the ◊Mercator projection, which dates from 1569. The weakness of these systems is that countries in different latitudes are disproportionately large, and lines of longitude and latitude appear distorted.

In 1973 German historian Arno Peters devised the ***Peters projection*** in which the countries of the world retain their relative areas. In 1992 the US physicist Mitchell Feigenbaum devised the ***optimal conformal projection***, using a computer program designed to take data about the boundary of a given area and calculate the projection that produces the minimum of inaccuracies.

The theory behind traditional map projection is that, if a light were placed at the centre of a transparent Earth, the surface features could be thrown as shadows on a piece of paper close to the surface. This paper may be flat and placed on a pole (azimuthal or zenithal), or may be rolled around the equator (cylindrical), or may be in the form of a tall cone resting on the equator (conical). The resulting maps differ from one another, distorting either area or direction, and each is suitable for a particular purpose. For example, projections distorting area the least are used for distribution maps, and those with least distortion of direction are used for navigation charts.

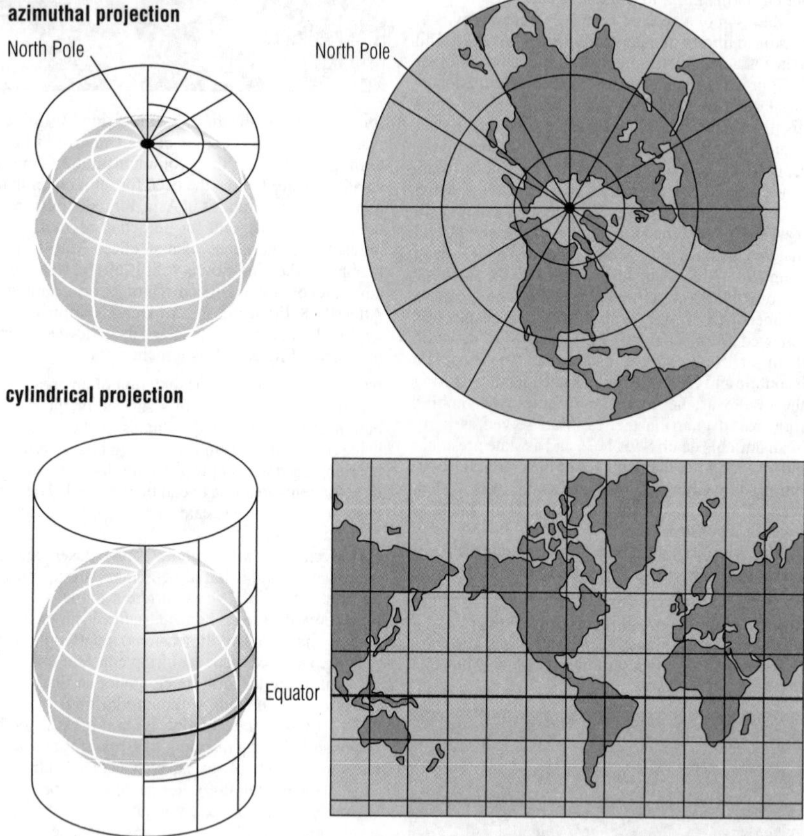

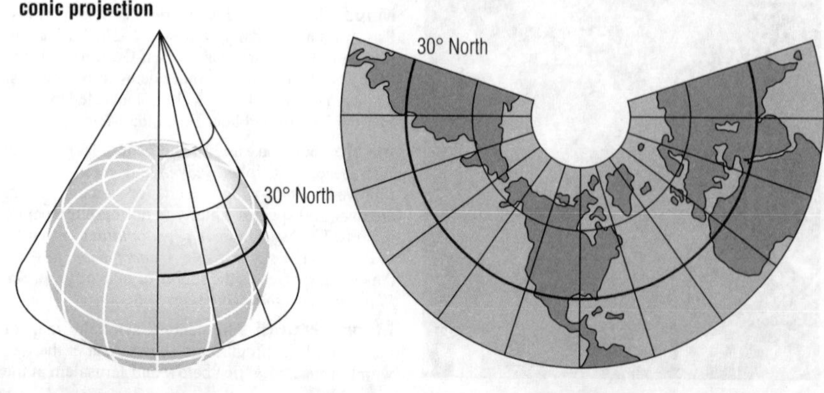

map projection Three widely used map projections. If a light were placed at the centre of a transparent Earth, the shapes of the countries would be thrown as shadows on a sheet of paper. If the paper is flat, the azimuthal projection results; if it is wrapped around a cylinder or in the form of a cone, the cylindrical or conic projections result.

Maputo formerly (until 1975) ***Lourenço Marques*** capital of Mozambique, and Africa's second-largest port, on Delagoa Bay; population (1993 est) 2,000,000. Linked by rail with Zimbabwe and South Africa, it is a major outlet for minerals, steel, textiles, processed foods, and furniture.

maquis mostly evergreen vegetation common in many Mediterranean countries, consisting of scrub woodland with many low-growing tangled bushes and shrubs, typically including species of broom, gorse, and heather.

Maquis French ◊resistance movement that fought against the German occupation during World War II.

Mara (Sanskrit 'killing') in Buddhism, a supernatural being who attempted to distract the Buddha from the meditations that led to his enlightenment. He embodies all distractions from the Buddhist path. In Hinduism, a goddess of death.

marabou stork *Leptoptilos crumeniferus* found in Africa. It is about 120 cm/4 ft tall, has a bald head, long heavy bill, and eats snakes, lizards, insects, and carrion. It has dark grey upperparts and white underparts, and has an inflatable throat pouch. The lack of feathers prevents blood clogging the plumage as it often feeds on carcasses left by predators such as lions.

Maracaña Stadium the world's largest football stadium, in Rio de Janeiro, Brazil, built 1950. It has a capacity of 175,000 but held a world record 199,854 spectators for the 1950 World Cup final between Brazil and Uruguay.

Maradona Diego Armando 1960– . Argentine footballer. One of the outstanding players of the 1980s, he won over 80 international caps, and helped his country to three successive ◊World Cup finals. He was South American footballer of the year 1979 and 1980. Despite his undoubted talent, his career was dogged by a series of drugs scandals, notably his disqualification from the 1994 World Cup after failing a drugs test.

Marat Jean Paul 1743–1793. French Revolutionary leader and journalist. He was elected to the National Convention 1792, where he carried on a long struggle with the right-wing ◊Girondins, ending in their overthrow May 1793. In July he was murdered by Charlotte ◊Corday, a member of the Girondins.

Maratha or ***Mahratta*** a people living mainly in Maharashtra, W India. There are about 40 million speakers of Marathi, a language belonging to the Indo-European family. The Maratha are mostly farmers, and practise Hinduism. In the 17th and 18th centuries the Maratha formed a powerful military confederacy in rivalry with the Mogul emperors. The latter's Afghan allies defeated the Maratha at Panipat 1761, and, after a series of wars with the British 1779–1871, most of their territory was annexed.

marathon athletics endurance race over 42.195 km/26 mi 385 yd. It was first included in the Olympic Games in Athens 1896. The distance varied until it was standardized 1924. More recently, races have been opened to wider participation, including social runners as well as those competing at senior level. The marathon derives its name from the story of Pheidippides, a Greek soldier who ran the distance of approximately 39 km/24 mi from the battlefield of Marathon to Athens with the news of a Greek victory over the Persians in 490 BC.

Leading marathons include the Boston Marathon 1897, New York Marathon 1970, Chicago Marathon 1977, and London Marathon 1981. In the 1980s, half marathons, over a distance of 21 km/13 mi 192.5 yd, became popular.

Marathon, Battle of battle at the start of the Persian Wars Sept 490 BC in which the Athenians and their allies from Plataea defeated the Persian king Darius' invasion force, on the Plain of Marathon about 40 km/25 mi northeast of Athens. The Persians were driven backwards into the sea and although most managed to re-embark into their ships, about 6,000 lay dead on the field, while Greek losses were under 200.

Marbella port and tourist resort on the Costa del Sol between Málaga and Algeciras in Andalucia, S Spain; population (1991) 80,645. There are three bullrings, a Moorish castle, and the remains of a medieval defensive wall.

marble rock formed by metamorphosis of sedimentary ◊limestone. It takes and retains a good polish, and is used in building and sculpture. In its pure form it is white and consists almost entirely of calcite $CaCO_3$. Mineral impurities give it various colours and patterns. Carrara, Italy, is known for white marble.

Marble Arch triumphal arch in London designed by John ◊Nash to commemorate Nelson's victories. Intended as a ceremonial entry to Buckingham Palace, in 1851 it was moved to Hyde Park at the end of Oxford Street.

Marburg disease or ***green monkey disease*** viral disease of central Africa, first occurring in Europe 1967 among research workers in Germany working with African green monkeys. Caused by a filovirus, it is characterized by haemorrhage of the mucous membranes, fever, vomiting, headache, and diarrhoea; mortality is high. It is a ◊haemorrhagic fever similar to Ebola virus disease.

Marc Franz 1880–1916. German Expressionist painter. He was associated with Wassily Kandinsky in founding the ◊*Blaue Reiter* movement. Animals played an essential part in his view of the world, and bold semi-abstracts of red and blue animals, particularly horses, are characteristic of his work.

Marceau Marcel 1923– . French mime artist. He is the creator of the clown-harlequin Bip and mime sequences such as 'Youth, Maturity, Old Age, and Death'.

Marchais Georges 1920–1997. Leader of the French Communist Party (PCF) 1972–94. Under his leadership, the party committed itself to a 'transition to socialism' by democratic means and entered into a union of the left with the Socialist Party (PS). This was severed 1977, and the PCF returned to a more orthodox pro-Moscow line, after which its share of the vote decreased.

Marche, Le (English ***the Marches***) region of E central Italy consisting of the provinces of Ancona, Ascoli Piceno, Macerata, and Pesaro e Urbino; capital Ancona; area 9,700 sq km/3,744 sq mi; population (1992 est) 1,434,000.

Marches boundary areas of England with Wales, and England with Scotland. In the Middle Ages these troubled frontier regions were held by lords of the Marches, sometimes called *marchiones* and later earls of March. The 1st Earl of March of the Welsh Marches was Roger de Mortimer (c. 1286–1330); of the Scottish Marches, Patrick Dunbar (died 1285).

March on Rome, the means by which Fascist leader Benito Mussolini came to power in Italy 1922. A protracted crisis in government and the threat of civil war enabled him to demand the formation of a Fascist government to restore order. On 29 Oct 1922, King Victor Emmanuel III invited Mussolini to come to Rome to take power. The 'march' was a propaganda myth: Mussolini travelled overnight by train from Milan to Rome, where he formed a government the following day, 30 Oct. Some 25,000 fascist Blackshirts were also transported to the city, where they marched in a ceremonial parade 31 Oct.

Marcian 396–457. Eastern Roman emperor 450–457. He was a general who married Pulcheria, sister of Theodosius II; he became emperor on Theodosius' death. He convened the Council of ◊Chalcedon (the fourth Ecumenical Council of the Christian Church) 451 and refused to pay tribute to Attila the Hun.

Marciano Rocky (Rocco Francis Marchegiano), known as the 'Brockton Blockbuster', 1923–1969. US boxer, world heavyweight champion 1952–56. He retired after 49 professional fights, the only heavyweight champion to retire undefeated.

Marconi Guglielmo 1874–1937. Italian electrical engineer and pioneer in the invention and development of radio. In 1895 he achieved radio communication over more than a mile, and in England 1896 he conducted successful experiments that led to the formation of the company that became Marconi's Wireless Telegraph Company Ltd. He shared the Nobel Prize for Physics 1909.

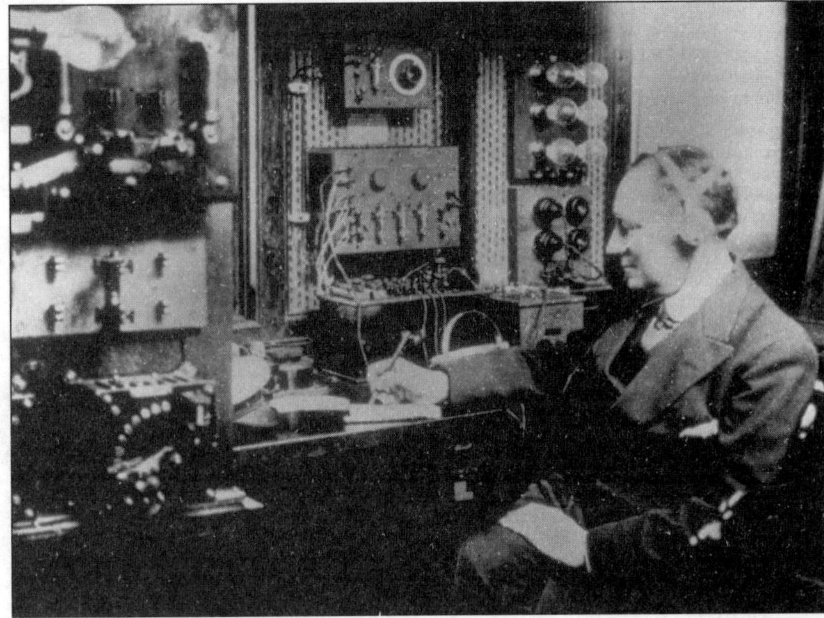

Marconi The Italian inventor Guglielmo Marconi on board his yacht *Elettra*, which was equipped as a floating laboratory. The equipment seen here was used to investigate new methods of maritime communication and navigation by wireless. *Marconi Company Ltd*

After reading about radio waves, Marconi built a device to convert them into electrical signals. He then tried to transmit and receive radio waves over increasing distances. In 1898 he successfully transmitted signals across the English Channel, and in 1901 established communication with St John's, Newfoundland, from Poldhu in Cornwall, and in 1918 with Australia.

Marconi Scandal scandal 1912 in which UK chancellor Lloyd George and two other government ministers were found by a French newspaper to have dealt in shares of the US Marconi company shortly before it was announced that the Post Office had accepted the British Marconi company's bid to construct an imperial wireless chain.

A parliamentary select committee, biased towards the Liberal government's interests, found that the other four wireless systems were technically inadequate and therefore the decision to adopt Marconi's tender was not the result of ministerial corruption. The scandal did irreparable harm to Lloyd George's reputation.

Marco Polo see ◊Polo, Marco.

Marco Polo bridge incident conflict 1937 between Chinese and Japanese army troops on the border of Japanese-controlled ◊Manchukuo and China that led to full-scale war between the two states. It lasted until the Japanese surrender 1945.

Marcos Ferdinand Edralin 1917–1989. Filipino right-wing politician, president 1965–86. His regime became increasingly repressive, with secret pro-Marcos groups terrorizing and executing his opponents. He was overthrown 1986 and forced into exile in Hawaii by a popular front led by Corazon ◊Aquino, widow of a murdered opposition leader, which obtained international and army support. He was backed by the USA when in power, but in 1988 US authorities indicted him and his wife Imelda Marcos for racketeering and embezzlement.

Marcos Imelda Romualdez 1930– . Filipino politician and socialite, wife of Ferdinand Marcos, in exile 1986–91 and known as the 'Iron Butterfly'. She was acquitted 1990 of defrauding US banks. Under indictment for misuse of Philippine state funds, she returned to Manila in 1991 and was an unsuccessful candidate in the 1992 presidential elections. She was convicted of corruption and sentenced to 18–24 years imprisonment 1993, but remained free on bail pending an appeal. In 1995 she was elected to the Philippines' House of Representatives by a landslide majority in her home province of Leyte.

Marcus Aurelius Antoninus adopted name of Marcus Annius Verus AD 121–180. Roman emperor from 161 and Stoic philosopher. He wrote the philosophical *Meditations*. Born in Rome, he was adopted by his uncle, the emperor Antoninus Pius, whom he succeeded in 161. He conceded an equal share in the rule to Lucius Verus (died 169).

Marcus Aurelius spent much of his reign warring against the Germanic tribes and died in Pannonia, where he had gone to drive back the invading Marcomanni.

Marcuse Herbert 1898–1979. German political philosopher, in the USA from 1934; his theories combining Marxism and Freudianism influenced radical thought in the 1960s. His books include *One-Dimensional Man* 1964.

Marcuse preached the overthrow of the existing social order by using the system's very tolerance to ensure its defeat; he was not an advocate of violent revolution. A refugee from Hitler's Germany, he became professor at the University of California at San Diego 1965.

Mardi Gras (French 'fat Tuesday' from the custom of using up all the fat in the household before the beginning of ◊Lent) Shrove Tuesday. A festival was traditionally held on this day in Paris, and there are carnivals in many parts of the world, including New Orleans, Louisiana; Italy; and Brazil.

Marduk in Babylonian mythology, the sun god, creator of Earth and humans.

mare (plural ***maria***) dark lowland plain on the Moon. The name comes from Latin 'sea', because these areas were once wrongly thought to be water.

Marengo, Battle of during the Napoleonic Wars, defeat of the Austrians 14 June 1800 by the French army under Napoleon Bonaparte, as part of his Italian campaign, near the village of Marengo in Piedmont, Italy. It was one of Napoleon's greatest victories which resulted in the Austrians ceding northern Italy to France. ▷*See feature on pp. 748–749.*

mare nostrum (Latin 'our sea') Roman name for the Mediterranean Sea.

Margaret (called ***the Maid of Norway***) 1283–1290. Queen of Scotland from 1285, the daughter of Eric II, King of Norway, and Princess Margaret of Scotland. When only two years old she became queen of Scotland on the death of her grandfather, Alexander III, but died in the Orkneys on the voyage from Norway to her kingdom.

Her great-uncle Edward I of England arranged her marriage to his son Edward, later Edward II. Edward declared himself overlord of Scotland by virtue of the marriage treaty, and 20 years of civil war and foreign intervention followed.

Margaret Rose 1930– . Princess of the UK, younger daughter of George VI and sister of Elizabeth II. In 1960 she married Anthony Armstrong-Jones, later created Lord Snowdon, but they were divorced 1978. Their children are David, Viscount Linley (1961–) and Lady Sarah Armstrong-Jones (1964–).

'I have spent more than half a lifetime trying to express the tragic moment.'

MARCEL MARCEAU
Quoted in the *Guardian* 11 Aug 1988

Margaret of Anjou 1430–1482. Queen of England from 1445, wife of ◊Henry VI of England. After the outbreak of the Wars of the ◊Roses 1455, she acted as the leader of the Lancastrians, but was defeated and captured at the battle of Tewkesbury

Let them eat cake.

MARIE ANTOINETTE
Attributed remark, on being told that the poor had no bread

1471 by Edward IV. Her one object had been to secure the succession of her son, Edward (born 1453), who was killed at Tewkesbury. After five years' imprisonment Margaret was allowed in 1476 to return to her native France.

Margaret, St c. 1045–1093. Queen of Scotland, the granddaughter of King Edmund Ironside of England. She went to Scotland after the Norman Conquest, and soon after married Malcolm III. The marriage of her daughter Matilda to Henry I united the Norman and English royal houses. Through her influence, the Lowlands, until then purely Celtic, became largely anglicized. She was canonized 1251 in recognition of her benefactions to the church.

margarine butter substitute made from animal fats and/or vegetable oils. The French chemist Hippolyte Mège-Mouries invented margarine 1889. Today, margarines are usually made with vegetable oils, such as soya, corn, or sunflower oil, giving a product low in saturated fats (see ◊polyunsaturate) and fortified with vitamins A and D.

Margate town and seaside resort on the north coast of Kent, SE England, on the Isle of Thanet; one of the original ◊Cinque Ports; population (1991) 56,700. Industries include textiles and scientific instruments. It developed as a seaside resort at the end of the 18th century, and has a fine promenade and beach.

margay small cat *Felis wiedi* found from southern USA to South America in forested areas. It is about 60 cm/2 ft long with a 40 cm/1.3 ft tail, has a rounded head, and has black spots and blotches on a yellowish-brown coat.

marginal cost or ***contribution cost*** for a business, the cost of producing an extra unit of output. For example, if a bakery increased its production from 10,000 loaves a day to 11,000 loaves a day, and its costs increased from £2,000 to £2,100, then the marginal cost of the extra 1,000 loaves would be £100. So the marginal cost of a loaf would be 10p.

marginal land in farming, poor-quality land that is likely to yield a poor return. It is the last land to be brought into production and the first land to be abandoned. Examples are desert fringes in Africa and mountain areas in the UK.

margrave German title (equivalent of marquess) for the 'counts of the march', who guarded the frontier regions of the Holy Roman Empire from Charlemagne's time. Later the title was used by other territorial princes. Chief among these were the margraves of Austria and of Brandenburg.

Margrethe II 1940– . Queen of Denmark from 1972, when she succeeded her father Frederick IX. In 1967, she married the French diplomat Count Henri de Laborde de Monpezat, who took the title Prince Hendrik. Her heir is Crown Prince Frederick (1968–).

marguerite European plant *Leucanthemum vulgare* of the daisy family Compositae. It is a shrubby perennial and bears white daisylike flowers. Marguerite is also the name of a cultivated variety of ◊chrysanthemum.

Marguerite of Navarre also known as ***Margaret d'Angoulême*** 1492–1549. Queen of Navarre from 1527, French poet, and author of the *Heptaméron* 1558, a collection of stories in imitation of Boccaccio's *Decameron*. The sister of Francis I of France, she was born in Angoulême. Her second husband 1527 was Henri d'Albret, king of Navarre.

Mariana Islands or ***Marianas*** archipelago in the NW Pacific E of the Philippines, divided politically into ◊***Guam*** (an unincorporated territory of the USA) and the ◊***Northern Mariana Islands*** (a commonwealth of the USA with its own internal government).

Mariana Trench lowest region on the Earth's surface; the deepest part of the sea floor. The trench is 2,400 km/1,500 mi long and is situated 300 km/200 mi E of the Mariana Islands, in the NW Pacific Ocean. Its deepest part is the gorge known as the Challenger Deep, which extends 11,034 m/36,210 ft below sea level.

Maria Theresa 1717–1780. Empress of Austria from 1740, when she succeeded her father, the Holy Roman emperor Charles VI; her claim to the throne was challenged and she became embroiled, first in

Mariana Islands

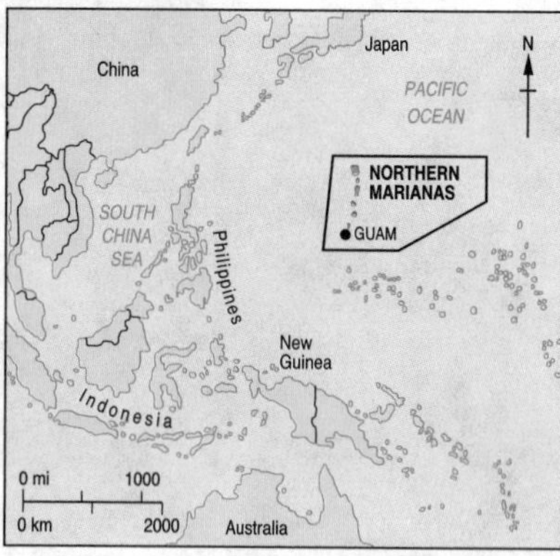

the War of the ◊Austrian Succession 1740–48, then in the ◊Seven Years' War 1756–63; she remained in possession of Austria but lost Silesia. The rest of her reign was peaceful and, with her son Joseph II, she introduced social reforms.

She married her cousin Francis of Lorraine 1736, and on the death of her father became archduchess of Austria and queen of Hungary and Bohemia. Her claim was challenged by Charles of Bavaria, who was elected emperor 1742, while Frederick of Prussia occupied Silesia. The War of the Austrian Succession followed, in which Austria was allied with Britain, and Prussia with France; when it ended 1748, Maria Theresa retained her heritage, except that Frederick kept Silesia, while her husband had succeeded Charles as emperor 1745. Intent on recovering Silesia, she formed an alliance with France and Russia against Prussia; the Seven Years' War, which resulted, exhausted Europe and left the territorial position as before. After 1763 she pursued a consistently peaceful policy, concentrating on internal reforms; although her methods were despotic, she fostered education, codified the laws, and abolished torture. She also expelled the Jesuits. In these measures she was assisted by her son, Joseph II, who became emperor 1765, and succeeded her in the Habsburg domains.

Marie 1875–1938. Queen of Romania. She was the daughter of the duke of Edinburgh, second son of Queen Victoria of England, and married Prince Ferdinand of Romania in 1893 (he was king 1922–27). She wrote a number of literary works, notably *Story of My Life* 1934–35. Her son Carol became king of Romania, and her daughters, Elisabeth and Marie, queens of Greece and Yugoslavia respectively.

Marie Antoinette 1755–1793. Queen of France from 1774. She was the daughter of Empress Maria Theresa of Austria, and married ◊Louis XVI of France 1770. Her reputation for extravagance helped provoke the ◊French Revolution of 1789. She was tried for treason Oct 1793 and guillotined.

Marie Antoinette influenced her husband to resist concessions in the early days of the Revolution – for example, ◊Mirabeau's plan for a constitutional settlement. She instigated the disastrous flight to Varennes, which discredited the monarchy, and welcomed foreign intervention against the Revolution, betraying French war strategy to the Austrians 1792.

Marie de' Medici 1573–1642. Queen of France, wife of Henry IV from 1600, and regent (after his murder) for their son Louis XIII. She left the government to her favourites, the Concinis, until Louis XIII seized power and executed them 1617. She was banished but, after she led a revolt 1619, ◊Richelieu effected her reconciliation with her son. When she attempted to oust him again 1630, she was exiled.

Mari E L autonomous republic of the Russian Federation
area 23,200 sq km/8,900 sq mi
capital Yoshkar-Ola
physical the Volga flows through the SW; 60% is forested; it is W of the Ural Mountains
industries timber, paper, grain, flax, potatoes, fruit
population (1992) 762,000; about 43% are ethnic Mari
history the Mari were conquered by Russia 1552. Mari was made an autonomous region 1920 and became an autonomous republic 1936.

Marie Louise 1791–1847. Queen consort of Napoleon I from 1810 (after his divorce from Josephine), mother of Napoleon II. She was the daughter of Francis I of Austria (see Emperor ◊Francis II) and on Napoleon's fall returned with their son to Austria, where she was granted the duchy of Parma 1815.

marigold any of several plants of the family Compositae, especially the genus *Tagetes*, including pot marigold *Calendula officinalis* and the tropical American *T. patula*, commonly known as French marigold.

marijuana dried leaves and flowers of the hemp plant ◊cannabis, used as a drug; it is illegal in most countries. Mexico is the world's largest producer.

marimba bass ◊xylophone of Latin American origin with wooden rather than metal tubular resonators.

Mariner spacecraft series of US space probes that explored the planets Mercury, Venus, and Mars 1962–75. *Mariner 1* (to Venus) had a failed launch. *Mariner 2* 1962 made the first fly-by of Venus, at 34,000 km/21,000 mi, confirmed the existence of ◊solar wind, and measured Venusian temperature. *Mariner 3* did not achieve its intended trajectory to Mars. *Mariner 4* 1965 passed Mars at a distance of 9,800 km/6,100 mi, and took photographs, revealing a dry, cratered surface. *Mariner 5* 1967 passed Venus at 4,000 km/2,500 mi, and measured Venusian temperature, atmosphere, mass, and diameter. *Mariner 6* and *7* 1969 photographed Mars' equator and southern hemisphere respectively, and also measured temperature, atmospheric pressure and composition, and diameter. *Mariner 8* (to Mars) had a failed launch. *Mariner 9* 1971 mapped the entire Martian surface, and photographed Mars' moons. Its photographs revealed the changing of the polar caps, and the extent of volcanism, canyons, and features, which suggested that there might once have been water on Mars. *Mariner 10* 1974–75 took close-up photographs of Mercury and Venus, and measured temperature, radiation, and magnetic fields. *Mariner 11* and *12* were renamed *Voyager 1* and *2* (see ◊Voyager probes).

marines fighting force that operates both on land and at sea. The British ***Corps of Royal Marines*** (1664) is primarily a military force also trained for fighting at sea, and providing commando units, landing craft, crews, and frogmen. The ***US Marine Corps*** (1775) is constituted as an arm of the US Navy. It is made up of infantry and air support units trained and equipped for amphibious landings under fire.

Marinetti (Emilio) Filippo Tommaso 1876–1944. Italian author. In 1909 he published *Manifesto del Futurismo*, the first manifesto of ◊Futurism, exhorting the youth of Italy to break with tradition in art, poetry, and the novel and face the challenges of a new machine age. His best-known work is the *Manifesto technico della letteratura futuristica/Technical Manifesto of Futurist Literature* 1912.

marionette type of ◊puppet, a jointed figure controlled from above by wires or strings. Intricately crafted marionettes were used in Burma (now Myanmar) and Ceylon (now Sri Lanka) and later at the courts of Italian princes in the 16th–18th centuries.

Maritain Jacques 1882–1973. French philosopher. Originally a disciple of Henri ◊Bergson, he later became the best-known of the neo-Thomists, applying the methods of Thomas ◊Aquinas to contemporary problems. Maritain distinguished three types of knowledge: scientific, metaphysical, and mystical. His works include *La philosophie bergsonienne/Bergsonian Philosophy* 1914 and *Introduction à la Philosophie/Introduction to Philosophy* 1920.

maritime law that part of the law dealing with the sea: in particular, fishing areas, ships, and navigation. Seas are divided into internal waters governed by a state's internal laws (such as harbours, inlets); ◊territorial waters (the area of sea adjoining the coast over which a state claims rights); the continental shelf (the seabed and subsoil that the coastal state is entitled to exploit beyond the territorial waters); and the high seas, where international law applies.

Marinetti A photograph of the Italian writer Marinetti (centre). Though he looks like a dapper businessman, Marinetti was an impassioned cultural revolutionary, calling for the destruction of traditional art and the creation of a new art based on permanent revolution and change. His views, particularly his belief in the value of war, became popular with the Fascists. *Corbis*

Marius Gaius c. 157–86 BC. Roman general and politician. He was elected consul seven times, the first time in 107 BC. He defeated the Cimbri and the Teutons (Germanic tribes attacking Gaul and Italy) 102–101 BC. Marius tried to deprive ◊Sulla of the command in the east against ◊Mithridates and, as a result, civil war broke out 88 BC. Sulla marched on Rome, and Marius fled to Africa, but later returned and created a reign of terror in Rome.

Marivaux Pierre Carlet de Chamblain de 1688–1763. French novelist and dramatist. His sophisticated comedies deal primarily with love and include *Le Jeu de l'amour et du hasard/The Game of Love and Chance* 1730 and *Les Fausses Confidences/False Confidences* 1737. He wrote two novels, *La Vie de Marianne/The Life of Marianne* 1731–41 and *Le Paysan parvenu/The Fortunate Villager* 1735–36, both unfinished.

Marivaux was a master of brilliant dialogue, full of veiled avowals and subtle indications, and he gave the word *marivaudage* (oversubtle lovers' conversation) to the French language.

marjoram aromatic herb of the mint family Labiatae. Wild marjoram *Origanum vulgare* is found both in Europe and Asia and has become naturalized in the Americas; the culinary sweet marjoram *O. majorana* is widely cultivated.

Mark in Celtic legend, king of Cornwall, uncle of ◊Tristan, and suitor and husband of ◊Isolde.

Mark Antony (Marcus Antonius) c. 83–30 BC. Roman politician and soldier. He served under Julius ◊Caesar in Gaul, and was consul with him in 44, when he tried to secure for Caesar the title of king. After Caesar's assassination, he formed the Second Triumvirate with Octavian (later ◊Augustus) and Lepidus. In 42 he defeated Brutus and Cassius at Philippi. He took Egypt as his share of the empire and formed a liaison with ◊Cleopatra, but in 40 he returned to Rome to marry Octavia, the sister of Octavian. In 32 the Senate declared war on Cleopatra, and Antony, who had combined forces with Cleopatra, was defeated by Octavian at the battle of Actium 31 BC. He returned to Egypt and committed suicide.

market any situation where buyers and sellers are in contact with each other. This could be a street market or it could be a world market where buyers and sellers communicate via letters, faxes, telephones, and representatives. In a perfect or ***free market***, there are many buyers and sellers, so that no single buyer or seller is able to influence the price of the product; there is therefore perfect competition in the market. In an ***imperfect market*** either a few buyers or sellers (or even just one) dominates the market.

market economy economy in which most resources are allocated through markets rather than through state planning. See ◊free enterprise.

market forces in economics, the forces of demand (a want backed by the ability to pay) and supply (the willingness and ability to supply).

market gardening farming system that specializes in the commercial growing of vegetables, fruit, or flowers. It is an ◊intensive agriculture with crops often being grown inside greenhouses on small farms. Market gardens may be located within easy access of markets, on the fringes of urban areas.

marketing promoting goods and services to consumers. The factors that help a firm to sell its products are known collectively as the marketing mix. Four elements – the four Ps – are normally distinguished: getting the right product to the market, at the right price; ensuring that the promotion in terms of advertising and marketing for the product is right; and ensuring that the product is distributed to the most convenient place for customers to buy it.

In the 20th century, marketing has played an increasingly larger role in determining company policy, influencing product development, pricing, methods of distribution, advertising, and promotion techniques.

market research process of gaining information about customers in a market through field research or desk research. ***Field research*** involves collecting primary data by interviewing customers or completing questionnaires. ***Desk research*** involves collecting secondary data by looking at information and statistics collected by others and published, for example, by the government.

markhor large wild goat *Capra falconeri*, with spirally twisted horns and long shaggy coat. It is found in the Himalayas.

Markievicz Constance Georgina, Countess Markievicz (born Gore Booth) 1868–1927. Irish nationalist who married the Polish count Markievicz 1900. Her death sentence for taking part in the Easter Rising of 1916 was commuted, and after her release from prison 1917 she was elected to the Westminster Parliament as a Sinn Féin candidate 1918 (technically the first British woman member of Parliament), but did not take her seat.

Markova Alicia. Adopted name of Lilian Alicia Marks 1910– . English ballet dancer. She danced with ◊Diaghilev's company 1925–29 and created a number of roles in Frederick ◊Ashton's early ballets, such as *Façade* 1931. She was the first resident ballerina of the Vic-Wells Ballet 1933–35, partnered Anton ◊Dolin in their own Markova–Dolin Ballet Company 1935–38, and danced with the Ballets Russes de Monte Carlo 1938–41, American Ballet Theater, USA, 1941–46, and the London Festival Ballet 1950–52. A dancer of delicacy and lightness, she is associated with the great classical ballets such as *Giselle*.

Markov chain in statistics, an ordered sequence of discrete states (random variables) $x_1, x_2, ..., x_i, ..., x_n$ such that the probability of x_i depends only on n and/or the state x_{i-1} which has preceded it. If independent of n, the chain is said to be homogeneous. It was formulated by Russian mathematician Andrei Markov (1856–1922).

Marks Simon, 1st Baron Marks of Broughton 1888–1964. English chain-store magnate. His father, Polish immigrant Michael Marks, had started a number of 'penny bazaars' with Yorkshireman Tom Spencer 1887; Simon Marks entered the business 1907 and built up a national chain of Marks and Spencer stores.

Mark, St lived 1st century AD. In the New Testament, Christian apostle and evangelist whose name is given to the second Gospel. It was probably written AD 65–70, and used by the authors of the first and third Gospels. He is the patron saint of Venice, and his emblem is a winged lion; feast day 25 April.

'Suffer the little children to come unto me.'

ST MARK
New Testament, Mark 10:14

marl crumbling sedimentary rock, sometimes called ***clayey limestone***, including various types of calcareous ◊clays and fine-grained ◊limestones. Marls are often laid down in freshwater lakes and are usually soft, earthy, and of a white, grey, or brownish colour. They are used in cement-making and as fertilizer.

Marlborough market town in Wiltshire, England, on the river Kennet, 122 km/76 mi W of London; population (1991) 6,400. There is engineering, tanning, and tourism. It is the site of Marlborough College (1843), a public school.

Marlborough John Churchill, 1st Duke of Marlborough 1650–1722. English soldier, created a duke 1702 by Queen Anne. He was granted the Blenheim mansion in Oxfordshire in recognition of his services, which included defeating the French army outside Vienna in the Battle of ◊Blenheim 1704, during the War of the ◊Spanish Succession.

In 1688 he deserted his patron, James II, for William of Orange, but in 1692 fell into disfavour for Jacobite intrigue. He had married Sarah Jennings (1660–1744), confidante of the future Queen Anne. He achieved further victories in Belgium at the battles of ◊Ramillies 1706 and Oudenaarde 1708, and in France at ◊Malplaquet 1709. However, the return of the Tories to power and his wife's quarrel with the queen led to his dismissal 1711 and his flight to Holland to avoid charges of corruption. He returned 1714.

Marley Bob (Robert Nesta) 1945–1981. Jamaican reggae singer and songwriter. A Rastafarian, his songs, many of which were topical and political, popularized reggae worldwide in the 1970s. They include 'Get Up, Stand Up' 1973 and 'No Woman No Cry' 1974; his albums include *Natty Dread* 1975 and *Exodus* 1977.

Marley Jamaican singer and guitarist Bob Marley, the first reggae artist to enjoy international success. A committed Rastafarian, he wrote of social and moral issues. In the 1970s, when he had become a national hero, he survived an attempt on his life. He was one of the major figures in the development of reggae, his style increasingly influenced by rock and African music. *Topham*

marlin The blue marlin is a very large, deep-shouldered seafish with a streamlined body. Its upper jaw is elongated into a distinct, spikelike snout. It may reach weights of as much as 900 kg/2,000 lb and is prized by game fishers. It is found throughout the warm and temperate seas and oceans of the world.

The core of Marley's band the Wailers was formed around 1960, and they began making local hits – 'Simmer Down' 1963, 'Rude Boy' 1965, 'Stir It Up' 1967, 'Trench Town Rock' 1971 – combining rock steady (a form of ska), soul, and rock influences. *Catch a Fire* 1972 was a seminal reggae album, but the international breakthrough came with *Burnin'* 1973, containing the song 'I Shot the Sheriff'. *Punky Reggae Party* 1977 was a nod to their British punk fans. Marley toured Africa 1978 and began to incorporate African elements in his music. His last album was *Uprising* 1980.

marlin or ***spearfish*** any of several genera of open-sea fishes known as billfishes, of the family Istiophoridae, order Perciformes. Some 2.5 m/7 ft long, they are found in warmer waters, have elongated snouts, and high-standing dorsal fins. Members of the family include the sailfish *Istiophorus platypterus*, the fastest of all fishes over short distances – reaching speeds of 100 kph/62 mph – and the blue marlin *Makaira nigricans*, highly prized as a 'game' fish.

'Stand still you ever-moving spheres of heaven, / That time may cease, and midnight never come.'
CHRISTOPHER MARLOWE
Doctor Faustus

Marlowe Christopher 1564–1593. English poet and dramatist. His work includes the blank-verse plays *Tamburlaine the Great* in two parts 1587–88, *The Jew of Malta* about 1591, *Edward II* about 1592 and *Dr Faustus* about 1594, the poem *Hero and Leander* 1598, and a translation of parts of ◊Ovid's *Amores*. Marlowe transformed the new medium of English blank verse into a powerful, melodic form of expression.

He was born in Canterbury and studied at Cambridge University, where he is thought to have become a government agent. His life was turbulent, with a brief imprisonment in connection with a man's death in a brawl (of which he was cleared), and a charge of atheism. He was murdered in a Deptford tavern, allegedly in a dispute over the bill, but it may have been a political killing.

Marlowe's work is remarkable for its varied, and even conflicting moods. *Hero and Leander* and the early play *Dido, Queen of Carthage* exhibit a sensuous sweetness and charm which is as peculiarly Marlovian as the mighty rhetoric and over-reaching egotism of *Tamburlaine* or *Dr Faustus*. In *The Jew of Malta* Machiavellian heroism stands side by side with farcical melodrama, while in *Dr Faustus* comic slapstick is followed by the thrilling poetry of the hero's final speeches.

Marmara, Sea of small inland sea separating Turkey in Europe from Turkey in Asia, connected through the Bosporus with the Black Sea, and through the Dardanelles with the Aegean; length 275 km/170 mi, breadth up to 80 km/50 mi.

marmoset small tree-dwelling monkey in the family Callithricidae, found in South and Central America. Most species have characteristic tufted ears, clawlike nails, and a handsome tail, and some only reach a body length of 18 cm/7 in. The tail is not prehensile. Some are known as tamarins.

'An optimist is a guy that has never had much experience.'
DON MARQUIS
'certain maxims of archy', *archy and mehitabel*

marmot any of several large burrowing rodents of the genus *Marmota*, in the squirrel family Sciuridae. There are about 15 species. They are found throughout Canada and the USA, and from the Alps to the Himalayas. Marmots live in colonies, make burrows (one to each family), and hibernate. In North America they are called ***woodchucks*** or ***groundhogs***.

Marne river in France which rises in the plateau of Langres and joins the Seine at Charenton near Paris; length 5,251 km/928 mi. It gives its name to the *départements* of Marne, Haute Marne, Seine-et-Marne, and Val de Marne.

Marne, Battles of the in World War I, two unsuccessful German offensives in northern France. In the ***First Battle*** 6–9 Sept 1914 German advance was halted by French and British troops under the overall command of the French general Jospeh Joffre; in the ***Second Battle*** 15 July–4 Aug 1918, the German advance was defeated by British, French, and US troops under the French general Henri Pétain, and German morale crumbled.

Maronite member of a Christian sect deriving from refugee Monothelites (Christian heretics) of the 7th century. They were subsequently united with the Roman Catholic Church and number about 400,000 in Lebanon and Syria, with an equal number scattered in S Europe and the Americas.

maroon (Spanish *cimarrón* 'wild, untamed') in the West Indies and Surinam, a freed or escaped African slave. Maroons were organized and armed by the Spanish in Jamaica in the late 17th century and early 18th century. They harried the British with guerrilla tactics. A peace treaty was signed 1739 between the Maroons and the British, granting the Maroons land and exemption from taxes.

Marprelate controversy pamphleteering attack on the clergy of the Church of England 1588 and 1589 made by a Puritan writer or writers, who took the pseudonym of ***Martin Marprelate***. The pamphlets were printed by John Penry, a Welsh Puritan. His press was seized, and he was charged with inciting rebellion and hanged 1593.

Marquand J(ohn) P(hillips) 1893–1960. US writer. Author of a series of stories featuring the Japanese detective Mr Moto, he later made his reputation with gently satirical novels of Boston society, including *The Late George Apley* 1937 (Pulitzer prize) and *H M Pulham, Esq* 1941.

Marquesas Islands (French ***Iles Marquises***) island group in ◊French Polynesia, lying N of the Tuamotu Archipelago; area 1,270 sq km/490 sq mi; population (1988) 7,500. The administrative headquarters is Atuona on Hiva Oa. The islands were annexed by France 1842.

marquess or ***marquis*** title and rank of a nobleman who in the British peerage ranks below a duke and above an earl. The wife of a marquess is a marchioness.

marquetry inlaying of various woods, bone, or ivory, usually on furniture, to create ornate patterns and pictures. ***Parquetry*** is the term used for geometrical inlaid patterns. The method is thought to have originated in Germany or Holland.

Márquez Gabriel García. See ◊García Márquez, Colombian novelist.

Marquis Don(ald Robert Perry) 1878–1937. US author. He is chiefly known for his humorous writing, including *Old Soak* 1921, which portrays a hard-drinking comic, and *archy and mehitabel* 1927, verse adventures typewritten by a literary cockroach.

marmoset The golden lion tamarin, a member of the marmoset family, is one of three species of tamarin found in the rainforests of SE Brazil. Tamarins live in family groups, in dense vegetation, 3–10 m/10–33 ft above the ground. They are gravely endangered by the loss of primary tropical forest.

Marrakesh historic city in Morocco in the foothills of the Atlas Mountains, about 210 km/130 mi S of Casablanca; population (1982) 439,700; urban area (1990) 665,000. It is a tourist centre, and has textile, leather, and food processing industries. Founded 1062, it has a medieval palace and mosques, and was formerly the capital of Morocco.

marram grass coarse perennial grass *Ammophila arenaria*, flourishing on sandy areas. Because of its tough, creeping rootstocks, it is widely used to hold coastal dunes in place.

Marrano (Spanish *marrano* 'pig') Spanish or Portuguese Jew who, during the 14th and 15th centuries, converted to Christianity to escape death or persecution at the hands of the ◊Inquisition. Many continued to adhere secretly to Judaism and carry out Jewish rites. During the Spanish Inquisition thousands were burned at the stake as 'heretics'.

marriage legally or culturally sanctioned union of one man and one woman (monogamy); one man and two or more women (polygamy); one woman and two or more men (polyandry). The basis of marriage varies considerably in different societies (romantic love in the West; arranged marriages in some other societies), but most marriage ceremonies, contracts, or customs involve a set of rights and duties, such as care and protection, and there is generally an expectation that children will be born of the union to continue the family line and maintain the family property. In the 1990s the concept of marriage was extended in some countries to include the blessing or registration of homosexual relationships.

In different cultures and communities there are various conventions and laws that limit the choice of a marriage partner. Restrictive factors include: age limits, below which no marriage is valid; degrees of consanguinity or other special relationships within which marriage is either forbidden or enjoined; economic factors such as ability to pay a dowry; rank, caste, or religious differences or expectations; medical requirements, such as the blood tests of some US states; the necessity of obtaining parental, family, or community consent; the negotiations of a marriage broker in some cultures, as in Japan or formerly among Jewish communities; colour – for example, marriage was illegal until 1985 between 'European' and 'non-European' people in South Africa, until 1967 between white and black people in some southern US states, and between white and Asian people in some western US states.

rights In Western cultures, social trends have led to increased legal equality for women within marriage: in England married women were not allowed to hold property in their own name until 1882; in California community property laws entail the equal division of all assets between the partners on divorce. Other legal changes have made ◊divorce easier, notably in the USA and increasingly in the UK, so that remarriage is more and more frequent for both sexes within the lifetime of the original partner.

law In most European countries and in the USA civil registration of marriage, as well as (or instead of) a religious ceremony, is obligatory. Common-law marriages (that is, cohabitation as man and wife without a legal ceremony) are recognized (for inheritance purposes) in, for example, Scotland and some states of the USA. As a step to international agreement on marriage law, the United Nations in 1962 adopted a convention on consent to marriage, minimum age for marriage, and registration.

In England marriages can be effected according to the rites of the Church of England or those of other faiths, or in a superintendent registrar's office.

marrow trailing vine *Cucurbita pepo*, family Cucurbitaceae, producing large pulpy fruits, used as vegetables and in preserves; the young fruits of one variety are known as courgettes.

Marryat Frederick (Captain) 1792–1848. English naval officer and writer. He was the originator of the British sea story. His adventure stories, taken from personal experience, are full of life, humour, and stirring narrative; they include *Peter Simple* 1834 and *Mr Midshipman Easy* 1836. He also wrote children's books, including *The Children of the New Forest* 1847.

Mars Mars as seen by a Viking space probe on its approach to the red planet. *National Aeronautical Space Agency*

Mars fourth planet from the Sun. It is much smaller than Venus or Earth, with a mass 0.11 that of Earth. Mars is slightly pear-shaped, with a low, level northern hemisphere, which is comparatively uncratered and geologically 'young', and a heavily cratered 'ancient' southern hemisphere
mean distance from the Sun 227.9 million km/141.6 million mi
equatorial diameter 6,780 km/4,210 mi
rotation period 24 hr 37 min
year 687 Earth days
atmosphere 95% carbon dioxide, 3% nitrogen, 1.5% argon, and 0.15% oxygen. Red atmospheric dust from the surface whipped up by winds of up to 450 kph/280 mph accounts for the light pink sky. The surface pressure is less than 1% of the Earth's atmospheric pressure at sea level.
surface The landscape is a dusty, red, eroded lava plain. Mars has white polar caps (water ice and frozen carbon dioxide) that advance and retreat with the seasons.
satellites two small satellites: ◊Phobos and Deimos.

There are four enormous volcanoes near the equator, of which the largest is Olympus Mons 24 km/15 mi high, with a base 600 km/375 mi across, and a crater 65 km/40 mi wide. To the east of the four volcanoes lies a high plateau cut by a system of valleys, Valles Marineris, some 4,000 km/2,500 mi long, up to 200 km/120 mi wide and 6 km/4 mi deep; these features are apparently caused by faulting and wind erosion. Recorded temperatures vary from −100°C/−148°F to 0°C/32°F.

Mars may approach Earth to within 54.7 million km/34 million mi. The first human-made object to orbit another planet was *Mariner 9*. *Viking 1* and *2*, which landed, also provided much information. Studies in 1985 showed that enough water might exist to sustain prolonged missions by space crews.

In 1996 NASA scientists revealed that analysis of Martian rock discovered in Antarctica suggested that simple forms of life may have existed on Mars 3 billion years ago. The rock, which entered the Earth's atmosphere in the form of a meteorite 12,000 years ago, was probably broken from the surface of Mars when the planet collided with a large object in space.

Mars in Roman mythology, the god of war, depicted as a fearless warrior. The month of March is named after him. He is equivalent to the Greek Ares.

Marsala port in W Sicily, Italy, notable for the sweet fortified wine of the same name; population (1980) 85,000. The nationalist leader Giuseppe ◊Garibaldi landed here 1860 at the start of his campaign to capture Sicily for Italy.

Marsalis Branford 1960– . US saxophonist. Born in New Orleans, he was taught by his father Ellis Marsalis, and played alto in Art Blakey's Jazz Messengers 1981, alongside his brother Wynton Marsalis. He was tenor/soprano lead saxophonist on Wynton's 1982 world tour, and has since recorded with Miles Davis, Tina Turner, and Dizzy Gillespie. His first solo recording was *Scenes in the City* 1983.

Marsalis Wynton 1961– . US trumpet player. He has recorded both classical and jazz music. He was a member of Art Blakey's Jazz Messengers 1980–82 and also played with Miles Davis before forming his own quintet. At one time this included his brother Branford Marsalis on saxophone.

'Marseillaise, La' French national anthem; the words and music were composed 1792 as a revolutionary song by the army officer Claude Joseph Rouget de Lisle (1760–1836).

Marseille (English ***Marseilles***) chief seaport of France, industrial centre (chemicals, oil refining, metallurgy, shipbuilding, food processing), and capital of the *département* of Bouches-du-Rhône, on the Golfe du Lion, Mediterranean Sea; population (1990) 807,700.

It is surrounded by hills and connected with the river Rhône by a canal, and there are several offshore islands including If. Its university was founded 1409. In 1991 a grotto was discovered near Marseille, accessible only by an underwater passage. It contains prehistoric wall paintings showing people and animals, which may date from 20,000–12,000 BC; at that time the cave would have been accessible by land as the sea-level was much lower.

Marsalis US virtuoso saxophonist Branford Marsalis. He has recorded with jazz greats Miles Davis and Dizzy Gillespie as well as pop stars Sting and Tina Turner. He has recorded arrangements of classical pieces by French and Russian composers with the English Chamber Orchestra. *CBS*

history Marseille was founded by mariners of Phocaea in Asia Minor 600 BC. Under the Romans it was a free city, and then, after suffering successive waves of invaders, became in the 13th century an independent republic, until included in France 1481. Much of the old quarter was destroyed by Germany 1943.

marsh low-lying wetland. Freshwater marshes are common wherever groundwater, surface springs, streams, or run-off cause frequent flooding or more or less permanent shallow water. A marsh is alkaline whereas a ◊bog is acid. Marshes develop on inorganic silt or clay soils. Rushes are typical marsh plants. Large marshes dominated by papyrus, cattail, and reeds, with standing water throughout the year, are commonly called ◊swamps. Near the sea, ◊salt marshes may form.

Marsh (Edith) Ngaio 1899–1982. New Zealand detective fiction writer. Her first detective novel *A Man Lay Dead* 1934 introduced her protagonist Chief Inspector Roderick Alleyn.

Marsh Rodney William 1947– . Australian cricketer who holds the world record for a wicket-keeper with 355 dismissals in Test cricket. A Western Australian, he originally played for his state as a batsman. As wicket-keeper, he claimed 355 victims in 96 tests from 1970 to 1984, many from the bowling of Dennis Lillee. He was the first player to reach a Test double of 3,000 runs and 300 dismissals.

marshal title given in some countries to a high officer of state. Originally it meant one who tends horses, in particular one who shoes them. The ◊Earl Marshal in England organizes state ceremonies; the office is hereditarily held by the duke of Norfolk. The corresponding officer in Scotland was the Earl Marischal.

marshal highest military rank in the British Royal Air Force. It corresponds to admiral of the fleet in the navy and field marshal in the army.

Marshall Alfred 1842–1924. English economist, a pioneer of ◊neoclassical economics. He stressed the importance of supply and demand for the determination of prices in markets, introducing the concept of elasticity of demand relative to price. He derived the relationship between demand for a product and its price from the concept of marginal utility, the extra satisfaction gained by a consumer from an additional purchase. His ideas are set out in *Principles of Economics* 1890.

Marshall George Catlett 1880–1959. US general and diplomat. He was army Chief of Staff in World War II, secretary of state 1947–49, and secretary of defence Sept 1950–Sept 1951. He foresaw the inevitability of US involvement in the war and prepared the army well for it. He initiated the ◊***Marshall Plan*** 1947 and received the Nobel Peace Prize 1953.

Marshall John Ross 1912–1988. New Zealand National Party politician, notable for his negotiations of a free-trade agreement with Australia. He was deputy to K J Holyoake as prime minister and succeeded him Feb–Nov 1972.

Marshall Islands country in the W Pacific Ocean, part of Micronesia, occupying 31 atolls (the Ratak and Ralik chains). *See country box on p. 678.*

Marshall Plan programme of US economic aid to Europe, set up at the end of World War II, totalling $13,000 billion 1948–52. Officially known as the European Recovery Programme, it was announced by Secretary of State George C ◊Marshall in a speech at Harvard June 1947, but it was in fact the work of a State Department group led by Dean ◊Acheson. The perceived danger of communist takeover in postwar Europe was the main reason for the aid effort.

Marshall Space Flight Center NASA installation at Huntsville, Alabama, where the series of ◊Saturn rockets and the space-shuttle engines were developed. It also manages various payloads for the space shuttle, including the ◊Spacelab space station.

marsh gas gas consisting mostly of ◊methane. It is produced in swamps and marshes by the action of bacteria on dead vegetation.

MARSHALL ISLANDS
Republic of the

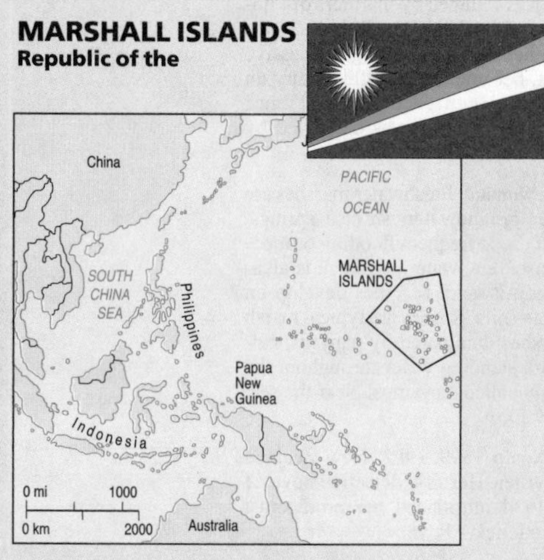

area 181 sq km/70 sq mi
capital Dalap-Uliga-Darrit (on Majuro atoll)
physical features comprises the Ratak and Ralik island chains in the W Pacific, which together form an archipelago of 31 coral atolls, 5 islands, and 1,152 islets
head of state and government Imata Kabua from 1997
political system liberal democracy
administrative divisions each inhabited atoll has its own system of local government
political parties no organized party system, but in 1991 an opposition grouping, the Ralik Ratak Democratic Party, was founded to oppose the ruling group
population 54,000 (1994 est)
population growth rate 2.9% (1990–95)
ethnic distribution 97% Marshallese, of predominantly Micronesian descent
literacy rate 93%
language Marshallese, English (both official)
religions Christian, mainly Protestant, and Baha'i
currency US dollar
GDP (US $) 69 million (1992)
growth rate 0.1% (1992)
exports copra, phosphates, fish, coconuts, tomatoes, melons, breadfruit; tourism is important

HISTORY
after c. 1000 BC Micronesians first settled the islands.
1529 Visited by Spanish navigator Miguel de Saavedra and thereafter came under Spanish influence.
1875 Spanish rule formally declared in face of increasing encroachment by German traders.
1885 German protectorate established.
1914 Seized by Japan on the outbreak of World War I.
1920–44 Administered under League of Nations mandate by Japan and vigorously colonized.
1944 Japanese removed after heavy fighting with US troops during World War II.
1946–63 Eniwetok and Bikini atolls used for US atom-bomb tests; islanders later demanded rehabilitation and compensation for the damage.
1947 Became part of United Nations (UN) Pacific Islands Trust Territory, administered by the USA.
1979 Amata Kabua elected president as internal self-government established.
1986 Compact of Free Association with USA granted islands self-government, with USA retaining responsibility for defence and security until 2001.
1990 UN trust status terminated.
1991 Independence agreed with Kabua as president; UN membership granted.
1996 Amata Kabua died.
1997 Imata Kabua, his cousin, elected president.

SEE ALSO Bikini; Eniwetok; Pacific Islands

'The country in town.'
MARTIAL *Epigrammata*

marsh marigold plant *Caltha palustris* of the buttercup family Ranunculaceae, also known as the kingcup. It grows in moist sheltered spots and has five-sepalled flowers of a brilliant yellow.

Marsilius of Padua c. 1270–c. 1342. Italian scholar and jurist. He studied and taught in Paris and in 1324 collaborated with John of Jandun (c. 1286–1328) in writing the *Defensor pacis/Defender of the Peace*, a plea for the subordination of the ecclesiastical to the secular power and for the right of the people to choose their own government. He played a part in the establishment of the Roman republic 1328 and was made archbishop of Milan.

Mars Observer NASA space probe launched 1992 to orbit Mars and survey the planet, its atmosphere, and the polar caps over two years. The probe was also scheduled to communicate information from the robot vehicles delivered by Russia's Mars 94 mission. The $1 billion project miscarried, however, when the probe unaccountably stopped transmitting Aug 1993, three days before it was due to drop into orbit.

Mars Pathfinder US spacecraft that landed in the Ares Vallis region of ◊Mars 4 July 1997. It carried a small six-wheeled roving vehicle called ***Sojourner*** which examined rock and soil samples around the landing site. Mars Pathfinder was the first to use air bags instead of retro-rockets to cushion the landing.

Marston John 1576–1634. English satirist and dramatist. His early plays, the revenge tragedies *Antonio and Mellida* and *Antonio's Revenge* 1599, were followed by a number of satirical comedies distinguished by their harsh and often sombre qualities. The first of these was *What You Will* 1601; *The Malcontent* 1604 and *The Dutch Courtesan* 1605 were among the most notable.

Marston also collaborated with dramatists George ◊Chapman and Ben ◊Jonson in *Eastward Hoe* 1605, which satirized the Scottish followers of James I, and for which the authors were imprisoned.

Marston Moor, Battle of battle fought in the English Civil War 2 July 1644 on Marston Moor, 11 km/7 mi W of York. The Royalists were conclusively defeated by the Parliamentarians and Scots.

The Royalist forces were commanded by Prince Rupert and the Duke of Newcastle; their opponents by Oliver Cromwell and Lord Leven. Lord Fairfax, on the right of the Parliamentarians, was routed, but Cromwell's cavalry charges were decisive.

'Is it to be understood that the principles of the Declaration of Independence bear no relation to half of the human race?'
HARRIET MARTINEAU 'Marriage' *Society in America*

marsupial (Greek *marsupion* 'little purse') mammal in which the female has a pouch where she carries her young (born tiny and immature) for a considerable time after birth. Marsupials include omnivorous, herbivorous, and carnivorous species, among them the kangaroo, wombat, opossum, phalanger, bandicoot, dasyure, and wallaby.

Martello tower circular tower for coastal defence. Formerly much used in Europe, many were built along the English coast, especially in Sussex and Kent, in 1804, as a defence against the threatened French invasion. The name is derived from a tower on Cape Mortella, Corsica, which was captured by the British with great difficulty 1794, and was taken as a model. They are round towers of solid masonry, sometimes moated, with a flat roof for mounted guns.

marten small bushy-tailed carnivorous mammal of the genus *Martes* in the weasel family Mustelidae. Martens live in North America, Europe, and temperate regions of Asia, and are agile climbers of trees. The ***sable*** *M. zibellina* lives in E Siberia, and provides the most valued fur. The largest marten is the ***fisher*** *M. pennanti* of North America, with black fur and reaching 125 cm/4 ft in length. The ***pine marten*** *M. martes*, Britain's rarest mammal, has long, brown fur and is about 75 cm/2.5 ft long.

Martens Wilfried 1936– . Prime minister of Belgium 1979–92, member of the Social Christian Party (CVP). He was president of the Dutch-speaking CVP 1972–79 and, as prime minister, headed several coalition governments in the period 1979–92, when he was replaced by Jean-Luc ◊Dehaene heading a new coalition.

Martí José Julian 1853–1895. Cuban revolutionary. Active in the Cuban independence movement from boyhood, he was deported to Spain 1871, returning 1878. Exiled again for continued opposition, he fled to the USA 1880, from where he organized resistance to Spanish rule. He was killed in battle at Dos Ríos, soon after proclaiming the uprising which led to Cuban independence.

Martí was chief of the Cuban Revolutionary Party formed 1892, and united Cubans in exile. In 1959 Fidel Castro cited him as the 'intellectual author' of the revolution, and he remains a national hero.

Martial (Marcus Valerius Martialis) c. AD 41–c. 104. Latin poet and epigrammatist. His poetry, often obscene, is keenly observant of all classes in contemporary Rome. Of his works the following survive: about 33 poems from *Liber Spectaculorum*, published AD 80 to commemorate the opening of the Colosseum; two collections of short mottoes entitled *Xenia* and *Apophoreta*, AD 84–85; and 12 books of *Epigrams*, published AD 86–102.

martial arts any of several styles of armed and unarmed combat developed in the East from ancient techniques and arts. Common martial arts include ◊aikido, ◊judo, ◊jujitsu, ◊karate, ◊kendo, and ◊kung fu.

martial law replacement of civilian by military authorities in the maintenance of order. In Britain, the legal position of martial law is ill-defined but, in effect, when war or rebellion is in progress in an area, the military authorities maintain order by summary means.

martin any of several species of birds in the swallow family, Hirundinidae, in the order Passeriformes. The European ***house martin*** *Delichon urbica*, a summer migrant from Africa, is blue-black above and white below, distinguished from the swallow by its shorter, less forked tail, and white band across the lower back. It is 12 cm/5 in long. Its cuplike mud nest is usually constructed under the eaves of buildings. Other species include the brownish European ***sand martin*** *Riparia riparia*, also a migrant from Africa, which tunnels to make a nest in sandy banks, and the North American ***purple martin*** *Progne subis*.

Martin John 1789–1854. English Romantic painter. He painted grandiose landscapes and ambitious religious subjects which – characterized by massive perspectives, gigantic crags, and towering battlements – have a nightmarish quality. *The Great Day of His Wrath* (Tate Gallery, London) is typical of his apocalyptic style.

Martin (John) Leslie 1908– . English architect. He was co-editor (with Naum ◊Gabo and Ben ◊Nicholson) of the review *Circle*, which helped to introduce the Modern Movement to England. With Peter Moro (1911–) and Robert Matthew (1905–1975), he designed the Royal Festival Hall, London, 1951. He was Professor of Architecture at Cambridge University 1956–72. In 1991 he received a RIBA award for his series of buildings for the Gulbenkian Foundation, Lisbon (completed 1984), which span a period of 30 years.

Martin five popes, including:

Martin V (born Oddone Colonna) 1368–1431. Pope from 1417. A member of the Roman family of Colonna, he was elected during the Council of Constance, and ended the Great Schism between the rival popes of Rome and Avignon.

Martin du Gard Roger 1881–1958. French novelist. He realistically recorded the way of life of the bourgeoisie in the eight-volume *Les Thibault/ The World of the Thibaults* 1922–40, which follows the story of two families, one Catholic and the other Protestant. His style is lucid, detailed, and restrained, and he places his narrative against an objectively researched background of contemporary events. Nobel Prize for Literature 1937.

Martineau Harriet 1802–1876. English journalist, economist, and novelist. She wrote popular works on economics; several novels, including *Deerbrook* 1839; children's stories, including *Feats on the Fiord* 1844; and articles in favour of the abolition of slavery. Her *Illustrations of Political Economy* 1832–34 consist of theoretical tracts roughly disguised as stories which reveal her passion for social reform. *Poor Laws and Paupers Illustrated* followed 1833–34. Other works include *Society in America* 1837.

Martinique French island in the West Indies (Lesser Antilles)

area 1,079 sq km/417 sq mi
capital Fort-de-France
features several active volcanoes; Napoleon's empress Josephine was born in Martinique, and her childhood home is now a museum
industries sugar, cocoa, rum, bananas, pineapples
population (1990) 359,600
language French (official), Creole
history Martinique was reached by Spanish navigators 1493, became a French colony 1635, an overseas department 1946, and from 1974 also an administrative region of France.

Martinique

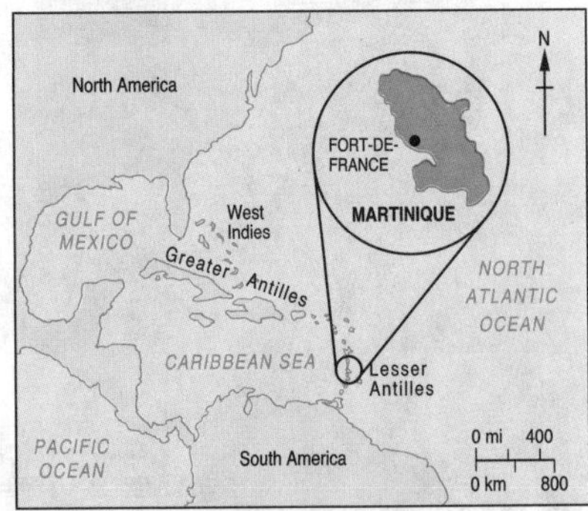

Martins Peter 1946– . Danish-born US dancer, choreographer, and ballet director. He was principal dancer with the New York City Ballet (NYCB) from 1969, its joint ballet master (with Jerome Robbins) from 1983, and its director from 1990. He is especially noted for his partnership with Suzanne Farrell, with whom he danced Balanchine's *Jewels* 1967. He retired from performing 1983, after partnering Farrell in *The Nutcracker*, to concentrate on choreography.

Martins trained at the Royal Danish Ballet School, joining the company 1965. He created roles in, among others, Robbins' *Goldberg Variations* 1971 and Balanchine's *Stravinsky Violin Concerto* and *Duo Concertante* both 1972, and has choreographed many ballets, for example, *Calcium Night Light* 1978.

Martin, St c. 316–c. 400. Bishop of Tours, France, from about 371, and founder of the first monastery in Gaul. He is usually represented as tearing his cloak to share it with a beggar. His feast day is Martinmas, 11 Nov.

Martinů Bohuslav Jan 1890–1959. Czech composer. He settled in New York after the Nazi occupation of Czechoslovakia 1939. His music is richly expressive, and has great vitality. His works include the operas *Julietta* 1937 and *The Greek Passion* 1959, symphonies, and chamber music.

martyr (Greek 'witness') one who voluntarily suffers death for refusing to renounce a religious faith. The first recorded Christian martyr was St Stephen, who was killed in Jerusalem shortly after the apostles began to preach.

Marvell Andrew 1621–1678. English metaphysical poet and satirist. His poems include 'To His Coy Mistress' written 1650–52 and 'An Horatian Ode upon Cromwell's Return from Ireland' 1650. He was committed to the Parliamentary cause, and was member of Parliament for Hull from 1659. He devoted his last years mainly to verse satire and prose works attacking aspects of the state and government, such as *An Account of the Growth of Popery and Arbitrary Government* 1677, a scathing review of Charles II's reign.

His reputation in his own day was as a champion of liberty and toleration, and as a polemicist. Today his reputation rests mainly on a small number of skilful and graceful but perplexing and intriguing poems, which were published posthumously as *Miscellaneous Poems* 1681. They include love lyrics, pastorals, and religious poems, executed with a compelling mixture of lyric grace and dialectical urgency and complexity.

'But at my back / I always hear / Time's wingèd chariot hurrying near. / And yonder all before us lie / Deserts of vast eternity.'

Andrew Marvell
'To His Coy Mistress'

Marvin Lee 1924–1987. US film actor. He began his career playing violent, often psychotic villains and progressed to playing violent, occasionally psychotic heroes. His work includes *The Big Heat* 1953, *The Killers* 1964, and *Cat Ballou* 1965.

Marx Karl Heinrich 1818–1883. German philosopher, economist, and social theorist whose account of change through conflict is known as historical, or dialectical, materialism (see ◊Marxism). His *Das Kapital/Capital* 1867–95 is the fundamental text of Marxist economics, and his systematic theses on class struggle, history, and the importance of economic factors in politics have exercised an enormous influence on later thinkers and political activists.

In 1844 Marx began his lifelong collaboration with Friedrich ◊Engels, with whom he developed the Marxist philosophy, first formulated in their joint works *Die heilige Familie/The Holy Family* 1844 and *Die deutsche Ideologie/German Ideology* 1846 (which contains the theory demonstrating the material basis of all human activity: 'Life is not determined by consciousness, but consciousness by life'). Both joined the Communist League, a German refugee organization, and in 1847–48 they prepared its programme, *The Communist Manifesto*. In the wake of the 1848 revolution, Marx was expelled from Prussia 1849.

He then settled in London, where he wrote *Die Klassenkämpfe in Frankreich/Class Struggles in France* 1849, *Die Achtzehnte Brumaire des Louis Bonaparte/The 18th Brumaire of Louis Bonaparte* 1852, *Zur Kritik der politischen Ökonomie/Critique of Political Economy* 1859, and his monumental work *Das Kapital/Capital*. In 1864 the International Working Men's Association was formed, whose policy Marx, as a member of the general council, largely controlled. Although he showed extraordinary tact in holding together its diverse elements, it collapsed 1872 owing to Marx's disputes with the anarchists, including the Russian ◊Bakunin.

Marx German social theorist Karl Marx spent more than half his life in London, where he studied in the British Library and wrote several books. His most famous work, *Das Kapital/Capital*, was interpreted and edited for publication by his lifelong friend Friedrich Engels, who had supported Marx and his family for many years. *Corbis*

Marx Brothers team of US film comedians: Leonard ***Chico*** (from the 'chicks' – women – he chased) 1891–1961; Adolph, the silent ***Harpo*** (from the harp he played) 1888–1964; Julius ***Groucho*** (from his temper) 1890–1977; Milton ***Gummo*** (from his gumshoes, or galoshes) c. 1892–1977, who left the team before they began making films; and Herbert ***Zeppo*** (born at the time of the first zeppelins) 1901–1979, part of the team until 1935. They made a total of 13 zany films 1929–49 including *Animal Crackers* 1930, *Monkey Business* 1931, *Duck Soup* 1933, *A Day at the Races* 1937, *A Night at the Opera* 1935, and *Go West* 1940.

Marxism philosophical system, developed by the 19th-century German social theorists ◊Marx and ◊Engels, also known as ***dialectical materialism***, under which matter gives rise to mind (materialism) and all is subject to change (from dialectic; see ◊Hegel). As applied to history, it supposes that the succession of feudalism, capitalism, socialism, and finally the classless society is inevitable. The stubborn resistance of any existing system to change necessitates its complete overthrow in the class struggle – in the case of capitalism, by the proletariat – rather than gradual modification.

Social and political institutions progressively change their nature as economic developments transform material conditions. The orthodox belief is that each successive form is 'higher' than the last; perfect socialism is seen as the ultimate rational system, and it is alleged that the state would then wither away. Marxism has proved one of the most powerful and debated theories in modern history, inspiring both dedicated exponents (Lenin, Trotsky, Stalin, Mao) and bitter opponents. It is the basis of ◊communism.

Marxism–Leninism term used by the Soviet dictator Stalin and his supporters to define their own views as the orthodox position of ◊Marxism as a means of refuting criticism. It has subsequently been employed by other communist parties as a yardstick for ideological purity.

Mary Queen of Scots 1542–1587. Queen of Scotland 1542–67. Also known as ***Mary Stuart***, she was the daughter of James V. Mary's connection with the English royal line from Henry VII made her a threat to Elizabeth I's hold on the English throne, especially as she represented a champion of the Catholic cause. She was married three times. After her forced abdication she was imprisoned but escaped 1568 to England. Elizabeth I held her prisoner, while the Roman Catholics, who regarded Mary as rightful queen of England, formed many conspiracies to place her on the throne, and for complicity in one of these she was executed.

Mary's mother was the French Mary of Guise. Born in Linlithgow (now in Lothian region,

'One morning I shot an elephant in my pajamas. How he got into my pajamas I'll never know.'

Groucho Marx
Animal Crackers, script by Morrie Ryskind

Marx Brothers US film and radio comedians; from top left Zeppo, Groucho, Chico, and Harpo. Their inspired, anarchic clowning lifted their films far above the frail plot lines. *Sachem*

❛Dirty British coaster with a salt-caked smoke stack, / Butting through the Channel in the mad March days.❜

JOHN MASEFIELD
'Cargoes'

Scotland), Mary was sent to France, where she married the dauphin, later Francis II. After his death she returned to Scotland 1561, which, during her absence, had become Protestant. She married her cousin, the Earl of ◊Darnley, 1565, but they soon quarrelled, and Darnley took part in the murder of Mary's secretary, ◊Rizzio. In 1567 Darnley was assassinated as the result of a conspiracy formed by the Earl of ◊Bothwell, possibly with Mary's connivance, and shortly after Bothwell married her. A rebellion followed; defeated at Carberry Hill, Mary abdicated and was imprisoned. She escaped 1568, raised an army, and after its defeat at Langside fled to England, only to be imprisoned again. A plot against Elizabeth I devised by Anthony Babington led to her trial and execution at Fotheringay Castle, Northamptonshire, 1587.

Mary (Hebrew ***Miriam***) in the New Testament, the mother of Jesus through divine intervention (see ◊Annunciation), wife of ◊Joseph. The Roman Catholic Church maintains belief in her ◊Immaculate Conception and bodily assumption into heaven, and venerates her as a mediator. Feast day of the Assumption is 15 Aug.

Mary Duchess of Burgundy 1457–1482. Daughter of Charles the Bold, Duke of Burgundy. She married Maximilian of Austria 1477, thus bringing the Low Countries into the possession of the Habsburgs and, ultimately, of Spain.

Mary Queen 1867–1953. Consort of George V of the UK. The daughter of the Duke and Duchess of Teck, the latter a grand-daughter of George II, in 1891 she became engaged to the Duke of Clarence, eldest son of the Prince of Wales (later Edward VII). After his death 1892, she married 1893 his brother George, Duke of York, who succeeded to the throne 1910.

Mary I (called ***Bloody Mary***) 1516–1558. Queen of England from 1553. She was the eldest daughter of Henry VIII by Catherine of Aragon. When Edward VI died, Mary secured the crown without difficulty in spite of the conspiracy to substitute Lady Jane ◊Grey. In 1554 Mary married Philip II of Spain, and as a devout Roman Catholic obtained the restoration of papal supremacy and sanctioned the persecution of Protestants. She was succeeded by her half-sister Elizabeth I.

Mary II 1662–1694. Queen of England, Scotland, and Ireland from 1688. She was the Protestant elder daughter of the Catholic ◊James II, and in 1677 was married to her cousin ◊William of Orange. After the 1688 revolution she accepted the crown jointly with William. During his absences from England she took charge of the government, and showed courage and resource when invasion seemed possible 1690 and 1692.

Maryland state of E USA; nicknamed Old Line State/Free State
area 31,600 sq km/12,198 sq mi
capital Annapolis
cities Baltimore, Silver Spring, Dundalk, Bethesda
features Chesapeake Bay, an inlet of the Atlantic Ocean; Assateague Island national seashore, a 60-km/37-mi barrier island; Annapolis, a world yachting centre, with the Maryland State House; Baltimore, with the Peale Museum (1814, the oldest museum in the USA) and the Basilica of the Assumption (1812, the oldest Roman Catholic cathedral in the USA); horse racing (the Preakness Stakes at Baltimore); the United States Naval Academy, Annapolis (1845); Johns Hopkins University, with a famous medical school, and the Peabody Institute for music; St John's College, Annapolis (1784)

Maryland

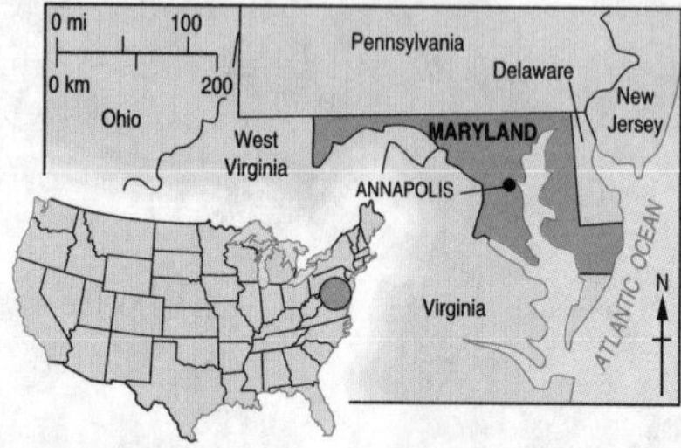

industries poultry, dairy products, machinery, steel, cars and parts, electric and electronic equipment, chemicals, fish and shellfish
population (1991) 4,860,000
history one of the original 13 states, first settled by English Catholics 1634; it became a state 1788. During the Civil War the state was largely occupied by Union troops because of its strategic location near Washington DC, and the Confederate armies three times invaded Maryland. In recent times the state has prospered from the growth of the federal government in nearby Washington and the redevelopment of Baltimore, whose port ranks second in handling foreign shipping.

Mary Magdalene, St lived 1st century AD. In the New Testament, a woman whom Jesus cured of possession by evil spirits. She was present at the Crucifixion and burial, and was the first to meet the risen Jesus. She is often identified with the woman of St Luke's gospel who anointed Jesus' feet, and her symbol is a jar of ointment; feast day 22 July.

Mary of Guise (or Mary of Lorraine) 1515–1560. French wife of James V of Scotland from 1538, and from 1554 regent of Scotland for her daughter ◊Mary Queen of Scots. A Catholic, she moved from reconciliation with Scottish Protestants to repression, and died during a Protestant rebellion in Edinburgh.

Mary of Modena (born Marie Beatrice d'Este) 1658–1718. Queen consort of England and Scotland. She was the daughter of the Duke of Modena, Italy, and married James, Duke of York, later James II, 1673. The birth of their son James Francis Edward Stuart was the signal for the revolution of 1688 that overthrew James II. Mary fled to France.

Mary Rose greatest warship of Henry VIII of England, which sank off Southsea, Hampshire, 19 July 1545. The wreck was located 1971, and raised for preservation in dry dock in Portsmouth harbour 1982. To prevent the wreck from drying out and crumbling it is sprayed continuously with cold water. In 1994 work began on coating the timber with waxy polymers to preserve it and enable controlled drying.

Masaccio (Tommaso di Giovanni di Simone Guidi) 1401–c. 1428. Florentine painter, one of the major figures of the early Italian Renaissance. His frescoes in the Brancacci Chapel of Sta Maria del Carmine, Florence, 1425–28 show a decisive break with traditional styles. He was the first painter to apply the scientific laws of perspective, newly discovered by the architect Brunelleschi, and achieved a sense of space and volume that gives his pictures a sculptural quality.

The frescoes in the Brancacci Chapel include scenes from the life of St Peter, notably *The Tribute Money*, and a moving account of *Adam and Eve's Expulsion from Paradise*. They have a monumental grandeur, without trace of Gothic decorative detail. Marking a return to the style of ◊Giotto, Masaccio's figures have solidity and weight and are clearly set in three-dimensional space.

Other works are the *Trinity* about 1428 (Sta Maria Novella, Florence) and the polyptych for the Carmelite church in Pisa 1426 (divided between National Gallery, London; Staatliche Museen, Berlin; Museo di Capodimonte, Naples). Although brief, his career marks a turning point in Italian art.

Masada rock fortress 396 m/1,300 ft above the western shore of the Dead Sea, Israel, site of the Hebrews' final stand in their revolt against the Romans (AD 66–73). After withstanding a year-long siege, the Hebrew population of 953 committed mass suicide rather than be conquered and enslaved. The site was excavated 1963–65, including the palace of Herod, and is now an Israeli national monument.

Masai an E African people whose territory is divided between Tanzania and Kenya, and who number about 250,000. They were originally warriors and nomads, breeding humped zebu cattle, but some have adopted a more settled life. Their cooperation is being sought by the Kenyan authorities to help in wildlife conservation. They speak a Nilotic language belonging to the Nilo-Saharan family.

Masaryk Tomáš Garrigue 1850–1937. Czechoslovak nationalist politician. He directed the revolutionary movement against the Austrian Empire, founding with Eduard Beneš and Stefanik the Czechoslovak National Council, and in 1918 was elected first president of the newly formed Czechoslovak Republic. Three times re-elected, he resigned 1935 in favour of Beneš.

After the communist coup 1948, Masaryk was systematically removed from public memory in order to reverse his semi-mythological status as the forger of the Czechoslovak nation.

Masaccio *The Virgin and Child 1426 by Masaccio (National Gallery, London). Though this picture seems formal and traditional, it was in its day revolutionary for Masaccio's use of perspective (newly discovered by his friend Brunelleschi), his firm modelling of the figures, and the realism with which he depicted both the Virgin and the Child.*
Corbis

Mascagni Pietro 1863–1945. Italian composer. His one-act opera *Cavalleria rusticana/Rustic Chivalry* was first produced in Rome 1890 in the new verismo or realistic style.

Masefield John 1878–1967. English poet and novelist. His early years in the merchant navy inspired *Salt Water Ballads* 1902 and two further volumes of poetry, and several adventure novels; he also wrote children's books, such as *The Midnight Folk* 1927 and *The Box of Delights* 1935, and plays. *The Everlasting Mercy* 1911, characterized by its forcefully colloquial language, and *Reynard the Fox* 1919 are long verse narratives. His other works include the novels *Jim Davis* 1911 and *Sard Harker* 1924, and the play *The Tragedy of Nan* 1908. *Collected Poems* was first published 1923. He was poet laureate from 1930.

Masekela Hugh 1939– . South African trumpet player. Exiled from his homeland 1960–90, he has recorded jazz, rock, and mbaqanga (township jive). His albums include *Techno-Bush* 1984. An opponent of apartheid, he left South Africa with his wife, singer Miriam ◊Makeba.

maser (acronym for ***microwave amplification by stimulated emission of radiation***) in physics, a high-frequency microwave amplifier or oscillator in which the signal to be amplified is used to stimulate excited atoms into emitting energy at the same frequency. Atoms or molecules are raised to a higher energy level and then allowed to lose this energy by radiation emitted at a precise frequency. The principle has been extended to other parts of the electromagnetic spectrum as, for example, in the ◊laser.

The two-level ammonia-gas maser was first suggested 1954 by US physicist Charles Townes at Columbia University, New York, and independently the same year by Nikolai Basov and Aleksandr Prokhorov in Russia. The solid-state three-level maser, the most sensitive amplifier known, was envisaged by Nicolaas Bloembergen (1920–) at Harvard 1956. The ammonia maser is used as a frequency standard oscillator (see ◊clock), and the three-level maser as a receiver for satellite communications and radio astronomy.

Maserati Italian racing-car company founded 1926 by the six Maserati brothers. The most outstanding Maserati was the 250F Grand Prix car, which the Argentine Juan Manuel Fangio drove during his world-championship-winning year 1957. The company withdrew from Grand Prix racing at the end of 1957.

Maseru capital of Lesotho, S Africa, on the Caledon River; population (1992 est) 367,000. Founded 1869, it is a centre for trade and diamond processing.

Mashraq (Arabic 'east') the Arab countries of the E Mediterranean: Egypt, Sudan, Jordan, Syria, and Lebanon. The term is contrasted with ◊Maghreb, comprising the Arab countries of NW Africa.

Masire Quett Ketumile Joni 1925– . President of Botswana from 1980. In 1962, with Seretse ◊Khama, he founded the Botswana Democratic Party (BDP) and in 1965 was made deputy prime minister. After independence 1966, he became vice president and, on Khama's death 1980, president, continuing a policy of nonalignment. A centrist, he has helped Botswana become one of the most stable states in Africa.

mask artificial covering for part or all of the face, or for the whole head, associated with ritual or theatrical performances in many cultures. Theatrical traditions using masks include ancient Greek drama (full head masks), Japanese Nō (facial masks), and the Italian commedia dell'arte (caricatured half-masks). In the 20th century masked performance has been re-explored in experimental and mainstream theatrical productions.

In many cultures masks are an important aspect of the religious and social life of the society. They often take the form of animals, sometimes representing totemic ancestors, human beings, or spirits, and can be realistic or abstract. The form of mask is often determined by tradition; in some the mask itself is sacred and is thought to have supernatural powers, in others the wearer is thought to be possessed by the spirit represented by the mask.

Death or funerary masks, made in the likeness of the dead person, are often associated with a belief in the return of the spirit.

Maskelyne Nevil 1732–1811. English astronomer, Astronomer Royal 1765–1811. He made observations to investigate the reliability of the lunar distance method for determining longitude at sea. In 1774 he estimated the mass of the Earth by noting the deflection of a plumb line near Mount Schiehallion in Perthshire, Scotland. He began publication 1766 of the *Nautical Almanac*. This contained astronomical tables and navigational aids, and was probably his most enduring contribution to astronomy.

masochism desire to subject oneself to physical or mental pain, humiliation, or punishment, for erotic pleasure, to alleviate guilt, or out of destructive impulses turned inwards. The term is derived from Leopold von Sacher-Masoch (1836–1895).

Mason James Neville 1909–1984. English film actor. He portrayed romantic villains in British films of the 1940s. After *Odd Man Out* 1947 he worked in the USA, often playing intelligent but troubled, vulnerable men, notably in *A Star Is Born* 1954. He returned to Europe 1960, where he made *Lolita* 1962, *Georgy Girl* 1966, and *Cross of Iron* 1977. Other films include *The Wicked Lady* 1946, *Five Fingers* 1952 and *North by Northwest* 1959. His final role was in *The Shooting Party* 1984.

Mason–Dixon Line in the USA, the boundary line between Maryland and Pennsylvania (latitude 39° 43′ 26.3″ N), named after Charles Mason (1730–1787) and Jeremiah Dixon (died 1777), English astronomers and surveyors who surveyed it 1763–67. It was popularly seen as dividing the North from the South.

masonry the craft of constructing stonework walls. The various styles of masonry include random rubblework, irregular stones arranged according to fit; coursed rubblework, irregular stones placed in broad horizontal bands, or courses; ashlar masonry, smooth, square-cut stones arranged in courses; Cyclopean masonry, large polygonal stones cut to fit each other; and rustification, large stones separated by deep joints and chiselled or hammered into a variety of styles. Rustification is usually employed at the base of buildings, on top of an ashlar base, to give an appearance of added strength.

Masai The Masai, Kenya. There are around 250,000 Masai living in Tanzania and Kenya. *Image Select (UK) Ltd*

masque spectacular and essentially aristocratic entertainment with a fantastic or mythological theme in which music, dance, and extravagant costumes and scenic design figured larger than plot. Originating in Italy, where members of the court actively participated in the performances, the masque reached its height of popularity at the English court between 1600 and 1640, with the collaboration of Ben ◊Jonson as writer and Inigo ◊Jones as stage designer. John Milton also wrote masque verses. Composers included Thomas Campion, John Coperario, Henry Lawes, William Byrd, and Henry Purcell.

The masque had great influence on the development of ballet and opera, and the elaborate frame in which it was performed developed into the proscenium arch.

mass in physics, the quantity of matter in a body as measured by its inertia. Mass determines the acceleration produced in a body by a given force acting on it, the acceleration being inversely proportional to the mass of the body. The mass also determines the force exerted on a body by ◊gravity on Earth, although this attraction varies slightly from place to place. In the SI system, the base unit of mass is the kilogram.

At a given place, equal masses experience equal gravitational forces, which are known as the weights of the bodies. Masses may, therefore, be compared by comparing the weights of bodies at the same place.

Mass in Christianity, the celebration of the ◊Eucharist.

Mass in music, the setting of the invariable parts of the Christian Mass, that is the *Kyrie*, *Gloria*, *Credo*, *Sanctus* with *Benedictus*, and *Agnus Dei*. A notable example is J S Bach's *Mass in B Minor*.

Massachusetts state of the northeastern USA; nicknamed Bay State/Old Colony State
area 21,500 sq km/8,299 sq mi
capital Boston
towns and cities Worcester, Springfield, New Bedford, Brockton, Cambridge
population (1991) 5,996,000
features the Berkshire Hills; Cape Cod national seashore; the islands of Nantucket and Martha's Vineyard, former whaling ports; Plymouth, with Mayflower II; Minute Man national historical park and battlefields of Lexington and Concord; Salem, site of 1690s witch trials; New Bedford Whaling Museum; Hancock Shaker Village; Provincetown, with the Pilgrim Monument commemorating the landing of the Pilgrims 1620; Harvard University (Harvard College 1636), and Massachusetts Institute of Technology (MIT) in Cambridge; Mount Holyoake College (1837), the first women's college in the USA; Tanglewood Music Festival, summer home of the Boston Symphony Orchestra; the Museum of Fine Arts and the Isabella Stewart Gardner Museum, Boston; National Basketball Hall of Fame, Springfield
industries electronic, communications, and optical equipment; precision instruments; nonelectrical machinery; fish; cranberries; dairy products
history one of the original 13 states, it was first settled 1620 by the Pilgrims at Plymouth. After the ◊Boston Tea Party 1773, the American Revolution began at Lexington and Concord 19 April 1775, and the British evacuated Boston the following year. Massachusetts became a state 1788.

Massachusetts

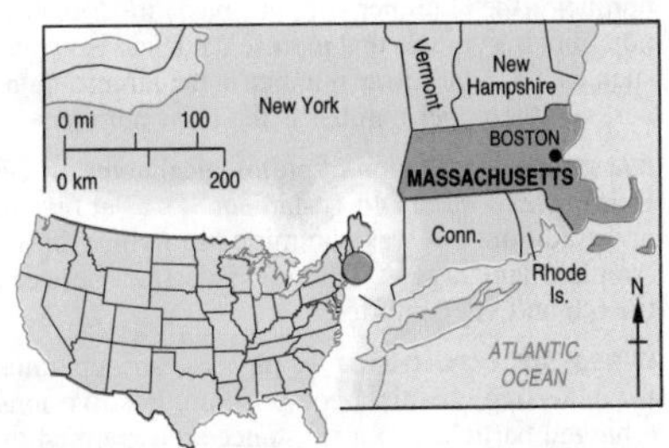

mass action, law of in chemistry, a law stating that at a given temperature the rate at which a chemical reaction takes place is proportional to the product of the active masses of the reactants. The active mass is taken to be the molar concentration of the each reactant.

massage manipulation of the soft tissues of the body, the muscles, ligaments, and tendons, either to encourage the healing of specific injuries or to produce the general beneficial effects of relaxing muscular tension, stimulating blood circulation, and improving the tone and strength of the skin and muscles. The benefits of massage were known to the ancient Chinese, Egyptian, and Greek cultures. The techniques most widely practised today were developed by the Swedish physician Per Henrik Ling (1776–1838).

He that would govern others, first should be / The master of himself.

Philip Massinger *The Bondman*

Massawa chief port and naval base of Eritrea, on the Red Sea, with salt production and pearl fishing; population (1989) 19,400. It is one of the hottest inhabited places in the world, the temperature reaching 46°C/115°F in May. Massawa was an Italian possession 1885–1941.

Masséna André 1758–1817. Marshal of France. He served in the French Revolutionary Wars and under the emperor Napoleon was created marshal 1804, duke of Rivoli 1808, and prince of Essling 1809. He was in command in Spain 1810–11 in the Peninsular War and was defeated by British troops under Wellington.

mass–energy equation Albert ◊Einstein's equation $E = mc^2$, denoting the equivalence of mass and energy, where E is the energy in joules, m is the mass in kilograms, and c is the speed of light, in a vacuum, in metres per second.

Massenet Jules Emile Frédéric 1842–1912. French composer of operas. His work is characterized by prominent roles for females, sincerity, and sentimentality. Notable works are *Manon* 1884, *Le Cid* 1885, and *Thaïs* 1894; among other works is the orchestral suite *Scènes pittoresques* 1874.

Massey (Charles) Vincent 1887–1967. Canadian Liberal Party politician. He was the first Canadian to become governor general of Canada (1952–59).

Massey William Ferguson 1856–1925. New Zealand politician, prime minister 1912–25. He led the Reform Party, an offshoot of the Conservative Party, and as prime minister before World War I concentrated on controlling militant unions and the newly formed Federation of Labour.

Massif Central mountainous plateau region of S central France; area 93,000 sq km/36,000 sq mi, highest peak Puy de Sancy, 1,886 m/6,188 ft. It is a source of hydroelectricity.

Massine Léonide. Adopted name of Leonid Fyodorovich Miassin 1895–1979. Russian choreographer and dancer with the Ballets Russes. He was a creator of comedy in ballet and also symphonic ballet using concert music. His works include the first Cubist-inspired ballet, *Parade* 1917, *La Boutique fantasque* 1919, and *The Three-Cornered Hat* 1919.

He succeeded Mikhail ◊Fokine at the Ballets Russes and continued with the company after Sergei ◊Diaghilev's death, later working in both the USA and Europe.

Massinger Philip 1583–1640. English dramatist. He was the author of *A New Way to Pay Old Debts* c. 1625. He collaborated with John ◊Fletcher and Thomas ◊Dekker, and has been credited with a share in writing Shakespeare's *Two Noble Kinsmen* and *Henry VIII*.

mass number or ***nucleon number*** sum (symbol A) of the numbers of protons and neutrons in the nucleus of an atom. It is used along with the ◊atomic number (the number of protons) in ◊nuclear notation: in symbols that represent nuclear isotopes, such as $^{14}_{6}C$, the lower number is the atomic number, and the upper number is the mass number.

Massorah collection of philological notes on the Hebrew text of the Old Testament. It was at first an oral tradition, but was committed to writing in the Aramaic language at Tiberias, Palestine, between the 6th and 9th centuries.

mass spectrometer in physics, an apparatus for analysing chemical composition. Positive ions (charged particles) of a substance are separated by an electromagnetic system, which permits accurate measurement of the relative concentrations of the various ionic masses present, particularly isotopes.

Master of the King's/Queen's Musick honorary appointment to the British royal household, the holder composing appropriate music for state occasions. The first was Nicholas Lanier, appointed by Charles I 1626; later appointments have included Edward Elgar and Arthur Bliss. The present holder, Malcolm ◊Williamson, was appointed 1975.

Master of the Rolls English judge who is the president of the civil division of the Court of Appeal, besides being responsible for ◊Chancery records and for the admission of solicitors.

mastiff breed of powerful dog, usually fawn in colour, that was originally bred in Britain for hunting purposes. It has a large head, wide-set eyes, and broad muzzle. It can grow up to 90 cm/36 in at the shoulder, and weigh 100 kg/220 lb.

mastodon any of an extinct family (Mastodontidae) of mammals of the elephant order (Proboscidae). They differed from elephants and mammoths in the structure of their grinding teeth. There were numerous species, among which the American mastodon *Mastodon americanum*, about 3 m/10 ft high, of the Pleistocene era, is well known. They were hunted by humans for food.

Mastroianni Marcello 1924– . Italian film actor. He was popular for his carefully understated roles as an unhappy romantic lover in such films as Antonioni's *La notte/The Night* 1961. He starred in several films with Sophia Loren, including *Una giornata speciale/A Special Day* 1977, and worked with Fellini in *La dolce vita* 1960, *8½* 1963, and *Ginger and Fred* 1986.

Masur Kurt 1927– . German conductor, music director of the New York Philharmonic from 1990. His speciality is late Romantic and early 20th-century repertoire, in particular Mendelssohn, Liszt, Bruch, and Prokofiev.

He was conductor of the Dresden Philharmonic Orchestra 1955–58 and 1967–72, before making his London debut 1973 with the New Philharmonia. He was prominent in the political campaigning that took place prior to German unification.

Matabeleland western portion of Zimbabwe between the Zambezi and Limpopo rivers, inhabited by the Ndebele people
area 181,605 sq km/70,118 sq mi
towns and cities Bulawayo
features rich plains watered by tributaries of the Zambezi and Limpopo, with mineral resources
language Matabele
famous people Joshua Nkomo
history Matabeleland was granted to the British South Africa Company 1889 and occupied 1893 after attacks on white settlements in Mashonaland; in 1923 it was included in Southern Rhodesia. It is now divided into two administrative regions (Matabeleland North and Matabeleland South). Joshua Nkomo was accused of plotting to overthrow the post-independence government of Zimbabwe and then expelled from the cabinet 1981. Zimbabwe African People's Union (ZAPU) supporters, mostly drawn from the Ndebele people, began a loosely organized armed rebellion against the Zimbabwe African National Union (ZANU) government of Robert Mugabe. The insurgency was brought to an end 1988, when a unity agreement was reached between ZANU and ZAPU and Nkomo was appointed minister of state in the office of vice president.

Matadi chief port of the Democratic Republic of Congo on the River Congo/Zaïre, 115 km/70 mi from its mouth, linked by oil pipelines with the capital Kinshasa; population (1991 est) 172,900.

Mata Hari stage name of Margaretha Geertruida Zelle 1876–1917. Dutch courtesan, dancer, and probable spy. In World War I she had affairs with highly placed military and government officials on both sides and told Allied secrets to the Germans. She may have been a double agent, in the pay of both France and Germany. She was shot by the French on espionage charges.

maté dried leaves of the Brazilian ◊holly *Ilex paraguensis*, an evergreen shrub that grows in Paraguay and Brazil. The roasted, powdered leaves are made into a tea.

materialism philosophical theory that there is nothing in existence over and above matter and matter in motion. Such a theory excludes the possibility of deities. It also sees mind as an attribute of the physical, denying idealist theories that see mind as something independent of body; for example, Descartes' theory of 'thinking substance'.

Like most other philosophical ideas, materialism probably arose among the early Greek thinkers. The Stoics and the Epicureans were materialists, and so were the ancient Buddhists. Among later materialists have been the English philosopher Thomas Hobbes, the French Denis Diderot, the German dramatist Georg Büchner, and the German scientist Ernst Haeckel; in the UK, David Hume, J S Mill, Thomas Huxley, and Herbert Spencer showed materialist tendencies.

Mata Hari Dutch-born spy Mata Hari. After the break-up of her marriage to a Dutch army officer, she became a dancer in Paris where she adopted the stage name of Mata Hari ('eye of the day' in Malay). During World War I she sold Allied secrets to the Germans, and was shot as a spy by the French. *Corbis*

mathematics science of relationships between numbers, between spatial configurations, and abstract structures. The main divisions of ***pure mathematics*** include geometry, arithmetic, algebra, calculus, and trigonometry. Mechanics, statistics, numerical analysis, computing, the mathematical theories of astronomy, electricity, optics, thermodynamics, and atomic studies come under the heading of ***applied mathematics***.
early history Prehistoric human beings probably learned to count at least up to ten on their fingers. The Chinese, Hindus, Babylonians, and Egyptians all devised methods of counting and measuring that were of practical importance in their everyday lives. The first theoretical mathematician is held to be Thales of Miletus (c. 580 BC) who is believed to have proposed the first theorems in plane geometry. His disciple ◊Pythagoras established geometry as a recognized science among the Greeks.

The later school of Alexandrian geometers (4th and 3rd centuries BC) included ◊Euclid and ◊Archimedes. Our present decimal numerals are based on a Hindu–Arabic system that reached Europe about AD 100 from Arab mathematicians of the Middle East such as ◊Khwārizmī.
Europe Western mathematics began to develop from the 15th century. Geometry was revitalized by the invention of coordinate geometry by René Descartes 1637; Blaise Pascal and Pierre de Fermat developed probability theory; John Napier invented logarithms; and Isaac Newton and Gottfried Leibniz invented calculus, later put on a more rigorous footing by Augustin Cauchy. In Russia, Nikolai Lobachevsky rejected Euclid's parallelism and developed a non-Euclidean geometry; this was subsequently generalized by Bernhard Riemann and later utilized by Einstein in his theory of relativity. In the mid-19th century a new major theme emerged: investigation of the logical foundations of mathematics. George Boole showed how logical arguments could be expressed in algebraic symbolism. Gottlob Frege and Giuseppe Peano considerably developed this symbolic logic.
the present In the 20th century, mathematics has become much more diversified. Each specialist subject is being studied in far greater depth and advanced work in some fields may be unintelligible to researchers in other fields. Mathematicians working in universities have had the economic freedom to pursue the subject for its own sake. Nevertheless, new branches of mathematics have been developed

MATHEMATICS: TIMELINE

BC	
c. 2500	The people of Mesopotamia (now Iraq) developed a positional numbering (place-value) system, in which the value of a digit depends on its position in a number.
c. 2000	Mesopotamian mathematicians solved quadratic equations (algebraic equations in which the highest power of a variable is 2).
876	A symbol for zero was used for the first time, in India.
c. 550	Greek mathematician Pythagoras formulated a theorem relating the lengths of the sides of a right-angled triangle. The theorem was already known by earlier mathematicians in China, Mesopotamia, and Egypt.
c. 450	Hipparcos of Metapontum discovered that some numbers are irrational (cannot be expressed as the ratio of two integers).
300	Euclid laid out the laws of geometry in his book *Elements*, which was to remain a standard text for 2,000 years.
c. 230	Eratosthenes developed a method for finding all prime numbers.
c. 100	Chinese mathematicians began using negative numbers.
c. 190	Chinese mathematicians used powers of 10 to express magnitudes.
AD	
c. 210	Diophantus of Alexandria wrote the first book on algebra.
c. 600	A decimal number system was developed in India.
829	Persian mathematician Muhammad ibn-Mūsā al-Khwārizmī published a work on algebra that made use of the decimal number system.
1202	Italian mathematician Leonardo Fibonacci studied the sequence of numbers (1, 1, 2, 3, 5, 8, 13, 21, ...) in which each number is the sum of the two preceding ones.
1550	In Germany, Rheticus published trigonometrical tables that simplified calculations involving triangles.
1614	Scottish mathematician John Napier invented logarithms, which enable lengthy calculations involving multiplication and division to be carried out by addition and subtraction.
1623	Wilhelm Schickard invented the mechanical calculating machine.
1637	French mathematician and philosopher René Descartes introduced coordinate geometry.
1654	In France, Blaise Pascal and Pierre de Fermat developed probability theory.
1666	Isaac Newton developed differential calculus, a method of calculating rates of change.
1675	German mathematician Gottfried Wilhelm Leibniz introduced the modern notation for integral calculus, a method of calculating volumes.
1679	Leibniz introduced binary arithmetic, in which only two symbols are used to represent all numbers.
1684	Leibniz published the first account of differential calculus.
1718	Jakob Bernoulli in Switzerland published his work on the calculus of variations (the study of functions that are close to their minimum or maximum values).
1746	In France, Jean le Rond d'Alembert developed the theory of complex numbers.
1747	D'Alembert used partial differential equations in mathematical physics.
1798	Norwegian mathematician Caspar Wessel introduced the vector representation of complex numbers.
1799	Karl Friedrich Gauss of Germany proved the fundamental theorem of algebra: the number of solutions of an algebraic equation is the same as the exponent of the highest term.
1810	In France, Jean Baptiste Joseph Fourier published his method of representing functions by a series of trigonometric functions.
1812	French mathematician Pierre Simon Laplace published the first complete account of probability theory.
1822	In the UK, Charles Babbage began construction of the first mechanical computer, the difference machine, a device for calculating logarithms and trigonometric functions.
1827	Gauss introduced differential geometry, in which small features of curves are described by analytical methods.
1829	In Russia, Nikolai Ivanonvich Lobachevsky developed hyperbolic geometry, in which a plane is regarded as part of a hyperbolic surface, shaped like a saddle. In France, Evariste Galois introduced the theory of groups (collections whose members obey certain simple rules of addition and multiplication).
1844	French mathematician Joseph Liouville found the first transcendental number, which cannot be expressed as an algebraic equation with rational coefficients. In Germany, Hermann Grassmann studied vectors with more than three dimensions.
1854	George Boole in the UK published his system of symbolic logic, now called Boolean algebra.
1858	English mathematician Arthur Cayley developed calculations using ordered tables called matrices.
1865	August Ferdinand Möbius in Germany described how a strip of paper can have only one side and one edge.
1892	German mathematician Georg Cantor showed that there are different kinds of infinity and studied transfinite numbers.
1895	Jules Henri Poincaré published the first paper on topology, often called 'the geometry of rubber sheets'.
1931	In the USA, Austrian-born mathematician Kurt Gödel proved that any formal system strong enough to include the laws of arithmetic is either incomplete or inconsistent.
1937	English mathematician Alan Turing published the mathematical theory of computing.
1944	John Von Neumann and Oscar Morgenstern developed game theory in the USA.
1945	The first general purpose, fully electronic digital computer, ENIAC (electronic numerator, integrator, analyser, and computer), was built at the University of Pennsylvania, USA.
1961	Meteorologist Edward Lorenz at the Massachusetts Institute of Technology, USA, discovered a mathematical system with chaotic behaviour, leading to a new branch of mathematics – chaos theory.
1962	Benoit Mandelbrot in the USA invented fractal images, using a computer that repeats the same mathematical pattern over and over again.
1975	US mathematician Mitchell Feigenbaum discovered a new fundamental constant (approximately 4.669201609103), which plays an important role in chaos theory.
1980	Mathematicians worldwide completed the classification of all finite and simple groups, a task that took over a hundred mathematicians more than 35 years to complete and whose results took up more than 14,000 pages in mathematical journals.
1989	A team of US computer mathematicians at Amdahl Corporation, California, discovered the highest known prime number (it contains 65,087 digits).
1993	British mathematician Andrew Wiles published a 1,000-page proof of Fermat's last theorem, one of the most baffling challenges in pure mathematics.
1996	Wiles's revised proof of Fermat's last theorem was accepted.

which are of great practical importance and which have basic ideas simple enough to be taught in secondary schools. Probably the most important of these is the mathematical theory of statistics in which much pioneering work was done by Karl Pearson. Another new development is operations research, which is concerned with finding optimum courses of action in practical situations, particularly in economics and management. As in the late medieval period, commerce began to emerge again as a major impetus for the development of mathematics.

Higher mathematics has a powerful tool in the high-speed electronic computer, which can create and manipulate mathematical 'models' of various systems in science, technology, and commerce.

Modern additions to school syllabuses such as sets, group theory, matrices, and graph theory are sometimes referred to as 'new' or 'modern' mathematics.

Mather Cotton 1663–1728. American theologian and writer. He was a Puritan minister in Boston, and wrote over 400 works of history, science, annals, and theology, including *Magnalia Christi Americana/The Great Works of Christ in America* 1702, a vast compendium of early New England history and experience. Mather appears to have supported the Salem witch-hunts.

Matilda ***the Empress Maud*** 1102–1167. Claimant to the throne of England. On the death of her father, Henry I, 1135, the barons elected her cousin Stephen to be king. Matilda invaded England 1139, and was crowned by her supporters 1141. Civil war ensued until Stephen was finally recognized as king 1153, with Henry II (Matilda's son) as his successor.

Matilda was recognized during the reign of Henry I as his heir. She married first the Holy Roman emperor Henry V and, after his death, Geoffrey Plantagenet, Count of Anjou (1113–1151).

Matisse Henri Emile Benoît 1869–1954. French painter, sculptor and illustrator. Matisse was one of the most original creative forces in early 20th-century art. He was a leading figure in ◊Fauvism and later developed a style characterized by strong, sinuous lines, surface pattern, and brilliant colour. *The Dance* 1910 (The Hermitage, St Petersburg) is characteristic. Later works include pure abstracts, as in his collages of coloured paper shapes (*gouaches découpées*).

Influenced by Impressionism and then Post-Impressionism, by 1905 he had developed his Fauvist style of strong, expressive colours. Largely unaffected by Cubism and other strident forms of modern art, he concentrated on the decorative effects of colour, line and form, a vivid example being *The Red Room* 1908–09 (Hermitage, St Petersburg).

As early as 1899 he made sculptures and in later years resumed the practice of free and unconventional modelling, his best-known works being the series in bronze relief, *The Back* 1909–29. As a graphic artist he produced etchings, lithographs, and wood-engravings and illustrated Mallarmé's poems, James Joyce's *Ulysses*, and other works. As a designer he produced sets and costumes for Diaghilev's Ballets Russes. He also designed and built the chapel for the Dominicans of Vence, near Nice, consecrated 1951, a late work of importance in applying an entirely modern decorative sense to a religious interior.

Matlock spa town with warm springs, on the river Derwent, administrative headquarters of Derbyshire, England; population (1990 est) 15,000. Formerly known as a centre for hydropathic treatment, it manufactures textiles and high-tech products and caters for tourists.

matriarchy theoretical form of society where domestic and political life is dominated by women, where kinship is traced exclusively through the female line, and where religion is centred around the cult of a mother goddess. Its opposite concept is that of patriarchy.

Matriarchy and patriarchy are oversimplifications of the distribution of familial and political power between the sexes. The concept persists largely through a confusion with matrilineal descent, where kinship is reckoned through females, and with matrilocal residence, where men reside in their wives' homes or villages after marriage. Matrilineal societies with matrilocal residence do exist, for example the Minangkabau of Indonesia.

matrix in biology, usually refers to the ◊extracellular matrix.

matrix in mathematics, a square ($n \times n$) or rectangular ($m \times n$) array of elements (numbers or algebraic variables). They are a means of condensing information about mathematical systems and can be used for, among other things, solving simultaneous linear equations (see ◊simultaneous equations and ◊transformation).

Matsuyama largest city on Shikoku Island, Japan; population (1994) 456,000. Industries include agricultural machinery, textiles, and chemicals. There is a feudal fortress (1634).

❛No man can serve two masters ... Ye cannot serve God and mammon.❜

St Matthew
New Testament, Matthew 6:24

matter in physics, anything that has mass and can be detected and measured. All matter is made up of ◊atoms, which in turn are made up of ◊elementary particles; it exists ordinarily as a solid, liquid, or gas. The history of science and philosophy is largely taken up with accounts of theories of matter, ranging from the hard 'atoms' of Democritus to the 'waves' of modern quantum theory.

Matterhorn (French ***le Cervin***, Italian ***il Cervino***) mountain peak in the Alps on the Swiss-Italian border; 4,478 m/14,690 ft. It was first climbed 1865 by English mountaineer Edward Whymper (1840–1911); four members of his party of seven were killed when a rope broke during their descent.

Matthau Walter. Stage name of Walter Matuschanskavasky 1920– . US character actor. He was impressive in both comedy and dramatic roles. He gained film stardom in the 1960s after his stage success in *The Odd Couple* 1965. His many films include *Kotch* 1971, *Charley Varrick* 1973, *The Bad News Bears* 1976, *JFK* 1991, *Grumpy Old Men* 1993, *Short Cuts* 1994, and *A Weekend in the Country* 1995.

Matthews Stanley 1915– . English footballer who played for Stoke City, Blackpool, and England. An outstanding right-winger, he was nicknamed 'the Wizard of the Dribble' because of his ball control. He played nearly 700 Football League games, and won 54 international caps. He was the first Footballer of the Year 1948 (again 1963), the first European Footballer of the Year 1956, and the first footballer to be knighted for services to the game 1965.

❛It is not true that suffering ennobles the character; happiness does that sometimes, but suffering, for the most part, makes men petty and vindictive.❜

Somerset Maugham
The Moon and Sixpence

Matthew, St lived 1st century AD. Christian apostle and evangelist, the traditional author of the first Gospel. He is usually identified with Levi, who was a tax collector in the service of Herod Antipas, and was called by Jesus to be a disciple as he sat by the Lake of Galilee receiving customs dues. His emblem is a man with wings; feast day 21 Sept.

Matthias Corvinus c. 1440–1490. King of Hungary from 1458. His aim of uniting Hungary, Austria, and Bohemia involved him in long wars with Holy Roman emperor Frederick III and the kings of Bohemia and Poland, during which he captured Vienna (1485) and made it his capital. His father was János ◊Hunyadi.

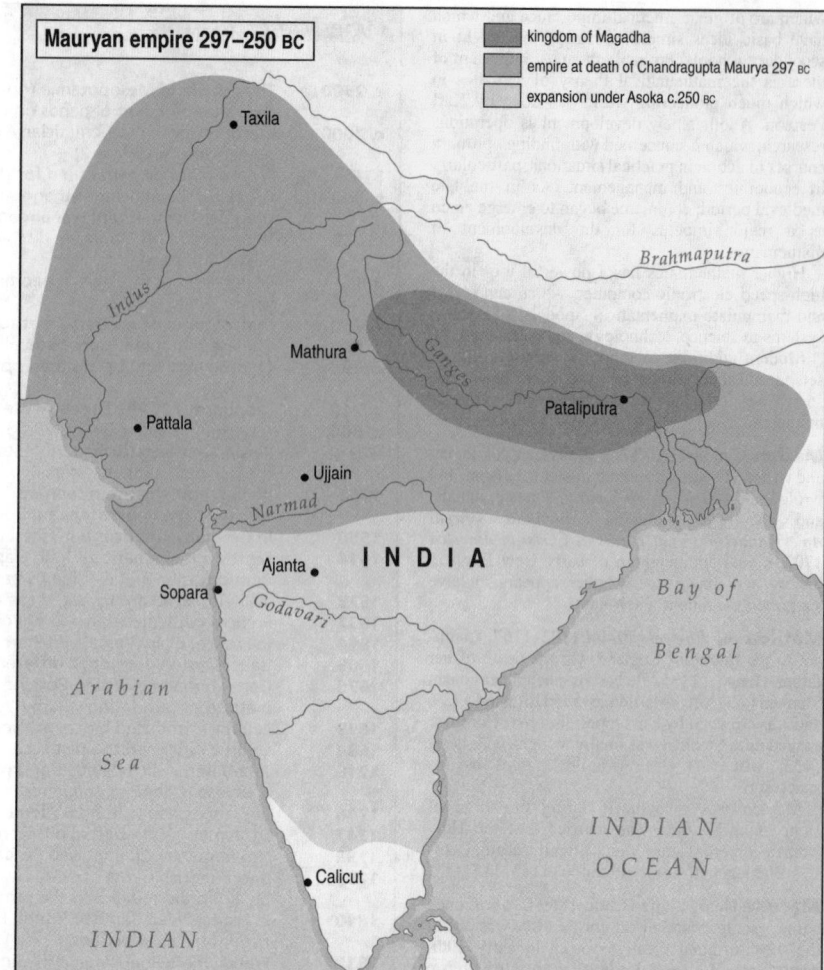

Mauryan empire 297–250 BC

kingdom of Magadha
empire at death of Chandragupta Maurya 297 BC
expansion under Asoka c.250 BC

Taxila
Brahmaputra
Indus
Mathura
Ganges
Pataliputra
Pattala
Ujjain
Narmada
INDIA
Ajanta
Sopara
Godavari
Bay of Bengal
Arabian Sea
INDIAN OCEAN
Calicut
INDIAN OCEAN
LANKA
0 400 mi
0 600 km

Matura Mustapha 1939– . Trinidad-born British dramatist. Cofounder of the Black Theatre Cooperative 1978, his plays deal with problems of ethnic diversity and integration. These include *As Time Goes By* 1971, *Play Mas* 1974, and *Meetings* 1981. Other works include *Playboy of the West Indies* 1984 and *Trinidad Sisters* 1988 (adaptations of plays by Synge and Chekhov respectively), and *The Coup* 1991.

matzo or ***matza*** (Yiddish) unleavened bread eaten during the ◊Passover.

Mauchly John William 1907–1980. US physicist and engineer who, in 1946, constructed the first general-purpose computer, the ENIAC, in collaboration with John Eckert (1919–1995). In 1949 Mauchly and Eckert designed a small-scale binary computer, BINAC, which was faster and cheaper to use. Punched cards were replaced with magnetic tape, and the computer stored programs internally. Their company was bought by Remington Rand 1950, and they built the UNIVAC 1 computer 1951 for the US census.

Maufe Edward Brantwood 1883–1974. English architect. His works include the Runnymede Memorial and Guildford Cathedral.

Mauger Ivan Gerald 1939– . New Zealand speedway star. He won the world individual title a record six times 1968–79.

Maugham (William) Somerset 1874–1965. English writer. His work includes the novels *Of Human Bondage* 1915, *The Moon and Sixpence* 1919, and *Cakes and Ale* 1930; the short-story collections *Ashenden* 1928 and *Rain and Other Stories* 1933; and the plays *Lady Frederick* 1907 and *Our Betters* 1917. There were new editions of *Collected Stories* 1900 and *Selected Plays* 1991. A penetrating observer of human behaviour, his writing is essentially anti-romantic and there is a vein of cynicism running through his work.

Maugham was born in Paris. He studied medicine at St Thomas's Hospital, London, and drew upon his medical experiences in his first novel, *Liza of Lambeth* 1897. The success of that novel, and of *Mrs Craddock* 1902, made him decide upon a literary career. During World War I Maugham was a secret agent in Switzerland and Russia, and his *Ashenden* spy stories are based on this experience.

Mau Mau Kenyan secret guerrilla movement 1952–60, an offshoot of the Kikuyu Central Association banned in World War II. Its aim was to end British colonial rule. This was achieved 1960 with the granting of Kenyan independence and the election of Jomo Kenyatta as Kenya's first prime minister.

Mauna Kea astronomical observatory in Hawaii, USA, built on a dormant volcano at 4,200 m/13,784 ft above sea level. Because of its elevation high above clouds, atmospheric moisture, and artificial lighting, Mauna Kea is ideal for infrared astronomy. The first telescope on the site was installed 1970.

Telescopes include the 2.24 m/88 in University of Hawaii reflector 1970. Three telescopes were erected 1979: the 3.8 m/150 in United Kingdom

Mauritania The W African republic of Mauritania was a prosperous region in medieval times. This 16th-century mosque at Chinguitti, the seventh holy city of Islam, where caravans would gather before setting out for Mecca, is a reminder that the city was once an important centre of Islamic learning. *UNESCO*

Infrared Telescope (UKIRT) (also used for optical observations); the 3 m/120 in NASA Infrared Telescope Facility (IRTF); and the 3.6 m/142 in Canada–France–Hawaii Telescope (CFHT), designed for optical and infrared work. The 15 m/50 ft diameter UK/Netherlands James Clerk Maxwell Telescope (JCMT) is the world's largest telescope specifically designed to observe millimetre wave radiation from nebulae, stars, and galaxies. The JCMT is operated via satellite links by astronomers in Europe. The world's largest optical telescope, the ◊Keck Telescope, is also situated on Mauna Kea.

Mauna Loa active volcano rising to a height of 4,169 m/13,678 ft on the Pacific island of Hawaii; it has numerous craters, including the second-largest active crater in the world.

Maundy Thursday in the Christian church, the Thursday before Easter. The ceremony of washing the feet of pilgrims on that day was instituted in commemoration of Jesus' washing of the apostles' feet and observed from the 4th century to 1754. In Britain it was performed by the English sovereigns until the time of William III, and Maundy money is still presented by the sovereign to poor people each year.

Maupassant (Henry René Albert) Guy de 1850–1893. French author. He established a reputation with the short story 'Boule de suif/Ball of Fat' 1880 and wrote some 300 short stories in all. His novels include *Une Vie/A Woman's Life* 1883 and *Bel-Ami* 1885.

Mauriac François 1885–1970. French novelist. His novels are studies, from a Roman Catholic standpoint, of the psychological and moral problems of the Catholic and provincial middle class, usually set in his native city of Bordeaux and the Landes region of SW France. *Le Baiser au lépreux/A Kiss for the Leper* 1922 describes the conflict of an unhappy marriage, while the irreconcilability of Christian practice and human nature is examined in *Fleuve de feu/River of Fire* 1923, *Le Désert de l'amour/The Desert of Love* 1925, and *Thérèse Desqueyroux* 1927. Nobel Prize for Literature 1952.

Mauritania country in NW Africa, bounded NE by Algeria, E and S by Mali, SW by Senegal, W by the Atlantic Ocean, and NW by Western Sahara. *See country box below.*

Mauritius island country in the Indian Ocean, E of Madagascar. *See country box on p. 686.*

Maurois André. Pen name of Emile Herzog 1885–1967. French writer and biographer. During World War I he was attached to the British Army as a liaison officer, and the essays in *Les Silences du Colonel Bramble* 1918 and *Les Discours du Docteur O'Grady* 1920 offer humorously sympathetic observations on the British character. His other works include the semi-autobiographical *Bernard Quesnay* 1926 and a large number of distinguished biographies intended to read as novels, such as *Ariel, ou la vie de Shelley* 1923, *La Vie de Disraëli* 1927, *Byron* 1930, *Voltaire* 1932, *Dickens* 1934, *Lélia, ou la vie de George Sand* 1952, *Olympia, ou la vie de Victor Hugo* 1953, and *Les Trois Dumas* 1957.

Mauryan dynasty Indian dynasty c. 321–c. 185 BC, founded by ***Chandragupta Maurya*** (321–c. 279 BC). Under Emperor ◊Aśoka most of India was united for the first time, but after his death in 232 the empire was riven by dynastic disputes. Reliant on a highly organized aristocracy and a centralized administration, it survived until the assassination of Emperor Brihadratha 185 BC and the creation of the Sunga dynasty.

mausoleum large, free-standing, sumptuous tomb. The term derives from the magnificent sepulchral monument built for King Mausolus of Caria (died 353 BC) by his wife Artemisia at Halicarnassus in Asia Minor (modern-day Bodrum in Anatolia, Turkey); it was considered one of the ◊Seven Wonders of the World.

Mauthausen German ◊concentration camp near Linz, Austria, established 1941. Although not actually an extermination camp, an estimated 180,000 prisoners died there.

maxim saying or proverb that gives moral guidance or a piece of advice on the way to live (e.g. 'Better late than never').

Maximilian 1832–1867. Emperor of Mexico 1864–67. He accepted that title when the French emperor Napoleon III's troops occupied the country, but encountered resistance from the deposed president Benito ◊Juárez. In 1866, after the French troops withdrew on the insistence of the USA, Maximilian was captured by Mexican republicans and shot.

Maximilian I 1459–1519. Holy Roman emperor from 1493, the son of Emperor Frederick III. He had acquired the Low Countries through his marriage to Mary of Burgundy 1477. He married his son Philip I (the Handsome) to the heiress to the Spanish throne, and undertook long wars with Italy and Hungary in attempts to extend Habsburg power. He was the patron of the artist Dürer.

maximum and minimum in ◊coordinate geometry, points at which the slope of a curve representing a ◊function changes from positive to negative (maximum), or from negative to positive (minimum). A tangent to the curve at a maximum or minimum has zero gradient.

Maxima and minima can be found by differentiating the function for the curve and setting the differential to zero (the value of the slope at the turning point). For example, differentiating the function for the ◊parabola $y = 2x^2 - 8x$ gives $dy/dx = 4x - 8$. Setting this equal to zero gives $x = 2$, so that $y = -8$ (found by substituting $x = 2$ into the parabola equation). Thus the function has a minimum at the point $(2, -8)$. *See illustration on following page.*

maxwell c.g.s. unit (symbol Mx) of magnetic flux (the strength of a ◊magnetic field in an area multiplied by the area). It is now replaced by the SI unit, the ◊weber (one maxwell equals 10^{-8} weber).

Maxwell (Ian) Robert (born Jan Ludvik Hoch) 1923–1991. Czech-born British publishing and

> *The whole island ... was adorned with an air of perfect elegance, the scenery, if I may use such an expression, appeared to the sight harmonious.*
>
> On **Mauritius**
> Charles Darwin
> *Voyage of the Beagle* 1839

MAURITANIA
Islamic Republic of

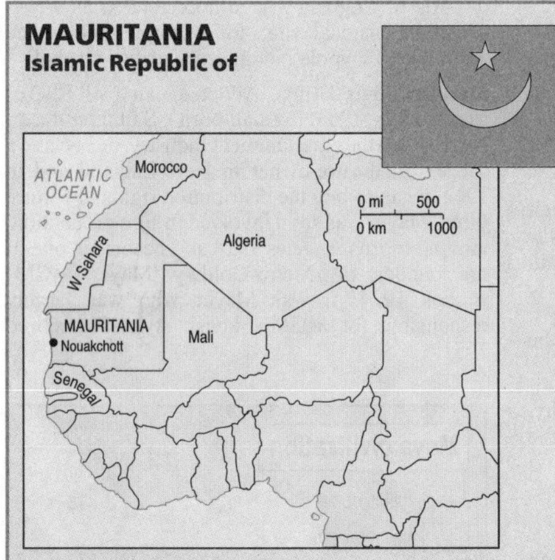

national name *République Islamique Arabe et Africaine de Mauritanie*
area 1,030,700 sq km/397,850 sq mi
capital Nouakchott (port)
major towns/cities Kaédi, Kiffa, Rosso
major ports Nouâdhibou
physical features valley of river Senegal in S; remainder arid and flat
head of state Maaoya Sid'Ahmed Ould Taya from 1984
head of government Cheik el Avia Ould Muhammad Khouna from 1996
political system emergent democratic republic
administrative divisions 12 regions and the capital district
political parties Democratic and Social Republican Party (PRDS), centre-left, militarist; Rally for Democracy and National Unity (RDNU), centrist; Mauritian Renewal Party (MPR), centrist; Umma, Islamic fundamentalist
population 2,274,000 (1995 est)
population growth rate 2.5% (1990–95); 2.5% (2000–05)
ethnic distribution over 80% of the population is of Moorish or Moorish-black origin; about 18% is black African (concentrated in the S); there is a small European minority
life expectancy 46 (men), 50 (women)
literacy rate men 47%, women 21%
languages French and Hasaniya Arabic (both official), black African languages including Pulaar, Soninke, and Wolof
religion Sunni Muslim
currency ouguiya
GDP (US $) 1.02 billion (1994)
growth rate 4.6% (1994)
exports iron ore, fish, gypsum

HISTORY
early Christian era A Roman province with the name Mauritania, after the Mauri, its Berber inhabitants who became active in the long-distance salt trade.
7th–11th Cs Eastern Mauritania was incorporated in the larger Ghana Empire, centred on Mali to the E, but with its capital at Kumbi in SE Mauritania. The Berbers were reduced to vassals and converted to Islam in the 8th century.
11th–12th Cs The area's Sanhadja Berber inhabitants, linked to the Morocco-based Almoravid Empire, destroyed the Ghana Empire and spread Islam among neighbouring peoples.
13th–15th Cs Southeastern Mauritania formed part of Muslim Mali Empire, which extended to the E and S.
1441 Coast visited by Portuguese, who founded the port of Arguin and captured Africans to sell as slaves.
15th–16th Cs Eastern Mauritania formed part of Muslim Songhai Empire, which spread across the western Sahel, and Arab tribes immigrated into the area.
1817 Formerly disputed by European nations, the Senegal Treaty recognized the coastal region as a French sphere of influence.
1903 Formally became a French protectorate.
1920 Became a French colony, within French West Africa.
1960 Independence achieved, with Moktar Ould Daddah, the leader of the Mauritanian People's Party (PPM), as president. New capital built at Nouakchott.
1968 Underlying tensions between agriculturalist black population of the S and the economically dominant semi-nomadic Arabo-Berber peoples, or Moors, of desert N became more acute after Arabic was made an official language (with French).
1976 Western Sahara, to the NW, ceded by Spain to Mauritania and Morocco. Mauritania occupied the southern area and Morocco the mineral-rich N. Polisario Front formed in Sahara to resist this occupation and guerrilla war broke out, with the Polisario receiving backing from Algeria and Libya.
1978 Daddah deposed in bloodless coup; replaced by Col Mohamed Khouna Ould Haidalla in military government.
1979 Peace accord signed with Polisario Front in Algiers, in which Mauritania, crippled by the cost of the military struggle over a largely uninhabited area, renounced its claims to southern Western Sahara (Tiris el Gharbia region) and recognized the Polisario regime; diplomatic relations restored with Algeria.
1981 Diplomatic relations with Morocco broken after it annexed the southern Western Sahara.
1984 Haidalla overthrown by Col Maaoya Sid'Ahmed Ould Taya.
1985 Relations with Morocco restored.
1989 Violent clashes in Mauritania and Senegal between Moors and black Africans, chiefly of Senegalese origins; over 50,000 Senegalese were expelled.
1991 Amnesty for political prisoners. Calls for resignation of President Taya. Political parties legalized and new multiparty constitution approved in referendum.
1992 First multiparty elections largely boycotted by opposition; Taya and his Social Democratic Republican Party (DSRP) re-elected. Diplomatic relations with Senegal resumed.
1996 Cheikh el Avia Ould Muhammad appointed prime minister.

SEE ALSO Berber; Ghana, ancient; Mali Empire; Western Sahara

MAURITIUS
Republic of

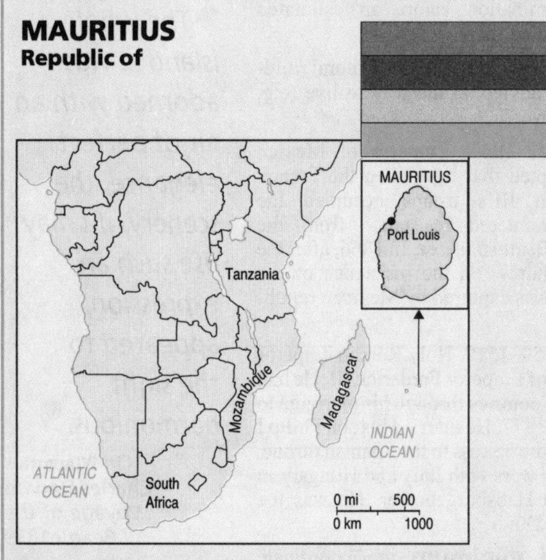

area 1,865 sq km/720 sq mi; the island of Rodrigues is part of Mauritius; there are several small island dependencies
capital Port Louis (port)
major towns/cities Beau Bassin-Rose Hill, Curepipe, Quatre Bornes, Vacoas-Phoenix
physical features mountainous, volcanic island surrounded by coral reefs
head of state Cassam Uteem from 1992
head of government Navim Ramgoolam from 1995
political system liberal democratic republic
administrative divisions nine districts
political parties Mauritius Socialist Movement (MSM), moderate socialist-republican; Mauritius Labour Party (MLP), democratic socialist, Hindu-oriented; Mauritius Social Democratic Party (PMSD), conservative, Francophile; Mauritius Militant Movement (MMM), Marxist-republican; Organization of Rodriguan People (OPR), left of centre
population 1,129,000 (1996 est)
population growth rate 1.1% (1990–95); 1.1% (2000–05)
ethnic distribution five principal ethnic groups: French, black Africans, Indians, Chinese, and Mulattos (or Creoles). Indo-Mauritians predominate, constituting 67% of the population, followed by Creoles (29%), Sino-Mauritians (3.5%), and Europeans (0.5%)
life expectancy 68 (men), 73 (women)
literacy rate 83%
languages English (official), French, creole, Indian languages
religions Hindu, Christian (mainly Roman Catholic), Muslim
currency Mauritian rupee
GDP (US $) 3.4 billion (1994)
growth rate 5.7% (1994 est)
exports sugar, knitted goods, tea, toys and games, sporting goods, sunglasses, watches, jewellery. Tourism is important

HISTORY
1598 Previously uninhabited, the island was discovered by the Dutch and named after Prince Morris of Nassau.
1710 The Dutch colonists withdrew.
1721 Reoccupied by the French East India Company, who renamed it Île de France, and established sugar-cane and tobacco plantations worked by imported African slaves.
1814 Ceded to Britain by the Treaty of Paris.
1835 Slavery abolished, and indentured Indian and Chinese labourers were imported to work the sugar-cane plantations, which were later hit by competition from beet sugar.
1903 Formerly administered with Seychelles, it became a single colony.
1936 Mauritius Labour Party (MLP) founded, drawing strong support from sugar workers.
1957 Internal self-government granted.
1968 Independence achieved from Britain within the Commonwealth, with Seewoosagur Ramgoolam of the centrist Indian-dominated MLP as prime minister.
1971 State of emergency temporarily imposed as a result of industrial unrest.
1982 Aneerood Jugnauth, of the moderate socialist Mauritius Socialist Movement (MSM) became prime minister, pledging a programme of nonalignment, nationalization, and the creation of a republic.
1992 Mauritius became a republic, within the Commonwealth, with Cassam Uteem elected president.
1995 MLP and cross-community Mauritian Militant Movement (MMM) coalition won landslide election victory; Navim Ramgoolam (MLP) became prime minister.

newspaper proprietor who owned several UK national newspapers, including the *Daily Mirror*, the Macmillan Publishing Company, and the New York *Daily News*. At the time of his death the Maxwell domain carried debts of about $3.9 billion.

In late 1991 Maxwell, last seen on his yacht off the Canary Islands, was found dead at sea. His sons Kevin and Ian were named as his successors. After his death it was revealed that he had been involved in fraudulent practices for much of his career. In 1991 the Serious Fraud Office started an investigation into pension fund losses following reports of transfers of over £400 million from the Maxwell pension funds to the private Maxwell firms, to offset mounting company losses, affecting more than 30,000 current and future pensioners. Kevin and Ian Maxwell were arrested and charged in 1992, and in 1996 were cleared of all charges to defraud the Maxwell pension funds, following an eight-month trial that cost £25 million.

> *‘The definition of a specialist as one who ‘knows more and more about less and less’ is good and true.’*
>
> CHARLES H MAYO
> *Modern Hospital*
> Sept 1938

Maxwell James Clerk 1831–1879. Scottish physicist. His main achievement was in the understanding of ◊electromagnetic waves: ***Maxwell's equations*** bring together electricity, magnetism, and light in one set of relations. He studied gases, optics, and the sensation of colour, and his theoretical work in magnetism prepared the way for wireless telegraphy and telephony.

In developing the kinetic theory of gases, Maxwell gave the final proof that heat resides in the motion of molecules. Studying colour vision, he explained how all colours could be built up from mixtures of the primary colours red, green, and blue. Maxwell confirmed English physicist Thomas ◊Young's theory that the eye has three kinds of receptors sensitive to the primary colours, and showed that colour blindness is due to defects in the receptors. In 1861 he produced the first colour photograph to use a three-colour process.

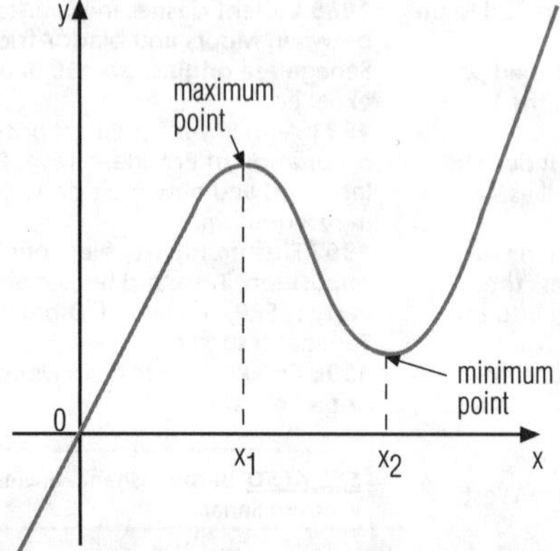

maximum and minimum A maximum point on a curve is higher than the points immediately on either side of it; it is not necessarily the highest point on the curve. Similarly, a minimum point is lower than the points immediately on either side.

Maxwell–Boltzmann distribution in physics, a statistical equation describing the distribution of velocities among the molecules of a gas. It is named after James Maxwell and Ludwig Boltzmann, who derived the equation, independently of each other, in the 1860s.

One form of the distribution is $n = Ne(-E/RT)$, where N is the total number of molecules, n is the number of molecules with energy in excess of E, T is the absolute temperature (temperature in kelvin), R is the ◊gas constant, and e is the exponential constant.

May Thomas Erskine, 1st Baron Farnborough 1815–1886. English constitutional jurist. He was Clerk of the House of Commons from 1871 until 1886, when he was created Baron Farnborough. He wrote a practical *Treatise on the Law, Privileges, Proceedings, and Usage of Parliament* 1844, the authoritative work on parliamentary procedure.

maya (Sanskrit ‘illusion’) in Hindu philosophy, mainly in the *Vedānta*, the cosmos which Isvara, the personal expression of Brahman, or the ◊atman, has called into being. This is real, yet also an illusion, since its reality is not everlasting.

Maya member of a Native American civilization originating in the Yucatán Peninsula in Central America about 2600 BC, with later sites in Mexico, Guatemala, and Belize, and enjoying a classical period AD 325–925, after which it declined. Today they are Roman Catholic, and number 8–9 million (1994 est). They live in Yucatán, Guatemala, Belize, and W Honduras. Many still speak Maya, a member of the Totonac-Mayan (Penutian) language family, as well as Spanish. In the 1980s more than 100,000 Maya fled from Guatemala to Mexico.

Maya beliefs are based on land, which was held in common until the arrival of the Spanish. They constructed stone buildings and stepped pyramids without metal tools; used hieroglyphic writing in manuscripts, of which only three survive; were skilled potters, weavers, and farmers; and regulated their rituals and warfare by observations of the planet Venus.

Mayakovsky Vladimir Vladimirovich 1893–1930. Russian Futurist poet. He combined revolutionary propaganda with efforts to revolutionize poetic technique in his poems *150,000,000* 1920 and *V I Lenin* 1924. His satiric play *The Bedbug* 1928 was taken in the West as an attack on philistinism in the USSR.

Mayan art see ◊pre-Columbian art.

Mayapán ancient Mayan city 55 km/35 mi SE of Mérida, in modern Mexico. Mayapán was the dominant religious and political centre of the Yucatán region 1200–1450.

May Day first day of May. In many countries it is a national holiday in honour of labour; see also ◊Labour Day. Traditionally the first day of summer, in parts of England it is still celebrated as a pre-Christian magical rite; for example, the dance around the maypole (an ancient fertility symbol).

Mayer Louis B(urt). Adopted name of Eliezer Mayer 1885–1957. Russian-born US film producer. Attracted to the entertainment industry, he became a successful theatre-owner in New England and in 1914 began to buy the distribution rights to feature films. Mayer was soon involved in film production, moving to Los Angeles 1918 and becoming one of the founders of ◊Metro-Goldwyn-Mayer (MGM) studios 1924. It was Mayer who was largely responsible for MGM's lavish style. He retired 1951.

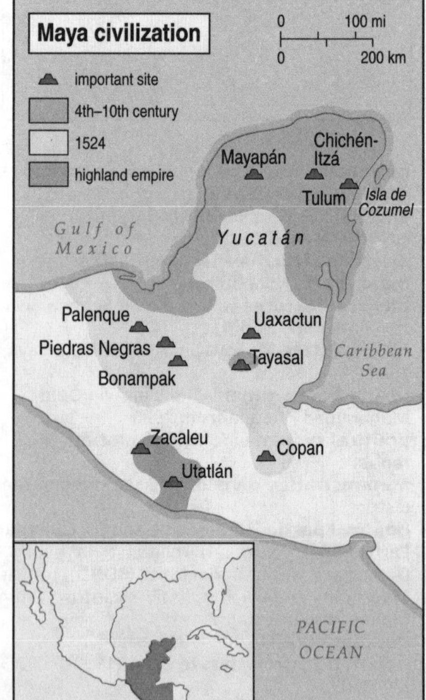

mayfly any insect of the order Ephemerida (Greek *ephemeros* 'lasting for a day', an allusion to the very brief life of the adult). The larval stage, which can last a year or more, is passed in water, the adult form developing gradually from the nymph through successive moults.

May 4th Movement Chinese student-led nationalist movement ignited by demonstrations in Beijing 1919. It demanded that China's unpopular warlord government reject the decision by the Versailles peace conference to confirm Japan's rights over the Shandong peninsula that had been asserted in Japan's Twenty-one demands 1915.

The students won mass workers' support in Beijing, a boycott of Japanese goods, and stimulated an intellectual revolution, the New Culture movement. Influenced by Marxist and liberal ideas, this led to the subsequent creation of the Chinese Communist Party. The 70th anniversary of the May 4th Movement was marked by mass prodemocracy demonstrations in ◊Tiananmen Square, Beijing, 1989.

Mayhew Patrick (Barnabas Burke) 1929– . British lawyer and Conservative politician, Northern Ireland secretary 1992–97. He was appointed Solicitor General 1983 and four years later Attorney General, becoming the government's chief legal adviser. His appointment as Northern Ireland secretary came at a propitious time and within two years he had witnessed the voluntary cessation of violence by both Republicans and Loyalists, but allegations of unnecessary delays in the peace process led to the resumption of IRA violence Feb 1996. He left the Northern Ireland office after the Labour victory in the 1997 general election.

Maynard Smith John 1920– . British biologist. He applied ◊game theory to animal behaviour and developed the concept of the ◊evolutionary stable strategy as a mathematical technique for studying the evolution of behaviour. His books include *The Theory of Evolution* 1958 and *Evolution and the Theory of Games* 1982.

Mayo county of the Republic of Ireland, in the province of Connacht; county town Castlebar; area 5,400 sq km/2,084 sq mi; population (1991) 110,700. It has wild Atlantic coast scenery. Features include Lough Conn; Achill Island; Croagh Patrick 765 m/2,510 ft, the mountain where St Patrick spent the 40 days of Lent in 441, climbed by pilgrims on the last Sunday of July each year; and the village of Knock, where two women claimed a vision of the Virgin with two saints 1879, now a site of pilgrimage. Industries include sheep and cattle farming, salmon fishing, potatoes, oats, and pigs.

mayor title of head of urban administration. In England, Wales, and Northern Ireland, the mayor is the principal officer of a district council that has been granted district-borough status under royal charter. In the USA a mayor is the elected head of a city or town. In 1996 the Labour Party floated proposals for directly elected mayors in Britain.

Mayotte or ***Mahore*** island group of the ◊Comoros, off the east coast of Africa, a *collectivité territoriale* of France by its own wish. The two main islands are Grande Terre and Petite Terre
area 374 sq km/144 sq mi
capital Dzaoudzi
industries coffee, copra, vanilla, fishing
language French, Swahili
population (1994 est) 109,600
history a French colony 1843–1914, and later, with the Comoros, an overseas territory of France. In 1974, Mayotte voted to remain a French dependency, and was accepted as a member of the United Nations 1975.

Mazarin Jules (born Giulio Raimondo Mazzarini) 1602–1661. French politician who succeeded Richelieu as chief minister of France 1642. His attack on the power of the nobility led to the ◊Fronde and his temporary exile, but his diplomacy achieved a successful conclusion to the Thirty Years' War, and, in alliance with Oliver Cromwell during the British protectorate, he gained victory over Spain.

Mazowiecki Tadeusz 1927– . Polish politician, founder member of ◊Solidarity, and Poland's first postwar noncommunist prime minister 1989–90. Forced to introduce unpopular economic reforms, he was knocked out in the first round of the 1990 presidential elections, resigning in favour of his former colleague Lech ◊Wałesa. In 1994 he formed the centrist Freedom Union (UW).

Maya The pyramid of Kukulcan or Quetzalcoatl, known as the Castillo, which stands in the centre of the main plaza of the ancient Mayan city of Chichen Itzá. This magnificent temple pyramid is built in nine tiers with a staircase on each side, and at the spring and autumn equinoxes the light falls such that the impression is given of a great serpent descending from the temple. *Corbis*

mazurka any of a family of traditional Polish dances from the 16th century, characterized by foot-stamping and heel-clicking, together with a turning movement. The music for the mazurka is in triple time (3/4), with dotted rhythms and the accentuation of weak beats, on which phrases also begin and end.

Mazzini Giuseppe 1805–1872. Italian nationalist. He was a member of the revolutionary society, the Carbonari, and founded in exile the nationalist movement Giovane Italia (Young Italy) 1831. Returning to Italy on the outbreak of the 1848 revolution, he headed a republican government established in Rome, but was forced into exile again on its overthrow 1849. He acted as a focus for the movement for Italian unity (see ◊Risorgimento).

Mbabane capital (since 1902) of Swaziland, 160 km/100 mi W of Maputo, in the Dalgeni Hills; population (1992) 42,000. Mining and tourism are important.

MBE abbreviation for ***Member of the Order of the British Empire***, an honour first awarded 1917.

Mbeki Thabo 1942– . South African politician, first executive deputy president from 1994 and leader of the ◊African National Congress (ANC) from 1997. In 1989 he played an important role in the constitutional talks with the de Klerk government which eventually led to the adoption of a nonracial political system.

Mboya Tom (Thomas Joseph) 1930–1969. Kenyan politician, a founder of the Kenya African National Union (◊KANU), and minister of economic affairs from 1964 until his assassination.

MCC abbreviation for ***Marylebone Cricket Club***.

McGahern John 1934– . Irish novelist. He won early acclaim for *The Barracks* 1963, a study of the mind of a dying woman. His books explore Irish settings and issues as in *Amongst Women* 1991, about an ageing member of the IRA. His other works include *The Dark* 1965, *Nightlines* 1970, *The Leavetaking*, and *The High Ground* 1985.

McGrath John Peter 1935– . Scottish dramatist and director. He founded the socialist 7:84 Theatre Companies in England 1971 and Scotland 1973, and is the author of such plays as *Events Guarding the Bofors Gun* 1966; *The Cheviot, the Stag, and the Black, Black Oil* 1973, about the economic exploitation of the Scottish highlands; and *The Garden of England* 1985. He has published two books arguing the case for popular and radical theatre: *A Good Night Out* 1981 and *The Bone Won't Break* 1990.

MDMA (3,4-methylenedio-xymethamphetamine) psychedelic drug, also known as ◊ecstasy.

ME abbreviation for ***Middle English***, the period of the English language from 1050 to 1550.

ME abbreviation for ***myalgic encephalomyelitis*** (also known as ***chronic fatigue syndrome*** or ***post-viral fatigue syndrome***) a debilitating condition still not universally accepted as a genuine disease. The condition occurs after a flulike attack and has a diffuse range of symptoms. These strike and recur for years and include extreme fatigue, muscular pain, weakness, poor balance and coordination, joint pains, gastric upset, and depression.

Outbreaks of ME have been documented worldwide for more than 50 years. Recent research suggests that ME may be the result of chronic viral infection, leaving the sufferer exhausted, debilitated, and with generally lowered resistance. Differences have been seen in brainwave patterns in patients. There is no definitive treatment, but with time the symptoms become less severe.

mead alcoholic drink made from honey and water fermented with yeast, often with added spices. It was known in ancient times and was drunk by the Greeks, Britons, and Norse.

Mead Margaret 1901–1978. US anthropologist who popularized cultural relativity and challenged the conventions of Western society with *Coming of Age in Samoa* 1928 and subsequent works. Her fieldwork was later criticized. She was a popular speaker on civil liberties, ecological sanity, feminism, and population control.

'Human beings do not carry civilization in their genes.'

MARGARET MEAD
Quoted in *New York Times Magazine* April 1964

Mead Controversial US anthropologist Margaret Mead compared the adolescence of American girls with that of their Samoan counterparts in her famous book *Coming of Age in Samoa*. In *Sex and Temperament in Three Primitive Societies* she described her fieldwork in Bali, Samoa, and New Guinea. *Corbis*

‘If politics is the art of the possible, research is surely the art of the soluble.’

PETER MEDAWAR
Art of the Soluble

Meade Richard John Hannay 1938– . British equestrian in three-day events. He won three Olympic gold medals 1968 and 1972, and was twice a world champion. He is associated with horses such as Cornishman, Laureston, and The Poacher, and has won all the sport's major honours.

mean in mathematics, a measure of the average of a number of terms or quantities. The simple ***arithmetic mean*** is the average value of the quantities, that is, the sum of the quantities divided by their number. The ***weighted mean*** takes into account the frequency of the terms that are summed; it is calculated by multiplying each term by the number of times it occurs, summing the results and dividing this total by the total number of occurrences. The ***geometric mean*** of *n* quantities is the *n*th root of their product. In statistics, it is a measure of central tendency of a set of data.

meander loop-shaped curve in a river flowing across flat country. As a river flows, any curve in its course is accentuated by the current. The current is fastest on the outside of the curve where it cuts into the bank; on the curve's inside the current is slow and deposits any transported material. In this way the river changes its course across the flood plain.

mean deviation in statistics, a measure of the spread of a population from the ◊mean. Thus if there are *n* observations with a mean of *m*, the mean deviation is the sum of the moduli (absolute values) of the differences of the observation values from *m*, divided by *n*.

mean free path in physics, the average distance travelled by a particle, atom, or molecule between successive collisions. It is of importance in the ◊kinetic theory of gases.

mean life in nuclear physics, the average lifetime of a nucleus of a radioactive isotope equal to 1.44 times the ◊half-life. See ◊radioactivity.

means test method of assessing the amount to be paid in ◊social security benefits, which takes into account all sources of personal or family income.

measles acute virus disease (rubeola), spread by airborne infection. Symptoms are fever, severe catarrh, small spots inside the mouth, and a raised, blotchy red rash appearing for about a week after two weeks' incubation. Prevention is by vaccination.

In industrialized countries it is not usually a serious disease, though serious complications may develop. More than 1 million children a year die of measles (1995); a high percentage of them are Third World children.

meat flesh of animals taken as food, in Western countries chiefly from domesticated herds of cattle, sheep, pigs, and poultry. Major exporters include Argentina, Australia, New Zealand, Canada, the USA, and Denmark (chiefly bacon). The practice of cooking meat is at least 600,000 years old. More than 40% of the world's grain is now fed to animals.

Animals have been hunted for meat since the beginnings of human society. The domestication of animals for meat began during the ◊Neolithic era in the Middle East about 10,000 BC.

Meat is wasteful in production (the same area of grazing land would produce far greater food value in cereal crops). The consumption of meat in 1989 was 111 kg/244 lb per person in the USA, 68 kg/150 lb in the UK, 30 kg/66 lb in Japan, 6 kg/13 lb in Nigeria, and 1 kg/2.2 lb in India. Research suggests that, in a healthy diet, consumption of meat (especially with a high fat content) should not exceed the Japanese level.

To supply the British market 1994, 3 million cattle, 14 million pigs, 19 million sheep, and 670 million chickens were slaughtered for food.

Meath county of the Republic of Ireland, in the province of Leinster; county town Trim; area 2,340 sq km/903 sq mi; population (1991) 105,600. Tara Hill, 155 m/509 ft high, was the site of a palace and coronation place of many kings of Ireland (abandoned in the 6th century) and St Patrick preached here. Sheep, cattle, oats, and potatoes are produced.

Mecca (Arabic ***Makkah***) city in Saudi Arabia and, as birthplace of Muhammad, the holiest city of the Islamic world; population (1986) 618,000. In the centre of Mecca is the Great Mosque, in the courtyard of which is the ◊Kaaba, the sacred shrine containing the black stone believed to have been given to Abraham by the angel Gabriel. It also contains the well Zam-Zam, associated by tradition with the biblical characters Hagar and Ishmael. Most pilgrims come via the port of ◊Jiddah.

mechanical advantage (MA) in physics, the number of times the load moved by a machine is greater than the effort applied to that machine. In equation terms: MA = load/effort. The exact value of a working machine's MA is always less than its predicted value because there will always be some frictional resistance that increases the effort necessary to do the work.

mechanics branch of physics dealing with the motions of bodies and the forces causing these motions, and also with the forces acting on bodies in ◊equilibrium. It is usually divided into ◊dynamics and ◊statics. ***Quantum mechanics*** is the system based on the ◊quantum theory, which has superseded Newtonian mechanics in the interpretation of physical phenomena on the atomic scale.

mechanization the use of machines in place of manual labour or the use of animals. Until the 1700s there were few machines available to help people in the home, on the land, or in industry. There were no factories, only cottage industries, in which people carried out work, such as weaving, in their own homes for other people. The 1700s saw a long series of inventions, initially in the textile industry, that ushered in a machine age and brought about the ◊Industrial Revolution.

Among the first inventions in the textile industry were those made by John Kay (1704–c. 1780) (flying shuttle, 1773), James ◊Hargreaves (spinning jenny, 1764), and Richard ◊Arkwright (water frame, 1769). Arkwright pioneered the mechanized factory system by installing many of his ◊spinning machines in one building and employing people to work them.

mechanized infantry combat vehicle (MICV) tracked military vehicle designed to fight as part of an armoured battle group; that is, with tanks. It is armed with a quick-firing cannon and one or more machine guns. MICVs have replaced armoured personnel carriers. The British Army's MICV is the Warrior and the US Army's equivalent is the Bradley.

Mechnikov Ilya Ilich 1845–1916. Russian-born French zoologist who discovered the function of white blood cells and ◊phagocytes (amoebalike blood cells that engulf foreign bodies). He also described how these ‘scavenger cells’ can attack the body itself (autoimmune disease). He shared the Nobel Prize for Physiology or Medicine 1908.

Meciar Vladimir 1942– . Slovak politician, prime minister of the Slovak Republic Jan 1993–March 1994 and again from Oct 1994. He held a number of posts under the Czechoslovak communist regime until, as a dissident, he was expelled from the party 1970. He joined the Public Against Violence (PAV) movement 1989, campaigning for a free Czechoslovakia, then, as leader of the Movement for a Democratic Slovakia (HZDS) from 1990, sought an independent Slovak state. Under the federal system, Meciar became prime minister of the Slovak Republic 1990 and the new state's first prime minister Jan 1993. He resigned March 1994 after a no-confidence vote in parliament, but was returned as premier Oct 1994 following a general election victory.

With his Czech counterparts Meciar played an important role in ensuring that the ‘velvet revolution’ of 1989 was translated into a similarly bloodless ‘velvet divorce’.

Mecklenburg–West Pomerania (German ***Mecklenburg-Vorpommern***) administrative *Land* (state) of Germany

area 22,887 sq km/8,840 sq mi
capital Schwerin
towns and cities Rostock, Wismar, Stralsund, Neubrandenburg
products fish, ships, diesel engines, electronics, plastics, chalk
population (1994 est) 1,843,000
history the state was formerly the two grand duchies of Mecklenburg-Schwerin and Mecklenburg-Strelitz, which became free states of the Weimar Republic 1918–34, and were joined 1946 with part of Pomerania to form a region of East Germany. In 1952 it was split into the districts of Rostock, Schwerin, and Neubrandenburg. Following German reunification 1990, the districts were abolished and Mecklenburg–West Pomerania was reconstructed as one of the five new states of the Federal Republic.

medals and decorations coinlike metal pieces, struck or cast to commemorate historic events; to mark distinguished service, whether civil or military (in the latter case in connection with a particular battle, or for individual feats of courage, or for service over the period of a campaign); or as a badge of membership of an order of knighthood, society, or other special group.

Medan seaport and economic centre of the island of Sumatra, Indonesia; population (1990) 1,885,000. It trades in rubber, tobacco, and palm oil.

Medawar Peter Brian 1915–1987. British immunologist who, with Macfarlane ◊Burnet, discovered that the body's resistance to grafted tissue is undeveloped in the newborn child, and studied the way it is acquired. They shared a Nobel prize 1960. Medawar's work has been vital in understanding the phenomenon of tissue rejection following ◊transplantation.

Medea in Greek mythology, the sorceress daughter of the king of Colchis. When ◊Jason reached Colchis, she fell in love with him, helped him acquire the ◊Golden Fleece, and they fled together. When Jason later married Creusa, daughter of the king of Corinth, Medea killed his bride with the gift of a poisoned garment, and then killed her own two children by Jason.

Medellín industrial city (textiles, chemicals, engineering, coffee) in the Central Cordillera, Colombia, 1,538 m/5,048 ft above sea level; population (1994) 1,608,000. It is the second city and main textile and gold and silver mining centre of Colombia, and the drug capital of South America. Other industries include coffee growing.

media (singular ***medium***) means of communication; the mass media comprise the broadcast media of radio and ◊television, and the print media of ◊newspapers and ◊magazines.

median in mathematics and statistics, the middle number of an ordered group of numbers. If there is no middle number (because there is an even number of terms), the median is the ◊mean (average) of the two middle numbers. For example, the median of the group 2, 3, 7, 11, 12 is 7; that of 3, 4, 7, 9, 11, 13 is 8 (the average of 7 and 9).

In geometry, the term refers to a line from the vertex of a triangle to the midpoint of the opposite side.

medical ethics moral guidelines for doctors governing good professional conduct. The basic aims are considered to be doing good, avoiding harm, preserving the patient's autonomy, telling the truth, and pursuing justice. Ethical issues provoke the most discussion in medicine where these five aims cannot be simultaneously achieved – for example, what is ‘good’ for a child may clash with his or her autonomy or that of the parents.

Traditionally these principles have been set out in the Hippocratic Oath (introduced by Greek physician ◊Hippocrates and including such injunctions as the command to preserve confidentiality, to help the sick to the best of one's ability, and to refuse fatal draughts), but in the late 20th century rapidly advancing technology has raised the question of how far medicine should intervene in natural processes.

Medicaid US health care programme, introduced in 1965 by President Lyndon B Johnson, as part of his ‘Great Society’ welfare programme. Medicaid provides health care for the poor and unemployed, and is administered by the states and jointly funded by the state and federal governments. During the 1980s, under the Republican presidencies of Ronald Reagan and George Bush, federal spending on Medicaid was progressively reduced. Under the terms of the 1996 Welfare Reform Act, approved by the Democrat President Bill Clinton, states were given the power to deny Medicaid to non-citizens, and future legal immigrants will be denied Medicaid during their first five years in the USA.

Medicare US federally administered and financed health care insurance programme, providing medical benefits to citizens over the age of 65. Originally proposed by President John F Kennedy, as part of his 'New Frontier' programme to attack poverty, it was introduced by President Lyndon B Johnson in 1965. Unlike Medicaid, Medicare largely escaped cutbacks in federal spending during the Republican Reagan presidency of the 1980s.

Medici noble family of Florence, the city's rulers from 1434 until they died out 1737. Family members included ◊Catherine de' Medici, Pope ◊Leo X, Pope ◊Clement VII, and ◊Marie de' Medici.

Medici Cosimo de' 1389–1464. Italian politician and banker. Regarded as the model for Machiavelli's *The Prince*, he dominated the government of Florence from 1434 and was a patron of the arts. He was succeeded by his inept son Piero de' Medici (1416–1469).

Medici Cosimo de' 1519–1574. Italian politician, ruler of Florence; duke of Florence from 1537 and 1st grand duke of Tuscany from 1569.

Medici Ferdinand de' 1549–1609. Italian politician, grand duke of Tuscany from 1587.

Medici Giovanni de' 1360–1429. Italian entrepreneur and banker, with political influence in Florence as a supporter of the popular party. He was the father of Cosimo de' Medici.

Medici Lorenzo de', ***the Magnificent*** 1449–1492. Italian politician, ruler of Florence from 1469. He was also a poet and a generous patron of the arts.

medicine the practice of preventing, diagnosing, and treating disease, both physical and mental; also any substance used in the treatment of disease. The basis of medicine is anatomy (the structure and form of the body) and physiology (the study of the body's functions).

In the West, medicine increasingly relies on new drugs and sophisticated surgical techniques, while diagnosis of disease is more and more by noninvasive procedures. The time and cost of Western-type medical training makes it inaccessible to many parts of the Third World; where health care of this kind is provided it is often by auxiliary medical helpers trained in hygiene and the administration of a limited number of standard drugs for the prevalent diseases of a particular region. ▷*See feature on pp. 1024–1025.*

medicine, alternative forms of medical treatment that do not use synthetic drugs or surgery in response to the symptoms of a disease, but aim to treat the patient as a whole (◊holism). The emphasis is on maintaining health (with diet and exercise) and on dealing with the underlying causes rather than just the symptoms of illness. It may involve the use of herbal remedies and techniques like ◊acupuncture, ◊homoeopathy, and ◊chiropractic. Some alternative treatments are increasingly accepted by orthodox medicine, but the absence of enforceable standards in some fields has led to the proliferation of eccentric or untrained practitioners.

MEDICINE, WESTERN: TIMELINE

c. 400 BC	Hippocrates recognized that disease had natural causes.
c. AD 200	Galen consolidated the work of the Alexandrian doctors.
1543	Andreas Vesalius gave the first accurate account of the human body.
1628	William Harvey discovered the circulation of the blood.
1768	John Hunter began the foundation of experimental and surgical pathology.
1785	Digitalis was used to treat heart disease; the active ingredient was isolated 1904.
1798	Edward Jenner published his work on vaccination.
1877	Patrick Manson studied animal carriers of infectious diseases.
1882	Robert Koch isolated the bacillus responsible for tuberculosis.
1884	Edwin Klebs isolated the diphtheria bacillus.
1885	Louis Pasteur produced a vaccine against rabies.
1890	Joseph Lister demonstrated antiseptic surgery.
1895	Wilhelm Röntgen discovered X-rays.
1897	Martinus Beijerinck discovered viruses.
1899	Felix Hoffman developed aspirin; Sigmund Freud founded psychiatry.
1900	Karl Landsteiner identified the first three blood groups, later named A, B, and O.
1910	Paul Ehrlich developed the first specific antibacterial agent, Salvarsan, a cure for syphilis.
1922	Insulin was first used to treat diabetes.
1928	Alexander Fleming discovered penicillin.
1932	Gerhard Domagk discovered the first antibacterial sulphonamide drug, Prontosil.
1937	Electro-convulsive therapy (ECT) was developed.
1940s	Lithium treatment for manic-depressive illness was developed.
1950s	Antidepressant drugs and beta-blockers for heart disease were developed. Manipulation of the molecules of synthetic chemicals became the main source of new drugs. Peter Medawar studied the body's tolerance of transplanted organs and skin grafts.
1950	Proof of a link between cigarette smoking and lung cancer was established.
1953	Francis Crick and James Watson announced the structure of DNA. Jonas Salk developed a vaccine against polio.
1958	Ian Donald pioneered diagnostic ultrasound.
1960s	A new generation of minor tranquillizers called benzodiazepines was developed.
1967	Christiaan Barnard performed the first human heart-transplant operation.
1971	Viroids, disease-causing organisms even smaller than viruses, were isolated outside the living body.
1972	The CAT scan, pioneered by Godfrey Hounsfield, was first used to image the human brain.
1975	César Milstein developed monoclonal antibodies.
1978	World's first 'test-tube baby' was born in the UK.
1980s	AIDS (acquired immune-deficiency syndrome) was first recognized in the USA. Barbara McClintock's discovery of the transposable gene was recognized.
1980	The World Health Organization reported the eradication of smallpox.
1983	The virus responsible for AIDS, now known as human immunodeficiency virus (HIV), was identified by Luc Montagnier at the Institut Pasteur, Paris; Robert Gallo at the National Cancer Institute, Maryland, USA discovered the virus independently 1984.
1984	The first vaccine against leprosy was developed.
1987	The world's longest-surviving heart-transplant patient died in France, 18 years after his operation.
1989	Grafts of fetal brain tissue were first used to treat Parkinson's disease.
1990	Gene for maleness discovered by UK researchers.
1991	First successful use of gene therapy (to treat severe combined immune deficiency) was reported in the USA.
1996	US companies began testing different kinds of artificial blood in humans.
1998	The US Food and Drug Administration approved the drug Viagra for the treatment of impotence in May; Sept, approved UK but not available on NHS.

Medici Lorenzo de' Medici ('the Magnificent'), 15th century ruler of Florence, grandson of Cosimo. One of the greatest Renaissance princes, his court was a centre of the arts. He was patron to artists such as Botticelli (who painted his famous allegory *Primavera* for Lorenzo) and Ghirlandaio, architects such as Brunelleschi, and the sculptors Donatello and the della Robbias. Lorenzo himself was a noted poet. *Corbis*

medieval art painting and sculpture of the Middle Ages in Europe and parts of the Middle East, dating roughly from the 3rd century to the emergence of the Renaissance in Italy in the 1400s. This includes early Christian, Byzantine, Celtic, Anglo-Saxon, and Carolingian art. The Romanesque style was the first truly international style of medieval times, superseded by Gothic in the late 12th century. Religious sculpture, frescoes, and manuscript illumination proliferated; panel painting was introduced only towards the end of the Middle Ages.

early Christian art (3rd–5th centuries AD) This dates from when Christianity was made one of the official religions of the Roman state. Churches were built and artistic traditions adapted to the portrayal of the new Christian saints and symbols. Roman burial chests (*sarcophagi*) were adopted by the Christians and the imagery of pagan myths was gradually transformed into biblical themes.

Byzantine art (4th–15th centuries) This developed in the Eastern Empire, centred on Byzantium (modern Istanbul).

The use of mosaic associated with Byzantine art also appears in church decoration in the West. In Ravenna, for example, churches of the 5th and 6th centuries present powerful religious images on walls and vaults in brilliant, glittering colour and a bold, linear style. The Byzantine style continued for many centuries in icon painting in Greece and Russia.

Celtic and Anglo-Saxon art (4th–9th centuries) Stemming from the period when S Europe was overrun by Germanic tribes from the north, this early medieval art consists mainly of portable objects, such as articles for personal use or adornment. Among the invading tribes, the Anglo-Saxons, particularly those who settled in the British Isles, excelled in metalwork and jewellery, often in gold with garnet or enamel inlays, ornamented with highly stylized, plant-based interlace patterns with animal motifs. This type of ornament was translated into manuscript illumination produced in Christian monasteries, such as the decorated pages of the Northumbrian 7th-century *Lindisfarne Gospels* (British Museum, London) or the Celtic 8th-century *Book of Kells* (Trinity College, Dublin, Ireland).

Carolingian art (late 8th–early 9th centuries) Carolingian art centred around manuscript painting, which flourished in Charlemagne's empire, drawing its inspiration from the late Classical artistic traditions of the early Christian, Byzantine, and Anglo-Saxon styles. Several monasteries produced richly illustrated prayer books and biblical texts. Carved ivories and delicate metalwork, especially for bookcovers, were also produced.

Romanesque or Norman art (10th–12th centuries) This is chiefly evident in church architecture and church sculpture, on capitals and portals, and in

To be or not to be is not a question of compromise. Either you be or you don't be.

GOLDA MEIR
On the future of Israel, quoted in the *New York Times* 12 Dec 1974

manuscript illumination. Romanesque art was typified by the rounded arch, and combined naturalistic elements with the fantastic, poetical, and pattern-loving Celtic and Germanic traditions. Imaginary beasts and medieval warriors mingle with biblical themes. Fine examples remain throughout Europe, from N Spain and Italy to France, the Germanic lands of the Holy Roman Empire, England, and Scandinavia.

Gothic art (late 12th–15th centuries) Gothic art developed as large cathedrals were built in Europe. Sculptural decoration in stone became more monumental, and stained glass filled the tall windows, as at Chartres Cathedral, France. Figures were also carved in wood. Court patronage produced exquisite small ivories, goldsmiths' work, devotional books illustrated with miniatures, and tapestries depicting romantic tales. Panel painting, initially on a gold background, evolved in N Europe into the more realistic ◊International Gothic style. In Italy fresco painting made great advances; a seminal figure in this development was the artist Giotto di Bondone, whose work is seen as proto-Renaissance.

Medina (Arabic ***Madinah***) Saudi Arabian city, about 355 km/220 mi N of Mecca; population (1986 est) 500,000. It is the second holiest city in the Islamic world, and is believed to contain the tomb of Muhammad. It produces grain and fruit.

meditation act of spiritual contemplation, practised by members of many religions or as a secular exercise. It is a central practice in Buddhism (the Sanskrit term is *Samādhi*) and the movement for ◊transcendental meditation.

Mediterranean Sea inland sea separating Europe from N Africa, with Asia to the E; extreme length 3,700 km/2,300 mi; area 2,966,000 sq km/1,145,000 sq mi. It is linked to the Atlantic Ocean (at the Strait of Gibraltar), Red Sea, and Indian Ocean (by the Suez Canal), Black Sea (at the Dardanelles and Sea of Marmara). The main subdivisions are the Adriatic, Aegean, Ionian, and Tyrrhenian seas. It is highly polluted.

The Mediterranean is almost tideless, and is saltier and warmer than the Atlantic; shallows from Sicily to Cape Bon (Africa) divide it into an east and a west basin. Dense salt water forms a permanent deep current out into the Atlantic.

medlar small shrub or tree *Mespilus germanica* of the rose family Rosaceae. Native to SE Europe, it is widely cultivated for its fruit, resembling a small brown-green pear or quince. These are palatable when decay has set in.

Médoc French district bordering the Gironde in Aquitaine region, N of Bordeaux. It is famed for its claret wines, Margaux and St Julien being two well-known names. Lesparre and Pauillac are the chief towns.

medulla central part of an organ. In the mammalian kidney, the medulla lies beneath the outer cortex and is responsible for the reabsorption of water from the filtrate. In plants, it is a region of packing tissue in the centre of the stem. In the vertebrate brain, the medulla is the posterior region responsible for the coordination of basic activities, such as breathing and temperature control.

medusa the free-swimming phase in the life cycle of a coelenterate, such as a ◊jellyfish or ◊coral. The other phase is the sedentary polyp.

Medusa in Greek mythology, a mortal woman who was transformed into a ◊Gorgon. Medusa was slain by ◊Perseus; the winged horse ◊Pegasus was supposed to have sprung from her blood. Her head was so hideous – even in death – that any beholder was turned to stone.

Medway river of SE England, rising in Sussex and flowing through Kent and the Medway towns (Chatham, Gillingham, Rochester) to Sheerness, where it enters the Thames; it is about 96 km/60 mi long. In local tradition it divides the 'Men of Kent', who live to the east, from the 'Kentish Men', who live to the west.

Mee Margaret Ursula 1909–1988. English botanical artist. In the 1950s she went to Brazil, where she accurately and comprehensively painted many plant species of the Amazon basin. She is thought to have painted more species than any other botanical artist.

meerschaum aggregate of minerals, usually the soft white clay mineral ***sepiolite***, hydrous magnesium silicate. It floats on water and is used for making pipe bowls.

mega- prefix denoting multiplication by a million. For example, a megawatt (MW) is equivalent to a million watts.

megabyte (MB) in computing, a unit of memory equal to 1,024 ◊kilobytes. It is sometimes used, less precisely, to mean 1 million bytes.

megalith prehistoric stone monument of the late Neolithic or early Bronze Age. Most common in Europe, megaliths include single, large uprights (***menhirs***, for example, the Five Kings, Northumberland, England); ***rows*** (for example, Carnac, Brittany, France); ***circles***; and the remains of burial chambers with the covering earth removed, looking like a hut (***dolmens***, for example Kits Coty, Kent, England).

megamouth deep-sea shark *Megachasma pelagios*, which feeds on plankton. It has a bulbous head with protruding jaws and blubbery lips, is 4.5 m/15 ft long, and weighs 750 kg/1,650 lb.

megapode chickenlike bird of the family Megapodiidae, order Galliformes found in the Malay Archipelago and Australia. Megapodes pile up large mounds of vegetable matter, earth, and sand 4 m/13 ft across, in which to deposit their eggs. They cover the eggs and leave them to be incubated by the heat produced by the rotting vegetation. There are 19 species, characterized by very large feet.

megaton one million (10^6) tons. Used with reference to the explosive power of a nuclear weapon, it is equivalent to the explosive force of one million tons of trinitrotoluene (TNT).

megavitamin therapy the administration of large doses of vitamins to combat conditions considered wholly or in part due to their deficiency. The treatment has proved effective with addicts, schizophrenics, alcoholics, and depressives.

Meghalaya state of NE India
area 22,400 sq km/8,648 sq mi
capital Shillong
features mainly agricultural and comprises tribal hill districts
industries potatoes, cotton, jute, fruit, timber, mineral extraction (including 95% of India's sillimanite)
minerals coal, limestone, white clay, corundum, sillimanite
population (1994 est) 1,960,000, mainly Khasi, Jaintia, and Garo
religion Hindu 70%
language various.

Megiddo site of a fortress town in N Israel, where Thothmes III defeated the Canaanites; the Old Testament figure Josiah was killed in battle about 609 BC; and in World War I the British field marshal Allenby broke the Turkish front 1918. It is identified with ◊Armageddon.

Mehmet Ali or ***Muhammad Ali*** 1769–1849. Pasha (governor) of Egypt from 1805, and founder of the dynasty that ruled until 1953. An Albanian in the Ottoman service, he had originally been sent to Egypt to fight the French. As pasha, he established a European-style army and navy, fought his Turkish overlord 1831 and 1839, and conquered Sudan.

Mehta Zubin 1936– . Indian-born US conductor, music director of the New York Philharmonic from 1978. He specializes in robust, polished interpretations of 19th- and 20th-century repertoire, including contemporary US composers.

Meier Richard Alan 1934– . US architect. His white designs spring from the poetic Modernism of the ◊Le Corbusier villas of the 1920s. Originally one of the New York Five, Meier has remained closest to its purist ideals. His abstract style is at its most mature in the Museum für Kunsthandwerk (Museum of Arts and Crafts), Frankfurt, Germany, which was completed 1984.

Earlier schemes are the Bronx Developmental Centre, New York, 1970–76, and the Athenaeum–New Harmony, Indiana, 1974. He is the architect for the Getty Museum, Los Angeles.

Meiji Mutsuhito 1852–1912. Emperor of Japan from 1867, under the regnal era name Meiji ('enlightened'). During his reign – the ***Meiji era*** – Japan became a world industrial and naval power. His ministers abolished the feudal system and discrimination against the lowest caste, established state schools, reformed the civil service, and introduced conscription, the Western calendar, and other measures to modernize Japan, including a constitution 1889.

He took the personal name Mutsuhito when he became crown prince 1860. He was the son of Emperor Kōmei (reigned 1846–67), who was a titular ruler in the last years of the ◊Tokugawa shogunate.

Mein Kampf (German 'my struggle') book dictated by Adolf ◊Hitler to Rudolf Hess 1923–24 during their imprisonment for attempting the 1923 Munich beer-hall putsch (an attempt to overthrow the government of Bavaria). Part autobiography, part political philosophy, the book presents Hitler's ideas of German expansion, anticommunism, and anti-Semitism. It was published in two volumes, 1925 and 1927.

meiosis in biology, a process of cell division in which the number of ◊chromosomes in the cell is halved. It only occurs in ◊eukaryotic cells, and is part of a life cycle that involves sexual reproduction because it allows the genes of two parents to be combined without the total number of chromosomes increasing.

In sexually reproducing ◊diploid animals (having two sets of chromosomes per cell), meiosis occurs during formation of the ◊gametes (sex cells, sperm and egg), so that the gametes are ◊haploid (having only one set of chromosomes). When the gametes unite during ◊fertilization, the diploid condition is restored. In plants, meiosis occurs just before spore formation. Thus the spores are haploid and in lower plants such as mosses they develop into a haploid plant called a gametophyte which produces the gametes (see ◊alternation of generations). See also ◊mitosis.

Meir Golda (born Mabovitch, later Myerson) 1898–1978. Israeli Labour (*Mapai*) politician. Born in Russia, she emigrated to the USA 1906, and in 1921 went to Palestine. She was foreign minister 1956–66 and prime minister 1969–74. Criticism of the Israelis' lack of preparation for the 1973 Arab-Israeli War led to election losses for Labour and, unable to form a government, she resigned.

Meissen city in the state of Saxony, Germany, on the river Elbe; known for Meissen or Dresden porcelain from 1710; population (1983) 38,908.

Meissen Harlequin Bowing Low 1745, Wadsworth Atheneum, Hartford, Connecticut. The Meissen porcelain factory produced its finest work in the middle of the 18th century, when expertise in decoration combined with skill in modelling. The company's tableware and ornaments were exported all over Europe. *Corbis*

Meistersinger (German 'master singer') one of a group of German lyric poets, singers, and musicians of the 14th–16th centuries, who formed guilds for the revival of minstrelsy. Hans Sachs (1494–1576) was a Meistersinger, and Wagner's opera *Die Meistersinger von Nürnberg/The Mastersingers of Nuremberg* 1868 depicts the tradition.

Meitner Lise 1878–1968. Austrian-born Swedish physicist who worked with German radiochemist Otto Hahn (1879–1968) and was the first to realize that they had inadvertently achieved the fission of uranium. They also discovered ◊protactinium 1918. She refused to work on the atom bomb.

Mekele capital of Tigré region, N Ethiopia; population (1992) 113,000. It trades in salt, incense, and resin.

Mekong river rising as the Za Qu in Tibet and flowing to the South China Sea, through a vast delta (about 200,000 sq km/77,000 sq mi); length 4,425 km/2,750 mi.

melamine $C_3N_6H_6$ ◊thermosetting ◊polymer based on urea–formaldehyde. It is extremely resistant to heat and is also scratch-resistant. Its uses include synthetic resins.

Melanchthon Philip. Assumed name of Philip Schwarzerd 1497–1560. German theologian who helped Martin Luther prepare a German translation of the New Testament. In 1521 he issued the first systematic formulation of Protestant theology, reiterated in the Confession of ◊Augsburg 1530.

Melanesia islands in the SW Pacific between Micronesia to the N and Polynesia to the E, embracing all the islands from the New Britain archipelago to Fiji Islands. ▷ *See feature on pp. 806–807.*

Melanesian the indigenous inhabitants of Melanesia; any of the Pacific peoples of Melanesia. The Melanesian languages belong to the ◊Austronesian family.

melanin brown pigment that gives colour to the eyes, skin, hair, feathers, and scales of many vertebrates. In humans, melanin helps protect the skin against ultraviolet radiation from sunlight. Both genetic and environmental factors determine the amount of melanin in the skin.

melanism black coloration of animal bodies caused by large amounts of the pigment melanin. Melanin is of significance in insects, because melanic ones warm more rapidly in sunshine than do pale ones, and can be more active in cool weather. A fall in temperature may stimulate such insects to produce more melanin. In industrial areas, dark insects and pigeons match sooty backgrounds and escape predation, but they are at a disadvantage in rural areas where they do not match their backgrounds. This is known as industrial melanism.

melanoma highly malignant tumour of the melanin-forming cells (melanocytes) of the skin. It develops from an existing mole in up to two thirds of cases, but can also arise in the eye or mucous membranes. Malignant melanoma is the most dangerous of the skin cancers; it is associated with brief but excessive exposure to sunlight. It is easily treated if caught early but deadly once it has spread. There is a genetic factor in some cases.

Once rare, this disease is increasing at the rate of 7% in most countries with a predominantly fair-skinned population, owing to the increasing popularity of holidays in the sun. Most at risk are those with fair hair and light skin, and those who have had a severe sunburn in childhood. It strikes about 3,000 people a year in the UK, killing 1,250.

Melba Nellie. Adopted name of Helen Porter Mitchell 1861–1931. Australian soprano. Her recordings of Italian and French romantic opera, including a notable *Lucia di Lammermoor*, are distinguished by a radiant purity and technical finesse.

Peach melba (half a peach plus vanilla ice cream and melba sauce, made from sweetened, fresh raspberries) and melba toast (crisp, thin toast) are named after her.

Melbourne capital of Victoria, Australia, near the mouth of the river Yarra; population (1993) 3,189,200. Industries include engineering, shipbuilding, electronics, chemicals, food processing, clothing, and textiles.

Founded 1835, it grew in the wake of the gold rushes, and was the seat of the Commonwealth government 1901–27. It is the country's second largest city, with three universities, and was the site of the 1956 Olympics.

Melbourne (Henry) William Lamb, 2nd Viscount Melbourne 1779–1848. British Whig politician. Home secretary 1830–34, he was briefly prime minister in 1834 and again 1835–41. Accused in 1836 of seducing Caroline Norton (1808–1877), he lost the favour of William IV.

Melbourne was married 1805–25 to Lady Caroline Ponsonby (novelist Lady Caroline Lamb, 1785–1828). He was an adviser to the young Queen Victoria.

Melbourne Cup Australian horse race, raced over 3.2 km/2 mi at Flemington Park, Victoria, on the first Tuesday in Nov. It was inaugurated 1861.

Melchite (Syriac 'royalist') or ***Melkite***, member of a Christian church in Syria, Egypt, Lebanon, and Israel. The Melchite Church was founded in Syria in the 6th–7th centuries and is now part of the Eastern Orthodox Church. The Melchites accepted Byzantine rule at the Council of Chalcedon 451 (unlike the

Mekong

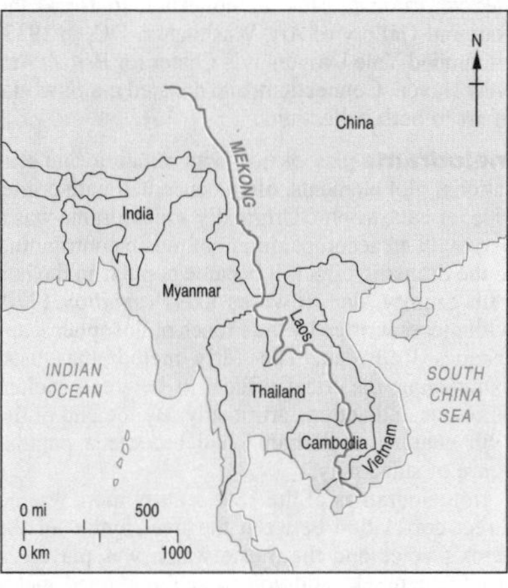

◊Maronites). In 1754 some Melchites broke away to form a ◊Uniate Church with Rome.

Meleager c. 140–170 BC. Greek philosopher and epigrammatist. Born at Gadara in the Decapolis, he was educated at Tyre, but spent the remainder of his life on the island of Kos. He compiled an anthology of epigrams, known as the *Garland*, for which he wrote an introduction, comparing each poet to an appropriate flower. His own epigrams are mostly erotic, and combine sophistication with feeling.

Melgarejo Mariano c. 1820–1871. Bolivian dictator and most notorious of the caudillos (dictatorial leaders) who dominated 19th-century Bolivia. He sold disputed land to Brazil, allowed Chilean businessmen to exploit Bolivian nitrate deposits, and seized large tracts of Indian land in the Altiplano (high plateau) to be sold to the highest bidder. Melgarejo seized power 1864 and survived a series of rebellions before he was overthrown by the last in a series of military uprisings seven years later.

Méliès Georges 1861–1938. French film pioneer. From 1896 to 1912 he made over 1,000 films, mostly fantasies (including *Le Voyage dans la lune/A Trip to the Moon* 1902). He developed trick effects, slow motion, double exposure, and dissolves, and in 1897 built Europe's first film studio at Montreuil.

Beginning his career as a stage magician, Méliès' interest in cinema was sparked by the Lumière brothers' cinematograph, premiered 1895. He constructed a camera and founded a production company, Star Film, but failed to develop as a filmmaker and went bankrupt 1913.

'Unlike so many who find success, she remained a 'dinkum hard-swearing Aussie' to the end.'

On DAME NELLIE MELBA
Arnold Haskell
Waltzing Matilda

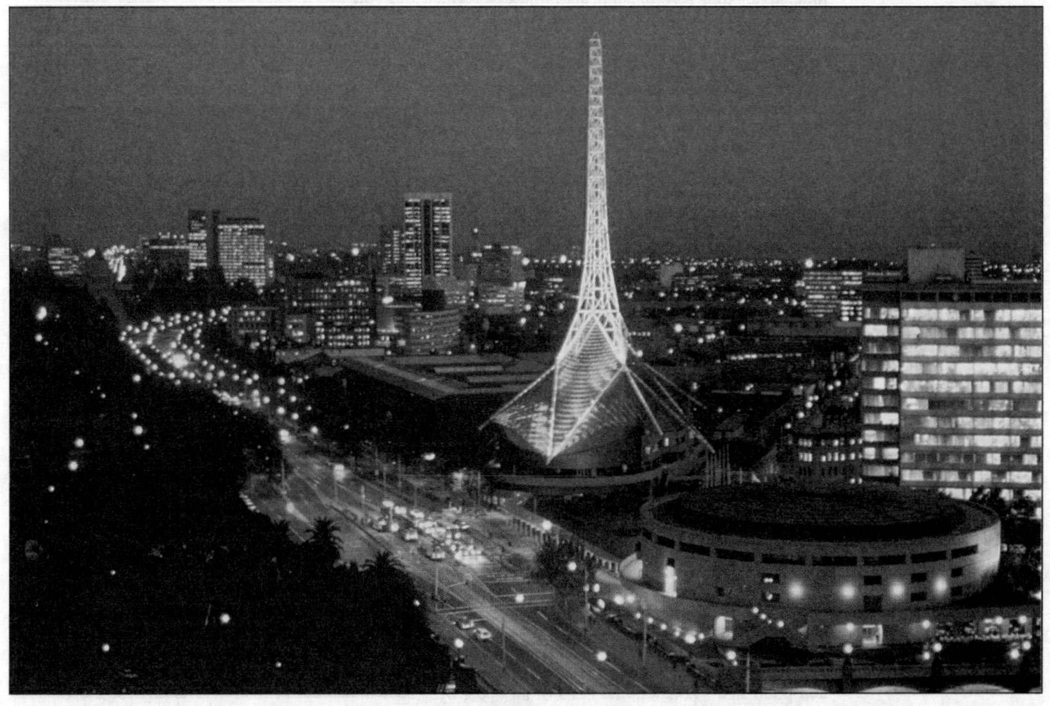

Melbourne A night view of Melbourne, the capital of Victoria, Australia. The tower that stands over the new arts centre is clearly visible. Melbourne is the second largest Australian city – two-thirds of the population of the state of Victoria live here – and it is an important cultural centre, with three universities. *Australian Overseas Information Office*

Life is all memory except for the one present moment that goes by you so quick you hardly catch it going.

On MEMORY
Tennessee Williams
The Milk Train Doesn't Stop Here Anymore

Mellon Andrew William 1855–1937. US financier who donated his art collection to found the National Gallery of Art, Washington DC, in 1937. He funded Yale University's Center for British Art, New Haven, Connecticut, and donated major works of art to both collections.

melodrama play or film with romantic and sensational plot elements, often concerned with crime, vice, or catastrophe. Originally a melodrama was a play with an accompaniment of music contributing to the dramatic effect. It became popular in the late 18th century, due to works like *Pygmalion* 1770, with pieces written by the French philosopher Jean-Jacques Rousseau. The early melodramas used extravagant theatrical effects to heighten violent emotions and actions artificially. By the end of the 19th century, melodrama had become a popular genre of stage play.

In melodramas of the 18th century there was no direct correlation between the free rhythm of the actor's voice and the music which was played in strict ◊metre. In addition to self-contained melodramas, some operas of the period included scenes of this style, as in the grave-digging scene in Beethoven's *Fidelio* 1805. Schoenberg developed the genre in his *Pierrot lunaire* 1912, by the inclusion of semi-musical speech called *Sprechgesang* (German 'speech-song').

Beginning with the early work of ◊Goethe and ◊Schiller, melodrama was popularized in France by Pixérécourt (1773–1844), whose *L'Enfant de mystère* was first introduced to England in an unauthorized translation by Thomas Holcroft as *A Tale of Mystery* 1802. Melodramas were frequently played against a Gothic background of mountains or ruined castles.

melody (Greek *melos* 'song') in music, a distinctive sequence of notes sounded consecutively within an orderly pitch structure such as a scale or a mode. A melody may be a tune in its own right, or it may form a theme running through a longer piece of music.

melon any of several large, juicy (95% water), thick-skinned fruits of trailing plants of the gourd family Cucurbitaceae. The muskmelon *Cucumis melo* and the large red watermelon *Citrullus vulgaris* are two of the many edible varieties.

Melrose town and administrative headquarters of Scottish Borders, Scotland; population (1991) 2,300. The heart of Robert I the Bruce is buried here and the ruins of Melrose Abbey 1136 are commemorated in verse by Sir Walter Scott.

meltdown the melting of the core of a nuclear reactor, due to overheating. To prevent such accidents all reactors have equipment intended to flood the core with water in an emergency. The reactor is housed in a strong containment vessel, designed to prevent radiation escaping into the atmosphere. The result of a meltdown would be an area radioactively contaminated for 25,000 years or more.

At Three Mile Island, Pennsylvania, USA, in March 1979, a partial meltdown occurred caused by a combination of equipment failure and operator error, and some radiation was released into the air. In April 1986, a reactor at Chernobyl, near Kiev, Ukraine, exploded, causing a partial meltdown of the core. Radioactive ◊fallout was detected as far away as Canada and Japan.

melting point temperature at which a substance melts, or changes from solid to liquid form. A pure substance under standard conditions of pressure (usually one atmosphere) has a definite melting point. If heat is supplied to a solid at its melting point, the temperature does not change until the melting process is complete. The melting point of ice is 0°C or 32°F.

Melton Mowbray market town in Leicestershire, England, on the river Eye; population (town, 1991) 24,350; (local authority district, 1994) 46,600. A fox-hunting and horse-breeding centre, it is also known for pork pies and Stilton cheeses. Britain's newest coalmine, Ashfordby Colliery, is here.

Melville Herman 1819–1891. US writer. His novel *Moby-Dick* 1851 was inspired by his whaling experiences in the South Seas and is considered to be one of the masterpieces of American literature. *Billy Budd, Sailor*, completed just before his death and published 1924, was the basis of an opera by Benjamin ◊Britten 1951. Although most of his works were unappreciated during his lifetime, today he is one of the most highly regarded of US authors.

Melville was born in Albany, New York. His family was left destitute when his father became bankrupt and died when Melville was 12. He went to sea as a cabin boy 1839, and later used that experience as a basis for *Redburn* 1849. His next voyage in 1841 from Fairhaven to the Pacific in a whaler, the *Acushnet*, gave him much material for *Moby Dick*. He deserted ship when it reached the Marquesas Islands, was captured by cannibals, and wrote about them in *Typee* 1846, his first published work. Escaping in an Australian whaler, the *Lucy Ann*, he was put ashore at Tahiti as one of a mutinous crew and later made the Society Islands the subject of his second book *Omoo* 1847. Sailing from there to Honolulu, he went home as a seaman in the frigate *United States*. of which he wrote in *White-Jacket* 1850.

Melville published a collection of short stories *The Piazza Tales* 1856, and an unsuccessful satire, *The Confidence Man* 1857. He worked in the New York customs office 1866–85, and published several volumes of verse, including *Battle Pieces* 1866, and *Clarel* 1876. He did not produce any prose from 1857 until *Billy Budd*. A friend of Nathaniel Hawthorne, he explored the dark, troubled side of American experience in novels of unusual form and great philosophical power.

membrane in living things, a continuous layer, made up principally of fat molecules, that encloses a ◊cell or ◊organelles within a cell. Small molecules, such as water and sugars, can pass through the cell membrane by ◊diffusion. Large molecules, such as proteins, are transported across the membrane via special channels, a process often involving energy input. The ◊Golgi apparatus within the cell is thought to produce certain membranes.

memento mori (Latin) a reminder of death.

Memling (or ***Memlinc***) Hans c. 1430–1494. Flemish painter. He was probably a pupil of van der ◊Weyden, but his style is calmer and softer. He painted religious subjects and also portraits, including *Tommaso Portinari and His Wife* about 1480 (Metropolitan Museum of Art, New York).

His works, which were highly regarded in Renaissance Italy, where they influenced Perugino and others, include: *The Mystic Marriage of St Catherine* (Hospital of St John, Bruges); the Donne Triptych (National Gallery, London), which includes both a self-portrait and a portrait of the English donor, Sir John Donne; *Bathsheba* (Staatsgalerie, Stuttgart), a life-sized nude; and such fine portraits as that of Guillaume Moreel and his wife (Musée des Beaux-Arts, Brussels).

Memling A detail from *The Adoration of the Magi* by Hans Memling (Prado, Madrid). A prolific and popular artist, Memling acquired an international reputation, his works being particularly admired in Italy. *Corbis*

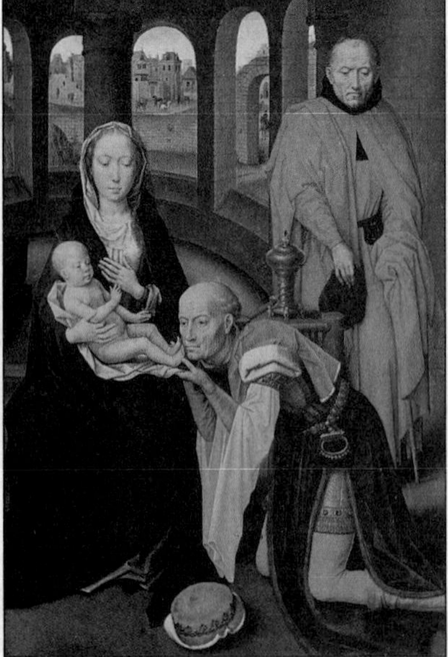

Memorial Day in the USA, a day of remembrance (formerly Decoration Day) instituted 1868 for those killed in the US Civil War. Since World War I it has been observed as a national holiday on the last Monday in May, traditionally falling on 30 May, in remembrance of all Americans killed in war.

memory ability to store and recall observations and sensations. Memory does not seem to be based in any particular part of the brain; it may depend on changes to the pathways followed by nerve impulses as they move through the brain. Memory can be improved by regular use as the connections between ◊nerve cells (neurons) become 'well-worn paths' in the brain. Events stored in ***short-term memory*** are forgotten quickly, whereas those in ***long-term memory*** can last for many years, enabling recall of information and recognition of people and places over long periods of time.

Short-term memory is the most likely to be impaired by illness or drugs whereas long-term memory is very resistant to such damage. Memory changes with age and otherwise healthy people may experience a natural decline after the age of about 40. Research is just beginning to uncover the biochemical and electrical bases of the human memory.

memory in computing, the part of a system used to store data and programs either permanently or temporarily. There are two main types: immediate access memory and backing storage. Memory capacity is measured in ◊bytes or, more conveniently, in kilobytes (units of 1,024 bytes) or megabytes (units of 1,024 kilobytes).

Immediate access memory, or ***internal memory***, describes the memory locations that can be addressed directly and individually by the central processing unit. It is either read-only (stored in ROM, PROM, and EPROM chips) or read/write (stored in RAM chips). Read-only memory stores information that must be constantly available and is unlikely to be changed. It is nonvolatile – that is, it is not lost when the computer is switched off. Read/write memory is volatile – it stores programs and data only while the computer is switched on.

Backing storage, or ***external memory***, is nonvolatile memory, located outside the central processing unit, used to store programs and data that are not in current use. Backing storage is provided by such devices as magnetic ◊discs (floppy and hard discs), ◊magnetic tape (tape streamers and cassettes), optical discs (such as ◊CD-ROM), and bubble memory (a memory device based on the creation of small bubbles on a magnetic surface).

Memphis ruined city beside the Nile, 19 km/12 mi SW of Cairo, Egypt. Once the centre of the worship of Ptah, it was the earliest capital of a united Egypt under King Menes about 3050 BC, and acted intermittently as capital until c. 1300 BC.

Memphis was later used as a stone quarry, but the 'cemetery city' of Sakkara survives, with the step pyramid built for King Zoser by ◊Imhotep, probably the world's oldest stone building.

Memphis industrial port city (pharmaceuticals, food processing, cotton, timber, tobacco) on the Mississippi River, in Tennessee, USA; population (1992) 610,300. The French built a fort here 1739, but Memphis was not founded until 1819. Its musical history includes Beale Street, home of the blues composer W C Handy, and Graceland, home of Elvis Presley; its recording studios and record companies (Sun 1953–68, Stax 1960–75) made it a focus of the music industry.

Menai Strait (Welsh ***Afon Menai***) channel of the Irish Sea, dividing Anglesey from the Welsh mainland; about 22 km/14 mi long, up to 3 km/2 mi wide. It is crossed by Thomas Telford's suspension bridge 1826 (reconstructed 1940) and Robert Stephenson's tubular rail bridge 1850.

Menander c. 342–291 BC. Greek comic dramatist. Previously only known by reputation and some short fragments, Menander's comedy *Bad-Tempered Man* 316 BC, was discovered 1957 on Egyptian papyrus. Substantial parts of *The Samian Woman*, *The Arbitration*, *The Unkindest Cut*, and *The Shield* are also extant. His comedies, with their wit and ingenuity of plot often concerning domestic intrigue, were adapted by the Roman comic dramatists ◊Plautus and ◊Terence.

Mencius Latinized name of Mengzi c. 372–c. 289 BC. Chinese philosopher and moralist in the tradition of orthodox Confucianism. He considered human nature innately good, although this goodness required cultivation, and based his conception of morality on this conviction. He spent 20 years searching (unsuccessfully) for a ruler to put into practice his enlightened political programme. His teachings are preserved as the *Book of Mengzi*.

Mencken H(enry) L(ouis) 1880–1956. US essayist and critic. He was known as 'the sage of Baltimore'. His unconventionally phrased, satiric contributions to the periodicals *The Smart Set* and *American Mercury* (both of which he edited) aroused controversy.

Mende a W African people living in the rainforests of central east Sierra Leone and W Liberia. They number approximately 1 million. The Mende are farmers as well as hunter-gatherers.

Mendel Gregor Johann 1822–1884. Austrian biologist, founder of ◊genetics. His experiments with successive generations of peas gave the basis for his theory of particulate inheritance rather than blending, involving dominant and recessive characters; see ◊Mendelism. His results, published 1865–69, remained unrecognized until the early 20th century.

From his findings Mendel formulated his law of segregation and law of independent assortment of characters, which are now recognized as two of the fundamental laws of heredity.

mendelevium synthesized, radioactive metallic element of the ◊actinide series, symbol Md, atomic number 101, relative atomic mass 258. It was first produced by bombardment of Es-253 with helium nuclei. Its longest-lived isotope, Md-258, has a half-life of about two months. The element is chemically similar to thulium. It was first synthesized in 1955.

Mendeleyev Dmitri Ivanovich 1834–1907. Russian chemist who framed the periodic law in chemistry 1869, which states that the chemical properties of the elements depend on their relative atomic masses. This law is the basis of the ◊periodic table of the elements, in which the elements are arranged by atomic number and organized by their related groups.

Mendeleyev was the first chemist to understand that all elements are related members of a single ordered system. From his table he predicted the properties of elements then unknown, of which three (gallium, scandium, and germanium) were discovered in his lifetime.

Mendelism in genetics, the theory of inheritance originally outlined by Austrian biologist Gregor Mendel. He suggested that, in sexually reproducing species, all characteristics are inherited through indivisible 'factors' (now identified with ◊genes) contributed by each parent to its offspring.

Mendelssohn (-Bartholdy) (Jakob Ludwig) Felix 1809–1847. German composer, also a pianist and conductor. His music has a lightness and charm of Classical music, applied to Romantic and descriptive subjects. Among his best-known works are *A Midsummer Night's Dream* 1827; the *Fingal's Cave* overture 1832; and five symphonies, which include the 'Reformation' 1830, the 'Italian' 1833, and the 'Scottish' 1842. He was instrumental in promoting the revival of interest in J S Bach's music.

Mendes Chico (Filho Francisco) 1944–1988. Brazilian environmentalist and labour leader. Opposed to the destruction of Brazil's rainforests, he organized itinerant rubber tappers into the Workers' Party (PT) and was assassinated by Darci Alves, a cattle rancher's son. Of 488 similar murders in land conflicts in Brazil 1985–89, his was the first to come to trial.

Mendès-France Pierre 1907–1982. French prime minister and foreign minister 1954–55. He extricated France from the war in Indochina, and prepared the way for Tunisian independence.

mendicant order religious order dependent on alms. In the Roman Catholic Church there are four orders of mendicant friars: Franciscans, Dominicans, Carmelites, and Augustinians. Buddhist monks and nuns (bhikkus and bhikkunis) are also traditionally dependent on alms.

Mendip Hills or *Mendips* range of limestone hills in S England, stretching nearly 40 km/25 mi SE–NW from Wells in Somerset towards the Bristol Channel. There are many cliffs, scars, and caverns, notably Cheddar Gorge. The highest peak is Blackdown (326 m/1,068 ft).

Mendoza capital of the Argentine province of the same name; population (1991) 121,700; metropolitan area (1992 est) 801,900. Founded 1561, it developed because of its position on the Trans-Andean railway; it lies at the centre of a wine-producing area.

Mendoza Antonio de c. 1490–1552. First Spanish viceroy of New Spain (Mexico) 1535–51. He attempted to develop agriculture and mining and supported the church in its attempts to convert the Indians. The system he established lasted until the 19th century. He was subsequently viceroy of Peru 1551–52.

Menelaus in Greek mythology, king of Sparta, son of Atreus, brother of ◊Agamemnon, and husband of ◊Helen. With his brother he was joint leader of the Greek expedition against ◊Troy.

Menem Carlos (Saul) 1935– . Argentine politician, president from 1989; leader of the Peronist (Justicialist Party) movement. As president, he introduced sweeping privatization and public spending cuts, released hundreds of political prisoners jailed under the Alfonsín regime, and sent two warships to the Gulf to assist the USA against Iraq in the 1992 Gulf War (the only Latin American country to offer support to the USA). He also improved relations with the UK.

Menes lived c. 3050 BC. Traditionally, the first king (pharaoh) of the first dynasty of ancient Egypt. He is said to have founded Memphis and organized worship of the gods.

Mengistu Haile Mariam 1937– . Ethiopian soldier and socialist politician, head of state 1977–91 (president 1987–91). He seized power in a coup, and instituted a regime of terror to stamp out any effective opposition. Confronted with severe problems of drought and secessionist uprisings, he survived with help from the USSR and the West until his violent overthrow by rebel forces. He was granted asylum in Zimbabwe and in 1995 he was tried in absentia on charges of mass murder, relating to the assassination of Emperor Selassie and the deaths of thousands of his political opponents.

menhir (Breton 'long stone') prehistoric standing stone; see ◊megalith.

Ménière's disease or ***Ménière's syndrome*** recurring condition of the inner ear affecting mechanisms of both hearing and balance. It usually develops in the middle or later years. Symptoms, which include deafness, ringing in the ears, nausea, vertigo, and loss of balance, may be eased by drugs, but there is no cure.

meningitis inflammation of the meninges (membranes) surrounding the brain, caused by bacterial or viral infection. Bacterial meningitis, though treatable by antibiotics, is the more serious threat. Diagnosis is by ◊lumbar puncture.

The severity of the disease varies from mild to rapidly lethal, and symptoms include fever, headache, nausea, neck stiffness, delirium, and (rarely) convulsions. Many common viruses can cause the occasional case of meningitis, although not usually in its more severe form. The treatment for viral meningitis is rest. Around 3,000 cases are recorded in the UK each year, mostly in children and teenagers.

meniscus in physics, the curved shape of the surface of a liquid in a thin tube, caused by the cohesive effects of ◊surface tension (capillary action). When the walls of the container are made wet by the liquid, the meniscus is concave, but with highly viscous liquids (such as mercury) the meniscus is convex. Meniscus is also the name of a concavo-convex or convexo-concave ◊lens.

Mennonite member of a Protestant Christian sect, originating as part of the ◊Anabaptist movement in Zürich, Switzerland, 1523. Members refuse to hold civil office or do military service, and reject infant baptism. They were named Mennonites after Menno Simons (1496–1559), leader of a group in Holland. Persecution drove other groups to Russia and North America.

menopause in women, the cessation of reproductive ability, characterized by menstruation (see ◊menstrual cycle) becoming irregular and eventually ceasing. The onset is at about the age of 50, but varies greatly. Menopause is usually uneventful, but some women suffer from complications such as flushing, excessive bleeding, and nervous disorders. Since the 1950s, ◊hormone-replacement therapy (HRT), using ◊oestrogen alone or with progestogen, a synthetic form of ◊progesterone, has been developed to counteract such effects.

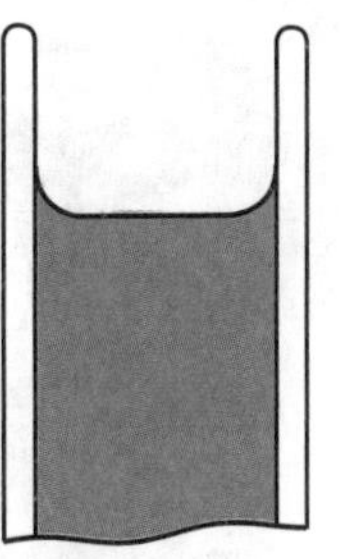

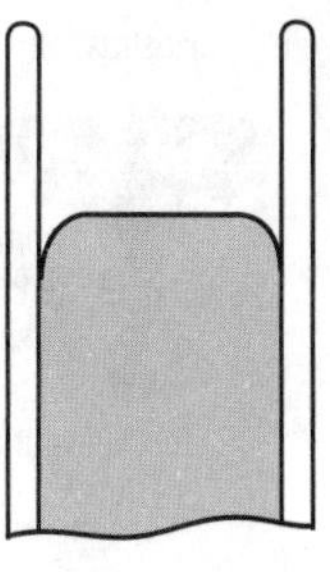

meniscus The curved shape, or meniscus, of a liquid surface is caused by the attraction or repulsion between liquid and container molecules.

Long-term use of HRT was previously associated with an increased risk of cancer of the uterus, and of clot formation in the blood vessels, but newer formulations using natural oestrogens are not associated with these risks. Without HRT there is increased risk of ◊osteoporosis (thinning of the bones) leading to broken bones, which may be indirectly fatal, particularly in the elderly.

menorah seven-branched candlestick symbolizing Judaism and the state of Israel. Also, the candelabrum (having seven branches and a *shammes*, or extra candle with which to light the others) used on ◊Hanukkah.

Menorca Spanish form of ◊Minorca, one of the Balearic Islands.

Menotti Gian Carlo 1911– . Italian-born US composer. He created small-scale realist operas in tonal idiom, including *The Medium* 1946, *The Telephone* 1947, *The Consul* 1950, *Amahl and the Night Visitors* 1951 (the first opera to be written for television), and *The Saint of Bleecker Street* 1954. He has also written orchestral and chamber music. He was co-librettist with Samuel Barber for the latter's *Vanessa* and *A Hand of Bridge*.

Mensa International organization founded in the UK 1945 with membership limited to those passing an 'intelligence' test. It has been criticized by many who believe that intelligence is not satisfactorily measured by IQ (intelligence quotient) tests alone. In recent years, Mensa has started to fund special schools and activities for children with high-IQ in the UK.

Menshevik (Russian *menshinstvo* 'minority') member of the minority of the Russian Social Democratic Party, who split from the ◊Bolsheviks 1903. The Mensheviks believed in a large, loosely organized party and that, before socialist revolution could occur in Russia, capitalist society had to develop further. During the Russian Revolution they had limited power and set up a government in Georgia, but were suppressed 1922.

menstrual cycle cycle that occurs in female mammals of reproductive age, in which the body is prepared for pregnancy. At the beginning of the cycle, a Graafian (egg) follicle develops in the ovary, and the inner wall of the uterus forms a soft spongy lining. The egg is released from the ovary, and the uterus lining (endometrium) becomes vascularized (filled with blood vessels). If fertilization does not occur, the corpus luteum (remains of the Graafian follicle) degenerates, and the uterine lining breaks down, and is shed. This is what causes the loss of blood that marks menstruation. The cycle then begins again. Human menstruation takes place from puberty to menopause, except during pregnancy, occurring about every 28 days.

The cycle is controlled by a number of ◊hormones, including ◊oestrogen and ◊progesterone. If fertilization occurs, the corpus luteum persists and goes on producing progesterone. *See illustration on following page.*

mental disability arrested or incomplete development of mental capacities. It can be very mild, but in more severe cases is associated with social problems and difficulties in living independently. A person may be born with a mental disability (for example, ◊Down's syndrome) or may acquire it

'If, after I depart this vale, you ever remember me and have thought to please my ghost, forgive some sinner and wink your eye at some homely girl.'

H L Mencken

Smart Set Dec 1922

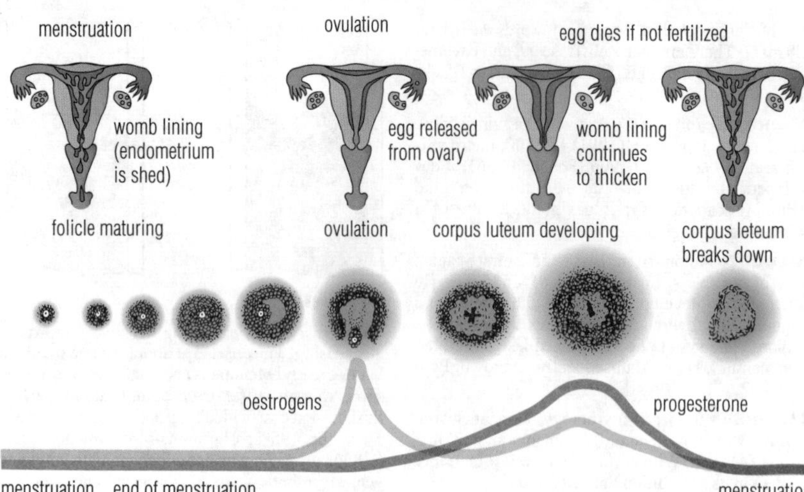

menstrual cycle From puberty to the menopause, most women produce a regular rhythm of hormones that stimulate the various stages of the menstrual cycle. The change in hormone levels may cause premenstrual tension.

through brain damage. Between 90 and 130 million people in the world suffer from such disabilities.

Clinically, mental disability is graded as profound, severe, moderate, or mild, roughly according to ◊IQ and the sufferer's ability to cope with everyday tasks. Among its many causes are genetic defect (◊phenylketonuria), chromosomal errors (Down's syndrome), infection before birth (◊rubella) or in infancy (◊meningitis), trauma (brain damage at birth or later), respiratory difficulties at the time of birth, toxins (lead poisoning), physical deprivation (lack of, or defective, ◊thyroid tissue, as in cretinism), and gross psychological deprivation.

mental illness disordered functioning of the mind. Since normal working cannot easily be defined, the borderline between mild mental illness and normality is a matter of opinion (not to be confused with normative behaviour; see ◊norm). It is broadly divided into two categories: ◊neurosis, in which the patient remains in touch with reality; and ◊psychosis, in which perception, thought, and belief are disordered.

menthol pungent, waxy, crystalline alcohol $C_{10}H_{19}OH$, derived from oil of peppermint and used in medicines and cosmetics.

Mentor in Homer's *Odyssey*, an old man, adviser to ◊Telemachus in the absence of his father ◊Odysseus. His form is often taken by the goddess Athena.

menu in computing, a list of options, displayed on screen, from which the user may make a choice – for example, the choice of services offered to the customer by a bank cash dispenser: withdrawal, deposit, balance, or statement. Menus are used extensively in ◊graphical user interface (GUI) systems, where the menu options are often selected using a ◊mouse.

Menuhin Yehudi, Baron Menuhin 1916–1999. US-born violinist and conductor. His solo repertoire extends from Vivaldi to Enescu. He recorded the Elgar Violin Concerto 1932 with the composer conducting, and commissioned the Sonata for violin solo 1944 from an ailing Bartók. He has appeared in concert with sitar virtuoso Ravi Shankar, and with jazz violinist Stephane Grappelli.

He made his debut with an orchestra at the age of 11 in New York. A child prodigy, he achieved great depth of interpretation, and was often accompanied on the piano by his sister Hephzibah (1921–1981). In 1959 he moved to London, becoming a British subject 1985. He founded the Yehudi Menuhin School of Music, Stoke d'Abernon, Surrey, 1963.

Menzies Robert Gordon 1894–1978. Australian politician, leader of the United Australia (now Liberal) Party and prime minister 1939–41 and 1949–66. His critics argued that he did not show enough interest in Asia, and supported the USA and white African regimes too uncritically (he followed America's lead in committing Australia to the Vietnam War). His defenders argued that he provided stability in domestic policy and national security.

Meo or *Miao* another name (sometimes considered derogatory) for the ◊Hmong, a SE Asian people.

MEP abbreviation for ***member of the ◊European Parliament***.

Mephistopheles or *Mephisto*, another name for the ◊devil, or an agent of the devil, associated with the ◊Faust legend.

Mercalli scale scale used to measure the intensity of an ◊earthquake. It differs from the ◊Richter scale, which measures magnitude. It is named after the Italian seismologist Giuseppe Mercalli (1850–1914). *See list of tables on p. 1177.*

Mercator Gerardus, Latinized form of Gerhard Kremer 1512–1594. Flemish mapmaker who devised the first modern atlas, showing ***Mercator's projection*** in which the parallels and meridians on maps are drawn uniformly at 90°. It is often used for navigational charts, because compass courses can be drawn as straight lines, but the true area of countries is increasingly distorted the further north or south they are from the equator. For other types, see ◊map projection.

Mercedes-Benz German car-manufacturing company created by a merger of the Daimler and Benz factories 1926. The first cars to carry the Mercedes name were those built by Gottlieb ◊Daimler 1901. In the 1930s, Mercedes-Benz dominated Grand Prix races. The W196, which made its debut 1954, was one of the finest racing cars of the postwar era. Following a disaster at Le Mans 1955, when 80 spectators lost their lives after an accident involving a Mercedes, the company withdrew from motor sport until 1989.

Menuhin The violinist and conductor Yehudi Menuhin in 1991. At the age of 16 he played Elgar's Violin Concerto with the 75-year-old composer as conductor, and since then has inspired several composers to write for him. During recent years he has turned increasingly to conducting. *EMI*

mercenary soldier hired by the army of another country or by a private army. Mercenary military service originated in the 14th century, when cash payment on a regular basis was the only means of guaranteeing soldiers' loyalty. In the 20th century mercenaries have been common in wars and guerrilla activity in Asia, Africa, and Latin America.

Most famous of the mercenary armies was the Great Company of the 14th century, which was in effect a glorified protection racket, comprising some 10,000 knights of all nationalities and employing condottieri, or contractors, to serve the highest bidder. By the end of the 14th century, condottieri and freelances were an institutionalized aspect of warfare. In the 18th century, Swiss cantons and some German states regularly provided the French with troops for mercenary service as a means of raising money; they were regarded as the best forces in the French army. Britain employed 20,000 German mercenaries to make up its numbers during the Seven Years' War 1756–63 and used Hessian forces during the American Revolution 1775–83.

Article 47 of the 1977 Additional Protocols to the Geneva Convention stipulates that 'a mercenary shall not have the right to be a combatant or a prisoner of war' but leaves a party to the Protocols the freedom to grant such status if so wished.

Mercer David 1928–1980. English dramatist. He first became known for his television plays, including *A Suitable Case for Treatment* 1962, filmed as *Morgan, A Suitable Case for Treatment* 1966; stage plays include *After Haggerty* 1970.

Merchant Ismail 1936– . Indian film producer, known for his stylish collaborations with James ◊Ivory on films including *Shakespeare Wallah* 1965, *The Europeans* 1979, *Heat and Dust* 1983, *A Room with a View* 1987, *Maurice* 1987, *Howards End* 1992, and *The Remains of the Day* 1993.

merchant bank financial institution that specializes in corporate finance and financial and advisory services for business. Originally developed in the UK in the 19th century, merchant banks now offer many of the services provided by the commercial banks. Traditionally, the merchant banks have been situated in the City of London, but in recent years some have opened in major provincial cities and overseas.

merchant navy the passenger and cargo ships of a country. Most are owned by private companies. To avoid strict regulations on safety, union rules on crew wages, and so on, many ships are today registered under 'flags of convenience', that is, flags of countries that do not have such rules. During wartime, merchant shipping may be drafted by the national government for military purposes.

Types of ship include: tramps either in home coastal trade, or carrying bulk cargoes worldwide; tankers the largest ships afloat, up to 500,000 tonnes/492,000 tons and 380 m/1,245 ft long, and other vessels carrying specialized cargo; cargo liners combining cargo and passenger traffic on short or world voyages. Passenger-only liners enjoyed a revival in the 1980s.

Merchants Adventurers English trading company founded 1407, which controlled the export of cloth to continental Europe. It comprised guilds and traders in many N European ports. In direct opposition to the Hanseatic League, it came to control 75% of English overseas trade by 1550. In 1689 it lost its charter for furthering the traders' own interests at the expense of the English economy. The company was finally dissolved 1806.

Mercia Anglo-Saxon kingdom that emerged in the 6th century. By the late 8th century it dominated all England south of the Humber, but from about 825 came under the power of ◊Wessex. Mercia eventually came to denote an area bounded by the Welsh border, the river Humber, East Anglia, and the river Thames.

Merckx Eddie 1945– . Belgian cyclist known as 'the Cannibal'. He won the Tour de France a joint record five times 1969–74. Merckx turned professional 1966 and won his first classic race, the

Milan–San Remo, the same year. He went on to win 24 classics as well as the three major tours (of Italy, Spain, and France) a total of 11 times. He was world professional road-race champion three times and in 1971 won a record 54 races in the season. He retired in 1977.

Mercosur (Spanish *Mercado del Sur* 'Market of the South') (South American Common Market) free-trade organization, founded 1991 on signature of the Asunción Treaty by Argentina, Brazil, Paraguay, and Uruguay, and formally inaugurated 1 Jan 1995. In June 1996 Chile and Bolivia were admitted as associate members. With a GNP of $800,000 million and a population of more than 190 million, Mercosur constitutes the world's fourth-largest free-trade bloc after the European Economic Area, the North American Free Trade Area, and the Asia-Pacific Economic Cooperation.

mercury (Latin *mercurius*) or ***quicksilver***, heavy, silver-grey, metallic element, symbol Hg (from Latin *hydrargyrum*), atomic number 80, relative atomic mass 200.59. It is a dense, mobile liquid with a low melting point (−38.87°C/−37.96°F). Its chief source is the mineral cinnabar, HgS, but it sometimes occurs in nature as a free metal. Its alloys with other metals are called amalgams (a silver-mercury amalgam is used in dentistry for filling cavities in teeth). Industrial uses include drugs and chemicals, mercury-vapour lamps, arc rectifiers, power-control switches, barometers, and thermometers.

Mercury is a cumulative poison that can contaminate the food chain, and cause intestinal disturbance, kidney and brain damage, and birth defects in humans. (The World Health Organization's 'safe' limit for mercury is 0.5 milligrams of mercury per kilogram of muscle tissue). The discharge into the sea by industry of organic mercury compounds such as dimethylmercury is the chief cause of mercury poisoning in the latter half of the 20th century.

The element was known to the ancient Chinese and Hindus, and is found in Egyptian tombs of about 1500 BC. It was named by the alchemists after the fast-moving god, for its fluidity.

Mercury in astronomy, the closest planet to the Sun. Its mass is 0.056 that of Earth. On its sunward side the surface temperature reaches over 400°C/752°F, but on the 'night' side it falls to −170°C/−274°F
mean distance from the Sun 58 million km/36 million mi
equatorial diameter 4,880 km/3,030 mi
rotation period 59 Earth days
year 88 Earth days
atmosphere Mercury has an atmosphere with minute traces of argon and helium
surface composed of silicate rock often in the form of lava flows. In 1974 the US space probe *Mariner 10* showed that Mercury's surface is cratered by meteorite impacts
satellites none

Its largest known feature is the Caloris Basin, 1,400 km/870 mi wide. There are also cliffs hundreds of kilometres long and up to 4 km/2.5 mi high, thought to have been formed by the cooling of the planet billions of years ago. Inside is an iron core three-quarters of the planet's diameter, which produces a magnetic field 1% the strength of Earth's.

Mercury in Roman mythology, a god, identified with the Greek ◊Hermes, and like him represented with winged sandals and a winged staff entwined with snakes. He was the messenger of the gods, and was associated particularly with commerce.

mercury fulminate highly explosive compound used in detonators and percussion caps. It is a grey, sandy powder and extremely poisonous.

Mercury project US project to put a human in space in the one-seat Mercury spacecraft 1961–63. The first two Mercury flights, on Redstone rockets, were short flights to the edge of space and back. The orbital flights, beginning with the third in the series (made by John Glenn (1921–)), were launched by Atlas rockets.

Meredith George 1828–1909. English novelist and poet. His realistic psychological novel *The Ordeal of Richard Feverel* 1859 engendered both scandal and critical praise. His best-known novel, *The Egoist* 1879, is superbly plotted and dissects the hero's self-centredness with merciless glee. The sonnet sequence *Modern Love* 1862 reflects the failure of his own marriage to the daughter of Thomas Love ◊Peacock. Other novels include *Evan Harrington* 1861, *Diana of the Crossways* 1885, and *The Amazing Marriage* 1895. *Poems and Lyrics of the Joy of Earth* 1883 was a further notable book of verse.

> 'Speech is the small change of silence.'
>
> **George Meredith** *The Ordeal of Richard Feverel*

merganser any of several diving ducks of the genus *Mergus* with long, slender, serrated bills for catching fish. Most have crested heads. They are widely distributed in the northern hemisphere.

merger the linking of two or more companies, either by creating a new organization by consolidating the original companies or by absorption by one company of the others. Unlike a takeover, which is not always a voluntary fusion of the parties, a merger is the result of an agreement.

Mérida capital of Yucatán state, Mexico, a centre of the sisal industry; population (1990) 556,800. It was founded 1542, and has a cathedral 1598. Its port on the Gulf of Mexico is Progreso.

meridian half a ◊great circle drawn on the Earth's surface passing through both poles and thus through all places with the same longitude. Terrestrial longitudes are usually measured from the Greenwich Meridian.

An astronomical meridian is a great circle passing through the celestial pole and the zenith (the point immediately overhead).

Mérimée Prosper 1803–1870. French author. Among his works are the short novels *Mateo Falcone* 1829, *Colomba* 1841, *Carmen* 1846 (the basis for Bizet's opera), and the *Lettres à une inconnue/ Letters to an Unknown Girl* 1873. Romantically set in foreign and less civilized countries, his stories nevertheless have a realistic background of local colour and atmosphere.

His literary career began with six dramatic pieces which he attributed to an imaginary Spanish actress, Clara Gazul (*Le Théâtre de Clara Gazul/The Theatre of Clara Gazul* 1825).

merino breed of sheep. Its close-set, silky wool is highly valued. The merino, originally from Spain, is now found all over the world, and is the breed on which the Australian wool industry is built.

meristem region of plant tissue containing cells that are actively dividing to produce new tissues (or have the potential to do so). Meristems found in the tip of roots and stems, the apical meristems, are responsible for the growth in length of these organs. The ◊cambium is a lateral meristem that is responsible for increase in girth in perennial plants. Some plants also have intercalary meristems, as in the stems of grasses, for example; these are responsible for their continued growth after cutting or grazing.

meritocracy system (of, for example, education or government) in which selection is by performance or competitive examinations. Such a system favours intelligence and ability rather than social position or wealth.

Merleau-Ponty Maurice 1908–1961. French philosopher, one of the most significant contributors to ◊phenomenology after Edmund ◊Husserl. He attempted to move beyond the notion of a pure experiencing consciousness, arguing in *The Phenomenology of Perception* 1945 that perception is intertwined with bodily awareness and with language. In his posthumously published work *The Visible and the Invisible* 1964, he argued that our experience is inherently ambiguous and elusive and that the traditional concepts of philosophy are therefore inadequate to grasp it.

merlin small ◊falcon *Falco columbarius*, order Falconiformes, of Eurasia and North America, where it is also called ***pigeon hawk***. The male, 26 cm/10 in long, has a grey-blue back and reddish-brown barred front; the female, 32 cm/13 in long, is brown with streaks. They fly relatively low over the ground when hunting and 'stoop' quickly onto their prey, which consists mainly of small birds.

Merlin legendary magician and counsellor to King ◊Arthur. Welsh bardic literature has a cycle of poems attributed to him, and he may have been a real person. He is said to have been buried in a cave in the park of Dynevor Castle, Dyfed.

MERLIN array radiotelescope network centred on ◊Jodrell Bank, N England.

mermaid mythical sea creature (the male is a ***merman***), having a human head and torso and a fish's tail. The dugong and seal are among suggested origins for the idea.

Meroë ancient city in Sudan, on the Nile near Khartoum, capital of Nubia from about 600 BC to AD 350. Tombs and inscriptions have been excavated, and iron-smelting slag heaps have been found.

Merovingian dynasty 5th–8th centuries. Frankish dynasty, named after its founder, ***Merovech*** (5th century AD). His descendants ruled France from the time of Clovis (481–511) to 751.

Mersey river in NW England; length 112 km/ 70 mi. Formed by the confluence of the Goyt and Tame rivers at Stockport, it flows W to join the Irish Sea at Liverpool Bay. It is linked to the Manchester Ship Canal.

Mersey beat pop music of the mid-1960s that originated in the northwest of England. It was also known as the Liverpool sound or ◊beat music in the UK. It was almost exclusively performed by all-male groups, the most popular being the Beatles.

Merseyside metropolitan county of NW England, created 1974; in 1986, most of the functions of the former county council were transferred to metropolitan district councils
area 650 sq km/251 sq mi
towns and cities Liverpool, Bootle, Birkenhead, St Helens, Wallasey, Southport
features river Mersey; Merseyside Innovation Centre (MIC), linked with Liverpool University and Polytechnic; Prescot Museum of clock- and watch-making; Speke Hall (Tudor), and Croxteth Hall and Country Park
industries chemicals, electrical goods, vehicles
population (1991) 1,403,600

Merthyr Tydfil industrial town (light engineering, electrical goods) on the river Taff and, from 1996, unitary authority of Wales (*see United Kingdom map*); population (1991) 39,500. It was formerly a centre of the Welsh coal and steel industries.

Merton outer borough of SW Greater London; population (1991) 168,500. It includes the suburbs of ◊Wimbledon, Mitcham, and Morden
features Augustinian priory, founded 1114, where Thomas à Becket and Walter de Merton, founder of Merton College, Oxford, were educated (it was demolished at the dissolution and the stones used by Henry VIII to build Nonsuch Palace); Merton Place, where Admiral Nelson lived; Merton Park, laid out in the mid-19th century, claimed as the forerunner of garden suburbs; part of Wimbledon Common, includes Caesar's Camp – an Iron Age fort; All England Lawn Tennis Club (1877).

mesa (Spanish 'table') flat-topped, steep-sided plateau, consisting of horizontal weak layers of rock topped by a resistant formation; in particular, those found in the desert areas of the USA and Mexico. A small mesa is called a butte.

mescaline psychedelic drug derived from a small, spineless cactus *Lophophora williamsii* of N Mexico and the southwestern USA, known as ◊peyote. The tops (called mescal buttons), which scarcely appear above ground, are dried and chewed, or added to alcoholic drinks. It is used by some North American Indians in religious rites.

Meskhetian a community of Turkish descent that formerly inhabited Meskhetia, on the then Turkish-Soviet border. They were deported by Stalin 1944 to Kazakhstan and Uzbekistan, and have campaigned since then for a return to their homeland.

Mesmer Friedrich Anton (or Franz) 1734–1815. Austrian physician, an early experimenter in ◊hypnosis, which was formerly (and popularly) called 'mesmerism' after him. He claimed to reduce people to trance state by consciously exerted 'animal magnetism', their willpower being entirely subordinated to his. Expelled by the police from Vienna, he created a sensation in Paris in 1778, but was denounced as a charlatan in 1785.

mesmerism former term for ◊hypnosis, after Austrian physician Friedrich Mesmer.

Mesolithic the Middle Stone Age developmental stage of human technology and of ◊prehistory.

meson in physics, a group of unstable subatomic particles made up of two indivisible elementary particles called ◊quarks. It has a mass intermediate between that of the electron and that of the proton, is found in cosmic radiation, and is emitted by nuclei under bombardment by very high-energy particles. The mesons form a subclass of the hadrons and include the kaons and pions.

mesophyll the tissue between the upper and lower epidermis of a leaf blade (◊lamina), consisting of parenchyma-like cells containing numerous ◊chloroplasts. In many plants, mesophyll is divided into two distinct layers. The ***palisade mesophyll*** is usually just below the upper epidermis and is composed of regular layers of elongated cells. Lying below them is the ***spongy mesophyll***, composed of loosely arranged cells of irregular shape. This layer contains fewer chloroplasts and has many intercellular spaces for the diffusion of gases (required for ◊respiration and ◊photosynthesis), linked to the outside by means of ◊stomata.

Mesopotamia the land between the Tigris and Euphrates rivers, now part of Iraq. The civilizations of Sumer and Babylon flourished here. Sumer (3500 BC) may have been the earliest urban civilization.

Mesopotamian art the art of the ancient civilizations which grew up in the area around the Tigris and Euphrates rivers, now in Iraq. Mesopotamian art, which was largely used to glorify powerful dynasties, achieved great richness and variety.

Sumerian (3500–2300 BC) The first of the powerful Mesopotamian civilizations, Sumer was concentrated in the cities of Ur, Eridu, and Uruk in southern Mesopotamia. The Sumerians built temples on top of vast ziggurats (stepped towers) and also vast, elaborately decorated palaces. Sculptures include erect, stylized figures carved in marble and characterized by clasped hands and huge eyes; those found in the Abu Temple, Tell Asmar, date from 2700 BC. Earlier sculptures in alabaster, such as the *Female Head* 3000 BC (Iraq Museum, Baghdad), show a greater naturalism and sensitivity. Inlay work is seen in the *Standard of Ur* 2500 BC, a box decorated with pictures in lapis lazuli, shell, and red sandstone. The Sumerians, who invented writing about 3000 BC, produced many small, finely carved cylindrical seals made of marble, alabaster, carnelian, lapis lazuli, and stone.

Akkadian (2300–2150 BC) The Akkadian invaders quickly assimilated Sumerian styles. The stele (decorated upright slab) *Victory of Naram-Sin* 2200 BC (Louvre, Paris), carved in relief, depicts a military campaign of the warlike Akkadians. The technical and artistic sophistication of bronze sculpture is illustrated by the *Head of an Akkadian King* 2200 BC (Iraq Museum, Baghdad).

Assyrian (1400–600 BC) The characteristic Assyrian art form was narrative relief sculpture, which was used to decorate palaces, for example, the Palace of Ashurbanipal (7th century BC). Its dramatic and finely carved reliefs, including dramatic scenes of a lion hunt, are in the British Museum, London. Winged bulls with human faces, carved partially in the round, stood as sentinels at the royal gateways (Louvre, Paris).

Mesopotamia An ancient clay model made in southern Mesopotamia about 1600–1900 BC, depicting a four-wheeled chariot. *Corbis*

Babylonian (625–538 BC) Babylon, although it had ancient traditions, came to artistic prominence in the 6th century BC, when it flourished under King Nebuchadnezzar II. He built the ◊Hanging Gardens of Babylon, a series of terraced gardens. The Babylonians practised all the Mesopotamian arts and excelled in brightly coloured glazed tiles, used to create relief sculptures. An example is the Ishtar Gate (about 575 BC) from the Temple of Bel, the biblical Tower of Babel (Pergamon Museum, Berlin, and Metropolitan Museum of Art, New York).

mesosphere layer in the Earth's ◊atmosphere above the stratosphere and below the thermosphere. It lies between about 50 km/31 mi and 80 km/50 mi above the ground.

Mesozoic era of geological time 245–65 million years ago, consisting of the Triassic, Jurassic, and Cretaceous periods. At the beginning of the era, the continents were joined together as Pangaea; dinosaurs and other giant reptiles flourished; and ferns, horsetails, and cycads thrived in a warm climate worldwide. By the end of the Mesozoic era, the continents had begun to assume their present positions, flowering plants were dominant, and many of the large reptiles and marine fauna were becoming extinct.

Messerschmitt Willy (Wilhelm Emil) 1898–1978. German aeroplane designer whose Me-109 was a standard Luftwaffe fighter in World War II, and whose Me-262 (1944) was the first mass-produced jet fighter. Messerschmitt aeroplanes were characterized by simple concept, minimum weight and aerodynamic drag, and the possibility of continued development.

Messiaen Olivier Eugène Prosper Charles 1908–1992. French composer, organist, and teacher. His music is mystical in character, vividly coloured, and incorporates transcriptions of birdsong. Among his works are the *Quartet for the End of Time* 1941, the large-scale *Turangalîla Symphony* 1949, and solo organ and piano pieces. As a teacher at the Paris Conservatoire from 1942, he influenced three generations of composers.

Messiah (from Hebrew *māshīach* 'anointed') in Judaism and Christianity, the saviour or deliverer. Jews from the time of the Old Testament exile in Babylon have looked forward to the coming of the Messiah. Christians believe that the Messiah came in the person of ◊Jesus, and hence called him the Christ.

Messier Charles 1730–1817. French astronomer. He discovered 15 comets and in 1784 published a list of 103 star clusters and nebulae. Objects on this list are given M (for Messier) numbers, which astronomers still use today, such as M1 (the Crab nebula) and M31 (the Andromeda galaxy).

Messina, Strait of channel in the central Mediterranean separating Sicily from mainland Italy; in Greek legend a monster (Charybdis), who devoured ships, lived in the whirlpool on the Sicilian side, and another (Scylla), who devoured sailors, in the rock on the Italian side.

metabolism the chemical processes of living organisms enabling them to grow and to function. It involves a constant alternation of building up (anabolism) and breaking down (catabolism). For example, green plants build up complex organic substances from water, carbon dioxide, and mineral salts (photosynthesis); by digestion animals partially break down complex organic substances, ingested as food, and subsequently resynthesize them for use in their own bodies.

metal any of a class of chemical elements with certain chemical characteristics (◊metallic character) and physical properties: they are good conductors of heat and electricity; opaque but reflect light well; malleable, which enables them to be cold-worked and rolled into sheets; and ductile, which permits them to be drawn into thin wires.

Metallic elements compose about 75% of the 111 elements shown in the ◊periodic table of the elements. They form alloys with each other, ◊bases with the hydroxyl radical (OH), and replace the hydrogen in an ◊acid to form a salt. The majority are found in nature in the combined form only, as compounds or mineral ores; about 16 of them also occur in the elemental form, as ◊native metals. Their chemical properties are largely determined by the extent to which their atoms can lose one or more electrons and form positive ions (cations).

Metals have been put to many uses, both structural and decorative, since prehistoric times, and the Copper Age, Bronze Age, and Iron Age are named after the metal that formed the technological base for that stage of human evolution.

commercial use The following are widely used in commerce: ***precious metals*** – gold, silver, and platinum, used principally in jewellery; ***heavy metals*** – iron, copper, zinc, tin, and lead, the common metals of engineering; ***rarer heavy metals*** – nickel, cadmium, chromium, tungsten, molybdenum, manganese, cobalt, vanadium, antimony, and bismuth, used principally for alloying with the heavy metals; ***light metals*** – aluminium and magnesium; ***alkali metals*** – sodium, potassium, and lithium; and ***alkaline-earth metals*** – calcium, barium, and strontium, used principally for chemical purposes.

Other metals have come to the fore because of special nuclear requirements – for example, technetium, produced in nuclear reactors, is corrosion-inhibiting; zirconium may replace aluminium and magnesium alloy in canning uranium in reactors.

metal detector electronic device for detecting metal, usually below ground, developed from the wartime mine detector. In the head of the metal detector is a coil, which is part of an electronic circuit. The presence of metal causes the frequency of the signal in the circuit to change, setting up an audible note in the headphones worn by the user. They are used to survey areas for buried metallic objects, occasionally by archaeologists. However, their indiscriminate use by treasure hunters has led to their being banned on recognized archaeological sites in some countries.

metal fatigue condition in which metals fail or fracture under relatively light loads, when these loads are applied repeatedly. Structures that are subject to flexing, such as the airframes of aircraft, are prone to metal fatigue.

metallic bond the force of attraction operating in a metal that holds the atoms together. In the metal the ◊valency electrons are able to move within the crystal and these electrons are said to be delocalized. Their movement creates short-lived, positively charged ions. The electrostatic attraction between the delocalized electrons and the ceaselessly forming ions constitutes the metallic bond.

metallic character chemical properties associated with those elements classed as metals. These properties, which arise from the element's ability to lose electrons, are: the displacement of hydrogen from dilute acids; the formation of basic oxides; the formation of ionic chlorides; and their reducing reaction, as in the ◊thermite process (see ◊reduction).

metallic glass substance produced from metallic materials (non-corrosive alloys rather than simple metals) in a liquid state which, by very rapid cooling, are prevented from reverting to their regular metallic structure. Instead they take on the properties of glass, while retaining the metallic properties of malleability and relatively good electrical conductivity.

metalloid or ***semimetal*** any chemical element having some of but not all the properties of metals; metalloids are thus usually electrically semiconducting. They comprise the elements germanium, arsenic, antimony, and tellurium.

metallurgy the science and technology of producing metals, which includes extraction, alloying, and hardening. Extractive, or ***process, metallurgy*** is concerned with the extraction of metals from their ◊ores and refining and adapting them for use. ***Physical metallurgy*** is concerned with their properties and application. ***Metallography*** establishes the microscopic structures that contribute to hardness, ductility, and strength.

Metals can be extracted from their ores in three main ways: ***dry processes***, such as smelting, volatilization, or amalgamation (treatment with mercury); ***wet processes***, involving chemical reactions; and ***electrolytic processes***, which work on the principle of ◊electrolysis.

The foundations of metallurgical science were laid about 3500 BC in Egypt, Mesopotamia, China, and India, where the art of ◊smelting metals from ores was discovered, starting with the natural alloy bronze. Later, gold, silver, copper, lead, and tin were worked in various ways, although they had been cold-hammered as native metals for thousands of years. The smelting of iron was discovered about 1500 BC. The Romans hardened and tempered iron into steel, using ◊heat treatment. From then until about AD 1400, advances in metallurgy came into Europe by way of Arabian chemists. ◊Cast iron began to be made in the 14th century in a crude blast furnace. The demands of the Industrial Revolution led to an enormous increase in ◊wrought iron production. The invention by British civil engineer Henry Bessemer of the ◊Bessemer process in 1856 made cheap steel available for the first time, leading to its present widespread use and the industrial development of many specialized steel alloys.

metamorphic rock rock altered in structure and composition by pressure, heat, or chemically active fluids after original formation. (If heat is sufficient to melt the original rock, technically it becomes an igneous rock upon cooling.) The term was coined in 1833 by Scottish geologist Charles Lyell (1797–1875).

There are two main types of metamorphism. ***Thermal metamorphism***, or contact metamorphism, is brought about by the baking of solid rocks in the vicinity of an igneous intrusion (molten rock, or magma, in a crack in the Earth's crust). It is responsible, for example, for the conversion of limestone to marble. ***Regional metamorphism*** results from the heat and intense pressures associated with the movements and collision of tectonic plates (see ◊plate tectonics). It brings about the conversion of shale to slate, for example.

metamorphosis period during the life cycle of many invertebrates, most amphibians, and some fish, during which the individual's body changes from one form to another through a major reconstitution of its tissues. For example, adult frogs are produced by metamorphosis from tadpoles, and butterflies are produced from caterpillars following metamorphosis within a pupa.

In classical thought and literature, metamorphosis is the transformation of a living being into another shape, either living or inanimate (for example ◊Niobe). The Roman poet ◊Ovid wrote about this theme.

metaphor (Greek 'transfer') figure of speech using an analogy or close comparison between two things that are not normally treated as if they had anything in common. Metaphor is a common means of extending the uses and references of words. See also ◊simile.

If we call people cabbages or foxes, we are indicating the opinion that they share certain qualities with those vegetables or animals: an inert quality in the case of cabbages, a cunning quality in the case of foxes. This may lead to calling people 'foxy' and saying 'He really foxed them that time', meaning that he tricked them. Such usages are metaphorical.

Metaphysical painting (Italian *pittura metafisica*) Italian painting style, conceived 1917 by Giorgio de ◊Chirico and Carlo Carrà (1881–1966), which sought to convey a sense of mystery through the use of dreamlike imagery. Reacting against both Cubism and Futurism, it anticipated Surrealism in the techniques it employed, notably the incongruous juxtaposition of familiar objects. Though short-lived – it had disbanded by the early 1920s – its influence was considerable.

Metaphysical poets group of early 17th-century English poets whose work is characterized by ingenious, highly intricate wordplay and unlikely or paradoxical imagery. They used rhetorical and literary devices, such as paradox, hyperbole, and elaborately developed conceits, in such a way as to engage the reader by their humour, strangeness, or sheer outrageousness. Among the exponents of this genre are John ◊Donne, George ◊Herbert, Andrew ◊Marvell, Richard Crashaw (c. 1613–1649), and Henry Vaughan (1622–1695). As originally used, the term 'metaphysical' implied a criticism of these poets; Samuel ◊Johnson, for example, complained that their poetry was laden with too much far-fetched learning. A revival of interest in their work was prompted by T S ◊Eliot's essay 'The Metaphysical Poets' 1921.

metaphysics branch of philosophy that deals with first principles, in particular 'being' (ontology) and 'knowing' (◊epistemology), and that is concerned with the ultimate nature of reality. It has been maintained that no certain knowledge of metaphysical questions is possible.

Epistemology, or the study of how we know, lies at the threshold of the subject. Metaphysics is concerned with the nature and origin of existence and of mind, the interaction between them, the meaning of time and space, causation, determinism and free will, personality and the self, arguments for belief in God, and human immortality. The foundations of metaphysics were laid by ◊Plato and ◊Aristotle. St Thomas ◊Aquinas, basing himself on Aristotle, produced a metaphysical structure that is accepted by the Catholic church. The subject has been advanced by René Descartes, Baruch Spinoza, Gottfried Leibniz, George Berkeley, David Hume, John Locke, Immanuel Kant, G W F Hegel, Arthur Schopenhauer, and Karl Marx; and in the 20th century by Henri Bergson, F H Bradley, Benedetto Croce, John McTaggart, Alfred North Whitehead, and Ludwig Wittgenstein.

Metastasio pen name of Pietro Armando Dominico Trapassi 1698–1782. Italian poet and librettist. In 1730 he became court poet to Charles VI in Vienna. Acknowledged as the leading librettist of his day, he created 18th-century Italian ◊*opera seria* (serious opera). His chief dramatic works are *Didone abbandonata*, *Catone in Utica*, *Olimpiade*, and *La clemenza di Tito*. Among the composers who used his work were Scarlatti, Handel, J C Bach, Mozart, and Gluck.

Metaxas Ioannis 1870–1941. Greek general and politician, born in Ithaca. He restored ◊George II (1890–1947) as king of Greece, under whom he established a dictatorship as prime minister from 1936, and introduced several necessary economic and military reforms. He led resistance to the Italian invasion of Greece in 1940, refusing to abandon Greece's neutral position.

metazoa another name for animals. It reflects an earlier system of classification, in which there were two main divisions within the animal kingdom, the multicellular animals, or metazoa, and the single-celled 'animals' or protozoa. The ◊protozoa are no longer included in the animal kingdom.

metempsychosis another word for ◊reincarnation.

meteor flash of light in the sky, popularly known as a ***shooting*** or ***falling star***, caused by a particle of dust, a meteoroid, entering the atmosphere at speeds up to 70 kps/45 mps and burning up by friction at a height of around 100 km/60 mi. On any clear night, several sporadic meteors can be seen each hour.

Several times each year the Earth encounters swarms of dust shed by comets, which give rise to a meteor shower. This appears to radiate from one particular point in the sky, after which the shower is named; the Perseid meteor shower in Aug appears in the constellation Perseus. A brilliant meteor is termed a fireball.

meteor-burst communications technique for sending messages by bouncing radio waves off the trails of ◊meteors. High-speed computer-controlled equipment is used to sense the presence of a meteor and to broadcast a signal during the short time that the meteor races across the sky. The technique offers a communications link that is difficult to jam, undisturbed by storms on the Sun, and would not be affected by nuclear war.

meteorite piece of rock or metal from space that reaches the surface of the Earth, Moon, or other body. Most meteorites are thought to be fragments from asteroids, although some may be pieces from the heads of comets. Most are stony, although some are made of iron and a few have a mixed rock-iron composition. Stony meteorites can be divided into two kinds: chondrites and achondrites. ***Chondrites*** contain chondrules, small spheres of the silicate minerals olivine and orthopyroxene, and comprise 85% of meteorites. ***Achondrites*** do not contain chondrules. Meteorites provide evidence for the nature of the Solar System and may be similar to the Earth's core and mantle, neither of which can be observed directly.

Thousands of meteorites hit the Earth each year, but most fall in the sea or in remote areas and are never recovered. The largest known meteorite is one composed of iron, weighing 60 tonnes, which lies where it fell in prehistoric times at Grootfontein, Namibia. Meteorites are slowed down by the Earth's atmosphere, but if they are moving fast enough they can form a ◊crater on impact. Meteor Crater in Arizona, about 1,200 m/4,000 ft in diameter and 200 m/650 ft deep, is the site of a meteorite impact about 50,000 years ago.

meteorite A piece of meteorite that fell in the English Midlands in the late 1960s. Earth is struck by many meteorites every year but most fail to penetrate the atmosphere without being incinerated. *Image Select (UK) Ltd*

meteorology scientific observation and study of the ◊atmosphere, so that ◊weather can be accurately forecast.

Data from meteorological stations and weather satellites are collated by computer at central agencies, and forecast and weather maps based on current readings are issued at regular intervals. Modern analysis, employing some of the most powerful computers, can give useful forecasts for up to six days ahead.

At meteorological stations readings are taken of the factors determining weather conditions: atmospheric pressure, temperature, humidity, wind (using the ◊Beaufort scale), cloud cover (measuring both type of cloud and coverage), and precipitation such as rain, snow, and hail (measured at 12-hour intervals). ◊Satellites are used either to relay information transmitted from the Earth-based stations, or to send pictures of cloud development, indicating wind patterns, and snow and ice cover.

history Apart from some observations included by Aristotle in his book *Meteorologia*, meteorology did not become a precise science until the end of the 16th century, when Galileo and the Florentine academicians constructed the first thermometer of any importance, and when Evangelista Torricelli in 1643 discovered the principle of the barometer. Robert ◊Boyle's work on gases, and that of his assistant, Robert ◊Hooke, on barometers, advanced the physics necessary for the understanding of the weather. Gabriel ◊Fahrenheit's invention of a superior mercury thermometer provided further means for temperature recording.

weather maps In the early 19th century a chain of meteorological stations was established in France, and weather maps were constructed from the data collected. The first weather map in England, showing the trade winds and monsoons, was made 1688, and the first telegraphic weather report appeared 31 Aug 1848. The first daily telegraphic weather map was prepared at the Great Exhibition 1851, but the Meteorological Office was not established in London until 1855. The first regular daily collections of weather observations by telegraph and the first British daily weather reports were made 1860, and the first daily printed maps appeared 1868.

collecting data Observations can be collected not only from land stations, but also from weather ships, aircraft, and self-recording and automatic transmitting stations, such as the ◊radiosonde. ◊Radar may be used to map clouds and storms. Satellites have played an important role in televising pictures of global cloud distribution.

As well as supplying reports for the media, the Meteorological Office in Bracknell, near London, does specialist work for industry, agriculture, and transport. Kew is the main meteorological observatory in the British Isles, but other observatories are at Eskdalemuir in the southern uplands of Scotland, Lerwick in the Shetlands, and Valentia in SW Ireland. Climatic information from British climatological reporting stations is published in the Monthly Weather Report, and periodically in tables of averages and frequencies.

Mexico has a faint, physical smell of her own, as each human being has. And this is a curious, inexplicable scent, in which there are resin and perspiration, and sunburned earth, and urine, among other things.

On MEXICO
D H Lawrence
Mornings in Mexico
1927

meter any instrument used for measurement. The term is often compounded with a prefix to denote a specific type of meter: for example, ammeter, voltmeter, flowmeter, or pedometer.

methanal (common name ***formaldehyde***) HCHO gas at ordinary temperatures, condensing to a liquid at −21°C/−5.8°F. It has a powerful, penetrating smell. Dissolved in water, it is used as a biological preservative. It is used in the manufacture of plastics, dyes, insulating foam, and in medicine.

methane CH_4 the simplest hydrocarbon of the paraffin series. Colourless, odourless, and lighter than air, it burns with a bluish flame and explodes when mixed with air or oxygen. It is the chief constituent of natural gas and also occurs in the explosive firedamp of coal mines. Methane emitted by rotting vegetation forms marsh gas, which may ignite by spontaneous combustion to produce the pale flame seen over marshland and known as ◊will-o'-the-wisp.

Methane causes about 38% of the warming of the globe through the ◊greenhouse effect; weight for weight it is 60–70 times more potent than carbon dioxide at trapping solar radiation in the atmosphere and so heating the planet. The amount of methane in the air is predicted to double over the next 60 years. An estimated 15% of all methane gas into the atmosphere is produced by cows and other cud-chewing animals, and 20% is produced by termites that feed on soil.

methanogenic bacteria one of a group of primitive microorganisms, the ◊Archaea. They give off methane gas as a by-product of their metabolism, and are common in sewage treatment plants and hot springs, where the temperature is high and oxygen is absent. Archaeons were originally classified as bacteria, but were found to be unique 1996 following the gene sequencing of the deep-sea vent *Methanococcus jannaschii*.

methanoic acid (common name ***formic acid***) HCOOH, a colourless, slightly fuming liquid that freezes at 8°C/46.4°F and boils at 101°C/213.8°F. It occurs in stinging ants, nettles, sweat, and pine needles, and is used in dyeing, tanning, and electroplating.

methanol (common name ***methyl alcohol***) CH_3OH the simplest of the alcohols. It can be made by the dry distillation of wood (hence it is also known as wood alcohol), but is usually made from coal or natural gas. When pure, it is a colourless, flammable liquid with a pleasant odour, and is highly poisonous. Methanol is used to produce formaldehyde (from which resins and plastics can be made), methyl-ter-butyl ether (MTB, a replacement for lead as an octane-booster in petrol), vinyl acetate (largely used in paint manufacture), and petrol.

Method US adaptation of ◊Stanislavsky's teachings on acting and direction, in which importance is attached to the psychological building of a role rather than the technical side of its presentation. Emphasis is placed on improvisation, aiming for a spontaneous and realistic style of acting. One of the principal exponents of the Method was the US actor and director Lee Strasberg, who taught at the Actors Studio theatre workshop in New York.

Methodism evangelical Protestant Christian movement that was founded by John ◊Wesley 1739 within the Church of England, but became a separate body 1795. The Methodist Episcopal Church was founded in the USA 1784. There are over 50 million Methodists worldwide.

Methodist doctrines are contained in Wesley's sermons and 'Notes on the New Testament'. A series of doctrinal divisions in the early 19th century were reconciled by a conference in London 1932 that brought Wesleyan methodists, primitive methodists, and United methodists into the Methodist Church. The church government is presbyterian in Britain and episcopal in the USA. Supreme authority is vested in the annual conference (50% ministers, 50% lay people); members are grouped under 'class leaders' and churches into 'circuits'.

Methodius, St c. 825–884. Greek Christian bishop, who with his brother ◊Cyril translated much of the Bible into Slavonic. Feast day 14 Feb.

Methuselah in the Old Testament, Hebrew patriarch who lived before the Flood; his lifespan of 969 years makes him a byword for longevity.

methyl alcohol common name for ◊methanol.

methylated spirit alcohol that has been rendered undrinkable, and is used for industrial purposes, as a fuel for spirit burners or a solvent.

methyl benzene alternative name for ◊toluene.

methyl orange $C_{14}H_{14}N_3NaO_3S$ orange-yellow powder used as an acid–base indicator in chemical tests, and as a stain in the preparation of slides of biological material. Its colour changes with pH; below pH 3.1 it is red, above pH 4.4 it is yellow.

metre in music, the timescale represented by the beat. Metre is regular, whereas rhythm is irregular. Metre can be simple as in 2/4, 4/8, and so on, where each beat divides into two sub-beats; compound metre as in 6/8, 9/8, 12/16, and so on, consists of sub-beats of 'compounded' or aggregated in units of three. The numerical sign for metre is a time signature, of which the upper number represents the number of beats in the bar, the lower number the type of beat, expressed as a fraction of a unit (semibreve). Hence 3/4 is three crotchet (quarter-note) beats to the bar and 6/8 is two beats each of three quavers (eighth notes).

metre in poetry, the recurring pattern of stressed and unstressed syllables in a line of ◊verse. The unit of metre is a foot.

Metre is classified by the number of feet to a line: a minimum of two and a maximum of eight. A line of two feet is a dimeter. They are then named, in order, trimeter, tetrameter, pentameter, hexameter, heptameter, and octameter.

metre SI unit (symbol m) of length, equivalent to 1.093 yards. It is defined by scientists as the length of the path travelled by light in a vacuum during a time interval of 1/299,792,458 of a second.

metric system system of weights and measures developed in France in the 18th century and recognized by other countries in the 19th century. In 1960 an international conference on weights and measures recommended the universal adoption of a revised International System (Système International d'Unités, or SI), with seven prescribed 'base units': the metre (m) for length, kilogram (kg) for mass, second (s) for time, ampere (A) for electric current, kelvin (K) for thermodynamic temperature, candela (cd) for luminous intensity, and mole (mol) for quantity of matter.

Two supplementary units are included in the SI system – the radian (rad) and steradian (sr) – used to measure plane and solid angles. In addition, there are recognized derived units that can be expressed as simple products or divisions of powers of the basic units, with no other integers appearing in the expression; for example, the watt.

Some non-SI units, well established and internationally recognized, remain in use in conjunction with SI: minute, hour, and day in measuring time; multiples or submultiples of base or derived units which have long-established names, such as tonne for mass, the litre for volume; and specialist measures such as the metric carat for gemstones. *See list of tables on p. 1177.*

Metro-Goldwyn-Mayer (MGM) US film-production company 1924–1970s. MGM was formed by the amalgamation of the Metro Picture Corporation, the Goldwyn Picture Corporation, and Louis B Mayer Pictures. One of the most powerful Hollywood studios of the 1930s–1950s, it produced such prestige films as *David Copperfield* 1935 and *The Wizard of Oz* 1939. Among its stars were Greta Garbo, Clark Gable, and Elizabeth Taylor.

metropolitan (Greek 'mother-state, capital') in the Christian church generally, a bishop who has rule over other bishops (termed suffragans). In the Eastern Orthodox Church, a metropolitan has a rank between an archbishop and a ◊patriarch. In the Church of England, the archbishops of York and Canterbury are both metropolitans.

metropolitan county in England, a group of six counties established under the Local Government Act 1972 in the largest urban areas outside London: Tyne and Wear, South Yorkshire, Merseyside, West Midlands, Greater Manchester, and West Yorkshire. Their elected assemblies (county councils) were abolished 1986 when most of their responsibilities reverted to the metropolitan district councils.

Metropolitan Museum of Art, New York one of the world's greatest art collections, including both ancient and modern works of art. Founded 1870 and opened 1880, it possesses vast collections covering many periods and styles. It has been enriched by the legacies of private collectors such as Benjamin Altman and Henry Frick, thus acquiring some of the finest examples of the work of Rembrandt, Frans Hals, and other European masters.

Metropolitan Opera Company foremost opera company in the USA, founded 1883 in New York City. The Metropolitan Opera House (opened 1883) was demolished 1966, and the company moved to the new Metropolitan Opera House at the Lincoln Center.

Metternich Klemens Wenzel Nepomuk Lothar, Prince von Metternich 1773–1859. Austrian politician, the leading figure in European diplomacy after the fall of Napoleon. As foreign minister 1809–48 (as well as chancellor from 1821), he tried to maintain the balance of power in Europe, supporting monarchy and repressing liberalism. ▷ *See feature on pp. 748–749.*

Meuse (Dutch ***Maas***) river flowing through France, Belgium, and the Netherlands; length 900 km/560 mi. It was an important line of battle in both world wars. It gives its name to a French *département*.

Mexican Empire short-lived empire 1822–23 following the liberation of Mexico from Spain. The empire lasted only eight months, under the revolutionary leader Agustín de ◊Iturbide. He was forced to abdicate and was shot by republican leaders Guadalupe Victoria and Santa Anna. Victoria became the first president of Mexico.

Mexican War war between the USA and Mexico 1846–48, begun in territory disputed between Texas (annexed by the USA 1845 but claimed by Mexico) and Mexico. It began when General Zachary Taylor invaded New Mexico after efforts to purchase what are now California and New Mexico failed. Mexico City was taken 1847, and under the Treaty of Guadaloupe Hidalgo that ended the war, the USA acquired New Mexico and California, as well as clear title to Texas in exchange for $15 million.

Mexico country in the North American continent, bounded N by the USA, E by the Gulf of Mexico, SE by Belize and Guatemala, and SW and W by the Pacific Ocean. It is the northernmost country in ◊Latin America. *See country box opposite.*

Mexico City (Spanish ***Ciudad de México***) capital, industrial (iron, steel, chemicals, textiles), and cultural centre of Mexico, 2,255 m/7,400 ft above sea level on the southern edge of the central plateau; population (1994) 15,500,000. It is thought to be one of the world's most polluted cities because of its position in a volcanic basin; pollutants gather and cause a smog cloud. Notable buildings include the 16th-century cathedral, the national palace, national library, Palace of Justice, and national university; the Ministry of Education has murals 1923–27 by Diego Rivera.

The city dates from about 1325, when the Aztec capital Tenochtitlán was founded on an island in Lake Texcoco. This city was levelled 1521 by the Spaniards, who in 1522 founded a new city on the site. It was the location of the 1968 Summer Olympics. In 1985 over 2,000 people were killed by an earthquake.

Meyerbeer Giacomo. Adopted name of Jakob Liebmann Meyer Beer 1791–1864. German composer. His spectacular operas include *Robert le Diable* 1831 and *Les Huguenots* 1836. From 1826 he lived mainly in Paris, returning to Berlin after 1842 as musical director of the Royal Opera.

Meyerhold Vsevolod Yemilyevich 1874–1940. Russian actor and director. He developed a system of actor training known as biomechanics, which combined insights drawn from sport, the circus, and modern studies of time and motion. He produced the Russian poet Mayakovsky's futurist *Mystery-Bouffe* 1918 and 1921, and *The Bed Bug* 1929.

mezuza in Judaism, a small box containing a parchment scroll inscribed with a prayer, the Shema from Deuteronomy 6:4–9; 11:13–21, which is found on the doorpost of every home and every room in a Jewish house, except the bathroom.

mezzanine (Italian *mezzano* 'middle') architectural term for a storey with a lower ceiling placed between two main storeys, usually between the ground and first floors of a building.

mezzogiorno (Italian 'midday') hot, impoverished area of S Italy, comprising six regions and the islands of Sardinia and Sicily. Agriculture is the chief mainstay of a generally poor economy; the main products are grains, vegetables, grapes, and olives. The region's economic, educational, and income levels are much lower than that of N Italy.

mezzo-soprano female singing voice between contralto and soprano.

mezzotint (Italian 'half tint') print produced by a method of etching in density of tone rather than line, popular in the 18th and 19th centuries when it was largely used for the reproduction of paintings, especially portraits. A copper or steel plate is roughened with a finely-toothed tool known as a 'rocker' to raise an even, overall burr (rough edge), which will hold ink. At this point the plate would print a rich, even black, so areas of burr are carefully smoothed away with a 'scraper' to produce a range of lighter tones. Primarily a reproductive technique, mezzotint declined rapidly with the invention of photography.

Mezzotint was invented by Ludwig Von Siegen of Utrecht (1609–1675). Another pioneer in the medium was Prince Rupert, nephew of Charles I of England, who was also responsible for initiating the first Englishman, William Sherwin, in the art, established by a dated mezzotint portrait of Charles II (1669). Many of the earliest practitioners were English, and by the end of the 17th century it was generally known as *la manière anglaise*.

Mfecane in African history, a series of disturbances in the early 19th century among communities in what is today the eastern part of South Africa. They arose when chief ◊Shaka conquered the Nguni peoples between the Tugela and Pongola rivers, then created by conquest a centralized, militaristic Zulu kingdom from several communities, resulting in large-scale displacement of people.

mg symbol for ***milligram***.

MHD abbreviation for ◊***magnetohydrodynamics***.

mho SI unit of electrical conductance, now called the ◊siemens; equivalent to a reciprocal ohm.

mi symbol for ◊***mile***.

MI5 abbreviation for ***Military Intelligence, section five***, the counter-intelligence agency of the British ◊intelligence services.

MI6 abbreviation for ***Military Intelligence, section six***, the secret intelligence agency of the British ◊intelligence services which operates largely under Foreign Office control.

Miami industrial city (food processing, transportation and electronic equipment, clothing, and machinery) and port in Florida, USA; population (1992) 367,000. It is the hub of finance, trade, and

MEXICO
United States of

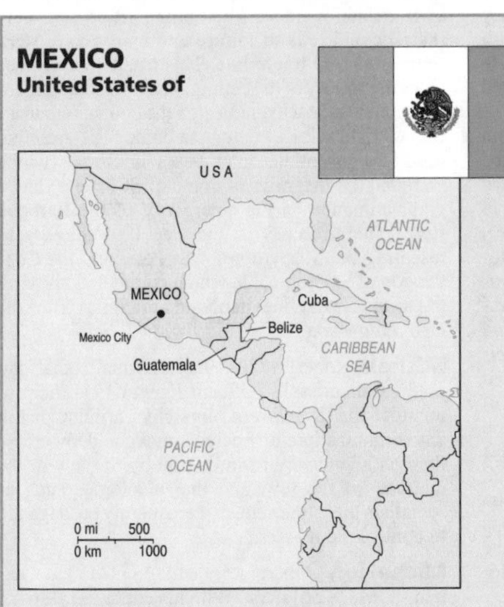

national name *Estados Unidos Mexicanos*
area 1,958,201 sq km/756,198 sq mi
capital Mexico City
major towns/cities Guadalajara, Monterrey, Puebla de Zaragoza
major ports 49 ocean ports
physical features partly arid central highlands; Sierra Madre mountain ranges E and W; tropical coastal plains; volcanoes, including Popocatepetl; Rio Grande
head of state Ernesto Zedillo Ponce de Leon from 1994
head of government Ernesto Zedillo Ponce de Leon from 1994
political system federal democratic republic
administrative divisions 31 states and a Federal District
political parties Institutional Revolutionary Party (PRI), moderate, left-wing; National Action Party (PAN), moderate, Christian, centre-right; Party of the Democratic Revolution (PRD), centre-left
armed forces 175,000; rural defence militia of 14,000 (1994)
conscription one year, part-time (conscripts selected by lottery)
defence spend (% GDP) 0.7 (1994)
education spend (% GNP) 4.9 (1992)
health spend (% GDP) 1.6 (1990)
death penalty only for exceptional crimes; last execution 1937
population 98,553,000 (1998 est)
population growth rate 2.1% (1990–95); 1.5% (2000–05)
age distribution (% of total population) <15 35.9%, 15–65 59.9%, >65 4.2% (1995)
ethnic distribution around 60% mestizo (mixed Native American and Spanish descent), 30% Native Americans, remainder mainly of European origin
population density (per sq km) 47 (1994)
urban population (% of total) 75 (1995)
labour force 37% of population: 28% agriculture, 24% industry, 48% services (1990)
unemployment 10.7% (1992 est)
child mortality rate (under 5, per 1,000 live births) 36 (1997)
life expectancy 67 (men), 74 (women)
education (compulsory years) 6
literacy rate 90% (men), 85% (women)
languages Spanish (official), Nahuatl, Maya, Zapoteco, Mixteco, Otomi
religion Roman Catholic
TV sets (per 1,000 people) 193 (1996)
currency Mexican peso
GDP (US $) 404.2 billion (1997)
GDP per capita (PPP) (US $) 6,780 (1995)
growth rate 3.5% (1994)
average annual inflation 7.0% (1994); 47.1% (1985–93)
major trading partners USA, Japan, Spain, France, Germany, Brazil, Canada
resources petroleum, natural gas, zinc, salt, silver, copper, coal, mercury, manganese, phosphates, uranium, strontium sulphide, flourite
industries motor vehicles, food processing, iron and steel, chemicals, beverages, electrical machinery, electronic goods, petroleum refinery, cement, metals and metal products, tourism
exports petroleum and petroleum products, engines and spare parts for motor vehicles, motor vehicles, electrical and electronic goods, fresh and preserved vegetables, coffee, cotton. Principal market: USA 74.5% (1993)
imports motor vehicle chassis, industrial machinery and equipment, iron and steel, telecommunications apparatus, organic chemicals, cereals and cereal preparations, petroleum and petroleum products. Principal source: USA 70.7% (1993)
arable land 11.8%
agricultural products maize, wheat, sorghum, barley, rice, beans, potatoes, coffee, cotton, sugar cane, fruit and vegetables; livestock raising and fisheries

HISTORY
c. 2600 BC Mayan civilization originated in Yucatán peninsula.
1000–500 BC Zapotec civilization developed around Monte Albán in S Mexico.
4th–10th Cs AD Mayan Empire at its height.
10th–12th Cs Toltecs ruled much of Mexico from their capital at Tula.
12th C Aztecs migrated south into valley of Mexico.
c. 1325 Aztecs began building their capital Tenochtitlán on site of present-day Mexico City.
15th C Montezuma I built up the Aztec Empire in central Mexico.
1519–21 Hernán Cortes conquered Aztec Empire and secured Mexico for Spain.
1520 Montezuma II, last king of the Aztecs, killed.
1535 Mexico became Spanish viceroyalty of New Spain; plantations and mining developed.
1519–1607 Indigenous population reduced from 21 million to 1 million, due mainly to lack of resistance to diseases transported from Old World.
1821 Independence proclaimed by Augustín de Iturbide with support of church and landowners.
1822 Iturbide overthrew provisional government and proclaimed himself Emperor Augustín I.
1824 Federal republic established amid continuing public disorder.
1824–55 Military rule of Antonio López de Santa Anna, who imposed stability (he became president 1833).
1846–48 Mexican War: Mexico lost California and New Mexico to USA.
1848 Revolt of Mayan Indians suppressed.
1855 Benito Juárez aided overthrow of Santa Anna's dictatorship.
1857–60 Sweeping liberal reforms and anti-clerical legislation introduced by Juárez led to civil war with the conservatives.
1861 Mexico suspended payment on foreign debt leading to French military intervention; Juárez resisted with US support.
1864 Supported by conservatives, France installed Archduke Maximilian of Austria as emperor of Mexico.
1867 Maximilian shot by republicans as French troops withdrew; Juárez resumed presidency.
1872 Death of Juárez.
1876 General Porfirio Diaz established dictatorship; Mexican economy modernized through foreign investment.
1911 Revolution overthrew Diaz; liberal president Francisco Madero introduced radical land reform and labour legislation but political disorder increased.
1914 and 1916–17 US military intervention to quell disorder.
1917 New constitution, designed to ensure permanent democracy, adopted with encouragement by USA.
1924–35 Government dominated by anti-clerical General Plutarco Calles, who introduced further social reforms.
1929 Foundation of National Revolutionary Party (PRFN).
1938 President Lázaro Cárdenas nationalized all foreign-owned oil wells in face of US opposition.
1942 Mexico declared war on Germany and Japan (and so regained favour of USA).
1946 PRFN renamed PRI.
1946–52 Miguel Alemán first of succession of authoritarian PRI presidents to seek moderation and stability rather than further radical reform.
1960s Rapid industrial growth partly financed by borrowing.
1976 Discovery of huge oil reserves in SE state of Chiapas; oil production tripled in six years.
1982 Falling oil prices caused grave financial crisis; Mexico defaulted on debt.
1985 Earthquake in Mexico City killed thousands.
1994 Uprising in Chiapas by Zapatista National Liberation Army (EZLN), seeking rights for the Mayan Indian population; Mexico formed North American Free Trade Area with USA and Canada.
1995 Government agreed to offer greater autonomy to Mayan Indians in Chiapas.
1996 Short-lived peace talks with EZLN; violent attacks against government by new leftist Popular Revolutionary Army (EPR) increased.
1997 PRI lost its assembly majority. Zapatista National Liberation Front (FZLN) formed, a civilian counterpart to the EZLN.
1998 Lapsed peace accord with Zapatist rebels reactivated.

SEE ALSO Aztec; Maya; Yucatán

air transport for the USA, Latin America, and the Caribbean. There has been an influx of immigrants from Cuba, Haiti, Mexico, and South America since 1959.

The first permanent non-Indian settlement dates from the 1870s. In 1896 a railway was extended to Miami, and the city was subsequently promoted as a tourist resort for its beaches. It is also a centre for oceanographic research.

Miandad Javed 1957– . Pakistani Test cricketer, his country's leading run-maker. He scored a century on his Test debut in 1976 and has since become one of a handful of players to make 100 Test appearances. He has captained his country and helped Pakistan to win the 1992 World Cup. He made his highest score of 311 when aged 17.

mica group of silicate minerals that split easily into thin flakes along lines of weakness in their crystal structure (perfect basal cleavage). They are glossy, have a pearly lustre, and are found in many igneous and metamorphic rocks. Their good thermal and electrical insulation qualities make them valuable in industry. A common example of mica is muscovite (white mica), $KAl_2Si_3AlO_{10}(OH,F)_2$.

Micah lived 8th century BC. In the Old Testament, a Hebrew prophet whose writings denounced the oppressive ruling class of Judah and demanded justice.

Michael in the Old Testament, an archangel, referred to as the guardian angel of Israel. In the New Testament Book of Revelation he leads the hosts of heaven to battle against Satan. In paintings, he is depicted with a flaming sword and sometimes a pair of scales. Feast day 29 Sept (Michaelmas).

Michael Mikhail Fyodorovich Romanov 1596–1645. Tsar of Russia from 1613. He was elected tsar by a national assembly, at a time of chaos and foreign invasion, and was the first of the Romanov dynasty, which ruled until 1917.

Michael 1921– . King of Romania 1927–30 and 1940–47. The son of Carol II, he succeeded his grandfather as king 1927 but was displaced when his father returned from exile 1930. In 1940 he was proclaimed king again on his father's abdication, overthrew 1944 the fascist dictatorship of Ion Antonescu (1882–1946), and enabled Romania to share in the victory of the Allies at the end of World War II. He abdicated and left Romania 1947. In 1997 he was allowed to return.

michaelmas daisy popular name for species of ◊aster, family Compositae, and also for the sea aster or starwort.

Michaelmas Day in Christian church tradition, the festival of St Michael and all angels, observed 29 Sept.

Michelangelo properly Michelangelo di Lodovico Buonarroti 1475–1564. Italian sculptor, painter, architect, and poet. He was active in his native Florence and in Rome. His giant talent dominated the High Renaissance. The marble *David* 1501–04 (Accademia, Florence) set a new standard in nude sculpture. His massive figure style was translated into fresco in the Sistine Chapel 1508–12 and 1536–41 (Vatican). Other works in Rome include the dome of St Peter's basilica. His influence, particularly on the development of ◊Mannerism, was profound.

At 13 Michelangelo became an apprentice to the successful painter Domenico Ghirlandaio. He also studied Giotto and the frescoes of Masaccio in the Brancacci Chapel. Chosen as one of the young artists whom Lorenzo de' Medici allowed to work in the school and the collection of classical sculpture in the Medici gardens, he was encouraged to develop his natural gift and liking for sculpture. In rivalry with the antique, he produced the *Head of a Faun* that delighted his patron and the relief *Battle of Centaurs and Lapiths* (Florence, Casa Buonarotti). The Medicean atmosphere of Platonic philosophy and classical study typical of the Renaissance made a lasting impression on him, though after the death of Lorenzo 1492, and in the now uneasy political atmosphere of Florence, he was seized by a presentiment of disaster, and fled to Bologna. He returned to Florence after a year to find it changed by the stern theocracy of Savonarola.

He went to Rome 1496, aged 21, where a Cupid in which he had counterfeited the antique attracted notice, and during five years' stay he produced two famous works of sculpture, strangely contrasting in style and spirit, his *Bacchus* (Florence, Museum) and *Pietà* (St Peter's, Rome). He returned to Florence 1501 and was next occupied by the famous and colossal *David*. Michelangelo had not abandoned painting altogether – the *Entombment* and *Madonna and Child with St John and Angels* (National Gallery) have been regarded as works of about his 20th year; the Holy Family (Uffizi) of 1503 was a masterpiece executed for his and Raphael's patron Angelo Doni; and in 1504 he was commissioned to paint a large fresco in the council hall of the new Florentine Republic as a companion piece to the *Battle of Anghiari* by Leonardo da Vinci. Michelangelo chose an incident from the Battle of Cascina during the Pisan War when Florentine soldiers had been surprised by the enemy while bathing. Both artists left their work unfinished, though Michelangelo, while he seems to have disliked Leonardo personally, may well have learned from the latter's cartoon a new energy of movement and intensity of expression. He was, however, summoned to Rome by Julius II to work on the famous tomb on which he was to toil at intervals during 40 years.

A fresh project of the impetuous Pope was among the circumstances first diverting him from the task: the decoration of the vaulting of the Sistine Chapel. Though reluctant, Michelangelo accepted the challenge, and in an astonishingly short space of time, working without assistants and under difficult conditions, painted the famous ceiling. A tremendous biblical symphony, it interprets the Creation of the World and of Man, the Fall, and the Flood in nine great compositions flanked by the figures of prophets and sibyls, and with supporting 'slaves' or 'atlases'. The conception is conveyed with the utmost force and lucidity by the human figure and gesture alone, as in the magnificent *Creation of Adam*. Michelangelo was then 37.

He went back to sculpture to become again involved in the 'tragedy of the tomb'. It was not until 1545 that it was finished, on a less ambitious scale than had been planned, only the figure of Moses being the artist's own work. He was commissioned 1520 by Clement VII, to design the Medici supulchral chapel in San Lorenzo, Florence. This, with its famous figures of Day and Night, Morning and Evening, was finished 1535. In 1534 he was required by Clement VII to devote himself to painting the altar wall of the Sistine Chapel, which had previously been decorated by Perugino. He took the Last Judgement as his subject and in six years produced his overwhelming masterpiece. It was in a different key from either the wall frescoes of other painters in the chapel or Michelangelo's own earlier work on the ceiling. It is sombrely majestic and tells of torture and martyrdom, stern retribution and tragic fate. This tragic masterpiece lacks the beauty of the ceiling, yet in its command of movement in space it indicated the course Italian art was to follow for a century to come. The architectural designs of his later years in Rome (which included the magnificent dome of St Peter's) had a great influence on the emergence of the Baroque style. Two frescoes in the Capella Paolina representing the Martyrdom of St Peter and the Conversion of St Paul, 1549, which completed his work in painting, were inevitably an anticlimax after the *Last Judgement*.

Michelangelo Michelangelo's reclining statue representing *Night*, from the Medici Chapel, Florence. This was from a series of four statues representing the times of the day. *Day* and *Night* were placed on the tomb of Giuliano de' Medici, while *Dawn* and *Dusk* adorned the sarcophagus of Lorenzo de' Medici. *Corbis*

Michels Robert 1876–1936. German social and political theorist. In *Political Parties* 1911, he propounded the 'iron law of oligarchy', arguing that in any organization or society, even a democracy, there is a tendency towards rule by the few in the interests of the few, and that ideologies such as socialism and communism were merely propaganda to control the masses.

Michelson Albert Abraham 1852–1931. German-born US physicist. With his colleague Edward Morley (1838–1923), he performed in 1887 the ***Michelson–Morley experiment*** to detect the motion of the Earth through the postulated ether (a medium believed to be necessary for the propagation of light). The failure of the experiment indicated the nonexistence of the ether, and led Albert ◊Einstein to his theory of ◊relativity. Michelson was the first American to be awarded a Nobel prize, in 1907.

He invented the ***Michelson ◊interferometer*** to detect any difference in the velocity of light in two directions at right angles. The negative result of the Michelson–Morley experiment demonstrated that the velocity of light is constant whatever the motion of the observer.

Michelucci Giovanni 1891–1990. Italian architect. A leading exponent of ◊Rationalism in the 1930s, he produced numerous urban projects characterized by a restrained Modernism, for example, the Sta Maria Novella Station in Florence 1934–37. He departed from his Rationalist principles in his design for the church of S Giovanni 1961 by the Autostrada del Sole near Florence, a fluid, sculptural composition in poured concrete.

Michigan state in N central USA; nicknamed Wolverine State/Great Lake State
area 151,600 sq km/58,518 sq mi
capital Lansing
cities Detroit, Grand Rapids, Flint
features Great Lakes: Superior, Michigan, Huron, and Erie; Porcupine Mountains; Muskegon, Grand, St Joseph, and Kalamazoo rivers; over 50% forested; the Upper Peninsula, connected to the rest of the state since 1957 by the Mackinac Bridge (pronounced Mackinaw); the Keweenaw Peninsula, the source of much of the world's copper 1840s–1960s; Detroit, with the Detroit Institute of Art (1885), and the Henry Ford Museum; University of Michigan, Ann Arbor
products motor vehicles and equipment; nonelectrical machinery; iron and steel; chemicals; pharmaceuticals; dairy products
population (1991) 9,368,000
history temporary posts established in early 17th century by French explorers Brulé, Marquette,

Michigan

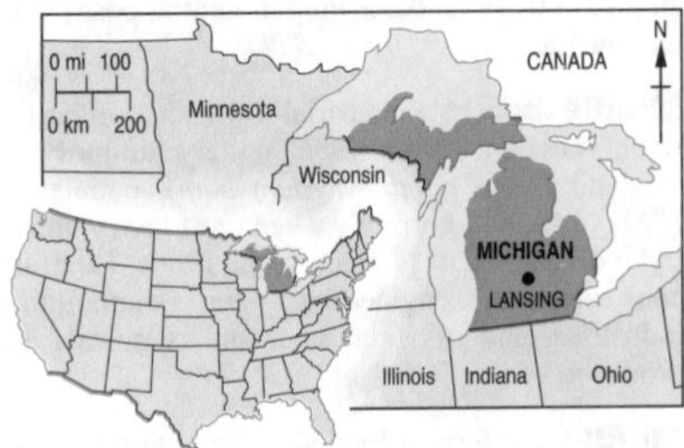

Joliet, and La Salle; first settled 1668 at Sault Sainte Marie; present-day Detroit settled 1701; passed to the British 1763 and to the USA 1796; statehood achieved 1837.

Michigan, Lake lake in N central USA, one of the Great Lakes; area 58,000 sq km/22,390 sq mi. Chicago and Milwaukee are its main ports. Lake Michigan is joined to Lake Huron by the Straits of Mackinac. Green Bay is the largest inlet.

Mickey Mouse cartoon character created 1928 by US animator Walt Disney, characterized by black disc-shaped ears and white gloves. He made his film debut in *Plane Crazy* and starred in the first synchronized sound cartoon, *Steamboat Willie* 1928. The comic book *Mickey Mouse Weekly* started 1936 and ran 920 issues. Mickey Mouse also appeared in the feature-length animated films *Fantasia* 1940, *Fun and Fancy Free* 1947, and *The Simple Things* 1953.

Mickiewicz Adam Bernard 1798–1855. Polish revolutionary poet. His *Pan Tadeusz* 1832–34 is Poland's national epic. He died in Constantinople while raising a Polish corps to fight against Russia in the Crimean War.

micro- prefix (symbol μ) denoting a one-millionth part (10^{-6}). For example, a micrometre, μm, is one-millionth of a metre.

microbe another name for ◊microorganism.

microbiological warfare use of harmful microorganisms as a weapon. See ◊biological warfare.

microbiology the study of microorganisms, mostly viruses and single-celled organisms such as bacteria, protozoa, and yeasts. The practical applications of microbiology are in medicine (since many microorganisms cause disease); in brewing, baking, and other food and beverage processes, where the microorganisms carry out fermentation; and in genetic engineering, which is creating increasing interest in the field of microbiology.

microchip popular name for the silicon chip, or ◊integrated circuit.

microclimate the climate of a small area, such as a woodland, lake, or even a hedgerow. Significant differences can exist between the climates of two neighbouring areas – for example, a town is usually warmer than the surrounding countryside (forming a heat island), and a woodland cooler, darker, and less windy than an area of open land. Microclimates play a significant role in agriculture and horticulture, as different crops require different growing conditions.

microcomputer or ***micro*** or ***personal computer*** small desktop or portable computer, typically designed to be used by one person at a time, although individual computers can be linked in a network so that users can share data and programs. Its central processing unit is a ◊microprocessor, contained on a single integrated circuit.

Microcomputers are the smallest of the four classes of computer (the others are ◊supercomputer, ◊mainframe, and ◊minicomputer). The first commercially available microcomputer, the Altair 8800, appeared in 1975.

microfiche sheet of film on which printed text is photographically reduced. See ◊microform.

microform generic name for media on which text or images are photographically reduced. The main examples are ***microfilm*** (similar to the film in an ordinary camera) and ***microfiche*** (flat sheets of film, generally 105 mm/4 in × 148 mm/6 in, holding the equivalent of 420 standard pages). Microform has the advantage of low reproduction and storage costs, but it requires special devices for reading the text. It is widely used for archiving and for storing large volumes of text, such as library catalogues.

micrometer instrument for measuring minute lengths or angles with great accuracy; different types of micrometer are used in astronomical and engineering work.

micrometre one-millionth of a ◊metre (symbol μm).

Micronesia group of islands in the Pacific Ocean lying N of ◊Melanesia, including the Federated States of Micronesia, Palau, Kiribati, the Mariana and Marshall Islands, Nauru, and Tuvalu. ▷*See feature on pp. 806–807.*

Micronesia Federated States of, country in the W Pacific Ocean, forming part of the archipelago of the Caroline Islands, 800 km/497 mi E of the Philippines. *See country box below.*

Micronesian inhabitants of Micronesia; people of a Micronesian culture or descent. Their languages belong to the Austronesian family.

microorganism or ***microbe*** living organism invisible to the naked eye but visible under a microscope. Microorganisms include viruses and single-celled organisms such as bacteria, protozoa, yeasts, and some algae. The study of microorganisms is known as microbiology.

microphone primary component in a sound-reproducing system, whereby the mechanical energy of sound waves is converted into electrical signals by means of a ◊transducer. One of the simplest is the telephone receiver mouthpiece, invented by Scottish–US inventor Alexander Graham Bell in 1876; other types of microphone are used with broadcasting and sound-film apparatus.

Telephones have a ***carbon microphone***, which reproduces only a narrow range of frequencies. For live music, a ***moving-coil microphone*** is often used. In it, a diaphragm that vibrates with sound waves moves a coil through a magnetic field, thus generating an electric current. The ***ribbon microphone*** combines the diaphragm and coil. The ***condenser microphone*** is most commonly used in recording and works by a ◊capacitor.

microprocessor complete computer ◊central processing unit contained on a single ◊integrated circuit, or chip. The appearance of the first microprocessor 1971 designed by Intel for a pocket calculator manufacturer heralded the introduction of the microcomputer. The microprocessor has led to a dramatic fall in the size and cost of computers, and ◊dedicated computers can now be found in washing machines, cars, and so on. Examples of microprocessors are the Intel Pentium family and the IBM/Apple Power PC.

micropropagation the mass production of plants by placing tiny pieces of plant tissue in sterile glass containers along with nutrients. Perfect clones of superplants are produced in sterile cabinets, with filtered air and carefully controlled light, temperature, and humidity. The system is used for the house-plant industry and for forestry.

micropyle in flowering plants, a small hole towards one end of the ovule. At pollination the pollen tube growing down from the ◊stigma eventually passes through this pore. The male gamete is contained within the tube and is able to travel to the egg in the interior of the ovule. Fertilization can then take place.

microscope instrument for magnification with high resolution for detail. Optical and electron microscopes are the ones chiefly in use; other types include acoustic, ◊scanning tunnelling, and ◊atomic force microscopes. In 1988 a scanning tunnelling microscope was used to photograph a single protein molecule for the first time.

MICRONESIA
Federated States of

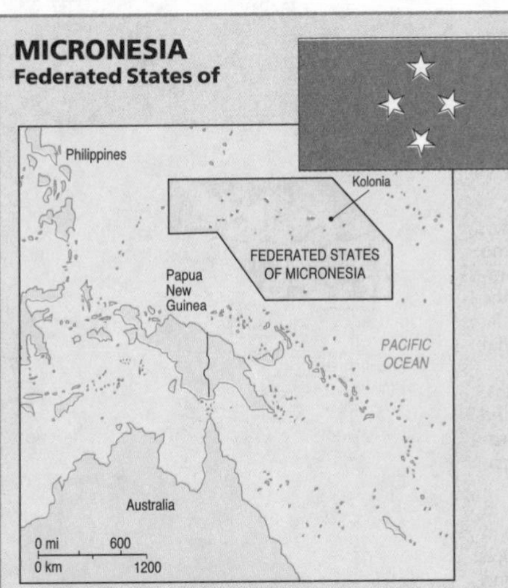

area 700 sq km/270 sq mi
capital Kolonia, in Pohnpei state
major towns/cities Weno, in Chuuk state; Lelu, in Kosrae state
major ports Teketik, Lepukos, Okak, Colonia
physical features an archipelago of 607 equatorial, volcanic islands in the W Pacific
head of state and government Bailey Olter from 1991
political system democratic federal state
political parties no formally organized political parties
administrative divisions state legislatures
population 121,000 (1994 est)
population growth rate 2.8% (1990–95)
ethnic distribution main ethnic groups are the Trukese (41%) and Pohnpeian (26%), both Micronesian
literacy 78%
languages English (official) and eight local languages
religion Christianity (mainly Roman Catholic in Yap state, Protestant elsewhere)
currency US dollar
GDP (US $) 254 million (1992)
growth rate 1.0% (1992)
exports copra, fish products, bananas, citrus fruit, peppers. Tourism is important

HISTORY
c. 1000 BC Micronesians first settled the islands.
1525 Portuguese navigators first visited Yap and Ulithi islands in the Carolines (Micronesia).
later 16th C Fell under Spanish influence.
1874 Spanish rule formally declared in face of increasing encroachment by German traders.
1885 Yap seized by German naval forces, but restored to Spain after arbitration by Pope Leo XIII on condition that Germany was allowed freedom of trade.
1899 Purchased for $4.5 million by Germany from Spain, after the latter's defeat in the Spanish-American War.
1914 Occupied by Japan on the outbreak of World War I.
1919 Administered under League of Nations mandate by Japan, and vigorously colonized.
1944 Occupied by USA after Japanese forces defeated in World War II.
1947 Administered by USA as part of the United Nations (UN) Trust Territory of the Pacific Islands, under the name of the Federated States of Micronesia (FSM).
1979 Constitution adopted, establishing a federal system for its four constituent states (Yap, Chuuk, Pohnpei, and Kosrae) and internal self-government.
1986 Compact of Free Association entered into with USA, granting the islands self-government with USA retaining responsibility for defence and security until 2001.
1990 UN trust status terminated.
1991 Independence agreed, with Bailey Olter as president. Entered into UN membership.

SEE ALSO Pacific Islands

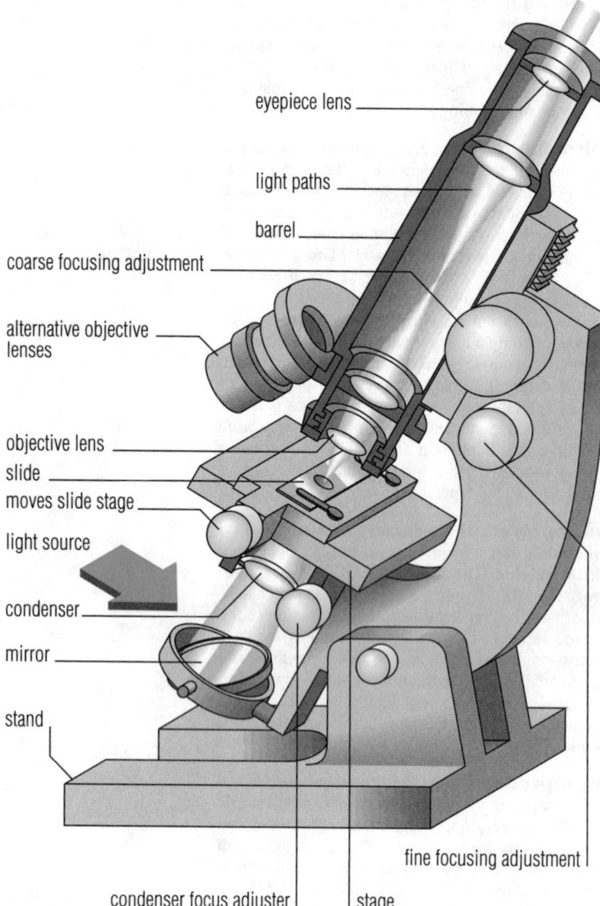

microscope Terms used to describe an optical microscope. In essence, the optical microscope consists of an eyepiece lens and an objective lens, which are used to produce an enlarged image of a small object by focusing light from a light source. Optical microscopes can achieve magnifications of up to 1,500–2,000. Higher magnifications and resolutions are obtained by electron microscopes.

The ***optical microscope*** usually has two sets of glass lenses and an eyepiece. It was invented 1609 in the Netherlands by Zacharias Janssen (1580–c. 1638). ***Fluorescence microscopy*** makes use of fluorescent dyes to illuminate samples, or to highlight the presence of particular substances within a sample. Various illumination systems are also used to highlight details.

The ◊***transmission electron microscope***, developed from 1932, passes a beam of electrons, instead of a beam of light, through a specimen. Since electrons are not visible, the eyepiece is replaced with a fluorescent screen or photographic plate; far higher magnification and resolution are possible than with the optical microscope.

The ◊***scanning electron microscope*** (SEM), developed in the mid-1960s, moves a fine beam of electrons over the surface of a specimen, the reflected electrons being collected to form the image. The specimen has to be in a vacuum chamber.

The ***acoustic microscope*** passes an ultrasonic (ultrahigh-frequency sound) wave through the specimen, the transmitted sound being used to form an image on a computer screen.

The ***scanned-probe microscope***, developed in the late 1980s, runs a probe, with a tip so fine that it may consist only of a single atom, across the surface of the specimen.

In the ***scanning tunnelling microscope***, an electric current that flows through the probe is used to construct an image of the specimen.

In the ***atomic force microscope***, the force felt by the probe is measured and used to form the image. These instruments can magnify a million times and give images of single atoms.

Microsoft US software corporation, now the world's largest supplier. Microsoft's first major product was ◊MS-DOS, written for IBM, but it has increased its hold on the personal computer market with the release of ◊Windows and related applications. Microsoft was founded by Bill ◊Gates and Paul Allen 1975. Together with Intel, the company supplied operating systems and computer chips for almost 90% of the world's personal computers 1997. A US federal probe into charges that Microsoft was engaging in anticompetitive behaviour was carried out 1990–93, from which date the US Justice Department launched its own investigations. Under a settlement reached 1994, Microsoft agreed to end the practice of demanding a licensing fee from computer makers on certain models of processor irrespective of the software to be installed. In 1997 Microsoft was accused of breaking this settlement, however, the US government suffered a major legal defeat in late June 1998, when an appeal court ruled that Microsoft was quite within its right to combine its Internet browser with its operating system.

microsurgery part or all of an intricate surgical operation performed with the aid of a binocular microscope, using miniaturized instruments. Sewing of the nerves and blood vessels is done with a nylon thread so fine that it is only just visible to the naked eye.

microtubules tiny tubes found in almost all cells with a nucleus. They help to define the shape of a cell by forming scaffolding for cilia and they also form the fibres of mitotic spindle (see ◊mitosis).

microwave ◊electromagnetic wave with a wavelength in the range 0. 3 to 30 cm/0.1 in to 12 in, or 300–300,000 megahertz (between radio waves and ◊infrared radiation). Microwaves are used in radar, in radio broadcasting, and in microwave heating and cooking.

microwave heating heating by means of microwaves. Microwave ovens use this form of heating for the rapid cooking or reheating of foods, where heat is generated throughout the food simultaneously. If food is not heated completely, there is a danger of bacterial growth that may lead to food poisoning. Industrially, microwave heating is used for destroying insects in grain and enzymes in processed food, pasteurizing and sterilizing liquids, and drying timber and paper.

MICV abbreviation for ◊***mechanized infantry combat vehicle***.

Midas in Greek mythology, a king of Phrygia who was granted the gift of converting all he touched to gold. He soon regretted his gift, as his food and drink were also turned to gold. For preferring the music of Pan to that of Apollo, he was given ass's ears by the latter.

MIDAS acronym for ***Missile Defence Alarm System***.

Mid-Atlantic Ridge ◊ocean ridge, formed by the movement of plates described by ◊plate tectonics, that runs along the centre of the Atlantic Ocean, parallel to its edges, for some 14,000 km/8,800 mi – almost from the Arctic to the Antarctic. The Mid-Atlantic Ridge is central because the ocean crust beneath the Atlantic Ocean has continually grown outwards from the ridge at a steady rate during the past 200 million years. Iceland straddles the ridge and was formed by volcanic outpourings.

Middle Ages period of European history between the fall of the Roman Empire in the 5th century and the Renaissance in the 15th. Among the period's distinctive features were the unity of W Europe within the Roman Catholic Church, the feudal organization of political, social, and economic relations, and the use of art for largely religious purposes.

It can be divided into three subperiods:

the ***early Middle Ages***, 5th–11th centuries, when Europe was settled by pagan Germanic tribes who adopted the vestiges of Roman institutions and traditions, were converted to Christianity by the church (which had preserved Latin culture after the fall of Rome), and who then founded feudal kingdoms;

the ***high Middle Ages***, 12th–13th centuries, which saw the consolidation of feudal states, the expansion of European influence during the ◊Crusades, the flowering of ◊scholasticism and monasteries, and the growth of population and trade;

the ***later Middle Ages***, 14th–15th centuries, when Europe was devastated by the ◊Black Death and incessant warfare, ◊feudalism was transformed under the influence of incipient nation-states and new modes of social and economic organization, and the first voyages of discovery were made.

Middle East indeterminate area now usually taken to include the Balkan States, Egypt, and SW Asia. Until the 1940s, this area was generally called the Near East, and the term Middle East referred to the area from Iran to Burma (now Myanmar).

Middle Kingdom period of Egyptian history embracing the 11th and 12th dynasties (roughly 2040–1640 BC); Chinese term for China and its empire until 1912, describing its central position in the Far East.

Middlesbrough industrial town and port on the river Tees, and, from 1996, unitary authority of England (*see United Kingdom map*); population (1991) 140,900. Formerly a centre of heavy industry, it diversified its products in the 1960s. There are constructional, engineering, and shipbuilding industries, and iron and steel and chemicals are produced.

Middlesex former English county, absorbed by Greater London 1965. It was settled in the 6th century by Saxons, and its name comes from its position between the kingdoms of the East and West Saxons. Contained within the Thames basin, it provided good agricultural land before it was built over. The name is still used, as in Middlesex County Cricket Club.

Middleton Thomas c. 1570–1627. English dramatist. He produced numerous romantic plays, tragedies, and realistic comedies, both alone and in collaboration, including *A Fair Quarrel* 1617, *The Changeling* 1622, and *The Spanish Gypsy* 1623 with William ◊Rowley; *The Roaring Girl* 1611 with Thomas ◊Dekker; *The Widow* about 1616 with Ben ◊Jonson; and (alone) *Women Beware Women* 1621. He also composed many pageants and masques.

His most characteristic feature, whether in comedy or tragedy, is the precise, detached, but extremely powerful observation of the frailties of human character. His work shows a particular sympathy with and insight into female psychology.

Middle Way the path to enlightenment, taught by the Buddha, which avoids the extremes of indulgence and asceticism.

midge common name for many insects resembling ◊gnats, generally divided into biting midges (family Ceratopogonidae) that suck blood, and non-biting midges (family Chironomidae).

Mid-Atlantic Ridge The Mid-Atlantic Ridge is the boundary between the crustal plates that form America, and Europe and Africa. An oceanic ridge cannot be curved since the material welling up to form the ridge flows at a right angle to the ridge. The ridge takes the shape of small straight sections offset by fractures transverse to the main ridge.

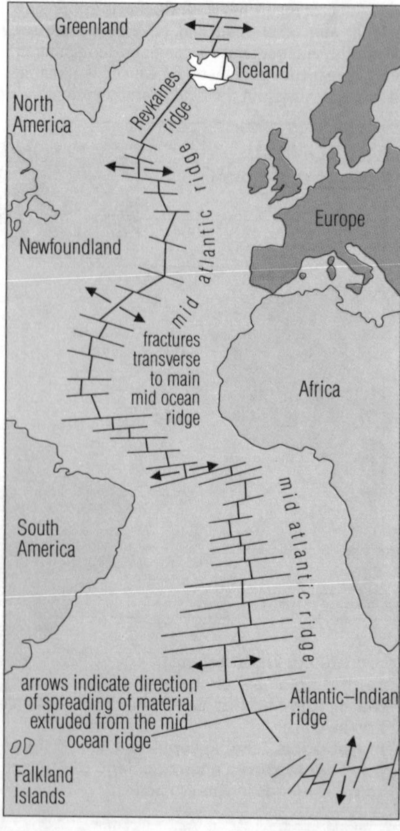

Mid Glamorgan (Welsh ***Morgannwg Ganol***) former county of S Wales, created 1974, abolished 1996.

Midgley Mary 1919– . English moral philosopher who used studies of animal behaviour (ethology) to support broadly Aristotelian ethics. She has also argued that our moral concern should extend to animals. Her publications include *Beast and Man: The Roots of Human Nature* 1978, *Animals and Why They Matter* 1983, and *Wickedness: a Philosophical Enquiry* 1984.

MIDI (acronym for ***musical instrument digital interface***) manufacturer's standard allowing different pieces of digital music equipment used in composing and recording to be freely connected. The information-sending device (any electronic instrument) is called a controller, and the reading device (such as a computer) the sequencer. Pitch, dynamics, decay rate, and stereo position can all be transmitted via the interface. A computer with a MIDI interface can input and store the sounds produced by the connected instruments, and can then manipulate these sounds in many different ways. For example, a single keystroke may change the key of an entire composition.

Midi-Pyrénées region of SW France, comprising the *départements* of Ariège, Aveyron, Haute-Garonne, Gers, Lot, Hautes-Pyrénées, Tarn, and Tarn-et-Garonne; capital Toulouse; area 45,300 sq km/17,486 sq mi; population (1990) 2,430,700. The region includes several spa towns (including Lourdes), winter resorts, and prehistoric caves; it produces fruit, wine, and livestock
history occupied by the Basques since prehistoric times, this region once formed part of the prehistoric province of Gascony that was taken by the English 1154, recaptured by the French 1453, inherited by Henry of Navarre, and reunited with France 1607.

Midland Bank the UK's third-largest clearing bank. It was founded 1836 and took its present name 1923.

Midlands area of England corresponding roughly to the Anglo-Saxon kingdom of ◊Mercia. The ***E Midlands*** comprises Derbyshire, Leicestershire, Northamptonshire, and Nottinghamshire. The ***W Midlands*** covers the metropolitan county of ◊West Midlands created from parts of Staffordshire, Warwickshire, and Worcestershire; and (often included) the ***S Midlands*** comprising Bedfordshire, Buckinghamshire, and Oxfordshire.

Midlothian local authority of Scotland created 1996 (*see United Kingdom map*).

midnight sun the constant appearance of the Sun (within the Arctic and Antarctic circles) above the ◊horizon during the summer.

Midrash (Hebrew 'inquiry') medieval Hebrew commentaries on the Bible, in the form of sermons, in which allegory and legendary illustration are used. They were compiled mainly in Palestine between AD 400 and 1200.

midshipman trainee naval officer. In the UK, a midshipman has either completed the first year at the Royal Naval College, Dartmouth, or is in his first year with the fleet, after which he becomes an acting sublieutenant.

Midway, Battle of in World War II, decisive US naval victory over Japan June 1942 off Midway Islands, northwest of Hawaii. The Midway victory was one of the most important battles of the Pacific war – Japanese naval air superiority was destroyed in one day, putting an end to Japanese expansion and placing them on the defensive thereafter.

Midway Islands two islands in the Pacific, 1,800 km/1,120 mi NW of Honolulu; area 5 sq km/2 sq mi; population (1980) 500. They were annexed by the USA 1867, and are now administered by the US Navy.

Midwest or ***Middle West*** large area of the northern central USA. It is loosely defined, but is generally taken to comprise the states of Illinois, Iowa, Wisconsin, Minnesota, Nebraska, Kansas, Missouri, North Dakota, and South Dakota and the portions of Montana, Wyoming, and Colorado that lie east of the Rocky Mountains. Ohio, Michigan, and Indiana are often variously included as well. Traditionally its economy is divided between agriculture and heavy industry. The main urban Midwest centre is Chicago.

midwifery assistance of women in childbirth. Traditionally, it was undertaken by experienced specialists; in modern medical training it is a nursing speciality for practitioners called midwives.

Mies van der Rohe Ludwig 1886–1969. German architect. A leading exponent of the ◊International Style, he practised in the USA from 1937. He succeeded Walter ◊Gropius as director of the ◊Bauhaus 1929–33. He designed the bronze-and-glass Seagram building in New York City 1956–59 and numerous apartment buildings. From 1938 to 1958 he was professor at the Illinois Technical Institute, for which he designed a new campus on characteristically functional lines from 1941. He also designed the National Gallery, Berlin, 1963–68.

mifepristone (formerly ***RU486***) anti-progesterone drug used, in combination with a ◊prostaglandin, to procure early ◊abortion (up to the tenth week in pregnancy). It is administered only in hospitals or recognized clinics and a success rate of 95% is claimed. Formerly known as RU486, it was developed and first used in France in 1989. It was licensed in the UK in 1991.

Mifune Toshiro 1920– . Japanese film actor. He appeared in many films directed by Akira ◊Kurosawa, including *Rashōmon* 1950, *Shichinin no samurai/Seven Samurai* 1954, and *Throne of Blood* 1957. He has occasionally appeared in European and American films: *Grand Prix* 1966, *Hell in the Pacific* 1969.

mignonette sweet-scented plant *Reseda odorata*, native to N Africa, bearing yellowish-green flowers in racemes (along the main stem), with abundant foliage; it is widely cultivated. It was brought to England about 1752; related species are found in the wild.

migraine acute, sometimes incapacitating headache (generally only on one side), accompanied by nausea, that recurs, often with advance symptoms such as flashing lights. Italian researchers found in 1998, that 48% of migraine sufferers harboured the bacterium *Helicobacter pylori* and that symptoms were alleviated following antiboitics to eradicate *H. pylori*. An allergic reaction to certain foods is also probable.

migrant labour people who leave their homelands to work elsewhere, usually because of economic or political pressures.

The world's pool of legal and illegal immigrants is a significant economic and social force. About 7 million migrants were employed in the Middle East during the 1970s and early 1980s, but the subsequent decline in jobs had severe financial consequences for India and Sri Lanka, who supplied the workers. S Europe has also been a traditional source of migrant workers.

migration Migrating flamingoes in Kenya. It is not well understood how birds navigate during their migration. Even young birds can migrate by a route they have never flown before. It has been suggested that parts of the necessary knowledge may be inherited. *Image Select (UK) Ltd*

migration the movement, either seasonal or as part of a single life cycle, of certain animals, chiefly birds and fish, to distant breeding or feeding grounds. The precise methods by which animals navigate and know where to go are still obscure. *See feature on pp. 704–705.*

Mihailović Draža (Dragoljub) 1893–1946. Yugoslav soldier, leader of the guerrilla ◊Chetniks of World War II, a nationalist resistance movement against the German occupation. His feud with Tito's communists led to the withdrawal of Allied support and that of his own exiled government from 1943. He turned for help to the Italians and Germans, and was eventually shot for treason.

mikado (Japanese 'honourable palace gate') title until 701 of the Japanese emperor, when it was replaced by the term *tennō* ('heavenly sovereign').

Mikes George 1912– . Hungarian-born English writer. The best known of his many humorous books are the shrewdly comic descriptions of national types and foibles, such as *How to be an Alien* 1946, *Über Alles* 1953, *Switzerland for Beginners* 1962, and *Land of the Rising Yen* 1970. Other books are *Shakespeare and Myself* 1952, *How to be Inimitable* 1960, *How to be Affluent* 1966, and *The Spy who Died of Boredom* 1973.

Milan (Italian ***Milano***) industrial city (aircraft, cars, locomotives, textiles), financial and cultural centre, capital of Lombardy, and second largest city in Italy; population (1992) 1,358,600
features the Gothic cathedral, built about 1450, crowned with pinnacles, can hold 40,000 worshippers; the Pinacoteca di Brera art gallery; Leonardo da Vinci's *Last Supper* 1495–97 in the refectory of Sta Maria della Grazie; La Scala opera house (Italian *Teatro alla Scala*) 1778; an annual trade fair
history settled by the Gauls in the 5th century BC, it was conquered by the Roman consul Marcellus 222 BC to become the Roman city of *Mediolanum*. Under Diocletian, in AD 286 Milan was capital of the Western empire. Destroyed by Attila the Hun 452, and again by the Goths 539, the city regained its power through the political importance of its bishops. It became an autonomous commune 1045; then followed a long struggle for supremacy in Lombardy.

cont. on p. 706

Marathon Journeys of the Animal World

By spending its summers in the arctic and its winters in the antarctic, the arctic tern takes full advantage of the long hours of daylight. This enables it to profit from the summer increase in the numbers of small sea creatures on which it feeds, as well as having maximum daylight in which to catch them. *Tony Stone*

How can we best define migration? It is not simply a long journey – when an albatross flies north in search of food it is foraging, not migrating. Migrating animals, by contrast, rarely stop to feed or rest. They are persistent and hard to distract, as if they were compelled to keep moving. Migrants seem to have a destination in mind, and only rest when they have reached it.

Why do animals migrate?

Most animals have to cope with seasonal changes in their environment. Migrations, which have evolved over millions of years, are adaptations to such changes that compel animals to move to the right place for breeding, feeding, and growing. The journeys are long simply because these chosen places may be thousands of kilometres apart. This accounts for the migration of whales, which have to migrate from the cooler polar regions of the ocean which are the best for feeding, to the warmer equatorial regions which are good for breeding and rearing young. The grey whale *Eschristus robustus*, one of the baleens, breeds in the calm lagoons of Mexico, but in spring, when the calves are strong, starts a great journey north to the Arctic. Including the autumnal return trip, this is a migration of 18,000 km/11,250 mi, full of danger from predators – including, until recently, people, but now mainly killer whales. However, the rich feeding grounds of the Arctic make the risks worth taking.

Several generations of monarch butterflies are required to complete the 6,000 km/3,728 mi round trip of their migration. Their journey begins in Mexico each spring, with subsequent generations arriving in Canada in summer and returning to Mexico to begin the cycle again. *Bryan Ceney*

Butterflies: a family affair

One of the world's most spectacular and impressive migrations is another lengthy round trip, this time between Mexico and Canada, but undertaken by a far smaller animal, the monarch butterfly *Danaus plexippus*. Remarkably, the monarch relies on several generations to get the journey done, perhaps because a butterfly is after all a very fragile animal. Winters are spent in just a few areas of the central Mexican hills, where the monarchs hibernate in vast groups that contain millions of individuals. When spring arrives, the monarchs become active, mate, and fly north, crossing into the southern states of the USA. The eggs are laid and the adults rest and feed, their work done. When the eggs hatch, however, this new generation continues the flight north, perhaps reaching as far as Washington DC. Another generation will be needed before the final destination – Canada – is reached. Most remarkable though is the return journey south, all 3,000 km/1,864 mi of it, back to Mexico. This is the task of the young born during the Canadian summer, butterflies whose great-grandparents had left Mexico six months before, never to see it again.

Cyclic migration: the grass is greener

The brindled gnu or wildebeest *Connochaetes taurinus* of the Serengeti plains use migration to ensure a year-round food supply. From December to April, grass and water are plentiful in the southeastern plains; it is here that the calves are born and reared. But in May and June the plains become dry, the grass disappears, and the waterholes dry up. Now both adults and young are in danger, and the animals' behaviour changes. Instead of foraging, they gather in larger and larger groups, finally setting off for Lake Victoria, hundreds of kilometres to the north. No obstacle can stop the movement of these vast and spectacular herds. Despite exhaustion, the dangers of fast-flowing rivers, and attacks from lions and cheetahs, the gnu move

A leatherback turtle makes her way back to the ocean after laying her eggs. She may have travelled thousands of miles to find a suitable sandy beach, but after digging a hole, laying her eggs, and covering them with sand, she will return to the sea and leave the eggs to hatch and the young to find their way to the sea unaided. *Corbis*

steadily northwards, arriving at Lake Victoria in August. Here, grass is more plentiful and the animals can feed. In November, great storm clouds arrive, moving south; this is the signal for the return migration. Following the rain, the gnu head back to their favoured breeding grounds, where the grass is once more richly growing.

Record-breaking flights: pole to pole

Of all the migrating animals, the arctic tern *Sterna paradisaea* travels the furthest, migrating 25,000 km/15,625 mi in just one year. This long-distance flyer breeds in the Arctic, incubating its eggs and feeding its chicks during the summer months. When autumn arrives, however, in a feat of extraordinary endurance, the terns fly south to the tropics, cross the equator, and continue on to the Antarctic. They spend the winter here, taking advantage of the rich food supply near the edge of the ice-pack. Yet, when spring arrives, the terns depart; they head north once more, arriving back in the Arctic in early summer, ready for the breeding season.

Using smell as a guide

The Atlantic salmon *Salmo salar* makes the toughest of journeys, but makes it only once. Far out in the ocean, maturing salmon use their sense of smell to find their way to the home estuary, detecting scents encountered only once before, when they themselves hatched in the ancestral river. After entering the estuary, the salmon swim upstream, resting only when they reach the river's upper stretches, perhaps a hundred kilometres inland. Here, in freezing cold water, the females release their eggs, and the males their sperm. Exhausted and in poor condition, the adults mostly soon die, and through decomposition release nutrients that contribute to the health of the river and therefore of their young. For the newly hatched fish, the migratory force develops as quickly as their size, and after a few months they set off down-river, in search of the open ocean. A few years later, they will follow exactly their parents' route back to the river to breed.

The leatherback's favourite beach

Like the salmon, the leatherback turtle *Dermochelys coriacea* migrates great distances to find a breeding ground. Again like the salmon, the choice of location is astonishingly precise. Although the leatherback is found throughout the tropics, and travels widely, the females are very particular about where to lay their eggs. Leatherbacks have been known to migrate 6,000 km/3,750 mi, returning to a tropical beach from feeding grounds in Labrador or Norway. It is on these beaches, between April to July, that the leatherbacks emerge at night, hauling themselves out of the sea and burying their eggs, before disappearing once more into the ocean.

Migration: the art of finding your way

These spectacular journeys by birds, mammals, fish, and reptiles require at least a sense of direction. In some cases, however, something more complex is involved: navigation. Navigation is knowing where to go, even without any signal from your final destination. Leatherback turtles navigate by the contours of underwater mountains and valleys. Fish such as eels and salmon probably rely partly on currents and on changes in the composition and temperature of the sea in particular locations – though, for salmon, the sense of smell appears to be vital, as they get lost if their nostrils are blocked. The brindled gnu also uses its sense of smell, as well as sight.

Most striking, however, is the migration of young birds that have never flown a route before and are unaccompanied by adults. Migrating terns, warblers, and swallows travel vast distances. They cannot do it just by following landmarks: they travel at night, and cross oceans where little visual information is available. How do they do this?

Some scientists now believe that birds inherit, as part of their genetic code, an overall 'sky chart' of their journey that is triggered into use when they become aware of how the local sky pattern, above the place in which they hatch, fits into it. They probably use this sky chart in combination with a 'reading' of the Earth's magnetic field through an inbuilt 'magnetic compass', which is a tiny mass of tissue between their eyes and brain. It is also known that birds can detect patterns of polarized light in the sky, and use this for help in finding their way. Among migrating animals, it is the birds that can justly claim to be the master navigators.

STEPHEN WEBSTER

Salmon leaping up a waterfall in Alaska, USA. After spending up to four years as adults in the sea, salmon head back to fresh water to breed, always returning to the exact river where they first hatched. In their determination to complete their journey they may leap up waterfalls as much as 3 m/10 ft high. After spawning they die. *Corbis*

SEE ALSO
navigation, biological

Gnu migrating through Kenya. Gnu are grazing animals that inhabit African grassland. They have long manes and tails, and short curved horns. *Image Select (UK) Ltd*

❝Ask yourself whether you are happy, and you cease to be so.❞
JOHN STUART MILL
Autobiography

The city was taken by ◊Frederick (I) Barbarossa 1162; it was ruled by the Ghibelline Visconti dynasty 1277–1450, when Francesco Sforza seized control and became duke. The Sforza court marked the high point of Milan as a cultural and artistic centre. Control of the city passed to Louis XII of France 1499, and in 1535 it was annexed by Spain, beginning a long decline. The city was ceded to Austria by the Treaty of ◊Utrecht 1714, and in the 18th century began a period of intellectual enlightenment. Milan was in 1796 taken by Napoleon, who made it the capital of the Cisalpine Republic 1799, and in 1805 capital of the kingdom of Italy until 1814, when it reverted to the Austrians. In 1848, Milan rebelled unsuccessfully (the *Cinque Giornate*/Five Days), and in 1859 was joined to Piedmont.

Milankovitch hypothesis the combination of factors governing the occurrence of ◊ice ages proposed in 1930 by the Yugoslav geophysicist M Milankovitch (1879–1958). These include the variation in the angle of the Earth's axis, and the geometry of the Earth's orbit around the Sun.

mildew any fungus that appears as a destructive growth on plants, paper, leather, or wood when exposed to damp; such fungi usually form a thin white coating.

mile imperial unit of linear measure. A statute mile is equal to 1,760 yards (1.60934 km), and an international nautical mile is equal to 2,026 yards (1,852 m).

Mile End area of the East End of London, England, in the district of Stepney, now part of the London borough of Tower Hamlets. Mile End Green (now Stepney Green) was the scene of Richard II's meeting with the rebel peasants 1381.

Miles Bernard James, Baron Miles 1907–1991. English actor and producer. He appeared on stage as Briggs in *Thunder Rock* 1940 and Iago in *Othello* 1942, and his films include *Great Expectations* 1947. He founded a trust that in 1959 built the City of London's first new theatre for 300 years, the Mermaid.

Miletus ancient Greek city on the W coast of modern Turkey with a port that eventually silted up. It was famous for its woollen goods, and traded with the whole Mediterranean coast from the Mycenean period until the Roman empire.

milfoil another name for the herb ◊yarrow. Water milfoils, plants of the genus *Miriophyllum*, are unrelated; they have whorls of fine leaves and grow underwater.

Milford Haven (Welsh ***Aberdaugleddau***) seaport in Dyfed, SW Wales, on the estuary of the east and west Cleddau rivers; population (1991) 13,200. It has oil refineries, and a terminal for giant tankers linked by pipeline with Llandarcy, near Swansea. There is a fishing industry.

Milhaud Darius 1892–1974. French composer and pianist. A member of the group of composers known as *Les Six*, he was extremely prolific in a variety of styles and genres, influenced by jazz, the rhythms of Latin America, and electronic composition. He is noted for his use of ◊polytonality (the simultaneous existence of two or more keys), as in the *Saudades do Brasil* 1921 for orchestra and *L'Homme et son désir* 1918. Other works include the operas *Christophe Colombe/Christopher Columbus* 1928 and *Bolívar* 1943, and the jazz ballet *La Création du monde* 1923. He lived in both France and the USA.

Militant Tendency in British politics, left-wing faction originally within the Labour Party, aligned with the publication *Militant*. It became active in the 1970s, with radical socialist policies based on Trotskyism (see ◊Trotsky), and gained some success in local government, for example in the inner-city area of Liverpool. In the mid-1980s the Labour Party considered it to be a separate organization within the party and banned it.

military-industrial complex conjunction of the military establishment and the arms industry, both inflated by Cold War demands. The phrase was first used by US president and former general Dwight D Eisenhower in 1961 to warn Americans of the potential misplacement of power.

The British military industry accounts for 11% of total industrial production and the Ministry of Defence is British industry's biggest customer. Exports are worth about £2–£3 billion a year; the government keeps British arms sales secret despite publicly calling for a United Nations register. Britain is the world's largest exporter of arms. Military and related industries employ about 600,000 people.

❝I only know that summer sang in me / A little while, that in me sings no more.❞
EDNA ST VINCENT MILLAY
sonnet 19,
The Harp-Weaver and Other Poems

Milky Way A satellite trail in the Milky Way. The Milky Way, a spiral galaxy, is about 100,000 light years in diameter, and contains about 100 billion stars. Our Solar System is about 25,000 light years out from its centre. *Image Select (UK) Ltd*

militia body of civilian soldiers, usually with some military training, who are on call in emergencies, distinct from professional soldiers. In Switzerland, the militia is the national defence force, and every able-bodied man is liable for service in it. In the UK the ◊***Territorial Army*** and in the USA the ◊***National Guard*** have supplanted earlier voluntary militias.

milk secretion of the ◊mammary glands of female mammals, with which they suckle their young (during ◊lactation). Over 85% is water, the remainder comprising protein, fat, lactose (a sugar), calcium, phosphorus, iron, and vitamins. Milk composition varies among species; human milk contains less protein and more lactose than that of cows. The milk of cows, goats, and sheep is often consumed by humans, but regular drinking of milk after infancy is principally a Western practice.

Skimmed milk is what remains when the cream has been separated from milk. It is readily dried and is available in large quantities at low prices, so it is often sent as food aid to Third World countries. ***Evaporated milk*** is milk reduced by heat until it reaches about half its volume. ***Condensed milk*** is concentrated to about a third of its original volume with added sugar. The average consumption of milk in the UK is about 2.5–3 1/4–5 pt per week.

Milky Way faint band of light crossing the night sky, consisting of stars in the plane of our Galaxy. The name Milky Way is often used for the Galaxy itself. It is a spiral ◊galaxy, 100,000 light years in diameter and 2,000 light years thick, containing at least 100 billion ◊stars. The Sun is in one of its spiral arms, about 25,000 light years from the centre, not far from its central plane.

The densest parts of the Milky Way, towards the Galaxy's centre, lie in the constellation ◊Sagittarius. In places, the Milky Way is interrupted by lanes of dark dust that obscure light from the stars beyond, such as the Coalsack ◊nebula in ◊Crux (the Southern Cross). It is because of these that the Milky Way is irregular in width and appears to be divided into two between Centaurus and Cygnus.

Mill James 1773–1836. Scottish philosopher and political thinker who developed the theory of ◊utilitarianism. He is remembered for his political articles, and for the rigorous education he gave his son John Stuart Mill. Associated for most of his working life with the East India Company, he wrote a vast *History of British India* 1817–18. He was one of the founders of University College, London, together with his friend and fellow utilitarian Jeremy Bentham.

Mill John Stuart 1806–1873. English philosopher and economist who wrote *On Liberty* 1859, the classic philosophical defence of liberalism, and *Utilitarianism* 1863, a version of the 'greatest happiness for the greatest number' principle in ethics. His progressive views inspired *On the Subjection of Women* 1869.

He was born in London, the son of James Mill. In 1822 he entered the East India Company, where he remained until retiring in 1858. In 1826, as described in his *Autobiography* 1873, he passed through a mental crisis; he found his father's bleakly intellectual Utilitarianism emotionally unsatisfying and abandoned it for a more human philosophy influenced by the poet S T Coleridge. Mill sat in Parliament as a Radical 1865–68 and introduced a motion for women's suffrage.

In *Utilitarianism*, he states that actions are right if they bring about happiness and wrong if they bring about the reverse of happiness. *On Liberty* moved away from the Utilitarian notion that individual liberty was necessary for economic and governmental efficiency and advanced the classical defence of individual freedom as a value in itself and the mark of a mature society; this change can be traced in the later editions of *Principles of Political Economy* 1848. His philosophical and political writings include *A System of Logic* 1843 and *Considerations on Representative Government* 1861.

Millais John Everett 1829–1896. English painter, a founder member of the ◊Pre-Raphaelite Brotherhood (PRB) 1848. Among his well-known works are *Ophelia* 1852 (National Gallery, London), and *Autumn Leaves* 1856 (City Art Galleries, Manchester). By the late 1860s he had left the PRB, and he developed a far more conventional style that appealed strongly to Victorian tastes.

During the 1850s, inspired by the Pre-Raphaelite doctrine of 'truth to nature', he produced some of his best work, including *Ophelia* and *Christ in the House of His Parents* 1850 (Tate Gallery, London) (which caused an outcry on its first showing, since its realistic detail was considered unfitting to a sacred subject). Revolutionary in their time, such works were controversial, being championed by John Ruskin and soundly abused by Charles Dickens. Other works in the Pre-Raphaelite style are *Lorenzo and Isabella* 1849 (Walker Gallery, Liverpool), depicting the banquet scene from Keat's 'Isabella'; *The Return of the Dove to the Ark* 1851; *Mariana of the Moated Grange* 1851; *Ophelia*; and the popular *The Order of Release* 1853.

By the 1860s however, Millais was beginning to abandon the Pre-Raphaelite manner, developing an academic style in which popular sentiment plays a leading part, as in *The Boyhood of Raleigh* 1870 (Tate Gallery, London), and *Bubbles* 1885, which was used as an advertisement by the Pears soap company.

Millay Edna St Vincent 1892–1950. US poet. She wrote romantic, emotional verse, including *Renascence and Other Poems* 1917 and *The Harp-Weaver and Other Poems* 1923 (Pulitzer prize 1924).

millefiore (Italian 'a thousand flowers') ornamental glassmaking technique. Coloured glass rods are arranged in bundles so that the cross-section forms a pattern. When the bundle is heated and drawn out thinly, the design becomes reduced in scale. Slices of this are used in glass-bead manufacture and can be set side by side and fused into metalware.

millennium period of 1,000 years. Some quasi-Christian sects, such as Jehovah's Witnesses, believe that Jesus will return to govern the Earth in person at the next millennium, the 6001st year after the creation (as located by Archbishop Usher at 4004 BC). This belief, millenarianism, also called chiliasm (from the Greek for 1,000), was widespread in the early days of Christianity. As hopes were disappointed, belief in the imminence of the second coming tended to fade, but millenarian views have been expressed at periods of great religious excitement, such as the Reformation.

Millennium Bug crisis facing some computer systems in the year 2000 because they are unable to operate normally when faced with the unfamiliar date format.

Millennium Dome giant structure serving as the centrepiece of Great Britain's Millennium Festival celebrating the year 2000. Located on a 732,483 sq m/181 acre site in Greenwich, London, the Dome is on the Greenwich Prime Meridian (0° longitude). The Dome is 320 m/1,050 ft in diameter, 50 m/164 ft in height, and covers an area of 80,425 sq m/19.86 acres.

Miller (Alton) Glenn 1904–1944. US trombonist and bandleader. He was an exponent of the big-band swing sound from 1938. He composed his signature tune 'Moonlight Serenade' (a hit 1939). Miller became leader of the US Army Air Force Band in Europe 1942, made broadcasts to troops throughout the world during World War II, and disappeared without trace on a flight between England and France.

Miller Arthur 1915– . US dramatist. His plays deal with family relationships and contemporary American values, and include *Death of a Salesman* 1949 (Pulitzer prize), and *The Crucible* 1953, based on the Salem witch trials and reflecting the communist witch-hunts of Senator Joe ◊McCarthy. He was married 1956–61 to the film star Marilyn Monroe, for whom he wrote the film *The Misfits* 1960.

Miller One of the most acclaimed US playwrights of the 20th century, Arthur Miller has sought to find an authentic form of modern tragedy – an engaged and committed drama which does justice both to social themes and to the moral and psychological complexity of the individual. *Penguin Books Ltd*

More recent work includes *The American Clock* 1979 on the 1930s depression, *The Ride Down Mount Morgan* 1991, and *Broken Glass* 1994, on anti-semitism in the 1930s.

Miller Henry Valentine 1891–1980. US writer. From 1930 to 1940 he lived a bohemian life in Paris, where he wrote his fictionalized, sexually explicit, autobiographical trilogy *Tropic of Cancer* 1934, *Black Spring* 1936, and *Tropic of Capricorn* 1938. They were banned in the USA and England until the 1960s.

His autobiographical *The Rosy Crucifixion* trilogy, consisting of *Sexus* 1949, *Plexus* 1949, and *Nexus* 1957, was published as a whole in the USA 1965. Inspired by Surrealism, Miller was a writer of exuberant and comic prose fuelled by anarchist passion, and was later adopted as a guru by the followers of the ◊Beat Generation.

Miller Stanley Lloyd 1930– . US chemist. In the early 1950s, under laboratory conditions, he tried to recreate the formation of life on Earth. To water under a gas mixture of methane, ammonia, and hydrogen, he added an electrical discharge. After a week he found that amino acids, the ingredients of protein, had been formed.

Miller William 1801–1880. Welsh crystallographer, developer of the ***Miller indices***, a coordinate system of mapping the shapes and surfaces of crystals.

millet any of several grasses, family Gramineae, of which the grains are used as a cereal food and the stems as fodder. Species include *Panicum miliaceum*, extensively cultivated in the warmer parts of Europe, and *Sorghum bicolor*, also known as ◊durra.

Millet Jean François 1814–1875. French artist. A leading member of the ◊Barbizon School, he painted scenes of peasant life and landscapes. *The Angelus* 1859 (Musée d'Orsay, Paris) and *The Gleaners* (Louvre, Paris) 1857 were widely reproduced in his day.

Born in Normandy of a peasant family, he went to Paris to study in 1837. After a long struggle to earn a living by painting shepherdesses and nude bathers in the 18th-century *style galant*, he found his true vein in *The Winnower* of 1848. He settled at the village of Barbizon 1849, with his second wife and growing family, and there, still in poverty, devoted himself exclusively to the paintings of peasant life for which he is famous, such as *The Reapers* 1854, *The Gleaners* 1857, and *The Angelus* 1859.

Typically, his paintings and drawings convey the sombre melancholy of a peasant existence, a melancholy often emphasized by a twilight atmosphere. Though later dismissed as sentimental, such works were among the first to try to convey the dignity of rural life.

Millett Kate 1934– . US radical feminist lecturer, writer, and sculptor whose book *Sexual Politics* 1970 was a landmark in feminist thinking. She was a founding member of the National Organization of Women (NOW).

milli- prefix (symbol m) denoting a one-thousandth part (10^{-3}). For example, a millimetre, mm, is one thousandth of a metre.

millibar unit of pressure, equal to one-thousandth of a ◊bar.

Millikan Robert Andrews 1868–1953. US physicist, awarded a Nobel prize 1923 for his determination of ◊Planck's constant (a fundamental unit of quantum theory) 1916 and the ◊electric charge on an electron 1913.

His experiment to determine the electronic charge involved observing oil droplets, charged by external radiation, falling under gravity between two horizontal metal plates connected to a high-voltage supply. By varying the voltage, he was able to make the electrostatic field between the plates balance the gravitational field so that some droplets became stationary and floated. If a droplet of weight W is held stationary between plates separated by a distance d and carrying a potential difference V, the charge, e, on the drop is equal to Wd/V.

millilitre one-thousandth of a litre (ml), equivalent to one cubic centimetre (cc).

millimetre of mercury unit of pressure (symbol mmHg), used in medicine for measuring blood pressure defined as the pressure exerted by a column of mercury one millimetre high, under the action of gravity.

millipede any arthropod of the class Diplopoda. It has a segmented body, each segment usually bearing two pairs of legs, and the distinct head bears a pair of short clubbed antennae. Most millipedes are no more than 2.5 cm/1 in long; a few in the tropics are 30 cm/12 in. They live in damp, dark places, feeding mainly on rotting vegetation. Some species injure crops by feeding on tender roots, and some produce a poisonous secretion in defence.

Mills C(harles) Wright 1916–1962. US sociologist whose concern for humanity, ethical values, and individual freedom led him to criticize the US establishment. Originally in the liberal tradition, Mills later adopted Weberian and even Marxist ideas. He aroused considerable popular interest in sociology with such works as *White Collar* 1951; *The Power Elite* 1956, depicting the USA as ruled by businessmen, military experts, and politicians; and *Listen, Yankee* 1960.

Mills John Lewis Ernest Watts 1908– . English actor. A very versatile performer, he appeared in films such as *In Which We Serve* 1942, *The Rocking Horse Winner* 1949, *The Wrong Box* 1966, and *Oh! What a Lovely War* 1969. He received an Academy Award for *Ryan's Daughter* 1970. He is the father of the actresses Hayley Mills and Juliet Mills.

Mills Brothers US vocal group that specialized in close-harmony vocal imitations of instruments. Formed 1922, the group first broadcast on radio 1925, and continued to perform until the 1950s. Their 70 hits include 'Lazy River' 1948 and 'You Always Hurt the One You Love' 1944.

Milne A(lan) A(lexander) 1882–1956. English writer. His books for children were based on the teddy bear and other toys of his son Christopher Robin (*Winnie-the-Pooh* 1926 and *The House at Pooh Corner* 1928). He also wrote children's verse (*When We Were Very Young* 1924 and *Now We Are Six* 1927). He was an accomplished dramatist whose plays included *Toad of Toad Hall* 1929, an adaptation of Kenneth ◊Grahame's *The Wind in the Willows*.

Milošević Slobodan 1941– . Serbian communist politician, party chief and president of Serbia 1986–97; re-elected Dec 1990 in multiparty elections and again Dec 1992, and president of Yugoslavia from 1997. Milošević wielded considerable influence over the Serb-dominated Yugoslav federal army during the 1991–92 civil war and continued to back Serbian militia in ◊Bosnia-Herzegovina 1992–94, although publicly disclaiming any intention to 'carve up' the newly independent republic. Widely believed to be the instigator of the conflict, Milošević changed tactics from 1993, adopting the public persona of peacemaker and putting pressure on his allies, the Bosnian Serbs, to accept negotiated peace terms; this contributed to the Dayton peace accord for Bosnia-Herzegovina Nov 1995. However, in 1998 he faced international condemnation again for the brutal treatment by Serbian forces of ethnic Albanians in the province of Kosovo.

Miłosz Czesław 1911– . Polish-American writer. He became a diplomat before defecting and becoming a US citizen. His poetry in English translation, classical in style, includes *Selected Poems* 1973 and *Bells in Winter* 1978. His collection of essays 'The Captive Mind' 1953 concerns the impact of communism on Polish intellectuals. Among his novels are *The Seizure of Power* 1955, *The Issa Valley* 1981, and *The Land of Ulro* 1984. Nobel Prize for Literature 1980.

Milstein César 1927– . Argentine-born British molecular biologist who developed ◊monoclonal antibodies, giving immunity against specific diseases. He shared the Nobel Prize for Physiology or Medicine 1984 with Georges Köhler (1946–1995) and Niels Jerne (1911–1994).

Milton John 1608–1674. English poet and prose writer. His epic ◊*Paradise Lost* 1667 is one of the landmarks of English literature. Early poems, including *Comus* (a masque performed 1634) and *Lycidas* (an elegy, 1638), showed Milton's superlative lyric gift. Latin secretary to Oliver ◊Cromwell during the Commonwealth period, he also wrote many pamphlets and prose works, including *Areopagitica* 1644, which opposed press censorship. His early poems have a baroque exuberance, a rich and sensuous use of imagery and cadence, while his later works are more sober.

'A salesman is got to dream, boy. It comes with the territory.'
ARTHUR MILLER
Death of a Salesman

'If men cease to believe that they will one day become gods then they will surely become worms.'
HENRY MILLER
The Colossus of Maroussi

'O dark, dark, dark, amid the blaze of noon, / Irrecoverably dark, total eclipse / Without all hope of day!'
JOHN MILTON
Samson Agonistes

Milton A portrait of English poet John Milton by Jonathan Richardson. Milton's poetic career was interrupted by the exigencies of the English civil war, during which he wrote a number of pamphlets concerned with religious, civil, and domestic liberties. A passionate supporter of republicanism, Milton devoted his life to poetry following the Restoration. *Corbis*

Born in Cheapside, London, and educated at Cambridge, Milton was a scholarly poet, ambitious to match the classical epics, and with strong theological views. Of polemical temperament, he published prose works on republicanism and church government. His middle years were devoted to the Puritan cause and writing pamphlets, including *The Doctrine and Discipline of Divorce* 1643, which may have been based on his own experience of marital unhappiness. From 1649 he was Latin secretary to Cromwell and the Council of State. His assistants, as his sight failed, included Andrew ◊Marvell. *Paradise Lost* and the less successful sequel *Paradise Regained* 1671 were written when he was blind and in some political danger (after the restoration of Charles II), as was the dramatic poem *Samson Agonistes* 1671.

Milton Keynes industrial ◊new town and, from 1997, unitary authority of England (*see United Kingdom map*); population (1991) 176,300. It was developed as a new town 1967 around the old village of the same name, following a grid design by Richard Llewelyn-Davies; it is the headquarters of the Open University (founded 1969). Industries include electronics, clothing, and machinery.

Milwaukee industrial port (meatpacking, brewing, engineering, machinery, electronic and electrical equipment, chemicals) in Wisconsin, USA, on Lake Michigan; population (1992) 617,000. The site was settled 1818 and drew a large influx of German immigrants, beginning in the 1840s.

mime type of acting in which gestures, movements, and facial expressions replace speech. It has developed as a form of theatre, particularly in France, where Marcel ◊Marceau and Jean Louis ◊Barrault have continued the traditions established in the 19th century by Deburau and the practices of the ◊commedia dell'arte in Italy. In ancient Greece, mime was a crude, realistic comedy with dialogue and exaggerated gesture.

mimosa The fluffy ball-like pompons of *Mimosa albida* from Mexico are typical of the genus. Many mimosa flowers are sweetly scented and very attractive to bees. *Premaphotos Wildlife*

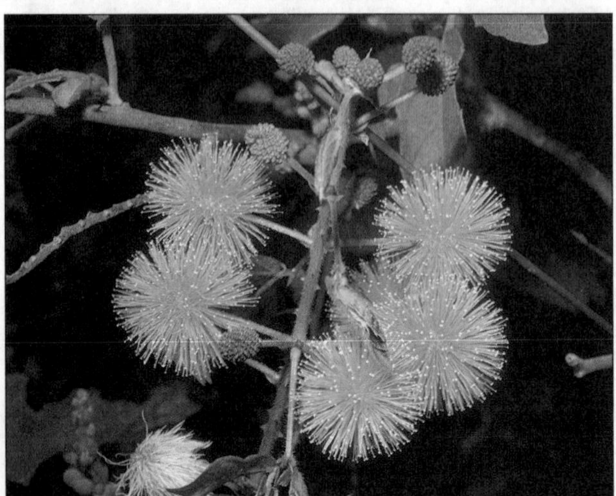

mimicry imitation of one species (or group of species) by another. The most common form is ***Batesian mimicry*** (named after English naturalist H W ◊Bates), where the mimic resembles a model that is poisonous or unpleasant to eat, and has aposematic, or warning, coloration; the mimic thus benefits from the fact that predators have learned to avoid the model. Hoverflies that resemble bees or wasps are an example. Appearance is usually the basis for mimicry, but calls, songs, scents, and other signals can also be mimicked.

mimosa tree, shrub, or herb of the genus *Mimosa* of the family Mimosaceae, found in tropical and subtropical regions. All bear small, fluffy, golden, ball-like flowers.

min. abbreviation for ***minute*** (time).

Minamoto or ***Genji*** ancient Japanese clan, the members of which were the first ruling shoguns 1192–1219. Their government was based in Kamakura, near present-day Tokyo. After the death of the first shogun, Minamoto Yoritomo (1147–1199), the real power was exercised by the regent for the shogun; throughout the Kamakura period (1192–1333), the regents were of the Hōjō family, a branch of the ◊Taira.

Minangkabau an Indonesian people of W Sumatra. In addition to approximately 3 million Minangkabau in W Sumatra, there are sizeable communities in the major Indonesian cities. The Minangkabau language belongs to the Austronesian family.

Minas Gerais state in SE Brazil; centre of the country's iron ore, coal, diamond and gold mining industries; area 587,172 sq km/226,710 sq mi; capital Belo Horizonte; population (1991) 16,956,900.

mind in philosophy, the presumed mental or physical being or faculty that enables a person to think, will, and feel; the seat of the intelligence and of memory; sometimes only the cognitive or intellectual powers, as distinguished from the will and the emotions.

Mind may be seen as synonymous with the merely random chemical reactions within the brain, or as a function of the brain as a whole, or (more traditionally) as existing independently of the physical brain, through which it expresses itself, or even as the only reality, matter being considered the creation of intelligence. The relation of mind to matter may be variously regarded. Traditionally, materialism identifies mental and physical phenomena equally in terms of matter and motion. Dualism holds that mind and matter exist independently side by side. Idealism maintains that mind is the ultimate reality and that matter does not exist apart from it.

Mindanao second-largest island of the Philippines. The indigenous peoples are the Lumad and Moro; area 94,627 sq km/36,526 sq mi; population (1990) 14,298,000. Towns and cities include Davao and Zamboanga. Industries include pineapples, coffee, rice, coconut, rubber, hemp, timber, nickel, gold, steel, chemicals, and fertilizer. The island is mainly mountainous rainforest; the active volcano Apo reaches 2,954 m/9,600 ft, and the island is subject to severe earthquakes.

mine explosive charge on land or sea, or in the atmosphere, designed to be detonated by contact, vibration (for example, from an enemy engine), magnetic influence, or a timing device. Countermeasures include metal detectors (useless for plastic types), specially equipped helicopters, and (at sea) ◊minesweepers. Mines were first used at sea in the early 19th century, during the Napoleonic Wars; landmines came into use during World War I to disable tanks. Landmines are simple to make but very difficult to clear once an area has been mined. Once laid, they continue to pose a threat to civilians years after the conflict has ended. In December 1997 in Ottawa, Canada, 125 states, including Britain, signed a treaty to ban the use, production, transfer and stock-piling of anti-personnel landmines. The International Campaign to Ban Landmines, an umbrella organization of 120 groups that that had been supported by the late Princess Diana, was instrumental in this achievement.

It is estimated that each year the 110 million landmines in use around the world kill 10,000 people and maim 14,000 more. Russia has agreed to sign the treaty later, after ratification by the required 40 states, but the United States will not since the treaty failed to include a nine-year waiver for the landmines that protect US troops stationed in South Korea. China, India, Pakistan, North and South Korea, Israel, Egypt, Syria, Iran, Iraq, and Kuwait are also prominent non-signatories.

mineral naturally formed inorganic substance with a particular chemical composition and a regularly repeating internal structure. Either in their perfect crystalline form or otherwise, minerals are the constituents of ◊rocks. In more general usage, a mineral is any substance economically valuable for mining (including coal and oil, despite their organic origins).

Mineral forming processes include: melting of pre-existing rock and subsequent crystallization of a mineral to form magmatic or volcanic rocks; weathering of rocks exposed at the land surface, with subsequent transport and grading by surface waters, ice or wind to form sediments; and recrystallization through increasing temperature and pressure with depth to form metamorphic rocks.

Minerals are usually classified as magmatic, sedimentary, or metamorphic. The magmatic minerals include the feldspars, quartz, pyroxenes, amphiboles, micas, and olivines that crystallize from silica-rich rock melts within the crust or from extruded lavas. The most commonly occurring sedimentary minerals are either pure concentrates or mixtures of sand, clay minerals, and carbonates (chiefly calcite, aragonite, and dolomite). Minerals typical of metamorphism include andalusite, cordierite, garnet, tremolite, lawsonite, pumpellyite, glaucophane, wollastonite, chlorite, micas, hornblende, staurolite, kyanite, and diopside.

mineral extraction recovery of valuable ores from the Earth's crust. The processes used include open-cast mining, shaft mining, and quarrying, as well as more specialized processes such as those used for oil and sulphur (see, for example, ◊Frasch process).

mineralogy study of minerals. The classification of minerals is based chiefly on their chemical composition and the kind of chemical bonding that holds these atoms together. The mineralogist also studies their crystallographic and physical characters, occurrence, and mode of formation.

mineral oil oil obtained from mineral sources, for example coal or petroleum, as distinct from oil obtained from vegetable or animal sources.

mineral salt in nutrition, a simple inorganic chemical that is required by living organisms. Plants usually obtain their mineral salts from the soil, while animals get theirs from their food. Important mineral salts include iron salts (needed by both plants and animals), magnesium salts (needed mainly by plants, to make chlorophyll), and calcium salts (needed by animals to make bone or shell). A ◊trace element is required only in tiny amounts.

mineral water water with mineral constituents gathered from the rocks with which it comes in contact, and classified by these into earthy, brine, and oil mineral waters; also water with artificially added minerals and, sometimes, carbon dioxide.

Many people believe that mineral waters have curative powers, the types of these medicinal waters being alkaline (Vichy), bitter (Seidlitz), chalybeate (iron: Tunbridge Wells) salt (Droitwich), earthy (Bath), sulphurous (Saratoga Springs), and special varieties, such as barium (Harrogate). The most widely sold mineral water is Perrier, from the French village of Vergèze in W Provence.

Minerva in Roman mythology, the goddess of intelligence, and of handicrafts and the arts, equivalent to the Greek ◊Athena. From the earliest days of ancient Rome, there was a temple to her on the Capitoline Hill, near the Temple of Jupiter.

minesweeper small naval vessel for locating and destroying mines at sea. A typical minesweeper weighs about 725 tonnes, and is built of reinforced plastic (immune to magnetic and acoustic mines).

Ming dynasty 14th–17th centuries. Chinese dynasty 1368–1644, based in Nanjing. During the rule 1402–24 of Yongle (or Yung-lo), there was territorial expansion into Mongolia and Yunnan in the SW. The administrative system was improved, public works were carried out, and foreign trade was developed. Art and literature flourished and distinctive blue and white porcelain was produced.

The Ming dynasty was founded by Zhu Yuanzhang (or Chu Yuan-chang) (1328–1398), a rebel leader who captured the ◊Yuan capital Khanbaligh (modern Beijing) 1368. He set up his headquarters in Nanjing and proclaimed himself Emperor Hong

Wu. From the late 16th century, the Ming faced the threat of attack from the NE by Japan, which invaded its tributary Korea 1592. Population pressure also led to peasant rebellions, and decline came with the growth of eunuch power, pressure from Mongols in the N, and an increasing burden of taxes.

Mingus Charles 1922–1979. US jazz bassist and composer. He played with Louis Armstrong, Duke Ellington, and Charlie Parker. His experimentation with ◊atonality and dissonant effects opened the way for the new style of free collective jazz improvisation of the 1960s.

Based on the West Coast until 1951, Mingus took part in the development of cool jazz. Subsequently based in New York, he worked with a number of important musicians and expanded the scope of the bass as a lead instrument. Recordings include *Pithecanthropus Erectus* 1956 and *Mingus at Monterey* 1964.

miniature painting painting on a very small scale, notably early manuscript illumination, and later miniature portraits, sometimes set in jewelled cases, and Islamic paintings. Hans Holbein the Younger introduced miniature portrait painting into England, the form reaching its height in the works of ◊Hilliard in the 16th century, though continuing well into the 19th century. There was also a very strong tradition of miniature portrait painting in France. Miniatures by Islamic artists flourished in India and Persia, their subjects often bird and flowers, or scenes from history and legend, rather than portraits (◊Islamic art).

English miniatures Hans Holbein painted portrait miniatures while in England 1531–43, using ◊gouache on playing cards. The form was later perfected by such artists as Nicholas Hilliard, who set the portraits, which were worn as jewellery, in exquisite frames of precious metal. Later English miniaturists include Hilliard's pupil Isaac Oliver (c. 1560–1617) and Isaac's son, Peter Oliver; Samuel Cooper (1609–1672), who was called a 'van Dyck in little'; and Richard Cosway (1742–1821), whose miniatures for snuffbox lids were famous.

French miniatures The earliest French miniaturists were Jean and François ◊Clouet, and a number of specialists practised the art in France in the 17th and 18th centuries, while such well-known painters as Largillierre, Boucher, and Prud'hon produced some minatures. Petitot (1607–1691) is noted for miniatures executed in enamel for Louis XIV.

Leading French miniaturists of the late 18th century were Jean Baptiste Jacques Augustin (1759–1832) and Jean Baptiste Isabey (1757–1855), a favourite of the Napoleonic court. Friedrich Fuger (1751–1818), a German artist who worked for the Austrian court, is sometimes known as 'the Cosway of Vienna'.

minicomputer multiuser computer with a size and processing power between those of a ◊mainframe and a ◊microcomputer. Nowadays almost all minicomputers are based on ◊microprocessors. Minicomputers are often used in medium-sized businesses and in university departments handling ◊database or other commercial programs and running scientific or graphical applications.

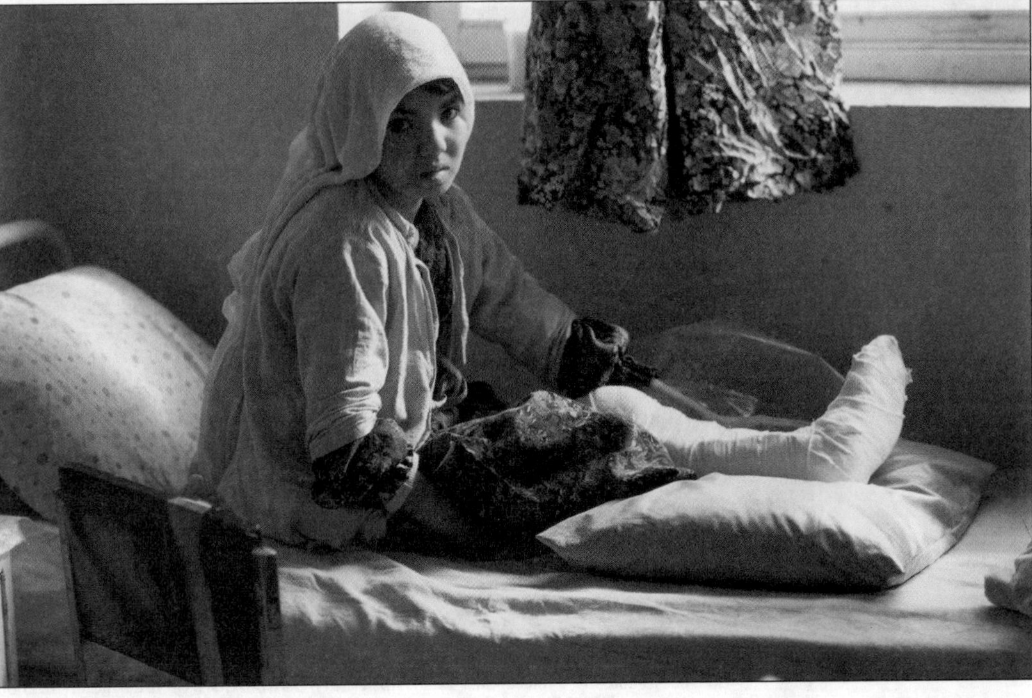

mine A young woman wounded by an anti-personnel mine in February 1996 at the Red Cross Hospital in Kabul, Afghanistan. Anti-personnel mines are currently one of the most prevalent types of mine in use worldwide. *Peter Turnley/Corbis*

Minimalism movement in abstract art (mostly sculpture) and music towards severely simplified composition. Minimal art developed in the USA in the 1950s in reaction to ◊Abstract Expressionism, shunning its emotive approach in favour of impersonality and elemental, usually geometric, shapes. It has found its fullest expression in sculpture, notably in the work of Carl Andre (1935–), who employs industrial materials in modular compositions. In music, from the 1960s, it manifested itself in large-scale statements, usually tonal or even diatonic, and highly repetitive, based on a few 'minimal' musical ideas. Major Minimalist composers are Steve ◊Reich and Philip ◊Glass.

minimum wage minimum level of pay for workers, usually set by government. Minimum wages are argued by some economists to cause unemployment because if wages were allowed to fall below the minimum wage level, some employers would be prepared to take on more employees. In June 1998 the UK government announced a minimum wage of £3.60 per hour for those aged 21 and over.

mineral The crystalline structure of olivine (magnesium iron silicate, $(Mg,Fe)_2SiO_4$) is clearly visible under a polarized microscope. It is a rock-forming mineral abundant in gabbros and basalts. *Corel*

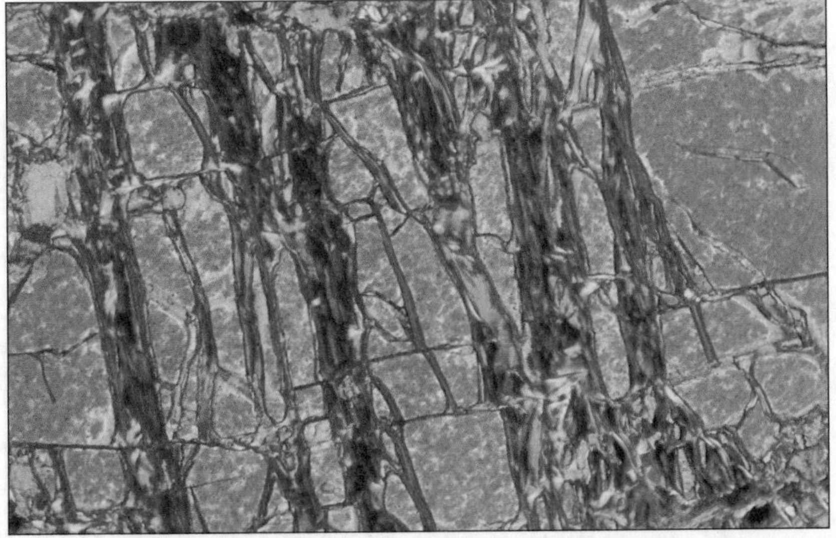

mining extraction of minerals from under the land or sea for industrial or domestic uses. Exhaustion of traditionally accessible resources has led to development of new mining techniques; for example, extraction of oil from offshore deposits and from land shale reserves. Technology is also under development for the exploitation of minerals from entirely new sources such as mud deposits and mineral nodules from the sea bed.

Mud deposits are laid down by hot springs (about 350°C/660°F): sea water penetrates beneath the ocean floor and carries copper, silver, and zinc with it on its return. Such springs occur along the midocean ridges of the Atlantic and Pacific and in the geological rift between Africa and Arabia under the Red Sea.

Mineral nodules form on the ocean bed and contain manganese, cobalt, copper, molybdenum, and nickel; they stand out on the surface, and 'grow' by only a few millimetres every 100,000 years. *See illustration on following page.*

mink two species of carnivores of the weasel family, genus *Mustela*, usually found in or near water. They have rich, brown fur, and are up to 50 cm/1.6 ft long with bushy tails 20 cm/8 in long. They live in Eurasia (*M. lutreola*) and North America (*M. vison*). The demand for their fur led to the establishment from the 1930s of mink ranches to breed the animals in a wide range of fur colours.

Minneapolis city in Minnesota, USA, forming with St Paul the Twin Cities area; population (1992) 362,700; metropolitan area (1992) 2,618,000. It is at the head of navigation of the Mississippi River. Industries include food processing and the manufacture of machinery, electrical and electronic equipment, precision instruments, transport machinery, and metal and paper products.

> *'Minneapolis and St Paul ... are divided by the Mississippi River, and united by the belief that the inhabitants of the other side of the river are inferior.'*
>
> On MINNEAPOLIS AND ST PAUL
> Trevor Fishlock
> *Americans and Nothing Else*

Minnelli Liza May 1946– . US actress and singer. The daughter of Judy ◊Garland and director Vincente Minnelli, she achieved stardom in the Broadway musical *Flora, the Red Menace* 1965 and in the film *Cabaret* 1972. Her subsequent films include *New York, New York* 1977 and *Arthur* 1981.

Minnelli Vincente 1910–1986. US film director. He specialized in musicals and occasional melodramas. His most successful films, such as *Meet Me in St Louis* 1944 and *Lust for Life* 1956, display great visual flair.

Minnesota state in N midwest USA; nicknamed Gopher State/North Star State
area 218,700 sq km/84,418 sq mi
capital St Paul
towns and cities Minneapolis, Duluth, Bloomington, Rochester
features more than 15,000 lakes; 260 km/160 mi of

mining Workers in a tin mine in Bolivia. Mining is a hazardous occupation and the majority of mining accidents are associated with the haulage equipment. Miners are prone to black lung or pneumoconiosis due to the dusty conditions in which they work. *United Nations/Image Select (UK) Ltd*

Lake Superior rocky shoreline; Minneapolis, with the Walker Art Center with the Minneapolis Sculpture Garden, the Falls of St Anthony on the Mississippi River, and the Minnehaha Falls (made famous by Longfellow in *The Song of Hiawatha*); St Paul, with the Cathedral of St Paul, the state capitol (with a dome 68 m/223 ft high, the world's largest unsupported marble dome); the Iron Range; Greyhound Origin Center at Hibbing, where the Greyhound bus system began; the Mayo Clinic, Rochester
products cereals, soya beans, livestock, meat and dairy products, iron ore (about two-thirds of US output), nonelectrical machinery, electronic equipment
population (1991) 4,432,000
history first European exploration, by French fur traders, in the 17th century; region claimed for France by Daniel Greysolon, Sieur Duluth, 1679; part E of Mississippi River ceded to Britain 1763 and to the USA 1783; part W of Mississippi passed to the USA under the Louisiana Purchase 1803; became a territory 1849; statehood achieved 1858.

Minnesota

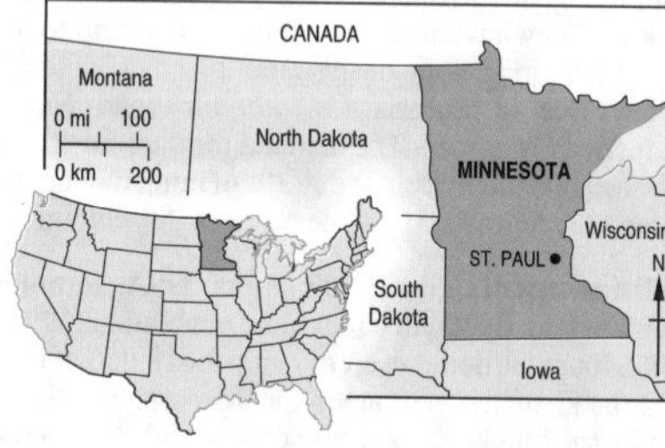

minnow various small freshwater fishes of the carp family (Cyprinidae), found in streams and ponds worldwide. Most species are small and dully coloured, but some are brightly coloured. They feed on larvae and insects.

Minoan art art of Bronze Age Crete, about 2300–1100 BC. It is of a high aesthetic standard, reflecting the artistic orientation and zest for life of the Minoan people. Its fine pottery, painted in a fresh, spontaneous style with plant and animal motifs curving to suit the form of the vases, comes in various styles but is best represented by 'light-on-dark' and Kamares-style (polychrome on a dark background) ware. Its magnificent palaces, such as Knossos, Phaestos, and Mallia, were decorated with cheerful ◊frescoes depicting scenes from everyday life, plants, birds, leaping fish, and dolphins; fragments remain, such as the lily fresco from Ambisos (Iráklion Museum, Crete). The culture came to an end when, after the eruption of the volcano on Thera (now Santorini) and the destruction of the Minoan centre on that island, the ◊Mycenaeans gained control in the Aegean.

Minoan civilization Bronze Age civilization on the Aegean island of Crete. The name is derived from Minos, the legendary king of Crete. The civilization is divided into three main periods: early Minoan, about 3000–2000 BC; middle Minoan, about 2000–1550 BC; and late Minoan, about 1550–1050 BC.

With the opening of the Bronze Age, about 3000 BC, the Minoan culture proper began. Each period was marked by cultural advances in copper and bronze weapons, pottery of increasingly intricate design, frescoes, and the construction of palaces and fine houses at Phaistos and Mallia, in addition to ◊Knossos. About 1400 BC, in the late Minoan period, the civilization was suddenly destroyed by earthquake or war. A partial revival continued until about 1100.

The earlier (Linear A) of two languages used in Crete remains undeciphered; Linear B, which is also found at sites on the mainland of Greece, was deciphered by Michael ◊Ventris.

In religion the Minoans seem to have worshipped principally a great mother goddess with whom was associated a young male god. The tales of Greek mythology about Rhea, the mother of Zeus, and the birth of Zeus himself in a Cretan cave seem to be based on Minoan religion.

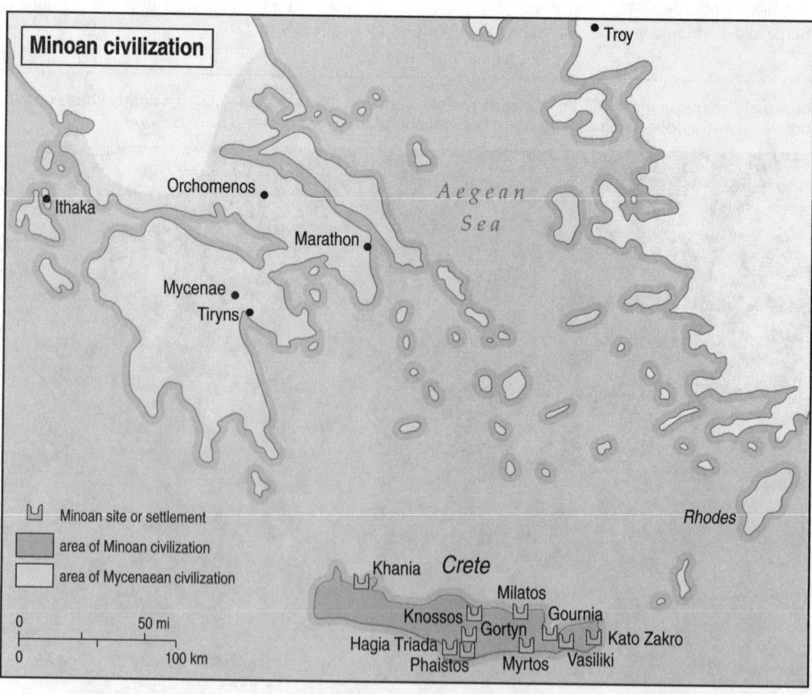

minor legal term for those under the age of majority, which varies from country to country but is usually between 18 and 21. In many European countries, including Britain (from 1970), and in the USA (from 1971 for voting) the age of majority is 18. Most civic and legal rights and duties only accrue at the age of majority: for example, the rights to vote, to make a will, and (usually) to make a fully binding contract, and the duty to act as a juror.

Minorca (Spanish ***Menorca***) second largest of the ◊Balearic Islands in the Mediterranean. Because of its unique ecology, the island was designated a Biosphere Reserve by UNESCO in 1993, and in 1995 a large area in the northeast of the island was declared a national park of Spain, ensuring the protection of a wide variety of fauna and flora, especially bird species
area 689 sq km/266 sq mi
towns and cities Mahon, Ciudadela, Mercadal, Ferrerias, Fornells
products leather goods; costume jewellery; cheese and dairy products; tourism is important
population (1990 est) 62,000.

Minority Rights Group international human-rights organization established 1965 to increase awareness of minority issues. It publishes reports on minority groups worldwide, produces educational material for schools, and makes representations at the United Nations. Its headquarters are in London.

minor planet another name for an ◊asteroid.

Minos in Greek mythology, a king of Crete (son of Zeus and Europa), who demanded a yearly tribute of young men and girls from Athens for the ◊Minotaur. After his death, he became a judge in ◊Hades.

Minotaur in Greek mythology, a monster, half man and half bull, offspring of Pasiphaë, wife of King Minos of Crete, and a bull. It lived in the Labyrinth at Knossos, and its victims were seven girls and seven youths, sent in annual tribute by Athens, until ◊Theseus killed it, with the aid of Ariadne, the daughter of Minos.

Minsk or ***Mensk*** industrial city (machinery, textiles, leather; a centre of the Russian computer industry) and capital of Belarus; population (1991) 1,633,600. Minsk dates from the 11th century and has in turn been held by Lithuania, Poland, Sweden, and Russia before Belarus became an independent republic 1991. The city was devastated by Napoleon 1812 and heavily damaged by German forces 1944.

Minsmere coastal marshland bird reserve (1948) near Aldeburgh, Suffolk, attracting a greater number of species than any other in Britain, and containing the Scrape, an artificial breeding habitat.

mint The water mint *Mentha aquatica*. As its name suggests, water mint grows in marshes and fens, producing small pink flowers from July to Oct. Mints have a wide range of uses in cooking and medicine. *Premaphotos Wildlife*

minster in the UK, a church formerly attached to a monastery: for example, York Minster. Originally the term meant a monastery, and in this sense it is often preserved in place names, such as Westminster.

mint in botany, any aromatic plant, genus *Mentha*, of the family Labiatae, widely distributed in temperate regions. The plants have square stems, creeping rootstocks, and spikes of small flowers, usually pink or purplish. Mints include garden mint *M. spicata* and peppermint *M. piperita*.

mint in economics, a place where coins are made under government authority. In Britain, the official mint is the Royal Mint; the US equivalent is the Bureau of the Mint. The UK Royal Mint also manufactures coinages, official medals, and seals for Commonwealth and foreign countries.

For centuries in the Tower of London, the Royal Mint was housed in a building on Tower Hill from 1810 until the new Royal Mint was opened at Llantrisant, near Cardiff, Mid Glamorgan, in 1968. The nominal head is the Master Worker and Warden, who is the chancellor of the Exchequer, but the actual chief is the Deputy Master and Comptroller, a permanent civil servant.

Mintoff Dom(inic) 1916– . Labour prime minister of Malta 1955–58 and 1971–84. He negotiated the removal of British and other foreign military bases 1971–79 and made treaties with Libya.

Minton Thomas 1765–1836. English potter. He first worked under the potter Josiah Spode, but in 1789 established himself at Stoke-on-Trent as an engraver of designs (he originated the 'willow pattern') and in the 1790s founded a pottery there, producing high-quality bone china, including tableware.

minuet French country dance in three time adapted as a European courtly dance of the 17th century. The music was later used as the third movement of a classical four-movement symphony where its gentle rhythm provides a foil to the slow second movement and fast final movement.

minute unit of time consisting of 60 seconds; also a unit of angle equal to one sixtieth of a degree.

Minuteman in weaponry, a US three-stage intercontinental ballistic missile (ICBM) with a range of about 8,000 km/5,000 mi. In US history the term was applied to members of the citizens' militia in the 1770s. These volunteer soldiers had pledged to be available for battle at a 'minute's notice' during the ◊American Revolution.

Miocene ('middle recent') fourth epoch of the Tertiary period of geological time, 23.5–5.2 million years ago. At this time grasslands spread over the interior of continents, and hoofed mammals rapidly evolved.

mips (acronym for ***million instructions per second***) in computing, a measure of the speed of a processor. It does not equal the computer power in all cases. The original IBM PC had a speed of one-quarter mips, but now 50 mips PCs and 100 mips workstations are available.

Mir (Russian 'peace' or 'world') Soviet space station, the core of which was launched 20 Feb 1986. It is intended to be a permanently occupied space station. *Mir* weighs almost 21 tonnes, is approximately 13.5 m/44 ft long, and has a maximum diameter of 4.15 m/13.6 ft. It carries a number of improvements over the earlier ◊Salyut series of space stations, including six docking ports; four of these can have scientific and technical modules attached to them. The first of these was the *Kvant* (quantum) astrophysics module, launched 1987. This had two main sections: a main experimental module, and a service module that would be separated in orbit. The experimental module was 5.8 m/19 ft long and had a maximum diameter matching that of *Mir*. When attached to the *Mir* core, *Kvant* added a further 40 cu m/1,413 cu ft of working space to that already there. Among the equipment carried by *Kvant* were several X-ray telescopes and an ultraviolet telescope. In June 1995 the US space shuttle *Atlantis* docked with *Mir*, exchanging crew members.

Mira or ***Omicron Ceti*** brightest long-period pulsating ◊variable star, located in the constellation ◊Cetus. Mira was the first star discovered to vary periodically in brightness. It has a periodic variation between third or fourth magnitude and ninth magnitude over an average period of 331 days. It can sometimes reach second magnitude and once almost attained first magnitude 1779. At times it is easily visible to the naked eye, being the brightest star in that part of the sky, while at others it cannot be seen without a telescope.

Mirabeau Honoré Gabriel Riqueti, Comte de 1749–1791. French politician, leader of the National Assembly in the French Revolution. He wanted to establish a parliamentary monarchy on the English model. From May 1790 he secretly acted as political adviser to the king.

miracle play another name for ◊mystery play.

mirage illusion seen in hot weather of water on the horizon, or of distant objects being enlarged. The effect is caused by the ◊refraction, or bending, of light. Light rays from the sky bend as they pass through the hot layers of air near the ground, so that they appear to come from the horizon. Because the light is from a blue sky, the horizon appears blue and watery. If, during the night, cold air collects near the ground, light can be bent in the opposite direction, so that objects below the horizon appear to float above it. In the same way, objects such as trees or rocks near the horizon can appear enlarged.

Miranda Carmen. Stage name of Maria de Carmo Miranda da Cunha 1909–1955. Portuguese dancer and singer. She lived in Brazil from childhood, moving to Hollywood 1939. Her Hollywood musicals include *Down Argentine Way* 1940 and *The Gang's All Here* 1943. Her hallmarks were extravagant costumes and headgear adorned with tropical fruits, a staccato singing voice, and fiery temperament.

Mirandola Italian 15th-century philosopher. See ◊Pico della Mirandola.

Miró Joan 1893–1983. Spanish painter and sculptor, a major figure in ◊Surrealism. In the mid-1920s he developed an abstract style, lyrical and often witty, with amoeba shapes, some linear, some highly coloured, generally floating on a plain background. *Birth of the World* 1925 (Museum of Modern Art New York) is typical of his more abstract works.

His paintings before 1922 combine the influence of ◊Cubism with an emblematic treatment of detail. In 1924 he joined the Surrealists, and increasingly a strong element of fantasy entered his work, as in the painting *The Hunter* 1923–24 (Museum of Modern Art, New York), an elaborate composition full of strange creatures and erotic imagery. He also made more abstract paintings in which rudimentary signs are set against a background of drips and splashes, anticipating ◊Abstract Expressionism.

During the 1930s he was deeply affected by the Spanish Civil War and his style became more sober, probing, and at times savage. After World War II he produced larger abstracts, experimented with printmaking and sculpture (sometimes using everyday objects), and produced ceramic murals (including two in the UNESCO building in Paris, 1958). He also designed stained glass and sets for the ballet impresario Sergei Diaghilev.

Mirren Helen 1945– . English actress. She has played both modern and classical stage roles. Her Shakespearean roles include Lady Macbeth and Isabella in *Measure for Measure*. Her films include *The Long Good Friday* 1981 and *Cal* 1984; and *Prime Suspect* 1990 for television.

mirror any polished surface that reflects light; often made from 'silvered' glass (in practice, a mercury-alloy coating of glass). A plane (flat) mirror produces a same-size, erect 'virtual' image located behind the mirror at the same distance from it as the object is in front of it. A spherical concave mirror produces a reduced, inverted real image in front or an enlarged, erect virtual image behind it (as in a shaving mirror), depending on how close the object is to the mirror. A spherical convex mirror produces a reduced, erect virtual image behind it (as in a car's rear-view mirror).

MIRV abbreviation for ***multiple independently targeted re-entry vehicle***, used in ◊nuclear warfare.

miscarriage spontaneous expulsion of a fetus from the womb before it is capable of independent survival. Often, miscarriages are due to an abnormality in the developing fetus.

misdemeanour in US law, an offence less serious than a ◊felony. A misdemeanour is an offence punishable by a relatively insevere penalty, such as a fine or short term in prison or a term of community service, while a felony carries more severe penalties, such as a term of imprisonment of a year or more up to the death penalty. In Britain the term is obsolete.

mise en scène (French 'stage setting') in cinema, the composition and content of the frame in terms of background scenery, actors, costumes, props, camera movement, and lighting.

Mishima Yukio. Pen name of Hiraoka Kimitake 1925–1970. Japanese novelist. His work often deals with sexual desire and perversion, as in *Confessions of a Mask* 1949 and *The Temple of the Golden Pavilion* 1956. He committed hara-kiri (ritual suicide) as a protest against what he saw as the corruption of the nation and the loss of the samurai warrior tradition.

Mishnah (Hebrew '(teaching by) repetition') or ***Mishna*** collection of commentaries on written Hebrew law, consisting of discussions between rabbis, handed down orally from their inception in AD 70 until about 200, when, with the *Gemara* (the main body of rabbinical debate on interpretations of

Minoan civilization A large Minoan jar decorated with scroll and floral motifs. The term 'Minoan' comes from Minos, the legendary king of Crete, and is applied to the culture of the island in ancient times, particularly from about 2500 BC to 1100 BC. During this time it was the major civilization in the Mediterranean, evidently peaceful and prosperous. It was probably destroyed partly by earthquake and partly by invasion. *Corbis*

❛The Nile of the Western Hemisphere.❜

On the Mississippi River
John Gunther
Inside USA

the Mishnah), it was committed to writing to form the *Talmud*.

Miskito a Native American people of Central America, living mainly in the area of Central America that is now Nicaragua.

misrepresentation in law, an untrue statement of fact, made in the course of negotiating a contract, that induces one party to enter into the contract. The remedies available for misrepresentation depend on whether the representation is found to be fraudulent, negligent, or innocent.

missal in the Roman Catholic Church, a service book containing the complete office of Mass for the entire year. A simplified missal in the vernacular was introduced 1969 (obligatory from 1971): the first major reform since 1570.

missile rocket-propelled weapon, which may be nuclear-armed (see ◊nuclear warfare). Modern missiles are often classified as surface-to-surface missiles (SSM), air-to-air missiles (AAM), surface-to-air missiles (SAM), or air-to-surface missiles (ASM). A ***cruise missile*** is in effect a pilotless, computer-guided aircraft; it can be sea-launched from submarines or surface ships, or launched from the air or the ground.

Rocket-propelled weapons were first used by the Chinese about AD 1100, and were encountered in the 18th century by the British forces. The rocket missile was then re-invented in England around 1805, and remained in use with various armies in the 19th century. The first wartime use of a long-range missile was against England in World War II, by the jet-powered German V1 (*Vergeltungswaffe*, 'revenge weapon' or Flying Bomb), a monoplane (wingspan about 6 m/18 ft, length 8.5 m/26 ft); the first rocket-propelled missile with a preset guidance system was the German V2, also launched by Germany against Britain in World War II.

Modern missiles are also classified as strategic or tactical: strategic missiles are the large, long-range ***intercontinental ballistic missiles*** (ICBMs, capable of reaching targets over 5,500 km/3,400 mi), and tactical missiles are the short-range weapons intended for use in limited warfare (with a range under 1,100 km/680 mi).

Not all missiles are large; many are small enough to be carried by one person. The Stinger, for example, is an anti-aircraft missile fired by a single soldier from a shoulder-held tube. Most fighter aircraft are equipped with missiles to use against enemy aircraft or against ground targets. Other small missiles are launched from a type of truck, called a MLRS (multiple-launch rocket system), that can move around a battlefield. Ship-to-ship missiles like the Exocet have proved very effective in naval battles.

The vast majority of missiles have systems that guide them to their target. The guidance system may consist of radar and computers, either in the missile or on the ground. These devices track the missile and determine the correct direction and distance required for it to hit its target. In the radio-guidance system, the computer is on the ground, and guidance signals are radio-transmitted to the missile. In the inertial guidance system, the computer is on board the missile. Some small missiles have heat-seeking devices fitted to their noses to seek out the engines of enemy aircraft, or are guided by laser light reflected from the target. Others (called TOW missiles) are guided by signals sent along wires that trail behind the missile in flight.

missile An air-to-air missile launched from a fighter aircraft. Missiles of this type are generally heat seeking. The first such missile manufactured was the American Sidewinder, so named because it owed much of its design to the rattlesnake's heat-seeking sensory system. *Image Select (UK) Ltd*

mission organized attempt to spread a religion. Throughout its history Christianity has been the most assertive of missionary religions; Islam has also played a missionary role. Missionary activity in the Third World has frequently been criticized for its disruptive effects on indigenous peoples and their traditional social, political, and cultural systems.

Mississippi river in the USA, the main arm of the great river system draining the USA between the Appalachian and the Rocky mountains. The length of the Mississippi is 3,780 km/2,350 mi; with its tributary the Missouri 6,020 km/3,740 mi.

Mississippi (river)

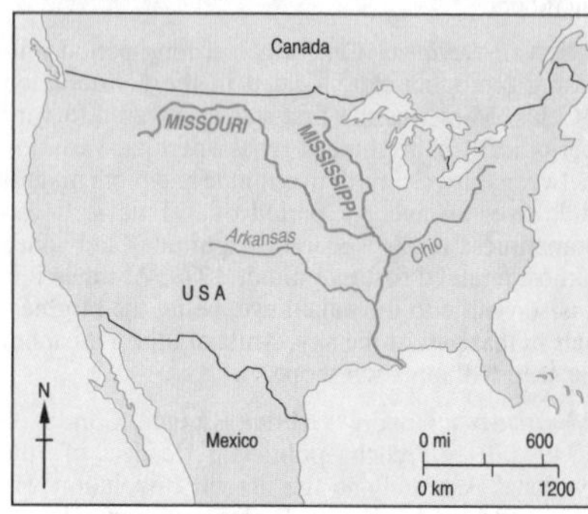

The Mississippi rises in the lake region of N Minnesota, with St Anthony Falls at Minneapolis. Below the tributaries Minnesota, Wisconsin, Des Moines, and Illinois, the confluence of the Missouri and Mississippi occurs at St Louis. Turning at the Ohio junction, it passes Memphis, and takes in the St Francis, Arkansas, Yazoo, and Red tributaries before reaching its delta on the Gulf of Mexico beyond New Orleans.

Mississippi state in SE USA; nicknamed Magnolia State/Bayou State
area 123,600 sq km/47,710 sq mi
capital Jackson
towns and cities Biloxi, Meridian, Hattiesburg
features Mississippi, Pearl, and Big Black rivers; Mississippi Delta; Gulf Islands national seashore; Jackson, with many Greek Revival buildings; Oxford, with the Center for Study of Southern Culture in Barnard Observatory (with the world's largest blues archive); Natchez, with cotton plantation mansions built in the first half of the 19th century; Vicksburg national military park (Civil War site); Emerald Mound, an Native American mound dating from c. 1300; Civil War sites at Corinth; University of Mississippi (1848); Elvis Presley's birthplace at Tupelo; the Coca Cola museum, Vicksburg
products cotton, rice, soya beans, chickens, fish and shellfish, lumber and wood products, petroleum and natural gas, transportation equipment, chemicals
population (1991) 2,595,000
history first explored by Hernando de Soto for Spain 1540; settled by the French 1699, the English 1763; ceded to USA 1798; statehood achieved 1817. After secession from the Union during the Civil War, it was readmitted 1870.

Mississippi (state)

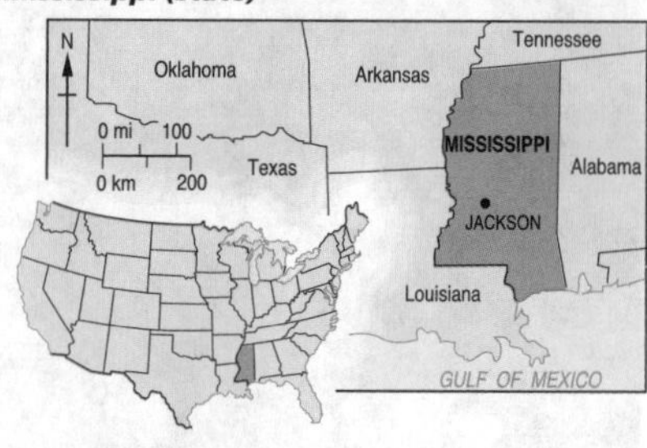

Mississippian US term for the Lower or Early ◊Carboniferous period of geological time, 363–323 million years ago. It is named after the state of Mississippi.

Missolonghi (Greek ***Mesolóngion***) town in W central Greece and Eubrea region, on the north shore of the Gulf of Patras; population (1981) 10,200. It was several times under siege by the Turks in the wars of 1822–26.

Missouri major river in the central USA, a tributary of the Mississippi, which it joins N of St Louis; length 4,320 km/2,683 mi.

Missouri state in central USA; nicknamed Show Me State/Bullion State
area 180,600 sq km/69,712 sq mi
capital Jefferson City
towns and cities St Louis, Kansas City, Springfield, Independence
features Ozark Mountains and the Lake of the Ozarks; Missouri and Mississippi rivers; St Louis, with the Gateway Arch (1966, 192 m/630 ft high), St Louis Art Museum, and Cathedral of St Louis; the Pony Express national memorial, and the birthplace of Jesse James, in St Joseph; Ste Genevieve, the oldest permanent settlement in Missouri; the Carver national monument; the Mark Twain home and museum, Hannibal; Harry S Truman library and museum, Independence; Fulton, site of Winston Churchill's 'Iron Curtain' speech 1946, with collection of Churchilliana in the Church of St Mary the Virgin, Aldermanbury; Nelson-Atkins Museum of Art, Kansas City; St Louis Symphony Orchestra; 'Bible Belt' centred on Springfield
products meat and other processed food, aerospace and transport equipment, lead, zinc
population (1991) 5,158,000
history explored by Hernando de Soto for Spain 1541; acquired by the USA under the Louisiana Purchase 1803; achieved statehood 1821, following the Missouri Compromise of 1820.

Missouri Compromise in US history, the solution by Congress (1820–21) of a sectional crisis caused by the 1819 request from Missouri for admission to the Union as a slave state, despite its proximity to existing nonslave states. The compromise was the simultaneous admission of Maine as a nonslave state to keep the same ratio.

Mistinguett stage name of Jeanne Marie Bourgeois 1873–1956. French actress and dancer. A leading music-hall artist in Paris from 1899, she appeared in revues at the Folies-Bergère, Casino de Paris, and Moulin Rouge. She was known for the song 'Mon Homme' and her partnership with Maurice Chevalier.

mistletoe parasitic evergreen unisexual plant *Viscum album*, native to Europe. It grows on trees as a branched bush with translucent white berries.

Missouri

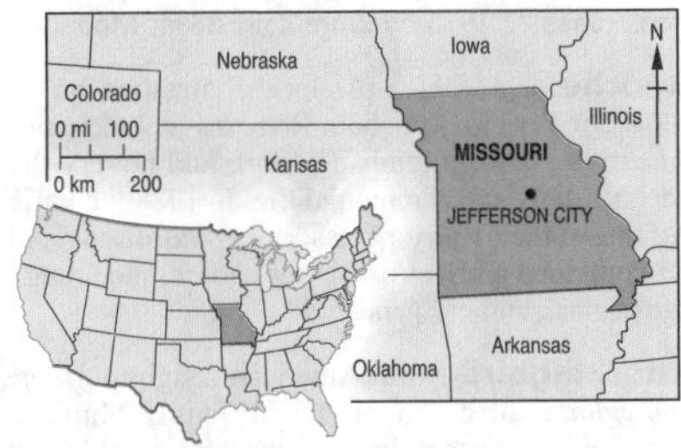

Used in many Western countries as a Christmas decoration, it also featured in ◊Druidism.

mistral cold, dry, northerly wind that occasionally blows during the winter on the Mediterranean coast of France, particularly concentrated along the Rhône valley. It has been known to reach a velocity of 145 kph/90 mph.

Mistral Gabriela. Pen name of Lucila Godoy de Alcayaga 1889–1957. Chilean poet. She wrote *Sonnets of Death* 1915 and was awarded the Nobel Prize for Literature 1945. She was consul of Chile in Spain, and represented her country at the League of Nations and the United Nations.

Mitchell Arthur 1934–1990. US dancer. He was director of the Dance Theater of Harlem, which he founded 1968 with Karel Shook (1920–). Mitchell was a principal dancer with the New York City Ballet 1956–68, creating many roles in Balanchine's ballets, such as *Agon* 1967.

Mitchell Joni. Adopted name of Roberta Joan Anderson 1943– . Canadian singer, songwriter, and guitarist. She began in the 1960s folk style and subsequently incorporated elements of rock and jazz with confessional, sophisticated lyrics. Her albums include *Blue* 1971 and *Hejira* 1976.

Mitchell Juliet 1940– . British psychoanalyst and writer. Her article in *New Left Review* 1966 entitled 'Women: The Longest Revolution' was one of the first attempts to combine socialism and feminism, using Marxist theory to explain the reasons behind women's oppression. She published *Women's Estate* 1971 and *Psychoanalysis and Feminism* 1974.

Mitchell Margaret 1900–1949. US novelist. She was born in Atlanta, Georgia, which is the setting for her one book, the bestseller *Gone With the Wind* 1936 (Pulitzer prize), a story of the US Civil War. It was filmed 1939 starring Vivien Leigh and Clark Gable.

Mitchum Robert Charles Duran 1917–1997. US film actor. A star for more than 30 years, he was equally at home as the relaxed modern hero or psychopathic villain. His films include *Out of the Past* 1947, *The Night of the Hunter* 1955, and *The Friends of Eddie Coyle* 1973.

mite minute ◊arachnid comprising, with the ◊ticks, the order Acarina. Some mites are free-living scavengers or predators; a number live in cheese, flour, and other foodstuffs. Some are parasitic, such as the itch mite *Sarcoptes scabiei*, which burrows in skin causing scabies in humans and mange in dogs, and the red mite *Dermanyssus gallinae*, which sucks blood from poultry and other birds. Others parasitize plants.

Mitford sisters the six daughters of British aristocrat 2nd Lord Redesdale, including: ***Nancy*** (1904–1973), author of the semi-autobiographical *The Pursuit of Love* 1945 and *Love in a Cold Climate* 1949, and editor and part author of the satirical essays collected in *Noblesse Oblige* 1956 elucidating 'U' (upper-class) and 'non-U' behaviour; ***Diana*** (1910–), who married Oswald ◊Mosley; ***Unity*** (1914–1948), who became an admirer of Hitler; and ***Jessica*** (1917–1996), author of the autobiographical *Hons and Rebels* 1960 and *The American Way of Death* 1963.

Mithras in Persian mythology, the god of light. Mithras represented the power of goodness, and promised his followers compensation for present evil after death. He was said to have captured and killed the sacred bull from whose blood all life sprang. Mithraism was introduced into the Roman Empire 68 BC. By about AD 250, it rivalled Christianity in strength.

Mithridates VI Eupator (called ***the Great***) c. 120–63 BC. King of Pontus (on the Black Sea coast of modern Turkey), who became the greatest obstacle to Roman expansion in the E. He massacred 80,000 Romans in overrunning the rest of Asia Minor and went on to invade Greece. He was defeated by ◊Sulla in the First Mithridatic War 88–84; by ◊Lucullus in the Second 83–81; and by ◊Pompey in the Third 74–64.

mitochondria (singular ***mitochondrion***) membrane-enclosed organelles within ◊eukaryotic cells, containing enzymes responsible for energy production during ◊aerobic respiration. These rodlike or spherical bodies are thought to be derived from free-living bacteria that, at a very early stage in the history of life, invaded larger cells and took up a symbiotic way of life inside. Each still contains its own small loop of DNA called mitochondrial DNA, and new mitochondria arise by division of existing ones.

mitosis in biology, the process of cell division by which identical daughter cells are produced. During mitosis the DNA is duplicated and the chromosome number doubled, so new cells contain the same amount of DNA as the original cell.

The genetic material of ◊eukaryotic cells is carried on a number of ◊chromosomes. To control movements of chromosomes during cell division so that both new cells get the correct number, a system of protein tubules, known as the spindle, organizes the chromosomes into position in the middle of the cell before they replicate. The spindle then controls the movement of chromosomes as the cell goes through the stages of division: interphase, prophase, metaphase, anaphase, and telophase. See also ◊meiosis.

Mitre Bartólomé 1821–1906. Argentine president 1862–68. In 1852 he helped overthrow the dictatorial regime of Juan Manuel de Rosas, and in 1861 helped unify Argentina. Mitre encouraged immigration and favoured growing commercial links with Europe. He is seen as a symbol of national unity.

Mitsotakis Constantine 1918– . Greek politician, leader of the conservative New Democracy Party (ND) 1984–93, prime minister 1990–93. Minister for economic coordination 1965 (a post he held again 1978–80), he was arrested by the military junta 1967, but escaped and lived in exile until 1974. In 1980–81 he was foreign minister. He resigned the leadership of the ND after its 1993 election defeat.

Mitterrand François 1916–1996. French socialist politician, president 1981–95. He held ministerial posts in 11 governments 1947–58, and founded the French Socialist Party (PS) 1971. In 1985 he introduced proportional representation, allegedly to weaken the growing opposition from left and right. From 1982 his administrations combined economic orthodoxy with social reform.

Mitterrand studied law and politics in Paris. During World War II he was prominent in the Resistance after initially being a supporter of Marshal Pétain's Vichy regime. He entered the National Assembly as a centre-left deputy for Nièvre. Opposed to General de Gaulle's creation of the Fifth Republic 1958, he formed the centre-left anti-Gaullist Federation of the Left in the 1960s. In 1971 he became leader of the new PS. An electoral union with the Communist Party 1972–77 established the PS as the most popular party in France.

As president, his programme of reform was hampered by deteriorating economic conditions after 1983. When the socialists lost their majority 1986, he was compelled to work with a right-wing prime minister, Jacques Chirac, and grew in popularity. He defeated Chirac to secure a second term in the presidential election 1988. In 1993 he entered a second term of 'cohabitation' with the conservative prime minister Edouard Balladur. However, whereas he was able to enhance his reputation when 'cohabiting' with Chirac, his popularity waned and his influence weakened in contrast with the successful premiership of Balladur. Towards the end of his presidency his failing health further weakened his hold on power.

Mix Tom (Thomas) 1880–1940. US film actor. He was the most colourful cowboy star of silent films. At their best, his films, such as *The Range Riders* 1910 and *King Cowboy* 1928, were fast-moving and full of impressive stunts. His talkies include *Destry Rides Again* 1932 and *The Miracle Rider* 1935.

mixed economy type of economic structure that combines the private enterprise of capitalism with a degree of state monopoly. In mixed economies, governments seek to control the public services, the basic industries, and those industries that cannot raise sufficient capital investment from private sources. Thus a measure of economic planning can be combined with a measure of free enterprise. A notable example was US President F D Roosevelt's ◊New Deal in the 1930s.

Mixtec ancient civilization of pre-colonial Mexico. The Mixtecs succeeded the ◊Zapotecs in the valley of Oaxaca. They founded new towns, including Tilatongo and Teozacualco, and partially rebuilt some Zapotec cities. The Mixtecs produced historical records which contain biographies of rulers and noblemen and trace Mixtec history back to AD 692. They were skilled in the use of metals, including gold and silver.

mixture in chemistry, a substance containing two or more compounds that still retain their separate physical and chemical properties. There is no chemical bonding between them and they can be separated from each other by physical means (compare ◊compound).

Miyake Issey 1938– . Japanese fashion designer. Active in Paris from 1965, he showed his first collection in New York and Tokyo 1971, and has been showing in Paris since 1973. His 'anti-fashion' looks combined Eastern and Western influences: a variety of textured and patterned fabrics were layered and wrapped round the body to create linear and geometric shapes.

mite The African giant red velvet mite (family Trombidiidae) can be found wandering around in semi-arid areas after rains. The similar looking but much smaller red earth mite *Trombidium holocericeum* is common in gardens in the British Isles. There are some 20,000 species of mite, adapted to a very broad range of conditions and habitats. *Premaphotos Wildlife*

'Frankly, my dear, I don't give a damn.'

MARGARET MITCHELL
Gone with the Wind

Mitterrand French socialist politician François Mitterrand was an anti-Gaullist during the 1960s and committed to major economic and social reforms at the beginning of his presidency 1981. Although it proved impossible to carry through these reforms, he preserved his position by the skilled political manoeuvring for which he had been named 'the fox'. In 1989 he was widely criticized for the vast sums spent on celebrating the bicentenary of the French Revolution. *French Embassy*

Miyamoto Musashi c. 1584–1645. Japanese samurai. His manual on military strategy and sword fighting, *Gorinsho/The Book of Five Rings* 1645, became popular in English translation 1974 in the USA as a guide to business success. He was a painter as well as a fencer, and spent his life travelling in Japan in search of Zen enlightenment.

Mizoguchi Kenji 1898–1956. Japanese film director. *Ugetsu Monogatari* 1953 confirmed his international reputation. Notable for his sensitive depiction of female psychology, he also directed *The Poppies* 1935, *Sansho daiyu/Sansho the Bailiff* 1954, and *Street of Shame* 1956.

Mizoram state of NE India
area 21,100 sq km/8,145 sq mi
capital Aizawl
products rice, hand-loom weaving
population (1994 est) 775,000
religion 84% Christian
history made a Union Territory 1972 from the Mizo Hills District of Assam. Rebels carried on a guerrilla war 1966–76, but 1976 acknowledged Mizoram as an integral part of India. It became a state 1986.

Mkapa Benjamin William 1938– . Tanzanian politician, president from 1995. He became press secretary to President Julius Nyere 1974 and went on to hold a number of posts in government, including foreign affairs minister 1977–80 and 1984–91. He succeeded Ali Hassan Mwinyi as president.

ml symbol for ***millilitre***.

Mladic Ratko 1943– . Bosnian Serb general, leader of the Bosnian Serb army 1992–96. His ruthless conduct in the civil war in Bosnia led to his being indicted for war crimes by the United Nations War Crimes Commission 1995.

A general in the former Yugoslav Federal Army, when Yugoslavia broke up he became one of the leaders of the Serbian population in Bosnia, and was appointed military commander of the Republika Srbska by its president Radovan Karadžić 1992. He took part in the 1994 peace talks. In Nov 1996 he was dismissed as army chief by Bosnian Serb president Biljana Plavsic.

MLR abbreviation for ◊***minimum lending rate***.

mm symbol for ***millimetre***.

Mmabatho or ***Sun City*** capital of North West Province, South Africa; population (1991) 13,300. It is a casino resort frequented by many white South Africans.

mnemonic verbal device to aid memory; often a short sentence or a rhyme (such as 'i before e except after c').

Mnouchkine Ariane 1939– . French theatre director. She founded the Théâtre du Soleil 1964. After 1968, the company began to devise its own material, firstly with *The Clowns* 1969, which was followed by *1789* 1970, an exploration of the French Revolution, and *L'Age d'or* 1975, concerning the exploitation of immigrant workers.

moa extinct flightless kiwi-like bird, order Dinornithiformes, which lived in New Zealand. There were 19 species; they varied from 0.5 to 3.5 m/2 to 12 ft, with strong limbs, a long neck, and no wings. The last moa was killed in the 1800s.

Moab ancient country in Jordan east of the southern part of the river Jordan and the Dead Sea. The inhabitants were closely akin to the Hebrews in culture, language, and religion, but were often at war with them, as recorded in the Old Testament. Moab eventually fell to Arab invaders. The Moabite Stone, discovered 1868 at Dhiban, dates from the 9th century BC and records the rising of Mesha, King of Moab, against Israel.

Mobile industrial city (meat-packing, paper, cement, clothing, chemicals) and only seaport in Alabama, USA; population (1992) 201,900. Founded 1702 by the French a little to the N of the present city, Mobile was capital of the French colony of Louisiana until 1763. It was then British until 1780, and Spanish to 1813.

mobile ion in chemistry, an ion that is free to move; such ions are only found in the aqueous solutions or melts (molten masses) of an ◊electrolyte. The mobility of the ions in an electrolyte is what allows it to conduct electricity.

mobile phone in computing, cordless telephone linked to a digital cellular radio network. Mobile phones can connect to the Internet via a datacard, which converts computer data into a form that can be passed over the network and vice versa. Users can connect them to a ◊laptop computer and others incorporate a full pocket organizer. A trend for greater integration of phone and computer emerged 1996.

Möbius August Ferdinand 1790–1868. German mathematician and theoretical astronomer, discoverer of the Möbius strip and considered one of the founders of ◊topology. Möbius formulated his barycentric calculus in 1818, a mathematical system in which numerical coefficients were assigned to points. The position of any point in the system could be expressed by varying the numerical coefficients of any four or more noncoplanar points.

Möbius strip structure made by giving a half twist to a flat strip of paper and joining the ends together. It has certain remarkable properties, arising from the fact that it has only one edge and one side. If cut down the centre of the strip, instead of two new strips of paper, only one long strip is produced.

Mobutu Sese Seko Kuku Ngbeandu Wa Za Banga 1930–1997. Zairean president 1965–1997. He assumed the presidency in a coup, and created a unitary state under a centralized government. He abolished secret voting in elections 1976 in favour of a system of acclamation at mass rallies. The harshness of some of his policies and charges of corruption attracted international criticism. In 1991 opposition leaders forced Mobutu to agree formally to give up some of his powers, but the president continued to oppose constitutional reform initiated by his prime minister, Etienne Tshisekedi. Despite his opposition, a new transitional constitution was adopted 1994. In 1996–97, rebel forces led by Laurent Kabila made great advances against government forces. In May 1997 Mobutu fled the country and Kabila declared himself president, renaming the country the Democratic Republic of Congo.

Mobutu Sese Seko, Lake lake on the border of Uganda and Zaire in the Great ◊Rift Valley; area 4,275 sq km/1,650 sq mi. The first European to see it was the British explorer Samuel ◊Baker, who named it Lake Albert after the Prince Consort. It was renamed 1973 by Zaire's president Mobutu.

Moche or ***Mochica*** pre-Inca civilization on the coast of Peru AD 100–800. Remains include cities, massive platform tombs (*adobe*), and pottery that details daily and ceremonial life. In 1988 the burial of one of their warrior-priest rulers was discovered. It contained a priceless treasure hoard, including a gold mask and ear pendants.

mockingbird North American songbird *Mimus polyglottos* of the mimic thrush family Mimidae, order Passeriformes, found in the USA and Mexico. About 25 cm/10 in long, it is brownish grey, with white markings on the black wings and tail. It is remarkable for its ability to mimic the songs of other species.

mock orange or ***syringa*** deciduous shrub of the genus *Philadelphus*, family Philadelphaceae, including *P. coronarius*, which has white, strongly scented flowers, resembling those of the orange.

mod British youth subculture that originated in London and Brighton in the early 1960s around the French view of the English; it was revived in the late 1970s. Mods were fashion-conscious, speedy, and upwardly mobile; they favoured scooters and soul music.

MOD abbreviation for ***Ministry of Defence***.

mode in mathematics, the element that appears most frequently in a given set of data. For example, the mode for the data 0, 0, 9, 9, 9, 12, 87, 87 is 9.

model simplified version of some aspect of the real world. Models are produced to show the relationships between two or more factors, such as land use and the distance from the centre of a town. Because models are idealized, they give only a general guide to what may happen.

Model Parliament English parliament set up 1295 by Edward I; it was the first to include representatives from outside the clergy and aristocracy, and was established because Edward needed the support of the whole country against his opponents: Wales, France, and Scotland. His sole aim was to raise money for military purposes, and the parliament did not pass any legislation.

modem Modems are available in various forms: microcomputers may use an external device connected through a communications port, or an internal device, which takes the form of an expansion board inside the computer. Notebook computers use an external modem connected via a special interface card.

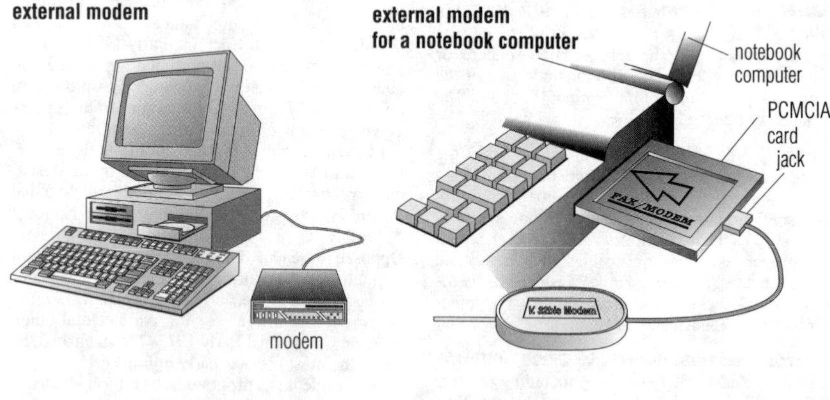

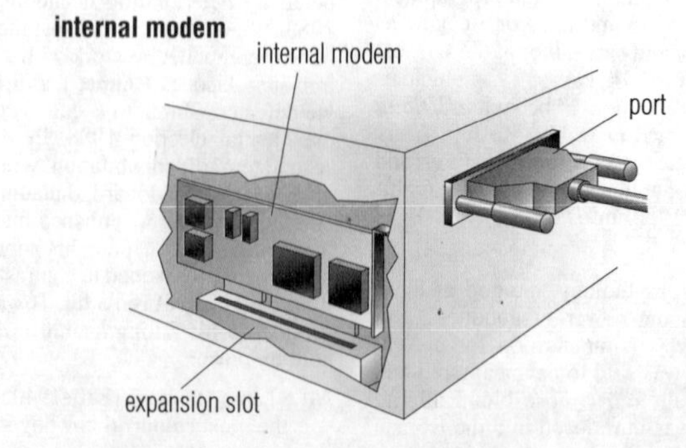

modem (acronym for ***modulator/demodulator***) device for transmitting computer data over telephone lines. Such a device is necessary to convert the ◊digital signals produced by computers to ◊analogue signals which are used on the telephone network. The modem converts the digital signals to analogue, and back again. Modems are used for linking remote terminals to central computers and enable computers to communicate with each other anywhere in the world.

Modena city in Emilia, Italy, capital of the province of Modena, 37 km/23 mi NW of Bologna; population (1992) 177,000. Products include vehicles, glass, pasta, and sausages. It has a 12th-century cathedral, a 17th-century ducal palace, and a university (1683), known for its medical and legal faculties.

moderator in a ◊nuclear reactor, a material such as graphite or heavy water used to reduce the speed of high-energy neutrons. Neutrons produced by nuclear fission are fast-moving and must be slowed to initiate further fission so that nuclear energy continues to be released at a controlled rate.

modern dance 20th-century dance idiom that evolved in opposition to traditional ballet by those seeking a freer and more immediate means of dance expression. Leading exponents include Martha ◊Graham and Merce ◊Cunningham in the USA, Isadora ◊Duncan and Mary Wigman (1886–1973) in Europe.

Modern dance was pioneered by US women seeking individual freedom but it is from Ruth St Denis and Ted Shawn's ◊Denishawn School of Dancing and Related Arts in Los Angeles 1915, that the first generation of modern dance – Martha Graham, Doris Humphrey, and Charles Weidman – emerged. In the UK, the London Contemporary Dance Theatre and school was set up 1966–67 and flourished under the artistic direction of Graham's pupil, Robert Cohan. The school is the only European institute authorized to teach Graham Technique. In 1966, the Ballet Rambert became a modern-dance company. In Germany, the originators of a modernist movement known as *Ausdruckstanz* were Emile Jaques-Dalcroze and Rudolf von Laban. The leading exponents, Mary Wigman, Harald Kreutzberg, and Kurt Jooss, had some influence on modern dance through their visits to the USA and through Hanya Holm (born 1893), a former Wigman dancer who settled and taught in New York, and with whom the choreographer/producer, Alwin Nikolais (1912–1993), was originally associated. Recent experimental work is known as new dance or ◊avant-garde dance.

Modernism in the arts, a general term used to describe the 20th century's conscious attempt to break with the artistic traditions of the 19th century; it is based on a concern with form and the exploration of technique as opposed to content and narrative. In the visual arts, direct representationalism gave way to abstraction (see ◊abstract art); in literature, writers experimented with alternatives to orthodox sequential storytelling, such as ◊stream of consciousness; in music, the traditional concept of key was challenged by ◊atonality; and in architecture, Functionalism ousted decorativeness as a central objective (see ◊Modern Movement).

Modernism in the Church of England, a development of the 20th-century liberal church movement, which attempts to reconsider Christian beliefs in the light of modern scientific theories and historical methods, without abandoning the essential doctrines. Similar movements exist in many Nonconformist churches and in the Roman Catholic Church. Modernism was condemned by Pope Pius X in 1907.

Modern Jazz Quartet US jazz group specializing in group improvisation, formed 1952 (disbanded 1974 and re-formed 1981). Noted for elegance and mastery of form, the quartet has sometimes been criticized for being too 'classical'.

Modern Movement the dominant movement in 20th-century architecture, which grew out of the technological innovations of 19th-century ◊Industrial architecture, crystallized in the ◊International Style of the 1920s and 1930s, and has since developed various regional trends, such as ◊Brutalism. 'Truth to materials' and 'form follows function' are its two most representative dicta, although neither allows for the modernity of large areas of contemporary architecture, concerned with proportion, human scale, and attention to detail. Currently, architectural ◊Post-Modernism, a reaction to the movement, is developing alongside such Modernist styles as ◊High Tech.

The Modern Movement gained momentum after World War II when its theories, disseminated through the work of CIAM (Congrès Internationaux d'Architecture Moderne, a loose association of architects founded 1928), were influential in the planning and rebuilding of European cities. The work of ◊Le Corbusier is perhaps most representative of the underlying principles of the movement; other notable early Modernists include Adolf ◊Loos, Peter ◊Behrens, Walter ◊Gropius, and ◊Mies van der Rohe.

Modigliani *Portrait of a Polish Woman* 1919 by Amadeo Modigliani, Louis E Stern Collection, Philadelphia Museum of Art, Pennsylvania, USA. Forced to abandon sculpture because the stone-dust exacerbated the tuberculosis that eventually killed him, Modigliani spent the rest of his life painting. His portraits have a sculptural quality. *Corbis*

Modigliani Amedeo 1884–1920. Italian painter and sculptor, active in France from 1906. He is best known for graceful nudes and portraits. His paintings – for example, the portrait of his mistress Jeanne Hébuterne, painted 1919 (Guggenheim Museum, New York) – have a distinctive style, the forms elongated and sensual.

The study of African tribal masks inspired the bold elongation and simplification of his sculptured heads, as in *Stone Head* 1911 (Philadelphia Museum of Art, Pensylvania). His paintings showed the same influences, though in their subtle colour and their senstive linear design they reveal his sympathy with Italian Renaissance art, particularly that of ◊Botticelli. Typical are the portrait *Lunia Czechowska* 1916 (Musée de Peinture, Grenoble), and the nude *Standing Nude (Elvira)* 1918 (Kunstmuseum, Bern).

modular course in education, a course, usually leading to a recognized qualification, that is divided into short and often optional units, which are assessed as they are completed. An accumulation of modular credits may then lead to the award of a qualification such as a degree, a BTEC diploma, or a GCSE pass. Modular schemes are becoming increasingly popular as a means of allowing students to take a wider range of subjects.

modulation in music, movement from one ◊key to another. In classical dance music, modulation is a guide to phrasing rhythm to the step pattern. Electronic modulation of live or prerecorded instrumental sound is also used to create unusual timbres.

modulation in radio transmission, the variation of frequency, or amplitude, of a radio carrier wave, in accordance with the audio characteristics of the speaking voice, music, or other signal being transmitted. See ◊pulse-code modulation, ◊AM (amplitude modulation), and ◊FM (frequency modulation).

module in construction, a standard or unit that governs the form of the rest. For example, Japanese room sizes are traditionally governed by multiples of standard tatami floor mats; today prefabricated buildings are mass-produced in a similar way. The components of a spacecraft are designed in coordination; for example, for the *Apollo* Moon landings the craft comprised a command module (for working, eating, sleeping), service module (electricity generators, oxygen supplies, manoeuvring rocket), and lunar module (to land and return the astronauts).

modulus in mathematics, a number that divides exactly into the difference between two given numbers. Also, the multiplication factor used to convert a logarithm of one base to a logarithm of another base.

modus operandi (Latin) a method of operating.

modus vivendi (Latin 'way of living') a compromise between opposing points of view.

Mogadishu or ***Mugdisho*** capital and chief port of Somalia; population (1987 est) 1,000,000. It is a centre for oil refining, food processing, and uranium mining. During the struggle to overthrow President Barre and the ensuing civil war 1991–92, much of the city was devastated and many thousands killed. From 1992 UN peacekeeping troops (including a large contingent of US Marines) were stationed in the city to monitor a cease-fire and to protect relief operations. However, mounting clashes between UN and Somali rebel forces 1993 resulted in the withdrawal of most US troops 1994.

Mogul dynasty N Indian dynasty 1526–1858, established by ◊Babur, Muslim descendant of Tamerlane, the 14th-century Mongol leader. The Mogul emperors ruled until the last one, ◊Bahadur Shah II, was dethroned and exiled by the British; they included ◊Akbar, ◊Aurangzeb, and ◊Shah Jahan. The Moguls established a more extensive and centralized empire than their Delhi sultanate forebears, and the Mogul era was one of great artistic achievement as well as urban and commercial development.

When Akbar died 1605 the Mogul empire had a population of 70–100 million, but it was at its largest under Aurangzeb (ruled 1658–1707), who briefly subdued the Deccan and the south-central states of Bijapur and Golconda. However, Mogul authority never extended into the far south and,

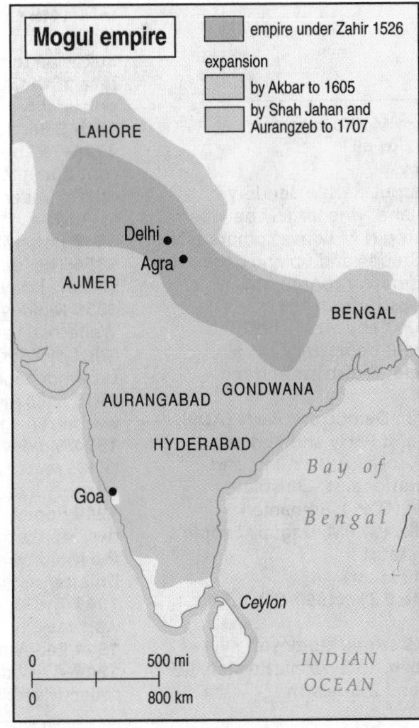

The Mojave is a big desert and a frightening one. It's as though nature tested man for endurance and constancy to prove whether he was good enough to get to California.

On the MOJAVE DESERT
John Steinbeck
Travels with Charley

although more bureaucratized than the Delhi sultanate, power waxed and waned between central and local rulers.

MOH abbreviation for ***Medical Officer of Health***.

Mohács, Battle of Turkish victory over a Hungarian army 29 Aug 1526; the battle marked the end of the medieval kingdom of Hungary. King Louis II of Hungary's 25,000-strong army was attacked by a Turkish army of about 100,000 troops under Suleiman the Magnificent and totally destroyed; 24,000 Hungarians were killed, including Louis. This left the road to Buda open, and the Turks sacked the city 12 Sept 1526.

Mohács, a port on the river Danube in Hungary, was to be the scene of an important defeat for the Turks under Mohammed IV 12 Aug 1687 by a combined Austrian and Hungarian army under Charles of Lorraine. This battle effectively meant the end of Turkish expansion into Europe.

mohair (Arabic *mukhayyar* 'goat') yarn made from the long, lustrous hair of the ◊Angora goat or rabbit, loosely woven with cotton, silk, or wool to produce a fuzzy texture. Commercial mohair is now obtained from cross-bred animals, pure-bred supplies being insufficient to satisfy demand.

Mohammed alternative form of ◊Muhammad, founder of Islam.

Mohammedanism misnomer for ◊Islam, the religion founded by Muhammad.

Mohawk a Native American people, part of the ◊Iroquois confederation, who lived in the Mohawk Valley, New York, and now live on reservations in Ontario, Quebec, and New York State, as well as among the general population. Their language belongs to the Macro-Siouan group.

Mohenjo Daro ('mound of the dead') site of a city about 2500–1600 BC on the lower Indus River, NW Pakistan, where excavations from the 1920s have revealed the ◊Indus Valley civilization, to which the city of ◊Harappa also belongs.

Mohican and Mohegan or ***Mahican*** two closely related Native American peoples, speaking an Algonquian language, who formerly occupied the Hudson Valley and parts of Connecticut, respectively.

Moholy-Nagy Laszlo 1895–1946. Hungarian-born painter, sculptor and photographer. Inspired by ◊Constructivism, he made abstract sculptures from the early 1920s and from 1923–29 taught at the Bauhaus school in Weimar and later in the USA. He experimented with a wide range of media, materials, and techniques, including the use of photographic techniques to achieve non-naturalistic effects.

He worked in Paris, London and Amsterdam as well as in Germany, and in 1937 moved to the USA, where he spent the rest of his life. His commitment to innovation is reflected in the range of his works: in the books *Painting, Photography, Film* 1925 and *The New Vision* 1929; in his documentary film *Berlin Still Life* 1926; and in his experiments with kinetic sculpture during the 1920s, and with what he called 'space modulators' – sculptures made of plexiglas and other materials – during the 1930s.

Mohorovičić discontinuity also *Moho* or ***M-discontinuity*** boundary that separates the Earth's crust and mantle, marked by a rapid increase in the speed of earthquake waves. It follows the variations in the thickness of the crust and is found approximately 32 km/20 mi below the continents and about 10 km/6 mi below the oceans. It is named after the Yugoslav geophysicist Andrija Mohorovičić (1857–1936), who suspected its presence after analysing seismic waves from the Kulpa Valley earthquake 1909.

Mohs Friedrich 1773–1839. German mineralogist who 1812 devised Mohs' scale of minerals, classified in order of relative hardness.

Mohs' scale scale of hardness for minerals (in ascending order): 1 talc; 2 gypsum; 3 calcite; 4 fluorite; 5 apatite; 6 orthoclase; 7 quartz; 8 topaz; 9 corundum; 10 diamond. The scale is useful in mineral identification because any mineral will scratch any other mineral lower on the scale than itself, and similarly it will be scratched by any other mineral higher on the scale. *See list of tables on p. 1177.*

Moi Daniel arap 1924– . Kenyan politician, president from 1978. Leader of Kenya African National Union (KANU), he became minister of home affairs 1964, vice president 1967, and succeeded Jomo Kenyatta as president. After 1988 his rule became increasingly authoritarian and he was widely criticized for Kenya's poor human-rights record. In 1991 he promised an eventual introduction of multiparty politics. In 1992 he was elected president in the first free elections amid widespread accusations of vote rigging.

Mojave Desert arid region in S California, USA, part of the Great Basin; area 38,500 sq km/15,000 sq mi. The US military has appropriated thousands of square kilometres for bombing ranges and test stations, including Edwards Air Force Base, a landing place for space shuttles.

moksha (Sanskrit 'liberation') in Hinduism, liberation from the cycle of reincarnation and from the illusion of ◊maya.

molar one of the large teeth found towards the back of the mammalian mouth. The structure of the jaw, and the relation of the muscles, allows a massive force to be applied to molars. In herbivores the molars are flat with sharp ridges of enamel and are used for grinding, an adaptation to a diet of tough plant material. Carnivores have sharp powerful

MOLDOVA
Republic of

0 mi 500
0 km 1000
Ukraine
MOLDOVA
Chişinău
Romania
BLACK SEA

national name *Republica Moldoveneasca*
area 33,700 sq km/13,012 sq mi
capital Chişinău (Kishinev)
major towns/cities Tiraspol, Beltsy, Bendery
physical features hilly land lying largely between the rivers Prut and Dniester; N Moldova comprises the level plain of the Beltsy Steppe and uplands; the climate is warm and moderately continental
head of state Petru Lucinschi from 1997
head of government Ion Cebuc from 1997
political system emergent democracy
administrative divisions 38 districts and ten cities
political parties Agrarian Democratic Party (ADP), nationalist, centrist; Socialist Party and Yedinstvo/Unity Movement, reform-socialist; Peasants and Intellectuals, Romanian nationalist; Christian Democratic Popular Front (CDPF), Romanian nationalist; Gagauz-Khalky (GKPM; Gagauz People's Movement), Gagauz separatist
population 4,432,000 (1995 est)
population growth rate 0.3% (1990–95); 0.5% (2000–05)
ethnic distribution 65% ethnic Moldovan (Romanian), 14% Ukrainian, 13% ethnic Russian, 4% Gagauzi, 2% Bulgarian, and 2% Jewish
life expectancy 65 (men), 72 (women)
literacy rate 96%
language Moldovan
religion Russian Orthodox
currency leu
GDP (US $) 3.67 billion (1994)
growth rate −22.0% (1994)
exports wine, tobacco, canned goods

HISTORY
AD 106 The current area covered by Moldova, which lies chiefly between the Prut river, bordering Romania in the W, and the Dniester river, with Ukraine in the E, was conquered by the Roman Emperor Trajan and became part of the Roman province of Dacia. It was known in earlier times as Bessarabia.
mid-14th C Formed part of an independent Moldovan principality, which included areas, such as Bukovina to the W, that are now part of Romania.
late 15th C Under Stephen IV 'the Great' the principality reached the height of its power.
16th C Became a tributary of the Ottoman Turks.
1774–75 The Moldovan principality, though continuing to recognize Turkish overlordship, was placed under Russian protectorship; Bukovina was lost to Austria.
1812 Bessarabia ceded to tsarist Russia.
1856 The remainder of the Moldovan principality became largely independent of Turkish control.
1859 Moldovan Assembly voted to unite with Wallachia, to the SW, to form the state of Romania, ruled by Prince Alexandru Ion Cuza. The state became fully independent 1878.
1918 Following the Russian Revolution, Bessarabia was seized and incorporated within Romania.
1924 Moldovan autonomous Soviet Socialist Republic (SSR) created, as part of the Soviet Union, comprising territory E of the Dniester river.
1940 Romania returned Bessarabia, E of the Prut river, to the Soviet Union, which divided it between the Moldovan SSR and Ukraine, with the Trans-Dniester region transferred from Ukraine to Moldova.
1941 The Moldovan SSR occupied by Romania and its wartime ally Germany.
1944 Red Army reconquered Bessarabia.
1946–47 Widespread famine as agriculture was collectivized; rich farmers and intellectuals liquidated.
1950 Immigration by settlers from Russia and Ukraine as industries were developed.
late 1980s Upsurge in Moldovan nationalism, encouraged by the *glasnost* initiative of the reformist Soviet leader Mikhail Gorbachev.
1988 Moldavan Movement in Support of Perestroika (economic restructuring) campaigned for accelerated political reform.
1989 Nationalist demonstrations in Kishinev (now Chişinău). Moldovan Popular Front (MPF) founded; Moldovan made the state language. Campaigns for autonomy among ethnic Russians, strongest in the industrialized Trans-Dniester region, and the Turkish-speaking but Orthodox Christian Gagauz minority in the SW.
1990 MPF polled strongly in parliamentary elections and Mircea Snegur, a reform-nationalist communist, became president. Economic and political sovereignty declared.
1991 Independence declared and Communist Party outlawed after conservative coup in Moscow against Gorbachev; joined the Commonwealth of Independent States (CIS). Insurrection in the Trans-Dniester region.
1992 Admitted into United Nations (UN) and the Conference on Security and Cooperation in Europe (CSCE; now the Organization on Security and Cooperation in Europe, OSCE); peace agreement signed with Russia to end civil war in Trans-Dniester, giving special status to the region. MPF-dominated government fell; 'Government of national accord' formed, headed by Andrei Sangheli and dominated by the ADP.
1993 New currency, the leu, introduced. Privatization programme launched and closer ties established with Russia.
1994 Parliamentary elections won by ADP. Plebiscite rejected nationalist demands for merger with Romania. Russia agreed to withdraw Trans-Dniester troops by 1997.
1995 Joined Council of Europe; economic growth resumed.

SEE ALSO Bessarabia; Ottoman Empire; Russia; Union of Soviet Socialist Republics molars called ***carnassials***, which are adapted for cutting meat.

molarity in chemistry, ◊concentration of a solution expressed as the number of ◊moles in grams of solute per cubic decimetre of solution.

molar solution in chemistry, solution that contains one ◊mole of a substance per litre of solvent.

molar volume volume occupied by one ◊mole (the molecular mass in grams) of any gas at standard temperature and pressure, equal to 2.24136×10^{-2} m^3.

molasses thick, usually dark, syrup obtained during the refining of sugar (either cane or beet) or made from varieties of sorghum. Fermented sugar-cane molasses produces rum; fermented beet-sugar molasses yields ethyl alcohol.

Mold (Welsh ***Yr Wyddgrung***) market town on the river Alyn and from 1996, administrative headquarters of Flintshire, Wales; population (1991) 8,750. It has light industries.

Moldavia former principality in E Europe, on the river Danube, occupying an area divided today between Moldova and Romania. It was independent between the 14th and 16th centuries, when it became part of the Ottoman Empire. In 1861 Moldavia was united with its neighbouring principality Wallachia as Romania. In 1940 the eastern part, ◊Bessarabia, became part of the USSR, whereas the western part remained in Romania.

Moldavian the majority ethnic group living in Moldova, comprising almost two-thirds of the population; also, inhabitants of the Romanian province of Moldavia. The Moldavian language is a dialect of Romanian, and belongs to the Romance group of the Indo-European family.

Moldova or ***Moldavia*** country in E central Europe, bounded N, S, and E by Ukraine, and W by Romania. *See country box opposite.*

mole burrowing insectivore of the family Talpidae, order Insectivora. Moles grow to 18 cm/7 in, and have acute senses of hearing, smell, and touch, but poor vision. They have short, muscular forelimbs and shovel-like, clawed front feet for burrowing, and eat insects, grubs, and worms. Their soft and velvety fur lies without direction to enable them to move forwards or backwards within their tunnels. Moles are very voracious and cannot live more than a few hours without food.

mole person working subversively within an organization. The term has come to be used broadly for someone who gives out ('leaks') secret information in the public interest; it originally meant a person who spends several years working for a government department or a company with the intention of passing secrets to an enemy or a rival.

mole SI unit (symbol mol) of the amount of a substance. It is defined as the amount of a substance that contains as many elementary entities (atoms, molecules, and so on) as there are atoms in 12 g of the ◊isotope carbon-12. One mole of an element that exists as single atoms weighs as many grams as its ◊atomic number (so one mole of carbon weighs 12 g), and it contains 6.022045×10^{23} atoms, which is ◊Avogadro's number.

molecular biology study of the molecular basis of life, including the biochemistry of molecules such as DNA, RNA, and proteins, and the molecular structure and function of the various parts of living cells.

molecular clock use of rates of ◊mutation in genetic material to calculate the length of time elapsed since two related species diverged from each other during evolution. The method can be based on comparisons of the DNA or of widely occurring proteins, such as haemoglobin. This information can be compared with the evidence obtained from palaeontology to reconstruct evolutionary events.

molecular mass (also known as relative molecular mass) the mass of a molecule, calculated relative to one-twelfth the mass of an atom of carbon-12. It is found by adding the relative atomic masses of the atoms that make up the molecule.

molecular solid in chemistry, solid composed of molecules that are held together by relatively weak ◊intermolecular forces. Such solids are low-melting and tend to dissolve in organic solvents. Examples of molecular solids are sulphur, ice, sucrose, and solid carbon dioxide.

molecule group of two or more ◊atoms bonded together. A molecule of an element consists of one or more like ◊atoms; a molecule of a compound consists of two or more different atoms bonded together. Molecules vary in size and complexity from the hydrogen molecule (H_2) to the large macromolecules of proteins. They are held together by ionic bonds, in which the atoms gain or lose electrons to form ◊ions, or by covalent bonds, where electrons from each atom are shared in a new molecular orbital.

According to the molecular or ◊kinetic theory of matter, molecules are in a state of constant motion, the extent of which depends on their temperature, and exert forces on one another.

The shape of a molecule profoundly affects its chemical, physical, and biological properties. Optical ◊isomers (molecules that are mirror images of each other) rotate plane ◊polarized light in opposite directions; isomers of drug molecules may have different biological effects; and ◊enzyme reactions are crucially dependent on the shape of the enzyme and the substrate on which it acts.

The symbolic representation of a molecule is known as its formula. The presence of more than one atom is denoted by a subscript figure – for example, one molecule of the compound water, having two atoms of hydrogen and one atom of oxygen, is shown as H_2O.

mole rat, naked small subterranean mammal *Heterocephalus glaber*, almost hairless, with a disproportionately large head but the smallest brain relative to body size of any small mammal. The mole rat is of importance to zoologists as one of the very few mammals that are eusocial, that is, living in colonies with sterile workers and one fertile female.

Molière pen name of Jean-Baptiste Poquelin 1622–1673. French satirical dramatist and actor. Modern French comedy developed from his work. After the collapse of the Paris-based Illustre Théâtre (of which he was one of the founders), Molière performed in the provinces 1645–58. In 1655 he wrote his first play, *L'Etourdi/The Blunderer*, and on his return to Paris produced *Les Précieuses ridicules/The Affected Ladies* 1659. His satires include *L'Ecole des femmes/The School for Wives* 1662, *Le Misanthrope* 1666, *Le Bourgeois Gentilhomme/The Would-Be Gentleman* 1670, and *Le Malade imaginaire/The Imaginary Invalid* 1673. Other satiric plays include *Tartuffe* 1664 (banned for attacking the hypocrisy of the clergy; revised 1667; banned again until 1699), *Le Médecin malgré lui/Doctor in Spite of Himself* 1666, and *Les Femmes savantes/The Learned Ladies* 1672.

Molière's art marked a new departure in the French theatre away from reliance on classical Greek themes. In his comedies the ideal hero of classical tragedy gave way to the flawed human individual with all his or her foibles and vices. Molière's chief aim seems to have been to amuse by depicting things as they really were, in strict truthfulness to life. It is uncertain whether he had any deliberate moral designs on his audiences by his exposure of hypocrisy and cant. However, there is little room for sympathy in the amusement evoked by his characters, and this made Molière vulnerable to many attacks (from which he was protected by Louis XIV).

'We should look long and carefully at ourselves before we think about judging other people.'

Molière
Le Misanthrope

Molinos Miguel de 1640–1697. Spanish mystic and Roman Catholic priest. He settled in Rome and wrote several devotional works in Italian, including the *Guida spirituale/Spiritual Guide* 1675, which aroused the hostility of the Jesuits. In 1687 he was sentenced to life imprisonment. His doctrine is known as ◊quietism.

mollusc any invertebrate of the phylum Mollusca with a body divided into three parts, a head, a foot, and a visceral mass. The majority of molluscs are marine animals, but some inhabit fresh water, and a few are terrestrial. They include bivalves, mussels, octopuses, oysters, snails, slugs, and squids. The body is soft, limbless, and cold-blooded. There is no internal skeleton, but many species have a hard shell covering the body.

The shell can take a variety of forms: univalve (snail), bivalve (clam), chambered (nautilus), and many other variations. In some cases (for example cuttlefish and squid), the shell is internal. Every mollusc has a fold of skin, the mantle, which covers the whole body or the back only, and secretes the calcareous substance forming the shell.

Shellfish (oysters, mussels, clams) are commercially valuable, especially when artificially bred and 'farmed'. The Romans, and in the 17th century the Japanese, experimented with advanced methods of farming shellfish, and raft culture of oysters is now widely practised. The cultivation of pearls began in the 1890s and became an important export industry after World War I.

Molly Maguires, the in US history, a secret Irish coalminers' organization in the 1870s that staged strikes and used violence against coal-company officials and property in the anthracite fields of Pennsylvania, prefiguring a long period of turbulence in industrial relations. The movement was infiltrated by ◊Pinkerton agents (detectives), and 1876 trials led to convictions and executions.

mollusc Prior to mating, Roman snails *Helix pomatia* engage in a courtship dance during which each participant shoots a 'love dart' into the other's body. *Premaphotos Wildlife*

"Colour is my obsession, joy and torment."

Claude Monet
Quoted in *Claude Monet: Les Nymphéas* 1926

Moloch or ***Molech*** in the Old Testament, a Phoenician deity worshipped in Jerusalem in the 7th century BC, to whom live children were sacrificed by fire.

Molotov Vyacheslav Mikhailovich. Assumed name of V M Skriabin 1890–1986. Soviet communist politician. He was chair of the Council of People's Commissars (prime minister) 1930–41 and foreign minister 1939–49 and 1953–56. He negotiated the 1939 nonaggression treaty with Germany (the ◊Ribbentrop–Molotov pact), and, after the German invasion 1941, the Soviet partnership with the Allies. His postwar stance prolonged the Cold War and in 1957 he was expelled from the government for Stalinist activities.

Molotov cocktail or ***petrol bomb*** home-made weapon consisting of a bottle filled with petrol, plugged with a rag as a wick, ignited, and thrown as a grenade. Resistance groups during World War II named them after the Soviet foreign minister Molotov.

Moltke Helmuth Carl Bernhard, Count von Moltke 1800–1891. Prussian general. He became chief of the general staff 1857, and was responsible for the Prussian strategy in the wars with Denmark 1863–64, Austria 1866, and France 1870–71.

Moluccas another name for ◊Maluku, a group of Indonesian islands.

molybdenite molybdenum sulphide, MoS_2, the chief ore mineral of molybdenum. It possesses a hexagonal crystal structure similar to graphite, has a blue metallic lustre, and is very soft (1–1.5 on Mohs' scale).

molybdenum (Greek *malybdos* 'lead') heavy, hard, lustrous, silver-white, metallic element, symbol Mo, atomic number 42, relative atomic mass 95.94. The chief ore is the mineral molybdenite. The element is highly resistant to heat and conducts electricity easily. It is used in alloys, often to harden steels. It is a necessary trace element in human nutrition. Producing countries include Canada, the USA, and Norway.

Molyneaux Jim (James Henry) 1920– . Northern Ireland Unionist politician, leader of the Official Ulster Unionist Party (the largest Northern Ireland party) 1979–95. A member of the House of Commons 1970–1997, he temporarily relinquished his seat 1983–85 in protest at the ◊Anglo-Irish Agreement. He resigned as party leader 1995. Although a fervent supporter of the union between Britain and Northern Ireland, he was regarded as one of the more moderate Loyalists.

Momaday N(avarre) Scott 1934– . US writer of Kiowa descent. He won a Pulitzer prize for his novel *House Made of Dawn* 1968, about a young Native American at home in neither white nor his ancestral society. He was professor of English at Stanford University 1972–81.

Mombasa industrial port (oil refining, cement) in Kenya (serving also Uganda and Tanzania), built on Mombasa Island and adjacent mainland; population (1989) 465,000. It was founded by Arab traders in the 11th century and was an important centre for ivory and slave trading until the 16th century.

moment of a force in physics, measure of the turning effect, or torque, produced by a force acting on a body. It is equal to the product of the force and the perpendicular distance from its line of action to the point, or pivot, about which the body will turn. Its unit is the newton metre. If the magnitude of the force is F newtons and the perpendicular distance is d metres then the moment is given by:

$$\text{moment} = Fd$$

moment of inertia in physics, the sum of all the point masses of a rotating object multiplied by the squares of their respective distances from the axis of rotation. It is analogous to the ◊mass of a stationary object or one moving in a straight line.

In linear dynamics, Newton's second law of motion states that the force F on a moving object equals the products of its mass m and acceleration a ($F = ma$); the analogous equation in rotational dynamics is $T = I\alpha$, where T is the torque (the turning effect of a force) that causes an angular acceleration α and I is the moment of inertia. For a given object, I depends on its shape and the position of its axis of rotation.

momentum the product of the mass of a body and its velocity. If the mass of a body is m kilograms and its velocity is v m s^{-1}, then its momentum is given by:

$$\text{momentum} = mv$$

Its unit is the kilogram metre-per-second (kg m s^{-1}) or the newton second.

The momentum of a body does not change unless a resultant or unbalanced force acts on that body (see ◊Newton's laws of motion).

According to Newton's second law of motion, the magnitude of a resultant force F equals the rate of change of momentum brought about by its action, or:

$$F = (mv - mu)/t$$

where mu is the initial momentum of the body, mv is its final momentum, and t is the time in seconds over which the force acts. The change in momentum, or impulse (the product of a force and the time over which it acts), produced can therefore be expressed as:

$$\text{impulse} = mv - mu) = Ft$$

The law of conservation of momentum is one of the fundamental concepts of classical physics. It states that the total momentum of all bodies in a closed system is constant and unaffected by processes occurring within the system.

Momoyama in Japanese history, the period 1568–1616 or 1573–1603. During this time three great generals, Oda Nobunaga (1534–1582), ◊Toyotomi Hideyoshi, who invaded Korea 1592, and ◊Tokugawa Ieyasu, successively held power; Ieyasu established the Tokugawa shogunate. Portuguese missionaries and traders were an influence at this time, and ◊Japanese art, architecture (castles), and the tea ceremony flourished. The period is named after a castle built by Hideyoshi in Fushimi, central Honshu.

Mon (or ***Talaing***) a minority ethnic group living in the Irrawaddy delta region of lower Myanmar (Burma) and Thailand. The Mon founded the city of Pegu in 573 and established kingdoms in the area in the 7th century, but much of their culture was absorbed by invaders such as the Toungoo 1539, and Alaungpaya, founder of the Konbaung dynasty, 1757.

Mona Latin name for ◊Anglesey, an island off the coast of Wales.

Monaco small sovereign state forming an enclave in S France, with the Mediterranean Sea to the south. *See country box opposite.*

monad philosophical term deriving from the work of Gottfried Leibniz, suggesting a soul or metaphysical unit that has a self-contained life. The monads are independent of each other but coordinated by a 'pre-established harmony'.

Monagas José Tadeo 1784–1868. Venezuelan president 1847–51 and 1855–58, a hero of the independence movement. Monagas wanted to create a separate state in E Venezuela called Oriente, leading an uprising in 1831 against President José Antonio Páez (1790–1873). He called it off in return for a pardon for his rebels. The Liberal Monagas clan gained power after the fall 1847 of Páez's Conservative oligarchy. Monagas's brother José Gregorio was president 1851–55, and their 'Liberal oligarchy' was marked by a series of revolts led by Páez's supporters and by the disillusionment of their Liberal backers. José Tadeo was forced to resign 1858.

Monaghan (Irish ***Mhuineachain***) county of the Republic of Ireland, in the province of Ulster; county town Monaghan; area 1,290 sq km/498 sq mi; population (1991) 51,300. Products include cereals, linen, potatoes, and cattle. The county is low and rolling, and includes the rivers Finn and Blackwater.

Mona Lisa, the (also known as *La Gioconda*) oil painting by ◊Leonardo da Vinci 1503–05 (Louvre, Paris), a portrait of the wife of a Florentine official, Francesco del Giocondo, which, according to ◊Vasari, Leonardo worked on for four years. It was the first Italian portrait to extend below waist level, setting a precedent for composition that was to dominate portraiture until the 19th century. In the *Mona Lisa* Leonardo brought his technique of *sfumato* (avoiding sharp outlines through gentle gradations of colour) to perfection. ▷ *See feature on pp. 626–627.*

Monarchianism form of belief in the Christian Trinity that emphasizes the undifferentiated unity of God. It was common in the early 3rd century.

monasticism devotion to religious life under vows of poverty, chastity, and obedience, known to Judaism (for example ◊Essenes), Buddhism, and other religions, before Christianity. In Islam, the Sufis formed monastic orders from the 12th century.

monazite mineral, $(Ce,La,Th)PO_4$, yellow to red, valued as a source of ◊lanthanides or rare earths, including cerium and europium; generally found in placer deposit (alluvial) sands.

Monck or ***Monk*** George, 1st Duke of Albemarle 1608–1670. English soldier. During the English Civil War he fought for King Charles I, but after being captured changed sides and took command of the Parliamentary forces in Ireland. Under Oliver ◊Cromwell he became commander in chief in Scotland, and in 1660 he led his army into England and brought about the restoration of Charles II.

Mond Ludwig 1839–1909. German-born British chemist who invented a process for recovering sulphur during the manufacture of alkali. He gave his name to a method of extracting nickel from nickel carbonyl, one of its volatile organic compounds.

Monday second day of the week, following Sunday. The name derives from its having been considered sacred to the Moon (Old English *Mōnandaeg* and Latin *Lunae dies*).

Mondrian Piet (Pieter Cornelis Mondriaan) 1872–1944. Dutch painter. A founder member of the De ◊Stijl movement, he was the chief exponent of Neo-Plasticism, a rigorous abstract style based on the use of simple geometric forms and pure colours. Typically his works are frameworks of horizontal and vertical lines forming rectangles of white, red, yellow, and blue, as in *Composition in Red, Yellow and Blue* 1920 (Stedelijk, Amsterdam).

Born in Amersfoort, he studied art in Amsterdam and in 1911 went to Paris where he was strongly influenced by ◊Cubism. Returning to the Netherlands during World War I, he executed a series of still lifes and landscapes to refine his ideas, ultimately developing a pure abstract style. He lived in Paris 1919–38, then in London, and from 1940 in New York. His aesthetic theories – which were in part based on the spiritualist theories of the Theosophists – were published in the journal *De Stijl* from 1917, in *Neo-plasticism* 1920, and in the essay 'Plastic Art and Pure Plastic Art' 1937. From the New York period his *Broadway Boogie-Woogie* 1942–43 (Museum of Modern Art, New York) reflects a late preoccupation with jazz rhythms.

Monet Claude 1840–1926. French painter. He was a pioneer of Impressionism and a lifelong exponent of its ideals; his painting *Impression, Sunrise* 1872 gave the movement its name. In the 1870s he began painting the same subjects at different times of day to explore the ever-changing effects of light on colour and form; the *Haystacks* and *Rouen Cathedral* series followed in the 1890s, and from 1899 he painted a series of *Water Lilies* in the garden of his house at Giverny, Normandy (now a museum).

Monet spent his youth in Le Havre. He painted with Renoir, Sisley, and Bazille in the forest of Fontainebleau and until 1870 was engaged in perfecting a new approach to which the realism of Courbet and the direct method of Manet both contributed, as may be seen in *Les Femmes au Jardin*, 1867 (Louvre, Paris), and *La Plage à Trouville*, 1870 (Tate Gallery, London). A wartime interlude followed, spent in Holland and London, where he admired the works of Turner. He worked at Argenteuil 1872–78, where he had a floating studio, his mature method of rendering light in colour being now fully developed. His *Impression* in the exhibition of 1874, in which he and his friends appeared as a fairly homogeneous group, brought the term Impressionism into currency for the first time. He painted at Vétheuil 1878–83, and afterwards settled at Giverny, where in the garden of his house he painted his last remarkable studies of water lilies. Almost abstract visions of colour, these studies have been hailed in recent years as outstanding examples of pure painting.

MONACO
Principality of

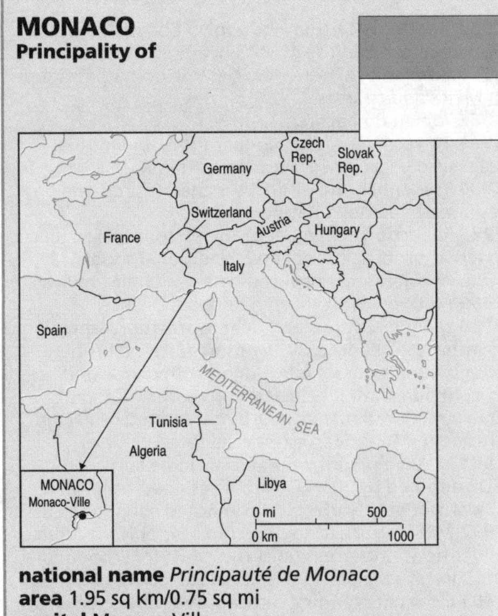

national name *Principauté de Monaco*
area 1.95 sq km/0.75 sq mi
capital Monaco-Ville
major towns/cities Monte Carlo, La Condamine; heliport Fontvieille
physical features steep and rugged; surrounded landwards by French territory; being expanded by filling in the sea
head of state Prince Rainier III from 1949
head of government Paul Dijoud from 1994
political system constitutional monarchy under French protectorate
administrative divisions no local or regional government
political parties no formal parties, but lists of candidates: Liste Campora, moderate, centrist; Liste Medecin, moderate, centrist
population 31,000 (1993 est)
population growth rate 1.2% (1990–95)
ethnic distribution 58% French; 19% Monegasque
literacy rate 99% (1985)
languages French (official), English, Italian
religion Roman Catholic
currency French franc
GDP (US $) 596 million (1992)
growth rate 0.8% (1992)
exports some light industry; economy dependent on tourism and gambling

HISTORY
1191 The Genoese took control of Monaco, which had formerly been part of the Holy Roman Empire.
1297 Came under the rule of the Grimaldi dynasty, the current ruling family, who initially allied themselves to the French.
1524–1641 Came under Spanish protection.
1793 Annexed by France during the French Revolutionary Wars. One member of the ruling family was guillotined; the rest were imprisoned.
1815 Placed under the protection of Sardinia.
1848 The towns of Menton and Roquebrune, which had formed the greater part of the principality, seceded and later became part of France.
1861 Franco-Monagesque treaty restored Monaco's independence under French protection; casino built.
1865 Customs union established with France.
1918 France given a veto over succession to the throne and established that if the reigning prince dies without leaving a male heir, Monaco is to be incorporated into France.
1941–45 Occupied successively by the Italians and Germans during World War II.
1949 Prince Rainier III ascended the throne.
1956 Prince Rainier married US actress Grace Kelly.
1958 Birth of male heir, Prince Albert.
1959 Constitution of 1911 suspended and National Council dissolved.
1962 New, more liberal constitution adopted and National Council restored.
1982 Princess Grace died in a car accident.
1993 Joined the United Nations.

monetarism economic policy that proposes control of a country's money supply to keep it in step with the country's ability to produce goods, with the aim of curbing inflation. Cutting government spending is advocated, and the long-term aim is to return as much of the economy as possible to the private sector, allegedly in the interests of efficiency. Monetarism was first advocated by the economist Milton Friedman and the Chicago school of economists.

Unemployment may result from some efforts to withdraw government 'safety nets', but monetarists claim it is less than eventually occurs if the methods of ◊Keynesian economics are adopted. Monetarist policies were widely adopted in the 1980s in response to the inflation problems caused by spiralling oil prices in 1979. See also ◊deregulation, ◊privatization.

monetary policy economic policy aimed at controlling the amount of money in circulation, usually through controlling the level of lending or credit. Increasing interest rates is an example of a contractionary monetary policy, which aims to reduce inflation by reducing the rate of growth of spending in the economy.

money any common medium of exchange acceptable in payment for goods or services or for the settlement of debts; legal tender. Money is usually coinage (invented by the Chinese in the second millennium BC) and paper notes (used by the Chinese from about AD 800). Developments such as the cheque and credit card fulfil many of the traditional functions of money. In 1994 Mondex electronic money was introduced experimentally in Swindon, Wiltshire, England.

money market institution that deals in gold and foreign exchange, and securities in the short term. Long-term transactions are dealt with on the capital market. There is no physical marketplace, and many deals are made by telephone or telex.

money supply quantity of money in circulation in an economy at any given time. It can include notes, coins, and clearing-bank and other deposits used for everyday payments. Changes in the quantity of lending are a major determinant of changes in the money supply. One of the main principles of ◊monetarism is that increases in the money supply in excess of the rate of economic growth are the chief cause of inflation.

In Britain there are several definitions of money supply. M0 was defined as notes and coins in circulation, together with the operational balance of clearing banks with the Bank of England. The M1 definition encompasses M0 plus current account deposits; M2, now rarely used, covers the M1 items plus deposit accounts; M3 covers M2 items plus all other deposits held by UK citizens and companies in the UK banking sector. In May 1987 the Bank of England introduced new terms including M4 (M3 plus building society deposits) and M5 (M4 plus Treasury bills and local authority deposits).

Mongol any of the various Mongol (or Mongolian) ethnic groups of Central Asia. Mongols live in Mongolia, Russia, Inner Mongolia (China), Tibet, and Nepal. The Mongol language belongs to the Altaic family; some groups of Mongol descent speak languages in the Sino-Tibetan family, however.

The Mongols are primarily pastoral nomads, herding sheep, horses, cattle, and camels. Traditionally they moved with their animals in summer to the higher pastures, returning in winter to the lower steppes. The government of Mongolia now encourages more sedentary forms of pastoralism, and winter quarters are often more permanent. Many Mongols are Buddhist, although the Mongolian government has been communist since 1924.

Mongol Empire empire established by ◊Genghis Khan, who extended his domains from Russia to N China and became khan of the Mongol tribes 1206. His grandson ◊Kublai Khan conquered China and used foreigners (such as the Venetian traveller Marco Polo) as well as subjects to administer his empire. The Mongols lost China 1368 and suffered defeats in the west 1380; the empire broke up soon afterwards.

Mongolia country in E Central Asia, bounded N by Russia and S by China. *See country box on p. 720.*

Mongolia, Inner (Chinese ***Nei Mongol***) autonomous region of NE China from 1947
area 450,000 sq km/173,700 sq mi
capital Hohhot
features strategic frontier area with Russia; known for Mongol herders, who are now becoming settled farmers
physical grassland and desert
products cereals under irrigation; coal; reserves of rare earth oxides europium, and yttrium at Bayan Obo
population (1990) 21,110,000.

mongolism former name (now considered offensive) for ◊Down's syndrome.

Mongoloid former racial classification, based on physical features, used to describe people of E Asian and North American origin; see ◊race.

mongoose any of various carnivorous mammals of the family Viverridae, especially the genus *Herpestes*. The Indian mongoose *H. mungo* is greyish in colour and about 50 cm/1.5 ft long, with a long tail. It may be tamed and is often kept for its ability to kill snakes. *See illustration on following page.*

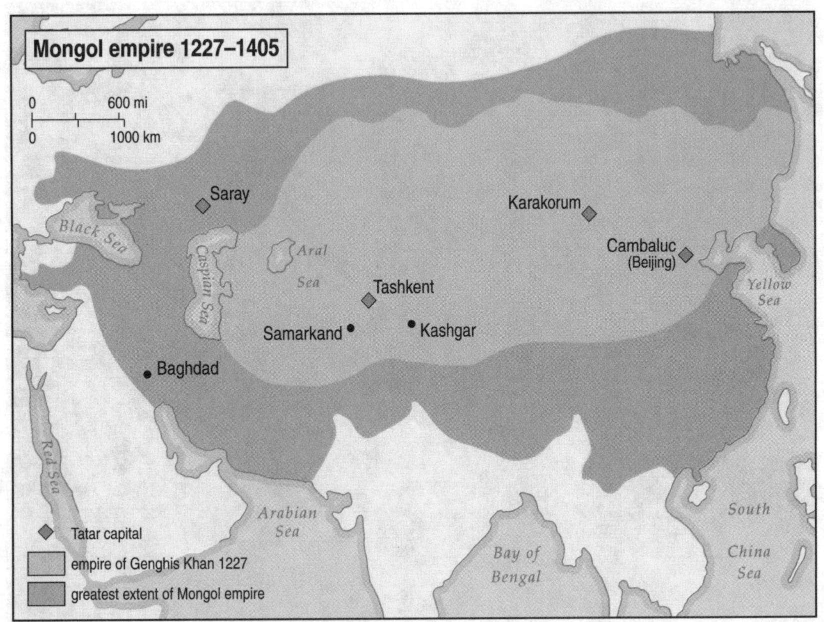

MONGOLIA

State of (*Outer Mongolia* until 1924; *People's Republic of Mongolia* until 1991)

national name *Mongol Uls*
area 1,565,000 sq km/604,480 sq mi
capital Ulaanbaatar (Ulan Bator)
major towns/cities Darhan, Choybalsan, Erdenet
physical features high plateau with desert and steppe (grasslands); Altai Mountains in SW; salt lakes; part of Gobi Desert in SE; contains both the world's southernmost permafrost and northernmost desert
head of state Natsagiyn Bagabandi from 1997
head of government Tsakhiagiin Elbegdorj from 1998
political system emergent democracy
administrative divisions 18 provinces and one municipality
political parties Mongolian People's Revolutionary Party (MPRP), reform-socialist (ex-communist); Mongolian National Democratic Party (MNDP), traditionalist, promarket economy; Union Coalition (UC, comprising the MNPD and the Social Democratic Party (SDP)), democratic, promarket economy
population 2,515,000 (1996 est)
population growth rate 2.0% (1990–95); 1.9% (2000–05)
ethnic distribution 90% Mongol, 4% Kazakh, 2% Chinese, and 2% Russian
life expectancy 62 (men), 65 (women)
literacy rate 90%
languages Khalkha Mongolian (official), Chinese, Russian, and Turkic languages
religion officially none (Tibetan Buddhist Lamaism suppressed 1930s)
currency tugrik
GDP (US $) 700 million (1994)
growth rate 2.1% (1994)
exports meat and hides, minerals, wool, livestock, grain, cement, timber

HISTORY

AD 1206 Nomadic Mongol tribes united by Genghis Khan to form the nucleus of a vast Mongol Empire which, stretching across central Asia, reached its zenith under Genghis Khan's grandson, Kublai Khan.
late 17th C Conquered by China to become the province of Outer Mongolia.
1911 Independence proclaimed by Mongolian nationalists after Chinese 'republican revolution'; Tsarist Russia helped Mongolia to secure autonomy, under a traditionalist Buddhist monarchy in the form of a reincarnated lama.
1915 Chinese sovereignty reasserted.
1921 Chinese rule overthrown with Soviet help.
1924 People's Republic proclaimed on the death of the king, when the monarchy was abolished; defeudalization programme launched, entailing collectivization of agriculture and suppression of Lama Buddhism.
1932 Armed antigovernment uprising suppressed with Soviet assistance; 100,000 killed in purges.
1946 China recognized Mongolia's independence.
1952 Death of Marshal Horloogiyn Choybalsan, the dominant force in the MPRP since 1939.
1958 Yumjaagiyn Tsedenbal became dominant figure in MPRP and country.
1962 Joined Comecon.
1966 20-year friendship, cooperation, and mutual-assistance pact signed with Soviet Union (USSR).
1984 Tsedenbal, the effective leader, retired and replaced by Jambyn Batmunkh.
1987 Reduction in number of Soviet troops; Mongolia's external contacts broadened, traditional social customs tolerated, encouraging a nationalist revival.
1989 Further Soviet troop reductions.
1990 Demonstrations and democratization campaign launched, influenced by events in eastern Europe; Batmunkh resigned and charged with corruption. Ex-communist MPRP elected in first free multiparty elections; Punsalmaagiyn Ochirbat indirectly elected president. Mongolian script readopted.
1991 Massive privatization programme launched. GDP declined by 10%. Ochirbat resigned from MPRP in wake of anti-Gorbachev attempted coup in USSR.
1992 MPRP returned to power in assembly elections under new, non-communist constitution. Economic situation worsened; GDP again declined by 10%.
1993 Ochirbat won first direct presidential elections.
1996 Economy showed signs of revival. Union Coalition won assembly elections, defeating MPRP and ending 75 years of communist rule. Defence cooperation agreement signed with USA. Mendsayhany Enhsayhan became prime minister.
1997 Ex-communist Natsagiyn Bagabandi elected MPRP chairman. Economic 'shock therapy' programme, supervised by IMF and World Bank, created unemployment and made government unpopular. Bagabandi elected president. Mongolia first country to abolish all taxes and tariffs on trade.
1998 National Democratic Party leader Tsakhiagiin Elbegdorj became prime minister.

SEE ALSO Genghis Khan; Lamaism; Mongol

'*Do not hack me as you did my Lord Russell.*'
James, Duke of Monmouth
To his executioner

monism in philosophy, the theory that reality is made up of only one substance. This view is usually contrasted with ◊dualism, which divides reality into two substances, matter and mind. The Dutch philosopher Baruch Spinoza saw the one substance as God or Nature. Monism is also sometimes used as a description of a political system in which only one party is permitted to operate.

monitor any of various lizards of the family Varanidae, found in Africa, S Asia, and Australasia. Monitors are generally large and carnivorous, with well-developed legs and claws and a long powerful tail that can be swung in defence. They include the Komodo dragon, the largest of all lizards, and also the slimmer Salvador's monitor *Varanus salvadorii*, which may reach 2.5 m/8 ft.

monk man belonging to a religious order under the vows of poverty, chastity, and obedience, and living under a particular rule; see ◊monasticism.

Monk Thelonious Sphere 1917–1982. US jazz pianist and composer. He took part in the development of ◊bebop. He had a highly idiosyncratic style, but numbers such as 'Round Midnight' and 'Blue Monk' have become standards. Monk worked in Harlem, New York, during the Depression, and became popular in the 1950s.

monkey any of the various smaller, mainly tree-dwelling anthropoid primates, excluding humans and the ◊apes. The 125 species live in Africa, Asia, and tropical Central and South America. Monkeys eat mainly leaves and fruit, and also small animals. Several species are endangered due to loss of forest habitat, for example the woolly spider monkey and black saki of the Amazonian forest.

Old World monkeys, family Cercopithecidae, of tropical Africa and Asia are distinguished by their close-set nostrils and differentiated thumbs, some also having cheek pouches and rumps with bare patches (callosities) of hardened skin. They include ◊baboons, ◊langurs, ◊macaques, and guenons.

New World monkeys of Central and South America are characterized by wide-set nostrils, and some have highly sensitive prehensile tails. They include two families:

(1) the family Cebidae, which includes the larger species saki, capuchin, squirrel, howler, and spider monkeys;

(2) the family Callithricidae, which includes the small ◊marmosets and tamarins.

mongoose The ring-tailed mongoose *Galidia elegans* is found in Madagascar where it is active by day in both wet and dry forests. Like many mongooses, it has a very varied diet, including birds' eggs, snails, insects, lizards, and small mammals. *Premaphotos Wildlife*

monkey puzzle or ***Chilean pine*** coniferous evergreen tree *Araucaria araucana* (see ◊araucaria), native to Chile; it has whorled branches covered in prickly leaves of a leathery texture.

Monmouth (Welsh ***Trefynwy***) market town in Monmouthshire, Wales, at the confluence of the rivers Wye and Monnow; population (1991) 75,000. There is some light industry. Henry V was born in the now ruined castle.

Monmouth James Scott, 1st Duke of Monmouth 1649–1685. Claimant to the English crown, the illegitimate son of Charles II and Lucy Walter. After James II's accession 1685, Monmouth landed in England at Lyme Regis, Dorset, claimed the crown, and raised a rebellion, which was crushed at ◊Sedgemoor in Somerset. He was executed with 320 of his accomplices.

When ◊James II converted to Catholicism, the Whig opposition attempted unsuccessfully to secure Monmouth the succession to the crown by the Exclusion Bill, and having become implicated in a Whig conspiracy, the ◊Rye House Plot 1683, he fled to Holland.

Monmouthshire unitary authority of Wales created 1996 (*see United Kingdom map*).

monocarpic or ***hapaxanthic*** term describing plants that flower and produce fruit only once during their life cycle, after which they die.

monkey Temminck's red colobus monkey *Colobus badius temmincki* from the forests of W Africa is a typical Old World member of the family Cercopithecidae. *Premaphotos Wildlife*

monoclonal antibody (MAB) antibody produced by fusing an antibody-producing lymphocyte with a cancerous myeloma (bone-marrow) cell. The resulting fused cell, called a hybridoma, is immortal and can be used to produce large quantities of a single, specific antibody. By choosing antibodies that are directed against antigens found on cancer cells, and combining them with cytotoxic drugs, it is hoped to make so-called magic bullets that will be able to pick out and kill cancers.

The full potential of these biological missiles, developed by César ◊Milstein and others at Cambridge University, England, 1975, is still under investigation. However, they are already in use in blood-grouping, in pinpointing viruses and other sources of disease, in tracing cancer sites, and in developing vaccines.

monocotyledon angiosperm (flowering plant) having an embryo with a single cotyledon, or seed leaf (as opposed to ◊dicotyledons, which have two). Monocotyledons usually have narrow leaves with parallel veins and smooth edges, and hollow or soft stems. Their flower parts are arranged in threes. Most are small plants such as orchids, grasses, and lilies, but some are trees such as palms.

monoculture farming system where only one crop is grown. In the developing world this is often a ◊cash crop, grown on ◊plantations, for example, sugar and coffee. Cereal crops in the industrialized world are also frequently grown on a monoculture basis; for example, wheat in the Canadian prairies.

monkey puzzle The monkey-puzzle tree has a regular dome-shaped crown of downwards-pointing branches set with pointed leaves. Its name derives from the belief that monkeys have difficulty climbing it. It is the nearest living example of the trees of the Carboniferous period, about 300 million years ago, which gave us our coal.

Monoculture allows the farmer to tailor production methods to the requirements of one crop, but it is a high-risk strategy since the crop may fail (because of pests, disease, or bad weather) and world prices for the crop may fall. Monoculture without ◊crop rotation is likely to result in reduced soil quality despite the addition of artificial fertilizers, and it contributes to ◊soil erosion.

Monod Jacques Lucien 1910–1976. French biochemist who shared the 1965 Nobel Prize for Physiology or Medicine with his co-workers André Lwoff (1902–) and François ◊Jacob for research in genetics and microbiology.

monoecious having separate male and female flowers on the same plant. Monoecism is a way of avoiding self-fertilization.

monogamy practice of having only one husband or wife at a time in ◊marriage.

monohybrid inheritance pattern of inheritance seen in simple ◊genetics experiments, where the two animals (or two plants) being crossed are genetically identical except for one gene.

This gene may code for some obvious external features such as seed colour, with one parent having green seeds and the other having yellow seeds. The offspring are monohybrids, that is, hybrids for one gene only, having received one copy of the gene from each parent. Known as the F1 generation, they are all identical, and usually resemble one parent, whose version of the gene (the dominant ◊allele) masks the effect of the other version (the recessive allele). Although the characteristic coded for by the recessive allele (for example, green seeds) completely disappears in this generation, it can reappear in offspring of the next generation if they have two recessive alleles. On average, this will occur in one out of four offspring from a cross between two of the monohybrids. The next generation (called F2) show a 3:1 ratio for the characteristic in question, 75% being like the original parent with the recessive allele.

monolith (Greek *monos* 'sole', *lithos* 'stone') single isolated stone or column, usually standing and of great size, used as a form of monument. Some are natural features, such as the Buck Stone in the Forest of Dean, England; others may be quarried, resited, finished, or carved; those in Egypt c. 3000 BC take the form of ◊obelisks. They are found in Europe, South America, N Africa, and the Middle East.

monologue one person speaking, though the term is generally understood to mean a virtuoso solo performance. Literary monologues are often set pieces in which a character reveals his or her personality, sometimes unintentionally (as in the dramatic monologue, a poem consisting of a speech by a single character); in drama the soliloquy performs a similar function.

monomer chemical compound composed of simple molecules from which ◊polymers can be made. Under certain conditions the simple molecules (of the monomer) join together (polymerize) to form a very long chain molecule (macromolecule) called a polymer. For example, the polymerization of ethene (ethylene) monomers produces the polymer polyethene (polyethylene).

$$2nCH_2 = CH_2 \rightarrow (CH_2\text{–}CH_2\text{–}CH_2\text{–}CH_2)_n$$

Monophysite (Greek 'one-nature') member of a group of Christian heretics of the 5th–7th centuries who taught that Jesus had one nature, in opposition to the orthodox doctrine (laid down at the Council of Chalcedon 451) that he had two natures, the human and the divine. Monophysitism developed as a reaction to ◊Nestorianism and led to the formal secession of the Coptic and Armenian churches from the rest of the Christian church. Monophysites survive today in Armenia, Syria, and Egypt.

Monopolies and Mergers Commission (MMC) UK government body re-established 1973 under the Fair Trading Act and, since 1980, embracing the Competition Act. Its role is to investigate and report when there is a risk of creating a monopoly by a company merger or takeover, or when a newspaper or newspaper assets are transferred. It also investigates companies, nationalized industries, or local authorities that are suspected of operating in a noncompetitive way.

monopoly in economics, the domination of a market for a particular product or service by a single ◊company, which can therefore restrict competition and keep prices high. In practice, a company can be said to have a monopoly when it controls a significant proportion of the market (technically an oligopoly). In communist countries the state itself has the overall monopoly; in capitalist ones some services, such as transport or electricity supply, may be state monopolies.

In the UK, monopoly was originally a royal grant of the sole right to manufacture or sell a certain article. The Fair Trading Act 1973 defines a monopoly supplier as one having 'a quarter of the market', and the Monopolies and Mergers Commission controls any attempt to reach this position (in the USA 'antitrust laws' are similarly used). The Competition Act of 1980 covers both private monopolies and possible abuses in the public sector.

monorail railway that runs on a single rail; the cars can be balanced on it or suspended from it. It was invented 1882 to carry light loads, and when run by electricity was called a 'telpher'. Today most monorails are of the straddle type, where the passenger cars run on top of the rail. They are used to transport passengers between terminals at some airports.

monosaccharide or ***simple sugar*** ◊carbohydrate that cannot be hydrolysed (split) into smaller carbohydrate units. Examples are glucose and fructose, both of which have the molecular formula $C_6H_{12}O_6$.

monosodium glutamate (MSG)$NaC_5H_8NO_4$ a white, crystalline powder, the sodium salt of glutamic acid (an ◊amino acid found in proteins that plays a role in the metabolism of plants and animals). It has no flavour of its own, but enhances the flavour of foods such as meat and fish. It is used to enhance the flavour of many packaged and 'fast foods', and in Chinese cooking. It occurs naturally in soybeans and seaweed.

monotheism belief or doctrine that there is only one God; the opposite of polytheism. See also ◊religion.

Monothelite member of a group of Christian heretics of the 7th century who sought to reconcile the orthodox and ◊Monophysite theologies by maintaining that, while Christ possessed two natures, he had only one will. Monothelitism was condemned as a heresy by the Third Council of Constantinople 680.

monotreme any member of the order Monotremata, the only living egg-laying mammals, found in Australasia. They include the echidnas and the platypus.

Monroe James 1758–1831. 5th president of the USA 1817–25, a Democratic Republican. He served in the American Revolution, was minister to France 1794–96, and in 1803 negotiated the ◊Louisiana Purchase. He was secretary of state 1811–17. His name is associated with the ◊Monroe Doctrine.

Monroe Marilyn. Stage name of Norma Jean Mortenson or Baker 1926–1962. US film actress. The voluptuous blonde sex symbol of the 1950s, she made adroit comedies such as *Gentlemen Prefer Blondes* 1953, *How to Marry a Millionaire* 1953, *The Seven Year Itch* 1955, *Bus Stop* 1956, and *Some Like It Hot* 1959. Born in Los Angeles to a single mother often confined in mental institutions, she had a wretched childhood and married for the first time at the age of 16. Her second husband was baseball star Joe DiMaggio, and her third was playwright Arthur ◊Miller, who wrote *The Misfits* 1960 for her, a serious film that became her last. She committed suicide, taking an overdose of sleeping pills. *See illustration on following page.*

Monroe Doctrine declaration by US president James Monroe 1823 that any further European colonial ambitions in the western hemisphere would be threats to US peace and security, made in response to proposed European intervention against newly independent former Spanish colonies in South America. In return for the absence of such European ambitions, the USA would not interfere in European affairs. The doctrine, subsequently broadened, has been a recurrent theme in US foreign policy, although it has no basis in US or international law.

Monrovia capital and port of Liberia; population (1992) 490,000. Industries include rubber, cement, and petrol processing. It was founded 1821 for slaves repatriated from the USA.

Monroe US film actress Marilyn Monroe in the film *Gentlemen Prefer Blondes* 1953. An orphan, she married a local policeman at 16, before her astonishing rise to stardom in such films as *Some Like it Hot* 1959. From that point her life, and tragic death, became a public spectacle. *British Film Institute*

'Civility costs nothing and buys everything.'

MARY WORTLEY MONTAGU
Letter to the Countess of Bute 1756

Mons (Flemish ***Bergen***) industrial city (coal mining, textiles, sugar) and capital of the province of Hainaut, Belgium; population (1995 est) 92,700. The military headquarters of NATO is at nearby Chièvres-Casteau.

In World War I, it was the site of the Battle of Mons between British and German forces Aug 1914. A planned attack on the German armies invading Belgium fell apart when French reserve troops did not arrive and those French troops that were present abandoned the British flank, leaving them open to encirclement. The British were forced to retreat onto one defensive line after another until the Germans overstretched their supply lines.

monsoon wind pattern that brings seasonally heavy rain to S Asia; it blows towards the sea in winter and towards the land in summer. The monsoon may cause destructive flooding all over India and SE Asia from April to Sept.

monstera or ***Swiss cheese plant*** evergreen climbing plant, genus *Monstera*, of the arum family Araceae, native to tropical America. *M. deliciosa* is cultivated as a house plant. Areas between the veins of the leaves dry up, creating deep marginal notches and ultimately holes.

montage in cinema, the juxtaposition of several images or shots to produce an independent meaning. The term is also used more generally to describe the whole process of editing or a rapidly edited series of shots. It was coined by the Russian director Sergei ◊Eisenstein.

Montagnard member of a group in the legislative assembly and National Convention convened after the ◊French Revolution. They supported the more extreme aims of the revolution, and were destroyed as a political force after the fall of Robespierre 1794.

Montagu Edward John Barrington Douglas Scott, 3rd Baron Montagu of Beaulieu 1926– . British car enthusiast, founder of the Montagu Motor Museum at Beaulieu, Hampshire, and chair of English Heritage (formerly Historic Buildings and Monuments Commission) 1983–92.

Montagu Lady Mary Wortley, (born Pierrepont) 1689–1762. English society hostess. She was well known in literary circles, associating with writers such as English poet Alexander Pope, with whom she later quarrelled. Her witty and erudite letters were renowned. She introduced inoculation against smallpox into Britain.

'If you press me to say why I loved him, I feel that it can only be expressed by replying 'Because it was him; because it was me'.'

MICHEL EYQUEM DE MONTAIGNE
Explaining his friendship with Etienne de La Boëtie, *Essays*

Montaigne Michel Eyquem de 1533–1592. French writer. He is regarded as the creator of the essay form. In 1580 he published the first two volumes of his *Essais*; the third volume appeared 1588, and the definitive edition was issued posthumously 1595. In his writings Montaigne considers all aspects of life from an urbanely sceptical viewpoint. He is critical of human pride and suspicious of philosophy and religion, seeking his own independent path to self-knowledge. ◊Descartes, ◊Pascal, and Francis ◊Bacon are among the thinkers who have been challenged and stimulated by his work, and through the translation by John Florio 1603, he influenced Shakespeare and other English writers.

Montana state in western USA, on the Canadian border; nicknamed Treasure State
area 318,100 sq km/147,143 sq mi
capital Helena
towns and cities Billings, Great Falls, Butte
physical mountainous forests in the W, rolling grasslands in the E
features Missouri, Yellowstone, and Little Bighorn rivers; Glacier national park, on the Continental Divide; part of Yellowstone national park; Missouri Headwaters state park; National Bison Range; Little Bighorn Battlefield national monument, the site of Custer's last stand, 1876; the Museum of the Plains Indians, Browning; gold rush mansions in Helena
products wheat (under irrigation), cattle, coal, copper, oil, natural gas, lumber, wood products
population (1991) 808,000
history explored for France by Verendrye early 1740s; passed to the USA 1803 in the Louisiana Purchase; first settled 1809; W Montana obtained from Britain in the Oregon Treaty 1846; influx of gold-seeking immigrants mid-19th century; fierce Indian wars 1867–77, which included 'Custer's last stand' with the Sioux; achieved statehood 1889.

Montana

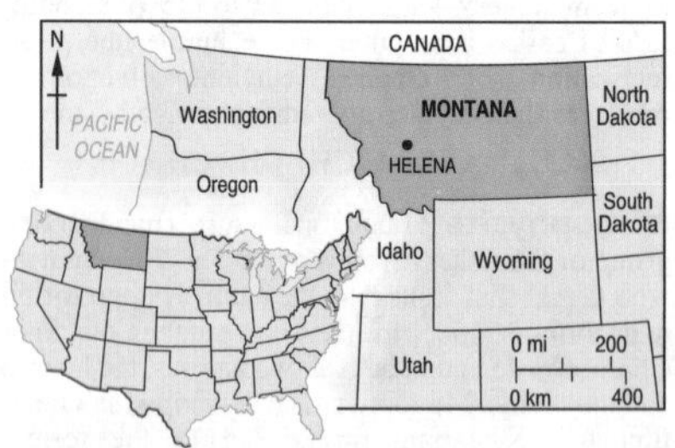

Montana Joe 1956– . US football player who has appeared in four winning Super Bowls as quarterback for the San Francisco 49ers 1982, 1985, 1989, and 1990, winning the Most Valuable Player award in 1982, 1985, and 1990. He threw a record five touchdown passes in the 1990 Super Bowl. He joined the Kansas City Chiefs 1993.

He was the leading passer in the National Football Conference 1981, 1984, and 1985 in the National Football League 1987, setting league records for touchdowns thrown (31) and consecutive completions (22). In the 1989 Super Bowl, he set a record for passing yardage and the most passes without an interception (33).

Montand Yves. Stage name of Ivo Livi 1921–1991. Italian-born French actor and singer who became known for his music-hall performances, and who later achieved fame in the thriller *Le Salaire de la peur/The Wages of Fear* 1953 and continued to be popular in French and American films, including *Let's Make Love* 1960 (with Marilyn Monroe), *Z* 1968, *Le Sauvage/The Savage* 1976, *Jean de Florette* 1986, and *Manon des sources* 1986.

Montanism movement within the early Christian church that strove to return to the purity of primitive Christianity. It originated in Phrygia in about 156 with the teaching of a prophet named Montanus, and spread to Anatolia, Rome, Carthage, and Gaul. The theologian ◊Tertullian was a Montanist.

Mont Blanc (Italian ***Monte Bianco***) highest mountain in the ◊Alps, between France and Italy; height 4,807 m/15,772 ft. It was first climbed 1786 by Jacques Balmat and Michel Paccard of Chamonix.

montbretia European plant *Tritonia crocosmiflora* of the iris family Iridaceae, native to South Africa, with orange or reddish flowers on long stems.

Montcalm-Gozon Louis-Joseph de, Marquis de Montcalm 1712–1759. French general, appointed military commander in Canada 1756. He won a succession of victories over the British during the French and Indian War, but was defeated in 1759 by James ◊Wolfe at Quebec on the Plains of Abraham, where both he and Wolfe were killed; this battle marked the end of French rule in Canada.

Monte Carlo town and luxury resort in the principality of ◊Monaco, situated on a rocky promontory NE of Monaco town; population (1988 est) 28,000. It is known for its Casino (1878) designed by architect Charles Garnier, and the Monte Carlo car rally and Monaco Grand Prix.

Montego Bay port and resort on the northwest coast of Jamaica; population (1991) 83,400. The fine beaches and climate attract tourists.

Montenegrin Slavic inhabitants of Montenegro (Yugoslavia) whose culture has much in common with the Serbs.

Montenegro (Serbo-Croatian ***Crna Gora***) constituent republic of Yugoslavia
area 13,800 sq km/5,327 sq mi
capital Podgorica
towns and cities Cetinje
features smallest of the republics; Skadarsko Jezero (Lake Scutari) shared with Albania; Mount Lovćen (1,749 m/5,738 ft)
physical mountainous and ◊karst region in SW; forests and grasslands in E
population (1991) 615,300, including c. 397,000 Montenegrins, 79,500 Muslims, and 39,500 Albanians
language Serbian variant of Serbo-Croat
religion Serbian Orthodox
history part of ◊Serbia from the late 12th century, it became independent (under Venetian protection) after Serbia was defeated by the Turks 1389. It was forced to accept Turkish suzerainty in the late 15th century, but was never completely subdued by Turkey. It was ruled by bishop princes until 1851, when a monarchy was founded, and became a sovereign principality under the Treaty of Berlin 1878. Montenegro participated in the Balkan Wars 1912 and 1913. It was overrun by Austria in World War I, and in 1918 voted to become part of Serbia. In 1946 Montenegro became a republic of Yugoslavia. In the 1991 conflict with Slovenia and Croatia, it sided with Serbia. In a referendum 1992 Montengrins voted to remain part of the Yugoslav federation; the referendum was boycotted by Montenegro's Muslim and Albanian communities.

Montespan Françoise-Athénaïs de Rochechouart, Marquise de Montespan 1641–1707. Mistress of Louis XIV of France from 1667. They had seven children, for whom she engaged as governess the future Madame de ◊Maintenon, who later supplanted her.

Montesquieu Charles Louis de Secondat, Baron de la Brède 1689–1755. French philosophical historian, author of *Lettres persanes/Persian Letters* 1721. *De l'Esprit des lois/The Spirit of the Laws* 1748, a 31-volume philosophical disquisition on politics and sociology as well as legal matters, advocated the separation of powers within government, a doctrine that became the basis of liberal constitutions.

Montesquieu arrived at the concept of the separation of powers – that is, of the legislative, executive, and judicial functions – from the viewpoint of the Tory opposition to Robert Walpole and the Whigs in the UK, where he lived 1729–31.

Montessori Maria 1870–1952. Italian educationist. Working with mentally disabled children, she developed the ***Montessori method***, an educational system for all children based on an informal approach, incorporating instructive play and allowing children to develop at their own pace. She wrote *The Montessori Method* 1912 and *The Secret of Childhood* 1936.

Monteux Pierre 1875–1964. French conductor. Ravel's *Daphnis and Chloe* and Stravinsky's *The Rite of Spring* were first performed under his direction. He conducted Diaghilev's Ballets Russes 1911–14 and 1917, and the San Francisco Symphony Orchestra 1935–52.

Monteverdi Claudio Giovanni Antonio 1567–1643. Italian composer. He contributed to the development of the opera with *La favola d'Orfeo/The Legend of Orpheus* 1607 and *L'incoronazione di Poppea/The Coronation of Poppea* 1642. He also wrote madrigals, motets, and sacred music, notably the *Vespers* 1610.

Born in Cremona, he was in the service of the Duke of Mantua about 1591–1612, and was director of music at St Mark's, Venice, from 1613. He was first to use an orchestra and to reveal the dramatic possibilities of the operatic form. His first opera *Orfeo* was produced for the carnival at Mantua 1607.

Montevideo capital and chief port (grain, meat products, hides) of Uruguay, on the Río de la Plata; population (1992) 1,383,700. Industries include meat packing, tanning, footwear, flour milling, and textiles

history Founded by the Spanish in 1726 as a defence against the attacks by the Portuguese from Brazil. It has been the capital of Uruguay since 1830

features A cathedral, built from 1790 to 1804, on the Plaza Constitucíon; the University of Uruguay, founded in 1849; museums of fine art and history in the park El Prado; a popular summer resort.

Montez Lola. Stage name of Maria Dolores Eliza Rosanna Gilbert 1818–1861. Irish actress and dancer. She appeared on the stage as a Spanish dancer, and in 1847 became the mistress of King Ludwig I of Bavaria, whose policy she dictated for a year. Her liberal sympathies led to her banishment through Jesuit influence in 1848. She died in poverty in the USA.

Montezuma II 1466–1520. Aztec emperor 1502–20. When the Spanish conquistador Cortés invaded Mexico, Montezuma was imprisoned and killed during the Aztec attack on Cortés's force as it tried to leave Tenochtitlán, the Aztec capital city.

Montfort Simon de Montfort, 1st Earl of Leicester c. 1208–1265. English politician and soldier. From 1258 he led the baronial opposition to Henry III's misrule during the second ◊Barons' War and in 1264 defeated and captured the king at Lewes, Sussex. In 1265, as head of government, he summoned the first parliament in which the towns were represented; he was killed at the Battle of Evesham during the last of the Barons' Wars.

Born in Normandy, the son of ***Simon de Montfort*** (about 1160–1218) who led a crusade against the Albigenses, he arrived in England in 1230, married Henry III's sister, and was granted the earldom of Leicester.

Montgolfier Joseph Michel (1740–1810) and Jacques Etienne (1745–1799) French brothers whose hot-air balloon was used for the first successful human flight 21 Nov 1783. On 5 June 1783 they first sent up a balloon filled with hot air. After further experiments with wood-fuelled fabric-and-paper balloons, and one crewed ascent in a tethered balloon, they sent up two people who travelled for 20 minutes above Paris, a journey of 9 km/6 mi. The Montgolfier experiments greatly stimulated scientific interest in aviation.

Montgomery state capital of Alabama, USA, on the Alabama River; population (1992) 192,100

Montenegro The port of Kolos, Montenegro, Yugoslavia. Montenegro and Serbia are the only two republics which remain as Yugoslavia. Like the other republics which broke away in the early 1990s, Montenegro displays a wealth of cultural influences, including Roman, Byzantine, Turkish, and Venetian. *UNESCO*

history the site was inhabited by prehistoric Indian mound builders, and later there were Indian villages. The present city dates from 1819, when two settlements were amalgamated. The Confederate States of America met and organized themselves here 1861; Montgomery is therefore regarded as the Cradle of the Confederacy. After the American Civil War it developed as a market for cotton, cattle, and timber. The 1955 Montgomery Bus Boycott, which began when a black passenger, Rosa Parks, refused to give up her seat to a white person, led to the nullification of the bus-segregation laws; this was a landmark in the civil rights campaign.

features first White House of the Confederacy 1835; State Archives and History Museum; Civil Rights Memorial, commemorating Martin Luther King's marches 1965 to protest against violent attacks on black people registering to vote; annual American Shakespeare festival.

Montgomery Bernard Law, 1st Viscount Montgomery of Alamein 1887–1976. British field marshal. In World War II he commanded the 8th Army in N Africa in the Second Battle of El ◊Alamein 1942. As commander of British troops in N Europe from 1944, he received the German surrender 1945.

At the start of World War II he commanded part of the British Expeditionary Force in France 1939–40 and took part in the evacuation from Dunkirk. In Aug 1942 he took command of the 8th Army, then barring the German advance on Cairo; the victory of El ◊Alamein in Oct turned the tide in N Africa and was followed by the expulsion of Field Marshal Rommel from Egypt and rapid Allied advance into Tunisia. In Feb 1943 Montgomery's forces came under US general Eisenhower's command, and they took part in the conquest of Tunisia and Sicily and the invasion of Italy.

Montgomery was promoted to field marshal in 1944. He commanded the Allied armies during the opening phase of the invasion of France in Jun 1944, and from Aug the British and imperial troops that liberated the Netherlands, overran N Germany, and entered Denmark. At his 21st Army Group headquarters on Lüneburg Heath, he received the German surrender on 4 May 1945. He was in command of the British occupation force in Germany until Feb 1946, when he was appointed chief of the Imperial General Staff. In 1948 he became permanent military chair of the Commanders-in-Chief Committee for W European defence, and 1951–58 was deputy Supreme Commander Europe.

> *In defeat unbeatable: in victory unbearable.*
>
> On Viscount Montgomery
> Winston Churchill quoted in Marsh *Ambrosia and Small Beer*

month unit of time based on the motion of the Moon around the Earth. The time from one new or full Moon to the next (the ***synodic*** or ***lunar month***) is 29.53 days. The time for the Moon to complete one orbit around the Earth relative to the stars (the ***sidereal month***) is 27.32 days. The ***solar month*** equals 30.44 days, and is exactly one-twelfth of the solar or tropical year, the time taken for the Earth to orbit the Sun. The ***calendar month*** is a human invention, devised to fit the calendar year.

Montgomery British general Bernard Montgomery in Nov 1942, after he had taken command of the British 8th Army in N Africa. A month later the 8th Army defeated Rommel's army at El Alamein. *Library of Congress*

Monti Eugenio 1928– . Italian bobsleigh driver who won Olympic gold medals in two- and four-crew bobs in 1968, and between 1957 and 1968 won 11 world titles. His two-person successes were shared with the brakemen Renzo Alvera and Sergio Siorpaes, both Italian. On his retirement in 1968 Monti became manager to the Italian team.

Montmartre district of Paris, France, dominated by the basilica of Sacré Coeur 1875. It is situated in the N of the city on a hill 120 m/400 ft. It is known for its nightlife and artistic associations and is a popular tourist site.

Montparnasse district of Paris, France, formerly frequented by artists and writers. It is situated in the W of the city. The Pasteur Institute is also here.

Montpellier industrial city (electronics, medical research, engineering, textiles, food processing, and a trade in wine and brandy), capital of ◊Languedoc-Roussillon, France; population (1990) 210,900. There is a 14th-century cathedral and a university (1229), noted for its medical school.

Montréal inland port, industrial city (aircraft, chemicals, oil and petrochemicals, flour, sugar, brewing, meat packing) of Quebec, Canada, on Montréal Island at the junction of the Ottawa and St Lawrence rivers; population (1991) 1,017,700
features Mont Réal (Mount Royal, 230 m/753 ft) overlooks the city; an artificial island in the St Lawrence (site of the international exhibition 1967); three universities; except for Paris, the world's largest French-speaking city
history Jacques ◊Cartier reached the site 1535, Samuel de ◊Champlain established a trading post 1611, and the original Ville Marie (later renamed Montréal) was founded 1642 by Paul de Chomédy, Sieur de Maisonneuve (1612–1676). It was the last town surrendered by France to Britain 1760. Nevertheless, when troops of the rebel Continental Congress occupied the city 1775–76, the citizens refused to be persuaded to join the future USA in its revolt against Britain.

Montréal Protocol international agreement, signed 1987, to stop the production of chemicals that are ◊ozone depleters by the year 2000. Originally the agreement was to reduce the production of ozone depleters by 35% by 1999. The green movement criticized the agreement as inadequate, arguing that an 85% reduction in ozone depleters would be necessary just to stabilize the ozone layer at 1987 levels. The protocol (under the Vienna Convention for the Protection of the Ozone Layer) was reviewed 1992. Amendments added another 11 chemicals to the original list of eight chemicals suspected of harming the ozone layer. A controversial amendment concerns a fund established to pay for the transfer of ozone-safe technology to poor countries.

Montrose James Graham, 1st Marquess and 5th Earl of Montrose 1612–1650. Scottish soldier, son of the 4th earl of Montrose. He supported the ◊Covenanters against Charles I, but after 1640 changed sides. Defeated in 1645 at Philiphaugh, he escaped to Norway. Returning in 1650 to raise a revolt, he survived shipwreck only to have his weakened forces defeated, and (having been betrayed to the Covenanters) was hanged in Edinburgh.

Moon The far side of the Moon photographed from the Apollo 13 spacecraft 1970. The lunar landscape has been fashioned by the impact of countless meteorites. The bright-rayed crater seen here was caused by a relatively recent impact (still many millions of years ago). The darker areas are thought to be far older craters which have filled with lava welling up from the Moon's interior. *National Aeronautical Space Agency*

Mont St Michel islet off the coast of NW France converted to a peninsula by an artificial causeway; it has a Benedictine monastery, founded 708.

Montserrat volcanic island in the West Indies, one of the Leeward group, a British crown colony; capital Plymouth; area 110 sq km/42 sq mi; population (1991) 11,957. Practically all buildings were destroyed by Hurricane Hugo Sept 1989.

Montserrat produces cotton, cotton-seed, coconuts, citrus and other fruits, and vegetables. Its first European visitor was Christopher ◊Columbus 1493, who named it after the mountain in Spain. It was first colonized by English and Irish settlers who moved from St Christopher 1632. It was held by the French until ceded to Britain 1783. It became part of the colony of the Leeward Islands 1871, and a British crown colony 1956.

Montserrat (Spanish *monte serrado* 'serrated mountain') isolated mountain in NE Spain, height 1,240 m/4,070 ft, so called because its uneven outline of eroded pinnacles resembles the edge of a saw. There is a monastery dating from 880. According to legend, St Peter hid an image of the Virgin Mary on the mountain at the time of the Moorish invasion, which was later discovered by shepherds.

Monument, the a tower commemorating the Great Fire of London 1666, near the site of the house in Pudding Lane where the conflagration began. It was designed by Christopher ◊Wren and completed 1677.

moon in astronomy, any natural ◊satellite that orbits a planet. Mercury and Venus are the only planets in the Solar System that do not have moons.

Moon natural satellite of Earth, 3,476 km/2,160 mi in diameter, with a mass 0.012 (approximately one-eightieth) that of Earth. Its surface gravity is only 0.16 (one-sixth) that of Earth. Its average distance from Earth is 384,400 km/238,855 mi, and it orbits in a west-to-east direction every 27.32 days (the sidereal month). It spins on its axis with one side permanently turned towards Earth. The Moon has no atmosphere or water.
phases The Moon is illuminated by sunlight, and goes through a cycle of phases of shadow, waxing from new (dark) via first quarter (half Moon) to full, and waning back again to new every 29.53 days (the synodic month, also known as a lunation). On its sunlit side, temperatures reach 110°C/230°F, but during the two-week lunar night the surface temperature drops to −170°C/−274°F.
origins The origin of the Moon is still open to debate. Scientists suggest the following theories: that it split from the Earth; that it was a separate body captured by Earth's gravity; that it formed in orbit around Earth; or that it was formed from debris thrown off when a body the size of Mars struck Earth.
research The far side of the Moon was first photographed from the Soviet *Lunik, 3* Oct 1959. Much of our information about the Moon has been derived from this and other photographs and measurements taken by US and Soviet Moon probes, from geological samples brought back by US Apollo astronauts and by Soviet Luna probes, and from experiments set up by the US astronauts 1969–72. In 1995 NASA announced plans to send a new probe to the Moon in 1997 to search for surface ice and to monitor escaping gas as a measure of tectonic activity.
composition The Moon's composition is rocky, with a surface heavily scarred by ◊meteorite impacts that have formed craters up to 240 km/150 mi across. Seismic observations indicate that the Moon's surface extends downwards for tens of kilometres; below this crust is a solid mantle about 1,100 km/688 mi thick, and below that a silicate core, part of which may be molten. Rocks brought back by astronauts show the Moon is 4.6 billion years old, the same age as Earth. It is made up of the same chemical elements as Earth, but in different proportions, and differs from Earth in that most of the Moon's surface features were formed within the first billion years of its history when it was hit repeatedly by meteorites. The youngest craters are surrounded by bright rays of ejected rock. The largest scars have been filled by dark lava to produce the lowland plains called seas, or maria (plural of ◊mare). One of the Moon's easiest features to observe is the mare Plato, which is about 100 km/62 mi in diameter and 2,700 m/8,860 ft deep, and at times is visible with the naked eye alone.

Moon Sun Myung 1920– . Korean industrialist and founder of the ◊Unification Church (***Moonies***) 1954. From 1973 he launched a major mission in the USA and elsewhere. The church has been criticized for its manipulative methods of recruiting and keeping members. Moon has allegedly been associated with extreme right-wing organizations, arms manufacture, and the Korean Central Intelligence Agency. He was convicted of tax fraud in the USA 1982.

Moon William 1818–1894. English inventor of the ***Moon alphabet*** for the blind. Devised in 1847, it uses only nine symbols in different orientations. From 1983 it has been possible to write it with a miniature typewriter.

Moonie popular name for a follower of the ◊Unification Church, a religious sect founded by Sun Myung Moon.

Moon probe crewless spacecraft used to investigate the Moon. Early probes flew past the Moon or crash-landed on it, but later ones achieved soft landings or went into orbit. Soviet probes included the Luna/Lunik series. US probes (Ranger, Surveyor, Lunar Orbiter) prepared the way for the Apollo crewed flights.

The first space probe to hit the Moon was the Soviet *Luna 2*, on 13 Sept 1959 (*Luna 1* had missed the Moon eight months earlier). In Oct 1959, *Luna 3* sent back the first photographs of the Moon's far side. *Luna 9* was the first probe to soft-land on the Moon, on 3 Feb 1966, transmitting photographs of the surface to Earth. *Luna 16* was the first probe to return automatically to Earth carrying Moon samples, in Sept 1970, although by then Moon rocks had already been brought back by US ◊Apollo astronauts. *Luna 17* landed in Nov 1970 carrying a lunar rover, Lunokhod, which was driven over the Moon's surface by remote control from Earth.

The first successful US Moon probe was *Ranger 7*, which took close-up photographs before it hit the Moon on 31 July 1964. *Surveyor 1*, on 2 June 1966, was the first US probe to soft-land on the lunar surface. It took photographs, and later Surveyors analysed the surface rocks. Between 1966 and 1967 a series of five Lunar Orbiters photographed the entire Moon in detail, in preparation for the Apollo landings 1969–72.

In March 1990 Japan put a satellite, *Hagoromo*, into orbit around the Moon. *Hagoromo* weighs only 11 kg/26 lb and was released from a larger Japanese space probe.

moonstone translucent, pearly variety of potassium sodium ◊feldspar, found in Sri Lanka and Myanmar, and distinguished by a blue, silvery, or red opalescent tint. It is valued as a gem.

moor stretch of land, usually at a height, which is characterized by a vegetation of heather, coarse grass, and bracken. A moor may be poorly drained and contain boggy hollows.

Moor any of the NW African Muslims, of mixed Arab and Berber origin, who conquered Spain and ruled its southern part from 711 to 1492, when they were forced to renounce their faith and became Christian (they were then known as *Moriscos*). The name (English form of Latin *Maurus*) was originally applied to an inhabitant of the Roman province of Mauritania, in NW Africa.

Moore Bobby (Robert Frederick) 1941–1993. English footballer who led the England team to victory against West Germany in the 1966 World Cup final. A superb defender, he played 108 games for England 1962–70 (until 1978, a world-record number of international appearances) and was captain 90 times. His Football League career, spent at West Ham 1968–74 and Fulham 1974–77, spanned 19 years and 668 matches.

Moore Brian 1921–1999. Irish-born novelist. He emigrated to Canada 1948 and then to the USA 1959. His books include *Judith Hearne* 1955, *The Temptation of Eileen Hughes* 1981, *Black Robe* 1985, *The Colour of Blood* 1987, *No Other Life* 1993, and *The Statement* 1995. Catholicism, obsession, and the contrast between dreams and reality are recurrent and powerful themes, depicted with stylistic economy and realism.

Moore Dudley Stuart John 1935– . English actor, comedian, and musician. He was formerly teamed with the comedian Peter Cook. Moore became a Hollywood star after appearing in *'10'* 1979. His other films, mostly comedies, include *Bedazzled* 1968, *Arthur* 1981, *Santa Claus* 1985, and *Blame it on the Bellboy* 1992. He is also an accomplished musician and has given classical piano concerts.

Moore Gerald 1899–1987. English pianist. He was renowned as an accompanist to Elizabeth Schwarzkopf, Kathleen Ferrier, Heddle Nash, and other singers, a role he raised to equal partnership.

Moore Henry (Spencer) 1898–1986. English sculptor. His recurring subjects include the reclining nude, mother-and-child groups, the warrior, and interlocking abstract forms. Many of his post-1945 works are in bronze or marble, including monumental semi-abstracts such as *Reclining Figure* 1957–58 (outside the UNESCO building, Paris), and often designed to be placed in landscape settings. He is considered one of the leading artists of the 20th century.

Moore's work of the 1920s was based on the human figure and laid stress on truth to material and retaining the shape of the original block, as in *Reclining Figure* 1929 (Leeds City Art Gallery). This, like much of his work then, was strongly influenced by ancient Mexican art. During the 1930s he was also influenced both by the Surrealists, particularly Giacometti, and by abstract artists. Their combined impact can be seen in sculptures such as *The Bride* 1940 (Museum of Modern Art, New York), in which a series of strings which define space are stretched across a biomorphic form (which has affinities with sculpture by Hans Arp and Barbara ◊Hepworth). Semi-abstract work suggesting organic structures recurs in the latter half of the century, for example in the interwoven bonelike forms of the *Hill Arches* and the bronze *Sheep Pieces* 1970s, set in fields by his studio in Hertfordshire, England.

Moore Marianne Craig 1887–1972. US poet. She edited the literary magazine *The Dial* 1925–29, and published several volumes of witty and intellectual verse, including *Observations* 1924, *What are Years* 1941, and *A Marianne Moore Reader* 1961. She also published translations and essays. Her work is noted for its observation of detail.

Moore Thomas 1779–1852. Irish poet. Among his works are the verse romance *Lalla Rookh* 1817 and *Irish Melodies* 1807–34, for which the music was arranged by John Stevenson (1761–1833); the songs include 'The Minstrel Boy' and ''Tis the Last Rose of Summer'. Moore also showed himself to be a master of satire in *Intercepted Letters; or Two-penny Post-bag* 1813.

moorhen marsh bird *Gallinula chloropus* of the rail family Rallidae, order Gruiformes, common in water of swamps, lakes, and ponds in Eurasia, Africa, and North and South America. It is about 33 cm/13 in long, and mainly brown and grey, but with a red bill and forehead, and a vivid white underside to the tail.

moose North American name for ◊elk.

moped lightweight motorcycle with pedals. Early mopeds (like the autocycle) were like motorized bicycles, using the pedals to start the bike and assist propulsion uphill. The pedals have little function in many mopeds today.

moquette textile woven in the same manner as velvet (with cut or uncut pile) from coarse wool and linen yarns, usually for upholstery or carpeting. By introducing rods during weaving, the thread is raised in loops. Moquette was made from the Middle Ages onwards in many parts of Europe, notably the Low Countries.

moraine rocky debris or ◊till carried along and deposited by a ◊glacier. Material eroded from the side of a glaciated valley and carried along the glacier's edge is called a ***lateral moraine***; that worn from the valley floor and carried along the base of the glacier is called a ***ground moraine***. Rubble dropped at the snout of a melting glacier is called a ***terminal moraine***.

morality play didactic medieval European verse drama, in part a development of the ◊mystery play (or miracle play), in which human characters are replaced by personified virtues and vices, the limited humorous elements being provided by the Devil. In England, morality plays, such as *Everyman*, flourished in the 15th century. They exerted an influence on the development of Elizabethan drama and comedy.

Moral Rearmament (MRA) international movement calling for 'moral and spiritual renewal', founded by the Christian evangelist F N D Buchman in 1938 (as a successor to the Oxford Group, founded in the 1920s). It based its teachings on the 'Four Absolutes' (honesty, purity, unselfishness, love). Later, as the MRA (1938), it became more involved in political and social issues, particularly during the Cold War period when its anticommunist orientation found a receptive climate.

Moravia (Czech ***Morava***) area of central Europe, forming two regions of the Czech Republic:

South Moravia (Czech ***Jihomoravský***)
area 15,030 sq km/5,802 sq mi
capital Brno
population (1991) 2,048,900
North Moravia (Czech ***Severomoravský***)
area 11,070 sq km/4,273 sq mi
capital Ostrava
population (1991) 1,961,500
features (N and S) river Morava; 25% forested
products maize, grapes, wine in the S; wheat, barley, rye, flax, sugar beet in the N; coal and iron
history part of the Avar territory since the 6th century; conquered by Charlemagne's Holy Roman Empire. In 874 the kingdom of Great Moravia was founded by the Slavic prince Sviatopluk, who ruled until 894. It was conquered by the Magyars 906, and became a fief of Bohemia 1029. It was passed to the Habsburgs 1526, and became an Austrian crown land 1849.

It became part of the new republic of Czechoslovakia 1918, forming a province until 1949. From 1960 it was divided into two administrative regions, North and South Moravia; part of the Czech Republic from 1993.

Moravia Alberto. Pen name of Alberto Pincherle 1907–1991. Italian novelist. His first successful novel was *Gli indifferenti/The Time of Indifference* 1929, but its criticism of Mussolini's regime led to the government censoring his work until after World War II. Later books include *Agostino* 1944, *La romana/Woman of Rome* 1947, *Racconti Romani/Roman Tales* 1954, *La ciociara/Two Women* 1957, *La noia/The Empty Canvas* 1961 (a study of an artist's obsession with his model), *L'attenzione/The Lie* 1965, and *La vita interiore/Time of Desecration* 1978. Moravia was particularly successful when describing the ideological vacuum and corruption of the upper and middle classes.

Moravian member of a Christian Protestant sect, the ***Moravian Brethren***. An episcopal church that grew out of the earlier Bohemian Brethren, it was established by the Lutheran Count Zinzendorf in Saxony 1722.

Persecution of the Bohemian Brethren began 1620, and they were held together mainly by the leadership of their bishop, Comenius (Jan Komensky (1592–1670)). Driven out of Bohemia in 1722, they spread into Germany, England, and North America. In 1732 missionary work began. There are about 63,000 Moravians in the USA, and small congregations in the UK and the rest of Europe.

Moray another spelling of ◊Murray, regent of Scotland 1567–70.

Moray local authority of Scotland created 1996 (*see United Kingdom map*).

Moray Firth North Sea inlet in Scotland, between Burghead (Grampian Region) and Tarbat Ness (Highland Region), 38 km/15 mi wide at its entrance. The city of Inverness is situated at the head of the Firth.

Mordovia another name for ◊Mordvinia, an autonomous republic of the Russian Federation.

Mordred in Arthurian legend, nephew and final opponent of King ◊Arthur. What may be an early version of his name (Medraut) appears with Arthur in annals from the 10th century, listed under the year AD 537.

Mordvin Finnish people inhabiting the middle Volga Valley in W Asia. They are known to have lived in the region since the 1st century AD. There are 1 million speakers of Mordvin scattered throughout W Russia, about one-third of whom live in the Mordvinian republic. Mordvin is a Finno-Ugric language belonging to the Uralic family.

Mordvinia or ***Mordovia*** autonomous republic of central Russian Federation
area 26,200 sq km/10,100 sq mi
capital Saransk
physical river Sura on the E; forested in the W
industries sugar beet, grains, potatoes; sheep and dairy farming; timber, furniture, and textiles
population (1986) 964,000
language Russian, Mordvin
history Mordvinia was conquered by Russian princes during the 13th century. It was made an autonomous region 1930, and an Autonomous Soviet Socialist Republic 1934. It remained an autonomous republic of Russia after the dissolution of the Soviet Union 1991.

More (St) Thomas 1478–1535. English politician and author. From 1509 he was favoured by ◊Henry VIII and employed on foreign embassies. He was a member of the privy council from 1518 and Lord Chancellor from 1529 but resigned over Henry's break with the pope. For refusing to accept the king as head of the church, he was executed. The title of his political book *Utopia* 1516 has come to mean any supposedly perfect society.

More studied Greek, Latin, French, theology, and music at Oxford, and law at Lincoln's Inn, London, and was influenced by the humanists John Colet and ◊Erasmus. In Parliament from 1504, he was made Speaker of the House of Commons in 1523. He was knighted in 1521, and on the fall of Cardinal Wolsey became Lord Chancellor, but resigned in 1532 because he could not agree with the king on his ecclesiastical policy and marriage with Anne Boleyn. In 1534 he refused to take the oath of supremacy to Henry VIII as head of the church, and after a year's imprisonment in the Tower of London he was executed.

Among Thomas More's writings are the Latin *Utopia* 1516, sketching an ideal commonwealth; the English *Dialogue* 1528, a theological argument against the Reformation leader Tyndale; and a *History of Richard III*. He was also a patron of artists, including ◊Holbein. More was canonized in 1935.

Moreau Jeanne 1928– . French actress. She has appeared in international films, often in passionate, intelligent roles. Her work includes *Les Amants/The Lovers* 1958, *Jules et Jim/Jules and Jim* 1961, *Chimes at Midnight* 1966, and *Querelle* 1982.

Morecambe town and resort in Lancashire, England, on Morecambe Bay, conjoined with the port of Heysham, which has a ferry service to Ireland; joint population (1991) 46,700. Industries include shrimp fishing, clothing, plastics, and engineering. There are oil wells, and natural gas 50 km/30 mi offshore.

morel any edible mushroom of the genus *Morchella*. The common morel *M. esculenta* grows in Europe and North America. The yellowish-brown

'Tis the last rose of summer / Left blooming alone; / All her lovely companions / Are faded and gone.
THOMAS MOORE
''Tis the Last Rose'

As time requireth, a man of marvellous mirth and pastimes, and sometimes of as sad gravity, as who say: a man for all seasons.
On THOMAS MORE
Robert Whittington
Vulgaria II

morel Most morels, such as this common morel *Morchella esculenta*, appear in spring, in contrast to the majority of fungi which appear in autumn when rotting vegetation provides nutrients. *Premaphotos Wildlife*

Morocco is like a tree nourished by roots deep in the soil of Africa which breathes through foliage rustling in the winds of Europe … Horizontally it looks to the East, with which it is bound by ties of religion and culture.

On **Morocco**
King Hassan II of Morocco, *The Challenge*

cap is pitted like a sponge and about 2.5 cm/1 in long. It is used for seasoning gravies, soups, and sauces and is second only to the truffle as the world's most sought-after mushroom.

Morelos José María 1765–1815. Mexican priest and revolutionary. A mestizo (person with Spanish American and Native American parents), Morelos followed independence campaigner Miguel Hidalgo y Costilla (1753–1811), intending to be an army chaplain, but he displayed military genius and came to head his own forces. The independence movement was stalled for five years after his death.

He sought to rescue the revolution from chaos and violence, and to widen its political base. However, the Creoles failed to respond. After four major campaigns against the Spaniards, he was captured, stripped of the priesthood by the Inquisition, and executed.

Morgagni Giovanni Battista 1682–1771. Italian anatomist who developed the view that disease was not an imbalance of the body's humours but a result of alterations in the organs. His work *De sedibus et causis morborum per anatomen indagatis/On the Seats and Causes of Diseases as Investigated by Anatomy* 1761 formed the basis of ◊pathology.

Morgan Henry c. 1635–1688. Welsh buccaneer in the Caribbean. He made war against Spain, capturing and sacking Panama 1671. In 1675 he was knighted and appointed lieutenant governor of Jamaica.

Morgan J(ohn) P(ierpont) 1837–1913. US financier and investment banker whose company became the most influential private banking house after the Civil War, being instrumental in the formation of many trusts to stifle competition. He set up the US Steel Corporation 1901 and International Harvester 1902.

Have nothing in your houses that you do not know to be useful, or believe to be beautiful.

William Morris
Hopes and Fears for Art

Morgan Thomas Hunt 1866–1945. US geneticist who helped establish that the ◊genes are located on the chromosomes, discovered sex chromosomes, and invented the techniques of genetic mapping. He was the first to work on the fruit fly *Drosophila*, which has since become a major subject of genetic studies. Nobel Prize for Physiology or Medicine 1933.

Morgan horse breed of riding and driving show horse originating in the USA in the 1780s from a single stallion named *Justin Morgan* after his owner. They are marked by high, curved necks and high stepping action. The breed is valued for its strength, endurance, and speed.

Morgan le Fay in the romance and legend of the English king ◊Arthur, an enchantress and healer, ruler of ◊Avalon and sister of the king, whom she tended after his final battle. In some versions of the legend she is responsible for the suspicions held by the king of his wife ◊Guinevere.

Morisot Berthe Marie Pauline 1841–1895. French painter, the first woman to join the Impressionist movement. Taught by ◊Corot, she was also much influenced by ◊Manet and, in the 1880s, ◊Renoir. She specialized in sensitive pictures of women and children, as in *The Cradle* 1872 (Impressionist Museum, Paris).

Born into a wealthy family in Bourges, she was granddaughter of the Rococo artist Fragonard. She

morning glory **The morning glory is a vinelike climbing plant that bears large, purplish-blue, trumpet-shaped flowers. Its seeds were once used by the Central American Indians, the Aztecs, to induce hallucinations during religious ceremonies. Nowadays, it is grown as an ornamental.**

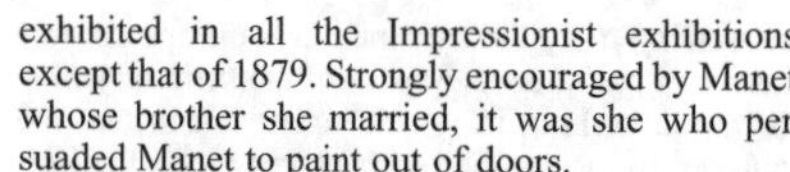

exhibited in all the Impressionist exhibitions, except that of 1879. Strongly encouraged by Manet, whose brother she married, it was she who persuaded Manet to paint out of doors.

Morley Thomas c. 1557–c. 1602. English composer. He wrote consort music, madrigals, and airs including the lute song 'It was a lover and his lass' for Shakespeare's play *As You Like It* 1599. He edited a collection of Italian madrigals *The Triumphs of Oriana* 1601, and published an influential keyboard tutor *A Plaine and Easie Introduction to Practicall Musicke* 1597.

Mormon or ***Latter-day Saint*** member of a Christian sect, the ***Church of Jesus Christ of Latter-day Saints***, founded at Manchester, New York, in 1830 by Joseph ◊Smith. According to Smith, Mormon was an ancient prophet in North America whose *Book of Mormon*, of which Smith claimed divine revelation, is accepted by Mormons as part of the Christian scriptures. It is a missionary church with headquarters in Utah and a worldwide membership of about 6 million.

The Mormon Church has two orders of priesthood, 'Melchisedek' dealing with religious and 'Aaron' with temporal matters. Mormons believe in the authority of their scriptures (the *Bible*, the *Book of Mormon*, and *Doctrine and Covenants*) and in the supreme value of personal revelation, especially that received by the president of the sect. The millennium is expected, and baptism by proxy is practised on behalf of the dead. They advocate a strict sexual morality, large families, and respect for authority. The consumption of alcohol, coffee, tea, and tobacco is forbidden. Polygamy was officially practised until 1890, when the Church decided to conform to the law.

morning glory any twining or creeping plant of the genus *Ipomoea*, especially *I. purpurea*, family Convolvulaceae, native to tropical America, with dazzling blue flowers.

Moro Aldo 1916–1978. Italian Christian Democrat politician. Prime minister 1963–68 and 1974–76, he was expected to become Italy's president, but he was kidnapped and shot by Red Brigade urban guerrillas.

Moroccan Crises two periods of international tension 1905 and 1911 following German objections to French expansion in Morocco. Their wider purpose was to break up the Anglo-French entente 1904, but both crises served to reinforce the entente and isolate Germany. The first was resolved at the Algeciras Conference. The second brought Europe to the brink of war and is known as the ◊Agadir Incident.

Morocco country in NW Africa, bounded N and NW by the Mediterranean Sea, E and SE by Algeria, and S by Western Sahara. *See country box opposite.*

Moroni capital of the Comoros Republic, on Njazidja (Grand Comore); population (1992) 22,000. It has a small natural harbour from which coffee, cacao, and vanilla are exported.

morpheme basic unit of language; morphemes are the building blocks of which a language is constructed. They are the smallest units of grammatical analysis and include prefixes, suffixes, verb endings, and root words.

Morpheus in Greek and Roman mythology, the god of dreams, son of Hypnos or Somnus, god of sleep.

morphine narcotic alkaloid $C_{17}H_{19}NO_3$ derived from ◊opium and prescribed only to alleviate severe pain. Its use produces serious side effects, including nausea, constipation, tolerance, and addiction, but it is highly valued for the relief of the terminally ill.

morphing the metamorphosis of one shape or object into another by computer-generated animation. First used in filmmaking 1990, it transformed cinema special effects. Conventional animation is limited to two dimensions; morphing enables the creation of three-dimensional transformations.

To create such effects, the start and end of the transformation must be specified on screen using a wire-frame model that mathematically defines the object. To make the object three-dimensional, the wire can be extruded from a cross-section or turned as on a lathe to produce an evenly turned surface. This is then rendered, or filled in and shaded. Once the beginning and end objects have been created the computer can calculate the morphing process.

morphogen in medicine, one of a class of substances believed to be present in the growing embryo, controlling its growth pattern.

morphology in biology, the study of the physical structure and form of organisms, in particular their soft tissues.

morphology in the study of language, the analysis of the formation of words, the breaking-down of a language into ◊morphemes.

Morricone Ennio 1928– . Italian composer of film music. His atmospheric scores for 'spaghetti Westerns', notably the Clint ◊Eastwood movies *A Fistful of Dollars* 1964 and *The Good, the Bad, and the Ugly* 1966, were widely imitated. His highly ritualized, incantatory style pioneered the use of amplified instruments and solo voices, using studio special effects.

Morrigan in Celtic mythology, a goddess of war and death who could take the shape of a crow.

Morris Jan 1926– . English travel writer and journalist. Her books display a zestful, witty, and knowledgeable style and offer vivid sense impressions combined with deftly handled historical perspectives. These books include *Coast to Coast* 1956, *Venice* 1960, *Oxford* 1965, *Farewell the Trumpets* 1978, and *Among the Cities* 1985. Born James Morris, her adoption of female gender is described in *Conundrum* 1974.

Morris Mark 1956– . US choreographer and dancer. His ballets merge various styles ranging from avant-garde, ballet, folk, and jazz dance. He was artistic director of the Théâtre de la Monnaie in Brussels 1988–91. He is the director of his own company in New York.

Morris Thomas, Jr 1851–1875. British golfer, one of the first great champions. He was known as 'Young Tom' to distinguish him from his father (known as 'Old Tom'). Morris Jr won the British Open four times between 1868 and 1872.

Morris William 1834–1896. English artist, designer, and writer. A founder of the ◊Arts and Crafts movement, he condemned 19th-century mechanization and sought a revival of traditional crafts, such as furniture making, book illustration, fabric design, and so on. He linked this to a renewal of society based on Socialist principles.

Morris was born in Walthamstow, near London, and studied at Oxford, where he formed a lasting friendship with the Pre-Raphaelite artist Edward ◊Burne-Jones and was influenced by the art critic John Ruskin and the painter and poet Dante Gabriel ◊Rossetti. In 1861 he cofounded a company, Morris, Marshall, Faulkner and Company ('the Firm') to design and produce furniture, carpets, and decorative wallpapers in which Rossetti, Burne-Jones, and other artists were partners. With an interest in medieval and oriental sources, he designed wallpaper, tapestry, fabric, carpets, furniture, and stained glass. He also designed windows for Middleton Cheney Parish Church 1864, and centralized his weaving and dyeing works at Merton Abbey in 1880, where William de Morgan joined him to produce tiles and ruby-lustre ware.

A leading Socialist, he joined the Social Democratic Federation 1883, but left it 1884 because he found it too moderate, and set up the Socialist League. To this period belong the critical and sociological studies *Signs of Change* 1888 and *Hopes and Fears for Art* 1892. His utopian views found their most enduring expression in the prose fantasy *News from Nowhere* 1891.

Other literary works include *The Defence of Guenevere and other Poems* 1858, *The Life and Death of Jason* 1867, *The Earthly Paradise* 1868–70, and *Love is Enough* 1875, in which year he also made a translation in verse of Virgil's *Aeneid*. Travels in Iceland led to the writing of *Three Northern Love Stories* and the epic of *Sigurd the Volsung* 1876. His translation of the *Odyssey* in verse appeared in 1887. A series of prose romances include the *House of Wolfings* 1889, and *The Well at the World's End* 1896.

In 1890 he set up the Kelmscott Press, for which he designed type and decorations, the most famous product being the *Kelmscott Chaucer*. The Press had a major impact on printing and book design.

morris dance English folk dance. In early times it was usually performed by six men, one of whom wore girl's clothing while another portrayed a horse. The others wore costumes decorated with bells. Morris dancing probably originated in pre-Christian ritual dances and is still popular in the UK and USA.

Morrison Herbert Stanley, Baron Morrison of Lambeth 1888–1965. British Labour politician. He was a founder member and later secretary of the London Labour Party 1915–45, and a member of the London County Council 1922–45. He entered Parliament in 1923, and organized the Labour Party's general election victory in 1945. He was twice defeated in the contest for leadership of the party, once to Clement Attlee in 1932, and then to Hugh Gaitskell 1955. A skilful organizer, he lacked the ability to unite the party.

He was minister of transport 1929–31, home secretary 1940–45, Lord President of the Council and leader of the House of Commons 1945–51, and foreign secretary March–Oct 1951.

Morrison Toni Chloe Anthony, (born Wofford) 1931– . US novelist. Her fiction records black life in the South, including *Song of Solomon* 1978, *Tar Baby* 1981, *Beloved* 1987, based on a true story about infanticide in Kentucky, which won a Pulitzer prize 1988, and *Jazz* 1992. Nobel Prize for Literature 1993.

Morrison Van (George Ivan) 1945– . Northern Irish singer and songwriter. His jazz-inflected Celtic soul style was already in evidence on *Astral Weeks* 1968 and has been highly influential. Among other albums are *Tupelo Honey* 1971, *Veedon Fleece* 1974, and *Avalon Sunset* 1989.

Morrissey stage name of Steven Patrick Morrissey 1959– . English rock singer and lyricist. He was a founder member of the rock group the Smiths 1982–87 and subsequently a solo artist. His lyrics reflect on everyday miseries or glumly celebrate the England of his childhood. Solo albums include *Viva Hate* 1987 and *Your Arsenal* 1992.

Morrissey The lyrics of English singer Morrissey have a melancholy social realism. He has drawn inspiration from English popular culture from music hall to 1960s soap opera. His self-deprecating humour and use of a natural vernacular in songwriting distinguished his work from the outset. *HMV*

Morse Samuel Finley Breese 1791–1872. US inventor. In 1835 he produced the first adequate electric telegraph (see ◊telegraphy), and in 1843 was granted $30,000 by Congress for an experimental line between Washington DC and Baltimore. With his assistant Alexander Bain (1810–1877) he invented the Morse code. *See illustration on following page.*

Morse code international code for transmitting messages by wire or radio using signals of short (dots) and long (dashes) duration, originated by US inventor Samuel Morse for use on his invention, the telegraph (see ◊telegraphy). The letters SOS (3 short, 3 long, 3 short) form the international distress signal, being distinctive and easily transmitted (popularly but erroneously save our souls). By radio telephone the distress call is 'Mayday', for similar reasons (popularly alleged to derive from French *m'aidez*, help me). *See illustration on following page.*

mortar method of projecting a bomb via a high trajectory at a target up to 6–7 km/3–4 mi away. A mortar bomb is stabilized in flight by means of tail

MOROCCO
Kingdom of

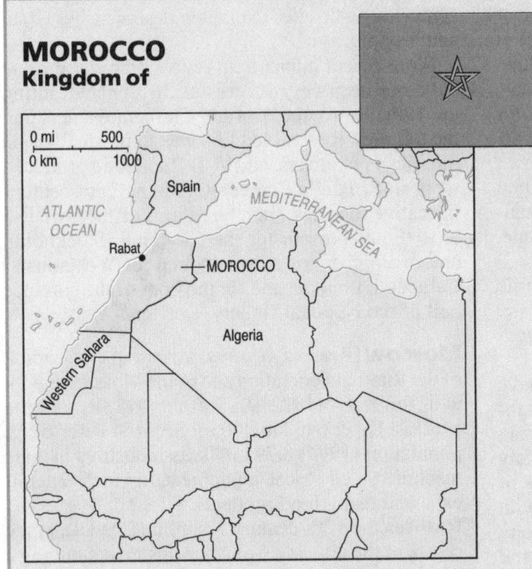

national name *al-Mamlaka al-Maghrebia*
area 458,730 sq km/177,070 sq mi (excluding Western Sahara)
capital Rabat
major towns/cities Marrakesh, Fez, Meknès
major ports Casablanca, Tangier, Agadir
physical features mountain ranges, including the Atlas Mountains NE–SW; fertile coastal plains in W
head of state Hassan II from 1961
head of government Abderrahmane Yousoufi from 1998
political system constitutional monarchy
administrative divisions 49 provinces and prefectures with seven economic regions
political parties Constitutional Union (UC), right-wing; National Rally of Independents (RNI), royalist; Popular Movement (MP), moderate, centrist; Istiqlal, nationalist, centrist; Socialist Union of Popular Forces (USFP), progressive socialist; National Democratic Party (PND), moderate, nationalist
armed forces 195,500; paramilitary forces of 42,000 (1994)
conscription 18 months
defence spend (% GDP) 4.3 (1994)
education spend (% GNP) 5.8 (1992)
health spend (% GDP) 0.9 (1990)
death penalty retained and used for ordinary crimes
population 27,021,000 (1996 est)
population growth rate 2.1% (1990–95); 1.6% (2000–05)
age distribution (% of total population) <15 36.1%, 15–65 59.8%, >65 4.1% (1995)
ethnic distribution majority indigenous Berbers; sizeable Jewish minority
population density (per sq km) 59 (1994)
urban population (% of total) 48 (1995)
labour force 38% of population: 45% agriculture, 25% industry, 31% services (1990)
unemployment 16% (1994)
child mortality rate (under 5, per 1,000 live births) 56 (1994)
life expectancy 62 (men), 65 (women)
education (compulsory years) 6
literacy rate 61% (men), 38% (women)
languages Arabic (official) 75%, Berber 25%, French, Spanish
religion Sunni Muslim
TV sets (per 1,000 people) 74 (1992)
currency dirham (DH)
GDP (US $) 30.8 billion (1994)
GDP per capita (PPP) (US $) 3,270 (1993)
growth rate 11.8% (1994)
average annual inflation 5.1% (1994); 5.3% (1985–93)
major trading partners France, Spain, USA, Japan, UK, Italy, Iran
resources phosphate rock and phosphoric acid, coal, iron ore, barytes, lead, copper, manganese, zinc, petroleum, natural gas, fish
industries phosphate products (chiefly fertilizers), petroleum refinery, food processing, textiles, clothing, leather goods, paper and paper products, tourism
exports phosphates and phosphoric acid, mineral products, seafoods and seafood products, citrus fruit, tobacco, clothing, hosiery. Principal market: France 33.2% (1993)
imports crude petroleum, raw materials, wheat, chemicals, sawn wood, consumer goods. Principal source: France 23% (1993)
arable land 20.7%
agricultural products wheat, barley, sugar beet, citrus fruits, tomatoes, potatoes; fishing (chiefly seafoods)

HISTORY
10th–3rd Cs BC Phoenicians from Tyre settled along N coast.
1st C AD NW Africa became Roman province of Mauritania.
5th–6th Cs Invaded by Vandals and Visigoths.
682 Start of Arab conquest, followed by spread of Islam.
8th C King Idris I established small Arab kingdom.
1056–1146 Empire embracing Morocco and parts of Algeria and Spain created by Almoravids, a Berber dynasty based at Marrakesh.
1122–1268 After a civil war, the Almohads, a rival Berber dynasty, overthrew the Almoravids; Almohads extended empire but later lost most of Spain.
1258–1358 Beni Merin dynasty supplanted Almohads.
14th C Moroccan Empire fragmented into separate kingdoms, based in Fez and Marrakesh.
15th C Spain and Portugal occupied Moroccan ports; expulsion of Muslims from Spain 1492.
16th C Saadian dynasty restored unity of Morocco and resisted Turkish invasion.
1649 Foundation of current Alaouite dynasty of sultans; Morocco remained independent and isolated kingdom.
1856 Under British pressure, sultan opened Morocco to European commerce.
1860 Spain invaded Morocco, which was forced to cede the SW region of Ifni.
1905 Major international crisis caused by German objections to increasing French influence in Morocco.
1911 Agadir Crisis: further German objections to French imperialism in Morocco overcome by territorial compensation in central Africa.
1912 Morocco divided into French and Spanish protectorates; sultan reduced to puppet ruler.
1921 Moroccan rebels, the Riffs, led by Abd el-Krim, defeated large Spanish force at Anual.
1923 City of Tangier separated from Spanish Morocco and made a neutral international zone.
1926 French forces crushed Riff revolt.
1944 Nationalist party, Istiqlal, founded to campaign for full independence.
1948 Consultative assemblies introduced.
1953–55 Serious anti-French riots.
1956 French and Spanish forces withdrew; Morocco regained effective independence under Sultan Muhammad V, who took title of king 1957.
1961 Muhammad V succeeded by Hassan II.
1962 First constitution adopted; replaced 1970 and 1972.
1965–77 King Hassan suspended constitution and ruled by decree.
1969 Spanish overseas province of Ifni returned to Morocco.
1975 Spain withdrew from Western Sahara, leaving Morocco and Mauritania to divide it between themselves.
1976 Polisario Front, supported by Algeria, began guerrilla war in Western Sahara with aim of securing its independence as Sahrahwi Arab Democratic Republic.
1979 Mauritania withdrew from its portion of Western Sahara, which Morocco annexed after major battles with Polisario.
1984 Morocco signed a mutual defence with Libya, which had previously supported Polisario.
1991 UN-sponsored cease-fire came into effect in Western Sahara.
1992 Constitution amended in attempt to increase influence of parliament.
1994 Abd-al Latif Filali became prime minister.
1996 New two-chamber assembly approved.
1997 Assembly elections proved inconclusive.
1998 Prime Minister Abderrahmane Yousoufi formed centre-left coalition.

SEE ALSO Almoravid; Western Sahara

Morse US artist and inventor Samuel Morse, shown next to a printing telegraph. Backed by $30,000 from Congress, Morse erected the first telegraph line between Baltimore and Washington and sent the first message on 11 May 1844. His invention was such a success that within four years of Morse's first public demonstration, America had five thousand miles of telegraph wire. *Ann Ronan/Image Select (UK) Ltd*

fins. The high trajectory results in a high angle of attack and makes mortars more suitable than artillery for use in built-up areas or mountains; mortars are not as accurate, however.

mortgage transfer of property, usually a house, as a security for repayment of a loan. The loan is normally repaid to a bank or building society over a period of years. Mortgage debt in the UK 1995 amounted to £370 billion.

Morse code

A	B	C	D	E	F
.-	-...	-.-.	-..	.	..-.
G	**H**	**I**	**J**	**K**	**L**
--.	....	..	.---	-.-	.-..
M	**N**	**O**	**P**	**Q**	**R**
--	-.	---	.--.	--.-	.-.
S	**T**	**U**	**V**	**W**	**X**
...	-	..-	...-	.--	-..-
		Y	**Z**		
		-.--	--..		
1	**2**	**3**	**4**	**5**	
.----	..---	...--	....-	.....	
6	**7**	**8**	**9**	**0**	
-....	--...	---..	----.	-----	

mortgage tax relief subsidy given to people who have taken out a mortgage. They are allowed to claim the interest on the mortgage as an income tax allowance. If the income tax rate is 25%, it effectively reduces interest on the loan by one-quarter. Mortgage tax relief provides an incentive for people to buy houses.

Mortimer John Clifford 1923– . English barrister and writer. His works include the plays *The Dock Brief* 1958 and *A Voyage Round My Father* 1970, the novel *Paradise Postponed* 1985, and the television series *Rumpole of the Bailey*, from 1978, centred on a fictional barrister.

Mortimer Roger de, 8th Baron of Wigmore and 1st Earl of March c. 1287–1330. English politician and adventurer. He opposed Edward II and with Edward's queen, Isabella, led a rebellion against him 1326, bringing about his abdication. From 1327 Mortimer ruled England as the queen's lover, until Edward III had him executed.

Morton Henry Vollam 1892–1979. English journalist and travel writer. He was the author of the *In Search of ...* series published during the 1950s. His earlier travel books include *The Heart of London* 1925, *In the Steps of the Master* 1934, *Through Lands of the Bible* 1938, and *Middle East* 1941. Later works include *This is Rome* 1960 and *H V Morton's England* 1975.

Morton Jelly Roll. Stage name of Ferdinand Joseph La Menthe Morton 1885–1941. US New Orleans-style jazz pianist, singer, and composer. Influenced by Scott Joplin, he was a pioneer in the development of jazz from ragtime to swing by improvising and imposing his own personality on the music. His 1920s band was called the Red Hot Peppers.

mosaic design or picture, usually for a floor or wall, produced by setting small pieces (*tesserae*) of marble, glass, or other materials in a cement ground. The ancient Greeks were the first to use large-scale mosaic (in the Macedonian royal palace at Pella, for example). Mosaic was commonly used by the Romans for their baths and villas (a well-known example being at Hadrian's Villa in Tivoli) and reached its highest development in the early Byzantine period (for example,in the church of S Vitale, Ravenna).

earliest forms Mosaic was used in Mesopotamia and Ancient Egypt for ornament on a small scale. Jewellery and movable objects, such as the *Standard* of Ur (British Museum), are examples.

Roman Mosaic pavement, which seems to have originated with the ancient Greeks, reached its highest development among the Romans. Roman mosaic varies from the formal pattern to elaborately pictorial effect. Famous examples are the doves of Pliny at Hadrian's villa, Tivoli, represented with great delicacy of colouring, and the mosaic copy from Pompeii of the battle between Alexander and Darius, after the painter Philoxenos. In Britain, mosaic floors often survive on the sites of Roman villas.

Byzantine In the Byzantine period, mosaic in the form of coloured and gilded glass was impressively used for mural decoration on a large scale. The richness of gold leaf, calculated irregularities of surface, and the juxtaposition of different colours are combined with a great simplicity of form. Mosaic remained the dominant form of mural 'painting' until the rise of fresco in Italy.

In Rome the early Christian mosaics in the churches of Sta Costanza 4th Century and Sta Maria Maggiore 4th–5th centuries are the first great examples of religious composition. In Ravenna there are the famous masterpieces of the church of S Vitale 6th century representing the Emperor Justinian, the Empress Theodora, and their attendants. Other masterpieces at Ravenna are Sant' Apollinare Nuovo and the tomb of Galla Placidia. In the cathedral of Torcello, near Venice, there are mosaics dating from the 12th century.

Other important examples are the mosaics found in Istanbul (Constantinople) in the cathedral of Sta Sophia (now Hagia Sophia) 6th century, and the church of Kariye Camii 13th century. In Greece there are mosaics in the church of S Demetrios, Salonika 7th century; in the church of Daphni (between Athens and Eleusis) 11th century; and, near Athens, at Hosias Lukas 11th century. In Kiev in Russia there are important mosaics dating from the 11th century.

Byzantine artists worked in many centres, not only in Greece and Italy, but also in Palermo and Monreale in Sicily (which saw a great flowering of mosaic painting in the 12th century), Cologne, Cordova, Jerusalem and Damascus.

later mosaics In modern times the art of mosaic seems to have been well preserved only in Venice. There both Byzantine tradition and later developments are represented in St Mark's Cathedral, which has a sequence of work from the 12th to 18th centuries, with later examples designed by Titian and Tiepolo.

More recent attempts to revive pictorial mosaic have not been very successful. In England during the 19th century the Arts and Crafts movement and the ◊Gothic Revival led to some some small-scale mosaics in churches, and W B Richmond produced work in St Paul's Cathedral. Among 20th-century figurative mosaics, there are those of the Swedish artist Einar Forseth for the City Hall, Stockholm, and of English artist Boris Anrep for Westminster Cathedral, London, and for the floor of the entrance hall of the National Gallery, London.

mosaic A Roman mosaic of a charioteer, at Trier. The Romans frequently used mosaic in their baths and villas. *Philip Sauvain*

Moscow (Russian ***Moskva***) industrial city, capital of the Russian Federation and of the Moskva region, and formerly (1922–91) of the USSR, on the Moskva River 640 km/400 mi SE of St Petersburg; population (1994) 8,793,000. Its industries include machinery, electrical equipment, textiles, chemicals, and many food products

features the 12th-century Kremlin (Citadel), at the centre of the city, is a walled enclosure containing a number of historic buildings, including three cathedrals, one of them the burial place of the tsars; the Ivan Veliki tower, a 90 m/300 ft bell tower with two golden domes, commissioned by Boris Godunov to provide work during the great famine 1600; various palaces, including the former imperial palace; museums; and the Tsar Kolokol, the world's largest bell (200 tonnes) 1735. The walls of the Kremlin are crowned by 18 towers and have five gates. Red Square, used for political demonstrations and processions, contains St Basil's Cathedral, the state department store GUM, and Lenin's tomb. The former headquarters of the former ◊KGB, with Lubyanka Prison behind it, is in Dzerzhinsky Square; the underground railway was opened 1935.

The former Russian parliament building, made of white marble and known as the 'White House', was built in 1981 as the headquarters of the Russian Republic. It is on the Moskva River, near the Kutuzovsky Bridge. The building was under siege for two weeks 1993 following the dissolution of parliament by President Yeltsin. The Russian parliament, now known as the State Duma, moved 1994 to the former headquarters of Gos-Plan, the central planning agency of the former USSR.

Institutions include Moscow University 1755 and People's Friendship University (for foreign students) 1953; the Academy of Sciences, which moved from Leningrad (now St Petersburg) 1934; Tretyakov Gallery of Russian Art 1856; Moscow State Circus. Moscow is the seat of the patriarch of the Russian Orthodox church. On the city outskirts is Star City (Zvezdnoy Gorodok), the space centre. Moscow is the largest industrial centre of the Commonwealth of Independent States, linked with Stavropol by oil pipeline 480 km/300 mi, built 1957.

history Moscow, founded as the city-state of Muscovy 1127, was destroyed by the Mongols during the 13th century, but rebuilt 1294 by Prince Daniel (died 1303) as the capital of his principality. During the 14th century, it was under the rule of ◊Alexander Nevski, Ivan I (1304–1341), and Dmitri Donskai (1350–1389) , and became the foremost political power in Russia, and its religious capital. It was burned 1571 by the khan of the Crimea, and ravaged by fire 1739, 1748, and 1753; in 1812 it was burned by its own citizens to save it from Napoleon's troops, or perhaps by accident.

It became capital of the Russian Soviet Federated Social Republic (RSFSR) 1918, and of the Union of Soviet Socialist Republics (USSR) 1922. In World War II Hitler's troops were within 30 km/20 mi of Moscow on the northwest by Nov 1941, but the stubborn Russian defence and severe winter weather forced their withdrawal in Dec.

In 1993 it was the scene of an armed uprising led by parliamentary leaders opposed to the constitutional reforms of Russia's president, Boris Yeltsin; after several days of rioting, during which the coup leaders barricaded themselves within the Russian parliament building, order was restored by troops loyal to the president.

Moselle or ***Mosel*** river in W Europe some 515 km/320 mi long; it rises in the Vosges Mountains, France, and is canalized from Thionville to its confluence with the ◊Rhine at Koblenz in Germany. It gives its name to the *départements* of Moselle and Meurthe-et-Moselle in France. Vineyards along the Moselle in Germany produce popular white wines.

Moses lived c. 13th century BC. Hebrew lawgiver and judge who led the Israelites out of Egypt to the promised land of Canaan. On Mount Sinai he claimed to have received from Jehovah the oral and written Law, including the Ten Commandments engraved on tablets of stone. The first five books of the Old Testament – in Judaism, the *Torah* – are ascribed to him.

According to the Torah, the infant Moses was hidden among the bulrushes on the banks of the Nile when the pharaoh commanded that all newborn male Hebrew children should be destroyed. He was found by a daughter of Pharaoh, who reared him. Eventually he became the leader of the Israelites in their Exodus from Egypt and their 40 years' wandering in the wilderness. He died at the age of 120, after having been allowed a glimpse of the Promised Land from Mount Pisgah.

Moses 'Grandma' (born Anna Mary Robertson) 1860–1961. US painter. She was self-taught, and painted naive and colourful scenes from rural American life. Her first solo exhibition 'What a Farmwife Painted' was held in New York 1940.

Moses Ed(win Corley) 1955– . US track athlete and 400 metres hurdler. Between 1977 and 1987 he ran 122 races without defeat. He first broke the world record in 1976, and set a time of 47.02 seconds 1983. He was twice Olympic champion and twice world champion.

Moslem alternative spelling of ***Muslim***, a follower of ◊Islam.

Mosley Oswald (Ernald) 1896–1980. British politician, founder of the British Union of Fascists (BUF) 1932. He was a member of Parliament 1918–31, then led the BUF until his internment 1940–43 during World War II. In 1946 Mosley was denounced when it became known that Italy had funded his prewar efforts to establish ◊fascism in Britain, but in 1948 he resumed fascist propaganda with his Union Movement, the revived BUF.

mosque (Arabic *mesjid*) in Islam, a place of worship. Chief features are: the dome; the minaret, a balconied turret from which the faithful are called to prayer; the *mihrab*, or prayer niche, in one of the interior walls, showing the direction of the holy city of Mecca; and an open court surrounded by porticoes. The earliest mosques were based on the plan of Christian basilicas, although different influences contributed towards their architectural development (see ◊Islamic architecture). Mosques vary a great deal in style in various parts of the world.

mosquito any fly of the family Culicidae. The female mosquito has needlelike mouthparts and sucks blood before laying eggs. Males feed on plant juices. Some mosquitoes carry diseases such as ◊malaria. Human odour in general is attractive to mosquitos, also lactic acid in sweat and heat at close range. Natural mosquito repellents include lavender oil, citronella (from lemon grass), thyme, and eucalyptus oils.

Mosquito Coast Caribbean coast of Honduras and Nicaragua, characterized by swamp, lagoons, and tropical rainforest. The territory is inhabited by Miskito Indians, Garifunas, and Zambos, many of whom speak English. Between 1823 and 1860 Britain maintained a protectorate over the Mosquito Coast which was ruled by a succession of 'Mosquito Kings'.

moss small nonflowering plant of the class Musci (10,000 species), forming with the ◊liverworts and the ◊hornworts the order Bryophyta. The stem of each plant bears ◊rhizoids that anchor it; there are no true roots. Leaves spirally arranged on its lower portion have sexual organs at their tips. Most mosses flourish best in damp conditions where other vegetation is thin.

Moss Stirling 1929– . English racing-car driver. Despite being one of the best-known names in British motor racing, Moss never won the world championship. He was runner-up on four occasions, losing to Juan Manuel Fangio (1911–1995) in 1955, 1956, and 1957, and to fellow Briton Mike Hawthorn (1929–1959) in 1958. A bad accident at Goodwood in 1962 ended his career but he maintained contact with the sport and in recent years has taken part in sports-car races.

Mössbauer effect the recoil-free emission of gamma rays from atomic nuclei under certain conditions. The effect was discovered 1958 by German physicist Rudolf Mössbauer (1929–), for which he shared the 1961 Nobel Prize for Physics. It was used 1960 to provide the first laboratory test of Einstein's general theory of relativity.

The absorption and subsequent re-emission of a gamma ray by an atomic nucleus usually causes it to recoil, so affecting the wavelength of the emitted ray. Mössbauer found that at low temperatures, crystals will absorb gamma rays of a specific wavelength and resonate so that the crystal as a whole recoils while individual nuclei do not. The wavelength of the re-emitted gamma rays is therefore virtually unaltered by recoil and may be measured to a high degree of accuracy. Changes in the wavelength may therefore be studied as evidence of the effect of, say, neighbouring electrons or gravity. For example, the effect provided the first verification of the general theory of relativity by showing that gamma-ray wavelengths become longer in a gravitational field, as predicted by Einstein.

Mossi the majority ethnic group living in Burkina Faso. Their social structure, based on a monarchy and aristocracy, was established during the 13th–14th centuries. The Mossi have been prominent traders, using cowrie shells as currency. There are about 4 million speakers of Mossi, a language belonging to the Gur branch of the Niger–Congo family.

Mostar industrial town (aluminium, tobacco) in Bosnia-Herzegovina, known for its grapes and wines; population (1991) 126,000. The eastern, mainly Muslim sector of the town was under siege by Bosnian Croat forces 1993–94.

motet sacred, polyphonic music for unaccompanied voices in a form that originated in 13th-century Europe.

moth any of the various families of mainly night-flying insects of the order Lepidoptera, which also includes the butterflies. Their wings are covered with microscopic scales. The mouthparts are formed into a sucking proboscis, but certain moths have no functional mouthparts, and rely upon stores of fat and other reserves built up during the caterpillar stage. At least 100,000 different species of moth are known.

Moths feed chiefly on the nectar of flowers, and other fluid matter; some, like the hawk moths, frequent flowers and feed while hovering. The females of some species (such as bagworm moths) have wings either absent or reduced to minute flaps. Moths vary greatly in size. In many cases the males are smaller and more brightly coloured than the females.

The minute Nepticulidae sometimes have a wingspread less than 3 mm/0.1 in, while the giant Noctuid or owlet moth *Erebus agrippina* measures about 280 mm/11 in across. The largest British moths are the death's head and convolvulus hawk moths, which have a wingspread ranging from 114 mm/4.5 in to 133 mm/5.25 in.

motherboard ◊printed circuit board that contains the main components of a microcomputer.

moth Not all moths are night-flying. The burnet moths (family Zygaenidae), such as this *Zygaena praslini* from Israel, are active exclusively by day when they can exhibit their aposematic (warning) colours. *Premaphotos Wildlife*

Moses Moses before the burning bush. The story is told in the Old Testament book of Exodus that Moses saw a bush that was on fire but did not burn up. God spoke to Moses from the bush and told him to lead the Israelites out of Egypt. *Corbis*

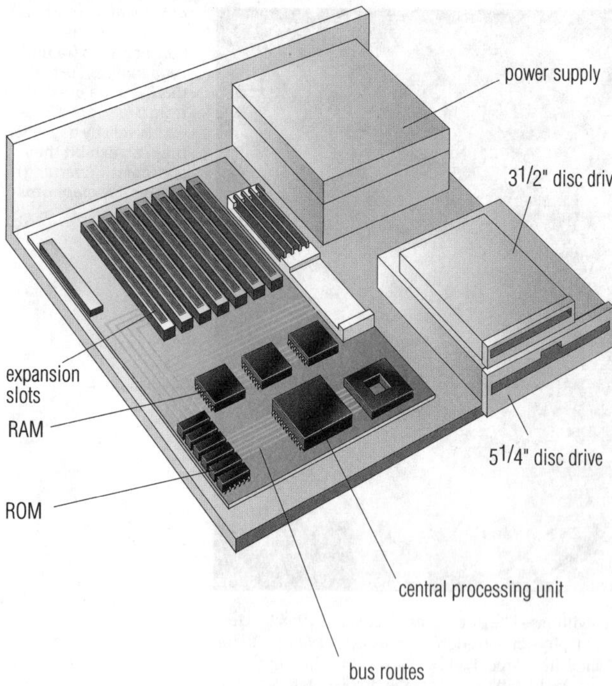

motherboard The position of a motherboard within a computer's system unit. The motherboard contains the central processing unit, Random Access Memory (RAM) chips, Read Only Memory (ROM), and a number of expansion slots.

mother-of-pearl or ***nacre*** the smooth lustrous lining in the shells of certain molluscs – for example pearl oysters, abalones, and mussels. It is used commercially for jewellery and decorations. Mother-of-pearl consists of calcium carbonate. See ◊pearl.

Mother's Day day set apart in the USA, UK, and many European countries for honouring mothers. It is thought to have originated in Grafton, West Virginia, USA, in 1908 when Anna Jarvis observed the anniversary of her mother's death. In the UK it is known as Mothering Sunday and observed on the fourth Sunday of Lent; in the USA, Australia, and Canada, on the second Sunday in May.

Motherwell Robert Burns 1915–1991. US painter. He was associated with the New York school of ◊action painting. Borrowing from Picasso, Matisse, and the Surrealists, Motherwell's style of Abstract Expressionism retained some suggestion of the figurative. His works include the *Elegies to the Spanish Republic* 1949–76, a series of over 100 paintings devoted to the Spanish Civil War.

Motherwell and Wishaw industrial town and administrative headquarters of North Lanarkshire, Scotland, SE of Glasgow; population (1991) 60,500. The two burghs were amalgamated 1920. Formerly a coal-mining town, its industries include iron and engineering, although the Ravenscraig iron and steel works closed 1992.

motility the ability to move spontaneously. The term is often restricted to those cells that are capable of independent locomotion, such as spermatozoa. Many single-celled organisms are motile, for example, the amoeba.

motorcycle racing Motorcycle racing in the World Superbikes Championships. The most famous motorcycle contests are the Tourist Trophy races, which have been held on the Isle of Man each June since 1907. *Image Select (UK) Ltd*

motion picture US term for film; see ◊cinema.

motor anything that produces or imparts motion; a machine that provides mechanical power – for example, an ◊electric motor. Machines that burn fuel (petrol, diesel) are usually called engines, but the internal-combustion engine that propels vehicles has long been called a motor, hence 'motoring' and 'motorcar'. Actually the motor is a part of the car engine.

motorboat small, waterborne craft for pleasure cruising or racing, powered by a petrol, diesel, or gas-turbine engine. A boat not equipped as a motorboat may be converted by a detachable outboard motor. For increased speed, such as in racing, motorboat hulls are designed to skim the water (aquaplane) and reduce frictional resistance. Plastics, steel, and light alloys are now used in construction as well as the traditional wood.

In recent designs, drag is further reduced with hydrofins and ◊hydrofoils, which enable the hull to rise clear of the water at normal speeds. Notable events in motorboat or 'powerboat' racing include the American Gold Cup 1947 (over a 145 km/90 mi course) and the Round-Britain race 1969.

motorcar another term for ◊car.

motorcycle or ***motorbike*** two-wheeled vehicle propelled by a ◊petrol engine. The first successful motorized bicycle was built in France 1901, and British and US manufacturers first produced motorbikes 1903.

In 1868 Ernest and Pierre Michaux in France experimented with a steam-powered bicycle, but the steam power unit was too heavy and cumbersome. Gottlieb ◊Daimler, a German engineer, created the first motorcycle when he installed his lightweight petrol engine in a bicycle frame 1885. Daimler soon lost interest in two wheels in favour of four and went on to pioneer the ◊car.

The first really successful two-wheel design was devised by Michael and Eugene Werner in France 1901. They adopted the classic motorcycle layout with the engine low down between the wheels. Harley Davidson in the USA and Triumph in the UK began manufacture 1903. Road races like the Isle of Man TT (Tourist Trophy), established 1907, helped improve motorcycle design and it soon evolved into more or less its present form.

Until the 1970s British manufacturers predominated but today Japanese motorcycles, such as Honda, Kawasaki, Suzuki, and Yamaha, dominate the world market. They make a wide variety of machines, from ◊mopeds (lightweights with pedal assistance) to streamlined superbikes capable of speeds up to 250 kph/160 mph. There is still a smaller but thriving Italian motorcycle industry, making more specialist bikes. Laverda, Moto Guzzi, and Ducati continue to manufacture in Italy.

The lightweight bikes are generally powered by a two-stroke petrol engine (see ◊two-stroke cycle), while bikes with an engine capacity of 250 cc or more are generally four-strokes (see ◊four-stroke cycle). However, many special-use larger bikes (such as those developed for off-road riding and racing) are two-stroke. Most motorcycles are air-cooled – their engines are surrounded by metal fins to offer a large surface area – although some have a water-cooling system similar to that of a car. Most small bikes have single-cylinder engines, but larger machines can have as many as six. The single-cylinder engine is economical and was popular in British manufacture, then the Japanese developed multiple-cylinder models, but there has recently been some return to single-cylinder engines. In the majority of bikes a chain carries the drive from the engine to the rear wheel, though some machines are now fitted with shaft drive.

motorcycle racing speed contests on motorcycles. It has many different forms: ***road racing*** over open roads; ***circuit racing*** over purpose-built tracks; ***speedway*** over oval-shaped dirt tracks; ***motocross*** over natural terrain, incorporating hill climbs; and ***trials***, also over natural terrain, but with the addition of artificial hazards.

For finely tuned production machines, there exists a season-long world championship Grand Prix series with various categories for machines with engine sizes 125 cc–500 cc. Major events are the world championship, which has been in existence since 1949 (the ◊blue riband event is the 500 cc class), and the Isle of Man Tourist Trophy, the principal race of which is the Senior TT. The first motorcycle race was in Richmond, Surrey in 1897. The Isle of Man TT races were inaugurated in 1907 and are held over the island's roads.

motor effect tendency of a wire carrying an electric current in a magnetic field to move. This effect is used in the ◊electric motor. It also explains why streams of electrons produced, for instance, in a television tube can be directed by electromagnets.

motoring law law affecting the use of vehicles on public roads. It covers the licensing of vehicles and drivers, and the criminal offences that can be committed by the owners and drivers of vehicles.

In Britain, all vehicles are subject to road tax and (when over a certain age) to an annual safety check (MOT test). Anyone driving on a public road must have a valid driving licence for that kind of vehicle. There is a wide range of offences: from parking in the wrong place to causing death by dangerous driving. Offences are punishable by fixed penalties: fines; endorsement of the offender's driving licence; disqualification from driving for a period; or imprisonment, depending on the seriousness of the offence. Courts must disqualify drivers convicted of driving while affected by alcohol. Licence endorsements carry penalty points (the number depending on the seriousness of the offence) which are totted up. Once a driver acquires more than 12 points, the court must disqualify him or her from driving.

motor nerve in anatomy, any nerve that transmits impulses from the central nervous system to muscles or organs. Motor nerves cause voluntary and involuntary muscle contractions, and stimulate glands to secrete hormones.

motor neurone disease or ***amyotrophic lateral sclerosis*** chronic disease in which there is progressive degeneration of the nerve cells which instigate movement. It leads to weakness, wasting, and loss of muscle function and usually proves fatal within two to three years of onset. Motor neurone disease occurs in both hereditary and sporadic forms but its causes remain unclear. In Britain some 1,200 new cases are diagnosed each year.

motor racing competitive racing of motor vehicles. It has forms as diverse as hill-climbing, stock-car racing, rallying, sports-car racing, and Formula One Grand Prix racing. The first organized race was from Paris to Rouen 1894.

Purpose-built circuits include: Brands Hatch, Brooklands (to 1939), Donington, Silverstone, UK; Hockenheim, Nurburgring, Germany; Monza, Imola, Italy; Indianapolis, USA; Interlagos, Brazil. Street circuits include Detroit, USA, and Monte Carlo, Monaco. In Grand Prix racing (instituted 1906) a world championship for drivers has been in existence since 1950, and for constructors since 1958. The first six drivers and cars in each race are awarded points from ten to one, and the cumulative total at the end of a season (normally 16 races) decides the winners. Other leading events apart from the world championship are the ◊Le Mans Grand Prix d'Endurance, first held 1923, and the Indianapolis 500, first held 1911.

Rally-driving events include the Monte Carlo Rally, the Acropolis Rally, and the Lombard–RAC Rally (formerly the RAC International Rally of Great Britain), first held 1927. Road races such as the *Targa Florio* and *Mille Miglia* were tests of a driver's skill and a machine's durability in the 1920s, 1930s, and 1950s, until they were judged to be too dangerous to be held on public roads.

Specialist makes of car include Bugatti, BRM, Mercedes-Benz, Alfa Romeo, Auto Union, Ferrari, Porsche, Lotus, Brabham, Williams, and McLaren. There are also races for modified mass-produced cars; time-checked events, often across continents, are popular, the toughest being the Safari Rally, run every Easter. *See list of tables on p. 1177.*

motorway main road for fast motor traffic, with two or more lanes in each direction, and with special access points (junctions) fed by slip roads. The first motorway (85 km/53 mi) ran from Milan to Varese, Italy, and was completed 1924; by 1939 some 500 km/300 mi of motorway (*autostrada*) had been built. In Germany some 2,100 km/1,310 mi of *Autobahnen* had been completed by 1942. After World War II motorways were built in a growing number of countries, for example the USA, France, and the UK. The most ambitious building programme was in the USA, which by 1974 had 70,800 km/44,000 mi of 'expressway'.

The first motorway in the UK, the Preston bypass (now part of the M6) was opened 1958, and the first section of the M1 was opened 1959.

Motown first black-owned US record company, founded in Detroit (Mo(tor) Town) 1959 by Berry Gordy, Jr (1929–). Its distinctive, upbeat sound (exemplified by the Four Tops and the ◊Supremes) was a major element in 1960s pop music. The Motown sound was created by in-house producers and songwriters such as Smokey Robinson and the team of Holland–Dozier–Holland; performers included Stevie Wonder, Marvin Gaye, and the Temptations. Its influence faded after the company's move to Los Angeles 1971, but it still served as a breeding ground for such singers as Lionel Richie (1950–) and Michael Jackson. Gordy sold Motown to the larger MCA company 1988.

mouflon sheep *Ovis ammon* found wild in mountain areas of Cyprus, Corsica, and Sardinia. It has woolly underfur in winter, but this is covered by heavy guard hairs. The coat is brown with white belly and rump. Males have strong, curving horns.

mould mainly saprophytic fungi (see ◊fungus) living on foodstuffs and other organic matter, a few being parasitic on plants, animals, or each other. Many moulds are of medical or industrial importance; for example, penicillin.

moulding use of a pattern, hollow form, or matrix to give a specific shape to something in a plastic or molten state. It is commonly used for shaping plastics, clays, and glass. When metals are used, the process is called ◊casting.

In ***injection moulding***, molten plastic, for example, is injected into a water-cooled mould and takes the shape of the mould when it solidifies. In ***blow moulding***, air is blown into a blob of molten plastic inside a hollow mould. In ***compression moulding***, synthetic resin powder is simultaneously heated and pressed into a mould.

Moulins capital of the *département* of Allier, Auvergne, central France; main industries are cutlery, textiles, and glass; population (1990) 23,400. Moulins was capital of the old province of Bourbonnais 1368–1527.

moulting periodic shedding of the hair or fur of mammals, feathers of birds, or skin of reptiles. In mammals and birds, moulting is usually seasonal and is triggered by changes of day length. The term is also often applied to the shedding of the ◊exoskeleton of arthropods, but this is more correctly called ecdysis.

Moundbuilder member of any of the various Native American peoples of the Midwest and the South who built earth mounds, from about 300 BC. Some mounds were linear and pictographic in form, such as the Great Serpent Mound in Ohio, with truncated pyramids and cones for the platforms of chiefs' houses and temples. The ◊Hopewell and ◊Natchez were Moundbuilders. The Moundbuilders were in decline by the time of the Spanish invasion, but traces of their culture live on in the folklore of the Choctaw and ◊Cherokee Indians.

mountain natural upward projection of the Earth's surface, higher and steeper than a hill. The process of mountain building (orogeny) consists of volcanism, folding, faulting, and thrusting, resulting from the collision and welding together of two tectonic plates (see ◊plate tectonics). This process deforms the rock and compresses it between the two plates into mountain chains.

mountain ash or ***rowan*** flowering tree *Sorbus aucuparia* of the family Rosaceae. It grows to 15 m/50 ft and has pinnate leaves and large clusters of whitish flowers, followed by scarlet berries.

mountain ash The mountain ash, or rowan, is native to Europe and W Asia. The tree has divided leaves with small toothed leaflets and red berries and grows to a height of 18 m/60 ft.

mountain biking recreational sport that enjoyed increasing popularity in the 1990s. Mountain bikes were developed from the rugged 'clunkers' ridden by a small group of off-road riders on the steep, rocky hillsides of Marin County, California, in the mid-1970s. The fashion spread and the first mass-produced model appeared in the USA 1981, and in the UK 1984. Sometimes known as all-terrain bikes, or ATBs, mountain bikes have toughened frames with high ground clearance; wide tyres with a knobbly tread; wide, flat handlebars; powerful brakes (usually cantilevered); and a wide range of gears (typically 18 or 21).

National mountain-bike championships have been held in the USA since 1983 and in the UK since 1984. The first world championship was held in France 1987. The sport was included as an Olympic event for the first time at Atlanta 1996.

mountaineering art and practice of mountain climbing. For major peaks of the Himalayas it was formerly thought necessary to have elaborate support from Sherpas (local people), fixed ropes, and oxygen at high altitudes (siege-style climbing). In the 1980s the Alpine style was introduced. This dispenses with these aids, and relies on human ability to adapt, Sherpa-style, to high altitude.

In 1854 Wetterhorn, Switzerland, was climbed by Alfred Wills, thereby founding the sport; 1865 Matterhorn, Switzerland–Italy, by Edward ◊Whymper; 1897 Aconcagua, Argentina, by Zurbriggen; 1938 Eiger (north face), Switzerland, by Heinrich Harrer; 1953 Everest, Nepal–Tibet, by Edmund ◊Hillary and Norgay ◊Tenzing; 1981 Kongur, China, by Chris ◊Bonington.

mountain gorilla highly endangered ape subspecies *Gorilla gorilla beringei* found in bamboo and rainforest on the Rwanda, Zaire, and Uganda borders in central Africa, with a total population of around 600 (1995). It is threatened by deforestation and illegal hunting for skins and the zoo trade.

mountain lion another name for ◊puma.

Mountbatten Louis Francis Albert Victor Nicholas, 1st Earl Mountbatten of Burma 1900–1979. British admiral and administrator. In World War II he became chief of combined operations 1942 and commander in chief in SE Asia 1943. As last viceroy and governor general of India 1947–48, he oversaw that country's transition to independence. He was killed by an Irish Republican Army bomb aboard his yacht in the Republic of Ireland.

As chief of combined operations 1942 he was criticized for the heavy loss of Allied lives in the disastrous Dieppe raid. In SE Asia he concentrated on the reconquest of Burma, although the campaign was actually conducted by General ◊Slim. Mountbatten accepted the surrender of 750,000 Japanese troops in his area of command at a formal parade in Singapore Sept 1945. He was chief of UK Defence Staff 1959–65.

'I can't think of a more wonderful thanksgiving for the life I have had than that everyone should be jolly at my funeral.'

LOUIS MOUNTBATTEN
Quoted in R Hough *Mountbatten*

Mounties popular name for the ***Royal Canadian Mounted Police***, known for their uniform of red jacket and broad-brimmed hat. Their Security Service, established 1950, was disbanded 1981 and replaced by the independent Canadian Security Intelligence Service.

Mount Palomar astronomical observatory, 80 km/50 mi NE of San Diego, California, USA. It has a 5-m/200-in diameter reflector called the Hale. Completed 1948, it was the world's premier observatory during the 1950s.

Mount Stromlo Observatory astronomical observatory established in Canberra, Australia, in 1923. Important observations have been made there on the Magellanic Clouds, which can be seen clearly from southern Australia.

Mount Wilson site near Los Angeles, California, of the 2.5 m/100 in Hooker telescope, opened 1917, with which Edwin Hubble discovered the expansion of the universe. Two solar telescopes in towers 18.3 m/60 ft and 45.7 m/150 ft tall, and a 1.5 m/60 in reflector opened 1908, also operate there.

mouse in zoology, one of a number of small rodents with small ears and a long, thin tail, belonging largely to the Old World family Muridae. The house mouse *Mus musculus* is distributed worldwide. It is 75 mm/3 in long, with a naked tail of equal length, and has a grey-brown body. Common in Britain is the wood mouse *Apodemus sylvaticus*, richer in colour, and normally shy of human habitation. The tiny harvest mouse *Micromys minutus*, 65–75 mm/2.5–3 in long, makes spherical nests of straw supported on grass stems.

mouse in computing, an input device used to control a pointer on a computer screen. It is a feature of ◊graphical user interface (GUI) systems. The mouse is about the size of a pack of playing cards, is connected to the computer by a wire, and incorporates one or more buttons that can be pressed. Moving the mouse across a flat surface causes a corresponding movement of the pointer. In this way, the operator can manipulate objects on the screen and make menu selections.

Mice work either mechanically (with electrical contacts to sense the movement in two planes of a ball on a level surface), or optically (photocells detecting movement by recording light reflected from a grid on which the mouse is moved).

mousebird bird of the order Coliiformes, including a single family (Coliidae) of small crested species peculiar to Africa. They have hairlike feathers, long tails, and mouselike agility.

Moustier, Le rock-shelter in the Dordogne, SW France, with prehistoric remains, giving the name ***Mousterian*** to the flint-tool culture of Neanderthal peoples (100,000–40,000 years ago); the earliest ritual burials are linked with Mousterian settlements.

mouth cavity forming the entrance to the digestive tract. In land vertebrates, air from the nostrils enters the mouth cavity to pass down the trachea. The mouth in mammals is enclosed by the jaws, cheeks, and palate.

mouth organ any of a family of small portable wind instruments originating in Eastern and South Asia. The compact ***harmonica***, or European mouth organ, developed by Charles Wheatstone 1829, has tuned metal free reeds of variable length contained in a narrow rectangular box and is played by blowing and sucking air while moving the instrument from side to side through the lips. As the ***mouth harp***, the mouth organ is a staple instrument in country and western music. As a melody instrument

MOUNTAIN: HIGHEST MOUNTAINS

Name	Height (m/ft)	Location
Everest	8,850/29,030	China–Nepal
K2	8,610/28,250	Kashmir–Jammu
Kangchenjunga	8,590/28,170	India–Nepal
Lhotse	8,500/27,890	China–Nepal
Kangchenjunga S Peak	8,470/27,800	India–Nepal
Makalu I	8,470/27,800	China–Nepal
Kangchenjunga W Peak	8,420/27,620	India–Nepal
Lhotse E Peak	8,380/27,500	China–Nepal
Dhaulagiri	8,170/26,810	Nepal
Cho Oyu	8,150/26,750	China–Nepal
Manaslu	8,130/26,660	Nepal
Nanga Parbat	8,130/26,660	Kashmir–Jammu
Annapurna I	8,080/26,500	Nepal
Gasherbrum I	8,070/26,470	Kashmir–Jammu
Broad-highest	8,050/26,400	Kashmir–Jammu
Gasherbrum II	8,030/26,360	Kashmir–Jammu
Gosainthan	8,010/26,290	China
Broad-middle	8,000/26,250	Kashmir–Jammu
Gasherbrum III	7,950/26,090	Kashmir–Jammu
Annapurna II	7,940/26,040	Nepal
Nanda Devi	7,820/25,660	India
Rakaposhi	7,790/25,560	Kashmir
Kamet	7,760/25,450	India
Ulugh Muztagh	7,720/25,340	Tibet
Tirich Mir	7,690/25,230	Pakistan

heights are given to the nearest 10 m

❛I thank God for graciously granting me the opportunity ... of learning that death is the key which unlocks the door to our true happiness.❜

WOLFGANG AMADEUS MOZART
Letter to his father
4 April 1787

it achieved concert status through the virtuosity of Larry Adler.

moving-coil meter instrument used to detect and measure electrical current. A coil of wire pivoted between the poles of a permanent magnet is turned by the motor effect of an electric current (by which a force acts on a wire carrying a current in a magnetic field). The extent to which the coil turns can then be related to the magnitude of the current.

Mowlam Mo (Marjorie) 1949– . British Labour politician, secretary of state for Northern Ireland from 1997. She joined Labour's shadow cabinet, covering Northern Ireland 1988–89, Trade and Industry 1989–92, the Citizen's Charter and Women's Affairs 1992–93, National Heritage 1993–94, and Northern Ireland again 1994–97. As secretary of state for Northern Ireland in 1997, she made an immediate impact on politics in the province, initiating a non-ministerial dialogue with Sinn Féin. Her willingness to 'take risks' to promote the peace process, including a January 1998 visit to convicted loyalist terrorists in Maze prison, helped bring about the 1998 Good Friday Agreement, paving the way for the election of a power-sharing Northern Ireland assembly.

Mozambique country in SE Africa, bounded N by Zambia, Malawi, and Tanzania; E and S by the Indian Ocean; SW by South Africa and Swaziland; and W by Zimbabwe. *See country box below.*

Mozart (Johann Chrysostom) Wolfgang Amadeus 1756–1791. Austrian composer and performer who showed astonishing precocity as a child and was an adult virtuoso. He was trained by his father, Leopold Mozart (1719–1787). From an early age he composed prolifically, his works including 27 piano concertos, 23 string quartets, 35 violin sonatas, and 41 symphonies including the E flat K543, G minor K550, and C major K551 ('Jupiter') symphonies, all composed 1788. His operas include *Idomeneo* 1780, *Entführung aus dem Serail/The Abduction from the Seraglio* 1782, *Le Nozze di Figaro/The Marriage of Figaro* 1786, *Don Giovanni* 1787, *Così fan tutte/Thus Do All Women* 1790, and *Die Zauberflöte/The Magic Flute* 1791. Together with Haydn, Mozart's music marks the height of the Classical age in its purity of melody and form.

Mozart's career began when, with his sister, Maria Anna, he was taken on a number of tours 1762–79, visiting Vienna, the Rhineland, Holland, Paris, London, and Italy. He had already begun to compose. In 1772 he was appointed master of the archbishop of Salzburg's court band but he found the post uncongenial and in 1781 was suddenly dismissed. He married Constanze Weber 1782, settled in Vienna, and embarked on a punishing freelance career as concert pianist, composer, and teacher that brought lasting fame but only intermittent financial security. His *Requiem*, unfinished at his death, was completed by a pupil.

His works were catalogued chronologically 1862 by the musicologist Ludwig von Köchel (1800–1877) whose system of numbering – giving each work a 'Köchel number', for example K354 – remains in use in modified form.

mp in chemistry, abbreviation for ***melting point***.

MP abbreviation for ***member of Parliament***.

mpg abbreviation for ***miles per gallon***.

mph abbreviation for ***miles per hour***.

Mphahlele Es'kia (Ezekiel) 1919– . South African literary critic, journalist, and novelist. He is best known for his influential autobiography *Down Second Avenue* 1959.

MPLA (abbreviation for ***Movimento Popular de Libertaçaõ de Angola***/Popular Movement for the Liberation of Angola) socialist organization founded in the early 1950s that sought to free Angola from Portuguese rule 1961–75 before being involved in the civil war against its former allies ◊UNITA and FNLA 1975–76. The MPLA gained control of the country 1976 and in 1977 renamed itself the People's Movement for the Liberation of Angola-Workers' Party (***MPLA-PT***). It won the first multiparty elections 1992, but UNITA disputed the result and guerrilla activity continued, escalating into full-scale civil war 1993. A peace agreement was signed with UNITA 1994.

Mpumalanga formerly ***Eastern Transvaal*** province of the Republic of South Africa from 1994, formerly part of Transvaal province
area 81,816 sq km/31,589 sq mi
capital Nelspruit
features Limpopo River, Vaal River
industries farming, coal
population (1995 est) 3,007,100
languages Siswati 40%, Zulu 28%, Afrikaans 9%.

MRBM abbreviation for ***medium-range ballistic missile***.

MSc in education, abbreviation for the degree of ***Master of Science***.

MS-DOS (abbreviation for ***Microsoft Disc Operating System***) computer ◊operating system produced by Microsoft Corporation, widely used on ◊microcomputers with Intel x 86 and Pentium family microprocessors. A version called PC-DOS is sold by IBM specifically for its personal computers. MS-DOS and PC-DOS are usually referred to as DOS. MS-DOS first appeared 1981.

MS(S) abbreviation for ***manuscript(s)***.

MU in economics, abbreviation for ***monetary unit***.

Mubarak Hosni 1928– . Egyptian politician, president from 1981. Vice president to Anwar Sadat from 1975, Mubarak succeeded him on his assassination. He has continued to pursue Sadat's moderate policies, and has significantly increased the freedom of the press and of political association, while trying to repress the growing Islamic fundamentalist movement. He was re-elected (uncontested) 1987 and 1993. He survived an assassination attempt 1995. He played a part in arranging the Middle East peace conference Nov 1991.

Mucha Alphonse Maria 1860–1939. Czech painter and designer, one of the leading figures of ◊Art Nouveau. His posters and decorative panels brought him international fame, presenting idealized images of young women with long, flowing hair, within a patterned flowered border. His early theatre posters were done for the actress Sarah Bernhardt, notably the lithograph *Gismonda* 1894. He also designed textiles, furniture, ceramic plaques, and exhibition displays, and in 1900–01 a jewellery boutique for Georges Fouquet in Paris (now demolished).

MOZAMBIQUE
People's Republic of

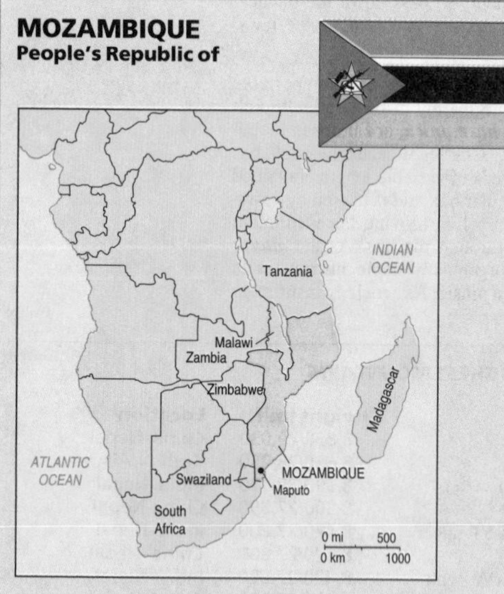

national name *República Popular de Moçambique*
area 799,380 sq km/308,561 sq mi
capital (and chief port) Maputo
major towns/cities Nampula
major ports Beira, Nacala, Quelimane
physical features mostly flat tropical lowland; mountains in W; rivers Zambezi and Limpopo
head of state Joaquim Alberto Chissano from 1986
head of government Pascoal Mocumbi from 1994
political system emergent democratic republic
administrative divisions 11 provinces
political parties National Front for the Liberation of Mozambique (Frelimo), free market; Renamo, or Mozambique National Resistance (MNR), former rebel movement, right of centre
population 17,796,000 (1996 est)
population growth rate 2.4% (1990–95); 2.8% (2000–05)
ethnic distribution the majority belong to local groups, the largest being the Makua-Lomue, who comprise about 38% of the population; the other significant group is the Tsonga (24%)
life expectancy 47 (men), 50 (women)
literacy rate men 45%, women 21%
languages Portuguese (official), 16 African languages
religions animist, Roman Catholic, Muslim
currency metical
GDP (US $) 1.46 billion (1994)
growth rate 5.0% (1994)
exports prawns, cashews, sugar, cotton, tea, petroleum products, copra

HISTORY
1st–4th Cs AD Bantu-speaking peoples settled in Mozambique.
8th–15th C Arab gold traders established independent city-states on the coast.
1498 Portuguese navigator Vasco da Gama was the first European visitor; at this time the most important local power was the Maravi kingdom of the Mwene Matapa peoples, who controlled much of the Zambezi basin.
1626 The Mwene Matapa formally recognized Portuguese sovereignty; gold and ivory resources were exploited by slave labour and private agricultural estates set up by Portuguese soldiers.
late 17th C Portuguese pushed temporarily S of Zambezi by the ascendant Rozwi kingdom.
1752 First Portuguese colonial governor appointed; slave trade outlawed.
late 19th C Concessions given by Portugal to private companies to develop and administer parts of Mozambique.
1930 More centralized Portuguese rule established by the Colonial Act, which ended concessions to monopolistic companies and forged closer integration with Lisbon.
1951 Became an overseas province of Portugal and, economically, a cheap labour reserve for South Africa's mines.
1962 Frelimo (Front for the Liberation of Mozambique) established in exile in Tanzania by Marxist guerrillas, including Samora Machel, to fight for independence.
1964 Fighting broke out between Frelimo forces and Portuguese troops, starting a ten-year liberation war; Portugal despatched 70,000 troops to Mozambique.
1969 Eduardo Mondlane, leader of Frelimo, was assassinated.
1975 Following revolution in Portugal, independence achieved as a socialist republic, with Machel as president, Joaquim Chissano as prime minister, and Frelimo as the sole legal party; Portuguese settlers left the country. Lourenço Marques renamed Maputo. Key enterprises nationalized.
1977 Renamo resistance group formed, with covert backing of South Africa.
1979 Machel encouraged the Patriotic Front guerrillas in Rhodesia to accept the Lancaster House Agreement, creating Zimbabwe.
1983 Good relations restored with Western powers.
1984 Nkomati Accord of nonaggression signed with South Africa.
1986 Machel killed in air crash near South African border; succeeded by Chissano.
1988 Tanzanian troops withdrawn from Mozambique.
1989 Renamo continued attacks on government facilities and civilians.
1990 One-party rule officially ended, and Frelimo abandoned Marxist-Leninism and embraced the market economy.
1992 Peace accord signed with Renamo.
1993 Price riots in Maputo as IMF-promoted reforms to restructure the economy devastated by war and drought were implemented.
1994 Demobilization of contending armies completed. Chissano and Frelimo re-elected in first multiparty elections; Renamo (now a political party) agreed to co-operate with government.
1995 Mozambique admitted to Commonwealth.

Mubarak **Hosni Mubarak, President of Egypt, addressing the United Nations General Assembly 1989. Mubarak has pursued an even-handed approach to international relations, remaining friendly with the USA while improving relationships with other Arab states, which had been damaged by the signing of the Egyptian-Israeli peace treaty of 1979.** *United Nations*

Muckrakers, the movement of US writers and journalists about 1880–1914 who aimed to expose political, commercial, and corporate corruption, and record frankly the age of industrialism, urban poverty, and conspicuous consumption. Novelists included Frank Norris, Theodore Dreiser, Jack London, and Upton Sinclair. The muckrakers were closely associated with ◊Progressivism.

Major figures of the earlier period include Rebecca Harding Davis, Henry George (*Progress and Poverty* 1879), and Henry Demarest Lloyd (1847–1903). Later the movement included Lincoln Steffens (1866–1936) (*The Shame of the Cities* 1904), Ida M Tarbell, and Thorstein Veblen (*The Theory of the Leisure Class* 1904).

mucus lubricating and protective fluid, secreted by mucous membranes in many different parts of the body. In the gut, mucus smooths the passage of food and keeps potentially damaging digestive enzymes away from the gut lining. In the lungs, it traps airborne particles so that they can be expelled.

Muddy Waters adopted name of McKinley Morganfield 1915–1983. US blues singer, songwriter, and guitarist. He was a central figure in the development of electric urban blues in the 1950s. Many of his songs have become rhythm-and-blues standards, including 'Hoochie Coochie Man' 1954 and 'Got My Mojo Workin'' 1957. From 1950 for two decades Muddy Waters recorded for the Chess label, and scored R & B hits with, among others, 'Louisiana Blues' 1951, 'Mannish Boy' 1955, and 'Close to You' 1958. He was an influence on bands like the Rolling Stones, who took their name from his 1950 song.

mudfish another name for ◊bowfin.

mudnester any of an Australian group of birds that make their nests from mud, including the apostle bird *Struthidea cinerea*, the white-winged chough *Corcorax melanorhamphos*, and the magpie lark *Grallina cyanoleuca*.

mudpuppy brownish salamander of the genus *Necturus* in the family Proteidae. There are five species, living in fresh water in North America. They all breathe in water using external gills. *N. maculatus* is about 20 cm/8 in long.

mudskipper fish of the goby family, genus *Periophthalmus*, found in brackish water and shores in the tropics, except for the Americas. It can walk or climb over mudflats, using its strong pectoral fins as legs, and has eyes set close together on top of the head. It grows up to 30 cm/12 in long.

muezzin (Arabic) a person whose job is to perform the call to prayer five times a day from the minaret of a Muslim mosque.

mufti Muslim legal expert who guides the courts in their interpretation. In Turkey the ***grand mufti*** had supreme spiritual authority until the establishment of the republic in 1924.

Mugabe Robert (Gabriel) 1925– . Zimbabwean politician, prime minister from 1980 and president from 1987. He was in detention in Rhodesia for nationalist activities 1964–74, then carried on guerrilla warfare from Mozambique. As leader of ◊ZANU he was in an uneasy alliance with Joshua ◊Nkomo of ZAPU (Zimbabwe African People's Union) from 1976. In 1985 he postponed the introduction of a multiparty state for five years. His failure to anticipate and respond to the 1991–92 drought in southern Africa adversely affected his popularity, but he was re-elected, unchallenged, 1996.

Muggeridge (Thomas) Malcolm 1903–1990. English journalist and author. He worked for the *Guardian*, the *Calcutta Statesman*, the London *Evening Standard*, and the *Daily Telegraph* before becoming editor of *Punch* 1953–57.

Mugabe **Zimbabwean politician Robert Mugabe. As leader of the ZANU wing of the Patriotic Front he played a leading role in the historic Lancaster House negotiations, which brought to an end white minority rule in the former British colony of Rhodesia in 1980. He was Zimbabwe's first prime minister 1980, and in 1987 became president.** *Topham*

mugwump (from an Indian word meaning 'chief') in US political history, a colloquial name for the Republicans who voted in the 1884 presidential election for Grover Cleveland, the Democratic candidate, rather than for their Republican nominee, James G Blaine (1830–1893). Blaine was accused of financial improprieties, and the reform-minded mugwumps were partly responsible for his defeat. The term has come to mean a politician who remains neutral on divisive issues.

mudskipper **Mudskippers use their fins as rudimentary legs. They often leave the waters of the mangrove swamps and tidal flats of the Indian and Pacific Oceans where they live, to lie on the mud or climb on exposed mangrove roots. Alert to danger, they quickly skip away when disturbed.**

Muhammad (Arabic 'praised') or ***Mohammed, Mahomet*** c. 570–632. Founder of Islam, born in Mecca on the Arabian peninsula. In about 616 he began to preach the worship of one God, who allegedly revealed to him the words of the Koran (it was later written down by his followers) through the angel Jibra'el (Gabriel). Muhammad fled from persecution to the town now known as Medina in 622: the flight, ***Hijrah*** or ***Hegira***, marks the beginning of the Islamic era.

Muhammad was originally a shepherd and trader. He married Khadija, a widow, in 595, spent time in meditation, and received his first revelation in 610. The series of revelations continued throughout his life. At first he doubted their divine origin but later he began to teach others, who wrote down the words of his revelations; they were collected after his death to form the Koran.

The move to Medina resulted in the first Islamic community, which for many years fought battles against fierce opposition from Mecca and from neighbouring tribes. In 630 the Muslim army defeated that of Mecca and the city came under Muslim rule. By the time of Muhammad's death in 632, Islam had spread throughout the Arabian peninsula. After his death, the leadership of the Muslims was disputed.

Muslims believe that Muhammad was the final prophet, although they recognize other, earlier prophets, including Ibrahim (Abraham) and Isa (Jesus). Muhammad is not worshipped, but honoured by the words 'Peace be upon him' whenever Muslims mention his name.

'An orgy looks particularly alluring seen through the mists of righteous indignation.'

MALCOLM MUGGERIDGE
'Dolce Vita in a Cold Climate'

Muir Edwin 1887–1959. Scottish poet. *First Poems* 1925 was published after an extended period of travel and residence in Europe, which also resulted in translations of ◊Kafka and Lion Feuchtwanger (1884–1958), in collaboration with his wife, the novelist Willa Anderson (1890–1970). Dreams, myths, and menaces coexist in his poetry and his notable *Autobiography* 1954 explores similar themes. *Complete Poems* was published 1992.

Muir Jean Elizabeth 1933–1996. English fashion designer. She worked for Jaeger 1956–61 and set up her own fashion house 1961. In 1991 she launched a knitwear collection. Her clothes are characterized by soft, classic, tailored shapes in leathers and soft fabrics.

Mujaheddin (Arabic *mujahid* 'fighters', from *jihad* 'holy war') Islamic fundamentalist guerrillas of contemporary Afghanistan and Iran.

Muhammad **The prophet Muhammad, from a miniature in the Royal Asiatic Society. Muhammad's preaching was seen as a threat to Mecca's trade and prosperity. When it became dangerous for him to remain in Mecca, he fled by night to a community of Muslim converts at Medina. Eight years later, after much fighting, he re-entered Mecca and began spreading Islam further.** *Corbis*

mulberry The juicy, purplish-black fruit of the black mulberry resembles a blackberry and makes a fine preserve. Male and female flowers grow on separate bushes but the fruits form on the female trees whether or not they have been fertilized.

Mukalla seaport capital of the Hadhramaut coastal region of S Yemen; on the Gulf of Aden 480 km/300 mi E of Aden; population (1995 est) 154,400.

Mukden, Battle of Japanese victory over the Russians during the ◊Russo-Japanese War, Feb–March 1905, outside Mukden (now called Shenyang), capital city of Manchuria. This was the last major battle of the war – the Russian defeat finally persuaded the Tsar to accept US mediation June 1905.

Mukden was later the scene of a surprise attack (the 'Mukden incident') 18 Sept 1931 by the Japanese on the Chinese garrison, which marked the beginning of their invasion of China.

mulberry any tree of the genus *Morus*, family Moraceae, consisting of a dozen species. It is native to W Asia and has heart-shaped, toothed leaves, and spikes of whitish flowers. It is widely cultivated for its fruit, which resembles a raspberry. The leaves of the Asiatic white mulberry *M. alba* are used to feed silkworms.

Mulberry Harbour prefabricated floating harbour, used on D-day in World War II, to assist in the assault on the German-held French coast of Normandy. Two were built in the UK and floated across the English Channel.

Muldoon Robert David 1921–1992. New Zealand National Party politician, prime minister 1975–84. He pursued austere economic policies such as a wage-and-price policy to control inflation.

He was minister of finance 1967–72, and in 1974 became leader of the National Party. As prime minister he sought to introduce curbs on trade unions, was a vigorous supporter of the Western alliance, and a proponent of reform of the international monetary system.

mule hybrid animal, usually the offspring of a male ass and a female horse.

Mull second largest island of the Inner Hebrides, Strathclyde Region, Scotland; area 950 sq km/367 sq mi; population (1991) 2,700. It is mountainous, and is separated from the mainland by the Sound of Mull. There is only one town, Tobermory. The economy is based on fishing, forestry, tourism, and some livestock.

Mullard Radio Astronomy Observatory radio observatory of the University of Cambridge, England. Its main instrument is the Ryle Telescope, eight dishes 12.8 m/42 ft wide in a line of 5 km/3 mi long, opened 1972.

mullein any plant of the genus *Verbascum*, family Scrophulariaceae. The great mullein *Verbascum thapsus* has lance-shaped leaves 30 cm/12 in or more in length, covered in woolly down, and a large spike of yellow flowers. It is found in Europe and Asia and is naturalized in North America.

Every generation revolts against its fathers and makes friends with its grandfathers.
LEWIS MUMFORD
The Brown Decade

Müller Heiner 1929– . German dramatist. His scripts have played a leading role in contemporary avant-garde theatre in Germany and abroad. Early political works, showing the influence of Brecht, (*The Scab* 1950, *The Correction* 1958) were followed by *Mauser* 1970, *Cement* 1972 (on the Russian revolution), *Hamletmachine* 1977, and *Medea-material* 1982.

Muller Hermann Joseph 1890–1967. US geneticist who discovered 1926 that mutations can be artificially induced by X-rays. This showed that mutations are nothing more than chemical changes. He was awarded the Nobel Prize for Physiology or Medicine 1946.

Muller pressed for safety regulations to ensure that people who were regularly exposed to X-rays were adequately protected. He also opposed nuclear-bomb tests.

Müller Johannes Peter 1801–1858. German comparative anatomist whose studies of nerves and sense organs opened a new chapter in physiology by demonstrating the physical nature of sensory perception. His name is associated with a number of discoveries, including the Müllerian ducts in the mammalian fetus and the lymph heart in frogs.

Müller Paul Herman 1899–1965. Swiss chemist who discovered the first synthetic contact insecticide, ◊DDT, 1939. For this he was awarded a Nobel prize 1948.

mullet two species of fish. The ***red mullet*** *Mullus surmuletus* is found in the Mediterranean and warm Atlantic as far north as the English Channel. It is about 40 cm/16 in long, red with yellow stripes, and has long barbels round the mouth. The ***grey mullet*** *Crenimugil labrosus* lives in ponds and estuaries. It is greyish above, with longitudinal dark stripes, and grows to 60 cm/24 in.

Mulligan Gerry (Gerald) 1927–1996. US jazz saxophonist, arranger, and composer. Spanning the bebop and cool jazz movements, he worked with trumpeter Miles Davis on the seminal *Birth of the Cool* album 1950 and led his own quartet from 1951, which briefly featured Chet Baker on trumpet. Mulligan is chiefly associated with the West Coast jazz style. An outstanding baritone-sax player, he has worked with many great names in jazz, including bandleader Stan Kenton (for whom he wrote arrangements) and pianist Thelonius Monk.

Mullingar county town of County Westmeath, Republic of Ireland; population (1991) 30,300. It is a cattle market and trout-fishing centre.

Mulroney Brian 1939– . Canadian politician, Progressive Conservative Party leader 1983–93, prime minister 1984–93. He achieved a landslide in the 1984 election, and won the 1988 election on a platform of free trade with the USA, but with a reduced majority. Opposition within Canada to the 1987 Meech Lake agreement, a prerequisite to signing the 1982 Constitution, continued to plague Mulroney in his second term. A revised reform package 1992 failed to gain voters' approval, and in 1993 he was forced to resign the leadership of the Conservative Party.

multicultural education education aimed at preparing children to live in a multiracial society by giving them an understanding of the culture and history of different ethnic groups. The initiative for multicultural teaching in the UK rose out of the *Swann Report* 1985 against racism and racial disadvantage in schools.

multilateralism trade among more than two countries without discrimination over origin or destination and regardless of whether a large trade gap is involved. Unlike ◊bilateralism, multilateralism does not require the trade flow between countries to be of the same value.

multimedia computerized method of presenting information by combining audio and video components using text, sound, and graphics (still, animated, and video sequences). For example, a multimedia database of musical instruments may allow a user not only to search and retrieve text about a particular instrument but also to see pictures of it and hear it play a piece of music. Multimedia applications emphasize interactivity between the computer and the user.

As graphics, video, and audio are extremely demanding of storage space, multimedia PCs are usually fitted with ◊CD-ROM drives because of the high storage capacity of CD-ROM discs. In the mid-1990s developments in compression techniques and software made it possible to incorporate multimedia elements into Internet Web sites.

multinational corporation company or enterprise operating in several countries, usually defined as one that has 25% or more of its output capacity located outside its country of origin.

multiple birth in humans, the production of more than two babies from one pregnancy. Multiple births can be caused by more than two eggs being produced and fertilized (often as the result of hormone therapy to assist pregnancy), or by a single fertilized egg dividing more than once before implantation. See also ◊twin.

multiple independently targeted re-entry vehicle (MIRV) nuclear-warhead-carrying part of a ballistic ◊missile that splits off in midair from the main body. Since each is individually steered and controlled, MIRVs can attack separate targets over a wide area.

Multiple Mirror Telescope telescope on Mount Hopkins, Arizona, USA, opened 1979, consisting of six 1.83 m/72 in mirrors mounted in a hexagon, the light-collecting area of which equals that of a single mirror of 4.5 m/176 in diameter. It is planned to replace the six mirrors with a single mirror 6.5 m/256 in wide.

multiple proportions, law of in chemistry, the principle that if two elements combine with each other to form more than one compound, then the ratio of the masses of one of them that combine with a particular mass of the other is a small whole number.

multiple sclerosis (MS) or ***disseminated sclerosis*** incurable chronic disease of the central nervous system, occurring in young or middle adulthood. Most prevalent in temperate zones, it affects more women than men. It is characterized by degeneration of the myelin sheath that surrounds nerves in the brain and spinal cord. Depending on where the demyelination occurs – which nerves are affected – the symptoms of MS can mimic almost any neurological disorder. Typically seen are unsteadiness, ataxia (loss of muscular coordination), weakness, speech difficulties, and rapid involuntary movements of the eyes. The course of the disease is episodic, with frequent intervals of remission. Its cause is unknown, but it may be initiated in childhood by some environmental factor, such as infection, in genetically susceptible people.

multiplexer in telecommunications, a device that allows a transmission medium to carry a number of separate signals at the same time – enabling, for example, several telephone conversations to be carried by one telephone line, and radio signals to be transmitted in stereo.

multistage rocket rocket launch vehicle made up of several rocket stages (often three) joined end to end. The bottom stage fires first, boosting the vehicle to high speed, then it falls away. The next stage fires, thrusting the now lighter vehicle even faster. The remaining stages fire and fall away in turn, boosting the vehicle's payload (cargo) to an orbital speed that can reach 28,000 kph/17,500 mph.

multitasking or ***multiprogramming*** in computing, a system in which one processor appears to run several different programs (or different parts of the same program) at the same time. All the programs are held in memory together and each is allowed to run for a certain period. The ability to multitask depends on the ◊operating system rather than the type of computer.

Muluzi Bakili 1943– . Malawi politician, president from 1994. Muluzi formed the United Democratic Front (UDF) 1992 when President ◊Banda agreed to end one-party rule, and went on to win almost half of the presidential votes. Since taking office, he has applied his business experience to the task of liberalizing trade and reviving the economy.

Mumford Lewis 1895–1990. US urban planner and social critic, concerned with the adverse effect of technology on contemporary society. His books, including *Technics and Civilization* 1934 and *The Culture of Cities* 1938, discussed the rise of cities and proposed the creation of green belts around large conurbations. His view of the importance of an historical perspective in urban planning for the future is reflected in his major work *The City in History* 1961.

mummers' play or ***St George play*** British folk drama enacted in dumb show by a masked cast, performed on Christmas Day to celebrate the death of the old year and its rebirth as the new year. The plot usually consists of a duel between St George and an infidel knight, in which one of them is killed but later revived by a doctor.

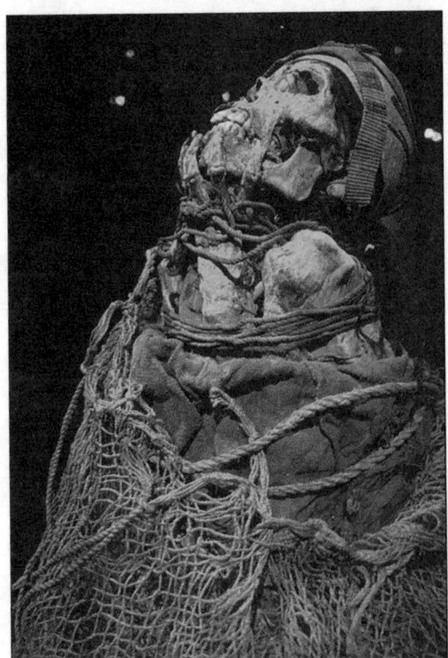

mummy The embalmed body of a priest in the Museo del Oro, Bogotá, Colombia. The full mummification process involved the removal of the brain and internal organs before the body was treated with various natural preservatives and wrapped in layers of bandages. Through X-ray studies, genetic tests, and radiocarbon dating, mummies can be an important source of medical and cultural information about ancient peoples. *Sally Jenkins*

mummy any dead body, human or animal, that has been naturally or artificially preserved. Natural mummification can occur through freezing (for example, mammoths in glacial ice from 25,000 years ago), drying, or preservation in bogs or oil seeps. Artificial mummification may be achieved by embalming (for example, the mummies of ancient Egypt) or by freeze-drying (see ◊cryonics).

mumps or ***infectious parotitis*** virus infection marked by fever, pain, and swelling of one or both parotid salivary glands (situated in front of the ears). It is usually shortlived in children, although meningitis is a possible complication. In adults the symptoms are more serious and it may cause sterility in men.

Mumps is the most common cause of ◊meningitis in children, but it follows a much milder course than bacterial meningitis, and a complete recovery is usual. Rarely, mumps meningitis may lead to deafness. An effective vaccine against mumps, measles, and rubella (MMR vaccine) is now offered for children aged 18 months.

Munch Edvard 1863–1944. Norwegian painter and graphic artist, a major influence on ◊Expressionism. His highly charged paintings, characterized by strong colours and distorted forms, often focus on intense emotional states, as in one of his best-known works *The Scream* 1893. His works brought a new urgency and power to the two themes that dominated late 19th-century ◊decadence, death and sexuality.

He studied in Paris and Berlin, and his major works date from the period 1892–1908, when he lived mainly in Germany. Influenced first by the Symbolists and then by van Gogh and Gauguin, he soon developed his own expressive style, reducing his compositions to broad areas of strong colour with sinuous contours emphasized by heavy brushstrokes, distorting faces and figures. His first show in Berlin 1892 made a great impact on young German artists. The *Frieze of Life* 1890s, a sequence of symbolic paintings, includes some of his most characteristic images.

In 1908 he suffered a nervous breakdown and returned to Norway. Later works include a series of murals 1910–15 in the assembly halls of Oslo University.

Münchhausen Karl Friedrich Hieronymus, Freiherr (Baron) von Münchhausen 1720–1797. German soldier. He served with the Russian army against the Turks, and after his retirement 1760 told exaggerated stories of his adventures. This idiosyncrasy was utilized by the German writer Rudolph Erich Raspe (1737–1794) in his extravagantly fictitious *Baron Munchausen's Narrative of his Marvellous Travels and Campaigns in Russia* 1785, which he wrote in English while living in London. The book was subsequently enlarged by the insertion of stories culled from various sources.

Münchhausen's syndrome emotional disorder in which a patient feigns or invents symptoms to secure medical treatment. It is the chronic form of factitious disorder (a fictional illness that satisfies an emotional or psychological need at a particular time), which is more common, and probably underdiagnosed. In some cases the patient will secretly ingest substances to produce real symptoms. It was named after the exaggerated tales of Baron Münchhausen.

Munda any one of several groups living in NE and central India, numbering about 5 million (1983). Their most widely spoken languages are Santali and Mundari, languages of the Munda group, an isolated branch of the Austro-Asiatic family. The Mundas were formerly nomadic hunter-gatherers, but now practise shifting cultivation. They are Hindus, but retain animist beliefs.

Mungo, St another name for St ◊Kentigern, first bishop of Glasgow.

Munich (German ***München***) industrial city (brewing, printing, precision instruments, machinery, electrical goods, textiles), capital of Bavaria, Germany, on the river Isar; population (1993) 1,256,300

features Munich owes many of its buildings and art treasures to the kings ◊Ludwig I and Maximilian II of Bavaria. The cathedral is late 15th century. The Alte Pinakothek contains paintings by old masters, and the Neue Pinakothek, modern paintings; there is the Bavarian National Museum, the Bavarian State Library, and the Deutsches Museum (science and technology). The university, founded at Ingolstadt 1472, was transferred to Munich 1826; to the NE at Garching there is a nuclear research centre

history dating from the 12th century, Munich became the residence of the dukes of Wittelsbach in the 13th century, and the capital of independent Bavaria. It was the scene of the November revolution of 1918, the 'Soviet' republic of 1919, and the Hitler putsch of 1923. It became the centre of the Nazi movement, and the Munich Agreement of 1938 was signed there. When the 1972 Summer Olympics were held in Munich, 11 Israeli athletes were killed by Palestine Liberation Organization terrorists.

Munich Agreement pact signed on 29 Sept 1938 by the leaders of the UK (Neville ◊Chamberlain), France (Edouard ◊Daladier), Germany (Hitler), and Italy (Mussolini), under which Czechoslovakia was compelled to surrender its Sudeten-German districts (the Sudetenland) to Germany. Chamberlain claimed it would guarantee 'peace in our time', but it did not prevent Hitler from seizing the rest of Czechoslovakia in March 1939. After World War II the Sudetenland was returned to Czechoslovakia, and over 2 million German-speaking people were expelled from the country.

Munch *Two Girls in a Garden* 1905 by Edvard Munch, Boymans-van Beuningen, Rotterdam, Netherlands. Munch left Norway in 1889 and spent several years abroad, first in Paris, then in Berlin, returning to Norway in 1908 after a nervous breakdown. During this time he was influenced by Van Gogh, and also developed his Expressionist style. *Corbis*

Municipal Corporations Act English act of Parliament 1835 that laid the foundations of modern local government. The act made local government responsible to a wider electorate of ratepayers through elected councils. Boroughs incorporated in this way were empowered to take on responsibility for policing, public health, and education, and were also subject to regulation and auditing which served to reduce corruption. Similar acts were passed for Scotland (1833) and Ireland (1840).

Munster southern province of the Republic of Ireland, comprising the counties of Clare, Cork, Kerry, Limerick, North and South Tipperary, and Waterford; area 24,140 sq km/9,318 sq mi; population (1991) 1,008,400. It was a kingdom until the 12th century, and was settled in plantations by the English from 1586.

Münster industrial city (wire, cement, iron, brewing, and distilling) in North Rhine–Westphalia, NW

Munich Agreement British prime minister Neville Chamberlain with Daladier, Hitler and Mussolini at the conference which proclaimed the Munich Agreement. The pact did not prevent German aggression in Europe and World War II broke out a year later. *Image Select (UK) Ltd*

❛There are those who do not dislike wrong rumours if they are about the right men.❜

LADY MURASAKI
The Tale of Genji

Germany, formerly the capital of Westphalia; population (1993) 267,000. The Treaty of Westphalia was signed simultaneously here and at Osnabrück 1648, ending the Thirty Years' War. Badly damaged in World War II, its ancient buildings, including the 15th-century cathedral and town hall, have been restored or rebuilt.

Munternia Romanian name of ◊Wallachia, a former province of Romania.

muntjac small deer, genus *Muntiacus*, found in SE Asia. There are about six species. Males have short spiked antlers and two sharp canine teeth forming tusks. They are sometimes called 'barking deer' because of their voices. Muntjac live mostly in dense vegetation and do not form herds. Some have escaped from parks in central England and have become established in the wild.

muon an ◊elementary particle similar to the electron except for its mass which is 207 times greater than that of the electron. It has a half-life of 2 millionths of a second, decaying into electrons and ◊neutrinos. The muon was originally thought to be a ◊meson and is thus sometimes called a mu meson, although current opinion is that it is a ◊lepton.

Murakami Haruki 1949– . Japanese novelist and translator. He is one of Japan's best-selling writers, influenced by 20th-century US writers and popular culture. His dreamy, gently surrealist novels include *A Wild Sheep Chase* 1982 and *Norwegian Wood* 1987.

mural painting (Latin *murus* 'wall') decoration of the wall either by painting on the surface, or on a canvas which is subsequently affixed in position, the latter being a method frequently used in modern times. In painting directly on the wall, various media have been used, principal among them being fresco, though tempera, encaustic and oil also have their examples. Mural painting is found in all periods of art, but mainly, as distinct from the domestic easel picture, in palaces, churches or the interiors of buildings of public use or significance.

Two main forms can be distinguished: that which emphasizes the flatness of the wall surface and is conceived in large areas of flat colour, as in ancient Egypt, Crete, or in the work of Puvis de Chavannes; and that which gives the illusion of imaginary perspective, breaking down the flatness of the wall, as in Pompeian wall-painting, Baroque painting or the Rococo style as represented by Tiepolo.

❛Writing is like getting married. One should never commit oneself until one is amazed at one's luck.❜

IRIS MURDOCH
The Black Prince

Murasaki Shikibu c. 978–c. 1015. Japanese writer. She was a lady at the court. Her masterpiece of fiction, *The Tale of Genji* c. 1010, is one of the classic works of Japanese literature, and may be the world's first novel. She was a member of the Fujiwara clan, but her own name is not known; scholars have given her the name Murasaki after a character in the book. It deals with upper-class life in Heian Japan, centring on the affairs of Prince Genji. A portion of her diary and a number of poems also survive.

Murat Joachim 1767–1815. King of Naples 1808–15. An officer in the French army, he was made king by Napoleon, but deserted him in 1813 in the vain hope that Austria and Great Britain would recognize him. In 1815 he attempted unsuccessfully to make himself king of all Italy, but when he landed in Calabria in an attempt to gain the throne he was captured and shot.

Murayama Tomiichi 1924– . Japanese trade unionist and politician, leader of the Social Democratic Party (SDPJ) 1993–96, prime minister 1994–96. At the age of 70, Murayama became Japan's first socialist prime minister for more than 30 years. His emergence as a major figure followed months of virtual chaos in Japanese politics, during which two prime ministers resigned. Despite losses for the SDPJ in upper house elections 1995, his administration survived until Jan 1996; he resigned from the SDPJ leadership Sept 1996.

Murchison Roderick Impey 1792–1871. Scottish geologist responsible for naming the ◊Silurian period (in his book *The Silurian System* 1839). Expeditions to Russia 1840–45 led him to define another worldwide system, the Permian, named after the strata of the Perm region.

❛Monopoly's a terrible thing, till you have it.❜

RUPERT MURDOCH
Quoted in *New Yorker* 1979

Murcia autonomous region of SE Spain; area 11,300 sq km/4,362 sq mi; population (1991) 1,045,600. It includes the cities Murcia and Cartagena, and produces esparto grass, lead, zinc, iron, and fruit.

Murcia industrial city (silk, metal, glass, textiles, pharmaceuticals), capital of the Spanish province of Murcia, on the river Segura; population (1994) 342,000. Murcia was founded 825 on the site of a Roman colony by 'Abd-ar-Rahman II, caliph of Córdoba. It has a university and 14th-century cathedral.

murder unlawful killing of one person by another. In the USA, first-degree murder requires proof of premeditation; second-degree murder falls between first-degree murder and ◊manslaughter. In British law murder is committed only when the killer acts with malice aforethought, that is, intending either to kill or to cause serious injury, or realizing that this would probably result. It is punishable by life imprisonment. It is the most serious form of ◊homicide.

Murdoch (Jean) Iris 1919–1999. English novelist, born in Dublin. Her novels combine philosophical speculation with often outrageous situations and tangled human relationships. They include *The Sandcastle* 1957, *The Bell* 1958, *The Sea, The Sea* 1978 (Booker Prize), *Nuns and Soldiers* 1980, *The Message to the Planet* 1989, *The Green Knight* 1993, and *Jackson's Dilemma* 1995.

Her first work was a philosophical study, *Sartre, Romantic Rationalist* 1953, and she has since published other works of philosophy, including *Metaphysics as a Guide to Morals* 1992.

Murdoch (Keith) Rupert 1931– . Australian-born US media magnate with worldwide interests. His UK newspapers, generally right-wing, include the *Sun*, the *News of the World*, and *The Times*; in the USA, he has a 50% share of 20th Century Fox, six Metromedia TV stations, and newspaper and magazine publishing companies. He purchased a 50% stake in a Hungarian tabloid, *Reform*, from 1989.

His newspapers (which also include *Today* and the *Sunday Times*) and 50% of Sky Television, the UK's first satellite television service, are controlled by News International, a wholly owned subsidiary of the Australian-based News Corporation. In Nov 1990 Sky Television and its rival company British Satellite Broadcasting merged to form British Sky Broadcasting (BSkyB). Over 70% of newspapers sold in Australia are controlled by Murdoch.

Murillo Bartolomé Esteban c. 1618–1682. Spanish painter. Active mainly in Seville, he painted sentimental pictures of the Immaculate Conception, and also specialized in studies of street urchins. His *Self-Portrait* about 1672 (National Gallery, London) is generally considered to be one of his finest works.

Born in Seville, he remained in the city during his years of success, and founded the Academy of Seville 1660. In 1670 he declined the honour of becoming court painter to Charles II. In his early days he painted many pictures of peasant and street urchin types, but his later works were mainly religious and executed in his soft and melting *estilo vaporoso*, as in the *Immaculate Conception* (Prado, Madrid), a favoured theme, of which there are many versions. The *Melon Eaters* (Munich, Alte Pinakothek) and *Two Peasant Boys* (Dulwich Picture Gallery, London) are notable examples of his naturalism, traceable to Ribera and Velázquez but not free from the sentimentality which makes his religious works unpalatable to modern taste. The dramatized genre of his *Prodigal Son* series shows his later work at its best.

Murmansk seaport in NW Russian Federation, on the Barents Sea; population (1994) 444,000. It is the largest city in the Arctic, Russia's most important fishing port, and the base of naval units and the icebreakers that keep the Northeast Passage open.

Murnau F W. Adopted name of Friedrich Wilhelm Plumpe 1889–1931. German silent-film director. He was known for his expressive images and 'subjective' use of a moving camera in *Der letzte Mamm/The Last Laugh* 1924. Other films include *Nosferatu* 1922 (a version of the Dracula story), *Sunrise* 1927, and *Tabu* 1931.

Muromachi in Japanese history, the period 1392–1568, comprising the greater part of the rule of the ◊Ashikaga shoguns; it is named after the area of Kyoto where their headquarters were sited.

Murphy Eddie (Edward Regan) 1951– . US film actor and comedian. His first film, *48 Hours* 1982, introduced the street-wise, cocksure character that has become his speciality. His other films include *Trading Places* 1983, *Beverly Hills Cop* 1984, *Vampire in Brooklyn* 1995, and *The Nutty Professor* 1996.

Murray principal river of Australia, 2,575 km/1,600 mi long. It rises in the Australian Alps near Mount Kosciusko and flows W, forming the boundary between New South Wales and Victoria, and reaches the sea at Encounter Bay, South Australia. With its main tributary, the Darling, it is 3,750 km/2,330 mi long.

Murray (George) Gilbert (Aimé) 1866–1957. Australian-born British scholar. Author of *History of Ancient Greek Literature* 1897, he became known for verse translations of the Greek dramatists, notably of Euripides, which rendered the plays more accessible to readers. He was professor of Greek at Glasgow University 1889–99 and at Oxford 1908–36.

Murray James Augustus Henry 1837–1915. Scottish philologist. He was the first editor of the *Oxford English Dictionary* (originally the *New English Dictionary*) from 1878 until his death; the first volume was published 1884.

Murray James Stuart, 1st Earl of Murray, or Moray 1531–1570. Regent of Scotland from 1567, an illegitimate son of James V. He was one of the leaders of the Scottish Reformation, and after the deposition of his half-sister ◊Mary Queen of Scots, he became regent. He was assassinated by one of her supporters.

Murray Les(lie) A(llan) 1938– . Australian poet. His poetry, adventurous, verbally inventive, deeply serious, has appeared in collections such as *The Vernacular Republic: Poems 1961–1981* 1982, *The People's Otherworld* 1983, *The Australian Seasons* 1985, and *Translations from the Natural World* 1993. He has emerged as a determined advocate of the virtues and values of rural life.

Murrayfield Scottish rugby football ground and home of the national team. It staged its first international in 1925 when Scotland beat England 14–11. The capacity is approximately 70,000. Over 100,000 fans are reputed to have been in the ground for the match against Wales in 1975.

Murrow Edward R(oscoe) 1908–1965. US broadcast journalist who covered World War II from London for the Columbia Broadcasting System (CBS).

Murrumbidgee river of New South Wales, Australia; length 1,690 km/1,050 mi. It rises in the Australian Alps, flows N to the Burrinjuck reservoir, and then W to meet the river ◊Murray.

Murry John Middleton 1889–1957. English writer. He produced studies of Dostoevsky, Keats, Blake, and Shakespeare; poetry; and an autobiographical novel, *Still Life*, 1916. In 1913 he married the writer Katherine Mansfield, whose biography he wrote.

Musashi Miyamotosee ◊Miyamoto Musashi, Japanese samurai.

Muscat or ***Masqat*** capital of Oman, E Arabia, adjoining the port of Matrah, which has a deep-water harbour; combined population (1993) 40,900. It produces natural gas and chemicals.

muscle contractile animal tissue that produces locomotion and power, and maintains the movement of body substances. Muscle is made of long cells that can contract to between one-half and one-third of their relaxed length.

Striped (or striated) muscles are activated by ◊motor nerves under voluntary control; their ends are usually attached via tendons to bones.

Involuntary or ***smooth*** muscles are controlled by motor nerves of the ◊autonomic nervous system, and are located in the gut, blood vessels, iris, and various ducts.

Cardiac muscle occurs only in the heart, and is also controlled by the autonomic nervous system.

muscovite white mica, $KAl_2Si_3AlO_{10}(OH,F)_2$, a common silicate mineral. It is colourless to silvery white with shiny surfaces, and like all micas it splits into thin flakes along its one perfect cleavage. Muscovite is a metamorphic mineral occurring mainly

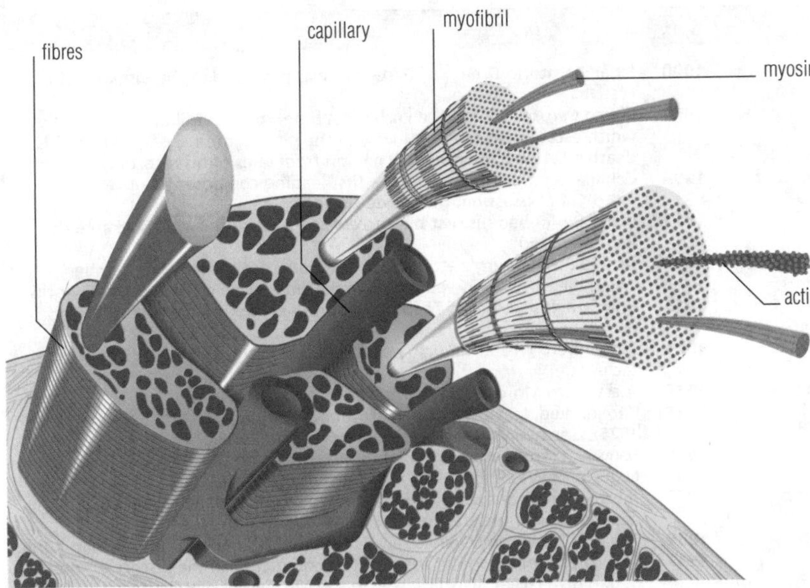

muscle Muscles make up 35–45% of our body weight; there are over 650 skeletal muscles. Muscle cells may be up to 20 cm/0.8 in long. They are arranged in bundles, fibres, fibrils, and myofilaments.

in schists; it is also found in some granites, and appears as shiny flakes on bedding planes of some sandstones.

muscular dystrophy any of a group of inherited chronic muscle disorders marked by weakening and wasting of muscle. Muscle fibres degenerate, to be replaced by fatty tissue, although the nerve supply remains unimpaired. The commonest form, Duchenne muscular dystrophy, strikes boys (1 in 3,000), usually before the age of four. The child develops a waddling gait and an inward curvature (lordosis) of the lumbar spine. The muscles affected by dystrophy and the rate of progress vary. There is no cure, but physical treatments can minimize disability. Death usually occurs before the age of 20.

Muse in Greek mythology, one of the nine daughters of Zeus and Mnemosyne (goddess of memory) and inspirers of creative arts: Calliope, epic poetry; Clio, history; Erato, love poetry; Euterpe, lyric poetry; Melpomene, tragedy; Polyhymnia, sacred song; Terpsichore, dance; Thalia, comedy; and Urania, astronomy.

Museum of Modern Art, New York leading US art museum devoted to art of the late 19th and early 20th centuries. Opened 1929, it has amassed an exceptional collection of modern works, including collections of films and photographs.

Museveni Yoweri Kaguta 1945– . Ugandan general and politician, president from 1986. He led the opposition to Idi Amin's regime 1971–78 and was minister of defence 1979–80 but, unhappy with Milton Obote's autocratic leadership, formed the National Resistance Army (NRA). When Obote was ousted in a coup in 1985, Museveni entered into a brief power-sharing agreement with his successor, Tito Okello, before taking over as president. Museveni leads a broad-based coalition government, and in 1993 reinstated the country's four tribal monarchies.

Musgrave Thea 1928– . Scottish composer. Her works, in a conservative modern idiom, include concertos for horn, clarinet, and viola; string quartets; and operas, including *Mary, Queen of Scots* 1977.

Musgrave Ranges Australian mountain ranges on the border between South Australia and the Northern Territory; the highest peak is Mount Woodruffe at 1,525 m/5,000 ft. The area is an Aboriginal reserve.

mushroom fruiting body of certain fungi, consisting of an upright stem and a spore-producing cap with radiating gills on the undersurface. There are many edible species belonging to the genus *Agaricus*. See also ◊fungus and ◊toadstool.

music art of combining sounds into a coherent perceptual experience, typically in accordance with conventional patterns and for an aesthetic purpose. Music is generally categorized as classical, ◊jazz, ◊pop music, ◊country and western, and so on.

The Greek word *mousikē* covered all the arts presided over by the ◊Muses. The various civilizations of the ancient and modern world developed their own musical systems. Eastern music recognizes subtler distinctions of pitch than does Western music and also differs from Western music in that the absence, until recently, of written notation ruled out the composition of major developed works; it fostered melodic and rhythmic patterns, freely interpreted (as in the Indian raga) by virtuosos.

Middle Ages The documented history of Western music since Classical times begins with the liturgical music of the medieval Catholic Church, derived from Greek and Hebrew antecedents. The four scales, or modes, to which the words of the liturgy were chanted were traditionally first set in order by St Ambrose AD 384. St Gregory the Great added four more to the original Ambrosian modes, and this system forms the basis of Gregorian ◊plainsong, still used in the Roman Catholic Church. The organ was introduced in the 8th century, and in the 9th century harmonized music began to be used in churches, with notation developing towards its present form.

In the 11th century counterpoint was introduced, notably at the monastery of St Martial, Limoges, France, and in the late 12th century at Notre Dame in Paris (by Léonin and Perotin). In the late Middle Ages the Provençal and French ◊troubadours and court composers, such as Machaut, developed a secular music, derived from church and folk music (see also ◊Minnesingers).

15th and 16th centuries Europe saw the growth of contrapuntal or polyphonic music. One of the earliest composers was the English musician John Dunstable, whose works inspired the French composer Guillaume Dufay, founder of the Flemish school; its members included Dufay's pupil Joannes Okeghem and the Renaissance composer Josquin Desprez. Other composers of this era were Palestrina from Italy, Roland de Lassus from Flanders, Victoria from Spain, and Thomas Tallis and William Byrd from England. ◊Madrigals were developed in Italy by members of the Flemish school and later by native composers, including Giovanni Gabrieli; they were written during the Elizabethan age in England by such composers as Thomas Morley, Orlando Gibbons, and Thomas Weelkes (c. 1575–1623). Notable composers of organ music were Antonio de Cabezon (1500–1566) in Spain and Andrea Gabrieli (c. 1533–1586) in Italy.

17th-century The Florentine Academy (Camerata), a group of artists and writers, aimed to revive the principles of Greek tragedy. This led to the invention of dramatic recitative and the beginning of opera. Claudio Monteverdi was an early operatic composer; by the end of the century the form had evolved further in the hands of Alessandro Scarlatti in Italy and Jean-Baptiste Lully in France. In England the outstanding composer of the period was Henry Purcell. ◊Oratorio was developed in Italy by Giacomo Carissimi (1605–1674); in Germany, Heinrich Schütz produced a new form of sacred music.

18th century The early part of the century was dominated by J S Bach and Georg Friedrich Handel. Bach was a master of harmony and counterpoint. Handel is renowned for his dramatic oratorios. In France, their most important contemporaries were François Couperin in keyboard music and Jean-Philippe Rameau in grand opera and ballet; the later operas of Christoph Willibald von Gluck, with their emphasis on dramatic expression, saw a return to the principles of Monteverdi. The modern orchestra evolved out of various movements of the mid-1700s, notably that led by Johann Stamitz (1717–1757) at Mannheim. Bach's sons C P E Bach and J C Bach reacted against contrapuntal forms and developed sonata form, the basis of the classical sonata, quartet, and symphony. In these types of composition, mastery of style was achieved by the Viennese composers Franz Haydn and Wolfgang Mozart. With Ludwig van Beethoven, music assumed new dynamic and expressive functions.

19th century Romantic music, represented in its early stages by Carl Weber, Franz Schubert, Robert Schumann, Felix Mendelssohn, and Frédéric Chopin, tended to be subjectively emotional. Orchestral colour was increasingly exploited – most notably by Hector Berlioz – and harmony became more chromatic. Nationalism became prominent at this time, as evidenced by the intense Polish nationalism of Chopin; the exploitation of Hungarian music by Franz Liszt; the works of the Russians Nikolai Rimsky-Korsakov, Alexander Borodin, Modest Mussorgsky, and, less typically, Peter Tchaikovsky; the

‘Music, the greatest good that mortals know, / And all of heaven we have below.’

On MUSIC
Joseph Addison *Song for St Cecilia's Day*

mushroom The flesh of the red-staining mushroom *Agaricus langei*, a tasty edible species which appears in woodlands in autumn, turns red when cut or bruised. *Premaphotos Wildlife*

MUSIC, WESTERN: TIMELINE

AD 590 St Gregory the Great was elected pope. Under his rule, music attained new heights, initiating Gregorian chant.
1026 The Italian monk Guido d'Arezzo completed his treatise *Micrologus*. He founded modern notation and tonic sol-fa.
1207 Minnesingers (singer songwriters) Walther von der Vogelweide, Tannhäuser, and Wolfram von Eschenbach competed in a song contest at Wartburg Castle, later celebrated in Richard Wagner's opera *Die Meistersinger von Nürnberg*.
c.1240 The earliest known canon, *Sumer is Icumen In*, was composed.
1280 *Carmina Burana*, a collection of students' songs, was compiled in Benediktbuern, Bavaria; Carl Orff was later inspired by their subject matter.
1288 France's greatest troubadour, Adam de la Halle, died in Naples, Italy.
1320 *Ars nova*, a tract by the French composer Philippe de Vitry, gave its name to a new, more graceful era in music.
1364 Music's first large-scale masterpiece, the *Notre Dame Mass* of Guillaume de Machaut, was performed in Reims to celebrate the coronation of Charles V of France.
1453 John Dunstable, England's first composer of significance, died in London.
1473 The earliest known printed music, the *Collectorium super Magnificat* by Johannes Gerson, was published in Esslingen, near Stuttgart, Germany.
1521 Josquin Desprez, the leading musician of his time, died in Condé-sur-Escaut, Burgundy.
1550s Production of violins began at the workshop of Andrea Amati in Cremona.
1575 Thomas Tallis and William Byrd jointly published their *Cantiones sacrae*, a collection of 34 motets.
1576 Hans Sachs, the most famous of the Meistersinger (mastersinger) poets and composers, died in Nuremberg.
1597 The first opera, *La Dafne* by Jacopo Peri, was staged privately at the Corsi Palazzo in Florence.
1610 Claudio Monteverdi's *Vespers* was published in Venice.
1637 The world's first opera house opened in Venice.
1644 Antonio Stradivari was born. More than 600 of his violins, made in Cremona, survived into the 20th century.
1672 The violinist John Banister inaugurated the first season of public concerts in London.
1709 Bartolemmeo Cristofori unveiled the first fortepiano in Florence.
1721 J S Bach completed his six *Brandenburg Concertos* for Baroque orchestra.
1722 Jean-Philippe Rameau's book *Traité de l'harmonie* was published, founding modern harmonic theory.
1725 Antonio Vivaldi's orchestral suite *The Four Seasons* was published in Amsterdam.
1742 Georg Friedrich Handel's *Messiah* received its world premiere in Dublin, Ireland.
1753 C P E Bach wrote his influential treatise 'The Essay on the True Art of Playing Keyboard Instruments'.
1757 Johann Stamitz died in Mannheim, Rhine Palatinate, where he had made important contributions to the development of the symphony and raised the status of the orchestra.
1761 Franz Joseph Haydn took up liveried service as vice kapellmeister with the aristocratic Esterházy family, to whom he was connected until his death 1809.
1788 Wolfgang Amadeus Mozart completed his last three symphonies, numbers 39–41, in six weeks.
1798 The *Allgemeine Musikalische Zeitung*, a journal of music criticism, was first published in Leipzig, Germany.
1805 Ludwig van Beethoven's 'Eroica' Symphony was first performed; it vastly expanded the horizons of orchestral music.
1814 Johann Maelzel invented the metronome.
1815 Franz Schubert's output for this year included two symphonies, two masses, 20 waltzes, and 145 songs.
1821 Carl Weber's *Der Freischütz/The Marksman* introduced heroic German Romanticism to opera.
1828 The limits of instrumental virtuosity were redefined by the violinist Niccolò Paganini's Vienna debut.
1830 Hector Berlioz's dazzlingly avant-garde and programmatic *Symphonie fantastique* startled Paris concertgoers.
1831 Grand opera was inaugurated with *Robert le diable* by Giacomo Meyerbeer.
1839 Verdi's first opera, *Oberto*, was produced at La Scala, Milan.
1842 The Vienna Philharmonic Orchestra gave its first concerts.
1854 In Weimar, Germany, Franz Liszt conducted the premieres of his first symphonic poems.
1865 Richard Wagner's opera *Tristan and Isolde* scaled new heights of expressiveness using unprecedented chromaticism. Schubert's *Unfinished Symphony* (1822) was premiered in Vienna.
1875 The first of a series of collaborations between Arthur Sullivan and the librettist W S Gilbert, *Trial by Jury*, was given its premiere.
1876 Wagner's *The Ring of the Nibelung* was produced in Bayreuth. Johannes Brahms's *First Symphony* was performed in Karlsruhe.
1883 The Metropolitan Opera House opened in New York with a production of Charles Gounod's *Faust*.
1885 Liszt composed *Bagatelle without Tonality* (his *Faust Symphony* of 1857 opened with a 12-note row).
1894 Claude Debussy's *Prélude à l'après-midi d'un faune* anticipated 20th-century composition with its use of the whole-tone scale.
1895 Henry Wood conducted the first Promenade Concert at the Queen's Hall in London.
1899 Scott Joplin's *Maple Leaf Rag* was published in Sedalia, Missouri.
1900 Elgar's oratorio *Dream of Gerontius* was produced at the Birmingham Festival.
1902 Enrico Caruso recorded ten arias in a hotel room in Milan, the success of which established the popularity of the phonograph. By the time of his death 1921 he had earned $2 million from sales of his recordings.
1908 Camille Saint-Saëns became the first leading composer to write a film score, for *L'Assassinat du duc de Guise*.
1911 Irving Berlin had his first big success as a songwriter with 'Alexander's Ragtime Band'.
1912 Arnold Schoenberg's atonal *Pierrot lunaire*, for reciter and chamber ensemble, foreshadowed many similar small-scale quasi-theatrical works.
1913 Igor Stravinsky's ballet *The Rite of Spring* precipitated a riot at its premiere in Paris.
1921 Schoenberg wrote the first works based entirely on twelve-note serial technique.
1922 Alessandro Moreschi, last of the castrati, died in Rome.
1924 Puccini died, leaving his opera *Turandot* unfinished (completed by Alfano 1926). Gershwin's *Rhapsody in Blue* was premiered.
1925 Louis Armstrong made his first jazz records with the Hot Five. Duke Ellington's Washingtonians also started recording.
1927 Jerome Kern's *Show Boat*, with libretto by Oscar Hammerstein II, laid the foundations of the US musical.
1930 The BBC Symphony Orchestra was founded in London under Adrian Boult.
1937 Arturo Toscanini, one of the greatest conductors in the history of music, began his 17-year association with the NBC Symphony Orchestra.
1938 Sergei Prokofiev's score for Sergei Eisenstein's *Alexander Nevsky* raised film music to new levels.
Big-band music became popular.
1939 Elisabeth Lutyens was one of the first English composers to use 12-note composition in her *Chamber Concerto No 1* for nine instruments.
1940 Walt Disney's *Fantasia* introduced classical music, conducted by Leopold Stokowski, to a worldwide audience of filmgoers.
1940s Bebop jazz was initiated. The jazz greats Charlie Parker and Dizzy Gillespie first recorded together. Big bands, such as those led by Duke Ellington and Glen Miller, reached their height of popularity.
1942 In Chicago, John Cage conducted the premiere of his *Imaginary Landscape No 3*, scored for marimbula, gongs, tin cans, buzzers, plucked coil, electric oscillator, and generator.
1945 Bartók composed his final work, the *Third Piano Concerto*, and died later the same year in New York. Britten's *Peter Grimes* was premiered.
1954 Karlheinz Stockhausen's *Electronic Studies* for magnetic tape were broadcast in Cologne. Edgard Varèse's *Déserts*, the first work to combine instruments and prerecorded magnetic tape, was performed in Paris. Elvis Presley made his first rock-and-roll recordings in Memphis, Tennesee.
1955 Pierre Boulez's *Le Marteau sans maître*, for contralto and chamber ensemble, was performed in Baden-Baden. Its formidable serial technique and exotic orchestration were acclaimed by the avant-garde. The Miles Davis Quintet with John Coltrane united two of the most important innovators in jazz.
1956 The first annual Warsaw autumn festival of contemporary music was held. This became important for the promotion of Polish composers such as Witold Lutosławski and Krzystof Penderecki.
1957 Leonard Bernstein's *West Side Story* was premiered in New York. A computer, programmed at the University of Illinois by Lejaren Hiller and Leonard Isaacson, composed the *Illiac Suite* for string quartet.
1963 Dmitry Shostakovich's opera *Lady Macbeth of Mezensk*, earlier banned and condemned in the Soviet newspaper *Pravda* 1936, was produced in a revised version as *Katerina Ismaylova*.
1965 Robert Moog invented a synthesizer that considerably widened the scope of electronic music. The film soundtrack of *The Sound of Music*, with music by Rodgers and lyrics by Hammerstein, was released, and stayed in the sales charts for the next two years. Bob Dylan turned to electric instrumentation on *Highway 61 Revisited*.
1967 The Beatles' album *Sgt Pepper's Lonely Hearts Club Band*, which took over 500 hours to record, was released. The first Velvet Underground album was released. Psychedelic rock spread from San Francisco, and hard rock developed in the UK and the USA.
1969 Peter Maxwell Davies's theatre piece *Eight Songs for a Mad King*, for vocalist and six instruments, was premiered.
1971 B B King's popular *Live at the Regal* proved the continuing tradition of the blues.
1972 Bob Marley's LP *Catch a Fire* began the popularization of reggae beyond Jamaica.
1976 Philip Glass's opera *Einstein on the Beach*, using the repetitive techniques of minimalism, was given its first performance in Paris. Punk rock arrived with the Sex Pistols' 'Anarchy in the UK'.
1977 The Institute for Research and Coordination of Acoustics and Music (IRCAM) was founded in Paris under the direction of Pierre Boulez, for visiting composers to make use of advanced electronic equipment.
1981 MTV (Music Television) started broadcasting nonstop pop videos on cable in the USA, growing into a worldwide network in the following decade.
1983 Olivier Messiaen's only opera, *Saint François d'Assise*, was given its first performance in Paris. Lutosławski's *Third Symphony* was premiered to worldwide acclaim by the Chicago Symphony Orchestra under Georg Solti. Compact discs were launched.
1986 Paul Simon's *Graceland* album drew on and popularized world music.
1991 US rap group NWA declared not obscene by a UK court. Various attempts, especially in the USA, to limit freedom of speech in popular music were generally unsuccessful.
1997 'Candle in the Wind "97"' Elton John's tribute to Diana, Princess of Wales, became the best-selling single of all time.

works of the Czechs Antonin Dvořák and Bedřich Smetana; the Norwegian Edvard Grieg; and the Spaniards Isaac Albéniz, Enrique Granados, and Manuel de Falla. Revolutionary changes were brought about by Richard Wagner in the field of opera, although traditional Italian lyricism continued in the work of Gioacchino Rossini, Giuseppe Verdi, and Giacomo Puccini. Wagner's contemporary Johannes Brahms stood for Classical discipline of form combined with Romantic feeling. The Belgian César Franck, with a newly chromatic idiom, also renewed the tradition of polyphonic writing.

20th century Around 1900 a reaction against Romanticism became apparent in the impressionism of Claude Debussy and Maurice Ravel, and the exotic chromaticism of Igor Stravinsky and Alexander Scriabin. In Austria and Germany, the tradition of Anton Bruckner, Gustav Mahler, and Richard Strauss faced a disturbing new world of atonal expressionism in Arnold Schoenberg, Alban Berg, and Anton von Webern.

After World War I Neo-Classicism, represented by Stravinsky, Sergei Prokofiev, and Paul Hindemith, attempted to restore 18th-century principles of objectivity and order while maintaining a distinctively 20th-century tone. In Paris *Les Six* adopted a more relaxed style, while composers further from the cosmopolitan centres of Europe, such as Sir Edward Elgar, Frederick Delius, and Jean Sibelius, continued loyal to the Romantic symphonic tradition. The rise of radio and recorded media created a new mass market for classical and Romantic music, but one which was initially resistant to music by contemporary composers. Organizations such as the International Society for Contemporary Music became increasingly responsible for ensuring that new music continued to be publicly performed. Interest in English folk music was revived by the work of Gustav Holst and Ralph Vaughan-Williams.

Among other important contemporary composers are Béla Bartók and Zoltán Kodály in Hungary; Olivier Messiaen in France; Luigi Dallapiccola and Luciano Berio in Italy; Dmitri Shostakovich in Russia; and Sir Arthur Bliss, Aaron Copland, Edmund Rubbra, Sir William Walton, Samuel Barber, Benjamin Britten, and Michael Tippett in England and the USA.

modern developments The second half of the 20th century has seen dramatic changes in the nature of composition and in the instruments used to create sounds. The recording studio has facilitated the development of concrete music based on recorded natural sounds, and electronic music, in which sounds are generated electrically, developments implying the creation of music as a finished object without the need for interpretation by live performers. Chance music, promoted by John Cage, introduced the notion of a music designed to provoke unforeseen results and thereby make new connections; aleatoric music, developed by Pierre Boulez, introduced performers to freedom of choice from a range of options. In Germany, the avant-garde works of Karlheinz Stockhausen have introduced new musical sounds and compositional techniques. Since the 1960s the computer has become a focus of attention for developments in the synthesis of musical tones, and also in the automation of compositional techniques, most notably at Stanford University and MIT in the USA, and at IRCAM in Paris.

musical 20th-century form of dramatic musical performance, combining elements of song, dance, and the spoken word, often characterized by lavish staging and large casts. It developed from the operettas and musical comedies of the 19th century.

The ***operetta*** is a light-hearted entertainment with extensive musical content: Jacques Offenbach, Johann Strauss, Franz Lehár, and Gilbert and Sullivan all composed operettas. The ***musical comedy*** is an anglicization of the French *opéra bouffe*, of which the first was *A Gaiety Girl* 1893, mounted by George Edwardes (1852–1915) at the Gaiety Theatre, London. Typical musical comedies of the 1920s were *Rose Marie* 1924 by Rudolf Friml (1879–1972); *The Student Prince* 1924 and *The Desert Song* 1926, both by Sigmund Romberg (1887–1951); and *No, No, Nanette* 1925 by Vincent Youmans (1898–1946). The 1930s and 1940s were an era of sophisticated musical comedies with many filmed examples and a strong US presence (Irving Berlin, Jerome Kern, Cole Porter, and George Gershwin). In England Noël Coward and Ivor Novello also wrote musicals.

In 1943 Rodgers and Hammerstein's *Oklahoma!* introduced an integration of plot and music, which was developed in Lerner and Loewe's *My Fair Lady* 1956 and Leonard Bernstein's *West Side Story* 1957. Sandy Wilson's *The Boy Friend* 1953 revived the British musical and was followed by hits such as Lionel Bart's *Oliver!* 1960. Musicals began to branch into religious and political themes with *Oh, What a Lovely War* 1963, produced by Joan Littlewood and Charles Chiltern, and the Andrew Lloyd Webber musicals *Jesus Christ Superstar* 1971 and *Evita* 1978. Another category of musical, substituting a theme for conventional plotting, includes Stephen Sondheim's *Company* 1970, Hamlisch and Kleban's *A Chorus Line* 1975, and Lloyd Webber's *Cats* 1981, using verses by T S Eliot. In the 1980s 19th-century melodrama was popular, for example *Les Misérables* 1985 (first London performance) and *The Phantom of the Opera* 1986.

musical instrument digital interface manufacturer's standard for digital music equipment; see ◊MIDI.

music hall British light theatrical entertainment, in which singers, dancers, comedians, and acrobats perform in 'turns'. The music hall's heyday was at the beginning of the 20th century, with such artistes as Marie Lloyd, Harry Lauder, and George Formby. The US equivalent is vaudeville.

Many performers had a song with which they were associated, such as Albert Chevalier (1861–1923) ('My Old Dutch'), or a character 'trademark', such as Vesta Tilley's immaculate masculine outfit as Burlington Bertie. Later stars of music hall included Sir George Robey, Gracie Fields, the Crazy Gang, Ted Ray, and the US comedian Danny Kaye.

history Music hall originated in the 17th century, when tavern-keepers acquired the organs that the Puritans had banished from churches. On certain nights organ music was played, and this resulted in a weekly entertainment known as the 'free and easy'. Certain theatres in London and the provinces then began to specialize in variety entertainment. With the advent of radio and television, music hall declined, but in the 1960s and 1970s there was a revival in working men's clubs and in pubs.

music theatre staged performance of vocal music that deliberately challenges, in style and subject matter, traditional operatic pretensions. Drawing on English music-hall and European cabaret and *Singspiel* traditions, it flourished during the Depression of the 1920s and 1930s as working-class opera, for example the Brecht–Weill *Die Dreigroschenoper/The Threepenny Opera* 1928; in the USA as socially conscious musical, for example Gershwin's *Porgy and Bess* 1935; and on film, in René Clair's *Sous les Toits de Paris/Under the Roofs of Paris* 1930 (music composed by Raoul Moretti) and *A Nous la Liberté/Freedom for Us* 1931 (music by Georges Auric). Composers addressing a similar mood of social unrest in the years after 1968 include Henze (*Essay on Pigs* 1968), Berio (*Recital I* 1972), and Ligeti (*Le Grand Macabre/The Great Macabre*) 1978. Since 1970 music theatre has emerged as a favoured idiom for short-term community music projects produced by outreach departments of civic arts centres and opera houses.

Musil Robert 1880–1942. Austrian novelist. He was the author of the unfinished *Der Mann ohne Eigenschaften/The Man without Qualities* (three volumes) 1930–43. Its hero shares the author's background of philosophical study and scientific and military training, and is preoccupied with the problems of the self viewed from a mystic but agnostic viewpoint. Musil's analytic exploration of the motivation and the subconscious mind of his characters is reminiscent of James ◊Joyce, though in no way derivative.

musk in botany, perennial plant *Mimulus moschatus* of the family Scrophulariaceae; its small oblong leaves exude the musky scent from which it takes its name. Also any of several plants with a musky odour, including the musk mallow *Malva moschata* and the musk rose *Rosa moschata*.

musk deer any of three species of small deer of the genus *Moschus*, native to the mountains of central and NE Asia. A solitary animal, the musk deer is about 80–100 cm/30–40 in, sure-footed, and has large ears and no antlers. Males have long tusklike upper canine teeth. They are hunted and farmed for their musk (a waxy substance secreted by the male from an abdominal gland), which is used as medicine or perfume.

musk ox ruminant *Ovibos moschatus* of the family Bovidae, native to the Arctic regions of North America. It displays characteristics of sheep and oxen, is about the size of a small domestic cow, and has long brown hair. At certain seasons it exhales a musky odour.

muskrat rodent *Ondatra zibethicus* of the family Cricetidae, about 30 cm/12in long, living along streams, rivers, and lakes in North America. It has webbed hind feet, a side-to-side flattened tail, and shiny, light-brown fur. It builds up a store of food, plastering it over with mud, for winter consumption. It is hunted for its fur.

Muslim or ***Moslem***, a follower of ◊Islam.

Muslim Brotherhood Sunni Islamic movement founded in Egypt in 1928, active throughout the Arab world although banned in most countries. It aims at the establishment of a Muslim state governed by Islamic law. The movement, founded by Hasan al-Banna (1906–1949), also operates under different names, such as the ***People of the Call*** (Alh al-Da'wa) in Algeria and ***Islamic Party*** (al Hizb al-Islami) in Tunisia.

Muslim League Indian political organization. The All India Muslim League was founded 1906 under the leadership of the Aga Khan. In 1940 the league, led by Muhammad Ali ◊Jinnah, demanded an independent Muslim state. The ◊Congress Party and the Muslim League won most seats in the 1945 elections for an Indian central legislative assembly. In 1946 the Indian constituent assembly was boycotted by the Muslim League. It was partly the activities of the League that led to the establishment of Pakistan. ▷ *See feature on pp. 432–433.*

mussel one of a number of bivalve molluscs, some of them edible, such as *Mytilus edulis*, found in clusters attached to rocks around the N Atlantic and American coasts. It has a blue-black shell. The green-lipped mussel, found only off New Zealand, produces an extract that is used in the treatment of arthritis.

Musset (Louis Charles) Alfred de 1810–1857. French poet and playwright. He achieved success with the volume of poems *Contes d'Espagne et d'Italie/Stories of Spain and Italy* 1829. His autobiographical poem *Confessions d'un enfant du siècle/Confessions of a Child of the Century* 1835 recounts his broken relationship with the writer George ◊Sand. Typical of his work are the verse in *Les Nuits/Nights* 1835–37 and the short plays *Comédies et proverbes/Comedies and Proverbs* 1840. His play *Lorenzaccio* 1833 is a minor masterpiece.

Mussolini Benito Amilcare Andrea 1883–1945. Italian dictator 1925–43. As founder of the Fascist Movement (see ◊fascism) 1919 and prime minister from 1922, he became known as *Il Duce* ('the leader'). He invaded Ethiopia 1935–36, intervened in the Spanish Civil War 1936–39 in support of Franco, and conquered Albania 1939. In June 1940 Italy entered World War II supporting Hitler. Forced by military and domestic setbacks to resign 1943, Mussolini established a breakaway government in N Italy 1944–45, but was killed trying to flee the country.

Mussolini was born in the Romagna, the son of a blacksmith, and worked in early life as a teacher and journalist. He became active in the socialist movement, from which he was expelled 1914 for advocating Italian intervention in World War I. In 1919 he founded the Fascist Movement, whose programme combined violent nationalism with demagogic republican and anticapitalist slogans, and launched a campaign of terrorism against the socialists. This movement was backed by many landowners and industrialists and by the heads of the army and police, and in Oct 1922 Mussolini was in power as prime minister at the head of a coalition government. In 1925 he assumed dictatorial powers, and in 1926 all opposition parties were banned. During the years that followed, the political, legal, and education systems were remodelled on Fascist lines.

Mussolini's Blackshirt followers were the

> 'Fascism is a religion; the twentieth century will be known in history as the century of Fascism.'
>
> **Benito Mussolini**
> Quoted in
> George Seldes
> *Sawdust Caesar*

Mussolini Italian dictator Benito Mussolini. By 1930, when this picture was taken, he had been in power for eight years. Through vigorously suppressing opposition and introducing a wide range of popular reforms based on his notion of a corporate, authoritarian state he brought some stability to Italian political life. His expansionist foreign policy, however, though it offered to restore national pride, was to prove disastrous. *Topham*

forerunners of Hitler's Brownshirts, and his career of conquest drew him into close cooperation with Nazi Germany. Italy and Germany formed the ◊Axis alliance 1936. During World War II, Italian defeats in N Africa and Greece, the Allied invasion of Sicily, and discontent at home destroyed Mussolini's prestige, and in July 1943 he was compelled to resign by his own Fascist Grand Council. He was released from prison by German parachutists Sept 1943 and set up a 'Republican Fascist' government in N Italy. In April 1945 he and his mistress, Clara Petacci, were captured by partisans at Lake Como while heading for the Swiss border, and shot. Their bodies were taken to Milan and hung upside down in a public square.

Mussorgsky Modest Petrovich 1839–1881. Russian nationalist composer. He was a member of the group of five composers 'The Five'. His opera masterpiece *Boris Godunov* 1869, revised 1871–72, touched a political nerve and employed realistic transcriptions of speech patterns. Many of his works, including *Pictures at an Exhibition* 1874 for piano, were 'revised' and orchestrated by others, including Rimsky-Korsakov, Ravel, and Shostakovich, and some have only recently been restored to their original harsh beauty.

Mussorgsky resigned his commission in the army 1858 to concentrate on music while working as a government clerk. He was influenced by both folk music and literature. Among his other works are the incomplete operas *Khovanshchina* and *Sorochintsy Fair*, the orchestral *Night on the Bare Mountain* 1867, and many songs.

Mustafa Kemal Pasha Turkish leader who assumed the name of ◊Atatürk.

Muti The Italian conductor Riccardo Muti. He won the Guido Cantelli conducting prize 1967 and became principal conductor 1969 and musical director 1977 of the Florence Music Festival, Maggio Musicale. He made his operatic debut at Covent Garden 1977 with *Aïda*, and since then has worked with many leading orchestras and opera companies. *Sony Classical*

mustard any of several annual plants of the family Cruciferae, with sweet-smelling yellow flowers. Brown and white mustard are cultivated as a condiment in Europe and North America. The seeds of brown mustard *Brassica juncea* and white mustard *Sinapis alba* are used in the preparation of table mustard. ***English mustard*** is made from finely milled brown and white mustard seed to which turmeric is added as a colorant. French ***Dijon mustard*** contains brown mustard seed, verjuice (the juice of unripe grapes), oil, and white wine.

Mustique island in the Caribbean; see ◊St Vincent and the Grenadines.

mutagen any substance that increases the rate of gene ◊mutation. A mutagen may also act as a ◊carcinogen.

mutation in biology, a change in the genes produced by a change in the ◊DNA that makes up the hereditary material of all living organisms. Mutations, the raw material of evolution, result from mistakes during replication (copying) of DNA molecules. Only a few improve the organism's performance and are therefore favoured by ◊natural selection. Mutation rates are increased by certain chemicals and by radiation.

Common mutations include the omission or insertion of a base (one of the chemical subunits of DNA); these are known as ***point mutations***. Larger-scale mutations include removal of a whole segment of DNA or its inversion within the DNA strand. Not all mutations affect the organism, because there is a certain amount of redundancy in the genetic information. If a mutation is 'translated' from DNA into the protein that makes up the organism's structure, it may be in a nonfunctional part of the protein and thus have no detectable effect. This is known as a ***neutral mutation***. Some mutations do affect genes that control protein production or functional parts of protein, and most of these are lethal to the organism.

mute in music, any device used to dampen the vibration of an instrument and so affect the tone. Orchestral strings apply a form of clamp to the bridge. Brass instruments use the hand or a plug of metal or cardboard inserted in the bell.

Muti Riccardo 1941– . Italian conductor. Artistic director of La Scala, Milan, from 1986, he was conductor of the Philharmonia Orchestra, London, 1973–82 and the Philadelphia Orchestra from 1981. He is equally at home with opera or symphonic repertoire performed with bravura, energy, and scrupulous detail, and is known as a purist.

mutiny organized act of disobedience or defiance by two or more members of the armed services. In naval and military law, mutiny has always been regarded as one of the most serious of crimes, punishable in wartime by death. The last British soldier to be executed for mutiny was Private Jim Daly in India in 1920.

Effective mutinies in history include the ◊Indian Mutiny by Bengal troops against the British 1857 and the mutiny of some Russian soldiers in World War I who left the eastern front for home and helped to bring about the Russian Revolution of 1917. Most combatants in World War I suffered mutinies about the same time, the most serious outbreak affecting the French Army when whole battalions refused to fight. Several American units mutinied during the American Revolution and the War of 1812.

Mutiny Act in Britain, an act of Parliament, passed 1689 and re-enacted annually since then (since 1882 as part of the Army Acts), for the establishment and payment of a standing army. The act is intended to prevent an army from existing in peacetime without Parliament's consent.

Mutsuhito personal name of the Japanese emperor ◊Meiji.

mutton bird any of various shearwaters and petrels that breed in burrows on Australasian islands. The young are very fat, and are killed for food and oil.

mutual fund another name for ◊unit trust, used in the USA.

mutual induction in physics, the production of an electromotive force (emf) or voltage in an electric circuit caused by a changing ◊magnetic flux in a neighbouring circuit. The two circuits are often coils of wire, as in a ◊transformer, and the size of the induced emf depends largely on the numbers of turns of wire in each of the coils.

mutualism or ◊***symbiosis*** an association between two organisms of different species whereby both profit from the relationship.

Muybridge Eadweard. Adopted name of Edward James Muggeridge 1830–1904. English-born US photographer. He made a series of animal locomotion photographs in the USA in the 1870s and proved that, when a horse trots, there are times when all its feet are off the ground. He also explored motion in birds and humans.

Muzorewa Abel (Tendekayi) 1925– . Zimbabwean politician and Methodist bishop. He was president of the African National Council 1971–85 and prime minister of Rhodesia/Zimbabwe 1979–80. He was detained for a year in 1983–84. He was leader of the minority United Africa National Council, which merged with the Zimbabwe Unity Movement (ZUM) 1994. He pulled out of the 1996 presidential election contest at the last minute, claiming the electoral process was unfairly tilted in President Mugabe's favour.

Mwinyi Ali Hassan 1925– . Tanzanian socialist politician, succeeding Julius Nyerere as president 1985–95. He began a revival of private enterprise and control of state involvement and spending, and also instituted a multi-party political system 1995. However in Oct he lost the first free presidential elections.

Myanmar formerly (until 1989) ***Burma*** country in SE Asia, bounded NW by India and Bangladesh, NE by China, SE by Laos and Thailand, and SW by the Bay of Bengal. *See country box opposite.*

mycelium interwoven mass of threadlike filaments or ◊hyphae, forming the main body of most fungi. The reproductive structures, or 'fruiting bodies', grow from the mycelium.

Mycenae ancient Greek city in the E Peloponnese, which gave its name to the Mycenaean (Bronze Age) civilization. Its peak was 1400–1200 BC, when the Cyclopean walls (using close-fitting stones) were erected. The city ceased to be inhabited after about 1120 BC.

Mycenaean art art of Mycenae, from about 1580–1100 BC. It reflects the warlike preoccupations of the mainland Mycenean society, both in character and in the subjects portrayed. Fortified citadels were developed, such as that of Mycenae itself, which was entered through the Lion Gate, about 1330 BC, so called because of the massive lion figures, carved from stone, that adorned it. Stylized frescoes decorated its palaces and its pottery, typically dark-on-light, was centred on large bowls, or kraters, depicting scenes of warfare. Perhaps its overriding artistic contribution lies in its metalwork, principally in bronze and gold, for example the royal funeral mask (National Museum, Athens), about 1500 BC. Many of the ideas and art forms of the Mycenean and other early sea-faring civilizations influenced the Greeks (see ◊Greek art).

Mycenaean civilization Bronze Age civilization that flourished in Crete, Cyprus, Greece, the Aegean Islands, and W Anatolia about 2000–1100 BC, and reached its height 1450 BC. During this period, magnificent architecture and sophisticated artefacts were produced. Mycenaean civilization was strongly influenced by the ◊Minoan from Crete, from about 1600 BC. It continued to thrive, with its centre at Mycenae, after the decline of Crete in about 1400. It was finally overthrown by the Dorian invasions, about 1100. The system of government was by kings, who also monopolized priestly functions. The Mycenaeans have been identified with the ◊Achaeans of Homer; they may also have been the marauding ◊Sea Peoples of Egyptian records.

They used a form of Greek deciphered by Michael ◊Ventris called Linear B, which has been discovered on large numbers of clay tablets containing administrative records. Their palaces were large and luxurious, and their tombs (known as beehive tombs) were massive and impressive monuments. Pottery, frescoes, and metalwork reached a high artistic level. Evidence of the civilization was brought to light by the excavations of Heinrich ◊Schliemann at Troy, Mycenae, and Tiryns (a stronghold on the plain of Argolis) from 1870 onwards, and of Arthur ◊Evans in Crete from 1899. *See illustration on p. 742.*

THE AMBLE.
A HALF-STRIDE IN SIX PHASES.
Horse "Clinton."

Muybridge Series of photographs from Eadweard Muybridge's book *Animal Locomotion* 1877. Using a complex array of trip wires and cameras, Muybridge captured a wide variety of animal motion. He was also a pioneer of cinematography: he invented the zoopraxiscope, which used still images to give the impression of motion. *Ann Ronan/ Image Select (UK) Ltd*

mycorrhiza mutually beneficial (mutualistic) association occurring between plant roots and a soil fungus. Mycorrhizal roots take up nutrients more efficiently than non-mycorrhizal roots, and the fungus benefits by obtaining carbohydrates from the plant or tree.

myelin sheath insulating layer that surrounds nerve cells in vertebrate animals. It serves to speed up the passage of nerve impulses. Myelin is made up of fats and proteins and is formed from up to a hundred layers, laid down by special cells, the Schwann cells.

Myers F(rederic) W(illiam) H(enry) 1843–1901. English psychic researcher and classical scholar. He coined the word 'telepathy' and was a founder 1882 and one of the first presidents, 1900, of the Society for Psychical Research. His main works include *Essays Classical and Modern* 1883, *Phantasms of the Living* 1886, *Science and a Future Life* 1893, and the posthumous *Human Personality and its Survival of Bodily Death* 1903.

My Lai massacre killing of 109 civilians in My Lai, a village in South Vietnam, by US troops in March 1968. An investigation in 1969 produced enough evidence to charge 30 soldiers with war crimes, but the only soldier convicted was Lt William Calley, commander of the platoon.

mynah any of various tropical starlings, family Sturnidae, order Passeriformes, of SE Asia. The glossy blackhill mynah *Gracula religiosa* of India is a realistic mimic of sounds and human speech. It is up to 40 cm/16 in long with yellow wattles on the head, and a yellow bill and legs.

myoglobin globular protein, closely related to ◊haemoglobin and located in vertebrate muscle. Oxygen binds to myoglobin and is released only when the haemoglobin can no longer supply adequate oxygen to muscle cells.

myopia or ***short-sightedness*** defect of the eye in which a person can see clearly only those objects

MYANMAR

Union of (formerly *Burma*, until 1989)

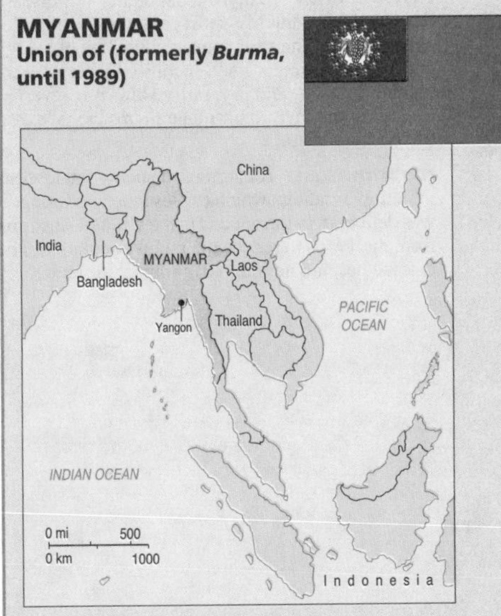

national name *Thammada Myanmar Naingngandaw*
area 676,577 sq km/261,228 sq mi
capital (and chief port) Yangon (formerly Rangoon)
major towns/cities Mandalay, Moulmein, Pegu, Bassein
physical features over half is rainforest; rivers Irrawaddy and Chindwin in central lowlands ringed by mountains in N, W, and E
head of state and government Than Shwe from 1992
political system military republic
administrative divisions seven states and seven provinces
political parties National Unity Party (NUP), military-socialist ruling party; National League for Democracy (NLD), pluralist opposition grouping
population 46,527,000 (1995 est)
population growth rate 2.1% (1990–95); 1.9% (2000–05)
ethnic distribution Burmans, who predominate the fertile central river valley and southern coastal and delta regions, constitute the ethnic majority, comprising 72% of the total population. Out of more than 100 minority communities, the most important are the Karen (7%), Shan (6%), Indians (6%), Chinese (3%), Kachin (2%), and Chin (2%). The indigenous minority communities, who predominate in mountainous border regions, show considerable hostility towards the culturally and politically dominant Burmans, undermining national unity
life expectancy 61 (men), 64 (women)
literacy rate men 89%, women 72%
languages Burmese (official), English
religions Hinayāna Buddhist 85%, animist, Christian, Muslim
currency kyat
GDP (US $) 55.2 billion (1993)
growth rate 6.8% (1994)
exports rice, rubber, jute, teak, jade, rubies, sapphires, pulses and beans

HISTORY

3rd C BC Sittoung valley settled by Mons; Buddhism introduced by missionaries from India.
3rd C AD Arrival of Burmans from Tibet.
1057 First Burmese Empire established by King Anawrahta, who conquered Thaton, established a capital inland at Pagan, and adopted Theravāda Buddhism.
1287 Pagan sacked by Mongols.
1531 Founding of Toungoo dynasty, which survived until the mid-18th century.
1755 Nation reunited by Alaungpaya, with the port of Rangoon as capital.
1824–26 First Anglo-Burmese war resulted in Arakan coastal strip, between Chittagong and Cape Negrais, being ceded to British India.
1852 Following defeat in second Anglo-Burmese war, Lower Burma, including Rangoon, was annexed by British.
1886 Upper Burma was ceded to British after defeat of Thibaw in third Anglo-Burmese war; British united Burma, which was administered as a province of British India.
1886–96 Guerrilla warfare waged against British in northern Burma.
early 20th C Developed as major rice, teak and, later, oil exporter, drawing in immigrant labourers and traders from India and China.
1937 Became a British crown colony in the Commonwealth, with a degree of internal self-government.
1942 Invaded and occupied by Japan, who installed an anti-British nationalist puppet government headed by Ba Maw.
1945 Liberated from Japanese control by the British, assisted by the nationalists Aung San and U Nu, formerly ministers in the puppet government, who had formed the socialist Anti Fascist People's Freedom League (AFPFL).
1947 Assassination of Aung San and six members of interim government by political opponents.
1948 Independence achieved from Britain as Burma, with U Nu as prime minister. Left the Commonwealth. Quasi-federal state established.
1958–60 Administered by emergency government, formed by army chief of staff Genreal Ne Win.
1962 General Ne Win re-assumed power in a left-wing army coup, and proceeded to abolish the federal system, crippling the economy.
1973–74 Adopted presidential-style 'civilian' constitution.
1975 Opposition National Democratic Front formed by regionally-based minority groups, who mounted guerrilla insurgencies.
1987 Student demonstrations in Rangoon as food shortages worsened.
1988 Government resigned after violent student demonstrations and workers' riots. General Saw Maung seized power in military coup believed to have been organized by the ousted Ne Win; over 2,000 killed.
1989 Martial law declared; thousands arrested including advocates of democracy and human rights. Country renamed Myanmar and capital Yangon.
1990 Landslide victory for opposition National League for Democracy (NLD) in general election ignored by military junta; NLD leaders U Nu and Suu Kyi, the daughter of Aung San, placed under house arrest. Breakaway opposition group formed 'parallel government'.
1991 Martial law and human-rights abuses continued. Government crackdown on Karen ethnic rebels in the SE. Suu Kyi, still imprisoned, awarded Nobel Prize for Peace. Pogrom against Muslim community in Arakan province in SW Myanmar. Western countries imposed sanctions.
1992 Saw Maung replaced by Than Shwe. Several political prisoners liberated. Martial law lifted, but restrictions on political freedom remained.
1993 Cease-fire agreed with Kachin rebels in the NE.
1995 Karen rebels forced to flee to Thailand after further military crackdown. Suu Kyi released from house arrest, but her appointment as NLD leader declared illegal. NLD boycotted constitutional convention.
1996 Karen rebels agreed to peace talks. Suu Kyi held first party congress since her release; 200 supporters detained by government.
1997 Admission to Association of South East Asian Nations (ASEAN) granted, despite US sanctions for human-rights abuses. Currency under threat from speculators.

SEE ALSO Aung San; Burman; Karen; Suu Kyi, Aung San

Mycenaean civilization Two Mycenaean idols. Little is known in detail about the Mycenaean civilization, but its culture forms the background to the story of the Trojan war as told by Homer. Agamemnon, who led the Greek forces against the Trojans, was king of Mycenae. *Corbis*

that are close up. It is caused either by the eyeball being too long or by the cornea and lens system of the eye being too powerful, both of which cause the images of distant objects to be formed in front of the retina instead of on it. Nearby objects are sharply perceived. Myopia can be corrected by suitable glasses or contact lenses.

myopia, low-luminance poor night vision. About 20% of people have poor vision in twilight and nearly 50% in the dark. Low-luminance myopia does not show up in normal optical tests, but in 1989 a method was developed of measuring the degree of blurring by projecting images on a screen using a weak laser beam.

Myrdal (Karl) Gunnar 1898–1987. Swedish economist, author of many works on development economics. He shared a Nobel prize in 1974.

myrmecophyte plant that lives in association with a colony of ants and possesses specialized organs in which the ants live. For example, *Myrmecodia*, an epiphytic plant from Malaysia, develops root tubers containing a network of cavities inhabited by ants.

Myrmidon in Greek mythology, one of the soldiers of the Greek warrior ◊Achilles, whom he commanded at the siege of Troy in Homer's *Iliad*. They came from Thessaly, in N Greece.

Myron c. 500–440 BC. Greek sculptor. A late contemporary of ◊Phidias, he is known to have made statues of the athletes Timanthes (456) and Lycinus (448), excelling in the representation of movement. His bronze *Discobolus/Discus-Thrower* and *Athene and Marsyas*, much admired in his time, are known through Roman copies, which confirm his ancient reputation for brilliant composition and naturalism.

myrrh gum resin produced by small trees of the genus *Commiphora* of the bursera family, especially *C. myrrha*, found in Ethiopia and Arabia. In ancient times it was used for incense and perfume and in embalming.

myrtle evergreen shrub of the Old World genus *Myrtus*, family Myrtaceae. The commonly cultivated Mediterranean myrtle *M. communis* has oval opposite leaves and white flowers followed by purple berries, all of which are fragrant.

mystery play or ***miracle play*** medieval religious drama based on stories from the Bible. Mystery plays were performed around the time of church festivals, reaching their height in Europe during the 15th and 16th centuries. A whole cycle running from the Creation to the Last Judgement was performed in separate scenes on mobile wagons by various town guilds, usually on the festival of Corpus Christi in mid-summer. Four English cycles survive: Coventry, Wakefield (or Townley), Chester, and York.

mystery religion any of various cults of the ancient world, open only to the initiated; for example, the cults of Demeter (see ◊Eleusinian Mysteries), Dionysus, Cybele, Isis, and Mithras. Underlying some of them is a fertility ritual, in which a deity undergoes death and resurrection and the initiates feed on the flesh and blood to attain communion with the divine and ensure their own life beyond the grave. The influence of mystery religions on early Christianity was considerable.

mysticism religious belief or spiritual experience based on direct, intuitive communion with the divine. It does not always involve an orthodox deity, though it is found in all the main religions – for example, kabbalism in Judaism, Sufism in Islam, and the bhakti movement in Hinduism. The mystical experience is often rooted in asceticism and can involve visions, trances, and ecstasies; many religious traditions prescribe meditative and contemplative techniques for achieving mystical experience. Official churches fluctuate between acceptance of mysticism as a form of special grace, and suspicion of it as a dangerous deviation, verging on the heretical.

mythology body of traditional stories symbolically underlying a given culture. These stories describe gods and other supernatural beings with whom humans may have relationships, and are often intended to explain the workings of the universe, nature, or human history. Ancient mythologies, with the names of the chief god of each, include those of Egypt (Osiris), Greece (Zeus), Rome (Jupiter), India (Brahma), and the Teutonic peoples (Odin or Woden).

myxoedema thyroid-deficiency disease developing in adult life, most commonly in middle-aged women. The symptoms include loss of energy and appetite, weight gain, inability to keep warm, mental dullness, and dry, puffy skin. It is reversed by giving the thyroid hormone thyroxine. See also ◊hypothyroidism.

myxomatosis contagious, usually fatal, virus infection of rabbits which causes much suffering. It was deliberately introduced in the UK and Australia from the 1950s to reduce the rabbit population. The disease has had no long-term impact in the UK.

NAACP abbreviation for ◊***National Association for the Advancement of Colored People***, a US civil-rights organization.

Nabis, les (Hebrew 'prophets') group of French painters formed towards the end of the 19th century in an effort to clarify modern purpose in painting. Paul Sérusier, a follower of Gauguin, invented the name, Nabiim ('the divinely inspired'). He was joined by Maurice Denis, who became the theoretician of the movement, Paul Ranson, K X Roussel, Pierre Bonnard, Edouard Vuillard, and Félix Vallotton. Reacting against Impressionism, they sought to give ideas aesthetic form (see ◊Symbolism).The movement is of note as part of the ferment of ideas that preceded Fauvism and Cubism.

Nabokov Vladimir Vladimirovich 1899–1977. Russian-born US writer. He left Russia 1917 and began writing in English in the 1940s. His most widely known book is *Lolita* 1955, the story of the middle-aged Humbert Humbert's infatuation with a precocious girl of 12. His other books, remarkable for their word play and ingenious plots, include *Laughter in the Dark* 1938, *The Real Life of Sebastian Knight* 1945, *Pnin* 1957, and his memoirs *Speak, Memory* 1947.

nacre another name for ◊mother-of-pearl.

Nadar Adopted name of Gaspard-Félix Tournachon 1820–1910. French portrait photographer and caricaturist. He took the first aerial photographs (from a balloon 1858) and was the first to take flash photographs (using magnesium bulbs).

Nader Ralph 1934– . US lawyer and consumer advocate. Called the 'scourge of corporate morality', he led many major consumer campaigns. His book *Unsafe at Any Speed* 1965 led to US car-safety legislation. In 1996 he was nominated for president of the Green Party at the organization's first ever political convention in the USA.

Nabokov Novelist Vladimir Nabokov spent all his adult life in exile. Born to a noble and wealthy family in Russia, he moved to Germany after the Russian Revolution, then, fleeing the Nazis, to the USA, and finally to Switzerland. Themes of estrangement and social isolation or, in the case of *Lolita*, perversity are integral to his finely styled novels. *Topham.*

Nagasaki The devastation caused by the atomic bomb dropped 9 Aug 1945. A vast area was obliterated, heat and shock waves killing many thousands, massive doses of neutron and gamma radiation causing thousands of further deaths over the next few decades. The hills surrounding the city helped to contain the explosion and so prevented even worse devastation. *Library of Congress*

nadir the point on the celestial sphere vertically below the observer and hence diametrically opposite the zenith. The term is used metaphorically to mean the low point of a person's fortunes.

naevus mole, or patch of discoloration on the skin which has been present from birth. There are many different types of naevi, including those composed of a cluster of small blood vessels, such as the 'strawberry mark' (which usually disappears early in life), and the 'port-wine stain'.

A naevus of moderate size is harmless, and such marks can usually be disguised cosmetically unless they are extremely disfiguring, when they can sometimes be removed by cutting out, burning with an electric needle, freezing with carbon dioxide snow, or by argon laser treatment. In rare cases a mole may be a precursor of a malignant ◊melanoma. Any changes in a mole, such as enlargement, itching, soreness, or bleeding, should be reported to a doctor.

NAFTA acronym for ◊***North American Free Trade Agreement***.

Naga any of the various peoples who inhabit the highland region near the Indian/Myanmar (Burma) border; they number approximately 800,000. These peoples do not possess a common name; some of the main groups are Ao, Konyak, Sangtam, Lhota, Sema, Rengma, Chang, and Angami. They live by farming, hunting, and fishing. Their languages belong to the Sino-Tibetan family.

Nagaland state of NE India, bordering Myanmar (Burma) on the east
area 16,600 sq km/6,409 sq mi
capital Kohima
industries rice, tea, coffee, paper, sugar
population (1994 est) 1,410,000
history formerly part of Assam, the area was seized by Britain from Burma (now Myanmar) 1826. After India attained independence 1947, there was Naga guerrilla activity against the Indian government; the state of Nagaland was established 1963 in response to demands for self-government, but fighting continued sporadically. A peace accord was struck with the guerrillas 1975 but fighting resumed 1980. Charges of serious human-rights violations have been filed against Indian forces operating in the area. The Naga guerrillas have links with other rebel groups in NE India, but there is conflict between groups over protection money from the heroin trade, transport, and banking; by Aug 1993 they had forced the closure of 57 of the 63 bank branches in Nagaland and held hundreds of lorries to ransom on the Nagaland–Assam border.

Nagasaki industrial port (coal, iron, shipbuilding) on Kyushu Island, Japan; population (1994) 438,000. Nagasaki was the only Japanese port open to European trade from the 16th century until 1859. An atom bomb was dropped on it by the USA 9 Aug 1945.

Three days after ◊Hiroshima, the second atom bomb was dropped here at the end of World War II. Of Nagasaki's population of 212,000, 73,884 were killed and 76,796 injured, not counting the long-term victims of radiation.

Nagorno-Karabakh (Russian 'mountainous Qarabagh') autonomous region of ◊Azerbaijan
area 4,400 sq km/1,700 sq mi
capital Stepanakert
industries cotton, grapes, wheat, silk
population (1990) 192,400 (77% Armenian, 22% Azeri), the Christian Armenians forming an enclave within the predominantly Shi'ite Muslim Azerbaijan
history the region formed part of Armenia until the 7th century, but was subsequently taken by the Arabs. An autonomous protectorate after the Russian Revolution 1917, it was annexed to Azerbaijan 1923 against the wishes of the largely Christian-Armenian population. From 1989, when the local council declared its intention to transfer control of the region to Armenia, the enclave was racked by fighting between local Armenian troops (reputedly backed by Armenia) and Azeri forces, both attempting to assert control. After a declaration of independence by the region's parliament Dec 1991, the conflict intensified and by June 1993 Armenian forces had overrun much of Nagorno-Karabakh. By Feb 1994, 18,000 Armenians and 5,000 Azeri were reported to have been killed in the conflict, and one million people made refugees. By 1996, Nagorno-Karabakh was effectively an independent state, with its own president.

Nagoya industrial seaport (cars, textiles, clocks) on Honshu Island, Japan; population (1994) 2,091,000. It has a shogun fortress 1610 and a notable Shinto shrine, Atsuta Jingu.

Nagpur industrial city (textiles, metals) in Maharashtra, India, on the river Pench; population (1991) 1,661,000. Pharmaceuticals, cotton goods, and hosiery are produced, and oranges are traded. Nagpur was founded in the 18th century, and was the former capital of Berar and Madhya Pradesh states.

Nagy Imre 1895–1958. Hungarian politician, prime minister 1953–55 and 1956. He led the Hungarian revolt against Soviet domination in 1956, for which he was executed.

Nahayan Sheik Sultan bin Zayed al- 1918– . Emir of Abu Dhabi from 1969, when he deposed his brother, Sheik Shakhbut. He was elected president of the supreme council of the United Arab Emirates 1971. In 1991 he was implicated, through his majority ownership, in the international financial scandals associated with the Bank of Commerce and Credit International (BCCI), and in 1994 approved a payment by Abu Dhabi of $1.8 billion to BCCI creditors.

Nahuatl any of a group of Mesoamerican Indian peoples (Mexico and Central America), of which the best-known group were the Aztecs. The Nahuatl are the largest ethnic group in Mexico, and their languages, which belong to the Uto-Aztecan

'I am sufficiently proud of my knowing something to be modest about my not knowing all.'

Vladimir Nabokov *Lolita*

'I'm the kind of writer that people think other people are reading.'

V S Naipaul
Quoted in *Radio Times* 1979

(Aztec-Tanoan) family, are spoken by over a million people today.

naiad in classical mythology, a water nymph. Naiads lived in rivers and streams; ◊Nereids in the sea.

Naipaul V(idiadhar) S(urajprasad) 1932– . Trinidadian novelist living in Britain. His novels include *A House for Mr Biswas* 1961, *The Mimic Men* 1967, *A Bend in the River* 1979, *Finding the Centre* 1984, and *A Way in the World* 1994. His brother ***Srinivasa ('Shiva') Naipaul*** (1945–1985) was also a novelist (*Fireflies* 1970) and journalist.

Nairobi capital of Kenya, in the central highlands at 1,660 m/5,450 ft; population (1989) 1,346,000. It has light industry and food processing. It is the headquarters of the United Nations Environment Programme, and has the UN Centre for Human Settlements.

Nairobi was founded 1899. It has the International Louis Leakey Institute for African Prehistory 1977, and the International Primate Research Institute is nearby.

naive art fresh, childlike style of painting, employing bright colours and strong, rhythmic designs, usually the work of artists with no formal training. Outstanding naive artists include Henri Rousseau and Camille Bombois (1883–1970) in France, and Alfred Wallis (1855–1942) in England. The term is also used to describe the work of trained artists who employ naive techniques and effects, for example, L S Lowry.

Najibullah Ahmadzai 1947–1996. Afghan communist politician, leader of the People's Democratic Party of Afghanistan (PDPA) from 1986, and state president 1986–92. Although his government initially survived the withdrawal of Soviet troops Feb 1989, continuing pressure from the Mujaheddin forces resulted in his eventual overthrow. In the spring of 1992, he was captured while attempting to flee the country and placed under United Nations protection, pending trial by an Islamic court. However, in Sept 1996 he was executed by the ◊Talibaan (Islamic student army) who had seized governmental control of most of Afghanistan.

Nakasone Yasuhiro 1917– . Japanese conservative politician, leader of the Liberal Democratic Party (LDP) and prime minister 1982–87. He stepped up military spending and increased Japanese participation in international affairs, with closer ties to the USA. He was forced to resign his party post May 1989 as a result of having profited from insider trading in the Recruit scandal. After serving a two-year period of atonement, he rejoined the LDP April 1991.

Nakhichevan autonomous republic forming part of Azerbaijan, even though it is entirely outside the Azerbaijan boundary, being separated from it by Armenia; area 5,500 sq km/2,120 sq mi; population (1994) 315,000. Industries include cotton, tobacco, fruit, silk, and meat packing. Taken by Russia in 1828, it was annexed to Azerbaijan in 1924. Some 85% of the population are Muslim Azeris who maintain strong links with Iran to the south. Nakhichevan has been affected by the Armenia–Azerbaijan conflict; many Azeris have fled to Azerbaijan, and in Jan 1990 frontier posts and border fences with Iran were destroyed. In May 1992 Armenian forces made advances in the region, but Azeri forces soon regained control. The republic has sought independence from Azerbaijan.

Namib Desert coastal desert region in Namibia between the Kalahari Desert and the Atlantic Ocean. Its aridity is caused by the descent of dry air cooled by the cold Benguela current along the coast. The sand dunes of the Namib Desert are among the tallest in the world, reaching heights of 370 m/1,200 ft. ▷ *See feature on pp. 308–309.*

Namibia formerly (to 1968) ***South West Africa*** country in SW Africa, bounded N by Angola and Zambia, E by Botswana and South Africa, and W by the Atlantic Ocean. *See country box below.*

Nanak 1469–c. 1539. Indian guru and founder of Sikhism, a religion based on the unity of God and the equality of all human beings. He was strongly opposed to caste divisions.

Greatly influenced by Islamic mysticism (Sufism), Nanak preached a new path of release from the Hindu cycle of rebirth and caste divisions through sincere meditation on the name of God. He is revered by Sikhs ('disciples') as the first of their ten gurus (religious teachers). At 50, after many years travelling and teaching, he established a new town in the Punjab called Kartarpur, where many people came to live as his disciples. On his deathbed, Guru Nanak announced his friend Lehna as his successor, and gave him the name Angad ('part of me').

Nana Sahib Popular name for Dandhu Panth 1820–c. 1859. The adopted son of a former peshwa (chief minister) of the ◊Maratha people of central India, he joined the rebels in the ◊Indian Mutiny 1857–58, and was responsible for the massacre at Kanpur when safe conducts given to British civilians were broken and many women and children massacred. After the failure of the mutiny he took refuge in Nepal.

Nancarrow Conlon 1912–1997. US composer. He settled in Mexico 1940. Using a player-piano as a form of synthesizer, punching the rolls by hand, he experimented with mathematically derived combinations of rhythm and tempo in *37 Studies for Piano-Player* 1950–68, works of a hypnotic persistence that aroused the admiration of a younger generation of minimalist composers.

Nanchang industrial city (textiles, glass, porcelain, soap), capital of Jiangxi province, China,

NAMIBIA
Republic of (formerly *South West Africa*, until 1968)

area 824,300 sq km/318,262 sq mi
capital Windhoek
major towns/cities Swakopmund, Rehoboth, Rundu
major ports Walvis Bay
physical features mainly desert (Namib and Kalahari); Orange River; Caprivi Strip links Namibia to Zambezi River; includes the enclave of Walvis Bay (area 1,120 sq km/432 sq mi)
head of state Sam Nujoma from 1990
head of government Hage Geingob from 1990
political system democratic republic
administrative divisions 13 regions
political parties South West Africa People's Organization (SWAPO), socialist Ovambo-oriented; Democratic Turnhalle Alliance (DTA), moderate, multiracial coalition; United Democratic Front (UDF), disaffected ex-SWAPO members; National Christian Action (ACN), white conservative
population 1,540,000 (1995 est)
population growth rate 2.7% (1990–95); 2.5% (2000–05)
ethnic distribution 85% black African, of which 51% belong to the Ovambo tribe; the remainder includes the pastoral Nama and hunter-gatherer groups. There is a 6% white minority
life expectancy 58 (men), 60 (women)
literacy rate 38%
languages English (official), Afrikaans, German, indigenous languages
religions mainly Christian (Lutheran, Roman Catholic, Dutch Reformed Church, Anglican)
currency Namibia dollar
GDP (US $) 2.88 billion (1994)
growth rate 5.4% (1994)
exports diamonds, uranium, copper, lead, zinc, cattle, fish, meat products

HISTORY
1480s Coast visited by European explorers.
16th C Bantu-speaking Herero migrated into NW and Ovambo settled in northernmost areas.
1840s Rhenish Missionary Society began to spread German influence; Jonkar Afrikaner conquest state dominant in southern Namibia.
1884 Germany annexed most of the area, terming it South West Africa, with Britain incorporating a small enclave around Walvis Bay in the Cape Colony of South Africa.
1892 German farmers arrived to settle in the region.
1903–04 Uprisings by long-settled indigenous peoples, including the Herero, brutally repressed by Germans, with over half the local communities slaughtered.
1908 Diamonds discovered, leading to a larger European influx.
1915 German colony invaded and seized by South Africa during World War I and the Ovambo, in the N, were conquered.
1920 Administered by South Africa, under League of Nations mandate.
1946 Full incorporation in South Africa refused by United Nations (UN).
1949 White voters in South West Africa were given representation in the South African parliament.
1960 Radical wing of SWAPO, led by Sam Nujoma, forced into exile.
1964 UN voted to end South Africa's mandate, but South Africa refused to relinquish control or soften its policies towards the economically disenfranchised black majority population.
1966 South Africa's racist apartheid laws extended to the country; 60% of land was allocated to whites, who formed 10% of the population.
1968 South West Africa redesignated Namibia by UN. South West Africa People's Organization (SWAPO), campaigning for racial equality and full independence since the late 1950s, drew strong support from the Ovambo people of the N and began an armed guerrilla struggle against South African rule, establishing the People's Liberation Army of Namibia (PLAN).
1971 Prolonged general strike by black Namibian contract workers.
1973 The UN recognized SWAPO as the 'authentic representative of the Namibian people'.
1975–76 Establishment of new Marxist regime in independent Angola strengthened the position of the SWAPO guerrilla movement, but also led to increased military involvement of South Africa in the region.
1978 UN Security Council Resolution 435 for the granting of full independence accepted by South Africa and then rescinded.
1983 Direct rule reimposed by Pretoria after the resignation of the Democratic Turnhalle Alliance (DTA), a conservative administration dominated by whites.
1985 South Africa installed a new puppet administration, the Transitional Government of National Unity (TGNU), which tried to reform the apartheid system, but was not recognized by the UN.
1988 Peace talks between South Africa, Angola, and Cuba led to agreement on troop withdrawals and full independence for Namibia.
1989 UN peacekeeping force stationed to oversee free elections to an assembly to draft a new constitution; SWAPO won the elections.
1990 Liberal multiparty constitution adopted; independence achieved. Sam Nujoma, SWAPO's former guerrilla leader, elected president. Joined Commonwealth.
1993 South Africa, with its new multiracial government, relinquished claim to Walvis Bay sovereignty. Namibia dollar launched with South African rand parity.
1994 SWAPO won assembly elections and Nujoma re-elected president.

SEE ALSO apartheid; ; Khoikhoi; League of Nations; SWAPO; Walvis Bay

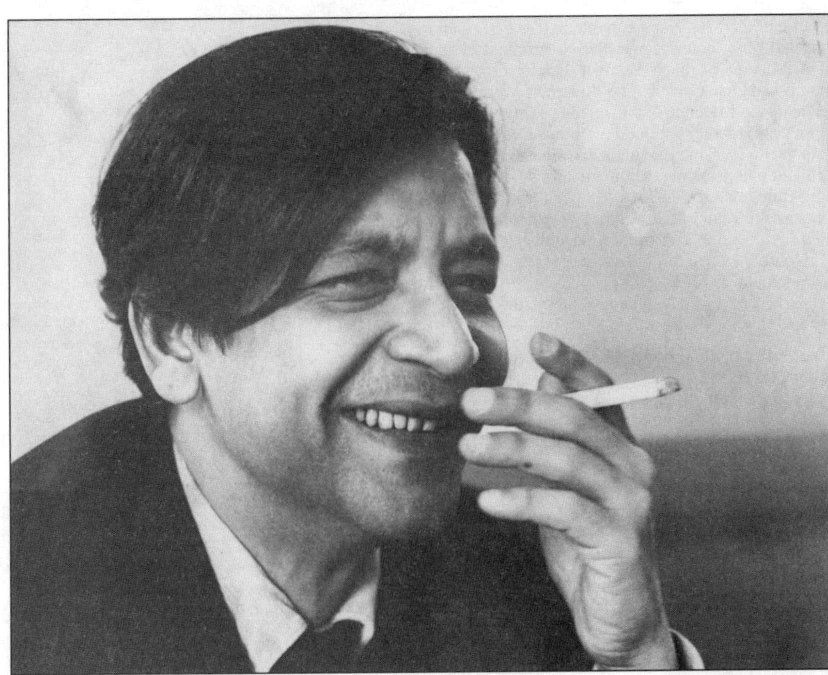

Naipaul West Indian-born British writer V S Naipaul, a prolific novelist as well as travel writer and author of works of political journalism. His novels deal with recurrent themes concerning the melancholy side of human nature and the experience of alienation. *Corbis*

about 260 km/160 mi SE of Wuhan; population (1993) 1,420,000.

Nanchang is a road and rail junction. It was originally a walled city built in the 12th century. The first Chinese Communist uprising took place here 1 Aug 1927.

Nancy capital of the *département* of Meurthe-et-Moselle and of the region of Lorraine, France, on the Meurthe River 280 km/175 mi E of Paris; population (1990) 102,400. Nancy dates from the 11th century.

Nanda Devi peak in the Himalayas, Uttar Pradesh, N India; height 7,817 m/25,645 ft. Until Kanchenjunga was absorbed into India, Nanda Devi was the country's highest mountain.

Nanga Parbat peak in the Himalayan Karakoram Mountains of Kashmir; height 8,126 m/26,660 ft.

Nanni di Banco This life-size marble group of *Four Crowned Saints* was made by the Florentine sculptor Nanni di Banco in about 1415. It depicts four Christian sculptors who according to legend worked in ancient Rome and preferred to die rather than betray their religion by making a statue of a heathen god. The dignified figures of the saints are influenced by Roman sculpture. *Corbis*

Nanjing or *Nanking* capital of Jiangsu province, China, 270 km/165 mi NW of Shanghai; centre of industry (engineering, shipbuilding, oil refining), commerce, and communications; population (1993) 2,430,000. The bridge 1968 over the river Chang Jiang is the longest in China at 6,705 m/22,000 ft.

The city dates from the 2nd century BC, perhaps earlier. It received the name Nanjing ('southern capital') under the Ming dynasty (1368–1644) and was the capital of China 1368–1421, 1928–37, and 1946–49.

Nanni di Banco c. 1384–1421. Florentine sculptor. He worked on several of the great civic commissions of 15th-century Florence. He remained independent of Donatello's sculptural innovations, using conservative techniques to create classical imagery. His major work, commissioned for a niche at Orsanmichele, is Quattro Santi Coronati, created in about 1413.

His relief *Assumption* 1414–21 over the Porta della Mandorla of Florence Cathedral prefigures Baroque style. But for an early death, his career might have rivalled Donatello's.

Nanning industrial river port, capital of Guangxi Zhuang autonomous region, China, on the You Jiang River; population (1993) 960,000. It was a supply town during the Vietnam War and the Sino-Vietnamese confrontation 1979.

nano- prefix used in ◊SI units of measurement, equivalent to a one-billionth part (10^{-9}). For example, a nanosecond is one-billionth of a second.

nanotechnology experimental technology using individual atoms or molecules as the components of minute machines, measured by the nanometre, or millionth of a millimetre. Nanotechnology research in the 1990s focused on testing molecular structures and refining ways to manipulate atoms using a scanning tunnelling microscope. The ultimate aim is to create very small computers and molecular machines which could perform vital engineering or medical tasks.

The ◊scanning electron microscope can be used to see and position single atoms and molecules, and to drill holes a nanometre (billionth of a metre) across in a variety of materials. The instrument can be used for ultrafine etching; the entire 28 volumes of the *Encyclopedia Britannica* could be engraved on the head of a pin. In the USA a complete electric motor has been built, which is less than 0.1 mm across with a top speed of 600,000 rpm. It is etched out of silicon, using the ordinary methods of chip manufacturers.

Nansen Fridtjof 1861–1930. Norwegian explorer and scientist. In 1893, he sailed to the Arctic in the *Fram*, which was deliberately allowed to drift north with an iceflow. Nansen, accompanied by F Hjalmar Johansen (1867–1923), continued north on foot and reached 86° 14′ N, the highest latitude then attained. After World War I, Nansen became League of Nations high commissioner for refugees. Nobel Peace Prize 1923.

The Nansen passport issued to stateless persons is named after him.

Nantes industrial port in W France on the Loire River, capital of Pays de la Loire region; industries include oil, sugar refining, textiles, soap, and tobacco; population (1990) 252,000. It has a cathedral 1434–1884 and a castle founded 938.

Nantes, Edict of decree by which Henry IV of France granted religious freedom to the ◊Huguenots 1598. It was revoked 1685 by Louis XIV.

Nantucket island and resort in Massachusetts, USA, south of Cape Cod, 120 sq km/46 sq mi. In the 18th–19th centuries, Nantucket was a whaling port; it is now a popular summer resort because of its excellent beaches.

'Almost part and parcel of the ocean; as much in league with the waters as Venice, its very buildings seasoned with tar and the salt winds.'

On **Nantucket**
James Morris *Coast to Coast*

napalm fuel used in flamethrowers and incendiary bombs. Produced from jellied petrol, it is a mixture of naphthenic and palmitic acids. Napalm causes extensive burns because it sticks to the skin even when aflame. It was widely used by the US Army during the Vietnam War, and by Serb forces in the civil war in Bosnia-Herzegovina.

naphtha the mixtures of hydrocarbons obtained by destructive distillation of petroleum, coal tar, and shale oil. It is a raw material for the petrochemical and plastics industries. The term was originally applied to naturally occurring liquid hydrocarbons.

naphthalene $C_{10}H_8$ solid, white, shiny, aromatic hydrocarbon obtained from coal tar. The smell of moth-balls is due to their napthalene content. It is used in making indigo and certain azo dyes, as a mild disinfectant, and as an insecticide.

Napier John, 8th Laird of Merchiston 1550–1617. Scottish mathematician who invented ◊logarithms 1614 and 'Napier's bones', an early mechanical calculating device for multiplication and division.

It was Napier who first used and then popularized the decimal point to separate the whole number part from the fractional part of a number.

Napier Robert Cornelis, 1st Baron Napier of Magdala 1810–1890. British field marshal. Knighted for his services in relieving Lucknow during the ◊Indian Mutiny, he took part in capturing Peking (Beijing) 1860 during the war against China in 1860. He was commander in chief in India 1870–76 and governor of Gibraltar 1876–82.

Naples (Italian ***Napoli***) industrial port (shipbuilding, cars, textiles, paper, food processing) and capital of Campania, Italy, on the Tyrrhenian Sea; population (1992) 1,071,700. To the S is the Isle of Capri, and behind the city is Mount Vesuvius, with the ruins of Pompeii at its foot.

Naples is the third-largest city of Italy, and as a port second in importance only to Genoa. Buildings include the royal palace, the San Carlo Opera House, the Castel Nuovo (1283), and the university (1224).

The city began as the Greek colony Neapolis in the 6th century BC and was taken over by Romans 326 BC; it became part of the Kingdom of the Two ◊Sicilies 1140 and capital of the Kingdom of Naples 1282. *See illustration on following page.*

Naples, Kingdom of the southern part of Italy, alternately independent and united with ◊Sicily in the Kingdom of the Two Sicilies.

Naples was united with Sicily 1140–1282, first under Norman rule 1130–94, then Hohenstaufen 1194–1266, then Angevin from 1268; apart from Sicily, but under continued Angevin rule to 1435; reunited with Sicily 1442–1503, under the house of Aragon to 1501; a Spanish Habsburg possession 1504–1707 and Austrian 1707–35; under Spanish Bourbon rule 1735–99. The Neapolitan Republic was established 1799 after Napoleon had left Italy for Egypt, but fell after five months to the forces of reaction under Cardinal Ruffo, with the British admiral Nelson blockading the city by sea; many prominent citizens were massacred after the capitulation. The Spanish Bourbons were restored 1799, 1802–05, and 1815–60, when Naples joined the Kingdom of Italy.

Naples The Galleria Umberto I in Naples, built in the late 1880s by Emmanuele Rocco, forms the main shopping centre of the city. In his use of High Renaissance architectural detail and ironwork and glass vaulting, Rocco united tradition and modernity. *Italian State Tourist Office*

Napoleon I French emperor Napoleon Bonaparte. Napoleon seized power in France in 1799, after the French Revolution, and conquered most of Europe from 1803. He died in exile on the island of St Helena, off the west coast of Africa. *Corbis*

Napoleon I (Napoleon Bonaparte) 1769–1821. Emperor of the French 1804–14 and 1814–15. A general from 1796 in the ◊Revolutionary Wars, in 1799 he overthrew the ruling Directory (see ◊French Revolution) and made himself dictator. From 1803 he conquered most of Europe (the Napoleonic Wars) and installed his brothers as puppet kings (see ◊Bonaparte). After the Peninsular War and retreat from Moscow 1812, he was forced to abdicate 1814 and was banished to the island of Elba. In March 1815 he reassumed power but was defeated by British and Prussian forces at the Battle of ◊Waterloo and exiled to the island of St Helena, 1,900 km/1,200 mi west of Africa, where he died. His body was brought back 1840 to be interred in the Hôtel des Invalides, Paris.

Napoleon, born in Ajaccio, Corsica, received a commission in the artillery 1785 and first distinguished himself at the siege of ◊Toulon 1793. Having suppressed a royalist uprising in Paris 1795, he was given command against the Austrians in Italy and defeated them at Lodi, Arcole, and Rivoli 1796–97. Egypt, seen as a halfway house to India, was overrun and Syria invaded, but his fleet was destroyed by the British admiral ◊Nelson at the Battle of the Nile. Napoleon returned to France and carried out a coup against the government of the Directory to establish his own dictatorship, nominally as First Consul. The Austrians were again defeated at Marengo 1800 and the coalition against France shattered, a truce being declared 1802. A plebiscite the same year made him consul for life. In 1804 a plebiscite made him emperor.

While retaining and extending the legal and educational reforms of the Jacobins, Napoleon replaced the democratic constitution established by the Revolution with a centralized despotism, and by his ◊concordat with Pius VII conciliated the Catholic church. The *Code Napoléon* remains the basis of French law. ▷ *See feature on pp. 748–749.*

Napoleon II (born François Charles Joseph Bonaparte) 1811–1832. Title given by the Bonapartists to the son of Napoleon I and ◊Marie Louise; until 1814 he was known as the king of Rome and after 1818 as the duke of Reichstadt. After his father's abdication 1814 he was taken to the Austrian court, where he spent the rest of his life.

Napoleon III (born Charles Louis Napoleon Bonaparte) 1808–1873. Emperor of the French 1852–70, known as ***Louis-Napoleon***. After two attempted coups (1836 and 1840) he was jailed, then went into exile, returning for the revolution of 1848, when he became president of the Second Republic but proclaimed himself emperor 1852. In 1870 he was manoeuvred by the German chancellor Bismarck into war with Prussia (see ◊Franco-Prussian war); he was forced to surrender at Sedan, NE France, and the empire collapsed.

The son of Louis Bonaparte and Hortense de Beauharnais, brother and step-daughter respectively of Napoleon I, he led two unsuccessful revolts against the French king Louis Philippe, at Strasbourg 1836 and at Boulogne 1840. After the latter he was imprisoned. Escaping in 1846, he lived in London until 1848. He was elected president of the newly established French republic in Dec, and set himself to secure a following by posing as the champion of order and religion against the revolutionary menace. He secured his re-election by a military coup d'état 1851, and a year later was proclaimed emperor. Hoping to strengthen his regime by military triumphs, he joined in the Crimean War 1854–55, waged war with Austria 1859, winning the Battle of Solferino, annexed Savoy and Nice 1860, and attempted unsuccessfully to found a vassal empire in Mexico 1863–67. In so doing he aroused the mistrust of Europe and isolated France.

At home, his regime was discredited by its notorious corruption; republican and socialist opposition grew, in spite of severe repression, and forced Napoleon, after 1860, to make concessions in the direction of parliamentary government. After losing the war with Prussia he withdrew to England, where he died. His son by Empress ◊Eugénie, ***Eugène Louis Jean Joseph Napoleon***, Prince Imperial (1856–79), was killed fighting with the British army against the Zulus in Africa.

Napoleonic Wars series of European wars (1803–15) conducted by Napoleon I following the ◊Revolutionary Wars, aiming for French conquest of Europe. ▷ *See feature on pp. 748–749.*

Narayanan, Kocheril Raman 1920– . Indian politician and public servant, president from 1997. A Harijan ('untouchable') from the S Indian state of Kerala, after a career chiefly as a diplomat, he became Vice-President in 1992 and, in July 1997, was indirectly elected, with cross-party support, as the country's first ever dalit president.

narcissism in psychology, an exaggeration of normal self-respect and self-involvement which may amount to mental disorder when it precludes relationships with other people.

narcissus any bulbous plant of the genus *Narcissus*, family Amaryllidaceae. Species include the daffodil, jonquil, and narcissus. All have flowers with a cup projecting from the centre.

Narcissus in Greek mythology, a beautiful youth who rejected the love of the nymph ◊Echo and was condemned to fall in love with his own reflection in a pool. He pined away and in the place where he died a flower sprang up that was named after him.

narcotic pain-relieving and sleep-inducing drug. The term is usually applied to heroin, morphine, and other opium derivatives, but may also be used for other drugs which depress brain activity, including anaesthetic agents and ◊hypnotics.

Napoleon III Nephew of Napoleon Bonaparte, Napoleon III, Emperor of the French. Allying himself with Britain during the Crimean War, he secured the Treaty of Paris that brought peace 1856. However, finding himself isolated during the Franco-Prussian War, the emperor was captured and exiled to Britain. *Philip Sauvain*

Narmada River river that rises in the Maikala range in Madhya Pradesh state, central India, and flows 1,245 km/778 mi WSW to the Gulf of Khambat, an inlet of the Arabian Sea. Forming the traditional boundary between Hindustan and Deccan, the Narmada is a holy river of the Hindus.

India's Narmada Valley Project is one of the largest and most controversial river development projects in the world. Between 1990 and 2040 it is planned to build 30 major dams, 135 medium-sized dams, and 3,000 smaller dams in a scheme that will involve moving 1 million of the valley's population of 20 million people. In April 1993 the Indian government withdrew from the loan agreement with the World Bank to fund the Narmada Valley Project.

narwhal toothed whale *Monodon monoceros*, found only in the Arctic Ocean. It grows to 5 m/16 ft long, has a grey and black body, a small head, and short flippers. The male has a single spirally fluted tusk that may be up to 2.7 m/9 ft long.

NASA acronym for ***National Aeronautics and Space Administration***, US government agency for spaceflight and aeronautical research, founded 1958 by the National Aeronautics and Space Act. Its headquarters are in Washington DC and its main installation is at the ◊Kennedy Space Center in Florida. NASA's early planetary and lunar programs included Pioneer spacecraft from 1958, which gathered data for the later crewed missions, the most famous of which took the first people to the Moon in *Apollo 11* on 16–24 July 1969.

In the early 1990s, NASA moved towards lower-budget 'Discovery missions', which should not exceed a budget of $150 million (excluding launch costs), nor a development period of three years.

Naseby, Battle of decisive battle of the English Civil War 14 June 1645, when the Royalists, led by Prince Rupert, were defeated by the Parliamentarians ('Roundheads') under Oliver Cromwell and General Fairfax. It is named after the nearby village of Naseby, 32 km/20 mi south of Leicester.

Nash (Frederic) Ogden 1902–1971. US poet and wit. He published numerous volumes of humorous, quietly satirical light verse, characterized by unorthodox rhymes and puns. They include *I'm a Stranger Here Myself* 1938, *Versus* 1949, and *Bed Riddance* 1970. Most of his poems first appeared in the *New Yorker* magazine.

Nash John 1752–1835. English architect. First attracting attention for designing country houses, he later laid out Regent's Park, London, Trafalgar Square and St James's Park under the patronage of the Prince of Wales (later George IV). Between

1811 and 1821 he planned Regent Street (later rebuilt), repaired and enlarged Buckingham Palace (for which he designed Marble Arch), and rebuilt the Royal Pavilion, Brighton, in oriental style.

Nash, John F(orbes), Jr 1928– . US mathematician. His doctoral thesis, 'Noncooperative Games' was published in the early 1950s and is regarded as laying the mathematical foundations for game theory. This field of analysis uses mathematics to predict how people will behave in all kinds of situations, including rivalries.

Nash Paul 1889–1946. English painter. He was an official war artist in World Wars I and II. In the 1930s he was one of a group of artists promoting avant-garde style, and was deeply influenced by Surrealism. Two works which illustrate the visionary quality of his paintings are *Totes Meer/Dead Sea* 1940–41 (Tate Gallery, London) and *Solstice of the Sunflower* 1945 (National Gallery of Canada, Ottawa). 'Structural purpose' was an aim which led him into many forms of design, for textiles, ceramics, the stage and the book, but the Surrealist trend of the 1930s and the exhibition of 1936 brought out an imaginative and poetic feeling already apparent in his oils and watercolours.

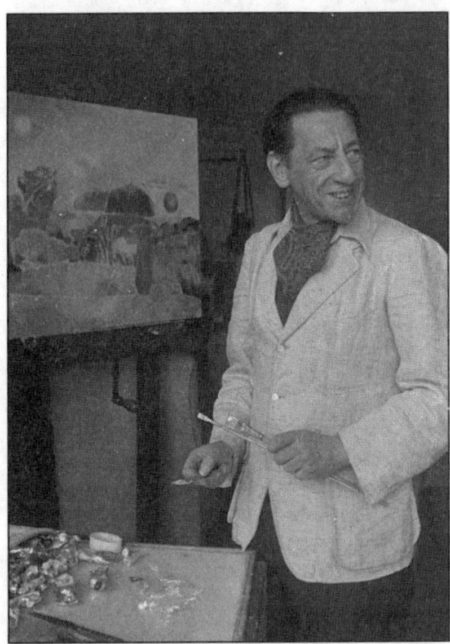

Nash English artist Paul Nash. A leading figure in English avant-garde art in the 1930s and 1940s, Nash used French Surrealism to revitalize the British landscape tradition. *Corbis*

Nashe Thomas 1567–1601. English poet, satirist, and anti-Puritan pamphleteer. He was drawn into the Martin ◊Marprelate controversy (a pamphleteering attack on the clergy of the Church of England by Puritans), and wrote at least three attacks on the Martinists. Among his later works are the satirical *Pierce Pennilesse, his Supplication to the Divell* 1592 and the religious *Christes Teares over Jerusalem* 1593.

Nashville port on the Cumberland River and capital of Tennessee, USA; population (1992) 495,000. It is a banking and commercial centre, and has large printing, music-publishing, and recording industries.

history Nashville was settled 1779. The Confederate army was defeated here 1864. From 1963 it has been officially called Nashvill-Davidson city.

industries Nashville is the capital of country music and the birthplace of the 'Nashville sound', and there are many printing and music-publishing firms and recording studios. *Grand Ole Opry*, the oldest radio show in the United States, started here 1925, and is broadcast from Opry USA. RCA Studio B, the Country Music Hall of Fame and Museum, and the Ryman Auditorium and Museum (home of Grand Ole Opry 1943–74), are here. Most of the Bibles in the United States are printed here, and it is the headquarters of the United Methodist Publishing House, and of the United Methodist Church and the Southern Baptist Convention.

Nassau capital and port of the Bahamas, on New Providence Island; population (1980) 135,000.

English settlers founded it in the 17th century, and it was a supply base for Confederate blockade runners during the American Civil War.

Nasser Gamal Abdel 1918–1970. Egyptian politician, prime minister 1954–56 and from 1956 president of Egypt (the United Arab Republic 1958–71). In 1952 he was the driving power behind the Neguib coup, which ended the monarchy. His nationalization of the Suez Canal 1956 led to an Anglo-French invasion and the ◊Suez Crisis, and his ambitions for an Egyptian-led union of Arab states led to disquiet in the Middle East (and in the West). Nasser was also an early and influential leader of the nonaligned movement.

nastic movement plant movement that is caused by an external stimulus, such as light or temperature, but is directionally independent of its source, unlike ◊tropisms. Nastic movements occur as a result of changes in water pressure within specialized cells or differing rates of growth in parts of the plant.

Examples include the opening and closing of crocus flowers following an increase or decrease in temperature (thermonasty), and the opening and closing of evening-primrose *Oenothera* flowers on exposure to dark and light (photonasty).

nasturtium any plant of the genus *Nasturtium*, family Cruciferae, including watercress *N. officinale*, a perennial aquatic plant of Europe and Asia, grown as a salad crop. It also includes plants of the South American family Tropaeolaceae, including the cultivated species *Tropaeolum majus*, with orange or scarlet flowers, and *T. minus*, which has smaller flowers.

Natal former province of South Africa to 1994, bounded on the east by the Indian Ocean. In 1994 it became part of ◊KwaZulu Natal Province.

Called Natal ('of [Christ's] birth') because Vasco da Gama reached it on Christmas Day 1497, the region was part of the British Cape Colony 1843–1856, when it was made into a separate colony.

Zululand was annexed to Natal 1897, and the districts of Vrijheid, Utrecht, and part of Wakkerstroom were transferred from the Transvaal to Natal 1903; the colony became a part of the Union of South Africa 1910. In 1993 nearly 2,000 people were killed in political violence in Natal, compared with 1,300 people in 1992 and just under 1,000 in 1991. A state of emergency was imposed in Natal in the run-up to the first multiracial elections 1994, after escalating violence by the Zulu-based ◊Inkatha party threatened to derail the election process.

Nataraja ('Lord of the Dance') in Hinduism, a title of ◊Siva.

Natchez Native American people of the Mississippi area, one of the Moundbuilder group of peoples. They had a highly developed caste system unusual in North America, headed by a ruler priest (the 'Great Sun'). Members of the highest caste always married members of the lowest caste. The system lasted until French settlers colonized the area 1731. Only a few Natchez now survive in Oklahoma. Their Muskogean language is extinct.

national anthem patriotic song for official occasions. The US national anthem, 'The Star-Spangled Banner', was written 1814 by Francis Scott Key (1779–1843) and was adopted officially 1931. In Britain 'God Save the King/Queen' has been accepted as such since 1745, although both music and words are of much earlier origin. The German anthem 'Deutschland über Alles/Germany before Everything' is sung to music by Haydn. The French national anthem, the ◊'Marseillaise', dates from 1792.

Countries within the Commonwealth retain 'God Save the King/Queen' as the 'royal anthem', adopting their own anthem as a mark of independence. The anthem of united Europe is Schiller's 'Ode to Joy' set by Beethoven in his Ninth Symphony.

National Assembly for Wales 60-seat devolved body, based in Cardiff, taking over the functions of the Welsh Office, and spending its £7 billion budget. The assembly is due to be elected in 1999, with a third of its seats being selected by proportional representation. A new building, designed by the architect Richard ◊Rogers, is to be built at Cardiff Bay to house the assembly.

National Association for the Advancement of Colored People (NAACP) US civil-rights organization dedicated to ending inequality and segregation for African-Americans through nonviolent protest. Founded 1910, its first aim was to eradicate lynching. The NAACP campaigned to end segregation in state schools; it funded test cases that eventually led to the Supreme Court decision 1954 outlawing school segregation, although it was only through the ◊civil-rights movement of the 1960s that desegregation was achieved.

The NAACP was founded by a group of white liberals, including William Walling, Oswald Villard, social worker Jane Addams, philosopher John Dewey, and novelist William Dean Howells. The organization has been criticized by militants and black separatists for its moderate stance and its commitment to integration.

national curriculum in the UK from 1988, a course of study in ten subjects common to all primary and secondary state schools. The national curriculum is divided into three core subjects – English, maths, and science – and seven foundation subjects: geography, history, technology, a foreign language (for secondary school pupils), art, music, and physical education. There are four stages, on completion of which the pupil's work is assessed: ages 5–7, 7–11, 11–14, and 14–16.

national debt debt incurred by the central government of a country to its own people and institutions and also to overseas creditors. A government can borrow from the public by means of selling interest-bearing bonds, for example, or from abroad. Traditionally, a major cause of

cont. on p. 750

Brightness falls from the air; / Queens have died young and fair; / Dust hath closed Helen's eye.

Thomas Nashe
'In Time of Pestilence'

Nasser Egyptian president Gamal Nasser is greeted by delirious crowds on his return to Cairo during the Suez Crisis. The nationalization of the Suez Canal by Nasser in contradiction of British interests was greeted by the Egyptians as the first assertion of national pride for millennia. *Corbis*

The Napoleonic Adventure

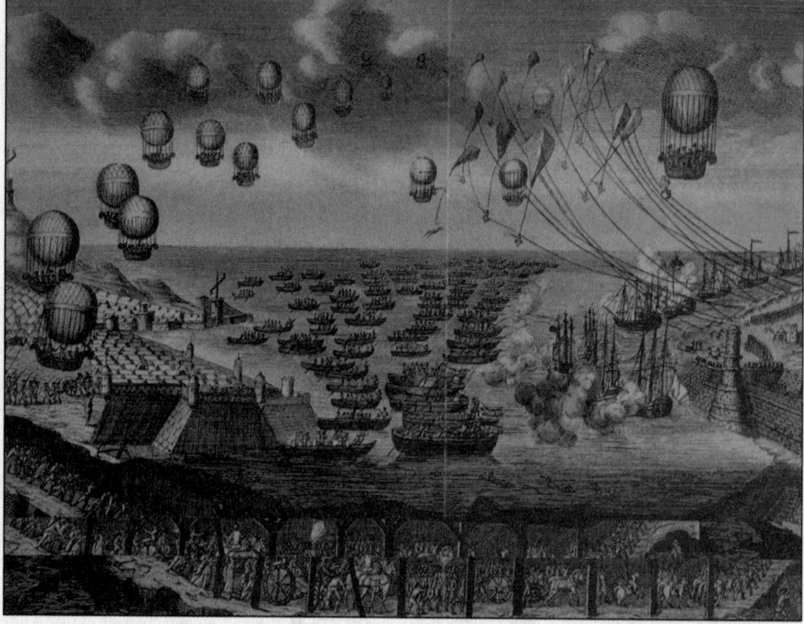

Fears of a French invasion abounded – this 1804 print shows how Napoleon could overcome the natural defence line of the Channel. The idea of a Channel tunnel for peaceful purposes had been mooted just two years earlier by a French engineer, Albert Mathieu-Favier; but discussions with British politicians were halted at the outbreak of war in 1803. *Philip Sauvain*

Napoleon has often been called a warmonger, but he did not start the great conflict that bears his name. Europe had been at war seven years before he took power in France in 1799, and at least some of the conflict's origins go back over a century. In the long term, these wars were the last round in a long struggle for power between Britain and France, which stretched back to the late 17th century. In the short term, it was a continuation of the war between the French revolutionaries and the other European states, begun in 1792. Napoleon inherited these two conflicts, neither of which he had provoked, but he had to deal with them quickly, for France faced defeat in 1799.

Napoleon triumphs, 1799–1807

Napoleon fought his first campaign as leader of France with the tired, weakened armies he inherited from the revolutionaries. In 1800 he defeated an Austrian army in N Italy at the battle of Marengo, and knew he was lucky that the war ended quickly. All the great powers were exhausted by this time, France as much as the rest, and a general peace was soon agreed, rounded off in 1802 by the Treaty of Amiens with Britain. Britain and France returned to war after only eighteen months, but the fighting was confined to naval warfare, and the continent was at peace until 1805.

While the other European rulers only toyed with projects for reform, Napoleon used these years of peace to reform France in ways that made it better able to wage war. He trained a massive army to high standards of military efficiency, and placed it under several dynamic generals. Morale and tactics were the key, for the Napoleonic army's weapons were little different to those of its opponents. It was raised to invade England, but all hope of this was ended on 21 Oct 1805 when the British, under Admiral Nelson, defeated the French navy at the battle of Trafalgar.

Napoleon's years of preparation were not wasted, however. When he crowned himself 'Emperor of the French' in May 1804, it seemed only a provocative gesture to the rest of Europe; but the great military victories of the next three years made his title a reality. In 1805, incited by Britain, both Russia and Austria declared war on Napoleon. Had they known the new power of his army, they may not have been so easily led. Napoleon shattered their armies at the battles of Ulm and Austerlitz, and a humiliating peace was imposed on Francis II, the Holy Roman and Austrian Emperor. Napoleon then reorganized Italy and W Germany as he pleased, bringing many German princes – and their armies – under his command.

Prussia had kept out of the wars since 1795, but in 1806 Britain bullied her into fighting Napoleon. Promises of help from Russia came to nothing,and Prussia went to war almost alone. Napoleon feared the Prussian army, but he swept it aside at the twin battles of Jena and Auerstadt on 14 Oct. Then, Russian help finally arrived. In 1807 this led Napoleon into a bitter, inconclusive campaign against the young tsar, Alexander I. After two battles, at Friedland and Eylau, Napoleon and Alexander decided they could not defeat each other, and virtually declared themselves joint overlords of Europe. Napoleon then persuaded Alexander to join his economic blockade of Britain. Victory seemed complete, but the blockade soon led Napoleon into a new round of wars.

From triumph to disaster, 1808–1812

Spain was France's traditional ally, but she had been unable to enforce the blockade or to make a useful contribution to the war effort; so, when squabbling broke out within the Spanish royal family in 1808, Napoleon seized the opportunity to invade and put his brother Joseph on the Spanish throne. This led to a widespread popular revolt, which soon developed into a 'guerrilla' war against Napoleon – the first time this military term was used. When he tried to do the same to the Portuguese, a small British army led by Arthur Wellesley – the future Duke of Wellington – came to the rescue.

The resistance in Spain gave the Austrians new heart, but Napoleon defeated them at Wagram in July 1809. The Austrian foreign minister, Metternich, saw that alliance with France was his only option, and this was sealed by Napoleon's marriage to Marie-Louise, the daughter of Francis II. No one could stop this, but neither could Napoleon defeat Britain. Nor could he get Alexander to enforce the blockade. In 1812, still fighting in Spain, Napoleon assembled a massive army from all over Europe and prepared to invade Russia.

The defeat of Napoleon: the Great Alliance of 1812–1814

Although Napoleon was able to defeat the Russians in battle, the price was high, as at Borodino where his losses were horrific. As he advanced on Moscow, deep into Russia, Cossack cavalry and Russian peasants plundered the supply bases he had set up for his planned retreat. When winter came, Napoleon's army, already weakened, was caught without supplies.

Napoleon and Alexander I of Russia, as depicted by the English caricaturist James Gillray. After inconclusive battles in 1807, Napoleon and the Russian tsar decided to join forces against the rest of Europe – but it was not, Gillray suggests, a partnership of equals. By 1812, the alliance had collapsed and Napoleon's army invaded Russia. *Corbis*

Arthur Wellesley, 1st Duke of Wellington, an 1814 portrait by Thomas Lawrence. After a successful campaign against the French in Spain and Portugal, Wellington – known as 'the Iron Duke' – met Napoleon for the first time at Waterloo 1815, where he finally crushed the French emperor's attempt to regain his former power. *ET Archive*

This should have been the end of Napoleon, but the Russians hesitated to push west and the Austrians still feared him. While they waited, Napoleon raised a new army, reinforced from Spain. Metternich saw he could not persuade Napoleon to discuss peace, and Austria joined the war. By 1813, the Prussians had reformed their army; led by Blucher and Yorck it was a much more formidable opponent than in 1806. Napoleon was defeated by a combination of the Prussian, Austrian, and Russian armies at the 'Battle of Nations' at Leipzig in Oct 1813. He was driven back to France, and his German allies turned on him. Wellington swept a weakened French army from Spain, and France was invaded from the east and the south.

Napoleon waged a brilliant defensive war to save France, but he was now outnumbered, and Britain promised almost unlimited funds to continue the war. He abdicated in April 1814, and was exiled to Elba. Louis XVIII was restored to the throne, and the allies met at Vienna to discuss how best to dismantle Napoleon's empire. In March 1815 Napoleon returned from exile and seized power in France, but his recovery was shortlived – Wellington and Blucher defeated him at Waterloo, Belgium, in June of the same year. The 'Napoleonic adventure' was over.

August 1813: the commanders of the Allied forces of Austria, Prussia, and Russia prepare to attack Dresden, which had been captured by the French. Despite heavy artillery bombardment and a much smaller force – around 80,000 French, against nearly 200,000 – Allies Napoleon successfully counterattacked and forced the Allies to withdraw. *Corbis*

Napoleon's legacy

Napoleon's military career was dazzling, but France was not strong enough to support his wars for long. Good organization could not compensate for a declining population or a largely rural economy. Britain was more industrialized and had the ability to finance the other powers' wars against Napoleon; Russia and Austria had larger populations; Prussia created an army equal in quality to Napoleon's. Talleyrand resigned as Napoleon's foreign minister in1807, because he believed that the blockade could not work and that Napoleon's power was overstretched. He was right. After 1815, France was never again the greatest military power in Europe, although Napoleon had shown how a state could organize itself for major war, and how armies should wage such wars. In the end, Napoleon's lasting achievement was not his victories but the effective systems of administration and law that he laid down, and which helped to bring Europe into the modern era.

MICHAEL BROERS

SEE ALSO
Napoleon I; Nations, Battle of the; Waterloo, Battle of; Francis II; Alexander I

‘Nationalism is an infantile sickness. It is the measles of the human race.’

On NATIONALISM
Albert Einstein, letter to G S Viereck 1921

national debt was the cost of war but in recent decades governments have borrowed heavily in order to finance development or nationalization, to support an ailing currency, or to avoid raising taxes.

Government budgets are often planned with a deficit that is funded by overseas borrowing. In the 1980s most governments adopted monetary policies designed to limit their borrowing requirements, both to reduce the cost of servicing the debt and because borrowing money tends to cause inflation.

In Britain the national debt is managed by the Bank of England, under the control of the Treasury. The first issue of government stock in Britain was made in 1693, to raise a loan of £1 million. Historically, increases of the national debt have been caused by wartime expenditure; thus after the War of the Spanish Succession 1701–14 it reached £54 million. By 1900 it reached £610 million but World War I forced it up, by 1920, to £7,828 million and World War II, by 1945, to £21,870,221,651. Since then other factors have increased the national debt, including nationalization expenditure and overseas borrowing to support the pound.

National Economic Development Council (NEDC) known as ‘*Neddy*’, the UK forum for economic consultation between government, management, and trade unions. It examines the country's economic and industrial performance, in both the public and private sectors, and seeks agreement on ways to improve efficiency. It was established 1962; its role diminished during the 1980s.

National Front in the UK, extreme right-wing political party founded 1967. Some of its members had links with the National Socialist Movement of the 1960s (see ◊Nazism).

National Gallery London art gallery housing the British national collection of pictures by artists no longer living, founded 1824. Its collection covers all major pre-20th-century periods and schools, but it is unique in its collection of Italian Gothic and Renaissance works, which is more comprehensive than any other collection outside Italy.

In 1824, Parliament voted £57,000 for the purchase of 38 pictures from the collection of John Julius Angerstein (1735–1823), a wealthy merchant, plus £3,000 for the maintenance of the building in Pall Mall, London, where they were housed. The present building in Trafalgar Square was designed by William Wilkins and opened 1838: there have been several extensions, including the Sainsbury Wing, designed by US architect Robert Venturi, which opened July 1991.

National Guard ◊militia force recruited by each state of the USA. The volunteer National Guard units are under federal orders in emergencies, and under the control of the governor in peacetime, and are now an integral part of the US Army.

National Heritage, Department for (DNH) UK government department established 1992. It is responsible for broadcasting and the media, the arts, libraries, museums and galleries, architectural and archaeological heritage, tourism, sport and recreation, and the national lottery.

national income the total income of a state in one year, including both the wages of individuals and the profits of companies. It is equal to the value of the output of all goods and services during the same period. National income is equal to gross national product (the value of a country's total output) minus an allowance for replacement of ageing capital stock.

national insurance in the UK, state social-security scheme that provides child allowances, maternity benefits, and payments to the unemployed, sick, and retired, and also covers medical treatment. It is paid for by weekly or monthly contributions from employees and employers.

National Insurance Act UK act of Parliament 1911, introduced by Lloyd George, Liberal chancellor, which first provided insurance for workers against ill health and unemployment.

nationalism in music, the adoption by 19th-century composers of folk idioms with which an audience untrained in the classics could identify. Nationalism was encouraged by governments in the early 20th century for propaganda purposes in times of war and political tension. Composers of nationalist music include Smetana, Sibelius, Grieg, Dvořák, Nielsen, Kodály, Copland, Elgar, Shostakovich, and Stephen Foster.

nationalism in politics, a movement that consciously aims to unify a nation, create a state, or liberate it from foreign or imperialistic rule. Nationalist movements became a potent factor in European politics during the 19th century; since 1900 nationalism has become a strong force in Asia and Africa and in the late 1980s revived strongly in E Europe.

Stimulated by the French Revolution, movements arose in the 19th century in favour of national unification in Germany and Italy and national independence in Ireland, Italy, Belgium, Hungary, Bohemia, Poland, Finland, and the Balkan states. Revival of interest in the national language, history, traditions, and culture has accompanied and influenced most political movements. See also ◊African nationalism.

In political terms, nationalism can be pursued as an ideology that stresses the superiority of a nation and its inhabitants compared with other nations and peoples. Most countries enjoy, and wish to demonstrate, national pride but – carried to an extreme – nationalism can produce dangerous regimes and political systems.

nationalization policy of bringing a country's essential services and industries under public ownership. It was pursued, for example, by the UK Labour government 1945–51. Subsequently the trend towards nationalization has slowed and in many countries (the UK, France, and Japan) reversed (◊privatization). Assets in the hands of foreign governments or companies may also be nationalized; for example, Iran's oil industry (see ◊Abadan), the ◊Suez Canal, and US-owned fruit plantations in Guatemala, all in the 1950s.

national park land set aside and conserved for public enjoyment. The first was Yellowstone National Park, USA, established 1872. National parks include not only the most scenic places, but also places distinguished for their historic, prehistoric, or scientific interest, or for their superior recreational assets. They range from areas the size of small countries to pockets of just a few hectares. In the UK national parks are not wholly wilderness or conservation areas, but merely places where planning controls on development are stricter than elsewhere.

National Party of Australia Australian political party, favouring free enterprise and seeking to promote the interests of people outside the major metropolitan areas. It holds the balance of power between Liberals and Labor. It was formed 1916 as the Country Party of Australia and adopted its present name 1982. It gained strength following the introduction of proportional representation 1918 and was in coalition with the Liberals 1949–83. Its leader since 1990 has been Tim Fischer and its federal president John Paterson. In 1996 it entered into a coalition with the Liberal Party led by Prime Minister John Howard.

National Portrait Gallery London art gallery containing portraits of distinguished British men and women. It was founded 1856 and moved to its present building in St Martin's Place, Trafalgar Square, in 1896. In addition to paintings, there are drawings, cartoons, sculptures, and photographs on display.

Overall the collection has over 8,000 original paintings, drawings, and sculptures, and photographs of noted figures from Tudor times onwards, together with an archive and reference library.

National Rivers Authority (NRA) UK government agency launched 1989. It is responsible for managing water resources, investigating and regulating pollution, and taking over flood controls and land drainage from the former ten regional water authorities of England and Wales. Following a judicial review of the authority 1991 for allegedly failing to carry out its statutory duty to protect rivers and seas from pollution, river quality improved by 26% 1993–96. The NRA has granted licences to many UK companies to discharge polluting materials (a total of 12,000 licensed pipelines), and has in most cases failed to prosecute when the companies have exceeded their discharge limit.

In April 1996 the NRA, having begun to establish a reputation for being supportive to wildlife projects and tough on polluters, was replaced by the Environment Agency.

National Savings several government savings schemes in the UK, including the National Savings Bank (NSB), which operates through the Post Office; National Savings Certificates; and British Savings Bonds.

National Security Agency (NSA) largest and most secret of US intelligence agencies. Established 1952 to intercept foreign communications as well as to safeguard US transmissions, the NSA collects and analyses computer communications, telephone signals, and other electronic data, and gathers intelligence. Known as the Puzzle Palace, its headquarters are at Fort Meade, Maryland (with a major facility at Menwith Hill, England). It operates outside normal channels of government accountability, and its budget (also secret) is thought to exceed several billion dollars.

National Security Council US federal executive council that was established under the National Security Act of 1947. The membership includes the president, vice-president, and secretaries of state and defence. Their special advisers include the head of the Joint Chiefs of Staff and the director of the Central Intelligence Agency. The national security adviser heads the council's staff.

national security directive in the USA, secret decree issued by the president that can establish national policy and commit federal funds without the knowledge of Congress, under the National Security Act 1947. The National Security Council alone decides whether these directives may be made public; most are not. The directives have been criticized as unconstitutional, since they enable the executive branch of government to make laws.

history In 1950 President Truman issued a secret directive for covert operations to foment ‘unrest and revolt’ in the Eastern bloc. J F Kennedy authorized an invasion of Cuba by this means (see ◊Bay of Pigs), and Lyndon Johnson approved military incursions into Laos during the Vietnam War. The US invasion of Grenada and the allocation of $19 million for the Central Intelligence Agency to start arming and training Contras in Central America were also authorized by national security directives.

national service ◊conscription into the armed services in peacetime.

National Socialism official name for the ◊Nazi movement in Germany; see also ◊fascism.

National Theatre, Royal British national theatre company established 1963, and the complex, opened 1976, that houses it on London's South Bank. The national theatre of France is the ◊Comédie Française, founded 1680.

National Trust British trust founded 1895 for the preservation of land and buildings of historic interest or beauty, incorporated by an Act of Parliament 1907. It is the largest private landowner in Britain. The National Trust for Scotland was established 1931.

The total income of the National Trust 1990 was £104 million, making it the top-earning charity in the UK. Its most popular property in 1991 was Polesden Lacey in Surrey, with 205,000 visitors.

In 1994 the Trust in England, Wales and Northern Ireland owned 545 miles of coastline and 20,000 buildings.

national vocational qualification (NVQ) in the UK, a certificate of attainment of a standardized level of skill and competence. A national council for NVQs was set up 1986 in an effort by the government in cooperation with employers to rationalize the many unrelated vocational qualifications then on offer. The Scottish equivalent is SVQ.

In 1991 NVQs were established in colleges of further education, with companies arranging them for employees; points are awarded for previous experience. Qualifications gained are roughly equivalent to the GCSE, A-level, and degree system of academic qualifications.

National Westminster Tower building designed by Richard Seifert, located in the City of London, England. It is 183 m/600 ft high and has 49 storeys. Seen from above it resembles the National Westminster Bank's logo. It was completed in 1979 at a cost of £72 million, and was London's tallest building until 1991.

Nation of Islam original name of the group popularly known as the ◊Black Muslims, now the title of a 100,000-member splinter group faithful to the Black Muslims' original principles led by Louis ◊Farrakhan. Members strive to improve their social and religious position in society, and the group has won praise for its work in deprived areas, although its reputation has been tarnished by Farrakhan's anti-Semitic and anti-white beliefs. In Oct 1995 the group demonstrated its political strength by organizing the 'Million Man March' – a march of around 400,000 black men in Washington DC.

Native American one of the aboriginal peoples of the Americas. The Asian ancestors of the Native Americans are thought to have entered North America at the end of the last ice age, 14,000–15,000 years ago, when the Bering Land Bridge was exposed by the lowered sea level between Siberia and Alaska. The earliest well-dated archaeological sites in North America are about 13,000–14,000 years old. In South America they are about 12,000–13,000 years old.

Hunting, fishing, and moving camp throughout the Americas, the migrants inhabited both continents and settled all the ecological zones. Traditionally, Native Americans were agriculturalists and were the first cultivators of maize, potatoes, sweet potatoes, manioc, peanuts, peppers, tomatoes, pumpkins, cacao, and chicle. They also grew tobacco, coca, peyote, and cinchona (the last three are sources of cocaine, mescalin, and quinine respectively). The Spanish introduced horses about 1600, which by about 1750 allowed many tribes to invade the prairies to hunt bison. Almost everything necessary for everyday life was made from local materials. However, trade networks existed between Native Americans, and between Native Americans and Europeans for European goods. The most important trade items were blankets, beads, guns and gunpowder, and iron and copper.

It is estimated that there were just over 200 Native American groups in the 1600s. By the 1970s there were 173. Nearly 90% now live west of the Mississippi. The relatively small number in the east is the result of disease, warfare, massacres by colonists, and the destruction of wild animals on which populations depended, but mainly by the US government's policy of forced migration westwards, beginning with the Indian Removal Act 1830. In North America, most Native Americans were living on reservations by 1887.

In South America the Native Americans were massacred by the Spanish, died from new diseases and serious famines, and were forced to work as slaves in Spanish mines. Interbreeding with the Spanish produced a mestizo population. In Brazil, the modern population is the result of interbreeding between Native Americans, Portuguese immigrants, and slaves imported from Africa to work on the sugar plantations. In the 19th century many of the remaining indigenous people were decimated by disease and had their land expropriated for huge cattle ranches.

Native American and Inuit art the art of the North American indigenous peoples. The first Arctic cultures were established on the continent around 12,000 years ago. Remains of prehistoric cultures have been found, but the finer Native American artefacts belong to the last 2000 years. Generally, the arts of the different tribes were determined by materials available, lifestyle (whether settled or nomadic), and religion (almost invariably shamanistic). Most ethnographic collections include Native American artworks; notable are those at the Museum of the American Indian, New York, and the Museum of Mankind, London.

Arctic Inuit art (from about 25,000 BC) This is rich in carvings, particularly of bone and walrus ivory. Alaskan Inuit produced shaman masks and decorated sealskin for clothes, tents, and canoes.

Northwest Coast Indian art (about 3000 BC–AD 1800) The wealth of natural resources in the area is reflected in an abundance of diverse artefacts, such as totem poles, canoes, and masks. Highly stylized animal motifs decorate both wood and blanket weaving, a notable example of the latter being *chilkat*. The arts of the Kwakiutl and Tlingit Indians express social status as well as religious beliefs.

Southwest Coast Indian art (about 1000 BC–AD 1800) The lifestyle of more settled cultures is reflected. Early cliff palace complexes, such as Mesa Verde, Colorado, 12th century, gave way to pueblo (village) life by the 14th century. *Mimbres* pottery and murals from kivas (underground ceremonial rooms) are characteristic of the pueblo culture. The Navaho Indians executed stylized sand paintings and blanket weaving, employing an elaborate symbolism and complex, often geometrical, designs. The masks and dolls of Kachina have found favour with Western collectors. The Museum of the American Indian in Santa Fe, New Mexico, has a good collection of artefacts from the area.

Eastern Woodlands Indian art (700 BC–AD 1500) This was dominated first by the Adena culture, then by the Hopewell culture. Both built great earthen mounds, such as the Serpent Mound in Ohio, for ceremonial purposes, and made jewellery in copper and motifs in cut foil. The Hopewell culture was technically more proficient and made human effigies in pottery and sleek animal carvings in stone. Between AD 800–1500, the area was dominated by the Mississippians, an agrarian society which built large city complexes similar to those of Central America (see ◊pre-Columbian art). Their art is represented in shell-carving and trophy-head vessels. The Iroquois culture excelled in decorative beadwork and quillwork, pottery, and dramatic masks for the 'false face' ceremonies of their shamanistic cult.

The Great Plains Indian art (250 BC–1500 AD) This was the product of mostly nomadic peoples, such as the Sioux and the Crow. Theirs was a portable art, with buckskin clothes and tents decorated with beadwork and quillwork in highly stylized designs. Some painted robes and tents have survived, for instance a Crow tepee lining showing cowboys fighting Indians, 19th century, (Smithsonian Institute, Washington).

native metal or ***free metal*** any of the metallic elements that occur in nature in the chemically uncombined or elemental form (in addition to any combined form). They include bismuth, cobalt, copper, gold, iridium, iron, lead, mercury, nickel, osmium, palladium, platinum, ruthenium, rhodium, tin, and silver. Some are commonly found in the free state, such as gold; others occur almost exclusively in the combined state, but under unusual conditions do occur as native metals, such as mercury. Examples of native nonmetals are carbon and sulphur.

nativity Christian festival celebrating a birth: Christmas is celebrated 25 Dec from AD 336 in memory of the birth of Jesus in Bethlehem; Nativity of the Virgin Mary is celebrated 8 Sept by the Catholic and Eastern Orthodox churches; Nativity of John the Baptist is celebrated 24 June by the Catholic, Eastern Orthodox, and Anglican churches.

NATO abbreviation for ◊***North Atlantic Treaty Organization***.

natural in music, a sign cancelling a sharp or flat. A natural trumpet or horn is an instrument without valves, thus restricted to playing natural harmonics.

Natural Environment Research Council (NERC) UK organization established by royal charter 1965 to undertake and support research in the earth sciences, to give advice both on exploiting natural resources and on protecting the environment, and to support education and training of scientists in these fields of study.

Research areas include geothermal energy, industrial pollution, waste disposal, satellite surveying, acid rain, biotechnology, atmospheric circulation, and climate. Research is carried out principally within the UK but also in Antarctica and in many Third World countries. It comprises 13 research bodies.

Within the NERC, the research bodies are: Freshwater Biological Association, British Geological Survey, Institute of Hydrology, Plymouth Marine Laboratory, Institute of Oceanographic Sciences, Deacon Laboratory, Proudman Oceanographic Laboratory, Institute of Virology, Institute of Terrestrial Ecology, Scottish Marine Biological Association, Sea Mammal Research Unit, Unit of Comparative Plant Ecology, and the NERC Unit for Thematic Information Systems.

natural frequency the frequency at which a mechanical system will vibrate freely. A pendulum, for example, always oscillates at the same frequency when set in motion. More complicated systems, such as bridges, also vibrate with a fixed natural frequency. If a varying force with a frequency equal to the natural frequency is applied to such an object the vibrations can become violent, a phenomenon known as ◊resonance.

NATIVE AMERICANS: MAJOR ETHNIC GROUPS

North America	
Arctic	Inuit, Aleut
Subarctic	Algonquin, Cree, Ottawa
NE woodlands	Huron, Iroquois, Mohican, Shawnee (Tecumseh)
SE woodlands	Cherokee, Choctaw, Creek, Hopewell, Natchez, Seminole
Great Plains	Blackfoot, Cheyenne, Comanche, Pawnee, Sioux
NW coast	Chinook, Tlingit, Tsimshian
Desert West	Apache, Navajo, Pueblo, Hopi, Mojave, Shoshone
Central America	Maya, Toltec, Aztec, Mexican
South America	
Eastern	Carib, Xingu
Central	Guaraní, Miskito
Western	Araucanian, Aymara, Chimú, Inca, Jivaro, Quechua

natural gas mixture of flammable gases found in the Earth's crust (often in association with petroleum). It is one of the world's three main fossil fuels (with coal and oil). Natural gas is a mixture of ◊hydrocarbons, chiefly methane, with ethane, butane, and propane. Natural gas is usually transported from its source by pipeline, although it may be liquefied for transport and storage and is, therefore, often used in remote areas where other fuels are scarce and expensive. Prior to transportation, butane and propane are removed and liquefied to form 'bottled gas'. Liquefied natural gas has potential as a fuel for land transport, as it has low emissions. Bus trials began in the UK 1995.

In the UK from the 1970s natural gas from the North Sea has superseded coal gas, or town gas, both as a domestic fuel and as an energy source for power stations. ▷*See feature on pp. 360–361.*

naturalism in the arts generally, an approach that advocates the factual and realistic representation of the subject of a painting or novel with no stylization.

Specifically, naturalism refers to a movement in literature and drama that originated in France in the late 19th century with the writings of Emile ◊Zola and the brothers ◊Goncourt. Similar to ◊realism in that it was concerned with everyday life, naturalism also held that people's fates were determined by heredity, environment, and social forces beyond their control.

Zola, the chief theorist of the movement, demonstrates the characteristic accuracy of reportage in his Rougon-Macquart sequence of novels (1871–93),

nativity *The Nativity* 1470–75 by the Italian painter Piero della Francesca (National Gallery, London). One of the central events of the Christian story, the nativity became one of the most familiar and best-loved images in western art. The challenge for the artist was to depict the humbleness of the setting – a mere stable – while clearly indicating the sacredness of the event. *Corbis*

which shows the working of heredity and environment in one family. Other naturalist writers include Guy de Maupassant and Alphonse Daudet in France, Gerhart Hauptmann in Germany, and Theodore Dreiser in the USA.

natural justice the concept that there is an inherent quality in law that compares favourably with arbitrary action by a government. It is largely associated with the idea of the rule of law. For natural justice to be present, it is generally argued that no one should be a judge in his or her own case, and that each party in a dispute has an unalienable right to be heard and to prepare their case thoroughly (the rule of *audi alterem partem*).

natural logarithm in mathematics, the ◊exponent of a number expressed to base e, where e represents the ◊irrational number 2.71828... .

Natural ◊logarithms are also called Napierian logarithms, after their inventor, the Scottish mathematician John Napier.

natural radioactivity radioactivity generated by those radioactive elements that exist in the Earth's crust. All the elements from polonium (atomic number 84) to uranium (atomic number 92) are radioactive.

◊Radioisotopes of some lighter elements are also found in nature (for example potassium-40). See ◊background radiation.

natural selection the process whereby gene frequencies in a population change through certain individuals producing more descendants than others because they are better able to survive and reproduce in their environment.

The accumulated effect of natural selection is to produce ◊adaptations such as the insulating coat of a polar bear or the spadelike forelimbs of a mole. The process is slow, relying firstly on random variation in the genes of an organism being produced by ◊mutation and secondly on the genetic ◊recombination of sexual reproduction. It was recognized by Charles Darwin and English naturalist Alfred Russel Wallace as the main process driving ◊evolution.

Nature Conservancy Council (NCC) former name of UK government agency divided 1991 into English Nature, Scottish Natural Heritage, and the Countryside Council for Wales.

The NCC was established by act of Parliament 1973 (Nature Conservancy created by royal charter 1949) with the aims of designating and managing national nature reserves and other conservation areas; identifying Sites of Special Scientific Interest; advising government ministers on policies; providing advice and information; and commissioning or undertaking relevant scientific research. In 1991 the Nature Conservancy Council was dissolved and its three regional bodies became autonomous agencies.

nature–nurture controversy or ***environment–heredity controversy*** long-standing dispute among philosophers and psychologists over the relative importance of environment, that is, upbringing, experience, and learning ('nurture'), and heredity, that is, genetic inheritance ('nature'), in determining the make-up of an organism, as related to human personality and intelligence.

nature reserve area set aside to protect a habitat and the wildlife that lives within it, with only restricted admission for the public. A nature reserve often provides a sanctuary for rare species. The world's largest is Etosha Reserve, Namibia; area 99,520 sq km/38,415 sq mi.

naturopathy in alternative medicine, facilitating of the natural self-healing processes of the body. Naturopaths are the general practitioners (GPs) of alternative medicine and often refer clients to other specialists, particularly in manipulative therapies, to complement their own work of seeking, through diet, the prescription of natural medicines and supplements, and lifestyle counselling, to restore or augment the vitality of the body and thereby its optimum health.

Nauru island country in Polynesia, SW Pacific, W of Kiribati. *See country box below.*

nautical mile unit of distance used in navigation, an internationally agreed-on standard (since 1959) equalling the average length of one minute of arc on a great circle of the Earth, or 1,852 m/6,076.12 ft. The term formerly applied to various units of distance used in navigation. In the UK the nautical mile was formerly defined as 6,082 ft.

nautilus shelled ◊cephalopod, genus *Nautilus*, found in the Indian and Pacific oceans. The pearly nautilus *N. pompilius* has a chambered spiral shell about 20 cm/8 in in diameter. Its body occupies the outer chamber. The nautilus has a large number of short, grasping tentacles surrounding a sharp beak.

The living nautiluses are representatives of a group common 450 million years ago.

Paper nautilus is another name for the ◊argonaut, a type of octopus.

Navajo or *Navaho* (Tena ***Navahu*** 'large planted field') a Native American people related to the Apache, and numbering about 200,000, mostly in Arizona. They speak an Athabaskan language, belonging to the Na-Dené family. The Navajo were traditionally cultivators; many now herd sheep and earn an income from tourism, making and selling rugs, blankets, and silver and turquoise jewellery. The Navajo refer to themselves as *Dineh*, 'people'.

They were attacked by Kit Carson (1809–1868) and US troops 1864, and were rounded up and exiled. Their reservation, created 1868, is the largest in the USA (65,000 sq km/25,000 sq mi), and is mainly in NE Arizona but extends into NW New Mexico and SE Utah. Some uranium and natural gas is extracted on their reservation.

Navarino, Battle of during the Greek war of liberation, destruction 20 Oct 1827 of a joint Turkish–Egyptian fleet by by the combined fleets of the British, French, and Russians under Vice-Admiral Edward Codrington (1770–1851). The destruction of their fleet left the Turks highly vulnerable in Greece as they had no protection to their rear and no supply line, and this proved to be the decisive battle of the war. Navarino is the Italian and historic name of Pylos Bay, Greece, on the SW coast of the Peloponnese.

Navarre (Spanish ***Navarra***) autonomous mountain region of N Spain, including Monte Adi 1,503 m/4,933 ft; area 10,400 sq km/4,014 sq mi; population (1992) 519,200. Its capital is Pamplona.
history part of the medieval kingdom of ◊Navarre. Estella, to the SW, where Don Carlos was proclaimed king 1833, was a centre of agitation by the ◊Carlists.

Navarre, Kingdom of former kingdom comprising the Spanish province of Navarre and part of what is now the French *département* of Basses-Pyrénées. It resisted the conquest of the ◊Moors and was independent until it became French 1284 on the marriage of Philip IV to the heiress of Navarre. In 1479 Ferdinand of Aragon annexed Spanish Navarre, with French Navarre going to Catherine of Foix (1483–1512), who kept the royal title. Her grandson became Henry IV of France, and Navarre was absorbed in the French crown lands 1620.

nave in architecture, the central part of a church, between the choir and the entrance.

navel or ***umbilicus*** small indentation in the centre of the abdomen of mammals, marking the site of attachment of the ◊umbilical cord, which connects the fetus to the ◊placenta.

navigation the science and technology of finding the position, course, and distance travelled by a ship, plane, or other craft. Traditional methods include the magnetic ◊compass and ◊sextant. Today the gyrocompass is usually used, together with highly sophisticated electronic methods, employing beacons of radio signals, such as Decca, Loran, and Omega. Satellite navigation uses satellites that broadcast time and position signals.

The US ◊global positioning system (GPS) was introduced 1992. When complete, it will feature 24 Navstar satellites that will enable users (including

---

NAURU
Republic of

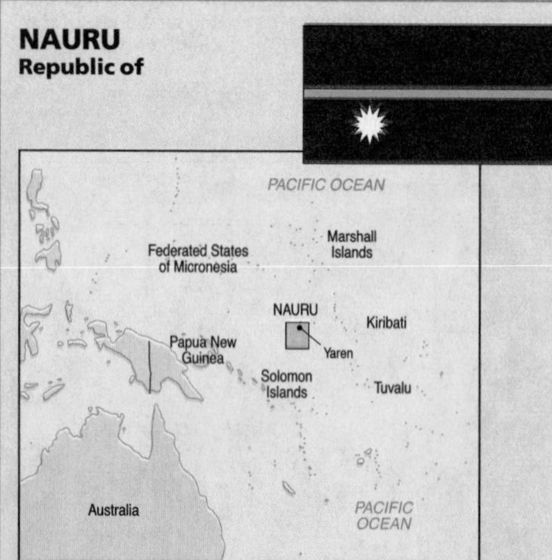

national name *Naoero*
area 21 sq km/8 sq mi
capital (seat of government) Yaren District
physical features tropical coral island in SW Pacific; plateau encircled by coral cliffs and sandy beaches
head of state and government Kinza Klodimar from 1997
political system liberal democracy
administrative divisions 14 districts, grouped into eight divisions
political parties candidates are traditionally elected as independents, grouped into pro- and anti-government factions; Democratic Party of Nauru (DPN), only formal political party, anti-government
population 11,000 (1996 est)
population growth rate 2.6% (1990–95)
ethnic distribution about 87% of European origin (mostly British), about 9% Maori, and about 2% Pacific Islander
literacy rate 99%
languages Nauruan (official), English
religions Protestant, Roman Catholic
currency Australian dollar
GDP (US $) 100 million (1993)
exports phosphates

HISTORY
1798 British whaler Capt John Fearn first visited Nauru and named it 'Pleasant Island'.
1830s–80s The island was a haven for white runaway convicts and deserters.
1888 Annexed by Germany at the request of German settlers who sought protection from local clan unrest.
1899 Phosphate deposits were discovered and mining began eight years later, with indentured Chinese labourers brought in to work the British Australian-owned mines.
1914 Occupied by Australia on outbreak of World War I.
1920 Administered by Australia on behalf of itself, New Zealand, and the UK until independence, except 1942–43, when occupied by Japan, and two-thirds of the population were deported briefly to Micronesia.
1951 Local Government Council set up to replace Council of Chiefs.
1956 Hammer DeRoburt became head chief of Nauru.
1968 Independence achieved, with 'special member' British Commonwealth status. Hammer DeRoburt elected president.
1976 Bernard Dowiyogo elected president as criticism mounted of DeRoburt's personal style of government.
1978 DeRoburt re-elected.
1986 DeRoburt briefly replaced as president by opposition leader Kennan Adeang.
1987 Adeang established the Democratic Party of Nauru.
1989 DeRoburt replaced by Kenas Aroi, who was later succeeded by Dowiyogo.
1992 DeRoburt died.
1994 Australia agreed to out-of-court settlement of A$107 million, payable over 20 years, for environmental damage caused by phosphate mining which had left 80% of land agriculturally barren.
1995 Lagumot Harris replaced Dowiyogo as president.
1997 Kinza Klodimar became president after new general election.

SEE ALSO Pacific Islands

eventually motorists and walkers) to triangulate their position (from any three satellites) to within 15 m/50 ft.

In 1992, 85 nations agreed to take part in trials of a new navigation system which makes use of surplus military space technology left over from the Cold War. The new system, known as FANS or Future Navigation System, will make use of the 24 Russian Glonass satellites and the 24 US GPS satellites. Small computers will gradually be fitted to civil aircraft to process the signals from the satellite, allowing aircraft to navigate with pinpoint accuracy anywhere in the world. The signals from at least three satellites will guide the craft to within a few metres of accuracy. FANS will be used in conjunction with four Inmarsat satellites to provide worldwide communications between pilots and air-traffic controllers.

Navigation Acts in British history, a series of acts of Parliament passed from 1381 to protect English shipping from foreign competition and to ensure monopoly trading between Britain and its colonies. The last was repealed 1849 (coastal trade exempt until 1853). The Navigation Acts helped to establish England as a major sea power, although they led to higher prices. They ruined the Dutch merchant fleet in the 17th century, and were one of the causes of the ◊American Revolution. ▷*See feature on pp. 32–33.*

1650 'Commonwealth Ordinance' forbade foreign ships to trade in English colonies.
1651 Forbade the importation of goods except in English vessels or in vessels of the country of origin of the goods. This act led to the Anglo-Dutch War 1652–54.
1660 All colonial produce was required to be exported in English vessels.
1663 Colonies were prohibited from receiving goods in foreign (rather than English) vessels.

navigation, biological the ability of animals or insects to navigate. Although many animals navigate by following established routes or known landmarks, many animals can navigate without such aids; for example, birds can fly several thousand miles back to their nest site, over unknown terrain.

Such feats may be based on compass information derived from the position of the Sun, Moon, or stars, or on the characteristic patterns of Earth's magnetic field.

Biological navigation refers to the ability to navigate both in long-distance ◊migrations and over shorter distances when foraging (for example, the honey bee finding its way from the hive to a nectar site and back). Where reliant on known landmarks, birds may home on features that can be seen from very great distances (such as the cloud caps that often form above isolated mid-ocean islands). Even smells can act as a landmark. Aquatic species like salmon are believed to learn the characteristic taste of the river where they hatch and return to it, often many years later. Brain cells in some birds have been found to contain ◊magnetite and may therefore be sensitive to the Earth's magnetic field.

Navratilova Czech-born tennis player Martina Navratilova, the world's top-ranked female player 1979 and 1982–86. She became a US citizen 1981 and set the professional women's record with 74 consecutive victories 1984. For some years her only rival was the popular US player Chris Evert. *Topham*

Navratilova Martina 1956– . Czech tennis player who became a naturalized US citizen 1981. The most outstanding woman player of the 1980s, she had 55 Grand Slam victories by 1991, including 18 singles titles. She won the Wimbledon singles title a record nine times, including six in succession 1982–87. She was defeated by Conchita Martinez in the final of her last Wimbledon as a singles player 1994.

Navratilova won her first Wimbledon title in 1976 (doubles with Chris Evert). Between 1974 and 1988 she won 52 Grand Slam titles (singles and doubles), second only to Margaret ◊Court.

navy fleet of ships, usually a nation's ◊warships and the organization to maintain them.

In the early 1990s, the UK had a force of small carriers, destroyers, frigates, and submarines.

Nazarbayev Nursultan 1940– . President of Kazakhstan from 1990. In the Soviet period he was prime minister of the republic 1984–89 and leader of the Kazakh Communist Party 1989–91, which established itself as the independent Socialist Party of Kazakhstan Sept 1991. He is an advocate of free-market policies, and yet also enjoys the support of the environmentalist lobby.

Nazareth town in Galilee, N Israel, SE of Haifa; population about 64,000. According to the New Testament, it was the boyhood home of Jesus.

Nazi member of the *Nationalsozialistische Deutsche Arbeiterpartei*, usually abbreviated to the Nazi Party. The party was based on the ideology of Nazism.

Nazism ideology based on racism, nationalism, and the supremacy of the state over the individual. The German Nazi party, the *Nationalsozialistische Deutsche Arbeiterpartei* (National Socialist German Workers' Party), was formed from the German Workers' Party (founded 1919) and led by Adolf ◊Hitler 1921–45.

During the 1930s, many similar parties were created throughout Europe and the USA, although only those of Austria, Hungary, and Sudetenland were of major importance. These parties collaborated with the German occupation of Europe 1939–45. After the Nazi atrocities of World War II (see ◊SS, ◊concentration camp, ◊Holocaust), the party was banned in Germany, but today parties with Nazi or neo-Nazi ideologies exist in many countries.

N'djamena capital of Chad, at the confluence of the Chari and Logone rivers, on the Cameroon border; population (1993) 531,000.

Founded 1900 by the French at the junction of caravan routes, it was used 1903–12 as a military centre against the kingdoms of central Sudan. Its name until 1973 was Fort Lamy.

Ndola mining centre and chief city of the Copperbelt province of central Zambia; population (1990) 376,000.

N'Dour Youssou 1959– . Senegalese singer, songwriter, and musician. His fusion of traditional *mbalax* percussion music with bluesy Arab-style vocals, accompanied by African and electronic instruments, became popular in the West in the 1980s on albums such as *Immigrés* 1984 with the band Le Super Etoile de Dakar.

Neagh, Lough lake in Northern Ireland, 25 km/15 mi W of Belfast; area 396 sq km/153 sq mi. It is the largest lake in the British Isles.

Neagle Anna, (born (Florence) Marjorie Robertson) 1904–1986. English actress. She was made a star by her producer-director husband Herbert Wilcox (1890–1977). Her films include *Nell Gwyn* 1934, *Victoria the Great* 1937, and *Odette* 1950.

Neanderthal hominid of the Mid-Late Palaeolithic, named after the Neander Tal (valley) near Düsseldorf, Germany, where a skeleton was found 1856. *Homo sapiens neanderthalensis* lived from about 150,000 to 35,000 years ago and was similar

Nazi An election poster for the German National Socialists from 1931. It reads, 'Work, Freedom and Bread!' The National Socialists came to power in Germany 1933. *Philip Sauvain*

in build to present-day people, but slightly smaller, stockier, and heavier-featured with a strong jaw and prominent brow ridges on a sloping forehead. The condition of the Neanderthal teeth that have been found suggests that they were used as clamps for holding objects with the hands. Neanderthals lived in Europe, the Middle East, and Africa. They looked after their disabled and buried their dead ritualistically. ▷*See feature on pp. 518–519.*

Neath Port Talbot unitary authority of Wales created 1996 (*see United Kingdom map*).

Neave Airey Middleton Sheffield 1916–1979. British intelligence officer and Conservative member of Parliament 1953–79, a close adviser to former prime minister Margaret Thatcher. During World War II he escaped from Colditz, a German high-security prison camp. As shadow undersecretary of state for Northern Ireland from 1975, he became a target for extremist groups and was assassinated by an Irish terrorist bomb.

Nebraska state in central USA; nicknamed Cornhusker State/Blackwater State
area 200,400 sq km/77,354 sq mi
capital Lincoln
towns and cities Omaha, Grand Island, North Platte
population (1991) 1,593,000
features Rocky Mountain foothills; tributaries of the Missouri; prairies; a 206-km/128-mi stretch of the Oregon Trail, including Scotts Bluff national monument, Chimney Rock national historic site, and Courthouse and Jail Rocks; Mission River; Platte River, with the Platte River Whooping Crane Habitat; Nebraska national forest; Buffalo Bill Ranch state historical park; Willa Cather Historical Center and Cather Memorial Prairie, Red Cloud; Homestead national monument; Boys Town, founded 1917 for homeless boys; Fremont and Elkhorn Valley Railroad; Strategic Air Command Museum, Bellevue.
industries cereals, livestock, processed foods, fertilizers, oil, natural gas
famous people Fred Astaire, William Jennings Bryan, Johnny Carson, Willa Cather, Henry Fonda, Harold Lloyd, Malcolm X
history exploited by French fur traders in the early 1700s; ceded to Spain by France 1763; retroceded to

Nebraska

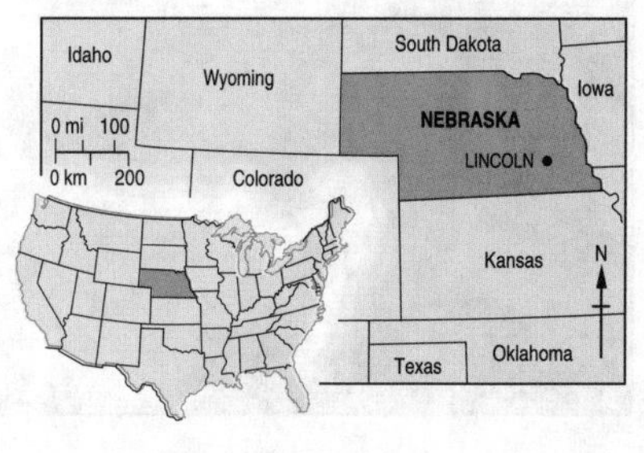

'One's first and constant emotion here is of thankfulness that Jesus was reared amidst such natural beauty.'

On **Nazareth**
Harriet Martineau
Eastern Life Past and Present 1848

‘I have only one eye, I have a right to be blind sometimes: ... I really do not see the signal!’

Horatio Nelson
At the Battle of Copenhagen 1801

France 1801; part of the Louisiana Purchase 1803; explored by Lewis and Clark 1804–06; first settlement at Bellevue 1823; became a territory 1854 and a state 1867 after the Union Pacific began its transcontinental railroad at Omaha 1865.

Nebuchadnezzar or *Nebuchadrezzar II* c. 630–c. 562 BC. King of Babylonia from 604 BC. Shortly before his accession he defeated the Egyptians at Carchemish and brought Palestine and Syria into his empire. Judah revolted, with Egyptian assistance, 596 and 587–586 BC; on both occasions he captured Jerusalem and took many Hebrews into captivity. He largely rebuilt Babylon and constructed the hanging gardens.

nebula cloud of gas and dust in space. Nebulae are the birthplaces of stars, but some nebulae are produced by gas thrown off from dying stars (see ◊planetary nebula; ◊supernova). Nebulae are classified depending on whether they emit, reflect, or absorb light.

An ***emission nebula***, such as the ◊Orion nebula, glows brightly because its gas is energized by stars that have formed within it. In a ***reflection nebula***, starlight reflects off grains of dust in the nebula, such as surround the stars of the ◊Pleiades cluster. A ***dark nebula*** is a dense cloud, composed of molecular hydrogen, which partially or completely absorbs light behind it. Examples include the Coalsack nebula in ◊Crux and the Horsehead nebula in Orion. ▷ *See feature on pp. 70–71.*

Necker Jacques 1732–1804. French politician. As finance minister 1776–81, he attempted reforms, and was dismissed through Queen Marie Antoinette's influence. Recalled 1788, he persuaded Louis XVI to summon the States General (parliament), which earned him the hatred of the court, and in July 1789 he was banished. The outbreak of the French Revolution with the storming of the Bastille forced his reinstatement, but he resigned Sept 1790.

necrosis death or decay of tissue in a particular part of the body, usually due to bacterial poisoning or loss of local blood supply.

nectar sugary liquid secreted by some plants from a nectary, a specialized gland usually situated near the base of the flower. Nectar often accumulates in special pouches or spurs, not always in the same location as the nectary. Nectar attracts insects, birds, bats, and other animals to the flower for ◊pollination and is the raw material used by bees in the production of honey.

nectarine smooth, shiny-skinned variety of ◊peach, usually smaller than other peaches and with firmer flesh. It arose from a natural mutation.

NEDC abbreviation for ◊***National Economic Development Council***.

Needham Joseph 1900–1995. English biochemist and sinologist, historian of Chinese science. He worked first on problems in embryology. In the 1930s he learned Chinese and began to collect material. The first volume of his *Science and Civilization in China* was published 1954 and by 1990 sixteen volumes had appeared.

needlefish any bony fish of the marine family Belonidae, with an elongated body and long jaws lined with many sharp teeth.

Needles, the group of rocks in the sea near the Isle of ◊Wight, S England

Nefertiti or *Nofretete* queen of Egypt and wife of the pharaoh ◊Akhenaton.

negative/positive in photography, a reverse image, which when printed is again reversed, restoring the original scene. It was invented by Fox ◊Talbot about 1834.

Negev desert in S Israel that tapers to the port of Eilat. It is fertile under irrigation, and minerals include oil and copper.

negligence in law, doing some act that a ‘prudent and reasonable’ person would not do, or omitting to do some act that such a person would do. Negligence may arise in respect of a person's duty towards an individual or towards other people in general. Breach of the duty of care that results in reasonably foreseeable damage is a tort.

Contributory negligence is a defence sometimes raised where the defendant to an action for negligence claims that the plaintiff by his own negligence contributed to the cause of the action.

Negro term formerly used to refer to the indigenous people of Africa south of the Sahara, today distributed around the world. The term generally preferred today is ◊black.

Nehru Jawaharlal 1889–1964. Indian nationalist politician, prime minister from 1947. Before the partition (the division of British India into India and Pakistan), he led the socialist wing of the nationalist ◊Congress Party, and was second in influence only to Mahatma Gandhi. He was imprisoned nine times by the British 1921–45 for political activities. As prime minister from the creation of the dominion (later republic) of India in Aug 1947, he originated the idea of nonalignment (neutrality towards major powers). His daughter was Prime Minister Indira Gandhi. His sister, Vijaya Lakshmi Pandit (1900–1990) was the UN General Assembly's first female president (1953–54). ▷ *See feature on pp. 432–433.*

Nehru Report constitution drafted for India 1928. After Indian nationalists rejected the Simon Commission (a British group set up 1927 to examine the working of government in India and recommend future policy), an all-party committee was set up, chaired by Motilal Nehru (1861–1931), to map out a constitution. Established to counter British charges that Indians could not find a constitutional consensus among themselves, it advocated that India be given dominion status of complete internal self-government. Many members of the Congress preferred complete independence to dominion status, and in 1929 announced a campaign of ◊civil disobedience to support their demands.

Nelson Horatio, 1st Viscount Nelson 1758–1805. English admiral. He joined the navy in 1770. In the Revolutionary Wars against France he lost the sight in his right eye 1794 and lost his right arm 1797. He became a national hero, and rear admiral, after the victory off Cape St Vincent, Portugal. In 1798 he tracked the French fleet to Aboukir Bay where he almost entirely destroyed it. In 1801 he won a decisive victory over Denmark at the Battle of ◊Copenhagen, and in 1805, after two years of blockading Toulon, another over the Franco-Spanish fleet at the Battle of ◊Trafalgar, near Gibraltar.

Nelson was almost continuously on active service in the Mediterranean 1793–1800, and lingered at Naples for a year, during which he helped to crush a democratic uprising and fell completely under the influence of Lady ◊Hamilton. In 1800 he returned to England and soon after separated from his wife, Frances Nisbet (1761–1831). In 1803 he received the Mediterranean command and in 1805 defeated the combined French and Spanish fleets off Cape Trafalgar. Nelson himself was mortally wounded. He is buried in St Paul's Cathedral, London. ▷ *See feature on pp. 748–749.*

nematode unsegmented worm of the phylum Nematoda. Nematodes are pointed at both ends, with a tough, smooth outer skin. They include many free-living species found in soil and water, including the sea, but a large number are parasites, such as the roundworms and pinworms that live in humans, or the eelworms that attack plant roots. They differ from ◊flatworms in that they have two openings to the gut (a mouth and an anus).

Most nematode species are found in deep-sea sediment. Around 4,000 marine species are known, but a 1995 study by the Natural History Museum, based on the analysis of sediment from 17 seabed sites worldwide, estimated that nematodes may make up as much as 75% of all species, with an estimated 100 million species.

Nemerov Howard Stanley 1920– . US poet, critic, and novelist. He published his poetry collection *Guide to the Ruins* 1950, a short-story collection *A Commodity of Dreams* 1959, and *Collected Poems* 1977, which won both the National Book Award and a Pulitzer prize 1978. Later poetry includes *Trying Conclusions* 1991.

Nemesis in Greek mythology, the goddess of retribution, who especially punished hubris (Greek *hybris*), violent acts carried through in defiance of the gods and human custom.

neo- (Greek *neos* ‘new’) prefix used to indicate a revival or development of an older form, often in a different spirit. Examples include neo-Marxism and neo-Darwinism.

neoclassical economics school of economic thought based on the work of 19th-century economists such as Alfred Marshall, using marginal theory (the study of the effect of increasing a factor by one more unit) to modify classical economic theories, and placing greater emphasis on mathematical techniques and theories of the firm. Neoclassicists believed competition to be the regulator of economic activity that would establish equilibrium between demand and supply through the operation of market forces.

Neoclassical economics was criticized by the English economist John Maynard Keynes for its analysis of output and employment in the whole economy. The US economist Milton ◊Friedman reasserted neoclassical principles of macroeconomics.

Neo-Classicism movement in art, architecture, and design in Europe and North America about 1750–1850, characterized by a revival of Classical Greek and Roman styles. Leading figures of the movement were the architects Claude-Nicolas Ledoux and Robert Adam; the painters Jacques-Louis David, Jean Ingres, and Anton Mengs; the sculptors Antonio Canova, John Flaxman, Bertel Thorvaldsen, and Johann Sergel; and the designers Josiah Wedgwood, George Hepplewhite, and Thomas Sheraton.

Neo-Classicism superseded the Rococo style and was inspired both by the excavation of the Roman towns of Pompeii and Herculaneum and by the theories of the cultural studies of the German art

Nehru The Indian politician and prime minister Jawaharlal Nehru, with his daughter Indira Gandhi 1940. Nehru played an important part in the negotiations for an independent India, and became its first prime minister 1947. *Image Select (UK) Ltd*

historian Johann J Winckelmann (which revived Greek styles). Winckelmann identified the most important elements of Classical art as being 'noble simplicity and calm grandeur'. Neo-Classical artists sought to capture these qualities by conscious emulation of Classical styles and subject matter. They took themes from Homer and Plutarch and were influenced by John Flaxman's austere linear illustrations for the *Iliad* and *Odyssey*.

neocolonialism disguised form of ◊imperialism, by which a country may grant independence to another country but continue to dominate it by control of markets for goods or raw materials. Many developing countries, heavily dependent on leading industrial nations, are subject to this new form of imperialism, with significant proportions of their national product being allocated to payment of interest on accumulated foreign debts.

neo-Darwinism the modern theory of ◊evolution, built up since the 1930s by integrating the 19th-century English scientist Charles ◊Darwin's theory of evolution through natural selection with the theory of genetic inheritance founded on the work of the Austrian biologist Gregor ◊Mendel.

Neo-Darwinism asserts that evolution takes place because the environment is slowly changing, exerting a selection pressure on the individuals within a population. Those with characteristics that happen to adapt to the new environment are more likely to survive and have offspring and hence pass on these favourable characteristics. Over time the genetic make-up of the population changes and ultimately a new species is formed.

neodymium yellowish metallic element of the ◊lanthanide series, symbol Nd, atomic number 60, relative atomic mass 144.24. Its rose-coloured salts are used in colouring glass, and neodymium is used in lasers.

It was named in 1885 by Austrian chemist Carl von Welsbach (1858–1929), who fractionated it away from didymium (originally thought to be an element but actually a mixture of rare-earth metals consisting largely of neodymium, praesodymium, and cerium).

Neo-Expressionism art movement, at its height in Germany and Italy in the 1970s and 1980s, which championed the revival of representational art (using images that can be recognized from the real world), expressive brushwork, and a concern with narrative and history at the expense of Minimalist and Conceptual art forms. Leading exponents include Anselm Kiefer (1945–), Georg Baselitz (1928–), and Francesco Clemente (1952–). In Italy the movement is known as *Transavanguardia* and in the USA as Bad Painting.

Neo-Impressionism movement in French painting in the 1880s, an extension of Impressionist technique. It drew on contemporary theories on colour and perception, building up form and colour by painting dots side by side. Georges ◊Seurat was the chief exponent; his minute technique became known as ◊Pointillism. Paul Signac and Camille Pissarro practised the style for a few years.

Neolithic last period of the ◊Stone Age, characterized by settled communities based on agriculture and domesticated animals, and identified by sophisticated, finely honed stone tools, and ceramic wares. The earliest Neolithic communities appeared about 9000 BC in the Middle East, followed by Egypt, India, and China. In Europe farming began in about 6500 BC in the Balkans and Aegean, spreading north and east by 1000 BC.

neon (Greek *neon* 'new') colourless, odourless, nonmetallic, gaseous element, symbol Ne, atomic number 10, relative atomic mass 20.183. It is grouped with the ◊inert gases, is non-reactive, and forms no compounds. It occurs in small quantities in the Earth's atmosphere. Neon was discovered by Scottish chemist William Ramsay and the Englishman Morris Travers.

neo-Nazism the upsurge in racial and political intolerance in Eastern and Western Europe of the early 1990s. In Austria, Belgium, France, Germany, Russia, and Italy, the growth of extreme right-wing political groupings, coupled with racial violence, particularly in Germany, has revived memories of the Nazi period in Hitler's Germany. Ironically, the liberalization of politics in the post-Cold War world has unleashed anti-liberal forces hitherto checked by authoritarian regimes.

neoplasm (Greek 'new growth') any lump or tumour, which may be benign or malignant (cancerous).

neo-Platonism school of philosophy that flourished during the declining centuries of the Roman Empire (3rd–6th centuries AD). Neo-Platonists argued that the highest stage of philosophy is attained not through reason and experience, but through a mystical ecstasy. Many later philosophers, including Nicholas of Cusa, were influenced by neo-Platonism.

neoprene synthetic rubber, developed in the USA 1931 from the polymerization of chloroprene. It is much more resistant to heat, light, oxidation, and petroleum than is ordinary rubber.

Neo-Rationalism in architecture, a movement originating in Italy in the 1960s which rejected the functionalist and technological preoccupations of mainstream Modernism, advocating a rationalist approach to design based on an awareness of formal properties. It developed in the light of a re-evaluation of the work of Giuseppe ◊Terragni led by Aldo Rossi (1931–), and gained momentum through the work of Giorgio Grassi (1935–). Characterized by elemental forms and an absence of detail, the style has adherents throughout Europe and the USA.

Neo-Realism movement in Italian cinema that emerged in the 1940s. It is characterized by its naturalism, social themes, frequent use of non-professional actors, and the visual authenticity achieved through location filming. Exponents include the directors de Sica, Visconti, and Rossellini.

neoteny in biology, the retention of some juvenile characteristics in an animal that seems otherwise mature. An example is provided by the axolotl, a salamander that can reproduce sexually although still in its larval form.

Nepal landlocked country in the Himalayan mountain range in Central Asia, bounded N by Tibet (an autonomous region of China), E, S, and W by India. *See country box on p. 756.*

neper unit used in telecommunications to express a ratio of powers and currents. It gives the attenuation of amplitudes as the natural logarithm of the ratio.

nephritis or ***Bright's disease*** general term used to describe inflammation of the kidney. The degree of illness varies, and it may be acute (often following a recent streptococcal infection), or chronic, requiring a range of treatments from antibiotics to ◊dialysis or transplant.

nephron microscopic unit in vertebrate kidneys that forms urine. A human kidney is composed of over a million nephrons. Each nephron consists of a knot of blood capillaries called a glomerulus, contained in the Bowman's capsule, and a long narrow tubule enmeshed with yet more capillaries. Waste materials and water pass from the bloodstream into the tubule, and essential minerals and some water are reabsorbed from the tubule back into the bloodstream. The remaining filtrate (urine) is passed out from the body.

Neptune in astronomy, the eighth planet in average distance from the Sun. It is a giant gas (hydrogen, helium, methane) planet, with a mass 17.2 times that of Earth. It has the highest winds in the Solar System.

mean distance from the Sun 4.4 billion km/2.794 billion mi

equatorial diameter 48,600 km/30,200 mi

rotation period 16 hr 7 min

Neo-Classicism The remains of a church in Essex, England, known as Mistley Towers, designed by Robert Adam. When asked to build a church in about 1774, Adam added these two square towers to the existing church. They are adorned with free-standing columns and topped with domes. This is typical of the Neo-Classical style of architecture of the second half of the 18th century, of which Adam was a leading exponent. *Corbis*

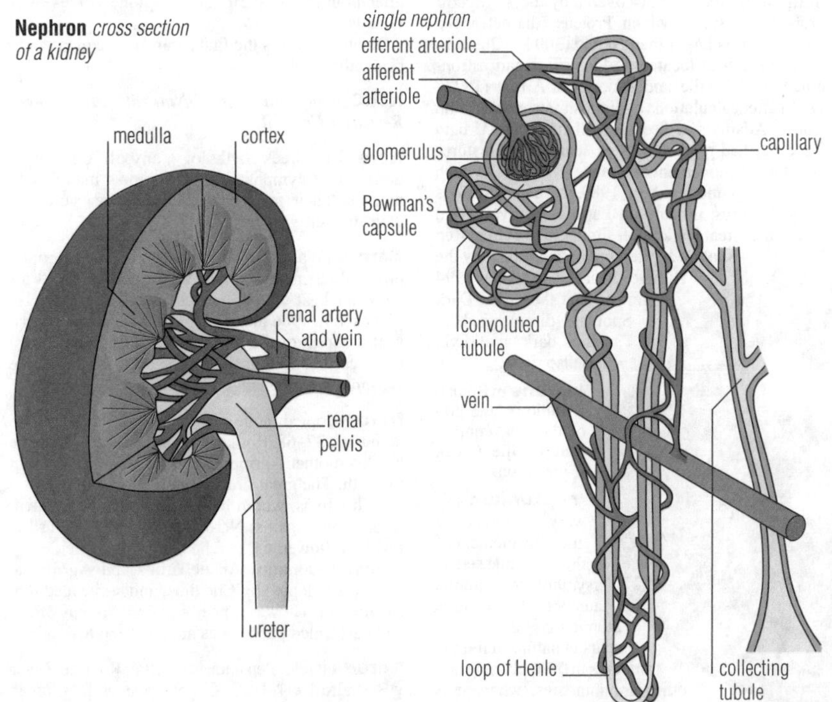

nephron The kidney (left) contains more than a million filtering units, or nephrons (right), consisting of the glomerulus, Bowman's capsule, and the loop of Henle. Blood flows through the glomerulus – a tight knot of fine blood vessels from which water and metabolic wastes filter into the tubule. This filtrate flows through the convoluted tubule and loop of Henle where most of the water and useful molecules are reabsorbed into the blood capillaries. The waste materials are passed to the collecting tubule as urine.

NEPAL
Kingdom of

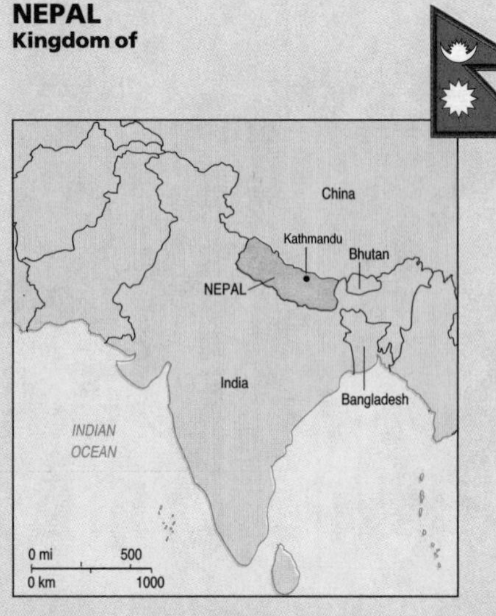

national name *Nepal Adhirajya*
area 147,181 sq km/56,850 sq mi
capital Kathmandu
major towns/cities Pátan, Moráng, Bhádgáon
physical features descends from the Himalayan mountain range in N through foothills to the river Ganges plain in S; Mount Everest, Mount Kangchenjunga
head of state King Birendra Bir Bikram Shah Dev from 1972
head of government Surya Bahadur Thapa from 1997
political system constitutional monarchy
administrative divisions 14 locally administered zones
political parties Nepali Congress Party (NCP), left of centre; United Nepal Communist Party (UNCP; Unified Marxist–Leninist), left-wing; Rashtriya Prajatantra Party (RPP), monarchist
population 21,918,000 (1995 est)
population growth rate 2.6% (1990–95); 2.4% (2000–05)
ethnic distribution 80% of Indo-Nepalese origin, including the Gurkhas, Paharis, Newars, and Tharus; 20% of Tibeto-Nepalese descent (concentrated in the N and E)
life expectancy 54 (men), 53 (women)
literacy rate men 38%, women 13%
languages Nepali (official); 20 dialects spoken
religions Hindu 90%; Buddhist, Muslim, Christian
currency Nepalese rupee
GDP (US $) 4.04 billion (1994)
growth rate 11.1% (1994)
exports jute, rice, timber, oilseed, ghee, potatoes, medicinal herbs, hides and skins, cattle

HISTORY
8th C BC Katmandu Valley occupied by Ahirs (shepherd kings), Tibeto-Burman migrants from N India.
5th C BC In Lumbini in the far S, Prince Siddhartha Gautama, the historic Buddha, was born.
AD 300 The Licchavis dynasty immigrated from India and introduced the caste system.
13th–16th Cs Dominated by the Malla dynasty, who were great patrons of the arts.
1768 Nepal emerged as unified kingdom after the ruler of the principality of the Gurkhas in the W, King Prithwi Narayan Shah, conquered the Katmandu Valley.
1792 Nepal's expansion was halted by defeat at the hands of the Chinese in Tibet; a commercial treaty was signed with Britain.
1815–16 Anglo-Nepali 'Gurkha War'; Nepal became a British-dependent buffer state with a British resident stationed in Kathmandu.
1846 Fell under sway of the Rana family, who became hereditary chief ministers, dominating a powerless monarchy and isolating Nepal from the outside world.
1923 Full independence formally recognized by Britain.
1951 Monarchy restored to power and the Ranas overthrown in 'palace revolution' supported by the Nepali Congress Party (NCP).
1959 Constitution created elected legislature.
1960–61 Parliament dissolved by King Mahendra; political parties banned after the NCP's pro-India socialist leader B P Koirala had become prime minister.
1962 New constitution provided for a tiered, traditional system of indirectly elected local councils (*panchayats*) and an appointed prime minister.
1972 King Mahendra died and was succeeded by his son, King Birendra Bikram Shah Dev.
1980 Constitutional referendum held following popular agitation led by B P Koirala resulted in introduction of direct, but nonparty, elections to National Assembly.
1983 Overthrow of monarch-supported prime minister by directly elected deputies to the National Assembly.
1986 New assembly elections returned a majority opposed to *panchayat* system of partyless government.
1988 Strict curbs placed on opposition activity; over 100 supporters of banned NCP arrested; censorship imposed.
1989 Border blockade imposed by India during treaty dispute.
1990 *Panchayat* system collapsed after mass NCP-led violent prodemocracy demonstrations; new democratic constitution introduced, and the ban on political parties lifted.
1991 Nepali Congress Party, led by Girija Prasad Koirala, won general election.
1992 Communists led anti-government demonstrations in Kathmandu and Pátan.
1994 Koirala's government defeated on 'no-confidence' motion; parliament dissolved. After new elections, minority communist government formed under Man Mohan Adhikari.
1995 Parliament dissolved by King Birendra at Prime Minister Adhikari's request; Sher Bahadur Deuba (NCP) became prime minister.
1997 Lokendra Bahadur Chand became prime minister, leading a coalition government.

SEE ALSO caste; Gurkha; Hinduism

Nero A coin from the reign of the Roman emperor Nero. Nero became emperor through the efforts of his ambitious mother; he later had her, and others, murdered to further his own ambitions. Yet throughout his life he had a genuine enthusiasm for the arts, writing poetry, and putting on theatrical performances, which the Romans considered beneath the dignity of an emperor. *Corbis*

year 164.8 Earth years
atmosphere methane in its atmosphere absorbs red light and gives the planet a blue colouring.
surface hydrogen, helium and methane. Its interior is believed to have a central rocky core covered by a layer of ice.
satellites Neptune has three faint rings and of its eight moons, two (◊Triton and Nereid) are visible from Earth. Six were discovered by the *Voyager 2* probe in 1989, of which Proteus (diameter 415 km/260 mi) is larger than Nereid (300 km/200 mi).

Neptune was located 1846 by German astronomers J G ◊Galle and Heinrich d'Arrest (1822–1875) after calculations by English astronomer John Couch Adams and French mathematician Urbain Leverrier had predicted its existence from disturbances in the movement of Uranus. *Voyager 2*, which passed Neptune in Aug 1989, revealed various cloud features, notably an Earth-sized oval storm cloud, the Great Dark Spot, similar to the Great Red Spot on Jupiter, but images taken by the Hubble Space Telescope 1994 showed that the Great Dark Spot has disappeared. A smaller dark spot DS2 has also gone.

Neptune in Roman mythology, the god of the sea, equivalent of the Greek ◊Poseidon.

neptunium silvery, radioactive metallic element of the ◊actinide series, symbol Np, atomic number 93, relative atomic mass 237.048. It occurs in nature in minute amounts in ◊pitchblende and other uranium ores, where it is produced from the decay of neutron-bombarded uranium in these ores. The longest-lived isotope, Np-237, has a half-life of 2.2 million years. The element can be produced by bombardment of U-238 with neutrons and is chemically highly reactive.

It was first synthesized in 1940 by US physicists E McMillan (1907–) and P Abelson (1913–), who named it for the planet Neptune (since it comes after uranium as the planet Neptune comes after Uranus).

Neptunium was the first ◊transuranic element to be synthesized.

NERC abbreviation for ◊***Natural Environment Research Council***.

Nereid in Greek mythology, any of 50 sea goddesses, or ◊nymphs, who sometimes mated with mortals. Their father was Nereus, a sea god, and their mother was Doris.

Nernst (Walther) Hermann 1864–1941. German physical chemist who won a Nobel prize 1920 for work on heat changes in chemical reactions. He proposed in 1906 the principle known as the Nernst heat theorem or the third law of thermodynamics: chemical changes at the temperature of ◊absolute zero involve no change of ◊entropy (disorder).

Nero Adopted name of Lucius Domitius Ahenobarbus AD 37–68. Roman emperor from 54. In 59 he had his mother Agrippina and his wife Octavia put to death. The great fire at Rome 64 was blamed on the Christians, whom he subsequently persecuted. In 65 a plot against Nero was discovered. Further revolts followed 68, and he committed suicide.

Son of Domitius Ahenobarbus and Agrippina, Nero was adopted by Claudius, and succeeded him as emperor. He was a poet and connoisseur of art, and performed publicly as an actor and a singer.

Neruda Pablo. Pen name of Neftalí Ricardo Reyes y Basualto 1904–1973. Chilean poet and diplomat. His work includes lyrics and the epic poem of the American continent *Canto General* 1950. He was awarded the Nobel Prize for Literature 1971. He served as consul and ambassador to many countries.

Nerva (Marcus Cocceius Nerva) AD c. 30–98. Roman emperor. He was proclaimed emperor on Domitian's death AD 96, and introduced state loans for farmers, family allowances, and allotments of land to poor citizens in his sixteen-month reign.

Neruda Chilean poet and diplomat Pablo Neruda. A political activist, he joined the Communist Party and supported the Communist president Salvador Allende. He travelled widely, and visited Russia, China, and E Europe 1948–52 when the Communist Party in Chile was outlawed. His writings are both personal and political. *Corbis*

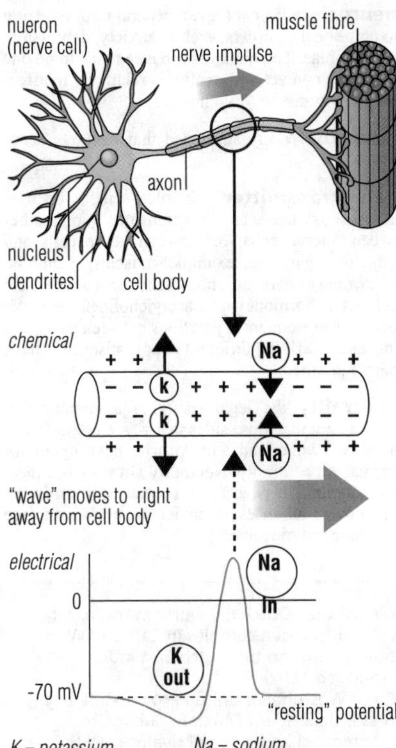

nerve cell **The anatomy and action of a nerve cell. The nerve cell or neuron consists of a cell body with the nucleus and projections called dendrites which pick up messages. An extension of the cell, the axon, connects one cell to the dendrites of the next. When a nerve cell is stimulated, waves of sodium (Na^+) and potassium (K^+) ions carry an electrical impulse down the axon.**

nerve bundle of nerve cells enclosed in a sheath of connective tissue and transmitting nerve impulses to and from the brain and spinal cord. A single nerve may contain both ◊motor and sensory nerve cells, but they function independently.

nerve cell or ***neuron*** elongated cell, the basic functional unit of the ◊nervous system that transmits information rapidly between different parts of the body. Each nerve cell has a cell body, containing the nucleus, from which trail processes called dendrites, responsible for receiving incoming signals. The unit of information is the nerve impulse, a travelling wave of chemical and electrical changes involving the membrane of the nerve cell. The cell's longest process, the ◊axon, carries impulses away from the cell body.

The impulse involves the passage of sodium and potassium ions across the nerve-cell membrane. Sequential changes in the permeability of the membrane to positive sodium (Na^+) ions and potassium (K^+) ions produce electrical signals called action potentials. Impulses are received by the cell body and passed, as a pulse of electric charge, along the axon. The axon terminates at the ◊synapse, a specialized area closely linked to the next cell (which may be another nerve cell or a specialized effector cell such as a muscle). On reaching the synapse, the impulse releases a chemical ◊neurotransmitter, which diffuses across to the neighbouring cell and there stimulates another impulse or the action of the effector cell.

Nerve impulses travel quickly – in humans, they may reach speeds of 160 m/525 ft per second.

Nervi Pier Luigi 1891–1979. Italian engineer. He used soft steel mesh within ◊concrete to give it flowing form; for example, the Turin exhibition hall 1948–49, consisting of a single undulating large-span roof, the UNESCO building in Paris 1953–58, with Marcel Breuer and Bernard-Louis Zehrfuss (1911–), and the cathedral at New Norcia, near Perth, Australia, 1960. He was the structural engineer on the Pirelli skyscraper project of Gio Ponti (1891–1979) in Milan 1958.

nervous breakdown popular term for a reaction to overwhelming psychological stress. There is no equivalent medical term. People said to be suffering from a nervous breakdown may be suffering from a neurotic illness, such as depression or anxiety, or a psychotic illness, such as schizophrenia.

nervous system the system of interconnected ◊nerve cells of most invertebrates and all vertebrates. It is composed of the ◊central and ◊autonomic nervous systems. It may be as simple as the nerve net of coelenterates (for example, jellyfishes) or as complex as the mammalian nervous system, with a central nervous system comprising ◊brain and ◊spinal chord and a peripheral nervous system connecting up with sensory organs, muscles, and glands.

human nervous system The human nervous system represents the product of millions of years of evolution, particularly in the degree of encephalization or brain complexity. It can be divided into central and peripheral parts for descriptive purposes, although there is both anatomical and functional continuity between the two parts. The central nervous system consists of the brain and the spinal cord. The peripheral nervous system is not so clearly subdivided, but its anatomical parts are: (1) the spinal nerves; (2) the cranial nerves; and (3) the autonomic nervous system.

Nesbit E(dith) 1858–1924. English author of children's books. She wrote *The Story of the Treasure Seekers* 1899 and *The Railway Children* 1906. Her stories often have a humorous magical element, as in *Five Children and It* 1902 and *The Phoenix and the Carpet* 1904. *The Treasure Seekers* is the first of several books about the realistically squabbling Bastable children; it was followed by *The Would-be Goods* 1901 and *The New Treasure Seekers* 1904. Nesbit was a Fabian socialist. She supported her family (including her husband's children by other women) by writing.

Ness, Loch lake in Highland Region, Scotland, forming part of the Caledonian Canal; 36 km/22.5 mi long, 229 m/754 ft deep. There have been unconfirmed reports of a Loch Ness monster since the 15th century. The monster is worth £5 million a year to Scottish tourism.

Nestlé multinational corporation, the world's largest packaged-food company, best known for producing chocolate, coffee, and baby milk (the marketing of which in the Third World has been criticized as inappropriate). The company's market value 1991 was estimated at £7.8 billion, and it employed 199,000 people.

Nestorianism Christian doctrine held by the Syrian ecclesiastic Nestorius (died c. 457), patriarch of Constantinople 428–431. He asserted that Jesus had two natures, human and divine. He was banished for maintaining that Mary was the mother of the man Jesus only, and therefore should not be called the mother of God. Today the Nestorian Church is found in small communities in Syria, Iraq, Iran, and India.

Nestorius and his followers fled from persecution in the Byzantine Empire after the Council of Ephesus 431 banned him and his teachings. They migrated to Persia and from there launched one of the most significant missionary movements. By the end of the 8th century they had spread to China and from Central Asia through Afghanistan to India, probably becoming the most numerous church in the world by the 9th century.

However, the Mongol invasions and the consolidation of Islam throughout these areas have now reduced this church to its present-day numbers of around 100,000.

Net, the abbreviation for the ◊Internet. The term is often used to denote the entire community of people with with computer access to the Internet.

Netanyahu Bibi (Binjamin) 1949– . Israeli right-wing politician and diplomat, leader of the Likud (Consolidation Party) from 1993 and prime minister from 1996. A hard-line politician, he succeeded Yitzak ◊Shamir to the Likud leadership in 1993 following the party's 1992 electoral defeat. He is Israel's first directly-elected prime minister.

He served in the Israeli embassy in Washington 1982–84 and was a principal representative at the United Nations in New York 1984–88. As deputy foreign minister in the Likud-led government of Shamir, he was the chief Israeli spokesperson in the 1991–92 Middle East peace talks. His elevation to the post of prime minister 1996 raised doubts about the Middle East peace process because of his hard-line stance.

net assets either the total ◊assets of a company less its current liabilities (that is, the capital employed) or the total assets less current liabilities, debt capital, long-term loans and provisions, which would form the amount available to ordinary shareholders if the company were to be wound up.

netball game developed from basketball, played by two teams of seven players each on a hard court 30.5 m/100 ft long and 15.25 m/50 ft wide. At each end is a goal, consisting of a post 3.05 m/10 ft high, at the top of which is attached a circular hoop and net. The object of the game is to pass an inflated spherical ball through the opposing team's net. The ball is thrown from player to player; no contact is allowed between players, who must not run with the ball.

Netherlands, the country in W Europe on the North Sea, bounded E by Germany and S by Belgium. *See country box on p. 758.*

Netherlands Antilles two groups of Caribbean islands, overseas territories of the Netherlands with full internal autonomy, comprising ◊Curaçao and Bonaire off the coast of Venezuela (◊Aruba is considered separately), and St Eustatius, Saba, and the southern part of St Maarten in the Leeward Islands, 800 km/500 mi to the NE

area 797 sq km/308 sq mi
capital Willemstad on Curaçao
industries oil from Venezuela refined here; tourism is important; rum; small manufacturing industries
language Dutch (official), Papiamento, English
population (1993 est) 197,100.

Netherlands Antilles

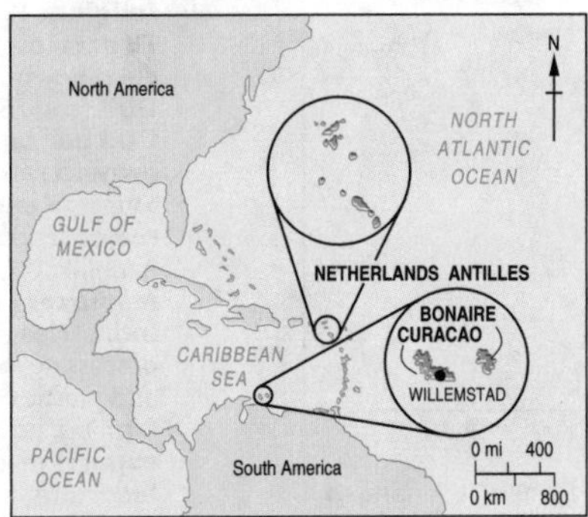

netiquette (derived from ***Internet etiquette***) behaviour guidelines evolved by users of the ◊Internet. The rules of netiquette include: no messages typed in upper case (considered to be the equivalent of shouting); new users, or new members of a ◊newsgroup, should read the frequently asked questions (FAQ) file before asking a question; no advertising via USENET newsgroups.

nettle any plant of the genus *Urtica*, family Urticaceae. Stinging hairs on the generally ovate leaves contain nerve toxins, which penetrate the skin and cause inflammation. The common nettle *U. dioica* grows on waste ground in Europe and North America, where it was introduced.

nettle rash popular name for the skin disorder ◊urticaria.

network in computing, a method of connecting computers so that they can share data and peripheral devices, such as printers. The main types are classified by the pattern of the connections – star or ring network, for example – or by the degree of geographical spread allowed; for example, ***local area networks*** (LANs) for communication within a room or building, and ***wide area networks*** (WANs) for more remote systems. Internet is the computer network that connects major English-speaking institutions throughout the world, with around 12 million users. Janet (joint academic network), a variant of Internet, is used in Britain. SuperJanet, launched 1992, is an extension of this that can carry 1,000 million bits of information per second. *See illustrations on p. 759.*

Neubrandenburg former district of East Germany which, since 1990, has been absorbed into the state of Mecklenburg–West Pomerania, Germany.

neuralgia sharp or burning pain originating in a nerve and spreading over its area of distribution. Trigeminal neuralgia, a common form, is a severe pain on one side of the face.

neural network artificial network of processors that attempts to mimic the structure of nerve cells (neurons) in the human brain. Neural networks may be electronic, optical, or simulated by computer software.

A basic network has three layers of processors: an input layer, an output layer, and a 'hidden' layer in between. Each processor is connected to every other in the network by a system of 'synapses'; every processor in the top layer connects to every one in the hidden layer, and each of these connects to every processor in the output layer. This means that each nerve cell in the middle and bottom layers receives input from several different sources; only when the amount of input exceeds a critical level does the cell fire an output signal.

The chief characteristic of neural networks is their ability to sum up large amounts of imprecise data and decide whether they match a pattern or not. Networks of this type may be used in developing robot vision, matching fingerprints, and analysing fluctuations in stock-market prices. However, it is thought unlikely by scientists that such networks will ever be able accurately to imitate the human brain, which is very much more complicated; it contains around 10 billion nerve cells, whereas current artificial networks contain only a few hundred processors.

neurasthenia obsolete term for nervous exhaustion, covering mild ◊depression and various symptoms of ◊neurosis. Formerly thought to be a bodily malfunction, it is now generally considered to be mental in origin. Dating from the mid-19th century, the term became widely used to describe the symptoms of soldiers returning from the front in World War I.

neuritis peripheral nerve inflammation caused by injury, poisoning, or disease, and accompanied by sensory and motor changes in the area of the affected nerve.

neurology medical speciality concerned with the study and treatment of disorders of the brain, spinal cord, and peripheral nerves.

neuron another name for a ◊nerve cell.

neurosis in psychology, a general term referring to emotional disorders, such as anxiety, depression, and phobias. The main disturbance tends to be one of mood; contact with reality is relatively unaffected, in contrast to ◊psychosis.

neurotoxin any substance that destroys nerve tissue.

neurotransmitter chemical that diffuses across a ◊synapse, and thus transmits impulses between ◊nerve cells, or between nerve cells and effector organs (for example, muscles). Common neurotransmitters are noradrenaline (which also acts as a hormone) and acetylcholine, the latter being most frequent at junctions between nerve and muscle. Nearly 50 different neurotransmitters have been identified.

neutrality the legal status of a country that decides not to choose sides in a war. Certain states, notably Switzerland and Austria, have opted for permanent neutrality. Neutrality always has a legal connotation. In peacetime, neutrality towards the big power alliances is called nonalignment (see ◊nonaligned movement).

NETHERLANDS

Kingdom of the (popularly referred to as *Holland*)

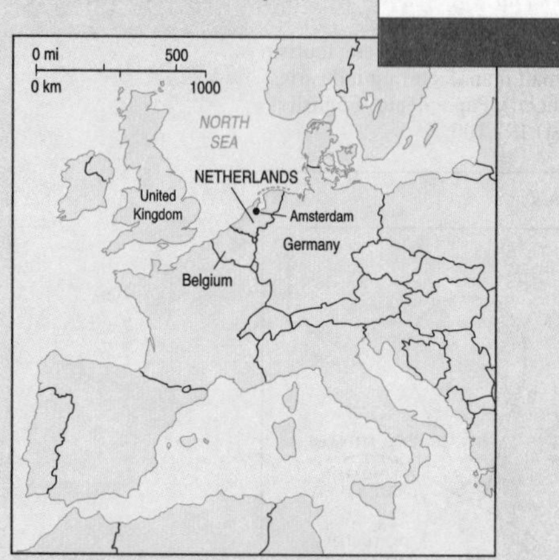

national name *Koninkrijk der Nederlanden*
area 41,863 sq km/16,169 sq mi
capital Amsterdam
major towns/cities The Hague (seat of government), Utrecht, Eindhoven, Maastricht
major ports Rotterdam
physical features flat coastal lowland; rivers Rhine, Scheldt, Maas; Frisian Islands
territories Aruba, Netherlands Antilles (Caribbean)
head of state Queen Beatrix Wilhelmina Armgard from 1980
head of government Wim Kok from 1994
political system constitutional monarchy
administrative divisions 12 provinces
political parties Christian Democratic Appeal (CDA), Christian, right of centre; Labour Party (PvdA), democratic socialist, left of centre; People's Party for Freedom and Democracy (VVD), liberal, free enterprise; Democrats 66 (D66), ecologist, centrist; Political Reformed Party (SGP), moderate Calvinist; Evangelical Political Federation (RPF), radical Calvinist; Reformed Political Association (GPV), fundamentalist Calvinist; Green Left, ecologist; General League of the Elderly (AOV), pensioner-oriented
armed forces 70,100 (1994)
conscription none
defence spend (% GDP) 2.1 (1994)
education spend (% GNP) 5.9 (1992)
health spend (% GDP) 6.8 (1993)
death penalty abolished 1982
population 15,575,000 (1996 est)
population growth rate 0.7% (1990–95); 0.3% (2000–05)
age distribution (% of total population) <15 18.4%, 15–65 68.4%, >65 13.2% (1995)
ethnic distribution primarily Germanic, with some Gallo-Celtic mixtures; sizeable minority of Indonesians and Surinamese
population density (per sq km) 377 (1994)
urban population (% of total) 89 (1995)
labour force 46% of population: 5% agriculture, 26% industry, 70% services (1990)
unemployment 7% (1995)
child mortality rate (under 5, per 1,000 live births) 8 (1993)
life expectancy 74 (men), 81 (women)
education (compulsory years) 11
literacy rate 99%
language Dutch
religions Roman Catholic, Dutch Reformed Church
TV sets (per 1,000 people) 488 (1992)
currency guilder
GDP (US $) 392.4 billion (1996)
GDP per capita (PPP) (US $) 19,341 (1995)
growth rate 2.4% (1994/95)
average annual inflation 2.2% (1995)
major trading partners EU (principally Germany, Benelux, UK, France, and Italy), USA
resources petroleum, natural gas
industries electrical machinery, metal products, food processing, electronic equipment, chemicals, rubber and plastic products, petroleum refinery, dairy farming, horticulture, diamond cutting
exports machinery and transport equipment, foodstuffs, live animals, petroleum and petroleum products, natural gas, chemicals, plants and cut flowers, plant-derived products. Principal market: Germany 28.8% (1993)
imports electrical machinery, cars and other vehicles, mineral fuels, metals and metal products, plastics, paper and cardboard, clothing and accessories. Principal source: Germany 25.2% (1993)
arable land 24.3% (1993)
agricultural products sugar beet, potatoes, wheat, barley, flax, fruit, vegetables, flowers; dairy farming

HISTORY

55 BC Julius Caesar brought lands S of Rhine under Roman rule.
4th C AD Region overrun by Franks and Saxons.
7th–8th Cs Franks subdued Saxons N of the Rhine, imposing Christianity.
843–12th Cs Division of Holy Roman Empire: the Netherlands repeatedly partitioned, not falling clearly into either French or German kingdoms.
12th–14th Cs Local feudal lords, led by count of Holland and bishop of Utrecht, became practically independent; Dutch towns became prosperous trading centres, usually ruled by small groups of merchants.
15th C Low Countries (Holland, Belgium, and Flanders) came under rule of dukes of Burgundy.
1477 Low Countries passed by marriage to Habsburgs.
1555 The Netherlands passed to Spain upon division of Habsburg domains.
1568 The Dutch rebelled under leadership of William the Silent, Prince of Orange, and fought a long war of independence.
1579 Union of Utrecht: seven northern rebel provinces formed United Provinces.
17th C 'Golden Age': Dutch led world in trade, art, and science, and founded colonies in East and West Indies, primarily through the Dutch East India Company, founded 1602.
1648 Treaty of Westphalia: United Provinces finally recognized as independent Dutch Republic.
1652–54 Commercial and colonial rivalries led to naval war with England.
1652–72 Johann de Witt ruled Dutch Republic as premier after conflict between republicans and House of Orange.
1665–67 Second Anglo-Dutch war.
1672–74 Third Anglo-Dutch war.
1672 William of Orange became stadholder (ruling as chief magistrate) of the Dutch Republic, an office which became hereditary in the Orange family.
1672–78 The Netherlands fought to prevent domination by King Louis XIV of France.
1688–97 and 1701–13 War with France resumed.
18th C Exhausted by war, the Netherlands ceased to be a Great Power.
1795 Revolutionary France conquered the Netherlands and established the Batavian Republic.
1806 Napoleon made his brother Louis king of Holland.
1810 France annexed the Netherlands.
1815 Northern and southern Netherlands (Holland and Belgium) unified as Kingdom of the Netherlands under King William I of Orange, who also became grand duke of Luxembourg.
1830 Southern Netherlands rebelled and declared independence as Belgium.
1848 Liberal constitution adopted.
1890 Queen Wilhelmina succeeded to throne; dynastic link with Luxembourg broken.
1894–96 Dutch suppressed colonial revolt in Java.
1914–18 Netherlands neutral during World War I.
1940–45 Occupied by Germany during World War II.
1948 The Netherlands formed Benelux customs union with Belgium and Luxembourg; Queen Wilhelmina abdicated in favour of her daughter Juliana.
1949 Became a founding member of North Atlantic Treaty Organization (NATO); most of Dutch East Indies became independent as Indonesia.
1953 Dykes breached by storm; nearly two thousand people and tens of thousands of cattle died in flood.
1954 Remaining Dutch colonies achieved internal self-government.
1958 The Netherlands became a founding member of European Economic Community (EEC).
1963 Dutch colony of Western New Guinea ceded to Indonesia.
1975 Dutch Guiana became independent as Surinam.
1980 Queen Juliana abdicated in favour of her daughter Beatrix.
1994 Following inconclusive general election, three-party coalition formed under PvdA leader Wim Kok.
1998 Gains for Labour in May general election.

SEE ALSO Belgium; East India Company, Dutch; Luxembourg; Orange, House of

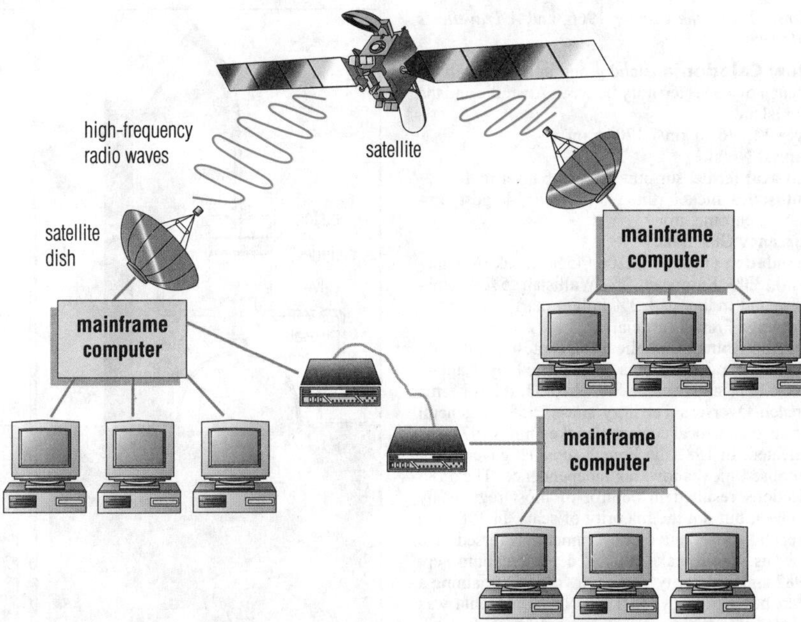

network A wide area network is used to connect remote computers via telephone lines or satellite links. The ISDN (Integrated Services Digital Network) telecommunications network allows high-speed transfer of digital data.

neutralization in chemistry, a process occurring when the excess acid (or excess base) in a substance is reacted with added base (or added acid) so that the resulting substance is neither acidic nor basic.

In theory neutralization involves adding acid or base as required to achieve ◊pH7. When the colour of an ◊indicator is used to test for neutralization, the final pH may differ from pH7 depending upon the indicator used.

neutral oxide oxide that has neither acidic nor basic properties (see ◊oxide). Neutral oxides are only formed by ◊nonmetals. Examples are carbon monoxide, water, and nitrogen(I) oxide.

neutrino in physics, any of three uncharged ◊elementary particles (and their antiparticles) of the ◊lepton class, having a mass too close to zero to be measured. The most familiar type, the antiparticle of the electron neutrino, is emitted in the beta decay of a nucleus. The other two are the muon and tau neutrinos.

US physicists at Los Alamos National Laboratory announced 1995 that neutrinos have a mass of up to 5 electronvolts (one hundred-thousandth of the mass of an electron).

Neutrinos created by the Big Bang number 300 for every 1 cu cm/0.061 cu in of space. A million neutrinos a second are emitted by every 1 cm^2/0.155 in^2.

neutron one of the three main subatomic particles, the others being the proton and the electron. The neutron is a composite particle, being made up of three ◊quarks, and therefore belongs to the ◊baryon group of the ◊hadrons. Neutrons have about the same mass as protons but no electric charge, and occur in the nuclei of all atoms except hydrogen. They contribute to the mass of atoms but do not affect their chemistry.

For instance, the ◊isotopes of a single element differ only in the number of neutrons in their nuclei but have identical chemical properties. Outside a nucleus, a free neutron is unstable, decaying with a half-life of 11.6 minutes into a proton, an electron, and an antineutrino. The neutron was discovered by the British chemist James Chadwick 1932.

neutron beam machine nuclear reactor or accelerator producing a stream of neutrons, which can 'see' through metals. It is used in industry to check molecular changes in metal under stress.

neutron bomb or ***enhanced radiation weapon*** small hydrogen bomb for battlefield use that kills by radiation, with minimal damage to buildings and other structures. See ◊nuclear warfare.

neutron star very small, 'superdense' star composed mostly of ◊neutrons. They are thought to form when massive stars explode as ◊supernovae, during which the protons and electrons of the star's atoms merge, owing to intense gravitational collapse, to make neutrons. A neutron star may have the mass of up to three Suns, compressed into a globe only 20 km/12 mi in diameter.

If its mass is any greater, its gravity will be so strong that it will shrink even further to become a ◊black hole. Being so small, neutron stars can spin very quickly. The rapidly flashing radio stars called ◊pulsars are believed to be neutron stars. The flashing is caused by a rotating beam of radio energy similar in behaviour to a lighthouse beam of light. *See illustration on following page.*

'Neutrinos, they are very small. / They have no charge and have no mass / And do not interact at all.'

On NEUTRINOS
John Updike
'Cosmic Gall'

Nevada state in western USA; nicknamed Silver State/Sagebrush State
area 286,400 sq km/110,550 sq mi
capital Carson City
towns and cities Las Vegas, Reno
population (1991) 1,284,000
physical Mojave Desert; lakes: Tahoe, Pyramid, Mead; mountains and plateaus alternating with valleys
environment decontamination project underway after the discovery that plutonium and other radioactive materials are leaking out through cracks in the rocks around an underground nuclear weapons testing site, ground water and wild animals near the site have been found to be contaminated
features the most arid state; Great Basin national park, with Wheeler Peak (3,981 m/13,061 ft), and the Lehman Caves; Red Rock Canyon; Hoover Dam and Lake Mead (the largest artificial lake in the W hemisphere); Valley of Fire state park, with Pueblo Indian rock drawings and brightly coloured rock formations; Virginia City national historic district; legal gambling and prostitution in some counties; Las Vegas, a gambling resort, with casino hotels on the Las Vegas Strip, the easiest place to get married in the USA, with 25 chapels along the Strip and hotel chapels; Reno, with the Reno Arch proclaiming it 'The Biggest Little City in the World'
industries mercury, barite, gold
history explored by Kit Carson and John C Fremont 1843–45; ceded to the USA after the Mexican War 1848; first permanent settlement a Mormon trading post 1848. Discovery of silver (the Comstock Lode) 1858 led to rapid population growth and statehood 1864.

network Local area networks can be connected together via a ring circuit or in a star arrangement. In the ring arrangement, signals from a terminal or peripheral circulate around the ring to reach the terminal or peripheral addressed. In the star arrangement, signals travel via a central controller.

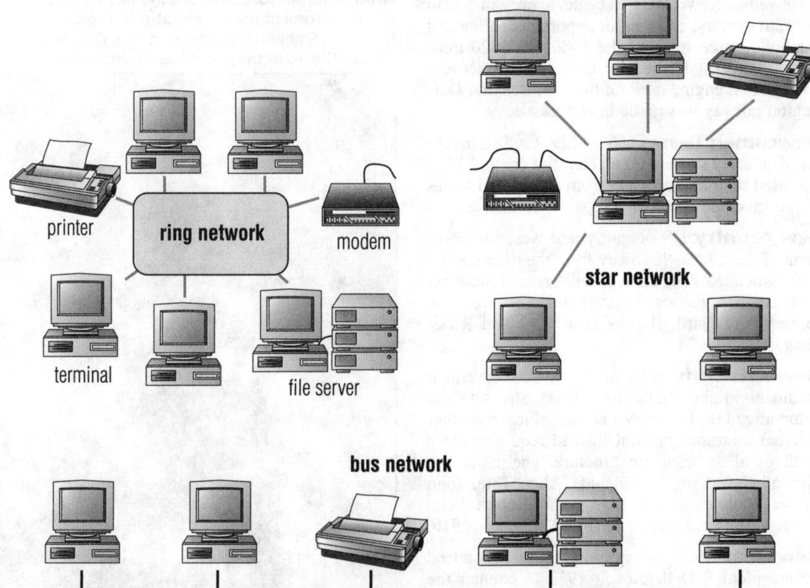

Nevada

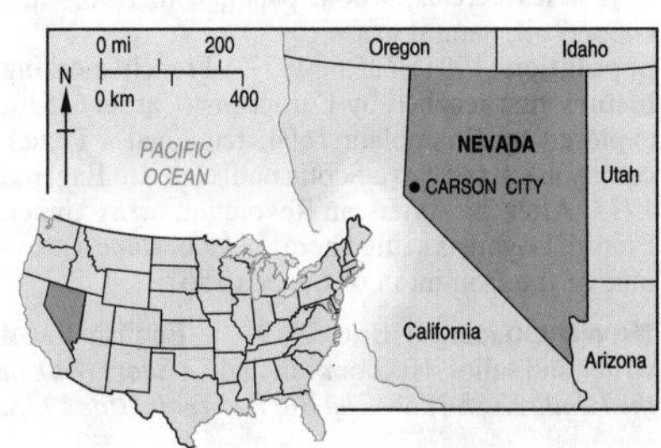

Neville Brothers, the US rhythm-and-blues group, exponents of the New Orleans style, internationally successful from the 1980s. There are four Neville brothers, the eldest of whom has been active from the 1950s in various musical ventures. Albums include *Yellow Moon* 1989.

new age movement of the late 1980s characterized by an emphasis on the holistic view of body and mind, alternative (or complementary) medicines, personal growth therapies, and a loose mix of theosophy, ecology, oriental mysticism, and a belief in the dawning of an astrological age of peace and harmony.

Drawing on the hippie counterculture of the 1960s, new-age ideas include ◊monism and ◊pantheism, preferring intuition and direct experience to rationality and science. Critics of new-age thinking

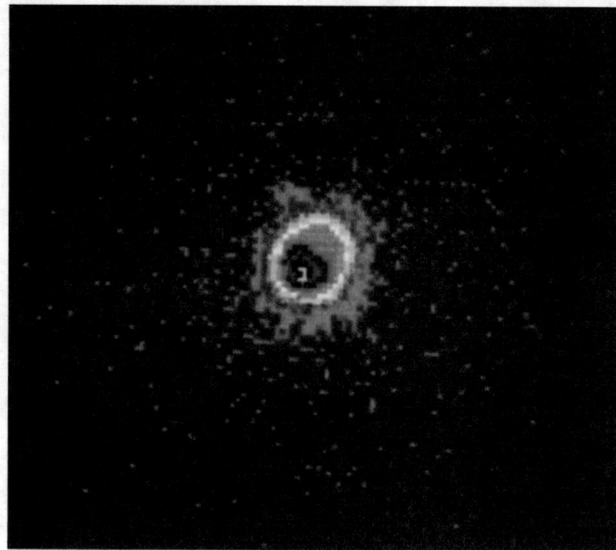

neutron star Cygnus X-2, a neutron star. A neutron star is a very small, dense star that is formed when a star explodes and its protons and electrons merge under the force of gravity to make neutrons. *Image Select (UK) Ltd*

argue that it is so eclectic that it is incoherent. Nonetheless, new-age principles have inspired many business organizations to decentralize and produce less rigid management hierarchies. The rise of European ◊Green parties provided the new-age philosophy with a practical and political forum for its ideas.

new-age music instrumental or ambient music, often semi-acoustic or electronic; less insistent than rock and less difficult than jazz. Clean production, undemanding compositions, and a soft, gentle sound characterize new age.

Widespread from the 1980s, new-age music originated in the mid-1970s with English composer Brian Eno (1948–) who released such albums as *Music for Airports* 1979.

Newark largest city (industrial and commercial) of New Jersey, USA; population (1992) 267,850. Industries include electrical equipment, machinery, chemicals, paints, canned meats. The city dates from 1666, when a settlement called Milford was made on the site.

New Britain largest island in the ◊Bismarck Archipelago, part of Papua New Guinea; capital Rabaul; population (1990) 312,000. Two volcanoes erupted Sept 1994, covering Rabaul in ash and mud, but there were no deaths. The previous eruption was 1937.

New Brunswick maritime province of E Canada
area 73,400 sq km/28,332 sq mi
capital Fredericton
towns and cities St John, Moncton
features Grand Lake, St John River; Bay of Fundy
industries cereals, wood, paper, fish, lead, zinc, copper, oil, natural gas
population (1991) 725,600; 37% French-speaking
history first reached by Europeans (Cartier) 1534; explored by Champlain 1604; remained a French colony as part of Nova Scotia until ceded to England 1713. After the American Revolution many United Empire Loyalists settled here, and it became a province of the Dominion of Canada 1867.

Newby (George) Eric 1919– . English travel writer and sailor. His books include *A Short Walk in the Hindu Kush* 1958, *The Big Red Train Ride* 1978, *Slowly Down the Ganges* 1966, and *A Traveller's Life* 1985.

New Brunswick

New Caledonia island group in the S Pacific, a French overseas territory between Australia and the Fiji Islands
area 18,576 sq km/7,170 sq mi
capital Nouméa
physical fertile, surrounded by a barrier reef
industries nickel (the world's third-largest producer), chrome, iron
currency CFP franc
population (1989) 164,200 (45% Kanak (Melanesian), 33% European, 7% Wallisian, 5% Vietnamese and Indonesian, 3% Polynesian)
language French (official)
religion Roman Catholic 60%, Protestant 30%
history New Caledonia was visited by Captain Cook 1774 and became French 1853. It has been a French Overseas Territory since 1958. A general strike to gain local control of nickel mines 1974 was defeated. In 1981 the French socialist government promised moves towards independence. The 1985 elections resulted in control of most regions by Kanaks, but not the majority of seats. In 1986 the French conservative government reversed the reforms. The Kanaks boycotted a referendum Sept 1987 and a majority were in favour of remaining a French dependency. In 1988 New Caledonia was divided into three autonomous provinces. In 1989 the leader of the Socialist National Liberation front (the most prominent separatist group), Jean-Marie Tjibaou, was murdered. A referendum on full independence is scheduled for 1998. The French high commissioner is Didier Cultiaux. ▷ *See feature on pp. 806–807.*

Newcastle industrial port (iron, steel, chemicals, textiles, ships) in New South Wales, Australia; population (1993) 454,800. Coal was discovered nearby 1796. A penal settlement was founded 1804.

Newcastle Thomas Pelham-Holles, 1st Duke of Newcastle 1693–1768. British Whig politician, prime minster 1754–56 and 1757–62. He served as secretary of state for 30 years from 1724, then succeeded his younger brother, Henry ◊Pelham, as prime minister 1754. In 1756 he resigned as a result of setbacks in the Seven Years' War, but returned to office 1757 with ◊Pitt the Elder (1st Earl of Chatham) taking responsibility for the conduct of the war.

Newcastle upon Tyne city in NE England on the river Tyne opposite Gateshead; population (1991) 281,700. It is the administrative centre of Tyne and Wear and regional centre of NE England. It is a centre for retail, commerce, communications, and the arts. The University of Newcastle was founded 1963, and the University of Northumbria 1992.
industries engineering (including offshore technology); food processing; brewing; electronics. Only 1% of the workforce is now in heavy industry, 80% are in the public or service sectors.
history It stands on the site of a Roman settlement, *Pons Aelius*. Newcastle first began to trade in coal in the 13th century, and was an important coaling and shipbuilding centre until the 1980s. In 1826 ironworks were established by George ◊Stephenson, and the first engine used on the Stockton and Darlington railway was made in Newcastle.

Newcomen Thomas 1663–1729. English inventor of an early steam engine. His 'fire engine' 1712 was used for pumping water from mines until James ◊Watt invented one with a separate condenser.

new country US ◊country and western movement of the 1980s–90s away from the overproduction associated with the Nashville record industry. New country generated successful crossover performers like Garth Brooks (1961–) and Ricky Skaggs (1954–).

New Criticism in literature, a US movement dominant in the 1930s and 1940s, stressing the autonomy of the text without biographical and other external interpolation, but instead requiring close readings of its linguistic structure. The major figures of New Criticism include Allen Tate, John Crowe Ransom (1888–1974), and Robert Penn Warren. The term was coined by J E Spingarn 1910.

New Deal in US history, programme introduced by President F D Roosevelt 1933 to counter the Great Depression, including employment on public works, farm loans at low rates, and social reforms such as old-age and unemployment insurance, prevention of child labour, protection of employees against unfair practices by employers, and loans to local authorities for slum clearance.

The Public Works Administration was given $3.3 billion to spend on roads, public buildings, and similar developments. The Agricultural Adjustment Administration raised agricultural prices by restriction of output. In 1935 Harry L Hopkins (1890–1946) was put in charge of a new agency, the Works Progress Administration (WPA), which in addition to taking over the public works created something of a cultural revolution with its federal theatre, writers', and arts projects. When the WPA was disbanded 1943 it had found employment for 8.5 million people.

Some of the provisions of the New Deal were

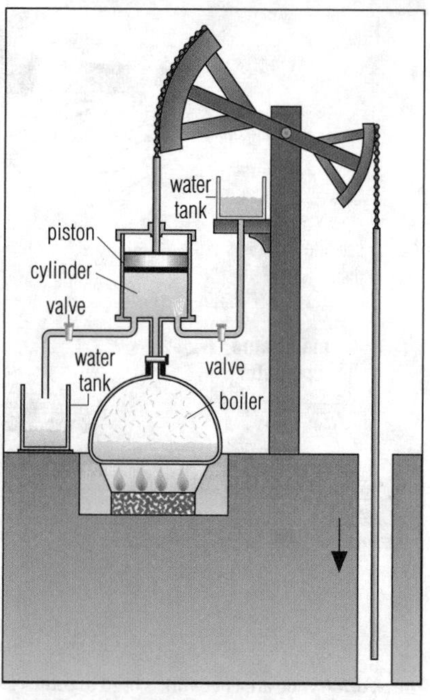

Newcomen Thomas Newcomen's steam engine, invented 1712, was the first practical steam engine and was used to power pumps in the tin mines of Cornwall and the coal mines of N England. Steam from the boiler entered the cylinder as the piston moved up (pulled by the weight of a wooden beam). Water from a tank was then sprayed into the cylinder, condensing the steam and creating a vacuum so that air pressure forced down the piston and activated the pump.

New Deal A trainee of the Civilian Conservation Corps, an organization run along military lines which offered work to young men (c. 1935). The Corps was one of the organizations created under President Franklin D Roosevelt's New Deal, in a bid to cure the ills of the Great Depression. *Corbis*

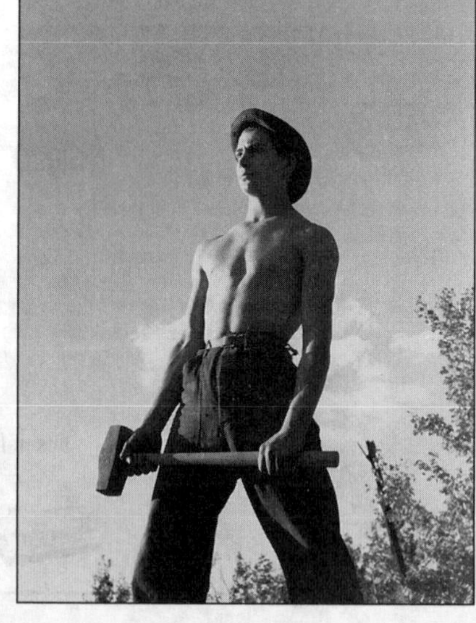

'I pledge you – I pledge myself – to a new deal for the American people.'

NEW DEAL
Franklin D Roosevelt
speech 1932

declared unconstitutional by the Supreme Court 1935–36. The New Deal encouraged the growth of trade-union membership, brought previously unregulated areas of the US economy under federal control, and revitalized cultural life and community spirit. Although full employment did not come until World War II, the New Deal did bring political stability to the industrial-capitalist system.

New Delhi city adjacent to Old Delhi on the Yamuna River in the Union Territory of Delhi, N India; population (1991) 301,000. It is the administrative centre of Delhi, and was designated capital of India by the British 1911. Largely designed by British architect Edwin Lutyens, New Delhi was officially inaugurated after its completion 1931. Chemicals, textiles, machine tools, electrical goods, and footwear are produced.

New Democratic Party (NDP) Canadian political party, moderately socialist, formed 1961 by a merger of the Labour Congress and the Cooperative Commonwealth Federation. Its leader is Alexa McDonough.

New Economic Policy (NEP) economic policy of the USSR 1921–29 devised by the Soviet leader Lenin. Rather than requisitioning all agricultural produce above a stated subsistence allowance, the state requisitioned only a fixed proportion of the surplus; the rest could be traded freely by the peasant. The NEP thus reinstated a limited form of free-market trading, although the state retained complete control of major industries.

The NEP was introduced in March 1921 after a series of peasant revolts and the Kronstadt uprising (a revolt by sailors of the Russian Baltic Fleet). Aimed at re-establishing an alliance with the peasantry, it began as an agricultural measure to act as an incentive for peasants to produce more food. The policy was ended in 1928 by Stalin's first Five-Year Plan, which began the collectivization of agriculture.

New England district of N New South Wales, Australia, especially the tableland area of Glen Innes and Armidale.

New England region of NE USA, comprising the states of Maine, New Hampshire, Vermont, Massachusetts, Rhode Island, and Connecticut. It is a geographic region rather than a political entity, with an area of 172,681 sq km/66,672 sq mi. Boston is the principal urban centre of the region, and Harvard and Yale are its major universities.

Originally settled by Pilgrims and Puritans from England, the area is still heavily forested and the economy relies on tourism and services as well as industry.

New Forest ancient forest in ◊Hampshire, S England. Its legal boundary encloses 38,000 ha (1995), of which 8,400 ha is enclosed plantation, and 20,000 ha is common land, including ancient woodland, heath, grassland, and bog. At least 46 rare plants are found in the New Forest, as well as more than half of Britain's species of butterflies, moths, and beetles.

Newfoundland breed of large dog said to have originated in Newfoundland. Males can grow to 70 cm/27.5 in tall, and weigh 65 kg/145 lb; the females are slightly smaller. They have an oily, water-repellent undercoat and are excellent swimmers. Gentle in temperament, they have a dense, flat coat, usually dull black.

Newfoundlands that are black and white or brown and white are called Landseers.

Newfoundland Canadian province on the Atlantic Ocean
area 405,700 sq km/156,600 sq mi
capital St John's
towns and cities Corner Brook, Gander
physical Newfoundland island and ◊Labrador on the mainland on the other side of the Straits of Belle Isle; rocky
features Grand Banks section of the continental shelf rich in cod; home of the Newfoundland and Labrador dogs
industries newsprint, fish products, hydroelectric power, iron, copper, zinc, uranium, offshore oil
population (1991) 571,600
history colonized by Vikings about AD 1000; Newfoundland was reached by the English, under the Italian navigator Giovanni ◊Caboto, 1497. It was the first English colony, established 1583. French

Newfoundland

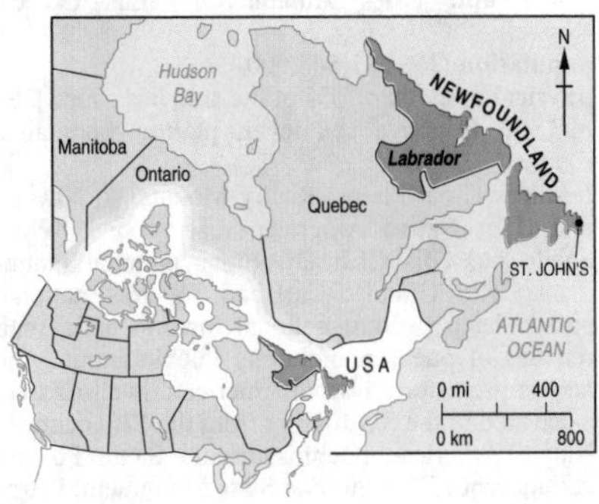

settlements were made and British sovereignty was not recognized until 1713; France retained the offshore islands of St Pierre and Miquelon. Internal self-government was achieved 1855. In 1934, as Newfoundland had fallen into financial difficulties, administration was vested in a governor and a special commission. A 1948 referendum favoured federation with Canada and the province joined Canada 1949.

New Guinea island in the SW Pacific, N of Australia, comprising Papua New Guinea and the Indonesian province of Irian Jaya; total area about 885,780 sq km/342,000 sq mi. Part of the Dutch East Indies from 1828, West Irian was ceded by the United Nations to Indonesia 1963.
history The western half of New Guinea was annexed by the Dutch 1828. In 1884 the area of Papua on the southeast coast was proclaimed a protectorate by the British, and in the same year Germany took possession of the northeast quarter of New Guinea. Under Australian control 1914–21, German New Guinea was administered as a British mandate and then united with Papua 1945. Papua and New Guinea jointly gained full independence as Papua New Guinea 1975. The Dutch retained control over the western half of the island (West Irian) after Indonesia gained its independence 1949, but were eventually forced to transfer administrative responsibility to Indonesia 1963. Tension between Papua New Guinea and Indonesia has heightened as a result of a growing number of border incidents involving Indonesian troops and Irianese separatist guerrillas. At the same time large numbers of refugees have fled eastwards into Papua New Guinea from West Irian. Its tropical rainforest and the 0.5 million hunter-gatherers who inhabit it are under threat from logging companies and resettlement schemes. ▷ *See feature on pp. 806–807.*

Newham inner borough of E Greater London, N of the river Thames. It includes the districts of East and West Ham and the northern part of Woolwich
features site of former Royal Docks: Victoria (1855), Albert (1880), and King George V (1921); post-war tower blocks (collapse of Ronan Point 1968 led to official enquiry)
population (1991) 200,200
famous people Dick Turpin, Gerard Manley Hopkins
history From 1671 onwards the borough was associated with the Quakers – from 1704 there was a meeting house in Plaistow, which the Gurneys, Frys, and Barclays attended; it was closed 1924.

New Hampshire state in NE USA; nicknamed Granite State
area 24,000 sq km/9,264 sq mi
capital Concord
towns and cities Manchester, Nashua
population (1991) 1,105,000

New Hampshire

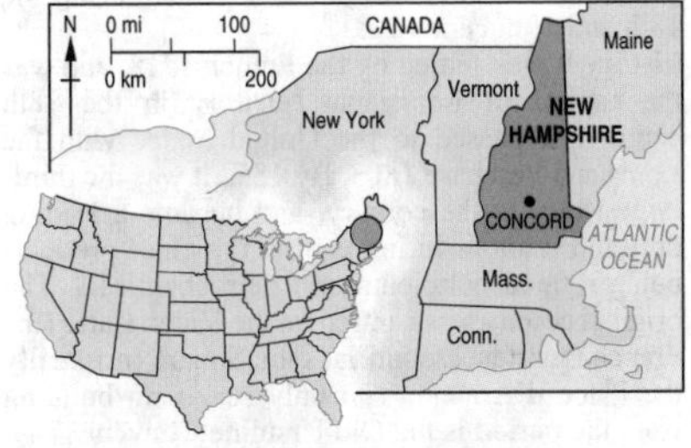

features the Connecticut River, forming the boundary with Vermont; the White Mountains, the highest mountains in New England, including Mount Washington (1,917 m/6,288 ft) with its cog railway (1869, the world's first mountain climbing railway), Dartmouth College (1769), at Hanover, with murals by the Mexican artist Orozco in the Baker Memorial Library; farm at Derry, home of the poet Robert Frost, who wrote 'New Hampshire' (1923); home of Mary Baker Eddy, founder of Christian Science, at Concord.
industries dairy, poultry, fruits, and vegetables; electrical and other machinery; pulp and paper
famous people Mary Baker Eddy, Robert Frost
history settled as a fishing colony near Rye and Dover 1623; separated from Massachusetts colony 1679. As leaders in the Revolutionary cause, its leaders received the honour of being the first to declare independence from Britain 4 July 1776. It became a state 1788, one of the original 13 states.

New Haven city and port in Connecticut, USA, on Long Island Sound; population (1992) 124,000. Yale University, third oldest in the USA, was founded here 1701 and named after Elihu Yale (1648–1721), an early benefactor. New Haven was founded 1683 by English Protestants.

New Hebrides former name (to 1980) of ◊Vanuatu, a country in the S Pacific.

Ne Win ('Brilliant Sun') Adopted name of Maung Shu Maung 1911– . Myanmar (Burmese) politician, prime minister 1958–60, ruler from 1962 to 1974, president 1974–81, and chair until 1988 of the ruling Burma Socialist Programme Party (BSPP). His domestic 'Burmese Way to Socialism' policy programme brought the economy into serious decline.

Active in the nationalist movement during the 1930s, Ne Win joined the Allied forces in the war against Japan in 1945 and held senior military posts before becoming prime minister in 1958. After leading a coup in 1962, he ruled the country as chair of the revolutionary council until 1974, when he became state president. Although he stepped down as president 1981, he continued to dominate political affairs, but was forced to resign as BSPP leader 1988 after riots in Rangoon (now Yangon).

New Jersey

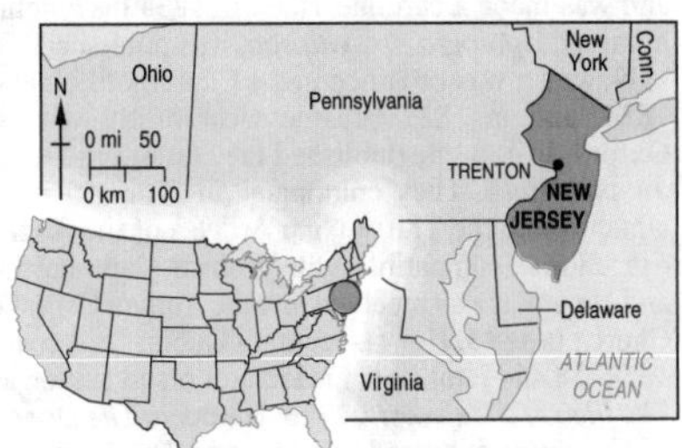

New Jersey state in NE USA; nicknamed Garden State
area 20,200 sq km/7,797 sq mi
capital Trenton
towns and cities Newark, Jersey City, Paterson, Elizabeth
population (1991) 7,760,000
features the most densely populated state in the USA; c. 200 km/125 mi of Jersey Shore, including gambling casinos, amusement piers, and the boardwalk (the first elevated wooden walkway in USA, 1870) in Atlantic City, and the Victorian beach resort of Cape May, the state's oldest resort; Delaware Water Gap National Recreation Area; Edison national historic site, Menlo Park; Walt Whitman House, Camden; Princeton University (1746), with the Institute for Advanced Study; Rutgers University; Statue of Liberty national monument (shared with New York)
industries fruits and vegetables, fish and shellfish, chemicals, pharmaceuticals, soaps and cleansers, transport equipment, petroleum refining
famous people Stephen Crane, Thomas Edison, Thomas Paine, Paul Robeson, Frank Sinatra, Bruce Springsteen, Woodrow Wilson
history colonized in the 17th century by the Dutch (New Netherlands); ceded to England 1664; became a state 1787. It was one of the original 13 states.

'There is a sumptuous variety about the New England weather ... I have counted one hundred and thirty-six different kinds of weather inside of four-and-twenty hours.'

On the weather in **New England**
Mark Twain, speech at dinner of New England Society, 22 Dec 1876

'It looked to me like a town spending the summer months in the country.'

On **New Haven**
Alexander Mackay
The Western World

Newman One of the leaders of the Oxford Movement, John Henry Newman was author of the well-known hymn 'Lead, kindly Light'. He was a popular preacher during his 15 years as vicar of St Mary the Virgin, Oxford. He preached his last sermon, on 'Development in Christian Doctrine', on 2 Feb 1843, then resigned and two years later became a Catholic. *Corbis*

"There is on the globe one single spot, the possessor of which is our natural and habitual enemy. It is New Orleans, through which the produce of three eighths of our territory must pass to market."

On New Orleans Thomas Jefferson, letter to Robert R Livingstone, US minister to France, 18 April 1802

Newlands John Alexander Reina 1837–1898. English chemist who worked as an industrial chemist; he prepared in 1863 the first ◊periodic table of the elements arranged in order of relative atomic masses, and pointed out 1865 the 'law of octaves' whereby every eighth element has similar properties. He was ridiculed at the time, but five years later Russian chemist Dmitri ◊Mendeleyev published a more developed form of the table, also based on atomic masses, which forms the basis of the one used today (arranged by atomic number).

Newlyn seaport near Penzance, Cornwall, England, which gave its name to the Newlyn School of artists 1880–90, including Stanhope Forbes (1857–1947). The Ordnance Survey relates heights in the UK to mean sea level here.

Newman John Henry 1801–1890. English Roman Catholic theologian. While still an Anglican, he wrote a series of *Tracts for the Times*, which gave their name to the Tractarian Movement (subsequently called the ◊Oxford Movement) for the revival of Catholicism. He became a Catholic 1845 and was made a cardinal 1879. In 1864 his autobiography, *Apologia pro vita sua*, was published.

Newman was ordained in the Church of England 1824, and in 1827 became vicar of St Mary's, Oxford. In 1833 he published the first of the *Tracts for the Times*. They culminated in *Tract 90* 1841 which found the Thirty-Nine Articles of the Anglican church compatible with Roman Catholicism, and Newman was received into the Roman Catholic Church in 1845. He was rector of Dublin University 1854–58 and published his lectures on education as *The Idea of a University* 1873. His poem *The Dream of Gerontius* appeared in 1866, and *The Grammar of Assent*, an analysis of the nature of belief, in 1870. He wrote the hymn 'Lead, kindly light' 1833.

Newman Paul 1925– . US actor and director. He was one of Hollywood's leading male stars of the 1960s and 1970s, initially often as an alienated figure, and later in character roles of many kinds. His films include *Somebody Up There Likes Me* 1956, *Cat on a Hot Tin Roof* 1958, *The Hustler* 1961, *Sweet Bird of Youth* 1962, *Hud* 1963, *Cool Hand Luke* 1967, *Butch Cassidy and the Sundance Kid* 1969, *The Sting* 1973, *The Verdict* 1983, *The Color of Money* 1986 (for which he won an Academy Award), *Mr and Mrs Bridge* 1991, and *The Hudsucker Proxy* 1994.

He directed his wife Joanne Woodward in *Rachel, Rachel* 1968 and other films and is noted as a race-car driver and for his philanthropic activities.

Newmarket town in Suffolk, E England, a centre for horse racing since James I's reign, notably the 1,000 and 2,000 Guineas, the Cambridgeshire, and the Cesarewitch. It is the headquarters of the Jockey Club, and a bookmaker who is 'warned off Newmarket Heath' is banned from all British racecourses. The National Horseracing Museum (1983) and the National Stud are here. Products include caravans and electronic equipment.

New Mexico state in southwestern USA; nicknamed Land of Enchantment
area 315,000 sq km/121,590 sq mi
capital Santa Fe
towns and cities Albuquerque, Las Cruces, Roswell
population (1991) 1,548,000
physical more than 75% of the area lies over 1,200 m/3,900 ft above sea level; plains, mountains, caverns
features Great Plains; Rocky Mountains; Navaho and Hopi Native American reservations; White Sands and Gila Cliff Dwellings national monuments; Rio Grande; Carlsbad Caverns national park; Chaco Culture national historic park, with remains of pueblos, including Pueblo Bonito, the largest prehistoric Native American dwelling ever excavated in the SW, dating from the 12th century; Native American pueblos around Santa Fe and Albuquerque; Fort Sumner State Monument; Petroglyph national monument, with over 17,000 ancient rock drawings; Pecos national historic park; Albuquerque, dating from 1706, with San Felipe de Neri church, and the Indian Pueblo Cultural Center, with the largest collection of Native American arts and crafts in the SW; Santa Fe, with Spanish mission-style architecture, the pueblo-style Palace of the Governors, St Francis Cathedral, museums of Native American arts, the Institute of American Indian Arts, and San Miguel Mission (1625), the oldest church still in use in the USA; Taos art centre; Kit Carson home and museum, Taos; Ranchos de Taos, with San Francisco de Asis Church, an early mission church; Los Alamos National Laboratory, an atomic and space research centre; White Sands Missile Range (also used by space shuttle); Kiowa Ranch, site of D H Lawrence's stay in the Sangre de Cristos Mountains; Santa Fe Opera Company, which performs in an outdoor theatre in the Sangre de Cristo Mountains
products uranium, potash, copper, oil, natural gas, petroleum and coal products; sheep farming; cotton; pecans; vegetables
famous people Billy the Kid, Kit Carson, Georgia O'Keeffe
history explored by Francisco de Coronado for Spain 1540–42; Spanish settlement 1598 on the Rio Grande; Santa Fe founded 1610; most of New Mexico ceded to the USA by Mexico 1848; became a state 1912. The first atomic bomb, a test device, was exploded in the desert near Alamogordo 16 July 1945. Oil and gas development and tourism now contribute to the state economy.

New Mexico

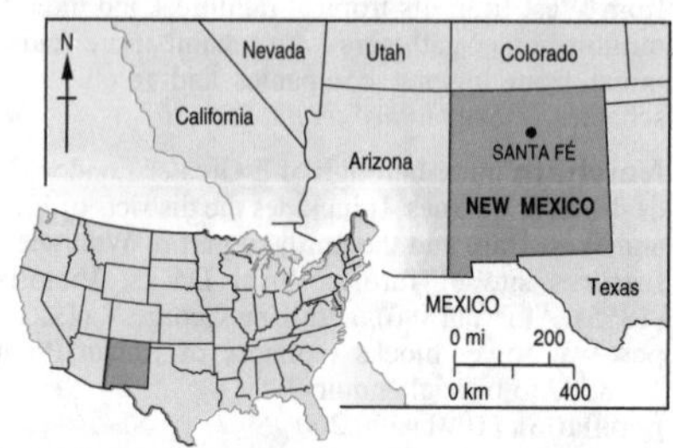

New Model Army army created 1645 by Oliver Cromwell to support the cause of Parliament during the English ◊Civil War. It was characterized by organization and discipline. Thomas Fairfax was its first commander.

New Orleans commercial and manufacturing city and port on the Mississippi River, linked to the Gulf of Mexico, in Louisiana, USA; population (1992) 489,600; metropolitan area (1992) 1,303,000. New Orleans is regarded as the traditional birthplace of jazz, which is thought to have started in Congo Square, developing out of the singing and voodoo rhythms popular with the large gatherings of slaves which took place during the 18th and 19th centuries.
history It was settled by the French 1718, and was the capital of Louisiana Territory in the 18th century. It passed to the United States with the Louisiana Purchase 1803. By 1852 it was the third-largest city in the country, and became a leading port and manufacturing centre, the chief products being refined petroleum and petrochemicals. The original colony was centred on the Vieux Carré (the French Quarter) around Jackson Square (originally the Place d'Armes). The only surviving building from the period is the Old Ursuline Convent 1749.

Centroport USA, a 30-year plan, was launched 1970 with the intention of moving port activities from the Mississippi River to the Gulf of Mexico in order to develop residential and recreational areas on the river front.
features The French Quarter is famous for its French Creole restaurants and jazz clubs. 18th century sites include Lafitte's Blacksmith Shop 1772, St Louis Cemetery No. 1 1789, the St Louis Cathedral 1794, and the First Skyscraper 1795–1811, originally three stories high. The Historic New Orleans Collection includes the Merieult house, with archives relating to the history of the city. The Voodoo Museum includes memorabilia of the voodoo queen, Marie Laveau. The Municipal Auditorium, in Louis Armstrong Park, is on the site of Congo Square; the principal venue for traditional jazz is Preservation Hall.

The New Orleans Museum of Art is in City Park. The Old US Mint is part of the Louisiana State Museum, which houses the Jazz and Mardi Gras exhibits, and A Streetcar Named Desire (from the old Desire line, the inspiration for the Tennesee Williams play). The Superdome sports palace is one of the largest enclosed stadiums in the world

New Photography German photographic movement of the 1930s, led by Albert Renger-Patzsch (1897–1966), that aimed to depict modern life in a direct and objective manner. In its anti-Pictorialism and emphasis on clarity, it paralleled the ◊'f/64' group in the USA.

Newport river port, administrative headquarters of the Isle of Wight, England; population (1991) 20,600. Charles I was imprisoned in nearby Carisbrooke Castle.

Newport (Welsh ***Casnewydd***) seaport on the river Usk and, from 1996, unitary authority of Wales (*see United Kingdom map*); population (1994 est) 111,000. There is a steelworks at nearby Llanwern, and a high-tech complex at Cleppa Park. Other industries include engineering, chemicals, fertilizers, aluminium, and electronics. The Newport Transporter Bridge was built 1906.

Newport Riots violent demonstrations by the ◊Chartists in 1839 in Newport, Wales, in support of the Peoples' Charter. violent demonstrations by the ◊Chartists in 1839 in Newport, Wales, in support of the Peoples' Charter. They were suppressed with the loss of 20 lives.

news agency business handling news stories and photographs that are then sold to newspapers and magazines. International agencies include the Associated Press (AP, 1848), Agence France-Presse (AFP, 1944), United Press International (UPI, 1907), and Reuters.

newsgroup discussion group on the ◊Internet. Newsgroups are organized in seven broad categories: ***comp.*** – computers and programming; ***news.*** – newsgroups themselves; ***rec.*** – sports and hobbies; ***sci.*** – scientific research and ideas; ***talk.*** – discussion groups; and ***misc.*** – everything else. In addition, there are alternative hierarchies such as the wide-ranging and anarchic ***alt.*** (alternative). Within these categories there is a hierarchy of subdivisions.

New South Wales state of SE Australia
area 801,600 sq km/309,418 sq mi
capital Sydney
towns and cities Newcastle, Wollongong, Broken Hill
physical Great Dividing Range (including Blue Mountains) and part of the Australian Alps (including Snowy Mountains and Mount Kosciusko); Riverina district, irrigated by the Murray-Darling-Murrumbidgee river system; other main rivers Lachlan, Macquarie-Bogan, Hawkesbury, Hunter, Macleay, and Clarence
features a radio telescope at Parkes; Siding Spring Mountain 859 m/2,817 ft, NW of Sydney, with telescopes that can observe the central sector of the Galaxy. ◊Canberra forms an enclave within the state, and New South Wales administers the dependency of Lord Howe Island
products cereals, fruit, sugar, tobacco, wool, meat, hides and skins, gold, silver, copper, tin, zinc, coal; hydroelectric power from the Snowy River
population (1992) 5,958,700; 60% in Sydney
history called New Wales by English explorer Capt ◊Cook, who landed at Botany Bay 1770 and thought that the coastline resembled that of Wales.

New South Wales

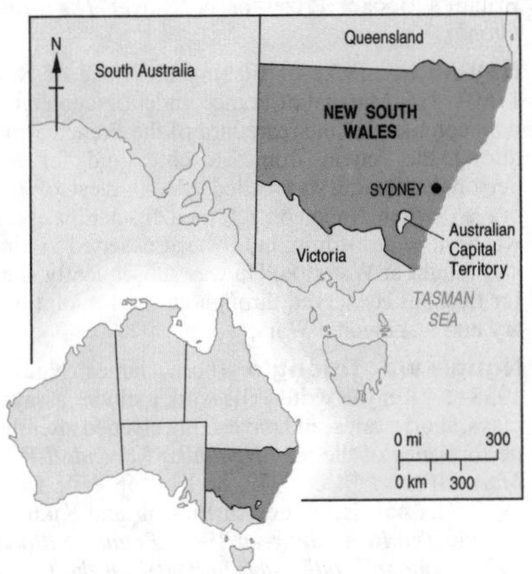

It was a convict settlement 1788–1850; opened to free settlement by 1819; achieved self-government 1856; and became a state of the Commonwealth of Australia 1901. Since 1973 there has been decentralization to counteract the pull of Sydney, and the New England and Riverina districts have separatist movements. During the first weeks of Jan 1994, bush fires ravaged 965 km/600 mi of the state's eastern coastline, burning 770,000 hectares/1.9 million acres and claiming four lives.

newspaper daily or weekly publication in the form of folded sheets containing news and comment. News-sheets became commercial undertakings after the invention of printing and were introduced 1609 in Germany, 1616 in the Netherlands. In 1622 the first newspaper appeared in English, the *Weekly News*, edited by Nicholas Bourne and Thomas Archer. Improved ◊printing (steam printing 1814, the rotary press 1846 USA and 1857 UK), newsprint (paper made from wood-pulp, used in the UK from the 1880s), and a higher literacy rate led to the growth of newspapers. In recent years, production costs have fallen with the introduction of new technology. The oldest national newspaper in the UK is *The Observer* 1791; the highest circulation UK newspaper is the Sunday *News of the World* (nearly 5 million copies weekly). The world's most widely read newspaper is Japan's *Yomiuri Shimbun*, with a daily circulation of 10 million.

history One of the earliest newspapers, the Roman *Acta Diurna*, said to have been started by the emperor Julius Caesar, contained announcements of marriages, deaths, and military appointments, and was posted in public places. In England by 1645 there were 14 news weeklies on sale in London, but the first daily was the subsidized progovernment *Daily Courant* 1702. Arrests, seizure of papers, and prosecution for libel or breach of privilege were employed by the government against opposition publications, and taxes and restrictions were imposed 1700–1820 in direct relation to the growth of radical opinion. The last of these taxes, stamp duty, was abolished 1855.

A breakthrough was the Linotype machine that cast whole lines of type, introduced in Britain 1896; and better train services made national breakfast-time circulation possible. There were nine evening papers in the London area at the end of the 19th century, and by 1920, 50% of British adults read a daily paper; by 1947, just before the introduction of television, the average adult read 1.2 daily papers and 2.3 Sunday papers; in 1988, 67% of adults read a daily paper.

The first generation of press barons, ◊Beaverbrook, ◊Northcliffe, and ◊Rothermere in the UK, and ◊Hearst in the USA, used their power to propagate their own political opinions. Newspaper proprietors now may own papers that espouse conflicting viewpoints. For commercial reasons, diminishing choice and increasing monopoly occurs throughout Europe and the USA. Some countries, such as Sweden, have a system of government subsidies to encourage competition.

Newspapers in the first half of the 20th century reinforced the traditional model of British society, being aimed at upper, middle, or working-class readers. During World War II and until 1958, newsprint rationing prevented market forces from killing off the weaker papers. Polarization into 'quality' and 'tabloid' newspapers followed. Papers with smaller circulation, such as *The Times* and the *Independent*, survive because their readership is comparatively well off, so advertising space can be sold at higher rates. The *Guardian* is owned by a non-profit trust. The sales of the mass-circulation papers are boosted by lotteries and photographs of naked women; their news content is small.

British newspapers cover a political spectrum from the moderate left to the far right. Investigative reporting is restricted by stringent laws of libel and contempt of court and by the Official Secrets Act. The Press Council was established 1953 to foster 'integrity and a sense of responsibility to the public', but had no power to enforce its recommendations. In Dec 1989 all major national newspapers agreed on a new code of conduct to prevent possible new legislation by instituting a right of reply, a readers' representative, and prompt correction of mistakes, resulting in the Press Complaints Commission a voluntary regulatory body, from 1991.

New Style the Western or Gregorian ◊calendar introduced in 1582 and now used throughout most of the world.

newt small salamander, of the family Salamandridae, order Urodela, found in Eurasia, NW Africa, and North America.

The European newts, such as the smooth newt *Triturus vulgaris*, live on land for part of the year but enter a pond or lake to breed in the spring.

Britain has three native newt species: the endangered great crested or warty newt *Triturus cristatus*; the palmate newt *T. helveticus*; and the common or smooth newt *T. vulgaris*.

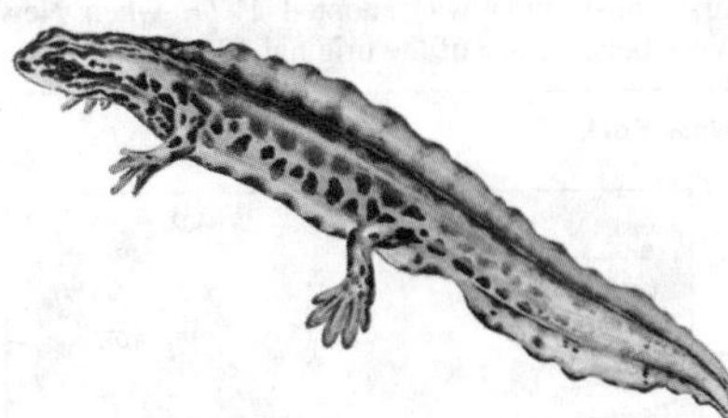

newt The crested newt, shown here, develops a crest of skin along the back in the spring mating season. All male newts are brightly coloured at this time. The European newts, such as the smooth newt, live on land for part of the year but enter a pond or lake to breed in the spring.

New Technology Telescope optical telescope that forms part of the ◊European Southern Observatory, La Silla, Chile; it came into operation 1991. It has a thin, lightweight mirror, 3.38 m/141 in across, which is kept in shape by computer-adjustable supports to produce a sharper image than is possible with conventional mirrors. Such a system is termed active optics.

New Testament the second part of the ◊Bible, recognized by the Christian church from the 4th century as sacred doctrine. The New Testament includes the Gospels, which tell of the life and teachings of Jesus, the history of the early church, the teachings of St Paul, and mystical writings. It was written in Greek during the 1st and 2nd centuries AD, and the individual sections have been ascribed to various authors by biblical scholars.

newton SI unit (symbol N) of ◊force. One newton is the force needed to accelerate an object with mass of one kilogram by one metre per second per second. The weight of a medium size (100 g/3 oz) apple is one newton.

Newton Isaac 1642–1727. English physicist and mathematician who laid the foundations of physics as a modern discipline. During 1665–66, he discovered the binomial theorem, differential and integral calculus, and that white light is composed of many colours. He developed the three standard laws of motion and the universal law of gravitation, set out in *Philosophiae naturalis principia mathematica* 1687 (usually referred to as the *Principia*).

Newton's greatest achievement was to demonstrate that scientific principles are of universal application. He clearly defined the nature of mass, weight, force, inertia, and acceleration.

Newton An engraving of English scientist and mathematician Isaac Newton, who developed the theory of gravitation and the three laws of motion that bear his name. *Ann Ronan/Image Select (UK) Ltd*

In 1679 Newton calculated the Moon's motion on the basis of his theory of gravity and also found that his theory explained the laws of planetary motion that had been derived by German astronomer Johannes ◊Kepler on the basis of observations of the planets.

I seem to have been only a boy playing on the sea-shore, and diverting myself in now and then finding a smoother pebble or a prettier shell than ordinary, whilst the great ocean of truth lay all undiscovered before me.

Isaac Newton
Quoted in L T More *Isaac Newton*

Newton Aycliffe town in Durham, England, on the river Skerne; population (1991) 25,100. It was designated a new town 1947. Industries include the manufacture of washing machines, lawn mowers, electrical and telephone equipment, and vehicle axles.

Newtonian physics physics based on the concepts of the English scientist Isaac ◊Newton, before the formulation of quantum theory or relativity theory.

Newton's laws of motion in physics, three laws that form the basis of Newtonian mechanics. (1) Unless acted upon by an unbalanced force, a body at rest stays at rest, and a moving body continues moving at the same speed in the same straight line. (2) An unbalanced force applied to a body gives it an acceleration proportional to the force and in the direction of the force. (3) When a body A exerts a force on a body B, B exerts an equal and opposite force on A; that is, to every action there is an equal and opposite reaction.

Newton's rings in optics, an ◊interference phenomenon seen (using white light) as concentric rings of spectral colours where light passes through a thin film of transparent medium, such as the wedge of air between a large-radius convex lens and a flat glass plate. With monochromatic light (light of a single wavelength), the rings take the form of alternate light and dark bands. They are caused by interference (interaction) between light rays reflected from the plate and those reflected from the curved surface of the lens.

new town centrally planned urban area. In the UK, new towns such as Milton Keynes and Stevenage were built after World War II to accommodate the overspill from cities and large towns, at a time when the population was rapidly expanding and inner-city centres had either decayed or been destroyed. In 1976 the policy, which had been criticized for disrupting family groupings and local communities, and furthering the decay of city centres, was abandoned.

New towns are characterized by a regular street pattern and the presence of a number of self-contained neighbourhood units, consisting of houses, shops, and other local services. Modern industrial estates are located on the outskirts of towns where they are well served by main roads and motorways.

New Wave (French *nouvelle vague*) movement in French cinema in the late 1950s and the 1960s characterized by an unconventional use of both camera and editing and by inventive and experimental manipulation of story line. Directors associated with the movement include Claude Chabrol, Jean-Luc Godard, and François Truffaut.

New Wave in pop music, a style that evolved parallel to punk in the second half of the 1970s. It shared the urban aggressive spirit of punk but was musically and lyrically more sophisticated; examples are the early work of Elvis Costello and

New York A view over New York City from the World Trade Center towers. In the distance is the Empire State Building, which at 381 m/1,250 ft was the tallest building in the world at the time it was built 1931. *Image Select (UK) Ltd*

Talking Heads. New Wave underwent a revival in the 1990s.

New World the Americas, so called by the first Europeans who reached them. The term also describes animals and plants of the western hemisphere.

New York largest city in the USA, industrial port (printing, publishing, clothing), cultural, financial, and commercial centre, in southern New York State, at the junction of the Hudson and East rivers and including New York Bay. It comprises the boroughs of the Bronx, Brooklyn, Manhattan, Queens, and Staten Island; population (1991, metropolitan area) 8,600,000, white 43.2%, black 25.2%, Hispanic 24.4%. New York is also known as the Big Apple.

features The Statue of Liberty stands on Liberty Island in the inner harbour of New York Bay. Manhattan skyscrapers include the twin towers of the World Trade Center (412 m/1,350 ft), the Art Deco Empire State Building (381 m/1,250 ft), and the Chrysler Building; the headquarters of the United Nations is also here. St Patrick's Cathedral is 19th-century Gothic.

There are a number of art galleries, among them the Frick Collection, the Metropolitan Museum of Art (with a medieval crafts department, the Cloisters), the Museum of Modern Art, and the Guggenheim, designed by Frank Lloyd Wright. Columbia University (1754) is one of a number of institutions of higher education.

Central Park is the largest park.

history The Italian navigator Giovanni da Verrazano (c. 1485–c. 1528) reached New York Bay 1524, and Henry Hudson explored it 1609. The Dutch established a settlement on Manhattan 1624, named New Amsterdam from 1626; this was captured by the English 1664 and renamed New York. During the American Revolution, British troops occupied New York 1776–84; it was the capital of the USA 1785–89. The five boroughs were linked 1898 to give the city its present extent. The largest power failure in history took place 9 Nov 1965, blacking out all New York City as well as parts of other states and parts of Canada.

A mountain here is only beautiful if it has good grass on it. ... If it is good for sheep, it is beautiful, magnificent, and all the rest of it; if not, it is not worth looking at.

On **New Zealand**
Samuel Butler *A First Year in Canterbury Settlement* 1863

New York state in northeast USA; nicknamed Empire State/Excelsior State

area 127,200 sq km/49,099 sq mi

capital Albany

towns and cities New York, Buffalo, Rochester, Yonkers, Syracuse

population (1991) 18,058,000

physical mountains: Adirondacks, Catskills; lakes: Champlain, Placid, Erie, Ontario; rivers: Mohawk, Hudson, St Lawrence (with Thousand Islands); Niagara Falls; Long Island; New York Bay

features New York City; Erie Canal; Lake Placid, site of 1980 Winter Olympics; Long Island, including the Hamptons; Fire Island national seashore; Hudson Valley; Finger Lakes; Fort Ticonderoga; Statue of Liberty national monument; Franklin Delano Roosevelt national historic site and Roosevelt Library, Hyde Park; home of Theodore Roosevelt, Oyster Bay; Washington Irving's home at Philipsburg Manor; colleges: Columbia University (1745), Cornell University, Vassar College, New York University, Colgate, CUNY, SUNY, Rensselaer Polytech, Pratt, Juilliard, and the Eastman School of Music; West Point Military Academy (1801); the world's largest museum of photography, in George Eastman House, home of the founder of Eastman Kodak Company, in Rochester; Corning Museum of Glass; the National Baseball Hall of Fame, Cooperstown; Fenimore House (commemorating J F ◊Cooper), Cooperstown; Saratoga Springs, with medicinal springs, National Museum of Dance, and Performing Arts Centre (summer home of the Philadelphia Orchestra and the New York City Ballet); Woodstock (scene of 1969 concert); horse racing at Belmont, Aqueduct, Saratoga Springs; United Nations headquarters

products dairy products, apples, clothing, periodical and book printing and publishing, electronic components and accessories, office machines and computers, communications equipment, motor vehicles and equipment, pharmaceuticals, aircraft and parts

famous people James Fenimore Cooper, George Gershwin, Washington Irving, Henry James, Herman Melville, Arthur Miller, Franklin D Roosevelt, Theodore Roosevelt, Walt Whitman

history explored by Giovanni da Verrazano for France 1524; explored by Samuel de Champlain for France and Henry Hudson for the Netherlands 1609; colonized by the Dutch from 1614; first permanent settlement at Albany (Fort Orange) 1624; Manhattan Island purchased by Peter Minuit 1625; New Amsterdam annexed by the English 1664. The first constitution was adopted 1777, when New York became one of the original 13 states.

New York

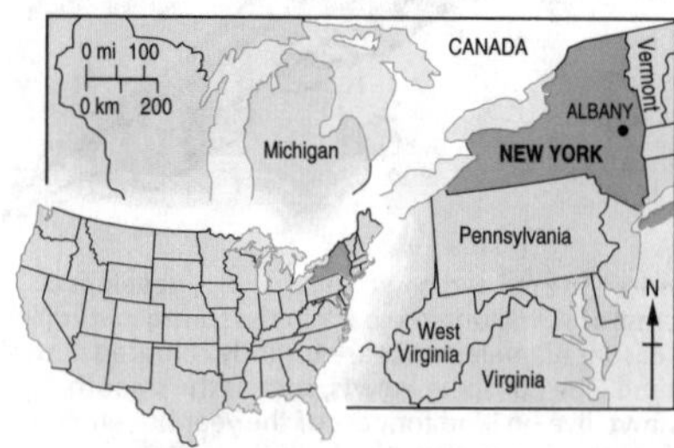

New Zealand or ***Aotearoa*** country in the SW Pacific Ocean, SE of Australia, comprising two main islands, North Island and South Island, and other small islands. *See country box opposite.*

New Zealand literature prose and poetry of New Zealand. Among interesting pioneer records of the mid- to late 19th century are those of Edward Jerningham Wakefield and F E Maning; and *A First Year in Canterbury Settlement* by Samuel ◊Butler. Earliest of the popular poets was Thomas Bracken, author of the New Zealand national song, followed by native-born Jessie Mackay and W Pember Reeves, though the latter is better known as the author of the prose account of New Zealand *The Long White Cloud*; and Ursula Bethell (1874–1945).

In the 20th century New Zealand literature gained an international appeal with the short stories of Katherine ◊Mansfield, produced an exponent of detective fiction in Dame Ngaio ◊Marsh, and struck a specifically New Zealand note in *Tutira, the Story of a New Zealand Sheep Station* 1926, by W H Guthrie Smith (1861–1940). Poetry of a new quality was written by R A K Mason (1905–1971) in the 1920s, and in the 1930s by a group of which A R D Fairburn (1904–1957), with a witty conversational turn, and Allen Curnow, poet, critic, and anthologist, are the most striking. In fiction the 1930s were remarkable for the short stories of Frank Sargeson and Roderick Finlayson (1904–), and the talent of John Mulgan (1911–1945), who is remembered both for his novel *Man Alone* and for his posthumous factual account of World War II, in which he died, *Report on Experience* 1947. Kendrick Smithyman (1922–) struck a metaphysical note in poetry, James K Baxter (1926–1972) published fluent lyrics, and Janet Frame has a brooding depth of meaning in such novels as *The Rainbirds* 1968 and *Intensive Care* 1970. In 1985 Keri Hulme won Britain's Booker Prize for her novel *The Bone People.*

It is merely a great deal of water falling over some cliffs. But it is very remarkably that.

On **Niagara Falls**
Rupert Brooke *Letters from America*

Ney Michel. Duke of Elchingen, Prince of Ney 1769–1815. Marshal of France under ◊Napoleon I, who commanded the rearguard of the French army during the retreat from Moscow, and for his personal courage was called 'the bravest of the brave'. When Napoleon returned from Elba, Ney was sent to arrest him, but instead deserted to him and fought at Waterloo. He was subsequently shot for treason. He served throughout the Revolutionary and Napoleonic Wars.

Ngugi wa Thiong'o (born James Ngugi) 1938– . Kenyan writer. His work includes essays, plays, short stories, and novels. Imprisoned after the performance of the play *Ngaahika Ndeenda/I Will Marry When I Want* 1977, he lived in exile from 1982. His novels, written in English and Kikuyu, include *The River Between* 1965, *Petals of Blood* 1977, *Caitaani Mutharaba-ini/Devil on the Cross* 1982, and *Matigari* 1989, and deal with colonial and post-independence oppression.

niacin one of the 'B group' vitamins; see ◊nicotinic acid.

Niagara Falls two waterfalls on the Niagara River, on the Canada–USA border, between lakes Erie and Ontario and separated by Goat Island. The American Falls are 51 m/167 ft high, 330 m/1,080 ft wide; Horseshoe Falls, in Canada, are 49 m/160 ft high, 790 m/2,600 ft across.

On the west bank of the river is Niagara Falls, a city in Ontario, Canada; population (1981) 71,000; on the east bank is Niagara Falls, a city in New York State, USA; population (1990) 61,800. Their economies are based on hydroelectric generating plants, diversified industry, and tourism.

Niamey river port and capital of ◊Niger; population (1988) 398,000. It produces textiles, chemicals, pharmaceuticals, and foodstuffs.

Nibelungenlied (*Song of the Nibelung*) anonymous 12th-century German epic poem, derived from older sources. The composer Richard Wagner made use of the legends in his *Ring* cycle.

◊Siegfried, possessor of the Nibelung treasure, marries Kriemhild (sister of Gunther of Worms) and wins Brunhild as a bride for Gunther. However, Gunther's vassal Hagen murders Siegfried, and Kriemhild achieves revenge by marrying Etzel (Attila) of the Huns, at whose court both Hagen and Gunther are killed.

Nicaea ruined city (modern Iznik) in Turkey, capital of the ancient kingdom of Bithynia. It was the site of the Council of Nicaea AD 325 and of another ecumenical council AD 787. Between 1205 and 1261 it was the seat of the Byzantine emperors, and in 1330 it was conquered by Turkish forces.

Nicaea, Council of Christian church council held in Nicaea (now Iznik, Turkey) in 325, called by the Roman emperor Constantine. It condemned ◊Arianism as heretical and upheld the doctrine of the Trinity in the ◊Nicene Creed.

Nicaragua country in Central America, between the Pacific Ocean and the Caribbean Sea, bounded N by Honduras and S by Costa Rica. *See country box on p. 766.*

Nicaragua, Lake lake in Nicaragua, the largest in Central America; area 8,250 sq km/3,185 sq mi.

Nicaraguan Revolution the revolt 1978–79 in Nicaragua, led by the socialist Sandinistas against the US-supported right-wing dictatorship established by Anastasio ◊Somoza. His son, President Anastasio (Debayle) Somoza (1925–1980), was forced into exile 1979 and assassinated in Paraguay. The Sandinista National Liberation Front (FSLN) was named after Augusto César Sandino, a guerrilla leader killed by the US-trained National Guard 1934.

Nice city on the French Riviera; population (1990) 345,700. Founded in the 3rd century BC, it repeatedly changed hands between France and the Duchy of Savoy from the 14th to the 19th century. In 1860 it was finally transferred to France.

Chocolate and perfume are made here. Chapels in the nearby village of Vence have been decorated by the artists Marc Chagall and Henri Matisse, and Nice has a Chagall museum. The Nice Carnival takes place during the three weeks leading up to Shrove Tuesday.

NEW ZEALAND
Dominion of

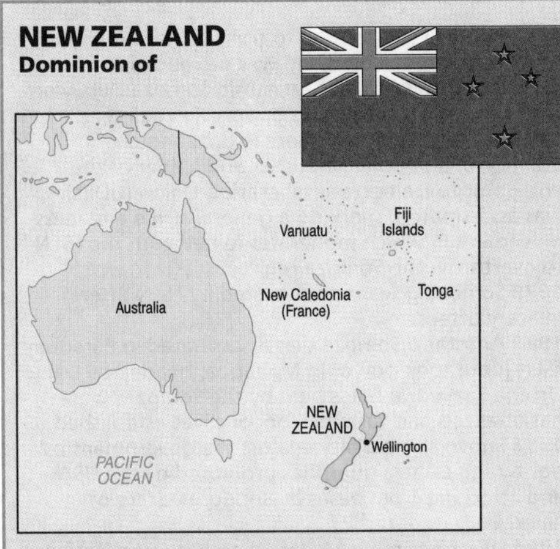

area 268,680 sq km/103,777 sq mi
capital (and port) Wellington
major towns/cities Hamilton, Palmerston North, Christchurch, Dunedin
major ports Auckland
physical features comprises North Island, South Island, Stewart Island, Chatham Islands, and minor islands; mainly mountainous; Ruapehu in the North Island, 2,797 m/9,180 ft, highest of three active volcanoes; geysers and hot springs of the Rotorua district; Lake Taupo (616 sq km/238 sq mi), source of Waikato River; Kaingaroa state forest. In the South Island are the Southern Alps and Canterbury Plains
territories Tokelau (three atolls transferred 1926 from former Gilbert and Ellice Islands colony); Niue Island (one of the Cook Islands, separately administered from 1903: chief town Alafi); Cook Islands are internally self-governing but share common citizenship with New Zealand; Ross Dependency in Antarctica
head of state Elizabeth II from 1952 represented by governor general Catherine Tizard from 1990
head of government Jenny Shipley from 1997
political system constitutional monarchy
administrative divisions 93 counties, 12 regions, and six territorial authorities
political parties Labour Party, moderate, left of centre; New Zealand National Party, free enterprise, centre-right; Alliance Party bloc, left of centre, ecologists; New Zealand First Party (NZFP), centrist; United New Zealand Party (UNZ), centrist
armed forces 10,000; 2,650 regular reserves and 5,200 territorial reserves (1994)
conscription none
defence spend (% GDP) 1.1 (1994)
education spend (% GNP) 7.1 (1992)
health spend (% GDP) 5.9 (1993)
death penalty abolished 1989
population 3,602,000 (1996 est)
population growth rate 1.2% (1990–95); 0.8% (2000–05)
age distribution (% of total population) <15 23.4%, 15–65 65.3%, >65 11.3% (1995)
ethnic distribution around 87% of European origin, about 9% Maori, and 2% Pacific Islander
population density (per sq km) 3 (1994)
urban population (% of total) 86 (1995)
labour force 48% of population: 10% agriculture, 25% industry, 65% services (1990)
unemployment 6.3% (1995)
child mortality rate (under 5, per 1,000 live births) 9 (1993)
life expectancy 73 (men), 79 (women)
education (compulsory years) 11
literacy rate 99%
languages English (official), Maori
religion Christian
TV sets (per 1,000 people) 443 (1992)
currency New Zealand dollar
GDP (US $) 65 billion (1996)
GDP per capita (PPP) (US $) 16,746 (1995)
growth rate 2.2% (1994/95)
average annual inflation 2.3% (1995); 4.6% (1984–94)
major trading partners Australia, USA, Japan, UK
resources coal, clay, limestone, dolomite, natural gas, hydroelectric power, pumice, iron ore, gold, forests
industries food processing, machinery, textiles and clothing, fishery, wood and wood products, paper and paper products, metal products; farming, particularly livestock and dairying, cropping, fruit-growing, and horticulture
exports meat, dairy products, wool, fish, timber and wood products, fruit and vegetables, aluminium, machinery. Principal market: Australia 21% (1994)
imports machinery and mechanical appliances, vehicles and aircraft, petroleum, fertilizer, consumer goods. Principal source: Australia 21.5% (1994)
arable land 9% (1993)
agricultural products barley, wheat, maize, fodder crops, exotic timber, fruit (kiwi and apple)

HISTORY
1642 Dutch explorer Abel Tasman reached New Zealand but indigenous Maoris prevented him from going ashore.
1769–1777 English explorer James Cook surveyed coastline of islands.
1815 First British missionaries arrived.
1826 New Zealand Company founded in London to establish settlement.
1840 Treaty of Waitangi: Maoris accepted British sovereignty; colonization began and large-scale sheep farming developed.
1845–47 Maori revolt against loss of land.
1851 Became separate colony (was originally part of Australian colony of New South Wales).
1852 Colony procured constitution after dissolution of New Zealand Company; self-government fully implemented 1856.
1860–72 Second Maori revolt led to concessions, including representation in parliament.
1891 New Zealand took part in Australasian Federal Convention in Sydney but rejected idea of joining Australian Commonwealth.
1893 Became first country to give women the right to vote in parliamentary elections.
1898 Liberal government under Richard Seddon introduced pioneering old-age pension scheme.
1899–1902 Volunteers from New Zealand fought alongside imperial forces in Boer War.
1907 New Zealand achieved dominion status within British Empire.
1912–25 Government of Reform Party, led by William Massey, reflected interests of North Island farmers and strongly supported imperial unity.
1914–18 130,000 New Zealanders fought for the British Empire in World War I.
1916 Labour Party of New Zealand established.
1931 Statute of Westminster affirmed equality of status between Britain and dominions, effectively granting independence to New Zealand.
1935–49 Labour governments of Michael Savage and Peter Fraser introduced social reforms and encouraged state intervention in industry.
1936 Liberal Party merged with Reform Party to create National Party.
1939–45 New Zealand troops fought in World War II, notably in Crete, N Africa, and Italy.
1947 Parliament confirmed independence of New Zealand within British Commonwealth.
1951 New Zealand joined Australia and USA in ANZUS Pacific security treaty.
1965–72 New Zealand took part in Vietnam War.
1973 British entry into European Economic Community (EEC) forced New Zealand to seek closer trading relations with Australia.
1985 Non-nuclear military policy led to disagreements with France and USA.
1986 USA suspended defence obligations to New Zealand after it banned entry of US warships.
1988 Free-trade agreement signed with Australia.
1991 Alliance Party formed to challenge two-party system.
1992 Ban on entry of US warships lifted.
1996 National Party retained power by forming coalition with United Party. Inconclusive general election result later in year.
1997 Resignation of Jim Bolger forced by Jenny Shipley, who was elected in Dec as prime minister.
1998 A rift between Shipley and her deputy Winston Peters, of the New Zealand First party, led to calls for an election.

SEE ALSO Maori

Nicene Creed one of the fundamental ◊creeds of Christianity, promulgated by the Council of ◊Nicaea 325.

niche in ecology, the 'place' occupied by a species in its habitat, including all chemical, physical, and biological components, such as what it eats, the time of day at which the species feeds, temperature, moisture, the parts of the habitat that it uses (for example, trees or open grassland), the way it reproduces, and how it behaves.

It is believed that no two species can occupy exactly the same niche, because they would be in direct competition for the same resources at every stage of their life cycle.

Nichiren 1222–1282. Japanese Buddhist monk, founder of the sect that bears his name. The sect bases its beliefs on the *Lotus Sūtra*, which Nichiren held to be the only true revelation of the teachings of Buddha, and repetition of the sūtra's title to attain enlightenment.

Nicholas I 1796–1855. Tsar of Russia from 1825. His Balkan ambitions led to war with Turkey 1827–29 and the Crimean War 1853–56.

Nicholas II 1868–1918. Tsar of Russia 1894–1917. He was dominated by his wife, Tsarina ◊Alexandra, who was under the influence of the religious charlatan ◊Rasputin. His mismanagement of the Russo-Japanese War and of internal affairs led to the revolution of 1905, which he suppressed, although he was forced to grant limited constitutional reforms. He took Russia into World War I in 1914, was forced to abdicate in 1917 after the ◊Russian Revolution, and was executed with his family.

Nicholas, St also known as ***Santa Claus*** lived 4th century AD. In the Christian church, patron saint of Russia, children, merchants, sailors, and pawnbrokers; bishop of Myra (now in Turkey). His legendary gifts of dowries to poor girls led to the custom of giving gifts to children on the eve of his feast day, 6 Dec, still retained in some countries, such as the Netherlands; elsewhere the custom has been transferred to Christmas Day. His emblem is three balls.

Nichols Peter Richard 1927– . English dramatist. His first stage play, *A Day in the Death of Joe Egg* 1967, explored the life of a couple with a paraplegic child, while *The National Health* 1969 dramatized life in the face of death from cancer. *Privates on Parade* 1977, about the British army in Malaya, was followed by the middle-class comedy *Passion Play* 1981.

Nicholson Ben(jamin Lauder) 1894–1982. English abstract artist. After early experiments influenced by ◊Cubism and the Dutch ◊De Stijl group, Nicholson developed an elegant style of geometrical reliefs, notably a series of white reliefs (1933–38).

He studied briefly at the Slade School of Art,

Nicholas II Tsar Nicholas II of Russia, held prisoner by the Bolsheviks Aug 1917. His autocratic style, resistance to reform, and the ill-managed wars against Japan and Germany helped to bring about the Russian Revolution. Within a year of this photograph being taken, he and his family had been shot.

NICARAGUA
Republic of

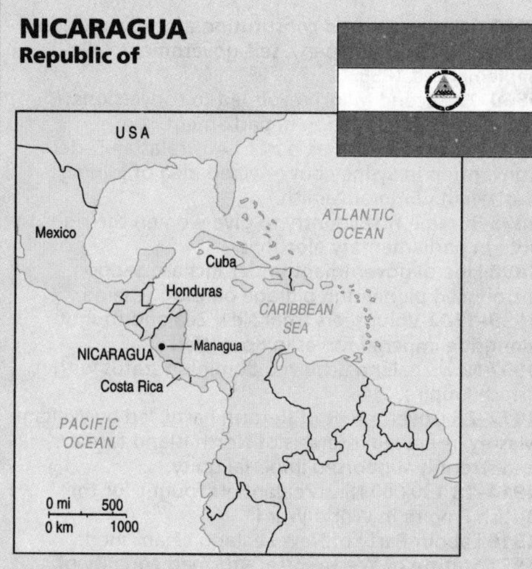

national name *República de Nicaragua*
area 127,849 sq km/49,363 sq mi
capital Managua
major towns/cities León, Granada
major ports Corinto, Puerto Cabezas, El Bluff
physical features narrow Pacific coastal plain separated from broad Atlantic coastal plain by volcanic mountains and lakes Managua and Nicaragua; one of world's most active earthquake regions
head of state and government Arnoldo Aleman from 1996
political system emergent democracy
administrative divisions 16 departments
political parties Sandinista National Liberation Front (FSLN), Marxist-Leninist; Opposition Political Alliance (APO, formerly National Opposition Union: UNO), loose US-backed coalition
population 4,238,000 (1996 est)
population growth rate 3.7% (1990–95); 2.8% (2000–05)
ethnic distribution over 70% of mixed Indian, Spanish, and African origin; about 9% African; 5% Indian
life expectancy 65 (men), 68 (women)
literacy rate 81%
languages Spanish (official), Indian, English
religion Roman Catholic 95%
currency cordoba
GDP (US $) 1.8 billion (1994 est)
growth rate 2.5% (1994)
exports coffee, cotton, sugar, bananas, meat, chemical products

HISTORY
10th C AD Indians from Mexico and Mesoamerica migrated to Nicaragua's Pacific lowlands.
1522 Visited by Spanish explorer Gil Gonzalez de Avila, who named the area Nicaragua after the local Indian chief, Nicarao.
1523–24 Colonized by the Spanish, under Francisco Hernandez de Cordoba, who was attracted by local gold deposits and founded the cities of Granada and León.
17th–18th Cs The British were a dominant force on the Caribbean side of Nicaragua, while Spain controlled the Pacific lowlands.
1821 Independence achieved from Spain; Nicaragua was initially part of the Mexican Empire.
1823 Became part of United Provinces (Federation) of Central America, also embracing Costa Rica, El Salvador, Guatemala, and Honduras.
1838 Became fully independent when it seceded from the Federation.
1857–93 Ruled by a succession of Conservative Party governments.
1860 The British ceded control over the Caribbean ('Mosquito') Coast to Nicaragua.
1893 The Liberal Party leader, José Santos Zelaya, deposed the Conservative president and established a dictatorship which lasted until overthrown by US marines in 1909.
1912–25 At the Nicaraguan government's request, with the political situation deteriorating, the USA established military bases and stationed marines.
1927–33 Re-stationed US marines faced opposition from an anti-American guerrilla group led by Augusto César Sandino, who was assassinated in 1934 on the orders of the commander of the US-trained National Guard, General Anastasio Somoza Garcia.
1937 General Anastasio Somoza elected president; start of near-dictatorial rule by Somoza family, which amassed a huge personal fortune.
1956 General Somoza assassinated and succeeded as president by his elder son, Luis Somoza Debayle.
early 1960s FSLN formed to fight Somoza regime.
1967 Luis Somoza died and was succeeded as president by his brother Anastasio Somoza Debayle, who headed an even more oppressive regime.
1978 Nicaraguan Revolution: Pedro Joaquin Chamorro, a popular publisher and leader of the anti-Somoza Democratic Liberation Union (UDEL), was assassinated, sparking a general strike and mass movement in which moderates joined with the FSLN to overthrow the Somoza regime.
1979 Somoza government ousted by FSLN after military offensive.
1980 Anastasio Somoza was assassinated in Paraguay; FSLN junta took power in Managua, headed by Daniel Ortega Saavedra; lands held by the Somozas were nationalized and farming cooperatives established.
1982 Subversive activity against the government by right-wing Contra guerrillas promoted by the USA and attacking from bases in Honduras. State of emergency declared.
1984 US troops mined Nicaraguan harbours. Action condemned by World Court 1986 and $17 billion in reparations ordered. FSLN won assembly elections.
1985 Denunciation of Sandinista government by US president Ronald Reagan, who vowed to 'remove it' and imposed a US trade embargo.
1987 Central American peace agreement cosigned by Nicaraguan leaders.
1988 Peace agreement failed. Nicaragua held talks with Contra rebel leaders. Hurricane left 180,000 people homeless.
1989 Demobilization of rebels and release of former Somozan supporters; cease-fire ended but economy was in ruins after the Contra war; 60% unemployment.
1990 FSLN defeated by the right-of-centre National Opposition Union (UNO), a US-backed coalition; Violeta Barrios de Chamorro, widow of the murdered Pedro Joaquin Chamorro, elected president. Antigovernment riots.
1992 Around 16,000 made homeless by earthquake.
1994 Peace accord with remaining Contra rebels.
1996 Right-wing candidate Arnoldo Aleman won presidential elections.
1998 Over 2,800 killed in flooding and landslides after Hurricane Mitch caused extensive damage to transport network, agriculture and property.

SEE ALSO Contra; Nicaraguan Revolution; United Provinces of Central America

London, and travelled in Europe and the USA 1912–18. He married the painter Winifred Nicholson (1893–1981) 1920, and the sculptor Barbara ◊Hepworth 1934. In later years he was a leading member of the St Ives School.

His championship of abstract art extended to publications such as *Circle* 1937, an international review of ◊Constructivism, and the book *Notes on Abstract Art* 1941.

Nicholson Jack 1937– . US film actor. In the late 1960s, he captured the mood of nonconformist, uncertain young Americans in such films as *Easy Rider* 1969 and *Five Easy Pieces* 1970. He subsequently became a mainstream Hollywood star, appearing in *Chinatown* 1974, *One Flew over the Cuckoo's Nest* (Academy Award) 1975, *The Shining* 1979, *Terms of Endearment* (Academy Award) 1983, *Batman* 1989, and *A Few Good Men* 1992.

He has directed several films, including *The Two Jakes* 1990, a sequel to *Chinatown*.

Nichrome trade name for a series of alloys containing mainly nickel and chromium, with small amounts of other substances such as iron, magnesium, silicon, and carbon. Nichrome has a high melting point and is resistant to corrosion. It is therefore used in electrical heating elements and as a substitute for platinum in the ◊flame test.

nickel hard, malleable and ductile, silver-white metallic element, symbol Ni, atomic number 28, relative atomic mass 58.71. It occurs in igneous rocks and as a free metal (◊native metal), occasionally occurring in fragments of iron-nickel meteorites. It is a component of the Earth's core, which is held to consist principally of iron with some nickel. It has a high melting point, low electrical and thermal conductivity, and can be magnetized. It does not tarnish and therefore is much used for alloys, electroplating, and for coinage.

It was discovered in 1751 by Swedish mineralogist Axel Cronstedt (1722–1765) and the name given as an abbreviated form of *kopparnickel*, Swedish 'false copper', since the ore in which it is found resembles copper but yields none.

nickel ore any mineral ore from which nickel is obtained. The main minerals are arsenides such as chloanthite ($NiAs_2$), and the sulphides millerite (NiS) and pentlandite $(Ni,Fe)_9S_8$, the commonest ore. The chief nickel-producing countries are Canada, Russia, Kazakhstan, Cuba, and Australia.

Nicklaus Jack William 1940– . US golfer, nicknamed 'the Golden Bear'. He won a record 20 major titles, including 18 professional majors between 1962 and 1986.

Nicklaus played for the US Ryder Cup team six times 1969–81 and was nonplaying captain 1983 and 1987 when the event was played over the course he designed at Muirfield Village, Ohio.

He was voted the 'Golfer of the Century' 1988.

Nicobar Islands group of Indian islands, part of the Union Territory of ◊Andaman and Nicobar Islands.

Nicolle Charles Jules Henri 1866–1936. French bacteriologist whose discovery in 1909 that typhus is transmitted by the body louse made the armies of World War I introduce delousing as a compulsory part of the military routine. Nobel Prize for Physiology or Medicine 1928.

Nicosia (Greek ***Lefkosia***, Turkish ***Lefkosha***) capital of Cyprus, with leather, textile, and pottery industries; population (1993) 177,000. Nicosia was the residence of Lusignan kings of Cyprus 1192–1475. The Venetians, who took Cyprus 1489, surrounded Nicosia with a high wall, which still exists; the city fell to the Turks 1571. It was again partly taken by the Turks in the invasion 1974.

In 1995 the Greek Cypriot national assembly voted unanimously to change the divided city's name to Lefkosia. Turkish Cypriots already referred to their half of the city as Lefkosha.

nicotine $C_{10}H_{14}N_2$ ◊alkaloid (nitrogenous compound) obtained from the dried leaves of the tobacco plant *Nicotiana tabacum* and used as an insecticide. A colourless oil, soluble in water, it turns brown on exposure to the air.

Nicotine in its pure form is one of the most powerful poisons known. It is the component of cigarette smoke that causes physical addiction. It is named after a 16th-century French diplomat, Jacques Nicot, who introduced tobacco to France.

nicotine patch plastic patch impregnated with nicotine that is stuck on to the skin to help the wearer give up smoking tobacco. Nicotine seeps out at a controlled rate onto the skin and is absorbed into the blood, thereby relieving the wearer's physical craving for the drug. The amount administered is reduced over time as the wearer proceeds from high-dose to low-dose patches.

Nicotine patches are more effective when combined with counselling because, although they can alleviate physical dependence on nicotine, they do not alter the habits that can make the wearer yearn for a cigarette. Very high doses of nicotine, such as those produced when wearing more than one patch at a time, can produce side effects such as vomiting, disturbed vision, and – in extreme cases – heart attacks.

nicotinic acid or ***niacin*** water-soluble ◊vitamin ($C_5H_5N.COOH$) of the B complex, found in meat, fish, and cereals; it can also be formed in small amounts in the body from the essential ◊amino acid tryptophan. Absence of nicotinic acid from the diet leads to the disease ◊pellagra.

Niebuhr Reinhold 1892–1971. US Protestant theologian, a Lutheran minister. His *Moral Man and Immoral Society* 1932 attacked depersonalized modern industrial society but denied the possibility of fulfilling religious and political utopian aspirations, a position that came to be known as Christian Realism. Niebuhr was a pacifist, activist, and socialist but advocated war to stop totalitarianism in the 1940s.

niello black substance made by melting powdered silver, copper, sulphur, and often borax. It is used as a filling for incised decoration on silver and fixed by the application of heat.

Niello was used to decorate objects in ancient Egypt, in the Bronze Age Aegean, in the European Middle Ages, and in much Anglo-Saxon metalwork. It reached its height of technical and artistic excellence in the early Renaissance in Italy, especially in Florence. It was much used in 19th-century Russia, where it is known as *tula* work.

nielsbohrium name proposed by Soviet scientists for the element currently known as ◊unnilpentium (atomic number 105), to honour Danish physicist Niels Bohr.

Nielsen Carl August 1865–1931. Danish composer. His works combine an outward formal strictness with an inner waywardness of tonality and structure. They include the Neo-Classical opera *Maskarade/Masquerade* 1906, a *Wind Quintet* 1922, six programmatic symphonies, numerous songs, and incidental music on Danish texts. He also composed concertos for violin 1911, flute 1926, and clarinet 1928; chamber music; and piano works.

Niemeyer (Soares Filho) Oscar 1907– . Brazilian architect. He was joint designer of the United Nations headquarters in New York 1947 and from 1957 architect of many public buildings in the capital, Brasília. His idiosyncratic interpretation of the Modernist idiom uses symbolic form to express the function of a building; for example, the Catholic Cathedral in Brasília.

Niemöller (Friedrich Gustav Emil) Martin 1892–1984. German Christian Protestant pastor. He was imprisoned in a concentration camp 1938–45 for campaigning against Nazism in the German church. He was president of the World Council of Churches 1961–68.

Niepce Joseph Nicéphore 1765–1833. French pioneer of photography. Niepce invented heliography, a precursor of photography that fixed images onto pewter plates coated with pitch and required eight-hour exposures. He produced the world's first photograph from nature 1826 and later collaborated with ◊Daguerre on the faster daguerreotype process.

Nietzsche Friedrich Wilhelm 1844–1900. German philosopher who rejected the accepted absolute moral values and the 'slave morality' of Christianity. He argued that 'God is dead' and therefore people were free to create their own values. His ideal was the *Übermensch*, or 'Superman', who would impose his will on the weak and worthless. Nietzsche claimed that knowledge is never objective but always serves some interest or unconscious purpose.

His insights into the relation between thought and language were a major influence on philosophy. Although he has been claimed as a precursor by Nazism, many of his views are incompatible with totalitarian ideology. He is a profoundly ambivalent thinker whose philosophy can be appropriated for many purposes.

He published *Morgenröte/The Dawn* 1880–81, *Die fröhliche Wissenschaft/The Gay Science* 1881–82, *Also sprach Zarathustra/Thus Spoke Zarathustra* 1883–85, *Jenseits von Gut und Böse/Between Good and Evil* 1885–86, *Zur Genealogie der Moral/Towards a Genealogy of Morals* 1887, and *Ecce Homo* 1888.

Niger landlocked country in NW Africa, bounded N by Algeria and Libya, E by Chad, S by Nigeria and Benin, and W by Burkina Faso and Mali. *See country box below.*

Niger third-longest river in Africa, 4,185 km/2,600 mi. It rises in the highlands bordering Sierra Leone and Guinea, flows NE through Mali, then SE through Niger and Nigeria to an inland delta on the Gulf of Guinea. Its flow has been badly affected by the expansion of the Sahara Desert. It is sluggish and frequently floods its banks. It was explored by the Scotsman Mungo Park 1795–96.

Niger-Congo languages the largest group of languages in Africa. It includes about 1,000 languages and covers a vast area south of the Sahara desert, from the W coast to the E, and down the E coast as far as South Africa. It is divided into groups and subgroups; the most widely spoken Niger-Congo languages are Swahili (spoken on the E coast), the members of the Bantu group (southern Africa), and Yoruba (Nigeria).

Nigeria country in W Africa on the Gulf of Guinea, bounded N by Niger, E by Chad and Cameroon, and W by Benin. *See country box on p. 768.*

nightingale songbird *Luscinia megarhyncos* of the thrush family Muscicapidae, with a song of great beauty, heard at night as well as by day. About 16.5 cm/6.5 in long, it is dull brown with a reddish-brown rounded tail; the breast is dull greyish-white, tinting to brown. It migrates in summer to Europe and winters in Africa. It feeds on insects, small animals, and occasionally fruit. It has a huge musical repertoire, built from about 900 melodic elements.

The female is slightly smaller than the male, but exhibits no definite distinction of plumage. The nest is often made on the ground, of dry grass and leaves, and in it are laid 4–6 olive-green eggs. The male's song continues until the young are hatched.

L. luscinia, the thrush nightingale of eastern Europe, is a louder but not such a sweet songster. Both species also sing in their winter ranges in Africa.

Nightingale Florence 1820–1910. English nurse, the founder of nursing as a profession. She took a team of nurses to Scutari (now Üsküdar, Turkey) in 1854 and reduced the ◊Crimean War hospital death rate from 42% to 2%. In 1856 she founded the Nightingale School and Home for Nurses in London. *See illustration on following page.*

nightjar any of about 65 species of night-hunting birds forming the family Caprimulgidae, order Caprimulgiformes. They have wide, bristly mouths for catching flying insects. Their distinctive calls have earned them such names as whippoorwill and church-will's-widow. Some US species are called nighthawks.

Nighthawk most commonly refers to the Chordeiles species of North America, including *Chordeiles minor* which breeds widely as far north as southern Alaska, and migrates south to Argentina.

The European nightjar *Caprimulgus europaeus* is about 28 cm/11 in long. It is patterned in shades of

'Morality is the herd instinct in the individual.'

FRIEDRICH NIETZSCHE
The Joyous Science

'West and East Nigeria are as different as Ireland from Germany. The North is as different from either as China.'

On NIGERIA
Obafemi Awolowo, quoted in John Gunther *Inside Africa*

NIGER
Republic of

ATLANTIC OCEAN
0 mi 500
0 km 1000
Algeria
Libya
Mali
NIGER
Niamey
Chad
Burkina Faso
Benin
Nigeria

national name *République du Niger*
area 1,267,000 sq km/489,188 sq mi
capital Niamey
major towns/cities Zinder, Maradi, Tahoua, Agadez
physical features desert plains between hills in N and savanna in S; river Niger in SW, Lake Chad in SE
head of state Ibrahim Barre Mainassara from 1996
head of government Amadou Boubacar Cisse from 1997
political system transitional
administrative divisions seven departments
political parties National Movement for a Development Society (MNSD–Nassara), left of centre; Alliance of the Forces for Change (AFC), left-of-centre coalition; Party for Democracy and Socialism–Tarayya (PNDS–Tarayya), left of centre
population 9,465,000 (1996 est)
population growth rate 3.4% (1990–95); 3.2% (2000–05)
ethnic distribution three ethnic groups make up over 75% of the population: the Hausa (mainly in central areas and the S), Djerma-Songhai (SW), and Beriberi-Manga (E); there is also a significant number of the mainly nomadic Fulani people, and the Tuareg in the N
life expectancy 45 (men), 48 (women)
literacy rate men 40%, women 17%
languages French (official), Hausa, Djerma, and other minority languages
religions Sunni Muslim; also Christian, and traditional animist beliefs
currency franc CFA
GDP (US $) 1.54 billion (1994)
growth rate 2.6% (1994)
exports peanuts, livestock, gum arabic, uranium

HISTORY
10th–13th Cs Kanem-Bornu Empire flourished in the SE, near Lake Chad, spreading Islam from the 11th century.
15th C Tuareg sultanate of Agades dominant in the N.
17th C The Songhai-speaking Djerma established an empire on the Niger river.
18th C The powerful Gobir kingdom was founded by the Hausa people, who had migrated from S in the 14th century.
late 18th–early 19th Cs Visited by European explorers, including the Scot, Mungo Park; Sultanate of Sokoto formed by the Islamic revivalist Fulani, who had defeated the Hausa in a jihad (holy war).
1890s French conquered the region and ended the local slave trade.
1904 Became part of French West Africa, although Tuareg resistance continued until 1922.
1946 Became a French overseas territory, with its own territorial assembly and representation in the French Parliament.
1958 Became autonomous republic within French community.
1960 Achieved full independence; Hamani Diori of the Niger Progressive Party (NPP) elected president, but maintained close ties with France.
1971 Uranium production commenced.
1974 Diori ousted in army coup led by Lt-Col Seyni Kountché after long Sahel drought had led to civil disorder; military government launched drive against corruption.
1977 Cooperation agreement signed with France.
1984 Partial privatization of state firms as a result of further drought and increased government indebtedness as world uranium prices slumped.
1987 Kountché died and was replaced by General Ali Saibu.
1989 Ali Saibu elected president without opposition.
1991 Saibu stripped of executive powers, and transitional government formed amid student and industrial unrest.
1992 Transitional government collapsed amid economic problems and ethnic unrest among secessionist-minded Tuaregs in N. Referendum approved of new multiparty constitution.
1993 The Alliance of the Forces for Change (AFC) left-of-centre coalition won absolute majority in assembly elections. Mahamane Ousmane, a Muslim Hausa, elected president in first free presidential election.
1994 Peace agreement with northern Tuareg.
1995 AFC coalition won general election with reduced majority.
1996 President Ousmane ousted in military coup led by Ibrahim Barre Mainassara. Civilian government restored with Boukary Adji as premier; Mainassara formerly elected president amidst claims of electoral fraud.
1997 Amadou Boubacar Cisse appointed prime minister.

Nightingale **Although nursing was thought to be totally unsuitable work for a woman of the Victorian middle classes, Florence Nightingale (seen in this 1859 photograph) was unwavering in her determination to transform both the standard of care that nurses provided and their professional status. The publicity surrounding her work in the Crimean War as 'the Lady with the Lamp' allowed her to achieve both aims.** ***St Thomas's Library***

brown, and well camouflaged. It is a summer visitor to Europe, and winters in tropical Africa.

Night Journey or *al-Miraj* (Arabic 'the ascent') in Islam, the journey of the prophet Muhammad, guided by the archangel Gabriel, from Mecca to Jerusalem, where he met the earlier prophets, including Adam, Moses, and Jesus; he then ascended to paradise, where he experienced the majesty of Allah, and was also shown hell.

nightshade any of several plants in the family Solanaceae, which includes the black nightshade *Solanum nigrum*, bittersweet or woody nightshade *S. dulcamara*, and deadly nightshade or ◊belladonna.

nihilism the rejection of all traditional values, authority, and institutions. The term was coined 1862 by Ivan Turgenev in his novel *Fathers and Sons*, and was adopted by the ◊Nihilists, the Russian radicals of the period. Despairing of reform, they saw change as possible only through the destruction of morality, justice, marriage, property, and the idea of God. Since then nihilism has come to mean a generally negative and destructive outlook.

Nihilist member of a group of Russian revolutionaries in the reign of Alexander II 1855–81. Despairing of reform, they saw change as possible only through the destruction of morality, justice, marriage, property, and the idea of God. In 1878 the Nihilists launched a guerrilla campaign leading to the murder of the tsar 1881.

Nijinksa Bronislava 1891–1972. Russian choreographer and dancer. Nijinksa was the first major female choreographer to work in classical ballet, creating several dances for Diaghilev's Ballets Russes, including *Les Noces* 1923, a landmark in 20th-century modernist dance. She was the sister of Vaslav ◊Nijinsky, continuing his revolutionary ideas of kinetic movement in dance. Other pieces include *Les Biches* 1924.

She joined the Ballets Russes as a dancer 1909, leaving when her brother was fired, to return as choreographer 1921. She staged the fairy dances in Max Reinhardt's film *A Midsummer Night's Dream* 1935.

Nijinsky Vaslav Fomich 1890–1950. Russian dancer and choreographer. Noted for his powerful but graceful technique, he was a legendary member of ◊Diaghilev's Ballets Russes, for whom he choreographed Debussy's *Prélude à l'après-midi d'un faune* 1912 and *Jeux* 1913, and Stravinsky's *Le Sacre du printemps/The Rite of Spring* 1913.

Nijinsky also took lead roles in ballets such as *Petrushka* 1911. He rejected conventional forms of classical ballet in favour of free expression. His sister was the choreographer Bronislava Nijinska.

Nike in Greek mythology, the goddess of victory, represented as 'winged', as in the statue from Samothrace in the Louvre, Paris. One of the most beautiful architectural monuments of Athens was the temple of Nike Apteros.

Nile river in Africa, the world's longest, 6,695 km/4,160 mi. The Blue Nile rises in Lake Tana, Ethiopia, the White Nile at Lake Victoria, and they join at Khartoum, Sudan. The river enters the Mediterranean Sea at a vast delta in N Egypt.

Its remotest headstream is the Luvironza, in Burundi. The Nile proper begins on leaving Lake Victoria above Owen Falls. From Lake Victoria it flows over rocky country, and there are many cataracts and rapids, including the Murchison Falls, until it enters Lake Mobutu (Albert). From here it flows across flat country and in places spreads out to form lakes. At Lake No it is joined by the Bahr el Ghazal, and from this point to Khartoum it is called the White Nile. At Khartoum it is joined by the Blue Nile, which rises in the Ethiopian highlands, and 320 km/200 mi below Khartoum it is joined by the

NIGERIA
Federal Republic of

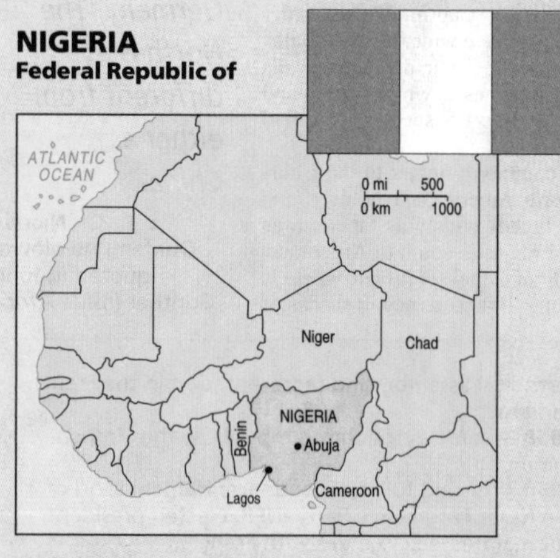

area 923,773 sq km/356,576 sq mi
capital Abuja
major towns/cities Ibadan, Ogbomosho, Kano
major ports Lagos, Port Harcourt, Warri, Calabar
physical features arid savanna in N; tropical rainforest in S, with mangrove swamps along the coast; river Niger forms wide delta; mountains in SE
head of state and government Olesegun Obasanjo from 1999
political system military republic
administrative divisions 30 states and a Federal Capital Territory
political parties Social Democratic Party (SDP), left of centre; National Republican Convention (NRC), right of centre (all parties dissolved on resumption of military rule 1992)
armed forces 76,500 (1994)
conscription none
defence spend (% GDP) 3.1 (1994)
education spend (% GNP) 0.5 (1992)
health spend (% GDP) 1.2 (1990)
death penalty retained and used for ordinary crimes
population 110,532,000 (1998 est)
population growth rate 3.0% (1990–95); 2.7% (2000–05)
age distribution (% of total population) <15 46.5%, 15–65 51.7%, >65 2.8% (1995)
ethnic distribution over 250 tribal groups; major tribes include the Hausa and Fulani in the N, the Yoruba in the S, and the Ibo in the E
population density (per sq km) 117 (1994)
urban population (% of total) 39 (1995)
labour force 40% of population: 43% agriculture, 7% industry, 50% services (1990)
unemployment 3.4% (1992)
child mortality rate (under 5, per 1,000 live births) 141 (1997)
life expectancy 51 (men), 54 (women)
education (compulsory years) 6
literacy rate 62% (men), 40% (women)
languages English (official), Hausa, Ibo, Yoruba
religions Sunni Muslim 50% (in N), Christian 40% (in S), local religions 10%
TV sets (per 1,000 people) 33 (1992)
currency naira
GDP (US $) 36.5 billion (1997)
GDP per capita (PPP) (US $) 1,540 (1993)
growth rate 1.3% (1994)
average annual inflation 57% (1994); 28.7% (1985–93)
major trading partners Germany, UK, USA, France, Spain, the Netherlands, Italy
resources petroleum, natural gas, coal, tin, iron ore, uranium, limestone, marble, forest
industries food processing, brewing, petroleum refinery, iron and steel, motor vehicles (using imported components), textiles, cigarettes, footwear, pharmaceuticals, pulp and paper, cement
exports petroleum, cocoa beans, rubber, palm products, urea and ammonia, fish. Principal market: USA 45.3% (1993)
imports machinery and transport equipment, basic manufactures, cereals, chemicals, foodstuffs. Principal source: Germany 16.2% (1993)
arable land 32.3% (1993)
agricultural products cocoa, groundnuts, oil palm, rubber, rice, maize, taro, yams, cassava, sorghum, millet, plantains; livestock (principally goats, sheep, cattle, and poultry) and fisheries

HISTORY
4th C BC–2nd C AD Highly organized Nok culture flourished in N Nigeria.
9th C NE Nigeria became part of the empire of Kanem-Bornu, based around Lake Chad.
11th C Creation of Hausa states, including Kano and Katsina.
13th C Arab merchants introduced Islam in N.
15th C Empire of Benin at its height in S; first contact with European traders.
17th C Oyo Empire dominant in SW; development of slave trade in Niger delta.
1804–17 Islamic Fulani (or Sokoto) Empire established in N.
1861 British traders procured Lagos; spread of Christian missionary activity in S.
1884–1904 Britain occupied most of Nigeria by stages.
1914 N and S protectorates united; growth of railway network and trade.
1951 Introduction of elected representation led to formation of three regional political parties.
1954 New constitution increased powers of regions.
1958 Oil discovered in SE.
1960 Achieved independence from Britain, within the Commonwealth; breakdown of law and order amid growing ethnic and regional conflict.
1963 Became a republic, with Nnamdi Azikiwe as president.
1966 General Aguiyi-Ironsi of Ibo tribe seized power and imposed unitary government; massacre of Ibo by Hausa in N; General Gowon seized power and restored federalism.
1967 Conflict over oil revenues led to secession of eastern region as independent Ibo state of Biafra; ensuing civil war claimed up to a million lives.
1970 Surrender of Biafra and end of civil war; development of oil industry financed more effective central government.
1975 Gowon ousted in military coup; second coup put General Olusegun Obasanjo in power.
1979 Civilian rule restored under President Shehu Shagari.
1983 Bloodless coup staged by Maj-Gen Muhammadu Buhari; economy suffered from falling oil prices.
1985 Buhari replaced by Maj-Gen Ibrahim Babangida; Islamic northerners dominant in regime.
1989 Ban on political activity lifted; two official non-regional political parties created.
1992 Multiparty elections won by Babangida's SDP.
1993 Moshood Abiola (SDP) won first free presidential election; results suspended. General Sani Abacha restored military rule and dissolved political parties.
1995 Commonwealth membership suspended in protest at human-rights abuses by military regime.
1998 Elections boycotted by Abacha opponents. Abacha died; Abdusalam Abubakar became president.
1999 Retired general Olesegun Obasanjo became president following a presidential election.

SEE ALSO Benin; Biafra, Republic of

Nijinska Russian dancer and choreographer Bronislava Nijinska, whose career was overshadowed by her brother Vaslav Nijinsky. She choreographed one of the first 'feminist' ballets, *Les Biches* (1924) for the Ballets Russes, and she allowed female dancers a freer style of movement. She eventually settled in California where she trained many dancers in her Los Angeles school. *Corbis*

Atbara. From Khartoum to Aswan there are six cataracts. The Nile is navigable to the second cataract, a distance of 1,545 km/960 mi. The delta of the Nile is 190 km/120 mi wide. From 1982 Nile water has been piped beneath the Suez Canal to irrigate ◊Sinai. The water level behind the Aswan Dam fell from 170 m/558 ft in 1979 to 150 m/492 ft in 1988, threatening Egypt's hydroelectric power generation. The 1988 water level was the lowest in a century.

Nile, Battle of the alternative name for the Battle of ◊Aboukir Bay.

nilgai large antelope *Boselaphus tragocamelus* native to India. The bull has short conical horns and is bluish-grey. The female is brown.

Nîmes capital of Gard *département*, Languedoc-Roussillon, S France; population (1990) 133,600. Roman remains include an amphitheatre dating from the 2nd century and the Pont du Gard (aqueduct). The city gives its name to the cloth known as denim (*de Nîmes*).

Nin Anaïs 1903–1977. French-born US novelist and diarist. Her extensive and impressionistic diaries, published 1966–76, reflect her interest in dreams, which along with psychoanalysis are recurring themes of her gently erotic novels (such as *House of Incest* 1936 and *A Spy in the House of Love* 1954). Her correspondence with Henry Miller was published 1985.

Born in Paris, she started out as a model and dancer, but later took up the study of psychoanalysis. She emigrated to the USA 1940, becoming a prominent member of Greenwich Village literary society in New York.

Nile

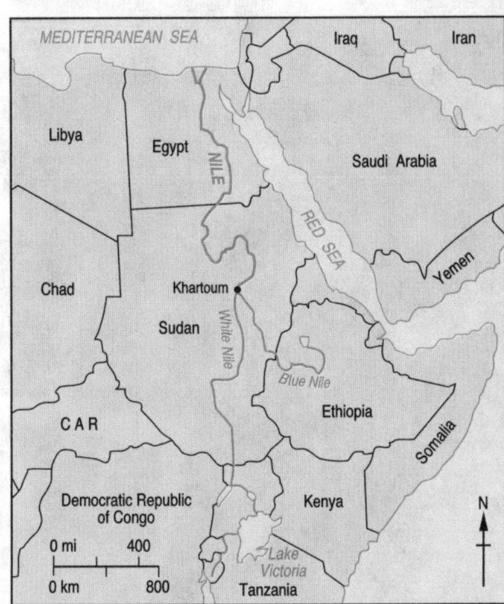

Nineteen Propositions demands presented by the English Parliament to Charles I 1642. They were designed to limit the powers of the crown, and their rejection represented the beginning of the Civil War.

Nineveh capital of the Assyrian Empire from the 8th century BC until its destruction by the Medes under King Cyaxares in 612 BC. It was situated on the river Tigris (opposite the present city of Mosul, Iraq) and was adorned with palaces.

Ningxia or ***Ningxia Hui*** autonomous region (formerly ***Ninghsia-Hui***) of NW China
area 170,000 sq km/65,620 sq mi
capital Yinchuan
physical desert plateau
products cereals and rice under irrigation; coal
population (1990) 4,655,000.

ninja (Japanese, from *ninjutsu* 'the art of invisibility') member of a body of trained assassins in feudal Japan, whose martial-arts skills were greatly feared. Popular legend had it that they were able to make themselves invisible.

Niobe in Greek mythology, the daughter of Tantalus and wife of Amphion, the king of Thebes. She was contemptuous of the goddess Leto for having produced only two children, Apollo and Artemis. She died of grief when her own 12 offspring were killed by them in revenge, and was changed to stone by Zeus.

niobium soft, grey-white, somewhat ductile and malleable, metallic element, symbol Nb, atomic number 41, relative atomic mass 92.906. It occurs in nature with tantalum, which it resembles in chemical properties. It is used in making stainless steel and other alloys for jet engines and rockets and for making superconductor magnets.

Niobium was discovered in 1801 by English chemist Charles Hatchett (1765–1847), who named it columbium (symbol Cb), a name that is still used in metallurgy. In 1844 it was renamed after Niobe by German chemist Heinrich Rose (1795–1864) because of its similarity to tantalum (Niobe is the daughter of Tantalus in Greek mythology).

Nippon English transliteration of the Japanese name for ◊Japan.

nirvana (Sanskrit 'a blowing out') in Buddhism, the attainment of perfect serenity, compassion, and wisdom by the eradication of all desires.

Nirvana US rock group 1986–94 who popularized a hard-driving, dirty sound, a tuneful ◊grunge, exemplified by their second album, *Nevermind* 1991, and its hit single 'Smells Like Teen Spirit'.

Nirvana formed in Washington State 1986–88 around singer, songwriter, and guitarist Kurt Cobain (1967–1994). Between their debut album *Bleach* 1989 and their 1991 breakthrough, the line-up was stripped to a three-piece. Their songs combined the hooks and dynamics of classic pop with the abrasive aesthetics of grunge. Their other albums were *In Utero* 1993 and *Unplugged* 1994. The group disbanded with Cobain's suicide in 1994.

Nissan Motor Company Japanese car manufacturer founded 1934. Its production of motor vehicles, initially marketed under the name of Datsun and then as Nissan, was more than 1.5 million in 1988.

nitrate salt or ester of nitric acid, containing the NO_3^- ion. Nitrates are used in explosives, in the chemical and pharmaceutical industries, in curing meat (see ◊nitre), and as fertilizers. They are the most water-soluble salts known and play a major part in the nitrogen cycle. Nitrates in the soil, whether naturally occurring or from inorganic or organic fertilizers, can be used by plants to make proteins and nucleic acids. However, runoff from fields can result in ◊nitrate pollution.

nitrate pollution the contamination of water by nitrates. Increased use of artificial fertilizers and land cultivation means that higher levels of nitrates are being washed from the soil into rivers, lakes, and aquifers. There they cause an excessive enrichment of the water (◊eutrophication), leading to a rapid growth of algae, which in turn darkens the water and reduces its oxygen content. The water is expensive to purify and many plants and animals die. High levels are now found in drinking water in arable areas. These may be harmful to newborn babies, and it is possible that they contribute to stomach cancer, although the evidence for this is unproven.

Nîmes The Maison Carrée, or temple, at Nîmes in S France is one of the best preserved Roman buildings outside Italy. The Carré d'Art, the new arts centre built by the English architect Norman Foster, offers a modern variation on the classical colonnade and portico. *Sir Norman Foster and Partners*

nitre or ***saltpetre*** potassium nitrate, KNO_3, a mineral found on and just under the ground in desert regions; used in explosives. Nitre occurs in Bihar, India, Iran, and Cape Province, South Africa. The salt was formerly used for the manufacture of gunpowder, but the supply of nitre for explosives is today largely met by making the salt from nitratine (also called Chile saltpetre, $NaNO_3$). Saltpetre is a ◊preservative and is widely used for curing meats.

nitric acid or ***aqua fortis*** HNO_3 fuming acid obtained by the oxidation of ammonia or the action of sulphuric acid on potassium nitrate. It is a highly corrosive acid, dissolving most metals, and a strong oxidizing agent. It is used in the nitration and esterification of organic substances, and in the making of sulphuric acid, nitrates, explosives, plastics, and dyes.

nitrification process that takes place in soil when bacteria oxidize ammonia, turning it into nitrates. Nitrates can be absorbed by the roots of plants, so this is a vital stage in the ◊nitrogen cycle.

nitrite salt or ester of nitrous acid, containing the nitrite ion (NO_2^-). Nitrites are used as preservatives (for example, to prevent the growth of botulism spores) and as colouring agents in cured meats such as bacon and sausages.

nitrogen (Greek *nitron* 'native soda', sodium or potassium nitrate) colourless, odourless, tasteless, gaseous, nonmetallic element, symbol N, atomic number 7, relative atomic mass 14.0067. It forms almost 80% of the Earth's atmosphere by volume and is a constituent of all plant and animal tissues (in proteins and nucleic acids). Nitrogen is obtained for industrial use by the liquefaction and fractional distillation of air. Its compounds are used in the manufacture of foods, drugs, fertilizers, dyes, and explosives.

Nitrogen has been recognized as a plant nutrient, found in manures and other organic matter, from early times, long before the complex cycle of ◊nitrogen fixation was understood. It was isolated in 1772 by English chemist Daniel Rutherford (1749–1819) and named in 1790 by French chemist Jean Chaptal (1756–1832).

nitrogen cycle the process of nitrogen passing through the ecosystem. Nitrogen, in the form of inorganic compounds (such as nitrates) in the soil, is absorbed by plants and turned into organic compounds (such as proteins) in plant tissue. A proportion of this nitrogen is eaten by ◊herbivores, with some of this in turn being passed on to the carnivores, which feed on the herbivores. The nitrogen is ultimately returned to the soil as excrement and when organisms die and are converted back to inorganic form by ◊decomposers.

Although about 78% of the atmosphere is nitrogen, this cannot be used directly by most organisms.

'The alien and mysterious Nile, that gigantic serpent that winds so fabulously, so ungraspably, back through history.'

On the river **Nile**
Rose Macaulay
Pleasures of Ruins
1953

nitrogen cycle The nitrogen cycle is one of a number of cycles during which the chemicals necessary for life are recycled. The carbon, sulphur, and phosphorus cycles are others. Since there is only a limited amount of these chemicals in the Earth and its atmosphere, the chemicals must be continuously recycled if life is to go on.

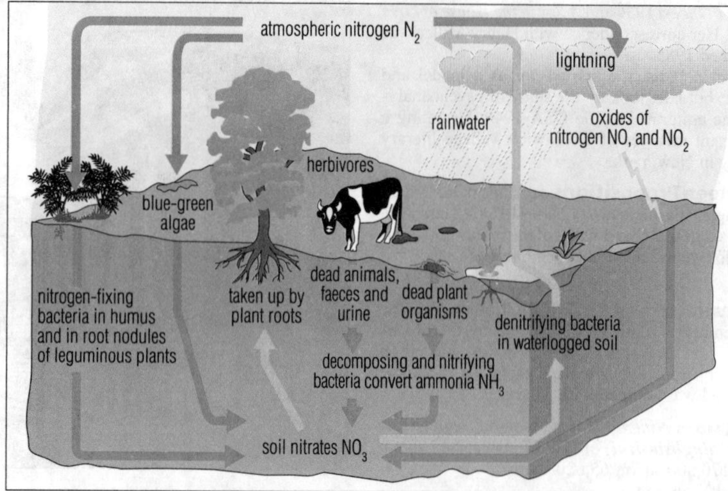

However, certain bacteria and cyanobacteria (see ◊blue-green algae) are capable of nitrogen fixation. Some nitrogen-fixing bacteria live mutually with leguminous plants (peas and beans) or other plants (for example, alder), where they form characteristic nodules on the roots. The presence of such plants increases the nitrate content, and hence the fertility, of the soil.

nitrogen fixation the process by which nitrogen in the atmosphere is converted into nitrogenous compounds by the action of microorganisms, such as cyanobacteria (see ◊blue-green algae) and bacteria, in conjunction with certain ◊legumes. Several chemical processes duplicate nitrogen fixation to produce fertilizers; see ◊nitrogen cycle.

nitrogen oxide any chemical compound that contains only nitrogen and oxygen. All nitrogen oxides are gases. Nitrogen monoxide and nitrogen dioxide contribute to air pollution. See also ◊nitrous oxide.

Nitrogen oxide was discovered during the 1980s to act as a chemical messenger in small quantities within the human body, despite being toxic at higher concentrations, and its rapid reaction with oxygen. The medical condition of septic shock is linked to overproduction by the body of nitrogen oxide. Nitrogen oxide has an unpaired electron, which can be removed to produce the nitrosyl ion, NO^+.

Nitrogen monoxide (NO), or nitric oxide, is a colourless gas released when metallic copper reacts with concentrated ◊nitric acid. It is also produced when nitrogen and oxygen combine at high temperature. On contact with air it is oxidized to nitrogen dioxide.

Nitrogen dioxide (nitrogen(IV) oxide, NO_2) is a brown, acidic, pungent gas that is harmful if inhaled and contributes to the formation of ◊acid rain, as it dissolves in water to form nitric acid. It is the most common of the nitrogen oxides and is obtained by heating most nitrate salts (for example lead(II) nitrate, $Pb(NO_3)_2$). If liquefied, it gives a colourless solution (N_2O_4). It has been used in rocket fuels.

nitroglycerine $C_3H_5(ONO_2)_3$ flammable, explosive oil produced by the action of nitric and sulphuric acids on glycerol. Although poisonous, it is used in cardiac medicine. It explodes with great violence if heated in a confined space and is used in the preparation of dynamite, cordite, and other high explosives.

It was invented by the Italian Ascanio Soberro in 1846, and is unusual among explosives in that it is a liquid. Nitroglycerine is an effective explosive because it has low ◊activation energy, and produces little smoke when burned. However, it was initially so reactive it was virtually unusable. Alfred ◊Nobel's innovation was to purify nitroglycerine (using water, with which it is immiscible, to dissolve the impurities), and thereby make it more stable.

‘There can be no whitewash at the White House.’

Richard Nixon
On Watergate, television speech
30 April 1973

nitrous acid HNO_2 weak acid that, in solution with water, decomposes quickly to form nitric acid and nitrogen dioxide.

nitrous oxide or ***dinitrogen oxide*** N_2O colourless, nonflammable gas that, used in conjunction with oxygen, reduces sensitivity to pain. In higher doses it is an anaesthetic. Well tolerated, it is often combined with other anaesthetic gases to enable them to be used in lower doses. It may be self-administered; for example, in childbirth. It is a greenhouse gas; about 10% of nitrous oxide released into the atmosphere comes from the manufacture of nylon. It used to be known as ‘laughing gas’.

Nitrous oxide was inhaled as a recreational drug at 19th-century ‘ether frolics’.

Niven (James) David (Graham) 1910–1983. Scottish-born US film actor. In Hollywood from the 1930s, his films include *Wuthering Heights* 1939, *Around the World in 80 Days* 1956, *Separate Tables* 1958 (Academy Award), *The Guns of Navarone* 1961, and *The Pink Panther* 1964. He published two best-selling volumes of autobiography, *The Moon's a Balloon* 1972 and *Bring on the Empty Horses* 1975.

Nixon Richard Milhous 1913–1994. 37th president of the USA 1969–74, a Republican. He attracted attention as a member of the Un-American Activities Committee 1948, and was vice president to Eisenhower 1953–61. As president he was responsible for US withdrawal from Vietnam, and the normalization of relations with communist China, but at home his culpability in the cover-up of the ◊Watergate scandal and the existence of a ‘slush fund’ for political machinations during his re-election campaign 1972 led to his resignation 1974 when threatened with ◊impeachment.

Nixon entered Congress 1947, and rose to prominence during the McCarthyite era of the 1950s. He was senator for California from 1951 until elected vice president. He lost the 1960 presidential election to J F Kennedy.

presidency He did not seek presidential nomination 1964, but in a ‘law and order’ campaign defeated vice president Humphrey 1968 in one of the most closely contested elections in US history. Facing a Democratic Congress, Nixon sought to extricate the US from the war in Vietnam. He formulated the Nixon Doctrine 1969, abandoning close involvement with Asian countries, but escalated the war in Cambodia by massive bombing.

resignation Nixon was re-elected 1972 in a landslide victory over George McGovern, and immediately faced allegations of irregularities and illegalities conducted on his behalf in his re-election campaign and within the White House. Despite his success in extricating the US from Vietnam, congressional and judicial investigations, along with press exposures of the Watergate affair, undermined public support. He resigned 1974, the first and only US president to do so, under threat of impeachment on three counts: obstruction of the administration of justice in the investigation of Watergate; violation of constitutional rights of citizens, for example attempting to use the Internal Revenue Service, Federal Bureau of Investigation, and Central Intelligence Agency as weapons against political opponents; and failure to produce ‘papers and things’ as ordered by the Judiciary Committee.

He was granted a pardon 1974 by President Ford and turned to lecturing and writing.

Nizhni-Novgorod formerly (1932–90) ***Gorky*** city in central Russian Federation; population (1990) 1,443,000. Cars, locomotives, and aircraft are manufactured here.

Nkomo Joshua 1917– . Zimbabwean politician, vice president from 1988. As president of ZAPU (Zimbabwe African People's Union) from 1961, he was a leader of the black nationalist movement against the white Rhodesian regime. He was a member of Robert ◊Mugabe's cabinet 1980–82 and from 1987.

After completing his education in South Africa, Joshua Nkomo became a welfare officer on Rhodesian Railways and later organizing secretary of the Rhodesian African Railway Workers' Union. He entered politics 1950, and was president of the ANC in S Rhodesia 1957–59. In 1961 he created ZAPU, of which he was president.

Arrested along with other black African politicians, he was kept in detention 1963–1974. After his release he joined forces with Robert Mugabe as a joint leader of the Patriotic Front 1976, opposing the white-dominated regime of Ian Smith. Nkomo took part in the Lancaster House Conference, which led to Rhodesia's independence as the new state of Zimbabwe, and became a cabinet minister and vice president.

Nkrumah Kwame 1909–1972. Ghanaian nationalist politician, prime minister of the Gold Coast (Ghana's former name) 1952–57 and of newly independent Ghana 1957–60. He became Ghana's first president 1960 but was overthrown in a coup 1966. He remained in exile in Guinea, where he was made a co-head of state until his death, but was posthumously ‘rehabilitated’ 1973. His policy of ‘African socialism’ led to links with the communist bloc.

Nō or ***Noh*** classical, aristocratic Japanese drama which developed from the 14th to the 16th centuries and is still performed. There is a repertory of some 250 pieces, of which five, one from each of the several classes devoted to different subjects, may be put on in a performance lasting a whole day. Dance, mime, music, and chanting develop the mythical or historical themes. All the actors are men, some of whom wear masks and elaborate costumes; scenery is limited. Nō influenced ◊kabuki drama.

Nō developed from popular rural entertainments and religious performances staged at shrines and temples by travelling companies. The leader of one of these troupes, Kan'ami (1333–1384), and his son and successor Zeami (1363–1443) wrote a number of Nō plays and are regarded as the founders of the form. The plots often feature a ghost or demon seeking rest or revenge, but the aesthetics are those of Zen Buddhism. Symbolism and suggestion take precedence over action, and the slow, stylized dance is the strongest element. Flute, drums, and chorus supply the music.

Nkrumah Kwame Nkrumah, seen here addressing the United Nations General Assembly 1961, led Ghana to independence 1957 and became the country's first president. Called ‘the Ghandi of Africa’, he was prominent in the anticolonial and Pan African movements of the 1950s and 1960s. *United Nations*

Noah in the Old Testament, the son of Lamech and father of Shem, Ham, and Japheth, who, according to God's instructions, built a ship, the ark, so that he and his family and specimens of all existing animals might survive the ◊Flood. There is also a Babylonian version of the tale, the *Epic of* ◊*Gilgamesh*.

Nobel Alfred Bernhard 1833–1896. Swedish chemist and engineer. He invented ◊dynamite in 1867, gelignite 1875, and ballistite, a smokeless gunpowder, in 1887. Having amassed a large fortune from the manufacture of explosives and the exploitation of the Baku oilfields in Azerbaijan, near the Caspian Sea, he left this in trust for the endowment of five ◊Nobel prizes.

nobelium synthesized, radioactive, metallic element of the ◊actinide series, symbol No, atomic number 102, relative atomic mass 259. It is synthesized by bombarding curium with carbon nuclei.

It was named in 1957 after the Nobel Institute in Stockholm, Sweden, where it was claimed to have been first synthesized. Later evaluations determined that this was in fact not so, as the successful 1958 synthesis at the University of California at Berkeley produced a different set of data. The name was not, however, challenged. In 1992 the International Unions for Pure and Applied Chemistry and Physics (IUPAC and IUPAP) gave credit to Russian scientists in Dubna for the discovery of nobelium.

Nobel prize annual international prize. *See list of tables on p. 1177.*

noble gas alternative name for ◊inert gas.

noble gas structure the configuration of electrons in noble or ◊inert gases (helium, neon, argon, krypton, xenon, and radon).

This is characterized by full electron shells around the nucleus of an atom, which render the element stable. Any ion, produced by the gain or loss of electrons, that achieves an electronic configuration similar to one of the inert gases is said to have a noble gas structure.

noble savage, the ◊Enlightenment idea of the virtuous innocence of 'savage' (aboriginal or non-Westernized) peoples, often embodied in the Native American, and celebrated by the writers J J Rousseau, Chateaubriand (in the novel *Atala* 1801), and James Fenimore Cooper.

nocturne in music, a reflective character piece, often for piano, introduced by John Field (1782–1837) and adopted by Chopin.

node in physics, a position in a ◊standing wave pattern at which there is no vibration. Points at which there is maximum vibration are called antinodes. Stretched strings, for example, can show nodes when they vibrate. Guitarists can produce special effects (◊harmonics) by touching a sounding string lightly to produce a node.

nodule in geology, a lump of mineral or other matter found within rocks or formed on the seabed surface; ◊mining technology is being developed to exploit them.

Nofretete alternative name for ◊Nefertiti, queen of Egypt.

Noguchi Hideyo, (born Noguchi Seisaku) 1876–1928. Japanese bacteriologist who studied syphilitic diseases, snake venoms, trachoma, and poliomyelitis. He discovered the parasite of yellow fever, a disease from which he died while working in British W Africa.

noise in pop music, a style that relies heavily on feedback, distortion, and dissonance. A loose term that came into use in the 1980s with the slogan 'noise annoys', it has been applied to ◊hardcore punk, ◊grunge, and industrial music (which uses electronic distortion, metal percussion, and industrial tools to achieve deafening, discordant effects), among others.

noise unwanted sound. Permanent, incurable loss of hearing can be caused by prolonged exposure to high noise levels (above 85 decibels). Over 55 decibels on a daily outdoor basis is regarded as an unacceptable level.

In scientific and engineering terms, a noise is any form of random, unpredictable signal.

Noise is a recognized form of pollution, but is difficult to actually measure, because the annoyance or discomfort caused varies between individuals. If the noise is in a narrow frequency band, temporary hearing loss can occur even though the level is below 85 decibels or exposure is only for short periods. Lower levels of noise are an irritant, but seem not to increase fatigue or affect efficiency to any great extent. Loss of hearing is a common complaint of people working on factory production lines or in the construction and road industry. Minor psychiatric disease, stress-related ailments including high blood pressure, and disturbed sleep patterns are regularly linked to noise, although the causal links are in most cases hard to establish. Loud noise is a major pollutant in towns and cities. ***electronic noise*** takes the form of unwanted signals generated in electronic circuits and in recording processes by stray electrical or magnetic fields, or by temperature variations. In electronic recording and communication systems, 'white noise' frequently appears in the form of high frequencies, or hiss. The main advantages of digital systems are their relative freedom from such noise and their ability to recover and improve noise-affected signals.

Nolan Sidney Robert 1917–1992. Australian artist. Largely self-taught, he created atmospheric paintings of the outback, exploring themes from Australian history such as the life of the outlaw Ned Kelly. His work, along with that of ◊Drysdale and others, marked the beginning of modernism in Australian art.

Nolde Emil. Adopted name of Emil Hansen 1867–1956. German Expressionist painter and graphic artist. Nolde studied in Paris and Dachau, joined the group of artists known as *die* ◊*Brücke* 1906–07, and visited Polynesia 1913; he then became almost a recluse in NE Germany.

He painted biblical subjects marked by a barbaric intensity of colour, still lifes, and studies of the landscape of his native region on the German–Danish border. His work includes brilliant watercolours.

Nom Chinese-style characters used in writing the Vietnamese language. Nom characters were used from the 13th century for Vietnamese literature, but were replaced in the 19th century by a romanized script known as Quoc Ngu. The greatest Nom writer was the poet Nguyen Du.

nomad person whose way of life involves movement from place to place. Nomads fall into two main groups: herders (see ◊nomadic pastoralism and hunter-gatherers; peoples who move from place to place selling their skills or trading are also nomads; for example, the ◊Romany people.

Both hunter-gatherers and pastoralists are threatened by enclosure of land and by habitat degradation and destruction, as well as by the social and economic pressures of a money economy. Remaining examples of hunter-gatherers are the Australian Aborigines, many Amazon Indian peoples, and the Kung and San of the Kalahari Desert in S Africa.

nomadic pastoralism farming system where animals (cattle, goats, camels) are taken to different locations in order to find fresh pastures. It is practised in the developing world; out of an estimated 30–40 million (1990) nomadic pastoralists worldwide, most are in central Asia and the Sahel region of W Africa. Increasing numbers of cattle may lead to overgrazing of the area and ◊desertification.

The increasing enclosure of land has reduced the area available for nomadic pastoralism and, as a result, this system of farming is under threat. The movement of farmers in this way contrasts with sedentary agriculture, in which the farmer remains settled in one place. ▷ *See feature on pp. 308–309.*

nominalism in philosophy, the theory that objects of general terms (such as 'red' and 'dog') have nothing in common except the general term. Nominalists deny that the meaning of a general term is an independently accessible thing, concept, or ◊universal. Nominalists also deny that any particular thing has an independently real essence (all that makes a thing what it is and is indispensable to the thing).

Consequently, nominalism makes our classifications arbitrary. The opposite of nominalism is realism, and the dispute between these two theories has continued since at least the 11th century. Leading nominalists include William of Occam, Thomas Hobbes, Nelson Goodman, and W V O Quine.

Nomura Securities the world's largest financial institution, an investment house handling about 20% of all transactions on the Tokyo stock exchange. In 1991 Nomura admitted to paying Y16.5 billion in compensation to favoured clients (including companies in London and Hong Kong) for losses sustained on the stock market since the beginning of 1990, resulting in tax evasion of Y9 billion. It was also shown to have links with organized crime.

Nomura's profits were down by 54% in 1990. In Jan 1991, its average daily earnings in commission were Y405 million. A criminal investigation into Nomura for allegedly manipulating the share price of the Tokyu railway group on behalf of a retired *yakuza* (gangster syndicate) boss began in July 1991.

nonaligned movement countries adopting a strategic and political position of neutrality ('nonalignment') towards major powers, specifically the USA and former USSR. Although originally used by poorer states, the nonaligned position was later adopted by oil-producing nations. Its members hold more than half the world's population and 85% of

Nō Highly formalized theatre, Japanese Nō is performed on a raised, almost bare stage covered by a temple-style roof. The audience is seated on two sides of the stage and the masked actors, their movements slow and stylized, are supported by four musicians and a small chorus. *Japan National Tourist Organization*

'Probably the greatest concentration of talent and genius in this house except for perhaps those times when Thomas Jefferson ate alone.'

On a White House dinner for **Nobel prizewinners**
John Kennedy quoted in the *New York Times* 30 April 1962

oil resources, but only 7% of global GDP (1995). The origins of the movement can be traced back to the conference of Afro-Asian nations that was held in Bandung, Indonesia 1955.

With the end of the Cold War, the chief issues promoted by the movement have been international action against poverty, environmental destruction, nuclear testing, and drug-trafficking. The eleventh conference, held Oct 1995 at Cartagena, Columbia, was attended by delegates and heads of state from 113 developing countries, including the South African president Nelson ◊Mandela, the Cuban president Fidel ◊Castro, and the leader of the Palestine Liberation Organization (PLO) Yassir ◊Arafat.

Nonconformist in religion, originally a member of the Puritan section of the Church of England clergy who, in the Elizabethan age, refused to conform to certain practices, for example the wearing of the surplice and kneeling to receive Holy Communion.

After 1662 the term was confined to those who left the church rather than conform to the Act of Uniformity requiring the use of the Prayer Book in all churches. It is now applied mainly to members of the Free churches.

noncooperation movement or *satyagraha* in India, a large-scale civil disobedience campaign orchestrated by Mahatma ◊Gandhi 1920 following the ◊Amritsar Massacre April 1919. Based on a policy of peaceful non-cooperation, the strategy was to bring the British administrative machine to a halt by the total withdrawal of Indian support. The campaign made little impression on the British government. When it became violent, Gandhi called off further demonstrations. Its most successful aspect was that it increased political awareness among the Indian people.

Nonjuror any of the priests of the Church of England who, after the revolution of 1688, refused to take the oaths of allegiance to William and Mary. They continued to exist as a rival church for over a century, and consecrated their own bishops, the last of whom died 1805.

nonmetal one of a set of elements (around 20 in total) with certain physical and chemical properties opposite to those of metals. Nonmetals accept electrons (see ◊electronegativity) and are sometimes called electronegative elements.

Nono Luigi 1924–1990. Italian composer. He wrote attenuated pointillist works such as *Il canto sospeso/Suspended Song* 1955–56 for soloists, chorus, and orchestra, in which influences of Webern and Gabrieli are applied to issues of social conscience. After the opera *Intolleranza 1960/Intolerance 1960* his style became more richly expressionist, and his causes more overtly polemical.

nonrenewable resource natural resource, such as coal or oil, that takes thousands or millions of years to form naturally and can therefore not be replaced once it is consumed. The main energy sources used by humans are nonrenewable; ◊renewable resources, such as solar, tidal, and geothermal power, have so far been less exploited.

Nonrenewable resources have a high carbon content because their origin lies in the photosynthetic activity of plants millions of years ago. The fuels release this carbon back into the atmosphere as carbon dioxide. The rate at which such fuels are being burnt is thus resulting in rise in the concentration of carbon dioxide in the atmosphere. ▷ *See features on pp. 360–361 and pp. 858–859.*

‘Some odd transitory phenomenon of cross-breeding ... produced the only body of men who were all lords, and who in their collective action showed continually nothing but genius.’

On the **Normans**
Hilaire Belloc *Hills and the Sea*

nonsteroidal anti-inflammatory drug full name of ◊NSAID.

noradrenaline in the body, a ◊catecholamine that acts directly on specific receptors to stimulate the sympathetic nervous system. Released by nerve stimulation or by drugs, it slows the heart rate mainly by constricting arterioles (small arteries) and so raising blood pressure. It is used therapeutically to treat ◊shock.

Nordenskjöld Nils Adolf Erik 1832–1901. Swedish explorer. He made voyages to the Arctic with the geologist Torell and in 1878–79 discovered the Northeast Passage. He published the results of his voyages in a series of books, including *Voyage of the Vega round Asia and Europe* 1881.

Nordic ethnic designation for any of the various Germanic peoples, especially those of Scandinavia. The physical type of Caucasoid described under that term is tall, long-headed, blue-eyed, fair of skin and hair. The term is no longer in current scientific use.

Nord-Pas-de-Calais region of N France; area 12,400 sq km/4,786 sq mi; population (1990) 3,965,100. Its capital is Lille, and it consists of the *départements* of Nord and Pas-de-Calais.

Pas-de-Calais is the French term for the Straits of Dover, between the English Channel and the North Sea.

Nore, the sandbank at the mouth of the river Thames, England; site of the first lightship 1732.

Norfolk county of E England
area 5,360 sq km/2,069 sq mi (*see United Kingdom map*)
towns and cities Norwich (administrative headquarters), King's Lynn; resorts: Great Yarmouth, Cromer, Hunstanton
features low-lying with the Fens in the W and the ◊Norfolk Broads in the E; rivers: Ouse, Yare, Bure, Waveney; Halvergate Marshes wildlife area; traditional reed thatching; Grime's Graves (Neolithic flint mines); shrine of Our Lady of Walsingham, a medieval and present-day centre of pilgrimage; Blickling Hall (Jacobean); residence of Elizabeth II at Sandringham (built 1869–71)
products cereals, turnips, sugar beets, turkeys, geese; offshore natural gas; fishing centred on Great Yarmouth
population (1991) 745,600.

Norfolk Miles Francis Stapleton Fitzalan-Howard, 17th Duke of Norfolk 1915– . Earl marshal of England, and premier duke and earl; seated at Arundel Castle, Sussex, England. As earl marshal, he is responsible for the organization of ceremonial on major state occasions.

Norfolk Broads area of some 12 interlinked freshwater lakes in E England, created about 600 years ago by the digging-out of peat deposits; the lakes are used for boating and fishing. Chemical pollution has destroyed much of the wildlife.

Norfolk Island Pacific island territory of Australia, S of New Caledonia
area 40 sq km/15 sq mi
products citrus fruit, bananas; tourist industry
population (1991) 1,912
history reached by English explorer Capt Cook 1774; settled 1856 by descendants of the mutineers of the *Bounty* (see ◊Bligh) from ◊Pitcairn Island; Australian territory from 1914; largely self-governing from 1979.

Noriega Manuel (Antonio Morena) 1940– . Panamanian soldier and politician, effective ruler of Panama from 1983, as head of the National Guard, until deposed by the USA 1989. An informer for the US Central Intelligence Agency, he was known to be involved in drug trafficking as early as 1972. He enjoyed US support until 1987. In the 1989 US invasion of Panama, he was forcibly taken to the USA. He was tried and convicted of trafficking 1992.

norm informal guideline about what is, or is not, considered normal social behaviour (as opposed to rules and laws, which are formal guidelines). Such shared values and expectations may be measured by statistical sampling and vary from one society to another and from one situation to another; they range from crucial taboos, such as those against incest or cannibalism, to trivial customs and traditions, such as the correct way to hold a fork. Norms play a key part in social control and social order.

normal distribution curve the bell-shaped curve that results when a normal distribution is represented graphically by plotting the distribution $f(x)$ against x. The curve is symmetrical about the mean value.

Norman any of the descendants of the Norsemen (to whose chief, Rollo, Normandy was granted by Charles III of France 911) who adopted French language and culture. During the 11th and 12th centuries they conquered England 1066 (under William the Conqueror), Scotland 1072, parts of Wales and Ireland, S Italy, Sicily, and Malta, and took a prominent part in the Crusades.

They introduced feudalism, Latin as the language of government, and Norman French as the language of literature. Church architecture and organization were also influenced by the Normans, although they ceased to exist as a distinct people after the 13th century.

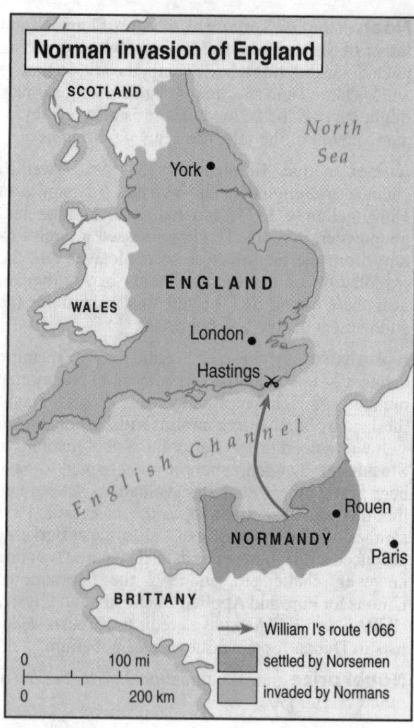

Norman Greg 1955– . Australian golfer, nicknamed ‘the Great White Shark’. After many wins in his home country, he enjoyed success on the European PGA Tour before joining the US Tour. He has won the World Match-Play title three times.

Norman Jessye 1945– . US soprano. She is acclaimed for majestically haunting interpretations of German opera and lieder (songs), notably Wagner, Mahler, and Richard Strauss, but is equally at home with Ravel and Chausson songs and gospel music.

Norman architecture English term for ◊Romanesque, the style of architecture used in England in the 11th and 12th centuries. Norman buildings are massive, with round arches (although trefoil arches are sometimes used for small

Norman architecture The nave of Durham cathedral, England. Dating from the 12th century, Durham cathedral is one of the finest examples of Norman architecture. This picture clearly shows two typical features of the Norman style, massive piers and round arches. *Corbis*

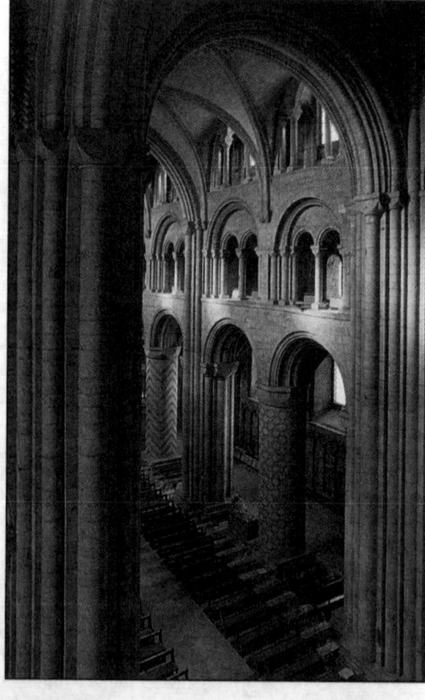

openings). Buttresses are of slight projection, and vaults are barrel-roofed. Examples in England include the Keep of the Tower of London and parts of the cathedrals of Chichester, Gloucester, and Ely.

Normandy former duchy of NW France now divided into two regions: ◊Haute-Normandie and ◊Basse-Normandie. Normandy was named after the Viking Norsemen (Normans), the people who conquered and settled in the area in the 9th century. As a French duchy it reached its peak under William the Conqueror and was renowned for its centres of learning established by Lanfranc and St Anselm. Normandy was united with England 1100–35. England and France fought over it during the Hundred Years' War, England finally losing it 1449 to Charles VII. In World War II the Normandy beaches were the site of the Allied invasion on D-day, 6 June 1944.

The main towns are Alençon, Bayeux, Caen, Cherbourg, Dieppe, Deauville, Lisieux, Le Havre, and Rouen. Features of Normandy include the painter Monet's restored home and garden at Giverny; Mont St Michel; Château Miromesnil, the birthplace of de Maupassant; Victor Hugo's house at Villequier; and ◊Calvados apple brandy.

Normandy landings alternative name for ◊D-day.

Norman French form of French used by the Normans in Normandy from the 10th century, and by the Norman ruling class in England after the Conquest 1066. It remained the language of the English court until the 15th century, the official language of the law courts until the 17th century, and is still used in the Channel Islands.

Norn in Scandinavian mythology, any of three goddesses of fate – the goddess of the past (Urd), the goddess of the present (Verdandi), and the goddess of the future (Skuld).

Norris Frank (Benjamin Franklin) 1870–1902. US novelist. A naturalist writer, he wrote *McTeague* 1899, about a brutish San Francisco dentist and the love of gold (filmed as *Greed* 1923). He completed only two parts of his projected trilogy, the *Epic of Wheat*: *The Octopus* 1901, dealing with the struggles between wheat farmers, and *The Pit* 1903, describing the Chicago wheat exchange.

Norsemen early inhabitants of Norway. The term Norsemen is also applied to Scandinavian ◊Vikings who during the 8th–11th centuries raided and settled in Britain, Ireland, France, Russia, Iceland, and Greenland.

North Frederick, 2nd Earl of Guilford, known as Lord North 1732–1792. British Tory politician. He entered Parliament in 1754, became chancellor of the Exchequer in 1767, and was prime minister in a government of Tories and 'king's friends' from 1770. His hard line against the American colonies was supported by George III, but in 1782 he was forced to resign by the failure of his policy. In 1783 he returned to office in a coalition with Charles ◊Fox. After its defeat, he retired from politics.

North Oliver 1943– . US Marine lieutenant colonel. In 1981 he joined the staff of the National Security Council (NSC), where he supervised the mining of Nicaraguan harbours 1983, an air-force bombing raid on Libya 1986, and an arms-for-hostages deal with Iran 1985, which, when uncovered 1986 (◊Irangate), forced his dismissal and trial.

After Irangate, North was convicted on felony charges of obstructing Congress, mutilating government documents, and taking an illegal gratuity. In Sept 1991, all charges against him were dropped on the grounds that, since his evidence before Congressional committees July 1987 had been widely televised, it was impossible to give him a fair trial. He was unsuccessful as Virginia's Republican candidate for the Senate in the 1994 midterm elections.

North Thomas c. 1535–c. 1601. English translator. His version of ◊Plutarch's *Lives* 1579 was the source for Shakespeare's Roman plays.

North Africa Campaign Allied military campaign 1940–42 during World War II. Shortly after Italy declared war on France and Britain June 1940, an Italian offensive was launched from Libya towards Egypt and the Suez Canal. In Dec 1940 Britain launched a successful counter-offensive and captured Cyrenaica. Following agreement between Mussolini and Hitler, the German Afrika korps was established under General Rommel. During 1941 and early 1942 the Axis powers advanced, recaptured Tobruk, and crossed the Egyptian border before halting at El Alamein. The British 8th Army under General Montgomery won a decisive Allied victory against Rommel's forces at El Alamein on 4 Nov 1942, followed by advances across Libya from Tunisia. British and US troops advanced from French NW Africa and the Allied armies in N Africa converged on Tunis. After a last-ditch defence, the Axis forces surrendered in May 1943.

Northallerton market town, administrative headquarters of North Yorkshire, England; industries include tanning, flour-milling, trailer-manufacturing, and light engineering; population (1991) 13,800.

North America third largest of the continents (including Greenland and Central America), and over twice the size of Europe

area 24,000,000 sq km/9,400,000 sq mi (*see map on following page*)

largest cities (population over 1 million) Mexico City, New York, Chicago, Toronto, Los Angeles, Montréal, Guadalajara, Monterrey, Philadelphia, Houston, Guatemala City, Vancouver, Detroit, San Diego, Dallas

features Lake Superior (the largest body of fresh water in the world); Grand Canyon on the Colorado River; Redwood National Park, California, has some of the world's tallest trees; San Andreas Fault, California; deserts: Death Valley, Mojave, Sonoran; rivers (over 1,600 km/1,000 mi) include Mississippi, Missouri, Mackenzie, Rio Grande, Yukon, Arkansas, Colorado, Saskatchewan-Bow, Columbia, Red, Peace, Snake

physical occupying the northern part of the landmass of the western hemisphere between the Arctic Ocean and the tropical southeast tip of the isthmus that joins Central America to South America; the northernmost point on the mainland is the tip of Boothia Peninsula in the Canadian Arctic; the northernmost point on adjacent islands is Cape Morris Jesup on Greenland; the most westerly point on the mainland is Cape Prince of Wales, Alaska; the most westerly point on adjacent islands is Attu Island in the Aleutians; the most easterly point on the mainland lies on the southeast coast of Labrador; the highest point is Mount McKinley, Alaska, 6,194 m/20,320 ft; the lowest point is Badwater in Death Valley −86 m/−282 ft.

Perhaps the most dominating characteristic is the western cordillera running parallel to the coast from Alaska to Panama; it is called the ◊Rocky Mountains in the USA and Canada and its continuation into Mexico is called the ◊Sierra Madre. The cordillera is a series of ranges divided by intermontane plateaus and takes up about one-third of the continental area.

To the east of the cordillera lie the Great Plains, the agricultural heartland of North America, which descend in a series of steps to the depressions occupied by the ◊Great Lakes in the east and the Gulf of Mexico coastal lowlands in the southeast. The Plains are characterized by treeless expanses crossed by broad, shallow river valleys. To the north and east of the region lie the Laurentian Highlands of Canada, an ancient plateau or shield area. Glaciation has deeply affected its landscape. In the east are the Appalachian Mountains, flanked by the narrow coastal plain which widens further south. Erosion here has created a line of planed crests, or terraces, at altitudes between 300–1,200 m/985–3,935 ft. This has also formed a ridge-and-valley topography which was an early barrier to continental penetration. The Fall Line is the abrupt junction of plateau and coastal plain in the east.

Low plains on the Atlantic coast are indented by the Gulf of St Lawrence, Bay of Fundy, Delaware Bay, and Chesapeake Bay; the St Lawrence and Great Lakes form a rough crescent (with Lake Winnipeg, Lake Athabasca, the Great Bear, and the Great Slave lakes) around the exposed rock of the great Canadian/Laurentian shield, into which Hudson Bay breaks from the north; Greenland (the largest island in the world next to Australia) is a high, ice-covered plateau with a deeply indented coastline of fjords.

North America has one of the longest rivers in the world (the Mississippi) and also a drainage system with one of the greatest water capacities (the St Lawrence–Great Lakes). The chief continental divide is the western cordillera and because rivers rising on the east slopes have a long way to go to the sea, it follows that the drainage basins of these large rivers (such as the Mackenzie) are enormous. Whilst the rivers flowing east are the largest, the rivers flowing west (the Colorado, Columbia, and the Frazer), cutting through the western cordillera, are the most spectacular. They are also an important source of hydroelectric power.

Lakes also abound, mainly as a result of glaciation. Arctic Canada is covered with the remains of an immense glacial lake (Lake Agassiz) and also the results of ice damming the drainage of water to the open sea, such as the Great Slave and Bear lakes. The ice sheet deepened the basins but the early lakes drained south into the Mississippi–Ohio system, and not until the final retreat of the ice did the lakes seek the lowest outlet east through the St Lawrence

climate with a N–S length of over 8,000 km/4,970 mi, North America has a wide range of climates, and resultant soil and vegetation zoning. About one-third of the continent has a dry climate, chiefly in the southwest, where the tropical continental air mass and the rainshadow effect of the western cordillera coincide. The Great Plains area can be classed as semi-arid. The larger rivers act as funnels for storms. The Arctic zone includes the Canadian Shield and Alaska and is dominated by polar air masses; only in June–Sept do temperatures rise above freezing. The cool temperate zone stretches south of this from Newfoundland to Alaska and is dominated by the polar continental air mass bringing long, severe winters. Spring and autumn frosts are hazardous to crops. The warm temperate zone covers the Mississippi lowlands and the SE USA and is dominated by the Gulf tropical air mass. Winters are mild and the frost-free season lasts over 200 days. The SW USA has a Mediterranean-type climate, with dry summers and mild winters.

products with abundant resources and an ever-expanding home market, the USA's fast-growing industrial and technological strength has made it less dependent on exports and a dominant economic power throughout the continent. Canada is the world's leading producer of nickel, zinc, uranium, potash, and linseed, and the world's second largest producer of asbestos, silver, titanium, gypsum, sulphur, and molybdenum; Mexico is the world's leading producer of silver and the fourth largest oil producer; the USA is the world's leading producer of salt and the second largest producer of oil and cotton; nearly 30% of the world's beef and veal is produced in North America

population (1990 est) 395 million, rising to an estimated 450 million by the year 2000; annual growth rate from 1980 to 1985: Canada 1.08%, USA 0.88%, Mexico 2.59%, Honduras 3.39%; the Native American, Inuit, and Aleut peoples are now a minority within a population predominantly of European immigrant origin. Many Africans were brought in as part of the slave trade

language English predominates in Canada, the USA, and Belize; Spanish is the chief language of the countries of Latin America and a sizeable minority in the USA; French is spoken by about 25% of the population of Canada, and by people of the French *département* of St Pierre and Miquelon; indigenous non-European minorities, including the Inuit of Arctic Canada, the Aleuts of Alaska, North American Indians, and the Maya of Central America, have their own languages and dialects

religion Christian and Jewish religions predominate; 97% of Latin Americans, 47% of Canadians, and 21% of those living in the USA are Roman Catholic.

North American Free Trade Agreement (NAFTA) trade agreement between the USA, Canada, and Mexico, agreed in Aug 1992 and effective from Jan 1994. The first trade pact of its kind to link two highly-industrialized countries to a developing one, it created a free market of 375 million people, with a total GDP of $6.8 trillion (equivalent to 30% of the world's GDP). Tariffs were to be progressively eliminated over a 10–15 year period and investment into low-wage Mexico by Canada and the USA progressively increased. Chile was invited to join in Dec 1994.

The origins of NAFTA lay in a bilateral Free Trade Agreement (FTA) between the USA and Canada, effective from 1989. In May 1997, at a meeting of 34 of the hemisphere's political leaders (only Cuba was absent) in Belo Horizonte, Brazil, it was agreed to negotiate a Free Trade Area of the Americas (FTAA) by 2005.

‘The traveller who desires to tell his experience of North America must write of people rather than of things.’

On North America
Anthony Trollope
North America

North and Central America

Northampton administrative centre of Northamptonshire, England, on the river Nene; population (1991) 180,600. Boots and shoes (of which there is a museum) are still made, but engineering has superseded them as the chief industry; other industries include food processing, brewing, the manufacture of shoe machinery, cosmetics, leather goods, and motor car accessories. It was designated a new town 1968.

Northamptonshire county of central England
area 2,370 sq km/915 sq mi (*see United Kingdom map*)
towns and cities Northampton (administrative headquarters), Kettering
features rivers Welland and Nene; Canons Ashby, Tudor house, home of the Drydens for 400 years; churches with broached spires
industries cereals, cattle, sugar beet, shoemaking, food processing, printing, engineering
population (1991) 578,800
famous people Richard III, Robert Browne, John Dryden.
history The site of the victory of Oliver Cromwell at the Battle of Naseby 1645.

North Atlantic Drift warm ◊ocean current in the N Atlantic Ocean; an extension of the ◊Gulf Stream. It flows east across the Atlantic and has a mellowing effect on the climate of NW Europe, particularly the British Isles and Scandinavia.

North Atlantic Treaty agreement signed 4 April 1949 by Belgium, Canada, Denmark, France, Iceland, Italy, Luxembourg, the Netherlands, Norway, Portugal, the UK, the USA; Greece, Turkey 1952; West Germany 1955; and Spain 1982. They agreed that 'an armed attack against one or more of them in Europe or North America shall be considered an attack against them all'. The North Atlantic Treaty Organization (NATO) is based on this agreement.

North Atlantic Treaty Organization (NATO) association set up in April 1949 in response to the Soviet blockade of Berlin, to provide for the collective defence of the major W European and North American states against the perceived threat from the USSR. The collapse of communism in eastern Europe from 1989 prompted the most radical review of its policy and defence strategy since its inception. After the E European ◊Warsaw Pact was disbanded in 1991, an adjunct to NATO, the ***North Atlantic Cooperation Council*** (NACC), was established, including all the former Soviet republics, with the aim of building greater security in Europe. In 1992 it was agreed that the ◊Conference on Security and Cooperation in Europe would in future authorize all NATO's military responses within Europe.

At the 1994 Brussels summit a 'partnership for peace' (PFP) programme was formally launched, inviting former members of the Warsaw Pact and ex-Soviet republics to take part in a wide range of military cooperation arrangements, including training alongside NATO members and opening up defence plans. Romania was the first to join, followed by Estonia, Lithuania, and Poland; Russia agreed to participate in 1995. By 1996 the partnership included 27 countries, comprising the 15 former Soviet republics, Austria, Hungary, the Slovak Republic, Bulgaria, Malta, Albania, the Czech Republic, the Former Yugoslav Republic of Macedonia, Finland, and Sweden.

In May 1997, a NATO–Russia security pact, called the Founding Act on Mutual Relations, Cooperation and Security, was signed in Paris by all 16 NATO heads of government and Russian President Yeltsin. The charter gave Russia an assurance that NATO had no intention of siting nuclear weapons or allowing major troop deployments on the territories of new eastern European member-states.

NATO's chief body is the Council of Foreign Ministers (who have representatives in permanent session), and there is an international secretariat in Brussels, Belgium, and also the Military Committee consisting of the Chiefs of Staff. The military headquarters SHAPE (Supreme Headquarters Allied Powers, Europe) is in Chièvres, near Mons, Belgium. In Dec 1995, Spain's former foreign minister, Javier Solana, became NATO's secretary-general designate, replacing Willy Claes, who resigned to face trial in Belgium on corruption charges.

Both the Supreme Allied Commanders (Europe and Atlantic) are from the USA, but there is also an Allied Commander, Channel (a British admiral). In 1960 a permanent multinational ***Allied Mobile Force*** (AMF) was established with headquarters in Heidelberg, Germany, to move immediately to any NATO country under threat of attack. France withdrew from the military integration (not the alliance) in 1966, but rejoined the decision-making military committee (remaining outside the integrated structure) in 1995; Greece withdrew politically but not militarily in 1974. In 1980 Turkey was opposed to Greek re-entry because of differences over rights in the Aegean Sea. NATO has encountered numerous problems since its inception over such issues as the dominant position of the USA, the presence in Europe of US nuclear weapons, burden sharing, and standardization of weapons. It engaged in its first major combat action in Aug–Sept 1995 in Bosnia-Herzegovina.

In May 1991 a meeting of NATO defence ministers endorsed the creation of a UK-commanded, 100,000-strong 'rapid-reaction corps' as the core of a new, streamlined military structure, based on mobile, multinational units adaptable to post-Cold War contingencies. The new force was to be used solely inside NATO territory, unless otherwise agreed by all members of the alliance. In Dec 1995 a 60,000-strong, NATO-led 'International Implementation Force' was sent to Bosnia-Herzegovina to police the Dayton peace settlement. The USA supplied one-third of the troops for the mission, termed 'Joint Endeavour'.

In March 1999 NATO launched air strikes against Serbia in response to repression by Serbia of ethnic Albanians in Kosovo.

The UK's annual contribution to NATO is around £160 million.

North Ayrshire local authority of Scotland created 1996 (*see United Kingdom map*).

North Brabant (Dutch ***Noord Brabant***) southern province of the Netherlands, lying between the Maas River (Meuse) and Belgium
area 4,940 sq km/1,907 sq mi
capital 's-Hertogenbosch
towns and cities Breda, Eindhoven, Tilburg
population (1995 est) 2,276,200
physical former heathland is now under mixed farming
industries brewing, engineering, microelectronics, textile manufacture.

North Carolina

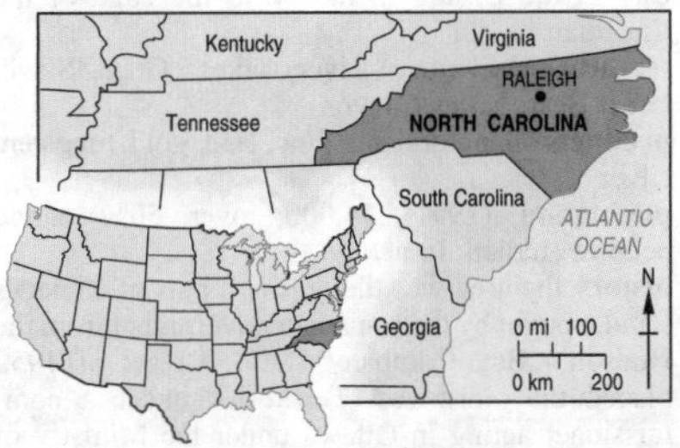

North Cape (Norwegian ***Nordkapp***) cape in the Norwegian county of Finnmark; the most northerly point of Europe.

North Carolina state in E USA; nicknamed Tar Heel State/Old North State
area 136,400 sq km/52,650 sq mi
capital Raleigh
towns and cities Charlotte, Greensboro, Winston-Salem
features Great Smoky Mountain national park; Blue Ridge Mountains, with Blowing Rock (1,200 m/4,000 ft); Cape Hatteras national seashore, with marshland and sandy beaches (Cape Hatteras Lighthouse, 63 m/208 ft, is the tallest in the USA); the Wright Brothers national memorial, Kill Devil Hills, the site of Wilbur and Orville Wrights' first powered flight from the sand dunes at Kitty Hawk; University of North Carolina (the Chapel Hill campus, founded 1795, was the first state university in the USA);
industries tobacco, corn, soya beans, livestock, poultry, textiles, clothing, cigarettes, furniture, chemicals, machinery
population (1991) 6,737,000
famous people Billy Graham, O Henry, Jesse Jackson, Thomas Wolfe
history after England's Roanoke Island colony was unsuccessful 1585 and 1587, permanent settlement was made 1663; it was one of the original 13 states 1789.

Northcliffe Alfred Charles William Harmsworth, 1st Viscount Northcliffe 1865–1922. British newspaper proprietor, born in Dublin. Founding the *Daily Mail* 1896, he revolutionized popular journalism, and with the *Daily Mirror* 1903 originated the picture paper. In 1908 he also obtained control of *The Times*.

North Dakota state in N USA; nicknamed Flickertail State/Sioux State
area 183,100 sq km/70,677 sq mi
capital Bismarck
towns and cities Fargo, Grand Forks, Minot
features Red River Valley; Missouri River; the Badlands, so called because the pioneers had great difficulty in crossing them, with Theodore Roosevelt national park, and Painted Canyon; Lake Sakakawea; Devils Lake, breeding ground for migratory waterfowl; Pembina Gorge; Garrison Dam power plant on the Missouri River; the geographical centre of North America at Rugby; Knife River Native American villages national historic site; frontier forts, including Fort Buford (1866), where the Sioux leader Sitting Bull was imprisoned, and Fort Abercrombie; Fort Abraham Lincoln state park, including Custer House; Bismarck, with art deco state capitol, and the Victorian former Governor's Mansion; International Peace Garden, on Canadian border; 90% of the land is cultivated.
industries cereals, meat products, farm equipment
population (1991) 635,000
famous people Maxwell Anderson, Louis L'Amour
history explored by La Verendrye's French Canadian expedition 1738–40; acquired by the USA partly in the Louisiana Purchase 1803 and partly by treaty with Britain 1813. The earliest settlement was Pembina 1812, by Scottish and Irish families, and North Dakota became a state 1889, attracting many German and Norwegian settlers.

North Dakota

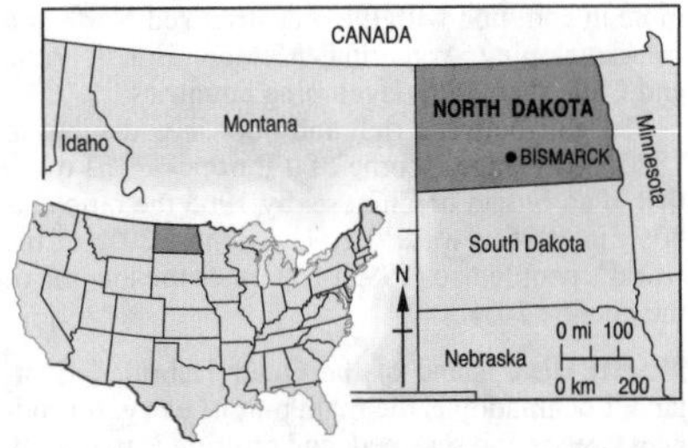

North-East India area of India (Meghalaya, Assam, Mizoram, Tripura, Manipur, Nagaland, and Arunachal Pradesh) linked with the rest of India only by a narrow corridor. There is opposition to immigration from Bangladesh and the rest of India, and demand for secession.

North East Lincolnshire unitary authority of England created 1996 (*see United Kingdom map*).

Northeast Passage sea route from the N Atlantic, around Asia, to the N Pacific, pioneered by Swedish explorer Nils ◊Nordenskjöld 1878–79 and developed by the USSR in settling N Siberia from 1935. Russia owns offshore islands and claims it as an internal waterway; the USA claims that it is international.

Northern Cape province of the Republic of South Africa from 1994, formerly part of Cape Province, including the former independent homeland of Venda
area 363,389 sq km/140,305 sq mi
capital Kimberley
features largest and most sparsely populated province
industries diamonds, iron, manganese, asbestos, cotton
population (1995 est) 742,000
languages Afrikaans 65%, Setswana (Tswana) 22%, Xhosa 4%.

Northern Ireland see ◊Ireland, Northern.

Northern Ireland Office (NIO) UK government department established 1972. It is responsible for direct government of Northern Ireland, including administration of security, law and order, and economic, industrial, and social policies.

northern lights common name for the ◊aurora borealis.

Northern Mariana Islands archipelago in the NW Pacific, with ◊Guam known collectively as the Mariana Islands. The Northern Marianas are a commonwealth in union with the USA.
area 471 sq km/182 sq mi
capital Garapan on Saipan
physical 16 islands and atolls extending 560 km/350 mi N of Guam
political system liberal democracy
political parties Democratic Party, centre-left; Republican Party, right of centre; Territorial Party, nationalist
currency US dollar
population (1995 est) 47,200
language English
religion mainly Roman Catholicism
history came under Spanish control 1565; sold to Germany 1899; came under Japanese control 1914 and Japanese rule under a League of Nations mandate 1921. Taken by US marines in World War II, the islands became a UN Trust Territory administered by the USA 1947 and a US commonwealth territory 1978. Granted internal self-government and full US citizenship 1986. UN Trusteeship status ended 22 Dec 1990.

Northern Province (formerly ***Northern Transvaal***) province of the Republic of South Africa from 1994, formerly part of Transvaal
area 119,606 sq km/46,180 sq mi
capital Pietersburg
industries copper, asbestos, iron, diamonds, wheat, maize, tobacco, groundnuts, tourism. Most men in rural areas are migrant workers in Gauteng province
population (1995 est) 5,397,200
languages Sepedi (North Sotho) 56%, Shangaan 22%, Venda 12%

Northern Rhodesia former name (to 1964) of ◊Zambia, a country in Africa.

Northern Territory territory of Australia
area 1,346,200 sq km/519,633 sq mi
capital Darwin (chief port)
towns and cities Alice Springs
features mainly within the tropics, although with wide range of temperature; very low rainfall, but artesian bores are used; Macdonnell Ranges (Mount Zeil 1,510 m/4,956 ft); ◊Cocos and ◊Christmas Islands included in the territory 1984; 50,000–60,000-year-old rock paintings of animals, birds, and fish in Kakadu National Park
industries beef cattle, prawns, bauxite (Gove), gold and copper (Tennant Creek), uranium (Ranger)
population (1993) 169,300
government there is an administrator and a legislative assembly, and the territory is also represented in the federal parliament
history originally part of New South Wales, it was annexed 1863 to South Australia but from 1911 until 1978 (when self-government was introduced) was under the control of the Commonwealth of Australia government. Mineral discoveries on land occupied by Aborigines led to a royalty agreement 1979. *See illustrations on following page.*

Northern Territory

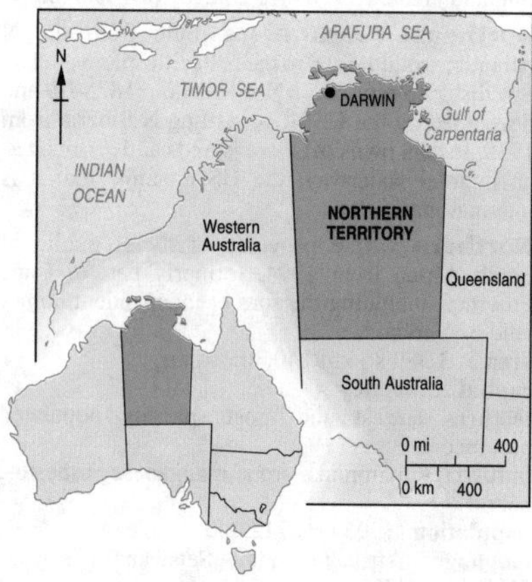

Northern Transvaal former name of ◊Northern Province, a province of the Republic of South Africa.

North Holland (Dutch *Noord Holland*) low-lying coastal province of the Netherlands occupying the peninsula jutting northward between the North Sea and the IJsselmeer
area 2,670 sq km/1,031 sq mi
population (1995 est) 2,463,600
capital Haarlem
towns and cities Amsterdam, Hilversum, Den Helder, the cheese centres Alkmaar and Edam
physical most of the province is below sea level, protected from the sea by a series of sand dunes and artificial dykes
products flower bulbs, grain, and vegetables
history once part of the former county of Holland that was divided into two provinces (North and South) 1840.

North Island smaller of the two main islands of ◊New Zealand.

North Korea see ◊Korea, North.

North Lanarkshire local authority of Scotland created 1996 (*see United Kingdom map*).

North Lincolnshire unitary authority of England created 1996 (*see United Kingdom map*).

North Pole the northern point where an imaginary line penetrates the Earth's surface by the axis about which it revolves; see also ◊pole and ◊Arctic.

North Rhine–Westphalia (German *Nordrhein-Westfalen*) administrative *Land* of Germany
area 34,100 sq km/13,163 sq mi
capital Düsseldorf
towns and cities Cologne, Essen, Dortmund, Duisburg, Bochum, Wuppertal, Bielefeld, Bonn, Gelsenkirchen, Münster, Mönchengladbach
features valley of the Rhine; Ruhr industrial district
industries iron, steel, coal, lignite, electrical goods, fertilizers, synthetic textiles
population (1994 est) 17,759,000
religion 53% Roman Catholic, 42% Protestant
history see ◊Westphalia.

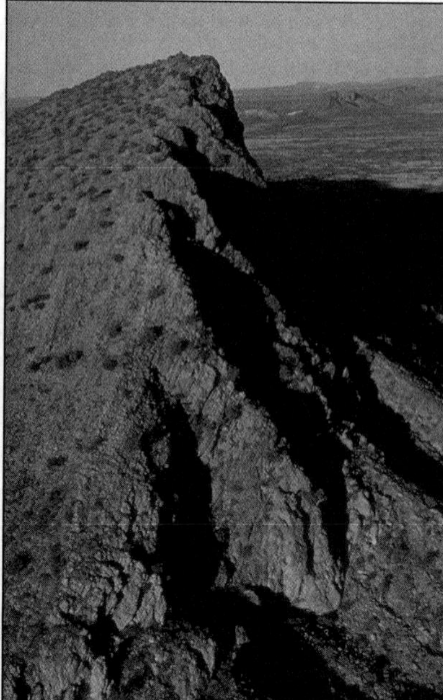

Northern Territory Most of the Northern Territory in Australia occupies a large plateau. It includes Arnhem Land in the N and the Macdonnell Ranges in the S, and contains Australia's largest Aborigine population with 20,000 people (about 30% of the total) living on 15 reservations. *Australian Overseas Information Service*

Northrop John Howard 1891–1987. US chemist. In the 1930s he crystallized a number of enzymes, including pepsin and trypsin, showing conclusively that they were proteins. He shared the 1946 Nobel Prize for Chemistry with Wendell Stanley (1904–1971) and James Sumner (1887–1955).

North Sea sea to the E of Britain and bounded by the coasts of Belgium, the Netherlands, Germany, Denmark, and Norway; part of the Atlantic Ocean; area 523,000 sq km/202,000 sq mi; average depth 55 m/180 ft, greatest depth 660 m/2,165 ft. In the NE it joins the Norwegian Sea, and in the S it meets the Strait of Dover. It has 300 oil platforms, 10,000 km of gas pipeline (gas was discovered 1965), and fisheries (especially mackerel and herring).

In 1995 there were 164 million people living around the North Sea, with a further 50 million visiting each year. There are 400,000 sailings resulting in 150 accidents annually.

In 1987, Britain dumped more than 4,700 tonnes of sewage sludge into the North Sea; Britain agreed 1994 to stop the dumping of sludge by 1998 (5% of sewage released is untreated). Britain is also responsible for the highest input of radioactive isotopes, atmospheric nitrogen, and hydrocarbons. In 1991 the North Sea received more than 2 million tonnes of liquid chemical waste. The effects of pollution are most noted along the east coast of the North Sea. The North Sea is heavily polluted with oil and toxic metals (such as cadmium) and chemicals (such as tributyl tin and polychlorinated biphenyl). Overfishing is a growing problem, and many remaining fish are deformed or diseased.

North Somerset unitary authority of England created 1996 (*see United Kingdom map*).

North–South divide geographical division of the world that theoretically demarcates the rich from the poor. The South includes all of Asia except Japan, Australia, New Zealand, Brunei, and the South East Asian 'dragons' of Hong Kong, South Korea, Malaysia, Singapore, Taiwan, and Thailand; all of Africa; the Middle East, except the oil-rich UAE, Qatar, Saudi Arabia, and Bahrain; and Central and South America. The North includes Europe; the USA, except Bermuda and the Bahamas; Canada; and the European republics of the former Soviet Union. Newly industrialized countries such as South Korea and Taiwan now have more in common with the industrialized North and fast-developing Argentina, Mexico, Brazil, Peru, and Chile than with developing countries.

The gulf between rich and poor is widening: in 1880 the average income of a European was twice that of an Indian or Chinese; by 1965 the ratio was 40:1; in 1995 it was 70:1. The richest 20% of the world's people had (1992) 150 times the income of the poorest 20%.

North Uist island of the Outer Hebrides, Scotland. Lochmaddy is the main port of entry. It produces tweeds and seaweed, and crofting is practised.

Northumberland county of N England
area 5,030 sq km/1,942 sq mi (*see United Kingdom map*)
towns and cities Morpeth (administrative headquarters), Berwick-upon-Tweed, Hexham
features Cheviot Hills; rivers: Tweed, upper Tyne; Northumberland National Park in the west; Holy Island; the Farne island group; part of Hadrian's Wall and Housestead's Fort; Alnwick and Bamburgh castles; Thomas ◊Bewick museum; large moorland areas are used for military manoeuvres; Longstone Lighthouse from which Grace Darling rowed to the rescue is no longer inhabited, the crew having been replaced by an automatic light; wild white cattle of Chillingham; Kielder Water (1982), the largest artificial lake in N Europe
industries sheep, fishing
population (1991) 304,700
famous people Thomas Bewick, Grace Darling, Jack and Bobby Charlton.

Northumberland John Dudley, Duke of Northumberland c. 1502–1553. English politician, son of the privy councillor Edmund Dudley (beheaded 1510), and chief minister until Edward VI's death 1553. He tried to place his daughter-in-law Lady Jane ◊Grey on the throne, and was executed on Mary I's accession.

Northumbria Anglo-Saxon kingdom that covered NE England and SE Scotland, comprising the 6th-century kingdoms of Bernicia (Forth–Tees) and Deira (Tees–Humber), united in the 7th century. It accepted the supremacy of Wessex 827 and was conquered by the Danes in the late 9th century.

Influenced by Irish missionaries, it was a cultural and religious centre until the 8th century with priests such as Bede, Cuthbert, and Wilfrid.

North West province of the Republic of South Africa from 1994
area 118,710 sq km/45,834 sq mi
capital Mmabatho
features includes part of the former independent homeland of Bophuthatswana
industries platinum, chrome, iron, groundnuts
population (1995 est) 3,351,800
languages Setswana (Tswana) 63%, Xhosa 14%, Sesotho (Sotho) 8%

North-West Frontier Province province of Pakistan; capital Peshawar; area 74,500 sq km/28,757 sq mi; population (1985) 12,287,000. It was a province of British India 1901–47. It includes the strategic Khyber Pass, the site of constant struggle between the British Raj and the ◊Pathan warriors. In the 1980s it had to accommodate a stream of refugees from neighbouring Afghanistan.

Northwest Ordinances US Congressional legislation 1784–87 setting out procedures for the sale and settlement of lands still occupied by American Indians. The land, between the Great Lakes and the Mississippi and Ohio rivers, was to be formed into townships and sold at minimum $1 per acre. The sales revenue was the first significant source of income for the new federal government.

The 1787 Ordinance guaranteed freedom of religion for settlers, prohibited slavery in the new territory, and outlined procedures for the organization into states for eventual admission to the Union.

Northwest Passage Atlantic–Pacific sea route around the north of Canada. Canada, which owns offshore islands, claims it as an internal waterway; the USA insists that it is an international waterway and sent an icebreaker through without permission 1985.

Early explorers included Englishmen Martin ◊Frobisher and, later, John Franklin, whose failure to return 1847 led to the organization of 39 expeditions in the next ten years. John Ross reached Lancaster Sound 1818 but mistook a bank of cloud for a range of mountains and turned back. R McClune explored the passage 1850–53 although he did not cover the whole route by sea. The polar explorer Roald ◊Amundsen was the first European to sail through 1903–06.

Northwest rebellion revolt against the Canadian government March–May 1885 by the métis (people of mixed French Canadian and Native American descent). Led by their political leader Louis ◊Riel and his military lieutenant Gabriel Dumont (1838–1906), the métis population of what is now Saskatchewan rebelled after a number of economic and political grievances were ignored by the government.

Fearing a full-scale Indian uprising, troops were quickly despatched west along the newly completed transcontinental railway and the rebellion was suppressed. Riel was tried and hanged Nov 1885.

Northwest Territories territory of Canada
area 3,426,300 sq km/1,322,552 sq mi
capital Yellowknife
physical extends into the Arctic Circle, to Hudson's Bay in the E, and in the W to the edge of the Canadian Shield
features Mackenzie River; lakes: Great Slave, Great Bear; Miles Canyon
products oil, natural gas, zinc, lead, gold, tungsten, silver
population (1991) 54,000; over 50% native peoples (Indian, Inuit)
history the area was the northern part of Rupert's Land, bought by the Canadian government from the Hudson's Bay Company 1869. An act of 1952 placed the Northwest Territories under a commissioner acting in Ottawa under the Ministry of

Northwest Territories

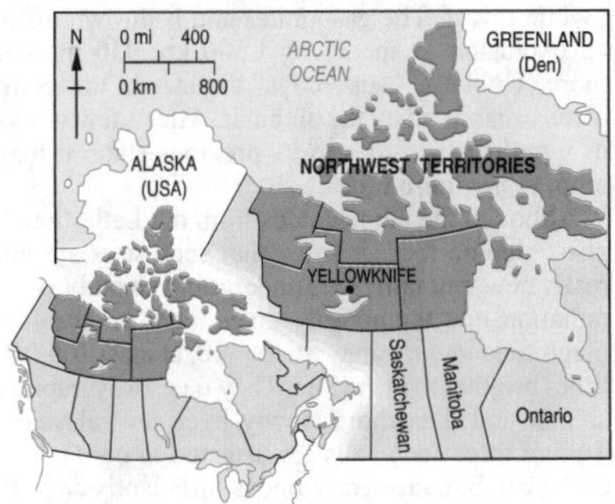

Northern Affairs and Natural Resources. In 1990 territorial control of over 350,000 sq km/135,000 sq mi of the Northwest Territories was given to the ◊Inuit, and in 1992 the creation of an Inuit autonomous homeland, Nunavut, was agreed in a regional referendum.

North Yorkshire county of NE England, created 1974 from most of the North Riding and parts of East and West Ridings of Yorkshire
area 8,320 sq km/3,212 sq mi
towns and cities Northallerton (administrative headquarters); resorts: Harrogate, Scarborough, Whitby
features England's largest county; including part of the Pennines, the Vale of York, and the Cleveland Hills and North Yorkshire Moors, which form a national park (within which is Fylingdales radar station to give early warning – 4 minutes – of nuclear attack); Rievaulx Abbey; Yorkshire Dales National Park (including Swaledale, Wensleydale, and Bolton Abbey in Wharfedale); rivers: Derwent, Ouse; Fountains Abbey near Ripon, with Studley Royal Gardens; Castle Howard, designed by Vanbrugh, has Britain's largest collection of 18th–20th-century costume; largest accessible cavern in Britain, the Battlefield Chamber, Ingleton
industries cereals, wool and meat from sheep, dairy products, coal, electrical goods, footwear, clothing, vehicles, plastics, foodstuffs
famous people Alcuin, Guy Fawkes, W H Auden.

Norway country in NW Europe, on the Scandinavian peninsula, bounded E by Sweden, NE by Finland and Russia, S by the North Sea, W by the Atlantic Ocean, and N by the Arctic Ocean. *See country box below.*

Norwegian people of Norwegian culture. There are 4–4.5 million speakers of Norwegian (including some in the USA), a Germanic language belonging to the Indo-European family. The seafaring culture of the Norwegians can be traced back to the Viking age from about AD 800–1050, when people of Norwegian descent settled Iceland and Greenland, and voyaged to Vinland (coast of Newfoundland).

The Norwegians have a long tradition of woodworking going back to the Vikings and are known for their stave (timber) churches.

Norwich cathedral city in Norfolk, E England, on the river Wensum; administrative headquarters of Norfolk; population (1991) 120,900. Industries include financial services, shoes, clothing, chemicals, confectionery, engineering, printing, and insurance. It has a Norman castle, a 15th-century Guildhall, 32 medieval churches, Tudor houses, and a Georgian Assembly House. Its City Hall dates from 1938; the Castle Mall Shopping Centre was completed 1993. It is the largest medieval walled city in England.

The cathedral was founded 1096. The castle has a collection of paintings by the Norwich School (John Sell ◊Cotman and John ◊Crome). The University of East Anglia (1963), designed by Denys Lasdun, has the Sainsbury Centre for Visual Arts (Norman Foster) on its campus. The Sainsbury Laboratory (1987), in association with the John Innes Institute, was founded here to study the molecular causes of disease. Norwich became an important textile centre at the end of the 16th century, after the arrival of Dutch weavers.

Norwich School English regional school of landscape painters, inspired by the 17th-century Dutch realist tradition of landscape painting,

NORWAY
Kingdom of

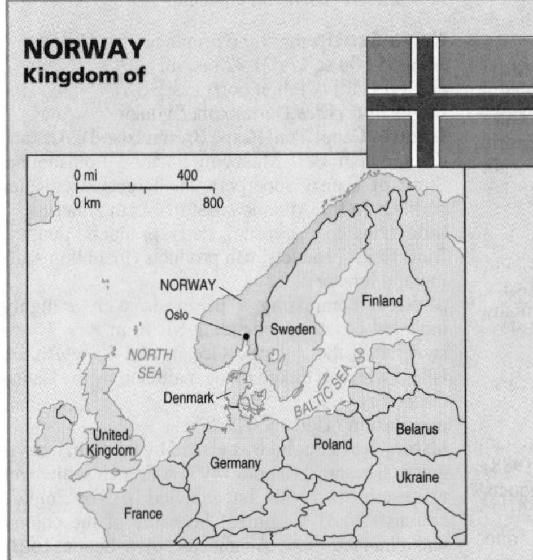

national name *Kongeriket Norge*
area 387,000 sq km/149,421 sq mi (includes Svalbard and Jan Mayen)
capital Oslo
major towns/cities Bergen, Trondheim, Stavanger
physical features mountainous with fertile valleys and deeply indented coast; forests cover 25%; extends N of Arctic Circle
territories dependencies in the Arctic (Svalbard and Jan Mayen) and in Antarctica (Bouvet and Peter I Island, and Queen Maud Land)
head of state Harald V from 1991
head of government Kjell Magne Bondevik from 1997
political system constitutional monarchy
administrative divisions 19 counties
political parties Norwegian Labour Party (DNA), moderate left of centre; Conservative Party, progressive, right of centre; Christian People's Party (KrF), Christian, centre-left; Centre Party (Sp), left of centre, rural-oriented; Progress Party (FrP), right-wing, populist
armed forces 33,500 (1994); Home Guard 79,000 (1995); fast mobilization reserve 282,000 (1995)
conscription 12 months, with 4–5 refresher training periods
defence spend (% GDP) 3.1 (1994)
education spend (% GNP) 8.4 (1992)
health spend (% GDP) 7.6 (1993)
death penalty abolished 1979
population 4,337,000 (1995 est)
population growth rate 0.5% (1990–95); 0.3% (2000–05)
age distribution (% of total population) <15 19.5%, 15–65 64.7%, >65 15.9% (1995)
ethnic distribution majority of Nordic descent; Lapp minority in the far N
population density (per sq km) 13 (1994)
urban population (% of total) 73 (1995)
labour force 50% of population: 6% agriculture, 25% industry, 68% services (1990)
unemployment 4.9% (1995)
child mortality rate (under 5, per 1,000 live births) 8 (1993)
life expectancy 74 (men), 81 (women)
education (compulsory years) 9
literacy rate 99%
languages Norwegian (official); there are Saami- (Lapp) and Finnish-speaking minorities
religion Evangelical Lutheran (endowed by state)
TV sets (per 1,000 people) 424 (1992)
currency Norwegian krone
GDP (US $) 146.6 billion (1995)
GDP per capita (PPP) (US $) 23,202 (1995)
growth rate 3.7% (1994/95)
average annual inflation 1.4% (1994); 3.0% (1984–94)
major trading partners EU (principally UK and Germany), Sweden, USA, Japan
resources petroleum, natural gas, iron ore, iron pyrites, copper, lead, zinc, forests
industries mining, fishery, food processing, non-electric machinery, metals and metal products, paper products, printing and publishing, shipbuilding, chemicals
exports petroleum, natural gas, fish products, non-ferrous metals, wood pulp and paper. Principal market: UK 25% (1993)
imports machinery and transport equipment, chemicals, clothing, fuels and lubricants, iron and steel, office machines and computers, telecommunications and sound apparatus and equipment. Principal source: Sweden 20% (1993)
arable land 2.7% (1993)
agricultural products wheat, barley, oats, potatoes, fruit; fishing industry, including fish farming

HISTORY
5th C First small kingdoms established by the Goths.
c. 900 Harald Fairhair created a united Norwegian kingdom; it dissolved after his death.
8th–11th Cs Vikings from Norway raided and settled in many parts of Europe.
c. 1016–28 Olav II (St Olav) reunited the kingdom and introduced Christianity.
1217–63 Haakon VI established royal authority over nobles and church and made the monarchy hereditary.
1263 Iceland submitted to authority of king of Norway.
1397 Union of Kalmar: Norway, Denmark, and Sweden united under a single monarch.
15th C Norway, the weakest of the three kingdoms, was increasingly treated as an appendage of Denmark.
1523 Secession of Sweden further undermined Norway's status.
16th C Introduction of sawmill precipitated development of timber industry and growth of export trade.
1661 Denmark restored formal equality of status to Norway as a twin kingdom.
18th C Norwegian merchants profited from foreign wars which increased demand for naval supplies.
1814 Treaty of Kiel: Denmark ceded Norway (minus Iceland) to Sweden; Norway retained its own parliament but cabinet appointed by king of Sweden.
19th C Economic decline followed slump in timber trade due to Canadian competition; expansion of merchant navy and whaling industry.
1837 Democratic local government introduced.
1884 Achieved internal self-government when king of Sweden made Norwegian cabinet accountable to Norwegian parliament.
1895 Start of constitutional dispute over control of foreign policy: Norway's demand for a separate consular service refused by Sweden.
1905 Union with Sweden dissolved; Norway achieved independence under King Haakon VII.
1907 Norway became first European country to grant women the right to vote in parliamentary elections.
early 20th C Development of industry based on hydro-electric power; long period of Liberal government committed to neutrality and moderate social reform.
1935 First Labour government took office.
1940–45 German occupation with Vidkun Quisling as puppet leader.
1945–65 Labour governments introduced economic planning and permanent price controls.
1949 Became a founding member of North Atlantic Treaty Organization (NATO).
1952 Joined Nordic Council.
1957 Olaf V succeeded his father King Haakon VII.
1960 Joined European Free Trade Association (EFTA).
1972 National referendum rejected membership of European Economic Community (EEC).
1975 Export of North Sea oil began.
1981 Gro Harlem Brundtland (Labour) became Norway's first woman prime minister.
1982 Kare Willoch formed first Conservative government since 1928.
1986 Falling oil prices caused recession; Labour re-elected under Brundtland.
1991 Olaf V succeeded by his son Harald V.
1994 National referendum rejected membership of European Union (formerly EC).
1996 Brundtland resigned; succeeded by Thorbjoern Jagland.
1997 Jagland failed to win decisive majority in general election. Kjell Magne Bondevik became prime minister.

SEE ALSO Denmark; Sweden; Viking

nose The structure of the nose. The organs of smell are confined to a small area in the roof of the nasal cavity. The olfactory cells are stimulated when certain molecules reach them. Smell is one of our most subtle senses: tens of thousands of smells can be distinguished. By comparison, taste, although closely related to smell, is a crude sensation. All the subtleties of taste depend upon smell.

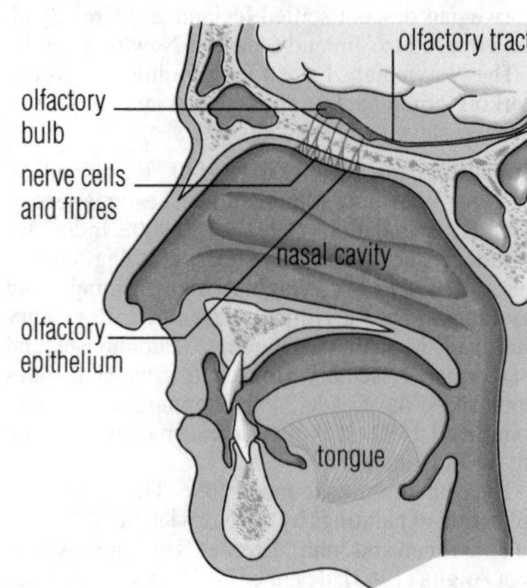

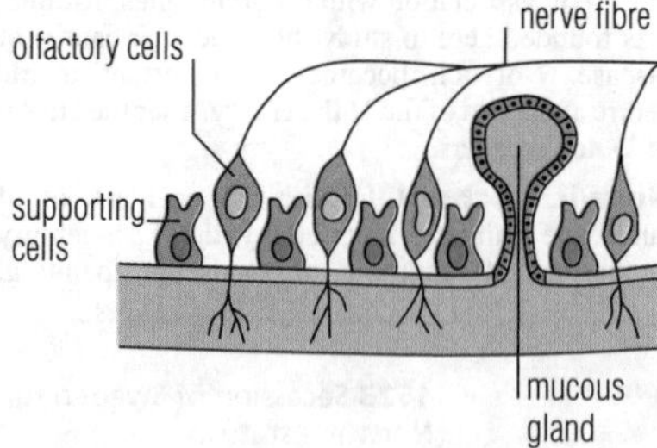

notably the work of ◊Ruisdael. Founded 1803, the school was made up of both professional and amateur artists and flourished until the 1830s. Its leading members were John Sell ◊Cotman and John ◊Crome.

nose in humans, the upper entrance of the respiratory tract; the organ of the sense of smell. The external part is divided down the middle by a septum of ◊cartilage. The nostrils contain plates of cartilage that can be moved by muscles and have a growth of stiff hairs at the margin to prevent foreign objects from entering. The whole nasal cavity is lined with a mucous membrane (a thin skin that secretes mucus) that warms and moistens the air as it enters and ejects dirt. In the upper parts of the cavity the membrane contains 50 million olfactory receptor cells (cells sensitive to smell).

nosebleed or ***epistaxis*** bleeding from the nose. It may be caused by injury, infection, high blood pressure, or some disorders of the blood. Although usually minor and easily controlled, the loss of blood may occasionally be so rapid as to be life-threatening, particularly in small children. Most nosebleeds can be stopped by simply squeezing the nose for a few minutes with the head held forwards, but in exceptional cases transfusion may be required and the nose may need to be packed with ribbon gauze or cauterized.

nosocomial description of any infection acquired in a hospital or other medical facility, whether its effects are seen during the patient's stay or after discharge. Widely prevalent in some hospitals, nosocomial infections threaten patients who are seriously ill or whose immune systems have been suppressed. The threat is compounded by the prevalence of drug-resistant ◊pathogens endemic to the hospital environment.

Nostradamus Latinized name of Michel de Nôtredame 1503–1566. French physician and astrologer who was consulted by Catherine de' Medici and Charles IX of France. His book of prophecies in verse, *Centuries* 1555, makes cryptic predictions about world events up to the year 3797.

notary public legal practitioner who attests or certifies deeds and other documents. British diplomatic and consular officials may exercise notarial functions outside the UK.

notation in dance, the codification and recording of dances by symbols. There are several dance notation systems; prominent among them is Labanotation.

notation a system representing music graphically as successive values in pitch and time. By 1700 modern notation had displaced ◊plainsong and tablature notations, making possible the coordination under one system of orchestras of increasing size, and also making possible the composition of large-scale musical forms. Notation embodies the assumption that pitch and time are uniform and continuous, hence it relates to the development of keyboard instruments, the tempered scale, and chronometric time-keeping.

note in music, the written symbol indicating pitch and duration, the sound of which is a tone.

notochord the stiff but flexible rod that lies between the gut and the nerve cord of all embryonic and larval chordates, including the vertebrates. It forms the supporting structure of the adult lancelet, but in vertebrates it is replaced by the vertebral column, or spine.

Nottingham industrial city (engineering, coal mining, bicycles, textiles, knitwear, pharmaceuticals, tobacco, lace, electronics) and administrative headquarters of Nottinghamshire, England; population (1991) 263,500. Nottingham was founded by the Danes. The English Civil War began here 1642.

Features include the university (1881), the Playhouse (opened 1963), and the Theatre Royal. Nearby are Newstead Abbey, home of Byron, and D H Lawrence's home at Eastwood.

Nottinghamshire county of central England
area 2,160 sq km/834 sq mi (*see United Kingdom map*)
towns and cities Nottingham (administrative headquarters), Mansfield, Worksop, Newark
features river Trent; the remaining areas of Sherwood Forest (home of ◊Robin Hood), formerly a royal hunting ground, are included in the 'Dukeries'; Cresswell Crags (remains of prehistoric humans); D H Lawrence commemorative walk from Eastwood (where he lived) to Old Brinsley Colliery
industries cereals, cattle, sheep, light engineering, footwear, limestone, coal mining, ironstone, oil, cigarettes, tanning, furniture, pharmaceuticals, typewriters, gypsum, gravel. There are many orchards, and there is market gardening
population (1991) 980,600
famous people William Booth, D H Lawrence, Alan Sillitoe.

Nouakchott capital of Mauritania, 270 mi/435 km NE of Dakar, Senegal; population (1988) 393,000. It is the largest city in the Sahara. Products include salt, cement, and insecticides.

It was a coastal village on the desert trail from Dakar, and was chosen as capital 1957. It grew rapidly in the 1970s as refugees poured in during the Saharan drought. The port exports petroleum and copper.

Nouméa port and capital on the southwest coast of New Caledonia; population (1992) 65,000.

nouveau roman (French 'new novel') experimental literary form produced in the 1950s by French novelists including Alain Robbe-Grillet and Nathalie Sarraute. In various ways, these writers seek to eliminate character, plot, and authorial subjectivity in order to present the world as a pure, solid 'thing in itself'.

Robbe-Grillet's *Le Voyeur* 1955 and Sarraute's *Le Planetarium* 1959 are critically successful examples. Michel Butor, Claude Ollier, and Marguerite Duras also contributed to this form, which is sometimes labelled the 'anti-novel' because of its subversion of traditional methods.

Nouvel Jean 1945– . French architect. He uses the language of ◊High Tech building in novel and highly distinctive ways. His celebrated Institut du Monde Arabe, Paris, 1981–87, adapts traditional Islamic motifs to technological ends: mechanized irises, for instance, control the penetration of daylight.

nouvelle cuisine (French 'new cooking') contemporary French cooking style that avoids traditional rich sauces, emphasizing fresh ingredients and attractive presentation. The phrase was coined in the British magazine *Harpers & Queen* in June 1975.

nova (plural ***novae***) faint star that suddenly erupts in brightness by 10,000 times or more, remains bright for a few days, and then fades away and is not seen again for very many years, if at all. Novae are believed to occur in close ◊binary star systems, where gas from one star flows to a companion ◊white dwarf. The gas ignites and is thrown off in an explosion at speeds of 1,500 kps/930 mps or more. Unlike a ◊supernova, the star is not completely disrupted by the outburst. After a few weeks or months it subsides to its previous state; it may erupt many more times.

Although the name comes from the Latin 'new', photographic records show that such stars are not really new, but faint stars undergoing an outburst of radiation that temporarily gives them an absolute magnitude in the range −6 to −10, at least 100,000 times brighter than the Sun. They fade away, rapidly at first and then more slowly over several years. Two or three such stars are detected in our Galaxy each year, but on average one is sufficiently close to us to become a conspicuous naked-eye object only about once in ten years. Novae very similar to those appearing in our own Galaxy have also been observed in other galaxies.

Novalis Pen name of Friedrich Leopold von Hardenberg 1772–1801. Pioneer German Romantic poet. He wrote *Hymnen an die Nacht/Hymns to the Night* 1800, prompted by the death of his fiancée Sophie von Kühn. Feeling himself ecstatically united with his dead beloved, he tried to free his spirit from material things, and many of his poems contain a note of mysticism. He left two unfinished romances, *Die Lehrlinge zu Sais/The Novices of Sais* and *Heinrich von Ofterdingen*.

Nova Scotia maritime province of E Canada
area 55,500 sq km/21,423 sq mi
capital Halifax (chief port)
towns and cities Dartmouth, Sydney
features Cabot Trail (Cape Breton Island); Alexander Graham Bell Museum; Fortress Louisbourg; Strait of Canso Superport, the largest deepwater harbour on the Atlantic coast of North America
industries coal, gypsum, dairy products, poultry, fruit, forest products, fish products (including scallop and lobster)
physical comprising a peninsula with a highly indented coastline extending SE from New Brunswick into the Atlantic Ocean, and Cape Breton Island which is linked to the mainland by the Canso Causeway
population (1991) 897,500
history Nova Scotia was visited by the Italian navigator Giovanni ◊Caboto 1497. A French settlement was established 1604, but expelled 1613 by English colonists from Virginia. The name of the colony was changed from Acadia to Nova Scotia 1621. England and France contended for possession of the territory until Nova Scotia (which then included present-day New Brunswick and Prince Edward Island) was ceded to Britain 1713; Cape Breton Island remained French until 1763. Nova Scotia was one of the four original provinces of the Dominion of Canada.

Nova Scotia

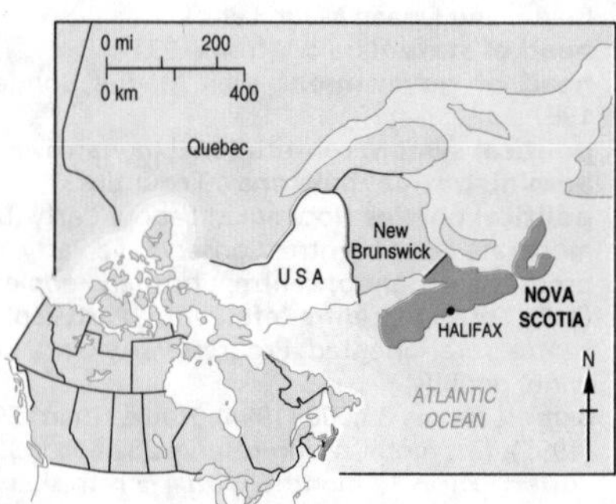

novel extended fictional prose narrative, often including the psychological development of the central characters and of their relationship with a broader world. The modern novel took its name and inspiration from the Italian *novella*, the short tale of varied character which became popular in the late 13th century. As the main form of narrative fiction in the 20th century, the novel is frequently classified according to genres and subgenres such as the ◊historical novel, ◊detective fiction, ◊fantasy, and ◊science fiction.

❛The only reason for the existence of a novel is that it does attempt to represent life.❜

On the NOVEL
Henry James, 'The Art of Fiction' *Partial Portraits*

origins The European novel is said to have originated in Greece in the 2nd century BC. Ancient Greek examples include the *Daphnis and Chloë* of Longus; almost the only surviving Latin work that could be called a novel is the *Golden Ass* of Apuleius (late 2nd century), based on a Greek model. There is a similar, but until the 19th century independent, tradition of prose narrative including psychological development in the Far East, notably in Japan, with, for example, the 11th-century *Tale of Genji* by Murasaki Shikibu.

development A major period of the novel's development came during the late Italian Renaissance, when the stimulus of foreign travel, increased wealth, and changing social patterns produced a greater interest in the events of everyday life, as opposed to religious teaching, legends of the past, or fictional fantasy. The works of the Italian writers Boccaccio and Matteo Bandello (1485–1561) were translated into English in such collections as William Painter's *Palace of Pleasure* 1566–67, and inspired the Elizabethan novelists, including John Lyly, Philip Sidney, Thomas Nash, and Thomas Lodge.

In Spain, Cervantes' *Don Quixote* 1604 contributed to the development of the novel through its translation into other European languages, but the 17th century was dominated by the French romances of Gauthier de Costes de la Calprenède (1614–1663) and Madelaine de Scudéry (1607–1691), although William Congreve and Aphra Behn continued the English tradition. With the growth of literacy, the novel rapidly developed from the 18th century to become, in the 20th century, the major literary form.

Novello Ivor. Stage name of Ivor Novello Davies 1893–1951. Welsh composer and actor-manager. He wrote popular songs, such as 'Keep the Home Fires Burning', in World War I, and musicals in which he often appeared as the romantic lead, including *Glamorous Night* 1925, *The Dancing Years* 1939, and *Gay's the Word* 1951.

Noverre Jean-Georges 1727–1810. French choreographer, writer, and ballet reformer. He promoted *ballet d'action* (with a plot) and simple, free movement, and is often considered the creator of modern classical ballet. *Les Petits Riens* 1778 was one of his works.

Novgorod industrial city (chemicals, engineering, clothing, brewing) on the Volkhov River, NW Russian Federation; a major trading city in medieval times; population (1994) 233,000.

Novgorod was the original capital of the Russian state, founded at the invitation of the people of the city by the Viking (Varangian) chieftain Rurik 862. In 882 the capital of the principality moved to Kiev. Until the 13th century, it flourished as a major commercial centre (with a monopoly on the Russian fur trade) for trade with Scandinavia, the Byzantine empire, and the Muslim world. (It was known in Russia as 'Lord Novgorod the Great' because of its position on the trade route between the Baltic and Black Seas.) It became one of the principal members of the ◊Hanseatic League, but its economy had already started to decline. It came under the control of Ivan the Great III 1478 and was sacked by Ivan the Terrible 1570.

Novgorod school Russian school of icon and mural painters active from the late 14th to the 16th century in Novgorod, inspired by the work of the refugee Byzantine artist Theophanes the Greek (c. 1330–1405). Russian artists imitated his linear style, but their work became increasingly stilted and mannered.

Novi Sad industrial and commercial city (pottery and cotton), capital of the autonomous province of Vojvodina in N Serbia, Yugoslavia, on the river Danube; population (1991) 179,600. Products include leather, textiles, and tobacco.

Novocaine trade name of ***procaine***, the first synthetic local anaesthetic, invented 1905. It is now seldom used, having been replaced by agents such as lignocaine. It is as effective as cocaine, formerly used as a painkiller, when injected, but only one third as toxic and not habit-forming.

NSAID (abbreviation for ***nonsteroidal anti-inflammatory drug***) any of a class of drugs used in the long-term treatment of rheumatoid ◊arthritis and osteoarthritis; they act to reduce swelling and pain in soft tissues. Bleeding into the digestive tract is a serious side effect: NSAIDs should not be taken by persons with peptic ulcers.

NSPCC abbreviation for ***National Society for the Prevention of Cruelty to Children*** (UK).

NT abbreviation for ◊*Northern Territory*, Australia.

Nu U (Thakin) 1907–1995. Myanmar politician, prime minister of Burma (now Myanmar) for most of the period from 1947 to the military coup of 1962. He was the country's first democratically elected prime minister Exiled from 1966, U Nu returned to the country 1980 and, in 1988, helped found the National League for Democracy opposition movement.

Nuba a minority ethnic group living in S Sudan, numbering about 1 million (1991). They speak related dialects of Nubian, which belongs to the Chari-Nile family. Forced Islamization threatens their cultural identity, and thousands were killed in the Sudan civil war.

The Nuba farm terraced fields in the Nuba mountains, to the west of the White Nile. Army massacres, forced 'disappearances', and extrajudicial executions took place in the late 1980s and early 1990s, as the Muslim Sudanese of the north attempted to dominate the south, and many Nuba were driven from their homes.

Nubia former African country now divided between Egypt and Sudan; it gives its name to the Nubian Desert S of Lake Nasser. Ancient Egypt, which was briefly ruled by Nubian kings in the 8th–7th centuries BC, knew the north as Wawat and the south as Kush, with the dividing line roughly at Dongola. Egyptian building work in the area included temples at ◊Abu Simbel, Philae, and a defensive chain of forts that established the lines of development of medieval fortification. Nubia's capital about 600 BC–AD 350 was Meroe, near Khartoum. About AD 250–550 most of Nubia was occupied by the X-group people, of whom little is known; their royal mound tombs (mistaken by earlier investigations for natural mounds created by wind erosion) were excavated in the 1930s by W B ◊Emery, and many horses and attendants were found to have been slaughtered to accompany the richly jewelled dead.

nuclear arms verification the process of checking the number and types of nuclear weapons held by a country in accordance with negotiated limits. The chief means are: ***reconnaissance satellites*** that detect submarines or weapon silos, using angled cameras to give three-dimensional pictures of installations, penetrating camouflage by means of scanners, and partially seeing through cloud and darkness by infrared devices; ***telemetry*** or radio transmission of instrument readings; ***interception*** to get information on performance of weapons under test; ***on-site inspection*** by experts visiting bases, launch sites, storage facilities, and test sites in another country; ***radar tracking*** of missiles in flight; ***seismic monitoring*** of underground tests, in the same way as with earthquakes. This is not accurate and on-site inspection is needed. Tests in the atmosphere, space, or the oceans are forbidden, and the ban is accepted because explosions are not only dangerous to all but immediately detectable.

nuclear energy or ***atomic energy*** energy released from the inner core, or ◊nucleus, of the atom. Energy produced by nuclear ◊fission (the splitting of uranium or plutonium nuclei) has been harnessed since the 1950s to generate electricity, and research continues into the possible controlled use of ◊nuclear fusion (the fusing, or combining, of atomic nuclei).

In nuclear power stations, fission takes place in a ◊nuclear reactor. The nuclei of uranium or, more rarely, plutonium are induced to split, releasing large amounts of heat energy. The heat is then removed from the core of the reactor by circulating gas or water, and used to produce the steam that drives alternators and turbines to generate electrical power. Unlike fossil fuels, such as coal and oil, which must be burned in large quantities to produce energy, nuclear fuels are used in very small amounts and supplies are therefore unlikely to be exhausted in the foreseeable future. However, the use of nuclear energy has given rise to concern over safety. Anxiety has been heightened by accidents such as the one at Chernobyl, Ukraine, in 1986. There has also been mounting concern about the production and disposal of toxic nuclear waste, which may have an active life of several thousand years, and the cost of maintaining nuclear power stations and decommissioning them at the end of their lives. ▷*See feature on pp. 360–361.*

Nova Scotia Ile Sainte Croix, the first French settlement of Acadia. Britain and France contested ownership of the peninsula until British possession 1713. *Philip Sauvain*

nuclear fusion process whereby two atomic nuclei are fused, with the release of a large amount of energy. Very high temperatures and pressures are thought to be required in order for the process to happen. Under these conditions the atoms involved are stripped of all their electrons so that the remaining particles, which together make up a plasma, can come close together at very high speeds and overcome the mutual repulsion of the positive charges on the atomic nuclei. At very close range the strong nuclear force will come into play, fusing the particles together to form a larger nucleus. As fusion is accompanied by the release of large amounts of energy, the process might one day be harnessed to form the basis of commercial energy production. Methods of achieving controlled fusion are therefore the subject of research around the world.

Fusion is the process by which the Sun and the other stars produce their energy.

nuclear magnetic resonance (NMR) in medicine, scanning technique used to produce images of the organs in the body. It is another term for ◊magnetic resonance imaging (MRI).

nuclear notation method used for labelling an atom according to the composition of its nucleus. The atoms or isotopes of a particular element are represented by the symbol ${}^{A}_{Z}X$ where A is the mass number of their nuclei, Z is their atomic number, and X is the chemical symbol for that element.

nuclear physics study of the properties of the nucleus of the ◊atom, including the structure of nuclei; nuclear forces; the interactions between particles and nuclei; and the study of radioactive decay. The study of elementary particles is ◊particle physics.

nuclear reaction reaction involving the nuclei of atoms. Atomic nuclei can undergo changes either as a result of radioactive decay, as in the decay of radium to radon (with the emission of an alpha particle) or as a result of particle bombardment in a machine or device, as in the production of cobalt-60 by the bombardment of cobalt-59 with neutrons.

$$ {}^{226}_{88}\mathrm{Ra} \rightarrow {}^{222}_{86}\mathrm{Rn} + {}^{4}_{2}\mathrm{He} $$
$$ {}^{59}_{27}\mathrm{Co} + {}^{1}_{0}\mathrm{n} \rightarrow {}^{60}_{27}\mathrm{Co} + \gamma $$

Nuclear ◊fission and nuclear ◊fusion are examples of nuclear reactions. The enormous amounts of energy released arise from the mass–energy relation put forward by Einstein, stating that $E = mc^2$ (where E is energy, m is mass, and c is the velocity of light).

In nuclear reactions the sum of the masses of all the products (on the atomic mass unit scale) is less than the sum of the masses of the reacting particles. This lost mass is converted to energy according to Einstein's equation.

'There is no evil in the atom; only in men's souls.'

On NUCLEAR ENERGY
Adlai Stevenson, speech in Hartford, Connecticut, 18 Sept 1952

nuclear reactor device for producing ◊nuclear energy in a controlled manner. There are various types of reactor in use, all using nuclear fission. In a ***gas-cooled reactor***, a circulating gas under pressure

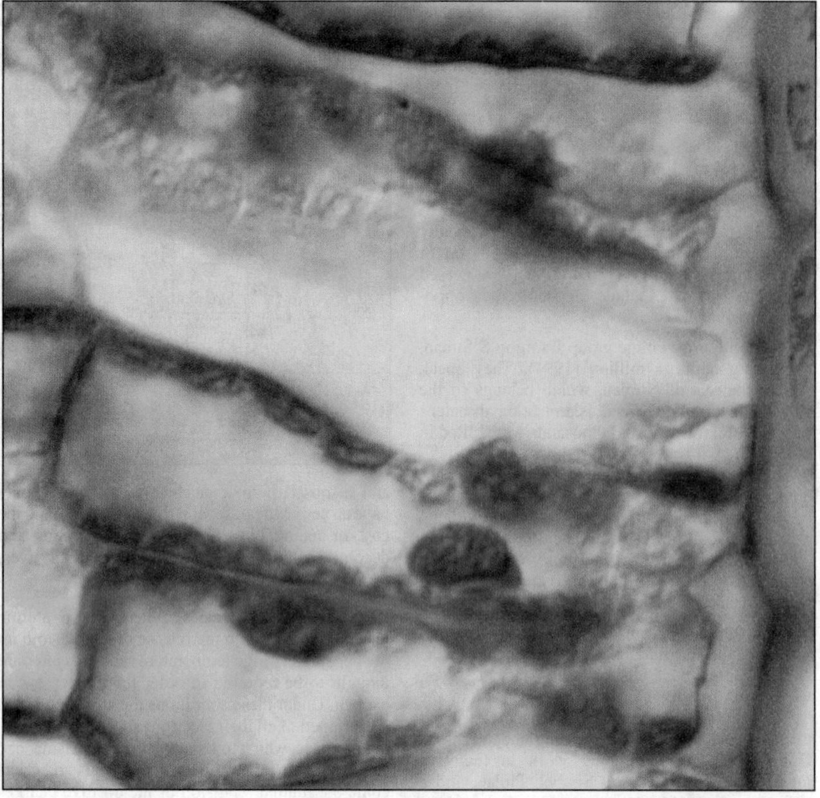

nucleus The nuclei of these plant cells are clearly visible as densely coloured oval structures in each cell, magnified under the electron microscope. *Corbis*

(such as carbon dioxide) removes heat from the core of the reactor, which usually contains natural uranium. The efficiency of the fission process is increased by slowing neutrons in the core by using a ◊moderator such as carbon. The reaction is controlled with neutron-absorbing rods made of boron. An ***advanced gas-cooled reactor*** (AGR) generally has enriched uranium as its fuel. In the USA the ***direct cycle gas turbine*** is favoured. It has modular construction, enriched uranium fuel, and is cooled by helium. A ***water-cooled reactor***, such as the steam-generating heavy water (deuterium oxide) reactor, has water circulating through the hot core. The water is converted to steam, which drives turbo-alternators for generating electricity. The most widely used reactor is the ***pressurized-water reactor*** (PWR), which contains a sealed system of pressurized water that is heated to form steam in heat exchangers in an external circuit. The ***fast reactor*** has no moderator and uses fast neutrons to bring about fission. It uses a mixture of plutonium and uranium oxide as fuel. When operating, uranium is converted to plutonium, which can be extracted and used later as fuel. It is also called the fast breeder because it produces more plutonium than it consumes. Heat is removed from the reactor by a coolant of liquid sodium.

Public concern over the safety of nuclear reactors has been intensified by explosions and accidental release of radioactive materials. The safest system allows for the emergency cooling of a reactor by automatically flooding an overheated core with water. Other concerns about nuclear power centre on the difficulties of reprocessing nuclear fuel and disposing safely of nuclear waste, and the cost of maintaining nuclear power stations and of decommissioning them at the end of their lives. The break up of the former Soviet Union raised concerns about the ability of the new nation states to safely manage ageing reactors. In 1989, the UK government decided to postpone the construction of new nuclear power stations; in the USA, no new stations have been commissioned in over a decade. Rancho Seco, near Sacramento, California, was the first nuclear power station to be closed, by popular vote, in 1989. Sweden is committed to decommissioning its reactors. Some countries, such as France, are pressing ahead with their nuclear programmes.

nuclear safety measures to avoid accidents in the operation of nuclear reactors and in the production and disposal of nuclear weapons and of ◊nuclear waste. There are no guarantees of the safety of any of the various methods of disposal.

Major nuclear accidents include:

Windscale (now Sellafield), Cumbria, England. In 1957, fire destroyed the core of a reactor, releasing large quantities of radioactive fumes into the atmosphere.

Ticonderoga, 130 km/80 mi off the coast of Japan. In 1965 a US Navy Skyhawk jet bomber fell off the deck of this ship, sinking in 4,900 m/16,000 ft of water. It carried a one-megaton hydrogen bomb. The accident was only revealed in 1989.

Three Mile Island, Harrisburg, Pennsylvania, USA. In 1979, a combination of mechanical and electrical failure, as well as operator error, caused a pressurized water reactor to leak radioactive matter.

Church Rock, New Mexico, USA. In July 1979, 380 million litres/100 million gallons of radioactive water containing uranium leaked from a pond into the Rio Purco, causing the water to become over 6,500 times as radioactive as safety standards allow for drinking water.

Chernobyl, Ukraine. In April 1986 there was an explosive leak, caused by overheating, from a non-pressurized boiling-water reactor, one of the largest in Europe. The resulting clouds of radioactive material spread as far as the UK. 31 people were killed in the explosion, and thousands of square kilometres of land were contaminated by fallout. By 1992, seven times as many children in the Ukraine and Belarus were contracting thyroid cancer as before the accident, the incidence of leukemia was rising, and it was estimated that more than 6,000 people had died as a result of the accident, and that the death toll in the Ukraine alone would eventually reach 40,000.

Tomsk, Siberia. In April 1993 a tank exploded at a uranium reprocessing plant, sending a cloud of radioactive particles into the air.

nuclear warfare war involving the use of nuclear weapons. Nuclear-weapons research began in Britain 1940, but was transferred to the USA after it entered World War II. The research programme, known as the Manhattan Project, was directed by J Robert Oppenheimer. The worldwide total of nuclear weapons in 1990 was about 50,000, and the number of countries possessing nuclear weapons stood officially at five – USA, USSR, UK, France, and China.

atom bomb The original weapon relied on use of a chemical explosion to trigger a chain reaction. The first test explosion was at Alamogordo, New Mexico, 16 July 1945; the first use in war was by the USA against Japan 6 Aug 1945 over Hiroshima and three days later at Nagasaki.

hydrogen bomb A much more powerful weapon than the atom bomb, it relies on the release of thermonuclear energy by the condensation of hydrogen nuclei to helium nuclei (as happens in the Sun). The first detonation was at Eniwetok Atoll, Pacific Ocean, 1952 by the USA.

neutron bomb or *e*nhanced *r*adiation *w*eapon (ERW) A very small hydrogen bomb that has relatively high radiation but relatively low blast, designed to kill (in up to six days) by a brief neutron radiation that leaves buildings and weaponry intact.

nuclear methods of attack Methods used now include aircraft bombs, missiles (long- or short-range, surface to surface, air to surface, and surface to air), depth charges, and high-powered landmines ('atomic demolition munitions') to destroy bridges and roads.

The major subjects of disarmament negotiations are intercontinental ballistic missiles (ICBMs), which have from 1968 been equipped with clusters of warheads (which can be directed to individual targets) and are known as multiple independently targetable re-entry vehicles (MIRVs). The 1980s US-designed MX (Peacekeeper) carries up to ten warheads in each missile. In 1989, the UK agreed to purchase submarine-launched Trident missiles from the USA. Each warhead has eight independently targetable re-entry vehicles (each nuclear-armed) with a range of about 6,400 km/4,000 mi to eight separate targets within about 240 km/150 mi of the central aiming point. The Trident system was scheduled to enter service within the Royal Navy in the mid-1990s.

nuclear methods of defence Methods include: antiballistic missile (ABM) Earth-based systems with two types of missile, one short-range with high acceleration, and one comparatively long-range for interception above the atmosphere; ◊Strategic Defense Initiative (announced by the USA 1983 to be operative from 2000, but cancelled 1993; popularly known as the 'Star Wars' programme) 'directed energy weapons' firing laser beams would be mounted on space stations, and by burning holes in incoming missiles would either collapse them or detonate their fuel tanks. The UK nuclear warhead programme costs £607 million a year.

nuclear waste the radioactive and toxic by-products of the nuclear-energy and nuclear-weapons industries. Nuclear waste may have an active life of several thousand years. Reactor waste is of three types: ***high-level*** spent fuel, or the residue when nuclear fuel has been removed from a reactor and reprocessed; ***intermediate***, which may be long-or short-lived; and ***low-level***, but bulky, waste from reactors, which has only short-lived radioactivity. Disposal, by burial on land or at sea, has raised problems of safety, environmental pollution, and security. In absolute terms, nuclear waste cannot be safely relocated or disposed of.

The issue of nuclear waste is becoming the central controversy threatening the future of generating electricity by nuclear energy. The dumping of nuclear waste at sea officially stopped 1983, when a moratorium was agreed by the members of the London Dumping Convention (a United Nations body that controls disposal of wastes at sea). Covertly, the USSR continued dumping, and deposited thousands of tonnes of nuclear waste and three faulty reactors in the sea 1964–86. The USSR and the Russian Federation between them dumped an estimated 12 trillion becquerels of radioactivity in the sea 1959–93. Russia has no way of treating nuclear waste and in 1993 announced its intention of continuing to dump it in the sea, in violation of international conventions, until 1997. Twenty reactors from Soviet nuclear-powered ships were dumped off the Arctic and Pacific coasts 1965–93, and some are leaking. Fish-spawning grounds off Norway are threatened by plutonium from abandoned Soviet nuclear warheads.

Waste from a site where uranium is mined or milled may have an active life of several thousand years, and spent (irradiated) fuel is dangerous for tens of thousands of years. Sea disposal has occurred at many sites, for example 450 km/300 mi off Land's End, England, but there is no guarantee of the safety of this method of disposal, even for low-activity waste. There have been proposals to dispose of high-activity waste in old mines, granite formations, and specially constructed bunkers. The

nuclear reactor Construction workers building the pile cap of an advanced gas-cooled reactor (AGR) in Hartlepool, NE England. One of the latest designs in nuclear reactors, AGRs are thought to be far safer than earlier models. *AEA Technology*

most promising proposed method is by vitrification into solid glass cylinders, which would be placed in titanium-cobalt alloy containers and deposited on dead planets in space. Beneath the sea the containers would start to corrode after 1,000 years, and the cylinders themselves would dissolve within the next 1,000 years. About one-third of the fuel from nuclear reactors becomes spent each year. It is removed to a reprocessing plant where radioactive waste products are chemically separated from remaining uranium and plutonium, in an expensive and dangerous process. This practice increases the volume of radioactive waste more than a hundred times.

nuclear winter possible long-term effect of a widespread nuclear war. In the wake of the destruction caused by nuclear blasts and the subsequent radiation, it has been suggested that atmospheric pollution by dust, smoke, soot, and ash could prevent the Sun's rays from penetrating for a period of time sufficient to eradicate most plant life on which other life depends, and create a new Ice Age.

Even after it had settled, ash would still reflect the Sun's rays and delay the planet's return to normal warmth. Insects, grasses, and sea life would have the best prospects of survival, as well as microorganisms. The cold would be intense, and a great increase in snow and ice worldwide would occur.

nucleic acid complex organic acid made up of a long chain of ◊nucleotides, present in the nucleus and sometimes the cytoplasm of the living cell. The two types, known as ◊DNA (deoxyribonucleic acid) and ◊RNA (ribonucleic acid), form the basis of heredity. The nucleotides are made up of a sugar (deoxyribose or ribose), a phosphate group, and one of four purine or pyrimidine bases. The order of the bases along the nucleic acid strand contains the genetic code.

nucleolus in biology, a structure found in the nucleus of eukaryotic cells. It produces the RNA that makes up the ◊ribosomes, from instructions in the DNA.

nucleon in particle physics, either a ◊proton or a ◊neutron, when present in the atomic nucleus. Nucleon number is an alternative name for the ◊mass number of an atom.

nucleotide organic compound consisting of a purine (adenine or guanine) or a pyrimidine (thymine, uracil, or cytosine) base linked to a sugar (deoxyribose or ribose) and a phosphate group. ◊DNA and ◊RNA are made up of long chains of nucleotides.

nucleus in biology, the central, membrane-enclosed part of a eukaryotic cell, containing the chromosomes.

nucleus in physics, the positively charged central part of an ◊atom, which constitutes almost all its mass. Except for hydrogen nuclei, which have only protons, nuclei are composed of both protons and neutrons. Surrounding the nuclei are electrons, of equal and opposite charge to that of the protons, thus giving the atom a neutral charge.

The nucleus was discovered by New Zealand physicist Ernest Rutherford in 1911 as a result of experiments in passing alpha particles through very thin gold foil.

A few of the particles were deflected back, and Rutherford, astonished, reported: 'It was almost as if you fired a 15-inch shell at a piece of tissue paper and it came back and hit you!' The deflection, he deduced, was due to the positively charged alpha particles being repelled by approaching a small but dense positively charged nucleus.

nuclide in physics, a species of atomic nucleus characterized by the number of protons (Z) and the number of neutrons (N). Nuclides with identical proton number but differing neutron number are called ◊isotopes.

Nuffield William Richard Morris, 1st Viscount Nuffield 1877–1963. English manufacturer and philanthropist. Starting with a small cycle-repairing business, in 1910 he designed a car that could be produced cheaply, and built up Morris Motors Ltd at Cowley, Oxford. He endowed Nuffield College, Oxford, 1937 and the Nuffield Foundation 1943.

nuisance in law, interference with enjoyment of, or rights over, land. There are two kinds of nuisance. Private nuisance affects a particular occupier of land, such as noise from a neighbour; the aggrieved occupier can apply for an ◊injunction and claim ◊damages. Public nuisance affects an indefinite number of members of the public, such as obstructing the highway; it is a criminal offence. In this case, individuals can claim damages only if they are affected more than the general public.

Having contaminated the water supply in Camelford, Cornwall, England, the South West Water Authority was in 1991 fined £10,000 for causing a public nuisance.

Nujoma Sam 1929– . Namibian left-wing politician, founder and leader of ◊SWAPO (the South-West Africa People's Organization) from 1959, president from 1990. He was exiled in 1960 and controlled guerrillas from Angolan bases until the first free elections were held 1989, taking office early the following year.

Nuku'alofa capital and port of Tonga on Tongatapu Island; population (1989) 29,000.

numbat or ***banded anteater*** Australian marsupial anteater *Myrmecobius fasciatus*. It is brown with white stripes on the back and has a long tubular tongue to gather termites and ants. The body is about 25 cm/10 in long, and the tongue can be extended 10 cm/4 in. It is distinct from other marsupials in that it has no pouch.

number symbol used in counting or measuring. In mathematics, there are various kinds of numbers. The everyday number system is the decimal ('proceeding by tens') system, using the base ten. ◊***Real numbers*** include all rational numbers (integers, or whole numbers, and fractions) and irrational numbers (those not expressible as fractions). ◊***Complex numbers*** include the real and imaginary numbers (real-number multiples of the square root of -1). The ◊binary number system, used in computers, has two as its base. The natural numbers (the set of numbers used for counting) 0, 1, 2, 3, 4, 5, 6, 7, 8, and 9, give a counting system that, in the decimal system, continues 10, 11, 12, 13, and so on. These are whole numbers (integers), with fractions represented as, for example, ¼, ½, ¾, or as decimal fractions (0.25, 0.5, 0.75). They are also ***rational numbers***. ***Irrational numbers*** cannot be represented in this way and require symbols, such as $\sqrt{2}$, π, and e. They can be expressed numerically only as the (inexact) approximations 1.414, 3.142, and 2.718 (to three places of decimals) respectively. The symbols π and e are also examples of ***transcendental numbers***, because they (unlike $\sqrt{2}$) cannot be derived by solving a ◊polynomial equation (an equation with one ◊variable quantity) with rational ◊coefficients (multiplying factors). Complex numbers, which include the real numbers as well as

Nuffield English car manufacturer and philanthropist Lord Nuffield. He began his career manufacturing bicycles 1895 with just £5 of capital. *Philip Sauvain*

imaginary numbers, take the general form $a + bi$, where $i = \sqrt{-1}$ (that is, $i^2 = -1$), and a is the real part and bi the imaginary part.

evolution of number systems The ancient Egyptians, Greeks, Romans, and Babylonians all evolved number systems, although none had a zero, which was introduced from India by way of Arab mathematicians in about the 8th century AD and allowed a place-value system to be devised on which the decimal system is based. Other number systems have since evolved and have found applications. For example, numbers to base two (binary numbers), using only 0 and 1, are commonly used in digital computers to represent the two-state 'on' or 'off' pulses of electricity. Binary numbers were first developed by German mathematician Gottfried Leibniz in the late 17th century. *See list of tables on p. 1177.*

numerator the number or symbol that appears above the line in a vulgar fraction. For example, the numerator of 5/6 is 5. The numerator represents the fraction's dividend and indicates how many of the equal parts indicated by the denominator (number or symbol below the line) comprise the fraction.

nun (Latin *nonna* 'elderly woman') woman belonging to a religious order under the vows of poverty, chastity, and obedience, and living under a particular rule. Christian convents are ruled by a superior (often elected), who is subject to the authority of the bishop of the diocese or sometimes directly to the pope. See ◊monasticism.

Nunavut (Inuit 'our land') semi-autonomous Inuit homeland in Northwest Territories, Canada, extending over 2,000,000 sq km/772,000 sq mi. In a regional plebiscite May 1992, its creation in 1999 was approved by a narrow majority, after representatives of the 17,000 Inuit had negotiated hunting and fishing rights in the area. A final land claims agreement, signed May 1993 on Baffin Island (proposed capital of Nunavut), gave the Inuit outright ownership of 353,610 sq km/136,493 sq mi of the land, and mineral rights to 36,257 sq km/13,995 sq mi.

Núñez Rafael 1825–1894. Colombian president 1880–82 and 1884–94, responsible for a new,

Nuremberg trials The defendants' dock at the main Nuremberg trials – the first two figures in the front row are Hermann Goering and Rudolf Hess. The charges against the officials of the German Third Reich were 'crimes against humanity' and 'violations of the rules of war'. Some jurists argue that there was no legal basis for such charges and that the trials were in effect the punishment of the vanquished by the victors. *Library of Congress*

authoritarian constitution 1886. A doctrinaire Liberal in the 1850s, he held several government posts, and was a foreign diplomat 1863–74.

Nuremberg (German *Nürnberg*) industrial city (electrical and other machinery, precision instruments, textiles, toys) in Bavaria, Germany; population (1993) 499,800. From 1933 the Nuremberg rallies were held here, and in 1945 the Nuremberg trials of war criminals.

Created an imperial city 1219, it has an 11th–16th-century fortress and many medieval buildings (restored after destruction of 75% of the city in World War II), including the home of the 16th-century composer Hans Sachs (1494–1576), where the ◊Meistersinger met. The artist Albrecht Dürer was born in Nuremberg; his birthplace is now a museum.

Nuremberg rallies annual meetings 1933–38 of the German ◊Nazi Party. They were characterized by extensive torchlight parades, marches in party formations, and mass rallies addressed by Nazi leaders such as Hitler and Goebbels.

Nuremberg trials after World War II, the trials of the 24 chief ◊Nazi war criminals Nov 1945–Oct 1946 by an international military tribunal consisting of four judges and four prosecutors: one of each from the USA, UK, USSR, and France. An appendix accused the German cabinet, general staff, high command, Nazi leadership corps, ◊SS, ◊Sturmabteilung, and ◊Gestapo of criminal behaviour.

Nureyev Rudolf Hametovich 1938–1993. Russian dancer and choreographer. A soloist with the Kirov Ballet, he defected to the West during a visit to Paris 1961. Mainly associated with the Royal Ballet (London) and as Margot ◊Fonteyn's principal partner, he was one of the most brilliant dancers of the 1960s and 1970s. Nureyev danced in such roles as Prince Siegfried in *Swan Lake* and Armand in *Marguerite and Armand*, which was created especially for Fonteyn and Nureyev. He also danced and acted in films and on television and choreographed several ballets. It was due to his enormous impact on the ballet world that the male dancer's role was elevated to the equivalent of the ballerina's.

nuthatch The European nuthatch is one of about 25 species of nuthatch. They are robust little birds, with strong legs and sharp claws to help them climb. They run up and down branches and tree trunks, looking for food.

Nurmi Paavo Johannes 1897–1973. Finnish long distance runner, known as the 'Flying Finn'. He won nine Olympic gold medals, including five at the 1924 Games, and broke 20 world records in 16 separate events ranging from the 1,500 metres to the 20,000 metres. Through his achievements and his scientific approach to training and racing he transformed competitive running in the 1920s.

nursery school or ***kindergarten*** educational establishment for children aged three to five. The first was established in Germany 1836 by Friedrich ◊Froebel. Provision of nursery education varies widely between countries. In the UK, fewer than half of three- and four-year olds have nursery education. In France, all children attend a state-run *école maternelle* from the age of three. In Japan, education is compulsory only from the age of six, but 90% of children attend a private nursery school from the age of three.

nursing care of the sick, the very young, the very old, and the disabled. Organized training originated 1836 in Germany, and was developed in Britain by the work of Florence ◊Nightingale, who, during the Crimean War, established standards of scientific, humanitarian care in military hospitals. Nurses give day-to-day care and carry out routine medical and surgical duties under the supervision of medical staff.

nut any dry, single-seeded fruit that does not split open to release the seed, such as the chestnut. A nut is formed from more than one carpel, but only one seed becomes fully formed, the remainder aborting. The wall of the fruit, the pericarp, becomes hard and woody, forming the outer shell.

Examples of true nuts are the acorn and hazelnut. The term also describes various hard-shelled fruits and seeds, including almonds and walnuts, which are really the stones of ◊drupes, and brazil nuts and shelled peanuts, which are seeds. The kernels of most nuts provide a concentrated, nutritious food, containing vitamins, minerals, and enzymes, about 50% fat, and 10–20% protein, although a few, such as chestnuts, are high in carbohydrates and have only a moderate protein content of 5%. World production in the mid-1980s was about 4 million tonnes per year.

nutation in astronomy, a slight 'nodding' of the Earth in space, caused by the varying gravitational pulls of the Sun and Moon. Nutation changes the angle of the Earth's axial tilt (average 23.5°) by about 9 seconds of arc to either side of its mean position, a complete cycle taking just over 18.5 years.

nutation in botany, the spiral movement exhibited by the tips of certain stems during growth; it enables a climbing plant to find a suitable support. Nutation sometimes also occurs in tendrils and flower stalks.

The direction of the movements, clockwise or anticlockwise, is usually characteristic for particular species.

nutcracker jay-like bird of the genus *Nucifraga*, in the crow family Corvidae, order Passeriformes. There are two species: one in the Old World and one in the New World.

The Old World nutcracker *N. caryocatactes* is found in areas of coniferous forest in Asia and parts of Europe, particularly in mountains. About 30 cm/1 ft long, it has a brown back, with a long white spot on each feather, dark brown head, white tipped outer tailfeathers, black feet and a powerful black bill. It feeds on conifer seeds. The nest is a big, clumsy structure, and in it about three eggs are laid, which are very light green, spotted with pale brown. Irregularly, there is a mass migration of nutcrackers from Siberia to W Europe.

nuthatch small bird of the family Sittidae, order Passeriformes, with a short tail and pointed beak. Nuthatches climb head first up, down, and around tree trunks and branches, foraging for insects and their larvae.

The European nuthatch *Sitta europaea* has a blue-grey back and buff breast; the throat is white, and the tailfeathers have white tips. It is fairly common in the southern half of England and in Europe, and is a climber, feeding mainly on nuts. The bill is powerful and wedge-shaped, and is used to force away the bark in the search for insects, as well as to break nuts. The nest is built in a hole in a tree, and 5–8 white eggs with reddish-brown spots are laid in early summer.

nutmeg kernel of the seed of the evergreen tree *Myristica fragrans*, native to the Maluku. Both the nutmeg and its secondary covering, known as mace, are used as spice in cookery.

nutrition the strategy adopted by an organism to obtain the chemicals it needs to live, grow, and reproduce. Also, the science of food, and its effect on human and animal life, health, and disease. Nutrition involves the study of the basic nutrients required to sustain life, their bioavailability in foods and overall diet, and the effects upon them of cooking and storage. It is also concerned with dietary deficiency diseases.

There are six classes of nutrients: water, carbohydrates, proteins, fats, vitamins, and minerals.

NVQ abbreviation for ◊***national vocational qualification***.

nyala antelope *Tragelaphus angasi* found in the thick bush of southern Africa. About 1 m/3 ft at the shoulder, it is greyish-brown with thin vertical white stripes. Males have horns up to 80 cm/2.6 ft long.

Nyerere Tanzanian president Julius Nyerere, speaking at a summit on nuclear disarmament in India, Jan 1985. Under Nyerere, the Tanganyika African National Union won electoral successes 1958 and 1960, which led to his becoming prime minister in 1961. He was then president of Tanzania 1964–1985. *Corbis*

Nyasa former name for Lake ◊Malawi.

Nyasaland former name (to 1964) for ◊Malawi.

Nyerere Julius Kambarage 1922– . Tanzanian socialist politician, president 1964–85. He devoted himself from 1954 to the formation of the Tanganyika African National Union and subsequent campaigning for independence. He became chief minister 1960, was prime minister of Tanganyika 1961–62, president of the newly formed Tanganyika Republic 1962–64, and first president of Tanzania 1964–85.

nylon synthetic long-chain polymer similar in chemical structure to protein. Nylon was the first all-synthesized fibre, made from petroleum, natural gas, air, and water by the Du Pont firm in 1938. It is used in the manufacture of moulded articles, textiles, and medical sutures. Nylon fibres are stronger and more elastic than silk and are relatively insensitive to moisture and mildew. Nylon is used for hosiery and woven goods, simulating other materials such as silks and furs; it is also used for carpets. It was developed 1937 by the US chemist W H Carothers and his associates.

Nyman Michael 1944– . English composer. His highly stylized music is characterized by processes of gradual modification by repetition of complex musical formulae (known as minimalism). His compositions include scores for English filmmaker Peter Greenaway and New Zealand filmmaker Jane Campion (*The Piano* 1993); a chamber opera, *The Man Who Mistook His Wife for a Hat* 1989; and three string quartets.

nymph The nymph of the grasshopper *Taeniopoda auricornis* is like a small wingless version of the adult. However, as in many other insects which develop via nymphs, the adult is very differently coloured from any of the preceding nymphal stages. *Premaphotos Wildlife*

nymph in entomology, the immature form of insects that do not have a pupal stage; for example, grasshoppers and dragonflies. Nymphs generally resemble the adult (unlike larvae), but do not have fully formed reproductive organs or wings.

nymph in Greek mythology, a guardian spirit of nature. Hamadryads or dryads guarded trees; naiads, springs and pools; oreads, hills and rocks; and Nereids, the sea.

oak any tree or shrub of the genus *Quercus* of the beech family Fagaceae, with over 300 known species widely distributed in temperate zones. Oaks are valuable for timber, the wood being durable and straight-grained. Their fruits are called acorns.

The English oak *Q. robur*, also found in mainland Europe, grows to 36 m/120 ft with a girth of 15 m/50 ft. Other European varieties are the evergreen oak *Q. ilex*, the Turkey oak *Q. cerris*, and the cork oak *Q. suber*, of the W Mediterranean region; valuable New World timber oaks are the white oak *Q. alba* and the evergreen live oak *Q. virginiana*.

Oak wilt, the result of a symbiotic partnership between a beetle and a fungus, resembles Dutch ◊elm disease and is virulent.

Oakland industrial port (vehicles, textiles, chemicals, food processing, shipbuilding) in California, USA, on the east coast of San Francisco Bay; population (1992) 373,200. It is linked by bridge (1936) with San Francisco. A major earthquake 1989 buckled the bay bridge and an Oakland freeway section, causing more than 60 deaths.

oarfish any of a family *Regalecidae* of deep-sea bony fishes, found in warm parts of the Atlantic, Pacific, and Indian oceans. Oarfish are large, up to 9 m/30 ft long, elongated, and compressed, with a fin along the back and a manelike crest behind the head. They have a small mouth, no teeth or scales, and large eyes.

oarweed or ***tangleweed*** any of several large, coarse, brown seaweeds (algae) found on the lower shore and below, especially *Laminaria digitata*. This species has fronds 1–2 m/3–6 ft long, a thick stalk, and a frond divided into flat fingers. In Japan and Korea it is cultivated and harvested commercially.

oasis area of land made fertile by the presence of water near the surface in an otherwise arid region. The occurrence of oases affects the distribution of plants, animals, and people in the desert regions of the world. ▷ *See feature on pp. 308–309.*

oat type of grass, genus *Avena*, a cereal food. The plant has long, narrow leaves and a stiff straw stem; the panicles of flowers, and later of grain, hang downwards. The cultivated oat *Avena sativa* is produced for human and animal food.

Oates Joyce Carol 1938– . US writer. Her novels are often aggressive, realistic descriptions of the forces of darkness and violence in modern culture. A prolific writer, she uses a wide range of genres and settings including the comedy *Unholy Loves* 1979, the Gothic horror of *A Bloodsmoor Romance* 1982, and the thriller *Kindred Passions* 1987. Her other novels include *A Garden of Earthly Delights* 1967, *them* 1969, and *Because It Is Bitter, and Because It Is My Heart* 1990.

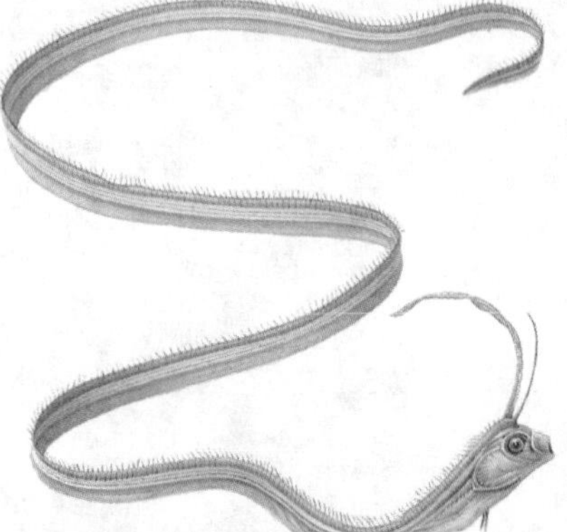

oarfish The oarfish is a strange-looking deep-sea fish found in warm parts of the Atlantic, Pacific, and Indian oceans. It grows up to 9 m/30 ft long. Its silver body is compressed and the dorsal fin forms a manelike crest behind the head.

Oates Laurence Edward Grace 1880–1912. British Antarctic explorer who accompanied Robert Falcon ◊Scott on his second expedition to the South Pole. On the return journey, suffering from frostbite, he went out alone into the blizzard to die rather than delay the others.

Oates Titus 1648–1705. English conspirator. A priest, he entered the Jesuit colleges at Valladolid, Spain, and St Omer, France, as a spy 1677–78, and on his return to England announced he had discovered a 'Popish Plot' to murder Charles II and re-establish Catholicism. Although this story was almost entirely false, many innocent Roman Catholics were executed during 1678–80 on Oates's evidence. In 1685 Oates was flogged, pilloried, and imprisoned for perjury. He was pardoned and granted a pension after the revolution of 1688.

oath solemn promise to tell the truth or perform some duty, combined with a declaration naming a deity or something held sacred. In English courts witnesses normally swear to tell the truth holding a ◊New Testament in their right hand. In the USA witnesses raise their right hand in taking the oath. People who object to the taking of oaths, such as ◊Quakers and atheists, give a solemn promise to tell the truth. Jews swear holding the Torah (Pentateuch), with their heads covered. Muslims and Hindus swear by their respective sacred books.

Oaxaca capital of a state of the same name in the Sierra Madre del Sur mountain range, central Mexico; population (1990) 212,900. Industries include food processing, textiles, and handicrafts.

Ob

Ob river in Asian Russia, flowing 3,380 km/2,100 mi from the Altai Mountains through the W Siberian Plain to the Gulf of Ob in the Arctic Ocean. With its main tributary, the Irtysh, it is 5,600 km/3,480 mi long. Although frozen for half the year, and subject to flooding, the Ob is a major transport route. Novosibirsk and Barnaul are the main ports.

OBE abbreviation for ***Officer of the Order of the British Empire***, a British honour.

obelisk tall, tapering column of stone, much used in ancient Egyptian and Roman architecture. Examples are Cleopatra's Needles 1475 BC, one of which is in London, another in New York.

Oberammergau village in Bavaria, Germany, 72 km/45 mi SW of Munich; population (1980) 5,000. A Christian ◊passion play has been performed here every ten years since 1634 (except during the world wars) to commemorate the ending of the Black Death plague.

Oberon in folklore, king of the elves or fairies and, according to the 13th-century French romance *Huon of Bordeaux*, an illegitimate son of Julius Caesar. Shakespeare used the character in *A Midsummer Night's Dream*.

Oberon Merle. Stage name of Estelle Merle O'Brien Thompson 1911–1979. Indian-born British actress. (She claimed to be Tasmanian.) She starred in several films by Alexander Korda (to whom she was briefly married 1939–45), including *The Scarlet Pimpernel* 1935. She played Cathy to Laurence Olivier's Heathcliff in *Wuthering Heights* 1939, and after 1940 worked in the USA.

obesity condition of being overweight (generally, 20% or more above the desirable weight for one's sex, build, and height). Obesity increases susceptibility to disease, strains the vital organs, and reduces life expectancy; it is usually remedied by controlled weight loss, healthy diet, and exercise.

obi or ***obeah*** form of witchcraft practised in the West Indies. It combines elements of Christianity and African religions, such as snake worship.

oboe musical instrument of the woodwind family, a refined treble shawm (a double-reed conical bore musical instrument) of narrow tapering bore and exposed double reed. The oboe was developed by the Hotteterre family of makers about 1700 and was incorporated in the court ensemble of Louis XIV. In C, it has a rich tone of elegant finish. Oboe concertos have been composed by Vivaldi, Albinoni, Richard Strauss, and others. Heinz Holliger is a modern virtuoso oboist.

Obote (Apollo) Milton 1924– . Ugandan politician who led the independence movement from 1961. He became prime minister 1962 and was president 1966–71 and 1980–85, being overthrown by first Idi ◊Amin and then by Lt-Gen Tito Okello.

Obrenovich Serbian dynasty that ruled 1816–42 and 1859–1903. The dynasty engaged in a feud with the rival house of Karageorgevich, which obtained the throne by the murder of the last Obrenovich 1903.

obscenity law law established by the Obscene Publications Act 1959 prohibiting the publishing of any material that tends to deprave or corrupt. In Britain, obscene material can be, for example, pornographic, violent, or can encourage drug taking. Publishing includes distribution, sale, and hiring of the material. There is a defence in support of the public good if the defendant can produce expert evidence to show that publication was in the interest of, for example, art, science, or literature.

observatory site or facility for observing astronomical or meteorological phenomena. The earliest recorded observatory was in Alexandria, N Africa, built by Ptolemy Soter in about 300 BC. The modern observatory dates from the invention of the telescope. Observatories may be ground-based, carried on aircraft, or sent into orbit as satellites, in space stations, and on the space shuttle.

The erection of observatories was revived in W Asia about AD 1000, and extended to Europe. The observatory built on the island of Hven (now Ven) in Denmark 1576 for Tycho Brahe (1546–1601) was elaborate, but survived only to 1597. It was followed by those in Paris 1667, Greenwich (the ◊Royal Greenwich Observatory) 1675, and Kew, England. Most early observatories were near towns, but with the advent of big telescopes, clear skies with little background light, and hence high, remote sites, became essential.

The most powerful optical telescopes covering the sky are at ◊Mauna Kea, Hawaii; ◊Mount Palomar, California; ◊Kitt Peak National Observatory, Arizona; La Palma, Canary Islands; Cerro Tololo Inter-American Observatory, and the ◊European Southern Observatory, Chile; ◊Siding Spring Mountain, Australia; and ◊Zelenchukskaya in the Caucasus.

Radio astronomy observatories include ◊Jodrell Bank, Cheshire, England; the ◊Mullard Radio Astronomy Observatory, Cambridge, England; ◊Arecibo, Puerto Rico; ◊Effelsberg, Germany; and ◊Parkes, Australia. The ◊Hubble Space Telescope was launched into orbit April 1990.

obsession persistently intruding thought, emotion, or impulse, often recognized by the sufferer as irrational, but nevertheless causing distress. It may be a brooding on destiny or death, or chronic doubts interfering with everyday life (such as fearing the gas is not turned off and repeatedly checking), or an impulse leading to repetitive action, such as continually washing one's hands.

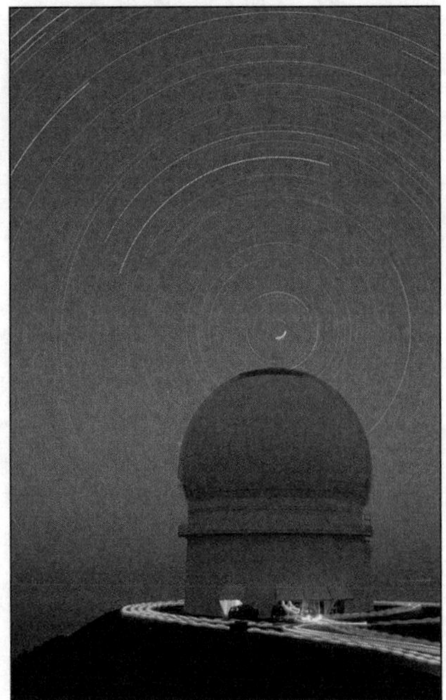

observatory A time-lapse photograph showing star trails over a telescope dome at Mauna Kea Observatory, Hawaii. Bright stars form arcs around the Pole Star above the Canada-France-Hawaii Telescope on the summit of Mauna Kea. Vehicle headlights leave glowing tracks around the base of the building. *Corbis*

obsidian black or dark-coloured glassy volcanic rock, chemically similar to ◊granite, but formed by cooling rapidly on the Earth's surface at low pressure. The glassy texture is the result of rapid cooling, which inhibits the growth of crystals. Obsidian was valued by the early civilizations of Mexico for making sharp-edged tools and ceremonial sculptures.

obstetrics medical speciality concerned with the management of pregnancy, childbirth, and the immediate postnatal period.

O'Casey Sean. Adopted name of John Casey 1884–1964. Irish dramatist. His early plays are tragicomedies, blending realism with symbolism and poetic with vernacular speech: *The Shadow of a Gunman* 1922, *Juno and the Paycock* 1925, and *The Plough and the Stars* 1926. Later plays include *Red Roses for Me* 1946 and *The Drums of Father Ned* 1960. He also wrote a six-volume autobiography.

Occam William of, or ***Ockham*** c. 1300–1349. English philosopher and scholastic logician who revived the fundamentals of nominalism. As a Franciscan monk he defended evangelical poverty against Pope John XXII, becoming known as the Invincible Doctor. He was imprisoned in Avignon, France, on charges of heresy 1328 but escaped to Munich, Germany, where he died. The principle of reducing assumptions to the absolute minimum is known as Occam's razor.

occult (Latin 'hidden from general view') vague term describing a wide range of activities connected with the supernatural, from seances to black magic, from reading one's horoscope in the newspaper to child abuse. The term has come to have a largely sinister connotation and association with Satanism and witchcraft. The occult sciences include the study and practice of such paranormal phenomena as telepathy and clairvoyance.

occultation in astronomy, the temporary obscuring of a star by a body in the solar system. Occultations are used to provide information about changes in an orbit, and the structure of objects in space, such as radio sources.

The exact shapes and sizes of planets and asteroids can be found when they occult stars. The rings of Uranus were discovered when that planet occulted a star 1977.

occupational psychology study of human behaviour at work. It includes dealing with problems in organizations, advising on management difficulties, and investigating the relationship between humans and machines (as in the design of aircraft controls; see also ◊ergonomics). Another area is ◊psychometrics and the use of assessment to assist in selection of personnel.

ocean great mass of salt water. Strictly speaking three oceans exist – the Atlantic, Indian, and Pacific – to which the Arctic is often added. They cover approximately 70% or 363,000,000 sq km/ 140,000,000 sq mi of the total surface area of the Earth. Water levels recorded in the world's oceans have shown an increase of 10–15 cm/4–6 in over the past 100 years.

depth (average) 3,660 m/12,000 ft, but shallow ledges (continental shelves) 180 m/600 ft run out from the continents, beyond which the continental slope reaches down to the ◊abyssal zone, the largest area, ranging from 2,000–6,000 m/6,500–19,500 ft. Only the ◊deep-sea trenches go deeper, the deepest recorded being 11,034 m/36,201 ft (by the *Vityaz*, USSR) in the Mariana Trench of the W Pacific 1957

features deep trenches (off E and SE Asia, and western South America), volcanic belts (in the W Pacific and E Indian Ocean), and ocean ridges (in the mid-Atlantic, E Pacific, and Indian Ocean)

temperature varies on the surface with latitude (−2°C to +29°C); decreases rapidly to 370 m/1,200 ft, then more slowly to 2,200 m/7,200 ft; and hardly at all beyond that

water contents salinity averages about 3%; minerals commercially extracted include bromine, magnesium, potassium, salt; those potentially recoverable include aluminium, calcium, copper, gold, manganese, silver.

pollution Oceans have always been used as a dumping area for human waste, but as the quantity of waste increases, and land areas for dumping it diminish, the problem is exacerbated. Today ocean pollutants include airborne emissions from land (33% by weight of total marine pollution); oil from both shipping and land-based sources; toxins from industrial, agricultural, and domestic uses; sewage; sediments from mining, forestry, and farming; plastic litter; and radioactive isotopes. Thermal pollution by cooling water from power plants or other industry is also a problem, killing coral and other temperature-sensitive sedentary species.

oceanarium large display tank in which aquatic animals and plants live together much as they would in their natural environment. The first oceanarium was created by the explorer and naturalist W Douglas Burden 1938 in Florida, USA.

ocean current fast-flowing ◊current of seawater generated by the wind or by variations in water density between two areas. Ocean currents are partly responsible for transferring heat from the equator to the poles and thereby evening out the global heat imbalance.

Ocean Drilling Program (ODP, formerly the ***Deep-Sea Drilling Project***) 1968–1985) research project initiated in the USA 1968 to sample the rocks of the ocean ◊crust. Initially under the direction of Scripps Institution of Oceanography, the project was planned and administered by the Joint Oceanographic Institutions for Deep Earth Sampling (JOIDES). The operation became international in 1975, when Britain, France, West Germany, Japan, and the USSR also became involved.

Oceania the groups of islands in the southern and central Pacific Ocean, comprising all those intervening between the southeastern shores of Asia and the western shores of America. See ◊Australasia and Oceania.

Oceanic art the art of the native peoples of Australia and the South Pacific Islands, including New Guinea and New Zealand, have little historical depth, despite the classifying work of modern anthropology. Of the little that remains from the prehistoric period, an outstanding example is the sculpture of ◊Easter Island, huge standing figures, possibly representing ancestors. Melanesian art – little of which remains in the islands – has inspired such Western artists as ◊Ernst, ◊Brancusi, ◊Giacometti, and Henry ◊Moore, among others. Most Oceanic arts are considered primitive in that until recently the indigenous cultures possessed no metal, and cutting tools were of stone or shell. For Australian aboriginal art, see ◊Australian art. ▷ *See feature on pp. 806–807.*

OCEANS AND SEAS

	Area in sq km/sq mi	Average depth in m/ft
Pacific Ocean	166,242,000/64,186,300	3,939/12,925
Atlantic Ocean	86,557,000/33,420,000	3,575/11,730
Indian Ocean	73,427,500/28,350,500	3,840/12,598
Arctic Ocean	13,224,000/5,105,700	1,038/3,407
South China Sea	2,975,000/1,148,500	1,464/4,802
Caribbean Sea	2,516,000/971,400	2,575/8,448
Mediterranean Sea	2,510,000/969,100	1,501/4,926
Bering Sea	2,261,061/873,000	1,491/4,893
Gulf of Mexico	1,508,000/582,100	1,614/5,297
Sea of Okhotsk	1,392,000/537,500	973/3,192
Sea of Japan	1,013,000/391,100	1,667/5,468
Hudson Bay	730,000/281,900	93/305
East China Sea	665,000/256,600	189/620
Andaman Sea	565,000/218,100	1,118/3,667
Black Sea	508,000/196,100	1,190/3,906
Red Sea	453,000/174,900	538/1,764
North Sea	427,000/164,900	94/308
Baltic Sea	382,000/147,500	55/180
Yellow Sea	294,000/113,500	37/121
Persian Gulf	230,000/88,800	100/328
Gulf of St Lawrence	162,000/62,530	810/2,660
Gulf of California	153,000/59,100	724/2,375
English Channel	89,900/34,700	54/177
Irish Sea	88,550/34,200	60/197
Bass Strait	75,000/28,950	70/230

oceanography study of the oceans. Its subdivisions deal with each ocean's extent and depth, the water's evolution and composition, its physics and chemistry, the bottom topography, currents and wind effects, tidal ranges, the biology, and the various aspects of human use.

Oceanography involves the study of water movements – currents, waves, and tides – and the chemical and physical properties of the seawater. It deals with the origin and topography of the ocean floor – ocean trenches and ridges formed by ◊plate tectonics, and continental shelves from the submerged portions of the continents. Computer simulations are widely used in oceanography to plot the possible movements of the waters, and many studies are carried out by remote sensing.

ocean ridge mountain range on the seabed indicating the presence of a constructive plate margin (where tectonic plates are moving apart and magma rises to the surface; see ◊plate tectonics). Ocean ridges, such as the ◊Mid-Atlantic Ridge, consist of many segments offset along transform ◊faults, and can rise thousands of metres above the surrounding seabed.

Ocean ridges usually have a ◊rift valley along their crests, indicating where the flanks are being pulled apart by the growth of the plates of the ◊lithosphere beneath. The crests are generally free of sediment; increasing depths of sediment are found with increasing distance down the flanks.

ocean trench deep trench in the seabed indicating the presence of a destructive margin (produced by the movements of ◊plate tectonics). The subduction or dragging downwards of one plate of the ◊lithosphere beneath another means that the ocean floor is pulled down. Ocean trenches are found around the edge of the Pacific Ocean and the NE Indian Ocean; minor ones occur in the Caribbean and near the Falkland Islands.

Ocean trenches represent the deepest parts of the ocean floor, the deepest being the ◊Mariana Trench which has a depth of 11,034 m/36,201 ft. At depths of below 6 km/3.6 mi there is no light and very high pressure; ocean trenches are inhabited by crustaceans, coelenterates (for example, sea anemones), polychaetes (a type of worm), molluscs, and echinoderms.

ocelot wild cat *Felis pardalis* of the southwestern USA, Mexico, and Central and South America, up to 1 m/3 ft long with a 45 cm/1.5 ft tail. It weighs about 18 kg/40 lb and has a pale yellowish coat marked with longitudinal stripes and blotches. Hunted for its fur, it is close to extinction. *See illustration on following page.*

Ockham William of, English philosopher; see ◊Occam.

O'Connell Daniel 1775–1847. Irish politician, called 'the Liberator'. Although ineligible, as a Roman Catholic, to take his seat, he was elected member of Parliament for County Clare 1828 and so

'There's no reason to bring religion into it. I think we ought to have as great a regard for religion as we can, so as to keep it out of as many things as possible.'

Sean O'Casey
The Plough and the Stars

ocelot **In some parts of its range the beautifully marked ocelot has been hunted almost to extinction for its pelt. It inhabits the thick forests of the central Americas where it hunts mainly at night for small mammals and birds. It is a comparatively small cat reaching no more than 1 m/3.3 ft in length.**

forced the government to grant Catholic emancipation. In Parliament he cooperated with the Whigs in the hope of obtaining concessions until 1841, when he launched his campaign for repeal of the union.

In 1823 O'Connell founded the Catholic Association to press Roman Catholic claims. His reserved and vacillating leadership and conservative outlook on social questions alienated his most active supporters, who broke away and formed the nationalist ◊Young Ireland movement.

O'Connor (Mary) Flannery 1925–1964. US novelist and short-story writer. Her works have a great sense of evil and sin, and often explore the religious sensibility of the Deep South, as in her novels *Wise Blood* 1952 and *The Violent Bear It Away* 1960. Her work exemplifies the postwar revival of the ◊Gothic novel in Southern US fiction.

Her collections of short stories include *A Good Man Is Hard to Find* 1955, *Everything That Rises Must Converge* 1965, and *Flannery O'Connor: Collected Works* 1988.

octahedron, regular regular solid with eight faces, each of which is an equilateral triangle. It is one of the five regular polyhedra or Platonic solids. The figure made by joining the midpoints of the faces is a perfect cube and the vertices of the octahedron are themselves the midpoints of the faces of a surrounding cube. For this reason, the cube and the octahedron are called dual solids.

octal number system number system to the base eight, used in computing. The highest digit that can appear in the octal system is seven. Normal decimal, or base-ten, numbers may be considered to be written under column headings based on the number ten. The octal number system is sometimes used by computer programmers as an alternative to the ◊hexadecimal number system. *See list of tables on p. 1177.*

octane rating numerical classification of petroleum fuels indicating their combustion characteristics.

The efficient running of an ◊internal combustion engine depends on the ignition of a petrol–air mixture at the correct time during the cycle of the engine. Higher-rated petrol burns faster than lower-rated fuels.

octave in music, a span of eight notes as measured on the white notes of a piano keyboard. It corresponds to the consonance of first and second harmonics.

octet rule in chemistry, rule stating that elements combine in a way that gives them the electronic structure of the nearest ◊inert gas. All the inert gases except helium have eight electrons in their outermost shell, hence the term octet.

October Revolution second stage of the ◊Russian Revolution 1917, when, on the night of 24 Oct (6 Nov in the Western calendar), the Bolshevik forces under Trotsky, and on orders from Lenin, seized the Winter Palace and arrested members of the Provisional Government. The following day the Second All-Russian Congress of Soviets handed over power to the Bolsheviks.

❛Go out and fight so life shouldn't be printed on dollar bills.❜

Clifford Odets
Awake and Sing

octopus any of an order (Octopoda) of ◊cephalopods, genus *Octopus*, having a round or oval body and eight arms with rows of suckers on each. They occur in all temperate and tropical seas, where they feed on crabs and other small animals.

Octopuses can vary their coloration according to their background and can swim using their arms as well as by a type of jet propulsion by means of their funnel. They are as intelligent as some vertebrates and not easily stimulated to aggression. Octopuses are shy creatures that release clouds of ink when frightened.

The common octopus *O. vulgaris* may reach 2 m/6 ft, and the rare, deep-sea giant octopus *O. apollyon* may span more than 10 m/32 ft. There are a few species of Australian blue-ringed octopods, genus *Hapalochlaena*; they can kill a human being in 15 minutes as a result of their venomous bite.

Oddsson David 1948– . Icelandic politician, prime minister from 1991. A member of the right-of-centre Independence Party, he was made vice chairman of the party 1989 and chairman 1991, when he succeeded Thorsteinn Pálsson as premier. Outside of politics, he has an established reputation as a stage and TV dramatist.

ode lyric poem of complex form. Odes originated in ancient Greece, where they were chanted to a musical accompaniment. Classical writers of odes include Sappho, Pindar, Horace, and Catullus. English poets who adopted the form include Spenser, Milton, Dryden, and Keats.

Oder (Polish ***Odra***) European river flowing N from the Czech Republic to the Baltic Sea (the Neisse River is a tributary); length 885 km/550 mi.

Oder–Neisse Line border between Poland and East Germany agreed at the Potsdam Conference 1945 at the end of World War II, named after the two rivers that formed the frontier.

Odessa seaport in Ukraine, on the Black Sea, capital of Odessa region; population (1992) 1,096,000. Products include chemicals, pharmaceuticals, and machinery.

Odessa was founded by Catherine II 1795 near the site of an ancient Greek settlement. Occupied by Germany 1941–44, it suffered severe damage under the Soviet scorched-earth policy and from German destruction.

Odets Clifford 1906–1963. US dramatist. He was associated with the Group Theatre and the most renowned of the social-protest dramatists of the Depression era. His plays include *Waiting for Lefty* 1935, about a taxi drivers' strike, *Awake and Sing* 1935, *Golden Boy* 1937, and *The Country Girl* 1950. In the late 1930s he went to Hollywood and became a successful film writer and director, but he continued to write plays.

Odin chief god of Scandinavian mythology, the ***Woden*** or ***Wotan*** of the Germanic peoples. A sky god, he lives in Asgard, at the top of the world-tree, and from the Valkyries (the divine maidens) receives the souls of half of the heroic slain warriors, feasting with them in his great hall, Valhalla; the rest are feasted by Freya, his wife. The son of Odin and Freya is Thor. Wednesday is named after Odin.

Odoacer c. 433–493. King of Italy from 476, when he deposed Romulus Augustulus, the last Roman emperor. He was a leader of the barbarian mercenaries employed by Rome. He was overthrown and killed by Theodoric the Great, king of the Ostrogoths.

Odo of Bayeux c. 1030–1097. French bishop, co-regent of England, who probably commissioned the ◊Bayeux Tapestry. He was the son of Duke Robert the Devil of Normandy and half-brother of William the Conqueror, from whom he received his bishopric 1049. His service at the Battle of ◊Hastings won him the earldom of Kent 1067 and vast English estates, making him one of the richest men in Europe. During William's absence in Normandy 1067 he shared the regency of England with William Fitzosborne and remained prominent in the royal administration until 1082.

Odysseus chief character of Homer's *Odyssey*, king of the island of Ithaca; he is also mentioned in the *Iliad* as one of the leaders of the Greek forces at the siege of Troy. Odysseus was distinguished among Greek leaders for his cleverness and cunning. He appears in other later tragedies.

Odyssey Greek epic poem; the product of an oral tradition, it was probably written before 700 BC and is attributed to ◊Homer. It describes the voyage home of Odysseus after the fall of Troy, and the vengeance he takes with his son Telemachus on the suitors of his wife Penelope on his return. During his ten-year wanderings, he encounters the Cyclops, the enchantress Circe, Scylla and Charybdis, and the Sirens.

OECD abbreviation for ◊***Organization for Economic Cooperation and Development***.

oedema any abnormal accumulation of fluid in tissues or cavities of the body; waterlogging of the tissues due to excessive loss of ◊plasma through the capillary walls. It may be generalized (the condition once known as dropsy) or confined to one area, such as the ankles.

Oedipus in Greek mythology, king of Thebes who unwittingly killed his father, Laius, and married his mother, Jocasta, in fulfilment of a prophecy. When he learned what he had done, he put out his eyes. His story was dramatized by the Greek tragedian ◊Sophocles.

Left to die at birth because Laius had been warned by an oracle that his son would kill him, Oedipus was saved and brought up by the king of Corinth. Oedipus later killed Laius in a quarrel (without recognizing him). Because Oedipus saved Thebes from the Sphinx, he was granted the Theban kingdom and Jocasta (wife of Laius and his own mother) as his wife. After four children had been born, the truth was discovered. Jocasta hanged herself, Oedipus blinded himself, and as an exiled wanderer was guided by his daughter, Antigone, to a final resting place at Colonus, near Athens.

Oedipus complex in psychology, the unconscious antagonism of a son to his father, whom he sees as a rival for his mother's affection. For a girl antagonistic to her mother, as a rival for her father's affection, the term is Electra complex. The terms were coined by Sigmund ◊Freud. Freud saw this as a universal part of childhood development, which in most children is resolved during late childhood. Contemporary theory places less importance on the Oedipus/Electra complex than did Freud and his followers.

oersted c.g.s. unit (symbol Oe) of ◊magnetic field strength, now replaced by the SI unit ampere per metre. The Earth's magnetic field is about 0.5 oersted; the field near the poles of a small bar magnet is several hundred oersteds; and a powerful ◊electromagnet can have a field strength of 30,000 oersteds.

Oersted Hans Christian 1777–1851. Danish physicist who founded the science of electromagnetism. In 1820 he discovered the ◊magnetic field associated with an electric current.

oesophagus muscular tube by which food travels from mouth to stomach. The human oesophagus is about 23 cm/9 in long. Its extends downwards from the ◊pharynx, immediately behind the windpipe. It is lined with a mucous membrane which secretes lubricant fluid to assist the downward movement of food (◊peristalsis).

oestrogen any of a group of hormones produced by the ◊ovaries of vertebrates; the term is also used for various synthetic hormones that mimic their effects. The principal oestrogen in mammals is oestradiol. Oestrogens control female sexual development, promote the growth of female secondary sexual characteristics, stimulate egg production, and, in mammals, prepare the lining of the uterus for pregnancy.

Oestrogens are used therapeutically for some hormone disorders and to inhibit lactation; they also form the basis of oral contraceptives. US researchers 1995 observed that oestrogen plays a role in the healing of damaged blood vessels. It has also been found that women recover more quickly from strokes if given a low oestrogen dose.

oestrus in mammals, the period during a female's reproductive cycle (also known as the oestrus cycle or ◊menstrual cycle) when mating is most likely to occur. It usually coincides with ovulation.

O'Faolain Sean (born John Whelan) 1900–1991. Irish novelist, short-story writer, critic, and biographer. His first book was *Midsummer Night Madness and Other Stories* 1932, after which he wrote *A Nest of Simple Folk* 1933, the first of his three novels. He also wrote biographies of Daniel ◊O'Connell 1938, ◊de Valera (beside whom he had fought in the Irish Republican Army) 1939, and Cardinal ◊Newman 1952. He founded the influential Irish literary journal *The Bell* 1940, and edited it until 1946. *Collected Short Stories* was published 1980–82.

Offa died c. 796. King of Mercia, England, from 757. He conquered Essex, Kent, Sussex, and Surrey; defeated the Welsh and the West Saxons; and established Mercian supremacy over all England south of the river Humber.

Offaly county of the Republic of Ireland, in the province of Leinster, between Galway on the W and Kildare on the E; county town Tullamore; area 2,000 sq km/772 sq mi; population (1991) 58,500. It is low-lying, with part of the Bog of Allen to the N. Features include the rivers Shannon (along the western boundary), Brosna, Clodagh, and Broughill and the Slieve Bloom mountains in the SE. Peat is used to fuel power stations; products include oats, barley, wheat, and cattle.

Offa's Dyke defensive earthwork along the Welsh border, of which there are remains from the mouth of the river Dee to that of the river Severn. It represents the boundary secured by ◊Offa's wars with Wales. The dyke covered a distance of 240 km/149 mi, of which 130 km/81 mi are still standing.

Offenbach Jacques 1819–1880. French composer. He wrote light opera, initially for presentation at the *Bouffes parisiens*. Among his works are *Orphée aux enfers/Orpheus in the Underworld* 1858, revised 1874, *La Belle Hélène* 1864, and *Les Contes d'Hoffmann/The Tales of Hoffmann* 1881.

Offenbach *The German-born composer Jacques Offenbach (1819–1880), from a chromolithograph of 1912. After moving to Paris as a teenager, he later became a leading composer of opéras-comiques. Wagner, never renowned for his humour, did not appreciate being parodied in Le Carnaval des revues. Image Select (UK) Ltd*

Official Secrets Act UK act of Parliament 1989, prohibiting the disclosure of confidential material from government sources by employees; it remains an absolute offence for a member or former member of the security and intelligence services (or those working closely with them) to disclose information about their work. There is no public-interest defence, and disclosure of information already in the public domain is still a crime. Journalists who repeat disclosures may also be prosecuted.

offset printing the most common method of ◊printing, which uses smooth (often rubber) printing plates. It works on the principle of ◊lithography: that grease and water repel one another.

The printing plate is prepared using a photographic technique, resulting in a type image that attracts greasy printing ink. On the printing press the plate is wrapped around a cylinder and wetted and inked in turn. The ink adheres only to the type area, and this image is then transferred via an intermediate blanket cylinder to the paper.

O'Flaherty Liam 1896–1984. Irish author. He is best known for his short stories published in volumes such as *Spring Sowing* 1924, *The Tent* 1926, and *Two Lovely Beasts* 1948. His novels, set in County Mayo, are less poetic and more violent than his stories; they include *Thy Neighbour's Wife* 1923, *The Informer* 1925 (Tait Black Memorial Prize), *Skerrett* 1932, and *Famine* 1937. *The Short Stories* (new edition) was published 1986. O'Flaherty's writings have a strength acquired from his sense of primeval humanity beneath the layers of civilization.

Ogaden desert region in Harar province, SE Ethiopia, that borders on Somalia. It is a desert plateau, rising to 1,000 m/3,280 ft, inhabited mainly by Somali nomads practising arid farming. The area became one of five new autonomous provinces created in Ethiopia 1987.

A claim to the area was made by Somalia in the 1960s, resulting in guerrilla fighting and major Somali advances during 1977. By 1980 Ethiopia, backed by the USSR and Cuba, was again in virtual control of the area, but armed clashes continued. In 1988 diplomatic relations were restored between Ethiopia and Somalia and troops were withdrawn from their shared border. Internal troubles in Somalia 1990 created a large refugee population in E Ogaden.

Oglethorpe James Edward 1696–1785. English soldier and colonizer of Georgia. He served in parliament for 32 years and in 1732 obtained a charter for the colony of Georgia, USA, intended as a refuge for debtors and for European Protestants.

Ogoni an ethnic minority of about 500,000 (1990) occupying an impoverished area of about 350 square miles in the Niger river delta of Nigeria. They speak Khana, Gokama, and Eleme languages which form a distinct branch of the Benue-Congo language family. They are fishermen and farmers, yams being the principal crop. In 1958 oil was discovered under their land. In protest at the pollution from the oil wells and their lack of any benefit from oil revenues they petitioned the Nigerian government for political autonomy in 1990 and 1992.

The Ogoniland resistance organization was founded 1990. The Ogoni claim that their land was heavily polluted by the Shell oil company's activities and oil spills, and that by 1995 more than 1,800 people had been killed by Nigerian troops who regard them as secessionists. The activist and environmental campaigner Ken Saro-Wiwa (1941–95), who had led the campaign for Ogoni self-determination, was executed along with eight colleagues by the Nigerian military government in 1995, prompting the Commonwealth to suspend Nigeria's membership. Shell withdrew from Ogoniland in 1993 following sabotage of its pipelines.

Ogun state of SW Nigeria; area 16,762 sq km/6,474 sq mi; capital Abeokuta; population (1991) 2,338,600.

O'Hara Frank 1926–1966. US poet and art critic. He was the leading member of the New York School of poets (others include John Ashbery, Kenneth Koch (1925–), and James Schuyler (1923–)), whose work was based on an immediate and autobiographical relationship to city life. His work includes *Lunch Poems* 1964.

He also wrote essays and criticism collected in *Standing Still in New York* and *Art Chronicles* both 1975.

O'Higgins Bernardo 1778–1842. Chilean revolutionary, known as 'the Liberator of Chile'. He was a leader of the struggle for independence from Spanish rule 1810–17 and head of the first permanent national government 1817–23.

Ohio river in the USA, 1,580 km/980 mi long; it is formed by the union of the Allegheny and Monongahela at Pittsburgh, Pennsylvania, and flows SW until it joins the river Mississippi at Cairo, Illinois.

Ohio state in N central USA; nicknamed Buckeye State
area 107,100 sq km/41,341 sq mi
capital Columbus
towns and cities Cleveland, Cincinnati, Dayton, Akron, Toledo, Youngstown, Canton
population (1991) 10,939,000
features Lake Erie; Ohio River; Serpent Mound, an embankment built by Hopewell American Indians c. 2nd–1st centuries BC; Mound City Group, 23 prehistoric mounds, a burial ground of the Hopewell American Indians; Cleveland, with the Old Arcade (1890), the Cleveland Museum of Art, and the Rock and Roll Hall of Fame and Museum (1995); Cincinnati, with the Cincinnati Art Museum, Museum Center at Union Terminal, the Carew Tower, and Omni Netherland Plaza Hotel; Columbus, with German Village (built by 19th-century immigrants); Dayton, with the Wright Brothers Bicycle Shop and the Wright Memorial, and the US Air Force Museum; the National Afro-American Museum and Cultural Center, Canton; Oberlin College (1833), the first coeducational college in the USA; the Cleveland Orchestra; the Cincinnati Symphony Orchestra
industries coal, cereals, livestock, dairy foods, machinery, chemicals, steel, motor vehicles, automotive and aircraft parts, rubber products, office equipment, refined petroleum
famous people Thomas Edison, John Glenn, Paul Newman, General Sherman, Orville Wright; seven presidents (Garfield, Grant, Harding, Harrison, Hayes, McKinley, and Taft)
history explored for France by La Salle 1669; ceded to Britain by France 1763; first settled at Marietta (capital of the Northwest Territory) by Europeans 1788; became a state 1803.

Ohio

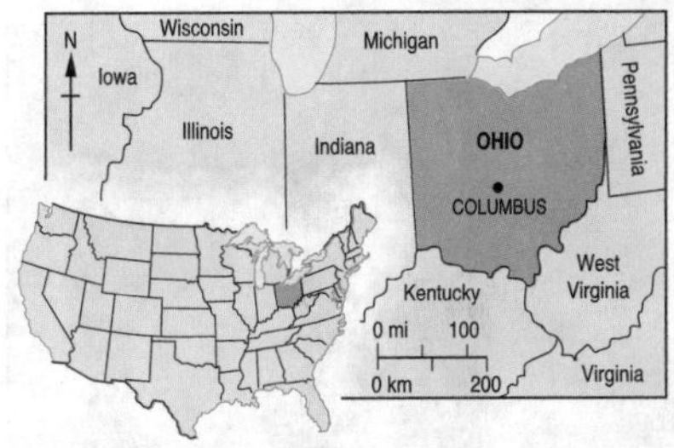

ohm SI unit (symbol ω) of electrical ◊resistance (the property of a conductor that restricts the flow of electrons through it). It was originally defined with reference to the resistance of a column of mercury, but is now taken as the resistance between two points when a potential difference of one volt between them produces a current of one ampere.

Ohm Georg Simon 1789–1854. German physicist who studied electricity and discovered the fundamental law that bears his name. The SI unit of electrical resistance, the ohm, is named after him, and the unit of conductance (the inverse of resistance) was formerly called the mho, which is 'ohm' spelled backwards.

Ohm's law law that states that the current flowing in a metallic conductor maintained at constant temperature is directly proportional to the potential difference (voltage) between its ends. The law was discovered by German physicist Georg Ohm 1827.

If a current of I amperes flows between two points in a conductor across which the potential difference is V volts, then V/I is a constant called the ◊resistance R ohms between those two points. Hence:

$$V/I = R$$
$$\text{or } V = IR$$

Not all conductors obey Ohm's law; those that do are called ohmic conductors.

OIC abbreviation for ◊***Organization of the Islamic Conference***.

oil flammable substance, usually insoluble in water, and composed chiefly of carbon and hydrogen. Oils may be solids (fats and waxes) or liquids. The three main types are: ***essential oils***, obtained from plants; ***fixed oils***, obtained from animals and plants; and ***mineral oils***, obtained chiefly from the refining of ◊petroleum.

Essential oils are volatile liquids that have the odour of their plant source and are used in perfumes, flavouring essences, and in ◊aromatherapy. Fixed oils are mixtures of ◊lipids, of varying consistency, found in both animals (for example, fish oils) and plants (in nuts and seeds); they are used as foods and as lubricants, and in the making of soaps, paints, and varnishes. Mineral oils are composed of a mixture of hydrocarbons, and are used as fuels and lubricants. *See illustration on following page.*

oil, cooking fat that is liquid at room temperature, extracted from the seeds or fruits of certain

oil A production platform in British Petroleum's Magnus oilfield in the North Sea. Development of the North Sea oilfields was accelerated by the 1973 oil crisis. Poor weather conditions and deep, stormy waters combine to make oil extraction difficult, dangerous, and expensive. *British Petroleum*

plants and used for frying, salad dressings, and sauces and condiments such as mayonnaise and mustard. Plants used for cooking oil include sunflower, olive, maize (corn), soya, peanut, and rape. Vegetable oil is a blend of more than one type of oil. Most oils are hot-pressed and refined, a process that leaves them without smell or flavour. Cold-pressed, unrefined oils keep their flavour. Oils are generally low in cholesterol and contain a high proportion of polyunsaturated or monounsaturated fatty acids, although all except soya and corn oil become saturated when heated.

oil crop plant from whose seeds vegetable oils are pressed. Cool temperate areas grow rapeseed and linseed; warm temperate regions produce sunflowers, olives, and soya beans; tropical regions produce groundnuts (peanuts), palm oil, and coconuts. Some of the major vegetable oils, such as soya bean oil, peanut oil, and cottonseed oil, are derived from crops grown primarily for other purposes. Most vegetable oils are used as both edible oils and as ingredients in industrial products such as soaps, varnishes, printing inks, and paints.

oil paint painting medium in which ground pigment is bound with oil, usually linseed. Oil paint was in decorative use as early as the 5th century, but its artistic application is usually credited to the early-15th-century Flemish painter, Jan van Eyck. Passing from Flanders to Rome, it quickly succeeded tempera as the standard medium. Capable of the greatest flexibility and luminosity, oil paint has since the 16th century been considered pre-eminent among painting media, although ◊acrylic paint may prove in time to be a rival.

oil palm African ◊palm tree *Elaeis guineensis*, the fruit of which yields valuable oils, used as food or processed into margarine, soaps, and livestock feeds.

'It is part of the High Plains, wide and flat. If you raise your arms, they touch the sky, and if you spread them, they reach the end of the earth.'

On **Oklahoma**
Douglas Reed
Far and Wide

oil spill oil released by damage to or discharge from a tanker or oil installation. An oil spill kills all shore life, clogging up the feathers of birds and suffocating other creatures. At sea toxic chemicals leach into the water below, poisoning sea life. Mixed with dust, the oil forms globules that sink to the seabed, poisoning sea life there as well. Oil spills are broken up by the use of detergents but such chemicals can themselves damage wildlife. The annual spillage of oil is 8 million barrels a year. At any given time tankers are carrying 500 million barrels.

In March 1989 the *Exxon Valdez* (belonging to the ◊Exxon Corporation) spilled oil in Alaska's Prince William Sound, covering 12,400 sq km/4,800 sq mi and killing at least 34,400 sea birds, 10,000 sea otters, and up to 16 whales. The incident led to the US Oil Pollution Act of 1990, which requires tankers operating in US waters to have double hulls.

The world's largest oil spill was in the Persian Gulf in Feb 1991 as a direct result of hostilities during the ◊Gulf War. Around 6–8 million barrels of oil were spilled, polluting 675 km/420 mi of Saudi coastline. In some places, the oil was 30 cm/12 in deep in the sand. ▷ *See feature on pp. 858–859.*

Oise European river that rises in the Ardennes plateau, Belgium, and flows SW through France for 300 km/186 mi to join the Seine about 65 km/40 mi below Paris. It gives its name to a French *département* in Picardie.

Oistrakh David Fyodorovich 1908–1974. Soviet violinist. He was celebrated for performances of both standard and contemporary Russian repertoire. Shostakovich wrote both his violin concertos for him. His son ***Igor*** (1931–) is equally renowned as a violinist.

okapi ruminant *Okapia johnstoni* of the giraffe family, although with much shorter legs and neck, found in the tropical rainforests of central Africa. Purplish brown with a creamy face and black and white stripes on the legs and hindquarters, it is excellently camouflaged. Okapis have remained virtually unchanged for millions of years. Now only a few hundred are thought to survive.

Okavango Swamp marshy area in NW Botswana, fed by the Okavango River, which rises in Angola and flows SE about 1,600 km/1,000 mi. It is an important area for wildlife.

O'Keeffe Georgia 1887–1986. US painter. She is known chiefly for her large, semi-abstract studies of flowers and bones, such as *Black Iris* 1926 (Metropolitan Museum of Art, New York) and the *Pelvis Series* of the 1940s. She was married 1924–46 to photographer and art exhibitor Alfred ◊Stieglitz, in whose gallery her work was first shown.

Her mature style stressed contours and subtle tonal transitions, which often transformed the subject into a powerful and erotic abstract image. In 1946 she settled in New Mexico, where the desert landscape inspired many of her paintings.

O'Keeffe US painter Georgia O'Keeffe at an exhibition of her work *Life and Death*, 1931. Her clear, precise paintings, often featuring bones and flowers, have an eerie Surrealist quality. *Corbis*

Okinawa group of islands, forming part of the Japanese ◊Ryukyu Islands in the W Pacific; the largest island is Okinawa
area 2,250 sq km/869 sq mi
capital Naha
features Okinawa, the largest island of the group (area 1,176 sq km/453 sq mi; population (1990) 105,852), has a large US military base
population (1995) 1,274,000
history virtually all buildings were destroyed in World War II. The principal island, Okinawa, was captured by the USA in the Battle of Okinawa 1 April–21 June 1945, with 47,000 US casualties (12,000 dead) and 60,000 Japanese (only a few hundred survived as prisoners). During the invasion over 150,000 Okinawans, mainly civilians, died; many were massacred by Japanese forces. The island was returned to Japan 1972.

okapi The okapi has a prehensile tongue which is used to pick tasty leaves. The tongue is so long that the animal uses it to clean its eyes and eyelids. The okapi is found in the tropical forests of Zaire.

Oklahoma state in S central USA; nicknamed Sooner State
area 181,100 sq km/69,905 sq mi
capital Oklahoma City
towns and cities Tulsa, Lawton, Norman, Enid
features Arkansas, Red, and Canadian rivers; Wichita Mountains Wildlife Refuge; Ouachita national forest; Tallgrass Prairie Reserve; Grand Lake o'the Cherokees; Salt Plains national wildlife refuge, with whooping cranes and bald eagles; a large Native American population, mainly in the E; Fort Sill Military Reservation (1869), where Geronimo died 1909; Tahlequah, headquarters of the Cherokee Nation, with the Cherokee National Museum; Anadarko, with the Southern Plains Indian Museum and Craft Centre, the National Hall of Fame for famous Native Americans, and Indian City USA; Spiro Mounds Archaeological state park, with the remains of earth mounds lived in by the Spiro 900–1400; Guthrie; Dog Iron Ranch and Will Rogers Birthplace; Will Rogers Memorial; Oklahoma City, including the Oklahoma state capitol (with oil wells in its grounds), Harn Homestead and 1889er Museum, and the National Cowboy Hall of Fame and Western Heritage Center; Tulsa, with art deco architecture from the 1920s, and the Gilcrease Museum (with a collection of Native American art); Bartlesville, with the Frank Phillips home (1909) and the Price Tower (1956, designed by Frank Lloyd Wright); Woolacre Museum, a wildlife reserve with a museum of the West
industries cereals, peanuts, cotton, livestock, oil, natural gas, helium, machinery and other metal products
population (1990) 3,145,600
famous people John Berryman, Ralph Ellison, Woody Guthrie, Mickey Mantle, Will Rogers, Jim Thorpe
history explored for Spain by Francisco de Coronado 1541; most acquired by the USA from France with the ◊Louisiana Purchase 1803.

Part of the present state formed the Territory of Oklahoma from 1890, and was thrown open to settlers with lotteries and other hurried methods of distributing land. Together with what remained of Indian Territory, it became a state 1907.

Oklahoma City industrial city (oil refining, machinery, aircraft, telephone equipment), capital of Oklahoma, USA, on the Canadian River;

Oklahoma

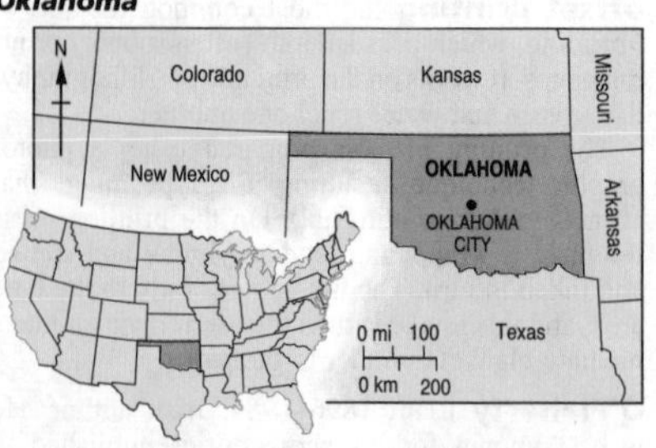

population (1992) 454,000. On 22 April 1889, a tent city of nearly 10,000 inhabitants was set up overnight as the area was opened to settlement. In 1910 Oklahoma City had 64,000 people and became the state capital.

okra plant *Hibiscus esculentus* belonging to the Old World hibiscus family. Its red-and-yellow flowers are followed by long, sticky, green fruits known as ladies' fingers or bhindi. The fruits are cooked in soups and stews.

Okri Ben 1959– . Nigerian novelist, broadcaster, and journalist. His novel *The Famished Road* won the UK Booker Prize 1991. He published his first book *Flowers and Shadows* 1980, and wrote his second, *The Landscapes Within* 1982, while still a student at university in Essex, England.

Olaf five kings of Norway, including:

Olaf (I) Tryggvesson c. 969–1000. King of Norway from 995. He began the conversion of Norway to Christianity and was killed in a sea battle against the Danes and Swedes.

Olaf (II) Haraldsson c. 995–1030. King of Norway from 1015. He offended his subjects by his centralizing policy and zeal for Christianity, and was killed in battle by Norwegian rebel chiefs backed by ◊Canute of Denmark. He was declared the patron saint of Norway 1164.

Olaf V 1903–1991. King of Norway from 1957, when he succeeded his father, Haakon VII.

After the German invasion of Norway 1940 Olav, as crown prince, became a rallying point for his compatriots by holding out against German air raids for two months and later, in exile in England, playing an important part in liaison with resistance movements in Norway as well as building up the Free Norwegian forces in Britain.

Olazabal Jose Maria 1966– . Spanish golfer, one of the leading players on the European circuit. After a distinguished amateur career he turned professional 1986. He was a member of the European Ryder Cup teams 1987, 1989, 1991, and 1993 and won the US Masters 1994.

old age later years of life. The causes of progressive degeneration of bodily and mental processes associated with it are still not precisely known, but every one of the phenomena of ◊ageing can occur at almost any age, and the process does not take place throughout the body at an equal rate. Geriatrics is the branch of medicine dealing with the diagnosis and treatment of disease in the elderly.

Old Bailey popular name for the Central Criminal Court in London, situated in a street of that name in the City of London, off Ludgate Hill.

Old Catholic one of various breakaway groups from Roman Catholicism, including those in the Netherlands (such as the Church of Utrecht, who separated from Rome 1724 after accusations of ◊Jansenism); and groups in Austria, Czechoslovakia, Germany, and Switzerland, who rejected the proclamation of ◊papal infallibility of 1870. Old Catholic clergy are not celibate.

Oldenbarneveldt Johan van 1547–1619. Dutch politician, a leading figure in the Netherlands' struggle for independence from Spain. He helped William the Silent negotiate the Union of Utrecht 1579.

As leader of the Republican party he opposed the war policy of stadholder (magistrate) Maurice of Orange and negotiated a 12-year truce with Spain 1609. His support of the Remonstrants (Arminians) in the religious strife against Maurice and the Gomarists (Calvinists) effected his downfall and he was arrested and executed.

Oldenburg Claes Thure 1929– . US Pop artist. He organized ◊happenings and made assemblages (works of art constructed from atypical materials), but is best known for 'soft sculptures', gigantic replicas of everyday objects and foods, made of stuffed canvas or vinyl. One characteristic work is *Lipstick* 1969 (Yale University).

Old English general name for the range of dialects spoken by Germanic settlers in England between the 5th and 11th centuries AD, also known as ◊Anglo-Saxon. The literature of the period includes *Beowulf*, an epic in West Saxon dialect. Other Old English literature includes shorter poems such as 'The Wanderer' and 'The Seafarer', prose chronicles, Bible translations, spells, and charms. See also ◊English language.

Old English literature poetry and prose in the various dialects of Old English written between AD 449 and 1066. Poetry (alliterative, without rhyme) was composed and delivered orally, much has therefore been lost. What remains owes its survival to monastic scribes who favoured verse with a Christian motivation or flavour. Prose in Old English was a later achievement, essentially beginning in the reign of Alfred the Great.

The greatest surviving epic poem is ◊*Beowulf* c. 700, which recounts the hero's battles with mythical foes such as the man-eating Grendel and his mother. *Widsith/The Wanderer, Finnsburgh* (about a tragic battle), and *Waldhere* (fragments of a lost epic), all mid-7th century, also belong to the the earlier centuries and express the bleakness and melancholy of life. *The Battle of Maldon* written soon after the event 991, extols heroic values of courage in defeat.

One of the earliest attributed short poems consists of six lines by ◊Caedmon the herder, reputedly inspired to sing about the Creation by a vision. 'The Dream of the Rood' c. 698 shows the cult of the Cross, as does ◊Cynewulf's 'Elene'. Elegies, including 'The Seafarer' written before 940, express the sense of loneliness in exile and an inflexible Fate.

Prose in Old English dates from Alfred the Great's translations of St Gregory, Boethius, and Bede's *History of the English Peoples* (first published in Latin 731), translated between 871 and 899). Historical writing began with the *Anglo-Saxon Chronicle*, at first brief notes of yearly events but later a dignified and even poetic narrative. The existing version of the Chronicle dates from King Alfred's reign and was compiled from earlier records (now lost) purporting to go back to the time of Adam. Dating from the 10th and 11th centuries are sermons by ◊Aelfric, a Dorset monk who also translated the Old Testament, and those by the prelate Wulfstan (died 1023). Some spells and riddles have also survived.

Oldham industrial town in Greater Manchester, England; population (1991) 211,400. Industries include textiles and textile machinery, plastics, electrical goods, and electronic equipment. It was traditionally a cotton-spinning town.

Old Testament Christian term for the Hebrew ◊Bible, which is the first part of the Christian Bible. It contains 39 (according to Christianity) or 24 (according to Judaism) books, which include the origins of the world, the history of the ancient Hebrews and their covenant with God, prophetical writings, and religious poetry. The first five books (*The five books of Moses*) are traditionally ascribed to Moses and known as the Pentateuch (by Christians) or the ◊Torah (by Jews).

The language of the original text was Hebrew, dating from the 12th–2nd centuries BC. The earliest known manuscripts containing part of the text were found among the ◊Dead Sea Scrolls. The traditional text (translated first into Greek and then other languages) was compiled by rabbinical authorities around the 2nd century AD.

Old Trafford two sporting centres in Manchester, England. Old Trafford football ground is the home of Manchester United FC and was opened 1910. The record attendance is 76,692, although its capacity is now reduced to 50,726. It was used for the 1966 World Cup competition and has also hosted one FA Cup Final and two FA Cup Final replays. Old Trafford cricket ground was opened 1857 and has staged Test matches regularly since 1884. The ground capacity is 40,000.

Olduvai Gorge deep cleft in the Serengeti steppe, Tanzania, where Louis and Mary ◊Leakey found prehistoric stone tools in the 1930s. They discovered Pleistocene remains of prehumans and gigantic animals 1958–59. The gorge has given its name to the Olduvai culture, a simple stone-tool culture of prehistoric hominids, dating from 2–0.5 million years ago. ▷ *See feature on pp. 518–519.*

Old World the continents of the eastern hemisphere, so called because they were familiar to Europeans before the Americas. The term is used as an adjective to describe animals and plants that live in the eastern hemisphere.

oleander or ***rose bay*** evergreen Mediterranean shrub *Nerium oleander* of the dogbane family Apocynaceae, with pink or white flowers and aromatic leaves that secrete the poison oleandrin.

oligarchy rule of the few, in their own interests. It was first identified as a form of government by the Greek philosopher Aristotle. In modern times there have been a number of oligarchies, sometimes posing as democracies; the paramilitary rule of the ◊Duvalier family in Haiti, 1957–86, is an example.

Oligocene third epoch of the Tertiary period of geological time, 35.5–3.25 million years ago. The name, from Greek, means 'a little recent', referring to the presence of the remains of some modern types of animals existing at that time.

oligopoly in economics, a situation in which a few companies control the major part of a particular market. For example, in the UK the two largest soap-powder companies, Procter & Gamble and Unilever, control over 85% of the market. In an oligopolistic market, firms may well join together in a ◊cartel, colluding to fix high prices. This collusion, an example of a restrictive trade practice, is illegal in the UK and the European Union.

oligosaccharide ◊carbohydrate comprising a few ◊monosaccharide units linked together. It is a general term used to indicate that a carbohydrate is larger than a simple di- or trisaccharide but not as large as a polysaccharide.

olive evergreen tree *Olea europaea* of the family Oleaceae. Native to Asia but widely cultivated in Mediterranean and subtropical areas, it grows up to 15 m/50 ft high, with twisted branches and opposite, lance-shaped silvery leaves. The white flowers are followed by green oval fruits that ripen a bluish black. They are preserved in brine or oil, dried, or pressed to make olive oil. The oil, which is a pale, greenish yellow and chiefly composed of glycerides, is widely consumed; it is also used in soaps and ointments, and as a lubricant.

olive branch ancient symbol of peace; in the Bible (Genesis 9), an olive branch is brought back by the dove to Noah to show that the flood has abated.

olivenite basic copper arsenate, $Cu_2AsO_4(OH)$, occurring as a mineral in olive-green prisms.

Oliver King (Joseph) 1885–1938. US jazz cornet player, bandleader, and composer. His work with Louis Armstrong 1922–24, on numbers like 'Canal Street Blues', took jazz beyond the confines of early Dixieland. His other compositions include 'Snake Rag' 1923 and 'Dr Jazz' 1927.

Olives, Mount of range of hills E of Jerusalem, associated with the Christian religion: a former chapel (now a mosque) marks the traditional site of Jesus' ascension to heaven, with the Garden of Gethsemane at its foot.

Olivetti Italian office-machinery and furniture company, based in Ivrea, a small town near Milan. Formed 1908 by Camillo Olivetti (1868–1943), the company is known for its high design standards, sustained through relationships with some of this century's leading designers.

Olivier Laurence Kerr. Baron Olivier 1907–1989. English actor and director. For many years associated with the Old Vic theatre, he was director of the National Theatre company 1962–73. His stage roles include Henry V, Hamlet, Richard III, and Archie Rice in John Osborne's *The Entertainer* 1957 (filmed 1960). His acting and direction of filmed versions of Shakespeare's plays received critical acclaim for example, *Henry V* 1944 and *Hamlet* 1948 (Academy Award).

> *'What is acting but lying and what is good acting but convincing lying?'*
>
> LAURENCE OLIVIER *Autobiography*

olivine greenish mineral, magnesium iron silicate, $(Mg,Fe)_2SiO_4$. It is a rock-forming mineral, present in, for example, peridotite, gabbro, and basalt. Olivine is called peridot when pale green and transparent, and used in jewellery.

olm cave-dwelling aquatic salamander *Proteus anguinus*, the only European member of the family Proteidae, the other members being the North American mudpuppies. Olms are found in underground caves along the Adriatic seaboard in Italy, Croatia, and Yugoslavia. The adult is permanently larval in form, about 25 cm/10 in long, almost blind, with external gills and under-developed limbs. See ◊neoteny.

Olmec first civilization of Mesoamerica and thought to be the mother culture of the Mayans. It

Olivier English actor and director Laurence Olivier holding the skull of Yorick in a 1948 production of *Hamlet*. During a career that spanned nearly 60 years, Olivier played both Shakespearean and modern roles and appeared in a number of films. He was director of the Old Vic, London, the Chichester Festival Theatre, and the National Theatre, London. *Corbis*

developed in the coastal zone S of Vera Cruz and in adjacent Tabasco 1200–400 BC. The Olmecs built a large clay pyramid and several smaller mounds on the island of La Venta. Some gigantic stone heads, vestiges of their religion, also remain.

Olson Charles John 1910–1970. US poet and theoretician. He was a leader of the ◊Black Mountain school of experimental poets and originator of the theory of 'composition by field'.

Olympia ancient sanctuary in the W Peloponnese, Greece, with a temple of Zeus, and the stadium (for foot races, boxing, wrestling) and hippodrome (for chariot and horse races), where the original Olympic Games, founded 776 BC, were held every four years. The gold and ivory statue of Zeus that was here, made by ◊Phidias, was one of the ◊Seven Wonders of the World.

Olympic Games sporting contests originally held in Olympia, ancient Greece, every four years during a sacred truce; records were kept from 776 BC. Women were forbidden to be present, and the male contestants were naked. The ancient Games were abolished AD 394. The present-day games have been held every four years since 1896. Since 1924 there has been a separate winter Games programme; from 1994 the winter and summer Games are held two years apart.

The first modern Games were held in Athens, Greece. They were revived by Frenchman Pierre de Fredi, Baron de Coubertin (1863–1937), and have been held every four years with the exception of 1916, 1940, and 1944, when the two world wars intervened. At the first revived Games, 245 competitors represented 14 nations in nine sports. At Atlanta, USA, in 1996, over 10,000 athletes represented 197 countries in 29 sports. There were 271 events compared to 43 at Athens in 1896. *See list of tables on p. 1177.*

Olympus (Greek ***Olimbos***) any of several mountains in Greece and elsewhere, one of which is Mount Olympus in N Thessaly, Greece, 2,918 m/9,577 ft high. In ancient Greece it was considered the home of the gods.

Om sacred word in Hinduism, used to begin prayers and placed at the beginning and end of books. It is composed of three syllables, symbolic of the Hindu Trimurti, or trinity of gods.

Omagh county town of County ◊Tyrone, Northern Ireland, in the foothills of the Sperrin Mountains, on the River Strule, 48 km/30 mi south of Londonderry; population (1991) 17,300. Industries include dairy produce, food processing, footwear, shirt manufacturing, and engineering.

Omagh became the scene of a terrorist attack when a republican car bomb exploded on 15 August 1998 in a busy shopping area, killing 29 people.

Oman country at the SE end of the Arabian peninsula, bounded W by the United Arab Emirates, Saudi Arabia, and Yemen, SE by the Arabian Sea, and NE by the Gulf of Oman. *See country box below.*

Omar alternative spelling of ◊Umar, 2nd caliph of Islam.

Omar Khayyám c. 1050–c. 1123. Persian astronomer, mathematician, and poet. In the West, he is chiefly known as a poet through Edward ◊Fitzgerald's version of 'The Rubaiyat of Omar Khayyám' 1859. Khayyám was born in Nishapur. He founded a school of astronomical research and assisted in reforming the calendar. The result of his observations was the *Jalālī* era, begun 1079. He wrote a study of algebra, which was known in Europe as well as in the East.

ombudsman (Swedish 'commissioner') official who acts on behalf of the private citizen in investigating complaints against the government. The post is of Scandinavian origin; it was introduced in Sweden 1809, Denmark 1954, and Norway 1962, and spread to other countries from the 1960s.

Omdurman city in Sudan, on the White Nile, a suburb of Khartoum; population (1989) 526,300. It was the residence of the Sudanese sheik known as the Mahdi 1884–98.

Omdurman, Battle of victory 2 Sept 1898 of British and Egyptian troops under General Horatio Kitchener over Sudanese tribesmen (Dervishes) led by the Khalifa Abdullah el Taashi. The Khalifa escaped, to be pursued and later brought to battle and killed.

O'Meara, Mark 1957– . US golfer who in 1998 at the age of 41 won the US Masters and the British Open; he also won the World Matchplay championship and was voted Player of the Year by the US PGA Tour. By November 1998 he had won 21 tournaments worldwide, and stood in fourth position in the all-time US PGA Tour career money list, having earned $10,293,473 in prize money. He appeared in the US Ryder Cup team in 1985, 1989, 1991, and 1997.

Omega Workshops group of early 20th-century English artists, led by Roger ◊Fry, who brought them together to design and make interiors, furnishings, and craft objects. The workshops, 1913–20, included members of the ◊Bloomsbury Group, such as Vanessa Bell, Duncan Grant, Wyndham Lewis, and Henri Gaudier-Brzeska.

omnivore animal that feeds on both plant and animal material. Omnivores have digestive adaptations intermediate between those of ◊herbivores and ◊carnivores, with relatively unspecialized digestive systems and gut microorganisms that can digest a variety of foodstuffs. Examples include the chimpanzee, the cockroach, and the ant.

Omsk industrial city (agricultural and other machinery, food processing, sawmills, oil refining) in the Russian Federation, capital of Omsk region, W Siberia; population (1994) 1,161,000. Its oil refineries are linked with Tuimazy in the Bashkir republic by a 1,600-km/1,000-mi pipeline.

OMAN
Sultanate of

national name *Saltanat 'Uman*
area 272,000 sq km/105,000 sq mi
capital Muscat
major towns/cities Salalah, Nizwa
major ports Mina Qaboos, Mina Raysut
physical features mountains to N and S of a high arid plateau; fertile coastal strip; Jebel Akhdar highlands; Kuria Muria islands
head of state and government Qaboos bin Said from 1970
political system absolute monarchy
administrative divisions 41 provinces
political parties none
population 2,302,000 (1996 est)
population growth rate 4.2% (1990–95); 3.7% (2000–05)
ethnic distribution predominantly Arab, with substantial Iranian, Baluchi, Indo-Pakistani, and East African minorities
life expectancy 66 (men), 70 (women)
literacy rate 35%
languages Arabic (official), English, Urdu, other Indian languages
religions Ibadhi Muslim 75%, Sunni Muslim, Shi'ite Muslim, Hindu
currency Omani rial
GDP (US $) 11.62 billion (1994)
growth rate 3.5% (1994)
exports oil, dates, silverware, copper, fish

HISTORY
c. 3000 BC Archaeological evidence suggests Oman may have been the semilegendary Magan, a thriving seafaring state at the time of the Sumerian Civilization of Mesopotamia (the Tigris and Euphrates region of Iraq).
9th C BC Migration of Arab clans to Oman, notably the Qahtan family from SW Arabia and the Nizar from NW Arabia, between whom rivalry has continued.
4th C BC–AD 800 North Oman under Persian control.
AD 630 Converted to Islam.
751 Julanda ibn Masud was elected imam (spiritual leader); Oman remained under imam rule until 1154.
1151 Dynasty established by Banu Nabhan.
1428 Dynastic rule came under challenge from the imams.
1507 Coastal area, including port city of Muscat, fell under Portuguese control.
1650 Portuguese ousted by Sultan ibn Sayf, a powerful Ya'ariba leader.
early 18th C Civil war between the Hinawis (descendants of the Qahtan) and the Ghafiris (descendants of the Nizar).
1749 Independent Sultanate of Muscat and Oman established by Ahmad ibn Said, founder of the Al Bu Said dynasty that still rules Oman.
first half of 19th C Muscat and Oman was most powerful state in Arabia, ruling Zanzibar until 1861, and coastal parts of Persia, Kenya, and Pakistan; came under British protection.
1951 The Sultanate of Muscat and Oman achieved full independence from Britain. Treaty of Friendship with Britain signed.
1964 Oil discovered, leading to transformation of undeveloped kingdom into modern state.
1970 After 38 years' rule, Sultan Said bin Taimur replaced in bloodless coup by his son Qaboos bin Said. Name changed to Sultanate of Oman and moderization programme launched.
1975 Left-wing rebels in Dhofar in the S, who had been supported by South Yemen, defeated with UK military assistance, ending a ten-year insurrection.
1981 Consultative Council set up; Oman played key role in establishment of six-member Gulf Cooperation Council.
1982 Memorandum of Understanding with UK signed, providing for regular consultation on international issues.
1991 Joined US-led coalition opposing Iraq's occupation of Kuwait.
1994 Proposal to allow women members of parliament.

onager wild ass *Equus hemionus* found in W Asia. Onagers are sandy brown, lighter underneath, and about the size of a small horse.

Onassis Aristotle Socrates 1906–1975. Turkish-born Greek shipowner. In 1932 he started what became the largest independent shipping line and during the 1950s he was one of the first to construct supertankers. In 1968 he married Jacqueline Kennedy, widow of US president John F Kennedy.

onchocerciasis or ***river blindness*** disease found in tropical Africa and Central America. It is transmitted by bloodsucking black flies, which infect the victim with parasitic filarial worms (genus *Onchocerca*), producing skin disorders and intense itching; some invade the eyes and may cause blindness.

oncogene gene carried by a virus that induces a cell to divide abnormally, giving rise to a cancer. Oncogenes arise from mutations in genes (proto-oncogenes) found in all normal cells. They are usually also found in viruses that are capable of transforming normal cells to tumour cells. Such viruses are able to insert their oncogenes into the host cell's DNA, causing it to divide uncontrollably. More than one oncogene may be necessary to transform a cell in this way.

oncology medical speciality concerned with the diagnosis and treatment of ◊neoplasms, especially cancer.

onco-mouse mouse that has a human ◊oncogene (gene that can cause certain cancers) implanted into its cells by genetic engineering. Such mice are used to test anticancer treatments and were patented (see ◊patent) within the USA by Harvard University in 1988, thereby protecting its exclusive rights to produce the animal and profit from its research.

ondes Martenot (French 'Martenot waves') electronic musical instrument invented by Maurice Martenot (1898–1980), a French musician, teacher, and writer who first demonstrated his invention 1928 at the Paris Opéra. A melody of considerable range and voicelike timbre is produced by sliding a contact along a conductive ribbon, the left hand controlling the tone colour.

Onega, Lake second-largest lake in Europe, NE of St Petersburg, partly in Karelia, in the Russian Federation; area 9,600 sq km/3,710 sq mi. The Onega Canal, along its S shore, is part of the Mariinsk system linking St Petersburg with the river Volga.

O'Neill Eugene Gladstone 1888–1953. US playwright. He is widely regarded as the greatest US dramatist. His plays, although tragic, are characterized by a down-to-earth quality and are often experimental in form, influenced by German Expressionism, Strindberg, and Freud. They were a radical departure from the romantic and melodramatic American theatre entertainments. They include the Pulitzer prize-winning plays *Beyond the Horizon* 1920 and *Anna Christie* 1921, as well as *The Emperor Jones* 1920, *The Hairy Ape* 1922, *Desire Under the Elms* 1924, *The Iceman Cometh* 1946, and the posthumously produced autobiographical drama *A Long Day's Journey into Night* 1956 (written 1941), also a Pulitzer prize winner. He was awarded the Nobel Prize for Literature 1936.

O'Neill Terence. Baron O'Neill of the Maine 1914–1990. Northern Irish Unionist politician. In the Ulster government he was minister of finance 1956–63, then prime minister 1963–69. He resigned when opposed by his party on measures to extend rights to Roman Catholics, including a universal franchise.

one-party state state in which one political party dominates, constitutionally or unofficially, to the point where there is no effective opposition. There may be no legal alternative parties; for example, in Cuba. In other instances, a few token members of an opposition party may be tolerated, as in Mexico; or one party may be permanently in power with no elections.

onion bulbous plant *Allium cepa* of the lily family Liliaceae. Cultivated from ancient times, it may have originated in Asia. The edible part is the bulb, containing an acrid volatile oil and having a strong flavour. The onion is a biennial, the common variety producing a bulb in the first season and seeds in the second.

O'Neill The US playwright Eugene O'Neill. He followed a varied career before becoming involved in theatre, but became an acclaimed dramatist and won four Pulitzer Prizes and the Nobel Prize for Literature. *Corbis*

on line in computing, connected, so that data can be transferred, for example, to a printer or from a network. The opposite is off line.

on-line system in computing, originally a system that allows the computer to work interactively with its users, responding to each instruction as it is given and prompting users for information when necessary. Since almost all the computers used now work this way, 'on-line system' is now used to refer to large database, electronic mail, and conferencing systems accessed via a dial-up ◊modem.

onomatopoeia (Greek 'name-making') ◊figure of speech that copies natural sounds. For example, the word 'cuckoo' imitates the sound that the cuckoo makes. Such words as *bang*, *crash*, *ripple*, *smash*, *splash*, and *thump* are said to be onomatopoeic.

Ontario province of central Canada
area 1,068,600 sq km/412,480 sq mi
capital Toronto
towns and cities Hamilton, Ottawa (federal capital), London, Windsor, Kitchener, St Catharines, Oshawa, Thunder Bay, Sudbury
features Black Creek Pioneer Village; ◊Niagara Falls; richest, chief manufacturing, most populated, and leading cultural province of English-speaking Canada
industries nickel, iron, gold, forest products, motor vehicles, iron, steel, paper, chemicals, copper, uranium
population (1991) 10,085,000
history first explored by the French in the 17th century, it came under British control 1763 (Treaty of Paris).

An attempt 1841 to form a merged province with French-speaking Quebec failed, and Ontario became a separate province of Canada 1867. Under the protectionist policies of the new federal government, Ontario gradually became industrialized and urban. Since World War II, more than 2 million immigrants, chiefly from Europe, have settled in Ontario.

Ontario

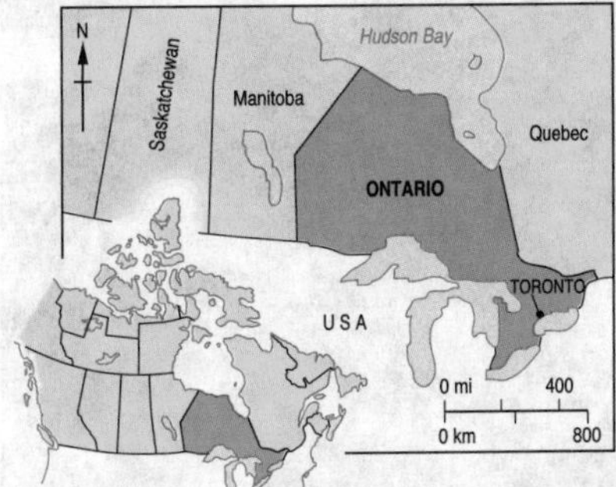

Ontario, Lake smallest and easternmost of the Great Lakes, on the US-Canadian border; area 19,200 sq km/7,400 sq mi. It is connected to Lake Erie by the Welland Canal and the Niagara River, and drains into the St Lawrence River. Its main port is Toronto.

on-the-job training training in the workplace, as opposed to off-the-job training where training takes place outside the workplace at, for example, a college or training institute. Youth Training in the UK offers a mixture of on-the-job and off-the-job training.

On the Road novel 1957 by US writer Jack ◊Kerouac. A lyrical, freewheeling, picaresque account of his real-life adventures with Neal Cassady (1920–1968), written with the jazz rhythms of 'spontaneous bop prosody', it became the bible of the ◊Beat Generation.

ontogeny process of development of a living organism, including the part of development that takes place after hatching or birth.

ontology branch of philosophy concerned with the study of being. In the 20th century, the German philosopher Martin ◊Heidegger distinguished between an 'ontological' enquiry (an enquiry into 'Being') and an 'ontic' enquiry (an enquiry into a specific kind of entity).

onyx semiprecious variety of chalcedonic ◊silica (SiO_2) in which the crystals are too fine to be detected under a microscope, a state known as cryptocrystalline. It has straight parallel bands of different colours: milk-white, black, and red. Sardonyx, an onyx variety, has layers of brown or red carnelian alternating with lighter layers of onyx. It can be carved into cameos.

oolite limestone made up of tiny spherical carbonate particles, called ooliths, cemented together. Ooliths have a concentric structure with a diameter up to 2 mm/0.08 in. They were formed by chemical precipitation and accumulation on ancient sea floors. The surface texture of oolites is rather like that of fish roe. The late Jurassic limestones of the British Isles are mostly oolitic in nature.

Oort Jan Hendrik 1900–1992. Dutch astronomer. In 1927, he calculated the mass and size of our Galaxy, the ◊Milky Way, and the Sun's distance from its centre, from the observed movements of stars around the Galaxy's centre. In 1950 Oort proposed that comets exist in a vast swarm, now called the ◊Oort cloud, at the edge of the Solar System.

In 1944 Oort's student Hendrik van de Hulst (1918–) calculated that hydrogen in space would emit radio waves at 21 cm/8.3 in wavelength, and in the 1950s Oort's team mapped the spiral structure of the Milky Way from the radio waves given out by interstellar hydrogen.

Oort cloud spherical cloud of comets beyond Pluto, extending out to about 100,000 astronomical units (1.5 light years) from the Sun. The gravitational effect of passing stars and the rest of our Galaxy disturbs comets from the cloud so that they fall in towards the Sun on highly elongated orbits, becoming visible from Earth. As many as 10 trillion comets may reside in the Oort cloud, named after Dutch astronomer Jan Oort who postulated it 1950.

ooze sediment of fine texture consisting mainly of organic matter found on the ocean floor at depths greater than 2,000 m/6,600 ft. Several kinds of ooze exist, each named after its constituents. ***Siliceous ooze*** is composed of the ◊silica shells of tiny marine plants (diatoms) and animals (radiolarians). ***Calcareous ooze*** is formed from the ◊calcite shells of microscopic animals (foraminifera) and floating algae (coccoliths).

opal form of hydrous ◊silica ($SiO_2.nH_2O$), often occurring as stalactites and found in many types of rock. The common opal is translucent, milk-white, yellow, red, blue, or green, and lustrous. Precious opal is opalescent, the characteristic play of colours being caused by close-packed silica spheres diffracting light rays within the stone.

Opal is cryptocrystalline, that is, the crystals are too fine to be detected under an optical microscope.

"An unalterable and unquestioned law of the musical world required that the German text of French operas sung by Swedish artists should be translated into Italian for the clearer understanding of English-speaking audiences."

On **OPERA**
Edith Wharton
The Age of Innocence
1920

Opals are found in Hungary; New South Wales, Australia (black opals were first discovered there 1905); and Mexico (red fire opals).

Op art (abbreviation for ***Optical art***) movement in abstract art during the late 1950s and 1960s, in which colour and pattern were used to create optical effects, particularly the illusion of movement. Exponents include Victor ◊Vasarély and Bridget ◊Riley.

OPEC acronym for ◊***Organization of Petroleum-Exporting Countries***.

opencast mining or ***open-pit mining*** or ***strip mining*** mining at the surface rather than underground. Coal, iron ore, and phosphates are often extracted by opencast mining. Often the mineral deposit is covered by soil, which must first be stripped off, usually by large machines such as walking draglines and bucket-wheel excavators. The ore deposit is then broken up by explosives.

One of the largest excavations in the world has been made by opencast mining at the Bingham Canyon copper mine in Utah, USA, measuring 790 m/2,590 ft deep and 3.7 km/2.3 mi across.

Open College in the UK, a network launched by the Manpower Services Commission 1987 to enable people to gain and update technical and vocational skills by means of distance teaching, such as correspondence, radio, and television.

open-door policy economic philosophy of equal access by all nations to another nation's markets.

open-hearth furnace method of steelmaking, now largely superseded by the ◊basic-oxygen process. It was developed in 1864 in England by German-born William and Friedrich Siemens, and improved by Pierre and Emile Martin in France in the same year. In the furnace, which has a wide, saucer-shaped hearth and a low roof, molten pig iron and scrap are packed into the shallow hearth and heated by overhead gas burners using preheated air.

open learning teaching available to students without pre-qualifications by means of flexible attendance at an institution, often including teaching by correspondence, radio, television, or tape, for example, in Britain, the Open University and Open College.

open shop factory or other business employing men and women not belonging to trade unions, as opposed to the ◊closed shop, which employs trade unionists only.

Open University institution established in the UK 1969 to enable mature students without qualifications to study to degree level without regular attendance. Open University teaching is based on a mixture of correspondence courses, TV and radio lectures and demonstrations, personal tuition organized on a regional basis, and summer schools.

opera dramatic musical work in which singing takes the place of speech. In opera the music accompanying the action has paramount importance, although dancing and spectacular staging may also play their parts. Opera originated in late 16th-century Florence when the musical declamation, lyrical monologues, and choruses of Classical Greek drama were reproduced in current forms.

early development One of the earliest opera composers was Jacopo Peri, whose *Euridice* influenced Claudio Monteverdi, the first great master of the operatic form. Initially solely a court entertainment, opera soon became popular, and in 1637 the first public opera house was opened in Venice. It spread to other Italian towns, to Paris (about 1645), and to Vienna and Germany, where it remained Italian at the courts but became partly German at Hamburg from about 1680.

In the later 17th century the elaborately conventional aria, designed to display the virtuosity of the singer, became predominant, overshadowing the dramatic element. Composers of this type of opera included Pier Cavalli, Pietro Antonio Cesti (1623–1669), and Alessandro Scarlatti. In France opera was developed by Jean-Baptiste Lully and Jean-Philippe Rameau, and in England by Henry Purcell, but the Italian style retained its ascendancy, as exemplified by Georg Handel.

Comic opera (opera buffa) was developed in Italy by such composers as Giovanni Battista Pergolesi (1710–1736), while in England *The Beggar's Opera* 1728 by John Gay started the vogue of the ballad opera, using popular tunes and spoken dialogue. *Singspiel* was the German equivalent (although its music was newly composed). A lessening of artificiality began with Christoph Willibald von Gluck, who insisted on the pre-eminence of the dramatic over the purely vocal element. Wolfgang Mozart learned much from Gluck in writing his serious operas, but excelled in Italian opera buffa. In works such as *The Magic Flute*, he laid the foundations of a purely German-language opera, using the *Singspiel* as a basis. This line was continued by Ludwig van Beethoven in *Fidelio* and by the work of Carl Weber, who introduced the Romantic style for the first time in opera.

developments into the 19th century The Italian tradition, which placed the main stress on vocal display and melodic suavity (*bel canto*), continued unbroken into the 19th century in the operas of Gioacchino Rossini, Gaetano Donizetti, and Vincenzo Bellini. It is in the Romantic operas of Weber and Giacomo Meyerbeer that the work of Richard Wagner has its roots. Dominating the operatic scene of his time, Wagner attempted to create, in his 'music-dramas', a new art form, and completely transformed the 19th-century conception of opera. In Italy, Giuseppe Verdi assimilated, in his mature work, much of the Wagnerian technique, without sacrificing the Italian virtues of vocal clarity and melody. This tradition was continued by Giacomo Puccini. In French opera in the mid-19th century, represented by such composers as Léo Delibes, Charles Gounod, Camille Saint-Saëns, and Jules Massenet, the drama was subservient to the music. Comic opera (*opéra comique*), as represented in the works of André Gréry (1741–1813) and, later, Daniel Auber, became a popular genre in Paris. More serious artistic ideals were put into practice by Hector Berlioz in *The Trojans*, but the merits of his work were largely unrecognized in his own time.

George Bizet's *Carmen* began a trend towards realism in opera; his lead was followed in Italy by Pietro Mascagni, Ruggero Leoncavallo, and Puccini. Claude Debussy's *Pelléas et Mélisande* represented a reaction against the over-emphatic emotionalism of Wagnerian opera. National operatic styles were developed in Russia by Mikhail Glinka, Nikolai Rimsky-Korsakov, Modest Mussorgsky, Alexander Borodin, and Peter Tchaikovsky, and in Bohemia by Bedřich Smetana and, later, Dvořák and Janáček. Several composers of light opera emerged, including Arthur Sullivan, Franz Lehár, Jacques Offenbach, and Johann Strauss.

20th-century opera In the 20th century the Viennese school produced an outstanding opera in Alban Berg's *Wozzeck*, and the Romanticism of Wagner was revived by Richard Strauss in *Der Rosenkavalier*. Other 20th-century composers of opera include George Gershwin, Leonard Bernstein, and John Adams in the USA; Roberto Gerhard, Michael Tippett, Benjamin Britten, and Harrison Birtwistle in the UK; Arnold Schoenberg, Paul Hindemith, and Hans Henze in Germany; Luigi Dallapiccola and Goffreddo Petrassi in Italy; and the Soviet composers Sergey Prokofiev and Dmitry Shostakovich. The operatic form has developed in many different directions, for example, towards oratorio in Igor Stravinsky's *Oedipus Rex* 1925, and towards cabaret and music-theatre, as represented by the works of Kurt Weill.

opera buffa (Italian 'comic opera') type of humorous opera with characters taken from everyday life. The form began as a musical intermezzo in the 18th century and was then adopted in Italy and France for complete operas. An example is Rossini's *The Barber of Seville*.

opéra comique (French 'comic opera') opera that includes text to be spoken, not sung; Bizet's *Carmen* is an example. Of the two Paris opera houses in the 18th and 19th centuries, the Opéra (which aimed at setting a grand style) allowed no spoken dialogue, whereas the Opéra Comique did.

opera seria (Italian 'serious opera') type of opera distinct from opera buffa, or humorous opera. Common in the 17th and 18th centuries, it tended to treat classical subjects in a formal style, with most of the singing being by solo voices. Examples include many of Handel's operas based on mythological subjects.

operating system (OS) in computing, a program that controls the basic operation of a computer. A typical OS controls the peripheral devices (such as keyboards and printers), organizes the filing system, provides a means of communicating with the operator, and runs other programs.

Some operating systems were written for specific computers, but some are accepted standards, such as MS-DOS for microcomputers, and UNIX for workstations, minicomputers, and supercomputers as well as desktop PCs and mainframes.

operetta light form of opera, with music, dance, and spoken dialogue. The story line is romantic and sentimental, often employing farce and parody. Its origins lie in the 19th-century *opéra comique* and is intended to amuse. Examples of operetta are Jacques Offenbach's *Orphée aux enfers/Orpheus in the Underworld* 1858, Johann Strauss' *Die Fledermaus/The Flittermouse* 1874, and Gilbert and Sullivan's *The Pirates of Penzance* 1879 and *The Mikado* 1885.

operon group of genes that are found next to each other on a chromosome, and are turned on and off as an integrated unit. They usually produce enzymes that control different steps in the same biochemical pathway. Operons were discovered 1961 (by the

opencast mining
Attempts are made to re-green mines once they are taken out of production, as at this partially waterfilled opencast lignite mine near Leipzig, Germany. The water will attract birds and amphibians, and grasses, shrubs, and trees will eventually grow. The contours of the land however, will always bear witness to its industrial past.
Corbis

opium The opium poppy *Papaver somniferum*, native to Asia, has been widely cultivated since antiquity. The opium is obtained from the latex of the poppy, which is secreted when the poppy head is cut. *Premaphotos Wildlife*

French biochemists François Jacob and Jacques Monod) in bacteria.

Ophiuchus large constellation along the celestial equator (see ◊celestial sphere), known as the serpent bearer because the constellation ◊Serpens is wrapped around it. The Sun passes through Ophiuchus each Dec, but the constellation is not part of the zodiac. Ophiuchus contains ◊Barnard's star.

ophthalmology medical speciality concerned with diseases of the eye and its surrounding tissues.

Ophuls Max. Adopted name of Max Oppenheimer 1902–1957. German film director. His style is characterized by an ironic, bittersweet tone and intricate camera movement. He worked in Europe and the USA, attracting much critical praise for such films as *Letter from an Unknown Woman* 1948, *La Ronde* 1950, and *Lola Montes* 1955.

opiate, endogenous naturally produced chemical in the body that has effects similar to morphine and other opiate drugs; a type of neurotransmitter. Examples include ◊endorphins and ◊encephalins.

opinion poll attempt to measure public opinion by taking a survey of the views of a representative sample of the electorate; the science of opinion sampling is called psephology. Most standard polls take random samples of around a thousand voters, which gives results that should be accurate to within three percentage points, 95% of the time. The first accurately sampled opinion poll was carried out by George ◊Gallup during the US presidential election 1936.

opium drug extracted from the unripe seeds of the opium poppy *Papaver somniferum* of SW Asia. An addictive ◊narcotic, it contains several alkaloids, including morphine, one of the most powerful natural painkillers and addictive narcotics known, and codeine, a milder painkiller.

Heroin is a synthetic derivative of morphine and even more powerful as a drug. Opium is still sometimes given as a tincture, dissolved in alcohol and known as laudanum. Opium also contains the highly poisonous alkaloid thebaine.

Opium Wars two wars, the First Opium War 1839–42 and the Second Opium War 1856–60, waged by Britain against China to enforce the opening of Chinese ports to trade in opium. Opium from British India paid for Britain's imports from China, such as porcelain, silk, and, above all, tea.

The First Opium War, between Britain and China, resulted in the cession of Hong Kong to Britain and the opening of five treaty ports. Other European states were also subsequently given concessions. The Second Opium War followed between Britain and France in alliance against China, when there was further Chinese resistance to the opium trade. China was forced to give the European states greater trading privileges, at the expense of its people.

opossum any of a family (Didelphidae) of marsupials native to North and South America. Most opossums are tree-living, nocturnal animals, with prehensile tails, and hands and feet well adapted for grasping. They range from 10 cm/4 in to 50 cm/20 in in length and are insectivorous, carnivorous, or, more commonly, omnivorous. The name is also popularly applied to some of the similar-looking phalangers found in Australia.

Oppenheimer J(ulius) Robert 1904–1967. US physicist. As director of the Los Alamos Science Laboratory 1943–45, he was in charge of the development of the atom bomb (the Manhattan Project). When later he realized the dangers of radioactivity, he objected to the development of the hydrogen bomb, and was alleged to be a security risk 1953 by the US Atomic Energy Commission (AEC).

Investigating the equations describing the energy states of the atom, Oppenheimer showed in 1930 that a positively charged particle with the mass of an electron could exist. This particle was detected in 1932 and called the ◊positron.

opposition in astronomy, the moment at which a body in the Solar System lies opposite the Sun in the sky as seen from the Earth and crosses the ◊meridian at about midnight. Although the inferior planets (whose orbits lie within that of the Earth) cannot come to opposition, it is the best time for observation of the superior planets as they can then be seen all night.

Opposition, Leader of His/Her Majesty's in UK politics, official title (from 1937) of the leader of the largest opposition party in the House of Commons. Since 1989 the post has received a government salary, starting at £98,000 (from 1997).

optical aberration see ◊aberration, optical.

optical activity in chemistry, the ability of certain crystals, liquids, and solutions to rotate the plane of ◊polarized light as it passes through them. The phenomenon is related to the three-dimensional arrangement of the atoms making up the molecules concerned.

optical character recognition (OCR) in computing, a technique for inputting text to a computer by means of a document reader. First, a scanner produces a digital image of the text; then character-recognition software makes use of stored knowledge about the shapes of individual characters to convert the digital image to a set of internal codes that can be stored and processed by computer.

optical disc in computing, a storage medium in which laser technology is used to record and read large volumes of digital data. Types include ◊CD-ROM, ◊WORM, and erasable optical disc.

optical fibre very fine, optically pure glass fibre through which light can be reflected to transmit images or data from one end to the other. Although expensive to produce and install, optical fibres can carry more data than traditional cables, and are less susceptible to interference.

Optical fibres are increasingly being used to replace metal communications cables, the messages being encoded as digital pulses of light rather than as fluctuating electric current. Current research is investigating how optical fibres could replace wiring inside computers. Bundles of optical fibres are also used in endoscopes to inspect otherwise inaccessible parts of machines or of the living body (see ◊endoscopy).

optical illusion scene or picture that fools the eye. An example of a natural optical illusion is that the Moon appears bigger when it is on the horizon than when it is high in the sky, owing to the ◊refraction of light rays by the Earth's atmosphere. *See illustration on following page.*

optical instrument instrument that makes use of one or more lenses or mirrors, or of a combination of these, in order to change the path of light rays and produce an image. Optical instruments such as magnifying glasses, ◊microscopes, and ◊telescopes are used to provide a clear, magnified image of the very small or the very distant. Others, such as ◊cameras, photographic enlargers, and film

Oppenheimer US physicist J Robert Oppenheimer led the Manhattan Project, which produced the atomic bomb. When later he opposed the construction of the hydrogen bomb and advocated the international control of atomic energy, he was accused of communist sympathies. A man of wide learning, he wrote several nontechnical books, including *Science and the Common Understanding* 1954. *Sachem*

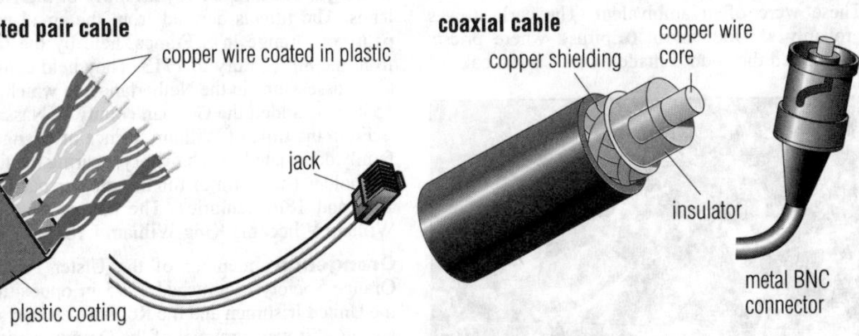

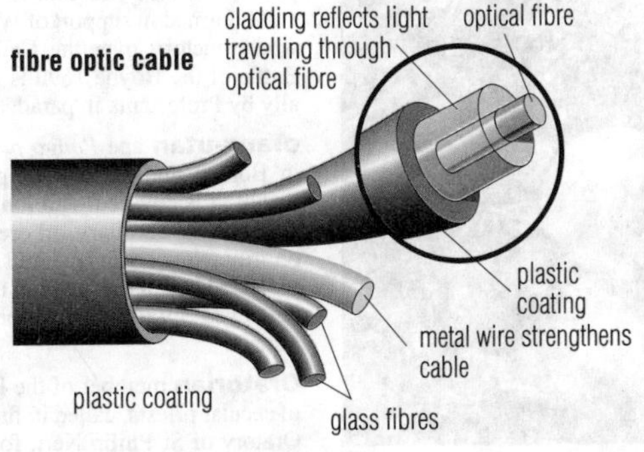

optical fibre The major differences in construction between twisted pair (telephone), coaxial (Ethernet), and fibre optic cable.

optical illusion A fantascope, a toy which relies on an optical illusion for its effect. When the picture is spun and its reflection viewed in a mirror, the man and dog appear to move. *Image Select (UK) Ltd*

projectors, may be used to store or reproduce images.

optic nerve large nerve passing from the eye to the brain, carrying visual information. In mammals, it may contain up to a million nerve fibres, connecting the sensory cells of the retina to the optical centres in the brain. Embryologically, the optic nerve develops as an outgrowth of the brain.

optics branch of physics that deals with the study of ◊light and vision – for example, shadows and mirror images, lenses, microscopes, telescopes, and cameras. For all practical purposes light rays travel in straight lines, although Albert ◊Einstein demonstrated that they may be 'bent' by a gravitational field. On striking a surface they are reflected or refracted with some absorption of energy, and the study of this is known as geometrical optics.

opting out in UK education, schools that choose to be funded directly from the Department of Education and Science are said to be opting out of local-authority control. The Education Act 1988 gave this option to all secondary schools and the larger primary schools, and in 1990 it was extended to all primary schools.

option in business, a contract giving the owner the right (as opposed to the obligation, as with futures contracts; see ◊futures trading) to buy or sell a specific quantity of a particular commodity or currency at a future date and at an agreed price, in return for a premium. The buyer only can decide not to exercise the option if it would prove disadvantageous, but in this case would lose the premium paid.

opuntia any cactus of the genus *Opuntia* of plants to which the ◊prickly pear belongs. They all have showy flowers and fleshy, jointed stems.

Opus Dei (Latin 'God's work') Roman Catholic institution advocating holiness in everyday life. Founded in Madrid 1928, and still powerful in Spain, it has (1993) more than 1,000 priests and 75,000 lay members of both sexes in more than 80 countries. Opus Dei has been the subject of controversy because of allegations about secret right-wing involvement in politics, finance, and education. It was founded by José Maria Escriva de Balaguer (1902–1975), who was beatified 1992.

oracle Greek sacred site where answers (also called oracles) were given by priests of a deity to enquirers about personal affairs or state policy. These were often ambivalent. The earliest was probably at Dodona (in ◊Epirus), where priests interpreted the sounds made by the sacred oaks of ◊Zeus, but the most celebrated was that of Apollo at ◊Delphi.

orange Frost-free winters are necessary for the successful growth of orange trees as flowers and fruits are borne continuously throughout the year. These oranges are part of Spain's annual production of 2.5 million metric tons. *Spanish Tourist Office*

oral literature stories that are or have been transmitted in spoken form, such as public recitation, rather than through writing or printing. Most pre-literate societies have had a tradition of oral literature, including short folk tales, legends, myths, proverbs, and riddles as well as longer narrative works; and most of the ancient epics – such as the Greek *Odyssey* and the Mesopotamian *Gilgamesh* – seem to have been composed and added to over many centuries before they were committed to writing.

Some ancient stories from oral traditions were not written down as literary works until the 19th century, such as the Finnish *Kalevala* (1835–49); many fairy tales, such as those collected in Germany by the Grimm brothers, also come into this category. Much of this sort of folk literature may have been consciously embellished and altered, as happened in 19th-century Europe for nationalistic purposes.

Oral literatures have continued to influence the development of national written literatures in the 20th century, particularly in Africa, central Asia, and Australia.

Oran (Arabic ***Wahran***) seaport in Algeria; population (1989) 664,000. Products include iron, textiles, footwear, and processed food; the port trades in grain, wool, vegetables, and native esparto grass. Oran was part of the Ottoman Empire, except when it was under Spanish rule 1509–1708 and 1732–91. It was occupied by France 1831. After the surrender of France to Germany 1940, the French warships in the naval base of Mers-el-Kebir nearby were put out of action by the British navy to prevent them from falling into German hands.

orange any of several evergreen trees of the genus *Citrus*, family Rutaceae, which bear blossom and fruit at the same time. Thought to have originated in SE Asia, orange trees are commercially cultivated in Spain, Israel, the USA, Brazil, South Africa, and elsewhere. The sweet orange *C. sinensis* is the one commonly eaten fresh; the Jaffa, blood, and navel orange are varieties of this species.

Tangerines and mandarins belong to a related species *C. reticulata*. The sour orange or Seville *C. aurantium* is the bitter orange used in making marmalade. Oranges yield several essential oils.

Orange river in South Africa, rising on the Mont aux Sources in Lesotho and flowing W to the Atlantic Ocean; length 2,100 km/1,300 mi. It runs along the southern boundary of the Orange Free State and was named 1779 after William of Orange. Water from the Orange is diverted via the Orange-Fish River Tunnel (1975) to irrigate the semi-arid Eastern Cape Province.

Orange Free State former name of ◊Free State, a province of the Republic of South Africa.

Orange, House of royal family of the Netherlands. The title is derived from the small principality of Orange in S France, held by the family from the 8th century to 1713. They held considerable possessions in the Netherlands, to which, after 1530, was added the German county of Nassau.

From the time of William, Prince of Orange, the family dominated Dutch history, bearing the title of stadholder (magistrate) for the greater part of the 17th and 18th centuries. The son of Stadholder William V became King William I 1815.

Orangeman member of the Ulster Protestant Orange Society established 1795 in opposition to the United Irishmen and the Roman Catholic secret societies. It was a revival of the Orange Institution 1688, formed in support of William (III) of Orange, whose victory over the Catholic James II at the Battle of the Boyne 1690 is commemorated annually by Protestants in parades on 12 July.

orang-utan ape *Pongo pygmaeus*, found solely in Borneo and Sumatra. Up to 1.65 m/5.5 ft in height, it is covered with long, red-brown hair and mainly lives a solitary, arboreal life, feeding chiefly on fruit. Now an endangered species, it is officially protected because its habitat is being systematically destroyed by ◊deforestation. Less than 30,000 remain.

Oratorian member of the Roman Catholic order of secular priests, called in full Congregation of the Oratory of St Philip Neri, formally constituted by Philip Neri 1575 in Rome, and characterized by the degree of freedom allowed to individual communities.

oratorio dramatic, non-scenic musical setting of religious texts, scored for orchestra, chorus, and solo voices. Its origins lie in the *Laude spirituali* performed by St Philip Neri's Oratory in Rome in the 16th century, followed by the first definitive oratorio in the 17th century by Cavalieri. The form reached perfection in such works as J S Bach's *Christmas Oratorio*, and Handel's *Messiah*.

The term is sometimes applied to secular music drama in which there is little or no stage action, as in Stravinsky's *Oedipus Rex* 1926–27 and Messiaen's *St François d'Assise* 1975–83. In the earliest oratorios there was often an element of ritual and spatial dramatization, and Bach himself introduced audience participation with the chorales of his *St Matthew Passion*.

orbit path of one body in space around another, such as the orbit of Earth around the Sun, or the Moon around Earth. When the two bodies are similar in mass, as in a ◊binary star, both bodies move around their common centre of mass. The movement of objects in orbit follows Johann ◊Kepler's laws, which apply to artificial satellites as well as to natural bodies.

As stated by the laws, the orbit of one body around another is an ellipse. The ellipse can be highly elongated, as are comet orbits around the Sun, or it may be almost circular, as are those of some planets. The closest point of a planet's orbit to the Sun is called perihelion; the most distant point is aphelion. (For a body orbiting the Earth, the closest and furthest points of the orbit are called perigee and apogee.)

orbital, atomic region around the nucleus of an atom (or, in a molecule, around several nuclei) in which an ◊electron is most likely to be found. According to ◊quantum theory, the position of an electron is uncertain; it may be found at any point. However, it is more likely to be found in some places than in others, and it is these that make up the orbital.

orchestra group of musicians playing together on different instruments. In Western music, an orchestra typically contains various bowed string instruments and sections of wind, brass, and percussion. The size and format may vary according to the needs of composers.

The term was originally used in Greek theatre for the semicircular space in front of the stage, and was adopted in 17th-century France to refer first to the space in front of the stage where musicians sat, and later to the musicians themselves.

The string section is commonly divided into two groups of violins (first and second), violas, cellos, and double basses. The woodwind section became standardized by the end of the 18th century, when it consisted of two each of flutes, oboes, clarinets, and bassoons, to which were later added piccolo, cor anglais, bass clarinet, and double bassoon. At that time, two timpani and two horns were also standard, and two trumpets were occasionally added. During the 19th century, the brass section was gradually expanded to include four horns, three trumpets, three trombones, and tuba. To the percussion section a third timpano was added, and from Turkey came the bass drum, side drum, cymbals, and triangle. One or more harps became common and, to maintain balance, the number of string instruments to a part also increased. Other instruments used in the orchestra include xylophone, celesta, glockenspiel, piano (which superseded the harpsichord in the late 18th century), and organ. The orchestra used to be conducted by means of a violin bow, but by Felix Mendelssohn's time the baton was implemented.

orchestration scoring of a composition for orchestra; the choice of instruments of a score expanded for orchestra (often by another hand). A work may be written for piano, and then transferred to an orchestral score.

orchid any plant of the family Orchidaceae, which contains at least 15,000 species and 700 genera, distributed throughout the world except in the coldest areas, and most numerous in damp equatorial regions. The flowers are the most evolved of the plant kingdom, have three sepals and three petals and are sometimes solitary, but more usually borne in spikes, racemes, or panicles, either erect or drooping.

The lowest petal of each flower, the labellum, is usually large, and may be spurred, fringed, pouched, or crested. Many tropical orchids are epiphytes attached to trees, but temperate orchids commonly grow on the ground. Such orchids include the spotted orchid *Dactylorhiza maculata* and other British species.

ordeal, trial by in tribal societies and in Europe in medieval times, a method of testing the guilt of an accused person based on the belief in heaven's protection of the innocent. Examples of such ordeals include walking barefoot over heated iron, dipping the hand into boiling water, and swallowing consecrated bread (causing the guilty to choke). In Europe the practice originated with the Franks in the 8th century, and survived until the 13th century.

order in classical architecture, the ◊column (including capital, shaft, and base) and the ◊entablature, considered as an architectural whole. The five orders are Doric, Ionic, Corinthian, Tuscan, and Composite.

The earliest order was the Doric (without a base), which originated before the 5th century BC, soon followed by the Ionic (with scroll-like capitals), which was first found in Asia Minor. The Corinthian (with leaves in the capitals) dates from the end of the 5th century BC, while the Composite appears first on the arch of Titus in Rome AD 82. No Tuscan columns survive from antiquity, although the order was thought to originate in Etruscan times.

order in biological classification, a group of related ◊families. For example, the horse, rhinoceros, and tapir families are grouped in the order Perissodactyla, the odd-toed ungulates, because they all have either one or three toes on each foot. The names of orders are not shown in italic (unlike genus and species names) and by convention they have the ending '-formes' in birds and fish; '-a' in mammals, amphibians, reptiles, and other animals; and '-ales' in fungi and plants. Related orders are grouped together in a ◊class.

Order of Merit British order of chivalry founded 1902 by Edward VII and limited in number to 24 at any one time within the British Isles, plus additional honorary OMs for overseas peoples. It ranks below a knighthood. There are two types of OM, military and civil.

ordinal number in mathematics, one of the series first, second, third, fourth, ... Ordinal numbers relate to order, whereas ◊cardinal numbers (1, 2, 3, 4, ...) relate to quantity, or count.

ordinary share type of ◊share in a company. Ordinary shareholders receive a variable rate of ◊dividend. When company profits are high, the dividends will be high also. If the company is doing badly, it may well reduce or even stop paying any dividend to ordinary shareholders. Ordinary shareholders have only second claim on dividends after preference shareholders, who receive a fixed rate of dividend.

ordinate in ◊coordinate geometry, the y coordinate of a point; that is, the vertical distance of the point from the horizontal or x-axis. For example, a point with the coordinates (3,4) has an ordinate of 4. See ◊abscissa.

ordination religious ceremony by which a person is accepted into the priesthood or monastic life in various religions. Within the Christian church, ordination authorizes a person to administer the sacraments.

ordination of women Many Protestant denominations, such as the Methodists and Baptists, ordain women as ministers, as do many churches in the Anglican Communion. In 1988 the first female bishop was elected within the Anglican Communion (in Massachusetts, USA). The Anglican church in England and Australia voted in favour of the ordination of women priests Nov 1992, and the first women priests were ordained in England 1994. The Roman Catholic and Eastern Orthodox churches refuse to ordain women.

Ordnance Survey (OS) official body responsible for the mapping of Britain. It was established 1791 as the Trigonometrical Survey to continue work initiated 1784 by Scottish military surveyor General William Roy (1726–1790). Its first accurate maps appeared 1830, drawn to a scale of 1 in to the mile (1:63,000). In 1858 the OS settled on a scale of 1:2,500 for the mapping of Great Britain and Ireland (higher for urban areas, lower for uncultivated areas).

Subsequent revisions and editions include the 1:50,000 Landranger series 1971–86. In 1989, the OS began using a computerized system for the creation and continuous revision of maps. Customers can now have maps drafted to their own specifications, choosing from over 50 features (such as houses, roads, and vegetation).

Ordovician period of geological time 510–439 million years ago; the second period of the ◊Palaeozoic era. Animal life was confined to the sea: reef-building algae and the first jawless fish are characteristic.

ore body of rock, a vein within it, or a deposit of sediment, worth mining for the economically valuable mineral it contains. The term is usually applied to sources of metals. Occasionally metals are found uncombined (native metals), but more often they occur as compounds such as carbonates, sulphides, or oxides. The ores often contain unwanted impurities that must be removed when the metal is extracted.

Commercially valuable ores include bauxite (aluminium oxide, Al_2O_3) hematite (iron(III) oxide, Fe_2O_3), zinc blende (zinc sulphide, ZnS), and rutile (titanium dioxide, TiO_2).

oregano any of several perennial herbs of the Labiatae family, especially the aromatic *Origanum vulgare*, also known as wild marjoram. It is native to the Mediterranean countries and W Asia and naturalized in the Americas. Oregano is extensively used to season Mediterranean cooking.

Oregon state in NW USA, on the Pacific coast; nicknamed Beaver State
area 251,500 sq km/97,079 sq mi
capital Salem
towns and cities Portland, Eugene
population (1990) 2,842,300
features Columbia and Snake rivers; the fertile Willamette River valley; Crater Lake national park (the deepest lake in the USA, 589 m/1,933 ft), formed as a result of the eruption of Mount Mazama; Newberry national volcanic monument; Oregon Caves national monument; Cascade Mountains; Pacific coast; vineyards; Mount Hood national forest (Mount Hood 3,427 m/11,245 ft); High Desert Museum, Bend, with a living exhibit of plants and animals native to the arid region of the Pacific Northwest; Portland, with Yamhill and Skidmore national historic districts, End of the Trail Interpretative Center (the history of the Oregon Trail), the McLoughlin historic district, with Victorian buildings, including the John McLoughlin House national historic site (1846), Pittock Mansion (1909), Portland Art Museum, Chinatown, Forest Park (15,000 acres, the largest urban wilderness in the USA), and Washington Park Rose Garden and Japanese Garden; Fort Clatsop national memorial, commemorating the first sight of the Pacific by Lewis and Clark 1805; Hoover-Minthorne House (1881), the boyhood home of President Herbert Hoover; Willamette University, Salem (1842), the oldest college in the West; Reed College (1909); the Oregon Shakespeare Festival, Ashland
industries wheat, livestock, timber, electronics
famous people Linus Pauling, Ursula LeGuin
history settled 1811 by the Pacific Fur Company, Oregon Territory included Washington until 1853; Oregon became a state 1859. The Oregon Trail (3,200 km/2,000 mi from Independence, Missouri, to the Columbia river) was the pioneer route across the USA 1841–60.

Oregon

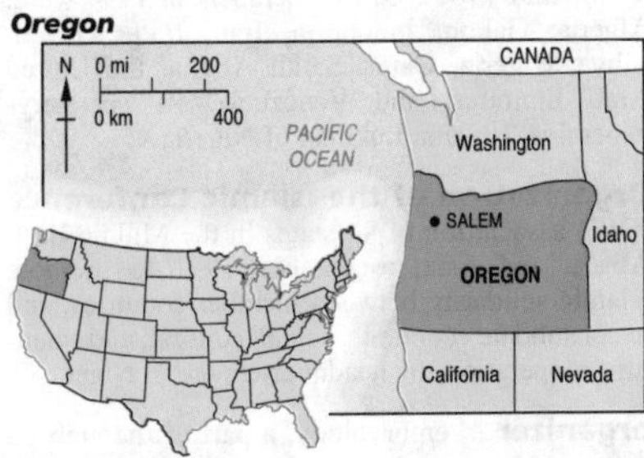

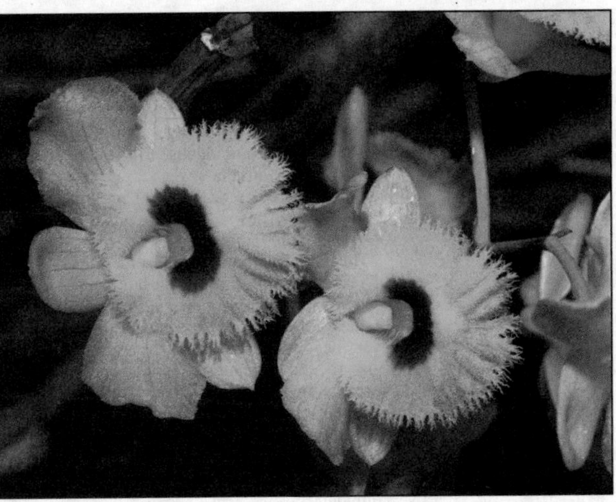

orchid *Dendrobium fimbriatum* var. *occulatum* is one of the most attractive members of the orchid genus. Originally from India, it now grows wild in other parts of the tropics. *Premaphotos Wildlife*

Orellana Francisco de c. 1500–c. 1549. Spanish explorer who travelled with Francesco ◊Pizarro from Guayaquil, on the Pacific coast of South America, to Quito in the Andes. He was the first person known to have navigated the full length of the Amazon from the Napo River to the Atlantic Ocean 1541–43.

Orenburg city in S central Russian Federation, on the Ural River; population (1994) 558,000. It is a trading and mining centre and capital of Orenburg region. It dates from the early 18th century and was called Chkalov 1938–57 in honour of Soviet aviator Valeri Chkalov (1904–1938).

Oresteia trilogy of tragic Greek plays by ◊Aeschylus – *Agamemnon*, *Libation-Bearers*, and *Eumenides* – which won first prize at the festival of Dionysus at Athens 458 BC. Their subject is the murder of Agamemnon by his wife Clytemnestra and the consequent vengeance of their son Orestes and daughter Electra.

Orestes in Greek mythology, the son of ◊Agamemnon and ◊Clytemnestra, who killed his mother on the instructions of Apollo because she and her lover Aegisthus had murdered his father, and was then hounded by the ◊Furies until he was purified, and acquitted of the crime of murder.

orfe fish *Leuciscus idus* of the carp family. It grows up to 50 cm/1.7 ft, and feeds on small aquatic animals. The species is generally greyish-black, but an ornamental variety is orange. It lives in rivers and lakes of Europe and NW Asia.

Orff Carl 1895–1982. German composer. An individual stylist, his work is characterized by sharp dissonances and percussion. Among his compositions are the cantata ◊*Carmina Burana* 1937 and the opera *Antigone* 1949.

organ in biology, part of a living body, such as the liver or brain, that has a distinctive function or set of functions.

organ musical wind instrument of ancient origin. It produces sound from pipes of various sizes under applied pressure and has keyboard controls. Apart from its continued use in serious compositions and for church music, the organ has been adapted for light entertainment.

The organ developed from the panpipes and hydraulis (water organ), and is mentioned in writings as early as the 3rd century BC. Organs were imported to France from Byzantium in the 8th and 9th centuries, after which their manufacture in Europe began. The electric tone-wheel organ was invented 1934 by the US engineer Laurens Hammond (1895–1973). Other types of electric organ were developed in the 1960s.

organelle discrete and specialized structure in a living cell; organelles include mitochondria, chloroplasts, lysosomes, ribosomes, and the nucleus.

organic chemistry branch of chemistry that deals with carbon compounds. Organic compounds form the chemical basis of life and are more abundant than inorganic compounds. In a typical organic compound, each carbon atom forms bonds covalently with each of its neighbouring carbon atoms in a chain or ring, and additionally with other atoms, commonly hydrogen, oxygen, nitrogen, or sulphur.

The basis of organic chemistry is the ability of carbon to form long chains of atoms, branching chains, rings, and other complex structures. Compounds containing only carbon and hydrogen are known as hydrocarbons.

Organic chemistry is largely the chemistry of a great variety of homologous series – those in which the molecular formulae, when arranged in ascending order, form an arithmetical progression. The physical properties undergo a gradual change from one member to the next.

The linking carbon atoms that form the backbone of an organic molecule may be built up from beginning to end without branching; or may throw off branches at one or more points. Sometimes, however, the ropes of carbon atoms curl round and form rings (cyclic compounds), usually of five, six, or seven atoms. Open-chain and cyclic compounds may be classified as ◊aliphatic or ◊aromatic depending on the nature of the bonds between their atoms. Compounds containing oxygen, sulphur, or nitrogen within a carbon ring are called heterocyclic compounds.

Many organic compounds (such as proteins and carbohydrates) are made only by living organisms, and it was once believed that organic compounds could not be made by any other means. This was disproved when Wöhler synthesized urea, but the name 'organic' (that is 'living') chemistry has remained in use. Many organic compounds are derived from petroleum, which represents the chemical remains of millions of microscopic marine organisms.

In inorganic chemistry, a specific formula usually represents one substance only, but in organic chemistry, it is exceptional for a molecular formula to represent only one substance. Substances having the same molecular formula are called isomers, and the relationship is known as isomerism.

Hydrocarbons form one of the most prolific of the many organic types; fuel oils are largely made up of hydrocarbons. Typical groups containing only carbon, hydrogen, and oxygen are alcohols, aldehydes, ketones, ethers, esters, and carbohydrates. Among groups containing nitrogen are amides, amines, nitro-compounds, amino acids, proteins, purines, alkaloids, and many others, both natural and artificial. Other organic types contain sulphur, phosphorus, or halogen elements.

The most fundamental of all natural processes are oxidation, reduction, hydrolysis, condensation, polymerization, and molecular rearrangement. In nature, such changes are often brought about through the agency of promoters known as enzymes, which act as catalytic agents in promoting specific reactions. The most fundamental of all natural processes is synthesis, or building up. In living plant and animal organisms, the energy stored in carbohydrate molecules, derived originally from sunlight, is released by slow oxidation and utilized by the organisms. The complex carbohydrates thereby revert to carbon dioxide and water, from where they were built up with absorption of energy. Thus, a so-called carbon food cycle exists in nature. In a corresponding nitrogen food cycle, complex proteins are synthesized in nature from carbon dioxide, water, soil nitrates, and ammonium salts, and these proteins ultimately revert to the elementary raw materials from which they came, with the discharge of their energy of chemical combination.

organic compound in chemistry, a class of compounds that contain carbon. The original distinction between organic and inorganic compounds was based on the belief that the molecules of living systems were unique, and could not be synthesized in the laboratory. Today it is routine to manufacture thousands of organic chemicals both in research and in the drug industry. Certain simple compounds of carbon, such as carbonates, oxides of carbon, carbon disulphide, and carbides are usually treated in inorganic chemistry.

organic farming farming without the use of synthetic fertilizers (such as ◊nitrates and phosphates) or ◊pesticides (herbicides, insecticides, and fungicides) or other agrochemicals (such as hormones, growth stimulants, or fruit regulators).

In place of artificial fertilizers, compost, manure, seaweed, or other substances derived from living things are used (hence the name 'organic'). Growing a crop of a nitrogen-fixing plant such as lucerne, then ploughing it back into the soil, also fertilizes the ground. Some organic farmers use naturally occurring chemicals such as nicotine or pyrethrum to kill pests, but control by non-chemical methods is preferred. Those methods include removal by hand, intercropping (planting with companion plants which deter pests), mechanical barriers to infestation, crop rotation, better cultivation methods, and ◊biological control. Weeds can be controlled by hoeing, mulching (covering with manure, straw, or black plastic), or burning off. Organic farming methods produce food with minimal pesticide residues and greatly reduce pollution of the environment. They are more labour intensive, and therefore more expensive, but use less fossil fuel. Soil structure is greatly improved by organic methods, and recent studies show that a conventional farm can lose four times as much soil through erosion as an organic farm, although the loss may not be immediately obvious.

Organization for Economic Cooperation and Development (OECD) international organization of 30 industrialized countries that provides a forum for discussion and coordination of member states' economic and social policies. Founded 1961, with its headquarters in Paris, the OECD superseded the Organization for European Economic Cooperation, which had been established 1948 to implement the ◊Marshall Plan. The Commission of the European Union also participates in the OECD's work.

Organization for Security and Cooperation in Europe (OSCE) international forum to reach agreement in security, economics, science, technology, and human rights. It was originally known (until 1994) as the Conference on Security and Cooperation in Europe (CSCE), and first met at the ◊Helsinki Conference in Finland 1975. By mid-1995, having admitted the former republics of the USSR, as well as other new nations from the former communist bloc (with the exception of Yugoslavia whose membership was suspended in July 1992), its membership had risen to 53 states.

Organization of African Unity (OAU) association established 1963 to eradicate colonialism and improve economic, cultural, and political cooperation in Africa. The secretary general is Salim Ahmed Salim of Tanzania. Its headquarters are in Addis Ababa, Ethiopia. There are now 53 members representing virtually the whole of central, southern, and northern Africa.

Organization of American States (OAS) association founded 1948 by a charter signed by representatives of 30 North, Central, and South American states. It aims to maintain peace and solidarity within the hemisphere, and is also concerned with the social and economic development of Latin America. The secretary-general is Cesar Gauiria Trujillo of Colombia.

Organization of Arab Petroleum Exporting Countries (OAPEC) body established 1968 to safeguard the interests of its members and encourage economic cooperation within the petroleum industry. Its members are Algeria, Bahrain, Egypt, Iraq, Kuwait, Libya, Qatar, Saudi Arabia, Syria, and the United Arab Emirates accounting for more than a quarter of world oil output; its headquarters are in Kuwait.

Organization of Petroleum-Exporting Countries (OPEC) body established 1960 to coordinate price and supply policies of oil-producing states. Its concerted action in raising prices in the 1970s triggered worldwide recession but also lessened demand so that its influence was reduced by the mid-1980s. OPEC members in 1994 were: Algeria, Gabon, Indonesia, Iran, Iraq, Kuwait, Libya, Nigeria, Qatar, Saudi Arabia, the United Arab Emirates, and Venezuela. Its secretary-general is Rilwana Lukman of Nigeria.

Organization of the Islamic Conference (OIC) association of 44 states in the Middle East, Africa, and Asia, established 1971 to promote Islamic solidarity between member countries, and to consolidate economic, social, cultural, and scientific cooperation. Its headquarters are in Niger.

organizer in embryology, a part of the embryo that causes changes to occur in another part, through ◊induction, thus 'organizing' development and ◊differentiation.

orienteering sport of cross-country running and route-finding. Competitors set off at one-minute intervals and have to find their way, using map and compass, to various checkpoints (approximately 0.8 km/0.5 mi apart), where their control cards are marked. World championships have been held since 1966.

original sin Christian doctrine that the ◊Fall of Man rendered humanity predisposed to sin and unable to achieve salvation except through divine grace and the redemptive power of Jesus.

Orinoco river in N South America, flowing for about 2,400 km/1,500 mi through Venezuela and forming for about 320 km/200 mi the boundary with Colombia; tributaries include the Guaviare, Meta, Apure, Ventuari, Caura, and Caroni. It is navigable by large steamers for 1,125 km/700 mi from its Atlantic delta; rapids obstruct the upper river.

oriole brightly-coloured songbird. Orioles are members of two families: New World orioles belong to the family Icteridae, and Old World orioles are members of the family Oriolidae. They eat insects, seeds, and fruit. New World orioles belong to the family Icteridae.

oriole Most dictionaries suggest that the name 'oriole' comes from the Latin word *aureolus* meaning 'golden'. Indeed, many of the 28 species in the oriole family are combinations of golden yellow and black. Orioles are related to starlings and drongos and are found in Eurasia and a limited area of Africa. The golden oriole is found in Europe.

Orion in astronomy, a very prominent constellation in the equatorial region of the sky (see ◊celestial sphere), identified with the hunter of Greek mythology.

The bright stars Alpha (◊Betelgeuse), Gamma (Bellatrix), Beta (◊Rigel), and Kappa Orionis mark the shoulders and legs of Orion. Between them the belt is formed by Delta, Epsilon, and Zeta, three second-magnitude stars equally spaced in a straight line. Beneath the belt is a line of fainter stars marking Orion's sword. One of these, Theta, is not really a star but the brightest part of the ◊Orion nebula.

Orion nebula luminous cloud of gas and dust 1,500 light years away, in the constellation Orion, from which stars are forming. It is about 15 light years in diameter, and contains enough gas to make a cluster of thousands of stars. At the nebula's centre is a group of hot young stars, called the Trapezium, which make the surrounding gas glow. The nebula is visible to the naked eye as a misty patch below the belt of Orion.

Orissa state of NE India
area 155,700 sq km/60,115 sq mi
capital Bhubaneswar
towns and cities Cuttack, Rourkela
features mainly agricultural; Chilka Lake with fisheries and game; temple of Jagannath or Juggernaut at Puri
industries rice, wheat, oilseed, sugar, timber, chromite (95% of India's output), dolomite, graphite, iron
population (1994 est) 33,795,000
language Oriya (official)
religion 90% Hindu
history administered by the British 1803–1912 as a

subdivision of Bengal, it joined with Bihar to become a province. In 1936 Orissa became a separate province, and in 1948–49 its area was almost doubled before its designation as a state 1950.

Orkney Causeway or ***Churchill Barriers*** construction in N Scotland put up in World War II, completed 1943, joining four of the Orkney Islands. It was built to protect the British fleet from intrusion through the eastern entrances to Scapa Flow.

The Orkney Causeway links the east mainland with the islands of Lambholm, Glimsholm, Burray, and South Ronaldsay.

Orkney Islands island group off the northeast coast of Scotland; also Scottish local authority (unchanged in reorganization 1996)
area 970 sq km/375 sq mi (*see United Kingdom map*)
towns and cities Kirkwall (administrative headquarters), on Mainland (Pomona)
features comprises about 90 islands and islets, low-lying and treeless; mild climate owing to the Gulf Stream; Skara Brae, a well-preserved Neolithic village on Mainland. On the island of Hoy is an isolated stack known as the Old Man of Hoy. The population, long falling, has in recent years risen as the islands' remoteness from the rest of the world attracts new settlers. Scapa Flow, between Mainland and Hoy, was a naval base in both world wars, and the German fleet scuttled itself here 21 June 1919
industries fishing and farming, beef cattle, poultry, fish curing, woollen weaving, wind power (Burgar Hill has the world's most productive wind-powered generator; a 300 KW wind turbine with blades 60 m/197 ft diameter, capable of producing 20% of the islands' energy needs)
population (1993) 19,760
famous people Edwin Muir, John Rae
history The population is of Scandinavian descent. Harald I (Fairhair) of Norway conquered the islands 876; they were pledged to James III of Scotland 1468 for the dowry of Margaret of Denmark and annexed by Scotland (the dowry unpaid) 1472.

Orlando industrial city in Florida, USA; population (1992) 174,200. It is a winter resort and tourist centre, with Walt Disney World and the Epcot Center nearby. Electronic and aerospace equipment are manufactured in the city, and citrus-fruit products are processed here. Educational institutions include the University of Central Florida. Orlando was settled 1843. The city was named 1857 after Orlando Reeves, a soldier killed in a clash with Indians.

Orlando furioso poem 1516 by the Italian Renaissance writer Ariosto, published 1532 as a sequel to Boiardo's *Orlando innamorato* 1487. The poem describes the unrequited love of Orlando for Angelica, set against the war between Saracens (Arabs) and Christians during Charlemagne's reign. It influenced Shakespeare, Byron, and Milton, and is considered to be the greatest poem of the Italian Renaissance.

Orléans industrial city of France, on the river Loire; 115 km/70 mi SW of Paris; population (1990) 108,000. It is the capital of Loiret *département*. Industries include engineering and food processing.

Orléans, of pre-Roman origin and formerly the capital of the old province of Orléanais, is associated with Joan of Arc, who liberated it from English rule 1429.

Orly suburb of Paris in the *département* of Val-de-Marne; population (1990) 21,800. Orly international airport is the busiest in France.

ormolu (French *or moulu* 'ground gold') alloy of copper, zinc, and sometimes tin, used for furniture decoration.

ornithology study of birds. It covers scientific aspects relating to their structure and classification, and their habits, song, flight, and value to agriculture as destroyers of insect pests. Worldwide scientific banding (or the fitting of coded rings to captured specimens) has resulted in accurate information on bird movements and distribution. There is an International Council for Bird Preservation with its headquarters at the Natural History Museum, London.

orogeny or ***orogenesis*** the formation of mountains. It is brought about by the movements of the rigid plates making up the Earth's crust (described by ◊plate tectonics). Where two plates collide at a destructive margin rocks become folded and lifted to form chains of fold mountains (such as the ◊young fold mountains of the Himalayas).

Orpheus mythical Greek poet and musician. The son of Apollo and a muse, he married Eurydice, who died from the bite of a snake. Orpheus went down to Hades to bring her back and her return to life was granted on condition that he walk ahead of her without looking back. He did look back and Eurydice was irretrievably lost. In his grief, he offended the ◊maenad women of Thrace, and was torn to pieces by them.

Orphism French style of abstract painting, derived from ◊Cubism, in which colour harmonies take precedence over form. The term 'Orphic Cubism' (later Orphism) was first used by the poet Guillaume Apollinaire 1913 to describe the mystical, visionary qualities he perceived in the first nonobjective (nonrepresentational) works of Robert ◊Delaunay. These sought to develop a visual equivalent to music through the interplay of light and colour on pure abstract form.

Orphism ancient Greek mystery cult, of which the Orphic hymns formed a part. Secret rites, accompanied by a harsh lifestyle, were aimed at securing immortality. Remains of an Orphic temple were found 1980 at Hungerford, Berkshire, England.

orrery mechanical device for demonstrating the motions of the heavenly bodies. Invented about 1710 by George Graham, it was named after his patron, the 4th Earl of Orrery. It is the forerunner of the planetarium.

orris root underground stem of a species of ◊iris grown in S Europe. Violet-scented, it is used in perfumery and herbal medicine.

Ortega Saavedra Daniel 1945– . Nicaraguan socialist politician, head of state 1981–90. He was a member of the Sandinista Liberation Front (FSLN) which overthrew the regime of Anastasio Somoza 1979, later becoming its secretary general. US-sponsored ◊Contra guerrillas opposed his government from 1982.

A participant in underground activities against the Somoza regime from an early age, Ortega was imprisoned and tortured several times. He became a member of the national directorate of the FSLN and fought in the two-year campaign for the ◊Nicaraguan Revolution. Ortega became a member of the junta of national reconstruction, and its coordinator two years later. The FSLN won the free 1984 elections, but in Feb 1990, Ortega lost the presidency to US-backed Violeta Chamorro. He was also defeated in the 1996 presidential election.

Ortega y Gasset José 1883–1955. Spanish philosopher and critic. He considered communism and fascism the cause of the downfall of Western civilization. His *Toward a Philosophy of History* 1941 contains philosophical reflections on the state and an interpretation of the meaning of human history.

'War is not an instinct but an invention.'
José Ortega y Gasset
Revolt of the Masses, epilogue

orthochromatic photographic film or paper of decreased sensitivity, which can be processed with a red safelight. Using it, blue objects appear lighter and red ones darker because of increased blue sensitivity.

orthodontics branch of ◊dentistry concerned with ◊dentition, and with treatment of any irregularities, such as correction of malocclusion (faulty position of teeth).

Orthodox Church or ***Eastern Orthodox Church*** or ***Greek Orthodox Church*** federation of self-governing Christian churches mainly found in E and SE Europe and parts of Asia. The centre of worship is the Eucharist. There is a married clergy, except for bishops; the Immaculate Conception is not accepted. The highest rank in the church is that of ecumenical patriarch, or bishop of Istanbul.

There are (1990) about 130 million adherents.

The church's teaching is based on the Bible, and the ◊Nicene Creed (as modified by the Council of Constantinople 381) is the only confession of faith used. The celebration of the Eucharist has changed little since the 6th century. The ritual is elaborate, and accompanied by singing in which both men and women take part, but no instrumental music is used.

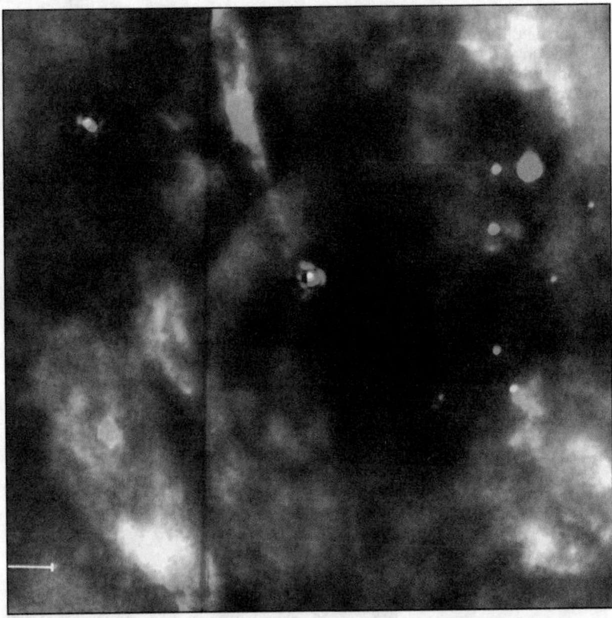

Orion nebula The Orion Nebula pictured by the Hubble Space Telescope. The nebula surrounds the three stars that depict the sword in the constellation Orion, the hunter of Greek mythology. The jet structure visible in the photograph was identified by the space telescope. *Image Select (UK) Ltd*

Besides the seven sacraments, the prayer book contains many other services for daily life.

Its adherents include Greeks, Russians, Romanians, Serbians, Bulgarians, Georgians, and Albanians. In the last 200 years the Orthodox Church has spread into China, Korea, Japan, and the USA, as well as among the people of Siberia and central Asia.

orthopaedics (Greek *orthos* 'straight'; *pais* 'child') medical speciality concerned with the correction of disease or damage in bones and joints.

ortolan songbird *Emberiza hortulana* of the bunting family Emberizidae, order Passeriformes, common in Europe and W Asia, migrating to Africa in the winter. The upper surface is reddish-brown with black streaks, the throat yellow, the head grey, and the underparts greenish-olive. The nest is made in the undergrowth, on the ground or on banks. Long considered a delicacy among gourmets, it has become rare and is now a protected species.

Orton Joe (John Kingsley) 1933–1967. English dramatist. In his black comedies, surreal and violent action takes place in genteel and unlikely settings. Plays include *Entertaining Mr Sloane* 1964, *Loot* 1966, and *What the Butler Saw* 1968. His diaries deal frankly with his personal life. He was murdered by his lover Kenneth Halliwell.

Orvieto town in Umbria, Italy, NE of Lake Bolsena, population (1990) 21,580. Built on the site of Volsinii, an Etruscan town destroyed by the Romans 280 BC, Orvieto has many Etruscan remains. The name is from Latin *Urbs Vetus* meaning 'old town'.

Orwell George. Pen name of Eric Arthur Blair 1903–1950. English author. His books include the satirical fable *Animal Farm* 1945 (an attack on the Soviet Union and Stalin), which included such slogans as 'All animals are equal, but some are more equal than others', and the prophetic *Nineteen Eighty-Four* 1949 (targeting contemporary Cold-War politics), which portrays the catastrophic excesses of state control over the individual. Other works include *Down and Out in Paris and London* 1933. He also wrote numerous essays. Orwell was distrustful of all political parties and ideologies and a deep sense of social conscience and antipathy towards political dictatorship characterize his work.

'It is only because miners sweat their guts out that superior persons can remain superior.'
George Orwell
The Road to Wigan Pier

oryx any of the genus *Oryx* of large antelopes native to Africa and Asia. The Arabian oryx *O. leucoryx*, at one time extinct in the wild, has been successfully reintroduced into its natural habitat using stocks bred in captivity.

The scimitar-horned oryx *O. tao* of the Sahara is also rare. Beisaoryx *O. beisa* in E Africa and gemsbok *O. gazella* in the Kalahari are more common. In profile the two long horns appear as one, which may have given rise to the legend of the unicorn. *See illustration on following page.*

Osaka industrial port (iron, steel, shipbuilding, chemicals, textiles) on Honshu Island, Japan;

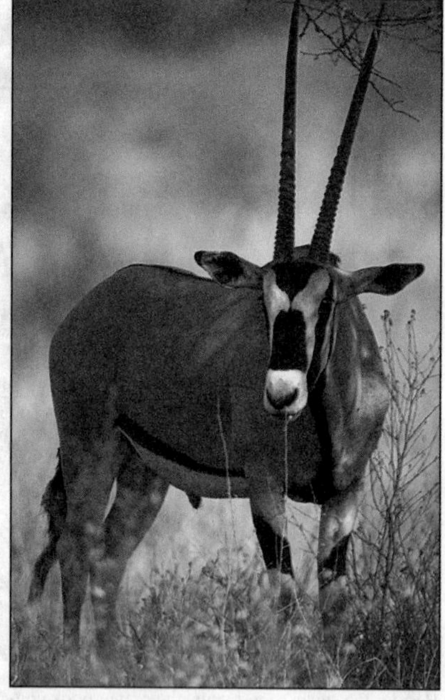

oryx A male oryx in a Kenyan wildlife reserve. Oryx live in arid regions, where they are able to survive without drinking water, obtaining sufficient moisture from the vegetation they eat. In the past they formed large herds, but hunting has reduced their numbers. *Corbis*

population (1994) 2,481,000. It is the oldest city of Japan and was at times the seat of government in the 4th–8th centuries.

Lying on a plain sheltered by hills and opening onto Osaka Bay, Osaka is honeycombed with waterways. It is a tourist centre for Kyoto and the Seto Inland Sea and is linked with Tokyo by fast electric train (travelling up to 200 kph/124 mph). An underground shopping and leisure centre (1951) has been used as a model for others throughout Japan. It was a mercantile centre in the 18th century, and in the 20th century set the pace for Japan's revolution based on light industries.

Osborne John James 1929–1994. English dramatist. He became one of the first ◊Angry Young Men (anti-establishment writers of the 1950s) of British theatre with his debut play, *Look Back in Anger* 1956. Other plays include *The Entertainer* 1957, *Luther* 1960, *Inadmissible Evidence* 1964, *A Patriot for Me* 1965, *West of Suez* 1971, and *Watch It Come Down* 1976. With *Déjà-Vu* 1992 he returned unsuccessfully to Jimmy Porter, the hero of the epoch-making *Look Back in Anger*.

Oscar in cinema, popular name for ◊Academy Award.

Oscar I 1799–1859. King of Sweden and Norway from 1844, when he succeeded his father, Charles XIV. He established freedom of the press, and supported Denmark against Germany 1848.

Oscar II 1829–1907. King of Sweden and Norway 1872–1905, king of Sweden until 1907. He was the younger son of Oscar I, and succeeded his brother Charles XV. He tried hard to prevent the separation of his two kingdoms but relinquished the throne of Norway to Haakon VII 1905.

He was an international arbitrator in Samoa, Venezuela, and the Anglo-American dispute.

oscillating universe in astronomy, a theory that states that the gravitational attraction of the mass within the universe will eventually slow down and stop the expansion of the universe. The outward motions of the galaxies will then be reversed, eventually resulting in a 'Big Crunch' where all the matter in the universe would be contracted into a small volume of high density. This could undergo a further ◊Big Bang, thereby creating another expansion phase. The theory suggests that the universe would alternately expand and collapse through alternate Big Bangs and Big Crunches.

oscillator any device producing a desired oscillation (vibration). There are many types of oscillator for different purposes, involving various arrangements of thermionic ◊valves or components such as ◊transistors, inductors, ◊capacitors, and ◊resistors.

oscillograph instrument for displaying or recording the values of rapidly changing oscillations, electrical or mechanical.

oscilloscope or ***cathode-ray oscilloscope*** (CRO) instrument used to measure electrical voltages that vary over time and to display the waveforms of electrical oscillations or signals, by means of the deflection of a beam of ◊electrons. Readings are displayed graphically on the screen of a ◊cathode-ray tube.

'They spend their time mostly looking forward to the past.'

JOHN OSBORNE
Look Back in Anger

osier any of several trees and shrubs of the willow genus *Salix*, cultivated for basket making; in particular, *S. viminalis*.

Osiris ancient Egyptian god, the embodiment of goodness, who ruled the underworld after being killed by ◊Set. The sister-wife of Osiris was ◊Isis or Hathor, and their son ◊Horus captured his father's murderer. The pharaohs were thought to be his incarnation.

Oslo capital and industrial port (textiles, engineering, timber) of Norway; population (1991) 461,600. The first recorded settlement was made in the 11th century by Harald III Hardrada, but after a fire 1624, it was entirely replanned by Christian IV and renamed Christiania 1624–1924.

The port is built at the head of Oslo fjord, which is kept open in winter by icebreakers. There is a Viking museum, the 13th-century Akershus Castle, a 17th-century cathedral, and the National Gallery, which includes many paintings by Edvard Munch.

Osman I or ***Uthman I*** 1259–1326. Turkish ruler from 1299. He began his career in the service of the Seljuk Turks, but in 1299 he set up a kingdom of his own in Bithynia, NW Asia, and assumed the title of sultan. He conquered a great part of Anatolia, so founding a Turkish empire. His successors were known as 'sons of Osman', from which the term ◊Ottoman Empire is derived.

osmium (Greek *osme* 'odour') hard, heavy, bluish-white, metallic element, symbol Os, atomic number 76, relative atomic mass 190.2. It is the densest of the elements, and is resistant to tarnish and corrosion. It occurs in platinum ores and as a free metal (see ◊native metal) with iridium in a natural alloy called osmiridium, containing traces of platinum, ruthenium, and rhodium. Its uses include pen points and light-bulb filaments; like platinum, it is a useful catalyst.

osmoregulation process whereby the water content of living organisms is maintained at a constant level. If the water balance is disrupted, the concentration of salts will be too high or too low, and vital functions, such as nerve conduction, will be adversely affected.

osmosis movement of solvent (usually water) through a semipermeable membrane separating solutions of different concentrations. The solvent passes from a less concentrated solution to a more concentrated solution until the two concentrations are equal. Applying external pressure to the solution on the more concentrated side arrests osmosis, and is a measure of the osmotic pressure of the solution.

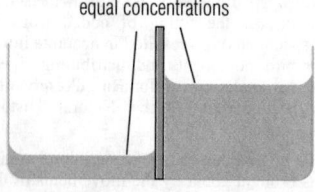

Many cell membranes behave as semipermeable membranes, and osmosis is a vital mechanism in the transport of fluids in living organisms – for example, in the transport of water from the roots up the stems of plants.

osprey bird of prey *Pandion haliaetus*, the single member of the family Pandionidae, order Falconiformes; sometimes erroneously called 'fish hawk'. To catch fish, it plunges feet first into the water. Dark brown above and a striking white below, the osprey measures 60 cm/2 ft with a 2 m/6 ft wingspan. The nest is often made in trees near the seashore or lakeside. In it are laid two or three white eggs, blotched with crimson. Ospreys occur on all continents except Antarctica and have faced extinction in several areas of habitation.

Ossa, Mount the highest peak on the island of Tasmania, Australia; height 1,617 m/5,250 ft.

Ossetia region in the Caucasus, on the border between Russia and Georgia. It is inhabited by the Ossets, who speak the Iranian language Ossetic, and who were conquered by the Russians 1802.

Some live in ◊Alania (formerly North Ossetia), an autonomous republic in the SW Russian Federation. The rest live in ◊South Ossetia, an autonomous region of the Georgian republic. The region has been the scene of Osset–Georgian interethnic conflict since 1989. More than 100,000 Ossets from South Ossetia moved to Alania 1989–92, in turn causing the Ingush there to flee to Ingushetia.

The Ossets demanded that South Ossetia be upgraded to an autonomous republic as a preliminary to reunification with Alania, and in Sept 1990 declared the region independent of the USSR (a claim rejected by President Gorbachev). Separatist moves were violently suppressed by Georgian authorities and states of emergency imposed following clashes between police and Ossets. During 1991 several hundred lives were claimed in interethnic gun battles. The violence escalated June 1992, when armed South Ossetian nationalists launched a drive to unite the two regions, spreading violence to Alania and heightening tensions between Georgia and Russia.

A peace accord reached 24 June had little effect, but in July 1992 a cease-fire was agreed and Georgian and Russian peacekeeping troops were deployed. In Sept 1996 Ludvig Chibirov was elected president of South Ossetia in elections declared illegal by the Georgian government.

Ossian (Celtic ***Oisin***) legendary Gaelic hero and bard, claimed by both Ireland and Scotland. He is sometimes represented as the son of ◊Finn Mac Cumhaill, about 250, and as having lived to tell the tales of Finn and the Ulster heroes to St Patrick, about 400. The publication 1760 of James ◊Macpherson's poems, attributed to Ossian, made Ossian's name familiar throughout Europe.

ossification or ***osteogenesis*** process whereby bone is formed in vertebrate animals by special cells (osteoblasts) that secrete layers of ◊extracellular matrix on the surface of the existing ◊cartilage. Conversion to bone occurs through the deposition of calcium phosphate crystals within the matrix.

Ostend (Flemish ***Oostende***) seaport and pleasure resort in W Flanders, Belgium; 108 km/67 mi NW of Brussels; population (1995 est) 68,900. There are large docks, and the Belgian fishing fleet has its headquarters here. There are ferry links to Dover and Folkestone, England. It was occupied by the Germans 1914–18 and developed as an important naval base.

osteoarthritis degenerative form of arthritis which tends to affect larger, load-bearing joints such as the knee and hip. It appears in later life, especially in joints that have been subject to earlier stress or damage; one or more joints stiffen and may give considerable pain. It occurs most in people over middle age and the elderly, and is more common in men than women. Joint replacement surgery is nearly always successful. See also ◊rheumatoid arthritis.

osteology part of the science of ◊anatomy, dealing with the structure, function, and development of bones.

osteomyelitis infection of bone, with spread of pus along the marrow cavity. Now quite rare, it may follow from a compound fracture (where broken bone protrudes through the skin), or from infectious disease elsewhere in the body. It is more common in children whose bones are not yet fully grown.

osmosis Apparatus for measuring osmotic pressure. In 1877 German physicist Wilhelm Pfeffer used this apparatus to make the first ever measurement of osmotic pressure and show that osmotic pressure varies according to temperature and the strength of the solute (dissolved substance).

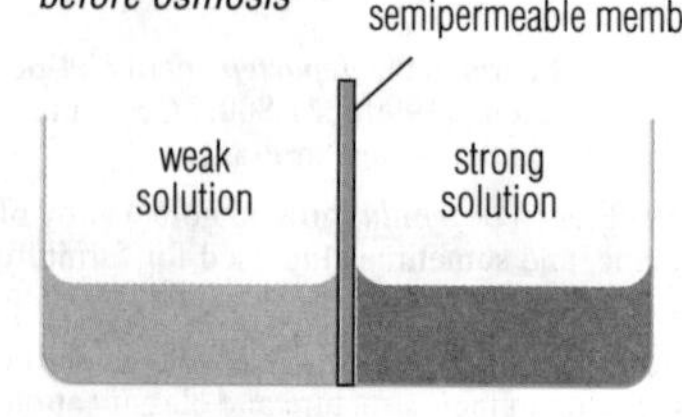

ostrich The ostrich cannot fly but it is the fastest animal on two legs. It can run at speeds up to 70 kph/44 mph. The ostrich lays the largest eggs of any bird, each egg being up to 20 cm/8 in long, weighing 1.3 kg/3 lb, and having the volume of 40 chicken's eggs.

osteopathy system of alternative medical practice that relies on physical manipulation to treat mechanical stress. It was developed over a century ago by US physician Andrew Taylor Still, who maintained that most ailments can be prevented or cured by techniques of spinal manipulation.

osteoporosis disease in which the bone substance becomes porous and brittle. It is common in older people, affecting more women than men. It may be treated with calcium supplements and etidronate. Approximately 1.7 million people worldwide, mostly women, suffer hip fractures, mainly due to osteoporosis. A single gene was discovered 1993 to have a major influence on bone thinning.

Ostia ancient Roman town near the mouth of the Tiber. Founded about 330 BC, it was the port of Rome and had become a major commercial centre by the 2nd century AD. It was abandoned in the 9th century. The present-day seaside resort Ostia Mare is situated nearby.

ostrich large flightless bird *Struthio camelus*, found in Africa. The single species forms the order Struthioniformes. The male may be about 2.5 m/8 ft tall and weigh 135 kg/300 lb, and is the largest living bird. It has exceptionally strong legs and feet (two-toed) that enable it to run at high speed, and are also used in defence. It lives in family groups of one cock with several hens, each of which lays about 14 eggs.

Ostrovsky Alexander Nikolaevich 1823–1886. Russian dramatist. He was a founder of the modern Russian theatre. He dealt satirically with the manners of the merchant class in numerous plays, for example *The Bankrupt* (or *It's All in the Family*) 1849. His best-known play is a family tragedy, *The Storm* 1860. His fairy-tale play *The Snow Maiden* 1873 inspired the composers Tchaikovsky and Rimsky-Korsakov.

Ostwald (Friedrich) Wilhelm 1853–1932. Latvian-born German chemist who devised the Ostwald process (the oxidation of ammonia over a platinum catalyst to give nitric acid). His work on catalysts laid the foundations of the petrochemical industry. Nobel Prize for Chemistry 1909.

O'Sullivan, Sonia 1969– . Irish athlete. A brilliant and versatile middle and long distance runner equally strong on the track or in cross-country. In 1998 she won both the short and long distance events at the World Cross-Country Championships in Marrakesh, Morocco, and then, at the European Championships in Budapest, Hungary, she won golds at 5,000 and 10,000 metres.

Oswald, St c. 605–642. King of Northumbria from 634, after killing the Welsh king Cadwallon. He became a Christian convert during exile on the Scottish island of Iona. With the help of St Aidan he furthered the spread of Christianity in N England. Oswald was defeated and killed by King Penda of Mercia. His feast day is 9 Aug.

Othman alternative spelling of ◊Uthman, third caliph of Islam.

Otis Elisha Graves 1811–1861. US engineer who developed a lift that incorporated a safety device, making it acceptable for passenger use in the first skyscrapers. The device, invented 1852, consisted of vertical ratchets on the sides of the lift shaft into which spring-loaded catches would engage and lock the lift in position in the event of cable failure.

otitis inflammation of the ear. *Otitis externa*, occurring in the outer ear canal, is easily treated with antibiotics. Inflamed conditions of the middle ear (*otitis media*) or inner ear (*otitis interna*) are more serious, carrying the risk of deafness and infection of the brain. Treatment is with antibiotics or, more rarely, surgery.

O'Toole Peter Seamus 1932– . Irish-born English actor. He made his name as *Lawrence of Arabia* 1962, and then starred in such films as *Becket* 1964 and *The Lion in Winter* 1968. Subsequent appearances include *The Ruling Class* 1972, *The Stuntman* 1978, and *High Spirits* 1988.

otosclerosis overgrowth of bone in the middle ear causing progressive deafness. This inherited condition is gradual in onset, developing usually before middle age. It is twice as common in women as in men. Surgery is necessary to remove the diseased bone and reconstruct the ossicular chain.

Ottawa capital of Canada, in E Ontario, on the hills overlooking the Ottawa River and divided by the Rideau Canal into the Upper (western) and Lower (eastern) towns; population (1991) 314,000, metropolitan area (with adjoining Hull, Quebec) 819,000. Industries include timber, pulp and paper, engineering, food processing, and publishing. It was founded 1826–32 as Bytown, in honour of John By (1781–1836), whose army engineers were building the Rideau Canal. It was renamed 1854 after the Outaouac Indians.

Features include the National Museum, National Art Gallery, Observatory, Rideau Hall (the governor general's residence), and the National Arts Centre 1969 (with an orchestra and English/French theatre). In 1858 it was chosen by Queen Victoria as the country's capital.

otter any of various aquatic carnivores of the weasel family, found on all continents except Australia. Otters have thick, brown fur, short limbs, webbed toes, and long, compressed tails. They are social, playful, and agile.

The otter of Europe and Asia *Lutra lutra* has a broad head, an elongated body covered by grey-brown fur, short legs, and webbed feet. Including a 45 cm/1.5 ft tail, it measures over 1 m/3.5 ft. It lives on fish. There are a number of American species, including the larger *L. canadensis* of North America, the sea otter *Enhydra lutris* of the N Pacific, and the giant otter *Pteronura brasiliensis* of South America.

Otto four Holy Roman emperors, including:

Otto I 912–973. Holy Roman emperor from 962. He restored the power of the empire, asserted his authority over the pope and the nobles, ended the Magyar menace by his victory at the Lechfeld 955, and refounded the East Mark, or Austria, as a barrier against them.

Otto IV c. 1182–1218. Holy Roman emperor, elected 1198. He engaged in controversy with Pope Innocent III, and was defeated by the pope's ally, Philip of France, at Bouvines 1214.

Otto cycle alternative name for the ◊four-stroke cycle, introduced by the German engineer Nikolaus Otto (1832–1891) in 1876. It improved on existing piston engines by compressing the fuel mixture in the cylinder before it was ignited.

Ottoman Empire Muslim empire of the Turks 1300–1920, the successor of the ◊Seljuk Empire. It was founded by ◊Osman I and reached its height with ◊Suleiman in the 16th century. Its capital was Istanbul (formerly Constantinople).

At its greatest extent the Ottoman Empire's boundaries were Europe as far as Hungary, part of S Russia, Iran, the Palestinian coastline, Egypt, and N Africa. From the 17th century it was in decline. There was an attempted revival and reform under the Young Turk party 1908, but the regime crumbled when Turkey sided with Germany in World War I. The sultanate was abolished by Kemal Atatürk 1922; the last sultan was Muhammad VI. *See illustration on following page.*

Otway Thomas 1652–1685. English dramatist. His plays include the tragedies *Alcibiades* 1675, *Don Carlos* 1676, *The Orphan* 1680, and *Venice Preserv'd* 1682.

Ouagadougou capital and industrial centre of Burkina Faso; population (1991 est) 634,000. Products include textiles, vegetable oil, and soap. The city has the palace of Moro Naba, emperor of the Mossi people, a neo-Romanesque cathedral, and a central avenue called the Champs Elysées.

Oudh region of N India, now part of Uttar Pradesh. An independent kingdom before it fell under Mogul rule, Oudh regained independence 1732–1856, when it was annexed by Britain. Its capital was Lucknow, centre of the ◊Indian Mutiny 1857–58. In 1877 it was joined with Agra, from 1902 as the

otter A North American river otter eating a trout. Freshwater otters are just as agile on land as in water, and feed on a variety of small creatures including mice, fish, frogs, and water voles. Their numbers have declined dramatically in the 20th century because of pollution and destruction of their natural habitat, and trapping for their fur. *Corbis*

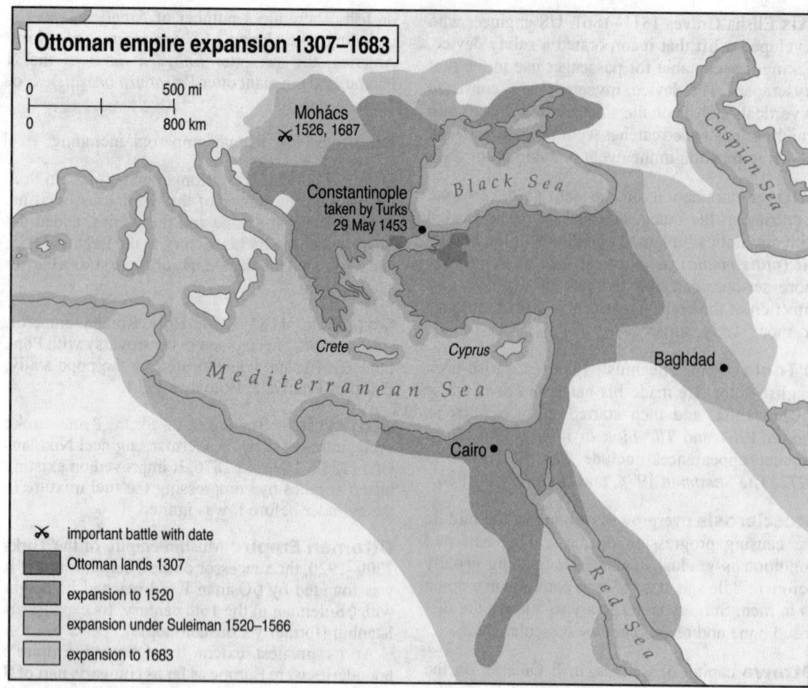

United Provinces of Agra and Oudh, renamed Uttar Pradesh 1950.

Oughtred William 1575–1660. English mathematician, credited as the inventor of the slide rule 1622. His major work *Clavis mathematicae/The Key to Mathematics* 1631 was a survey of the entire body of mathematical knowledge of his day. It introduced the '×' symbol for multiplication, as well as the abbreviations 'sin' for sine and 'cos' for cosine.

ounce another name for the snow ◊leopard.

ounce unit of mass, one-sixteenth of a pound ◊avoirdupois, equal to 437.5 grains (28.35 g); also one-twelfth of a pound troy, equal to 480 grains. The fluid ounce is a measure of capacity. In the UK it is equivalent to one-twentieth of a pint; in the USA to one-sixteenth of a pint.

Ouse (Celtic 'water') any of several British rivers: The Great Ouse rises in Northamptonshire and winds its way across 250 km/160 mi to enter the Wash N of King's Lynn. A large sluice across the Great Ouse, near King's Lynn, was built as part of extensive flood-control works 1959. The Little Ouse flows for 38 km/24 mi along part of the Norfolk–Suffolk border and is a tributary of the Great Ouse. The Yorkshire Ouse is formed by the junction of the Ure and Swale near Boroughbridge and joins the river Trent to form the Humber. The Sussex Ouse rises between Horsham and Cuckfield and flows through the South Downs to enter the English Channel at Newhaven.

Ouspensky Peter Demianovich 1878–1947. Russian mystic. He became a disciple of the occultist George ◊Gurdjieff 1914 but broke with him 1924. He expanded Gurdjieff's ideas in terms of other dimensions of space and time. His works include *In Search of the Miraculous*.

outback the inland region of Australia. Its main inhabitants are Aborigines, miners (including opal miners), and cattle ranchers. Its harsh beauty has been recorded by such artists as Sidney Nolan.

outlawry in medieval England, a declaration that a criminal was outside the protection of the law, with his or her lands and goods forfeited to the crown, and all civil rights being set aside. It was a lucrative royal 'privilege'; ◊Magna Carta restricted its use, and under Edward III it was further modified. Some outlaws, such as ◊Robin Hood, became popular heroes.

Time the devourer of things.

OVID
Metamorphoses

output device in computing, any device for displaying, in a form intelligible to the user, the results of processing carried out by a computer. The most common output devices are the ◊VDU (visual display unit, or screen) and the printer. Other output devices include graph plotters, speech synthesizers, and COM (computer output on microfilm/microfiche).

Oval, the cricket ground in Kennington, London, England, the home of Surrey County Cricket Club. It was the venue for the first test match between England and Australia 1880.

ovary in female animals, the organ that generates the ◊ovum. In humans, the ovaries are two whitish rounded bodies about 25 mm/1 in by 35 mm/1.5 in, located in the lower abdomen to either side of the uterus. Every month, from puberty to the onset of the menopause, an ovum is released from the ovary. This is called ovulation, and forms part of the ◊menstrual cycle. In botany, an ovary is the expanded basal portion of the ◊carpel of flowering plants, containing one or more ◊ovules. It is hollow with a thick wall to protect the ovules. Following fertilization of the ovum, it develops into the fruit wall or pericarp.

The ovaries of female animals secrete the hormones responsible for the secondary sexual characteristics of the female, such as smooth, hairless facial skin and enlarged breasts. An ovary in a half-grown human fetus contains 5 million eggs, and so the unborn baby already possesses the female genetic information for the next generation.

In botany, the relative position of the ovary to the other floral parts is often a distinguishing character in classification; it may be either inferior or superior, depending on whether the petals and sepals are inserted above or below.

overfishing fishing at rates result in a net population decline. For example, in the North Atlantic, herring has been fished to the verge of extinction and the cod and haddock populations are severely depleted. In the Third World, use of huge factory ships, often by fisheries from industrialized countries, has depleted stocks for local people who cannot obtain protein in any other way. See also ◊fishing and fisheries.

Ecologists have long been concerned at the wider implications of overfishing, in particular the devastation wrought on oceanic ◊food chains. The United Nations Food and Agriculture Organization estimates that worldwide overfishing has damaged oceanic ecosystems to such an extent that potential catches are on average reduced by 20%. With better management of fishing programmes the fishing catch could in principle be increased; it is estimated that, annually, 20 million tonnes of fish are discarded from fishing vessels at sea, because they are not the species sought.

overhead in economics, fixed costs in a business that do not vary in the short term. These might include property rental, heating and lighting, insurance, and administration costs.

Overijssel province of the E central Netherlands, containing the rivers rivers IJssel and Vecht; area 3,340 sq km/1,289 sq mi; population (1995 est) 1,050,400. Its capital is Zwolle; other towns and cities include Enschede, Hengelo, Deventer. Its industries are livestock, dairy products, and textiles.

overlander one of the Australian drovers in the 19th century who opened up new territory by driving their cattle through remote areas to new stations, or to market, before the establishment of regular stock routes.

Overlord, Operation Allied invasion of Normandy 6 June 1944 (◊D-day), during World War II.

overpopulation too many people for the resources available in an area (such as food, land, and water). The consequences were first set out by English economist Thomas ◊Malthus at the start of the population explosion. Although there is often a link between overpopulation and population density (the number of people living in a given area), high densities will not always result in overpopulation. In many countries, resources are plentiful and the ◊infrastructure and technology are well developed. This means that a large number of people can be supported by a small area of land.

Overseas Development Administration (ODA) see ◊International Development Department (IDD).

overtone note that has a frequency or pitch that is a multiple of the fundamental frequency, the sounding body's ◊natural frequency. Each sound source produces a unique set of overtones, which gives the source its quality or timbre.

overture in music, the opening piece of a concert or opera, having the dual function of settling the audience and allowing the conductor and musicians to become acquainted with the ◊acoustic of a concert auditorium. The use of an overture in opera began during the 17th century; the 'Italian' overture consisting of two quick movements separated by a slow one, and the 'French' of a quick movement between two in slower tempo.

Ovid (Publius Ovidius Naso) 43 BC–AD 17. Latin poet. His poetry deals mainly with the themes of love (*Amores* 20 BC, *Ars amatoria/The Art of Love* 1 BC), mythology (*Metamorphoses* AD 2), and exile (*Tristia* AD 9–12). Born at Sulmo, Ovid studied rhetoric in Rome in preparation for a legal career, but soon turned to literature. In 8 BC he was banished by Augustus to Tomi, on the Black Sea, where he died. Sophisticated, ironical, and self-pitying, his work was highly influential during the Middle Ages and Renaissance.

oviparous method of animal reproduction in which eggs are laid by the female and develop

Owen English poet Wilfred Owen. Admired for the bleak realism of his World War I poetry, Owen's work exemplifies his horror at the brutalities of warfare. He fought on the Somme, won the Military Cross, and was killed in action in 1918, one week before the Armistice. *Corbis*

outside her body, in contrast to ovoviviparous and viviparous. It is the most common form of reproduction.

ovoviviparous method of animal reproduction in which fertilized eggs develop within the female (unlike oviparous), and the embryo gains no nutritional substances from the female (unlike viviparous). It occurs in some invertebrates, fishes, and reptiles.

ovulation in female animals, the process of releasing egg cells (ova) from the ◊ovary. In mammals it occurs as part of the ◊menstrual cycle.

ovule structure found in seed plants that develops into a seed after fertilization. It consists of an ◊embryo sac containing the female gamete (◊ovum or egg cell), surrounded by nutritive tissue, the nucellus. Outside this there are one or two coverings that provide protection, developing into the testa, or seed coat, following fertilization.

ovum (plural *ova*) female gamete (sex cell) before fertilization. In animals it is called an egg, and is produced in the ovaries. In plants, where it is also known as an egg cell or oosphere, the ovum is produced in an ovule. The ovum is nonmotile. It must be fertilized by a male gamete before it can develop further, except in cases of ◊parthenogenesis.

Owen David Anthony Llewellyn 1938– . British politician, Labour foreign secretary 1977–79. In 1981 he was one of the founders of the ◊Social Democratic Party (SDP), and became its leader 1983. Opposed to the decision of the majority of the party to merge with the Liberals 1987, Owen stood down, but emerged 1988 as leader of a rump SDP, which was eventually disbanded 1990. In 1992 he became the European Union mediator in the peace talks on Bosnia-Herzegovina; he resigned from the post 1995.

Owen, Michael 1979– . English footballer. A striker of exceptional pace, he made his full England debut in February 1998 at the age of 18 years 59 days, then three months later became England's youngest ever goalscorer. He scored two goals at the 1998 World Cup finals, including what was widely regarded as the goal of the tournament against Argentina. Owen made his first team debut for Liverpool in May 1997, and in his first full season (1997–98) finished as the Premier League's equal top scorer with 18 goals.

Owen Robert 1771–1858. British socialist, born in Wales. In 1800 he became manager of a mill at New Lanark, Scotland, where by improving working and housing conditions and providing schools he created a model community. His ideas stimulated the cooperative movement (the pooling of resources for joint economic benefit).

Owens US track and field athlete Jesse Owens in training at the Berlin Olympics 1936. An outstanding athlete, Owens broke many world records and his domination of the Berlin Olympics did much to discredit Nazi propaganda on the racial superiority of the 'Aryan'. *Topham*

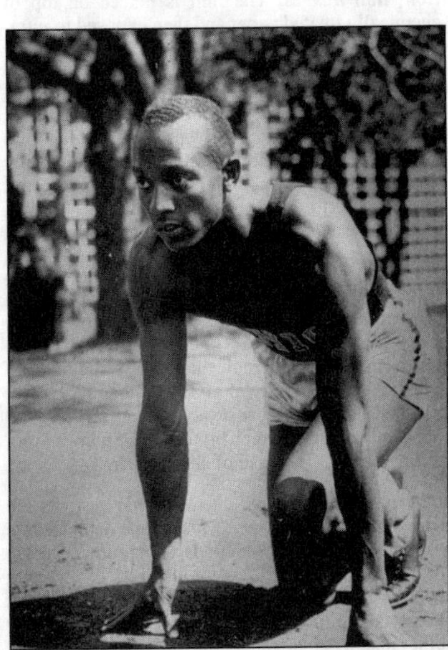

ox Since the earliest days of civilization oxen have been used for a wide variety of tasks requiring strength and stamina. Here, in India, they are being used to dehusk the rice crop with a concrete roller. *Premaphotos Wildlife*

◊From 1817 Owen proposed that 'villages of cooperation', self-supporting communities run on socialist lines, should be founded; these, he believed, would ultimately replace private ownership. His later attempt to run such a community in the USA (called New Harmony) failed.

Owen Wilfred Edward Salter 1893–1918. English poet. His verse, owing much to the encouragement of Siegfried ◊Sassoon, is among the most moving of World War I poetry; it shatters the illusion of the glory of war, revealing its hollowness and cruel destruction of beauty. Only four poems were published during his lifetime; he was killed in action a week before the Armistice. Sassoon posthumously collected and edited his *Poems* 1920. Among the best known are 'Dulce et Decorum Est' and 'Anthem for Doomed Youth', published 1921.

Owens Jesse (James Cleveland) 1913–1980. US track and field athlete who excelled in the sprints, hurdles, and the long jump. At the 1936 Berlin Olympics he won four gold medals. His triumph so angered Hitler that he is said to have stormed out of the stadium. Owens held the world long-jump record for 25 years 1935–60. At Ann Arbor, Michigan, on 25 May 1935, he broke six world records in less than an hour.

owl bird of the order Strigiformes, found worldwide. They are mainly nocturnal birds of prey, with hooked beaks, mobile heads and contracted necks, soundless flight, acute hearing, and forward-facing immobile eyes, surrounded by 'facial discs' of rayed feathers. Owls comprise two families: typical owls, family Strigidae, of which there are about 120 species; and barn owls, family Tytonidae, of which there are 10 species.

They feed mainly on rodents, but reptiles, fish, and insects are also eaten, and some species have been observed to feed on carrion. All species lay white eggs, and begin incubation as soon as the first is laid. They regurgitate indigestible remains of their prey in pellets (castings).

ox castrated male of domestic species of cattle, used in developing countries for ploughing and other agricultural purposes. Also the extinct wild ox or ◊aurochs of Europe, and extant wild species such as buffaloes and yaks.

oxalic acid $(COOH)_2.2H_2O$ white, poisonous solid, soluble in water, alcohol, and ether. Oxalic acid is found in rhubarb, and its salts (oxalates) occur in wood sorrel (genus *Oxalis*, family Oxalidaceae) and other plants. It also occurs naturally in human body cells. It is used in the leather and textile industries, in dyeing and bleaching, ink manufacture, metal polishes, and for removing rust and ink stains.

oxbow lake curved lake found on the flood plain of a river. Oxbows are caused by the loops of ◊meanders being cut off at times of flood and the river subsequently adopting a shorter course. In the USA, the term bayou is often used.

Oxenstjerna Axel Gustafsson, Count Oxenstjerna 1583–1654. Swedish politician, chancellor from 1612. He pursued Gustavus Adolphus's foreign policy, acted as regent for Queen Christina, and maintained Swedish interests during and after the Thirty Years' War. Count 1645.

Oxfam (abbreviation for ***Oxford Committee for Famine Relief***) charity working to relieve poverty and famine worldwide. It was established in the UK 1942 by Canon Theodore Richard Milford (1896–1987), initially to assist the starving people of Greece. Its director from 1992 is David Bryer (1944–).

Oxford university city and administrative centre of Oxfordshire in S central England, at the confluence of the rivers Thames (called the Isis around Oxford) and Cherwell; population (1991) 110,000. Oxford University has 39 colleges, the oldest being University College (1249). Industries include motor vehicles at Cowley, steel products, electrical goods, paper, publishing, and English language schools. Tourism is important.

features Christ Church cathedral (12th century), the Divinity School and Duke Humphrey's Library (1488), the Sheldonian Theatre, designed by Christopher ◊Wren 1663–69, the Ashmolean museum (1845). Other museums include the University Museum, designed by Benjamin Woodward 1855–60, the Pitt-Rivers Museum, and the Museum of Modern Art. Merton College has the 14th-century Mob Quad and library; St John's College has the Canterbury Quad (1636) and gardens laid out by 'Capability' Brown; 17th-century Bodleian Library. The Bate Collection of Historical Instruments is housed at the Faculty of Music. On 1 May (May morning) madrigals are sung at the top of Magdalen College tower. St Giles fair takes place every September.

history The town was first occupied in Saxon times as a fording point, and is first mentioned in written records in the Anglo-Saxon Chronicle of 912. The University of Oxford, the oldest in England, is first mentioned in the 12th century, when its growth was encouraged by the influx of English students expelled from Paris 1167. Most of the university's buildings were built during the 15th, 16th, and 17th centuries. Oxford's earliest colleges were University College 1249, Balliol 1263, and Merton 1264. *See illustration on following page.*

What passing-bells for these that die as cattle?

WILFRED OWEN
'Anthem for Doomed Youth' 1917

And that sweet City with her dreaming spires, / She needs not June for beauty's heightening.

On OXFORD
Matthew Arnold
'Thyrsis' 1867

owl The barn-owl family can be distinguished from other owl groups by its heart-shaped face, relatively small eyes, and long slender legs. The long, hooked beak is usually concealed by feathers. All barn owls are hunters by night.

Oxford View of Oxford's High Street from the tower of Magdalen College. The distinctive dome of the Radcliffe Camera (part of the Bodleian Library) can be seen on the skyline. Oxford's oldest college, University College (founded 1249), is located in the High Street. *Sally Jenkins*

During the Civil War, the university supported the Royalist cause while the city declared for Parliament. Oxford became the headquarters of the king and court 1642, but yielded to the Parliamentary commander in chief, General Fairfax, 1646. After the Restoration the university settled down into the ease of the 18th century, interrupted only by political disputes and the Methodist movement.

By the beginning of the 20th century, the city had experienced rapid expansion and industrialization, and printing and publishing industries had become firmly established. In the 1920s the English industrial magnate William Morris (1877–1963), later Lord Nuffield, began a motor-car industry at Cowley, just outside the city, which became the headquarters of the Austin-Rover group.

Oxford Movement also known as ***Tractarian Movement*** or ***Catholic Revival*** movement that attempted to revive Catholic religion in the Church of England. Cardinal Newman dated the movement from ◊Keble's sermon in Oxford 1833. The Oxford Movement by the turn of the century had transformed the Anglican communion, and survives today as Anglo-Catholicism.

Oxfordshire county of S central England
area 2,610 sq km/1,007 sq mi (*see United Kingdom map*)
towns and cities Oxford (administrative headquarters), Abingdon, Banbury, Henley-on-Thames, Witney, Woodstock
features river Thames and tributaries; Cotswolds and Chiltern Hills; Vale of the White Horse (chalk hill figure at Uffington, 114 m/374 ft long); Oxford University; Blenheim Palace, Woodstock (started 1705 by Vanbrugh with help from Nicholas Hawksmoor, completed 1722), with landscaped grounds by Capability ◊Brown; early 14th-century Broughton Castle; Rousham Park (1635), remodelled by William ◊Kent 1738–40, with landscaped garden; Ditchley Park, designed by James ◊Gibbs 1720; Europe's major fusion project JET (Joint European Torus) at the UK Atomic Energy Authority's fusion laboratories at Culham; The Manor House, Kelmscott (country house of William Morris, leader of the Arts and Crafts movement)
industries cereals, cars, paper, bricks, cement
population (1991) 553,800
famous people William Davenant, Flora Thompson, Winston Churchill, William Morris (founder of Morris Motors Ltd, and of Nuffield College, Oxford 1937).

Oxford University oldest British university, established during the 12th century, the earliest existing college being founded 1249. After suffering from land confiscation during the Reformation, it was reorganized by Elizabeth I 1571. In 1995 there were 10,500 undergraduate and 4,400 postgraduate students.

Besides the 39 colleges, notable academic buildings are the Bodleian Library (including the New Bodleian, opened 1946, with a capacity of 5 million books), the Divinity School, the Radcliffe Camera, and the Sheldonian Theatre. The university is governed by the Congregation of the University; Convocation, composed of masters and doctors, has a delaying power. Normal business is conducted by the Hebdomadal Council.

oxidation in chemistry, the loss of ◊electrons, gain of oxygen, or loss of hydrogen by an atom, ion, or molecule during a chemical reaction. Oxidation may be brought about by reaction with another compound (oxidizing agent), which simultaneously undergoes ◊reduction, or electrically at the anode (positive electrode) of an electrolytic cell.

oxidation in earth science, a form of chemical weathering caused by the chemical reaction that takes place between certain iron-rich minerals in rock and the oxygen in water. It tends to result in the formation of a red-coloured soil or deposit. The inside walls of canal tunnels and bridges often have deposits formed in this way.

oxidation number Roman numeral often seen in a chemical name, indicating the ◊valency of the element immediately before the number. Examples are lead(II) nitrate, manganese(IV) oxide, and potassium manganate(VII).

oxide compound of oxygen and another element, frequently produced by burning the element or a compound of it in air or oxygen.

Oxides of metals are normally ◊bases and will react with an acid to produce a ◊salt in which the metal forms the cation (positive ion). Some of them will also react with a strong alkali to produce a salt in which the metal is part of a complex anion (negative ion; see ◊amphoteric). Most oxides of nonmetals are acidic (dissolve in water to form an ◊acid). Some oxides display no pronounced acidic or basic properties.

oxpecker or ***tick-bird*** African bird *Buphagus africana*, of the starling family Sturnidae, order Passeriformes. It clambers about the bodies of large mammals, feeding on ticks and other parasites. It is generally seen in groups of seven or eight, attending a herd of buffaloes or antelopes, and may help to warn the host of approaching dangers.

oxyacetylene torch gas torch that burns ethyne (acetylene) in pure oxygen, producing a high-temperature (3,000°C/5,400°F) flame. It is widely used in welding to fuse metals. In the cutting torch, a jet of oxygen burns through metal already melted by the flame.

oxygen (Greek *oxys* 'acid'; *genes* 'forming') colourless, odourless, tasteless, nonmetallic, gaseous element, symbol O, atomic number 8, relative atomic mass 15.9994. It is the most abundant element in the Earth's crust (almost 50% by mass), forms about 21% by volume of the atmosphere, and is present in combined form in water and many other substances. Oxygen is a by-product of ◊photosynthesis and the basis for ◊respiration in plants and animals.

Oxygen is very reactive and combines with all other elements except the ◊inert gases and fluorine. It is present in carbon dioxide, silicon dioxide (quartz), iron ore, calcium carbonate (limestone). In nature it exists as a molecule composed of two atoms (O_2); single atoms of oxygen are very short-lived owing to their reactivity. They can be produced in electric sparks and by the Sun's ultraviolet radiation in space, where they rapidly combine with molecular oxygen to form ozone (an allotrope of oxygen).

The element was first identified by English chemist Joseph Priestley 1774 and independently in the same year by Swedish chemist Karl Scheel. It was named by French chemist Antoine Lavoisier 1777.

oxygen debt physiological state produced by vigorous exercise, in which the lungs cannot supply all the oxygen that the muscles need.

oxymoron (Greek 'sharply dull' or 'pointedly foolish') ◊figure of speech involving the combination of two or more words that are normally opposites, in order to startle. *Bittersweet* is an oxymoron, as are *cruel to be kind* and *beloved enemy.*

oxytocin hormone that stimulates the uterus in late pregnancy to initiate and sustain labour. After birth, it stimulates the uterine muscles to contract, reducing bleeding at the site where the placenta was attached.

Intravenous injections of oxytocin may be given to induce labour, improve contractions, or control haemorrhage after birth. It is also secreted during lactation. Oxytocin sprayed in the nose a few minutes before nursing improves milk production. It is secreted by the ◊pituitary gland.

oyster bivalve ◊mollusc constituting the Ostreidae, or true oyster, family, having the upper valve flat, the lower concave, hinged by an elastic ligament. The mantle, lying against the shell, protects the inner body, which includes respiratory, digestive, and reproductive organs. Oysters commonly change their sex annually or more frequently; females may discharge up to a million eggs during a spawning period.

Among the species commercially exploited for food are the North American eastern oyster *Crassostrea virginica* of the Atlantic coast and the European oyster *Ostrea edulis*. Valuable ◊pearls are not obtained from members of the true oyster family; they occur in pearl oysters (family Pteriidae).

oyster catcher chunky shorebird of the family Haematopodidae, order Charadriiformes, with a laterally flattened, heavy bill that can pry open mollusc shells.

The common oyster catcher of European coasts, *Haemotopus ostralegus*, is about 40 cm/16 in long, black and white, with a long red beak to open shellfish, but both marine and terrestrial worms and insects are also consumed. The nest is usually a rough structure without lining. In it are laid three or four large eggs of a buff or stone colour, blotched with dark brown or black. Both sexes appear to share the duties of incubation. The young in their thick down are able to run about when only a few hours old, and in 5–6 weeks are able to fly. By the end of July the birds congregate in large flocks on the coast.

The black and white American oyster catcher *Haematopus palliatus* is found on the Atlantic and S Pacific coasts.

Özal Turgut 1927–1993. Turkish Islamic right-wing politician, prime minister 1983–89, president 1989–93. He was responsible for improving his country's relations with Greece, but his prime objective was to strengthen Turkey's alliance with the USA. In 1980 he was deputy to prime minister Bülent Ulusu under the military regime of Kenan Evren, and, when political pluralism returned 1983, he founded the Islamic, right-of-centre Motherland Party (ANAP) and led it to victory in the elections of that year. In the 1987 general election he retained his majority and Nov 1989 replaced Evren as Turkey's first civilian president for 30 years. He was succeeded by Süleiman Demirel.

Ozalid process trademarked copying process used to produce positive prints from drawn or printed materials or film, such as printing proofs from film images. The film is placed on top of chemically treated paper and then exposed to ultraviolet light. The image is developed dry using ammonia vapour.

Ozark Mountains area in the USA (shared by Arkansas, Illinois, Kansas, Mississippi, Oklahoma) of ridges, valleys, and streams; highest point only 700 m/2,300 ft; area 130,000 sq km/50,000 sq mi. This heavily forested region between the Missouri and Arkansas rivers has agriculture and lead and zinc mines.

ozone O_3 highly reactive pale-blue gas with a penetrating odour. Ozone is an allotrope of oxygen (see ◊allotropy), made up of three atoms of oxygen. It is formed when the molecule of the stable form of oxygen (O_2) is split by ultraviolet radiation or electrical discharge. It forms the ◊ozone layer in the upper atmosphere, which protects life on Earth from ultraviolet rays, a cause of skin cancer.

ozone depleter any chemical that destroys the ozone in the stratosphere. Most ozone depleters are chemically stable compounds containing chlorine or bromine, which remain unchanged for long enough to drift up to the upper atmosphere. The best known are ◊chlorofluorocarbons (CFCs), but many other ozone depleters are known, including halons, used in some fire extinguishers; methyl chloroform and carbon tetrachloride, both solvents; some CFC substitutes; and the pesticide methyl bromide. ▷ *See feature on pp. 858–859.*

ozone layer thin layer of the gas ◊ozone in the upper atmosphere that shields the Earth from harmful ultraviolet rays. A continent-sized hole has formed over Antarctica as a result of damage to the ozone layer. This has been caused in part by ◊chlorofluorocarbons (CFCs), but many reactions destroy ozone in the stratosphere: nitric oxide, chlorine, and bromine atoms are implicated.

At ground level, ozone can cause asthma attacks, stunted growth in plants, and corrosion of certain materials. It is produced by the action of sunlight on air pollutants, including car exhaust fumes, and is a major air pollutant in hot summers. Ozone is a powerful oxidizing agent and is used industrially in bleaching and air conditioning.

Ozu Yasujiro 1903–1963. Japanese film director. He became known in the West only in his last years. *Tokyo Monogatari/Tokyo Story* 1953 has low camera angles and a theme of middle-class family life, which typify his work. His other major films include *Late Spring* 1949 and *Autumn Afternoon* 1962.

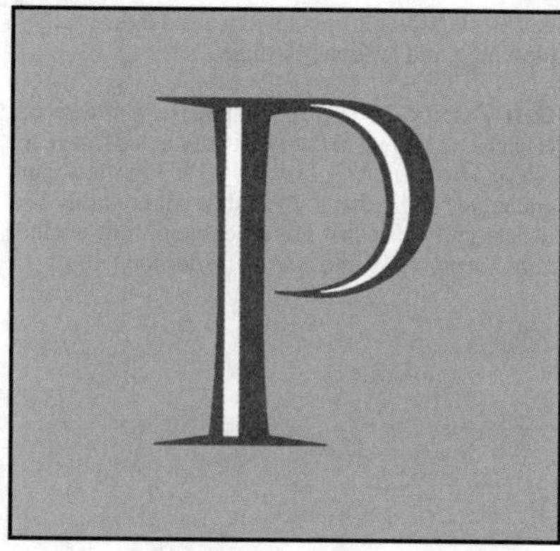

Pabst G(eorg) W(ilhelm) 1885–1967. German film director. His films include *Die Büchse der Pandora/Pandora's Box* and *Das Tagebuch einer Verlorenen/The Diary of a Lost Girl* 1929, both starring Louise ◊Brooks, the antiwar story *Westfront 1918* 1930, and *Die Dreigroschenoper/The Threepenny Opera* 1931.

paca large, tailless, nocturnal, burrowing ◊rodent of the genus *Cuniculus*, in the family Dasyproctidae, which also includes the agoutis. The paca, about 60 cm/2 ft long, is native to Central and South America.

Pacaraima, Sierra mountain range along the Brazil–Venezuela frontier, extending into Guyana; length 620 km/385 mi; highest point Mount Roraima, a plateau about 50 sq km/20 sq mi, 2,810 m/9,222 ft above sea level, surrounded by cliffs 300 m/1,000 ft high, at the conjunction of the three countries. Formed 300 million years ago, it has unique fauna and flora, because of its isolation, consisting only of grasses, bushes, flowers, insects, and small amphibians.

pacemaker or ***sinoatrial node*** (SA node) in vertebrates, a group of muscle cells in the wall of the heart that contracts spontaneously and rhythmically, setting the pace for the contractions of the rest of the heart. The pacemaker's intrinsic rate of contraction is increased or decreased, according to the needs of the body, by stimulation from the ◊autonomic nervous system. The term also refers to a medical device implanted under the skin of a patient whose heart beats inefficiently. It delivers minute electric shocks to stimulate the heart muscles at regular intervals and restores normal heartbeat.

The latest pacemakers are powered by radioactive isotopes for long life and weigh no more than 15 g/0.5 oz.

Pacific Islands former (1947–1990) United Nations ◊trust territory in the W Pacific captured from Japan during World War II. The territory comprised over 2,000 islands and atolls and was assigned to the USA 1947. The islands were divided into four governmental units: the Northern Mariana Islands (except Guam) which became a self-governing commonwealth in union with the USA 1975 (inhabitants granted US citizenship 1986); the ◊Marshall Islands, the Federated States of ◊Micronesia, and the Republic of ◊Palau (formerly also known as Belau) became self-governing 1979–80, signing agreements of free association with the USA 1986. In Dec 1990 the United Nations Security Council voted to dissolve its trusteeship over the islands with the exception of Palau. The Marshall Islands and the Federated States of Micronesia were granted UN membership 1991.

Pacific Islands Commission association of Pacific states formed as an offshoot of the South Pacific Commission 1971 and known until 1997 as the South Pacific Forum. It aims to discuss common interests and develop common policies, both social and economic. Members include Australia, Cook Islands, Fiji Islands, Kiribati, Marshall Islands, Micronesia, New Zealand, Papua New Guinea, Samoa, Solomon Islands, Tonga, Tuvalu, United Kingdom, United States, and Vanuatu.

In 1985 the forum adopted the ◊Rarotonga Treaty for creating a nuclear-free zone in the Pacific and in 1996 the UK, France, and USA endorsed this aim. Its secretary-general is George Sokoma.

‘That great sea, miscalled the Pacific.’

On the Pacific Ocean
Charles Darwin
Voyage of the Beagle
1839

Pacific Ocean world's largest ocean, extending from Antarctica to the Bering Strait; area 166,242,500 sq km/64,170,000 sq mi; average depth 4,188 m/13,749 ft; greatest depth of any ocean 11,034 m/36,210 ft in the ◊Mariana Trench.

Pacific peoples inhabitants of the islands of the Pacific Ocean, conventionally excluding those of Australia, New Zealand, Indonesia, and the Philippines. They number nearly 7 million and speak over 1,200 different languages, most of which have fewer than 5,000 speakers. They are customarily categorized into three ethnic and geographic groups: Melanesians, Micronesians, and Polynesians. ▷ *See feature on pp. 806–807.*

Pacific Security Treaty military alliance agreement between Australia, New Zealand, and the USA, signed 1951. Military cooperation between the USA and New Zealand has been restricted by the latter's policy of banning ships that might be carrying nuclear weapons or nuclear power sources.

pacifism belief that violence, even in self-defence, is unjustifiable under any conditions and that arbitration is preferable to war as a means of solving disputes. In the East, pacifism has roots in Buddhism, and nonviolent action was used by Mahatma ◊Gandhi in the struggle for Indian independence.

Pacino Al(redo) James 1940– . US film actor. He has played powerful, introverted but violent roles in films such as *The Godfather* 1972, *Serpico* 1973, and *Scarface* 1983. *Dick Tracy* 1990 added comedy to his range of acting styles. More recent roles include *Glengarry Glen Ross* 1992 and *Scent of a Woman* 1992, for which he won an Academy Award.

Packer Kerry Francis Bullmore 1937– . Australian media proprietor. He is chair of Consolidated Press Holdings (CPH), which he privatized in 1983, a conglomerate founded by his father which produces such magazines as the *Australian Women's Weekly* and the *Bulletin*. CPH also has interests in radio and television stations. In 1977 he created World Series Cricket, which introduced one-day matches and coloured kit to the game.

Padang port on the west coast of Sumatra, Indonesia; population (1990) 477,300. The Dutch secured trading rights here 1663. The port trades in copra, coffee, and rubber.

Paderewski Ignacy Jan 1860–1941. Polish pianist, composer, and politician. After his debut in Vienna 1887, he became celebrated in Europe and the USA as an interpreter of the piano music of Chopin and as composer of the nationalist *Polish Fantasy* 1893 for piano and orchestra and the *'Polonia' Symphony* 1903–09.

During World War I he helped organize the Polish army in France; in 1919 he became prime minister of the newly independent Poland, which he represented at the Peace Conference, but continuing opposition forced him to resign the same year. He resumed a musical career 1922, was made president of the Polish National Council in Paris 1940, and died in New York.

Padua (Italian ***Padova***) city in N Italy, 45 km/28 mi W of Venice; population (1992) 213,700. The astronomer Galileo taught at the university, founded 1222. The 13th-century Palazzo della Ragione, the basilica of Sant' Antonio, and the botanical garden laid out 1545 are notable. Padua is the birthplace of the Roman historian Livy and the painter Andrea Mantegna.

paediatrics or ***pediatrics*** medical speciality concerned with the care of children.

Paestum ancient Greek city, near Salerno in S Italy. It was founded about 600 BC as the Greek colony Posidonia, and a number of Doric temples remain.

Pagan archaeological site in Myanmar, on the Irrawaddy River, with the ruins of the former capital (founded 847, taken by the Mongol leader Kublai Khan 1287). These include Buddhist pagodas, shrines, and temples with wall paintings of the great period of Burmese art (11th–13th centuries), during which the Pagan state controlled much of Burma (now Myanmar).

pagan (Latin *paganus* 'a person from the countryside') usually, a member of one of the pre-Christian cultures of N Europe, primarily Celtic or Norse, linked to the stone circles and to an agricultural calendar of which the main festivals are the summer and winter solstices and Beltane, the spring festival.

The term was and often still is used as a dismissive phrase, signifying ignorance or 'primitive' religion. It can cover a range of activities, largely agricultural and closely associated with veneration of nature. In the 8th–12th centuries the Church set itself to eradicate the rural practices which were found to be continuing even after the population had officially converted to Christianity. This gave paganism a strong anti-Christian emphasis, which is one of its attractions for some people today.

Paganini Niccolò 1782–1840. Italian violinist and composer. He was a concert soloist from the age of nine. A prodigious technician, he drew on folk and gypsy idioms to create the modern repertoire of virtuoso techniques.

His dissolute appearance, wild love life, and amazing powers of expression, even on a single string, fostered rumours of his being in league with the devil. His compositions include six concertos and various sonatas and variations for violin and orchestra, sonatas for violin and guitar, and guitar quartets.

Pagnol Marcel Paul 1895–1974. French film director, producer, author, and playwright. His work includes *Fanny* 1932 and *Manon des sources* 1952 (novels, filmed 1986). His autobiographical *La Gloire de mon père/My Father's Glory* 1957 was filmed 1991. He regarded the cinema as recorded theatre; thus his films, although strong on character and background, fail to exploit the medium fully as an independent art form.

pagoda Buddhist structure common in China, Japan, and Korea, built to contain a relic or sutra (collection of recorded Buddhist dialogues and discourses). Pagodas have three, five, or seven storeys (in exceptional cases more), crowned by a tall spire (*sōrin*). There is generally no room inside, so that a pagoda is essentially just a stack of roofs, not a functioning building. Deriving from the Indian ◊stupa, the pagoda came to resemble a Chinese watchtower; the shape also has symbolic meaning.

Pahang state of E Peninsular Malaysia; capital Kuantan; area 36,000 sq km/13,896 sq mi; population (1993) 1,056,100. It is mountainous and forested and produces rubber, tin, gold, and timber. There is a port at Tanjung Gelang. Pahang is ruled by a sultan.

Pahlavi dynasty Iranian dynasty founded by Reza Khan (1877–1944), an army officer who seized control of the government 1921 and was proclaimed shah 1925. During World War II,

Paine The title page of Thomas Paine's pamphlet *Common Sense*. Written in America in 1776, it advocated independence and resistance to Britain and encouraged the American Revolution. *Corbis*

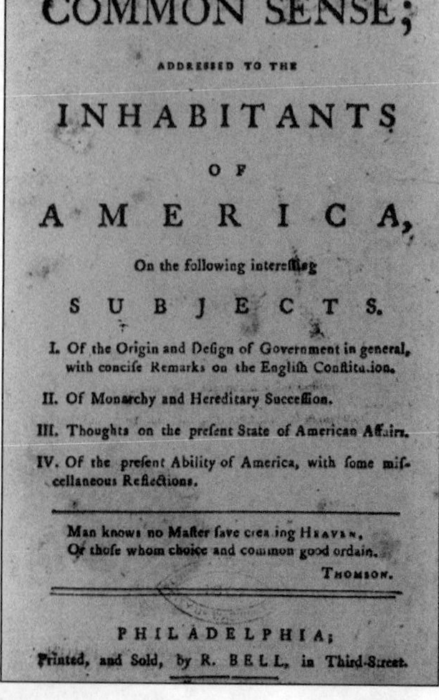

COMMON SENSE;

ADDRESSED TO THE

INHABITANTS

OF

AMERICA,

On the following interesting

SUBJECTS.

I. Of the Origin and Design of Government in general, with concise Remarks on the English Constitution.

II. Of Monarchy and Hereditary Succession.

III. Thoughts on the present State of American Affairs.

IV. Of the present Ability of America, with some miscellaneous Reflections.

Man knows no Master save creating Heaven,
Or those whom choice and common good ordain.

Thomson.

PHILADELPHIA;
Printed, and Sold, by R. BELL, in Third-Street.

Britain and the USSR were nervous about his German sympathies and occupied Iran 1941–46. They compelled him to abdicate 1941 in favour of his son Muhammad Reza Shah Pahlavi, who took office in 1956, with US support, and was deposed in the Islamic revolution of 1979.

pain sense that gives an awareness of harmful effects on or in the body. It may be triggered by stimuli such as trauma, inflammation, and heat. Pain is transmitted by specialized nerves and also has psychological components controlled by higher centres in the brain. Drugs that control pain are known as painkillers or ◊analgesics.

A pain message to the brain travels along the sensory nerves as electrical impulses. When these reach the gap between one nerve and another, biochemistry governs whether this gap is bridged and may also either increase or decrease the attention the message receives or modify its intensity in either direction. The main type of pain transmitter is known simply as 'substance P', a neuropeptide concentrated in a certain area of the spinal cord. Substance P has been found in fish, and there is also evidence that the same substances that cause pain in humans (for example, bee venom) cause a similar reaction in insects and arachnids (for instance, spiders).

Since the sensation of pain is transmitted by separate nerves from that of fine touch, it is possible in diseases such as syringomyelia to have no sense of pain in a limb, yet maintain a normal sense of touch. Such a desensitized limb is at great risk of infection from unnoticed cuts and abrasions.

Paine Thomas 1737–1809. English left-wing political writer. He was active in the American and French revolutions. His pamphlet *Common Sense* 1776 ignited passions in the American Revolution; others include *The Rights of Man* 1791 and *The Age of Reason* 1793. He advocated republicanism, deism, the abolition of slavery, and the emancipation of women.

Paine, born in Thetford, Norfolk, was a friend of US scientist and politician Benjamin Franklin. He went to America 1774, where he fought for the colonists in the revolution. In 1787 he returned to Britain. *The Rights of Man* is an answer to the conservative theorist Burke's *Reflections on the Revolution in France*. In 1792, Paine was indicted for treason and escaped to France, to represent Calais in the National Convention. Narrowly escaping the guillotine, he regained his seat after the fall of Robespierre. Paine returned to the USA 1802 and died in New York.

painkiller drug or agent that relieves pain. See ◊analgesic.

paint any of various materials used to give a protective and decorative finish to surfaces or for making pictures. A paint consists of a pigment suspended in a vehicle, or binder, usually with added solvents. It is the vehicle that dries and hardens to form an adhesive film of paint. Among the most common kinds are cellulose paints (or lacquers), oil-based paints, emulsion (water-based) paints, and special types such as enamels and primers.

Lacquers consist of a synthetic resin (such as an

cont. on p. 808

'The sublime and the ridiculous are often so nearly related, that it is difficult to class them separately.'

THOMAS PAINE
The Age of Reason

PAINTING: TIMELINE OF WESTERN PAINTING

27000–13000 BC	Cave art in south-west Europe expressed the concerns of hunters.
3000–100	Egyptian wall paintings combined front, three-quarter and side views of the human body in a flat 'diagrammatic' style.
2000–1450	The Minoan civilization, based at Knossos in Crete, evolved bright wall paintings.
1000–400	Greek painting by the finest artists survived mainly as vase decorations.
AD 79	Volcanic ash from Vesuvius preserved fine examples of Roman domestic painting and mosaics.
230–450	Early Christian murals painted in catacombs and as mosaics in churches.
330–1453	Byzantine art expressed Orthodox Christian values in formalized mosaics and painted icons.
680–800	Celtic Christian art illuminated religious texts such as the *Lindisfarne Gospel* and the *Book of Kells*.
1290–1337	Italian painting emerged from the Byzantine style with the new depth and realism of Giotto, the first great painter of the Italian Renaissance period.
1315–1425	Italian Gothic and then International Gothic evolved an elegant and decorative style.
1420–1492	Fra Angelico, Piero della Francesca, and Botticelli brought a new freshness of vision to Italian painting.
1425–50	A new and vivid realism, owing much to the established use of high-quality oil paints, appears in the early Renaissance painters of the North such as Jan van Eyck.
c. 1428	Masaccio incorporated Brunelleschi's laws of perspective in his grand and austere *Holy Trinity*, creating an illusion of depth never seen before in painting.
1470–1569	The Northern Renaissance produced a series of disparate geniuses, including Dürer, Bosch, and Brueghel, who expressed the religious anxieties of the age.
1472–1519	Leonardo da Vinci brought a new sense of mystery and psychological depth to painting.
1500–1564	Michelangelo rediscovered classical grandeur and harnessed it to Christian subjects as in the Sistine Chapel frescoes.
1504–1520	Raphael's short career expressed the Florentine Renaissance ideals with an unsurpassed harmony.
1506–1594	The Venetian Renaissance is manifested in the warm sensuality of Titian, Giorgione, Tintoretto, and Veronese.
1520–1600	Mannerists, such as Romano, Pontormo and Parmigianino, applied the discoveries of the High Renaissance in more stylized forms.
1525–1792	The tradition of portrait painting in Britain began with Holbein and continued to Reynolds and Gainsborough.
1560–1609	Caravaggio, a master of dramatic light and shade, led the way towards the Baroque style.
1570–1682	The great age of Spanish painting lasted from the tortured religious idealism of El Greco through to Velázquez.
1577–1640	Rubens was the supreme master of the Baroque grand style.
1620–1670	Dutch genre painting produced masters of portraiture, interiors, landscapes, and still life.
1624–82	Poussin and Claude established the idealized classical landscape painting.
1626–1669	Rembrandt brought an unparalled psychological and emotional depth to biblical scenes and portraits.
1706–1806	The elegance of French rococo was captured by Watteau, Boucher, and Fragonard.
1780–1851	The Romantic spirit was expressed in the vision of painters such as Goya, Turner, Constable, and Delacroix.
1780–1867	Ingres and David sustained the classicism of the French revolutionary and post-revolutionary periods.
1840–1877	Courbet developed a radical realism in his work.
1863	Eschewing half-tones and contemporary pictorial conventions, Manet heralded a new era in art.
1870–1890	Symbolists and Pre-Raphaelites portrayed visionary ideas through the use of symbols and rich colours.
1874	Monet, Renoir, and Degas exhibited at the first Impressionist exhibiton with paintings composed of broken surfaces of light.
1883–1891	Seurat carried the discoveries of the Impressionists further with his pointillist techniques of dots of colour.
1883–1903	Gauguin's spiritual and sensual odyssey to Tahiti looked forward to expressionism and fauvism.
1885–90	Van Gogh's personal vision invested ordinary scenes with unparalleled emotion and spirituality through broad strokes of bright colour.
1886–1906	Cézanne created a new kind of painting with solid forms built with a mosaic of brush strokes. His concentration on geometric forms inspired the Cubist movement.
1892–1926	Munch, and later the Expressionists, used colour and form to express their inner emotions.
1905	Matisse and the Fauves showed compositions where form was defined by subjective choice of colour.
1907	*Les Demoiselles d'Avignon* by Picasso heralded the Cubist movement by rejecting conventional naturalistic representation from only one viewpoint and conventional ideas of beauty.
1910–1914	Kandinsky developed a purely abstract art.
1913	The Armory Show in New York is often regarded as the beginning of public interest in progressive art in the USA.
1913–1944	A geometrical abstract art was developed by Malevitch, Tatlin, Rodchenko, and Mondrian.
from 1914	Duchamp and the Dadaists brought an anarchist element to painting that questioned traditional notions of art.
1914–1940	Klee's figurative painting was built out of abstract patterns.
from 1924	Surrealist painters, notably Dali, Magritte, and Miro, reached for unconscious sources of inspiration.
1940s	Abstract Expressionism, developed in New York by Jackson Pollock and Arshile Gorky, added the element of uninhibited expression to pure abstraction.
from World War II	Painting became increasingly pluralistic, with a broad range of styles flourishing, including abstract and figurative.
late 1940s–1950s	European postwar anxiety found expression in the *art brut* of Jean Dubuffet (France), and the Expressionism of the COBRA group, including Karel Appel (Holland).
late 1950s–1960s	Pop Art returned to representation, drawing on popular images and commercial techniques. Artists included Richard Hamilton (UK), David Hockney (UK), Jasper Johns (USA), and Andy Warhol (USA).
from late 1950s	The broadly based 'London School' continued British figurative tradition: Francis Bacon, Frank Auerbach, and Lucien Freud.
from 1960s	In the USA, super-Realist artists (Malcolm Morley and Richard Estes) strove for a photographic realism. Op art extended the range of abstraction, with Bridget Riley (UK) a leading figure.
mid-1970s–1980s	In the USA, graffiti, seen as an urban folk art, exploited by artists such as Keith Haring and Jean-Michel Basquiat.
late 1970s–1980s	Neo-Expressionism flourished in Germany (Anselm Keifer and Georg Baselitz), Italy (Francesco Clemente and Enzo Cucchi), and the USA (Julian Schnabel).
1980s–1990s	A multiplicity of styles – drawing on a broad range of sources, from pop culture to old masters – was common.

The Peoples of the Pacific

Native fishing boats, Moorea, Tahiti. Outriggers provide stabilization in the open ocean. Similar vessels up to 30 m/100 ft long were used to colonize the Pacific. *Corel*

Yam house, Kuiyawa Village, Trobriand Islands, New Guinea. Yams, the dietary staple, are stored in purpose-built houses erected in the centres of circular villages. The largest belongs to the headman who receives yams in tribute from his many in-laws. *Corel*

The peopling of the Pacific

The Pacific was first populated 35,000 to 50,000 years ago, when lower sea levels permitted hunter-gatherers to migrate to present-day Australia and New Guinea. There they became isolated when sea levels rose, some 8,000 to 10,000 years ago. The origins of the Micronesians and Polynesians are debated, but speakers from Madagascar to Easter Island all belong to the Austronesian (Malay-Polynesian) language family, which is believed to have originated in southeast Asia between 5,000 and 6,500 years ago. Genetic and archaeological data also suggest an Asian origin.

The eastward migration of people across the Pacific has been traced by finds of pottery belonging to a distinctive style (called 'Lapita'). The Marshall Islands were reached by about 2000 BC, Fiji by 1500 BC, Tonga and Samoa by 1200 BC, the Cook Islands by 200 BC, Easter Island by 400 AD, New Zealand by 750 AD, and Hawaii by 1000 AD.

The settlement of Polynesia ranks as one of the most remarkable navigational feats in history. Using the rising and setting points of stars for direction, and the winds and swells to maintain their course, Polynesian navigators sailed across 3,200 km/2,000 mi of open ocean in dugout canoes, locating islands that were sometimes no more than a kilometre in diameter. By the time European explorers entered the Pacific in the 16th century, almost all the habitable islands had been settled for hundreds of years.

The stone heads (maoi) of Easter Island. The largest of the statues weighs 80 tons and is 11 m/37 ft high. Most had separate stone topknots and inlaid eyes, and many stood on ceremonial platforms with burial chambers beneath. *Corel*

The coming of the Europeans

The Portuguese and Spanish were the first to venture into the Pacific, followed by Dutch, British, and French explorers. By the end of the 19th century, almost the entire Pacific was divided among the major European powers and the USA.

Europeans had a disastrous impact on the indigenous populations. Relatively mild diseases, such as measles, almost wiped out entire populations lacking immunity. The Chamorro of Guam, for example, dwindled from a population of over 80,000 to under 5,000 between 1668 and 1740. Missionaries had a similar effect on the cultures. Most Pacific peoples had been Christianized by 1900, resulting in the destruction of traditional religious sites and artefacts, and the abandonment of ancestral ceremonies and traditional crafts. Missionaries also dismissed the supernatural sanctions that had supported political leadership and social morality. Today, few features of the indigenous religions and cultures remain.

Cultures under threat

Migration has become a way of life for many people in the Pacific. The search for employment in port towns, island capitals, and military centres has emptied many smaller islands, causing overcrowding on larger islands and in many urban centres, which suffer from poor housing, inadequate sanitation, and high crime and unemployment rates. Many islanders have migrated to Pacific countries with greater employment opportunities, which has eased urban congestion but led to large expatriate populations. There are, for example, twice as many Cook Islanders living in New

Eighteenth-century French print of a Polynesian in costume. The skirt was probably made of bark cloth and the feathered headdress worn only for ceremonial purposes. *Corbis*

Zealand and Australia as in the Cook Islands. Most emigrants send money home to relatives.

Colonization and migration have produced a complex mix of cultures and languages in the Pacific. In some island states, such as Hawaii, New Caledonia, and Fiji, the indigenous populations are outnumbered by newcomers. The profusion of languages has led to the rapid spread of European colonial languages, especially English. Formal education is almost always in the old colonial language and this, along with radio and television, has jeopardized the continued existence of many local languages. Their extinction would signal the final demise of Pacific cultures. Nationalistic sentiment and tourism, however, especially in New Caledonia, Easter Island, Tahiti, French Polynesia, and Hawaii, have led to a cultural resurgence in some areas.

Melanesians

Melanesia – Greek for 'black islands' because of the dark skin colour of the people – comprises nearly 95% of the land surface in the Pacific and over 85% of the population. It is dominated by New Guinea, where the diverse natural environments have resulted in a wide variety of cultures and languages; more than 700 languages, most belonging to the Papuan language family, are spoken in New Guinea and surrounding islands.

Melanesians are primarily gardeners, with taro, yams, and sweet potatoes being the chief crops, and pigs providing the main source of protein. Melanesian societies are far more egalitarian than elsewhere in the Pacific, power and status being acquired through individual achievement. For example, the local chief, or 'big man', who is still a prominent figure in Melanesian society, acquires his position of leadership by accumulating wealth through ceremonial exchanges of pigs, money, and food; by some skill, such as public speaking; or by his success in warfare – raids on neighbouring tribes were common in the interior of New Guinea until recently.

Melanesian religion is animistic and characterized by ancestor and spirit cults, secret societies, elaborate initiation ceremonies, sorcery, and totemism. These beliefs and practices are reflected in their art, which is typified by exaggerated natural forms with prominent sexual motifs, and colourful, demonic-looking ritual masks. Cult objects are made to contain *mana*, a sacred supernatural power possessed, in varying degrees, by all things, both animate and inanimate – a belief common throughout the Pacific.

Micronesians

Barely 400,000 people inhabit the tiny volcanic islands and atolls of Micronesia, yet there are between eight and ten cultural and linguistic regions. Micronesians traditionally live by growing garden crops, especially on the volcanic islands, and by fishing. They were skilled traders and navigators and even in prehistoric times a chain of communication existed between the islands.

The degree of social stratification in Micronesian societies varied considerably. In the Caroline Islands, for example, hereditary chiefs had little wealth or power and individual achievement could raise a person above his or her hereditary rank. In Yap, however, tribes were hierarchically ranked and chiefs, who received tribute from their subjects, were owed considerable deference. The Micronesians believed in several high gods, ancestral spirits, and a large number of local spirits which performed specific functions. Their art typically combined extreme functional simplicity and high-quality finish with little decoration.

Polynesians

Polynesia ('many islands') occupies a rough triangle formed by Hawaii, Easter Island, and New Zealand. Culturally the most homogeneous of the three groups, Polynesians live mainly by fishing. Polynesian art is highly decorative and is typified by the featherwork of Hawaii. Traditional Polynesian society was highly stratified and hereditary chiefs were extremely powerful. They are still influential where indigenous people remain in the majority. Chiefs were regarded as descendants of deified ancestors and as possessing a great measure of *mana*, which had to be protected by the observance of a multitude of *tapu* – taboos, or avoidance rules. The Polynesian universe was peopled with a variety of spiritual beings, from great gods to local deities, all of which required worship in specific ways, often involving human sacrifice.

On Easter Island, the most intriguing Polynesian Island, over 800 huge carved statues were erected between AD 1000 and 1600. An unusual script discovered on the island was deciphered in 1996; it tells the story of creation and indicates that the Easter Islanders were the first Pacific people to write.

Sepik club house, New Guinea. In many Sepik River societies the men live separately from women in huge club houses which serve as a focus for ritual and military unity. *Corel*

Karawan painted woman, New Guinea. In many New Guinea societies the body is the focus of art. Faces and bodies are painted in symbolic designs and elaborate wigs, headdresses, and costumes are worn. *Corel*

CHRIS HOLDSWORTH

SEE ALSO
Australasia–Oceania; Melanesia; Micronesia; Polynesia

acrylic resin or cellulose acetate) dissolved in a volatile organic solvent, which evaporates rapidly to give a very quick-drying paint. A typical ***oil-based paint*** has a vehicle of a natural drying oil (such as linseed oil), containing a prime pigment of iron, lead, titanium, or zinc oxide, to which coloured pigments may be added. The finish – gloss, semi-matt, or matt – depends on the amount of inert pigment (such as clay or silicates). Oil-based paints can be thinned, and brushes cleaned, in a solvent such as turpentine or white spirit (a petroleum product). ***Emulsion paints***, sometimes called latex paints, consist of pigments dispersed in a water-based emulsion of a polymer (such as polyvinyl chloride [PVC] or acrylic resin). They can be thinned with water, which can also be used to wash the paint out of brushes and rollers. ***Enamels*** have little pigment, and they dry to an extremely hard, high-gloss film. ***Primers*** for the first coat on wood or metal, on the other hand, have a high pigment content (as do undercoat paints). Aluminium or bronze powder may be used for priming or finishing objects made of metal.

painting the application of coloured pigment to a surface. The chief methods of painting are: ***tempera*** emulsion painting, with a gelatinous (for example, egg yolk) rather than oil base – known in ancient Egypt; ***fresco*** watercolour painting on plaster walls – the palace of Knossos, Crete, contains examples from about 2,000 BC; ***ink*** developed in China for calligraphy in the Sung period and highly popular in Japan from the 15th century; ***oil*** ground pigments in linseed, walnut, or other oil, it spread from N to S Europe in the 15th century; ***watercolour*** pigments combined with gum arabic and glycerol, which are diluted with water – the method was developed in the 15th–17th centuries for wash drawings; ***acrylic*** synthetic pigments developed after World War II, the colours are very hard and brilliant.

For the history of painting see ◊medieval art; ◊Chinese art, and so on. Individual painters and art movements are listed alphabetically. ▷ *See feature on pp. 200–201 and timeline on p. 805.*

Paisley Ian (Richard Kyle) 1926– . Northern Ireland politician, cleric, and leader of the Democratic Unionist Party (DUP) from 1971. An imposing and deeply influential member of the Protestant community, he is staunchly committed to the union with the UK. His political career has been one of high drama, marked by protests, resignations, fierce oratory, and a pugnacious and forthright manner.

Paisley was born in Armagh, and was educated at South Wales Bible College and the Reformed Presbyterian Theological College in Belfast. In 1951 he

PAKISTAN
Islamic Republic of

national name *Islami Jamhuriya e Pakistan*
area 796,100 sq km/307,295 sq mi; one-third of Kashmir under Pakistani control
capital Islamabad
major towns/cities Lahore, Rawalpindi, Faisalabad, Hyderabad
major ports Karachi, Port Qasim
physical features fertile Indus plain in E, Baluchistan plateau in W, mountains in N and NW; the 'five rivers' (Indus, Jhelum, Chenab, Ravi, and Sutlej) feed the world's largest irrigation system; K2 mountain; Khyber Pass
head of state Rafiq Tarar from 1997
head of government Nawaz Sharif from 1997
political system emergent democracy
administrative divisions four provinces, the Federal Capital Territory, and the federally-administered tribal areas
political parties Islamic Democratic Alliance (IDA), conservative; Pakistan People's Party (PPP), moderate, Islamic, socialist; Pakistan Muslim League (PML), Islamic conservative (contains pro- and anti-government factions); Pakistan Islamic Front (PIF), Islamic fundamentalist, right-wing; Awami National Party (ANP), left-wing; National Democratic Alliance (NDA) bloc, left of centre; Mohajir National Movement (MQM), Sind-based *mohajir* settlers (Muslims previously living in India); Movement for Justice, reformative, anti-corruption
armed forces 587,000; paramilitary forces 275,000 (1994)
conscription none
defence spend (% GDP) 6.9 (1994)
education spend (% GNP) 2.7 (1992)
health spend (% GDP) 1.8 (1990)
death penalty retained and used for ordinary crimes
population 148,166,000 (1998 est)
population growth rate 2.8% (1990–95); 2.7% (2000–05)
age distribution (% of total population) <15 44.3%, 15–65 52.7%, >65 3.0% (1995)
ethnic distribution four principal, regionally-based, antagonistic communities: Punjabis in the Punjab; Sindhis in Sind; Baluchis in Baluchistan; and the Pathans (Pushtans) in the Northwest Frontier Province
population density (per sq km) 172 (1994)
urban population (% of total) 35 (1995)
labour force 35% of population: 52% agriculture, 19% industry, 30% services (1990)
unemployment 10% (1991 est)
child mortality rate (under 5, per 1,000 live births) 99 (1997)
life expectancy 63 (men), 65 (women)
education (years) 5–12 (not compulsory, but free)
literacy rate 47% (men), 21% (women)
languages Urdu (official); English, Punjabi, Sindhi, Pashto, Baluchi, other local dialects
religions Sunni Muslim 75%, Shi'ite Muslim 20%; also Hindu, Christian, Parsee, Buddhist
TV sets (per 1,000 people) 18 (1992)
currency Pakistan rupee
GDP (US $) 64.3 billion (1997)
GDP per capita (PPP) (US $) 2,160 (1993)
growth rate 3.1% (1994)
average annual inflation 12.5% (1994); 8.0% (1985–93)
major trading partners Japan, USA, Germany, UK, Saudi Arabia
resources iron ore, natural gas, limestone, rock salt, gypsum, silica, coal, petroleum, graphite, copper, manganese, chromite
industries textiles (principally cotton), food processing, petroleum refinery, leather production, soda ash, sulphuric acid, bicycles
exports cotton, textiles, petroleum and petroleum products, clothing and accessories, leather, rice, food and live animals. Principal market: USA 13.9% (1993)
imports machinery and transport equipment, mineral fuels and lubricants, chemicals and related products, edible oil. Principal source: Japan 15.9% (1993)
arable land 26.1% (1993)
agricultural products cotton, rice, wheat, maize, sugar cane

HISTORY

2500–1600 BC The area was the site of the Indus Valley civilization, a sophisticated, city-based ancient culture.
327 BC Invaded by Alexander the Great of Macedonia.
1st–2nd Cs North Pakistan was the heartland of the Kusana Empire, formed by invaders from Central Asia.
8th C First Muslim conquests, in Baluchistan and Sind, followed by increasing immigration by Muslims from the W, from the 10th century.
1206 Establishment of the Delhi Sultanate, stretching from NW Pakistan and across northern India.
16th C Sikh religion developed in Punjab.
16th–17th Cs Lahore served intermittently as a capital city for the Mogul Empire, which stretched across the northern half of the Indian subcontinent.
1843–49 Sind and Punjab annexed by the British and incorporated within the empire of 'British India'.
late 19th C Major canal irrigation projects in West Punjab and the northern Indus Valley drew in settlers from the E, as wheat and cotton production expanded.
1933 The name 'Pakistan' (Urdu for 'Pure Nation') invented by Choudhary Rahmat Ali, as Muslims within British India began to campaign for the establishment of an independent Muslim territory that would embrace the four provinces of Sind, Baluchistan, Punjab, and the Northwest Frontier.
1940 The All-India Muslim League (established 1906), led by Karachi-born Muhammad Ali Jinnah, endorsed the concept of a separate nation for Muslims in the Lahore Resolution.
1947 Independence achieved from Britain, as dominion within the Commonwealth. Pakistan, which included East Bengal, a Muslim-dominated province more than 1,600 km/1,000 mi from Punjab, was formed following the partition of British India. Large-scale and violent cross-border migrations of Muslims, Hindus, and Sikhs followed, and a brief border war with India over disputed Kashmir.
1956 Proclaimed a republic.
1958 Military rule imposed by General Ayub Khan.
1965 Border war with India over disputed territory of Kashmir.
1969 Power transferred to General Yahya Khan following strikes and riots.
1970 A general election produced a clear majority in East Pakistan for the pro-autonomy Awami League, led by Sheikh Mujibur Rahman, and in West Pakistan for the Islamic socialist Pakistan People's Party (PPP), led by Zulfiqar Ali Bhutto.
1971 East Pakistan secured independence, as Bangladesh, following a civil war with decisive military support from India. Power was transferred from the military to the populist Bhutto in Pakistan.
1977 Bhutto overthrown in military coup by General Zia ul-Haq following months of civil unrest; martial law imposed.
1979 Bhutto executed for alleged murder; tight political restrictions imposed by Zia regime.
1980 3 million refugees fled to the Northwest Frontier Province and Baluchistan as a result of the Soviet invasion of Afghanistan.
1981 Broad-based Opposition Movement for the Restoration of Democracy formed. Islamization process pushed forward by government.
1985 Martial law and ban on political parties lifted.
1986 Agitation for free elections launched by Benazir Bhutto, the daughter of Zulfiqar Ali Bhutto.
1988 Islamic legal code, the Shari'a, introduced; Zia killed in a military plane crash. Benazir Bhutto became prime minister after the now centrist PPP won the general election.
1989 Tension with India increased by outbreaks of civil war in Kashmir. Pakistan rejoined the Commonwealth, which it had left in 1972.
1990 Bhutto dismissed as prime minister by President Ghulam Ishaq Khan on charges of incompetence and corruption. The conservative Islamic Democratic Alliance (IDA), led by Nawaz Sharif, won general election and launched a privatization and economic deregulation programme.
1993 Khan and Sharif resigned, ending months of political stalemate and unrest; Benazir Bhutto and PPP re-elected. Farooq Leghari (PPP) elected president.
1994 Escalation in regional sectarian violence between Shiah and Sunni Muslims, centred in Karachi.
1996 Justice Movement formed by former cricket captain Imran Khan. Benazir Bhutto dismissed by Leghari amid allegations of corruption and mismanagement. Meraj Khalid appointed interim prime minister.
1997 Landslide victory for right-of-centre Pakistan Muslim League in general election, returning Nawaz Sharif to power as prime minister. Clashes with the judiciary; resignation of President Leghari. Rafiq Tarat elected president.
1998 First ever nuclear tests carried out, in response to similar tests by India.

SEE ALSO Bangladesh; India; Kashmir

established the Free Presbyterian Church in Belfast. When Catholic civil-rights agitation began to flourish in the 1960s, Paisley organized numerous marches and speeches in opposition, which led to his imprisonment for six weeks in 1968 for unlawful assembly. In April 1970, Paisley won the seat for Bannside in Northern Ireland's Stormont assembly, and he won the North Antrim seat two months later. The following year, he established the DUP as a hardline rival to the ruling dominant Ulster Unionist Party. He was influential in the actions of the Ulster Workers' Council and their general strike which destroyed the Sunningdale Power Sharing Initiative in 1974. Paisley's powerful speeches and image of strength won him great support within the Protestant community and he scored overwhelming victories in the 1979 and 1984 European elections. Throughout the 1980s, Paisley stuck rigidly to his 'no surrender' policies, resigning his seat 1985 in protest at the Anglo-Irish Agreement. He re-entered Parliament early the following year. His Presbyterian beliefs are inextricably bound up with his political aims, and in 1988 he was ejected from the European Parliament for interrupting an address by Pope John Paul II.

He has opposed the 1998 Good Friday Agreement on power-sharing in Northern Ireland and in the May 1998 referendum his North Antrim constituency was the only one of Northern Ireland's 18 seats in which there was a majority against the accord. He now leads the opposition to the agreement within the new Northern Ireland Assembly.

Pakistan country in S Asia, stretching from the Himalayas to the Arabian Sea, bounded W by Iran, NW by Afghanistan, NE and E by India. *See country box opposite.*

Pakula Alan J(ay) 1928–1998. US film director and producer, his compelling films include *Klute* 1971, *The Parallax View* 1974, and *All the President's Men* 1976. His later work includes *Sophie's Choice* 1982 and *Presumed Innocent* 1990.

PAL (abbreviation for ***phase alternation by line***) the coding system for colour-television broadcasting adopted by the UK, West Germany, the Netherlands, and Switzerland 1967. NTSC (National Television System Committee) is the system which operates in America. See ◊television.

Palaeocene (Greek 'old' + 'recent') first epoch of the Tertiary period of geological time, 65–56.5 million years ago. Many types of mammals spread rapidly after the disappearance of the great reptiles of the Mesozoic. Flying mammals replaced the flying reptiles, swimming mammals replaced the swimming reptiles, and all the ecological niches vacated by the reptiles were adopted by mammals.

Palaeolithic the Old Stone Age period, the earliest stage of human technology; see ◊prehistory.

palaeomagnetism science of the reconstruction of the Earth's ancient magnetic field and the former positions of the continents from the evidence of remnant magnetization in ancient rocks; that is, traces left by the Earth's magnetic field in ◊igneous rocks before they cool. Palaeomagnetism shows that the Earth's magnetic field has reversed itself – the magnetic north pole becoming the magnetic south pole, and vice versa – at approximate half-million-year intervals, with shorter reversal periods in between the major spans.

Starting in the 1960s, this known pattern of magnetic reversals was used to demonstrate seafloor spreading or the formation of new ocean crust on either side of mid-oceanic ridges. As new material hardened on either side of a ridge, it would retain the imprint of the magnetic field, furnishing datable proof that material was spreading steadily outward. Palaeomagnetism is also used to demonstrate ◊continental drift by determining the direction of the magnetic field of dated rocks from different continents.

palaeontology in geology, the study of ancient life, encompassing the structure of ancient organisms and their environment, evolution, and ecology, as revealed by their ◊fossils. The practical aspects of palaeontology are based on using the presence of different fossils to date particular rock strata and to identify rocks that were laid down under particular conditions; for instance, giving rise to the formation of oil.

The use of fossils to trace the age of rocks was pioneered in Germany by Johann Friedrich Blumenbach (1752–1830) at Göttingen, followed by Georges ◊Cuvier and Alexandre Brongniart (1770–1847) in France 1811.

The term palaeontology was first used in 1834, during the period when the first ◊dinosaur remains were discovered. ▷ *See feature on pp. 518–519.*

Palaeozoic era of geological time 570–245 million years ago. It comprises the Cambrian, Ordovician, Silurian, Devonian, Carboniferous, and Permian periods. The Cambrian, Ordovician, and Silurian constitute the Lower or Early Palaeozoic; the Devonian, Carboniferous, and Permian make up the Upper or Late Palaeozoic. The era includes the evolution of hard-shelled multicellular life forms in the sea; the invasion of land by plants and animals; and the evolution of fish, amphibians, and early reptiles. The earliest identifiable fossils date from this era.

palate in mammals, the roof of the mouth. The bony front part is the hard palate, the muscular rear part the soft palate. Incomplete fusion of the two lateral halves of the palate (◊cleft palate) causes interference with speech.

Palatinate (called the ***Pfalz*** in Germany) historic division of Germany, dating from before the 8th century. It was ruled by a count palatine (a count with royal prerogatives) and varied in size.

When the Palatinate was attached to Bavaria 1815 it consisted of two separate parts: Rhenish (or Lower) Palatinate on the Rhine (capital Heidelberg), and Upper Palatinate (capital Amberg on the Vils) 210 km/130 mi to the E. In 1946 Rhenish Palatinate became an administrative division of the *Land* (German region) of Rhineland-Palatinate, with its capital at Neustadt; Upper Palatinate remained an administrative division of Bavaria, with its capital at Regensburg.

Palatine one of the seven hills on which ancient Rome was built. According to tradition it was the site of the original settlement. It was the residence of many leading citizens under the republic, and the site of the imperial palaces of Augustus, Tiberius, Nero, Domitian, and their successors.

Palau (also known as ***Belau***) country comprising more than 350 islands and atolls (mostly uninhabited) in the W Pacific Ocean. *See country box below.*

Palembang oil-refining city in Indonesia, capital of S Sumatra province; population (1990) 1,084,500. Palembang was the capital of a sultanate when the Dutch established a trading station here 1616.

Palermo capital and seaport of Sicily; population (1992) 696,700. Industries include shipbuilding, steel, glass, and chemicals. It was founded by the Phoenicians in the 8th century BC.

Palestine (Arabic *Falastin* 'Philistine') historic geographical area at the E end of the Mediterranean sea, also known as the Holy Land because of its historic and symbolic importance for Jews, Christians, and Muslims. Early settlers included the Canaanites, Hebrews, and Philistines. Over the centuries it became part of the Egyptian, Assyrian, Babylonian, Macedonian, Ptolemaic, Seleucid, Roman, Byzantine, Arab, and Ottoman empires. Today, it comprises parts of modern Israel, and Jordan.

Palestinian Arabs include 2,400,000 in the West Bank, E Jerusalem, and the Gaza Strip (1994). In 1993, more than 750,000 Palestinian children under the age of 16 were living in refugee camps. Under the 1993 Oslo Accord, interim Palestinian self-rule was introduced in the Gaza Strip and West Bank town of Jericho; an agreement signed May 1995 in Cairo marked the beginning of a permanent pact on Palestinian self-rule. In Jan 1996 Yassir Arafat, the leader of the Palestine Liberation Organization (PLO), was elected president of the Palestinian National Council.

Palestine Liberation Organization (PLO) Arab organization founded 1964 to bring about an independent state in Palestine. It consists of several distinct groupings, the chief of which is al-◊Fatah, led by Yassir ◊Arafat, the president of the PLO from 1969. The PLO's original main aim was the

> *'The word Palestine always brought to my mind a vague suggestion of a country as large as the United States. … I suppose it was because I could not conceive of a small country having so large a history.'*
>
> On PALESTINE
> Mark Twain
> *The Innocents Abroad*

PALAU
Republic of (also known as *Belau*)

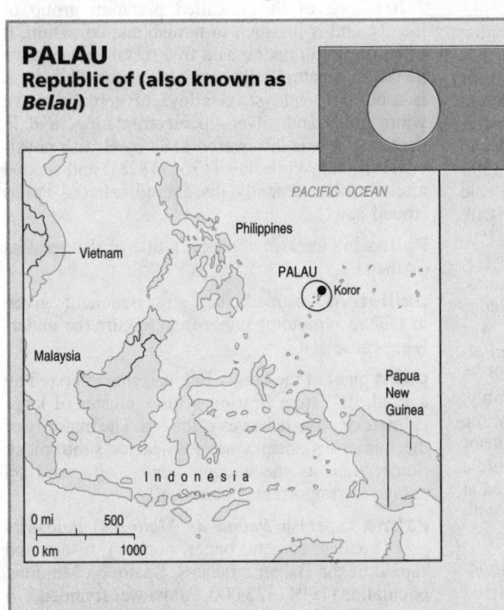

area 508 sq km/196 sq mi
capital Koror (on Koror Island)
physical features more than 350 islands, mostly uninhabited, islets and atolls in the West Pacific Ocean; warm, humid climate, susceptible to typhoons
head of state and government Kuniwo Nakamura from 1992
political system liberal democracy
administrative divisions 16 states
political parties there are no formally organized political parties
population 17,000 (1996 est)
population growth rate 2.3% (1990–95)
ethnic distribution predominantly Micronesian
languages Palauan and English
religion Christian, principally Roman Catholic
currency US dollar
GDP (US $) 82 million (1994 est)
products copra, fish products

HISTORY
c. 1000 BC Micronesians first settled the islands.
1543 First visited by Spanish navigator Ruy Lopez de Villalobos.
16th C Colonized by Spain.
later 16th C Fell under Spanish influence.
1899 Purchased from Spain by Germany.
1914 Occupied by Japan at the outbreak of World War I.
1920 Administered by Japan under League of Nations mandate.
1944 Occupied by USA after Japanese removed during World War II.
1947 Became part of the United Nations (UN) Pacific Islands Trust Territory, administered by USA.
1981 Acquired autonomy as the Republic of Belau (Palau) under a constitution which prohibited the entry, storage, or disposal of nuclear or biological weapons.
1982 Compact of Free Association signed with USA, providing for the right to maintain US military facilities in return for economic aid. However, the compact could not come into force since it contradicted the constitution, which could only be amended by a 75% vote in favour.
1985 President Haruo Remeliik assassinated; succeeded by Lazarus Salii.
1988 President Salii committed suicide and was succeeded by Ngiratkel Etpison.
1992 Kuniwo Nakamura elected president.
1993 Referendum approved constitutional amendment allowing implementation of Compact of Free Association with USA.
1994 Independence achieved; UN membership granted.

SEE ALSO Pacific Islands

PALESTINE: TIMELINE

c. 1000 BC	Hebrew leader King David formed a united Kingdom of Israel.
922	Kingdom of Israel split into Israel in the north and Judah in the south after the death of King Solomon.
722	Israel conquered by Assyrians.
586	Judah conquered by Babylonians who destroyed Jerusalem and forced many Jews into exile in Babylon.
539	Palestine became part of Persian Empire.
536	Jews allowed to return to Jerusalem.
332	Conquest by Alexander the Great.
168	Maccabean revolt against Seleucids restored independence.
63	Conquest by Roman Empire.
AD 70	Romans destroyed Jerusalem following Jewish revolt.
636	Conquest by the Muslim Arabs made Palestine, a target for the Crusades.
1516	Conquest by the Ottoman Turks.
1880–1914	Jewish immigration increased as a result of pogroms in Russia and Poland.
1897	At the first Zionist Congress, Jews called for a permanent homeland in Palestine.
1909	Tel Aviv, the first all-Jewish town in Palestine, was founded.
1917	The Balfour Declaration expressed the British government's support for the establishment of a Jewish national homeland in Palestine.
1917–18	The Turks were driven out by the British under Field Marshal Allenby in World War I.
1922	A League of Nations mandate (which incorporated the Balfour Declaration) placed Palestine under British administration.
1936–39	Arab revolt took place, fuelled by Jewish immigration (300,000 people 1920–39).
1937	The Peel Commission report recommended the partition of Palestine into Jewish and Arab states.
1939–45	Arab and Jewish Palestinians served in the Allied forces in World War II.
1946	Resentment of immigration restrictions led to acts of anti-British violence by Jewish guerrilla groups.
1947	The United Nations (UN) approved Britain's plan for partition.
1948	A Jewish state of Israel was proclaimed 14 May (eight hours before Britain's renunciation of the mandate was due). A series of Arab-Israeli Wars resulted in Israeli territorial gains and the occupation of other parts of Palestine by Egypt and Jordan. Many Palestinian Arabs were displaced.
1964	The Palestinian Liberation Organization (PLO) was formed and a guerrilla war was waged against the Jewish state.
1974	The PLO became the first nongovernmental delegation to be admitted to a plenary session of the UN General Assembly.
1987	The Intifada, a popular uprising against Israeli occupation, began.
1988	PLO leader Yassir Arafat renounced terrorism; the USA agreed to meetings.
1989	Israeli prime minister Yitzhak Shamir proposed Palestinian elections in the West Bank/Gaza Strip.
1991	Gulf War against Iraq's annexation of Kuwait caused diplomatic reconsideration of a Palestinian state in an effort to stabilize the Middle East. A peace conference in Spain included Israel and Arab states.
1993	Historic accord of mutual recognition signed by Israel and PLO (the Oslo Accord), outlining plans for interim Palestinian self-rule in Gaza Strip and West Bank town of Jericho and for phased withdrawal of Israeli troops.
1995	By the end of Dec Israeli troops had withdrawn from six West Bank cities.
1996	Yassir Arafat elected president of the self-governing Palestinian National Council.
1998	Agreement was reached at Wye Plantation, Maryland, for further withdrawal by Israel from the West Bank. Terrorist acts by Hamas and Islamic Jihad, and intransigent Netanyahu government freeze peace process.

destruction of the Israeli state, but over time it changed to establishing a Palestinian state alongside that of Israel, and in 1993 a peace agreement based on mutual recognition was reached with Israel.

In 1994 Arafat returned to Gaza and Jericho to head an interim civilian administration, the Palestinian National Authority, and in 1995 agreement was reached with Israel on its withdrawal from Palestinian areas in the West Bank. In Jan 1996 Arafat was elected president of the Palestinian National Council (PNC) and, as such, effectively the president of the embryonic state of Palestine. Members of Arafat's al-Fatah faction, some campaigning as independents, won an estimated 75% of seats. The peace agreement was jeopardized by mounting tensions with Israel from 1996, and outbreaks of violence on both sides.

Beirut, Lebanon, became PLO headquarters 1970–71 after its defeat in the Jordanian civil war. In 1974 the PLO became the first nongovernmental delegation to be admitted to a session of the United Nations General Assembly. When Israel invaded Lebanon 1982 the PLO had to abandon its headquarters there; it moved to Tunis, Tunisia. PLO members who remained in Lebanon after the expulsion were later drawn into the internal conflict (see ◊Arab-Israeli Wars). In 1987 the outbreak of the Palestinian uprising (◊Intifada) was followed by King Hussein's renunciation of any Jordanian claim to the West Bank. In 1988, the Palestine National Council voted to create a state of Palestine, but at the same time endorsed United Nations resolution 242, recognizing Israel's right to exist.

Discussions with the US government began for the first time when Arafat renounced terrorism as a policy. The Israeli prime minister Yitzhak Shamir proposed Palestinian elections in the West Bank and Gaza Strip 1989. Under the terms of the Sept 1993 Israeli-PLO accord, limited Palestinian self-rule was established in the Gaza Strip and West Bank town of Jericho. Autonomy arrangements for Palestinian areas of the West Bank were agreed 1995, and the militant fundamentalist group Hamas, which had maintained a campaign of violence within Israel in opposition to the 1993 accord, was invited to talks on self-rule. The status of the Palestine Liberation Organization was upgraded in July 1998 by the United Nations General Assembly. Under the proposals, passed by a large majority, the PLO is able to take part in debates, co-sponsor resolutions, and raise points of order when Middle East affairs are being discussed. Israel protested at the move. The PLO signed a cooperation pact with Jordan Jan 1995.

Palestrina Giovanni Pierluigi da c. 1525–1594. Italian composer. He wrote secular and sacred choral music, and is regarded as the most perfect exponent of Renaissance ◊counterpoint. Apart from motets and madrigals, he also wrote 105 masses, including *Missa Papae Marcelli*.

Paley William 1743–1805. English Christian theologian and philosopher. He put forward the argument from design theory, which reasons that the complexity of the universe necessitates a superhuman creator and that the existence of this being (God) can be deduced from a 'design' seen in all living creatures. His views were widely held until challenged by Charles ◊Darwin. His major treatises include *The Principles of Moral and Political Philosophy* 1785, *A View of the Evidences of Christianity* 1794, and *Natural Theology* 1802.

Pali ancient Indo-European language of N India, related to Sanskrit, and a classical language of Buddhism.

palindrome word, sentence, or verse that reads the same backwards as forwards (ignoring word breaks and punctuation). 'Madam, in Eden, I'm Adam.' 'Ten animals I slam in a net.'

palisade cell cylindrical cell lying immediately beneath the upper epidermis of a leaf. Palisade cells normally exist as one closely packed row and contain many chloroplasts. During the hours of daylight palisade cells are photosynthetic, using the energy of the sun to create carbohydrates from water and carbon dioxide.

Palk Strait channel separating SE India from the island of Sri Lanka; it is 53 km/33 mi at the widest point.

Palladian style of architecture influenced by the work of the great Italian Renaissance architect Andrea ◊Palladio. An early exponent was Inigo ◊Jones, who introduced Palladianism to England in the 1600s. The true Palladian revival, however, did not begin until the early 18th century when Richard Boyle ◊Burlington and Colen ◊Campbell 'rediscovered' the Palladio–Jones link. Campbell's Mereworth Castle in Kent, 1722–25, is an example of the style.

In Russia the Scottish-born Charles Cameron (1740–1812) was the principal exponent of Palladianism, while in the USA the style was adopted by Thomas Jefferson, third president of the United States, who designed his own house, Monticello, 1769, and the University of Virginia, Charlottesville, 1817–26.

Palladio Andrea 1508–1580. Italian Renaissance architect who created harmonious and balanced classical structures. He designed numerous palaces and country houses in and around Vicenza, Italy, making use of Roman classical forms, symmetry, and proportion. The Villa Malcontenta and the Villa Rotonda are examples of houses designed from 1540 for patrician families of the Venetian Republic. He also designed churches in Venice and published his studies of classical form in several illustrated books.

palladium lightweight, ductile and malleable, silver-white, metallic element, symbol Pd, atomic number 46, relative atomic mass 106.4.

It is one of the so-called platinum group of metals, and is resistant to tarnish and corrosion. It often occurs in nature as a free metal (see ◊native metal) in a natural alloy with platinum. Palladium is used as a catalyst, in alloys of gold (to make white gold) and silver, in electroplating, and in dentistry. It was discovered 1803 by British physicist William Wollaston (1766–1828), and named after the then recently discovered asteroid Pallas (found 1802).

Pallas in Greek mythology, a title of the goddess ◊Athena.

palliative in medicine, any treatment given to relieve symptoms rather than to cure the underlying cause.

palm plant of the family Palmae, characterized by a single tall stem bearing a thick cluster of large palmate or pinnate leaves at the top. The majority of the numerous species are tropical or subtropical. Some, such as the coconut, date, sago, and oil palms, are important economically.

Palma (Spanish ***Palma de Mallorca***) industrial port (textiles, cement, paper, pottery), resort, and capital of the Balearic Islands, Spain, on Majorca; population (1994) 322,000. Palma was founded 276 BC as a Roman colony. It has a Gothic cathedral, begun 1229.

Palme (Sven) Olof Joachim 1927–1986. Swedish social-democratic politician, prime minister 1969–76 and 1982–86. As prime minister he carried

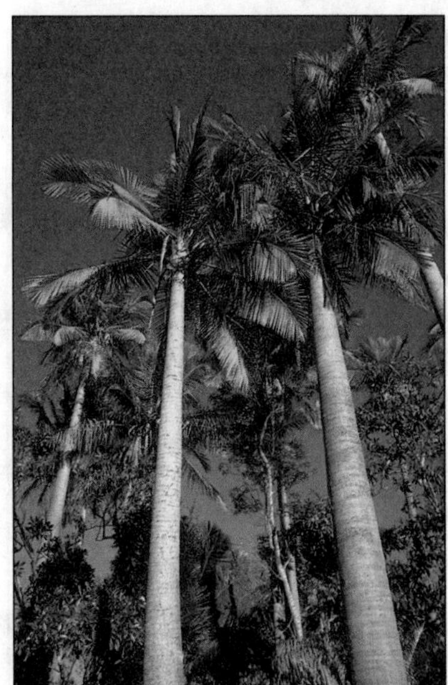

palm **The island of Madagascar is one of the richest areas of the world for palms. It has over 130 species, more than the whole of Africa. Most of them are endemic, including this *Ravenea rivularis* which grows on river banks in the S of the island. *Premaphotos Wildlife***

out constitutional reforms, turning the Riksdag into a single-chamber parliament and stripping the monarch of power, and was widely respected for his support of developing countries. He was assassinated Feb 1986, allegedly by South African secret servicemen.

Palmer Arnold Daniel 1929– . US golfer who helped to popularize the professional sport in the USA in the 1950s and 1960s. He won the Masters 1958, 1960, 1962, and 1964; the US Open 1960; and the British Open 1961 and 1962.

Palmer Samuel 1805–1881. English landscape painter and etcher. He lived in Shoreham, Kent, 1826–35 with a group of artists who were all followers of William Blake and referred to themselves as 'the Ancients'. Palmer's small pastoral scenes, mostly painted in watercolour and sepia, have an intense, visionary quality.

Palmerston Henry John Temple, 3rd Viscount Palmerston 1784–1865. British politician. He was prime minister 1855–58, when he rectified Aberdeen's mismanagement of the Crimean War, suppressed the Indian Mutiny, and carried through the Second Opium War; and 1859–65, when he almost involved Britain in the American Civil War on the side of the South. Initially a Tory, in Parliament from 1807, he was secretary-at-war 1809–28. He broke with the Tories 1830 and sat in the Whig cabinets of 1830–34, 1835–41, and 1846–51 as foreign secretary.

Palm Sunday in the Christian calendar, the Sunday before Easter and first day of Holy Week, commemorating Jesus' entry into Jerusalem, when the crowd strewed palm leaves in his path.

Palmyra ancient city and oasis in the desert of Syria, about 240 km/150 mi NE of Damascus. Palmyra, the biblical Tadmor, was flourishing by about 300 BC. It was destroyed AD 272 after Queen Zenobia had led a revolt against the Romans. Extensive temple ruins exist, and on the site is a village called Tadmor.

Pamirs central Asian plateau mainly in Tajikistan, but extending into China and Afghanistan, traversed by mountain ranges. Its highest peak is Kommunizma Pik (Communism Peak 7,495 m/24,600 ft) in the Akademiya Nauk range.

Pampas flat, treeless, Argentine plains, lying between the Andes Mountains and the Atlantic Ocean and rising gradually from the coast to the lower slopes of the mountains. The E Pampas contain large cattle ranches and the flax- and grain-growing area of Argentina; the W Pampas are arid and unproductive.

pampas grass any grass of the genus *Cortaderia*, native to South America, especially *C. argentea*, which is grown in gardens and has tall leaves and large panicles of white flowers.

Pan in Greek mythology, the god of flocks and herds (Roman Sylvanus), shown as a man with the horns, ears, and hoofed legs of a goat, and playing a shepherd's panpipe (or syrinx).

pan-Africanism anticolonial movement that believed in the innate unity of all black Africans and their descendants overseas, and advocated a united Africa (see ◊African nationalism). It was founded 1900 at the first Pan-African Conference in London. Since 1958 pan-Africanism has become partially absorbed into wider movements of the developing world.

Support for the movement was fuelled by the Italian invasion of Ethiopia 1933. By the time of the sixth Pan-African Conference 1945, national independence dominated the agenda and the conference was attended by several future African leaders, including Kwame Nkrumah of Ghana and Jomo Kenyatta of Kenya. In 1963, the ◊Organization of African Unity was founded to foster cooperation among the newly independent African nations and to continue to fight colonialism, especially in South Africa.

Pan-Africanist Congress (PAC) South African political party, formed as a militant black nationalist group 1959, when it broke away from the African National Congress (ANC), promoting a black-only policy for Africa. PAC was outlawed 1960–90; its military wing was called Poqo ('we alone'). It suspended its armed struggle 1994, and transformed itself into a political party to contest the first multiracial elections. It is more radical than the ANC, advocating a radical redistribution of land and a state-run economy.

Panama country in Central America, on a narrow isthmus between the Caribbean and the Pacific Ocean, bounded W by Costa Rica and E by Colombia. *See country box on p. 812.*

Palmerston **British Tory politician Lord Palmerston, a member of parliament for 58 years, nine of them as prime minister. As foreign secretary, his abrasive style of diplomacy and his arrogance with colleagues earned him the nickname 'Lord Pumice-stone'. *Image Select (UK) Ltd***

Panama Canal canal across the Panama isthmus in Central America, connecting the Pacific and Atlantic oceans; length 80 km/50 mi, with 12 locks. Built by the USA 1904–14 after an unsuccessful attempt by the French, it was formally opened 1920. The Panama Canal Zone was acquired 'in perpetuity' by the USA 1903, comprising land extending about 5 km/3 mi on either side of the canal. The zone passed to Panama 1979, and control of the canal itself was ceded to Panama by the USA Jan 1990 under the terms of the Panama Canal Treaty 1977. The Canal Zone has several US military bases.

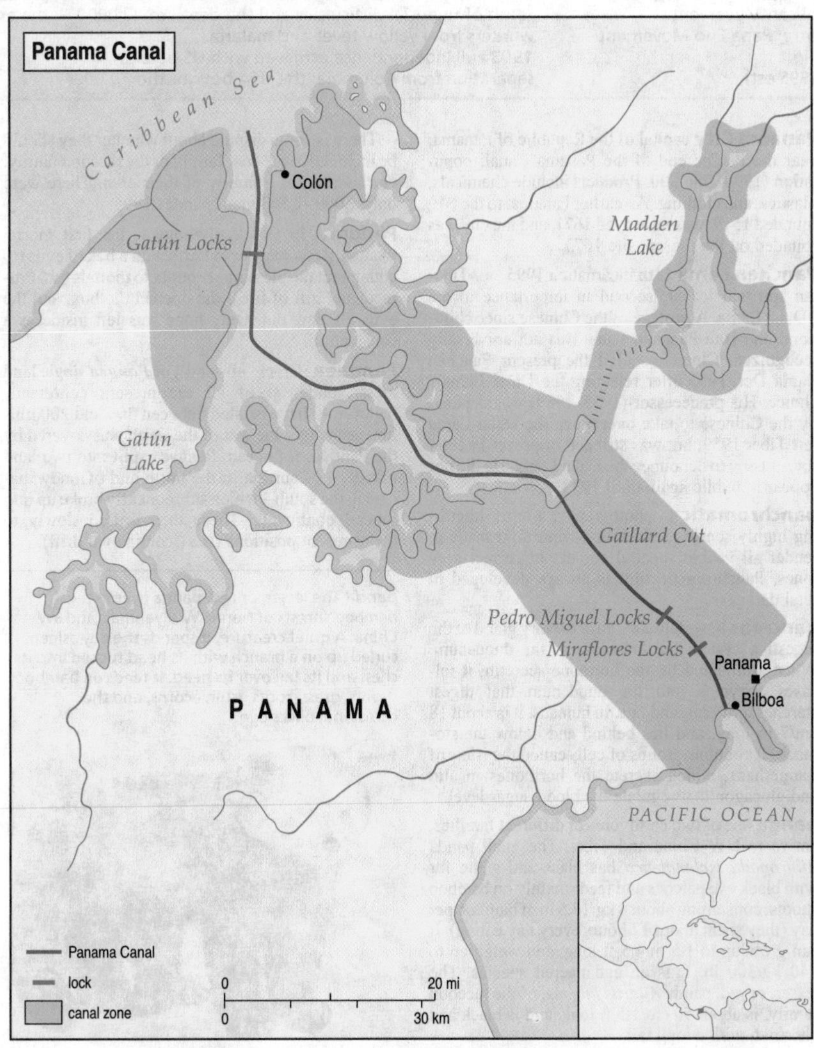

PANAMA
Republic of

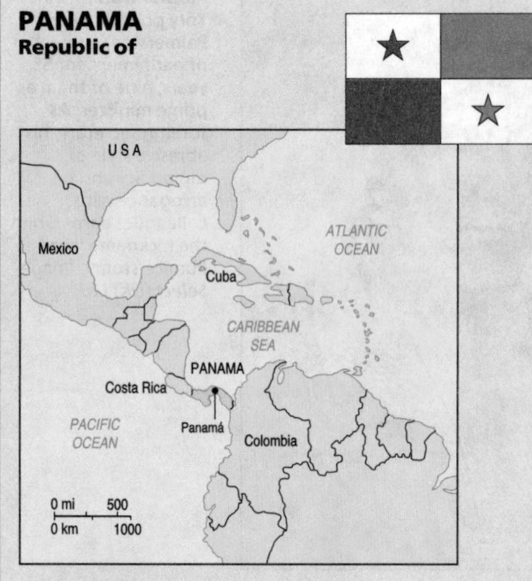

national name *República de Panamá*
area 77,100 sq km/29,768 sq mi
capital Panamá (Panama City)
major towns/cities San Miguelito, David
major ports Colón, Cristóbal, Balboa
physical features coastal plains and mountainous interior; tropical rainforest in E and NW; Pearl Islands in Gulf of Panama; Panama Canal
head of state and government Ernesto Pérez Balladares from 1994
political system emergent democratic republic
administrative divisions nine provinces and three autonomous Indian reservations
political parties Democratic Revolutionary Party (PRD), right-wing; Arnulfista Party (PA), left of centre; Authentic Liberal Party (PLA), left of centre; Nationalist Liberal Republican Movement (MOLIRENA), right of centre; Papa Ego Movement (MPE), moderate, centre-left
population 2,631,000 (1995 est)
population growth rate 1.9% (1990–95); 1.4% (2000–05)
ethnic distribution about 70% mestizos (of Spanish–American and American–Indian descent), 14% West Indian, 10% white American or European, and 6% Indian
life expectancy 71 (men), 75 (women)
literacy rate men 88%, women 88%
languages Spanish (official), English
religion Roman Catholic
currency balboa
GDP (US $) 6.97 billion (1994)
growth rate 4.7% (1994)
exports bananas, petroleum products, copper, shrimps, sugar, coffee, timber

HISTORY
1502 Visited by the Spanish explorer Rodrigo de Bastidas, at which time it was inhabited by Cuna, Choco, Guaymi, and other Indian groups.
1513 Spanish conquistador Vasco Nunez de Balboa explored the Pacific Ocean from the Darien isthmus; he was made governor of Panama (meaning 'abundance of fish'), but was later executed as a result of Spanish court intrigue.
1519 A Spanish city was established at Panama, which became part of the Spanish viceroyalty of New Andalucia (later New Granada).
1572–95 and 1668–71 Spanish settlements sacked by the British buccaneers Francis Drake and Henry Morgan.
1821 Achieved independence from Spain; joined confederacy of Gran Colombia, which included Colombia, Venezuela, Ecuador, Peru, and Bolivia.
1830 Gran Colombia split up and Panama became part of Colombia.
1846 Treaty signed with the USA allowing it to construct a railway across the isthmus.
1880s French attempt to build a Panama canal connecting the Atlantic and Pacific Oceans failed as a result of financial difficulties and the death of 22,000 workers from yellow fever and malaria.
1903 Full independence achieved with US help on separation from Colombia; the USA bought the rights to build the Panama Canal, and were given control of a ten-mile strip, the Canal Zone, in perpetuity.
1914 Panama Canal opened.
1939 Panama's status as a US protectorate was terminated by mutual agreement.
1968–81 Military rule of General Omar Torrijos Herrera, leader of the National Guard, who deposed the elected president and launched a costly programme of economic modernization.
1979 Ratification of the USA–Panama treaties, transferring the canal to Panama (effective from 2000), with the USA guaranteeing its protection and an annual payment.
1984 Nicolás Ardito Barletta of the right-wing Democratic Revolutionary Party (PRD) was elected president by a narrow margin.
1985 Barletta resigned and was replaced by Eric Arturo del Valle, to the dissatisfaction of the USA.
1987 General Manuel Noriega (head of the National Guard and effective ruler since 1983) resisted calls for his removal, despite suspension of US military and economic aid.
1988 Del Valle replaced by Manuel Solis Palma after trying to oust Noriega. Noriega, charged with drug smuggling by the USA, declared a state of emergency after the coup against him failed.
1989 Assembly elections declared invalid when won by the opposition. 'State of war' with the USA announced, and the US invasion (codenamed 'Operation Just Cause') deposed Noriega; 4,000 Panamanians died in the fighting. Guillermo Endara, who had won earlier elections, was installed as president in Dec.
1991 Attempted antigovernment coup foiled. Constitutional reforms approved by assembly, including abolition of a standing army; privatization programme introduced.
1992 Noriega found guilty of drug offences and given a 40-year prison sentence in USA. Referendum rejected proposed constitutional reforms.
1994 Ernesto Pérez Balladares (PRD) elected president. Constitution amended by assembly, and the army formally abolished.

'Is not a woman's life, is not her health, are not her limbs more valuable than panes of glass? There is no doubt of that, but most important of all, does not the breaking of glass produce more effect upon the Government?'

EMMELINE PANKHURST
Speech 16 Feb 1912

Panama City capital of the Republic of Panama, near the Pacific end of the Panama Canal; population (1990) 584,800. Products include chemicals, plastics, and clothing. An earlier Panama, to the NE, founded 1519, was destroyed 1671, and the city was founded on the present site 1673.

Panchen Lama 11th incarnation 1995– . Tibetan spiritual leader, second in importance to the ◊Dalai Lama. A protégé of the Chinese since childhood, the 10th Panchen Lama was not universally recognized. China installed the present Panchen Lama Dec 1995 after rejecting the Dalai Lama's choice. His predecessor (1935–1989) was deputed by the Chinese to take over when the Dalai Lama left Tibet 1959, but was stripped of power in 1964 for refusing to denounce the Dalai Lama. He did not appear in public again until 1978.

panchromatic in photography, a term describing highly sensitive black-and-white film made to render all visible spectral colours in correct grey tones. Panchromatic film is always developed in total darkness.

pancreas in vertebrates, an accessory gland of the digestive system located close to the duodenum. When stimulated by the hormone secretin, it releases enzymes into the duodenum that digest starches, proteins, and fats. In humans, it is about 18 cm/7 in long, and lies behind and below the stomach. It contains groups of cells called the islets of Langerhans, which secrete the hormones insulin and glucagon that regulate the blood sugar level.

panda one of two carnivores of different families, native to NW China and Tibet. The giant panda *Ailuropoda melanoleuca* has black-and-white fur with black eye patches and feeds mainly on bamboo shoots, consuming about 8 kg/17.5 lb of bamboo per day (they spent about 12 hours every day eating). It can grow up to 1.5 m/4.5 ft long, and weigh up to 140 kg/300 lb. It is an endangered species. The lesser, or red, panda *Ailurus fulgens*, of the raccoon family, is about 50 cm/1.5 ft long, and is black and chestnut, with a long tail.

There is some dispute about whether they should be included in the bear family or the raccoon family, or classified as a family of their own. There were only 1,000–1,500 giant pandas 1995.

Pandora in Greek mythology, the first mortal woman. Zeus sent her to Earth with a box of evils (to counteract the blessings brought to mortals by ◊Prometheus' gift of fire); she opened the box, and the evils all flew out. Only hope was left inside as a consolation.

Pangaea (Greek 'all-land') or ***Pangea*** single land mass, made up of all the present continents, believed to have existed between 300 and 200 million years ago; the rest of the Earth was covered by the Panthalassa ocean. Pangaea split into two land masses – ◊Laurasia in the north and ◊Gondwanaland in the south – which subsequently broke up into several continents. These then drifted slowly to their present positions (see ◊continental drift).

panda The lesser, or red, panda lives in the bamboo forests of Nepal, W Myanmar, and SW China. A quiet creature, it spends the day asleep, curled up on a branch with its head tucked into its chest and its tail over its head. It feeds on bamboo shoots, grass, roots, fruit, acorns, and the occasional bird's egg.

The existence of a single 'supercontinent' was proposed by German meteorologist Alfred Wegener 1912.

pangolin or ***scaly anteater*** toothless mammal of tropical Africa and SE Asia. They are long-tailed and covered with large, overlapping scales, except on the muzzle, sides of the head, throat, chest, and belly. They have an elongated skull and a long, extensible tongue. Pangolins measure 30–100 cm/12–39 in long, exclusive of the prehensile tail, which is about twice as long as the body.

Some are arboreal and others are terrestrial. All live on ants and termites. Pangolins comprise the order Pholidota. There is only one genus (*Manis*) and family Manidae, with seven species.

Panipat, Battles of three decisive battles in the vicinity of this Indian town, about 120 km/75 mi north of Delhi: 1526, when ◊Babur, great-grandson of the Mongol conqueror Tamerlane, defeated the emperor of Delhi and founded the Mogul empire; 1556, won by his descendant ◊Akbar; 1761, when the ◊Marathas were defeated by ◊Ahmad Shah Durrani of Afghanistan.

Pankhurst Emmeline, (born Goulden) 1858–1928. English suffragette. Founder of the Women's Social and Political Union 1903, she launched the militant suffragette campaign 1905. In 1926 she joined the Conservative Party and was a prospective Parliamentary candidate.

She was supported by her daughters ***Christabel Pankhurst*** (1880–1958), political leader of the movement, and ***Sylvia Pankhurst*** (1882–1960). The latter was imprisoned nine times under the 'Cat and Mouse Act', and was a pacifist in World War I.
▷ *See feature on pp. 1152–1153.*

pansy cultivated violet derived from the European wild pansy *Viola tricolor*, and including many different varieties and strains. The flowers are usually purple, yellow, cream, or a mixture, and there are many highly developed varieties bred for size, colour, or special markings. Several of the 400 different species are scented.

The wild pansy is also called heartsease.

Panthalassa ocean that covered the surface of the Earth not occupied by the world continent ◊Pangaea between 300 and 200 million years ago.

pantheism (Greek *pan* 'all'; *theos* 'God') doctrine that regards all of reality as divine, and God as present in all of nature and the universe. It is expressed in Egyptian religion and Brahmanism; stoicism, neo-Platonism, Judaism, Christianity, and Islam can be interpreted in pantheistic terms. Pantheistic philosophers include Giordano Bruno, Baruch Spinoza, J G Fichte, F W J Schelling, and G W F Hegel.

pantheon originally a temple for worshipping all the gods, such as that in ancient Rome, rebuilt by the emperor Hadrian AD 118–about 128, and still used as a church. In more recent times, the name has been used for a building where famous people are buried (as in the Panthéon, Paris).

The Pantheon in Rome has an enormous concrete dome spanning 43.2 m/142 ft.

panther another name for the ◊leopard.

pantomime in the British theatre, a traditional Christmas entertainment. It has its origins in the harlequin spectacle of the 18th century and burlesque of the 19th century, which gave rise to the tradition of the principal boy being played by an actress and the dame by an actor. The harlequin's role diminished altogether as themes developed on folk tales such as 'The Sleeping Beauty' and 'Cinderella', and with the introduction of additional material such as popular songs, topical comedy, and audience participation.

pantothenic acid water-soluble ◊vitamin ($C_9H_{17}NO_5$) of the B complex, found in a wide variety of foods. Its absence from the diet can lead to dermatitis, and it is known to be involved in the breakdown of fats and carbohydrates. It was first isolated from liver in 1933.

panzer (German 'armour') German mechanized units in World War II created by Heinz Guderain. A Panzer army was a mechanized unit based on a core of tanks and supported by infantry, artillery, and service troops in vehicles capable of accompanying the tanks.

Paolozzi Eduardo Luigi 1924– . Scottish sculptor and graphic artist. He was an important figure in the Pop-art movement in London in the 1950s and 1960s. In his early sculptures he typically assembled bronze casts of machinery to create sinister, robotlike figures. *Cyclops* 1957 (Tate Gallery, London) and *Jason* 1956 (Museum of Modern Art, New York) are examples. From the 1960s his work became more abstract and lighter in mood.

papal infallibility doctrine formulated by the Roman Catholic Vatican Council 1870, which stated that the pope, when speaking officially on certain doctrinal or moral matters, was protected from error by God, and therefore such rulings could not be challenged.

Papal States area of central Italy in which the pope was temporal ruler from 756 until the unification of Italy 1870.

Papandreou Andreas 1919–1996. Greek socialist politician, founder of the Pan-Hellenic Socialist Movement (PASOK); prime minister 1981–89, and 1993–96. He lost the 1989 election after being implicated in an alleged embezzlement scandal, involving the diversion of funds to the Greek government from the Bank of Crete, headed by George Koskotas. In Jan 1992 a trial cleared Papandreou of all corruption charges.

papaya tropical tree *Carica papaya* of the family Caricaceae, native from Florida to South America. Varieties are grown throughout the tropics. The edible fruits resemble a melon, with orange-coloured flesh and numerous blackish seeds in the central cavity; they may weigh up to 9 kg/20 lb.

The fruit juice and the tree sap contain papain, an enzyme used to tenderize meat and aid digestion.

The name pawpaw is also used for this tree, but in the USA the ◊pawpaw is the tree *Asimina triloba*, of the custard-apple family.

Papeete capital and port of French Polynesia on the NW coast of Tahiti; population (1992) 24,200. Products include vanilla, copra, and mother-of-pearl.

paper thin, flexible material made in sheets from vegetable fibres (such as wood pulp) or rags and used for writing, drawing, printing, packaging, and various household needs. The name comes from papyrus, a form of writing material made from water reed, used in ancient Egypt. The invention of true paper, originally made of pulped fishing nets and rags, is credited to Tsai Lun, Chinese minister of agriculture, AD 105.

Paper came to the West with Arabs who had learned the secret from Chinese prisoners of war in Samarkand in 768. It spread from Morocco to Moorish Spain and to Byzantium in the 11th century, then to the rest of Europe. All early paper was handmade within frames.

With the spread of literacy there was a great increase in the demand for paper which led to the invention, by Louis Robert (1761–1828) in 1799, of a machine to produce a continuous reel of paper. The process was developed and patented in 1801 by François Didot, Robert's employer. Today most paper is made from wood pulp on a Fourdrinier machine, then cut to size; some high grade paper is still made from esparto or rag. Paper products absorb 35% of the world's annual commercial wood harvest; recycling avoids some of the enormous waste of trees, and most papermakers plant and replant their own forests of fast-growing stock.

papier mâché (French 'chewed paper') craft technique that involves building up layer upon layer of pasted paper, which is then baked or left to harden. Used for trays, decorative objects, and even furniture, it is often painted, lacquered, or decorated with mother-of-pearl.

Papineau Louis Joseph 1786–1871. Canadian politician. He led a mission to England to protest against the planned union of Lower Canada (Quebec) and Upper Canada (Ontario), and demanded economic reform and an elected provincial legislature. In 1835 he gained the cooperation of William Lyon Mackenzie (1795–1861) in Upper Canada, and in 1837 organized an unsuccessful rebellion of the French against British rule in Lower Canada. He fled the country, but returned 1847 to sit in the United Canadian legislature until 1854.

Pap test or ***Pap smear*** common name for ◊cervical smear.

Papua New Guinea country in the SW Pacific, comprising the eastern part of the island of New Guinea, the Bismarck Archipelago, and part of the Solomon Islands. *See country box on p. 814.*

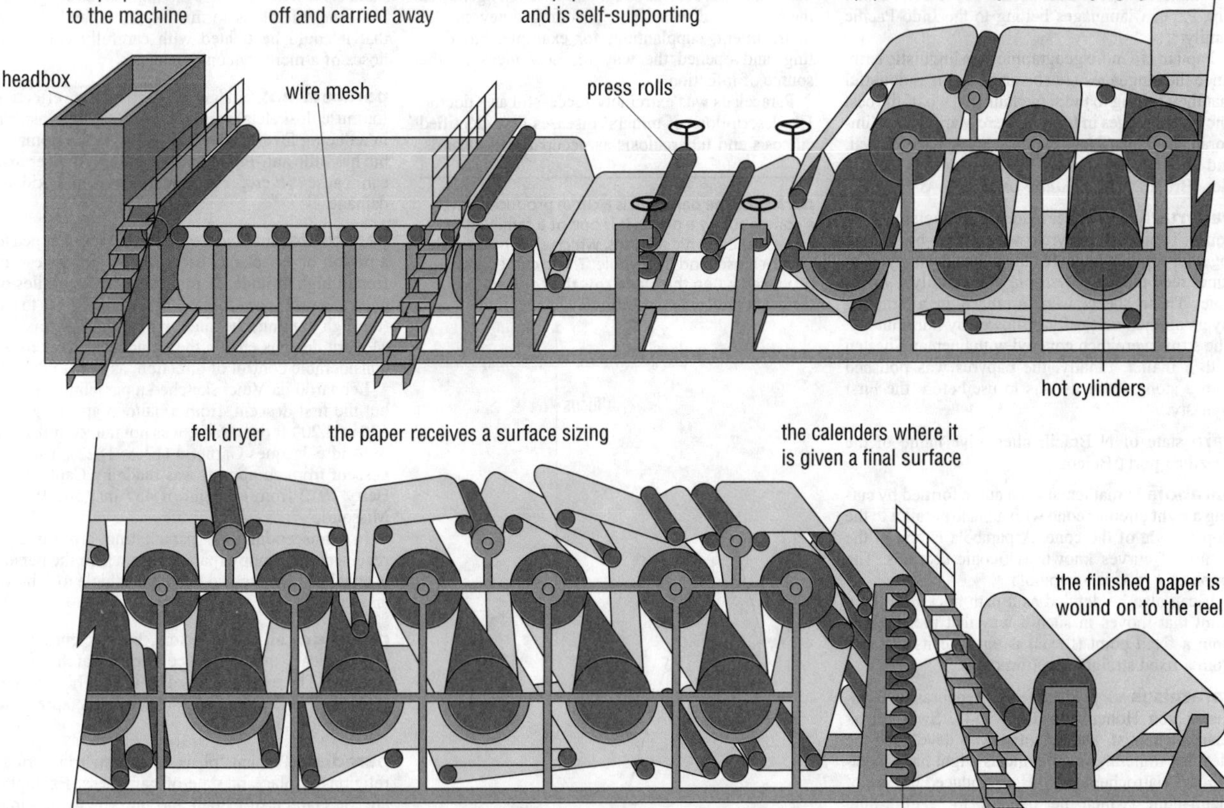
the pulp flows on to the machine
the free water is drawn off and carried away
the paper has now formed and is self-supporting
the paper enters the system of drying cylinders
headbox
wire mesh
press rolls
hot cylinders
felt dryer
the paper receives a surface sizing
the calenders where it is given a final surface
the finished paper is wound on to the reel
calender stacks

paper Today's fully automatic papermaking machines can be 200 m/640 ft long and produce over 1,000 m/3,200 ft of paper in a minute. The most common type of papermaking machine is the Fourdrinier, named after two British stationer brothers who invented it in 1803. Their original machine deposited the paper on pieces of felt, after which it was finished by hand.

PAPUA NEW GUINEA

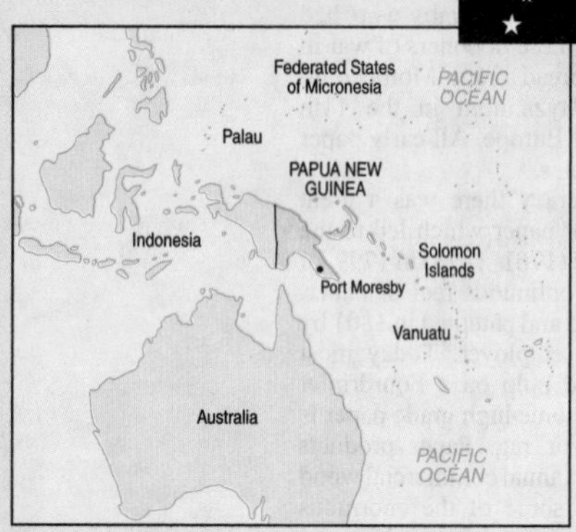

area 462,840 sq km/178,656 sq mi
capital Port Moresby (on E New Guinea)
major towns/cities Lae, Madang, Wewak
major ports Rabaul
physical features mountainous; swamps and plains; monsoon climate; includes tropical islands of New Ireland, New Britain, and Bougainville; Admiralty Islands, D'Entrecasteaux Islands, and Louisiade Archipelago; active volcanoes Vulcan and Tavurvur
head of state Queen Elizabeth II of Britain, represented by governor general Silas Atopare from 1997
head of government Bill Skate from 1997
political system liberal democracy
administrative divisions 19 provinces and a National Capital District
political parties Papua New Guinea Party (Pangu Pati: PP), urban- and coastal-oriented nationalist; People's Democratic Movement (PDM), 1985 breakaway from the PP; National Party (NP), highlands-based, conservative; Melanesian Alliance (MA), Bougainville-based, pro-autonomy, left of centre; People's Progress Party (PPP), conservative; People's Action Party (PAP), right of centre
population 4,400,000 (1996 est)
population growth rate 2.3% (1990–95); 2.1% (2000–05)
ethnic distribution mainly Melanesian, particularly in coastal areas; inland (on New Guinea and larger islands), Papuans predominate. On the outer archipelagos and islands, mixed Micronese-Melanesians are found. A small Chinese minority also exists
life expectancy 55 (men), 57 (women)
literacy rate men 65%, women 38%
languages English (official); pidgin English, 715 local languages
religions Protestant, Roman Catholic, local faiths
currency kina
GDP (US $) 5.4 billion (1994)
growth rate 3.5% (1994)
exports copra, coconut oil, palm oil, tea, copper, gold, coffee, cocoa beans, timber, petroleum

HISTORY
c. 3000 BC New settlement of Austronesian (Melanesian) immigrants.
1526 Visited by the Portuguese navigator Jorge de Menezes, who named the main island the Ilhos dos Papua after the 'frizzled' hair of the inhabitants.
1545 The Spanish navigator Ynigo Ortis de Retez gave the island the name of New Guinea.
17th C Regularly visited by Dutch merchants.
1828 Dutch East India Company incorporated western part of New Guinea into the Netherlands East Indies (becoming Irian Jaya, in Indonesia).
1884 NE New Guinea annexed by Germany; SE claimed by Britain.
1906 Britain transferred its rights to Australia, which renamed the lands Papua.
1914 German New Guinea occupied by Australia at the outbreak of World War I; from the merged territories Papua New Guinea was formed.
1920–42 Held as a League of Nations mandate by Australia.
1942–45 Occupied by Japan, who lost 150,000 troops resisting Allied counterattack.
1947 Held as a United Nations Trust Territory by Australia.
1951 Legislative Council established.
1964 Elected House of Assembly formed.
1967 Pangu Party (Pangu Pati; PP) formed to campaign for home rule.
1975 Independence achieved from Australia, within the Commonwealth, with Michael Somare (PP) as prime minister.
1980 Sir Julius Chan of the People's Progress Party (PPP) became prime minister.
1982 Somare returned to power.
1985 Somare challenged by Paias Wingti, the deputy prime minister, who later left the PP and formed the People's Democratic Movement (PDM); he became head of a five-party coalition government.
1988 Wingti defeated on no-confidence vote; replaced by Rabbie Namaliu (PP), heading coalition government. Joined Solomon Islands and Vanuatu to form Spearhead Group, aiming to preserve Melanesian cultural traditions.
1989 State of emergency imposed on copper-rich Bougainville in response to separatist violence.
1990 Bougainville Revolutionary Army (BRA) issued unilateral declaration of independence.
1991 Economic boom as gold production doubled.
1992 Wingti appointed premier, heading a three-party coalition.
1994 Wingti replaced as premier by Sir Julius Chan. Short-lived peace agreement with BRA.
1996 Prime minister of Bougainville murdered, jeopardizing peace process.
1997 Army and police mutinied following government's use of mercenaries against secessionist rebels. Prime Minister Chan forced to resign but returned after being cleared of corruption charges. Chan's coalition polled badly in general election; Bill Skate (PDM) appointed prime minister. Silas Ajtopare appointed governor general.
1998 Truce with Bougainville secessionists. Hundreds died when tsunami destroyed villages on north coast.

SEE ALSO Australasia–Oceania; Pacific peoples

Papuan native to or inhabitant of Papua New Guinea; speaker of any of various Papuan languages, used mainly on the island of New Guinea, although some 500 are used in New Britain, the Solomon Islands, and the islands of the SW Pacific. The Papuan languages belong to the Indo-Pacific family.

Papuan is a more geographic than linguistic term, since the languages are so varied that it is doubtful that they belong to the same family. Two of the best known languages in Irian Jaya are Marind and Nimborau. In Papua New Guinea, Enga, Kate, Kiwai, and Orokoto are spoken, while Baining is used in New Britain. ▷ *See feature on pp. 806–807.*

papyrus type of paper made by the ancient Egyptians. Typically papyrus was made by gluing together some 20 sheets of the pith of the papyrus or paper reed plant *Cyperus papyrus*, family Cyperaceae. These sheets were arranged in alternating layers aligned vertically, followed by horizontally. The strips were then covered with linen and beaten with a mallet. Finally, the papyrus was polished with a stone. Papyrus was in use before the First Dynasty.

Pará state of N Brazil; alternative name of the Brazilian port ◊Belém.

parabola in mathematics, a curve formed by cutting a right circular cone with a plane parallel to the sloping side of the cone. A parabola is one of the family of curves known as ◊conic sections. The graph of $y = x^2$ is a parabola.

It can also be defined as a path traced out by a point that moves in such a way that the distance from a fixed point (focus) is equal to its distance from a fixed straight line (directrix).

Paracelsus adopted name of Theophrastus Bombastus von Hohenheim 1493–1541. Swiss physician, alchemist, and scientist who developed the idea that minerals and chemicals might have medical uses (iatrochemistry). He introduced the use of ◊laudanum (which he named) for pain-killing purposes. His rejection of traditional lore and insistence on the value of observation and experimentation make him a leading figure in early science.

Overturning the contemporary view of illness as an imbalance of the four humours (see ◊humours, theory of), Paracelsus sought an external agency as the source of disease. This encouraged new modes of treatment, supplanting, for example, bloodletting, and opened the way for new ideas on the source of infection.

Paracelsus was extremely successful as a doctor. His descriptions of miners' diseases first identified silicosis and tuberculosis as occupational hazards. He recognized goitre as endemic and related to minerals in drinking water, and originated a medical account of chorea, rather than believing this nervous disease to be caused by possession by spirits. Paracelsus was the first to distinguish the congenital from the infectious form of syphilis, and showed that it could be treated with carefully controlled doses of a mercury compound.

parabola The parabola is a curve produced when a cone is cut by a plane. It is one of a family of curves called conic sections, which also includes the circle, ellipse, and hyperbole. These curves are produced when the plane cuts the cone at different angles and positions.

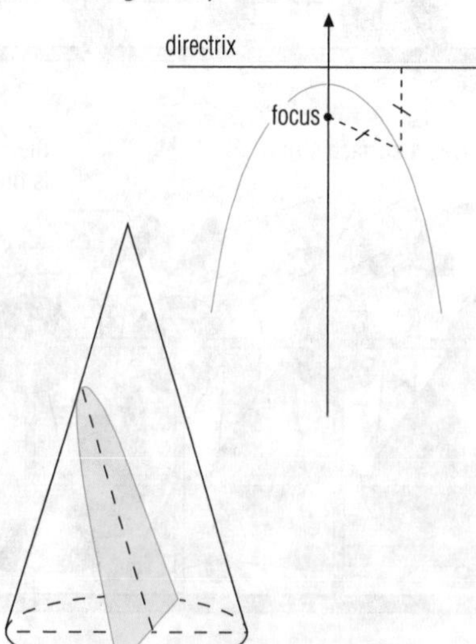

paracetamol analgesic, particularly effective for musculoskeletal pain. It is as effective as aspirin in reducing fever, and less irritating to the stomach, but has little anti-inflammatory action. An overdose can cause severe, even fatal, liver and kidney damage.

parachute any canopied fabric device strapped to a person or a package, used to slow down descent from a high altitude, or returning spent missiles or parts to a safe speed for landing, or sometimes to aid (through braking) the landing of a plane or missile. Modern designs enable the parachutist to exercise considerable control of direction, as in ◊skydiving.

Leonardo da Vinci sketched a parachute design, but the first descent, from a balloon at a height of 670 m/2,200 ft over Paris, was not made until 1797 by André-Jacques Garnerin (1769–1823). The first descent from an aircraft was made by Capt Albert Berry 1912 from a height of 457 m/1,500 ft over Missouri.

In parascending the parachuting procedure is reversed, the canopy (parafoil) to which the person is attached being towed behind a vehicle to achieve an ascent.

paradigm all those factors, both scientific and sociological, that influence the research of the scientist. The term, first used by the US historian of science T S ◊Kuhn, has subsequently spread to social studies and politics.

paradise (Persian 'pleasure garden') in various religions, a place or state of happiness. Examples are the Garden of ◊Eden and the Messianic kingdom; the Islamic paradise of the Koran is a place of sensual pleasure.

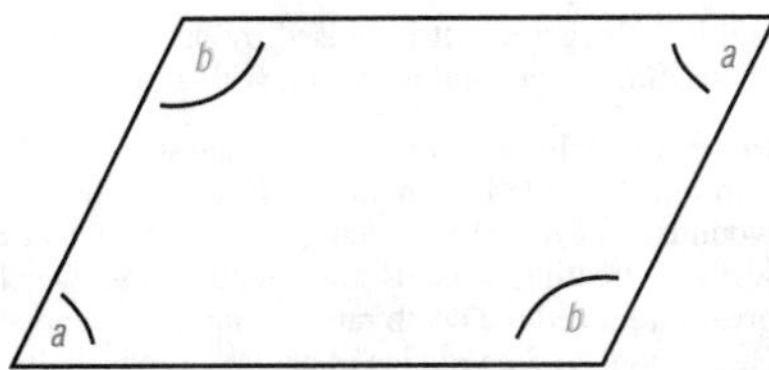

(i) opposite sides and angles are equal

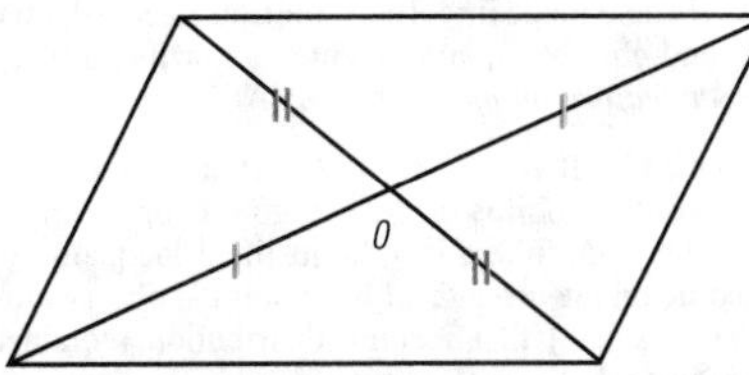

(ii) diagonals bisect each other at *0*

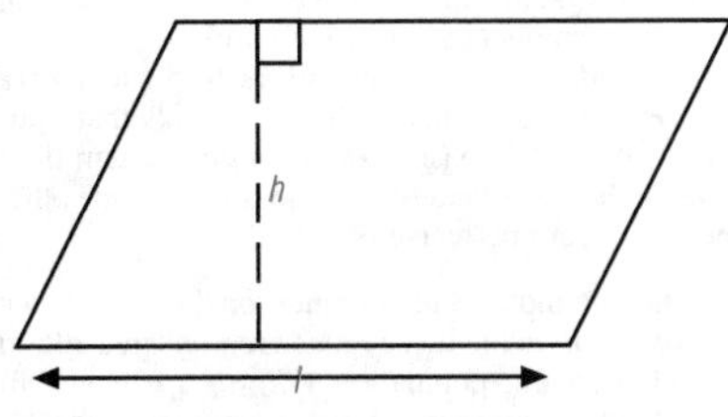

(iii) area of a parallelogram *l* x *h*

parallelogram Some properties of a parallelogram.

Paradise Lost epic poem in 12 books, by John ◊Milton, first published 1667. The poem describes the Fall of Man and the battle between God and Satan, as enacted through the story of Adam and Eve in the Garden of Eden. A sequel, *Paradise Regained*, was published 1671 and relates the temptation of Christ in the wilderness.

paradox statement that seems contradictory but contains an element of truth. The truth is emphasized by the unexpected form of expression. The Bible is a rich source of paradox: 'Love your enemies'; 'The first shall be last and the last shall be first.'

Paraguay landlocked country in South America, bounded NE by Brazil, S by Argentina, and NW by Bolivia. *See country box below.*

paraffin common name for ◊alkane, any member of the series of hydrocarbons with the general formula C_nH_{2n+2}. The lower members are gases, such as methane (marsh or natural gas). The middle ones (mainly liquid) form the basis of petrol, kerosene, and lubricating oils, while the higher ones (paraffin waxes) are used in ointment and cosmetic bases. The fuel commonly sold as paraffin in Britain is more correctly called kerosene.

parakeet any of various small long-tailed ◊parrots, order Psittaciformes, with a moderate beak. They include the ring-necked parakeets, genus *Psittacula*, which are very common in India and Africa, and ◊cockatiels, and ◊budgerigars, natives of Australia. The king parakeet is about the size of a magpie and has a red head and breast and green wings.

parallax the change in the apparent position of an object against its background when viewed from two different positions. In astronomy, nearby stars show a shift owing to parallax when viewed from different positions on the Earth's orbit around the Sun. A star's parallax is used to deduce its distance.

parallel lines and parallel planes in mathematics, straight lines or planes that always remain a constant distance from one another no matter how far they are extended. This is a principle of Euclidean geometry. Some non-Euclidean geometries, such as elliptical and hyperbolic geometry, however, reject Euclid's parallel axiom.

parallelogram in mathematics, a quadrilateral (four-sided plane figure) with opposite pairs of sides equal in length and parallel, and opposite angles equal. The diagonals of a parallelogram bisect each other. Its area is the product of the length of one side and the perpendicular distance between this and the opposite side. In the special case when all four sides are equal in length, the parallelogram is known as a rhombus, and when the internal angles are right angles, it is a rectangle or square.

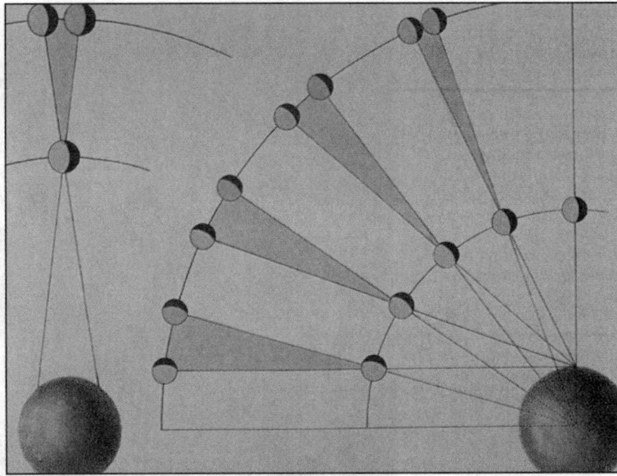

parallax A diagram showing planetary parallax, 1845. The parallax – the apparent shift of a body's position when measured from two different positions on the Earth – is used to calculate the body's distance. *Image Select (UK) Ltd*

parallelogram of forces in physics and applied mathematics, a method of calculating the resultant (combined effect) of two different forces acting together on an object. Because a force has both magnitude and direction it is a ◊vector quantity and can be represented by a straight line. A second force acting at the same point in a different direction can be represented by another line drawn at an angle to the first. By completing the parallelogram (of which the two lines are sides) a diagonal may be drawn from the original angle to the opposite corner to represent the resultant force vector.

paralysis loss of voluntary movement due to failure of nerve impulses to reach the muscles involved. It may result from almost any disorder of the nervous system, including brain or spinal cord injury, poliomyelitis, stroke, and progressive conditions such as a tumour or multiple sclerosis. Paralysis may also involve loss of sensation due to sensory nerve disturbance.

Infantile paralysis is an old-fashioned term for ◊polio; paralysis agitans is ◊Parkinson's disease.

PARAGUAY
Republic of

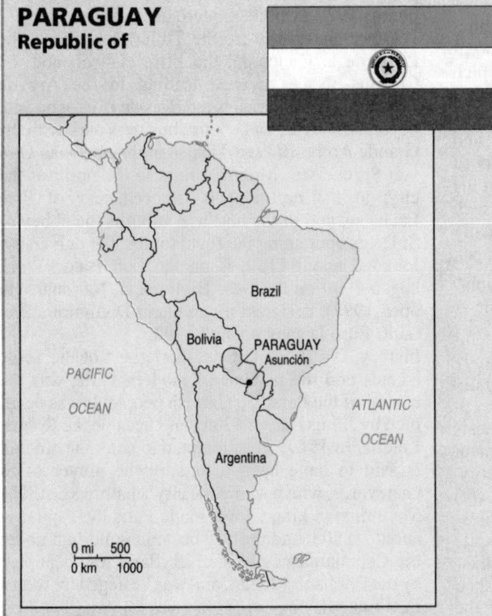

national name *República del Paraguay*
area 406,752 sq km/157,006 sq mi
capital (and port) Asunción
major towns/cities Ciudad del Este, Pedro Juan Caballero
major ports Concepción
physical features low marshy plain and marshlands; divided by Paraguay River; Paraná River forms SE boundary
head of state and government Raul Cubas from 1998
political system emergent democratic republic
administrative divisions 19 departments
political parties National Republican Association (Colorado Party), right of centre; Authentic Radical Liberal Party (PLRA), centrist; National Encounter, right of centre; Radical Liberal Party (PLR), centrist; Liberal Party (PL), centrist
population 4,957,000 (1996 est)
population growth rate 2.8% (1990–95); 2.3% (2000–05)
ethnic distribution predominantly mixed-race mestizos; less than 5% Spanish or Indian
life expectancy 65 (men), 70 (women)
literacy rate men 92%, women 88%
languages Spanish 6% (official), Guarani 90%
religions Roman Catholic (official religion); Mennonite, Anglican
currency guaraní
GDP (US $) 7.88 billion (1994)
growth rate 3.5% (1994)
exports cotton, soya beans, timber, vegetable oil, maté, hides, meat

HISTORY
1526 Visited by Italian navigator Sebastian Cabot, who travelled up Paraná river; at this time the E of the country had long been inhabited by Guarani-speaking Amerindians, who gave the country its name, which means 'land with an important river'.
1537 The Spanish made an alliance with the Guarani Indians against the hostile Chaco Indians, enabling them to colonize the interior plains; Asunción was founded by the Spanish.
1609 Jesuits arrived from Spain to convert the local population to Roman Catholicism and administer the country.
1767 Jesuit missionaries expelled.
1776 Formerly part of the Spanish Viceroyalty of Peru, which covered much of South America, became part of Viceroyalty of La Plata, with its capital at Buenos Aires (Argentina).
1808 With the Spanish monarchy overthrown by Napoleon Bonaparte, the La Plata Viceroyalty became autonomous, but Paraguayans revolted against rule from Buenos Aires.
1811 Independence achieved from Spain.
1814 Under the dictator General José Gaspar Rodriguez Francia ('El Supremo'), Paraguay became an isolated state.
1840 Francia was succeeded by his nephew, Carlos Antonio Lopez, who opened the country to foreign trade and whose son, Francisco Solano Lopez, as president from 1862, built up a powerful army.
1865–70 War with Argentina, Brazil, and Uruguay over access to the sea; less than half the population survived and 150,000 sq km/58,000 sq mi of territory lost; President Lopez killed.
later 1880s The conservative Colorado Party and the Liberal Party were founded.
1912 The Liberal leader Edvard Schaerer came to power, ending decades of political instability.
1932–35 Territory in the W won from Bolivia during the Chaco War (settled by arbitration 1938).
1940–48 Presidency of autocratic General Higinio Morínigo.
1948–54 Political instability; six different presidents.
1954 General Alfredo Stroessner seized power in a coup, and ruled as a ruthless autocrat, suppressing civil liberties; received initial US backing as economy expanded.
1989 Stroessner ousted in coup led by Gen Andrés Rodríguez. Rodríguez elected as president; the right-of-centre military-backed Colorado Party won the assembly elections.
1992 New democratic constitution adopted.
1993 Colorado Party won most seats in first free multiparty elections, but no overall majority; its candidate, Juan Carlos Wasmosy, won first free presidential elections.
1998 Despite claims of fraud, Colorado Party candidate Raul Cubas elected president.

parasite The larvae of many parasitic wasps develop inside the bodies of other insects. These larvae of the braconid wasp *Apanteles glomeratus* are boring their way out through the skin of their host, a caterpillar of the large white butterfly *Pieris brassicae*, in order to pupate. Parasites such as these, which normally kill their host, are sometimes distinguished from 'true' parasites. *Premaphotos Wildlife*

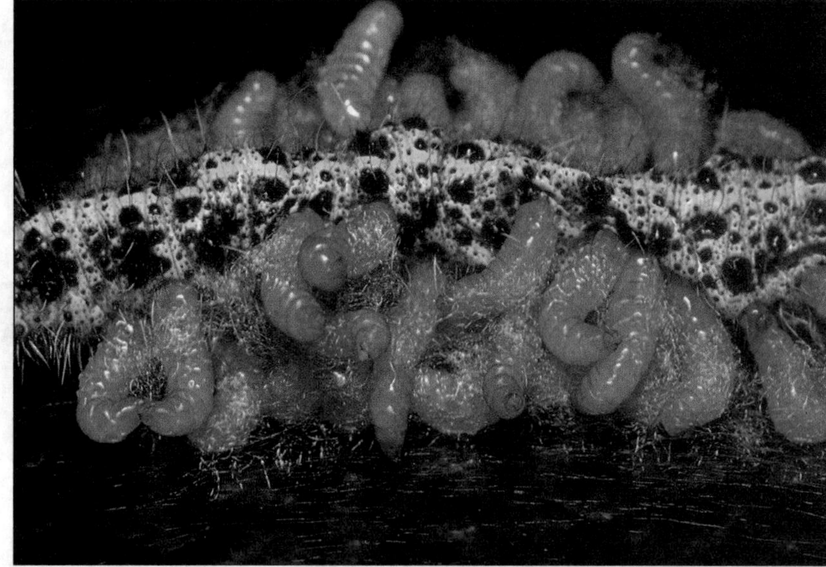

'Give me fruitful error any time, full of seeds, bursting with its own corrections. You can keep your sterile truth for yourself.'

VILFREDO PARETO
Mind and Society

Paramaribo port and capital of Surinam, South America, 24 km/15 mi from the sea on the river Suriname; population (1993 est) 201,100. Products include coffee, fruit, timber, and bauxite.
history originally a Native American village, it was settled by the French in about 1640. The British Lord Willoughby of Parham founded the first successful colony in 1651. It was ceded to the Dutch in the Treaty of Breda of 1667 in exchange for New Amsterdam, now New York, and remained under Dutch rule until 1975 except for two periods during the Napoleonic Wars (1799–1802 and 1804–1815).
features Dutch colonial architecture; 17th-century Fort Zeelandia.

paramilitary uniformed, armed force found in many countries, occupying a position between the police and the military. In France such a force is called the Gendarmerie and in Germany the Federal Border Guard. In recent years the term has been extended to include illegal organizations of a terrorist nature.

Paramount Studios US film production and distribution company, founded 1912 as the Famous Players Film Company by Adolph Zukor (1873–1976). In 1914 it merged with the distribution company Paramount Pictures. A major studio from the silent days of cinema, Paramount was adept at discovering new talent and Cecil B de Mille made many of his films for the studio. In 1966 the company was taken over by Gulf and Western Industries. In recent years it has produced such successful films as *Grease* 1978 and *Raiders of the Lost Ark* 1981.

Paris The church of Sacré Coeur in Paris. It stands on the heights of Montmartre and is one of the most important landmarks of the city. *Image Select (UK) Ltd*

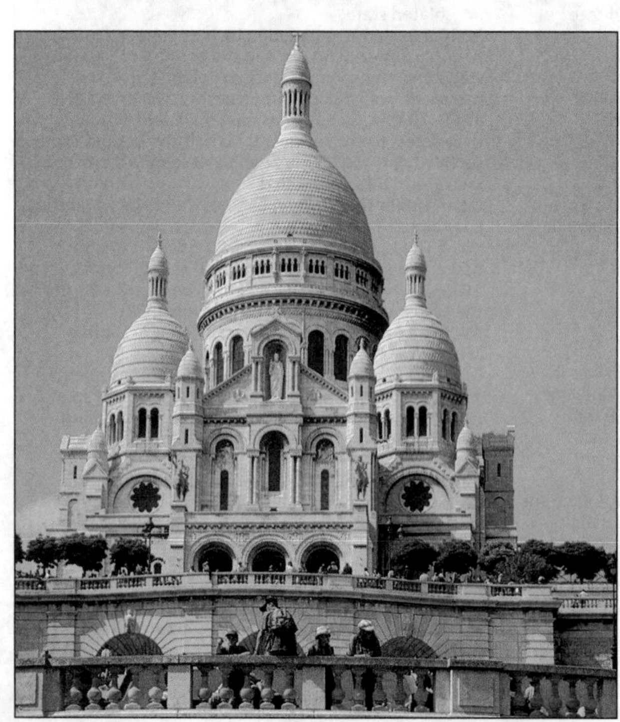

paranoia mental disorder marked by ◊delusions of grandeur or persecution. In popular usage, paranoia means baseless or exaggerated fear and suspicion.

In chronic paranoia, patients exhibit a rigid system of false beliefs and opinions, believing themselves, for example, to be followed by the secret police, to be loved by someone at a distance, or to be of great importance or in special relation to God. There are no hallucinations and patients are in other respects normal.

In paranoid states, the delusions of persecution or grandeur are present but not systematized.

In paranoid ◊schizophrenia, the patient suffers from many unsystematized and incoherent delusions, is extremely suspicious, and experiences hallucinations and the feeling that external reality has altered.

paranormal not within the range of, or explicable by, established science. Paranormal phenomena include ◊extrasensory perception (ESP) which takes in clairvoyance, precognition, and telepathy; telekinesis, the movement of objects from one position to another by human mental concentration; and mediumship, supposed contact with the spirits of the dead, usually via an intermediate 'guide' in the other world. ◊Parapsychology is the study of such phenomena. Paranormal phenomena are usually attributed to the action of an unknown factor, ◊psi.

paraplegia paralysis of the lower limbs, involving loss of both movement and sensation; it is usually due to spinal injury.

parapsychology (Greek *para* 'beyond') study of ◊paranormal phenomena, which are generally subdivided into two types: ◊extrasensory perception (ESP), or the paracognitive; and psychokinesis (PK), telekinesis, or the paraphysical – movement of an object without use of physical force or energy.

The first Society for Psychical Research was established in London 1882 by scientists, philosophers, classical scholars, and spiritualists. Despite continued scepticism within the scientific establishment, a chair of parapsychology was established 1984 at Edinburgh University, endowed by the Hungarian author Arthur Koestler.

parasite organism that lives on or in another organism (called the host) and depends on it for nutrition, often at the expense of the host's welfare. Parasites that live inside the host, such as liver flukes and tapeworms, are called endoparasites; those that live on the exterior, such as fleas and lice, are called ectoparasites.

parathyroid one of a pair of small ◊endocrine glands. Most tetrapod vertebrates, including humans, possess two such pairs, located behind the ◊thyroid gland. They secrete parathyroid hormone, which regulates the amount of calcium in the blood.

paratyphoid fever infectious disease of the intestinal tract, similar to ◊typhoid fever but milder and less dangerous. It is caused by bacteria of the genus *Salmonella* and is treated with antibiotics.

Paré Ambroise c. 1509–1590. French surgeon who introduced modern principles to the treatment of wounds. As a military surgeon, Paré developed new ways of treating wounds and amputations, which greatly reduced the death rate among the wounded. He abandoned the practice of cauterization (sealing with heat), using balms and soothing lotions instead, and used ligatures to tie off blood vessels. Paré eventually became chief surgeon to Charles IX. He also made important contributions to dentistry and childbirth, and invented an artificial hand. ▷*See feature on pp. 1024–1025.*

Pareto Vilfredo 1848–1923. Italian economist and political philosopher. A vigorous opponent of socialism and liberalism, he justified inequality of income on the grounds of his empirical observation (Pareto's law) that income distribution remained constant whatever efforts were made to change it.

Pareto was born in Paris. He produced the first account of society as a self-regulating and interdependent system that operates independently of human attempts at voluntary control.

A founder of welfare economics, he put forward a concept of 'optimality', which contends that optimum conditions exist in an economic system if no one can be made better off without at least one other person becoming worse off.

Paris port and capital of France, on the river Seine; *département* in the Île de France region; area 105 sq km/40.5 sq mi; population *Ville de Paris* (1990) 2,152,000; *agglomération parisienne* (1990) 9,300,000. It is the core of a highly centralized national administration.
features The river Seine is spanned by 32 bridges, the oldest of which is the Pont Neuf 1578. Churches include Notre Dame cathedral built 1163–1250; the Invalides, housing the tomb of Napoleon; the Gothic Sainte-Chapelle; and the 19th-century basilica of Sacré-Coeur, 125 m/410 ft high. Notable buildings include the Palais de Justice, the Hôtel de Ville, and the Luxembourg Palace and Gardens. The former palace of the Louvre (with its glass pyramid entrance by I M Pei 1989) is one of the world's major art galleries; the Musée d'Orsay 1986 has Impressionist and other paintings from the period 1848–1914; the Pompidou Centre (Beaubourg) 1977 exhibits modern art.

Other landmarks are the Tuileries Gardens, the Place de la Concorde, the Eiffel Tower, and the Champs-Elysées avenue leading to the Arc de Triomphe. To the west is the Bois de Boulogne and, beyond the river, La Défense business park with the Grande Arche 1989 by Danish architect Johan Otto von Sprekelsen; Montmartre is in the north of the city; to the northeast is the cemetery of Père Lachaise, and in the northern suburbs the abbey of St Denis containing the royal tombs; the university, founded about 1150, is on the Left Bank. Work began 1990 on the New Bibliotèque Nationale (to open 1997), designed by architect Dominique Perrault. Euro Disney opened 1992.
history The Île de la Cité, the largest of the Seine islands and the nucleus of modern Paris, was the capital of the Parisii, a Gaulish people. It was occupied by Julius Caesar 53 BC, and became the Roman Lutetia. In 451 Attila attempted to enter the city but is said to have been halted by the prayer of St Geneviève, who became the city's patron saint. The Merovingian king Clovis made Paris the capital in about AD 508, and the city became important under the Capetian kings 987–1328. Paris was occupied by the English 1420–36, and was besieged by Henry IV 1590–94.

The Bourbon kings did much to beautify the city. Louis XIV built many magnificent buildings but lost the loyalty of the populace by moving the court to Versailles. The French Revolution began in Paris 1789 with the storming and destruction of the Bastille. Napoleon I, as emperor from 1804, undertook to modernize the city and added new boulevards, bridges, and triumphal arches, as did Napoleon III. Paris was the centre of the revolutions of 1789–94, 1830, and 1848. The medieval heart of the city was redesigned by the French administrator Baron Haussmann 1853–70 and the modern layout of boulevards, avenues, and parks established. It was besieged by Prussia 1870–71, and by government troops during the Commune period (local socialist government) March–May 1871.

During World War I it suffered from air raids and bombardment, and in World War II it was occupied by German troops June 1940–Aug 1944. The German commandant, General Cholitz, ignored Hitler's order to defend Paris at all costs to avoid causing large-scale damage to the city. Large-scale architectural projects of note were again undertaken during the presidency of François Mitterrand 1981–95.

Paris in Greek mythology, a prince of Troy whose abduction of Helen, wife of King Menelaus of Sparta, caused the Trojan War. Helen was promised to him by the goddess Aphrodite as a bribe, in his judgement between her beauty and that of two other goddesses, Hera and Athena. Paris killed the Greek hero Achilles by shooting an arrow into his heel, but was himself killed by Philoctetes before the capture of Troy.

Paris Matthew c. 1200–1259. English chronicler. He entered St Albans Abbey 1217, and wrote a valuable history of England up to 1259.

Paris Commune name given to two separate periods in the history of Paris:

The Paris municipal government 1789–94 was established after the storming of the ◊Bastille and remained powerful in the French Revolution until the fall of Robespierre 1794.

The provisional national government 18 March–May 1871 was formed while Paris was besieged by the German troops during the Franco-Prussian War. It consisted of socialists and left-wing republicans, and is often considered the first socialist government in history. Elected after the right-wing National Assembly at Versailles tried to disarm the National Guard, it fell when the Versailles troops captured Paris and massacred 20,000–30,000 people 21–28 May.

parish in Britain, a subdivision of a county often coinciding with an original territorial subdivision in Christian church administration, served by a parish church. In the US, the parish is an ecclesiastical unit committed to one minister or priest.

The origins of the parish lie in early medieval Italian cities, and by the 12th century most of Christian Europe was divided into parishes.

parish council unit of local government in England and Wales, based on church parishes. In Wales they are commonly called community councils.

Parish councils provide and maintain monuments, playing fields, footpaths, and churchyards, administer local charities, may impose a limited local rate, are elected every four years, and function in parishes of 200 or more electors. Parish councils were established by the Local Government Act 1894, but most of their legal powers were abolished by the 1972 Local Government Act.

Paris, Treaty of any of various peace treaties signed in Paris, including: 1763 ending the ◊Seven Years' War; 1783 recognizing American independence; 1814 and 1815 following the abdication and final defeat of ◊Napoleon I; 1856 ending the ◊Crimean War; 1898 ending the ◊Spanish-American War; 1919–20 the conference preparing the Treaty of ◊Versailles at the end of World War I was held in Paris; 1947 after World War II, the peace treaties between the ◊Allies and Italy, Romania, Hungary, Bulgaria, and Finland; 1951 treaty signed by France, West Germany, Italy, Belgium, Netherlands, and Luxembourg, embodying the Schuman Plan to set up a single coal and steel authority; 1973 ending US participation in the ◊Vietnam War.

parity of a number, the state of being either even or odd. In computing, the term refers to the number of 1s in the binary codes used to represent data. A binary representation has even parity if it contains an even number of 1s and odd parity if it contains an odd number of 1s.

For example, the binary code 1000001, commonly used to represent the character 'A', has even parity because it contains two 1s, and the binary code 1000011, commonly used to represent the character 'C', has odd parity because it contains three 1s.

parity in economics, equality of price, rate of exchange, wages, and buying power. Parity ratios may be used in the setting of wages to establish similar status to different work groups. Parity in international exchange rates means that those on a par with each other share similar buying power. In the USA, agricultural output prices are regulated by a parity system.

Park Mungo 1771–1806. Scottish explorer who traced the course of the Niger River 1795–97. He disappeared and probably drowned during a second African expedition 1805–06. He published *Travels in the Interior of Africa* 1799.

Park spent 18 months in the Niger Basin while tracing the river. Even though he did not achieve his goal of reaching Timbuktu, he proved that it was feasible to travel through the interior of Africa.

Park Chung Hee 1917–1979. President of South Korea 1963–79. Under his rule South Korea had one of the world's fastest-growing economies, but recession and his increasing authoritarianism led to his assassination 1979.

Parker Charlie, (Charles Christopher 'Bird', 'Yardbird') 1920–1955. US alto saxophonist and jazz composer. He was associated with the trumpeter Dizzy Gillespie in developing the ◊bebop style. His skilful improvisations inspired performers on all jazz instruments.

Parker was born in Kansas City, a hub of jazz music. The young Parker studied the work of saxophonist Lester ◊Young and played in several conventional jazz and dance bands. Joining the Earl Hines Orchestra 1942–43 brought him into collaboration with Gillespie, and in their early recordings together ('Salt Peanuts', 'Groovin' High' 1945) bebop began to take shape. 'Ko-Ko' and 'Billie's Bounce' 1945 were recorded with a group that included Miles Davis on trumpet. Among other Parker compositions are 'Yardbird Suite' and 'Ornithology' (late 1940s). Parker was also very influential as a live performer; primitive bootleg tapes were made by fans, and live albums include *Quintet of the Year* 1953, again with Gillespie.

Parker Dorothy, (born Rothschild) 1893–1967. US writer and wit. She was a leading member of the literary circle known as the Algonquin Round Table. She reviewed for the magazines *Vanity Fair* and the *New Yorker*, and wrote wittily ironic verses, collected in several volumes including *Enough Rope* 1927, and *Not So Deep as a Well* 1936. Her short stories include the collections 'Laments for Living' 1930, and 'Here Lies' 1939. She also wrote screenplays in Hollywood, having moved there from New York City along with other members of her circle.

Parker US writer and wit Dorothy Parker in a photograph taken in the 1920s. For over 40 years she wrote reviews, stories, and light verse which provided a sharp, merciless, and wholly disenchanted view of American life. *Corbis*

Parkes site in New South Wales of the Australian National Radio Astronomy Observatory, featuring a radio telescope of 64 m/210 ft aperture, run by the Commonwealth Scientific and Industrial Research Organization.

Parkinson Cyril Northcote 1909–1993. English writer and historian, celebrated for his study of public and business administration, *Parkinson's Law* 1958, which included the dictum: 'Work expands to fill the time available for its completion.'

Parkinson Norman. Adopted name of Ronald William Smith 1913–1990. English fashion and portrait photographer. He caught the essential glamour of each decade from the 1930s to the 1980s. Long associated with the magazines *Vogue* and *Queen*, he was best known for his colour work, and from the late 1960s took many official portraits of the royal family.

Parkinson's disease or *parkinsonism* or *paralysis agitans* degenerative disease of the brain characterized by a progressive loss of mobility, muscular rigidity, tremor, and speech difficulties. The condition is mainly seen in people over the age of 50.

Parkinson's disease destroys a group of cells called the *substantia nigra* ('black substance') in the upper part of the ◊brainstem. These cells are concerned with the production of a neurotransmitter known as dopamine, which is essential to the control of voluntary movement. The almost total loss of these cells, and of their chemical product, produces the disabling effects. A defective gene responsible for 1 in 20 cases was identified 1992.

The disease occurs in two forms: multiple system atrophy (MSA), which is a failure of the central nervous system and accounts for 1 in 5 cases; and pure autonomic failure (PAF), a deficit in the peripheral nerves. Symptoms, particularly in the early stages, can be identical.

The introduction of the drug ◊L-dopa in the 1960s seemed at first the answer to Parkinson's disease. However, it became evident that long-term use brings considerable problems. At best, it postpones the terminal phase of the disease. Brain grafts with dopamine-producing cells were pioneered in the early 1980s, and attempts to graft Parkinson's patients with fetal brain tissue have been made. This experimental surgery brought considerable improvement to some PAF patients, but is ineffective in the MSA form. In 1989 a large US study showed that the drug deprenyl may slow the rate at which disability progresses in patients with early Parkinson's disease.

parliament (French 'speaking') legislative body of a country. The world's oldest parliament is the Icelandic Althing, which dates from about 930. The UK Parliament is usually dated from 1265. The legislature of the USA is called ◊Congress and comprises the ◊House of Representatives and the ◊Senate.

In the UK, Parliament is the supreme legislature, comprising the ◊House of Commons and the ◊House of Lords. The origins of Parliament are in the 13th century, but its powers were not established until the late 17th century. The powers of the Lords were curtailed 1911, and the duration of parliaments was fixed at five years, but any parliament may extend its own life, as happened during both world wars. The UK Parliament meets in the Palace of Westminster, London.

history Parliament originated under the Norman kings as the Great Council of royal tenants-in-chief, to which in the 13th century representatives of the shires were sometimes summoned. The Parliament summoned by Simon de Montfort 1265 (as head of government in the Barons' War) set a precedent by including representatives of the boroughs as well as the shires. Under Edward III the burgesses and knights of the shires began to meet separately from the barons, thus forming the House of Commons.

By the 15th century Parliament had acquired the right to legislate, vote, and appropriate supplies, examine public accounts, and impeach royal ministers. The powers of Parliament were much diminished under the Yorkists and Tudors but under Elizabeth I a new spirit of independence appeared. The revolutions of 1640 and 1688 established parliamentary control over the executive and judiciary, and finally abolished all royal claim to tax or legislate without parliamentary consent. During these struggles the two great parties (Whig and Tory) emerged, and after 1688 it became customary for the sovereign to choose ministers from the party dominant in the Commons. The English Parliament was united with the Scottish 1707, and with the Irish 1801–1922. The ◊franchise was extended to the middle classes 1832, to the urban working classes

'There's a hell of a distance between wise-cracking and wit. Wit has truth in it; wise-cracking is simply callisthenics with words.'

DOROTHY PARKER
Paris Review
Summer 1956

'Work expands so as to fill the time available for its completion.'

C NORTHCOTE PARKINSON
Parkinson's Law

1867, to agricultural labourers 1884, and to women 1918 and 1928. The duration of parliaments was fixed at three years 1694, at seven 1716, and at five 1911. Payment of MPs was introduced 1911. A public bill that has been passed is an ◊act of Parliament.

parliamentary reform acts UK acts of Parliament 1918, 1928, and 1971. The 19th century witnessed the gradual reform of the voting system in Britain and suffrage was extended in the 20th century. In 1918 the Representation of the People Act gave the vote in the UK to men over 21 years and to women over 30. In 1928 a further act gave women the vote from the age of 21. In 1971 the voting age for men and women was lowered to the age of 18.

Parliament, European governing body of the European Union (formerly the European Community); see ◊European Parliament.

Parliament, Houses of building where the UK legislative assembly meets. The present Houses of Parliament in London, designed in Gothic Revival style by the architects Charles Barry and A W Pugin, were built 1840–60, the previous building having burned down 1834. It incorporates portions of the medieval Palace of Westminster.

The Commons debating chamber was destroyed by incendiary bombs 1941: the rebuilt chamber (opened 1950) is the work of architect Giles Gilbert Scott and preserves its former character.

Parma city in Emilia-Romagna, N Italy; population (1992) 170,600. Industries include food processing, textiles, and engineering.

Founded by the Etruscans, it was the capital of the duchy of Parma 1545–1860. It has given its name to Parmesan cheese.

Parmenides c. 510–450 BC. Greek pre-Socratic philosopher, head of the Eleatic school (so called after Elea in S Italy). Against Heraclitus's doctrine of Becoming, Parmenides advanced the view that nonexistence was impossible, that everything was permanently in a state of being. Parmenides saw speculation and reason as more important than the evidence of the senses.

Parnassiens, Les school of French poets which flourished 1866–76, including ◊Leconte de Lisle, Heredia (1842–1905), Sully-Prudhomme (1839–1907), François-Edouard Coppée (1842–1908), Léon Dierx (1838–1912), Louis Menard (1822–1901), and Albert Merat (1840–1909). It was named after *Le Parnasse contemporain*, a periodical devoted to poetry, and advocated 'art for art's sake' in opposition to the ideas of the Romantics.

The Parnassians were much influenced by the scientific and philosophical climate of their times, in particular by scientific positivism. Their aim was to create poetry that was impersonal and intellectual in tone, not subjective and sentimental, and impeccable in form.

Parnassus mountain in central Greece, height 2,457 m/8,200 ft, revered by the ancient Greeks as the abode of Apollo and the Muses. The sacred site of Delphi lies on its southern flank.

Parnell Charles Stewart 1846–1891. Irish nationalist politician. He supported a policy of obstruction and violence to attain ◊Home Rule, and became the president of the Nationalist Party 1877. In 1879 he approved the ◊Land League, and his attitude led to his imprisonment 1881. His career was ruined 1890 when he was cited as co-respondent in a divorce case.

Parnell, born in County Wicklow, was elected member of Parliament for Meath 1875. He welcomed Gladstone's Home Rule Bill, and continued his agitation after its defeat 1886. In 1887 his reputation suffered from an unfounded accusation by *The Times* of complicity in the murder of Lord Frederick ◊Cavendish, chief secretary to the Lord-lieutenant of Ireland. Three years later came the adultery scandal, and for fear of losing the support of Gladstone, Parnell's party deposed him. He died suddenly of rheumatic fever at the age of 45. ▷*See feature on pp. 550–551.*

parrot **The grey parrot of the lowland forest and savanna of Kenya and Tanzania. Large flocks roost together in the trees at the forest edge, or on small river or lake islands. At sunrise, the birds fly off in pairs to search for food. They eat seeds, nuts, berries, and fruit, particularly the fruit of the oil palm.**

parole conditional release of a prisoner from jail. The prisoner remains on licence until the date release would have been granted, and may be recalled if the authorities deem it necessary.

In the UK, the granting of parole is discretionary and is usually considered after one-third of the prisoner's sentence has been served. The Criminal Justice Bill 1991 provided for prisoners serving less than four years to be released after half their sentence had been served, and others after two-thirds of their sentence.

parquetry geometric version of ◊marquetry: a decorative veneer applied to furniture and floors, composed of shaped pieces of wood or other suitable materials, such as bone, horn, or ivory, to form a geometric pattern or mosaic.

Parquetry was first practised in Germany and the Low Countries; it was introduced from there to France in the 17th century, and to England around 1675.

Parr Catherine 1512–1548. Sixth wife of Henry VIII of England. She had already lost two husbands when in 1543 she married Henry VIII. She survived him, and in 1547 married Lord Seymour of Sudeley (1508–1549).

parrot tropical bird found mainly in Australia and South America. These colourful birds have been valued as pets in the Western world for many centuries. Parrots have the ability to imitate human speech. They are mainly vegetarian, and range in size from the 8.5 cm/3.5 in pygmy parrot to the 100 cm/40 in Amazon parrot. The smaller species are commonly referred to as ◊parakeets. The plumage is often very colourful, and the call is usually a harsh screech. In most species the sexes are indistinguishable. Several species are endangered. Parrots are members of the family Psittacidae, of the order Psittaciformes.

Parrots all have powerful hooked bills and feet adapted for tree climbing. The bill, with its elongated tip, is well adapted in most parrots for tearing up fruit and cracking nuts, and in a number of species the tongue is highly specialized for extracting honey by means of a brushlike tip.

unusual parrots The ◊kakapo of New Zealand is flightless and usually lives on the ground, though it can still climb trees. The ◊kea, another New Zealand parrot, differs from the rest of the group in having developed carnivorous habits.

Parry William Edward 1790–1855. English admiral and Arctic explorer. He made detailed charts during explorations of the Northwest Passage (the sea route between the Atlantic and Pacific oceans) 1819–20, 1821–23, and 1824–25. He made an attempt to reach the North Pole 1827. The Parry Islands, Northwest Territories, Canada, are named after him.

parsec in astronomy, a unit (symbol pc) used for distances to stars and galaxies. One parsec is equal to 3.2616 ◊light years, 2.063×10^5 ◊astronomical units, and 3.086×10^{13} km.

It is the distance at which a star would have a ◊parallax (apparent shift in position) of one second of arc when viewed from two points the same distance apart as the Earth's distance from the Sun; or the distance at which one astronomical unit subtends an angle of one second of arc.

Parsee (Persian *parsi* 'Persian') or ***Parsi*** follower of the religion ◊Zoroastrianism. The Parsees fled from Persia after its conquest by the Arabs, and settled in India in the 8th century AD. About 100,000 Parsees now live mainly in Bombay State.

Parsifal in Germanic mythology, one of the knights who sought the ◊Holy Grail; the father of ◊Lohengrin.

parsley biennial herb *Petroselinum crispum* of the carrot family, Umbelliferae, cultivated for flavouring and its nutrient properties, being rich in vitamin C and minerals. Up to 45 cm/1.5 ft high, it has pinnate, aromatic leaves and yellow umbelliferous flowers.

parsnip temperate Eurasian biennial *Pastinaca sativa* of the carrot family Umbelliferae, with a fleshy edible root.

Parsons Charles Algernon 1854–1931. English engineer who invented the Parsons steam ◊turbine 1884, a landmark in marine engineering and later universally used in electricity generation to drive an alternator.

Parsons developed more efficient screw propellers for ships and suitable gearing to widen the turbine's usefulness, both on land and sea. He also designed searchlights and optical instruments, and developed methods for the production of optical glass.

Parsons Talcott 1902–1979. US sociologist who attempted to integrate all the social sciences into a science of human action. He was converted to ◊functionalism under the influence of the anthropologist Bronislaw Malinowski.

In *The Social System* 1951, Parsons argued that the crucial feature of societies, as of biological organisms, is homeostasis (maintaining a stable state), and that their parts can be understood only in terms of the whole.

parthenocarpy in botany, the formation of fruits without seeds. This phenomenon, of no obvious benefit to the plant, occurs naturally in some plants, such as bananas. It can also be induced in some fruit crops, either by breeding or by applying certain plant hormones.

parthenogenesis development of an ovum (egg) without any genetic contribution from a male. Parthenogenesis is the normal means of reproduction in a few plants (for example, dandelions) and animals (for example, certain fish). Some sexually reproducing species, such as aphids, show parthenogenesis at some stage in their life cycle to accelerate reproduction to take advantage of good conditions.

Parthenon temple of Athena Parthenos ('the Virgin') on the Acropolis at Athens; built 447–438 BC by Callicrates and Ictinus under the supervision of the sculptor ◊Phidias, and the most perfect example of Doric architecture. In turn a Christian church and a Turkish mosque, it was then used as a gunpowder store, and reduced to ruins when the Venetians bombarded the Acropolis 1687. The ◊Elgin marbles were removed from the Parthenon in the early 19th century and are now in the British Museum, London.

Parthia ancient country in W Asia in what is now NE Iran, capital Ctesiphon. Parthian ascendancy began with the Arsacid dynasty in 248 BC, and reached the peak of its power under Mithridates I in the 2nd century BC; the region was annexed to Persia under the Sassanians AD 226.

Parthian horse riders feigned retreat and shot their arrows unexpectedly backwards, hence the use of 'Parthian shot' to mean a remark delivered in parting. Parthian administration was influenced by the Seleucid empire in Syria and later they successfully resisted the Romans.

particle detector one of a number of instruments designed to detect subatomic particles and track their paths; they include the ◊cloud chamber, ◊bubble chamber, ◊spark chamber, and multiwire chamber.

The earliest particle detector was the cloud chamber, which contains a super-saturated vapour in which particles leave a trail of droplets, in much the same way that a jet aircraft leaves a trail of vapour in the sky. A bubble chamber contains a superheated liquid in which a particle leaves a trail of bubbles. A spark chamber contains a series of closely-packed parallel metal plates, each at a high voltage. As particles pass through the chamber, they leave a visible spark between the plates. A modern multiwire chamber consists of an array of fine, closely-packed wires, each at a high voltage. As a particle passes through the chamber, it produces an electrical signal in the wires. A computer analyses the signal and reconstructs the path of the particles. Multiwire detectors can be used to detect X-ray and gamma rays, and are used as detectors in ◊positron emission tomography (PET).

particle physics study of the particles that make up all atoms, and of their interactions. More than 300 subatomic particles have now been identified by physicists, categorized into several classes according to their mass, electric charge, spin, magnetic moment, and interaction. Subatomic particles include the ◊elementary particles (◊quarks, ◊leptons, and ◊gauge bosons), which are believed to be indivisible and so may be considered the fundamental units of matter; and the ◊hadrons (baryons, such as the proton and neutron, and mesons), which are composite particles, made up of two or three quarks.

The proton, electron, and neutrino are the only stable particles (the neutron being stable only when in the atomic nucleus). The unstable particles decay rapidly into other particles, and are known from experiments with particle accelerators and cosmic radiation. See ◊atomic structure.

Pioneering research took place at the Cavendish laboratory, Cambridge, England. In 1897 English physicist Joseph John Thomson discovered that all atoms contain identical, negatively charged particles (◊electrons), which can easily be freed. By 1911 New Zealand physicist Ernest Rutherford had shown that the electrons surround a very small, positively-charged ◊nucleus. In the case of hydrogen, this was found to consist of a single positively charged particle, a ◊proton. The nuclei of other elements are made up of protons and uncharged particles called ◊neutrons.

1932 also saw the discovery of a particle (whose existence had been predicted by British theoretical physicist Paul Dirac in 1928) with the mass of an electron, but an equal and opposite charge – the ◊positron. This was the first example of ◊antimatter; it is now believed that almost all particles have corresponding antiparticles. In 1934 Italian–US physicist Enrico Fermi argued that a hitherto unsuspected particle, the ◊neutrino, must accompany electrons in beta-emission.

particles and fundamental forces By the mid-1930s, four types of fundamental ◊force interacting between particles had been identified. The ◊electromagnetic force acts between all particles with electric charge, and is thought to be related to the exchange between these particles of ◊gauge bosons called ◊photons, packets of electromagnetic radiation.

In 1935 Japanese physicist Hideki Yukawa suggested that the ◊strong nuclear force (binding protons and neutrons together in the nucleus) was transmitted by the exchange of particles with a mass about one-tenth of that of a proton; these particles, called ◊pions (originally pi mesons), were found by British physicist Cecil Powell in 1946. Yukawa's theory was largely superseded from 1973 by the theory of ◊quantum chromodynamics, which postulates that the strong nuclear force is transmitted by the exchange of gauge bosons called ◊gluons between the quarks and antiquarks making up protons and neutrons. Theoretical work on the ◊weak nuclear force began with Enrico Fermi in the 1930s. The existence of the gauge bosons that carry this force, the ◊weakons (W and Z particles), was confirmed in 1983 at CERN, the European nuclear research organization. The fourth fundamental force, ◊gravity, is experienced by all matter; the postulated carrier of this force has been named the ◊graviton.

leptons The electron, muon, tau, and their neutrinos comprise the ◊leptons – particles with half-integral spin that 'feel' the weak nuclear force but not the strong force. The muon (found by US physicist Carl Anderson in cosmic radiation in 1937) produces the muon neutrino when it decays; the tau, a surprise discovery of the 1970s, produces the tau neutrino when it decays.

mesons and baryons The hadrons (particles that 'feel' the strong nuclear force) were found in the 1950s and 1960s. They are classified into ◊mesons, with whole-number or zero spins, and ◊baryons (which include protons and neutrons), with half-integral spins. It was shown in the early 1960s that if hadrons of the same spin are represented as points on suitable charts, simple patterns are formed. This symmetry enabled a hitherto unknown baryon, the omega-minus, to be predicted from a gap in one of the patterns; it duly turned up in experiments.

quarks In 1964, US physicists Murray Gell-Mann and George Zweig suggested that all hadrons were built from three 'flavours' of a new particle with half-integral spin and a charge of magnitude either ⅓ or ⅔ that of an electron; Gell-Mann named the particle the quark. Mesons are quark–antiquark pairs (spins either add to one or cancel to zero), and baryons are quark triplets. To account for new mesons such as the psi (J) particle the number of quark flavours had risen to six by 1985.

particle, subatomic in physics, a particle that is smaller than an atom; see ◊particle physics.

partisan member of an armed group that operates behind enemy lines or in occupied territories during wars. The name 'partisans' was first given to armed bands of Russians who operated against Napoleon's army in Russia during 1812, but has since been used to describe Russian, Yugoslav, Italian, Greek, and Polish Resistance groups against the Germans during World War II. In Yugoslavia the communist partisans under their leader, Tito, played a major role in defeating the Germans.

part of speech grammatical function of a word, described in the grammatical tradition of the Western world, based on Greek and Latin. The four major parts of speech are the noun, verb, adjective, and adverb; the minor parts of speech vary according to schools of grammatical theory, but include the article, conjunction, preposition, and pronoun.

In languages like Greek and Latin, the part of speech of a word tends to be invariable (usually marked by an ending, or ◊inflection); in English, it is much harder to recognize the function of a word simply by its form.

Some English words may have only one function (for example, *and* as a conjunction). Others may have several functions (for example, *fancy*, which is a noun in the phrase 'flights of *fancy*', a verb in '*Fancy* that!' and an adjective in 'a *fancy* hat').

Parton Dolly Rebecca 1946– . US country singer and songwriter. Her combination of cartoonlike sex-symbol looks and intelligent, assertive lyrics made her popular beyond the genre, with hits like 'Jolene' 1974, but deliberate crossover attempts were less successful. She has also appeared in films, beginning with *9 to 5* 1980.

partridge any of various medium-sized ground-dwelling fowl of the family Phasianidae, order Galliformes, that also includes pheasants, quail, and chickens. Partridges are Old World birds, some of which have become naturalized in North America.

Partridges pair early in the year. The nest is made on the ground and contains 10–20 olive brown eggs. The young remain with their parents for some months, forming coveys of about 20 birds.

Two species common in the UK are the grey partridge *Perdix perdix*, with mottled brown back, grey speckled breast, and patches of chestnut on the sides, and the French partridge *Alectoris rufa*, distinguished by its red legs, bill, and eyelids. The back is plain brown, the throat white edged with black, and the sides barred chestnut and black. The wings are rounded and short. *See illustration on following page.*

Parvati in Hindu mythology, the consort of Siva in one of her gentler manifestations, and the mother of Ganesa, the god of prophecy; she is said to be the daughter of the Himalayas.

PASCAL (French acronym for ***program appliqué à la selection et la compilation automatique de la littérature***) a high-level computer-programming language. Designed by Niklaus Wirth (1934–) in the 1960s as an aid to teaching programming, it is still widely used as such in universities, and as a good general-purpose programming language. Most professional programmers, however, now use ◊C or C++. Pascal was named after 17th-century French mathematician Blaise Pascal.

pascal SI unit (symbol Pa) of pressure, equal to one newton per square metre. It replaces ◊bars and millibars (10^5 Pa equals one bar). It is named after the French mathematician Blaise Pascal.

Pascal Blaise 1623–1662. French philosopher and mathematician. He contributed to the development of hydraulics, the ◊calculus, and the mathematical theory of ◊probability.

In mathematics, Pascal is known for his work on conic sections and, with Pierre de Fermat, on the probability theory. In physics, Pascal's chief work concerned fluid pressure and hydraulics. Pascal's principle states that the pressure everywhere in a fluid is the same, so that pressure applied at one point is transmitted equally to all parts of the container. This is the principle of the hydraulic press and jack.

Pascal's triangle is a triangular array of numbers in which each number is the sum of the pair of numbers above it. When plotted at equal distances along a horizontal axis, the numbers in the rows give the binomial probability distribution (with equal probability of success and failure) of an event, such as the result of tossing a coin. *See illustration on following page.*

parthenogenesis During spring and summer female aphids such as this *Macrosiphum cholodkovskyi* produce a continuous succession of offspring by parthenogenesis, but mate and lay eggs before the onset of winter. *Premaphotos Wildlife*

Parthenon Seriously damaged by war during the 17th century, and stripped of its sculptured friezes in the 19th century, the temple of the Parthenon in Athens is now being seriously damaged by atmospheric pollution. Dedicated to Athena, the goddess who protected Athens, it was built on the Acropolis in the 5th century BC, the golden age of ancient Greek civilization. *UNESCO*

partridge Partridges are native to Europe and Asia, and have been introduced to North America. This French or red-legged partridge *Alectoris rufa* has been widely introduced into the British Isles. Like all partridges, it nests on the ground. *Premaphotos Wildlife*

‘In the field of observation, chance favours only the prepared mind.’

LOUIS PASTEUR
Lecture, 1854

Pascal In Pascal's triangle, each number is the sum of the two numbers immediately above it, left and right – for example, 2 is the sum of 1 and 1, and 4 is the sum of 3 and 1. Furthermore, the sum of each row equals a power of 2 – for example, the sum of the 3rd row is $4 = 2^2$; the sum of the 4th row is $8 = 2^3$.

1
1 1
1 2 1
1 3 3 1
1 4 6 4 1
1 5 10 10 5 1
1 6 15 20 15 6 1
1 7 21 35 35 21 7 1

pas de deux (French ‘step for two’) dance for two performers. Codified by Marius ◊Petipa into the *grand pas de deux*, the dance opens with the ballerina and her male partner dancing together. It continues with display solos, firstly for the man and then the woman, and ends with the two dancing together again.

Pashto language or ***Pushto*** or ***Pushtu*** Indo-European language, the official language of Afghanistan, also spoken in N Pakistan.

Pasiphae in Greek mythology, the wife of King Minos of Crete and mother of Phaedra and of the ◊Minotaur, the monstrous offspring of her sexual union with a bull sent from the sea by the god Poseidon.

Pasolini Pier Paolo 1922–1975. Italian film director, poet, and novelist. His early work is coloured by his experience of life in the poor districts of Rome, where he lived from 1950. From his Marxist viewpoint, he illustrates the decadence and inequality of society, set in a world ravaged by violence and sexuality. Among his films are *Il vangelo secondo Mateo/The Gospel According to St Matthew* 1964, *The Decameron* 1970, *I racconti de Canterbury/The Canterbury Tales* 1972, and *Salò/Salo – The 120 Days of Sodom* 1975, which included explicit scenes of sexual perversion.

Pasolini's writings include the novels *Ragazzi di vita/The Ragazzi* 1955 and *Una vita violenta/A Violent Life* 1959, filmed with success as *Accattone* 1961.

pasqueflower plant *Pulsatilla vulgaris* of the buttercup family. A low-growing hairy perennial, it has feathery leaves and large purple bell-shaped flowers that start erect, then droop. Found in Europe and Asia, it is characteristic of grassland on limy soil.

Passchendaele, Battle of in World War I, successful but costly British operation to capture the Passchendaele ridge in western Flanders, part of the third battle of ◊Ypres Oct–Nov 1917; British casualties numbered nearly 400,000. The name is often erroneously applied to the whole of the battle of Ypres, but Passchendaele was in fact just part of that battle.

Control of the ridge, some 60 m/200 ft high, gave the Germans command of the Allied lines. Hence, its capture was an important target of the British strategy during the third battle of Ypres. It was re-taken by the Germans March 1918 and recovered again by the Belgians Oct 1918.

passion flower climbing plant of the tropical American genus *Passiflora*, family Passifloraceae. It bears distinctive flower heads comprising a saucer-shaped petal base, a fringelike corona, and a central stalk bearing the stamens and ovary. Some species produce edible fruit.

passion play play representing the death and resurrection of Jesus, performed on Good Friday throughout medieval Europe. It has its origins in medieval ◊mystery plays. Traditionally, a passion play takes place every ten years at ◊Oberammergau, Germany.

passive smoking inhalation of tobacco smoke from other people's cigarettes; see ◊smoking.

pass laws South African laws that required the black population to carry passbooks (identity documents) at all times and severely restricted freedom of movement. The laws, a major cause of discontent, formed a central part of the policies of ◊apartheid. They were repealed 1986.

Passover also called ***Pesach*** in Judaism, an eight-day spring festival which commemorates the exodus of the Israelites from Egypt and the passing over by the Angel of Death of the Jewish houses, so that only the Egyptian firstborn sons were killed, in retribution for Pharaoh's murdering of all Jewish male infants.

pasta food made from a dough of durum-wheat flour or semolina, water, and, sometimes egg, and cooked in boiling water. It is usually served with a sauce. Pasta is available either fresh or dried. It may be creamy yellow or coloured green with spinach or red with tomato. Pasta has been used in Italian cooking since the Middle Ages.

Italian pasta shapes include narrow strands (spaghetti, vermicelli), flat sheets or ribbons (lasagne, tagliatelle, fettucine), shell-shaped (conchiglie, lumache), butterfly-shaped (farfalle), tubular (cannelloni, macaroni, penne), and twisted (fusilli). Some varieties are sold ready stuffed with a meat, cheese, herb, or vegetable filling (ravioli, agnolotti, tortellini). Some types of Far Eastern pasta are made from buckwheat.

passion flower These climbing, vinelike plants derive their name from the ‘passion’ or sufferings of Jesus at the crucifixion. Spanish missionaries to South America, where many species grow, thought the flowers resembled the crown of thorns and the wounds on Jesus' body. Some species are cultivated for their edible fruits or decorative flowers.

pastel sticklike drawing or painting material consisting of ground pigment bound with gum; also works produced in this medium. Pastel is a form of painting in dry colours and produces a powdery surface, which is delicate and difficult to conserve. Exponents include Rosalba Carriere (1675–1785), La Tour, Chardin, Degas, and Mary Cassatt.

The use of coloured chalks has a long history, and many European old masters used them to heighten the effect of a drawing (for example Holbein in his portrait drawings). Red, black, and white chalks were used with beautiful effect by Watteau. The more elaborate pastel painting was popularized in 18th-century France by the Venetian painter Rosalba Carriera. Quentin de la Tour is its most famous exponent. In more modern times it has been practised by Degas, Toulouse-Lautrec, Millet and Whistler, Degas finding pastel especially congenial in some of his most beautiful ballet scenes and in his nude studies, on account of the swift and free handling it allowed, and the fresh and luminous effects it produced.

Pasteur Louis Pasteur, from a cartoon in *Vanity Fair* 1877. He is shown with two of the rabbits used for his research on rabies which led to the production of a vaccine against the disease. *Image Select (UK) Ltd*

Pasternak Boris Leonidovich 1890–1960. Russian poet and novelist. His novel *Dr Zhivago* 1957 was banned in the USSR as a ‘hostile act’, and was awarded a Nobel prize (which Pasternak declined). The ban on *Dr Zhivago* has since been lifted and Pasternak has been posthumously rehabilitated.

Pasteur Louis 1822–1895. French chemist and microbiologist who discovered that fermentation is caused by microorganisms and developed the germ theory of disease. He also created a vaccine for ◊rabies, which led to the foundation of the Pasteur Institute in Paris 1888.

Pasteur saved the French silkworm industry by identifying two microbial diseases that were decimating the worms. He discovered the pathogens responsible for ◊anthrax and chicken cholera, and developed vaccines for these diseases. He inspired his pupil Joseph ◊Lister's work in antiseptic surgery. ***Pasteurization*** to make dairy products free from the tuberculosis bacteria is based on his discoveries. See also ◊food technology.

pasteurization treatment of food to reduce the number of microorganisms it contains and so protect consumers from disease. Harmful bacteria are killed and the development of others is delayed. For milk, the method involves heating it to 72°C/161°F for 15 seconds followed by rapid cooling to 10°C/50°F or lower. The process also kills beneficial bacteria and reduces the nutritive property of milk.

The experiments of Louis Pasteur on wine and beer in the 1850s and 1860s showed how heat treatment slowed the multiplication of bacteria and thereby the process of souring. Pasteurization of milk made headway in the dairy industries of Scandinavia and the USA before 1900 because of the realization that it also killed off bacteria associated with the diseases of tuberculosis, typhoid, diphtheria, and dysentery.

pastoral(e) work of art, literature, music, or a musical play that depicts the countryside or rural life, often in an idyllic way. Pastoral scenes were popular in classical Greece and Rome (for instance, Virgil's *Eclogues*), and again in the 15th to 18th centuries (for example, ◊Handel's masque *Acis and Galatea* 1718). They were frequently peopled with shepherds and shepherdesses or with mythological figures, such as nymphs and satyrs.

pastoral farming the rearing or keeping of animals in order to obtain meat or other products, such as milk, skins, and hair. Animals can be kept in one place or periodically moved (◊nomadic pastoralism).

Patagonia geographic area of South America, S of latitude 40° S, with sheep farming, and coal and oil resources. Uranium ore deposit was found in 1993. Sighted by Ferdinand Magellan 1520, it was claimed by both Argentina and Chile until divided between them 1881.

Pataliputra ancient N Indian city, founded c. 490 BC as a small fort (Pataligrama) near the river Ganges within ◊Magadha *janapada* (kingdom). It became the capital for both the Mauryan dynasty under Chandragupta and, later, of the imperial Guptas. During the reign of Emperor Aśoka in the 3rd century BC, it was the world's largest city, with a population of 150,000–300,000. As Patna, it remains an important regional centre.

patchouli soft-wooded E Indian shrub *Pogostemon heyneanus* of the mint family Labiateae, source of the perfume patchouli.

patella or ***kneecap*** flat bone embedded in the knee tendon of birds and mammals, which protects the joint from injury.

patent or ***letters patent*** documents conferring the exclusive right to make, use, and sell an invention for a limited period. Ideas are not eligible; neither is anything not new. The earliest known patent for an invention in England is dated 1449 (granted by Henry VI for making stained glass for Eton College).

The purpose of patenting is to encourage business to take the risk of breaking new ground; it also has the effect of spreading technological knowledge, because the details of the invention have to be made public.

The UK Patent Office was set up 1852, and is based in Newport, Wales. It protects patents (in the UK only) for 20 years, and also deals with designs and trademarks. The Patents Act 1977 requires that an invention should be new, should not be obvious, and should be capable of industrial application. In order to be registered it must also be accompanied by a specification. The British Technology Group (BTG) was set up 1967 to protect and commercialize the inventions of research bodies such as universities and polytechnics.

In the USA the period of patent is 17 years. Each patent application is checked to ensure that it does not conflict with any other application, and applicants may be challenged to prove the precedence of their inventions.

Pater Walter Horatio 1839–1894. English scholar, essayist and art critic. He published *Studies in the History of the Renaissance* 1873, which expressed the idea of 'art for art's sake' that influenced the ◊Aesthetic Movement. His other works include the novel *Marius the Epicurean* 1885, in which the solitary hero, living under the Roman imperium of Marcus Aurelius, meditates on beauty, Paganism, and Christianity; *Imaginary Portraits* 1887; *Appreciations with an Essay on Style* 1889; and *Plato and Platonism* 1893. *Greek Studies* and *Miscellaneous Studies* appeared posthumously 1895.

Pathan a people of NW Pakistan and Afghanistan, numbering about 14 million (1984). The majority are Sunni Muslims. The Pathans speak Pashto, a member of the Indo-Iranian branch of the Indo-European family.

The Pathans comprise distinct groups, some living as nomads with herds of goats and camels, while others are farmers. Formerly a constant threat to the British Raj, the Pakistani Pathans are now claiming independence, with the Afghani Pathans, in their own state of ◊Pakhtoonistan, although this has not yet been recognized.

Pathé Charles 1863–1957. French film pioneer. He began his career selling projectors 1896 and with the profits formed Pathé Frères with his brothers. In 1901 he embarked on film production and by 1908 had become the world's biggest producer, with branches worldwide. He also developed an early colour process and established a weekly newsreel, *Pathé Journal*. During World War I he faced stiff competition from the USA, and his success in Europe suffered as a consequence of the war. In 1929 he handed over control of his company, which continued to produce a large number of films after his retirement.

Pathé *An item from the Pathé weekly newsreel reporting Neville Chamberlain's return from the Munich conference Sept 1938. Image Select (UK) Ltd*

pathetic fallacy in the arts, the presentation of natural events and objects as controlled by human emotions, so that in some way they express human sorrow or joy ('a brave little snowdrop'; 'the heavens smiled on our enterprise'). The phrase was coined by the English critic John ◊Ruskin in *Modern Painters* 1843–60, to describe the ascription of human feelings to the outside world.

pathogen (Greek 'disease producing') in medicine, any microorganism that causes disease. Most pathogens are ◊parasites, and the diseases they cause are incidental to their search for food or shelter inside the host. Nonparasitic organisms, such as soil bacteria or those living in the human gut and feeding on waste foodstuffs, can also become pathogenic to a person whose immune system or liver is damaged. The larger parasites that can cause disease, such as nematode worms, are not usually described as pathogens.

pathology medical speciality concerned with the study of disease processes and how these provoke structural and functional changes in the body.

patina effect produced on bronze by oxidation, which turns the surface green, and by extension any lacquering or finishing technique, other than gilding, applied to bronze objects. Patina can also mean the surface texture of old furniture, silver, and antique objects.

Patmos Greek island in the Aegean Sea, one of the Dodecanese; the chief town is Hora. St John is said to have written the New Testament Book of Revelation while in exile here.

Patna capital of Bihar state, India, on the river Ganges; population (1991) 917,000. It has remains of a hall built by the emperor Aśoka in the 3rd century BC, when it was called ◊Pataliputra.

Paton Alan Stewart 1903–1988. South African writer. His novel *Cry, the Beloved Country* 1948 focused on racial inequality in South Africa. Later books include the study *Land and People of South Africa* 1956 and *The Long View* 1968; *Debbie Go Home* 1961 (short stories); political and social studies; and his autobiography *Towards the Mountain* 1980.

Patou Jean 1880–1936. French clothes designer. He opened a fashion house 1919 and was an overnight success. His swimsuits and innovative designs were popular in the 1920s and he dominated both the couture and the ready-to-wear sectors of the fashion world until his death. He had a great influence on the designers he employed, many of whom went on to make names for themselves.

Patras (Greek ***Pátrai***) industrial city (hydroelectric installations, textiles, paper) in the NW Peloponnese region, Greece, on the Gulf of Patras; population (1991) 155,200. The ancient Patrai, it is the only one of the 12 cities of the ancient Greek province of ◊Achaea to survive.

patriarch (Greek 'ruler of a family') in the Old Testament, one of the ancestors of the human race, and especially those of the ancient Hebrews, from Adam to Abraham, Isaac, Jacob, and his sons (who became patriarchs of the Hebrew tribes). In the Eastern Orthodox Church, the term refers to the leader of a national church.

patriarchy (Greek 'rule of the father') form of social organization in which a man heads and controls the family unit. By extension, in a patriarchal society men also control larger social and working groups as well as government. The definition has been broadened by feminists to describe the dominance of male values throughout society.

patrician member of a privileged class in ancient Rome, which originally dominated the ◊Senate. During the 5th and 4th centuries BC many of the rights formerly exercised by the patricians alone were extended to the plebeians, and patrician descent became a matter of prestige.

Patrick, St c. 389–c. 461. Patron saint of Ireland. Born in Britain, probably in S Wales, he was carried off by pirates to six years' slavery in Antrim, Ireland, before escaping either to Britain or Gaul – his poor Latin suggests the former – to train as a missionary. He is variously said to have landed again in Ireland 432 or 456, and his work was a vital factor in the spread of Christian influence there. His symbols are snakes and shamrocks; feast day 17 March.

Patriot missile ground-to-air medium-range missile system used in air defence. It has high-altitude coverage, electronic jamming capability, and excellent mobility. US Patriot missiles were tested in battle against Scud missiles fired by the Iraqis in the 1991 Gulf War. They successfully intercepted 24 Scud missiles out of about 85 attempts.

patronage power to give a favoured appointment to an office or position in politics, business, or the church; or sponsorship of the arts. Patronage was for centuries bestowed mainly by individuals (in Europe often royal or noble) or by the church. In the 20th century, patrons have tended to be political parties, the state, and – in the arts – private industry and foundations.

In Britain, where it was nicknamed 'Old Corruption', patronage existed in the 16th century, but was most common from the Restoration of 1660 to the 19th century, when it was used to manage elections and ensure party support. Patronage was used not only for the preferment of friends, but also as a means of social justice, often favouring, for example, the families of those in adversity. Political patronage has largely been replaced by a system of meritocracy (in which selection is by open competition rather than by personal recommendation).

Patronage survives today in the political honours system (awards granted to party supporters) and the appointment of university professors, leaders of national corporations, and government bodies or quangos, which is often by invitation rather than by formal application. Selection on grounds other than solely the basis of ability lives on today with the practice of positive discrimination.

Patten Chris(topher Francis) 1944– . British Conservative politician, governor of Hong Kong 1992–97. He was Conservative Party chair 1990–92, orchestrating the party's campaign for the 1992 general election, in which he lost his parliamentary seat. He accepted the governorship of Hong Kong for the crucial five years prior to its transfer to China. His prodemocracy, anti-Chinese stance won the backing of many Hong Kong residents, but was criticized by members of its business community.

Patterson P J (Percival James) 1935– . Jamaican politician and lawyer, prime minister from 1992. In spite of financial scandal and his subsequent resignation from the post of finance minister 1991, he was elected prime minister by an overwhelming majority 1992 and successfully fought a general election in the following year.

'To burn always with this hard, gemlike flame, to maintain this ecstasy, is success in life.'

Walter Pater
Studies in the History of the Renaissance

When I was a child, I spake as a child, I understood as a child, I thought as a child; but when I became a man, I put away childish things.

St Paul
New Testament
1 Corinthians 13:11

Patton George Smith 1885–1945. US general in World War II, known as 'Blood and Guts'. During World War I, he formed the first US tank force and led it in action 1918. He was appointed to command the 2nd Armored Division 1940 and became commanding general of the First Armored Corps 1941. In 1942 he led the Western Task Force that landed at Casablanca, Morocco. After commanding the 7th Army in the invasion of Sicily, he led the 3rd Army across France and into Germany, and in 1945 took over the 15th Army.

Paul 1901–1964. King of the Hellenes (Greece) from 1947, when he succeeded his brother George II. He was the son of Constantine I. In 1938 he married Princess Frederika (1917–), daughter of the Duke of Brunswick.

Paul six popes, including:

Paul VI Giovanni Battista Montini 1897–1978. Pope from 1963. His encyclical *Humanae Vitae/Of Human Life* 1968 reaffirmed the church's traditional teaching on birth control, thus following the minority report of the commission originally appointed by Pope John rather than the majority view.

He was born near Brescia, Italy. He spent more than 25 years in the Secretariat of State under Pius XI and Pius XII before becoming archbishop of Milan in 1954. In 1958 he was created a cardinal by Pope John, and in 1963 he succeeded him as pope, taking the name of Paul as a symbol of ecumenical unity.

Paul I 1754–1801. Tsar of Russia from 1796, in succession to his mother Catherine II. Mentally unstable, he pursued an erratic foreign policy and was assassinated.

Pauling Linus Carl 1901–1994. US theoretical chemist and biologist whose ideas on chemical bonding are fundamental to modern theories of molecular structure. He also investigated the properties and uses of vitamin C as related to human health. He won the Nobel Prize for Chemistry 1954 and the Nobel Peace Prize 1962, having campaigned for a nuclear test-ban treaty.

We are condemned to kill time: thus we die little by little.

Octavio Paz
Cuento de los Jardines

Pauling's work on the nature of the chemical bond included much new information about interatomic distances. Applying his knowledge of molecular structure to proteins in blood, he discovered that many proteins have structures held together with hydrogen bonds, giving them helical shapes.

He was a pioneer in the application of quantum mechanical principles to the structures of molecules, relating them to interatomic distances and bond angles by X-ray and electron diffraction, magnetic effects, and thermochemical techniques. In 1928, Pauling introduced the concept of hybridization of bonds. This provided a clear basic insight into the framework structure of all carbon compounds, that is, of the whole of organic chemistry. He also studied electronegativity of atoms and polarization (movement of electrons) in chemical bonds. Electronegativity values can be used to show why certain substances, such as hydrochloric acid, are acid, whereas others, such as sodium hydroxide, are alkaline. Much of this work was consolidated in his book *The Nature of the Chemical Bond* 1939.

Pauling Double Nobel prize-winning American chemist Linus Pauling. Pauling won the prize for Chemistry in 1954 following his work investigating the nature of the chemical bond. In 1962 he also won the Peace prize following his campaign for a nuclear test ban treaty. *Image Select (UK) Ltd*

Paul, St c. AD 3–c. AD 68. Christian missionary and martyr; in the New Testament, one of the apostles and author of 13 epistles. Originally opposed to Christianity, he took part in the stoning of St Stephen. He is said to have been converted by a vision on the road to Damascus. After his conversion he made great missionary journeys, for example to Philippi and Ephesus, becoming known as the Apostle of the Gentiles (non-Jews). His emblems are a sword and a book; feast day 29 June.

The Jewish form of his name is Saul. He was born in Tarsus (now in Turkey), son of well-to-do Pharisees, and had Roman citizenship. On his return to Jerusalem after his missionary journeys, he was arrested, appealed to Caesar, and (as a citizen) was sent to Rome for trial about 57 or 59. After two years in prison, he may have been released before his final arrest and execution under the emperor Nero.

St Paul's theology was rigorous on such questions as sin and atonement, and his views on the role of women were adopted by the Christian church generally.

Pausanias lived 2nd century AD. Greek geographer, author of a valuably accurate description of Greece compiled from his own travels, *Description of Greece*, also translated as *Itinerary of Greece*.

pavane or ***pavan*** a slow, stately court dance in double time, of Paduan origin, especially popular in Italy and France in the 16th and 17th centuries. Music composed for or derived from the pavane is often coupled with that composed for a galliard, a spirited 16th-century court dance in triple time. Composers include Dowland and Byrd, more recently Ravel, whose *Pavane pour une infante défunte/Pavane for a Dead Infanta* for piano 1899 was orchestrated 1905.

Pavarotti Luciano 1935– . Italian tenor. He has an impressive dynamic range. His operatic roles have included Rodolfo in *La Bohème*, Cavaradossi in *Tosca*, the Duke of Mantua in *Rigoletto*, and Nemorino in *L'Elisir d'amore*. He gave his first performance in the title role of *Otello* in Chicago, USA, 1991. He has done much to popularize opera, performing to wide audiences outside the opera houses including open-air concerts in New York and London city parks.

He collaborated with José Carreras and Placido Domingo in a recording of operatic hits coinciding with the World Cup soccer series in Rome 1990; his rendition of 'Nessun Dorma' from Puccini's *Turandot* was adopted as the theme music for the series.

Pavese Cesare 1908–1950. Italian poet, translator, and novelist. Imprisoned for anti-Fascist journalism, he published his poems *Lavorare stanca/Hard Labour* 1936 on his release. His sensitive translations and critical writings introduced Italian readers to modern English and American writers, notably Joyce and Melville. These writers influenced his fascination with myth, symbol, and archetype.

Pavlov Ivan Petrovich 1849–1936. Russian physiologist who studied conditioned reflexes in animals (see ◊conditioning). His work had a great impact on behavioural theory (see ◊behaviourism) and learning theory. Nobel Prize for Physiology or Medicine 1904.

Pavlova Anna 1881–1931. Russian dancer. Prima ballerina of the Imperial Ballet from 1906, she left Russia 1913, and went on to become one of the world's most celebrated exponents of classical ballet. With London as her home, she toured extensively with her own company, influencing dancers worldwide with roles such as Mikhail ◊Fokine's *The Dying Swan* solo 1907. She was opposed to the modern reforms of Diaghilev's Ballets Russes, adhering strictly to conservative aesthetics.

pawnbroker one who lends money on the security of goods held. The traditional sign of the premises of a pawnbroker is three gold balls, the

Pavarotti The tenor Luciano Pavarotti. The greatest lyric tenor of his generation, Pavarotti has built upon his fame earned in the opera house by giving frequent recitals to mass audiences at outdoor arenas and other venues, and by recording 'Nessun Dorma' for the 1990 World Cup. *Polygram*

symbol used in front of the houses of the medieval Lombard merchants of Italy.

pawpaw or ***papaw*** small tree *Asimina triloba* of the custard-apple family Annonaceae, native to the eastern USA. It bears oblong fruits 13 cm/5 in long with yellowish, edible flesh. The name pawpaw is also used for the ◊papaya.

Pax in Roman mythology, the goddess of peace, equivalent to the Greek ◊Irene.

Paxton Joseph 1801–1865. English architect. He was also garden superintendent to the Duke of Devonshire from 1826. He designed the Great Exhibition building 1851 (the Crystal Palace), which was revolutionary in its structural use of glass and iron.

Pay-As-You-Earn (PAYE) system of tax collection in the UK in which ◊income tax is deducted on a regular basis by the employer from wages before they are paid. PAYE tax deductions are calculated so that when added up they will approximately equal the total amount of tax likely to be due in that year. In the USA this is called withholding tax.

paymaster-general head of the Paymaster-General's Office, the British government department (established 1835) that acts as paying agent for most other departments.

Pays de la Loire agricultural region of W France, comprising the *départements* of Loire-Atlantique, Maine-et-Loire, Mayenne, Sarthe, and Vendée; capital Nantes; area 32,100 sq km/12,391 sq mi; population (1990) 3,059,100. Industries include shipbuilding and wine production.

Paz (Estenssoro) Victor 1907– . President of Bolivia 1952–56, 1960–64, and 1985–89. He founded and led the Movimiento Nacionalista Revolucionario (MNR) which seized power 1952. His regime extended the vote to Indians, nationalized the country's largest tin mines, embarked on a programme of agrarian reform, and brought inflation under control.

Paz Octavio 1914–1998. Mexican poet and essayist. His works reflect many influences, including Marxism, Surrealism, and Aztec mythology. His long poem *Piedra del sol/Sun Stone* 1957 uses contrasting images, centring upon the Aztec Calendar Stone (representing the Aztec universe), to symbolize the loneliness of individuals and their search for union with others. Nobel Prize for Literature 1990.

pea climbing plant *Pisum sativum*, family Leguminosae, with pods of edible seeds, grown since prehistoric times for food. The pea is a popular vegetable and is eaten fresh, canned, dried, or frozen. The sweet pea *Lathyrus odoratus* of the same

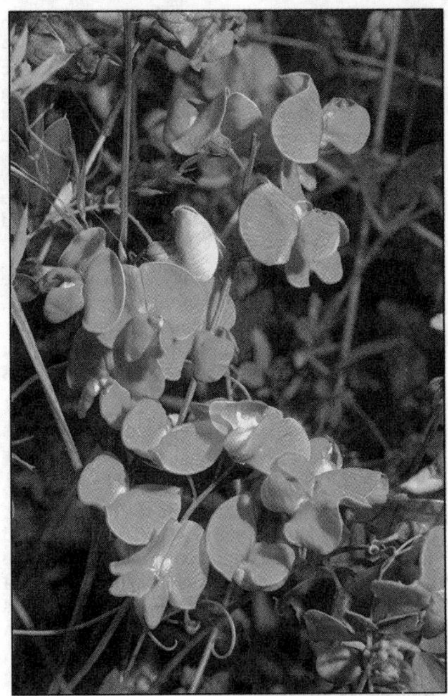

pea The Fyfield pea *Lathyrus tuberosus* is one of a number of large-flowered peas that are now widely grown as ornamental flowers. *Premaphotos Wildlife*

family is grown for its scented, butterfly-shaped flowers.

Peace Corps US organization of trained men and women, established by President Kennedy 1961. The Peace Corps provides skilled volunteer workers for developing countries, especially in the fields of teaching, agriculture, and health, for a period of two years.

Living among the country's inhabitants, workers are paid only a small allowance to cover their basic needs and maintain health. The organization provides around 6,500 volunteers in 94 countries each year; over 140,000 people have been involved since 1961 (1995). The Peace Corps was inspired by the British programme Voluntary Service Overseas.

peace movement collective opposition to war. The Western peace movements of the late 20th century can trace their origins to the pacifists of the 19th century and conscientious objectors during World War I (see ◊pacifism). The campaigns after World War II have tended to concentrate on nuclear weapons, but there are numerous organizations devoted to peace, some wholly pacifist, some merely opposed to escalation.

Opposition to the Vietnam War was a focus of the peace movement in the late 1960s and early 1970s, especially in the USA but also in countries that supported the US role in Vietnam militarily (Australia) or politically (the UK). Support for nuclear disarmament has been strong in Australia and New Zealand.

peach tree *Prunus persica*, family Rosaceae. It has ovate leaves and small, usually pink, flowers. The yellowish edible fruits have thick velvety skins; the nectarine is a smooth-skinned variety.

peacock technically, the male of any of various large ◊pheasants, order Galliformes. The name is most often used for the common peacock *Pavo cristatus*, a bird of the pheasant family, native to S Asia. It is rather larger than a pheasant. The male has a large fan-shaped tail, brightly coloured with blue, green, and purple 'eyes' on a chestnut background, that is raised during courtship displays. The female (peahen) is brown with a small tail.

The hen lays 4–8 eggs in the spring, and incubation takes 30 days. She remains with her chicks eight months. The green peacock, *P. muticus*, native to SE Asia, breeds freely with the common peacock. A third species, *Afropavus congensis*, was discovered in the late 1930s in the Congo forests. These are much smaller than the common peacock and do not have erectile tail coverts.

Peacock Thomas Love 1785–1866. English satirical novelist and poet. His unique whimsical novels are full of paradox, prejudice, curious learning, and witty dialogue, interspersed with occasional poems, and he satirizes contemporary ideas, outlooks, and attitudes in a prevailing comic tone. They include *Headlong Hall* 1816, *Melincourt* 1817, and *Nightmare Abbey* 1818, which has very little plot, consisting almost entirely of conversation expressing points of view on contemporary controversies and society.

He published two romances, *Maid Marian* 1822 and *Misfortunes of Elphin* 1829, but returned to the form of *Headlong Hall* with his last and best novels, *Crotchet Castle* 1831 and *Gryll Grange* 1860.

Peak District tableland of the S Pennines in NW Derbyshire, England. It is a tourist region and a national park (1951). The highest point is Kinder Scout, 636 m/2,088 ft.

Peake Mervyn Laurence 1911–1968. English writer and illustrator. His novels include the grotesque fantasy trilogy *Titus Groan* 1946, *Gormenghast* 1950, and *Titus Alone* 1959, together creating an allegory of the decline of modern civilization. He illustrated most of his own work and produced drawings for an edition of *Treasure Island* 1949, and other works. Among his collections of verse are *The Glassblowers* 1950 and the posthumous *A Book of Nonsense* 1972. He also wrote a play, *The Wit to Woo*, 1957.

peanut or ***groundnut*** or ***monkey nut*** South American vinelike annual plant *Arachis hypogaea*, family Leguminosae. After flowering, the flower stalks bend and force the pods into the earth to ripen underground. The nuts are a staple food in many tropical countries and are widely grown in the S USA. They yield a valuable edible oil and are the basis for numerous processed foods.

pear tree *Pyrus communis*, family Rosaceae, native to temperate regions of Eurasia. It has a succulent edible fruit, less hardy than the apple.

pearl shiny, hard, rounded abnormal growth composed of nacre (or mother-of-pearl), a chalky substance. Nacre is secreted by many molluscs, and deposited in thin layers on the inside of the shell around a parasite, a grain of sand, or some other irritant body. After several years of the mantle (the layer of tissue between the shell and the body mass) secreting this nacre, a pearl is formed.

Although commercially valuable pearls are obtained from freshwater mussels and oysters, most precious pearls come from the various species of the family Pteriidae (the pearl oysters) found in tropical waters off N and W Australia, off the Californian coast, in the Persian Gulf, and in the Indian Ocean. Because of their rarity, large mussel pearls of perfect shape are worth more than those from oysters.

Artificial pearls were first cultivated in Japan in 1893. A tiny bead of shell from a clam, plus a small piece of membrane from another pearl oyster's mantle (to stimulate the secretion of nacre) is inserted in oysters kept in cages in the sea for three years, and then the pearls are harvested.

peanut The peanut, groundnut, or monkey nut is a leguminous perennial plant belonging to the pea family, native to South America. After flowering, its pods bury themselves in the ground where the fruits ripen. The plant is widely cultivated for the kernels which are rich in oil and protein.

Pearl Harbor US Pacific naval base in Oahu, Hawaii, USA, the scene of a Japanese aerial attack 7 Dec 1941, which brought the USA into World War II. The attack took place while Japanese envoys were holding so-called peace talks in Washington. More than 2,000 members of the US armed forces were killed, and a large part of the US Pacific fleet was destroyed or damaged.

The local commanders Admiral Kimmel and Lt-Gen Short were relieved of their posts and held responsible for the fact that the base was totally unprepared at the time of the attack, but recent information indicates that warnings of the attack given to the USA (by British intelligence and others) were withheld from Kimmel and Short by President Roosevelt. US public opinion was very much against entering the war, and Roosevelt wanted an excuse to change popular sentiments and take the USA into the war. The Japanese, angered by US embargoes of oil and other war material and convinced that US entry into the war was inevitable, had hoped to force US concessions. Instead, the attack galvanized public opinion and raised anti-Japanese sentiment to fever pitch.

Pearl Islands group of some 180 islands in the Gulf of Panama, Central America. The main islands are San Miguel (the largest), San José, and Pedro González. The main industries are pearl fishing and sea angling.

Pears Peter Neville Luard 1910–1986. English tenor. He was the life companion of Benjamin ◊Britten and with him co-founded the Aldeburgh Festival. He inspired and collaborated with Britten in a rich catalogue of song cycles and operatic roles, exploiting a distinctively airy and luminous tone, from the title role in *Peter Grimes* 1947 to Aschenbach in *Death in Venice* 1973.

Pearse Patrick Henry 1879–1916. Irish poet. He was prominent in the Gaelic revival, a leader of the ◊Easter Rising 1916. Proclaimed president of the provisional government, he was court-martialled and shot after its suppression.

'The mountain sheep are sweeter, / But the valley sheep are fatter; / We therefore deemed it meeter / To carry off the latter.'

THOMAS LOVE PEACOCK
'The War-Song of Dinas Vawr'

Pearl Harbor USS *West Virginia* after the surprise Japanese attack on the US naval base at Pearl Harbor in Hawaii 7 Dec 1941. Despite its devastating impact, the attack was not the success it might have been since most of the US aircraft carriers, of vital importance in a Pacific war, were out of the harbour on manoeuvres. *Library of Congress*

❛The right Hon. Gentleman caught the Whigs bathing, and walked away with their clothes.❜

On **Robert Peel**
Benjamin Disraeli, speech in House of Commons 28 Feb 1845

Pearson Karl 1857–1936. British statistician who followed Francis ◊Galton in introducing statistics and probability into genetics and who developed the concept of eugenics (improving the human race by selective breeding).

Pearson introduced in 1900 the χ^2 (chi-squared) test to determine whether a set of observed data deviates significantly from what would have been predicted by a 'null hypothesis' (that is, totally at random). He demonstrated that it could be applied to examine whether two hereditary characteristics (such as height and hair colour) were inherited independently.

Pearson Lester Bowles 1897–1972. Canadian politician, leader of the Liberal Party from 1958, prime minister 1963–68. As foreign minister 1948–57, he represented Canada at the United Nations, playing a key role in settling the ◊Suez Crisis 1956. Nobel Peace Prize 1957.

Pearson served as president of the General Assembly 1952–53 and helped to create the UN Emergency Force (UNEF) that policed Sinai following the Egypt–Israel war of 1956. As prime minister, he led the way to formulating a national medicare (health insurance) law.

Peary Robert Edwin 1856–1920. US polar explorer who, after several unsuccessful attempts, became the first person to reach the North Pole on 6 April 1909. In 1988 an astronomer claimed Peary's measurements were incorrect.

Peasants' Revolt the rising of the English peasantry in June 1381, the result of economic, social, and political disillusionment. It was sparked off by the imposition of a new poll tax, three times the rates of those imposed in 1377 and 1379. Led by Wat ◊Tyler and John ◊Ball, rebels from SE England marched on London and demanded reforms. The authorities put down the revolt by deceit and force.

Following the plague of the Black Death, a shortage of agricultural workers led to higher wages. The Statute of Labourers, enacted 1351, attempted to return wages to pre-plague levels. When the third poll tax was enforced 1381, riots broke out all over England, especially in Essex and Kent. Wat Tyler and John Ball emerged as leaders and the rebels went on to London, where they continued plundering, burning John of Gaunt's palace at the Savoy, and taking the prisons at Newgate and Fleet. The young king Richard II attempted to appease the mob, who demanded an end to serfdom and feudalism. The rebels then took the Tower of London and murdered Archbishop Sudbury and Robert Hales. Again the king attempted to make peace at Smithfield, but Tyler was stabbed to death by William Walworth, the Lord Mayor of London. The king made concessions to the rebels, and they dispersed, but the concessions were revoked immediately.

peat fibrous organic substance found in bogs and formed by the incomplete decomposition of plants such as sphagnum moss. N Asia, Canada, Finland, Ireland, and other places have large deposits, which have been dried and used as fuel from ancient times. Peat can also be used as a soil additive.

Peat bogs began to be formed when glaciers retreated, about 9,000 years ago. They grow at the rate of only a millimetre a year, and large-scale digging can result in destruction both of the bog and of specialized plants growing there.

A number of ancient corpses, thought to have been the result of ritual murders, have been found preserved in peat bogs, mainly in Scandinavia. In 1984, Lindow Man, dating from about 500 BC, was found in mainland Britain, near Wilmslow, Cheshire. In 1990 the third largest peat bog in Britain, on the borders of Shropshire and Clwyd, was bought by the Nature Conservancy Council, the largest purchase ever made by the NCC.

Peel Robert Peel, shown here in a contemporary illustration, was the founder in 1834 of the modern Conservative Party. He later split the party over the Corn Laws. *Philip Sauvain*

pecan nut-producing ◊hickory tree *Carya illinoensis* or *C. pecan*, native to central USA and N Mexico and now widely cultivated. The tree grows to over 45 m/150 ft, and the edible nuts are smooth-shelled, the kernel resembling a smoothly ovate walnut.

peccary one of two species of the New World genus *Tayassu* of piglike hoofed mammals. A peccary has a gland in the middle of its back which secretes a strong-smelling substance. Peccaries are blackish in colour, covered with bristles, and have tusks that point downwards. Adults reach a height of 40 cm/16 in, and a weight of 25 kg/60 lb.

Peck (Eldred) Gregory 1916– . US film actor. He specialized in strong, upright characters, but also had a gift for light comedy. His films include *Spellbound* 1945, *Duel in the Sun* 1946, *Gentleman's Agreement* 1947, *Roman Holiday* 1953, *To Kill a Mockingbird* 1962, for which he won an Academy Award, and (cast against type as a Nazi doctor) *The Boys from Brazil* 1974.

Peckinpah Sam (David Samuel) 1926–1984. US film director. Mainly Westerns, his films were usually associated with slow-motion, blood-spurting violence. His best work, such as *The Wild Bunch* 1969, exhibits a magisterial grasp of staging and construction.

pectoral relating to the upper area of the thorax associated with the muscles and bones used in moving the arms or forelimbs, in vertebrates. In birds, the *pectoralis major* is the very large muscle used to produce a powerful downbeat of the wing during flight.

pediment in architecture, the triangular structure crowning the portico of a Classical building. The pediment was a distinctive feature of Greek temples.

Pedro I 1798–1834. Emperor of Brazil 1822–31. The son of John VI of Portugal, he escaped to Brazil on Napoleon's invasion, and was appointed regent 1821. He proclaimed Brazil independent 1822 and was crowned emperor, but abdicated 1831 and returned to Portugal.

Pedro II 1825–1891. Emperor of Brazil 1831–89. He proved an enlightened ruler, but his antislavery measures alienated the landowners, who compelled him to abdicate.

Peeblesshire former county of S Scotland, included from 1975 in Borders Region; Peebles was the county town.

Peel Robert 1788–1850. British Conservative politician. As home secretary 1822–27 and 1828–30, he founded the modern police force and in 1829 introduced Roman Catholic emancipation. He was prime minister 1834–35 and 1841–46, when his repeal of the ◊Corn Laws caused him and his followers to break with the party.

peepul another name for the ◊bo tree.

peerage in the UK, holders, in descending order, of the titles of duke, marquess, earl, viscount, and baron. Some of these titles may be held by a woman in default of a male heir. In the late 19th century the peerage was augmented by the Lords of Appeal in Ordinary (the nonhereditary life peers) and, from 1958, by a number of specially created life peers of either sex (usually long-standing members of the House of Commons). Since 1963 peers have been able to disclaim their titles, usually to enable them to take a seat in the Commons (where peers are disqualified from membership).

peer group in the social sciences, people who have a common identity based on such characteristics as similar social status, interests, age, or ethnic group. The concept has proved useful in analysing the power and influence of co-workers, school friends, and ethnic and religious groups in socialization and social behaviour.

Pegasus in astronomy, a constellation of the northern hemisphere, near Cygnus, and represented as the winged horse of Greek mythology.

Pegasus in Greek mythology, the winged horse that sprang from the blood of the Gorgon Medusa. He was transformed into a constellation.

Hippocrene, the spring of the Muses on Mount Helicon, is said to have sprung from a blow of his hoof.

pegmatite extremely coarse-grained ◊igneous rock of any composition found in veins; pegmatites are usually associated with large granite masses.

Pegu city in S Myanmar on the river Pegu, NE of Yangon; population (1983) 254,762. It was founded 573 and was once an important seaport. It is the site of the celebrated Shwemawdaw pagoda, 99 m/324 ft high and said to contain two of the Buddha's hairs. It was almost completely destroyed by an earthquake 1930 and was rebuilt after World War II. The town also contains the statue of the Reclining Buddha, 55 m/181 ft long.

Pei Ieoh Ming 1917– . Chinese-born US Modernist architect. He is noted for his innovative High-Tech structures, particularly the use of glass walls. His projects include the 70-storey Bank of China, Hong Kong, 1987 – Asia's tallest building at 368 m/1,209 ft – and the glass pyramid in front of the Louvre, Paris, 1989.

Pei became a US citizen 1948. Other works by him are Dallas City Hall, Texas; East Building, National Gallery of Art, Washington DC 1978; John F Kennedy Library Complex and the John Hancock Tower, Boston 1979; and the National Airlines terminal at Kennedy Airport, New York.

Peiping name (meaning 'northern peace') 1928–49 of ◊Beijing in China.

Peirce Charles Sanders 1839–1914. US philosopher and logician, founder of ◊pragmatism (which he later called pragmaticism), who argued that genuine conceptual distinctions must be correlated with some differences of practical effect. He wrote extensively on the logic of scientific enquiry, suggesting that truth could be conceived of as the object of an ultimate consensus.

pekan or ***fisher marten*** North American marten (carnivorous mammal) *Martes penanti* about 1.2 m/4 ft long, with a doglike face, and brown fur with white patches on the chest. It eats porcupines.

Peking alternative transcription of ◊Beijing, the capital of China.

pekingese breed of small long-haired dog first bred at the Chinese court as the 'imperial lion dog'. It has a flat skull and flat face, is typically less than 25 cm/10 in tall, and weighs less than 5 kg/11 lb.

Peking man Chinese representative of an early species of human, found as fossils, 500,000–750,000 years old, in the cave of Choukoutien 1927 near Beijing (Peking). Peking man used chipped stone tools, hunted game, and used fire. Similar varieties of early human have been found in Java and E Africa. Their classification is disputed: some anthropologists classify them as *Homo erectus*, others as *Homo sapiens pithecanthropus*. ▷ *See feature on pp. 518–519.*

Pelagius c. 360–c. 420. British theologian. He taught that each person possesses free will (and hence the possibility of salvation), denying Augustine's doctrines of predestination and original sin. Cleared of heresy by a synod in Jerusalem 415, he was later condemned by the pope and the emperor.

pelargonium flowering plant of the genus *Pelargonium* of the geranium family Geraniaceae, grown extensively in gardens, where it is familiarly known as the geranium. Ancestors of the garden hybrids came from southern Africa.

Pelé Adopted name of Edson Arantes do Nascimento 1940– . Brazilian soccer player. A prolific goal scorer, he appeared in four World Cup competitions 1958–70 and led Brazil to three championships (1958, 1962, 1970). He spent most of his playing career with the Brazilian team Santos, before ending it with the New York Cosmos in the USA.

Pelée, Mont volcano on the island of Martinique in the West Indies; height 1,350 m/4,428 ft. It destroyed the town of St Pierre during its eruption 1902.

Pelham Henry 1696–1754. English Whig politician. He held a succession of offices in Robert Walpole's cabinet 1721–42, and was prime minister 1743–54. An able financier and peace-loving statesman, his influence in the House of Commons was based on systematic corruption rather than ability.

The younger son of Thomas, 1st Baron Pelham, Henry Pelham was educated at Westminster and Oxford. After a short military career, he won the Seaford by-election 1717. Pelham later became member of Parliament for Sussex and was appointed secretary for war 1724. As secretary, Pelham proved valuable as a mediator between his brother, Thomas Pelham-Holles, 1st Duke of ◊Newcastle, and Walpole, whose mutual jealousy led to frequent disputes. In 1730 he was promoted to the post of paymaster of the forces.

Pelham was appointed First Lord of the Treasury and chancellor of the Exchequer 1743, despite the opposition of Walpole's successor John Carteret (1690–1763). The following years were thus spent in collusion with Newcastle, counteracting the Hanoverian policy of Carteret, who was seeking to attain Tory support. Pelham's period in office was one of general pacification. Opposition (including that of King George II) was overcome, an alliance being forged with the Dutch 1744 and then peace concluded with the French in the treaty of Aix-la-Chapelle 1748. This having been established, Pelham devoted himself wholeheartedly to the reduction of national expenditure and the reorganization of the finances.

pelican large water bird of family Pelecanidae, order Pelecaniformes, remarkable for the pouch beneath the bill, which is used as a fishing net and temporary store for catches of fish. Some species grow up to 1.8 m/6 ft and have wingspans of 3 m/ 10 ft.

The legs are short and the feet large, with four webbed toes; the tail is short and rounded, and the neck long. The wings are long and expansive, and the birds are capable of rapid flight. The species are widely distributed, frequenting the seashore and margins of lakes, and feeding almost exclusively on fish, which are deposited in the pouch for subsequent digestion.

Pelion mountain in Thessaly, Greece, near Mount Ossa; height 1,548 m/5,079 ft. In Greek mythology it was the home of the centaurs, creatures half-human and half-horse.

pelican A brown pelican on its nest in Louisiana, USA. This is the smallest of the eight species of pelican, growing to around 127 cm/50 in. It is the only pelican that dives from the air to catch its food – the others simply use their capacious bills as scoops to take fish out of the water. *Corbis*

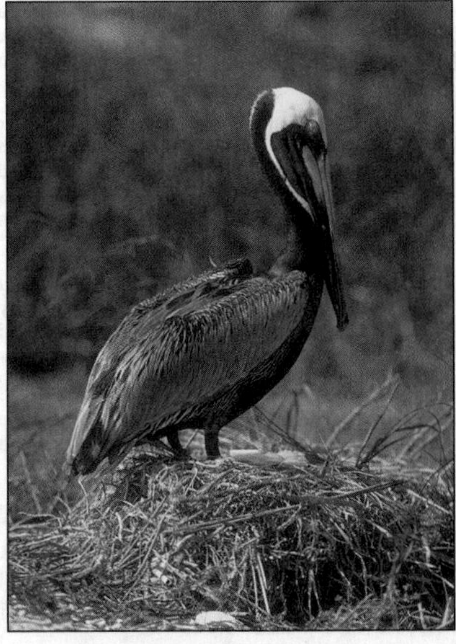

Pella capital of the ancient kingdom of ◊Macedonia. Excavations have revealed many elaborate mosaics at its site, 40 km/25 mi NW of Thessaloniki. It declined after the defeat of Macedonia by Rome 168 BC, and later became a Roman colony.

pellagra chronic disease mostly seen in subtropical countries in which the staple food is maize. It is caused by deficiency of ◊nicotinic acid (one of the B vitamins), which is contained in protein foods, beans and peas, and yeast. Symptoms include diarrhoea, skin eruptions, and mental disturbances.

pellitory-of-the-wall plant *Parietaria judaica* of the nettle family, found growing in cracks in walls and rocks and also on banks, in W and S Europe; it is widely cultivated in gardens. The stems are up to 1 m/3 ft and reddish, the leaves lance-shaped, and the greenish male and female flowers are separate but on the same plant.

Peloponnese (Greek ***Peloponnesos***) peninsula forming the S part of Greece; area 21,549 sq km/8,318 sq mi; population (1991) 1,077,000. It is joined to the mainland by the narrow isthmus of Corinth and is divided into the nomes (administrative areas) of Argolis, Arcadia, Achaea, Elis, Corinth, Lakonia, and Messenia, representing its seven ancient states. It is divided into two regions; Greece West (including Achaea and Elis), and Peloponnese (including Argolis, Arcadia, Corinth, Lakonia, and Messenia).

Peloponnesian War conflict between Athens and Sparta, backed by their respective allies, 431–404 BC, originating in suspicions about the ambitions of the Athenian leader Pericles. It was ended by the Spartan general Lysander's capture of the Athenian fleet in 405, and his starving the Athenians into surrender in 404. Sparta's victory meant the destruction of the political power of Athens.

pelota or *jai alai* ('merry festival') very fast ball game of Basque derivation, popular in Latin American countries and in the USA where it is a betting sport. It is played by two, four, or six players, in a walled court, or *cancha*, and somewhat resembles squash, but each player uses a long, curved, wickerwork basket, or *cesta*, strapped to the hand, to hurl the ball, or pelota, against the walls.

Peltier effect in physics, a change in temperature at the junction of two different metals produced when an electric current flows through them. The extent of the change depends on what the conducting metals are, and the nature of change (rise or fall in temperature) depends on the direction of current flow. It is the reverse of the ◊Seebeck effect. It is named after the French physicist Jean Charles Peltier (1785–1845) who discovered it 1834.

pelvis in vertebrates, the lower area of the abdomen featuring the bones and muscles used to move the legs or hindlimbs. The pelvic girdle is a set of bones that allows movement of the legs in relation to the rest of the body and provides sites for the attachment of relevant muscles.

Pembrokeshire unitary authority of Wales created 1996 *(see United Kingdom map)*.

penal colony settlement established to receive transported convicts and built in part through convict labour. Examples include a British settlement in New South Wales, Australia, 1788–1857; Devil's Island, a former French penal colony off the South American coast; and the Soviet gulags.

penance Roman Catholic sacrament, involving confession of sins and receiving absolution, and works performed (or punishment self-inflicted) in atonement for sin. Penance is worked out nowadays in terms of good deeds rather than routine repetition of prayers.

Penang (Malay ***Pulau Pinang***) state in W Peninsular Malaysia, formed of Penang Island, Province Wellesley, and the Dindings on the mainland; area 1,030 sq km/398 sq mi; capital Penang (George Town); population (1993) 1,141,500. Penang Island was bought by Britain from the ruler of Kedah 1785; Province Wellesley was acquired 1800.

penates the household gods of a Roman family; see ◊lares and penates.

Penda c. 577–654. King of Mercia, an Anglo-Saxon kingdom in England, from about 632. He raised Mercia to a powerful kingdom, and defeated and killed two Northumbrian kings, Edwin 632 and ◊Oswald 642. He was killed in battle by Oswy, king of Northumbria.

Penderecki Krzysztof 1933– . Polish composer. His expressionist works, such as the *Threnody for the Victims of Hiroshima* 1961 for strings, employ cluster and percussion effects. He later turned to religious subjects and a more orthodox style, as in the *Magnificat* 1974 and the *Polish Requiem* 1980–83. His opera *The Black Mask* 1986 uncovered a new vein of surreal humour.

pendulum weight (called a 'bob') swinging at the end of a rod or cord. The regularity of a pendulum's swing was used in making the first really accurate clocks in the 17th century. Pendulums can be used for measuring the acceleration due to gravity (an important constant in physics). Specialized pendulums are used to measure velocities (ballistic pendulum) and to demonstrate the Earth's rotation (Foucault's pendulum).

Penelope in Greek mythology, the wife of Odysseus, the king of Ithaca; their son was Telemachus. While Odysseus was absent at the siege of Troy she kept her many suitors at bay by asking them to wait until she had woven a shroud for her father-in-law, but unravelled her work each night. When Odysseus returned, after 20 years, he and Telemachus killed her suitors.

penguin marine flightless bird, family Spheniscidae, order Sphenisciformes, mostly black and white, found in the southern hemisphere. They comprise 18 species in six genera. Males are usually larger than the females. Penguins range in size from 40 cm/1.6 ft to 1.2 m/4 ft tall, and have thick feathers to protect them from the intense cold. They are awkward on land (except on snow slopes down which they propel themselves at a rapid pace), but their wings have evolved into flippers, making them excellent swimmers. Penguins congregate to breed in 'rookeries', and often spend many months incubating their eggs while their mates are out at sea feeding. They feed on a mixture of fish, squid, and krill.

The wing is long and has no covert or quill feathers, and always remains open. The feathers are tiny, with very broad shafts and but little vane or web. The legs of the birds are placed far back, and in the water the feet are stretched out straight behind and held motionless, the wings working rapidly as if being used in flight. Moult in penguins is general and areas of feathers are lost at once. It is usually a rapid process unlike the ordered progressive moult of flying birds. Penguins generally moult once a year, and have to stay out of the water during this time, without feeding.

The nest is often no more than a slight hollow in the ground, but some penguins, especially the Adelie penguins *Pygoscelis adeliae*, collect stones, with which they bank the nest round. One or two eggs are laid, and both birds, but chiefly the male, attend to their incubation.

They are very social birds, living together, and usually breed in vast colonies, always returning to the same rookery (breeding group). The young gather in groups while the parents are foraging for food. When the parents return, the chicks often have to chase for food, with the stronger chick being fed first. They spend much time preening themselves and each other (allopreening).

penicillin any of a group of ◊antibiotic (bacteria killing) compounds obtained from filtrates of moulds of the genus *Penicillium* (especially *P. notatum*) or produced synthetically. Penicillin was the first antibiotic to be discovered (by Alexander ◊Fleming); it kills a broad spectrum of bacteria, many of which cause disease in humans.

The use of the original type of penicillin is limited by the increasing resistance of ◊pathogens and by allergic reactions in patients. Since 1941, numerous other antibiotics of the penicillin family have been discovered which are more selective against, or resistant to, specific microorganisms.

peninsula land surrounded on three sides by water but still attached to a larger landmass. Florida, USA, is an example.

Peninsular War war 1808–14 caused by the French emperor Napoleon's invasion of Portugal and Spain. British expeditionary forces under Sir Arthur Wellesley (Duke of ◊Wellington),

Peninsular War Satirical cartoon depicting French emperor Napoleon with his brother Joseph Bonaparte, king of Spain, pondering the events of 1808. *Philip Sauvain*

combined with Spanish and Portuguese resistance, succeeded in defeating the French at Vimeiro 1808, Talavera 1809, Salamanca 1812, and Vittoria 1813. The results were inconclusive, and the war was ended by Napoleon's abdication.

1807 Portugal was occupied by the French.

1808 Napoleon placed his brother Joseph Bonaparte on the Spanish throne. Armed revolts followed all over Spain and Portugal. A British force under Sir Arthur Wellesley was sent to Portugal and defeated the French at Vimeiro; Wellesley was then superseded, and the French were allowed to withdraw.

1809 Wellesley took a new army to Portugal, and advanced on Madrid, but after defeating the French at Talavera had to retreat.

1810–11 Wellesley (now Viscount Wellington) stood on the defensive.

1812 Wellington won another victory at Salamanca, occupied Madrid, and forced the French to evacuate S Spain.

1813 Wellington's victory at Vittoria drove the French from Spain.

1814 Wellington invaded S France. The war was ended by Napoleon's abdication. ▷ *See feature on pp. 748–749.*

> *It is a reproach to religion and government to suffer so much poverty and excess.*
>
> **William Penn**
> *Reflexions and Maxims*

penis male reproductive organ containing the ◊urethra, the channel through which urine and ◊semen are voided. It transfers sperm to the female reproductive tract to fertilize the ovum. In mammals, the penis is made erect by vessels that fill with blood, and in most mammals (but not humans) is stiffened by a bone.

Snakes and lizards have a paired structure that serves as a penis; other reptiles have a single organ. A few birds, mainly ducks and geese, also have a type of penis, as do snails, barnacles, and some other invertebrates. Many insects have a rigid, non-erectile male organ, usually referred to as an intromittent organ.

Penn Irving 1917– . US fashion, advertising, portrait, editorial, and fine art photographer. In 1948 he made the first of many journeys to Africa and the Far East, resulting in a series of portrait photographs of local people, avoiding sophisticated technique. He was associated for many years with *Vogue* magazine in the USA.

Penn William 1644–1718. English member of the Society of Friends (Quakers), born in London. He joined the Society 1667, and in 1681 obtained a grant of land in America (in settlement of a debt owed by the king to his father) on which he established the colony of ◊Pennsylvania as a refuge for persecuted Quakers.

Pennines mountain system, 'the backbone of England', broken by a gap through which the river Aire flows to the E and the Ribble to the W; length (Scottish border to the Peaks in Derbyshire) 400 km/250 mi. It is the watershed for the main rivers of NE England. The rocks are carboniferous limestone and millstone grit, the land high moorland and fell.

Britain's first long-distance footpath was the Pennine Way, opened 1965.

Pennsylvania state in NE USA; nicknamed Keystone State
area 117,400 sq km/45,316 sq mi
capital Harrisburg
towns and cities Philadelphia, Pittsburgh, Erie, Allentown, Scranton
features Allegheny Mountains; Ohio, Susquehanna, and Delaware rivers; Allegheny national forest; the Poconos, a mountainous wilderness on the Delaware River; Poconos resort region; Pennsylvania Dutch country (the name comes from Deutsch, meaning German), settled in the 18th century by German immigrants escaping religious persecution, and the home of sects, including the Amish in Lancaster County; Hans Herr House (1719), former Mennonite meeting place, the best example of early German architecture in North America; Hershey, the 'Chocolate Town', founded by Milton S Hershey 1903, including Hersheypark and Hershey's Chocolate World

Pennsylvania

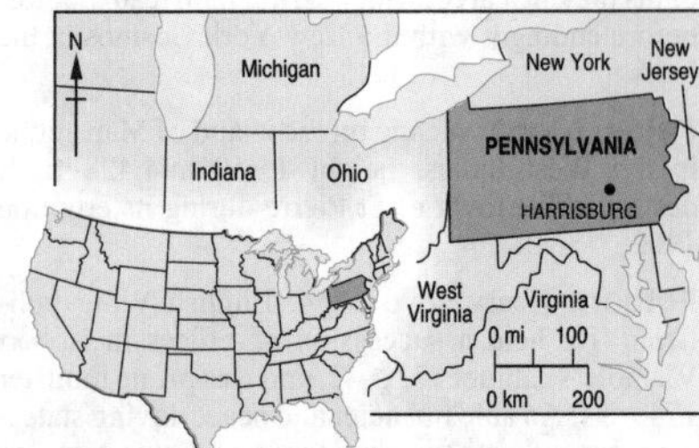

industries hay, cereals, mushrooms, cattle, poultry, dairy products, cement, coal, steel, petroleum products, pharmaceuticals, motor vehicles and equipment, electronic components, textiles
population (1990) 11,881,600
famous people Marian Anderson, Stephen Foster, Benjamin Franklin, George C Marshall, Robert E Peary, Gertrude Stein, John Updike, Andy Warhol
history founded and named by William ◊Penn 1682, following a land grant by Charles II. The Declaration of Independence was proclaimed in Philadelphia, and many important battles of the American Revolution were fought here 1777–78. It was one of the original 13 states.

Pennsylvanian US term for the Upper or Late ◊Carboniferous period of geological time, 323–290 million years ago; it is named after the US state.

pennyroyal European perennial plant *Mentha pulegium* of the mint family, with oblong leaves and whorls of purplish flowers. It is found growing in wet places on sandy soil.

pentadactyl limb typical limb of the mammals, birds, reptiles, and amphibians. These vertebrates (animals with backbone) are all descended from primitive amphibians whose immediate ancestors were fleshy-finned fish. The limb which evolved in those amphibians had three parts: a 'hand/foot' with five digits (fingers/toes), a lower limb containing two bones, and an upper limb containing one bone.

This basic pattern has persisted in all the terrestrial vertebrates, and those aquatic vertebrates (such as seals) which are descended from them. Natural selection has modified the pattern to fit different ways of life. In flying animals (birds and bats) it is greatly altered and in some vertebrates, such as whales and snakes, the limbs are greatly reduced or lost. Pentadactyl limbs of different species are an example of ◊homologous organs.

Pentagon the headquarters of the US Department of Defense, Arlington, Virginia from 1947. One of the world's largest office buildings (five-sided with a pentagonal central court), it houses the administrative and command headquarters for the US armed forces and has become synonymous with the military establishment bureaucracy.

In 1994 the estimated budget for the Pentagon's intelligence services was $13.2 billion; the three intelligence agencies included in the budget were the National Security Agency, which conducts electronic eavesdropping; the National Reconnaissance Office, which builds spy satellites; and the Defense Intelligence Agency, which manages Pentagon intelligence.

pentagon five-sided plane figure. The regular pentagon has ◊golden section proportions between its sides and diagonals. The five-pointed star formed by drawing all the diagonals of a regular pentagon is called a pentagram. This star has further golden sections.

pentanol $C_5H_{11}OH$ (common name ***amyl alcohol***) clear, colourless, oily liquid, usually having a characteristic choking odour. It is obtained by the fermentation of starches and from the distillation of petroleum.

Pentateuch Greek (and Christian) name for the first five books of the Bible, ascribed to Moses, and called the ◊Torah by Jews.

pentathlon five-sport competition. Pentathlon consists of former military training pursuits: swimming, fencing, running, horsemanship, and shooting. Formerly a five-event track and field competition for women, it was superseded by the seven-event heptathlon 1981.

Penn William Penn, the founder of the Pennsylvania Colony, establishing friendly relations with Native American tribes, 1682. An English Quaker who had fled persecution, Penn was determined to make the colony – which he called a 'Holy Experiment' – a model of tolerance and harmony. *Corbis*

Pentecost in Judaism, the festival of *Shavuot*, celebrated on the 50th day after ◊Passover in commemoration of the giving of the Ten Commandments to Moses on Mount Sinai, and the end of the grain harvest; in the Christian church, Pentecost is the day on which the apostles experienced inspiration of the Holy Spirit, commemorated on Whit Sunday.

Pentecostal movement Christian revivalist movement inspired by the baptism in the Holy Spirit with 'speaking in tongues' experienced by the apostles at the time of Pentecost. It represents a reaction against the rigid theology and formal worship of the traditional churches.

Pentecostalists believe in the literal word of the Bible and disapprove of alcohol, tobacco, dancing and theatre. It is an intensely missionary faith, and recruitment has been rapid since the 1960s: worldwide membership is more than 10 million.

The Pentecostal movement dates from 4 April 1906 when members of the congregation of the Azusa Street Mission in Los Angeles experienced 'baptism in the Spirit'. The services are informal, with gospel music and exclamations of 'Hallelujah'.

The movement spread, and took hold in revivalist areas of Wales and N England, but was less successful there than in Scandinavia, South America, and South Africa. In the USA, where the largest grouping is the Assemblies of God, members of the movement total more than 0.5 million. Black and white denominations within the US Pentecostal church voted Oct 1994 to create a national multiracial association, ending 88 years of racial segregation within the movement.

Pentium microchip produced by Intel 1993. The Pentium was designed to take advantage of PCI local bus architecture, which increases the bandwidth available between devices. It was the first 64-bit microprocessor (see ◊bit). The Pentium Pro was launched Nov 1995. It is a 64-bit microprocessor containing 5.5 million transistors compared with Pentium's 3.1 million, and can execute 166 million instructions per second, with a clock speed of up to 200 MHz (megahertz).

Pentland Firth channel separating the Orkney Islands from N Scotland.

penumbra the region of partial shade between the totally dark part (umbra) of a shadow and the fully illuminated region outside. It occurs when a source of light is only partially obscured by a shadow-casting object. The darkness of a penumbra varies gradually from total darkness at one edge to full brightness at the other. In astronomy, a penumbra is a region of the Earth from which only a partial ◊eclipse of the Sun or Moon can be seen.

peony any perennial plant of the genus *Paeonia*, family Paeoniaceae, remarkable for their brilliant flowers. Most popular are the common peony *P. officinalis*, the white peony *P. lactiflora*, and the taller tree peony *P. suffruticosa*.

People's Charter the key document of ◊Chartism, a movement for reform of the British political system in the 1830s. It was used to mobilize working-class support following the restricted extension of the franchise specified by the 1832 Reform Act. It was drawn up in Feb 1837.

The campaign failed but within 70 years four of its six objectives: universal male suffrage, abolition of property qualifications for members of Parliament, payment of MPs, and voting by secret ballot had been realized.

Pepin the Short c. 714–c. 768. King of the Franks from 751. The son of Charles Martel, he acted as Mayor of the Palace to the last Merovingian king, Childeric III, deposed him and assumed the royal title himself, founding the ◊Carolingian dynasty. He was ◊Charlemagne's father.

pepper climbing plant *Piper nigrum* native to the E Indies, of the Old World pepper family Piperaceae. When gathered green, the berries are crushed to release the seeds for the spice called black pepper. When the berries are ripe, the seeds are removed and their outer skin is discarded, to produce white pepper. Chilli pepper, cayenne or red pepper, and the sweet peppers used as a vegetable come from ◊capsicums native to the New World.

peppermint perennial herb *Mentha piperita* of the mint family, native to Europe, with ovate, aromatic leaves and purple flowers. Oil of peppermint is used in medicine and confectionery.

pepsin enzyme that breaks down proteins during digestion. It requires a strongly acidic environment and is present in the stomach.

peptide molecule comprising two or more ◊amino acid molecules (not necessarily different) joined by peptide bonds, whereby the acid group of one acid is linked to the amino group of the other (–CO.NH). The number of amino acid molecules in the peptide is indicated by referring to it as a di-, tri-, or polypeptide (two, three, or many amino acids).

Proteins are built up of interacting polypeptide chains with various types of bonds occurring between the chains. Incomplete hydrolysis (splitting up) of a protein yields a mixture of peptides, examination of which helps to determine the sequence in which the amino acids occur within the protein.

Pepys Samuel 1633–1703. English naval administrator and diarist. His *Diary* 1660–69 is a unique record of the daily life of the period, the historical events of the Restoration, the manners and scandals of the court, naval administration, and Pepys's own interests, weaknesses, and intimate feelings. Written in shorthand, it was not deciphered until 1825.

Pepys entered the Navy Office 1660 and was secretary to the Admiralty 1672–79. He was imprisoned 1679 in the Tower of London on suspicion of being connected with the Popish Plot (see Titus ◊Oates). In 1684 he was reinstated as secretary to the Admiralty, but finally resigned his post after the 1688 Revolution. He published *Memoires of the Navy* 1690. Pepys abandoned writing his diary because he believed, mistakenly, that his eyesight was about to fail – in fact, it continued to serve him for 30 or more years of active life.

The original manuscript of the *Diary*, preserved in Cambridge together with other papers, is in six volumes, containing more than 3,000 pages. Highlights include his accounts of the Great Plague of London 1665, the Fire of London 1666, and the sailing up the Thames of the Dutch fleet 1667.

Pepys A portrait of the English diarist Samuel Pepys 1666 by John Hayls, National Portrait Gallery, London. The private diaries of Pepys, who was an energetic public servant, express a relish for life and its full range of experiences. His account of the last great plague epidemic 1665 and of the Fire of London 1666 are particularly valuable as social history. *Topham*

Perak state of W Peninsular Malaysia; capital Ipoh; area 21,000 sq km/8,106 sq mi; population (1993) 2,222,400. It produces tin and rubber. The government is a sultanate. The other principal city is Taiping.

percentage way of representing a number as a ◊fraction of 100. Thus 45 percent (45%) equals $^{45}/_{100}$, and 45% of 20 is $^{45}/_{100} \times 20 = 9$. In general, if a quantity x changes to y, the percentage change is $100(x - y)/x$. Thus, if the number of people in a room changes from 40 to 50, the percentage increase is $(100 \times 10)/40 = 25\%$. To express a fraction as a percentage, its denominator must first be converted to 100 – for example, $^1/_8 = 12.5/100 = 12.5\%$. The use of percentages often makes it easier to compare fractions that do not have a common denominator.

Perceval Spencer 1762–1812. British Tory politician. He became chancellor of the Exchequer 1807 and prime minister 1809. He was shot in the lobby of the House of Commons 1812 by a merchant who blamed government measures for his bankruptcy.

perch any of the largest order of spiny-finned bony fishes, the Perciformes, with some 8,000 species. This order includes the sea basses, cichlids, damselfishes, mullets, barracudas, wrasses, and gobies. Perches of the freshwater genus *Perca* are found in Europe, Asia, and North America. They have varied shapes and are usually a greenish colour. They are very prolific, spawning when about three years old, and have voracious appetites.

The common perch *P. fluviatilis* is olive green or yellowish in colour, with dark vertical bands. It can be 50 cm/1.6 ft long but is usually less. It is a predator found in still water and rivers. The American yellow perch *P. flavescens* is slightly smaller.

percussion instrument musical instrument played by being struck with the hand or a beater. Percussion instruments can be divided into those that can be tuned to produce a sound of definite pitch, such as the timpani, tubular bells, glockenspiel, and xylophone, and those of indefinite pitch, including bass drum, tambourine, triangle, cymbals, and castanets.

The ***timpano*** is a hemispherical bowl of metal with a membrane stretched across the rim, affixed and tuned by screwtaps; ***tubular bells*** are suspended on a frame; the ***glockenspiel*** (German 'bell play') is a small keyboard of aluminium alloy keys; the ***xylophone*** has hardwood rather than metal bars.

The ***snare drum*** is a shallow double-sided drum on the underside of which gut coils or metal springs are secured by a clamp and rattle against the underside when the drum is beaten, while the ***bass drum*** produces the lowest sound in the orchestra; the ***tambourine*** has a wooden hoop with a membrane stretched across it, and has metal discs suspended in the rim; a ***triangle*** is formed from a suspended triangular-shaped steel bar, played by striking it with a separate bar of steel – the sound produced can be clearly perceived even when played against a full orchestra; ***cymbals*** are two brass dishes struck together; ***castanets*** are two hollow shells of wood struck together; and the ***gong*** is a suspended disc of metal struck with a soft hammer.

Percy Henry 'Hotspur' 1364–1403. English soldier, son of the 1st Earl of Northumberland. In repelling a border raid, he defeated the Scots at Homildon Hill in Durham 1402. He was killed at the battle of Shrewsbury while in revolt against Henry IV.

perennating organ in plants, that part of a ◊biennial plant or herbaceous perennial that allows it to survive the winter; usually a root, tuber, rhizome, bulb, or corm.

perennial plant plant that lives for more than two years. Herbaceous perennials have aerial stems and leaves that die each autumn. They survive the winter by means of an underground storage (perennating) organ, such as a bulb or rhizome. Trees and shrubs or woody perennials have stems that persist above ground throughout the year, and may be either ◊deciduous or ◊evergreen. See also ◊annual plant, ◊biennial plant.

Peres Shimon 1923– . Israeli socialist politician, prime minister 1984–86 and 1995–96. Peres was prime minister, then foreign minister, under a power-sharing agreement with the leader of the Consolidation Party (Likud), Yitzhak ◊Shamir. From 1989 to 1990 he was finance minister in a Labour–Likud coalition. As foreign minister in Yitzhak Rabin's Labour government from 1992, he negotiated the 1993 peace agreement with the Palestine Liberation Organization (PLO). He was awarded the 1994 Nobel Prize for Peace jointly with Israeli prime minister, Rabin, and PLO leader, Yassir Arafat.

Following the assassination of Rabin Nov 1995, Peres succeeded him as prime minister, and pledged to continue with the peace process in which they had

'To think how fine they show on the stage by candle-light, and how poor things they are to look now too near-hand, is not pleasant at all.'

SAMUAL PEPYS
On actors, *Diary*
19 March 1666

Peres Israeli politician Shimon Peres, leader of the Labour Party 1977–92, and prime minister 1984–86 under a power-sharing agreement with Yitzhak Shamir of the Likud Party. His plans for peace with the Palestinians were often thwarted by his inability to form a Labour government, though as foreign minister he was able to negotiate the 1993 peace accord with the PLO. *Associated Press/ Topham*

both been so closely involved, but in May 1996 was defeated in Israel's first direct elections for prime minister.

Peres emigrated from Poland to Palestine 1934, but was educated in the USA. In 1959 he was elected to the Knesset (Israeli parliament). He was leader of the Labour Party 1977–92, when he was replaced by Rabin.

perestroika (Russian 'restructuring') in Soviet politics, the wide-ranging economic and political reforms initiated from 1985 by Mikhail Gorbachev, finally leading to the demise of the Soviet Union. Originally, in the economic sphere, *perestroika* was conceived as involving 'intensive development' concentrating on automation and improved labour efficiency. It evolved to attend increasingly to market indicators and incentives ('market socialism') and the gradual dismantling of the Stalinist central-planning system, with decision-taking being devolved to self-financing enterprises. ▷ *See feature on pp. 1090–1091.*

Perey Marguérite (Catherine) 1909–1975. French nuclear chemist who discovered the radioactive element francium in 1939. Her career, which began as an assistant to Marie ◊Curie 1929, culminated with her appointment as professor of nuclear chemistry at the University of Strasbourg 1949 and director of its Centre for Nuclear Research 1958.

Pergamum The acropolis of the ancient city of Pergamum, near Bergama, W Turkey. Flourishing during the Hellenistic period, 3rd–2nd centuries BC, Pergamum became famous for its architecture, its parchment books (the word parchment is derived from the city's name), and its vast library. *Turkish Embassy*

Pérez de Cuéllar Javier 1920– . Peruvian diplomat, secretary general of the United Nations 1982–91. He raised the standing of the UN by his successful diplomacy in ending the Iran–Iraq War 1988 and securing the independence of Namibia 1989. He was a candidate in the 1995 presidential elections, but was defeated by his opponent Alberto Fujimori.

A delegate to the first UN General Assembly 1946–47, he subsequently held several ambassadorial posts. He was unable to resolve the Gulf conflict resulting from Iraq's invasion of Kuwait 1990 before combat against Iran by the UN coalition began Jan 1991, but later in 1991 he negotiated the release of Western hostages held in Beirut.

Pérez Jiménez Marcos 1914– . Venezuelan president 1952–58. He led the military junta that overthrew the Acción Democrática government of Rómulo Gallegos 1948, was made provisional president 1952, and approved as constitutional president by Congress 1953. His regime had a reputation as the most repressive in Venezuelan history. It also encouraged European immigration and undertook massive public works in the capital, Caracas.

performance art staged artistic events, sometimes including music, painting, and sculpture. During the 20th century performance has played a part in several artistic movements, in particular Futurism, Dada, and the Bauhaus. Performance art flourished in the 1960s in ◊happenings, body art, and ◊Conceptual art, and since then has largely been absorbed by pop music.

performing right permission to perform ◊copyright musical or dramatic works in public; this is subject to licence and the collection of fees. The first performing right society was established 1851 in France. In the UK the Copyright Act 1842 was the first to encompass musical compositions. The agent for live performances is the Performing Right Society, founded 1914; the rights for recorded or broadcast performance are administered by the Mechanical Copyright Protection Society, founded 1924.

Italy introduced a performing-right society 1882, Germany 1915. The US organizations are ASCAP (American Society of Composers, Authors, and Publishers) and BMI (Broadcast Music Incorporated). National societies now collect on behalf of other countries as well as for their own members.

perfume fragrant essence used to scent the body, cosmetics, and candles. More than 100 natural aromatic chemicals may be blended from a range of 60,000 flowers, leaves, fruits, seeds, woods, barks, resins, and roots, combined by natural animal fixatives and various synthetics. Favoured ingredients include ◊balsam, ◊civet (from the African civet cat) hyacinth, jasmine, lily of the valley, musk (from the ◊musk deer), orange blossom, rose, and tuberose.

Culture of the cells of fragrant plants, on membranes that are constantly bathed in a solution to carry the essential oils away for separation, is now being adopted to reduce costs.

Pergamum ancient Greek city in W Asia Minor, which became the capital of an independent kingdom 283 BC under the Attalid dynasty. As the ally of Rome it achieved great political importance in the 2nd century BC, and became a centre of art and culture. It was the birthplace of the physician ◊Galen. Close to its site is the modern Turkish town of Bergama.

Pergau Dam hydroelectric dam on the Pergau River in Malaysia, near the Thai border. Building work began 1991 with money from the UK foreign aid budget. Concurrently, the Malaysian government bought around £1 billion worth of arms from the UK. The suggested linkage of arms deals to aid become the subject of a UK government enquiry from March 1994. In Nov 1994 a High Court ruled as illegal British foreign secretary Douglas Hurd's allocation of £234 million towards the funding of the dam, on the grounds that it was not of economic or humanitarian benefit to the Malaysian people.

peri in Persian myth, a beautiful, harmless being, ranking between angels and evil spirits. Peris were ruled by Eblis, the greatest of evil spirits.

Peri Jacopo 1561–1633. Italian composer. He served the Medici family, the rulers of Florence. His experimental melodic opera *Euridice* 1600 established the opera form and influenced Monteverdi. His first opera, *Dafne* 1597, is now lost.

pericarp wall of a ◊fruit. It encloses the seeds and is derived from the ◊ovary wall. In fruits such as the acorn, the pericarp becomes dry and hard, forming a shell around the seed. In fleshy fruits the pericarp is typically made up of three distinct layers.

Pericles c. 495–429 BC. Athenian politician who was effective leader of the city from 443 BC and under whom Athenian power reached its height. His policies helped to transform the Delian League (the alliance between the Athenians and the Ionian Greeks) into an Athenian empire, but the disasters of the ◊Peloponnesian War led to his removal from office 430 BC. Although quickly reinstated, he died soon after.

peridot pale-green, transparent gem variety of the mineral ◊olivine.

peridotite rock consisting largely of the mineral olivine; pyroxene and other minerals may also be present. Peridotite is an ultramafic rock containing less than 45% silica by weight. It is believed to be one of the rock types making up the Earth's upper mantle, and is sometimes brought from the depths to the surface by major movements, or as inclusions in lavas.

perigee the point at which an object, travelling in an elliptical orbit around the Earth, is at its closest to the Earth. The point at which it is furthest from the Earth is the apogee.

periglacial bordering a glacial area but not actually covered by ice, or having similar climatic and environmental characterisitics, such as mountainous areas. Periglacial areas today include parts of Siberia, Greenland, and North America. The rock and soil in these areas is frozen to a depth of several metres (◊permafrost) with only the top few centimetres thawing during the brief summer. The vegetation is characteristic of ◊tundra.

During the last ice age all of southern England was periglacial. Weathering by ◊freeze-thaw (the alternate freezing and thawing of ice in rock cracks) would have been severe, and solifluction (the downhill movement of topsoil that has become saturated with water) would have taken place on a large scale, causing wet topsoil to slip from valley sides.

perihelion the point at which an object, travelling in an elliptical orbit around the Sun, is at its closest to the Sun. The point at which it is furthest from the Sun is the aphelion.

perimeter or ***boundary*** line drawn around the edge of an area or shape. For example, the perimeter of a rectangle is the sum of its four sides; the perimeter of a circle is known as its circumference.

period another name for menstruation; see ◊menstrual cycle.

period in physics, the time taken for one complete cycle of a repeated sequence of events. For example, the time taken for a pendulum to swing from side to side and back again is the period of the pendulum. The period is the reciprocal of the ◊frequency.

periodic table of the elements in chemistry, a table in which the elements are arranged in order of their atomic number. The table summarizes the major properties of the elements and enables predictions to be made about their behaviour.

There are striking similarities in the chemical properties of the elements in each of the vertical columns (called groups), which are numbered I–VII and 0 to reflect the number of electrons in the outermost unfilled shell and hence the maximum ◊valency. A gradation of properties may be traced along the horizontal rows (called periods). Metallic character increases across a period from right to left, and down a group. A large block of elements, between groups II and III, contains the transition elements, characterized by displaying more than one valency state.

These features are a direct consequence of the electronic (and nuclear) structure of the atoms of the elements. The relationships established between the positions of elements in the periodic table and their major properties has enabled scientists to predict the properties of other elements – for example, technetium, atomic number 43, first synthesized 1937.

The first periodic table was devised by Russian chemist Dmitri Mendeleyev 1869, the elements being arranged by atomic mass (rather than atomic number) in accordance with Mendeleyev's statement 'the properties of elements are in periodic dependence upon their atomic weight'. *See illustration on pp. 830–831.*

periodontal disease (formerly known as ***pyorrhoea***) disease of the gums and bone supporting the teeth, caused by the accumulation of plaque and microorganisms; the gums recede, and the teeth eventually become loose and may drop out unless treatment is sought. Bacteria can eventually erode the bone that supports the teeth, so that surgery becomes necessary.

peripheral device in computing, any item connected to a computer's ◊cental processing unit (CPU). Typical peripherals include keyboard, mouse, monitor, and printer.

periscope optical instrument designed for observation from a concealed position such as from a submerged submarine. In its basic form it consists of a tube with parallel mirrors at each end, inclined at 45° to its axis. The periscope attained prominence in naval and military operations of World War I.

Although most often thought of as a submarine observation device, periscopes were widely used in the trenches during World War I to allow observation without exposing the observer, and special versions were also developed to be attached to rifles.

peristalsis wavelike contractions, produced by the contraction of smooth muscle, that pass along tubular organs, such as the intestines. The same term describes the wavelike motion of earthworms and other invertebrates, in which part of the body contracts as another part elongates.

peristyle in architecture, a range of columns surrounding a building or open courtyard.

peritoneum membrane lining the abdominal cavity and digestive organs of vertebrates. Peritonitis, inflammation within the peritoneum, can occur due to infection or other irritation. It is sometimes seen following a burst appendix and quickly proves fatal if not treated.

periwinkle in botany, any of several trailing blue-flowered evergreen plants of the genus *Vinca* of the dogbane family Apocynaceae. They range in length from 20 cm/8 in to 1 m/3 ft.

The related Madagascar periwinkle *Catharanthus roseus* produces chemicals that inhibit the division of cells and are used to treat leukaemia.

periwinkle in zoology, any marine snail of the family Littorinidae, found on the shores of Europe and E North America. Periwinkles have a conical spiral shell, and feed on algae.

perjury the offence of deliberately making a false statement on ◊oath when appearing as a witness in legal proceedings, on a point material to the question at issue. In Britain and the USA it is punishable by a fine, imprisonment, or both.

Perkins Anthony 1932–1992. US film actor. He is remembered as the mother-fixated psychopath Norman Bates in Alfred Hitchcock's *Psycho* 1960 and *Psycho II* 1982. He played shy but subtle roles in *Friendly Persuasion* 1956, *The Trial* 1962, and *The Champagne Murders* 1967. He also appeared on the stage in London and New York.

Perlis border state of Peninsular Malaysia, NW Malaysia; capital Kangar; area 800 sq km/309 sq mi; population (1993) 187,600. It produces rubber, rice, coconuts, and tin. Perlis is ruled by a raja. It was transferred by Siam to Britain 1909.

Perm industrial city (shipbuilding, oil refining, aircraft, chemicals, sawmills), and capital of Perm region, N Russian Federation, on the Kama near the Ural Mountains; population (1994) 1,086,000. It was called Molotov 1940–57.

permafrost condition in which a deep layer of soil does not thaw out during the summer. Permafrost occurs under ◊periglacial conditions. It is claimed that 26% of the world's land surface is permafrost. It gives rise to a poorly drained form of grassland typical of N Canada, Siberia, and Alaska known as ◊tundra.

Permian period of geological time 290–245 million years ago, the last period of the Palaeozoic era. Its end was marked by a significant change in marine life, including the extinction of many corals and trilobites. Deserts were widespread, terrestrial amphibians and mammal-like reptiles flourished, and cone-bearing plants (gymnosperms) came to prominence. In the oceans, 49% of families and 72% of genera vanished in the late Permian. On land, 78% of reptile families and 67% of amphibian families disappeared.

Pernambuco state of NE Brazil, on the Atlantic coast; area 98,281 sq km/37,946 sq mi; population (1991) 7,122,500. The capital is Recife (former name Pernambuco). There are highlands, and the coast is low and humid. Cotton, sugar, and tropical fruit are produced.

Perón (María Estela) Isabel, (born Martínez) 1931– . President of Argentina 1974–76, and third wife of Juan Perón. She succeeded him after he died in office, but labour unrest, inflation, and political violence pushed the country to the brink of chaos. Accused of corruption, she was held under house arrest for five years. She went into exile in Spain.

Perón Evita (María Eva), (born Duarte) 1919–1952. Argentine populist leader. A successful radio actress, she married Juan ◊Perón in 1945. When he became president the following year, she became his chief adviser and virtually ran the health and labour ministries, devoting herself to helping the poor, improving education, and achieving women's suffrage. She was politically astute and sought the vice-presidency 1951, but was opposed by the army and withdrew.

Perón Juan Domingo 1895–1974. Argentine politician, dictator 1946–55 and from 1973 until his

periwinkle A plant native to central and S Europe and N Africa, the greater periwinkle *Vinca major* is now widespread in the British Isles as an escapee, usually on grass verges outside gardens. It flowers from March to July. *Premaphotos Wildlife*

peripheral device Some of the types of peripheral device that may be connected to a computer include printers, scanners, and modems.

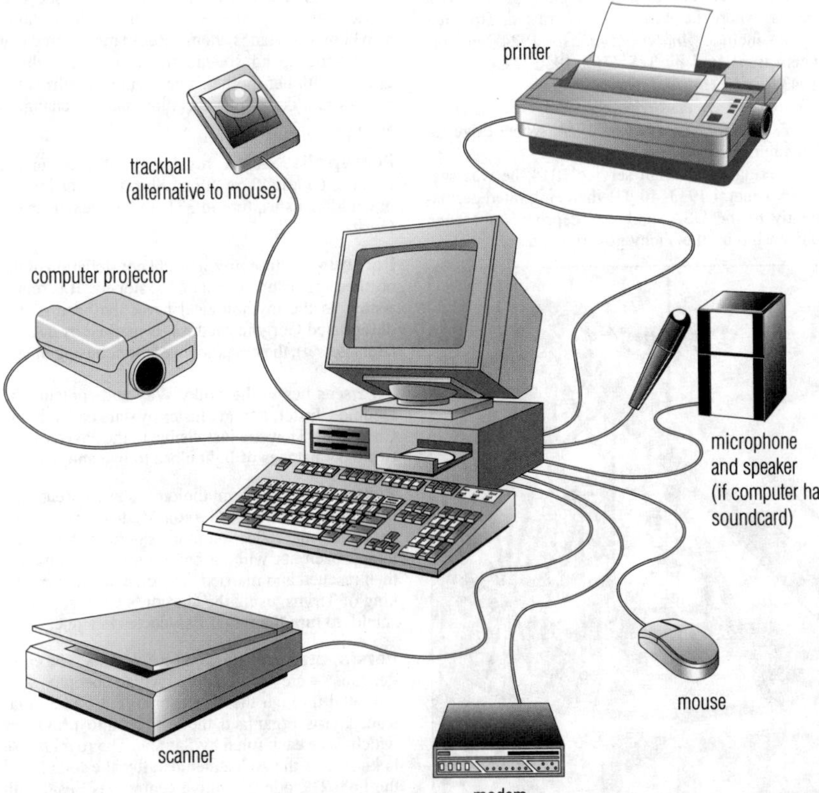

❛Just ahead rose what looked like a lot of battered ninepins on the top of a shaky table. This was Persepolis.❜

On **Persepolis**
John Foster Fraser
Round the World on a Wheel

death. His populist appeal to the poor was enhanced by the charisma and political work of his second wife Eva (Evita) Perón. After her death in 1952 his popularity waned and he was deposed in a military coup 1955. He returned from exile to the presidency 1973, but died in office 1974, and was succeeded by his third wife Isabel Perón.

A professional army officer, Perón took part in the right-wing military coup that toppled Argentina's government 1943 and his popularity with the *descamisados* ('shirtless ones') led to his election as president 1946. He instituted social reforms, but encountered economic difficulties.

Perpendicular period of English Gothic architecture lasting from the end of the 14th century to the mid-16th century. It is characterized by window tracery consisting chiefly of vertical members, two or four arc arches, lavishly decorated vaults, and the use of traceried panels. Examples include the choir, transepts, and cloister of Gloucester Cathedral, about 1331–1412, and King's College Chapel, Cambridge, built in three phases 1446–61, 1477–85, and 1508–15.

perpendicular in mathematics, at a right angle; also, a line at right angles to another or to a plane. For a pair of skew lines (lines in three dimensions that do not meet), there is just one common perpendicular, which is at right angles to both lines; the nearest points on the two lines are the feet of this perpendicular.

perpetual motion the idea that a machine can be designed and constructed in such a way that, once started, it will continue in motion indefinitely without requiring any further input of energy (motive power). Such a device contradicts the two laws of thermodynamics that state that (1) energy can neither be created nor destroyed (the law of conservation of energy) and (2) heat cannot by itself flow from a cooler to a hotter object. As a result, all practical (real) machines require a continuous supply of energy, and no heat engine is able to convert all the heat into useful work.

Perrault Charles 1628–1703. French writer who published a collection of fairy tales, *Contes de ma mère l'oye/Mother Goose's Fairy Tales* 1697. These are based on traditional stories and include 'The Sleeping Beauty', 'Little Red Riding Hood', 'Blue Beard', 'Puss in Boots', and 'Cinderella'.

Perry Fred (Frederick John) 1909–1995. English lawn-tennis player, the last Briton to win the men's singles at Wimbledon, 1936. He also won the world table-tennis title 1929. Perry later became a television commentator and a sports-goods manufacturer.

Perry Matthew (Calbraith) 1794–1858. US naval officer, commander of the expedition of 1853 that reopened communication between Japan and the outside world after 250 years' isolation. Evident military superiority enabled him to negotiate the Treaty of Kanagawa 1854, giving the USA trading rights with Japan.

Perse Saint-John. Pen name of (Marie René Auguste) Alexis Saint-Léger 1887–1975. French poet and diplomat. He was a US citizen from 1940. His first book of verse, *Eloges/Eloges and Other Poems* 1911, reflects the ambience of the West Indies, where he was born and raised. His later works include *Anabase/Anabasis* 1924, an epic poem translated by T S Eliot 1930, *Pluies/Rains* 1943, *Exil/Exile and Other Poems* 1944, *Vents/Winds* 1946, *Amers/Seamarks* 1957, *Oiseaux/Birds* 1962, and *Honneur/Honour* 1964. Nobel Prize for Literature 1960.

Entering the foreign service 1914, he was secretary general 1933–40. He then emigrated permanently to the USA, and was deprived of French citizenship by the Vichy government.

Persephone in Greek mythology, a goddess (Roman Proserpina), the daughter of Zeus and Demeter, and queen of the underworld. She was carried off to the underworld as the bride of Pluto, also known as Hades, though Zeus later ordered that she should spend six months of the year above ground with her mother. The myth symbolizes the growth and decay of vegetation and the changing seasons.

Persepolis ancient royal city of the Persian Empire, 65 km/40 mi NE of Shiraz. It was burned down after its capture in 331 BC by Alexander the Great.

Perseus in astronomy, a bright constellation of the northern hemisphere, near ◊Cassiopeia. It is represented as the mythological hero; the head of the decapitated Gorgon, Medusa, is marked by ◊Algol (Beta Persei), the best known of the eclipsing binary stars.

Perseus lies in the Milky Way and contains the Double Cluster, a twin cluster of stars called h and Chi Persei. They are just visible to the naked eye as two hazy patches of light close to one another.

Perseus in Greek mythology, son of Zeus and Danaë. He slew the ◊Gorgon Medusa and cut off her head – the reflection in his shield enabling him to approach her without being turned to stone. He then rescued and married Andromeda, and became king of Tiryns, using the Gorgon's head, set on his shield, to turn the tyrant Polydectes to stone.

Persia, ancient kingdom in SW Asia. The early Persians were a nomadic Aryan people who migrated through the Caucasus to the Iranian plateau. Cyrus organized the empire into provinces which were each ruled by Satraps. The royal house is known as the Achaemenids after the founder of the line. The administrative centre was Susa, with the royal palace at Persepolis.

element: 1 — atomic number; Hydrogen — name; H — symbol; 1.00794 — relative atomic mass

Period	I	II							
1	1 Hydrogen **H** 1.00794								
2	3 Lithium **Li** 6.941	4 Beryllium **Be**							
3	11 Sodium **Na** 22.98977	12 Magnesium **Mg** 24.305							
4	19 Potassium **K** 30.098	20 Calcium **Ca** 40.06	21 Scandium **Sc** 44.9559	22 Titanium **Ti** 47.90	23 Vanadium **V** 50.9414	24 Chromium **Cr** 51.996	25 Manganese **Mn** 54.9380	26 Iron **Fe** 55.847	27 Cobalt **Co** 58.9332
5	37 Rubidium **Rb** 85.4678	38 Strontium **Sr** 87.62	39 Yttrium **Y** 88.9059	40 Zirconium **Zr** 91.22	41 Niobium **Nb** 92.9064	42 Molybdenum **Mo** 95.94	43 Technetium **Tc** 97.9072	44 Ruthenium **Ru** 101.07	45 Rhodium **Rh** 102.9055
6	55 Caesium **Cs** 132.9054	56 Barium **Ba** 137.34	**La**	72 Hafnium **Hf** 178.49	73 Tantalum **Ta** 180.9479	74 Tungsten **W** 183.85	75 Rhenium **Re** 186.207	76 Osmium **Os** 190.2	77 Iridium **Ir** 192.22
7	87 Francium **Fr** 223.0197	88 Radium **Ra** 226.0254	**Ac**	104 Rutherfordium **Rf** 261.109	105 Dubnium **Db** 262.114	106 Seaborgium **Sg** 263.120	107 Bohrium **Bh** 262	108 Hassium **Hs** 265	109 Meitnerium **Mt** 266

Series						
Lanthanide series	57 Lanthanum **La** 138.9055	58 Cerium **Ce** 140.12	59 Praseodymium **Pr** 140.9077	60 Neodymium **Nd** 144.24	61 Promethium **Pm** 144.9128	62 Samarium **Sm** 150.36
Actinide series	89 Actinium **Ac** 227.0278	90 Thorium **Th** 232.0381	91 Protactinium **Pa** 231.0359	92 Uranium **U** 238.029	93 Neptunium **Np** 237.0482	94 Plutonium **Pu** 244.0642

periodic table of the elements The periodic table of the elements arranges the elements into horizontal rows (called periods) and vertical columns (called groups) according to their atomic numbers. The elements in a group or column all have similar properties – for example, all the elements in the far right-hand column are inert gases. Nonmetals are shown in blue, metals in grey, and the metalloid (metal-like) elements in yellow. The elements in white are called transition elements.

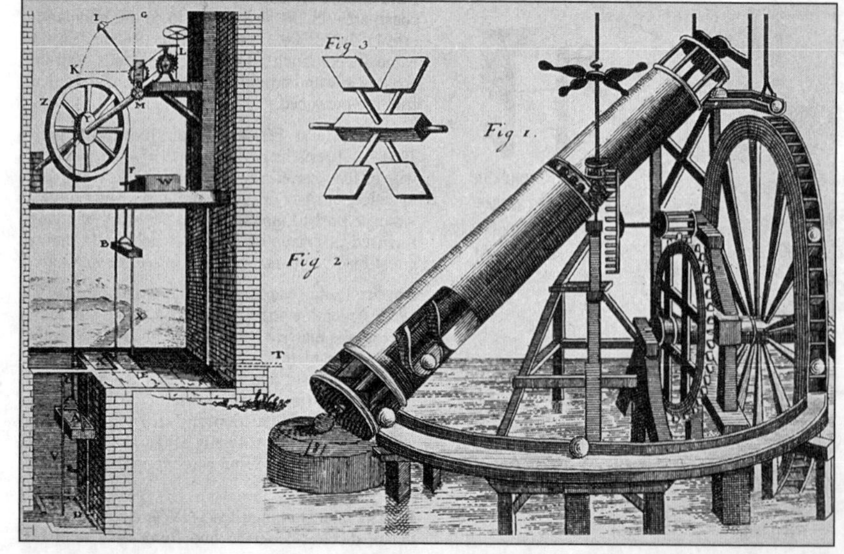

perpetual motion Perpetual motion machine designed in Hamburg around 1747. Iron balls drive the water wheel that, in turn operates an Archimedean screw that raises the balls up to the wheel again. The designer of the machine, Colonel Kranach, intended that the machine be used to operate pumps for mines. *Image Select (UK) Ltd*

			III	IV	V	VI	VII	0
								2 Helium **He** 4002.60
			5 Boron **B** 10.81	6 Carbon **C** 12.011	7 Nitrogen **N** 14.0067	8 Oxygen **O** 15.9994	9 Fluorine **F** 18.99840	10 Neon **Ne** 20.179
			13 Aluminium **Al** 26.98154	14 Silicon **Si** 28.066	15 Phosphorus **P** 30.9738	16 Sulphur **S** 32.06	17 Chlorine **Cl** 35.453	18 Argon **Ar** 39.948
28 Nickel **Ni** 58.70	29 Copper **Cu** 63.546	30 Zinc **Zn** 65.38	31 Gallium **Ga** 69.72	32 Germanium **Ge** 72.59	33 Arsenic **As** 74.9216	34 Selenium **Se** 78.96	35 Bromine **Br** 79.904	36 Krypton **Kr** 83.80
46 Palladium **Pd** 106.4	47 Silver **Ag** 107.868	48 Cadmium **Cd** 112.40	49 Indium **In** 114.82	50 Tin **Sn** 118.69	51 Antimony **Sb** 121.75	52 Tellurium **Te** 127.75	53 Iodine **I** 126.9045	54 Xenon **Xe** 131.30
78 Platinum **Pt** 195.09	79 Gold **Au** 196.9665	80 Mercury **Hg** 200.59	81 Thallium **Tl** 204.37	82 Lead **Pb** 207.37	83 Bismuth **Bi** 207.2	84 Polonium **Po** 210	85 Astatine **At** 211	86 Radon **Rn** 222.0176
110 Ununnilium **Uun** 269	111 Unununium **Uuu** 272							

63 Europium **Eu** 151.96	64 Gadolinium **Gd** 157.25	65 Terbium **Tb** 158.9254	66 Dysprosium **Dy** 162.50	67 Holmium **Ho** 164.9304	68 Erbium **Er** 167.26	69 Thulium **Tm** 168.9342	70 Ytterbium **Yb** 173.04	71 Lutetium **Lu** 174.97
95 Americium **Am** 243.0614	96 Curium **Cm** 247.0703	97 Berkelium **Bk** 247	98 Californium **Cf** 251.0786	99 Einsteinium **Es** 252.0828	100 Fermium **Fm** 257.0951	101 Mendelevium **Md** 258.0986	102 Nobelium **No** 259.1009	103 Lawrencium **Lr** 260.1054

Expansion led the Persians into conflicts with Greek cities, notably in the Ionian Revolt, Darius I's campaign that ended at the Athenian victory of Marathon (490 BC), and Xerxes I's full-blown invasion of the Greek mainland 480.

7th century BC The Persians were established in the present region of Fars, which then belonged to the Assyrians.

550 BC Cyrus the Great overthrew the empire of the Medes, to whom the Persians had been subject, and founded the Persian Empire.

539 BC Having conquered all Anatolia, Cyrus added Babylonia (including Syria and Palestine) to his empire.

525 BC His son and successor Cambyses conquered Egypt.

521–485 BC Darius I organized an efficient centralized system of administration and extended Persian rule east into Afghanistan and NW India and as far north as the Danube, but the empire was weakened by internal dynastic struggles.

499–449 BC The Persian Wars with Greece ended Persian domination of the Aegean seaboard.

330 BC Alexander the Great drove the Persians under Darius III (died 330 BC) into retreat at Gaugamela on the Tigris, marking the end of the Persian Empire and the beginning of the Hellenistic period under the Seleucids.

250 BC–AD 230 The Arsacid dynasty established Parthia as the leading power in the region.

224 The Sassanian Empire was established in Persia and annexed Parthia.

637 Arabs took the capital, Ctesiphon, and introduced Islam in place of Zoroastrianism.

For modern history see ◊Iran.

Persian inhabitants of Persia; now Iran. The Persians claim descent from Aryans who are thought to have migrated from S Russia around 2000 BC.

Persian art the arts of Persia (now Iran) from the 6th century BC. Subject to invasions from both East and West, Persia has over the centuries blended many influences to create a rich diversity of arts, styles, and techniques. Persian art is particularly noted for its architecture and production of exquisite miniatures.

Though Persia has been a centre of civilization for at least 7,000 years, it was during the Achaemenid dynasty (550–333 BC), when the first Persian empire was formed, that a unified style emerged, drawing on a wide range of influences. For example, the palace at Persepolis, begun by Darius I and completed by Xerxes, was decorated about 520 BC with relief friezes recalling Assyrian and Babylonian styles. The period also produced work in gold and silver, bronze castings, and inlay.

The conquest of Persia by Alexander the Great in the 4th century BC brought about a blending of Persian and Hellenistic styles, seen, for example, in the bronzes, pottery, and jewellery of the Parthians. The Sassanian dynasty (AD 224–642) was the richest period of artistic achievement, developing to the full a wide range of new and inherited styles and techniques. The Sassanians introduced silk to Persia; they produced exquisite jewellery, metalwork in silver, gold, and bronze, and ceramics; and they decorated their palaces with relief sculptures and mosaics. The innovative domes and arches they developed were later to have a profound influence on Islamic architecture.

After the Muslim invasion of the 7th century AD, Persia was brought within the sphere of Islamic styles and techniques, clearly reflected in the ceramics and ornate calligraphy which developed. During the Mongol Timurid dynasty (1369–1506) Chinese influences were apparent in the development of one of Persia's greatest artistic achievements, the miniature, which was used to illustrate books of poetry, history, and romances. By the 15th century a distinctively Persian style had evolved, characterized by firm lines, strong colours, and a lot of detail; its greatest exponent was Bihzad (c. 1450–1536). The Timurid dynasty also saw the use of coloured tiles to cover buildings, for example on the Blue Mosque of Tabriz.

The Safavid dynasty (1502–1736) produced miniatures, which now began to show the influence of Western styles; fine carpets – many of the finest Persian carpets are Safavid; fabrics, particularly silk; and metalwork. Palaces were decorated with murals. The Safavid dynasty marked the beginning of Persia's artistic decline, as European influences grew stronger.

Persian Gulf or ***Arabian Gulf*** large shallow inlet of the Arabian Sea; area 233,000 sq km/90,000 sq mi. It divides the Arabian peninsula from Iran and is linked by the Strait of Hormuz and the Gulf of Oman to the Arabian Sea. Oilfields surround it in the Gulf States of Bahrain, Iran, Iraq, Kuwait, Oman, Qatar, Saudi Arabia, and the United Arab Emirates.

Persian language language belonging to the Indo-Iranian branch of the Indo-European family; see ◊Farsi.

Persian literature before the Arab conquest Persian literature is represented by the sacred books of ◊Zoroastrianism known as the *Avesta* and later translated into Pahlavi, in which language there also appeared various secular writings. After the conquest the use of Arabic became widespread. The Persian language was revived during the 9th century, and the following centuries saw a succession of brilliant poets, including the epic writer Firdawsi, the didactic S'adi (1184–1291), the mystic Rumi (1207–1273), the lyrical Hâfiz, and Jami, who combined the gifts of his predecessors and is considered the last of the classical poets. Omar Khayyám, who is well known outside Iran, is considered less important there. In the 16th and 17th centuries many Persian writers worked in India, still using classical forms and themes.

The introduction of the printing-press in the 19th century made possible a new newspaper culture, although hampered by censorship and limited readership, through which much literary work was published. Histories and translations soon followed, in a prose increasingly open to Western influences. Persian poetry, strongly traditional, blending classical courtly idiom with popular ballad and lampoon, was widely diffused among an only partly literate audience which discouraged the development of

'No arm of the sea has been, or is of greater interest alike to the geologist and archeologist, the historian and geographer, the merchant and the student of strategy, than the inland water known as the Persian Gulf.'

On the PERSIAN GULF Arnold Wilson *The Persian Gulf*

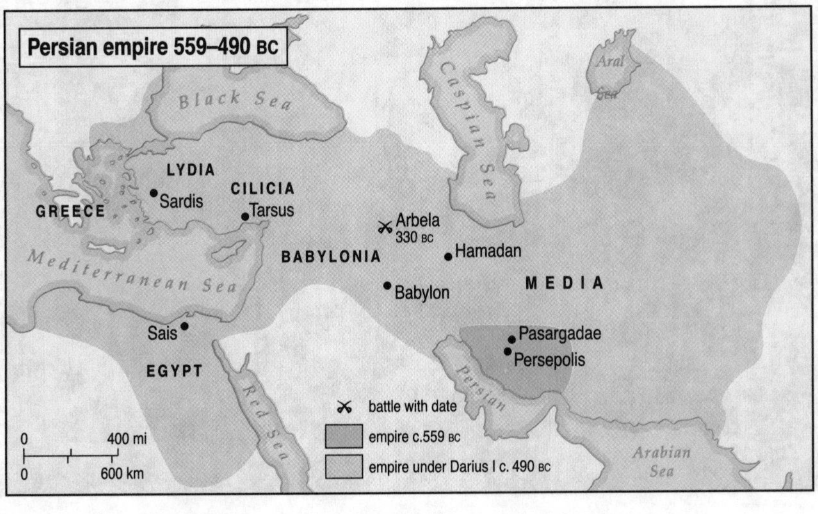

Persian empire 559–490 BC

battle with date

empire c.559 BC

empire under Darius I c. 490 BC

persimmon
Persimmon is the name given to the usually edible fruits of some species of the genus *Diospyros*. This genus includes various shrubs and trees native to the tropics and subtropical areas of the world. Persimmons are cultivated widely in Japan and China as ornamentals and for their fruits, some of which also produce a useful dye.

new forms despite the cautious innovations of Nīmā-yi Yūshīj (1895–1959). The alienation and isolation of the poet who has broken with tradition were poignantly expressed by the poetess and film-maker Furūgh Farrukhzād (1935–1967). Since the 1930s realist fiction has become established. After the Iranian revolution of 1979 some important works such as Shusha Guppy's autobiographical *The Blindfold Horse* 1988 were written and published abroad.

Persian Wars series of conflicts between Greece and Persia 499–449 BC. The eventual victory of Greece marked the end of Persian domination of the ancient world and the beginning of Greek supremacy.

persicaria plant *Polygonum persicaria* of the dock family, found growing in waste places and arable land, often near water. Sprawling, with lance-shaped, black-spotted leaves, it bears spikes of pink flowers.

Pale persicaria *P. lapathifolium* is slightly larger, with pale dots on the leaves, and heads of usually white flowers.

persimmon any tree of the genus *Diospyros* of the ebony family Ebenaceae, especially the common persimmon *D. virginiana* of the SE USA. Up to 19 m/60 ft high, the persimmon has alternate oval leaves and yellow-green unisexual flowers. The small, sweet, orange fruits are edible.

The Japanese persimmon *D. kaki* has larger fruits and is widely cultivated.

personal computer (PC) another name for ◊microcomputer. The term is also used, more specifically, to mean the IBM Personal Computer and computers compatible with it.

The first IBM PC was introduced in 1981; it had 64 kilobytes of random access memory (RAM) and one floppy-disc drive. It was followed in 1983 by the XT (with a hard-disc drive) and in 1984 by the AT (based on a more powerful ◊microprocessor). Many manufacturers have copied the basic design, which is now regarded as a standard for business microcomputers. Computers designed to function like an IBM PC are IBM-compatible computers.

personal digital assistant (PDA) handheld computer designed to store names, addresses, and diary information, and to send and receive faxes and e-mail. They aim to provide a more flexible and powerful alternative to the filofax or diary, but have met with limited success.

Some PDAs (such as Apple's Newton) can recognize the user's handwriting and store it as digital text (with variable accuracy).

personality individual's characteristic way of behaving across a wide range of situations. Two broad dimensions of personality are extroversion and neuroticism. A number of more specific personal traits have also been described, including ◊psychopathy (antisocial behaviour).

'I am what is mine. Personality is the original personal property.'
On PERSONALITY
Norman O Brown
Love's Body 1967

personality cult practice by which a leader is elevated to a pre-eminent status through a propaganda campaign. In the USSR, the cult of personality was developed by Joseph Stalin in the 1930s. More recently, both Mao Zedong in China and Kim Il Sung in North Korea used similar techniques to reinforce their leadership and power.

personification ◊figure of speech (poetic or imaginative expression) in which animals, plants, objects, and ideas are treated as if they were human or alive ('Clouds chased each other across the face of the Moon'; 'Nature smiled on their work and gave it her blessing'; 'The future beckoned eagerly to them').

Personification has an important relationship with ◊allegory, as many allegorical works, such as Bunyan's *Pilgrim's Progress*, include characters that are personifications of abstract qualities, such as Despair.

perspective the realistic representation of a three-dimensional object in two dimensions. In a perspective drawing, vertical lines are drawn parallel from the top of the page to the bottom. Horizontal lines, however, are represented by straight lines which meet at one of two perspective points. These perspective points lie to the right and left of the drawing at a distance which depends on the view being taken of the object.

Perspex trade name for a clear, lightweight, tough plastic first produced 1930. It is widely used for watch glasses, advertising signs, domestic baths, motorboat windscreens, aircraft canopies, and protective shields. Its chemical name is polymethylmethacrylate (PMMA). It is manufactured under other names: Lucite, Acrylite, and Rhoplex (in the USA), and Oroglas (in Europe).

perspiration excretion of water and dissolved substances from the ◊sweat glands of the skin of mammals. Perspiration has two main functions: body cooling by the evaporation of water from the skin surface, and excretion of waste products such as salts.

Persson Goran 1949– . Swedish politician, prime minister from 1996. He was elected to parliament 1979 and made leader of the Social Democratic Labour Party (SAP) 1996. He served as finance minister for a time, before succeeding Ingvar Carlsson as prime minister.

Perth capital of Western Australia, with its port at nearby Fremantle on the Swan River; population (1993) 1,221,200. Industries include textiles, cement, furniture, vehicles, and oil refining. It was founded 1829 and expanded after gold was discovered at Kalgoorlie 1893. It is the commercial and cultural centre of the state, and the headquarters of the Royal Perth Yacht Club, from which the America's Cup challenge was staged 1987.

Perth industrial town and administrative headquarters of Perth and Kinross, E Scotland, on the river Tay; population (1991) 41,500. It was the capital of Scotland from the 12th century until James I of Scotland was assassinated here 1437. Industries include dyeing, textiles, whisky distilling, and carpets.

Perth and Kinross local authority of Scotland created 1996 *(see United Kingdom map)*.

pertussis medical name for ◊whooping cough, an infectious disease mainly seen in children.

Peru country in South America, on the Pacific, bounded N by Ecuador and Colombia, E by Brazil and Bolivia, and S by Chile. *See country box opposite.*

Peru Current formerly known as Humboldt Current cold ocean ◊current flowing north from the Antarctic along the W coast of South America to S Ecuador, then west. It reduces the coastal temperature, making the W slopes of the Andes arid because winds are already chilled and dry when they meet the coast.

Perugia capital of Umbria, Italy, 520 m/1,700 ft above the river Tiber, about 137 km/85 mi N of Rome; population (1992) 146,200. Its industries include textiles, liqueurs, and chocolate. One of the 12 cities of the ancient country of Etruria, it surrendered to Rome 309 BC. There is a university, founded 1276; a municipal palace, built 1281; and a 15th-century cathedral.

Perugino Pietro. Original name of Pietro di Cristoforo Vannucci c. 1446–1523. Italian painter. He taught Raphael, who absorbed his graceful figure style. Perugino produced paintings for the lower walls of the Sistine Chapel of the Vatican 1481 and in 1500 decorated the Sala del Cambio in Perugia. A work typical in its gracefulness is the altarpiece *Virgin and Child with St Michael and St Raphael* c. 1498 (National Gallery, London).

Perugino may have been a pupil of ◊Piero della Francesca and was probably an assistant to Verrocchio, his style being formed at Florence. Frescoes in the Palazzo Communale at Perugia 1475 were an early undertaking. In 1480 he was one of the artists chosen by Sixtus IV to embellish his newly finished Sistine Chapel, his fresco of *The Delivery of the Keys to St Peter* showing that sense of space he was to transmit to his pupil Raphael, who worked under him at Florence 1500–04.

Among principal works were his frescoes for the Collegio del Cambio, Perugia, the *Crucifixion with Saints*, 1496 (Florence, Santa Maria Maddalena de' Pazzi), and the altarpiece *Virgin and Child with St Michael and St Raphael* (National Gallery, London), in which, it has been speculatively suggested, there is a trace of the young Raphael's handiwork. Its gentle and youthful human types and

Perugino *The Crucifixion with the Virgin, St John, St Jerome, and St Mary Magdalene* c. 1485 by Perugino, National Gallery of Art, Washington, USA. With their balanced, harmonious compositions, lucid space, and graceful, dignified figures, Perugino's works epitomize the ideals of the Classical Renaissance.

also its serene sky and background, receding space being emphasized by tall, thin trees, indicate clearly enough the source of Raphael's early style, though Perugino was left behind by the great onward movement of the Renaissance in which Raphael attained his full stature.

Perutz Max Ferdinand 1914– . Austrian-born British biochemist who shared the 1962 Nobel Prize for Chemistry with his co-worker John Kendrew (1917–) for work on the structure of the haemoglobin molecule.

perverting the course of justice in law, the criminal offence of acting in such a way as to prevent justice being done. Examples are tampering with evidence, misleading the police or a court, and threatening witnesses or jurors.

Pesach Jewish name for the ◊Passover festival.

Peshawar capital of North-West Frontier Province, Pakistan, 18 km/11 mi E of the Khyber Pass; population (1981) 555,000. Products include textiles, leather, and copper.

pest in biology, any insect, fungus, rodent, or other living organism that has a harmful effect on human beings, other than those that directly cause human diseases. Most pests damage crops or livestock, but the term also covers those that damage buildings, destroy food stores, and spread disease.

Pestalozzi Johann Heinrich 1746–1827. Swiss educationalist who advocated the French philosopher Jean-Jacques Rousseau's 'natural' principles (of natural development and the power of example), and described his own theories in *Wie Gertrude ihre Kinder lehrt/How Gertrude Teaches her Children* 1801. He stressed the importance of mother and home in a child's education.

pesticide any chemical used in farming, gardening, or indoors to combat pests. Pesticides are of three main types: insecticides (to kill insects), fungicides (to kill fungal diseases), and herbicides (to kill plants, mainly those considered weeds). Pesticides cause a number of pollution problems through spray drift onto surrounding areas, direct contamination of users or the public, and as residues on food.

The safest pesticides include those made from plants, such as the insecticides pyrethrum and derris. Pyrethrins are safe and insects do not develop resistance to them. Their impact on the environment is very small as the ingredients break down harmlessly.

More potent are synthetic products, such as chlorinated hydrocarbons. These products, including DDT and dieldrin, are highly toxic to wildlife and often to human beings, so their use is now restricted by law in some areas and is declining. Safer pesticides such as malathion are based on organic phosphorus compounds, but they still present hazards to health. The aid organization Oxfam estimates that pesticides cause about 10,000 deaths worldwide every year. In 1991 Central America was the world's highest consumer of pesticides per head of the population.

Pesticides were used to deforest SE Asia during the Vietnam War, causing death and destruction to the area's ecology and lasting health and agricultural problems.

Many pesticides remain in the soil, since they are not biodegradable, and are then passed on to foods. In the UK, more than half of all potatoes sampled 1995 contained residues of a storage pesticide; seven different pesticides were found in carrots, with concentrations up to 25 times the permitted level; and 40% of bread contained pesticide residues. There are around 4,000 cases of acute pesticide poisoning a year in the UK. ▷ *See feature on pp. 858–859.*

Pétain (Henri) Philippe 1856–1951. French general and right-wing politician. His defence of Verdun 1916 during World War I made him a national hero.

In 1917 Pétain was created French commander in chief, although he became subordinate to Marshal Foch 1918. He suppressed a rebellion in Morocco 1925–26. As a member of the Higher Council of National Defence he advocated a purely defensive military policy, and was strongly conservative in politics. He became head of state 16 June 1940 and signed an armistice with Germany 22 June, convinced that Britain was close to defeat and that France should get the best terms possible. Although his ◊Vichy government collaborated with the

PERU
Republic of

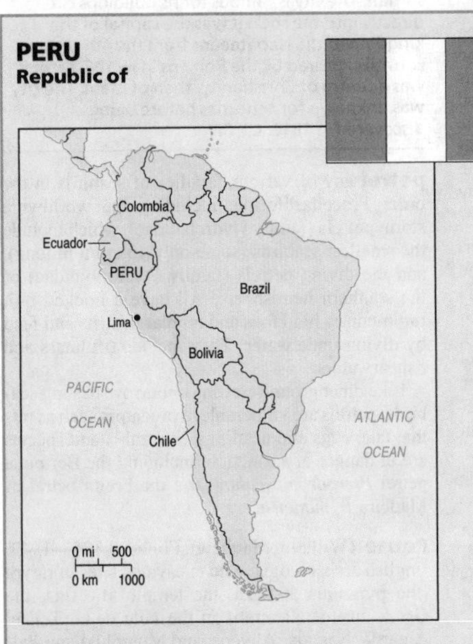

national name *República del Perú*
area 1,285,200 sq km/496,216 sq mi
capital Lima, including port of Callao
major towns/cities Arequipa, Iquitos, Chiclayo, Trujillo, Cuzco
physical features Andes mountains NW–SE cover 27% of Peru, separating Amazon river-basin jungle in NE from coastal plain in W; desert along coast N–S (Atacama Desert); Lake Titicaca
head of state Alberto Fujimori from 1990
head of government to be announced
political system democratic republic
administrative divisions 11 regions, the province of Callao, and 24 departments
political parties American Popular Revolutionary Alliance (APRA), moderate, left-wing; United Left (IU), left-wing; Change 90 (Cambio 90), centrist; New Majority (Nueva Mayoria), centrist; Popular Christian Party (PPC), right of centre; Liberal Party (PL), right-wing
population 23,780,000 (1995 est)
population growth rate 1.9% (1990–95); 1.7% (2000–05)
ethnic distribution about 45% South American Indian, 37% mestizo, 15% European, and 3% African
life expectancy 63 (men), 67 (women)
literacy rate men 92%, women 79%
languages Spanish, Quechua (both official), Aymara
religion Roman Catholic (state religion)
currency nuevo sol
GDP (US $) 50.08 billion (1994)
growth rate 12.9% (1994)
exports coca, coffee, alpaca, llama and vicuña wool, fish meal, fishery products, lead (largest producer in South America), copper, iron, oil

HISTORY
4000 BC Evidence of early settled agriculture in the Chicama Valley.
AD 700–1100 Period of Wari Empire, the first expansionist militarized empire in Andes.
1200 Manco Capac became first emperor of South American Indian Quechua-speaking Incas, who established a growing and sophisticated empire centred on the Andean city of Cuzco, and believed their ruler was descended from the sun.
late 15th C Inca Empire at its zenith, stretching from Quito in Ecuador to beyond Santiago in southern Chile; it superseded the Chimu civilization, which had flourished in Peru 1250–1470.
1532–33 Incas defeated by Spanish conquistadores, led by Francisco Pizarro, and king Atahualpa killed; came under Spanish rule, as part of Viceroyalty of Peru, with the capital in Lima, which was founded in 1535.
1541 Pizarro was assassinated as rivalries broke out among the conquistadores.
1780 Tupac Amaru, who claimed to be descended from the last Inca chieftain, led a failed native revolt against Spanish.
1810 Peru became headquarters for the Spanish government as European settlers rebelled elsewhere in Spanish America.
1820–22 Fight for liberation from Spanish rule led by General José de San Martin, and the Army of Andes which, after freeing Argentina and Chile, invaded S Peru.
1824 Became the last colony in Central and South America to achieve independence from Spain after attacks from the N by Field Marshal Sucre, acting for the freedom fighter Simón Bolívar.
1836–39 Failed attempts at union with Bolivia.
1845–62 Economic progress under rule of Gen Ramón Castilla.
1849–74 Around 80,000–100,000 Chinese labourers arrived in Peru to fill menial jobs such as collecting guano.
1866 Victorious naval war fought with Spain.
1879–83 Pacific War fought in alliance with Bolivia and over the nitrate fields of the Atacama Desert in the S; three provinces along the coastal S lost to Chile.
1902 Boundary dispute with Bolivia settled.
mid-1920s After several decades of civilian government, a series of right-wing dictatorships held power.
1927 Boundary dispute with Colombia settled.
1929 Tacna province, lost to Chile 1880, was returned.
1941 Brief war with Ecuador secured Amazonian territory.
1945 Civilian government, dominated by left-of-centre American Popular Revolutionary Alliance (APRA, formed 1924), came to power after free elections.
1948 Army coup installed a military government led by General Manuel Odría, who remained in power until 1956.
1963 Return to civilian rule, with centrist Fernando Belaúnde Terry as president.
1968 Return of military government in a bloodless coup by General Juan Velasco Alvarado, following industrial unrest. Populist land reform programme introduced.
1975 Velasco replaced, in a bloodless coup, by General Morales Bermúdez.
1980 Return to civilian rule, with Fernando Belaúnde as president; agrarian and industrial reforms pursued. Sendero Luminoso ('Shining Path') Maoist guerrilla group active.
1981 Boundary dispute with Ecuador renewed.
1985 Belaúnde succeeded by Social Democrat Alan García Pérez, who launched a campaign to remove military and police 'old guard'.
1987 President García delayed the nationalization of Peru's banks after a vigorous campaign against the proposal.
1988 García pressured to seek help from the International Monetary Fund (IMF) as economy deteriorated. Sendero Luminoso increased campaign of violence.
1990 Right-of-centre Alberto Fujimori, the son of Japanese immigrants, defeated ex-communist writer Vargas Llosa in presidential elections. Assassination attempt on president failed. Inflation 400%; privatization programme launched.
1992 Fujimori allied himself with the army and suspended the constitution, provoking international criticism. Sendero Luminoso leader arrested and sentenced to life imprisonment after a 'show trial'. New single-chamber legislature elected.
1993 New constitution adopted, enabling Fujimori to seek re-election.
1994 6,000 Sendero Luminoso guerrillas surrendered to the authorities.
1995 Border dispute with Ecuador resolved after armed clashes. Fujimori re-elected to second term. Controversial amnesty granted to those previously convicted of human-rights abuses.
1996 Armed Marxist guerrillas beseiged Japanese embassy in Lima, taking 500 people hostage.
1997 Hostage seige ended by government forces.

SEE ALSO Bolívar, Simón; Inca

Peter the Great Peter the Great, from an 18th-century mosaic. He was tsar of Russia from 1682, and instituted many reforms in the government, the administrative and legal systems, and the army. *Image Select (UK) Ltd*

Germans he dismissed his deputy Pierre Laval who wanted to side with the Axis powers Dec 1940. The Germans had Laval reinstated April 1942 and in Nov occupied the Vichy area of France, reducing Pétain's 'government' to a puppet regime. On the Allied invasion he was taken to Germany, but returned 1945 and was sentenced to death for treason, the sentence later being commuted to life imprisonment.

petal part of a flower whose function is to attract pollinators such as insects or birds. Petals are frequently large and brightly coloured and may also be scented. Some have a nectary at the base and markings on the petal surface, known as honey guides, to direct pollinators to the source of the nectar. In wind-pollinated plants, however, the petals are usually small and insignificant, and sometimes absent altogether. Petals are derived from modified leaves, and are known collectively as a corolla.

Some insect-pollinated plants also have inconspicuous petals, with large colourful ◊bracts (leaflike structures) or ◊sepals taking over their role, or strong scents that attract pollinators such as flies.

Peter (I) the Great 1672–1725. Tsar of Russia from 1682 on the death of his brother Tsar Feodor; he assumed control of the government 1689. He attempted to reorganize the country on Western lines; the army was modernized, a fleet was built, the administrative and legal systems were remodelled, education was encouraged, and the church was brought under state control. On the Baltic coast, where he had conquered territory from Sweden, Peter built his new capital, St Petersburg.

After a successful campaign against the Ottoman Empire 1696, he visited Holland and Britain to study Western techniques, and worked in Dutch and English shipyards. In order to secure an outlet to the Baltic, Peter undertook a war with Sweden 1700–21, which resulted in the acquisition of Estonia and parts of Latvia and Finland. A war with Persia 1722–23 added Baku to Russia.

'Imagine a temple cut out of the solid rock, … soaring upwards to the very top of the cliff in the most exquisite proportions and carved with groups of figures almost as fresh as when the chisel left them.'

On PETRA
Gertrude Bell, letter
29 March 1900

Peter II 1715–1730. Tsar of Russia from 1727. Son of Peter the Great, he had been passed over in favour of Catherine I 1725 but succeeded her 1727. He died of smallpox.

Peter III 1728–1762. Tsar of Russia 1762. Weak-minded son of Peter I's eldest daughter, Anne, he was adopted 1741 by his aunt ◊Elizabeth, Empress of Russia, and at her command married the future Catherine II 1745. He was deposed in favour of his wife and probably murdered by her lover, Alexius Orlov.

Peter I 1844–1921. King of Serbia from 1903. He was the son of Prince Alexander Karageorgevich and was elected king when the last Obrenovich king was murdered 1903. He took part in the retreat of the Serbian army 1915, and in 1918 was proclaimed first king of the Serbs, Croats, and Slovenes (renamed Yugoslavia in 1921).

Peter II 1923–1970. King of Yugoslavia 1934–45. He succeeded his father, Alexander I, and assumed the royal power after the overthrow of the regency 1941. He escaped to the UK after the German invasion, and married Princess Alexandra of Greece 1944. He was dethroned 1945 when Marshal Tito came to power and the Soviet-backed federal republic was formed.

Peterborough city in Cambridgeshire, England, on the river Nene, noted for its 12th-century cathedral; population (1991) 153,200, one of the fastest growing cities in Europe. It has an advanced electronics industry. Nearby Flag Fen disclosed 1985 a well-preserved Bronze Age settlement of 660 BC.

Peterborough Southern Township, the largest private-sector town in Europe, is planned for the S, threatening the world's largest colony of great crested newts in old clay pits.

Peterloo massacre the events in St Peter's Fields, Manchester, England, 16 Aug 1819, when an open-air meeting in support of parliamentary reform was charged by yeomanry and hussars. Eleven people were killed and 500 wounded. The name was given in analogy with the Battle of Waterloo.

Peter, St lived 1st century. Christian martyr, the author of two epistles in the New Testament and leader of the apostles. He is regarded as the first bishop of Rome, whose mantle the pope inherits. His real name was Simon, but he was nicknamed Kephas ('Peter', from the Greek for 'rock') by Jesus, as being the rock upon which he would build his church. His emblem is two keys; feast day 29 June.

Originally a fisherman of Capernaum, on the Sea of Galilee, Peter may have been a follower of John the Baptist, and was the first to acknowledge Jesus as the Messiah. Tradition has it that he later settled in Rome; he was martyred during the reign of the emperor Nero, perhaps by crucifixion. Bones excavated from under the Basilica of St Peter's in the Vatican 1968 were accepted as those of St Peter by Pope Paul VI.

Petipa Marius 1822–1910. French choreographer. He created some of the most important ballets in the classical repertory. For the Imperial Ballet in Russia he created masterpieces such as *Don Quixote* 1869, *La Bayadère* 1877, *The Sleeping Beauty* 1890, *Swan Lake* 1895 (with Ivanov), and *Raymonda* 1898.

A feature of Petipa's ballets were the ◊divertissements that brought the often thin storyline to a halt to allow the soloists a chance to display their virtuosity. These were contrasted with the shifting patterns and formations of the corps de ballet.

Petőfi Sándor 1823–1849. Hungarian nationalist poet. He published his first volume of poems 1844. He expressed his revolutionary ideas in the semi-autobiographical poem 'The Apostle', and died fighting the Austrians in the battle of Segesvár.

Petra (Arabic ***Wadi Musa***) ancient city carved out of the red rock at a site in Jordan, on the eastern slopes of the Wadi el Araba, 90 km/56 mi S of the Dead Sea. An Edomite stronghold and capital of the Nabataeans in the 2nd century, it was captured by the Roman emperor Trajan 106 and destroyed by the Arabs in the 7th century. It was forgotten in Europe until 1812 when the Swiss traveller Johann Ludwig Burckhardt (1784–1817) came across it.

Petrarch Francesco, (Italian *Petrarca*) 1304–1374. Italian poet, humanist, and leader of the revival of Classical learning. His *Il canzoniere/Songbook* (also known as *Rime Sparse/Scattered Lyrics*) contains madrigals, songs, and ◊sonnets in praise of his idealized love, 'Laura', whom he first saw 1327 (she was a married woman and refused to become his mistress). These were Petrarch's greatest contributions to Italian literature; they shaped the lyric poetry of the Renaissance and greatly influenced French and English love poetry. Although he did not invent the sonnet form, he was its finest early practitioner and the 'Petrarchan sonnet' was admired as an ideal model by later poets.

A passionate believer in the power of ancient literature to restore antique virtue, culture, and social order to a degraded age, he inspired the new feeling in Italy and Europe towards study of the classics and more than anyone else directed young scholars towards ancient learning. He was a friend of the poet ◊Boccaccio, and supported the political reformer Cola di ◊Rienzi's attempt to establish an ancient Roman-style republic 1347.

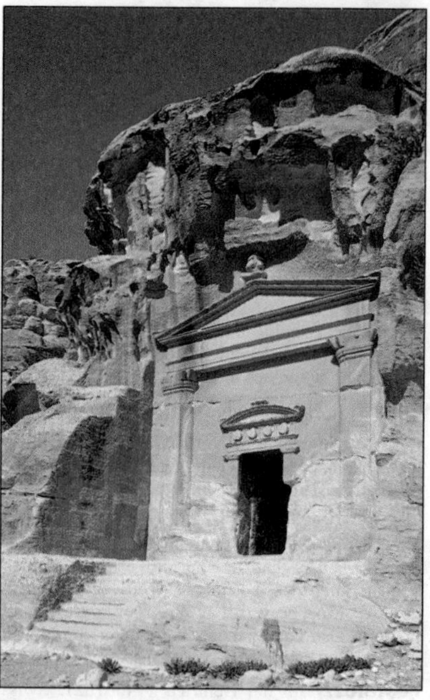

Petra Ruins near the ancient city of Petra in Jordan. The city is famous for its buildings cut directly into the rock. It was the capital of the kingdom of the Nabataeans from the 4th century BC until captured by the Romans in AD 106. Later it was a centre of Christianity, then of Islam. The city was unknown for centuries before being discovered in 1812. *Corbis*

petrel any of various families of seabirds in the order Procellariiforme, including the worldwide storm petrels (family Hydrobatidae), which include the smallest seabirds (some only 13 cm/5 in long), and the diving petrels (family Pelecanoididae) of the southern hemisphere. All have a hooked bill, rudimentary hind toes and tubular nostrils and feed by diving underwater. They include ◊fulmars and ◊shearwaters.

Like other ground-nesting or burrow-nesting seabirds, petrels are vulnerable to predators such as rats that take eggs and nestlings. Several island species are in danger of extinction, including the Bermuda petrel *Pterodroma cahow* and the Freira petrel of Madeira *P. madeira*.

Petrie (William Matthew) Flinders 1853–1942. English archaeologist who excavated sites in Egypt (the pyramids at Gîza, the temple at Tanis, the Greek city of Naucratis in the Nile delta, Tell el Amarna, Naqada, Abydos, and Memphis) and Palestine from 1880. Petrie's work was exacting and systematic, and he developed dating sequences of pottery styles that correlated with dynastic and predynastic events.

petrochemical chemical derived from the processing of petroleum (crude oil).

Petrochemical industries are those that obtain their raw materials from the processing of petroleum and natural gas. Polymers, detergents, solvents, and nitrogen fertilizers are all major products of the petrochemical industries. Inorganic chemical

petrel Like all petrels, the Madeiran fork-tailed petrel has globular salt glands close to the eyes. About 100 species of petrels are known, most of which range over the cold southern seas. They are highly social birds, nesting in large colonies and feeding together in large, floating 'rafts'.

products include carbon black, sulphur, ammonia, and hydrogen peroxide.

petrodollars in economics, dollar earnings of nations that make up the ◊Organization of Petroleum-Exporting Countries (OPEC).

Petrograd former name (1914–24) of St Petersburg, a city in Russia.

petrol mixture of hydrocarbons derived from petroleum, mainly used as a fuel for internal-combustion engines. It is colourless and highly volatile. Leaded petrol contains antiknock (a mixture of tetraethyl lead and dibromoethane), which improves the combustion of petrol and the performance of a car engine. The lead from the exhaust fumes enters the atmosphere, mostly as simple lead compounds. There is strong evidence that it can act as a nerve poison on young children and cause mental impairment. This has prompted a gradual switch to the use of unleaded petrol in the UK.

The changeover from leaded petrol gained momentum from 1989 owing to a change in the tax on petrol, making it cheaper to buy unleaded fuel. Unleaded petrol contains a different mixture of hydrocarbons, and has a lower ◊octane rating than leaded petrol. Leaded petrol cannot be used in cars fitted with a ◊catalytic converter.

In the USA, petrol is called gasoline, and unleaded petrol has been used for some years.

petrol engine the most commonly used source of power for motor vehicles, introduced by the German engineers Gottlieb Daimler and Karl Benz 1885. The petrol engine is a complex piece of machinery made up of about 150 moving parts. It is a reciprocating piston engine, in which a number of pistons move up and down in cylinders. The motion of the pistons rotate a crankshaft, at the end of which is a heavy flywheel. From the flywheel the power is transferred to the car's driving wheels via the transmission system of clutch, gearbox, and final drive.

The parts of the petrol engine can be subdivided into a number of systems. The fuel system pumps fuel from the petrol tank into the carburettor. There it mixes with air and is sucked into the engine cylinders. (With electronic fuel injection, it goes directly from the tank into the cylinders by way of an electronic monitor.) The ignition system supplies the sparks to ignite the fuel mixture in the cylinders. By means of an ignition coil and contact breaker, it boosts the 12-volt battery voltage to pulses of 18,000 volts or more. These go via a distributor to the spark plugs in the cylinders, where they create the sparks. (Electronic ignitions replace these parts.) Ignition of the fuel in the cylinders produces temperatures of 700°C/1,300°F or more, and the engine must be cooled to prevent overheating.

Most engines have a water-cooling system, in which water circulates through channels in the cylinder block, thus extracting the heat. It flows through pipes in a radiator, which are cooled by fan-blown air. A few cars and most motorbikes are air-cooled, the cylinders being surrounded by many fins to present a large surface area to the air. The lubrication system also reduces some heat, but its main job is to keep the moving parts coated with oil, which is pumped under pressure to the camshaft, crankshaft, and valve-operating gear.

petroleum or ***crude oil*** natural mineral oil, a thick greenish-brown flammable liquid found underground in permeable rocks. Petroleum consists of hydrocarbons mixed with oxygen, sulphur, nitrogen, and other elements in varying proportions. It is thought to be derived from ancient organic material that has been converted by, first, bacterial action, then heat and pressure (but its origin may be chemical also).

From crude petroleum, various products are made by distillation and other processes; for example, fuel oil, petrol, kerosene, diesel, and lubricating oil. Petroleum products and chemicals are used in large quantities in the manufacture of detergents, artificial fibres, plastics, insecticides, fertilizers, pharmaceuticals, toiletries, and synthetic rubber.

Petroleum was formed from the remains of marine plant and animal life which existed many millions of years ago (hence it is known as a fossil fuel). Some of these remains were deposited along with rock-forming sediments under the sea where they were decomposed anaerobically (without oxygen) by bacteria which changed the fats of the sediments into fatty acids which were then changed into an asphaltic material called kerogen. This was then converted over millions of years into petroleum by the combined action of heat and pressure.

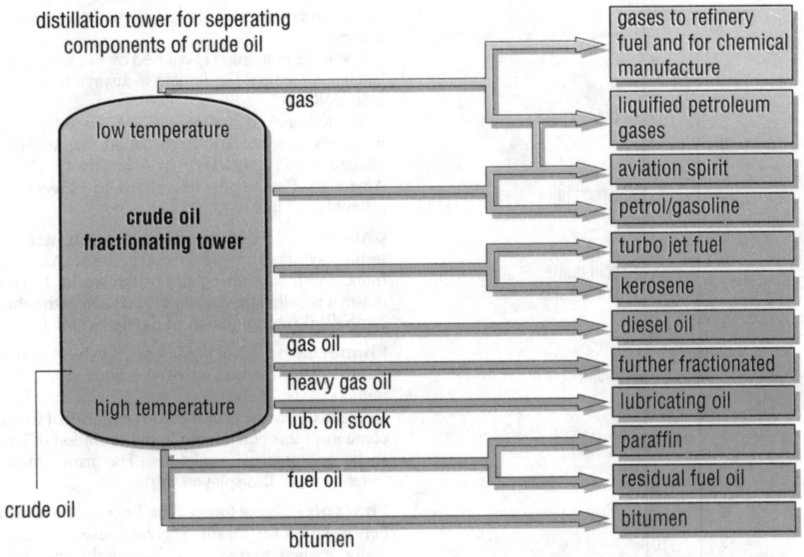

The modern oil industry originates in the discovery of oil in western Ontario in 1857 followed by Edwin Drake's discovery in Pennsylvania in 1859. Drake used a steam engine to drive a punching tool to 21 m below the surface where he struck oil and started an oil boom. Rapid development followed in other parts of the USA, Canada, Mexico, and then Venezuela where commercial production began in 1878. Oil was found in Romania in 1860, Iran in 1908, Iraq in 1923, Bahrain in 1932, and Saudi Arabia and Kuwait in 1938.

The USA led in production until the 1960s, when the Middle East outproduced other areas, their immense reserves leading to a worldwide dependence on cheap oil for transport and industry. In 1961 the Organization of the Petroleum Exporting Countries (OPEC) was established to avoid exploitation of member countries; after OPEC's price rises in 1973, the International Energy Agency (IEA) was established 1974 to protect the interests of oil-consuming countries. New technologies were introduced to pump oil from offshore and from the Arctic (the Alaska pipeline) in an effort to avoid a monopoly by OPEC. Global consumption of petroleum in 1993 was 23 billion barrels.

pollutionThe burning of petroleum fuel is one cause of air pollution. The transport of oil can lead to catastrophes – for example, the *Torrey Canyon* tanker lost off SW England 1967, which led to an agreement by the international oil companies 1968 to pay compensation for massive shore pollution. The 1989 oil spill in Alaska from the *Exxon Valdez* damaged the area's fragile environment, despite clean-up efforts. Drilling for oil involves the risks of accidental spillage and drilling-rig accidents. The problems associated with oil have led to the various alternative ◊energy technologies.

A new kind of bacterium was developed during the 1970s in the USA, capable of 'eating' oil as a means of countering oil spills.

distillation tower for seperating components of crude oil
low temperature
crude oil fractionating tower
high temperature
crude oil
gas
gas oil
heavy gas oil
lub. oil stock
fuel oil
bitumen
gases to refinery fuel and for chemical manufacture
liquified petroleum gases
aviation spirit
petrol/gasoline
turbo jet fuel
kerosene
diesel oil
further fractionated
lubricating oil
paraffin
residual fuel oil
bitumen

petroleum Refining petroleum using a distillation column. The crude petroleum is fed in at the bottom of the column where the temperature is high. The gases produced rise up the column, cooling as they travel. At different heights up the column, different gases condense to liquids called fractions, and are drawn off.

petrology branch of geology that deals with the study of rocks, their mineral compositions, and their origins.

Petronius Gaius, known as Petronius Arbiter, died 1st century. Roman author of the licentious romance *Satyricon*. He was a companion of the emperor Nero and supervisor of his pleasures.

'Beware of the dog.'

PETRONIUS *Satyricon*

Peugeot France's second-largest car manufacturer, founded 1885 when Armand Peugeot (1849–1915) began making bicycles; the company bought the rival firm Citroën 1974 and the European operations of the American Chrysler Company 1978.

In 1889 Armand Peugeot produced his first steam car and in 1890 his first petrol-driven car, with a Daimler engine. Peugeot's cars did well in races and were in demand from the public, and by 1900 he was producing a range of models. In the 1930s Peugeot sporting family cars sold widely. In 1978, after the acquisition of Chrysler in Europe, the Talbot marque was reintroduced.

Pevsner Nikolaus Bernhard Leon 1902–1983. Anglo-German art historian. Born in Leipzig, he fled from the Nazis to England. He became an authority on architecture, especially English. His *Outline of European Architecture* was published 1942 (followed by numerous other editions). In his series *The Buildings of England* (46 volumes) 1951–74, he built up a first-hand report on every notable building in the country.

pewter any of various alloys of mostly tin with varying amounts of lead, copper, or antimony. Pewter has been known for centuries and was once widely used for domestic utensils but is now used mainly for ornamental ware.

peyote spineless cactus *Lophopora williamsii* of N Mexico and the SW USA. It has white or pink

peyote Peyote cactus (mescal) *Lophophora williamsii* is found in Mexico and the SW USA. It is a spineless cactus which produces small pink flowers in Aug and Sept, after the arrival of the summer rains. *Premaphotos Wildlife*

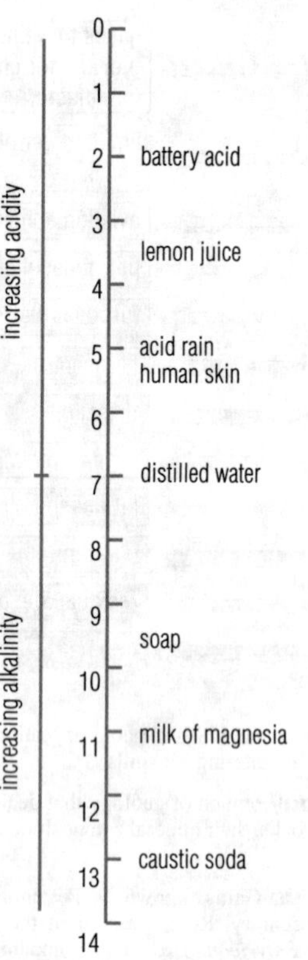

pH The pHs of some common substances. The lower the pH the more acid the substance.

flowers. Its buttonlike tops contain the hallucinogen mescaline, which is used by American Indians in religious ceremonies.

Pfalz German name of the historic division of Germany, the ◊Palatinate.

pH scale from 0 to 14 for measuring acidity or alkalinity. A pH of 7.0 indicates neutrality, below 7 is acid, while above 7 is alkaline. Strong acids, such as those used in car batteries, have a pH of about 2; strong alkalis such as sodium hydroxide are pH 13.

Acidic fruits such as citrus fruits are about pH 4. Fertile soils have a pH of about 6.5 to 7.0, while weak alkalis such as soap are 9 to 10.

Phaedrus c. 15 BC–c. AD 50. Roman fable writer. Born in Macedonia, he came to Rome as a slave in the household of Emperor Augustus, where he learnt Latin and was later freed. The allusions in his 97 fables (modelled on those of Aesop) caused him to be brought to trial by a minister of Emperor Tiberius. His work was popular in the Middle Ages.

Phaethon in Greek mythology, the son of Helios, the sun god, who was allowed for one day to drive the chariot of the Sun. Losing control of the horses, he almost set the Earth on fire and was killed by Zeus with a thunderbolt.

phage another name for a ◊bacteriophage, a virus that attacks bacteria.

phagocyte type of white blood cell, or ◊leucocyte, that can engulf a bacterium or other invading microorganism. Phagocytes are found in blood, lymph, and other body tissues, where they also ingest foreign matter and dead tissue. A ◊macrophage differs in size and life span.

Phalangist member of a Lebanese military organization (***Phalanges Libanaises***), since 1958 the political and military force of the ◊Maronite Church in Lebanon. The Phalangists' unbending right-wing policies and resistance to the introduction of democratic institutions were among the contributing factors to the civil war in Lebanon.

phalanx in ancient Greece and Macedon, a battle formation using up to 16 lines of infantry with pikes about 4 m/13 ft long, protected to the sides and rear by cavalry. It was used by Philip II and Alexander the Great of Macedon, and though more successful than the conventional ◊hoplite formation, it proved inferior to the Roman legion.

phalarope any of a genus *Phalaropus* of small, elegant shorebirds in the sandpiper family (Scolopacidae). They have the habit of spinning in the water to stir up insect larvae. They are native to North America, the UK, and the polar regions of Europe.

The male phalarope is courted by the female and hatches the eggs. The female is always larger and more colourful.

The red-necked phalarope *P. lobatus* and grey *P. fulicarius* visit the UK from the Arctic; Wilson's phalarope *P. tricolor* is exclusively North American. Phalaropes are related to plovers and resemble sandpipers.

phallus model of the male sexual organ, used as a fertility symbol in ancient Greece, Rome, Anatolia, India, and many other parts of the world. In Hinduism it is called the *lingam*, and is used as the chief symbolical representation of the deity Shiva.

Phanerozoic (Greek *phanero* 'visible') eon in Earth history, consisting of the most recent 570 million years. It comprises the Palaeozoic, Mesozoic, and Cenozoic eras. The vast majority of fossils come from this eon, owing to the evolution of hard shells and internal skeletons. The name means 'interval of well-displayed life'.

Pharaoh Hebrew form of the Egyptian royal title Per-'o. This term, meaning 'great house', was originally applied to the royal household, and after about 950 BC to the king.

Pharisee (Hebrew 'separatist') member of a conservative Jewish sect that arose in the 2nd century BC in protest against all movements favouring compromise with Hellenistic culture. The Pharisees were devout adherents of the law, both as found in the Torah and in the oral tradition known as the *Mishnah*.

They were opposed by the ◊Sadducees on several grounds: the Sadducees did not acknowledge the Mishnah; the Pharisees opposed Greek and Roman rule of their country; and the Pharisees held a number of beliefs – such as the existence of hell, angels, and demons, the resurrection of the dead, and the future coming of the Messiah – not found in the Torah.

The Pharisees rejected political action, and in the 1st century AD the left wing of their followers, the Zealots, broke away to pursue a revolutionary nationalist policy. After the fall of Jerusalem, Pharisee ideas became the basis of orthodox Judaism as the people were dispersed throughout the W Roman empire.

pharmacology study of the properties of drugs and their effects on the human body.

pharynx muscular cavity behind the nose and mouth, extending downwards from the base of the skull. Its walls are made of muscle strengthened with a fibrous layer and lined with mucous membrane. The internal nostrils lead backwards into the pharynx, which continues downwards into the oesophagus and (through the epiglottis) into the windpipe. On each side, a Eustachian tube enters the pharynx from the middle ear cavity.

The upper part (nasopharynx) is an airway, but the remainder is a passage for food. Inflammation of the pharynx is named pharyngitis.

phase in astronomy, the apparent shape of the Moon or a planet when all or part of its illuminated hemisphere is facing the Earth.

The Moon undergoes a full cycle of phases from new (when between the Earth and the Sun) through first quarter (when at 90° eastern elongation from the Sun), full (when opposite the Sun), and last quarter (when at 90° western elongation from the Sun). The Moon is gibbous (more than half but less than fully illuminated) when between first quarter and full or full and last quarter. Mars can appear gibbous at quadrature (when it is at right angles to the Sun in the sky). The gibbous appearance of Jupiter is barely noticeable. The planets whose orbits lie within that of the Earth can also undergo a full cycle of phases, as can an asteroid passing inside the Earth's orbit.

phase in chemistry, a physical state of matter: for example, ice and liquid water are different phases of water; a mixture of the two is termed a two-phase system.

phase in physics, a stage in an oscillatory motion, such as a wave motion: two waves are in phase when their peaks and their troughs coincide. Otherwise, there is a phase difference, which has consequences in ◊interference phenomena and ◊alternating current electricity.

pheasant any of various large, colourful Asiatic fowls of the family Phasianidae, order Galliformes, which also includes grouse, quail, and turkey. The typical pheasants are in the genus *Phasianus*, which has two species: the Japanese pheasant, *P. versicolor*, found in Japan, and the Eurasian ring-necked or common pheasant, *P. colchicus*, also introduced to North America. The genus is distinguished by the very long wedge-shaped tail and the absence of a crest. The plumage of the male common pheasant is richly tinted with brownish-green, yellow, and red markings, but the female is a camouflaged brownish colour. The nest is made on the ground. The male is polygamous.

Among the more exotically beautiful pheasants of other genera, often kept as ornamental birds, are the golden pheasant *Chrysolophus pictus* and Lady Amherst's pheasant *Chrysolophus amherstiae*, both from China, and the argus pheasant *Argusianus argus* of Malaysia, which has metallic spots or 'eyes' on the wings.

Reeves's pheasant *Symaticus reevesii*, a native of China, is over 2 m/6.6 ft in length, and has yellow and brown spangled plumage.

phenol member of a group of aromatic chemical compounds with weakly acidic properties, which are characterized by a hydroxyl (OH) group attached directly to an aromatic ring. The simplest of the phenols, derived from benzene, is also known as phenol and has the formula C_6H_5OH. It is sometimes called carbolic acid and can be extracted from coal tar.

Pure phenol consists of colourless, needle-shaped crystals, which take up moisture from the atmosphere. It has a strong and characteristic smell and was once used as an antiseptic. It is, however, toxic by absorption through the skin.

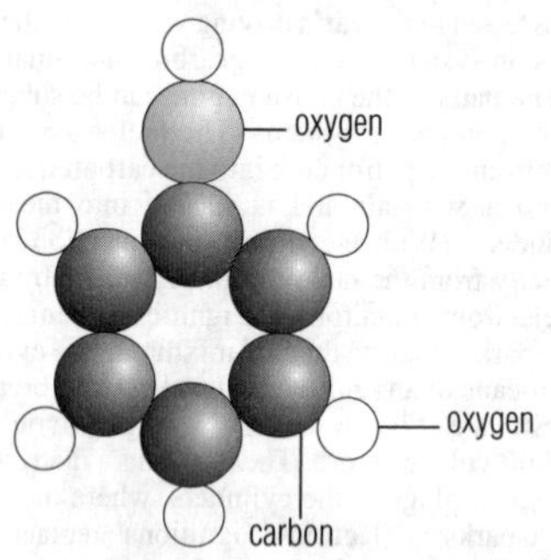

phenol The phenol molecule with its ring of six carbon atoms and a hydroxyl (OH) group attached. Phenol was first extracted from coal tar in 1834. It is used to make phenolic and epoxy resins, explosives, pharmaceuticals, perfumes, and nylon.

phenomenalism philosophical position that argues that statements about objects can be reduced to statements about what is perceived or perceivable. Thus English philosopher John Stuart Mill defined material objects as 'permanent possibilities of sensation'. Phenomenalism is closely connected with certain forms of ◊empiricism.

phenomenology the philosophical perspective, founded by the German philosopher Edmund ◊Husserl, that concentrates on phenomena as objects of perception (rather than as facts or occurrences that exist independently) in attempting to examine the ways people think about and interpret the world around them. It has been practised by the philosophers Martin Heidegger, Jean-Paul Sartre, and Maurice Merleau-Ponty.

In contrast to positivism or 'scientific' philosophy, phenomenology sees reality as essentially relative and subjective, and uses such tools as ethnomethodology and symbolic interactionism to focus on the structure of everyday life.

phenotype in genetics, visible traits, those actually displayed by an organism. The phenotype is not a direct reflection of the ◊genotype because some alleles are masked by the presence of other, dominant, alleles (see ◊dominance). The phenotype is further modified by the effects of the environment (for example, poor nutrition stunts growth).

phenylketonuria inherited metabolic condition in which the liver of a child cannot control the level of phenylalanine (an ◊amino acid derived from protein food) in the bloodstream. The condition must be detected promptly and a special diet started in the first few weeks of life if brain damage is to be avoided. Untreated, it causes stunted growth, epilepsy, and severe mental disability.

pheromone chemical signal (such as an odour) that is emitted by one animal and affects the behaviour of others. Pheromones are used by many animal species to attract mates.

Phidias or ***Pheidias*** lived mid-5th century BC. Greek sculptor. Active in Athens, he supervised the sculptural programme for the Parthenon (most of it is preserved in the British Museum, London, and known as the ◊Elgin marbles). He also executed the colossal statue of Zeus at Olympia, one of the ◊Seven Wonders of the World. No surviving sculptures can be credited to him with certainty.

He was a friend of the political leader Pericles, who made him superintendent of public works in Athens. Phidias executed for the Parthenon the statue of Athena in ivory and gold about 438 BC. Six years later, he was accused of impiety in having introduced his own and Pericles' likenesses on the shield of the goddess and of stealing the gold entrusted to him. He died either in prison or in exile.

Philadelphia ('the city of brotherly love') industrial city and financial centre, and the world's largest freshwater port, on the Delaware River at the junction of the Schuykill River, in Pennsylvania, USA; population (1992) 1,552,600; metropolitan area (1992) 5,939,000. Industries include refined oil, chemicals, textiles, processed food, printing and publishing, and transportation equipment.

history Founded 1682 as 'the city of brotherly love' by William Penn as a Quaker settlement, its religious tolerance made it the most populated city of the 13 colonies. It was the first capital of the US 1790–1800; the Constitution was drafted here 1787. The Centennial Exposition, the first international trade fair in the US, was held here 1876. Its population in 1950 was 2.1 million, but urban decay and the migration of industry led to a decline in population.

features Independence Square National Historic Park contains Independence Hall 1732, where the Declaration of Independence was adopted 4 July 1776 and the Constitution was adopted 17 September 1787. Congress hall, where the US Congress met 1790–1800 is in Independence Hall. Other landmarks include the Liberty Bell 1753, Christ Church 1754, Christ Church Burial Ground (with the grave of Benjamin Franklin), Carpenters Hall 1770, where the First Continental Congress convened 1774, Philosophical Hall 1785 (the headquarters of the American Philosophical Society, founded by Benjamin Franklin 1743), Betsy Ross House (where the first American flag was sewn) and Elfreth's Alley 1702 (the oldest residential street in continuous occupation in the United States). City Hall 1871–1900, with 642 rooms, a 37-ft bronze statue of William Penn, and a 30-mile view from the observation area, is the largest city hall in the United States. Penn's Landing, where William Penn landed 1682, is in a riverside park on the Delaware River waterfront.

The Philadelphia Museum of Art is world-famous, and the Pennsylvania Academy of the Fine Arts 1804 is the oldest art institution in the United States. The Rodin Museum has the best collection of Rodin sculptures outside France. Other museums include the Rosenbach Museum and Library 1863, the Academy of Natural Sciences 1868 (founded 1813), the first natural history museum in the United States, and the Franklin Institute. The Philadelphia Orchestra became famous under Leopold Stokowski and Eugene Ormandy. The University of Pennsylvania is here. Fairmount Park is the largest city park in the world. The United States Mint 1969 is the largest mint in the world.

philanthropy love felt by an individual towards humankind. It is expressed through acts of generosity and ◊charity and seeks to promote the greater happiness and prosperity of humanity.

The term derives from the Greek, but the notion of caring for more than oneself and one's immediate family is the basis for all civilizations. It can be found in the writings of ◊Confucius and ◊Mencius and it is a central tenet of Judaism, where it is considered not just a virtue but an obligation. To do good works and to relieve suffering is to recognize one's fellow beings equally as children of God. Philanthropy in the forms of charity and ◊aid has sometimes been accused of perpetuating poverty and inequality by victimizing the recipients rather than encouraging self-help.

philately the collection and study of postage stamps. It originated as a hobby in France about 1860.

Many countries earn extra revenue and cater to the philatelist by issuing sets of stamps to commemorate special events, anniversaries, and so on. There are many specialized fields of collection, from particular countries to specimens that have some defect; for example, contemporary issues that accidentally remain unperforated.

Philby Kim (Harold Adrian Russell) 1912–1988. British intelligence officer from 1940 and Soviet agent from 1933. He was liaison officer in Washington 1949–51, when he was confirmed to be a double agent and asked to resign. Named in 1963 as having warned Guy Burgess and Donald Maclean (similarly double agents) that their activities were known, he fled to the USSR and became a Soviet citizen and general in the KGB. A fourth member of the ring was Anthony Blunt.

Philby British double agent Kim Philby facing the press. Philby became a communist at Cambridge, like Burgess, Maclean, and Blunt. He worked for British Intelligence during and after World War II, and then at the British embassy in Washington, where he liaised with the CIA. During this time he was supplying secret intelligence information to the Russians. He was uncovered as a double agent in 1951 and asked to resign. He disappeared to the USSR in 1963. *Corbis*

Philip Duke of Edinburgh 1921– . Prince of the UK, husband of Elizabeth II, a grandson of George I of Greece and a great-great-grandson of Queen Victoria. He was born in Corfu, Greece, but brought up in England.

He was educated at Gordonstoun and Dartmouth Naval College. During World War II he served in the Mediterranean, taking part in the battle of Matapan, and in the Pacific. A naturalized British subject, taking the surname Mountbatten March 1947, he married Princess Elizabeth in Westminster Abbey 20 Nov 1947, having the previous day received the title Duke of Edinburgh. In 1956 he founded the Duke of Edinburgh's Award Scheme to encourage creative achievement among young people. He was created a prince of the UK 1957, and awarded the Order of Merit 1968.

Philip six kings of France, including:

Philip II (Philip Augustus) 1165–1223. King of France from 1180. As part of his efforts to establish a strong monarchy and evict the English from their French possessions, he waged war in turn against the English kings Henry II, Richard I (with whom he also went on the Third Crusade), and John (whom he defeated, along with Emperor Otto IV, at the decisive battle of Bouvines in Flanders 1214).

Philip IV the Fair 1268–1314. King of France from 1285. He engaged in a feud with Pope Boniface VIII and made him a prisoner 1303.

Clement V (1264–1314), elected pope through Philip's influence 1305, moved the papal seat to Avignon 1309 and collaborated with Philip to suppress the ◊Templars, a powerful order of knights. Philip allied with the Scots against England and invaded Flanders.

Philip VI 1293–1350. King of France from 1328, first of the house of Valois, elected by the barons on the death of his cousin, Charles IV. His claim was challenged by Edward III of England, who defeated him at Crécy 1346.

Philip II of Macedon 382–336 BC. King of ◊Macedonia from 359 BC. He seized the throne from his nephew, for whom he was regent, defeated the Greek city states at the battle of Chaeronea (in central Greece) 338 and formed them into a league whose forces could be united against Persia. He was assassinated while he was planning this expedition, and was succeeded by his son ◊Alexander the Great.

Philip's tomb was discovered at Vergina, N Greece, in 1978.

Philip five kings of Spain, including:

Philip (I) the Handsome 1478–1506. King of Castile from 1504, through his marriage 1496 to Joanna the Mad (1479–1555). He was the son of the Holy Roman emperor Maximilian I.

Philip II 1527–1598. King of Spain from 1556. He was born at Valladolid, the son of the Habsburg emperor Charles V, and in 1554 married Queen Mary of England. On his father's abdication 1556 he inherited Spain, the Netherlands, and the Spanish possessions in Italy and the Americas, and in 1580 he annexed Portugal. His intolerance and lack of understanding of the Netherlands drove them into revolt. Political and religious differences combined to involve him in war with England and, after 1589, with France. The defeat of the ◊Spanish Armada (the fleet sent to invade England in 1588) marked the beginning of the decline of Spanish power.

Philip V 1683–1746. King of Spain from 1700. A grandson of Louis XIV of France, he was the first Bourbon king of Spain. He was not recognized by the major European powers until 1713. See ◊Spanish Succession, War of the.

Philippines country in SE Asia, on an archipelago of more than 7,000 islands W of the Pacific Ocean and S of the SE Asian mainland. *See country box on p. 838.*

Philip Neri, St 1515–1595. Italian Roman Catholic priest who organized the Congregation of the Oratory (see ◊Oratorian). He built the oratory over the church of St Jerome, Rome, where prayer meetings were held and scenes from the Bible performed with music, originating the musical form ◊oratorio. Feast day 26 May.

Philippa of Hainault c. 1314–1369. Daughter of William III Count of Holland; wife of King Edward III of England, whom she married in York Minster 1328, and by whom she had 12 children (including Edward the Black Prince, Lionel Duke of Clarence, John Duke of Lancaster, Edmund Duke of York, and Thomas Duke of Gloucester). She was admired for her clemency and successfully pleaded for the lives of the six burghers of Calais who surrendered to save the town from destruction 1347.

Philippi ancient city of Macedonia founded by Philip of Macedon 358 BC. Near Philippi, Mark Antony and Augustus defeated Brutus and Cassius 42 BC, and the Roman colony was established. St Paul addressed a New Testament letter to the church in the city.

Philip, St lived 1st century AD. In the New Testament, one of the 12 apostles. He was an inhabitant of Bethsaida (N Israel), and is said to have worked as a missionary in Anatolia. Feast day 3 May.

Philip the Good 1396–1467. Duke of Burgundy from 1419. He engaged in the Hundred Years' War as an ally of England until he made peace with the French at the Council of Arras 1435. He made the Netherlands a centre of art and learning.

Philistine member of a seafaring people of non-Semitic origin who founded city-states on the Palestinian coastal plain in the 12th century BC, adopting a Semitic language and religion.

They were at war with the Israelites in the 11th–10th centuries BC (hence the pejorative use of their name in Hebrew records for anyone uncivilized in intellectual and artistic terms). They were largely absorbed into the kingdom of Israel under King David, about 1000 BC, and later came under Assyrian rule.

philology (Greek 'love of language') in historical ◊linguistics, the study of the development of languages. It is also an obsolete term for the study of literature.

In this sense the scholars of Alexandria, who edited the Greek epics of Homer, were philologists. The Renaissance gave great impetus to this kind of

'Philanthropic people lose all sense of humanity. It is their distinguishing characteristic.'

On PHILANTHROPY
Oscar Wilde
The Picture of Dorian Gray 1891

A little philosophy inclineth man's mind to atheism, but depth in philosophy bringeth men's minds about to religion.

On **Philosophy**
Francis Bacon
'Atheism' *Essays*, 1597

study. Dutch scholars took the lead in the 17th century while Richard Bentley made significant contributions in England. Comparative philology arose at the beginning of the 19th century from the study of Sanskrit, under Franz Bopp's (1791–1867) leadership. It was originally mainly concerned with the ◊Indo-European languages, but the Romantic movement greatly inspired the establishment of national philology throughout Europe and Asia.

Philosophes the leading intellectuals of pre-revolutionary 18th-century France, including Condorcet, Diderot, J J Rousseau, and Voltaire. Their role in furthering the principles of the Enlightenment and extolling the power of human reason made them question the structures of the *ancien régime*, and influenced the revolutionaries of 1789.

philosophy (Greek 'love of wisdom') systematic analysis and critical examination of fundamental problems such as the nature of reality, mind, perception, self, free will, causation, time and space, and moral judgements. Traditionally, philosophy has three branches: metaphysics (the nature of being), epistemology (theory of knowledge), and logic (study of valid inference). Modern philosophy also includes ethics, aesthetics, political theory, the philosophy of science, and the philosophy of religion.

In the ancient civilizations of India and China, various sages set out their views and reflections about life and ultimate reality; but philosophy as a systematic and rational endeavour originated in Greece in the 6th century BC with the Milesian school (Thales, Anaximander, Anaximenes). Both they and later pre-Socratics (Pythagoras, Xenophon, Parmenides, Zeno of Elea, Empedocles, Anaxagoras, Heraclitus, Democritus) were lively theorists, and ideas like atomism, developed by Democritus, occur in later schemes of thought.

Originally, philosophy included all intellectual endeavour, but over time traditional branches of philosophy have acquired their own status as separate areas of study. In the 5th century Socrates, foremost among the teachers known as the Sophists, laid the foundation of ethics; Plato evolved a system of universal ideas; Aristotle developed logic. Later schools include Epicureanism (Epicurus), stoicism (Zeno) and scepticism (Pyrrho); the eclectics – not a school, they selected what appealed to them from various systems (Cicero and Seneca); and the neo-Platonists, infusing a mystic element into the system of Plato (Philo, Plotinus and, as disciple, Julian the Apostate).

The close of the Athenian schools of philosophy by Justinian AD 529 marks the end of ancient philosophy, though the Roman philosopher Boethius passed on the outlines of Greek philosophy to the West. Greek thought also survived in the work of the Arab philosophers Avicenna and Averroes, and of the Jewish philosophers Avencebrol (1021–1058) and Maimonides. In the early medieval period, Johannes Scotus Erigena formulated a neo-Platonic system. The 12th century saw the recovery of the texts of Aristotle, which stimulated the scholastic philosophers, mainly concerned with the reconciliation of ancient philosophy with Christian belief – Anselm, Abelard, Albertus Magnus, Thomas Aquinas, his opponent Duns Scotus, and William of Occam.

In the 17th century, René Descartes, Gottfried Leibniz, and Baruch Spinoza mark the beginning of modern philosophy with their rationalism and faith in mathematical proof. In the 17th and 18th centuries, the British empiricists (John Locke, George Berkeley, David Hume) turned to science and sense experience for guidance on what can be known and how. The German philosopher Immanuel Kant tried to define what we can know and to rebut both scepticism and speculative metaphysics in his critical philosophy.

In the early 19th century, classical German idealists (J G Fichte, F W J Schelling, G W F Hegel) rejected Kant's limitation on human knowledge. Notable also in the 19th century are the pessimistic

PHILIPPINES
Republic of the

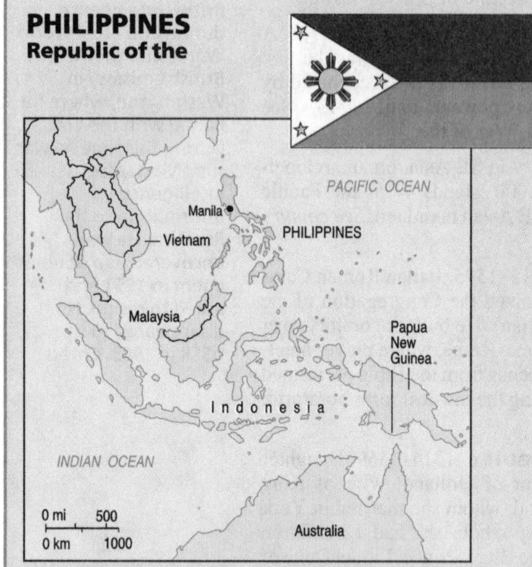

national name *Republika ng Pilipinas*
area 300,000 sq km/115,800 sq mi
capital (and chief port) Manila (on Luzon)
major towns/cities Quezon City (Luzon)
major ports Cebu, Davao (on Mindanao), Iloilo, Zamboanga (Mindanao)
physical features comprises over 7,000 islands; volcanic mountain ranges traverse main chain N–S; 50% still forested. The largest islands are Luzon 108,172 sq km/41,754 sq mi and Mindanao 94,227 sq km/36,372 sq mi; others include Samar, Negros, Palawan, Panay, Mindoro, Leyte, Cebu, and the Sulu group; Pinatubo volcano (1,759 m/5,770 ft); Mindanao has active volcano Apo (2,954 m/9,690 ft) and mountainous rainforest
head of state and government Joseph Estrada from 1998
political system emergent democracy
administrative divisions 15 regions (two of which are autonomous)
political parties Laban ng Demokratikong Pilipino (Democratic Filipino Struggle Party; LDP–DFSP), centrist, liberal-democrat coalition; Lakas ng Edsa (National Union of Christian Democrats; LNE–NUCD), centrist; Liberal Party, centrist; Nationalist Party (Nacionalista), right-wing; New Society Movement (NSM; Kilusan Bagong Lipunan), conservative, pro-Marcos; National Democratic Front, left-wing umbrella grouping, including the Communist Party of the Philippines (CPP); Mindanao Alliance, island-based decentralist body
armed forces 106,500; reserve forces 131,000; paramilitary forces around 60,000 (1994)
conscription none
defence spend (% GDP) 1.4 (1994)
education spend (% GNP) 2.9 (1992)
health spend (% GDP) 1.0 (1990)
death penalty retained in law, but considered abolitionist de facto; last execution 1976
population 69,282,000 (1996 est)
population growth rate 2.1% (1990–95); 1.8% (2000–05)
age distribution (% of total population) <15 38.3%, 15–65 58.3%, >65 3.4% (1995)
ethnic distribution comprises more than 50 ethnic communities, although 95% of the population is designated 'Filipino', an Indo-Polynesian ethnic grouping
population density (per sq km) 221 (1994)
urban population (% of total) 54 (1995)
labour force 40% of population: 46% agriculture, 15% industry, 39% services (1990)
unemployment 8.9% (1993)
child mortality rate (under 5, per 1,000 live births) 57 (1994)
life expectancy 63 (men), 67 (women)
education (compulsory years) 6
literacy rate 90% (men), 90% (women)
languages Tagalog (Filipino, official); English and Spanish; Cebuano, Ilocano, and more than 70 other indigenous languages
religions mainly Roman Catholic; Protestant, Muslim, local religions
TV sets (per 1,000 people) 45 (1992)
currency peso
GDP (US $) 64.16 billion (1994)
GDP per capita (PPP) (US $) 2,590 (1993)
growth rate 4.3% (1994)
average annual inflation 9.3% (1994)
major trading partners Japan, USA, Singapore, Taiwan, South Korea, Hong Kong
resources copper ore, gold, silver, chromium, nickel, coal, crude petroleum, natural gas, forests
industries food processing, petroleum refinery, textiles, chemical products, pharmaceuticals, electrical machinery (mainly telecommunications equipment), metals and metal products, tourism
exports electronic products (notably semiconductors and microcircuits), garments, agricultural products (particularly fruit and seafood), woodcraft and furniture, lumber, chemicals, coconut oil. Principal market: USA 36.8% (1994)
imports machinery and transport equipment, mineral fuels, basic manufactures, food and live animals, textile yarns, base metals, cereals and cereal preparations. Principal source: Japan 24.1% (1994)
arable land 18.4% (1993)
agricultural products rice, maize, cassava, coconuts, sugar cane, bananas, pineapples; livestock (chiefly pigs, buffaloes, goats, and poultry) and fisheries

HISTORY

14th C Traders from Malay peninsula introduced Islam and created Muslim principalities of Manila and Jolo.
1521 Portuguese navigator Ferdinand Magellan reached the islands, but was killed in a battle with the islanders.
1536 Philippines named after Charles V's son (later Philip II of Spain) by Spanish navigator Ruy López de Villalobos.
1565 Philippines conquered by Spanish army led by Miguel López de Lagazpi.
1571 Manila was made capital of the colony, which was part of the viceroyalty of Mexico.
17th C Spanish missionaries converted much of lowland population to Roman Catholicism.
1762–63 British occupied Manila.
1834 End of Spanish monopoly on trade; British and American merchants bought sugar and tobacco.
1896–97 Emilio Aguinaldo led revolt against Spanish.
1898 Spanish-American War: US navy destroyed Spanish fleet in Manila Bay; Aguinaldo declared independence, but Spain ceded Philippines to USA.
1898–1901 Nationalist uprising suppressed by US troops; 200,000 Filipinos killed.
1907 Americans set up elected legislative assembly.
1916 Bicameral legislature introduced on US model.
1935 Philippines gained internal self-government with Manuel Quezon as president.
1942–45 Occupied by Japan.
1946 Philippines achieved independence from USA under President Manuel Roxas; USA retained military bases and supplied economic aid.
1957–61 'Filipino First' policy introduced by President Carlos García to reduce economic power of Americans and Chinese; official corruption increased.
1965 Ferdinand Marcos elected president.
1972 Marcos declared martial law and ended freedom of press; economic development financed by foreign loans of which large sums were diverted by Marcos for personal use.
1981 Martial law officially ended but Marcos retained sweeping emergency powers.
1983 Opposition leader Benigno Aquino murdered at Manila airport.
1986 Marcos falsified election results. Corazon Aquino (widow of Benigno Aquino) used 'people's power' to force Marcos to flee country.
1987 'Freedom constitution' adopted; Aquino's People's Power won congressional elections.
1989 State of emergency declared after sixth coup attempt suppressed with US aid.
1991 Philippine senate called for withdrawal of US forces; US renewal of Subic Bay naval base lease rejected.
1992 Fidel Ramos elected to succeed Aquino; 'Rainbow Coalition' government formed.
1995 Imelda Marcos (widow of Ferdinand Marcos) elected to House of Representatives while on bail from prison.
1996 The LDP withdrew from coalition. Peace agreement between government and Moro National Liberation Front (MNLF) after 25 years of civil unrest on Mindanao.
1997 Preliminary peace talks between government and Muslim secessionist MILF. Major changes in political parties. Supreme Court rejected proposal to allow second presidential term.
1998 Joseph Estrada, the vice president, was elected president.

PHILOSOPHY: GREAT PHILOSOPHERS

Name	Dates	Nationality	Representative work
Heraclitus	c. 544–483 BC	Greek	*On Nature*
Parmenides	c. 510–c. 450 BC	Greek	fragments
Socrates	469–399 BC	Greek	–
Plato	428–347 BC	Greek	*Republic; Phaedo*
Aristotle	384–322 BC	Greek	*Nichomachaen Ethics; Metaphysics*
Epicurus	341–270 BC	Greek	fragments
Lucretius	c. 99–55 BC	Roman	*On the Nature of Things*
Plotinus	AD 205–270	Greek	*Enneads*
Augustine	354–430	N African	*Confessions; City of God*
Aquinas	c. 1225–1274	Italian	*Summa Theologica*
Duns Scotus	c. 1266–1308	Scottish	*Opus Oxoniense*
William of Occam	c. 1285–1349	English	*Commentary of the Sentences*
Nicholas of Cusa	1401–1464	German	*De Docta Ignorantia*
Giordano Bruno	1548–1600	Italian	*De la Causa, Principio e Uno*
Bacon	1561–1626	English	*Novum Organum; The Advancement of Learning*
Hobbes	1588–1679	English	*Leviathan*
Descartes	1596–1650	French	*Discourse on Method; Meditations on the First Philosophy*
Pascal	1623–1662	French	*Pensées*
Spinoza	1632–1677	Dutch	*Ethics*
Locke	1632–1704	English	*Essay Concerning Human Understanding*
Leibniz	1646–1716	German	*The Monadology*
Vico	1668–1744	Italian	*The New Science*
Berkeley	1685–1753	Irish	*A Treatise Concerning the Principles of Human Knowledge*
Hume	1711–1776	Scottish	*A Treatise of Human Nature*
Rousseau	1712–1778	French	*The Social Contract*
Diderot	1713–1784	French	*D'Alembert's Dream*
Kant	1724–1804	German	*The Critique of Pure Reason*
Fichte	1762–1814	German	*The Science of Knowledge*
Hegel	1770–1831	German	*The Phenomenology of Spirit*
Schelling	1775–1854	German	*System of Transcendental Idealism*
Schopenhauer	1788–1860	German	*The World as Will and Idea*
Comte	1798–1857	French	*Cours de philosophie positive*
Mill	1806–1873	English	*Utilitarianism*
Kierkegaard	1813–1855	Danish	*Concept of Dread*
Marx	1818–1883	German	*Economic and Philosophical Manuscripts*
Dilthey	1833–1911	German	*The Rise of Hermeneutics*
Pierce	1839–1914	US	*How to Make our Ideas Clear*
Nietzsche	1844–1900	German	*Thus Spake Zarathustra*
Bergson	1859–1941	French	*Creative Evolution*
Husserl	1859–1938	German	*Logical Investigations*
Russell	1872–1970	English	*Principia Mathematica*
Lukács	1885–1971	Hungarian	*History and Class Consciousness*
Wittgenstein	1889–1951	Austrian	*Tractatus Logico-Philosophicus; Philosophical Investigations*
Heidegger	1889–1976	German	*Being and Time*
Gadamer	1900–	German	*Truth and Method*
Sartre	1905–1980	French	*Being and Nothingness*
Merleau Ponty	1908–1961	French	*The Phenomenology of Perception*
Quine	1908–	US	*Word and Object*
Foucault	1926–1984	French	*The Order of Things*

atheism of Arthur Schopenhauer; the work of Friedrich Nietzsche and Søren Kierkegaard, which led towards 20th-century existentialism; the pragmatism of William James and John Dewey; and the neo-Hegelianism at the turn of the century (F H Bradley, T H Green, Josiah Royce).

Among 20th-century movements are logical positivism (Rudolf Carnap, Karl Popper, Alfred Ayer); neo-Thomism, the revival of the medieval philosophy of Aquinas (Jacques Maritain); existentialism (Martin Heidegger, Karl Jaspers, Jean-Paul Sartre); phenomenology (Edmund Husserl, Maurice Merleau-Ponty); and analytical and linguistic philosophy (Bertrand Russell, G E Moore, Ludwig Wittgenstein, Gilbert Ryle, Willard Quine). Under the influence of Russell's work on formal logic and Wittgenstein's *Philosophical Investigations*, English-speaking philosophers have paid great attention to the nature and limits of language, in particular in relation to the language used to formulate philosophical problems.

phlebitis inflammation of the wall of a vein. It is sometimes associated with ◊varicose veins or with a blockage by a blood clot (◊thrombosis), in which case it is more accurately described as thrombophlebitis.

Phlebitis may occur as a result of the hormonal changes associated with pregnancy, or due to long-term use of contraceptive pills, or following prolonged immobility (which is why patients are mobilized as soon as possible after surgery). If a major vein is involved, nearly always in a leg, the part beyond the blockage swells and may remain engorged for weeks. It is very painful. Treatment is with ◊anticoagulant drugs and sometimes surgery, depending on the cause.

phloem tissue found in vascular plants whose main function is to conduct sugars and other food materials from the leaves, where they are produced, to all other parts of the plant.

Phloem is composed of sieve elements and their associated companion cells, together with some sclerenchyma (tough, thick-walled cells) and parenchyma (loosely packed, more or less spherical cells with thin cellulose walls) cell types. Sieve elements are long, thin-walled cells joined end to end, forming sieve tubes; large pores in the end walls allow the continuous passage of nutrients. Phloem is usually found in association with ◊xylem, the water-conducting tissue, but unlike the latter it is a living tissue.

phlox any plant of the genus *Phlox*, native to North America and Siberia. Phloxes are small with alternate leaves and showy white, pink, red, or purple flowers.

The cultivated varieties derive from *P. drummondii*; they are half-hardy annuals with lanceolate (tapering) leaves.

Phnom Penh capital of Cambodia, on the Mekong River, 210 km/130 mi NW of Saigon; population (1994) 920,000. Industries include textiles and food-processing. It has been Cambodia's capital since the 15th century, and has royal palaces, museums, and pagodas.

On 17 April 1975 the entire population (about 3 million) was forcibly evacuated by the ◊Khmer Rouge communist movement as they captured the city; survivors later returned. In 1979 it was taken by the Vietnamese, who ousted Pol Pot and the Khmer Rouge; they withdrew 1989, and were banned 1994.

phobia excessive irrational fear of an object or situation – for example, agoraphobia (fear of open spaces and crowded places), acrophobia (fear of heights), and claustrophobia (fear of enclosed places). ◊Behaviour therapy is one form of treatment.

A specific phobia is a severe dislike of a particular thing, including objects, animals or situations. Specific phobias start in childhood (particularly animal phobias) and early adulthood. They are more common in women than men.

Complex phobias have more complicated contributing factors and include agoraphobia and social phobia. These phobias are more disabling. Agoraphobia typically starts between the ages of 18 and 28. Social phobia usually onsets between 11 and 16 years.

Phobos one of the two moons of Mars, discovered 1877 by the US astronomer Asaph Hall (1829–1907). It is an irregularly shaped lump of rock, cratered by ◊meteorite impacts. Phobos is 27 × 22 × 19 km/17 × 13 × 12 mi across, and orbits Mars every 0.32 days at a distance of 9,400 km/5,840 mi from the planet's centre. It is thought to be an asteroid captured by Mars' gravity.

Phoenicia ancient Greek name for N ◊Canaan on the E coast of the Mediterranean. The Phoenician civilization flourished from about 1200 until the capture of Tyre by Alexander the Great in 332 BC. Seafaring traders and artisans, they are said to have circumnavigated Africa and established colonies in Cyprus, N Africa (for example, Carthage), Malta, Sicily, and Spain. Their cities (Tyre, Sidon, and Byblos were the main ones) were independent states ruled by hereditary kings but dominated by merchant ruling classes.

The Phoenicians occupied the seaboard of Lebanon and Syria, north of Mount Carmel. Their exports included Tyrian purple dye and cloth, furniture (from the timber of Lebanon), and jewellery. Documents found 1929 at Ugarit on the Syrian coast give much information on their civilization; their deities included ◊Baal, Astarte or ◊Ishtar, and ◊Moloch. Competition from the colonies combined with attacks by the Sea Peoples, the Assyrians, and the Greeks on the cities in Phoenicia led to their ultimate decline.

In August 1996 Spanish archaeologists, working at Cerro del Villar to the west of Málaga, unearthed the site of a large Phoenician settlement dating from at least the eighth century BC, providing scholars with a greater insight into the lives of the Phoenicians.

phoenix mythical Egyptian bird that burned itself to death on a pyre every 500 years and rose rejuvenated from the ashes.

phlox *Phlox tenuifolia* from Arizona is one of many members of the genus growing in the deserts of the SW USA. Native to North America and Siberia, phlox is widely cultivated for its showy flowers. *Premaphotos Wildlife*

Phoenix capital of Arizona, USA; industrial city (steel, aluminium, electrical goods, food processing) and tourist centre on the Salt River; population (1992) 1,012,200.

Phoenix Park Murders the murder of several prominent members of the British government in Phoenix Park, Dublin on 6 May 1882. The murders threatened the cooperation between the Liberal government and the Irish nationalist members at Westminster which had been secured by the ◊Kilmainham Treaty.

The murders began with the stabbing of Thomas Burke, the permanent under-secretary for Ireland and Lord Frederick Cavendish, chief secretary to the viceroy. A murderous campaign was continued by the Irish National Invincibles until some members turned 'Queen's evidence'.

phon unit of loudness, equal to the value in decibels of an equally loud tone with frequency 1,000 Hz. The higher the frequency, the louder a noise sounds for the same decibel value; thus an 80-decibel tone with a frequency of 20 Hz sounds as loud as 20 decibels at 1,000 Hz, and the phon value of both tones is 20. An aircraft engine has a loudness of around 140 phons.

phoneme distinctive unit of sound from which a language is formed. For example, /t/ and /d/ are phonemes in English because they can be used to distinguish between two words, for example 'bad' and 'bat'.

Although the exact sound of /t/ varies with its phonetic context (phonetically, the /t/ in the words 'top' and 'stop' is different), these variants cannot be used to distinguish between two otherwise identical words. Sound variants that do not change meaning in a given language are called allophones. The study of phonemes is called phonology.

phonetics the identification, description, and classification of sounds used in articulate speech. These sounds are codified in the International Phonetic Alphabet (IPA), a highly modified version of the Roman alphabet.

The IPA is based on ordinary Roman letters, along with modified forms, letters from other alphabets, and some invented letters. There are also a number of accents and other diacritics. Each symbol stands for a particular sound, but the interpretation of a sequence of symbols also depends on a number of conventions and on the phonetic context.

phoney war the period in World War II between Sept 1939, when the Germans had occupied Poland, and April 1940, when the invasions of Denmark and Norway took place. During this time there were few signs of hostilities in Western Europe; indeed, Hitler made some attempts to arrange a peace settlement with Britain and France.

phosphate salt or ester of ◊phosphoric acid. Incomplete neutralization of phosphoric acid gives rise to acid phosphates (see ◊acid salts and ◊buffer). Phosphates are used as fertilizers, and are required for the development of healthy root systems. They are involved in many biochemical processes, often as part of complex molecules, such as ◊ATP.

phospholipid any ◊lipid consisting of a glycerol backbone, a phosphate group, and two long chains. Phospholipids are found everywhere in living systems as the basis for biological membranes.

One of the long chains tends to be hydrophobic and the other hydrophilic (that is, they interrelate with water in opposite ways). This means that phospholipids will line up the same way round when in solution.

phosphor any substance that is phosphorescent, that is, gives out visible light when it is illuminated by a beam of electrons or ultraviolet light. The television screen is coated on the inside with phosphors that glow when beams of electrons strike them. Fluorescent lamp tubes are also phosphor-coated. Phosphors are also used in Day-Glo paints, and as optical brighteners in detergents.

phosphorescence in physics, the emission of light by certain substances after they have absorbed energy, whether from visible light, other electromagnetic radiation such as ultraviolet rays or X-rays, or cathode rays (a beam of electrons). When the stimulating energy is removed phosphorescence ceases, although it may persist for a short time after (unlike ◊fluorescence, which stops immediately).

'The camera is an instrument that teaches people how to see without a camera.'

On PHOTOGRAPHY
Dorothea Lange
Quoted in
Los Angeles Times
1978

phosphoric acid acid derived from phosphorus and oxygen. Its commonest form (H_3PO_4) is also known as orthophosphoric acid, and is produced by the action of phosphorus pentoxide (P_2O_5) on water. It is used in rust removers and for rust-proofing iron and steel.

phosphorus (Greek *phosphoros* 'bearer of light') highly reactive, nonmetallic element, symbol P, atomic number 15, relative atomic mass 30.9738. It occurs in nature as phosphates (commonly in the form of the mineral ◊apatite), and is essential to plant and animal life. Compounds of phosphorus are used in fertilizers, various organic chemicals, for matches and fireworks, and in glass and steel.

Phosphorus was first identified 1674 by German alchemist Hennig Brand (c. 1630–?), who prepared it from urine. The element has three allotropic forms: a black powder; a white-yellow, waxy solid that ignites spontaneously in air to form the poisonous gas phosphorus pentoxide; and a red-brown powder that neither ignites spontaneously nor is poisonous.

photocell or *photoelectric cell* device for measuring or detecting light or other electromagnetic radiation, since its electrical state is altered by the effect of light. In a photoemissive cell, the radiation causes electrons to be emitted and a current to flow (◊photoelectric effect); a photovoltaic cell causes an ◊electromotive force to be generated in the presence of light across the boundary of two substances. A photoconductive cell, which contains a semiconductor, increases its conductivity when exposed to electromagnetic radiation.

Photocells are used for photographers' exposure meters, burglar and fire alarms, automatic doors, and in solar energy arrays.

photochemical reaction any chemical reaction in which light is produced or light initiates the reaction. Light can initiate reactions by exciting atoms or molecules and making them more reactive: the light energy becomes converted to chemical energy. Many photochemical reactions set up a ◊chain reaction and produce ◊free radicals.

This type of reaction is seen in the bleaching of dyes or the yellowing of paper by sunlight. It is harnessed by plants in ◊photosynthesis and by humans in ◊photography.

Chemical reactions that produce light are most commonly seen when materials are burned. Light-emitting reactions are used by living organisms in ◊bioluminescence. One photochemical reaction is the action of sunlight on car exhaust fumes, which results in the production of ◊ozone. Some large cities, such as Los Angeles, and Santiago, Chile, now suffer serious pollution due to photochemical smog.

photodiode semiconductor ◊*p–n* junction diode used to detect light or measure its intensity. The photodiode is encapsulated in a transparent plastic case that allows light to fall onto the junction. When this occurs, the reverse-bias resistance (high resistance in the opposite direction to normal current-flow) drops and allows a larger reverse-biased current to flow through the device. The increase in current can then be related to the amount of light falling on the junction.

Photodiodes that can detect small changes in light level are used in alarm systems, camera exposure controls, and optical communication links.

photoelectric cell alternative name for ◊photocell.

photoelectric effect in physics, the emission of ◊electrons from a substance (usually a metallic surface) when it is struck by ◊photons (quanta of electromagnetic radiation), usually those of visible light or ultraviolet radiation.

photography process for reproducing images on sensitized materials by various forms of radiant energy, including visible light, ultraviolet, infrared, X-rays, atomic radiations, and electron beams.

Photography was developed in the 19th century; among the pioneers were L J M ◊Daguerre in France and ◊Fox Talbot in the UK. Colour photography dates from the early 20th century.

The most familiar photographic process depends upon the fact that certain silver compounds (called halides) are sensitive to light. A photographic film is coated with these compounds and, in a camera, is exposed to light. An image, or picture, of the scene before the camera is formed on the film because the silver halides become activated (light-altered) where light falls but not where light does not fall. The image is made visible by the process of ◊developing, made permanent by fixing, and, finally, is usually printed on paper. Motion-picture photography uses a camera that exposes a roll of film to a rapid succession of views that, when developed, are projected in equally rapid succession to provide a moving image.

photogravure ◊printing process that uses a plate prepared photographically, covered with a pattern of recessed cells in which the ink is held. See ◊gravure.

photolysis chemical reaction that is driven by light or ultraviolet radiation. For example, the light reaction of ◊photosynthesis (the process by which green plants manufacture carbohydrates from carbon dioxide and water) is a photolytic reaction.

photometer instrument that measures luminous intensity, usually by comparing relative intensities from different sources. Bunsen's grease-spot photometer 1844 compares the intensity of a light source with a known source by each illuminating one half of a translucent area. Modern photometers use ◊photocells, as in a photographer's exposure meter. A photomultiplier can also be used as a photometer.

photomultiplier instrument that detects low levels of electromagnetic radiation (usually visible light or ◊infrared radiation) and amplifies it to produce a detectable signal.

One type resembles a ◊photocell with an additional series of coated ◊electrodes (dynodes) between the ◊cathode and ◊anode. Radiation striking the cathode releases electrons (primary emission) which hit the first dynode, producing yet more electrons (◊secondary emission), which strike the second dynode. Eventually this produces a measurable signal up to 100 million times larger than the original signal by the time it leaves the anode. Similar devices, called image intensifiers, are used in television camera tubes that 'see' in the dark.

photon in physics, the ◊elementary particle or 'package' (quantum) of energy in which light and other forms of electromagnetic radiation are emitted. The photon has both particle and wave properties; it has no charge, is considered massless but possesses momentum and energy. It is one of the ◊gauge bosons, a particle that cannot be subdivided, and is the carrier of the ◊electromagnetic force, one of the fundamental forces of nature.

According to ◊quantum theory the energy of a photon is given by the formula $E = hf$, where h is Planck's constant and f is the frequency of the radiation emitted.

photoperiodism biological mechanism that determines the timing of certain activities by responding to changes in day length. The flowering of many plants is initiated in this way. Photoperiodism in plants is regulated by a light-sensitive pigment, phytochrome. The breeding seasons of many temperate-zone animals are also triggered by increasing or declining day length, as part of their ◊biorhythms.

Autumn-flowering plants (for example, chrysanthemum and soya bean) and autumn-breeding mammals (such as goats and deer) require days that are shorter than a critical length; spring-flowering and spring-breeding ones (such as radish and lettuce, and birds) are triggered by longer days.

Photorealism or ***Superrealism*** or ***Hyperrealism*** style of painting and sculpture popular in the late 1960s and 1970s, especially in the USA, characterized by intense, photographic realism and attention to minute detail. The Photorealists' aim was to create a record of peoples, places, and objects that was dispassionate to the extent of being almost surreal. Leading exponents were US painters Chuck Close (1940–) and Richard Estes (1936–) and US sculptor Duane Hanson (1925–).

Derived from ◊Pop art, its practitioners exhibited a similar interest in contemporary mass culture and glossy, high-tech presentation techniques. Many Photorealists used photography extensively, either copying from prints or working from colour slides projected directly on to the canvas.

photosphere visible surface of the Sun, which emits light and heat. About 300 km/200 mi deep, it consists of incandescent gas at a temperature of 5,800K (5,530°C/9,980°F).

Rising cells of hot gas produce a mottling of the photosphere known as granulation, each granule being about 1,000 km/620 mi in diameter. The photosphere is often marked by large, dark patches called ◊sunspots.

photosynthesis process by which green plants trap light energy and use it to drive a series of chemical reactions, leading to the formation of carbohydrates. All animals ultimately depend on photosynthesis because it is the method by which the basic food (sugar) is created. For photosynthesis to occur, the plant must possess ◊chlorophyll and must have a supply of carbon dioxide and water. Actively photosynthesizing green plants store excess sugar as starch (this can be tested for in the laboratory using iodine).
chemical process The chemical reactions of photosynthesis occur in two stages. During the light reaction sunlight is used to split water (H_2O) into oxygen (O_2), protons (hydrogen ions, H^+), and electrons, and oxygen is given off as a by-product. In the dark reaction, for which sunlight is not required, the protons and electrons are used to convert carbon dioxide (CO_2) into carbohydrates ($C_m(H_2O)_n$). Photosynthesis depends on the ability of chlorophyll to capture the energy of sunlight and to use it to split water molecules. The initial charge separation occurs in less than a billionth of a second, a speed that compares with current computers.

Other pigments, such as ◊carotenoids, are also involved in capturing light energy and passing it on to chlorophyll. Photosynthesis by cyanobacteria was responsible for the appearance of oxygen in the Earth's atmosphere 2 billion years ago, and photosynthesis by plants maintains the oxygen level today. *See illustration on following page.*

phototropism movement of part of a plant toward or away from a source of light. Leaves are positively phototropic, detecting the source of light and orientating themselves to receive the maximum amount.

phrenology study of the shape and protuberances of the skull, based on the (now discredited) theory of the Austrian physician Franz Josef Gall that such features revealed measurable psychological and intellectual traits.

Phrygia former kingdom of W Asia covering the Anatolian plateau. It was inhabited in ancient times by an Indo-European people and achieved great prosperity in the 8th century BC under a line of kings bearing in turn the names Gordius and Midas, but then fell under Lydian rule. From Phrygia the cult of the Earth goddess Cybele was introduced into Greece and Rome.

phyllite ◊metamorphic rock produced under increasing temperature and pressure, in which minute mica crystals are aligned so that the rock splits along their plane of orientation, the resulting break being shiny and smooth. Intermediate between slate and schist, its silky sheen is an identifying characteristic.

phyllotaxis the arrangement of leaves on a plant stem. Leaves are nearly always arranged in a regular pattern and in the majority of plants they are inserted singly, either in a spiral arrangement up the stem, or on alternate sides. Other principal forms are opposite leaves, where two arise from the same node, and whorled, where three or more arise from the same node.

phylloxera plant-eating insect of the family Phylloxeridae, closely related to the aphids.

The grape, or vine phylloxera *Phylloxera vitifolia*, a native of North America, is a notorious pest of grapevines, forming galls on roots and leaves, which damage the plant. European vines are markedly susceptible and many French vineyards suffered from the arrival of the pest in Europe in the late 19th century, when nearly 2 million hectares of vineyards were destroyed.

Phylloxera is very resistant to treatment, as there are no natural enemies and it is difficult to treat with pesticide because of its depth within the soil. Phylloxera insects (hemipterans) may be destroyed by spraying with carbon disulphide or petroleum.

phylogeny historical sequence of changes that occurs in a given species during the course of its evolution. It was once erroneously associated with ontogeny (the process of development of a living organism).

PHOTOGRAPHY: TIMELINE

1515	Leonardo da Vinci described the camera obscura.
1750	The painter Canaletto used a camera obscura as an aid to his painting in Venice.
1790	Thomas Wedgwood in England made photograms – placing objects on leather, sensitized using silver nitrate.
1826	Nicéphore Niepce, a French doctor, produced the world's first photograph from nature on pewter plates with a camera obscura and an eight-hour exposure.
1838	As a result of his earlier collaboration with Niepce, L J M Daguerre produced the first daguerreotype camera photograph.
1839	Daguerre was awarded an annuity by the French government and his process given to the world.
1840	Invention of the Petzval lens, which reduced exposure time by 90%. Herschel discovered sodium thiosulphate as a fixer for silver halides.
1841	Fox Talbot's calotype process was patented – the first multicopy method of photography using a negative/positive process, sensitized with silver iodide.
1844–46	Fox Talbot published the first photographic book, *The Pencil of Nature*.
1845	Hill and Adamson began to use calotypes for portraits in Edinburgh.
1851	Fox Talbot used a one-thousandth of a second exposure to demonstrate high-speed photography. Invention of the wet-collodion-on-glass process and the waxed-paper negative. Photographs were displayed at the Great Exhibition in London.
1852	The London Society of Arts exhibited 779 photographs.
1855	Roger Fenton made documentary photographs of the Crimean War from a specially constructed caravan with portable darkroom.
1858	Nadar took the first aerial photographs from a balloon.
1859	Nadar in Paris made photographs underground using battery-powered arc lights.
1860	Queen Victoria was photographed by Mayall. Abraham Lincoln was photographed by Mathew Brady for political campaigning.
1861	The single-lens reflex plate camera was patented by Thomas Sutton. The principles of three-colour photography were demonstrated by Scottish physicist James Clerk Maxwell.
1870	Julia Margaret Cameron used long lenses for her distinctive portraits.
1871	Gelatin-silver bromide was developed.
1878	In the USA Eadweard Muybridge analysed the movements of animals through sequential photographs, using a series of cameras.
1879	The photogravure process was invented.
1880	A silver bromide emulsion was fixed with hypo. Photographs were first reproduced in newspapers in New York using the half-tone engraving process. The first twin-lens reflex camera was produced in London. Gelatin-silver chloride paper was introduced.
1884	George Eastman produced flexible negative film.
1889	The Eastman Company in the USA produced the Kodak No 1 camera and roll film, facilitating universal, hand-held snapshots.
1891	The first telephoto lens. The interference process of colour photography was developed by the French doctor Gabriel Lippmann.
1897	The first issue of Alfred Stieglitz's *Camera Notes* appeared in the USA.
1902	In Germany, Deckel invented a prototype leaf shutter and Zeiss introduced the Tessar lens.
1904	The autochrome colour process was patented by the Lumière brothers.
1905	Alfred Stieglitz opened the gallery '291' in New York promoting photography. Lewis Hine used photography to expose the exploitation of children in American factories, causing protective laws to be passed.
1907	The autochrome process began to be factory-produced.
1914	Oskar Barnack designed a prototype Leica camera for Leitz in Germany.
1924	Leitz launched the first 35mm camera, the Leica, delayed because of World War I. It became very popular with photojournalists because it was quiet, small, dependable, and had a range of lenses and accessories.
1929	Rolleiflex produced a twin-lens reflex camera in Germany.
1935	In the USA, Mannes and Godowsky invented Kodachrome transparency film, which produced sharp images and rich colour quality. Electronic flash was invented in the USA.
1936	*Life* magazine, significant for its photojournalism, was first published in the USA.
1938	*Picture Post* magazine was introduced in the UK.
1940	Multigrade enlarging paper by Ilford was made available in the UK.
1942	Kodacolour negative film was introduced.
1945	The zone system of exposure estimation was published in the book *Exposure Record* by Ansel Adams.
1947	Polaroid black-and-white instant process film was invented by Dr Edwin Land, who set up the Polaroid corporation in Boston, Massachusetts. The principles of holography were demonstrated in England by Dennis Gabor.
1955	Kodak introduced Tri-X, a black-and-white 200 ASA film.
1959	The zoom lens was invented by the Austrian firm of Voigtlander.
1960	The laser was invented in the USA, making holography possible. Polacolor, a self-processing colour film, was introduced by Polaroid, using a 60-second colour film and dye diffusion technique.
1963	Cibachrome, paper and chemicals for printing directly from transparencies, was made available by Ciba-Geigy of Switzerland. One of the most permanent processes, it is marketed by Ilford in the UK.
1966	The International Center of Photography was established in New York.
1969	Photographs were taken on the Moon by US astronauts.
1970	A charge-coupled device was invented at Bell Laboratories in New Jersey, USA, to record very faint images (for example in astronomy). Rencontres Internationales de la Photographie, the annual summer festival of photography with workshops, was founded in Arles, France.
1971	Opening of the Photographers' Gallery, London, and the Photo Archive of the Bibliothéque Nationale, Paris.
1972	The SX70 system, a single-lens reflex camera with instant prints, was produced by Polaroid.
1975	The Center for Creative Photography was established at the University of Arizona.
1980	Ansel Adams sold an original print, *Moonrise: Hernandez*, for $45,000, a record price, in the USA. *Voyager 1* sent photographs of Saturn back to Earth across space.
1983	The National Museum of Photography, Film and Television opened in Bradford, England.
1985	The Minolta Corporation in Japan introduced the Minolta 7000 – the world's first body-integral autofocus single-lens reflex camera.
1988	The electronic camera, which stores pictures on magnetic disc instead of on film, was introduced in Japan.
1990	Kodak introduced PhotoCD, which converts 35mm camera pictures (on film) into digital form and stores them on compact disc (CD) for viewing on TV.
1992	Japanese company Canon introduced a camera with autofocus controlled by the user's eye. The camera focuses on whatever the user is looking at. *Girl with a Leica* by Russian photographer Aleksandr Rodchenko sold for £115,500 at Christie's, London – a world-record price for a photograph.

photosynthesis
Process by which green plants and some bacteria manufacture carbohydrates from water and atmospheric carbon dioxide, using the energy of sunlight. Photosynthesis depends on the ability of chlorophyll molecules within plant cells to trap the energy of light to split water molecules, giving off oxygen as a by-product. The hydrogen of the water molecules is then used to reduce carbon dioxide to simple carbohydrates.

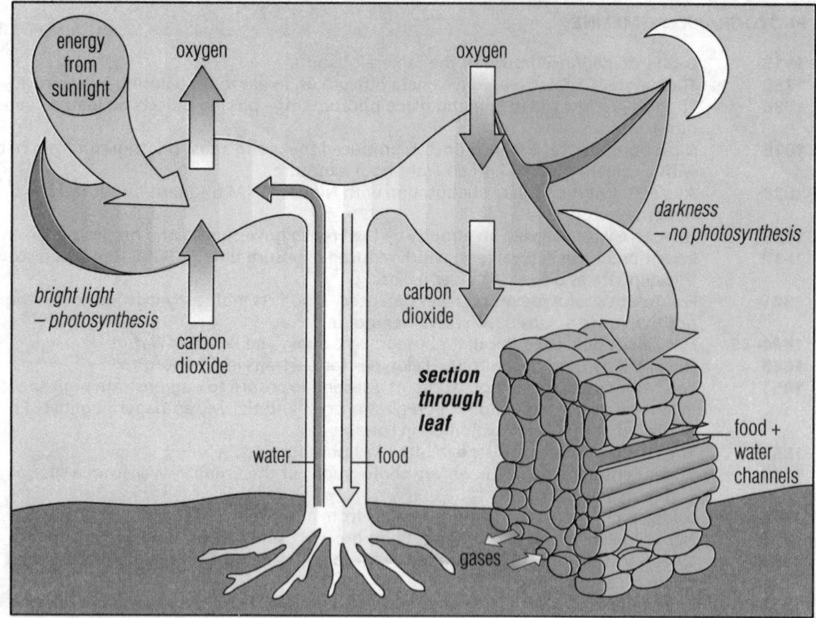

phylum (plural ***phyla***) major grouping in biological classification. Mammals, birds, reptiles, amphibians, fishes, and tunicates belong to the phylum Chordata; the phylum Mollusca consists of snails, slugs, mussels, clams, squid, and octopuses; the phylum Porifera contains sponges; and the phylum Echinodermata includes starfish, sea urchins, and sea cucumbers. In classifying plants (where the term 'division' often takes the place of 'phylum'), there are between four and nine phyla depending on the criteria used; all flowering plants belong to a single phylum, Angiospermata, and all conifers to another, Gymnospermata. Related phyla are grouped together in a ◊kingdom; phyla are subdivided into ◊classes.

There are 36 different phyla. The most recently identified is the Cycliophora described Dec 1995. It contains a single known species, *Symbion pandora*, that lives on lobsters.

physical chemistry branch of chemistry concerned with examining the relationships between the chemical compositions of substances and the physical properties that they display. Most chemical reactions exhibit some physical phenomenon (change of state, temperature, pressure, or volume, or the use or production of electricity), and the measurement and study of such phenomena has led to many chemical theories and laws.

physics branch of science concerned with the laws that govern the structure of the universe, and the investigation of the properties of matter and energy and their interactions. For convenience, physics is often divided into branches such as atomic physics, nuclear physics, particle physics, solid-state physics, molecular physics, electricity and magnetism, optics, acoustics, heat, thermodynamics, quantum theory, and relativity. Before the 20th century, physics was known as natural philosophy.

physiocrat member of a school of 18th-century French economists, including François Quesnay (1694–1774) and Mirabeau, who believed in the bounty of nature and the inherent goodness of man. They held that governments should intervene in society only where individuals' liberties were infringed. Otherwise there should be a *laissez-faire* system with free trade between states. The Scottish economist Adam Smith was much influenced by their ideas.

physiology branch of biology that deals with the functioning of living organisms, as opposed to anatomy, which studies their structures.

physiotherapy treatment of injury and disease by physical means such as exercise, heat, manipulation, massage, and electrical stimulation.

phytomenadione one form of vitamin K, a fat-soluble chemical found in green vegetables. It is involved in the production of prothrombin, which is essential in blood clotting. It is given to newborns to prevent potentially fatal brain haemorrhages.

pi symbol π, the ratio of the circumference of a circle to its diameter. The value of pi is 3.1415926, correct to seven decimal places. Common approximations to pi are $^{22}/_{7}$ and 3.14, although the value 3 can be used as a rough estimation.

Piaf Edith. Stage name of Edith Giovanna Gassion 1915–1963. French singer and songwriter, a cabaret singer in Paris from the late 1930s. She is remembered for the defiant song 'Je ne regrette rien/I Regret Nothing' and 'La Vie en rose' 1946.

Piaget Jean 1896–1980. Swiss psychologist whose studies of the development of thought processes in children have been influential in early-childhood research and on school curricula and teaching methods.

The subjects of Piaget's studies of intellectual development were his own children. He postulated four main stages in the development of mental processes: sensorimeter (birth to the age of two), preoperational (two to seven), concrete operational (seven to twelve), and formal operational, characterized by the development of logical thought.

piano or ***pianoforte*** (originally ***fortepiano***) stringed musical instrument played by felt-covered hammers activated from a keyboard. It is capable of dynamic gradation between soft (piano) and loud (forte) tones, hence its name. The first piano was constructed 1704 and introduced 1709 by Bartolommeo Cristofori, a harpsichord maker in Padua. Extensively developed during the 18th century, the piano attracted admiration among many composers, although it was not until 1768 that J C Bach gave one of the first public recitals on the instrument.

Further improvements in the keyboard action and tone by makers such as Broadwood, Erard, and Graf, together with a rapid expansion of published music by Haydn, Beethoven, Schubert, and others, led to the development of the powerfully resonant concert grand piano and the mass production of smaller upright pianos for the home.

Piano Renzo 1937– . Italian High Tech architect. With Richard ◊Rogers, he designed the Pompidou Centre, Paris, 1970–77. Among his other buildings are Kansai Airport, Osaka, Japan and a sports stadium in Bari, Italy, 1989, both employing new materials and making imaginative use of civil-engineering techniques.

PIC abbreviation for ◊***Pacific Islands Commission***.

Picardy (French ***Picardie***) region of N France, including Aisne, Oise, and Somme *départements*; area 19,400 sq km/7,488 sq mi; population (1990) 1,810,700. Its industries include chemicals and metals.

history In the 13th century the name Picardy was used to describe the feudal smallholdings N of Paris added to the French crown by Philip II. During the Hundred Years' War the area was hotly contested by France and England, but it was eventually occupied by Louis XI 1477. Picardy once more became a major battlefield in World War I.

picaresque (Spanish *pícaro* 'rogue') genre of novel that takes a rogue or villain for its central character, telling his or her story in episodic form. The genre originated in Spain and was popular in the 18th century in Britain. Daniel Defoe's *Moll Flanders*, Tobias Smollett's *Roderick Random*, Henry Fielding's *Tom Jones*, and Mark Twain's *Huckleberry Finn* are typical picaresque novels. The device of using an outsider gave the author the opportunity to give fresh moral insights into society.

Picasso Pablo Ruiz y 1881–1973. Spanish artist, chiefly active in France. He was one of the most inventive and prolific talents in 20th-century art. His Blue Period 1901–04 and Rose Period 1905–06 preceded the revolutionary *Les Demoiselles d'Avignon* 1907 (Museum of Modern Art, New York), which paved the way for ◊Cubism. In the early 1920s he was considered a leader of the Surrealist movement. From the 1930s his work included sculpture, ceramics, and graphic works in a wide variety of media. Among his best-known paintings is ◊*Guernica* 1937 (Prado, Madrid), a comment on the bombing of civilians in the Spanish Civil War.

He first went to Paris 1900 and settled there permanently 1904. To begin with his work was concerned with the social scene, after the fashion of Degas and Toulouse-Lautrec, but between 1901 and 1904 he turned to austere figure studies, blue being the dominant colour (Blue Period). Circus pictures followed, delicate and more varied in colour (Rose Period, 1905–06).

Between 1907 and 1909, with Georges◊Braque, he developed Cubism, from the study of Cézanne combined with that of Negro sculpture and primitive art. *Les Demoiselles d'Avignon*, 1907, marks the birth of the Cubist movement, to which Picasso adhered until 1914. Like Braque, he practised successively its 'analytic' form (construction in depth) and its 'synthetic' form (more decorative and two-dimensional in effect). A feature of his Cubist still life, 1912–14, was the use of 'collage'.

He reverted to a Neo-Classical style 1920–24, in painting and in outline etchings of classical themes. He met Diaghilev and designed the *décor* of a number of ballets 1917–1927. A new and imaginative phase of his art began c. 1925, and coincided with the development of Surrealism. The bull, a traditional Spanish emblem of conflict and tragedy,

Picasso Spanish painter and sculptor Pablo Picasso showed outstanding artistic talent from an early age and became one of the most original and influential figures of 20th century art. A prolific artist, he worked in a broad range of styles, and was particularly important in the development of Surrealism and Cubism. *Topham*

'I paint objects as I think them, not as I see them.'

Pablo Picasso
Quoted in J Golding *Cubism*

PHYSICS: TIMELINE

c. 400 BC	The first 'atomic' theory was put forward by Democritus.
c. 250	Archimedes' principle of buoyancy was established.
AD 1600	Magnetism was described by William Gilbert.
1608	Hans Lippershey invented the refracting telescope.
c. 1610	The principle of falling bodies descending to earth at the same speed was established by Galileo.
1642	The principles of hydraulics were put forward by Blaise Pascal.
1643	The mercury barometer was invented by Evangelista Torricelli.
1656	The pendulum clock was invented by Christiaan Huygens.
1662	Boyle's law concerning the behaviour of gases was established by Robert Boyle.
c. 1665	Isaac Newton put forward the law of gravity, stating that the Earth exerts a constant force on falling bodies.
1690	The wave theory of light was propounded by Christiaan Huygens.
1704	The corpuscular theory of light was put forward by Isaac Newton.
1714	The mercury thermometer was invented by Daniel Fahrenheit.
1764	Specific and latent heats were described by Joseph Black.
1771	The link between nerve action and electricity was discovered by Luigi Galvani.
c. 1787	Charles's law relating the pressure, volume, and temperature of a gas was established by Jacques Charles.
1795	The metric system was adopted in France.
1798	The link between heat and friction was discovered by Benjamin Rumford.
1800	Alessandro Volta invented the Voltaic cell.
1801	Interference of light was discovered by Thomas Young.
1808	The 'modern' atomic theory was propounded by John Dalton.
1811	Avogadro's hypothesis relating volumes and numbers of molecules of gases was proposed by Amedeo Avogadro.
1814	Fraunhofer lines in the solar spectrum were mapped by Joseph von Fraunhofer.
1815	Refraction of light was explained by Augustin Fresnel.
1820	The discovery of electromagnetism was made by Hans Oersted.
1821	The dynamo principle was described by Michael Faraday; the thermocouple was discovered by Thomas Seebeck.
1822	The laws of electrodynamics were established by André Ampère.
1824	Thermodynamics as a branch of physics was proposed by Sadi Carnot.
1827	Ohm's law of electrical resistance was established by Georg Ohm; Brownian movement resulting from molecular vibrations was observed by Robert Brown.
1829	The law of gaseous diffusion was established by Thomas Graham.
1831	Electromagnetic induction was discovered by Faraday.
1834	Faraday discovered self-induction.
1842	The principle of conservation of energy was observed by Julius von Mayer.
c. 1847	The mechanical equivalent of heat was described by James Joule.
1849	A measurement of speed of light was put forward by French physicist Armand Fizeau (1819–1896).
1851	The rotation of the Earth was demonstrated by Jean Foucault.
1858	The mirror galvanometer, an instrument for measuring small electric currents, was invented by William Thomson (Lord Kelvin).
1859	Spectrographic analysis was made by Robert Bunsen and Gustav Kirchhoff.
1861	Osmosis was discovered.
1873	Light was conceived as electromagnetic radiation by James Maxwell.
1877	A theory of sound as vibrations in an elastic medium was propounded by John Rayleigh.
1880	Piezoelectricity was discovered by Pierre Curie.
1887	The existence of radio waves was predicted by Heinrich Hertz.
1895	X-rays were discovered by Wilhelm Röntgen.
1896	The discovery of radioactivity was made by Antoine Becquerel.
1897	Joseph Thomson discovered the electron.
1899	Ernest Rutherford discovered alpha and beta rays.
1900	Quantum theory was propounded by Max Planck; the discovery of gamma rays was made by French physicist Paul-Ulrich Villard (1860–1934).
1902	Oliver Heaviside discovered the ionosphere.
1904	The theory of radioactivity was put forward by Rutherford and Frederick Soddy.
1905	Albert Einstein propounded his special theory of relativity.
1908	The Geiger counter was invented by Hans Geiger and Rutherford.
1911	The discovery of the atomic nucleus was made by Rutherford.
1913	The orbiting electron atomic theory was propounded by Danish physicist Niels Bohr.
1915	X-ray crystallography was discovered by William and Lawrence Bragg.
1916	Einstein put forward his general theory of relativity; mass spectrography was discovered by William Aston.
1924	Edward Appleton made his study of the Heaviside layer.
1926	Wave mechanics was introduced by Erwin Schrödinger.
1927	The uncertainty principle of quantum physics was established by Werner Heisenberg.
1931	The cyclotron was developed by Ernest Lawrence.
1932	The discovery of the neutron was made by James Chadwick; the electron microscope was developed by Vladimir Zworykin.
1933	The positron, the antiparticle of the electron, was discovered by Carl Anderson.
1934	Artificial radioactivity was developed by Frédéric and Irène Joliot-Curie.
1939	The discovery of nuclear fission was made by Otto Hahn and Fritz Strassmann.
1942	The first controlled nuclear chain reaction was achieved by Enrico Fermi.
1956	The neutrino, an elementary particle, was discovered by Clyde Cowan and Fred Reines.
1960	The Mössbauer effect of atom emissions was discovered by Rudolf Mössbauer; the first laser and the first maser were developed by US physicist Theodore Maiman (1927–).
1964	Murray Gell-Mann and George Zweig discovered the quark.
1967	Jocelyn Bell (now Bell Burnell) and Antony Hewish discovered pulsars (rapidly rotating neutron stars that emit pulses of energy).
1971	The theory of superconductivity was announced, where electrical resistance in some metals vanishes above absolute zero.
1979	The discovery of the asymmetry of elementary particles was made by US physicists James W Cronin and Val L Fitch.
1982	The discovery of processes involved in the evolution of stars was made by Subrahmanyan Chandrasekhar and William Fowler.
1983	Evidence of the existence of weakons (W and Z particles) was confirmed at CERN, validating the link between the weak nuclear force and the electromagnetic force.
1986	The first high-temperature superconductor was discovered, able to conduct electricity without resistance at a temperature of −238°C/−396°F.
1989	CERN's Large Electron Positron Collider (LEP), a particle accelerator with a circumference of 27 km/16.8 mi, came into operation.
1991	LEP experiments demonstrated the existence of three generations of elementary particles, each with two quarks and two leptons.
1995	Top quark discovered at Fermilab, the US particle-physics laboratory, near Chicago, USA. US researchers announced the discovery of a material which is superconducting at the temperature of liquid nitrogen – a much higher temperature than previously achieved. First atoms of antimatter (antihydrogen) produced at CERN. Scientists at the University of Colorado created a Bose–Einstein condensate, a new state of matter in which atoms fuse together and behave as if they were a single giant atom.

began to appear in paintings and etchings, and *Guernica*, painted 1937 during the Spanish Civil War (New York, Museum of Modern Art), was a fierce pictorial comment on a deplorable bombing incident, making use of this symbolism.

In later works he moved freely from one style and one medium to another, using all with astonishing freedom and virtuosity.

Piccard Auguste Antoine 1884–1962. Swiss scientist. In 1931–32, he and his twin brother, ***Jean Félix*** (1884–1963), made ascents to 17,000 m/55,000 ft in a balloon of his own design, resulting in useful discoveries concerning stratospheric phenomena such as ◊cosmic radiation. He also built and used, with his son ***Jacques Ernest*** (1922–), bathyscaphs for research under the sea.

piccolo woodwind instrument, the smallest member of the flute family, for which Vivaldi composed three concertos.

picketing gathering of workers and their trade-union representatives to try to persuade others to support them in an industrial dispute. They often carry signs attached to pickets, hence the term.

In the UK, the Employment Act 1980 restricted the right to picket to a striker's own place of work and outlawed secondary picketing (that is, at other workplaces).

Pickford Mary. Stage name of Gladys Mary Smith 1893–1979. Canadian-born US actress. The first star of the silent screen, she was known as 'America's Sweetheart', and played innocent ingenue roles into her thirties. In 1919 she formed United Artists with Charlie Chaplin, D W Griffith, and her second husband (1920–35) Douglas Fairbanks. Her films include *Rebecca of Sunnybrook Farm* 1917, *Pollyanna* 1920, *Little Lord Fauntleroy* 1921, and *Coquette* 1929, her first talkie (Academy Award). She was presented a special Academy Award 1976.

pickling method of preserving food by soaking it in acetic acid (found in vinegar), which stops the growth of moulds. In sauerkraut, lactic acid, produced by bacteria, has the same effect.

Pico della Mirandola Count Giovanni 1463–1494. Italian mystic philosopher. Born at Mirandola, of which his father was prince, he studied Hebrew, Chaldean, and Arabic, showing particular interest in the Jewish and theosophical system, the ◊kabbala. His attempt to reconcile the religious base of Christianity, Islam, and the ancient world earned Pope Alexander VI's disapproval.

Piero della Francesca *The Baptism of Christ* 1450s by Piero della Francesca (National Gallery, London). Piero della Francesca was among the most formal of 15th-century painters, his forms and compositions worked out mathematically. As a result, his works have a precise, still, and timeless quality that was meant to express the divine harmony of the universe. *Corbis*

Pict Roman term for a member of the peoples of N Scotland, possibly meaning 'painted' (tattooed). Of pre-Celtic origin, and speaking a Celtic language which died out in about the 10th century, the Picts are thought to have inhabited much of England before the arrival of the Celtic Britons. They were united with the Celtic Scots under the rule of Kenneth MacAlpin 844. Their greatest monument is a series of carved stones, whose symbols remain undeciphered.

PID (abbreviation for ***pelvic inflammatory disease***) serious gynaecological condition characterized by lower abdominal pain, malaise, and fever; menstruation may be disrupted; infertility may result. Treatment is with antibiotics. The incidence of the disease is twice as high in women using intrauterine contraceptive devices (IUDs).

PID is potentially life-threatening, and, while mild episodes usually respond to antibiotics, surgery may be necessary in cases of severe or recurrent pelvic infection. The bacterium *Chlamydia trachomatis* (see ◊chlamydia) has been implicated in a high proportion of cases. The condition is increasingly common.

pidgin English originally a trade jargon to establish contact between the British and the Chinese in the 19th century, but now commonly and loosely used to mean any kind of 'broken' or 'native' version of the English language.

Pidgin English originally referred to the trade jargon developed between the British and the Chinese in the 19th century (*pidgin* is believed to have been a Chinese pronunciation of the English word *business*). There have been many forms of pidgin English, often with common elements because of the wide range of contacts made by commercial shipping (see pidgin languages).

pidgin language any of various trade jargons, contact languages, or ◊lingua francas arising in ports and markets where people of different linguistic backgrounds meet for commercial and other purposes. Usually a pidgin language is a rough blend of the vocabulary of one (often dominant) language with the syntax or grammar of one or more other (often dependent) groups. Pidgin English in various parts of the world, *français petit negre*, and Bazaar Hindi or Hindustani are examples of pidgins that have served long-term purposes to the extent of being acquired by children as one of their everyday languages.

At this point they become ◊creole languages.

Piedmont (Italian ***Piemonte***) region of N Italy, bordering Switzerland to the N and France to the W, and surrounded, except to the E, by the Alps and the Apennines; area 25,400 sq km/9,804 sq mi; population (1992 est) 4,303,800. Its capital is Turin, and towns include Alessandria, Asti, Vercelli, and Novara. It also includes the fertile Po river valley. Products include fruit, grain, cattle, cars, and textiles. The movement for the unification of Italy started in the 19th century in Piedmont, under the house of Savoy.

Pierce Franklin 1804–1869. 14th president of the USA, 1852–56. A Democrat, he held office in the US House of Representatives 1833–37, and the US Senate 1837–42. Chosen as a compromise candidate of the Democratic party, he was elected president 1852. Despite his expansionist foreign policy, North–South tensions grew more intense, and Pierce was denied renomination 1856.

Piero della Francesca c. 1420–1492. Italian painter. Active in Arezzo and Urbino, he was one of the major artists of the 15th century. His work has a solemn stillness and unusually solid figures, luminous colour, and carefully calculated compositional harmonies. It includes several important fresco series, and panel paintings such as the *Flagellation of Christ* c. 1455 (Ducal Palace, Urbino), which is remarkable for its use of perspective.

Formal and austere, all his works, of whatever size or medium, show in their use of colour, perspective and composition a fascination with mathematical order. Among his great works include the fresco series *The Legend of the True Cross* (the church of San Francesco, Arezzo) 1452–60; the fresco *The Resurrection of Christ* (Pinacoteca, Sansepolcro); and the panel altarpiece *Madonna with the Duke of Urbino as Donor* (Brera, Milan). The two famous panel paintings in the National Gallery, London, the *Baptism of Christ* and the *Nativity*, though closely related in style, are considered to be an early and late work respectively.

His portraits include *Federigo da Montefeltro* c. 1470 and *Battista Sforza* c. 1470 (both Uffizi, Florence).

The oil method of these portraits suggests some acquaintance with Netherlandish painting, but in general the art of Piero is strongly individual in its poetry and contemplative spirit, and the feeling of intellectual force conveyed by its abstract treatment of space and form.

Piero di Cosimo c. 1462–c. 1521. Italian painter. He was known for his inventive pictures of mythological subjects, often featuring fauns and centaurs. *Mythological Scene* about 1510 (National Gallery, London) is typical. He also painted religious subjects and portraits.

The son of Lorenzo di Piero, he was the pupil of Cosimo Rosselli, whose Christian name he adopted. Though influenced by Signorelli and Leonardo, he had a personal and whimsical imagination, which gives a vivid life to his representations of the satyrs and centaurs of classical fable, and also shows itself in the various animals he introduced into his pictures.

His *Perseus and Andromeda* (Uffizi) presents a typically fantastic dragon, and his mythological picture, formerly known as *The Death of Procris* (National Gallery), like the work of his contemporary Botticelli in its delicate pathos, introduces, as well as its famous dog, a strange-looking faun.

Another distinctive masterpiece is the *Venus, Mars and Cupid* (Berlin). He assisted Cosimo Rosselli in his frescoes in the Sistine Chapel 1481–82. He was also the author of some strongly characterized portraits that have an element of Leonardesque caricature. He was the master of Andrea del Sarto.

Pietism religious movement within Lutheranism in the 17th century that emphasized spiritual and devotional faith rather than theology and dogma. It was founded by Philipp Jakob Spener (1635–1705), a minister in Frankfurt, Germany, who emphasized devotional meetings for 'groups of the Elect' rather than biblical learning; he wrote the *Pia Desideria* 1675.

pietra dura (Italian 'hard stone') Italian technique of inlaying furniture with semiprecious stones, such as agate or quartz, in a variety of colours, to create pictures or patterns.

Pietro da Cortona (Pietro Berrettini) 1596–1669. Italian painter and architect. He was a major influence in the development of the High Baroque. His enormous fresco *Allegory of Divine Providence* 1633–39 (Barberini Palace, Rome) glorifies his patron the pope and the Barberini family, and gives a convincing illusion of reality.

He studied at Cortona under a Florentine painter, Andrea Commodi, and then in Rome, where he attracted the notice of Urban VIII and enjoyed the patronage of a succession of pontiffs. 1620–1640 he produced paintings for the Marchese Sacchetti (Rome, Capitoline Gallery), frescoes for Cardinal Francesco Barberini in Sta Bibiana and other Roman churches, and his masterpiece, the allegorical ceiling painting for the Barberini Palace, 1633–39 (Rome, Galleria Nazionale), in which the illusionist effect of figures foreshortened and floating in space as seen from below was contrived with immense skill and daring.

piezoelectric effect property of some crystals (for example, quartz) to develop an electromotive force or voltage across opposite faces when subjected to tension or compression, and, conversely, to expand or contract in size when subjected to an electromotive force. Piezoelectric crystal ◊oscillators are used as frequency standards (for example, replacing balance wheels in watches), and for producing ultrasound.

The crystals are also used in gramophone pickups, transducers in ultrasonics, and certain gas lighters.

pig any even-toed hoofed mammal of the family Suidae. They are omnivorous, and have simple, non-ruminating stomachs and thick hides. The Middle Eastern wild boar *Sus scrofa* is the ancestor of domesticated breeds; it is 1.5 m/4.5 ft long and 1 m/3 ft high, with formidable tusks, but not naturally aggressive.

Wild pigs include the ◊babirusa and the ◊wart hog. The farming of domesticated pigs was practised during the Neolithic in the Middle East and China at least 11,000 years ago and the pig was a common farm animal in ancient Greece and Rome. Over 400 breeds evolved over the centuries, many of which have all but disappeared in more recent times with the development of intensive rearing systems. The Berkshire, Chester White, Poland, China, Saddleback, Yorkshire, Duroc, and Razorback are the main surviving breeds. Modern indoor rearing methods favour the large white breeds, such as the Chester White and the originally Swedish Landrace, over coloured varieties, which tend to be hardier and can survive better outdoors. Since 1960, hybrid pigs, produced by crossing two or more breeds, have become popular for their heavy but lean carcasses.

The Berkshire and Tamworth are now rare in the UK, but still widespread in Australia and New Zealand. About 30% of the pork and bacon consumed in the UK is imported from intensive farms in the Netherlands and Denmark.

pigeon or ***dove*** bird of the family Columbidae, order Columbiformes, distinguished by its large crop, which becomes glandular in the breeding season and secretes a milky fluid ('pigeon's milk') that aids digestion of food for the young. There are many species, and they are found worldwide.

New World species include the mourning-doves, which live much of the time on the ground. The fruit pigeons of Australasia and the Malay regions are beautifully coloured. In the USA, there were once millions of passenger pigeons *Ectopistes migratorius*, but they have been extinct since 1914.

species The collared dove *Streptopelia decaocto* has multiplied greatly in Europe since it first arrived from central Asia 1930. It is a sandy coloured bird with a black collar, edged in white around the back of the head, and lives in urban areas as well as the countryside. The stock-dove *Columba oenas* is similar to the rock dove, but the wood-pigeon, or ring-dove, *C. palumbus* is much larger and has white patches on the neck. The carrier pigeon is remarkable for the huge white wattle round the eyes and at the base of the beak. Other varieties of domesticated pigeon include pouter, fantail, and homer. The European turtle dove, with brown speckled wings and a long, dark tail, lives mostly on the ground.

pigeon hawk another name for the merlin, a small ◊falcon.

pigeon racing sport of racing pigeons against a clock. The birds are taken from their loft(s) and transported to a starting point, often hundreds of miles away. They have to return to their loft and a special clock times their arrival.

In shorter races pigeons failing to reach their destination average 10–20%; in longer races losses can be much higher.

In Britain the National Homing Union dates from 1896. Elizabeth II has a flight of pigeons which is looked after by a racing manager.

Piggott Lester Keith 1935– . English jockey. He adopted a unique high riding style and is renowned as a brilliant tactician. A champion jockey 11 times between 1960 and 1982, he has ridden a record nine ◊Derby winners. Piggott retired from riding 1985 and took up training, but returned to racing in 1990. He retired as a jockey for the second time Sept 1995.

He was associated with such great horses as Nijinsky, Sir Ivor, Roberto, Empery, and The Minstrel. Piggott won all the major races, including the English classics.

pig iron or ***cast iron*** the quality of iron produced in a ◊blast furnace. It contains around 4% carbon plus some other impurities.

pika or ***mouse-hare*** any small mammal of the family Ochotonidae, belonging to the order Lagomorpha (rabbits and hares). The single genus *Ochotona* contains about 15 species, most of which live in mountainous regions of Asia, although two species are native to North America.

Pikas have short, rounded ears, and most species are about 20 cm/8 in long, with greyish-brown fur and no visible tail. Their warning call is a sharp whistle. They are vegetarian and in late summer cut grasses and other plants and place them in piles to dry as hay, which is then stored for the winter.

pike any of a family Esocidae in the order Salmoniformes, of slender, freshwater bony fishes with narrow pointed heads and sharp, pointed teeth. The northern pike *Esox lucius*, of North America and Eurasia, may reach 2.2 m/7 ft and 9 kg/20 lb. Other kinds of pike include muskellunges, up to 2.2 m/7 ft long, and the smaller pickerels, both in the genus *Esox*.

pikeperch any of various freshwater members of the perch family, resembling pikes, especially the walleye *Stizostedion vitreum*, common in Europe, W Asia, and North America. It reaches over 1 m/3 ft.

Pilate Pontius died c. AD 36. Roman procurator of Judea AD 26–36. The New Testament Gospels describe his reluctant ordering of Jesus' crucifixion, but there has been considerable debate about his actual role in it.

Pilate was unsympathetic to the Jews; his actions several times provoked riots, and in AD 36 he was recalled to Rome to account for the brutal suppression of a Samaritan revolt. The Greek historian Eusebius says Pilate committed suicide after Jesus' crucifixion, but another tradition says he became a Christian, and he is regarded as a saint and martyr in the Ethiopian Coptic and Greek Orthodox churches.

pilchard any of various small, oily members of the herring family, Clupeidae, especially the commercial sardine of Europe *Sardina pilchardus*, and the California sardine *Sardinops sagax*.

pilgrimage journey to sacred places inspired by religious devotion. For Hindus, the holy places include Varanasi and the purifying river Ganges; for Buddhists, the places connected with the crises of Buddha's career; for the ancient Greeks, the shrines at Delphi and Ephesus, among others; for Jews, the sanctuary at Jerusalem; and for Muslims, Mecca.

Pilgrimage of Grace rebellion against Henry VIII of England 1536–37, originating in Yorkshire and Lincolnshire. The uprising was directed against the policies of the monarch (such as the dissolution of the monasteries and the effects of the enclosure of common land).

Pilgrims the emigrants who sailed from Plymouth, Devon, England, in the *Mayflower* on 16 Sept 1620 to found the first colony in New England at New Plymouth, Massachusetts. Of the 102 passengers fewer than a quarter were Puritan refugees.

The Pilgrims (also known as the Pilgrim Fathers) originally set sail in the *Mayflower* and *Speedwell* from Southampton on 5 Aug 1620, but had to put into Dartmouth when the *Speedwell* needed repair. Bad weather then drove them into Plymouth Sound, where the *Speedwell* was abandoned. They landed at Cape Cod in Dec, and about half their number died over the winter before they received help from the Indians; the survivors celebrated the first ◊Thanksgiving in the autumn of 1621.

Pill, the commonly used term for the contraceptive pill, based on female hormones. The combined pill, which contains synthetic hormones similar to oestrogen and progesterone, stops the production of eggs, and makes the mucus produced by the cervix hostile to sperm. It is the most effective form of contraception apart from sterilization, being more than 99% effective.

The minipill or progesterone-only pill prevents implantation of a fertilized egg into the wall of the uterus. The minipill has a slightly higher failure rate, especially if not taken at the same time each day, but has fewer side effects and is considered safer for long-term use. Possible side effects of the Pill include migraine or headache and high blood pressure. More seriously, oestrogen-containing pills can slightly increase the risk of a clot forming in the blood vessels. This risk is increased in women over 35 if they smoke. Controversy surrounds other possible health effects of taking the Pill. The evidence for a link with cancer is slight (and the Pill may protect women from some forms of cancer). Once a woman ceases to take it, there is an increase in the likelihood of conceiving identical twins.

pilotfish small marine fish *Naucrates ductor* of the family Carangidae, which also includes pompanos. It hides below sharks, turtles, or boats, using the shade as a base from which to prey on smaller fish. It is found in all warm oceans and grows to about 36 cm/1.2 ft.

pilot whale or ***black whale*** or ***social whale*** marine mammmal of the dolphin family, genus *Globiocephala*. It grows to about 8.5 m/28 ft and is black with a white streak on its belly and a broad, flat head. The pilot whale is more frequently stranded than any other species, and is found in almost every sea.

Piłsudski Józef (Klemens) 1867–1935. Polish nationalist politician, dictator from 1926. Born in Russian Poland, he founded the Polish Socialist Party 1892 and was twice imprisoned for anti-Russian activities. During World War I he commanded a Polish force to fight for Germany and evicted the Russians from E Poland but fell under suspicion of intriguing with the Allies and was imprisoned by the Germans 1917–18. When Poland became independent 1919, he was elected chief of state, and led a Polish attack on the USSR 1920, driving the Soviets out of Poland. He retired 1923, but in 1926 led a military coup that established his dictatorship until his death.

Piltdown man fossil skull fragments 'discovered' by Charles Dawson at Piltdown, E Sussex, England, in 1913, and believed to be the earliest European human remains until proved a hoax in 1953 (the jaw was that of an orang-utan).

pimento or ***allspice*** tree found in tropical parts of the New World. The dried fruits of the species *Pimenta dioica* are used as a spice. Also, a sweet variety of ◊capsicum pepper (more correctly spelled pimiento).

pimpernel any plant of the genus *Anagallis* of the primrose family Primulaceae comprising about 30 species mostly native to W Europe. The European scarlet pimpernel *A. arvensis* grows in cornfields, the flowers opening only in full sunshine. It is naturalized in North America.

PIN (acronym for ***personal identification number***) in banking, a unique number used as a password to establish the identity of a customer using an automatic cash dispenser. The PIN is normally encoded into the magnetic strip of the customer's bank card

pigeon The laughing dove *Stigmatopelia senegalensis* is found over the whole of Africa S of the Sahara and then eastwards as far as India. Throughout most of this region it is one of the most familiar garden birds, often becoming tame.

❛Anyone can be heroic from time to time, but a gentleman is something you have to be all the time.❜

Luigi Pirandello *The Pleasure of Honesty*

and is known only to the customer and to the bank's computer.

Pinatubo, Mount active volcano on Luzon Island, the Philippines, 88 km/55 mi N of Manila. Dormant for 600 years, it erupted June 1991, killing 343 people and leaving as many as 200,000 homeless. Surrounding rice fields were covered with 3 m/10 ft of volcanic ash.

Pindar c. 518–c. 438 BC. Greek lyric poet. He is noted for his surviving choral songs, or ◊odes, written in honour of victors in the Greek athletic games at Delphi, Olympia, Nemea, and the Isthmus of Corinth. Only fragments of his other works survive; these include hymns, processional songs, and dirges.

Pindling Lynden (Oscar) 1930– . Bahamian politician, prime minister 1967–92. After studying law in London, he returned to the island to join the newly formed Progressive Liberal Party and then became the first black prime minister of the Bahamas.

pine evergreen resinous tree of the genus *Pinus* with some 70–100 species, belonging to the Pinaceae, the largest family of conifers. The oldest living species is probably the bristlecone pine *P. aristata*, native to California, of which some specimens are said to be 4,600 years old.

The Scots pine *P. sylvestris* is grown commercially for soft timber and its yield of turpentine, tar, and pitch.

pineal body or ***pineal gland*** a cone-shaped outgrowth of the vertebrate brain. In some lower vertebrates, it develops a rudimentary lens and retina, which show it to be derived from an eye, or pair of eyes, situated on the top of the head in ancestral vertebrates. In fishes that can change colour to match their background, the pineal perceives the light level and controls the colour change. In birds, the pineal detects changes in daylight and stimulates breeding behaviour as spring approaches. Mammals also have a pineal gland, but it is located deeper within the brain. It secretes a hormone, melatonin, thought to influence rhythms of activity. In humans, it is a small piece of tissue attached by a stalk to the rear wall of the third ventricle of the brain.

pineapple plant *Ananas comosus* of the bromeliad family, native to South and Central America, but now cultivated in many other tropical areas, such as Hawaii and Queensland, Australia. The mauvish flowers are produced in the second year, and subsequently consolidate with their bracts into a fleshy fruit.

For export to world markets the fruits are cut unripe and lack the sweet juiciness typical of the canned pineapple (usually the smoother-skinned Cayenne variety), which is allowed to mature fully.

Pinero Arthur Wing 1855–1934. English dramatist. A leading exponent of the 'well-made' play, he enjoyed great contemporary success with his farces, beginning with *The Magistrate* 1885. More substantial social drama followed with *The Second Mrs Tanqueray* 1893, and comedies including *Trelawny of the 'Wells'* 1898.

pineapple With its large pineapplelike fruit, *Ananas ananassoides* from central Brazil is very closely related to the ancestor of the true pineapple, which is native to the same region. *Premaphotos Wildlife*

pinhole camera the simplest type of camera, in which a pinhole rather than a lens is used to form an image. Light passes through the pinhole at one end of a box to form a sharp inverted image on the inside surface of the opposite end. The image is equally sharp for objects placed at different distances from the camera because only one ray from a particular distance or direction can enter through the tiny pinhole, and so only one corresponding point of light will be produced on the image. A photographic film or plate fitted inside the box will, if exposed for a long time, record the image.

pink any annual or perennial plant of the genus *Dianthus* of the family Carophyllaceae. The stems have characteristically swollen nodes, and the flowers range in colour from white through pink to purple. Members of the pink family include carnations, sweet williams, and baby's breath *Gypsophila paniculata*.

Pinkerton Allan 1819–1884. US detective, born in Glasgow, Scotland. He founded Pinkerton's National Detective Agency 1852 and built up the federal secret service from the espionage system he developed during the American Civil War.

Pink Floyd British psychedelic rock group, formed 1965. The original members were Syd Barrett (1946–), Roger Waters (1944–), Richard Wright (1945–), and Nick Mason (1945–). Their albums include *The Dark Side of the Moon* 1973 and *The Wall* 1979, with its spin-off film starring Bob Geldof.

pinna in botany, the primary division of a ◊pinnate leaf. In mammals, the pinna is the external part of the ear.

pinnate leaf leaf that is divided up into many small leaflets, arranged in rows along either side of a midrib, as in ash trees (*Fraxinus*). It is a type of compound leaf. Each leaflet is known as a pinna, and where the pinnae are themselves divided, the secondary divisions are known as pinnules.

Pinochet (Ugarte) Augusto 1915– . Military ruler of Chile from 1973, when a coup backed by the US Central Intelligence Agency ousted and killed President Salvador Allende. Pinochet took over the presidency and governed ruthlessly, crushing all opposition. He was voted out of power when general elections were held Dec 1989 but remained head of the armed forces.

Pinochet's attempts to reassert political influence were firmly censured by President Patricio Aylwin in 1990, and by President Frei Ruiz-Tagle in 1995.

In April 1999 British home secretary Jack Straw authorized extradition proceedings against him, on a warrant by a Spanish lawyer investigating alleged crimes by him.

pint imperial dry or liquid measure of capacity equal to 20 fluid ounces, half a quart, one-eighth of a gallon, or 0.568 litre. In the US, a liquid pint is equal to 0.473 litre, while a dry pint is equal to 0.550 litre.

Pinter Harold 1930– . English dramatist, originally an actor. He specializes in the tragicomedy of the breakdown of communication, broadly in the tradition of the Theatre of the ◊Absurd – for example, *The Birthday Party* 1958 and *The Caretaker* 1960. Later plays include *The Homecoming* 1965, *Old Times* 1971, *Betrayal* 1978, and *Moonlight* 1993.

Pinturicchio (or ***Pintoricchio***) pseudonym of Bernardino di Betto c. 1454–1513. Italian painter. His chief works are the frescoes in the Borgia Apartments in the Vatican, painted in the 1490s, and in the Piccolomini Library of Siena Cathedral, 1503–08, illustrating the history of Pope Pius II.

Born in Perugia, he came to Rome 1481 as one of ◊Perugino's assistants in the decorating of the Sistine Chapel, Rome. He became very successful, his skill in large-scale narrative proving popular with both Church and nobility. An example of his work on a smaller scale is *The Return of Odysseus* (National Gallery, London).

pinworm ◊nematode worm *Enterobius vermicularis*, an intestinal parasite of humans.

Pinyin Chinese phonetic alphabet approved 1956 by the People's Republic of China, and used since 1979 in transcribing all names of people and places from Chinese ideograms into other languages using the English/Roman alphabet. For example, the former transcription Chou En-lai becomes Zhou Enlai, Hua Kuo-feng became Hua Guofeng, Teng Hsiao-ping became Deng Xiaoping, Peking became Beijing.

pion or ***pi meson*** in physics, a subatomic particle with a neutral form (mass 135 MeV) and a positively charged form (mass 139 MeV). The charged pion decays into muons and neutrinos and the neutral form decays into gamma-ray photons. They belong to the ◊hadron class of ◊elementary particles.

The mass of a positive pion is 273 times that of an electron; the mass of a neutral pion is 264 times that of an electron.

Pioneer probe any of a series of US Solar-System space probes 1958–78. The probes *Pioneer 4–9* went into solar orbit to monitor the Sun's activity during the 1960s and early 1970s. *Pioneer 5*, launched 1960, was the first of a series to study the solar wind between the planets. *Pioneer 10*, launched March 1972, was the first probe to reach Jupiter (Dec 1973) and to leave the Solar System 1983. *Pioneer 11*, launched April 1973, passed Jupiter Dec 1974, and was the first probe to reach Saturn (Sept 1979), before also leaving the Solar System.

Pioneer 10 and *11* carry plaques containing messages from Earth in case they are found by other civilizations among the stars. Pioneer Venus probes were launched May and Aug 1978. One orbited Venus, and the other dropped three probes onto the surface. The orbiter finally burned up in the atmosphere of Venus 1992. In 1992 *Pioneer 10* was more than 8 billion km/4.4 billion mi from the Sun. Both it and *Pioneer 11* were still returning data measurements of starlight intensity to Earth.

Pioneer 1, *2*, and *3*, launched 1958, were intended Moon probes, but *Pioneer 2*'s launch failed, and *1* and *3* failed to reach their target, although they did measure the ◊Van Allen radiation belts. *Pioneer 4* began to orbit the Sun after passing the Moon.

pipefish any of various long-snouted, thin, pipe-like marine fishes in the same family (Syngnathidae) as seahorses. The great pipefish *Syngnathus acus* grows up to 50 cm/1.6 ft, and the male has a brood pouch for eggs and developing young, which hatch as tiny versions of the adults in five to six weeks: there is no larval stage.

pipette device for the accurate measurement of a known volume of liquid, usually for transfer from one container to another, used in chemistry and biology laboratories.

A pipette is a glass tube, often with an enlarged bulb, which is calibrated in one or more positions, or it may be a plastic device with an adjustable plunger, fitted with one or more disposable plastic tips.

pipit any of various sparrow-sized ground-dwelling songbirds of the genus *Anthus* of the family Motacillidae, order Passeriformes.

The European meadow pipit *Anthus pratensis* is about the size of a sparrow and streaky brown, with a slender notched bill. It lives in open country and feeds on the ground. Other British species are the tree pipit, *A. trivialis*, and the rock pipit, *A. petrosus*.

piracy the taking of a ship, aircraft, or any of its contents, from lawful ownership, punishable under international law by the court of any country where the pirate may be found or taken. When the craft is taken over to alter its destination, or its passengers held to ransom, the term is ◊hijacking. Piracy is also used to describe infringement of ◊copyright.

Algiers (see ◊corsairs), the West Indies (see ◊buccaneers), the coast of Trucial Oman (the Pirate Coast), Chinese and Malay waters, and such hide-outs as Lundy Island, SW England, were pirate haunts for many years. Between the 16th and 18th centuries, the Barbary states of N Africa (Morocco, Algiers, Tunis, and Tripoli) were called the Pirate States. Piracy in the Atlantic reached a peak from the 1650s to the 1720s, when there were as many as 2,000 pirates. These were largely eliminated by the British Navy; over 400 men were hanged for piracy 1716–1726. The best-known contemporary account of piracy is Capt Charles Johnson's *General History of the Pyrates* 1724.

Modern communications and the complexities of supplying and servicing modern vessels tend to eliminate piracy, or confine it to the immediate vicinity of a harbour. However, incidents are increasing in the waters of Hong Kong, W Africa, and Brazil, and particularly in the SE Asian region, where piracy cost $200 million in 1990. In Indonesian territorial waters alone, 200 pirate attacks were reported in 1991. A pirate-monitoring and warning centre was opened in 1992 by the International Maritime Bureau; however piracy on the high seas almost doubled 1993–94 – the number of attempted boardings declined, but the number of successful boardings (60 ships), hijackings, and attacks in anchorages rose. Most targets were dry-cargo vessels.

Piraeus port of both ancient and modern Athens and main port of Greece, on the Gulf of Aegina; population (1991) 169,600. Constructed as the port of Athens about 493 BC, it was linked with that city by the Long Walls, a fortification protecting the approaches to Athens comprising three walls built 496–456 BC. After the destruction of Athens by Sulla 86 BC, Piraeus declined. Piraeus is now an industrial suburb of Athens.

Pirandello The Italian writer Luigi Pirandello. As well as ten plays and a number of full-length novels, Pirandello published many short stories exploring the themes of his plays, such as the relationship between appearance and reality, in greater depth. *Corbis*

Pirandello Luigi 1867–1936. Italian playwright, novelist, and short-story writer. His plays, which often deal with the themes of illusion and reality, and the tragicomic absurdity of life, include *Sei personaggi in cerca d'autore/Six Characters in Search of an Author* 1921, and *Enrico IV/Henry IV* 1922. The themes and innovative techniques of his plays anticipated the work of Brecht, O'Neill, Anouilh, and Genet. Among his novels are *L'esclusa/The Outcast* 1901, *Il fu Mattia Pascal/ The Late Mattia Pascal* 1904, and *I vecchi e i giovani/The Old and the Young* 1909. He also wrote many short stories, some of which are little more than anecdotes; 28 were dramatized. Nobel Prize for Literature 1934.

Piranesi Giambattista (Giovanni Battista) 1720–1778. Italian architect and graphic artist. He was an influential theorist of architecture, advocating imaginative use of Roman models. His series of etchings *Carceri d'Invenzione/Prisons of Invention* about 1745–61 depicts imaginary prisons, vast and gloomy.

Only one of his architectural designs was built: Sta Maria del Priorato, Rome. His powerful etchings of Roman antiquities evoked ruined grandeur; his *Vedute* (views of Rome), published from 1745, proved very popular. He was born in Venice.

piranha any South American freshwater fish of the genus *Serrusalmus*, in the same order as cichlids. They can grow to 60 cm/2 ft long, and have razor-sharp teeth; some species may rapidly devour animals, especially if attracted by blood.

Piran, St lived c. 500 AD. Christian missionary sent to Cornwall by St Patrick. There are remains of his oratory at Perranzabuloe, and he is the patron saint of Cornwall and its nationalist movement. Feast day 5 March.

pirouette in dance, a movement comprising one or more complete turns of the body on one leg with the other touching the supporting leg at the knee.

Pisa city in Tuscany, Italy; population (1991) 101,000. It has an 11th–12th-century cathedral. Its famous campanile, the Leaning Tower of Pisa (repaired 1990), is 55 m/180 ft high and about 5 m/16.5 ft out of perpendicular. It has foundations only about 3 m/10 ft deep.

Pisa was a maritime republic in the 11th–12th centuries. The university dates from 1338. The scientist Galileo was born here.

The Piazza dei Miracoli, the square in which the famous tower stands, is built on over 70 m/230 ft of alternating layers of clay and sand, and is slowly sinking with greater subsidence in certain areas; the tower leans because it was built on one of these areas. In 1995 a concrete ring was built around the base and anchored to a layer of sand at a depth of 50 m/164 ft.

Pisanello nickname of Antonio Pisano c. 1395–c. 1455. Italian painter and medallist. He painted religious works and portraits in the ◊International Gothic style, as in *Madonna and Child with St George and St Anthony Abbot* c. 1445 (National Gallery, London). He was also an outstanding portrait medallist. His frescoes in the Palazzo Ducale in Mantua were rediscovered after World War II.

His early life was spent at Verona, where he was trained in the ◊International Gothic style which flourished there. He was associated with one of the main Italian practitioners of the style, Gentile da Fabriano, completing frescoes (now destroyed) by Gentile, in Venice and Rome. As a painter and producer of portrait medallions he made a triumphal progress from one Italian court to another, working for the Gonzagas in Mantua, the Visconti in Pavia, Sigismondo Malatesta in Rimini, Lionello d'Este in Ferrara, and from 1448, for Alfonso of Aragon in Naples.

Pisano Nicola (died c. 1284) and his son ***Giovanni*** (died c. 1314). Italian sculptors and architects. Nicola initiated a revival of Classical forms, his best-known works being the pulpit of the Pisa Baptistry 1260, and the pulpit for Siena Cathedral 1265–68, on which his son Giovanni also worked. The sculptures of Giovanni, such as the pulpit for San Andrea, Pistoia, about 1300, are more emotional and expressive than his father's, showing the influence of French Gothic.

Pisces inconspicuous zodiac constellation, mainly in the northern hemisphere between ◊Aries and ◊Aquarius, near ◊Pegasus. It is represented as two fish tied together by their tails. The Circlet, a delicate ring of stars, marks the head of the western fish in Pisces. The constellation contains the vernal equinox, the point at which the Sun's path around the sky (the ecliptic) crosses the celestial equator (see ◊celestial sphere). The Sun reaches this point around 21 March each year as it passes through Pisces from mid-March to late April. In astrology, the dates for Pisces are between about 19 Feb and 20 March (see ◊precession).

piranha Red piranhas swim in shoals so large that they can devour even large animals quickly by their combined efforts. Their razor-sharp teeth and strong jaws can chop off pieces of flesh with great speed.

Piscis Austrinus or ***Southern Fish*** constellation of the southern hemisphere near ◊Capricornus. Its brightest star is the first-magnitude ◊Fomalhaut.

Pisistratus c. 605–527 BC. Athenian politician. Although of noble family, he assumed the leadership of the peasant party, and seized power 561 BC. He was twice expelled, but recovered power from 546 BC until his death. Ruling as a tyrant under constitutional forms, he was the first to have the Homeric poems written down, and founded Greek drama by introducing the Dionysiac peasant festivals into Athens.

Pissarro Camille 1830–1903. French painter. A leading member of the Impressionists, he experimented with various styles, including ◊Pointillism, in the 1880s. Though he is closely linked with pictures of the French countryside and peasant life, he also painted notable street scenes, as in *Boulevard Montmartre* 1897 (Hermitage, St Petersburg).

Born in the West Indies, he went to Paris 1855. He studied at the Académie Suisse, where he met Claude Monet, and was influenced by Corot and Courbet. His early work, subdued in tone and simple in composition, already showed the feeling of open air which he developed in country retreat at Pontoise and Louveciennes before 1870.

During the Franco-Prussian war 1870–01, when his house was occupied and most of his pictures destroyed, he was in England with Monet, living in south London and painting pictures of the Crystal Palace, Sydenham and Upper Norwood. On his return he pursued a course parallel with that of Monet in the rendering of light by colour, with blues, purples and greens prevailing.

Pisa The circular baptistry, marble-clad cathedral, and campanile (Leaning Tower of Pisa) form the most celebrated complex of Gothic architecture in Italy. *Italian State Tourist Office*

'The atrocious crime of being a young man … I shall neither attempt to palliate nor deny.'

William Pitt the Elder Speech in the House of Commons 27 Jan 1741

He settled at Eragny 1884 but made frequent visits to Le Havre, Rouen, and Paris, with views of the boulevards of the capital and of the waterfronts being the results, though his most typical paintings represent the quiet countryside and its peasants.

pistachio deciduous Eurasian tree *Pistacia vera* of the cashew family Anacardiaceae, with green nuts, which are eaten salted or used to enhance and flavour foods.

pistil general term for the female part of a flower, either referring to one single ◊carpel or a group of several fused carpels.

pistol any small ◊firearm designed to be fired with one hand. Pistols were in use from the early 15th century.

The problem of firing more than once without reloading was tackled by using many combinations of multiple barrels, both stationary and revolving. A breech-loading, multichambered revolver of as early as 1650 still survives; the first practical solution, however, was Samuel Colt's six-gun 1847. Behind a single barrel, a short six-chambered cylinder was rotated by cocking the hammer and a fresh round of ammunition brought into firing position. The automatic pistol, operated by gas or recoil, was introduced in Germany in the 1890s. Both revolvers and automatics remain in widespread military use.

piston barrel-shaped device used in reciprocating engines (steam, petrol, diesel oil) to harness power. Pistons are driven up and down in cylinders by expanding steam or hot gases. They pass on their motion via a connecting rod and crank to a crankshaft, which turns the driving wheels. In a pump or compressor, the role of the piston is reversed, being used to move gases and liquids. See also ◊internal-combustion engine.

pit bull terrier or ***American pit bull terrier*** variety of dog that was developed in the USA solely as a fighting dog. It usually measures about 50 cm/20 in at the shoulder and weighs roughly 23 kg/50 lb, but there are no established criteria since it is not recognized as a breed by either the American or British Kennel Clubs. Selective breeding for physical strength and aggression has created a dog unsuitable for life in the modern community.

Legislation in Britain 1989 and 1991 (see ◊dog, dangerous) has made it illegal to import, breed, or sell pit bull terriers. Further, they must be registered, kept muzzled and on a lead when in public places, and, in order to ensure the type dies out, they must also be neutered.

Pitcairn Islands British colony in Polynesia, 5,300 km/3,300 mi NE of New Zealand
area 27 sq km/10 sq mi
capital Adamstown
features the uninhabited Henderson Islands, an unspoiled coral atoll with a rare ecology, and tiny Ducie and Oeno islands, annexed by Britain 1902
industries fruit and souvenirs to passing ships
population (1994) 56
language English
government the governor is the British high commissioner in New Zealand
history settled 1790 by nine mutineers from the British ship the *Bounty* together with some Tahitians; their occupation remained unknown until 1808.

pitch in chemistry, a black, sticky substance, hard when cold, but liquid when hot, used for waterproofing, roofing, and paving. It is made by the destructive distillation of wood or coal tar, and has been used since antiquity for caulking wooden ships.

pitch in mechanics, the distance between the adjacent threads of a screw or bolt. When a screw is turned through one full turn it moves a distance equal to the pitch of its thread. A screw thread is a simple type of machine, acting like a rolled-up inclined plane, or ramp (as may be illustrated by rolling a long paper triangle around a pencil). A screw has a ◊mechanical advantage greater than one.

'Not merely a chip off the old 'block', but the old block itself.'

Edmund Burke, on **William Pitt the Younger's** first speech

pitch in music, the position of a note in the scale, dependent on the frequency of the predominant sound wave. In concert pitch, A above middle C (A4) is the reference tone to which instruments are tuned. Perfect pitch is an ability to name or reproduce any note heard or asked for; it does not necessarily imply high musical ability.

In a musical instrument, pitch is a consequence of design converting a continuous input of energy into a periodic output of pressure waves that the ear perceives as a tone of constant pitch. In string instruments, pitch depends on the length, composition, and tension of the string in vibration, transmitted to a resonating soundbox. Tuned percussion instruments generate pitch by a combination of natural reverberation of the vibrating body, and the natural frequency of any associated resonator, such as the shell of a drum or the soundboard of a piano. The fundamental pitch of a wind instrument (excepting free reeds) depends on the period of oscillation of the travelling pressure wave within the tube, and is a function of the length of the tube. In organ terminology, pipes are classified in wavelength pitch as 4-foot, 8-foot, 16-foot, depending on their octave range.

pitchblende or ***uraninite*** brownish-black mineral, the major constituent of uranium ore, consisting mainly of uranium oxide (UO_2). It also contains some lead (the final, stable product of uranium decay) and variable amounts of most of the naturally occurring radioactive elements, which are products of either the decay or the fissioning of uranium isotopes. The uranium yield is 50–80%; it is also a source of radium, polonium, and actinium. Pitchblende was first studied by Pierre and Marie ◊Curie, who found radium and polonium in its residues in 1898.

pitcher plant any of various insectivorous plants of the family Sarraceniaceae, especially the genera *Nepenthes* and *Sarracenia*, the leaves of which are shaped like a pitcher and filled with a fluid that traps and digests insects.

pitcher plant *Nepenthes madagascariensis* from open swamps in S Madagascar, one of two species of pitcher plants native to the island. The greatest variety of pitcher plants is found in Borneo, especially on Mount Kinabalu, where the largest pitcher plant *Nepenthes rajah* grows. *Premaphotos Wildlife*

Pitman Isaac 1813–1897. English teacher and inventor of Pitman's shorthand. He studied Samuel Taylor's scheme for shorthand writing, and in 1837 published his own system, *Stenographic Sound-hand*, fast, accurate, and adapted for use in many languages.

Pitot tube instrument that measures fluid (gas and liquid) flow. It is used to measure the speed of aircraft, and works by sensing pressure differences in different directions in the airstream.

It was invented in the 1730s by the French scientist Henri Pitot (1695–1771).

Pitt William, ***the Elder***, 1st Earl of Chatham 1708–1778. British Whig politician, 'the Great Commoner'. As paymaster of the forces 1746–55, he broke with tradition by refusing to enrich himself; he was dismissed for attacking the Duke of Newcastle, the prime minister. Recalled by popular demand to form a government on the outbreak of the Seven Years' War 1756, he was forced to form a coalition with Newcastle 1757. A 'year of victories' ensued 1759, and the French were expelled from India and Canada.

In 1761 Pitt wished to escalate the war by a declaration of war on Spain, George III disagreed and Pitt resigned, but was again recalled to form an all-party government 1766. He championed the Americans against the king, though rejecting independence, and collapsed during his last speech in the House of Lords – opposing the withdrawal of British troops – and died a month later.

Pitt William, ***the Younger*** 1759–1806. British Tory prime minister 1783–1801 and 1804–06. He raised the importance of the House of Commons, clamped down on corruption, carried out fiscal reforms, and effected the union with Ireland. He attempted to keep Britain at peace but underestimated the importance of the French Revolution and became embroiled in wars with France from 1793; he died on hearing of Napoleon's victory at Austerlitz.

pitta tropical bird of order Passeriformes, genus *Pitta*, forming the family Pittidae. Some 20 species are native to SE Asia, W Africa, and Australia. They have round bodies, big heads, are often brightly coloured, and are silent. They live on the ground and in low undergrowth, and can run from danger. They feed on insects.

Pittsburgh industrial city (machinery, chemicals) in the NE USA and the nation's largest inland port, where the Allegheny and Monongahela rivers join to form the Ohio River in Pennsylvania; population (1992) 366,850; metropolitan area (1992) 2,406,000.

Established by the French as Fort Duquesne 1750, the site was taken by the British 1758 and renamed Fort Pitt. The main growth of the city's iron and steel industry came after 1850. Pittsburgh was transformed from a smoky steelmaking city into chiefly a corporate service centre by urban redevelopment from the 1960s and the demise of heavy industry.

pituitary gland major ◊endocrine gland of vertebrates, situated in the centre of the brain. It is attached to the ◊hypothalamus by a stalk. The pituitary consists of two lobes. The posterior lobe is an extension of the hypothalamus, and is in effect nervous tissue. It stores two hormones synthesized in the hypothalamus: ◊ADH and ◊oxytocin. The anterior lobe secretes six hormones, some of which control the activities of other glands (thyroid, gonads, and adrenal cortex); others are direct-acting hormones affecting milk secretion and controlling growth.

Piura capital of the department of the same name in the arid NW of Peru, situated on the Piura River, 160 km/100 mi SW of Punta Pariñas; population (1993) 278,000. It is the westernmost point in South America and was founded 1532 by the Spanish conquistadors left behind by Francisco Pizarro. Cotton is grown in the surrounding area.

Pius 12 popes, including:

Pius IV 1499–1565. Pope from 1559, of the ◊Medici family. He reassembled the Council of Trent (see Counter-Reformation under ◊Reformation) and completed its work 1563.

Pius V 1504–1572. Pope from 1566. He excommunicated Elizabeth I of England, and organized the expedition against the Turks that won the victory of ◊Lepanto.

Pius VI (Giovanni Angelo Braschi) 1717–1799. Pope from 1775. He strongly opposed the French Revolution, and died a prisoner in French hands.

Pius VII 1742–1823. Pope from 1800. He concluded a concordat (papal agreement) with France 1801 and took part in Napoleon's coronation, but relations became strained. Napoleon annexed the papal states, and Pius was imprisoned 1809–14. After his return to Rome 1814, he revived the Jesuit order.

Pius IX 1792–1878. Pope from 1846. He never accepted the incorporation of the papal states and of

Rome in the kingdom of Italy. He proclaimed the dogmas of the Immaculate Conception of the Virgin 1854 and papal infallibility 1870; his pontificate was the longest in history.

Pius X (Giuseppe Melchiore Sarto) 1835–1914. Pope from 1903, canonized 1954. He condemned ◊Modernism in a manifesto 1907.

Pius XI (Achille Ratti) 1857–1939. Pope from 1922. He signed the concordat (papal agreement) with Mussolini 1929.

Pius XII (Eugenio Pacelli) 1876–1958. Pope from 1939. He was conservative in doctrine and politics, and condemned ◊Modernism. He proclaimed the dogma of the bodily assumption of the Virgin Mary 1950 and in 1951 restated the doctrine (strongly criticized by many) that the life of an infant must not be sacrificed to save a mother in labour. He was criticized for failing to speak out against atrocities committed by the Germans during World War II and has been accused of collusion with the Nazis.

pixel (derived from ***picture element***) single dot on a computer screen. All screen images are made up of a collection of pixels, with each pixel being either off (dark) or on (illuminated, possibly in colour). The number of pixels available determines the screen's resolution. Typical resolutions of microcomputer screens vary from 320 × 200 pixels to 640 × 480 pixels, but screens with 1,024 × 768 pixels are now common for high-quality graphic (pictorial) displays.

Pizarro Francisco c. 1475–1541. Spanish conquistador who took part in the expeditions of Vasco Núñez de Balboa and others. He began exploring the NW coast of South America 1524, and conquered Peru 1531 with 180 followers. The Inca king Atahualpa was seized and murdered. In 1535 Pizarro founded the Peruvian city of Lima. Internal feuding led to Pizarro's assassination.

Pizarro The Spanish conquistador Francisco Pizarro, who conquered Peru for Spain, defeating the Inca chiefs and capturing their cities. He founded the city of Lima 1535 as the new capital and established other cities along the coast. After an initial expedition to gather information about the Inca empire, he used brutal and treacherous means to crush their civilization. *Corbis*

pizzicato (Italian 'pinched') in music, an instruction to pluck a bowed stringed instrument (such as the violin) with the fingers.

It is heard to advantage in the *Pizzicato Polka* 1870 by Johann Strauss II and Josef Strauss and in the 'Playful Pizzicato' of Benjamin Britten's *Simple Symphony* 1933–34.

PKK abbreviation for ◊***Workers' Party of Kurdistan***, a Kurdish guerrilla organization.

Plaatje Solomon Tshekiso 1875–1932. Pioneer South African black community leader who was the first secretary general and founder of the ◊African National Congress 1912.

placebo (Latin 'I will please') any harmless substance, often called a 'sugar pill', that has no active ingredient, but may nevertheless bring about improvement in the patient's condition.

The use of placebos in medicine is limited to drug trials, where a placebo is given alongside the substance being tested, to compare effects. The 'placebo effect', first named in 1945, demonstrates the control mind exerts over matter, bringing changes in blood pressure, perceived pain, and rates of healing. Recent research points to the release of certain neurotransmitters in the production of the placebo effect.

placenta organ that attaches the developing ◊embryo or ◊fetus to the ◊uterus in placental mammals (mammals other than marsupials, platypuses, and echidnas). Composed of maternal and embryonic tissue, it links the blood supply of the embryo to the blood supply of the mother, allowing the exchange of oxygen, nutrients, and waste products. The two blood systems are not in direct contact, but are separated by thin membranes, with materials diffusing across from one system to the other. The placenta also produces hormones that maintain and regulate pregnancy. It is shed as part of the afterbirth.

It is now understood that a variety of materials, including drugs and viruses, can pass across the placental membrane. HIV, the virus that causes ◊AIDS, can be transmitted in this way.

The tissue in plants that joins the ovary to the ovules is also called a placenta.

placer deposit detrital concentration of an economically important mineral, such as gold, but also other minerals such as cassiterite, chromite, and platinum metals. The mineral grains become concentrated during transport by water or wind because they are more dense than other detrital minerals such as quartz, and (like quartz) they are relatively resistant to chemical breakdown. Examples are the Witwatersrand gold deposits of South Africa, which are gold- and uranium-bearing conglomerates laid down by ancient rivers, and the placer tin deposits of the Malay Peninsula.

plague term applied to any epidemic disease with a high mortality rate, but it usually refers to the bubonic plague. This is a disease transmitted by fleas (carried by the black rat) which infect the sufferer with the bacillus *Yersinia pestis*. An early symptom is swelling of lymph nodes, usually in the armpit and groin; such swellings are called 'buboes'. It causes virulent blood poisoning and the death rate is high.

Rarer but more virulent forms of plague are septicaemic and pneumonic; both still exert a formidable mortality. Outbreaks of plague still occur, mostly in poor countries, but never to the extent seen in the late Middle Ages.

plaice fish *Pleuronectes platessa* belonging to the flatfish group, abundant in the N Atlantic. It is white beneath and brownish with orange spots on the 'eyed' side. It can grow to 75 cm/2.5 ft long, and weigh about 2 kg/4.5 lb.

Plaid Cymru (Welsh 'Party of Wales') Welsh nationalist political party established 1925, dedicated to an independent Wales. In 1966 the first Plaid Cymru member of Parliament was elected; in the 1997 election four MP's were returned.

plain or ***grassland*** land, usually flat, upon which grass predominates. The plains cover large areas of the Earth's surface, especially between the deserts of the tropics and the rainforests of the equator, and have rain in one season only. In such regions the climate belts move north and south during the year, bringing rainforest conditions at one time and desert conditions at another. Temperate plains include the North European Plain, the High Plains of the USA and Canada, and the Russian Plain also known as the steppe.

plague An engraving depicting mass exodus into the country during the Great Plague of London. The epidemic was mainly curbed by the outbreak of the Great Fire 1666. *Image Select (UK) Ltd*

Plains Indian any of the Native American peoples of the Great Plains, which extend over 3,000 km/2,000 mi from Alberta to Texas. The Plains Indians were drawn from diverse linguistic stocks fringing the Plains but shared many cultural traits, especially the nomadic hunting of bison herds once horses became available in the 18th century. The various groups include Blackfoot, Cheyenne, Comanche, Pawnee, and the Dakota or Sioux.

plainsong ancient chant of the Christian church first codified by Ambrose, bishop of Milan, and then by Pope Gregory in the 6th century. See ◊Gregorian chant.

plaintiff in law, a person who brings a civil action in a court of law seeking relief (for example, damages).

Planck Max Karl Ernst 1858–1947. German physicist who framed the ◊quantum theory 1900. His research into the manner in which heated bodies radiate energy led him to report that energy is emitted only in indivisible amounts, called 'quanta', the magnitudes of which are proportional to the frequency of the radiation. His discovery ran counter to classical physics and is held to have marked the commencement of the modern science. Nobel Prize for Physics 1918.

Planck's constant in physics, a fundamental constant (symbol h) that relates the energy (E) of one quantum of electromagnetic radiation (the smallest possible 'packet' of energy; see ◊quantum theory) to the frequency (f) of its radiation by $E = hf$. Its value is 6.6261×10^{-34} joule seconds.

plane in botany, any tree of the genus *Platanus*. Species include the oriental plane *P. orientalis*, a favourite plantation tree of the Greeks and Romans and the American plane or buttonwood *P. occidentalis*. A hybrid of these two is the London plane *P.* × *acerifolia*, with palmate, usually five-lobed leaves, which is widely planted in cities for its resistance to air pollution. All species have pendulous burlike fruits and are capable of growing to 30 m/100 ft high.

planet (Greek 'wanderer') large celestial body in orbit around a star, composed of rock, metal, or gas. There are nine planets in the ◊Solar System: Mercury, Venus, Earth, Mars, Jupiter, Saturn, Neptune, Uranus, and Pluto. The inner four, called the terrestrial planets, are small and rocky, and include the planet Earth. The outer planets, with the exception of Pluto, are called the major planets, and consist of large balls of rock, liquid, and gas; the largest is

plane The plane tree is very tolerant of pollution and is widely grown in towns. It has flaky bark and burrlike fruit resembling drumsticks.

THE PLANETS

Planet	Main constituents	Atmosphere	Average distance from Sun million km	million mi	Time for one orbit (Earth years)	Diameter thousand km	thousand mi	Average density (density of water = 1 unit)
Mercury	rocky, ferrous	–	58	36	0.241	4.88	3.03	5.4
Venus	rocky, ferrous	carbon dioxide	108	67	0.615	12.10	7.51	5.2
Earth	rocky, ferrous	nitrogen, oxygen	150	93	1.00	12.76	7.92	5.5
Mars	rocky	carbon dioxide	228	141	1.88	6.78	4.21	3.9
Jupiter	liquid hydrogen, helium	–	778	483	11.86	142.80	88.73	1.3
Saturn	hydrogen, helium	–	1,427	886	29.46	120.00	74.56	0.7
Uranus	icy, hydrogen, helium	hydrogen, helium	2,870	1,783	84.00	50.80	31.56	1.3
Neptune	icy, hydrogen, helium	hydrogen, helium	4,497	2,794	164.80	48.60	30.20	1.8
Pluto	icy, rocky	methane	5,900	3,666	248.50	2.25	1.39	about 2

Jupiter, which contains a mass equivalent to 70% of all the other planets combined. Planets do not produce light, but reflect the light of their parent star.

As seen from the Earth, all the historic planets are conspicuous naked-eye objects moving in looped paths against the stellar background. The size of these loops, which are caused by the Earth's own motion round the Sun, are inversely proportional to the planet's distance from the Earth.

new discoveries In Oct 1995 Italian astronomers detected a new planet around 51 Pegasi in the constellation Pegasus. It has been named 51 Pegasi B and has a mass comparable to Jupiter. The discovery of three further new planets was announced at the American Astronomical Society meeting Jan 1996. All are outside the Solar System, but two are only about 35 light years from Earth and orbit stars visible with the naked eye. One, 70 Vir B, is in the constellation Virgo, and the other, 47 UMa B, is in Ursa Major. The third, β Pictoris, is about 50 light years away in the southern constellation Pictor.

In April 1996 another planet was discovered, orbiting Rho Cancri in the constellation Cancer. Yet another was found June 1996, this time orbiting the star Tau Bootis.

planetarium optical projection device by means of which the motions of stars and planets are reproduced on a domed ceiling representing the sky.

The planetarium of the Heureka Science Centre, Finland, opened 1989, is the world's first to use fibre optics.

planetary nebula shell of gas thrown off by a star at the end of its life. Planetary nebulae have nothing to do with planets. They were named by William Herschel, who thought their rounded shape resembled the disc of a planet. After a star such as the Sun has expanded to become a ◊red giant, its outer layers are ejected into space to form a planetary nebula, leaving the core as a ◊white dwarf at the centre.

planimeter simple integrating instrument for measuring the area of a regular or irregular plane surface. It consists of two hinged arms: one is kept fixed and the other is traced around the boundary of the area. This actuates a small graduated wheel; the area is calculated from the wheel's change in position.

plankton small, often microscopic, forms of plant and animal life that live in the upper layers of fresh and salt water, and are an important source of food for larger animals. Marine plankton is concentrated in areas where rising currents bring mineral salts to the surface.

plant organism that carries out ◊photosynthesis, has cellulose cell walls and complex cells, and is immobile. A few parasitic plants have lost the ability to photosynthesize but are still considered to be plants.

Plants are ◊autotrophs, that is, they make carbohydrates from water and carbon dioxide, and are the primary producers in all food chains, so that all animal life is dependent on them. They play a vital part in the carbon cycle, removing carbon dioxide from the atmosphere and generating oxygen. The study of plants is known as ◊botany.

levels of complexity Many of the lower plants (the algae and bryophytes) consist of a simple body, or thallus, on which the organs of reproduction are borne. Simplest of all are the threadlike algae, for example *Spirogyra*, which consist of a chain of cells.

The seaweeds (algae) and mosses and liverworts (bryophytes) represent a further development, with simple, multicellular bodies that have specially modified areas in which the reproductive organs are carried. Higher in the morphological scale are the ferns, club mosses, and horsetails (pteridophytes). Ferns produce leaflike fronds bearing sporangia on their undersurface in which the spores are carried. The spores are freed and germinate to produce small independent bodies carrying the sexual organs; thus the fern, like other pteridophytes and some seaweeds, has two quite separate generations in its life cycle (see ◊alternation of generations).

The pteridophytes have special supportive water-conducting tissues, which identify them as vascular plants, a group which includes all seed plants, that is the gymnosperms (conifers, yews, cycads, and ginkgos) and the angiosperms (flowering plants).

seed plants The seed plants are the largest group, and structurally the most complex. They are usually divided into three parts: root, stem, and leaves. Stems grow above or below ground. Their cellular structure is designed to carry water and salts from the roots to the leaves in the ◊xylem, and sugars from the leaves to the roots in the ◊phloem. The leaves manufacture the food of the plant by means of photosynthesis, which occurs in the ◊chloroplasts they contain. Flowers and cones are modified leaves arranged in groups, enclosing the reproductive organs from which the fruits and seeds result.

Plantagenet English royal house, reigning 1154–1399, whose name comes from the nickname of Geoffrey, Count of Anjou (1113–1151), father of Henry II, who often wore in his hat a sprig of broom, *planta genista*. In the 1450s, Richard, Duke of York, took 'Plantagenet' as a surname to emphasize his superior claim to the throne over Henry VI's.

plantain any plant of the genus *Plantago*, family Plantaginaceae. The great plantain *P. major* has oval leaves, grooved stalks, and spikes of green flowers with purple anthers followed by seeds, which are used in bird food.

The most common introduced species is *P. lanceolata*, native to Europe and Asia and a widespread weed in Australia, Europe, and America. Many other species are troublesome weeds. A type of ◊banana is also known as plantain.

plantation large farm or estate where commercial production of one crop – such as rubber (in Malaysia), palm oil (in Nigeria), or tea (in Sri Lanka) – is carried out. Plantations are usually owned by large companies, often ◊multinational corporations, and run by an estate manager. Many plantations were established in countries under colonial rule, using slave labour. ▷ *See feature on pp. 982–983.*

plant classification taxonomy or classification of plants. Originally the plant kingdom included bacteria, diatoms, dinoflagellates, fungi, and slime moulds, but these are not now thought of as plants. The groups that are always classified as plants are the bryophytes (mosses and liverworts), pteridophytes (ferns, horsetails, and club mosses), gymnosperms (conifers, yews, cycads, and ginkgos), and angiosperms (flowering plants). The angiosperms are split into monocotyledons (for example, orchids, grasses, lilies) and dicotyledons (for example, oak, buttercup, geranium, and daisy).

The basis of plant classification was established by the Swedish naturalist Carolus ◊Linnaeus. Among the angiosperms, it is largely based on the number and arrangement of the flower parts.

The unicellular algae, such as *Chlamydomonas*, are often now put with the protists (single-celled organisms) instead of the plants. Some classification schemes even classify the multicellular algae (seaweeds and freshwater weeds) in a new kingdom, the Protoctista, along with the protists.

plant hormone substance produced by a plant that has a marked effect on its growth, flowering, leaf fall, fruit ripening, or some other process. Examples include ◊auxin, ◊ethylene, and ◊cytokinin.

Unlike animal hormones, these substances are not produced by a particular area of the plant body, and they may be less specific in their effects. It has therefore been suggested that they should not be described as hormones at all.

plant propagation production of plants. Botanists and horticulturalists can use a wide variety of means for propagating plants. There are the natural techniques of ◊vegetative reproduction, together with cuttings, ◊grafting, and ◊micropropagation. The range is wide because most plant tissue, unlike animal tissue, can give rise to the complete range of tissue types within a particular species.

plaque any abnormal deposit on a body surface, especially the thin, transparent film of sticky protein (called mucin) and bacteria on tooth surfaces. If not removed, this film forms tartar (calculus), promotes tooth decay, and leads to gum disease. Another form of plaque is a deposit of fatty or fibrous material in the walls of blood vessels causing ◊atheroma.

plasma in biology, the liquid component of the ◊blood.

plasma in physics, an ionized gas produced at extremely high temperatures, as in the Sun and other stars, which contains positive and negative charges in equal numbers. It is a good electrical conductor. In thermonuclear reactions the plasma produced is confined through the use of magnetic fields.

plasmapheresis technique for acquiring plasma from blood. Blood is withdrawn from the patient and separated into its components (plasma and blood cells) by centrifugal force in a continuous-flow cell separator. Once separated, the plasma is available for specific treatments. The blood cells are transfused back into the patient.

plasmid small, mobile piece of ◊DNA found in bacteria and used in ◊genetic engineering. Plasmids are separate from the bacterial chromosome but still multiply during cell growth. Their size ranges from 3% to 20% of the size of the chromosome. There is usually only one copy of a single plasmid per cell, but occasionally several are found. Some plasmids carry 'fertility genes' that enable them to move from one bacterium to another and transfer genetic information between strains. Plasmid genes determine a wide variety of bacterial properties including resistance to antibiotics and the ability to produce toxins.

Plassey, Battle of British victory under Robert ◊Clive over the Nawab of Bengal, Suraja Dowla, 23 June 1757 which brought Bengal under the effective control of the East India Company and hence under British rule. The battle took place at the former village of Plassey, about 150 km/95 mi north of Calcutta. Suraj had taken Calcutta 1756 and carried out the notorious atrocity of the ◊Black Hole of Calcutta.

Although outnumbered, Clive won the battle with minimal losses through Suraj's impetuous squandering of his advantage in an all-out bombardment which exhausted his ammunition. Clive used the support of his Indian banker allies to buy the defection of Suraj's general Mir Jafar, who he then installed as nawab.

plaster of Paris form of calcium sulphate, obtained from gypsum; it is mixed with water for making casts and moulds.

plastic any of the stable synthetic materials that are fluid at some stage in their manufacture, when they can be shaped, and that later set to rigid or semi-rigid solids. Plastics today are chiefly derived from petroleum. Most are polymers, made up of long chains of identical molecules.

environmental influence Since plastics have afforded an economical replacement for ivory in the manufacture of piano keys and billiard balls, the industrial chemist may well have been responsible for the survival of the elephant.

Most plastics cannot be broken down by microorganisms, so cannot easily be disposed of. Incineration leads to the release of toxic fumes, unless carried out at very high temperatures.

plastic arts the arts that are produced by modelling or moulding, chiefly sculpture and ◊ceramics.

plastic surgery surgical speciality concerned with the repair of congenital defects and the reconstruction of tissues damaged by disease or injury, including burns. If a procedure is undertaken solely for reasons of appearance, for example, the removal of bags under the eyes or a double chin, it is called cosmetic surgery.

plastid general name for a cell ◊organelle of plants that is enclosed by a double membrane and contains a series of internal membranes and vesicles. Plastids contain ◊DNA and are produced by division of existing plastids. They can be classified into two main groups: the chromoplasts, which contain pigments such as carotenes and chlorophyll, and the leucoplasts, which are colourless; however, the distinction between the two is not always clear-cut.

◊Chloroplasts are the major type of chromoplast. They contain chlorophyll, are responsible for the green coloration of most plants, and perform ◊photosynthesis. Other chromoplasts give flower petals and fruits their distinctive colour. Leucoplasts are food-storage bodies and include amyloplasts, found in the roots of many plants, which store large amounts of starch.

Plataea, Battle of battle 479 BC, in which the Greeks defeated the Persians during the ◊Persian Wars.

plate or tectonic plate, one of several sections of ◊lithosphere approximately 100 km/60 mi thick and at least 200 km/120 mi across which together comprise the outermost layer of the Earth like the pieces of the cracked surface of a hard-boiled egg.

The plates are made up of two types of crustal material: oceanic crust (sima) and continental crust (sial), both of which are underlain by a solid layer of ◊mantle. Dense oceanic crust lies beneath Earth's oceans and consists largely of ◊basalt. Continental crust, which underlies the continents and their continental shelves, is thicker, less dense and consists of rocks rich in silica and aluminium.

Due to convection in the Earth's mantle (see ◊plate tectonics) these pieces of lithosphere are in motion, riding on a more plastic layer of the mantle, called the aesthenosphere. Mountains, volcanoes, earthquakes, and other geological features and phenomena all come about as a result of interaction between the plates.

plateau elevated area of fairly flat land, or a mountainous region in which the peaks are at the same height. An intermontane plateau is one surrounded by mountains. A piedmont plateau is one that lies between the mountains and low-lying land. A continental plateau rises abruptly from low-lying lands or the sea. Examples are the Tibetan Plateau and the Massif Central in France.

platelet tiny disc-shaped structure found in the blood, which helps it to clot. Platelets are not true cells, but membrane-bound cell fragments without nuclei that bud off from large cells in the bone marrow. They play a vital role in blood clotting as they release blood clotting factors at the site of a cut.

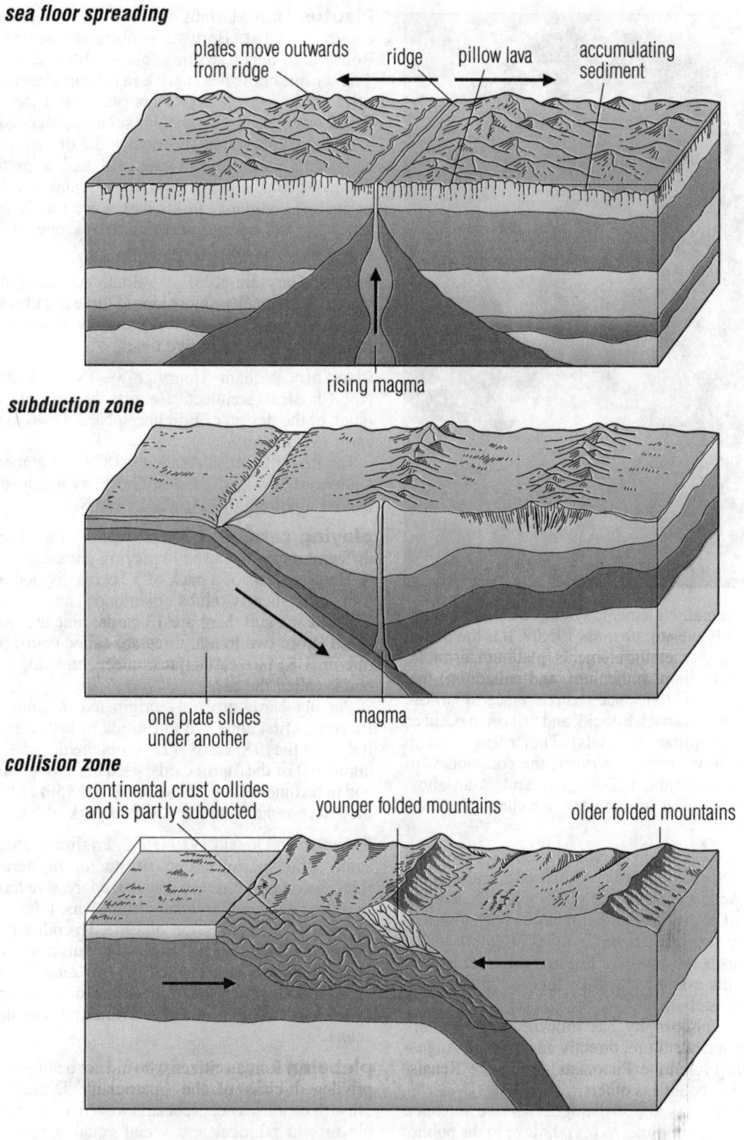

plate tectonics The three main types of action in plate tectonics. (top) Sea-floor spreading. The up-welling of magma forces apart the crust plates, producing new crust at the joint. Rapid extrusion of magma produces a domed ridge; more gentle spreading produces a central valley. (middle) The drawing downwards of an oceanic plate beneath a continent produces a range of volcanic fold mountains parallel to the plate edge. (bottom) Collision of continental plates produces immense fold mountains, such as the Himalayas. Younger mountains are found near the coast with older ranges inland. The size and shape of each plate is always changing as material is added at constructive margins and removed at destructive margins. The process is extremely slow, but it means that the tectonic history of the Earth cannot be traced back further than about 200 million years.

Over 12 clotting factors have been discovered and they produce a complex series of reactions which ultimately leads to fibrinogen, the inactive blood sealant always found in the plasma, being converted into fibrin. Fibrin aggregates into threads which form the fabric of a blood clot.

plate tectonics theory formulated in the 1960s to explain the phenomena of ◊continental drift and seafloor spreading, and the formation of the major physical features of the Earth's surface. The Earth's outermost layer is regarded as a jigsaw of rigid major and minor plates up to 100 km/62 mi thick, which move relative to each other, probably under the influence of convection currents in the mantle beneath. Major landforms occur at the margins of the plates, where plates are colliding or moving apart – for example, volcanoes, fold mountains, ocean trenches, and ocean ridges.

constructive margin Where two plates are moving apart from each other, molten rock from the mantle wells up in the space left between the plates and hardens to form new crust, usually in the form of an ocean ridge (such as the ◊Mid-Atlantic Ridge). The newly formed crust accumulates on either side of the ocean ridge, causing the seafloor to spread – for example, the floor of the Atlantic Ocean is growing by 5 cm/2 in each year because of the upwelling of new material at the Mid-Atlantic Ridge.

destructive margin Where two plates are moving towards each other, the denser of the two plates may be forced under the other into a region called the subduction zone. The descending plate melts to form a body of magma, which may then rise to the surface through cracks and faults to form volcanoes. If the two plates consist of more buoyant continental crust, subduction does not occur. Instead, the crust crumples gradually to form ranges of young fold mountains, such as the Himalayas in Asia, the Andes in South America, and the Rockies in North America.

conservative margin Sometimes two plates will slide past each other – an example is the San Andreas Fault, California, where the movement of the plates sometimes takes the form of sudden jerks, causing the earthquakes common in the San Francisco–Los Angeles area. Most of the earthquake and volcano zones of the world are, in fact, found in regions where two plates meet or are moving apart.

The concept of continental drift was first put forward in 1915 by the German geophysicist Alfred Wegener; plate tectonics was formulated by Canadian geophysicist John Tuzo Wilson (1908–) 1965 and has gained widespread acceptance among earth scientists.

In 1995 US and French geophysicists produced the first direct evidence that the Indo-Australian plate has split in two (in the middle of the Indian Ocean, just south of the equator). They believe the split began about 8 million years ago.

Plath Sylvia 1932–1963. US poet and novelist. Her powerful, highly personal poems, often expressing a sense of desolation, are distinguished by their intensity and sharp imagery. Her *Collected Poems* 1981 was awarded a Pulitzer prize. Her autobiographical novel *The Bell Jar* 1961 deals with the events surrounding a young woman's emotional breakdown.

Plath was awarded a Fulbright scholarship to study at Cambridge University, England. Here she met the poet Ted Hughes, whom she married 1956; they separated 1962. She committed suicide while living in London. Collections of her poems include *The Colossus* 1960 and *Ariel* 1965, published after her death. *See illustration on following page.*

platinum (Spanish *platina* 'little silver' (*plata* 'silver')) heavy, soft, silver-white, malleable and

Plath US poet Sylvia Plath, one of the finest poets of her generation. Though her themes were often those of alienation and despair – themes which made her a cult figure after her suicide at the age of 29 – she explored them with great wit, honesty, intelligence, and even humour. *Corbis*

ductile, metallic element, symbol Pt, atomic number 78, relative atomic mass 195.09. It is the first of a group of six metallic elements (platinum, osmium, iridium, rhodium, ruthenium, and palladium) that possess similar traits, such as resistance to tarnish, corrosion, and attack by acid, and that often occur as free metals (◊native metals). They often occur in natural alloys with each other, the commonest of which is osmiridium. Both pure and as an alloy, platinum is used in dentistry, jewellery, and as a catalyst.

‘Our object in the establishment of the state is the greatest happiness of the whole, and not that of any one class.’

PLATO
Republic IV

Plato c. 427–347 BC. Greek philosopher. He was a pupil of Socrates, teacher of Aristotle, and founder of the Academy school of philosophy. He was the author of philosophical dialogues on such topics as metaphysics, ethics, and politics. Central to his teachings is the notion of Forms, which are located outside the everyday world – timeless, motionless, and absolutely real.

Plato's philosophy has influenced Christianity and European culture, directly and through Augustine, the Florentine Platonists during the Renaissance, and countless others.

Of his work, some 30 dialogues survive, intended for performance either to his pupils or to the public. The principal figure in these ethical and philosophical debates is Socrates and the early ones employ the Socratic method, in which he asks questions and traps the students into contradicting themselves; for example, *Iron*, on poetry. Other dialogues include the *Symposium*, on love, *Phaedo*, on immortality, and *Apology and Crito*, on Socrates' trial and death. It is impossible to say whether Plato's Socrates is a faithful representative of the real man or an articulation of Plato's own thought.

Plato's philosophy rejects scientific rationalism (establishing facts through experiment) in favour of arguments, because mind, not matter, is fundamental, and material objects are merely imperfect copies of abstract and eternal ‘ideas’. His political philosophy is expounded in two treatises, *The Republic* and *The Laws*, both of which describe ideal states. Platonic love is inspired by a person's best qualities and seeks their development.

‘He whom the gods love dies young.’

PLAUTUS
Bacchides

platoon in the army, the smallest infantry subunit. It contains 30–40 soldiers and is commanded by a lieutenant or second lieutenant. There are three or four platoons in a company.

platypus monotreme, or egg-laying, mammal *Ornithorhynchus anatinus*, found in Tasmania and E Australia. Semiaquatic, it has small eyes and no external ears, and jaws resembling a duck's beak. It lives in long burrows along river banks, where it lays two eggs in a rough nest. It feeds on water worms and insects, and when full-grown is 60 cm/2 ft long.

According to research by Australian scientists 1995, platypuses locate their prey by detecting the small electric fields produced by their nerve and muscle activity.

platypus When the platypus was discovered 200 years ago, scientists thought the first specimens were fakes. It has some birdlike features, such as the duck's beak and webbed feet; it also lays eggs. The body has some reptilian characteristics, but is covered with hair like a mammal. Like a mammal, the platypus feeds its young with milk.

Plautus Titus Maccius c. 250–c. 184 BC. Roman comic dramatist. Born in Umbria, he settled in Rome and began writing plays about 224 BC. Twenty-one comedies survive in his name; 35 other titles are known. Many of his plays are based on Greek originals by playwrights such as ◊Menander, to which Plautus added his own brand of native wit and sharp character-drawing. He had a perfect command of language and metre, and enjoyed unrivalled popularity in his day; since the Renaissance he has been acknowledged as one of the greatest of ancient playwrights.

Player Gary Jim 1935– . South African golfer who won major championships in three decades and the first British Open 1959. A match-play specialist, he won the world title five times.

Playfair William Henry 1789–1857. Scottish Neo-Classical architect. He was responsible for much of the design of Edinburgh New Town in the early 19th century.

His Royal Scottish Academy 1822 and National Gallery of Scotland 1850 in Greek style helped to make Edinburgh the ‘Athens of the North’.

playing cards set of small pieces of card with different markings, used in playing games. A standard set consists of a pack of 52 cards divided into four suits: hearts, clubs, diamonds, and spades. Within each suit there are 13 cards: nine are numbered (from two to ten, three are called court, picture or (US) face cards (jack, queen, and king) and one is called the ace.

Playing cards probably originated in China or India, and first appeared in Europe in 14th-century Italy as the 78 cards (22 emblematic and 56 numerals) of the ◊tarot cards, used both for gaming and in fortune-telling. However, in the 15th century they were reduced to the standard pack of 52.

Pleasence Donald 1919–1995. English character actor, who specialized in sinister or mysterious roles; for example, as the devious, aggressive tramp in Pinter's *The Caretaker* 1960 which he also played in the film version of 1963. His other films include *Dr Crippen* 1962, Roman Polanski's *Cul de Sac* 1966, *Soldier Blue* 1970, *The Last Tycoon* 1976, and *The Eagle Has Landed* 1976. He was one of the most prolific of British film and television actors.

plebeian Roman citizen who did not belong to the privileged class of the ◊patricians. During the 5th–4th centuries BC, plebeians waged a long struggle to win political and social equality with the patricians, eventually securing admission to the offices formerly reserved for patricians.

plebiscite ◊referendum or direct vote by all the electors of a country or district on a specific question. Since the 18th century plebiscites have been employed on many occasions to decide to what country a particular area should belong; for example, in Upper Silesia and elsewhere after World War I, and in the Saar 1935.

The term fell into disuse during the 1930s, after the widespread abuse by the Nazis in Germany to legitimize their regime.

Pléiade, La group of seven poets in 16th-century France, led by Pierre ◊Ronsard, who aimed to break away from the medieval poetic tradition by seeking inspiration in Classical Greek and Latin works, and to make the French language a suitable medium for all literary purposes. The other poets, according to Ronsard, were Joaquim Du Bellay (c. 1522–1560), Jean Antoine de Baïf (1532–1589), Rémi Belleau (c. 1528–1577), Etienne Jodelle (1532–1573), Pontus de Tyard (1521–1605), and Jacques Peletier (1517–1582), but the name of the humanist scholar Jean Dorat (1508–1588) is sometimes substituted for that of Peletier. The views of the group were first set out in Du Bellay's *Défense et illustration de la langue française* 1549, and the name is derived from the seven stars of the Pleiades group.

Pleiades in astronomy, an open star cluster about 400 light years away in the constellation Taurus, represented as the Seven Sisters of Greek mythology. Its brightest stars (highly luminous, blue-white giants only a few million years old) are visible to the naked eye, but there are many fainter ones.

It is a young cluster, and the stars of the Pleiades are still surrounded by traces of the reflection ◊nebula from which they formed, visible on long-exposure photographs.

Pleiades in Greek mythology, the seven daughters of the giant Atlas who asked to be changed into a cluster of stars to escape the pursuit of the hunter Orion.

Pleistocene first epoch of the Quaternary period of geological time, beginning 1.64 million years ago and ending 10,000 years ago. The polar ice caps were extensive and glaciers were abundant during the ice age of this period, and humans evolved into modern *Homo sapiens sapiens* about 100,000 years ago.

plesiosaur prehistoric carnivorous marine reptile of the Jurassic and Cretaceous periods, which reached a length of 12 m/36 ft, and had a long neck and paddlelike limbs. The pliosaurs evolved from the plesiosaurs.

pleurisy inflammation of the pleura, the thin, secretory membrane that covers the lungs and lines the space in which they rest. Pleurisy is nearly always due to bacterial or viral infection, but may also be a complication of other diseases.

Normally the two lung surfaces move easily on one another, lubricated by small quantities of fluid. When the pleura is inflamed, the surfaces may dry up or stick together, making breathing difficult and painful. Alternatively, a large volume of fluid may collect in the pleural cavity, the space between the two surfaces, and pus may accumulate.

Plimsoll Samuel 1824–1898. English social reformer, born in Bristol. He sat in Parliament as a Radical 1868–80, and through his efforts the Merchant Shipping Act was passed in 1876, providing for Board of Trade inspection of ships, and the compulsory painting of a Plimsoll line to indicate safe loading limits.

Plimsoll line loading mark painted on the hull of merchant ships, first suggested by English politician Samuel Plimsoll. It shows the depth to which a vessel may be safely (and legally) loaded.

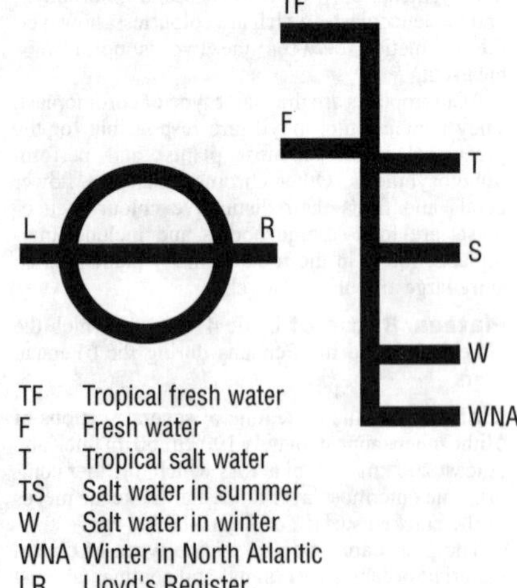

Plimsoll line The Plimsoll line on the hull of a ship indicates maximum safe loading levels for sea or fresh water, winter or summer, in tropical or northern waters.

Pliny the Elder (Gaius Plinius Secundus) c. AD 23–79. Roman scientific encyclopedist and historian. Many of his works have been lost, but in *Historia naturalis/Natural History*, probably completed AD 77, Pliny surveys all the known sciences of his day, notably astronomy, meteorology, geography, mineralogy, zoology, and botany.

Pliny states that he has covered 20,000 subjects of importance drawn from 100 selected writers, to whose observations he has added many of his own. Botany, agriculture, and horticulture appear to interest him most. To Pliny the world consisted of four elements: earth, air, fire, and water. The light substances were prevented from rising by the weight of the heavy ones, and vice versa. This is the earliest theory of gravity.

Pliny the Younger (Gaius Plinius Caecilius Secundus) c. AD 61–113. Roman administrator. He was the nephew of Pliny the Elder. His correspondence is of great interest; among his surviving letters are those describing the eruption of Vesuvius, his uncle's death, and his correspondence with the emperor ◊Trajan.

Pliocene ('almost recent') fifth and last epoch of the Tertiary period of geological time, 5.2–1.64 million years ago. The earliest hominid, the human-like ape *Australopithecines*, evolved in Africa.

pliosaur prehistoric carnivorous marine reptile, descended from the plesiosaurs, but with a shorter neck, and longer head and jaws. It was approximately 5 m/15 ft long. In 1989 the skeleton of one of a previously unknown species was discovered in N Queensland, Australia. A hundred million years ago, it lived in the sea that once covered the Great Artesian Basin.

PLO abbreviation for ◊***Palestine Liberation Organization***, founded 1964 to bring about an independent state of Palestine.

plot the storyline in a novel, play, film, or other work of fiction. A plot is traditionally a scheme of connected events.

Novelists sometimes subvert or ignore the reader's expectation of a causally linked story. James Joyce and Virginia Woolf wrote novels that explore the minutiae of a character's experience, rather than telling a tale. English novelist E M Forster defined it thus: The king died and then the queen died. The king died and then the queen died of grief at the king's death. The first is the beginning of a series of events; the second is the beginning of a plot.

Plough, the in astronomy, a popular name for the most prominent part of the constellation ◊Ursa Major.

plough agricultural implement used for tilling the soil. The plough dates from about 3500 BC, when oxen were used to pull a simple wooden blade, or ard. In about 500 BC the iron ploughshare came into use. By about AD 1000 horses as well as oxen were being used to pull wheeled ploughs, equipped with a ploughshare for cutting a furrow, a blade for forming the walls of the furrow (called a coulter), and a mouldboard to turn the furrow. In the 18th century an innovation introduced by Robert Ransome (1753–1830), led to a reduction in the number of animals used to draw a plough: from 8–12 oxen, or 6 horses, to a 2- or 4-horse plough.

Steam ploughs came into use in some areas in the 1860s, superseded half a century later by tractor-drawn ploughs. The modern plough consists of many 'bottoms', each comprising a curved ploughshare and angled mouldboard. The bottom is designed so that it slices into the ground and turns the soil over.

Plovdiv industrial city (textiles, chemicals, leather, tobacco) in Bulgaria, on the river Maritsa; population (1991) 379,000. Conquered by Philip of Macedon in the 4th century BC, it was known as Philippopolis ('Philip's city'). It was capital of Roman Thrace.

plover any shore bird of the family Charadriidae, order Charadriiformes, found worldwide. Plovers are usually black or brown above and white below, and have short bills. The European golden plover *Pluviatilis apricaria*, of heathland and sea coast, is about 28 cm/11 in long. In winter the upper parts are a sooty black with large yellow spots, and white throat and underparts, changing to black in the spring. It nests on the ground, laying four yellowish eggs blotched with brown.

The ringed plover *Charadrius hiaticula*, with a black and white face, and black band on the throat, is found on British shores, nesting in a scrape on a beach or amongst shingle. The largest of the ringed plovers is the killdeer *Charadrius vociferus*, so called because of its cry.

plucking in earth science, a process of glacial erosion. Water beneath a glacier will freeze fragments of loose rock to the base of the ice. When the ice moves, the rock fragment is 'plucked' away from the underlying bedrock. Plucking is thought to be responsible for the formation of steep, jagged slopes such as the backwall of the corrie and the downslope-side of the roche moutonnée.

plum tree *Prunus domestica*, bearing edible fruits that are smooth-skinned with a flat kernel. There are many varieties, including the Victoria, czar, egg-plum, greengage, and damson; the sloe *P. spinosa* is closely related. Dried plums are known as prunes.

plumbago alternative name for the mineral ◊graphite.

pluralism in political science, the view that decision-making in contemporary liberal democracies is the outcome of competition among several interest groups in a political system characterized by free elections, representative institutions, and open access to the organs of power. This concept is opposed by corporatism and other approaches that perceive power to be centralized in the state and its principal elites (the Establishment).

Plutarch c. AD 46–c. 120. Greek biographer and essayist. His *Parallel Lives* comprise paired biographies of famous Greek and Roman soldiers and politicians, followed by comparisons between the two. Thomas North's 1579 translation inspired Shakespeare's Roman plays.

Plutarch lectured on philosophy in Rome and was appointed procurator of Greece by Emperor Hadrian.

All men whilst they are awake are in one common world: but each of them, when he is asleep, is in a world of his own.

PLUTARCH
'Of Superstition', *Morals*

Pluto in astronomy, the smallest and, usually, outermost planet of the Solar System. The existence of Pluto was predicted by calculation by Percival Lowell and the planet was located by Clyde ◊Tombaugh in 1930. Its highly elliptical orbit occasionally takes it within the orbit of Neptune, as in 1979–99. Pluto has a mass about 0.002 of that of Earth.

mean distance from the Sun 5.8 billion km/3.6 billion mi
equatorial diameter 2,300 km/1,438 mi
rotation period 6.39 Earth days
year 248.5 Earth years
atmosphere Thin atmosphere with small amounts of methane gas
surface Low density, composed of rock and ice, primarily frozen methane. There is an ice cap at Pluto's north pole
satellites One moon, Charon.

Charon, Pluto's moon, was discovered 1978 by James Walter Christy (1938–). It is about 1,200 km/750 mi in diameter, half the size of Pluto, making it the largest moon in relation to its parent planet in the Solar System. It orbits about 20,000 km/12,500 mi from the planet's centre every 6.39 days – the same time that Pluto takes to spin on its axis. Charon is composed mainly of ice.

Pluto in Greek mythology, the lord of the underworld (Roman Dis), sometimes known as Hades. He was the brother of Zeus and Poseidon.

plutonic rock igneous rock derived from magma that has cooled and solidified deep in the crust of the Earth; granites and gabbros are examples of plutonic rocks.

plutonium silvery-white, radioactive, metallic element of the ◊actinide series, symbol Pu, atomic number 94, relative atomic mass 239.13. It occurs in nature in minute quantities in ◊pitchblende and other ores, but is produced in quantity only synthetically. It has six allotropic forms (see ◊allotropy) and is one of three fissile elements (elements capable of splitting into other elements – the others are thorium and uranium). The element has awkward physical properties and is the most toxic substance known.

Because Pu-239 is so easily synthesized from abundant uranium, it has been produced in large quantities by the weapons industry. It has a long half-life (24,000 years) during which time it remains highly toxic. Plutonium is dangerous to handle, difficult to store, and impossible to dispose of.

It was first synthesized in 1940 by Glenn Seaborg and his team at the University of California at Berkeley.

Plymouth city and seaport in Devon, England, at the mouth of the river Plym, with dockyard, barracks, and a naval base at Devonport; population (1981) 243,400. There are marine industries; clothing, radio equipment, and processed foods are produced. The city rises N of the Hoe headland where tradition has it that Francis ◊Drake played bowls as the Spanish Armada approached 1588. The *Mayflower* ◊Pilgrims sailed from here 1620.

The city centre was reconstructed after heavy bombing in World War II. The Eddystone Rocks lighthouse is 22 km/14 mi to the S.

Plymouth Brethren fundamentalist Christian Protestant sect characterized by extreme simplicity of belief, founded in Dublin about 1827 by the Reverend John Nelson Darby (1800–1882). The Plymouth Brethren have no ordained priesthood, affirming the ministry of all believers, and maintain no church buildings. They hold prayer meetings and Bible study in members' houses.

An assembly of Brethren was held in Plymouth 1831 to celebrate the sect's arrival in England, but by 1848 the movement had split into 'Open' and 'Closed' Brethren. The latter refuse communion with those not of their persuasion. A further subset of the Closed Brethren is the 'Exclusive' Brethren, who have strict rules regarding dress and conduct.

In the UK, the Plymouth Brethren are mainly found in the fishing villages of NE Scotland. There are some 65,000 in the USA, divided into eight separate groups. Worldwide membership is about 1.5 million (1993), including members in the Caribbean, India, and Myanmar.

plywood manufactured panel of wood widely used in building. It consists of several thin sheets, or plies, of wood, glued together with the grain (direction of the wood fibres) of one sheet at right angles to the grain of the adjacent plies. This construction gives plywood equal strength in every direction.

pneumatic drill drill operated by compressed air, used in mining and tunnelling, for drilling shot holes (for explosives), and in road repairs for breaking up pavements. It contains an air-operated piston that delivers hammer blows to the drill bit many times a second. The French engineer Germain Sommeiller (1815–1871) developed the pneumatic drill 1861 for tunnelling in the Alps.

pneumatophore erect root that rises up above the soil or water and promotes ◊gas exchange. Pneumatophores, or breathing roots, are formed by certain swamp-dwelling trees, such as mangroves, since there is little oxygen available to the roots in waterlogged conditions. They have numerous pores or ◊lenticels over their surface, allowing gas exchange.

pneumoconiosis disease of the lungs caused by an accumulation of dust, especially from coal, asbestos, or silica. Inhaled particles make the lungs gradually fibrous and the victim has difficulty breathing. Over many years the condition causes severe disability.

pneumonia inflammation of the lungs, generally due to bacterial or viral infection but also to particulate matter or gases. It is characterized by a build-up of fluid in the alveoli, the clustered air sacs (at the ends of the air passages) where oxygen exchange takes place.

Symptoms include fever and pain in the chest. With widespread availability of antibiotics, infectious pneumonia is much less common than it was. However, it remains a dire threat to patients whose immune systems are suppressed (including transplant recipients and AIDS and cancer victims) and to those who are critically ill or injured. Pneumocystis pneumonia is a leading cause of death in AIDS.

pneumothorax the presence of air in the pleural cavity, between a lung and the chest wall. It may be due to a penetrating injury of the lung or to lung disease, or it may occur without apparent cause (spontaneous pneumothorax) in an otherwise healthy person. Prevented from expanding normally, the lung is liable to collapse.

p–n junction diode in electronics, another name for ◊semiconductor diode.

Po longest river in Italy, flowing from the Cottian Alps to the Adriatic Sea; length 668 km/415 mi. Its valley is fertile and contains natural gas. The river is heavily polluted with nitrates, phosphates, and arsenic.

Pobeda, Pik highest peak in the Tian Shan mountain range on the Kyrgyz-Chinese border, at 7,439 m/24,406 ft.

Pocahontas Matoaka c. 1595–1617. Native American alleged to have saved the life of English colonist John Smith when he was captured by her father, Powhatan. She was kidnapped 1613 by an Englishman, Samuel Argall, and later married colonist John Rolfe (1585–1622) and was entertained as a princess at the English court of James I.

pochard any of various diving ducks found in Europe and North America, especially the genus

Everything in this district savours of the sea.

On PLYMOUTH
Maurice Baring
Round the World in Any Number of Days

pochard Native to the temperate regions of Asia and Europe, pochards live on inland waters, diving to feed on plants and invertebrates. Wild pochard overwinter in large numbers alongside the captive waterfowl at the Wildfowl Trust at Slimbridge in Gloucestershire, S England. *Premaphotos Wildlife*

Aythya. They feed largely on water plants. The nest is made in long grass on the borders of lakes and pools.

The male common pochard *Aythya ferina* has a red head, black breast, whitish body and wings with black markings, and is about 45 cm/1.5 ft long. The base and point of the bill are black, and the central portion pale blue. The female is greyish brown, with greyish white below, and a black bill. The canvasback *A. valisineria*, the redhead *A. americana*, the ring-necked *A. collaris*, and two species of scaup, *A. marila* and *A. affinis*, are all related New World species.

pod in botany, a type of fruit that is characteristic of legumes (plants belonging to the Leguminosae family), such as peas and beans. It develops from a single ◊carpel and splits down both sides when ripe to release the seeds.

Podgorica formerly (1946–92) ***Titograd*** capital of Montenegro, Yugoslavia; population (1993 est) 135,000. Industries include metalworking, furniture-making, and tobacco. It was damaged in World War II and after rebuilding was renamed in honour of Marshal Tito; it reverted to its original name with the collapse of communism. It was the birthplace of the Roman emperor Diocletian.

podzol or ***podsol*** type of light-coloured soil found predominantly under coniferous forests and on moorlands in cool regions where rainfall exceeds evaporation. The constant downward movement of water leaches nutrients from the upper layers, making podzols poor agricultural soils.

The leaching of minerals such as iron, lime, and alumina leads to the formation of a bleached zone, often also depleted of clay. These minerals can accumulate lower down the soil profile to form a hard, impermeable layer which restricts the drainage of water through the soil.

Poe US poet and short-story writer Edgar Allan Poe, photographed towards the end of his life. Poe's macabre and fantastic stories attracted the attention of Sigmund Freud and influenced a generation of poets and writers. His work continues to have a cult following. *Corbis*

Poe Edgar Allan 1809–1849. US writer and poet. His short stories are renowned for their horrific atmosphere, as in 'The Fall of the House of Usher' 1839 and 'The Masque of the Red Death' 1842, and for their acute reasoning (ratiocination), as in 'The Gold Bug' 1843 and 'The Murders in the Rue Morgue' 1841 (in which the investigators Legrand and Dupin anticipate Conan Doyle's Sherlock Holmes). His poems include 'The Raven' 1845. His novel *The Narrative of Arthur Gordon Pym of Nantucket* 1838 has attracted critical attention.

poet laureate poet of the British royal household, so called because of the laurel wreath awarded to eminent poets in the Graeco-Roman world. Early poets with unofficial status were John Skelton (c. 1460–1529), Samuel Daniel (1562–1619), Ben ◊Jonson, and William Davenant (1606–1668). John ◊Dryden was the first to receive the title by letters-patent 1668 and from then on the post became a regular institution. Ted ◊Hughes was appointed poet laureate 1984.

poetry the imaginative expression of emotion, thought, or narrative, frequently in metrical form and often using figurative language. Poetry has traditionally been distinguished from prose (ordinary written language) by rhyme or the rhythmical arrangement of words (◊metre).

A distinction is made between lyrical, or songlike, poetry (sonnet, ode, elegy, pastoral), and narrative, or story-telling, poetry (ballad, lay, epic). Poetic form has also been used as a vehicle for satire, parody, and expositions of philosophical, religious, and practical subjects. Traditionally, poetry has been considered a higher form of expression than prose. In modern times, the distinction is not always clear cut.

pogrom (Russian 'destruction') unprovoked violent attack on an ethnic group, particularly Jews, carried out with official sanction. The Russian pogroms against Jews began 1881, after the assassination of Tsar Alexander II, and again in 1903–06; persecution of the Jews remained constant until the Russian Revolution. Later there were pogroms in E Europe, especially in Poland after 1918, and in Germany under Hitler (see ◊Holocaust).

poikilothermy the condition in which an animal's body temperature is largely dependent on the temperature of the air or water in which it lives. It is characteristic of all animals except birds and mammals, which maintain their body temperatures by ◊homeothermy (they are 'warm-blooded').

Poikilotherms have behavioural means of temperature control; they can warm themselves up by basking in the sun, or shivering, and can cool themselves down by sheltering from the Sun under a rock or by bathing in water.

Poikilotherms are often referred to as 'cold-blooded animals', but this is not really correct: their internal temperatures, regulated by behavioural means, are often as high as those of birds and mammals during the times they need to be active for feeding and reproductive purposes, and may be higher, for example in very hot climates. The main difference is that their body temperatures fluctuate more than those of homeotherms.

Poincaré Jules Henri 1854–1912. French mathematician who developed the theory of differential equations and was a pioneer in ◊relativity theory. He suggested that Isaac ◊Newton's laws for the behaviour of the universe could be the exception rather than the rule. However, the calculation was so complex and time-consuming that he never managed to realize its full implication.

Poincaré Raymond Nicolas Landry 1860–1934. French politician, prime minister 1912–13, president 1913–20, and again prime minister 1922–24 (when he ordered the occupation of the Ruhr, Germany) and 1926–29.

poinsettia or ***Christmas flower*** winter-flowering shrub *Euphorbia pulcherrima*, with large red leaves encircling small greenish-yellow flowers. It is native to Mexico and tropical America and is a popular houseplant in North America and Europe.

point in geometry, a basic element, whose position in the Cartesian system may be determined by its ◊coordinates.

Mathematicians have had great difficulty in defining the point, as it has no size, and is only the place where two lines meet. According to the Greek mathematician Euclid: (i) a point is that which has no part; (ii) the straight line is the shortest distance between two points.

Pointe-Noire chief port of the Congo, formerly (1950–58) the capital; population (1992) 576,000. Industries include oil refining and shipbuilding.

pointer any of several breeds of gun dog, bred especially to scent the position of game and indicate it by standing, nose pointed towards it, often with one forefoot raised, in silence. English pointers have smooth coats, mainly white mixed with black, tan, or dark brown. They stand about 60 cm/24 in tall, and weigh 28 kg/62 lb.

A very similar breed, the German short-haired pointer, was developed in the 19th century to point and also to pursue game.

The Weimeraner is another pointing breed.

POETS LAUREATE OF THE UNITED KINGDOM

1668	John Dryden (1631–1700)
1689	Thomas Shadwell (1642?–1692)
1692	Nahum Tate (1652–1715)
1715	Nicholas Rowe (1674–1718)
1718	Laurence Eusden (1688–1730)
1730	Colley Cibber (1671–1757)
1757	William Whitehead (1715–1785)
1785	Thomas Warton (1728–1790)
1790	Henry James Pye (1745–1813)
1813	Robert Southey (1774–1843)
1843	William Wordsworth (1770–1850)
1850	Alfred, Lord Tennyson (1809–1892)
1896	Alfred Austin (1835–1913)
1913	Robert Bridges (1844–1930)
1930	John Masefield (1878–1967)
1968	Cecil Day Lewis (1904–1972)
1972	John Betjeman (1906–1984)
1984	Ted Hughes (1930–98)

pointillism in music, a form of 1950s ◊serialism in which melody and harmony are replaced by complexes of isolated tones. Pointillism was inspired by Webern and adopted by Messiaen, Boulez, Nono, Stockhausen, and Stravinsky.

Pointillism technique in oil painting developed in the 1880s by the Neo-Impressionist Georges Seurat. He used small dabs of pure colour laid side by side to create form and an impression of shimmering light when viewed from a distance.

poise c.g.s. unit (symbol P) of dynamic ◊viscosity (the property of liquids that determines how readily they flow). It is equal to one dyne-second per square centimetre. For most liquids the centipoise (one hundredth of a poise) is used. Water at 20°C/68°F has a viscosity of 1.002 centipoise.

poison or ***toxin*** any chemical substance that, when introduced into or applied to the body, is capable of injuring health or destroying life.

The liver removes some poisons from the blood. The majority of poisons may be divided into corrosives, such as sulphuric, nitric, and hydrochloric acids; irritants, including arsenic and copper sulphate; narcotics such as opium, and carbon monoxide; and narcotico-irritants from any substances of plant origin including carbolic acid and tobacco.

Corrosives all burn and destroy the parts of the body with which they come into contact; irritants have an irritating effect on the stomach and bowels; narcotics affect the brainstem and spinal cord, inducing a stupor; and narcotico-irritants can cause intense irritations and finally act as narcotics.

In noncorrosive poisoning every effort is made to remove the poison from the system as soon as possible, usually by gastric lavage (stomach 'washout'). For some corrosive and irritant poisons there are chemical antidotes, but for recently developed poisons in a new category (for example, the weedkiller paraquat) that produce proliferative changes in the system, there is no specific antidote. In the UK, the National Poisons Information Service, which was founded 1963, provides eight regional centres in major city hospitals, where data on cases of poisoning is collected.

Poisson Siméon Denis 1781–1840. French applied mathematician and physicist. In probability theory he formulated the Poisson distribution. Poisson's ratio in elasticity is the ratio of the lateral contraction of a body to its longitudinal extension. The ratio is constant for a given material.

Much of Poisson's work involved applying mathematical principles in theoretical terms to contemporary and prior experiments in physics, particularly with reference to electricity, magnetism, heat, and sound. Poisson was also responsible for a formulation of the 'law of large numbers' 1837.

Poitevin in English history, relating to the reigns of King John and King Henry III. The term is

derived from the region of France south of the Loire (Poitou), which was controlled by the English for most of this period.

Poitier Sidney 1924– . US actor and film director. He was Hollywood's first black star. His films as an actor include *Something of Value* 1957, *Lilies of the Field* 1963, *In the Heat of the Night* 1967, and *Sneakers* 1992, and as director *Stir Crazy* 1980.

Poitiers capital of Poitou-Charentes, W France; population (1990) 82,500. Products include chemicals and clothing. The Merovingian king Clovis defeated the Visigoths under Alaric here 507; ◊Charles Martel stemmed the Saracen advance 732, and ◊Edward the Black Prince of England defeated the French 1356.

Poitiers, Battle of during the Hundred Years' War, victory for Edward the Black Prince 13 Sept 1356 over King John II of France. King John, his son Philip, and 2,000 knights were taken prisoner, and about 3,000 French were killed.

Poitou-Charentes region of W central France, comprising the *départements* of Charente, Charente-Maritime, Deux-Sèvres, and Vienne; area 25,800 sq km/9,959 sq mi; population (1990) 1,595,100. Its capital is Poitiers. Industries include dairy products, wheat, chemicals, and metal goods; brandy is made at Cognac

history once part of the Roman province of Aquitaine, this region was captured by the Visigoths in the 5th century and taken by the Franks AD 507. The area was contested by the English and French until the end of the Hundred Years' War 1453, when it was incorporated into France by Charles II.

poker card game of US origin, in which two to eight people play (usually for stakes), and try to obtain a hand of five cards ranking higher than those of their opponents. The one with the highest scoring hand wins the central pool.

Poland country in E Europe, bounded N by the Baltic Sea, NE by Lithuania, E by Belarus and Ukraine, S by the Czech Republic and the Slovak Republic, and W by Germany. *See country box below.*

Polanski Roman 1933– . Polish film director. His films include *Repulsion* 1965, *Cul de Sac* 1966, *Rosemary's Baby* 1968, *Tess* 1979, *Frantic* 1988, *Bitter Moon* 1992, and *Death and the Maiden* 1995.

He suffered a traumatic childhood in Nazi-occupied Poland, and later his wife, actress Sharon Tate, was the victim of murder by the Charles Manson 'family'. He left the USA for Europe and his tragic personal life is perhaps reflected in a fascination with horror and violence in his work.

polar coordinates in mathematics, a way of defining the position of a point in terms of its distance r from a fixed point (the origin) and its angle θ to a fixed line or axis. The coordinates of the point are (r,θ).

Often the angle is measured in ◊radians, rather than degrees. The system is useful for defining positions on a plane in programming the operations of, for example, computer-controlled cloth- and metal-cutting machines.

Polaris or *Pole Star* or *North Star* bright star closest to the north celestial pole, and the brightest star in the constellation ◊Ursa Minor. Its position is indicated by the 'pointers' in ◊Ursa Major. Polaris is a yellow ◊supergiant about 500 light years away. It is also known as Alpha Ursae Minoris.

It currently lies within 1° of the north celestial pole; ◊precession (Earth's axial wobble) will bring Polaris closest to the celestial pole (less than 0.5° away) about AD 2100. Then its distance will start to increase, reaching 1° AD 2205 and 47° AD 28000. Other bright stars that have been, or will be close to the north celestial pole are Alpha Draconis (3000 BC), Gamma Cephei (AD 4000), Alpha Cephei (AD 7000), and ◊Vega (AD 14000).

'Take thy beak from out my heart, and take thy form from off my door! / Quoth the Raven, 'Nevermore'.'

EDGAR ALLAN POE
'The Raven'

POLAND
Republic of

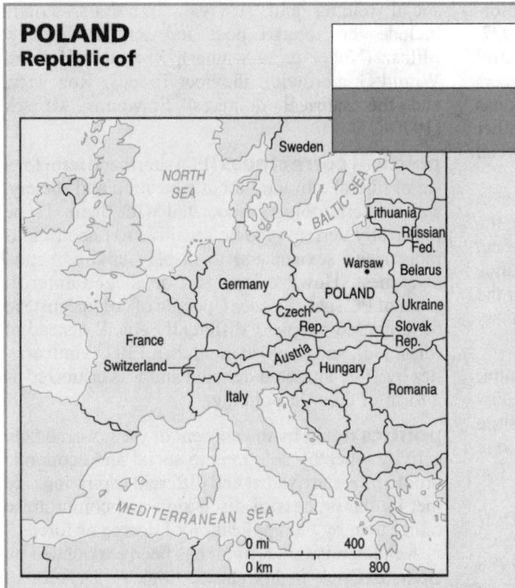

national name *Rzeczpospolita Polska*
area 312,683 sq km/120,628 sq mi
capital Warsaw
major towns/cities Lódź, Kraków (Cracow), Wrocl{sla}aw (Breslau), Poznań, Katowice, Bydgoszcz, Lublin
major ports Gdańsk (Danzig), Szczecin, Gdynia
physical features part of the great plain of Europe; Vistula, Oder, and Neisse rivers; Sudeten, Tatra, and Carpathian mountains on the S frontier
head of state Alexander Kwasniewski from 1995
head of government Jerzy Buzek from 1997
political system emergent democratic republic
administrative divisions 49 provinces
political parties Democratic Left Alliance (SLD), reform socialist (ex-communist); Polish Peasant Party (PSL), moderate, agrarian; Freedom Union (UW), moderate, centrist; Labour Union (UP), left-wing; Non-Party Bloc in Support of Reforms (BBWR), Christian Democrat, right of centre, pro-Wałesa; Confederation for an Independent Poland (KPN), right-wing; Solidarity Electoral Action (AWS), Christian right wing
population 38,601,000 (1996 est)
population growth rate 0.1% (1990–95); 0.3% (2000–05)
ethnic distribution 98% ethnic Western-Slav ethnic Poles; small ethnic German, Ukrainian, and Belarussian minorities
life expectancy 68 (men), 76 (women)
literacy 99%
languages Polish (official), German
religion Roman Catholic 95%
currency zloty
GDP (US $) 92.58 billion (1994)
growth rate 5.1% (1994)
exports coal, softwood timber, chemicals, machinery, ships, vehicles, meat, copper (Europe's largest producer), coke, sulphur, footwear

HISTORY
966 Polish Slavic tribes under Mieszko I, leader of the Piast dynasty, adopted Christianity and united the region around Poznań to form the first Polish state.
1241 Devastated by Mongols.
13th–14th Cs German and Jewish refugees settled among the Slav population.
1386 Jagellion dynasty came to power: a golden age for Polish culture.
1569 Poland united with Lithuania to become largest state in Europe.
1572 Jagellion dynasty became distinct; future kings were elected by the nobility and gentry, who formed a tenth of the population.
mid-17th C Defeat in war against Russia, Sweden, and Brandenburg (in Germany) set in a process of irreversible decline.
1772–95 Partitioned between Russia, which ruled the NE; Prussia, the W, including Pomerania; and Austria in the south-centre, including Galicia, where there was greatest autonomy.
1815 After Congress of Vienna, the Russian eastern portion of Poland was re-established as a kingdom within the Russian Empire.
1830 and 1863 Uprisings against repressive Russian rule.
1892 Nationalist Polish Socialist Party (PPS) founded.
1918 Independent Polish republic established after World War I, with Marshal Jozef Pilsudski, founder of the PPS, elected president.
1919–21 Abortive advance into Lithuania and Ukraine.
1926 Pilsudski seized full power in a coup and established an autocratic regime.
1935 On Pilsudski's death, a military regime held power under Marshal Smigly-Rydz.
1939 Invaded by Germany; W Poland was incorporated into the Nazi Reich (state) and the rest became a German colony; 6 million Poles – half of them Jews – were slaughtered in the next five years.
1944–45 Liberated from Nazi rule by Soviet Union's Red Army; boundaries redrawn westwards at Potsdam Conference. One half of 'old Poland', 180,000 sq km/70,000 sq mi in the E, was lost to the Soviet Union; 100,000 sq km/40,000 sq mi of ex-German territory in Silesia, along the Oder and Neisse rivers, was added, shifting the state 240 km/150 mi westwards; millions of Germans were expelled.
1947 Communist people's republic proclaimed after manipulated election.
1949 Joined Comecon.
early 1950s Harsh Stalinist rule under communist leader Boleslaw Bierut: nationalization; rural collectivization; persecution of Catholic Church members.
1955 Joined Warsaw Pact defence organization.
1956 Poznań strikes and riots. The moderate Wladyslaw Gomułka installed as Polish United Workers' Party (PUWP) leader.
1960s Private farming reintroduced and Catholicism tolerated.
1970 Gomułka replaced by Edward Gierek after Gdańsk riots against food price rises.
1970s Poland heavily indebted to foreign creditors after a failed attempt to boost economic growth.
1980 Solidarity, led by Lech Wałesa, emerged as a free trade union following Gdańsk disturbances.
1981 Martial law imposed by General Wojciech Jaruzelski, trade union activity banned and Solidarity leaders and supporters arrested.
1983 Martial law ended.
1984 Amnesty for 35,000 political prisoners.
1988 Solidarity-led strikes and demonstrations for pay increases. Reform-communist Mieczysław Rakowski became prime minister.
1989 Agreement to relegalize Solidarity, allow opposition parties, and adopt a more democratic constitution, after round-table talks involving Solidarity, the Communist Party, and the Catholic Church. Widespread success for Solidarity in first open elections for 40 years; noncommunist 'grand coalition' government formed, headed by Tadeusz Mazowiecki of Solidarity; economic austerity and free-market restructuring programme began.
1990 PUWP dissolved and re-formed as the Democratic Left Alliance (SLD). Wałesa was elected president and Jan Bielecki became prime minister.
1991 Shock therapy economic restructuring programme, including large-scale privatization, produced sharp fall in living standards and rise in unemployment rate to 11%. Unpopular Bielecki resigned and, after inconclusive elections, Jan Olszewski formed a fragile centre-right coalition government.
1992 Political instability continued, with Waldemar Pawlak, of the centre-left Polish Peasant Party (PSL), and Hanna Suchocka, of the centrist Democratic Union, successively replacing Olszewski as prime minister.
1993 Economy became the first in Central Europe to grow since collapse of communism. After new elections, Pawlak formed coalition government with ex-communist SLD, which pledged to continue to build a market-based economy and seek early entry into the European Union.
1994 Joined NATO 'partnership for peace' programme; last Russian troops left Poland.
1995 Ex-communist Jozef Oleksy replaced Pawlak as prime minister. Wałesa narrowly defeated by Alexander Kwasniewski, leader of the SLD, in presidential election.
1996 Oleksy resigned as prime minister amid allegations of spying for Russia's secret service; replaced by Wlodzimierz Cimoszewicz.
1997 General election won by Solidarity Electoral Action (AWS). Coalition government formed, led by Jerzy Buzek. EU membership talks begin.

SEE ALSO Solidarity; Union of Soviet Socialist Republics; Warsaw ghetto

❛Politics is not the art of the possible. It consists in choosing between the disastrous and the unpalatable.❜

On **POLITICS**
J K Galbraith, letter to President Kennedy
2 March 1962

polarized light light in which the electromagnetic vibrations take place in one particular plane. In ordinary (unpolarized) light, the electric fields vibrate in all planes perpendicular to the direction of propagation. After reflection from a polished surface or transmission through certain materials (such as Polaroid), the electric fields are confined to one direction, and the light is said to be linearly polarized. In circularly polarized and elliptically polarized light, the electric fields are confined to one direction, but the direction rotates as the light propagates. Polarized light is used to test the strength of sugar solutions, to measure stresses in transparent materials, and to prevent glare.

polarography electrochemical technique for the analysis of oxidizable and reducible compounds in solution. It involves the diffusion of the substance to be analyzed onto the surface of a small electrode, usually a bead of mercury, where oxidation or reduction occurs at an electric potential characteristic of that substance.

Polaroid camera instant-picture camera, invented by Edwin Land in the USA 1947. The original camera produced black-and-white prints in about one minute. Modern cameras can produce black-and-white prints in a few seconds, and colour prints in less than a minute. An advanced model has automatic focusing and exposure.

polar reversal change in polarity of Earth's magnetic field. Like all magnets, Earth's magnetic field has two opposing regions, or poles, one of attraction and one of repulsion, positioned approximately near geographical North and South Poles. During a period of normal polarity the region of attraction corresponds with the North Pole. Today, a compass needle, like other magnetic materials, aligns itself parallel to the magnetizing force and points to the North Pole. During a period of reversed polarity, the region of attraction would change to the South Pole and the needle of a compass would point south.

Studies of the magnetism retained in rocks at the time of their formation (like little compasses frozen in time) have shown that the polarity of the magnetic field has reversed repeatedly throughout geological time.

Polar reversals are a random process. Although the average time between reversals over the last ten million years has been 250,000 years, the rate of reversal has changed continuously over geological time. The most recent reversal was 700,000 years ago; scientists have no way of predicting when the next reversal will occur. The reversal process takes about a thousand years. Movements of Earth's molten ◊core are thought to be responsible for the magnetic field and its polar reversals. Dating rocks using distinctive sequences of magnetic reversals is called palaeomagnetic stratigraphy.

polder area of flat reclaimed land that used to be covered by a river, lake, or the sea. Polders have been artificially drained and protected from flooding by building dykes. They are common in the Netherlands, where the total land area has been increased by nearly one-fifth since AD 1200. Such schemes as the Zuider Zee project have provided some of the best agricultural land in the country.

pole either of the geographic north and south points of the axis about which the Earth rotates. The geographic poles differ from the magnetic poles, which are the points towards which a freely suspended magnetic needle will point.

In 1985 the magnetic north pole was some 350 km/218 mi NW of Resolute Bay, Northwest Territories, Canada. It moves northwards about 10 km/6 mi each year, although it can vary in a day about 80 km/50 mi from its average position. It is relocated every decade in order to update navigational charts.

Pole people of Polish culture from Poland and the surrounding area. There are 37–40 million speakers of Polish (including some in the USA), a Slavic language belonging to the Indo-European family. The Poles are predominantly Roman Catholic, though there is an Orthodox Church minority. They are known for their distinctive cooking, folk festivals, and folk arts.

polecat Old World weasel *Mustela putorius* with a brown back and dark belly and two yellow face patches. The body is about 50 cm/20 in long and it has a strong smell from anal gland secretions. It is native to Asia, Europe, and N Africa. In North America, ◊skunks are sometimes called polecats. A ferret is a domesticated polecat.

Almost extinct in Britain around 1915, the polecat has since increased in numbers. It breeds once or twice a year, producing up to eight young.

Pole Star another name for ◊Polaris, the northern pole star. There is no bright star near the southern celestial pole.

police civil law-and-order force. In the UK it is responsible to the Home Office, with 56 autonomous police forces, generally organized on a county basis; mutual aid is given in circumstances such as mass picketing in the 1984–85 miners' strike, but there is no national police force or police riot unit (such as the French CRS riot squad). The predecessors of these forces were the ineffective medieval watch and London's Bow Street runners, introduced 1749 by Henry ◊Fielding which formed a model for the London police force established by Robert ◊Peel's government 1829 (hence 'peelers' or 'bobbies'); the system was introduced throughout the country from 1856.

Landmarks include: Criminal Investigation Department detective branch of the London Metropolitan Police (New Scotland Yard) 1878, recruited from the uniformed branch (such departments now exist in all UK forces); women police 1919; motorcycle patrols 1921; two-way radio cars 1927; personal radio on the beat 1965; and Special Patrol Groups (SPG) 1970, squads of experienced officers concentrating on a specific problem (New York has the similar Tactical Patrol Force). Unlike most other police forces, the British are armed only on special occasions, but arms issues grow more frequent.

Other police forces include the Garda Síochána in the Republic of Ireland, the Carabinieri in Italy, the Guardia Civil in Spain, the Royal Canadian Mounted Police ('Mounties') in Canada, the Police Nationale (under the Ministry of the Interior) for the cities and the Gendarmerie (part of the army) elsewhere in France.

polio (*poliomyelitis*) viral infection of the central nervous system affecting nerves that activate muscles. The disease used to be known as infantile paralysis. Two kinds of vaccine are available, one injected (see ◊Salk) and one given by mouth. The Americas were declared to be polio-free by the Pan American Health Organization Oct 1994. In 1997 the World Health Organization reported that cases of polio had dropped by nearly 90% since 1988 when the organization began its programme to eradicate the disease by the year 2000. Most remaining cases are in Africa and southeast Asia (in 1998 India accounted for over 30% of the world's polio cases).

The polio virus is a common one and its effects are mostly confined to the throat and intestine, as with influenza or a mild digestive upset. There may also be muscle stiffness in the neck and back. Paralysis is seen in about 1% of cases, and the disease is life-threatening only if the muscles of the throat and chest are affected. Cases of this kind, once entombed in an 'iron lung', are today maintained on a respirator.

polis (Greek 'city') in ancient Greece, a city-state, the political and social centre of most larger Greek communities.

Membership of a polis as a citizen, participation in its cults and festivals, and the protection of its laws formed the basis of classical Greek civilization, which was marked by intense intercity rivalries and conflicts until the Hellenistic period.

Polish Corridor strip of land designated under the Treaty of ◊Versailles 1919 to give Poland access to the Baltic. It cut off East Prussia from the rest of Germany. Germany resented this partition and one of the primary causes of tension with Poland in the build-up to World War II was the German demand to be permitted to build a road and rail connection across the Corridor, in a zone to be granted extraterritorial rights, a demand which the Poles implacably refused. When Poland took over the southern part of East Prussia 1945, it was absorbed.

Polish language member of the Slavonic branch of the Indo-European language family, spoken mainly in Poland. Polish is written in the Roman and not the Cyrillic alphabet and its standard form is based on the dialect of Poznań in W Poland.

Polish literature a vernacular literature began to emerge in the 14th century and enjoyed a golden age in the 16th and 17th centuries under Renaissance influences, particularly apparent in the poetry of Jan Kochanowski (1530–1584). The tradition revived in the later 18th century, the era of the Enlightenment poet and pioneer novelist Ignacy Krasicki (1735–1801), and a Polish national theatre was opened 1765.

The domination of Poland by Austria, Russia, and Prussia towards the end of the 18th century and during the 19th century, and particularly the failure of the 1830 Polish insurrection, stimulated romantically tragic nationalism in major writers such as Adam ◊Mickiewicz, Juliusz Słowacki (1809–1849), and Zygmunt Krasiński (1812–1859). This theme also affected historical novelists such as Henryk Sienkiewicz (1846–1916). At the end of the 19th century there was a reaction against Naturalism and other orthodoxies in the 'Young Poland' movement 1890–1918, in theatre and fiction as well as poetry.

In the 20th century, political independence in the interwar years fostered writers as bewilderingly varied as the exuberant 'Skamander' group of poets and the fantastic, pessimistic philosopher and dramatist Stanisław Witkiewicz (1885–1939). Poland's tragic wartime and postwar experiences have given rise to poetry and prose registering social trauma and survival. Important writers include the veteran poet and scholar Czesław Miłosz (Nobel prize winner), Zbigniew Herbert, Witold Gombrowicz, the poet Tadeusz Rozewicz, and the satirical dramatist Sławomir Mrozek (1930–).

political correctness (PC) shorthand term for a set of liberal attitudes about education and society, and the terminology associated with them. To be politically correct is to be sensitive to unconscious racism and sexism and to display environmental awareness. However, the real or alleged enforcement of PC speech codes ('people of colour' instead of 'coloured people', 'differently abled' instead of 'disabled', and so on) at more than 130 US universities by 1991 attracted derision and was criticized as a form of thought-policing.

politics ruling by the consent of the governed; an activity whereby solutions to social and economic problems are arrived at and different aspirations are met by the process of discussion and compromise rather than by the application of decree or force.

A much misused term, it has been expounded by Bernard Crick in his classic book *In Defence of Politics* 1962. Its popular description as 'the art of the possible' was probably first used by Otto von ◊Bismarck of Prussia, in a recorded conversation in 1867. Both Bismarck and Crick made the point that politics is essentially an activity and not a science or set of rules. It is an activity based on diversity: diverse opinions about aims to be achieved and means to achieve them. Politics accepts this diversity as a fact of life and seeks to resolve conflicting views by discussion and compromise.

Polk James Knox 1795–1849. 11th president of the USA 1845–49, a Democrat, born in North Carolina. He allowed Texas admission to the Union, and forced the war on Mexico that resulted in the annexation of California and New Mexico.

polka Bohemian dance in quick duple time (2/4). Originating in the 19th century, it became popular throughout Europe. The basic step is a hop followed by three short steps. The polka spread with German immigrants to the USA, becoming a style of Texas country music. It was also used by European composers Smetana (in *The Bartered Bride* 1866, *Bohemian Dances* 1878), Dvořák, and others.

pollack marine fish *Pollachius virens* of the cod family, growing to 75 cm/2.5 ft, and found close to the shore on both sides of the N Atlantic.

Pollaiuolo Antonio del (c. 1432–1498) and Piero (c. 1441–1496) two Italian artists, brothers. They were active in Florence, both brothers being painters, sculptors, goldsmiths, engravers, and designers. Antonio, widely considered the better artist, is said to have been the first Renaissance artist to make a serious study of anatomy. The *Martyrdom of St Sebastian* about 1475 (National Gallery, London) is usually considered a joint work.

The brothers also executed two papal monuments to Popes Sixtus IV and Innocent VIII in St Peter's,

Polk As 11th president of the USA, James Polk settled the Oregon Boundary dispute with Britain and successfully conducted the Mexican War, which resulted in the annexation of California. Devoted to the Democratic principles of his predecessors, Thomas Jefferson and Andrew Jackson, Polk set up a revenue tariff and an independent treasury. *Library of Congress*

Rome. Piero's major individual work is his elegant series of *Virtues* 1469 (Uffizi, Florence). Antonio, who worked with ◊Ghiberti on the doors of the Baptistery, Florence, is best known for his engraving *The Battle of the Nude Gods* about 1465, which show his fascination with anatomy.

pollarding type of pruning whereby the young branches of a tree are severely cut back, about 2–4 m/6–12 ft above the ground, to produce a stumplike trunk with a rounded, bushy head of thin new branches. It is similar to ◊coppicing.

pollen the grains of ◊seed plants that contain the male gametes. In ◊angiosperms (flowering plants) pollen is produced within ◊anthers; in most ◊gymnosperms (cone-bearing plants) it is produced in male cones. A pollen grain is typically yellow and, when mature, has a hard outer wall. Pollen of insect-pollinated plants (see ◊pollination) is often sticky and spiny and larger than the smooth, light grains produced by wind-pollinated species.

pollen Pollination, the process by which pollen grains transfer their male nuclei (gametes) to the ovary of a flower. (1) The pollen grains land on the stigma and (2) form a pollen tube that (3) grows down into the ovary. The male nuclei travel along the pollen tube.

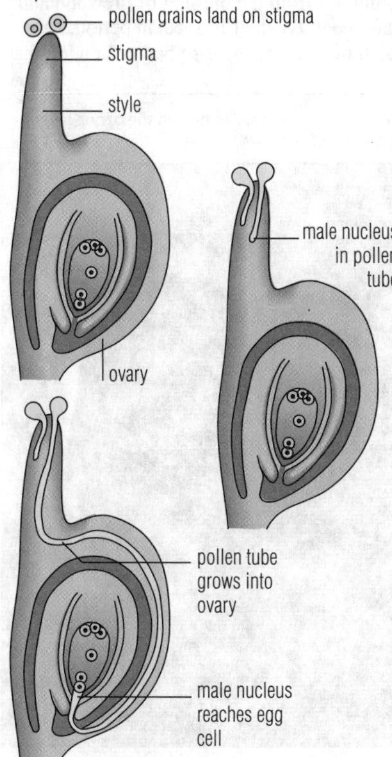

pollen tube outgrowth from a pollen grain that grows towards the ◊ovule, following germination of the grain on the ◊stigma. In ◊angiosperms (flowering plants) the pollen tube reaches the ovule by growing down through the ◊style, carrying the male gametes inside. The gametes are discharged into the ovule and one fertilizes the egg cell.

pollination the process by which pollen is transferred from one plant to another. The male ◊gametes are contained in pollen grains, which must be transferred from the anther to the stigma in ◊angiosperms (flowering plants), and from the male cone to the female cone in ◊gymnosperms (cone-bearing plants). Fertilization (not the same as pollination) occurs after the growth of the pollen tube to the ovary. Self-pollination occurs when pollen is transferred to a stigma of the same flower, or to another flower on the same plant; cross-pollination occurs when pollen is transferred to another plant. This involves external pollen-carrying agents, such as wind, water, insects, birds, bats, and other small mammals.

Animal pollinators carry the pollen on their bodies and are attracted to the flower by scent, or by the sight of the petals. Most flowers are adapted for pollination by one particular agent only. Bat-pollinated flowers tend to smell of garlic, rotting vegetation, or fungus. Those that rely on animals generally produce nectar, a sugary liquid, or surplus pollen, or both, on which the pollinator feeds. Thus the relationship between pollinator and plant is an example of mutualism, in which both benefit. However, in some plants the pollinator receives no benefit (as in ◊pseudocopulation), while in others, nectar may be removed by animals that do not effect pollination.

Pollock (Paul) Jackson 1912–1956. US painter. He was a pioneer of Abstract Expressionism and one of the foremost exponents of ◊action painting. His style is characterized by complex networks of swirling, interwoven lines of great delicacy and rhythmic subtlety.

In the early 1940s Pollock moved from a vivid Expressionist style, influenced by Mexican muralists such as Siqueiros (1896–1974) and by Surrealism, towards a semi-abstract style. The paintings of this period are colourful and vigorous, using enigmatic signs and mysterious forms. From 1947 he developed his more violently expressive abstracts, placing large canvases on the studio floor and dripping or hurling paint across them. He was soon recognized as the leading Abstract Expressionist and continued to develop his style, producing even larger canvases in the 1950s.

poll tax tax levied on every individual, without reference to income or property. Being simple to administer, it was among the earliest sorts of tax (introduced in England 1379), but because of its indiscriminate nature (it is a regressive tax, in that it falls proportionately more on poorer people) it has often proved unpopular. The community charge, a type of poll tax, was introduced in Scotland by the British government April 1989, and in England and Wales 1990, replacing the property-based local taxation (the ◊rates). Its unpopularity led to its replacement 1993–94 by a ◊council tax, based both on property values and on the size of households.

The poll tax of 1379 contributed to the ◊Peasants' Revolt of 1381 and was abolished in England 1698. In the USA it survived until 1964 when its use was declared unconstitutional in federal elections because of its frequent abuse as a tool for disenfranchising blacks.

pollution the harmful effect on the environment of by-products of human activity, principally industrial and agricultural processes – for example, noise, smoke, car emissions, chemical and radioactive effluents in air, seas, and rivers, pesticides, radiation, sewage (see ◊sewage disposal), and household waste. Pollution contributes to the ◊greenhouse effect. See also ◊air pollution.

Pollution control involves higher production costs for the industries concerned, but failure to implement adequate controls may result in irreversible environmental damage and an increase in the incidence of diseases such as cancer. Radioactive pollution results from inadequate ◊nuclear safety.

Transboundary pollution is when the pollution generated in one country affects another, for example as occurs with ◊acid rain. Natural disasters may also cause pollution; volcanic eruptions, for example, cause ash to be ejected into the atmosphere and deposited on land surfaces. ▷*See feature on pp. 858–859.*

Pollaiuolo *The Martyrdom of Saint Sabastian* 1475 by the Pollaiuolo brothers (National Gallery, London). The work of the Pollaiuolo reflect a new fascination with both the ancient world (the ruins on the left) and with the expressive potential of the human figure – in this picture the archers are arranged symmetrically, their poses reversed. *Corbis*

Pollux or ***Beta Geminorum*** the brightest star in the constellation ◊Gemini, and the 17th brightest star in the night sky. Pollux is a yellow star with a true luminosity 45 times that of the Sun. It is 35 light years away.

The first-magnitude Pollux and the second-magnitude ◊Castor, Alpha Geminorum, mark the heads of the Gemini twins. It is thought that the two stars may have changed their relative brightness since ◊Bayer named them, as Alpha is usually assigned to the brightest star in a constellation.

Pollux in Greek mythology, the twin brother of Castor (see ◊Castor and Pollux).

polo stick-and-ball game played between two teams of four on horseback. It originated in Iran, spread to India and was first played in England 1869. Polo is played on the largest field of any game, measuring up to 274 m/300 yd by 182 m/200 yd. A small solid ball is struck with the side of a longhandled mallet through goals at each end of the field. A typical match lasts about an hour, and is divided into 'chukkas' of 7½ minutes each. No pony is expected to play more than two chukkas in the course of a day. *See illustration on page 860.*

Polo Marco 1254–1324. Venetian traveller and writer. He joined his father (Niccolo) and uncle (Maffeo), who had travelled to China as merchants (1260–69), when they began a journey overland back to China (1271). Once there, he learned Mongolian and served the emperor Kubla Khan until he returned to Europe by sea 1292–95.

He was captured while fighting for Venice against Genoa, and, while in prison 1296–98, dictated an account of his travels. These accounts have

‘I have not told half of what I saw.’

Marco Polo
Last words

cont. on p. 860

Polluting the Planet

Major accidental oil spills, such as the one that soaked this cormorant, cause enormous damage and attract wide publicity. However, over a million tons of oil are deliberately discharged into the world's oceans each year by tankers carrying out routine cleaning of their tanks. *Corbis*

Polluting means, literally, destroying the purity or sanctity of something. The word has now become closely identified with the contamination of land, air, and water by a range of industrial by-products such as gases from factories and cars, and oil spills.

A pollutant is, most simply, something in the wrong place at the wrong time. Environmental pollutants damage wildlife and humans. Some particularly toxic substances, like poisons and some radioactive materials, are always likely to be pollutants. Other materials are harmless or even beneficial in most circumstances, and become pollutants only under certain conditions. For example, fertilizers make crops grow more quickly, but can also poison rivers and streams. Unfortunately, some of our most useful materials – including oil, plastics, and agricultural chemicals – can also be particularly damaging pollutants.

The natural history of pollution

Not all pollutants behave in the same way. Some act directly by harming or killing a plant or an animal. A seabird covered in oil is obviously in great distress, because oil destroys the waxy covering of its feathers, causing it to become waterlogged and often to drown or die of cold. Gases like sulphur dioxide, released from power stations and factories, kill many species of lichens and tree-living mosses: these have now all but disappeared in polluted areas. Pesticides caught by the wind can drift into surrounding woods and hedges and poison creatures that they were not intended to kill.

Other pollution impacts are more subtle. Scientists in Britain and the USA, investigating a decline in birds of prey during the 1960s, suspected that pesticides were to blame but could find no signs of direct poisoning. However, further research showed that organochlorine pesticides like DDT were causing birds to lay eggs with unnaturally thin shells. These tended to break open before the young birds could survive, causing a dramatic population crash, from which several species have still not recovered.

A similar picture emerged in studies of fish decline in lakes in Sweden and Norway. Sulphur and nitrogen oxides, released when coal and oil are burnt, can be chemically transformed to acids in the atmosphere and fall as mist, rain, and snow – commonly known as acid rain. In areas where the surrounding rock does not contain enough basic material to neutralize the acids, freshwater acidity increases; this has happened in much of Scandinavia. In most cases, adult fish were able to withstand the changes, but lost the ability to reproduce. Surviving fish grew to record size in the absence of competition for food but, with no young, entire populations disappeared in a single generation.

Other knock-on effects include loss of food. Research in England found that partridge chicks were dying because herbicides were drifting off agricultural fields and killing wild flowers in hedgerows. This in turn meant that plant-feeding insects disappeared, and the young partridges starved to death. Leaving an unsprayed strip at the edge of fields tripled the survival rate of the chicks.

Pollutants can also upset the balance of nature more indirectly. Artificial fertilizers and human sewage both damage freshwaters and shallow oceans, mainly by providing abundant food to rapidly reproducing algae, which grow to form a so-called algal bloom on the water surface. This reduces the amount of light reaching the bottom and interferes with the growth of other plants. When the algae die, the decomposition process takes up so much oxygen from the water that fish and other aquatic creatures may suffocate.

Living in a soup of pollution

Pollution has always been a feature of human society. Some pollutants occur naturally; for example, chemicals from volcanic explosions, and radiation released as radon gas from granitic rocks. However, humans have proved adept at increasing both the range and the amounts of pollutants. The Romans inadvertently poisoned themselves by using lead pipes to carry water. Early towns suffered heavy pollution from the burning of firewood and later coal. By the Elizabethan period, pollution had become so bad in London that

A satellite picture showing the damaged ozone layer over Antarctica. The hole in the ozone layer was first noticed in 1982, and has been growing ever since. *Image Select (UK) Ltd*

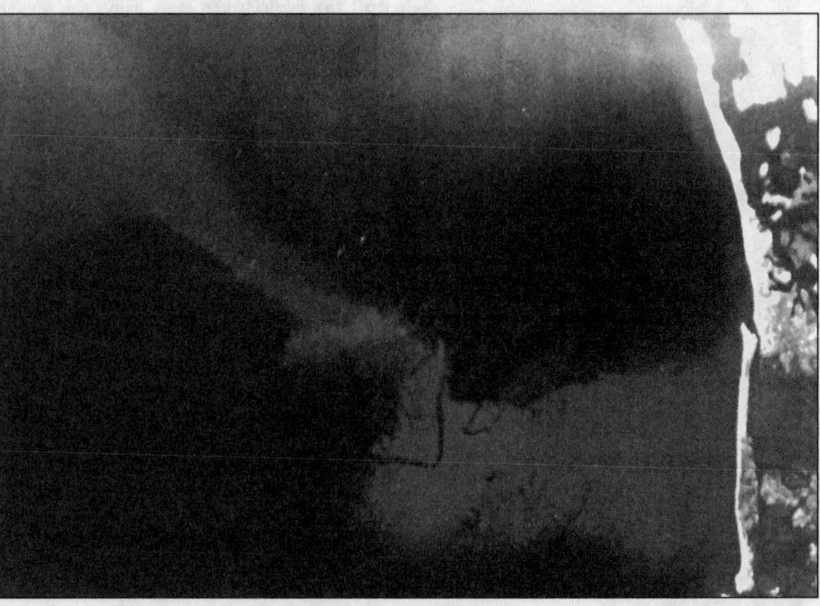

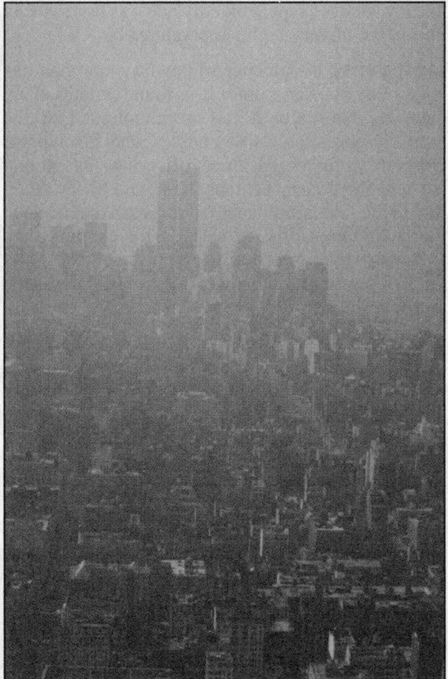

Smog over New York. Smog forms over many cities and is due, to a great extent, to pollution produced by the internal combustion engine. Catalytic converters to remove pollutants from vehicles' exhaust gases are being made mandatory in many countries in an attempt to reduce smog. *Image Select (UK) Ltd*

Litter left behind by climbing expeditions has become a problem even in the most remote mountains. *Image Select (UK) Ltd*

laws were introduced to control household fires; in 1661, the diarist John Evelyn attacked pollution in a pamphlet called *Fumifugium or the Smoake of London Dissipated*. In the following century, pollution increased rapidly with the beginnings of the Industrial Revolution.

Today, literally tens of thousands of pollutants are present in air, water, and soil and are incorporated into plant and animal tissues. Some of the constituents of this toxic cocktail combine to cause more damage than the sum of their individual effects. Pollution also often acts against a wider backdrop of environmental change. When the health of European trees started to decline unnaturally, many causes were suggested, including drought, acid rain, photochemical ozone, management changes, and pest attack. After 20 years of research, scientists have yet to reach a consensus, but it seems increasingly likely that many different factors are combining to injure the overall health of trees. While strong evidence links air pollution to tree decline in some areas, such as Poland and Slovakia, in other countries it is likely to be just one of a number of contributing elements.

Pollutants moving through the ecosystem

Pollution is no longer a local or even a national phenomenon. Able to survive almost indefinitely, some pollutants can spread around the world and cause damage far from their source. A major political problem has been created by the long-range transport of air pollutants, when one country suffers damage from pollution released in another. Similar journeys can be taken by water pollutants, which sometimes travel thousands of kilometres along rivers or in ocean currents.

Persistent pollutants can also be concentrated in the food chain. An animal at the top of the food chain – such as a large carnivorous mammal or a bird of prey – can accumulate pollutants from the bodies of many smaller animals, resulting in the build-up of dangerous levels. (This was the way in which DDT reached high enough levels in peregrines and sparrowhawks to cause eggshell thinning.)

Global hazards

Some pollution problems are truly global. The release of chlorofluorocarbons from aerosol canisters and halons from domestic refrigerators has caused a breakdown in the stratospheric ozone. This forms in a thin layer above the Earth and normally blocks out harmful wavelengths of radiation. All around the world, more people are suffering from skin cancer as a result of the damage to the ozone layer. Moreover, increased levels of such gases as carbon dioxide in the atmosphere may be changing the climate, with potentially catastrophic effects on crop production, sea levels, and climatic stability. Changes already seen around the world are consistent with global warming, including damaging levels of bleaching in coral reefs, extreme weather phenomena, and the melting of glaciers.

Air and water pollution from a pulp mill in Tacoma, Washington, USA. Legislation to control harmful emissions from factories is difficult to enforce, and there is always the threat of accidental spills. *Corbis*

Although great steps have been taken to control some dangerous forms of pollution, others remain hazardous, and new pollutants are constantly appearing. At the same time, we are learning more about their effects and methods of controlling them. One important development is the concept of critical load – the amount of a particular pollutant that can be absorbed by an ecosystem without causing any damage. Critical loads can be used to provide an early-warning system when pollution levels are becoming dangerously high.

Some pollutants can be controlled through technical innovations, but others are more intractable. In some cases, we may have to change our lifestyles to reduce pollution to acceptable levels.

NIGEL DUDLEY

SEE ALSO
acid rain; chlorofluorocarbon; global warming; oil spill; ozone layer; sewage disposal

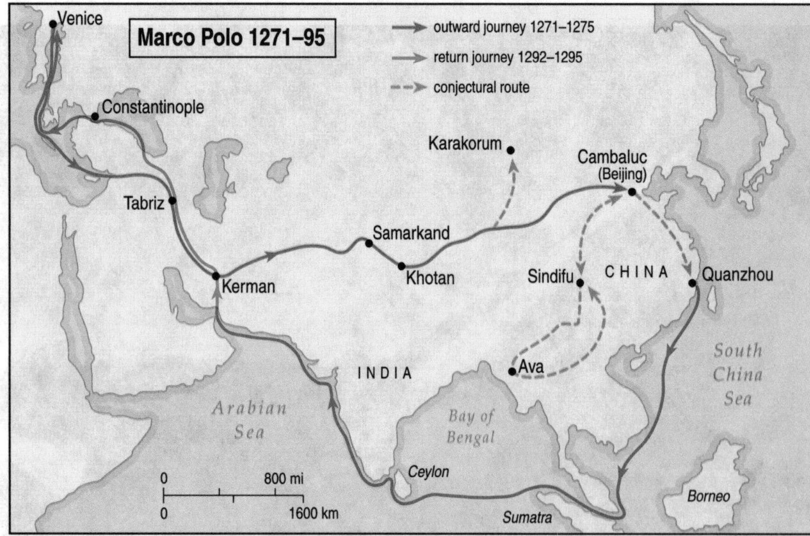

remained the primary source of information about the Far East until the 19th century.

polonaise Polish dance in stately 3/4 time that was common in 18th-century Europe. Chopin developed the polonaise as a pianistic form.

polonium radioactive, metallic element, symbol Po, atomic number 84, relative atomic mass 210. Polonium occurs in nature in small amounts and was isolated from ◊pitchblende. It is the element having the largest number of isotopes (27) and is 5,000 times as radioactive as radium, liberating considerable amounts of heat. It was the first element to have its radioactive properties recognized and investigated.

Polonium was isolated in 1898 from the pitchblende residues analyzed by French scientists Pierre and Marie ◊Curie, and named after Marie Curie's native Poland.

Pol Pot (also known as ***Saloth Sar***, ***Tol Saut***, and ***Pol Porth***) c. 1925–1998. Cambodian politician and leader of the Khmer Rouge communist movement that overthrew the government 1975. After widespread atrocities against the civilian population, his regime was deposed by a Vietnamese invasion 1979. Pol Pot continued to help lead the Khmer Rouge despite officially resigning from all positions in 1989.

Pol Pot was a member of the anti-French resistance under Ho Chi Minh in the 1940s. In 1975 he proclaimed Democratic Kampuchea with himself as premier. His policies were to evacuate cities and put people to work in the countryside. The Khmer Rouge also carried out a systematic extermination of the Western-influenced educated and middle classes (1–4 million). Pol Pot was tried and sentenced to a term of imprisonment 1997.

polo 16th-century Persian manuscript showing a game of polo. The game was first played in England in 1869. *Image Select (UK) Ltd*

poltergeist (German 'noisy ghost') unexplained phenomenon that invisibly moves objects or hurls them about, starts fires, or causes other mischief.

polyandry system whereby a woman has more than one husband at the same time. It is found in Madagascar, Malaysia, and certain Pacific isles, and among certain Inuit and Native American groups. In Tibet and parts of India, polyandry takes the form of the marriage of one woman to several brothers, as a means of keeping intact a family's heritage and property.

polyanthus cultivated variety of ◊primrose, with multiple flowers on one stalk, bred in a variety of colours.

Polybius c. 200–c. 118 BC. Greek politician and historian. He was involved with the ◊Achaean League against the Romans and, following the defeat of the Macedonians at Pydna 168 BC, he was taken as a political hostage to Rome. He returned to Greece 151 and was present at the capture of Carthage by his friend Scipio 146. The first part of his history of Rome in 40 books, covering the years 220–146, survives intact.

polychlorinated biphenyl (PCB) any of a group of chlorinated isomers of biphenyl $(C_6H_5)_2$. They are dangerous industrial chemicals, valuable for their fire-resisting qualities. They constitute an environmental hazard because of their persistent toxicity. Since 1973 their use has been limited by international agreement.

polyester synthetic resin formed by the ◊condensation of polyhydric alcohols (alcohols containing more than one hydroxyl group) with dibasic acids (acids containing two replaceable hydrogen atoms). Polyesters are thermosetting ◊plastics, used in making synthetic fibres, such as Dacron and Terylene, and constructional plastics. With glass fibre added as reinforcement, polyesters are used in car bodies and boat hulls.

polyethylene or ***polyethene*** polymer of the gas ethylene (technically called ethene, C_2H_4). It is a tough, white, translucent, waxy thermoplastic (which means it can be repeatedly softened by heating). It is used for packaging, bottles, toys, wood preservation, electric cable, pipes and tubing.

Polyethylene is produced in two forms: low-density polyethylene, made by high-pressure polymerization of ethylene gas, and high-density polyethylene, which is made at lower pressure by using catalysts. This form, first made 1953 by German chemist Karl Ziegler, is more rigid at low temperatures and softer at higher temperatures than the low-density type. Polyethylene was first made in the 1930s at very high temperatures by ICI.

polygamy the practice of having more than one spouse at the same time. It is found among many peoples. Normally it has been confined to the wealthy and to chiefs and nobles who can support several women and their offspring, as among ancient Egyptians, Teutons, Irish, and Slavs. Islam limits the number of legal wives a man may have to four. Certain Christian sects – for example, the Anabaptists of Münster, Germany, and the Mormons – have practised polygamy because it was the norm in the Old Testament.

polygon in geometry, a plane (two-dimensional) figure with three or more straight-line sides. Common polygons have names which define the number of sides (for example, triangle, quadrilateral, pentagon).

These are all convex polygons, having no interior angle greater than 180°. The sum of the internal angles of a polygon having n sides is given by the formula $(2n - 4) \times 90°$; therefore, the more sides a polygon has, the larger the sum of its internal angles and, in the case of a convex polygon, the more closely it approximates to a circle.

polygraph technical name for a ◊lie detector.

polyhedron in geometry, a solid figure with four or more plane faces. The more faces there are on a polyhedron, the more closely it approximates to a sphere. Knowledge of the properties of polyhedra is needed in crystallography and stereochemistry to determine the shapes of crystals and molecules.

There are only five types of regular polyhedron (with all faces the same size and shape), as was deduced by early Greek mathematicians; they are the tetrahedron (four equilateral triangular faces), cube (six square faces), octahedron (eight equilateral triangles), dodecahedron (12 regular pentagons) and icosahedron (20 equilateral triangles).

polymer compound made up of a large long-chain or branching matrix composed of many repeated simple units (monomers). There are many polymers, both natural (cellulose, chitin, lignin) and synthetic (polyethylene and nylon, types of plastic). Synthetic polymers belong to two groups: thermosoftening and thermosetting (see ◊plastic).

The size of the polymer matrix is determined by the amount of monomer used; it therefore does not form a molecule of constant molecular size or mass.

polymerization chemical union of two or more (usually small) molecules of the same kind to form a new compound. Addition polymerization produces simple multiples of the same compound. Condensation polymerization joins molecules together with the elimination of water or another small molecule.

Addition polymerization uses only a single monomer (basic molecule); condensation polymerization may involve two or more different monomers (co-polymerization).

polymorphism in genetics, the coexistence of several distinctly different types in a ◊population (groups of animals of one species). Examples include the different blood groups in humans, different colour forms in some butterflies, and snail shell size, length, shape, colour, and stripiness.

polymorphism in mineralogy, the ability of a substance to adopt different internal structures and external forms, in response to different conditions of temperature and/or pressure. For example, diamond and graphite are both forms of the element carbon, but they have very different properties and appearance.

Silica (SiO_2) also has several polymorphs, including quartz, tridymite, cristobalite, and stishovite (the latter a very high pressure form found in meteoritic impact craters).

Polynesia islands of Oceania E of 170° E latitude, including Hawaii, Kiribati, Tuvalu, Fiji Islands, Tonga, Tokelau, Samoa, Cook Islands, and French Polynesia.

Polynesian any of the seafaring peoples of Polynesia. They migrated by canoe from S Asia in about 2000 BC, peopling the islands of the S Pacific for about 2,000 years, and settling Hawaii last, from Tahiti. The Polynesian languages belong to the Oceanic branch of the Austronesian family.

main groups The main groups are Samoan

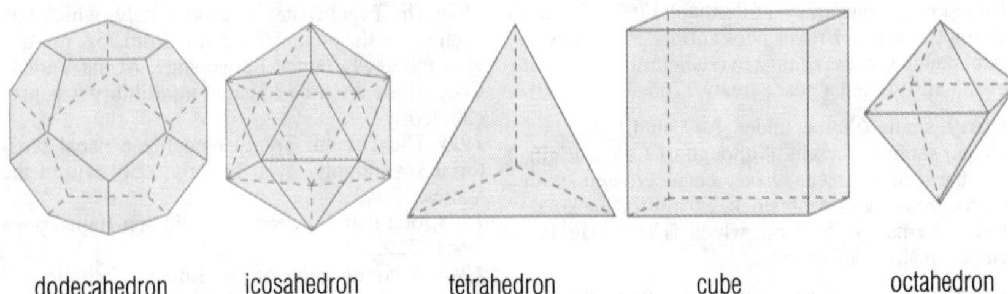

polyhedron The five regular polyhedra or Platonic solids.

(150,000), Maori of New Zealand (100,000), Tongan (75,000), Tahitian (50,000), Hawaian (7,500), Tuamotu (5,000), Raratongan of the Cook Islands (5,000), Uvea of the Wallis Islands (5,000), Marquesan (5,000) and Niuean (5,000).

The Polynesian islands usually support a mixed economy based on fishing, trading and cultivation, though the Maoris, who live far to the south, have adapted to a markedly different climatic zone. ▷ *See feature on pp. 806–807.*

Polynesian languages see ◊Malayo-Polynesian languages.

polynomial in mathematics, an algebraic expression that has one or more ◊variables (denoted by letters). A polynomial of degree one, that is, whose highest ◊power of x is 1, as in $2x + 1$, is called a linear polynomial; $3x^2 + 2x + 1$ is quadratic; $4x^3 + 3x^2 + 2x + 1$ is cubic.

polyp or ***polypus*** small 'stalked' benign tumour, usually found on mucous membrane of the nose or bowels. Intestinal polyps are usually removed, since some have been found to be precursors of cancer.

polyp in zoology, the sedentary stage in the life cycle of a coelenterate or cnidarian (such as a ◊coral or ◊jellyfish), the other being the free-swimming medusa.

polypeptide long-chain ◊peptide.

Polyphemus in Greek mythology, a son of Poseidon and a Cyclops (a one-eyed giant), who imprisoned ◊Odysseus and his companions in his cave on their homeward journey, and was finally blinded by them before they escaped. His story forms the subject of Book Eleven of Homer's *Odyssey*.

polyphony music combining two or more 'voices' or parts, each with an individual melody. A polyphony of widely separated groups is called antiphony.

polyploid in genetics, possessing three or more sets of chromosomes in cases where the normal complement is two sets (◊diploid). Polyploidy arises spontaneously and is common in plants (mainly among flowering plants), but rare in animals. Many crop plants are natural polyploids, including wheat, which has four sets of chromosomes per cell (durum wheat) or six sets (common wheat). Plant breeders can induce the formation of polyploids by treatment with a chemical, colchicine.

polypropylene plastic made by the polymerization, or linking together, of ◊propene molecules ($CH_2{=}CH_2$). It is used as a moulding material.

polysaccharide long-chain ◊carbohydrate made up of hundreds or thousands of linked simple sugars (monosaccharides) such as glucose and closely related molecules.

The polysaccharides are natural polymers. They either act as energy-rich food stores in plants (starch) and animals (glycogen), or have structural roles in the plant cell wall (cellulose, pectin) or the tough outer skeleton of insects and similar creatures (chitin). See also ◊carbohydrate.

polystyrene type of ◊plastic used in kitchen utensils or, in an expanded form, in insulation and ceiling tiles. CFCs are used to produce expanded polythene so alternatives are being sought.

polytechnic formerly, in the UK, an institution for higher education offering vocational and academic courses mainly at degree level.

In 1989 the polytechnics in England and Wales became independent corporations. In 1992 all polytechnics and some colleges of higher education became universities, and from 1993 all universities began to compete for funding on an equal basis. From 1992 public funds became the responsibility of the new Universities and Colleges Funding Council. Academic validation of courses was transferred from the Council for National Academic Awards to the individual institutions.

polytetrafluoroethene (PTFE) polymer made from the monomer tetrafluoroethene (CF_2CF_2). It is a thermosetting plastic with a high melting point that is used to produce 'non-stick' surfaces on pans and to coat bearings. Its trade name is Teflon.

polytheism the worship of many gods, as opposed to monotheism (belief in one god). Examples are the religions of ancient Egypt, Babylon, Greece, Rome, Mexico, and modern Hinduism.

Polythene trade name for a variety of ◊polyethylene.

polytonality in music, an overlapping of multiple parts in different keys, associated in particular with Darius ◊Milhaud whose miniature *Serenade* for orchestra 1917–22 combines up to six major keys. Two keys superimposed is bitonality.

The effect is akin to multiplexing, allowing the ear to fasten on any one line at will, but the combination effect is less coherent.

polyunsaturate type of ◊fat or oil containing a high proportion of triglyceride molecules whose ◊fatty acid chains contain several double bonds. By contrast, the fatty-acid chains of the triglycerides in saturated fats (such as lard) contain only single bonds. Medical evidence suggests that polyunsaturated fats, used widely in margarines and cooking fats, are less likely to contribute to cardiovascular disease than saturated fats, but there is also some evidence that they may have adverse effects on health.

The more double bonds the fatty-acid chains contain, the lower the melting point of the fat. Unsaturated chains with several double bonds produce oils, such as vegetable and fish oils, which are liquids at room temperature. Saturated fats, with no double bonds, are solids at room temperature. The polyunsaturated fats used for margarines are produced by taking a vegetable or fish oil and turning some of the double bonds to single bonds, so that the product is semi-solid at room temperature. This is done by bubbling hydrogen through the oil in the presence of a catalyst, such as platinum. The catalyst is later removed.

Monounsaturated oils, such as olive oil, whose fatty-acid chains contain a single double bond, are probably healthier than either saturated or polyunsaturated fats. Butter contains both saturated and unsaturated fats, together with ◊cholesterol, which also plays a role in heart disease.

polyurethane polymer made from the monomer urethane. It is a thermoset ◊plastic, used in liquid form as a paint or varnish, and in foam form for upholstery and in lining materials (where it may be a fire hazard).

polyvinyl chloride (PVC) a type of ◊plastic used for drainpipes, floor tiles, audio discs, shoes, and handbags.

pome type of ◊pseudocarp, or false fruit, typical of certain plants belonging to the Rosaceae family. The outer skin and fleshy tissues are developed from the ◊receptacle (the enlarged end of the flower stalk) after fertilization, and the five ◊carpels (the true fruit) form the pome's core, which surrounds the seeds. Examples of pomes are apples, pears, and quinces.

pomegranate deciduous shrub or small tree *Punica granatum*, family Punicaceae, native to SW Asia but cultivated widely in tropical and subtropical areas. The round, leathery, reddish-yellow fruit contains numerous seeds that can be eaten fresh or made into wine.

Pomerania (Polish ***Pomorze***, German ***Pommern***) region along the southern shore of the Baltic Sea, including the island of Rügen, divided between Poland and (west of the Oder–Neisse line) East Germany 1945–90, and the Federal Republic of Germany after reunification 1990. The chief port is Gdańsk. It was formerly a province of Germany.

An independent Slavic duchy in the 11th century, Pomerania was taken by Poland in the 12th century and divided into the principalities of West Pomerania and East Pomerania (or Pomerelia). West Pomerania became part of the Holy Roman Empire, while East Pomerania remained part of Poland until 1772, when it was ceded to Prussia.

pomeranian breed of toy dog, about 15 cm/6 in high, weighing about 3 kg/6.5 lb. It has long straight hair with a neck frill, and the tail is carried over the back.

polyp Corals such as this *Galaxea fascicularis* from the Indian Ocean off Kenya, E Africa, are composed of countless individual polyps. *Premaphotos Wildlife*

A statesman is a politician who places himself at the service of the nation. A politician is a statesman who places the nation at his service.

Georges Pompidou
Quoted in the *Observer* Dec 1973

Pompadour Jeanne Antoinette Poisson, Marquise de Pompadour, (known as Madame de Pompadour) 1721–1764. Mistress of ◊Louis XV of France from 1744, born in Paris. She largely dictated the government's ill-fated policy of reversing France's anti-Austrian policy for an anti-Prussian one. She acted as the patron of the Enlightenment philosophers Voltaire and Diderot.

Pompeii ancient city in Italy, near the volcano ◊Vesuvius, 21 km/13 mi SE of Naples.

In AD 63 an earthquake destroyed much of the city, which had been a Roman port and pleasure resort; it was completely buried beneath volcanic ash when Vesuvius erupted AD 79. Over 2,000 people were killed. Pompeii was rediscovered 1748 and the systematic excavation begun 1763 still continues.

Pompey the Great (Gnaeus Pompeius Magnus) 106–48 BC. Roman soldier and politician. From 60 BC to 53 BC, he was a member of the First Triumvirate with Julius ◊Caesar and Marcus Livius ◊Crassus.

Originally a supporter of ◊Sulla, Pompey became consul with Crassus in 70 BC. He defeated ◊Mithridates VI Eupator of Pontus, and annexed Syria and Palestine. He married Caesar's daughter Julia (died 54 BC) in 59 BC. When the Triumvirate broke down after 53 BC, Pompey was drawn into leadership of the senatorial faction. On the outbreak of civil war 49 BC he withdrew to Greece, was defeated by Caesar at Pharsalus 48 BC, and was murdered in Egypt.

Pompidou Georges Jean Raymond 1911–1974. French conservative politician, president 1969–74. He negotiated a settlement with the Algerians 1961 and, as prime minister 1962–68, with the students in the revolt of May 1968.

An adviser on General de Gaulle's staff 1944–46, Pompidou held administrative posts until he became director-general of the French House of Rothschild 1954, and even then continued in close association with de Gaulle, helping to draft the constitution of the Fifth Republic 1958–59. He was elected to the presidency on de Gaulle's resignation.

Ponce de León Juan c. 1460–1521. Spanish soldier and explorer. He is believed to have sailed with Columbus 1493, and served 1502–04 in Hispaniola. He conquered Puerto Rico 1508, and was made governor 1509. In 1513 he was the first European to reach Florida.

He returned to Spain 1514 to report his 'discovery' of Florida (which he thought was an island), and was given permission by King Ferdinand to colonize it. He died in Cuba from an arrow wound.

Pondicherry union territory of SE India; area 480 sq km/185 sq mi; population (1994 est) 894,000. Its capital is Pondicherry, and products include rice, peanuts, cotton, and sugar. Pondicherry was founded by the French 1674 and changed hands several times among the French, Dutch, and British before being returned to France 1814 at the close of the Napoleonic Wars. Together with Karaikal, Yanam, and Mahé (on the Malabar Coast) it formed a French colony until 1954 when all were transferred to the government of India; since 1962 they have formed the Union Territory of Pondicherry. Languages spoken include French, English, Tamil, Telegu, and Malayalam.

pond-skater water ◊bug (insect of the Hemiptera order with piercing mouth parts) that rows itself across the surface by using its middle legs. It feeds on smaller insects.

pondweed any aquatic plant of the genus *Potamogeton* that either floats on the water or is submerged. The leaves of floating pondweeds are broad and leathery, whereas leaves of the submerged forms are narrower and translucent; the flowers grow in green spikes.

Pontefract town in Wakefield borough, West Yorkshire, N England, 34 km/21 mi SW of York; population (1991) 28,400. Industries include coal, market gardening, and confectionery (liquorice Pontefract cakes). Features include the remains of the Norman castle where Richard II was murdered 1399.

Pontiac c. 1720–1769. Native American, chief of the Ottawa from 1755. Allied with the French forces during the French and Indian War, Pontiac was hunted by the British after the French withdrawal. He led the 'Conspiracy of Pontiac' 1763–64 in an attempt to resist British persecution. He achieved remarkable success against overwhelming odds, but eventually signed a peace treaty 1766.

When men grow virtuous in their old age, they only make a sacrifice to God of the devil's leavings.

Alexander Pope
Miscellany (with Jonathan Swift)

pony small ◊horse under 1.47 m/4.5 ft (14.2 hands) shoulder height. Although of Celtic origin, all the pony breeds have been crossed with thoroughbred and Arab stock, except for the smallest – the hardy Shetland, which is less than 105 cm/42 in shoulder height.

poodle breed of gun dog, including standard (above 38 cm/15 in at shoulder), miniature (below 38 cm/15 in), and toy (below 28 cm/11 in) varieties. The dense curly coat, usually cut into an elaborate style, is often either black or white, although greys and browns are also bred.

The poodle probably originated in Russia, was naturalized in Germany, where it was used for retrieving ducks and gained its name (from the German *pudeln*, 'to splash'), and became a luxury dog in France.

pool or ***pocket billiards*** game derived from ◊billiards and played in many different forms. Originally popular in the USA, it is now also played in Europe.

It is played with balls of different colours, each of which is numbered. The neutral ball (black) is the number eight ball. The most popular form of pool is eight-ball pool in which players have to sink all their own balls before the opponent, and then must sink the eight-ball to win the game. Other forms include sinking balls in numerical order (rotation), or sinking a designated ball into a designated pocket (straight pool).

Poole industrial town (chemicals, engineering, boat building, confectionery, pottery from local clay) and yachting centre on Poole Harbour, S England, 8 km/5 mi W of Bournemouth; population (1991) 133,000. It became a unitary authority of England 1997 *(see United Kingdom map).*

Poona former English spelling of ◊Pune, a city in India; after independence 1947 the form Poona was gradually superseded by Pune.

poor law English system for poor relief, established by the Poor Relief Act 1601. Each parish was responsible for its own poor, paid for by a parish tax. The care of the poor was transferred to the Ministry of Health 1918, but the poor law remained in force until 1930.

Pop Iggy. Stage name of James Newell Osterberg 1947– . US rock singer and songwriter. Initially known as Iggy Stooge, he was lead singer with a seminal garage band called the Stooges (1967–74), whose self-destructive proto-punk performances became legendary. His solo career began with *The Idiot* 1977 and *Lust for Life* 1977, composed and produced by David Bowie, who also contributed to *Blah, Blah, Blah* 1986.

Pop art movement of British and American artists in the mid-1950s and 1960s, reacting against the elitism of abstract art. Pop art imagery was drawn from advertising, comic strips, film, and television. Early exponents in the UK were Richard Hamilton, Peter Blake (1932–), and Eduardo Paolozzi, and in the USA Jasper Johns, Jim Dine, Andy Warhol, Roy Lichtenstein, and Claes Oldenburg. In its eclecticism and its sense of irony and playfulness, Pop art helped to prepare the way for the Post-Modernism of the 1970s and 1980s.

pope the bishop of Rome, head of the Roman Catholic Church, which claims he is the spiritual descendant of St Peter. Elected by the Sacred College of Cardinals, a pope dates his pontificate from his coronation with the tiara, or triple crown, at St Peter's Basilica, Rome. The pope had great political power in Europe from the early Middle Ages until the Reformation.

history

11th–13th centuries The papacy enjoyed its greatest temporal power under Gregory VII and Innocent III.

1309–78 The papacy came under French control (headquarters Avignon rather than Rome), 'the Babylonian Captivity'.

1378–1417 The 'Great Schism' followed, with rival popes in Avignon and Rome.

16th century Papal political power further declined with the withdrawal of allegiance by the Protestant states at the Reformation.

1870 The Papal States in central Italy, which had been under the pope's direct rule from 756, merged with the newly united Italian state. At the Vatican Council the doctrine of papal infallibility was proclaimed.

1929 The Lateran Treaty recognized papal territorial sovereignty, even in Italy, only within the Vatican City.

1978 John Paul II became the first non-Italian pope since 1522.

1982 A commission of the Roman Catholic and Anglican churches agreed that in any union between them, the pope would be 'universal primate'.

See list of tables on p. 1177.

Pope Alexander 1688–1744. English poet and satirist. He established his poetic reputation with the precocious *Pastorals* 1709 and *An Essay on Criticism* 1711, which were followed by a parody of the heroic epic, *The Rape of the Lock* 1712–14, *The Temple of Fame* 1715, and 'Eloisa to Abelard' 1717. His highly Neo-Classical translations of Homer's *Iliad* and *Odyssey* 1715–26 were very successful, but his edition of Shakespeare 1725 attracted scholarly ridicule, for which he revenged himself by a satire on scholarly dullness, *The Dunciad* 1728. His philosophical verse, including *An Essay on Man* 1733–34 and *Moral Essays* 1731–35, was influenced by the political philospher Henry ◊Bolingbroke. His finest mature works are his *Imitations of the Satires of Horace* 1733–38 and his personal letters.

Pope had a biting wit, expressed in the heroic couplet (two lines of five unstressed/stressed feet), of which he was a master. His couplets have an epigrammatic quality ('True wit is nature to advantage dressed/What oft was thought, but ne'er so well expressed'), and many of his observations have passed into the language as proverbs, for example 'A little learning is a dang'rous thing.' As a Catholic, he was subject to discrimination, and he was embittered by a deformity of the spine. Among his friends were the writers Jonathan ◊Swift, John ◊Arbuthnot, and John ◊Gay, and with them he was a member of the Scriblerus Club.

Popish Plot supposed plot to murder Charles II; see under Titus ◊Oates.

poplar deciduous tree of the genus *Populus* with characteristically broad leaves. The white poplar *P. alba* has a smooth grey trunk and leaves with white undersides. Other varieties are the aspen *P. tremula*, grey poplar *P. canescens*, and black poplar *P. nigra*. The latter was the only poplar in England in medieval times, but is now increasingly rare, with fewer than 1,000 trees remaining in Britain. It is distinctive for its bark, the most ragged of any British tree, and for its tall, leaning trunk.

pop music or ***popular music*** any contemporary music not categorizable as jazz or classical.

Characterized by strong rhythms of African origin, simple harmonic structures often repeated to strophic melodies, and the use of electrically amplified instruments, pop music generically includes the areas of rock, country and western, rhythm and blues, soul, and others. Pop became distinct from folk music with the advent of sound-recording techniques; electronic amplification and other technological innovations have played a large part in the creation of new styles. The traditional format is a song of roughly three minutes with verse, chorus, and middle eight bars.

Popper Karl Raimund 1902–1994. Austrian-born British philosopher of science. His theory of falsificationism says that although scientific generalizations cannot be conclusively verified, they can be conclusively falsified by a counterinstance; therefore, science is not certain knowledge but a series of 'conjectures and refutations', approaching, though never reaching, a definitive truth. For Popper, psychoanalysis and Marxism are unfalsifiable and therefore unscientific.

One of the most widely read philosophers of the century, Popper's book *The Open Society and its Enemies* 1945 became a modern classic. In it he investigated the long history of attempts to formulate a theory of the state. Animated by a dislike of the views of Freud and Marx, Popper believed he could show that their hypotheses about hidden social and psychological processes were unfalsifiable.

His major work on the philosophy of science is *The Logic of Scientific Discovery* 1935. Other works include *The Poverty of Historicism* 1957

Popper Austrian-born British philosopher Karl Popper. In his social philosophy, Popper has presented a defence of the liberal, 'open' society and a vigorous criticism of the totalitarian society in his influential work *The Open Society and Its Enemies* 1945. His social philosophy and his philosophy of science have essentially the same basis: only systems and theories that can be subjected to vigorous testing (verification) are sound. *Topham*

(about the philosophy of social science), *Conjectures and Refutations* 1963, and *Objective Knowledge* 1972.

poppy any plant of the genus *Papaver*, family Papaveraceae, that bears brightly coloured, often dark-centred, flowers and yields a milky sap. Species include the crimson European field poppy *P. rhoeas* and the Asian ◊opium poppies. Closely related are the California poppy *Eschscholtzia californica* and the yellow horned or sea poppy *Glaucium flavum*.

popular front political alliance of liberals, socialists, communists, and other centre and left-wing parties. This policy was propounded by the Communist International 1935 against fascism and was adopted in France and Spain, where popular-front governments were elected 1936; that in France was overthrown 1938 and the one in Spain fell with the defeat of the Republic in the Spanish Civil War 1939.

population in biology and ecology, a group of animals of one species, living in a certain area and able to interbreed; the members of a given species in a ◊community of living things.

population the number of people inhabiting a country, region, area, or town. Population statistics are derived from many sources; for example, through the registration of births and deaths, and from censuses of the population. The first national censuses were taken in 1800 and 1801 and provided population statistics for Italy, Spain, the UK, Ireland, and the USA; and the cities of London, Paris, Vienna, Berlin, and New York.

Since that time a growing number of countries have taken regular censuses, often at ten-yearly intervals, including Austria (1821), France (1821), China (1851), Russia (1861), Japan (1871), and India (1901). Although censuses are approximately accurate for wealthy industrial countries, this may not be the case with other countries. Between 1990 and 1995 world population increased by 1.7% a year (the number of elderly increased at 2.7% annually). In mid-1994 world population was 5.7 billion and increasing at the rate of 86 million per annum. According to a UN 'low variant' projection, the world population will be at least 7.9 billion by 2050, 9.8 billion by a mid-range projection, or 13 billion by high-range forecasts. In Sept 1994, a UN international conference on population and development was attended by politicians from 150 countries. It emphasized the importance of improving the position of women for effective population control, as well as improved sex education and contraception.

population control measures taken by some governments to limit the growth of their countries' populations by trying to reduce ◊birth rates. Propaganda, freely available contraception, and tax disincentives for large families are some of the measures that have been tried.

population cycle in biology, regular fluctuations in the size of a population, as seen in lemmings, for example. Such cycles are often caused by density-dependent mortality: high mortality due to overcrowding causes a sudden decline in the population, which then gradually builds up again. Population cycles may also result from an interaction between a predator and its prey.

Populism in US history, a late 19th-century political movement that developed out of farmers' protests against economic hardship. The Populist (or People's) Party was founded 1892 and ran several presidential candidates. It failed, however, to reverse increasing industrialization and the relative decline of agriculture in the USA.

porcelain (hardpaste) translucent ceramic material with a shining finish, see ◊pottery and porcelain.

porcupine any ◊rodent with quills on its body, belonging to either of two families: Old World porcupines (family Hystricidae), terrestrial in habit and having long black-and-white quills; or New World porcupines (family Erethizontidae), tree-dwelling, with prehensile tails and much shorter quills.

pornography obscene literature, pictures, photos, or films considered to be of no artistic merit and intended only to arouse sexual desire. Standards of what is obscene and whether a particular work has artistic value are subjective, hence there is often difficulty in determining whether a work violates the ◊obscenity laws. Opponents of pornography claim that it is harmful and incites violence to women and children.

porphyria group of rare genetic disorders caused by an enzyme defect. Porphyria affects the digestive tract, causing abdominal distress; the nervous system, causing psychotic disorder, epilepsy, and weakness; the circulatory system, causing high blood pressure; and the skin, causing extreme sensitivity to light. No specific treatments exist.

In porphyria the body accumulates and excretes (rather than utilizes) one or more porphyrins, the pigments that combine with iron to form part of the oxygen-carrying proteins haemoglobin and myoglobin; because of this urine turns reddish brown on standing. It is known as the 'royal disease' because sufferers are believed to have included Mary Queen of Scots, James I, and George III.

porphyry any ◊igneous rock containing large crystals in a finer matrix.

porpoise any small whale of the family Delphinidae that, unlike dolphins, have blunt snouts without beaks. Common porpoises of the genus *Phocaena* can grow to 1.8 m/6 ft long; they feed on fish and crustaceans.

Porsche Ferdinand 1875–1951. German car designer and engineer who designed the Volkswagen Beetle, first mass produced 1945. By 1972 more than 15 million had been sold, making it the world's most popular model. Porsche sports cars were developed by his son Ferry Porsche from 1948.

Ferdinand Porsche designed his first racing car in the mid-1930s, which was successfully developed by Auto-Union for their racing team. Ferry's Porsche Company produced Grand Prix cars, sports cars, and prototypes. Their Formula One racing car was not successful and it was at sports-car and Can-Am racing that they proved to be more dominant.

port in computing, a socket that enables a computer processor to communicate with an external device. It may be an ***input port*** (such as a joystick port), or an ***output port*** (such as a printer port), or both (an ***i/o port***).

Microcomputers may provide ports for cartridges, televisions and/or monitors, printers, and modems, and sometimes for hard discs and musical instruments (MIDI, the musical-instrument digital interface). Ports may be serial or parallel.

port point where goods are loaded or unloaded from a water-based to a land-based form of transport. Most ports are coastal, though inland ports on rivers also exist. Ports often have specialized equipment to handle cargo in large quantities (for example, container facilities).

port sweet red, tawny, or white dessert wine, fortified with brandy, made from grapes grown in the Douro basin of Portugal and exported from Oporto, hence the name.

Port Arthur former name (to 1905) of the port and naval base of Lüshun in NE China, now part of ◊Lüda.

Port-au-Prince capital and industrial port (sugar, rum, textiles, plastics) of Haiti; population (1992) 1,255,100. Founded by the French 1749, it was destroyed by earthquakes 1751 and 1770.

Port Elizabeth industrial port (engineering, steel, food processing) in Eastern Cape Province, South Africa, about 710 km/440 mi E of Cape Town on Algoa Bay; population (urban area, 1991) 853,200.

Porter Cole (Albert) 1892–1964. US composer and lyricist. He wrote mainly musical comedies. His witty, sophisticated songs like 'Let's Do It' 1928, 'I Get a Kick Out of You' 1934, and 'Don't Fence Me In' 1944 have been widely recorded and admired. His shows, many of which were made into films, include *The Gay Divorce* 1932 (filmed 1934 as *The Gay Divorcee*) and *Kiss Me Kate* 1948.

Porter Edwin Stratton 1869–1941. US director, a pioneer of silent films. His 1903 film *The Great Train Robbery* lasted an unprecedented 12 minutes and contained an early use of the close-up. More concerned with the technical than the artistic side of his films, which include *The Teddy Bears* 1907 and *The Final Pardon* 1912, Porter abandoned filmmaking 1916.

Porter Katherine Anne Maria Veronica Callista Russell 1890–1980. US writer. She published three volumes of short stories (*Flowing Judas* 1930, *Pale Horse, Pale Rider* 1939, and *The Leaning Tower* 1944); a collection of essays, *The Days Before* 1952; and the allegorical novel *Ship of Fools* 1962 (filmed 1965). Her *Collected Short Stories* 1965 won a Pulitzer prize.

Porter Rodney Robert 1917–1985. English biochemist. In 1962 he proposed a structure for human ◊immunoglobulin (antibody) in which the molecule was seen as consisting of four chains. He was awarded the 1972 Nobel Prize for Physiology or Medicine.

portico in architecture, a porch with a ◊pediment and columns.

Portland William Henry Cavendish Bentinck, 3rd Duke of Portland 1738–1809. British politician, originally a Whig, who in 1783 became nominal prime minister in the Fox–North coalition government. During the French Revolution he joined the Tories, and was prime minister 1807–09.

Port Louis capital of Mauritius, on the island's NW coast; population (1993) 144,250. Exports include sugar, textiles, watches, and electronic goods.

Port Moresby capital and port of Papua New Guinea on the S coast of New Guinea; population (1990) 193,200. In World War II it was a prime Japanese objective, since occupation would have meant control of N Australia, and was the target of a Japanese campaign from May 1942 but Allied forces successfully held out.

Pôrto (English ***Oporto***) industrial city (textiles, leather, pottery) in Portugal, on the river Douro, 5 km/3 mi from its mouth; population (1987) 350,000. It exports port wine; the suburb Vila Nova de Gaia on the S bank of the Douro is known for its port lodges. Pôrto is the second-largest city in Portugal and has a 12th-century cathedral.

Pôrto Alegre port and capital of Rio Grande do Sul state, S Brazil; population (1991) 1,254,600 (metropolitan area 3,757,500). It is a freshwater port for ocean-going vessels and is Brazil's major commercial centre.

'We may become the makers of our fate when we have ceased to pose as its prophets.'

KARL POPPER
The Open Society and Its Enemies

'In olden days a glimpse of stocking / Was looked on as something shocking / Now, heaven knows, / Anything goes.'

COLE PORTER
'Anything Goes'

"Every portrait that is painted with feeling is a portrait of the artist, not of the sitter."

On PORTRAITURE
Oscar Wilde
The Picture of Dorian Gray 1891

Port-of-Spain port and capital of Trinidad and Tobago, on the island of Trinidad; population (1990) 58,400. It has a cathedral (1813–28) and the San Andres Fort (1785).

Porton Down site of the Chemical and Biological Defence Establishment (until 1991 Chemical Defence Establishment) in Wiltshire, SW England. Its prime role is to conduct research into means of protection from chemical attack.

Porto Novo capital of Benin, W Africa; population (1994) 179,000. It was a former Portuguese centre for the slave and tobacco trade with Brazil and became a French protectorate 1863.

Although Porto Novo is the official capital, most political activity in Benin takes place in Cotonou.

portraiture in the visual arts, the creation of a likeness to someone. Such likenesses appear in many cultures but first flourished in the West in ancient Rome as statues and coins of the rich and the powerful. In Egypt in the 3rd century AD portraits painted in wax on the panels of mummy cases achieved a high degree of realism and frankness. Extinct during the Middle Ages, portraiture revived in the 14th century as patrons and donors began to appear in religious pictures.

The portrait complete in itself was produced both in Italy and the Netherlands in the 15th century, Italian artists favouring the profile (adaptation of the medallion), as in Piero della Francesca's portraits of the Duke of Urbino and his wife. The oil medium gave the great artists of the Renaissance the means of imparting a more lifelike aspect to the features, especially by means of light and shade (for example Leonardo's *Mona Lisa*), and this development, extending into the 17th century, made that period perhaps the greatest age of European portraiture, as exemplified by Rembrandt, Velázquez, Rubens, and Van Dyck.

The secular spirit of art after the Reformation and the establishment of settled monarchies in Europe both contributed to give portraiture special importance from the 16th century onwards, Hans Holbein the younger in England and the Clouets in France giving outstanding early examples. A long tradition in England found its greatest expression in the 18th century with Hogarth, Gainsborough, Reynolds, Romney, Ramsay, Raeburn, Lawrence, and others. A special growth was the intimate 'conversation piece'. The decline of portraiture began in the 19th century, two contributory factors being the rivalry of the camera and the preoccupation of many artists with ideas and styles that paid a decreasing attention to likeness – or at least to the requirements of the sitter – the portraits of Cézanne being an instance.

The self-portrait evolved as an independent genre during the Renaissance, reflecting both the growth of individualism and the greatly improved status of the artist. It is uncertain whether Jan van Eyck's *Man in a Red Turban* about 1433 (National Gallery, London) is a self-portrait; if it is, it is probably the first of its kind. Other examples include Dürer's *Self-portrait* 1493 (Louvre, Paris), Rembrandt's *Self-portrait* about 1659 (National Gallery of Art, Washington), and Van Gogh's *Self-portrait with Bandaged Ear* 1889 (Courtauld Institute Gallery, London).

Port Said port in Egypt, on reclaimed land at the N end of the ◊Suez Canal; population (1994) 526,000. During the 1967 Arab-Israeli War the city was damaged and the canal blocked; Port Said was evacuated by 1969 but by 1975 had been largely reconstructed.

Portsmouth city and naval port opposite the Isle of Wight; population (1991) 174,700. The naval dockyard was closed 1981 although some naval facilities remain. It is a continental ferry port. There are high-technology and manufacturing industries, including aircraft engineering, electronics, shipbuilding, and ship maintenance. It became a unitary authority of England 1997 *(see United Kingdom map)*.

It was already a port in the days of King Alfred, but in 1194 Richard I recognized its strategic importance and created a settlement on Portsea Island. The world's first dry dock was contructed here 1495. The Tudor warship *Mary Rose* and Admiral Horatio Nelson's flagship, HMS *Victory*, are exhibited here. The novelist Charles Dickens was born in the Portsmouth suburb of Landport. The diocese of Portsmouth was created 1927; the cathedral was enlarged with a new west front and consecrated 1991.

Port Talbot industrial port (tinplate, chemicals, and steel strip mill) and administrative headquarters of Neath Port Talbot, Wales; population (1991) 37,600. The port accommodates bulk carriers of iron ore.

Portugal country in SW Europe, on the Atlantic Ocean, bounded N and E by Spain. *See country box opposite.*

Portuguese inhabitants of Portugal. The Portuguese have a mixed cultural heritage that can be traced back to the Lusitanian Celts who were defeated by the Romans about 140 BC. In the 5th century AD the Suebi, a Germanic group, overran the Iberian peninsula, and were later subdued by the Visigoths. In the 8th century AD S Portugal was invaded by the Moors. The Portuguese are predominantly Roman Catholic.

Portuguese language member of the Romance branch of the Indo-European language family; spoken by 120–135 million people worldwide, it is the national language of Portugal, closely related to Spanish and strongly influenced by Arabic. Portuguese is also spoken in Brazil, Angola, Mozambique, and other former Portuguese colonies.

Portuguese literature under Provençal influence, medieval Portuguese literature produced popular ballads and troubadour songs.

The Renaissance provided a stimulus for the outstanding work of the dramatist Gil Vicente and of the lyric and epic poet ◊Camoëns. In the 17th and 18th centuries there was a decline towards mere formality, but the *Letters of a Portuguese Nun*, attributed to Marianna Alcoforado (1640–1723), were a poignant exception and found echoes in the modern revolutionary period. The outstanding writer of the 20th century was the poet Fernando Pessoa (1888–1935). Angola has developed its own school of Portuguese-African poetry.

Portuguese man-of-war any of a genus *Physalia* of phylum *Coelenterata* (see ◊coelenterate). They live in the sea, in colonies, and have a large air-filled bladder (or 'float') on top and numerous hanging tentacles made up of feeding, stinging, and reproductive individuals. The float can be 30 cm/1 ft long.

Poseidon in Greek mythology, the chief god of the sea (Roman Neptune), brother of Zeus and Pluto. The brothers dethroned their father, Kronos, and divided his realm, Poseidon taking the sea; he was also worshipped as god of earthquakes. His sons were the merman sea god ◊Triton and the Cyclops ◊Polyphemus.

positivism theory that confines genuine knowledge within the bounds of science and observation. The theory is associated with the French philosopher Auguste Comte and ◊empiricism. Logical positivism developed in the 1920s. It rejected any metaphysical world beyond everyday science and common sense, and confined statements to those of formal logic or mathematics.

positron in physics, the antiparticle of the electron; an ◊elementary particle having the same mass as an electron but exhibiting a positive charge. The positron was discovered in 1932 by US physicist Carl Anderson at Caltech, USA, its existence having been predicted by the British physicist Paul Dirac 1928.

positron emission tomography (PET) an imaging technique which enables doctors to observe the metabolic activity of the human body by following the progress of a radioactive chemical that has been inhaled or injected. PET, detecting ◊gamma radiation given out when ◊positrons emitted by the chemical are annihilated. The technique has been used to study a wide range of conditions, including schizophrenia, Alzheimer's disease and Parkinson's disease.

possible world in philosophy, a consistent set of propositions describing a logically, if not physically, possible state of affairs. The term was invented by German philosopher Gottfried ◊Leibniz, who argued that God chose to make real one world from an infinite range of possible worlds. Since God could only choose the best, our world is 'the best of all possible worlds'.

possum another name for the ◊opossum, a marsupial animal with a prehensile tail found in North, Central and South America. The name is also used for many of the smaller marsupials found in Australia.

postal service system for delivering mail. In Britain regular permanent systems were not created until the emergence of the modern nation state. Henry VIII in 1516 appointed Sir Brian Tuke as Master of the Posts, to maintain a regular service on the main roads from London. Postmasters (usually innkeepers) passed the mail to the next post, and supplied horses for the royal couriers. In 1635 a royal proclamation established the first public service. Private services were discouraged to avoid losing revenue for the state service and assisting treasonable activities, the latter point being stressed by the act establishing the Post Office, passed under Oliver ◊Cromwell in 1657. Mail coaches first ran in 1784, and in 1840 Rowland Hill's prepaid penny postage stamp, for any distance within the UK, led to a massive increase in use. Services were extended to registered post 1841; post boxes 1855; savings bank 1861; postcards 1870; postal orders 1881, parcel post 1883, air mail 1911, telephone 1912, data processing by computer 1967, and giro 1968. The Post Office also has responsibility for paying out social security and collecting revenue for state insurance schemes. In 1969 the original General Post Office ceased to be a government department, and in 1981 it split into two, the Post Office and the telecommunications corporation British Telecom (privatized 1984). The Post Office lost its monopoly 1987. International cooperation is through the Universal Postal Union, 1875, at Berne.

In the 1830s, a letter from England to India took from five to eight months to arrive; by the 1850s, this was reduced to 30–45 days; by 1870, a telegram could be sent in under five hours.

postcard card with space for a written message that can be sent through the mail without an envelope. The postcard's inventor was Emmanual Hermann, of Vienna, who in 1869 proposed a 'postal telegram', sent at a lower fee than a normal letter with an envelope. The first picture postcard was produced 1894.

The postcard, typically 14 × 9 cm/5½ × 3½ ins, rapidly gained popularity after the introduction of the picture postcard. From 1902 the address could be written on the back, leaving the whole of the front for the illustration. Subjects included topographical views, reproductions of paintings, photographs of film stars, and sentimental drawings; common in Britain was the seaside comic postcard, typically illustrated by Donald McGill (1875–1962).

poster public notice used for advertising or propaganda, often illustrated. The ancestors of the modern poster were the handbills, with woodcut illustrations, that were posted up in public places. One of the first English posters by a distinguished artist, Frederick Walker's design announcing *The Woman in White* (1871), was engraved on wood. An entirely new prospect with regard to both scale and colour, however, resulted from the use of colour lithography. By his brilliant exploitation of its pictorial possibilities, the French artist Jules Chéret may be called the 'father of the poster'. Influenced by him and by the simplified designs of Japanese prints, Toulouse-Lautrec achieved his great artistic triumphs in the colour lithographs he executed for various Parisian resorts. The purposes of art and propaganda coincided in the production of pictorial design simple and powerful enough to convey an immediate impact, a problem which artists were delighted to solve in the classic age of the poster, the 1890s. Aubrey Beardsley is an example, as are the 'Beggarstaff Brothers' (William Nicholson and James Pryde), whose telling simplicities of design evolved from pieces of coloured paper cut to shape and subsequently lithographed. Many famous artists have since designed posters for travel, commercial, and industrial organizations.

In England, for instance, E McKnight Kauffer, Sir Frank Brangwyn, Duncan Grant, Graham Sutherland, Paul Nash and John Minton, such organizations as London Transport, and Shell-Mex showed themselves to be enlightened patrons. Poster art flourished again in the 1960s with the advent of Psychedelic art, and artists such as Rick Griffin (1944–1991) and Stanley Mouse (1921–) in the USA, and Michael English (1942–) in the UK.

poste restante (French) a system whereby mail is sent to a certain post office and kept there until collected by the person to whom it is addressed.

Post-Impressionism movement in painting that followed ◊Impressionism in the 1880s and 1890s, incorporating various styles. The term was first used by the English critic Roger Fry 1910 to describe the works of Paul Cézanne, Vincent van Gogh, and Paul Gauguin. Although differing greatly in style and aims, these painters sought to go beyond Impressionism's concern with the ever-changing effects of light and to achieve a firmer pictorial construction. Subject matter also assumed importance.

In England, the movement was most strikingly represented in the work of the Camden Town Group, formed 1911.

Post-Modernism late 20th-century movement in architecture and the arts that rejects the preoccupation of ◊Modernism with purity of form and technique. Post-Modernists use an amalgam of style elements from the past, such as the Classical and the Baroque, and apply them to spare modern forms, often with ironic effect. Their slightly off-key familiarity creates a more immediate appeal than the austerities of Modernism. Exponents include the architects Robert ◊Venturi and Michael Graves (1934–) and the novelists David ◊Lodge and Thomas ◊Pynchon. In literary criticism and critical theory, Post-Modernism denotes a differently conceived resumption rather than a repudiation of Modernist radicalism.

postmortem (Latin 'after death') or ***autopsy*** dissection of a dead body to determine the cause of death.

postnatal depression mood change occurring in many mothers a few days after the birth of a baby, also known as 'baby blues'. It is usually a shortlived condition but can sometimes persist; one in five women suffer a lasting depression after giving birth. The most severe form of post-natal depressive illness, puerperal psychosis, requires hospital treatment.

In mild cases, antidepressant drugs and hormone treatment may help, although no link has been established between hormonal levels and postnatal depression. Research by UK psychologists 1996 showed that the mourning of a lost lifestyle may be a contributory factor.

Post Office (PO) government department or authority with responsibility for postal services; see ◊postal service. The Post Office has responsibility for paying out social security and collecting revenue for state insurance schemes. Post Office activities were divided 1981 and in 1984 telecommunications activities were privatized, forming a new company, British Telecom. Plans to privatize the Royal Mail, including customer services and parcel deliveries, were revived 1996.

potash general name for any potassium-containing mineral, most often applied to potassium carbonate (K_2CO_3) or potassium hydroxide (KOH). Potassium carbonate, originally made by roasting plants to ashes in earthenware pots, is commercially produced from the mineral sylvite (potassium chloride, KCl) and is used mainly in making artificial fertilizers, glass, and soap.

The potassium content of soils and fertilizers is also commonly expressed as potash, although in this case it usually refers to potassium oxide (K_2O).

potassium (Dutch *potassa* 'potash') soft, waxlike, silver-white, metallic element, symbol K (Latin *kalium*), atomic number 19, relative atomic

PORTUGAL
Republic of

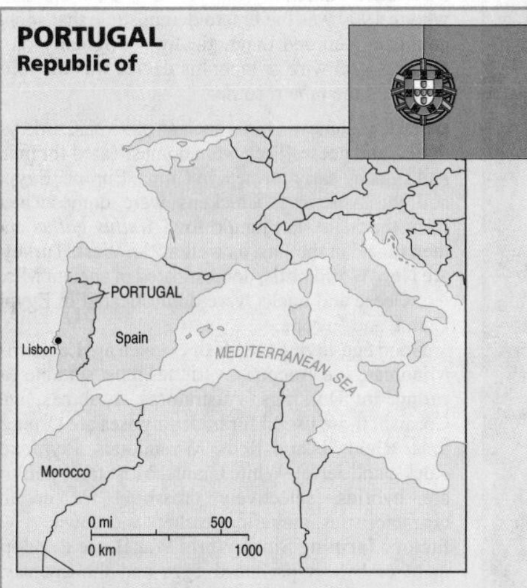

national name *República Portuguesa*
area 92,000 sq km/35,521 sq mi (including the Azores and Madeira)
capital Lisbon
major towns/cities Coimbra, Amadora
major ports Pôrto, Setúbal
physical features mountainous in the N (Serra da Estrêla mountains); plains in the S; rivers Minho, Douro, Tagus (Tejo), Guadiana
head of state Jorge Sampaio from 1996
head of government Antonio Guterres from 1995
political system democratic republic
administrative divisions 18 districts and two autonomous regions
political parties Social Democratic Party (PSD), moderate left of centre; Socialist Party (PS), centre-left; People's Party (PP), right-wing, anti-European integration
armed forces 50,700 (1995)
conscription 4–18 months
defence spend (% GDP) 2.6 (1994)
education spend (% GNP) 5.0 (1992)
health spend (% GDP) 4.1 (1993)
death penalty abolished 1976
population 9,808,000 (1996 est)
population growth rate −0.1% (1990–95); 0.0% (2000–05)
age distribution (% of total population) <15 18.8%, 15–65 67.0%, >65 14.1% (1995)
ethnic distribution most of the population is descended from the Caucasoid peoples who inhabited the whole of the Iberian peninsula in classical and pre-classical times; there are a number of minorities from Portugal's overseas possessions and former possessions
population density (per sq km) 106 (1994)
urban population (% of total) 36 (1995)
labour force 49% of population: 18% agriculture, 34% industry, 48% services (1990)
unemployment 7.2% (1995)
child mortality rate (under 5, per 1,000 live births) 11 (1993)
life expectancy 71 (men), 78 (women)
education (compulsory years) 9
literacy rate 89% (men), 82% (women)
language Portuguese
religion Roman Catholic 97%
TV sets (per 1,000 people) 188 (1992)
currency escudo
GDP (US $) 103.6 billion (1995)
GDP per capita (PPP) (US $) 12,841 (1995)
growth rate 2.5% (1994/95)
average annual inflation 5.1% (1995)
major trading partners EU (principally Spain, Germany, and France)
resources limestone, granite, marble, iron, tungsten, copper, pyrites, gold, uranium, coal, forests
industries textiles and clothing, footwear, paper pulp, cork items (world's largest producer of cork), chemicals, petroleum refinery, fish processing, viticulture, electrical appliances, ceramics, tourism
exports textiles, clothing, footwear, pulp and waste paper, wood and cork manufactures, tinned fish, electrical equipment, wine, refined petroleum. Principal market: Germany 19.6% (1993)
imports foodstuffs, machinery and transport equipment, crude petroleum, natural gas, textile yarn, coal, rubber, plastics, tobacco. Principal source: Spain 17.8% (1993)
arable land 25.5% (1993)
agricultural products wheat, maize, rice, potatoes, tomatoes, grapes, olives, fruit; fishing (1993 sardine catch was the world's largest at 88, 494 tons)

HISTORY
2nd C BC Roman conquest of Iberian peninsula.
5th C AD Iberia overrun by Vandals and Visigoths after fall of Roman Empire.
711 Visigoth kingdom overthrown by Muslims invading from N Africa.
997–1064 Christians re-settled northern area, which came under rule of Léon and Castile.
1139 Afonso I, son of Henry of Burgundy, defeated Muslims and the area became an independent kingdom.
1340 Final Muslim invasion defeated.
1373 Anglo-Portuguese alliance signed.
15th C Age of exploration: Portuguese mariners surveyed coast of Africa, opened sea route to India (Vasco da Gama), and reached Brazil (Pedro Cabral).
16th C 'Golden Age': Portugal flourished as commercial and colonial power.
1580 Philip II of Spain took throne of Portugal.
1640 Spanish rule overthrown in bloodless coup; duke of Braganza proclaimed as King John IV.
1668 Spain recognized Portuguese independence.
1755 Lisbon devastated by earthquake.
1755–77 Politics dominated by chief minister Sebastiao de Carlvalho, Marquis of Pombal, who introduced secular education and promoted trade.
1807 Napoleonic France invaded Portugal; Portuguese court fled to Brazil.
1807–11 In the Peninsular War British forces played leading part in liberating Portugal from French.
1820 Liberal revolution forced King John VI to return from Brazil and accept constitutional government.
1822 Brazil declared independence; first Portuguese constitution adopted.
1826 First constitution replaced by more conservative one.
1828 Dom Miguel blocked succession of his niece, Queen Maria, and declared himself absolute monarch; civil war ensued between liberals and conservatives.
1834 Queen Maria regained throne with British, French, and Brazilian help; constitutional government restored.
1840s Severe disputes between supporters of radical 1822 constitution and more conservative 1826 constitution.
1851 'Regeneration' to promote order and economic growth launched by duke of Saldanha after coup.
late 19th C Government faced severe financial difficulties; rise of socialist, anarchist, and republican parties.
1908 Assassination of King Carlos I.
1910 Portugal became republic after three-day insurrection forced King Manuel II to flee.
1911 New regime adopted liberal constitution, but republic proved unstable, violent, and corrupt.
1916–18 Portugal fought in World War I on Allied side.
1926–51 Popular military coup installed General António de Fragoso Carmona as president.
1928 António de Oliveira Salazar became finance minister and introduced successful reforms.
1932 Salazar became prime minister with dictatorial powers.
1933 Authoritarian 'Estado Novo' ('New State') constitution adopted; living conditions improved, but Salazar resisted political change at home and in colonies.
1949 Portugal became founding member of North Atlantic Treaty Organization (NATO).
1968 Salazar retired; succeeded by Marcello Caetano.
1974 Army seized power to end stalemate situation in African colonial wars; General Antó Ribeiro de Spínola became president; succeeded by General Francisco da Costa Gomes.
1975 Portuguese colonies achieved independence; Gomes narrowly averted communist coup.
1976 First free elections in 50 years resulted in minority government under socialist leader Mario Soares; General António Ramahlo Eanes won presidency.
1980 Francisco Balsemão (PSD) formed centre-party coalition.
1986 Soares became first civilian president in sixty years; Portugal joined European Community (EC).
1989 Social Democrat government started to dismantle socialist economy and privatize major industries.
1996 Jorge Sampaio (PS) elected president.

SEE ALSO Azores; Peninsular War

> "It is said that the effect of eating too much lettuce is 'soporific'."
> BEATRIX POTTER
> *The Tale of the Flopsy Bunnies*

mass 39.0983. It is one of the ◊alkali metals and has a very low density – it floats on water, and is the second lightest metal (after lithium). It oxidizes rapidly when exposed to air and reacts violently with water. Of great abundance in the Earth's crust, it is widely distributed with other elements and found in salt and mineral deposits in the form of potassium aluminium silicates.

Potassium is the main base ion of the fluid in the body's cells. Along with ◊sodium, it is important to the electrical potential of the nervous system and, therefore, for the efficient functioning of nerve and muscle. Shortage, which may occur with excessive fluid loss (prolonged diarrhoea, vomiting), may lead to muscular paralysis; potassium overload may result in cardiac arrest. It is also required by plants for growth. The element was discovered and named in 1807 by English chemist Humphry Davy, who isolated it from potash in the first instance of a metal being isolated by electric current.

potato perennial plant *Solanum tuberosum*, family Solanaceae, with edible tuberous roots that are rich in starch. Used by the Andean Indians for at least 2,000 years before the Spanish Conquest, the potato was introduced to Europe by the mid-16th century, and reputedly to England by the explorer Walter Raleigh.

Potemkin Grigory Aleksandrovich. Prince Potemkin 1739–1791. Russian politician. He entered the army and attracted the notice of Catherine II, whose friendship he kept throughout his life. He was an active administrator who reformed the army, built the Black Sea Fleet, conquered the Crimea 1783, developed S Russia, and founded the Kherson arsenal 1788 (the first Russian naval base on the Black Sea).

potential difference (pd) difference in the electrical potential (see ◊potential, electric) of two points, being equal to the electrical energy converted by a unit electric charge moving from one point to the other. The SI unit of potential difference is the volt (V). The potential difference between two points in a circuit is commonly referred to as voltage. See also ◊Ohm's law.

potential, electric in physics, the potential at a point is equal to the energy required to bring a unit electric charge from infinity to the point. The SI unit of potential is the volt (V). Positive electric charges will flow 'downhill' from a region of high potential to a region of low potential. See ◊potential difference.

potential energy ◊energy possessed by an object by virtue of its relative position or state (for example, as in a compressed spring). It is contrasted with kinetic energy, the form of energy possessed by moving bodies.

potentiometer in physics, an electrical ◊resistor that can be divided so as to compare, measure, or control voltages. In radio circuits, any rotary variable resistance (such as volume control) is referred to as a potentiometer.

A simple type of potentiometer consists of a length of uniform resistance wire (about 1 m/3 ft long) carrying a constant current provided by a battery connected across the ends of the wire. The source of potential difference (voltage) to be measured is connected (to oppose the cell) between one end of the wire, through a ◊galvanometer (instrument for measuring small currents), to a contact free to slide along the wire. The sliding contact is moved until the galvanometer shows no deflection. The ratio of the length of potentiometer wire in the galvanometer circuit to the total length of wire is then equal to the ratio of the unknown potential difference to that of the battery.

Potomac river in West Virginia, Virginia, and Maryland states, USA, rising in the Allegheny Mountains, and flowing SE through Washington DC, into Chesapeake Bay. It is formed by the junction of the N Potomac, about 153 km/95 mi long, and S Potomac, about 209 km/130 mi long, and is itself 459 km/285 mi long.

> "The trouble with words is that you never know whose mouths they have been in."
> DENNIS POTTER

Potsdam capital of the *Land* of Brandenburg, Germany, on the river Havel SW of Berlin; population (1993) 139,500. Products include textiles, pharmaceuticals, and electrical goods. A leading garrison town and Prussian military centre, Potsdam was restored to its position of capital of Brandenburg with the reunification of Germany 1990. The New Palace 1763–70 and Sans Souci were both built by Frederick the Great, and Hitler's Third Reich was proclaimed in the garrison church 21 March 1933. The Potsdam Conference took place here 1945.

Potsdam Conference conference held in Potsdam, Germany, 17 July–2 Aug 1945, between representatives of the USA, the UK, and the USSR. They established the political and economic principles governing the treatment of Germany in the initial period of Allied control at the end of World War II, and sent an ultimatum to Japan demanding unconditional surrender on pain of utter destruction.

Potter (Helen) Beatrix 1866–1943. English writer and illustrator of children's books. Her first book was *The Tale of Peter Rabbit* 1900, followed by *The Tailor of Gloucester* 1902, based on her observation of family pets and wildlife. Other books in the series include *The Tale of Mrs Tiggy-Winkle* 1904, *The Tale of Jeremy Fisher* 1906, and a sequel to Peter Rabbit, *The Tale of the Flopsy Bunnies* 1909. Her tales are told with a childlike wonder, devoid of sentimentality, and accompanied by delicate illustrations.

Potter Classic British children's author and illustrator Beatrix Potter. She stands at the door of the Cumbrian farm she bought 1905 with the revenue from her books. The tales of Tom Kitten, Jemima Puddleduck, and Samuel Whiskers were written and set here. *Topham*

Potter Dennis Christopher George 1935–1994. English playwright and journalist. He distinguished himself as the most important dramatist for television in its history, greatly extending the boundaries of the art-form. Plays include *Pennies from Heaven* 1978 (feature film 1981), *Brimstone and Treacle* 1976 (transmitted 1987, feature film 1982), and *The Singing Detective* 1986. His posthumous plays were *Cold Lazarus* and *Karaoke*, both 1995.

Potteries, the home of the china and earthenware industries, in central England. Wedgwood and Minton are factory names associated with the Potteries.

The Potteries lie in the upper Trent basin of N Staffordshire, covering the area around Stoke-on-Trent, and include the formerly separate towns of Burslem, Hanley, Longton, Fenton, and Tunstall.

pottery and porcelain ceramics in domestic and ornamental use, including ◊earthenware, ◊stoneware, and bone china (or softpaste porcelain). Made of 5% bone ash and china clay, bone china was first made in the West in imitation of Chinese porcelain. The standard British bone china was developed about 1800, with a body of clay mixed with ox bones; a harder version, called parian, was developed in the 19th century and was used for figurine ornaments.

Hardpaste porcelain is characterized by its hardness, ringing sound when struck, translucence, and shining finish, like that of a cowrie shell (Italian *porcellana*). It is made of kaolin and petuntse (fusible feldspar consisting chiefly of silicates reduced to a fine white powder); it is high-fired at 1,400°C/2,552°F. Porcelain first evolved from stoneware in China, about the 6th century AD. A formula for making porcelain was developed in the 18th century in Germany, also in France, Italy, and Britain. It was first produced in the USA in the early 19th century.

potto arboreal, nocturnal, African prosimian primate *Perodicticus potto* belonging to the ◊loris family. It has a thick body, strong limbs, and grasping feet and hands, and grows to 40 cm/16 in long, with horny spines along its backbone, which it uses in self-defence. It climbs slowly, and eats insects, snails, fruit, and leaves.

Poulenc Francis Jean Marcel 1899–1963. French composer and pianist. A self-taught composer of witty and irreverent music, he was a member of the group of French composers known as *Les Six*. Among his many works are the operas *Les Mamelles de Tirésias/The Breasts of Tiresias* 1947 and *Dialogues des Carmélites/Dialogues of the Carmelites* 1957, and the ballet *Les Biches/The Little Darlings* 1923.

Poulsen Valdemar 1869–1942. Danish engineer who in 1900 was the first to demonstrate that sound could be recorded magnetically – originally on a moving steel wire or tape; his device was the forerunner of the tape recorder.

poultry domestic birds such as chickens, turkeys, ducks, and geese. They were domesticated for meat and eggs by early farmers in China, Europe, Egypt, and the Americas. Chickens were domesticated from the SE Asian jungle fowl *Gallus gallus* and then raised in the East as well as the West. Turkeys are New World birds, domesticated in ancient Mexico. Geese and ducks were domesticated in Egypt, China, and Europe.

Good egg-laying breeds of chicken are Leghorns, Minorcas, and Anconas; varieties most suitable for eating are Dorkings, Australorps, Brahmas, and Cornish; those useful for both purposes are Orpingtons, Rhode Island Reds, Wyandottes, Plymouth Rocks, and Jersey White Giants. Most farm poultry are hybrids, selectively crossbred for certain characteristics, including feathers and down.

factory farming Since World War II, the development of battery-produced eggs and the intensive breeding of broiler fowls and turkeys has roused a public outcry against 'factory' methods of farming. The birds are often kept constantly in small cages, have their beaks and claws removed to prevent them from pecking their neighbours, and are given feed containing growth hormones and antibacterial drugs, which eventually make their way up the food chain to humans. Factory farming has led to a growing interest in deep-litter and free-range systems, although these account for only a small percentage of total production.

pound imperial unit (abbreviation lb) of mass. The commonly used avoirdupois pound, also called the imperial standard pound (7,000 grains/0.45 kg), differs from the pound troy (5,760 grains/0.37 kg), which is used for weighing precious metals. It derives from the Roman *libra*, which weighed 0.327 kg.

pound British standard monetary unit, issued as a gold sovereign before 1914, as a note 1914–83, and as a circular yellow metal-alloy coin from 1983. The pound is also the name given to the unit of currency in Egypt, Lebanon, Malta, Sudan, and Syria.

The edge inscriptions on the pound coin are: 1983 *Decus et tutamen* 'An ornament and a safeguard'; 1984 (Scottish) *Nemo me impune lacessit* 'No one injures me with impunity'; 1985 (Welsh) *Pleidiol wyf i'm gwlad* 'True am I to my country', from the national anthem.

The green pound is the European Union exchange rate for conversion of EU farm prices to sterling.

Pound Ezra Loomis 1885–1972. US poet and cultural critic. He is regarded as one of the most important figures of 20th-century literature, and his work revolutionized modern poetry. His *Personae* and *Exultations* 1909 established and promoted the principles of ◊Imagism, and influenced numerous poets, including T S ◊Eliot. His largest work was his series of *Cantos* 1925–69 (intended to number 100),

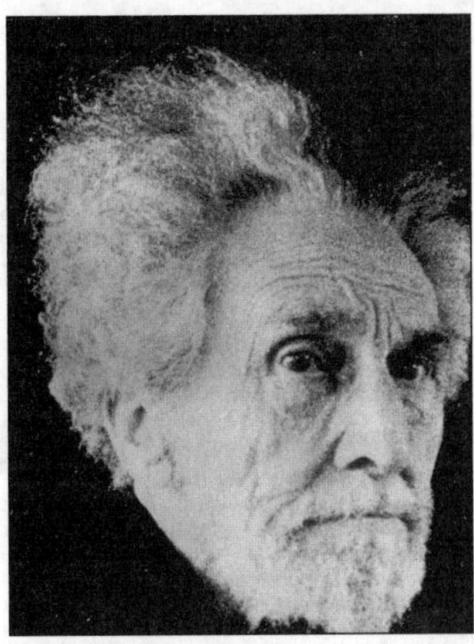

Pound US poet, translator, and critic Ezra Pound. One of the major figures of Modernism, Pound influenced T S Eliot, W B Yeats, James Joyce, William Carlos Williams, Wyndham Lewis, and others, and played a leading role in the development of imagism and Vorticism. His standing suffered after World War II because of his anti-Semitism and his support for Italian Fascism. *Topham*

a highly complex, eclectic collage, which sought to create a unifying, modern cultural tradition.

Born in Idaho, Pound was educated at Pennsylvania University and settled in Europe 1907. He lived in London 1909–21 and then moved to Paris 1921–25, where he became a friend of the writers Gertrude Stein and Ernest Hemingway. He then settled in Rapallo, Italy. His anti-Semitism and sympathy with the fascist dictator Mussolini led him to broadcast from Italy in World War II, and he was arrested by US troops 1945. Found unfit to stand trial, he was confined in a mental hospital until 1958.

poundal imperial unit (abbreviation pdl) of force, now replaced in the SI system by the ◊newton. One poundal equals 0.1383 newtons.

It is defined as the force necessary to accelerate a mass of one pound by one foot per second per second.

Poussin Nicolas 1594–1665. French painter. He was the foremost exponent of 17th-century Baroque Classicism. He painted several major religious works, but is best known for his mythological and literary scenes executed in an austere Classical style, for example, *Et in Arcadia Ego* 1638–39 (Louvre, Paris). His style had a profound effect on the development of French art.

Poussin spent most of his working life in Rome, though he was briefly court painter to Louis XIII of France 1640–43. Despite his absence, he managed to win a high reputation in France, his style eventually becoming the official style of the French Academy under Charles Le Brun (1619–1690). The restrained Classicism of this style, which in part reflects a contemporary interest in Stoic philosophy, has parallels in the Classical theatre of Corneille and Racine.

Among his major works are *The Inspiration of the Poet* 1636 (Louvre, Paris); *Bacchanalian Festival*, painted for Richelieu before 1641 (National Gallery, London); *The Golden Calf*, before 1634 (National Gallery, London); and *The Entombment* (National Gallery of Ireland). A superb self-portrait at the age of 56 is in the Louvre.

poverty condition where the basic needs of human beings (shelter, food, and clothing) are not being met. Over one-fifth of the world's population was living in extreme poverty 1995, of which around 70% were women. Nearly 13.5 million children under five die each year from poverty-related illness (measles, diarrhoea, malaria, pneumonia, and ◊malnutrition). There are different definitions of the standard of living considered to be the minimum adequate level (known as the poverty level). The European Union (EU) definition of poverty is an income of less than half the EU average (£150 a week in 1993). By this definition, there were 50 million poor in the EU 1993.

Absolute poverty, where people lack the necessary food, clothing, or shelter to survive, can be distinguished from relative poverty, which has been defined as the inability of a citizen to participate fully in economic terms in the society in which he or she lives. In many countries, absolute poverty is common and persistent, being reflected in poor nutrition, short life expectancy, and high levels of infant mortality. It may result from a country's complete lack of resources, or from inequitable distribution of wealth.

During the 1980s, the world's poorest 20% of people saw their share of global income reduced from 1.7% to 1.4%. In 1994, at least 1.1 billion people were subsisting on a cash income of less than $1 a day. Their total assets came to no more than $400 billion, compared with the $200 billion assets of the world's 160 billionaires.

poverty cycle set of factors or events by which poverty, once started, is likely to continue unless there is outside intervention. Once an area or a person has become poor, this tends to lead to other disadvantages, which may in turn result in further poverty. The situation is often found in inner city areas and shanty towns. Applied to countries, the poverty cycle is often called the development trap.

poverty trap situation where a person reduces his or her net income by taking a job, or gaining a higher wage, which disqualifies him/her from claiming social security benefits or raises his/her tax liability.

powder metallurgy method of shaping heat-resistant metals such as tungsten. Metal is pressed into a mould in powdered form and then sintered (heated to very high temperatures).

Powell Adam Clayton, Jr 1908–1972. US Democratic politician. A leader of New York's black community, he was elected to the city council 1941. He was appointed to the US Congress 1944, and later became chair of the House Education and Labor Committee. Following charges of corruption, he was denied his seat in Congress 1967. Re-elected 1968, he won back his seniority by a 1969 decision of the US Supreme Court.

Powell Anthony Dymoke 1905– . English novelist and critic. He wrote the series of 12 volumes *A Dance to the Music of Time* 1951–75 that begins shortly after World War I and chronicles a period of 50 years in the lives of Nicholas Jenkins and his circle of upper-class friends.

Powell Colin (Luther) 1937– . US general, chair of the Joint Chiefs of Staff from 1989–93 and, as such, responsible for the overall administration of the Allied forces in Saudi Arabia during the ◊Gulf War 1991. A Vietnam War veteran, he first worked in government 1972 and was national security adviser 1987–89.

Powell (John) Enoch 1912–1998. British Conservative politician. He was minister of health 1960–63, and contested the party leadership 1965. In 1968 he made a speech against immigration that led to his dismissal from the shadow cabinet. He resigned from the party 1974, and was Official Unionist Party member for South Down, Northern Ireland 1974–87.

Powell Michael Latham 1905–1990. English film director and producer. Some of his most memorable films were made in collaboration with Hungarian screenwriter Emeric ◊Pressburger.

They produced a succession of ambitious and richly imaginative films, including *A Matter of Life and Death* 1946, *Black Narcissus* 1947, and *The Red Shoes* 1948. Powell's films range from *The Life and Death of Colonel Blimp* 1943 to the opera movie *The Tales of Hoffman* 1951, but after the partnership with Pressburger was amicably dissolved, he went on to make generally less rewarding films. The most distinctive was the voyeuristic horror story *Peeping Tom* 1960.

Powell Mike 1963– . US long jumper who in 1991 broke US athlete Bob Beamon's world long-jump record of 8.90 m (which had stood since 1968) with a leap of 8.95 m. At the same time, he dealt Carl Lewis his first long-jump defeat since 1981. Powell also topped the world long-jump rankings in 1990.

Powell William 1892–1984. US film actor. He costarred with Myrna Loy in the *Thin Man* series 1934–1947. He also played suave leading roles in *My Man Godfrey* 1936, *Life with Father* 1947, and *Mister Roberts* 1955. He retired 1955.

power in mathematics, that which is represented by an ◊exponent or index, denoted by a superior small numeral. A number or symbol raised to the power of 2 – that is, multiplied by itself – is said to be squared (for example, 3^2, x^2), and when raised to the power of 3, it is said to be cubed (for example, 2^3, y^3).

power in optics, a measure of the amount by which a lens will deviate light rays. A powerful converging lens will converge parallel rays steeply, bringing them to a focus at a short distance from the lens. The unit of power is the dioptre, which is equal to the reciprocal of focal length in metres. By convention, the power of a converging (or convex) lens is positive and that of a diverging (or concave) lens negative.

power in physics, the rate of doing work or consuming energy. It is measured in watts (joules per second) or other units of work per unit time. If the work done or energy consumed is W joules and the time taken is t seconds, then the power P is given by the formula:

$$P = W/t$$

'One of the pleasures of middle age is to find out that one was right, and that one was much righter than one knew at say 17 or 23.'

Ezra Pound
ABC of Reading

'One of the worst things about life is not how nasty the nasty people are. You know that already. It is how nasty the nice people can be.'

Anthony Powell
A Dance to the Music of Time: The Kindly Ones

Poussin *The Birth of Venus* by the French artist Nicolas Poussin (Philadelphia Museum of Art). Poussin's Classicism – which dominated French painting throughout the 17th century – was an attempt to emulate the balance and harmony of late Renaissance art. A work such as this one, with its flying cupids and rearing horses, shows him at his most flamboyant. *Corbis*

power of attorney in law, legal authority to act on behalf of another, for a specific transaction, or for a particular period.

power station building where electrical energy is generated from a fuel or from another form of energy. Fuels used include fossil fuels such as coal, gas, and oil, and the nuclear fuel uranium. Renewable sources of energy include gravitational potential energy (energy possessed by an object when it is placed in a position from which, if it were free to do so, it would fall under the influence of gravity), used to produce ◊hydroelectric power; and ◊wind power.

The energy supply is used to turn ◊turbines either directly by means of water or wind pressure, or indirectly by steam pressure, steam being generated by burning fossil fuels or from the heat released by the fission of uranium nuclei. The turbines in their turn spin alternators, which generate electricity at very high voltage.

The world's largest power station is Turukhansk, on the Lower Tunguska river, Russia, with a capacity of 20,000 megawatts.

Powys unitary authority of Wales created 1996; former region of Wales 1974–96 *(see United Kingdom map).*

Powys John Cowper 1872–1963. English novelist. His mystic and erotic books include *Wolf Solent* 1929 and *A Glastonbury Romance* 1933; *Owen Glendower* 1940 is the most successful of his historical novels. He was one of six brothers, including ***Theodore Francis Powys*** (1875–1953) who is best known for the novel *Mr Weston's Good Wine* 1927, and ***Llewelyn Powys (1884–1939)*** who wrote essays, novels, and autobiographical works.

Poznań (German ***Posen***) industrial city (machinery, aircraft, beer) in W Poland; population (1993) 590,000. Founded 970, it was settled by German immigrants 1253 and passed to Prussia 1793; it was restored to Poland 1919.

PPP abbreviation for ◊***purchasing-power parity***.

PPP abbreviation for ***Point-to-Point Protocol***. In computing, one of two standard methods for connecting a computer to the Internet via a modem and line. PPP is faster and more versatile than its counterpart, SLIP (serial line Internet protocol), and performs its own error correction.

Prado (Real Museo de Pintura del Prado) Spanish art gallery containing the national collection of pictures. The building was designed as a natural history museum and begun 1785; it became an art gallery 1818 under Ferdinand VII.

It ranks as one of the world's greatest art collections and it is unquestionably the greatest collection of Spanish masters, Velázquez (over 60 works), El Greco, Zurbarán, Ribera, Murillo, and Goya being superbly represented.

The Spanish connection with the Netherlands helps to account for the especial richness of the Flemish School. It contains the greatest group of works by Bosch, whose strange genius was favoured by Philip II, some outstanding works by Pieter Brueghel, and over 60 works by Rubens. It also has a fine Adoration of the Magi by Memlinc, and Van der Weyden's *Descent from the Cross*.

The attachment of the Hapsburgs to Venetian art is evidenced by the wealth of paintings by Titian, Tintoretto, and Veronese. There are also paintings by Raphael, Rembrandt, Poussin, Claude, Dürer, Holbein, and Mor.

praetor in ancient Rome, a magistrate, elected annually, who assisted the ◊consuls (the chief magistrates) and presided over the civil courts. After a year in office, a praetor would act as a provincial governor for a further year.

pragmatism philosophical tradition that interprets truth in terms of the practical effects of what is believed and, in particular, the usefulness of these effects. The US philosopher Charles ◊Peirce is often accounted the founder of pragmatism; it was further advanced by William James.

Prague (Czech ***Praha***) city and capital of the Czech Republic on the river Vltava; population (1993) 1,217,300. Industries include cars, aircraft, chemicals, paper and printing, clothing, brewing, and food processing. It was the capital of Czechoslovakia 1918–93.

features Charles University 1348; Gothic cathedral of St Vitus; Prague castle (Prásky-Hrad); Malá Strana, with 17th- and 18th-century mansions; Old Town.

history

14th century Prague became important during the reign of Charles IV, king of Bohemia and Moravia, and Holy Roman Emperor; he established the university and laid out the New Town.

15th century Hussite wars held back development.

1620 Battle of the White Mountain took place near Prague; the Czechs were defeated, and were ruled by the Habsburgs until 1918.

1918 Czechoslovakia created; Prague became national capital.

1939 city occupied by Nazis.

1968 occupation by Soviet troops followed 'Prague Spring'.

1989 protests in Prague led to fall of Communist regime.

Prague Spring the 1968 programme of liberalization, begun under a new Communist Party leader in Czechoslovakia. In Aug 1968 Soviet tanks invaded Czechoslovakia and entered the capital Prague to put down the liberalization movement initiated by the prime minister Alexander Dubček, who had earlier sought to assure the Soviets that his planned reforms would not threaten socialism. Dubček was arrested but released soon afterwards. Most of the Prague Spring reforms were reversed.

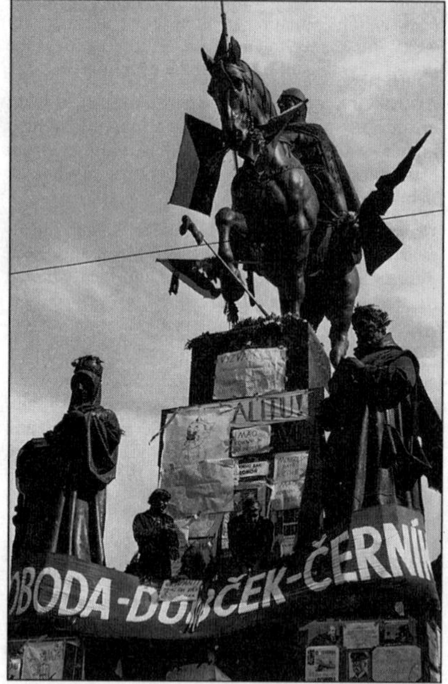

Prague Spring The attempts to liberalize the Czech regime in the spring of 1968, known as the Prague Spring, were spearheaded by Alexander Dubček, the General Secretary of the Communist Party. Here, student banners proclaim support for him. The reform movement was crushed on 20 Aug 1968, however, when Warsaw Pact forces invaded the country and restored hard-line Communism. *Corbis*

Praia port and capital of the Republic of Cape Verde, on the island of São Tiago (Santiago); population (1990) 61,700. Industries include fishing and shipping.

prairie the central North American plain, formerly grass-covered, extending over most of the region between the Rocky Mountains on the W and the Great Lakes and Ohio River on the E.

prairie dog any of the North American genus *Cynomys* of burrowing rodents in the squirrel family (Sciuridae). They grow to 30 cm/12 in, plus a short 8 cm/3 in tail. Their 'towns' can contain up to several thousand individuals. Their barking cry has given them their name. Persecution by ranchers has brought most of the five species close to extinction.

The prairie dog is also another term for the ◊marmot, a large burrowing rodent.

praise poem genre of traditional African literature which has influenced modern African poetry. Oral poets, particularly among southern African peoples such as the Xhosa, Tswana, Zulu, Sotho, and Shona, would recite poems in praise of chiefs, or prominent figures such as the Zulu hero Shaka, at formal gatherings. Such poems were often valued more for content than for execution. Many collections of transcripts have now been published, particularly since the 1960s.

Prakrit general name for the ancient Indo-European dialects of N India, contrasted with the sacred classical language Sanskrit. The word is itself Sanskrit, meaning 'natural', as opposed to *Sanskrit*, which means 'perfected'. The Prakrits are considered to be the ancestors of such modern N Indian languages as Hindi, Punjabi, and Bengali.

Prasad Rajendra 1884–1963. Indian politician. He was national president of the Indian National Congress several times between 1934 and 1948 and India's first president after independence 1950–62.

Prasad was trained as a lawyer, and was a loyal follower of Mahatma ◊Gandhi.

praseodymium (Greek *praseo* 'leek-green' + *dymium*) silver-white, malleable, metallic element of the ◊lanthanide series, symbol Pr, atomic number 59, relative atomic mass 140.907. It occurs in nature in the minerals monzanite and bastnaesite, and its green salts are used to colour glass and ceramics. It was named in 1885 by Austrian chemist Carl von Welsbach (1858–1929).

He fractionated it from dydymium (originally thought to be an element but actually a mixture of rare-earth metals consisting largely of neodymium, praseodymium, and cerium), and named it for its green salts and spectroscopic line.

prawn any of various ◊shrimps of the suborder Natantia ('swimming'), of the crustacean order Decapoda, as contrasted with lobsters and crayfishes, which are able to 'walk'. Species called prawns are generally larger than species called shrimps.

The common prawn *Leander serratus*, of temperate seas has a long saw-edged spike or rostrum just in front of its eyes, and antennae much longer than its body length. It is pinkish-orange when cooked. The larger Norway lobster or Dublin Bay prawn *Nephrops norwegicus* is sold as 'scampi'.

Praxiteles lived mid-4th century BC. Greek sculptor. His *Aphrodite of Cnidus* about 350 BC is thought to have initiated the tradition of life-size free-standing female nudes in Greek sculpture. It was destroyed by fire AD 475, but a Roman copy exists in the Vatican.

Praxiteles was active in Athens. He worked in a softer, more poetic style than his predecessors of the 5th century BC. His *Hermes*, a major work of the time, was found in Olympia 1877.

Precambrian in geology, the time from the formation of Earth (4.6 billion years ago) up to 570 million years ago. Its boundary with the succeeding Cambrian period marks the time when animals first developed hard outer parts (exoskeletons) and so left abundant fossil remains. Comprising about 85% of geological time, it is divided into two periods: the Archaean, in which no life existed, and the Proterozoic, in which there was life in some form.

precession slow wobble of the Earth on its axis, like that of a spinning top. The gravitational pulls of the Sun and Moon on the Earth's equatorial bulge cause the Earth's axis to trace out a circle on the sky every 25,800 years. The position of the celestial poles (see ◊celestial sphere) is constantly changing owing to precession, as are the positions of the equinoxes (the points at which the celestial equator intersects the Sun's path around the sky). The precession of the equinoxes means that there is a gradual westward drift in the ecliptic – the path that the Sun appears to follow – and in the coordinates of objects on the celestial sphere.

This is why the dates of the astrological signs of the zodiac no longer correspond to the times of year when the Sun actually passes through the constellations. For example, the Sun passes through Leo from mid-Aug to mid-Sept, but the astrological dates for Leo are between about 23 July and 22 Aug.

Precession also occurs in other planets. Uranus has the Solar System's fastest known precession (264 days) determined 1995.

precipitation in chemistry, the formation of an insoluble solid in a liquid as a result of a reaction within the liquid between two or more soluble substances. If the solid settles, it forms a precipitate; if the particles of solid are very small, they will remain in suspension, forming a colloidal precipitate (see ◊colloid).

precipitation in meteorology, water that falls to the Earth from the atmosphere. It includes rain, snow, sleet, hail, dew, and frost.

pre-Columbian architecture the architecture of the Central and South American civilizations that existed prior to the arrival of European colonizers in the 16th century.
Central American architecture Little evidence remains of pre-Mayan buildings, but the distinctive form of the pyramid – the focus of pre-Columbian ceremonial architecture – was in evidence by the 4th century BC, for example, at Cuicuilco, and well developed by AD 100, as in the Pyramid of the Sun at Teotihuacán, Mexico. Mesoamerican pyramids were different in form and function to those of the Egyptians. Instead of tombs, they were sites for ritual, usually topped by altars and with steeply sloping, stepped sides and rectangular or circular planforms. The Maya civilization, AD 300–900, left many imposing monuments, significant for their regular, symmetric form, stylized external decoration, and use of corbel arches and internal vaulting. Mayan sites include Chichén Itzá, Mexico, and Tikal, Guatemala. The Totonac, 5th–11th centuries, and Zapotec, 6th–7th centuries, were active during the latter part of the Mayan era and left their own monuments at Tajin and Monte Alban respectively. Arriving from the north in the 10th century, the Toltecs, 10th–12th centuries, took over Chichén Itzá and added many of their own structures, including the nine-tiered pyramid, the Castillo. At Tula, thought to be the Toltec capital, they employed free-standing columns – huge, sculpted figures of warriors and hunters – to support the roof of the temple of the god Quetzalcoatl. The architecture of the Aztecs, 14th–16th centuries, was influenced by Toltec culture but the sculpture that surrounded it had a more fluid and less stylized form. Their capital, Tenochtitlán, was levelled by the Spanish and is now the site of Mexico City, but they left many important buildings such as the double pyramid of Tenayuca, about 1450–1500. There was also a Mixtec civilization that evolved independently of the Aztecs. Few of their buildings remain but the Palace of the Columns at Mitla, AD 1000, is notable for the geometric patterns that cover its interior and exterior walls.
South American architecture Some monuments remain that predate Inca rule, such as the Temple of the Sun at Moche, about 200–600, a pyramidal stepped structure built by the Chavín peoples, and the Gateway of the Sun, Tiahuanaco, about 500–700, a richly carved monolithic structure. Between 1300–1400, a number of local cultures developed including those centred around Chan Chan and Cajamarquilla, towns laid out on a complex grid system composed of streets, pyramids, and reservoirs. The Inca civilization was formed about 1440 and came to dominate the region. Their architecture is best known for its use of huge masonry, laid without cement. The ancient capital of ◊Cuzco, 1200 onwards, has examples of this, as has the spectacularly sited ◊Machu Picchu, about 1500, high in the Andes. This late Inca city follows the typical pattern of the culture: a Sun Temple and palace situated on either side of a central plaza, a water system servicing baths and fountains, and terraced fields for step-cultivation descending the mountainside.

pre-Columbian art the art of the Central and South American civilizations that existed prior to the arrival of European colonizers in the 16th century.
Central American art The art of the Mesoamerican and Mexican cultures up to the Spanish conquest. The Olmec civilization, about 1200–600 BC, is characterized by jade figurines and heavy featured, colossal heads, resting mysteriously in the landscape. During the Classic Period, about AD 200–900, the dominant culture was Mayan, AD 300–900, of Yucatan, southern Mexico, and Guatemala. Its sculpture, mostly in relief, combined glyphs and stylized figures and was used to decorate architecture, such as the pyramid temple of Chichén Itzá; murals dating from about AD 750 were discovered when the city of Bonampak was excavated 1946. The Mayans were succeeded by more warlike, brutal societies governed by deities which demanded human sacrifice. The Toltecs, 10th–12th centuries, made colossal, blocklike sculptures, for example those employed as free-standing columns at Tula, Mexico. The Mixtecs developed a style of painting called 'Mixtec-Puebla', as seen in their murals and manuscripts ('codices'), in which all available space is covered by flat figures in geometric designs. The Aztec culture in Mexico produced some dramatically expressive work, such as the decorated skulls of captives and stone sculpture, a good example of which is *Tlazolteotl* (Woods Bliss Collection, Washington), a goddess in childbirth, AD 1300–1500.
South American art The art of the indigenous peoples of South America. The Chavín culture flourished in the Andean area (modern-day Peru) about 1000 BC, producing small sculpture and pottery, often human in form but with animal attributes, such as bird feet, reptilian eyes, or feline fangs. The Andean Mochicha peoples, about 100 BC–AD 700, were among the best artisans of the New World, producing delightful portrait vases (Moche ware), which, while realistic, are steeped in religious references, the significance of which is lost to us. They were also goldsmiths and weavers of outstanding talent. The short-lived Inca culture, about AD 1400–1580, of Peru and Bolivia, sculpted animal and human figurines, but is best known for its architecture at Andean sites such as Cuzco and Machu Picchu (see ◊pre-Columbian architecture).

predestination in Christian theology, the doctrine asserting that God has determined all events beforehand, including the ultimate salvation or damnation of the individual human soul. The concept of predestination is also found in Islam.

pre-eclampsia or *toxaemia of pregnancy* potentially serious condition developing in the third trimester and marked by high blood pressure and fluid retention. Arising from unknown causes, it disappears when pregnancy is over. It may progress to ◊eclampsia if untreated.

Preferential Trade Area for Eastern and Southern Africa (PTA) organization established 1981 with the object of increasing economic and commercial cooperation between member states, harmonizing tariffs, and reducing trade barriers, with the eventual aim of creating a common market. Members include (1997) Burundi, Comoros, Djibouti, Ethiopia, Kenya, Lesotho, Malawi, Mauritius, Rwanda, Somalia, Swaziland, Tanzania, Uganda, Zambia, and Zimbabwe. A free trade area, the Common Market for Eastern and Southern Africa (COMESA) was established by the PTA Nov 1993. The headquarters of the PTA are in Lusaka, Zambia.

pregnancy in humans, the period during which an embryo grows within the womb. It begins at conception and ends at birth, and the normal length is 40 weeks. Menstruation usually stops on conception. About one in five pregnancies fails, but most of these failures occur very early on, so the woman may notice only that her period is late. After the second month, the breasts become tense and tender, and the areas round the nipples become darker. Enlargement of the uterus can be felt at about the end of the third month, and thereafter the abdomen enlarges progressively. Foetal movement can be felt at about 18 weeks; a heart-beat may be heard during the sixth month. Pregnancy in animals is called ◊gestation.
complications Occasionally the fertilized egg implants not in the womb but in the ◊Fallopian tube (the tube between the ovary and the uterus), leading to an ectopic ('out of place') pregnancy. This will cause the woman severe abdominal pain and vaginal bleeding. If the growing fetus ruptures the tube, life-threatening shock may ensue. Toxaemia is characterized by rising blood pressure, and if untreated, can result in convulsions leading to coma.

According to 1996 WHO figures, 585,000 women die annually from pregnancy-related causes; 99% of these deaths occur in developing countries. The highest rate of maternal death is in Sierra Leone with 1,800 deaths per 100,000 live births, compared with an average of 27 for industrialized countries.

prehistoric art art that predates written records. The history of the fine arts, painting, engraving, and sculpture begins around 40,000 BC in the Palaeolithic period, or Old Stone Age. The oldest known rock engravings are in Australia, but within the next 30,000 years art occurs on every continent. The earliest surviving artefacts in Europe date from approximately 30,000 to 10,000 BC, a period of hunter-gatherer cultures. Extant small sculptures are generally of fecund female nudes and relate to the cult of the Mother Goddess, for example the *Willendorf Venus* (Kunsthistorisches Museum, Vienna) about 21,000 BC, which is carved from a small stone. The murals of the caves of ◊Lascaux, France, and ◊Altamira, Spain, depict animals such as bison, horses, and deer, as well as a few human figures. Executed in earth colours akin to ◊pastel technique, the murals are of a very high order and appear to have been done in near-impossible conditions, perhaps as a rite of initiation.

During the Neolithic period or New Stone Age 10,000–2,000 BC settled communities were established, which led to a greater technical and aesthetic sophistication in tools, ceramic vessels, jewellery, and human and animal figures. Human figures appear more often in wall paintings, and are skilfully composed into groups. The period 4,000–2,000 BC saw the erection of the great megalithic monuments, such as those at Carnac, France, and Stonehenge, England, and the production of ceramic pots and figurines with decorative elements that were later to be developed in the art of the Celts.

prehistoric life the diverse organisms that inhabited Earth from the origin of life about 3.5 billion years ago to the time when humans began to keep written records, about 3500 BC. During the

'There's a divinity that shapes our ends, / Rough-hew them how we will.'

On **PREDESTINATION**
William Shakespeare
Hamlet

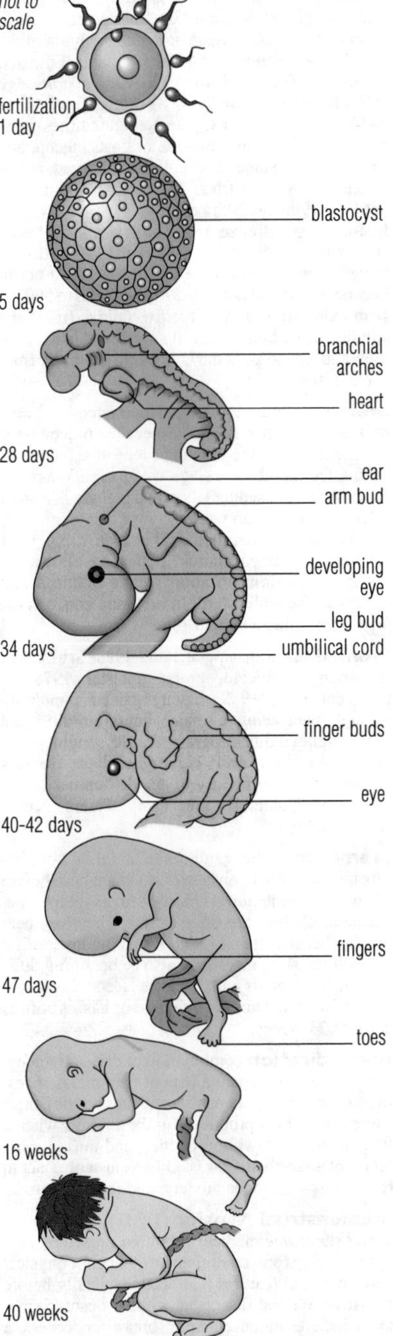

pregnancy The development of a human embryo. Division of the fertilized egg, or ovum, begins within hours of conception. Within a week a ball of cells – a blastocyst – has developed. After the third week, the embryo has changed from a mass of cells into a recognizable shape. At four weeks, the embryo is 3 mm/0.1 in long, with a large bulge for the heart and small pits for the ears. At six weeks, the embryo is 1.5 cm/0.6 in with a pulsating heart and ear flaps. At the eighth week, the embryo is 2.5 cm/1 in long and recognizably human, with eyelids, small fingers, and toes. From the end of the second month, the embryo is almost fully formed and further development is mainly by growth. After this stage, the embryo is termed a fetus.

course of evolution, new forms of life developed and many other forms, such as the dinosaurs, became extinct. Prehistoric life evolved over this vast timespan from simple bacteria-like cells in the oceans to algae and protozoans and complex multicellular forms such as worms, molluscs, crustaceans, fishes, insects, land plants, amphibians, reptiles, birds, and mammals. On a geological timescale human beings evolved relatively recently, about 4 million years ago, although the exact dating is a matter of some debate. See also ◊geological time.

prehistory human cultures before the use of writing. A classification system, the Three Age system, was devised 1816 by Danish archaeologist Christian Thomsen, based on the predominant materials used by early humans for tools and weapons: ◊Stone Age, ◊Bronze Age, ◊Iron Age. Knowledge of prehistory has been greatly advanced by the increase in data resulting from improved excavation, retrieval, analysis, and dating techniques.
Stone Age Stone was predominant for tools and weapons. The Stone Age is divided into: ***Old Stone Age*** (Palaeolithic) 3,500,000–8500 BC. Stone and bone tools were chipped into shape by early humans, or hominids, from Africa, Asia, the Middle East, and Europe as well as later Neanderthal and Cro-Magnon people; the only domesticated animals were dogs. Some Asians crossed the Bering land bridge to inhabit the Americas. Rock paintings were produced by 20,000 years ago in many parts of the world; for example, Altamira, Spain; Lascaux, France; S Africa; and Australia; ***Middle Stone Age*** (Mesolithic) and ***New Stone Age*** (Neolithic). Stone and bone tools were used. In Neolithic times, agriculture and the domestication of goats, sheep, and cattle began. Stone Age cultures survived in the Americas, Asia, Africa, Oceania, and Australia until the 19th and 20th centuries.
Bronze Age Bronze tools and weapons began approximately 5000 BC in the Far East, and continued in the Middle East until about 1200 BC; in Europe this period lasted from about 2000 to 500 BC.
Iron Age Iron was hardened (alloyed) by the addition of carbon, so that it superseded bronze for tools and weapons; in the Old World generally from about 1000 BC.

prelude in music, a composition intended as the preface to further music, especially preceding a ◊fugue, forming the opening piece of a ◊suite, or setting the mood for a stage work, as in Wagner's *Lohengrin*. As used by Chopin, a prelude is a short self-contained piano work.

A prelude is often rhetorical in style, mixing fast runs and sustained chords. It thereby allows the musicians to form an aural picture of the sound quality of the auditorium. In orchestra concerts the ◊overture fulfils a similar role.

Premadasa Ranasinghe 1924–1993. Sri Lankan right-wing politician, prime minister 1978–88, president from 1988, having gained popularity through overseeing a major house-building and poverty-alleviation programme. He sought peace talks with the Tamil Tiger guerrillas. He was assassinated in office by a suicide bomber in the centre of Colombo; the Tamil Tigers denied responsibility.

prematurity the condition of an infant born before the full term. In obstetrics, an infant born before 37 weeks' gestation is described as premature. Premature babies are often at risk. They lose heat quickly because they lack an insulating layer of fat beneath the skin; there may also be breathing difficulties. In hospitals with advanced technology, specialized neonatal units can save some babies born as early as 23 weeks.

premedication combination of drugs given before surgery to prepare a patient for general anaesthesia. One component (an anticholinergic) dries excess secretions produced by the airways when a tube is passed down the trachea, and during inhalation of anaesthetic gases. Other substances act to relax muscles, reduce anxiety, and relieve pain.

premenstrual tension (PMT) or ***premenstrual syndrome*** medical condition caused by hormone changes and comprising a number of physical and emotional features that occur cyclically before menstruation and disappear with its onset. Symptoms include mood changes, breast tenderness, a feeling of bloatedness, and headache.

Preminger Otto Ludwig 1906–1986. Austrian-born US film producer, director, and actor. His films include *Margin for Error* 1942, *Laura* 1944, *The Moon Is Blue* 1953, *The Man with the Golden Arm* 1955, *Anatomy of a Murder* 1959, *Advise and Consent* 1962, *Rosebud* 1974, and *The Human Factor* 1980. His films are characterized by an intricate technique of storytelling and a masterly use of the wide screen and the travelling camera.

Premium Savings Bond British government bond introduced 1956 whose purchaser is eligible for a prize-winning lottery. The prize money is funded from interest payable on the bond.

premolar in mammals, one of the large teeth toward the back of the mouth. In herbivores they are adapted for grinding. In carnivores they may be carnassials. Premolars are present in milk ◊dentition as well as permanent dentition.

Premonstratensian Roman Catholic monastic order founded 1120 by St Norbert (c. 1080–1134), a German bishop, at Prémontré, N France. Members were known as White Canons.

preparatory school fee-paying independent school. In the UK, it is a junior school that prepares children for entry to a senior school at about age 13. In the USA, it is a school that prepares students for university entrance at about age 18.

Pre-Raphaelite Brotherhood (PRB) group of British painters 1848–53; Dante Gabriel Rossetti, John Everett Millais, and Holman Hunt were founding members. They aimed to paint serious subjects, to study nature closely, and to shun the influence of the styles of painters after Raphael. Their subjects were mainly biblical and literary, painted with obsessive naturalism and attention to detail. Artists associated with the group include Edward Burne-Jones and William Morris.

A reaction against the triviality of early Victorian academic art, the Pre-Raphaelite Brotherhood was based partly on Ruskin's doctrine of 'truth to nature', and partly on the idea of return to pre-Renaissance ideals. The Brotherhood (PRB) did not last long, but Pre-Raphaelitism in a more extended sense had immense influence. Pre-Raphaelite disciples who produced notable works are W H Deverell, W L Windus, John Brett, W S Burton, and Robert Martineau. A second development, stimulated by Ruskin and Rossetti, was towards the revival of handicraft and the arts of design. It was first suggested by the abortive effort to decorate the Oxford Union with 'frescoes' 1857, in which Rossetti was assisted by William Morris, Burne-Jones, and others. The firm subsequently founded by Morris carried Pre-Raphaelite art into many fields of useful design.

presbyopia vision defect, an increasing inability with advancing age to focus on near objects. It is caused by thickening and loss of elasticity in the lens, which is no longer able to relax to the near-spherical shape required for near vision.

Presbyterianism system of Christian Protestant church government, expounded during the Reformation by John Calvin, which gives its name to the established Church of Scotland, and is also practised in England, Wales, Ireland, Switzerland, North America, and elsewhere. There is no compulsory form of worship and each congregation is governed by presbyters or elders (clerical or lay), who are of equal rank. Congregations are grouped in presbyteries, synods, and general assemblies.

Prescott John Leslie 1938– . British Labour Party politician, deputy leader from 1994, deputy prime minister as well as secretary for transport, environment, and the regions from 1997.

He was member of parliament for Kingston-on-Hull (East) 1970–83 and MP for Hull East from 1983. In 1975, he became a member of the European Parliament, despite being opposed to Britain's membership of the European Community.

prescription in medicine, an order written in a recognized form by a practitioner of medicine, dentistry, or veterinary surgery to a pharmacist for a preparation of medications to be used in treatment.

By tradition it used to be written in Latin, except for the directions addressed to the patient. It consists of (1) the superscription *recipe* ('take'), contracted to Rx; (2) the inscription or body, containing the names and quantities of the drugs to be dispensed; (3) the subscription, or directions to the pharmacist; (4) the signature, followed by directions to the patient; and (5) the patient's name, the date, and the practitioner's name.

preservative substance (◊additive) added to a food in order to inhibit the growth of bacteria, yeasts, moulds, and other microorganisms, and therefore extend its shelf life. The term sometimes refers to ◊anti-oxidants (substances added to oils and fats to prevent their becoming rancid) as well. All preservatives are potentially damaging to health if eaten in sufficient quantity. Both the amount used, and the foods in which they can be used, are restricted by law.

Alternatives to preservatives include faster turnover of food stocks, refrigeration, better hygiene in preparation, sterilization, and pasteurization (see ◊food technology).

preserve any food, usually fruit, that has been boiled with sugar, then bottled or canned; for example, jam, marmalade, lemon curd, glacé cherries, and mincemeat. Making preserves is an old method of storing fruit for long periods of time.

Jam is a conserve of fruit boiled with sugar; marmalade is jam made from citrus fruits; lemon-curd is made of lemons with eggs and butter; and mincemeat contains raisins, apples, currants, suet, and spices.

president in government, the usual title of the head of state in a republic; the power of the office may range from the equivalent of a constitutional monarch to the actual head of the government. For presidents of the USA, see ◊United States of America.

Presidential Medal of Freedom highest peacetime civilian award in the USA, instituted 1963, conferred annually on Independence Day by the president on those making significant contributions to the 'quality of American life'. It replaced the Medal of Freedom awarded from 1945 for acts and service aiding US security.

Presley Elvis Aron 1935–1977. US singer and guitarist, the most influential performer of the rock-and-roll era. With his recordings for Sun Records in Memphis, Tennessee, 1954–55 and early hits such as 'Heartbreak Hotel', 'Hound Dog', and 'Love Me Tender', all 1956, he created an individual vocal style, influenced by Southern blues, gospel music, country music, and rhythm and blues. His records continued to sell in their millions into the 1990s.

Presley was born in Tupelo, Mississippi. His first records were regional hits in the South, and he became a nationwide star 1956, Sun having sold his recording contract to RCA at the instigation of his

Presley US singer and film star Elvis Presley in 1957. He was then at the height of his success and still a symbol of rebellious youth. His image was remade in clean-cut patriotic mode in later films such as *GI Blues* 1960. *Topham*

new manager, the self-styled Colonel Tom Parker (1909–), a former carnival huckster. Of the four films Presley made in the 1950s, *Loving You* 1957 and *Jailhouse Rock* 1957 offer glimpses of the electrifying stage performer he then was. After his army service 1958–60, the album *Elvis Is Back* 1960 and some gospel-music recordings made that year were outstanding, but from then on his work deteriorated quickly. Parker pushed him into a demeaning career divided between Hollywood and Las Vegas. By the time of his death, Presley had long been a caricature. His early contribution to rock music was, however, inestimable, and his Memphis home, Graceland, draws millions of visitors each year.

Pressburger Emeric 1902–1988. Hungarian film producer, screenwriter, and director. He was known for his partnership with Michael ◊Powell. Forming the production company the Archers 1942, Powell and Pressburger collaborated on 14 films between 1942 and 1956, such as *The Red Shoes* 1948.

Press Council in the UK, an organization (1953–91) founded to preserve the freedom of the press, maintain standards, consider complaints, and report on monopoly developments. The Press Council was replaced by the Press Complaints Commission, which began operations in Jan 1991.

press, freedom of absence of political ◊censorship in the press or other media, a concept regarded as basic to Western democracy. Access to and expression of views are, however, in practice restricted by the commercial interests of the owners and advertisers.

press gang method used to recruit soldiers and sailors into the British armed forces in the 18th and early 19th centuries. In effect it was a form of kidnapping carried out by the services or their agents, often with the aid of armed men. This was similar to the practice of 'shanghaiing' sailors for duty in the merchant marine, especially in the Far East.

pressure in a fluid, the force that would act normally (at right angles) per unit surface area of a body immersed in the fluid. The SI unit of pressure is the pascal (Pa), equal to a pressure of one newton per square metre. In the atmosphere, the pressure declines with height from about 100 kPa at sea level to zero where the atmosphere fades into space. Pressure is commonly measured with a ◊barometer, ◊manometer, or Bourdon gauge. Other common units of pressure are the bar and the torr.

Absolute pressure is measured from a vacuum; gauge pressure is the difference between the absolute pressure and the local ◊atmospheric pressure. In a liquid, the pressure at a depth h is given by ρgh where ρ is the density and g is the acceleration of free fall.

pressure cooker closed pot in which food is cooked in water under pressure, where water boils at a higher temperature than normal boiling point (100°C/212°F) and therefore cooks food quickly. The modern pressure cooker has a quick-sealing lid and a safety valve that can be adjusted to vary the steam pressure inside.

The French scientist Denis Papin invented the pressure cooker in England in 1679.

pressurized water reactor (PWR) a ◊nuclear reactor design used in nuclear power stations in many countries, and in nuclear-powered submarines. In the PWR, water under pressure is the coolant and ◊moderator. It circulates through a steam generator, where its heat boils water to provide steam to drive power ◊turbines.

Prester John legendary Christian prince. During the 12th and 13th centuries, Prester John was believed to be the ruler of a powerful empire in Asia. From the 14th to the 16th century, he was generally believed to be the king of Abyssinia (now Ethiopia) in NE Africa.

Preston industrial town (textiles, chemicals, electrical goods, aircraft, plastics, engineering, and shipbuilding), and administrative headquarters of Lancashire, NW England, on the river Ribble, 34 km/21 mi S of Lancaster; population (1991) 126,100. Oliver Cromwell defeated the Royalists at Preston 1648. It is the birthplace of Richard Arkwright, inventor of cotton-spinning machinery, and was a centre of the cotton industry in the 18th century.

Prestonpans, Battle of battle 1745 in which Prince ◊Charles Edward Stuart's Jacobite forces defeated the English. It took place near the town of Prestonpans in Lothian region, E Scotland.

prestressed concrete developed form of ◊reinforced concrete in which tensioned steel cables enclosed in ducts take the place of steel reinforcement. This allows the most efficient use of the tensile strength of steel with the compressive strength of concrete. Its use was pioneered by the French engineer Eugène Freysinnet (1879–1962) in the 1920s.

pretender claimant to a throne. In British history, the term is widely used to describe the Old Pretender (◊James Edward Stuart) and the Young Pretender (◊Charles Edward Stuart).

Pretoria administrative capital of the Union of South Africa from 1910 and capital of Transvaal Province 1860–1994; population (1991) 1,080,200. Industries include engineering, chemicals, iron, and steel. Founded 1855, it was named after Boer leader Andries Pretorius (1799–1853).

Preval René 1943– . Haitian politician, president from 1996. A protegé of President Jean-Bertrand ◊Aristide, he was appointed prime minister 1991. He succeeded Aristide as president in the first peaceful handover of power to an elected president since the country's independence 1804. His opposition to the dictatorial ◊Duvalier regimes 1956–86 forced him into ten years of exile in the USA. He was chairman of the committee ('Pa Blie') responsible for investigating the disappearance of persons during the Duvalier regime.

Previn André George 1929– . German-born US conductor and composer. He was principal conductor of the London Symphony Orchestra 1968–79 and was appointed music director of Britain's Royal Philharmonic Orchestra 1985 (a post he relinquished the following year, staying on as principal conductor until 1991). He was also principal conductor of the Los Angeles Philharmonic 1986–89 and is now a guest conductor of many orchestras in Europe and the USA.

After early success as a composer and arranger for film, he studied conducting with Pierre Monteux 1951. His compositions include concertos for piano 1971 and guitar 1984; he has conducted Gershwin and Mozart concertos from the keyboard and recorded many US and British composers.

Priam in Greek mythology, the last king of Troy, husband of Hecuba and father of many sons and daughters, including ◊Cassandra, ◊Hector, and ◊Paris. He was killed by Pyrrhus, son of Achilles, when the Greeks entered the city of Troy concealed in a huge wooden horse which the Trojans believed to be a gift to the city.

Previn The conductor and pianist André Previn. He has had a long-lasting relationship with the London Symphony Orchestra, currently holding the position of Conductor Laureate. His many recordings include persuasive accounts of English music. *Polygram*

Priapus in Greek mythology, the god of fertility, son of Dionysus and Aphrodite, represented as grotesquely ugly, with an exaggerated phallus. He was later a Roman god of gardens, where his image was frequently used as a scarecrow.

prickly heat acute skin condition characterized by small white or red itchy blisters (miliaria), resulting from inflammation of the sweat glands in conditions of heat and humidity.

prickly pear cactus of the genus *Opuntia*, native to Central and South America, mainly Mexico and Chile, but naturalized in S Europe, N Africa, and Australia, where it is a pest. The common prickly pear *O. vulgaris* is low-growing, with flat, oval, stem joints, bright yellow flowers, and prickly, oval fruit; the flesh and seeds of the peeled fruit have a pleasant taste.

Pride's purge the removal of about 100 Royalists and Presbyterians of the English House of Commons from Parliament by a detachment of soldiers led by Col Thomas Pride (died 1658) in 1648. They were accused of negotiating with Charles I and were seen as unreliable by the army. The remaining members were termed the ◊Rump and voted in favour of the king's trial.

Pride (a former London drayman or brewer who rose to be a colonel in the Parliamentary army) acted as one of the judges at the trial and also signed the king's death warrant. He opposed the plan to make Cromwell king.

Priestley J(ohn) B(oynton) 1894–1984. English novelist and playwright. His first success was a novel about travelling theatre, *The Good Companions* 1929 (Tait Black Memorial Prize). He followed it with a realist novel about London life, *Angel Pavement* 1930. His career as a dramatist began with *Dangerous Corner* 1932, one of several plays in which time is a preoccupation. His best-known plays are the enigmatic *An Inspector Calls* 1945 and *The Linden Tree* 1948, a study of postwar social issues.

Priestley had a gift for family comedy, for example, the play *When We Are Married* 1938. He was also known for his wartime broadcasts and literary criticism, such as *Literature and Western Man* 1960. Later novels include *Festival at Farbridge* 1951 and *The Image Men* 1968.

Priestley Joseph 1733–1804. English chemist and Unitarian minister. He identified oxygen 1774 and several other gases. Dissolving carbon dioxide under pressure in water, he began a European craze for soda water.

Swedish chemist Karl Scheele (1742–1786) independently prepared oxygen in 1772, but his tardiness in publication resulted in Priestley being credited with the discovery.

Priestley discovered nitric oxide (nitrogen monoxide, NO) 1772 and reduced it to nitrous oxide (dinitrogen monoxide, N_2O). In the same year he became the first person to isolate gaseous ammonia by collecting it over mercury (previously ammonia was known only in aqueous solution). In 1774 he found a method for producing sulphur dioxide (SO_2).

Prigogine Ilya, Viscount Prigogine 1917– . Russian-born Belgian chemist who, as a highly original theoretician, has made major contributions to the field of ◊thermodynamics. Earlier theories had considered systems at or about equilibrium; Prigogine began to study 'dissipative' or nonequilibrium structures frequently found in biological and chemical reactions. Nobel Prize for Physics 1977.

primary in presidential election campaigns in the USA, a statewide ballot in which voters indicate their candidate preferences for the two main parties. Held in 41 states, primaries begin with New Hampshire in Feb and continue until June; they operate under varying complex rules.

Generally speaking, the number of votes received by a candidate governs the number of delegates who will vote for that person at the national conventions in July/Aug, when the final choice of candidate for both Democratic and Republican parties is made. Some delegates remain loyal to the last ballot, others make deals to benefit the state or local situation as the field of candidates narrows. Some primaries are 'closed', being restricted to actual members of the party, others are 'open' to any registered voter.

'It is hard to tell where the MCC ends and the Church of England begins.'

J B Priestley
Quoted in the *New Statesman* 20 July 1962

primate A young female grey langur *Presbytis entellus* with infant. Like most primates, langurs are adapted to living in trees and have forward-looking eyes and well-developed sight and hearing. Unlike most other mammals, primates are relatively unspecialized, depending instead on their brains for survival. *Premaphotos Wildlife*

primary education the education of children between the ages of 5 and 11 in the state school system in England and Wales, and up to 12 in Scotland.

100 million children in the world have no access to primary education, and many children leave primary school unable to read or write.

primary sexual characteristic in males, the primary sexual characteristic is the ◊testis; in females it is the ◊ovary. Both are endocrine glands that produce hormones responsible for secondary sexual characteristics, such as facial hair and a deep voice in males and breasts in females.

primate in the Christian church, the official title of an archbishop. The archbishop of Canterbury is the Primate of All England, and the archbishop of York the Primate of England.

primate in zoology, any member of the order of mammals that includes monkeys, apes, and humans (together called anthropoids), as well as lemurs, bushbabies, lorises, and tarsiers (together called prosimians).

Generally, they have forward-directed eyes, gripping hands and feet, opposable thumbs, and big toes. They tend to have nails rather than claws, with gripping pads on the ends of the digits, all adaptations to the arboreal, climbing mode of life.

In 1996 a new primate genus (probably extinct) was identified by a US anthropologist from a collection of bones believed to belong to a ◊potto. The animal has been named Pseudopotto martini.

prime minister or ***premier*** head of a parliamentary government, usually the leader of the largest party. In countries with an executive president, the prime minister is of lesser standing, whereas in those with dual executives, such as France, power is shared with the president. In federal countries, such as Australia, the head of the federal government has the title prime minister, while the heads of government of the states are called premiers. In Germany, the equivalent of the prime minister is known as the chancellor.

The first prime minister in Britain is usually considered to have been Robert ◊Walpole, but the office was not officially recognized until 1905. In some countries, such as Australia, a distinction is drawn between the prime minister of the whole country and the premier of an individual state. *See list of tables on p. 1177.*

PRIME NUMBERS

All the prime numbers between 1 and 1,000

2	3	5	7	11	13	17	19	23	29
31	37	41	43	47	53	59	61	67	71
73	79	83	89	97	101	103	107	109	113
127	131	137	139	149	151	157	163	167	173
179	181	191	193	197	199	211	223	227	229
233	239	241	251	257	263	269	271	277	281
283	293	307	311	313	317	331	337	347	349
353	359	367	373	379	383	389	397	401	409
419	421	431	433	439	443	449	457	461	463
467	479	487	491	499	503	509	521	523	541
547	557	563	569	571	577	587	593	599	601
607	613	617	619	631	641	643	647	653	659
661	673	677	683	691	701	709	719	727	733
739	743	751	757	761	769	773	787	797	809
811	821	823	827	829	839	853	857	859	863
877	881	883	887	907	911	919	929	937	941
947	953	967	971	977	983	991	997		

prime number number that can be divided only by 1 or itself, that is, having no other factors. There is an infinite number of primes, the first ten of which are 2, 3, 5, 7, 11, 13, 17, 19, 23, and 29 (by definition, the number 1 is excluded from the set of prime numbers). The number 2 is the only even prime because all other even numbers have 2 as a factor.

Over the centuries mathematicians have sought general methods (algorithms) for calculating primes, from Eratosthenes' sieve to programs on powerful computers.

The largest prime, $2^{859433}-1$ (258,716 digits long) was discovered 1993. It is the thirty-third Mersenne prime. All Mersenne primes are in the form 2^q-1, where q is also a prime.

Primitive Methodism Protestant Christian movement, an offshoot of Wesleyan ◊Methodism, that emerged in England 1811 when evangelical enthusiasts organized camp meetings at places such as Mow Cop, on the Cheshire–Staffordshire border, 1807. Inspired by American example, open-air sermons were accompanied by prayers and hymn singing. In 1932 the Primitive Methodists became a constituent of a unified Methodist church.

Primitivism the influence on modern art (Ernst Kirchner, Amedeo Modigliani, Pablo Picasso, Paul Gauguin, and others) of the indigenous arts of Africa, Oceania, the Americas, and also of Western folk art.

Primo de Rivera Miguel, Marqués de Estella 1870–1930. Spanish soldier and politician, dictator from 1923 as well as premier from 1925. He was captain-general of Catalonia when he led a coup against the ineffective monarchy and became virtual dictator of Spain with the support of Alfonso XIII. He resigned 1930.

primrose any plant of the genus *Primula*, family Primulaceae, with showy five-lobed flowers. The common primrose *P. vulgaris* is a woodland plant, native to Europe, bearing pale yellow flowers in spring. Related to it is the ◊cowslip.

prince royal or noble title. In Rome and medieval Italy it was used as the title of certain officials, for example, *princeps senatus* (Latin 'leader of the Senate'). The title was granted to the king's sons in 15th-century France, and in England from Henry VII's time.

The British sovereign's eldest son is normally created Prince of Wales.

Prince former stage name of Prince Rogers Nelson 1959– . US pop musician. He composes, arranges, and produces his own records and often plays all the instruments. His albums, including *1999* 1982 and *Purple Rain* 1984, contain elements of rock, funk, and jazz. His stage shows are energetic and extravagant. Prince has now changed his name to a symbol.

His band the Revolution broke up after four years 1986. His hits include 'Little Red Corvette' from *1999*, 'Kiss' from *Parade* 1986, and 'Sign O' The Times' from the album of the same name 1987.

Prince Edward Island province of E Canada
area 5,700 sq km/2,200 sq mi
capital Charlottetown
features Prince Edward Island National Park; Summerside Lobster Carnival
industries potatoes, dairy products, lobsters, oysters, farm vehicles
population (1991) 129,900
history first recorded visit by Cartier 1534, who called it Isle St-Jean; settled by French; taken by British 1758; annexed to Nova Scotia 1763; separate colony 1769; renamed after Prince Edward of Kent, father of Queen Victoria 1798; settled by Scottish 1803; joined Confederation 1873.

In the late 1980s, there was controversy about whether to build a bridge to the mainland.

Prince US pop musician Prince in concert at Madison Square Garden, New York, 1986. His highly original stage act, and a skilfully managed off-screen image, made him one of the best-known pop figures of the 1980s and 1990s. *Corbis*

Princess Royal title borne only by the eldest daughter of the British sovereign, granted by royal declaration. It was first borne by Mary, eldest daughter of Charles I, probably in imitation of the French court, where the eldest daughter of the king was styled 'Madame Royale'. The title is currently held by Princess Anne.

Princeton borough in Mercer County, W central New Jersey, USA, 80 km/50 mi SW of New York; population (1990) 13,200. It is the seat of Princeton University, founded 1746 at Elizabethtown and moved to Princeton 1756.

It is the site of an important battle of the American Revolution 1777.

Prince William Sound channel in the Gulf of Alaska, extending 200 km/125 mi NW from Kayak Island. In March 1989 the oil tanker *Exxon Valdez* ran aground here, spilling 12 million gallons of crude oil in one of the world's greatest oil-pollution disasters.

principal focus in optics, the point at which incident rays parallel to the principal axis of a ◊lens converge, or appear to diverge, after refraction. The distance from the lens to its principal focus is its ◊focal length.

principate (from Latin *princeps* 'first') in ancient Rome, an unofficial title for the rule of ◊Augustus and his successors, designating the emperor as the leading citizen.

printed circuit board (PCB) electrical circuit created by laying (printing) 'tracks' of a conductor such as copper on one or both sides of an insulating board. The PCB was invented in 1936 by Austrian scientist Paul Eisler, and was first used on a large scale in 1948.

Prince Edward Island

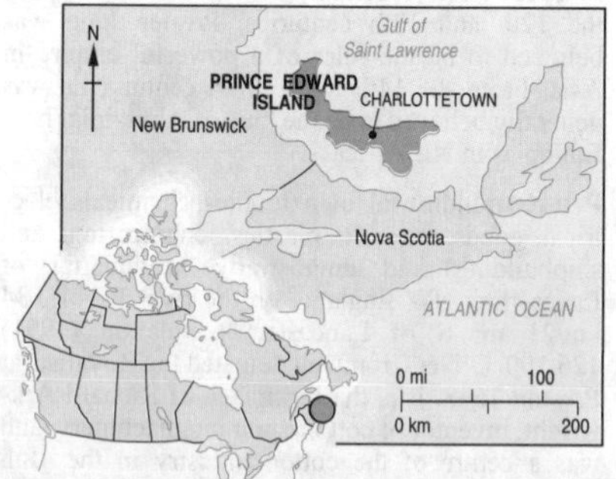

Components such as integrated circuits (chips), resistors and capacitors can be soldered to the surface of the board (surface-mounted) or, more commonly, attached by inserting their connecting pins or wires into holes drilled in the board. PCBs include ◊motherboards, expansion boards, and adaptors.

printer in computing, an output device for producing printed copies of text or graphics. Types include the daisywheel printer, which produces good-quality text but no graphics; the dot matrix printer, which produces text and graphics by printing a pattern of small dots; the ink-jet printer, which creates text and graphics by spraying a fine jet of quick-drying ink onto the paper; and the ◊laser printer, which uses electrostatic technology very similar to that used by a photocopier to produce high-quality text and graphics.

Printers may be classified as impact printers (such as daisywheel and dot-matrix printers), which form characters by striking an inked ribbon against the paper, and nonimpact printers (such as ink-jet and laser printers), which use a variety of techniques to produce characters without physical impact on the paper.

A further classification is based on the basic unit of printing, and categorizes printers as character printers, line printers, or page printers, according to whether they print one character, one line, or a complete page at a time.

printing reproduction of multiple copies of text or illustrative material on paper, as in books or newspapers, or on an increasing variety of materials; for example, on plastic containers. The first printing used woodblocks, followed by carved wood type or moulded metal type and hand-operated presses. Modern printing is effected by electronically controlled machinery. Current printing processes include electronic phototypesetting with ◊offset printing, and ◊gravure print.

origins In China the art of printing from a single wooden block was known by the 6th century AD, and movable type was being used by the 11th century. In Europe printing was unknown for another three centuries, and it was only in the 15th century that movable type was reinvented, traditionally by Johannes ◊Gutenberg in Germany. From there printing spread to Italy, France, and England, where it was introduced by William ◊Caxton.

steam power, linotype, and monotype There was no further substantial advance until, in the 19th century, steam power replaced hand-operation of printing presses, making possible long 'runs'; hand-composition of type (each tiny metal letter was taken from the case and placed individually in the narrow stick that carried one line of text) was replaced by machines operated by a keyboard. Linotype, a hot-metal process (it produced a line of type in a solid slug) used in newspapers, magazines, and books, was invented by Ottmar Mergenthaler 1886 and commonly used until the 1980s. The Monotype, used in bookwork (it produced a series of individual characters, which could be hand-corrected), was invented by Tolbert Lanston (1844–1913) in the USA 1889.

Important as these developments were, they represented no fundamental change but simply a faster method of carrying out the same basic typesetting operations. The actual printing process still involved pressing the inked type on to paper, by ◊letterpress.

20th-century developments In the 1960s, letterpress began to face increasing competition from ◊offset printing, a method that prints from an inked flat surface, and from the ◊gravure method (used for high-circulation magazines), which uses recessed plates. The introduction of electronic phototypesetting machines, also in the 1960s, allowed the entire process of setting and correction to be done in the same way that a typist operates, thus eliminating the hot-metal composing room (with its hazardous fumes, lead scraps, and noise) and leaving only the making of plates and the running of the presses to be done traditionally.

By the 1970s some final steps were taken to plateless printing, using various processes, such as a computer-controlled laser beam, or continuous jets of ink acoustically broken up into tiny equal-sized drops, which are electrostatically charged under computer control. Pictures can be fed into computer typesetting systems by optical scanners.

The first known English book to bear a date was the *Dictes of Sayengis of the Philosophers*, issued by Caxton from his press at Westminster 1477, although it is probable that it was not the first work printed there. Other notable British printers are William Caslon (1692–1766), considered the greatest English typefounder of the 18th century, and John ◊Baskerville. William Morris's designs for new types and decorated pages, produced at his Kelmscott Press from 1890, greatly influenced the work of other private presses.

printing A page from the *Hypnerotomachia Poliphili* pubished in Venice 1499 by Aldus Manutius. A humanist scholar and one of the most influential early printers, Aldus Manutius set up his Aldine Press in Venice in the 1490s, publishing low-cost editions of Greek and Latin classics renowned for their scholarship. He designed the first complete Greek font and in 1501 published the first book in italic type.

POLIPHILO QVIVI NARRA, CHE GLI PARVE ANCORA DI DORMIRE, ET ALTRONDE IN SOMNO RITROVARSE IN VNA CONVALLE, LAQVALE NEL FINE ERA SERATA DE VNA MIRABILE CLAVSVRA CVM VNA PORTENTOSA PYRAMIDE, DE ADMIRATIONE DIGNA, ET VNO EXCELSO OBELISCO DE SOPRA, LAQVALE CVM DILIGENTIA ET PIACERE SVBTILMENTE LA CONSIDEROE.

LA SPAVENTEVOLE SILVA, ET CONSTIPATO Nemore euaso, & gli primi altri lochi per el dolce somno che se hauea per le fesse & prosternate mēbre diffuso relicti, me ritrouai di nouo in uno piu delectabile sito assai piu che el praecedente. El quale non era de monti horridi, & crepidinose rupe intorniato, ne falcato di strumosi iugi. Ma compositamente de grate montagniole di non troppo altecia. Siluose di giouani quercioli, di roburi, fraxini & Carpini, & di frondosi Esculi, & Ilice, & di teneri Coryli, & di Alni, & di Tilie, & di Opio, & de infructuosi Oleastri, dispositi secondo laspecto de

printmaking creating a picture or design by printing from a plate (woodblock, stone, or metal sheet) that holds ink or colour. The oldest form of print is the woodcut, common in medieval Europe, followed by line ◊engraving (from the 15th century), and ◊etching (from the 17th century); coloured woodblock prints flourished in Japan from the 18th century. ◊Lithography was invented 1796.

prion (acronym for ***proteinaceous infectious particle***) exceptionally small microorganism, a hundred times smaller than a virus. Composed of protein, and without any detectable amount of nucleic acid (genetic material), it is thought to cause diseases such as scrapie in sheep, and certain degenerative diseases of the nervous system in humans. How it can operate without nucleic acid is not yet known.

The prion was claimed to have been discovered at the University of California 1982, when high protein was identified in infected cells. It was concluded that the protein was the infected particle, and it was named prion.

prior, prioress in a Christian religious community, the deputy of an abbot or abbess, responsible for discipline. In certain Roman Catholic orders, the prior or prioress is the principal of a monastery or convent.

Prior Matthew 1664–1721. British poet and diplomat. He was associated under the Whigs with the negotiation of the treaty of Ryswick 1697 ending the war with France, and, under the Tories, with that of Utrecht 1714 ending the War of the Spanish Succession. On the Whigs' return to power he was imprisoned by the government leader Walpole 1715–17. His gift as a writer was for light occasional verses, epigrams, and tales, in a graceful yet colloquial manner.

Pripet (Russian ***Pripyat***) river in E Europe, a tributary of the river Dnieper, which it joins 80 km/50 mi above Kiev, Ukraine, after a course of about 800 km/500 mi. The Pripet marshes near Pinsk were of strategic importance in both World Wars.

primrose The common primrose prefers damp woodland banks, but can also occur in dense stands on mountains and on open seaside cliffs. It is mainly pollinated by queen bumble bees. *Premaphotos Wildlife*

prism in mathematics, a solid figure whose cross section is constant in planes drawn perpendicular to its axis. A cube, for example, is a rectangular prism with all faces (bases and sides) the same shape and size.

A cylinder is a prism with a circular cross section.

prism in optics, a triangular block of transparent material (plastic, glass, silica) commonly used to 'bend' a ray of light or split a beam into its spectral colours. Prisms are used as mirrors to define the optical path in binoculars, camera viewfinders, and periscopes. The dispersive property of prisms is used in the ◊spectroscope.

prison place of confinement for those convicted of contravening the laws of the state; most countries claim to aim also at rehabilitation. The average number of people in prison in the UK (1990) was 43,300 (about 97 people per 100,000 of the population) with almost 20% of these under the age of 21. About 22% were on ◊remand (awaiting trial or sentence). Because of overcrowding in prisons, almost 2,000 prisoners were held in police cells. The US prison population 1993 was more than 1.3 million, of whom 60% were drug offenders.

Experiments have been made in Britain and elsewhere in 'open prisons' without bars, which included releasing prisoners in the final stages of their sentence to work in jobs outside the prison, and the provision of aftercare on release.

Attempts to deal with the increasing number of young offenders include, from 1982, accommodation in community homes in the case of minor offences, with (in more serious cases) 'short, sharp shock' treatment in detention centres (although the latter was subsequently found to have little effect on reconviction rates).

prison A London prison scene by the 19th-century French artist Gustave Doré. *Corbis*

'The printing press is either the greatest blessing or the greatest curse of modern times, one sometimes forgets which.'

On PRINTING
J M Barrie
Sentimental Tommy
1896

history (UK)
late 18th century Growth of criminal prisons as opposed to places of detention for those awaiting trial or confined for political reasons. Previously criminals had commonly been sentenced to death, mutilation, or transportation rather than imprisonment. One of the greatest reformers in Britain was John Howard, whose Prison Act 1778 established the principle of separate confinement combined with work in an attempt at reform (it was eventually carried out when Pentonville prison was built 1842).
19th century The Quaker Elizabeth Fry campaigned against the appalling conditions in early 19th-century prisons. Penal servitude was introduced 1857, as an additional deterrent, after the refusal of the colonies to accept transported convicts.
1948 Penal servitude and hard labour were finally abolished by the Criminal Justice Act 1948, so that there is only one form of prison sentence, namely imprisonment.
1967 Under the Criminal Justice Act 1967 courts may suspend prison sentences of two years or less, and, unless the offender has previously been in prison or ◊borstal, will normally do so; that is, the sentence comes into effect only if another offence is committed. Persistent offenders may receive an extended sentence for the protection of the public. After serving one-third of their sentence (minimum 12 months), selected prisoners may be released on parole.
1972 The Criminal Justice Act 1972 required the courts to consider information about an offender before sentencing them to prison for the first time, and introduced the concept of ◊community service to replace prison for nonviolent offenders, and of day-training centres for the social education under intensive supervision of those who could not integrate well into society.

prisoner of war (POW) person captured in war, who has fallen into the hands of, or surrendered to, an opponent. Such captives may be held in prisoner-of-war camps. The treatment of POWs is governed by the ◊Geneva Convention.

Priština capital of Kosovo autonomous province, S Serbia, Yugoslavia; population (1991) 108,000. Once capital of the medieval Serbian empire, it is now a trading centre.

Pritchett V(ictor) S(awdon) 1900–1997. English short-story writer, novelist, and critic. His style is often witty and satirical. Many of his short stories are set in London and SE England, among them *The Spanish Virgin* 1930, *Blind Love* 1969, and *The Camberwell Beauty* 1974. *The Complete Stories* was published 1990. His critical works include *The Living Novel* 1946 and biographies of the Russian writers ◊Turgenev 1977 and ◊Chekhov 1988.

Prithviraja Chauhan III Hindu ruler of Delhi and king of the Chauhan ◊Rajputs, who controlled the Delhi-Ajmer region of N central India. He commanded a coalition of Rajput forces which sought to halt Muhammad Ghuri's Turk-Muslim army at Tarain. Victorious in the first conflict 1191, he died heroically in the second Battle of Tarain 1192. He is immortalized in Hindi ballads and folk literature as a figure of romance and chivalry.

privacy the right of the individual to be free from secret surveillance (by scientific devices or other means) and from the disclosure to unauthorized persons of personal data, as accumulated in computer data banks. Always an issue complicated by considerations of state security, public welfare (in the case of criminal activity), and other factors, it has been rendered more complex by present-day technology.
computer data All Western countries now have computerized-data protection. In the USA the Privacy Act 1974 requires that there should be no secret data banks and that agencies handling data must ensure their reliability and prevent misuse (information gained for one purpose must not be used for another). The public must be able to find out what is recorded and how it is used, and be able to correct it. Under the Freedom of Information Act 1967, citizens and organizations have the right to examine unclassified files.

In Britain under the Data Protection Act 1984 a register is kept of all businesses and organizations that store and process personal information, and they are subject to a code of practice set out in the act.
media In the UK, a bill to curb invasions of privacy by the media failed to reach the statute book 1989. It would have enabled legal action against publication, or attempted publication, of private information without consent.

In the USA the media have a working rule that private information is made public only concerning those who have entered public life, such as politicians, entertainers, and athletes.

privateer privately owned and armed ship commissioned by a state to attack enemy vessels. The crews of such ships were, in effect, legalized pirates; they were not paid but received a share of the spoils. Privateering existed from ancient times until the 19th century, when it was declared illegal by the Declaration of Paris 1856.

private limited company a registered company which has limited liability (the shareholders cannot lose more than their original shareholdings), and a minimum of two shareholders and a maximum of fifty. It cannot offer its shares or debentures to the public and their transfer is restricted.

private school alternative name in the UK for a fee-paying ◊independent school.

private sector the part of the economy that is owned and controlled by private individuals and business organizations such as private and public limited companies. In a ◊free enterprise economy, the private sector is responsible for allocating most of the resources within the economy. This contrasts with the ◊public sector, where economic resources are owned and controlled by the state.

privatization policy or process of selling or transferring state-owned or public assets and services (notably nationalized industries) to private investors. Privatization of services involves the government contracting private firms to supply services previously supplied by public authorities.

In many cases the trend towards privatization has been prompted by dissatisfaction with the high level of subsidies being given to often inefficient state enterprise. The term 'privatization' is used even when the state retains a majority share of an enterprise.

The policy has been pursued by the post-1979 Conservative administration in the UK, and by recent governments in France, Japan (Nippon Telegraph and Telephone Corporation 1985, Japan Railways 1987, Japan Air Lines 1987), Italy, New Zealand and elsewhere. By 1988 the practice had spread worldwide, with communist countries such as China and Cuba selling off housing to private tenants.

privilege in law, a special right or immunity in connection with legal proceedings. Public-interest privilege may be claimed by the government seeking to preserve the confidentiality of state documents. Private privilege can only attach to an individual by virtue of rank or office; for example, for members of Parliament in defence of defamation proceedings.

privet any evergreen shrub of the genus *Ligustrum* of the olive family Oleaceae, with dark green leaves, including the European common privet *L. vulgare*, with white flowers and black berries, naturalized in North America, and the native North American California privet *L. ovalifolium*, also known as hedge privet.

Privy Council council composed originally of the chief royal officials of the Norman kings in Britain; under the Tudors and early Stuarts it became the chief governing body. It was replaced from 1688 by the ◊cabinet, originally a committee of the council, and the council itself now retains only formal powers in issuing royal proclamations and orders in council. Cabinet ministers are automatically members, and it is presided over by the Lord President of the Council.

privy purse personal expenditure of the British sovereign, which derives from his/her own resources (as distinct from the ◊civil list, which now finances only expenses incurred in pursuance of official functions and duties). The office that deals with this expenditure is also known as the Privy Purse.

Privy Seal, Lord until 1884, the UK officer of state in charge of the royal seal to prevent its misuse. The honorary title is now held by a senior cabinet minister who has special nondepartmental duties.

Prix Goncourt French literary prize for fiction, (founded by Edmond de ◊Goncourt 1903). *See list of tables on p. 1177.*

probability likelihood, or chance, that an event will occur, often expressed as odds, or in mathematics, numerically as a fraction or decimal.

In general, the probability that *n* particular events will happen out of a total of *m* possible events is n/m. A certainty has a probability of 1; an impossibility has a probability of 0. Empirical probability is defined as the number of successful events divided by the total possible number of events.

In tossing a coin, the chance that it will land 'heads' is the same as the chance that it will land 'tails', that is, 1 to 1 or even; mathematically, this probability is expressed as ½ or 0.5. The odds against any chosen number coming up on the roll of a fair die are 5 to 1; the probability is ⅙ or 0.1666 … . If two dice are rolled there are $6 \times 6 = 36$ different possible combinations. The probability of a double (two numbers the same) is 6/36 or ⅙ since there are six doubles in the 36 events: (1,1), (2,2), (3,3), (4,4), (5,5), and (6,6).

Probability theory was developed by the French mathematicians Blaise Pascal and Pierre de Fermat in the 17th century, initially in response to a request to calculate the odds of being dealt various hands at cards. Today probability plays a major part in the mathematics of atomic theory and finds application in insurance and statistical studies.

probate formal proof of a will. In the UK, if a will's validity is unquestioned, it is proven in 'common form'; the executor, in the absence of other interested parties, obtains at a probate registry a grant upon his or her own oath. Otherwise, it must be proved in 'solemn form': its validity established at a probate court (in the Chancery Division of the High Court), those concerned being made parties to the action.

probation in law, the placing of offenders under supervision of probation officers in the community, as an alternative to prison.

There are strict limits placed on travel, associations, and behaviour. Often an offender is required to visit a probation officer on a regular schedule. Failure to abide by the regulations can result in imprisonment.

Juveniles are no longer placed on probation, but under a 'supervision' order.

The probation service helps the families of those imprisoned, gives the prisoner supervisory aftercare on release, and assists in preventive measures to avoid family breakdown.

processor in computing, another name for the ◊central processing unit or ◊microprocessor of a computer.

proconsul Roman ◊consul (chief magistrate) who went on to govern a province when his term as consul ended.

Proconsul prehistoric ape skull found on Rusinga Island in Lake Victoria (Nyanza), E Africa, by Mary ◊Leakey. It is believed to be 20 million years old.

Procopius c. 495–565. Greek historian. As secretary to Justinian's general, Belisarius, he wrote a history of the campaigns of the Eastern Roman Empire against the Goths and the Vandals. He also wrote extensively on architecture, and was the author of *The Secret History*, a relatively scandalous account of the leading figures of the age.

Procrustes (Greek 'the stretcher') in Greek mythology, a robber who tied his victims to a bed; if they were too tall for it, he cut off the ends of their legs, and if they were too short, he stretched them.

procurator fiscal officer of a Scottish sheriff's court who (combining the role of public prosecutor and coroner) inquires into suspicious deaths and carries out the preliminary questioning of witnesses to crime.

Procyon or ***Alpha Canis Minoris*** brightest star in the constellation ◊Canis Minor and the eighth brightest star in the night sky. Procyon is a first-magnitude white star 11.4 light years from Earth, with a mass of 1.7 Suns. It has a ◊white dwarf companion that orbits it every 40 years.

The name, derived from Greek, means 'before the dog', and reflects the fact that in midnorthern latitudes Procyon rises shortly before ◊Sirius, the Dog Star. Procyon and Sirius are sometimes called 'the Dog Stars'. Both are relatively close to us and have white dwarf companions.

productivity, biological in an ecosystem, the amount of material in the food chain produced by the primary producers (plants) that is available for consumption by animals. Plants turn carbon dioxide and water into sugars and other complex carbon compounds by means of photosynthesis. Their net productivity is defined as the quantity of carbon compounds formed, less the quantity used up by the respiration of the plant itself.

Profumo John Dennis 1915– . British Conservative politician, secretary of state for war from 1960 to June 1963, when he resigned on the disclosure of his involvement with Christine Keeler, mistress also of a Soviet naval attaché. In 1982 Profumo became administrator of the social and educational settlement Toynbee Hall in London.

progesterone ◊steroid hormone that occurs in vertebrates. In mammals, it regulates the menstrual cycle and pregnancy. Progesterone is secreted by the corpus luteum (the ruptured Graafian follicle of a discharged ovum).

prognosis in medicine, prediction of the course or outcome of illness or injury, particularly the chance of recovery.

program in computing, a set of instructions that controls the operation of a computer. There are two main kinds: ◊applications programs, which carry out tasks for the benefit of the user – for example, word processing; and systems programs, which control the internal workings of the computer. A utility program is a systems program that carries out specific tasks for the user. Programs can be written in any of a number of ◊programming languages but are always translated into machine code before they can be executed by the computer.

programme music music that interprets a story, depicts a scene or painting, or illustrates a literary or philosophical idea, such as Richard Strauss's tone poem *Don Juan*. Programme music became popular in the Romantic era.

programming writing instructions in a programming language for the control of a computer. Applications programming is for end-user programs, such as accounts programs or word-processing packages. Systems programming is for operating systems and the like, which are concerned more with the internal workings of the computer.

programming language in computing, a special notation in which instructions for controlling a computer are written. Programming languages are designed to be easy for people to write and read, but must be capable of being mechanically translated (by a compiler or an interpreter) into the ◊machine code that the computer can execute. Programming languages may be classified as high-level languages or ◊low-level languages, according to how closely they reflect the machine codes of specific computers.

progression sequence of numbers each occurring in a specific relationship to its predecessor. An arithmetic progression has numbers that increase or decrease by a common sum or difference (for example, 2, 4, 6, 8); a geometric progression has numbers each bearing a fixed ratio to its predecessor (for example, 3, 6, 12, 24); and a harmonic progression has numbers whose reciprocals (the result of dividing the number into 1) are in arithmetical progression, for example 1, ½, ⅓, ¼.

progressive tax tax such that the higher the income of the taxpayer the greater the proportion or percentage paid in that tax. This contrasts with ◊regressive taxes where the proportion paid falls as income increases, and ◊proportional taxes where the proportion paid remains the same at all levels of income. Examples of progressive taxes in the UK include ◊income tax and capital gains tax.

Progressivism in US history, the name of both a reform movement and a political party, active in the two decades before World War I. Mainly middle-class and urban-based, Progressives secured legislation at national, state, and local levels to improve the democratic system, working conditions, and welfare provision.

Prohibition Detroit police inspecting illegal brewing equipment during Prohibition in the US. Despite a relentless campaign by the police and over 300,000 convictions, illegal drinking – and the organized crime that accompanied it – flourished during Prohibition. Some states and counties still maintain full or partial prohibition. *Library of Congress*

Prohibition in US history, the period 1920–33 when alcohol was illegal, representing the culmination of a long campaign by church and women's organizations, temperance societies, and the Anti-Saloon League. This led to bootlegging (the illegal distribution of liquor, often illicitly distilled), to the financial advantage of organized crime, and public opinion insisted on repeal 1933.

projectile particle that travels with both horizontal and vertical motion in the Earth's gravitational field. If the frictional forces of air resistance are ignored, the two components of its motion can be analyzed separately: its vertical motion will be accelerated due to its weight in the gravitational field; its horizontal motion may be assumed to be at constant velocity. In a uniform gravitational field and in the absence of frictional forces the path of a projectile is a parabola.

projection of the earth on paper, see ◊map projection.

prokaryote in biology, an organism whose cells lack organelles (specialized segregated structures such as nuclei, mitochondria, and chloroplasts). Prokaryote DNA is not arranged in chromosomes but forms a coiled structure called a nucleoid. The prokaryotes comprise only the bacteria and cyanobacteria (see ◊blue-green algae); all other organisms are eukaryotes.

Prokofiev Sergey Sergeyevich 1891–1953. Soviet composer. His music includes operas such as *The Love for Three Oranges* 1921; ballets for Sergei Diaghilev, including *Romeo and Juliet* 1935; seven symphonies including the *Classical Symphony* 1916–17; music for film, including Eisenstein's *Alexander Nevsky* 1938; piano and violin concertos; songs and cantatas (for example, that composed for the 30th anniversary of the October Revolution); and *Peter and the Wolf* 1936 for children, to his own libretto after a Russian folk tale.

Prokofiev was essentially a classicist in his use of form, but his extensive and varied output demonstrates great lyricism, humour, and skill. Born near Ekaterinoslav, he studied at St Petersburg under Rimsky-Korsakov and achieved fame as a pianist. He left Russia 1918 and lived for some time in the USA and in Paris, but returned 1927 and again 1935.

prolapse displacement of an organ due to the effects of strain in weakening the supporting tissues. The term is most often used with regard to the rectum (due to chronic bowel problems) or the uterus (following several pregnancies).

proletariat in Marxist theory, those classes in society that possess no property, and therefore depend on the sale of their labour or expertise (as opposed to the capitalists or bourgeoisie, who own the means of production, and the petty bourgeoisie, or working small-property owners). They are usually divided into the industrial, agricultural, and intellectual proletariat.

The term is derived from Latin 'proletarii', 'the class possessing no property', whose contribution to the state was considered to be their offspring, 'proles'.

promenade concert originally a concert where the audience was free to promenade (walk about) while the music was playing, now in the UK the name of any one of an annual BBC series (the 'Proms') at the Royal Albert Hall, London, at which part of the audience stands. They were originated by English conductor Henry Wood 1895.

Prometheus in Greek mythology, a ◊Titan who stole fire from heaven for the human race. In revenge, Zeus had him chained to a rock where an eagle came each day to eat his liver, which grew back each night, until he was rescued by the hero ◊Heracles.

promethium radioactive, metallic element of the ◊lanthanide series, symbol Pm, atomic number 61, relative atomic mass 145.

It occurs in nature only in minute amounts, produced as a fission product/by-product of uranium in ◊pitchblende and other uranium ores; for a long time it was considered not to occur in nature. The longest-lived isotope has a half-life of slightly more than 20 years.

Promethium is synthesized by neutron bombardment of neodymium, and is a product of the fission of uranium, thorium, or plutonium; it can be isolated in large amounts from the fission-product debris of uranium fuel in nuclear reactors. It is used in phosphorescent paints and as an X-ray source.

prominence bright cloud of gas projecting from the Sun into space 100,000 km/60,000 mi or more. Quiescent prominences last for months, and are held in place by magnetic fields in the Sun's corona. Surge prominences shoot gas into space at speeds of 1,000 kps/600 mps. Loop prominences are gases falling back to the Sun's surface after a solar ◊flare.

pronghorn ruminant mammal *Antilocapra americana* constituting the family Antilocapridae, native to the W USA. It is not a true antelope. It is light brown and about 1 m/3 ft high. It sheds its horns annually and can reach speeds of 100 kph/60 mph. The loss of prairies to agriculture, combined with excessive hunting, has brought this unique animal close to extinction. *See illustration on following page.*

proof spirit numerical scale used to indicate the alcohol content of an alcoholic drink. Proof spirit (or 100% proof spirit) acquired its name from a solution of alcohol in water which, when used to moisten gunpowder, contained just enough alcohol to permit it to burn.

In practice, the degrees proof of an alcoholic drink is based on the specific gravity of an aqueous solution containing the same amount of alcohol as the drink. Typical values are: whisky, gin, rum 70 degrees proof (40% alcohol); vodka 65 degrees proof; sherry 28 degrees proof; table wine 20 degrees proof; beer 4 degrees proof. The USA uses a different proof scale to the UK; a US whisky of 80 degrees proof on the US scale would be 70 degrees proof on the UK scale.

‘prohibition makes you / want to cry / into your beer and / denies you the beer / to cry into.’

On PROHIBITION
Don Marquis
archy and mehitabel
1927

pronghorn The pronghorn is unique in that it sheds annually the sheaths that cover the horns. The sheath, more prominent in the male pronghorn, appears to form part of the horn itself.

propaganda systematic spreading (propagation) of information or disinformation, usually to promote a religious or political doctrine with the intention of instilling particular attitudes or responses. As a system of disseminating information it was considered a legitimate instrument of government, but became notorious through the deliberate distortion of facts or the publication of falsehoods by totalitarian regimes, notably Nazi Germany.

The word is derived from the activities of a special sacred congregation of the Roman Catholic Church (*de propaganda fide*) which sought to spread the faith and recruit members.

propane C_3H_8 gaseous hydrocarbon of the ◊alkane series, found in petroleum and used as fuel.

propanol or ***propyl alcohol*** third member of the homologous series of ◊alcohols. Propanol is usually a mixture of two isomeric compounds (see ◊isomer): propan-1-ol ($CH_3CH_2CH_2OH$) and propan-2-ol ($CH_3CHOHCH_3$). Both are colourless liquids that can be mixed with water and are used in perfumery.

propanone CH_3COCH_3 (common name ***acetone***) colourless flammable liquid used extensively as a solvent, as in nail-varnish remover. It boils at 56.5°C/133.7°F, mixes with water in all proportions, and has a characteristic odour.

propellant substance burned in a rocket for propulsion. Two propellants are used: oxidizer and fuel are stored in separate tanks and pumped independently into the combustion chamber. Liquid oxygen (oxidizer) and liquid hydrogen (fuel) are common propellants, used, for example, in the space-shuttle main engines. The explosive charge that propels a projectile from a gun is also called a propellant.

propeller screwlike device used to propel some ships and aeroplanes. A propeller has a number of curved blades that describe a helical path as they rotate with the hub, and accelerate fluid (liquid or gas) backwards during rotation. Reaction to this backward movement of fluid sets up a propulsive thrust forwards. The marine screw propeller was developed by Francis Pettit Smith in the UK and Swedish-born John Ericson in the USA and was first used 1839.

propaganda World War I propaganda. Propaganda such as that shown here relies more on manipulating responses by using emotive images, than on spreading information. *Image Select (UK) Ltd*

propene $CH_3CH{:}CH_2$ (common name ***propylene***) second member of the alkene series of hydrocarbons. A colourless, flammable gas, it is widely used by industry to make organic chemicals, including polypropylene plastics.

propenoic acid $H_2C{:}CHCOOH$ (common name ***acrylic acid***) acid obtained from the aldehyde propenal (acrolein) derived from glycerol or fats. Glasslike thermoplastic resins are made by polymerizing ◊esters of propenoic acid or methyl propenoic acid and used for transparent components, lenses, and dentures. Other acrylic compounds are used for adhesives, artificial fibres, and artists' acrylic paint.

proper motion gradual change in the position of a star that results from its motion in orbit around our Galaxy, the Milky Way. Proper motions are slight and undetectable to the naked eye, but can be accurately measured on telescopic photographs taken many years apart.

Barnard's Star is the star with the largest proper motion, 10.3 arc seconds per year.

properties in chemistry, the characteristics a substance possesses by virtue of its composition.

Physical properties of a substance can be measured by physical means, for example boiling point, melting point, hardness, elasticity, colour, and physical state. Chemical properties are the way it reacts with other substances;whether it is acidic or basic, an oxidizing or a reducing agent, a salt, or stable to heat, for example.

Propertius Sextus c. 47–15 BC. Roman elegiac poet. A member of the literary circle of ◊Maecenas, he is best known for his highly personal love poems addressed to his mistress 'Cynthia'.

property the right to control the use of a thing (such as land, a building, a work of art, or a computer program). In English law, a distinction is made between real property, which involves a degree of geographical fixity, and personal property, which does not. Property is never absolute, since any society places limits on an individual's property (such as the right to transfer that property to another). Different societies have held widely varying interpretations of the nature of property and the extent of the rights of the owner of that property.

The debate about private and public property began with the Greeks. For Plato, an essential prerequisite for the guardians of his *Republic* was that they owned no property, while Aristotle saw private property as an equally necessary prerequisite for political participation. The story of Creation in the Bible was interpreted variously as a state of original communism destroyed by the Fall (by Thomas More in his *Utopia* 1516), and hence a justification of the monastic ideal, in which property is held in common, or as justifying the institution of private property, since Adam was granted dominion over all things in Eden. The philosopher John Locke argued that property rights to a thing are acquired by expending labour on it. Adam Smith saw property as a consequence of the transition of society from an initial state of hunting (in which property did not exist) to one of flock-rearing (which depended on property for its existence). Karl Marx contrasted an Asiatic mode of production, a mythical age in which all property was held in common, with the situation under capitalism in which the only 'property' of the worker, labour, was appropriated by the capitalist. One of Marx's achievements was to reawaken the debate over property in terms that are still being used today.

prophet person thought to speak from divine inspiration or one who foretells the future. In the Bible, the chief prophets were Elijah, Amos, Hosea, and Isaiah. In Islam, ◊Muhammad is believed to be the last and greatest of a long line of prophets beginning with Adam and including Moses and Jesus.

In the Bible, a prophet is any of the succession of saints and seers who preached and prophesied in the Hebrew kingdoms in Palestine from the 8th century BC until the suppression of Jewish independence in 586 BC, and possibly later. The prophetic books of the Old Testament constitute a division of the Hebrew Bible.

prophylaxis any measure taken to prevent disease, including exercise and ◊vaccination. Prophylactic (preventive) medicine is an aspect of public-health provision that is receiving increasing attention.

proportion the relation of a part to the whole (usually expressed as a fraction or percentage). In mathematics two variable quantities x and y are proportional if, for all values of x, $y = kx$, where k is a constant. This means that if x increases, y increases in a linear fashion.

A graph of x against y would be a straight line passing through the origin (the point $x = 0, y = 0$). y is inversely proportional to x if the graph of y against $1/x$ is a straight line through the origin. The corresponding equation is $y = k/x$. Many laws of science relate quantities that are proportional (for example, ◊Boyle's law).

proportional representation (PR) electoral system in which distribution of party seats corresponds to their proportion of the total votes cast, and minority votes are not wasted (as opposed to a simple majority, or 'first past the post', system). Forms include: the ***party list*** (PLS) or ***additional member system*** (AMS). As recommended by the Hansard Society 1976 for introduction in the UK, three-quarters of the members would be elected in single-member constituencies on the traditional majority-vote system, and the remaining seats be allocated according to the overall number of votes cast for each party (a variant of this, the additional member system, is used in Germany, where half the members are elected from lists by proportional representation, and half fight for single-member 'first past the post' constituencies).

The ***single transferable vote*** (STV), in which candidates are numbered in order of preference by the voter, and any votes surplus to the minimum required for a candidate to win are transferred to second preferences, as are second-preference votes from the successive candidates at the bottom of the poll until the required number of elected candidates is achieved (this is in use in the Republic of Ireland).

proportional tax tax such that the proportion or percentage paid in tax remains constant as income of the taxpayer changes. This contrasts with ◊regressive tax where the proportion paid falls as income increases, and ◊progressive tax where the proportion paid increases. ◊Value-added tax is often said to be an example of a proportional tax.

prop root or ***stilt root*** modified root that grows from the lower part of a stem or trunk down to the ground, providing a plant with extra support. Prop roots are common on some woody plants, such as mangroves, and also occur on a few herbaceous plants, such as maize. Buttress roots are a type of prop root found at the base of tree trunks, extended and flattened along the upper edge to form massive triangular buttresses; they are common on tropical trees.

propylene common name for ◊propene.

prose spoken or written language without metrical regularity; in literature, prose corresponds more closely to the patterns of everyday speech than ◊poetry.

In Western literature prose was traditionally used for what is today called nonfiction – that is, history, biography, essays, and so on – while verse was used for imaginative literature. Prose came into its own as a vehicle for fiction with the rise of the ◊novel in the 18th century. In modern literature, the distinction between verse and prose is not always clear cut.

prosecution in law, the party instituting legal proceedings. In the UK, the prosecution of a criminal case is begun by bringing the accused (defendant) before a magistrate, either by warrant or summons, or by arrest without warrant. Most criminal prosecutions are conducted by the ◊Crown Prosecution Service, although other government departments may also prosecute some cases; for example, the Department of Inland Revenue. An individual may bring a private prosecution, usually for assault.

Prosecution Service, Crown body established by the Prosecution of Offences Act 1985, responsible for prosecuting all criminal offences in England and Wales. It is headed by the Director of Public Prosecutions (DPP), and brings England and Wales in line with Scotland (see ◊procurator fiscal) in having a prosecution service independent of the police.

Proserpina in Roman mythology, the goddess of the underworld. Her Greek equivalent is ◊Persephone.

prosimian or ***primitive primate*** in zoology, any animal belonging to the suborder Strepsirhin of ◊primates. Prosimians are characterized by a wet nose with slitlike nostrils, the tip of the nose having a prominent vertical groove. Examples are lemurs, pottos, tarsiers, and the aye-aye.

Prost Alain Marie Pascal 1955– . French motor-racing driver who was world champion 1985, 1986, 1989, and 1993, and the first French world drivers' champion. To the end of the 1993 season he had won 51 Grand Prix from 199 starts. He retired 1993.

He raced in Formula One events from 1980 and had his first Grand Prix win in France 1981, driving a Renault. In 1984 he began driving for the McLaren team. He moved to Ferrari in 1990 for two years but was without a drive at the start of the 1992 season. He drove for Williams 1993, winning his fourth world championship before retiring at the end of the season.

prostaglandin any of a group of complex fatty acids present in the body that act as messenger substances between cells. Effects include stimulating the contraction of smooth muscle (for example, of the womb during birth), regulating the production of stomach acid, and modifying hormonal activity. In excess, prostaglandins may produce inflammatory disorders such as arthritis. Synthetic prostaglandins are used to induce labour in humans and domestic animals.

The analgesic actions of substances such as aspirin are due to inhibition of prostaglandin synthesis.

prostatectomy surgical removal of the ◊prostate gland. In many men over the age of 60 the prostate gland enlarges, causing obstruction to the urethra. This causes the bladder to swell with retained urine, leaving the sufferer more prone to infection of the urinary tract.

prostate gland gland surrounding and opening into the ◊urethra at the base of the ◊bladder in male mammals. The prostate gland produces an alkaline fluid that is released during ejaculation; this fluid activates sperm, and prevents their clumping together. Older men may develop benign prostatic hyperplasia, a painful condition in which the prostate becomes enlarged and restricts urine flow. This can cause further problems of the bladder and kidneys. It is treated by ◊prostatectomy.

prosthesis artificial device used to substitute for a body part which is defective or missing. Prostheses include artificial limbs, hearing aids, false teeth and eyes, heart ◊pacemakers and plastic heart valves and blood vessels.

prostitution receipt of money for sexual acts. Society's attitude towards prostitution varies according to place and period. In some countries, tolerance is combined with licensing of brothels and health checks on the prostitutes (both male and female). In the UK it is legal to be a prostitute, but soliciting for customers publicly, keeping a brothel, living on 'immoral earnings', and 'procuring' (arranging to make someone into a prostitute) and ◊kerb crawling (driving slowly seeking to entice someone into the car for sexual purposes) are illegal. In the USA, laws vary from state to state, with Nevada having legalized prostitution. Sex tourism is a big money-earner in parts of SE Asia, especially Thailand, attracting mostly men from N Europe, the USA, and Japan.

Laws vary in other European countries. For example, in France, Belgium, Italy, and Spain prostitution is tolerated but those who profit from it are repressed. In Denmark prostitution is authorized as a secondary activity. In Germany and the Netherlands a regulating system operates where prostitution is restricted to certain areas. In Greece, prostitution is considered a legal profession on condition that police authorization is obtained.

protactinium (Latin *proto* 'before' + actinium) silver-grey, radioactive, metallic element of the ◊actinide series, symbol Pa, atomic number 91, relative atomic mass 231.036. It occurs in nature in very small quantities, in ◊pitchblende and other uranium ores. It has 14 known isotopes; the longest-lived, Pa-231, has a half-life of 32,480 years.

The element was discovered in 1913 (Pa-234, with a half-life of only 1.2 minutes) as a product of uranium decay. Other isotopes were later found and the name was officially adopted in 1949, although it had been in use since 1918.

protease general term for a digestive enzyme capable of splitting proteins. Examples include pepsin, found in the stomach, and trypsin, found in the small intestine.

protectionism in economics, the imposition of heavy ◊duties or import ◊quotas by a government as a means of discouraging the import of foreign goods likely to compete with domestic products. Price controls, quota systems, and the reduction of surpluses are among the measures taken for agricultural products in the European Union.

protectorate formerly in international law, a small state under the direct or indirect control of a larger one. The 20th-century equivalent was a ◊trust territory. In English history the rule of Oliver and Richard ◊Cromwell 1653–59 is referred to as the Protectorate.

protein complex, biologically important substance composed of amino acids joined by ◊peptide bonds. Proteins are essential to all living organisms. As enzymes they regulate all aspects of metabolism. Structural proteins such as keratin and collagen make up the skin, claws, bones, tendons, and ligaments; muscle proteins produce movement; haemoglobin transports oxygen; and membrane proteins regulate the movement of substances into and out of cells. For humans, protein is an essential part of the diet, and is found in greatest quantity in soya beans and other grain legumes, meat, eggs, and cheese.

protein engineering the creation of synthetic proteins designed to carry out specific tasks. For example, an enzyme may be designed to remove grease from soiled clothes and remain stable at the high temperatures in a washing machine.

protein synthesis manufacture, within the cytoplasm of the cell, of the proteins an organism needs. The building blocks of proteins are ◊amino acids, of which there are 20 types. The pattern in which the amino acids are linked decides what kind of protein is produced. In turn it is the genetic code, contained within ◊DNA, that determines the precise order in which the amino acids are linked up during protein manufacture.

Interestingly, DNA is found only in the nucleus, yet protein synthesis occurs only in the cytoplasm. The information necessary for making the proteins is carried from the nucleus to the cytoplasm by another nucleic acid, ◊RNA.

Proterozoic eon of geological time, possible 3.5 billion to 570 million years ago, the second division of the Precambrian. It is defined as the time of simple life, since many rocks dating from this eon show traces of biological activity, and some contain the fossils of bacteria and algae.

Protestantism one of the main divisions of Christianity, which emerged from Roman Catholicism at the ◊Reformation. The chief denominations are the Anglican Communion (Episcopalian in the USA), Baptists, Lutherans, Methodists, Pentecostals, and Presbyterians, with a total membership of about 300 million.

Protestantism takes its name from the protest of Martin ◊Luther and his supporters at the Diet of Spires 1529 against the decision to reaffirm the edict of the Diet of Worms against the Reformation. Initially it denoted the position of the Lutherans as opposed to both Catholics and Reformed (Zwinglian or Calvinist), but it later came to be more generally applied.

The first conscious statement of Protestantism as a distinct movement was the Confession of Augsburg 1530. The chief characteristics of original Protestantism are the acceptance of the Bible as the only source of truth, the universal priesthood of all believers, and forgiveness of sins solely through faith in Jesus Christ. The Protestant church minimalises the liturgical aspects of Christianity and emphasizes the preaching and hearing of the word of God before sacramental faith and practice.

The many interpretations of doctrine and practice are reflected in the various denominations. The ecumenical movement of the 20th century has unsuccessfully attempted to reunite various Protestant denominations and, to some extent, the Protestant churches and the Catholic church. During the last 20 years there has been a worldwide upsurge in Christianity taking place largely outside the established church.

Proteus in Greek mythology, the warden of the sea beasts of the sea god Poseidon. He possessed the gift of prophecy and could transform himself into any form he chose to evade questioning.

prothallus in botany, a short-lived gametophyte of many ferns and other ◊pteridophytes (such as horsetails or clubmosses). It bears either the male or female sex organs, or both. Typically it is a small, green, flattened structure that is anchored in the soil by several ◊rhizoids (slender, hairlike structures, acting as roots) and needs damp conditions to survive. The reproductive organs are borne on the lower surface close to the soil. See also ◊alternation of generations.

protist in biology, a single-celled organism which has a eukaryotic cell, but which is not member of the plant, fungal, or animal kingdoms. The main protists are ◊protozoa.

Single-celled photosynthetic organisms, such as diatoms and dinoflagellates, are classified as protists or algae. Recently the term has also been used for members of the kingdom Protista, which features in certain five-kingdom classifications of the living world (see also ◊plant classification). This kingdom may include slime moulds, all algae (seaweeds as well as unicellular forms), and protozoa.

protocol in computing, an agreed set of standards for the transfer of data between different devices. They cover transmission speed, format of data, and the signals required to synchronize the transfer.

Protocols of Zion forged document containing supposed plans for Jewish world conquest, alleged to have been submitted by Theodor ◊Herzl to the first Zionist Congress at Basel 1897, and published in Russia 1905. Although proved to be a forgery 1921, the document was used by Hitler in his anti-Semitic campaign 1933–45.

proton (Greek 'first') in physics, a positively charged subatomic particle, a constituent of the nucleus of all atoms. It belongs to the ◊baryon subclass of the ◊hadrons. A proton is extremely long-lived, with a lifespan of at least 10^{32} years. It carries a unit positive charge equal to the negative

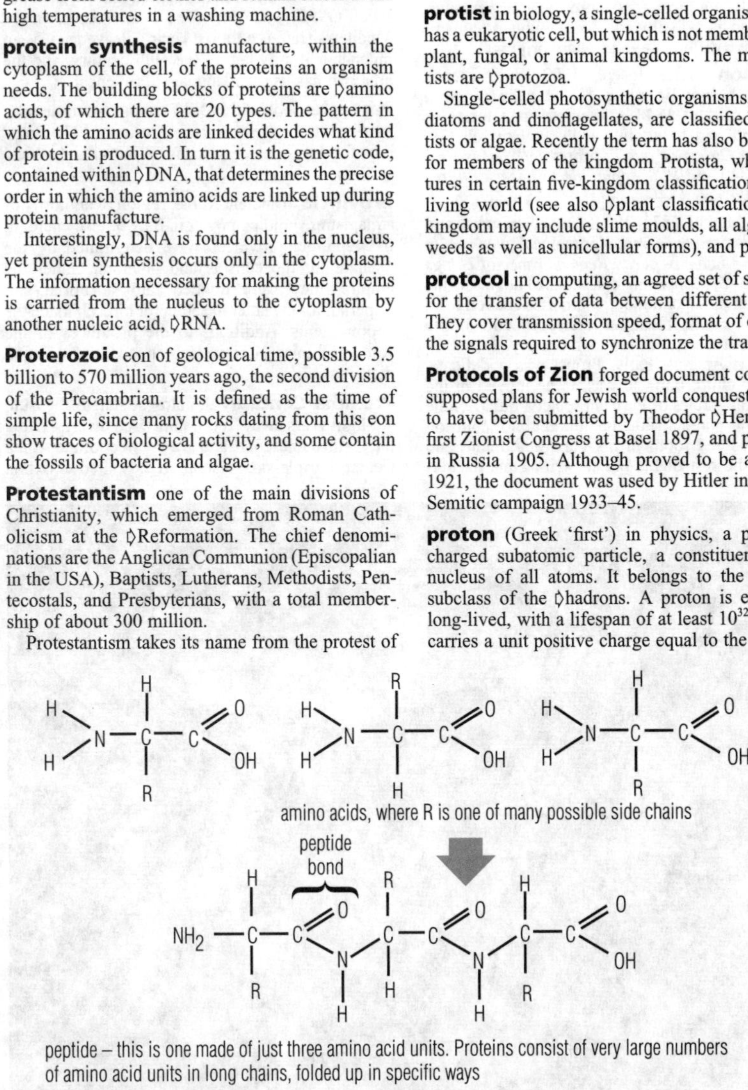

The chief contribution of Protestantism to human thought is its massive proof that God is a bore.

On **Protestantism**
H L Mencken
H L Mencken's Notebooks 1956

protein A protein molecule is a long chain of amino acids linked by peptide bonds. The properties of a protein are determined by the order, or sequence, of amino acids in its molecule, and by the three-dimensional structure of the molecular chain. The chain folds and twists, often forming a spiral shape.

Proust The French novelist Marcel Proust. In addition to his momentous *A la recherche du temps perdu* 1913–27, Proust wrote *Les plaisirs et les jours* 1896, *Pastiches et mélanges* 1919, and *Contre Sainte-Beuve* 1954. He also translated John Ruskin's *The Bible of Amiens* and *Sesame and Lilies* into French from 1899. *Corbis*

'Communism is inequality, but not as property is. Property is exploitation of the weak by the strong. Communism is exploitation of the strong by the weak.'

PIERRE-JOSEPH PROUDHON
What is Property? 1840

charge of an ◊electron. Its mass is almost 1,836 times that of an electron, or 1.67×10^{-27} kg. Protons are composed of two up ◊quarks and one down quark held together by ◊gluons. The number of protons in the atom of an element is equal to the atomic number of that element.

protoplasm contents of a living cell. Strictly speaking it includes all the discrete structures (organelles) in a cell, but it is often used simply to mean the jellylike material in which these float. The contents of a cell outside the nucleus are called ◊cytoplasm.

protozoa group of single-celled organisms without rigid cell walls. Some, such as amoeba, ingest other cells, but most are ◊saprotrophs or parasites. The group is polyphyletic (containing organisms which have different evolutionary origins).

Proudhon Pierre Joseph 1809–1865. French anarchist, born in Besançon. He sat in the Constituent Assembly of 1848, was imprisoned for three years, and had to go into exile in Brussels. He published *Qu'est-ce que la propriété/What is Property?* 1840 and *Philosophie de la misère/Philosophy of Poverty* 1846.

Proust Marcel 1871–1922. French novelist and critic. His immense autobiographical work *A la Recherche du temps perdu/Remembrance of Things Past* 1913–27, consisting of a series of novels, is the expression of his childhood memories coaxed from his subconscious; it is also a precise reflection of life in France at the end of the 19th century.

Born in Auteuil, Paris, Proust was a delicate, asthmatic child; until he was 35 he moved in the fashionable circles of Parisian society, but after the death of his parents 1904–05 he went into seclusion in a cork-lined room in his Paris apartment, and devoted the rest of his life to writing his masterpiece. Posthumous publications include the novel *Jean Santeuil* 1957, which seems to have been an early sketch for *A la recherche*, and *Contre Sainte-Beuve/By Way of Sainte-Beuve* 1954.

Prout William 1785–1850. British physician and chemist. In 1815 Prout published his hypothesis that the relative atomic mass of every atom is an exact and integral multiple of the mass of the hydrogen atom. The discovery of isotopes (atoms of the same element that have different masses) in the 20th century bore out his idea.

In 1827, Prout became the first scientist to classify the components of food into the three major divisions of carbohydrates, fats, and proteins.

Provençal language member of the Romance branch of the Indo-European language family, spoken in and around Provence in SE France. It is now regarded as a dialect or patois.

During the Middle Ages Provençal was in competition with French and was the language of the troubadours. It had a strong literary influence on such neighbouring languages as Italian, Spanish, and Portuguese. Since the 19th century, attempts have been made to revive it as a literary language.

Provençal literature Provençal literature originated in the 10th century and flowered in the 12th century with the work of the ◊troubadours, poet-musicians of the 12th–13th centuries. After the decline of the troubadours in the 13th century, Provençal virtually disappeared as a literary medium from the 14th until the 19th century, when Jacques Jasmin (1798–1864) and others paved the way for the Félibrige group of poets, of whom the greatest are Joseph Roumanille, Frédéric ◊Mistral, and Félix Gras (1844–1901).

Provence-Alpes-Côte d'Azur region of SE France, comprising the *départements* of Alpes-de-Haute-Provence, Hautes-Alpes, Alpes-Maritimes, Bouches-du-Rhône, Var, and Vaucluse; area 31,400 sq km/12,120 sq mi; capital Marseille; population (1990) 4,257,900. The Côte d'Azur, on the Mediterranean, is a tourist centre. Provence was an independent kingdom in the 10th century, and the area still has its own language, Provençal.

Proverbs book of the Old Testament traditionally ascribed to the Hebrew king ◊Solomon. The Proverbs form a series of maxims on moral and ethical matters.

provincia in ancient Rome, region of authority of a magistrate holding power in Italy or elsewhere. In the republic, provinces were determined by the ◊senate for the consuls and praetors. Under the empire, they were divided into senatorial and imperial; for the latter the emperor himself made the appointments. Additions to the provinces of the Roman empire effectively stopped after ◊Trajan died AD 117.

Proxima Centauri the closest star to the Sun, 4.2 light years away. It is a faint ◊red dwarf, visible only with a telescope, and is a member of the Alpha Centauri triple-star system. It is called Proxima because it is about 0.1 light years closer to us than its two partners.

Provence-Alpes-Côte d'Azur The village of Les Baux (formerly Les Beaux), situated on a limestone spur in the French *département* of Bouches-du-Rhône. Bauxite (the ore from which aluminium is made) was discovered nearby 1821 and was named after the village. *Sally Jenkins*

Prozac or ***fluoxetine*** antidepressant drug that functions mainly by boosting levels of the neurotransmitter ◊serotonin in the brain. Side effects include nausea and loss of libido. It is also used to treat some eating disorders, such as ◊bulimia. Prozac is controversial because it not only relieves depression but is also claimed, particularly in the USA, to make patients feel better than ever before, giving rise to the possibility of its future use as a personality 'improver' by healthy individuals.

Prud'hon Pierre Paul 1758–1823. French painter. One of the minor Romantic artists, opposed to the Neo-Classicism of Jacques-Louis ◊David, he is best known for his portraits and his mythological and allegorical subjects, such as *Love and Friendship* c. 1793 (Minneapolis Institute of Arts). He was patronized by Napoleon.

After winning the Prix de Rome 1784, Prud'hon visited Italy but, unlike his contemporary David, he was unaffected by the Neo-Classical vogue. His style, indebted to the Italian painter ◊Correggio, is an early expression of Romanticism.

Prunus genus of trees of the northern hemisphere, family Rosaceae, producing fruit with a fleshy, edible pericarp (outer wall). The genus includes plums, cherries, peaches, apricots, and also almonds.

Prussia N German state 1618–1945 on the Baltic coast. It was an independent kingdom until 1867, when it became, under Otto von ◊Bismarck, the military power of the North German Confederation and part of the German Empire 1871 under the Prussian king Wilhelm I. West Prussia became part of Poland under the Treaty of ◊Versailles, and East Prussia was largely incorporated into the USSR after 1945.

1618 Formed by the union of ◊Brandenburg and the duchy of Prussia (established 1525).

1640–88 The country's military power was founded by ◊Frederick William, the 'Great Elector'.

1701 Prussia became a kingdom under Frederick I.

1713–40 Frederick William I expanded the army.

1740–86 Silesia, East Frisia, and West Prussia were annexed by ◊Frederick II the Great.

1806 ◊Frederick William III was defeated at Jena by Napoleon Bonaparte.

1815 After the Congress of Vienna Prussia regained its lost territories and also acquired lands in the Rhineland and Saxony.

1848 The revolutions of 1848 overthrew the government but it was restored the following year.

1864 War with Denmark resulted in the acquisition of Schleswig.

1866 After the defeat of Austria, Prussia acquired Holstein and formed the North German Confederation with the territories of Hanover, Nassau, Frankfurt-am-Main, and Hesse-Cassel.

1871 After Prussia's victory in the Franco-Prussian War, the German Empire was proclaimed, under Bismarck's chancellorship, for Wilhelm I.

1918 Prussia became a republic after World War I.

1932 Prussia lost its local independence in Hitler's Germany and came under the control of the Reich.

1946 After World War II the Allies abolished Prussia altogether, dividing its territories among East and West Germany, Poland, and the USSR.

prussic acid former name for ◊hydrocyanic acid.

Prut river that rises in the Carpathian Mountains of SW Ukraine, and flows 900 km/565 mi to meet the Danube at Reni. For part of its course it follows the eastern frontier of Romania.

Przhevalsky Nikolai Mikhailovitch 1839–1888. Russian explorer and soldier. In 1870 he crossed the Gobi Desert to Beijing and then went on to the upper reaches of the Chang Jiang River. His attempts to penetrate Tibet as far as Lhasa failed on three occasions, but he continued to explore the mountain regions between Tibet and Mongolia, where he made collections of plants and animals, including a wild camel and a wild horse (the species is now known as Przhevalsky's horse).

The Kirghiz town of Karakol on the eastern shores of Lake Issyk Kul where he died was renamed Przewalski's in 1889.

psalm sacred poem or song of praise. The Book of Psalms in the Old Testament is divided into five books containing 150 psalms, traditionally ascribed to David, the second king of Israel. In the Christian church they may be sung antiphonally in ◊plainsong or set by individual composers to music in a great variety of styles, from Josquin Desprez's *De profundis* to Igor Stravinsky's *Symphony of Psalms* 1930.

PSBR abbreviation for ◊***public sector borrowing requirement***.

pseudocarp in botany, a fruitlike structure that incorporates tissue that is not derived from the ovary wall. The additional tissues may be derived from floral parts such as the ◊receptacle and ◊calyx. For example, the coloured, fleshy part of a strawberry develops from the receptacle and the true fruits are small ◊achenes – the 'pips' embedded in its outer surface. Rose hips are a type of pseudocarp that consists of a hollow, fleshy receptacle containing a number of achenes within. Different types of pseudocarp include pineapples, figs, apples, and pears.

A coenocarpium is a fleshy, multiple pseudocarp derived from an ◊inflorescence rather than a single flower. The pineapple has a thickened central axis surrounded by fleshy tissues derived from the receptacles and floral parts of many flowers. A fig is a type of pseudocarp called a syconium, formed from a hollow receptacle with small flowers attached to the inner wall. After fertilization the ovaries of the female flowers develop into one-seeded achenes.

Apples and pears are ◊pomes, another type of pseudocarp.

pseudocopulation attempted copulation by a male insect with a flower. It results in ◊pollination of the flower and is common in the orchid family, where the flowers of many species resemble a particular species of female bee. When a male bee attempts to mate with a flower, the pollinia (groups of pollen grains) stick to its body. They are transferred to the stigma of another flower when the insect attempts copulation again.

pseudomorph mineral that has replaced another *in situ* and has retained the external crystal shape of the original mineral.

psi in parapsychology, a hypothetical faculty common to humans and other animals said to be responsible for extrasensory perception, telekinesis, and other paranormal phenomena.

Psilocybe genus of mushroom with hallucinogenic properties, including the Mexican sacred mushroom *P. mexicana*, which contains compounds with effects similar to LSD (lysergic acid diethylamide, a hallucinogen). A related species *P. semilanceata* is found in N Europe.

psittacosis infectious acute or chronic disease, contracted by humans from birds (especially parrots), which produces pneumonialike symptoms. It is caused by a bacterium (*Chlamydia psittaci*, see ◊chlamydia) and treated with tetracycline.

psoriasis chronic, recurring skin disease characterized by raised, red, scaly patches, on the scalp, elbows, knees, and elsewhere. Tar preparations, steroid creams, and ultraviolet light are used to treat it, and sometimes it disappears spontaneously. Psoriasis may be accompanied by a form of arthritis (inflammation of the joints).

It is a common disease, sometimes running in families, and affecting 2% of the UK population.

Psyche late Greek personification of the soul as a winged girl or young woman. The goddess Aphrodite was so jealous of Psyche's beauty that she ordered her son Eros, the god of love, to make Psyche fall in love with the worst of men. Instead, he fell in love with her himself.

psychedelic drug any drug that produces hallucinations or altered states of consciousness. Such sensory experiences may be in the auditory, visual, tactile, olfactory, or gustatory fields or in any combination. Among drugs known to have psychedelic effects are LSD (lysergic acid diethylamide), mescaline, and, to a mild degree, marijuana, along with a number of other plant-derived or synthetically prepared substances.

psychedelic rock or ***acid rock*** pop music that usually involves advanced electronic equipment for both light and sound. The free-form improvisations and light shows that appeared about 1966, attempting to suggest or improve on mind-altering drug experiences, had by the 1980s evolved into stadium performances with lasers and other special effects.

psychiatry branch of medicine dealing with the diagnosis and treatment of mental disorder, normally divided into the areas of neurotic conditions, including anxiety, depression, and hysteria, and psychotic disorders, such as schizophrenia. Psychiatric treatment consists of drugs, analysis, or electroconvulsive therapy.

Psychiatrists are trained medical doctors (holding an MD degree) and may therefore prescribe drugs, whereas psychologists may hold a PhD but do not need a medical qualification to practise. See also ◊psychoanalysis.

psychoanalysis theory and treatment method for neuroses, developed by Sigmund ◊Freud in the 1890s. Psychoanalysis asserts that the impact of early childhood sexuality and experiences, stored in the ◊unconscious, can lead to the development of adult emotional problems. The main treatment method involves the free association of ideas, and their interpretation by patient and analyst, in order to discover these long-buried events and to grasp their significance to the patient, linking aspects of the patient's historical past with the present relationship to the analyst. Psychoanalytic treatment aims to free the patient from specific symptoms and from irrational inhibitions and anxieties.

concepts As a theoretical system, psychoanalysis rests on three basic concepts. The central concept is that of the unconscious, a reservoir within one's mental state which contains elements and experiences of which one is unaware, but which may to some extent be brought into preconscious and conscious awareness, or inferred from aspects of behaviour. The second and related basic concept is that of resistance, a process by which unconscious elements are forcibly kept out of the conscious awareness by an active repressive force. Freud came to experience the third basic concept in his work, known as transference, with his earliest patients, who transferred to him aspects of their past relationships with others, so that their relationship with him was coloured by their previous feelings. The analysis of the transference in all its manifestations has become a vital aspect of current psychoanalytic practice.

id, ego, and superego Freud proposed a model of human psychology based on the concept of the conflicting ◊id, ◊ego, and ◊superego. The id is the mind's instinctual element which demands pleasure and satisfaction; the ego is the conscious mind which deals with the demands of the id and superego; the superego is the ethical element which acts as a conscience and may produce feelings of guilt. The conflicts between these three elements can be used to explain a range of neurotic symptoms.

other schools In the early 1900s a group of psychoanalysts gathered around Freud. Some of these later broke away and formed their own schools, notably Alfred ◊Adler in 1911 and Carl ◊Jung in 1913. The significance of early infantile experience has been further elaborated in the field of child analysis, particularly in the work of Melanie ◊Klein and her students, who pay particular attention to the development of the infant in the first six to eight months of life.

psychology systematic study of human and animal behaviour. The first psychology laboratory was founded 1879 by Wilhelm ◊Wundt at Leipzig, Germany. The subject includes diverse areas of study and application, among them the roles of instinct, heredity, environment, and culture; the processes of sensation, perception, learning, and memory; the bases of motivation and emotion; and the functioning of thought, intelligence, and language. Significant psychologists have included Gustav Fechner, founder of psychophysics; Wolfgang Köhler, one of the ◊Gestalt or 'whole' psychologists; Sigmund Freud and his associates Carl Jung and Alfred Adler; William James, Jean Piaget; Carl Rogers; Hans Eysenck; J B Watson; and B F Skinner.

Experimental psychology emphasizes the application of rigorous and objective scientific methods to the study of a wide range of mental processes and behaviour, whereas social psychology concerns the study of individuals within their social environment; for example, within groups and organizations. This has led to the development of related fields such as occupational psychology, which studies human behaviour at work, and educational psychology. Clinical psychology concerns the understanding and treatment of mental health disorders, such as anxiety, phobias, or depression; treatment may include behaviour therapy, cognitive therapy, counselling, psychoanalysis, or some combination of these.

Modern studies have been diverse; for example, the psychological causes of obesity; the nature of religious experience; and the underachievement of women seen as resulting from social pressures. Other related subjects are the nature of sleep and dreams, and the possible extensions of the senses, which leads to the more contentious ground of ◊parapsychology. *See timeline on following page.*

psychometrics measurement of mental processes. This includes intelligence and aptitude testing to help in job selection and in the clinical assessment of cognitive deficiencies resulting from brain damage.

psychopathy personality disorder characterized by chronic antisocial behaviour (violating the rights of others, often violently) and an absence of feelings of guilt about the behaviour.

psychosis or ***psychotic disorder*** general term for a serious mental disorder where the individual commonly loses contact with reality and may experience hallucinations (seeing or hearing things that do not exist) or delusions (fixed false beliefs). For example, in a paranoid psychosis, an individual may believe that others are plotting against him or her. A major type of psychosis is ◊schizophrenia.

psychosomatic of a physical symptom or disease thought to arise from emotional or mental factors.

The term 'psychosomatic' has been applied to many conditions, including asthma, migraine, hypertension, and peptic ulcers. Whereas it is unlikely that these and other conditions are wholly due to psychological factors, emotional states such as anxiety or depression do have a distinct influence on the frequency and severity of illness.

psychotherapy any treatment for psychological problems that involves talking rather than surgery or drugs. Examples include ◊cognitive therapy and ◊psychoanalysis.

Ptah Egyptian god, the divine potter, a personification of the creative force. He was worshipped at ◊Memphis, and was often portrayed as a mummified man. He was said to be the father of ◊Imhotep, the physician and architect.

ptarmigan hardy, northern ground-dwelling bird of genus *Lagopus*, family Phasianidae (which also includes ◊grouse), with feathered legs and feet.

The willow ptarmigan *L. lagopus*, found in bushes and heather in northern parts of North America, Europe, and Asia, grows to 38 cm/15 in and turns white in the winter.

The rock ptarmigan *L. mutus* is found in mountainous areas above the tree line in N Europe. About 36 cm/1.2 ft long. It is an excellent instance of protective coloration, assimilating itself perfectly to its surroundings by the plumage changing with the season through white, grey, red or brown, except for

'Happiness is salutary for the body but sorrow develops the powers of the spirit.'

MARCEL PROUST
Remembrance of Things Past: Time Regained

ptarmigan This member of the grouse family inhabits the high mountains, remote forests, and tundra of northern latitudes around the world. It relies mainly on camouflage for defence and, in winter, turns from a speckled greyish brown to pure white with dark tail feathers. It feeds mainly on fruit, seeds, and buds.

PSYCHOLOGY: TIMELINE

1846	E H Weber reported on his pioneering quantitative investigations of touch in *On Touch and Common Sensibility*.
1860	G T Fechner published *Elements of Psychophysics*, in which he presented the first statistical treatment of psychological data.
1879	Wilhelm Wundt founded the first psychological laboratory in Leipzig.
1885	H Ebbinghaus published his experimental research into memory.
1890	William James published the first comprehensive psychology text, *Principles of Psychology*.
1895	Joseph Breuer and Sigmund Freud published *Studies on Hysteria*, containing the first writings on psychoanalysis.
1896	The first psychology clinic was founded by Lightner Witner at the University of Pennsylvania; the first use of the term 'clinical psychology'.
1900	Freud's *Interpretation of Dreams* published.
1905	Alfred Binet and Théodore Simon developed the first effective intelligence test.
1906	Ivan Pavlov first lectured in the West on conditioned reflexes in animals.
1908	The first textbook of social psychology was published by William McDougall and E A Ross.
1911	Max Wertheimer, Wolfgang Köhler, and Kurt Koffka founded the Gestalt School in Frankfurt.
1913	John B Watson's article 'Psychology as a behaviorist views it' was published and the behaviourist movement thus launched.
1923	Jean Piaget's *The Language and the Thought of the Child* published, the first of his many books on the development of thinking.
1927	C Spearman proposed in *The Abilities of Man* that intelligence comprises two kinds of factors, a general factor ('g') and specific factors.
1929	H Berger published his findings on the electroencephalogram (EEG).
1938	B F Skinner published *The Behavior of Organisms*, detailing his study of operant conditioning and his radical behaviourism.
1943	C L Hull published his influential book *Principles of Behavior*, the most rigorous account of conditioning and learning from the perspective of behaviourism.
1947	Hans Eysenck published *Dimensions of Personality*, a large-scale study of neuroticism and extroversion.
1948	Norbert Wiener coined the term 'cybernetics' and published *Cybernetics: Control and Communication in the Animal and Machine*.
1949	D O Hebb's *Organization of Behaviour* re-emphasized the role of central (brain) processes in the explanation of behaviour.
1950	Alan Turing proposed his test of whether a machine can be said to think, in the article 'Computing Machinery and Intelligence'. *The Authoritarian Personality* by Theodor Adorno and others published.
1953	E Aserinksy and N Kleitman published the first account of REM (rapid eye movement) sleep.
1957	Noam Chomsky published *Syntactic Structures*, a seminal work of psycholinguistics, which revolutionized the study of language. L Festinger published *A Theory of Cognitive Dissonance*.
1958	A Newell and H A Simon, with J C Shaw, published their article on human problem-solving, the first account of the information-processing approach to human psychology.
1958	Donald E Broadbent published *Perception and Communication*, a detailed account of information-processing psychology.
1960	G A Miller, E Galanter, and K Pribam applied the idea of a hierarchically structured computer program to the whole of psychology in their *Plans and the Structure of Behaviour*.
1961	A Newell and H A Simon published their pioneering computational model of human problem-solving, the General Problem Solver.
1962	M S Gazzaniga, J E Bogen, and R W Sperry first reported on the 'split brain' phenomenon in epileptic patients.
1963	Stanley Milgram published his first studies of obedience and the conditions under which individuals will inflict harm when so instructed.
1967	Konovski published *Integrative Activity of the Brain*, a melding of conditioning principles with sensation and motivation. Ulrich Neisser's *Cognitive Psychology* marked renewed interest in the study of cognition after years in which behaviourism had dominated.
1968	R C Atkinson and R M Shiffin developed their theory of interacting memory systems in cognitive processing.
1970	T Shallice and E K Warrington provided the first of much evidence from brain-damaged patients that short-term memory is parallel with long-term memory and is best viewed as a collection of separate processing modules.
1972	E Tulving distinguished episodic memory (for personal experience) and semantic memory (for general knowledge and facts about the world).
1983	J A Fodor published *The Modularity of Mind*, dividing the mind into independent cognitive processors and defining their activity.
1985	A new view of intelligence proposed by Robert J Sternberg in *Beyond IQ: A Triarchic Theory of Intelligence*.
1986	J L McClelland and D E Rumelhart developed complex computational networks using parallel processing to simulate human learning and categorization.
1989	The mathematician Roger Penrose, in *The Emperor's New Mind*, argued that the computational account of the mind is incomplete, particularly concerning consciousness.
1992	The philosopher John Searle, in *The Rediscovery of the Mind*, argued for the return of consciousness to its position as the central topic in psychology and cognitive science.

the wings, underparts and legs, which are always white. It hatches its young in June in a depression among moss and stones. The males are monogamous.

pteridophyte simple type of ◊vascular plant. The pteridophytes comprise four classes: the Psilosida, including the most primitive vascular plants, found mainly in the tropics; the Lycopsida, including the club mosses; the Sphenopsida, including the horsetails; and the Pteropsida, including the ferns. They do not produce seeds.

They are mainly terrestrial, non-flowering plants characterized by the presence of a vascular system; the possession of true stems, roots, and leaves; and by a marked ◊alternation of generations, with the sporophyte forming the dominant generation in the life cycle. The pteridophytes formed a large and dominant flora during the Carboniferous period, but many are now known only from fossils.

pterodactyl genus of ◊pterosaur.

pterosaur extinct flying reptile of the order Pterosauria, existing in the Mesozoic age. They ranged from the size of a starling to the 12 m/39 ft wingspan of *Arambourgiania philadelphiae*; the largest of the pterosaurs discovered so far. Some had horns on their heads that, when in flight, made a whistling to roaring sound.

Pterosaurs were formerly assumed to be smooth-skinned gliders, but recent discoveries show that at least some were furry, probably warm-blooded, and may have had muscle fibres and blood vessels on their wings, stiffened by moving the hind legs, thus allowing controlled and strong flapping flight.

Ptolemy (Claudius Ptolemaeus) c. AD 100–c. AD 170. Egyptian astronomer and geographer. His *Almagest* developed the theory that Earth is the centre of the universe, with the Sun, Moon, and stars revolving around it. In 1543 the Polish astronomer ◊Copernicus proposed an alternative to the Ptolemaic system. Ptolemy's *Geography* was a standard source of information until the 16th century.

The *Almagest* (he called it *Syntaxis*) contains all his works on astronomical themes, the only authoritative works until the time of ◊Copernicus. Probably inspired by ◊Plato, Ptolemy began with the premise that the Earth was a perfect sphere. All planetry orbits were circular, but those of Mercury and Venus, and possibly Mars (Ptolemy was not sure), were epicyclic (the planets orbited a point that itself was orbiting the Earth). The sphere of the stars formed a dome with points of light attached or pricked through.

Ptolemy dynasty of kings of Macedonian origin who ruled Egypt over a period of 300 years; they included:

Ptolemy I c. 367–283 BC. Ruler of Egypt from 323 BC, king from 304. He was one of ◊Alexander the Great's generals, and established the dynasty and Macedonian organization of the state in Alexandria.

Ptolemy II 308–246 BC. Ruler of Egypt 283–246 BC. He consolidated Greek control and administration, constructing a canal from the Red Sea to the Nile as well as the museum, library, and the Pharos (lighthouse) at Alexandria, one of the ◊Seven Wonders of the World. He was the son of Ptolemy I.

Ptolemy XIII 63–47 BC. Joint ruler of Egypt with his sister-wife ◊Cleopatra in the period preceding the Roman annexation of Egypt. He was killed fighting against Julius ◊Caesar.

ptomaine any of a group of toxic chemical substances (alkaloids) produced as a result of decomposition by bacterial action on proteins.

puberty stage in human development when the individual becomes sexually mature. It may occur from the age of ten upwards. The sexual organs take on their adult form and pubic hair grows. In girls, menstruation begins, and the breasts develop; in boys, the voice breaks and becomes deeper, and facial hair develops.

pubes lowest part of the front of the human trunk, the region where the external generative organs are situated. The underlying bony structure, the pubic arch, is formed by the union in the midline of the two pubic bones, which are the front portions of the hip bones. In women this is more prominent than in men, to allow more room for the passage of the child's head at birth, and it carries a pad of fat and connective tissue, the *mons veneris* (mount of Venus), for its protection.

public corporation company structure that is similar in organization to a public limited company but with no shareholder rights. Such corporations are established to carry out state-owned activities, but are financially independent of the state and are run by a board. The first public corporation to be formed in the UK was the Central Electricity Board in the 1920s.

public good in economics, a service, resource, or facility, such as street lighting, that is equally accessible to everyone for unlimited use.

Ptolemy Egyptian astronomer Ptolemy using a quadrant to observe the Moon, watched by Urania, the muse of astronomy. Ptolemy expounded the theory that the Earth is at the centre of the universe. From a print of 1508. *Image Select (UK) Ltd*

Public Health Acts 1848, 1872, 1875 in the UK, legislation enacted by Parliament to deal with squalor and disease and to establish a code of sanitary law. The first act, in 1848, established a central board of health with three members who were responsible to Parliament to impose local boards of health in districts where the death rate was above the national average and to make provision for other local boards of health to be established by petition. The 1872 act made it obligatory for every local authority to appoint a medical officer of health. The 1875 act consolidated previous acts and provided a comprehensive code for public health.

public inquiry in English law, a legal investigation where witnesses are called and evidence is produced in a similar fashion to a court of law. Inquiries may be held as part of legal procedure, or into a matter of public concern. The longest and most expensive inquiry ever held was the Sizewell B nuclear-plant inquiry, which lasted for two and a quarter years (approved 1987).

public lending right (PLR) method of paying a royalty to authors when books are borrowed from libraries, similar to a royalty on performance of a play or piece of music. Payment to the copyright holder for such borrowings was introduced in Australia 1974 and in the UK 1984.

public limited company (plc) registered company in which shares and debentures may be offered to the public. It must have a minimum of two shareholders and there is no upper limit. The company's financial records must be available for any member of the public to scrutinize, and the company's name must carry the words 'public limited company' or initials 'plc'. A public company can raise large sums of money to fuel its development and expansion by inviting the public to buy shares.

Public Order Act UK act of Parliament 1986 that abolished the common-law offences of riot, rout, unlawful assembly, and affray and created a new expanded range of statutory offences: riot, violent disorder, affray, threatening behaviour, and disorderly conduct. These are all arrestable offences that may be committed in both private and public places. Prosecution for riot requires the consent of the Director of Public Prosecutions.

public school in England and Wales, a prestigious fee-paying independent school. In Scotland, the USA, and many other English-speaking countries, a 'public' school is a state-maintained school, and independent schools are generally known as 'private' schools.

Some English public schools (for example Eton, Harrow, Rugby, Winchester) are ancient foundations, usually originally intended for poor male scholars; others developed in the 18th–19th centuries. Among those for girls are Roedean and Benenden. Many public schools are coeducational in the sixth form, and some boys' schools now admit girls at 13. Some discipline (less than formerly) is in the hands of senior boys and girls (prefects).

public sector the part of the economy that is owned and controlled by the state, namely central government, local government, and government enterprises. In a ◊command economy, the public sector allocates most of the resources in the economy. The opposite of the public sector is the ◊private sector, where resources are allocated by private individuals and business organizations.

public sector borrowing requirement (PSBR) amount of money needed by a government to cover any deficit in financing its own activities. It includes loans to local authorities and public corporations, and also the funds raised by local authorities and public corporations from other sources.

public sector debt repayment (PSDR) amount left over when government expenditure (◊public spending) is subtracted from government receipts. A PSDR enables a government to repay some of the ◊national debt.

public spending expenditure by government, covering the military, health, education, infrastructure, development projects, and the cost of servicing overseas borrowing.

A principal source of revenue to cover public expenditure is taxation. Most countries present their plans for spending in their annual budgets.

Puccini The composer Giacomo Puccini (1858–1924). One of the last great Romantic composers, Puccini also introduced 20th-century elements of realism (verismo) into his operas. Although his music was successful with the public, many critics have not been able to recognize his genius. *Image Select (UK) Ltd*

Puccini Giacomo (Antonio Domenico Michele Secondo Maria) 1858–1924. Italian opera composer. His music shows a strong gift for melody and dramatic effect and his operas combine exotic plots with elements of *verismo* (realism). They include *Manon Lescaut* 1893, *La Bohème* 1896, *Tosca* 1900, *Madame Butterfly* 1904, and the unfinished *Turandot* 1926.

puddle clay clay, with sand or gravel, that has had water added and mixed thoroughly so that it becomes watertight. The term was coined 1762 by the canal builder James Brindley, although the use of such clay in dams goes back to Roman times.

Pudovkin Vsevolod Illarionovich 1893–1953. Russian film director. His films include the silent *Mother* 1926, *The End of St Petersburg* 1927, and *Storm over Asia* 1928; and the sound films *Deserter* 1933 and *Suvorov* 1941.

Pueblo (Spanish 'village') a flat-roofed stone or adobe house, sometimes terraced, and several stories high. It is the communal dwelling house of the Hopi, Zuni, and other North American Indians of Arizona and New Mexico. In its capitalized form the word is also the generic name for the Native Americans themselves.

puerperal fever infection of the genital tract of the mother after childbirth, due to lack of aseptic conditions. Formerly often fatal, it is now rare and treated with antibiotics.

Puerto Rico the Commonwealth of; easternmost island of the Greater Antilles, situated between the US Virgin Islands and the Dominican Republic
area 9,000 sq km/3,475 sq mi
capital San Juan
towns and cities ports Mayagüez, Ponce
features volcanic mountains run E–W; the islands of Vieques and Culebra belong to Puerto Rico
exports sugar, tobacco, rum, pineapples, textiles, plastics, chemicals, processed foods, vegetables, coffee
currency US dollar
population (1992 est) 3,336,000
language Spanish and English (official)
religion Roman Catholic
government under the constitution of 1952, similar to that of the USA, with a governor elected for four years, and a legislative assembly with a senate and house of representatives. Residents are US citizens, represented in US Congress by an elected Resident Commissioner with a seat in the House of Representatives.
history visited 1493 by Columbus; annexed by Spain 1509; ceded to the USA after the ◊Spanish-American War 1898; known as Porto Rico ('Rich Port') 1898–1932; achieved commonwealth status with local self-government 1952.

puff adder variety of ◊adder, a poisonous snake.

puffball globulous fruiting body of certain fungi (see ◊fungus) that cracks with maturity, releasing the enclosed spores in the form of a brown powder; for example, the common puffball *Lycoperdon perlatum*.

puffer fish fish of the family Tetraodontidae. As a means of defence it inflates its body with air or water until it becomes spherical and the skin spines become erect. Puffer fish are mainly found in warm waters, where they feed on molluscs, crustaceans, and coral.

They vary in size, up to 50 cm/20 in long. The skin of some puffer fish is poisonous (25 times more toxic than cyanide). In Japan, where they are called *fugu*, they are prized as a delicacy after the poison has been removed. Nevertheless, the death of about 100 diners is recorded each year.

puffin any of various sea birds of the genus *Fratercula* of the ◊auk family, found in the N Atlantic and Pacific. The puffin is about 35 cm/14 in long,

puffball The common puffball is often found growing in clumps. It occurs in most woodlands during early autumn and is edible until mature. Superficially it is similar to several rather rarer species. *Premaphotos Wildlife*

puffin The puffin *Fratercula arctica* breeds in burrows in colonies distributed around the coast and islands of NW Europe. For breeding success it relies heavily upon shoals of sand eels that thrive in the waters in this area.

with a white face and front, red legs, and a large deep bill, very brightly coloured in summer. Having short wings and webbed feet, puffins are poor fliers but excellent swimmers. They nest in rock crevices, or make burrows, and lay a single egg.

The Atlantic, or common, puffin *F. arctica* has a distinctive striped bill. It breeds in the spring in colonies on islands, and spends the winter at sea.

pug breed of small dog with short wrinkled face, hanging ears, chunky body, and tail curled over the hip. It weighs 6–8 kg/13–18 lb. Its short coat may be black, beige or grey; the beige or grey dogs have black on the face and ears.

Puget Sound inlet of the Pacific Ocean on the west coast of Washington State, USA.

Pugin Augustus Welby Northmore 1812–1852. English architect. He collaborated with Charles ◊Barry in the detailed design of the Houses of Parliament. He did much to instigate the ◊Gothic Revival in England, largely through his book *Contrasts* 1836.

Puglia (English ***Apulia***) region of Italy, the SE 'heel'; area 19,300 sq km/7,450 sq mi; capital Bari; population (1992 est) 4,050,000. Products include wheat, grapes, almonds, olives, and vegetables. The main industrial centre is Taranto.

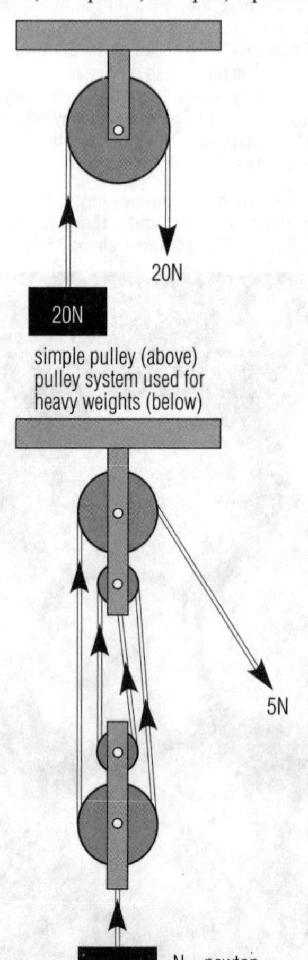

pulley The mechanical advantage of a pulley increases with the number of rope strands. If a pulley system has four ropes supporting the load, the mechanical advantage is four, and a 5 newton force will lift a 20 newton load.

P'u-i Henry, (or ***Pu-Yi***) 1906–1967. Last emperor of China (as Hsuan Tung) from 1908 until his deposition 1912; he was restored for a week 1917. After his deposition he chose to be called Henry. He was president 1932–34 and emperor 1934–45 of the Japanese puppet state of Manchukuo (see ◊Manchuria).

pūjā worship, in Hinduism, Buddhism, and Jainism.

Pulitzer Joseph 1847–1911. Hungarian-born US newspaper publisher. He acquired *The World* 1883 in New York City and, as a publisher, his format set the style for the modern newspaper. After his death, funds provided in his will established 1912 the school of journalism at Columbia University and the annual Pulitzer Prizes in journalism, literature, and music (from 1917). *See list of tables on p. 1177.*

pulley simple machine consisting of a fixed, grooved wheel, sometimes in a block, around which a rope or chain can be run. A simple pulley serves only to change the direction of the applied effort (as in a simple hoist for raising loads). The use of more than one pulley results in a mechanical advantage, so that a given effort can raise a heavier load.

The mechanical advantage depends on the arrangement of the pulleys. For instance, a block and tackle arrangement with three ropes supporting the load will lift it with one-third of the effort needed to lift it directly (if friction is ignored), giving a mechanical advantage of 3.

Pullman George Mortimer 1831–1897. US engineer and entrepreneur who developed the Pullman railway car from 1864. It was not the first sleeping carriage but it was the most luxurious. Pullman cars were initially staffed entirely by black porters whose only income was from tips.

pulsar celestial source that emits pulses of energy at regular intervals, ranging from a few seconds to a few thousandths of a second. Pulsars are thought to be rapidly rotating ◊neutron stars, which flash at radio and other wavelengths as they spin. They were discovered in 1967 by Jocelyn Bell Burnell (1943–) and Antony ◊Hewish at the Mullard Radio Astronomy Observatory, Cambridge, England. Over 500 radio pulsars are now known in our Galaxy, although a million or so may exist.

Pulsars slow down as they get older, and eventually the flashes fade. Of the 500 known radio pulsars, 20 are millisecond pulsars (flashing 1,000 times a second). Such pulsars are thought to be more than a billion years old. Two pulsars, one (estimated to be 1,000 years old) in the Crab nebula and one (estimated to be 11,000 years old) in the constellation Vela, give out flashes of visible light. ▷ *See feature on pp. 70–71.*

pulse impulse transmitted by the heartbeat throughout the arterial systems of vertebrates. When the heart muscle contracts, it forces blood into the ◊aorta (the chief artery). Because the arteries are elastic, the sudden rise of pressure causes a throb or sudden swelling through them. The actual flow of the blood is about 60 cm/2 ft a second in humans. The average adult pulse rate is generally about 70 per minute. The pulse can be felt where an artery is near the surface, for example in the wrist or the neck.

pulse crop such as peas and beans. Pulses are grown primarily for their seeds, which provide a concentrated source of vegetable protein, and make a vital contribution to human diets in poor countries where meat is scarce, and among vegetarians. Soya beans are the major temperate protein crop in the West; most are used for oil production or for animal feed. In Asia, most are processed into soya milk and beancurd. Peanuts dominate pulse production in the tropical world and are generally consumed as human food.

Pulses play a useful role in ◊crop rotation as they help to raise soil nitrogen levels as well as acting as break crops. In the mid-1980s, world production was about 50 million tonnes a year.

pulse-code modulation (PCM) in physics, a form of digital ◊modulation in which microwaves or light waves (the carrier waves) are switched on and off in pulses of varying length according to a binary code. It is a relatively simple matter to transmit data that are already in binary code, such as those used by computer, by these means. However, if an analogue audio signal is to be transmitted, it must first be converted to a pulse-amplitude modulated signal (PAM) by regular sampling of its amplitude. The value of the amplitude is then converted into a binary code for transmission on the carrier wave.

pulsed high frequency (PHF) instrumental application of high-frequency radio waves in short bursts to damaged tissue to relieve pain, reduce bruising and swelling, and speed healing.

puma also called cougar or mountain lion large wild cat *Felis concolar* found in North and South America. Tawny-coated, it is 1.5 m/4.5 ft long with a 1-m/3-ft tail. Cougars live alone, with each male occupying a distinct territory; they eat deer, rodents, and cattle. Although in some areas they have been hunted nearly to extinction, in California puma populations had grown by 1996, when numbers reached an estimated 5,000–6,000.

pumice light volcanic rock produced by the frothing action of expanding gases during the solidification of lava. It has the texture of a hard sponge and is used as an abrasive.

pump any device for moving liquids and gases, or compressing gases. Some pumps, such as the traditional lift pump used to raise water from wells, work by a reciprocating (up-and-down) action. Movement of a piston in a cylinder with a one-way valve creates a partial vacuum in the cylinder, thereby sucking water into it.

Gear pumps, used to pump oil in a car's lubrication system, have two meshing gears that rotate inside a housing, and the teeth move the oil. Rotary pumps contain a rotor with vanes projecting from it inside a casing, sweeping the oil round as they move.

pumped storage hydroelectric plant that uses surplus electricity to pump water back into a high-level reservoir. In normal working conditions the water flows from this reservoir through the ◊turbines to generate power for feeding into the grid. At times of low power demand, electricity is taken from the grid to turn the turbines into pumps that then pump the water back again. This ensures that there is always a maximum 'head' of water in the reservoir to give the maximum output when required.

pumpkin gourd *Cucurbita pepo* of the family Cucurbitaceae. The large, spherical fruit has a thick, orange rind, pulpy flesh, and many seeds.

punctuated equilibrium model evolutionary theory developed by Niles Eldredge and US palaeontologist Stephen Jay Gould 1972 to explain discontinuities in the fossil record. It claims that periods of rapid change alternate with periods of relative stability (stasis), and that the appearance of new lineages is a separate process from the gradual evolution of adaptive changes within a species.

The pattern of stasis and more rapid change is now widely accepted, but the second part of the theory remains unsubstantiated.

The turnover pulse hypothesis of US biologist Elisabeth Vrba postulates that the periods of rapid evolutionary change are triggered by environmental changes, particularly changes in climate.

punctuation system of conventional signs (punctuation marks) and spaces employed to organize written and printed language in order to make it as readable, clear, and logical as possible.

It contributes to the effective layout of visual language; if a work is not adequately punctuated, there may be problems of ambiguity and unclear association among words. Conventions of punctuation differ from language to language, and there are preferred styles in the punctuation of a language like English. Some people prefer a fuller use of punctuation, while others punctuate lightly; comparably, the use of punctuation will vary according to the kind of passage being produced: a personal letter, a newspaper article, and a technical report are all laid out and punctuated in distinctive ways.

Standard punctuation marks and conventions include the period (full stop or point), comma, colon, semicolon, exclamation mark (or point), question mark, apostrophe, hyphen, and parenthesis (including dashes, brackets, and the use of parenthetical commas).

Pune formerly ***Poona*** city in Maharashtra, India; population (1991) 2,494,000. Products include chemicals, rice, sugar, cotton, paper, and jewellery. Industries include cars, trucks, scooters, and motorbikes; pumps, cables, machinery, arms and ammunitions, cutting tools, televisions, boilers, and generators.

Punic Wars three wars between ◊Rome and ◊Carthage: First Punic War 264–241 BC, resulted in the defeat of the Carthaginians under ◊Hamilcar Barca and the cession of Sicily to Rome; Second Punic War 218–201 BC, Hannibal invaded Italy, defeated the Romans at Trebia, Trasimene, and at Cannae (under ◊Fabius Maximus), but was finally defeated himself by ◊Scipio Africanus Major at Zama (now in Algeria); Third Punic War 149–146 BC, ended in the destruction of Carthage, and its possessions becoming the Roman province of Africa.

Punjab (Sanskrit 'five rivers': the Indus tributaries Jhelum, Chenab, Ravi, Beas, and Sutlej) former state of British India, now divided between India and Pakistan. Punjab was annexed by Britain 1849 after the Sikh Wars (1845–46 and 1848–49), and formed into a province with its capital at Lahore. Under the British, W Punjab was extensively irrigated, and land was granted to Indians who had served in the British army.

Punjab state of NW India
area 50,400 sq km/19,454 sq mi
capital Chandigarh
towns and cities Amritsar, Jalandhar, Faridkot, Ludhiana
features mainly agricultural, crops chiefly under irrigation; longest life expectancy rates in India (59 for women, 64 for men); Harappa has ruins from the ◊Indus Valley civilization 2500 to 1600 BC
industry wheat, rice, textiles, sewing machines, sugar
population (1994 est) 21,695,000
language Punjabi
religion 60% Sikh, 30% Hindu; there is friction between the two groups
history in 1919 unrest led to the Punjab riots (see ◊Amritsar Massacre).

Punjab state of NE Pakistan
area 205,344 sq km/79,263 sq mi
capital Lahore
features wheat cultivation (by irrigation)
population (1981) 47,292,000
language Punjabi, Urdu
religion Muslim.

Punjabi the majority ethnic group living in the Punjab. Approximately 37 million live in the Pakistan half of Punjab, while another 14 million live on the Indian side of the border. In addition to Sikhs, there are Rajputs in Punjab, some of whom have adopted Islam. The Punjabi language belongs to the Indo-Iranian branch of the Indo-European family. It is considered by some to be a variety of Hindi, by others to be a distinct language.

Punjab massacres in the violence occurring after the partition of India 1947, more than a million people died while relocating in the Punjab. The eastern section became an Indian state, while the western area, dominated by the Muslims, went to Pakistan. Violence occurred as Muslims fled from eastern Punjab, and Hindus and Sikhs moved from Pakistan to India. ▷ *See feature on pp. 432–433.*

punk movement of disaffected youth of the late 1970s, manifesting itself in fashions and music designed to shock or intimidate. Punk rock began in the UK and stressed aggressive performance within a three-chord, three-minute format, as exemplified by the Sex Pistols.

Ostensibly a rejection of everything that had gone before, punk rock drew on more than a decade of US garage bands; reggae and rockabilly were also important influences on, for example, the Clash, the most successful British punk band. The punk movement brought more women into rock (for example, the Slits 1977–82) and was antiracist and anti-establishment. The musical limitations imposed by its insistence on amateurism and provoking outrage contributed to the decline of punk rock, but aspects live on in ◊hardcore punk and ◊grunge.

pupa nonfeeding, largely immobile stage of some insect life cycles, in which larval tissues are broken down, and adult tissues and structures are formed.

In many insects, the pupa is exarate, with the appendages (legs, antennae, wings) visible outside the pupal case; in butterflies and moths, it is called a chrysalis, and is obtect, with the appendages developing inside the case.

puppet figure manipulated on a small stage, usually by an unseen operator. The earliest known puppets are from 10th-century BC China. The types include finger or glove puppets and string marionettes (which reached a high artistic level in ancient Burma and Sri Lanka and in Italian princely courts from the 16th to 18th centuries, and for which the composer Franz Joseph Haydn wrote his operetta *Dido* 1778); shadow silhouettes (operated by rods and seen on a lit screen, as in Java); and bunraku (devised in Osaka, Japan), in which three or four black-clad operators on stage may combine to work each puppet about 1 m/3 ft high.

During the 16th and 17th centuries puppet shows became popular with European aristocracy and puppets were extensively used as vehicles for caricature and satire until the 19th century, when they were offered as amusements for children in parks. In the 1920s Sergei Obraztsov (1901–) founded the State Central Puppet Theatre in Moscow. Large-scale puppets have played an important role in street theatre since the 1960s as in Peter Schuman's Bread and Puppet Theater in the USA. In the 1970s interest was revived by television; for example, *The Muppet Show* (created by Jim ◊Henson), and, in the 1980s and 1990s, the satirical TV programme *Spitting Image*, which features puppets caricaturing public figures; these are created by Fluck and Law.

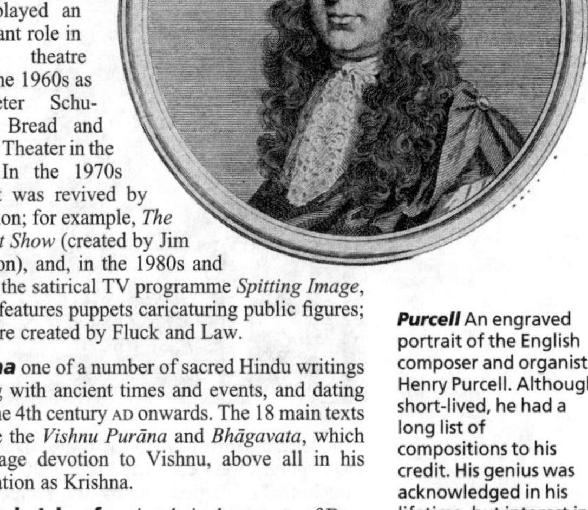

Purcell An engraved portrait of the English composer and organist Henry Purcell. Although short-lived, he had a long list of compositions to his credit. His genius was acknowledged in his lifetime, but interest in his music then declined until the later 19th century. The Purcell Society was founded in 1876 with the principal aim of publishing a complete edition of his work. *Corbis*

Purana one of a number of sacred Hindu writings dealing with ancient times and events, and dating from the 4th century AD onwards. The 18 main texts include the *Vishnu Purāna* and *Bhāgavata*, which encourage devotion to Vishnu, above all in his incarnation as Krishna.

Purbeck, Isle of peninsula in the county of Dorset, S England. Purbeck marble and china clay are obtained from the area, which includes Corfe Castle and Swanage.

Purcell Henry c. 1659–1695. English Baroque composer. His music balances high formality with melodic expression of controlled intensity, for example, the opera *Dido and Aeneas* 1689 and music for Dryden's *King Arthur* 1691 and for *The Fairy Queen* 1692. He wrote more than 500 works, ranging from secular operas and incidental music for plays to cantatas and church music.

purchasing-power parity (PPP) system for comparing standards of living between different countries. Comparing the ◊gross domestic product of different countries involves first converting them to a common currency (usually US dollars or pounds sterling), a conversion which is subject to large fluctuations with variations in exchange rates. Purchasing-power parity aims to overcome this by measuring how much money in the currency of those countries is required to buy a comparable range of goods and services.

purdah (Persian and Hindu 'curtain') seclusion of women practised by some Islamic and Hindu peoples. It had begun to disappear with the adoption of Western culture, but the fundamentalism of the 1980s revived it; for example, the wearing of the ◊chador (an all-enveloping black mantle) in Iran. The Koran enjoins only 'modesty' in dress.

Pure Land Buddhism dominant form of Buddhism in China and Japan. It emphasizes faith in and love of the Buddha Amitābha (Amida in Japan, Amituofo in China), the ideal 'Buddha of boundless light', who has vowed that all believers who call on his name will be reborn in his Pure Land, or Western Paradise, Sukhāvati. There are over 16 million Pure Land Buddhists in Japan.

Amidism developed in China in the 6th century, where the Pure Land school was founded by the monk T'an-Luan (476–542); it spread in Japan from the 10th century. The basic teachings are found in the *Sukhāvati vyūha/Pure Land Sūtras*. The prayer *Namu Amida Butsu* or *Nembutsu*, 'Homage to the Buddha Amitābha', was in some sects repeated for several hours a day. The True Pure Land school (Jōdo Shinshū), founded by the Japanese monk Shinran (1173–1262), held that a single, sincere invocation was enough and rejected monastic discipline and the worship of all other Buddhas; this has become the largest school in Japan. ▷ *See feature on pp. 162–163.*

purgatory in Roman Catholic belief, a purificatory state or place where the souls of those who have died in a state of grace can expiate their venial sins, with a limited amount of suffering.

purge removal (for example, from a political party) of suspected opponents or persons regarded

punk Guitarist Sid Vicious (left) and lead singer Johnny Rotten of the punk band The Sex Pistols, on their debut tour of the USA in 1978. The short-lived band epitomized the history of punk: 1978 was to be the band's third and final year. Vicious died the following year. *Corbis*

Puritan English Puritan family c. 1563. The term puritan is usually applied to those Protestants who wished to remain in the Church of England but wanted it to be further reformed after the break with Rome. It is often applied perjoratively to describe someone as sanctimonious and mean-spirited. *Philip Sauvain*

as undesirable (often by violent means). During the 1930s purges were conducted in the USSR under Joseph Stalin, carried out by the secret police against political opponents, Communist Party members, minorities, civil servants, and large sections of the armed forces' officer corps. Some 10 million people were executed or deported to labour camps from 1934 to 1938.

Purim Jewish festival celebrated in Feb or March (the 14th of Adar in the Jewish calendar), commemorating Esther, who saved the Jews from destruction in 473 BC during the Persian occupation.

Puritan from 1564, a member of the Church of England who wished to eliminate Roman Catholic survivals in church ritual, or substitute a presbyterian for an episcopal form of church government. The term also covers the separatists who withdrew from the church altogether. The Puritans were identified with the parliamentary opposition under James I and Charles I, and after the Restoration were driven from the church, and more usually known as ◊Dissenters or ◊Nonconformists.

'Habit is Heaven's own redress: it takes the place of happiness.'
ALEKSANDR PUSHKIN
Eugene Onegin

pus yellowish fluid that forms in the body as a result of bacterial infection; it includes white blood cells (leucocytes), living and dead bacteria, dead tissue, and serum. An enclosed collection of pus is called an abscess.

Pusan or ***Busan*** chief industrial port (textiles, rubber, salt, fishing) of Korea; population (1990) 3,797,600. It was invaded by the Japanese 1592 and opened to foreign trade 1883.

Pusey Edward Bouverie 1800–1882. English Church of England priest from 1828. In 1835 he joined J H ◊Newman in issuing the *Tracts for the Times*. After Newman's conversion to Catholicism, Pusey became leader of the High Church Party, or Puseyites, striving until his death to keep them from conversion.

Pushkin Aleksandr Sergeyevich 1799–1837. Russian poet and writer. His works include the novel in verse *Eugene Onegin* 1823–31 and the tragic drama *Boris Godunov* 1825. Pushkin's range was wide, and his willingness to experiment freed later Russian writers from many of the archaic conventions of the literature of his time.

Pushkin was born in Moscow. He was exiled 1820 for his political verse and in 1824 was in trouble for his atheistic opinions. He wrote ballads such as *The Gypsies* 1827, and the prose pieces *The Captain's Daughter* 1836 and *The Queen of Spades* 1834. He was mortally wounded in a duel with his brother-in-law.

'My belief is that no movie, nothing in life, leaves people neutral. You either leave them up or you leave them down.'
DAVID PUTTNAM
Quoted in the *International Herald Tribune* 23 Oct 1989

Pushtu another name for the ◊Pashto language of Afghanistan and N Pakistan.

Puskas Ferenc 1927– . Hungarian footballer. One of the world's greatest players, and a star of the outstanding Hungary team of the early 1950s, he scored 83 goals in 84 internationals between 1945 and 1956 before defecting to the West during the Hungarian Revolution. Joining Real Madrid in 1958, he went on to score 35 goals in 39 European Cup matches, including four in the 1960 final.

putrefaction decomposition of organic matter by microorganisms.

putsch a violent seizure of political power, such as Adolf Hitler and Erich von Ludendorff's abortive Munich beer-hall putsch Nov 1923, which attempted to overthrow the Bavarian government. The term is of Swiss–German origin.

Puttnam David Terence 1941– . English film producer. He played a major role in reviving the British film industry internationally in the 1980s. Films include *Chariots of Fire* 1981 (Academy Award for best film), *The Killing Fields* 1984, and *Memphis Belle* 1990. He was briefly head of Columbia Pictures in the mid-1980s.

Pu-Yi alternative transliteration of the name of the last Chinese emperor, Henry ◊P'u-i.

PVC abbreviation for ***polyvinylchloride***, a type of ◊plastic derived from vinyl chloride (CH_2:CHCl).

PWR abbreviation for ◊***pressurized water reactor***, a type of nuclear reactor.

pyelitis inflammation of the renal pelvis, the central part of the kidney where urine accumulates before discharge. It is caused by bacterial infection and is more common in women than in men.

Pygmalion in Greek mythology, a king of Cyprus who fell in love with an ivory statue he had carved. When Aphrodite brought it to life as a woman, Galatea, he married her.

Pygmy (sometimes ***Negrillo***) member of any of several groups of small-statured, dark-skinned peoples living in the equatorial jungles of the Central African Republic, Cameroon, Democratic Republic of Congo, Burundi, Gabon, Rwanda, Sudan, and Ethiopia. The most important groups are the Twa, Aka, Mbuti, Binga, Baka, Gelli Efé; their combined population is less than 200,000. They were probably the aboriginal inhabitants of the region, before the arrival of farming peoples from elsewhere. They live nomadically in small groups, as hunter-gatherers; they also trade with other, settled people in the area.

Pygmies have been known since ancient Egyptian and Greek times, and were mentioned in a letter to Pharo Phips 2360 BC. The word pygmy derives from a Greek word meaning 'fist', which was a measure equivalent to the length from the elbow to the fist.

Pyke Margaret 1893–1966. British birth-control campaigner. In the early 1930s she became secretary of the National Birth Control Association (later the Family Planning Association, FPA), and campaigned vigorously to get local councils to set up family-planning clinics. She became chair of the FPA in 1954.

pylon in modern usage, a steel lattice tower that supports high-tension electrical cables. In ancient Egyptian architecture, a pylon is one of a pair of inward-sloping towers that flank an entrance.

Pym John 1584–1643. English Parliamentarian, largely responsible for the petition of right 1628, which declared illegal taxation without parliamentary consent, imprisonment without trial, billeting of soldiers on private persons, and the use of martial law. As leader of the Puritan opposition in the ◊Long Parliament from 1640, he moved the impeachment of Charles I's advisers the Earl of Strafford and William Laud, drew up the ◊Grand Remonstrance, and was the chief of five members of Parliament Charles I wanted arrested 1642. The five hid themselves and then emerged triumphant when the king left London.

Pynchon Thomas 1937– . US novelist. With great stylistic verve, he created a bizarre, labyrinthine world in his books, the first of which was *V* 1963, a parodic detective story in pursuit of the endlessly elusive Lady V. It was followed by the shorter comic quest novel, *The Crying of Lot 49* 1966, before his gargantuan tour-de-force *Gravity's Rainbow* 1973, which represents a major achievement in 20th-century literature, with its fantastic imagery and esoteric language, drawn from mathematics and science.

Pyongyang capital and industrial city (coal, iron, steel, textiles, chemicals) of North Korea; population (1984) 2,640,000.

pyramid four-sided building with triangular sides. Pyramids were used in ancient Egypt to enclose a royal tomb; for example, the Great Pyramid of Khufu/Cheops at El Gîza, near Cairo, 230 m/755 ft square and 147 m/481 ft high. The three pyramids at Gîza were considered one of the ◊Seven Wonders of the World. In Babylon and Assyria, broadly stepped pyramids (◊ziggurats) were used as the base for a shrine to a god: the Tower of ◊Babel was probably one of these.

Truncated pyramidal temple mounds were also built by the ◊Mayas and ◊Aztecs of Central America, for example at Chichén Itzá and Cholula, near Mexico City, which is the world's largest in ground area (300 m/990 ft base, 60 m/195 ft high).

pyramid in geometry, a three-dimensional figure with triangular side-faces meeting at a common vertex (point) and with a ◊polygon as its base. The volume V of a pyramid is given by $V = \frac{1}{3}Bh$, where B is the area of the base and h is the perpendicular height.

Pyramids are generally classified by their bases. For example, the Egyptian pyramids have square bases, and are therefore called square pyramids. Triangular pyramids are also known as tetrahedra ('four sides').

Pyramus and Thisbe legendary Babylonian lovers whose story was retold by the Roman poet Ovid. Pursued by a lioness, Thisbe lost her veil, and when Pyramus arrived at their meeting place, he found it bloodstained. Assuming Thisbe was dead, he stabbed himself, and she, on finding his body, killed herself. In Shakespeare's *A Midsummer Night's Dream*, the 'rude mechanicals' perform the story as a farce for the nobles.

Pyrenees (French ***Pyrénées***; Spanish ***Pirineos***) mountain range in SW Europe between France and Spain; length about 435 km/270 mi; highest peak Aneto (French Néthon) 3,404 m/11,172 ft. ◊Andorra is entirely within the range. Hydroelectric power has encouraged industrial development in the foothills.

pyrethrum popular name for some flowers of the genus *Chrysanthemum*, family Compositae. The ornamental species *C. coccineum*, and hybrids derived from it, are commonly grown in gardens. Pyrethrum powder, made from the dried flower

pyramid Types of pyramid

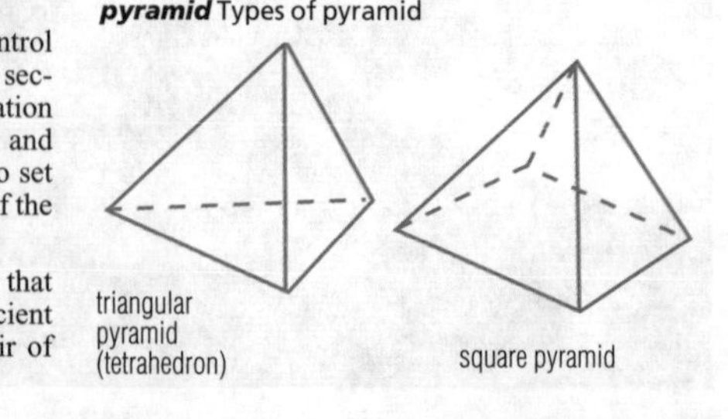

heads of some species, is a powerful contact pesticide for aphids and mosquitoes.

pyridine C_5H_5N a heterocyclic compound (see ◊cyclic compounds). It is a liquid with a sickly smell and occurs in coal tar. It is soluble in water, acts as a strong ◊base, and is used as a solvent, mainly in the manufacture of plastics.

pyridoxine or ***vitamin*** $B_6 C_8H_{11}NO_3$ water-soluble ◊vitamin of the B complex. There is no clearly identifiable disease associated with deficiency but its absence from the diet can give rise to malfunction of the central nervous system and general skin disorders. Good sources are liver, meat, milk, and cereal grains. Related compounds may also show vitamin B_6 activity.

pyrite iron sulphide FeS_2; also called fool's gold because of its yellow metallic lustre. Pyrite has a hardness of 6–6.5 on the Mohs' scale. It is used in the production of sulphuric acid.

pyroclastic in geology, pertaining to fragments of solidified volcanic magma, ranging in size from fine ash to large boulders, that are extruded during an explosive volcanic eruption; also the rocks that are formed by consolidation of such material. Pyroclastic rocks include tuff (ash deposit) and agglomerate (volcanic breccia).

pyroclastic deposit deposit made up of fragments of rock, ranging in size from fine ash to large boulders, ejected during an explosive volcanic eruption.

pyrolysis decomposition of a substance by heating it to a high temperature in the absence of air. The process is used to burn and dispose of old tyres, for example, without contaminating the atmosphere.

pyrometer in physics, any instrument used for measuring high temperatures by means of the thermal radiation emitted by a hot object. In a radiation pyrometer the emitted radiation is detected by a sensor such as a thermocouple. In an optical pyrometer the brightness of an electrically heated filament is matched visually to that of the emitted radiation. Pyrometers are especially useful for measuring the temperature of distant, moving or inaccessible objects.

pyroxene any one of a group of minerals, silicates of calcium, iron, and magnesium with a general formula $XYSi_2O_6$, found in igneous and metamorphic rocks. The internal structure is based on single chains of silicon and oxygen. Diopside (X = Ca, Y = Mg) and augite (X = Ca, Y = Mg,Fe,Al) are common pyroxenes. Jadeite ($NaAlSi_2O_6$), which is considered the more valuable form of jade, is also a pyroxene.

Pyrrho c. 360–c. 270 BC. Greek philosopher, founder of ◊Scepticism, who maintained that since certainty was impossible, peace of mind lay in renouncing all claims to knowledge.

Pyrrhus 319–272 BC. King of ◊Epirus, Greece, from 307, who invaded Italy 280, as an ally of the Tarentines against Rome. He twice defeated the Romans but with such heavy losses that a Pyrrhic victory has come to mean a victory not worth winning. He returned to Greece 275 after his defeat at Beneventum, and was killed in a riot in Argos.

Pythagoras c. 580–500 BC. Greek mathematician and philosopher who formulated ◊Pythagoras' theorem. Much of Pythagoras' work concerned numbers, to which he assigned mystical properties. For example, he classified numbers into triangular ones (1, 3, 6, 10, ...), which can be represented as a triangular array, and square ones (1, 4, 9, 16, ...), which form squares. He also observed that any two adjacent triangular numbers add to a square number (for example, $1 + 3 = 4; 3 + 6 = 9; 6 + 10 = 16$).

Pythagoras' theorem in geometry, a theorem stating that in a right-angled triangle, the area of the square on the hypotenuse (the longest side) is equal to the sum of the areas of the squares drawn on the other two sides. If the hypotenuse is h units long and the lengths of the other sides are a and b, then $h^2 = a^2 + b^2$. The theorem provides a way of calculating the length of any side of a right-angled triangle if the lengths of the other two sides are known. It is also used to determine certain trigonometrical relationships such as $\sin^2 \theta + \cos^2 \theta = 1$.

Pythagoras' theorem Pythagoras' theorem for right-angled triangles is likely to have been known long before the time of Pythagoras. It was probably used by the ancient Egyptians to lay out the pyramids.

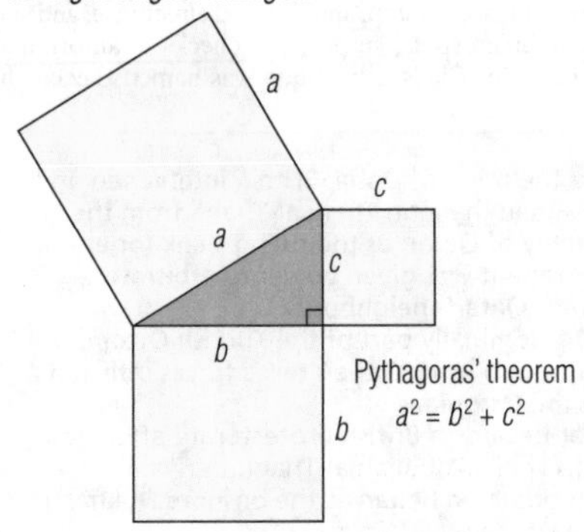

Pytheas lived 4th century BC. Greek navigator from Marseille who explored the coast of W Europe at least as far north as Denmark, sailed around Britain, and reached what he called ◊Thule, the most northern place known (possibly the Shetlands).

Pythia priestess of the god Apollo at the ◊oracle of Delphi in ancient Greece, and his medium. When consulted, her advice was interpreted by the priests of Apollo and shaped into enigmatic verses.

Pythian Games ancient Greek festival in honour of the sun god Apollo, celebrated near Delphi every four years.

python any constricting snake of the Old World subfamily Pythoninae of the family Boidae, which also includes ◊boas and the ◊anaconda. Pythons are found in the tropics of Africa, Asia, and Australia. Unlike boas, they lay eggs rather than produce living young. Some species are small, but the reticulated python *Python reticulatus* of SE Asia can grow to 10 m/33 ft.

A healthy adult can survive from six to twelve months without food. When food is scarce females do not ovulate so energy is not used up in reproducing.

python Pythons are non-venomous snakes, which kill their prey by constriction. They spend much of their lives in or near water, and can also climb by means of enlarged scales on their underside, which can grip the bark of trees. Some pythons have as many as 400 vertebrae, linked by ball-and-socket joints that allow great flexibility of movement. *Corbis*

pyx (Latin *pyxis* 'small box') in the Roman Catholic Church, the container used for the wafers of the sacrament.

Qaboos bin Said 1940– . Sultan of Oman, the 14th descendant of the Albusaid family. Opposed to the conservative views of his father, he overthrew him 1970 in a bloodless coup and assumed the sultanship. Since then he has followed more liberal and expansionist policies, while maintaining his country's position of international nonalignment.

Qaddafi alternative form of ◊Khaddhafi, Libyan leader.

Qadisiya, Battle of battle fought in S Iraq 637. A Muslim Arab force defeated a larger Zoroastrian Persian army and ended the ◊Sassanian Empire. The defeat is still resented in Iran, where Muslim Arab nationalism threatens to break up the Iranian state.

Qatar country in the Middle East, occupying Qatar peninsula in the Arabian Gulf, bounded SW by Saudi Arabia and S by United Arab Emirates. *See country box below.*

QC abbreviation for ◊*Queen's Counsel*.

qiblah direction in which Muslims face to pray: the direction of Mecca. In every mosque this is marked by a niche (mihrab) in the wall.

Qin dynasty China's first imperial dynasty 221–206 BC. It was established by ◊Shi Huangdi, ruler of the Qin, the most powerful of the Zhou era warring states. The power of the feudal nobility was curbed and greater central authority exerted over N central China, which was unified through a bureaucratic administrative system.

Writing and measurement systems were standardized, state roads and canals built, and border defence consolidated into what became known as the ◊Great Wall. On the debit side, the dynasty is identified with injustice, oppression, and a literary inquisition which came to be known as 'the burning of the books'.

Qinghai or ***Tsinghai*** province of NW China
area 721,000 sq km/278,306 sq mi
capital Xining
features mainly desert, with nomadic herders
industries oil, livestock, medical products
population (1990) 4,430,000; minorities include 900,000 Tibetans (mostly nomadic herders); Tibetan nationalists regard the province as being under colonial rule.

Qom or ***Qum*** holy city of Shi'ite Muslims, in central Iran, 145 km/90 mi S of Tehran; population (1991) 681,000. The Islamic academy of Madresseh Faizieh 1920 became the headquarters of Ayatollah ◊Khomeini.

quadrathon sports event in which the competitors must swim 2 miles (3.2 km), walk 30 miles (48 km), cycle 100 miles (161 km), and run 26.2 miles (42 km, a marathon) within 22 hours.

quadratic equation in mathematics, a polynomial equation of second degree (that is, an equation containing as its highest power the square of a variable, such as x^2). The general formula of such equations is $ax^2 + bx + c = 0$, in which a, b, and c are real numbers, and only the coefficient a cannot equal 0. In ◊coordinate geometry, a quadratic function represents a ◊parabola.

quadrature position of the Moon or an outer planet where a line between it and Earth makes a right angle with a line joining Earth to the Sun.

quadrilateral plane (two-dimensional) figure with four straight sides. The following are all quadrilaterals, each with distinguishing properties: square with four equal angles and sides, four axes of symmetry; rectangle with four equal angles, opposite sides equal, two axes of symmetry; rhombus with four equal sides, two axes of symmetry; parallelogram with two pairs of parallel sides, rotational symmetry; and trapezium one pair of parallel sides.

Quadruple Alliance in European history, three military alliances of four nations:
the Quadruple Alliance 1718 Austria, Britain, France, and the United Provinces (Netherlands) joined forces to prevent Spain from annexing Sardinia and Sicily.
the Quadruple Alliance 1813 Austria, Britain, Prussia, and Russia allied to defeat the French emperor Napoleon; renewed 1815 and 1818. See Congress of ◊Vienna.
the Quadruple Alliance 1834 Britain, France, Portugal, and Spain guaranteed the constitutional monarchies of Spain and Portugal against rebels in the Carlist War.

quaestor Roman magistrate whose duties were mainly concerned with public finances. The quaestors originated as assistants to the consuls. Both urban and military quaestors existed, the latter being attached to the commanding generals in the provinces.

quagga South African zebra that became extinct in the 1880s. It was brown, with a white tail and legs, and unlike surviving zebra species, had stripes only on its head, neck, and forequarters. An intriguing attempt to recreate the quagga by breeding from a zebra with poorly developed stripes began in 1991.

quail any of several genera of small ground-dwelling birds of the family Phasianidae, which also includes grouse, pheasants, bobwhites, and prairie chickens. Species are found in Africa, India, Australia, North America, and Europe. The common or European quail *Coturnix coturnix* is about 18 cm/7 in long, reddish-brown, with a white throat with a black patch at the bottom, and yellowish belly. It is found in Europe, Asia, and Africa, and has been introduced to North America. The nest is a small hollow in the ground, and in it are laid about ten yellowish-white eggs blotched with brown. The bird feeds upon grain seeds and insects.

Quaker popular name, originally derogatory, for a member of the Society of ◊Friends.

qualitative analysis in chemistry, a procedure for determining the identity of the component(s) of a single substance or mixture. A series of simple reactions and tests can be carried out on a compound to determine the elements present.

quango (acronym for ***quasi-autonomous non-governmental organization***) any administrative body that is nominally independent but relies on government funding. The creation of quangos aims to reduce the size of the central government machine. Examples are the Equal Opportunities Commission in the UK (established 1975); the Environmental Protection Agency in the USA (established 1970).

Quant Mary 1934– . English fashion designer. She popularized the miniskirt in the UK and was one of the first designers to make clothes specifically for the teenage and early twenties market, producing bold, simple outfits which were in tune with the 'swinging London' of the 1960s. Her designs were sharp, angular, and streetwise, and she combined spots, stripes, and checks in an original way. Her Chelsea boutique was named Bazaar. In

QATAR
State of

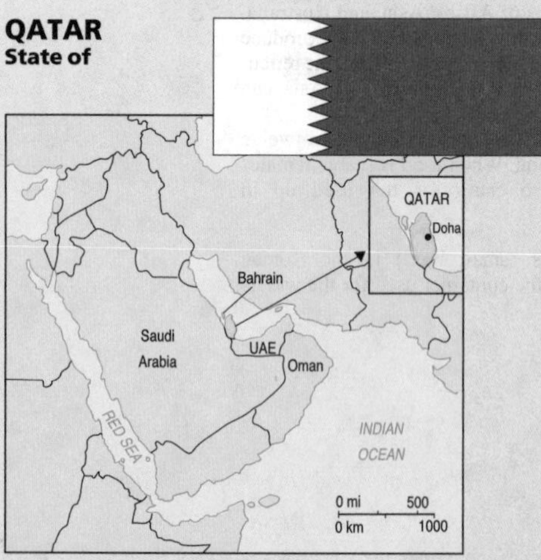

national name *Dawlat Qatar*
area 11,400 sq km/4,402 sq mi
capital (and chief port) Doha
major towns/cities Dukhan, centre of oil production; Halul, terminal for offshore oilfields
physical features mostly flat desert with salt flats in S
head of state and government Sheik Hamad bin Khalifa al-Thani from 1995
political system absolute monarchy
administrative divisions local government is the responsibility of the Minister of Municipal Affairs
political parties none
population 539,000 (1994 est)
population growth rate 2.5% (1990–95)
ethnic composition only about 25% of the population are indigenous Qataris, 40% being Arabs, and the others Pakistanis, Indians, and Iranians
life expectancy 68 (men), 73 (women)
literacy rate men 77%, women 73%
languages Arabic (official), English
religion Sunni Muslim
currency Qatari riyal
GDP (US $) 7.17 billion (1994)
growth rate –4.1% (1994)
exports oil, natural gas, petrochemicals, fertilizers, iron, steel

HISTORY
7th C AD Islam introduced.
8th C Developed into important trading centre during time of the Abbasid Empire.
1783 The al-Khalifa, who had migrated to NE Qatar from the W and N of the Arabian Peninsula, foiled a Persian invasion and moved their headquarters to Bahrain Island, while continuing to rule the area of Qatar.
1867–68 After the Bahrain-based al-Khalifa family had suppressed a revolt by their Qatari subjects, destroying the town of Doha, Britain intervened and installed Muhammad ibn Thani al-Thani, from the leading family of Qatar, as the ruling sheik (or emir). A British Resident was given power to arbitrate disputes with Qatar's neighbours.
1871–1914 Nominally part of the Turkish Ottoman Empire, although in 1893 the sheik's forces inflicted a defeat on the Ottomans.
1916 Qatar became a British protectorate after treaty signed with Sheik Adbullah al-Thani.
1949 Oil production began at the onshore Dukhan field in the W.
1960 Sheik Ahmad al-Thani became the new emir.
1968 Britain's announcement that it would remove its forces from the Persian Gulf by 1971 led Qatar to make an abortive attempt to arrange a federation of Gulf states.
1970 Constitution adopted, confirming the emirate as an absolute monarchy.
1971 Independence achieved from Britain.
1972 Emir Sheik Ahmad replaced in bloodless coup by his cousin, the Crown Prince and prime minister Sheik Khalifa ibn Hamad al-Thani.
1991 Forces joined United Nations coalition in Gulf War against Iraq.
1995 Sheik Khalifa ousted by his son Crown Prince Sheik Hamad bin Khalifa al-Thani.
1996 Announcement of plans to introduce democracy were followed by an assassination attempt on Sheik Hamad.

quagga A quagga, a South African zebra that became extinct in the latter half of the nineteenth century as a result of intensive hunting. They were only striped on the head, neck, and shoulders. *Image Select (UK) Ltd*

the 1970s she expanded into cosmetics and textile design.

quantitative analysis in chemistry, a procedure for determining the precise amount of a known component present in a single substance or mixture. A known amount of the substance is subjected to particular procedures.

Gravimetric analysis determines the mass of each constituent present; ◊volumetric analysis determines the concentration of a solution by ◊titration against a solution of known concentration.

quantity theory of money economic theory claiming that an increase in the amount of money in circulation causes a proportionate increase in prices. The theory dates from the 17th century and was elaborated by the US economist Irving Fisher (1867–1947). Supported and developed by Milton Friedman, it forms the theoretical basis of ◊monetarism.

quantum computing use of particles such as atoms, ions, and photons to perform computations, initially suggested by physicist Richard Feynman in 1982. In 1985, David Deutsch of the University of Oxford described a 'universal quantum computer' that would be able to perform feats beyond the capabilities of conventional computers. No such computer has been built to date, but quantum computing is though to show great promise in certain areas, such as cryptography.

quantum chromodynamics (QCD) in physics, a theory describing the interactions of ◊quarks, the ◊elementary particles that make up all ◊hadrons (subatomic particles such as protons and neutrons). In quantum chromodynamics, quarks are considered to interact by exchanging particles called gluons, which carry the ◊strong nuclear force, and whose role is to 'glue' quarks together.

The mathematics involved in the theory is complex, and, although a number of successful predictions have been made, the theory does not compare in accuracy with ◊quantum electrodynamics, upon which it is modelled. See ◊forces, fundamental.

quantum electrodynamics (QED) in physics, a theory describing the interaction of charged subatomic particles within electric and magnetic fields. It combines ◊quantum theory and ◊relativity, and considers charged particles to interact by the exchange of photons. QED is remarkable for the accuracy of its predictions; for example, it has been used to calculate the value of some physical quantities to an accuracy of ten decimal places, a feat equivalent to calculating the distance between New York and Los Angeles to within the thickness of a hair. The theory was developed by US physicists Richard Feynman and Julian Schwinger, and by Japanese physicist Sin-Itiro Tomonaga 1948.

quantum mechanics branch of physics dealing with the interaction of ◊matter and ◊radiation, the structure of the ◊atom, the motion of atomic particles, and with related phenomena (see ◊elementary particle and ◊quantum theory).

quantum number in physics, one of a set of four numbers that uniquely characterize an ◊electron and its state in an ◊atom. The ***principal quantum number*** n defines the electron's main energy level. The ***orbital quantum number*** l relates to its angular momentum. The ***magnetic quantum number*** m describes the energies of electrons in a magnetic field. The ***spin quantum number*** m_s gives the spin direction of the electron.

The principal quantum number, defining the electron's energy level, corresponds to shells (energy levels) also known by their spectroscopic designations K, L, M, and so on. The orbital quantum number gives rise to a series of subshells designated s, p, d, f, and so on, of slightly different energy levels. The magnetic quantum number allows further subdivision of the subshells (making three subdivisions p_x, p_y, and p_z in the p subshell, for example, of the same energy level). No two electrons in an atom can have the same set of quantum numbers (the Pauli (1900–1958) exclusion principle).

quantum theory or ***quantum mechanics*** in physics, the theory that ◊energy does not have a continuous range of values, but is, instead, absorbed or radiated discontinuously, in multiples of definite, indivisible units called quanta. Just as earlier theory showed how light, generally seen as a wave motion, could also in some ways be seen as composed of discrete particles (◊photons), quantum theory shows how atomic particles such as electrons may also be seen as having wavelike properties. Quantum theory is the basis of particle physics, modern theoretical chemistry, and the solid-state physics that describes the behaviour of the silicon chips used in computers.

The theory began with the work of Max Planck 1900 on radiated energy, and was extended by Albert Einstein to electromagnetic radiation generally, including light. Danish physicist Niels Bohr used it to explain the ◊spectrum of light emitted by excited hydrogen atoms. Later work by Erwin Schrödinger, Werner Heisenberg, Paul Dirac, and others elaborated the theory to what is called quantum mechanics (or wave mechanics).

quarantine (from French *quarantaine* '40 days') any period for which people, animals, plants, or vessels may be detained in isolation to prevent the spread of contagious disease.

quark in physics, the ◊elementary particle that is the fundamental constituent of all ◊hadrons (baryons, such as neutrons and protons, and mesons). There are six types, or 'flavours': up, down, top, bottom, strange, and charmed, each of which has three varieties, or 'colours': red, green, and blue (visual colour is not meant, although the analogy is useful in many ways). To each quark there is an antiparticle, called an antiquark. See ◊quantum chromodynamics.

quart imperial liquid or dry measure, equal to two pints or 1.136 litres. In the USA, a liquid quart is equal to 0.946 litre, while a dry quart is equal to 1.101 litres.

quartermaster in a military unit, usually a battalion, the officer in charge of its administration. In combat the quartermaster is responsible for supplying the unit with rations, fuel, and ammunition.

quarter session former local criminal court in England, replaced 1972 by crown courts (see also ◊law courts).

quartz crystalline form of ◊silica SiO_2, one of the most abundant minerals of the Earth's crust (12% by volume). Quartz occurs in many different kinds of rock, including sandstone and granite. It ranks 7 on the Mohs' scale of hardness and is resistant to chemical or mechanical breakdown. Quartzes vary according to the size and purity of their crystals. Crystals of pure quartz are coarse, colourless, transparent, show no cleavage, and fracture unevenly; this form is usually called rock crystal. Impure coloured varieties, often used as gemstones, include ◊agate, citrine quartz, and ◊amethyst. Quartz is also used as a general name for the cryptocrystalline and noncrystalline varieties of silica, such as chalcedony, chert, and opal.

Quartz is used in ornamental work and industry, where its reaction to electricity makes it valuable in electronic instruments (see ◊piezoelectric effect). Quartz can also be made synthetically. Crystals that would take millions of years to form naturally can now be 'grown' in pressure vessels to a standard that allows them to be used in optical and scientific instruments and in electronics, such as quartz wristwatches.

quartzite ◊metamorphic rock consisting of pure quartz sandstone that has recrystallized under increasing heat and pressure.

quasar (from ***quas***i-stell***ar*** object or QSO) one of the most distant extragalactic objects known, discovered 1963. Quasars appear starlike, but each emits more energy than 100 giant galaxies. They are thought to be at the centre of galaxies, their brilliance emanating from the stars and gas falling towards an immense ◊black hole at their nucleus.

Quasar light shows a large ◊red shift, indicating that they are very distant. Some quasars emit radio waves (see ◊radio astronomy), which is how they were first identified 1963, but most are radio-quiet. The furthest are over 10 billion light years away. ▷ *See feature on pp. 70–71.*

Quasimodo Salvatore 1901–1968. Italian poet. His early collections, such as *Acque e terre/Waters and Land* 1930, established his reputation as an exponent of 'hermetic' poetry, spare, complex, and private. Later collections, including *Nuove poesie/New Poetry* 1942 and *Il falso e vero verde/The False and True Green* 1956, reflect a growing preoccupation with the political and social problems of his time. Nobel prize 1959.

quassia any tropical American tree of the genus *Quassia*, family Simaroubaceae, with a bitter bark and wood. The heartwood of *Q. amara* is a source of quassiin, an infusion of which was formerly used as a tonic; it is now used in insecticides.

Quaternary period of geological time that began 1.64 million years ago and is still in process. It is divided into the ◊Pleistocene and ◊Holocene epochs.

Quatre Bras, Battle of battle fought 16 June 1815 during the Napoleonic Wars, in which the

'Poetry is the revelation of a feeling that the poet believes to be interior and personal but which the reader recognizes as his own.'

SALVATORE QUASIMODO
Speech 1960

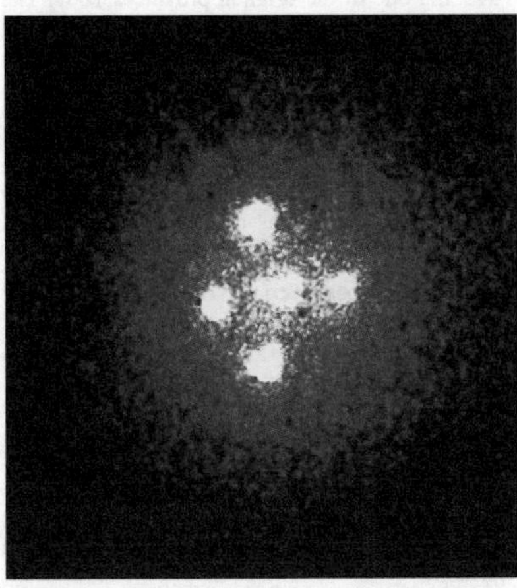

quasar A photographic image of the Einstein Cross quasar. Quasars, starlike extragalactic objects which contain very high levels of energy, were first discovered in 1963. *Image Select (UK) Ltd*

British commander Wellington defeated French forces under Marshal Ney. It is named after a hamlet in Brabant, Belgium, 32 km/20 mi SE of Brussels.

Quayle (John) Anthony 1913–1989. English actor and director. From 1948–56 he directed at the Shakespeare Memorial Theatre, and appeared as Falstaff in *Henry IV*, Petruchio in *The Taming of the Shrew*, and played the title role in *Othello*. He played nonclassical parts in *Galileo*, *Sleuth*, and *Old World*. He founded the Compass Company 1984. His numerous film appearances include *Lawrence of Arabia* 1962.

Quayle (James) Dan(forth) 1947– . US Republican politician, vice president 1989–93. A congressman for Indiana 1977–81, he became a senator 1981.

Quebec capital and industrial port (textiles, leather, timber, paper, printing, and publishing) of Quebec province, on the St Lawrence River, Canada; population (1991) 167,500, metropolitan area 645,550.

The city was founded by the French explorer Samuel de ◊Champlain 1608, and was a French colony 1608–1763. The British, under General ◊Wolfe, captured Quebec 1759 after a battle on the nearby Plains of Abraham; both Wolfe and the French commander ◊Montcalm were killed. Quebec is a centre of French culture, and there are two universities, Laval 1663 (oldest in North America) and Quebec 1969. Its picturesque old town survives below the citadel about 110 m/360 ft above the St Lawrence River.

Quebec

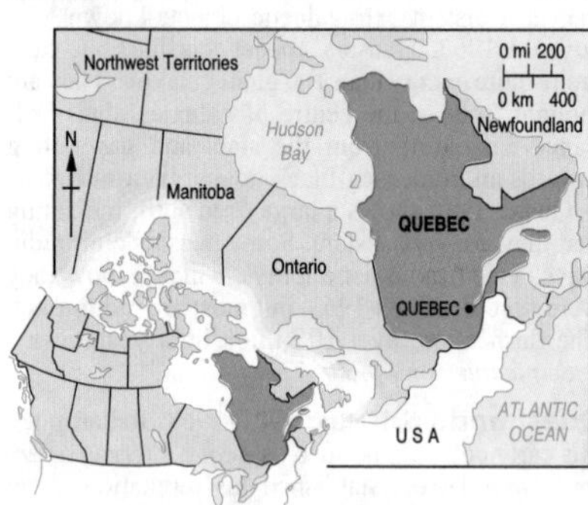

Quebec province of E Canada
area 1,540,700 sq km/594,710 sq mi
capital Quebec
towns and cities Montréal, Laval, Sherbrooke, Verdun, Hull, Trois-Rivières
features immense water-power resources (for example, the James Bay project)
industries iron, copper, gold, zinc, cereals, potatoes, paper, textiles, fish, maple syrup (70% of world's output)
population (1991) 6,811,800
language French (the only official language since 1974, although 17% speak English). Language laws 1989 prohibit the use of English on street signs
history known as New France 1534–1763; captured by the British and became province of Quebec 1763–90, Lower Canada 1791–1846, Canada East 1846–67; one of the original provinces 1867. The nationalist Parti Québecois won power 1976. In 1982, when Canada severed its last legal ties with the UK, Quebec opposed the new Constitution Act; the right of veto to constitutional change was proposed for all provinces of Canada 1987, but the agreement was not ratified by its 1990 deadline and support for Quebec's independence grew. In 1989 the Parti Québecois was defeated by the Liberal Party.

Quebec Conference two conferences of Allied leaders in the city of Quebec during World War II. The first conference 1943 approved British admiral Mountbatten as supreme Allied commander in SE Asia and made plans for the invasion of France, for which US general Eisenhower was to be supreme commander. The second conference Sept 1944 adopted plans for intensified air attacks on Germany, created a unified strategy against Japan, and established a postwar policy for a defeated Germany.

quebracho any of several South American trees, genus *Schinopsis*, of the cashew family Anacardiaceae, with very hard wood, chiefly the red quebracho *S. lorentzii*, used in tanning.

Quechua or ***Quichua*** or ***Kechua*** the largest group of Native Americans living in South America. The Quechua live in the Andean region. Their ancestors included the Inca, who established the Quechua language in the region, now the second official language of Peru and widely spoken as a lingua franca in Ecuador, Bolivia, Columbia, Argentina, and Chile; it belongs to the Andean-Equatorial family.

Queen British glam-rock group 1971–91 credited with making the first successful pop video, for their hit 'Bohemian Rhapsody' 1975. The operatic flamboyance of lead singer Freddie Mercury (1946–1991) was the cornerstone of their popularity. Among their other hits are 'We Will Rock You' 1977 and the rockabilly pastiche 'Crazy Little Thing Called Love' 1980.

Queen Anne style decorative art style in England 1700–20, characterized by plain, simple lines, mainly in silver and furniture.

Queens mainly residential borough and county at the west end of Long Island, New York City, USA; population (1980) 1,891,300.

Queensberry John Sholto Douglas, 8th Marquess of Queensberry 1844–1900. British patron of boxing. In 1867 he formulated the Queensberry Rules, which form the basis of today's boxing rules.

He was the father of Lord Alfred ◊Douglas and it was his misspelled insult to Oscar Wilde that set in motion the events leading to the playwright's imprisonment.

Queen's Counsel (QC) in England, a barrister appointed to senior rank by the Lord Chancellor. When the monarch is a king the term is King's Counsel (KC). A QC wears a silk gown, and takes precedence over a junior member of the Bar.

Queensland state in NE Australia
area 1,727,200 sq km/666,699 sq mi
capital Brisbane
towns and cities Townsville, Toowoomba, Cairns
features Great Dividing Range, including Mount Bartle Frere 1,657 m/5,438 ft; Great Barrier Reef (collection of coral reefs and islands about 2,000 km/1,250 mi long, off the east coast); Gold Coast, 32 km/20 mi long, S of Brisbane; Sunshine coast, a 100-km/60-mi stretch of coast N of Brisbane, between Rainbow Beach and Bribie Island
industries sugar, pineapples, beef, cotton, wool, tobacco, copper, gold, silver, lead, zinc, coal, nickel, bauxite, uranium, natural gas
population (1992) 3,030,500
history part of New South Wales until 1859, when it became self-governing. In 1989 the ruling National Party was defeated after 32 years in power and replaced by the Labor Party, who maintained power in the 1992 elections.

Queen's Proctor in England, the official representing the crown in matrimonial, probate, and admiralty cases. The Queen's Proctor's chief function is to intervene in divorce proceedings if it is discovered that material facts have been concealed from the court or that there has been collusion. When the monarch is a king the term is King's Proctor.

Queensland

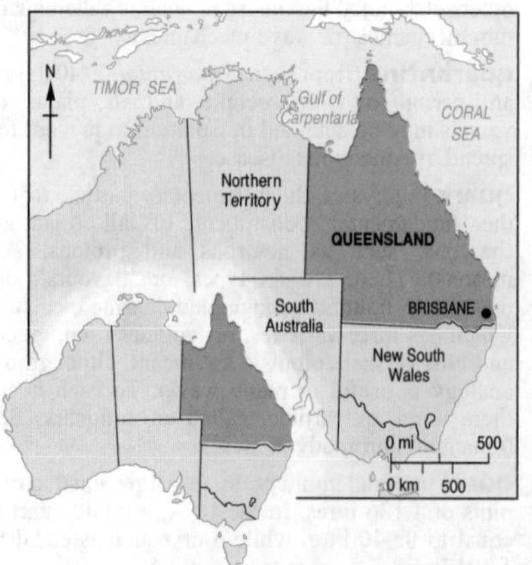

quetzal The long-tailed quetzal of Mexico and Central America was considered sacred by the ancient Maya and Aztecs. They associated the bird with the plumed serpent god Quetzalcoatl, and used its magnificent tail feathers in religious ceremonies.

quenching ◊heat treatment used to harden metals. The metals are heated to a certain temperature and then quickly plunged into cold water or oil.

quetzal long-tailed Central American bird *Pharomachus mocinno* of the ◊trogon family, order Trogoniformes. The male is brightly coloured, with green, red, blue, and white feathers. It has a train of blue-green plumes (tail coverts) that hang far beyond the true tail feathers. There is a crest on the head and decorative drooping feathers on the wings. It is about 1.3 m/4.3 ft long including tail. The female is smaller and lacks the tail and plumage.

The quetzal eats fruit, insects, and small frogs and lizards. It is the national emblem of Guatemala, and was considered sacred by the Mayans and the Aztecs. The quetzal's forest habitat is rapidly being destroyed, and hunting of birds for trophies or souvenirs also threatens its survival.

Quetzalcoatl in pre-Columbian cultures of Central America, a feathered serpent god of air and water. In his human form, he was said to have been fair-skinned and bearded and to have reigned on Earth during a golden age. He disappeared across the eastern sea, with a promise to return; the Spanish conquistador Hernán ◊Cortés exploited the myth in his own favour when he invaded. Ruins of Quetzalcoatl's temples survive in various ancient Mesoamerican ceremonial centres, including the one at Teotihuacán in Mexico. (See also ◊Aztec, ◊Mayan, and ◊Toltec civilizations.)

Quevedo y Villegas Francisco Gómez de 1580–1645. Spanish novelist and satirist. His picaresque novel *La vida del buscón/The Life of a Scoundrel* 1626 follows the tradition of the roguish hero who has a series of adventures. *Sueños/Visions* 1627 is a brilliant series of satirical portraits of contemporary society.

Quezon City former capital of the Philippines 1948–76, northeastern part of metropolitan

quince The quince is related to the japonica and other plants of the rose family. The common species has been grown in Europe since Roman times. The golden fruits are too hard and acidic to be eaten raw but are used to make jam or jellies.

◊Manila (the present capital), on Luzon Island; population (1990) 1,166,800. It was named after the Philippines' first president, Manuel Luis Quezon (1878–1944).

quicksilver another name for the element ◊mercury.

quietism religious attitude, displayed periodically in the history of Christianity, consisting of passive contemplation and meditation to achieve union with God. The founder of modern quietism was the Spanish priest ◊Molinos who published a *Guida Spirituale/Spiritual Guide* 1675.

Quiller-Couch Arthur Thomas 1863–1944. British scholar and writer who usually wrote under the pseudonym 'Q'. He edited several anthologies, including *The Oxford Book of English Verse* 1900, and wrote a number of critical studies, such as *On the Art of Writing* 1920. Among his novels are *The Splendid Spur* 1889 and *The Ship of Stars* 1899. He was professor of English literature at Cambridge University from 1912 until his death.

Quimby Fred(erick) 1886–1965. US film producer. He was head of MGM's short films department 1926–56. Among the cartoons produced by this department were the *Tom and Jerry* series and those directed by Tex Avery (1907–1980).

quince small tree *Cydonia oblonga*, family Rosaceae, native to W Asia. The bitter, yellow, pear-shaped fruit is used in preserves. Flowering quinces, genus *Chaenomeles*, are cultivated for their flowers.

quinine antimalarial drug extracted from the bark of the cinchona tree. Peruvian Indians taught French missionaries how to use the bark in 1630, but quinine was not isolated until 1820. It is a bitter alkaloid $C_{20}H_{24}N_2O_2$.

Other drugs against malaria have since been developed with fewer side effects, but quinine derivatives are still valuable in the treatment of unusually resistant strains.

Quinquagesima (Latin 'fiftieth') in the Christian church calendar, the Sunday before Lent and 50 days before Easter.

Quintana Roo state of Mexico, on the ◊Yucatán Peninsula; area 50,350 sq km/ 19,440 sq mi; population (1990) 493,300. Its capital is Chetumal. The chief products are chicle and copra, and there is sponge and turtle fishing. Most of the inhabitants are descendents of Maya Indians, and there are important archaeological remains of the Pre-Columbian Mayan Empire.

Quintero Serafin Alvárez and Joaquin Alvárez-Spanish dramatists; see ◊Alvárez Quintero.

Quintilian (Marcus Fabius Quintilianus) c. AD 35–c. 100. Roman rhetorician. Born at Calagurris, Spain, he was educated in Rome, but left early in Nero's reign. He returned to Rome in AD 68, where he quickly achieved fame and wealth as a teacher of rhetoric. He composed the *Institutio Oratoria/The Education of an Orator*, in which he advocated a simple and sincere style of public speaking. His moral tone is in striking contrast with the general degradation of his age.

Quirinal one of the seven hills on which ancient Rome was built. Its summit is occupied by a palace built 1574 as a summer residence for the pope and occupied 1870–1946 by the kings of Italy. The name Quirinal is derived from that of Quirinus, local god of the ◊Sabines.

Quisling Vidkun Abraham Lauritz Jonsson 1887–1945. Norwegian politician. Leader from 1933 of the Norwegian Fascist Party, he aided the Nazi invasion of Norway 1940 by delaying mobilization and urging non-resistance. He was made premier by Hitler 1942, and was arrested and shot as a traitor by the Norwegians 1945. His name became a generic term for a traitor who aids an occupying force.

Quito capital and industrial city (textiles, chemicals, leather, gold, silver) of Ecuador, about 3,000 m/9,850 ft above sea level; population (1990) 1,101,000. It is on a plateau in the Andes, on the slopes of the volcano Pichincha, which last erupted 1666. It has a temperate climate all year round.
history Quito was an ancient Indian settlement taken by the Incas in about 1470 and became the capital of the Inca Kingdom of Quito until it was captured by the Spanish in 1534. It is the oldest of the South American capitals.
features Spanish colonial architecture with balconied houses and fountains, and churches with wooden sculptures; religious buildings occupy a quarter of the space in the city; 17th-century cathedral; the art school, established by Franciscans in 1535, led to the flourishing of religious art throughout the Spanish colonial period; the burial place of Antonio José de Sucre.

Qumran or ***Khirbet Qumran*** archaeological site in Jordan, excavated from 1951, in the foothills NW of the Dead Sea. Originally an Iron Age fort (6th century BC), it was occupied in the late 2nd century BC by a monastic community, the ◊Essenes, until the buildings were burned by Romans AD 68. The monastery library once contained the ◊Dead Sea Scrolls, which had been hidden in caves for safekeeping and were discovered 1947.

Quorn mycoprotein, a tiny relative of mushrooms, that feeds on carbohydrates and grows prolifically in culture using a form of liquid fermentation. It is moist, looks like meat, and is used in cooking. It is rich in protein (12.3 g/100 g) and fibre (3.6 g/100 g) and low in fat (0.49 g/100 g).

quota in international trade, a limitation on the amount of a commodity that may be exported, imported, or produced. Restrictions may be imposed forcibly or voluntarily.

Quotas protect a home industry from an influx of cheap goods; prevent a heavy outflow of goods (usually raw materials) because there are insufficient numbers to meet domestic demand; allow for a new industry to develop before it is exposed to competition; or prevent a decline in the world price of a particular commodity.

QwaQwa former black homeland of South Africa in Orange Free State.

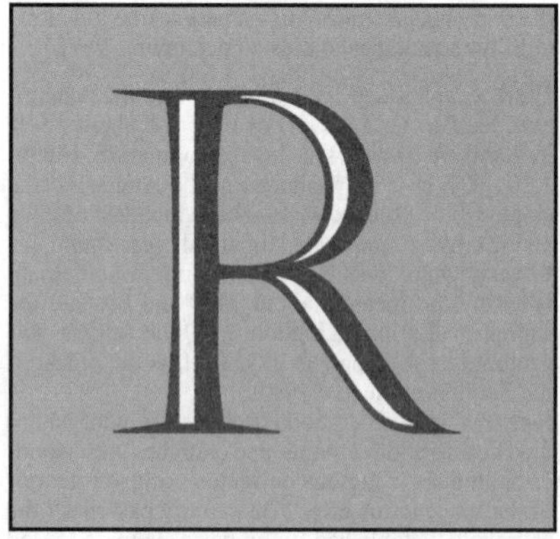

Rabat capital of Morocco, industrial port (cotton textiles, carpets, leather goods) on the Atlantic coast, 177 km/110 mi W of Fez; population (urban area, 1991) 519,000; Rabat-Salé 1,494,000. It is named after its original *ribat* or fortified monastery.

rabbi in Judaism, the chief religious leader of a synagogue or the spiritual leader (not a hereditary high priest) of a Jewish congregation; also, a scholar of Judaic law and ritual from the 1st century AD.

'Man never found the deities so kindly / As to assure him that he'd live tomorrow.'

FRANÇOIS RABELAIS
Pantagruel

rabbit any of several genera of hopping mammals of the order Lagomorpha, which together with ◊hares constitute the family Leporidae. Rabbits differ from hares in bearing naked, helpless young and in occupying burrows.

The European rabbit (*Oryctolagus cuniculus*) is the most common of the three species of Old World rabbit. Originally from S Europe and N Africa, it has now been introduced worldwide. New World cottontails (genus *Sylvilagus*), include 13 species native to North and South America.

Rabelais François c. 1495–1553. French satirist, monk, and physician. His name has become synonymous with bawdy humour. He was educated in the Renaissance humanist tradition and was the author of satirical allegories, including *La Vie inestimable de Gargantua/The Inestimable Life of Gargantua* 1535 and *Faits et dits héroïques du grand Pantagruel/Heroic Deeds and Sayings of the Great Pantagruel* 1533, about two giants (father and son).

'Crime has its degrees, as virtue does.'

JEAN RACINE
Phèdre

rabies (Greek 'fear of water') or ***hydrophobia*** viral disease of the central nervous system that can afflict all warm-blooded creatures. It is almost invariably fatal once symptoms have developed. Its transmission to humans is generally by a bite from an infected animal. Rabies continues to kill hundreds of thousands of people every year; almost all these deaths occur in Asia, Africa, and South America.

After an incubation period, which may vary from ten days to more than a year, symptoms of fever, muscle spasm, and delirium develop. As the disease progresses, the mere sight of water is enough to provoke convulsions and paralysis. Death is usual within four or five days from the onset of symptoms. Injections of rabies vaccine and antiserum may save those bitten by a rabid animal from developing the disease. Louis ◊Pasteur was the first to produce a preventive vaccine, and the Pasteur Institute was founded to treat the disease.

In France, Germany, Poland, Slovakia, Slovenia, Hungary, Austria and the Czech Republic, foxes are now vaccinated against rabies with capsules distributed by helicopter. In Britian, no human rabies has been transmitted since 1902. In September 1998 Britain announced that its quarantine regulations would be changing to allow animals from the European Union, and rabies-free islands, such as Australia and New Zealand, into the country without a period of quarantine. This would apply only to microchipped animals with vaccination certificates.

raccoon Raccoons are good climbers and spend much of their time in trees, usually near water. Their varied diet includes small aquatic animals such as frogs, crayfish, and fish. The common raccoon, found in N America from S Canada to the Panama canal, was adopted as a pet by the early settlers.

Rabin Yitzhak 1922–1995. Israeli Labour politician, prime minister 1974–77 and 1992–95. His policy of favouring Palestinian self-government in the occupied territories contributed to the success of the centre-left party in the 1992 elections. In Sept 1993 he signed a historic peace agreement with the Palestinian Liberation Organization (PLO), providing for a phased withdrawal of Israeli forces. He was awarded the 1994 Nobel Prize for Peace jointly with Israeli foreign minister Shimon Peres and PLO leader Yassir Arafat. He was shot and killed by a young Israeli extremist while attending a peace rally in Tel Aviv Nov 1995.

Rabuka Sitiveni 1948– . Fijian soldier and politician, prime minister from 1992. When the 1987 elections in Fiji produced an Indian-dominated government, Rabuka staged two successive coups (the first short-lived). Within months of the second, he stepped down, allowing a civilian government to take over. In 1992 he was nominated as the new Fijian premier.

raccoon any of several New World species of carnivorous mammals of the genus *Procyon*, in the family Procyonidae. The common raccoon *P. lotor* is about 60 cm/2 ft long, with a grey-brown body, a black-and-white ringed tail, and a black 'mask' around its eyes. The crab-eating raccoon *P. cancrivorus* of South America is slightly smaller and has shorter fur.

race in anthropology, term sometimes applied to a physically distinctive group of people, on the basis of their difference from other groups in skin colour, head shape, hair type, and physique. Formerly anthropologists divided the human race into three hypothetical racial groups: Caucasoid, Mongoloid, and Negroid. However, scientific studies have produced no proof of definite genetic racial divisions. Many anthropologists today, therefore, completely reject the concept of race, and social scientists tend to prefer the term ethnic group (see ◊ethnicity).

raceme in botany, a type of ◊inflorescence.

race-relations acts UK acts of Parliament 1965, 1968, and 1976 to combat discrimination. The Race Relations Act 1976 prohibits discrimination on the grounds of colour, race, nationality, or ethnic origin. Indirect as well as direct discrimination is prohibited in the provision of goods, services, facilities, employment, accommodation, and advertisements. The Commission for Racial Equality was set up under the act to investigate complaints of discrimination.

Rachmaninov Sergei Vasilevich 1873–1943. Russian composer, conductor, and pianist. After the 1917 Revolution he emigrated to the USA. His music is melodious and emotional and includes operas, such as *Francesca da Rimini* 1906, three symphonies, four piano concertos, piano pieces, and songs. Among his other works are the *Prelude in C-Sharp Minor* 1892 and *Rhapsody on a Theme of Paganini* 1934 for piano and orchestra.

Racine Jean Baptiste 1639–1699. French dramatist. He was an exponent of the classical tragedy in French drama, taking his subjects from Greek mythology and observing the rules of classical Greek drama. Most of his tragedies have women in the title role, for example *Andromaque* 1667, *Iphigénie* 1674, and *Phèdre* 1677.

An orphan, Racine was educated by Jansenists at Port Royal (see ◊Jansenism), but later moved away from an ecclesiastical career to success and patronage at court. His ingratiating flattery won him the success he craved 1677 when he was appointed royal historiographer. After the failure of *Phèdre* in the theatre he no longer wrote for the secular stage but, influenced by Madame de ◊Maintenon, wrote two religious dramas, *Esther* 1689 and *Athalie* 1691, which achieved posthumous success.

racism belief in, or set of implicit assumptions about, the superiority of one's own ◊race or ethnic group, often accompanied by prejudice against members of an ethnic group different from one's own. Racism may be used to justify ◊discrimination, verbal or physical abuse, or even genocide, as in Nazi Germany, or as practised by European settlers against American Indians in both North and South America.

Many social scientists believe that even where there is no overt discrimination, racism exists as an unconscious attitude in many individuals and societies, based on a stereotype or preconceived idea about different ethnic groups, which is damaging to individuals (both perpetrators and victims) and to society as a whole. See also ◊black, ◊ethnicity.

rackets or ***racquets*** indoor game played on an enclosed court. Although first played in the Middle Ages, rackets developed in the 18th century and was played against the walls of London buildings. It is considered the forerunner of many racket and ball games, particularly ◊squash. The game is played on a court usually 18.3 m/60 ft long by 9.1 m/30 ft wide, by two or four persons.

Rachmaninov Sergei Rachmaninov won the gold medal for composition at the Moscow Conservatoire, but his First Symphony was not a success, and he gave up composing for a time, but took it up again after a course of hypnosis. In the 1930s his music was banned in the Soviet Union as it was thought to represent 'the decadent attitude of the lower middle classes'. *Corbis*

rad unit of absorbed radiation dose, now replaced in the SI system by the ◊gray (one rad equals 0.01 gray), but still commonly used. It is defined as the dose when one kilogram of matter absorbs 0.01 joule of radiation energy (formerly, as the dose when one gram absorbs 100 ergs).

radar (acronym for ***radio direction and ranging***) device for locating objects in space, direction finding, and navigation by means of transmitted and reflected high-frequency radio waves.

The direction of an object is ascertained by transmitting a beam of short-wavelength (1–100 cm/½–40 in), short-pulse radio waves, and picking up the reflected beam. Distance is determined by timing the journey of the radio waves (travelling at the speed of light) to the object and back again. Radar is also used to detect objects underground, for example service pipes, and in archaeology. Contours of remains of ancient buildings can be detected down to 20 m/66 ft below ground. Radar is essential to navigation in darkness, cloud, and fog, and is widely used in warfare to detect enemy aircraft and missiles. To avoid detection, various devices, such as modified shapes (to reduce their radar cross-section), radar-absorbent paints and electronic jamming are used. To pinpoint small targets ◊laser 'radar' instead of microwaves has been developed. Radar is also used in ◊meteorology and ◊astronomy.

radar astronomy bouncing of radio waves off objects in the Solar System, with reception and analysis of the 'echoes'. Radar contact with the Moon was first made 1945 and with Venus 1961. The travel time for radio reflections allows the distances of objects to be determined accurately. Analysis of the reflected beam reveals the rotation period and allows the object's surface to be mapped. The rotation periods of Venus and Mercury were first determined by radar. Radar maps of Venus were obtained first by Earth-based radar and subsequently by orbiting space probes.

radian SI unit (symbol rad) of plane angles, an alternative unit to the ◊degree. It is the angle at the centre of a circle when the centre is joined to the two ends of an arc (part of the circumference) equal in length to the radius of the circle. There are 2π (approximately 6.284) radians in a full circle (360°). One radian is approximately 57°, and 1° is $\pi/180$ or approximately 0.0175 radians. Radians are commonly used to specify angles in ◊polar coordinates.

radiant heat energy that is radiated by all warm or hot bodies. It belongs to the ◊infrared part of the electromagnetic ◊spectrum and causes heating when absorbed. Radiant heat is invisible and should not be confused with the red glow associated with very hot objects, which belongs to the visible part of the spectrum.

Infrared radiation can travel through a vacuum and it is in this form that the radiant heat of the Sun travels through space. It is the trapping of this radiation by carbon dioxide and water vapour in the atmosphere that gives rise to the ◊greenhouse effect.

radiation in physics, emission of radiant ◊energy as particles or waves – for example, heat, light, alpha particles, and beta particles (see ◊electromagnetic waves and ◊radioactivity). See also ◊atomic radiation.

Of the radiation given off by the Sun, only a tiny fraction of it, called insolation, reaches the Earth's surface; much of it is absorbed and scattered as it passes through the ◊atmosphere. The radiation given off by the Earth itself is called ground radiation.

radiation biology study of how living things are affected by radioactive (ionizing) emissions (see ◊radioactivity) and by electromagnetic (nonionizing) radiation (◊electromagnetic waves). Both are potentially harmful and can cause mutations as well as leukaemia and other cancers; even low levels of radioactivity are very dangerous. Both are, however, used therapeutically, for example to treat cancer, when the radiation dose is very carefully controlled (◊radiotherapy or X-ray therapy).

Exposure to high levels of radioactive emissions produces radiation burns and radiation sickness, plus genetic damage (resulting in birth defects) and cancers in the longer term. Exposure to low-level ionizing radiation can also cause genetic damage and cancers, particularly leukaemia. ***Electromagnetic radiation*** is usually harmful only if exposure is to high-energy emissions, for example close to powerful radio transmitters or near radar-wave sources. Such exposure can cause organ damage, cataracts, loss of hearing, leukaemia and other cancers, or premature ageing. It may also affect the nervous system and brain. ***Background radiation*** is the natural radiation produced by cosmic rays and radioactive rocks such as granite, and this must be taken into account when calculating the effects of nuclear accidents or contamination from power stations.

radiation sickness sickness resulting from exposure to radiation, including X-rays, gamma rays, neutrons, and other nuclear radiation, as from weapons and fallout. Such radiation ionizes atoms in the body and causes nausea, vomiting, diarrhoea, and other symptoms. The body cells themselves may be damaged even by very small doses, causing leukaemia.

radiation units units of measurement for radioactivity and radiation doses. In SI units, the activity of a radioactive source is measured in becquerels (symbol Bq) where one becquerel is equal to one nuclear disintegration per second (an older unit is the curie). The exposure is measured in coulombs per kilogram ($C\ kg^{-1}$); the amount of ionizing radiation (x-rays or gamma-rays) which produces one coulomb of charge in one kilogram of dry air (replacing the roentgen). The absorbed dose of ionizing radiation is measured in grays (symbol Gy) where one gray is equal to one joule of energy being imparted to one kilogram of matter (the rad is the previously used unit). The dose equivalent, which is a measure of the effects of radiation on living organisms, is the absorbed dose multiplied by a suitable factor which depends upon the type of radiation. It is measured in sieverts (symbol Sv), where one sievert is a dose equivalent of one joule per kilogram (an older unit is the rem).

Radical in Britain, supporter of parliamentary reform before the Reform Bill 1832. As a group the Radicals later became the progressive wing of the Liberal Party. During the 1860s (led by Cobden, Bright, and J S Mill) they campaigned for extension of the franchise, free trade, and ◊*laissez faire*, but after 1870, under the leadership of Joseph Chamberlain and Charles Dilke, they adopted a republican and semi-socialist programme. With the growth of ◊socialism in the later 19th century, Radicalism ceased to exist as an organized movement.

In France, the Radical Party was a major force in the politics of the Third Republic, 1871–1940.

radical in chemistry, a group of atoms forming part of a molecule, which acts as a unit and takes part in chemical reactions without disintegration, yet often cannot exist alone; for example, the methyl radical $-CH_3$, or the carboxyl radical $-COOH$.

radical in politics, anyone with opinions more extreme than the main current of a country's major political party or parties. It is more often applied to those with left-wing opinions, although the radical right also exists.

radicle part of a plant embryo that develops into the primary root. Usually it emerges from the seed before the embryonic shoot, or plumule, its tip protected by a root cap, or calyptra, as it pushes through the soil. The radicle may form the basis of the entire root system, or it may be replaced by adventitious roots (positioned on the stem).

radio transmission and reception of radio waves. In radio transmission a microphone converts sound waves (pressure variations in the air) into ◊electromagnetic waves that are then picked up by a receiving aerial and fed to a loudspeaker, which converts them back into sound waves.

The theory of electromagnetic waves was first developed by Scottish physicist James Clerk ◊Maxwell 1864, given practical confirmation in the laboratory 1888 by German physicist Heinrich ◊Hertz, and put to practical use by Italian inventor Guglielmo ◊Marconi, who in 1901 achieved reception of a signal in Newfoundland transmitted from Cornwall, England.

To carry the transmitted electrical signal, an ◊oscillator produces a carrier wave of high frequency; different stations are allocated different transmitting carrier frequencies. A modulator superimposes the audiofrequency signal on the carrier. There are two main ways of doing this: ◊amplitude modulation (AM), used for long- and medium-wave broadcasts, in which the strength of the carrier is made to fluctuate in time with the audio signal; and ◊frequency modulation (FM), as used for VHF broadcasts, in which the frequency of the carrier is made to fluctuate. The transmitting aerial emits the modulated electromagnetic waves, which travel outwards from it.

In radio reception a receiving aerial picks up minute voltages in response to the waves sent out by a transmitter. A tuned circuit selects a particular frequency, usually by means of a variable ◊capacitor connected across a coil of wire. A demodulator disentangles the audio signal from the carrier, which is now discarded, having served its purpose. An amplifier boosts the audio signal for feeding to the loudspeaker. In a ◊superheterodyne receiver, the incoming signal is mixed with an internally-generated signal of fixed frequency so that the amplifier circuits can operate near their optimum frequency.

radioactive decay process of continuous disintegration undergone by the nuclei of radioactive elements, such as radium and various isotopes of uranium and the transuranic elements. This changes the element's atomic number, thus transmuting one element into another, and is accompanied by the emission of radiation. Alpha and beta decay are the most common forms.

In ***alpha decay*** (the loss of a helium nucleus – two protons and two neutrons) the atomic number decreases by two; in ***beta decay*** (the loss of an electron) the atomic number increases by one. Certain lighter artificially created isotopes also undergo radioactive decay. The associated radiation consists of alpha rays, beta rays, or gamma rays (or a combination of these), and it takes place at a constant rate expressed as a specific half-life, which is the time taken for half of any mass of that particular isotope to decay completely. Less commonly occurring decay forms include heavy-ion emission, electron capture, and spontaneous fission (in each of these the atomic number decreases). The original nuclide is known as the parent substance, and the product is a daughter nuclide (which may or may not be radioactive). The final product in all modes of decay is a stable element.

radioactive tracer any of various radioactive ◊isotopes used in labelled compounds; see ◊tracer.

radioactive waste any waste that emits radiation in excess of the background level. See ◊nuclear waste.

radioactivity spontaneous alteration of the nuclei of radioactive atoms, accompanied by the emission of radiation. It is the property exhibited by the radioactive ◊isotopes of stable elements and all isotopes of radioactive elements, and can be either natural or induced. See ◊radioactive decay.

Radioactivity establishes an equilibrium in parts of the nuclei of unstable radioactive substances, ultimately to form a stable arrangement of nucleons (protons and neutrons); that is, a non-radioactive (stable) element. This is most frequently accomplished by the emission of ◊alpha particles (helium nuclei); ◊beta particles (electrons and

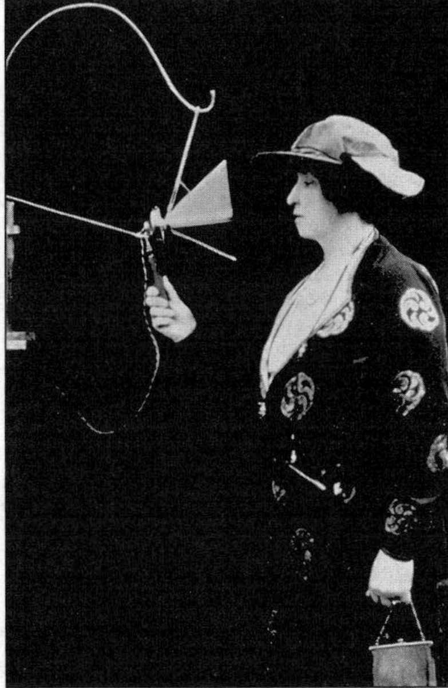

radio The opera singer Nellie Melba giving a song recital for radio 15 June 1920 at the Marconi Works in Chelmsford, SE England. This was Britain's first advertised public broadcast program. *Marconi Company Ltd*

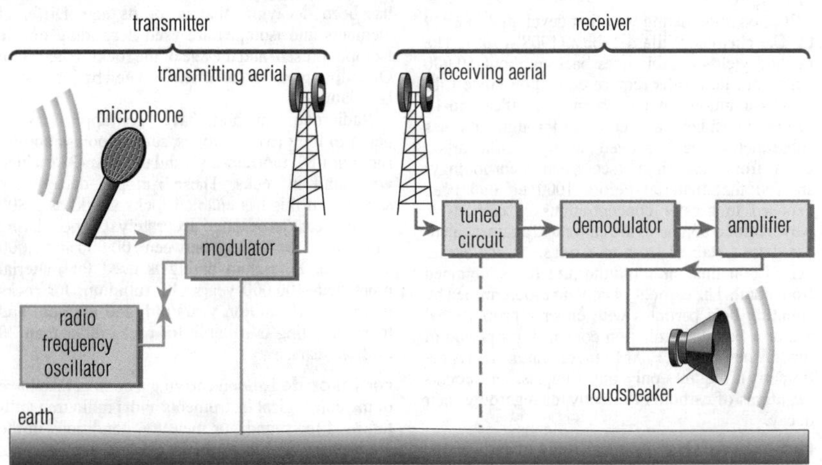

radio Radio transmission and reception. The radio frequency oscillator generates rapidly varying electrical signals, which are sent to the transmitting aerial. In the aerial, the signals produce radio waves (the carrier wave), which spread out at the speed of light. The sound signal is added to the carrier wave by the modulator. When the radio waves fall on the receiving aerial, they induce an electrical current in the aerial. The electrical current is sent to the tuning circuit, which picks out the signal from the particular transmitting station desired. The demodulator separates the sound signal from the carrier wave and sends it, after amplification, to the loudspeaker.

positrons); or ◊gamma radiation (electromagnetic waves of very high frequency). Alpha, beta, and gamma radiation are ionizing in their effect and are therefore dangerous to body tissues, especially if a radioactive substance is ingested or inhaled. It takes place either directly, through a one-step decay, or indirectly, through a number of decays that transmute one element into another. This is called a decay series or chain, and sometimes produces an element more radioactive than its predecessor.

The instability of the particle arrangements in the nucleus of a radioactive atom (the ratio of neutrons to protons and/or the total number of both) determines the lengths of the ◊half-lives of the isotopes of that atom, which can range from fractions of a second to billions of years. All isotopes of relative atomic mass 210 and greater are radioactive.

radio astronomy study of radio waves emitted naturally by objects in space, by means of a ◊radio telescope. Radio emission comes from hot gases (thermal radiation); electrons spiralling in magnetic fields (synchrotron radiation); and specific wavelengths (lines) emitted by atoms and molecules in space, such as the 21-cm/8-in line emitted by hydrogen gas.

Radio astronomy began 1932 when US astronomer Karl ◊Jansky detected radio waves from the centre of our Galaxy, but the subject did not develop until after World War II. Radio astronomy has greatly improved our understanding of the evolution of stars, the structure of galaxies, and the origin of the universe. Astronomers have mapped the spiral structure of the Milky Way from the radio waves given out by interstellar gas, and they have detected many individual radio sources within our Galaxy and beyond.

Among radio sources in our Galaxy are the remains of ◊supernova explosions, such as the ◊Crab nebula and ◊pulsars. Short-wavelength radio waves have been detected from complex molecules in dense clouds of gas where stars are forming. Searches have been undertaken for signals from other civilizations in the Galaxy, so far without success. Strong sources of radio waves beyond our Galaxy include ◊radio galaxies and ◊quasars. Their existence far off in the universe demonstrates how the universe has evolved with time. Radio astronomers have also detected weak background radiation thought to be from the ◊Big Bang explosion that marked the birth of the universe. ▷ *See feature on pp. 70–71.*

radio beacon radio transmitter in a fixed location, used in marine and aerial ◊navigation. Ships and aircraft pinpoint their positions by reference to continuous signals given out by two or more beacons.

radiocarbon dating or ***carbon dating*** method of dating organic materials (for example, bone or wood), used in archaeology. Plants take up carbon dioxide gas from the atmosphere and incorporate it into their tissues, and some of that carbon dioxide contains the radioactive isotope of carbon, carbon-14. This decays at a known rate (half of it decays every 5,730 years); the time elapsed since the plant died can therefore be measured in a laboratory. Animals take carbon-14 into their bodies from eating plant tissues and their remains can be similarly dated. After 120,000 years so little carbon-14 is left that no measure is possible (see ◊half-life).

Radiocarbon dating was first developed in 1949 by US chemist Willard Libby (1908–1980). The method yields reliable ages back to about 50,000 years, but its results require correction since Libby's assumption that the concentration of carbon-14 in the atmosphere was constant through time has subsequently been proved wrong. Radiocarbon dates from tree rings (see ◊dendrochronology) showed that material before 1000 BC had been exposed to greater concentrations of carbon-14. Now radiocarbon dates are calibrated against calendar dates obtained from tree rings, or, for earlier periods, against uranium/thorium dates obtained from coral. The carbon-14 content is determined by counting beta particles with either a proportional gas or a liquid scintillation counter for a period of time. A new advance, AMS (accelerator mass spectrometry), requires only tiny samples, and counts the atoms of carbon-14 directly, disregarding their decay.

radiochemistry chemical study of radioactive isotopes and their compounds (whether produced from naturally radioactive or irradiated materials) and their use in the study of other chemical processes.

When such isotopes are used in labelled compounds, they enable the biochemical and physiological functioning of parts of the living body to be observed. They can help in the testing of new drugs, showing where the drug goes in the body and how long it stays there. They are also useful in diagnosis – for example cancer, fetal abnormalities, and heart disease.

radio frequencies and wavelengths classification of, see ◊electromagnetic waves.

radio galaxy galaxy that is a strong source of electromagnetic waves of radio wavelengths. All galaxies, including our own, emit some radio waves, but radio galaxies are up to a million times more powerful. In many cases the strongest radio emission comes not from the visible galaxy but from two clouds, invisible through an optical telescope, that can extend for millions of light years either side of the galaxy. This double structure at radio wavelengths is also shown by some ◊quasars, suggesting a close relationship between the two types of object. In both cases, the source of energy is thought to be a massive black hole at the centre. Some radio galaxies are thought to result from two galaxies in collision or recently merged. ▷ *See feature on pp. 70–71.*

radiography branch of science concerned with the use of radiation (particularly ◊X-rays) to produce images on photographic film or fluorescent screens. X-rays penetrate matter according to its nature, density, and thickness. In doing so they can cast shadows on photographic film, producing a radiograph. Radiography is widely used in medicine for examining bones and tissues and in industry for examining solid materials; for example, to check welded seams in pipelines

radioisotope (contraction of ***radioactive isotope***) in physics, a naturally occurring or synthetic radioactive form of an element. Most radioisotopes are made by bombarding a stable element with neutrons in the core of a nuclear reactor. The radiations given off by radioisotopes are easy to detect (hence their use as ◊tracers), can in some instances penetrate substantial thicknesses of materials, and have profound effects (such as genetic ◊mutation) on living matter. Although dangerous, radioisotopes are used in the fields of medicine, industry, agriculture, and research.

radioisotope scanning use of radioactive materials (radioisotopes or radionucleides) to pinpoint disease. It reveals the size and shape of the target organ and whether any part of it is failing to take up radioactive material, usually an indication of disease.

radiology medical speciality concerned with the use of radiation, including X-rays, and radioactive materials in the diagnosis and treatment of injury and disease.

radiometric dating method of dating rock by assessing the amount of ◊radioactive decay of naturally occurring ◊isotopes. The dating of rocks may be based on the gradual decay of uranium into lead. The ratio of the amounts of 'parent' to 'daughter' isotopes in a sample gives a measure of the time it has been decaying, that is, of its age. Different elements and isotopes are used depending on the isotopes present and the age of the rocks to be dated. Once-living matter can often be dated by ◊radiocarbon dating.

Radiometric methods have been applied to the decay of long-lived isotopes, such as potassium-40, rubidium-87, thorium-232, and uranium-238 which are found in rocks. These isotopes decay very slowly and this has enabled rocks as old as 3,800 million years to be dated accurately. Carbon dating can be used for material between 100,000 and 1,000 years old. Potassium dating is used for material more than 100,000 years old, rubidium for rocks more than 10 million years old, and uranium and thorium dating is suitable for rocks older than 20 million years.

radiosonde balloon carrying a compact package of meteorological instruments and a radio transmitter, used to 'sound', or measure, conditions in the atmosphere. The instruments measure temperature, pressure, and humidity, and the information gathered is transmitted back to observers on the ground. A radar target is often attached, allowing the balloon to be tracked.

radio telescope instrument for detecting radio waves from the universe in ◊radio astronomy. Radio telescopes usually consist of a metal bowl that collects and focuses radio waves the way a concave mirror collects and focuses light waves. Radio telescopes are much larger than optical telescopes, because the wavelengths they are detecting are much longer than the wavelength of light. The largest single dish is 305 m/1,000 ft across, at Arecibo, Puerto Rico. ▷ *See feature on pp. 70–71.*

radiotherapy treatment of disease by ◊radiation from X-ray machines or radioactive sources. Radiation, which reduces the activity of dividing cells, is of special value for its effect on malignant tissues, certain nonmalignant tumours, and some diseases of the skin.

Generally speaking, the rays of the diagnostic X-ray machine are not penetrating enough to be efficient in treatment, so for this purpose more powerful machines are required, operating from 10,000 to over 30 million volts. The lower-voltage machines are similar to conventional X-ray machines; the higher-voltage ones may be of special design; for example, linear accelerators and betatrons. Modern radiotherapy is associated with fewer side effects than formerly, but radiotherapy to the head can cause temporary hair loss, and if the treatment involves the gut, diarrhoea and vomiting may occur. Much radiation now given uses synthesized ◊radioisotopes. Radioactive cobalt is the most useful, since it produces gamma rays, which are highly penetrating, and it is used instead of very high-energy X-rays.

radio wave electromagnetic wave possessing a long wavelength (ranging from about 10^{-3} to 10^4 m) and a low frequency (from about 10^5 to 10^{11} Hz). Included in the radio-wave part of the spectrum are ◊microwaves, used for both communications and for cooking; ultra high-and very high-frequency waves, used for television and FM (◊frequency modulation) radio communications; and short, medium, and long waves, used for AM (◊amplitude modulation) radio communications. Radio waves that are used for communications have all been modulated (see ◊modulation) to carry information. Certain astronomical objects emit radio waves, which may be detected and studied using ◊radio telescopes.

radish annual herb *Raphanus sativus*, family Cruciferae. It is native to Europe and Asia, and cultivated for its fleshy, pungent, edible root, which is usually reddish but sometimes white or black.

radium (Latin *radius* 'ray') white, radioactive, metallic element, symbol Ra, atomic number 88, relative atomic mass 226.02. It is one of the ◊alkaline-earth metals, found in nature in ◊pitchblende and other uranium ores. Of the 16 isotopes, the commonest, Ra-226, has a half-life of 1,620 years. The element was discovered and named in 1898 by Pierre and Marie ◊Curie, who were investigating the residues of pitchblende.

Radium decays in successive steps to produce radon (a gas), polonium, and finally a stable isotope of lead. The isotope Ra-223 decays through the uncommon mode of heavy-ion emission, giving off carbon-14 and transmuting directly to lead. Because radium luminesces, it was formerly used in paints that glowed in the dark; when the hazards of radioactivity became known its use was abandoned, but factory and dump sites remain contaminated and many former workers and neighbours contracted fatal cancers.

radius in biology, one of the two bones in the lower forearm of tetrapod (four-limbed) vertebrates.

radon colourless, odourless, gaseous, radioactive, nonmetallic element, symbol Rn, atomic number 86, relative atomic mass 222. It is grouped with the ◊inert gases and was formerly considered non-reactive, but is now known to form some compounds with fluorine. Of the 20 known isotopes, only three occur in nature; the longest half-life is 3.82 days (Rn-222).

Radon is the densest gas known and occurs in small amounts in spring water, streams, and the air, being formed from the natural radioactive decay of radium. Ernest Rutherford discovered the isotope

Rn-220 in 1899, and Friedrich Dorn (1848–1916) in 1900; after several other chemists discovered additional isotopes, William Ramsay and R W Whytlaw-Gray isolated the element, which they named niton in 1908. The name radon was adopted in the 1920s.

RAF abbreviation for ◊*Royal Air Force*.

Raffles (Thomas) Stamford 1781–1826. British colonial administrator, born in Jamaica. He served in the British ◊East India Company, took part in the capture of Java from the Dutch 1811, and while governor of Sumatra 1818–23 was responsible for the acquisition and founding of Singapore 1819.

Raffles Statue in Singapore of British colonial administrator Stamford Raffles, who founded Singapore 1819 and thereby secured British control of Malaya. He wrote a *History of Java* 1817 and was a keen natural history collector; he founded the Zoological Society of London 1826 and was its first president. *Corbis*

rafflesia or ***stinking corpse lily*** any parasitic plant without stems of the genus *Rafflesia*, family Rafflesiaceae, native to Malaysia, Indonesia, and Thailand. There are 14 species, several of which are endangered by logging of the forests where they grow; the fruit is used locally for medicine. The largest flowers in the world are produced by *R. arnoldiana*. About 1 m/3 ft across, they exude a smell of rotting flesh, which attracts flies to pollinate them.

Rafsanjani Hojatoleslam Ali Akbar Hashemi 1934– . Iranian politician and cleric, president from 1989. When his former teacher Ayatollah ◊Khomeini returned after the revolution of 1979–80, Rafsanjani became the speaker of the Iranian parliament and, after Khomeini's death, state president and effective political leader.

Rafsanjani kept in touch with his exiled mentor 1964–79 and was repeatedly imprisoned for fundamentalist political activity. His attitude became more moderate in the 1980s, and as president he normalized relations with the UK 1990. He was re-elected with a reduced majority 1993.

raga (Sanskrit *rāga* 'tone' or 'colour') in ◊Indian music, a scale of notes and style of ornament for music associated with a particular mood or time of day; the equivalent term in rhythm is tala. A choice of raga and tala forms the basis of improvised music; however, a written composition may also be based on (and called) a raga.

Raglan FitzRoy James Henry Somerset, 1st Baron Raglan 1788–1855. English general. He took part in the Peninsular War under Wellington, and lost his right arm at Waterloo. He commanded the British forces in the Crimean War from 1854. The raglan sleeve, cut right up to the neckline with no shoulder seam, is named after him.

Ragnarök in Norse mythology, the ultimate cataclysmic battle between gods and forces of evil, from which a new order will come. In Germanic mythology, this is known as Götterdämmerung.

ragtime syncopated music ('ragged time') in 2/4 rhythm, usually played on piano. It developed in the USA among black musicians in the late 19th century; it was influenced by folk tradition, minstrel shows, and marching bands, and was later incorporated into jazz. Scott ◊Joplin was a leading writer of ragtime pieces, called 'rags'.

ragwort any of several European perennial plants of the genus *Senecio*, family Compositae, usually with yellow-rayed flower heads; some are poisonous.

S. jacobaea is prolific on waste ground; it has bright yellow flowers and is poisonous.

Rahman Sheik Mujibur 1920–1975. Bangladeshi nationalist politician, president 1975. He was arrested several times for campaigning for the autonomy of East Pakistan. He won the elections 1970 as leader of the Awami League but was again arrested when negotiations with the Pakistan government broke down. After the civil war 1971, he became prime minister of the newly independent Bangladesh. He was presidential dictator Jan–Aug 1975, when he was assassinated.

Rahman Tunku (Prince) Abdul 1903–1990. Malaysian politician, first prime minister of independent Malaya 1957–63 and of Malaysia 1963–70. His achievement was to bring together the Malay, Chinese, and Indian peoples within the Alliance Party (which Rahman founded 1952), but in the 1960s he was accused of showing bias towards Malays. Ethnic riots followed in Kuala Lumpur 1969 and, after many attempts to restore better relations, the Tunku retired 1970. In his later years he voiced criticism of the authoritarian leadership of Mahathir bin Mohamed.

rail any wading bird of the family Rallidae, including the rails proper (genus *Rallus*), coots, moorhens, and gallinules. Rails have dark plumage, a short neck and wings, and long legs. They are 10–45 cm/4–18 in long.

Many oceanic islands have their own species of rail, often flightless, such as the Guam rail *R. owstoni* and Auckland Island rail *R. muelleri*. Several of these species have declined sharply, usually because of introduced predators such as rats and cats.

Railtrack government-owned public limited company responsible for the commercial operation of the railway network in Britain. It manages and charges private train operators for track access, train timetabling, and signalling operations, and leases station buildings to operators and franchisees. It also manages 14 major termini. In 1996 Railtrack was floated on the stock exchange, and its service companies sold into the private sector.

railway method of transport in which trains convey passengers and goods along a twin rail track. Following the work of English steam pioneers such as Scottish engineer James ◊Watt, English engineer George ◊Stephenson built the first public steam railway, from Stockton to Darlington, England, in 1825. This heralded extensive railway building in Britain, continental Europe, and North America, providing a fast and economical means of transport and communication.

growth years Four years after building the first steam railway, Stephenson opened the first steam passenger line, inaugurating it with his locomotive *Rocket*, which achieved speeds of 50 kph/30 mph. The railway construction that followed resulted in 250 separate companies in Britain, which resolved into four systems 1921 and became the nationalized British Railways 1948, known as British Rail from 1965. In North America the growth of railways during the 19th century made shipping from the central and western territories economical and helped the North to win the American Civil War; US rail travel reached its peak in 1929. Railways were extended into Asia, the Middle East, Africa, and Latin America in the late 19th century and were used for troop and supply transport in both world wars.

gauge Railway tracks were at first made of wood but later of iron or steel, with ties wedging them apart and relatively parallel. The distance between the wheels is known as the gauge. Since much of the early development of the railway took place in Tyneside, the gauge of local coal wagons, 1435 mm/4 ft 8.5 in, was adopted 1824 for most early railways. The main exception was the Great Western Railway (GWR) of Isambard Kingdom ◊Brunel, opened 1841, with a gauge of 2133 mm/7 ft. The narrow gauge won legal backing in the UK 1846, but parts of GWR carried on with Brunel's broad gauge until 1892. British engineers building railways overseas tended to use the narrow gauge, and it became the standard in the USA from 1885. The broad gauge, although expensive, offers a more comfortable journey.

rafflesia The rafflesia, or stinking corpse lily, is the largest flower of all, about 1 m/3 ft across and weighing 7 kg/15 lb. It gives off a smell of rotting meat to attract flies to pollinate it.

decline of railways With the increasing use of private cars and government-encouraged road haulage after World War II, and the demise of steam, rising costs on the railways meant higher fares, fewer passengers, and declining freight traffic. In the UK many rural rail services closed down on the recommendations of the Beeching Report 1963. In the 1970s, national railway companies began investing in faster intercity services: in the UK, the diesel high-speed train (HST) was introduced. Elsewhere such trains run on specially built tracks: for example, the Shinkansen (Japan) and ◊TGV (France) networks. *See timeline on p. 894.*

If God had intended us to fly, he'd never have given us the railways.

On RAILWAYS
Michael Flanders and Donald Swann
'By Air'

rain form of ◊precipitation in which separate drops of water fall to the Earth's surface from clouds. The drops are formed by the accumulation of fine droplets that condense from water vapour in the air. The condensation is usually brought about by rising and subsequent cooling of air.

Rain can form in three main ways – frontal (or cyclonic) rainfall, orographic (or relief) rainfall, and convectional rainfall. ***Frontal rainfall*** takes place at the boundary, or ◊front, between a mass of warm air from the tropics and a mass of cold air from the poles. The water vapour in the warm air is chilled and condenses to form clouds and rain. ***Orographic rainfall*** occurs when an airstream is forced to rise over a mountain range. The air becomes cooled and precipitation takes place. In the UK, the Pennine hills, which extend southwards from Northumbria to Derbyshire in N England, interrupt the path of the prevailing southwesterly winds, causing orographic rainfall. Their presence is partly responsible for the west of the UK being wetter than the east.

Convectional rainfall, associated with hot climates, is brought about by rising and abrupt cooling of air that has been warmed by the extreme heat of the ground surface. The water vapour carried by the air condenses and so rain falls heavily. Convectional rainfall is usually accompanied by a thunderstorm, and it can be intensified over urban areas due to higher temperatures.

rainbow arch in the sky displaying the colours of the ◊spectrum formed by the refraction and reflection of the Sun's rays through rain or mist. Its cause was discovered by Theodoric of Freiburg (c. 1250–1310) in the 14th century.

railway France's superfast TGV train, which runs on specially built tracks and began intercity operation in 1981. TGV trains travel from Brittany to SW France on high-speed tracks, and have reduced the travelling time between Bordeaux and Paris to 2 hr 58 min. *French Railways*

❛There is something in a tropical forest akin to the ocean in its effects on the mind. Man feels so completely his insignificance there, and the vastness of nature.❜

On RAINFORESTS
Henry Walter Bates
The Naturalist on the Amazons 1863

RAILWAYS: TIMELINE

1500s	Tramways – wooden tracks along which trolleys ran – were in use in mines.
1789	Flanged wheels running on cast-iron rails were first introduced; cars were still horse-drawn.
1804	Richard Trevithick built the first steam locomotive, and ran it on the track at the Pen-y-darren ironworks in South Wales.
1825	George Stephenson in England built the first public railway to carry steam trains – the Stockton and Darlington line – using his engine *Locomotion*.
1829	Stephenson designed his locomotive *Rocket*.
1830	Stephenson completed the Liverpool and Manchester Railway, the first steam passenger line. The first US-built locomotive, *Best Friend of Charleston*, went into service on the South Carolina Railroad.
1835	Germany pioneered steam railways in Europe, using *Der Adler*, a locomotive built by Stephenson.
1863	Robert Fairlie, a Scot, patented a locomotive with pivoting driving bogies, allowing tight curves in the track (this was later applied in the Garratt locomotives). London opened the world's first underground railway, powered by steam.
1869	The first US transcontinental railway was completed at Promontory, Utah, when the Union Pacific and the Central Pacific railroads met. George Westinghouse of the USA invented the compressed-air brake.
1879	Werner von Siemens demonstrated an electric train in Germany. Volk's Electric Railway along the Brighton seafront in England was the world's first public electric railway.
1883	Charles Lartique built the first monorail, in Ireland.
1885	The trans-Canada continental railway was completed, from Montréal in the east to Port Moody, British Columbia, in the west.
1890	The first electric underground railway opened in London.
1901	The world's longest-established monorail, the Wuppertal Schwebebahn, went into service in Germany.
1912	The first diesel locomotive took to the rails in Germany.
1938	The British steam locomotive *Mallard* set a steam-rail speed record of 203 kph/126 mph.
1941	Swiss Federal Railways introduced a gas-turbine locomotive.
1964	Japan National Railways inaugurated the 515 km/320 mi New Tokaido line between Osaka and Tokyo, on which the 210 kph/130 mph 'bullet' trains run.
1973	British Rail's High Speed Train (HST) set a diesel-rail speed record of 229 kph/142 mph.
1979	Japan National Railways' maglev test vehicle ML-500 attained a speed of 517 kph/321 mph.
1981	France's Train à Grande Vitesse (TGV) superfast trains began operation between Paris and Lyons, regularly attaining a peak speed of 270 kph/168 mph.
1987	British Rail set a new diesel-traction speed record of 238.9 kph/148.5 mph, on a test run between Darlington and York; France and the UK began work on the Channel Tunnel, a railway link connecting the two countries, running beneath the English Channel.
1988	The West German Intercity Experimental train reached 405 kph/252 mph on a test run between Würzburg and Fulda.
1990	A new rail-speed record of 515 kph/320 mph was established by a French TGV train, on a stretch of line between Tours and Paris.
1991	The British and French twin tunnels met to form the Channel Tunnel.
1993	British Rail privatization plans announced; government investment further reduced.
1994	Rail services started through the Channel Tunnel.
1996	Fire in the Channel Tunnel halted passenger services for two weeks. Tests began on a Japanese maglev supertrain designed for a 499 kph/310 mph link between Tokyo and Osaka, scheduled for 1999.

rainforest dense forest usually found on or near the ◊equator where the climate is hot and wet. Heavy rainfall results as the moist air brought by the converging tradewinds rises because of the heat. Over half the tropical rainforests are in Central and South America, the rest in SE Asia and Africa. They provide the bulk of the oxygen needed for plant and animal respiration. Tropical rainforests once covered 14% of the Earth's land surface, but are now being destroyed at an increasing rate as their valuable timber is harvested and the land cleared for agriculture, causing problems of ◊deforestation. Rainforests comprise about 50% of all growing wood on the planet, and harbour at least 40% of the Earth's species (plants and animals).

Tropical rainforests are characterized by a great diversity of species, usually of tall broad-leafed evergreen trees, with many climbing vines and ferns, some of which are a main source of raw materials for medicines. A tropical forest, if properly preserved, can yield medicinal plants, oils (from cedar, juniper, cinnamon, sandalwood), spices, gums, resins (used in inks, lacquers, linoleum), tanning and dyeing materials, forage for animals, beverages, poisons, green manure, rubber, and animal products (feathers, hides, honey). Other rainforests include montane, upper montane or cloud, mangrove, and subtropical.

Rainforests comprise some of the most complex and diverse ecosystems on the planet and help to regulate global weather patterns. When deforestation occurs, the microclimate of the mature forest disappears; soil erosion and flooding become major problems since rainforests protect the shallow tropical soils. Once an area is cleared it is very difficult for shrubs and bushes to re-establish because soils are poor in nutrients. This causes problems for plans to convert rainforests into agricultural land – after two or three years the crops fail and the land is left bare. Clearing of the rainforests may lead to a global warming of the atmosphere, and contribute to the ◊greenhouse effect. ▷*See feature on pp. 896–897.*

❛So the heart be right, it is no matter which way the head lies.❜

WALTER RALEIGH
When asked which way he preferred to lay his head on the block, quoted in W Stebbing
Sir Walter Raleigh

Rainier, Mount mountain in the Cascade Range, Washington State, USA; 4,392 m/14,415 ft, crowned by 14 glaciers and carrying dense forests on its slopes. It is a quiescent volcano. Mount Rainier national park was dedicated 1899.

Rais Gilles de 1404–1440. French marshal who fought alongside Joan of Arc. In 1440 he was hanged for the torture and murder of 140 children, but the court proceedings were irregular. He is the historical basis of the ◊Bluebeard character.

raisin dried grape, for eating as a fruit and also used in baking and confectionery. The chief kinds are the seedless raisin, the sultana, and the currant. The main producers are the Mediterranean area, California, Mexico, and Australia.

Raj, the the period of British rule in India before independence in 1947.

Rajasthan state of NW India
area 342,200 sq km/132,089 sq mi
capital Jaipur
features includes the larger part of the Thar Desert, where India's first nuclear test was carried out; in the SW is the Ranthambhor wildlife reserve, formerly the private hunting ground of the maharajahs of Jaipur, and rich in tiger, deer, antelope, wild boar, crocodile, and sloth bear
industries oilseed, cotton, sugar, asbestos, copper, textiles, cement, glass, gypsum, phosphate, silver
population (1994 est) 48,040,000
language Rajasthani, Hindi
religion 90% Hindu, 3% Muslim
history formed 1948; enlarged 1956.

Rajneesh meditation meditation based on the teachings of the Indian Shree Rajneesh (born Chaadra Mohan Jain), established in the early 1970s. Until 1989 he called himself Bhagwan (Hindi 'God'). His followers, who number about 0.5 million worldwide, regard themselves as sannyasin, or Hindu ascetics; they wear orange robes and carry a string of prayer beads. They are not expected to observe any specific prohibitions but to be guided by their instincts.

Rajneesh initially set up an ashram, or religious community, in Poona, NW India. He gained many followers, both Indian and Western, but his teachings also created considerable opposition, and in 1981 the Bhagwan moved his ashram to Oregon, USA, calling himself 'guru of the rich'. He was deported 1985 after pleading guilty to immigration fraud, and died 1990.

Rajput a Hindu people, predominantly soldiers and landowners, descended from 5th–7th-century warrior tribes of central Asia and now widespread over N India. The Rajput states of NW India are now merged in Rajasthan. The Rana family (ruling aristocracy of Nepal until 1951) was also Rajput. Rajastani languages belong to the Indo-Iranian branch of the Indo-European family.

Raleigh Walter, or ***Ralegh*** c. 1552–1618. English adventurer, writer, and courtier to Queen Elizabeth I. He organized expeditions to colonize North America 1584–87, all unsuccessful, and made exploratory voyages to South America 1595 and 1616. His aggressive actions against Spanish interests, including attacks on Spanish ports, brought him into conflict with the pacific James I. He was imprisoned for treason 1603–16 and executed on his return from an unsuccessful final expedition to South America. He is traditionally credited with introducing the potato to Europe and popularizing the use of tobacco.

Born in Devon, England, Raleigh became a confidant of Queen Elizabeth I and was knighted 1584. After initiating several unsuccessful attempts 1584–87 to establish a colony in North America (see ◊North Carolina), he led a gold-seeking expedition to the Orinoco River in South America 1595 (described in his *Discoverie of Guiana* 1596). He distinguished himself in expeditions against Spain in Cádiz 1596 and the Azores 1597.

After James I's accession to the English throne 1603, Raleigh was condemned to death on a charge of conspiracy, but was reprieved and imprisoned in the Tower of London, where he wrote his unfinished *History of the World*. Released 1616 to lead a second expedition to the Orinoco, which failed disastrously, he was beheaded on his return under the charges of his former sentence.

RAM (acronym for ***random-access memory***) in computing, a memory device in the form of a collection of integrated circuits (chips), frequently used in microcomputers. Unlike ◊ROM (read-only memory) chips, RAM chips can be both read from and written to by the computer, but their contents are lost when the power is switched off. Many modern commercial programs require a great deal of RAM to work efficiently. The 8 megabytes (MB) of RAM that most computers are sold with may not be enough: 16 MB is a minimum recommendation, and 32 MB, if you can afford it, will be ample for many years.

Rama incarnation of ◊Vishnu, the supreme spirit of Hinduism. He is the hero of the epic poem the *Rāmāyana*, and he is regarded as an example of morality and virtue.

Ramadan in the Muslim ◊calendar, the ninth month of the year. Throughout Ramadan a strict fast is observed during the hours of daylight; Muslims are encouraged to read the whole Koran in commemoration of the Night of Power (which falls during the month) when, it is believed, Muhammad first received his revelations from the angel Gabriel.

Ramakrishna Adopted name of Gadadhar Chatterjee 1836–1886. Hindu sage, teacher, and mystic (dedicated to achieving oneness with or a direct experience of God or some force beyond the normal world). Ramakrishna claimed that mystical experience was the ultimate aim of religions, and that all religions which led to this goal were equally valid.

Ramakrishna's most important follower, Swami Vivekananda (1863–1902), set up the Ramakrishna Society 1887, which now has centres for education, welfare, and religious teaching throughout India and beyond.

Rambert Marie. Adopted name of Cyvia Myriam Rambam 1888–1982. Polish-born British ballet dancer and teacher. One of the major innovative and influential figures in modern ballet, she worked with the Diaghilev ballet 1912–13, opened the Rambert School 1920, and in 1926 founded the Ballet Rambert which she directed. It became a modern-dance company from 1966 with Norman Morrice as director, and was renamed the Rambert Dance Company 1987. Rambert became a British citizen 1918.

Ram Das 1534–1581. Indian religious leader, fourth guru (teacher) of Sikhism 1574–81, who founded the Sikh holy city of Amritsar.

Rameau Jean-Philippe 1683–1764. French organist and composer. His *Traité de l'harmonie/Treatise on Harmony* 1722 established academic rules for harmonic progression, and his varied works include keyboard and vocal music and many operas, such as *Castor and Pollux* 1737.

Rameau The composer and theorist Jean-Philippe Rameau (1683–1764) as painted by Jacques Aved. Rameau's principal compositional accomplishments lie in the fields of keyboard music and opera. His treatise on harmony, a milestone during the period, held influence long after many of its principles were outdated. *Image Select (UK) Ltd*

Rameses alternative spelling of ◊Ramses, name of kings of ancient Egypt.

Ramgoolam Navin Chandra 1947– Mauritian politician, prime minister from 1995. He became leader of the centrist, Hindu-orientated Mauritius Labour Party (MLP) 1991, becoming its president soon afterwards. He is the son of Seewoosagur Ramgoolam, the country's first prime minister.

Ramillies, Battle of during the War of the ◊Spanish Succession, English and Dutch victory under the Duke of Marlborough over the French 23 May 1706, near Ramillies, 19 km/12 mi north of Namur, Belgium. The French lost all their artillery and some 15,000 casualties; English and Dutch losses were fewer than 4,000.

ramjet simple jet engine (see under ◊jet propulsion) used in some guided missiles. It only comes into operation at high speeds. Air is then 'rammed' into the combustion chamber, into which fuel is sprayed and ignited.

Ramos Fidel (Eddie) 1928– . Philippine politician, president from 1992–98. He was Corazon ◊Aquino's staunchest ally as defence secretary, and was later nominated her successor. As president, he launched a commission to consult with militant rebel groups, and, as part of a government move to end corruption and human-rights abuses, purged the police force. These and other initiatives won him popular support, and in the 1995 elections, with the economy booming, his supporters won a sweeping victory.

Ramphal Shridath Surendranath ('Sonny') 1928– . Guyanese politician. He was minister of foreign affairs and justice 1972–75 and secretary general of the British Commonwealth 1975–90.

Ramsay Allan 1713–1784. Scottish painter. Having studied in Edinburgh and then in Italy, he settled in London, becoming one of the most successful portrait painters of his day. He became artist to King George III 1760 and played an active role in London's literary and intellectual life. He is particularly noted for the charm of his female portraiture, as in his masterpiece of 1755 *The Artist's Wife*, the portrait of Margaret Lindsay, his second wife (National Gallery of Scotland, Edinburgh).

Ramsay Allan 1686–1758. Scottish poet. He published *The Tea-Table Miscellany* 1724–37 and *The Evergreen* 1724, collections of ancient and modern Scottish song, including revivals of the work of such poets as William Dunbar and Robert Henryson. He was the father of painter Allan Ramsay.

Ramsay William 1852–1916. Scottish chemist who, with Lord ◊Rayleigh, discovered argon 1894. In 1895 Ramsay produced helium and in 1898, in cooperation with Morris Travers (1872–1961), identified neon, krypton, and xenon. In 1903, with Frederick ◊Soddy, he noted the transmutation of radium into helium, which led to the discovery of the density and relative atomic mass of radium. Nobel prize 1904.

Ramses or ***Rameses*** 11 kings (pharaohs) of ancient Egypt, including:

Ramses II or ***Rameses II***; known as ***Ramses the Great*** king (pharaoh) of ancient Egypt about 1290–1224 BC, the son of Seti I. He campaigned successfully against the Hittites, and built two rock temples at ◊Abu Simbel in S Egypt.

Ramses III or ***Rameses III*** king (pharaoh) of ancient Egypt about 1194–1163 BC. He won victories over the Libyans and the ◊Sea Peoples and asserted his control over Palestine.

Ramsey Alf(red) Ernest 1920– . English football player and manager. England's most successful manager ever, he won the World Cup 1966. Of the 123 matches for which he was in charge of the national side between 1963 and 1974, England had 78 victories and only 13 defeats.

ranching commercial form of ◊pastoral farming that involves extensive use of large areas of land (◊extensive agriculture) for grazing cattle or sheep.

Ranches may be very large, especially where the soil quality is poor; for example, the estancias on the ◊Pampas grasslands in Argentina. Cattle have in the past been allowed to graze freely but more are now enclosed. In the Amazon some deforested areas have been given over to beef-cattle ranching. ▷ *See feature on pp. 896–897.*

random number one of a series of numbers having no detectable pattern. Random numbers are used in ◊computer simulation and ◊computer games. It is impossible for an ordinary computer to generate true random numbers, but various techniques are available for obtaining pseudo-random numbers – close enough to true randomness for most purposes.

rangefinder instrument for determining the range or distance of an object from the observer; used to focus a camera or to sight a gun accurately. A rangefinder camera has a rotating mirror or prism that alters the image seen through the viewfinder, and a secondary window. When the two images are brought together into one, the lens is sharply focused.

Rangoon former name (to 1989) of ◊Yangon, the capital of Myanmar (Burma).

Ranjit Singh 1780–1839. Indian maharajah. He succeeded his father as a minor Sikh leader 1792, and created a Sikh army that conquered Kashmir and the Punjab. In alliance with the British, he established himself as 'Lion of the Punjab', ruler of the strongest of the independent Indian states.

Rank J(oseph) Arthur, 1st Baron Rank 1888–1972. English film magnate. Having entered films 1933 to promote the Methodist cause, by the mid-1940s he controlled, through the Rank Organization, half the British studios and more than 1,000 cinemas. The Rank Organization still owns the Odeon chain of cinemas, although film is now a minor part of its activities.

Ransome Arthur Michell 1884–1967. English journalist (correspondent in Russia for the *Daily News* during World War I and the Revolution) and writer of adventure stories for children, such as *Swallows and Amazons* 1930 and *Peter Duck* 1932.

> ❛Better drowned than duffers if not duffers wont drown.❜
>
> ARTHUR RANSOME *Swallows and Amazons*

Rao P(amulaparti) V(enkata) Narasimha 1921– . Indian politician, prime minister of India 1991–96 and Congress leader 1991–96. He governed the state of Andhra Pradesh as chief minister 1971–73, and served in the cabinets of Indira and Rajiv Gandhi as minister of external affairs 1980–85 and 1988–90 and of human resources 1985–88. He took over Congress party leadership after the assassination of Rajiv Gandhi. Elected prime minister the following month, he instituted a market-centred and outward-looking reform of the economy. He survived a vote of no confidence 1993. After the Congress party was defeated in national elections May 1996, Rao resigned as prime minister. In Sept, he resigned as Congress leader as allegations mounted over his alleged involvement in political bribery.

Raoult François Marie 1830–1901. French chemist. In 1882, while working at the University of Grenoble, Raoult formulated one of the basic laws of chemistry. Raoult's law enables the relative molecular mass of a substance to be determined by noting how much of it is required to depress the freezing point of a solvent by a certain amount.

rape in law, sexual intercourse without the consent of the subject. Most cases of rape are of women by men.

In the UK from 1976 the victim's name may not be published, her sex history should not be in question, and her 'absence of consent' rather than (as previously required) proof of her 'resistance to violence' is the criterion of the crime. The anonymity of the accused is also preserved unless he is convicted. Rape within marriage became a criminal offence in England, Wales, and Northern Ireland 1991 (as was already the case in Scotland, the Republic of Ireland, New Zealand, Israel, and some states in the USA and Australia).

In Islamic law a rape accusation requires the support of four independent male witnesses. Rape and sexual abuse are systematically used in many countries, such as Pakistan, against women in police custody; and in warfare, to intimidate civilian populations and force ethnic groups to flee.

rape in botany, two plant species of the mustard family Cruciferae, *Brassica rapa* and *B. napus*, grown for their seeds, which yield a pungent edible oil. The common turnip is a variety of the former, and the swede turnip of the latter.

Oilseed rape, or canola, is the world's third most important oilseed crop. Plant breeders developed it from the 'weed' rapeseed, *B. napus oleifera*. Rape methyl ester provides a renewable replacement for diesel that emits fewer sooty particles and none of the acid-rain causing sulphur dioxide.

Raphael Sanzio (Raffaello Sanzio) 1483–1520. Italian painter and architect. One of the greatest artists of the High Renaissance, he painted portraits and mythological and religious works, noted for their harmony of colour and composition. He was active in Perugia, Florence, and (from 1508) Rome. Among his best-known and greatest works are *The Marriage of the Virgin* 1504 (Brera, Milan) and the fresco *The School of Athens* 1509–11 (Vatican, Rome).

Raphael was born in Urbino, the son of Giovanni Santi (died 1494), a court painter. In 1499 he went to Perugia, where he worked with ◊Perugino. During 1509–11, Pope Julius II commissioned him to decorate the papal apartments (the Stanze della Segnatura) in the Vatican. His last great work, *The Transfiguration* 1519–20, anticipates ◊Mannerism. *See illustration on p. 898.*

Rainforests

In many places along the Andean chain in the provinces of Salta, Tucuman, and Jujuy in Argentina, rainforest on the east-facing slopes turns rapidly into cactus-rich desert in the western rainshadow. *Premaphotos Wildlife*

Hoffmann's two-toed sloth in its characteristic upside-down position. Sloths are so well adapted to a life spent hanging from branches that they even give birth upside down. Although they cannot move quickly to escape predators, their claws are a powerful means of self-defence. *Corel*

Tropical rainforests are noisy. The air is full of sound: a continuous hum from countless cicadas, crickets, and bees forms the background to raucous bird cries. Huge trees stretch upwards, with irregularly shaped trunks and a thick covering of creepers. A dense canopy of thick, waxy leaves keeps out most of the sunlight.

This habitat, impenetrable and frequently dangerous to humans, is the focus of the greatest conservation effort in history. This is because rainforests contain more species of plants and animals than the rest of the world's ecosystems put together, and also store huge amounts of carbon in their vegetation so that their loss adds appreciably to the greenhouse effect.

Hot and cool rainforests

Forests with high rainfall and humidity are found in temperate as well as tropical regions. Tropical rainforests stretch around the equator, including the Amazon region of South America, the Congo basin in west Africa, parts of the Indian subcontinent, the archipelagos and islands of eastern Asia and the Pacific, and northern Queensland in Australia. Remaining temperate rainforests are found in Tasmania, northern New Zealand, central Asia, coastal Norway, and in a strip along the west coast of North America, from the Washington Cascade Mountains to the Tongass rainforest of Alaska.

Rich in biodiversity and human cultures

In a temperate forest, much of the organic matter remains in the soil, whereas in tropical rainforests there is far more biomass in the form of living material and the soil below can be quite poor; some tropical rainforests have been called 'jungles growing on deserts'. Some trees even have 'roots' on their branches to take nutrients from rotting vegetation caught in the canopy.

Rainforests are also extremely rich in species. Up to 300 different kinds of tree have been found in a single square kilometre of the Amazon, and scientists know that they have described only a fraction of the species of invertebrates and lower plants. In some rainforests, new mammals and birds are still being discovered.

Rainforests also provide homes for many unique human groups. Some peoples have inhabited particular forests for millennia, and have developed a sophisticated knowledge of their biology and ecology. Their way of life has changed little and is often based around philosophies and beliefs that are radically different from those of the civilizations beyond the forest edge. Many tropical groups first experience contact with Western society when forests are felled, and suffer persecution, introduction of diseases, and destruction of homelands. Throughout the world, indigenous groups are in conflict with loggers, settlers, and other short-term commercial interests; embattled peoples include the Dyak and Penan in Sarawak; the Lumad in the Philippines; tribal groups in the Chittagong Hill Tracts of Bangladesh; and the Waorani, Yanamami, and other groups in the Amazon.

A cornucopia for human development

The richness of the rainforests offers enormous opportunities to human society. Rainforests are the original source of many of our most important crops and vegetables, including rice, potatoes, cassava, tomatoes, peanuts, and Brazil nuts. At

A jaguar climbing a tree. Jaguars are excellent climbers, and often lie in wait for their prey in trees. Capybaras and wild pigs make up a large part of their diet. *Corel*

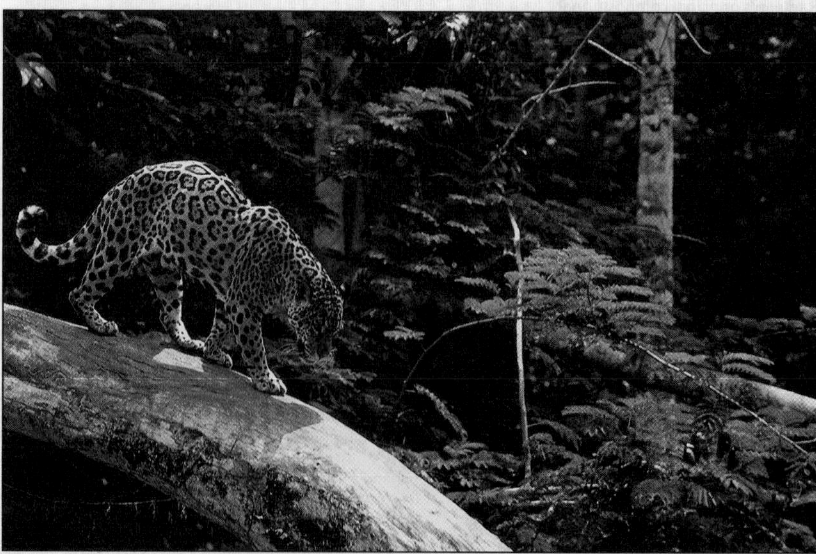

Yanomami Indians in a banana plantation. Dwindling numbers of these people, whose ancestors have lived in the rainforest for generations, are struggling to survive in the face of encroaching mining development in the Amazon region. *Survival International* [3]

Machu Picchu in Peru, the Incas built up an early gene bank of different tubers from all over the continent, including several that have become important commercial vegetables. Among medicines that originate from rainforest species are quinine, curare, and (from the Mexican yam) the modern contraceptive pill. A survey of 1,500 plants from Costa Rican rainforests found 15%) had properties that might be of use against cancer. Other important materials derived from rainforests include bamboo, rubber, coffee, cocoa, many vegetable oils, and rattan.

Thousands of other potentially useful plants have not yet been studied, and any single species is likely to have several applications; for example, the fruit, bark, leaves, and timber will all have different uses. In Kalimantan, Borneo, researchers found that local Dyak people use over 200 tree species for food, medicine, and materials. Like many rainforest communities, the Dyak practise low-level cultivation, particularly through establishing fruit gardens, patches of rainforest that appear natural but have undergone enrichment planting to make them extremely productive areas.

hawk moth A hawk moth *Batocnema coquereli* resting during daytime, in the rainforest. Hawk moths are some of the fastest flying of all insects, reaching speeds of over 53 kph/33 mph. *K G Preston-Mafham/ Premaphotos Wildlife*

Rainforests under threat

Currently, both tropical and temperate rainforests are under unprecedented threats. In a few decades, we risk losing ecosystems, species, and genetic diversity that have developed over millions of years, leading to the greatest rate of species extinction in the history of the planet – dwarfing even the loss of the dinosaurs.

Causes of loss are complex. Although population growth and agricultural expansion are often identified as the main problems, this is an oversimplification. Other factors range from commercial logging (both in felling forests and opening up areas to other forms of exploitation) to, perhaps, climate change. Oil companies have now leased virtually all remaining tropical forest areas for exploration and/or production, and drilling has caused damage in the Amazon, west Africa, and Papua New Guinea. Tropical forests are also harmed through mining for iron ore, gold, bauxite, copper, and uranium. Large hydroelectric projects have flooded forests in many countries. Some 72% of land clearance in the Amazon until 1980 was caused by the expansion of cattle ranching. Similar deforestation for ranching has taken place in Costa Rica and Honduras, also resulting in the marginalization of peasant producers.

In some countries, such as Nigeria, Ivory Coast, and Thailand, deforestation is already almost complete. In others, such as Zaire, Brazil, and parts of Indonesia, large areas of rainforest still remain, but are rapidly being lost. Although information remains poor, research by the United Nations Food and Agriculture Organization suggests that forest cover is falling in almost all the tropical countries of Africa, Asia, and Latin America, and in much of Oceania. Net losses occurred in at least 75 countries in 1990, and in 46 the rate of loss increased during the 1980s.

Efforts to save rainforests

As a result, governments, conservation organizations, and local communities are making efforts to save the world's rainforests – at least enough of them to preserve species and ecosystems. Steps include the creation of national parks and protected areas, and giving help to people who are often driven to exploit rainforests through the twin pressures of poverty and lack of land. Such conservation efforts succeed in practice only if local people support the initiatives. Changing management methods, including providing far greater control for communities to manage their own forest resources, is perhaps the best hope for long-term survival of these vital ecosystems.

Nigel Dudley

A blue-and-yellow macaw. The decline in numbers of these spectacular birds is a result of the destruction of the rainforest and the capture of young birds for sale as cage birds. *Corel*

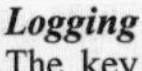

Logging

The key role that timber traders in Europe, Japan, and east Asia play in tropical forest loss has now been clearly identified. The global market for timber and especially for pulp is currently expanding. For example, pressure for logging has recently increased in Cameroon, and timber companies are moving into previously untouched areas of Guyana, Suriname, and Papua New Guinea. A study for the International Tropical Timber Organization found that 'the extent of tropical forest which is being deliberately managed at an operational level for the sustainable production of timber is, on a world scale, negligible'. Research in Malaysia found that for every 10% of trees extracted from an area, 55% were damaged. The World Wide Fund for Nature has identified commercial logging as a critical threat to those forests that are richest in wildlife.

Road construction in the Amazon, Brazil. The road itself is not the only threat to the indigenous peoples and wildlife – it will provide easier access for logging and mining, as well as bringing traffic pollution into the heart of the rainforest. *Survival International*

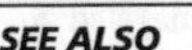

SEE ALSO
Amazon; biodiversity; deforestation; Yanamamo

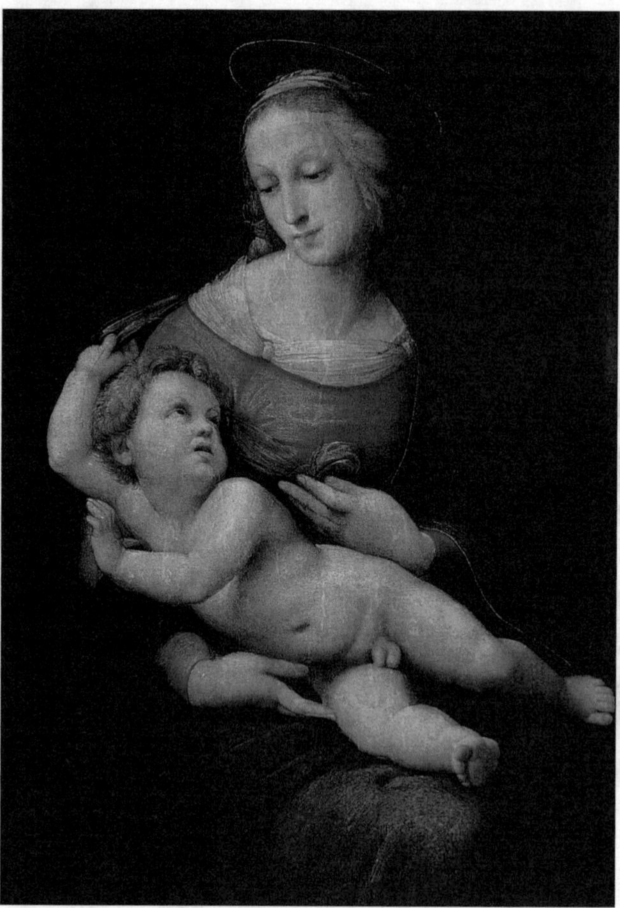

Raphael Sanzio The *Bridgewater Madonna* 1506–07, National Gallery of Scotland, Sutherland loan. The theme of the Virgin and Child inspired Raphael to create some of his best paintings; the subject is depicted with perfect Classical poise and conveys a religious sincerity and warmth. For centuries after his death, Raphael was considered the greatest painter of the Renaissance. *National Gallery of Scotland*

rap music rapid, rhythmic chant over a prerecorded repetitive backing track. Rap emerged in New York 1979 as part of the ◊hip-hop culture, although the macho, swaggering lyrics that initially predominated have roots in ritual boasts and insults. Different styles were flourishing by the 1990s, such as jazz rap, gangsta rap, and reggae rap. The strong political attack of Public Enemy made them one of the most influential rap groups.

rare-earth element alternative name for ◊lanthanide.

rare gas alternative name for ◊inert gas.

Rarotonga Treaty agreement that formally declares the South Pacific a nuclear-free zone. The treaty was signed 1987 by Australia, Fiji, Indonesia, New Zealand, and the USSR.

Ras el Khaimah or ***Ra's al Khaymah*** emirate on the Persian Gulf; area 1,690 sq km/652 sq mi; population (1985) 116,500. Products include oil, pharmaceuticals, and cement. It is one of the seven members of the ◊United Arab Emirates.

Rashdun the 'rightly guided ones', the first four caliphs (heads) of Islam: Abu Bakr, Umar, Uthman, and Ali.

Rasmussen Poul Nyrup 1943– . Danish economist and politician, prime minister from 1993. Leader of the Social Democrats from 1992, he succeeded Poul ◊ Schluter as prime minister, heading the first majority coalition government since 1982. He was returned to power in the 1994 general election.

raspberry prickly cane plant of the genus *Rubus* of the Rosaceae family, native to Eurasia and North America, with white flowers followed by red fruits. These are eaten fresh and used for jam and wine.

Rasputin (Russian 'dissolute'; born Grigory Efimovich Novykh) 1871–1916. Siberian Eastern Orthodox mystic. He acquired influence over the Tsarina ◊Alexandra, wife of ◊Nicholas II, and was able to make political and ecclesiastical appointments. His abuse of power and notorious debauchery (reputedly including the tsarina) led to his murder by a group of nobles.

Rasputin, the illiterate son of a peasant, began as a wandering 'holy man'. Through the tsarina's faith in his power to ease her son's suffering from haemophilia, he became a favourite at the court, where he instigated wild parties under the slogan 'Sin that you may obtain forgiveness'. A larger-than-life character, he even proved hard to kill: when poison had no effect, his assassins shot him and dumped him in the river Neva.

Rastafarianism religion originating in the West Indies, based on the ideas of Marcus ◊Garvey, who called on black people to return to Africa and set up a black-governed country there. When Haile Selassie (*Ras Tafari*, 'Lion of Judah') was crowned emperor of Ethiopia 1930, this was seen as a fulfilment of prophecy and some Rastafarians acknowledged him as an incarnation of God (*Jah*), others as a prophet. The use of ganja (marijuana) is a sacrament. There are no churches.

Rastafarians identify themselves with the Chosen People, the Israelites, of the Bible. Ethiopia is seen as the promised land, while all countries outside Africa are Babylon, the place of exile. Many Rastafarians do not cut their hair, because of biblical injunctions against this, but wear it instead in long dreadlocks, often covered in woollen hats in the Rastafarian colours of red, green, and gold. Food laws are very strict: for example, no pork or shellfish, no salt, milk, or coffee. Rastafarians use a distinct language, in particular using the term 'I and I' for 'we' to stress unity.

raster graphics computer graphics that are stored in the computer memory by using a map to record data (such as colour and intensity) for every ◊pixel that makes up the image. When transformed (enlarged, rotated, stretched, and so on), raster graphics become ragged and suffer loss of picture resolution, unlike ◊vector graphics. Raster graphics are typically used for painting applications, which allow the user to create artwork on a computer screen much as if they were painting on paper or canvas.

rat any of numerous long-tailed ◊rodents (especially of the families Muridae and Cricetidae) larger than mice and usually with scaly, naked tails. The genus *Rattus* in the family Muridae includes the rats found in human housing.

The ***brown rat*** *R. norvegicus* is about 20 cm/8 in long with a tail of almost equal length. It is believed to have originated in central Asia, and is now found worldwide after being transported from Europe by ships. The ***black rat*** *R. rattus*, responsible for the ◊plague, is smaller than the brown rat, but has larger ears and a longer, more pointed snout. It does not interbreed with brown rats.

rate of reaction the speed at which a chemical reaction proceeds. It is usually expressed in terms of the concentration (usually in ◊moles per litre) of a reactant consumed, or product formed, in unit time; so the units would be moles per litre per second (mol l^{-1} s^{-1}). The rate of a reaction may be affected by the concentration of the reactants, the temperature of the reactants, and the presence of a ◊catalyst. If the reaction is entirely in the gas state, the rate is affected by pressure, and, for solids, it is affected by the particle size.

◊Collision theory is used to explain these effects. Increasing the concentration or the pressure of a gas means there are more particles per unit volume, therefore there are more collisions and more fruitful collisions. Increasing the temperature makes the particles move much faster, resulting in more collisions per unit time and more fruitful collisions; consequently the rate increases.

rates in the UK, a local government tax levied on industrial and commercial property (business rates) and, until the introduction of the community charge (see ◊poll tax) 1989/90, also on residential property to pay for local amenities such as roads, footpaths, refuse collection and disposal, and community and welfare activities. The water companies also use a rating system to charge most householders for water supply.

The rate for a household with several wage-earners might be identical with that for a single person of retirement age, and rebates were given to ratepayers whose income fell below a certain level. The Conservative government, in power from 1979, curbed high-spending councils by cutting the government supplementary grant aid to them and limiting the level of rate that could be levied (rate-capping), and in 1989–90 replaced the rate with a community charge or poll tax on each individual (introduced in Scotland 1989 and England 1990). This in turn was superseded by a council tax 1993, based on property values but taking into account the number of occupiers.

Rathenau Walther 1867–1922. German politician. He was a leading industrialist and was appointed economic director during World War I, developing a system of economic planning in combination with capitalism. After the war he founded the Democratic Party, and became foreign minister 1922. The same year he signed the Rapallo Treaty of Friendship with the USSR, cancelling German and Soviet counterclaims for indemnities for World War I, and soon after was assassinated by right-wing fanatics.

rationalism in theology, the belief that human reason rather than divine revelation is the correct means of ascertaining truth and regulating behaviour. In philosophy, rationalism takes the view that self-evident a priori propositions (deduced by reason alone) are the sole basis of all knowledge. It is usually contrasted with ◊empiricism, which argues that all knowledge must ultimately be derived from the senses. The philosophers René Descartes, Gottfried Leibniz, and Baruch Spinoza are known as the continental rationalists, and are usually contrasted with the British empiricists.

Rationalism in architecture, an Italian movement of the 1920s which grew out of a reaction to the extremes of ◊Futurism. It was led by Gruppo 7, a loose association of young Italian architects, headed by Giuseppe ◊Terragni. The group's Rationalist approach aimed to restore a sense of mass and volume to modern architecture and resulted in a clear-cut, austere style, exemplified in Terragni's Casa del Fascio, Como, 1932–36. The work of the movement suffered from its association with Fascism, but was reappraised in the 1960s by the New York Five, in particular Peter ◊Eisenman. A parallel re-evaluation took place in Italy, culminating in the ◊Neo-Rationalism of Aldo Rossi (1931–) and Giorgio Grassi (1935–).

rational number in mathematics, any number that can be expressed as an exact fraction (with a denominator not equal to 0), that is, as $a \div b$ where a and b are integers. For example, $\frac{2}{1}$, $\frac{1}{4}$, $1\frac{5}{4}$, $-\frac{3}{5}$ are all rational numbers, whereas π (which represents the constant 3.141592 ...) is not. Numbers such as π are called ◊irrational numbers.

ratite flightless bird with a breastbone without the keel to which flight muscles are attached. Examples are ◊ostrich, ◊rhea, ◊emu, ◊cassowary, and ◊kiwi.

rat-tail or ***grenadier*** any fish of the family Macrouridae of deep-sea bony fishes. They have stout heads and bodies, and long tapering tails. They are common in deep waters on the continental slopes. Some species have a light-emitting organ in front of the anus.

Rattigan Terence Mervyn 1911–1977. English dramatist. His play *Ross* 1960 was based on the character of T E Lawrence (Lawrence of Arabia). Rattigan's work ranges from the comedy *French Without Tears* 1936 to the psychological intensity of *The Winslow Boy* 1946. Other plays include *The Browning Version* 1948 and *Separate Tables* 1954.

Rattle Simon 1955– . English conductor, principal conductor of the City of Birmingham Symphony Orchestra (CBSO) from 1979. He has built the CBSO into a world class orchestra, with a core repertoire of early 20th century music; he has also commissioned new works. A popular and dynamic conductor, he achieves a characteristically clear and precise sound.

rattlesnake any of various New World pit ◊vipers of the genera *Crotalus* and *Sistrurus* (the massasaugas and pygmy rattlers), distinguished by horny flat segments of the tail, which rattle when vibrated as a warning to attackers. They can grow to 2.5 m/8 ft long. The venom injected by some rattlesnakes can be fatal.

There are 31 species distributed from S Canada to central South America. The eastern diamondback *C. adamanteus* 0.9–2.5 m/2.8–8 ft long, is found in the flat pinelands of the southern USA.

Ratushinskaya Irina 1954– . Soviet dissident poet. Sentenced 1983 to seven years in a labour camp plus five years in internal exile for criticism of the Soviet regime, she was released 1986. Her strongly Christian work includes *Grey is the Colour of Hope* 1988.

Raunkiaer system method of classification devised by the Danish ecologist Christen Raunkiaer (1860–1938) whereby plants are divided into groups according to the position of their ◊perennating (overwintering) buds in relation to the soil surface. For example, plants in cold areas, such as the tundra, generally have their buds protected below ground, whereas in hot, tropical areas they are above ground and freely exposed. This scheme is useful for comparing vegetation types in different parts of the world.

The main divisions are phanerophytes with buds situated well above the ground; chamaephytes with buds borne within 25 cm/10 in of the soil surface; hemicryptophytes with buds at or immediately below the soil surface; and cryptophytes with their buds either beneath the soil (geophyte) or below water (hydrophyte).

Rauschenberg Robert, (born Milton Rauschenberg) 1925– . US Pop artist. He has created ◊happenings and multimedia works, called 'combined painting', such as *Monogram* 1959 (Moderna Museet, Stockholm), a stuffed goat daubed with paint and wearing a car tyre around its body. In the 1960s he returned to painting and used the silk-screen printing process to transfer images to canvas.

Ravel (Joseph) Maurice 1875–1937. French composer and pianist. His work is characterized by its sensuousness, exotic harmonics, and dazzling orchestral effects. Examples are the piano pieces *Pavane pour une infante défunte/Pavane for a Dead Infanta* 1899 and *Jeux d'eau/Waterfall* 1901, and the ballets *Daphnis et Chloë* 1912 and *Boléro* 1928.

Ravel The composer Maurice Ravel (1875–1937). Along with Debussy he was the leading impressionist composer. His works are often intricately crafted; Stravinsky compared him to a Swiss watchmaker. He was an innovator of pianistic and orchestral techniques, especially when evoking exotic musical ideas. *Image Select (UK) Ltd*

raven any of several large ◊crows, genus *Corvus*, of the Corvidae family, order Passeriformes. The common raven *C. corax* is about 60 cm/2 ft long with a wingspan of nearly 1 m/3 ft, and has black, lustrous plumage; the beak and mouth, tongue, legs, and feet are also black. It is a scavenger, and is found only in the northern hemisphere. The nest is built in cliffs or in the fork of a tall tree, and is a bulky structure. In it are laid four or five pale-green eggs spotted with brown. Incubation by the female lasts about 21 days.

Ravenna historical city and industrial port (petrochemical works) in Emilia-Romagna, Italy; population (1992) 137,100. It lies in a marshy plain and is known for its Byzantine churches with superb mosaics.
history Ravenna was a Roman port and naval station. It was capital of the Western Roman emperors 404–93, of ◊Theodoric the Great 493–526, and later of the Byzantine exarchs (bishops) 539–750.

Ravensbruck German ◊concentration camp for female prisoners in Mecklenburg, NW of Berlin, established 1936. Medical experiments were carried out on Polish women at the camp, and it was also the place of execution for Allied female agents.

Rawalpindi city in Punjab province, Pakistan, in the foothills of the Himalayas; population (1981) 928,400. Industries include oil refining, iron, chemicals, and furniture.

Rawlings Jerry (John) 1947– . Ghanaian politician, president from 1981. He first took power in a bloodless coup 1979, and, having returned power to a civilian government, staged another coup 1981. He then remained in power until 1992, when he was elected president under the new multiparty constitution. He was re-elected for a second term Dec 1996.

ray any of several orders (especially Ragiformes) of cartilaginous fishes with a flattened body, winglike pectoral fins, and a whiplike tail. Species include the stingray, for example the Southern stingray *Dasyatis americana*, which has a serrated, poisonous spine on the tail, and the ◊torpedo fish.

Ray John 1627–1705. English naturalist who devised a classification system accounting for some 18,000 plant species. It was the first system to divide flowering plants into ◊monocotyledons and ◊dicotyledons, with additional divisions made on the basis of leaf and flower characters and fruit types. Ray first set out his system in *Methodus plantarum nova* 1682. He also established the species as the fundamental unit of classification.

Ray Man. Adopted name of Emmanuel Rabinovich Rudnitsky 1890–1976. US photographer, painter, and sculptor. He was active mainly in France and was associated with the ◊Dada movement and then ◊Surrealism. One of his best-known sculptures is *Gift* 1921, a Surrealist ◊ready-made consisting of an iron on to which a row of nails has been glued.

Man Ray was born in Philadelphia, but lived mostly in Paris from 1921. He began as a painter and took up photography 1915, the year he met the Dada artist Marcel ◊Duchamp in New York. In 1922 he invented the rayograph, a black-and-white image obtained without a camera by placing objects on sensitized photographic paper and exposing them to light.

Ray Nicholas. Adopted name of Raymond Nicholas Kienzle 1911–1979. US film director. He was critically acclaimed for his socially aware dramas that concentrated on the individual as an outsider, such as *They Live by Night* 1948 and *Rebel Without a Cause* 1955. Other films include *In a Lonely Place* 1950 and *55 Days at Peking* 1963.

Ray Satyajit 1921–1992. Indian film director. He was internationally known for his trilogy of life in his native Bengal: *Pather Panchali*, *Unvanquished*, and *The World of Apu* 1955–59. Later films include *The Music Room* 1963, *Charulata* 1964, *The Chess Players* 1977, and *The Home and the World* 1984.

Rayleigh John William Strutt, 3rd Baron Rayleigh 1842–1919. English physicist who wrote the standard treatise *The Theory of Sound* (1877–78), experimented in optics and microscopy, and, with William ◊Ramsay, discovered argon. Nobel prize 1904.

Raynaud's disease chronic condition in which the blood supply to the extremities is reduced by periodic spasm of the blood vessels on exposure to cold. It is most often seen in young women.

rayon any of various shiny textile fibres and fabrics made from ◊cellulose. It is produced by pressing whatever cellulose solution is used through very small holes and solidifying the resulting filaments. A common type is ◊viscose, which consists of regenerated filaments of pure cellulose. Acetate and triacetate are kinds of rayon consisting of filaments of cellulose acetate and triacetate.

razorbill North Atlantic sea bird *Alca torda* of the auk family, order Charadriiformes, which breeds on cliffs and migrates south in winter. It is about 40 cm/16 in long, has a large curved beak, and is black above and white below. It uses its wings as paddles when diving. Razorbills make no nest; the female lays a single egg, which is white with brown markings. They are common off Newfoundland.

raspberry The wild raspberry *Rubus idaeus* grows in woods and on heathland, especially in hilly districts, throughout much of Europe (including Iceland) and Asia. *Premaphotos Wildlife*

razor-shell or ***razor-fish***; US name ***razor clam*** any bivalve mollusc in two genera *Ensis* and *Solen* with narrow, elongated shells, resembling an old-fashioned razor handle and delicately coloured. They can burrow rapidly into sand and are good swimmers.

reactance property of an alternating current circuit that together with any ◊resistance makes up the ◊impedance (the total opposition of the circuit to the passage of a current). The reactance of an inductance L is wL and that of the capacitance is $1/wC$. Reactance is measured in ◊ohms.

reaction in chemistry, the coming together of two or more atoms, ions, or molecules with the result that a chemical change takes place. The nature of the reaction is portrayed by a chemical equation.

reaction force in physics, the equal and opposite force described by Newton's third law of motion that arises whenever one object applies a force (action force) to another. For example, if a magnet attracts a piece of iron, then that piece of iron will also attract the magnet with a force that is equal in magnitude but opposite in direction. When any object rests on the ground the downwards contact force applied to the ground always produces an equal, upwards reaction force.

reactivity series chemical series produced by arranging the metals in order of their ease of reaction with reagents such as oxygen, water, and acids. This arrangement aids the understanding of the properties of metals, helps to explain differences between them, and enables predictions to be made about a metal's behaviour, based on a knowledge of its position or properties.

Ray The Dadaist artist Man Ray, photographed in Paris 1964, surrounded by his *objets d'art*. He gave these items the titles *Main-Ray*, *The Gift*, and *Person to Person* (the hand, the iron, and the shoe-trees respectively). *Corbis*

‘You know, by the time you reach my age, you've made plenty of mistakes if you've lived your life properly.’

RONALD REAGAN
Quoted in the *Observer* 1987

Read Herbert Edward 1893–1968. English art critic and poet. His reputation as a critic was established in the 1930s and 1940s, when he was a keen supporter of such artists as Henry ◊Moore, Barbara ◊Hepworth, and Ben ◊Nicholson. His many books and essays, which helped to make modern art accessible to a wider public, include *The Meaning of Art* 1931 and the influential *Education through Art* 1943.

Reading industrial town (biscuits, brewing, boat building, engineering, printing, electronics) on the river Thames; administrative headquarters of Berkshire, England; population (1991) 128,900. It is an agricultural and horticultural centre, and was extensively rebuilt after World War II. There is a 12th-century abbey where Henry I is buried.

ready-made in the visual arts, an object chosen at random by the artist, as opposed to being selected for any presumed aesthetic merit, and presented as a work of art. The concept was first launched by Marcel ◊Duchamp when he exhibited a bicycle wheel set on a stool 1913. Popular among Dadaists, ready-mades have been used to challenge the elitist qualities of fine art.

Although very similar to the found object (French *objet trouvé*) favoured by the Surrealists, ready-mades differ in that they are mass-manufactured items and are chosen entirely at random.

Reagan Ronald Wilson 1911– . 40th president of the USA 1981–89, a Republican. He was governor of California 1966–74, and a former Hollywood actor. Reagan was a hawkish and popular president. He adopted an aggressive policy in Central America, attempting to overthrow the government of Nicaragua, and invading Grenada 1983. In 1987, ◊Irangate was investigated by the Tower Commission; Reagan admitted that US–Iran negotiations had become an ‘arms for hostages deal’, but denied knowledge of resultant funds being illegally sent to the Contras in Nicaragua. He increased military spending (sending the national budget deficit to record levels), cut social programmes, introduced deregulation of domestic markets, and cut taxes. His ◊Strategic Defense Initiative (popularly called Star Wars), announced 1983, proved controversial owing to its cost and unfeasibility.

Having lost the Republican presidential nomination 1968 and 1976 to Nixon and Ford respectively, Reagan won it 1980 and defeated President Carter. He was wounded in an assassination attempt 1981. The invasion of Grenada generated a revival of national patriotism, and Reagan was re-elected by a landslide 1984. He was succeeded by Vice President George Bush.

realism in the arts and literature generally, an unadorned, naturalistic approach to subject matter. More specifically, Realism refers to a movement in mid-19th-century European art and literature, a reaction against Romantic and Classical idealization and a rejection of conventional academic themes (such as mythology, history, and sublime landscapes) in favour of everyday life and carefully observed social settings. The movement was particularly important in France, where it had political

Reagan Ronald Reagan, US president 1981–89. Despite, or perhaps because of, his fundamentalist rhetoric and his emphasis on high defence spending and military intervention, Reagan was a popular president and was easily re-elected 1984 for a second term. *Sachem*

Realism Gustave Courbet's *Self-Portrait with Pipe* 1846, Musée Fabre, Montpellier, France. Courbet painted things as he saw them, rejecting the traditional subjects such as classical mythology and religious themes. Critics often found his choice of subject offensive. *Corbis*

overtones; the painters Gustave ◊Courbet and Honoré ◊Daumier, two leading Realists, both used their art to expose social injustice.

In literature, realists include the novelists Honoré de Balzac, Gustave Flaubert, Stendhal, George Eliot, Theodor Fontane, Fyodor Dostoevsky, Nicolai Gogol, and Leo Tolstoy. Realism was superseded by ◊Impressionism in painting and ◊naturalism in literature.

realism in philosophy, the theory that ◊universals (properties such as ‘redness’) have an existence independent of the human mind. Realists hold that the essence of a thing (all that makes a thing what it is and is indispensable to the thing) is objectively given in nature, and that our classifications are not arbitrary. As such, realism is contrasted with nominalism, the theory that universals are merely names or general terms.

More generally, realism is any philosophical theory that emphasizes the existence of some kind of things or objects, in contrast to theories that dispense with the things in question in favour of words, ideas, or logical constructions. In particular, the term stands for the theory that there is a reality quite independent of the mind. In this sense, realism is opposed to idealism, the theory that only minds and their contents exist.

real number in mathematics, any of the ◊rational numbers (which include the integers) or ◊irrational numbers. Real numbers exclude ◊imaginary numbers, found in ◊complex numbers of the general form $a + bi$ where $i = \sqrt{-1}$, although these do include a real component a.

realpolitik (German *Realpolitik* ‘politics of realism’) belief that the pragmatic pursuit of self-interest and power, backed up by force when convenient, is the only realistic option for a great state. The term was coined 1859 to describe the German chancellor ◊Bismarck's policies.

real presence or ***transubstantiation*** in Christianity, the doctrine that Christ is really present in the consecrated ◊Eucharist. The Roman Catholic Church holds to a metaphysical theory, ◊transubstantiation, which is the doctrine that only the appearance of the consecrated bread and wine remains and that its actual substance becomes Christ's body and blood. The Lutheran churches hold to another metaphysical theory about it, consubstantiation, which is the doctrine that the substances of the bread and wine and of Christ's body and blood coexist in union with one another. The Anglican churches avoid metaphysical speculation about the real presence and regard it as a mystery.

real tennis racket and ball game played in France, from about the 12th century, over a central net in an indoor court, but with a sloping roof let into each end and one side of the court, against which the ball may be hit. The term ‘real’ here means ‘royal’, not ‘genuine’. Basic scoring is as for lawn ◊tennis, but with various modifications.

The oldest court still in use is the one installed by Henry VIII at Hampton Court, Richmond, London.

received pronunciation (RP) national and international English accent; the accent associated with Standard English. Spoken by royalty and representatives of the church, the government, and the law courts, RP is the language of official authority. See also ◊English language.

receiver in law, a person appointed by a court to collect and manage the assets of an individual, company, or partnership in serious financial difficulties. In the case of bankruptcy, the assets may be sold and distributed by a receiver to creditors.

receptacle the enlarged end of a flower stalk to which the floral parts are attached. Normally the receptacle is rounded, but in some plants it is flattened or cup-shaped. The term is also used for the region on that part of some seaweeds which becomes swollen at certain times of the year and bears the reproductive organs.

recession in economics, a fall in business activity lasting more than a few months, causing stagnation in a country's output. A serious recession is called a slump.

recessive gene in genetics, an ◊allele (alternative form of a gene) that will show in the ◊phenotype (observed characteristics of an organism) only if its partner allele on the paired chromosome is similarly recessive. Such an allele will not show if its partner is dominant, that is if the organism is ◊heterozygous for a particular characteristic. Alleles for blue eyes in humans, and for shortness in pea plants are recessive. Most mutant alleles are recessive and therefore are only rarely expressed (see ◊haemophilia and ◊sickle-cell disease).

recitative in opera and oratorio, sung narration partly modelled on the rhythms and inflections of natural speech. It is usually sparingly accompanied by harpsichord or organ.

recombinant DNA in genetic engineering, ◊DNA formed by splicing together genes from different sources into new combinations.

recombination in genetics, any process that recombines, or ‘shuffles’, the genetic material, thus increasing genetic variation in the offspring. The two main processes of recombination both occur during meiosis (reduction division of cells). One is crossing over, in which chromosome pairs exchange segments; the other is the random reassortment of chromosomes that occurs when each gamete (sperm or egg) receives only one of each chromosome pair.

Reconquista (Spanish ‘reconquest’) Christian defeat of the ◊Moors 9th–15th centuries, and their expulsion from Spain.

Spain was conquered by the Muslims between 711 and 728, and its reconquest began with Galicia, Leon, and Castile. By the 13th century, only Granada was left in Muslim hands, but disunity within the Christian kingdoms left it unconquered until 1492, when it fell to ◊Ferdinand and Isabella.

Reconstruction in US history, the period 1865–77 after the Civil War during which the nation was reunited under the federal government after the defeat of the Southern Confederacy.

Amendments to the US constitution, and to Southern state constitutions, conferred equal civil and political rights on blacks, although many Southern states, opposed to these radical Republican measures, still practised discrimination and segregation. During Reconstruction, industrial and commercial projects restored the economy of the South but failed to ensure racial equality, and the former slaves remained, in most cases, landless labourers, although emancipated slaves were assisted in finding work, shelter, and lost relatives through federal agencies. Reconstruction also resulted in an influx of Northern profiteers known as ◊carpetbaggers. Both the imposition of outside authority and the equal status conferred on former slaves combined to make Southerners bitterly resentful. Although Radical Republicans sought punitive measures against the South, they were restrained by President Abraham ◊Lincoln. When President Andrew ◊Johnson refused to agree to their programme, the Radicals contrived to bring about his impeachment, failing by one vote to convict him.

recorder in the English legal system, a part-time judge who usually sits in the ◊crown courts in less serious cases but may also sit in the county courts or the High Court. Recorders are chosen from barristers of standing and also, since the Courts Act of 1971, from solicitors. They may eventually become circuit judges.

recorder any of a widespread range of woodwind instruments of the whistle type which flourished in consort ensembles (chamber ensembles of instruments of uniform sonority) in the Renaissance and Baroque eras, along with viol consorts, as an instrumental medium for polyphonic music. A modern consort may include a sopranino in F5, soprano (descant) in C4, alto (treble) in F3, tenor in C3, bass in F2, and great bass in C2.

Early Renaissance recorders are of fairly wide bore and penetrating tone; late Renaissance and Baroque instruments are fipple flutes (flutes that have a plug inserted into the mouthpiece to direct the flow of air) of narrower bore and sweet to brilliant tone. The solo recorder remained a popular solo instrument into the 18th century, and the revival of popular interest in recorder playing after 1920, largely through the efforts of Arnold Dolmetsch (1858–1940), led to its wide adoption as a musical instrument for schools.

recording any of a variety of techniques used to capture, store and reproduce music, speech and other information carried by sound waves. A microphone first converts the sound waves into an electrical signal which varies in proportion to the loudness of the sound. The signal can be stored in digital or analogue form, or on magnetic tape.

In an ***analogue recording***, the pattern of the signal is copied into another form. In a gramophone record, for example, a continuous spiral groove is cut into a plastic disc by a vibrating needle. The recording is replayed by a stylus which follows the undulations in the groove, so reproducing the vibrations which are then converted to electrical signals by a ◊transducer in the head (often a ◊piezoelectric crystal). After amplification, the signals pass to one or more loudspeakers, which convert them into sound.

In a ***magnetic tape recording***, the signal is recorded as a pattern of magnetization on a plastic tape coated with a magnetic powder. When the tape is played back, the magnetic patterns create an electrical signal which, as with the gramophone record, is used to recreate the original sound.

In ***digital recording***, the signals picked up by the microphone are converted into a stream of numbers which can then be stored in several ways. The most well-known of these is the ◊compact disc, in which numbers are coded as a string of tiny pits pressed into a 12-cm plastic disc. When the recording is played back, using a laser, the exact values are retrieved and converted into a varying electrical signal and then back into sound.

rectangle quadrilateral (four-sided plane figure) with opposite sides equal and parallel and with each interior angle a right angle (90°). Its area A is the product of the length l and height h; that is, $A = l \times h$. A rectangle with all four sides equal is a ◊square. A rectangle is a special case of a ◊parallelogram. The diagonals of a rectangle are equal and bisect each other.

rectifier in electrical engineering, a device used for obtaining one-directional current (DC) from an alternating source of supply (AC). (The process is necessary because almost all electrical power is generated, transmitted, and supplied as alternating current, but many devices, from television sets to electric motors, require direct current.) Types include plate rectifiers, thermionic ◊diodes, and ◊semiconductor diodes.

rector Anglican priest, formerly entitled to the whole of the ◊tithes levied in the parish, as opposed to a vicar (Latin 'deputy') who was only entitled to part.

rectum lowest part of the large intestine of animals, which stores faeces prior to elimination (defecation).

recycling processing of industrial and household waste (such as paper, glass, and some metals and plastics) so that the materials can be reused. This saves expenditure on scarce raw materials, slows down the depletion of ◊nonrenewable resources, and helps to reduce pollution. Aluminium is frequently recycled because of its value and special properties that allow it to be melted down and repressed without loss of quality, unlike paper and glass, which deteriorate when recycled.

The USA recycles only around 13% of its waste, compared to around 33% in Japan. Most British recycling schemes are voluntary, and rely on people taking waste items to a central collection point. However, some local authorities, such as Leeds, now ask householders to separate waste before collection, making recycling possible on a much larger scale.

Red Army the army of the USSR until 1946; later known as the ***Soviet Army***. It developed from the Red Guards, volunteers who carried out the Bolshevik revolution, and received its name because it fought under the red flag, the international symbol of socialism. The Chinese revolutionary army was also called the Red Army.

red blood cell or ***erythrocyte*** the most common type of blood cell, responsible for transporting oxygen around the body. It contains haemoglobin, which combines with oxygen from the lungs to form oxyhaemoglobin. When transported to the tissues, these cells are able to release the oxygen because the oxyhaemoglobin splits into its original constituents.

Mammalian erythrocytes are disc-shaped with a depression in the centre and no nucleus; they are manufactured in the bone marrow and, in humans, last for only four months before being destroyed in the liver and spleen. Those of other vertebrates are oval and nucleated.

Redbridge outer borough of NE Greater London. It includes the suburbs of Ilford, Wanstead, and Woodford, and parts of Chigwell and Dagenham.
features Takes its name from old Red Bridge over river Roding; Leper Hospital, founded about 1140, with 14th-century chapel and 18th-century almshouses; Valentines (1696); Friends Burial Ground, Wanstead; part of Epping Forest; Hainault Forest
population (1991) 226,200
famous people William Penn, Richard Brinsley Sheridan, and Thomas Hood lived in Wanstead. Winston Churchill was member of Parliament for Woodford for 40 years.

Red Brigades (Italian *Brigate rosse*) extreme left-wing guerrilla groups active in Italy during the 1970s and early 1980s. They were implicated in many kidnappings and killings, some later attributed to right-wing *agents provocateurs*, including that of Christian Democrat leader Aldo Moro 1978.

Redcar and Cleveland unitary authority of England created 1996 *(see United Kingdom map)*.

Red Cross international relief agency founded by the Geneva Convention 1864 at the instigation of the Swiss doctor Henri ◊Dunant to assist the wounded and prisoners in war. Its symbol is a symmetrical red cross on a white ground. In addition to dealing with associated problems of war, such as refugees and the care of the disabled, the Red Cross is concerned with victims of natural disasters – floods, earthquakes, epidemics, and accidents. It was awarded the Nobel Peace Prize 1917 and 1944.

Prompted by war horrors described by Dunant, the Geneva Convention laid down principles to ensure the safety of ambulances, hospitals, stores, and personnel distinguished by the Red Cross emblem. The Muslim equivalent is the Red Crescent.

The British Red Cross Society was founded 1870, and incorporated 1908. It works in close association with the St John Ambulance Association.

red dwarf any star that is cool, faint, and small (about one-tenth the mass and diameter of the Sun). Red dwarfs burn slowly, and have estimated lifetimes of 100 billion years. They may be the most abundant type of star, but are difficult to see because they are so faint. Two of the closest stars to the Sun, ◊Proxima Centauri and ◊Barnard's Star, are red dwarfs.

Redford (Charles) Robert 1937– . US actor and film director. His blond good looks and versatility earned him his first starring role in *Barefoot in the Park* 1967, followed by *Butch Cassidy and the Sundance Kid* 1969 and *The Sting* 1973 (both with Paul ◊Newman). His other films as an actor include *All the President's Men* 1976, *Out of Africa* 1985, and *The Horse Whisperer* 1998.

red giant any large bright star with a cool surface. It is thought to represent a late stage in the evolution of a star like the Sun, as it runs out of hydrogen fuel at its centre. Red giants have diameters between 10 and 100 times that of the Sun. They are very bright because they are so large, although their surface temperature is lower than that of the Sun, about 2,000–3,000K (1,700–2,700°C/3,000°–5,000°F). See also Red ◊supergiants.

Redgrave Michael Scudamore 1908–1985. English actor. His stage roles included Hamlet and Lear (Shakespeare), Uncle Vanya (Chekhov), and the schoolmaster in Rattigan's *The Browning Version* (filmed 1951). On screen he appeared in *The Lady Vanishes* 1938, *The Importance of Being Earnest* 1952, and *Goodbye Mr Chips* 1969. He was the father of actresses Vanessa and Lynn Redgrave.

Redgrave Steven Geoffrey 1962– . English oarsman. Gold medallist at four successive Olympics, winning the coxed fours in 1984 and the coxless pairs in 1988, 1992, and 1996. He also won four gold medals at the World Championships 1986–93, gold at the World Indoor Championships in 1991. He was a member of the British coxless fours team which won a gold medal at the final of the inaugural World Cup Regatta in 1997. Rowing in UK's coxless four he won the World Championships in Cologne, Germany, in 1998.

Redgrave Vanessa 1937– . English actress. She has played Shakespeare's Lady Macbeth and

Red Cross A casualty of trench warfare being treated by a Red Cross team. The International Red Cross was awarded the Nobel Peace Prize 1917 and 1944. *Image Select (UK) Ltd*

Cleopatra on the stage, Ellida in Ibsen's *Lady From the Sea* 1976 and 1979, and Olga in Chekhov's *Three Sisters* 1990. She won an Academy Award for best supporting actress for her title role in the film *Julia* 1976; other films include *Wetherby* 1985 and *Howards End* 1992. She is active in left-wing politics.

Red Guard one of the school and college students, wearing red armbands, active in the ◊Cultural Revolution in China 1966–69. The armed workers who took part in the ◊Russian Revolution of 1917 were also called Red Guards.

red-hot poker any plant of the African genus *Kniphofia*, family Liliaceae, in particular *K. uvaria*, with a flame-coloured spike of flowers.

Redmond John Edward 1856–1918. Irish nationalist politician, leader of the Irish Parliamentary Party (IPP) 1900–18. He rallied his party after Charles Stewart ◊Parnell's imprisonment 1881, and came close to achieving Home Rule for all Ireland 1914. However, the pressure of World War I, Unionist intransigence, and the fallout of the 1916 ◊Easter Rising destroyed both his career and his party. ▷ *See feature on pp. 550–551.*

Redon Odilon 1840–1916. French painter and graphic artist. One of the major figures of ◊Symbolism, he is famous for his fantastic and dreamlike images. From 1890 onwards he produced oil paintings and pastels, brilliant in colour, including numerous flower pieces. His works anticipated ◊Surrealism.

Born in Bordeaux, he studied art there and in Paris, and first became noted for his highly original lithographs, inspired partly by the graphic work of Goya and partly by the writings of Edgar Allan Poe, Charles Baudelaire, and J K Huysmans.

redox reaction chemical change where one reactant is reduced and the other reactant oxidized. The reaction can only occur if both reactants are present and each changes simultaneously. For example, hydrogen reduces copper(II) oxide to copper while it is itself oxidized to water. The corrosion of iron and the reactions taking place in electric and electrolytic cells are just a few instances of redox reactions.

Red River either of two rivers in the USA. The Red River of the South is a western tributary of the ◊Mississippi River 1,638 km/1,018 mi long; so called because of the reddish soil sediment it carries. The stretch that forms the Texas–Oklahoma border is called Tornado Alley because of the storms caused by the collision in spring of warm air from the Gulf of Mexico with cold fronts from the N. The largest city on the river is Shreveport, Louisiana. The Red River of the North, about 877 km/545 mi long, runs from North Dakota into Manitoba, Canada, and through Winnipeg, emptying into Lake Winnipeg. The fertile soil of the river valley produces large yields of wheat and other crops.

Red River river in N Vietnam, 500 km/310 mi long, that flows into the Gulf of Tonkin. Its extensive delta is a main centre of population.

Red Sea submerged section of the Great ◊Rift Valley (2,000 km/1,200 mi long and up to 320 km/200 mi wide). Egypt, Sudan, Ethiopia, and Eritrea (in Africa) and Saudi Arabia (Asia) are on its shores.

redshank wading bird *Tringa totanus* of N Europe and Asia, a type of sandpiper. It nests in swampy areas, rarely in Europe, since most redshanks winter in the south. It is greyish and speckled black, and has long red legs.

red shift in astronomy, the lengthening of the wavelengths of light from an object as a result of the object's motion away from us. It is an example of the ◊Doppler effect. The red shift in light from galaxies is evidence that the universe is expanding.

Lengthening of wavelengths causes the light to move or shift towards the red end of the ◊spectrum, hence the name. The amount of red shift can be measured by the displacement of lines in an object's spectrum. By measuring the amount of red shift in light from stars and galaxies, astronomers can tell how quickly these objects are moving away from us. A strong gravitational field can also produce a red shift in light; this is termed gravitational red shift.

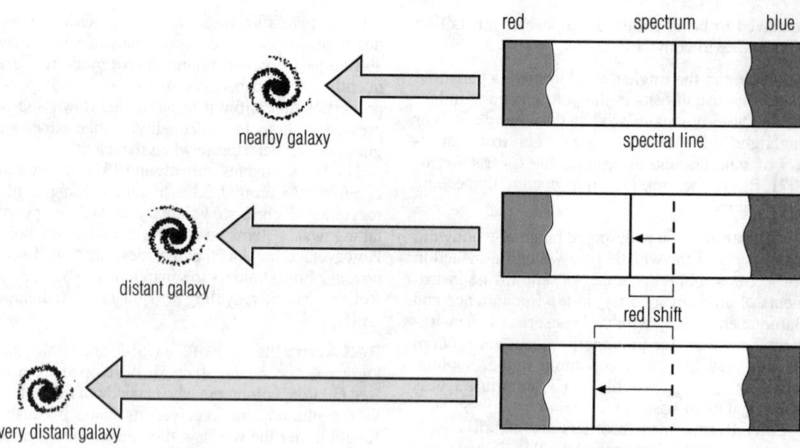

red shift The red shift causes lines in the spectra of galaxies to be shifted towards the red end of the spectrum. More distant galaxies have greater red shifts than closer galaxies. The red shift indicates that distant galaxies are moving apart rapidly, as the universe expands.

redstart any bird of the genus *Phoenicurus*, a member of the thrush family Muscicapidae, order Passeriformes. It winters in Africa and spends the summer in Eurasia. The American redstart *Setophaga ruticulla* belongs to the family Parulidae. The common redstart *P. phoenicurus*, is a summer visitor to Britain, nesting in hollow trees, where it lays about six greenish-blue eggs with red spots. Its upper parts are dark grey and the forehead pure white, the throat is black and the upper parts of the tail and tail coverts are rust red.

reduction in chemistry, the gain of electrons, loss of oxygen, or gain of hydrogen by an atom, ion, or molecule during a chemical reaction. Reduction may be brought about by reaction with another compound, which is simultaneously oxidized (reducing agent), or electrically at the cathode (negative electrode) of an electric cell.

redundancy loss of a person's job because the job no longer exists. This may be due to the business shrinking in size or going bankrupt, for example, due to a recession in the economy. The firm may have introduced labour-saving technology so that fewer workers are now needed to produce the same output as before. The firm may be changing its product mix, stopping or reducing production of one line but expanding elsewhere. The government provides a minimum standard of redundancy pay through the ◊national insurance fund. Some companies may pay redundancy rates well above the minimum. How much workers receive depends on age, weekly wage, and number of years of service with their present employer.

redwing type of thrush *Turdus iliacus*, family Muscicapidae, order Passeriformes. It is smaller than the song thrush, with reddish wing and body markings, and there is a distinct white line over the eye. It breeds in the north of Europe and Asia, flying south in winter.

redwood giant coniferous tree, one of the two types of ◊sequoia.

reed any of various perennial tall, slender grasses of wet or marshy environments; in particular, species of the genera *Phragmites* and *Arundo*; also the stalk of any of these plants. The common reed *P. australis* attains a height of 3 m/10 ft, having stiff, erect leaves and straight stems bearing a plume of purplish flowers.

Reed Carol 1906–1976. English film producer and director. He was an influential figure in the British film industry of the 1940s. His films include *Odd Man Out* 1946, *The Fallen Idol* 1948, *The Third Man* 1949, *Our Man in Havana* 1959, and the Academy Award-winning musical *Oliver!* 1968.

Odd Man Out, a brooding drama set in Belfast, was notable for its Expressionist imagery and an outstanding performance from James Mason as a wounded IRA man. Next came two features scripted by novelist and former film critic Graham Greene. *The Fallen Idol*, about a small boy trying to protect the family butler from a murder charge, earned Reed an Academy Award nomination, as did *The Third Man*, a stylish thriller about penicillin racketeering in postwar Vienna that, with its distinctive zither music and a towering performance by Orson Welles as Harry Lime, became an instant classic.

Reed Lou (Louis Firbank) 1942– . US rock singer, songwriter, and guitarist. He was a member (1965–70 and 1993) of the New York avant-garde group the Velvet Underground, perhaps the most influential band of the period. His solo work deals largely with urban alienation and angst, and includes the albums *Berlin* 1973, *Street Hassle* 1978, and *New York* 1989. His best-known recording is 'Walk on the Wild Side' from the album *Transformer* 1972.

reed instrument any of a class of wind instruments employing a single or double flexible reed, made of cane, metal, or plastic, which vibrates under pressure within an airtight enclosure (the mouth, bellows, airbag) and acts as a valve admitting pulses of pressurized air into a tubular resonator. Single-reed instruments, where the reed vibrates against the material of the instrument, include clarinets and saxophones; double-reeds, where the reeds vibrate against each other, include oboes, shawms, bagpipes, and bassoons. Most reed instruments incorporate finger holes to alter the pitch.

reel in cinema, a plastic or metal spool used for winding and storing film. As the size of reels became standardized it came to refer to the running time of the film: a standard 35-mm reel holds 313 m/900 ft of film, which runs for ten minutes when projected at 24 frames per second; hence a 'two-reeler' was a film lasting 20 minutes. Today's projectors, however, hold bigger reels.

referendum procedure whereby a decision on proposed legislation is referred to the electorate for settlement by direct vote of all the people. It is most frequently employed in Switzerland, the first country to use it, but has become increasingly widespread.

refining any process that purifies or converts something into a more useful form. Metals usually need refining after they have been extracted from their ores by such processes as ◊smelting. Petroleum, or crude oil, needs refining before it can be used; the process involves fractional ◊distillation, the separation of the substance into separate components or 'fractions'.

reflection the throwing back or deflection of waves, such as light or sound waves, when they hit a surface. The law of reflection states that the angle of incidence (the angle between the ray and a perpendicular line drawn to the surface) is equal to the angle of reflection (the angle between the reflected ray and a perpendicular to the surface).

reflex in animals, a very rapid involuntary response to a particular stimulus. It is controlled by the ◊nervous system. A reflex involves only a few nerve cells, unlike the slower but more complex responses produced by the many processing nerve cells of the brain.

A ***simple reflex*** is entirely automatic and involves no learning. Examples of such reflexes include the sudden withdrawal of a hand in response to a painful stimulus, or the jerking of a leg when the kneecap is tapped. Sensory cells (receptors) in the knee send signals to the spinal cord along a sensory nerve cell.

Within the spine a reflex arc switches the signals straight back to the muscles of the leg (effectors) via an intermediate nerve cell and then a motor nerve cell; contraction of the leg occurs, and the leg kicks upwards. Only three nerve cells are involved, and the brain is only aware of the response after it has taken place. Such reflex arcs are particularly common in lower animals, and have a high survival value, enabling organisms to take rapid action to avoid potential danger. In higher animals (those with a well-developed ◊central nervous system) the simple reflex can be modified by the involvement of the brain – for instance, humans can override the automatic reflex to withdraw a hand from a source of pain.

A ***conditioned reflex*** involves the modification of a reflex action in response to experience (learning). A stimulus that produces a simple reflex response becomes linked with another, possibly unrelated, stimulus. For example, a dog may salivate (a reflex action) when it sees its owner remove a tin-opener from a drawer because it has learned to associate that stimulus with the stimulus of being fed.

reflex camera camera that uses a mirror and prisms to reflect light passing through the lens into the viewfinder, showing the photographer the exact scene that is being shot. When the shutter button is released the mirror springs out of the way, allowing light to reach the film. The most common type is the single-lens reflex (◊SLR) camera. The twin-lens reflex (◊TLR) camera has two lenses: one has a mirror for viewing, the other is used for exposing the film.

reflexology in alternative medicine, manipulation and massage of the feet to ascertain and treat disease or dysfunction elsewhere in the body. Correspondence between reflex points on the feet and remote organic and physical functions were discovered early in the 20th century by US physician William Fitzgerald, who also found that pressure and massage applied to these reflex points beneficially affect the related organ or function.

Reform Acts UK acts of Parliament 1832, 1867, and 1884 that extended voting rights and redistributed parliamentary seats; the 1867 and 1884 acts are also known as ◊Representation of the People Acts. The ***1832 act*** abolished pocket and ◊rotten borough, redistributing seats on a more equitable basis in the counties and forming some new boroughs. The franchise was extended to male householders in property worth £10 a year or more in the boroughs and to owners of freehold property worth £2 a year, £10 copyholders, or £50 leaseholders in the counties. The ***1867 act*** redistributed seats from corrupt and small boroughs to the counties and large urban areas. It also extended the franchise in boroughs to male heads of households, and in counties to males who owned, or held on long leases, land worth £5 a year, or who occupied land worth £12 on which they paid poor rates. The ***1884 act*** extended the franchise to male agricultural labourers.

Reformation religious and political movement in 16th-century Europe to reform the Roman Catholic Church, which led to the establishment of Protestant churches. Anticipated from the 12th century by the Waldenses, Lollards, and Hussites, it was set off by German priest Martin ◊Luther 1517, and became effective when the absolute monarchies gave it support by challenging the political power of the papacy and confiscating church wealth.

Reformation A woodcarving by Lucas Cranach, showing the contrast between the Protestant and Roman Catholic churches. The Protestants, on the left, are described as following the true religion, by believing in salvation through Jesus Christ. *Philip Sauvain*

refraction the bending of a wave when it passes from one medium to another. Refraction occurs because waves travel at different velocities in different media.

refractive index measure of the refraction of a ray of light as it passes from one transparent medium to another. If the angle of incidence is *i* and the angle of refraction is *r*, the ratio of the two refractive indices is given by $n_1/n_2 = \sin i/\sin r$. It is also equal to the speed of light in the first medium divided by the speed of light in the second, and it varies with the wavelength of the light.

refractory (of a material) able to resist high temperature, for example ◊ceramics made from clay, minerals, or other earthy materials. Furnaces are lined with refractory materials such as silica and dolomite.

Alumina (aluminium oxide) is an excellent refractory, often used for the bodies of spark plugs. Titanium and tungsten are often called refractory metals because they are temperature resistant. Cermets are refractory materials made up of ceramics and metals.

refrigeration use of technology to transfer heat from cold to warm, against the normal temperature gradient, so that a body can remain substantially colder than its surroundings. Refrigeration equipment is used for the chilling and deep-freezing of food in ◊food technology, and in air conditioners and industrial processes.

Refrigeration is commonly achieved by a vapour-compression cycle, in which a suitable chemical (the refrigerant) travels through a long circuit of tubing, during which it changes from a vapour to a liquid and back again. A compression chamber makes it condense, and thus give out heat. In another part of the circuit, called the evaporator coils, the pressure is much lower, so the refrigerant evaporates, absorbing heat as it does so. The evaporation process takes place near the central part of the refrigerator, which therefore becomes colder, while the compression process takes place near a ventilation grille, transferring the heat to the air outside.

refugee person fleeing from oppressive or dangerous conditions (such as political, religious, or military persecution) and seeking refuge in a foreign country. An estimated average of 10,000 people a day become refugees.

The UK Asylum and Immigration Appeals Bill 1992 grants asylum to those refugees, as defined by the Geneva Convention, whose life and/or liberty are in danger in the country they have come from. It does not encompass those fleeing persecution or civil war.

Regency in Britain, the years 1811–20 during which ◊George IV (then Prince of Wales) acted as regent for his father ◊George III.

Regency style style of architecture and interior furnishings popular in England during the late 18th and early 19th centuries. It is characterized by restrained simplicity and the imitation of ancient classical elements, often Greek.

Architects of this period include Decimus Burton (1800–1881), Henry Holland (1746–1806), and John ◊Nash.

regeneration in biology, regrowth of a new organ or tissue after the loss or removal of the original. It is common in plants, where a new individual can often be produced from a 'cutting' of the original. In animals, regeneration of major structures is limited to lower organisms; certain lizards can regrow their tails if these are lost, and new flatworms can grow from a tiny fragment of an old one. In mammals, regeneration is limited to the repair of tissue in wound healing and the regrowth of peripheral nerves following damage.

Regensburg (English ***Ratisbon***) city in Bavaria, Germany, on the river Danube at its confluence with the Regen, 100 km/63 mi NE of Munich; population (1993) 125,000. It has many medieval buildings, including a Gothic cathedral 1275–1530.

history Regensburg stands on the site of a Celtic settlement dating from 500 BC. It became the Roman *Castra Regina* AD 179, the capital of the Eastern Frankish Empire, a free city 1245, and seat of the German *Diet* (parliament) 16th century–1806. It was included in Bavaria 1810.

regent person who carries out the duties of a sovereign during the sovereign's minority,

REFORMATION: TIMELINE

1517	Martin Luther's protest against the sale of indulgences began the Reformation in Europe.
1519	Ulrich Zwingli led the Reformation in Switzerland.
1529	The term 'Protestant' was first used.
1533	Henry VIII renounced papal supremacy and proclaimed himself head of the Church of England.
1541	The French theologian John Calvin established Presbyterianism in Geneva, Switzerland.
1559	The Protestant John Knox returned from exile to found the Church of Scotland.
1545–1563	The Counter-Reformation was initiated by the Roman Catholic Church at the Council of Trent. It aimed at reforming abuses and regaining the lost ground by using moral persuasion and extending the Spanish Inquisition to other countries.
1648	By the end of the Thirty Years' War, the present European alignment had been reached, with the separation of Catholic and Protestant churches.

incapacity, or lengthy absence from the country. In England since the time of Henry VIII, Parliament has always appointed a regent or council of regency when necessary. The years 1811–20 during which ◊George IV (then Prince of Wales) acted as regent for his father ◊George III is known as the Regency.

reggae predominant form of West Indian popular music of the 1970s and 1980s, characterized by a heavily accented offbeat and a thick bass line. The lyrics often refer to ◊Rastafarianism. Musicians include Bob ◊Marley, Lee 'Scratch' Perry (1940–) and the group Black Uhuru (1974–).

A fast reggae-rap style called ragga emerged in the early 1990s. Like rap texts, reggae lyrics tend to be political-historical, sexually explicit, or describe ghetto violence.

regiment military formation equivalent to a battalion in parts of the British army, and to a brigade in the armies of many other countries. In the British infantry, a regiment may include more than one battalion, and soldiers belong to the same regiment throughout their career.

regolith the surface layer of loose material that covers most bedrock. It consists of eroded rocky material, volcanic ash, river alluvium, vegetable matter, or a mixture of these known as ◊soil.

regressive tax tax such that the higher the income of the taxpayer the smaller the proportion or percentage paid in that tax. This contrasts with progressive taxes where the proportion paid rises as income increases, and proportional taxes where the proportion paid remains the same at all levels of income. Examples of regressive taxes in the UK are the ◊council tax and ◊excise duties.

Regulus or ***Alpha Leonis*** the brightest star in the constellation Leo, and the 21st brightest star in the night sky. First-magnitude Regulus has a true luminosity 100 times that of the Sun, and is 69 light years from Earth.

Regulus was one of the four royal stars of ancient Persia marking the approximate positions of the Sun at the equinoxes and solstices. The other three were ◊Aldebaran, ◊Antares, and ◊Fomalhaut.

Rehnquist William 1924– . Chief justice of the US ◊Supreme Court from 1986. Under his leadership, the Court has established a reputation for conservative rulings on such issues as abortion and capital punishment. Active within the Republican Party, Rehnquist was appointed head of the office of legal counsel by President Nixon in 1969 and controversially defended such measures as pre-trial detention and wiretapping. He became an associate justice of the Supreme Court in 1972. He was appointed chief justice by President Reagan.

Rehoboam King of Judah about 932–915 BC, son of Solomon. Under his rule the Jewish nation split into the two kingdoms of Israel and Judah. Ten of the tribes revolted against him and took Jeroboam as their ruler, leaving Rehoboam only the tribes of Judah and Benjamin.

Reich (German 'empire') three periods in European history. The First Reich was the Holy Roman Empire 962–1806, the Second Reich the German Empire 1871–1918, and the ◊Third Reich Nazi Germany 1933–45.

Reich Steve 1936– . US composer. His Minimalist music employs simple patterns carefully superimposed and modified to highlight constantly changing melodies and rhythms; examples are *Phase Patterns* for four electronic organs 1970, *Music for Mallet Instruments, Voices, and Organ* 1973, and *Music for Percussion and Keyboards* 1984.

Reich Wilhelm 1897–1957. Austrian physician who emigrated to the USA 1939. He combined ◊Marxism and ◊psychoanalysis to advocate the positive effects of directed sexual energies and sexual freedom. His works include *Die Sexuelle Revolution/The Sexual Revolution* 1936–45 and *Die Funktion des Orgasmus/The Function of the Orgasm* 1948.

Reichstag Fire burning of the German parliament building in Berlin 27 Feb 1933, less than a month after the Nazi leader Hitler became chancellor. The fire was used as a justification for the suspension of many constitutional guarantees and also as an excuse to attack the communists. There is still debate over whether the Nazis were involved in this crime, of which they were the main beneficiaries.

Reichstag Fire The German Parliament building (Reichstag) was set ablaze in Feb 1933. This enabled the Nazis to assume extra powers, declaring a state of emergency that lasted until the end of World War II. A Dutch man, Marinus van der Lubbe, was convicted of the arson and executed in 1934. *Corbis*

Reichstein Tadeus 1897–1996. Swiss biochemist who investigated the chemical activity of the adrenal glands. By 1946 Reichstein had identified a large number of steroids secreted by the adrenal cortex, some of which would later be used in the treatment of ◊Addison's disease. Reichstein shared the 1950 Nobel Prize for Physiology or Medicine with Edward ◊Kendall and Philip Hench (1896–1965).

Reims (English ***Rheims***) capital of Champagne-Ardenne region, France; population (1990) 185,200. It is the centre of the champagne industry and has textile industries. It was known in Roman times as *Durocorturum*. From 987 all but six French kings were crowned here. Ceded to England 1420 under the Treaty of Troyes, it was retaken by Joan of Arc, who had Charles VII consecrated in the 13th-century cathedral. In World War II, the German High Command formally surrendered here to US general Eisenhower 7 May 1945.

reincarnation belief that after death the human soul or the spirit of a plant or animal may live again in another human or animal. It is part of the teachings of many religions and philosophies; for example, ancient Egyptian and Greek (the philosophies of Pythagoras and Plato), Buddhism, Hinduism, Jainism, certain Christian heresies (such as the Cathars), and theosophy. It is also referred to as transmigration or metempsychosis.

reindeer or ***caribou*** deer *Rangifer tarandus* of Arctic and subarctic regions, common to North America and Eurasia. About 1.2 m/4 ft at the shoulder, it has a thick, brownish coat and broad hooves well adapted to travel over snow. It is the only deer in which both sexes have antlers; these can grow to 1.5 m/5 ft long, and are shed in winter.

The Old World reindeer have been domesticated by the Lapps of Scandinavia for centuries. There are two types of North American caribou: the large woodland caribou of the more southerly regions, and the barren-ground caribou of the far north. Reindeer migrate south in winter, moving in large herds. They eat grass, small plants, and lichens.

reinforced concrete material formed by casting ◊concrete in timber or metal formwork around a cage of steel reinforcement. The steel gives added strength by taking up the tension stresses, while the concrete takes up the compression stresses. Its technical potential was first fully demonstrated by François Hennebique (1842–1921) in the façade of the Charles VI Mill at Tourcoing, France, 1895.

Anatole de Baudot (1834–1915) and Victor Contamin (1840–1893) used it to architectural effect in the church of St Jean-de-Montmartre, Paris, 1894–1897. Eugène Freysinnet (1879–1962) demonstrated its structural versatility with his airship hangars at Orly 1916–24, while Auguste Perret (1874–1954) developed its architectural use in the church of Notre Dame deRaincy 1922–23. ◊Le Corbusier later explored its full technical, architectural, and decorative potential in two important projects: the Unité d'habitation, Marseilles, 1947–52, and Chandigarh, India, 1951–56.

Reinhardt Django (Jean Baptiste) 1910–1953. Belgian jazz guitarist and composer. He was co-leader, with Stephane Grappelli, of the Quintet du Hot Club de France 1934–39. He had a lyrical acoustic style and individual technique, and influenced many US musicians.

Reinhardt Max. Adopted name of Max Goldmann 1873–1943. Austrian producer and director. His Expressionist style was predominant in German theatre and film during the 1920s and 1930s. Directors such as Murnau and Lubitsch and stars such as Dietrich worked with him. He co-directed the film *A Midsummer Night's Dream* 1935, a play he directed in numerous stage productions.

In 1920 Reinhardt founded the Salzburg Festival. When the Nazis came to power, he lost his theatres and, after touring Europe as a guest director, went to the USA, where he produced and directed. He founded an acting school and theatre workshop in Hollywood.

relative atomic mass the mass of an atom relative to one-twelfth the mass of an atom of carbon-12. It depends primarily on the number of protons and neutrons in the atom, the electrons having negligible mass. If more than one ◊isotope of the element is present, the relative atomic mass is calculated by taking an average that takes account of the relative proportions of each isotope, resulting in values that are not whole numbers. The term atomic weight, although commonly used, is strictly speaking incorrect.

relative density the density (at 20°C/68°F) of a solid or liquid relative to (divided by) the maximum density of water (at 4°C/39.2°F). The relative density of a gas is its density divided by the density of hydrogen (or sometimes dry air) at the same temperature and pressure.

relative humidity the concentration of water vapour in the air. It is expressed as the ratio of the partial pressure of the water vapour to its saturated vapour pressure at the same temperature. The higher the temperature, the higher the saturated vapour pressure.

relative molecular mass the mass of a molecule, calculated relative to one-twelfth the mass of an atom of carbon-12. It is found by adding the relative atomic masses of the atoms that make up the molecule. The term molecular weight is often used, but strictly this is incorrect.

relativism philosophical position that denies the possibility of objective truth independent of some

reindeer The reindeer ranges over the tundra of N Europe and Asia, Alaska, Canada, and Greenland. It is a social animal, living in large herds containing thousands of individuals. Some herds migrate hundreds of kilometres from their breeding grounds on the tundra to their winter feeding grounds farther south.

specific social or historical context or conceptual framework.

relativity in physics, the theory of the relative rather than absolute character of motion and mass, and the interdependence of matter, time, and space, as developed by German-born US physicist Albert ◊Einstein in two phases:

special theory of relativity (1905) Starting with the premises that (1) the laws of nature are the same for all observers in unaccelerated motion, and (2) the speed of light is independent of the motion of its source, Einstein arrived at some rather unexpected consequences. Intuitively familiar concepts, like mass, length, and time, had to be modified. For example, an object moving rapidly past the observer will appear to be both shorter and heavier than when it is at rest (that is, at rest relative to the observer), and a clock moving rapidly past the observer will appear to be running slower than when it is at rest. These predictions of relativity theory seem to be foreign to everyday experience merely because the changes are quite negligible at speeds less than about 1,500 km s^{-1}, and they only become appreciable at speeds approaching the speed of light.

general theory of relativity (1915) The geometrical properties of space-time were to be conceived as modified locally by the presence of a body with mass. A planet's orbit around the Sun (as observed in three-dimensional space) arises from its natural trajectory in modified space-time; there is no need to invoke, as Isaac ◊Newton did, a force of ◊gravity coming from the Sun and acting on the planet. Einstein's general theory accounts for a peculiarity in the behaviour of the motion of the perihelion of the orbit of the planet Mercury that cannot be explained in Newton's theory. The new theory also said that light rays should bend when they pass by a massive object. The predicted bending of starlight was observed during the eclipse of the Sun 1919. A third corroboration is found in the shift towards the red in the spectra of the Sun and, in particular, of stars of great density – white dwarfs such as the companion of Sirius.

Einstein showed that, for consistency with the above premises (1) and (2), the principles of dynamics as established by Newton needed modification; the most celebrated new result was the equation $E = mc^2$, which expresses an equivalence between mass (m) and ◊energy (E), c being the speed of light in a vacuum. In 'relativistic mechanics', conservation of mass is replaced by the new concept of conservation of 'mass-energy'.

Although since modified in detail, general relativity remains central to modern ◊astrophysics and ◊cosmology; it predicts, for example, the possibility of ◊black holes. General relativity theory was inspired by the simple idea that it is impossible in a small region to distinguish between acceleration and gravitation effects (as in a lift one feels heavier when the lift accelerates upwards), but the mathematical development of the idea is formidable. Such is not the case for the special theory, which a nonexpert can follow up to $E = mc^2$ and beyond.

relaxin hormone produced naturally by women during pregnancy that assists childbirth. It widens the pelvic opening by relaxing the ligaments, inhibits uterine contractility, so preventing premature labour, and causes dilation of the cervix. A synthetic form was pioneered by the Howard Florey Institute in Australia, and this drug has possible importance in helping the birth process and avoiding surgery or forceps delivery.

relay in electrical engineering, an electromagnetic switch. A small current passing through a coil of wire wound around an iron core attracts an armature, whose movement closes a pair of sprung contacts to complete a secondary circuit, which may carry a large current or activate other devices. The solid-state equivalent is a thyristor switching device.

relic supposed part of some divine or saintly person, or something closely associated with them. Christian examples include the arm of St Teresa of Avila, the blood of St Januarius, and the True Cross. Buddhist relics include the funeral ashes of the historic Buddha, placed in a number of stupas or burial mounds.

In medieval times Christian relics were fiercely fought for, and there were a vast number of fakes. The cult was condemned by Protestant reformers but upheld by the Roman Catholic Church at the Council of Trent in the mid-16th century. Parallel nonreligious examples of the phenomenon include the display of the preserved body of Lenin in Moscow, Russia.

relief in sculpture, particularly architectural sculpture, carved figures and other forms that project from the background. The Italian terms *basso-rilievo* (low relief), *mezzo-rilievo* (middle relief), and *alto-rilievo* (high relief) are used according to the extent to which the sculpture projects. The French term *bas-relief* is commonly used to mean low relief.

religion (Latin *religare* 'to bind'; perhaps humans to God) code of belief or philosophy that often involves the worship of a ◊God or gods. Belief in a supernatural power is not essential (absent in, for example, Buddhism and Confucianism), but faithful adherence is usually considered to be rewarded; for example, by escape from human existence (Buddhism), by a future existence (Christianity, Islam), or by worldly benefit (Sōka Gakkai Buddhism). Among the chief religions are:

ancient and pantheist religions of Babylonia, Assyria, Egypt, Greece, and Rome;

oriental Hinduism, Buddhism, Jainism, Parseeism, Confucianism, Taoism, and Shinto;

'religions of a book' Judaism, Christianity (the principal divisions are Roman Catholic, Eastern Orthodox, and Protestant), and Islam (the principal divisions are Sunni and Shi'ite);

combined derivation these include Baha'ism, the Unification Church, and Mormonism.

Comparative religion studies the various faiths impartially, but often with the hope of finding common ground, to solve the practical problems of competing claims of unique truth or inspiration. The earliest known attempt at a philosophy of religious beliefs is contained in fragments written by Xenophanes in Greece 6th century BC, and later Herodotus and Aristotle contributed to the study. In 17th-century China, Jesuit theologians conducted comparative studies. Towards the end of the 18th century, English missionary schools in Calcutta compared the Bible with sacred Indian texts. The work of Charles Darwin in natural history and the growth of anthropology stimulated fresh investigation of religious beliefs; work by the Sanskrit scholar Max Müller (1823–1900), the Scottish anthropologist James Frazer, the German sociologist Max Weber, and the Romanian scholar Mircea Eliade has formed the basis for modern comparative religion. ▷ *See feature on pp. 162–163.*

Religion, Wars of series of civil wars 1562–89 in France between Catholics and (Protestant) Huguenots. Each side was led by noble families which competed for influence over a weakened monarchy. The most infamous event was the ◊Massacre of St Bartholomew 1572, carried out on the orders of the Catholic faction led by ◊Catherine de' Medici and the Duke of Guise. After 1584, the heir apparent to the French throne was the Huguenot Henry of Navarre. This prompted further hostilities, but after his accession as Henry IV 1589, he was able to maintain his hold on power, partly through military victory and partly by converting to Catholicism 1593. He introduced the Edict of Nantes 1598, guaranteeing freedom of worship throughout his kingdom.

religious education the formal teaching of religion in schools.

In voluntary-aided church schools in the UK, religious education (RE) syllabuses are permitted to follow the specific teachings of the church concerned; in other state schools, the syllabus is agreed between representatives of the local churches and the education authority. Until the introduction of the national curriculum from 1990, RE was the only compulsory subject. The law allows parents to withdraw their children from RE on conscientious grounds.

In the USA, religious education within the doctrines of a particular church is prohibited in public (state-maintained) schools because of the separation of church and state guaranteed under the first amendment to the constitution; however, the study of comparative religion is permitted.

rem acronym of ***roentgen equivalent man*** unit of radiation dose equivalent. The rem has now been replaced in the SI system by the ◊sievert (one rem equals 0.01 sievert), but remains in common use.

RELIGION: FOLLOWERS OF MAJOR FAITHS

Christianity	1,833,022,000
Islam	1,025,585,000
Hinduism	732,812,000
Buddhism	314,939,000
Sikhism	18,000,000
Judaism	17,822,000
Confucianism	8,028,000
Jainism	3,794,000
Baha'ism	3,517,000
Shinto	3,222,800

1992 figures

remand in law, the committing of an accused but not convicted person into custody or to release on bail pending a court hearing.

In the UK, remand in custody is made for not more than eight days at a time but can be renewed for further eight-day periods if the court so decides.

Remarque Erich Maria 1898–1970. German novelist. He was a soldier in World War I. His *All Quiet on the Western Front* 1929, one of the first anti-war novels, led to his being deprived of German nationality. He lived in Switzerland 1929–39, and then in the USA.

Rembrandt Harmensz van Rijn 1606–1669. Dutch painter and etcher. He was one of the most prolific and significant artists in Europe of the 17th century. Between 1629 and 1669 he painted about 60 penetrating self-portraits. He also painted religious subjects, and produced about 300 etchings and over 1,000 drawings. His major group portraits include *The Anatomy Lesson of Dr Tulp* 1632 (Mauritshuis, The Hague) and *The Night Watch* 1642 (Rijksmuseum, Amsterdam).

After studying in Leiden and for a few months in Amsterdam, Rembrandt began his career 1625 in Leiden, where his work reflected knowledge of Adam Elsheimer (1578–1610) and ◊Caravaggio, among others. He settled permanently in Amsterdam 1631 and obtained many commissions for portraits from wealthy merchants. The *Self-Portrait with Saskia* (his wife, Saskia van Uylenburgh) about 1634 (Gemäldegalerie, Dresden) displays their prosperity in warm tones and rich, glittering textiles.

Saskia died 1642. Rembrandt's fortunes began to decline and he became bankrupt 1656. His work became more sombre, revealing a deeper emotional content, and his portraits were increasingly melancholy; for example, *Jan Six* 1654 (Six Collection, Amsterdam).

Remembrance Sunday (known until 1945 as ***Armistice Day***) in the UK, national day of remembrance for those killed in both world wars and later

‘There is only one religion, though there are a hundred versions of it.’

On RELIGION
George Bernard Shaw
Arms and the Man, preface 1898

Rembrandt
Self-portrait 1659, by Rembrandt (National Gallery of Art, Washington DC). Rembrandt made no preliminary drawings for his paintings, but applied paint directly to a dark background, building up the light areas of his pictures with layers of paint and glazes. He excelled in portraits, particularly those of elderly people.
Corbis

conflicts, on the second Sunday of Nov. In Canada 11 Nov is Remembrance Day. The US equivalent is ◊Veterans Day.

Remington Philo 1816–1889. US inventor. He designed the breech-loading rifle that bears his name. He began manufacturing typewriters 1873, using the patent of Christopher ◊Sholes, and made improvements that resulted five years later in the first machine with a shift key, thus providing lower-case letters as well as capital letters.

The Remington rifle and carbine, which had a falling block breech and a tubular magazine, were developed in collaboration with his father Eliphalet Remington (1793–1861).

remix in pop music, the studio practice of reassembling a recording from all or some of its individual components, often with the addition of new elements. As a commercial concept, remixes accompanied the rise of the 12-inch single in the 1980s.

Issuing a recording in several different remixes ensures additional sales to collectors and increases airplay; remixes can be geared specifically to radio, dance clubs, and so on. Some record producers specialize in remixing.

Non-Stop Ecstatic Dancing 1981 by Soft Cell may have been the world's first all-remix LP. The British recording industry agreed 1990 not to issue more than five versions of any one record, following the release of a House of Love number in 11 versions. In 1987 Madonna became the first artist in the USA to release an album consisting entirely of remixes (*You Can Dance*).

remora any of a family of warm-water fishes that have an adhesive disc on the head, by which they attach themselves to whales, sharks, and turtles. These provide the remora with shelter and transport, as well as food in the form of parasites on the host's skin.

remotely piloted vehicle (RPV) crewless mini-aircraft used for military surveillance and to select targets in battle. RPVs barely show up on radar, so they can fly over a battlefield without being shot down, and they are equipped to transmit TV images to an operator on the ground. RPVs were used by the Allies in the 1991 Gulf War.

remote sensing gathering and recording information from a distance. Space probes have sent back photographs and data about planets as distant as Neptune. In archaeology, surface survey techniques provide information without disturbing subsurface deposits.

Satellites such as *Landsat* have surveyed all the Earth's surface from orbit. Computer processing of data obtained by their scanning instruments, and the application of so-called false colours (generated by the computer), have made it possible to reveal surface features invisible in ordinary light. This has proved valuable in agriculture, forestry, and urban planning, and has led to the discovery of new deposits of minerals.

REM sleep (acronym for ***rapid-eye-movement*** sleep) phase of sleep that recurs several times nightly in humans and is associated with dreaming. The eyes flicker quickly beneath closed lids.

Remus in Roman legend, one of two twins who were the eventual founders of Rome; see ◊Romulus.

Renaissance or ***Revival of Learning*** period in European cultural history that began in Italy around 1400 and lasted there until the end of the 16th century; elsewhere in Europe it flourished later, and lasted until the 17th century. Characteristic of the Renaissance is the exploration of the world and of the individual, and the rediscovery of pagan classical antiquity (led by Giovanni Boccaccio and Francesco Petrarch). Central to the Renaissance was ◊humanism, the belief in the active, rather than the contemplative life, and a faith in the republican ideal. The greatest expression of the Renaissance was in the arts and learning.

Leon Alberti, in his writings on painting, created both a method of painting – using perspective to create an illusion of a third dimension – and a classically inspired, nonreligious subject matter. In architecture, by his writing and his buildings he created a system of simple proportion that was to be followed for hundreds of years. Alberti's contemporaries Masaccio and Filippo Brunelleschi exemplified these ideas in painting and architecture respectively.

In the arts, critics regard the years 1490–1520 (the 'High Renaissance') as a peak, with the work of Leonardo da Vinci, Raphael Sanzio, and Michelangelo Buonarotti in painting, and Michelangelo and Donato Bramante in architecture. The high-point of Venetian painting was to come some years later, with Titian, Paolo Veronese, and Tintoretto. Leonardo has been described as a 'universal man' for his enormously wide-ranging studies, including painting, architecture, science, and engineering. The enormous achievements of creative artists was made possible by the patronage of wealthy ruling families such as the Sforza in Milan, and the Medici in Florence, by the ruling doge of Venice, or by popes, notably Julius II and Leo X. ▷ *See feature on pp. 626–627.*

In literature, both Boccaccio and Petrarch wrote major works in Italian rather than Latin, a trend continued by the creation of epic poems in the vernacular by Ludovico Ariosto and Torquato Tasso. Progress from the religious to the secular was seen in the creation of the first public libraries, and by the many translations from the classics published in Venice in the 16th century. In philosophy, the rediscovery of Greek thought took the form of ◊neo-Platonism in such figures as Marsilio Ficino. Niccolò Machiavelli in *The Prince* founded the modern study of politics.

Outside Italy, Renaissance art and ideas became widespread throughout Europe. Desiderius Erasmus, from the Netherlands, embodied humanist scholarship for northern Europe; Netherlandish painters include Albrecht Dürer and Hans Holbein. In France, Renaissance writers include François Rabelais, Joaquim Du Bellay, and Michel Eyquem de Montaigne; in Spain, Miguel de Cervantes, in Portugal, Luís Vaz de Camoëns, and in England William Shakespeare. The term 'Renaissance', to describe the period of cultural history, was invented by 19th-century historians. In the visual arts, the end of the High Renaissance is marked by a late-15th-century movement known as ◊Mannerism, a tendency to deliberate elongation of the body, and a wilful distortion of perspective; but the true end of the Renaissance ideal only came with the late-17th-century rise of the ◊enlightenment.

Renaissance architecture style of architecture which began in 15th-century Italy, based on the revival of classical, especially Roman, architecture developed by Brunelleschi. It is characterized by a concern with balance, clarity, and proportion, and by the external use of columns and fluted pilasters.

Many Roman buildings were still extant in Renaissance Italy and scholars studied their proportions and copied their decorative motifs. The architectural books of the Roman Vitruvius (1st century AD) were popularized by Leon Battista Alberti in his influential treatise *De re aedificatoria/On Architecture* 1486 but the first major work of the age was the successful construction by Brunelleschi of a dome 1420–34 on Florence Cathedral. Alberti himself designed a new façade for Santa Maria Novella, completed 1470, in Florence, and redesigned a church in Rimini subsequently called the Tempio Malatestiano, c. 1450. Bramante came closest to the recreation of classical ideas with works such as the Tempietto of San Pietro in Montorio, Rome, c. 1510 and the new basilica of St Peter's in Rome, begun 1506. Other Renaissance architects in Italy include Michelangelo, Giulio Romano, Palladio, Vignola, Sangallo, and Raphael.

As Renaissance architecture spread throughout the rest of Europe it often acquired a distinctively national character through the influence of indigenous styles. Renaissance architecture in England is exemplified by the Queen's House at Greenwich, London, built by Inigo Jones 1637 and in France by the Louvre Palace built for François I 1546. In Spain, a fusion of Renaissance and Gothic architectural forms led to the flamboyant style called Plateresque ('Manuellian' in Portugal), typified by the façade of the university at Salamanca, completed 1529.

Renaissance art movement in European art of the 15th and 16th centuries. It began in Florence, Italy, with the rise of a spirit of humanism and a new appreciation of the Classical Greek and Roman past. In painting and sculpture this led to greater naturalism and interest in anatomy and perspective. The 15th century is known as the Classical Renaissance. The High Renaissance (early 16th century) covers the careers of Leonardo da Vinci, Raphael, Michelangelo, and Titian in Italy and Dürer in Germany. Mannerism (roughly 1520s–90s) forms the final stage of the High Renaissance.

The Renaissance was heralded by the work of the early 14th-century painter Giotto in Florence, and in the early 15th century a handful of outstanding innovative artists emerged there: Masaccio (in painting), Donatello (in sculpture), and Brunelleschi (in architecture). At the same time the humanist philosopher, artist, and writer Leon Baptista Alberti recorded many of the new ideas in his treatises on painting, sculpture, and architecture. These ideas soon became widespread in Italy, and many new centres of patronage formed. In the 16th century Rome superseded Florence as the chief centre of activity and innovation, and became the capital of the High Renaissance. In northern Europe the Renaissance spirit is apparent in the painting of the van Eyck brothers in the early 15th century. Later, Dürer demonstrated a scientific and enquiring mind and, after his travels in Italy, brought many Renaissance ideas back to Germany. The Italian artists Cellini, Rosso Fiorentino, and Primaticcio took the Renaissance to France through their work at Fontainebleau. Hans Holbein the Younger carried some of the concerns of Renaissance art to England in the 16th century, but it was not until the 17th century that English taste was significantly affected.

Renault France's largest motor-vehicle manufacturer, founded 1898. In Nov 1994 the French government began to implement plans to privatize the company, which had been nationalized from 1944.

Louis Renault (1877–1944) formed the company with his brothers Fernand and Marcel. In 1899 they began motor racing, which boosted the sales of their cars, and by 1908 they were producing 5,000 cars a year. The company produced tanks for the French army in both world wars.

Renault Mary. Pen name of (Eileen) Mary Challans 1905–1983. English historical novelist. She specialized in stories about ancient Greece, with a trilogy on Theseus and two novels on Alexander the Great: *Fire from Heaven* 1970 and *The Persian Boy* 1972.

Rendell Ruth Barbara 1930– . English novelist and short-story writer. She is the author of a detective series featuring Chief Inspector Wexford. Her

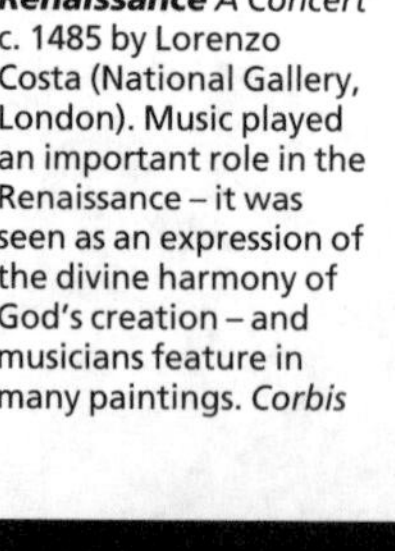

Renaissance *A Concert* c. 1485 by Lorenzo Costa (National Gallery, London). Music played an important role in the Renaissance – it was seen as an expression of the divine harmony of God's creation – and musicians feature in many paintings. *Corbis*

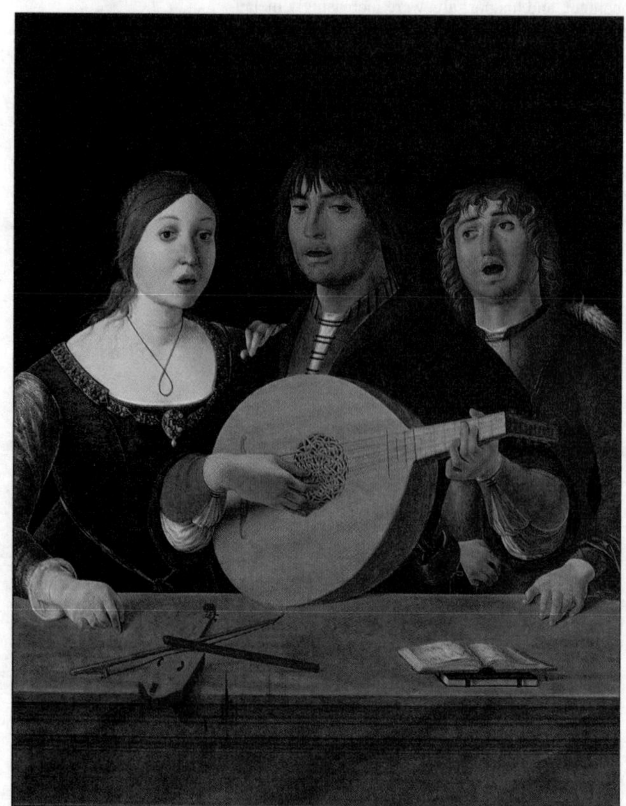

Rendell English novelist Ruth Rendell first achieved success with her series of detective novels written around the main character, Detective Chief Inspector Wexford. Obsessive love and personal inadequacy are frequent themes in her novels. She also writes under the pen name Barbara Vine. *Penguin Books*

psychological crime novels explore the minds of people who commit murder, often through obsession or social inadequacy, as in *A Demon in my View* 1976 and *Heartstones* 1987. She also writes under the pseudonym Barbara Vine.

René France-Albert 1935– . Seychelles left-wing politician. He became the country's first prime minister after independence and president from 1977 after a coup. He has followed a non-nuclear policy of nonalignment. In 1993 René and his party, the People's Progressive Front, won the country's first free elections in 16 years.

In 1964 René founded the left-wing Seychelles People's United Party, pressing for complete independence. When this was achieved 1976, he became prime minister and James Mancham, leader of the Seychelles Democratic Party, became president. René seized the presidency 1977 and set up a one-party state, but this was replaced by a multi-party constitution adopted 1993.

renewable energy power from any source that replenishes itself. Most renewable systems rely on ◊solar energy directly or through the weather cycle as ◊wave power, ◊hydroelectric power, or wind power via ◊wind turbines, or solar energy collected by plants (alcohol fuels, for example). In addition, the gravitational force of the Moon can be harnessed through ◊tidal power stations, and the heat trapped in the centre of the Earth is used via ◊geothermal energy systems. ▷ *See feature on pp. 360–361.*

renewable resource natural resource that is replaced by natural processes in a reasonable amount of time. Soil, water, forests, plants, and animals are all renewable resources as long as they are properly conserved. Solar, wind, wave, and geothermal energies are based on renewable resources.

Renfrewshire local authority of Scotland created 1996 *(see United Kingdom map)*.

Reni Guido 1575–1642. Italian painter. He was an important figure in the development of the ◊Baroque style. His best-known work is the fresco *Aurora* 1613–14 (Casino Rospigliosi, Rome), a work which shows the strong influence of the Classicism of the ◊Carracci.

He first studied in Bologna under the Flemish painter Denis Calvaert, but afterwards entered the academy of the Carracci and became one of the principal adherents of Annibale Carracci. He went to Rome about 1600, where, though belonging to an opposite camp, he seems to have been influenced to some extent by Caravaggio. He was, however, more greatly impressed by ◊Raphael Sanzio and antique sculpture, developing a sophisticated Classicism of his own.

Rennes industrial city (oil refining, chemicals, electronics, cars) and capital of Ille-et-Vilaine *département*, W France, at the confluence of the Ille and Vilaine, 56 km/35 mi SE of St Malo; population (1990) 203,500. It was the old capital of Brittany.

rennet extract, traditionally obtained from a calf's stomach, that contains the enzyme rennin, used to coagulate milk in the cheesemaking process. The enzyme can now be chemically produced.

Renoir Jean 1894–1979. French film director. His films, characterized by their humanism and naturalistic technique, include *Boudu sauvé des eaux/Boudu Saved from Drowning* 1932, *La Grande Illusion* 1937, and *La Règle du jeu/The Rules of the Game* 1939. In 1975 he received an honorary Academy Award for his life's work. He was the son of the painter Pierre-Auguste Renoir.

Renoir Pierre-Auguste 1841–1919. French Impressionist painter. He met Claude ◊Monet and Alfred ◊Sisley in the early 1860s, and together they formed the nucleus of ◊Impressionism. He developed a lively, colourful painting style with feathery brushwork (known as his 'rainbow style') and painted many scenes of everyday life, such as *The Luncheon of the Boating Party* 1881 (Phillips Collection, Washington DC), and also female nudes, such as *The Bathers* about 1884–87 (Philadelphia Museum of Art).

His early pictures show the influence of Gustave ◊Courbet, but after the Franco-Prussian War (in which he served as cuirassier), with Monet at the Paris suburb of Argenteuil, he produced riverscapes completely Impressionist in their atmospheric colour, such as the *Regatta, Argenteuil* 1874.

A reaction against Impressionism began in the 1880s after he had visited Italy, where he was influenced by the Graeco-Roman paintings from Pompeii at Naples, and by a stay at L'Estaque with ◊Cézanne (who was also concerned with solid and permanent qualities in painting). He now began to take a closer interest in ◊Ingres. A harder, linear manner resulted, as in *The Umbrellas* 1884 (National Gallery, London) and *The Bathers*.

reparation compensation paid by countries that start wars in which they are defeated, as by Germany in both world wars. Iraq is required to pay reparations, under the terms of a United Nations resolution, after its defeat in the 1991 Gulf War.

repetitive strain injury (RSI) inflammation of tendon sheaths, mainly in the hands and wrists, which may be disabling. It is found predominantly in factory workers involved in constant repetitive movements, and in those who work with computer keyboards. The symptoms include aching muscles, weak wrists, tingling fingers and in severe cases, pain and paralysis. Some victims have successfully sued their employers for damages. In the UK it is estimated that around 100,000 people a year visit their doctors because of upper limb injuries caused by RSI.

replication in biology, production of copies of the genetic material DNA; it occurs during cell division (◊mitosis and ◊meiosis). Most mutations are caused by mistakes during replication.

During replication the paired strands of DNA separate, exposing the bases. Nucleotides floating in the cell matrix pair with the exposed bases, adenine pairing with thymine, and cytosine with guanine.

reply, right of right of a member of the public to respond to a media statement. A statutory right of reply, enforceable by a Press Commission, as exists in many W European countries, failed to reach the statute book in the UK in 1989. There is no legal provision in the UK that any correction should receive the same prominence as the original statement and legal aid is not available in defamation cases, so that only the wealthy are able to sue. However, the major newspapers signed a Code of Practice in 1989 that promised some public protection.

repoussé relief decoration on metal, especially silver, brass, and copper, produced by hammering from the underside so that the decoration projects. It is the opposite of ◊chasing.

The technique was among the first to be developed by ancient metalworkers. Exceptionally fine examples are the Vapheio Cup made in Crete around 1500 BC (National Museum, Athens) and the Scythian animal reliefs of around 600–500 BC (Hermitage, St Petersburg).

Representation of the People Acts series of UK acts of Parliament from 1867 that extended voting rights, creating universal suffrage 1928. The 1867 and 1884 acts are known as the second and third ◊Reform Acts.

The 1918 act gave the vote to men over the age of 21 and women over the age of 30, and the 1928 act extended the vote to women over the age of 21. Certain people had the right to more than one vote; this was abolished by the 1948 act. The 1969 act reduced the minimum age of voting to 18.

repression in psychology, a mental process that ejects and excludes from consciousness ideas, impulses, or memories that would otherwise threaten emotional stability.

In the Austrian psychiatrist Sigmund Freud's early writing, repression is controlled by the censor, a hypothetical mechanism or agency that allows ideas, memories, and so on from the unconscious to emerge into consciousness only if distorted or disguised, as for example in dreams.

reproduction in biology, process by which a living organism produces other organisms similar to itself. There are two kinds: ◊asexual reproduction and ◊sexual reproduction. The ability to reproduce is considered one of the fundamental attributes of living things.

reptile any member of a class (Reptilia) of vertebrates. Unlike amphibians, reptiles have hard-shelled, yolk-filled eggs that are laid on land and from which fully formed young are born. Some snakes and lizards retain their eggs and give birth to live young. Reptiles are cold-blooded, and their skin is usually covered with scales. The metabolism is slow, and in some cases (certain large snakes) intervals between meals may be months. Reptiles date back over 300 million years.

The chief living orders are the Chelonia (tortoises and turtles), Crocodilia (alligators and crocodiles), and Squamata, divided into three suborders: Lacertilia (lizards), Ophidia or Serpentes (snakes), and Amphisbaenia (worm lizards). The order Rhynchocephalia has one surviving species, the lizardlike tuatara of New Zealand. Many extinct forms are known, including the orders Pterosauria, Plesiosauria, Ichthyosauria, and Dinosauria.

Repton Humphry 1752–1818. English garden designer. He worked for some years in partnership with English architect John ◊Nash. Repton preferred more formal landscaping than Capability ◊Brown, and was responsible for the landscaping of some 200 gardens and parks. He coined the term 'landscape gardening'.

republic country where the head of state is not a monarch, either hereditary or elected, but usually a president, whose role may or may not include political functions.

Republican Party one of the two main political parties of the USA, formed 1854. It is more right-wing than the Democratic Party, favouring capital and big business and opposing state subvention and federal controls. In the late 20th century most presidents have come from the Republican Party, but in Congress Republicans have generally been outnumbered. In 1992 Republican George Bush lost the presidency to Democrat Bill Clinton, who in 1996 was re-elected for a second term (the first Democrat to be elected to a second term since F D Roosevelt), although the Republicans retained control of Congress.

requiem in the Roman Catholic Church, a Mass for the dead. Musical settings include those by Palestrina, Mozart, Berlioz, Verdi, Fauré, and Britten.

requisition in UK property law, an application to HM Land Registry, the Land Charges Department, or a local authority for a certificate of official search to reveal whether or not land is affected by encumbrances, such as a mortgage or restrictive covenant.

reredos ornamental screen or wall-facing behind a church altar; see ◊altarpiece.

research the primary activity in science, a combination of theory and experimentation directed towards finding scientific explanations of phenomena. It is commonly classified into two types: pure research, involving theories with little apparent relevance to human concerns; and applied research, concerned with finding solutions to problems of social importance – for instance in medicine and engineering. The two types are linked in that theories developed from pure research may eventually be found to be of great value to society.

Scientific research is most often funded by government and industry, and so a nation's wealth and priorities are likely to have a strong influence on the kind of work undertaken.

In the UK, government expenditure on research and development in 1994–95 was £5.2 billion, a drop from the 1992 figure of £5.6 billion.

Reseda genus of 55 annual plants of the family Resedaceae, found in Britain, Europe, and around the Mediterranean. The garden ◊mignonette *R. odorata* is cultivated for its sweet-scented flowers, which are popular with bees and butterflies. The essential oil is extracted for use in perfumery. Two species commonly occur in Britain: the wild mignonette *R. lutea* and the dyer's rocket or weld *R. luteola*, which has been used for its yellow dye since antiquity.

reserve currency in economics, a country's holding of internationally acceptable means of payment (major foreign currencies or gold); central banks also hold the ultimate reserve of money for their domestic banking sector. On the asset side of company balance sheets, undistributed profits are listed as reserves.

reserves monies retained in case of emergency or to be used at a later date. Gold bullion and foreign currency reserves are held by a central bank such as the Bank of England. They are used to intervene in the foreign exchange market to change the exchange rate. If the Bank of England buys pounds sterling by selling some of its foreign currency reserves, the value of the pound should rise, and vice versa. In business, undistributed profits are listed as reserves on the asset side of company balance sheets.

residue in chemistry, a substance or mixture of substances remaining in the original container after the removal of one or more components by a separation process.

The nonvolatile substance left in a container after ◊evaporation of liquid, the solid left behind after removal of liquid by filtration, and the substances left in a distillation flask after removal of components by ◊distillation, are all residues.

resin substance exuded from pines, firs, and other trees in gummy drops that harden in air. Varnishes are common products of the hard resins, and ointments come from the soft resins.

Rosin is the solid residue of distilled turpentine, a soft resin. The name 'resin' is also given to many synthetic products manufactured by polymerization; they are used in adhesives, plastics, and varnishes.

resistance in physics, that property of a conductor that restricts the flow of electricity through it, associated with the conversion of electrical energy to heat; also the magnitude of this property. Resistance depends on many factors, such as the nature of the material, its temperature, dimensions, and thermal properties; degree of impurity; the nature and state of illumination of the surface; and the frequency and magnitude of the current. The SI unit of resistance is the ohm.

resistance movement opposition movement in a country occupied by an enemy or colonial power, especially in the 20th century; for example, the French resistance to Nazism in World War II (where the underground movement was called the *maquis*).

During World War II, resistance in E Europe took the form of ◊guerrilla warfare; for example, in Yugoslavia, Greece, Poland, and by ◊partisan bands behind the German lines in the USSR. In more industrialized countries, such as France, Belgium, and Czechoslovakia, sabotage in factories and on the railways, propaganda, and the assassination of Germans and collaborators were the main priorities.

resistivity in physics, a measure of the ability of a material to resist the flow of an electric current. It is numerically equal to the ◊resistance of a sample of unit length and unit cross-sectional area, and its unit is the ohm metre (symbol Ωm). A good conductor has a low resistivity (1.7×10^{-8} Ωm for copper); an insulator has a very high resistivity (10^{15} Ωm for polyethane).

resistor in physics, any component in an electrical circuit used to introduce ◊resistance to a current. Resistors are often made from wire-wound coils or pieces of carbon. ◊Rheostats and ◊potentiometers are variable resistors.

Resnais Alain 1922– . French film director. His work is characterized by the themes of memory and unconventional concepts of time. His films include *Hiroshima, mon amour* 1959, *L'Année dernière à Marienbad/Last Year at Marienbad* 1961, and *Providence* 1977.

resolution in computing, the number of dots per unit length in which an image can be reproduced on a screen or printer. A typical screen resolution for colour monitors is 75 dpi (dots per inch). A ◊laser printer will typically have a printing resolution of 300 dpi, and dot matrix printers typically have resolutions from 60 dpi to 180 dpi. Photographs in books and magazines have a resolution of 1,200 dpi or 2,400 dpi.

resonance rapid amplification of a vibration when the vibrating object is subject to a force varying at its ◊natural frequency. In a trombone, for example, the length of the air column in the instrument is adjusted until it resonates with the note being sounded. Resonance effects are also produced by many electrical circuits. Tuning a radio, for example, is done by adjusting the natural frequency of the receiver circuit until it coincides with the frequency of the radio waves falling on the aerial.

resources materials that can be used to satisfy human needs. Because human needs are diverse and extend from basic physical requirements, such as food and shelter, to ill-defined aesthetic needs, resources encompass a vast range of items. The intellectual resources of a society – its ideas and technologies – determine which aspects of the environment meet that society's needs, and therefore become resources. For example, in the 19th century, uranium was used only in the manufacture of coloured glass. Today, with the advent of nuclear technology, it is a military and energy resource.

Resources are often categorized into human resources, such as labour, supplies, and skills, and natural resources, such as climate, fossil fuels, and water. Natural resources are divided into ◊nonrenewable resources and ◊renewable resources.

respiration biochemical process whereby food molecules are progressively broken down (oxidized) to release energy in the form of ◊ATP. In most organisms this requires oxygen, but in some bacteria the oxidant is the nitrate or sulphate ion instead. In all higher organisms, respiration occurs in the ◊mitochondria. Respiration is also used to mean breathing, in which oxygen is exchanged for carbon dioxide in the lung alveoli, though this is more accurately described as a form of ◊gas exchange.

respiratory distress syndrome (RDS) formerly ***hyaline membrane disease*** condition in which a newborn baby's lungs are insufficiently expanded to permit adequate oxygenation. Premature babies are most at risk. Such babies survive with the aid of intravenous fluids and oxygen, sometimes with mechanically assisted ventilation.

Normal inflation of the lungs requires the presence of a substance called surfactant to reduce the surface tension of the alveoli (air sacs) in the lungs. In premature babies, surfactant is deficient and the lungs become hard and glassy. As a result, the breathing is rapid, laboured, and shallow, and there is the likelihood of ◊asphyxia. Artificial surfactant is administered to babies at risk.

respiratory surface area used by an organism for the exchange of gases, for example the lungs, gills or, in plants, the leaf interior. The gases oxygen and carbon dioxide are both usually involved in respiration and photosynthesis. Although organisms have evolved different types of respiratory surface according to need, there are certain features in common. These include thinness and moistness, so that the gas can dissolve in a membrane and then diffuse into the body of the organism. In many animals the gas is then transported away from the surface and towards interior cells by the blood.

rest mass in physics, the mass of a body when its velocity is zero. For subatomic particles, it is their mass at rest or at velocities considerably below that of light. According to the theory of ◊relativity, at very high velocities, there is a relativistic effect that increases the mass of the particle. the blood system.

Restoration in English history, the period when the monarchy, in the person of Charles II, was re-established after the English Civil War and the fall of the ◊Protectorate 1660.

Restoration comedy style of English theatre, dating from the Restoration (from 1660). It witnessed the first appearance of women on the English stage, most notably in the 'breeches part', specially created in order to costume the actress in male attire, thus revealing her figure to its best advantage. The genre placed much emphasis on wit and sexual intrigues. Examples include Wycherley's *The Country Wife* 1675, Congreve's *The Way of the World* 1700, and Farquhar's *The Beaux' Stratagem* 1707.

restriction enzyme bacterial ◊enzyme that breaks a chain of ◊DNA into two pieces at a specific point; used in ◊genetic engineering.

The point along the DNA chain at which the enzyme can work is restricted to places where a specific sequence of base pairs occurs. Different restriction enzymes will break a DNA chain at different points. The overlap between the fragments is used in determining the sequence of base pairs in the DNA chain.

restrictive covenant in law, an obligation created by deed that curtails the rights of an owner of land or leaseholder; for example, by prohibiting business use. Anyone acquiring the land or property will be bound by the terms of the covenant, which is

respiration The two phases of the process of respiration. Gas exchange occurs in the alveoli, tiny air tubes in the lungs.

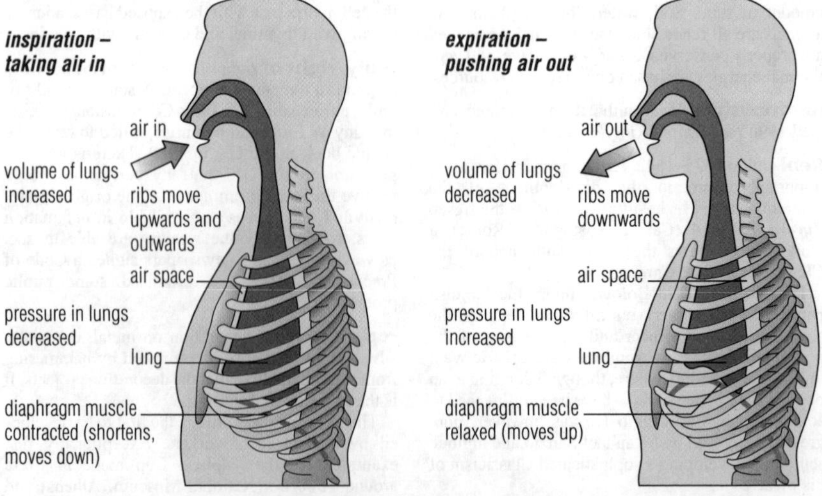

why restrictive covenants are said to 'run with the land'.

resurrection in Christian, Jewish, and Muslim belief, the rising from the dead that all souls will experience at the Last Judgement. The Resurrection also refers to Jesus rising from the dead on the third day after his crucifixion, a belief central to Christianity and celebrated at Easter.

resuscitation steps taken to revive anyone on the brink of death. The most successful technique for life-threatening emergencies, such as electrocution, near-drowning, or heart attack, is mouth-to-mouth resuscitation. Medical and paramedical staff are trained in cardiopulmonary resuscitation: the use of specialized equipment and techniques to attempt to restart the breathing and/or heartbeat and stabilize the patient long enough for more definitive treatment.

retail-price index (RPI) indicator of variations in the ◊cost of living, superseded in the USA by the consumer price index.

retina light-sensitive area at the back of the ◊eye connected to the brain by the optic nerve. It has several layers and in humans contains over a million rods and cones, sensory cells capable of converting light into nervous messages that pass down the optic nerve to the brain.

The rod cells, about 120 million in each eye, are distributed throughout the retina. They are sensitive to low levels of light, but do not provide detailed or sharp images, nor can they detect colour. The cone cells, about 6 million in number, are mostly concentrated in a central region of the retina called the fovea, and provide both detailed and colour vision. The cones of the human eye contain three visual pigments, each of which responds to a different primary colour (red, green, or blue). The brain can interpret the varying signal levels from the three types of cone as any of the different colours of the visible spectrum.

The image actually falling on the retina is highly distorted; research into the eye and the optic centres within the brain has shown that this poor quality image is processed to improve its quality. The retina can become separated from the wall of the eyeball as a result of a trauma, such as a boxing injury. It can be reattached by being 'welded' into place by a laser.

retinol or ***vitamin A*** fat-soluble chemical derived from β-carotene and found in milk, butter, cheese, egg yolk, and liver. Lack of retinol in the diet leads to the eye disease xerophthalmia.

retriever any of several breeds of hunting dogs, often used as guide dogs for the blind. The commonest breeds are the ***Labrador retriever***, large, smooth-coated, and usually black or yellow; and the ***golden retriever***, with either flat or wavy coat. They can grow to 60 cm/2 ft high and weigh 40 kg/90 lb.

Retrievers were originally developed for retrieving birds and other small game. Their gentle, even-tempered nature makes them popular companion dogs, and Labradors are also used in police work.

retrovirus any of a family of ◊viruses (Retroviridae) containing the genetic material ◊RNA rather than the more usual ◊DNA. For the virus to express itself and multiply within an infected cell, its RNA must be converted to DNA. It does this by using a built-in enzyme known as reverse transcriptase (since the transfer of genetic information from DNA to RNA is known as ◊transcription, and retroviruses do the reverse of this). Retroviruses include those causing ◊AIDS and some forms of leukaemia. See ◊immunity.

Retroviruses are used as vectors in ◊genetic engineering, but they cannot be used to target specific sites on the chromosome. Instead they incorporate their genes at random sites.

Retz Jean François Paul de Gondi, Cardinal de Retz 1614–1679. French politician. A priest with political ambitions, he stirred up and largely led the insurrection known as the ◊Fronde. After a period of imprisonment and exile he was restored to favour 1662 and created abbot of St Denis.

Réunion French island of the Mascarenes group, in the Indian Ocean, 650 km/400 mi E of Madagascar and 180 km/110 mi SW of Mauritius
area 2,512 sq km/970 sq mi
capital St Denis

Réunion

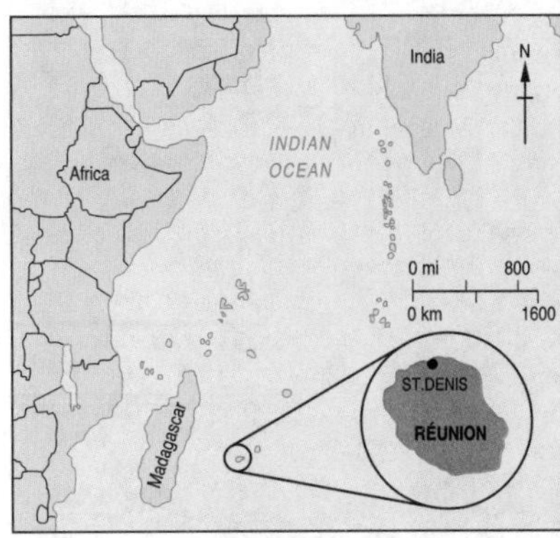

physical forested, rising in Piton de Neiges to 3,069 m/10,072 ft
features administers five uninhabited islands, also claimed by Madagascar
industries sugar, maize, vanilla, tobacco, rum
population (1995 est) 653,400
history explored by Portuguese (the first European visitors) 1513; annexed by Louis XIII of France 1642; overseas *département* of France 1946; overseas region 1972.

Reuter (Paul) Julius de, Baron Reuter. Adopted name of Israel Beer 1816–1899. German founder of the international news agency Reuters. He began a continental pigeon post 1849 at Aachen, Germany, and in 1851 set up a news agency in London. In 1858 he persuaded the press to use his news telegrams, and the service became worldwide.

Revelation last book of the New Testament, traditionally attributed to the author of the Gospel of St John but now generally held to be the work of another writer. It describes a vision of the end of the world, of the Last Judgement, and of a new heaven and earth ruled by God from Jerusalem.

revenge tragedy form of Elizabethan and Jacobean drama in which revenge provides the mainspring of the action. It is usually characterized by bloody deeds, intrigue, and high melodrama. It was pioneered by Thomas Kyd with *The Spanish Tragedy* c. 1588, Shakespeare's *Titus Andronicus* c. 1593, and Cyril Tourneur's *The Revenger's Tragedy* 1607. Its influence is apparent in tragedies such as Shakespeare's *Hamlet* and *Macbeth*.

Revere Paul 1735–1818. American revolutionary, a Boston silversmith, who carried the news of the approach of British troops to Lexington and Concord on the night of 18 April 1775 (see ◊American Revolution). On the next morning the first shots of the Revolution were fired at Lexington. Longfellow's poem 'The Midnight Ride of Paul Revere' commemorates the event.

reverse osmosis the movement of solvent (liquid) through a semipermeable membrane from a more concentrated solution to a more dilute solution. The solvent's direction of movement is opposite to that which it would experience during ◊osmosis, and is achieved by applying an external pressure to the solution on the more concentrated side of the membrane. The technique is used in desalination plants, when water (the solvent) passes from brine (a salt solution) into fresh water via a semipermeable filtering device.

reversible reaction chemical reaction that proceeds in both directions at the same time, as the product decomposes back into reactants as it is being produced. Such reactions do not run to completion, provided that no substance leaves the system. Examples include the manufacture of ammonia from hydrogen and nitrogen, and the oxidation of sulphur dioxide to sulphur trioxide.

revisionism political theory derived from Marxism that moderates one or more of the basic tenets of Karl Marx, and is hence condemned by orthodox Marxists.

The first noted Marxist revisionist was Eduard Bernstein, who in Germany in the 1890s questioned the inevitability of a breakdown in capitalism. After World War II the term became widely used by established communist parties, both in Eastern Europe and Asia, to condemn movements (whether more or less radical) that threatened the official party policy.

revolution any rapid, far-reaching, or violent change in the political, social, or economic structure of society. It is usually applied to political change: examples include the American Revolution, where the colonists broke free from their colonial ties and established a sovereign, independent nation; the French Revolution, where an absolute monarchy was overthrown by opposition from inside the country and a popular uprising; and the Russian Revolution, where a repressive monarchy was overthrown by those seeking to institute widespread social and economic changes based on a socialist model. In 1989–90 the Eastern Bloc nations demonstrated against and voted out the Communist Party, in many cases creating a prodemocracy revolution.

While political revolutions are often associated with violence, other types of change can have just as much impact on society. Most notable is the Industrial Revolution of the mid-18th century, which caused massive economic and social changes. In the 1970s and 1980s a high-tech revolution based on the silicon chip took place, facilitating the widespread use of computers.

Revolutionary Wars series of wars 1791–1802 between France and the combined armies of

> *'Revolutions have never lightened the burden of tyranny: they have only shifted it to another shoulder.'*
>
> On REVOLUTION
> George Bernard Shaw
> *Man and Superman*
> 1903

REVOLUTIONARY WARS: TIMELINE

1791	Emperor Leopold II and Frederick William II of Prussia issued the Declaration of Pillnitz, inviting the European powers to restore the French king Louis XVI to power.
1792	France declared war on Austria, which formed a coalition with Prussia, Sardinia, and (from 1793), Britain, Spain, and the Netherlands; victories for France at Valmy and Jemappes.
1793	French reverses until the reorganization by Lazare Carnot.
1795	Prussia, the Netherlands, and Spain made peace with France.
1796	Sardinia was forced to make peace by the Italian campaign of Napoleon I, then a commander.
1797	Austria was compelled to make peace with France under the Treaty of Campo-Formio.
1798	Napoleon's fleet, after its capture of Malta, was defeated by the British admiral Nelson in Egypt at the Battle of Aboukir Bay (Battle of the Nile), and Napoleon had to return to France without his army; William Pitt the Younger, Britain's prime minister, organized a new coalition with Russia, Austria, Naples, Portugal, and Turkey.
1798–99	The coalition mounted its major campaign in Italy (under the Russian field marshal Suvorov), but dissension led to the withdrawal of Russia.
1799	Napoleon, on his return from Egypt, reorganized the French army.
1800	Austrian army defeated by Napoleon at Marengo in NW Italy 14 June, and again 3 Dec (by General Moreau) at Hohenlinden near Munich; the coalition collapsed.
1801	Austria made peace under the Treaty of Lunéville; Sir Ralph Abercromby defeated the French army by land in Egypt at the Battle of Alexandria, but was himself killed.
1802	Treaty of Amiens truce between France and Britain, followed by the Napoleonic Wars.

revolutions of 1848 A scene from a barricaded street in Paris, 1848. In France, the catalyst for the revolutions in the rest of Europe, the monarchy was replaced by the Second Republic, with Louis Napoleon as president from 1852. *Philip Sauvain*

England, Austria, Prussia, and others, during the period of the ◊French Revolution and ◊Napoleon's campaign to conquer Europe.

revolutions of 1848 series of revolts in various parts of Europe against monarchical rule. Although some of the revolutionaries had republican ideas, many more were motivated by economic grievances. The revolution began in France with the overthrow of Louis Philippe and then spread to Italy, the Austrian Empire, and Germany, where the short-lived Frankfurt Parliament put forward ideas about political unity in Germany. None of the revolutions enjoyed any lasting success, and most were violently suppressed within a few months.

revolutions of 1989 popular uprisings in many countries of Eastern Europe against communist rule, prompted by internal reforms in the USSR that permitted dissent within its sphere of influence. By 1990 nearly all the Warsaw Pact countries had moved from one-party to pluralist political systems, in most cases peacefully but with growing hostility between various nationalist and ethnic groups.

Until the late 1980s, any discontent, however widespread, had been kept in check by the use or threat of military force controlled from Moscow. Mikhail Gorbachev's official encouragement of *perestroika* (radical restructuring) and *glasnost* (greater political openness), largely for economic reasons, allowed popular discontent to boil over. Throughout the summer and autumn of 1989 the Eastern European states broke away from the communist bloc, as the Soviet republics were to do during the next two years. ▷*See feature on pp. 1090–1091.*

Reye's syndrome rare disorder of the metabolism causing fatty infiltration of the liver and ◊encephalitis. It occurs mainly in children; its cause is uncertain although it has been linked with aspirin. The mortality rate is 50%.

Reykjavik capital (from 1918) and chief port of Iceland, on the SW coast; population (1994) 103,000. Fish processing is the main industry. Reykjavik is heated by underground mains fed by volcanic springs. It was a seat of Danish administration 1801–1918.

❝If you have great talents, industry will improve them: if you have but moderate abilities, industry will supply their deficiency.❞

JOSHUA REYNOLDS
Talk to students of the Royal Academy 11 Dec 1769

Reynolds Albert 1932– . Irish Fianna Fáil politician, Taoiseach (prime minister) 1992–94. He was minister for industry and commerce 1987–88 and minister of finance 1988–92. In Dec 1993 Reynolds and UK prime minister John Major issued a joint peace initiative for Northern Ireland, the Downing Street Declaration, which led to a cease-fire by both the Irish Republican Army (IRA) and the loyalist paramilitaries the following year.

Reynolds became party leader and prime minister Jan 1992, but his government was defeated on a vote of confidence Nov 1992. He succeeded in forming a Fianna Fáil–Labour coalition, but resigned as premier and party leader Nov 1994 after Labour disputed a judicial appointment he had made and withdrew from the coalition.

Reynolds Joshua 1723–1792. English painter. He was one of the greatest portrait painters of the 18th century. The principle exponent of the 'Grand Manner', a style based on Classical and Renaissance art, he often depicted his sitters in Classical terms, as in *Mrs Siddons as the Tragic Muse* 1784 (San Marino, California). His elegant portraits are mostly of wealthy patrons, though he also painted such figures as the writers Laurence Sterne and Dr Johnson, and the actor David Garrick.

Reynolds was active in London from 1752 and became the first president of the Royal Academy 1768. In his influential book *Discourses on Art*, based on lectures given at the Royal Academy 1769–91, he presented the theory of the Grand Manner, arguing that art should be based on the ideal rather than the realistic. He himself had been particularly influenced by Classical antiquity, but also by Michelangelo, Raphael, Titian, and Leonardo da Vinci. His own practice, however, often deviated from his precepts, some of his finest portraits combining elegance and Classical allusion with a keen awareness of individuality, as in his *Lord Heathfield* 1787 (National Gallery, London). In some works – such as his *Self-Portrait* about 1773 (Royal Academy, London) – he is much closer to ◊Rembrandt than to Renaissance artists.

Reynolds number number used in ◊fluid mechanics to determine whether fluid flow in a particular situation (through a pipe or around an aircraft body or a fixed structure in the sea) will be turbulent or smooth. The Reynolds number is calculated using the flow velocity, density and viscosity of the fluid, and the dimensions of the flow channel. It is named after British engineer Osborne Reynolds.

rhapsody in music, an instrumental ◊fantasia, often based on folk melodies, such as Liszt's *Hungarian Rhapsodies* 1853–54.

rhea one of two flightless birds of the family Rheidae, order Rheiformes. The common rhea *Rhea americana* is 1.5 m/5 ft high and is distributed widely in South America. The smaller Darwin's rhea *Pterocnemia pennata* occurs only in the south of South America and has shorter, feathered legs, and mottled plumage. Rheas differ from the ostrich in their smaller size and in having a feathered neck and head, three-toed feet, and no plumelike tail feathers.

Rhea in Greek mythology, a fertility goddess, one of the Titans, wife of Kronos and mother of several gods, including Zeus.

Rhee Syngman 1875–1965. Korean right-wing politician. A rebel under Chinese and Japanese rule, he became president of South Korea from 1948 until riots forced him to resign and leave the country 1960. He established a repressive dictatorship and was an embarrassing ally for the USA.

rhenium (Latin *Rhenus* 'Rhine') heavy, silver-white, metallic element, symbol Re, atomic number 75, relative atomic mass 186.2. It has chemical properties similar to those of manganese and a very high melting point (3,180°C/5,756°F), which makes it valuable as an ingredient in alloys. It was identified and named 1925 by German chemists W Noddack (1893–1960), I Tacke, and O Berg from the Latin name for the river Rhine.

rheostat in physics, a variable ◊resistor, usually consisting of a high-resistance wire-wound coil with a sliding contact. It is used to vary electrical resistance without interrupting the current (for example, when dimming lights). The circular type in electronics (which can be used, for example, as the volume control of an amplifier) is also known as a ◊potentiometer.

rhesus factor group of ◊antigens on the surface of red blood cells of humans which characterize the rhesus blood group system. Most individuals possess the main rhesus factor (Rh+), but those without this factor (Rh−) produce ◊antibodies if they come into contact with it. The name comes from rhesus monkeys, in whose blood rhesus factors were first found.

If an Rh− mother carries an Rh+ fetus, she may produce antibodies if fetal blood crosses the ◊placenta. This is not normally a problem with the first infant because antibodies are only produced slowly. However, the antibodies continue to build up after birth, and a second Rh+ child may be attacked by antibodies passing from mother to fetus, causing the child to contract anaemia, heart failure, or brain damage. In such cases, the blood of the infant has to be changed for Rh− blood; a badly affected fetus may be treated in the womb (see ◊fetal therapy). The problem can be circumvented by giving the mother anti-Rh globulin just after the first pregnancy, preventing the formation of antibodies.

rhesus monkey macaque monkey *Macaca mulatta* found in N India and SE Asia. It has a pinkish face, red buttocks, and long, straight, brown-grey hair. It can grow up to 60 cm/2 ft long, with a 20 cm/8 in tail.

rhetoric (Greek *rhetor* 'orator') traditionally, the art of public speaking and debate. Rhetorical skills are valued in such occupations as politics, teaching, law, religion, and broadcasting. Accomplished rhetoricians need not be sincere in what they say; they should, however, be effective, or at least entertaining.

rheumatic fever or ***acute rheumatism*** acute or chronic illness characterized by fever and painful swelling of joints. Some victims also experience involuntary movements of the limbs and head, a form of ◊chorea. It is now rare in the developed world.

Rheumatic fever, which strikes mainly children and young adults, is always preceded by a streptococcal infection such as ◊scarlet fever or a severe sore throat, usually occurring a couple of weeks beforehand. It is treated with bed rest, antibiotics, and painkillers. The most serious complication of rheumatic fever is damage to the heart and its valves, producing rheumatic heart disease many years later, which may lead to disability and death.

rheumatism nontechnical term for a variety of ailments associated with inflammation and stiffness of the joints and muscles. Acute rheumatism is better known as rheumatic fever.

rheumatoid arthritis inflammation of the joints; a chronic progressive disease, it begins with pain and stiffness in the small joints of the hands and feet and spreads to involve other joints, often with severe disability and disfigurement. There may also be damage to the eyes, nervous system, and other organs. The disease is treated with a range of drugs and with surgery, possibly including replacement of major joints.

Rheumatoid arthritis most often develops between the ages of 30 and 40, and is three times more common in women than men. It is an ◊autoimmune disease.

rhim or ***sand gazelle*** smallish gazelle *Gazella leptocerus* that has already disappeared over most of its former range of north Africa. Populations are fragmented and often isolated. It is one of several highly threatened gazelle species in northern Africa and the Sahara.

Rhine (German ***Rhein***, French ***Rhin***) European river rising in Switzerland and reaching the North Sea via Germany and the Netherlands; length 1,320 km/820 mi. Tributaries include the Moselle and the Ruhr. The Rhine is linked with the Mediterranean by the Rhine–Rhône Waterway, and with the Black Sea by the Rhine–Main–Danube Waterway.

Rhineland province of Prussia from 1815. Its unchallenged annexation by Nazi Germany 1936 was a harbinger of World War II.

rhinoceros The Indian rhinoceros *Rhinoceros unicornis*, the largest of the Asiatic species, weighs up to two tons and has only one horn. Its skin is deeply creased at the neck, shoulders, and legs, resembling armour plating. Now restricted to areas of Nepal, Assam, and Bengal, the Indian rhinoceros, like nearly all rhinoceroses, is an endangered species. *Premaphotos Wildlife*

Rhineland-Palatinate (German ***Rheinland-Pfalz***) administrative region (German *Land*) of Germany
area 19,800 sq km/7,643 sq mi
capital Mainz
towns and cities Ludwigshafen, Koblenz, Trier, Worms
physical wooded mountain country, river valleys of Rhine and Moselle
industries wine (75% of German output), tobacco, chemicals, machinery, leather goods, pottery
population (1994 est) 3,926,000
history formed 1946 of the Rhenish ◊Palatinate and parts of Hessen, Rhine province, and Hessen-Nassau.

rhinoceros odd-toed hoofed mammal of the family Rhinocerotidae. The one-horned Indian rhinoceros *Rhinoceros unicornis* is up to 2 m/6 ft high at the shoulder, with a tubercled skin, folded into shieldlike pieces; the African rhinoceroses are smooth-skinned and two-horned.

The African black rhinoceros *Diceros bicornis* is 1.5 m/5 ft high, with a prehensile upper lip for feeding on shrubs; the broad-lipped or 'white' rhinoceros *Ceratotherium simum* is actually slaty-grey, with a squarish mouth for browsing grass. They are solitary and vegetarian, with poor eyesight but excellent hearing and smell. An extinct hornless species, the baluchithere (genus *Baluchitherium*), reached 4.5 m/15 ft high.

Needless slaughter has led to the near extinction of all species of rhinoceros, particularly *R. sondaicus*, the related species of Javan rhinoceros and *Dicerorhinus sumatrensis*, the two-horned Sumatran rhinoceros.

rhizoid hairlike outgrowth found on the ◊gametophyte generation of ferns, mosses and liverworts. Rhizoids anchor the plant to the substrate and can absorb water and nutrients. They may be composed of many cells, as in mosses, where they are usually brownish, or may be unicellular, as in liverworts, where they are usually colourless.

Rhizoids fulfil the same functions as the ◊roots of higher plants but are simpler in construction.

rhizome or ***rootstock*** horizontal underground plant stem. It is a ◊perennating organ in some species, where it is generally thick and fleshy, while in other species it is mainly a means of ◊vegetative reproduction, and is therefore long and slender, with buds all along it that send up new plants.

The potato is a rhizome that has two distinct parts, the tuber being the swollen end of a long, cordlike rhizome.

Rhode Island smallest state of the USA, in New England; nicknamed Little Rhody or the Ocean State
area 3,100 sq km/1,197 sq mi
population (1990) 1,003,500
capital Providence
towns and cities Cranston, Newport, Woonsocket
features Narragansett Bay, one of the greatest sailing centres in the world, home of America's Cup yacht races; Block Island; 640 km/400 mi of coastline; Newport, with colonial waterfront and 19th-century mansions; the Friends Meeting House (1700), and the Touro Synagogue (1763), in Newport, both the oldest in the USA; Narragansett Native American monument at Sprague Park; Charlestown, with Native American church and burial ground; US Naval War College and Museum, Newport
industries electronics, machine tools, jewellery, textiles, silverware, rubber, and plastics. Agriculture is limited by the rocky terrain but is important in rural areas, the main crops being apples and potatoes
famous people George M Cohan, Anne Hutchinson, Matthew C Perry, Oliver Hazard Perry, Gilbert Stuart, Roger Williams
history founded 1636 by Roger Williams, exiled from Massachusetts Bay colony for religious dissent; one of the original 13 states. The principle trends in the 19th century were industrialization, immigration, and urbanization. Rhode Island is highly industrialized and the second most densely populated state; it suffers from high unemployment, low-wage manufacturing industries, and susceptibility to recessions.

Rhodes (Greek ***Ródhos***) Greek island, largest of the Dodecanese, in the E Aegean Sea
area 1,412 sq km/545 sq mi
capital Rhodes
industries grapes, olives
population (1981) 40,400
history settled by Greeks about 1000 BC; the ◊Colossus of Rhodes (fell 224 BC) was one of the ◊Seven Wonders of the World; held by the Knights Hospitallers of St John 1306–1522; taken from Turkish rule by the Italian occupation 1912; ceded to Greece 1947.

Rhode Island

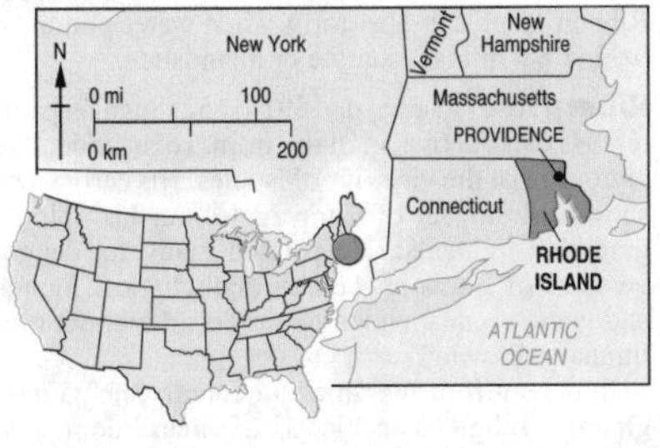

Rhodes Cecil John 1853–1902. South African politician, born in the UK, prime minister of Cape Colony 1890–96. Aiming at the formation of a South African federation and the creation of a block of British territory from the Cape to Cairo, he was responsible for the annexation of Bechuanaland (now Botswana) 1885. He formed the British South Africa Company 1889, which occupied Mashonaland and Matabeleland, thus forming Rhodesia (now Zambia and Zimbabwe).

Rhodes went to Natal 1870. As head of De Beers Consolidated Mines and Goldfields of South Africa Ltd, he amassed a large fortune. He entered the Cape legislature 1881, and became prime minister 1890, but the discovery of his complicity in the ◊Jameson Raid forced him to resign 1896. Advocating Anglo-Afrikaner cooperation, he was less alive to the rights of black Africans, despite the final 1898 wording of his dictum: 'Equal rights for every civilized man south of the Zambezi.'

The Rhodes scholarships were founded at Oxford University, UK, under his will, for students from the Commonwealth, the USA, and Germany.

'So little done, so much to do.'
CECIL RHODES
Last words

Rhodes Wilfred 1877–1973. English cricketer. He took more wickets than anyone else in the game – 4,187 wickets 1898–1930 – and also scored 39,802 first-class runs.

Playing for Yorkshire, Rhodes made a record 763 appearances in the county championship. He took 100 wickets in a season 23 times and completed the 'double' of 1,000 runs and 100 wickets in a season 16 times (both records). He played his 58th and final game for England, against the West Indies 1930, when he was 52 years old, the oldest ever Test cricketer.

Rhodes Zandra Lindsey 1940– . English fashion designer. She is known for the extravagant fantasy and luxury of her dress creations. She founded her own fashion house 1968.

She began by designing and printing highly individual textiles. Her fabrics – chiffon, silk, and tulle – are frequently handprinted with squiggles, zigzags, and other patterns. Her evening dresses are often characterized by their uneven handkerchief hems. She designs wedding and evening dresses embroidered in India, and saris for the top end of the Indian fashion market.

Rhodesia former name of ◊Zambia (Northern Rhodesia) and ◊Zimbabwe (Southern Rhodesia), in S Africa.

rhodium (Greek *rhodon* 'rose') hard, silver-white, metallic element, symbol Rh, atomic number 45, relative atomic mass 102.905. It is one of the so-called platinum group of metals and is resistant to tarnish, corrosion, and acid. It occurs as a free metal in the natural alloy osmiridium and is used in jewellery, electroplating, and thermocouples.

rhododendron any of numerous shrubs of the genus *Rhododendron* of the heath family Ericaceae. Most species are evergreen. The leaves are usually dark and leathery, and the large racemes of flowers occur in all colours except blue. They thrive on acid soils. ◊Azaleas belong to the same genus. *See illustration on following page.*

Rhodope Mountains range of mountains on the frontier between Greece and Bulgaria, rising to 2,925 m/9,497 ft at Musala.

rhombus in geometry, an equilateral (all sides equal) ◊parallelogram. Its diagonals bisect each other at right angles, and its area is half the product of the lengths of the two diagonals. A rhombus whose internal angles are 90° is called a ◊square.

Rhondda industrial town in Mid Glamorgan, Wales; population (1991) 59,900. Light industries have replaced coal mining, formerly the main source of employment in the area. The closure of the Maerdy mine (opened 1875) in 1990 ended mining in the valley. The Rhondda Heritage Park recreates a 1920s-style mining village for visitors.

Rhondda Cynon Taff unitary authority of Wales created 1996 *(see United Kingdom map.)*

Rhône river of S Europe; length 810 km/500 mi. It rises in Switzerland and flows through Lake Geneva to Lyon in France, where at its confluence with the Saône the upper limit of navigation is reached. The

rhododendron Native to Asia, rhododendrons are now widely cultivated in northern temperate regions as ornamentals. This *Rhododendron stenophyllum* is one of many members of the genus found on the shady forested slopes of Mount Kinabalu in Borneo. *Premaphotos Wildlife*

"A room is a place where you hide from the wolves outside and that's all any room is."

JEAN RHYS *Good Morning, Midnight*

river turns due south, passes Vienne and Avignon, and takes in the Isère and other tributaries. Near Arles it divides into the Grand and Petit Rhône, flowing respectively southeast and southwest into the Mediterranean west of Marseille. Here it forms a two-armed delta; the area between the tributaries is the marshy region known as the ◊Camargue. The river gives its name to a *département*.

Rhône-Alpes region of E France in the upper reaches of the Rhône; area 43,700 sq km/16,868 sq mi; population (1992) 5,344,000. It consists of the *départements* of Ain, Ardèche, Drôme, Isère, Loire, Rhône, Savoie, and Haute-Savoie. The capital is Lyon. There are several wine-producing areas, including Chenas, Fleurie, and Beaujolais. Industrial products include chemicals, textiles, and motor vehicles.

rhubarb perennial plant *Rheum rhaponticum* of the buckwheat family Polygonaceae, grown for its pink, edible leaf stalks. The leaves contain ◊oxalic acid, and are poisonous. There are also wild rhubarbs native to Europe and Asia.

rhyme identity of sound, usually in the endings of lines of verse, such as *wing* and *sing*. Avoided in Japanese, it is a common literary device in other Asian and European languages. Rhyme first appeared in Europe in late Latin poetry but was not used in Classical Latin or Greek.

rhyolite ◊igneous rock, the fine-grained volcanic (extrusive) equivalent of granite.

Rhys Jean. Adopted name of Ella Gwendolen Rees Williams 1894–1979. Dominican-born English novelist. Her works include *Wide Sargasso Sea* 1966, a recreation, set in a Caribbean island, of the life of the mad wife of Rochester from Charlotte Brontë's *Jane Eyre*.

rhythm and blues (R & B) US popular music of the 1940s–60s, which drew on swing and jump-jazz rhythms and blues vocals, and was an important influence on rock and roll. It diversified into soul, funk, and other styles. R & B artists include Bo Diddley, Jackie Wilson (1934–84), and Etta James (c. 1938–).

rhythm method method of natural contraception that relies on refraining from intercourse during ◊ovulation.

The time of ovulation can be worked out by the calendar (counting days from the last period), by temperature changes, or by inspection of the cervical mucus. All these methods are unreliable because it is possible for ovulation to occur at any stage of the menstrual cycle.

ria long narrow sea inlet, usually branching and surrounded by hills. A ria is deeper and wider towards its mouth, unlike a ◊fjord. It is formed by the flooding of a river valley due to either a rise in sea level or a lowering of a landmass.

rib long, usually curved bone that extends laterally from the ◊spine in vertebrates. Most fishes and many reptiles have ribs along most of the spine, but in mammals they are found only in the chest area. In humans, there are 12 pairs of ribs. The ribs protect the lungs and heart, and allow the chest to expand and contract easily.

At the rear, each pair is joined to one of the vertebrae of the spine. The upper seven ('true' or vertebro-sternal ribs) are joined by ◊cartilage directly to the breast bone (sternum). The next three ('false' or vertebro-costal ribs) are joined by cartilage to the end of the rib above. The last two ('floating ribs') are not attached at the front. The diaphragm and muscles between adjacent ribs are responsible for the respiratory movements which fill the lungs with air.

Ribbentrop Joachim von 1893–1946. German Nazi politician and diplomat. As foreign minister 1938–45, he negotiated the non-aggression pact between Germany and the USSR (the Ribbentrop–Molotov pact 1939). He was tried at Nuremberg as a war criminal 1946 and hanged.

Ribbentrop–Molotov pact nonaggression treaty signed by Germany and the USSR 23 Aug 1939. Under the terms of the treaty both countries agreed to remain neutral and to refrain from acts of aggression against each other if either went to war. Secret clauses allowed for the partition of Poland – German Nazi dictator Adolf Hitler was to acquire western Poland, Soviet dictator Joseph Stalin the eastern part. On 1 Sept 1939 Hitler invaded Poland. The pact ended when Hitler invaded Russia 22 June 1941. See also ◊World War II.

Ribble river in N England; length 120 km/75 mi. From its source in the Pennine hills, North Yorkshire, it flows S and SW past Preston, Lancashire, to join the Irish Sea in a wide estuary.

ribbon lake long, narrow lake found on the floor of a ◊glacial trough. A ribbon lake will often form in an elongated hollow carved out by a glacier, perhaps where it came across a weaker band of rock. Ribbon lakes can also form when water ponds up behind a terminal moraine or a landslide.

Ribera José (Jusepe) de 1591–1652. Spanish painter. He was active in Italy from 1616 under the patronage of the viceroys of Naples. His early work shows the impact of Caravaggio, but his colours gradually lightened. He painted many full-length versions of saints as well as mythological figures and genre scenes, which he produced without preliminary drawing.

In the spirit of his time and country, he painted gloomy religious subjects of martyrdom and torture, though these were varied by realistic studies of common types in which the 'naturalism' derived from Caravaggio was opposed to the 'idealism' of the School of Bologna. Though he never abandoned his brown shadows, he made some progress towards richness and luminosity of colour in his mature work, of which the *Martyrdom of St Bartholomew*, c. 1639 (Prado), is an example. One of his last paintings, the *Boy with a Club Foot*, 1652 (Louvre), is a masterpiece of realism, while such studies of types (represented as celebrities of antiquity) as his *Aesop* and *Archimedes* (Prado) are in a vein which Velázquez pursued.

riboflavin or ***vitamin*** B_2 ◊vitamin of the B complex important in cell respiration. It is obtained from eggs, liver, and milk. A deficiency in the diet causes stunted growth.

ribonucleic acid full name of ◊RNA.

ribosome in biology, the protein-making machinery of the cell. Ribosomes are located on the endoplasmic reticulum (ER) of eukaryotic cells, and are made of proteins and a special type of ◊RNA, ribosomal RNA. They receive messenger RNA (copied from the ◊DNA) and ◊amino acids, and 'translate' the messenger RNA by using its chemically coded instructions to link amino acids in a specific order, to make a strand of a particular protein.

Ricardo David 1772–1823. English economist. Among his discoveries were the principle of comparative advantage (that countries can benefit by specializing in goods they produce efficiently and trading internationally to buy others), and the law of diminishing returns (that continued increments of capital and labour applied to a given quantity of land will eventually show a declining rate of increase in output). He wrote *Principles of Political Economy* 1817.

Ricci Sebastiano 1659–1734. Venetian painter. Working in the style of ◊Veronese, he became one of the leading decorative painters of his day, working throughout Italy as well as in Vienna and London 1712–16. His *Resurrection* is in the chapel of the Royal Hospital, Chelsea, London.

Ricci's revival of the Venetian tradition of history painting was so successful that many of his paintings were indistinguishable from those of Veronese. His later works were influenced by the Rococo, his lighter palette paving the way for ◊Tiepolo.

rice principal cereal of the wet regions of the tropics; derived from grass of the species *Oryza sativa*, probably native to India and SE Asia. It is unique among cereal crops in that it is grown standing in water. The yield is very large, and rice is said to be the staple food of one-third of the world population.
cultivation Rice takes 150–200 days to mature in warm, wet conditions. During its growing period, it needs to be flooded either by the heavy monsoon rains or by adequate irrigation. This restricts the cultivation of swamp rice, the usual kind, to level land and terraces. A poorer variety, known as hill rice, is grown on hillsides.
nutrition Rice contains 8–9% protein. Brown, or unhusked, rice has valuable B-vitamins that are lost in husking or polishing. Most of the rice eaten in the world is, however, sold in polished form.
history Rice has been cultivated since prehistoric days in the East. New varieties with greatly increased protein content have been developed by gamma radiation for commercial cultivation, and yields are higher than ever before (see ◊green revolution).
by-products Rice husks when burned provide a ◊silica ash that, mixed with lime, produces an excellent cement.

Richard Cliff. Stage name of Harry Roger Webb 1940– . English pop singer. Initially influenced by Elvis Presley, he soon became a Christian family entertainer. One of his best-selling early records was 'Livin' Doll' 1959 and he had hits in the UK through the 1980s. His original backing group was the Shadows (1958–68 and later re-formed). During the 1960s, he starred in a number of musical films including *Summer Holiday* 1962.

Richard (I) the Lion-Heart (French *Coeur-de-Lion*) 1157–1199. King of England from 1189. He spent all but six months of his reign abroad. He was the third son of Henry II, against whom he twice rebelled. In the third ◊Crusade 1191–92 he won victories at Cyprus, Acre, and Arsuf (against ◊Saladin), but failed to recover Jerusalem. While returning overland he was captured by the Duke of Austria, who handed him over to the emperor Henry VI, and he was held prisoner until a large ransom was raised. He then returned briefly to England, where his brother John I had been ruling in his stead. His later years were spent in warfare in France, where he was killed. ▷ *See feature on pp. 280–281.*

Richard II or ***Richard of Bordeaux*** 1367–1400. King of England from 1377, effectively from 1389, son of Edward the Black Prince. He reigned in conflict with Parliament; they executed some of his associates 1388, and he executed some of the opposing barons 1397, whereupon he made himself absolute. Two years later, forced to abdicate in favour of ◊Henry IV, he was jailed and probably assassinated.

Richard was born in Bordeaux. He succeeded his grandfather Edward III when only ten, the government being in the hands of a council of regency. His fondness for favourites resulted in conflicts with Parliament, and in 1388 the baronial party, headed by the Duke of Gloucester, had many of his friends executed. Richard recovered control 1389, and ruled moderately until 1397, when he had Gloucester murdered and his other leading opponents executed or banished, and assumed absolute power. In 1399 his cousin Henry Bolingbroke, Duke of Hereford (later Henry IV), returned from exile to lead a revolt; Richard II was deposed by Parliament and imprisoned in Pontefract Castle, where he died mysteriously.

Richard III 1452–1485. King of England from 1483. The son of Richard, Duke of York, he was created Duke of Gloucester by his brother Edward IV, and distinguished himself in the Wars of the ◊Roses. On Edward's death 1483 he became protector to his nephew Edward V, and soon secured the crown for himself on the plea that Edward IV's sons were illegitimate. He proved a capable ruler, but the suspicion that he had murdered Edward V and his brother undermined his popularity. In 1485 Henry, Earl of Richmond (later ◊Henry VII), raised a rebellion, and Richard III was defeated and killed at ◊Bosworth.

Scholars now tend to minimize the evidence for his crimes as Tudor propaganda.

Richards Gordon 1904–1986. English jockey and trainer who was champion on the flat a record 26 times between 1925 and 1953.

He started riding 1920 and rode 4,870 winners from 21,834 mounts before retiring 1954 and taking up training. He rode the winners of all the classic races but only once won the Epsom ◊Derby (on Pinza 1953). In 1947 he rode a record 269 winners in a season and in 1933 at Nottingham/Chepstow he rode 11 consecutive winners.

Richards Viv (Isaac Vivian Alexander) 1952– . West Indian cricketer. He was captain of the West Indies team 1986–91. He has played for the Leeward Islands and, in the UK, for Somerset and Glamorgan. A prolific run-scorer, he holds the record for the greatest number of runs made in Test cricket in one calendar year (1,710 runs in 1976). He retired from international cricket after the West Indies tour of England 1991 and from first-class cricket at the end of the 1993 season.

Richardson Ralph David 1902–1983. English actor. He played many stage parts, including Falstaff (Shakespeare), Peer Gynt (Ibsen), and Cyrano de Bergerac (Rostand). He shared the management of the Old Vic theatre with Laurence Olivier 1944–50. In later years he revealed himself as an accomplished deadpan comic.

Later stage successes include David Storey's *Home* 1970 and Harold Pinter's *No Man's Land* 1976. His films include *Things to Come* 1936, *Richard III* 1956, *Our Man in Havana* 1959, *The Wrong Box* 1966, *The Bed Sitting Room* 1969, and *O Lucky Man!* 1973.

Richardson Samuel 1689–1761. English novelist. He was one of the founders of the modern novel. *Pamela* 1740–41, written in the form of a series of letters and containing much dramatic conversation, was sensationally popular all across Europe, and was followed by *Clarissa* 1747–48 and *Sir Charles Grandison* 1753–54.

Born in Derbyshire, Richardson was brought up in London and apprenticed to a printer. He set up his own business in London 1719, becoming printer to the House of Commons. All his six young children died, followed by his wife 1731, which permanently affected his health.

Richardson Tony (Cecil Antonio) 1928–1991. English director and producer. With George Devine he established the English Stage Company 1955 at the Royal Court Theatre, with productions such as John Osborne's *Look Back in Anger* 1956. His films include *Saturday Night and Sunday Morning* 1960, *A Taste of Honey* 1961, *The Loneliness of the Long Distance Runner* 1962, *Tom Jones* 1963, *Joseph Andrews* 1977, and *Blue Sky* 1991.

Richelieu Armand Jean du Plessis de 1585–1642. French cardinal and politician, who through the influence of ◊Marie de' Medici became chief minister under Louis XIII 1624. He aimed to make the monarchy absolute; he ruthlessly crushed opposition by the nobility and destroyed the political power of the ◊Huguenots, while leaving them religious freedom. Abroad, he sought to establish French supremacy by breaking the power of the Habsburgs; he therefore supported the Swedish king Gustavus Adolphus and the German Protestant princes against Austria and in 1635 brought France into the Thirty Years' War.

Richelieu French statesman and chief minister to Louis XIII, Cardinal Armand de Richelieu. Whilst tolerant of the religion of the Huguenots, Richelieu nevertheless sabotaged their military and political power, aiming to establish the absolute authority of the crown. *Image Select (UK) Ltd*

Richmond industrial city and port on the James River and capital of Virginia, USA; population (1992) 202,300. It is a major tobacco market and distribution, commercial, and financial centre of the surrounding region. Its diversified manufactures include tobacco products, chemicals, paper and printing, and textiles.

Richmond-upon-Thames outer borough of SW Greater London, the only London borough with land on both sides of the river Thames. It includes the districts of Kew, Teddington, Twickenham, and Hampton.

features Royal Botanic gardens, Kew; Richmond Park, 1,000 hectares/2470 acres, the largest urban park in Britain, enclosed by Charles I for hunting, with ancient oaks, deer, and White Lodge, home of the Royal Ballet School; Maids of Honour Row, Richmond (1724), terrace of four houses for maids of honour attending the princess of Wales; early 18th-century houses around Richmond green; gatehouse of former Richmond Palace; Richmond Theatre (1899); Garrick's Villa, Hampton, acquired by David Garrick 1754 and altered by Robert Adam; Old Court House, Hampton, last home of Christopher Wren; Faraday House, Hampton, home of Michael Faraday; Hampton Court Palace, begun by Thomas Wolsey in 1514; Bushy Park, acquired by Wolsey 1514, containing Bushey House, built 1665 and remodelled c.1720, which now houses the National Physical Laboratory; highest tidal point of river Thames at Teddington; Ham House, Petersham (1610), with 17th-century garden; Twickenham Rugby football ground; Eel Pie Island, favourite for boating parties; Barnes Common; 18th- and 19th-century Barnes terrace, facing river Thames

population (1991) 160,700

famous people Virginia and Leonard Woolf set up Hogarth Press here. Thomas Traherne and R D Blackmore lived in Teddington; Henry Fielding in Barnes.

Richter scale scale, ranging from 0 to 8 and above, based on measurement of seismic waves and used to determine the magnitude of an ◊earthquake at its epicentre. The magnitude of an earthquake differs from its intensity, measured by the ◊Mercalli scale, which is subjective and varies from place to place for the same earthquake. The scale is named after US seismologist Charles Richter. The greatest earthquake ever recorded, in 1920 in Gansu, China, measured 8.6 on the Richter scale. *See list of tables on p. 1177.*

Richthofen Manfred, Freiherr von, (the 'Red Baron') 1892–1918. German aviator. In World War I he commanded the 11th Chasing Squadron, known as Richthofen's Flying Circus, and shot down 80 aircraft before being killed in action.

Originally a cavalryman (Lancer) he transferred to the air corps and eventually became the most famous 'ace' of the German service. A phenomenal shot, he relied more upon that than upon any tactical skill, and by Feb 1917 had over 20 Allied aircraft to his credit.

ricin extremely toxic extract from the seeds of the ◊castor-oil plant. When incorporated into ◊monoclonal antibodies, ricin can attack cancer cells, particularly in the treatment of lymphoma and leukaemia.

rickets defective growth of bone in children due to an insufficiency of calcium deposits. The bones, which do not harden adequately, are bent out of shape. It is usually caused by a lack of vitamin D and insufficient exposure to sunlight. Renal rickets, also a condition of malformed bone, is associated with kidney disease.

riddle or ***conundrum*** verbal puzzle or question that offers clues rather than direct aids to solving it, and often involves unlikely comparisons. Riddles poems were common in Old English poetry.

In ancient literature, finding the answer to a riddle could be a matter of life and death. Oedipus, for example, became the ruler of the ancient Greek city of Thebes by solving the riddle of the Sphinx: 'What goes on four legs in the morning, two in the afternoon, and three in the evening?' The answer is a human being – crawling on all fours as a baby, and walking with a stick in old age.

Ridley Nicholas c. 1500–1555. English Protestant bishop. He became chaplain to Henry VIII 1541, and bishop of London 1550. He took an active part in the Reformation and supported Lady Jane Grey's claim to the throne. After Mary's accession he was arrested and burned as a heretic.

Rie Lucie, (born Gomperz) 1902–1995. Austrian-born potter. She worked in England from the 1930s. Her pottery, exhibited all over the world, is simple and pure in form, showing a debt to English potter Bernard ◊Leach.

Riefenstahl Leni (Berta Helene Amalie) 1902– . German filmmaker. Her film of the Nazi rallies at Nuremberg, *Triumph des Willens/Triumph of the Will* 1934, vividly illustrated Hitler's charismatic appeal but tainted her career. She followed this with a filmed two-part documentary on the 1936 Berlin Olympic Games – *Olympiad: Fest der Volker/Festival of the Nations* and *Olympiad: Fest der Schönheit/Festival of Beauty*.

Riel Louis 1844–1885. French-Canadian rebel, a champion of the Métis (an Indian-French people); he established a provisional government in Winnipeg in an unsuccessful revolt 1869–70 and was hanged for treason after leading a second revolt in Saskatchewan 1885.

‘Nothing is as dangerous for the state as those who would govern kingdoms with maxims found in books.’

ARMAND RICHELIEU
Political Testament

‘Richmond is Nature in a Court dress, but still Nature – ay, and very lovely Nature too.’

ON RICHMOND-UPON-THAMES
Mary Russell Mitford
A Visit to Richmond
1832

Riemann Georg Friedrich Bernhard 1826–1866. German mathematician whose system of non-Euclidean geometry, thought at the time to be a mere mathematical curiosity, was used by Albert ◊Einstein to develop his general theory of ◊relativity. Riemann made a breakthrough in conceptual understanding within several other areas of mathematics: the theory of functions, vector analysis, projective and differential geometry, and topology.

Riemann took into account the possible interaction between space and the bodies placed in it; until then, space had been treated as an entity in itself, and this new point of view was to become a central concept of 20th-century physics.

Rienzi Cola di c. 1313–1354. Italian political reformer. In 1347, he tried to re-establish the forms of an ancient Roman republic. His second attempt seven years later ended with his assassination.

Riesman David 1909– . US sociologist, author of *The Lonely Crowd: A Study of the Changing American Character* 1950. He made a distinction among 'inner-directed', 'tradition-directed', and 'other-directed' societies; the first using individual internal values, the second using established tradition, and the third, other people's expectations, to develop cohesiveness and conformity within a society.

Riff a ◊Berber people of N Morocco, who under ◊Abd al-Karim long resisted the Spanish and French.

Rifkind Malcolm Leslie 1946– . British lawyer and Conservative politician, foreign secretary from 1995–97. He was Scottish secretary 1986 and transport secretary 1990. As defence secretary 1992–95, he managed the 'peace dividend', with its inevitable rundown of parts of the armed forces, more successfully than some of his predecessors.

rifle ◊firearm that has spiral grooves (rifling) in its barrel. When a bullet is fired, the rifling makes it spin, thereby improving accuracy. Rifles were first introduced in the late 18th century.

It makes the Grand Canyon of the Colorado look like a line scratched with a toothpick.

On the GREAT RIFT VALLEY
John Gunther
Inside Africa

rift valley valley formed by the subsidence of a block of the Earth's ◊crust between two or more parallel ◊faults. Rift valleys are steep-sided and form where the crust is being pulled apart, as at ◊ocean ridges, or in the Great Rift Valley of E Africa.

Rift Valley, Great volcanic valley formed 10–20 million years ago by a crack in the Earth's crust and running about 8,000 km/5,000 mi from the Jordan Valley through the Red Sea to central Mozambique in SE Africa. It is marked by a series of lakes, including Lake Turkana, and volcanoes, such as Mount Kilimanjaro.

At some points its traces have been lost by erosion, but elsewhere, as in S Kenya, cliffs rise thousands of metres.

Riga capital and port of Latvia; population (1995) 840,000. A member of the ◊Hanseatic League from 1282, Riga has belonged in turn to Poland 1582, Sweden 1621, and Russia 1710. It was occupied by the Germans 1917 and then, after being seized by both Russian and German troops in the aftermath of World War I, became the capital of independent Latvia 1919–40. It was again occupied by Germany 1941–44, before being annexed by the USSR. It again became independent Latvia's capital 1991.

Rigel or ***Beta Orionis*** brightest star in the constellation Orion. It is a blue-white supergiant, with an estimated diameter 50 times that of the Sun. It is 900 light years from Earth, and is intrinsically the brightest of the first-magnitude stars, its luminosity being about 100,000 times that of the Sun. It is the seventh brightest star in the night sky.

right-angled triangle triangle in which one of the angles is a right angle (90°). It is the basic form of triangle for defining trigonometrical ratios (for example, sine, cosine, and tangent) and for which ◊Pythagoras' theorem holds true. The longest side of a right-angled triangle is called the hypotenuse; its area is equal to half the product of the lengths of the two shorter sides.

Spring has come again. The earth is like a child who knows poems.

RAINER MARIA RILKE
The Sonnets to Orpheus

right ascension in astronomy, the coordinate on the ◊celestial sphere that corresponds to longitude on the surface of the Earth. It is measured in hours, minutes, and seconds eastwards from the point where the Sun's path, the ecliptic, once a year intersects the celestial equator; this point is called the vernal equinox.

rights issue in finance, new shares offered to existing shareholders to raise new capital. Shareholders receive a discount on the market price while the company benefits from not having the costs of a relaunch of the new issue.

The amount of shares offered depends on the capital the company needs. In a 'one for one rights issue', a shareholder is offered one share for each that he or she already holds. For companies this is the least expensive way of raising more capital.

Rights of Man and the Citizen, Declaration of the historic French document. According to the statement of the French National Assembly 1789, these rights include representation in the legislature; equality before the law; equality of opportunity; freedom from arbitrary imprisonment; freedom of speech and religion; taxation in proportion to ability to pay; and security of property. In 1946 were added equal rights for women; right to work, join a union, and strike; leisure, social security, and support in old age; and free education.

right wing the more conservative or reactionary section of a political party or spectrum. It originated in the French national assembly 1789, where the nobles sat in the place of honour on the president's right, whereas the commons were on his left (hence ◊left wing).

Rigi mountain in central Switzerland, between lakes Lauerz, Lucerne, and Zug; height 1,800 m/5,908 ft. The cogwheel train to the top was the first in Europe.

rigor medical term for shivering or rigidity. Rigor mortis is the stiffness that ensues in a corpse soon after death, owing to chemical changes in muscle tissue.

Rig-Veda oldest of the ◊*Vedas*, the chief sacred writings of Hinduism. It consists of hymns to the Aryan gods, such as Indra, and to nature gods.

Riley Bridget Louise 1931– . English painter. A pioneer of ◊Op art, she developed her characteristic style in the early 1960s, arranging hard-edged black lines in regular patterns to create disturbing effects of scintillating light and movement. *Fission* 1963 (Museum of Modern Art, New York) is an example. In the late 1960s she introduced colour and experimented with silk-screen prints on Perspex, though she continued to create works in her familiar black-and-white style.

Rilke Rainer Maria 1875–1926. Austrian writer. His prose works include the semi-autobiographical *Die Aufzeichnungen des Malte Laurids Brigge/The Notebook of Malte Laurids Brigge* 1910. His verse is characterized by a form of mystic pantheism that seeks to achieve a state of ecstasy in which existence can be apprehended as a whole.

Rilke was born in Prague. He travelled widely and worked for a time as secretary to the sculptor Rodin. He died in Switzerland. His poetical works include *Die Sonnette an Orpheus/Sonnets to Orpheus* 1923 and *Duisener Elegien/Duino Elegies* 1923.

Rimbaud (Jean Nicolas) Arthur 1854–1891. French Symbolist poet. His verse was chiefly written before the age of 20, notably *Les Illuminations* published 1886. From 1871 he lived with the poet Paul ◊Verlaine.

Although the association ended after Verlaine attempted to shoot him, it was Verlaine's analysis of Rimbaud's work 1884 that first brought him recognition. Rimbaud then travelled widely, working as a trader in North Africa 1880–91.

Rimsky-Korsakov Nikolay Andreyevich 1844–1908. Russian nationalist composer. His operas include *The Maid of Pskov* 1873, *The Snow Maiden* 1882, *Mozart and Salieri* 1898, and *The Golden Cockerel* 1907, a satirical attack on despotism that was banned until 1909. Other works include the symphonic poem *Sadko* 1867, the programme symphony *Antar* 1869, and the symphonic suite *Scheherazade* 1888. He also completed works by other composers, for example Mussorgsky's *Boris Godunov*.

rinderpest acute viral disease of cattle (sometimes also of sheep and goats) characterized by fever and bloody diarrhoea, due to inflammation of the intestines. Rinderpest belongs to the Paramyxoviridae virus family and has a mortality rate of 95%. Its highest incidence is in the Horn of Africa where it kills 50–80% of cattle.

ring circuit household electrical circuit in which appliances are connected in series to form a ring with each end of the ring connected to the power supply.

ring ouzel mountain songbird *Turdus torquatus* with brownish-black plumage and a broad white patch on the throat. It nests in heather or on banks in moorland districts. It belongs to the thrush family Muscicapidae, order Passeriformes. It is resident in and a partial migrant to Britain. It is found mainly in northern and western districts.

ringworm any of various contagious skin infections due to related kinds of fungus, usually resulting in circular, itchy, discoloured patches covered with scales or blisters. The scalp and feet (athlete's foot) are generally involved. Treatment is with antifungal preparations.

Rinzai (Chinese ***Lin-ch'i***) school of Zen Buddhism introduced to Japan from China in the 12th century by the monk Eisai (1141–1215) and others. It emphasizes rigorous monastic discipline and sudden enlightenment by meditation on a *kōan* (paradoxical question).

Rio de Janeiro port and resort in east Brazil; population (1991) 5,480,800 (metropolitan area 10,389,400). Sugar Loaf Mountain stands at the entrance to the harbour. Rio was the capital of Brazil 1763–1960. The city is the capital of the state of Rio de Janeiro, which has a population of 13,267,100 (1987 est).

Some colonial churches and other buildings survive; there are modern boulevards, including the Avenida Rio Branco, and Copacabana is a luxurious beachside suburb. The name (Portuguese 'river of January') commemorates the arrival of Portuguese explorers 1 Jan 1502, but there is in fact no river.

Rio Grande river rising in the Rocky Mountains in S Colorado, USA, and flowing south to the Gulf of Mexico, where it is reduced to a trickle by irrigation demands on its upper reaches; length 3,050 km/1,900 mi. Its last 2,400 km/1,500 mi form the US–Mexican border (Mexican name ***Río Bravo del Norte***).

Rio Grande do Norte state of NE Brazil; area 53,000 sq km/20,460 sq mi; population (1991) 2,415,600. Its capital is Natal. Industries include agriculture and textiles; there is offshore oil.

Rio Grande do Sul most southerly state of Brazil, on the frontier with Argentina and Uruguay; area 282,184 sq km/108,993 sq mi; population (1991) 9,138,700. Its capital is Pôrto Alegre. Industries include agriculture and cattle, food processing, and textiles.

Rioja, La see ◊La Rioja, a region of Spain.

Río Negro river in South America, rising in E Colombia and joining the Amazon at Manáus, Brazil; length 2,250 km/1,400 mi.

riot disturbance caused by a potentially violent mob. In the UK, riots formerly suppressed under the Riot Act are now governed by the Public Order Act 1986. Methods of riot control include plastic bullets, stun bags (soft canvas pouches filled with buckshot which spread out in flight), water cannon, and CS gas (tear gas).

Riots in Britain include the Spitalfields weavers' riot 1736, the Gordon riots 1780, the Newport riots 1839, and riots over the Reform Bill in Hyde Park, London, 1866; in the 1980s inner-city riots occurred in Toxteth, Liverpool; St Paul's, Bristol; Broadwater Farm, Tottenham, and Brixton, London; and in 1990 rioting took place in London and several other cities after demonstrations against the ◊poll tax. Race-related riots erupted in Brixton again Dec 1995, arising from a demonstration after a black man died in police custody.

Riot Act in the UK, act of Parliament passed 1714 to suppress the ◊Jacobite disorders. If three or more persons assembled unlawfully to the disturbance of the public peace, a magistrate could read a proclamation ordering them to disperse ('reading the Riot Act'), after which they might be dispersed by force. It was superseded by the Public Order Act 1986, which was instituted in response to several inner-city riots in the early 1980s, and greatly extends police powers to control marches and demonstrations by rerouting them, restricting their size and duration, or by making arrests. Under the act a person is guilty of riot if in a crowd of 12 or more, threatening violence; the maximum sentence is ten years' imprisonment.

Ripon city and market town in North Yorkshire, England, on the river Ure; population (1991) 13,800. There is a cathedral 1154–1520; and the nearby 12th-century ruins of Fountains Abbey are among the finest monastic ruins in Europe.

Risorgimento 19th-century movement for Italian national unity and independence, begun 1815. Leading figures in the movement included ◊Cavour, ◊Mazzini, and ◊Garibaldi. Uprisings 1848–49 failed, but with help from France in a war against Austria – to oust it from Italian provinces in the north – an Italian kingdom was founded 1861. Unification was finally completed with the addition of Venetia 1866 and the Papal States 1870.

Rivadavia Bernardino 1780–1845. Argentine politician, first president of Argentina 1826–27. During his rule he made a number of social reforms including extending the franchise to all males over 20 and encouraging freedom of the press. Unable to control the provincial caudillos (dictatorial leaders), he was forced to resign and spent most of his remaining years in exile in Europe.

river long water course that flows down a slope along a channel. It originates at a point called its source, and enters a sea or lake at its mouth. Along its length it may be joined by smaller rivers called tributaries. The area of land drained by a river and its tributaries is called a drainage basin.

One way of classifying rivers is their stage of development. A youthful stream is typified by a narrow V-shaped valley with numerous waterfalls, lakes, and rapids. When maturity is reached the river is said to be graded; erosion and deposition are delicately balanced as the river meanders across the extensive floodplain. At this stage the floodplain is characterized by extensive ◊meanders, ◊ox-bow lakes, and ◊levées.

RIVERS, MAJOR

Name and location	Length (km/mi)
Nile (NE Africa)	6,695/4,160
Amazon (South America)	6,570/4,080
Chang Jiang (China)	6,300/3,900
Mississippi–Missouri (USA)	6,020/3,740
Ob–Irtysh (China/Kazakhstan/Russia)	5,600/3,480
Huang He (China)	5,464/3,395
Paraná (Brazil)	4,500/2,800
Zaïre (Africa)	4,500/2,800
Mekong (Asia)	4,425/2,750
Amur (Asia)	4,416/2,744
Lena (Russia)	4,400/2,730
Mackenzie (Canada)	4,241/2,635
Niger (Africa)	4,185/2,600
Yenisei (Russia)	4,100/2,550
Mississippi (USA)	3,780/2,350
Murray–Darling (Australia)	3,750/2,330
Missouri (USA)	3,725/2,328
Volga (Russia)	3,685/2,290
Euphrates (Iraq)	3,600/2,240
Madeira (Brazil)	3,240/2,013
São Francisco (Brazil)	3,199/1,988
Yukon (USA/Canada)	3,185/1,979
Indus (Tibet/Pakistan)	3,180/1,975
Syrdar'ya (Kazakhstan)	3,078/1,913
Rio Grande (USA/Mexico)	3,050/1,900
Purus (Brazil)	2,993/1,860
Danube (Europe)	2,858/1,776
Brahmaputra (Asia)	2,850/1,770
Japurá (Brazil)	2,816/1,750
Salween (Myanmar/China)	2,800/1,740
Tocantins (Brazil)	2,699/1,677
Zambezi (Africa)	2,650/1,650
Paraguay (Paraguay)	2,591/1,610
Nelson–Saskatchewan (Canada)	2,570/1,600
Orinoco (Venezuela)	2,560/1,591
Amu Darya (Tajikistan/Turkmenistan/Uzbekistan)	2,540/1,578
Ural (Russia/Kazakhstan)	2,534/1,575
Kolyma (Russia)	2,513/1,562
Ganges (India/Bangladesh)	2,510/1,560

Rio de Janeiro The peak of the Sugar Loaf Mountain towers above the high-rise buildings of Botafogo in the city of Rio de Janeiro, Brazil. Rio developed as a port exporting sugar, cocoa, and other crops. As exploration progressed, it grew wealthy trading in gold and diamonds from the interior. *Corbis*

Rivera Diego 1886–1957. Mexican painter. He was one of the most important muralists of the 20th century. An exponent of Social Realism, he received many public commissions for murals depicting the Mexican revolution, his vivid style influenced by Mexican folk art. A vast cycle on historical themes (National Palace, Mexico City) was begun 1929.

Born in Guanajuato, he studied art in Spain, France, and Mexico. In the 1930s he visited the USA and with Ben Shahn (1898–1969) produced murals for the Rockefeller Center, New York (later overpainted because he included a portrait of Lenin).

Rivera José Fructuoso c. 1788–1854. Uruguayan general and politician, president 1830–34, 1839–43. Rivera fought under José Artigas (1764–1850) and submitted to Brazilian occupation before rejoining the revolution 1825. When he became president his financial mismanagement and favouritism provoked open dissent. He led a revolt 1836 against his successor Manuel Oribe (1792–1857), during which he became the focus of the Colorado Party. During his second term in office he declared war on Argentina.

Rivera Primo de Spanish politician; see ◊Primo de Rivera.

river blindness another name for ◊onchocerciasis, a disease prevalent in some developing countries.

Riverina district of New South Wales, Australia, between the Lachlan and Murray rivers, through which runs the Murrumbidgee. On fertile land, artificially irrigated from the three rivers, wool, wheat, and fruit are produced.

riveting method of joining metal plates. A hot metal pin called a rivet, which has a head at one end, is inserted into matching holes in two overlapping plates, then the other end is struck and formed into another head, holding the plates tight. Riveting is used in building construction, boilermaking, and shipbuilding.

Riviera the Mediterranean coast of France and Italy from Marseille to La Spezia. The most exclusive stretch of the Riviera, with the finest climate, is the ◊Côte d'Azur, from Menton to St Tropez, which includes Monaco.

Riyadh (Arabic ***Ar Riyād***) capital of Saudi Arabia and of the Central Province, formerly the sultanate of Nejd, in an oasis, connected by rail with Dammam on the Arabian Gulf; population (1994) 1,500,000.

Outside the city are date gardens irrigated from deep wells. There is a large royal palace and an Islamic university (1950).

Rizzio David c. 1533–1566. Italian adventurer at the court of Mary Queen of Scots. After her marriage to ◊Darnley, Rizzio's influence over her incited her husband's jealousy, and he was murdered by Darnley and his friends.

RN abbreviation for ***Royal Navy***; see under ◊navy.

RNA (abbreviation for ***ribonucleic acid***) nucleic acid involved in the process of translating the genetic material ◊DNA into proteins. It is usually single-stranded, unlike the double-stranded DNA, and consists of a large number of nucleotides strung together, each of which comprises the sugar ribose, a phosphate group, and one of four bases (uracil, cytosine, adenine, or guanine). RNA is copied from DNA by the formation of ◊base pairs, with uracil taking the place of thymine.

RNA occurs in three major forms, each with a different function in the synthesis of protein molecules. Messenger RNA (mRNA) acts as the template for protein synthesis. Each ◊codon (a set of three bases) on the RNA molecule is matched up with the corresponding amino acid, in accordance with the ◊genetic code. This process (translation) takes place in the ribosomes, which are made up of proteins and ribosomal RNA (rRNA). Transfer RNA (tRNA) is responsible for combining with specific amino acids, and then matching up a special 'anticodon' sequence of its own with a codon on the mRNA.

Although RNA is normally associated only with the process of protein synthesis, it makes up the hereditary material itself in some viruses, such as ◊retroviruses.

roach any freshwater fish of the Eurasian genus *Rutilus*, of the carp family, especially *R. rutilus* of N Europe. It is dark green above, whitish below, with reddish lower fins; it grows to 35 cm/1.2 ft.

Roach Hal (Harald Eugene) 1892–1992. US film producer. He was active from the 1910s to the 1940s, producing many comedies. He worked with ◊Laurel and Hardy, and also produced films for Harold Lloyd and Charley Chase. His work includes *The Music Box* 1932, *Way Out West* 1936, and *Of Mice and Men* 1939.

road specially constructed route for wheeled vehicles to travel on. Reinforced tracks became necessary with the invention of wheeled vehicles in about 3000 BC and most ancient civilizations had some form of road network. The Romans developed engineering techniques that were not equalled for another 1,400 years.

Until the late 18th century most European roads were haphazardly maintained, making winter travel difficult. In the UK the turnpike system of collecting tolls created some improvement. The Scottish engineers Thomas Telford and John ◊McAdam

roadrunner The greater roadrunner is often seen on roads, as its name implies, and runs rapidly away if disturbed. It inhabits the semi-arid open country of the southwestern USA, and feeds on ground-dwelling insects, which it kills by a sudden pounce on the prey.

introduced sophisticated construction methods in the early 19th century. Recent developments have included durable surface compounds and machinery for rapid ground preparation. The ◊motorway is the most advanced form of road.

roadrunner crested North American ground-dwelling bird *Geococcyx californianus* of the ◊cuckoo family, found in the SW USA and Mexico. It can run at a speed of 25 kph/15 mph.

Robbe-Grillet Alain 1922– . French writer. He was the leading theorist of *le nouveau roman* ('the new novel'), for example his own *Les Gommes/The Erasers* 1953, *La Jalousie/Jealousy* 1957, and *Dans le Labyrinthe/In the Labyrinth* 1959, which concentrates on the detailed description of physical objects. He also wrote the script for the film *L'Année dernière à Marienbad/Last Year at Marienbad* 1961.

'Any institution which does not suppose the people good, and the magistrate corruptible, is a vicious one.'

MAXIMILIEN ROBESPIERRE
Declaration of the Rights of Man

Robben Island island in Table Bay, Cape Town, South Africa. It was used by the South African government to house political prisoners. Nelson ◊Mandela was imprisoned here 1964–82.

robbery in law, a variety of ◊theft: stealing from a person, using force, or the threat of force, to intimidate the victim.

Robbia, della Italian family of sculptors and architects. They were active in Florence. ***Luca della Robbia*** (1400–1482) created a number of major works in Florence, notably the marble *cantoria* (singing gallery) in the cathedral 1431–38 (Museo del Duomo), with lively groups of choristers. Luca also developed a characteristic style of glazed terracotta work.

Robbins Jerome 1918–1998. US dancer and choreographer. He was associate director of the New York City Ballet 1949–59 and 1969–83 (with George Balanchine). His ballets are internationally renowned and he is considered the greatest US-born ballet choreographer. His first, *Fancy Free* 1944, was a great success (and was adapted with Leonard Bernstein into the musical *On the Town* 1944). He also choreographed the musicals *The King and I* 1951, *West Side Story* 1957, and *Fiddler on the Roof* 1964.

Robert (I) the Devil Duke of Normandy from 1027. Also known as 'the Magnificent', he was the father of William the Conqueror, and was legendary for his cruelty. He became duke after the death of his brother Richard III, in which he may have been implicated.

Robert II c. 1054–1134. Eldest son of ◊William the Conqueror, succeeding him as Duke of Normandy (but not on the English throne) 1087. His brother ◊William II ascended the English throne, and they warred until 1096, after which Robert took part in the First Crusade. When his other brother ◊Henry I claimed the English throne 1100, Robert contested the claim and invaded England unsuccessfully 1101. Henry invaded Normandy 1106, and captured Robert, who remained a prisoner in England until his death.

Robinson US film actor Edward G Robinson (passenger) in *Little Caesar* 1930. He became famous playing gangsters in such films as *Little Caesar* and *Key Largo* 1948 (with Humphrey Bogart), though in his long career he played a wide variety of roles. Other films include *Double Indemnity* 1944, *Scarlet Street* 1945, and *The Cincinnati Kid* 1965. *British Film Institute*

Robert (I) the Bruce 1274–1329. King of Scotland from 1306, and grandson of Robert de Bruce (1210–1295). He shared in the national uprising led by William ◊Wallace and, after Wallace's execution 1305, rose once more against Edward I of England and was crowned at Scone 1306. He defeated Edward II at ◊Bannockburn 1314. In 1328 the Treaty of Northampton recognized Scotland's independence and Robert as king.

Robert II 1316–1390. King of Scotland from 1371. He was the son of Walter (1293–1326), steward of Scotland, who married Marjory, daughter of Robert the Bruce. He was the first king of the house of Stuart.

Robert III c. 1340–1406. King of Scotland from 1390, son of Robert II. He was unable to control the nobles, and the government fell largely into the hands of his brother, Robert, Duke of Albany (c. 1340–1420).

Roberts Charles George Douglas 1860–1943. Canadian poet, short-story writer, and novelist. He is known as 'the father of Canadian literature'. His early *Orion, and Other Poems* 1880 influentially demonstrated that Canadian poets could creatively assimilate Tennysonian Romanticism, but later volumes such as *The Vagrant of Time* 1927 developed a more modern idiom. His 24 volumes of short fiction, starting with *Earth's Enigmas* 1896, included some of the first and most realistic animal stories as well as tales of outdoor adventure.

Robeson Paul 1898–1976. US bass singer and actor. He appeared in Eugene O'Neill's play *The Emperor Jones* 1924 and the Jerome Kern musical *Show Boat* 1927, in which he sang 'Ol' Man River'. He played *Othello* 1930, and his films include *Sanders of the River* 1935 and *King Solomon's Mines* 1937.

An ardent advocate of black rights, he had his passport withdrawn 1950–58 after a highly public visit to Russia. His last years were spent in England.

Robespierre Maximilien François Marie Isidore de 1758–1794. French politician in the ◊French Revolution. As leader of the ◊Jacobins in the National Convention, he supported the execution of Louis XVI and the overthrow of the right-wing republican Girondins, and in July 1793 was elected to the Committee of Public Safety. A year later he was guillotined; many believe that he was a scapegoat for the Reign of ◊Terror since he ordered only 72 executions personally.

Robespierre, a lawyer, was elected to the National Assembly of 1789–91. His defence of democratic principles made him popular in Paris, while his disinterestedness won him the nickname of 'the Incorruptible'. His zeal for social reform and his attacks on the excesses of the extremists made him enemies on both right and left; a conspiracy was formed against him, and in July 1794 he was overthrown and executed by those who actually perpetrated the Reign of Terror.

robin migratory songbird *Erithacus rubecula* of the thrush family Muscicapidae, order Passeriformes, found in Europe, W Asia, Africa, and the Azores. About 13 cm/5 in long, both sexes are olive brown with a red breast. Two or three nests are constructed during the year in sheltered places, and from five to seven white freckled eggs are laid.

Robin Hood in English legend, an outlaw and champion of the poor against the rich, said to have lived in Sherwood Forest, Nottinghamshire, during the reign of Richard I (1189–99). He feuded with the sheriff of Nottingham, accompanied by Maid Marian and a band of followers known as his 'merry men' (including Little John, so-called because of his huge stature, Friar Tuck, a jovial cleric, and Alan a Dale). Traditionally he is a nobleman who remained loyal to Richard during his exile and opposed the oppression of King John. He appears in many popular ballads from the 13th century, but his first datable appearance is in William Langland's *Piers Plowman* in the late 14th century. He became popular in the 15th century.

robin Both sexes of the European robin *Erithacus rubecula* sport the characteristic red breast and it is impossible to distinguish between them. Robins are highly territorial, and fights to the death between males are not unusual. *Premaphotos Wildlife*

Robinson Edward G. Stage name of Emmanuel Goldenberg 1893–1973. US film actor. Born in Romania, he emigrated with his family to the USA 1903. He was noted for his gangster roles, such as *Little Caesar* 1930, but also gave strong performances in psychological dramas such as *Scarlet Street* 1945.

Robinson Edwin Arlington 1869–1935. US poet. His verse, dealing mainly with psychological themes in a narrative style, is collected in volumes such as *The Children of the Night* 1897, which established his reputation. He was awarded three Pulitzer Prizes for poetry: *Collected Poems* 1922, *The Man Who Died Twice* 1925, and *Tristram* 1928.

Robinson Mary 1944– . Irish Labour politician, president 1990–97. She became a professor of law at the age of 25. A strong supporter of women's rights, she has campaigned for the liberalization of Ireland's laws prohibiting divorce and abortion.

Robinson Robert 1886–1975. English chemist, Nobel prizewinner 1947 for his research in organic chemistry on the structure of many natural products, including flower pigments and alkaloids. He formulated the electronic theory now used in organic chemistry. His studies of the sex hormones, bile acids, and sterols were fundamental to the methods now used to investigate steroid compounds. His discovery that certain synthetic steroids could produce the same biological effects as the natural oestrogenic sex hormones paved the way for the contraceptive pill.

Robinson Smokey (William) 1940– . US singer, songwriter, and record producer. He was associated with ◊Motown records from its conception. He was lead singer of the Miracles 1957–72 (hits include 'Shop Around' 1961 and 'The Tears of a Clown' 1970) and his solo hits include 'Cruisin'' 1979 and 'Being With You' 1981. His light tenor voice and wordplay characterize his work.

Robinson Sugar Ray. Adopted name of Walker Smith 1920–1989. US boxer. He was world welterweight champion 1945–51; he defended his title five times. Defeating Jake LaMotta 1951, he took the middleweight title. He lost the title six times and won it seven times. He retired at the age of 45.

Robinson W(illiam) Heath 1872–1944. English cartoonist and illustrator. He made humorous drawings of bizarre machinery for performing simple tasks, such as raising one's hat. A clumsily designed apparatus is often described as a 'Heath Robinson' contraption.

robot any computer-controlled machine that can be programmed to move or carry out work. Robots are often used in industry to transport materials or to perform repetitive tasks. For instance, robotic arms, fixed to a floor or workbench, may be used to paint machine parts or assemble electronic circuits. Other robots are designed to work in situations that would be dangerous to humans – for example, in defusing bombs or in space and deep-sea exploration. Some robots are equipped with sensors, such as touch sensors and video cameras, and can be programmed to make simple decisions based on the sensory data received.

Rob Roy nickname of Robert MacGregor 1671–1734. Scottish Highland ◊Jacobite outlaw. After losing his estates, he lived by cattle theft and extortion. Captured, he was sentenced to transportation but pardoned 1727. He is a central character in Walter Scott's historical novel *Rob Roy* 1817.

Rochdale industrial town (textiles, machinery, asbestos) in Greater Manchester, England, on the river Roch 16 km/10 mi NE of Manchester; population (1991) 202,200. It was formerly an important cotton-spinning town. The so-called Rochdale Pioneers founded the first Co-operative Society in England, in Toad Lane, Rochdale, 1844. The singer Gracie Fields was born here and a theatre is named after her.

Rochester upon Medway city in Kent, England, on the Medway estuary; population (1991) 24,000. It was a Roman town, *Durobrivae*. It has a 12th-century Norman castle keep (the largest in England), a 12th–15th-century cathedral, and many timbered buildings. The Dickens Centre 1982 commemorates the town's links with the novelist Charles Dickens, whose home was at Gad's Hill.

rock constituent of the Earth's crust, composed of minerals and/or materials of organic origin consolidated into a hard mass as ◊igneous, ◊sedimentary, or ◊metamorphic rocks.

Rockall British islet in the Atlantic, 24 m/80 ft across and 22 m/65 ft high, part of the Hatton-Rockall bank, and 370 km/230 mi W of North Uist in the Hebrides. It is in a potentially rich oil/gas area. Formally annexed by Britain 1955, Denmark, Iceland, and Ireland challenge Britain's claims to mineral, oil, and fishing rights on Rockall.

rock and roll pop music born of a fusion of rhythm and blues and country and western and based on electric guitar and drums. In the mid-1950s, with the advent of Elvis Presley, it became the heartbeat of teenage rebellion in the West and also had considerable impact on other parts of the world. It found perhaps its purest form in late-1950s rockabilly; the blanket term 'rock' later came to comprise a multitude of styles.

Rockabilly developed in the US South with a strong country (hillbilly) element. The typical rockabilly singer was young, white, male, working class, and recorded for the Sun label in Memphis; among them were Elvis Presley, Johnny Cash, Roy Orbison, Jerry Lee Lewis, and Carl Perkins. Many rockabilly performers later became country singers.

The term 'rock and roll' was popularized by US disc jockey Alan Freed (1922–1965) from 1951. Leading rock-and-roll singers and songwriters of the 1950s included Chuck Berry, Little Richard, Jerry Lee Lewis, Buddy Holly, and Gene Vincent (1935–1971).

rock climbing sport originally an integral part of mountaineering. It began as a form of training for Alpine expeditions and is now divided into three categories: the outcrop climb for climbs of up to 30 m/100 ft; the crag climb on cliffs of 30–300 m/100–1,000 ft, and the big wall climb, which is the nearest thing to Alpine climbing, but without the hazards of snow and ice.

Rockefeller John D(avison) 1839–1937. US millionaire. He was the founder of Standard Oil 1870 (which achieved control of 90% of US refineries by 1882). He also founded the philanthropic Rockefeller Foundation 1913, to which his son ***John D(avison) Rockefeller Jr*** (1874–1960) devoted his life.

rocket projectile driven by the reaction of gases produced by a fast-burning fuel. Unlike jet engines, which are also reaction engines, modern rockets carry their own oxygen supply to burn their fuel and do not require any surrounding atmosphere.

Rockets have been valued as fireworks over the last seven centuries. The only form of propulsion available that can function in a vacuum, rockets are essential to exploration in outer space. ◊Multistage rockets have to be used, consisting of a number of rockets joined together. Two main kinds of rocket are used: one burns liquid propellants, the other solid propellants. The fireworks rocket uses gunpowder as a solid propellant. The ◊space shuttle's solid rocket boosters use a mixture of powdered aluminium in a synthetic rubber binder. Most rockets, however, have liquid propellants, which are more powerful and easier to control. Liquid hydrogen and kerosene are common fuels, while liquid oxygen is the most common oxygen provider, or oxidizer.

For warfare, rocket heads carry an explosive device; see ◊nuclear warfare and ◊missile.

Rockingham Charles Watson Wentworth, 2nd Marquess of Rockingham 1730–1782. British Whig politician, prime minister 1765–66 and 1782 (when he died in office); he supported the American claim to independence.

Rocky Mountains or ***Rockies*** largest North American mountain system. It extends from the junction with the Mexican plateau, north through the W central states of the USA, through Canada to the Alaskan border, and then forms part of the Continental Divide, which separates rivers draining into the Atlantic or Arctic oceans from those flowing toward the Pacific Ocean. Mount Elbert is the highest peak, 4,400 m/14,433 ft. Some geographers consider the Yukon and Alaska ranges as part of the system, making the highest point Mount Mckinley (Denali) 6,194 m/20,320 ft.

Many large rivers rise in the Rocky Mountains, including the Missouri. The Rocky Mountain national park (1915) in Colorado has more than 100 peaks over 3,350 m/11,000 ft; Mount Logan on the Canadian–Alaskan border is 5,951 m/19,524 ft. In the 1980s computer techniques enabled natural gas in large quantities to be located in the W Rockies.

Rococo movement in the arts and architecture in 18th-century Europe, tending towards lightness, elegance, delicacy, and decorative charm. The term 'Rococo' is derived from the French *rocaille* (rock- or shell-work), a style of interior decoration based on S-curves and scroll-like forms. Jean-Antoine Watteau's paintings and Sèvres porcelain belong to the French Rococo vogue. In the 1730s the movement became widespread in Europe, notably in the churches and palaces of S Germany and Austria. Chippendale furniture is an English example of the French Rococo style.

Other Rococo features include the use of fantastic ornament and pretty, naturalistic details. The architectural and interior design of the Amalienburg pavilion at Nymphenburg near Munich, Germany, and the Hôtel de Soubise pavilion in Paris are typical of the movement. The painters François Boucher and Jean Honoré Fragonard both painted typically decorative Rococo panels for Parisian *hôtels* (town houses).

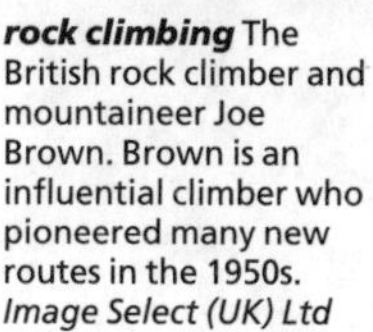

rock climbing The British rock climber and mountaineer Joe Brown. Brown is an influential climber who pioneered many new routes in the 1950s. *Image Select (UK) Ltd*

Rodchenko Alexander Mikhailovich 1891–1956. Russian avant-garde painter, designer, and photographer. The aim of his work, in all media, was to create a visual language that would reflect the new revolutionary times. His paintings were abstract works based on severe geometrical shapes; he made three-dimensional constructions of wood, cardboard, and metal. His photographs of everyday objects were presented in close-up, from strange angles or from high viewpoints; they document the early years of the Soviet era.

Roddick Anita Lucia 1943– . British entrepreneur, founder of the Body Shop, which now has branches worldwide. Roddick started with one shop in Brighton, England, 1976, selling only natural toiletries in refillable plastic containers.

rodent any mammal of the worldwide order Rodentia, making up nearly half of all mammal species. Besides ordinary 'cheek teeth', they have a single front pair of incisor teeth in both upper and lower jaw, which continue to grow as they are worn down.

They are often subdivided into three suborders: Sciuromorpha, including primitive rodents, with

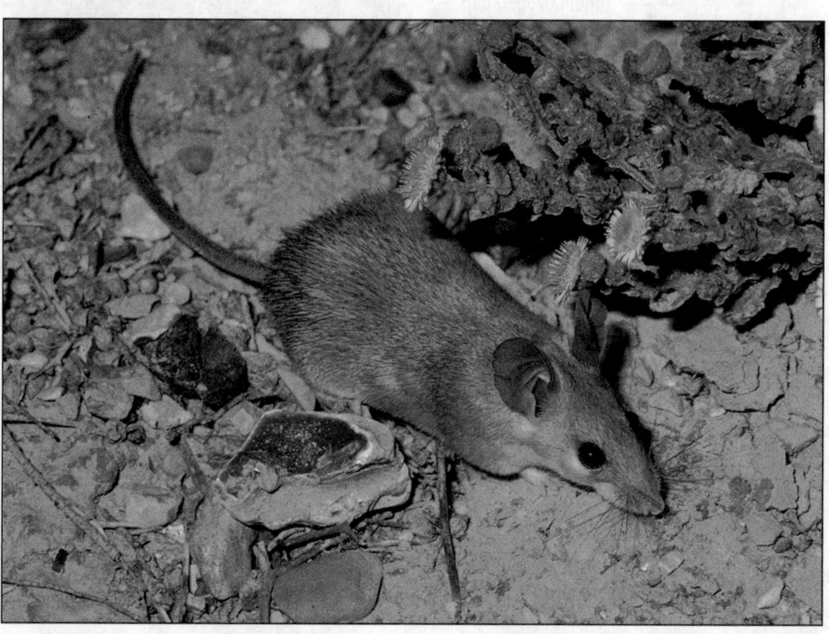

rodent Rodents, such as this Cairo spiny mouse *Acomys cahirinus* in Israel's Negev Desert, are particularly well adapted to the world's arid regions. Most desert rodents do not need access to free water but derive all the liquid they need from their food. *Premaphotos Wildlife*

'Form follows profit' is the aesthetic principle of our times.

RICHARD ROGERS
Quoted in *The Times* 13 Feb 1991

squirrels as modern representatives; Myomorpha, rats and mice and their relatives; and Hystricomorpha, including the Old World and New World porcupines and guinea pigs.

rodeo originally a practical means of rounding up cattle in North America. It is now a professional sport in the USA and Canada. Ranching skills such as bronco busting, bull riding, steer wrestling, and calf roping are all rodeo events.

Rodgers Richard Charles 1902–1979. US composer. He collaborated with librettist Lorenz Hart (1895–1943) on songs like 'Blue Moon' 1934 and musicals like *On Your Toes* 1936. With Oscar Hammerstein II, he wrote many musicals, including *Oklahoma!* 1943, *South Pacific* 1949, *The King and I* 1951, and *The Sound of Music* 1959.

Rodin (René François) Auguste 1840–1917. French sculptor. He is considered the greatest of his day. He freed sculpture from the idealizing conventions of the time by his realistic treatment of the human figure, introducing a new boldness of style and expression. Examples are *Le Penseur/The Thinker* 1904 (Musée Rodin, Paris), *Le Baiser/The Kiss* 1886 (marble version in the Louvre, Paris), and *The Burghers of Calais* 1884–86 (copy in Embankment Gardens, Westminster, London).

Rodin failed the entrance examination for the Ecole des Beaux Arts, and never attended. He started as a mason, began to study in museums, and in 1875 visited Italy, where he was inspired by the work of Michelangelo. His early statue *The Age of Bronze* 1877 (Musée Rodin, Paris) was criticized for its total naturalism and accuracy. In 1880 he began the monumental bronze *Gates of Hell* for the Ecole des Arts Décoratifs in Paris (inspired by Ghiberti's bronze doors in Florence), a project that occupied him for many years and was unfinished at his death. Many of the figures designed for the gate became independent sculptures. During the 1890s he received two notable commissions, for statues of the writers *Balzac* 1893–97 and *Victor Hugo* 1886–90 (both Musée Rodin, Paris).

Rodnina Irina Konstantinovna 1949– . Soviet ice skater. Between 1969 and 1980 she won 23 world, Olympic, and European gold medals in pairs competitions. Her partners were Alexei Ulanov and then Alexandr Zaitsev.

roebuck male of the Eurasian roe ◊deer.

Roeg Nicolas (Jack) 1928– . English film director and writer. He was formerly a cinematographer. His striking visual style is often combined with fractured, disturbing plots, as in *Performance* 1970, *Don't Look Now* 1973, *The Man Who Fell to Earth* 1976, and *The Witches* 1989.

His other films include *Walkabout* 1971, *Bad Timing* 1980, *Castaway* 1986, *Cold Heaven* 1990, *Heart of Darkness* 1993, and *Two Deaths* 1994.

roentgen or ***röntgen*** unit (symbol R) of radiation exposure, used for X-rays and gamma rays. It is defined in terms of the number of ions produced in one cubic centimetre of air by the radiation. Exposure to 1,000 roentgens gives rise to an absorbed dose of about 870 rads (8.7 grays), which is a dose equivalent of 870 rems (8.7 sieverts).

The annual dose equivalent from natural sources in the UK is 1,100 microsieverts.

Roger II 1095–1154. King of Sicily from 1130, the second son of Count Roger I of Sicily (1031–1101). By the time he was crowned king on the authority of Pope Innocent II (died 1143) he had achieved mastery over the whole of Norman Italy. He used his navy to conquer Malta and territories in North Africa, and to harass Byzantine possessions in the eastern Mediterranean. His Palermo court was a cultural centre where Latin, Greek, and Arab scholars mixed freely.

Rogers Carl Ransom 1902–1987. US psychologist who developed the client-centred approach to counselling and psychotherapy. This stressed the importance of clients making their own decisions and developing their own potential (self-actualization). He emphasized the value of genuine interest on the part of a therapist who is also accepting and empathetic. Rogers's views became widely employed.

Rogers Ginger. Stage name of Virginia Katherine McMath 1911–1995. US actress, dancer, and singer. She worked from the 1930s to the 1950s, often starring with Fred Astaire in such films as *Top Hat* 1935 and *Swing Time* 1936. Her other film work includes *Bachelor Mother* 1939 and *Kitty Foyle* 1940 (Academy Award). She later appeared in stage musicals.

Rogers first appeared with Astaire when both had secondary roles in *Flying Down to Rio* 1933. Their dance numbers together made them the most celebrated dance due in screen history.

Rogers Richard George 1933– . English High Tech architect. His works include the Pompidou Centre in Paris 1977 (jointly with Renzo ◊Piano), the Lloyd's of London building in London 1986, and the Reuters building at Blackwall Yard, London, 1992 (which won him a RIBA award).

Roget Peter Mark 1779–1869. English physician, one of the founders of the University of London, and author of a *Thesaurus of English Words and Phrases* 1852, a text constantly revised and still in print, offering synonyms.

Röhm Ernst 1887–1934. German leader of the Nazi Brownshirts, the SA (◊Sturmabteilung). On the pretext of an intended SA putsch (uprising) by the Brownshirts, the Nazis had some hundred of them, including Röhm, killed 29–30 June 1934. The event is known as the Night of the Long Knives.

Rohmer Eric. Adopted name of Jean-Maurice Henri Schérer 1920– . French film director, screenwriter, and critic. Part of the French New Wave, his films are often concerned with the psychology of self-deception. They include *Ma Nuit chez Maud/My Night at Maud's* 1969, *Le Genou de Claire/Claire's Knee* 1970, *Die Marquise von O/The Marquise of O* 1976, and *Conte d'été/A Tale of Summer* 1996.

Roh Tae-woo 1932– . South Korean right-wing politician and general, president 1988–93. He held ministerial office from 1981 under President Chun, and became chair of the ruling Democratic

rocket The three-stage Saturn V rocket used in the Apollo moonshots of the 1960s and 1970s. It stood 111 m/365 ft high, as tall as a 30-storey skyscraper, weighed 2,700 tonnes/3,000 tons when loaded with fuel, and developed a power equivalent to 50 Boeing 747 jumbo jets.

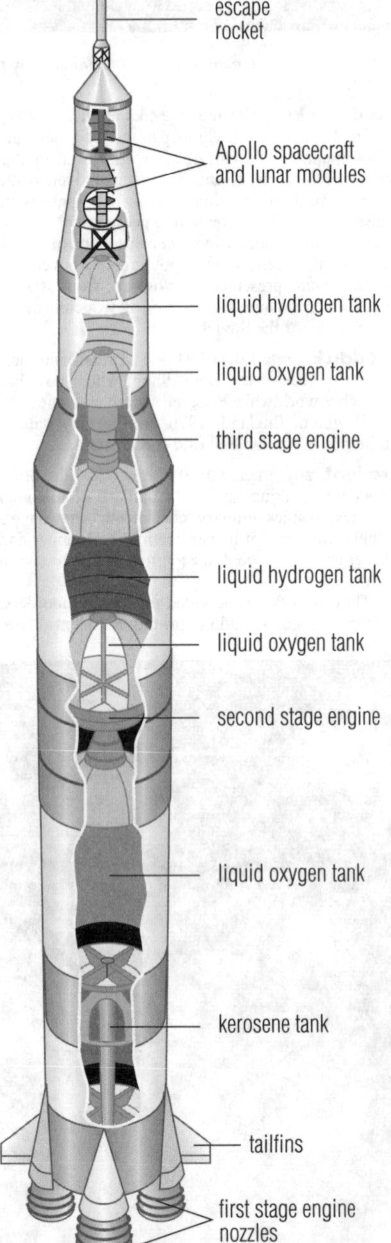

Rogers US psychologist Carl Rogers who developed client-centred psychotherapy which emphasizes the growth of an equal relationship between therapist and client and the mutual exploration of problems rather than the imposition of an outside set of attitudes or values. *Corbis*

Rodin Bronze statue *Le Penseur/The Thinker* (1904), Musée Rodin, Paris. This statue was originally conceived as a seated figure of Dante for Rodin's monumental set of doors, the *Gates of Hell*, which he never completed. *Sotheby's*

Justice Party 1985. He was elected president 1988, amid allegations of fraud and despite being connected with the massacre of about 2,000 anti-government demonstrators 1980. In Oct 1995 Roh admitted to secretly amassing a personal fortune during his term in office; he was arrested on corruption charges, along with former president Chun, and placed on trial 1996. He was found guilty and sentenced to 22 years' imprisonment (later reduced to 17 years).

Roland died c. 778. French hero. His real and legendary deeds of valour and chivalry inspired many medieval and later romances, including the 11th-century *Chanson de Roland* and Ariosto's *Orlando furioso*. A knight of ◊Charlemagne, Roland was killed 778 with his friend Oliver and the 12 peers of France at Roncesvalles (in the Pyrenees) by Basques. He headed the rearguard during Charlemagne's retreat from his invasion of Spain.

roller any brightly coloured bird of the Old World family Coraciidae, resembling crows but in the same order as kingfishers and hornbills. Rollers grow up to 32 cm/13 in long. The name is derived from the habit of some species of rolling over in flight.

Rolling Stones, the British band formed 1962, once notorious as the 'bad boys' of rock. Original members were Mick Jagger (1943–), Keith Richards (1943–), Brian Jones (1942–1969), Bill Wyman (1936–), Charlie Watts (1941–), and the pianist Ian Stewart (1938–1985). A rock-and-roll institution, the Rolling Stones were still performing and recording in the 1990s.

The Stones' earthy sound was based on rhythm and blues, and their rebel image was contrasted with the supposed wholesomeness of the early Beatles. Classic early hits include 'Satisfaction' 1965 and 'Jumpin' Jack Flash' 1968. The albums from *Beggars Banquet* 1968 to *Exile on Main Street* 1972 have been rated among their best work; others include *Some Girls* 1978, *Steel Wheels* 1989, and *Stripped* 1996.

Rollo First duke of Normandy c. 860–c. 932. Viking leader. He left Norway about 875 and marauded, sailing up the Seine to Rouen. He besieged Paris 886, and in 912 was baptized and granted the province of Normandy by Charles III of France. He was its duke until his retirement to a monastery 927. He was an ancestor of William the Conqueror.

Rolls, Master of the British judge; see ◊Master of the Rolls.

ROM (acronym for ***read-only memory***) in computing, a memory device in the form of a collection of integrated circuits (chips), frequently used in microcomputers. ROM chips are loaded with data and programs during manufacture and, unlike ◊RAM (random-access memory) chips, can subsequently only be read, not written to, by computer. However, the contents of the chips are not lost when the power is switched off, as happens in RAM.

Romagna area of Italy on the Adriatic coast, under papal rule 1278–1860 and now part of the region of ◊Emilia-Romagna.

Romains Jules. Pen name of Louis Henri Jean Farigoule 1885–1972. French novelist, playwright, and poet. His plays include the farce *Knock, ou le triomphe de la médecine/Dr Knock* 1923 and *Donogoo* 1930, and his novels include *Mort de quelqu'un/Death of a Nobody* 1911, *Les Copains/The Boys in the Back Room* 1913, and *Les Hommes de bonne volonté/Men of Good Will* (27 volumes) 1932–47. Romains developed the theory of Unanimism, which states that every group has a communal existence greater than that of the individual, which intensifies the individual's perceptions and emotions.

Roman architecture, ancient the architecture of the Roman Empire, spanning the period 4th century BC–5th century AD. In contrast to the linear emphasis of ◊Greek architecture, Roman architecture is noted for its development of the rounded form.

The Romans' mastery of concrete (used in combination with bricks) freed the ◊orders from their earlier structural significance and enabled the development of such rounded forms as the arch, vault, and dome. Arches and vaults were first employed in utilitarian structures; for example, bridges and aqueducts. Later they were used, together with the dome, in private and public buildings as a means of extending and diversifying the interior space.

Roman building types include the basilica, an oblong meeting hall with vaulted roof, often colonnaded; the thermae or bath houses with their complex spatial layout; and the triumphal arch, a purely ornamental structure. Rome has the richest collection of public buildings, notably the ◊Pantheon, built between 27 BC and AD 124, with its enormous concrete dome, the ◊Colosseum AD 70–80, numerous temples, and public baths such as those of Caracalla, about AD 215 onwards.

The ruins of Pompeii at the foot of Mount Vesuvius provide the most complete view of a Roman city, which was typically planned as a series of interlinked public spaces. Dwellings tend to look inwards towards an open atrium (inner court) and peristyle (colonnade surrounding the court).

Roman art sculpture and painting of ancient Rome, from the 4th century BC to the fall of the Western Empire 5th century AD. Much Roman art was intended for public education, notably the sculpted triumphal arches and giant columns, such as Trajan's Column AD 106–113, and portrait sculptures of soldiers, politicians, and emperors. Surviving mural paintings (in Pompeii, Rome, and Ostia) and mosaic decorations show Greek influence. Roman art was to prove of lasting inspiration in the West.

Realistic portrait sculpture was developed by the Romans. A cult of heroes began and in public places official statues were erected of generals, rulers, and philosophers. The portrait bust developed as a new art form from about 75 BC; these were serious, factual portraits of men to whose wisdom and authority (the busts implied) their subject nations should reasonably submit. Strict realism in portraiture gave way to a certain amount of Greek-style idealization in the propaganda statues of the emperors, befitting their semidivine status.

Narrative relief sculpture also flourished in Rome, linked to the need to commemorate military victories. These appeared on monumental altars, triumphal arches, and giant columns such as Trajan's Column, where his battles are recorded in relief like a cartoon strip winding its way around the column for about 200 m/655 ft. Gods and allegorical figures also featured with Rome's heroes on narrative relief sculptures, such as those on Augustus' giant altar to peace, the *Ara Pacis* 13–9 BC.

Very little Roman painting has survived; much of what has owes its survival to the volcanic eruption of Mount Vesuvius in AD 79 which buried the southern Italian towns of Pompeii and Herculaneum under ash, thus preserving the lively wall paintings that decorated the villas of an art-loving elite. Trompe l'oeil paintings and elements of still life were popular. A type of interior decoration known as Grotesque, rediscovered in Rome during the Renaissance, combined swirling plant motifs, strange animals, and tiny fanciful scenes.

The art of mosaic was found throughout the Roman Empire. It was introduced from Greece and used for floors as well as walls and vaults, in trompe l'oeil effects, geometric patterns, and scenes from daily life and mythology.

Roman Britain period in British history from the two expeditions by Julius Caesar 55 and 54 BC to the early 5th century AD. Roman relations with Britain began with Caesar's expeditions, but the actual conquest was not begun until AD 43. During the reign of the emperor Domitian, the governer of the province, Agricola, campaigned in Scotland. After several unsuccessful attempts to conquer Scotland, the northern frontier was fixed between the Solway and the Tyne at ◊Hadrian's Wall.

The process of Romanization was enhanced by the establishment of Roman colonies and other major urban centres. Most notable was the city of Colchester (Camulodunum), which was the location of the temple dedicated to the Divine Claudius, and the focus of the revolt of Boudicca. Other settlements included London, York, Chester, St Albans, Lincoln, and Gloucester, as well as the spa at Bath dedicated to the worship of Sulis Minerva, a combination of local and Roman deities. England was rapidly Romanized, but north of York few remains of Roman civilization have been found.

Roman Catholicism one of the main divisions of the Christian religion, separate from the Eastern

roller The lilac-breasted roller *Coracias caudata* is a common sight in thorn veld savannas from Natal province in South Africa northwards to Ethiopia and Somalia. Found especially in S Europe and Africa, rollers feed mainly on insects and lizards. They are noted for their aggression. *Premaphotos Wildlife*

'Every man who feels well is a sick man neglecting himself.'

JULES ROMAINS
Knock, or the Triumph of Medicine

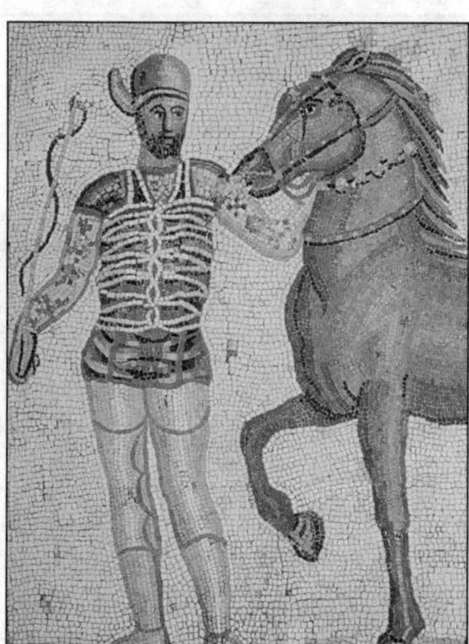

Roman art Detail from a mosaic showing a Roman coachman. Much surviving Roman art is in the form of mosaic, an art form that was introduced from Greece. *Corbis*

When one has travelled alone and on foot up and down the world, and seen its vastness and complexity, ... then one begins to understand the name of Rome.

On the **Roman Empire**
Hilaire Belloc
Hills and the Sea

ROMAN EMPERORS 27 BC–AD 285

Reign	Name
Julio-Claudian emperors	
27 BC–14 AD	Augustus
14–37	Tiberius I
37–41	Caligula (Gaius Caesar)
41–54	Claudius I
54–68	Nero
Civil wars	
68–69	Galba
69	Otho
69	Vitellius
Flavian emperors	
69–79	Vespasian
79–81	Titus
81–96	Domitian
96–98	Nerva
98–117	Trajan
117–38	Hadrian
Antonine emperors	
138–61	Antoninus Pius
161–69	Lucius Verus
Despotic emperors	
161–80	Marcus Aurelius
180–92	Commodus
193	Pertinax
193	Didius Julianus
The Severi	
193–211	Septimus Severus
211–17	Caracalla
217–18	Macrinus
218–22	Elagabalus
222–35	Severus Alexander
The soldier emperors	
235–38	Maximus I
238–44	Gordian III
244–49	Philip I, the Arab
249–51	Trajan Decius
251–53	Trebonianus Gallus
253–68	Gallienus
268–70	Claudius II
270–75	Aurelian
275–76	Tacitus
276	Florian
276–82	Probus
282–83	Carus
283–85	Carinus

Orthodox Church from 1054, and headed by the pope. For history and beliefs, see ◊Christianity. Membership is about 900 million worldwide, concentrated in S Europe, Latin America, and the Philippines.

The Protestant churches separated from the Catholic with the Reformation in the 16th century, to which the Counter-Reformation was the Catholic response. An attempt to update Catholic doctrines in the late 19th century was condemned by Pope Pius X 1907, and more recent moves have been rejected by John Paul II.

doctrine The focus of liturgical life is the Mass, or Eucharist, and attendance is obligatory on Sundays and Feasts of Obligation such as Christmas and Easter. The Roman Catholic differs from the other Christian churches in that it acknowledges the supreme jurisdiction of the pope, infallible when he speaks *ex cathedra* ('from the throne'); in the doctrine of the Immaculate Conception (which states that the Virgin Mary, the mother of Jesus, was conceived without the original sin with which all other human beings are born); and in according a special place to the Virgin Mary.

organization Since the Second Vatican Council 1962–66, major changes have taken place. They include the use of vernacular or everyday language instead of Latin in the liturgy, and increased freedom among the religious and lay orders. The pope has an episcopal synod of 200 bishops elected by local hierarchies to collaborate in the government of the church. The priesthood is celibate and there is a strong emphasis on the monastic orders. Great importance is also attached to ◊missionary work.

romance in literature, tales of love and adventure, in verse or prose, that became popular in France about 1200 and spread throughout Europe. There were Arthurian romances about the legendary King Arthur and his knights, and romances based on the adventures of Charlemagne and on classical themes. In the 20th century the term 'romantic novel' is often used disparagingly, to imply a contrast with a realist novel.

Romance languages branch of Indo-European languages descended from the Latin of the Roman Empire ('popular' or 'vulgar' as opposed to 'classical' Latin). The present-day Romance languages with national status are French, Italian, Portuguese, Romanian, and Spanish.

Romansch (or Rhaeto-Romanic) is a minority language of Switzerland and one of the four official languages of the country, while Catalan and Gallego (or Galician) in Spain, Provençal in France, and Friulian and Sardinian in Italy are recognized as distinct languages with strong regional and/or literary traditions of their own.

Roman Empire from 27 BC to the 5th century AD; see ◊Rome, ancient.

Romanesque architecture style of W European ◊architecture of the 10th to 12th centuries, marked by rounded arches, solid volumes, and emphasis on perpendicular elements. In England the style is also known as ◊Norman architecture.

Romanesque art European art of the 10th to 12th centuries; see ◊medieval art.

Romania country in SE Europe, bounded N and E by Ukraine, E by Moldova, SE by the Black Sea, S by Bulgaria, SW by Yugoslavia, and NW by Hungary. *See country box opposite.*

Romanian people of Romanian culture from Romania, Yugoslavia, Moldova, and the surrounding area. Historically the Romanians were known as Vlachs (German 'foreigner'). The religion of the Romanians is predominantly Romanian Orthodox, though there is a Greek Orthodox minority.

Romanian language member of the Romance branch of the Indo-European language family, spoken in Romania, Macedonia, Albania, and parts of N Greece. It has been strongly influenced by the Slavonic languages and by Greek. The Cyrillic alphabet was used until the 19th century, when a variant of the Roman alphabet was adopted. There are 20–25 million speakers of the Romanian language.

Roman law legal system of ancient Rome that is now the basis of ◊civil law, one of the main European legal systems.

It originated under the republic, was developed under the empire, and continued in use in the Byzantine Empire until 1453. The first codification was that of the 12 Tables (450 BC), of which only fragments survive. Roman law assumed its final form in the codification of Justinian AD 528–34. An outstanding feature of Roman law was its system of international law (*jus gentium*), applied in disputes between Romans and foreigners or provincials, or between provincials of different states.

Roman numerals ancient European number system using symbols different from Arabic numerals (the ordinary numbers 1, 2, 3, 4, 5, and so on). The seven key symbols in Roman numerals, as represented today, are I (1), V (5), X (10), L (50), C (100), D (500), and M (1,000). There is no zero, and therefore no place-value as is fundamental to the Arabic system. The first ten Roman numerals are I, II, III, IV (or IIII), V, VI, VII, VIII, IX, and X. When a Roman symbol is preceded by a symbol of equal or greater value, the values of the symbols are added (XVI = 16).

When a symbol is preceded by a symbol of less value, the values are subtracted (XL = 40). A horizontal bar over a symbol indicates a multiple of 1,000 ($\bar{X}$ = 10,000). Although addition and subtraction are fairly straightforward using Roman numerals, the absence of a zero makes other arithmetic calculations (such as multiplication) clumsy and difficult.

Romano GiulioSee ◊Giulio Romano, Italian painter and architect.

Romanov dynasty rulers of Russia from 1613 to the ◊Russian Revolution 1917. Under the Romanovs, Russia developed into an absolutist empire. The pattern of succession was irregular until 1797. The last tsar, Nicholas II, abdicated March 1917 and was murdered July 1918, together with his family. *See illustration on p. 922.*

Roman religion religious system that retained early elements of animism (with reverence for stones and trees) and totemism (see ◊Romulus and Remus), and had a strong domestic base in the ◊lares and penates, the cult of Janus and Vesta. It also had a main pantheon of gods derivative from the Greek one, which included Jupiter and Juno, Mars and Venus, Minerva, Diana, Ceres, and many lesser deities.

The deification of dead emperors served a political purpose and also retained the idea of family – that is, that those who had served the national family in life continued to care, as did one's ancestors, after their death. By the time of the empire, the educated classes tended towards stoicism or scepticism, but the following of mystery cults, especially within the army (see ◊Isis and ◊Mithraism), proved a strong rival to early Christianity.

Romansch member of the Romance branch of the Indo-European language family, spoken by some 50,000 people in the eastern cantons of Switzerland. It was accorded official status 1937 alongside French, German, and Italian. It is also known among scholars as Rhaeto-Romanic.

Romanticism in literature and the visual arts, a style that emphasizes the imagination, emotions, and creativity of the individual artist. Romanticism also refers specifically to late-18th- and early-19th-century European culture, as contrasted with 18th-century ◊Classicism.

Inspired by the ideas of Jean Jacques ◊Rousseau and by contemporary social change and revolution (US, French), Romanticism emerged as a reaction to 18th-century values, asserting emotion and intuition over rationalism, the importance of the individual over social conformity, and the exploration of natural and psychic wildernesses over classical restraint. Major themes of Romantic art and literature include a love of atmospheric landscapes; nostalgia for the past, particularly the

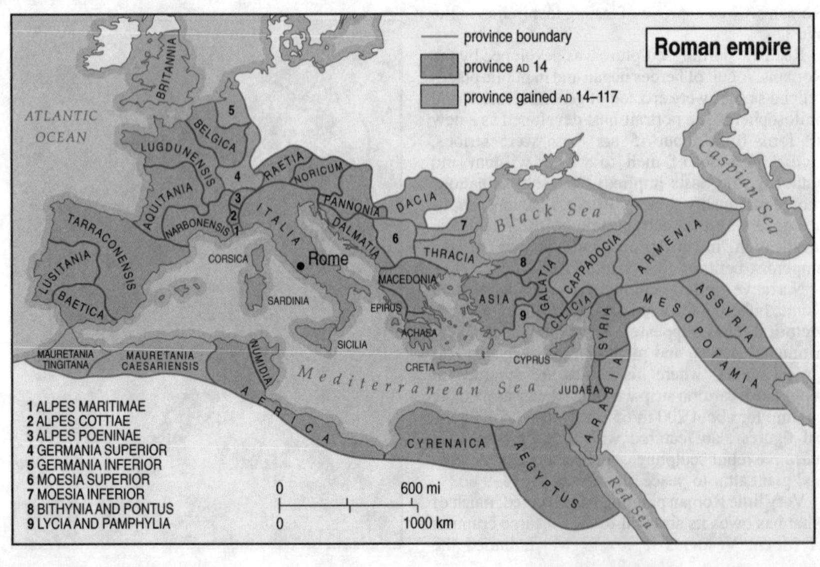

ROMANIA

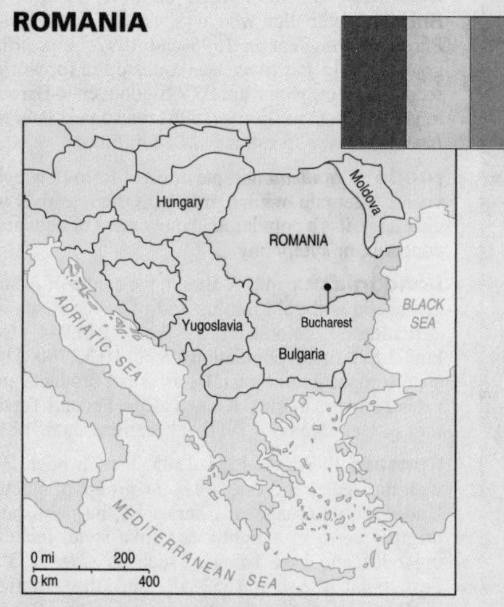

national name *România*
area 237,500 sq km/91,699 sq mi
capital Bucharest
major towns/cities Braşov, Timişoara, Cluj-Napoca, Iaşi
major ports Galaţi, Constanta, Brăila
physical features mountains surrounding a plateau, with river plains S and E. Carpathian Mountains, Transylvanian Alps; river Danube; Black Sea coast; mineral springs
head of state Emil Constantinescu from 1996
head of government Radu Vasile from 1998
political system emergent democratic republic
administrative divisions 40 counties and the municipality of Bucharest
political parties Democratic Convention of Romania (DCR), centre-right coalition; Social Democratic Union (SDU), reformist; Social Democracy Party of Romania (PSDR), social democrat; Romanian National Unity Party (RNUP), Romanian nationalist, right-wing, anti-Hungarian; Greater Romania Party (Romania Mare), far-right, ultranationalist, anti-Semitic; Democratic Party–National Salvation Front (DP–NSF), promarket; National Salvation Front (NSF), centre-left; Hungarian Democratic Union of Romania (HDUR), ethnic Hungarian; Christian Democratic–National Peasants' Party (CD–PNC), centre-right, promarket; Socialist Labour Party (SLP), ex-communist
population 22,655,000 (1996 est)
population growth rate −0.3% (1990–95); −0.2% (2000–05)
ethnic distribution 89% non-Slavic ethnic Romanian; substantial Hungarian, German, and Serbian minorities
life expectancy 69 (men), 74 (women)
literacy 96%
languages Romanian (official), Hungarian, German
religion mainly Romanian Orthodox
currency leu
GDP (US $) 30 billion (1994)
growth rate 3.5% (1994)
exports petroleum products and oilfield equipment, electrical goods, cars, cereals, equipment for chemical factories, ships

HISTORY

106 Formed the heartland of the ancient region of Dacia, which was conquered by Roman Emperor Trajan and became a province of the Roman Empire; Christianity introduced.
275 Taken from Rome by invading Goths.
4th–10th Cs Invaded by successive waves of Huns, Avars, Bulgars, Magyars, and Mongols.
c. 1000 Transylvania, in the N, became an autonomous province under the Hungarian crown.
late 13th–early 14th Cs Two Romanian principalities emerged, Wallachia in the S, around Bucharest (1290), and Moldova in the NE.
15th–16th Cs The formerly autonomous principalities of Wallachia, Moldova, and Transylvania became tributaries to the Ottoman Turks, despite peasant uprisings and resistance from Vlad Tepes ('the Impaler'), the ruling prince of Wallachia.
late 17th C Transylvania conquered by the Austrian Habsburgs.
1829 Wallachia and Moldova brought under tsarist Russian suzerainty.
1859 Under Prince Alexandru Ion Cuza, Moldova and Wallachia united to form a Romanian state.
1878 Romania's independence recognized by the Great Powers in the Congress of Berlin.
1881 Became a kingdom under Carol I.
1916–18 Fought on the Triple Entente side (Britain, France, and Russia) during World War I; acquired Transylvania and Bukovina, in the N, from the dismembered Austro-Hungarian Empire, and Bessarabia, in the E, from Russia.
1930 To counter fascist and antisemitic 'Iron Guard' mass movement, King Carol II abolished democratic institutions and established a dictatorship.
1940 Forced to surrender Bessarabia and N Bukovina, to the Soviet Union, and N Transylvania to Hungary; King Carol II abdicated, handing over effective power to General Ion Antonescu, who signed the Axis Pact with Germany.
1941–44 Fought on Germany's side against the Soviet Union; thousands of Jews massacred.
1944 Antonescu ousted; Romania joined the war against Germany.
1945 Occupied by Soviet Union; communist-dominated government installed.
1947 Paris Peace Treaty reclaimed Transylvania for Romania, but lost S Dobruja to Bulgaria and N Bukovina and Bessarabia to Soviet Union; King Michael, son of Carol II, abdicated and People's Republic proclaimed.
1948–49 New Soviet-style constitution; joined Comecon; nationalization and agricultural collectivization.
1955 Romania joined Warsaw Pact.
1958 Soviet occupation forces removed.
1965 Nicolae Ceauşescu replaced Gheorghe Gheorghiu-Dej as Romanian Communist Party leader, and pursued a foreign policy autonomous of Moscow, refusing to participate in Warsaw Pact manoeuvres.
1975 Ceauşescu made president.
1985–86 Winters of austerity and power cuts as Ceauşescu refused to liberalize the economy.
1987 Workers' demonstrations against austerity programme brutally crushed at Braşov.
1988–89 Relations with Hungary deteriorated over 'systematization programme', designed to forcibly resettle ethnic Hungarians in Transylvania.
1989 Bloody overthrow of Ceauşescu regime in 'Christmas Revolution'; Ceauşescu and wife tried and executed; estimated 10,000 dead in civil war. Power assumed by NSF, headed by Ion Iliescu.
1990 Securitate secret police replaced by new Romanian Intelligence Service; Eastern Orthodox Church and private farming re-legalized; systematization programme abandoned.
1991 Privatization law passed. Prime minister Petre Roman resigned following riots by striking miners; succeeded by Theodor Stolojan heading a new cross-party coalition government.
1992 NSF split; Iliescu re-elected president; Nicolai Vacaroiu appointed prime minister of minority coalition government.
1994 Military cooperation pact with Bulgaria. Far-right parties brought into governing coalition.
1996 Signs of economic growth; coalition government formed; Emil Constantinescu elected president; Victor Ciorbea appointed prime minister.
1997 Economic 'shock therapy' reform programme and drive against corruption. Sharp increase in inflation. Former King Michael returned from exile.
1998 Social Democrats withdrew support from ruling coalition. Ciorbea resigned as prime minister after budget blocked by Social Democrats. Radu Vaseil, of CD–PNC, became prime minister and Social Democrats resumed support of ruling coalition.

SEE ALSO: Ceauşescu, Nicolae; Moldavia; Ottoman Empire

Gothic; a love of the primitive, including folk traditions; cult of the hero figure, often an artist or political revolutionary; romantic passion; mysticism; and a fascination with death.

In literature, Romanticism is represented by Novalis, Clemens Brentano, Joseph Eichendorff, and Johann Tieck in Germany, who built on the work of the ◊*Sturm und Drang* movement; William Wordsworth, Samuel Taylor Coleridge, Percy Bysshe Shelley, Byron, and Walter Scott in Britain; and Victor Hugo, Alfonse de Lamartine, George Sand, and Alexandre Dumas *père* in France. The work of the US writers Edgar Allan Poe, Herman Melville, Henry Wadsworth Longfellow, and Walt Whitman reflects the influence of Romanticism.

In art, Caspar David Friedrich in Germany and J M W Turner in England are outstanding landscape painters of the Romantic tradition, while Henry Fuseli and William Blake represent a mystical and fantastic trend. The French painter Eugène Delacroix is often cited as the quintessential Romantic artist.

Romanticism in music, a preoccupation with subjective emotion expressed primarily through melody, a use of folk idioms, and a cult of the musician as visionary artist and hero (virtuoso). Often linked with nationalistic feelings, the Romantic movement reached its height in the late 19th century, as in the works of Robert Schumann and Richard Wagner.

The reaction against 18th-century Classical values first appears as imagery of untamed natural forces, in the hero figure of Mozart's opera *Don Giovanni* 1787 and Haydn's *Sturm und Drang* realization of *The Creation* 1797–98. The essentially private emotional world of Franz Schubert's and Schumann's lieder (songs) was rapidly transformed into the national mythic heroism of Richard Wagner and Giuseppe Verdi, experienced in the flesh in such virtuoso figures as Niccolò Paganini and Franz Liszt. Towards the end of the 19th century, however, the heroic ideal was increasingly challenged by intimations of fallibility, as in the antihero of Mussorgsky's opera *Boris Godunov* 1874, and by the cheerful cynicism of Richard Strauss's *Till Eulenspiegel* 1894–95. In the work of Gustav Mahler and Jean Sibelius, Romanticism became expansive and elegiac, finally petering out in the fragmentary idiom of Hollywood film romance.

Romany a nomadic people, also called *Gypsy* (a corruption of 'Egyptian', since they were erroneously thought to come from Egypt). They are now believed to have originated in NW India, and live throughout the world. The Romany language, spoken in several different dialects, belongs to the Indic branch of the Indo-European family.

Some Romany words correspond with words in Hindustani. All the countries through which the Romany people have passed have added to their word stock, but especially Greek and Slavonic.

Romanies may be descended from non-Muslim metalworkers. In the 14th century they settled in the Balkan peninsula, spread over Germany, Italy, and France, and arrived in England about 1500.

They were sold as slaves in some Balkan regions until the 19th century. During World War II, Nazi Germany tried to exterminate them (along with Jews, Slavs, homosexuals, and political prisoners).

They suffered a long period of persecution, including accusations of cannibalism and child-stealing. They are traditionally associated with music, various crafts, fortune-telling, and skills with horses. Attempts have been made to encourage them to settle, and to provide those still nomadic with official camp sites and educational facilities.

Rome (Italian ***Roma***) capital of Italy and of Lazio region, on the river Tiber, 27 km/17 mi from the Tyrrhenian Sea; population (1992) 2,723,300.

Rome has few industries but it is an important cultural, road, and rail centre. A large section of the population finds employment in government offices. Remains of the ancient city include the Forum, Colosseum, and Pantheon.

features East of the river are the seven hills on which Rome was originally built (Quirinal, Aventine, Caelian, Esquiline, Viminal, Palatine, and Capitol); to the west are the quarter of Trastevere, the residential quarters of the Prati, and the Vatican. Among ancient buildings and monuments are Castel Sant' Angelo (the mausoleum of the emperor Hadrian), the baths of Caracalla, the ◊Colosseum, and the Arch of Constantine. The Appian Way, bordered by ancient tombs, retains long sections of the old paving. Among the Renaissance palaces are the Lateran, Quirinal, Colonna, Borghese (now the Villa Umberto I), Barberini, and Farnese. The many

Romanov dynasty The last tsar of Russia, Nicholas II with his family c. 1914. His abdication in 1917 marked the end of the Romanov dynasty. The tsar and his family were murdered 1918 by Bolsheviks fearful of a successful counter-revolution. *Image Select (UK) Ltd*

churches of different periods include the five greater or patriarchal basilicas: San Giovanni; St Peter's (San Pietro), the largest church in the world, within the Vatican; San Paolo, founded by the emperor Constantine on St Paul's grave; Santa Maria Maggiore, with the city's highest campanile; and San Lorenzo. The Vatican Palace, which adjoins St Peter's, is the residence of the pope. Other ancient churches of interest are San Pietro in Vincoli (which houses the chains that fettered St Peter), Santa Maria in Cosmedin (built before the 6th century on the remains of a pagan temple), and the Pantheon (also built on pagan edifices).

history (For early history see ◊Rome, ancient.) After the deposition of the last emperor, Romulus Augustulus, 476, the papacy became the real ruler of Rome and from the 8th century was recognized as such. The Sack of Rome (1527) led to an era of rebuilding, and most of the great palaces and churches were built in the 16th and 17th centuries. As a result of the French Revolution, Rome temporarily became a republic 1798–99, and was annexed to the French Empire 1808–14, until the pope returned on Napoleon's fall. During the 1848–49 revolution, a republic was established under Giuseppe Mazzini's leadership, but, in spite of Giuseppe Garibaldi's defence, was overthrown by French troops. In 1870 Rome became the capital of Italy, the pope retiring into the Vatican until 1929 when the Vatican City was recognized as a sovereign state. The occupation of Rome by the Fascists 1922 marked the beginning of Mussolini's rule, but in 1943 Rome was occupied by Germany and then captured by the Allies 1944.

Rome, ancient civilization based in Rome, which lasted for about 800 years. Traditionally founded 753 BC, Rome became a republic 510 BC following the expulsion of the Etruscan king Tarquinius Superbus. From then, its history is one of almost continual expansion until the murder of Julius ◊Caesar and foundation of the empire under ◊Augustus and his successors. At its peak under ◊Trajan, the Roman Empire stretched from Britain to Mesopotamia and the Caspian Sea. A long train of emperors ruling by virtue of military, rather than civil, power marked the beginning of Rome's long decline; under ◊Diocletian the empire was divided into two parts – East and West – although temporarily reunited under ◊Constantine, the first emperor formally to adopt Christianity. The end of the Roman Empire is generally dated by the deposition of the last emperor in the west AD 476. The Eastern Empire continued until 1453 at ◊Constantinople.

The civilization of ancient Rome occupied first the Italian peninsula, then most of Europe, the Middle East, and North Africa. It influenced the whole of western Europe throughout the Middle Ages, the Renaissance, and beyond, in the fields of art and architecture, literature, law, and engineering, and through continued use by scholars of its language, ◊Latin. *See map and table on p. 920.*

❛No one can make you feel inferior without your consent.❜

Eleanor Roosevelt *Catholic Digest*

Rome–Berlin Axis another name for the ◊Axis alliance 1936–40 in World War II.

Rome, Sack of invasion and capture of the city of Rome AD 410 by the Goths, marking the effective end of the Roman Empire.

Rome, Treaties of two international agreements signed 25 March 1957 by Belgium, France, West Germany, Italy, Luxembourg, and the Netherlands, which established the European Economic Community (now ◊European Union) and the European Atomic Energy Commission (EURATOM).

Rommel Erwin Johannes Eugen 1891–1944. German field marshal. He served in World War I, and in World War II he played an important part in the invasions of central Europe and France. He was commander of the N African offensive from 1941 (when he was nicknamed 'Desert Fox') until defeated in the Battles of El ◊Alamein and he was expelled from Africa March 1943. Rommel was commander in chief for a short time against the Allies in Europe 1944 but (as a sympathizer with the ◊Stauffenberg plot against Hitler) was forced to commit suicide.

Romney George 1734–1802. English painter. Active in London from 1762, he became, with Thomas Gainsborough and Joshua Reynolds, one of the most successful portrait painters of the late 18th century. He painted several portraits of Lady Hamilton, Admiral Nelson's mistress.

His best work is to be found in the straightforward realism of *The Beaumont Family* (National Gallery, London) or the simple charm of *The Parson's Daughter* (Tate Gallery, London). His attempts to depict his subjects as mythological or allegorical figures such as 'Truth' or 'Beauty' – a genre in which Reynolds excelled – are generally thought less successful.

Romulus in Roman legend, founder and first king of Rome, the son of Mars and Rhea Silvia, daughter of Numitor, King of Alba Longa. Romulus and his twin brother Remus were thrown into the Tiber by their great-uncle Amulius, who had deposed Numitor, but were suckled by a she-wolf and rescued by a shepherd. On reaching adulthood they killed Amulius and founded Rome. Having murdered Remus, Romulus reigned alone until he disappeared in a storm; he was thereafter worshipped as a god under the name of Quirinus.

Romulus Augustulus c. AD 461–000. Last Roman emperor in the West. He was made emperor by his father the patrician Orestes about 475 but was compelled to abdicate 476 by Odoacer, leader of the barbarian mercenaries, who nicknamed him Augustulus (meaning 'Little Augustus'), because of his youth. Orestes was executed and Romulus Augustulus was sent to live on a pension in Campania. The date of his death is unknown.

Ronaldo Luiz de Nazario de Lima 1976 – . Brazilian footballer who was voted FIFA World Player of the Year in 1996 and 1997. A prolific goalscorer, he has twice been transferred for world record fees, moving from PSV Eindhoven to Barcelona for $13.25 million in 1996 , then a year later to Inter Milan for an estimated $18 million.

rondo or ***rondeau*** antique musical form in which verses alternate with a refrain. Often festive in character, it is a popular final movement of a sonata, concerto, or symphony.

Rondônia state in NW Brazil; the centre of Amazonian tin and gold mining and of experiments in agricultural colonization; area 243,044 sq km/93,876 sq mi; population (1991) 1,132,700. The state is mainly rainforest. Its principal products are rubber and brazil nuts. Known as the Federal Territory of Guaporé until 1956, it became a state 1981.

Ronsard Pierre de 1524–1585. French poet. He was the leader of the ◊*Pléiade* group of poets. Under the patronage of Charles IX, he published original verse in a lightly sensitive style, including odes and love sonnets, such as *Odes* 1550, *Les Amours/Lovers* 1552–53, and the 'Marie' cycle, *Continuation des amours/Lovers Continued* 1555–56.

röntgen alternative spelling for ◊roentgen, unit of X- and gamma-ray exposure.

Röntgen Wilhelm Konrad, (or ***Roentgen***) 1845–1923. German physicist. He discovered ◊X-rays 1895. While investigating the passage of electricity through gases, he noticed the ◊fluorescence of a barium platinocyanide screen. This radiation passed through some substances opaque to light, and affected photographic plates. Developments from this discovery revolutionized medical diagnosis. Nobel prize 1901.

rood alternative name for the cross of Christ, often applied to the large crucifix placed on a beam or screen at the entrance to the chancel of a church.

rook gregarious European ◊crow *Corvus frugilegus*. The plumage is black and lustrous and the face bare; the legs, toes, and claws are also black. A rook can grow to 45 cm/18 in long. Rooks nest in colonies (rookeries) at the tops of trees. They feed mainly on invertebrates found just below the soil surface. The last 5 mm/0.2 in of beak tip is mostly cartilage containing lots of nerve endings to enable the rook to feel for hidden food.

Roosevelt (Anna) Eleanor 1884–1962. US social worker, lecturer, and First Lady. Her newspaper column 'My Day', started 1935, was widely syndicated. She influenced ◊New Deal policies,

Röntgen German physicist Wilhelm Röntgen. Röntgen won the Nobel Prize for Physics in 1901 following his discovery of X-rays. The roentgen, named after him, is a unit of radiation exposure. *Image Select (UK) Ltd*

Roosevelt Eleanor Roosevelt broadcasts a message to the American people during World War II. An active campaigner on social welfare and humanitarian issues, she wrote many newspaper and magazine articles. Her books include *The Moral Basis of Democracy* 1940 and *The Autobiography of Eleanor Roosevelt* 1961. *Corbis*

especially supporting desegregation. She was a delegate to the UN general assembly and chair of the UN commission on human rights 1946–51, and helped to draw up the Declaration of Human Rights at the UN 1945. She was married to President Franklin D Roosevelt, and was the niece of Theodore ◊Roosevelt.

Roosevelt Franklin D(elano) 1882–1945. 32nd president of the USA 1933–45, a Democrat. He served as governor of New York 1929–33. Becoming president during the Great Depression, he launched the ◊New Deal economic and social reform programme, which made him popular with the people. After the outbreak of World War II he introduced ◊lend-lease for the supply of war materials and services to the Allies and drew up the ◊Atlantic Charter of solidarity. Once the USA had entered the war 1941, he spent much time in meetings with Allied leaders.

Born in Hyde Park, New York, of a wealthy family, Roosevelt was educated in Europe and at Harvard and Columbia universities, and became a lawyer. In 1910 he was elected to the New York state senate. He held the assistant secretaryship of the navy in Wilson's administrations 1913–21, and did much to increase the efficiency of the navy during World War I. He suffered from polio from 1921 but returned to politics, winning the governorship of New York State 1929. When he first became president 1933, Roosevelt inculcated a new spirit of hope. During the first hundred days of his administration, major legislation to facilitate industrial and agricultural recovery was enacted. The 1936 presidential election was won entirely on the record of the New Deal.

In his foreign policy, Roosevelt endeavoured to use his influence to restrain Axis aggression, and to establish 'good neighbour' relations with other countries in the Americas. Soon after the outbreak of war, he launched a vast rearmament programme, introduced conscription, and provided for the supply of armaments to the Allies on a 'cash-and-carry' basis. Roosevelt was eager for the USA to enter the war but was restrained by isolationist forces in Congress. In spite of strong opposition, he broke a long-standing precedent in running for a third term; he was re-elected 1940. The deaths at Pearl Harbor 7 Dec 1941 incited public opinion, and the USA entered the war. From this point on, Roosevelt concerned himself solely with the conduct of the war. He participated in the Washington 1942 and Casablanca 1943 conferences to plan the Mediterranean assault, and the conferences in ◊Quebec, Cairo, and ◊Tehran 1943, and ◊Yalta 1945, at which the final preparations were made for the Allied victory. He was re-elected for a fourth term 1944, but died 1945. *See illustration on following page.*

Roosevelt Theodore 1858–1919. 26th president of the USA 1901–09, a Republican. After serving as governor of New York 1898–1900 he became vice president to ◊McKinley, whom he succeeded as president on McKinley's assassination 1901. He campaigned against the great trusts (associations of enterprises that reduce competition), while carrying on a jingoist foreign policy designed to enforce US supremacy over Latin America.

Roosevelt, born in New York, was elected to the state legislature 1881. He was assistant secretary of the Navy 1897–98, and during the Spanish–American War 1898 commanded a volunteer force of 'rough riders'. At age 42, Roosevelt was the youngest person to become president of the USA. In office he became more liberal. He tackled business monopolies, initiated measures for the conservation of national resources, and introduced the Pure Food and Drug Act. He won the Nobel Peace Prize 1906 for his part in ending the Russo-Japanese war. Alienated after his retirement by the conservatism of his successor Taft, Roosevelt formed the Progressive or 'Bull Moose' Party. As their candidate he unsuccessfully ran for the presidency 1912. During World War I he strongly advocated US intervention.

root the part of a plant that is usually underground, and whose primary functions are anchorage and the absorption of water and dissolved mineral salts. Roots usually grow downwards and towards water (that is, they are positively geotropic and hydrotropic; see ◊tropism). Plants such as epiphytic orchids, which grow above ground, produce aerial roots that absorb moisture from the atmosphere. Others, such as ivy, have climbing roots arising from the stems, which serve to attach the plant to trees and walls.

The absorptive area of roots is greatly increased by the numerous slender root hairs formed near the tips. A calyptra, or root cap, protects the tip of the root from abrasion as it grows through the soil.

Symbiotic associations occur between the roots of certain plants, such as clover, and various bacteria that fix nitrogen from the air (see ◊nitrogen fixation). Other modifications of roots include ◊contractile roots, ◊pneumatophores, ◊taproots, and ◊prop roots.

root in language, the basic element from which a word is derived. The root is a ◊morpheme, a unit that cannot be subdivided. The Latin word *dominus* ('master'), for example, is a root from which many English words are derived, such as 'dominate', 'dominion', and 'domino'.

root crop plant cultivated for its swollen edible root (which may or may not be a true root). Potatoes are the major temperate root crop; the major tropical root crops are cassava, yams, and sweet potatoes. Root crops are second in importance only to cereals as human food. Roots have a high carbohydrate content, but their protein content rarely exceeds 2%. Consequently, communities relying almost exclusively upon roots may suffer from protein deficiency. Food production for a given area from roots is greater than from cereals.

root hair tiny hairlike outgrowth on the surface cells of plant roots that greatly increases the area available for the absorption of water and other materials. It is a delicate structure, which survives for a few days only and does not develop into a root.

New root hairs are continually being formed near the root tip, one of the places where plants show the most active growth to replace the ones that are lost. The majority of land plants have root hairs. The layer of the root's epidermis that produces root hairs is known as the piliferous layer.

root nodule clearly visible swelling that develops in the roots of members of the bean family, the Leguminosae. The cells inside this tumourous growth have been invaded by the bacteria Rhizobium, a soil microbe capable of converting gaseous nitrogen into nitrate. The nodule is therefore an association between a plant and a bacterium, with both partners benefiting. The plant obtains nitrogen compounds while the bacterium obtains nutrition and shelter.

Nitrogen fixation by bacteria is one of the main ways by which the nitrogen in the atmosphere is cycled back into living things. The economic value of the process is so great that research has been carried out into the possibility of stimulating the formation of root nodules in crops such as wheat, which do not normally form an association with rhizobium.

ROME, ANCIENT: TIMELINE

753 BC	According to tradition, Rome was founded.
510	The Etruscan dynasty of the Tarquins was expelled and a republic established, with power concentrated in patrician hands.
450	Publication of the law code contained in the Twelve Tables.
396	Capture of Etruscan Veii, 15 km/9 mi N of Rome.
387	Rome sacked by Gauls.
367	Plebeians gained the right to be consuls (the two chief magistrates, elected annually).
343–290	Sabines to the N, and the Samnites to the SE, were conquered.
338	Cities of Latium formed into a league under Roman control.
280–272	Greek cities in S Italy subdued.
264–241	First Punic War against Carthage, ending in a Roman victory and the annexation of Sicily.
238	Sardinia seized from Carthage.
226–222	Roman conquest of Cisalpine Gaul (Lombardy, Italy). More conflict with Carthage, which was attempting to conquer Spain.
218	Second Punic War. Hannibal crossed the Alps and invaded Italy, winning a series of brilliant victories.
202	Victory of General Scipio Africanus Major over Hannibal at Zama was followed by the surrender of Carthage and relinquishing of its Spanish colonies.
188	Peace of Apamea confined the rule of the Seleucid king Antiochus the Great to Asia.
168	Final defeat of Macedon by Rome.
146	After a revolt, Greece became in effect a Roman province. Carthage was destroyed and its territory annexed.
133	Tiberius Gracchus suggested agrarian reforms and was murdered by the senatorial party. Roman province of Asia formed from the kingdom of Pergamum, bequeathed to Rome by the Attalid dynasty.
123	Tiberius' policy adopted by his brother Gaius Gracchus, who was likewise murdered.
91–88	Social War: revolt by the Italian cities forced Rome to grant citizenship to all Italians.
87	While Sulla was repelling an invasion of Greece by King Mithridates of Pontus (in Asia Minor), Marius seized power.
82–79	Sulla returned and established a dictatorship ruled by terror.
70	Sulla's constitutional changes were reversed by Pompey and Crassus.
66–63	Pompey defeated Mithridates and annexed Syria.
60	The First Triumvirate was formed, an alliance between Pompey and the democratic leaders Crassus and Caesar.
51	Caesar conquered Gaul as far as the Rhine.
49	Caesar crossed the Rubicon, returned to Italy, and a civil war between him and Pompey's senatorial party began.
48	Pompey defeated at Pharsalus.
44	Caesar's dictatorship ended by his assassination.
43	Second Triumvirate formed by Octavian, Mark Antony, and Lepidus.
32	War between Octavian and Mark Antony.
31	Mark Antony defeated at Actium.
30	Egypt was annexed after the deaths of Mark Antony and Cleopatra.
27	Octavian took the name Augustus. He was by now absolute ruler, though in title he was only 'princeps' (first citizen).
AD 14	Augustus died. Tiberius proclaimed as his successor.
43	Claudius added Britain to the empire.
70	Jerusalem sacked by Titus.
96–180	The empire enjoyed a golden age under the Flavian and Antonine emperors Nerva, Trajan, Hadrian, Antoninus Pius, and Marcus Aurelius Antoninus.
115	Trajan conquered Parthia, achieving the peak of Roman territorial expansion.
180	Marcus Aurelius died, and a century of war and disorder followed, with a succession of generals being put on the throne by their armies.
212	Caracalla granted citizenship to the communities of the empire.
284–305	Diocletian reorganized the empire, dividing power between himself and three others (the Tetrarchy).
313	Constantine the Great recognized the Christians' right to freedom of worship by the Edict of Milan.
330	Constantine made Constantinople his new imperial capital.
395	The empire divided into eastern and western parts.
410	Visigoths sacked Rome. Roman legions withdrew from Britain.
451–52	Huns raided Gaul and Italy.
455	Vandals sacked Rome.
476	Last Western emperor, Romulus Augustulus, deposed.

Roosevelt The US president Franklin D Roosevelt 1936. Roosevelt, a Democrat, became the 32nd president of the USA 1933. His presidency saw the Great Depression, the launch of the New Deal, and World War II. *Image Select (UK) Ltd*

'It is beginning to be hinted that we are a nation of amateurs.'

ARCHIBALD ROSEBERY
Address 1900

ROSAT A cloud of hot gas in a small galaxy group photographed in the visible range of the spectrum by the ROSAT satellite. Three galaxies can be seen which together are known as the NGC2300 group. *Image Select (UK) Ltd*

rootstock another name for ◊rhizome, an underground plant organ.

rope stout cordage with circumference over 2.5 cm/1 in. Rope is made similarly to thread or twine, by twisting yarns together to form strands, which are then in turn twisted around one another in the direction opposite to that of the yarns. Although ◊hemp is still used to make rope, nylon is increasingly used.

rorqual any of a family (Balaenopteridae) of baleen ◊whales, especially the genus *Balaenoptera*, which includes the blue whale *B. musculus*, the largest of all animals, measuring 30 m/100 ft and more. The common rorqual or fin whale *B. physalus* is slate-coloured and not quite so long. Rorquals are long-bodied with pleated throats.

Rorschach test in psychology, a method of diagnosis involving the use of inkblot patterns that subjects are asked to interpret, to help indicate personality type, degree of intelligence, and emotional stability. It was invented by the Swiss psychiatrist Hermann Rorschach (1884–1922).

rosary string of beads used in a number of religions, including Buddhism, Christianity, and Islam. The term also refers to a form of prayer used by Catholics, consisting of 150 Ave Marias (prayers to the Virgin Mary) and 15 Paternosters (the Lord's Prayer) and Glorias, or to a string of 165 beads for keeping count of these prayers; it is linked with the adoration of the Virgin Mary.

Rosas Juan Manuel de 1793–1877. Argentine soldier, gaucho (cowboy), and dictator 1835–52. Rosas used his private gaucho army to overthrow the Liberal regime of Bernardino ◊Rivadavia 1827. A Buenos Aires Federalist, he was governor of that city 1829–32 and, when he was also dictator of Argentina, presided over a reign of terror. While appealing to the urban masses, he allowed huge land sales at absurdly low prices that benefited the landed aristocracy, including Rosas's wealthy Creole family. A manipulative and ruthless operator against centralists, he created a cult of personality which included his image being displayed on church altars.

ROSAT joint US/German/UK satellite launched 1990 to study cosmic sources of X-rays and extremely short ultraviolet wavelengths, named after Wilhelm Röntgen, the discoverer of X-rays.

Roscommon (originally Ros-Comain, 'wood around a monastery') county of the Republic of Ireland, in the province of Connacht; county town Roscommon; area 2,460 sq km/950 sq mi; population (1991) 51,900. It has rich pastures and is bounded on the east by the river Shannon, with lakes (Gara, Key, Allen) and bogs. There are the remains of a castle put up in the 13th century by English settlers. There is agriculture, especially cattle rearing.

rose any shrub or climber of the genus *Rosa*, family Rosaceae, with prickly stems and fragrant flowers in many different colours. Numerous cultivated forms have been derived from the Eurasian sweetbrier or eglantine *R. rubiginosa* and dogrose *R. canina*. There are many climbing varieties, but the forms more commonly cultivated are bush roses and standards (cultivated roses grafted on to a briar stem).

A Royal National Rose Society ruling 1979, received by the World Federation of Rose Societies, renamed the hybrid tea rose the larger flowered rose, and the floribunda became the cluster-flower rose. Individual names, such as Peace, were unchanged.

Roseau formerly ***Charlotte Town*** capital of ◊Dominica, West Indies, on the SW coast of the island; population (1981) 20,000.

rosebay willowherb common perennial weed. See ◊willowherb.

Rosebery Archibald Philip Primrose, 5th Earl of Rosebery 1847–1929. British Liberal politician. He was foreign secretary 1886 and 1892–94, when he succeeded Gladstone as prime minister, but his government survived less than a year. After 1896 his imperialist views gradually placed him further from the mainstream of the Liberal Party.

rosemary evergreen shrub *Rosemarinus officinalis* of the mint family Labiatae, native to the Mediterranean and W Asia, with small, scented leaves. It is widely cultivated as a culinary herb and for the aromatic oil extracted from the clusters of pale blue or purple flowers.

Rosenberg Alfred 1893–1946. German politician, born in Tallinn, Estonia. He became the chief Nazi ideologist and was minister for eastern occupied territories 1941–44. He was tried at ◊Nuremberg 1946 as a war criminal and hanged.

Rosenberg Julius (1918–1953) and Ethel Greenglass (1915–1953). US married couple, convicted of being leaders of a nuclear-espionage ring passing information from Ethel's brother via courier to the USSR. The Rosenbergs were executed after much public controversy and demonstration. They were the only Americans executed for espionage during peacetime.

Roses, Wars of the civil wars in England 1455–85 between the houses of ◊Lancaster (badge, red rose) and ◊York (badge, white rose), both of whom claimed the throne through descent from the sons of Edward III. As a result of ◊Henry VI's lapse into insanity 1453, Richard, Duke of York, was installed as protector of the realm. Upon his recovery, Henry forced York to take up arms in self-defence.

1455 Opened with battle of St Albans 22 May, a Yorkist victory.

1459–61 War renewed. Richard, Duke of York, killed 1460, but his son ◊Edward IV, having been proclaimed king, confirmed his position by a victory at Towton 29 March 1461.

1470 ◊Warwick (who had helped Edward to the throne) allied instead with Henry VI's queen, ◊Margaret of Anjou; Henry VI restored to the throne.

1471 Edward returned, defeated Warwick at Barnet 14 April and Margaret at Tewkesbury 4 May, her son killed, and her forces destroyed. Henry VI was murdered in the Tower of London.

1485 Yorkist regime ended with the defeat of ◊Richard III by the future ◊Henry VII at ◊Bosworth 22 Aug.

rosemary Rosemary is a bushy perennial shrub, often growing to a height of over 180 cm/6 ft. It has evergreen needles, dark green on top and silver underneath. It produces light-blue or purple flowers in early summer.

The name Wars of the Roses was given in the 19th century by novelist Walter Scott.

Rosetta Stone slab of basalt with inscriptions from 197 BC, found near the town of Rosetta, Egypt, 1799. Giving the same text in three versions – Greek, hieroglyphic, and demotic script – it became the key to deciphering other Egyptian inscriptions.

Discovered during the French Revolutionary Wars by one of Napoleon's officers in the town now called Rashid, in the Nile delta, the Rosetta Stone was captured by the British 1801, and placed in the British Museum 1802. Demotic is a cursive script (for quick writing) derived from Egyptian hieratic, which in turn is a more easily written form of hieroglyphic.

Rosh Hashanah two-day holiday that marks the start of the Jewish New Year (first new Moon after the autumn equinox), traditionally announced by blowing a ram's horn (a shofar).

Rosicrucians group of early 17th-century philosophers who claimed occult powers and employed the terminology of ◊alchemy to expound their mystical doctrines (said to derive from ◊Paracelsus). The name comes from books published 1614 and 1615, attributed to Christian Rosenkreutz ('rosy cross'), most probably a pen name but allegedly a writer living around 1460. Several societies have been founded in Britain and the USA that claim to be their successors, such as the Rosicrucian Fraternity (1614 in Germany, 1861 in the USA).

Ross James Clark 1800–1862. English explorer. He discovered the north magnetic pole 1831. He also went to the Antarctic 1839; Ross Island, Ross Sea, and Ross Dependency are named after him.

Ross Ronald 1857–1932. British physician and bacteriologist, born in India. From 1881 to 1899 he served in the Indian Medical Service, and during 1895–98 identified mosquitoes of the genus *Anopheles* as being responsible for the spread of malaria. Nobel prize 1902.

Ross Dependency all the Antarctic islands and territories between 160° E and 150° W longitude and S of 60° S latitude; it includes Edward VII Land, Ross Sea and its islands, and parts of Victoria Land. It is claimed by New Zealand

area 450,000 sq km/173,700 sq mi

features the Ross Ice Shelf (or Ross Barrier), a permanent layer of ice across the Ross Sea about 425 m/1,400 ft thick

population a few scientific bases with about 250 staff members, 12 of whom are present during winter

history given to New Zealand 1923. It is probable that marine organisms beneath the ice shelf had been undisturbed from the Pleistocene period until drillings were made 1976.

Rossellini Roberto 1906–1977. Italian film director. His World War II trilogy, *Roma città aperta/Rome, Open City* 1945, *Paisà/Paisan* 1946, and *Germania anno zero/Germany Year Zero* 1947, reflects his humanism, and is considered a landmark of European cinema.

He and actress Ingrid ◊Bergman formed a creative partnership which produced *Stromboli* 1949 and seven other films over a six-year period, which were neither critical nor box-office successes. After their divorce, Rossellini returned to form with *General della Rovere* 1959.

Rossetti Christina Georgina 1830–1894. English poet. She was the sister of Dante Gabriel ◊Rossetti and a devout High Anglican (see ◊Oxford movement). Her best-known work is *Goblin Market and Other Poems* 1862; among others are *The Prince's Progress* 1866, *Annus Domini* 1874, and *A Pageant* 1881.

Rossetti Dante Gabriel 1828–1882. English painter and poet. He was a founding member of the ◊Pre-Raphaelite Brotherhood (PRB) 1848. As well as romantic medieval scenes, he produced many idealized portraits of women, including the *Beata Beatrix* 1864. His verse includes 'The Blessed Damozel' 1850. His sister was the poet Christina ◊Rossetti.

He formed the PRB with the painters John Everett Millais and Holman Hunt but developed a broader style and a personal subject matter, related to his poetry. He was a friend of the critic John ◊Ruskin, who helped establish his reputation as a painter, and of William Morris and his wife Jane, who became Rossetti's lover and the subject of much of his work.

Rossini Gioacchino Antonio 1792–1868. Italian composer. His first success was the opera *Tancredi* 1813. In 1816 his opera buffa *Il barbiere di Siviglia/The Barber of Seville* was produced in Rome. During 1815–23 he produced 20 operas, and created (with Donizetti and Bellini) the 19th-century Italian operatic style.

After *Guillaume Tell/William Tell* 1829, Rossini gave up writing opera and his later years were spent in Bologna and Paris. Among the works of this period are the *Stabat Mater* 1842 and the piano music arranged for ballet by Respighi as *La Boutique fantasque/The Fantastic Toyshop* 1919.

Rossini The composer Gioacchino Rossini (1792–1868) in a cartoon by André Gill (1867). Most famous for the filigree of his comic operas, Rossini retired as a composer for the stage at the age of 37, *Guillaume Tell* being his last and one of his most successful operas. *Image Select (UK) Ltd*

Rosslare port in County Wexford, Republic of Ireland, 15 km/9 mi SE of Wexford; population (1986) 700. It was founded by the English 1210 and has been the Irish terminus of the ferry route from Fishguard from 1906.

Rostand Edmond 1868–1918. French poetic dramatist. He wrote *Cyrano de Bergerac* 1898 and *L'Aiglon* 1900 (based on the life of Napoleon III), in which Sarah Bernhardt played the leading role.

Rostock industrial port (electronics, fish processing, ship repair) in the *Land* of Mecklenburg–West

Roth A leading Jewish-American novelist, Philip Roth became established in the 1960s for his humorous yet biting portrayals of middle-class America. He is particularly known for his frank treatment of sexual relationships, as in *Portnoy's Complaint* 1969. *Topham*

Pomerania, Germany, on the river Warnow 13 km/8 mi S of the Baltic; population (1993) 239,700.

Founded 1189, in the 14th century Rostock became a powerful member of the ◊Hanseatic League. It was rebuilt in the 1950s and was capital of an East German district of the same name 1952–90.

Rostov-on-Don industrial port (shipbuilding, tobacco, cars, locomotives, textiles) in the SW Russian Federation, capital of Rostov region, on the river Don, 23 km/14 mi E of the Sea of Azov; population (1994) 1,023,000. Rostov dates from 1761 and is linked by river and canal with Volgograd on the river Volga.

Rostropovich Mstislav Leopoldovich 1927– . Russian cellist and conductor. He became an exile 1978 because of his sympathies with political dissidents. Prokofiev, Shostakovich, Khachaturian, and Britten wrote pieces for him. Since 1977 he has directed the National Symphony Orchestra, Washington, DC.

Roth Henry 1906–1995. US novelist. His first novel *Call it Sleep* 1934 was rediscovered in the 1960s, when it was hailed as a classic of US literature. In the late 1970s he began work on a 6-volume novel under the general title of *Mercy of a Rude Stream*. The first volume, *A Star Shines over Mt Morris Park*, appeared 1994.

Roth Philip Milton 1933– . US novelist. His witty, sharply satirical, and increasingly fantastic novels depict the moral and sexual anxieties of 20th-century Jewish-American life, most notably in *Goodbye Columbus* 1959 and *Portnoy's Complaint* 1969.

Roth's series of semi-autobiographical novels about a writer, Nathan Zuckerman, consist of *The Ghost Writer* 1979, *Zuckerman Unbound* 1981, *The Anatomy Lesson* 1984, and *The Counterlife* 1987. The novel *Operation Shylock: A Confession* 1993 is a fantasy about his fictional double; and his memoir *Patrimony* 1991 concerns his father's death.

Rotherham industrial town (pottery, glass, iron and steel, brassware, machinery, coal) in South Yorkshire, England, on the river Don, NE of Sheffield; population (1991) 251,600.

Rothermere Vere Harold Esmond Harmsworth, 3rd Viscount Rothermere 1925– . British newspaper proprietor. He became chair of Associated Newspapers 1971, controlling the right-wing *Daily Mail* (founded by his great-uncle Lord ◊Northcliffe) and *Mail on Sunday* (launched 1982), the London *Evening Standard*, and a string of regional newspapers.

Rothko Mark. Adopted name of Marcus Rothkovich 1903–1970. Russian-born US painter. He was a leading exponent of ◊Abstract Expressionism and a pioneer, towards the end of his life, of Colour Field painting. Typically, his works are canvases covered in large hazy rectangles of thin paint, the colours subtly modulated, as in *Light Red over Black* (Tate Gallery, London).

Born in Dvinsk, Russia, he went to the USA with his parents 1913. He received his only training at New York City's Art Students League. During the 1930s he painted for the Federal Arts Project and, with Adolph Gottlieb, founded the expressionist group The Ten. During the mid-1940s he painted in a style influenced by Surrealism but by the end of the decade he had evolved his distinctive manner employing flat areas of matt colour spread over large-scale canvases.

Rothschild European family active in the financial world for two centuries. ***Mayer Amschel*** (1744–1812) set up as a moneylender in Frankfurt-am-Main, Germany, and business houses were established throughout Europe by his ten children.

Nathan Meyer (1777–1836) settled in England, and his grandson ***Nathan Meyer*** (1840–1915) was created a baron in 1885. ***Lionel Walter*** (1868–1937) succeeded his father as 2nd Baron Rothschild and was an eminent naturalist. His daughter ***Miriam*** (1908–) is an entomologist, renowned for her studies of fleas. Of the French branch, Baron ***Eric de Rothschild*** (1940–) owns Château Lafite and Baron ***Philippe de Rothschild*** (1902–) owns Château Mouton-Rothschild, both leading red Bordeaux-producing properties in Pauillac, SW France.

rotifer any of the tiny invertebrates, also called 'wheel animalcules', of the phylum Rotifera. Mainly freshwater, some marine, rotifers have a ring of ◊cilia that carries food to the mouth and also provides propulsion. They are the smallest of multicellular animals – few reach 0.05 cm/0.02 in.

Rotorua town with medicinal hot springs and other volcanic activity in North Island, New Zealand, near Lake Rotorua; population (1993) 54,200.

rotten borough English parliamentary constituency, before the Great Reform Act 1832, that returned members to Parliament in spite of having small numbers of electors. Such a borough could easily be manipulated by those with sufficient money or influence.

Rotterdam industrial port in the Rhine-Maas delta of the Netherlands; the biggest oil-refining centre in the world, and one of its foremost ocean cargo ports. Other industries include brewing, distilling, shipbuilding, sugar and petroleum refining, margarine, and tobacco. It is linked by canal 1866–90 with the North Sea; population (1994) 598,500.

Rotterdam dates from the 12th century or earlier, but the centre was destroyed by German air attack 1940, and rebuilt; its notable art collections were saved. The philosopher Erasmus was born here.

Rottweiler breed of dog originally developed in Rottweil, Germany, as a herding and guard dog, and subsequently used as a police dog. Powerfully built, the dog is about 63–66 cm/25–27 in high at the shoulder, black with tan markings. It has a short coat and docked tail.

Although popular as a family pet in many countries, its natural guarding instincts and powerful bite have placed it at the centre of the debate concerning the regulation of dangerous dogs (see ◊dog, dangerous). However, the breed is not subject to the same legal restrictions as the ◊pit bull terrier.

Rouault Georges Henri 1871–1958. French painter, etcher, illustrator, and designer. He was one of the major religious artists of the 20th century. Early in his career he was associated with the ◊Fauves, but created his own highly distinctive style using rich, dark colours and heavy outlines.

His subjects include clowns, prostitutes, lawyers, and religious figures, as in *Christ Mocked* 1932 (Museum of Modern Art, New York).

He met ◊Matisse at the Ecole des Beaux-Arts and exhibited with him and the Fauves 1905, though he had more affinity with the German Expressionists than with his French contemporaries. His works convey both an acute awareness of suffering in the world and a deep religious belief: compassion in his depictions of clowns and prostitutes gives way to harsh social comment in his pictures of lawyers and judges, as in *Les Noces* (Tate Gallery, London).

Roubiliac Louis François, (or ***Roubillac***) c. 1705–1762. French sculptor. A Huguenot, he fled religious persecution to settle in England 1732. He

'When I am dead, my dearest, / Sing no sad songs for me.'

CHRISTINA ROSSETTI
Song

'I have been here before, / But when or how I cannot tell: / I know the grass beyond the door, / The sweet keen smell, / The sighing sound, the lights around the shore.'

DANTE GABRIEL ROSSETTI
'Sudden Light'

Laws are always useful to those who have possessions, and harmful to those who have nothing.

JEAN-JACQUES ROUSSEAU
The Social Contract

became a leading sculptor of the day, creating a statue of German composer Georg Handel for Vauxhall Gardens, London, 1737.

He also produced lively statues of historic figures, such as Newton, and an outstanding funerary monument, the *Tomb of Lady Elizabeth Nightingale* 1761.

Rouen industrial port (cotton textiles, electronics, distilling, oil refining) on the river Seine, in Seine-Maritime *département*, central N France; population (1990) 105,500.
history Rouen was the capital of ◊Normandy from 912. Lost by King ◊John 1204, it returned briefly to English possession 1419–49; Joan of Arc was burned in the square 1431. The novelist Flaubert was born here, and the hospital where his father was chief surgeon is now a Flaubert museum.

roughage alternative term for dietary ◊fibre, material of plant origin that cannot be digested by enzymes normally present in the human ◊gut.

roulette game of chance in which the players bet on a ball landing in the correct segment (numbered 0–36 and alternately coloured red and black) on a rotating wheel.

Bets can be made on a single number, double numbers, 3, 4, 6, 8, 12, or 24 numbers. Naturally the odds are reduced the more numbers are selected. Bets can also be made on the number being odd or even, between 1 and 18 or 19 and 36, or being red or black; the odds are even in each of those cases. The advantage is with the banker, however, because the 0 (zero) gives all stakes to the bank unless a player bets on 0. The play is under the control of a croupier.

rounders bat-and-ball game similar to ◊baseball but played on a much smaller pitch. The first reference to rounders was in 1744.

Roundhead member of the Parliamentary party during the English ◊Civil War 1640–60, opposing the royalist Cavaliers. The term referred to the short hair then worn only by men of the lower classes.

roup contagious respiratory disease of poultry and game birds. It is characterized by swelling of the head and purulent catarrh.

Rousseau Henri Julien Félix, 'Le Douanier' 1844–1910. French painter. A self-taught naive artist, he painted scenes of the Parisian suburbs, portraits, and exotic scenes with painstaking detail, as in *Tropical Storm with a Tiger* 1891 (National Gallery, London). He was much admired by artists such as Gauguin and Picasso, and writers such as the poet Apollinaire.

Rousseau served in the army for some years, then became a toll collector (hence *Le Douanier* 'the customs official'), and finally took up full-time painting 1885. He exhibited at the Salon des Indépendants 1886–1910 and was associated with the group led by Picasso and Apollinaire. His work has been seen as an anticipation of ◊Surrealism. Among his best-known works are *The Sleeping Gypsy* 1897 (Museum of Modern Art, New York), *The Snake Charmer* 1907 (Musée d'Orsay, Paris), and *The Football Players* 1908 (Guggenheim Museum, New York).

Rousseau Jean-Jacques 1712–1778. French social philosopher and writer. His book *Du Contrat social/Social Contract* 1762, emphasizing the rights of the people over those of the government, was a significant influence on the French Revolution. In the novel *Emile* 1762, he outlined a new theory of education.

Rousseau was born in Geneva, Switzerland. *Discourses on the Origins of Inequality* 1754 made his name: he denounced civilized society and postulated the paradox of the superiority of the '◊noble savage'. In *Social Contract* he rejected representative democracy in favour of direct democracy, modelled on the Greek polis and the Swiss canton, and stated that a government could be legitimately overthrown if it failed to express the general will of the people. Rousseau's ideas were widely condemned and he lived in exile in England for a year, helped by Scottish philosopher David Hume until they fell out.

Rousseau was a contributor to the ◊*Encyclopédie*; his *Confessions*, published posthumously 1782, was a frank account of his occasionally immoral life and was a founding work of autobiography.

rowan another name for the European ◊mountain ash tree.

Rowe Nicholas 1674–1718. English dramatist and poet. His dramas include *The Fair Penitent* 1703 and *The Tragedy of Jane Shore* 1714, in which English actress Mrs Siddons played. He edited Shakespeare, and was poet laureate from 1715.

rowing propulsion of a boat by oars, either by one rower with two oars (sculling) or by crews (two, four, or eight persons) with one oar each, often with a coxswain. Major events include the world championship, first held 1962 for men and 1974 for women, and the Boat Race (between England's Oxford and Cambridge universities), first held 1829.

Doggett's Coat and Badge 1715, begun for Thames watermen and also the first English race, still survives. Rowing as a sport began with the English Leander Club 1817, followed by the Castle Garden boat club, USA, 1834.

The Boat Race is rowed by crews from Oxford and Cambridge rowing clubs between Putney and Mortlake on the river Thames. The events of ◊Henley Royal Regatta, another major international event, also take place on the Thames.

Rowlandson Thomas 1757–1827. English painter and illustrator. He was one of the greatest caricaturists of 18th-century England. His fame rests on his humorous, often bawdy, depictions of the vanities and vices of Georgian England. He illustrated many books, including *Tour of Dr Syntax in Search of the Picturesque* 1809.

Rowlatt Bills in India 1919, peacetime extensions of restrictions introduced during World War I to counter the perceived threat of revolution. The planned legislation would inhibit individual rights and allow the Indian administration to arrest and detain people without a warrant. The bills were vigorously opposed by Indian nationalists, and the young Congress Party leader Mahatma ◊Gandhi called for a nationwide campaign for their repeal. Only one of the two bills was enacted, but it was never used and was later repealed.

Rowley William c. 1585–c. 1642. English actor and dramatist. He collaborated with Thomas ◊Middleton on *The Changeling* 1622 and with Thomas ◊Dekker and John ◊Ford on *The Witch of Edmonton* 1621.

Rowling Bill (Wallace Edward) 1927–1995. New Zealand Labour politician, party leader 1969–75, prime minister 1974–75.

Roxburgh former border county of Scotland, included 1975 in Borders Region. Jedburgh was the county town.

Rowntree B(enjamin) Seebohm 1871–1954. English entrepreneur and philanthropist. Much of the money he acquired as chair (1925–41) of the family firm of confectioners, H I Rowntree, he used to fund investigations into social conditions. His writings include *Poverty, A Study of Town Life* 1900. The three Rowntree Trusts, which were founded by his father Joseph Rowntree (1836–1925) in 1904, fund research into housing, social care, and social policy, support projects relating to social justice, and give grants to pressure groups working in these areas.

Royal Academy of Arts (RA) British society founded by George III in London 1768 to encourage painting, sculpture, and architecture; its first president was Joshua ◊Reynolds. It is now housed in Old Burlington House, Piccadilly. There is an annual summer exhibition for contemporary artists, and tuition is provided at the Royal Academy schools.

Royal Air Force (RAF) the ◊air force of Britain. The RAF was formed 1918 by the merger of the Royal Naval Air Service and the Royal Flying Corps.

royal assent in the UK, formal consent given by a British sovereign to the passage of a bill through Parliament, after which it becomes an ◊act of Parliament. The last instance of a royal refusal was the rejection of the Scottish Militia Bill of 1702 by Queen Anne.

Royal Ballet leading British ballet company and school, based at the Royal Opera House, Covent Garden, London. Until 1956 it was known as the Sadler's Wells Ballet. It was founded 1931 by Ninette ◊de Valois, who established her school and company at the Sadler's Wells Theatre. It moved to Covent Garden 1946. Frederick ◊Ashton became principal choreographer 1935, providing the company with its uniquely English ballet style. Leading dancers included Margot Fonteyn, Rudolf Nureyev, Alicia Markova, and Antoinette Sibley.

Royal Botanic Gardens, Kew botanic gardens in Richmond, Surrey, England, popularly known as ◊Kew Gardens.

Royal Canadian Mounted Police (RCMP) Canadian national police force, known as the ◊Mounties.

royal commission in the UK and Canada, a group of people appointed by the government (nominally by the sovereign) to investigate a matter of public concern and make recommendations on any actions to be taken in connection with it, including changes in the law. In cases where agreement on recommendations cannot be reached, a minority report can be submitted by dissenters.

Royal commissions are usually chaired by someone eminent in public life, often someone favourable to the government's position. No royal commissions were set up during the Thatcher administration (1979–90) but the practice was revived by her successor, John Major, who appointed a royal commission to investigate the judicial system 1990.

Royal Doulton British pottery firm. See Henry ◊Doulton.

Rowlandson *The Doctor Dismissing Death* 1788, a print by the English caricaturist Thomas Rowlandson. A prolific illustrator, and one of the finest caricaturists of his age, Rowlandson commented on all aspects of Georgian society. In this print he is being uncharacteristically charitable to doctors, who were a familiar target of 18th-century satire. *Corbis*

Royal Greenwich Observatory the national astronomical observatory of the UK, founded 1675 at Greenwich, SE London, England, to provide navigational information for sailors. After World War II it was moved to Herstmonceux Castle, Sussex; in 1990 it was transferred to Cambridge. It also operates telescopes on La Palma in the Canary Islands, including the 4.2-m/165-in William Herschel Telescope, commissioned 1987.

The observatory was founded by King Charles II. The eminence of its work resulted in Greenwich Time and the Greenwich Meridian being adopted as international standards of reference 1884.

Royal Horticultural Society British society established 1804 for the improvement of horticulture. The annual Chelsea Flower Show, held in the grounds of the Royal Hospital, London, is also a social event, and another flower show is held at Vincent Square, London. There are gardens, orchards, and trial grounds at Wisley, Surrey, and the Lindley Library has one of the world's finest horticultural collections.

royal household personal staff of a sovereign. In Britain the chief officers are the Lord Chamberlain, the Lord Steward, and the Master of the Horse. The other principal members of the royal family also maintain their own households.

Royal Institution of Great Britain organization for the promotion, diffusion, and extension of science and knowledge, founded in London 1799 by the Anglo-American physicist Count Rumford (1753–1814). English chemists Michael ◊Faraday and Humphry ◊Davy were among its directors.

Royal Marines British military force trained for amphibious warfare. See ◊marines.

Royal Opera House Britain's leading opera house, sited at Covent Garden, London.

The original theatre opened 1732, was destroyed by fire 1808 and reopened 1809. It was again destroyed by fire 1856, and the third and present building dates from 1858. It has been the home of the Royal Opera and the Royal Ballet since 1946.

royal prerogative powers, immunities, and privileges recognized in common law as belonging to the crown. Most prerogative acts in the UK are now performed by the government on behalf of the crown. The royal prerogative belongs to the Queen as a person as well as to the institution called the crown, and the award of some honours and dignities remain her personal choice. As by prerogative 'the king can do no wrong', the monarch is immune from prosecution.

Royal Shakespeare Company (RSC) British professional theatre company that performs Shakespearean and other plays. It was founded 1961 from the company at the Shakespeare Memorial Theatre 1932 (now the Royal Shakespeare Theatre) in Stratford-upon-Avon, Warwickshire, England, and produces plays in Stratford and the Barbican Centre in London.

The RSC initially presented mainly Shakespeare at Stratford; these productions were usually transferred to the Aldwych Theatre, London, where the company also performed modern plays and non-Shakespearean classics. In 1982 it moved into a permanent London headquarters at the Barbican. A second large theatre in Stratford, the Swan, opened 1986 with an auditorium similar to theatres of Shakespeare's day.

The first director of the RSC was Peter Hall. In 1968 Trevor Nunn replaced him, and in 1986 Nunn was succeeded by Terry Hands. Adrian Noble became director 1990.

Royal Society oldest and premier scientific society in Britain, originating 1645 and chartered 1662; Robert ◊Boyle, Christopher ◊Wren, and Isaac ◊Newton were prominent early members. Its Scottish equivalent is the Royal Society of Edinburgh 1783.

Royal Society for the Prevention of Cruelty to Animals (RSPCA) British organization formed 1824 to safeguard the welfare and best interests of animals; it promotes legislation, has an inspectorate to secure enforcement of existing laws, and runs clinics.

RSFSR abbreviation for ◊***Russian Soviet Federal Socialist Republic***, a republic of the former Soviet Union.

Rubens *Paris Awards the Golden Apple to Venus* (National Gallery, London), by the Flemish Baroque painter Rubens. Under his sure brushstrokes, Classical legends and allegorical scenes became as real and alive as his contemporary portraits. Rubens's vast output includes religious, mythological, and historical subjects, formal and informal portraits, and landscapes, all treated with masterly confidence and vitality. *Corbis*

RSPCA abbreviation for ◊***Royal Society for the Prevention of Cruelty to Animals***.

Ruanda part of the former Belgian territory of Ruanda-Urundi until it achieved independence as ◊Rwanda, a country in central Africa.

Ruapehu volcano in New Zealand, SW of Lake Taupo; the highest peak in North Island, 2,797 m/9,175 ft.

Rub' al Khali (Arabic 'empty quarter') vast sandy desert in S Saudi Arabia; area 650,000 sq km/250,000 sq mi. The British explorer Bertram Thomas (1892–1950) was the first European to cross it 1930–31.

rubber coagulated latex of a variety of plants, mainly from the New World. Most important is Para rubber, which derives from the tree *Hevea brasiliensis* of the spurge family. It was introduced from Brazil to SE Asia, where most of the world supply is now produced, the chief exporters being Peninsular Malaysia, Indonesia, Sri Lanka, Cambodia, Thailand, Sarawak, and Brunei. At about seven years the tree, which may grow to 20 m/60 ft, is ready for 'tapping'. Small incisions are made in the trunk and the latex drips into collecting cups. In pure form, rubber is white and has the formula $(C_5H_8)_n$.

Other sources of rubber are the Russian dandelion *Taraxacum koksagyz*, which grows in temperate climates and can yield about 45 kg/100 lb of rubber per tonne of roots, and guayule *Parthenium argentatum*, a small shrub of the Compositae family, which grows in SW USA and Mexico.

Early uses of rubber were limited by its tendency to soften on hot days and harden on colder ones, a tendency that was eliminated by Charles Goodyear's invention of ◊vulcanization 1839.

In the 20th century, world production of rubber has increased a hundredfold, and World War II stimulated the production of synthetic rubber to replace the supplies from Malaysian sources overrun by the Japanese. There are an infinite variety of synthetic rubbers adapted to special purposes, but economically foremost is SBR (styrene-butadiene rubber). Cheaper than natural rubber, it is preferable for some purposes; for example, on car tyres, where its higher abrasion-resistance is useful, and it is either blended with natural rubber or used alone for industrial moulding and extrusions, shoe soles, hoses, and latex foam.

rubber plant Asiatic tree *Ficus elastica* of the mulberry family Moraceae, native to Asia and N Africa, producing latex in its stem. It has shiny, leathery, oval leaves, and young specimens are grown as house plants.

Rubbra Edmund 1901–1986. English composer. He studied under German composer Gustav Holst and specialized in contrapuntal writing, as exemplified in his study *Counterpoint* 1960. His compositions include 11 symphonies, chamber music, and songs.

rubella technical term for ◊German measles.

Rubens Peter Paul 1577–1640. Flemish painter. He was one of the greatest figures of the ◊Baroque. Bringing the exuberance of Italian Baroque to N Europe, he created innumerable religious and allegorical paintings for churches and palaces. These show mastery of drama and movement in large compositions, and a love of rich colour and texture. He also painted portraits and, in his last years, landscapes. *The Rape of the Daughters of Leucippus* 1617 (Alte Pinakothek, Munich) is typical.

Rubens's energy was prodigious. In less than 40 years he produced more than 3,000 paintings. He created masterpieces in every genre: religious, for example *The Descent from the Cross* about 1611–14 (Antwerp Cathedral); portraiture, the so-called *Chapeau de pailles* about 1620 (National Gallery, London); peasant life, the *Kermesse* about 1622 (Louvre, Paris); allegory, *War and Peace* about 1629–30 (National Gallery, London); and landscape, the *Château de Steen* about 1635–37 (National Gallery, London).

Rubicon ancient name of the small river flowing into the Adriatic that, under the Roman Republic, marked the boundary between Italy proper and Cisalpine Gaul. When ◊Caesar led his army across it 49 BC, he therefore declared war on the republic; hence to 'cross the Rubicon' means to take an irrevocable step.

The Rubicon is believed to be the present-day Fiumicino, which flows into the Adriatic just north of Rimini.

rubidium (Latin *rubidus* 'red') soft, silver-white, metallic element, symbol Rb, atomic number 37, relative atomic mass 85.47. It is one of the ◊alkali metals, ignites spontaneously in air, and reacts violently with water. It is used in photocells and vacuum-tube filaments. Rubidium was discovered spectroscopically by German physicists Robert Bunsen and Gustav Kirchhoff 1861, and named after the red lines in its spectrum.

Rubik Ernö 1944– . Hungarian architect who invented the Rubik cube, a multicoloured puzzle that can be manipulated and rearranged in only one correct way, but about 43 trillion wrong ones. Intended to help his students understand three-dimensional design, it became a fad that swept around the world.

Rubinstein Artur 1887–1982. Polish-born US pianist. His early encounters with Joseph Joachim and the Belgian violinist, conductor, and composer Eugène Ysaÿe (1858–1931) link his interpretations of Beethoven, Mozart, and Chopin with the virtuoso Romantic tradition. He was also a noted interpreter of de Falla.

He studied in Warsaw and Berlin and for 85 of his 95 years appeared with the world's major symphony orchestras.

'The die is cast.'

Remark attributed to Julius Caesar on crossing the RUBICON

Rublev Andrei, or ***Rublyov*** c. 1360–c. 1430. Russian icon painter. He is considered the greatest exponent of the genre in Russia. Only one documented work of his survives, the *Old Testament Trinity* about 1411 (Tretyakov Gallery, Moscow). This shows a basically Byzantine style, but with a gentler expression.

He was probably the pupil at Moscow of Theophanes the Greek and Daniel Chyorny, with whom he collaborated. The two works which represent his genius are the fragments of a *Last Judgment*, 1408, in the Cathedral of Vladimir, and the Icon of the Holy Trinity (now in the Moscow Museum of History), a work of majestic simplicity and feeling far transcending the conventional icon.

ruby the red transparent gem variety of the mineral ◊corundum Al_2O_3, aluminium oxide. Small amounts of chromium oxide, Cr_2O_3, substituting for aluminium oxide, give ruby its colour. Natural rubies are found mainly in Myanmar (Burma), but rubies can also be produced artificially and such synthetic stones are used in ◊lasers.

rudd freshwater fish *Scardinius erythrophthalmus*, a type of minnow, belonging to the carp family Cypridae, common in lakes and slow rivers of Europe; now introduced in the USA. Brownish green above and silvery below, with red fins and golden eyes, it can reach a length of 45 cm/1.5 ft and a weight of 1 kg/2.2 lb.

Rudolf, Lake former name (to 1979) of Lake ◊Turkana in E Africa.

Rudolph 1858–1889. Crown prince of Austria, the only son of Emperor Franz Joseph. He married Princess Stephanie of Belgium in 1881, and they had one daughter, Elizabeth. In 1889 he and his mistress, Baroness Marie Vetsera, were found shot in his hunting lodge at Mayerling, near Vienna. The official verdict was suicide, although there were rumours that it was perpetrated by Jesuits, Hungarian nobles, or the baroness's husband.

Rudolph I 1218–1291. Holy Roman Emperor from 1273. Originally count of Habsburg, he was the first Habsburg emperor and expanded his dynasty by investing his sons with the duchies of Austria and Styria.

Rudolph II 1552–1612. Holy Roman Emperor from 1576, when he succeeded his father Maximilian II. His policies led to unrest in Hungary and Bohemia, which led to the surrender of Hungary to his brother Matthias 1608 and religious freedom for Bohemia.

rue shrubby perennial herb *Ruta graveolens*, family Rutaceae, native to S Europe and temperate Asia. It bears clusters of yellow flowers. An oil extracted from the strongly scented, blue-green leaves is used in perfumery.

ruff circular pleated or fluted collar of folded lawn or muslin worn by men and women in the 16th and 17th centuries. Before the introduction of starch in the 16th century, wires were used to support the folds.

ruff bird *Philomachus pugnax* of the sandpiper family Scolopacidae. The name is taken from the frill of erectile purple-black feathers developed in the breeding season around the neck of the male. The females (reeves) have no ruff; they lay four spotted green eggs in a nest of coarse grass made amongst reeds or rushes. The ruff is found across N Europe and Asia, and migrates south in winter. It is a casual migrant throughout North America.

Rugby market town and railway junction in Warwickshire, England; population (1991) 61,100. Rugby School 1567 established its reputation under headmaster Thomas ◊Arnold; it was described in Thomas ◊Hughes' semi-autobiographical classic *Tom Brown's Schooldays*. Rugby football originated here. Industries include engineering and cement.

rugby contact sport that originated at Rugby School, England, 1823 when a boy, William Webb Ellis, picked up the ball and ran with it while playing football (now soccer). Rugby is played with an oval ball. It is now played in two forms: Rugby League and Rugby Union.

Rugby League professional form of rugby football founded in England 1895 as the Northern Union when a dispute about pay caused northern clubs to break away from the Rugby Football Union. The game is similar to ◊Rugby Union, but the number of players was reduced from 15 to 13 in 1906, and other rule changes have made the game more open and fast-moving.

Major events include the Challenge Cup final, first held 1897 and since 1929 staged at Wembley Stadium, and the Premiership Trophy.

Rugby Union form of rugby in which there are 15 players on each side. Points are scored by 'tries', scored by 'touching down' the ball beyond the goal line or by kicking goals from penalties. The Rugby Football Union was formed 1871 and has its headquarters in England (Twickenham, Middlesex). Formerly an amateur game, the game's status was revoked Aug 1995 by the International Rugby Football Board, which lifted restrictions on players moving between rugby union and rugby league.

Major events include the World Cup; the International championship, a tournament between England, France, Ireland, Scotland, and Wales; County championship 1889; and Pilkington Cup, formerly the John Player Special Cup, the English club knockout tournament. *See list of tables on p. 1177.*

Ruhr river in Germany; it rises in the Rothaargebirge Mountains and flows west to join the Rhine at Duisburg. The Ruhr Valley (228 km/142 mi), a metropolitan industrial area (petrochemicals, cars, iron and steel at Duisburg and Dortmund), was formerly a coal-mining centre.

Ruisdael Jacob Isaakszoon van, or ***Ruysdael*** c. 1628–1682. Dutch artist. He is widely considered the greatest of the Dutch landscape painters. He painted scenes near his native town of Haarlem and in Germany, his works often concentrating on the dramatic aspects of nature. A notable example of his atmospheric style is *The Jewish Cemetery* about 1660 (Gemäldegalerie, Dresden).

Although he sometimes painted German and Scandinavian scenes, he is primarily an interpreter of typical Dutch landscape: of dunes, coastal gleams, low horizons over which great clouds sweep, and quiet patches of woodland with gnarled and weatherbeaten trees, his dark greens and greys infusing a personal and romantic melancholy. *Landscape with a Castle and Church* about 1668 (National Gallery, London) is typical.

Rum or ***Rhum*** island of the Inner Hebrides, Highland Region, Scotland, area 110 sq km/42 sq mi, a nature reserve from 1957. Askival is 810 m/2,658 ft high.

rum spirit fermented and distilled from sugar cane. Scummings from the sugar pans produce the best rum, molasses the lowest grade. Puerto Rico and Jamaica are the main producing countries.

rumba Latin American ballroom dance; the music for this. Rumba originated in Cuba and its rhythms are the basis of much Afro-Cuban music.

Rumford Benjamin Thompson, Count von Rumford 1753–1814. American-born British physicist and inventor. In 1798, impressed by the seemingly inexhaustible amounts of heat generated in the boring of a cannon, he published his theory that heat is a mode of vibratory motion, not a substance. Rumford devised domestic fireplaces incorporating all the features now considered essential in open fires and chimneys, such as the smoke shelf and damper.

Rumford spied for the British in the American Revolution, and was forced to flee from America to England 1776. He travelled in Europe, and was knighted and created a count of the Holy Roman Empire for services to the elector of Bavaria 1784.

ruminant any even-toed hoofed mammal with a rumen, the 'first stomach' of its complex digestive system. Plant food is stored and fermented before being brought back to the mouth for chewing (chewing the cud) and then is swallowed to the next stomach. Ruminants include cattle, antelopes, goats, deer, and giraffes, all with a four-chambered stomach. Camels are also ruminants, but they have a three-chambered stomach.

rummy card game in which the players score by obtaining cards either of the same denomination or in sequence in the same suit. It probably derives from mah-jongg.

Rump, the English parliament formed between Dec 1648 and Nov 1653 after ◊Pride's purge of the ◊Long Parliament to ensure a majority in favour of trying Charles I. It was dismissed 1653 by Cromwell, who replaced it with the ◊Barebones Parliament.

Reinstated after the Protectorate ended 1659 and the full membership of the Long Parliament was restored 1660, the Rump dissolved itself shortly afterwards and was replaced by the Convention Parliament, which brought about the restoration of the monarchy.

Rum Rebellion military insurrection in Australia 1808 when the governor of New South Wales, William ◊Bligh, was deposed by George Johnston, commander of the New South Wales Corps. This was a culmination of attempts by successive governors to curb the power and economic privileges of the Corps, which rested partly on the officers' trade in liquor. Bligh had particularly clashed with John MacArthur (1767–1834) and had arrested him on a charge of anti-government incitation. Johnston was persuaded to release MacArthur and then imprisoned the governor.

Runcie Robert Alexander Kennedy, Baron Runcie 1921– . English cleric, archbishop of Canterbury 1980–91, the first to be appointed on the suggestion of the Church Crown Appointments Commission (formed 1977) rather than by political consultation. He favoured ecclesiastical remarriage for the divorced and the eventual introduction of the ordination of women.

rugby Boys of Winchester College, England, playing Rugby football, 1866. The game takes its name from Rugby School, England, where it originated in 1823. *Image Select (UK) Ltd*

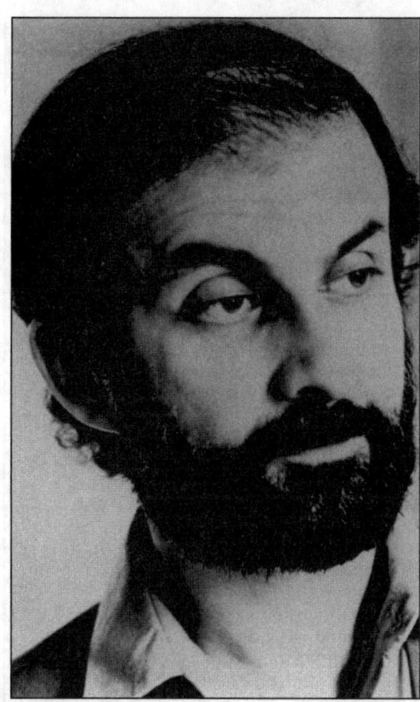

Rushdie Indian-born English writer Salman Rushdie. He was put under sentence of death when his novel *The Satanic Verses*, an imaginative exploration of verses omitted from the Koran, was condemned as blasphemous by the Muslim religious leader Ayatollah Khomeini. The violent response to the book – public demonstrations, the murder of several people associated with its publication – caused Rushdie, in hiding and under close guard, to undertake a profound reappraisal of his beliefs and in 1990 he converted to Islam. *Penguin Books Ltd*

Runcorn industrial town (chemicals) in Cheshire, NW England, 24 km/15 mi up the Mersey estuary from Liverpool; population (1991) 64,200. Designated a new town 1964, it has received Merseyside overspill. There are chemical and brewing industries.

Rundstedt (Karl Rudolf) Gerd von 1875–1953. German field marshal in World War II. Largely responsible for the German breakthrough in France 1940, he was defeated on the Ukrainian front 1941. As commander in chief in France from 1942, he resisted the Allied invasion 1944 and in Dec launched the temporarily successful Ardennes offensive.

rune character in the oldest Germanic script, chiefly adapted from the Latin alphabet, the earliest examples being from the 3rd century, and found in Denmark. Runes were scratched on wood, metal, stone, or bone.

runner or ***stolon*** in botany, aerial stem that produces new plants.

Runnymede meadow on the south bank of the river Thames near Egham, Surrey, England, where on 15 June 1215 King John put his seal to the ◊Magna Carta.

Runyon (Alfred) Damon 1880–1946. US journalist. Primarily a sports reporter, his short stories in 'Guys and Dolls' 1932 deal wryly with the seamier side of New York City life in his own invented jargon.

Rupert Prince, or ***Rupert of the Rhine*** 1619–1682. English Royalist general and admiral, born in Prague, son of the Elector Palatine Frederick V and James I's daughter Elizabeth. Defeated by Cromwell at ◊Marston Moor and ◊Naseby in the Civil War, he commanded a privateering fleet 1649–52, until routed by Admiral Robert Blake, and, returning after the Restoration, was a distinguished admiral in the Dutch Wars. He founded the ◊Hudson's Bay Company. Duke of Cumberland and Earl of Holderness 1644.

rupture in medicine, another name for ◊hernia.

Rusedski Greg(ory) (1973–) Canadian-born British tennis player. A left-hander renowned for his world record-breaking fast serves, who in September 1997 became the first Briton to reach a final of a Grand Slam men's singles tournament since Fred ◊Perry in 1936 when he was runner-up to Patrick Rafter in the US Open and took fourth place in the ATP world rankings, the highest position by a British male since the ranking system was introduced in 1973. He won the Paris Open in Nov 1998.

rush any grasslike plant of the genus *Juncus*, family Juncaceae, found in wet places in cold and temperate regions. The round stems and flexible leaves of some species have been used for making mats and baskets since ancient times.

Rushdie (Ahmed) Salman 1947– . British writer. He was born in India of a Muslim family. His novel *The Satanic Verses* 1988 (the title refers to verses deleted from the Koran) offended many Muslims with alleged blasphemy. In 1989 the Ayatollah Khomeini of Iran called for Rushdie and his publishers to be killed.

Rushdie was born in Bombay and later lived in Pakistan before moving to the UK. His earlier novels in the magic-realist style include *Midnight's Children* 1981, which deals with India from the date of independence and won the Booker Prize, and *Shame* 1983, set in an imaginary parallel of Pakistan. The furore caused by the publication of *The Satanic Verses* led to the withdrawal of British diplomats from Iran. In India and elsewhere, people were killed in demonstrations against the book and Rushdie was forced to go into hiding. *Haroun and the Sea of Stories*, a children's book, was published 1990, and the novel *The Moor's Last Sigh* 1995.

Rusk (David) Dean 1909–1994. US Democrat politician. He was secretary of state to presidents J F Kennedy and L B Johnson 1961–69, and became unpopular through his involvement with the ◊Vietnam War.

Ruskin John 1819–1900. English art and social critic. Much of his finest art criticism appeared in two widely influential works, *Modern Painters* 1843–60 and *The Seven Lamps of Architecture* 1849. He was a keen advocate of painters considered unorthodox at the time, such as J M W ◊Turner and members of the ◊Pre-Raphaelite Brotherhood. His later writings were concerned with social and economic problems.

Ruskin was one of the major figures of 19th-century British intellectual life. Like his contemporaries Thomas ◊Carlyle and Matthew ◊Arnold, he was an outspoken critic of Victorian society, and, like them, called for a renewal of British moral, intellectual, and artistic life. His early works were concerned with architecture and painting: his support both for the Pre-Raphaelite Brotherhood and the ◊Gothic Revival had a profound effect on Victorian art, architecture, and crafts.

Ruskin English art critic and social theorist John Ruskin at his home in the Lake District, about 1885. As the most important English art critic of the 19th century, he was a champion of both the Gothic Revival and Pre-Raphaelitism. As an influential social theorist, he was a relentless critic of 19th-century economic principles. *Corbis*

Russell Bertrand Arthur William, 3rd Earl Russell 1872–1970. British philosopher and mathematician. He contributed to the development of modern mathematical logic and wrote about social issues. His works include *Principia Mathematica* 1910–13 (with A N ◊Whitehead), in which he attempted to show that mathematics could be reduced to a branch of logic; *The Problems of Philosophy* 1912; and *A History of Western Philosophy* 1946. He was an outspoken liberal pacifist. Nobel Prize for Literature 1950.

Russell was born in Monmouthshire, the grandson of Prime Minister John Russell. He studied mathematics and philosophy at Trinity College, Cambridge, where he became a lecturer 1910. His pacifist attitude in World War I lost him the lectureship, and he was imprisoned for six months for an article he wrote in a pacifist journal. His *Introduction to Mathematical Philosophy* 1919 was written in prison. He and his wife ran a progressive school 1927–32. After visits to the USSR and China, he went to the USA 1938 and taught at many universities. In 1940, a US court disqualified him from teaching at City College of New York because of his liberal moral views. He later returned to England and resumed his fellowship at Trinity College.

Among his other works are *Principles of Mathematics* 1903, *Principles of Social Reconstruction* 1917, *Marriage and Morals* 1929, *An Enquiry into Meaning and Truth* 1940, *New Hopes for a Changing World* 1951, and *Autobiography* 1967–69.

Russell George William 1867–1935. Irish poet and essayist. An ardent nationalist, he helped found the Irish national theatre, and his poetry, published under the pseudonym 'AE', includes *Gods of War* 1915 and reflects his interest in mysticism and theosophy.

Russell Ken (Henry Kenneth Alfred) 1927– . English film director. His work, typified by stylistic extravagance, includes *Women in Love* 1969, *The Music Lovers* 1971, *Tommy* 1975, *Lisztomania* 1975, *Altered States* 1979, and *Gothic* 1986. Highly controversial, his work is often criticized for self-indulgence, containing gratuitous sex and violence, but is also regarded for its vitality and imagination. He has made television biographies of the lives of the composers Elgar, Delius, and Richard Strauss.

Russell William, Lord 1639–1683. British Whig politician. Son of the 1st Duke of Bedford, he was among the founders of the Whig Party, and actively supported attempts in Parliament to exclude the Roman Catholic James II from succeeding to the throne. In 1683 he was accused, on dubious evidence, of complicity in the ◊Rye House Plot to murder Charles II, and was executed. He used the courtesy title Lord Russell from 1678.

Russia originally the prerevolutionary Russian Empire (until 1917), now accurately restricted to the ◊Russian Federation.

Russian the majority ethnic group living in Russia. Russians are also often the largest minority in neighbouring republics. The ancestors of the Russians migrated from central Europe between the 6th and 8th centuries AD.

The Russian language is a member of the East Slavonic branch of the Indo-European language family and was the official language of the USSR, with 130–150 million speakers. It is written in the Cyrillic alphabet.

The people of Russia proper have traditionally referred to their language as Great Russian, in contrast with Ukrainian (which they call Little Russian) and the language of Byelorussia (White Russian). Ukrainians have traditionally objected to this usage, arguing that theirs is a distinct language. Even before the 1917 revolution, Russian language and culture was imposed on the country's minorities; this was to some extent reversed in the face of growing nationalist feeling in many of the republics of the USSR, and subsequently in those of the Russian Federation.

Russian art painting and sculpture of Russia, including art from the USSR 1917–91. For centuries Russian art was dominated by an unchanging tradition of church art inherited from Byzantium,

'I always claim the mission workers came out too early to catch any sinners on this part of Broadway. At such an hour the sinners are still in bed resting up from their sinning of the night before, so they will be in good shape for more sinning a little later on.'

Damon Runyon
'The Idyll of Miss Sarah Brown'

'When we build, let us think that we build for ever.'

John Ruskin
The Seven Lamps of Architecture

'A sense of duty is useful in work, but offensive in personal relations. People wish to be liked, not to be endured with patient resignation.'

Bertrand Russell
The Conquest of Happiness

responding slowly and hesitantly to Western influences. Briefly, in the early 20th century, it assumed a leading and influential role in European avant-garde art. However, official Soviet disapproval of this trend resulted in its suppression in favour of art geared to the glorification of workers.

10th–13th centuries Russian art was dominated by the Orthodox Church which drew on the traditions of Byzantine art, producing outstanding icons, carvings, metalwork, and embroidery.

13th–15th centuries The arts declined during the Mongol occupation (mid-13th century to the end of the 14th century) but revived during the 15th century. The development of the iconostasis (a screen, decorated with icons, which separates the altar from the body of the church) created new opportunities for painters. This period saw the rise of the Novgorod School, noted for its rich colours, and the exquisite icons of Ivan Rublev, the most important Russian icon painter.

16th–19th centuries Western styles were gradually absorbed, a process encouraged by Peter the Great and the Academy of Fine Arts in St. Petersburg, founded 1757, but no outstanding artists emerged as a result. The second half of the 19th century is characterised by the Social Realism of Ilya Repin.

early 20th century Towards the end of the 19th century the 'World of Art' movement, which sought to combine 19th-century aestheticism with a return to Russian folk traditions, produced richly coloured, highly detailed works which had a profound effect on book illustration and stage design. In 1899 Benois and Serge Diaghilev founded the review *Mir Iskoustva*, and from this stemmed the brilliant phase of Russian ballet design, in which the names of Benois, Leon Bakst, Nicolas Roerich, and others are eminent.

Several important collections of modern art, including works by Cézanne, Matisse, and Picasso, were built up by Russian merchants and frequent shows of European avant-garde work were organized in the major cities. Consequently, young Russian artists were often better informed concerning recent developments than were their European counterparts. Out of this knowledge grew genuinely Russian art, no longer relying upon Impressionism or Post-Impressionism.

Although working mainly in France and Germany, Marc Chagall took his subjects from Russian life and folklore, his highly personal idiom being far removed from current Russian styles. Wassily Kandinsky, who was to become the first truly abstract artist, left Russia 1896, though Russian folk culture played an important role in his development.

Thus the period 1910–18 shows a constant shifting of groups, all dominated by a desire for entirely abstract, nonrepresentational art. The artist most totally committed to abstract painting was Kasimir Malevich whose *Black Square* 1914 is the ultimate expression of his Suprematism school, which stressed the spiritual values of abstract art. In sculpture Constructivism became a major force, the attempts by Naum Gabo, Pevsner, Rodchenko, El Lizzitsky, and Tatlin to create an abstract sculpture from modern, often industrial, materials having a profound effect on the development of European sculpture. Other artists of the period include Natalya Goncharova and Mikhail Larionov, and the sculptor Archipenko. From 1914 to 1922 Kandinsky was again in Russia, playing a leading role in helping to reform Russian art schools and museums.

art and the Revolution For a brief period following the Revolution, these artists gained control of the art schools, establishing procedures which were greatly to influence the Bauhaus. These ideas travelled from Russia with Lissitzky and Gabo, when the official attitude changed, and the Communist Party decreed a return to Social Realism in art. Some artists rejected painting entirely, Tatlin turning to industrial design and architecture, whilst others, like Lissitzky, produced graphics and posters.

All the revolutionary artists took an active role in theatre, Malevich's most abstract works being first used as scenery for Kruchenikh's *Victory Over the Sun* 1913. After the revolution the 'Agitprop' train toured the country, with artists and actors performing simple plays and broadcasting propaganda. Their dream was an art larger than painting in which the people became active participants. Thus the storming of the Winter Palace was re-enacted three years later at the actual site and involved 6,000 participants. The stage director Vsevolod Meyerhold incorporated these ideas in the theatre itself, and had actors within, around, and above the audience, often dwarfed by huge abstract sets of canvas and wood. These effects culminated in the plays *The Magnanimous Cuckold* and *Tarelkin's Death* (both 1922). As with painting, the theatre was finally forbidden such adventurous approaches, and only in film did the original vitality survive with the works of the directors Vsevolod Pudovkin and also Serge Eisenstein.

Soviet art After the Russian revolution avant-garde art was suppressed by the state and replaced by Socialist Realism. The period 1922–27 was marked by the formation of groups of painters seeking a new style, such as the Association of Russian Revolutionary Artists (ARRA) whose members depicted themes from the revolution. Of these groups the leaders were Katzman, a founder of ARRA, a portrait-painter, and S Karpov. D Kardovski contributed a whole series of illustrations portraying the history of the revolution. The artist Lanser decorated one of the Moscow railway stations with paintings illustrating the work of Soviet construction. Stark realism characterizes the work of Soviet war artists generally. Some of the best examples of this realism are Gaponenko's *Slavholders*, Dormidontov's *Flames over Leningrad*, and Shmarinov's *We Shall Never Forget.*

RUSSIAN REVOLUTION: TIMELINE (WESTERN CALENDAR)

1894	Beginning of the reign of Tsar Nicholas II.
1898	Formation of the Social Democratic Party among industrial workers under the influence of Georgi Plekhanov and Lenin.
1901	Formation of the Socialist Revolutionary Party.
1903	Split in Social Democratic Party at the party's second congress (London Conference) into Bolsheviks and Mensheviks.
1905 Jan	'Bloody Sunday', where repression of workers in St Petersburg led to widespread strikes and the '1905 Revolution'.
Oct	Strikes and the first 'soviet' (local revolutionary council) in St Petersburg. October constitution provided for new parliament (Duma).
Dec	Insurrection of workers in Moscow. Punitive repression by the 'Black Hundreds'.
1914 July	Outbreak of war between Russia and the Central Powers.
1917 March	Outbreak of riots in Petrograd (St Petersburg). Tsar Nicholas abdicated. Provisional government established under Prince Lvov. Power struggles between government and Petrograd soviet.
April	Lenin arrived in Petrograd. He demanded the transfer of power to soviets; an end to the war; the seizure of land by the peasants; control of industry by the workers.
July	Bolsheviks attempted to seize power in Petrograd. Trotsky arrested and Lenin in hiding. Alexandr Kerensky became head of a provisional government.
Sept	Lavr Kornilov coup failed owing to strike by workers. Kerensky's government weakened.
Nov	Bolshevik Revolution. Military revolutionary committee and Red Guards seized government offices and the Winter Palace, arresting all the members of the provisional government. Second All-Russian Congress of Soviets created the Council of People's Commissars as new governmental authority, led by Lenin, with Trotsky as commissar for war and Stalin as commissar for national minorities. Land Decree ordered immediate distribution of land to the peasants. Banks were nationalized and national debt repudiated. Elections to the Constituent Assembly gave large majority to the Socialist Revolutionary Party; Bolsheviks a minority.
1918 Jan	Constituent Assembly met in Petrograd but almost immediately broken up by Red Guards.
March	Treaty of Brest-Litovsk marked the end of the war with the Central Powers but with massive losses of territory.
July	Murder of the tsar and his family.
1918–20	Civil War in Russia between Red Army led by Trotsky and White Russian forces. Red Army ultimately victorious.
6 July 1923	Constitution of USSR adopted.

Russian civil war bitter conflict of nearly three years (1918–21) which followed Russian setbacks in World War I and the upheavals of the 1917 Revolution. In Dec 1917 counterrevolutionary armies, the 'Whites', began to organize resistance to the October Revolution of 1917. The Red Army (Bolsheviks), improvized by Leon Trotsky, opposed them and civil war resulted. Hostilities continued for nearly three years with the Bolsheviks being successful.

The war was fought in the regions of the Caucasus and southern Russia, the Ukraine, the Baltic, northern Russia, and Siberia.

The Bolsheviks also had to fight against the armies of Latvia, Lithuania, Estonia, and Finland. In N Russia the British and French landed troops at Murmansk in June 1918, seized Archangel, and set up a puppet government. They continued outbursts of fighting against the Bolsheviks until Oct 1919. In Siberia, Admiral Kolchak, with the assistance of a Czech legion (composed of prisoners of war) and of Japanese forces that had landed at Vladivostok established a 'White' government at Omsk. Kolchak was captured and executed by the Bolsheviks Feb 1920. While each of the 'White' armies was engaged in an isolated operation, the Soviet forces were waging a single war. Trotsky was an active agent for the Bolsheviks in all the crucial operations of the war. The Bolsheviks put down peasant risings in 1920 and a mutiny by sailors at Kronstadt in 1921. The Bolsheviks were far superior to the Whites in both organization and propaganda. The

RUSSIAN RULERS 1547–1917

Ivan 'the Terrible'	1547–84
Theodore I	1584–98
Irina	1598
Boris Godunov	1598–1605
Theodore II	1605
Dimitri III	1605–06
Basil IV	1606–10
Michael Romanov	1613–45
Alexis	1645–76
Theodore III	1676–82
Peter I 'Peter the Great' and Ivan V (brothers)	1682–96
Peter I, as tsar	1689–1721
Peter I, as emperor	1721–25
Catherine I	1725–27
Peter II	1727–30
Anna Ivanovna	1730–40
Ivan VI	1740–41
Elizabeth	1741–62
Peter III	1762
Catherine II 'Catherine the Great'	1762–96
Paul I	1796–1801
Alexander I	1801–25
Nicholas I	1825–55
Alexander II	1855–81
Alexander III	1881–94
Nicholas II	1894–1917

last foreign forces left Soviet soil in 1922 when the Japanese evacuated Vladivostok. The Soviet government was recognized by Britain in 1924, and by the USA in 1933.

Russian Federation or ***Russia*** country in N Asia and E Europe, bounded N by the Arctic Ocean; E by the Bering Sea and the Sea of Okhotsk; W by Norway, Finland, the Baltic States, Belarus, and Ukraine; and S by China, Mongolia, Georgia, Azerbaijan, and Kazakhstan. *See country box on p. 932.*

Russian literature literary works produced in Russia and later in the USSR. The earliest known works are sermons and chronicles and the unique prose poem 'Tale of the Armament of Igor', belonging to the period in the 11th and 12th centuries when the centre of literary culture was Kiev. By the close of the 14th century leadership had passed to Moscow, which was isolated from developments in the West until the 18th century; notable works of this period are the political letters of Ivan the Terrible and traditional oral folk poems dealing with legendary and historical heroes, which were collected in the 18th and 19th centuries.

In the 19th century poetry reached its greatest heights with Alexander Pushkin and the tempestuously Byronic Mikhail Lermontov, while prose was dominated by Nikolai Gogol.

The golden age of the 19th-century Russian novel produced works by literary giants such as Ivan Turgenev, Ivan Goncharov, Fyodor Dostoevsky, and Leo Tolstoy. In their wake came the morbid Vsevolod Garshin and, in drama, the innovative genius of Anton Chekhov. Maxim Gorky rose above the pervasive pessimism of the 1880s.

Many writers left the country at the time of the Revolution, but in the 1920s two groups emerged: the militantly socialist LEF (Left Front of the Arts) led by the Futurist Vladimir Mayakovsky, and the fellow-travellers of NEP (New Economic Policy) including Boris Pasternak, Alexei Tolstoy, and Ilya Ehrenburg.

More freedom was allowed by the subsequent Realism movement, but during World War II censorship was again severe. In the thaw after Stalin's death Vladimir Dudintsev published his *Not by Bread Alone* 1956 and the journal *Novy Mir* encouraged bolder new writing, but this did not last. Landmark events included the controversy over the award of a Nobel prize to Pasternak. Some writers were imprisoned; others fled the country, including Anatoly Kuznetsov, whose novel *The Fire* 1969 obliquely criticized the regime, and Alexander Solzhenitsyn. The intellectual and cultural thaw under President Gorbachev heralded an era of literary revaluation as well as fresh discoveries of writers from the 1930s onwards. With the collapse of the Soviet Union, previously overshadowed or suspect national literatures in regions such as central Asia began to revive.

Russian Orthodox Church another name for the ◊Orthodox Church.

Russian revolution, 1905 political upheaval centred in and around St Petersburg, Russia 1905–1906, leading up to the February and October revolutions of 1917. On 22 Jan 1905 thousands of striking unarmed workers marched to Tsar Nicholas II's Winter Palace in St Petersburg, to ask for reforms-.Government troops fired on the crowd, killing many people. After this 'Bloody Sunday' slaughter the revolution gained strength, culminating in a general strike which paralysed the whole country in Oct 1905. Revolutionaries in St Petersburg formed a 'soviet' (council) called the Soviet of Workers' Deputies. Nicholas II then granted the Duma (parliament) the power to pass or reject proposed laws. Although these measures satisfied the liberal element, the revolution continued to gain ground and came to a head when the army crushed a serious uprising in Dec 1905.

Russian Revolution two revolutions of Feb and Oct 1917 (Julian ◊calendar) that began with the overthrow of the Romanov dynasty and ended with the establishment of a communist soviet (council) state, the Union of Soviet Socialist Republics (USSR).

The ***February Revolution*** (March by the Western calendar) arose because of food and fuel shortages, the ongoing repressiveness of the tsarist government, and military incompetence in World War I. Riots in Petrograd (as St Petersburg was named 1914–24) led to the abdication of Tsar Nicholas II and the formation of a provisional government under Prince Lvov. Lenin returned to Russia in April as head of the Bolsheviks. Alexandr Kerensky replaced Lvov as head of government in July. During this period, the Bolsheviks gained control of the soviets and advocated land reform and an end to their involvement in World War I.

Russian Revolution Street scene in Moscow during the 1917 Russian Revolution. The Bolsheviks seized power under Lenin after bloody battles such as this one. Shots are being fired from the public library and people are fleeing for their lives. *Corbis*

The ***October Revolution*** was a coup on the night of 25–26 Oct (6–7 Nov Western calendar). Bolshevik workers and sailors seized the government buildings and the Winter Palace, Petrograd. The second All-Russian Congress of Soviets, which met the following day, proclaimed itself the new government of Russia, and Lenin became leader. Bolsheviks soon took control of the cities, established worker control in factories, and nationalized the banks. The ◊Cheka (secret police) was set up to silence the opposition. The government concluded peace with Germany early in 1918 through the Treaty of ◊Brest-Litovsk, but civil war broke out in that year when anti-Bolshevik elements within the army attempted to seize power. The war lasted until 1922, when the Red Army, organized by Leon ◊Trotsky, finally overcame 'White' (tsarist) opposition, but with huge losses, after which communist control was complete.

Russian Soviet Federal Socialist Republic (RSFSR) the largest republic of the former Soviet Union; it became independent as the ◊Russian Federation 1991.

Russo-Japanese War war between Russia and Japan 1904–05, which arose from conflicting ambitions in Korea and ◊Manchuria, specifically, the Russian occupation of Port Arthur (modern Lüshun) 1897 and of the Amur province 1900. Japan successfully besieged Port Arthur May 1904–Jan 1905, took Mukden (modern Shenyang, see ◊Mukden, Battle of) on 29 Feb–10 March, and on 27 May defeated the Russian Baltic fleet, which had sailed halfway around the world to Tsushima Strait. A peace was signed 23 Aug 1905. Russia surrendered its lease on Port Arthur, ceded S Sakhalin to Japan, evacuated Manchuria, and recognized Japan's interests in Korea.

russula any fungus of the genus *Russula*, comprising many species. They are medium to large mushrooms with flattened caps, and many are brightly coloured.

R. emetica is a common species found in damp places under conifers. Up to 9 cm/3.5 in across; the cap is scarlet, fading to cherry, and the gills are white. This toadstool tastes acrid and causes vomiting eaten raw, but some russulas are edible.

rust in botany, common name for the minute parasitic fungi of the order Uredinales, which appear on the leaves of their hosts as orange-red spots, later becoming darker. The commonest is the wheat rust *Puccinia graminis*.

rust reddish-brown oxide of iron formed by the action of moisture and oxygen on the metal. It consists mainly of hydrated iron(III) oxide ($Fe_2O_3.H_2O$ and iron(III) hydroxide ($Fe(OH)_3$).

Rustaveli Shota c. 1172–c. 1216. Georgian poet. He was the author of the Georgian national epic *Vekhis-tqaosani/The Man (or Knight) in the Panther's Skin*, which draws on ancient Greek and Eastern philosophy in the celebration of heroism, courtly love, and comradeship.

Ruth in the Old Testament, ◊Moabite ancestor of David (king of Israel) by her second marriage to Boaz. When her first husband died, she preferred to stay with her mother-in-law Naomi, rather than return to her own people.

Ruth Babe (George Herman) 1895–1948. US baseball player, regarded by many as the greatest of all time. He played in ten ◊World Series and hit 714 home runs, a record that stood from 1935 to 1974 and led to the nickname 'Sultan of Swat'.

Ruth started playing 1914 as a pitcher-outfielder for the Boston Braves before moving to the Boston Red Sox later that year. He joined the New York Yankees 1920 and became one of the best hitters in the game. He hit 60 home runs in the 1927 season (a record beaten 1961 by Roger Maris). He is still the holder of the record for most bases in a season: 457 in 1921.

Ruthenia or ***Carpathian Ukraine*** region of central Europe, on the southern slopes of the Carpathian Mountains, home of the Ruthenes or Russniaks. Dominated by Hungary from the 10th century, it was part of Austria-Hungary until World War I. In 1918 it was divided between Czechoslovakia, Poland, and Romania; independent for a single day in 1938, it was immediately occupied by Hungary, captured by the USSR 1944 and incorporated

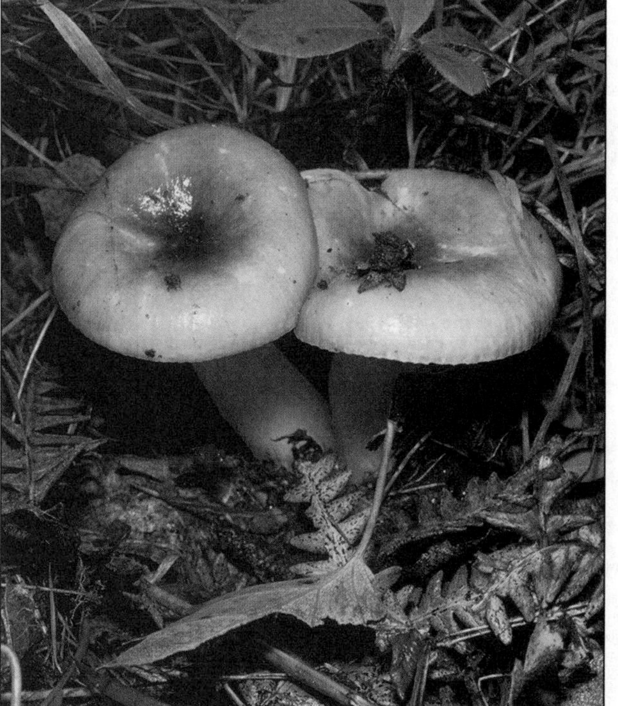

russula Like most members of the genus, the tooth-gilled russula *Russula fragilis* is brightly coloured and appears in autumn. Many species are superficially very similar and taste may play an important role in distinguishing between them. *Premaphotos Wildlife*

RUSSIAN FEDERATION

(formerly to 1991 *Russian Soviet Federal Socialist Republic (RSFSR)*)

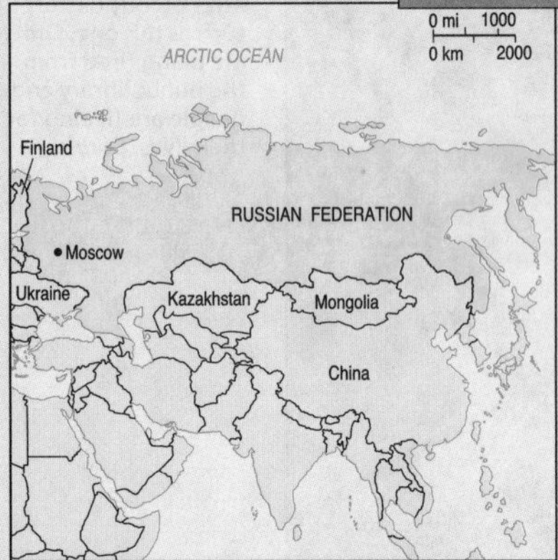

national name *Rossiskaya Federatsiya*
area 17,075,500 sq km/6,591,100 sq mi
capital Moscow
major towns/cities St Petersburg (Leningrad), Nizhni-Novgorod (Gorky), Rostov-on-Don, Samara (Kuibyshev), Tver (Kalinin), Volgograd, Vyatka (Kirov), Ekaterinburg (Sverdlovsk), Novosibirsk, Chelyabinsk, Kazan, Omsk
physical features fertile Black Earth district; extensive forests; the Ural Mountains with large mineral resources; Lake Baikal, world's deepest lake
head of state Boris Yeltsin from 1991
head of government Yevgeny Primakov from Aug 1998
political system emergent democracy
administrative divisions 21 republics, six territories, 49 provinces, 10 autonomous areas, two cities with federal status, and one autonomous region
political parties Russia is Our Home, centrist; Party of Unity and Accord (PRUA), moderate reformist; Communist Party of the Russian Federation (CPRF), left-wing, conservative (ex-communist); Agrarian Party, rural-based, centrist; Liberal Democratic Party, far-right, ultranationalist; Congress of Russian Communities, populist, nationalist; Russia's Choice, reformist, centre-right; Yabloko, gradualist free market; Russian Social Democratic People's Party (Derzhava), communist-nationalist; Patriotic Popular Union of Russia (PPUR), communist-led
armed forces 1,714,000; paramilitary forces of 280,000 (1994)
conscription two years
defence spend (% GDP) 9.6 (1994)
education spend (% GNP) 4.0 (1992)
health spend (% GDP) 2.9 (1992)
death penalty retained and used for ordinary crimes
population 146,861,000 (1998 est)
population growth rate –0.1% (1990–95); –0.2% (2000–05)
age distribution (% of total population) <15 21.1%, 15–65 66.9%, >65 12.1% (1995)
ethnic distribution predominantly ethnic (eastern Slav); significant Tatar, Ukranian, Chuvash, Belarussian, Bashkir, and Chechen minorities
population density (per sq km) 13 (1994)
urban population (% of total) 76 (1995)
labour force 52% of population: 14% agriculture, 42% industry, 45% services (1990)
unemployment 2.4% (1995)
child mortality rate (under 5, per 1,000 live births) 36 (1997)
life expectancy 62 (men), 74 (women)
education (compulsory years) 9
literacy rate 99%
language Russian
religion traditionally Russian Orthodox
TV sets (per 1,000 people) 370 (1992)
currency rouble
GDP (US $) 449.8 billion (1997)
GDP per capita (PPP) (US $) 4,190 (1997)
growth rate –15.0% (1994)
average annual inflation 294% (1994); 35.4% (1980–93)
major trading partners CIS republics, Germany, UK, China, USA, Japan, Italy
resources petroleum, natural gas, coal, peat, copper (world's fourth-largest producer), iron ore, lead, aluminium, phosphate rock, nickel, manganese, gold, diamonds, platinum, zinc, tin
industries cast iron, steel, rolled iron, synthetic fibres, soap, cellulose, paper, cement, machinery and transport equipment, glass, bricks, food processing, confectionery
exports mineral fuels, ferrous and non-ferrous metals and derivatives, precious stones, chemical products, machinery and transport equipment, weapons, timber and paper products. Principal market: Germany 14.7% (1994)
imports machinery and transport equipment, grain and foodstuffs, chemical products, textiles, clothing, footwear, pharmaceuticals, metals. Principal source: Germany 19.2% (1994)
arable land 8% (1993)
agricultural products grain, potatoes, flax, sunflowers, vegetables, fruit and berries, tea; livestock and dairy farming

HISTORY

9th–10th Cs Viking chieftains established own rule in Novgorod, Kiev, and other cities.
10th–12th Cs Kiev temporarily united the Russian peoples into its empire. Christianity introduced from Constantinople 988.
13th C Mongols (Golden Horde) overran the southern steppes 1223, compelling Russian princes to pay tribute.
14th C Byelorussia and Ukraine came under Polish rule.
1462–1505 Ivan the Great, grand duke of Muscovy, threw off Mongol yoke and united lands in NW.
1547–84 Ivan the Terrible assumed title of tsar and conquered Kazan and Astrakhan; colonization of Siberia began.
1613 First Romanov tsar, Michael, elected after period of chaos.
1667 Following a Cossack revolt, E Ukraine was reunited with Russia.
1682–1725 Peter the Great modernized the bureaucracy and army; he founded a navy and a new capital, St Petersburg, introduced Western education, and wrested the Baltic seaboard from Sweden.
1762–96 Catherine the Great annexed the Crimea and part of Poland and recovered W Ukraine and Byelorussia.
1798–1814 Russia intervened in Revolutionary and Napoleonic Wars (1798–1801, 1805–07); repelled Napoleon, and took part in his overthrow (1812–14).
1827–29 Russian attempts to dominate the Balkans led to war with Turkey.
1853–56 Crimean War.
1856–64 Caucasian War of conquest completed annexation of N Caucasus, causing more than a million people to emigrate.
1858–60 Treaties of Aigun 1858 and Peking 1860 imposed on China, annexing territories N of the Amur and E of the Ussuri rivers; Vladivostok founded on Pacific coast.
1861 Serfdom abolished (on terms unfavourable to peasants). Rapid growth of industry followed, a working-class movement developed, and revolutionary ideas spread, culminating in assassination of Alexander II 1881.
1877–78 Russo-Turkish War
1898 Social Democratic Party founded by Russian Marxists; split into Bolshevik and Menshevik factions 1903.
1904–05 Russo-Japanese War caused by Russian expansion in Manchuria.
1905 A revolution, though suppressed, forced the tsar to accept a parliament (Duma) with limited powers.
1914 Russo-Austrian rivalry in the Balkans was a major cause of outbreak of World War I; Russia fought in alliance with France and Britain.
1917 Russian Revolution: tsar abdicated, provisional government established; Bolsheviks seized power under Vladimir Lenin.
1918 Treaty of Brest-Litovsk ended war with Germany; murder of former tsar; Russian Empire collapsed; Finland, Poland, and Baltic States seceded.
1918–22 Civil War between Red Army, led by Leon Trotsky, and White Russian forces with foreign support; Red Army ultimately victorious; control regained over Ukraine, Caucasus, and Central Asia.
1922 Former Russian Empire renamed Union of Soviet Socialist Republics.
1924 Death of Lenin.
1928 Joseph Stalin absolute ruler after ousting Trotsky.
1928–33 First Five-Year Plan collectivized agriculture by force; millions died in famine.
1936–38 The Great Terror: Stalin executed his critics and imprisoned millions of people on false charges of treason and sabotage.
1939 Nazi-Soviet non-aggression pact; USSR invaded eastern Poland and attacked Finland.
1940 USSR annexed Baltic States.
1941–45 'Great Patriotic War' against Germany ended with Soviet domination of eastern Europe and led to 'Cold War' with USA and its allies.
1949 Council for Mutual Economic Assistance (COMECON) created to supervise trade in Soviet bloc.
1953 Stalin died; 'collective leadership' in power.
1955 Warsaw Pact created.
1956 Nikita Khrushchev made 'secret speech' criticizing Stalin; USSR invaded Hungary.
1957–58 Khrushchev ousted his rivals and became effective leader, introducing limited reforms.
1960 Rift between USSR and Communist China.
1962 Cuban missile crisis: Soviet nuclear missiles installed in Cuba; removed after ultimatum from USA.
1964 Khrushchev ousted by new 'collective leadership' headed by Leonid Brezhnev and Alexei Kosygin.
1968 USSR and allies invaded Czechoslovakia.
1970s 'Détente' with USA and western Europe.
1979 USSR invaded Afghanistan; fighting continued until Soviet withdrawal ten years later.
1982 Brezhnev died; Uri Andropov became leader.
1984 Andropov died; Konstantin Chernenko became leader.
1985 Chernenko died; Mikhail Gorbachev became leader and announced wide-ranging reform programme (*perestroika*).
1986 Chernobyl nuclear disaster.
1988 Special All-Union Party Congress approved radical constitutional changes and market reforms; start of open nationalist unrest in Caucasus and Baltic republics.
1989 Multi-candidate elections held in move towards 'socialist democracy'; collapse of Soviet satellite regimes in eastern Europe; end of Cold War.
1990 Anti-communists and nationalists polled strongly in multi-party local elections; Baltic and Caucasian republics defied central government; Boris Yeltsin became president of Russian Federation and left Communist Party.
1991 Unsuccessful coup by hardline communists; republics declared independence; dissolution of communist rule in Russian Federation; USSR replaced by Commonwealth of Independent States (CIS).
1992 Russia assumed former USSR seat on United Nations (UN) Security Council; new constitution devised; end of price controls.
1993 Power struggle between Yeltsin and Congress of People's Deputies; congress dissolved; attempted coup foiled; new parliament elected.
1994 Russia joined NATO 'Partnership for Peace'; Russian forces invaded breakaway republic of Chechnya.
1995 Bloody civil war in Chechnya continued.
1996 Re-election of President Yeltsin. Peace plan and final withdrawal of Russian troops from Chechnya.
1997 Peace treaty with Chechnya signed. Yeltsin agreed to expansion of NATO into central Europe, and signed agreement on cooperation with NATO. Russia gained effective admission to G-7 group. World Bank loan and International Monetary Fund (IMF) credit agreed in return for continuing economic reforms. Convention outlawing production and use of chemical weapons ratified by lower house of parliament. Major shake-up in finance ministry; Yeltsin's millionaire advisor, Boris Berezovsky, dismissed. Chechnya declared an Islamic republic.
1998 New rouble introduced. Yeltsin unexpectedly dismissed government and appointed inexperienced Sergei Kiriyenko prime minister. Interest rates raised to 150% as currency came under attack, but rouble was eventually devalued by 20% in Aug. Kriyenko sacked as prime minister but Duma refused to accept Yeltsin's nomination of Chernomyrdin to return as prime minister. Former communist spy chief, Yevgeny Primakov, became the new prime minister. Yeltsin's health deteriorated.

SEE ALSO: Cold War; Commonwealth of Independent States; Russian Revolution; Union of Soviet Socialist Republics

1945–47 (as the Transcarpathian Region) into Ukraine Republic, which became independent as Ukraine 1991.

ruthenium hard, brittle, silver-white, metallic element, symbol Ru, atomic number 44, relative atomic mass 101.07. It is one of the so-called platinum group of metals; it occurs in platinum ores as a free metal and in the natural alloy osmiridium. It is used as a hardener in alloys and as a catalyst; its compounds are used as colouring agents in glass and ceramics. It was discovered 1827 and named 1828 after its place of discovery, the Ural Mountains in Ruthenia (now part of Ukraine). Pure ruthenium was not isolated until 1845.

Rutherford Ernest, 1st Baron Rutherford of Nelson 1871–1937. New Zealand–born British physicist. He was a pioneer of modern atomic science. His main research was in the field of ◊radioactivity, and he discovered alpha, beta, and gamma rays. He was the first to recognize the nuclear nature of the atom 1911. Nobel prize 1908.

Rutherford produced the first artificial transformation, changing one element to another, 1919, bombarding nitrogen with alpha particles and getting hydrogen and oxygen. After further research he announced that the nucleus of any atom must be composed of hydrogen nuclei; at Rutherford's suggestion, the name 'proton' was given to the hydrogen nucleus 1920. He speculated that uncharged particles (neutrons) must also exist in the nucleus. In 1934, using heavy water, Rutherford and his co-workers bombarded deuterium with deuterons and produced tritium. This may be considered the first ◊nuclear fusion reaction.

Rutherford New Zealand-born physicist Ernest Rutherford. Rutherford described atomic structure. The vast majority of an atom's mass is made up of neutrons and protons which exist in an infinitesimally small nucleus. The nucleus is surrounded by space in which electrons orbit. *Image Select (UK) Ltd*

Rutherford Margaret 1892–1972. English film and theatre actress. She specialized in formidable yet jovially eccentric roles. She played Agatha Christie's Miss Marple in four films in the early 1960s and won an Academy Award for her role in *The VIPs* 1963.

rutherfordium synthesized radioactive element of the ◊transactinide series, symbol Rf, atomic number 106, relative atomic mass 263. It was first synthesized 1974 in the USA and given the temporary name unnilhexium. The discovery was not confirmed until 1993. It was officially named 1994 after New Zealand physicist Ernest ◊Rutherford.

rutile titanium oxide mineral, TiO_2, a naturally occurring ore of titanium. It is usually reddish brown to black, with a very bright (adamantine) surface lustre. It crystallizes in the tetragonal system. Rutile is common in a wide range of igneous and metamorphic rocks and also occurs concentrated in sands; the coastal sands of E and W Australia are a major source. It is also used as a pigment that gives a brilliant white to paint, paper, and plastics.

Rutland unitary authority of England created 1997 *(see United Kingdom map)*. Formerly the smallest English county, it was part of ◊Leicestershire 1974–97.

Rutskoi Aleksander 1947– . Russian politician, vice president of the Russian Federation 1991–93. During the abortive Aug 1991 coup he led the Russian delegation to rescue Soviet leader Mikhail Gorbachev from his forced confinement in the Crimea. In Sept 1993, with Rusian Khasbulatov (1943–), he led the insurrection against Russian president Boris Yeltsin. Both men were arrested and imprisoned but then released 1994 on the instructions of the federal assembly. Shortly after his release, Rutskoi, as leader of the Russian Social Democratic People's Party, professed his support for a reconstituted Soviet Union. In Aug 1996 Rutskoi became a leading member of the communist-led Patriotic Popular Union of Russia. He was elected governor of Kursk in SW Russia Oct 1996.

Ruysdael Jacob vansee ◊Ruisdael, Dutch painter.

Rwanda landlocked country in central Africa, bounded N by Uganda, E by Tanzania, S by Burundi, and W by the Democratic Republic of Congo. *See country box below.*

Ryazan industrial city (agricultural machinery, leather, shoes) dating from the 13th century, capital of Ryazan region, W Russia, on the river Oka SE of Moscow; population (1994) 526,000.

Ryder Albert Pinkham 1847–1917. US painter. He was one of the most original US artists of the 19th century. His romantic landscapes, moonlit seascapes, and depictions of scenes from Shakespeare and Wagner are intense, poetic, and dreamlike. His best-known work, *Death on a Pale Horse* about 1910 (Cleveland Museum of Art), has an eerie, haunted quality.

Ryder Cup golf tournament for professional men's teams from the USA and Europe. It is played

'All science is either physics or stamp collecting.'

Ernest Rutherford
Quoted in J B Birks *Rutherford at Manchester*

RWANDA
Republic of

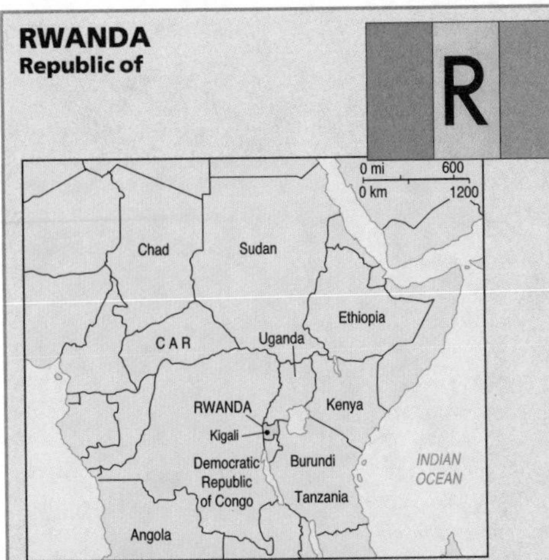

national name *Republika y'u Rwanda*
area 26,338 sq km/10,173 sq mi
capital Kigali
major towns/cities Butare, Ruhengeri, Gisenyi
physical features high savanna and hills, with volcanic mountains in NW; part of lake Kivu; highest peak Mount Karisimbi 4,507 m/14,792 ft; Kagera River (whose headwaters are the source of the Nile)
head of state Pasteur Bizimungu from 1994
head of government Pierre Celestin Rwigema from 1995
political system transitional
administrative divisions 11 prefectures
political parties National Revolutionary Development Movement (MRND), nationalist-socialist, Hutu-oriented; Social Democratic Party (PSD), left of centre; Christian Democratic Party (PDC), Christian, centrist; Republican Democratic Movement (MDR), Hutu nationalist; Liberal Party (PL), moderate centrist; Rwanda Patriotic Front (FPR), Tutsi-led but claims to be multiethnic
population 7,952,000 (1995 est)
population growth rate 2.6% (1990–95); 2.5% (2000–05)
ethnic distribution about 84% belongs to the Hutu tribe, most of the remainder being Tutsis; there are also Twa and Pygmy minorities
life expectancy 49 (men), 52 (women)
literacy rate men 64%, women 37%
languages Kinyarwanda, French (official); Kiswahili
religions Roman Catholic 54%, animist 23%, Protestant 12%, Muslim 9%
currency Rwanda franc
GDP (US $) 1.49 billion (1993)
growth rate −10.0% (1993)
exports coffee, tea, pyrethrum, tin, cotton

HISTORY
10th C onwards Hutu peoples settled in the region formerly inhabited by the hunter-gatherer Twa Pygmies, becoming peasant farmers.
14th C onwards The majority Hutu community came under the dominance of the cattle-owning Tutsi peoples, immigrants from the E, who became a semi-aristocracy and established control through land and cattle contracts.
15th C Ruganzu Bwimba, a Tutsi leader, founded a kingdom near Kigali.
17th C Central Rwanda and outlying Hutu communities subdued by the Tutsi mwami (king) Ruganzu Ndori.
late 19th C Under the great Tutsi king, Kigeri Rwabugiri, a unified state with a centralized military structure was established.
1890 Known as Ruandi, the Tutsi kingdom, along with neighbouring Burundi, came under nominal German control, as Ruanda-Urundi.
1916 Occupied by Belgium, during World War I.
1923 Belgium granted a League of Nations mandate to administer Ruanda-Urundi; they were to rule 'indirectly' through Tutsi chiefs.
1959 Interethnic warfare between Hutu and Tutsi, forcing mwami (king) Kigeri V into exile.
1961 Republic proclaimed after mwami deposed.
1962 Independence from Belgium achieved as Rwanda, with Hutu Grégoire Kayibanda as president; many Tutsis left the country.
1963 20,000 killed in interethnic clashes, after Tutsis exiled in Burundi had launched a raid.
1973 Kayibanda ousted in a military coup led by Hutu Maj-Gen Juvenal Habyarimana; this was caused by resentment of the Tutsis, who held some key government posts.
1981 Elections created a civilian legislation, but dominated by the Hutu socialist National Revolutionary Development Movement (MRND), in a one-party state.
1988 Hutu refugees from Burundi massacres streamed into Rwanda.
1990 Government attacked by Rwanda Patriotic Front (FPR), a Tutsi refugee military-political organization based in Uganda, which controlled parts of N Rwanda.
1992 Peace accord with FPR.
1993 United Nations mission sent to monitor peace agreement.
1994 President Habyarimana and Burundian Hutu president Ntaryamira killed in air crash; involvement of FPR suspected. Half a million killed in ensuing civil war, with many Tutsi massacred by Hutu death squads and exodus of 2 million refugees to neighbouring countries. Government fled as FPR forces closed in. French peacekeeping troops established a 'safe zone' in SW. Interim coalition government installed, with moderate Hutu and FPR leader, Pasteur Bizimungu, as president.
1995 War-crimes tribunal opened. Government human-rights abuses reported.
1996 Rwanda and Zaire on brink of war after Tutsi killings of Hutu in Zaire. Thousands of Hutu refugees allowed to return to Rwanda.
1997 Wave of Tutsi killings by Hutus.

SEE ALSO: Burundi; Hutu; Tutsi

At little, huddled, neighbourly Rye, even a white December sea-fog is a cosy and convenient thing.

On **Rye**
Henry James, letter
23 Dec 1900

The dogma of the Ghost in the Machine.

Gilbert Ryle
Concept of Mind

every two years, and the match is made up of a series of singles, foursomes, and fourballs played over three days.

Named after entrepreneur Samuel Ryder, who donated the trophy 1927, the tournament is played alternately in the USA and Great Britain. The match was between the USA and Great Britain 1927–71; USA v. Great Britain and Ireland 1973–77, and USA v. Europe from 1979. *See list of tables on p. 1177.*

rye cereal *Secale cereale* grown extensively in N Europe and other temperate regions. The flour is used to make dark-coloured ('black') breads. Rye is grown mainly as a forage crop, but the grain is also used to make whisky and breakfast cereals.

Rye town in East Sussex, England; population (1991) 3,700. It was formerly a flourishing port (and one of the ◊Cinque Ports), but silt washed down by the river Rother has left it 3 km/2 mi inland. The novelist Henry James lived here; another writer, E F Benson (who was mayor of Rye 1934–37), later lived in James's house.

ryegrass any of several species of grass belonging to the genus *Lolium*, widely grown as lawns and animal fodder. Perennial rye grass *L. perenne* grows to 90 cm/3 ft in height; it is native to Britain and Europe, and has been introduced to North America. Italian rye grass *L. multiflorum* and darnel *L. temulentum* are native to Europe and have been introduced elsewhere. The latter may become infected with a fungal parasite similar to ◊ergot, which causes abortion and blindness in cows.

Rye House Plot conspiracy 1683 by English Whig extremists against Charles II for his Roman Catholic leanings. They intended to murder Charles and his brother James, Duke of York, at Rye House, Hoddesdon, Hertfordshire, but the plot was betrayed. The Duke of ◊Monmouth was involved, and alleged conspirators, including Lord William ◊Russell and Algernon Sidney (1622–1683), were executed for complicity.

Rylance Mark 1960– . English actor and director, from 1995 the artistic director of Shakespeare's Globe Theatre, London. He received the 1994 Olivier Award for best actor for his role as Benedick in *Much Ado About Nothing*. Films include *Prospero's Books* 1991, *Angels and Insects* 1994, *Institute Bejamenta* 1994, and *Loving* 1995. In 1991 he formed his own theatre company, Phoebus Cart.

Ryle Gilbert 1900–1976. British philosopher. His *The Concept of Mind* 1949 set out to show that the distinction between an inner and an outer world in philosophy and psychology cannot be sustained. He ridiculed the mind–body dualism of the French philosopher René ◊Descartes as the doctrine of 'the Ghost in the Machine'.

Ryle Martin 1918–1984. English radio astronomer. At the Mullard Radio Astronomy Observatory, Cambridge, he developed the technique of sky-mapping using 'aperture synthesis', combining smaller dish aerials to give the characteristics of one large one. His work on the distribution of radio sources in the universe brought confirmation of the ◊Big Bang theory. In 1974 he won the Nobel Prize for Physics with his co-worker Antony ◊Hewish.

Ryukyu Islands southernmost island group of Japan, stretching towards Taiwan and including Okinawa, Miyako, and Ishigaki
area 2,254 sq km/870 sq mi
capital Naha, on Okinawa
features 73 islands, some uninhabited; subject to typhoons
industries sugar, pineapples, fish
population (1990) 1,500,000
history originally an independent kingdom; ruled by China from the late 14th century until seized by Japan 1609 and controlled by the Satsuma feudal lords until 1868, when the Japanese government took over. Chinese claims to the islands were relinquished 1895. In World War II the islands were taken by the USA 1945 (see under ◊Okinawa); northernmost group, Oshima, restored to Japan 1953, the rest 1972.

Ryzhkov Nikolai Ivanovich 1929– . Russian politician. He held governmental and party posts from 1975 before being brought into the Politburo and serving as prime minister 1985–90 under Gorbachev. A low-profile technocrat, Ryzhkov was the author of unpopular economic reforms. In June 1991, he unsuccessfully challenged Boris ◊Yeltsin for the presidency of the Russian Federation. He is a leading member of the Communist-led Patriotic Popular Union of Russia, formed Aug 1996.

Saami (or *Lapp*) a group of herding people living in N Scandinavia and the Kola Peninsula, and numbering about 46,000 (1983). Some are nomadic, others lead a more settled way of life. They live by herding reindeer, hunting, fishing, and producing handicrafts. Their language belongs to the Finno-Ugric family. Their religion is basically animist, but incorporates elements of Christianity.

Saarinen (Gottlieb) Eliel 1873–1950. Finnish-born US architect and town planner. He founded the Finnish Romantic school. His best-known European project is the Helsinki railway station 1905–14. In 1923 he emigrated to the USA, where he is remembered for his designs for the Cranbrook Academy of Art in Bloomfield Hills, Michigan, 1926–43, and Christ Church, Minneapolis, 1949.

Saarinen Eero 1910–1961. Finnish-born US architect. He was renowned for his wide range of innovative Modernist designs, experimenting with different structures and shapes. His works include the US embassy, London, 1955–61, the TWA Kennedy terminal, New York, 1956–62, and Dulles Airport, Washington DC, 1958–63. He collaborated on a number of projects with his father, Eliel Saarinen.

Saarland (French *Sarre*)*Land* (state) of Germany
area 2,570 sq km/992 sq mi
capital Saarbrücken
features one-third forest; crossed NW–S by the river Saar
industries cereals and other crops; cattle, pigs, poultry. Former flourishing coal and steel industries survive only by government subsidy
population (1994 est) 1,085,000
history in 1919 the Saar district was administered by France under the auspices of the League of Nations; a plebiscite returned it to Germany 1935; Hitler gave it the name Saarbrücken. Part of the French zone of occupation 1945, it was included in the economic union with France 1947. It was returned to Germany 1957.

Saatchi & Saatchi plc British advertising, communications, and consulting company. Founded by brothers Charles (1943–) and Maurice Saatchi (1946–) in 1970, by the mid-1980s it had become the world's largest advertising company. The Saatchi & Saatchi group changed its name 1995 to Cordiant plc, after the departure of the founding brothers to form the New Saatchi Agency.

Sabah self-governing state of the federation of Malaysia, occupying NE Borneo, forming (with Sarawak) East Malaysia
area 73,613 sq km/28,415 sq mi
capital Kota Kinabalu (formerly Jesselton)
physical chiefly mountainous (highest peak Mount Kinabalu 4,098 m/13,450 ft) and forested
industries hardwoods (25% of the world's supplies), rubber, fish, cocoa, palm oil, copper, copra, and hemp
population (1990) 1,736,900, of which the Kadazans form the largest ethnic group at 30%; also included are 250,000 immigrants from Indonesia and the Philippines
language Malay (official) and English
religion Sunni Muslim and Christian (the Kadazans, among whom there is unrest about increasing Muslim dominance)
government consists of a constitutional head of state with a chief minister, cabinet, and legislative assembly
history in 1877–78 the sultan of Sulu made concessions to the North Borneo Company, which was eventually consolidated with Labuan as a British colony 1946, and became the state of Sabah within Malaysia 1963. The Philippines advanced territorial claims on Sabah 1962 and 1968 on the grounds that the original cession by the sultan was illegal, Spain having then been sovereign in the area.

Sabah Sheik Jabir al-Ahmad al-Jabir al- 1928– . Emir of Kuwait from 1977. He suspended the national assembly 1986, after mounting parliamentary criticism, ruling in a feudal, paternalistic manner. On the invasion of Kuwait by Iraq 1990 he fled to Saudi Arabia, returning to Kuwait March 1991. In 1992 a reconstituted national assembly was elected.

Sabatier Paul 1854–1941. French chemist. He found in 1897 that if a mixture of ethylene and hydrogen was passed over a column of heated nickel, the ethylene changed into ethane. Further work revealed that nickel could be used to catalyse numerous chemical reactions. Nobel prize 1912.

Sabatini Gabriela 1970– . Argentine tennis player. In 1986 she became the youngest Wimbledon semifinalist for 99 years. She was ranked number three in the world behind Monica Seles and Steffi Graf 1991.

Sabbatarianism belief held by some Protestant Christians in the strict observance of the Sabbath, Sunday, following the fourth commandment of the ◊Bible. It began in the 17th century.

Sabbatarianism has taken various forms, including an insistence on the Sabbath's lasting a full 24 hours; prohibiting sports and games and the buying and selling of goods on the Sabbath; and ignoring public holidays when they fall on a Sunday.

Sabbath (Hebrew *shābath*, 'to rest') the seventh day of the week, commanded by God in the Old Testament as a sacred day of rest; in Judaism, from sunset Friday to sunset Saturday; in Christianity, Sunday (or, in some sects, Saturday).

Sabin Albert Bruce 1906–1993. Russian-born US microbiologist who developed a highly effective, live vaccine against polio. The earlier vaccine, developed by physicist Jonas ◊Salk, was based on heat-killed viruses. Sabin was convinced that a live form would be longer-lasting and more effective, and in 1957 he succeeded in weakening the virus so that it lost its virulence. The vaccine can be given by mouth.

Sabine member of an ancient people of central Italy, conquered by the Romans and amalgamated with them in the 3rd century BC. The so-called rape of the Sabine women – a mythical attempt by ◊Romulus in the early days of Rome to carry off the Sabine women to colonize the new city – is frequently depicted in art.

sable marten *Martes zibellina*, about 50 cm/20 in long and usually brown. It is native to N Eurasian forests, but now found mainly in E Siberia. The sable has diminished in numbers because of its valuable fur, which has long attracted hunters. Conservation measures and sable farming have been introduced to save it from extinction.

saccharide another name for a ◊sugar molecule.

saccharin or ***ortho-sulpho benzimide*** $C_7H_5NO_3S$ sweet, white, crystalline solid derived from coal tar and substituted for sugar. Since 1977 it has been regarded as potentially carcinogenic. Its use is not universally permitted and it has been largely replaced by other sweetening agents.

Sacco-Vanzetti case murder trial in Massachusetts, USA, 1920–21. Italian immigrants Nicola Sacco (1891–1927) and Bartolomeo Vanzetti (1888–1927) were convicted of murder during an alleged robbery. The conviction was upheld on appeal, with application for retrial denied. Prolonged controversy delayed execution until 1927. In 1977 the verdict was declared unjust because of the judge's prejudice against the anarchist views of the accused.

Sackville Thomas, 1st Earl of Dorset 1536–1608. English poet and politician. He collaborated with Thomas Norton on *Ferrex and Porrex* 1561, afterwards called *Gorboduc*. Written in blank verse, this was one of the earliest English tragedies. He also contributed to the influential *Mirror for Magistrates*, intended as a continuation of John ◊Lydgate's *Fall of Princes*. Dorset played a prominent part in the history of his time and held many high offices, including those of Lord Steward and Lord Treasurer.

Saarinen Finnish-born US architect Eero Saarinen originally trained as a sculptor and his buildings often exhibit a sculptural sense of form. The sweeping lines of his TWA Terminal Building (opened 1962) at JFK International Airport, New York, USA, clearly suggest flight. *Trans World Airlines Inc.*

Sackville-West Vita (Victoria Mary) 1892–1962. English writer. She was the wife of Harold Nicolson (1886–1968) from 1913; *Portrait of a Marriage* 1973 by their son Nigel Nicolson described their married life. Her novels include *The Edwardians* 1930 and *All Passion Spent* 1931; she also wrote the long pastoral poem *The Land* 1926. The fine gardens around her home at Sissinghurst, Kent, were created by her and her husband.

sacrament in Christian usage, observances forming the visible sign of inward grace. In the Roman Catholic Church there are seven sacraments: baptism, Holy Communion (Eucharist or Mass), confirmation, rite of reconciliation (confession and penance), holy orders, matrimony, and the anointing of the sick. Only the first two are held to be essential by the Church of England.

Sacramento industrial port and capital (since 1854) of California, USA, 130 km/80 mi NE of San Francisco; population (1992) 382,800; metropolitan area (1992) 1,563,000. It stands on the Sacramento River, which flows 615 km/382 mi through Sacramento Valley to San Francisco Bay. Industries include the manufacture of detergents and jet aircraft and food processing, including almonds, peaches, and pears.

Sacred Thread ceremony Hindu initiation ceremony that marks the passage to maturity for boys of the upper three castes; it usually takes place between the ages of five and twelve. It is regarded as a second birth, and the castes whose males are entitled to undergo the ceremony are called 'twice born'.

Sadat (Muhammad) Anwar 1918–1981. Egyptian politician. Succeeding ◊Nasser as president 1970, he restored morale by his handling of the Egyptian

'Always design a thing by considering it in its larger context – a chair in a room, a room in a house, a house in an environment, an environment in a city plan.'

EERO SAARINEN
Quoted in *Time* July 1956

Sadat Egyptian president Anwar Sadat. He was president from 1970 until he was assassinated by Islamic fundamentalists 1981. *Corbis*

‘The climate of Sahara is ... day after day, sunstroke after sunstroke with a frosty shadow between.’

On the **Sahara**
Ralph Waldo Emerson
Journals

campaign in the 1973 war against Israel. In 1974 his plan for economic, social, and political reform to transform Egypt was unanimously adopted in a referendum. In 1977 he visited Israel to reconcile the two countries, and shared the Nobel Peace Prize with Israeli prime minister Menachem Begin 1978. He was assassinated by Islamic fundamentalists.

Sadducee (Hebrew ‘righteous’) member of the ancient Hebrew political party and sect of ◊Judaism that formed in pre-Roman Palestine in the first century BC. They were the group of priestly aristocrats in Jerusalem until the final destruction of the Temple AD 70.

They opposed the ◊Pharisees and favoured Hellenization. They stood for the hereditary high priesthood, the Temple, and sacrifice. Sadducees denied the immortality of the soul and the existence of angels, and maintained the religious law in all its strictness. Many of their ideas and practices resurfaced in medieval Jewish sects after Pharisee ideas dominated the dispersed Jews of the Western Roman Empire.

Sade Donatien Alphonse François, Comte de, known as the ***Marquis de Sade*** 1740–1814. French writer. He was imprisoned for sexual offences and finally committed to an asylum. He wrote plays and novels dealing explicitly with a variety of sexual practices, including sadism, deriving pleasure or sexual excitement from inflicting pain on others.

sadism tendency to derive pleasure (usually sexual) from inflicting physical or mental pain on others. The term is derived from the Marquis de Sade.

Sadowa, Battle of (or ***Battle of Königgrätz***) Prussian victory over the Austrian army 13 km/8 mi NW of Hradec Kralove (German Königgrätz) 3 July 1866, ending the ◊Seven Weeks' War. It confirmed Prussian hegemony over the German states and led to the formation of the North German Confederation 1867. It is named after the nearby village of Sadowa (Czech Sadová) in the Czech Republic.

safety lamp portable lamp designed for use in places where flammable gases such as methane may be encountered; for example, in coal mines. The electric head lamp used as a miner's working light has the bulb and contacts in protected enclosures. The flame safety lamp, now used primarily for gas detection, has the wick enclosed within a strong glass cylinder surmounted by wire gauzes. English chemist Humphrey ◊Davy 1815 and English engineer George ◊Stephenson each invented flame safety lamps.

safflower Asian plant *Carthamus tinctorius*, family Compositae. It is thistlelike, and widely grown for the oil from its seeds, which is used in cooking, margarine, and paints and varnishes; the seed residue is used as cattle feed.

saffron plant *Crocus sativus* of the iris family, probably native to SW Asia, and formerly widely cultivated in Europe; also the dried orange-yellow ◊stigmas of its purple flowers, used for colouring and flavouring.

saga prose narrative written down in the 11th–13th centuries in Norway and Iceland. The sagas range from family chronicles, such as the *Landnamabok* of Ari (1067–1148), to legendary and anonymous works such as the *Njala* saga. Other sagas include the *Heimskringla* of Snorri Sturluson celebrating Norwegian kings, the *Sturlunga* of Sturla Thordsson (1214–1284), and the legendary and anonymous *Laxdaela* and *Grettla* sagas.

Sagan Carl Edward 1934–1996. US physicist and astronomer who popularized astronomy through writings and broadcasts. His main research was on planetary atmospheres. His books include *The Dragons of Eden: Speculations on the Evolution of Human Intelligence* 1978; *Broca's Brain: Reflections on the Romance of Science* 1979; *Cosmos* 1980, based on his television series of that name; and *Demon Haunted World* 1995, a polemic against pseudoscience.

Sagan also carried out research into the origins of life on Earth, the probable climatic effects of nuclear war, and the possibility of life on other planets.

sage perennial herb *Salvia officinalis* with grey-green aromatic leaves used for flavouring. It grows up to 50 cm/20 in high and has bluish-lilac or pink flowers.

Sagittarius bright zodiac constellation in the southern hemisphere, represented as a centaur aiming a bow and arrow at neighbouring Scorpius. The Sun passes through Sagittarius from mid-Dec to mid-Jan, including the winter solstice, when it is farthest south of the equator. The constellation contains many nebulae and ◊globular clusters, and open ◊star clusters. Kaus Australis and Nunki are its brightest stars. The centre of our Galaxy, the ◊Milky Way, is marked by the radio source Sagittarius A. In astrology, the dates for Sagittarius are about 22 Nov–21 Dec (see ◊precession).

sago starchy material obtained from the pith of the sago palm *Metroxylon sagu*. It forms a nutritious food and is used for manufacturing glucose and sizing textiles.

Sahara largest desert in the world, occupying 9,000,000 sq km/3,500,000 sq mi of N Africa from the Atlantic to the Nile, covering: W Egypt; part of W Sudan; large parts of Mauritania, Mali, Niger, and Chad; and southern parts of Morocco, Algeria, Tunisia, and Libya. Small areas in Algeria and Tunisia are below sea level, but it is mainly a plateau with a central mountain system, including the Ahaggar Mountains in Algeria, the Aïr Massif in Niger, and the Tibesti Massif in Chad, of which the highest peak is Emi Koussi, 3,415 m/11,208 ft.

Oases punctuate the caravan routes, now modern roads. Resources include oil and gas in the north. Satellite observations have established a pattern below the surface of dried-up rivers that existed 2 million years ago. Cave paintings confirm that 4,000 years ago running rivers and animal life existed. Satellite photos taken during the 1980s have revealed that the Sahara expands and contracts from one year to another depending on rainfall; that is, there is no continuous expansion, as had been feared. ▷ *See feature on pp. 308–309.*

Sahel (Arabic *sahil* ‘coast’) marginal area to the south of the Sahara, from Senegal to Somalia, where the desert is gradually encroaching. The desertification is partly due to climatic change but has also been caused by the pressures of a rapidly expanding population, which have led to overgrazing and the destruction of trees and scrub for fuelwood. In recent years many famines have taken place in the area.

saiga antelope *Saiga tartarica* of E European and W Asian steppes and deserts. Buff-coloured, whitish in winter, it stands 75 cm/30 in at the shoulder, with a body about 1.5 m/5 ft long. Its nose is unusually large and swollen, an adaptation which may help warm and moisten the air inhaled, and keep out the desert dust. The saiga can run at 80 kph/50 mph. Only the male has horns, which are straight and up to 30 cm/1 ft long.

The saiga is threatened by the demand for its horn for use in traditional Chinese medicine. Once a vanishing species, it is now protected.

Saigon former name (to 1976) of ◊Ho Chi Minh City, Vietnam.

Saigon, Battle of during the Vietnam War, battle 29 Jan–23 Feb 1968, when 5,000 Vietcong were expelled by South Vietnamese and US forces. The city was finally taken by North Vietnamese forces 30 April 1975, after South Vietnamese withdrawal from the central highlands.

saint holy man or woman respected for his or her wisdom, spirituality, and dedication to their faith. Within the Roman Catholic Church a saint is officially recognized through ◊canonization by the pope. Many saints are associated with miracles and canonization usually occurs after a thorough investigation of the lives and miracles attributed to them. For individual saints, see under forename; for example, ◊Paul, St.

In the Orthodox Church, saints are recognized by the patriarch and Holy Synod after recommendation by local churches. The term ‘saint’ is also used in Buddhism for individuals who have led a virtuous and holy life, such as Kūkai (774–835), also known as Kōbō Daishi, founder of the Japanese Shingon school of Buddhism.

St Albans city in Hertfordshire, England, on the river Ver, 40 km/25 mi NW of London; population (1991) 80,400. There are the ruins of the Roman city of Verulamium on Watling Street. A Benedictine abbey was founded 793 in honour of St Alban, and it became a cathedral 1878.

St Andrews town at the eastern tip of Fife, Scotland, 19 km/12 mi SE of Dundee; population (1991) 11,100. Its university (1411) is the oldest in Scotland, and the Royal and Ancient Club (1754) is the ruling body of golf.

There are four golf courses, all municipal; the Old Course dates from the 16th century. One of the earliest patrons was Mary Queen of Scots. St Andrews has been used to stage the British Open 24 times between 1873 and 1984.

St Bartholomew, Massacre of slaughter of ◊Huguenots (Protestants) in Paris, 24 Aug–17 Sept 1572, and until 3 Oct in the provinces. About 25,000 people are believed to have been killed.

After the failure of ◊Catherine de' Medici's plot to have Admiral Coligny (1519–1572) assassinated, she resolved to have all the Huguenot leaders killed, persuading her son Charles IX it was in the interest of public safety.

St Bernard breed of large, heavily built dog, named after the monks of Grand St Bernard Hospice, Switzerland, who kept them for finding lost travellers in the Alps and to act as guides. They are 70 cm/30 in high at the shoulder, and weigh about 70 kg/154 lb. They have pendulous ears and lips, large feet, and drooping lower eyelids. They are usually orange and white.

St Christopher–Nevis historical name of ◊St Kitts and Nevis.

St Elmo's fire bluish, flamelike electrical discharge that sometimes occurs above ships' masts and other pointed objects or about aircraft in stormy weather. Although high voltage, it is low current and therefore harmless. St Elmo (or St Erasmus) is the patron saint of sailors.

Saint-Exupéry Antoine Marie Roger de 1900–1944. French author and pilot. He wrote the autobiographical *Vol de nuit/Night Flight* 1931 and *Terre des hommes/Wind, Sand, and Stars* 1939. His children's book *Le Petit Prince/The Little Prince* 1943 is also an adult allegory.

St George's port and capital of Grenada, on the SW coast; population (1989) 35,700. It was founded 1650 by the French.

St Helena British island in the S Atlantic, 1,900 km/1,200 mi W of Africa, area 122 sq km/47 sq mi; population (1992) 5,700. Its capital is Jamestown, and it exports fish and timber. Ascension and Tristan da Cunha are dependencies.

St Helena became a British possession 1673, and a colony 1834. Napoleon died in exile here 1821.

St Helena

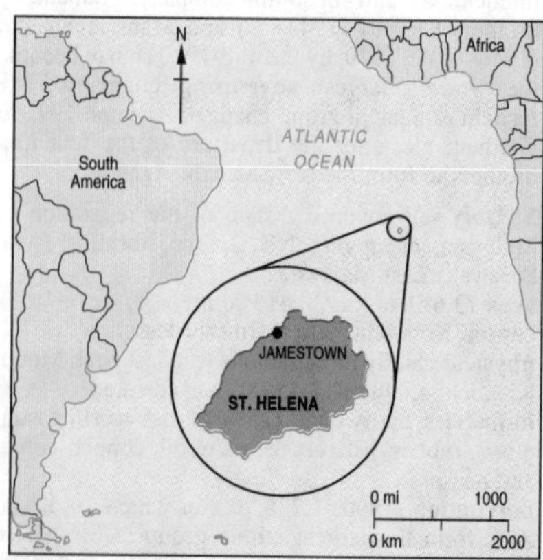

St Helens town in Merseyside, England, 19 km/12 mi NE of Liverpool, and connected to the river Mersey by canal; population (1991) 175,300. It is a leading centre for the manufacture of sheet glass. Other industries include bricks and tiles, engineering, pharmaceuticals, and brewing.

St Helens, Mount volcanic mountain in Washington State, USA. When it erupted 1980 after being quiescent since 1857, it devastated an area of

ST KITTS AND NEVIS
Federation of

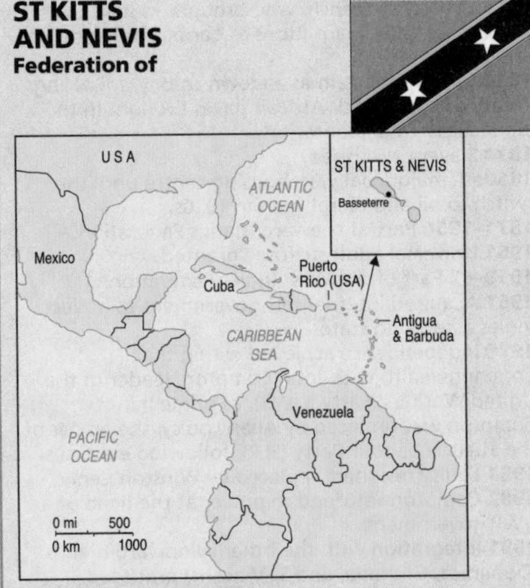

area 262 sq km/101 sq mi (St Kitts 168 sq km/65 sq mi, Nevis 93 sq km/36 sq mi)
capital and port Basseterre (on St Kitts)
major towns/cities Charlestown (largest on Nevis)
physical features both islands are volcanic; fertile plains on coast; black beaches
head of state Queen Elizabeth II of Britain from 1983 represented by governor general Clement Arrindell from 1983
head of government Denzil Douglas from 1995
political system federal constitutional monarchy
administrative divisions nine parishes on St Kitts; five on Nevis
political parties People's Action Movement (PAM), centre-right; Nevis Reformation Party (NRP), Nevis-separatist, centrist; Labour Party (SKLP), moderate left of centre
population 41,000 (1994 est)
population growth rate −0.3 (1990–95)
ethnic distribution almost entirely of African descent
life expectancy 69 (men), 72 (women)
literacy rate 92%
language English (official)
religions Anglican 36%, Methodist 32%, other Protestant 8%, Roman Catholic 10%
currency East Caribbean dollar
GDP (US $) 167 million (1993)
growth rate 4.5% (1993)
exports sugar, molasses, electronics, clothing

HISTORY
1493 Visited by the explorer Christopher Columbus, after whom the main island is named, but for next two centuries the islands were left in the possession of the indigenous Caribs.
1623 and 1628 St Christopher and Nevis islands successively settled by British as their first Caribbean colony, with 2,000 Caribs brutally massacred in 1626.
1783 In the Treaty of Versailles France, which had long disputed British possession, rescinded its claims to the islands, on which sugar-cane plantations developed, worked by imported African slaves.
1816 Anguilla was joined politically to the two islands.
1834 Abolition of slavery.
1871–1956 Part of the Leeward Islands Federation.
1932 Centre-left Labour Party founded to campaign for independence.
1937 Internal self-government granted.
1952 Universal adult suffrage granted.
1958–62 Part of the Federation of the West Indies.
1967 St Kitts, Nevis, and Anguilla achieved internal self-government, within the British Commonwealth, with Robert Bradshaw, Labour Party leader, as prime minister.
1970 NRP formed, calling for separation for Nevis.
1971 Anguilla returned to being a British dependency after rebelling against domination by St Kitts.
1978 Bradshaw died; succeeded by Paul Southwell.
1979 Southwell died; succeeded by Lee L Moore.
1980 People's Action Movement (PAM) and NRP centrist coalition government, led by Kennedy Simmonds, formed after inconclusive general election.
1983 Full independence achieved within the Commonwealth.
1993 Simmonds continued in office despite strong criticism of his leadership. Anti-government demonstrations followed inconclusive general election.
1994 Three-week state of emergency imposed after violent antigovernment riots by Labour Party supporters in Basseterre.
1995 Labour Party won general election; Denzil Douglas became prime minister.
1997 Nevis withdrew from the federation.

600 sq km/230 sq mi and its height was reduced from 2,950 m/9,682 ft to 2,560 m/8,402 ft.

St Helier resort and capital of Jersey, Channel Islands; population (1991) 28,100. The 'States of Jersey', the island legislature, sits here in the *salle des états*.

St Ives fishing port and resort in Cornwall; population (1991) 10,100. Its artists' colony, founded by Walter Sickert and James Whistler, later included Naum Gabo, Barbara ◊Hepworth (a museum and sculpture gardens commemorate her), and Ben Nicholson. A branch of the Tate Gallery opened here 1993, displaying works of art from the Tate's collection by artists connected with St Ives.

St James's Palace palace in Pall Mall, London, a royal residence 1698–1837.

St John, Order of (full title ***Knights Hospitallers of St John of Jerusalem***) oldest order of Christian chivalry, named after the hospital at Jerusalem founded about 1048 by merchants of Amalfi for pilgrims, whose travel routes the knights defended from the Muslims. Today there are about 8,000 knights (male and female), and the Grand Master is the world's highest-ranking Roman Catholic lay person. ▷*See feature on pp. 280–281.*

St John's port and capital of Antigua and Barbuda, on the NW coast of Antigua; population (1992) 38,000. It exports rum, cotton, and sugar.

St John's capital and chief port of Newfoundland, Canada; population (1986) 96,000, urban area 162,000. The main industry is fish processing; other products include textiles, fishing equipment, furniture, and machinery.

It was founded by English navigator Humphrey ◊Gilbert 1582. The inventor Guglielmo Marconi's first transatlantic radio message was received on Signal Hill 1901. Memorial University was founded 1925.

Saint-Just Louis Antoine Léon Florelle de 1767–1794. French revolutionary. A close associate of ◊Robespierre, he became a member of the Committee of Public Safety 1793, and was guillotined with Robespierre.

Elected to the National Convention 1792, he was its youngest member at 25 and immediately made his mark by a radical speech condemning King Louis XVI ('one cannot reign without guilt'). His later actions confirm the tone of his book *The Spirit of the Revolution* 1791 in which he showed his distrust of the masses and his advocacy of repression. On his appointment to the Committee of Public Safety he was able to carry out his theories by condemning 'not merely traitors, but the indifferent', including Danton and Lavoisier, although his own death was to follow within weeks.

St Kitts and Nevis country in the West Indies, in the E Caribbean Sea, part of the Leeward Islands. *See country box above.*

Saint-Laurent Yves Henri Donat Mathieu 1936– . French fashion designer. He has had an exceptional influence on fashion in the second half of the 20th century. He began working for Christian ◊Dior 1955 and succeeded him as designer on Dior's death 1957. He established his own label 1962 and a chain of boutiques called Rive Gauche 1966 selling his ready-to-wear line, and went on to create the first 'power-dressing' looks for men and women: classic, stylish city clothes.

St Lawrence river in E North America. From ports on the ◊Great Lakes it forms, with linking canals (which also give great hydroelectric capacity to the river), the St Lawrence Seaway for ocean-going ships, ending in the Gulf of St Lawrence. It is 745 mi/1,200 km long and is icebound for four months each year.

St Leger one of five principal horse races (classics) in Britain. The St Leger is held at Doncaster every Sept. It is a flat race over 2.8 km/3,060 yd, and is the last classic of the season. First held 1776, it is the oldest of the English classic races. Because of damage to the course, the 1989 race was held at Ayr, the first time Scotland had staged a classic.

St Louis city in Missouri, USA, on the Mississippi River; population (1992) 383,700; metropolitan area (1992) 2,519,000. Its products include aerospace equipment, aircraft, vehicles, chemicals, electrical goods, steel, and beer.

Founded as a French trading post 1764, it passed to the USA 1803 under the ◊Louisiana Purchase. The Gateway Arch 1965 is a memorial to the pioneers of the West, designed by architect Eero Saarinen.

St Lucia country in the West Indies, in the E Caribbean Sea, one of the Windward Islands. *See country box on p. 938.*

St Michael and St George British orders of ◊knighthood.

St Moritz winter sports centre in SE Switzerland; it contains the Cresta Run (built 1885) for toboggans, bobsleighs, and luges. It was the site of the Winter Olympics 1928 and 1948.

St Paul capital and industrial city of Minnesota, USA, adjacent to ◊Minneapolis; population (1992) 268,300. Industries include electronics, publishing and printing, chemicals, refined petroleum, machinery, and processed food.

St Paul's Cathedral cathedral church of the City of London, and the largest Protestant church in England. A Norman building, which had replaced the original Saxon church, was burned down in the Great Fire 1666; the present cathedral, designed by Christopher ◊Wren, was built 1675–1710.

St Petersburg capital of the St Petersburg region, Russian Federation, at the head of the Gulf of Finland; population (1994) 4,883,000. Industries include shipbuilding, machinery, chemicals, and textiles. It was renamed ***Petrograd*** 1914 and was called ***Leningrad*** 1924–91, when its original name was restored.

Built on a low and swampy site, St Petersburg is split up by the mouths of the river Neva, which connects it with Lake Ladoga. The climate is severe. The city became a seaport when it was linked with the Baltic by a ship canal built 1875–93. It is also linked by canal and river with the Caspian and Black seas, and in 1975 a seaway connection was completed via lakes Onega and Ladoga with the White Sea near Belomorsk, allowing naval forces to reach the Barents Sea free of NATO surveillance.
features Saint Petersburg is notable for its wide boulevards and the scale of its architecture. Most of its fine Baroque and Classical buildings of the 18th and early 19th centuries survived World War II. Museums include the Winter Palace, occupied by the Tsars until 1917, the Hermitage, and St Isaac's Cathedral. The univesity was founded 1819.
history Saint Petersburg was founded as an outlet to the Baltic 1703 by Peter the Great, who took up residence here 1712. It was capital of the Russian Empire 1709–1918 and the centre of all the main revolutionary movements from the Decembrist revolt 1825 up to the 1917 revolution.

During the German invasion in World War II the city withstood seige and bombardment 1941–1944. Most deaths (estimated at 1.3–1.5 million) resulted from famine and cold.

St Peter's Cathedral Roman Catholic cathedral church of the Vatican City State, Rome, built 1506–1626, chiefly by the architects Bramante and Michelangelo successively. The cathedral has an internal length of 180 m/600 ft and a width at the transepts of 135 m/450 ft. The dome has an internal diameter of 42 m/137 ft and rises externally 138 m/452 ft to the crowning cross of the lantern.

St Peter is the creation of the vision of Pope Julius II and the greatest architects of the Italian

ST LUCIA

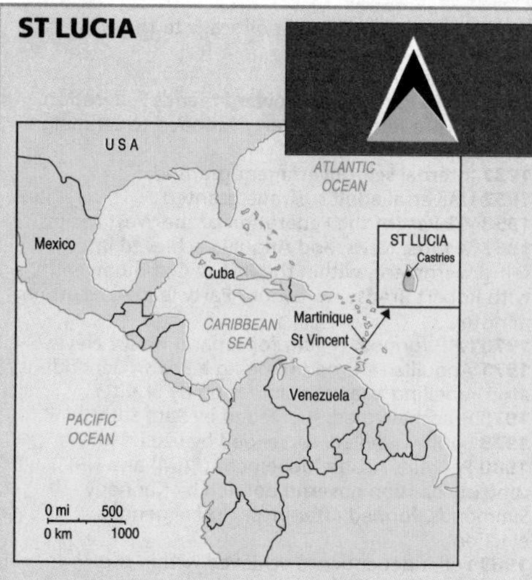

area 617 sq km/238 sq mi
capital Castries
major towns/cities Soufrière
major ports Vieux-Fort
physical features mountainous island with fertile valleys; mainly tropical forest; volcanic peaks; Gros and Petit Pitons

head of state Queen Elizabeth II of Britain from 1979, represented by governor general Stanislaus A James from 1992
head of government Kenny Anthony from 1997
political system constitutional monarchy
administrative divisions 16 parishes
political parties United Workers' Party (UWP), moderate left of centre; St Lucia Labour Party (SLP), moderate left of centre; Progressive Labour Party (PLP), moderate left of centre
population 141,000 (1994 est)
population growth rate 1.4% (1990–95)
ethnic distribution great majority of African descent
life expectancy 68 (men), 73 (women)
literacy rate 93%
languages English; French patois
religion Roman Catholic 90%
currency East Caribbean dollar
GDP (US $) 513 million (1994)
growth rate 2.2% (1994)
exports coconut oil, bananas, cocoa, copra

HISTORY
1502 Sighted by the explorer Christopher Columbus on St Lucia's day but not settled for more than a century due to the hostility of the island's Carib Indian inhabitants.
1635 Settled by French, who brought in slaves to work sugar-cane plantations as Carib community was annihilated.
1814 Ceded to Britain as a crown colony, following Treaty of Paris; black African slaves brought in to work sugar-cane plantations.
1834 Slavery abolished.
1860s A major coal warehousing centre until the switch to oil and diesel fuels in 1930s.
1871–1956 Part of Leeward Islands Federation.
1951 Universal adult suffrage granted.
1958–62 Part of the West Indies Federation.
1967 Acquired internal self-government as a West Indies associated state.
1979 Independence achieved within the Commonwealth with John Compton, leader of the United Workers' Party (UWP), as prime minister; Compton was replaced by Allan Louisy, the leader of the St Lucia Labour Party (SLP), following elections.
1981 Louisy resigned; replaced by Winston Cenac.
1982 Compton returned to power at the head of a UWP government.
1991 Integration with the other Windward Islands (Dominica, Grenada, and St Vincent) proposed.
1993 Unrest and strikes by farmers and agricultural workers as a result of depressed prices for the chief cash crop, bananas.
1997 SLP won general election; Kenny Anthony appointed prime minister.

Renaissance. In competition the design of Donato Bramante was selected, a Greek-cross plan with a dome related to the Pantheon in Athens. The foundation stone was laid 1506. Bramante died 1514 and, after a succession of architects, Michelangelo, better known as a painter and sculptor, succeeded Antonio da Sangallo in 1547, at the age of 72. He conceived the great dome. Carlo Maderno (1556–1629) lengthened the nave to a Latin cross and added the façade 1606–12. Finally, the Baroque architect Giovanni Bernini formed the elliptical entrance piazza from 1656 onwards.

St Pierre and Miquelon territorial dependency of France, eight small islands off the S coast of Newfoundland, Canada
area St Pierre group 26 sq km/10 sq mi; Miquelon-Langlade group 216 sq km/83 sq mi
capital St Pierre
features the last surviving remnant of France's North American empire
industries fish
currency French franc
population (1995) 6,760
language French
religion Roman Catholic
government French-appointed commissioner and elected local council; one representative in the National Assembly in France
history settled 17th century by Breton and Basque fisherfolk; French territory 1816–1976; overseas *département* until 1985; violent protests 1989 when France tried to impose its claim to a 320-km/200-mi fishing zone around the islands; Canada maintains that there is only a 19-km/12-mi zone.

Saint-Saëns (Charles) Camille 1835–1921. French composer, pianist and organist. Among his many lyrical Romantic pieces are concertos, the symphonic poem *Danse macabre* 1875, the opera *Samson et Dalila* 1877, and the orchestral *Carnaval des animaux/Carnival of the Animals* 1886.

Saint-Simon Claude Henri de Rouvroy, Comte de 1760–1825. French socialist who fought in the American Revolution and was imprisoned during the French Revolution. He advocated an atheist society ruled by technicians and industrialists in *Du système industriel/The Industrial System* 1821.

St Vincent and the Grenadines country in the West Indies, in the E Caribbean Sea, part of the Windward Islands. *See country box below.*

St Vitus' dance archaic name for Sydenham's ◊chorea, a transient disorder of childhood and adolescence, often associated with ◊rheumatic fever. St Vitus, martyred under the Roman emperor Diocletian, was the patron saint of dancers.

Sakha (formerly ***Yakutia***) autonomous republic in the Russian Federation, in Siberia
area 3,103,000 sq km/197,760 sq mi
capital Yakutsk
physical one of the world's coldest inhabited places; river Lena, the largest in Russia
industries furs, gold, natural gas, some agriculture in the S
population (1994) 1,060,700 (50% Russians, 33% Yakuts)
history the nomadic Yakuts were conquered by Russia in the 17th century; Yakutia was a Soviet Republic 1922–91.

It remained an autonomous republic within the Russian Federation after the collapse of the Soviet Union 1991. Underground nuclear blasts, atmospheric nuclear testing, and diamond and gold processing have all polluted the area.

Sakhalin (Japanese ***Karafuto***) island in the Pacific, N of Japan, that since 1947, with the Kurils,

ST VINCENT AND THE GRENADINES

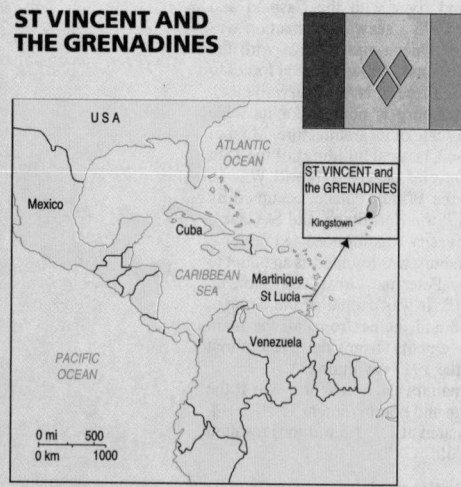

area 388 sq km/150 sq mi, including islets of the Northern Grenadines 43 sq km/17 sq mi
capital Kingstown
major towns/cities Georgetown, Chateaubelair
physical features volcanic mountains, thickly forested; La Soufrière volcano

head of state Queen Elizabeth II of Britain from 1979, represented by governor general David Jack from 1989
head of government James Mitchell from 1984
political system constitutional monarchy
administrative divisions five parishes
political parties New Democratic Party (NDP), right of centre; St Vincent Labour Party (SVLP), moderate left of centre
population 111,000 (1994 est)
population growth rate 0.9% (1990–95)
ethnic distribution largely of African origin; most of the original indigenous Caribs have disappeared
life expectancy 69 (men), 74 (women)
literacy rate 84%
languages English; French patois
religions Anglican, Methodist, Roman Catholic
currency East Caribbean dollar
GDP (US $) 256.6 million (1994)
growth rate 1.4% (1994)
exports bananas, taros, sweet potatoes, arrowroot, copra, eddoes and dasheen, tannias, tobacco, plantain, ginger

HISTORY
1498 The main island was visited by the explorer Christopher Columbus on St Vincent's day.
17th–18th Cs Possession disputed by France and Britain, with fierce resistance being met from the indigenous Carib community.
1783 Recognized as a British crown colony by the Treaty of Versailles.
1795–97 Carib uprising, with French support, resulted in the deportation of 5,000 to Belize and Honduras.
1834 Slavery abolished.
1902 Over 2,000 killed by the eruption of the La Soufrière volcano.
1951 Universal adult suffrage granted.
1958–62 Part of the West Indies Federation.
1969 Achieved internal self-government.
1979 Achieved full independence within the Commonwealth, with Milton Cato of the centre-left St Vincent Labour Party (SVLP) as prime minister.
1981 General strike against new industrial-relations legislation at a time of economic recession.
1984 James Mitchell, of the centre-right New Democratic Party (NDP), replaced Cato as prime minister.
1991 Integration with other Windward Islands (Dominica, Grenada, and St Lucia) proposed.

forms a region of Russia; capital Yuzhno-Sakhalinsk (Japanese ***Toyohara***); area 74,000 sq km/28,564 sq mi; population (1983) 660,000, including aboriginal ◊Ainu and Gilyaks. There are two parallel mountain ranges, rising to over 1,525 m/5,000 ft, which extend throughout its length, 965 km/600 mi.

The economy is based on dairy farming, leguminous crops, oats, barley, and sugar beet. In the milder south, there is also timber, rice, wheat, fish, some oil, and coal. The island was settled by both Russians and Japanese from the 17th century. In 1875 the south was ceded by Japan to Russia, but Japan regained it 1905, only to cede it again 1945. It has a missile base.

An earthquake measuring 7.5 on the Richter scale hit the island May 1995; worst affected was the city of Neftegorsk, where many poorly constructed buildings of the Soviet era collapsed, crushing their inhabitants.

Sakharov Andrei Dmitrievich 1921–1989. Soviet physicist. He was an outspoken human-rights campaigner, who with Igor Tamm (1895–1971) developed the hydrogen bomb. He later protested against Soviet nuclear tests and was a founder of the Soviet Human Rights Committee 1970, winning the Nobel Peace Prize 1975. For criticizing Soviet action in Afghanistan, he was in internal exile 1980–86.

Sakharov was elected to the Congress of the USSR People's Deputies 1989, where he emerged as leader of its radical reform grouping before his death later the same year.

Saki Pen name of H(ector) H(ugh) Munro 1870–1916. Burmese-born British writer. He produced ingeniously witty and bizarre short stories, often with surprise endings. He also wrote two novels, *The Unbearable Bassington* 1912 and *When William Came* 1913.

Sakkara or ***Saqqara*** village in Egypt, 16 km/10 mi S of Cairo, with 20 pyramids, of which the oldest (third dynasty) is the 'Step Pyramid' designed by ◊Imhotep, whose own tomb here was the nucleus of the Aesklepieion, a centre of healing in the ancient world.

Sakti the female principle in Hinduism.

Sakyamuni the historical ◊Buddha, called ***Shaka*** in Japan (because Gautama was of the Sakya clan).

Saladin or ***Sala-ud-din*** 1138–1193. Kurdish-born sultan of Egypt from 1175, in succession to the Atabeg of Mosul, on whose behalf he conquered Egypt 1164–74. He subsequently conquered Syria 1174–87 and precipitated the third ◊Crusade by his recovery of Jerusalem from the Christians 1187. Renowned for knightly courtesy, Saladin made peace with Richard I of England 1192. ▷*See feature on pp. 280–281.*

Salam Abdus 1926–1996. Pakistani physicist who proposed a theory linking the electromagnetic and weak nuclear forces. In 1979 he became the first person from his country to receive a Nobel prize, which he shared with US physicists Sheldon Glashow (1932–) and Steven Weinberg (1933–).

Salamanca, Battle of during the ◊Peninsular War, victory 22 July 1812 of the British led by the Duke of Wellington over the French under Marshal Auguste Marmont. The battle took place to the S of Salamanca, 170 km/105 mi NW of Madrid.

salamander tailed amphibian of the order Urodela. They are sometimes confused with ◊lizards, but unlike lizards they have no scales or claws. Salamanders have smooth or warty moist skin. The order includes some 300 species, arranged in nine families, found mainly in the northern hemisphere. Salamanders include hellbenders, mudpuppies, olms, waterdogs, sirens, mole salamanders, newts, and lungless salamanders (dusky, woodland, and spring salamanders).

They eat insects and worms, and live in water or in damp areas in the northern temperate regions, mostly feeding at night and hiding during the day, and often hibernating during the winter. Fertilization is either external or internal, often taking place in water. The larvae have external gills. Some remain in the larval form, although they become sexually mature and breed; this is called neoteny. The Mexican ◊axolotl and the mud puppy *Necturus maculosus* of North America are neotenic.

Salamis ancient city on the E coast of Cyprus, the capital under the early Ptolemies until its harbour silted up about 200 BC, when it was succeeded by Paphos in the southwest.

Salamis, Battle of in the Persian Wars, Greek naval victory over the Persians 480 BC in the Strait of Salamis W of Athens. Despite being heavily outnumbered, the Greeks inflicted a crushing defeat on the invading Persians which effectively destroyed their fleet.

salat the daily prayers that are one of the Five Pillars of ◊Islam. Muslims are required to pray five times a day, the first prayer being before dawn and the last after dusk. Times for prayer are signalled by a muezzin (caller). Prayer must be preceded by ritual washing and may be said in any clean place, facing the direction of Mecca. The prayers, which are recited in Arabic, follow a fixed series of words and movements.

Salazar António de Oliveira 1889–1970. Portuguese prime minister 1932–68 who exercised a virtual dictatorship. During World War II he maintained Portuguese neutrality but fought long colonial wars in Africa (Angola and Mozambique) that impeded his country's economic development as well as that of the colonies.

Saleh Ali Abdullah 1942– . Yemeni politician and soldier, president from 1990. He became president of North Yemen on the assassination of its president (allegedly by South Yemen extremists) 1978, and was re-elected to the post 1983 and 1988. In 1990 he was elected president of a reunified Yemen, but within three years differences between north and south had resurfaced and civil war re-erupted 1994. Saleh's army inflicted a crushing defeat on the southern forces of Vice President al-Baidh, who fled into exile, and a new ruling coalition was formed.

Salford industrial city in Greater Manchester, NW England, on the river Irwell and the Manchester Ship Canal; population (1991) 220,500. Industries include engineering, electrical goods, textiles, and chemicals. The artist L S Lowry was born and painted here.

Salic law law adopted in the Middle Ages by several European royal houses, excluding women from succession to the throne. The name derives mistakenly from the Salian or northern division of the Franks, who supposedly practised it. In Sweden 1980 such a provision was abrogated to allow Princess Victoria to become crown princess.

salicylic acid HOC_6H_4COOH the active chemical constituent of aspirin, an analgesic drug. The acid and its salts (salicylates) occur naturally in many plants; concentrated sources include willow bark and oil of wintergreen.

When purified, salicylic acid is a white solid that crystallizes into prismatic needles at 318°F/159°C. It is used as an antiseptic, in food preparation and dyestuffs, and in the preparation of aspirin.

Salieri Antonio 1750–1825. Italian composer. He taught Beethoven, Schubert, and Liszt, and was the musical rival of Mozart, whom it has been suggested, without proof, that he poisoned, at the emperor's court in Vienna, where he held the position of court composer.

Salinas de Gortari Carlos 1948– . Mexican politician, president 1988–94, a member of the dominant Institutional Revolutionary Party. During his presidency he was confronted with problems of drug trafficking and violent crime, including the murder of his nominated successor, Luis Donaldo Colosio, 1994. He went into exile 1995 after his brother Raúl was implicated in the assassination of another high-ranking PRI official and held in jail.

Salinger J(erome) D(avid) 1919– . US writer. He wrote the classic novel of mid-20th-century adolescence *The ◊Catcher in the Rye* 1951. He developed his lyrical Zen themes in *Franny and Zooey* 1961 and *Raise High the Roof Beam, Carpenters and Seymour: An Introduction* 1963, short stories about a Jewish family named Glass. A previously written story *Hapworth 16 1924* was published as a book 1996.

Salisbury city and market town in Wiltshire, S England, 135 km/84 mi SW of London; population (1991) 39,300. Salisbury is an agricultural centre, and industries include brewing. The cathedral of St Mary, built 1220–66, is an example of Early English architecture; its decorated spire 123 m/404 ft is the highest in England; its clock (1386) is one of the oldest still working. The cathedral library contains one of only four copies of the *Magna Carta*.

Another name for the modern city of Salisbury is New Sarum, Sarum being an abbreviated form of the medieval Latin corruption of the ancient Roman name Sorbiodonum. Old Sarum, site of an Iron Age fort, cathedral, and town on a 90-m/300-ft hill to the N, was abandoned 1220. Old Sarum was the most famous of the 'rotten boroughs' prior to the 1832 Reform Act.

salamander The fire salamander is seldom far from water, preferring moist areas. The bright markings warn predators of the salamander's poisonous body secretions, which burn the mouth and eyes of an attacker.

Salisbury Robert Cecil, 1st Earl of SalisburyTitle conferred on Robert ◊Cecil, secretary of state to Elizabeth I of England.

Salisbury Robert Arthur Talbot Gascoyne-Cecil, 3rd Marquess of Salisbury 1830–1903. British Conservative politician. He entered the Commons 1853 and succeeded to his title 1868. As foreign secretary 1878–80, he took part in the Congress of Berlin, and as prime minister 1885–86, 1886–92, and 1895–1902 gave his main attention to foreign policy, remaining also as foreign secretary for most of this time.

Salisbury Plain rolling plateau 775 sq km/300 sq mi between Salisbury and Devizes in Wiltshire, England. It rises to 235 m/770 ft in Westbury Down. ◊Stonehenge stands on Salisbury Plain. For many years it has been a military training area.

saliva in vertebrates, an alkaline secretion from the salivary glands that aids the swallowing and digestion of food in the mouth. In mammals, it contains the enzyme amylase, which converts starch to sugar. The salivary glands of mosquitoes and other blood-sucking insects produce ◊anticoagulants.

‘The cook was a good cook, as cooks go; and as cooks go she went.’

SAKI
'Reginald on Besetting Sins'

Salk Jonas Edward 1914–1995. US physician and microbiologist. In 1954 he developed the original vaccine that led to virtual eradication of paralytic ◊polio in industrialized countries. He was director of the Salk Institute for Biological Studies, University of California, San Diego, 1963–75.

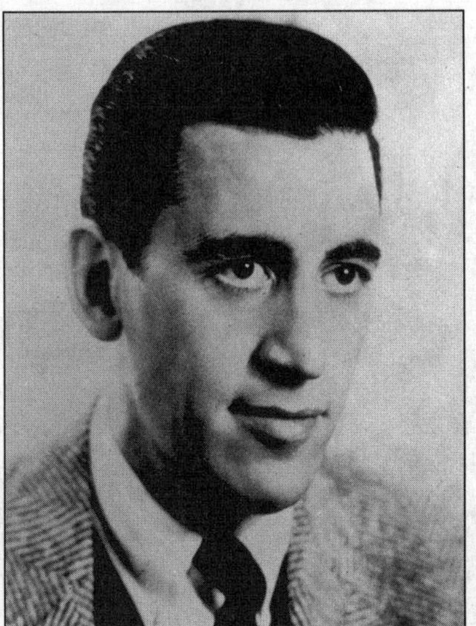

Salinger J D Salinger's first novel *The Catcher in the Rye* 1951, which describes an adolescent's rejection of the 'phony' world of adults, soon became a cult classic. *Penguin Books Ltd*

'Every war is easy to begin but difficult to stop; its beginning and end are not in the control of the same person.'

SALLUST
Jugurtha 83

Sallust Gaius Sallustius Crispus 86–c. 34 BC. Roman historian, a supporter of Julius Caesar. He wrote vivid accounts of ◊Catiline's conspiracy and the Jugurthine War.

salmon any of the various bony fishes of the family Salmonidae. More specifically the name is applied to several species of game fishes of the genera Salmo and Oncorhynchus of North America and Eurasia that mature in the ocean but, to spawn, return to the freshwater streams where they were born. Their normal colour is silvery with a few dark spots, but the colour changes at the spawning season, usually between Sept and Jan. The orange eggs, about 6 mm/0.25 in in diameter, are laid on the river bed, fertilized by the male, and then covered with gravel by the female. The incubation period is from five weeks to five months. ▷*See feature on pp. 704–705.*

salmonella any of a very varied group of bacteria, genus *Salmonella* that colonize the intestines of humans and some animals. Some strains cause typhoid and paratyphoid fevers, while others cause salmonella ◊food poisoning, which is characterized by stomach pains, vomiting, diarrhoea, and headache. It can be fatal in elderly people, but others usually recover in a few days without antibiotics. Most cases are caused by contaminated animal products, especially poultry meat.

'This is the place.'

On SALT LAKE CITY
Brigham Young
2 July 1847

salsa Latin big-band dance music popularized by Puerto Ricans in New York City in the 1970s–80s and by, among others, the Panamanian singer Rubén Blades (1948–).

salsify or ***vegetable oyster*** hardy biennial *Tragopogon porrifolius*, family Compositae. Its white fleshy roots and spring shoots are cooked and eaten.

salt in chemistry, any compound formed from an acid and a base through the replacement of all or part of the hydrogen in the acid by a metal or electropositive radical. Common salt is sodium chloride (see ◊salt, common).

A salt may be produced by chemical reaction between an acid and a base, or by the displacement of hydrogen from an acid by a metal. As a solid, the ions normally adopt a regular arrangement to form crystals. Some salts only form stable crystals as hydrates (when combined with water). Most inorganic salts readily dissolve in water to give an electrolyte (a solution that conducts electricity).

salt One of the world's largest saltpans, the Salar de Uyuni in Bolivia, covers over 12,000 sq km/4,635 sq mi. The salt was deposited when a vast lake which for thousands of years covered this part of the altiplano – a high plateau between two chains of the Andes – gradually dried up. *Sally Jenkins*

SALT abbreviation for ◊***Strategic Arms Limitation Talks***, a series of US–Soviet negotiations 1969–79.

saltbush drought-resistant plant of the goosefoot family Chenopodiaceae, especially the widespread genus *Atriplex* used as grazing plants in arid, saline, and alkaline parts of North America, Australia, and S Africa, and the Australian and New Zealand genus *Rhagodia*. Where saltbush is the predominant vegetation, as in SW South Australia, the area is referred to as the saltbush.

salt, common or ***sodium chloride*** NaCl white crystalline solid, found dissolved in sea water and as rock salt (the mineral halite) in large deposits and salt domes. Common salt is used extensively in the food industry as a preservative and for flavouring, and in the chemical industry in the making of chlorine and sodium.

Salt Lake City capital of Utah, USA, on the river Jordan, 18 km/11 mi SE of the Great Salt Lake; commercial centre and world capital of the Church of Jesus Christ of the Latter-day Saints (the ◊Mormon Church); population (1992) 165,900. The Great Salt Lake is eight times saltier than the ocean, and is second only to the Dead Sea. Speedway racing takes place on the Bonneville Salt Flats. Salt Lake City was chosen 1995 as the site for the 2002 Winter Olympic Games

history Salt Lake City was founded 1847 by Brigham Young and a group of Mormons escaping religious persecution. It passed to US sovereignty 1848, and became the territorial capital 1856. From 1862 it expanded, becoming a commercial centre for the mines and nearby farmlands, and the manufacturing industries of mining equipment, refined petroleum, metal goods, processed food, and textiles grew

features the city is dominated by Temple Square, with the Mormon Temple, the Assembly Hall 1882, and the Tabernacle (home of the world-famous Tabernacle Choir). Beehive House, the home of Brigham Young, dates from 1854. The Cathedral of St Mark 1871 is the oldest non-Mormon church in the city. The State Capitol 1915, built of Utah granite and marble, is a fine example of Renaissance Revival architecture.

salt marsh wetland with halophytic vegetation (tolerant to sea water). Salt marshes develop around estuaries and on the sheltered side of sand and shingle spits. Salt marshes usually have a network of creeks and drainage channels by which tidal waters enter and leave the marsh.

Typical plants of European salt marshes include salicornia, or saltwort, which has fleshy leaves like a succulent; sea lavender, sea pink, and sea aster. Geese such as brent, greylag, and bean are frequent visitors to salt marshes in winter, feeding on plant material.

saltpetre former name for potassium nitrate (KNO_3), the compound used in making gunpowder (from about 1500). It occurs naturally, being deposited during dry periods in places with warm climates, such as India.

saluki ancient breed of hunting dog resembling the greyhound. It is about 65 cm/26 in high and has a silky coat, which is usually fawn, cream, or white.

The saluki is a gazehound (hunts by sight) and is descended from the hound of the African desert Bedouins.

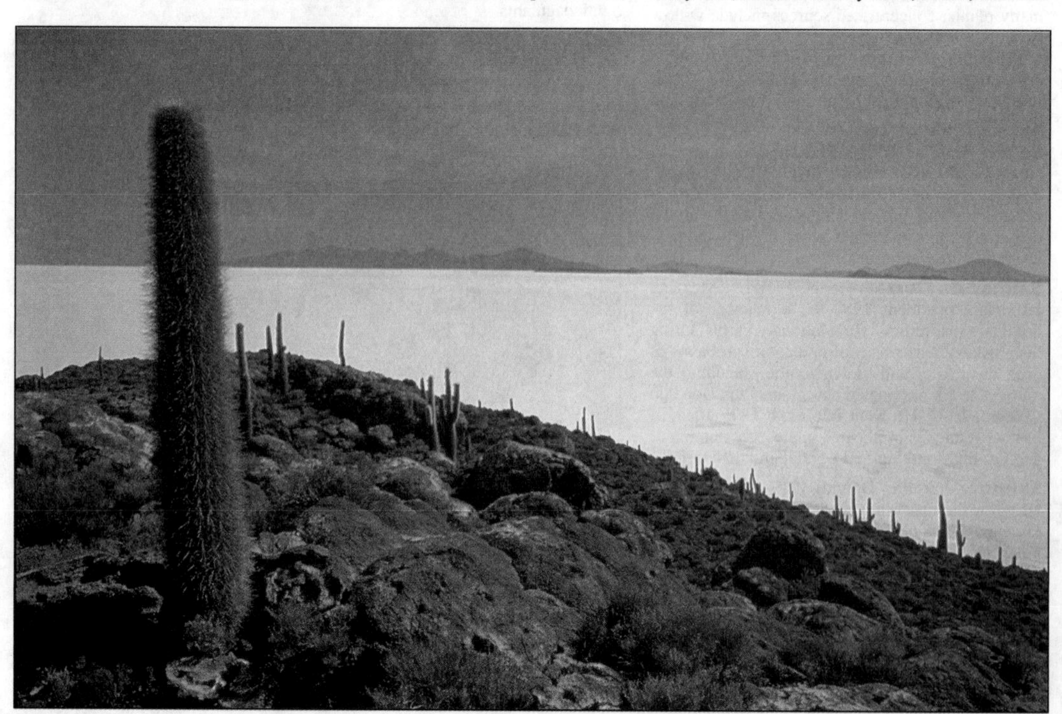

Salvador port and naval base, capital of Bahia state, NE Brazil, on the inner side of a peninsula separating Todos Santos Bay from the Atlantic Ocean; population (1991) 2,075,400 (metropolitan area 3,134,900). Products include cocoa, tobacco, and sugar. Founded 1510, it was the capital of Brazil 1549–1763.

Salvador, El republic in Central America; see ◊El Salvador.

Salvation Army Christian evangelical, social-service, and social-reform organization, originating 1865 in London, England, with the work of William ◊Booth. Originally called the Christian Revival Association, it was renamed the East London Christian Mission 1870 and from 1878 has been known as the Salvation Army, now a worldwide organization. It has military titles for its officials, is renowned for its brass bands, and its weekly journal is the *War Cry*.

Salyut (Russian 'salute') series of seven space stations launched by the USSR 1971–82. Salyut was cylindrical in shape, 15 m/50 ft long, and weighed 19 tonnes/21 tons. It housed two or three cosmonauts at a time, for missions lasting up to eight months.

Salyut 1 was launched 19 April 1971. It was occupied for 23 days in June 1971 by a crew of three, who died during their return to Earth when their ◊Soyuz ferry craft depressurized. In 1973 *Salyut 2* broke up in orbit before occupation. The first fully successful Salyut mission was a 14-day visit to *Salyut 3* July 1974. In 1984–85 a team of three cosmonauts endured a record 237-day flight in *Salyut 7*. In 1986 the Salyut series was superseded by ◊*Mir*, an improved design capable of being enlarged by additional modules sent up from Earth.

Crews observed Earth and the sky, and carried out processing of materials in weightlessness. The last in the series, *Salyut 7*, crashed to Earth Feb 1991, scattering debris in Argentina.

Salzburg capital of the state of Salzburg, W Austria, on the river Salzach; population (1991) 144,000. The city is dominated by the Hohensalzburg fortress. It is the seat of an archbishopric founded by St Boniface about 700 and has a 17th-century cathedral. Industries include stock rearing, dairy farming, forestry, and tourism. It is the birthplace of the composer Wolfgang Amadeus Mozart and an annual music festival has been held here since 1920. The Mozart Museum of Sound and Film opened 1991.

samara in botany, a winged fruit, a type of ◊achene.

Samara capital of Samara region, W central Russian Federation, and port at the junction of the rivers Samara and Volga, situated in the centre of the fertile middle Volga plain; population (1994) 1,223,000. Industries include aircraft, locomotives, cables, synthetic rubber, textiles, fertilizers, petroleum refining, and quarrying. It was called Kuibyshev from 1935, reverting to its former name Jan 1991. The city was provisional capital of the USSR 1941–43.

Samaria region of ancient Israel. The town of Samaria (now ***Sebastiyeh***) on the west bank of the river Jordan was the capital of Israel in the 10th–8th centuries BC. It was renamed Sebarte in the 1st century BC by the Roman administrator Herod the Great. Extensive remains have been excavated.

Samaritan members or descendants of the colonists forced to settle in Samaria (now N Israel) by the Assyrians after their occupation of the ancient kingdom of Israel 722 BC. Samaritans adopted a form of Judaism, but adopted only the Pentateuch, the five books of Moses of the Old Testament, and regarded their temple on Mount Gerizim as the true sanctuary. They remained a conservative, separate people and declined under Muslim rule, with only a few hundred, in a small community at Nablus, surviving today.

Samaritans voluntary organization aiding those tempted to suicide or despair, established in 1953 in the UK. Groups of lay people, often consulting with psychiatrists, psychotherapists, and doctors, offer friendship and counselling to those using their emergency telephone numbers, day or night. In July 1994 the Samaritans began operating an e-mail service.

samarium hard, brittle, grey-white, metallic element of the ◊lanthanide series, symbol Sm, atomic number 62, relative atomic mass 150.4. It is widely distributed in nature and is obtained commercially from the minerals monzanite and bastnaesite. It is used only occasionally in industry, mainly as a catalyst in organic reactions. Samarium was discovered by spectroscopic analysis of the mineral samarskite and named 1879 by French chemist Paul Lecoq de Boisbaudran (1838–1912) after its source.

Samarkand city in E Uzbekistan, capital of Samarkand region, near the river Zerafshan, 217 km/135 mi E of Bukhara; population (1990) 370,000. Industries include cotton-ginning, silk manufacture, and engineering.

Samarkand was the capital of the empire of ◊Tamerlane, the 14th-century Mongol ruler, who is buried here, and was once a major city on the ◊Silk Road. It was occupied by the Russians 1868 but remained a centre of Muslim culture until the Russian Revolution.

Samarra ancient town in Iraq, on the river Tigris, 105 km/65 mi NW of Baghdad; population about 62,000. Founded 836 by the Abbasid caliph Motassim, it was the Abbasid capital until 892 and is a place of pilgrimage for ◊Shi'ite Muslims. It is one of the largest archaeological sites in the world, and includes over 6,000 separate sites.

samba Latin American ballroom dance; the music for this. Samba originated in Brazil and became popular in the West in the 1940s. There are several different samba rhythms; the bossa nova is a samba–jazz fusion.

Samoa volcanic island chain in the SW Pacific. It is divided into Western Samoa and American Samoa. ▷ *See feature on pp. 806–807.*

Samoa, American group of islands 4,200 km/2,610 mi S of Hawaii, administered by the USA
area 200 sq km/77 sq mi
capital Pago Pago
features five volcanic islands, including Tutuila, Tau, and Swain's Island, and two coral atolls. National park (1988) includes prehistoric village of Saua, virgin rainforest, flying foxes
exports canned tuna, handicrafts, copra
currency US dollar
population (1993) 52,900
language Samoan and English
religion Christian
government as a non-self-governing territory of the USA, under Governor A P Lutali, it is constitutionally an unincorporated territory of the USA, administered by the Department of the Interior
history the islands were acquired by the USA Dec 1899 by agreement with Britain and Germany under the Treaty of Berlin. A constitution was adopted 1960 and revised 1967. Around 85,000 American Samoans were living in the USA in 1990.

Samoa country in the SW Pacific Ocean, in ◊Polynesia, NE of Fiji. *See country box below.*

samoyed breed of dog originating in Siberia. It weighs about 25 kg/60 lb and is 58 cm/23 in tall. It resembles a ◊chow chow, but has a more pointed face and a white or cream coat.

Sampaio Jorge 1940– . Portuguese lawyer and politician, president from 1996. A former leader and lifetime member of the Socialist Party (PS), he was mayor of Lisbon before defeating his opponent, former prime minister Cavaco Silva, in the 1996 presidential elections.

samphire or ***glasswort*** or ***sea asparagus*** perennial plant *Crithmum maritimum* found on sea cliffs in Europe. The aromatic leaves are fleshy and sharply pointed; the flowers grow in yellow-green umbels. It is used in salads, or pickled.

Sampras Pete 1971– . US tennis player. At the age of 19 years and 28 days, he became the youngest winner of the US Open 1990. A fine server and volleyer, Sampras also won the inaugural Grand Slam Cup in Munich 1990. In 1997 he won the men's singles at Wimbledon for the fourth time in five years. He finished 1997 at the top of the ATP men's world rankings for an unprecedented fifth consecutive year. In 1998 he won the Wimbledon tournament again, thus joining Sweden's Björn Borg as the only players to win five Wimbledon men's singles titles since the abolition of the Challenge Round in 1922.

Samson lived 11th century BC. In the Old Testament, a hero of Israel. He was renowned for exploits of strength against the Philistines, which ended when his lover Delilah had his hair, the source of his strength, cut off, as told in the Book of Judges.

Samsun Black Sea port and capital of a province of the same name in N Turkey; situated at the mouth of the Murat River in a tobacco-growing area; population (1990) 303,900. It is the site of the ancient city of Amisus.

Samuel lived 11th century BC. In the Old Testament, the last of the judges who ruled the ancient Hebrews before their adoption of a monarchy, and the first of the prophets; the two books bearing his name cover the story of Samuel and the reigns of kings Saul and David.

samurai member of the military caste in Japan from the mid-12th century until 1869, when the feudal system was abolished and all samurai pensioned off by the government. A samurai was an armed retainer of a *daimyō* (large landowner) with specific duties and privileges and a strict code of honour. A *rōnin* was a samurai without feudal allegiance.

From the 16th century, commoners were not allowed to carry swords, whereas samurai had two swords, and the higher class of samurai were permitted to fight on horseback. It is estimated that 8% of the population belonged to samurai families. A financial depression from about 1700 caused serious hardship to the samurai, beginning a gradual disintegration of their traditions and prestige, accelerated by the fall of the Tokugawa shogunate 1868, in which they had assisted. Under the new Meiji emperor, they were stripped of their role, and many rebelled. Their last uprising was the Satsuma Rebellion 1877–78.

San (formerly ***Bushman***) a small group of hunter-gatherer peoples living in and around the Kalahari Desert. Their language belongs to the ◊Khoisan family. ▷ *See feature on pp. 308–309.*

San'a capital of Yemen, SW Arabia, 320 km/200 mi N of Aden; population (1995) 972,000. A walled city, with fine mosques and traditional architecture, it is rapidly being modernized. Weaving and jewellery are local handicrafts.

Old San'a dates from the 14th and 15th centuries. It grew rich because of its position on one of the Arabian spice trade routes. UNESCO launched a campaign to restore and safeguard the old city 1984.

San Andreas fault fault stretching for 1,125 km/700 mi NW–SE through the state of California, USA. It marks a conservative plate margin, where two plates slide past each other (see ◊plate tectonics).

Friction is created as the coastal Pacific plate

SAMOA
Independent State of

Papua New Guinea
SAMOA
Indonesia
Apia
INDIAN OCEAN
Australia
PACIFIC OCEAN
New Zealand
0 mi 500
0 km 1000

national name *Malotutu'atasi o Samoa i Sisifo*
area 2,830 sq km/1,093 sq mi
capital and chief port Apia (on Upolu island)
physical features comprises South Pacific islands of Savai'i and Upolu, with two smaller tropical islands and uninhabited islets; mountain ranges on main islands; coral reefs; over half forested
head of state King Malietoa Tanumafili II from 1962
head of government Tofilau Eti Alesana from 1988
political system liberal democracy
administrative divisions 24 districts
political parties Human Rights Protection Party (HRPP), led by Tofilau Eti Alesana; Samoa Democratic Party (SDP), led by Le Tagaloa Pita; Samoa National Development Party (SNDP), led by Tupuola Taisi Efi and Va'ai Kolone. All 'parties' are personality-based groupings
population 166,000 (1996 est)
population growth rate 1.1% (1990–95)
ethnic distribution 90% of Samoan (Polynesian) origin; 10% Euronesian (mixed European and Polynesian)
life expectancy 64 (men), 69 (women)
literacy rate 92%
languages English, Samoan (official)
religions Congregationalist; also Roman Catholic, Methodist
currency tala, or Samoa dollar
GDP (US $) 415 million (1995)
growth rate −5.0% (1992)
exports coconut oil, copra, cocoa, fruit juice, cigarettes, timber, taro, coconut cream, beer

HISTORY
c. 1000 BC Settled by Polynesians from Tonga.
AD 950–1250 Samoa ruled by Tongan invaders and the Matai (chiefly) system was developed.
15th C United under the Samoan Queen Salamasina.
1722 Visited by Dutch traders.
1768 Visted by the French navigator Louis Antoine de Bougainville.
1830 Christian mission established and islanders were soon converted to Christianity.
1887–89 Samoan rebellion against German attempt to depose paramount ruler and install its own puppet regime.
1889 Under the terms of the Act of Berlin, Germany took control of the nine islands of Western Samoa, while the USA was granted American Samoa, and Britain Tonga and the Solomon Islands.
1900s More than 2,000 Chinese brought in to work coconut plantations.
1914 Occupied by New Zealand on the outbreak of World War I.
1918 Nearly a quarter of the population died in an influenza epidemic.
1920s Development of nationalist movement, the Mau, which resorted to civil disobedience.
1920–61 Administered by New Zealand under League of Nations and, later, United Nations mandate.
1959 Local government established, headed by chief minister Fiame Mata'afa Mulinu'u.
1961 Referendum favoured independence.
1962 Independence achieved within the Commonwealth, with Mata'afa as prime minister, a position he retained (apart from a short break 1970–73) until his death in 1975.
1976 Tupuola Taisi Efi became first nonroyal prime minister.
1982 Va'ai Kolone, the head of the opposition Human Rights Protection Party (HRPP), became prime minister, but was forced to resign over charges of electoral malpractice. The new HRPP leader, Tofilau Eti Alesana, became prime minister.
1985 Tofilau Eti Alesana resigned after opposition to budget; head of state invited Va'ai Kolone to lead the government.
1988 Elections produced a hung parliament, with first Tupuola Efi as prime minister and then Tofilau Eti Alesana.
1990 Universal adult suffrage introduced and power of the Matai (elected clan leaders) reduced.
1991 Fiame Naome became first woman in cabinet; major damage caused by 'Cyclone Val'.
1997 Changed name from Western Samoa to Samoa.

SEE ALSO Commonwealth, the British; League of Nations; Samoa, American

'More Mexican than American ... but picture postcard Mexican. ... you have the sensation in San Antonio by day of the rest of the world being deliciously excluded.'

On **San Antonio**
Graham Greene *The Lawless Roads 1939*

moves northwest, rubbing against the American continental plate, which is moving slowly southeast. The relative movement is only about 5 cm/2 in per year, which means that Los Angeles will reach San Francisco's latitude in 10 million years. The friction caused by the tectonic movement gives rise to frequent, destructive ◊earthquakes. For example, in 1906 an earthquake originating from the fault almost destroyed San Francisco and killed about 700 people.

San Antonio city in S Texas, USA; population (1992) 966,400. It is a commercial and financial centre; industries include aircraft maintenance, oil refining, and meat packing. Founded 1718, it grew up round the site of the ◊Alamo fort.

San Cristóbal capital of Tachira state, W Venezuela, near the Colombian border; population (1990) 220,700. It was founded by Spanish settlers 1561 and stands on the Pan-American Highway (the road linking the USA with Central and South America). It is the centre of the coffee-growing region.

sanction economic or military measure taken by a state or number of states to enforce international law. The first use of sanctions was the attempted economic boycott of Italy 1935–36 during the Abyssinian War by the League of Nations. Other examples are the measures taken against South Africa on human-rights grounds by the UN and other organizations from 1986; the economic boycott of Iraq 1990 in protest over its invasion of Kuwait, following resolutions passed by the UN; and the international sanctions against Serbia 1992–95 in protest against its backing of the Bosnian Serbs.

sand loose grains of rock, sized 0.0625–2.00 mm/0.0025–0.08 in in diameter, consisting most commonly of ◊quartz, but owing their varying colour to mixtures of other minerals. Sand is used in cement-making, as an abrasive, in glass-making, and for other purposes.

Sands are classified into marine, freshwater, glacial, and terrestrial. Some 'light' soils contain up to 50% sand. Sands may eventually consolidate into ◊sandstone.

'We cannot tear out a single page of our life, but we can throw the whole book in the fire.'

George Sand
Mauprat

Sand George. Pen name of Amandine Aurore Lucie Dupin 1804–1876. French author. Her prolific literary output was often autobiographical. In 1831 she left her husband after nine years of marriage and, while living in Paris as a writer, had love affairs with Alfred de Musset, Chopin, and others. Her first novel *Indiana* 1832 was a plea for women's right to independence.

sandalwood fragrant heartwood of any of certain Asiatic and Australian trees of the genus *Santalum*, family Santalaceae, used for ornamental carving, in perfume, and burned as incense.

sandbar ridge of sand built up by the currents across the mouth of a river or bay. A sandbar may be entirely underwater or it may form an elongated island that breaks the surface. A sandbar stretching out from a headland is a sand spit. Coastal bars can extend across estuaries to form bay bars.

Sandburg Carl August 1878–1967. US poet. He worked as a farm labourer and a bricklayer, and his poetry celebrates ordinary life in the USA, as in *Chicago Poems* 1916, *The People, Yes* 1936, and *Complete Poems* 1950 (Pulitzer prize). In free verse, it is reminiscent of Walt Whitman's poetry. Sandburg also wrote a monumental biography of Abraham Lincoln, *Abraham Lincoln: The Prairie Years* 1926 (two volumes) and *Abraham Lincoln: The War Years* 1939 (four volumes; Pulitzer prize). *Always the Young Strangers* 1953 is his autobiography.

sandgrouse any bird of the family Pteroclidae, order Columbiformes. They look like long-tailed grouse, but are actually closely related to pigeons. They live in warm, dry areas of Europe, Asia, and Africa and have long wings, short legs and bills, a wedge-shaped tail, and thick skin. They are sandy coloured and feed on vegetable matter and insects.

Sandgrouse may travel long distances to water to drink, and some carry water back to their young by soaking the breast feathers. The pin-tailed sandgrouse *Pterocles alchata* is a desert bird living in southern Europe, Africa, and Asia. Pallas's sandgrouse *Syrrhaptes paradoxus* is an occasional visitor to Britain.

sand hopper or ***beachflea*** any of various small crustaceans belonging to the order Amphipeda, with laterally compressed bodies, that live in beach sand and jump like fleas. The eastern sand hopper *Orchestia agilis* of North America is about 1.3 cm/0.5 in long.

San Diego city and US naval air station, on the Pacific Ocean, and on the border of Mexico, in California, USA; population (1992) 1,148,900; metropolitan area (1992) 2,601,000. San Diego is linked to Tijuana, Mexico, by a 26 km/16 mi transit line. It is an important Pacific Ocean fishing port. Manufacturing includes aerospace and electronic equipment, metal fabrication, printing and publishing, seafood canning, and shipbuilding
history San Diego's deep-water harbour was discovered by the Portuguese explorer Juan Rodríguez Cabrillo 1542. A Spanish mission and fort were established 1769. It was occupied by American troops during the Mexican war 1846. The establishment of military bases during World War II boosted the economy
features the city's Mexican and Spanish heritage is preserved in the Old Town San Diego State History Park, with the Casa de Machado y Stewart (an 1833 adobe), La Casa de Bandini (a hacienda), and La Casa de Estudillo (an 1829 adobe). The San Diego Aerospace Museum and the International Aerospace Hall of Fame reflect the city's importance as an aerospace centre.

Sandinista member of a Nicaraguan left-wing organization (Sandinist National Liberation Front, FSLN) named after Augusto César Sandino, a guerrilla leader killed 1934. It was formed 1962 and obtained widespread support from the trade unions, the church, and the middle classes, which enabled it to overthrow the regime of General Anastasio Somoza in July 1979. The FSLN dominated the Nicaraguan government and fought a civil war against US-backed Contra guerrillas until 1988. The FSLN was defeated in elections of 1990 by a US-backed coalition, but remained the party with the largest number of seats.

San Marino small landlocked country within NE Italy. *See country box below.*

sandpiper shorebird with a long, slender bill, which is compressed and grooved at the tip. They belong to the family Scolopacidae, which includes godwits, ◊curlews, and ◊snipes, order Charadriiformes.

The common sandpiper *Tringa hypoleucos* is a small graceful bird about 18 cm/7 in long with a short tail. The head and back are greenish-brown with irregular markings on the plumage; underparts are white. The wingspan measures about 35 cm/14 in. It is common in the northern hemisphere except North America and is a summer migrant to Britain frequenting tidal rivers from April to Sept. It has a rapid and easy flight, and is a skilful swimmer and diver, feeding on worms and small insects. Its nest is usually made in a bank or tuft of grasses, though sometimes the pretty yellowish-white eggs are laid on the ground.

sandstone ◊sedimentary rocks formed from the consolidation of sand, with sand-sized grains (0.0625–2 mm/0.0025–0.08 in) in a matrix or cement. Their principal component is quartz. Sandstones are commonly permeable and porous, and may form freshwater ◊aquifers. They are mainly used as building materials.

Sandstones are classified according to the matrix or cement material (whether derived from clay or silt; for example, as calcareous sandstone, ferruginous sandstone, siliceous sandstone).

Sandwich John Montagu, 4th Earl of Sandwich 1718–1792. British politician. He was an inept First Lord of the Admiralty 1771–82 during the American Revolution, and his corrupt practices were blamed for the British navy's inadequacies.

The Sandwich Islands (Hawaii) were named after him, as are sandwiches, which he invented so that he could eat without leaving the gaming table.

San Francisco chief Pacific port on the tip of a peninsula in San Fransisco Bay, in California, USA; population (1992) 728,900, metropolitan area of San Francisco and Oakland 3,686,600. The entrance to the bay was called the Golden Gate 1846, evoking the Golden Horn of Constantinople. The Golden Gate Strait is spanned by the world's second-longest single-span bridge, 1,280 m/

SAN MARINO
Most Serene Republic of

national name *Serenissima Repubblica di San Marino*
area 61 sq km/24 sq mi
capital San Marino
major towns/cities Serravalle (industrial centre)
physical features on the slope of Mount Titano
head of state and government two captains regent, elected for a six-month period
political system direct democracy
administrative divisions nine districts
political parties San Marino Christian Democrat Party (PDCS), Christian centrist; Progressive Democratic Party (PDP) (formerly the Communist Party: PCS), moderate left-wing; Socialist Party (PS), left of centre
population 25,000 (1994 est)
population growth rate 1.5% (1990–95)
ethnic distribution predominantly Italian
life expectancy 70 (men), 77 (women)
literacy rate 96%
language Italian
religion Roman Catholic 95%
currency Italian lira
GDP (US $) 480 million (1993)
growth rate 7.6% (1992)
exports wine, ceramics, paint, chemicals, building stone

HISTORY
c. AD 301 Founded as a republic (the world's oldest surviving) by St Marinus and a group of Christians who settled there to escape persecution.
12th C Self-governing commune.
1600 Statutes (constitution) provided for a parliamentary form of government, based around the Great and General Council.
1815 Independent status of the republic recognized by the Congress of Vienna.
1862 Treaty with Italy signed; independence recognized under Italy's protection.
1945–57 Communist-Socialist administration in power, eventually ousted in a bloodless 'revolution'.
1957–86 Governed by a series of left-wing and centre-left coalitions.
1971 Treaty with Italy renewed.
1986 Formation of Communist and centre-right Christian Democrat (PDCS) 'grand coalition'.
1992 Joined the United Nations. PDCS withdrew from 'grand coalition' to form alliance with Socialist Party.

sandpiper Like many waders, the wood sandpiper *Tringa glareola*, seen here in S Africa, overwinters in the warm tropical and subtropical zones. It migrates northwards into Europe and Asia during springtime to breed in swamps and bogs. *Premaphotos Wildlife*

4,200 ft. The strait gives access to San Francisco Bay. Manufactured goods include textiles, fabricated metal products, electrical equipment, petroleum products, chemicals, and pharmaceuticals. San Francisco is also a financial and trade centre; tourism is also important
history Francis Drake's ship, the *Golden Hind*, stopped here 1578 on its voyage round the world. A Spanish fort (the Presidio) and the San Francisco de Asis Mission were established 1776 and the first Spanish settlement 1835. The town was seized by the US army during the Mexican War 1846, and renamed San Francisco 1847. The 1848 Gold Rush led to a boom and in the later 19th century the city became the financial centre of the West. The city is on the ◊San Andreas fault, and was almost completely destroyed by an earthquake (equivalent to 8.3 on the Richter scale) and subsequent fire 1906. It was the main port for the war in the Pacific during World War II. Another earthquake (6.9 on the Richter scale) rocked the city 1989
features the Golden Gate National Recreation Area includes many historical landmarks. The city has 43 hills, including Nob Hill, on which stands Grace Cathedral 1929–64, with its replicas of Ghiberti's bronze doors to the baptistry of the Duomo in Florence, Italy. The Coit Tower is on the top of Telegraph Hill. Cable cars were developed 1872 to cope with the hills. The financial district has modern buildings, including the Transamerica Pyramid 1972.

Sanger Frederick 1918– . English biochemist. He was the first person to win a Nobel Prize for Chemistry twice: the first 1958 for determining the structure of ◊insulin, and the second 1980 for work on the chemical structure of ◊genes.

Sanger's second Nobel prize was shared with two US scientists, Paul ◊Berg and Walter ◊Gilbert, for establishing methods of determining the sequence of nucleotides strung together along strands of ◊RNA and DNA. He also worked out the structures of various enzymes and other proteins.

Sangha in Buddhism, the monastic orders, one of the Three Treasures of Buddhism (the other two are Buddha and the teaching, or dharma).

The term Sangha is sometimes used more generally by Mahāyāna Buddhists to include all followers including the laity.

San José capital of Costa Rica; population (1991 est) 299,400. Products include coffee, cocoa, and sugar cane. It was founded 1737 and has been the capital since 1823.

San José city in Santa Clara Valley, California, USA; population (1992) 801,300. It is the centre of 'Silicon Valley', the site of many high-technology electronic firms turning out semiconductors and other computer components. There are also electrical, aerospace, missile, rubber, metal, and machine industries, and it is a commercial and transportation centre for orchard crops and wines produced in the area. It was the first capital of California 1849–51.

San Juan capital of Puerto Rico; population (1990) 437,750. It is a port and industrial city. Products include chemicals, pharmaceuticals, machine tools, electronic equipment, textiles, plastics, and rum.

San Martín José de 1778–1850. South American revolutionary leader. He served in the Spanish army during the Peninsular War, but after 1812 he devoted himself to the South American struggle for independence, playing a large part in the liberation of Argentina, Chile, and Peru from Spanish rule.

San Pedro Sula main industrial and commercial city in NW Honduras, the second-largest city in the country; population (1991 est) 325,900. It trades in bananas, coffee, sugar, and timber, and manufactures textiles, plastics, furniture, and cement.

San Salvador capital of El Salvador 48 km/30 mi from the Pacific Ocean, at the foot of San Salvador volcano (2,548 m/8,360 ft); population (1992) 422,600. Industries include food processing and textiles. Since its foundation 1525, it has suffered from several earthquakes.

sans-culotte (French 'without knee breeches') in the French Revolution, a member of the working classes, who wore trousers, as opposed to the aristocracy and bourgeoisie, who wore knee breeches.

Sanskrit the dominant classical language of the Indian subcontinent, a member of the Indo-Iranian group of the Indo-European language family, and the sacred language of Hinduism. The oldest form of Sanskrit is Vedic, the variety used in the *Vedas* and *Upanishads* (about 1500–700 BC).

Classical Sanskrit was systematized by Panini and other grammarians in the latter part of the 1st millennium BC and became fixed as the spoken and written language of culture, philosophy, mathematics, law, and medicine. It is written in Devanagari script and is the language of the two great Hindu epics, the *Mahābhārata* and the *Rāmāyana*, as well as many other classical and later works. Sanskrit vocabulary has not only influenced the languages of India, Thailand, and Indonesia, but has also enriched several European languages, including English, with borrowed words as well as etymological bases.

Santa Ana periodic warm Californian ◊wind.

Santa Anna Antonio López de c. 1795–1876. Mexican revolutionary. He became general and dictator of Mexico for most of the years between 1824 and 1855. He led the attack on the ◊Alamo fort in Texas 1836.

A leader in achieving independence from Spain 1821, he pursued a chequered career of victory and defeat and was in and out of office as president or dictator for the rest of his life.

Santa Claus another name for Father Christmas; see St ◊Nicholas.

Santa Cruz Andrés 1792–1865. President of Bolivia 1829–34, 1839, 1841–44, and 1853–55. Strong-willed and conservative, he dabbled in political intrigue before and after his intermittent rule as dictator. He established order in the new state and increased expenditure on education and road building.

Santa Cruz de la Sierra capital of Santa Cruz department in E Bolivia, the second-largest city in the country; population (1992) 694,600. Sugar cane and cattle were the base of local industry until newly discovered oil and natural gas led to phenomenal growth.

Santa Cruz de Tenerife capital of Tenerife and of the Canary Islands; population (1994) 204,000. It is a fuelling port and cable centre. Industry also includes oil refining, pharmaceuticals, and trade in fruit. Santa Cruz was bombarded by the British admirals Blake 1657 and Nelson 1797 (the action in which he lost his arm).

Santa Fé de Bogotá capital of Santa Fé province, Argentina, on the Salado River 153 km/95 mi N of Rosario; population (1991) 395,000. It has shipyards and exports timber, cattle, and wool. It was founded 1573, and the 1853 constitution was adopted here.

Santa Fe capital of New Mexico, USA, on the Santa Fe River in the Rio Grande Valley, 65 km/40 mi W of Las Vegas; population (1990) 55,900, many Spanish-speaking. It is the cultural capital of the Southwest. Its chief industry is tourism
history founded by the Spanish 1610 on the site of a prehistoric Tiwa Indian Pueblo, it was evacuated 1680 following a Pueblo Indian revolt, but was retaken 1692. Many wagons passed through on the Santa Fe Trail in the 19th century. It was occupied by US troops 1846, and ceded to the United States 1848; it became the territorial capital 1851
features there is some traditional Spanish colonial and Pueblo Indian-style architecture, including the Palace of the Governors 1610 (restored as a museum 1914), the Chapel of San Miguel 1710, and the Cathedral of St Francis 1869. The San Miguel Mission, built around 1625 is the oldest church still in use in the United States. There are a number of pueblos near Santa Fe. Santa Fe is an important art centre, with many galleries. Museums include the Institute of American Indian Arts Museum, the Museum of International Folk Art, and the Wheelwright Museum of Navajo Art.

Santa Fe Trail US trade route 1821–80 from Independence, Missouri, to Santa Fe, New Mexico. Established by trader William Becknell, the trail passed through Raton Pass and between tributaries of the Kansas and Arkansas rivers. Later, to allow the passage of wheeled wagons, Becknell turned south and headed across the Cimarron Desert. This reduced the journey by 160 km/100 mi but increased the hardship and danger of Indian attack. The trade along the trail expanded to nearly 5,000 wagons carrying millions of dollars' worth of goods each year. It was rendered obsolete in 1880 when railway lines were extended to Santa Fe.

Santayana George, (originally Jorge Augustín Nicolás Ruiz de Santayana) 1863–1952. Spanish-born US philosopher and critic. He developed his philosophy based on naturalism and taught that everything has a natural basis.

Born in Madrid, Santayana grew up in Spain and the USA and graduated from Harvard University. He taught at Harvard 1889–1912. His books include *The Life of Reason* 1905–06, *Skepticism and Animal Faith* 1923, *The Realm of Truth* 1937, *Background of My Life* 1945; volumes of poetry; and the best-selling novel *The Last Puritan* 1935.

Santer Jacques 1937– . Luxembourg politician, prime minister 1984–94. A member of the European Parliament 1975–79, he succeeded Jacques Delors as president of the European Commission 1995.

Santiago capital of Chile, on the Mapocho River; population (1992) 4,385,500 (metropolitan area 5,180,800). Industries include textiles, chemicals, and food processing
history founded by the Spanish 1541, it became the capital of Chile 1818
features Spanish colonial architecture, including

'I am an idealist. I don't know where I'm going but I'm on the way.'
CARL SANDBURG
Incidentals

'Fanaticism consists in redoubling your effort when you have forgotten your aim.'
GEORGE SANTAYANA
The Life of Reason

Sapporo The city of Sapporo, on Hokkaido Island, Japan, developed rapidly in the 1870s, when Western influence was strong. The streets were laid out following Western architectural styles: broad, straight, tree-lined boulevards with fountains, gardens, and plazas. *Japan National Tourist Organization*

the Governor's Palace, cathedral, and churches; broad avenues.

Santiago de Compostela city in Galicia, Spain; population (1991) 105,500. The 11th-century cathedral was reputedly built over the grave of Sant Iago el Mayor (St ◊James the Great), patron saint of Spain, and was a world-famous centre for medieval pilgrims.

Santiago de Cuba port on the south coast of Cuba; population (1989) 405,400. Products include sugar, rum, and cigars.

Santiago de los Caballeros second-largest city in the Dominican Republic; population (1991 est) 375,000. It is a processing and trading centre for sugar, coffee, and cacao.

Santo Domingo capital and chief sea port of the Dominican Republic; population (1991 est) 2,055,000. Founded 1496 by Bartolomeo, brother of Christopher Columbus, it is the oldest colonial city in the Americas. Its cathedral was built 1515–40.

Santos the world's leading coffee-exporting port, in SE Brazil, 72 km/45 mi SE of São Paulo; population (1991) 546,600. The Brazilian soccer player Pelé played here for many years.

San Yu 1919–1996. Myanmar (Burmese) politician, president 1981–88. A member of the Revolutionary Council that came to power 1962, he became president 1981 and was re-elected 1985. He was forced to resign July 1988, along with Ne Win, after riots in Yangon (formerly Rangoon).

Saône river in E France, rising in the Vosges Mountains and flowing 480 km/300 mi to join the Rhône at Lyon.

São Paulo city in Brazil, 72 km/45 mi northwest of its port Santos; population (1992) 9,646,200 (metropolitan area 16,567,300). It is 900 m/3,000 ft above sea level, and 2° south of the Tropic of Capricorn. It is South America's leading industrial city, producing electronics, steel, and chemicals; it has meat-packing plants and is the centre of Brazil's coffee trade. It originated as a Jesuit mission 1554.

São Tomé port and capital of São Tomé e Príncipe, on the NE coast of São Tomé island, Gulf of Guinea; population (1991) 43,400. It exports cocoa and coffee.

São Tomé e Príncipe country in the Gulf of Guinea, off the coast of W Africa. *See country box opposite.*

sap the fluids that circulate through ◊vascular plants, especially woody ones. Sap carries water and food to plant tissues. Sap contains alkaloids, protein, and starch; it can be milky (as in rubber trees), resinous (as in pines), or syrupy (as in maples).

Sapir Edward 1884–1939. German-born US language scholar and anthropologist who initially studied the Germanic languages but later, under the influence of Franz Boas, investigated indigenous American languages. He is noted for the view now known as linguistic relativity: that people's ways of thinking are significantly shaped (and even limited) by the language(s) they use. His main work is *Language: An Introduction to the Study of Speech* 1921.

sapphire deep-blue, transparent gem variety of the mineral ◊corundum Al_2O_3, aluminium oxide. Small amounts of iron and titanium give it its colour. A corundum gem of any colour except red (which is a ruby) can be called a sapphire; for example, yellow sapphire.

Sappho c. 610–c. 580. Greek lyric poet. A native of Lesbos and contemporary of the poet Alcaeus (c. 611–c. 580 BC), she was famed for her female eroticism (hence the word lesbian). The surviving fragments of her poems express a keen sense of loss, and delight in the worship of the goddess ◊Aphrodite.

Sapporo capital of ◊Hokkaido prefecture, Japan; population (1994) 1,719,000. Industries include rubber and food processing. It is a winter sports centre and was the site of the 1972 Winter Olympics. Giant figures are sculpted in ice at the annual snow festival. The university was founded 1876 as the Sapporo Agricultural College.

saprotroph (formerly ***saprophyte***) organism that feeds on the excrement or the dead bodies or tissues of others. They include most fungi (the rest being parasites); many bacteria and protozoa; animals such as dung beetles and vultures; and a few unusual plants, including several orchids. Saprotrophs cannot make food for themselves, so they are a type of ◊heterotroph. They are useful scavengers, and in sewage farms and refuse dumps break down organic matter into nutrients easily assimilable by green plants.

Saracen ancient Greek and Roman term for an Arab, used in the Middle Ages by Europeans for all Muslims. The equivalent term used in Spain was ◊Moor.

Saragossa English spelling of ◊Zaragoza, a city in Spain.

Sarajevo capital of Bosnia-Herzegovina; population (1991) 526,000. Industries include engineering, brewing, chemicals, carpets, and ceramics. A Bosnian, Gavrilo Princip, assassinated Archduke ◊Franz Ferdinand here 1914, thereby precipitating World War I. From April 1992 the city was the target of a siege by Bosnian Serb forces in their fight to carve up the newly independent republic. A United Nations ultimatum and the threat of NATO bombing led to a cease-fire Feb 1994 and the effective end of the siege as Serbian heavy weaponry was withdrawn from the high points surrounding the city.

Sarawak state of Malaysia, on the NW corner of the island of Borneo
area 124,400 sq km/48,018 sq mi
capital Kuching
physical mountainous; the rainforest, which may be 10 million years old, contains several thousand tree species. A third of all its plant species are endemic to Borneo. 30% of the forest was cut down 1963–89; timber is expected to run out 1995–2001
industries timber, oil, rice, pepper, rubber, coconuts, and natural gas
population (1991) 1,669,000; 24 ethnic groups make up almost half this number
history Sarawak was granted by the Sultan of Brunei to English soldier James Brooke 1841, who became 'Rajah of Sarawak'. It was a British protectorate from 1888 until captured by the Japanese in World War II. It was a crown colony 1946–63, when it became part of Malaysia.

sarcoidosis chronic disease of unknown cause involving enlargement of the lymph nodes and the formation of small fleshy nodules in the lungs. It may also affect the eyes, and skin, and (rarely) other tissue. Many cases resolve spontaneously or may be successfully treated using ◊corticosteroids.

sarcoma malignant ◊tumour arising from the fat, muscles, bones, cartilage, or blood and lymph vessels and connective tissues. Sarcomas are much less common than ◊carcinomas.

sard yellow or red-brown variety of ◊chalcedony.

sardine common name for various small fishes (◊pilchards) in the herring family.

Sardinia (Italian ***Sardegna***) mountainous island, special autonomous region of Italy; area 24,100 sq km/9,303 sq mi; population (1992 est) 1,651,900. Its capital is Cagliari, and it exports cork and petrochemicals. It is the second-largest Mediterranean island and includes Costa Smeralda (Emerald Coast) tourist area in the NE and *nuraghi* (fortified Bronze Age dwellings). After centuries of foreign rule, Sardinia became linked 1720 with Piedmont, and this dual kingdom became the basis of a united Italy 1861.

Sardinia

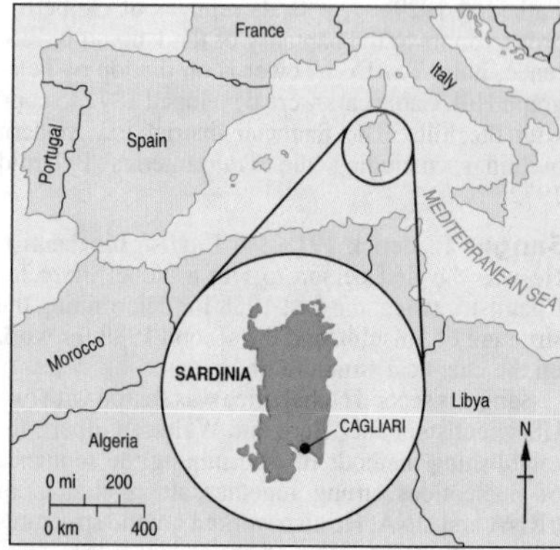

Sargent (Harold) Malcolm (Watts) 1895–1967. English conductor. He was professor at the Royal College of Music from 1923, chief conductor of the BBC Symphony Orchestra 1950–57, and continued as conductor in chief of the annual Henry Wood ◊promenade concerts at the Royal Albert Hall.

He championed Vaughan Williams and Holst and conducted the first performances of Walton's oratorio *Belshazzar's Feast* 1931 and opera *Troilus and Cressida* 1954.

Sargent John Singer 1856–1925. US portrait painter. He was born in Europe of American parents and settled in England 1885. He quickly became a fashionable and prolific painter, brilliantly depicting affluent late Victorian and Edwardian society, British and American. His *Madame X* 1884 (Metropolitan Museum of Art, New York) is one of his best-known works.

SÃO TOMÉ E PRÍNCIPE
Democratic Republic of

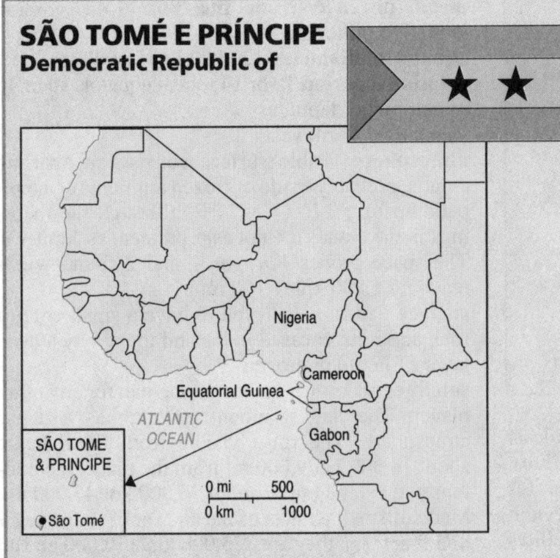

national name *República Democrática de São Tomé e Príncipe*
area 964 km/372 sq mi
capital São Tomé
major towns/cities São António
physical features comprises two main islands and several smaller ones, all volcanic; thickly forested and fertile
head of state Miguel Trovoada from 1991
head of government Carlos da Graca from 1994
political system emergent democratic republic
administrative divisions seven counties
political parties Movement for the Liberation of São Tomé e Príncipe–Social Democratic Party (MLSTP–PSD), nationalist socialist; Democratic Convergence Party–Reflection Group (PCD–GR), moderate left of centre; Independent Democratic Action (ADI), centrist
population 131,100 (1995 est)
population growth rate 2.2% (1990–95)
ethnic distribution predominantly African
life expectancy 62 (men), 62 (women)
literacy rate 63%
languages Portuguese (official), Fang (a Bantu language)
religions Roman Catholic 80%, animist
currency dobra
GDP (US $) 32.6 million (1993 est)
growth rate 1.5% (1993)
exports cocoa, copra, coffee, palm oil and kernels, bananas

HISTORY
1471 First visited by the Portuguese, who brought in convicts and slaves to work on sugar plantations in the formerly uninhabited islands.
1522 Became a province of Portugal.
1530 Slaves successfully revolted, forcing plantation owners to flee to Brazil; thereafter became a key staging post for Congo-Americas slave trade.
19th C Forced contract labour used to work coffee and cocoa plantations.
1953 More than 1,000 striking plantation workers gunned down by Portuguese troops.
1960 First political party formed, the forerunner of the socialist-nationalist Movement for the Liberation of São Tomé e Príncipe (MLSTP).
1974 Military coup in Portugal led to strikes, demonstrations, and army mutiny in São Tomé; thousands of Portuguese settlers fled the country.
1975 Independence achieved, with Manuel Pinto da Costa (MLSTP) as president; close links developed with communist bloc, and plantations nationalized.
1984 Formally declared a nonaligned state as economy deteriorated.
1988 Coup attempt against da Costa foiled by Angolan and East European troops.
1990 Influenced by collapse of communism in Eastern Europe, MLSTP abandoned Marxism; new pluralist constitution approved in referendum.
1991 In first multiparty elections, the ruling MLSTP lost its majority and the independent Miguel Trovoada, MLSTP prime minister before 1978, was elected president.
1994 MLSTP returned to power with Carlos da Graca as prime minister.
1995 Abortive coup by junior army officers; unemployment at 38% and foreign indebtedness $165 million.

Sargon I king of Akkad c. 2334–c. 2279 BC, and founder of the first Mesopotamian empire. Like Moses, he was said to have been found floating in a cradle on the local river, in his case the Euphrates.

Sargon II died 705. King of Assyria from 722 BC, who assumed the name of his predecessor. To keep conquered peoples from rising against him, he had whole populations moved from their homelands, including the Israelites from Samaria.

sarin poison gas 20 times more lethal to humans than potassium cyanide. It cripples the central nervous system, blocking the action of an enzyme that removes acetylcholine, the chemical that transmits signals. Sarin was developed in Germany during World War II.

Sarin was used 1995 in a terrorist attack on the Tokyo underground by a Japanese sect. It is estimated that the USA had a stockpile of 15,000 tonnes of sarin, and more than 1,000 US rockets with sarin warheads were found to be leaking 1995. There are no known safe disposal methods.

Sark one of the ◊Channel Islands, 10 km/6 mi E of Guernsey; area 5 sq km/2 sq mi; population (1991) 575. There is no town or village. It is divided into Great and Little Sark, linked by an isthmus, and is of great natural beauty. The Seigneurie of Sark was established by Elizabeth I, the ruler being known as Seigneur/Dame, and has its own parliament, the Chief Pleas. There is no income tax, divorce and cars are forbidden, and immigration is controlled.

Sarmiento Domingo Faustino 1811–1888. Argentina's first civilian president 1868–74, regarded as one of the most brilliant Argentines of the 19th century. An outspoken critic of the dictator Juan Manuel de ◊Rosas, Sarmiento spent many years in exile. As president, he doubled the number of schools, creating the best education system in Latin America, and encouraged the establishment of libraries and museums. He also expanded trade, extended railroad building, and encouraged immigration.

Sarney (Costa) José 1930– . Brazilian politician, member of the centre-left Democratic Movement (PMDB), president 1985–90, chairman of the Senate 1996.

Sarney was elected vice president 1985 and within months, on the death of President Neves, became head of state. Despite earlier involvement with the repressive military regime, he and his party won a convincing victory in the 1986 general election. In Dec 1989, Ferdinando Collor de Mello of the Party for National Reconstruction was elected to succeed Sarney in March 1990.

Saroyan William 1908–1981. US author. He wrote short stories, such as *The Daring Young Man on the Flying Trapeze* 1934, idealizing the hopes and sentiments of the 'little man'. His plays, preaching a gospel of euphoric enjoyment, include *The Time of Your Life* (Pulitzer prize; refused) 1939, about eccentricity; *My Heart's in the Highlands* 1939, about an uplifting bugle-player; *Love's Old Sweet Song* 1941, and *Talking to You* 1962. He published three volumes of autobiography, including *Obituaries* 1979.

Sarraute Nathalie Ilyanova, (born Tchernik) 1900– . Russian-born French novelist. Her books include *Portrait d'un inconnu/Portrait of a Man Unknown* 1948, *Les Fruits d'or/The Golden Fruits* 1964, and *Vous les entendez?/Do You Hear Them?* 1972. An exponent of the ◊*nouveau roman*, Sarraute bypasses plot, character, and style for the half-conscious interaction of minds.

Sartre Jean-Paul 1905–1980. French author and philosopher. He was a leading proponent of ◊existentialism. He published his first novel, *La Nausée/Nausea*, 1937, followed by the trilogy *Les Chemins de la liberté/Roads to Freedom* 1944–45 and many plays, including *Les Mouches/The Flies* 1943, *Huis clos/In Camera* 1944, and *Les Séquestrés d'Altona/The Condemned of Altona* 1960. *L'Etre et le néant/Being and Nothingness* 1943, his first major philosophical work, sets out a radical doctrine of human freedom. In the later work *Critique de la raison dialectique/Critique of Dialectical Reason* 1960 he tried to produce a fusion of existentialism and Marxism.

Sartre was born in Paris, and was the long-time companion of the feminist writer Simone de ◊Beauvoir. During World War II he was a prisoner for nine months, and on his return from Germany joined the Resistance. As a founder of existentialism, he edited its journal *Les Temps modernes/Modern Times*, and expressed its tenets in his novels and plays. According to Sartre, people have to create their own destiny without relying on powers higher than themselves. Awareness of this freedom takes the form of anxiety, and people therefore attempt to flee from awareness into what he terms *mauvaise foi* ('bad faith'); this is the theory he put forward in *L'Etre et le néant*. In *Les Mains sales/Crime passionel* 1948 he attacked aspects of communism while remaining generally sympathetic. In his later work Sartre became more sensitive to the social constraints on people's actions. He refused the Nobel Prize for Literature 1964 for 'personal reasons', but allegedly changed his mind later, saying he wanted it for the money.

SAS abbreviation for ◊***Special Air Service***.

Saskatchewan (Cree *Kis-is-ska-tche-wan* 'swift flowing') province of W Canada
area 652,300 sq km/251,788 sq mi
capital Regina
towns Saskatoon, Moose Jaw, Prince Albert
physical prairies in the south; to the north, forests, lakes, and subarctic tundra; Prince Albert National Park
industries more than 60% of Canada's wheat; oil, natural gas, uranium, zinc, potash (world's largest reserves), copper, helium (the only western reserves outside the USA)
population (1991) 995,300
history once inhabited by Indians speaking Athabaskan, Algonquin, and Sioux languages, who depended on caribou and moose in the north and buffalo in the south. French trading posts established about 1750; owned by Hudson's Bay Company, first permanent settlement 1774; ceded to Canadian government 1870 as part of Northwest Territories; became a province 1905.

Saskatchewan

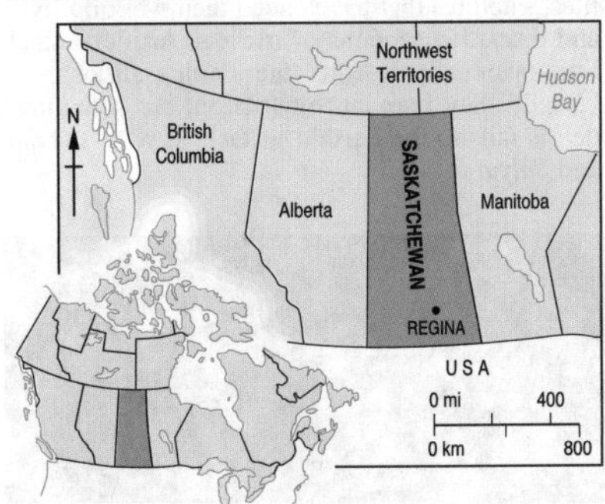

Sassanian Empire Persian empire founded AD 224 by Ardashir, a chieftain in the area of what is now Fars, in Iran, who had taken over ◊Parthia; it was named after his grandfather, Sasan. The capital was Ctesiphon, near modern ◊Baghdad, Iraq. After a rapid period of expansion, when it contested supremacy with Rome, it was destroyed 637 by Muslim Arabs at the Battle of ◊Qadisiya.

Sassau-Nguesso Denis 1943– . Congolese socialist politician, president 1979–92. He progressively consolidated his position within the ruling left-wing Congolese Labour Party (PCT), at the same time as improving relations with France and the USA. In 1990, in response to public pressure, he agreed that the PCT should abandon

'The world can survive very well without literature. But it can survive even more easily without man.'
Jean-Paul Sartre
Situations

LARGEST NATURAL PLANETARY SATELLITES

Planet	Satellite	Diameter (km/mi)	Mean distance from centre of primary planet (km/mi)	Orbital period (days)	Reciprocal mass (planet = 1)
Jupiter	Ganymede	5,262/3,300	1,070,000/664,898	7.16	12,800
Saturn	Titan	5,150/3,200	1,221,800/759,226	15.95	4,200
Jupiter	Callisto	4,800/3,000	1,883,000/1,170,096	16.69	17,700
Jupiter	Io	3,630/2,240	421,600/261,982	1.77	21,400
Earth	Moon	3,476/2,160	384,400/238,866	27.32	81.3
Jupiter	Europa	3,138/1,900	670,900/416,897	3.55	39,700
Neptune	Triton	2,700/1,690	354,300/220,162	5.88	770

'Soldiers are dreamers; when the guns begin / They think of firelit homes, clean beds, and wives.'

SIEGFRIED SASSOON 'Dreamers' 1918

Marxism-Leninism and that a multiparty system should be introduced.

Sassoon Siegfried Loraine 1886–1967. English writer. He wrote the autobiography *Memoirs of a Foxhunting Man* 1928. His *War Poems* 1919 express the disillusionment of his generation.

Educated at Cambridge, Sassoon enlisted in the army 1915, serving in France and Palestine. He published many volumes of poetry and three volumes of childhood autobiography, *The Old Century and Seven More Years* 1938, *The Weald of Youth* 1942, and *Siegfried's Journey* 1945. He wrote a biography of the novelist George Meredith 1948 and published *Collected Poems* 1961.

Satan a name for the ◊devil.

Satanism worship of the devil (Satan) instead of God, and the belief that doing so can bind a person to his power. The high point of Satanism is believed to be the Black Mass, a parody of the Christian Mass or Eucharist.

Accusations of Satanism are common in times of social and religious upheaval – such as the late 15th to late 17th centuries in Europe when the authority of first the Roman Catholic Church and then of the various major Protestant churches was questioned. There is little evidence that Satanism was ever actually practised, though in the 20th century Churches of Satan have emerged in the USA, which tend to be anti-Christian rather than overtly concerned with the propagation of evil.

'Satire is a sort of glass, wherein beholders do generally discover everybody's face but their own.'

On SATIRE Jonathan Swift *The Battle of the Books* 1704

satellite any small body that orbits a larger one, either natural or artificial. Natural satellites that orbit planets are called moons. The first artificial satellite, *Sputnik 1*, was launched into orbit around the Earth by the USSR 1957. Artificial satellites are used for scientific purposes, communications, weather forecasting, and military applications. The brightest artificial satellites can be seen by the naked eye.

At any time, there are several thousand artificial satellites orbiting the Earth, including active satellites, satellites that have ended their working lives, and discarded sections of rockets. Artificial satellites eventually re-enter the Earth's atmosphere. Usually they burn up by friction, but sometimes debris falls to the Earth's surface, as with ◊*Skylab* and *Salyut 7*.

satellite The Syncom IV-5 communications satellite in orbit around the Earth. *Image Select (UK) Ltd*

satellite television transmission of broadcast signals through artificial communications satellites. Mainly positioned in ◊geostationary orbit, satellites have been used since the 1960s to relay television pictures around the world. Higher-power satellites have more recently been developed to broadcast signals to cable systems or directly to people's homes.

Satie Erik (Alfred Leslie) 1866–1925. French composer. His piano pieces, such as the three *Gymnopédies* 1888, are precise and tinged with melancholy, and parody romantic expression with surreal commentary. His aesthetic of ironic simplicity, as in the *Messe des pauvres/Poor People's Mass* 1895, acted as a nationalist antidote to the perceived excesses of German Romanticism.

Mentor of the group of composers *Les Six*, he promoted the concept of *musique d'ameublement* ('furniture music'), anticipating the impact of radio. His *Parade* for orchestra 1917 includes a typewriter, and he invented a new style of film music for René Clair's *Entr'acte* 1924.

satire literary or dramatic work that ridicules human pretensions or exposes social evils. Satire is related to parody in its intention to mock, but satire tends to be more subtle and to mock an attitude or a belief, whereas parody tends to mock a particular work (such as a poem) by imitating its style, often with purely comic intent.

The Roman poets Juvenal and Horace wrote *Satires*, and the form became popular in Europe in the 17th and 18th centuries, used by Voltaire in France and by Alexander Pope and Jonathan Swift in England. Both satire and parody are designed to appeal to the intellect rather than the emotions and both, to be effective, require a knowledge of the original attitude, person, or work that is being mocked (although much satire, such as *Gulliver's Travels* by Swift, can also be enjoyed simply on a literal level).

satrap title of a provincial governor in ancient Persia. Under Darius I, the Persian Empire was divided between some 20 satraps, each owing allegiance only to the king. Later the term was used to describe any local ruler, often in a derogatory way.

satsuma small, hardy, loose-skinned orange *Citrus reticulata* of the tangerine family, originally from Japan. It withstands cold conditions well.

saturated compound organic compound, such as propane, that contains only single covalent bonds. Saturated organic compounds can only undergo further reaction by ◊substitution reactions, as in the production of chloropropane from propane.

saturated fatty acid ◊fatty acid in which there are no double bonds in the hydrocarbon chain.

saturated solution in physics and chemistry, a solution obtained when a solvent (liquid) can dissolve no more of a solute (usually a solid) at a particular temperature. Normally, a slight fall in temperature causes some of the solute to crystallize out of solution. If this does not happen the phenomenon is called supercooling, and the solution is said to be supersaturated.

Saturn in astronomy, the second-largest planet in the Solar System, sixth from the Sun, and encircled by bright and easily visible equatorial rings. Viewed through a telescope it is ochre. Its polar diameter is 12,000 km/7,450 mi smaller than its equatorial diameter, a result of its fast rotation and low density, the lowest of any planet. Its mass is 95 times that of Earth, and its magnetic field 1,000 times stronger.

mean distance from the Sun 1.427 billion km/0.886 billion mi

equatorial diameter 120,000 km/75,000 mi

rotational period 10 hr 14 min at equator, 10 hr 40 min at higher latitudes

year 29.46 Earth years

atmosphere visible surface consists of swirling clouds, probably made of frozen ammonia at a temperature of −170°C/−274°F, although the markings in the clouds are not as prominent as Jupiter's. The space probes *Voyager 1* and *2* found winds reaching 1,800 kph/1,100 mph

surface Saturn is believed to have a small core of rock and iron, encased in ice and topped by a deep layer of liquid hydrogen

satellites 18 known moons, more than for any other planet. The largest moon, ◊Titan, has a dense atmosphere. The rings visible from Earth begin about 14,000 km/9,000 mi from the planet's cloud-tops and extend out to about 76,000 km/47,000 mi. Made of small chunks of ice and rock (averaging 1 m/3 ft across), they are 275,000 km/170,000 mi rim to rim, but only 100 m/300 ft thick. The Voyager probes showed that the rings actually consist of thousands of closely spaced ringlets, looking like the grooves in a gramophone record.

Saturn in Roman mythology, the god of agriculture, identified by the Romans with the Greek god ◊Kronos. His period of rule was the ancient Golden Age. Saturn was dethroned by his sons Jupiter, Neptune, and Dis. At his festival, the Saturnalia in Dec, gifts were exchanged, and slaves were briefly treated as their masters' equals.

Saturn rocket family of large US rockets, developed by Wernher von Braun (1912–1977) for the ◊Apollo project. The two-stage *Saturn IB* was used for launching Apollo spacecraft into orbit around the Earth. The three-stage *Saturn V* sent Apollo spacecraft to the Moon, and launched the ◊*Skylab* space station. The liftoff thrust of a *Saturn V* was 3,500 tonnes. After Apollo and *Skylab*, the Saturn rockets were retired in favour of the ◊space shuttle.

satyagraha (Sanskrit 'insistence on truth') nonviolent resistance to British rule in India, as employed by Mahatma ◊Gandhi from 1918 to press for political reform; the idea owes much to the Russian writer Leo ◊Tolstoy. ▷*See feature on pp. 432–433.*

satyr in Greek mythology, a lustful, drunken woodland creature characterized by pointed ears, two horns on the forehead, and a tail. Satyrs attended the god of wine, ◊Dionysus. Roman writers confused satyrs with goat-footed fauns.

Satie Erik Satie, one of the great eccentrics of the history of music. As unconventional in art as in life, he lived alone, permitting no-one to enter his apartment, and he often gave his compositions bizarre titles. He is best known for his solo piano works. *Corbis*

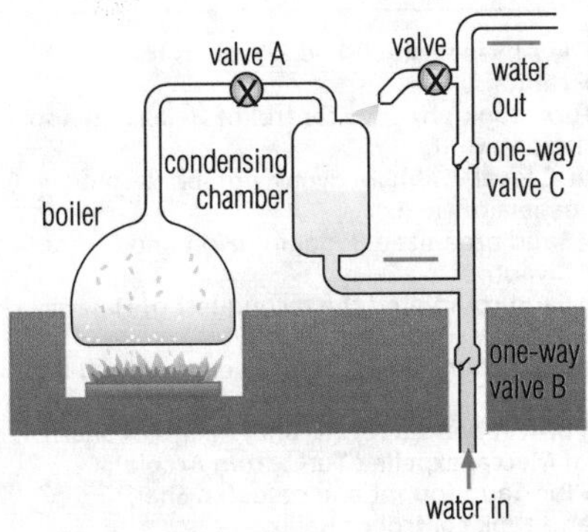

Savery Thomas Savery's steam pump, the 'Miners' Friend', has been described as the precursor of the steam engine. However, it achieved only limited success and was not adopted widely, probably because of faulty materials and poor workmanship.

Saudi Arabia country on the Arabian peninsula, stretching from the Red Sea in the W to the Arabian Gulf in the E, bounded N by Jordan, Iraq, and Kuwait; E by Qatar and United Arab Emirates; SE by Oman; and S by Yemen. *See country box on p. 948.*

Saul lived 11th century BC. in the Old Testament, the first king of Israel. He was anointed by Samuel and warred successfully against the neighbouring Ammonites and Philistines, but fell from God's favour in his battle against the Amalekites. He became jealous and suspicious of ◊David and turned against him and Samuel. After being wounded in battle with the Philistines, in which his three sons died, he committed suicide.

sausage tree tropical African tree *Kigelia pinnata*, family Bignoniaceae, up to 12 m/40 ft tall. Its gourdlike fruits hang from stalks and look like thick sausages, up to 60 cm/2 ft long and weighing 2–5 kg/5–12 lb. It has purplish flowers.

Saussure Ferdinand de 1857–1913. Swiss language scholar, a pioneer of modern linguistics and the originator of the concept of ◊structuralism as used in linguistics, anthropology, and literary theory.

He taught at the universities of Paris and Geneva. His early work, on the Indo-European language family, led to a major treatise on its vowel system. *Cours de linguistique générale/Course in General Linguistics* 1916 was posthumously derived mainly from his lecture notes by his students.

savanna or ***savannah*** extensive open tropical grasslands, with scattered trees and shrubs. Savannas cover large areas of Africa, North and South America, and N Australia. The soil is acidic and sandy and generally considered suitable only as pasture for low-density grazing.

A new strain of rice suitable for savanna conditions was developed 1992. It not only grew successfully under test conditions in Colombia but also improved pasture quality so grazing numbers could be increased twentyfold.

Savery Thomas c. 1650–1715. British engineer who invented the steam-driven water pump 1696. It was the world's first working steam engine, though the boiler was heated by an open fire. The pump used a boiler to raise steam, which was condensed (in a separate condenser) by an external spray of cold water. The partial vacuum created sucked water up a pipe; steam pressure was then used to force the water away, after which the cycle was repeated. Savery patented his invention 1698, but it appears that poor-quality work and materials made his engines impractical.

Save the Children Fund organization established 1919 to promote the rights of children to care, good health, material welfare, and moral, spiritual, and educational development. It operates in more than 50 Third World countries and the UK; projects include the provision of health care, education, community development, and emergency relief. Its headquarters are in London.

Savimbi Jonas Malheiro 1934– . Angolan soldier and right-wing revolutionary, founder and leader of the National Union for the Total Independence of Angola (UNITA). From 1975 UNITA, under Savimbi's leadership, tried to overthrow the government. A peace agreement was signed 1994; Savimbi rejected the offer of vice presidency in a coalition government 1996.

Savonarola Girolamo 1452–1498. Italian reformer, a Dominican friar and an eloquent preacher. His crusade against political and religious corruption won him popular support, and in 1494 he led a revolt in Florence that expelled the ruling Medici family and established a democratic republic. His denunciations of Pope ◊Alexander VI led to his excommunication 1497, and in 1498 he was arrested, tortured, hanged, and burned for heresy.

Savoy area of France between the Alps, Lake Geneva, and the river Rhône. A medieval duchy, it was made into the *départements* of Savoie and Haute-Savoie, in the Rhône-Alpes region.

history Savoy was a duchy from the 14th century, with the capital Chambéry. In 1720 it became a province of the kingdom of Sardinia which, with Nice, was ceded to France 1860 by Victor Emmanuel II (king of Italy from 1861) in return for French assistance in driving the Austrians from Italy.

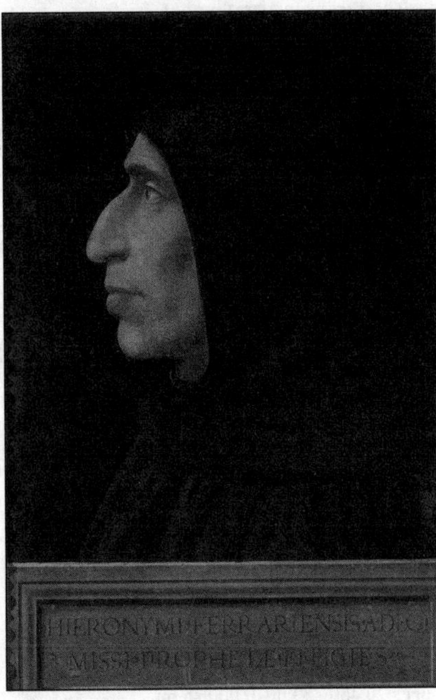

Savonarola Portrait of religious reformer Girolamo Savonarola by Fra Bartolomeo, 15th century, Convento di San Marco, Florence, Italy. After reforming the Dominican order in Tuscany, Savonarola went on to exert his puritan influence on Florentine society. Books and paintings were among the worldly goods burned at his public burnings of 'vanities'. *Corbis*

sawfish any fish of the order Pristiformes of large, sharklike ◊rays, characterized by a flat, sawlike snout edged with teeth. The common sawfish *Pristis pectinatus*, also called the smalltooth, is more than 6 m/19 ft long. It has some 24 teeth along an elongated snout (2 m/6 ft) that can be used as a weapon.

Sawfish have often been responsible for damaging underwater cables, and can injure humans when accidentally caught in fishing nets.

sawfly any of several families of insects of the order Hymenoptera, related to bees, wasps, and ants, but lacking a 'waist' on the body. The egg-laying tube (ovipositor) of the female is surrounded by a pair of sawlike organs, which it uses to make a slit in a plant stem to lay its eggs. Horntails are closely related.

Some species have sharp ovipositors that can drill into wood, such as the black and yellow European wood wasp *Uroceras gigas*, about 4 cm/1.5 in long, which bores into conifers. *See illustration on following page.*

Saw Maung 1929– . Myanmar (Burmese) soldier and politician. Appointed head of the armed forces in 1985 by ◊Ne Win, he led a coup to remove Ne Win's successor, Maung Maung, in 1988 and became leader of a totalitarian 'emergency government', which remained in office despite being defeated in the May 1990 election. In April 1992 he was replaced as chair of the ruling military junta, prime minister, and commander of the armed forces by Than Shwe.

Saturn Saturn taken by *Voyager 1* from a distance of 32 million miles on 5 October 1980. At this time the spacecraft was 940 million miles from Earth and six weeks away from its closest approach to Saturn. *NASA/Image Select (UK) Ltd*

Saxe (Hermann) Maurice, Comte de 1696–1750. Soldier, illegitimate son of the Elector of Saxony, who served under Prince Eugène of Savoy and was created marshal of France in 1743 for his exploits in the War of the Austrian Succession.

Saxe-Coburg-Gotha Saxon duchy. Albert, the Prince Consort of Britain's Queen Victoria, was a son of the 1st Duke, Ernest I (1784–1844), who was succeeded by Albert's elder brother, Ernest II (1818–1893). It remained the name of the British royal house until 1917, when it was changed to Windsor.

saxhorn family of brass musical instruments played with valves, invented 1845 by the Belgian Adolphe Sax (1814–1894); the ◊flugelhorn remains in current use.

saxifrage any plant of the genus *Saxifraga*, family Saxifragaceae, occurring in rocky, mountainous, and alpine situations in the northern hemisphere. They are low plants with groups of small white, pink, or yellow flowers. London pride *S. umbrosa x spathularis* is a common garden hybrid, with rosettes of fleshy leaves and clusters of white to pink, star-shaped flowers.

Saxon member of a Germanic tribe once inhabiting the Danish peninsula and N Germany. The Saxons migrated from their homelands in the early Middle Ages, under pressure from the Franks, and spread into various parts of Europe, including Britain (see ◊Anglo-Saxon). They also undertook piracy in the North Sea and the English Channel.

According to the English historian Bede, the Saxons arrived in Britain 449, and the archaeological evidence and sparse literary sources suggest the years around 450 as marking the end of their piratical raids, and the establishment of their first settlements in S England.

Saxony (German ***Sachsen***) administrative *Land* (state) of Germany
area 17,036 sq km/6,580 sq mi

sawfish Sawfishes are related to skates and rays. They are large, flattened fishes averaging 5 m/16 ft in length but maximum weights of more than 2,200 kg/5,000 lb have been recorded. Sawfishes use their elongated, toothed snouts to grub for molluscs and crustaceans on muddy seabeds.

SAUDI ARABIA
Kingdom of

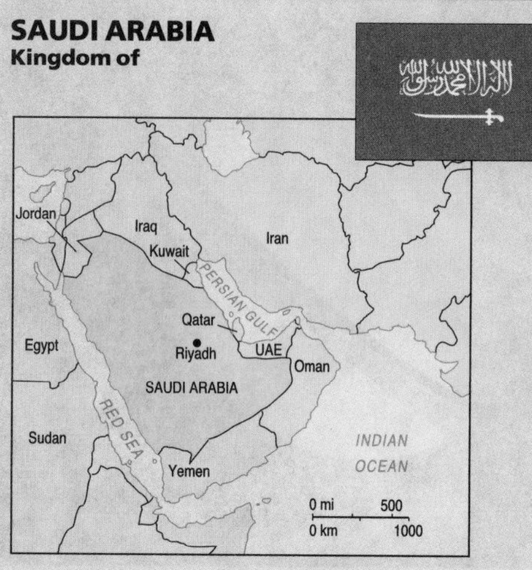

national name *Mamlaka al-'Arabiya as-Sa'udiya*
area 2,200,518 sq km/849,400 sq mi
capital Riyadh
major towns/cities Mecca, Medina, Taif
major ports Jiddah, Dammam, Jubail, Jizan, Yanbu
physical features desert, sloping to the Persian Gulf from a height of 2,750 m/9,000 ft in the W
head of state King Fahd Ibn Abdul Aziz from 1996
head of government King Fahd Ibn Abdul Aziz from 1996
political system absolute monarchy
administrative divisions 13 provinces
political parties none
armed forces 105,500 (1995); paramilitary forces 10,500; National Guard 77,000
conscription none
defence spend (% GDP) 11.2 (1994)
education spend (% GNP) 6.4 (1992)
health spend (% GDP) 3.1 (1990)
death penalty retained and used for ordinary crimes
population 20,786,000 (1998 est)
population growth rate 2.2% (1990–95); 3.1% (2000–05)
age distribution (% of total population) <15 41.9%, 15–65 55.4%, >65 2.7% (1995)
ethnic distribution around 90% Arab; 10% Afro-Asian
population density (per sq km) 8 (1994)
urban population (% of total) 80 (1995)
labour force 34% of population: 19% agriculture, 20% industry, 61% services (1990)
child mortality rate (under 5, per 1,000 live births) 36 (1994)
life expectancy 64 (men), 68 (women)
education (compulsory years) n/a
literacy 73% (men), 48% (women)
language Arabic
religions Sunni Muslim; there is a Shi'ite minority
TV sets (per 1,000 people) 263 (1996)
currency rial
GDP (US $) 145.8 billion (1997)
GDP per capita (PPP) (US $) 10,870 (1997)
growth rate 0.0% (1994)
average annual inflation 5.0% (1995); 2.1% (1980–93)
major trading partners USA, Japan, Germany, South Korea, France, Italy, Singapore, the Netherlands
resources petroleum, natural gas, iron ore, limestone, gypsum, marble, clay, salt, gold, uranium, copper, fish
industries petroleum and petroleum products, urea and ammonia fertilizers, steel, plastics, cement
exports crude and refined petroleum, petrochemicals, wheat. Principal market: Japan 17.1% (1994)
imports machinery and transport equipment, foodstuffs, beverages, tobacco, chemicals and chemical products, base metals and metal manufactures, textiles and clothing. Principal source: USA 20.6% (1993)
arable land 2% (1993)
agricultural products wheat, barley, sorghum, millet, tomatoes, dates, watermelons, grapes; livestock (chiefly poultry) and dairy products

HISTORY

622 Muhammad began to unite Arabs in Muslim faith.
7th–8th Cs Muslim Empire expanded, ultimately stretching from India to Spain, with Arabia itself being relegated to a subordinate part.
12th C Decline of Muslim Empire; Arabia grew isolated and internal divisions multiplied.
13th C Mameluke sultans of Egypt became nominal overlords of Hejaz in W Arabia.
1517 Hejaz became a nominal part of Ottoman Empire after Turks conquered Egypt.
18th C Al Saud family united tribesmen of Nejd in central Arabia in support of the Wahhabi religious movement.
c.1830 The Al Saud established Riyadh as the Wahhabi capital.
c.1870 Turks took effective control of Hejaz and also Hasa on Persian Gulf.
late 19th C Rival Wahhabi dynasty of Ibn Rashid became leaders of Nejd.
1902 Ibn Saud organized Bedouin revolt and regained Riyadh.
1913 Ibn Saud completed the reconquest of Hasa from Turks.
1915 Britain recognized Ibn Saud as emir of Nejd and Hasa.
1916–18 British-backed revolt, under aegis of Sharif Hussein of Mecca, expelled Turks from Arabia.
1919–25 Ibn Saud fought and defeated Sharif Hussein and took control of Hejaz.
1926 Proclamation of Ibn Saud as king of Hejaz and Nejd.
1932 Hejaz and Nejd renamed the United Kingdom of Saudi Arabia.
1933 Saudi Arabia allowed American-owned Standard Oil Company to prospect for oil, which was discovered in Hasa 1938.
1939–45 Although officially neutral in World War II, Saudi Arabia received subsidies from USA and Britain.
1940s Commercial exploitation of oil began, bringing great prosperity.
1953 Ibn Saud died; succeeded by his eldest son, Saud.
1964 King Saud forced to abdicate; succeeded by his brother, Faisal.
1975 King Faisal assassinated; succeeded by his half-brother, Khalid.
1982 King Khalid died; succeeded by his brother, Fahd.
1987 Rioting by Iranian pilgrims caused 400 deaths in Mecca and breach in diplomatic relations with Iran.
1990 Iraqi troops invaded Kuwait and massed on Saudi Arabian border, prompting King Fahd to call for assistance from US and UK forces.
1991 Saudi Arabia fought on Allied side against Iraq in Gulf War.
1992 Under international pressure to move towards democracy, King Fahd formed a 'consultative council' to assist in government of kingdom.
1995 King Fahd suffered a stroke and transferred power to Crown Prince Abdullah.
1996 King Fahd resumed power.

capital Dresden
towns Leipzig, Chemnitz, Zwickau
physical on the plain of the river Elbe north of the Erzgebirge mountain range
products electronics, textiles, vehicles, machinery, chemicals, coal
population (1994 est) 4,608,000
history conquered by Charlemagne 792, Saxony became a powerful medieval German duchy. The electors of Saxony were also kings of Poland 1697–1763. Saxony was part of East Germany 1946–90, forming a region with Anhalt.

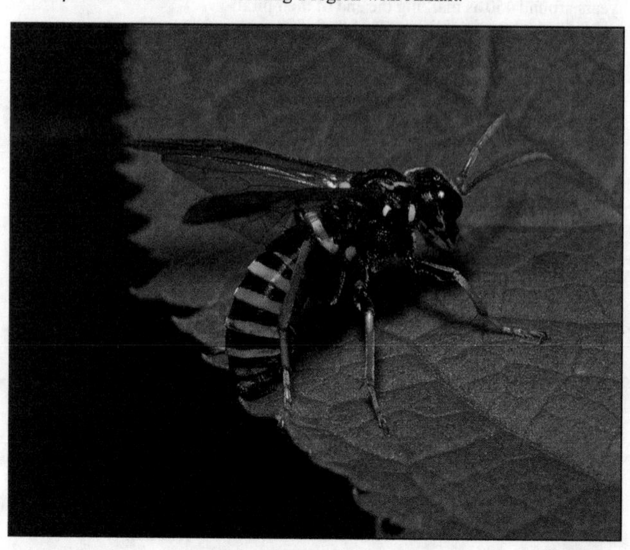

sawfly The sawlike ovipositor of this female *Thenthredo scrophulariae* sawfly is just visible beneath the tip of the abdomen as she cuts a slit into a leaf to insert her eggs. This species is an excellent wasp mimic. *Premaphotos Wildlife*

Saxony-Anhalt administrative *Land* (state) of Germany
area 20,450 sq km/10,000 sq mi
capital Magdeburg
towns Halle, Dessau
industries chemicals, electronics, rolling stock, footwear, cereals, vegetables
population (1994 est) 2,778,000
history Anhalt became a duchy 1863 and a member of the North German Confederation 1866. Between 1946 and 1990 it was joined to the former Prussian province of Saxony as a region of East Germany.

saxophone member of a hybrid brass instrument family of conical bore, with a single-reed woodwind mouthpiece and keyworks, invented about 1840 by Belgian instrumentmaker Adolphe Sax (1814–1894). Soprano, alto, tenor, and baritone forms remain current. The soprano saxophone is usually straight; the others are characteristically curved back at the mouthpiece and have an upturned bell. Initially a concert instrument of suave tone, the saxophone was incorporated into dance bands of the 1930s and 1940s, and assumed its modern guise as an abrasive solo jazz instrument after 1945. It has a voicelike ability to bend a note.

Sayers Dorothy L(eigh) 1893–1957. English writer of crime novels. Her stories feature the detective Lord Peter Wimsey and the heroine Harriet Vane, and include *Strong Poison* 1930, *The Nine Tailors* 1934, and *Gaudy Night* 1935. She also wrote religious plays for radio, and translations of Dante.

scabies contagious infection of the skin caused by the parasitic itch mite *Sarcoptes scabiei*, which burrows under the skin to deposit eggs. Treatment is by antiparasitic creams and lotions.

scabious any plant of the Eurasian genus *Scabiosa* of the teasel family Dipsacaceae, with many small, usually blue, flowers borne in a single head on a tall stalk. The small scabious *S. columbaria* and the Mediterranean sweet scabious *S. atropurpurea* are often cultivated. The field scabious *Knautia arvensis*, although of a different genus, is closely related.

Scafell Pike highest mountain in England, 978 m/3,210 ft. It is in Cumbria in the Lake District and is separated from Scafell (964 m/3,164 ft) by a ridge called Mickledore.

scalar quantity in mathematics and science, a quantity that has magnitude but no direction, as distinct from a ◊vector quantity, which has a direction as well as a magnitude. Temperature, mass, and volume are scalar quantities.

scale in chemistry, ◊calcium carbonate deposits that form on the inside of a kettle or boiler as a result of boiling ◊hard water.

scale in music, a sequence of pitches that establishes a key, and in some respects the character of a composition. A scale is defined by its starting note and may be major or minor depending on the order of intervals. A chromatic scale is the full range of 12 notes: it has no key because there is no fixed starting point. A whole-tone scale is a six-note scale and is also indeterminate in key: only two are possible. A diatonic scale has seven notes, a pentatonic scale has five.

scale insect any small plant-sucking insect, order Homoptera, of the superfamily Cocceidea. Some species are major pests – for example, the citrus mealy bug (genus *Pseudococcus*), which attacks citrus fruits in North America. The female is often wingless and legless, attached to a plant by the head and with the body covered with a waxy scale. The rare males are winged.

scallop any marine bivalve ◊mollusc of the family Pectinidae, with a fan-shaped shell. There are two 'ears' extending from the socketlike hinge. Scallops use water-jet propulsion to move through the water to escape predators such as starfish. The giant Pacific scallop found from Alaska to California can reach 20 cm/8 in width.

The St James's shell *Pecten jacobaeus* was used as a badge by medieval pilgrims to ◊Santiago de Compostela.

scaly anteater another name for the ◊pangolin.

Scandinavia peninsula in NW Europe, comprising Norway and Sweden; politically and culturally it also includes Denmark, Iceland, the Faroe Islands, and Finland. (See separate entries for all of these.)

scandium silver-white, metallic element of the ◊lanthanide series, symbol Sc, atomic number 21, relative atomic mass 44.956. Its compounds are found widely distributed in nature, but only in minute amounts. The metal has little industrial importance.

scanning in medicine, the noninvasive examination of body organs to detect abnormalities of structure or function. Detectable waves – for example, ◊ultrasound, gamma, or ◊X-rays – are passed through the part to be scanned. Their absorption pattern is recorded, analysed by computer, and displayed pictorially on a screen.

scanning electron microscope (SEM) electron microscope that produces three-dimensional images, magnified 10–200,000 times. A fine beam of electrons, focused by electromagnets, is moved, or scanned, across the specimen. Electrons reflected from the specimen are collected by a detector, giving rise to an electrical signal, which is then used to generate a point of brightness on a television-like screen. As the point moves rapidly over the screen, in phase with the scanning electron beam, an image of the specimen is built up.

scanning transmission electron microscope (STEM) electron microscope that combines features of the ◊scanning electron microscope (SEM) and the ◊transmission electron microscope (TEM). First built in the USA in 1966, the microscope has both the SEM's contrast characteristics and lack of aberrations and the high resolution of the TEM. Magnifications of over 90 million times can be achieved, enough to image single atoms.

scanning tunnelling microscope (STM) microscope that produces a magnified image by moving a tiny tungsten probe across the surface of the specimen. The tip of the probe is so fine that it may consist of a single atom, and it moves so close to the specimen surface that electrons jump (or tunnel) across the gap between the tip and the surface. The magnitude of the electron flow (current) depends on the distance from the tip to the surface, and so by measuring the current, the contours of the surface can be determined. These can be used to form an image on a computer screen of the surface, with individual atoms resolved. Magnifications up to 100 million times are possible.

scapolite group of white or greyish minerals, silicates of sodium, aluminium, and calcium, common in metamorphosed limestones and forming at high temperatures and pressures.

scapula or ***shoulder blade*** large, flat, triangular bone which lies over the second to seventh ribs on the back, forming part of the pectoral girdle, and assisting in the articulation of the arm with the chest region. Its flattened shape allows a large region for the attachment of muscles.

scarab any of a family Scarabaeidae of beetles, often brilliantly coloured, and including ◊cockchafers, June beetles, and dung beetles. The *Scarabeus sacer* was revered by the ancient Egyptians as the symbol of resurrection.

Scarborough spa and holiday resort in North Yorkshire, England; population (1991) 38,800. A ruined Norman castle overlooks the town, which is a touring centre for the Yorkshire Moors. It is the home town of British playwright Alan Ayckbourn.

Scargill Arthur 1938– . British trade-union leader. Elected president of the National Union of Mineworkers (NUM) 1981, he bitterly opposed the industrial policies of the Conservative government of Margaret Thatcher. The damaging strike of 1984–85 split the miners' movement. In 1995, criticizing what he saw as the Labour party's lurch to the right, he established the rival independent Socialist Labour Party. This proved to be largely ineffectual, and made little impact in consequent elections.

Scargill became a miner after leaving school and was soon a union and political activist, in the Young Communist League 1955–62, and then a member of the Labour Party from 1966 and president of the Yorkshire miners' union 1973–81. He became a fiery and effective orator. During the 1984–85 miners' strike he was criticised for not seeking an early NUM ballot to support the strike decision.

Scarlatti (Giuseppe) Domenico 1685–1757. Italian composer. The eldest son of Alessandro ◊Scarlatti, he lived most of his life in Portugal and Spain in the service of the Queen of Spain. He wrote over 500 sonatas for harpsichord, short pieces in ◊binary form demonstrating the new freedoms of keyboard composition and inspired by Spanish musical idioms.

Scarlatti (Pietro) Alessandro (Gaspare) 1660–1725. Italian Baroque composer. He was maestro di capella at the court of Naples and developed the opera form. He composed more than 100 operas, including *Tigrane* 1715, as well as church music and oratorios.

scarlet fever or ***scarlatina*** acute infectious disease, especially of children, caused by the bacteria in the *Streptococcus pyogenes* group. It is marked by fever, vomiting, sore throat, and a bright red rash spreading from the upper to the lower part of the body. The rash is followed by the skin peeling in flakes. It is treated with antibiotics.

scarp and dip in geology, the two slopes formed when a sedimentary bed outcrops as a landscape feature. The scarp is the slope that cuts across the bedding plane; the dip is the opposite slope which follows the bedding plane. The scarp is usually steep, while the dip is a gentle slope.

scattering in physics, the random deviation or reflection of a stream of particles or of a beam of radiation such as light.

Alpha particles scattered by a thin gold foil provided the first convincing evidence that atoms had very small, very dense, positive nuclei. From 1906 to 1908 Ernest Rutherford carried out a series of experiments from which he estimated that the closest approach of an alpha particle to a gold nucleus in a head-on collision was about 10^{-14} m. He concluded that the gold nucleus must be no larger than this. Most of the alpha particles fired at the gold foil passed straight through undeviated; however, a few were scattered in all directions and a very small fraction bounced back towards the source.

Light is scattered from a rough surface, such as that of a sheet of paper, by random reflection from the varying angles of each small part of the surface. This is responsible for the dull, flat appearance of such surfaces and their inability to form images (unlike mirrors). Light is also scattered by particles suspended in a gas or liquid. The red and yellow colours associated with sunrises and sunsets are due to the fact that red light is scattered to a lesser extent than is blue light by dust particles in the atmosphere. When the Sun is low in the sky, its light passes through a thicker, more dusty layer of the atmosphere, and the blue light radiated by it is scattered away, leaving the red sunlight to pass through to the eye of the observer.

scent gland gland that opens onto the outer surface of animals, producing odorous compounds that are used for communicating between members of the same species (◊pheromones), or for discouraging predators.

scepticism ancient philosophical view that absolute knowledge of things is ultimately unobtainable, hence the only proper attitude is to suspend judgement. Its origins lay in the teachings of the Greek philosopher Pyrrho, who maintained that peace of mind lay in renouncing all claims to knowledge.

It was taken up in a less extreme form by the Greek Academy in the 3rd and 2nd centuries BC. Academic sceptics claimed that although truth is finally unknowable, a balance of probabilities can be used for coming to decisions. The most radical form of scepticism is known as ◊solipsism, which maintains that the self is the only thing that can be known to exist.

Schelling Friedrich Wilhelm Joseph von 1775–1854. German philosopher who developed a 'philosophy of identity' (*Identitätsphilosophie*), in which subject and object are seen as united in the absolute. His early philosophy influenced G W F ◊Hegel, but his later work criticizes Hegel, arguing that being necessarily precedes thought.

Schelling began as a follower of J G Fichte, but moved away from subjective ◊idealism, which treats the external world as essentially immaterial.

Schengen Group association of states, within the European Union, that in theory adhere to the ideals of the Schengen Convention, notably the abolition of passport controls at common internal borders and the strengthening of external borders. The Convention, which went into effect on a three-month trial basis March 1995, was signed by

scarab This striking scarab beetle *Helictopleurus quadripunctatus* from the dry forests of Madagascar is one of many scarabs that collect and bury dung on which to rear their larvae. This particular species will utilize only the pellets of dung from the Verreaux's sifaka, a type of lemur. *Premaphotos Wildlife*

"Against stupidity the gods themselves struggle in vain."
Friedrich von Schiller *The Maid of Orleans*

Belgium, France, Germany, Luxembourg, and the Netherlands June 1990; Italy Nov 1990; Portugal and Spain June 1991; Greece Nov 1992; and Austria April 1995. In May 1995 several EU countries urged Italy to introduce tighter entry controls, believing that many illegal immigrants were entering the EU through Italy. The pact was renewed permanently June 1995 by all signatories except France, which invoked a clause allowing it to continue passport checks for a further six months; in March 1996, France again refused to implement the agreement due to concerns about the risk of drugs coming in from the Netherlands. In April 1996 five observer members were admitted: Denmark, Finland, Iceland, Norway and Sweden. The UK has not joined the agreement because of concerns over the removal of checks against drugs trafficking, terrorists and rabies.

scherzo (Italian 'joke') in music, a lively piece, usually in rapid triple (3/4) time; often used for the third movement of a symphony, sonata, or quartet as a substitute for the more stately ◊minuet and trio.

Schiaparelli Giovanni Virginio 1835–1910. Italian astronomer. He drew attention to linear markings on Mars, which gave rise to the popular belief that they were canals. The markings were soon shown by French astronomer Eugène Antoniadi (1870–1944) to be optical effects and not real lines. Schiaparelli also gave observational evidence for the theory that all meteor showers are fragments of disintegrating comets, and for this work he was awarded the Gold Medal of the Royal Astronomical Society 1873.

During his mapping of Mars, beginning 1877, Schiaparelli noted what his colleague in Rome, Pietro Secchi (1818–1878), had called 'channels' (*canali*). Schiaparelli adopted this term and also wrote of 'seas' and 'continents', but he made it quite clear that he did not mean the words to be taken literally. Nevertheless, fanciful stories of advanced life on Mars proliferated on the basis of the 'canals'.

"There is only one innate error, and that is that we are here in order to be happy."
Arthur Schopenhauer *The World as Will and Idea*

Schiele Egon 1890–1918. Austrian artist. Strongly influenced by ◊Art Nouveau, and in particular Gustav ◊Klimt, he developed an angular, contorted style, employing garish colours, that made him an important pioneer of ◊Expressionism. His subject matter includes portraits and openly erotic nudes.

Schiller Johann Christoph Friedrich von 1759–1805. German dramatist, poet, and historian. He wrote ◊*Sturm und Drang* ('storm and stress') verse and plays, including the dramatic trilogy *Wallenstein* 1798–99. He was an idealist, and much of his work concerns the aspiration for political freedom and the avoidance of mediocrity.

After the success of his play *Die Räuber/The Robbers* 1781, he completed the tragedies *Die Verschwörung des Fiesko zu Genua/Fiesco, or, the Genoese Conspiracy* (his first historical drama) and *Kabale und Liebe/Intrigue and Love* 1783. In 1787 he wrote his more mature blank-verse drama *Don Carlos* and the hymn 'An die Freude/Ode to Joy', later used by ◊Beethoven in his ninth symphony. As professor of history at Jena from 1789 he completed a history of the Thirty Years' War and developed a close friendship with ◊Goethe, after early antagonism. His essays on aesthetics include the piece of literary criticism *Über naive und sentimentalische Dichtung/Naive and Sentimental Poetry* 1795–96. Schiller became the foremost German dramatist with his classic dramas *Wallenstein*, *Maria Stuart* 1800, *Die Jungfrau von Orleans/The Maid of Orleans* 1801, and *Wilhelm Tell/William Tell* 1804.

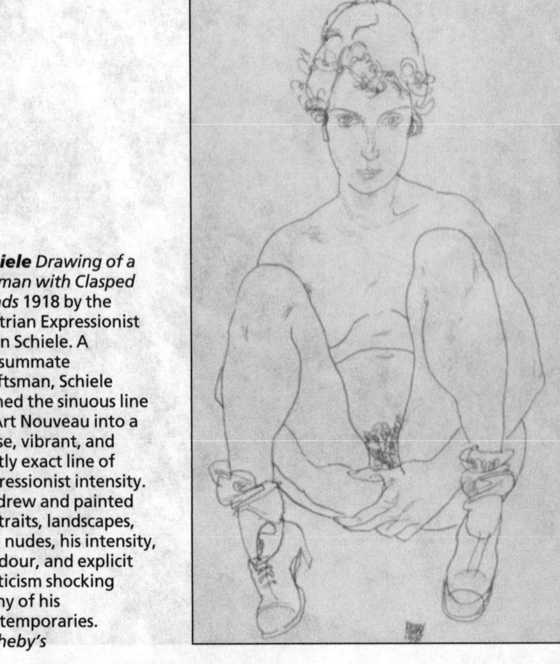

Schiele *Drawing of a Woman with Clasped Hands* 1918 by the Austrian Expressionist Egon Schiele. A consummate draftsman, Schiele turned the sinuous line of Art Nouveau into a tense, vibrant, and subtly exact line of Expressionist intensity. He drew and painted portraits, landscapes, and nudes, his intensity, candour, and explicit eroticism shocking many of his contemporaries. *Sotheby's*

schism formal split over a doctrinal difference between religious believers, as in the ◊Great Schism in the Roman Catholic Church; over the doctrine of papal infallibility, as with the Old Catholics in 1879; and over the use of the Latin Tridentine Mass 1988.

schist ◊metamorphic rock containing ◊mica or another platy or elongate mineral, whose crystals are aligned to give a foliation (planar texture) known as schistosity. Schist may contain additional minerals such as ◊garnet.

schizocarp dry ◊fruit that develops from two or more carpels and splits, when mature, to form separate one-seeded units known as mericarps.

The mericarps may be dehiscent, splitting open to release the seed when ripe, as in *Geranium*, or indehiscent, remaining closed once mature, as in mallow *Malva* and plants of the Umbelliferae family, such as the carrot *Daucus carota* and parsnip *Pastinaca sativa*.

schizophrenia mental disorder, a psychosis of unknown origin, which can lead to profound changes in personality, behaviour, and perception, including delusions and hallucinations. It is more common in males and the early-onset form is more severe than when the illness develops in later life. Modern treatment approaches include drugs, family therapy, stress reduction, and rehabilitation.

Schizophrenia implies a severe divorce from reality in the patient's thinking. Although the causes are poorly understood, it is now recognized as an organic disease, associated with structural anomalies in the brain. Canadian researchers 1995 identified a protein in the brain, PSA-NCAM, that plays a part in filtering sensory information. The protein is significantly reduced in the brains of schizophrenics, supporting the idea that schizophrenia occurs when the brain is overwhelmed by sensory information. There is also a genetic contribution.

Schlegel (Karl Wilhelm) Friedrich von 1772–1829. German literary critic. He was a founder of the Romantic movement, and a pioneer in the comparative study of languages.

Schlegel August Wilhelm von 1767–1845. German Romantic author and translator of Shakespeare. His 'Über dramatische Kunst und Literatur/Lectures on Dramatic Art and Literature' 1809–11 broke down the formalism of the old classical criteria of literary composition. Friedrich von Schlegel was his brother.

Schlesinger John Richard 1926– . English film and television director. He was responsible for such British films as *Billy Liar* 1963 and *Darling* 1965. His first US film, *Midnight Cowboy* 1969 (Academy Award), was a big commercial success and was followed by *Sunday, Bloody Sunday* 1971, *Marathon Man* 1976, *Yanks* 1979, and *Pacific Heights* 1990.

Schleswig-Holstein *Land* (state) of Germany
area 15,700 sq km/6,060 sq mi
capital Kiel
towns Lübeck, Flensburg, Schleswig
features river Elbe, Kiel Canal, Heligoland
industries shipbuilding, mechanical and electrical engineering, food processing
population (1994 est) 2,695,000
religion 87% Protestant; 6% Catholic
history Schleswig (Danish *Slesvig*) and Holstein were two duchies held by the kings of Denmark from 1460, but were not part of the kingdom; a number of the inhabitants were German, and Holstein was a member of the Confederation of the Rhine formed 1815. Possession of the duchies had long been disputed by Prussia, and when Frederick VII of Denmark died without an heir 1863, Prussia, supported by Austria, fought and defeated the Danes 1864, and in 1866 annexed the two duchies. A plebiscite held 1920 gave the northern part of Schleswig to Denmark, which made it the province of Haderslev and Aabenraa; the rest, with Holstein, remained part of Germany.

Schlieffen Plan military plan produced Dec 1905 by the German chief of general staff, General Count Alfred von Schlieffen (1833–1913), that formed the basis of German military planning before World War I, and inspired Hitler's plans for the conquest of Europe in World War II. It involved a simultaneous attack on Russia and France, the object being to defeat France quickly and then deploy all available resources against the Russians. The plan was altered by General von Moltke (1848–1916), who reduced the strength of the army's right wing and thus made it incapable of carrying out the Plan when it was implemented 1914.

Schliemann Heinrich 1822–1890. German archaeologist. He earned a fortune in business, retiring 1863 to pursue his lifelong ambition to discover a historical basis for Homer's *Iliad*. In 1870 he began excavating at Hissarlik, Turkey, a site which yielded the ruins of nine consecutive cities and was indeed the site of Troy. His later excavations were at Mycenae 1874–76, where he discovered the ruins of the ◊Mycenaean civilization.

Schlüter Poul Holmskov 1929– . Danish right-wing politician, leader of the Conservative People's Party (KF) from 1974 and prime minister 1982–93. His centre-right coalition survived the 1990 election and was reconstituted, with Liberal support. In Jan 1993 Schlüter resigned, accused of dishonesty over his role in an incident involving Tamil refugees. He was succeeded by Poul Nyrup ◊Rasmussen.

Schmidt Helmut Heinrich Waldemar 1918– . German socialist politician, member of the Social Democratic Party (SPD), chancellor of West Germany 1974–83. As chancellor, Schmidt introduced social reforms and continued Brandt's policy of Ostpolitik (reconciliation with Eastern Europe). With the French president Giscard d'Estaing, he instigated annual world and European economic summits. He was a firm supporter of ◊NATO and of the deployment of US nuclear missiles in West Germany during the early 1980s.

Schmidt Telescope reflecting telescope used for taking wide-angle photographs of the sky. Invented 1930 by Estonian astronomer Bernhard Schmidt (1879–1935), it has an added corrector lens to help focus the incoming light. Examples are the 1.2-m/48-in Schmidt telescope on ◊Mount Palomar and the UK Schmidt telescope, of the same size, at ◊Siding Spring.

Schnitzler Arthur 1862–1931. Viennese dramatist. A doctor with an interest in psychiatry, he was known for his psychological dramas exploring egotism, eroticism, and self-deception in Viennese bourgeois life. *Reigen/Merry-Go-Round* 1897, a cycle of dramatic dialogues depicting lust, caused a scandal when performed 1920 but made a successful French film as *La Ronde* 1950, directed by Max Ophuls. His novel *Leutnant Gustl* 1901 pioneered interior monologue in fiction.

Schoenberg Arnold Franz Walter 1874–1951. Austro-Hungarian composer, a US citizen from 1941. After Romantic early works such as *Verklärte Nacht/Transfigured Night* 1899 and the *Gurrelieder/Songs of Gurra* 1900–11, he experimented with ◊atonality (absence of key), producing works such as *Pierrot lunaire/Moonstruck Pierrot* 1912 for chamber ensemble and voice, before developing the ◊twelve-tone system of musical composition.

After 1918, Schoenberg wrote several Neo-Classical works for chamber ensembles. He taught at the Berlin State Academy 1925–33. The twelve-tone system was further developed by his pupils Alban ◊Berg and Anton ◊Webern. Driven from Germany by the Nazis, Schoenberg settled in the USA 1933, where he influenced music for films.

Scholastic Aptitude Test (SAT) in US education, national examination used as a college admissions test for high-school students. The SAT tests reasoning, maths, and use of the English language only, not knowledge of specific subjects.

scholasticism theological and philosophical systems and methods taught in the schools of

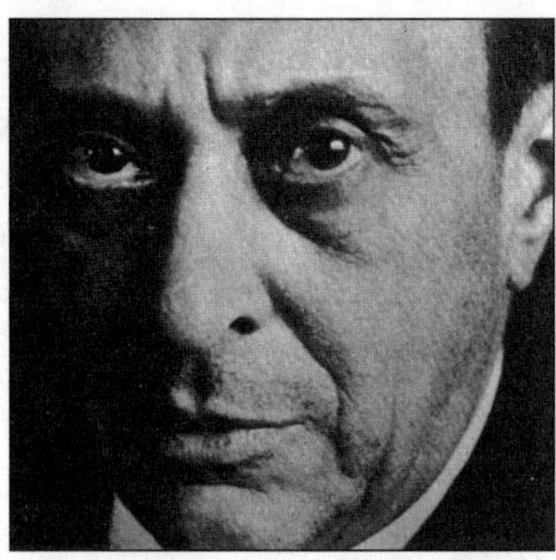

Schoenberg The composer Arnold Schoenberg (1874–1951) in his role as teacher at UCLA. After escaping the Nazis in 1933 he settled in the USA as a lecturer, eloquently preaching the laws of harmony despite his serialist compositional philosophy. *Larousse*

medieval Europe, especially in the 12th–14th centuries. Scholasticism tried to integrate orthodox Christian teaching with Aristotelian and some Platonic philosophy. The scholastic method involved surveying different opinions and the reasons given for them, and then attempting solutions of the problems raised, using logic and dialectic.

The 9th-century Platonist Johannes Scotus Erigena is sometimes regarded as an early scholastic. But scholasticism began at the end of the 11th century, when Roscellinus, a supporter of nominalism, and Anselm, a supporter of realism, disputed the nature of ◊universals. In the 12th century, the foundation of universities in Bologna, Paris, Oxford, and Cambridge, and the recovery of Greek philosophical texts, stimulated scholasticism.

The most important scholastic philosophers are, in the 13th century, Thomas Aquinas, whose works became classical texts of Catholic doctrine, and the Franciscan Duns Scotus; and in the 14th century William of Occam, who was the last major scholastic philosopher.

Schopenhauer Arthur 1788–1860. German philosopher. His *The World as Will and Idea* 1818, inspired by Immanuel Kant and ancient Hindu philosophy, expounded an atheistic and pessimistic world view: an irrational will is considered as the inner principle of the world, producing an ever-frustrated cycle of desire, of which the only escape is aesthetic contemplation or absorption into nothingness.

Having postulated a world of suffering and disappointment, he based his ethics on compassion. His notion of an irrational force at work in human beings strongly influenced both the philosopher Friedrich Nietzsche and the founder of psychiatry, Sigmund Freud.

Schreiner Olive Emilie Albertina 1855–1920. South African novelist and supporter of women's rights. Her autobiographical *The Story of an African Farm* 1883 describes life on the South African veld. Other works include *Trooper Peter Halket of Mashonaland* 1897, a fictional attack on the expansionist policies of Cecil Rhodes, and the feminist classic *Women and Labour* 1911.

Schrödinger Erwin 1887–1961. Austrian physicist. He advanced the study of wave mechanics to describe the behaviour of electrons in atoms. He produced in 1926 a solid mathematical explanation of the ◊quantum theory and the structure of the atom. Nobel prize 1933.

Schrödinger's mathematical description of electron waves superseded matrix mechanics, developed 1925 by Max ◊Born and Werner ◊Heisenberg, which also described the structure of the atom mathematically but, unlike wave mechanics, gave no picture of the atom. It was later shown that wave mechanics is equivalent to matrix mechanics.

Schroeder Gerhard 1944– . German politician, Social Democrat, Chancellor of Germany from 1998. Premier since 1990 of Lower Saxony, Germany's second-largest state, his re-election in March 1998, with an increased share of the vote, persuaded the SPD to select him to challenge Chancellor Helmut Kohl in the September 1998 general election. A moderate, media-skilled, populist politician, Schroeder has been described as a Eurosceptic.

Schubert Franz Peter 1797–1828. Austrian composer. His ten symphonies include the incomplete eighth in B minor (the 'Unfinished') and the 'Great' in C major. He wrote chamber and piano music, including the 'Trout Quintet', and over 600 lieder (songs) combining the Romantic expression of emotion with pure melody. They include the cycles *Die schöne Müllerin/The Beautiful Maid of the Mill* 1823 and *Die Winterreise/The Winter Journey* 1827.

Schumacher Fritz (Ernst Friedrich) 1911–1977. German economist. He believed that the increasing size of institutions, coupled with unchecked economic growth, creates a range of social and environmental problems. He argued his case in books like *Small is Beautiful* 1973, and established the Intermediate Technology Development Group 1965, which aims to give advice and assistance to the rural poor of developing countries on the appropriate choice of technologies.

Schumacher Michael 1969– . German motor-racing driver. He began his career in the Mercedes-Benz junior team; he joined the Jordan Formula One team 1991, but was poached by Benetton almost immediately. He won his first Grand Prix in Belgium 1992. Hailed by many as a gifted 'natural' driver, he won the world drivers' championship title for the first time 1994, and again 1995. He joined Ferrari at the end of the 1995 season. In July 1998 Schumacher won the British Grand Prix for the first time and signed a new £100 million contract with Ferrari that would keep him with the Italian team until 2002. At the end of the 1998 season he had a career total of 33 wins from 117 Grands Prix.

Schuman Robert 1886–1963. French politician. He was prime minister 1947–48, and as foreign minister 1948–53 he proposed in May 1950 a common market for coal and steel (the Schuman Plan), which was established as the European Coal and Steel Community 1952, the basis of the European Community (now the European Union).

Schumann Robert Alexander 1810–1856. German composer and writer. His songs and short piano pieces portray states of emotion with great economy. Among his compositions are four symphonies, a violin concerto, a piano concerto, sonatas, and song cycles, such as *Dichterliebe/Poet's Love* 1840. Mendelssohn championed many of his works.

Schuschnigg Kurt von 1897–1977. Austrian chancellor 1934–38, in succession to ◊Dollfuss. He tried in vain to prevent Nazi annexation (*Anschluss*) but in Feb 1938 he was forced to accept a Nazi minister of the interior, and a month later Austria was occupied and annexed by Germany. He was imprisoned in Germany until 1945, when he went to the USA; he returned to Austria 1967.

Schumann The composer Robert Schumann (1810–1856). After permanently damaging a finger as a result of over-practising, he gave up his career as a pianist to devote himself full-time to composition. His wife Clara was a fine pianist in her own right. *Image Select (UK) Ltd*

Schwarzenegger Arnold 1947– . Austrian-born US film actor. He was one of the biggest box-office attractions of the late 1980s and early 1990s. He starred in sword-and-sorcery films such as *Conan the Barbarian* 1982 and later graduated to large-scale budget action movies such as *Terminator* 1984, *Predator* 1987, *Terminator II* 1991, and *True Lies* 1994.

Schwarzkopf Norman, (nicknamed 'Stormin' Norman') 1934– . US general. He was supreme commander of the Allied forces in the ◊Gulf War 1991. He planned and executed a blitzkrieg campaign, 'Desert Storm', sustaining remarkably few Allied casualties in the liberation of Kuwait. He was a battalion commander in the Vietnam War and deputy commander of the 1983 US invasion of Grenada.

Schweitzer Albert 1875–1965. French Protestant theologian, organist, and missionary surgeon. He founded the hospital at Lambaréné in Gabon in 1913, giving organ recitals to support his work there. He wrote a life of German composer J S Bach and *Von reimarus zu Wrede/The Quest for the Historical Jesus* 1906. He was awarded the Nobel Peace Prize in 1952 for his teaching of 'reverence for life'.

Schwerin capital of the *Land* of Mecklenburg–West Pomerania, Germany, on the W shore of the lake of Schwerin; population (1993) 123,500. Products include machinery and chemicals.

Schwitters Kurt 1887–1948. German artist and poet. He was a leading member of the ◊Dada movement. His most important works are constructions and collages, which he called 'Merz', made from scraps and bric-a-brac of all kinds.

After an early Cubist phase, he became a founder-member of the Hanover Dada group 1919. He founded the influential Dada journal *Merz* 1923 and in the same year began his first of his *Merzbauen* ('Merz houses'), extensive constructions, some filling an entire building, of wood and scrap. Most were destroyed, though *Merz 32* 1924 has been kept in the Museum of Modern Art, New York.

He moved to Norway 1937 and, following the German invasion, to England 1940, where he spent the rest of his life.

sciatica persistent pain in the back and down the outside of one leg, along the sciatic nerve and its branches. Causes of sciatica include inflammation of the nerve or pressure of a displaced disc on a nerve root leading out of the lower spine.

science (Latin *scientia* 'knowledge') any systematic field of study or body of knowledge that aims, through experiment, observation, and deduction, to produce reliable explanation of phenomena, with reference to the material and physical world.

Activities such as healing, star-watching, and engineering have been practised in many societies since ancient times. Pure science, especially physics (formerly called natural philosophy), had traditionally been the main area of study for philosophers. The European scientific revolution between about 1650 and 1800 replaced speculative philosophy with a new combination of observation, experimentation, and rationality.

Today, scientific research involves an interaction between tradition, experiment and observation, and deduction. The subject area called philosophy of science investigates the nature of this complex interaction, and the extent of its ability to gain access to the truth about the material world. It has long been recognized that induction from observation cannot give explanations based on logic. In the 20th century Karl ◊Popper has described scientific method as a rigorous experimental testing of a scientist's ideas or hypotheses. The origin and role of these ideas, and their interdependence with observation, have been examined, for example, by the US thinker Thomas S ◊Kuhn, who places them in a historical and sociological setting. The sociology of science investigates how scientific theories and laws are produced, and questions the possibility of objectivity in any scientific endeavour. One controversial point of view is the replacement of scientific realism with scientific relativism, as proposed by Paul K ◊Feyerabend. Questions concerning the proper use of science and the role of science education are also restructuring this field of study.

Science is divided into separate areas of study, such as astronomy, biology, geology, chemistry, physics, and mathematics, although more recently

'My compositions spring from my sorrows. Those that give the world the greatest delight were born of my deepest griefs.'
FRANZ SCHUBERT
Diary 27 March 1824

'Reverence for Life.'
ALBERT SCHWEITZER
My Life and Thought

'Science is organized knowledge.'
On SCIENCE
Herbert Spencer
Education

O Caledonia! stern and wild, / Meet nurse for a poetic child!

On SCOTLAND
Walter Scott *The Lay of the Last Minstrel* 1805

attempts have been made to combine traditionally separate disciplines under such headings as ◊life sciences and ◊earth sciences. These areas are usually jointly referred to as the natural sciences. The physical sciences comprise mathematics, physics, and chemistry. The application of science for practical purposes is called technology. Social science is the systematic study of human behaviour, and includes such areas as anthropology, economics, psychology, and sociology.

science fiction or ***speculative fiction*** (also known as ***SF*** or ***sci-fi***) genre of fiction and film with an imaginary scientific, technological, or futuristic basis. It is sometimes held to have its roots in the works of Mary Shelley, notably *Frankenstein* 1818. Often taking its ideas and concerns from current ideas in science and the social sciences, science fiction aims to shake up standard perceptions of reality.

Science-fiction works often deal with alternative realities, future histories, robots, aliens, utopias and dystopias (often satiric), space and time travel, natural or human-made disasters, and psychic powers. Early practitioners were Jules Verne and H G Wells. In the 20th century the US pulp-magazine tradition of science fiction produced such writers as Arthur C Clarke, Isaac Asimov, Robert Heinlein, and Frank Herbert; a consensus of 'pure storytelling' and traditional values was disrupted by writers associated with the British magazine *New Worlds* (Brian Aldiss, Michael Moorcock, J G Ballard) and by younger US writers (Joanna Russ, Ursula Le Guin, Thomas Disch, Gene Wolfe) who used the form for serious literary purposes and for political and sexual radicalism. Thriving science-fiction traditions, only partly influenced by the Anglo-American one, exist in France, Germany, E Europe, and Russia.

Many mainstream writers have written science fiction, including Aldous Huxley (*Brave New World* 1932), George Orwell (*Nineteen Eighty-Four* 1949), and Doris Lessing (series of five books *Canopus in Argos: Archives* 1979–83).

Scientology (Latin *scire* 'to know' and Greek *logos* 'branch of learning') 'applied religious philosophy' based on ◊dianetics, founded in California 1954 by L Ron ◊Hubbard as the Church of Scientology. It claims to 'increase man's spiritual awareness', but its methods of recruiting and retaining converts have been criticized. Its headquarters from 1959 have been in Sussex, England.

scilla any bulbous plant of the genus *Scilla*, family Liliaceae, bearing blue, pink, or white flowers, and including the spring squill *S. verna*.

Scilly, Isles of or ***Scilly Isles/Islands***, or ***Scillies*** group of 140 islands and islets lying 40 km/25 mi SW of Land's End, England; administered by the Duchy of Cornwall; area 16 sq km/6.3 sq mi; population (1991) 2,050. The five inhabited islands are St Mary's, the largest, on which is Hugh Town, capital of the Scillies; Tresco, the second largest, with subtropical gardens; St Martin's, noted for beautiful shells; St Agnes; and Bryher.

Products include vegetables and early spring flowers, and tourism is important. The islands have remains of Bronze Age settlements. The numerous wreck sites off the islands include many of the 1707 fleet of Sir Cloudesley Shovell (1650–1707). The Isles of Scilly are an important birdwatching centre with breeding sea birds in the summer and rare migrants in the spring and autumn.

scintillation counter instrument for measuring very low levels of radiation. The radiation strikes a scintillator (a device that emits a unit of light when a charged elementary particle collides with it), whose light output is 'amplified' by a ◊photomultiplier; the current pulses of its output are in turn counted or added by a scaler to give a numerical reading.

Scipio Publius Cornelius 185–129 BC. Roman general, father of Scipio Africanus Major. Elected consul 218, during the Second ◊Punic War, he was defeated by Hannibal at Trebia and killed by the Carthaginians in Spain.

Scipio Africanus Major Publius Cornelius 236–c. 183 BC. Roman general. He defeated the Carthaginians in Spain 210–206 BC, invaded Africa 204 BC, and defeated Hannibal at Zama 202 BC.

Scipio Africanus Minor Publius Cornelius c. 185–129 BC. Roman general, the adopted grandson of Scipio Africanus Major, also known as Scipio Aemilianus. He destroyed Carthage 146, and subdued Spain 133. He was opposed to his brothers-in-law, the Gracchi (see ◊Gracchus).

sclerosis any abnormal hardening of body tissues, especially the nervous system or walls of the arteries. See ◊multiple sclerosis and ◊atherosclerosis.

Scofield (David) Paul 1922– . English actor. His wide-ranging roles include the drunken priest in Graham Greene's *The Power and the Glory* 1956, Lear in *King Lear* 1962, and Salieri in Peter Shaffer's *Amadeus*. He appeared as Sir Thomas More in both stage and film versions of Robert Bolt's *A Man for All Seasons* (stage 1960–61, film 1966).

scoliosis lateral (sideways) deviation of the spine. It may be congenital or acquired (through bad posture, illness, or other deformity); or it may be idopathic (of unknown cause). Treatments include mechanical or surgical correction, depending on the cause.

Scone site of ancient palace where most of the Scottish kings were crowned on the Stone of Destiny (now in the Coronation Chair at Westminster, London). The village of Scone is in Tayside, Scotland, N of Perth.

scorpion any arachnid of the order Scorpiones, common in the tropics and subtropics. Scorpions have four pairs of walking legs, large pincers, and long tails ending in upcurved poisonous stings, though the venom is not usually fatal to a healthy adult human. Some species reach 25 cm/10 in. There are about 600 different species.

They are nocturnal in habit, hiding during the day beneath stones and under the loose bark of trees. The females are viviparous (producing live young), the eggs being hatched in the enlarged oviducts. Scorpions sometimes prey on each other, but their main food is the woodlouse. They seize their prey with their powerful claws or palpi. They are also able to survive for a long time without eating.

scorpion fly any insect of the order Mecoptera. They have a characteristic downturned beak with jaws at the tip, and many males have a scorpion-like upturned tail, giving them their common name. Most feed on insects or carrion. They are an ancient group with relatively few living representatives.

Scorpius bright zodiacal constellation in the southern hemisphere between ◊Libra and ◊Sagittarius, represented as a scorpion. The Sun passes briefly through Scorpius in the last week of Nov. The heart of the scorpion is marked by the bright red supergiant star ◊Antares. Scorpius contains rich ◊Milky Way star fields, plus the strongest ◊X-ray source in the sky, Scorpius X-1. The whole area is rich in clusters and nebulae. In astrology, the dates for Scorpius are about 24 Oct–21 Nov (see ◊precession).

Scorsese Martin 1942– . US director, screenwriter, and producer. His films concentrate on complex characterization and the themes of alienation and guilt. Drawing from his Italian-American Catholic background, his work often deals with sin and redemption, as in his first major film *Boxcar Bertha* 1972. His influential, passionate, and forceful movies includes *Mean Streets* 1973, *Taxi Driver* 1976, *Raging Bull* 1980, *The Last Temptation of Christ* 1988, *GoodFellas* 1990, *Cape Fear* 1991, and *The Age of Innocence* 1993.

Scot inhabitants of Scotland, part of Britain; or people of Scottish descent. Originally the Scots were a Celtic (Gaelic) people of N Ireland who migrated to Scotland in the 5th century.

Scotland (Roman ***Caledonia***) the northernmost part of Britain, formerly an independent country, now part of the UK
area 78,470 sq km/30,297 sq mi
capital Edinburgh
towns Glasgow, Dundee, Aberdeen
features the Highlands in the north (with the Grampian Mountains); central Lowlands, including valleys of the Clyde and Forth, with most of the country's population and industries; Southern Uplands (including the Lammermuir Hills); islands of the Orkneys, Shetlands, and Western Isles
industry electronics, marine and aircraft engines, oil, natural gas, chemicals, textiles, clothing, printing, paper, food processing, tourism, whisky, coal, computer industries
currency pound sterling
population (1993 est) 5,120,000
languages English; Scots, a lowland dialect (derived from Northumbrian Anglo-Saxon); Gaelic spoken by 1.3%, mainly in the Highlands
religions Presbyterian (Church of Scotland), Roman Catholic
famous people Robert Bruce, Walter Scott, Robert Burns, Robert Louis Stevenson, Adam Smith
government Scotland sends 72 members to the UK Parliament at Westminster. In 1996, the former Scottish regions were abolished and 32 local authorities were created (*see list of tables on p. 1177 and United Kingdom map*). There is a differing legal system to England (see ◊Scottish law) and a movement for an independent or devolved Scottish assembly.

Scotland Yard, New headquarters of the ◊Criminal Investigation Department (CID) of Britain's London Metropolitan Police, established in 1878. It is named from its original location in Scotland Yard, off Whitehall.

Scots language the form of the English language as traditionally spoken and written in Scotland, regarded by some scholars as a distinct language. Scots derives from the Northumbrian dialect of Anglo-Saxon or Old English, and has been a literary language since the 14th century.

It is also known as Inglis (now archaic, and a variant of 'English'), ◊Lallans ('Lowlands'), Lowland Scots (in contrast with the Gaelic of the Highlands and Islands), and 'the Doric' (as a rustic language in contrast with the 'Attic' or 'Athenian' language of Edinburgh's literati, especially in the 18th century). It is also often referred to as Broad Scots in contrast to the anglicized language of the middle classes.

Scots has been spoken in SE Scotland since the 7th century. During the Middle Ages it spread to the far north, blending with the Norn dialects of Orkney and Shetland (once distinct varieties of Norse). Scots has a wide range of poetry, ballads, and prose records, including two national epic poems: John Barbour's *Brus* and Blind Harry's *Wallace*. With the transfer of the court to England upon the Union of the Crowns 1603 and the dissemination of the King James Bible, Scots ceased to be a national and court language, but has retained its vitality among the general population and in various literary and linguistic revivals.

Scott (George) Gilbert 1811–1878. English architect. As the leading practical architect of the

SCOTLAND: KINGS AND QUEENS 1005–1603

From the unification of Scotland to the union of the crowns of Scotland and England

Date of accession	Name
1005	Malcolm II
1034	Duncan I
1040	Macbeth
1057	Malcolm III Canmore
1093	Donald III Donalbane
1094	Duncan II
1094	Donald III (restored)
1097	Edgar
1107	Alexander I
1124	David I
1153	Malcolm IV
1165	William the Lion
1214	Alexander II
1249	Alexander III
1286	Margaret of Norway
1292	John Baliol
1296	annexed to England
1306	Robert I the Bruce
1329	David II
1371	Robert II
1390	Robert III
1406	James I
1437	James II
1460	James III
1488	James IV
1513	James V
1542	Mary
1567	James VI
1603	union of crowns

SCOTLAND: TIMELINE

3,000 BC	Neolithic settlements included Beaker people and Skara Brae on Orkney.
1st millennium BC	The Picts reached Scotland from mainland Europe.
1st C AD	Picts prevented Romans from penetrating far into Scotland.
122–128	Hadrian's Wall built to keep northern tribes out of England.
500	The Scots, a Gaelic-speaking tribe from Ireland, settled in the Kingdom of Dalriada (Argyll).
563	St Colomba founded the monastery on Iona and began to convert the Picts to Christianity.
9th C	Norsemen conquered Orkney, Shetland, Western Isles, and much of Highlands.
c. 843	Kenneth McAlpin unified the Scots and Picts and became first king of Scotland.
1040	King Duncan murdered by Macbeth.
1263	Scots defeated Norwegian invaders at Battle of Largs.
1295	First treaty between Scotland and France (the Auld Alliance).
1296	Edward I of England invaded and declared himself King of Scotland.
1297	William Wallace and Andrew Moray defeated English at Battle of Stirling Bridge.
1314	Robert the Bruce defeated the English at Battle of Bannockburn.
1328	Scottish independence recognized by England.
1371	Robert II became first king of the House of Stuart.
1513	Battle of Flodden: Scots defeated by the English and James IV killed.
1542	Mary, Queen of Scots, succeeded to throne when less than a week old.
1540s	John Knox introduced Calvinism to Scotland.
1557	The First Covenant established the Protestant faith in Scotland.
1567	Queen Mary abdicated, later fleeing to England, where she was beheaded in 1587.
1603	Union of crowns: James VI of Scotland became James I of England.
1638	Scots rebelled after National Covenant condemned Charles I's changes to church ritual.
1643	Solemn League and Covenant allied the Scots with Parliament in the English Civil War.
1650	Cromwell invaded and defeated the Scots at Dunbar.
1679	Presbyterian Covenanters defeated by Episcopalians at Battle of Bothwell Brig.
1689	Jacobite victory at Killiecrankie, but rebellion against William III collapsed soon after.
1692	Campbells massacred the Macdonalds at Glencoe.
1698	Unsuccessful Scottish colony founded at Darien in Central America.
1707	Act of Union united the Scottish and English Parliaments.
1715	'The Fifteen': Jacobite rebellion in support of James Edward Stuart.
1745	'The Forty-Five': Charles Edward Stuart led Jacobite rebels as far south as Derby.
1746	Jacobites defeated at Battle of Culloden by English forces under Duke of Cumberland.
1747	Act of Prescription banned Highland costume until repeal in 1782.
c. 1780–1860	Highland clearances: crofters evicted to make way for sheep.
1822	George IV made state visit to Scotland.
1843	The Disruption: 400 ministers left the Church of Scotland to form the Free Church of Scotland.
1885	Scottish Office created.
1886	Crofters Act provided security of tenure for crofters.
1926	Scottish Secretary upgraded to Secretary of State.
1928	National Party of Scotland formed (became Scottish National Party 1932).
1939	Headquarters of Scottish Office moved from London to Edinburgh.
1945	First Scottish Nationalist MP elected.
1970s	Aberdeen became centre of North Sea oil development.
1979	Referendum failed to approve devolution of power to a Scottish Assembly.
1990	'Constitutional Convention' of Labour and Liberal Parties demanded a Scottish Parliament.
1994	Scottish Grand Committee of MPs given additional powers.
1996	Local government reform: local authorities replaced regional and district councils.
1997	Referendum approved devolution.

mid-19th-century ◊Gothic Revival in England, Scott was responsible for the building or restoration of many public buildings and monuments, including the Albert Memorial 1863–72, the Foreign Office in Whitehall 1862–73, and the St Pancras Station Hotel 1868–74, all in London.

Scott Giles Gilbert 1880–1960. English architect. He was the grandson of Gilbert Scott. He designed Liverpool Anglican Cathedral (begun 1903; completed 1978), Cambridge University Library 1931–34, Battersea Power Station 1932–34, and Waterloo Bridge, London, 1939–45. He supervised the rebuilding of the House of Commons after World War II.

Scott Paul Mark 1920–1978. English novelist. He was the author of *The Raj Quartet* consisting of *The Jewel in the Crown* 1966, *The Day of the Scorpion* 1968, *The Towers of Silence* 1972, and *A Division of the Spoils* 1975, dealing with the British Raj in India. Other novels include *Staying On* 1977, which is set in post-independence India.

Scott Ridley 1939– . English film director and producer. His work includes some of the most visually spectacular and influential films of the 1980s and 1990s, such as *Alien* 1979 and *Blade Runner* 1982. Criticized for sacrificing storyline and character development in favour of ornate sets, Scott replied with *Thelma and Louise* 1991, a carefully wrought story of female bonding and adventure.

Scott Robert Falcon, (known as ***Scott of the Antarctic***) 1868–1912. English explorer who commanded two Antarctic expeditions, 1901–04 and 1910–12. On 18 Jan 1912 he reached the South Pole, shortly after the Norwegian Roald ◊Amundsen, but on the return journey he and his companions died in a blizzard only a few miles from their base camp. His journal was recovered and published 1913.

Born in Devonport, he entered the navy 1882. With Scott on the final expedition were Edward Wilson (1872–1912), Laurence ◊Oates, H R Bowers, and E Evans. The Scott Polar Research Institute in Cambridge was founded 1920 out of funds donated by the public following Scott's death, as a memorial to him and his companions. It houses a small museum and library, and carries out research into all aspects of the Antarctic and Arctic regions.

Scott Walter 1771–1832. Scottish novelist and poet. His first works were translations of German ballads and collections of Scottish ballads, which he followed with narrative poems of his own, such as *The Lay of the Last Minstrel* 1805 and *Marmion* 1808. He gained a European reputation for his historical novels such as *Waverley* 1814, *The Heart of Midlothian* 1818, and *Ivanhoe* 1819, all published anonymously. His last years were marked by frantic writing to pay off his debts, after the bankruptcy of the printing and publishing business of which he was a partner.

Scott exerted a strong influence on the imaginative life of his country. He stimulated an interest in Scottish history and materially affected the literary movement of his time: his unconventional manner of writing and his total freedom from the academic point of view were largely instrumental in arousing the French Romantic movement which produced such writers as Victor Hugo, Alfred de Musset, and Théophile Gautier, and such painters as Corot and Millet. Scott was also the creator of the historical novel, combining naturalness and realism with the historical and romantic element of adventure and the marvels of superstition.

'The hour is come, but not the man.'

Walter Scott
The Heart of Midlothian

Scottish Borders local authority of Scotland; previously Borders (1975–96), renamed in local government reorganization
area 4,700 sq km/1,815 sq mi
towns and cities Newtown St Boswells (administrative headquarters), Hawick, Jedburgh
features river Tweed; Lammermuir, Moorfoot, and Pentland hills; home of the novelist Walter Scott at Abbotsford; Dryburgh Abbey, burial place of Field Marshal Haig and Scott; ruins of 12th-century Melrose Abbey
industries knitted goods, tweed, electronics, timber
population (1991) 103,900
famous people Duns Scotus, James Murray, Mungo Park.

Scottish Gaelic language see ◊Gaelic language.

Scottish Gaelic literature the earliest examples of Scottish Gaelic prose belong to the period 1000–1150, but the most significant early original composition is the history of the MacDonalds in the Red and Black Books at Clanranald. The first printed book in Scottish Gaelic was a translation of Knox's Prayer Book 1567. Prose Gaelic is at its best in the folk tales, proverbs, and essays by writers such as Norman MacLeod in the 19th and Donald Lamont in the 20th century.

Scottish Gaelic poetry falls into two main categories. The older, syllabic verse was composed by professional bards. The chief sources of our knowledge of this are the Book of the Dean of Lismore (16th century), which is also the main early source for the Ossianic ballads; the panegyrics in the Books of Clanranald; and the Fernaig manuscript. Modern Scottish Gaelic stressed poetry began in the 17th

Scott Scottish novelist and poet Sir Walter Scott, whose early romantic ballads made him the most popular author of his day after Byron. *Waverley* 1814 was the first in a long series of historical novels which Scott wrote anonymously until 1827. He was created a baronet in 1820. *Corbis*

century but reached its zenith during the Jacobite period with Alexander MacDonald, Duncan Macintyre, Rob Donn, and Dugald Buchanan. Only William Livingstone (1808–1870) kept alive the old nationalistic spirit in the 19th century. During and after World War II a new school emerged, including Somhairle MacGilleathain, George Campbell-Hay, and Ruaraidh MacThómais.

Scottish law the legal system of Scotland. Owing to its separate development, Scotland has a system differing from the rest of the UK, being based on ◊civil law. Its continued separate existence was guaranteed by the Act of Union with England in 1707.

In the latter part of the 20th century England adopted some features already existing in Scottish law, for example, majority jury verdicts and the replacement of police prosecution by a system of public prosecution (see under ◊procurator fiscal). There is no separate system of ◊equity. The supreme civil court is the House of Lords, below which comes the ◊Court of Session, and then the sheriff court (in some respects similar to the English county court, but with criminal as well as civil jurisdiction). More serious criminal cases are heard by the High Court of Justiciary which also sits as a Court of Criminal Appeal (with no appeal to the Lords). Juries have 15 members, and a verdict of 'not proven' can be given. There is no coroner, inquiries into deaths being undertaken by the procurator fiscal.

Scout member of a worldwide youth organization that emphasizes character, citizenship, and outdoor life. It was founded (as the Boy Scouts) in England 1908 by Robert ◊Baden-Powell. His book *Scouting for Boys* 1908 led to the incorporation in the UK of the Boy Scout Association by royal charter 1912.

There are four branches: Beaver Scouts (aged 6–8), Cub Scouts (aged 8–10½), Scouts (10½–15½), and Venture Scouts (15½–20). Around a third of all Venture Scouts are girls and in 1990 younger girls were admitted to the Scouts (see also ◊Girl Guides). In 1987 there were 560,000 Cubs and Scouts and 640,000 Brownies and Guides. In 1966 the rules of the Boy Scout Association (now the Scout Association) were revised to embody a more adult and 20th-century image, and the dress was updated; for example, the traditional shorts were exchanged for long trousers.

scrapie fatal disease of sheep and goats that attacks the central nervous system, causing deterioration of the brain cells, and leading to the characteristic staggering gait and other behavioural abnormalities, before death. It is caused by the presence of an abnormal version of the brain protein PrP and is related to ◊bovine spongiform encephalopathy, the disease of cattle known as 'mad cow disease', and Creutzfeldt–Jakob disease in humans.

In 1996 Dutch researchers announced a test for detecting abnormal PrP in the tonsils of affected sheep before the symptoms of scrapie become apparent.

screamer any South American marsh-dwelling bird of the family Anhimidae, order Anseriformes; there are only three species, all in the genus *Anhima*. They are about 80 cm/30 in long, with short curved beaks, long toes, dark plumage, spurs on the fronts of the wings, and a crest or horn on the head.

Screamers wade in wet forests and marshes, although their feet are scarcely webbed. They are related to ducks and are placed in the same order. The horned screamer *A. cornuta* is found in certain parts of Central and South America, and has glossy black plumage with a white abdomen; it has a long, slender, yellowish horn on its head.

scree pile of rubble and sediment that collects at the foot of a mountain range or cliff. The rock fragments that form scree are usually broken off by the action of frost (◊freeze-thaw weathering).

With time, the rock waste builds up into a heap or sheet of rubble that may eventually bury even the upper cliffs, and the growth of the scree then stops. Usually, however, erosional forces remove the rock waste so that the scree stays restricted to lower slopes.

screening or ***health screening*** the systematic search for evidence of a disease, or of conditions that may precede it, in people who are at risk but not suffering from any symptoms. The aim of screening is to try to limit ill health from preventable diseases that might otherwise go undetected in the early stages. Examples are hypothyroidism and phenylketonuria, for which all newborn babies in Western countries are screened; breast cancer (◊mammography) and cervical cancer; and stroke, for which high blood pressure is a known risk factor.

Scriabin alternative transcription of ◊Skryabin, Russian composer.

scrofula tuberculosis of the lymph glands, especially of the neck, marked by enlargement, abscess formation, and scarring. Treatment is with drugs. Scrofula, which mostly affects children and young adults, is uncommon outside the Third World.

scuba (acronym for ***self-contained underwater breathing apparatus***) another name for ◊aqualung.

sculpture artistic shaping of materials such as wood, stone, clay, metal, and, more recently, plastic and other synthetics. The earliest prehistoric human artefacts include sculpted stone figurines, and all ancient civilizations have left behind examples of sculpture. Many indigenous cultures have maintained rich traditions of sculpture. Those of Africa (see ◊African art), South America, and the Caribbean in particular have been influential in the development of contemporary Western sculpture.

Historically, most sculpture has been religious in intent. Chinese, Japanese, and Indian sculptures are usually Buddhist or Hindu images. African, Native American, and Oceanic sculptures reflect spirit cults and animist beliefs.

There are two main techniques traditionally employed in sculpture: carving, involving the cutting away of hard materials such as wood or stone to reveal an image; and modelling, involving the building up of an image from malleable materials, such as clay or wax, which may then be cast in bronze.

ancient sculpture Egyptian and Mesopotamian sculpture took the form of monumental ◊reliefs in palace and temple decoration. Standing sculptures of the period were intended to be seen only from the front and sides. The first sculptures in the round (to be seen from all sides) were Greek. The development of vigorous poses and emotional expressiveness elevated Greek sculpture to the pinnacle of artistic achievement (see ◊Phidias, ◊Praxiteles, and ◊Parthenon), and much of subsequent Western sculpture has been imitative of Greek ideals. Lifelike portrait sculpture was introduced by the Romans.

medieval sculpture Sculpture of the medieval period is epitomized by niche figures carved in stone for churches (for example, Chartres Cathedral, France) and by delicate ivory carvings. The work of Nicola Pisano began a great tradition of Italian sculpture.

Renaissance sculpture Greek supremacy was challenged by the reintroduction of free-standing sculptures, notably Michelangelo's *David* 1501–04, and by superlative bronze casting, for example, Donatello's equestrian monument of *Gattamelata* 1447–50 (Piazza del Santo, Padua). In the work of Lorenzo Ghiberti, Luca della Robbia, and Andrea del Verrocchio, figure sculpture attained a new dignity and power. The work of Benvenuto Cellini and Giovanni Bologna (1524–1608) exemplified the Mannerist style.

Baroque and Rococo sculpture Relief rather than free-standing sculptures came to the fore. The limpid virtuosity of such sculptors as Giovanni Bernini seemed to defy the nature of the materials they used. The style was represented in France by Etienne Falconet, and in Spain by Alonso Cano.

Neo-Classical sculpture Sculpture of the 18th century concentrated on smooth perfection of form and surface, notably the work of Antonio Canova. The last great exponent of sculpture in the Classical tradition was Auguste Rodin. The work of Aristide Maillol and Antoine Bourdelle (1861–1929) emphasized formal qualities, rejecting both realism and Impressionism.

20th century Sculptors such as Henry Moore, Barbara Hepworth, and Jacob Epstein used traditional materials and techniques to create forms inspired by 'primitive' art and nature. The work of Amedeo Modigliani and Henri Gaudier-Brzeska also reflects such influences. Abstract sculpture was pioneered by Alexander Archipenko and Ossip Zadkine, both exponents of Cubism, and Constantin Brancusi and Alberto Giacometti.Followers of the nonrepresentational school include Jacques Lipchitz, Jean Arp, Naum Gabo and Antoine Pevsner (pioneers of Russian Constructivism), Reg Butler, and Anthony Caro. Among more traditional sculptors whose work powerfully expresses the modern idiom are Marino Marini in Italy and Frank Dobson (1888–1963) in England.

Other sculptors have broken with the past entirely, rejecting both carving and modelling. Today the term sculpture applies to the mobiles of Alexander Calder, assemblages (works constructed of atypical materials), ◊environment sculpture and ◊earthworks (pioneered by Carl André), and 'installations'.

scurvy disease caused by deficiency of vitamin C (ascorbic acid), which is contained in fresh vegetables and fruit. The signs are weakness and aching joints and muscles, progressing to bleeding of the gums and other spontaneous haemorrhage, and drying-up of the skin and hair. It is reversed by giving the vitamin.

scurvy grass The small white flowers of the common scurvy grass *Cochlearia officinalis* appear over a remarkably long season, from April to Sept. This species prefers dry rocks and banks near the sea. Other scurvy grasses favour wet tidal mud or even inland mountain tops. *Premaphotos Wildlife*

SCULPTURE: TIMELINE OF WESTERN SCULPTURE

c. 25,000 BC	Small clay models and carvings such as *The Venus of Willendorf*, probably a magic fertility symbol, made by palaeolithic peoples.
4500–400	Western Asian civilizations, including those based at Ur, Nineveh, and Persepolis, developed majestic carvings and reliefs.
2700–2300	Figurines produced by the Cycladic culture.
c. 2530	*The Sphinx*, one of the world's largest sculptures, built in the Egyptian Old Kingdom.
2000–1450	The Minoan civilization, based at Knossos in Crete, produced the *bull's head* sacrificial vessel.
from 2000	Oceanic culture carved the giant Easter Island statues.
1500–1200	Mycenaean civilization expressed itself in violent images and work in gold.
1379–1361	Heads of Nefertiti and Akhenaten carved in the Egyptian New Kingdom.
c. 500	Traditional Celtic curvilinear plants, animals, and abstract designs flowered again with early British and Irish Christianity. Central and West African sculpture developed. Ancient Greek statues attained a naturalistic style, while Etruscans adapted the Greek style freely yet more crudely.
460–450	Myron's *The Discus Thrower*, a Greek bronze now surviving only in the form of a Roman marble copy, achieved a striking naturalism and sense of movement.
c. 490–417	The sculptor Phidias supervised the reliefs for the Parthenon in Athens.
c. 400	The Olmecs in Central America created colossal stone heads and fine sculptures in jade, bronze, and clay.
350–330	Praxiteles executed the famous *Aphrodite of Knidos*, the first Greek life-size free-standing female nude.
323–31	The Hellenistic period achieved more complex forms with the *Venus de Milo*, the *Winged Victory of Samothrace*, *Dying Gaul*, and *Laocoön*.
75	Portrait busts (a new form), monuments, and sarcophagi celebrated the achievements of great Romans.
106–113 AD	*Trajan's Column* was the most complex example of Roman monumental art.
330–1453	Byzantine Christianity, established in the eastern Roman Empire, Russia, and Greece, specifically excluded religious sculpture.
from 580	Japanese Buddhist and later portrait sculpture flourished.
780–1050	The Carolingian and Ottonian period revived Roman aims.
800–1275	The Romanesque style, epitomized in the work of Gislebertus at Autun, united Celtic and Roman forms in early stone churches.
c. 1154	Chartres Cathedral marked the triumph of the spiritualized Gothic style, incorporating new serenity in the portrayal of figures.
1258–1314	Pulpits carved by the Pisano brothers developed a more classical form of Gothic church sculpture.
1380–1406	Claus Sluter achieved a new psychological realism in work on Philip the Bold's tomb.
1404–1452	Ghiberti sculpted the panels for the four great bronze doors for the Baptistery in Florence. He began the first pair in the graceful International Gothic style, but his second pair, *The Gates of Paradise*, represent a masterpiece of the Early Renaissance.
1430–32	Donatello, a pupil of Ghiberti, developed a new vital realism in sculpture. His *David* became the first free-standing life-size bronze since antiquity.
1502–04	Michelangelo's *Pietà*, completed during the Italian High Renaissance, revealed the artist's grandeur of vision, portraying a Christian subject with all the magnificence of rediscovered classical form.
1540–1600	Cellini achieved fame as a goldsmith and sculptor in the Mannerist style.
1587–95	Giambologna's *Rape of the Sabines* was a high point of Mannerist movement and the first statue requiring to be seen from all angles.
1615–1680	Bernini produced light and fluid forms that seemed to defy the weight of the marble in the High Baroque style.
1787–1793	Canova's *Cupid and Psyche* expressed the neoclassical ideal of the late 18th century.
1875–1898	In works such as *The Kiss*, *Balzac*, and *The Thinker*, Rodin's romanticism dissolved the classical tradition of sculpture.
1880	Degas's only displayed piece, *The Little 14-year-old Dancer*, was acclaimed as the first modern sculpture.
1906–10	Brancusi evolved a simplified, abstract vocabulary for modern sculpture.
1900–1931	Matisse's sculptures revealed formal simplifications that parallel his paintings.
1913	Boccioni developed Futurist sculpture, which aimed to express movement and the space around objects.
1913–1940	Jacob Epstein's achievement in sculpture embraced vorticism, expressionist portraits, and religious monuments.
1912–1966	Marcel Duchamp revolutionized traditional notions of art and artist by incorporating ready-made and found objects.
1916–24	Dadaists such as Schwitters and Arp included found objects, collage, and unorthodox materials for their anarchistic work.
1909–1973	Picasso's career as a sculptor paralleled and complemented that of his painting throughout his many styles.
c. 1920	Rodchenko, El Lissitzky, Tatlin, Gabo, and Pevsner developed a constructivist art to express revolutionary ideals.
1924–1986	Henry Moore explored the human form, in varying degrees of abstraction, often in monumental pieces.
from 1924	Arp, Ernst, and Miro developed sculpture as a surrealist medium.
from 1928	Wire and mobile sculptures created by Calder. Kinetic sculpture subsequently developed from the mid-1950s by Tinguely and Takis.
1931–75	Barbara Hepworth developed Brancusi's process of simplification into the realms of pure form.
1933–65	In the USA, David Smith pursued metal sculpture in the wake of Picasso's experiments, an approach further developed by Caro since the 1960s.
1935–66	Giacometti's slender, rough figures expressed the alienation of modern mid-century humans.
1950s	Marino Marini worked on the 'Horse and Rider' theme; Jean Tinguely made machines that self-destructed; Eduardo Paolozzi created robotlike figures; and Louise Levelson created assemblages.
1960s	Minimalism: Carl Andre (industrial bricks and timber) and Donald Judd (metal boxes). Environments: George Segal (life-size plaster casts of people). Pop art: Claes Oldenburg (huge replicas of everyday objects). Process art: Eva Hesse (hanging sculptures made of latex, cheesecloth, or string). David Smith began *Cubi* series. Anthony Caro used metal industrial materials, such as mesh and girders.
1970s	Concept art: Christo (wrapped buildings and areas in plastic sheets). Land (Earth) art: Richard Long (lines of stones set out in remote locations). Mixed media: Judy Chicago (tables set with ceramics and embroidered and woven cloth).
1980s–1990s	Pluralism continued, with all major forms and styles (land art, Minimalism, Surrealism) having exponents. Neo-expressionist: Georg Baselitz (carvings in wood). Kitsch: Jeff Koons (pop culture images in porcelain). Damien Hirst: *Away from the Flock* 1994 (a lamb in a tank of formaldehyde).

scurvy grass plant *Cochlearia officinalis* of the crucifer family, growing on salt marshes and banks by the sea in the northern hemisphere. Shoots may grow low, or more erect up to 50 cm/20 in, with rather fleshy heart-shaped leaves; flowers are white or mauve and four-petalled. The edible, sharp-tasting leaves are a good source of vitamin C and were formerly eaten by sailors as a cure for scurvy.

scutage in medieval Europe, a feudal tax imposed on knights as a substitute for military service. It developed from fines for non-attendance at musters under the Carolingians, but in England by the 12th century it had become a purely fiscal measure designed to raise money to finance mercenary armies, reflecting the decline in the military significance of feudalism.

Scylla and Charybdis in Greek mythology, a sea monster and a whirlpool, between which ◊Odysseus had to sail. Later writers located them in the Straits of Messina, between Sicily and Italy.

Scythia region north of the Black Sea between the Carpathian Mountains and the river Don, inhabited by the Scythians 7th–1st centuries BC. From the middle of the 4th century, they were slowly superseded by the Sarmatians. The Scythians produced ornaments and vases in gold and electrum with animal decoration. Although there is no surviving written work, there are spectacular archaeological remains, including vast royal burial mounds which often contain horse skeletons.

SDI abbreviation for ◊***Strategic Defense Initiative***.

SDLP abbreviation for ◊***Social Democratic Labour Party***, a Northern Ireland political party.

SDP abbreviation for ◊***Social Democratic Party***, former British political party.

sea anemone invertebrate marine animal of the phylum Cnidaria with a tubelike body attached by the base to a rock or shell. The other end has an open 'mouth' surrounded by stinging tentacles, which capture crustaceans and other small organisms. Many sea anemones are beautifully coloured, especially those in tropical waters.

Seaborg Glenn Theodore 1912–1999. US nuclear chemist. For his discovery of plutonium and research on the ◊transuranic elements, he shared a Nobel prize 1951 with his co-worker Edwin McMillan (1907–1991).

seaborgium name given briefly to element 106 1994. In October 1994 IUPAC changed the name to ◊rutherfordium following a new ruling that no element could be named after a living person.

sea cucumber any echinoderm of the class Holothuroidea with a cylindrical body that is tough-skinned, knobbed, or spiny. The body may be several feet in length. Sea cucumbers are sometimes called 'cotton-spinners' from the sticky filaments they eject from the anus in self-defence.

The dried flesh of sea cucumbers is a delicacy in Japan and Taiwan, and overfishing has threatened some populations. A high density is vital to sustain a population as they reproduce by releasing sperm or ova into the water; other sea cucumbers must also be releasing sperm or ova nearby.

seafloor spreading growth of the ocean ◊crust outwards (sideways) from ocean ridges. The concept of seafloor spreading has been combined with that of continental drift and incorporated into ◊plate tectonics.

Seafloor spreading was proposed 1960 by US geologist Harry Hess (1906–1969), based on his observations of ocean ridges and the relative youth of all ocean beds. In 1963, British geophysicists Fred Vine and Drummond Matthews observed that the floor of the Atlantic Ocean was made up of rocks that could be arranged in strips, each strip being magnetized either normally or reversely (due to changes in the Earth's polarity when the North Pole becomes the South Pole and vice versa, termed ◊polar reversal). These strips were parallel and formed identical patterns on both sides of the ocean ridge. The implication was that each strip was formed at some stage in geological time when the magnetic field was polarized in a certain way. The

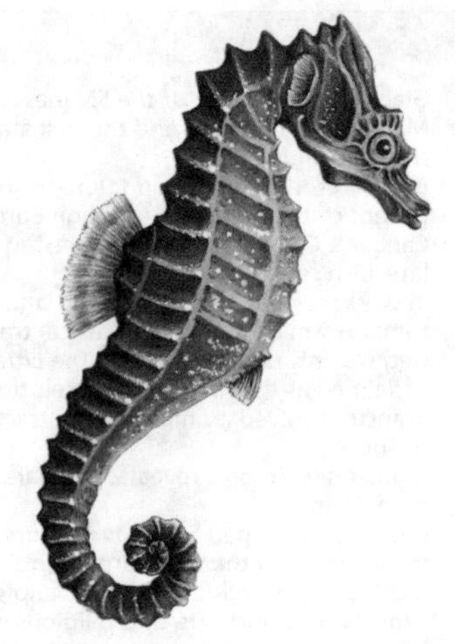

sea horse The dwarf sea horse swims in an upright position, propelled by gentle movements of its dorsal fin. It is found in the W Atlantic Ocean from Florida to the Caribbean.

Seattle is a comparatively new-looking city that covers an old frontier town like frosting on a cake.

On SEATTLE
Winthrop Sargeant in the *New Yorker* 26 June 1978

seafloor magnetic-reversal patterns could be matched to dated magnetic reversals found in terrestrial rock. It could then be shown that new rock forms continuously and spreads away from the ocean ridges, with the oldest rock located farthest away from the midline. The observation was made independently 1963 by Canadian geologist Lawrence Morley, studying an ocean ridge in the Pacific near Vancouver Island. Confirmation came when sediments were discovered to be deeper further away from the oceanic ridge, because the rock there had been in existence longer and had had more time to accumulate sediment.

seagull see ◊gull.

sea horse any marine fish of several related genera, especially *Hippocampus*, of the family Syngnathidae, which includes the ◊pipefishes. The body is small and compressed and covered with bony plates raised into tubercles or spines. The tail is prehensile, and the tubular mouth sucks in small shellfish and larvae as food. The head and foreparts, usually carried upright, resemble those of a horse. They swim vertically and beat their fins up to 70 times a second.

Unusually for fish, sea horses are monogamous and have a relatively long courtship, from 3–7 days. The female deposits her eggs, from dozens to hundreds, in a special pouch in the male. The male fertilizes the eggs whilst they are in his pouch, and nourishes them for six weeks or so until they are finally released as young fish.

seakale perennial plant *Crambe maritima* of the family Cruciferae. In Europe the young shoots are cultivated as a vegetable.

seal aquatic carnivorous mammal of the families Otariidae and Phocidae (sometimes placed in a separate order, the Pinnipedia). The eared seals or sea lions (Otariidae) have small external ears, unlike the true seals (Phocidae). Seals have a streamlined body with thick blubber for insulation, and front and hind flippers. They are able to close their nostrils as they dive, and obtain oxygen from their blood supply while under water. They feed on fish, squid, or crustaceans, and are commonly found in Arctic and Antarctic seas, but also in Mediterranean, Caribbean, and Hawaiian waters.

seal mark or impression made in a block of wax to authenticate letters and documents. Seals were used in ancient China and are still used in China, Korea, and Japan. In medieval England, the great seal of the nation was kept by the chancellor. The privy seal of the monarch was initially kept for less serious matters, but by the 14th century it had become the most important seal.

sea lily any ◊echinoderm of the class Crinoidea. In most, the rayed, cuplike body is borne on a sessile stalk (permanently attached to a rock) and has feathery arms in multiples of five encircling the mouth. However, some sea lilies are free-swimming and unattached.

sea lion any of several genera of ◊seals of the family Otariidae (eared seals), which also includes the fur seals. These streamlined animals have large fore flippers which they use to row themselves through the water. The hind flippers can be turned beneath the body to walk on land.

Sealyham breed of terrier dog, named after the place in Pembrokeshire, Wales, where it originated in the 19th century as a cross between the Welsh and Jack Russell terriers. It has a coarse white coat and reaches a height of 30 cm/12 in.

sea mouse any of a genus *Aphrodite* of large marine ◊annelid worms (polychaetes), with oval bodies covered in bristles and usually found on muddy sea floors.

The bristle worm *A. aculeata* is up to 20 cm/8 in long, with an oval body, flattened beneath and covered above with a mat of grey bristles, with iridescent bristles showing at the edges.

Sea Peoples unidentified seafaring warriors who may have been Achaeans, Etruscans, or ◊Philistines, who ravaged and settled the Mediterranean coasts in the 12th–13th centuries BC. They were defeated by Ramses III of Egypt 1191 BC.

seaplane aeroplane capable of taking off from, and landing on, water. There are two major types, floatplanes and flying boats. The floatplane is similar to an ordinary aeroplane but has floats in place of wheels; the flying boat has a broad hull shaped like a boat and may also have floats attached to the wing tips.

Seaplanes depend on smooth water for a good landing, and since World War II few have been built, although they were widely used in both world wars and the first successful international airlines, such as Pan Am, relied on a fleet of flying boats in the 1920s and 1930s.

sea potato yellow-brown sea urchin *Echinocardium cordatum* covered in short spines, and found burrowing in sand from the lower shore downwards.

search engine in computing, remotely accessible program to help users find information on the Internet. Commercial search engines such as AltaVista and Lycos comprise databases of documents, ◊URLs, USENET articles and more, which can be searched by keying in a key word or phrase. The databases are compiled by a mixture of automated agents registering their sites.

sea slug any of an order (Nudibranchia) of marine gastropod molluscs in which the shell is reduced or absent. The order includes some very colourful forms, especially in the tropics. They are largely carnivorous, feeding on hydroids and ◊sponges.

Most are under 2.5 cm/1 in long, and live on the sea bottom or on vegetation, although some live in open waters. Tentacles on the back help take in oxygen.

season period of the year having a characteristic climate. The change in seasons is mainly due to the change in attitude of the Earth's axis in relation to the Sun, and hence the position of the Sun in the sky at a particular place. In temperate latitudes four seasons are recognized: spring, summer, autumn (fall), and winter. Tropical regions have two seasons – the wet and the dry. Monsoon areas around the Indian Ocean have three seasons: the cold, the hot, and the rainy.

The northern temperate latitudes have summer when the southern temperate latitudes have winter, and vice versa. During winter, the Sun is low in the sky and has less heating effect because of the oblique angle of incidence and because the sunlight has further to travel through the atmosphere. The differences between the seasons are more marked inland than near the coast, where the sea has a moderating effect on temperatures. In polar regions the change between summer and winter is abrupt; spring and autumn are hardly perceivable. In tropical regions, the belt of rain associated with the trade winds moves N and S with the Sun, as do the dry conditions associated with the belts of high pressure near the tropics. The monsoon's three seasons result from the influence of the Indian Ocean on the surrounding land mass of Asia in that area.

seasonal affective disorder (SAD) form of depression which occurs in winter and is relieved by the coming of spring. Its incidence decreases closer to the equator. One type of SAD is associated with increased sleeping and appetite.

It has been suggested that SAD may be caused by changes in the secretion of melatonin, a hormone produced by the ◊pineal body in the brain. Melatonin secretion is inhibited by bright daylight.

sea squirt or ***tunicate*** any solitary or colonial-dwelling saclike ◊chordate of the class Ascidiacea. A pouch-shaped animal attached to a rock or other base, it draws in food-carrying water through one siphon and expels it through another after straining it through numerous gill slits. The young are free-swimming tadpole-shaped organisms, which, unlike the adults, have a ◊notochord. Sea squirts have transparent or translucent tunics made of cellulose. They vary in size from a few millimetres to 30 cm/12 in in length and are cylindrical, circular, or irregular in shape. Their defences against predators include sulphuric acid secretion and the accumulation of vanadium, a toxic heavy metal.

SEATO abbreviation for ◊***Southeast Asia Treaty Organization***.

Seattle port on Lake Washington, USA; the largest city in the Pacific Northwest; population (1992) 519,600, metropolitan area with Everett (1990) 2,559,200. Industries include the aerospace industry, timber, banking and insurance, paper industries, electronics, and ocean science, there is a large fishing fleet, and coffee is an important product.

history first settled 1851, Seattle grew as a sawmill

sea lion This South American sea lion bull *Otaria flavescens* will have to win many bloody fights with rival males in order to establish and maintain his harem of females. He mates with them on a regular basis, and fasts totally during his reign as master of the harem. *Premaphotos Wildlife*

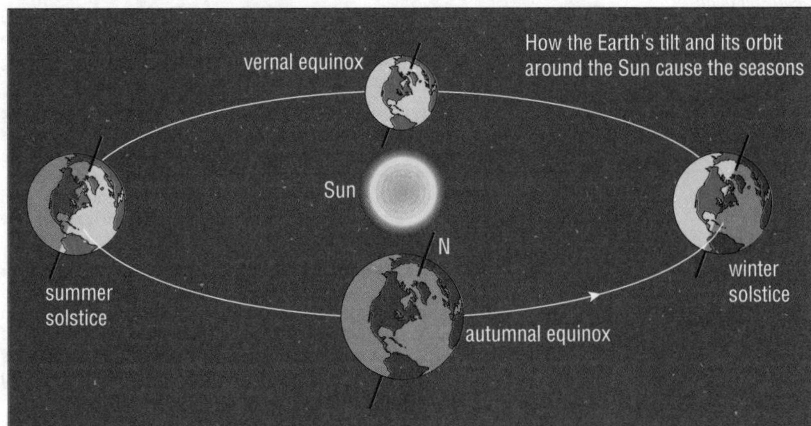

season The cause of the seasons. As the Earth orbits the Sun, its axis of rotation always points in the same direction. This means that, during the northern hemisphere summer solstice (21 June), the Sun is overhead in the northern hemisphere. At the northern hemisphere winter solstice (22 December), the Sun is overhead in the southern hemisphere.

centre. It developed into a major seaport after the Lake Washington Ship Canal was opened 1916. The economy boomed during World War II.
features Mount Baker-Snoqualmie National Forest on the slopes of the Cascade Mountains; Fort Lawton 1897 and Sand Point naval Base are here.

sea urchin any of various orders of the class Echinoidea among the ◊echinoderms. They all have a globular body enclosed with plates of lime and covered with spines. Sometimes the spines are anchoring organs, and they also assist in locomotion. Sea urchins feed on seaweed and the animals frequenting them, and some are edible.

sea water the water of the seas and oceans, covering about 70% of the Earth's surface and comprising about 97% of the world's water (only about 3% is fresh water). Sea water contains a large amount of dissolved solids, the most abundant of which is sodium chloride (almost 3% by mass); other salts include potassium chloride, bromide, and iodide, magnesium chloride, and magnesium sulphate. It also contains a large amount of dissolved carbon dioxide, and thus acts as a carbon 'sink' that may help to reduce the greenhouse effect.

seaweed any of a vast collection of marine and freshwater, simple, multicellular plant forms belonging to the ◊algae and found growing from about high-water mark to depths of 100–200 m/300–600 ft. Some have holdfasts, stalks, and fronds, sometimes with air bladders to keep them afloat, and are green, blue-green, red, or brown. Many seaweeds have traditionally been gathered for food, such as purple laver *Porphyra umbilicalis*, green laver *Ulva lactuca*, and carragheen moss *Chondrus crispus*.

Sebastiano del Piombo (Sebastiano Luciani) c. 1485–1547. Italian painter of the High Renaissance. Born in Venice, he was a pupil of ◊Giorgione and developed a similar style. In 1511 he moved to Rome, where his friendship with Michelangelo (and rivalry with Raphael) inspired him to his finest works, such as *The Raising of Lazarus* 1517–19 (National Gallery, London).

Sebastian, St died c. 258. Roman soldier. He was traditionally a member of Emperor Diocletian's bodyguard until his Christian faith was discovered. He was condemned to be killed by arrows. Feast day 20 Jan.

Sebastopol alternative spelling of ◊Sevastopol, a port in Ukraine.

sebum oily secretion from the sebaceous glands that acts as a skin lubricant. ◊Acne is caused by inflammation of the sebaceous glands and over-secretion of sebum.

secession (Latin *secessio*) in politics, the withdrawal from a federation of states by one or more of its members, as in the secession of the Confederate states from the Union in the USA 1860, Singapore from the Federation of Malaysia 1965, and Croatia and Slovenia from the Yugoslav Federation 1991.

second basic ◊SI unit (symbol sec or s) of time, one-sixtieth of a minute. It is defined as the duration of 9,192,631,770 cycles of regulation (periods of the radiation corresponding to the transition between two hyperfine levels of the ground state) of the cesium-133 isotope. In mathematics, the second is a unit (symbol ″) of angular measurement, equalling one-sixtieth of a minute, which in turn is one-sixtieth of a degree.

secondary education in the UK, ◊education from the age of 11 (12 in Scotland) until school-leaving at 16 or later.

secondary emission in physics, an emission of electrons from the surface of certain substances when they are struck by high-speed electrons or other particles from an external source. It can be detected with a ◊photomultiplier.

secondary growth or ***secondary thickening*** increase in diameter of the roots and stems of certain plants (notably shrubs and trees) that results from the production of new cells by the ◊cambium. It provides the plant with additional mechanical support and new conducting cells, the secondary ◊xylem and ◊phloem. Secondary growth is generally confined to ◊gymnosperms and, among the ◊angiosperms, to the dicotyledons. With just a few exceptions, the monocotyledons (grasses, lilies) exhibit only primary growth, resulting from cell division at the apical ◊meristems.

secondary modern school in the UK, a secondary school that normally takes children who have failed to gain a ◊grammar school place, in those few areas that retain academic selection at 11 or 12.

secondary sexual characteristic in biology, an external feature of an organism that is indicative of its gender (male or female), but not the reproductive organs themselves. They include facial hair in men and breasts in women, combs in cockerels, brightly coloured plumage in many male birds, and manes in male lions. In many cases, they are involved in displays and contests for mates and have evolved by ◊sexual selection. Their development is stimulated by sex hormones.

Second Front in World War II, battle line opened against Germany on 6 June 1944 by the Allies (Britain and the USA). See ◊D-day. Following Germany's invasion of the USSR June 1941 (the 'first front'), Soviet leader Josef Stalin constantly pressured Britain to invade the European mainland, to relieve pressure on Soviet forces.

Second World War alternative name for ◊World War II, 1939–45.

secretary bird ground-hunting, long-legged, mainly grey-plumaged bird of prey *Sagittarius serpentarius*. It is about 1.2 m/4 ft tall, with an erectile head crest tipped with black. It is protected in southern Africa because it eats poisonous snakes.

It gets its name from the fact that its head crest supposedly looks like a pen behind a clerk's ear. It is the only member of the family Sagittariidae, in the same order (Falconiformes) as vultures, eagles, and hawks.

secretary of state in the UK, a title held by a number of ministers; for example, the secretary of state for foreign and commonwealth affairs.

Originally the title was given under Elizabeth I of England to each of two officials conducting the royal correspondence. In the USA the secretary of state deals with foreign affairs.

secretin ◊hormone produced by the small intestine of vertebrates that stimulates the production of digestive secretions by the pancreas and liver.

secretion in biology, any substance (normally a fluid) produced by a cell or specialized gland, for example, sweat, saliva, enzymes, and hormones. The process whereby the substance is discharged from the cell is also known as secretion.

secret police any state security force that operates internally, against political dissenters or subversives; for example, the US ◊Federal Bureau of Investigation and the UK ◊Special Branch.

secret service any government ◊intelligence organization. In the USA the Secret Service is a law-enforcement unit of the Treasury Department and provides the president's bodyguard.

secret society society with membership by invitation only, often involving initiation rites, secret rituals, and dire punishments for those who break the code. Often founded for religious reasons or mutual benefit, some have become the province of corrupt politicians or gangsters, like the ◊Mafia, ◊Ku Klux Klan, and the ◊Triad. See also ◊freemasonry.

sect small ideological group, usually religious in nature, that may have moved away from a main group, often claiming a monopoly of access to truth or salvation. Sects are usually highly exclusive. They demand strict conformity, total commitment to their code of behaviour, and complete personal involvement, sometimes to the point of rejecting mainstream society altogether in terms of attachments, names, possessions, and family.

Most sects are short-lived, either because their appeal dies out and their members return to mainstream society, or because their appeal spreads and they become part of mainstream society (for example, Christianity began as a small sect in Roman-ruled Palestine).

secularization the process through which religious thinking, practice, and institutions lose their religious and/or social significance. The concept is based on the theory, held by some sociologists, that as societies become industrialized their

Sebastiano del Piombo *The Raising of Lazarus* 1517–19 by Sebastiano del Piombo (National Gallery, London). Sebastiano del Piombo's finest work, this huge picture shows him combining a richness of colour derived from his training in Venice, with a grandeur of form derived from Michelangelo. *Corbis*

religious morals, values, and institutions give way to secular ones and some religious traits become common secular practices.

Securities and Exchange Commission (*SEC*) official US agency created 1934, under Joseph P ◊Kennedy, to ensure full disclosure to the investing public and protection against malpractice in the securities (stocks and bonds) and financial markets (such as insider trading, the illegal use of privileged information when dealing on a stock exchange).

Securities and Investment Board UK body with the overall responsibility for policing financial dealings in the City of London. Introduced in 1987 following the deregulation process of the so-called ◊Big Bang, it acts as an umbrella organization to such self-regulating bodies as the Stock Exchange.

Security Council the most important body of the United Nations; see ◊United Nations.

sedative any drug that has a calming effect, reducing anxiety and tension. Sedatives will induce sleep in larger doses. Examples are ◊barbiturates, ◊narcotics, and ◊benzodiazepines.

sedge any perennial grasslike plant of the family Cyperaceae, especially the genus *Carex*, usually with three-cornered solid stems, common in low water or on wet and marshy ground.

Sedgemoor, Battle of in English history, a battle 6 July 1685 in which ◊Monmouth's rebellion was crushed by the forces of James II, on a tract of marshy land 5 km/3 mi SE of Bridgwater, Somerset.

sediment any loose material that has 'settled' – deposited from suspension in water, ice, or air, generally as the water current or wind speed decreases. Typical sediments are, in order of increasing coarseness, clay, mud, silt, sand, gravel, pebbles, cobbles, and boulders.

Sediments differ from sedimentary rocks in which deposits are fused together in a solid mass of rock by a process called lithification. Pebbles are cemented into ◊conglomerates; sands become sandstones; muds become mudstones or shales; peat is transformed into coal.

sedimentary rock rock formed by the accumulation and cementation of deposits that have been laid down by water, wind, ice, or gravity. Sedimentary rocks cover more than two-thirds of the Earth's surface and comprise three major categories: clastic, chemically precipitated, and organic (or biogenic). Clastic sediments are the largest group and are composed of fragments of pre-existing rocks; they include clays, sands, and gravels.

Chemical precipitates include some limestones and evaporated deposits such as gypsum and halite (rock salt). Coal, oil shale, and limestone made of fossil material are examples of organic sedimentary rocks.

Most sedimentary rocks show distinct layering (stratification), caused by alterations in composition or by changes in rock type. These strata may become folded or fractured by the movement of the Earth's crust, a process known as deformation.

sedition in the UK, the offence of inciting unlawful opposition to the crown and government. Unlike ◊treason, sedition does not carry the death penalty.

It includes attempting to bring into contempt or hatred the person of the reigning monarch, the lawfully established government, or either house of Parliament; inciting a change of government by other than lawful means; and raising discontent between different sections of the sovereign's subjects. Today any criticism aimed at reform is allowable.

Seebeck effect in physics, the generation of a voltage in a circuit containing two different metals, or semiconductors, by keeping the junctions between them at different temperatures. Discovered by the German physicist Thomas Seebeck (1770–1831), it is also called the thermoelectric effect, and is the basis of the ◊thermocouple. It is the opposite of the ◊Peltier effect (in which current flow causes a temperature difference between the junctions of different metals).

seed the reproductive structure of higher plants (◊angiosperms and ◊gymnosperms). It develops from a fertilized ovule and consists of an embryo and a food store, surrounded and protected by an outer seed coat, called the testa. The food store is contained either in a specialized nutritive tissue, the ◊endosperm, or in the ◊cotyledons of the embryo itself. In angiosperms the seed is enclosed within a ◊fruit, whereas in gymnosperms it is usually naked and unprotected, once shed from the female cone. Following ◊germination the seed develops into a new plant.

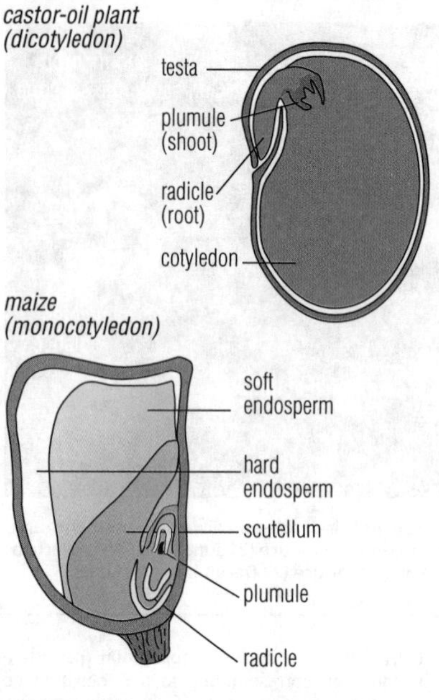

Seeds may be dispersed from the parent plant in a number of different ways. Agents of dispersal include animals, as with ◊burs and fleshy edible fruits, and wind, where the seed or fruit may be winged or plumed. Water can disperse seeds or fruits that float, and various mechanical devices may eject seeds from the fruit, as in the pods of some leguminous plants (see ◊legume).

seed The structure of seeds. The castor is a dicotyledon, a plant in which the developing plant has two leaves, developed from the cotyledon. In maize, a monocotyledon, there is a single leaf developed from the scutellum.

seed plant any seed-bearing plant; also known as a spermatophyte. The seed plants are subdivided into two classes: the ◊angiosperms, or flowering plants, and the ◊gymnosperms, principally the cycads and conifers. Together, they comprise the major types of vegetation found on land.

Angiosperms are the largest, most advanced, and most successful group of plants at the present time, occupying a highly diverse range of habitats. There are estimated to be about 250,000 different species. Gymnosperms differ from angiosperms in their ovules which are borne unprotected (not within an ◊ovary) on the scales of their cones.

The arrangement of the reproductive organs, and their more simplified internal tissue structure, also distinguishes them from the flowering plants. In contrast to the gymnosperms, the ovules of angiosperms are enclosed within an ovary and many species have developed highly specialized reproductive structures associated with ◊pollination by insects, birds, or bats.

Segovia Andrés 1893–1987. Spanish virtuoso guitarist. He transcribed J S Bach for guitar and Ponce, Castelnuovo-Tedesco, de Falla, and Villa-Lobos composed some of their best-known music for him. Segovia's artistry did much to rehabilitate the guitar as a concert instrument and to promote the music of Spain. He taught lutenist Julian Bream and guitarist John Williams.

Seifert Jaroslav 1901–1986. Czech poet. He won state prizes under the communists, but became an original member of the Charter 77 human-rights movement. His works include *Mozart in Prague* 1970, *Umbrella from Piccadilly* 1978, and *The Prague Column* 1979. Nobel prize 1984.

Seikan Tunnel the world's longest underwater tunnel, opened 1988, linking the Japanese islands of Hokkaido and Honshu, which are separated by the Tsungaru Strait; length 51.7 km/32.3 mi.

Seine French river rising on the Langres plateau NW of Dijon, and flowing 774 km/472 mi NW to join the English Channel near Le Havre, passing through Paris and Rouen.

seismograph instrument used to record the activity of an ◊earthquake. A heavy inert weight is suspended by a spring and attached to this is a pen that is in contact with paper on a rotating drum. During an earthquake the instrument frame and drum move, causing the pen to record a zigzag line on the paper; the pen does not move.

seismology study of earthquakes and how their shock waves travel through the Earth. By examining the global pattern of waves produced by an earthquake, seismologists can deduce the nature of the materials through which they have passed. This leads to an understanding of the Earth's internal structure.

On a smaller scale artificial earthquake waves, generated by explosions or mechanical vibrators, can be used to search for subsurface features in, for example, oil or mineral exploration. Earthquake waves from underground nuclear explosions can be distinguished from natural waves by their shorter wavelength and higher frequency.

Selangor state of the Federation of Malaysia; area 7,956 sq km/3,071 sq mi; population (1993 est) 1,981,200. It was under British protection from 1874 and was a federated state 1895–1946. The capital was transferred to Shah Alam from Kuala Lumpur 1973. Klang is the seat of the sultan and a centre for rubber-growing and tin-mining; Port Kelang (or Port Klang), formerly Port Swettenham, exports tin and rubber.

select committee any of several long-standing committees of the UK House of Commons, such as the Environment Committee and the Treasury and Civil Service Committee. These were intended to restore parliamentary control of the executive, improve the quality of legislation, and scrutinize public spending and the work of government departments. Select committees represent the major parliamentary reform of the 20th century, and a possible means – through their all-party membership – of avoiding the automatic repeal of one government's measures by its successor.

Selene in Greek mythology, the goddess of the Moon. She was the daughter of a ◊Titan, and the sister of Helios and Eos. In later times she was identified with ◊Artemis.

selenium (Greek *Selene* 'Moon') grey, nonmetallic element, symbol Se, atomic number 34, relative atomic mass 78.96. It belongs to the sulphur group and occurs in several allotropic forms that differ in their physical and chemical properties. It is an essential trace element in human nutrition. Obtained from many sulphide ores and selenides, it is used as a red colouring for glass and enamel.

Seles Monica 1973– . US lawn-tennis player, born in the former Yugoslavia. She won her first Grand Slam title, the French Open, at the age of 16. She dominated the major events in 1991 but withdrew from Wimbledon and consequently missed the chance to achieve the Grand Slam. In 1991 she became the youngest woman player ever to achieve number-one ranking.

In 1993 she was stabbed by a fan of her rival, Steffi Graf, on court during the Hamburg Open. The enforced break from the game meant her missing most major tournaments 1993–95. She beat Martina Navratilova July 1995 in her first public match since the stabbing.

Seleucus I Nicator c. 358–280 BC. Macedonian general under Alexander the Great and founder of the Seleucid Empire. After Alexander's death 323 BC, Seleucus became governor and then (312 BC) ruler of Babylonia, founding the city of Seleucia on the river Tigris. He conquered Syria and had himself crowned king 306 BC, but his expansionist policies brought him into conflict with the Ptolemies of Egypt, and he was assassinated. He was succeeded by his son Antiochus I.

Seljuk Empire empire of the Turkish people (converted to Islam during the 7th century) under the leadership of the invading Tatars or Seljuk Turks. The Seljuk Empire 1055–1243 included Iran, Iraq, and most of Anatolia and Syria. It was a loose confederation whose centre was in Iran, jointly ruled by members of the family and led by a great sultan exercising varying degrees of effective power. It was succeeded by the ◊Ottoman Empire.

Sellafield site of a nuclear power station on the coast of Cumbria, NW England. It was known as Windscale until 1971, when the management of the site was transferred from the UK Atomic Energy Authority to British Nuclear Fuels Ltd. It reprocesses more than 1,000 tonnes of spent fuel from nuclear reactors annually and is the world's greatest discharger of radioactive waste.

In 1990 a scientific study revealed an increased risk of leukaemia in children whose fathers worked at Sellafield 1950–85. In 1996, British Nuclear Fuels was fined £25,000 after admitting 'serious and significant' failures in safety that left a Sellafield plant worker contaminated with radioactivity. In 1998, the Norwegian environment minister called for a ban on the release of technetium-99 into the sea from Sellafield. For accidents, see ◊nuclear safety.

Sellers Peter, (originally Richard Henry Sellers) 1925–1980. English comedian and film actor. He made his name in the madcap British radio programme *The Goon Show* 1949–60. His films include *The Ladykillers* 1955, *I'm All Right Jack* 1960, *Dr Strangelove* 1964, five *Pink Panther* films 1964–78 (as the bumbling Inspector Clouseau), and *Being There* 1979.

Selwyn Lloyd (John) Selwyn Brooke Lloyd, Baron Selwyn Lloyd 1904–1978. British Conservative politician. He was foreign secretary 1955–60 and chancellor of the Exchequer 1960–62. He was responsible for the creation of the National Economic Development Council, but the unpopularity of his policy of wage restraint in an attempt to defeat inflation forced his resignation. He was Speaker of the House of Commons 1971–76.

Selznick David O(liver) 1902–1965. US film producer. His early work includes *King Kong*, *Dinner at Eight*, and *Little Women* all 1933. His independent company, Selznick International (1935–40), made such lavish films as *Gone With the Wind* 1939, *Rebecca* 1940, and *Duel in the Sun* 1946. His last film was *A Farewell to Arms* 1957.

semantics the branch of ◊linguistics dealing with the meaning of words.

semaphore visual signalling code in which the relative positions of two moveable pointers or hand-held flags stand for different letters or numbers. The system is used by ships at sea and for railway signals.

Semarang port in N Java, Indonesia; population (1990) 1,005,300. There is a shipbuilding industry, and exports include coffee, teak, sugar, tobacco, kapok, and petroleum from nearby oilfields.

Semele in Greek mythology, the daughter of ◊Cadmus of Thebes and mother of Dionysus by Zeus. At Hera's suggestion she demanded that Zeus should appear to her in all his glory, but when he did so she was consumed by lightning.

semelparity in biology, the occurrence of a single act of reproduction during an organism's lifetime. Most semelparous species produce very large numbers of offspring when they do reproduce, and normally die soon afterwards. Examples include the Pacific salmon and the pine looper moth. Many plants are semelparous, or ◊monocarpic. Repeated reproduction is called ◊iteroparity.

semen fluid containing ◊sperm from the testes and secretions from various sex glands (such as the prostate gland) that is ejaculated by male animals during copulation. The secretions serve to nourish and activate the sperm cells, and prevent them clumping together.

semiconductor material with electrical conductivity intermediate between metals and insulators and used in a wide range of electronic devices. Certain crystalline materials, most notably silicon and germanium, have a small number of free electrons that have escaped from the bonds between the atoms. The atoms from which they have escaped possess vacancies, called holes, which are similarly able to move from atom to atom and can be regarded as positive charges. Current can be carried by both electrons (negative carriers) and holes (positive carriers). Such materials are known as intrinsic semiconductors.

Conductivity can be enhanced by doping the material with small numbers of impurity atoms which either release free electrons (making an n-type semiconductor with more electrons than holes) or capture them (a p-type semiconductor with more holes than electrons). When p-type and n-type materials are brought together to form a p-n junction, an electrical barrier is formed which conducts current more readily in one direction than the other. This is the basis of the ◊semiconductor diode, used for rectification, and numerous other devices including ◊transistors, rectifiers, and ◊integrated circuits (silicon chips).

semiconductor diode or ***p–n junction diode*** in electronics, a two-terminal semiconductor device that allows electric current to flow in only one direction, the forward-bias direction. A very high resistance prevents current flow in the opposite, or reverse-bias, direction. It is used as a ◊rectifier, converting alternating current (AC) to direct current (DC).

semiology or ***semiotics*** the study of the function of signs and symbols in human communication, both in language and by various nonlinguistic means. Beginning with the notion of the Swiss linguist Ferdinand de ◊Saussure that no word or other sign (signifier) is intrinsically linked with its meaning (signified), it was developed as a scientific discipline, especially by Claude ◊Lévi-Strauss and Roland ◊Barthes.

Semiotics has combined with structuralism in order to explore the 'production' of meaning in language and other sign systems and has emphasized the conventional nature of this production.

Semiramis lived 9th century BC. Greek name for Sammuramat, an Assyrian queen, later identified with the chief Assyrian goddess ◊Ishtar.

Semite any of the peoples of the Middle East originally speaking a Semitic language, and traditionally said to be descended from Shem, a son of Noah in the Bible. Ancient Semitic peoples include the Hebrews, Ammonites, Moabites, Edomites, Babylonians, Assyrians, Chaldaeans, Phoenicians, and Canaanites. The Semitic peoples founded the monotheistic religions of Judaism, Christianity, and Islam.

Semitic languages branch of the ◊Hamito-Semitic language.

Semtex plastic explosive, manufactured in the Czech Republic. It is safe to handle (it can only be ignited by a detonator) and difficult to trace, since it has no smell. It has been used by extremist groups in the Middle East and by the IRA in Northern Ireland.

Senanayake Don Stephen 1884–1952. First prime minister of independent Sri Lanka (formerly Ceylon) 1948–52. Active in politics from 1915, he became leader of the United National Party and negotiated independence from Britain 1947. A devout Buddhist, he promoted Sinhalese-Tamil racial harmony and rural development.

Senanayake Dudley Shelton 1911–1973. Prime minister of Sri Lanka 1952–53, 1960, and 1965–70; son of Don Senanayake, he sought to continue his father's policy of communal reconciliation.

Senate in ancient Rome, the 'council of elders'. Originally consisting of the heads of patrician families, it was recruited from ex-magistrates and persons who had rendered notable public service, but was periodically purged by the censors. Although nominally advisory, it controlled finance and foreign policy. Sulla doubled its size to 600.

Sendak Maurice Bernard 1928– . US writer and book illustrator. His children's books with their deliberately arch illustrations include *Where the Wild Things Are* 1963, *In the Night Kitchen* 1970, and *Outside Over There* 1981.

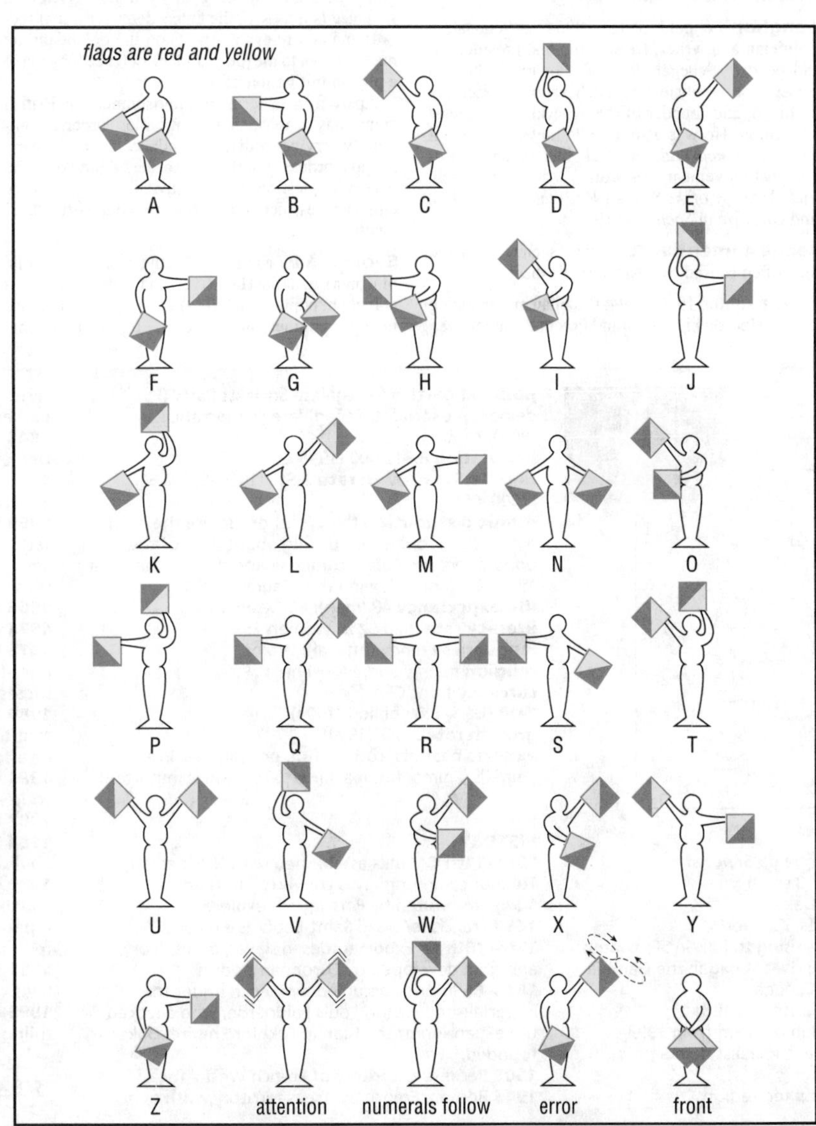

semaphore The semaphore signals for the letters of the alphabet and some special signals.

Live among men as if God beheld you; speak to God as if men were listening.

SENECA
Epistles

Sendero Luminoso (Shining Path) Maoist guerrilla group active in Peru, formed 1980 to overthrow the government; until 1988 its activity was confined to rural areas. In 1992 they stepped up their campaign in response to a crackdown imposed by Peruvian president Fujimori, which led to the arrest (and subsequent life imprisonment) of their leader, Abimael Guzman Reynoso (1934–), along with other leading members of the group. During 1994, more than 6,000 of the organization's guerrillas surrendered to the authorities.

Seneca Lucius Annaeus c. 4 BC–AD c. 65. Roman stoic playwright, author of essays and nine tragedies. He was tutor to the future emperor Nero but lost favour after Nero's accession to the throne and was ordered to commit suicide. His tragedies were accepted as classical models by 16th-century dramatists.

Senefelder (Johann Nepomuk Franz) Alois 1771–1834. Austrian engraver and playwright, born in Prague. Working as an actor and playwright, he is thought to have invented the printing technique of ◊lithography about 1796, possibly as a way of reproducing his own plays.

Senegal country in W Africa, on the Atlantic Ocean, bounded N by Mauritania, E by Mali, S by Guinea and Guinea-Bissau, and enclosing the Gambia on three sides. *See country box below.*

Senegal river in W Africa, formed by the confluence of the Bafing and Bakhoy rivers and flowing 1,125 km/700 mi NW and W to join the Atlantic Ocean near St Louis, Senegal. In 1968 the Organization of Riparian States of the River Senegal (Guinea, Mali, Mauritania, and Senegal) was formed to develop the river valley, including a dam for hydroelectric power and irrigation at Joina Falls in Mali; its headquarters is in Dakar. The river gives its name to the Republic of Senegal.

Senghor Léopold Sédar 1906– . Senegalese politician and writer. He was the first president of independent Senegal 1960–80. Previously he was Senegalese deputy to the French National Assembly 1946–58, and founder of the Senegalese Progressive Union. He was also a well-known poet and a founder of *négritude*, a black literary and philosophical movement. His works, written in French, include *Songs of the Shade* 1945, *Ethiopiques* 1956, and *On African Socialism* 1961.

senile dementia ◊dementia associated with old age, often caused by ◊Alzheimer's disease.

Senna Ayrton 1960–1994. Brazilian motor-racing driver. He won his first Grand Prix in Portugal 1985 and won 41 Grand Prix in 161 starts, including a record six wins at Monaco. Senna was world champion in 1988, 1990, and 1991. He was killed at the 1994 San Marino Grand Prix at Imola.

Sennacherib died 681 BC. King of Assyria from 705 BC. Son of ◊Sargon II, he rebuilt the city of Nineveh on a grand scale, sacked Babylon 689, and defeated ◊Hezekiah, King of Judah, but failed to take Jerusalem. He was assassinated by his sons, and one of them, Esarhaddon, succeeded him.

Sennett Mack. Stage name of Michael Sinnott 1880–1960. Canadian-born US film producer. He was originally an actor. In 1911 he founded the Keystone production company, responsible for slapstick silent films featuring the Keystone Kops, Fatty Arbuckle, and Charlie Chaplin. He did not make the transition to sound with much enthusiasm and retired 1935. His films include *Tillie's Punctured Romance* 1914, *The Shriek of Araby* 1923, and *The Barber Shop* (sound) 1933.

sense organ any organ that an animal uses to gain information about its surroundings. All sense organs have specialized receptors (such as light receptors in the eye) and some means of translating their response into a nerve impulse that travels to the brain. The main human sense organs are the eye, which detects light and colour (different wavelengths of light); the ear, which detects sound (vibrations of the air) and gravity; the nose, which detects some of the chemical molecules in the air; and the tongue, which detects some of the chemicals in food, giving a sense of taste. There are also many small sense organs in the skin, including pain, temperature, and pressure sensors, contributing to our sense of touch.

sentence in law, the judgement of a court stating the punishment to be imposed following a plea of guilty or a finding of guilt by a jury. Before a sentence is imposed, the antecedents (criminal record) and any relevant reports on the defendant are made known to the judge and the defence may make a plea in mitigation of the sentence.

Apart from a term of imprisonment, a British court may impose fines, probation orders, community-service orders, attendance-centre orders, hospital orders, guardianship orders, ◊bind over the person in question, and (for juveniles only) enforce either a care order or detention in a young offenders' institution.

Seoul or ***Sŏul*** capital of South ◊Korea (Republic of Korea), near the Han River, and with its chief port at Inchon; population (1994) 11,500,000. Industries include engineering, textiles, food processing, electrical and electronic equipment, chemicals, and machinery.

It was the capital of Korea 1392–1910, and has universities and a 14th-century palace. It was the site of the 1988 Summer Olympics.

sepal part of a flower, usually green, that surrounds and protects the flower in bud. The sepals are derived from modified leaves, and are collectively known as the ◊calyx.

In some plants, such as the marsh marigold *Caltha palustris*, where true ◊petals are absent, the sepals are brightly coloured and petal-like, taking over the role of attracting insect pollinators to the flower.

separation of powers limiting the powers of government by separating governmental functions into the executive, legislative, and judiciary. The concept has its fullest practical expression in the the US constitution (see ◊federalism).

Sephardi (plural ***Sephardim***) Jews descended from those expelled from Spain and Portugal in the 15th century, or from those forcibly converted during the Inquisition to Christianity (Marranos). Many settled in N Africa and in the Mediterranean countries, as well as in the Netherlands, England, and Dutch colonies in the New World. Sephardim speak Ladino, a 15th-century Romance dialect, as well as the language of their nation.

sepia brown pigment produced from the black fluid of cuttlefish. After 1870 it replaced the use of bistre (made from charred wood) in wash drawings due to its warmer range of colours. Sepia fades rapidly in bright light.

Sepoy Rebellion alternative name for the ◊Indian Mutiny, a revolt of Indian soldiers (sepoys) against the British in India 1857–58.

septicaemia general term for any form of ◊blood poisoning.

septic shock life-threatening fall in blood pressure caused by blood poisoning (septicaemia). Toxins produced by bacteria infecting the blood induce a widespread dilation of the blood vessels throughout the body, and it is this that causes the patient's collapse (see ◊shock). Septic shock can occur following bowel surgery, after a penetrating wound to the abdomen, or as a consequence of infection of the urinary tract. It is usually treated in an intensive care unit and has a high mortality rate.

Septuagint (Latin *septuagint*, seventy) the oldest Greek version of the Old Testament or Hebrew Bible, traditionally made by 70 scholars.

SENEGAL
Republic of

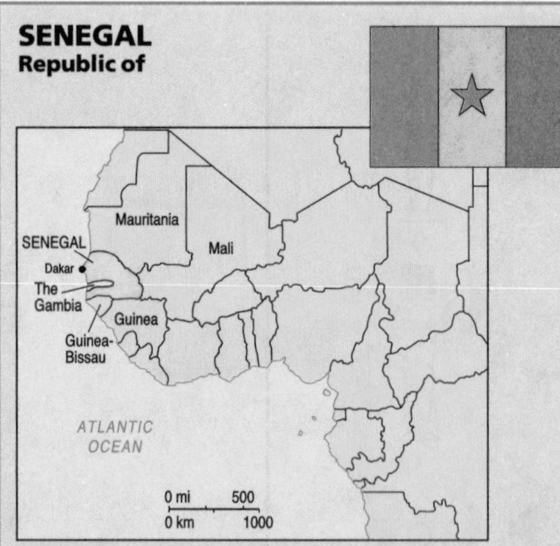

national name *République du Sénégal*
area 196,200 sq km/75,753 sq mi
capital (and chief port) Dakar
major towns/cities Thiès, Kaolack
physical features plains rising to hills in SE; swamp and tropical forest in SW; river Senegal; the Gambia forms an enclave within Senegal
head of state Abdou Diouf from 1981
head of government Habib Thiam from 1993
political system emergent socialist democratic republic
administrative divisions ten regions
political parties Senegalese Socialist Party (PS), democratic socialist; Senegalese Democratic Party (PDS), centrist
population 8,312,000 (1995 est)
population growth rate 2.5% (1990–95); 2.6% (2000–05)
ethnic distribution the Wolof group are the most numerous peoples, comprising about 36% of the population; the Fulani comprise about 21%; the Serer 19%; the Diola 7%; and the Mandingo 6%
life expectancy 48 (men), 50 (women)
literacy rate men 52%, women 25%
languages French (official); Wolof
religion mainly Sunni Muslim
currency franc CFA
GDP (US $) 3.88 billion (1994)
growth rate 2.0% (1994)
exports peanuts, cotton, fish, phosphates, live animals, animal fat, machinery. Tourism is important

HISTORY
10th–11th Cs Links established with N Africa; the Tukolor community was converted to Islam.
1445 First visited by Portuguese explorers.
1659 French founded Saint-Louis as a colony.
17th–18th Cs Export trades in slaves, gums, ivory, and gold developed by European traders.
1854–65 Interior occupied by French under their imperialist governor, Louis Faidherbe, who checked the expansion of the Islamic Tukulor Empire; Dakar founded.
1902 Became a territory of French West Africa.
1946 Became French overseas territory, with own territorial assembly and representation in French parliament.
1948 Leopold Sedar Senghor founded the Senegalese Democratic Bloc to campaign for independence.
1959 Formed the Federation of Mali with French Sudan.
1960 Independence achieved and withdrew from the federation. Senghor, leader of the socialist Senegalese Progressive Union (UPS), became president.
1966 UPS declared the only legal party.
1974 Pluralist system re-established.
1976 UPS reconstituted as Socialist Party (PS). Prime Minister Abdou Diouf nominated as Senghor's successor.
1980 Senghor resigned; succeeded by Diouf. Troops sent to defend Gambia against suspected Libyan invasion.
1981 Military help again sent to Gambia to thwart coup attempt.
1982 Confederation of Senegambia came into effect.
1983 Diouf re-elected. Post of prime minister abolished.
1989 Diplomatic links with Mauritania severed after 450 died in violent clashes; over 50,000 people repatriated from both countries. Senegambia federation abandoned.
1992 Post of prime minister reinstated. Diplomatic links with Mauritania re-established.
1993 Assembly and presidential elections won by ruling PS.

SEE ALSO Senghor, Léopold Sédar

sequencing in biochemistry, determining the sequence of chemical subunits within a large molecule. Techniques for sequencing amino acids in proteins were established in the 1950s, insulin being the first for which the sequence was completed. The ◊Human Genome Project is attempting to determine the sequence of the 3 billion base pairs within human ◊DNA.

sequoia two species of conifer in the redwood family Taxodiaceae, native to W USA. The redwood *Sequoia sempervirens* is a long-lived timber tree, and one specimen, the Howard Libbey Redwood, is the world's tallest tree at 110 m/361 ft, with a circumference of 13.4 m/44 ft. The giant sequoia *Sequoiadendron giganteum* reaches up to 30 m/100 ft in circumference at the base, and grows almost as tall as the redwood. It is also (except for the bristlecone pine) the oldest living tree, some specimens being estimated at over 3,500 years of age.

sequoia The sequoia, or California redwood, is the tallest and largest tree. Twenty homes, a church, a mansion, and a bank have been built from the timber of one redwood.

Sequoya George Guess c. 1770–1843. Native American scholar and leader. After serving with the US army in the Creek War 1813–14, he made a study of his own Cherokee language and created a syllabary which was approved by the Cherokee council 1821. This helped thousands of Indians towards literacy and resulted in the publication of books and newspapers in their own language. Sequoya went on to write down ancient tribal history. In later life he became political representative of the Western tribes in Washington, negotiating for the Indians when the US government forced resettlement in Indian territory in the 1830s.

seraph (plural ***seraphim***) in Christian and Judaic belief, an ◊angel of the highest order. They are mentioned in the book of Isaiah in the Old Testament.

Serapis ancient Graeco-Egyptian god, a combination of Apis and Osiris, invented by the Ptolemies; his finest temple was the Serapeum in Alexandria.

Serb Yugoslavia's largest ethnic group, found mainly in Serbia, but also in the neighbouring independent republics of Bosnia-Herzegovina and Croatia. Their language is generally recognized to be the same as Croat and is hence known as ◊Serbo-Croatian.

The Serbs are predominantly Greek Orthodox Christians and write in a Cyrillic script. Although they are closely related linguistically to the Croats, there are cultural differences and long-standing enmities, which resurfaced with the outbreak of civil war 1991. In the province of Kosovo, the Serbs are in conflict with Yugoslavian Albanians, who comprise the majority.

Serbia (Serbo-Croatian ***Srbija***) constituent republic of Yugoslavia, which includes Kosovo and Vojvodina
area 88,400 sq km/34,122 sq mi
capital Belgrade
physical fertile Danube plains in the north, mountainous in the south (Dinaric Alps, Sar Mountains, N Albanian Alps, Balkan Mountains); rivers Sava, Tisza, Morava
features includes the former autonomous provinces of ◊Kosovo, capital Priština, of which the predominantly Albanian population demands unification with Albania, and ◊Vojvodina, capital Novi Sad, largest town Subotica, with a predominantly Serbian population and a large Hungarian minority
population (1991) 9,791,400
language the Serbian variant of Serbo-Croatian
religion Serbian Orthodox
history The Serbs settled in the Balkans in the 7th century and became Christians in the 9th century. They were united as one kingdom about 1169; the Serbian hero Stephan Dushan (1331–1355) founded an empire covering most of the Balkans. After their defeat at Kosovo 1389 they came under the domination of the Turks, who annexed Serbia 1459. Uprisings 1804–16, led by Kara George and Milosh Obrenovich, forced the Turks to recognize Serbia as an autonomous principality under Milosh. The assassination of Kara George on Obrenovich's orders gave rise to a long feud between the two houses. After a war with Turkey 1876–78, Serbia became an independent kingdom. On the assassination of the last Obrenovich 1903 the Karageorgevich dynasty came to the throne.

The two Balkan Wars 1912–13 greatly enlarged Serbia's territory at the expense of Turkey and Bulgaria. Serbia's designs on Bosnia-Herzegovina, backed by Russia, led to friction with Austria, culminating in the outbreak of war 1914. Serbia was overrun 1915–16 and was occupied until 1918, when it became the nucleus of the new kingdom of the Serbs, Croats, and Slovenes, and subsequently ◊Yugoslavia. Rivalry between Croats and Serbs continued within the republic. During World War II Serbia was under a puppet government set up by the Germans (94% of Serbian Jews were killed 1941–44); after the war it became a constituent republic of Yugoslavia.

Serbia formally annexed Kosovo and Vojvodina Sept 1990. In 1991 civil war in Yugoslavia arose from the Slobodan ◊Milošević nationalist government attempting the forcible annexation of Serb-dominated regions in Croatia. In Oct 1991 Milošević renounced territorial claims on Croatia pressured by threats of European Community (EC, now European Union) and United Nations (UN) sanctions, but the fighting continued until a ceasefire was agreed Jan 1992. EC recognition of Slovenia's and Croatia's independence in Jan 1992 and Bosnia-Herzegovina's in April left Serbia dominating a greatly reduced 'rump' Yugoslavia. Serbia's continued backing of Bosnian Serbs in their fight to partition Bosnia-Herzegovina led to international sactions on Serbia. Under pressure from the UN, Milošević ordered a blockade of the Bosnian Serbs and from Sept 1995 Serbia played a key role in the Dayton peace accord for Bosnia-Herzegovina.

The Socialist authorities refused to recognize opposition victories in November 1996 municipal elections. Serbia was denied access to the International Monetary Fund, and the EU continued to deny the country preferential trade terms. On 4 Feb 1997, following 78 days of protests, Milošević apparently surrendered, ordering his government to recognize opposition victories.

Despite the 1996–97 winter civil unrest, Milošević was elected in July 1997 to the Yugoslav presidency (the only post open to him under constitutional rules) for the following four years. Fighting erupted 1998 in the province of Kosovo between Serb paramilitary forces and ethnic Albanians. In May NATO announced a ban on investment in Serbia. Despite sanctions, both President Milošević and the Albanian leader in Kosovo, Ibrahim Rugova, rejected the possibility of settlement talks. In Jan 1999 after a massacre of 45 Albanian villagers, airstrikes by NATO were threatened unless the two sides agreed to attend talks in Paris.

At the end of March 1999 NATO forces launched air strikes against Yugoslavia in an attempt to force Serbia to halt its repression of ethnic Albanians in Kosovo. Targets were hit throughout Serbia and there was widespread destruction of Serbian infrastructure.

Serbo-Croatian (or ***Serbo-Croat***) the most widely spoken language in Yugoslavia and its former constituent republics, it is a member of South Slavonic branch of the Indo-European family, and has over 17 million speakers.

sere plant ◊succession developing in a particular habitat. A lithosere is a succession starting on the surface of bare rock. A hydrosere is a succession in shallow freshwater, beginning with planktonic vegetation and the growth of pondweeds and other aquatic plants, and ending with the development of swamp. A plagiosere is the sequence of communities that follows the clearing of the existing vegetation.

serfdom the legal and economic status of peasants under ◊feudalism. Serfs could not be sold like slaves, but they were not free to leave their master's estate without his permission. They had to work the lord's land without pay for a number of days every week and pay a percentage of their produce to the lord every year. They also served as soldiers in the event of conflict. Serfs also had to perform extra labour at harvest time and other busy seasons; in return they were allowed to cultivate a portion of the estate for their own benefit.

In England serfdom died out between the 14th and 17th centuries, but it lasted in France until 1789, in Russia until 1861, and in most other European countries until the early 19th century.

serialism in music, a later form of the ◊twelve-tone system of composition. It usually refers to post-1950 compositions in which further aspects such as dynamics, durations, and attacks are brought under serial control. These other series may consist of fewer than 12 degrees while some pitch series can go higher.

Serlio Sebastiano 1475–1554. Italian architect and painter. He was the author of *L'Architettura* 1537–51, which set down practical rules for the use of the Classical orders.

Serpens constellation on the celestial equator (see ◊celestial sphere), represented as a serpent coiled around the body of ◊Ophiuchus. It is the only constellation divided into two halves: Serpens Caput, the head (on one side of Ophiuchus), and Serpens Cauda, the tail (on the other side). Its main feature is the Eagle nebula.

serpentine group of minerals, hydrous magnesium silicate, $Mg_3Si_2O_5(OH)_4$, occurring in soft ◊metamorphic rocks and usually dark green. The fibrous form chrysotile is a source of ◊asbestos; other forms are antigorite and lizardite. Serpentine minerals are formed by hydration of ultramafic rocks during metamorphism. Rare snake-patterned forms are used in ornamental carving.

Serpent Mound earthwork built by Hopewell Indians in the 2nd–1st centuries BC in Ohio, USA. It is 405 m/1,330 ft long, 1.3 m/4 ft high, and about 6 m/19 ft across and may have been constructed in the shape of a snake for religious purposes.

serum clear fluid that separates out from clotted blood. It is blood plasma with the anticoagulant proteins removed, and contains ◊antibodies and other proteins, as well as the fats and sugars of the blood. It can be produced synthetically, and is used to protect against disease.

serval African wild cat *Felis serval*. It is a slender, long-limbed cat, about 1 m/3 ft long, with a yellowish-brown, black-spotted coat. It has large, sensitive ears, with which it locates its prey, mainly birds and rodents.

Servetus Michael (Miguel Serveto) 1511–1553. Spanish Christian Anabaptist theologian and physician. He was a pioneer in the study of the circulation of the blood and found that it circulates to the lungs from the right chamber of the heart. He was burned alive by the church reformer Calvin in Geneva, Switzerland, for publishing attacks on the doctrine of the Trinity.

service tree deciduous Eurasian tree *Sorbus domestica* of the rose family Rosaceae, with alternate pinnate leaves, white flowers, and small, edible, oval fruit. The European wild service tree *Sorbus torminalis* has oblong rather than pointed leaflets. It is related to the ◊mountain ash.

servomechanism automatic control system used in aircraft, motor cars, and other complex machines.

sesame annual plant *Sesamum indicum* of the family Pedaliaceae, probably native to SE Asia. It produces oily seeds used for food and soap making.

sessile in botany, a leaf, flower, or fruit that lacks a stalk and sits directly on the stem, as with the sessile acorns of certain ◊oaks. In zoology, it is an animal that normally stays in the same place, such as a barnacle or mussel. The term is also applied to the eyes of ◊crustaceans when these lack stalks and sit directly on the head.

Session, Court of one of the civil courts in Scotland; see ◊Court of Session.

Sessions Roger Huntington 1896–1985. US composer. His international Modernist style secured an American platform for serious German influences, including Hindemith and Schoenberg, and offered an alternative to the lightweight, fashionable Modernism of Milhaud and Paris. An able symphonist, his works include *The Black Maskers* (incidental music) 1923, eight symphonies, and *Concerto for Orchestra* 1971.

set or ***class*** in mathematics, any collection of defined things (elements), provided the elements are distinct and that there is a rule to decide whether an element is a member of a set. It is usually denoted by a capital letter and indicated by curly brackets {}.

For example, L may represent the set that consists of all the letters of the alphabet. The symbol $\in$ stands for 'is a member of'; thus $p \in L$ means that p belongs to the set consisting of all letters, and $4 \notin L$ means that 4 does not belong to the set consisting of all letters.

There are various types of sets. A finite set has a limited number of members, such as the letters of the alphabet; an infinite set has an unlimited number of members, such as all whole numbers; an empty or null set has no members, such as the number of people who have swum across the Atlantic Ocean, written as {} or $\varnothing$; a single-element set has only one member, such as days of the week beginning with M, written as {Monday}. Equal sets have the same members; for example, if W = {days of the week} and S = {Sunday, Monday, Tuesday, Wednesday, Thursday, Friday, Saturday}, it can be said that $W = S$. Sets with the same number of members are equivalent sets. Sets with some members in common are intersecting sets; for example, if R = {red playing cards} and F = {face cards}, then R and F share the members that are red face cards. Sets with no members in common are disjoint sets. Sets contained within others are subsets; for example, V = {vowels} is a subset of L = {letters of the alphabet}.

Sets and their interrelationships are often illustrated by a ◊Venn diagram.

Set in Egyptian mythology, the god of night, the desert, and of all evils. Portrayed as a grotesque animal, Set was the murderer of ◊Osiris.

setter any of various breeds of gun dog, called 'setters' because they were trained to crouch or 'set' on the sight of game to be pursued. They stand about 66 cm/26 in high and weigh about 25 kg/55 lb. They have a long, smooth coat, feathered tails, and spaniel-like faces.

The Irish setter is a rich red, the English setter is usually white with black, tan, or liver markings, and the Gordon setter is black and brown.

Settlement, Act of in Britain, a law passed 1701 during the reign of King William III, designed to ensure a Protestant succession to the throne by excluding the Roman Catholic descendants of James II in favour of the Protestant House of Hanover. Elizabeth II still reigns under this act.

Seurat Georges Pierre 1859–1891. French artist. One of the major Post-Impressionists, he originated, with Paul ◊Signac, the technique of ◊Pointillism (painting with small dabs rather than long brushstrokes). One of his best-known works is *A Sunday Afternoon on the Island of La Grande Jatte* 1886 (Art Institute of Chicago).

At the age of 16 Seurat went to the Ecole des Beaux-Arts, showing a remarkable early proficiency in figure drawing. Artists whose work he studied closely were Delacroix, whose frescoes at St Sulpice made him realize the significance of colour; and Piero della Francesca, whose sense of formal and geometrical beauty he shared.

Although fascinated by the Impressionists' use of colour, he rejected what he considered to be their lack of form, and sought to create a perfectly ordered art based on scientific principles. His Pointillism was based on scientific research on the perception of colour. One of the first major results of his new art was his *Bathers at Asnières* 1884 (National Gallery, London), which combines the atmospheric effect of Impressionist painting with a new solidity of form and composition.

Sevastopol or ***Sebastopol*** Black Sea port, resort, and fortress in the Crimea, Ukraine; population (1992) 371,000. It was the base of the former Soviet Black Sea fleet. It also has shipyards and a winemaking industry. Founded by Catherine II 1784, it was successfully besieged by the English and French in the Crimean War (Oct 1854–Sept 1855), and in World War II by the Germans (Nov 1941–July 1942), but was retaken by Soviet forces 1944.

Seven against Thebes in Greek mythology, the attack of seven captains led by Adrastus, king of Argos, on the seven gates of ancient Thebes, prompted by the rivalry between the two sons of Oedipus, Polynices and ◊Eteocles, for the kingship of Thebes. In the event, the two brothers died by each other's hands. The subject of tragedies by ◊Aeschylus and ◊Euripides (*The Phoenician Women*), and of the epic *Thebaïd* by the Roman poet Statius, it forms the background to other Greek tragedies by ◊Sophocles (*Antigone, Oedipus at Colonus*) and Euripides (*Suppliant Women*).

seven deadly sins in Christian theology, anger, avarice, envy, gluttony, lust, pride, and sloth (or dejection). These vices are considered fundamental to all other sins.

Seventh-Day Adventist or ***Adventist*** member of the Protestant religious sect of the same name. It originated in the USA in the fervent expectation of Christ's Second Coming, or advent, that swept across New York State following William Miller's prophecy that Christ would return on 22 Oct 1844. When this failed to come to pass, a number of Millerites, as his followers were called, reinterpreted his prophetic speculations and continued to maintain that the millennium was imminent. Adventists observe Saturday as the Sabbath and emphasize healing and diet; many are vegetarians. The sect has 36,920 organized churches and almost 8 million members in 210 countries and territories (1995).

Seven Weeks' War war 1866 between Austria and Prussia, engineered by the German chancellor ◊Bismarck. It was nominally over the possession of ◊Schleswig-Holstein, but it was actually to confirm Prussia's superseding Austria as the leading German state. The Prussian victory at the Battle of ◊Sadowa was the culmination of General von Moltke's victories.

Seven Wonders of the World in antiquity, the ◊pyramids of Egypt, the ◊Hanging Gardens of Babylon, the temple of Artemis at ◊Ephesus, the statue of Zeus at ◊Olympia, the Mausoleum at ◊Halicarnassus, the ◊Colossus of Rhodes, and the Pharos (lighthouse) at Alexandria.

Seven Years' War (in North America known as the ***French and Indian War***) war 1756–63 arising from the conflict between Austria and Prussia, and between France and Britain over colonial supremacy. Britain and Prussia defeated France, Austria, Spain, and Russia; Britain gained control of India and many of France's colonies, including Canada.

Spain ceded Florida to Britain in exchange for Cuba. Fighting against great odds, Prussia was eventually successful in becoming established as one of the great European powers. The war ended with the Treaty of Paris 1763, signed by Britain, France, and Spain.

severe combined immune deficiency (SCID) rare condition caused by a gene malfunction in which a baby is born unable to produce the enzyme ADA. Without ADA the T cells involved in fighting infection are poisoned; untreated infants usually die before the age of two. The child must be kept within a germ-free 'bubble', a transparent plastic tent, until a matched donor can provide a bone-marrow transplant (bone marrow is the source of disease-fighting cells in the body).

Severn river of Wales and England, rising on the NE side of Plynlimmon, N Wales, and flowing 338 km/210 mi through Shrewsbury, Worcester, and Gloucester to the Bristol Channel. It is the longest river in Great Britain. The Severn bore is a tidal wave up to 2 m/6 ft high.

S England and S Wales are linked near Chepstow by a rail tunnel (1873–85) over the Severn, and the Severn Bridge, a suspension road bridge (1966). A second road bridge is under construction.

Severn

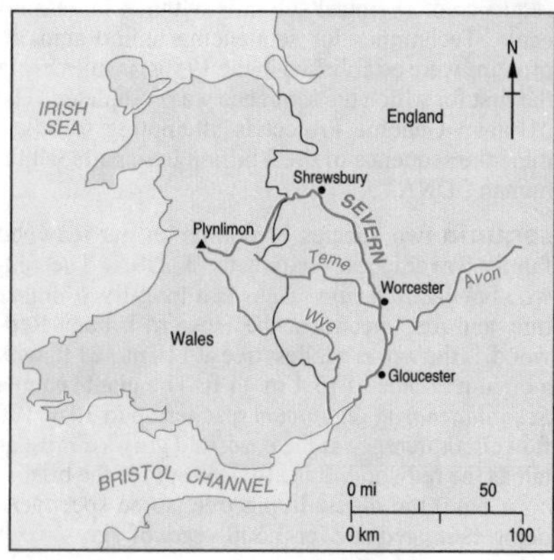

Severus Lucius Septimius 146–211. Roman emperor. He held a command on the Danube when in 193 the emperor Pertinax was murdered. Proclaimed emperor by his troops, Severus had to fight campaigns against his rivals, Pescennius Niger in Syria (died 194 AD) and Clodius Albinus, who was defeated at Lyons 197 AD. Severus was an able administrator. He was born in N Africa at ◊Leptis Magna, and was the only African to become emperor. He died at York while campaigning in Britain against the Caledonians.

Sévigné Marie de Rabutin-Chantal, Marquise de Sévigné 1626–1696. French writer. In her letters to her daughter, the Comtesse de Grignan, she paints a vivid picture of contemporary customs and events.

Seville (Spanish ***Sevilla***) city in Andalusia, Spain, on the Guadalquivir River, 96 km/60 mi N of Cadiz; population (1994) 714,000. Products include machinery, spirits, porcelain, pharmaceuticals, silk, and tobacco.

Formerly the centre of a Moorish kingdom, it has a 12th-century alcazar, or fortified palace, and a 15th–16th-century Gothic cathedral. Seville was the birthplace of the artists Murillo and Velázquez. The international trade fair Expo 92 celebrated the 500th anniversary of Europeans reaching the New World.

Sèvres fine porcelain produced at a factory in Sèvres, France (now a Paris suburb), since the early 18th century. It is characterized by the use of intensely coloured backgrounds (such as pink and royal blue), against which flowers are painted in elaborately embellished frames, often in gold.

It became popular after the firm's patronage by Louis XV's mistress, Madame de ◊Pompadour. The state porcelain factory was established in the park of St-Cloud 1756, and it is also the site of a national museum of ceramics.

Sèvres, Treaty of the last of the treaties that ended World War I. Negotiated between the Allied powers and the Ottoman Empire, it was finalized Aug 1920 but never ratified by the Turkish government.

The treaty reduced the size of Turkey by making concessions to the Greeks, Kurds, and Armenians, as well as ending Turkish control of Arab lands. Its terms were rejected by the newly created nationalist government and the treaty was never ratified. It was superseded by the Treaty of Lausanne in 1923.

sewage disposal the disposal of human excreta and other waterborne waste products from houses, streets, and factories. Conveyed through sewers to sewage works, sewage has to undergo a series of treatments to be acceptable for discharge into rivers or the sea, according to various local laws and ordinances. Raw sewage, or sewage that has not been treated adequately, is one serious source of water pollution and a cause of ◊eutrophication.

In the industrialized countries of the West, most industries are responsible for disposing of their own wastes. Government agencies establish industrial waste-disposal standards. In most countries, sewage works for residential areas are the responsibility of local authorities. The solid waste (sludge) may be spread over fields as a fertilizer or, in a few countries, dumped at sea. A significant proportion of bathing beaches in densely populated regions have unacceptably high bacterial content, largely as a result of untreated sewage being discharged into

Sèvres Biscuit porcelain figurines produced at the royal porcelain factory in Sèvres, France, 1765. The factory opened 1756 and was patronized by Madame de Pompadour, the mistress of Louis XV. These figurines are typical of the light and charming Rococo style of the 18th century. *Corbis*

rivers and the sea. Strict European rules phased out sea dumping in 1998.

The use of raw sewage as a fertilizer (long practised in China) has the drawback that disease-causing microorganisms can survive in the soil and be transferred to people or animals by consumption of subsequent crops. Sewage sludge is safer, but may contain dangerous levels of heavy metals and other industrial contaminants. In Britain in 1998 550,000 tonnes of sludge was spread on agricultural land.

Sewell Anna 1820–1878. English author. Her only published work, *Black Beauty* 1877, tells the life story of a horse. Her aim in writing the book was 'to induce kindness, sympathy, and understanding treatment of horses'.

Disabled by a childhood accident, her regular outings in a horse-drawn carriage provided material for the book. She wrote *Black Beauty* during the last years of her life when she was confined indoors.

sex determination process by which the sex of an organism is determined. In many species, the sex of an individual is dictated by the two sex chromosomes (X and Y) it receives from its parents. In mammals, some plants, and a few insects, males are XY, and females XX; in birds, reptiles, some amphibians, and butterflies the reverse is the case. In bees and wasps, males are produced from unfertilized eggs, females from fertilized eggs.

Environmental factors can affect some fish and reptiles, such as turtles, where sex is influenced by the temperature at which the eggs develop. In 1991 it was shown that maleness is caused by a single gene, 14 base pairs long, on the Y chromosome.

sex hormone steroid hormone produced and secreted by the gonads (testes and ovaries). Sex hormones control development and reproductive functions and influence sexual and other behaviour.

sexism belief in (or set of implicit assumptions about) the superiority of one's own sex, often accompanied by a stereotype or preconceived idea about the opposite sex. Sexism may also be accompanied by ◊discrimination on the basis of sex, generally as practised by men against women. ▷ *See feature on pp. 1152–1153.*

sex linkage in genetics, the tendency for certain characteristics to occur exclusively, or predominantly, in one sex only. Human examples include red-green colour blindness and haemophilia, both found predominantly in males. In both cases, these characteristics are ◊recessive and are determined by genes on the ◊X chromosome.

Since females possess two X chromosomes, any such recessive ◊allele on one of them is likely to be masked by the corresponding allele on the other. In males (who have only one X chromosome paired with a largely inert ◊Y chromosome) any gene on the X chromosome will automatically be expressed. Colour blindness and haemophilia can appear in females, but only if they are ◊homozygous for these traits, due to inbreeding, for example.

Sex Pistols, the UK punk-rock group (1975–78) that became notorious under the guidance of their manager Malcolm McLaren (1946–). Their first singles, 'Anarchy in the UK' 1976 and 'God Save the Queen' 1977, unbridled attacks on contemporary Britain, made the Pistols into figures the media loved to hate.

sextant navigational instrument for determining latitude by measuring the angle between some heavenly body and the horizon. It was invented 1730 by John Hadley (1682–1744) and can be used only in clear weather.

When the horizon is viewed through the right-hand side horizon glass, which is partly clear and partly mirrored, the light from a star can be seen at the same time in the mirrored left-hand side by adjusting an index mirror. The angle of the star to the horizon can then be read on a calibrated scale.

sexually transmitted disease (STD) any disease transmitted by sexual contact, involving transfer of body fluids. STDs include not only traditional ◊venereal disease, but also a growing list of conditions, such as ◊AIDS and scabies, which are known to be spread primarily by sexual contact. Other diseases that are transmitted sexually include viral ◊hepatitis. The World Health Organization estimate that there are 356,000 new cases of STDs daily worldwide (1995).

sexual reproduction reproductive process in organisms that requires the union, or ◊fertilization, of gametes (such as eggs and sperm). These are usually produced by two different individuals, although self-fertilization occurs in a few ◊hermaphrodites such as tapeworms. Most organisms other than bacteria and cyanobacteria (◊blue-green algae) show some sort of sexual process. Except in some lower organisms, the gametes are of two distinct types called eggs and sperm. The organisms producing the eggs are called females, and those producing the sperm, males. The fusion of a male and female gamete produces a zygote, from which a new individual develops.

The alternatives to sexual reproduction are parthenogenesis and asexual reproduction by means of ◊spores.

sexual selection process similar to ◊natural selection but relating exclusively to success in finding a mate for the purpose of sexual reproduction and producing offspring. Sexual selection occurs when one sex (usually but not always the female) invests more effort in producing young than the other. Members of the other sex compete for access to this limited resource (usually males competing for the chance to mate with females).

Sexual selection often favours features that increase a male's attractiveness to females (such as the pheasant's tail) or enable males to fight with one another (such as a deer's antlers). More subtly, it can produce hormonal effects by which the male makes the female unreceptive to other males, causes the abortion of fetuses already conceived, or removes the sperm of males who have already mated with a female.

Seychelles country in the Indian Ocean, off E Africa, N of Madagascar. *See country box on p. 964.*

Seyfert galaxy galaxy whose small, bright centre is caused by hot gas moving at high speed around a massive central object, possibly a ◊black hole. Almost all Seyferts are spiral galaxies. They seem to be closely related to ◊quasars, but are about 100 times fainter. They are named after their discoverer Carl Seyfert (1911–1960).

Seymour Jane c. 1509–1537. third wife of Henry VIII, whom she married 1536. She died soon after the birth of her son Edward VI.

Sezession (German 'secession') name given to various groups of German and Austrian artists in the 1890s who 'seceded' from official academic art institutions in order to found new schools of painting. The first was in Munich 1892; the next, linked with the paintings of Gustav ◊Klimt and the Art Nouveau movement, was the Vienna Sezession 1897; the Berlin Sezession, led by the Impressionist Max Liebermann (1847–1935), followed 1899.

In 1910 the members of the group *die ◊Brücke* formed the Neue Sezession when they were rejected by Berlin's first Sezession.

Sfax (Arabic ***Safaqis***) port and second-largest city in Tunisia; population (1994) 230,900. It is the capital of Sfax district, on the Gulf of Gabès, and lies about 240 km/150 mi SE of Tunis. Products include leather, soap, and carpets; there are also salt works and phosphate workings nearby. Exports include phosphates, olive oil, dates, almonds, esparto grass, and sponges.

Sforza Italian family that ruled the duchy of Milan 1450–99, 1512–15, and 1522–35. Its court was a centre of Renaissance culture and its rulers prominent patrons of the arts.

SGML (***Standard Generalized Markup Language***) ◊International Standards Organization standard describing how the structure (features such as headers, columns, margins, and tables) of a text can be identified so that it can be used in applications such as ◊desktop publishing and ◊electronic publishing. ◊HTML and VRML are both types of SGML.

female reproductive system

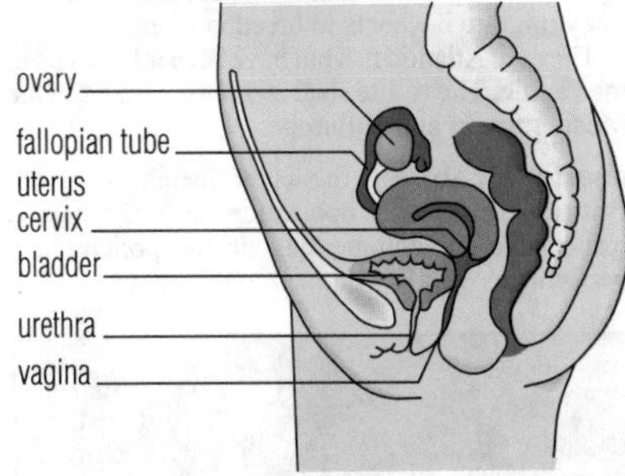

male reproductive system

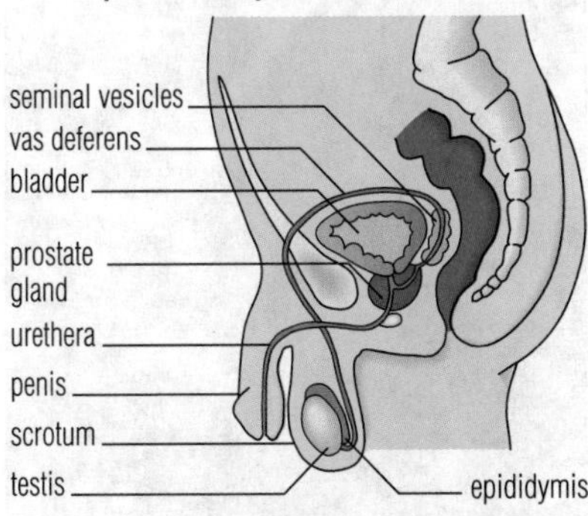

sexual reproduction The human reproductive organs. In the female, gametes called ova are released regularly in the ovaries after puberty. The Fallopian tubes carry the ova to the uterus or womb, in which the baby will develop. In the male, sperm is produced inside the testes after puberty; about 10 million sperm cells are produced each day, enough to populate the world in six months. The sperm duct or vas deferens, a continuation of the epididymis, carries sperm to the urethra during ejaculation.

SEYCHELLES
Republic of

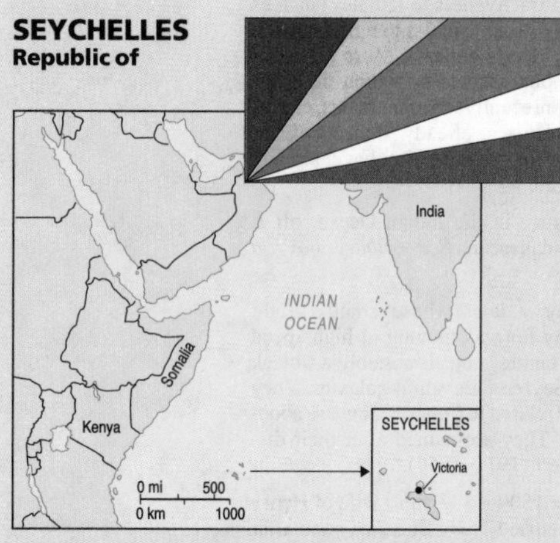

area 453 sq km/175 sq mi
capital and chief port Victoria (on Mahé island)
major towns/cities Cascade, Port Glaud, Misere
physical features comprises two distinct island groups: one, the Granitic group, concentrated, the other, the Outer or Coralline group, widely scattered; totals over 100 islands and islets
head of state and government France-Albert René from 1977
political system emergent democracy
administrative divisions none; centrally administered
political parties Seychelles People's Progressive Front (SPPF), nationalist socialist; Democratic Party (DP), left of centre
population 74,000 (1996 est)
population growth rate 1.1% (1990–95)
ethnic distribution predominantly Creole (of mixed African and European descent); small European minority (mostly French and British)
life expectancy 66 years
literacy rate 89%
languages creole (Asian, African, European mixture) 95%, English, French (all official)
religion Roman Catholic
currency Seychelles rupee
GDP (US $) 474.6 million (1994 est)
growth rate −3.0% (1994)
exports copra, cinnamon, coconuts, fish, shark fins, canned tuna

HISTORY
early 16 C First sighted by European navigators.
1744 Became a French colony.
1756 Claimed as a French possession and named after an influential French family.
1770s French colonists brought African slaves to settle the previously uninhabited islands; plantations established.
1794 Captured by British during French Revolutionary Wars.
1814 Ceded by France to Britain; incorporated as a dependency of Mauritius.
1835 Slavery abolished by the British, leading to an influx of liberated slaves from Mauritius and Chinese and Indian immigrants.
1903 Became a British crown colony, separate from Mauritius.
1963–64 First political parties formed.
1976 Independence achieved from Britain as a republic within the Commonwealth, with a moderate, James Mancham, of the centre-right Seychelles Democratic Party (SDP) as president.
1977 The more radical France-Albert René ousted Mancham in an armed bloodless coup and took over presidency; white settlers emigrated.
1979 The nationalistic socialist Seychelles People's Progressive Front (SPPF) became sole legal party under new constitution; became a nonaligned state.
1981 Attempted coup by South African mercenaries thwarted.
1991 Multiparty politics promised.
1993 New multiparty constitution adopted. René defeated Mancham, who had returned from exile, in competitive presidential elections; the SPPF won parliamentary elections.
1998 President René re-elected. SPUP won assembly elections.

Every man loves what he is good at.
THOMAS SHADWELL
A True Widow

Shaanxi or ***Shensi*** province of NW China
area 195,800 sq km/75,579 sq mi
capital Xian
towns Yan'an
physical mountains; Huang He Valley, one of the earliest settled areas of China
industries iron, steel, mining, textiles, fruit, tea, rice, wheat
population (1990) 32,470,000.

Shackleton Ernest Henry 1874–1922. Irish Antarctic explorer. In 1907–09, he commanded an expedition that reached 88° 23′ S latitude, located the magnetic South Pole, and climbed Mount ◊Erebus.

He was a member of Scott's Antarctic expedition 1901–04, and also commanded the expedition 1914–16 to cross the Antarctic, when he had to abandon his ship, the *Endurance*, crushed in the ice of the Weddell Sea. He died on board the *Quest* on his fourth expedition 1921–22 to the Antarctic.

shad any of several marine fishes, especially the genus *Alosa*, the largest (60 cm/2 ft long and 2.7 kg/6 lb in weight) of the herring family (Clupeidae). They migrate in shoals to breed in rivers.

They are Atlantic fish but have been introduced to the Pacific. The twaite shad *A. fallax* is found in the Mediterranean and N Europe.

shadow cabinet the chief members of the British parliamentary opposition, each of whom is responsible for commenting on the policies and performance of a government ministry.

Shackleton Irish Antarctic explorer Ernest Shackleton. In 1907–09 he led an expedition that came within 160 km/100 mi of the South Pole. In 1914–16, when his ship the *Endurance* was crushed in the ice, he led an arduous journey of 1,280 km/800mi to seek help for his men stranded on Elephant Island. *Topham*

Shadwell Thomas c. 1642–1692. English dramatist and poet. His plays include *Epsom-Wells* 1672 and *Bury-Fair* 1689.

He was involved in a violent feud with the poet ◊Dryden, whom he attacked in *The Medal of John Bayes* 1682 and succeeded as poet laureate 1689.

Shaffer Peter Levin 1926– . English dramatist. His psychological dramas include *Five Finger Exercise* 1958, the historical epic *The Royal Hunt of the Sun* 1964, *Equus* 1973, *Amadeus* 1979, about the envy provoked by the composer Mozart, and *Gift of the Gorgon* 1993.

Shaftesbury market town and agricultural centre in Dorset, England, 30 km/19 mi SW of Salisbury; population (1991) 6,200. King Alfred is said to have founded an abbey on the site 880; Canute died at Shaftesbury 1035.

Shaftesbury Anthony Ashley Cooper, 1st Earl of Shaftesbury 1621–1683. English politician, a supporter of the Restoration of the monarchy. He became Lord Chancellor 1672, but went into opposition 1673 and began to organize the ◊Whig Party. He headed the Whigs' demand for the exclusion of the future James II from the succession, secured the passing of the Habeas Corpus Act 1679, then, when accused of treason 1681, fled to Holland.

Shaftesbury Anthony Ashley Cooper, 7th Earl of Shaftesbury 1801–1885. British Tory politician. He strongly supported the Ten Hours Act of 1847 and other factory legislation, including the 1842 act forbidding the employment of women and children underground in mines. He was also associated with the movement to provide free education for the poor.

shag waterbird *Phalacrocorax aristoclis*, order Pelecaniformes, related to the ◊cormorant. It is smaller than the cormorant, with a green tinge to its plumage and in the breeding season has a crest. Its food consists mainly of sand eels for which it dives, staying underwater for up to 54 seconds. It breeds on deeply fissured cliffs, and on rocky parts of isolated islands.

shah (more formally, ***shahanshah*** 'king of kings') traditional title of ancient Persian rulers, and also of those of the recent ◊Pahlavi dynasty in Iran.

Shah Jahan 1592–1666. Mogul emperor of India from 1628, under whom the dynasty reached its zenith. Succeeding his father ◊Jahangir, he extended Mogul authority into the Deccan plateau (E India), subjugating Ahmadnagar, Bijapur, and Golconda 1636, but lost Kandahar in the NW to the Persians 1653. His reign marked the high point of Indo-Muslim architecture, with Delhi being rebuilt as Shahjahanabad, while the Taj Mahal and Pearl Mosque were constructed at Agra.

On falling seriously ill 1658 he was dethroned and imprisoned by his son ◊Aurangzeb.

Shaka or ***Chaka*** c. 1787–1828. Zulu chief who formed a Zulu empire in SE Africa. He seized power from his half-brother 1816 and then embarked on a bloody military campaign to unite the Zulu clans. He was assassinated by his two half-brothers.

His efforts to unite the Zulu peoples of Nguni (the area that today forms the South African province of Natal) initiated the period of warfare known as the ◊Mfecane.

Shaker member of the Christian sect of the ***United Society of Believers in Christ's Second Appearing***, called Shakers because of their ecstatic shakings in worship. The movement was founded by James and Jane Wardley in England about 1747, and taken to North America 1774 by Ann Lee (1736–1784).

They anticipated modern spiritualist beliefs, but their doctrine of celibacy led to their virtual

Shah Jahan The ruthless Mogul emperor Shah Jahan. A patron of architecture, the reign of Shah Jahan produced such celebrated examples of Indo-Muslim designs as the Taj Mahal mausoleum, built in memory of the emperor's favourite wife. *Philip Sauvain*

extinction. Shaker furniture has been admired in the 20th century for its simple and robust design.

Shakespeare William 1564–1616. English dramatist and poet. He is considered the greatest English dramatist. His plays, written in blank verse with some prose, can be broadly divided into lyric plays, including *Romeo and Juliet* and *A Midsummer Night's Dream*; comedies, including *The Comedy of Errors*, *As You Like It*, *Much Ado About Nothing*, and *Measure For Measure*; historical plays, such as *Henry VI* (in three parts), *Richard III*, and *Henry IV* (in two parts), which often showed cynical political wisdom; and tragedies, including *Hamlet*, *Othello*, *King Lear*, and *Macbeth*. He also wrote numerous sonnets.

Born in Stratford-on-Avon, the son of a wool dealer, he was educated at the grammar school, and in 1582 married Anne Hathaway (1556–1623). They had a daughter, Susanna, 1583, and in 1585 twins, Hamnet (died 1596) and Judith. By 1592 Shakespeare was established in London as an actor and a dramatist, and from 1594 he was an important member of the Lord Chamberlain's Company of actors. In 1598 the Company tore down their regular playhouse, the Theatre, and used the timber to build the ◊Globe Theatre in Southwark. Shakespeare became a 'sharer' in the venture, which entitled him to a percentage of the profits. In 1603 the Company became the King's Men. By this time Shakespeare was the leading playwright of the company and one of its business directors; he also continued to act. He retired to Stratford about 1610, where he died on 23 April 1616. He was buried in the chancel of Holy Trinity, Stratford.

early plays The plays written around 1589–94 include the three parts of *Henry VI*; the comedies *The Comedy of Errors*, *The Taming of the Shrew*, and *The Two Gentlemen of Verona*; the Senecan revenge tragedy *Titus Andronicus*; *Richard III*; and the comedy *Love's Labour's Lost*, satirizing the explorer Walter Raleigh's circle.

lyric plays The lyric plays *Romeo and Juliet*, *A Midsummer Night's Dream*, and *Richard II* (which explores the relationship between the private man and the public life of the state) 1594–97 were followed by *King John* and *The Merchant of Venice* 1596–97. The Falstaff plays of 1597–1600 – *Henry IV*, *Henry V* (a portrait of King Hal as the ideal soldier-king), and *The Merry Wives of Windsor* brought his fame to its height. The period ended with the lyrically witty *Much Ado About Nothing*, *As You Like It*, and *Twelfth Night*, about 1598–1601.

tragedies and late plays With *Hamlet* begins the period of the great tragedies, 1601–08: *Othello*, *King Lear*, *Macbeth*, *Timon of Athens*, *Antony and Cleopatra*, and *Coriolanus*. This 'darker' period is also reflected in the comedies *Troilus and Cressida* (a sardonic exploration of the concept of chivalric honour in relation to sexual conduct and the war between Greece and Troy), *All's Well That Ends Well*, and *Measure for Measure* around 1601–04. Plays of around 1608–11 – *Cymbeline*, *The Winter's Tale*, and *The Tempest* – form the mature romance or 'reconciliation' plays of the end of his career.

During 1613 it is thought that Shakespeare collaborated with John ◊Fletcher on *Henry VIII* and *The Two Noble Kinsmen*.

SHAKESPEARE: THE PLAYS

Title	Performed/ written (approximate)
Early plays	
Henry VI Part I	1589–92
Henry VI Part II	1589–92
Henry VI Part III	1589–92
The Comedy of Errors	1592–93
The Taming of the Shrew	1593–94
Titus Andronicus	1593–94
The Two Gentlemen of Verona	1594–95
Love's Labours Lost	1594–95
Romeo and Juliet	1594–95
Histories	
Richard III	1592–93
Richard II	1595–97
King John	1596–97
Henry IV Part I	1597–98
Henry IV Part II	1597–98
Henry V	1599
Roman plays	
Julius Caesar	1599–1600
Antony and Cleopatra	1607–08
Coriolanus	1607–08
The 'great' or 'middle' comedies	
A Midsummer Night's Dream	1595–96
The Merchant of Venice	1596–97
Much Ado About Nothing	1598–99
As You Like It	1599–1600
The Merry Wives of Windsor	1600–01
Twelfth Night	1601–02
The great tragedies	
Hamlet	1601–02
Othello	1604–05
King Lear	1605–06
Macbeth	1605–06
Timon of Athens	1607–08
The 'dark' comedies	
Troilus and Cressida	1601–02
All's Well That Ends Well	1602–03
Measure for Measure	1604–05
Late plays	
Pericles	1608–09
Cymbeline	1609–10
The Winter's Tale	1610–11
The Tempest	1611–12
Henry VIII	1612–13

Shakespeare The English dramatist and poet William Shakespeare. This portrait appeared on the title page of the edition of his works published 1623. *Philip Sauvain*

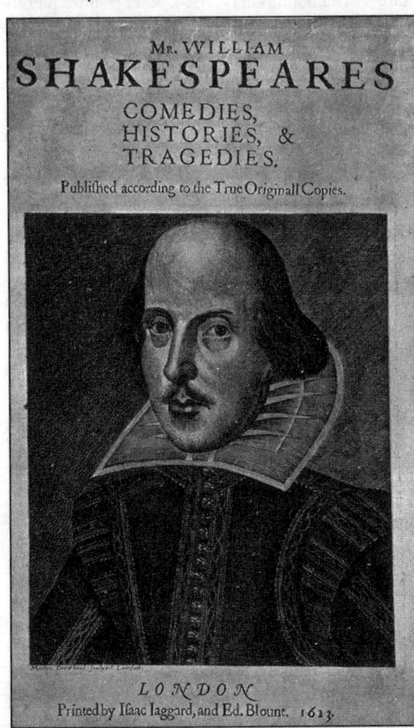
Mr. WILLIAM
SHAKESPEARES
COMEDIES,
HISTORIES, &
TRAGEDIES.
Publiſhed according to the True Originall Copies.
LONDON
Printed by Iſaac Iaggard, and Ed. Blount. 1623.

shale fine-grained and finely layered ◊sedimentary rock composed of silt and clay. It is a weak rock, splitting easily along bedding planes to form thin, even slabs (by contrast, mudstone splits into irregular flakes). Oil shale contains kerogen, a solid bituminous material that yields ◊petroleum when heated.

shallot small onion *Allium ascalonicum* in which bulbs are clustered like garlic; used for cooking and in pickles.

Shalmaneser five Assyrian kings, including Shalmaneser III, king of Assyria 859–824 BC, who pursued an aggressive policy and brought Babylon and Israel under the domination of Assyria.

shaman (Tungu *samân*) ritual leader who acts as intermediary between society and the supernatural world in many indigenous cultures of Asia, Africa, and the Americas. Also known as a medicine man, seer, or sorcerer, the shaman is expected to use special powers to cure illness and control good and evil spirits.

Shamir Yitzhak Yernitsky 1915– . Polish-born Israeli right-wing politician; prime minister 1983–84 and 1986–92; leader of the Likud (Consolidation Party) until 1993. He was foreign minister under Menachem Begin 1980–83, and again foreign minister in Shimon ◊Peres's unity government 1984–86.

shamrock several trifoliate plants of the family Leguminosae, including ◊clovers. St Patrick is said to have used one to illustrate the doctrine of the Holy Trinity, and it was made the national badge of Ireland. Irish people wear shamrocks on St Patrick's Day, 17 March.

Shan people of the mountainous borderlands separating Thailand, Myanmar (Burma), and China. They are related to the Laos and Thais, and their language belongs to the Sino-Tibetan family.

Shandong or ***Shantung*** province of NE China
area 153,300 sq km/59,174 sq mi
capital Jinan
towns ports: Yantai, Weihai, Qingdao, Shigiusuo
features crossed by the Huang He River and the ◊Grand Canal; Shandong Peninsula
industries cereals, cotton, wild silk, varied minerals, wine
population (1990) 83,430,000.

Shang dynasty or ***Yin dynasty*** China's first fully authenticated dynasty, c. 1500–c. 1066 BC, which saw the start of the Bronze Age. Shang rulers dominated the Huang He (Yellow River) plain of N China, developing a complex agricultural civilization which used a written language.

Shanghai port on the Huang-pu and Wusong rivers, Jiangsu province, China, 24 km/15 mi from the Chang Jiang estuary; population (1993) 8,760,000, the largest city in China. The municipality of Shanghai has an area of 5,800 sq km/2,239 sq mi and a population of 13,342,000. Industries include textiles, paper, chemicals, steel, agricultural machinery, precision instruments, shipbuilding, flour and vegetable-oil milling, and oil refining. It handles about 50% of China's imports and exports.

Shanghai is reckoned to be the most densely populated area in the world, with an average of 6 sq m/65 sq ft of living space and 2.2 sq m/2.6 sq yd of road per person.

features notable buildings include the Jade Buddha Temple 1882; the former home of the revolutionary ◊Sun Yat-sen; the house where the First National Congress of the Communist Party of China met secretly 1921; and the house, museum, and tomb of the writer Lu Xun

history Shanghai was a city from 1360 but became significant only after 1842, when the treaty of Nanking opened it to foreign trade. In the 1920s, about 40,000 foreigners lived in Shanghai, more than 2% of the total population; in 1925 the electorate consisted of 2,742 voters, of which 1,000 were British. The Municipal Council issued a de facto unilateral declaration of independence 1925. The international settlement then developed, which remained the commercial centre of the city after the departure of European interests 1943–46.

Shankar Ravi 1920– . Indian composer and musician. A virtuoso of the ◊sitar, he has been influential in popularizing Indian music in the West. He has composed two concertos for sitar and orchestra 1971 and 1981, and film music, including scores for Satyajit Ray's *Pather Panchali* 1955 and Richard Attenborough's *Gandhi* 1982, and founded music schools in Bombay and Los Angeles.

Shannon longest river in Ireland, rising in County Cavan and flowing 386 km/240 mi through loughs Allen and Ree and past Athlone, to reach the Atlantic Ocean through a wide estuary below Limerick. It is also the greatest source of electric power in the republic, with hydroelectric installations at and above Ardnacrusha, 5 km/3 mi N of Limerick.

Shantung alternative transliteration of the Chinese province of ◊Shandong.

Shanxi or ***Shansi*** or ***Shensi*** province of NE China
area 157,100 sq km/60,641 sq mi
capital Taiyuan
towns Datong
features a drought-ridden plateau, partly surrounded by the ◊Great Wall
industries coal, iron, fruit
population (1990) 28,180,000
history saw the outbreak of the Boxer Rebellion 1900.

'Men's evil manners live in brass; their virtues / We write in water.'

WILLIAM SHAKESPEARE
Henry VIII IV

'Our image has undergone a change from David fighting Goliath to being Goliath.'

YITZHAK SHAMIR
On Israel, quoted in the *Observer* Jan 1989

Do not do unto others as you would they should do unto you. Their tastes may not be the same.

George Bernard Shaw *Maxims for Revolutionists*

share in finance, that part of the capital of a company held by a member (shareholder). Shares may be numbered and are issued as units of definite face value; shareholders are not always called on to pay the full face value of their shares, though they bind themselves to do so.

Preference shares carry a fixed rate of dividend and have first claim on the profits of the company; ordinary shares have second claim, and if profits have been good may attract a higher dividend than the preference shares; deferred shares rank for dividend only after the rights of preference and ordinary shareholders have been satisfied. Fully paid-up shares can be converted by the company into stock.

sharecropping farming someone else's land, where the farmer gives the landowner a proportion of the crop instead of money. This system of rent payment was common in the USA, especially the South, until after World War II. It is still common in parts of the developing world; for example, in India. Often the farmer is left with such a small share of the crop that he or she is doomed to poverty.

Shari'a the law of ◊Islam believed by Muslims to be based on divine revelation, and drawn from a number of sources, including the Koran, the Hadith, and the consensus of the Muslim community. Under this law, *qisās*, or retribution, allows a family to exact equal punishment on an accused; *diyat*, or blood money, is payable to a dead person's family as compensation.

From the latter part of the 19th century, the role of the Shari'a courts in the majority of Muslim countries began to be taken over by secular courts, and the Shari'a to be largely restricted to family law. Modifications of Koranic maxims have resulted from the introduction of Western law; for example, compensation can now be claimed only after a conviction by a criminal court.

shark any member of various orders of cartilaginous fishes (class Chondrichthyes), found throughout the oceans of the world. There are about 400 known species of shark. They have tough, usually grey, skin covered in denticles (small toothlike scales). A shark's streamlined body has side pectoral fins, a high dorsal fin, and a forked tail with a large upper lobe. Five open gill slits are visible on each side of the generally pointed head. Most sharks are fish-eaters, and a few will attack humans. They range from several feet in length to the great white shark *Carcharodon carcharias*, 9 m/30 ft long, and the harmless plankton-feeding whale shark *Rhincodon typus*, over 15 m/50 ft in length. Their eyes, though lacking acuity of vision or sense of colour, are highly sensitive to light. Their sense of smell is so acute that one-third of the brain is given up to interpreting its signals; they can detect blood in the water up to 1 km/1,100 yd away. They also respond to electrical charges emanating from other animals.

Relatively few attacks on humans lead to fatalities, and research suggests that the attacking sharks are not searching for food, but attempting to repel perceived rivals from their territory.

shark The great white shark lives by hunting and scavenging in the warmer oceans and coastal waters of the world. Sharks have no swim bladder, so must swim constantly to stay afloat, though their oil-rich livers help to prevent them sinking. *Corbis*

Sharman Helen 1963– . The first Briton to fly in space, chosen from 13,000 applicants for a 1991 joint UK–Soviet space flight. Sharman, a research chemist, was launched on 18 May 1991 in *Soyuz TM-12* and spent six days with Soviet cosmonauts aboard the *Mir* space station.

Sharp Cecil James 1859–1924. English collector and compiler of folk dance and song. His work ensured that the English folk-music revival became established in school music throughout the English-speaking world.

He led a movement to record a threatened folk-song tradition for posterity, publishing *English Folk Song* 1907 (two volumes). In the USA he tracked down survivals of English song in the Appalachian Mountains and elsewhere.

Sharpeville black township in South Africa, 65 km/40 mi S of Johannesburg and N of Vereeniging; 69 people were killed here when police fired on a crowd of anti-apartheid demonstrators 21 March 1960. The massacre took place during a campaign launched by the Pan-Africanist Congress against the pass laws (laws requiring nonwhite South Africans to carry identity papers).

On the anniversary of the massacre 1985, during funerals of people who had been killed protesting against unemployment, 19 people were shot by the police at Langa near Port Elizabeth.

Shastri Lal Bahadur 1904–1966. Indian politician, prime minister 1964–66. He campaigned for national integration, and secured a declaration of peace with Pakistan at the Tashkent peace conference 1966.

Before independence, he was imprisoned several times for civil disobedience. Because of his small stature, he was known as 'the Sparrow'.

Shatt-al-Arab ('river of Arabia') (Persian Arvand) waterway formed by the confluence of the rivers ◊Euphrates and ◊Tigris; length 190 km/120 mi to the Persian Gulf. Basra, Khorramshahr, and Abadan stand on it.

Its lower reaches form a border of disputed demarcation between Iran and Iraq. In 1975 the two countries agreed on the deepest water line as the frontier, but Iraq repudiated this 1980; the dispute was a factor in the Iran–Iraq war 1980–88.

Shaw George Bernard 1856–1950. Irish dramatist. He was also a critic and novelist, and an early member of the socialist ◊Fabian Society. His plays combine comedy with political, philosophical, and polemic aspects, aiming to make an impact on his audience's social conscience as well as their emotions. They include *Arms and the Man* 1894, *Devil's Disciple* 1897, *Man and Superman* 1903, *Pygmalion* 1913, and *St Joan* 1923. Nobel prize 1925.

Shaw was born in Dublin, and went to London 1876, where he became a brilliant debater and supporter of the Fabians, and worked as a music and drama critic. He wrote five unsuccessful novels before his first play, *Widowers' Houses*, was privately produced 1892. Attacking slum landlords, it allied him with the realistic, political, and polemical movement in the theatre, pointing to people's responsibility to improve themselves and their social environment. His first public production was *Arms and the Man*, a cynical view of war.

The 'anti-romantic' comedy *Pygmalion*, first performed 1913, was written for the actress Mrs Patrick Campbell (1865–1940) (and after Shaw's death converted to a musical as *My Fair Lady*).

Shearer Alan 1970– . English footballer. In 1996 he was transferred to Newcastle United from Blackburn Rovers for what was then a world record fee of £15 million. A strongly-built centre-forward, he made his England debut in 1992 and by the end of October 1998 had scored 22 goals in 46 internationals.

Although he scored a hat trick on his league debut for Southampton at the age of 17 it was not until he joined Blackburn Rovers in July 1992 that he established his reputation as a prolific goal scorer. He scored over 30 league goals in three consecutive seasons. In the 1996 European Championships, he finished as the tournament's top scorer with five goals.

shearwater any sea bird of the genus *Puffinus*. All the species are oceanic, and either dark above and white below or all dark. Shearwaters are members of the same family (Procellariidae), as the diving ◊petrels, order Procellariiformes. They get their name from their habit of skimming low over the sea on still wings.

The sooty shearwater *P. griseus* is common on both North Atlantic coasts. The muttonbird or whalebird *P. tenuirostris* breeds in Australia but for the rest of the year moves over the Pacific; it is killed for meat and oil.

Sheba ancient name for S ◊Yemen (Sha'abijah). It was once renowned for gold and spices. According to the Old Testament, its queen visited Solomon; until 1975 the Ethiopian royal house traced its descent from their union.

Shechem ancient town in Palestine, capital of Samaria. In the Old Testament, it is the traditional burial place of Joseph; nearby is Jacob's well. Shechem was destroyed about AD 67 by the Roman emperor Vespasian; on its site stands Nablus (a corruption of Neapolis) built by the Roman emperor ◊Hadrian.

sheep any of several ruminant, even-toed, hoofed mammals of the family Bovidae. Wild species survive in the uplands of central and E Asia, N Africa, S Europe and North America. The domesticated breeds are all classified as *Ovis aries*. Various breeds of sheep are reared worldwide for meat, wool, milk, and cheese, and for rotation on arable land to maintain its fertility.

Domestic sheep are descended from wild sheep of the Neolithic Middle East. The original species may be extinct but was probably closely related to the surviving mouflon *O. musimom* of Sardinia and Corsica. The dozens of different breeds known across the world were developed to suit different requirements and a range of geographical and climatic conditions.

sheepdog any of several breeds of dog, bred originally for herding sheep. The dog now most commonly used by shepherds and farmers in Britain to tend sheep is the border collie. Non-pedigree dogs of the border collie type, though more variable in size and colour, are referred to as working sheepdogs. Other recognized British breeds are the ◊Old English and Shetland sheepdogs. Many countries have their own breeds of sheepdog, such as the Belgian sheepdog, Australian kelpie, and Hungarian puli.

Sheffield industrial city on the river Don, South Yorkshire, England; population (1991) 501,200. From the 12th century, iron smelting was the chief industry, and by the 14th century, Sheffield cutlery, silverware, and plate were made. During the Industrial Revolution the iron and steel industries developed rapidly. It now produces alloys and special steels, cutlery of all kinds, permanent magnets, drills, and precision tools. Other industries include electroplating, type-founding, and the manufacture of optical glass.

The parish church of St Peter and St Paul (14th–15th centuries) is the cathedral of Sheffield, bishopric established 1914. Mary Queen of Scots was imprisoned in Sheffield 1570–84, part of the time in the Norman castle, which was captured by the Parliamentarians 1644 and subsequently destroyed.

sheik leader or chief of an Arab family or village; also Muslim title meaning 'religious scholar'.

Shelburne William Petty, 2nd Earl of Shelburne 1737–1805. British Whig politician. He was an opponent of George III's American policy, and as prime minister in 1783, he concluded peace with the United States of America.

shelduck duck *Tadorna tadorna* of family Anatidae, order Anseriformes. It has a dark-green head and red bill, with the rest of the plumage strikingly marked in black, white, and chestnut. The drake is about 60 cm/24 in long. Widely distributed in Europe and Asia, it lays 10–12 white eggs in rabbit burrows on sandy coasts, and is usually seen on estuary mudflats.

shelf sea relatively shallow sea, usually no deeper than 200 m/650 ft, overlying the continental shelf around the coastlines. Most fishing and marine mineral exploitations are carried out in shelf seas.

shell the hard outer covering of a wide variety of invertebrates. The covering is usually mineralized, normally with large amounts of calcium. The shell of birds' eggs is also largely made of calcium.

shellac resin derived from secretions of the ◊lac insect.

Shelley Mary Wollstonecraft, (born Godwin) 1797–1851. English writer. She was the daughter of Mary Wollstonecraft and William Godwin. In 1814

Shelley English Romantic poet Percy Bysshe Shelley, whose creativity was fuelled by his radical thinking and eccentric behaviour. Shelley attempted to establish radical communes in Devon and Wales before eloping with 16-year-old Harriet Westbrook. His second marriage to Mary Wollstonecraft Godwin was marked by tragedy – two of his children died in infancy and Mary suffered a nervous breakdown. *Corbis*

she eloped with the poet Percy Bysshe Shelley, whom she married 1816. Her novels include ◊*Frankenstein* 1818, *The Last Man* 1826, and *Valperga* 1823.

Shelley Percy Bysshe 1792–1822. English lyric poet. He was a leading figure in the Romantic movement. Expelled from Oxford University for atheism, he fought all his life against religion and for political freedom. This is reflected in his early poems such as *Queen Mab* 1813. He later wrote tragedies including *The Cenci* 1818, lyric dramas such as *Prometheus Unbound* 1820, and lyrical poems such as 'Ode to the West Wind'. He drowned while sailing in Italy.

Born near Horsham, Sussex, he was educated at Eton public school and University College, Oxford, where his collaboration in a pamphlet *The Necessity of Atheism* 1811 caused his expulsion. While living in London he fell in love with 16-year-old Harriet Westbrook, whom he married 1811. He visited Ireland and Wales, writing pamphlets defending vegetarianism and political freedom, and in 1813 published privately *Queen Mab*, a poem with political freedom as its theme. Meanwhile he had become estranged from his wife and in 1814 left England with Mary Wollstonecraft Godwin, whom he married after Harriet drowned herself 1816. *Alastor*, written 1815, was followed by the epic *The Revolt of Islam*, and by 1818 Shelley was living in Italy. Here he produced *The Cenci*; the satire on Wordsworth, *Peter Bell the Third* 1819; and *Prometheus Unbound*. Other works of the period are 'Ode to the West Wind' 1819; 'The Cloud' and 'The Skylark', both 1820; 'The Sensitive Plant' and 'The Witch of Atlas'; 'Epipsychidion' and, on the death of the poet Keats, 'Adonais' 1821; the lyric drama *Hellas* 1822; and the prose *Defence of Poetry* 1821. In July 1822 Shelley was drowned while sailing near Viareggio, and his ashes were buried in Rome.

shellfish popular name for molluscs and crustaceans, including the whelk and periwinkle, mussel, oyster, lobster, crab, and shrimp.

Shenyang industrial city and capital of Liaoning province, China; population (1993) 3,860,000. It was the capital of the Manchu emperors 1625–44; their tombs are nearby.

Captured by the Manchus in the 16th century and given the name of Mukden, it was their capital 1625–44, until replaced by Peking. It was taken by the Japanese in the Battle of Mukden 20 Feb-10 March 1905. It regained its ancient Chinese name of Shenyang after the Chinese Revolution 1911, when it became the seat of the Manchurian warlords. It was retaken by the Japanese 1931. Occupied by the Chinese nationalists 1945, it fell to the communists 1948 and was renamed Shenyang 1949.

Shenzen special economic zone established 1980 opposite Hong Kong on the coast of Guangdong province, S China; population (1993) 2.4 million. Its status provided much of the driving force of its spectacular development in the 1980s when its population rose from 20,000 in 1980 to 600,000 in 1989. Part of the population is 'rotated': newcomers from other provinces return to their homes after a few years spent learning foreign business techniques.

Shepard Alan Bartlett 1923–1998. US astronaut, the fifth person to walk on the Moon. He was the first American in space, as pilot of the suborbital *Mercury-Redstone 3* mission on board the *Freedom 7* capsule May 1961, and commanded the *Apollo 14* lunar landing mission 1971.

Shepard Sam, (originally Samuel Shepard Rogers) 1943– . US dramatist and actor. His work combines colloquial American dialogue with striking visual imagery, and includes *The Tooth of Crime* 1972 and *Buried Child* 1978, for which he won a Pulitzer prize. He has acted in a number of films, including *The Right Stuff* 1983, *Fool for Love* 1986, based on his play of the same name, and *Steel Magnolias* 1989, and directed the film *Silent Tongue* 1994.

shepherd's purse annual plant *Capsella bursa-pastoris* of the Cruciferae family, distributed worldwide in temperate zones. It is a persistent weed with white flowers followed by heart-shaped, seed-containing pouches from which its name derives.

Sheraton Thomas 1751–1806. English designer of elegant inlaid furniture. He was influenced by his predecessors ◊Hepplewhite and ◊Chippendale. He published the *Cabinet-maker's and Upholsterer's Drawing Book* 1791.

Sheridan Philip Henry 1831–1888. Union general in the American ◊Civil War. Recognizing Sheridan's aggressive spirit, General Ulysses S ◊Grant gave him command of his cavalry 1864, and soon after of the Army of the Shenandoah Valley, Virginia. Sheridan laid waste to the valley, cutting off grain supplies to the Confederate armies. In the final stage of the war, Sheridan forced General Robert E ◊Lee to retreat to Appomattox and surrender.

Sheridan Richard Brinsley 1751–1816. Irish dramatist and politician. His social comedies include *The Rivals* 1775, celebrated for the character of Mrs Malaprop, and *The School for Scandal* 1777. He also wrote a burlesque, *The Critic* 1779. In 1776 he became lessee of the Drury Lane Theatre. He became a member of Parliament 1780.

He entered Parliament as an adherent of Charles ◊Fox. A noted orator, he directed the impeachment of the former governor general of India, Warren Hastings, and was treasurer to the Navy 1806–07. His last years were clouded by the burning down of his theatre 1809, the loss of his parliamentary seat 1812, and by financial ruin and mental breakdown.

sheriff (Old English *scīr* 'shire', *gerēfa* 'reeve') in England and Wales, the crown's chief executive officer in a county for ceremonial purposes; in Scotland, the equivalent of the English county-court judge, but also dealing with criminal cases; and in the USA the popularly elected head law-enforcement officer of a county, combining judicial authority with administrative duties.

Sherman William Tecumseh 1820–1891. Union general in the American ◊Civil War. In 1864 he captured and burned Atlanta; continued his march eastward, to the sea, laying Georgia waste; and then drove the Confederates northward. He was US Army Chief of Staff 1869–83.

Sherpa people in NE Nepal related to the Tibetans and renowned for their mountaineering skill. They frequently work as support staff and guides for climbing expeditions. A Sherpa, Tensing Norgay, was one of the first two people to climb to the summit of Everest.

Sherrington Charles Scott 1857–1952. English neurophysiologist who studied the structure and function of the nervous system. *The Integrative Action of the Nervous System* 1906 formulated the principles of reflex action. Nobel Prize for Physiology or Medicine 1932.

Sherwood Forest hilly stretch of parkland in W Nottinghamshire, England, area about 520 sq km/ 200 sq mi. Formerly a royal forest, it is associated with the legendary outlaw ◊Robin Hood.

Shetland Islands islands off the N coast of Scotland, beyond the Orkney Islands; also Scottish local authority
area 1,400 sq km/541 sq mi (*see United Kingdom map*)
towns Lerwick (administrative headquarters), on Mainland, largest of 19 inhabited islands
features over 100 islands including Muckle Flugga (latitude 60° 51′ N) the northernmost of the British Isles
industries processed fish, handknits from Fair Isle and Unst, miniature Shetland ponies, herring fishing, salmon farming, cattle and sheep farming; large oil and gas fields west of Shetland; Europe's largest oil port is Sullom Voe, Mainland; production at Foinaven oilfield, the first to be developed in Atlantic waters, was scheduled to begin 1996
population (1991) 22,500
language dialect derived from Norse, the islands having been a Norse dependency from the 9th century until 1472 when they were annexed by Scotland.

Shevardnadze Edvard Amvrosievich 1928– . Georgian politician, Soviet foreign minister 1985–91, head of the state of Georgia from 1992. A supporter of Mikhail ◊Gorbachev, he became in 1985 a member of the Politburo, working for détente and disarmament. In July 1991, he resigned from the Communist Party (CPSU) and, along with other reformers, established the Democratic Reform Movement. In Oct 1992 he was elected speaker of parliament (equivalent to president). He survived an assassination attempt 1995.

Shiah see ◊Shi'ite.

shiatsu in alternative medicine, Japanese method of massage derived from ◊acupuncture and sometimes referred to as 'acupressure', which treats organic or physiological dysfunctions by applying finger or palm pressure to parts of the body remote from the affected part.

shield in technology, any material used to reduce the amount of radiation (electrostatic, electromagnetic, heat, nuclear) reaching from one region of space to another, or any material used as a protection against falling debris, as in tunnelling.

Electrical conductors are used for electrostatic shields, soft iron for electromagnetic shields, and poor conductors of heat for heat shields. Heavy materials such as lead and concrete are used for protection against X-rays and nuclear radiation. See also ◊biological shield and ◊heat shield.

shifting cultivation farming system where farmers move on from one place to another when the land becomes exhausted. The most common form is slash-and-burn agriculture: land is cleared by burning, so that crops can be grown. After a few years, soil fertility is reduced and the land is abandoned. A new area is cleared while the old land recovers its fertility.

Slash-and-burn is practised in many tropical forest areas, such as the Amazon region, where yams, cassava, and sweet potatoes can be grown. This system works well while population levels are low, but where there is ◊overpopulation, the old land will be reused before soil fertility has been restored. A variation of this system, found in parts of Africa, is rotational bush fallowing that involves a more permanent settlement and crop rotation.

Shi Huangdi or ***Shih Huang Ti*** c. 259–c. 210 BC. Emperor of China. He succeeded to the throne of the state of Qin 246 BC and had reunited China as an empire by 228 BC. He burned almost all existing books 213 to destroy ties with the past; rebuilt the ◊Great Wall of China; and was buried in Xian, Shaanxi province, in a tomb complex guarded by 10,000 life-size terracotta warriors (excavated in the 1980s). He had so overextended his power that the dynasty and the empire collapsed with the death of his weak successor in 207.

Shi'ite or ***Shiah*** member of a sect of ◊Islam that believes that ◊Ali was ◊Muhammad's first true successor. The Shi'ites are doctrinally opposed to the Sunni Muslims. They developed their own law differing only in minor directions, such as inheritance and the status of women. In Shi'ism, the clergy are empowered to intervene between God and humans, whereas among the Sunni, the relationship with God is direct and the clergy serve as advisers.

'Poets are the unacknowledged legislators of the world.'
PERCY BYSSHE SHELLEY
Defence of Poetry

'When a heroine goes mad she always goes into white satin.'
RICHARD BRINSLEY SHERIDAN
The Critic

The Shi'ites are prominent in Iran, the Lebanon, and Indo-Pakistan, and are also found in Iraq and Bahrain.

Breakaway subsects include the Alawite sect, to which the ruling party in Syria belongs; and the Ismaili sect, with the Aga Khan IV (1936–) as its spiritual head. The term Shi'ite originally referred to shi'a ('the partisans') of Ali.

In the aftermath of the Gulf War 1991, many thousands of Shi'ites in Iraq were forced to take refuge in the marshes of S Iraq, after unsuccessfully rebelling against Saddam Hussein. Shi'ite sacred shrines were desecrated and atrocities committed by the armed forces on civilians.

Shijiazhuang or ***Shihchiachuang*** city and major railway junction in Hebei province, China; population (1993) 1,210,000. Industries include textiles, chemicals, printing, and light engineering.

Shikoku smallest of the four main islands of Japan, S of Honshu, E of Kyushu; area 18,800 sq km/7,257 sq mi; population (1995) 4,183,000; chief town Matsuyama. Products include rice, wheat, soya beans, sugar cane, orchard fruits, salt, and copper.

It has a mild climate, and annual rainfall in the south can reach 266 cm/105 in. The highest point is Mount Ishizuchi (1,980 m/6,498 ft).

shingles common name for ◊herpes zoster, a disease characterized by infection of sensory nerves, with pain and eruption of blisters along the course of the affected nerves.

Shinto (Chinese *shin tao* 'way of the gods') the indigenous religion of Japan. It combines an empathetic oneness with natural forces and loyalty to the reigning dynasty as descendants of the Sun goddess, Amaterasu-Omikami. An aggressive nationalistic form of Shinto, known as State Shinto, was developed under the Emperor Meiji (1868–1912) and remained official until 1945, when it was discarded.

Shinto is the Chinese transliteration of the Japanese *Kami-no-Michi*. Shinto ceremonies appeal to the kami, the mysterious forces of nature manifest in topographical features such as mountains, trees, stones, springs, and caves. Shinto focuses on purity, devotion, and sincerity; aberrations can be cleansed through purification rituals. In addition, purification procedures make the worshipper presentable and acceptable when making requests before the kami.

Shinto's holiest shrine is at Ise, on Ise Bay, SE Honshu, where in the temple of the Sun goddess is preserved the mirror that she is supposed to have given to Jimmu, the legendary first emperor, in the 7th century BC. The oldest-established shrine (perhaps 4th century) and second in importance is Izumo Taisha Jinja near Izumo in W Honshu. All the kami are said to gather there each year in Oct.

There is no Shinto philosophical literature, though there are texts on mythologies, ceremonial and administrative procedures, religious laws, and chronicles of ruling families and temple construction. Shinto has no doctrine and no fixed system of ethics. Believers made no images of gods until the introduction of Buddhism, with which Shinto has coexisted syncretically since the 8th century. There have also been attempts to synthesize it with Confucian ethics.

shinty (Gaelic *camanachd*) stick-and-ball game resembling hurling, popular in the Scottish Highlands. It is played between teams of 12 players each, on a field 132–183 m/144–200 yd long and 64–91 m/70–99 yd wide. A curved stick (*caman*) is used to propel a leather-covered cork and worsted ball into the opposing team's goal (*hail*). The premier tournament, the Camanachd Cup, was instituted 1896.

ship large seagoing vessel. The Greeks, Phoenicians, Romans, and Vikings used ships extensively for trade, exploration, and warfare. The 14th century was the era of European exploration by sailing ship, largely aided by the invention of the compass. In the 15th century Britain's Royal Navy was first formed, but in the 16th–19th centuries Spanish and Dutch fleets dominated the shipping lanes of both the Atlantic and Pacific.

The ultimate sailing ships, the fast US and British tea clippers, were built in the 19th century. Also in the 19th century, iron was first used for some shipbuilding instead of wood. Steam-propelled ships of the late 19th century were followed by compound engine and turbine-propelled vessels from the early 20th century.

origins The earliest vessels were rafts or dug-out canoes, many of which have been found in Britain, and date from prehistoric times. The Greeks and Phoenicians built wooden ships, propelled by oar or sail. The Romans and Carthaginians built war galleys equipped with rams and several tiers of rowers. The double-ended oak ships of the Vikings were built for rough seas.

development of sailing ships The invention of the stern rudder during the 12th century, together with the developments made in sailing during the Crusades, enabled the use of sails to almost completely supersede that of oars. Following the invention of the compass, and with it the possibilities of exploration, the development of sailing ships advanced quickly during the 14th century.

In the 1840s iron began replacing wood in shipbuilding, pioneered by British engineer Isambard Kingdom ◊Brunel's *Great Britain* 1845. Throughout the 19th century, improvements were made in warships, including the evolution of the elliptical stern. However, increased rivalry between US and British owners for possession of the Chinese and Indian tea trade led to improvements also being made to the merchant vessel.

The first clipper, the *Ann McKim*, was built in Baltimore 1832, and Britain soon adopted this type of fast-sailing ship. One of the finest of the tea clippers, the *Sir Launcelot*, was built 1865 and marked the highest development of the sailing ship. The US ship *Champion of the Seas* was one of the fastest of its time, averaging speeds of 20 knots.

steamships The first steamship to cross the Atlantic was the Dutch vessel *Curaçao*, a wooden paddler built at Dover 1826, which left Rotterdam April 1827, and took one month to cross. The next transatlantic steamer, the *Royal William*, crossed from Quebec to London in 17 days 1833.

Britain's entry into the transatlantic efforts began with ◊Brunel's *Great Western* paddle-steamer,

SHIPS: TIMELINE

8000–7000 BC	Reed boats were developed in Mesopotamia and Egypt; dugout canoes were used in NW Europe.
4000–3000	The Egyptians used single-masted square-rigged ships on the Nile.
1200	The Phoenicians built keeled boats with hulls of wooden planks.
1st C BC	The Chinese invented the rudder.
AD 200	The Chinese built ships with several masts.
200–300	The Arabs and Romans developed fore-and-aft rigging that allowed boats to sail across the direction of wind.
800–900	Square-rigged Viking longboats crossed the North Sea to Britain, the Faroe Islands, and Iceland.
1090	The Chinese invented the magnetic compass.
1400–1500	Three-masted ships were developed in W Europe, stimulating voyages of exploration.
1620	Dutch engineer Cornelius Drebbel invented the submarine.
1776	US engineer David Bushnell built a hand-powered submarine, *Turtle*, with buoyancy tanks.
1777	The first boat with an iron hull was built in Yorkshire, England.
1783	Frenchman Jouffroy d'Abbans built the first paddle-driven steamboat.
1802	Scottish engineer William Symington launched the first stern paddle-wheel steamer, the *Charlotte Dundas*.
1807	The first successful steamboat, the *Clermont*, designed by US engineer and inventor Robert Fulton, sailed between New York and Albany.
1836	The screw propeller was patented, by Francis Pettit Smith in the UK.
1838	British engineer Isambard Kingdom Brunel's *Great Western*, the first steamship built for crossing the Atlantic, sailed from Bristol to New York in 15 days.
1845	*Great Britain*, also built by Isambard Kingdom Brunel, became the first propeller-driven iron ship to cross the Atlantic.
1845	The first clipper ship, *Rainbow*, was launched in the USA.
1863	*Plongeur*, the first submarine powered by an air-driven engine, was launched in France.
1866	The British clippers *Taeping* and *Ariel* sailed, laden with tea, from China to London in 99 days.
1886	German engineer Gottlieb Daimler built the first boat powered by an internal-combustion engine.
1897	English engineer Charles Parson fitted a steam turbine to *Turbinia*, making it the fastest boat of the time.
1900	Irish-American John Philip Holland designed the first modern submarine *Holland VI*, fitted with an electric motor for underwater sailing and an internal-combustion engine for surface travel; E Forlanini of Italy built the first hydrofoil.
1902	The French ship *Petit-Pierre* became the first boat to be powered by a diesel engine.
1955	The first nuclear-powered submarine, *Nautilus*, was built in the USA; the hovercraft was patented by British inventor Christopher Cockerell.
1959	The first nuclear-powered surface ship, the Soviet ice-breaker *Lenin*, was commissioned; the US *Savannah* became the first nuclear-powered merchant (passenger and cargo) ship.
1980	Launch of the first wind-assisted commercial ship for half a century, the Japanese tanker *Shin-Aitoku-Maru*.
1983	German engineer Ortwin Fries invented a hinged ship designed to bend into a V-shape in order to scoop up oil spillages in its jaws.
1989	*Gentry Eagle* set a record for the fastest crossing of the Atlantic in a power vessel, taking 2 days, 14 hours, and 7 minutes.
1990	*Hoverspeed Great Britain*, a wave-piercing catamaran, crossed the Atlantic in 3 days, 7 hours, and 52 minutes, setting a record for the fastest crossing by a passenger vessel. The world's largest car and passenger ferry, the *Silja Serenade*, entered service between Stockholm and Helsinki, carrying 2,500 passengers and 450 cars.
1992	Japanese propellerless ship *Yamato* driven by magnetohydrodynamics completed its sea trials. The ship used magnetic forces to suck in and eject sea water like a jet engine.
1997	Launch of *Carnival Destiny*, the biggest ever cruise ship – as long as three football pitches, taller than the Statue of Liberty, and too wide to pass through the Panama Canal. US researchers tested a new type of submersible (small submarine) with wings, which can turn, dive, and roll like an airplane.

which achieved recognition when it completed the journey from Bristol to New York in 15 days – three days faster than a clipper. The first great iron steamship, *Rainbow*, was launched 1838.

In 1862 the Cunard Company obtained permission to fit mail steamers with propellers, which suffered less from the rolling of the ship, and the paddle-wheel was relegated to comparatively smooth water. The opening of the Suez Canal 1869, together with the simultaneous introduction of the compound engine, raised steamships to superiority over sailing ships. In 1902 the turbine engine was introduced an this was followed by the introduction of the internal combustion engine.

tankers Following World War II, when reconstruction and industrial development created a great demand for oil, the tanker was developed to carry supplies to the areas of consumption. The prolonged closure of the Suez Canal after 1967 and the great increase in oil consumption led to the development of the very large tanker, or 'supertanker'.

More recently ◊hovercraft and ◊hydrofoil boats have been developed for specialized purposes, particularly as short-distance ferries.

Shipley Jenny 1952– . New Zealand politician, prime minister from 1997. She joined the National Party at the age of 23 and was elected to the House of Representatives in 1987, having farmed for 15 years after a short career in teaching. She held various ministerial posts in Jim Bolger's government, and in Nov 1997 she challenged his leadership, and was elected to replace him Dec 1997.

ship money tax for support of the navy, levied on the coastal districts of England in the Middle Ages. Ship money was declared illegal by Parliament 1641.

Shiraz ancient walled city of S Iran, the capital of Fars province; population (1991) 965,000. It is known for its wines, carpets, and silverwork and for its many mosques.

shire administrative area formed in Britain for the purpose of raising taxes in Anglo-Saxon times. By AD 1000 most of S England had been divided into shires with fortified strongholds at their centres. The Midland counties of England are still known as the Shires; for example Derbyshire, Nottinghamshire, and Staffordshire.

Shiva alternative spelling of ◊Siva, Hindu god.

shock in medicine, circulatory failure marked by a sudden fall of blood pressure and resulting in pallor, sweating, fast (but weak) pulse, and sometimes complete collapse. Causes include disease, injury, and psychological trauma.

In shock, the blood pressure falls below that necessary to supply the tissues of the body, especially the brain. Treatment depends on the cause. Rest is needed, and, in the case of severe blood loss, restoration of the normal circulating volume.

shock wave narrow band or region of high pressure and temperature in which the flow of a fluid changes from subsonic to supersonic. Shock waves are produced when an object moves through a fluid at a supersonic speed. See ◊sonic boom.

shoebill or ***whale-headed stork*** large, grey, long-legged, swamp-dwelling African bird *Balaeniceps rex*. Up to 1.5 m/5 ft tall, it has a large wide beak 20 cm/8 in long, with which it scoops fish, molluscs, reptiles, and carrion out of the mud. It is the only species in the family Balaenicipitidae of the order Ciconiiformes.

Shoemaker Willie (William Lee) 1931– . US jockey 1949–90. He rode 8,833 winners from 40,351 mounts and his earnings exceeded $123 million. He retired Feb 1990 after finishing fourth on Patchy Groundfog at Santa Anita, California.

He was the leading US jockey ten times. Standing 1.5 m/4 ft 11 in tall, he weighed about 43 kg/95 lb.

shogun in Japanese history, title of a series of military strongmen 1192–1868 who relegated the emperor's role to that of figurehead. Technically an imperial appointment, the office was treated as hereditary and was held by the ◊Minamoto clan 1192–1219, by the ◊Ashikaga 1336–1573, and by the ◊Tokugawa 1603–1868. The shogun held legislative, judicial, and executive power.

The emperor had been a national and religious figurehead rather than a direct ruler since the rise of the Fujiwara clan in the 9th century, but the exercise of power had been by officials of the court rather than of the army. The title of *seii-tai-shōgun*, 'barbarian-subduing commander', first given 794 to one of the imperial guards appointed to lead an expedition against the Ainu people, had before 1192 entailed only temporary military command. The *bakufu* (shogunate), the administrative structure set up by the first Minamoto shogun, gradually extended its area of operations to all aspects of government.

Sholes Christopher Latham 1819–1890. American printer and newspaper editor who, in 1867, invented the first practicable typewriter in association with Carlos Glidden and Samuel Soulé. In 1873, they sold their patents to Remington & Sons, a firm of gunsmiths in New York, who developed and sold the machine commercially. In 1878 Sholes developed a shift-key mechanism that made it possible to touch-type.

Sholokhov Mikhail Aleksandrovich 1905–1984. Russian novelist. His *And Quiet Flows the Don* 1926–40, hailed in the Soviet Union as a masterpiece of ◊Socialist Realism, depicts the Don Cossacks through World War I and the Russian Revolution. His authorship of the novel was challenged by Alexander ◊Solzhenitsyn. Nobel prize 1965.

Shona a Bantu-speaking people of S Africa, comprising approximately 80% of the population of Zimbabwe. They also occupy the land between the Save and Pungure rivers in Mozambique, and smaller groups are found in South Africa, Botswana, and Zambia. The Shona are mainly farmers, living in scattered villages. The Shona language belongs to the Niger-Congo family.

shoot in botany, the parts of a ◊vascular plant growing above ground, comprising a stem bearing leaves, buds, and flowers. The shoot develops from the plumule of the embryo.

shooting star another name for a ◊meteor.

shop steward trade-union representative in a 'shop', or department of a factory, elected by his or her fellow workers. Shop stewards are unpaid and usually conduct union business in their own time. They recruit for the union, inspect contribution cards, and report grievances to the district committee. They represent their members' interests to employers through the process of ◊collective bargaining.

This form of organization originated in the engineering industry and has spread to all large industrial undertakings.

shorthand any system of rapid writing, such as the abbreviations practised by the Greeks and Romans. The first perfecter of an entirely phonetic system was Isaac ◊Pitman, by which system speeds of about 300 words a minute are said to be attainable.

The earliest recorded instance of shorthand being used is the system used by the historian Xenophon to write the memoirs of Socrates. The art of shorthand died out in the Middle Ages because of its imagined associations with witchcraft.

Stenotype machines, using selective keyboards enabling several word contractions to be printed at a time, are equally speedy and accurate. Abbreviations used can be transferred by the operator to a television screen, enabling the deaf to follow the spoken word.

Short Parliament the English Parliament that was summoned by Charles I on 13 April 1640 to raise funds for his war against the Scots. It was succeeded later in the year by the ◊Long Parliament.

When it became clear that the parliament opposed the war and would not grant him any money, he dissolved it 5 May and arrested some of its leaders.

short-sightedness nontechnical term for ◊myopia.

short story short work of prose fiction, which typically either sets up and resolves a single narrative point or depicts a mood or an atmosphere. The two seminal figures in the development of the modern short story are Guy de Maupassant and Anton Chekhov. Other outstanding short-story writers are Rudyard Kipling, Saki, Edgar Allan Poe, Ernest Hemingway, Isaac Babel, Katherine Mansfield, Jorge Luis Borges, and Sherwood Anderson.

Shostakovich Dmitry Dmitriyevich 1906–1975. Soviet composer. His music is tonal, expressive, and sometimes highly dramatic; it was not always to official Soviet taste. He wrote 15 symphonies, chamber and film music, ballets, and operas, the latter including *Lady Macbeth of Mtsensk* 1934, which was suppressed as 'too divorced from the proletariat', but revived as *Katerina Izmaylova* 1963.

shot put or ***putting the shot*** in athletics, the sport of throwing (or putting) overhand from the shoulder a metal ball (or shot). Standard shot weights are 7.26 kg/16 lb for men and 4 kg/8.8 lb for women.

shoveler fresh-water duck *Anas clypeata*, family Anatidae, order Anseriformes, so named after its long and broad flattened beak used for filtering out small organisms from sand and mud. The male has a green head, white and brown body plumage, black and white wings, greyish bill, orange feet, and can grow up to 50 cm/20 in long. The female is speckled brown. Spending the summer in N Europe or North America, it winters further south.

show trial public and well-reported trial of people accused of crimes against the state. In the USSR in the 1930s and 1940s, Stalin carried out show trials against economic saboteurs, Communist Party members, army officers, and even members of the Bolshevik leadership. Andrei Vyshinksy was the Soviet prosecutor for many of the most notorious show trials of the 1930s.

Shrapnel Henry 1761–1842. British army officer who invented shells containing bullets, to increase the spread of casualties, first used 1804; hence the word shrapnel to describe shell fragments.

shrew insectivorous mammal of the family Soricidae, order Insectivora, found in the Americas and Eurasia. It is mouselike, but with a long nose and pointed teeth. Its high metabolic rate means that it must eat almost constantly. The common shrew *Sorex araneus* is about 7.5 cm/3 in long with a long, supple, pointed snout bearing numerous stiff hairs projecting beyond the lower jaw; its fur is reddish-grey above and greyish beneath. It has glands which secrete a strong, unpleasant odour as a means of defence. It feeds on insects, worms, and often on members of its own kind killed after a fight. *See illustration on following page.*

Shrewsbury market town on the river Severn, Shropshire, England; population (1991) 90,900. It is the administrative headquarters of Shropshire. To the E is the site of the Roman city of Viroconium (larger than Pompeii). In the 5th century, as Pengwern, Shrewsbury was capital of the kingdom of Powys, which later became part of Mercia. The castle dates from 1070.

In the Battle of Shrewsbury 1403, Henry IV defeated the rebels led by Hotspur (Sir Henry ◊Percy). The city declined an invitation 1539, at the dissolution of the monasteries, to become a cathedral city.

shrike or ***butcher-bird*** bird of the family Laniidae, of which there are over 70 species, living mostly in Africa, but also in Eurasia and North America. They often impale insects and small vertebrates on thorns. They can grow to 35 cm/14 in long, have grey, black, or brown plumage, sharply clawed feet, and hooked beaks.

The great grey shrike *Lanius excubitor* is a regular winter visitor to Britain. It is about 25 cm/10 in long. The lesser grey shrike *L. minor* resembles its larger relation and is an occasional visitor. The other visiting species is *L. senator*, the woodchat shrike, a black-backed bird about 18 cm/7 in long. *See illustration on following page.*

shrimp crustacean related to the ◊prawn. It has a cylindrical, semi-transparent body, with ten jointed legs. Some shrimps grow up to 25 cm/10 in long.

The European common shrimp *Crangon vulgaris* is greenish, translucent, has its first pair of legs ending in pincers, possesses no rostrum (the beak-like structure which extends forwards from the head in some crustaceans), and has comparatively shorter antennae than the prawn.

Synalpheus regalis, a shrimp that lives within sponges in the coral reefs of Belize, was discovered in 1996 to live in social colonies with a structure resembling that of social insects, such as ants. All are the offspring of a single reproductive female; care of young is cooperative; and larger individuals act to defend the colony.

shrew A bush veld elephant shrew from S Africa. Elephant shrews, which are found only in Africa, typically have a highly mobile and flexible elephantlike snout which is used for seeking out termites, the main food of many species. From mouse- to rat-sized, they have long legs and soft fur and are active in daytime. *Premaphotos Wildlife*

Shropshire county of W England. Sometimes abbreviated to ***Salop***, it was officially known by this name from 1974 until local protest reversed the decision 1980
area 3,490 sq km/1,347 sq mi (*See United Kingdom map*)
towns Shrewsbury (administrative headquarters), Telford, Oswestry, Ludlow
features bisected, on the Welsh border, NW–SE by the river Severn; Ellesmere, the largest of several lakes; the Clee Hills rise to about 610 m/1,800 ft in the SW; Ironbridge Gorge open-air museum of industrial archaeology, with the Iron Bridge (1779), the world's first cast-iron bridge
industries chiefly agricultural: sheep and cattle, cereals, sugar beet. It is the main iron-producing county in England
population (1991) 406,400
famous people Charles Darwin, A E Housman, Wilfred Owen, Gordon Richards
history Shropshire became a county in the 10th century, as part of the kingdom of Mercia in its defence against the Danes. During the Middle Ages, it was part of the Welsh Marches and saw much conflict between the lords of the Marches and the Welsh.

Shrove Tuesday in the Christian calendar, the day before the beginning of Lent. It is also known as Mardi Gras. In the UK, it is called Pancake day, after the custom of eating rich food before the Lenten fast.

shrub perennial woody plant that typically produces several separate stems, at or near ground level, rather than the single trunk of most trees. A shrub is usually smaller than a tree, but there is no clear distinction between large shrubs and small trees.

Shushkevich Stanislav 1934– . Belarus politician, president 1991–94. He was elected to parliament as a nationalist 'reform communist' 1990 and played a key role in the creation of the Commonwealth of Independent States as the successor to the Soviet Union. A supporter of free-market reforms, he opposed alignment of Belarus's economic and foreign policy with that of neighbouring Russia.

shrike The great grey shrike. Shrikes are often referred to as 'butcher birds' because of their habit of impaling their prey on thorns in a gruesome larder. Shrikes are found in a variety of habitats in many parts of the world. As well as insects, shrikes will attack and kill small mammals, reptiles, amphibians, and even other birds.

SI abbreviation for ***Système International d'Unités*** (French 'International System of Metric Units'); see ◊SI units.

sial in geochemistry and geophysics, the substance of the Earth's continental ◊crust, as distinct from the ◊sima of the ocean crust. The name, now used rarely, is derived from ***si***lica and ***al***umina, its two main chemical constituents. Sial is often rich in granite.

siamang the largest ◊gibbon *Symphalangus syndactylus*, native to Malaysia and Sumatra. Siamangs have a large throat pouch to amplify the voice, making the territorial 'song' extremely loud.

They are black-haired, up to 90 cm/3 ft tall, with very long arms (a span of 150 cm/5 ft).

Sibelius Jean Julius Christian 1865–1957. Finnish composer. His works include nationalistic symphonic poems such as *En saga* 1893 and *Finlandia* 1900, a violin concerto 1904, and seven symphonies.

He studied the violin and composition at Helsinki and went on to Berlin and Vienna. In 1940 he abruptly ceased composing and spent the rest of his life as a recluse. Restoration of many works to their original state has helped to dispel his conservative image and reveal unexpectedly radical features.

Siberia Asian region of Russia, extending from the Ural Mountains to the Pacific Ocean
area 12,050,000 sq km/4,650,000 sq mi
towns Novosibirsk, Omsk, Krasnoyarsk, Irkutsk
features long and extremely cold winters; the world's largest remaining native forests, covering about 5,000,000 sq km/1,930,000 sq mi, continue to be cut down; the world's largest cat, the Siberian tiger, although an endangered species, is hunted for its bones, which are used in traditional medicine.
industries hydroelectric power from rivers Lena, Ob, and Yenisei; forestry; mineral resources, including gold, diamonds, oil, natural gas, iron, copper, nickel, cobalt
history overrun by Russia in the 17th century, Siberia was used from the 18th century to exile political and criminal prisoners. The first Trans-Siberian Railway 1892–1905 from St Petersburg (via Omsk, Novosibirsk, Irkutsk, and Khabarovsk) to Vladivostok, approximately 8,700 km/5,400 mi, began to open it up. A popular front was formed 1988, campaigning for ecological and political reform.

Sibyl in Roman mythology, one of many prophetic priestesses, notably one from Cumae near Naples. She offered to sell to the legendary king of Rome, ◊Tarquinius Superbus, nine collections of prophecies, the Sibylline Books, but the price was too high. When she had destroyed all but three, he bought those for the identical price, and they were kept for consultation in emergency at Rome.

Sichuan or ***Szechwan*** province of central China
area 569,000 sq km/219,634 sq mi
capital Chengdu
towns Chongqing
features surrounded by mountains, it was the headquarters of the Nationalist government 1937–45, and China's nuclear research centres are here. It is China's most populous administrative area
industries rice, coal, oil, natural gas
population (1990) 106,370,000.

Sicily (Italian ***Sicilia***) the largest Mediterranean island, an autonomous region of Italy; area 25,700 sq km/9,920 sq mi; population (1992) 4,997,700. Its capital is Palermo, and towns include the ports of Catania, Messina, Syracuse, and Marsala. It exports Marsala wine, olives, citrus, refined oil and petrochemicals, pharmaceuticals, potash, asphalt, and marble. The region also includes the islands of ◊Lipari, Egadi, Ustica, and Pantelleria. Etna, 3,323 m/10,906 ft high, is the highest volcano in Europe; its last major eruption was in 1971.
history conquered by most of the major powers of the ancient world, Sicily flourished under the Greeks who colonized the island during the 8th–5th centuries BC. It was invaded by Carthage and became part of the Roman Empire 241 BC–AD 476. In the Middle Ages it was ruled successively by the Arabs; the Normans 1059–1194, who established the Kingdom of the Two Sicilies (that is, Sicily and the southern part of Italy); the German emperors; and then the Angevins, until the popular revolt known as the Sicilian Vespers 1282.

Spanish rule was invited and continued in varying forms, with a temporary displacement of the Spanish Bourbons by Napoleon, until ◊Garibaldi's invasion 1860 resulted in the two Sicilies being united with Italy 1861. In World War II Sicily was the launch point for the Allied invasion of Italy 1943.

sick building syndrome malaise diagnosed in the early 1980s among office workers and thought to be caused by such pollutants as formaldehyde (from furniture and insulating materials), benzene (from paint), and the solvent trichloroethene, concentrated in air-conditioned buildings. Symptoms include headache, sore throat, tiredness, colds, and flu. Studies have found that it can cause a 40% drop in productivity and a 30% rise in absenteeism.

Work on improving living conditions of astronauts showed that the causes were easily and inexpensively removed by potplants in which interaction is thought to take place between the plant and microorganisms in its roots. Among the most useful are chrysanthemums (counteracting benzene), English ivy and the peace lily (trichloroethene), and the spider plant (formaldehyde).

Sickert Walter Richard 1860–1942. English artist. His works are broadly Impressionist in style, their

Sibelius The composer Jean Sibelius (1865–1957). Most of his works date from after 1897, when the Finnish government voted to give him an annual grant to enable him to compose full-time. He was an ardent nationalist, transferring his passion for Finland into his music. *Image Select (UK) Ltd*

most familiar subjects being the rather shabby music halls, streets, and interiors of late Victorian and Edwardian London. *Ennui* about 1913 (Tate Gallery, London) is a typical interior painting. His work inspired the ◊Camden Town Group.

Sickert learned his craft from James Whistler in London and then from Degas in Paris. Though often described as an Impressionist, he was only so to the same limited extent as Degas, constructing pictures from swift notes made on the spot, and never painting in the open air.

He worked in Dieppe 1885–1905, with occasional visits to Venice, and produced music-hall paintings and views of Venice and Dieppe in dark, rich tones. In his 'Camden Town' period 1905–14, he explored the little back rooms, shabby lodging houses, and dingy streets of N London. His zest for urban life and his personality drew together a group of younger artists who formed the nucleus of the Camden Town Group, which played a leading role in bringing Post-Impressionism into English art.

sickle-cell disease hereditary chronic blood disorder common among people of black African descent; also found in the E Mediterranean, parts of the Persian Gulf, and in NE India. It is characterized by distortion and fragility of the red blood cells, which are lost too rapidly from the circulation. This often results in ◊anaemia.

People with this disease have abnormal red blood cells (sickle cells), containing a defective ◊haemoglobin. The presence of sickle cells in the blood is called sicklemia. The disease is caused by a recessive allele. Those with two copies of the allele suffer debilitating anaemia; those with a single copy paired with the normal allele, suffer with only mild anaemia and have a degree of protection against ◊malaria because fewer normal red blood cells are available to the parasites for infection.

Siddons Sarah, (born Kemble) 1755–1831. English actress. Her majestic presence made her suited to tragic and heroic roles such as Lady Macbeth, Zara in Congreve's *The Mourning Bride*, and Constance in *King John*.

She toured the provinces with her father Roger Kemble (1721–1802), until she appeared in London to immediate acclaim in Otway's *Venice Preserv'd* 1774. This led to her appearing with David ◊Garrick at Drury Lane. She retired 1812.

sidereal period the orbital period of a planet around the Sun, or a moon around a planet, with reference to a background star. The sidereal period of a planet is in effect a 'year'. A ◊synodic period is a full circle as seen from Earth.

sidewinder rattlesnake *Crotalus cerastes* that lives in the deserts of the SW USA and Mexico, and moves by throwing its coils into a sideways 'jump' across the sand. It can grow up to 75 cm/30 in long.

Siding Spring Mountain peak 400 km/250 mi NW of Sydney, site of the UK Schmidt Telescope, opened 1973, and the 3.9-m/154-in Anglo-Australian Telescope, opened 1975, which was the first big telescope to be fully computer-controlled. It is one of the most powerful telescopes in the southern hemisphere.

Sidney Philip 1554–1586. English poet and soldier. He wrote the sonnet sequence *Astrophel and Stella* 1591, *Arcadia* 1590, a prose romance, and *Apologie for Poetrie* 1595, the earliest work of English literary criticism.

Sidney was born in Penshurst, Kent. He entered Parliament 1581. In 1585 he was made governor of Vlissingen in the Netherlands, and died at Zutphen, fighting the Spanish.

SIDS acronym for *s*udden *i*nfant *d*eath *s*yndrome, the technical name for ◊cot death.

Siegfried legendary Germanic and Norse hero. His story, which may contain some historical elements, occurs in the German ◊*Nibelungenlied/Song of the Nibelung* and in the Norse *Elder* or *Poetic* ◊*Edda* and the prose *Völsunga Saga* (in the last two works, the hero is known as Sigurd). Siegfried wins Brunhild for his liege lord and marries his sister, but is eventually killed in the intrigues that follow. He is the hero of the last two operas in Wagner's *The Ring of the Nibelung* cycle.

Siegfried Line in World War I, a defensive line established 1917 by the Germans in France, really a subdivision of the main ◊Hindenburg Line; in World War II, the Allies' name for the West Wall, a German defensive line established along its western frontier, from the Netherlands to Switzerland.

siemens SI unit (symbol S) of electrical conductance, the reciprocal of the ◊resistance of an electrical circuit. One siemens equals one ampere per volt. It was formerly called the mho or reciprocal ohm.

Siena city in Tuscany, Italy; population (1991) 58,400. Founded by the Etruscans, it has medieval sculpture including works in the 13th-century Gothic cathedral by ◊Pisano and Donatello, and many examples of the Sienese school of painting that flourished from the 13th to the 16th centuries. The *Palio* ('banner', in reference to the prize) is a dramatic and dangerous horse race in the main square, held annually (2 July and 16 August) since the Middle Ages.

history Siena was politically unstable internally as well as being involved in external warfare for most of the period 1355–1559. The city was governed by Visconti of Milan 1399–1404; by the pope 1458–63; under heavy Spanish influence from the 1520s to 1552 and directly by Spain 1555–57; it was then sold to Cosimo de' Medici, Duke of Florence.

Sierra Leone country in W Africa, on the Atlantic Ocean, bounded N and E by Guinea and SE by Liberia. *See country box on p. 972.*

Sierra Madre chief mountain system of Mexico, consisting of three ranges, enclosing the central plateau of the country; highest point Pico de Orizaba 5,700 m/18,700 ft. The Sierra Madre del Sur ('of the south') runs along the SW Pacific coast.

Sierra Nevada mountain range of S Spain; highest point Mulhacén 3,481 m/11,425 ft.

Sierra Nevada mountain range in E California; highest point Mount Whitney 4,418 m/14,500 ft. The Sierra Nevada includes the King's Canyon, Sequoia, and Yosemite Valley national parks.

About 640 km/400 mi in length, the Sierra Nevada separates California from the rest of the continent. In 1848 settlers found gold in its western foothills, touching off the great 1849 gold rush. Silver mines have been opened on its east side.

sievert SI unit (symbol Sv) of radiation dose equivalent. It replaces the rem (1 Sv equals 100 rem). Some types of radiation do more damage than others for the same absorbed dose – for example, an absorbed dose of alpha radiation causes 20 times as much biological damage as the same dose of beta radiation. The equivalent dose in sieverts is equal to the absorbed dose of radiation in grays multiplied by the relative biological effectiveness. Humans can absorb up to 0.25 Sv without immediate ill effects; 1 Sv may produce radiation sickness; and more than 8 Sv causes death.

Siena Still medieval and Renaissance in character, the centre of Siena, Italy, is dominated by the 14th-century tower of the town hall, which overlooks the Campo, the city's main square. *Edith Harkness*

Sieyès Emmanuel-Joseph 1748–1836. French cleric and constitutional theorist who led the bourgeois attack on royal and aristocratic privilege in the States General (parliament) 1788–89. Active in the early years of the French Revolution, he later retired from politics, but re-emerged as an organizer of the coup that brought Napoleon I to power in 1799.

Sigismund 1368–1437. Holy Roman Emperor from 1411. He convened and presided over the Council of Constance 1414–18, where he promised protection to the religious reformer ◊Huss, but imprisoned him after his condemnation for heresy and acquiesced in his burning. King of Bohemia from 1419, he led the military campaign against the ◊Hussites.

Sigma Octantis the star closest to the south celestial pole (see ◊celestial sphere), in effect the southern equivalent of ◊Polaris, although far less conspicuous. Situated just less than 1° from the south celestial pole in the constellation Octans, Sigma Octantis is 120 light years away.

Signac Paul 1863–1935. French artist. Associated with ◊Seurat in the development of ◊Pointillism, he is best known for his landscapes and seascapes painted in mosaic-like blocks of pure colour. One of his most striking works is his *Portrait of Félix Fénéon* 1980 (J Logan Collection, New York).

His first works were strongly influenced by the Impressionism of Monet, but in 1884, when he joined with Seurat in founding the Salon des Artistes Indépendants, he became a passionate and lifelong advocate of Pointillism. He produced many striking landscapes and seascapes of the Normandy, Brittany, and Mediterranean coasts, his love of ships and the sea finding expression in many watercolours as well as oils. His book *D'Eugène Delacroix au Néo-Impressionisme/From Delacroix to Neo-Impressionism* 1899 was the fullest statement of Pointillist aesthetics.

Sigurd hero of Norse legend; see ◊Siegfried.

Sihanouk Norodom 1922– . Cambodian politician, king 1941–55 and from 1993. He was prime minister 1955–70, when his government was overthrown in a military coup led by Lon Nol. With Pol Pot's resistance front, he overthrew Lon Nol 1975 and again became prime minister 1975–76, when he was forced to resign by the ◊Khmer Rouge. Based in North Korea, he became the recognized head of the Democratic Kampuchea government in exile 1982. He returned from exile Nov 1991 under the auspices of a United Nations-brokered peace settlement to head a coalition intended to comprise all Cambodia's warring factions (the Khmer Rouge, however, continued fighting). His son, Prince Norodam Ranariddh became prime minister July 1993 and Sihanouk was re-elected king after the 1993

'Who shoots at the mid-day sun, though he be sure he shall never hit the mark; yet as sure he is he shall shoot higher than who aims but at a bush.'

PHILIP SIDNEY
Arcadia

SIERRA LEONE
Republic of

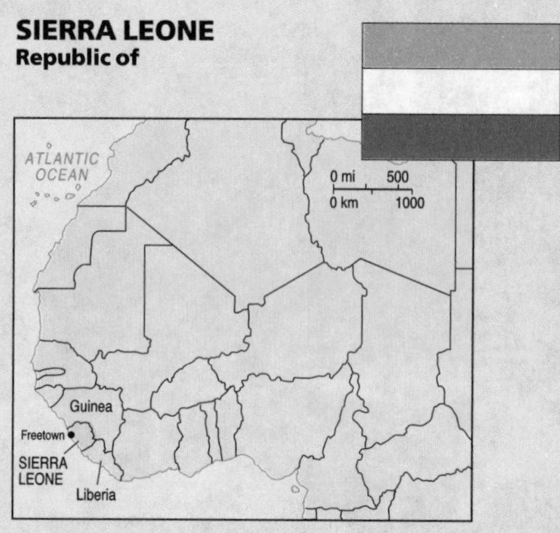

area 71,740 sq km/27,710 sq mi
capital Freetown
major towns/cities Koidu, Bo, Kenema, Makeni
major ports Bonthe-Sherbro
physical features mountains in E; hills and forest; coastal mangrove swamps
head of state and government Ahmad Tejan Kabbah from 1997
political system transitional
administrative divisions three provinces, plus the Western area, including Freetown
political parties All People's Congress (APC), moderate socialist; United Front of Political Movements (UNIFORM), centre-left. Party political activity suspended from 1992
population 4,509,000 (1995 est)
population growth rate 2.4% (1990–95); 2.3% (2000–05)
ethnic distribution 18 ethnic groups, 3 of which (the Mende, Tenne, and Limbe) comprise almost 70% of the population
life expectancy 41 (men), 45 (women); the lowest in the world
literacy rate men 30%, women 11%
languages English (official), Krio (a creole language)
religions animist 52%, Muslim 39%, Protestant 6%, Roman Catholic 2% (1980 est)
currency leone
GDP (US $) 843 million (1994)
growth rate −4.0% (1994)
exports cocoa, coffee, diamonds, bauxite, rutile, cassava, gold

HISTORY
15th C Formerly populated by the Bulom, Krim, and Gola peoples, the Mende, Temne, and the Fulani from Senegal now moved into the region; the Portuguese, who named the area Serra Lyoa, established a coastal fort, trading manufactured goods for slaves and ivory.
17th C English trading posts established on Bund and York islands.
1787–92 English abolitionists and philanthropists bought land to establish a settlement for liberated and runaway African slaves (including 1,000 rescued from Canada), known as Freetown.
1808 Became a British colony and Freetown a base for British naval operations against the slave trade, after parliament declared it illegal.
1896 Hinterland conquered and declared a British protectorate.
1951 First political party, Sierra Leone People's Party (SLPP), formed by Dr Milton Margai, who became 'leader of government business', in 1953.
1961 Independence achieved within the Commonwealth, with Margai as prime minister.
1964 Milton Margai died and was succeeded by his half-brother, Albert Margai.
1965 Free-trade area pact signed with Guinea, Liberia, and Ivory Coast.
1967 Election won by the All People's Congress (APC), led by Siaka Stevens, but disputed by the army, who set up a National Reformation Council and forced the governor general to leave the country.
1968 Army revolt; Stevens prime minister again.
1971 New constitution made Sierra Leone a republic, with Stevens as president.
1978 New constitution; APC the only legal party.
1985 Stevens retired; succeeded as president and APC leader by Maj-Gen Joseph Momoh.
1991 Referendum endorsed multiparty politics and new constitution. Liberian-based rebel group began guerrilla activities.
1992 President Momoh overthrown by military and party politics suspended as National Provisional Ruling Council established under Capt Valentine Strasser; 500,000 Liberians fled to Sierra Leone as a result of civil war.
1995 Ban on political parties lifted. Coup attempt foiled.
1996 Strasser overthrown by deputy, Julius Maada Bio, who was replaced as president by Ahmad Tejan Kabbah after multiparty elections.
1997 President Kabbah's civilian government restored after military coup.
1999 A Nigerian-led peace-keeping force, ECOMOG, fought with anti-government rebels loyal to jailed rebel leader Foday Sankoh.

elections, in which the royalist party won a majority; in 1996, however, it was announced that he was suffering from a brain tumour and may abdicate.

Sikhism religion professed by 14 million Indians, living mainly in the Punjab. Sikhism was founded by Nanak (1469–c. 1539). Sikhs believe in a single God who is the immortal creator of the universe and who has never been incarnate in any form, and in the equality of all human beings; Sikhism is strongly opposed to caste divisions.

Their holy book is the *Guru Granth Sahib*. Guru Gobind Singh (1666–1708) instituted the *Khanda-di-Pahul*, the baptism of the sword, and established the Khalsa ('pure'), the company of the faithful. The Khalsa wear the five Ks: *kes*, long hair; *kangha*, a comb; *kirpan*, a sword; *kachh*, short trousers; and *kara*, a steel bracelet. Sikh men take the last name 'Singh' ('lion') and women 'Kaur' ('princess').

Sikhs believe that human beings can make themselves ready to find God by prayer and meditation but can achieve closeness to God only as a result of God's *nadar* (grace). Sikhs believe in ◊reincarnation and that the ten human gurus were teachers through whom the spirit of Guru Nanak was passed on to live today in the *Guru Granth Sahib* and the Khalsa.

history On Nanak's death he was followed as guru by a succession of leaders who converted the Sikhs (the word means 'disciple') into a military confraternity which established itself as a political power.

Upon the partition of India many Sikhs migrated from W to E Punjab, and in 1966 the efforts of Sant Fateh Singh (c. 1911–1972) led to the creation of a Sikh state within India by partition of the Punjab.

However, the Akali separatist movement agitates for a completely independent Sikh state, Khalistan, and a revival of fundamentalist belief, and was headed from 1978 by Sant Jarnail Singh Bhindranwale, killed in the siege of the Golden Temple, ◊Amritsar. In retaliation for this, the Indian prime minister Indira Gandhi was assassinated in Oct of the same year by her Sikh bodyguards. Heavy rioting followed, in which 1,000 Sikhs were killed. Mrs Gandhi's successor, Rajiv Gandhi, reached an agreement for the election of a popular government in the Punjab and for state representatives to the Indian parliament with the moderate Sikh leader Sant Harchand Singh Longowal, who was himself killed 1985 by Sikh extremists.

Sikh Wars two wars in India between the Sikhs and the British:

The ***First Sikh War 1845–46*** followed an invasion of British India by Punjabi Sikhs. The Sikhs were defeated and part of their territory annexed.

The ***Second Sikh War 1848–49*** arose from a Sikh revolt in Multan. They were defeated, and the British annexed the Punjab.

Sikkim or ***Denjong*** state of NE India; formerly a protected state, it was absorbed by India 1975, the monarchy being abolished. China does not recognize India's sovereignty
area 7,100 sq km/2,741 sq mi
capital Gangtok
features Mount Kangchenjunga; wildlife including birds, butterflies, and orchids
industries rice, grain, tea, fruit, soya beans, carpets, cigarettes, lead, zinc, copper
population (1994 est) 444,000
language Bhutia, Lepecha, Khaskura (Nepali) – all official
religion Mahāyāna Buddhism, Hinduism
history ruled by the Namgyol dynasty from the 14th century to 1975, when the last chogyal, or king, was deposed. Allied to Britain 1886, Sikkim became a protectorate of India 1950 and a state of India 1975.

Sikorski Wladyslaw Eugeniusz 1881–1943. Polish general and politician; prime minister 1922–23, and 1939–43 of the Polish government in exile in London during World War II. He was killed in an aeroplane crash near Gibraltar in controversial circumstances.

He was in Paris when the Germans took Poland and became commander in chief of the Free Polish Forces, who he took to the UK 1940. Following the German invasion of the USSR 1941, he concluded an agreement with the USSR to re-establish Poland's pre-war boundaries, but the treatment of Polish prisoners in Soviet hands soured relations. The revelation of the Katyn Wood massacre 1943 nearly caused a serious rift, only averted by strong intervention from Churchill. Following his death, the government-in-exile's influence seriously declined.

Sikorsky Igor Ivan 1889–1972. Ukrainian-born US engineer. He built the first successful helicopter 1939 (commercially produced from 1943). His first biplane flew 1910, and in 1929 he began to construct multi-engined flying boats.

The first helicopter was followed by a whole series of production designs using one, then two, piston engines. During the late 1950s piston engines were replaced by the newly developed gas-turbine engines.

silage fodder preserved through controlled fermentation in a ◊silo, an airtight structure that presses green crops. It is used as a winter feed for livestock. The term also refers to stacked crops that may be preserved indefinitely.

Silbury Hill steep, rounded artificial mound (40 m/130 ft high) of the Neolithic period, dating to 2660 BC, in Wiltshire, near ◊Avebury, England. Excavation has shown it not to be a barrow (grave), as was previously thought.

Silchester archaeological site, a major town in Roman Britain. It is 10 km/6 mi N of Basingstoke, Hampshire.

Silesia region of Europe that has long been disputed because of its geographical position, mineral resources, and industrial potential; now in Poland and the Czech Republic with metallurgical industries and a coalfield in Polish Silesia. Dispute began in the 17th century with claims on the area by both Austria and Prussia. It was seized by Prussia's Frederick the Great, which started the War of the ◊Austrian Succession; this was finally recognized by Austria 1763, after the Seven Years' War. After World War I, it was divided 1919 among newly formed Czechoslovakia, revived Poland, and Germany, which retained the largest part. In 1945, after World War II, all German Silesia east of the Oder-Neisse line was transferred to Polish administration; about 10 million inhabitants of German origin, both there and in Czechoslovak Silesia, were expelled.

The chief towns (with their German names) are: Wroclaw (Breslau), Katowice (Kattowitz), Zabrze (Hindenburg), Chorzow (Königshütte), Gliwice (Gleiwitz), and Bytom (Beuthen) in Poland, and Opava (Troppau) in the Czech Republic.

silhouette profile or shadow portrait filled in with black or a dark colour. A common pictorial technique in Europe in the late 18th and early 19th centuries, it was named after Etienne de Silhouette (1709–1767), a French finance minister who made paper cut-outs as a hobby.

silica silicon dioxide, SiO_2, the composition of the most common mineral group, of which the most familiar form is quartz. Other silica forms are ◊chalcedony, chert, opal, tridymite, and cristobalite.

Common sand consists largely of silica in the form of quartz.

silicate one of a group of minerals containing silicon and oxygen in tetrahedral units of SiO_4, bound together in various ways to form specific

Silbury Hill Silbury Hill, in Wiltshire, southern England. It is the largest prehistoric artificial mound in Europe, at approximately 40 m/131 ft high. It was built around 2600 BC, and is closely associated with the nearby stone circle at Avebury, and barrow tombs, but its exact function is unknown. *Corbis*

structural types. Silicates are the chief rock-forming minerals. Most rocks are composed, wholly or in part, of silicates (the main exception being limestones). Glass is a manufactured complex polysilicate material in which other elements (boron in borosilicate glass) have been incorporated.

Generally, additional cations are present in the structure, especially Al^{3+}, Fe^{2+}, Mg^{2+}, Ca^{2+}, Na^{+}, K^{+}, but quartz and other polymorphs of SiO_2 are also considered to be silicates; stishovite (a high pressure form of SiO_2) is a rare exception to the usual tetrahedral coordination of silica and oxygen.

In orthosilicates, the oxygens are all ionically bonded to cations such as Mg^{2+} or Fe^{2+} (as olivines), and are not shared between tetrahedra. All other silicate structures involve some degree of oxygen sharing between adjacent tetrahedra. For example, beryl is a ring silicate based on tetrahedra linked by sharing oxygens to form a circle. Pyroxenes are single chain silicates, with chains of linked tetrahedra extending in one direction through the structure; amphiboles are similar but have double chains of tetrahedra. In micas, which are sheet silicates, the tetrahedra are joined to form continuous sheets that are stacked upon one another. Framework silicates, such as feldspars and quartz, are based on three-dimensional frameworks of tetrahedra in which all oxygens are shared.

silicon (Latin *silicium* 'silica') brittle, nonmetallic element, symbol Si, atomic number 14, relative atomic mass 28.086. It is the second-most abundant element (after oxygen) in the Earth's crust and occurs in amorphous and crystalline forms. In nature it is found only in combination with other elements, chiefly with oxygen in silica (silicon dioxide, SiO_2) and the silicates. These form the mineral ◊quartz, which makes up most sands, gravels, and beaches.

Pottery glazes and glassmaking are based on the use of silica sands and date from prehistory. Today the crystalline form of silicon is used as a deoxidizing and hardening agent in steel, and has become the basis of the electronics industry because of its ◊semiconductor properties, being used to make 'silicon chips' for microprocessors.

silicon chip ◊integrated circuit with microscopically small electrical components on a piece of silicon crystal only a few millimetres square. One may contain more than a million components. A chip is mounted in a rectangular plastic package and linked via gold wires to metal pins, so that it can be connected to a printed circuit board for use in electronic devices, such as computers, calculators, television sets, car dashboards, and domestic appliances.

Silicon Valley nickname given to Santa Clara County, California, since the 1950s the site of many high-technology electronic firms, whose prosperity is based on the silicon chip.

silicosis chronic disease of miners and stone cutters who inhale ◊silica dust, which makes the lung tissues fibrous and less capable of aerating the blood. It is a form of ◊pneumoconiosis.

silk in UK law, a ◊Queen's Counsel, a senior barrister entitled to wear a silk gown in court.

silk fine soft thread produced by the larva of the ◊silkworm moth when making its cocoon. It is soaked, carefully unwrapped, and used in the manufacture of textiles. The introduction of synthetics originally harmed the silk industry, but rising standards of living have produced an increased demand for real silk. It is manufactured in China, India, Japan, and Thailand.

Silk Road ancient and medieval overland route of about 6,400 km/4,000 mi by which silk was brought from China to Europe in return for trade goods; it ran west via the Gobi Desert, Samarkand, and Antioch to Mediterranean ports in Greece, Italy, the Middle East, and Egypt. Buddhism came to China via this route, which was superseded from the 16th century by sea trade.

silk-screen printing or ***serigraphy*** method of ◊printing based on stencilling. It can be used to print on most surfaces, including paper, plastic, cloth, and wood. An impermeable stencil (either paper or photosensitized gelatin plate) is attached to a finely meshed silk screen that has been stretched on a wooden frame, so that the ink passes through to the area beneath only where an image is required. The design can also be painted directly on the screen with varnish. A series of screens can be used to add successive layers of colour to the design.

The process was developed in the early 20th century for commercial use and adopted by many artists from the 1930s onwards, most notably Andy Warhol.

silkworm usually the larva of the common silkworm moth *Bombyx mori*. After hatching from the egg and maturing on the leaves of white mulberry trees (or a synthetic substitute), it spins a protective cocoon of fine silk thread 275 m/900 ft long. To keep the thread intact, the moth is killed before emerging from the cocoon, and several threads are combined to form the commercial silk thread woven into textiles.

Other moths produce different fibres, such as tussah from *Antheraea mylitta*. The raising of silkworms is called sericulture and began in China about 2000 BC. Chromosome engineering and artificial selection practised in Japan have led to the development of different types of silkworm for different fibres. *See illustration on following page.*

sill sheet of igneous rock created by the intrusion of magma (molten rock) between layers of pre-existing rock. (A ◊dyke, by contrast, is formed when magma cuts *across* layers of rock.) An example of a sill in the UK is the Great Whin Sill, which forms the ridge along which Hadrian's Wall was built.

A sill is usually formed of dolerite, a rock that is extremely resistant to erosion and weathering, and often forms ridges in the landscape or cuts across rivers to create ◊waterfalls.

sillimanite aluminium silicate, Al_2SiO_5, a mineral that occurs either as white to brownish prismatic crystals or as minute white fibres. It is an indicator of high temperature conditions in metamorphic rocks formed from clay sediments. Andalusite, kyanite, and sillimanite are all polymorphs of Al_2SiO_5.

Sillitoe Alan 1928– . English novelist. He wrote *Saturday Night and Sunday Morning* 1958, about a working-class man in Nottingham, Sillitoe's home town. He also wrote *The Loneliness of the Long Distance Runner* 1959, *Life Goes On* 1985, many other novels, and poems, plays, and children's

'The Loneliness of the Long-Distance Runner.'

ALAN SILLITOE
Book title

silicon chip A microchip surrounded by granulated sugar to illustrate its size. The pins around the chip are used to connect it into a printed circuit board that could then be used to control the function of any electrical machine which requires a programme. *Image Select (UK) Ltd*

silkworm Not a worm, the so-called silkworm is in fact the larva of a moth. Various species of the moth families Bombycidae and Saturniidae spin silken cocoons in which to pupate but the Chinese silkworm moth produces so much that it has been the basis of the eastern silk cloth industry for at least 2,000 years. Traditionally, the larvae are fed on white mulberry leaves.

books. His autobiography *Life Without Armour* appeared 1995.

silo in farming, an airtight tower in which ◊silage is made by the fermentation of freshly cut grass and other forage crops. In military technology, a silo is an underground chamber for housing and launching a ballistic missile.

silt sediment intermediate in coarseness between clay and sand; its grains have a diameter of 0.002–0.02 mm/0.00008–0.0008 in. Silt is usually deposited in rivers, and so the term is often used generically to mean a river deposit, as in the silting-up of a channel.

Silurian period of geological time 439–409 million years ago, the third period of the Palaeozoic era. Silurian sediments are mostly marine and consist of shales and limestone. Luxuriant reefs were built by coral-like organisms. The first land plants began to evolve during this period, and there were many ostracoderms (armoured jawless fishes). The first jawed fishes (called acanthodians) also appeared.

silver white, lustrous, extremely malleable and ductile, metallic element, symbol Ag (from Latin *argentum*), atomic number 47, relative atomic mass 107.868. It occurs in nature in ores and as a free metal; the chief ores are sulphides, from which the metal is extracted by smelting with lead. It is one of the best metallic conductors of both heat and electricity; its most useful compounds are the chloride and bromide, which darken on exposure to light and are the basis of photographic emulsions.

Silver is used ornamentally, for jewellery and tableware, for coinage, in electroplating, electrical contacts, and dentistry, and as a solder. It has been mined since prehistory; its name is an ancient non-Indo-European one, *silubr*, borrowed by the Germanic branch as *silber*.

silverfish wingless insect, a type of ◊bristletail.

silver plate silverware made by depositing a layer of silver on another metal, usually copper, by the process of ◊electroplating.

silverpoint drawing instrument consisting of silver wire encased in a holder, used on paper prepared with opaque white. Because it has a limited range and cannot be erased, silverpoint was rapidly superseded by the graphite pencil in the 18th century. An example of silverpoint is Dürer's *Self-portrait* 1484 (Albertina, Vienna).

The ground was composed of powdered bones and gumwater, giving an ivory finish, though in Italy, and especially in Florence, tinted grounds were favoured. Being indelible and not liable to smudge, the silverpoint was convenient for the sketchbook, as in that which Dürer took with him on his visit to the Netherlands. Lead, copper, and gold metalpoints were also used, but silver was most popular in the 15th and 16th centuries.

sima in geochemistry and geophysics, the substance of the Earth's oceanic ◊crust, as distinct from the ◊sial of the continental crust. The name, now used rarely, is derived from *si*lica and *ma*gnesia, its two main chemical constituents.

Simenon Georges Joseph Christian 1903–1989. Belgian crime writer. Initially a pulp fiction writer, in 1931 he created Inspector Maigret of the Paris Sûreté who appeared in a series of detective novels.

Simeon Stylites, St c. 390–459. Syrian Christian ascetic who practised his ideal of self-denial by living for 37 years on a platform on top of a high pillar (Greek *stulos*). Feast day 5 Jan.

simile (Latin 'likeness') ◊figure of speech that in English uses the conjunctions *like* and *as* to express comparisons between two things of different kinds ('run like the devil'; 'as deaf as a post'). It is sometimes confused with ◊metaphor. The simile makes an explicit comparison, while the metaphor's comparison is implicit.

Not every comparison that uses the words *like* or *as* is a simile; for example, 'the city of Bristol is like Bordeaux' literally compares two ports. In 'the city of Bristol is like a fine old ship' a more imaginative comparison (not city with city, but city with ship) creates an analogical link between less obvious contexts, and is a simile.

Simitis Costas (Constantine) 1936– . Greek politician, prime minister from 1996. Entering parliament 1985, he served under Andreas Papandreou as minister of agriculture 1981–85, minister of national economy 1985–89, minister of education 1989–93, and was responsible for industry, energy, technology, and commerce from 1993. In 1996 he was chosen by the ruling Panhellenic Socialist Movement (PASOK) to replace Papandreou on the latter's resignation 1996.

Simon (Marvin) Neil 1927– . US dramatist and screenwriter. His stage plays (which were made into films) include the wryly comic *Barefoot in the Park* 1963 (filmed 1967), *The Odd Couple* 1965 (filmed 1968), and *The Sunshine Boys* 1972 (filmed 1975), and the more serious, autobiographical trilogy *Brighton Beach Memoirs* 1983 (filmed 1986), *Biloxi Blues* 1985 (filmed 1988), and *Broadway Bound* 1986 (filmed 1991). He has also written screenplays and co-written musicals, including *Sweet Charity* 1966, *Promises, Promises* 1968, and *They're Playing Our Song* 1978.

Simon Paul 1942– . US pop singer and songwriter. In a folk-rock duo with Art Garfunkel (1942–), he had such hits as 'Mrs Robinson' 1968 and 'Bridge Over Troubled Water' 1970. Simon's solo work includes the critically acclaimed album *Graceland* 1986, for which he drew on Cajun and African music.

simony in the Christian church, the buying and selling of church preferments, now usually regarded as a sin. First condemned 451, it remained widespread until the Reformation.

Simon US singer and songwriter Paul Simon. As a duo, he and Art Garfunkel had hits such as 'The Sound of Silence' 1965, and Simon wrote songs for the film *The Graduate* 1967. He launched his solo career 1970 and has produced several successful albums including *Paul Simon* 1972, *Hearts and Bones* 1983, *Graceland* 1986 (featuring African musicians), and *The Rhythm of the Saints* 1990. *Topham*

The term is derived from Simon Magus (Acts 8) who offered money to the Apostles for the power of the Holy Ghost.

simple harmonic motion (SHM) oscillatory or vibrational motion in which an object (or point) moves so that its acceleration towards a central point is proportional to its distance from it. A simple example is a pendulum, which also demonstrates another feature of SHM, that the maximum deflection is the same on each side of the central point.

A graph of the varying distance with respect to time is a sine curve, a characteristic of the oscillating current or voltage of an alternating current (AC), which is another example of SHM.

Simplon (Italian ***Sempione***) Alpine pass Switzerland–Italy. The road was built by Napoleon 1800–05; the Simplon Tunnel, built in 1906, is 19.8 km/12.3 mi, one of Europe's longest.

Simpson James Young 1811–1870. Scottish physician, the first to use ether as an anaesthetic in childbirth 1847, and the discoverer, later the same year, of the anaesthetic properties of chloroform, which he tested by experiments on himself.

Simpson O(renthal) J(ames) 1947– . former professional American football player, film and TV actor, and sports commentator. In 1995 he was charged with two counts of first-degree murder relating to the 1994 fatal stabbings of his wife Nicole and her friend Ronald Goldman; he was found not guilty Oct 1995. A civil lawsuit, brought by the families of the victims, 1996 concluded that he was guilty.

Simpson Wallis Warfield, Duchess of Windsor 1896–1986. US socialite, twice divorced. She married ◊Edward VIII 1937, who abdicated in order to marry her. He was given the title Duke of Windsor by his brother, George VI, who succeeded him.

Simpson Desert desert area in Australia, chiefly in Northern Territory; area 145,000 sq km/56,000 sq mi. The desert was named after a president of the South Australian Geographical Society who financed its exploration.

simultaneous equations in mathematics, one of two or more algebraic equations that contain two or more unknown quantities that may have a unique solution. For example, in the case of two linear equations with two unknown variables, such as (i) $x + 3y = 6$ and (ii) $3y - 2x = 4$, the solution will be those unique values of x and y that are valid for both equations. Linear simultaneous equations can be solved by using algebraic manipulation to eliminate one of the variables, ◊coordinate geometry, or matrices (see ◊matrix).

sin transgression of the will of God or the gods, as revealed in the moral code laid down by a particular religion. In Roman Catholic theology, a distinction is made between mortal sins, which, if unforgiven, result in damnation, and venial sins, which are less serious. In Islam, the one unforgivable sin is shirk, denial that Allah is the only god.

In Christian belief, humanity is in a state of original sin and therefore in need of redemption through the crucifixion of Jesus. The sacrament of ◊penance is seen as an earthly means of atonement for sin. The ◊seven deadly sins are the vices leading to sin.

Sinai Egyptian peninsula, at the head of the Red Sea; area 65,000 sq km/25,000 sq mi. Resources include oil, natural gas, manganese, and coal; irrigation water from the river Nile is carried under the Suez Canal.

Sinai was occupied by Israel 1967–82. After the Battle of Sinai 1973, Israel began a gradual withdrawal from the area, under the disengagement agreement 1975 and the Camp David peace treaty 1979, and restored the whole of Sinai to Egyptian control by April 1982.

Sinai, Battle of battle 6–24 Oct 1973 during the Yom Kippur War between Israel and Egypt. It was one of the longest tank battles in history. Israeli troops crossed the Suez Canal 16 Oct, cutting off the Egyptian 3rd Army.

Sinai, Mount (Arabic ***Gebel Mûsa***) mountain near the tip of the Sinai Peninsula; height 2,285 m/7,500 ft. According to the Old Testament this is where ◊Moses received the Ten Commandments from God.

Sinan 1489–1588. Ottoman architect. He was chief architect to Suleiman the Magnificent from

Sinatra US singer and film actor Frank Sinatra. Affectionately known as 'Old Blue Eyes', Sinatra began his career as a crooner in the 1930s and in the 1940s appeared in film musicals such as *Anchors Aweigh* 1945 and *On the Town* 1949. His first role as a dramatic actor was in *From Here to Eternity* 1953. *Topham*

1538. Among the hundreds of buildings he designed are the Suleimaniye mosque complex in Istanbul 1551–58 and the Selimiye mosque in Adrinople (now Edirne) 1569–74.

Sinatra Frank (Francis Albert) 1915–1998. US singer and film actor. Celebrated for his phrasing and emotion, especially on love ballads, he is particularly associated with the song 'My Way'. His films from 1941 include *From Here to Eternity* 1953 (Academy Award), *Guys and Dolls* 1955, and *Some Came Running* 1959.

Sinclair Upton Beall 1878–1968. US novelist. His polemical concern for social reform was reflected in his prolific output of documentary novels. His most famous novel, *The Jungle* 1906, is an important example of naturalistic writing, which exposed the horrors of the Chicago meat-packing industry and led to a change in food-processing laws. His later novels include *King Coal* 1917, *Oil!* 1927, and his 11-volume Lanny Budd series 1940–53, including *Dragon's Teeth* 1942, which won a Pulitzer prize.

Sind province of SE Pakistan, mainly in the Indus delta
area 140,914 sq km/54,393 sq mi
capital and chief seaport Karachi
population (1992 est) 25,730,000
language 60% Sindi; others include Urdu, Punjabi, Baluchi, Pashto
features Sukkur Barrage, which enables water from the Indus River to be used for irrigation
history annexed 1843, it became a province of British India, and part of Pakistan on independence. There is agitation for its creation as a separate state, Sindhudesh.

Sindhi the majority ethnic group living in the Pakistani province of Sind. The Sindhi language is spoken by about 15 million people. Since the partition of India and Pakistan 1947, large numbers of Urdu-speaking refugees have moved into the region from India, especially into the capital, Karachi.

sine in trigonometry, a function of an angle in a right-angled triangle which is defined as the ratio of the length of the side opposite the angle to the length of the hypotenuse (the longest side).

sine rule in trigonometry, a rule that relates the sides and angles of a triangle, stating that the ratio of the length of each side and the sine of the angle opposite is constant (twice the radius of the circumscribing circle). If the sides of a triangle are *a*, *b*, and *c*, and the angles opposite are *A*, *B*, and *C*, respectively, then the sine rule may be expressed as

$$a/\sin A = b/\sin B = c/\sin C.$$

sinfonietta orchestral work that is of a shorter, lighter nature than a ◊symphony, for example Janáček's *Sinfonietta* 1926. It is also the name for a small-scale orchestra specializing in such works, for example the London Sinfonietta.

Singapore country in SE Asia, off the tip of the Malay Peninsula. *See country box on p. 976.*

Singapore City capital of Singapore, on the SE coast of the island of Singapore; population (1993) 2,874,000. It is an oil refining centre and port.

Singer Isaac Bashevis 1904–1991. Polish-born US novelist and short-story writer. He lived in the USA from 1935. His works, written in Yiddish, often portray traditional Jewish life in Poland and the USA, and the loneliness of old age. They include *The Family Moskat* 1950 and *Gimpel the Fool and Other Stories* 1957. Nobel prize 1978.

Written in an often magical storytelling style, his works combine a deep psychological insight with dramatic and visual impact. Many of his novels were written for serialization in New York Yiddish newspapers. Among his works are *The Slave* 1960, *Shosha* 1978, *Lost in America* 1981, *The Image and Other Stories* 1985, and *The Death of Methuselah* 1988. He also wrote plays and books for children.

Singer Isaac Merrit 1811–1875. US inventor of domestic and industrial sewing machines. Within a few years of opening his first factory 1851, he became the world's largest sewing-machine manufacturer (despite infringing the patent of Elias Howe (1819–1867)), and by the late 1860s more than 100,000 Singer sewing machines were in use in the USA alone.

Singh, Gobind see ◊Gobind Singh, Sikh guru.

Singh Vishwanath Pratap 1931– . Indian politician, prime minister 1989–90. As a member of the Congress (I) Party, he held ministerial posts under Indira Gandhi and Rajiv Gandhi, and from 1984 led an anti-corruption drive. When he unearthed an arms-sales scandal 1988, he was ousted from the government and party and formed a broad-based opposition alliance, the ◊Janata Dal, which won the 1989 election. Mounting caste and communal conflict split the Janata Dal and forced him out of office Nov 1990.

Single European Act 1986 update of the Treaty of ◊Rome (signed in 1957) that provides a legal basis for action by the European Union in matters relating to the environment. The act requires that environmental protection shall be a part of all other Union policies. Also, it allows for agreement by a qualified majority on some legislation, whereas before such decisions had to be unanimous.

Single European Market single market for all member countries of the European Union (formerly the European Community), which was established under the Single European Act 1987 and came into operation 1 Jan 1993. The market aims to create 'an area without internal frontiers in which the free movement of goods, persons, services, and capital is ensured'.

The single market has led to the removal of customs barriers (although some check points remain, particularly at airports) and is one more step towards the creation of a genuine economic, monetary, and according to its most ardent advocates, political union.

single parent a parent who is responsible for raising children alone; 80–90 % are women. Some women choose to have children on their own but the majority become single parents after separation or the death of their partner. Most single parents live below the poverty level and rely on state benefits for income.

In the UK, single-parent families increased from 8% of families in 1971 to 21% in 1992. Between 1970 and 1995, the number of single parents in the USA doubled.

singularity in astrophysics, the point in ◊space–time at which the known laws of physics break down. Singularity is predicted to exist at the centre of a black hole, where infinite gravitational forces compress the infalling mass of a collapsing star to infinite density. According to the Big Bang model of the origin of the universe, it is the point from which the expansion of the universe began.

Sinhalese the majority ethnic group of Sri Lanka (70% of the population). Sinhalese is the official language of Sri Lanka; it belongs to the Indo-Iranian branch of the Indo-European family, and is written in a script derived from the Indian Pali form. The Sinhalese are Buddhists. Trading and fishing remain important activities in coastal regions, while further inland rice is cultivated in irrigated fields. Since 1971 they have been involved in a violent struggle with the Tamil minority, who are seeking independence.

Sinn Féin (Gaelic 'we ourselves') Irish political party founded 1905, whose aim is the creation of a united republican Ireland. The driving political force behind Irish nationalism between 1916 and 1921, Sinn Féin returned to prominence with the outbreak of violence ('the Troubles') in ◊Northern Ireland in the late 1960s, when it split into 'Provisional' and 'Official' wings at the same time as the ◊Irish Republican Army (IRA), with which it is closely associated. From the late 1970s 'Provisional' Sinn Féin assumed a more active political role, putting up candidates to stand in local and national elections. Sinn Féin won two seats in the 1997 UK general election and one seat in the 1997 Irish general election. Gerry ◊Adams became party president in 1978. Sinn Féin participated in the multi-party negotiations (known as the Stormont Talks) and became a signatory of the agreement reached on Good Friday, 10 April 1998. The party gained 17.6% of votes in the June 1998 elections to the 108-seat Belfast assembly. In September a historic meeting between Gerry Adams and the Ulster Unionist leader, David Trimble, took place at Stormont; Sinn Féin also agreed to appoint a contact with the international body overseeing the decommissioning of arms – the party's chief negotiator, Martin McGuinness. ◊*See feature on pp. 550–551.*

Sino-Japanese Wars two wars waged by Japan against China 1894–95 and 1931–45 to expand to the mainland. Territory gained in the First Sino-Japanese War (Korea) and in the 1930s (Manchuria, Shanghai) was returned at the end of World War II.

First Sino-Japanese War 1894–95. Under the treaty of Shimonoseki, Japan secured the 'independence' of Korea, cession of Taiwan and the nearby Pescadores Islands, and the Liaodong peninsula (for a naval base). France, Germany, and Russia pressured Japan into returning the last-named, which Russia occupied 1896 to establish Port Arthur (now Lüda); this led to the Russo-Japanese War 1904–05.

Second Sino-Japanese War 1931–45.
1931–32 The Japanese occupied Manchuria, which they formed into the puppet state of Manchukuo.

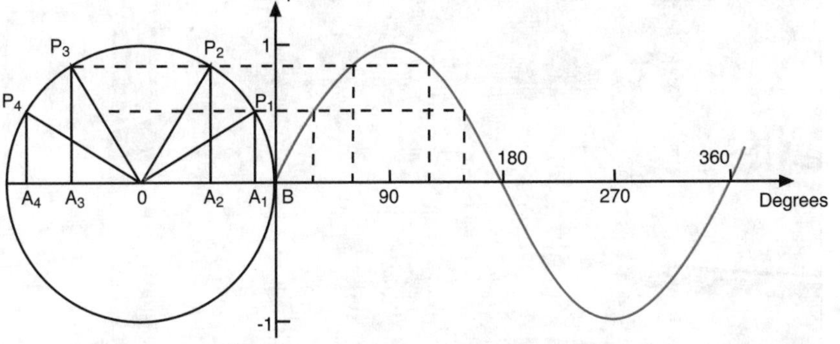

sine Constructing a sine wave. Within a circle of unit radius (left), the height P_1A_1 equals the sine of angle P_1OA_1. This fact and the equalities below the circle allow a sine curve to be drawn, as on the right.

SINGAPORE
Republic of

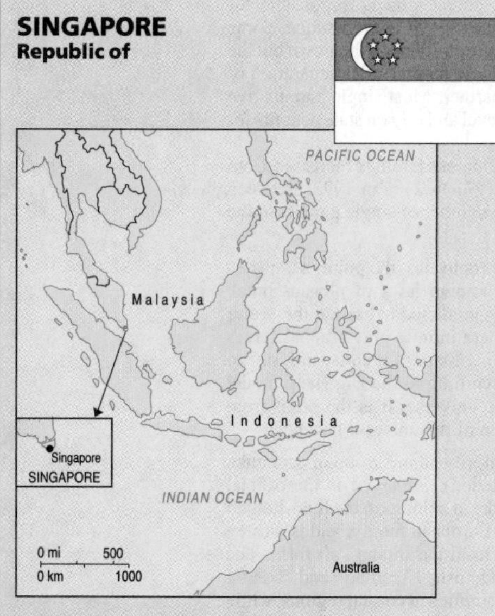

area 622 sq km/240 sq mi
capital Singapore City
major towns/cities Jurong, Changi
physical features comprises Singapore Island, low and flat, and 57 small islands; Singapore Island is joined to the mainland by causeway across Strait of Johore; temperature range 21°–34°C/69°–93°F
head of state Ong Teng Cheong from 1993
head of government Goh Chok Tong from 1990
political system liberal democracy with strict limits on dissent
administrative divisions five districts
political parties People's Action Party (PAP), conservative, free market, multi-ethnic; Workers' Party (WP), socialist; Singapore Democratic Party (SDP), liberal pluralist
armed forces 54,000; 210,000 reserves (1995)
conscription two years
defence spend (% GDP) 4.8 (1994)
education spend (% GNP) 4.4 (1985)
health spend (% GDP) 1.1 (1990)
death penalty retained and used for ordinary crimes
population 2,848,000 (1995 est)
population growth rate 1.0% (1990–95); 0.6% (2000–05)
age distribution (% of total population) <15 22.7%, 15–65 70.5%, >65 6.7% (1995)
ethnic distribution 77% of Chinese ethnic descent, predominantly Hokkien, Teochew, and Cantonese; 15% Malay; and 7% Indian, chiefly Tamil
population density (per sq km) 4,564 (1994)
urban population (% of total) 100 (1995)
labour force 49% of population: 0% agriculture, 36% industry, 64% services (1990)
unemployment 2.6% (1994)
child mortality rate (under 5, per 1,000 live births) 6 (1994)
life expectancy 72 (men), 77 (women)
education (compulsory years) 6
literacy rate 88%
languages Malay (national tongue), Chinese, Tamil, English (all official)
religions Buddhist, Taoist, Muslim, Hindu, Christian
TV sets (per 1,000 people) 379 (1992)
currency Singapore dollar
GDP (US $) 68.82 billion (1994)
GDP per capita (PPP) (US $) 19,350 (1993)
growth rate 10.1% (1994)
average annual inflation 3.1% (1994); 1.8% (1985–93)
major trading partners Japan, Malaysia, USA, Hong Kong, Thailand
resources granite
industries electrical machinery (particularly radios and televisions), petroleum refinery and petroleum products, transport equipment (especially shipbuilding), chemicals, metal products, machinery, food processing, clothing, finance and business services
exports electrical and non-electrical machinery, transport equipment, petroleum products, chemicals, rubber, foodstuffs, clothing, metal products, iron and steel, orchids and other plants, aquarium fish. Principal market: Malaysia 19.7% (1994)
imports electrical and non-electrical equipment, crude petroleum, transport equipment, chemicals, food and live animals, textiles, scientific and optical instruments, paper and paper products. Principal source: Japan 22% (1994)
arable land 1.6% (1993)
agricultural products vegetables, plants, orchids; poultry and fish production

HISTORY
12th C First trading settlement established on Singapore Island.
14th C Settlement destroyed, probably by Javanese Empire of Mahapahit.
1819 Stamford Raffles of British East India Company obtained Singapore from sultan of Johore.
1826 Straits Settlements formed from British possessions of Singapore, Penang, and Malacca ruled by governor of Bengal.
1832 Singapore became capital of Straits Settlements; the port prospered, attracting Chinese and Indian immigrants.
1851 Responsibility for Straits Settlements fell to governor general of India.
1858 The British government, through the India Office, took over administration of Straits Settlements.
1867 Straits Settlements became crown colony of the British Empire.
1922 Singapore chosen as principal British military base in Far East.
1942 Japan captured Singapore, taking 70,000 British and Australian prisoners.
1945 British rule restored after defeat of Japan.
1946 Singapore became separate crown colony.
1959 Internal self-government achieved as State of Singapore with Lee Kuan Yew (PAP) as prime minister.
1960s Rapid development as leading commercial and financial centre.
1963 Singapore combined with Federation of Malaya, Sabah, and Sarawak to form Federation of Malaysia.
1965 Became independent republic after withdrawing from Federation of Malaysia in protest at alleged discrimination against ethnic Chinese.
1971 Last remaining British military bases closed.
1984 Two opposition members elected to national assembly for first time.
1986 Opposition leader convicted of perjury and prohibited from standing for election.
1988 Ruling PAP won all but one of available assembly seats; increasingly authoritarian rule.
1990 Lee Kuan Yew retired from premiership after 31 years; succeeded by Goh Chok Tong.
1992 Lee Kuan Yew surrendered PAP leadership to Goh Chok Tong.
1993 Ong Teng Cheong elected president with increased powers.
1996 Constitutional change introduced, allowing better representation of minority races.

They also attacked Shanghai, and moved into NE China.
1937 Chinese leaders Chiang Kai-shek and Mao Zedong allied to fight the Japanese; war was renewed as the Japanese overran NE China and seized Shanghai and Nanjing.
1938 Japanese capture of Wuhan and Guangzhou was followed by the transfer of the Chinese capital to Chongqing; a period of stalemate followed.
1941 Japanese attack on the USA (see ◊Pearl Harbor) led to the extension of lend-lease aid to China and US entry into war against Japan and its allies.
1944 A Japanese offensive threatened Chongqing.
1945 The Chinese received the Japanese surrender at Nanjing in Sept, after the Allies had concluded World War II.

Sino-Japanese Wars Drawing of a battle at sea between Japan and China at the beginning of the First Sino-Japanese War. The Chinese showed little resistance and the campaign was shortlived, with Japan achieving control of Korea. *Philip Sauvain*

Sino-Tibetan languages group of languages spoken in SE Asia. This group covers a large area, and includes Chinese and Burmese, both of which have numerous dialects. Some classifications include the Tai group of languages (including Thai and Lao) in the Sino-Tibetan family.

Sinuiju capital of North Pyongan province, near the mouth of the Yalu River, North Korea; population (1984) 754,000. It was founded 1910.

sinusitis painful inflammation of one of the sinuses, or air spaces, that surround the nasal passages. Most cases clear with antibiotics and nasal decongestants, but some require surgical drainage.

Sinusitis most frequently involves the maxillary sinuses, within the cheek bones, producing pain around the eyes, toothache, and a nasal discharge.

Sioux (or ***Dakota***) a group of Native American ◊Plains Indians, now living on reservations in South Dakota and Nebraska, and among the general public. Their language belongs to the Macro-Siouan family.

When gold was discovered in their treaty territory, the USA sent in troops to remove them 1876. Under chiefs Crazy Horse and Sitting Bull they defeated General George Custer at Little Bighorn, Montana; as a result, Congress abrogated the Fort Laramie Treaty of 1868 (which had given the Sioux a large area in the Black Hills of Dakota). Gold, uranium, coal, oil, and natural gas have been found there since, and the Sioux pressed for and were awarded $160 million compensation 1980.

siphon tube in the form of an inverted U with unequal arms. When it is filled with liquid and the shorter arm is placed in a tank or reservoir, liquid flows out of the longer arm provided that its exit is below the level of the surface of the liquid in the tank.

The liquid flows through the siphon because low pressure develops at the apex as liquid falls freely down the long arm.

The difference between the pressure at the tank surface (atmospheric pressure) and the pressure at the apex causes liquid to rise in the short arm to replace that falling from the long arm.

Siraj-ud-Daula 1728–1757. Nawab of Bengal, India, from April 1756. He captured Calcutta from the British in June 1756 and imprisoned some of the British in the ◊Black Hole of Calcutta (a small room in which a number of them died), but was defeated in 1757 by Robert ◊Clive, and lost Bengal to the British at the Battle of ◊Plassey. He was killed in his capital, Murshidabad.

siren in Greek mythology, a sea ◊nymph who lured sailors to their deaths along rocky coasts by her singing. ◊Odysseus, in order to hear the sirens safely, tied himself to the mast of his ship and stuffed his crew's ears with wax.

The Argonauts escaped them because the singing of Orpheus surpassed that of the sirens.

Sirius or ***Dog Star*** or ***Alpha Canis Majoris*** the brightest star in the night sky, 8.6 light years from Earth in the constellation ◊Canis Major. Sirius is a white star with a mass 2.3 times that of the Sun, a diameter 1.8 times that of the Sun, and a luminosity of 23 Suns. It is orbited every 50 years by a ◊white dwarf, Sirius B, also known as the Pup.

Sirius is a double star with an orbital period of 50 years. Its eighth-magnitude companion is sometimes known as 'the Dark Companion' as it was first detected by Friedrich ◊Bessel from its gravitational effect on the proper motion of Sirius. It was seen for the first time 1862 but it was only in the 1920s that it was recognized as the first known example of a white dwarf.

sirocco hot, normally dry and dust-laden wind that blows from the deserts of N Africa across the Mediterranean into S Europe. It occurs mainly in the spring. The name 'sirocco' is also applied to any hot oppressive wind.

sisal strong fibre made from various species of ◊agave, such as *Agave sisalina*.

siskin North American finch *Carduelis pinus* with yellow markings or greenish-yellow bird *Carduelis spinus* about 12 cm/5 in long, found in Eurasia. They are members of the finch family Fringillidae, order Passeriformes.

C. spinus is frequently seen in Britain where it breeds, mainly in coniferous woods. In winter it is often to be seen with the redpoll in deciduous woods, especially alder.

Sisley Alfred 1839–1899. French Impressionist painter, born in Paris of English parents. Lyrical and harmonious, his landscapes are distinctive for their lightness of touch and subtlety of tone. Among his works are *The Square at Argenteuil* 1872 and *The Canal* 1872 (both Louvre, Paris).

His father was a wealthy English businessman in Paris. Sisley was sent to England at the age of 18, destined for a commercial career, but he was afterwards allowed to study art, and worked in the studio of Charles Gleyre, where he met Monet and Renoir. He devoted himself exclusively to landscape, exhibited at the first Impressionist exhibition of 1874, and is a close partner of Monet in atmospheric colour.

Sistine Chapel chapel in the Vatican, Rome, begun under Pope Sixtus IV in 1473 by Giovanni del Dolci, and decorated by (among others) Michelangelo. Built to the proportions of Solomon's temple in the Old Testament (its height one-half and its width one-third of its length), it has frescoes on the walls (emphasizing the authority and legality of the papacy) by ◊Botticelli and ◊Ghirlandaio and, on the altar wall and ceiling, by ◊Michelangelo. It houses the conclave that meets to select a new pope.

Sisulu Walter Max Ulyate 1912– . South African civil-rights activist, one of the first full-time secretary generals of the African National Congress (ANC), in 1964, with Nelson Mandela. He was imprisoned following the 1964 Rivonia Trial for opposition to the apartheid system and released, at the age of 77, as a gesture of reform by President F W ◊de Klerk 1989. In 1991, when Mandela became ANC president, Sisulu became his deputy.

Sisyphus in Greek mythology, a king of Corinth who, as punishment for his evil life, was condemned in the underworld to roll a huge stone uphill; it always fell back before he could reach the top.

Sita in Hinduism, the wife of Rama, an avatar (manifestation) of the god Vishnu; a character in the *Rāmāyana* epic, characterized by chastity and kindness.

sitar Indian stringed instrument, of the lute family. It has a pear-shaped body and long neck supported by an additional gourd resonator at the opposite end. A principal solo instrument, it has seven metal strings extending over movable frets and two concealed strings that provide a continuous drone. It is played with a plectrum, producing a luminous and supple melody responsive to nuances of pressure. Its most celebrated exponent in the West has been Ravi Shankar.

sitatunga herbivorous antelope *Tragelaphus spekei* found in several swamp regions in Central Africa. Its hooves are long and splayed to help progress on soft surfaces. It grows to about 1.2 m/4 ft high at the shoulder; the male has thick horns up to 90 cm/3 ft long. Males are dark greyish-brown, females and young are chestnut, all with whitish markings on the rather shaggy fur.

Site of Special Scientific Interest (SSSI) in the UK, land that has been identified as having animals, plants, or geological features that need to be protected and conserved. From 1991 these sites were designated and administered by English Nature, Scottish Natural Heritage, and the Countryside Council for Wales.

Although SSSIs enjoy some legal protection, this does not in practice always prevent damage or destruction by development, farming, public access and neglect. A report by English Nature estimated a quarter of the total area of SSSI's, over 1 million acres, had been damaged by acid rain. Around 1% of SSSIs are irreperably damaged each year.

Sitting Bull (Indian name ***Tatanka Iyotake***) c. 1834–1890. Native American chief who agreed to ◊Sioux resettlement 1868. When the treaty was broken by the USA, he led the Sioux against Lieutenant Colonel ◊Custer at the Battle of the ◊Little Bighorn 1876.

He was pursued by the US Army and forced to flee to Canada. He was allowed to return 1881, and he toured in the Wild West show of 'Buffalo Bill' ◊Cody. He settled on a Dakota reservation and was killed during his arrest on suspicion of involvement in Indian agitations.

Sitwell Edith Louisa 1887–1964. English poet. Her series of poems *Façade* was performed as recitations to the specially written music of William ◊Walton from 1923. Her verse has an imaginative and rhythmic intensity.

SI units (French ***Système International d'Unités***) standard system of scientific units used by scientists worldwide.

Introduced in 1960, it replaced the m.k.s. system (based on metre, kilogram, and second), the c.g.s. system (centimetre, gram, and second), and the f.p.s. system (foot, pound, and second). It is based on seven basic units: the metre (m) for length, kilogram (kg) for mass, second (s) for time, ampere (A) for electrical current, kelvin (K) for temperature, mole (mol) for amount of substance, and candela (cd) for luminosity. *See list of tables on p. 1177.*

Siva (Sanskrit 'propitious') or ***Shiva*** in Hinduism, the third chief god (with Brahma and Vishnu). As Mahadeva (great lord), he is the creator, symbolized by the phallic *lingam*, who restores what as Mahakala he destroys. He is often sculpted as Nataraja, performing his fruitful cosmic dance.

His consort or female principle (*sakti*) is Parvati, otherwise known as Durga or Kali.

Sivaji or ***Shivaji*** 1627–1680. Founder of the ◊Maratha state in W India, which lasted until 1818. He came from a Maratha noble family, and gained a reputation as a skilled warrior and defender of Hindu interests in successful confrontations with the Muslim rulers of Bijapur and the emperor Aurangzeb. He was crowned rajah (king) 1674 and remains a Hindu hero.

Sivaji was a superb organizer, setting up an equitable land system which helped to finance his military exploits. He was an innovative fighter, using guerrilla tactics of speed and surprise.

Six Acts in British history, acts of Parliament passed 1819 by Lord Liverpool's Tory administration to curtail political radicalism in the aftermath of the ◊Peterloo massacre and during a period of agitation for reform when ◊habeas corpus was suspended and the powers of magistrates extended.

The acts curtailed the rights of the accused by stipulating trial within a year; increased the penalties for seditious libel; imposed a newspaper stamp duty on all pamphlets and circulars containing news; specified strict limitations on public meetings; banned training with guns and other arms; and empowered magistrates to search and seize arms.

Six Articles act introduced by Henry VIII in England in 1539 to settle disputes over dogma in the English church.

The articles affirmed belief in transubstantiation, communion in one kind only, auricular confession, monastic vows, celibacy of the clergy, and private masses; those who rejected transubstantiation were to be burned at the stake. The act was repealed in 1547, replaced by 42 articles in 1551, and by an act of Thirty-Nine Articles in 1571.

Six-Day War another name for the third ◊Arab-Israeli War.

sixth form in UK education, an inclusive term used for pupils who study for one or two years beyond school-leaving age in order to gain ◊A level or other post-16 qualifications. In many areas, sixth-form education is concentrated in sixth-form or tertiary colleges.

Sixtus five popes, including:

Sixtus IV (born Francesco della Rovere) 1414–1484. Pope from 1471. He built the Sistine Chapel in the Vatican, which is named after him.

Sixtus V (born Felice Peretti) 1521–1590. Pope from 1585. He supported the Spanish Armada against Britain and the Catholic League against Henry IV of France.

Sjælland or ***Zealand*** main island of Denmark, on which Copenhagen is situated; area 7,000 sq km/2,700 sq mi; population (1995) 2,157,700. It is low-lying with an irregular coastline. The chief industry is dairy farming.

Skara Brae well-preserved Neolithic village, dating to the third millennium BC, built of stone slabs on the island of Orkney, Scotland.

skate any of several species of flatfish of the ray group. The common skate *Raja batis* is up to 1.8 m/6 ft long and greyish, with black specks. Its egg cases ('mermaids' purses') are often washed ashore by the tide.

skateboard single flexible board mounted on wheels and steerable by weight positioning. As a land alternative to surfing, skateboards developed in California in the 1960s and became a worldwide craze in the 1970s. Skateboarding is practised in urban environments and has enjoyed a revival since the late 1980s.

skating self-propulsion on ice by means of bladed skates, or on other surfaces by skates with small rollers (wheels of wood, metal, or plastic).

The chief competitive ice-skating events are figure skating, for singles or pairs, ice-dancing, and simple speed skating. The first world ice-skating championships were held in 1896.

Ice-skating became possible as a world sport from the opening of the first artificial ice rink in London, England, 1876. Figure skating includes both compulsory figures and freestyle combinations to music; ice-dancing has developed into a choreographed combination of ballet and popular dance movements welded to an artistic whole, as exemplified by John Curry and the team of Jayne Torvill and Christopher Dean.

The roller skate was the invention of James L Plympton, who opened the first rink in Newport, Rhode Island, USA, 1866; events are as for ice-skating with European and world championships.

skeleton the rigid or semirigid framework that supports and gives form to an animal's body, protects its internal organs, and provides anchorage points for its muscles. The skeleton may be composed of bone and cartilage (vertebrates), chitin (arthropods), calcium carbonate (molluscs and other invertebrates), or silica (many protists). The human skeleton is composed of 206 bones, with the

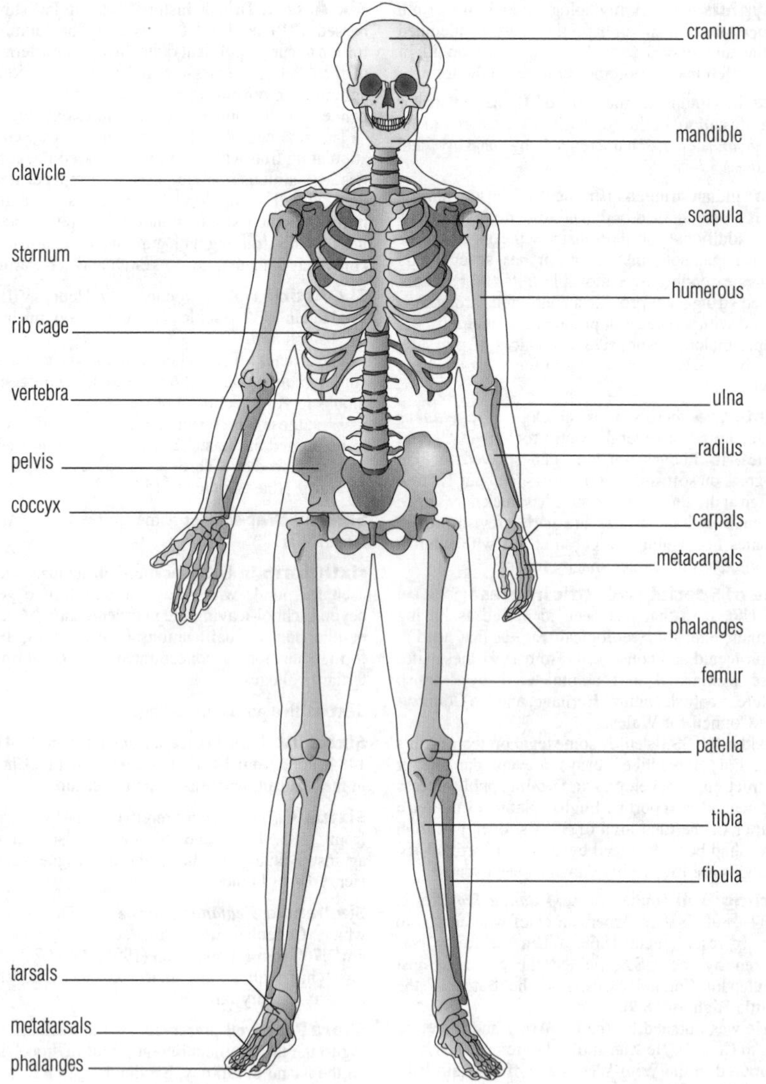

skeleton The human skeleton is made up of 206 bones and provides a strong but flexible supportive framework for the body.

◊vertebral column (spine) forming the central supporting structure.

A skeleton may be internal, forming an ◊endoskeleton, or external, forming an ◊exoskeleton, as in the shells of insects or crabs. Another type of skeleton, found in invertebrates such as earthworms, is the hydrostatic skeleton. This gains partial rigidity from fluid enclosed within a body cavity. Because the fluid cannot be compressed, contraction of one part of the body results in extension of another part, giving peristaltic motion.

skiffle British popular music style, introduced by singer and banjo player Lonnie Donegan (1931–) in the mid-1950s, using improvised percussion instruments such as tea chests and washboards. Donegan popularized US folk songs like 'Rock Island Line' 1953 (a hit 1955 UK and 1956 USA) and 'Cumberland Gap' 1957. Skiffle gave way to beat music in the early 1960s.

skiing self-propulsion on snow by means of elongated runners (skis) for the feet, slightly bent upward at the tip. It is a popular recreational sport, as cross-country ski touring or as downhill runs on mountain trails; events include downhill; slalom, in which a series of turns between flags have to be negotiated; cross-country racing; and ski jumping, when jumps of over 150 m/490 ft are achieved from ramps up to 90 m/295 ft high. Speed-skiing uses skis approximately one-third longer and wider than normal with which speeds of up to 200 kph/125 mph have been recorded. Recently, snowboarding (or monoboarding), the use of a single, very broad ski, similar to a surf board, used with the feet facing the front and placed together, has become increasingly popular.

Skiing was known as a means of transportation across snow in N Europe and Asia from about 3000 BC, but developed into a sport when innovations in ski design made it possible to manoeuvre more accurately, around 1896. Ski resorts then began as a winter holiday business in Europe and the USA, but not until the 1970s did skiing become a recreation for any but the wealthy or those who lived in ski conditions. The Alpine World Cup was first held 1967.

skin the covering of the body of a vertebrate. In mammals, the outer layer (epidermis) is dead and its cells are constantly being rubbed away and replaced from below; it helps to protect the body from infection and to prevent dehydration. The lower layer (dermis) contains blood vessels, nerves, hair roots, and sweat and sebaceous glands, and is supported by a network of fibrous and elastic cells. The medical speciality concerned with skin diseases is called dermatology.

Skin grafting is the repair of injured skin by placing pieces of skin, taken from elsewhere on the body, over the injured area.

skink lizard of the family Scincidae, a large family of about 700 species found throughout the tropics and subtropics. The body is usually long and the legs are reduced. Some skinks are legless and rather snakelike. Many are good burrowers, or can 'swim' through sand, like the sandfish genus *Scincus* of N Africa. Some skinks lay eggs, others bear live young.

Skinks include the three-toed skink *Chalcides chalcides* of S Europe and NW Africa, up to 40 cm/16 in long, of which half is tail, and the stump-tailed skink *Tiligua rugosus* of Australia, which stores fat in its triangular tail, looks the same at either end, and feeds on fruit as well as small animals.

Skinner B(urrhus) F(rederic) 1904–1990. US psychologist. He was a radical behaviourist who rejected mental concepts, seeing the organism as a 'black box' where internal processes are not significant in predicting behaviour. He studied operant conditioning (influencing behaviour patterns by reward or punishment) and held that behaviour is shaped and maintained by its consequences.

The 'Skinner box' is an enclosed environment in which the process of learned behaviour can be observed. In it, a rat presses a lever, and learns to repeat the behaviour because it is rewarded by food. Skinner also designed a 'baby box', a controlled, soundproof environment for infants. His own daughter was partially reared in such a box until the age of two.

skittles or ***ninepins*** game in which nine wooden pins, arranged in a diamond-shaped frame at the end of an alley, are knocked down in three rolls from the other end of the alley with a wooden ball. Two or more players can compete. Skittles resembles ◊tenpin bowling.

A smaller version called table skittles is played indoors on a table using a pivoted ball attached to a pole by a chain.

Skopje capital and industrial city of the Former Yugoslav Republic of Macedonia; population

skin The skin of an adult man covers about 1.9 sq m/20 sq ft; a woman's skin covers about 1.6 sq m/17 sq ft. During our lifetime, we shed about 18 kg/40 lb of skin.

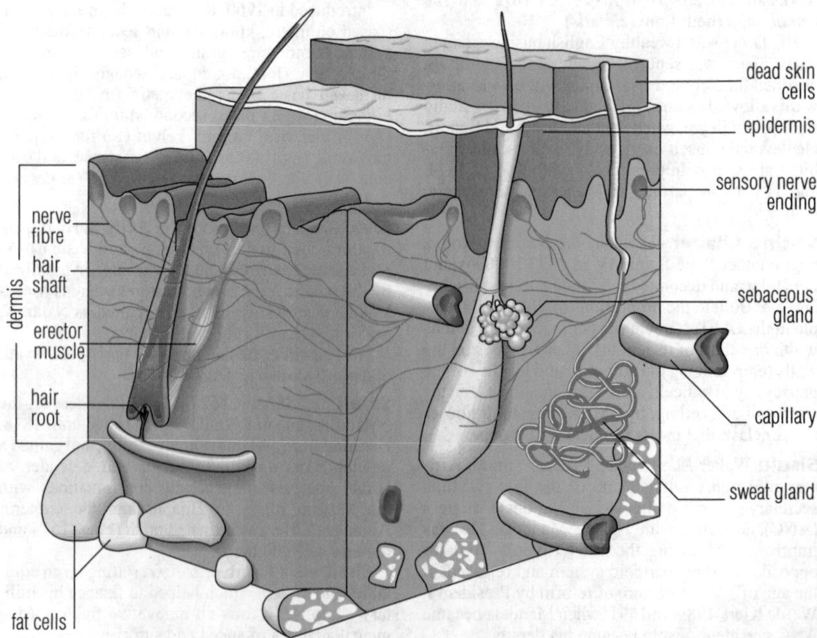

(1991) 563,300. Industries include iron, steel, chromium mining, and food processing.

history it stands on the site of an ancient town destroyed by an earthquake in the 5th century. The city was taken in 1282 by the Serbian king Milutin, who made it his capital, and in 1392 by the Turks, when it became part of the Ottoman Empire. Captured by Serbia during the Balkan Wars of 1912–13, it became part of Yugoslavia in 1929. Again destroyed by an earthquake 1963, Skopje was rebuilt on a safer site nearby. It is an Islamic centre.

Skryabin Alexander Nikolayevich, or ***Scriabin*** 1872–1915. Russian composer and pianist. His visionary tone poems such as *Prometheus* 1911, and symphonies such as *Divine Poem* 1903, employed unusual scales and harmonies.

skua dark-coloured gull-like seabird, living in Arctic and Antarctic waters. Skuas can grow up to 60 cm/2 ft long, with long, well-developed wings and short, stout legs; in colour they are greyish above and white below. They are aggressive scavengers, and seldom fish for themselves but force gulls to disgorge their catch, and also eat chicks of other birds. Skuas are in the family Stercorariidae, order Charadriiformes.

skull in vertebrates, the collection of flat and irregularly shaped bones (or cartilage) that enclose the brain and the organs of sight, hearing, and smell, and provide support for the jaws. In most mammals, the skull consists of 22 bones joined by fibrous immobile joints called sutures. The floor of the skull is pierced by a large hole (*foramen magnum*) for the spinal cord and a number of smaller apertures through which other nerves and blood vessels pass.

The skull comprises the cranium (brain case) and the bones of the face, which include the upper jaw, enclosing the sinuses, and form the framework for the nose, eyes, and the roof of the mouth cavity. The lower jaw is hinged to the middle of the skull at its lower edge. The opening to the middle ear is located near the jaw hinge. The plate at the back of the head is jointed at its lower edge with the upper section of the spine. Inside, the skull has various shallow cavities into which fit different parts of the brain. *See illustration on following page.*

skunk North American mammal of the weasel family. The common skunk *Mephitis mephitis* has a long, arched body, short legs, a bushy tail, and black fur with white streaks on the back. In self-defence, it discharges a foul-smelling fluid.

skydiving sport of freefalling from an aircraft at a height of up to 3,650m/12,000 ft, performing aerobatics, and opening a parachute when 600 m/2,000 ft from the ground.

Skye largest island of the Inner Hebrides, off the W coast of Scotland; area 1,740 sq km/672 sq mi; population (1991) 8,900.

It is separated from the mainland by the Sound of Sleat. The chief port is Portree. The economy is based on crofting, tourism, and livestock. The Skye Bridge, a privately financed toll bridge to the island, was completed 1995.

Bonnie Prince Charlie (◊Charles Edward Stuart) took refuge here after the Battle of ◊Culloden.

Skylab US space station, launched 14 May 1973, made from the adapted upper stage of a Saturn V rocket. At 75 tonnes/82.5 tons, it was the heaviest object ever put into space, and was 25.6 m/84 ft long. *Skylab* contained a workshop for carrying out experiments in weightlessness, an observatory for monitoring the Sun, and cameras for photographing the Earth's surface.

Damaged during launch, it had to be repaired by the first crew of astronauts. Three crews, each of three astronauts, occupied *Skylab* for periods of up to 84 days, at that time a record duration for human spaceflight. *Skylab* finally fell to Earth on 11 July 1979, dropping debris on Western Australia.

skylark a type of ◊lark.

skyscraper building so tall that it appears to 'scrape the sky', developed 1868 in New York, USA, where land prices were high and the geology allowed such methods of construction. Skyscrapers are now found in cities throughout the world. One of the world's tallest free-standing structures is the CN (Canadian National) Tower, Toronto, at 555 m/1,821 ft. In Manhattan, New York, are the Empire State Building 1931 (102 storeys and 381 m/1,250 ft high) and the twin towers of the World Trade Center 1970–74 (415 m/1,361 ft), but these are surpassed by the Sears Tower in Chicago 1973 (443 m/1,454 ft).

Chicago has many of the earliest skyscrapers, such as the Home Insurance Building 1883–85, which was built ten storeys high with an iron and steel frame. A rigid steel frame is the key to skyscraper construction, taking all the building loads. The walls simply 'hang' from the frame (see ◊curtain wall), and they can thus be made from relatively flimsy materials such as glass and aluminium. *See list of tables on p. 1177.*

Slade Felix 1790–1868. English art collector. He bequeathed his collections of engravings, glass, and pottery to the British Museum, and endowed Slade professorships in fine art at Oxford, Cambridge, and University College, London. The Slade School of Fine Arts, opened 1871, is a branch of University College.

slag in chemistry, the molten mass of impurities that is produced in the smelting or refining of metals.

The slag produced in the manufacture of iron in a ◊blast furnace floats on the surface above the molten iron. It contains mostly silicates, phosphates, and sulphates of calcium. When cooled, the solid is broken up and used as a core material in the foundations of roads and buildings.

slaked lime $Ca(OH)_2$ (technical name ***calcium hydroxide***) substance produced by adding water to quicklime (calcium oxide, CaO). Much heat is given out and the solid crumbles as it absorbs water. A solution of slaked lime is called ◊limewater.

slander spoken defamatory statement; if written, or broadcast on radio or television, it constitutes ◊libel.

In the UK slanders are generally actionable only if pecuniary loss has been suffered, except where, for example, the slander implies that a person is incapable of his or her profession. As in the case of libel, the slander must be made to some person other than the person defamed for it to be actionable.

slang very informal language usage that often serves to promote a feeling of group membership. It is not usually accepted in formal speech or writing and includes expressions that may be impolite or taboo in conventional communication.

Forms of slang develop among particular groups, for example soldiers, teenagers, and criminals, and are often extended into more general use because social conditions make them fashionable or people have grown accustomed to using them. Some types of slang are highly transient; others may last across generations and gain currency in the standard language.

slash and burn simple agricultural method whereby natural vegetation is cut and burned, and the clearing then farmed for a few years until the soil loses its fertility, whereupon farmers move on and leave the area to regrow. Although this is possible with a small, widely dispersed population, it becomes unsustainable with more people and is now a form of ◊deforestation.

slate fine-grained, usually grey metamorphic rock that splits readily into thin slabs along its ◊cleavage planes. It is the metamorphic equivalent of ◊shale.

Slate is highly resistant to atmospheric conditions and can be used for writing on with chalk (actually gypsum). Quarrying slate takes such skill and time that it is now seldom used for roof and sill material except in restoring historic buildings.

Slav an Indo-European people in central and E Europe, the Balkans, and parts of N Asia, speaking closely related ◊Slavonic languages. The ancestors of the Slavs are believed to have included the Sarmatians (an Indo-European nomadic people) and ◊Scythians. Moving west from Central Asia, they settled in E and SE Europe during the 2nd and 3rd millennia BC.

The present Slavonic nations emerged around the 5th and 6th centuries AD. By the 7th century they were the predominant population of E and SE Europe. During the 9th century they adopted Christianity, and in the course of the Middle Ages were expelled from the area of former East Germany.

slavery the enforced servitude of one person (a slave) to another or one group to another. A slave has no personal rights and is the property of another person through birth, purchase, or capture.

Chattel slavery involves outright ownership of the slave by a master, but there are forms of partial slavery where an individual is tied to the land, or to another person, by legal obligations, as in ◊serfdom or ◊indentured labour.

Slavery goes back to prehistoric times but declined in Europe after the fall of the Roman Empire. During the imperialism of Spain, Portugal, and Britain in the 16th–18th centuries and in the American South in the 17th–19th centuries, slavery became a mainstay of an agricultural factory economy, with millions of Africans sold to work on plantations in North and South America. Millions more died in the process, but the profits from this trade were enormous. Slavery was abolished in the British Empire 1833 and in the USA at the end of the Civil War 1863–65.

Although outlawed in most countries, various forms of slavery continue to exist – as evidenced by the steps taken by international organizations such as the League of Nations between the world wars and the United Nations since 1945 to curb such practices. ▷ *See feature on pp. 982–983.*

Slavonia region of E Croatia bounded by the Sava, Drava, and Danube rivers; Osijek is the largest town. E and W Slavonia declared themselves autonomous provinces of Serbia following Croatia's declaration of independence from Yugoslavia 1991, and the region was the scene of fierce fighting between Croatian forces and Serb-dominated Yugoslav federal troops 1991–92. After the ceasefire 1992, 10,000 UN troops were deployed in E and W Slavonia and contested Krajina. Rebel Serbs in Croatia agreed Nov 1995 to return the region of E Slavonia to Croatian control.

Slavonic languages or ***Slavic languages*** branch of the Indo-European language family spoken in central and E Europe, the Balkans, and parts of N Asia. The family comprises the southern group (Slovene, Serbo-Croatian, Macedonian, and Bulgarian); the western group (Czech and Slovak,

Slang is a language that rolls up its sleeves, spits on its hands and goes to work.

On SLANG
Carl Sandburg quoted in the *New York Times* 13 Feb 1959

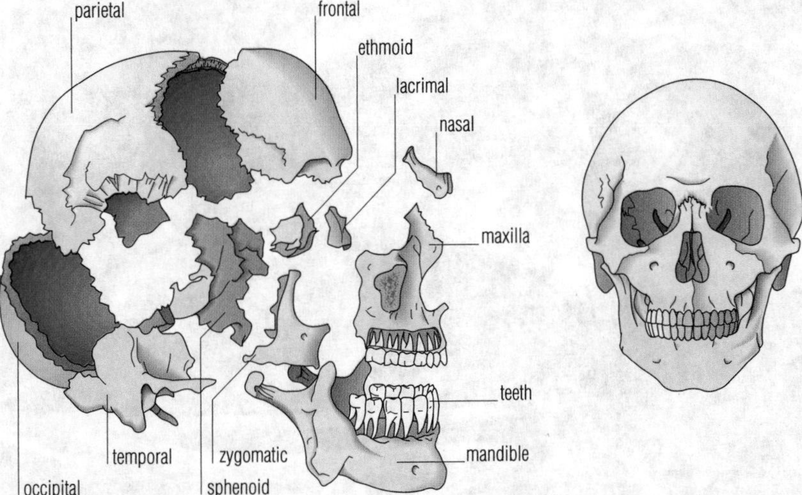

skull The skull is a protective box for the brain, eyes, and hearing organs. It is also a framework for the teeth and flesh of the face. The cranium has eight bones: occipital, two temporal, two parietal, frontal, sphenoid, and ethmoid. The face has 14 bones, the main ones being two maxillae, two nasal, two zygoma, two lacrimal, and the mandible.

slime mould The plasmodial slime mould *Badhamia* on a log. The slime mould is able to move very slowly along the log in search of food. *K G Preston-Mafham/Premaphotos Wildlife*

Sorbian in Germany, and Polish and its related dialects); and the eastern group (Russian, Ukrainian, and Belarusian).

There is such a high degree of uniformity among the Slavic languages that scholars speak of a 'dialect continuum' in which the users of one variety understand fairly well much of what is said in other varieties. Some Slavic languages, like Polish, are written in the Roman alphabet while others, like Russian, use the Cyrillic alphabet.

'In a battle nothing is ever as good or as bad as the first reports of excited men would have it.'

WILLIAM SLIM
Unofficial History

sleep state of natural unconsciousness and activity that occurs at regular intervals in most mammals and birds, though there is considerable variation in the amount of time spent sleeping. Sleep differs from hibernation in that it occurs daily rather than seasonally, and involves less drastic reductions in metabolism. The function of sleep is unclear. People deprived of sleep become irritable, uncoordinated, forgetful, hallucinatory, and even psychotic.

In humans, sleep is linked with hormone levels and specific brain electrical activity, including delta waves, quite different from the brain's waking activity. REM (rapid eye movement) phases, associated with dreams, occur at regular intervals during sleep, when the eyes move rapidly beneath closed lids.

sleeping pill any ◊sedative that induces sleep; in small doses, such drugs may relieve anxiety.

sleeping sickness or ***trypanosomiasis*** infectious disease of tropical Africa, a form of ◊trypanosomiasis. Early symptoms include fever, headache, and chills, followed by ◊anaemia and joint pains. Later, the disease attacks the central nervous system, causing drowsiness, lethargy, and, if left untreated, death. Sleeping sickness is caused by either of two trypanosomes, *Trypanosoma gambiense* or *T. rhodesiense*. Control is by eradication of the tsetse fly, which transmits the disease to humans. Sleeping sickness in cattle is called nagana.

Sleep Wayne 1948– . English dancer. He was a principal dancer with the Royal Ballet 1973–83. He formed his own company, Dash, 1980, and in 1983 adapted his TV *Hot Shoe Show* for the stage, fusing classical, modern, jazz, tap, and disco. He also acted in the musical *Cats* 1981.

slide rule mathematical instrument with pairs of logarithmic sliding scales, used for rapid calculations, including multiplication, division, and the extraction of square roots. It has been largely superseded by the electronic calculator.

It was invented 1622 by the English mathematician William Oughtred. A later version was devised by the French army officer Amédée Mannheim (1831–1906).

Sligo county of the Republic of Ireland, in the province of Connacht, situated on the Atlantic coast of NW Ireland; area 1,800 sq km/695 sq mi; population (1991) 54,700. It is hilly. There is livestock and dairy farming.

Slim William Joseph, 1st Viscount Slim 1891–1970. British field marshal in World War II. He served in the North Africa campaign 1941 then commanded the 1st Burma Corps 1942–45, stemming the Japanese invasion of India, and then forcing them out of Burma (now Myanmar) 1945. He was governor general of Australia 1953–60.

slime mould or ***myxomycete*** extraordinary organism that shows some features of ◊fungus and some of ◊protozoa. Slime moulds are not closely related to any other group, although they are often classed, for convenience, with the fungi. There are two kinds, cellular slime moulds and plasmodial slime moulds, differing in their complex life cycles.

Cellular slime moulds go through a phase of living as single cells, looking like amoebae, and feed by engulfing the bacteria found in rotting wood, dung, or damp soil. When a food supply is exhausted, up to 100,000 of these amoebae form into a colony resembling a single sluglike animal and migrate to a fresh source of bacteria. The colony then takes on the aspect of a fungus, and forms long-stalked fruiting bodies which release spores. These germinate to release amoebae, which repeat the life cycle.

Plasmodial slime moulds have a more complex life cycle involving sexual reproduction. They form a slimy mass of protoplasm with no internal cell walls, which slowly spreads over the bark or branches of trees.

slip decoration traditional decoration for earthenware with designs trailed in a thin, smooth mixture of clay and water (slip) or incised through a coating of slip. It is usually finished with a transparent lead glaze.

White trailed slip is characteristic of the early earthenware made by Reginald Wells (1877–1951). The English potter Bernard Leach used trailed slip designs on *raku* ware when he worked in Japan in the early 20th century and revived the technique of moulding plates with slip decorations in the UK in the 1920s.

Sloane Hans 1660–1753. British physician, born in County Down, Ireland. He settled in London, and in 1721 founded the Chelsea Physic Garden. He was president of the Royal College of Physicians 1719–35, and in 1727 succeeded the physicist Isaac ◊Newton as president of the Royal Society. His library, which he bequeathed to the nation, formed the nucleus of the British Museum.

sloe fruit of the ◊blackthorn.

sloth slow-moving South American mammal, about 70 cm/2.5 ft long, family Bradypodidae, order Edentata. Sloths are greyish brown and have small rounded heads, rudimentary tails, and prolonged forelimbs. Each foot has long curved claws adapted to clinging upside down from trees. On the ground the animals cannot walk, but drag themselves along. They are vegetarian.

The hair is brown, long, coarse and shaggy. An alga lives in it, and in damp weather turns the hair green, which helps the animal to blend in with its leafy background. Sloths are nocturnal animals. They usually live alone in the treetops, eating leaves. They give birth to one young at a time, which spends its first few weeks clinging to its mother's hair.

Slovakia one of the two republics that formed the Federative Republic of Czechoslovakia. Settled in the 5th–6th centuries by Slavs; it was occupied by the Magyars in the 10th century, and was part of the kingdom of Hungary until 1918, when it became a province of Czechoslovakia. Slovakia was a puppet state under German domination 1939–45, and was abolished as an administrative division in 1949. Its capital and chief town was Bratislava. It was re-established as a sovereign state, the ◊Slovak Republic, after the break-up of Czechoslovakia 1993.

Slovak literature The literature of the Slovak republic and people. Slovakian emerged as a literary language only in the 18th century. It served as a

slow-worm The normal coloration for the slow-worm (or blind worm) *Anguis fragilis* is a mixture of fawns and brown, but some are a dark blue-grey colour with paler blue spotting. Living on heathland and in open woods, they are found in many parts of Europe. *Premaphotos Wildlife* medium for literary patriots such as L'udovít Štur (1815–1856), and came of age in the 20th century in fine lyric poetry such as that of Ivan Krasko (1876–1958), a symbolist, and Vojtech Mihálik (1926–).

Like ◊Czech literature, Slovak literature suffered repression under the communist regime of Czechoslovakia 1948–89 but is enjoying a revival since the secession of the independent Slovak republic 1993.

Slovak Republic landlocked country in central Europe, bounded N by Poland, E by the Ukraine, S by Hungary, W by Austria, and NW by the Czech Republic. *See country box below.*

Slovene the Slavic people of Slovenia and parts of the Austrian Alpine provinces of Styria and Carinthia. There are 1.5–2 million speakers of Slovene, a language belonging to the South Slavonic branch of the Indo-European family. The Slovenes use the Roman alphabet and the majority belong to the Roman Catholic Church.

Slovenia or ***Slovenija*** country in S central Europe, bounded N by Austria, E by Hungary, W by Italy, and S by Croatia. *See country box on p. 984.*

Slovo Joe 1926–1995. South African lawyer and politician, general secretary of the South African Communist Party 1986–91, Chief of Staff of Umkhonto we Sizwe (Spear of the Nation), the armed wing of the African National Congress (ANC) 1985–87, and minister of housing in President Mandela's government 1994–95. He was one of the most influential figures in the ANC, and spent 27 years in exile.

slow-worm harmless species of lizard *Anguis fragilis*, once common in Europe, now a protected species in Britain. Superficially resembling a snake, it is distinguished by its small mouth and movable eyelids. It is about 30 cm/1 ft long, and eats worms and slugs.

SLR abbreviation for ***single-lens reflex***, a type of ◊camera in which the image can be seen through the lens before a picture is taken. A small mirror directs light entering the lens to the viewfinder.

When a picture is taken the mirror moves rapidly aside to allow the light to reach the film. The SLR allows different lenses, such as close-up or zoom lenses, to be used because the photographer can see exactly what is being focused on.

slug air-breathing gastropod related to the snails, but with absent or much reduced shell. Slugs are often a pest to crops and garden plants. *See illustration on p. 984.*

Sluis, Battle of (or ***Sluys***)1340 naval victory for England over France which marked the beginning of the Hundred Years' War. England took control of the English Channel and seized 200 great ships from the French navy of Philip IV; there were 30,000 French casualties.

slurry form of manure composed mainly of liquids. Slurry is collected and stored on many farms, especially when large numbers of animals are kept in factory units (see ◊factory farming). When slurry tanks are accidentally or deliberately breached, large amounts can spill into rivers, killing fish and causing ◊eutrophication. Some slurry is spread on fields as a fertilizer.

Sluter Claus c. 1380–1406. N European Gothic sculptor. Probably of Dutch origin, he was active in Dijon, France. His work includes the *Well of Moses* about 1395–1403 (now in the grounds of a hospital in Dijon) and the kneeling mourners for the tomb of his patron Philip the Bold, Duke of Burgundy (Dijon Museum and Cleveland Museum, Ohio). In its striking realism, his work marks a break with the ◊International Gothic style prevalent at the time.

small arms one of the two main divisions of firearms: guns that can be carried by hand. The first small arms were portable handguns in use in the late 14th century, supported on the ground and ignited by hand. Today's small arms range from breech-loading single-shot rifles and shotguns to sophisticated automatic and semiautomatic weapons.

The matchlock, which evolved during the 15th century, used a match of tow and saltpetre gripped by an S-shaped lever, which was rocked towards the touch hole with one finger, enabling the gun to be held, aimed, and fired in much the same way as today. The match was replaced by the wheel lock, about 1515, in which a shower of sparks was produced by a spring-drawn steel wheel struck by iron pyrites. This cumbersome and expensive mechanism evolved into the simpler flintlock in about 1625, operated by flint striking steel and in general use for 200 years until a dramatic advance, the 'percussion cap', invented 1810, removed the need for external igniters. From then on, weapons were fired by a small explosive detonator placed behind or within the base of the bullet, struck by a built-in hammer.

The principles of rifling, breech-loading, and the repeater, although known since the 16th century, were not successfully exploited until the 19th century. An early rifle with bolt action was the Lee-Metford 1888, followed by the Lee-Enfield, both having a magazine beneath the breech, containing a number of cartridges. A modified model is still used by the British army. US developments favoured the repeater (such as the Winchester) in which the fired case was extracted and ejected, the hammer cocked, and a new charge inserted into the chamber, all by one reciprocation of a finger lever. In the semiautomatic, part of the explosion energy performs the same operations: the Garand, long used by the US army, is of this type. Completely automatic weapons were adopted during World War II. Improvements since then have concentrated on making weapons lighter and faster-firing, as with the M-16, extensively used by US troops in the Vietnam War.

There are only two sorts of people in life you can trust – good Christians and good Communists.

Joe Slovo
Quoted in the *Independent* 4 Nov 1988

SLOVAK REPUBLIC

Slovak Republic

national name *Slovenská Republika*
area 49,035 sq km/18,940 sq mi
capital Bratislava
major towns/cities Košice, Nitra, Prešov, Banská Bystrica, Zilina, Trnava
physical features Western range of the Carpathian Mountains including Tatra and Beskids in N; Danube plain in S; numerous lakes and mineral springs
head of state vacant from March 1998.
head of government Vladimir Meciar from 1994
political system emergent democracy
administrative divisions four regions
political parties Movement for a Democratic Slovakia (MDS), centre-left, nationalist-populist; Democratic Union of Slovakia (DUS), centrist; Christian Democratic Movement (KSDH), right of centre; Slovak National Party (SNP), nationalist; Party of the Democratic Left (PDL), reform socialist, (ex-communist); Association of Workers' of Slovakia, left-wing; Hungarian Coalition, ethnic Hungarian
population 5,347,000 (1996 est)
population growth rate 0.4% (1990–95); 0.4% (2000–05)
ethnic distribution 87% ethnic Slovak, 11% ethnic Hungarian (Magyar); small Czech, Moravian, Silesian, and Romany communities
life expectancy 68 (men), 75 (women)
literacy 100%
language Slovak (official)
religions Roman Catholic (over 50%), Lutheran, Reformist, Orthodox
currency Slovak koruna (based on Czechoslovak koruna)
GDP (US $) 12.37 billion (1994)
growth rate 4.2% (1994)
exports iron ore, copper, mercury, magnesite, armaments, chemicals, textiles, machinery

HISTORY
9th C Part of the kingdom of Greater Moravia, in the Czech lands to the W, founded by the Slavic Prince Sviatopluk; Christianity adopted.
906 Came under Magyar (Hungarian) domination and adopted Roman Catholicism.
1526 Came under Austrian Habsburg rule.
1867 With creation of dual Austro-Hungarian monarchy, came under separate Hungarian rule; a policy of forced Magyarization stimulated a revival of Slovak national consciousness.
1918 Austro-Hungarian Empire dismembered; Slovaks joined Czechs to form independent state of Czechoslovakia. Slovak-born Tomas Masaryk remained president until 1935, but political and economic power became concentrated in the Czech lands.
1939 Germany annexed Czechoslovakia; became an Axis puppet state under the Slovak autonomist leader Monsignor Jozef Tiso; Jews persecuted.
1944 Popular revolt against German rule (the 'Slovak Uprising').
1945 Liberated from German rule by Soviet troops; Czechoslovakia re-established.
1948 Communists assumed power in Czechoslovakia.
1950s Heavy industry introduced into previously rural Slovakia; Slovak nationalism and the Catholic Church forcibly suppressed.
1968–69 'Prague Spring' political reforms introduced by the Slovak-born Communist Party leader Alexander Dubček; Warsaw Pact forces invaded Czechoslovakia to stamp out the reforms; the Slovak Socialist Republic, with autonomy over local affairs, created under new federal constitution; the Slovak-born Gustáv Husák became Communist Party leader in Czechoslovakia.
1989 Prodemocracy demonstrations in Bratislava; new political parties, including the centre-left People Against Violence (PAV), formed and later legalized; Communist Party stripped of powers; new government formed, with ex-dissident playwright Václav Havel as president.
1990 Slovak nationalists polled strongly in multiparty elections, with Vladimir Meciar (PAV) becoming prime minister.
1991 Increasing Slovak separatism, as the economy, exposed to market forces, deteriorated. Meciar formed the PAV splinter group, Movement for a Democratic Slovakia (HZDS), pledging greater autonomy for Slovakia. Pro-Meciar rallies in Bratislava followed his dismissal.
1992 Meciar returned to power following electoral victory for HZDS. Slovak parliament's declaration of sovereignty led to resignation of Havel; 'velvet divorce' agreement on separate Czech and Slovak states established a free-trade customs union.
1993 Slovak Republic entered United Nations and Council of Europe as a sovereign state, with Meciar prime minister and Michal Kovac, formerly of the HZDS, president.
1994 Joined NATO's 'Partnership for Peace' programme. Meciar ousted on a no-confidence vote, but later returned after new elections, heading a 'red-brown' coalition government that included ultranationalists and socialists.
1995 Second wave of mass privatization postponed; Slovak made sole official language; Treaty of Friendship and Cooperation signed with Hungary, easing tensions among Hungarian minority community.
1997 Referendum on NATO membership and direct presidential elections declared invalid.
1998 Presidency vacant; presidential powers assumed by Prime Minister Meciar, after failure to elect new president.

SEE ALSO Austro-Hungarian Empire; Czechoslovakia; Czech Republic

The Abolition of Slavery

A 19th-century illustration of two men being taken captive to be sold as slaves in the Gambia. Millions of Africans were sent to North and South America to work as slaves in the 17th–19th centuries. *Philip Sauvain*

An escaped slave, Frederick Douglass (born Frederick Augustus Washington Bailey) played a major role in fighting for the abolition of slavery in the southern states of the USA. His volumes of autobiography gave a vivid and moving account of slavery, and countered the argument that slaves were born intellectually inferior. *Library of Congress*

The slave trade between Africa and the Americas began in the 16th century as European settlers started to colonize the New World. By the time the Atlantic slave trade was abolished in the 19th century, around 11–12 million African men, women, and children had been transported to the American slave colonies – some 70% of them destined, initially, for the sugar fields of Brazil and the West Indies. By 1820, only 2 million of the 12 million people who had migrated to the Americas since Columbus were Europeans; the rest were Africans.

The profit motive

The labour of black slaves opened frontiers, converting the fertile wilderness of the New World to profitable agriculture. Harvests of sugar, rum, tobacco, rice, and other staples found a ready and ever-growing European market. The beneficiaries were the white settlers of the New World (among them, the English, Spanish, and Danish) and their European investors. Profits helped the colonial societies to establish themselves and also flowed back to Europe. Slave-grown sugar transformed the Western diet, creating a taste for sweet drinks and food; the use of tobacco spread ever wider. Later, slave-grown cotton helped to clothe the Western world.

Slavery's economic and social benefits appeared to be so obvious, so universal, that initial ethical doubts were rapidly overcome. Who could deny that slavery brought prosperity to all involved – except, of course, to the slaves? Few spoke against it, and their voices were usually drowned by the clamour for yet more slave-grown profit.

The seeds of opposition

George Fox, the founder of the Quakers, had denounced slavery as early as the 1670s. In the 1700s, Quakers on both sides of the Atlantic – who were few in number but often held economically powerful positions – followed his lead. In the mid-1700s, the writers of the Enlightenment, arguing for the expansion of social and political rights, raised both moral and economic questions about slavery. The framing of the American Constitution, following American independence from Britain in 1776, also put slavery in the spotlight: how did it fit into a new society committed to democratic ideals? Even the profit argument for slavery came under fire with Adam Smith's *The Wealth of Nations* (1776), which firmly established the importance of a free trade system – the very opposite of the slave trade, which had traditionally been highly protected.

There was no sign, however, that slavery would simply fade away; on the contrary, it thrived. In the USA the rise of the cotton industry in the new states led to the revival of slavery: from around 698,000 slaves in 1790 the number had risen to almost 4 million by 1860.

Mounting pressure for reform

The effective attack on slavery came, ironically, from Britain – the country that had perfected the Atlantic slave system. The British had shipped more Africans

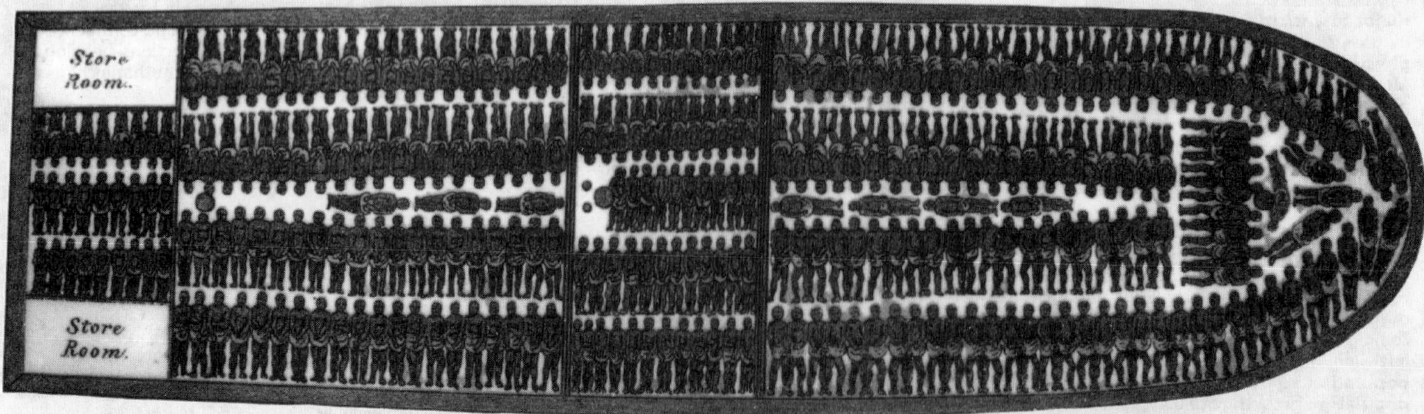

The inhuman conditions on a 19th-century slave ship are seen in this lithograph showing how the greatest number of people could be packed into one deck of such a ship. Fresh air and sanitation were almost non-existent, disease travelled rapidly among the slaves, and many of them died. *Corbis*

across the Atlantic than any other nation: about 2 million in the course of the 18th century alone, on some 11,000 voyages.

Few parts of Britain were not involved in this trade. Ships carrying local produce sailed from the major ports (Liverpool, London, Bristol, Glasgow) to West Africa. There, the ships' cargo was exchanged for Africans who had been purchased by local slave traders. The slaves were then transported to the Americas where they were sold to work on the plantations. To complete the triangular trade, the ships were loaded with sugar, cotton, and tobacco bought in return for the slaves, and returned to Europe.

Britain's efficient ports proved to be the Atlantic slave trade's Achilles' heel. They provided the opportunity for slavery's opponents to regulate – and ultimately to ban – the carrying of slaves. In 1787, Quakers launched a campaign to improve conditions on the slave ships. While the campaigners gained particularly strong support from members of Nonconformist chapels and women, they also reached a wider, increasingly literate public who were shocked by exposures published in the popular press. Thousands of antislave trade petitions flooded into Parliament.

The move towards abolition faltered temporarily towards the end of the 18th century with government fears of social upheaval, following the French Revolution and the 1791 slave rebellion in Haiti. But in 1807, in the face of fierce opposition from slave-traders and plantation owners, the British finally abolished their slave trade.

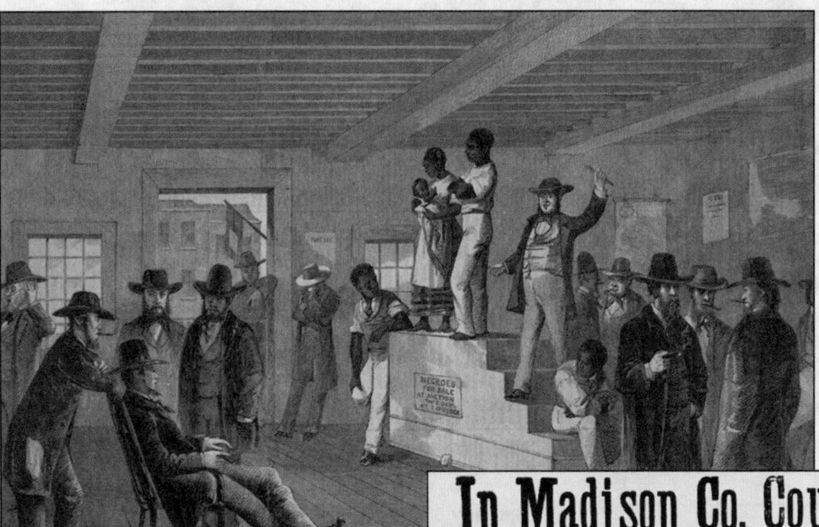

Slaves were often sold by advertised auction – the illustration shows one held in 1861, at which around 50 men and women were sold for prices ranging from $488 to $1450. *Auction: Image Select (UK) Ltd; advertisement: Corbis*

In Madison Co. Court!

LARGE SALE OF

LAND AND NEGROES

Petition for Sale of Land and Slaves.

Albert G. McClellan and others
vs.
Mary Vaden and husband, G. W. Vaden and others, distributees of Isabella McClellan, dec'd.

In the above cause, the undersigned, Clerk of the County Court of Madison county, Tenn., as commissioner, will expose to public sale on Saturday, 24th of March next, at the Court house, in the town of Jackson, that most desirable and conveniently situated Tract of Land, known as the McClellan farm, contianing

1000 ACRES.

in one body, and lying within a mile and a half of the town of Jackson. Also, at the same time and place,

18 Or 20 NEGROES,

consisting of men, women and children. The land will be divided into tracts previous to the day of sale, and each division will be sold seperately.

Terms of sale.—Land on a credit of one and two years, and the negroes upon a credit of 12 months from the day of sale. Notes, with good security, will be required of purchasers, and lien retained on both land and negroes for the purchase money. Title t. the land and negroes indisputable.

P. C. McCOWAT,

An end to slavery?

Although the slave trade had ended, there were still 600,000 slaves working on British-owned plantations in the West Indies. The campaigners had hoped that, by cutting off the supply of new slaves, they would force the plantation owners to treat their slaves better. But major slave rebellions (Barbados 1816, Demerara 1823, and Jamaica 1831–32) told of continuing repression and the slaves' resistance to bondage.

From the mid-1820s the British antislavery campaign revived, once again driven forward by Nonconformists and women. The impact of Christian missionaries in the Caribbean also played a part as black Christians demanded their freedom. When slavery was finally abolished in the British Empire, partially in 1833 and completely in 1838, the slave owners were compensated for their loss by a total of £20 million. The slaves had to be content with just their freedom.

A leading member of the Evangelical Movement, which sought to promote Christian values in late 18th–early 19th-century English society, William Wilberforce fought from 1788 to abolish British involvement in the slave trade. Having achieved this in 1807, he began campaigning for the abolition of the slave trade abroad and the total abolition of slavery. Slavery in the British Empire ended in 1833, the year of his death. *Corbis*

Slavery and the American Civil War

Having won the battle at home, British abolitionists turned their attention to the USA, and in particular the cotton-growing Southern states. American antislavery became a crusade, with abolitionists criss-crossing the Atlantic as they built up the pressure for change. But the supporters of slavery dug in, convinced of their own moral, religious, and economic justification. Proslavery arguments had taken on a racist veneer, but their basis remained economic: slave-based cotton was profitable. Moreover, the fight against slavery was seen as an attack on the Southern way of life itself.

This siege mentality led to the South's secession from the Union, and the American Civil War. Although the war was about secession, the conflict focused on the issue of slavery. In the disruptions of the war, many American slaves took the opportunity to flee from their former masters. In January 1863 US president Abraham Lincoln issued the Emancipation Proclamation, granting freedom to all slaves in the rebellious states; and, two years later, the Thirteenth Amendment to the American Constitution confirmed freedom throughout the USA.

After abolition

Slavery lived on in Cuba and Brazil until the 1880s. In the British Empire, the Foreign Office and the Royal Navy imposed a slavery ban on often reluctant societies with all the vigour of a poacher turned gamekeeper. The West has turned its back on its long and ignoble slave-trading past. Slavery still survives in societies where deep-seated social and religious practice, combined with wretched poverty, conspire to prolong it. But few slave systems can compare with the Atlantic slave trade, which effectively transformed the face of three continents.

JAMES WALVIN

SEE ALSO

black; Brown, John; Civil War, American; Emancipation Proclamation; Lincoln, Abraham; Toussaint L'Ouverture; Willberforce, William

SLOVENIA
Republic of

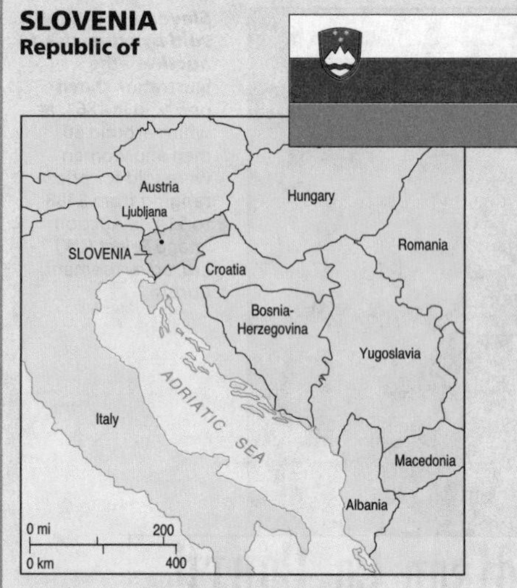

national name *Republika Slovenija*
area 20,251 sq km/7,817 sq mi
capital Ljubljana
major towns/cities Maribor, Kranj, Celji
major ports Koper
physical features mountainous; Sava and Drava rivers
head of state Milan Kučan from 1990
head of government Janez Drnovšek from 1992
political system emergent democracy
administrative divisions 62 districts
political parties Slovenian Christian Democrats (SKD), right of centre; Slovenian People's Party (SPP), conservative; Liberal Democratic Party of Slovenia (LDS), centrist; Slovenian Nationalist Party (SNS), right-wing nationalist; Democratic Party of Slovenia (LDP), left of centre; United List of Social Democrats (ZLSD) left of centre, ex-communist
population 1,946,000 (1995 est)
population growth rate 0.3% (1990–95); −0.1% (2000–05)
ethnic distribution 98% of Slovene origin, 3% ethnic Croat, and 2% Serb
life expectancy 67 (men), 75 (women)
literacy rate 99%
language Slovene, resembling Serbo-Croat, written in Roman characters
religion Roman Catholic
currency tolar
GDP (US $) 14.03 billion (1994)
growth rate 5.5% (1994)
exports grain, sugar beet, livestock, timber, cotton and woollen textiles, steel, vehicles, pharmaceuticals, cosmetics

HISTORY
1st C BC Came under Roman rule.
AD 395 In division of Roman Empire, stayed in W half, along with Croatia and Bosnia.
6th C Settled by the Slovene South Slavs.
7th C Adopted Christianity as Roman Catholics.
8th–9th Cs Under the successive rule of the Franks and dukes of Bavaria.
907–55 Came under Hungarian domination.
1335 Absorbed in the Austro-Hungarian Habsburg Empire, as part of the Austrian crownlands of Carniola, Styria, and Carinthia.
1848 Slovene struggle for independence began.
1918 On the collapse of Habsburg Empire, Slovenia united with Serbia, Croatia, and Montenegro to form the 'Kingdom of Serbs, Croats and Slovenes', under Serbian Karageorgevic dynasty.
1929 The kingdom became known as Yugoslavia.
1941–45 Occupied by the Axis powers, Nazi Germany, and Italy during World War II; anti-Nazi Slovene Liberation Front formed and became allies of Marshal Tito's communist-led Partisans.
1945 Became a constituent republic of Yugoslav Socialist Federal Republic.
mid-1980s The Slovenian Communist Party liberalized itself and agreed to free elections. Yugoslav counterintelligence (KOV) began repression.
1989 Constitution changed to allow secession from federation.
1990 Nationalist Democratic Opposition of Slovenia (DEMOS) coalition secured victory in first multiparty parliamentary elections; Milan Kučan, a reform communist, became president. Sovereignty declared. Independence overwhelmingly approved in referendum.
1991 Seceded from Yugoslav federation, along with Croatia; 100 killed after Yugoslav federal army intervened; cease-fire brokered by European Community (EC) brought withdrawal of Yugoslav army.
1992 Janez Drnovšek, a centrist Liberal Democrat, appointed prime minister; independence recognized by EC and USA. Admitted into United Nations. Liberal Democrats and Christian Democrats won assembly elections.
1996 Governing coalition weakened by withdrawal of ZLSD. LDS failed to win overall majority in assembly elections.

SEE ALSO Austro-Hungarian Empire; Croatia; Serbia; Yugoslavia

smallpox acute, highly contagious viral disease, marked by aches, fever, vomiting, and skin eruptions leaving pitted scars. Widespread vaccination programmes have eradicated this often fatal disease.

It was endemic in Europe until the development of vaccination by Edward ◊Jenner about 1800, and remained so in Asia, where a virulent form of the disease (variola major) entailed a fatality rate of 30% until the World Health Organization (WHO) campaign from 1967, which resulted in its virtual eradication by 1980. The campaign was estimated to have cost $300 million/£200 million, and was the organization's biggest health success to date.

smart drug any drug or combination of nutrients (vitamins, amino acids, minerals, and sometimes herbs) said to enhance the functioning of the brain, increase mental energy, lengthen the span of attention, and improve the memory. As yet there is no scientific evidence to suggest that these drugs have any significant effect on healthy people.

The description is also applied to existing drugs claimed to improve mental performance but which are legally prescribed for other purposes. These include beta-blockers (prescribed for some heart disease), phenytoin (epilepsy), and L-dopa (Parkinson's disease).

smart weapon programmable bomb or missile that can be guided to its target by laser technology, TV homing technology, or terrain-contour matching (TERCOM). A smart weapon relies on its pinpoint accuracy to destroy a target rather than on the size of its warhead.

Smart weapons were first used on the battlefield in the Gulf War 1991.

smell sense that responds to chemical molecules in the air. It works by having receptors for particular chemical groups, into which the airborne chemicals must fit to trigger a message to the brain.

A sense of smell is used to detect food and to communicate with other animals (see ◊pheromone and ◊scent gland). Humans can distinguish between about 10,000 different smells. Aquatic animals can sense chemicals in water, but whether this sense should be described as 'smell' or 'taste' is debatable. See also ◊nose; ◊sense organ.

smelt small fish, usually marine, although some species are freshwater. They occur in Europe and North America. The most common European smelt is the sparling *Osmerus eperlanus*.

smelting processing a metallic ore in a furnace to produce the metal. Oxide ores such as iron ore are smelted with coke (carbon), which reduces the ore into metal and also provides fuel for the process.

A substance such as limestone is often added during smelting to facilitate the melting process and to form a slag, which dissolves many of the impurities present.

Smetana Bedřich 1824–1884. Bohemian composer. He established a Czech nationalist style in, for example, the operas *Prodaná Nevěsta/The Bartered Bride* 1866 and *Dalibor* 1868, and the symphonic suite *Má Vlast/My Country* 1875–80. He conducted the National Theatre of Prague 1866–74.

Smith Adam 1723–1790. Scottish economist. He is often regarded as the founder of political economy. His *The Wealth of Nations* 1776 defined national wealth in terms of consumable goods and the labour that produces them, rather than in terms of bullion, as prevailing economic theories assumed. The ultimate cause of economic growth is explained by the division of labour – dividing a production process into several repetitive operations, each carried out by different workers, is more efficient. Smith advocated the free working of individual enterprise, and the necessity of 'free trade'. In *Theory of Moral Sentiments* 1759, Smith argued that the correct way to discern the morally right is to ask what a hypothetical impartial spectator would regard as fitting or proper.

Smith Bessie (Elizabeth) 1894–1937. US jazz and blues singer. Known as the 'Empress of the Blues',

slug A number of slugs, such as this giant *Trichotoxon* species from Kenya, engage in an elaborate courtship ritual, caressing and mouthing one another's faces before eventually mating. *Premaphotos Wildlife*

Smith US jazz and blues singer Bessie Smith in a photograph from the 1920s. Her sense of phrasing and rhythm, together with her effortless ability to improvise, made her one of the greatest of all jazz artists. *Corbis*

she established herself in the 1920s after she was discovered by Columbia Records. She made over 150 recordings accompanied by such greats as Louis Armstrong and Benny Goodman.

Her popularity waned in the Depression, and she died after a car crash when she was refused admission to a whites-only hospital.

Smith Ian (Douglas) 1919– . Rhodesian politician. He was a founder of the Rhodesian Front 1962 and prime minister 1964–79. In 1965 he made a unilateral declaration of Rhodesia's independence and, despite United Nations sanctions, maintained his regime with tenacity.

In 1979 he was succeeded as prime minister by Bishop Abel Muzorewa, when the country was renamed Zimbabwe. He was suspended from the Zimbabwe parliament April 1987 and resigned in May as head of the white opposition party. In 1992 he helped found a new opposition party, the United Front.

Smith John 1580–1631. English colonist. After an adventurous early life he took part in the colonization of Virginia, acting as president of the North American colony 1608–09. He explored New England in 1614, which he named, and published pamphlets on America and an autobiography. His trade with the Indians may have kept the colonists alive in the early years.

During an expedition among the American Indians he was captured, and his life is said to have been saved by the intervention of the chief's daughter ◊Pocahontas.

Smith John 1938–1994. British Labour politician, party leader 1992–94. He was trade and industry secretary 1978–79 and from 1979 held various shadow cabinet posts, culminating in that of shadow chancellor 1987–92. As leader of the opposition, he won a reputation as a man of transparent honesty and a formidable parliamentarian.

His sudden death from a heart attack shocked British politicians of all parties.

Smith John Maynard. British biologist, see ◊Maynard Smith.

Smith Joseph 1805–1844. US founder of the ◊Mormon religious sect.

Born in Vermont, he received his first religious call in 1820, and in 1827 claimed to have been granted the revelation of the *Book of Mormon* (an ancient American prophet), inscribed on gold plates and concealed a thousand years before in a hill near Palmyra, New York State. He founded the Church of Jesus Christ of Latter-day Saints in Fayette, New York, 1830. The Mormons were persecuted for their beliefs and Smith was killed by an angry mob in Illinois.

Smith Maggie (Margaret Natalie Cross) 1934– . English actress. She is notable for her commanding presence, fluting voice, and throwaway lines. Her films include *The Prime of Miss Jean Brodie* 1969 (Academy Award), *California Suite* 1978, *A Private Function* 1984, *A Room with a View* and *The Lonely Passion of Judith Hearne* both 1987, and *Sister Act* 1992.

Smith Stevie (Florence Margaret) 1902–1971. English poet and novelist. She published her first book, *Novel on Yellow Paper*, 1936, and her first collection of poems, *A Good Time Was Had by All*, 1937. She wrote a further eight volumes of eccentrically direct verse illustrated with her equally eccentric line drawings, including *Not Waving but Drowning* 1957, and two more novels. *Collected Poems* was published 1975.

Smithson Alison Margaret (born Gill) (1928–1993) and Peter Denham (1923–) English architects, teachers, and theorists. They are known for their development in the 1950s and 1960s of the style known as ◊Brutalism, for example, Hunstanton School, Norfolk, 1954. Notable among their other designs are the Economist Building, London, 1964, and Robin Hood Gardens, London, 1968–72.

Their style reflected the influence of ◊Le Corbusier and ◊Mies van der Rohe in its symmetry and clarity of form.

smog natural fog containing impurities, mainly nitrogen oxides (NO_x) and volatile organic compounds (VOCs) from domestic fires, industrial furnaces, certain power stations, and internal-combustion engines (petrol or diesel). It can cause substantial illness and loss of life, particularly among chronic bronchitics, and damage to wildlife.

Photochemical smog is mainly prevalent in the summer as it is caused by chemical reaction between strong sunlight and vehicle exhaust fumes. Such smogs create a build-up of ozone and nitrogen oxides which cause adverse symptoms, including coughing and eye irritation, and in extreme cases can kill.

The London smog of 1952 lasted for five days and killed more than 4,000 people from heart and lung diseases. The use of smokeless fuels, the treatment of effluent, and penalties for excessive smoke from poorly maintained and operated vehicles can be effective in reducing smog but it still occurs in many cities throughout the world. ▷ *See feature on pp. 858–859.*

smokeless fuel fuel that does not give off any smoke when burned, because all the carbon is fully oxidized to carbon dioxide (CO_2). Natural gas, oil, and coke are smokeless fuels.

smoking method of preserving fresh oily meats (such as pork and goose) or fish (such as herring and salmon). Before being smoked, the food is first salted or soaked in brine, then hung to dry. Meat is hot-smoked over a fast-burning wood fire, which is covered with sawdust, producing thick smoke and partly cooking the meat. Fish may be hot-smoked or cold-smoked over a slow-burning wood fire, which does not cook it. Modern refrigeration techniques mean that food does not need to be smoked to help it keep, so factory-smoked foods tend to be smoked just enough to give them a smoky flavour, with colours added to give them the appearance of traditionally smoked food.

smoking inhaling the fumes from burning substances, generally ◊tobacco in the form of ◊cigarettes. The practice can be habit-forming and is dangerous to health, since carbon monoxide and other toxic materials result from the combustion process. A direct link between lung cancer and tobacco smoking was established 1950; the habit is also linked to respiratory and coronary heart diseases. In the West, smoking is now forbidden in many public places because even passive smoking – breathing in fumes from other people's cigarettes – can be harmful.

health risks The National Health Service spends up to £500 million a year caring for people with severe illnesses directly related to smoking. Approximately 50% of smokers die as a result of smoking-related diseases.

passive smoking Cigarette smoke contains at least 40 known ◊carcinogens. US research shows that one carcinogen, found only in tobacco products, can be detected in the urine of nonsmokers after exposure for 90 minutes to conditions typical of a smoky room. In May 1996 it was reported by US researchers that 88% of US nonsmokers have detectable levels of the nicotine breakdown product cotinine in their blood. Studies show that passive smoking is a cause of lung cancer. Children whose parents smoke suffer an increased risk of asthma and respiratory infections. It is estimated that around 30,000 nonsmokers die annually as a result of passive smoking.

Smollett Tobias George 1721–1771. Scottish novelist. He wrote the picaresque novels *Roderick Random* 1748, *Peregrine Pickle* 1751, *Ferdinand Count Fathom* 1753, *Sir Launcelot Greaves* 1760–62, and *Humphrey Clinker* 1771. His novels are full of gusto and vivid characterization.

smut in botany, any parasitic ◊fungus of the order Ustilaginales, which infects flowering plants, particularly cereal grasses.

Smuts Jan Christian 1870–1950. South African politician and soldier; prime minister 1919–24 and 1939–48. He supported the Allies in both world wars and was a member of the British imperial war cabinet 1917–18.

During the Second ◊South African War (1899–1902) Smuts commanded the Boer forces in his native Cape Colony. He subsequently worked for reconciliation between the Boers and the British. On the establishment of the Union of South Africa, he became minister of the interior 1910–12 and defence minister 1910–20. During World War I he commanded the South African forces in E Africa 1916–17. He was prime minister 1919–24 and minister of justice 1933–39; on the outbreak of World War II he succeeded General Hertzog as premier. He was made a field marshal in 1941.

Smyrna ancient city near the modern Turkish port of ◊Izmir. The earliest remains date from the 3rd millennium BC, and excavations have revealed that by the 8th century BC the city had a circuit of defensive walls. This is one of the earliest signs of the revival of Greek culture after the collapse of the ◊Mycenaean civilization.

snail air-breathing gastropod mollusc with a spiral shell. There are thousands of species, on land and in water. The typical snails of the genus *Helix* have two species in Europe. The common garden snail *H. aspersa* is very destructive to plants.

The Roman snail *H. pomatia* is farmed for the gourmet food market. Overcollection has depleted the population. The French eat as much as 5 kg/11 lb of snails a head each year.

snake reptile of the suborder Serpentes of the order Squamata, which also includes lizards. Snakes are characterized by an elongated limbless body, possibly evolved because of subterranean ancestors. One of the striking internal modifications is the absence or greatly reduced size of the left lung. The skin is covered in scales, which are markedly wider underneath where they form. There are 3,000 species found in the tropical and temperate zones, but none in New Zealand, Ireland, Iceland, and near the poles. All snakes are carnivorous, and often camouflaged for better concealment in hunting as well as for their own protection. In all except a few species, scales are an essential aid to locomotion.

senses Detailed vision is limited at a distance, though movement is immediately seen; hearing is restricted to ground vibrations (sound waves are not perceived); the sense of touch is acute; besides the sense of smell through the nasal passages, the flickering tongue picks up airborne particles which are then passed to special organs in the mouth for investigation; and some (rattlesnakes) have a cavity between eye and nostril which is sensitive to infrared rays (useful in locating warm-blooded prey in the dark).

reproduction Some are oviparous and others ovoviviparous, that is, the eggs are retained in the oviducts until development is complete; in both cases the young are immediately self-sufficient.

species The majority of snakes belong to the Colubridae, chiefly harmless, such as the common grass snake of Europe, but including the deadly African boomslang *Dispholidus typus*. The venomous families include the Elapidae, comprising the true ◊cobras, the New World coral snakes, and the Australian taipan, copper-head, and death adder; the Viperidae (see ◊viper); and the Hydrophiidae, aquatic sea-snakes.

‘To found a great empire for the sole purpose of raising up a people of customers, may at first sight appear a project fit only for a nation of shopkeepers. It is, however, a project altogether unfit for a nation of shopkeepers; but extremely fit for a nation that is governed by shopkeepers.’

ADAM SMITH
The Wealth of Nations

‘I was much too far out all my life / And not waving but drowning.’

STEVIE SMITH
‘Not Waving but Drowning’

Among the more primitive snakes are the Boidae, which still show links with the lizards and include the boa constrictor, anaconda, and python.

Snake tributary of the Columbia River, in NW USA; length 1,670 km/1,038 mi. It flows 65 km/40 mi through Hell's Canyon, one of the deepest gorges in the world.

snapdragon perennial herbaceous plant of the genus *Antirrhinum*, family Scrophulariaceae, with spikes of brightly coloured two-lipped flowers.

Snell's law of refraction in optics, the rule that when a ray of light passes from one medium to another, the sine of the angle of incidence divided by the sine of the angle of refraction is equal to the ratio of the indices of refraction in the two media. For a ray passing from medium 1 to medium 2:

$$n_2/n_1 = \sin i/\sin r$$

where n_1 and n_2 are the refractive indices of the two media. The law was devised by the Dutch physicist, Willebrord Snell.

snipe marsh bird of the family Scolopacidae, order Charadriiformes closely related to the ◊woodcock. Snipes use their long, straight bills to probe marshy ground for worms, insects, and molluscs. Their nests are made on the grass, and they lay four eggs.

The cry of the birds resembles the sound 'scape-scape', and during the breeding season they make a peculiar drumming or bleating noise in their downward flight. A gamebird, the snipe has a swift and darting flight, making it a difficult target.

snooker indoor game derived from ◊billiards (via ◊pool). It is played with 22 balls: 15 red, one each of yellow, green, brown, blue, pink, and black, and one white cueball. A tapered pole (cue) is used to move the balls across the table. Red balls are worth one point when sunk, while the coloured balls have ascending values from two points for the yellow to seven points for the black. The world professional championship was first held in 1927. The world amateur championship was first held 1963.

The game was invented by British army officers serving with the Devonshire Regiment in Jubbulpore, India, in 1875 and derived from the game of black pool. It did not gain popularity until the 1920s when Joe ◊Davis introduced new techniques. Since then it has become one of the biggest television sports in the UK and is gaining popularity across Europe, the Far East, and North America. A season-long series of ranking tournaments culminates in the World Professional Championship at the Crucible Theatre, Sheffield, England, every April or May.

snoring loud noise during sleep made by vibration of the soft palate (the rear part of the roof of the mouth), caused by streams of air entering the nose and mouth at the same time. It is most common when the nose is partially blocked.

snowboarding art of riding across snow standing on a snowboard, a wide single ski resembling a small surf board, though with bindings to secure the feet. Snowboards can be ridden at speed on downhill runs and slalom courses, as in Alpine skiing, or used to perform jumps and other manoeuvres, a discipline known as freestyle or halfpipe riding (a halfpipe being a banked course carved out of snow). It was included for the first time at the Winter Olympic Games in 1998.

Snowdon (Welsh ***Y Wyddfa***) highest mountain in Wales, 1,085 m/3,560 ft above sea level. It consists of a cluster of five peaks. At the foot of Snowdon are the Llanberis, Aberglaslyn, and Rhyd-ddu passes. A rack railway ascends to the summit from Llanberis. Snowdonia, the surrounding mountain range, was made a national park 1951. It covers 2,188 sq km/845 sq mi of mountain, lakes, and forest land.

Snowdon Anthony Charles Robert Armstrong-Jones, 1st Earl of Snowdon 1930– . English photographer. He is especially known for his portraits. He was consultant to the Council of Industrial Design and editorial adviser to *Design Magazine* 1961–87; artistic adviser to Sunday Times Publications 1962–90; and photographer for the *Telegraph Magazine* from 1990. He has also made several films for television. In 1960 he married Princess Margaret; they were divorced 1978.

‘There is no such thing as Society. There are individual men and women, and there are families.’

On SOCIETY Margaret Thatcher quoted in *Woman's Own* 31 Oct 1987

snowdrop bulbous plant *Galanthus nivalis*, family Amaryllidaceae, native to Europe, with white, bell-shaped flowers, tinged with green, in early spring.

Snowy Mountains range in the Australian Alps, chiefly in New South Wales, near which the Snowy River rises both river and mountains are known for a hydroelectric and irrigation system.

snuff finely powdered ◊tobacco for sniffing up the nostrils (or sometimes chewed or rubbed on the gums) as a stimulant or sedative. Snuff taking was common in 17th-century England and the Netherlands, and spread in the 18th century to other parts of Europe, but was largely superseded by cigarette smoking.

Snyder Gary Sherman 1930– . US poet. He was a key figure in the poetry renaissance in San Francisco during the 1950s. He combined an early interest in ecological issues with studies of Japanese, Chinese and Native American cultures and myths. Associated with the ◊Beat Generation of writers, he was the protagonist of Jack Kerouac's novel *The Dharma Bums* 1958. Snyder's works include *Earth House Hold* 1969, the Pulitzer prize-winning poetry collection *Turtle Island* 1974, and *No Nature* 1992.

Soane John 1753–1837. English architect. His refined Neo-Classical designs anticipated contemporary taste. He designed his own house in Lincoln's Inn Fields, London, 1812–13, now the Soane Museum.

soap mixture of the sodium salts of various ◊fatty acids: palmitic, stearic, and oleic acid. It is made by the action of sodium hydroxide (caustic soda) or potassium hydroxide (caustic potash) on fats of animal or vegetable origin. Soap makes grease and dirt disperse in water in a similar manner to a ◊detergent.

soapstone compact, massive form of impure ◊talc.

Soares Mario Alberto Nobre Lopes 1924– . Portuguese socialist politician, president 1986–96. Exiled 1970, he returned to Portugal 1974, and, as leader of the Portuguese Socialist Party, was prime minister 1976–78. He resigned as party leader 1980, but in 1986 he was elected Portugal's first socialist president.

Sobchak Anatoly 1937– . Soviet centrist politician, mayor of St Petersburg 1990–96, cofounder of the Democratic Reform Movement (with former foreign minister ◊Shevardnadze), and member of the Soviet parliament 1989–91. He prominently resisted the abortive anti-Gorbachev attempted coup of Aug 1991.

Sobers Garry (Garfield St Auburn) 1936– . West Indian Test cricketer, arguably the world's finest ever all rounder. He held the world individual record for the highest Test innings with 365 not out, until beaten by Brian Lara 1994. He played county cricket for Nottinghamshire and, in a match against Glamorgan at Swansea 1968, he became the first to score six sixes in an over in first-class cricket. He played for the West Indies on 93 occasions, and was captain 39 times.

Sobieski John. Alternative name for ◊John III, king of Poland.

Social and Liberal Democrats official name for the British political party formed 1988 from the former Liberal Party and most of the Social Democratic Party. The common name for the party is the Liberal Democrats. Its leader (from July 1988) is Paddy ◊Ashdown.

social behaviour in zoology, behaviour concerned with altering the behaviour of other individuals of the same species. Social behaviour allows animals to live harmoniously in groups by establishing hierarchies of dominance to discourage disabling fighting. It may be aggressive or submissive (for example, cowering and other signals of appeasement), or designed to establish bonds (such as social grooming or preening).

The social behaviour of mammals and birds is generally more complex than that of lower organisms, and involves relationships with individually recognized animals. Thus, courtship displays allow individuals to choose appropriate mates and form the bonds necessary for successful reproduction. In the social systems of bees, wasps, ants, and termites, an individual's status and relationships with others are largely determined by its biological form, as a member of a caste of workers, soldiers, or reproductives; see ◊eusociality.

Social Chapter chapter of the 1991 ◊Maastricht Treaty on European Union relating to social policy. It required European Community (EC) member states to adopt common social policies and was intended to implement the Community Charter of the Fundamental Social Rights of Workers, which was adopted by 11 EC member states, but opposed by British prime minister Margaret Thatcher, at a summit meeting in Strasbourg Dec 1989. In the face of continued UK opposition, member states were given freedom of choice over whether or not to adopt it; only the UK declined to sign up to it. However, the British Labour Party and Liberal Democrats were committed to adopting it and the 1997 Labour government confirmed its intention to do so.

social contract the idea that government authority derives originally from an agreement between ruler and ruled in which the former agrees to provide order in return for obedience from the latter. It has been used to support both absolutism (Thomas ◊Hobbes) and democracy (John ◊Locke, Jean-Jacques ◊Rousseau).

The term was revived in the UK in 1974 when a head-on clash between the Conservative government and the trade unions resulted in a general election which enabled a Labour government to take power. It now denotes an unofficial agreement (hence also called 'social compact') between a government and organized labour that, in return for control of prices, rents, and so on, the unions would refrain from economically disruptive wage demands.

social Darwinism see ◊Darwinism, social.

social democracy political ideology or belief in the gradual evolution of a democratic ◊socialism within existing political structures. The earliest was the German Sozialdemokratische Partei (SPD) 1891 (today one of the two main German parties), which had been created 1875 by the amalgamation of other groups including August Bebel's earlier German Social Democratic Workers' Party, founded 1869. Parties along the lines of the German model were founded in the last two decades of the 19th century in a number of countries, including Austria, Belgium, the Netherlands, Hungary, Poland, and Russia. The British Labour Party is in the social democratic tradition.

Social Democratic Labour Party (SDLP) Northern Irish left-of-centre political party, formed 1970. It aims ultimately at Irish unification, but has distanced itself from violent tactics, adopting a constitutional, conciliatory role.

The SDLP, led by John Hume (1937–), was responsible for setting up the New Ireland Forum (a meeting between politicians of the Irish Republic and Northern Ireland) 1983, and for initiating talks with the leader of Sinn Féin (the political wing of the IRA), Gerry Adams, 1993, which prompted a joint UK-Irish peace initiative and set in motion a Northern Ireland cease-fire 1994–96.

Social Democratic Party (SDP) British centrist political party 1981–90, formed by members of Parliament who resigned from the Labour Party. The 1983 and 1987 general elections were fought in alliance with the Liberal Party as the Liberal/SDP Alliance. A merger of the two parties was voted for by the SDP 1987, and the new party became the ◊Social and Liberal Democrats, leaving a rump SDP that folded 1990.

social history branch of history that documents the living and working conditions of people rather than affairs of state. In recent years, television programmes, books, and museums have helped to give social history a wide appeal.

History became a serious branch of study in the 18th century, but was confined to ancient civilizations and to recent political and religious history. Only in the early 20th century did historians begin to study how people lived and worked in the past.

socialism movement aiming to establish a classless society by substituting public for private ownership of the means of production, distribution, and exchange. The term has been used to describe positions as widely apart as anarchism and social democracy. Socialist ideas appeared in classical times; in early Christianity; among later Christian sects such as the ◊Anabaptists and ◊Diggers; and, in the 18th and early 19th centuries, were put forward as systematic political aims by Jean-Jacques Rousseau, Claude Saint-Simon, François Fourier, and Robert Owen, among others. See also Karl ◊Marx and Friedrich ◊Engels.

The late 19th and early 20th centuries saw a division between those who reacted against Marxism leading to social-democratic parties and those who emphasized the original revolutionary significance of Marx's teachings. Weakened by these divisions, the second ◊International (founded 1889) collapsed in 1914, right-wing socialists in all countries supporting participation in World War I while the left opposed it. The Russian Revolution took socialism from the sphere of theory to that of practice, and was followed in 1919 by the foundation of the Third International, which completed the division between right and left. This lack of unity, in spite of the temporary successes of the popular fronts in France and Spain in 1936–38, facilitated the rise of fascism and Nazism.

After World War II socialist and communist parties tended to formal union in Eastern Europe, although the rigid communist control that ensued was later modified in some respects in, for example, Poland, Romania, and Yugoslavia. Subsequent tendencies to broaden communism were suppressed in Hungary (1956) and Czechoslovakia (1968). In 1989, however, revolutionary change throughout Eastern Europe ended this rigid control; this was followed in 1991 by the disbanding of the Soviet Communist Party and the ensuing disintegration of the Soviet Union.

Socialist Realism artistic doctrine established by the USSR during the 1930s, setting out the optimistic, socialist terms in which society should be portrayed in works of art. It applied to music and the visual arts as well as writing.

The policy was used as a means of censoring artists whose work, it was felt, did not follow the approved Stalinist party line, or was too 'Modern'. The policy was relaxed after Stalin's death but remained somewhat in force until the dissolution of the USSR 1991. Artists whose work was censured in this way included the composer Dmitri Shostakovich and the writers Alexander Solzhenitsyn and Mikhail Sholokhov.

Social Realism in painting, art that realistically depicts subjects of social concern, such as poverty and deprivation. Those described as Social Realists include: in the USA, members of the Ashcan School and Ben Shahn; in the UK, the 'kitchen-sink group', for example John Bratby; and in Mexico, the muralists José Orozco and Diego Rivera.

social science the group of academic disciplines that investigate how and why people behave the way they do, as individuals and in groups. The term originated with the 19th-century French thinker Auguste ◊Comte. The academic social sciences are generally listed as sociology, economics, anthropology, political science, and psychology.

Western thought about society has been influenced by the ideas and insights of such great theorists as Plato, Aristotle, Machiavelli, Rousseau, Hobbes, and Locke. The study of society, however, can be traced to the great intellectual period of the 18th century called the Enlightenment, and to the industrial and political revolutions of the 18th and 19th centuries, to the moral philosophy of ◊positivism. Comte attempted to establish the study of society as a scientific discipline, capable of precision and prediction in the same way as natural science, but it overlaps extensively with such subject areas as history, geography, law, philosophy, and even biology.

social security state provision of financial aid to alleviate poverty. The term 'social security' was first applied officially in the USA, in the Social Security Act 1935. In Britain it was first used officially 1944, and following the ◊Beveridge Report 1942 a series of acts was passed from 1945 to widen the scope of social security. Basic entitlements of those paying National Insurance contributions in Britain include an old-age pension, unemployment benefit, widow's pension, and payment during a period of sickness in one's working life. Other benefits include family credit, child benefit, and attendance allowance for those looking after sick or disabled people.

In the USA the term 'social security' usually refers specifically to old-age pensions. The federal government is responsible for social security (Medicare, retirement, survivors', and disability insurance); unemployment insurance is covered by a joint federal-state system for industrial workers; and welfare benefits are the responsibility of individual states, with some federal assistance.

society the organization of people into communities or groups. Social science, in particular sociology, is the study of human behaviour in a social context. Various aspects of society are discussed under ◊class, ◊community, ◊culture, ◊kinship, ◊norms, and ◊status.

Society Islands (French ***Archipel de la Société***) archipelago in ◊French Polynesia, divided into the Windward Islands and the Leeward Islands; area 1,685 sq km/650 sq mi; population (1988) 162,600. The administrative headquarters is Papeete on ◊Tahiti. The ***Windward Islands*** (French *Iles du Vent*) have an area of 1,200 sq km/460 sq mi and a population (1988) of 140,300. They comprise Tahiti, Moorea (area 132 sq km/51 sq mi; population 7,000), Maio (or Tubuai Manu; 9 sq km/3.5 sq mi; population 200), and the smaller Tetiaroa and Mehetia. The ***Leeward Islands*** (French *Iles sous le Vent*) have an area of 404 sq km/156 sq mi and a population of 22,200 (1988). They comprise the volcanic islands of Raiatea (including the main town of Uturoa), Huahine, Bora-Bora, Maupiti, Tahaa, and four small atolls. Claimed by France 1768, the group became a French protectorate 1843 and a colony 1880.

Society of Jesus official name of the Roman Catholic order commonly known as the ◊Jesuits.

sociobiology study of the biological basis of all social behaviour, including the application of population genetics (the study of the way in which the frequencies of different variants of a gene change in populations of organisms) to the evolution of behaviour. It builds on the concept of inclusive fitness, introduced by New Zealand biologist W D Hamilton, which emphasizes that the evolutionary function of behaviour is to allow an organism to contribute as many of its own ◊alleles as it can to future generations: this idea is encapsulated in the British zoologist Richard Dawkins's notion of the 'selfish gene'.

sociology systematic study of the origin and constitution of human society, in particular of social order and social change, social conflict and social problems. It studies institutions such as the family, law, and the church, as well as concepts such as norm, role, and culture. Sociology attempts to study human behaviour in its social environment according to certain underlying moral, philosophical, and political codes of behaviour. In particular, it investigates how societies reproduce themselves, develop and change, and also the nature, causes, and effects of social relations and interaction among individuals, and between individuals and groups. It is concerned with the regularities and patterns of human behaviour, and with such things as the family, law, the church, class, ethnicity and race, gender, poverty, politics, aggression, marriage, education, communication, work, social change, urbanism, health, and social movements.

Socrates c. 469–399 BC. Athenian philosopher. He wrote nothing but was immortalized in the dialogues of his pupil Plato. In his desire to combat the scepticism of the ◊sophists, Socrates asserted the possibility of genuine knowledge. In ethics, he put forward the view that the good person never knowingly does wrong. True knowledge emerges through dialogue and systematic questioning and an abandoning of uncritical claims to knowledge.

The effect of Socrates' teaching was disruptive since he opposed tyranny. Accused in 399 on charges of impiety and corruption of youth, he was condemned by the Athenian authorities to die by drinking hemlock.

soda lime powdery mixture of calcium hydroxide and sodium hydroxide or potassium hydroxide, used in medicine and as a drying agent.

Soddy Frederick 1877–1956. English physical chemist who pioneered research into atomic disintegration and coined the term ◊isotope. He was awarded a Nobel prize 1921 for investigating the origin and nature of isotopes.

The displacement law, introduced by Soddy in 1913, explains the changes in atomic mass and atomic number for all the radioactive intermediates in the decay processes.

After his chemical discoveries, Soddy spent some 40 years developing a theory of 'energy economics', which he called 'Cartesian economics'. He argued for the abolition of debt and compound interest, the nationalization of credit, and a new theory of value based on the quantity of energy contained in a thing.

sodium soft, waxlike, silver-white, metallic element, symbol Na (from Latin *natrium*), atomic number 11, relative atomic mass 22.989. It is one of the ◊alkali metals and has a very low density, being light enough to float on water. It is the sixth-most abundant element (the fourth-most abundant metal) in the Earth's crust. Sodium is highly reactive, oxidizing rapidly when exposed to air and reacting violently with water. Its most familiar compound is sodium chloride (common salt), which occurs naturally in the oceans and in salt deposits left by dried-up ancient seas.

Other sodium compounds used industrially include ◊sodium hydroxide, ◊sodium carbonate, ◊sodium hydrogencarbonate, sodium nitrate (saltpetre, $NaNO_3$, used as a fertilizer), and sodium thiosulphate (hypo, $Na_2S_2O_3$, used as a photographic fixer). Thousands of tons of these are manufactured annually.

Socrates A bust of the Greek philosopher Socrates. His views are recorded in Plato's *The Republic*, in which Socrates describes the ideal state, where the cultivation of truth, beauty, and goodness achieves perfection. *Corbis*

sodium carbonate or ***soda ash*** Na_2CO_3 anhydrous white solid. The hydrated, crystalline form ($Na_2CO_3.10H_2O$) is also known as washing soda.

It is made by the ◊Solvay process and used as a mild alkali, as it is hydrolysed in water.

$$CO_3^{2-}{}_{(aq)} + H_2O_{(l)} \rightarrow HCO_3^-{}_{(aq)} + OH^-{}_{(aq)}$$

It is used to neutralize acids, in glass manufacture, and in water softening.

sodium chloride or ***common salt*** or ***table salt*** NaCl white, crystalline compound found widely in nature. It is a a typical ionic solid with a high melting point (801°C/1,474°F); it is soluble in water, insoluble in organic solvents, and is a strong electrolyte when molten or in aqueous solution. Found in concentrated deposits, it is widely used in the food industry as a flavouring and preservative, and in the chemical industry in the manufacture of sodium, chlorine, and sodium carbonate.

sodium hydrogencarbonate chemical name for ◊bicarbonate of soda.

sodium hydroxide or ***caustic soda*** NaOH the commonest alkali. The solid and the solution are corrosive. It is used to neutralize acids, in the manufacture of soap, and in oven cleaners. It is prepared industrially from sodium chloride by the ◊electrolysis of concentrated brine.

Sodom and Gomorrah two ancient cities in the Dead Sea area of the Middle East, recorded in the Old Testament (Genesis) as being destroyed by fire and brimstone for their wickedness.

sodomy another term for ◊buggery.

Sofia or ***Sofiya*** capital of Bulgaria since 1878; population (1991) 1,221,000. Industries include textiles, rubber, machinery, and electrical equipment. It lies at the foot of the Vitosha Mountains.

history Sofia was of great importance in Roman times, when it was known as Serdica, especially under the emperor Constantine in the 4th century AD. As part of the Byzantine Empire, it was of strategic importance as it was on the road linking Constantinople and Belgrade. It was captured by the Turks 1382 and became part of the Ottoman Empire until chosen as capital of the newly independent state of Bulgaria 1878.

features 4th-century rotunda of St George's church; ruins of Serdica; 6th-century church of Sveta Sofia; 13th-century Boyana church; Banya bashi mosque 1576; Alexsandar Nevski memorial church 1924; mausoleum of Georgi Dimitrov 1949.

softball bat and ball game, a form of ◊baseball played with similar equipment. The two main differences are the distances between the bases (18.29 m/60 ft) and that the ball is pitched underhand in softball. There are two forms of the game, fast pitch and slow pitch; in the latter the ball must be delivered to home plate in an arc that must not be less than 2.4 m/8 ft at its height. The fast-pitch world

'No evil can befall a good man either in life or death.'

SOCRATES
Attributed remark, in Plato *Apology* 41

championship was instituted 1965 for women, 1966 for men; it is now contested every four years.

software in computing, a collection of programs and procedures for making a computer perform a specific task, as opposed to ◊hardware, the physical components of a computer system. Software is created by programmers and is either distributed on a suitable medium, such as the floppy disc, or built into the computer in the form of firmware (programs held permanently in a computer's ROM chips). Examples of software include ◊operating systems, compilers, and applications programs, such as payrolls. No computer can function without some form of software.

softwood any coniferous tree, or the wood from it. In general this type of wood is softer and easier to work, but in some cases less durable, than wood from flowering (or angiosperm) trees.

soil loose covering of broken rocky material and decaying organic matter overlying the bedrock of the Earth's surface. Various types of soil develop under different conditions: deep soils form in warm wet climates and in valleys; shallow soils form in cool dry areas and on slopes. Pedology, the study of soil, is significant because of the relative importance of different soil types to agriculture.

The organic content of soil is widely variable, ranging from zero in some desert soils to almost 100% in peats.

soil erosion the wearing away and redistribution of the Earth's soil layer. It is caused by the action of water, wind, and ice, and also by improper methods of ◊agriculture. If unchecked, soil erosion results in the formation of deserts (◊desertification). It has been estimated that 20% of the world's cultivated topsoil was lost between 1950 and 1990.

If the rate of erosion exceeds the rate of soil formation (from rock and decomposing organic matter), then the land will become infertile. The removal of forests (◊deforestation) or other vegetation often leads to serious soil erosion, because plant roots bind soil, and without them the soil is free to wash or blow away, as in the American ◊dust bowl. The effect is worse on hillsides, and there has been devastating loss of soil where forests have been cleared from mountainsides, as in Madagascar.

Improved agricultural practices such as contour ploughing are needed to combat soil erosion. Windbreaks, such as hedges or strips planted with coarse grass, are valuable, and organic farming can reduce soil erosion by as much as 75%.

Soil degradation and erosion are becoming as serious as the loss of the rainforest. It is estimated that more than 10% of the world's soil lost a large amount of its natural fertility during the latter half of the 20th century. Some of the worst losses are in Europe, where 17% of the soil is damaged by human activity such as mechanized farming and fallout from acid rain. Mexico and Central America have 24% of soil highly degraded, mostly as a result of deforestation.

soil mechanics branch of engineering that studies the nature and properties of the soil. Soil is investigated during construction work to ensure that it has the mechanical properties necessary to support the foundations of dams, bridges, and roads.

Sokoto state in Nigeria, established 1976; capital Sokoto; area 102,500 sq km/39,565 sq mi; population (1991) 4,392,400. It was a Fula sultanate (an empire founded by people of Fulani extraction) from the 16th century until occupied by the British 1903.

sol ◊colloid of very small solid particles dispersed in a liquid that retains the physical properties of a liquid.

solar energy energy derived from the Sun's radiation. The amount of energy falling on just 1 sq km/0.3861 sq mi is about 4,000 megawatts, enough to heat and light a small town. In one second the Sun gives off 13 million times more energy than all the electricity used in the USA in one year. Solar heaters have industrial or domestic uses. They usually consist of a black (heat-absorbing) panel containing pipes through which air or water, heated by the Sun, is circulated, either by thermal ◊convection or by a pump.

Solar energy may also be harnessed indirectly using solar cells (photovoltaic cells) made of panels of ◊semiconductor material (usually silicon), which generate electricity when illuminated by sunlight. Swiss researchers announced a cheaper and more efficient solar cell in 1998. Based on titanium dioxide, it is twice as efficient as former cells. Despite their low running costs, their high installation cost and low power output have meant that solar cells have found few applications outside space probes and artificial satellites. Solar heating is, however, widely used for domestic purposes in many parts of the world, and is an important nonpolluting and renewable source of energy.

In March 1996 the first solar power plant capable of storing heat was switched on in California's Mojave Desert. Solar 2, part of a three-year government sponsored project, consists of 2,000 motorized mirrors that focus the Sun's rays on to a 91-m/300 ft metal tower containing molten nitrate salt. When the salt reaches 565°C/1049/°F it boils water to drive a 10-megawatt steam turbine. The molten salt retains its heat for up to 12 hours.

▷ *See feature on pp. 360–361.*

solar radiation radiation given off by the Sun, consisting mainly of visible light, ◊ultraviolet radiation, and ◊infrared radiation, although the whole spectrum of ◊electromagnetic waves is present, from radio waves to X-rays. High-energy charged particles such as electrons are also emitted, especially from solar ◊flares. When these reach the Earth, they cause magnetic storms (disruptions of the Earth's magnetic field), which interfere with radio communications.

Solar System the ◊Sun (a star) and all the bodies orbiting it: the nine ◊planets (Mercury, Venus, Earth, Mars, Jupiter, Saturn, Uranus, Neptune, and Pluto), their moons, the asteroids, and the comets. The Sun contains 99.86% of the mass of the Solar System.

The Solar System gives every indication of being a strongly unified system having a common origin and development. It is isolated in space; all the planets go round the Sun in orbits that are nearly circular and coplanar, and in the same direction as the Sun itself rotates; moreover this same pattern is continued in the regular system of satellites that accompany Jupiter, Saturn, and Uranus. It is thought to have formed by condensation from a cloud of gas and dust in space about 4.6 billion years ago.

solar wind stream of atomic particles, mostly protons and electrons, from the Sun's corona, flowing outwards at speeds of between 300 kps/200 mps and 1,000 kps/600 mps.

The fastest streams come from 'holes' in the Sun's corona that lie over areas where no surface activity occurs. The solar wind pushes the gas of comets' tails away from the Sun, and 'gusts' in the solar wind cause geomagnetic disturbances and aurorae on Earth.

solder any of various alloys used when melted for joining metals such as copper, its common alloys (brass and bronze), and tin-plated steel, as used for making food cans.

Soft solders (usually alloys of tin and lead, sometimes with added antimony) melt at low temperatures (about 200°C/392°F), and are widely used in the electrical industry for joining copper wires. Hard (or brazing) solders, such as silver solder (an alloy of copper, silver, and zinc), melt at much higher temperatures and form a much stronger joint. ◊Printed circuit boards for computers are assembled by soldering.

A necessary preliminary to making any solder joint is thorough cleaning of the surfaces of the metal to be joined (to remove oxide) and the use of a flux (to prevent the heat applied to melt the solder from reoxidizing the metal).

sole flatfish found in temperate and tropical waters. The common sole *Solea solea*, also called Dover sole, is found in the southern seas of NW Europe. Up to 50 cm/20 in long, it is a prized food fish, as is the sand or French sole *Pegusa lascaris* further south.

solenodon rare insectivorous shrewlike mammal, genus *Solenodon*. There are two species, one each on Cuba and Hispaniola. They are about 30 cm/12 in long with a 25 cm/10 in naked tail, shaggy hair, long, pointed snouts, and strong claws, and

Solar System Most of the objects in the Solar System lie close to the plane of the ecliptic. The planets are tiny compared to the Sun. If the Sun were the size of a basketball, the planet closest to the Sun, Mercury, would be the size of a mustard seed 15 m/48 ft from the Sun. The most distant planet, Pluto, would be a pinhead 1.6 km/1 mi away from the Sun. The Earth, which is the third planet out from the Sun, would be the size of a pea 32 m/100 ft from the Sun.

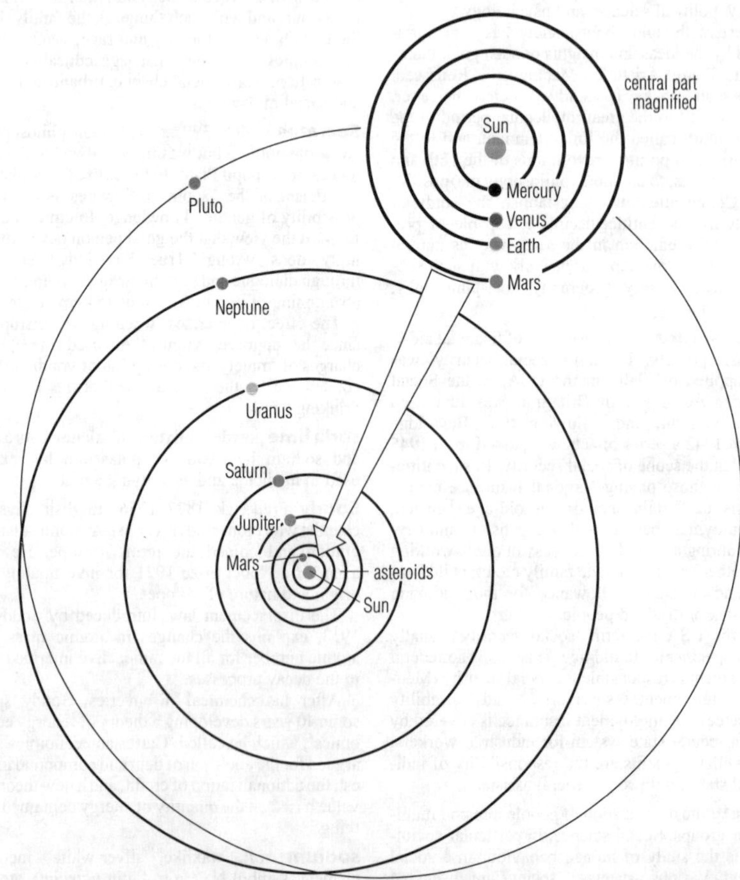

they produce venomous saliva. They are slow-moving, come out mostly at night, and eat insects, worms, and other invertebrate animals. They are threatened with extinction owing to introduced predators.

solenoid coil of wire, usually cylindrical, in which a magnetic field is created by passing an electric current through it (see ◊electromagnet). This field can be used to move an iron rod placed on its axis. Mechanical valves attached to the rod can be operated by switching the current on or off, so converting electrical energy into mechanical energy. Solenoids are used to relay energy from the battery of a car to the starter motor by means of the ignition switch.

Solent, the channel between the coast of Hampshire, England, and the Isle of ◊Wight. It is now a yachting centre.

sol-fa short for ***tonic sol-fa***, a method of teaching music, usually singing, systematized by John Curwen (1816–1880). The notes of a scale are named by syllables (doh, ray, me, fah, soh, lah, te, with the ◊key indicated) to simplify singing by sight.

solicitor in the UK, a member of one of the two branches of the English legal profession, the other being a ◊barrister. A solicitor is a lawyer who provides all-round legal services (making wills, winding up estates, conveyancing, divorce, and litigation). A solicitor cannot appear at High Court level, but must brief a barrister on behalf of his or her client. Solicitors may become circuit judges and recorders.

Solicitor General in the UK, a law officer of the Crown, deputy to the ◊Attorney General, a political appointee with ministerial rank.

In the USA, the second-ranking member of the US Department of Justice, charged with representing the federal government before the US Supreme Court, and any other courts, and who must approve any appeal the federal government might take to an appellate court.

solid in physics, a state of matter that holds its own shape (as opposed to a liquid, which takes up the shape of its container, or a gas, which totally fills its container). According to ◊kinetic theory, the atoms or molecules in a solid are not free to move but merely vibrate about fixed positions, such as those in crystal lattices.

Solidarity (Polish *Solidarność*) national confederation of independent trade unions in Poland, formed under the leadership of Lech ◊Wałesa Sept 1980. An illegal organization from 1981 to 1989, it was then elected to head the Polish government. Divisions soon emerged in the leadership and in 1990 its political wing began to fragment; Wałesa resigned as chairman in Dec of that year, when he was sworn in as president of Poland. In the Sept 1993 elections Solidarity gained less than 5% of the popular vote.

solipsism in philosophy, a view that maintains that the self is the only thing that can be known to exist. It is an extreme form of ◊scepticism. The solipsist sees himself or herself as the only individual in existence, assuming other people to be a reflection of his or her own consciousness.

Solomon c. 974–c. 937 BC. In the Old Testament, third king of Israel, son of David by Bathsheba. During a peaceful reign, he was famed for his wisdom and his alliances with Egypt and Phoenicia. The much later biblical Proverbs, Ecclesiastes, and Song of Songs are attributed to him. He built the temple in Jerusalem with the aid of heavy taxation and forced labour, resulting in the revolt of N Israel. The so-called King Solomon's Mines at Aqaba, Jordan (copper and iron), are of later date.

Solomon Islands country in the SW Pacific Ocean, E of New Guinea, comprising many hundreds of islands, the largest of which is Guadalcanal. *See country box on p. 990.*

Solomon's seal any perennial plant of the genus *Polygonatum* of the lily family Liliaceae, native to Europe and found growing in moist, shady woodland areas. They have bell-like white or greenish-white flowers drooping from the leaf axils of arching stems, followed by blue or black berries.

Solon c. 638–c. 558 BC. Athenian statesman. As one of the chief magistrates about 594 BC, he carried out the cancellation of all debts from which land or liberty was the security and the revision of the constitution that laid the foundations of Athenian democracy.

solstice either of the days on which the Sun is farthest north or south of the celestial equator each year. The summer solstice, when the Sun is farthest north, occurs around 21 June; the winter solstice around 22 Dec.

Solti Georg 1912–1997. Hungarian-born British conductor. He was music director at the Royal Opera House, Covent Garden, London, 1961–71, and became director of the Chicago Symphony Orchestra 1969. He was also principal conductor of the London Philharmonic Orchestra 1979–83.

solubility measure of the amount of solute (usually a solid or gas) that will dissolve in a given amount of solvent (usually a liquid) at a particular temperature. Solubility may be expressed as grams of solute per 100 grams of solvent or, for a gas, in parts per million (ppm) of solvent.

solution two or more substances mixed to form a single, homogenous phase. One of the substances is the solvent and the others (solutes) are said to be dissolved in it.

The constituents of a solution may be solid, liquid, or gaseous. The solvent is normally the substance that is present in greatest quantity; however, if one of the constituents is a liquid this is considered to be the solvent even if it is not the major substance.

solution in earth science, the dissolving in water of minerals within a rock. It may result in weathering (for example, by carbonation, in which rainwater absorbs carbon dioxide from the atmosphere and forms a weak carbonic acid which can dissolve certain minerals in rocks) and erosion (when flowing water passes over rocks). Solution commonly affects limestone and chalk, and may be responsible for forming features such as sink holes (funnel-shaped hollows in limestone).

Solvay process industrial process for the manufacture of sodium carbonate. It is a multistage process in which carbon dioxide is generated from limestone and passed through ◊brine saturated with ammonia. Sodium hydrogen carbonate is isolated and heated to yield sodium carbonate. All intermediate by-products are recycled so that the only ultimate by-product is calcium chloride.

solvent substance, usually a liquid, that will dissolve another substance (see ◊solution). Although the commonest solvent is water, in popular use the term refers to low-boiling-point organic liquids, which are harmful if used in a confined space. They can give rise to respiratory problems, liver damage, and neurological complaints.

Typical organic solvents are petroleum distillates (in glues), xylol (in paints), alcohols (for synthetic and natural resins such as shellac), esters (in lacquers, including nail varnish), ketones (in cellulose lacquers and resins), and chlorinated hydrocarbons (as paint stripper and dry-cleaning fluids). The fumes of some solvents, when inhaled (◊glue-sniffing), affect mood and perception. In addition to damaging the brain and lungs, repeated inhalation of solvent from a plastic bag can cause death by asphyxia.

Solway Firth inlet of the Irish Sea, formed by the estuaries of the rivers Eden and Esk, at the western end of the border between England and Scotland.

Solyman I alternative spelling of ◊Suleiman, Ottoman sultan.

Solzhenitsyn Alexander Isayevich 1918– . Soviet novelist. He became a US citizen 1974. He was in prison and exile 1945–57 for anti-Stalinist comments. Much of his writing is semi-autobiographical and highly critical of the system, including *One Day in the Life of Ivan Denisovich* 1962, which deals with the labour camps under Stalin, and *The Gulag Archipelago* 1973, an exposé of the whole Soviet labour-camp network. This led to his expulsion from the USSR 1974. In 1991, cleared of the original charges of treason, he returned to Russia. He was awarded a Nobel prize 1970.

Somali a group of E African peoples from the Horn of Africa. Although the majority of Somalis live in the Somali Republic, there are minorities in

Solomon's seal Angular Solomon's seal *Polygonatum odoratum* is distributed over much of Europe as far east as the W Himalayas, although in warmer countries it is restricted to mountainous areas. In the British Isles it is a very localized plant found in woods on limestone, flowering in June and July. *Premaphotos Wildlife*

Solidarity A demonstrator wearing a Solidarity T-shirt leads a May Day Solidarity demonstration in Warsaw, Poland. Solidarity was formed in 1980 in response to a period of industrial unrest, to coordinate trade union activities and negotiate with the government. It was illegal 1981–89, but was then elected to head the Polish government in 1989. *Corbis*

'When you've robbed a man of everything he's no longer in your power – he's free again.'

ALEXANDER SOLZHENITSYN
The First Circle

SOLOMON ISLANDS

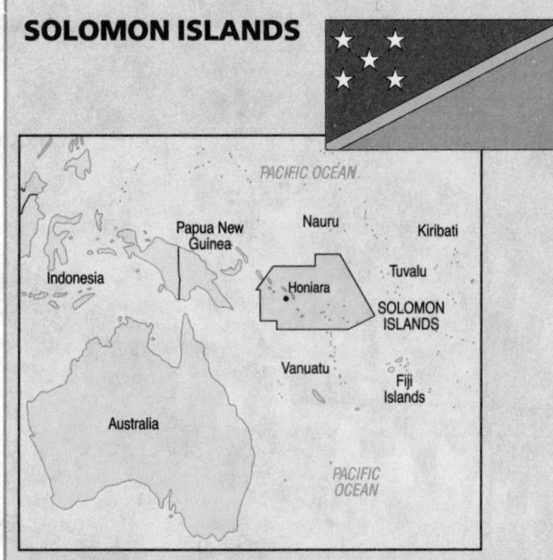

area 27,600 sq km/10,656 sq mi
capital and port Honiara (on Guadalcanal)
major towns/cities Gizo
major ports Yandina
physical features comprises all but the northernmost islands (which belong to Papua New Guinea) of a Melanesian archipelago stretching nearly 1,500 km/900 mi. The largest is Guadalcanal (area 6,500 sq km/2,510 sq mi); others are Malaita, San Cristobal, New Georgia, Santa Isabel, Choiseul; mainly mountainous and forested
head of state Elizabeth II represented by governor general Moses Pitakaka from 1994
head of government Bartholomew Ulufa'alu from 1997
political system constitutional monarchy
administrative divisions four districts
political parties Group for National Unity and Reconciliation (GNUR), centrist coalition; National Coalition Partners (NCP), broad-based coalition
population 391,000 (1996 est)
population growth rate 3.3% (1990–95); 3.1% (2000–05)
ethnic distribution 93% Melanesian, 4% Polynesian, 1.5% Micronesian, 0.7% European, and 0.2% Chinese
life expectancy 66 (men), 71 (women)
literacy rate 24%
languages English (official); there are some 120 Melanesian dialects spoken by 85% of the population, and Papuan and Polynesian languages
religions Anglican, Roman Catholic, South Sea Evangelical, other Protestant
currency Solomon Island dollar
GDP (US $) 246 million (1993)
growth rate 4.0% (1993)
exports fish products, palm oil, copra, cocoa, timber, wood products, tuna

HISTORY

1568 The islands, rumoured in South America to be the legendary gold-rich 'Islands of Solomon', were first sighted by Spanish navigator Alvaro de Mendana, journeying from Peru.
1595 and 1606 Unsuccessful Spanish efforts to settle the islands, which had long been peopled by Melanesians.
later 18th C Visited again by Europeans.
1840s Christian missions established.
1870s Development of copra export trade and shipment of islanders to work on sugar-cane plantations in Australia and Fiji.
1886 Northern Solomon Islands became a German protectorate.
1893 Southern Solomon Islands placed under British protection.
1899 Germany ceded its Solomon Islands possessions to Britain in return for British recognition of its claims to Western Samoa.
1900 A unified British Solomon Islands Protectorate was formed and was placed under the jurisdiction of the Western Pacific High Commission (WPHC), with its headquarters in Fiji.
1942–43 Occupied by Japan and became site of fierce fighting, especially on Guadalcanal, which was recaptured by US forces, with the loss of 21,000 Japanese and 5,000 US troops.
1943–50 Development of Marching Rule (Ma'asina Ruru) cargo cult populist movement on Malaita island, campaigning for self-rule.
1945 Headquarters of WPHC moved to Honiara.
1960 Legislative and executive councils established by constitution.
1974 Became substantially self-governing, with Solomon Mamaloni of the centre-left People's Progressive Party (PPP) as chief minister.
1976 Became fully self-governing, with Peter Kenilorea of the right-of-centre Solomon Islands United Party (SIUPA) as chief minister.
1978 Independence achieved from Britain within the Commonwealth, with Kenilorea as prime minister.
1981 Mamaloni (PPP) became prime minister, pledging to decentralize power.
1984 Kenilorea returned to power, heading a coalition government.
1986 Kenilorea resigned after allegations of corruption; replaced by his deputy, Ezekiel Alebua.
1988 Kenilorea elected deputy prime minister. Joined Vanuatu and Papua New Guinea to form the Spearhead Group, aiming to preserve Melanesian cultural traditions.
1989 Mamaloni, now leader of the People's Alliance Party (PAP), appointed prime minister.
1990 Mamaloni resigned as PAP party leader, but continued as head of a government of national unity, which included Keniloea as foreign minister.
1993 New Mamaloni-led coalition won largest number of seats in general election, but Francis Billy Hilly, an independent politician, appointed prime minister.
1994 Billy Hilly resigned; Mamaloni returned to power.
1997 Bartholomew Ulufa'alu elected prime minister.

SEE ALSO Australasia and Oceania; Pacific Islands

Ethiopia and Kenya. Their Cushitic language belongs to the Hamitic branch of the Afro-Asiatic family.

Somalia country in NE Africa (the Horn of Africa), on the Indian Ocean, bounded NW by Djibouti, W by Ethiopia, and SW by Kenya. *See country box opposite.*

Somaliland region of Somali-speaking peoples in E Africa including the former British Somaliland Protectorate (established 1887) and Italian Somaliland (made a colony 1927, conquered by Britain 1941 and administered by Britain until 1950) – which both became independent 1960 as the Somali Democratic Republic, the official name for ◊Somalia – and former French Somaliland, which was established 1888, became known as the Territory of the Afars and Issas 1967, and became independent as ◊Djibouti 1977.

Somerset county of SW England
area 3,460 sq km/1,336 sq mi (*see United Kingdom map*)
towns Taunton (administrative headquarters); Wells, Bridgwater, Glastonbury, Yeovil
features rivers Avon, Parret, and Exe; marshy coastline on the Bristol Channel; Mendip Hills (including Cheddar Gorge and Wookey Hole, a series of limestone caves where Stone Age flint implements and bones of extinct animals have been found); Quantock Hills; Exmoor; Blackdown Hills
industries engineering, dairy products, cider, food processing, textiles
population (1991) 460,400
famous people John Pym, Henry Fielding, Ernest Bevin.
history James II defeated the Duke of Monmouth at the Battle of Sedgemoor 1685.

Somerset Edward Seymour, 1st Duke of Somerset c. 1506–1552. English politician. Created Earl of Hertford after Henry VIII's marriage to his sister Jane, he became Duke of Somerset and protector (regent) for Edward VI in 1547. His attempt to check ◊enclosure (the transfer of land from common to private ownership) offended landowners and his moderation in religion upset the Protestants, and he was beheaded on a fake treason charge in 1552.

Shall I compare thee to a summer's day? / Thou art more lovely and more temperate: / Rough winds do shake the darling buds of May, / And summer's lease hath all too short a date.

SONNET
William Shakespeare
Sonnet 18

Somme river in N France, on which Amiens and Abbeville stand; length 240 km/150 mi. It rises in Aisne *département* and flows W through Somme *département* to the English Channel.

Somme, Battle of the Allied offensive in World War I July–Nov 1916 on the river Somme in N France, during which severe losses were suffered by both sides. It was planned by the Marshal of France, Joseph Joffre, and UK commander in chief Douglas Haig; the Allies lost over 600,000 soldiers and advanced 13 km/8 mi. It was the first battle in which tanks were used. The German offensive around St Quentin March–April 1918 is sometimes called the Second Battle of the Somme.

Somoza Debayle Anastasio 1925–1980. Nicaraguan soldier and politician, president 1967–72 and 1974–79. The second son of Anastasio Somoza García, he succeeded his brother Luis Somoza Debayle (1922–1967; president 1956–63) as president of Nicaragua in 1967, to head an even more oppressive regime. He was removed by Sandinista guerrillas in 1979, and assassinated in Paraguay 1980.

Somoza García Anastasio 1896–1956. Nicaraguan soldier and politician, president 1937–47 and 1950–56. A protégé of the USA, who wanted a reliable ally to protect their interests in Central America, he was virtual dictator of Nicaragua from 1937 until his assassination in 1956. He exiled most of his political opponents and amassed a considerable fortune in land and businesses. Members of his family retained control of the country until 1979, when they were overthrown by popular forces.

sonar (acronym for ***sound navigation and ranging***) method of locating underwater objects by the reflection of ultrasonic waves. The time taken for an acoustic beam to travel to the object and back to the source enables the distance to be found since the velocity of sound in water is known. Sonar devices, or echo sounders, were developed 1920, and are the commonest means of underwater navigation.

sonata (Italian 'sounded') in music, an essay in instrumental composition for a solo player or a small ensemble and consisting of a single movement or series of movements. The name signifies that the work is not beholden to a text or existing dance form, but is self-sufficient.

sonata form in music, rules determining the structure of a ◊sonata first movement, typically divided into exposition, development, and recapitulation sections. It introduced the new possibility of open and continuous development to an 18th-century music previously limited to closed dance routines. It provides the framework for first movements in general, including symphonies, concertos, and string quartets.

Sondheim Stephen Joshua 1930– . US composer and lyricist. He wrote the lyrics of Leonard Bernstein's *West Side Story* 1957 and composed witty and sophisticated musicals, including *A Little Night Music* 1973, *Pacific Overtures* 1976, *Sweeney Todd* 1979, *Into the Woods* 1987, and *Sunday in the Park with George* 1989.

song a setting of words to music for one or more singers, with or without instrumental accompaniment. Song may be sacred, for example a psalm, motet, or cantata, or secular, for example a folk song or ballad. In verse song, the text changes in mood while the music remains the same; in ◊lied and other forms of art song, the music changes in response to the emotional development of the text.

song cycle sequence of songs related in mood and sung as a group, used by romantic composers such as Schubert, Schumann, and Wolf.

Song dynasty or ***Sung dynasty*** lived 10th–13th centuries. Chinese imperial family 960–1279, founded by northern general Taizu (Zhao Kuangyin 928–76). A distinction is conventionally made between the Northern Song period 960–1126, when the capital was at Kaifeng, and Southern Song 1127–1279, when it was at Hangzhou (Hangchow). A stable government was supported by a thoroughly centralized administration. The dynasty was eventually ended by Mongol invasion.

During the Song era, such technologies as shipbuilding, firearms, clock-making, and the use of the compass far outstripped those of Europe. Painting, poetry, and ceramics flourished, as did economic development, particularly in the rice-growing SE. NE China remained independent of the Song, being ruled by the ◊Liao and ◊Jin dynasties.

Songhai Empire former kingdom of NW Africa, founded in the 8th century, which developed into a powerful Muslim empire under the rule of Sonni Ali (reigned 1464–92). It superseded the ◊Mali Empire and extended its territory, occupying an area that included parts of present-day Guinea, Burkina Faso, Senegal, Gambia, Mali, Mauritania, Niger, and Nigeria. In 1591 it was invaded and overthrown by Morocco.

sonic boom noise like a thunderclap that occurs when an aircraft passes through the ◊sound barrier, or begins to travel faster than the speed of sound. It happens when the cone-shaped shock wave caused by the plane touches the ground.

sonnet fourteen-line poem of Italian origin introduced to England by Thomas ◊Wyatt in the form used by Petrarch (rhyming *abba abba cdcdcd* or *cdecde*) and followed by Milton and Wordsworth; Shakespeare used the form *abab cdcd efef gg*.

In the final couplet Shakespeare summed up the argument of the sonnet or introduced a new, perhaps contradictory, idea. The difference in the rhyme scheme of the first eight lines (the octet) and the last six (the sestet) reflected a change in mood or direction of the Petrarchan sonnet.

Sons of Liberty in American colonial history, the name adopted by those colonists opposing the ◊Stamp Act of 1765. Merchants, lawyers, farmers, artisans, and labourers joined what was an early instance of concerted resistance to British rule, causing the repeal of the act in March 1766. ▷ *See feature on pp. 32–33.*

Sontag Susan 1933– . US critic, novelist, and screenwriter. Her novel *The Benefactor* appeared 1963, and she established herself as a critic with the influential cultural essays of 'Against Interpretation' 1966 and 'Styles of Radical Will' 1969. More recent studies are *On Photography* 1976, the powerful *Illness as Metaphor* 1978, and *Aids and its Metaphors* 1989.

Sony Japanese electronics hardware company that produced the Walkman, the first easily portable cassette player with headphones, 1980. It diversified into entertainment by the purchase of CBS Records 1988 and Columbia Pictures 1989. It also manufactures computing games consoles. During the 1970s Sony developed the Betamax video-cassette format, which technicians rated as more advanced than the rival VHS system developed by the Matsushita corporation, but the latter eventually triumphed in the marketplace.

sophist (Greek *sophistes* 'wise man') in ancient Greece, one of a group of 5th-century BC itinerant lecturers on culture, rhetoric, and politics. Sceptical about the possibility of achieving genuine knowledge, they applied bogus reasoning and were concerned with winning arguments rather than establishing the truth. ◊Plato regarded them as dishonest and sophistry came to mean fallacious reasoning. In the 2nd century AD the term was linked to the art of public speaking.

Sophocles c. 496–406 BC. Athenian dramatist. He is attributed with having developed tragedy by introducing a third actor and scene-painting, and ranked with ◊Aeschylus and ◊Euripides as one of the three great tragedians. He wrote some 120 plays, of which seven tragedies survive. These are *Antigone* 443 BC, *Oedipus the King* 429, *Electra* 410, *Ajax*, *Trachiniae*, *Philoctetes* 409 BC, and *Oedipus at Colonus* 401 (produced after his death).

Sophocles lived in Athens when the city was ruled by Pericles, a period of great prosperity; he was a devout man, and assumed public office. A regular winner of dramatic competitions, he first defeated Aeschylus at the age of 27. In his tragedies heroic determination leads directly to violence unless, as in *Philoctetes* and *Oedipus at Colonus*, it contains an element of resignation. Among his other works are a lost treatise on the chorus, and a large surviving fragment of one of his satyr-dramas, *Ichneutai*.

soprano in music, the highest range of the female voice, stretching from around D4 to A6. Some operatic roles require the extended upper range of a *coloratura* soprano, reaching to around F6, for example Kiri ◊Te Kanawa.

sopranino describes an instrument of higher range than soprano. An alternative term is *piccolo*.

Sopwith Thomas Octave Murdoch 1888–1989. English designer of the Sopwith Camel biplane, used in World War I, and joint developer of the Hawker Hurricane fighter plane used in World War II.

From a Northumbrian engineering family, Sopwith gained a pilot's licence 1910 and soon after set a British aerial duration record for a flight of 3 hours 12 minutes. In 1912 he founded the Sopwith Aviation Company, which in 1920 he wound up and reopened as the Hawker Company, after the chief test pilot Harry Hawker. The Hawker Company was responsible for the Hawker Hart bomber, the Hurricane, and eventually the vertical take-off ◊Harrier jump jet.

sorbic acid $CH_3CH{:}CHCH{:}CHCOOH$ tasteless acid found in the fruit of the mountain ash (genus *Sorbus*) and prepared synthetically. It is widely used in the preservation of food – for example, cider, wine, soft drinks, animal feeds, bread, and cheese.

Sorbonne common name for the University of Paris, originally a theological institute founded 1253 by Robert de Sorbon, chaplain to Louis IX.

Richelieu ordered the reconstruction of the buildings in 1626, which were again rebuilt 1885. In 1808, the Sorbonne became the seat of the Académie of Paris and of the University of Paris. It is the most prestigious French university.

Sorbus genus of deciduous trees and shrubs of the northern hemisphere, family Rosaceae, including American and Eurasian ◊mountain ash species; the latter include ◊whitebeam and ◊service tree.

sorghum or ***great millet*** or ***Guinea corn*** any cereal grass of the genus *Sorghum*, native to Africa but cultivated widely in India, China, the USA, and

'Interpretation is the revenge of the intellect upon art.'

SUSAN SONTAG
Against Interpretation

'None love the messenger who brings bad news.'

SOPHOCLES
Antigone

SOMALIA

Somali Democratic Republic

national name *Jamhuriyadda Dimugradiga ee Soomaaliya*
area 637,700 sq km/246,220 sq mi
capital and port Mogadishu
major towns/cities Hargeisa
major ports Berbera, Marka, Kismayo
physical features mainly flat, with hills in N
(interim) head of state and government Hussein Aidid from 1996
political system transitional
administrative divisions 18 regions (agreed 1993)
political parties parties are mainly clan-based and include the United Somali Congress (USC), Hawiye clan; Somali Patriotic Movement (SPM), Darod clan; Somali Southern Democratic Front (SSDF), Majertein clan; Somali Democratic Alliance (SDA), Gadabursi clan; United Somali Front (USF), Issa clan; Somali National Movement (SNM) based in self-proclaimed Somaliland Republic
population 9,250,000 (1995 est)
population growth rate 1.3% (1990–95); 3.0% (2000–05)
ethnic distribution 98% indigenous Somali (about 84% Hamitic and 14% Bantu); population is divided into around 100 clans
life expectancy 45 (men), 49 (women)
literacy rate men 36%, women 14%
languages Somali, Arabic (both official), Italian, English
religion Sunni Muslim
currency Somali shilling
GDP (US $) 996 million (1993)
growth rate −12.0% (1992)
exports livestock, skins, hides, bananas, fruit

HISTORY
8th–10th Cs Arab ancestors of Somali clan families migrated to the region and introduced Sunni Islam; coastal trading cities, including Mogadishu, were formed by Arabian immigrants and developed into sultanates.
11th–14th C Southward and westward movement of Somalis and Islamization of Christian Ethiopian interior.
early 16th C Portuguese contacts with coastal region.
1820s First British contacts with N Somalia.
1884–87 British protectorate of Somaliland established in the N.
1889 Italian protectorate of Somalia established in the S.
1927 Italian Somalia became a colony and part of Italian East Africa from 1936.
1941 Italian Somalia occupied by Britain during World War II.
1943 Somali Youth League (SYL) formed as nationalist party.
1950 Italy resumed control over Italian Somalia under a UN trusteeship.
1960 Independence achieved from Italy and Britain as Somalia, with Aden Abdullah Osman as president.
1963 Border dispute with Kenya; diplomatic relations broken with Britain for five years.
1967 Dr Abdirashid Ali Shermarke (SYL) became president.
1969 President Ibrahim Egal assassinated in army coup led by Maj-Gen Muhammad Siad Barre; constitution suspended, political parties banned, Supreme Revolutionary Council set up, and socialist-Islamic state formed.
1972 20,000 died in severe drought.
1978 Defeated in eight-month war with Ethiopia fought on behalf of Somali guerrillas in Ogaden to the SW. Armed insurrection began in the N and hundreds of thousands became refugees.
1979 New constitution for socialist one-party state dominated by Somali Revolutionary Socialist Party (SRSP).
1982 Antigovernment Ethiopian-backed Somali National Movement (SNM) formed in the N. Oppressive countermeasures by government.
late 1980s Guerrilla activity increased in the N as civil war intensified.
1991 Mogadishu captured by rebels; Barre fled; Ali Mahdi Muhammad named president; free elections promised. Secession of NE Somalia, as the Somaliland Republic, announced but not recognized internationally.
1992 Widespread famine. Western food-aid convoys hijacked by 'warlords'. United Nations (UN) peacekeeping troops, led by US Marines, sent in to protect relief operations.
1993 Leaders of armed factions (excepting Somaliland-based faction) agreed to federal system of government. US-led UN forces destroyed headquarters of warlord General Muhammad Farah Aidid after killing of Pakistani peacekeepers.
1994 Ali Mahdi Muhammad and Aidid signed truce. Majority of Western peacekeeping troops withdrawn, but clan-based fighting continued.
1995 Last UN peacekeepers withdrawn.
1996 Aidid killed in renewed faction fighting; his son Hussein Aidid succeeded him, as interim president.
1997 Peace agreement signed between rival factions.

SEE ALSO British Somaliland; Italian Somaliland

sorghum Sorghum is a type of grass that was originally cultivated in Africa to provide grain for animal fodder and to make flour for bread or porridge. There are other kinds of sorghums which have been used to provide hay, molasses or syrup, and even brushes and brooms.

S Europe. The seeds are used for making bread. ◊Durra is a member of the genus.

Around 58 million tonnes of sorghum are grown worldwide on 44 million hectares. It is vulnerable to the fungus ◊ergot, which can destroy whole crops. In 1994 a simple fungicidal spray of garlic and water was found to be nearly 100% successful in combatting ergot.

sorrel (Old French *sur* 'sour') any of several plants of the genus *Rumex* of the buckwheat family Polygonaceae. *R. acetosa* is grown for its bitter salad leaves. ◊Dock plants are of the same genus.

sorus in ferns, a group of sporangia, the reproductive structures that produce ◊spores. They occur on the lower surface of fern fronds.

Sōseki Natsume. Pen name of Natsume Kinnosuke 1867–1916. Japanese novelist. His works are deep psychological studies of urban intellectual lives. Strongly influenced by English literature, his later works are somewhat reminiscent of Henry James; for example, the unfinished *Meian/Light and Darkness* 1916. Sōseki is regarded as one of Japan's greatest writers.

Sotho a large ethnic group in southern Africa, numbering about 7 million (1987) and living mainly in Botswana, Lesotho, and South Africa. The Sotho are predominantly farmers, living in small village groups. They speak a variety of closely related languages belonging to the Bantu branch of the Niger-Congo family. With English, Sotho is the official language of Lesotho.

soul according to many religions, an intangible part of a human being that survives the death of the physical body. Judaism, Christianity, and Islam all teach that at the end of the world each soul will be judged and assigned to heaven or hell on its merits.

According to orthodox Jewish doctrine, most souls first spend time in purgatory to be purged of their sins, and are then removed to paradise. In Christianity the soul is that part of the person that can be redeemed from sin through divine grace.

In other religions, such as Hinduism, the soul is thought to undergo ◊reincarnation until the individual reaches enlightenment and is freed from the cycle of rebirth. According to the teachings of Buddhism, no permanent self or soul exists.

soul music emotionally intense style of ◊rhythm and blues sung by, among others, Sam Cooke, Aretha Franklin, and Al Green (1946–). A synthesis of blues, gospel music, and jazz, it emerged in the 1950s. Sometimes all popular music made by African-Americans is labelled soul music.

Soult Nicolas Jean de Dieu 1769–1851. Marshal of France. He held commands in Spain in the Peninsular War, where he sacked the port of Santander 1808, and was Chief of Staff at the Battle of ◊Waterloo. He was war minister 1830–40.

sound physiological sensation received by the ear, originating in a vibration that communicates itself as a pressure variation in the air and travels in every direction, spreading out as an expanding sphere. All sound waves in air travel with a speed dependent on the temperature; under ordinary conditions, this is about 330 m/1,070 ft per second. The pitch of the sound depends on the number of vibrations imposed on the air per second, but the speed is unaffected. The loudness of a sound is dependent primarily on the amplitude of the vibration of the air.

The lowest note audible to a human being has a frequency of about 20 ◊hertz (vibrations per second), and the highest one of about 20,000 Hz; the lower limit of this range varies little with the person's age, but the upper range falls steadily from adolescence onwards.

Sound, the (Swedish and Danish ***Øresund***) strait dividing SW Sweden from Denmark and linking the ◊Kattegat strait and the Baltic Sea; length 113 km/70 mi; width between 5–60 km/3–37 mi.

sound barrier concept that the speed of sound, or sonic speed (about 1,220 kph/760 mph at sea level), constitutes a speed limit to flight through the atmosphere, since a badly designed aircraft suffers severe buffeting at near sonic speed owing to the formation of shock waves. US test pilot Chuck Yeager first flew through the 'barrier' in 1947 in a Bell X-1 rocket plane. Now, by careful design, such aircraft as Concorde can fly at supersonic speed with ease, though they create in their wake a ◊sonic boom.

Souphanouvong Prince 1902–1995. Laotian politician, president 1975–86. After an abortive revolt against French rule in 1945, he led the guerrilla organization Pathet Lao (Land of the Lao), and in 1975 became the first president of the Republic of Laos.

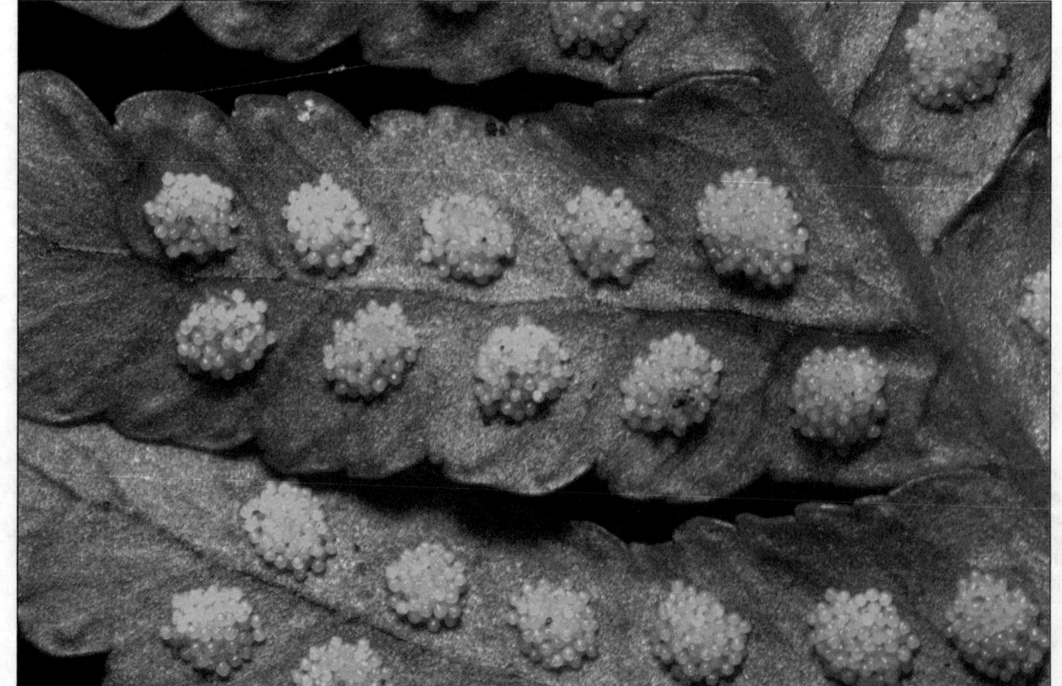

sorus Heaps of bright yellow spore-producing sporangia grouped to form sori are clearly visible beneath this frond of common polypody fern. *Premaphotos Wildlife*

Sousa John Philip 1854–1932. US bandmaster, and composer of marches. He wrote 'The Stars and Stripes Forever!' 1897.

sousaphone large bass ◊tuba designed to wrap round the player in a circle and having a forward-facing bell. The form was suggested by US bandmaster John Sousa. Today sousaphones are largely fabricated in lightweight fibreglass.

South Africa country on the southern tip of Africa, bounded N by Namibia, Botswana, and Zimbabwe and NE by Mozambique and Swaziland. *See country box opposite.*

South African literature the founder of South African literature in English was Thomas Pringle (1789–1834), who published lyric poetry and the prose *Narrative of a Residence in South Africa*. More recent poets are Roy Campbell and Francis C Slater (1876–1959). The first work of South African fiction to receive attention outside the country was Olive Schreiner's *Story of an African Farm* 1883. Later writers include Sarah Gertrude Millin, Pauline Smith (1882–1959), William Plomer, Laurens van der Post, Alan Paton, Nadine Gordimer (winner of the Nobel Prize for Literature 1991), and playwright Athol Fugard.

Original writing in ◊Afrikaans developed rapidly after the South African War, and includes works by the satirical sketch and story writer C J Langenhoven and the student of wildlife 'Sangiro' (A A Peinhar), author of *The Adventures of a Lion Family*, which became popular in English translation.

See also ◊African literature.

South African Wars two wars between the Boers (settlers of Dutch origin) and the British; essentially fought for the gold and diamonds of the Transvaal.

The ***War of 1881*** was triggered by the attempt of the Boers of the ◊Transvaal to reassert the independence surrendered 1877 in return for British aid against African peoples. The British were defeated at Majuba, and the Transvaal again became independent.

The ***War of 1899–1902***, also known as the ***Boer War***, was preceded by the armed Jameson Raid into the Boer Transvaal; a failed attempt, inspired by the Cape Colony prime minister Rhodes, to precipitate a revolt against Kruger, the Transvaal president. The *uitlanders* (non-Boer immigrants) were still not given the vote by the Boers, negotiations failed, and the Boers invaded British territory, besieging Ladysmith, Mafeking (now Mafikeng), and Kimberley. The war ended with the Peace of Vereeniging following the Boer defeat.

British commander ◊Kitchener countered Boer guerrilla warfare by putting the noncombatants who supported them into concentration camps, where about 26,000 women and children died of sickness.

South America fourth largest of the continents, nearly twice as large as Europe (13% of the world's land surface), extending south from ◊Central America

area 17,864,000 sq km/6,900,000 sq mi

largest cities (population over 3.5 million) Buenos Aires, São Paulo, Rio de Janeiro, Bogotá, Santiago, Lima, Caracas

features Lake Titicaca (the world's highest navigable lake); La Paz (highest capital city in the world); Atacama Desert; Inca ruins at Machu Picchu; rivers include the Amazon (world's largest and second longest), Paraná, Madeira, São Francisco, Purús, Paraguay, Orinoco, Araguaia, Negro, Uruguay

physical occupying the southern part of the landmass of the western hemisphere, the South American continent stretches from Point Gallinas on the Caribbean coast of Colombia to Cape Horn at the southern tip of Horn Island, which lies adjacent to Tierra del Fuego; the most southerly point on the mainland is Cape Froward on the Brunswick peninsula, S Chile; at its maximum width (5,120 km/3,200 mi) the continent stretches from Point Pariñas, Peru, in the extreme west to Point Coqueiros, just north of Recife, Brazil, in the east; five-sixths of the continent lies in the southern hemisphere and two-thirds within the tropics.

The continent can be divided into the following physical regions: (1) the Andes mountain system, which consists of extensive chains of parallel folded mountains, formed during the subsidence of the bed of the Pacific Ocean; (2) the uplifted remains of the old continental mass, with interior plains at an elevation of 610–1,520 m/2,000–5,000 ft, which are found in the east and northeast, in the Brazilian Highlands (half the area of Brazil) and Guiana Highlands; (3) the plain of the Orinoco River, which is an alluvial tropical lowland lying between the Venezuelan Andes and the Guiana Highlands; (4) the tropical Amazon Plain, which stretches over 3,200 km/2,000 mi from the eastern foothills of the Andes to the Atlantic Ocean, separating the Brazilian and Guiana highlands; (5) the Pampa-Chaco plain of Argentina, Paraguay, and Bolivia, which occupies a former bay of the Atlantic Ocean that has been filled with sediment brought down from the surrounding highlands; and (6) the Patagonian Plateau in the south, which consists of a series of terraces that rise from the Atlantic Ocean to the foothills of the Andes

climate the distribution of rainfall in South America is affected by three factors: (1) the areas of high pressure over the South Atlantic and the South Pacific between latitudes 20° and 40°; (2) the tropical continental region of low pressure in the Upper Amazon basin; and (3) the direction of the ocean currents which wash both east and west coasts, together with a cold current that clings to the coast along most of the west coast. The continent's summer rainfall is of a monsoonal type, but differs from that of Asia in that there is no movement outwards of high-pressure air owing to the continent being as a whole warmer than the surrounding seas during all seasons

industries South America produces 44% of the world's coffee (Brazil, Colombia), 22% of its cocoa (Brazil), 35% of its citrus fruit, meat (Argentina, Brazil), soya beans (Argentina, Brazil), cotton (Brazil), and linseed (Argentina); Argentina is the world's second-largest producer of sunflower seed; Brazil is the world's largest producer of bananas, its second-largest producer of tin, and its third-largest producer of manganese, tobacco, and mangoes; Peru is the world's second-largest producer of silver; Chile is the world's largest producer of copper

SOUTH AFRICA
Republic of

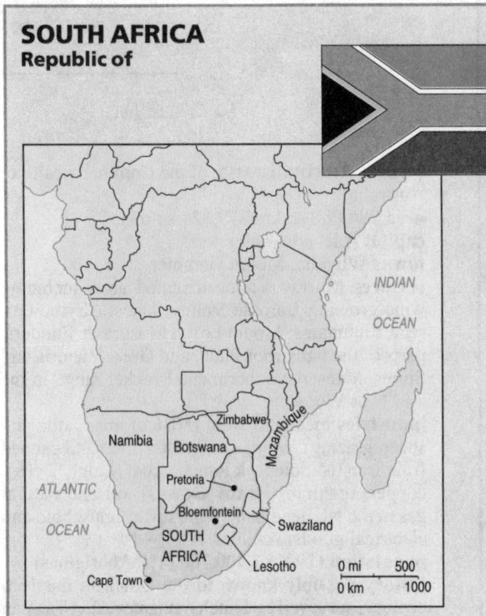

national name *Republiek van Suid-Afrika*
area 1,222,081 sq km/471,723 sq mi
capital and port Cape Town (legislative), Pretoria (administrative), Bloemfontein (judicial)
major towns/cities Johannesburg
major ports Durban, Port Elizabeth, East London
physical features southern end of large plateau, fringed by mountains and lowland coastal margin; Drakensberg Mountains, Table Mountain; Limpopo and Orange rivers
territories Marion Island and Prince Edward Island in the Antarctic
head of state Nelson Mandela from 1994
head of government Nelson Mandela from 1994
political system liberal democracy
administrative divisions nine provinces
political parties African National Congress (ANC), left of centre; National Party (NP), right of centre; Inkatha Freedom Party (IFP), centrist, multiracial (formerly Zulu nationalist); Freedom Front (FF), right-wing; Democratic Party (DP), moderate, centre-left, multiracial; Pan-Africanist Congress (PAC), black, left-wing; African Christian Democratic Party (ACDP), Christian, right of centre
armed forces 78,500 (1994)
conscription none
defence spend (% GDP) 3.3 (1994)
education spend (% GNP) 7.0 (1992)
health spend (% GDP) 3.2 (1990)
death penalty for exceptional crimes only (from 1995)
population 42,834,000 (1998 est)
population growth rate 2.2% (1990–95); 2.1% (2000–05)
age distribution (% of total population) <15 37.3%, 15–65 58.3%, >65 4.4% (1995)
ethnic distribution 73% of the population is black African, 15% white (of European descent), 9% of mixed African–European descent, and 3% Asian; 20% of the population live in shanty towns
population density (per sq km) 33 (1994)
urban population (% of total) 51 (1995)
labour force 39% of population: 14% agriculture, 32% industry, 55% services (1990)
unemployment 29% (early 1995)
child mortality rate (under 5, per 1,000 live births) 68 (1994)
life expectancy whites 73, blacks 57 (1994)
education (compulsory years) 10
literacy rate 70%
languages English and Afrikaans (both official); main African languages: Xhosa, Zulu, and Sesotho (all official)
religions Dutch Reformed Church and other Christian denominations, Hindu, Muslim
TV sets (per 1,000 people) 98 (1992)
currency rand
GDP (US $) 129.1 billion (1997)
GDP per capita (PPP) (US $) 3,127 (1993)
growth rate 2.3% (1994)
average annual inflation 9.0% (1994); 14.4% (1985–93)
major trading partners Germany, UK, USA, Japan, Switzerland
resources gold (world's largest producer), coal, platinum, iron ore, diamonds, chromium, manganese, limestone, asbestos, fluorspar, uranium, copper, lead, zinc, petroleum, natural gas
industries chemicals, petroleum and coal products, gold, diamonds, food processing, transport equipment, iron and steel, metal products, machinery, fertilizers, textiles, paper and paper products, clothing, wood and cork products
exports metals and metal products, gold, precious and semiprecious stones, mineral products and chemicals, natural cultured pearls, machinery and mechanical appliances, wool, maize, fruit, sugar. Principal market: Switzerland 10% (1993)
imports machinery and electrical equipment, transport equipment, chemical products, mechanical appliances, textiles and clothing, vegetable products, wood, pulp, paper and paper products. Principal source: Germany 17.2% (1994)
arable land 10.1% (1993)
agricultural products maize, sugar cane, sorghum, fruits, wheat, groundnuts, grapes, vegetables; livestock rearing, wool production

HISTORY
1652 The Dutch East India Company established a colony at Cape Town as a port of call.
1795 Britain occupied the Cape after France conquered the Netherlands.
1814 Britain bought Cape Town and the hinterland from the Netherlands for £6 million.
1820s Zulu people established a military kingdom under Shaka.
1836–38 The Great Trek: 10,000 Dutch settlers (known as Boers, meaning 'farmers') migrated north to escape British rule.
1843 Britain established the colony of Natal on the E coast.
1852–54 Britain recognized the Boer republics of the Transvaal and Orange Free State.
1872 The Cape became a self-governing colony within the British Empire.
1877 Britain annexed the Transvaal.
1879 Zulu War: Britain destroyed the power of the Zulus.
1881 First Boer War: Transvaal Boers defeated British at Majuba Hill and regained independence.
1886 Discovery of gold on the Witwatersrand attracted many migrant miners (uitlanders) to Transvaal, which denied them full citizenship.
1895 Jameson Raid: uitlanders, backed by Cecil Rhodes, tried to overthrow President Paulus Kruger of Transvaal.
1899–1902 Second South African War (also known as the Boer War): dispute over rights of uitlanders led to conflict which ended with British annexation of the Boer republics.
1907 Britain granted internal self-government to Transvaal and Orange Free State on whites-only franchise.
1910 Cape Colony, Natal, Transvaal, and Orange Free State formed the Union of South Africa, with Louis Botha as prime minister.
1912 General Barry Hertzog founded (Boer) Nationalist Party; ANC formed to campaign for rights of black majority.
1914 Boer revolt in Orange Free State suppressed; South African troops fought for the British Empire in World War I.
1919 Jan Smuts succeeded Botha as premier; South West Africa (Namibia) became a South African mandate.
1924 Hertzog became prime minister, aiming to sharpen racial segregation and loosen ties to British Empire.
1939–45 Smuts led South Africa into World War II despite neutralism of Hertzog; South African troops fought with the Allies in the Middle East, East Africa, and Italy.
1948 Racial policy of apartheid ('separateness') adopted when National Party (NP) took power under Daniel Malan; continued by his successors Johannes Strijdom 1954–58, Hendrik Verwoerd 1958–66, B J Vorster 1966–78, and P J Botha 1978–89.
1950 Entire population classified by race; Group Areas Act segregated blacks and whites; ANC responded with campaign of civil disobedience.
1960 70 black demonstrators killed at Sharpville; ANC banned.
1961 South Africa left the Commonwealth and became a republic.
1964 ANC leader Nelson Mandela sentenced to life imprisonment.
1967 Terrorism Act introduced indefinite detention without trial.
1970s Over 3 million people forcibly resettled in black 'homelands'.
1976 Over 600 killed in clashes between black protesters and security forces in Soweto.
1984 New constitution gave segregated representation to coloureds and Asians, but continued to exclude blacks.
1985 Growth of violence in black townships led to proclamation of state of emergency.
1986 USA and Commonwealth imposed limited economic sanctions against South Africa.
1989 F W de Klerk succeeded P W Botha as president; public facilities desegregated; many ANC activists released.
1990 Ban on ANC lifted; Mandela released; talks began between government and ANC; daily average of 35 murders; Namibia became independent.
1991 De Klerk repealed remaining apartheid laws; sanctions lifted; severe fighting between ANC and the Zulu Inkatha movement.
1993 Interim majority-rule constitution adopted; de Klerk and Mandela agreed to form government of national unity after free elections.
1994 ANC victory in first non-racial elections; Mandela became president; Commonwealth membership restored.
1996 De Klerk withdrew NP from coalition after new constitution failed to provide for power-sharing after 1999.
1997 New constitution signed by President Mandela. F W de Klerk announced his retirement from politics. Thabo Mbeki succeeded Mandela as president of ANC.
1998 Truth and Reconciliation Commission published report on apartheid.

SEE ALSO African National Congress; Afrikaner; apartheid; Mandela, Nelson; South African Wars

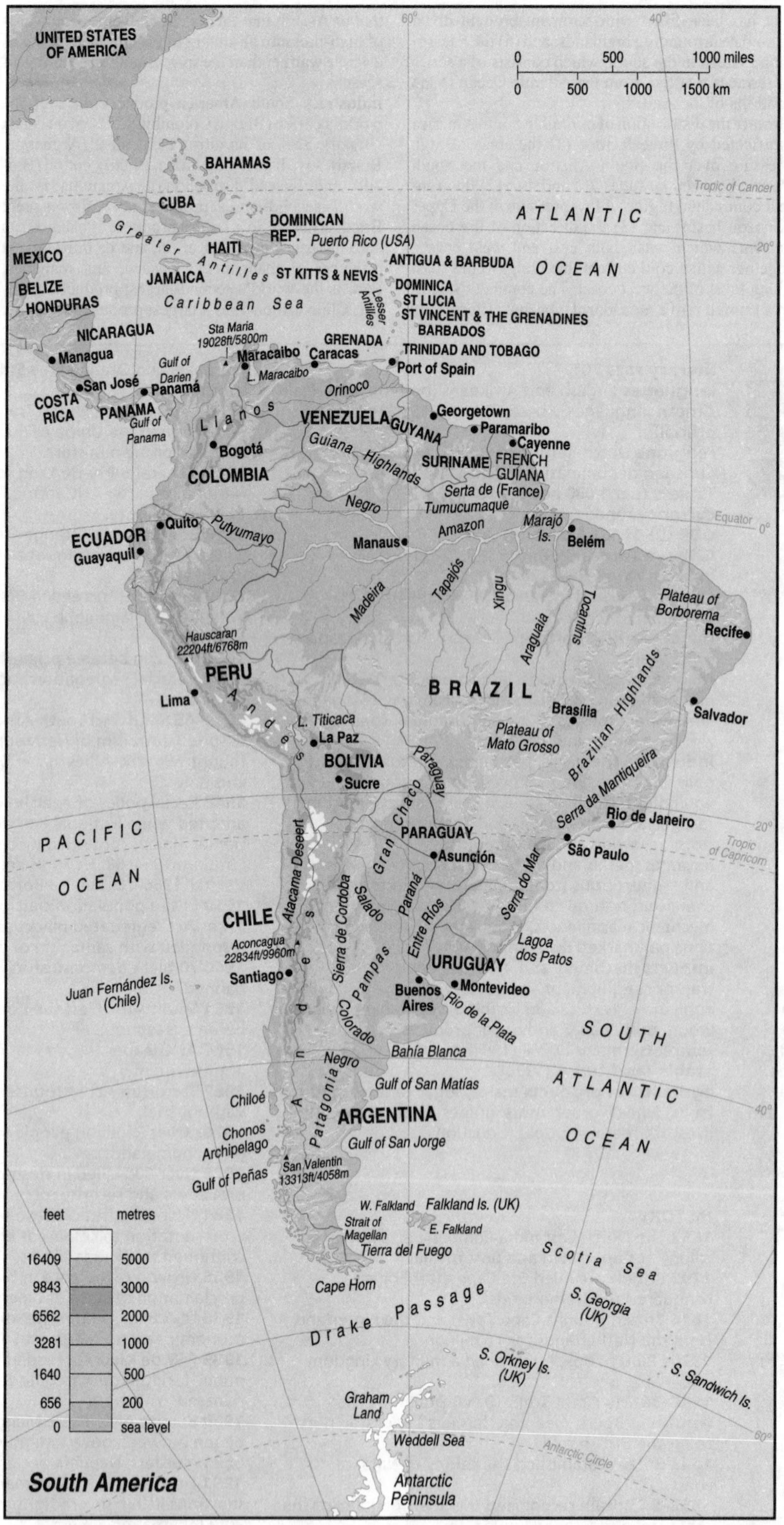

population (1988) 285 million, rising to 550 million (est) by the year 2000; annual growth rate from 1980 to 1985, 2.3%
language Spanish, Portuguese (chief language in Brazil), Dutch (Surinam), French (French Guiana), Native American languages; Hindi, Javanese, and Chinese spoken by descendants of Asian immigrants to Surinam and Guyana; a variety of Creole dialects spoken by those of African descent
religion 90–95% Roman Catholic; local animist beliefs among Amerindians; Hindu and Muslim religions predominate among the descendants of Asian immigrants in Surinam and Guyana.

Southampton seaport and, from 1997, unitary authority of England, on Southampton Water (*see United Kingdom map*); population (1991) 196,800. Industries include marine engineering, chemicals, plastics, flour-milling, cables, electrical goods, and tobacco. It is a major passenger and container port. There is an oil refinery at Fawley.

The *Mayflower* originally set sail from here en route to North America 1620 (bad weather forced the ship into Plymouth and hence the ship finally sailed from there), as did the *Titanic* on its fateful maiden voyage 1912. The ◊Ordnance Survey is located here.

Southampton Henry Wriothesley, 3rd Earl of Southampton 1573–1624. English courtier, patron of Shakespeare. Shakespeare dedicated *Venus and Adonis* and *The Rape of Lucrece* to him and may have addressed him in the sonnets.

South Australia

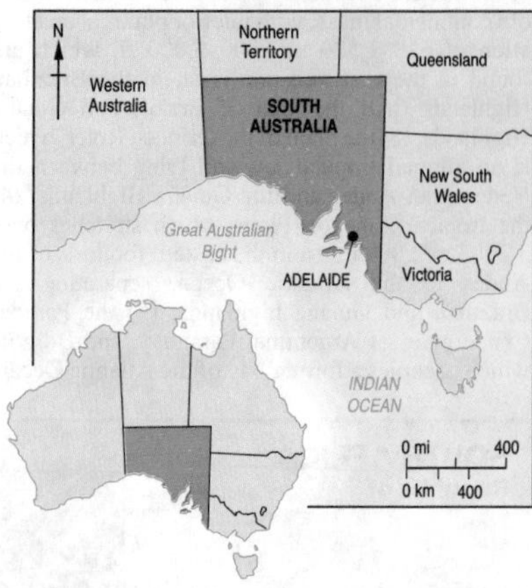

South Australia state of the Commonwealth of Australia
area 984,000 sq km/379,824 sq mi
capital Adelaide (chief port)
towns Whyalla, Mount Gambier
features Murray Valley irrigated area, including wine-growing Barossa Valley; lakes: ◊Eyre, Torrens; mountains: Mount Lofty, Musgrave, Flinders; parts of the Nullarbor Plain, and Great Victoria and Simpson deserts; experimental rocket range in the arid N at Woomera
industries meat and wool (80% of area cattle and sheep grazing), wines and spirits, dried and canned fruit, iron (Middleback Range), coal (Leigh Creek), copper, uranium (Roxby Downs), oil and natural gas in the NE, lead, zinc, iron, opals, household and electrical goods, vehicles
population (1991) 1,400,700 (1% Aborigines)
history possibly known to the Dutch in the 16th century; surveyed by Dutch navigator Abel Tasman 1644; first European settlement 1834; province 1836; became a state 1901.

South Ayrshire local authority of Scotland created 1996 (*see United Kingdom map*).

South Carolina state in SE USA; nicknamed Palmetto State
area 80,600 sq km/31,112 sq mi
capital Columbia
towns Charleston, Greenville-Spartanburg
population (1991) 3,560,000
features large areas of woodland; subtropical climate in coastal areas; the Grand Strand, a resort area with 89 km/55 mi of beach; semi-tropical islands including Kiawah, Seabrook, and Isle of Palms; Frances Marion national forest; Boone Hall Plantation (1681, with the original slave quarters, reputedly the inspiration for Tara in the film version of *Gone with the Wind*); Fort Sumter national monument
industries tobacco, soya beans, lumber, textiles, clothing, paper, wood pulp, chemicals, nonelectrical machinery, primary and fabricated metals
famous people John C Calhoun, 'Dizzy' Gillespie
history first Spanish settlers 1526; Charles I gave the area (known as Carolina) to Robert Heath (1575–1649), attorney general 1629; one of the original 13 states 1776; joined the Confederacy 1860; readmitted to Union 1868.

South Dakota state in W USA; nicknamed Coyote or Sunshine State
area 199,800 sq km/77,123 sq mi
capital Pierre
cities Sioux Falls, Rapid City, Aberdeen
physical Great Plains; Black Hills, with Mount Rushmore; Badlands
features Black Hills national forest, with granite Mount Rushmore, on whose face giant relief portrait heads of former presidents Washington, Jefferson, Lincoln, and T Roosevelt are carved; the Badlands national park; the Missouri River; Wind Cave national park
industries cereals, hay, livestock, gold (second-largest US producer), meat products
population (1991) 703,000
famous people Crazy Horse, Sitting Bull, Ernest O Lawrence
history claimed by French 18th century; first white settlements 1794; passed to the USA as part of the Louisiana Purchase 1803; became a state 1889.

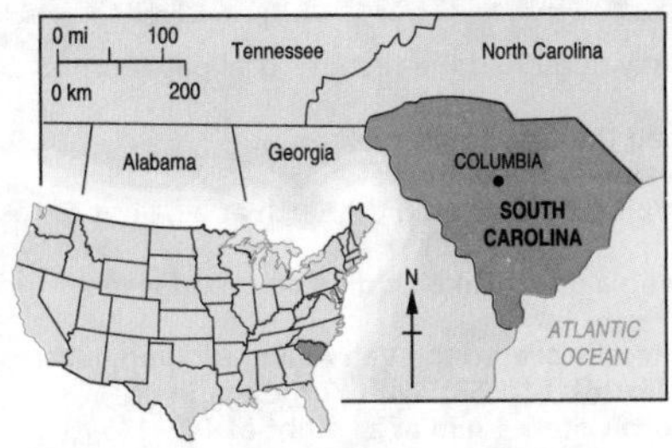

South Carolina

Southeast Asia Treaty Organization (SEATO) collective military system 1954–77 established by Australia, France, New Zealand, Pakistan, the Philippines, Thailand, the UK, and the USA, with Vietnam, Cambodia, and Laos as protocol states. After the Vietnam War, SEATO was phased out.

Its nonmilitary aspects were assumed by the ◊Association of Southeast Asian Nations (ASEAN).

Southend-on-Sea resort in Essex, England, on the Thames estuary, the nearest seaside resort to London; population (1991) 158,500. The shallow water of the Thames estuary enabled the building of a pier 2 km/1.25 mi long, the longest in the world.

Southern Cross popular name for the constellation ◊Crux.

Southerne Thomas 1660–1746. English playwright and poet. He was the author of the tragicomedies *Oroonoko* 1695–96 and *The Fatal Marriage* 1694.

southern lights common name for the ◊aurora australis, coloured light in southern skies.

Southern Ocean corridor linking the Pacific, Atlantic, and Indian oceans, all of which receive cold polar water from the world's largest ocean surface current, the Antarctic Circumpolar Current, which passes through the Southern Ocean.

Southey Robert 1774–1843. English poet and author. He is sometimes regarded as one of the 'Lake poets', more because of his friendship with Samuel Taylor ◊Coleridge and William ◊Wordsworth and residence in Keswick, in the English Lake District, than for any Romantic influence in his work. In 1813 he became poet laureate, but he is better known for his *Life of Nelson* 1813 and for his letters.

He was an early admirer of the French Revolution, whose aims he supported in the epic poem *Joan of Arc* 1796. He joined with Coleridge in planning the utopian 'Pantisocracy', a scheme for a radical community in the USA, which came to nothing, and married Edith Fricker 1795. He later abandoned his revolutionary views, and from 1808 contributed regularly to the Tory *Quarterly Review*. He wrote long epic poems reflecting the contemporary fashion for exotic melodrama, and short poems including 'The Battle of Blenheim' and 'The Inchcape Rock'.

South Georgia island in the S Atlantic, a British crown colony administered, with the South Sandwich Islands, from the Falkland Islands by a commissioner; area 3,757 sq km/1,450 sq mi. The average temperature on the island is −2°C/28.4°F.

There has been no permanent population since the whaling station was abandoned 1966. South Georgia lies 1,300 km/800 mi SE of the Falkland Islands, of which it was a dependency until 1985. The British Antarctic Survey has a station on nearby Bird Island.

South Georgia was visited by Capt James Cook 1775. The explorer Edward Shackleton is buried here. The chief settlement, Grytviken, was established as a whaling station 1904 and abandoned 1966; it was reoccupied by a small military garrison after the Falklands War 1982.

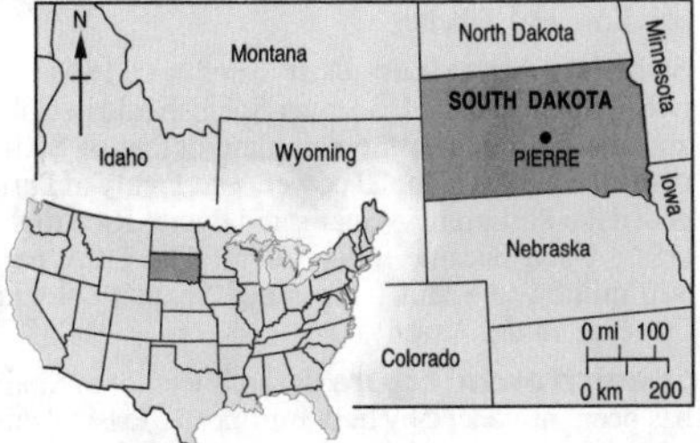

South Dakota

South Glamorgan (Welsh ***De Morgannwg***) former county of S Wales, created 1974, abolished 1996.

South Gloucestershire unitary authority of England created 1996 (*see United Kingdom map*).

South Holland (Dutch ***Zuid Holland***) low-lying coastal province of the Netherlands, between the provinces of North Holland and Zeeland
area 2,910 sq km/1,123 sq mi
capital The Hague
towns Rotterdam, Dordrecht, Leiden, Delft, Gouda
industries bulbs, horticulture, livestock, dairy products, chemicals, textiles
population (1995 est) 3,325,100
history once part of the former county of Holland, which was divided into two provinces 1840.

South Korea see ◊Korea, South.

South Lanarkshire local authority of Scotland created 1996 (*see United Kingdom map*).

South Ossetia autonomous region of the Georgian republic; population (1990) 99,800; capital Tshkinvali, population (1989) 34,000. See ◊Ossetia.

South Pacific Commission (SPC) former name of the ◊Pacific Islands Commission (PIC).

South Pacific Forum (SPF) former name of the ◊Pacific Islands Commission (PIC).

South Sea Bubble financial crisis in Britain in 1720. The South Sea Company, founded 1711, which had a monopoly of trade with South America, offered in 1719 to take over more than half the national debt in return for further concessions. Its 100 shares rapidly rose to 1,000, and an orgy of speculation followed. When the 'bubble' burst, thousands were ruined.

The discovery that cabinet ministers had been guilty of corruption led to a political crisis. Robert Walpole became prime minister, protected the royal family and members of the government from scandal, and restored financial confidence.

South, the historically, the states of the USA bounded on the N by the ◊Mason–Dixon Line, the Ohio River, and the E and N borders of Missouri, with an agrarian economy based on plantations worked by slaves, and which seceded from the Union 1861, beginning the American Civil War, as the ◊Confederacy. The term is now loosely applied in a geographical and cultural sense, with Texas often regarded as part of the Southwest rather than the South. See also ◊North–South divide.

South Uist island in the Outer Hebrides, Scotland, separated from North Uist by the island of Benbecula. There is a guided-missile range here.

Southwark inner borough of S Greater London. It includes the districts of Camberwell, ◊Dulwich, and Walworth.
features large Roman baths complex, about AD 120, and fine wall paintings have been excavated; Southwark Cathedral (1220), earliest Gothic church in London, with nave built in the 1890s (formerly a parish church, it became a cathedral 1905); inns and alehouses, including the Tabard Inn, where Chaucer's pilgrims met, and the George Inn (1677), the last galleried inn in London; formerly seven prisons, including the Clink and the Marshalsea; site of Globe Theatre (built on Bankside 1599 by Burbage, Shakespeare, and others, burned down 1613, rebuilt 1995); the International Shakespeare Globe Centre is planned to open 1999; Imperial War Museum; Dulwich Picture Gallery; Horniman Museum; Elephant and Castle public house, Walworth; Labour Party headquarters in Walworth Road; former Bankside power station to be transformed into the Tate Gallery of Modern Art (Swiss architects Herzog and de Meuron)
famous people John Harvard (1607–1638), founder of Harvard College, Massachusetts, USA – he is commemorated in Harvard Chapel, Southwark Cathedral; Joseph Chamberlain
population (1991) 218,500.

South Yorkshire metropolitan county of NE England, created 1974; in 1986, most of the functions of the former county council were transferred to the metropolitan district councils
area 1,560 sq km/602 sq mi
towns Barnsley, Sheffield, Doncaster, Rotherham
features river Don; part of Peak District National Park; the 1995 Millennium Commission award will enable the Earth Centre for environmental research to be built near Doncaster
industries metal work, coal, dairy, sheep, arable farming
population (1991) 1,262,600
famous people Ian Botham, Arthur Scargill.

Soutine Chaïm 1893–1943. Lithuanian-born French painter. An important French Expressionist, he used brilliant colours and thick, energetically applied paint to create his landscapes and portraits, such as *Page Boy* 1927 (Albright-Knox Art Gallery, Buffalo, New York).

Born in Smilovitchi, Lithuania, he studied briefly at the art school in Vilna, and then found his way to Paris, where he lived a poverty-stricken life among painters and poets. He developed his distinctive style 1919–21 after studying at the Ecole des Beaux-Arts, Paris. He was a close friend of the painter ◊Modigliani, on whose death he retired for a while to Céret, painting tormented canvases. After 1923, however, when Zborowski, the dealer to whom Modigliani had introduced him, arranged an exhibition, he had a measure of success in Paris.

sovereign British gold coin, introduced by Henry VII, which became the standard monetary unit in 1817. Minting ceased for currency purposes in the UK in 1914, but the sovereign continued to be used as 'unofficial' currency in the Middle East. It was minted for the last time in 1987 and has now been replaced by the Britannia.

The value is notionally 1, but the actual value is that of the weight of the gold at current rates.

Like the Mexican 50-peso piece, US 20-dollar piece, and South African krugerrand, sovereigns are bought by investors suspicious of falling values of paper currencies.

sovereignty absolute authority within a given territory. The possession of sovereignty is taken to be the distinguishing feature of the state, as against other forms of community. The term has an internal aspect, in that it refers to the ultimate source of authority within a state, such as a parliament or monarch, and an external aspect, where it denotes the independence of the state from any outside authority.

soviet (Russian 'council') originally a strike committee elected by Russian workers in the 1905 revolution; in 1917 these were set up by peasants, soldiers, and factory workers. The soviets sent delegates to the All-Russian Congress of Soviets to represent their opinions to a future government. They were later taken over by the ◊Bolsheviks.

Soviet Central Asia former name (to 1991) of the ◊Central Asian Republics.

Soviet Union alternative name for the former ◊Union of Soviet Socialist Republics (USSR).

Soweto (acronym for ***South West Township***) racially segregated urban settlement in South Africa, SW of Johannesburg; population (1991) 597,000. It experienced civil unrest during the ◊apartheid regime.

It began as a shanty town in the 1930s and is now the largest black city in South Africa, but until 1976 its population could have status only as temporary residents, serving as a workforce for Johannesburg. There were serious riots June 1976, sparked by a ruling that Afrikaans be used in African schools here; the riots were violently suppressed, with 176 people killed and more than 1,000 injured. Reforms followed, but riots flared up again 1985 and continued until the multiracial elections April 1994.

soya bean leguminous plant *Glycine max*, native to E Asia, in particular Japan and China. Originally grown as a forage crop, it is increasingly used for human consumption in cooking oils and margarine, as a flour, soya milk, soy sauce, or processed into tofu, miso, or textured vegetable protein.

Soya is the richest natural vegetable food. The dried bean is 18–22% fat, 35% carbohydrate, and one hectare of soya beans yields 162 kg/357 lb of protein (compared with 9 kg/20 lb per hectare for beef). There are more than 1,000 varieties. The plant has been cultivated in Asia for about 5,000 years, and first became known in Europe when brought back from Japan by German botanist Engelbert Kaenfer in 1692. Today the USA produces more than Asia and many crops are genetically modified.

Soyinka Wole. Pen name of Akinwande Oluwole 1934– . Nigerian author and dramatist. His plays explore Yoruba myth, ritual, and culture, with the early *Swamp Dwellers* 1958 and *The Lion and the Jewel* 1959, culminating with *A Dance of the Forests* 1960. Tragic inevitability is the theme of *Madmen and Specialists* 1970 and of *Death and the King's Horseman* 1976, but he has also written sharp satires, from *The Jero Plays* 1960 and 1973 to the indictment of African dictatorship in *A Play of Giants* 1984. He was the first African to receive the Nobel Prize for Literature, 1986. His anthology *From Zia with Love*, appeared 1992.

Soyuz (Russian 'union') Soviet series of spacecraft, capable of carrying up to three cosmonauts. Soyuz spacecraft consist of three parts: a rear section containing engines; the central crew compartment; and a forward compartment that gives additional room for working and living space. They are now used for ferrying crews up to space stations, though they were originally used for independent space flight.

Soyuz 1 crashed on its first flight April 1967, killing the lone pilot, Vladimir Komarov. The *Soyuz 11* 1971 had three deaths on re-entry. In 1975 the Apollo–Soyuz test project resulted in a successful docking in orbit.

Spaak Paul-Henri 1899–1972. Belgian socialist politician. From 1936 to 1966 he held office almost continuously as foreign minister or prime minister. He was an ardent advocate of international peace.

space or ***outer space*** the void that exists beyond Earth's atmosphere. Above 120 km/75 mi, very little atmosphere remains, so objects can continue to move quickly without extra energy. The space between the planets is not entirely empty, but filled with the tenuous gas of the ◊solar wind as well as dust specks.

space-frame in architecture, a lightweight, triangulated, structural framework, designed to be of uniform load resistance and used principally in large-span constructions, such as exhibition halls, stadia, and aircraft hangars. The Eiffel Tower, Paris, 1889, is a space-frame of riveted steel beams. A contemporary development is Buckminster Fuller's ◊geodesic dome, a shell-like space-frame covered in plastic, plywood, or metal sheeting.

Spacelab small space station built by the European Space Agency, carried in the cargo bay of the US space shuttle, in which it remains throughout each flight, returning to Earth with the shuttle. Spacelab consists of a pressurized module in which astronauts can work, and a series of pallets, open to the vacuum of space, on which equipment is mounted.

Spacelab is used for astronomy, Earth observation, and experiments utilizing the conditions of weightlessness and vacuum in orbit. The pressurized module can be flown with or without pallets, or the pallets can be flown on their own, in which case the astronauts remain in the shuttle's own crew compartment. All the sections of Spacelab can be reused many times. The first Spacelab mission, consisting of a pressurized module and pallets, lasted ten days Nov–Dec 1983.

space probe any instrumented object sent beyond Earth to collect data from other parts of the Solar System and from deep space. The first probe was the Soviet *Lunik 1*, which flew past the Moon 1959. The first successful planetary probe was the US *Mariner 2*, which flew past Venus 1962, using ◊transfer orbit. The first space probe to leave the Solar System was *Pioneer 10* 1983. Space probes include *Galileo*, *Giotto*, *Magellan*, *Mars Observer*, *Ulysses*, the ◊Moon probes, and the Mariner, Pioneer, Viking, and Voyager series.

SPACE FLIGHT: TIMELINE

1903	Russian scientist Konstantin Tsiolkovsky published the first practical paper on astronautics.
1926	US engineer Robert Goddard launched the first liquid-fuel rocket.
1937–45	In Germany, Wernher von Braun developed the V2 rocket.
1957	4 Oct: The first space satellite, *Sputnik 1* (USSR) orbited the Earth at a height of 229–898 km/142–558 mi in 96.2 min. 3 Nov: *Sputnik 2* was launched carrying a dog, 'Laika'; it died on board seven days later.
1958	31 Jan: *Explorer 1*, the first US satellite, discovered the Van Allen radiation belts.
1961	12 April: the first crewed spaceship, *Vostok 1* (USSR), with Yuri Gagarin on board, was recovered after a single orbit of 89.1 min at a height of 142–175 km/88–109 mi.
1962	20 Feb: John Glenn in *Friendship 7* (USA) became the first American to orbit the Earth. *Telstar* (USA), a communications satellite, sent the first live television transmission between the USA and Europe.
1963	16–19 June: Valentina Tereshkova in *Vostok 1* (USSR) became the first woman in space.
1967	27 Jan: US astronauts Virgil Grissom, Edward White, and Roger Chaffee were killed during a simulated countdown when a flash fire swept through the cabin of *Apollo 1*. 24 April: Vladimir Komarov was the first person to be killed on a mission, when his ship, *Soyuz 1* (USSR), crash-landed on the Earth.
1969	20 July: Neil Armstrong of *Apollo 11* (USA) was the first person to walk on the Moon.
1970	10 Nov: *Luna 17* (USSR) was launched; its space probe, *Lunokhod*, took photographs and made soil analyses of the Moon's surface.
1971	19 April: *Salyut 1* (USSR), the first orbital space station, was established; it was later visited by the *Soyuz 11* crewed spacecraft.
1973	*Skylab 2*, the first US orbital space station, was established.
1975	15–24 July: *Apollo 18* (USA) and *Soyuz 19* (USSR) made a joint flight and linked up in space.
1979	The European Space Agency's satellite launcher, *Ariane 1*, was launched.
1981	12 April: The first reusable crewed spacecraft, the space shuttle *Columbia* (USA), was launched.
1986	Space shuttle *Challenger* (USA) exploded shortly after take-off, killing all seven crew members.
1988	US shuttle programme resumed with launch of *Discovery*. Soviet shuttle *Buran* was launched from the rocket *Energiya*. Soviet cosmonauts Musa Manarov and Vladimir Titov in space station *Mir* spent a record 365 days 59 min in space.
1990	April: Hubble Space Telescope (USA) was launched from Cape Canaveral.
1991	5 April: The Gamma Ray Observatory was launched from the space shuttle *Atlantis* to survey the sky at gamma-ray wavelengths.
1992	Dec: Space shuttle *Endeavour* successfully carried out mission to replace the Hubble Space Telescope's solar panels and repair its mirror.
1995	June: the US space shuttle *Atlantis* docked with *Mir*, exchanging crew members.
1996	19 Feb: tenth anniversary of launch of *Mir* space station. 4 June: spectacular failure of maiden flight of European Space Agency's Ariane 5 rocket, destroying four scientific satellites called Cluster. 31 July: landing accident destroyed Clipper Graham, a US experimental unmanned single-stage reusable rocket.
1998	*Deep Space I*, launched in 1998 is the first spacecraft to steer itself across the Solar System.

space shuttle reusable crewed spacecraft. The first was launched 12 April 1981 by the USA. It was developed by NASA to reduce the cost of using space for commercial, scientific, and military purposes. After leaving its payload in space, the space-shuttle orbiter can be flown back to Earth to land on a runway, and is then available for reuse.

Four orbiters were built: *Columbia*, *Challenger*, *Discovery*, and *Atlantis*. *Challenger* was destroyed in a midair explosion just over a minute after its tenth launch 28 Jan 1986, killing all seven crew members, the result of a failure in one of the solid rocket boosters. Flights resumed with redesigned boosters in Sept 1988. A replacement orbiter, *Endeavour*, was built, which had its maiden flight in May 1992.

space station any large structure designed for human occupation in space for extended periods of time. Space stations are used for carrying out astronomical observations and surveys of Earth, as well as for biological studies and the processing of materials in weightlessness. The first space station was ◊*Salyut 1*, and the USA has launched ◊*Skylab*. The first components of the international space station, a joint project by 16 nations, were launched Dec 1998.

space-time in physics, combination of space and time used in the theory of ◊relativity. When developing relativity, Albert Einstein showed that time was in many respects like an extra dimension (or direction) to space. Space and time can thus be considered as entwined into a single entity, rather than two separate things.

Space-time is considered to have four dimensions: three of space and one of time. In relativity theory, events are described as occurring at points in space-time. The general theory of relativity describes how space-time is distorted by the presence of material bodies, an effect that we observe as gravity.

spadix in botany, an ◊inflorescence consisting of a long, fleshy axis bearing many small, stalkless flowers. It is partially enclosed by a large bract or ◊spathe. A spadix is characteristic of plants belonging to the family Araceae, including the arum lily *Zantedeschia aethiopica*.

Spain country in SW Europe, on the Iberian Peninsula between the Atlantic Ocean and the Mediterranean Sea, bounded N by France and W by Portugal. *See country box on p. 998 and tables on p. 999.*

spaniel any of several breeds of small and medium-sized gundog, characterized by large, drooping ears and a wavy, long, silky coat. Spaniels are divided into two groups: those that are still working gundogs – Clumber, cocker, Irish water, springer, and Sussex – and the toy breeds that are kept as pets – including the Japanese, King Charles, papillon, and Tibetan.

Spanish-American War brief war 1898 between Spain and the USA over Spanish rule in Cuba and the Philippines; the complete defeat of Spain made the USA a colonial power. The Treaty of Paris ceded the Philippines, Guam, and Puerto Rico to the USA; Cuba became independent. The USA paid $20 million to Spain. This ended Spain's colonial presence in the Americas.

Spanish architecture the architecture of Spain has been influenced by both European Classical and Islamic traditions.

space shuttle The launch of a space shuttle. These reusable crewed spacecraft were developed by NASA as a cost-cutting exercise. *Image Select (UK) Ltd*

early Christian (5th–8th centuries) The Visigoths invaded Spain 415 and were later converted to Christianity. Their small churches, few of which remain, are indebted to Roman architecture and have parallels with the early French Romanesque style. Fine examples are San Juan de Banos 661 and San Pedro de Nave about 7th century.

Muslim (8th–15th centuries) The Muslims invaded 711, quickly capturing most of the country. In Córdoba, the Great Mosque, a huge rectangular hall with a proliferation of columns, was begun 786 and worked on over the next 200 years. Elsewhere in Muslim-occupied Spain architecture developed in unique response to its environment, characterized by a particularly delicate decorative style. In the fortified palaces of the Alcázar, Seville, 1350–69, and the Alhambra, Granada, built mainly 1248–1354, a vocabulary of water gardens, courtyards, colourful tilework, and elaborate stalactite decoration is used.

Romanesque (11th–12th centuries) Romanesque church building began in Catalonia from the 11th century and developed along the pilgrimage routes from France. The cathedral of Santiago de Compostela (begun about 1075) is a fine example, with its barrel-vaulted roof and huge, sculpted Pórtico de la Gloria.

Gothic (13th–16th centuries) In the 12th century, the Cistercian order brought the Gothic style to Spain and by the following century the style of northern French Gothic cathedrals had been adopted, as in Burgos Cathedral (begun 1221). The Catalan version of Gothic proved the most distinctive, introducing a high wide nave, as at Sta Maria, Barcelona (begun 1298). Later cathedrals, such as that in Seville (begun 1402), show German influence in their use of rib-vaulting but this is tempered by unique ground plans owing much to Islamic mosque architecture.

Renaissance (16th century) The Italian Renaissance reached Spain in the 16th century. The finest example of the High Renaissance is the Escorial (begun 1563), the huge palace, monastery, and church built for Phillip II, largely designed by Juan de Herrera (1530–1597). This structure is more severe than most other Spanish Renaissance architecture, which is characterized by richly decorative work in a style known as Plateresque, as in the façade of Salamanca University 1514.

Baroque (17th–18th centuries) An interest in surface decoration, reflecting the Muslim past, re-emerged in the late-17th-century Spanish variation of Baroque, Churrigueresque, of which the west front of the cathedral of Santiago de Compostela (begun 1738), is a fine example. José Benito de Churriguera and Narciso Tomè (active 1715–1742) were both active in this style.

Neo-Classicism (18th century) During the latter part of the 18th century a severe Neo-Classicism was developed in such works as the portico of Pamplona Cathedral 1783 by Ventura Rodríguez (1717–1783).

Art Nouveau (late 19th–early 20th century) The industrialization of Catalan provided Spain with a distinctive late-19th-century architecture, a variation of Art Nouveau known as Modernismo. Connected in part to a growth in Catalan nationalism, it is best represented in the works of Lluis Doménech i Montaner (1850–1923), who built the Palau de la Música Catalana 1905–08, and of Antonio Gaudí, who designed the Church of the Holy Family (begun 1883) and the Casa Milá 1905–10, both in Barcelona.

20th century Under Franco, Spain retreated from its European connections into a provincialism that was echoed in its architecture. Since the restoration of democracy numerous designers of international importance have emerged. Among these are the Neo-Classicist Ricardo Bofill, now practising largely in France, who built the Antigone development in Montpelier 1992, the architect and engineer Santiago Calatrava, and Rafael Moneo (1937–), who was the architect responsible for the Museum of Archaeology at Mérida 1986.

Spanish Armada fleet sent by Philip II of Spain against England in 1588 in response to the English army supporting the Netherlands in their revolt against Spain. Consisting of 130 ships, it sailed from Lisbon and carried on a running fight up the Channel with the English fleet of 197 small ships under Howard of Effingham and Francis ◊Drake. The Armada anchored off Calais but fire ships forced it to put to sea, and a general action followed off Gravelines. What remained of the Armada escaped around the N of Scotland and W of Ireland, suffering many losses by storm and shipwreck on the way. Only about half the original fleet returned to Spain.

Spanish art painting and sculpture of Spain. Spanish art has been fashioned by both European and Islamic traditions, with notable regional adaptations. Whatever the source of its influences, Spanish art has always transformed styles and given them a distinctively Spanish character.

historical background Spain was under Roman dominance 218 BC–AD 414, and there are extensive Roman architectural remains and some mosaics and fragments of mural painting survive. The region was overrun by the Visigoths 414 and by the Arabs 711. The Visigoths contributed little to artistic development, crudely carrying on Roman traditions. The Arab civilization was brilliant and played an important part in the development of Spanish art and architecture.

9th–10th centuries The origins of painting in Spain are traced in illuminated manuscripts and in the remains of mural decoration. Many manuscripts survive from the 9th and 10th centuries, reflecting strong Islamic and Byzantine influence in the style known as Mozarabic – the first genuinely Spanish national art.

11th–13th centuries In the north of Spain, particularly in Catalonia, the Romanesque style took root and brought Spain more into the mainstream of European artistic development. Bold and colourful church frescoes were its finest expression – Spain has more surviving examples of fresco painting from that time than any other country. In the south, occupied by the Moors 711–1492, Islamic influence predominated.

13th–14th centuries During this Gothic phase in Spanish art, the influence of Italian art, particularly the painting style of Siena, became pronounced. It can be seen clearly in the work of Ferrer Bassa, the first great identifiable Spanish painter and the founder of the Catalan school. An important school of manuscript illuminators grew up at the court of Alfonso X of Castile (reigned 1252–82), reflecting the French influence which became important in the early Gothic period.

15th century The unification of Spain 1472 brought about a rapid development in the arts, largely due to the royal patronage of Ferdinand and Isabella. A Hispano-Flemish style flourished, based largely on Flemish painting (in particular the works of van Eyck and van der Weyden) but also on Moorish traditions. Fernando Gallego (c. 1440–after 1507) and Luis Dalmau (active 1428–60) were among its finest exponents. The influence of the Italian Renaissance can be seen in the works of the court painter Pedro Berruguete.

16th century The full impact of the Italian Renaissance is evident in the paintings of Luis de Morales (died 1586), who was strongly influenced by Leonardo da Vinci, and the paintings and sculptures of Alonso Berruguete (the first important Spanish sculptor). The outstanding artist of the late 16th century – the first great figure in Spanish art – was El Greco, a Cretan whose Mannerist style drew on

spadix The numerous tiny stalkless flowers on the spadix of the sweet flag *Acorus calamus*. A plant of watersides, the sweet flag is native to S Asia and North America but is now widely naturalized in Europe, including the British Isles. *Premaphotos Wildlife*

SPAIN
Kingdom of

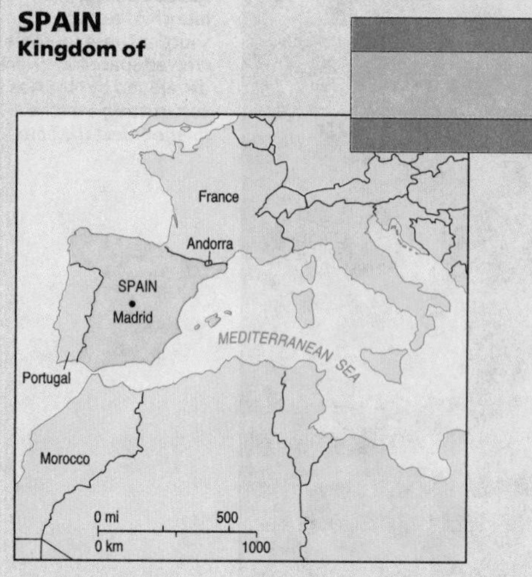

national name *Reino de España*
area 504,732 sq km/194,827 sq mi
capital Madrid
major towns/cities Zaragoza, Seville, Murcia, Córdoba
major ports Barcelona, Valencia, Cartagena, Málaga, Cádiz, Vigo, Santander, Bilbao
physical features central plateau with mountain ranges, lowlands in S; rivers Ebro, Douro, Tagus, Guadiana, Guadalquivir; Iberian Plateau (Meseta); Pyrenees, Cantabrian Mountains, Andalusian Mountains, Sierra Nevada
territories Balearic and Canary Islands; in N Africa: Ceuta, Melilla, Alhucemas, Chafarinas Is, Peñón de Vélez
head of state King Juan Carlos I from 1975
head of government José Maria Aznar from 1996
political system constitutional monarchy
administrative divisions 17 autonomous communities (contain 50 provinces)
political parties Socialist Workers' Party (PSOE), democratic socialist; Popular Party (PP), centre-right
armed forces 206,500 (1994)
conscription nine months
defence spend (% GDP) 1.6 (1994)
education spend (% GNP) 4.6 (1992)
health spend (% GDP) 5.7 (1993)
death penalty abolished 1995
population 39,134,000 (1998 est)
population growth rate 0.2% (1990–95); 0.0% (2000–05)
age distribution (% of total population) <15 16.5%, 15–65 68.6%, >65 14.9% (1995)
ethnic distribution mostly of Moorish, Roman, and Carthaginian descent
population density (per sq km) 78 (1994)
urban population (% of total) 76 (1995)
labour force 41% of population: 12% agriculture, 33% industry, 55% services (1990)
unemployment 22.9% (1995)
child mortality rate (under 5, per 1,000 live births) 9 (1997)
life expectancy 75 (men), 81 (women)
education (compulsory years) 10
literacy rate 97% (men), 93% (women)
languages Spanish (Castilian, official), Basque, Catalan, Galician
religion Roman Catholic
TV sets (per 1,000 people) 509 (1996)
currency peseta
GDP (US $) 531.3 billion (1997)
GDP per capita (PPP) (US $) 14,216 (1995)
growth rate 3.0% (1994/95)
average annual inflation 4.2% (1995)
major trading partners EU (principally Germany, France, Italy, and the UK), USA, Japan
resources coal, lignite, anthracite, copper, iron, zinc, uranium, potassium salts
industries machinery, motor vehicles, textiles, footwear, chemicals, electrical appliances, wine, olive oil, fishery products, steel, cement, tourism
exports motor vehicles, machinery and electrical equipment, vegetable products, metals and their manufactures, foodstuffs. Principal market: France 20% (1993)
imports machinery and transport equipment, electrical equipment, petroleum and petroleum products, chemicals, consumer goods. Principal source: Germany 16.2% (1993)
arable land 29.7% (1993)
agricultural products barley, wheat, sugar beet, vegetables, citrus fruit, grapes, olives; fishing (one of world's largest fishing fleets)

HISTORY
2nd C BC Roman conquest of the Iberian peninsula, which became the province of Hispania.
5th C AD After the fall of the Roman Empire, Iberia was overrun by Vandals and Visigoths.
711 Muslims invaded from N Africa and overthrew Visigoth kingdom.
9th C Christians in northern Spain formed kingdoms of Asturias, Aragon, Navarre, and Léon, and county of Castile.
10th C Abd-al-Rahman III established caliphate of Córdoba; Muslim culture at its height in Spain.
1230 Léon and Castile united under Ferdinand III, who drove the Muslims from most of southern Spain.
14th C Spain consisted of Christian kingdoms of Castile, Aragon, and Navarre, and the Muslim emirate of Granada.
1469 Marriage of Ferdinand of Aragon and Isabella of Castile; kingdoms united on their accession 1479.
1492 Conquest of Granada ended Muslim rule in Spain.
1494 Treaty of Tordesillas; Spain and Portugal divided newly discovered America; Spain became a world power.
1519–56 Emperor Charles V was both King of Spain and Archduke of Austria; he also ruled Naples, Sicily, and the Low Countries; Habsburgs dominant in Europe.
1555 Charles V divided his domains between Spain and Austria before retiring; Spain retained the Low Countries and southern Italy as well as South American colonies.
1568 Dutch rebelled against Spanish rule; Spain recognized independence of Dutch Republic 1648.
1580 Philip II of Spain inherited the throne of Portugal, where Spanish rule lasted until 1640.
1588 The Spanish Armada: attempt to invade England defeated.
17th C Spanish power declined amid wars, corruption, inflation, and loss of civil and religious freedom.
1701–14 War of the Spanish Succession: allied powers fought France to prevent Philip of Bourbon inheriting throne of Spain.
1713–14 Treaties of Utrecht and Rastat: Bourbon dynasty recognized, but Spain lost Gibraltar, southern Italy, and Spanish Netherlands.
1793 Spain declared war on revolutionary France; reduced to a French client state 1795.
1808 Napoleon installed his brother Joseph as King of Spain.
1808–14 Peninsular War: British forces played a large part in liberating Spain and restoring Bourbon dynasty.
1810–30 Spain lost control of its South American colonies.
1833–39 Carlist civil war: Don Carlos (backed by conservatives) unsuccessfully contested the succession of his niece Isabella II (backed by liberals).
1870 Offer of Spanish throne to Leopold of Hohenzollern-Sigmaringen sparked Franco-Prussian War.
1873–74 First republic ended by military coup which restored Bourbon dynasty with Alfonso XII.
1898 Spanish-American War: Spain lost Cuba and Philippines.
1923–30 Dictatorship of General Primo de Rivera with support of Alfonso XIII.
1931 Proclamation of Second Republic, initially dominated by anticlerical radicals and socialists.
1933 Moderates and Catholics won elections; insurrection by socialists and Catalans 1934.
1936 Left-wing Popular Front narrowly won fresh elections; General Francisco Franco launched military rebellion.
1936–39 Spanish Civil War: Nationalists (with significant Italian and German support) defeated Republicans (with limited Soviet support); Franco became dictator of nationalist-fascist regime.
1941 Though officially neutral in World War II, Spain sent 40,000 troops to fight USSR.
1955 Spain admitted to the United Nations (UN).
1975 Death of Franco; succeeded by King Juan Carlos I.
1978 Referendum endorsed democratic constitution.
1982 Socialists took office under Felipe González; Spain joined the North Atlantic Treaty Organization (NATO); Basque separatist organization (ETA) stepped up terrorist campaign.
1986 Spain joined the European Economic Community (EEC).
1996 José Maria Aznar formed a minority PP government.
1997 23 Basque nationalist leaders jailed for terrorist activities.

SEE ALSO Civil War, Spanish; Spanish Armada; Spanish Succession, War of the

both Greek icon painting and the Venetian school. Other important painters of the 16th century were Juan de Juanes (c. 1523–1579), Juan de las Roelas (c. 1558–1625), and Luis de Vargas.

17th century This period, which marked the transition from Mannerist to Baroque, was dominated by sombre and intense religious art in a realist style. Painters include Ribera, Morillo, Zurbarán, Juan de Valdés Leal (1622–1690), Ribalta, and – the towering figure of the age – Velázquez.

Alonso Cano and Montañés (1568–1649) were the leading sculptors during the 17th century, the period when painted wooden statues, expressive of intense religious fervour, were a popular art form.

18th–19th centuries With the advent of the Bourbons in the 18th century, foreign influence again made itself felt. A succession of foreign painters were established at the court, and regional characteristics tended to wane as Madrid grew in importance. Spanish individualism asserted itself once more in Goya, who completely dominated 18th-century Spanish art. His work exerted a great influence on European art in the 19th century, a period during which Spanish art declined, though Esquivel (1806–1857), López y Portaña, and Mariano Fortuny (1838–1874) produced notable work.

20th century Spanish art became an important force in European art. Major figures, many of whom worked abroad, include Juan Gris, Joan Miró, Salvador Dali, and Picasso, widely regarded as the most innovative artist of the century. Antoni Tàpies and Modesto Cuizart (born 1925) are among the leading Spanish artists of the second half of the 20th century.

Spanish Civil War 1936–39. See ◊Civil War, Spanish.

Spanish fly alternative name for a European blister ◊beetle *Lytta vesicatoria*, once used in powdered form as a dangerous diuretic and supposed aphrodisiac.

Spanish language member of the Romance branch of the Indo-European language family, traditionally known as Castilian and originally spoken only in NE Spain. As the language of the court, it has been the standard and literary language of the Spanish state since the 13th century. It is now a world language, spoken in Mexico and all South and Central American countries (except Brazil, Guyana, Surinam, and French Guiana) as well as in the Philippines, Cuba, Puerto Rico, and much of the USA.

Castilian Spanish has never succeeded in supplanting such regional languages as Basque, Gallego or Galician, and Catalan. Because of the long Muslim dominance of the S Iberian peninsula, Spanish has been considerably influenced by Arabic.

Spanish literature of the classical Spanish epics, the 12th-century *El cantar de mio Cid* is the only complete example. The founder of Castilian prose was King Alfonso X, El Sabio (the Wise). The first true poet was the 14th-century satirist Juan Ruiz (c. 1283–1350), archpriest of Hita. To the 15th century belong the Marquis of Santillana (Iñigo López de Mendoza), poet, critic, and collector of proverbs; chivalric romances, such as the *Amadis de Gaula*; ballads dealing with the struggle against the Moors; and the *Celestina*, a novel in dramatic form.

SPAIN: RULERS FROM 1516

Reign	Name
House of Habsburg	
1516–56	Charles I
1556–98	Philip II
1598–1621	Philip III
1621–65	Philip IV
1665–1700	Charles II
House of Bourbon	
1700–46	Philip V
1746–59	Ferdinand VI
1759–88	Charles III
1788–1808	Charles IV
1808	Ferdinand VII (deposed)
1808–13	Joseph Napoleon*
1813–33	Ferdinand VII (restored)
1833–68	Isabel II
1868–70	provisional government
1870–73	Amadeus I ** (abdicated)
1873–74	first republic
1874–86	Alfonso XII
1886–1931	Alfonso XIII (deposed)
1931–39	second republic
1939–75	fascist state, General Francisco Franco, head of state
1975–	Juan Carlos I

* House of Bonaparte
** House of Savoy

The golden age of the 15th–16th centuries produced poets such as the lyrical Garcilaso de la Vega; the mystics Santa Teresa and Luis de León; and the satirist Francisco de Quevedo. In fiction there developed the pastoral romance, for example Jorge de Montemayor's *Diana*; the picaresque novel, established by the anonymous *Lazarillo del Tormes*; and the work of Cervantes.

In the 18th century the Benedictine Benito J Feijoo introduced scientific thought to Spain, and French influence emerged in the comedies of Leandro F de Moratín (1760–1828) and others. Among 19th-century novelists were Pedro de Alarcón and Vicente Blasco Ibáñez.

The 'Generation of 1898' included the Nobel prize-winning poet Juan Ramón Jiménez. The next generation included novelist Camilo José Cela and the Nobel prizewinning poet Vincente Aleixandre; and the dramatist Federico García Lorca. The Civil War and the strict censorship of the Franco government disrupted mid-20th-century literary life, but later names include the novelist Juan Goytisolo (1931–); and the poet José Hierro (1922–).

Spanish Main common term for the Caribbean Sea in the 16th–17th centuries, but more properly the South American mainland between the river Orinoco and Panama.

Spanish Succession, War of the war 1701–14 of Britain, Austria, the Netherlands, Portugal, and Denmark (the Allies) against France, Spain, and Bavaria. It was caused by Louis XIV's acceptance of the Spanish throne on behalf of his grandson, Philip, in defiance of the Partition Treaty of 1700, under which it would have passed to Archduke Charles of Austria (later Holy Roman Emperor Charles VI).

Peace was made by the Treaties of Utrecht 1713 and Rastatt 1714. Philip V was recognized as king of Spain, thus founding the Spanish branch of the Bourbon dynasty. Britain received Gibraltar, Minorca, and Nova Scotia; and Austria received Belgium, Milan, and Naples.

1704 The French marched on Vienna to try to end the war, but were defeated at Blenheim by the Duke of ◊Marlborough and ◊Eugène of Savoy.
1705 The Allies invaded Spain, twice occupying Madrid but failing to hold it.
1706 Marlborough was victorious over the French (under Villeroi) at Ramillies 23 May, in Brabant, Belgium.
1708 Marlborough and Eugène were victorious over the French (under the Duke of Burgundy and ◊Vendôme) at Oudenaarde (near Ghent, Belgium) 30 June–11 July.
1709 Marlborough was victorious with Eugène over the French (under Villars) at Malplaquet 11 Sept.
1713 Treaties of Utrecht and *1714* Rastat under which the Allies recognized Philip as king of Spain, but Gibraltar, Minorca, and Nova Scotia were ceded to Britain, and Belgium, Milan, and Naples to Austria.

Spark Muriel Sarah, (born Camberg) 1918– . Scottish novelist. She is a Catholic convert, and her enigmatic satires include *The Ballad of Peckham Rye* 1960, *The Prime of Miss Jean Brodie* 1961, *The Only Problem* 1984, and *Symposium* 1990. *See illustration on following page.*

spark chamber electronic device for recording tracks of charged subatomic particles, decay products, and rays. In combination with a stack of photographic plates, a spark chamber enables the point where an interaction has taken place to be located, to within a cubic centimetre. At its simplest, it consists of two smooth threadlike ◊electrodes that are positioned 1–2 cm/0.5–1 in apart, the space between being filled by an inert gas such as neon. Sparks jump through the gas along the ionized path created by the radiation. See ◊particle detector.

SPAIN: TERRITORIAL DIVISIONS

Regions and provinces	Area (sq km/sq mi)
Andalusia	
Almería, Cádiz, Córdoba, Granada, Huelva, Jaén, Málaga, Sevilla	87,300/33,698
Aragon	
Huesca, Teruel, Zaragoza	47,700/18,412
Asturias	10,600/4,092
Balearic Islands	5,000/1,930
Basque Country	
Alava, Guipúzcoa, Vizcaya	7,300/2,818
Canary Islands	
Las Palmas, Santa Cruz de Tenerife	7,300/2,818
Cantabria	5,300/2,046
Castilla–La Mancha	
Albacete, Ciudad Real, Cuenca, Guadalajara, Toledo	79,200/30,571
Castilla–León	
Avila, Burgos, León, Palencia, Salamanca, Segovia, Soria, Valladolid, Zamora	94,100/36,323
Catalonia	
Barcelona, Gerona, Lérida, Tarragona	31,900/12,313
Extremadura	
Badajoz, Cáceres	41,600/16,058
Galicia	
La Coruña, Lugo, Orense, Pontevedra	29,400/11,348
Madrid	8,000/3,088
Murcia	11,300/4,362
Navarra	10,400/4,014
La Rioja	5,000/1,930
Valencian Community	
Alicante, Castellón, Valencia	23,300/8,994
Ceuta	18/7
Melilla	14/5
TOTAL	504,732/194,827

spark plug plug that produces an electric spark in the cylinder of a petrol engine to ignite the fuel mixture. It consists essentially of two electrodes insulated from one another. High-voltage (18,000 V) electricity is fed to a central electrode via the distributor. At the base of the electrode, inside the cylinder, the electricity jumps to another electrode earthed to the engine body, creating a spark. See also ◊ignition coil.

sparrow any of a family (Passeridae) of small Old World birds of the order Passeriformes with short, thick bills, but applied particularly to the different members of the genus *Passer* in the family Ploceidae, order Passeriformes.

Many numbers of the New World family Emberizidae, which includes ◊warblers, orioles, and buntings, are also called sparrows; for example, the North American song sparrow *Melospize melodia*.

The house sparrow *Passer domesticus* has brown-black marked plumage, and a black chest and eyestripe in the male. It is inconspicuous, intelligent, and adaptable, with a cheery chirp and untidy nesting habits, using any scrap materials to hand for the nest. In diet it is omnivorous, feeding on insects and their larvae in spring and summer, and on grain in winter.

sparrow hawk small woodland ◊hawk *Accipiter nisus*, of the family Falconidae, order Falconiformes, found in Eurasia and N Africa. It is bluish-grey, with brown and white markings, and has a long tail and short wings. The male grows to 28 cm/11 in long, and the female to 38 cm/15 in. It hunts small birds and mice.

Sparta ancient Greek city-state in the S Peloponnese (near Sparte), developed from Dorian settlements in the 10th century BC. The Spartans, known for their military discipline and austerity, took part in the ◊Persian and ◊Peloponnesian Wars.

The Dorians formed the ruling race in Sparta, the original inhabitants being divided into *perioeci* (tributaries without political rights) and helots or serfs. The state was ruled by two hereditary kings, and under the constitution attributed to Lycurgus all citizens were trained for war from childhood. As a result, the Spartans became proverbial for their indifference to pain or death, their contempt for luxury and the arts, and their harsh treatment of the helots. They distinguished themselves in the Persian and Peloponnesian wars, but defeat by the Thebans in 371 BC marked the start of their decline.

'I am putting old heads on your young shoulders ... and all my pupils are the crème de la crème.'

Muriel Spark
The Prime of Miss Jean Brodie

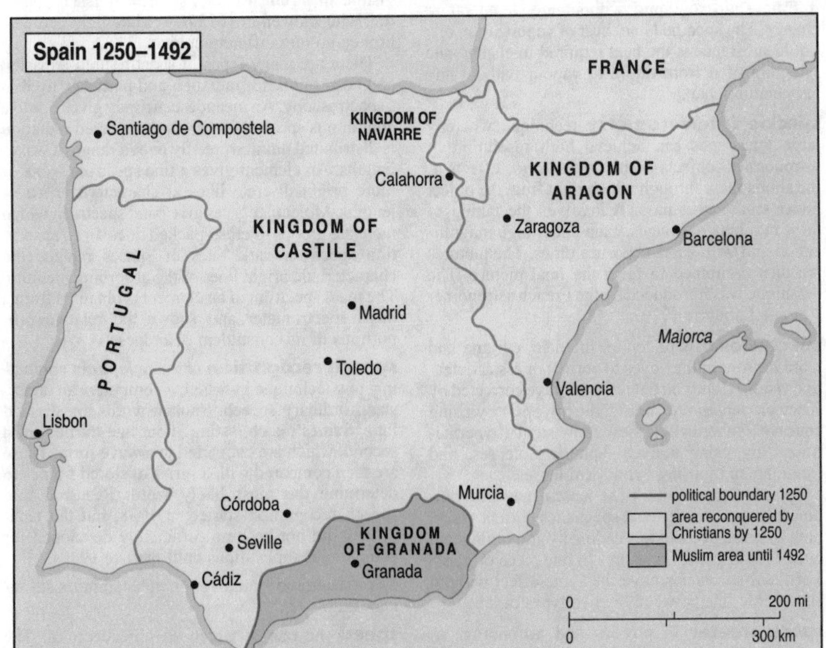

Spark Scottish novelist Muriel Spark. Her novels, which are witty, finely structured satires, blend fantasy and sharply observed realism to express essentially spiritual themes. She has also written biographies and poetry. *Penguin Books Ltd*

The ancient city was destroyed by the Visigoths in 396 AD.

Spartacist member of a group of left-wing radicals in Germany at the end of World War I, founders of the Spartacus League, which became the German Communist Party in 1919. The league participated in the Berlin workers' revolt of Jan 1919, which was suppressed by the Freikorps on the orders of the socialist government. The agitation ended with the murder of Spartacist leaders Karl Liebknecht (1871–1919) and Rosa ◊Luxemburg.

Spartacus died 71 BC. Thracian gladiator. In 73 BC he led a revolt of gladiators and slaves in Capua, near Naples, and swept through southern Italy and Cisalpine Gaul. He was eventually caught by Roman general ◊Crassus 71 BC. The fate of Spartacus is not known, although his followers were executed in mass crucifixions.

spathe in flowers, the single large bract surrounding the type of inflorescence known as a ◊spadix. It is sometimes brightly coloured and petal-like, as in the brilliant scarlet spathe of the flamingo plant *Anthurium andreanum* from South America; this serves to attract insects.

Speaker presiding officer charged with the preservation of order in the legislatures of various countries. In the UK the equivalent of the Speaker in the House of Lords is the Lord Chancellor; in the House of Commons the Speaker is elected for each parliament, usually on an agreed basis among the parties, but often holds the office for many years. The original appointment dates from 1377. In 1992 Betty ◊Boothroyd became the first female Speaker of the House of Commons.

The chair of the US House of Representatives also has the title of Speaker, who is second in line of succession to the presidency in the event of death or incapacitation of the president and vice-president.

spearmint perennial herb *Mentha spicata* of the mint family Labiatae, with aromatic leaves and spikes of purple flowers, used for flavouring food.

Special Air Service (SAS) specialist British regiment recruited from regiments throughout the army. It has served in Malaysia, Oman, Yemen, the Falklands, Northern Ireland, and during the 1991 Gulf War, as well as against international urban guerrillas, as in the siege of the Iranian embassy in London 1980.

The SAS was founded in Egypt 1941 by Col David Stirling to raid German and Italian airfields in N Africa. It also operated behind the lines in Italy and France 1943–44 and Germany 1945. Disbanded at the end of World War II, it was revived from 1952 to carry out special operations. Its headquarters is at Bradbury Lines near Hereford on the Welsh border. Members are anonymous. Their motto is 'Who dares wins' under a winged dagger.

Special Branch section of the British police originally established 1883 to deal with Irish Fenian activists. All 42 police forces in Britain now have their own Special Branches. They act as the executive arm of MI5 (British ◊intelligence) in its duty of preventing or investigating espionage, subversion, and sabotage; carry out duties at air and sea ports in respect of naturalization and immigration; and provide armed bodyguards for public figures.

special drawing right (SDR) the right of a member state of the ◊International Monetary Fund to apply for money to finance its balance of payments deficit. Originally, the SDR was linked to gold and the US dollar. After 1974 SDRs were defined in terms of a 'basket' of the 16 currencies of countries doing 1% or more of the world's trade. In 1981 the SDR was simplified to a weighted average of US dollars, French francs, German marks, Japanese yen, and UK pounds sterling.

special education education, often in separate 'special schools', for children with specific physical or mental problems or disabilities.

In the UK, the 1981 Education Act encouraged local authorities to integrate as many children with special needs into mainstream schools as was practicable but did not recommend the complete closure of special schools.

species in biology, a distinguishable group of organisms that resemble each other or consist of a few distinctive types (as in ◊polymorphism), and that can all interbreed to produce fertile offspring. Species are the lowest level in the system of biological classification.

Related species are grouped together in a genus. Within a species there are usually two or more separate ◊populations, which may in time become distinctive enough to be designated subspecies or varieties, and could eventually give rise to new species. Around 1.4 million species have been identified so far, of which 750,000 are insects, 250,000 are plants, and 41,000 are vertebrates. In tropical regions there are roughly two species for each temperate-zone species. It is estimated that one species becomes extinct every day through habitat destruction.

A native species is a species that has existed in that country at least from prehistoric times; a naturalized species is one known to have been introduced by humans from another country, but which now maintains itself; while an exotic species is one that requires human intervention to survive.

specific gravity alternative term for ◊relative density.

specific heat capacity in physics, quantity of heat required to raise unit mass (1 kg) of a substance by one ◊kelvin (1°C). The unit of specific heat capacity in the SI system is the ◊joule per kilogram kelvin ($J\ kg^{-1}\ K^{-1}$).

specific latent heat in physics, the heat that changes the physical state of a unit mass (one kilogram) of a substance without causing any temperature change.

The specific latent heat of fusion of a solid substance is the heat required to change one kilogram of it from solid to liquid without any temperature change. The specific latent heat of vaporization of a liquid substance is the heat required to change one kilogram of it from liquid to vapour without any temperature change.

speckle interferometry technique whereby large telescopes can achieve high resolution of astronomical objects despite the adverse effects of the atmosphere through which light from the object under study must pass. It involves the taking of large numbers of images, each under high magnification and with short exposure times. The pictures are then combined to form the final picture. The technique was introduced by the French astronomer Antoine Labeyrie 1970.

spectacles pair of lenses fitted in a frame and worn in front of the ◊eyes to correct or assist defective vision. Common defects of the eye corrected by spectacle lenses are short sight (myopia) by using concave (spherical) lenses, long sight (hypermetropia) by using convex (spherical) lenses, and astigmatism by using cylindrical lenses.

Spherical and cylindrical lenses may be combined in one lens. Bifocal spectacles correct vision both at a distance and for reading by combining two lenses of different curvatures in one piece of glass. Varifocal spectacles have the same effect without any visible line between the two types of lens.

spectrometer in physics and astronomy, an instrument used to study the composition of light emitted by a source. The range, or ◊spectrum, of wavelengths emitted by a source depends upon its constituent elements, and may be used to determine its chemical composition.

The simpler forms of spectrometer analyse only visible light. A collimator receives the incoming rays and produces a parallel beam, which is then split into a spectrum by either a ◊diffraction grating or a prism mounted on a turntable. As the turntable is rotated each of the constituent colours of the beam may be seen through a telescope, and the angle at which each has been deviated may be measured on a circular scale. From this information the wavelengths of the colours of light can be calculated.

Spectrometers are used in astronomy to study the electromagnetic radiation emitted by stars and other celestial bodies. The spectral information gained may be used to determine their chemical composition, or to measure the ◊red shift of colours associated with the expansion of the universe and thereby calculate the speed with which distant stars are moving away from the Earth. ▷*See feature on pp. 70–71.*

spectrometry in analytical chemistry, a technique involving the measurement of the spectrum of energies (not necessarily electromagnetic radiation) emitted or absorbed by a substance. Emission spectroscopy is the study of the characteristic series of sharp lines in the spectrum produced when an ◊element is heated. Thus an unknown mixture can be analysed for its component elements. Related is absorption spectroscopy, dealing with atoms and molecules as they absorb energy in a characteristic way. Again, dark lines can be used for analysis. More detailed structural information can be obtained using infrared spectroscopy (concerned with molecular vibrations) or nuclear magnetic resonance (NMR) spectroscopy (concerned with interactions between adjacent atomic nuclei). Supersonic jet laser beam spectroscopy enables the isolation and study of clusters in the gas phase. A laser vaporizes a small sample, which is cooled in helium, and ejected into an evacuated chamber. The jet of clusters expands supersonically, cooling the clusters to near absolute zero, and stabilizing them for study in a ◊mass spectrometer.

spectroscopy study of spectra (see ◊spectrum) associated with atoms or molecules in solid, liquid, or gaseous phase. Spectroscopy can be used to identify unknown compounds and is an invaluable tool in science, medicine, and industry (for example, in checking the purity of drugs).

spectrum (plural ***spectra***) in physics, an arrangement of frequencies or wavelengths when electromagnetic radiations are separated into their constituent parts. Visible light is part of the electromagnetic spectrum and most sources emit waves over a range of wavelengths that can be broken up or 'dispersed'; white light can be separated into red, orange, yellow, green, blue, indigo, and violet. The visible spectrum was first studied by Isaac ◊Newton, who showed in 1672 how white light could be broken up into different colours.

There are many types of spectra, both emission and absorption, for radiation and particles, used in ◊spectroscopy. An incandescent body gives rise to a continuous spectrum where the dispersed radiation is distributed uninterruptedly over a range of wavelengths. An element gives a line spectrum – one or more bright discrete lines at characteristic wavelengths. Molecular gases give band spectra in which there are groups of close-packed lines. In an absorption spectrum dark lines or spaces replace the characteristic bright lines of the absorbing medium. The mass spectrum of an element is obtained from a mass spectrometer and shows the relative proportions of its constituent ◊isotopes.

speech recognition or ***voice input*** in computing, any technique by which a computer can understand ordinary speech. Spoken words are divided into 'frames', each lasting about one-thirtieth of a second, which are converted to a wave form. These are then compared with a series of stored frames to determine the most likely word. Research into speech recognition started in 1938, but the technology did not become sufficiently developed for commercial applications until the late 1980s.

speed common name for ◊amphetamine, a stimulant drug.

speed the rate at which an object moves. The average speed v of an object may be calculated by

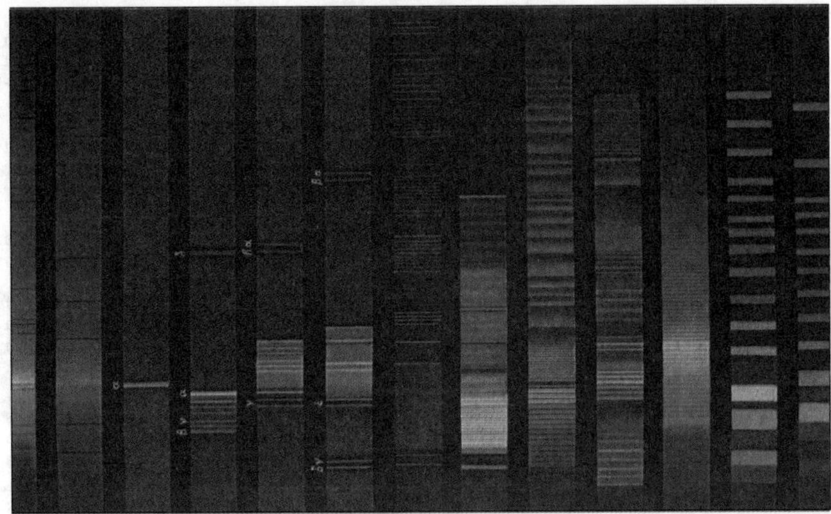

spectrum Spectra from various light sources including the Sun and stars, with carbon arc comparison spectrum. From Amédée Guillemin 'Forces of Nature' 1873. *Image Select (UK) Ltd*

dividing the distance *s* it has travelled by the time *t* taken to do so, and may be expressed as:

$$v = s/t$$

The usual units of speed are metres per second or kilometres per hour.

Speed is a scalar quantity in which direction of motion is unimportant (unlike the vector quantity ◊velocity, in which both magnitude and direction must be taken into consideration).

speed of light speed at which light and other ◊electromagnetic waves travel through empty space. Its value is 299,792,458 m/186,281 mi per second. The speed of light is the highest speed possible, according to the theory of ◊relativity, and its value is independent of the motion of its source and of the observer. It is impossible to accelerate any material body to this speed because it would require an infinite amount of energy.

speed of sound speed at which sound travels through a medium, such as air or water. In air at a temperature of 0°C/32°F, the speed of sound is 331 m/1,087 ft per second. At higher temperatures, the speed of sound is greater; at 18°C/64°F it is 342 m/1,123 ft per second.

It is greater in liquids and solids; for example, in water it is around 1,440 m/4,724 ft per second, depending on the temperature.

speedometer instrument attached to the transmission of a vehicle by a flexible drive shaft, which indicates the speed of the vehicle in miles or kilometres per hour on a dial easily visible to the driver.

speedway sport of motorcycle racing on a dirt track. Four riders compete in each heat over four laps. A series of heats make up a match or competition. In Britain there are two leagues, the British League and the National League. World championships exist for individuals, pairs (first held 1970), four-rider teams (first held 1960), long-track racing, and ice speedway.

The first organized races were in Australia 1923 and the first track in Britain was at Droylsden, near Manchester, 1927.

speedwell any flowering plant of the genus *Veronica* of the snapdragon family Scrophulariaceae. Of the many wild species, most are low-growing with small, bluish flowers.

The creeping common speedwell *V. officinalis* grows in dry, grassy places, heathland, and open woods throughout Europe, with oval leaves and spikes of lilac flowers.

Speenhamland system method of poor relief in England started by Berkshire magistrates in 1795, whereby wages were supplemented from the poor-rates. However, it encouraged the payment of low wages and was superseded by the 1834 ◊Poor Law.

Speer Albert 1905–1981. German architect and minister in the Nazi government during World War II. He was appointed Hitler's architect and, like his counterparts in Fascist Italy, chose an overblown Classicism to glorify the state, for example, his plan for the Berlin and Nuremberg Party Congress Grounds 1934. He built the New Reich Chancellery, Berlin, 1938–39 (now demolished) but his designs for an increasingly megalomaniac series of buildings in a stark Classical style were never realized, notably the Great Assembly Hall for Berlin.

Speke John Hanning 1827–1864. British explorer. He joined British traveller Richard ◊Burton on an African expedition in which they reached Lake Tanganyika 1858; Speke became the first European to see Lake ◊Victoria.

His claim that it was the source of the Nile was disputed by Burton, even after Speke and James Grant (1827–1892) made a second confirming expedition 1860–63. Speke accidentally shot himself, in England, the day before he was due to debate the matter publicly with Burton.

speleology scientific study of caves, their origin, development, physical structure, flora, fauna, folklore, exploration, mapping, photography, cave-diving, and rescue work. Potholing, which involves following the course of underground rivers or streams, has become a popular sport.

Speleology first developed in France in the late 19th century, where the Société de Spéléologie was founded in 1895.

Spence Basil Urwin 1907–1976. Scottish architect. His works include Coventry Cathedral 1951 and the British embassy in Rome. He was professor of architecture at the Royal Academy, London, 1961–68.

Spencer Herbert 1820–1903. English philosopher. He wrote *Social Statics* 1851, expounding his *laissez-faire* views on social and political problems. In 1862 he began his ten-volume *System of Synthetic Philosophy*, in which he extended Charles ◊Darwin's theory of evolution to the entire field of human knowledge. The chief of the ten volumes are *First Principles* 1862 and *Principles of Biology* 1864–67, *Principles of Sociology* 1876–96, and *Principles of Ethics* 1879–93.

Spencer Stanley 1891–1959. English painter. He was born and lived in Cookham-on-Thames, Berkshire, S England, and recreated the Christian story in a Cookham setting. Typically his works combine a dry, meticulously detailed, and often humorous depiction of everyday life with an elaborate religious symbolism, as in *The Resurrection, Cookham* 1924–26 (Tate Gallery, London).

He studied at the Slade School 1910–1914, and served in World War I. His military service produced its effect on his painting, particularly evident in his greatest work, the mural paintings of the Memorial Chapel, All Soul's, at Burghclere, Hampshire. The side walls of the chapel depict crowded and active scenes of military life, while the east wall shows the Resurrection (a recurrent theme in Spencer).

Among his other major works are *Christ Carrying the Cross* 1920 (Tate Gallery, London). More intimate scenes are depicted in *Self-portrait with Patricia Preece* 1936 (Fitzwilliam Museum, Cambridge) and *The Dustman, or The Lovers* 1934 (Laing Art Gallery, Newcastle upon Tyne).

Spender Stephen Harold 1909–1995. English poet and critic. His earlier poetry has a left-wing political content, as in *Twenty Poems* 1930, *Vienna* 1934, *The Still Centre* 1939, and *Poems of Dedication* 1946. Other works include the verse drama *Trial of a Judge* 1938, the autobiography *World within World* 1951, and translations. His *Journals 1939–83* were published 1985.

Educated at University College, Oxford, he founded with Cyril Connolly the magazine *Horizon* (of which he was co-editor 1939–41) and was co-editor of *Encounter* 1953–67. He became professor of English at University College, London, 1970.

Spengler Oswald 1880–1936. German philosopher whose *Decline of the West* 1918 argued that civilizations go through natural cycles of growth and decay. He was admired by the Nazis.

Spenser Edmund c. 1552–1599. English poet. He has been called the 'poet's poet' because of his rich imagery and command of versification. His major work is the moral allegory *The ◊Faerie Queene*, of which six books survive (three published 1590 and three 1596). Other books include *The Shepheard's Calendar* 1579, *Astrophel* 1586, the love sonnets *Amoretti*, and the marriage poem *Epithalamion* 1595.

Born in London and educated at Cambridge University, in 1580 he became secretary to the Lord Deputy in Ireland and at Kilcolman Castle completed the first three books of *The Faerie Queene*. In 1598 the castle was burned down by rebels, and Spenser and his family narrowly escaped. He died in London, and was buried in Westminster Abbey.

sperm or ***spermatozoon*** in biology, the male ◊gamete of animals. Each sperm cell has a head capsule containing a nucleus, a middle portion containing ◊mitochondria (which provide energy), and a long tail (flagellum). See ◊sexual reproduction.

In most animals, the sperm are motile, and are propelled by a long flagellum, but in some (such as crabs and lobsters) they are nonmotile. Sperm cells are produced in the testes (see ◊testis). From there they pass through the sperm ducts via the seminal vesicles and the ◊prostate gland, which produce fluids called semen that give the sperm cells energy and keep them moving after they leave the body. Hundreds of millions of sperm cells are contained in only a small amount of semen. The human sperm is 0.005 mm/0.0002 in long and can survive inside the female for 2–9 days. Mammalian sperm have receptor cells identical to some of those found in the lining of the nose. These may help in navigating towards the egg.

The term is sometimes applied to the motile male gametes (◊antherozoids) of lower plants.

spermaceti glistening waxlike substance, not a true oil, contained in the cells of the huge, almost rectangular 'case' in the head of the sperm whale, amounting to about 2.8 tonnes/3 tons. It rapidly changes in density with variations in temperature. It was formerly used in lubricants and cosmetics, but in 1980 a blend of fatty acids and esters from tallow and coconut oil was developed as a substitute.

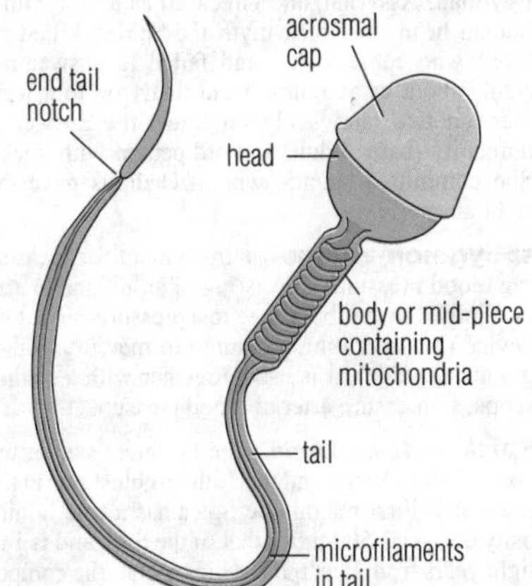

sperm Only a single sperm is needed to fertilize a female egg, or ovum. Yet up to 500 million may start the journey towards the egg. Once a sperm has fertilized an egg, the egg's wall cannot be penetrated by other sperm. The unsuccessful sperm die after about three days.

'No one can be perfectly free till all are free; no one can be perfectly moral till all are moral; no one can be perfectly happy till all are happy.'

HERBERT SPENCER *Social Statics*

'Christian theology is the grandmother of Bolshevism.'

OSWALD SPENGLER *Hour of Decision*

spider Of the three main spider groups it is the so-called true spiders (suborder Labidognatha) which contains by far the greatest number of species. The brightly marked orb web spider *Araneus discolor* from South America is a member of this group. *Premaphotos Wildlife*

spermatophore small capsule containing ◊sperm and other nutrients produced in invertebrates, newts, and cephalopods.

spermatophyte in botany, another name for a ◊seed plant.

spermicide any cream, jelly, pessary, or other preparation that kills the ◊sperm cells in semen. Spermicides are used for contraceptive purposes, usually in combination with a ◊condom or ◊diaphragm. Spermicide used alone is only 75% effective in preventing pregnancy.

Spey river in Highland and Grampian regions, Scotland, rising SE of Fort Augustus, and flowing 172 km/107 mi to the Moray Firth between Lossiemouth and Buckie. It has salmon fisheries at its mouth.

sphalerite mineral composed of zinc sulphide with a small proportion of iron, formula (Zn,Fe)S. It is the chief ore of zinc. Sphalerite is brown with a nonmetallic lustre unless an appreciable amount of iron is present (up to 26% by weight). Sphalerite usually occurs in ore veins in limestones, where it is often associated with galena. It crystallizes in the cubic system but does not normally form perfect cubes.

sphere in mathematics, a perfectly round object with all points on its surface the same distance from the centre. This distance is the radius of the sphere. For a sphere of radius r, the volume $V = \frac{4}{3}\pi r^3$ and the surface area $A = 4\pi r^2$.

sphincter ring of muscle, such as is found at various points in the ◊alimentary canal, that contracts and relaxes to open and close the canal and control the movement of food. The pyloric sphincter, at the base of the stomach, controls the release of the gastric contents into the ◊duodenum. After release the sphincter contracts, closing off the stomach. The external anal sphincter closes the ◊anus; the internal anal sphincter constricts the rectum; the sphincter vesicae controls the urethral orifice of the bladder. In the eye the sphincter pupillae contracts the pupil in response to bright light.

Sphinx mythological creature, represented in Egyptian, Assyrian, and Greek art as a lion with a human head. In Greek myth the Sphinx killed all those who came to her and failed to answer her riddle about what animal went firstly on four legs, then on two, and lastly on three: the answer is humanity (baby, adult, and old person with stick). She committed suicide when ◊Oedipus gave the right answer.

‘I wanted the water to mean shark. The horizon to mean shark. I wanted the shark's presence to be felt everywhere.’

STEVEN SPIELBERG
On his film *Jaws*

sphygmomanometer instrument for measuring blood pressure. Consisting of an inflatable arm cuff joined by a rubber tube to a pressure-recording device (incorporating a column of mercury with a graduated scale), it is used, together with a stethoscope, to measure arterial blood pressure.

Spica or ***Alpha Virginis*** the brightest star in the constellation Virgo and the 16th brightest star in the night sky. First-magnitude Spica has a true luminosity of over 1,500 times that of the Sun, and is 140 light years from Earth. It is a binary star, the components of which orbit each other every four days.

spice any aromatic vegetable substance used as a condiment and for flavouring food. Spices are mostly obtained from tropical plants, and include pepper, nutmeg, ginger, and cinnamon. They have little food value but increase the appetite and may facilitate digestion.

Spice Girls British vocal pop quintet. They achieved rapid success with simultaneous hits in the UK and the USA with their debut single 'Wannabe' in 1996. Their next three singles all also debuted at number one in the UK, a feat never before achieved. Group members are Melanie Janine Brown (1975–), Victoria Addams (1975–), Emma Lee Bunton (1976–), Melanie Jayne Chisholm (1974–), and Geri Estelle ◊Halliwell (1972–) who left the group in 1998. Their songs combine dance and funk rhythms with lyrics extolling the virtues of what the group call 'girl power'.

spicules, solar in astronomy, short-lived jets of hot gas in the upper chromosphere (the layer of mostly hydrogen gas above the visible surface) of the Sun. Spiky in appearance, they move at high velocities along lines of magnetic force to which they owe their shape, and last for a few minutes each. Spicules appear to disperse material into the ◊corona.

spider any arachnid (eight-legged animal) of the order Araneae. There are about 30,000 known species, mostly a few centimetres in size, although a few tropical forms attain great size, for example, some bird-eating spiders attain a body length of 9 cm/3.5 in. Spiders produce silk, and many spin webs to trap their prey. They are found everywhere in the world except Antarctica. Many species are found in woods and dry commons; a few are aquatic.

Spiders are predators; they bite their prey, releasing a powerful toxin from poison glands which causes paralysis, together with digestive juices. They then suck out the juices and soft parts. Spiders are oviparous (egg-laying), and the female encloses her eggs in a silken bag.

spider plant African plant of the genus *Chlorophytum* of the lily family. Two species, *C. comosum* and *C. elatum*, are popular house plants. They have long narrow variegated leaves and produce flowering shoots from which the new plants grow. The flowers are small and white. Spider plants absorb toxins from the air and therefore have a purifying action on the local atmosphere.

Spielberg Steven 1947– . US film director, writer, and producer. His credits include such phenomenal box-office successes as *Jaws* 1975, *Close Encounters of the Third Kind* 1977, *Raiders of the Lost Ark* 1981, *ET* 1982, and *Jurassic Park* (winner of three Academy Awards) and *Schindler's List*, based on Thomas Keneally's novel, which won seven Academy Awards, including those for Best Picture and Best Director, 1993. Immensely popular, his films often combine heartfelt sentimentality and a childlike sensibility.

He also directed *Indiana Jones and the Temple of Doom* 1984, *The Color Purple* 1985, *Empire of the Sun* 1987, *Indiana Jones and the Last Crusade* 1989, and *Hook* 1991.

Spielberg US film director, writer, and producer Steven Spielberg holding his Oscars for Best Picture and Best Director 1993. The awards were given for *Schindler's List*, based on Thomas Keneally's true story of the Holocaust in which German businessman Oskar Schindler saved the lives of over 1,000 Polish Jews by employing them in his factory. The film was widely acclaimed and brought a new depth to Spielberg's reputation. *Topham*

spikelet in botany, one of the units of a grass ◊inflorescence. It comprises a slender axis on which one or more flowers are borne.

Each individual flower or floret has a pair of scalelike bracts, the glumes, and is enclosed by a membranous lemma and a thin, narrow palea, which may be extended into a long, slender bristle, or awn.

spikenard Himalayan plant *Nardostachys jatamansi* of the valerian family Valerianaceae; its underground stems give a perfume used in Eastern aromatic oils. Also, a North American plant *Aralia racemosa* of the ginseng family, with fragrant roots.

Spillane Mickey (Frank Morrison) 1918– . US crime novelist. He began by writing for pulp magazines and became an internationally best-selling author with books featuring private investigator Mike Hammer, a violent vigilante who wages an amoral war on crime. His most popular novels include *I, the Jury* 1947 and *Kiss Me Deadly* 1953 (both made into films in the *noir* style in the 1950s).

spin in physics, the intrinsic angular ◊momentum of a subatomic particle, nucleus, atom, or molecule, which continues to exist even when the particle comes to rest.

A particle in a specific energy state has a particular spin, just as it has a particular electric charge and mass. According to ◊quantum theory, this is restricted to discrete and indivisible values, specified by a spin ◊quantum number. Because of its spin, a charged particle acts as a small magnet and is affected by magnetic fields.

spina bifida congenital defect in which part of the spinal cord and its membranes are exposed, due to incomplete development of the spine (vertebral column).

Spina bifida, usually present in the lower back, varies in severity. The most seriously affected babies may be paralysed below the waist. There is also a risk of mental retardation and death from hydrocephalus, which is often associated. Surgery is performed to close the spinal lesion shortly after birth, but this does not usually cure the disabilities caused by the condition. Spina bifida can be diagnosed prenatally.

spinach annual plant *Spinacia oleracea* of the goosefoot family Chenopodiaceae. It is native to Asia and widely cultivated for its leaves, which are eaten as a vegetable.

spinal cord major component of the ◊central nervous system in vertebrates, encased in the spinal column. It consists of bundles of nerves enveloped in three layers of membrane (the meninges).

spinal tap another term for ◊lumbar puncture, a medical test.

spine backbone of vertebrates. In most mammals, it contains 26 small bones called vertebrae, which enclose and protect the spinal cord (which links the peripheral nervous system to the brain).

The spine articulates with the skull, ribs, and hip bones, and provides attachment for the back muscles.

In humans it is made up of individual vertebrae, separated by intervertebral discs. In the adult there are seven cervical vertebrae in the neck; twelve thoracic in the upper trunk; five lumbar in the lower back; the sacrum (consisting of five rudimentary vertebrae fused together, joined to the hipbones); and the coccyx (four vertebrae, fused into a tailbone). The human spine has four curves (front to rear), which allow for the increased size of the chest and pelvic cavities, and permit springing, to minimize jolting of the internal organs.

spinel any of a group of 'mixed oxide' minerals consisting mainly of the oxides of magnesium and aluminium, $MgAl_2O_4$ and $FeAl_2O_4$. Spinels crystallize in the cubic system, forming octahedral crystals. They are found in high-temperature igneous and metamorphic rocks. The aluminium oxide spinel contains gem varieties, such as the ruby spinels of Sri Lanka and Myanmar (Burma).

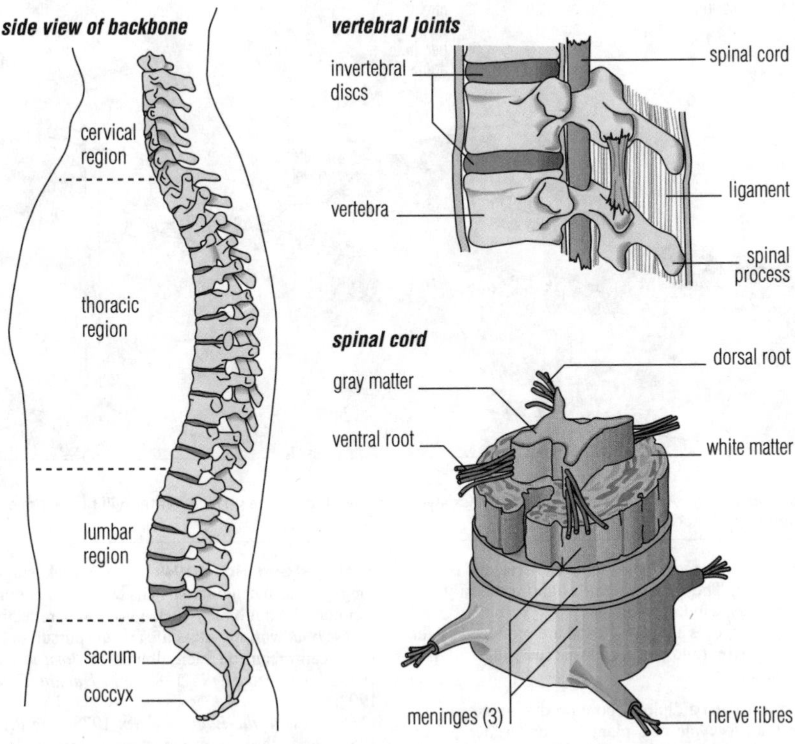

spine The human spine extends every night during sleep. During the day, the cartilage discs between the vertebra are squeezed when the body is in a vertical position, standing or sitting, but at night, with pressure released, the discs swell and the spine lengthens by about 8 mm/0.3 in.

spinet 17th-century laterally tapered domestic keyboard instrument of up to a three-and-a-half octave range, having a plucking action and single strings. It was the precursor of the ◊harpsichord.

spinifex spiny grass of the genus *Spinifex* chiefly of Australia, often useful for binding sand on the seashore. It is found on the sand dunes of the coasts of all states. The term also refers to the genus *Triodia*, spiny-leaved, tussock-forming grasses of inland Australia.

spinning art of drawing out and twisting fibres (originally wool or flax) into a long thread, or yarn, by hand or machine. Synthetic fibres are extruded as a liquid through the holes of a spinneret.

Originally, some 9,000 years ago, spinning was done by hand using a distaff (a cleft stick holding a bundle of fibres) and a weighted spindle, which was spun to twist the thread. In the 1300s the spinning wheel came to Europe, though it had been in use earlier in the East. In about 1764 in England James ◊Hargreaves built the spinning jenny, a machine that could spin 8, then 16, bobbins at once. Later, Samuel ◊Crompton's spinning mule 1779 had a moving carriage carrying the spindles; this is still in use today.

Spinoza Benedict, or Baruch 1632–1677. Dutch philosopher. He believed in a rationalistic pantheism that owed much to René ◊Descartes's mathematical appreciation of the universe. Mind and matter are two modes of an infinite substance that he called God or Nature, good and evil being relative. He was a determinist, believing that human action was motivated by self-preservation.

Ethics 1677 is his main work. *A Treatise on Religious and Political Philosophy* 1670 was the only one of his works published during his life, and was attacked by Christians. He was excommunicated by the Jewish community in Amsterdam on charges of heretical thought and practice 1656. He was a lens-grinder by trade.

spiny anteater alternative name for ◊echidna.

spiracle in insects, the opening of a ◊trachea, through which oxygen enters the body and carbon dioxide is expelled. In cartilaginous fishes (sharks and rays), the same name is given to a circular opening that marks the remains of the first gill slit.

In tetrapod vertebrates, the spiracle of early fishes has evolved into the Eustachian tube, which connects the middle ear cavity with the pharynx.

spiraea any herbaceous plant or shrub of the genus *Spiraea*, family Rosaceae, which includes many cultivated species with ornamental panicles of flowers.

spirit strong ◊alcoholic beverage, other type of ◊alcohol, or ◊white spirit.

spiritualism belief in the survival of the human personality and in communication between the living and those who have 'passed on'. The spiritualist movement originated in the USA in 1848. Adherents to this religious denomination practise mediumship, which claims to allow clairvoyant knowledge of distant events and spirit healing. The writer Arthur Conan Doyle and the Victorian prime minister Gladstone were converts.

In the UK the Society for Psychical Research was founded in 1882 by W H Myers and Henry Sidgwick (1838–1900) to investigate the claims of spiritualism. Spiritualists include Daniel Home, the scientists Oliver Lodge and William Crookes, and Air Marshal Lord Dowding.

spirochaete spiral-shaped bacterium. Some spirochaetes are free-living in water, others inhabit the intestines and genital areas of animals. The sexually transmitted disease syphilis is caused by a spirochaete.

spit ridge of sand or shingle projecting from the land into a body of water. It is deposited by waves carrying material across the mouth of an inlet. Deposition in the brackish water behind a spit may result in the formation of a ◊salt marsh.

Spitsbergen mountainous island with a deeply indented coastline in the Arctic Ocean, the main island in the Norwegian archipelago of ◊Svalbard, 657 km/408 mi N of Norway; area 39,043 sq km/15,075 sq mi. Fishing, hunting, and coal mining are the chief economic activities. The Norwegian Polar Research Institute operates an all-year scientific station on the west coast. Mount Newton rises to 1,713 m/5,620 ft.

spittle alternative name for ◊saliva and ◊cuckoo spit.

spittlebug alternative name for ◊froghopper.

Spitz Mark Andrew 1950– . US swimmer. He won a record seven gold medals at the 1972 Olympic Games, all in world record times.

He won 11 Olympic medals in total (four in 1968) and set 26 world records between 1967 and 1972. After retiring in 1972 he became a movie actor.

spleen organ in vertebrates, part of the reticuloendothelial system, which helps to process ◊lymphocytes. It also regulates the number of red blood cells in circulation by destroying old cells, and stores iron. It is situated on the left side of the body, behind the stomach.

splenectomy surgical removal of the ◊spleen. It may be necessary following injury to the spleen, or in the course of some blood diseases.

Split (Italian ***Spalato***) port in Croatia, on the Adriatic coast; population (1991) 189,400. Industries include engineering, cement, and textiles. Split was bombed during 1991 as part of Yugoslavia's blockade of the Croatian coast.

Spock Benjamin McLane 1903–1998. US paediatrician and writer on child care. His *Common Sense Book of Baby and Child Care* 1946 urged less rigidity in bringing up children than had been advised by previous generations of writers on the subject, but this was misunderstood as advocating permissiveness. He was also active in the peace movement, especially during the Vietnam War.

In his later work he stressed that his common-sense approach had not implied rejecting all discipline, but that his main aim was to give parents the confidence to trust their own judgement rather than rely on books by experts who did not know a particular child.

Spode Josiah 1754–1827. English potter. Around 1800, he developed bone porcelain (made from bone ash, china stone, and china clay), which was produced at all English factories in the 19th century. Spode became potter to King George III 1806.

spoils system in the USA, the granting of offices and favours among the supporters of a party in office. The spoils system, a type of patronage, was used by President Jackson in the 1830s in particular, and by Republican administrations after the Civil War. The practice remained common in the 20th century in US local government.

The term is derived from a speech after an election victory by Secretary of State William Marcy: 'To the victor belong the spoils of the enemy.'

sponge any saclike simple invertebrate of the phylum Porifera, usually marine. A sponge has a hollow body, its cavity lined by cells bearing flagellae, whose whiplike movements keep water circulating, bringing in a stream of food particles. The body walls are strengthened with protein (as in the bath sponge) or small spikes of silica, or a framework of calcium carbonate.

A deep-sea sponge found 1994 is the first carnivorous sponge to be identified. The 15-mm/0.6-in

'We feel and know that we are eternal.'
BENEDICT SPINOZA *Ethics*

spinet The spinet refers to a small kind of harpsichord in which, as the illustration shows, the strings are perpendicular to the keys instead of parallel. It was similar or identical to the virginal and almost invariably had only one manual.
Antique Instruments

high sponge, of the family Cladorhizidae, traps small crustaceans by entangling them in thin filaments. Epithelial cells then migrate towards the prey and envelop it.

spontaneous combustion burning that is not initiated by the direct application of an external source of heat. A number of materials and chemicals, such as hay and sodium chlorate, can react with their surroundings, usually by oxidation, to produce so much internal heat that combustion results.

Special precautions must be taken for the storage and handling of substances that react violently with moisture or air. For example, phosphorus ignites spontaneously in the presence of air and must therefore be stored under water; sodium and potassium are stored under kerosene in order to prevent their being exposed to moisture.

spontaneous generation or ***abiogenesis*** erroneous belief that living organisms can arise spontaneously from non-living matter. This survived until the mid-19th century, when the French chemist Louis Pasteur demonstrated that a nutrient broth would not generate microorganisms if it was adequately sterilized. The theory of ◊biogenesis holds that spontaneous generation cannot now occur; it is thought, however, to have played an essential role in the origin of ◊life on this planet 4 billion years ago.

spoonbill any of several large wading birds of the ibis family Threskiornithidae, order Ciconiiformes, characterized by a long, flat bill, dilated at the tip in the shape of a spoon. Spoonbills are white or pink, and up to 90 cm/3 ft tall. Their feet are adapted for wading, and the birds obtain their food, consisting chiefly of fish, frogs, molluscs, and crustaceans, from shallow water.

The Eurasian spoonbill *Platalea leucorodia* of Europe, S Asia, and Africa is found in shallow open water, which it sifts for food.

spoonerism exchange of elements in a flow of words. Usually a slip of the tongue, a spoonerism can also be contrived for comic effect (for example 'a troop of Boy Scouts' becoming 'a scoop of Boy Trouts'). William Spooner (1844–1930) gave his name to the phenomenon.

Spooner was Warden of New College, Oxford, 1903–24, and was credited with many real or apocryphal slips of the tongue. He is rumoured to have told a lazy student: 'You have tasted two whole worms, hissed all my mystery lectures, and have been caught fighting a liar in the quad.'

sporangium structure in which ◊spores are produced.

spore small reproductive or resting body, usually consisting of just one cell. Unlike a ◊gamete, it does not need to fuse with another cell in order to develop into a new organism. Spores are produced by the lower plants, most fungi, some bacteria, and certain protozoa. They are generally light and easily dispersed by wind movements.

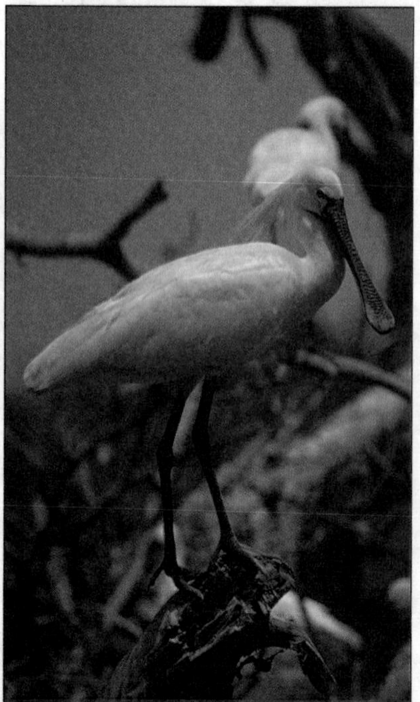

spoonbill The Eurasian spoonbill *Platalea leucordia* in a nesting colony in S India. The spoon-shaped bill is used for sifting fish and crustaceans from the shallow waters of lakes and estuaries. The untidy nest of sticks may be made on the ground or, as here, in trees. *Premaphotos Wildlife*

spring Springs occur where water-laden rock layers (aquifers) reach the surface. Water will flow from a well whose head is below the water table.

Plant spores are haploid and are produced by the sporophyte, following ◊meiosis; see ◊alternation of generations.

sporophyte diploid spore-producing generation in the life cycle of a plant that undergoes ◊alternation of generations.

Spratly Islands (Chinese ***Nanshan Islands***) disputed group of small islands, coral reefs, and sandbars dispersed over a distance of 965 km/600 mi in the South China Sea. The islands are of strategic importance, commanding the sea passage from Japan to Singapore, and in 1976 oil was discovered.

Used as a submarine base by the Japanese during World War II, the islands are claimed in whole or part by the People's Republic of China, Taiwan, Malaysia, Brunei, the Philippines, and Vietnam.

spreadsheet in computing, a program that mimics a sheet of ruled paper, divided into columns and rows. The user enters values in the sheet, then instructs the program to perform some operation on them, such as totalling a column or finding the average of a series of numbers. Highly complex numerical analyses may be built up from these simple steps.

Spreadsheets are widely used in business for forecasting and financial control. The first spreadsheet program, Software Arts' VisiCalc, appeared 1979. The best known include ◊Lotus 1–2–3 and Microsoft Excel.

spring in geology, a natural flow of water from the ground, formed at the point of intersection of the water table and the ground's surface. The source of water is rain that has percolated through the overlying rocks. During its underground passage, the water may have dissolved mineral substances that may then be precipitated at the spring (hence, a mineral spring).

A spring may be continuous or intermittent, and depends on the position of the water table and the topography (surface features).

Spring Richard ('Dick') 1950– . Irish Labour Party leader from 1982. He entered into coalition with Garret ◊FitzGerald's Fine Gael 1982 as deputy prime minister (with the posts of minister for the environment 1982–83 and minister for energy 1983–87). In 1993 he became deputy prime minister to Albert ◊Reynolds in a Fianna Fáil–Labour Party coalition, with the post of minister for foreign affairs. He withdrew from the coalition Nov 1994 in protest over a judicial appointment made by Reynolds, and the following month formed a new coalition with Fine Gael.

springbok South African antelope *Antidorcas marsupialis* about 80 cm/30 in at the shoulder, with head and body 1.3 m/4 ft long. It may leap 3 m/10 ft or more in the air when startled or playing, and has a fold of skin along the middle of the back which is raised to a crest in alarm. Springboks once migrated in herds of over a million, but are now found only in small numbers where protected.

Springsteen Bruce 1949– . US rock singer, songwriter, and guitarist. His music combines melodies in traditional rock idiom and reflective lyrics about working-class life and the pursuit of the American dream on such albums as *Born to Run* 1975, *Born in the USA* 1984, and *Human Touch* 1992.

Darkness at the Edge of Town 1978, *The River* 1980, and the solo acoustic *Nebraska* 1982 reinforced his reputation as a songwriter. His vast stadium concerts with the E Street Band were marked by his ability to overcome the distance between audience and artist, making him one of rock's finest live performers.

spruce coniferous tree of the genus *Picea* of the pine family, found over much of the northern hemisphere. Pyramidal in shape, spruces have rigid, prickly needles and drooping, leathery cones.

Some are important forestry trees, such as the sitka spruce *P. sitchensis*, native to W North America, and the Norway spruce *P. abies*, now planted widely in North America.

spruce Spruces are evergreen trees of the pine family. They have hard sharp needles and soft leathery cones hanging from the branches. Perhaps the most familiar is the traditional Christmas tree, the Norway spruce.

Sputnik (Russian 'fellow traveller') series of ten Soviet Earth-orbiting satellites. *Sputnik 1* was the first artificial satellite, launched 4 Oct 1957. It weighed 84 kg/185 lb, with a 58 cm/23 in diameter, and carried only a simple radio transmitter which allowed scientists to track it as it orbited Earth. It burned up in the atmosphere 92 days later. Sputniks were superseded in the early 1960s by the Cosmos series.

Sputnik 2, launched 3 Nov 1957, weighed about 500 kg/1,100 lb including the dog Laika, the first living creature in space. Unfortunately, there was no way to return the dog to Earth, and it died in space. Later Sputniks were test flights of the ◊Vostok spacecraft.

square in geometry, a quadrilateral (four-sided) plane figure with all sides equal and each angle a right angle. Its diagonals bisect each other at right angles. The area A of a square is the length l of one side multiplied by itself ($A = l \times l$).

Also, any quantity multiplied by itself is termed a square, represented by an ◊exponent of power 2; for example, $4 \times 4 = 4^2 = 16$ and $6.8 \times 6.8 = 6.8^2 = 46.24$.

square root in mathematics, a number that when squared (multiplied by itself) equals a given number. For example, the square root of 25 (written $\sqrt{25}$) is ± 5, because $5 \times 5 = 25$, and $(-5) \times (-5) = 25$. As an ◊exponent, a square root is represented by ½, for example, $16^{1/2} = 4$.

Negative numbers (less than 0) do not have square roots that are ◊real numbers. Their roots are represented by ◊complex numbers, in which the square root of -1 is given the symbol i (that is, $\pm i^2 = -1$). Thus the square root of -4 is $\sqrt{[(-1) \times 4]} = \sqrt{-1} \times \sqrt{4} = 2i$.

squash or ***squash rackets*** racket-and-ball game usually played by two people on an enclosed court, derived from ◊rackets. Squash became a popular sport in the 1970s and later gained competitive status. There are two forms of squash: the American form, which is played in North and some South American countries, and the English, which is played mainly in Europe and Commonwealth countries such as Pakistan, Australia, and New Zealand.

In singles squash under the American rules, the court is 10 m/32 ft long and 5.6 m/18 ft 6 in wide. The front and side walls are 4.9 m/16 ft high and the back wall is 2 m/6 ft 6 in high. In doubles it measures 25 ft/7.6 m by 45 ft/13.7 m.

In English singles, the court is 10 m/32 ft long and 6.4 m/21 ft wide. The front wall is 5 m/15 ft high, and the back wall is 2.1 m/7 ft high. The side walls slant down from 15 ft at the front to 7 ft at the back. Doubles squash is played by two teams of two players each on a larger court.

A small rubber ball is hit against a wall (the front wall) and, when serving, must be above a line about 1.83 m/6 ft high. Thereafter the ball must be hit alternately against the front wall, within certain limitations, but rebounds off the other three walls are permitted. The object is to win points by playing shots the opponent cannot return to the wall.

squill bulb-forming perennial plant of the genus *Scilla*, family Liliaceae, found growing in dry places near the sea in W Europe. Cultivated species usually bear blue flowers either singly or in clusters at the top of the stem.

The spring squill *S. verna* has narrow, grasslike leaves, sometimes curled; violet-blue six-petalled flowers appear in early summer, two to twelve on a dense spike. The autumn squill *S. autumnalis* is somewhat similar, but flowers in autumn before the emergence of leaves.

squint or ***strabismus*** common condition in which one eye deviates in any direction. A squint may be convergent (with the bad eye turned inwards), divergent (outwards), or, in rare cases, vertical. A convergent squint is also called cross-eye.

There are two types of squint: paralytic, arising from disease or damage involving the extraocular muscles or their nerve supply; and nonparalytic, which may be inherited or due to some refractive error within the eye. Nonparalytic (or concomitant) squint is the typical condition seen in small children. It is treated by corrective glasses, exercises for the eye muscles, or surgery.

squirrel rodent of the family Sciuridae. Squirrels are found worldwide except for Australia, Madagascar, and polar regions. Some are tree dwellers; these generally have bushy tails, and some, with membranes between their legs, are called ◊flying squirrels. Others are terrestrial, generally burrowing forms called ground squirrels; these include chipmunks, gophers, marmots, and prairie dogs.

The red squirrel *Sciurus vulgaris* is found throughout Europe and N Asia. It is about 23 cm/9 in long (plus 18 cm/7 in tail), with red fur and a bushy tail. It rears its young in stick nests, or 'dreys'. Although it is less active in winter, it does not hibernate, burying nuts as a winter store. In Britain, the red squirrel has been replaced in most areas by the introduced grey squirrel *S. carolinensis* from North America; in 1996 there were only 160,000 red squirrels remaining, compared with 2.5 million greys.

Sri Lanka island in the Indian Ocean, off the SE coast of India. *See country box on following page.*

Srinagar summer capital of the state of ◊Jammu and Kashmir, India; population (1991) 595,000. It is a beautiful resort, intersected by waterways, and has carpet, papier mâché, and leather industries.

SS (German *S*chutz-*S*taffel 'protective squadron') Nazi elite corps established 1925. Under ◊Himmler its 500,000 membership included the full-time Waffen-SS (armed SS), which fought in World War II, and spare-time members. The SS performed state police duties and was brutal in its treatment of the Jews and others in the concentration camps and occupied territories. It was condemned as an illegal organization at the Nuremberg Trials of war criminals.

SSSI abbreviation for ◊***Site of Special Scientific Interest***.

stability measure of how difficult it is to move an object from a position of balance or ◊equilibrium with respect to gravity.

stabilizer one of a pair of fins fitted to the sides of a ship, especially one governed automatically by a ◊gyroscope mechanism, designed to reduce side-to-side rolling of the ship in rough weather.

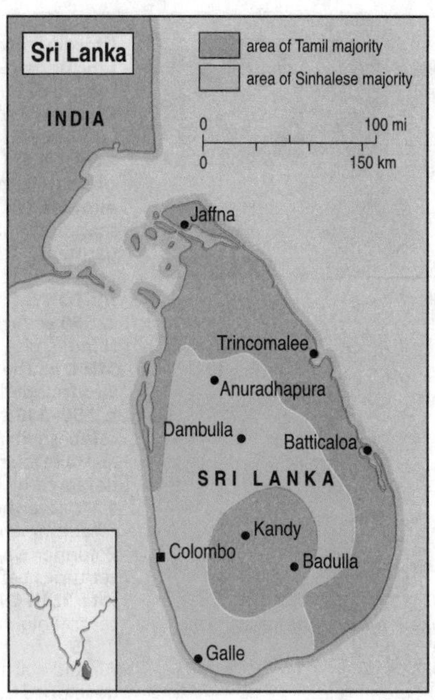

stack isolated pillar of rock that has become separated from a headland by ◊coastal erosion. It is usually formed by the collapse of an ◊arch. Further erosion will reduce it to a stump, which is exposed only at low tide.

Examples of stacks in the UK are the Needles, off the Isle of Wight, which are formed of chalk.

Staël Anne Louise Germaine Necker, Madame de 1766–1817. French author. She wrote semi-autobiographical novels such as *Delphine* 1802 and *Corinne* 1807, and the critical work *De l'Allemagne* 1810, on German literature. She was banished from Paris by Napoleon 1803 because of her advocacy of political freedom.

Staffa uninhabited island in the Inner Hebrides, W of Mull. It has a rugged coastline and many caves, including ◊Fingal's Cave.

Staffordshire county of W central England
area 2,720 sq km/1,050 sq mi (*see United Kingdom map*)
towns Stafford (administrative headquarters), Stoke-on-Trent, Newcastle-under-Lyme
features largely flat; river Trent and its tributaries; Cannock Chase; Keele University 1962; Staffordshire bull terriers
industries china and earthenware in the Potteries and the upper Trent basin, especially Wedgwood; dairy farming; coal mining
population (1991) 1,031,100
famous people Arnold Bennett, Peter de Wint, Robert Peel, Josiah Wedgwood.

stained glass pieces of coloured glass held in place by thin strips of metal (usually lead) to form pictures in a window. One of the great medieval arts, it developed with the increase of window space in the Gothic church, and to some extent serves the same purpose as a wall-painting, with the added richness given by translucence and the variations of light piercing through from outside.
early The first references to stained glass appear in literature from the 10th century. Early windows consisted of a mosaiclike arrangement of pieces of brightly coloured glass stained all the way through; pictorial subjects were introduced later.
medieval By the middle of the 12th century, incidents in the life of Jesus or of one of the saints were commonly depicted. Much of the most beautiful glass belongs to the 12th and 13th centuries.
16th–19th centuries In the mid-16th century a new technique was introduced, the painting of glass in enamels. This method produced imitations of oil painting, in which the true nature and brilliance of the art of stained glass was lost. The revival conducted in the 19th century by William ◊Morris and Edward ◊Burne-Jones produced windows of interesting design, though lacking the splendour of the Middle Ages.

squill The blue flowers of the spring squill *Scilla verna* often carpet the short grassland sward on clifftops around the coasts of W Europe. Some species are cultivated for the garden. *Premaphotos Wildlife*

SRI LANKA
Democratic Socialist Republic of (formerly to 1972 *Ceylon*)

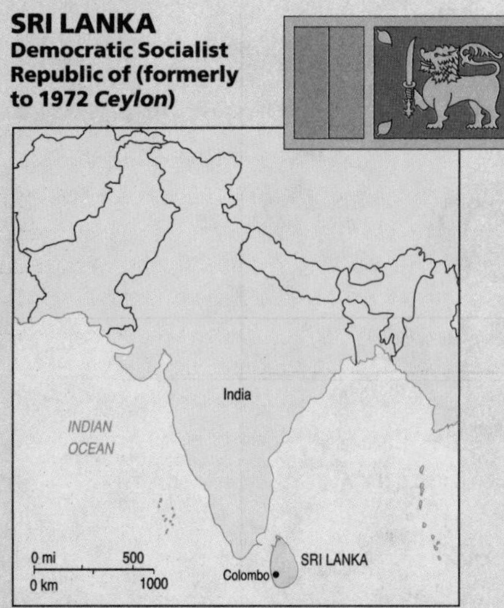

national name *Sri Lanka Prajathanthrika Samajawadi Janarajaya*
area 65,600 sq km/25,328 sq mi
capital (and chief port) Colombo
major towns/cities Kandy
major ports Jaffna, Galle, Negombo, Trincomalee
physical features flat in N and around the coast; hills and mountains in S and central interior
head of state Chandrika Bandaranaike Kumaratunga from 1994
head of government Sirimavo Bandaranaike from 1994
political system liberal democratic republic
administrative divisions eight provincial councils; 68 district councils
political parties United National Party (UNP), right of centre; Sri Lanka Freedom Party (SLFP), left of centre; Democratic United National Front (DUNF), centre-left; Tamil United Liberation Front (TULF), Tamil autonomy (banned from 1983); Eelam People's Revolutionary Liberation Front (EPRLF), Indian-backed Tamil-secessionist 'Tamil Tigers'; People's Liberation Front (JVP), Sinhalese-chauvinist, left-wing (banned 1971–77 and 1983–88)
population 18,100,000 (1996 est)
population growth rate 1.3% (1990–95); 1.1% (2000–05)
ethnic distribution 73% Sinhalese, 19% Tamil, and 7% Moors or Muslims (concentrated in the E); the Tamil community is divided between the long settled 'Sri Lankan Tamils' (11% of the population), who reside in northern and eastern coastal areas, and the more recent immigrant 'Indian Tamils' (8%), who settled in the Kandyan highlands during the 19th and 20th centuries
life expectancy 70 (men), 74 (women)
literacy rate men 93%, women 84%
languages Sinhala, Tamil, English
religions Buddhist 69%, Hindu 15%, Muslim 8%, Christian 7%
currency Sri Lankan rupee
GDP (US $) 11,71 billion (1994)
growth rate 5.6% (1994)
exports tea, rubber, coconut products, graphite, sapphires, rubies, other gemstones, textiles and garments

HISTORY
c. 550 BC Arrival of the Sinhalese, led by Vijaya, from N India, displacing the long-settled Veddas.
5th C BC The Sinhalese kingdom of Anuradhapura was founded by King Pandukabaya.
c. 250–210 BC Buddhism, brought from India, became established in Sri Lanka.
AD 992 Downfall of Anuradhapura kingdom, defeated by the South Indian Colas.
1070 Overthrow of Colas by Vijayabahu I and establishment of the Sinhalese kingdom of Polonnaruva, which survived for more than two centuries before a number of regional states arose.
late 15th C Kingdom of Kandy established in the central highlands.
1505 Arrival of Portuguese navigator Lorenço de Almeida, attracted by the spice trade that had been developed by Arab merchants who had called the island Serendip.
1597–1618 Portuguese controlled most of Sri Lanka, with the exception of Kandy.
1658 Dutch conquest of Portuguese territories.
1795–98 British conquest of Dutch territories.
1802 Treaty of Amiens recognized the island as the British colony of Ceylon.
1815 British won control of Kandy, becoming the first European power to rule the whole island.
1830s Immigration of S Indian Hindu Tamil labourers to work the central coffee plantations.
1880s Tea and rubber become the chief cash crops after blight ended the production of coffee.
1919 Formation of the Ceylon National Congress to campaign for self rule; increasing conflicts between Sinhalese majority community and Tamil minority.
1931 Universal adult suffrage introduced for elected legislature and executive council in which power was shared with the British.
1948 Ceylon achieved independence from Britain within the Commonwealth.
1949 Indian Tamils disenfranchised.
1956 Sinhala established as the official language; Solomon Bandaranaike became prime minister.
1959 Bandaranaike assassinated.
1960 Sirimavo Bandaranaike, the widow of Solomon, won the general election and formed the SLFP government, which nationalized the oil industry.
1965 General election won by UNP and Dudley Senanayake became prime minister.
1970 Sirimavo Bandaranaike returned to power as prime minister, leading a United Front government.
1971 Sinhalese Marxist uprising, led by students and the People's Liberation Army (JVP).
1972 Socialist Republic of Sri Lanka proclaimed, and Buddhism given 'foremost place' in the new state, antagonizing Tamils.
1976 Tamil United Liberation Front formed to fight for an independent Tamil state ('Eelam') in N and E Sri Lanka.
1978 Presidential constitution adopted by new free-market government headed by Junius Jayawardene of the UNP.
1983 Ethnic riots as Tamil guerrilla violence escalated; state of emergency imposed; more than 1,000 Tamils killed by Sinhalese mobs.
1987 President Jayawardene and Indian prime minister Rajiv Gandhi signed Colombo Accord aimed at creating new provincial councils, disarming the Tamil militants ('Tamil Tigers'), and stationing a 7,000-strong Indian Peace Keeping Force. Violence continued despite cease-fire policed by Indian troops.
1988 Left-wing JVP guerrillas campaigned against Indo-Sri Lankan peace pact. Prime Minister Ranasinghe Premadasa elected president.
1989 Dingiri Banda Wijetunga became prime minister. Leaders of the Tamil Tigers and the banned Sinhala extremist JVP assassinated.
1990 Indian peacekeeping force withdrawn. Violence continued, with death toll exceeding 1,000 a month.
1991 Defence minister Ranjan Wijeratne assassinated; Sri Lankan army killed 2,552 Tamil Tigers at Elephant Pass in the northern Jaffna region. Impeachment motion against President Premadasa failed. A new party, the Democratic National United Front (DUNF), formed by former members of the UNP.
1992 Several hundred Tamil Tiger rebels killed in army offensive, code-named 'Strike Force Two'.
1993 DUNF leader and President Premadasa assassinated by Tamil Tiger terrorists; succeeded by Dingiri Banda Wijetunge.
1994 UNP narrowly defeated in general election; Chandrika Kumaratunga became prime minister of SLFP-led left-of-centre coalition. Peace talks opened with Tamil Tigers. Kumaratunga elected first female president; her mother, Sirimavo Bandaranaike, became prime minister.
1995 Renewed bombing campaign by Tamil Tigers. Major offensive drove out Tamil Tigers from Jaffna city.
1996 State of emergency extended nationwide after Tamils bombed the capital. Government forces launched new major offensive against Tamil Tigers.
1997 Major offensive launched against Tamil separatists. Bomb attack and clashes with Tamil separatists threatened to derail government's peace initiative.
1998 Tamil Tigers outlawed after bombing of Sri Lanka's holiest Buddhist site.

SEE ALSO Bandaranaike; Sinhalese; Tamil; Tamil Tigers

stainless steel widely used ◊alloy of iron, chromium, and nickel that resists rusting. Its chromium content also gives it a high tensile strength. It is used for cutlery and kitchen fittings, and in surgical instruments. Stainless steel was first produced in the UK 1913 and in Germany 1914.

Stakhanov Aleksei Grigorievich 1906–1977. Soviet miner who exceeded production norms; he gave his name to the Stakhanovite movement of the 1930s, when workers were offered incentives to simplify and reorganize work processes in order to increase production.

stalactite and stalagmite cave structures formed by the deposition of calcite dissolved in ground water. Stalactites grow downwards from the roofs or walls and can be icicle-shaped, straw-shaped, curtain-shaped, or formed as terraces. Stalagmites grow upwards from the cave floor and can be conical, fir-cone-shaped, or resemble a stack of saucers. Growing stalactites and stalagmites may meet to form a continuous column from floor to ceiling.

Stalactites are formed when ground water, hanging as a drip, loses a proportion of its carbon dioxide into the air of the cave. This reduces the amount of calcite that can be held in solution, and a small trace of calcite is deposited. Successive drips build up the stalactite over many years. In stalagmite formation the calcite comes out of the solution because of agitation – the shock of a drop of water hitting the floor is sufficient to remove some calcite from the drop. The different shapes result from the splashing of the falling water.

‘History shows that there are no invincible armies.’

Joseph Stalin
Speech on the Soviet Union's declaration of war on Germany 1941

Stalin Joseph. Adopted name (Russian 'steel') of Joseph Vissarionovich Djugashvili 1879–1953. Soviet politician. A member of the October Revolution Committee 1917, Stalin became general secretary of the Communist Party 1922. After ◊Lenin's death 1924, Stalin sought to create 'socialism in one country' and clashed with ◊Trotsky, who denied the possibility of socialism inside Russia until revolution had occurred in W Europe. Stalin won this ideological struggle by 1927, and a series of five-year plans was launched to collectivize industry and agriculture from 1928. All opposition was eliminated in the Great Purge 1936–38. During World War II, Stalin intervened in the military direction of the campaigns against Nazi Germany. He managed to not only bring the USSR through the war but helped it emerge as a superpower, although only at an immense cost in human suffering to his own people. After the war, Stalin quickly turned E Europe into a series of Soviet satellites and maintained an autocratic rule domestically. His role was denounced after his death by Khrushchev and other members of the Soviet regime.

Stalin was born in Georgia, the son of a shoemaker. Educated for the priesthood, he was expelled from his seminary for Marxist propaganda. He became a member of the Social Democratic Party 1898, and joined Lenin and the Bolsheviks 1903. He was repeatedly exiled to Siberia 1903–13. He then became a member of the Communist Party's Politburo (executive committee), and sat on the October Revolution committee. Stalin rapidly consolidated a powerful following (including Molotov); in 1921 he became commissar for nationalities in the Soviet government, responsible for the decree granting equal rights to all peoples of the Russian Empire, and was appointed general secretary of the Communist Party 1922.

Stalingrad former name (1925–61) of the Russian city of ◊Volgograd.

Stalingrad, Siege of in World War II, German siege of Soviet city of Stalingrad (now Volgograd) Aug 1942–Jan 1943. The siege of Stalingrad was a horrific campaign, with both sides sustaining heavy casualties – the Germans lost 400,000 troops while there were 750,000 Soviet military casualties and an unknown number of civilian deaths.The Germans were finally driven out by a massive Soviet counterattack launched Nov 1942.

stamen male reproductive organ of a flower. The stamens are collectively referred to as the

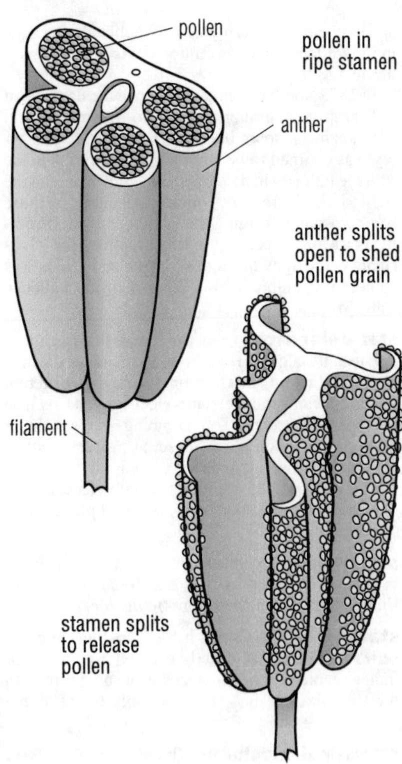

stamen The stamen is the male reproductive organ of a flower. It has a thin stalk called a filament with an anther at the tip. The anther contains pollen sacs, which split to release tiny grains of pollen.

◊androecium. A typical stamen consists of a stalk, or filament, with an anther, the pollen-bearing organ, at its apex, but in some primitive plants, such as *Magnolia*, the stamen may not be markedly differentiated.

The number and position of the stamens are significant in the classification of flowering plants. Generally the more advanced plant families have fewer stamens, but they are often positioned more effectively so that the likelihood of successful pollination is not reduced.

Stamford Bridge, Battle of battle 25 Sept 1066 at Stamford Bridge, a crossing of the Derwent 14 km/9 mi northeast of York, at which ◊Harold II defeated and killed Harold Hardraada, king of Norway, and Tostig, the English king's exiled brother. Harold then marched south to face the Normans at the Battle of ◊Hastings.

Stamp Act UK act of Parliament in 1765 that sought to raise enough money from the American colonies to cover the cost of their defence.

Refusal to use the required tax stamps and a blockade of British merchant shipping in the colonies forced repeal of the act the following year. It helped to precipitate the ◊American Revolution.

The act provoked vandalism and looting in America, and the Stamp Act Congress in Oct of that year (the first intercolonial congress) declared the act unconstitutional, with the slogan 'No taxation without representation', because the colonies were not represented in the British Parliament.

standard atmosphere alternative term for ◊atmosphere, a unit of pressure.

standard form or ***scientific notation*** method of writing numbers often used by scientists, particularly for very large or very small numbers. The numbers are written with one digit before the decimal point and multiplied by a power of 10. The number of digits given after the decimal point depends on the accuracy required. For example, the ◊speed of light is 2.9979×10^8 m/1.8628×10^5 mi per second.

standard gravity acceleration due to gravity, generally taken as 9.81274 m/32.38204 ft per second per second. See also ◊*g* scale.

standard of living in economics, the measure of consumption and welfare of a country, community, class, or person. Individual standard-of-living expectations are heavily influenced by the income and consumption of other people in similar jobs.

Universal measures of standards of living cannot be applied to individuals. National income and gross national product, which measure a country's wealth, do not take into account unpaid work (housework and family labour) or quality of life and do not show the distribution of wealth or reflect the particular national or individual aspirations, duties, or responsibilities, which differ widely from person to person, class to class, and country to country.

standing crop in ecology, the total number of individuals of a given species alive in a particular area at any moment. It is sometimes measured as the weight (or ◊biomass) of a given species in a sample section.

standing wave in physics, a wave in which the positions of ◊nodes (positions of zero vibration) and antinodes (positions of maximum vibration) do not move. Standing waves result when two similar waves travel in opposite directions through the same space.

For example, when a sound wave is reflected back along its own path, as when a stretched string is plucked, a standing wave is formed. In this case the antinode remains fixed at the centre and the nodes are at the two ends. Water and ◊electromagnetic waves can form standing waves in the same way.

Stanford Charles Villiers 1852–1924. Irish composer and teacher. He was a leading figure in the 19th-century renaissance of British music. His many works include operas such as *Shamus O'Brien* 1896, seven symphonies, chamber music, and church music. Among his pupils were Vaughan Williams, Gustav Holst, and Frank Bridge.

Stanislavsky Konstantin Sergeivich Alekseyev 1863–1938. Russian actor, director, and teacher of acting. He rejected the declamatory style of acting in favour of a more realistic approach, concentrating on the psychological basis for the development of character. The Actors Studio workshop is based on his methods. As a director, he is acclaimed for his productions of the great plays of ◊Chekhov.

Stanislavsky co-founded the Moscow Art Theatre 1898 and directed productions of Chekhov and Gorky. His ideas, which were described in the autobiography *My Life in Art* 1924 and the manuals *An Actor Prepares* 1936, *Building a Character* 1950, and *Creating a Role* 1961, had considerable influence on acting techniques in Europe and the USA.

Stansted London's third international airport, in Essex, England. The original runway was built by US forces during World War II and became operational 1944.

As a civilian airport from 1957, offering limited international service, it featured in three government inquiries before the 1985 decision to make it London's third airport. The passenger terminal, opened March 1991 and designed by Norman Foster, is the centrepiece of a £400 million development, which took the airport's annual capacity to 8 million passengers.

Stanley town on E Falkland, capital of the ◊Falkland Islands; population (1991) 1,557. After changing its name only once between 1843 and 1982, it was renamed five times in the space of six weeks during the Falklands War April–June 1982.

Stanley Henry Morton. Adopted name of John Rowlands 1841–1904. Welsh-born US explorer and journalist who made four expeditions to Africa. He and David ◊Livingstone met at Ujiji 1871 and explored Lake Tanganyika. He traced the course of the river Congo/Zaïre to the sea 1874–77, established the Congo Free State (Democratic Republic of Congo) 1879–84, and charted much of the interior 1887–89.

Stanley worked his passage over to America when he was 18. He fought on both sides in the US Civil War. He worked for the *New York Herald* from 1867, and in 1871 he was sent by the editor James Gordon Bennett (1795–1872) to find the ailing Livingstone, which he did on 10 Nov. From Africa he returned to the UK and was elected to Parliament 1895.

Stanton Elizabeth, (born Cady) 1815–1902. US feminist. With Susan B ◊Anthony, she founded the National Woman Suffrage Association 1869, the first women's movement in the USA, and was its first president. She and Anthony wrote and compiled the *History of Women's Suffrage* 1881–86. Stanton also worked for the abolition of slavery.

She organized the International Council of Women in Washington DC. Her publications include *Degradation of Disenfranchisement* and *Solitude of Self* 1892, and in 1885 and 1898 she published a two-part feminist critique of the Bible: *The Woman's Bible*.

staphylococcus spherical bacterium that occurs in clusters. It is found on the skin and mucous membranes of humans and other animals. It can cause abscesses and systemic infections that may prove fatal.

Staphylococcus aureus is a very common bacterium, present in the nose in 30% of people. Normally it gives no trouble, but, largely due to over-prescribing of antibiotics, strains have arisen that are resistant to the drugs used to treat them, principally methicillin, a semi-synthetic form of penicillin. Methicillin-resistant *S. aureus* (MRSA) strains represent a serious hazard to the critically ill or immunosuppressed.

MRSA normally responds to two antibiotics which are considered too toxic for use in any but life-threatening infections (vancomycin and teicoplanin) but it still causes fatalities.

star luminous globe of gas, mainly hydrogen and helium, which produces its own heat and light by nuclear reactions. Although stars shine for a very long time – many billions of years – they are not eternal, and have been found to change in appearance at different stages in their lives.

The smallest mass possible for a star is about 8% that of the Sun (80 times that of ◊Jupiter), otherwise nuclear reactions do not occur. Objects with less than this critical mass shine only dimly, and are termed brown dwarfs.

STAR: NEAREST STARS

Star	Distance (light years)
Proxima Centauri	4.2
Alpha Centauri A	4.3
Alpha Centauri B	4.3
Barnard's Star	6.0
Wolf 359	7.7
Lalande 21185	8.2
UV Ceti A	8.4
UV Ceti B	8.4
Sirius A	8.6
Sirius B	8.6
Ross 154	9.4
Ross 249	10.4

starch widely distributed, high-molecular-mass ◊carbohydrate, produced by plants as a food store; main dietary sources are cereals, legumes, and tubers, including potatoes. It consists of varying proportions of two ◊glucose polymers (◊polysaccharides): straight-chain (amylose) and branched (amylopectin) molecules.

Purified starch is a white powder used to stiffen textiles and paper and as a raw material for making various chemicals. It is used in the food industry as a thickening agent. Chemical treatment of starch gives rise to a range of 'modified starches' with varying properties. Hydrolysis (splitting) of starch by acid or enzymes generates a variety of 'glucose syrups' or 'liquid glucose' for use in the food industry. Complete hydrolysis of starch with acid generates the ◊monosaccharide glucose only. Incomplete hydrolysis or enzymic hydrolysis yields a mixture of glucose, maltose, and non-hydrolysed fractions called dextrins.

Star Chamber in English history, a civil and criminal court, named after the star-shaped ceiling decoration of the room in the Palace of Westminster, London, where its first meetings were held. Created in 1487 by Henry VII, the Star Chamber comprised some 20 or 30 judges. It was abolished 1641 by the ◊Long Parliament.

The Star Chamber became notorious under Charles I for judgements favourable to the king and to Archbishop ◊Laud (for example, the branding on both cheeks of William Prynne in 1637 for seditious

'Dr Livingstone, I presume?'
HENRY MORTON STANLEY
On meeting David Livingstone at Lake Tanganyika Nov 1871

'The Bible and the Church have been the greatest stumbling blocks in the way of women's emancipation.'
ELIZABETH CADY STANTON
Free Thought Sept 1896

starfish The large starfish *Stichaster striatus* on the rocky Pacific coastline of Peru. Starfish live along shorelines and on seabeds, feeding mainly on molluscs and crustaceans. They have the ability to regenerate an arm if one is broken off. *Premaphotos Wildlife*

libel). Under the Thatcher government 1979–90 the term was revived for private ministerial meetings at which disputes between the Treasury and high-spending departments were resolved.

‘The beckoning counts, and not the clicking latch behind you.’

FREYA STARK
Quoted in the *Sunday Telegraph* 1993

star cluster group of related stars, usually held together by gravity. Members of a star cluster are thought to form together from one large cloud of gas in space. Open clusters such as the ◊Pleiades contain from a dozen to many hundreds of young stars, loosely scattered over several light years. ◊Globular clusters are larger and much more densely packed, containing perhaps 100,000 old stars.

The more conspicuous clusters were originally catalogued with the nebulae, and are usually known by their Messier or NGC numbers. A few clusters like the Pleiades, Hyades, and Praesepe are also known by their traditional names.

starfish or ***sea star*** any ◊echinoderm of the subclass Asteroidea with arms radiating from a central body. Usually there are five arms, but some species have more. They are covered with spines and small pincerlike organs. There are also a number of small tubular processes on the skin surface that assist in locomotion and respiration. Starfish are predators, and vary in size from 1.2 cm/0.5 in to 90 cm/3 ft.

Some species use their suckered tube feet to pull open the shells of bivalve molluscs, then evert their stomach to surround and digest the animal inside. The poisonous and predatory crown-of-thorns of the Pacific is very destructive to coral and severely damaged Australia's Great Barrier Reef when it multiplied prolifically in the 1960s–70s. Another outbreak along the Great Barrier Reef was officially declared 1996.

star fruit fruit of the carambola tree.

starling The superb starling *Spreo superbus* from Kenya is one of numerous brilliantly plumaged members of the family to be found in tropical Africa. Like the European starling, several of these beautiful African species, including the one pictured, become very tame and are often found around human habitation. *Premaphotos Wildlife*

Stark Freya Madeline 1893–1993. English traveller, mountaineer, and writer who for a long time worked in South America. Often travelling alone in dangerous territories, she described her explorations in the Middle East in many books, including *The Valley of the Assassins* 1934, *The Southern Gates of Arabia* 1936, and *A Winter in Arabia* 1940.

starling any member of a large widespread Old World family (Sturnidae) of chunky, dark, generally gregarious birds of the order Passeriformes. The European starling *Sturnus vulgaris*, common in N Eurasia, has been naturalized in North America from the late 19th century. The black, speckled plumage is glossed with green and purple. The feathers on the upper parts are tipped with buff, and the wings are greyish-black, with a reddish-brown fringe. The female is less glossy and lustrous than the male. Its own call is a bright whistle, but it is a mimic of the songs of other birds. It is about 20 cm/8 in long.

Strikingly gregarious in feeding, flight, and roosting, it often becomes a pest in large cities, where it becomes attached to certain buildings as ‘dormitories’, returning each night from omnivorous foraging in the countryside, feeding principally on worms, snails, and insects. Nests are made almost anywhere, and about five pale blue eggs are laid. If disturbed, starlings have been known to lay eggs in the nests of other birds before starting a new nest with their mate elsewhere.

Star of David (Hebrew ‘shield of David’) or ***Magen David*** six-pointed star (made with two equilateral triangles), a symbol of Judaism since the 17th century. It is the central motif on the flag of Israel, and, since 1897, the emblem of Zionism.

START acronym for ◊***Strategic Arms Reduction Talks***.

Star Wars popular term for the ◊Strategic Defense Initiative announced by US president Reagan in 1983.

state territory that forms its own domestic and foreign policy, acting through laws that are typically decided by a government and carried out, by force if necessary, by agents of that government. It can be argued that growth of regional international bodies such as the European Union (formerly the European Community) means that states no longer enjoy absolute sovereignty.

The so-called states of the USA, which are to some degree subject to the will of the federal government, are not states in international terms, nor are colonial or similar possessions, which, too, are subject to an overriding authority.

In 1995 there were 192 sovereign nation states in the world, 40 of which were less than 20 years old.

State Department (Department of State) US government department responsible for ◊foreign relations, headed by the ◊secretary of state, the senior cabinet officer of the executive branch.

states' rights interpretation of the US constitution that emphasizes the powers retained by individual states and minimizes those given to the federal government. The dividing line between state and national sovereignty was left deliberately vague in the Philadelphia convention devising the constitution 1787.

In 1832 South Carolina developed the doctrine of nullification, claiming the right to overrule federal laws against its own interests. The practice of slavery was claimed to be among a state's rights in the years leading up to the American Civil War, and the right to secede from the Union was claimed by those southern states forming the Confederacy at its outbreak. More recently, federal support for civil-rights campaigns during the 1950s and 1960s was sometimes inhibited by a reluctance to challenge states' rights.

static electricity ◊electric charge that is stationary, usually acquired by a body by means of electrostatic induction or friction. Rubbing different materials can produce static electricity, as seen in the sparks produced on combing one's hair or removing a nylon shirt. In some processes static electricity is useful, as in paint spraying where the parts to be sprayed are charged with electricity of opposite polarity to that on the paint droplets, and in ◊xerography.

statics branch of mechanics concerned with the behaviour of bodies at rest and forces in equilibrium, and distinguished from ◊dynamics.

stations of the Cross in the Christian church, a series of 14 crosses, usually each with a picture or image, depicting the 14 stages in Jesus' journey to the Crucifixion. They are commonly found on the walls of churches.

statistical mechanics branch of physics in which the properties of large collections of particles are predicted by considering the motions of the constituent particles. It is closely related to ◊thermodynamics.

statistics branch of mathematics concerned with the collection and interpretation of data. For example, to determine the ◊mean age of the children in a school, a statistically acceptable answer might be obtained by calculating an average based on the ages of a representative sample, consisting, for example, of a random tenth of the pupils from each class. ◊Probability is the branch of statistics dealing with predictions of events.

Statius c. 45–96. Roman poet. He was the author of the *Silvae*, occasional poems of some interest; the epic *Thebaïd*, which tells the story of the sons of Oedipus; and an unfinished epic *Achilleïs*. He was admired by Dante and Chaucer.

status in the social sciences, an individual's social position, or the esteem in which he or she is held by others in society. Both within and between most occupations or social positions there is a status hierarchy. Status symbols, such as insignia of office or an expensive car, often accompany high status.

The two forms of social prestige may be separate or interlinked. Formal social status is attached to a certain social position, occupation, role, or office. Informal social status is based on an individual's own personal talents, skills, or personality. Sociologists distinguish between ascribed status, which is bestowed by birth, and achieved status, the result of one's own efforts.

The German sociologist Max Weber analysed social stratification in terms of three separate but interlinked dimensions: class, status, and power. Status is seen as a key influence on human behaviour, on the way people evaluate themselves and others.

Stauffenberg Claus von 1907–1944. German colonel in World War II who, in a conspiracy to assassinate Hitler (the ◊July Plot, planted a bomb in the dictator's headquarters conference room in the Wolf's Lair at Rastenburg, East Prussia, 20 July 1944. Hitler was merely injured, and Stauffenberg and 200 others were later executed by the Nazi regime.

staurolite silicate mineral, $(Fe,Mg)_2(Al,Fe)_9Si_4O_{20}(OH)_2$. It forms brown crystals that may be twinned in the form of a cross. It is a useful indicator of medium grade (moderate temperature and pressure) metamorphism in metamorphic rocks formed from clay sediments.

Stavropol territory of the Russian Federation, lying N of the Caucasus Mountains; area 80,600 sq km/31,128 sq mi; population (1991 est) 2,926,500.

The capital is Stavropol. Irrigated land produces grain and sheep are also reared. There are natural gas deposits.

Stavropol formerly (1935–43) ***Voroshilovsk*** town SE of Rostov, in the N Caucasus, SW Russian Federation; population (1994) 337,000. Founded 1777 as a fortress town, it is now a market centre for an agricultural area and makes agricultural machinery, textiles, and food products.

STD abbreviation for ◊sexually transmitted disease.

steady-state theory in astronomy, a rival theory to that of the ◊Big Bang, which claims that the universe has no origin but is expanding because new matter is being created continuously throughout the universe. The theory was proposed 1948 by Hermann ◊Bondi, Thomas Gold (1920–), and Fred ◊Hoyle, but was dealt a severe blow in 1965 by the discovery of ◊cosmic background radiation (radiation left over from the formation of the universe) and is now largely rejected.

stealth technology methods used to make an aircraft as invisible as possible, primarily to radar detection but also to detection by visual means and heat sensors. This is achieved by a combination of aircraft-design elements: smoothing off all radar-reflecting sharp edges; covering the aircraft with radar-absorbent materials; fitting engine coverings that hide the exhaust and heat signatures of the aircraft; and other, secret technologies.

The US F-117A stealth fighter-bomber was used successfully during the 1991 Gulf War to attack targets in Baghdad completely undetected.

steam in chemistry, a dry, invisible gas formed by vaporizing water.

The visible cloud that normally forms in the air when water is vaporized is due to minute suspended water particles. Steam is widely used in chemical and other industrial processes and for the generation of power.

steam engine engine that uses the power of steam to produce useful work. It was the principal power source during the British Industrial Revolution in the 18th century. The first successful steam engine was built 1712 by English inventor Thomas Newcomen at Dudley, West Midlands; it was developed further by Scottish mining engineer James Watt from 1769 and by English mining engineer Richard Trevithick, whose high-pressure steam engine 1802 led to the development of the steam locomotive.

In Newcomen's engine, steam was admitted to a cylinder as a piston moved up, and was then condensed by a spray of water, allowing air pressure to force the piston downwards. James Watt improved Newcomen's engine in 1769 by condensing the steam outside the cylinder (thus saving energy formerly used to reheat the cylinder) and by using steam to force the piston upwards. Watt also introduced the double-acting engine, in which steam is alternately sent to each side of the piston. The compound engine (1781) uses the exhaust from one cylinder to drive the piston of another. A later development was the steam ◊turbine, still used today to power ships and generators in power stations. In other contexts, the steam engine was superseded by the ◊internal-combustion engine.

stearic acid $CH_3(CH_2)_{16}COOH$ saturated long-chain ◊fatty acid, soluble in alcohol and ether but not in water. It is found in many fats and oils, and is used to make soap and candles and as a lubricant. The salts of stearic acid are called stearates.

stearin mixture of stearic and palmitic acids, used to make soap.

steel alloy or mixture of iron and up to 1.7% carbon, sometimes with other elements, such as manganese, phosphorus, sulphur, and silicon. The USA, Russia, Ukraine, and Japan are the main steel producers. Steel has innumerable uses, including ship and car manufacture, skyscraper frames, and machinery of all kinds.

Steels with only small amounts of other metals are called carbon steels. These steels are far stronger than pure iron, with properties varying with the composition. Alloy steels contain greater amounts of other metals. Low-alloy steels have less than 5% of the alloying material; high-alloy steels have more. Low-alloy steels containing up to 5% silicon with relatively little carbon have a high electrical resistance and are used in power transformers and motor or generator cores, for example. Stainless steel is a high-alloy steel containing at least 11% chromium. Steels with up to 20% tungsten are very hard and are used in high-speed cutting tools. About 50% of the world's steel is now made from scrap.

Steel is produced by removing impurities, such as carbon, from raw or pig iron, produced by a ◊blast furnace. The main industrial process is the ◊basic–oxygen process but the open-hearth process is also used, and high-quality steel is made in an electric furnace.

steel band musical ensemble common in the West Indies, consisting mostly of percussion instruments made from oil drums that give a sweet, metallic ringing tone.

Steele Richard 1672–1729. Irish essayist. He founded the journal *The Tatler* 1709–11, in which Joseph ◊Addison collaborated. They continued their joint work in *The Spectator*, also founded by Steele, 1711–12, and *The Guardian* 1713. He also wrote plays, such as *The Conscious Lovers* 1722.

Steen Jan Havickszoon c. 1626–1679. Dutch painter. He painted humorous genre scenes, mainly set in taverns or bourgeois households, as well as portraits and landscapes. An example is *The Prince's Birthday* (Rijksmuseum, Amsterdam).

He studied under Nicholas Knupfer (1603–1660), Adriaen van Ostade, and Jan van Goyen, whose daughter he married. He worked in The Hague, Delft (where he had a brewery), and Leiden, where in his later years he kept an inn. His great sensitivity as an artist – he had a real gift of composition and colour – saved his humorous genre scenes from triviality. He also produced historical and religious works, and was one of the most prolific painters of the period.

Steichen Edward Jean 1879–1973. Luxembourg-born US photographer, who with Alfred ◊Stieglitz helped to establish photography as an art form. His style evolved during his career from painterly impressionism to realism.

He recorded both world wars, and was also an innovative fashion and portrait photographer.

Steiger Rod(ney Stephen) 1925– . US character actor. Of the ◊Method school, his films includes *On the Waterfront* 1954, *The Pawnbroker* 1965, *In the Heat of the Night* 1967 (Academy Award), and the title role in *W C Fields and Me* 1976.

Stein Gertrude 1874–1946. US writer. She influenced authors Ernest ◊Hemingway, Sherwood Anderson (1876–1941), and F Scott ◊Fitzgerald with her radical prose style. Drawing on the stream-of-consciousness psychology of William James and on the geometry of Cézanne and the Cubist painters in Paris, she evolved a 'continuous present' style made up of constant repetition and variation of simple phrases. Her work includes the self-portrait *The Autobiography of Alice B Toklas* 1933.

Born in Allegheny, Pennsylvania, Stein went to Paris 1903 after medical school at Johns Hopkins University and lived there, writing and collecting art, for the rest of her life. In her home she held court to a 'lost generation' of expatriate US writers and modern artists (Picasso, Matisse, Braque, Gris). She also wrote *Three Lives* 1910, *The Making of Americans* 1925, *Composition as Explanation* 1926, *Tender Buttons* 1914, *Mrs Reynolds* 1952.

Stein Gertrude Stein, influential US novelist. *Topham*

Steinbeck US novelist John Steinbeck in 1968. As a young man, Steinbeck worked for some years as a casual labourer and some of his finest fiction is based on his encounters with the migrant workers of California's farming valleys. His critical reputation declined in the early 1960s, although novels such as *The Grapes of Wrath* 1939 won him the Nobel Prize for Literature 1962. *Topham*

Steinbeck John Ernst 1902–1968. US novelist. His realist novels, such as *In Dubious Battle* 1936, *Of Mice and Men* 1937, and *The Grapes of Wrath* 1939 (Pulitzer prize; filmed 1940), portray agricultural life in his native California, where migrant farm labourers from the Oklahoma dust bowl struggled to survive. Nobel prize 1962.

Born in Salinas, California, Steinbeck worked as a labourer to support his writing career, and his experiences supplied him with authentic material for his books. He first achieved success with *Tortilla Flat* 1935, a humorous study of the lives of Monterey *paisanos* (farmers). His early naturalist works are his most critically acclaimed. Later books include *Cannery Row* 1944, *The Wayward Bus* 1947, *East of Eden* 1952, *Once There Was a War* 1958, *The Winter of Our Discontent* 1961, and *Travels with Charley* 1962. He also wrote screenplays for films, notably *Viva Zapata!* 1952. His best-known short story is the fable 'The Pearl'.

'There are three kinds of lies: lies, damned lies, and statistics.'

On STATISTICS
Mark Twain
Autobiography

Steinem Gloria 1934– . US journalist and liberal feminist. She emerged as a leading figure in the US women's movement in the late 1960s. She was also involved in radical protest campaigns against racism and the Vietnam War. She cofounded the Women's Action Alliance 1970 and *Ms* magazine. In 1983 a collection of her articles was published as *Outrageous Acts and Everyday Rebellions.* ▷*See feature on pp. 1152–1153.*

Steiner (Francis) George 1929– . French-born US critic and writer. His books, which focus on the relationships between the arts, culture, and society, include *The Death of Tragedy* 1960, *In Bluebeard's Castle* 1971, a novella about Hitler, *The Portage to San Cristobal of A.H.* 1981, and *Proofs and Three Parables* 1993.

Steiner Rudolf 1861–1925. Austrian philosopher, occultist, and educationalist. He formulated his own mystic and spiritual teaching, which he called ◊anthroposophy. This rejected materialism and aimed to develop the whole human being, intellectually, socially, and, above all, spiritually. A number of Steiner schools (or Waldorf) schools follow a curriculum for children from the nursery-school stage to the age of 17. The curriculum lays a strong emphasis on artistic creativity and intuitive thinking but also permits pupils to take state exams in traditional academic subjects.

Stella Frank Philip 1936– . US painter. He was a pioneer of the severe, hard-edged geometric trend in abstract art that followed ◊Abstract Expressionism.

'I know this – a man got to do what he got to do.'

JOHN STEINBECK
The Grapes of Wrath

Stephenson English engineer George Stephenson. A mining engineer who educated himself at night school, Stephenson made many important improvements to steam engine design. His famous locomotive *Rocket* 1829 was adopted for use on the Liverpool and Manchester Railway 1830. *Topham*

From around 1960 he also experimented with shaped canvases.

Born in Malden, Massachusetts, he studied at Princeton University. In the late 1950s he abandoned Abstract Expressionism and in 1960 came to prominence when he exhibited large-scale paintings consisting of thin regular white stripes on black. From 1960 to 1962 he worked in metallic paint, again using thin stripes which repeated the non-rectangular shape of the support. Later paintings by Stella employ a wider range of colour, the choice of which emphasizes the flatness of the painting, which is then contradicted by the use of overlapping shapes.

stem main supporting axis of a plant that bears the leaves, buds, and reproductive structures; it may be simple or branched. The plant stem usually grows above ground, although some grow underground, including ◊rhizomes, ◊corms, ◊rootstocks, and ◊tubers. Stems contain a continuous vascular system that conducts water and food to and from all parts of the plant.

The point on a stem from which a leaf or leaves arise is called a node, and the space between two successive nodes is the internode. In some plants, the stem is highly modified; for example, it may form a leaf-like ◊cladode or it may be twining (as in many climbing plants), or fleshy and swollen to store water (as in cacti and other succulents). In plants exhibiting ◊secondary growth, the stem may become woody, forming a main trunk, as in trees, or a number of branches from ground level, as in shrubs.

One can acquire everything in solitude except character.

STENDHAL *On Love*

Stendhal Pen name of Marie Henri Beyle 1783–1842. French novelist. His novels *Le Rouge et le Noir/The Red and the Black* 1830 and *La Chartreuse de Parme/The Charterhouse of Parma* 1839 were pioneering works in their treatment of disguise and hypocrisy and outstanding for their psychological analysis; a review of the latter by fellow novelist ◊Balzac 1840 furthered Stendhal's reputation, but he was not fully understood during his lifetime.

His critical works include *Histoire de la peinture en Italie/History of Painting in Italy* 1817, *Rome, Naples et Florence/Rome, Naples and Florence* 1817, *Racine et Shakespeare/Racine and Shakespeare* 1823–25, and *Promenades dans Rome/A Roman Journal* 1829. His unfinished novel *Lucien Leuwen* was published 1894. Although he shared many of the literary ideas of the Romantics, he remained fiercely independent.

Desire of knowledge, like the thirst of riches, increases ever with the acquisition of it.

LAURENCE STERNE *Tristram Shandy*

Stephen c. 1097–1154. King of England from 1135. A grandson of William the Conqueror, he was elected king 1135, although he had previously recognized Henry I's daughter ◊Matilda as heiress to the throne. Matilda landed in England 1139, and civil war disrupted the country until 1153, when Stephen acknowledged Matilda's son, Henry II, as his own heir.

Stephen I (St Stephen of Hungary) c. 975–c. 1038. King of Hungary from 997, when he succeeded his father. He completed the conversion of Hungary to Christianity and was canonized in 1803.

Stephen, St lived c. AD 35. The first Christian martyr; he was stoned to death. Feast day 26 Dec.

Stephenson George 1781–1848. English engineer. He built the first successful steam locomotive. He also invented a safety lamp independently of Humphrey ◊Davy in 1815. He was appointed engineer of the Stockton and Darlington Railway, the world's first public railway, in 1821, and of the Liverpool and Manchester Railway in 1826. In 1829 he won a prize with his locomotive *Rocket*.

Stephenson Robert 1803–1859. English civil engineer. He constructed railway bridges such as the high-level bridge at Newcastle-upon-Tyne, England, and the Menai and Conway tubular bridges in Wales. He was the son of George Stephenson.

steppe the temperate grasslands of Europe and Asia. Sometimes the term refers to other temperate grasslands and semi-arid desert edges.

steradian SI unit (symbol sr) of measure of solid (three-dimensional) angles, the three-dimensional equivalent of the ◊radian. One steradian is the angle at the centre of a sphere when an area on the surface of the sphere equal to the square of the sphere's radius is joined to the centre.

stereophonic sound system of sound reproduction using two complementary channels leading to two loudspeakers, which gives a more natural depth to the sound. Stereo recording began with the introduction of two-track magnetic tape in the 1950s. See ◊hi-fi.

sterilization the killing or removal of living organisms such as bacteria and fungi. A sterile environment is necessary in medicine, food processing, and some scientific experiments. Methods include heat treatment (such as boiling), the use of chemicals (such as disinfectants), irradiation with gamma rays, and filtration.

sterilization any surgical operation to terminate the possibility of reproduction. In women, this is normally achieved by sealing or tying off the ◊Fallopian tubes (tubal ligation) so that fertilization can no longer take place. In men, the transmission of sperm is blocked by ◊vasectomy.

Sterilization may be encouraged by governments to limit population growth or as part of a selective-breeding policy (see ◊eugenics).

sterling silver ◊alloy containing 925 parts of silver and 75 parts of copper. The copper hardens the silver, making it more useful.

Sternberg Josef von 1894–1969. Austrian film director. He lived in the USA from childhood. He is best remembered for his seven films with Marlene Dietrich, including *Der blaue Engel/The Blue Angel* 1930, *Blonde Venus* 1932, and *The Devil Is a Woman* 1935, all of which are marked by his expressive use of light and shadow.

Sterne Laurence 1713–1768. Irish writer. He created the comic anti-hero Tristram Shandy in *The Life and Opinions of Tristram Shandy, Gent* 1759–67, an eccentrically whimsical and bawdy novel which foreshadowed many of the techniques and devices of 20th-century novelists, including James Joyce. His other works include *A Sentimental Journey through France and Italy* 1768.

Sterne, born in Clonmel, Ireland, took orders 1737 and became vicar of Sutton-in-the-Forest, Yorkshire, the following year. In 1741 he married Elizabeth Lumley, producing an unhappy union largely because of his infidelity. He had a sentimental love affair with Eliza Draper, of which the *Letters of Yorick to Eliza* 1775 is a record.

sternum or ***breastbone***, the large flat bone, 15–20 cm/5.9–7.8 in long in the adult, at the front of the chest, joined to the ribs. It gives protection to the heart and lungs. During open-heart surgery the sternum must be split to give access to the thorax.

steroid in biology, any of a group of cyclic, unsaturated alcohols (lipids without fatty acid components), which, like sterols, have a complex molecular structure consisting of four carbon rings. Steroids include the sex hormones, such as ◊testosterone, the corticosteroid hormones produced by the ◊adrenal gland, bile acids, and ◊cholesterol.

The term is commonly used to refer to ◊anabolic steroid. In medicine, synthetic steroids are used to treat a wide range of conditions.

Steroids are also found in plants. The most widespread are the brassinosteroids, necessary for normal plant growth.

stethoscope instrument used to ascertain the condition of the heart and lungs by listening to their action. It consists of two earpieces connected by flexible tubes to a small plate that is placed against the body. It was invented in 1819 in France by René Théophile Hyacinthe ◊Laënnec.

Stevenage town in Hertfordshire, England, 45 km/28 mi N of London; population (1991) 76,100. Dating from medieval times, in 1946 Stevenage was the first place to be designated a new town (to accommodate overspill). Industries include aircraft manufacture, electrical and plastic goods, and missiles.

Stevens Siaka Probin 1905–1988. Sierra Leone politician, president 1971–85. He was the leader of the moderate left-wing All People's Congress (APC), from 1978 the country's only legal political party.

Stevens became prime minister in 1968 and in 1971, under a revised constitution, became Sierra Leone's first president. He created a one-party state based on the APC, and remained in power until his retirement at the age of 80.

Stevens Wallace 1879–1955. US poet. An insurance company executive, he was not recognized as a major poet until late in life. His volumes

Stephenson High level bridge over the River Tyne in Newcastle built by Robert Stephenson 1846–49. The bridge carried track for the North British Railway. *Image Select (UK) Ltd*

of poems include *Harmonium* 1923, *The Man with the Blue Guitar* 1937, and *Transport to Summer* 1947. *The Necessary Angel* 1951 is a collection of essays. An elegant and philosophical poet, he won a Pulitzer prize 1954 for his *Collected Poems*.

Stevenson Robert Louis Balfour 1850–1894. Scottish novelist and poet. He wrote the adventure novel *Treasure Island* 1883. Later works included the novels *Kidnapped* 1886, *The Master of Ballantrae* 1889, *The Strange Case of Dr Jekyll and Mr Hyde* 1886, and the anthology *A Child's Garden of Verses* 1885.

Stevenson was born in Edinburgh. He studied at the university there and qualified as a lawyer, but never practised. Early works include *An Island Voyage* 1878 and *Travels with a Donkey* 1879. In 1879 he met the American Fanny Osbourne in France and followed her to the USA, where they married 1880. In the same year they returned to Britain, and he subsequently published a volume of stories, *The New Arabian Nights* 1882, and essays. The humorous *The Wrong Box* 1889 and the novels *The Wrecker* 1892 and *The Ebb-tide* 1894 were written in collaboration with his stepson, Lloyd Osbourne (1868–1920). In 1890 he settled at Vailima, in Samoa, where he sought a cure for his tuberculosis.

Stewart Alec James 1963– . English cricketer. A stylish right-handed batsman who plays county cricket for Surrey. He made his test debut in 1990 and was appointed England captain in May 1998.

Stewart Jackie (John Young) 1939– . Scottish motor-racing driver. Until surpassed by Alain ◊Prost (France) 1987, Stewart held the record for the most Formula One Grand Prix wins (27). His first win was in 1965, and he started in 99 races.

Stewart James Maitland 1908–1997. US actor. He made his Broadway debut 1932 and soon after worked in Hollywood. Speaking with a soft, slow drawl, he specialized in the role of the stubbornly honest, ordinary American in such films as *Mr Smith Goes to Washington* 1939, *The Philadelphia Story* 1940 (Academy Award), *It's a Wonderful Life* 1946, *Harvey* 1950, *The Man from Laramie* 1955, and *Anatomy of a Murder* 1959. His films with director Alfred Hitchcock include *Rope* 1948, *Rear Window* 1954, *The Man Who Knew Too Much* 1956, and *Vertigo* 1958.

stick insect insect of the order Phasmida, closely resembling a stick or twig. The eggs mimic plant seeds. Many species are wingless. The longest reach a length of 30 cm/1 ft.

Fossilized eggs were identified 1995, and are thought to be around 44 million years old.

stickleback any fish of the family Gasterosteidae, found in marine and fresh waters of the northern hemisphere. It has a long body that can grow to 18 cm/7 in. The spines along a stickleback's back take the place of the first dorsal fin, and can be raised to make the fish difficult to eat for predators. After the eggs have been laid the female takes no part in rearing the young: the male builds a nest for the eggs, which he then guards and rears for the first two weeks.

Stieglitz Alfred 1864–1946. US photographer. After forming the Photo Secession group in 1903, he started up the magazine *Camera Work*. Through exhibitions at his gallery '291' in New York he helped to establish photography as an art form. His works include *Winter, Fifth Avenue* 1893 and *Steerage* 1907. In 1924 he married the painter Georgia O'Keeffe, who was the model in many of his photographs.

stigma in a flower, the surface at the tip of a ◊carpel that receives the ◊pollen. It often has short outgrowths, flaps, or hairs to trap pollen and may produce a sticky secretion to which the grains adhere.

stigmata impressions or marks corresponding to the five wounds Jesus received at his crucifixion, which are said to have appeared spontaneously on St Francis and other saints.

Stijl, De (Dutch 'the style') influential movement in art, architecture, and design founded 1917 in the Netherlands. Attempting to bring art and design together in a single coherent system, the members of De Stijl developed an austere simplification of style, based on simple geometrical shapes and primary colour. Its best-known member was the abstract painter Piet ◊Mondrian.

The influence of De Stijl was deeply felt in architecture and design during the 1930s. The architects Walter ◊Gropius and ◊Le Corbusier, for example, were attracted by its comprehensiveness and radical simplicity, and it stimulated the direction of study at the ◊Bauhaus.

Its name came from the journal *De Stijl* ('Style'), founded 1917 by a group of Dutch artists. The movement has also been called 'Neo-Plasticism', from a pamphlet of that name published by the artists in Paris 1920. The leading figures of De Stijl were Mondrian, the architect and painter Theo van Doesburg (1883–1931), and the architect Jacobus Oud (1890–1963).

Stilicho Flavius AD 365–408. Roman general of ◊Vandal origin, who campaigned successfully against the Visigoths and Ostrogoths. He virtually ruled the western empire as guardian of Honorius (son of ◊Theodosius I) from 395, but was later executed on Honorius' orders.

still life in painting and graphic art, a depiction of inanimate objects.

A feature of painting since classical times, still life developed as an independent genre in the 17th century, flourishing first in Holland, where the Reformation had discouraged religious imagery and artists were seeking new subjects. Early examples often combine a sheer delight in the appearance of things with religious or moral symbolism. One of the first true still lifes is Caravaggio's *Basket of Fruit* 1596 (Pinacoteca Ambrosiana, Milan). Other examples include Chardin's *Skate, Cat and Kitchen Utensils* 1728 (Louvre, Paris) and Morandi's *Still Life* 1946 (Tate Gallery, London).

Stilwell Joseph Warren, ('Vinegar Joe') 1883–1946. US general in World War II. In 1942 he became US military representative in China, when he commanded the Chinese forces cooperating with the British (with whom he quarrelled) in Burma (now Myanmar); he later commanded all US forces in China, Burma, and India until recalled to the USA 1944 after differences over nationalist policy with the ◊Guomindang (nationalist) leader Chiang Kai-shek. Subsequently he commanded the US 10th Army on the Japanese island of Okinawa.

stimulant any substance that acts on the brain to increase alertness and activity; for example, ◊amphetamine. When given to children, stimulants may have a paradoxical, calming effect. Stimulants cause liver damage, are habit-forming, have limited therapeutic value, and are now prescribed only to treat narcolepsy (a neurological disorder characterized by an abnormal tendency to fall asleep) and severe obesity.

Sting Stage name of Gordon Sumner 1951– . English pop singer, songwriter, bass player, and actor. As a member of the trio Police 1977–83, he had UK number-one hits with 'Message in a Bottle' 1979, 'Walking on the Moon' 1979, and 'Every Breath You Take' 1983. In his solo career he has often drawn on jazz, as on the albums *The Dream of Blue Turtles* 1985, *Nothing Like the Sun* 1987, and *Soul Cages* 1991. More recent albums include *Ten Summoner's Tales* 1993 and *Mercury Falling* 1996.

stinkhorn The phallic resemblance of the European stinkhorn *Phallus impudicus* is obvious. Hordes of flies are attracted to the fetid blackish-olive spore-containing mucus that coats the head of the fungus. The spores are widely distributed in the flies' droppings. *Premaphotos Wildlife*

stinkhorn any foul-smelling fungus of the European genus *Phallus*, especially *P. impudicus*; they first appear on the surface as white balls.

stinkwood any of various trees with unpleasant-smelling wood. The S African tree *Ocotea bullata*, family Lauraceae, has offensive-smelling wood when newly felled, but fine, durable timber used for furniture. Another stinkwood is *Gustavia augusta* from tropical America.

'For my part, I travel not to go anywhere, but to go. I travel for travel's sake. The great affair is to move.'

ROBERT LOUIS STEVENSON
Travels with a Donkey

stipule outgrowth arising from the base of a leaf or leaf stalk in certain plants. Stipules usually occur in pairs or fused into a single semicircular structure.

They may have a leaf-like appearance, as in goosegrass *Galium aparine*, be spiny, as in false acacia *Robina*, or look like small scales. In some species they are large, and contribute significantly to the photosynthetic area, as in the garden pea *Pisum sativum*.

Stirling town on the river Forth, created a unitary authority of Scotland 1996 (*see United Kingdom map*)

population (1991) 30,500

industries manufacture of agricultural machinery, textiles, chemicals, carpets

features summer programme of historical theatre; Scottish Wool Centre at Aberfoyle, showing the history of the wool and textile industries in Scotland, opened 1993. The castle, which guarded a key

stigma In many cactus flowers the multilobed stigma (which receives the pollen grains) protrudes well up above the anthers (which produce the pollen grains). In most yellow-flowered species of *Notocactus*, such as this *N. mammulosus*, the stigma is red. *Premaphotos Wildlife*

God knows what their use was. They are hard to tell but may be old.

On **Stonehenge**
Samuel Pepys *Diary*
11 June 1668

crossing of the river, predates the 12th century and was long a Scottish royal residence.

history William Wallace won a victory at Stirling bridge 1297. Edward II of England (in raising a Scottish siege of the town) went into battle at Bannockburn 1314 and was defeated by Robert I the Bruce.

Stirling James Frazer 1926–1992. Scottish architect. He was possibly the most influential of his generation. While in partnership with James Gowan (1924–), he designed the Leicester University Engineering Building 1959–63 in a Constructivist vein. He later adopted a more eclectic approach, exemplified in his considered masterpiece, the Staatsgalerie, Stuttgart, Germany, 1977–83, which blended Constructivism, Modernism, and several strands of Classicism. He also designed the Clore Gallery 1982–86 to house the Tate Collection of the Tate Gallery, London.

stoat carnivorous mammal *Mustela erminea* of the northern hemisphere, in the weasel family, about 37 cm/15 in long including the black-tipped tail. It has a long body and a flattened head. The upper parts and tail are red-brown, and the underparts are white. In the colder regions, the coat turns white (ermine) in winter. Its young are called kits.

The stoat is an efficient predator, killing its prey (typically rodents and rabbits) by biting the back of the neck. It needs to consume the equivalent of almost a third of its body weight each day. Females are about half the size of males, and males and females live in separate territories. Stoats live in Europe, Asia, and North America; they have been introduced to New Zealand.

stock in botany, any of several herbaceous plants of the genus *Matthiola* of the Crucifer family, commonly grown as garden ornamentals. Many cultivated varieties, including simple-stemmed, queen's, and ten-week, have been derived from the wild stock *M. incana*; *M. bicornis* becomes aromatic at night and is known as night-scented (or evening) stock.

stock-car racing sport popular in the UK and USA, but in two different forms. In the UK, the cars are 'old bangers', which attempt to force the other cars off the track or to come to a standstill.

This format is known in the USA as 'demolition derbies'. In the USA, stock cars are high-powered sports cars that race on purpose-built tracks at distances up to 640–800 km/400–500 mi.

stock exchange institution for the buying and selling of stocks and shares (securities). The world's largest stock exchanges are London, New York (Wall Street), and Tokyo. The oldest stock exchanges are Antwerp 1460, Hamburg 1558, Amsterdam 1602, New York 1790, and London 1801. The former division on the London Stock Exchange between brokers (who bought shares from jobbers to sell to the public) and jobbers (who sold them only to brokers on commission, the 'jobbers' turn') was abolished in 1986.

By value, more than half the shares traded on the London stock exchange 1993 were overseas shares.

Stock Exchange Automated Quotation (SEAQ) computerized system of share-price monitoring. From Oct 1987, SEAQ began displaying market makers' quotations for UK stocks, having been operational previously only for overseas equities.

Stockhausen Karlheinz 1928– . German composer of avant-garde music. He has continued to explore new musical sounds and compositional techniques since the 1950s. His major works include *Gesang der Jünglinge* 1956, *Kontakte* 1960 (electronic music), and *Sirius* 1977.

Since 1977 all his works have been part of *LICHT*, a cycle of seven musical ceremonies intended for performance on the evenings of a week. He has completed *Donnerstag* 1980, *Samstag* 1984, *Montag* 1988, and *Dienstag* 1992. Earlier works include *Klavierstücke I–XIV* 1952–85, *Momente* 1961–64, and *Mikrophonie I* 1964.

An impersonal and scientific knowledge of the structure of our bodies is the surest safeguard against prurient curiosity and lascivious gloating.

Marie Stopes
Married Love 1918

Stockholm capital and industrial port of Sweden; population (1994 est) 703,600. It is built on a number of islands. Industries include engineering, brewing, electrical goods, paper, textiles, and pottery.

A network of bridges links the islands and the mainland; an underground railway was completed 1957. The 18th-century royal palace stands on the site of the 13th-century fortress that defended the trading settlements of Lake Mälar, around which the town first developed. The old town is well preserved and has a church (1264). The town hall was designed by Ragnar Östberg 1923. The new city has been developed since 1950 with contemporary architecture. Most of Sweden's educational institutions are in Stockholm (including the ◊Nobel Institute). The warship *Wasa* (built for King Gustavus Adolphus, 69 m/75 yd long and 52 m/57 yd high), which sank in the harbour 1628, was raised 1961 and is preserved in a museum.

During the 17th century, the city was the capital of Sweden's Baltic empire.

Stockport town in Greater Manchester, England; population (1994) 120,000. The rivers Tame and Goyt join here to form the Mersey. Industries include electronics, chemicals, engineering, textile and electrical machinery, hats, paper, plastics, and still some cotton textiles.

stocks and shares investment holdings (securities) in private or public undertakings. Although distinctions have become blurred, in the UK stock usually means fixed-interest securities – for example, those issued by central and local government – while ◊shares represent a stake in the ownership of a trading company which, if they are ordinary shares, yield to the owner dividends reflecting the success of the company. In the USA the term stock generally signifies what in the UK is an ordinary share.

Stockton-on-Tees town and port on the river Tees, created a unitary authority of England 1996 (*see United Kingdom map*); population (1991) 170,200. There are ship-repairing, steel, and chemical industries, and it was the starting point for the world's first passenger railway 1825.

It has the oldest railway-station building in the world, and there are many Georgian buildings.

stoicism (Greek *stoa* 'porch') Greek school of philosophy, founded about 300 BC by Zeno of Citium. The stoics were pantheistic materialists who believed that happiness lay in accepting the law of the universe. They emphasized human brotherhood, denounced slavery, and were internationalist. The name is derived from the porch on which Zeno taught.

In the 3rd and 2nd centuries BC, stoics took a prominent part in Greek and Roman revolutionary movements. After the 1st century BC stoicism became the philosophy of the Roman ruling class and lost its revolutionary significance; outstanding stoics of this period were Seneca, Epictetus, and Marcus Aurelius Antoninus.

Stoke-on-Trent city on the river Trent, created a unitary authority of England 1997 (*see United Kingdom map*); population (1991) 244,600. It is the heart of the ◊Potteries, a major ceramic centre, and the largest clay producer in the world. Other industries include steel, chemicals, engineering machinery, paper, and rubber. Pit closures 1992–93 have led to a decline in coal mining.

Stoke was formed 1910 from Burslem, Hanley, Longton, Stoke-upon-Trent, Fenton, and Tunstall. The ceramics factories of ◊Minton and ◊Wedgwood are here. The Gladstone Pottery Museum is the only working pottery museum.

Stoker Bram (Abraham) 1847–1912. Irish novelist, actor, theatre manager, and author. His novel ◊*Dracula* 1897 crystallized most aspects of the traditional vampire legend and became the source for all subsequent fiction and films on the subject.

Stoker wrote a number of other stories and novels of fantasy and horror, such as *The Lady of the Shroud* 1909. A civil servant 1866–78, he subsequently became business manager to the theatre producer Henry Irving.

STOL (acronym for ***short takeoff and landing***) aircraft fitted with special devices on the wings (such as sucking flaps) that increase aerodynamic lift at low speeds. Small passenger and freight STOL craft may become common with the demand for small airports, especially in difficult terrain.

stolon in botany, a type of ◊runner.

stoma (plural ***stomata***) in botany, a pore in the epidermis of a plant. Each stoma is surrounded by a pair of guard cells that are crescent-shaped when the stoma is open but can collapse to an oval shape, thus closing off the opening between them. Stomata allow the exchange of carbon dioxide and oxygen (needed for ◊photosynthesis and ◊respiration) between the internal tissues of the plant and the outside atmosphere. They are also the main route by which water is lost from the plant, and they can be closed to conserve water, the movements being controlled by changes in turgidity of the guard cells.

stomach the first cavity in the digestive system of animals. In mammals it is a bag of muscle situated just below the diaphragm. Food enters it from the oesophagus, is digested by the acid and ◊enzymes secreted by the stomach lining, and then passes into the duodenum. Some plant-eating mammals have multichambered stomachs that harbour bacteria in one of the chambers to assist in the digestion of ◊cellulose.

Stone Age the developmental stage of humans in ◊prehistory before the use of metals, when tools and weapons were made chiefly of stone, especially flint. The Stone Age is subdivided into the Old or Palaeolithic, the Middle or Mesolithic, and the New or Neolithic. The people of the Old Stone Age were hunters and gatherers, whereas the Neolithic people took the first steps in agriculture, the domestication of animals, weaving, and pottery.

stonechat small insectivorous ◊thrush *Saxicola torquata*, family Muscicapidae, order Passeriformes, frequently found in Eurasia and Africa on

stoma The stomata, tiny openings in the epidermis of a plant, are surrounded by pairs of crescent-shaped cells, called guard cells. The guard cells open and close the stoma by changing shape.

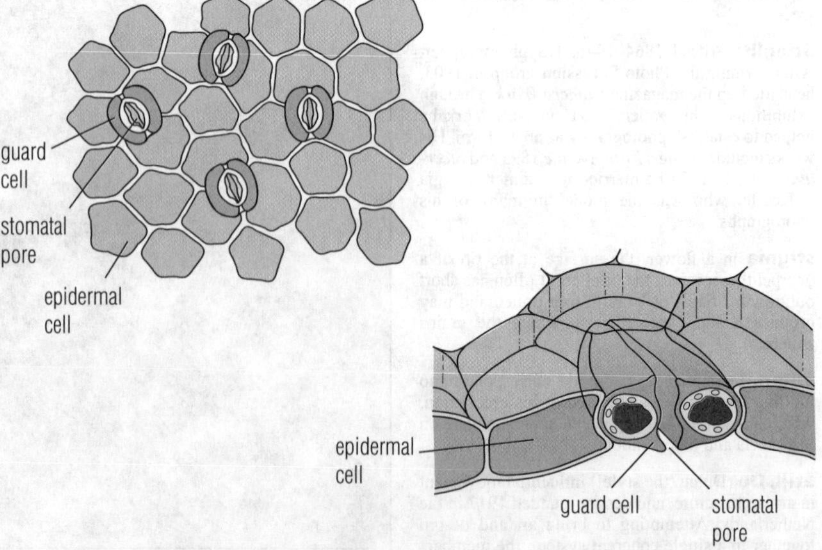

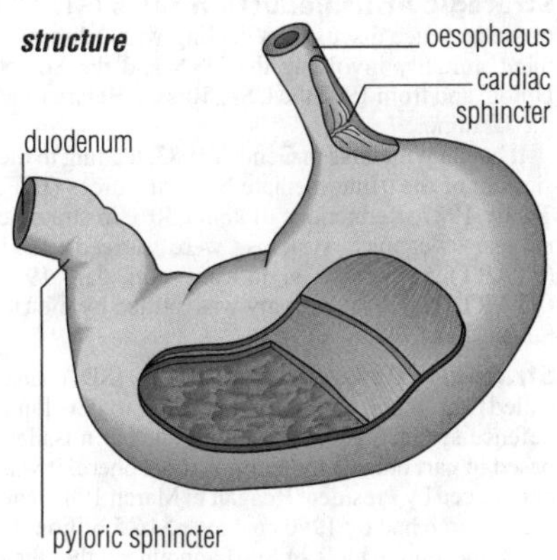

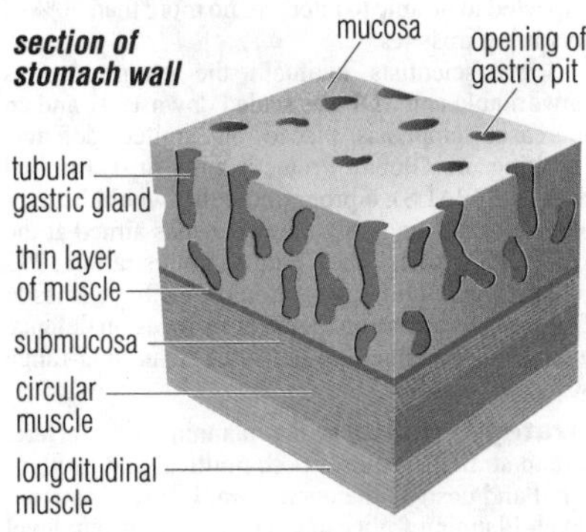

stomach The human stomach can hold about 1.5 l/2.6 pt of liquid. The digestive juices are acidic enough to dissolve metal. To avoid damage, the cells of the stomach lining are replaced quickly – 500,000 cells are replaced every minute, and the whole stomach lining every three days.

open land with bushes. The male has a black head and throat, tawny breast, and dark back; the female is browner. It is about 13 cm/5 in long.

stonecrop any of several plants of the genus *Sedum* of the orpine family Crassulaceae, a succulent herb with fleshy leaves and clusters of starlike flowers. Stonecrops are characteristic of dry, rocky places and some grow on walls.

Biting stonecrop *S. acre* is a low-growing evergreen with bright yellow flowers in early summer. It lives on dry grassland, shingle, and on walls in Europe, N Asia, and N Africa. It gets its name from its peppery taste.

stonefish any of a family (Synanceiidae) of tropical marine bony fishes with venomous spines and bodies resembling encrusted rocks. The species *Synanceia verrucosa* lives in shallow waters of the Indian and Pacific Oceans. It is about 35 cm/14 in long; its poisonous spines have been known to kill a human.

stonefly any insect of the order Plecoptera, with a long tail and antennae and two pairs of membranous wings. Stoneflies live near fresh water. There are over 1,300 species.

Stonehenge megalithic monument dating from about 2000 BC on Salisbury Plain, Wiltshire, England. It consisted originally of a circle of 30 upright stones, their tops linked by lintel stones to form a continuous circle about 30 m/100 ft across. Within the circle was a horseshoe arrangement of five trilithons (two uprights plus a lintel, set as five separate entities), and a so-called 'altar stone' – an upright pillar – on the axis of the horseshoe at the open, NE end, which faces in the direction of the rising sun.

The local sandstone, or sarsen, was used for the uprights, which measure 5.5 by 2 m/18 by 7 ft and weigh some 26 tonnes each. To give true perspective, they were made slightly convex. A secondary circle, inside the sarsen circle, and the horseshoe were built of bluestones, originally brought from Pembrokeshire, Wales.

Stonehenge is one of a number of prehistoric structures on Salisbury Plain, including about 400 round ◊barrows, Durrington Walls (once a structure similar to that in Avebury), Woodhenge (a henge, or enclosure, once consisting of great wooden posts), and the Cursus (a pair of banked ditches, about 100 m/300 ft apart, which run straight for some 3 km/2 mi; dated 4th millennium BC). The purpose of these is unknown but may have been ritual.

Although Stonehenge is far older than ◊Druidism, an annual Druid ceremony is held there at the summer solstice.

stoneware very hard, opaque, water-resistant pottery made of non-porous clay with feldspar and a high silica content, fired to the point of vitrification (1,200–1,280° C/2,192–2,336° F).

Glazing decorates and gives it a smooth finish; it usually fires to shades of grey or buff, though some

stonecrop Biting stonecrop *Sedum acre*, a succulent that grows well on chalk and limestone. Called 'biting stonecrop' and 'wall pepper' because of the sharp taste of its leaves, it has a variety of uses in herbal medicine. It is often encouraged to grow on walls.

red stonewares do exist. The earliest examples are Chinese, from the 10th to 3rd centuries BC.

From the 9th century AD stoneware was made in N Europe; in Britain from the late 17th century.

Stopes Marie Charlotte Carmichael 1880–1958. Scottish birth-control campaigner. With her husband H V Roe (1878–1949), an aircraft manufacturer, she founded Britain's first birth-control clinic in London 1921. She wrote plays and verse as well as the best-selling manual *Married Love* 1918, in which she urged women to enjoy sexual intercourse within their marriage, a revolutionary view for the time.

Stoppard Tom, (originally Thomas Straussler) 1937– . Czechoslovak-born British dramatist. His works use wit and wordplay to explore logical and philosophical ideas. His play *Rosencrantz and Guildenstern are Dead* 1967 was followed by comedies including *The Real Inspector Hound* 1968, *Jumpers* 1972, *Travesties* 1974, *Dirty Linen* 1976, *The Real Thing* 1982, *Hapgood* 1988, *Arcadia* 1993, and *Indian Ink* 1995. He has also written for radio, television, and the cinema. A recent success was the award-winning film *Shakespeare in Love* 1998.

'Life is a gamble, at terrible odds – if it was a bet, you wouldn't take it.'

TOM STOPPARD *Rosencrantz and Guildenstern Are Dead*

stork any of the 17 species of the Ciconiidae, a family of long-legged, long-necked wading birds with long, powerful wings, and long conical bills used for spearing prey. Some species grow up to 1.5 m/5 ft tall.

Species include the Eurasian white stork *Ciconia ciconia*, which is encouraged to build on rooftops as a luck and fertility symbol. It feeds on reptiles, small mammals, and insects. Its plumage is greyish white, its quills and longest feathers on the wing coverts black, and the beak and legs red. It migrates to

Stonehenge The stone circle of Stonehenge in southern England. The earliest erections at Stonehenge date from about 3000 BC. The Stonehenge complex, which includes a long avenue and other nearby circles, is thought to have been used to predict various astronomical events and to have been important in worship of the sky and the sun. The building of the main part, about 2000 BC, would have required complex organization, and coincided with the beginnings of chiefdoms in Britain. *Corbis*

Stowe Harriet Beecher Stowe, author of *Uncle Tom's Cabin* 1851–52. With its vivid depiction of the suffering of families torn apart by slavery, the novel greatly influenced the abolitionist cause. *Library of Congress*

'Do you know who made you?' 'Nobody, as I knows on,' said the child, with a short laugh. ... 'I 'spect I grow'd.'

HARRIET BEECHER STOWE
Uncle Tom's Cabin

The first view of the Avon and of the town where Shakespeare was born gave me those feelings which men of enthusiasm have on seeing remarkable places. Cicero had them when he walked at Athens.

On STRATFORD-UPON-AVON
James Boswell's journal 6 Sept 1769

Africa in winter. The jabiru *Jabiru mycteria* of the Americas is up to 1.5 m/5 ft high, and is white plumaged, with a black and red head. In the black stork *C. nigra*, the upper surface is black and the lower parts are white. It is widely found in southern and central Europe, Asia, and parts of Africa. The ◊ibis, ◊heron, and ◊spoonbill are related birds.

storm surge abnormally high tide brought about by a combination of a deep atmospheric depression (very low pressure) over a shallow sea area, high spring tides, and winds blowing from the appropriate direction. A storm surge can cause severe flooding of lowland coastal regions and river estuaries.

Bangladesh is particularly prone to surges, being sited on a low-lying ◊delta where the Indian Ocean funnels into the Bay of Bengal. In May 1991, 125,000 people were killed there in such a disaster. In Feb 1953 more than 2,000 died when a North Sea surge struck the Dutch and English coasts.

Stowe Harriet Elizabeth Beecher 1811–1896. US suffragist, abolitionist, and author. Her antislavery novel ◊*Uncle Tom's Cabin* was first published serially 1851–52. The inspiration came to her in a vision 1848, and the book brought immediate success.

Born in Litchfield, Connecticut, Stowe was a daughter of Congregationalist minister Lyman ◊Beecher, and in 1836 married C E Stowe, a professor of theology. Her first publication was *The Mayflower* 1843. *Uncle Tom's Cabin* was radical in its time and did much to spread antislavery sentiment, but in the 20th century was criticized for sentimentality and racism.

strabismus technical term for a ◊squint.

Strabo c. 63 BC–AD c. 24. Greek geographer and historian who travelled widely to collect first-hand material for his *Geography*.

Strachey (Giles) Lytton 1880–1932. English critic and biographer. He was a member of the ◊Bloomsbury Group of writers and artists. His *Landmarks in French Literature* was written 1912. The mocking and witty treatment of Cardinal Manning, Florence Nightingale, Thomas Arnold, and General Gordon in *Eminent Victorians* 1918 won him recognition. His biography of *Queen Victoria* 1921 was more affectionate.

Stradivari Antonio, (Latin form ***Stradivarius***) c. 1644–1737. Italian stringed instrumentmaker, generally considered the greatest of all violinmakers. He was born in Cremona and studied there with Niccolò Amati (1596–1684). He produced more than 1,100 instruments from his family workshops, over 600 of which survive.

The secret of his skill is said to be in the varnish but is probably a combination of fine proportioning and ageing.

Strafford Thomas Wentworth, 1st Earl of Strafford 1593–1641. English politician. He was originally an opponent of Charles I, but from 1628 he was on the Royalist side. He ruled despotically as Lord Deputy of Ireland 1632–39, when he returned to England as Charles's chief adviser and received an earldom. He was impeached in 1640 by Parliament, abandoned by Charles as a scapegoat, and beheaded.

strain in the science of materials, the extent to which a body is distorted when a deforming force (stress) is applied to it. It is a ratio of the extension or compression of that body (its length, area, or volume) to its original dimensions (see ◊Hooke's law. For example, linear strain is the ratio of the change in length of a body to its original length.

Straits Settlements former province of the ◊East India Company 1826–58, a British crown colony 1867–1946; it comprised Singapore, Malacca, Penang, Cocos Islands, Christmas Island, and Labuan.

Strasberg Lee, (originally Israel Strassberg) 1901–1982. US actor and artistic director of the Actors Studio workshop from 1948. He developed Method acting from ◊Stanislavsky's system; pupils have included Marlon Brando, Paul Newman, Julie Harris, Kim Hunter, Geraldine Page, Al Pacino, and Robert De Niro.

Strasbourg city on the river Ill, in Bas-Rhin *département*, capital of Alsace, France; population (1990) 255,900. Industries include car manufacture, tobacco, printing and publishing, and preserves. The ◊Council of Europe meets here, and sessions of the European Parliament alternate between Strasbourg and Luxembourg.

Seized by France 1681, it was surrendered to Germany 1870–1919 and 1940–44. It has a 13th-century cathedral.

strata (singular ***stratum***) layers or beds of sedimentary rock.

Strategic Arms Limitation Talks (SALT) series of US-Soviet discussions 1969–79 aimed at reducing the rate of nuclear-arms build-up (as opposed to ◊disarmament, which would reduce the number of weapons, as discussed in Strategic Arms Reduction Talks (START)). Treaties in the 1970s sought to prevent the growth of nuclear arsenals.

The talks, delayed by the Soviet invasion of Czechoslovakia 1968, began in 1969 between the US president Lyndon Johnson and the Soviet leader Brezhnev. Neither the SALT I accord (effective 1972–77) nor SALT II called for reductions in nuclear weaponry, merely a limit on the expansion of these forces. SALT II was mainly negotiated by US president Ford before 1976 and signed by Soviet leader Brezhnev and US president Carter in Vienna in 1979. It was never fully ratified because of the Soviet occupation of Afghanistan, although the terms of the accord were respected by both sides until US president ◊Reagan exceeded its limitations during his second term 1985–89. SALT talks were superseded by START negotiations under Reagan, and the first significant reductions began under Soviet president Gorbachev.

Strategic Arms Reduction Talks (START) phase in peace discussions dealing with ◊disarmament, initially involving the USA and the Soviet Union, and from 1992 the USA, Russia, Belarus and the Ukraine.

It began with talks in Geneva 1983, leading to the signing of the ◊Intermediate Nuclear Forces (INF) Treaty 1987. Reductions of about 30% in strategic nuclear weapons systems were agreed 1991 (START) and more significant cuts Jan 1993 (START II); the latter treaty was ratified by the US Senate Jan 1996.

Strategic Defense Initiative (SDI) also called ***Star Wars***, attempt by the USA to develop a defence system against incoming nuclear missiles, based in part outside the Earth's atmosphere. It was announced by President Reagan in March 1983, and the research had by 1990 cost over $16.5 billion. In 1988, the Joint Chiefs of Staff announced that they expected to be able to intercept no more than 30% of incoming missiles.

Some scientists maintain the programme is unworkable and SDI was scaled down 1991 and an increased emphasis placed on limited defence, resulting in Global Protection Against Limited Strikes (GPALS), a programme that would be capable of destroying only a few missiles aimed at the USA and its allies. The Clinton administration 1993 renamed the SDI Organization the Ballistic Missile Defense Organization to reflect its focus on defence against short-range missiles rather than long-range strategic missiles.

strategy, military the planning of warfare. Grand strategy requires both political and military input and designs the overall war effort at national level. Planning for a campaign at army-group level or above is strategy proper. Operational strategy involves military planning at corps, divisional, and brigade level. Tactics is the art of warfare at unit level and below; that is, the disposition of relatively small numbers of soldiers over relatively small distances.

Stratford-upon-Avon market town on the river Avon, in Warwickshire, England; population (1991) 22,200. It is the birthplace of William ◊Shakespeare and has the Royal Shakespeare Theatre 1932, the Swan Theatre, and The Other Place.

The theatre replaced an earlier building 1877–79 that burned down 1926. Shakespeare's birthplace contains relics of his life and times. His grave is in the parish church; the cottage of his wife Anne Hathaway (1556–1623) is nearby.

Stratford receives over 2 million tourists a year. Industries include canning, aluminium ware, and boat building.

Strathclyde former region of Scotland, created 1975, abolished 1996.

stratigraphy branch of geology that deals with the sequence of formation of ◊sedimentary rock layers and the conditions under which they were formed. Its basis was developed by William Smith (1769–1839), a British canal engineer. Stratigraphy in the interpretation of archaeological excavations

Strafford Execution of the Earl of Strafford, Charles I's chief adviser, on Tower Hill, 1641 after an etching by Wenceslaus Hollar. Upon hearing that Charles had signed his death warrant at Parliament's insistence, Strafford famously commented 'Put not your trust in princes'. *Philip Sauvain*

provides a relative chronology for the levels and the artefacts within them. The basic principle of superimposition establishes that upper layers or deposits have accumulated later in time than the lower ones.

stratosphere that part of the atmosphere 10–40 km/6–25 mi from the Earth's surface, where the temperature slowly rises from a low of −55°C/−67°F to around 0°C/32°F. The air is rarefied and at around 25 km/15 mi much ◊ozone is concentrated.

Strauss Johann (Baptist) 1825–1899. Austrian conductor and composer. He was the son of composer Johann Strauss (1804–1849). In 1872 he gave up conducting and wrote operettas, such as *Die Fledermaus/The Flittermouse* 1874, and numerous waltzes, such as *The Blue Danube* and *Tales from the Vienna Woods*, which gained him the title 'the Waltz King'.

Strauss Richard (Georg) 1864–1949. German composer and conductor. He followed the German Romantic tradition but had a strongly personal style, characterized by his bold, colourful orchestration. He first wrote tone poems such as *Don Juan* 1889, *Till Eulenspiegel's Merry Pranks* 1895, and *Also sprach Zarathustra/Thus Spake Zarathustra* 1896. He then moved on to opera with *Salome* 1905 and *Elektra* 1909, both of which have elements of polytonality. He reverted to a more traditional style with *Der Rosenkavalier/The Knight of the Rose* 1909–10.

Stravinsky Igor 1882–1971. Russian composer, later of French (1934) and US (1945) nationality. He studied under ◊Rimsky-Korsakov and wrote the music for the Diaghilev ballets *The Firebird* 1910, *Petrushka* 1911, and *The Rite of Spring* 1913 (controversial at the time for their unorthodox rhythms and harmonies). His versatile work ranges from his Neo-Classical ballet *Pulcinella* 1920 to the choral-orchestral *Symphony of Psalms* 1930. He later made use of serial techniques in such works as the *Canticum Sacrum* 1955 and the ballet *Agon* 1953–57.

Stravinsky The composer Igor Stravinsky (1882–1971), painted by J E Blanche. Along with Schoenberg he was the most important composer of the early 20th century. He did not embrace serial technique until late in his career, his earlier works favouring first a rhythmically vital dissonant style and then neo-classicism. *Image Select (UK) Ltd*

Straw Jack 1946– . British Labour politician and lawyer, home secretary from 1997. He became MP for Blackburn in 1979. He first joined Labour's front bench team in 1980, and was shadow education secretary 1987–92, shadow environment secretary 1992–94, and shadow home secretary 1994–97. As home secretary, Straw followed prime minister Tony Blair's lead in announcing that he would be 'tough on crime and tough on the causes of crime'.

strawberry low-growing perennial plant of the genus *Fragaria*, family Rosaceae, widely cultivated for its red, fleshy fruits, which are rich in vitamin C. Commercial cultivated forms bear one crop of fruit in summer and multiply by runners. Alpine garden varieties are derived from the wild strawberry *F. vesca*, which has small aromatic fruit.

streaming in education, the practice of dividing pupils for all classes according to an estimate of their overall ability, with arrangements for 'promotion' and 'demotion' at the end of each academic year.

In the UK, rigid streaming was unusual in secondary education in the 1980s, and had disappeared from primary education.

streamlining shaping a body so that it offers the least resistance when travelling through a medium such as air or water. Aircraft, for example, must be carefully streamlined to reduce air resistance, or ◊drag. High-speed aircraft must have swept-back wings, supersonic craft a sharp nose and narrow body.

stream of consciousness narrative technique in which a writer presents directly the uninterrupted flow of a character's thoughts, impressions, and feelings, without the conventional devices of dialogue and description. It first came to be widely used in the early 20th century. Leading exponents have included the novelists Virginia Woolf, James Joyce, and William Faulkner.

Streep Meryl (Mary Louise) 1949– . US actress. A leading star of the 1980s and 1990s, she is known for her strong character roles, portrayed with emotionally dramatic intensity, and her accomplished facility with a wide variety of accents. Her films include *The Deer Hunter* 1978, *Kramer vs Kramer* 1979 (Academy Award for best supporting actress), *The French Lieutenant's Woman* 1981, *Sophie's Choice* 1982 (Academy Award), *Out of Africa* 1985, *Ironweed* 1988, *A Cry in the Dark* 1989, and the comedy *Death Becomes Her* 1992.

Streisand Barbra Joan 1942– . US singer and actress who became a film star in *Funny Girl* 1968 (Academy Award). Her subsequent films include *What's Up Doc?* 1972, *The Way We Were* 1973, and *A Star Is Born* 1979. She directed, produced, and starred in *Yentl* 1983 and *Prince of Tides* 1991.

strength of acids and bases in chemistry, the ability of ◊acids and ◊bases to dissociate (split into two or more smaller products) in solution with water, and hence to produce a low or high ◊pH respectively. A strong acid is fully dissociated in aqueous solution, whereas a weak acid is only partly dissociated. Since the dissociation of acids generates hydrogen ions, a solution of a strong acid will have a high concentration of hydrogen ions and therefore a low pH. A strong base will have a high pH, whereas a weaker base will not dissociate completely and will have a pH of nearer 7.

streptokinase enzyme produced by *Streptococcus* bacteria that is capable of digesting fibrin, the protein making up blood clots. It is used to treat pulmonary ◊embolism and heart attacks, reducing mortality.

streptomycin antibiotic drug discovered in 1944, active against a wide range of bacterial infections.

It is derived from a soil bacterium *Streptomyces griseus* or synthesized. It is rarely used in the UK, except to treat organisms resistant to other drugs, because of serious side effects, including ear and kidney damage.

Stresemann Gustav 1878–1929. German politician, chancellor in 1923 and foreign minister from 1923 to 1929 of the Weimar Republic. During World War I he was a strong nationalist but his views became more moderate under the Weimar Republic. His achievements included reducing the amount of war reparations paid by Germany after the Treaty of Versailles 1919; negotiating the Locarno Treaties 1925; and negotiating Germany's admission to the League of Nations. He shared the 1926 Nobel Peace Prize with Aristide Briand.

stress in psychology, any event or situation that makes heightened demands on a person's mental or emotional resources. Stress can be caused by overwork, anxiety about exams, money, or job security, unemployment, bereavement, poor relationships, marriage breakdown, sexual difficulties, poor living or working conditions, and constant exposure to loud noise.

stridulatory organs In katydids such as this European great green bush cricket *Tettigonia viridissima*, the male stridulates by rubbing a toothed vein on the left forewing (the file) against a hardened area (the scraper) on the rear edge of the right forewing. Most katydids call at night; the sound is sharp and penetrating. *Premaphotos Wildlife*

Many changes that are apparently 'for the better', such as being promoted at work, going to a new school, moving to a new house, and getting married, are also a source of stress. Stress can cause, or aggravate, physical illnesses, among them psoriasis, eczema, asthma, and stomach and mouth ulcers. Apart from removing the source of stress, acquiring some control over it and learning to relax when possible are the best treatments.

stress and strain in the science of materials, measures of the deforming force applied to a body (stress) and of the resulting change in its shape (◊strain). For a perfectly elastic material, stress is proportional to strain (◊Hooke's law).

stride piano jazz piano style alternating left-hand chords with single bass notes; it was popularized in the 1930s by such musicians as Fats ◊Waller.

stridulatory organs in insects, organs that produce sound when rubbed together. Crickets rub their wings together, but grasshoppers rub a hind leg against a wing. Stridulation is thought to be used for attracting mates, but may also serve to mark territory.

‘Work brings inspiration, if inspiration is not discernible at the beginning.’

IGOR STRAVINSKY
Chronicle of My Life

strike stoppage of work by employees, often as members of a trade union, to obtain or resist change in wages, hours, or conditions. A lockout is a weapon of an employer to thwart or enforce such change by preventing employees from working. Another measure is work to rule, when production is virtually brought to a halt by strict observance of union rules.

Strikes may be 'official' (union-authorized) or 'wildcat' (undertaken spontaneously), and may be accompanied by a sit-in or work-in, the one being worker occupation of a factory and the other continuation of work in a plant the employer wishes to close. In a 'sympathetic' strike, action is in support of other workers on strike elsewhere, possibly in a different industry.

See also ◊general strike and ◊industrial relations.

Strindberg (Johan) August 1849–1912. Swedish dramatist and novelist. His plays are in a variety of styles including historical dramas, symbolic dramas (the two-part *Dödsdansen/The Dance of Death* 1901), and 'chamber plays' such as *Spöksonaten/The Ghost [Spook] Sonata* 1907. *Fadren/The Father* 1887 and *Fröken Julie/Miss Julie* 1888 are among his best-known works.

Born in Stockholm, he lived mainly abroad after 1883, having been unsuccessfully prosecuted for blasphemy 1884 following publication of his short stories *Giftas/Marrying*. *See illustration on following page.*

‘Antipathy, dissimilarity of views, hate, contempt, can accompany true love.’

AUGUST STRINDBERG
The Son of a Servant

string instrument musical instrument that produces a sound when a stretched string is made to vibrate. Today the strings are made of gut, metal, and Pearlon (a plastic). Types of string instruments include: bowed, the violin family and viol family; plucked, the guitar, ukelele, lute, sitar, harp, banjo,

Strindberg Swedish playwright August Strindberg experimented with almost every style available to him, ranging from historical dramas, through mysticism, romanticism, naturalism, and social satire. He has been criticized for his anti-Semitism and opposition to democracy and the emancipation of women. *Corbis*

and lyre; plucked mechanically, the harpsichord; struck mechanically, the piano and clavichord; and hammered, the dulcimer.

string quartet ◊chamber music ensemble consisting of first and second violins, viola, and cello. The 18th-century successor to the domestic viol consort, the string quartet with its stronger and more rustic tone formed the basis of the symphony orchestra. Important composers for the string quartet include Haydn (more than 80 string quartets), Mozart (27), Schubert (20), Beethoven (17), Dvořák (8), and Bartók (6).

String-quartet music evolved from the decorative but essentially vocal style of viol music into a vigorously instrumental style exploiting the instruments' full expressive potential. The older hierarchy of solo and accompanying voices also changed to a concertante style offering solo opportunities for each player, a trend accelerated by the adoption of shriller metal strings in the 19th century.

strobilus in botany, a reproductive structure found in most ◊gymnosperms and some ◊pteridophytes, notably the club mosses. In conifers the strobilus is commonly known as a ◊cone.

stroboscope instrument for studying continuous periodic motion by using light flashing at the same frequency as that of the motion; for example, rotating machinery can be optically 'stopped' by illuminating it with a stroboscope flashing at the exact rate of rotation.

Stroessner Alfredo 1912– . Military leader and president of Paraguay 1954–89. As head of the armed forces from 1951, he seized power in a coup in 1954 sponsored by the right-wing ruling Colorado Party. Accused by his opponents of harsh repression, his regime spent heavily on the military to preserve his authority. Despite criticisms of his government's civil-rights record, he was re-elected seven times and remained in office until ousted in an army-led coup 1989, after which he gained asylum in Brazil.

Stroheim Erich von. Assumed name of Erich Oswald Stroheim 1885–1957. Austrian actor and director. In Hollywood from 1914, he was successful as an actor in villainous roles. His career as a director, which produced films such as *Foolish Wives* 1922, was wrecked by his extravagance (*Greed* 1923) and he returned to acting in such films as *La Grande Illusion* 1937 and *Sunset Boulevard* 1950.

stroke or ***cerebrovascular accident*** or ***apoplexy*** interruption of the blood supply to part of the brain due to a sudden bleed in the brain (cerebral haemorrhage) or ◊embolism or ◊thrombosis. Strokes vary in severity from producing almost no symptoms to proving rapidly fatal. In between are those (often recurring) that leave a wide range of impaired function, depending on the size and location of the event.

Strokes involving the right side of the brain, for example, produce weakness of the left side of the body. Some affect speech. Around 80% of strokes are ischaemic strokes, caused by a blood clot blocking an artery transporting blood to the brain. Transient ischaemic attacks, or 'mini-strokes', with effects lasting only briefly (less than 24 hours), require investigation to try to forestall the possibility of a subsequent full-blown stroke.

The disease of the arteries that predisposes to stroke is ◊atherosclerosis. High blood pressure (◊hypertension) is also a precipitating factor – a worldwide study 1995 estimated that high blood pressure before middle age gives a tenfold increase in the chance of having a stroke later in life.

Strokes can sometimes be prevented by surgery (as in the case of some ◊aneurysms), or by use of ◊anticoagulant drugs or vitamin E or daily aspirin to minimize the risk of stroke due to blood clots. According to the results of a US trial announced Dec 1995, the clot-buster (clot-dissolving) drug tPA, if administered within three hours of a stroke, can cut the number of stroke victims experiencing lasting disability by 50%.

Stromboli Italian island in the Tyrrhenian Sea, one of the ◊Lipari Islands; area 12 sq km/5 sq mi. It has an active volcano, 926 m/3,039 ft high. The island produces Malmsey wine and capers.

strong nuclear force one of the four fundamental ◊forces of nature, the other three being the electromagnetic force, gravity, and the weak nuclear force. The strong nuclear force was first described by Japanese physicist Hideki Yukawa 1935. It is the strongest of all the forces, acts only over very small distances (within the nucleus of the atom), and is responsible for binding together ◊quarks to form ◊hadrons, and for binding together protons and neutrons in the atomic nucleus. The particle that is the carrier of the strong nuclear force is the ◊gluon, of which there are eight kinds, each with zero mass and zero charge.

strontium soft, ductile, pale-yellow, metallic element, symbol Sr, atomic number 38, relative atomic mass 87.62. It is one of the ◊alkaline-earth metals, widely distributed in small quantities only as a sulphate or carbonate. Strontium salts burn with a red flame and are used in fireworks and signal flares.

The radioactive isotopes Sr-89 and Sr-90 (half-life 25 years) are some of the most dangerous products of the nuclear industry; they are fission products in nuclear explosions and in the reactors of nuclear power plants. Strontium is chemically similar to calcium and deposits in bones and other tissues, where the radioactivity is damaging. The element was named in 1808 by English chemist Humphry Davy, who isolated it by electrolysis, after Strontian, a mining location in Scotland where it was first found.

strophanthus any tropical plant of the genus *Strophanthus* of the dogbane family Apocynaceae, native to Africa and Asia. Seeds of the handsome climber *S. gratus* yield a poison, strophantin, used on arrows in hunting, and in medicine as a heart stimulant.

structuralism 20th-century philosophical movement that has influenced such areas as linguistics, anthropology, and literary criticism. Inspired by the work of the Swiss linguist Ferdinand de Saussure, structuralists believe that objects should be analysed as systems of relations, rather than as positive entities.

Saussure proposed that language is a system of arbitrary signs, meaning that there is no intrinsic link between the 'signifier' (the sound or mark) and the 'signified' (the concept it represents). Hence any linguistic term can only be defined by its differences from other terms. His ideas were taken further by Roman Jakobson (1896–1982) and the Prague school of linguistics, and were extended into a general method for the social sciences by the French anthropologist Claude Lévi-Strauss. The French writer Roland Barthes took the lead in applying the ideas of structuralism to literary criticism, arguing that the critic should identify the structures within a text that determine its possible meanings, independently of any reference to the real. This approach is radicalized in Barthes's later work and in the practice of 'deconstruction', pioneered by the French philosopher Jacques Derrida. Here the text comes to be viewed as a 'decentred' play of structures, lacking any ultimately determinable meaning.

strychnine $C_{21}H_{22}O_2N_2$ bitter-tasting, poisonous alkaloid. It is a poison that causes violent muscular spasms, and is usually obtained by powdering the seeds of plants of the genus *Strychnos* (for example *S. nux vomica*). Curare is a related drug.

Stuart or ***Stewart*** royal family who inherited the Scottish throne in 1371 and the English throne in 1603, holding it until 1714, when Queen Anne died without heirs and the house of Stuart was replaced by the house of ◊Hanover.

Stuart John McDouall 1815–1866. Scottish-born Australian explorer. He went with Charles ◊Sturt on his 1844 expedition, and in 1860, after two unsuccessful attempts, crossed the centre of Australia from Adelaide in the southeast to the coast of Arnhem Land. He almost lost his life on the return journey.

Stubbs George 1724–1806. English artist. He is renowned for his paintings of horses. After the publication of his book of engravings *The Anatomy of the Horse* 1766, he was widely commissioned as an animal painter. The dramatic *Lion Attacking a Horse* 1770 (Yale University Art Gallery, New Haven, Connecticut) and the peaceful *Reapers* 1786 (Tate Gallery, London) show the variety of mood in his painting.

stucco durable plaster finish for exterior walls, composed of sand and lime. In the 18th and 19th centuries stucco was used extensively to add dignity to brick buildings, by giving the illusion that they were built of stone. The stucco would be moulded, coursed, or coloured to imitate ashlar ◊masonry. John ◊Nash used stucco to create the illusory stone palaces that surround Regents Park, London (begun 1811).

Stud, National British establishment founded 1915, and since 1964 located at ◊Newmarket, Suffolk, where stallions are kept for visiting mares in order to breed racehorses. It is now maintained by the Horserace Betting Levy Board.

stupa domed structure built to house a Buddhist or Jain relic. The stupa originated in India around 1000 BC from burial monuments and is usually a hemisphere crowned by a spire. In the Far East the stupa developed into the ◊pagoda.

sturgeon any of a family (Acipenseridae) of large, primitive, bony fishes with five rows of bony plates, small sucking mouths, and chin barbels used for exploring the bottom of the water for prey.

The beluga sturgeon *Huso huso* of the Caspian Sea can reach a length of 8 m/25 ft and weigh 1,500 kg/3,300 lb. The common sturgeon *Acipenser sturio* of the Atlantic and Mediterranean reaches a length of 3.5 m/12 ft.

Sturluson Snorri 1179–1241. Icelandic author. He wrote the Old Norse poems called ◊Eddas and the *Heimskringla*, a saga chronicle of Norwegian kings until 1177.

Sturmabteilung (German 'storm section') (SA) German militia, also known as Brownshirts, of the ◊Nazi Party, established 1921 under the leadership of Ernst ◊Röhm, in charge of physical training and political indoctrination.

Originally uniformed stewards to organize demonstrations, they became street brawlers who dealt with any political opposition to party rallies. When the Nazis gained power 1933 their strength was about 400,000 and they considered themselves the rival to the German Army. At the instigation of the Army and ◊SS leaders, Hitler had all the SA's leaders murdered 30 June 1933, the 'Night of the Long Knives', and the organization disbanded.

Sturm und Drang (German 'storm and stress') German early Romantic movement in literature and music, from about 1775, concerned with the depiction of extravagant passions. Writers associated with the movement include Johann Gottfried von Herder, Johann Wolfgang von Goethe, and Friedrich von Schiller. The name is taken from a play by Friedrich von Klinger 1776.

Sturt Charles 1795–1869. British explorer and soldier. In 1828 he sailed down the Murrumbidgee River in SE Australia to the estuary of the Murray in circumstances of great hardship, charting the entire river system of the region.

Born in India, he served in the army, and in 1827 discovered with the Australian explorer Hamilton Hume the river ◊Darling. Drawn by his concept of a great inland sea, he set out for the interior in 1844, crossing what is now known as the Sturt Desert, but failing to penetrate the Simpson Desert.

Stuttgart capital of Baden-Württemberg, on the river Neckar, Germany; population (1993) 598,000.

Industries include the manufacture of vehicles and electrical goods, foodstuffs, textiles, papermaking and publishing; it is a fruit-growing and wine-producing centre. There are two universities. It is the headquarters of the US European Command (Eucom).

Stuttgart was founded in the 10th century. The philosopher Hegel was born here.

style in flowers, the part of the ◊carpel bearing the ◊stigma at its tip. In some flowers it is very short or completely lacking, while in others it may be long and slender, positioning the stigma in the most effective place to receive the pollen.

Usually the style withers after fertilization but in certain species, such as traveller's joy *Clematis vitalba*, it develops into a long feathery plume that aids dispersal of the fruit.

Style, Old and New forms of dating, see ◊calendar.

Styria (German ***Steiermark***) Alpine state of SE Austria; area 16,400 sq km/6,330 sq mi; population (1994) 1,204,000. Its capital is Graz, and its industries include iron, steel, lignite, vehicles, electrical goods, and engineering. An independent state from 1056 until it passed to the ◊Habsburgs in the 13th century, it was annexed by Germany 1938.

Styron William Clark 1925– . US novelist. His novels *Lie Down in Darkness* 1951, *The Confessions of Nat Turner* 1967 (Pulitzer prize), and *Sophie's Choice* 1979 (filmed 1982) all won critical and popular acclaim. *Confessions* caused controversy and protest from black critics for its fictionalization of the leader of a slave revolt in 19th-century Virginia. *A Tidewater Morning* appeared 1993.

Styx in Greek mythology, the river surrounding the underworld.

Suárez González Adolfo 1932– . Spanish politician, prime minister 1976–81. A friend of King Juan Carlos, he was appointed by the king to guide Spain into democracy after the death of the fascist dictator Franco.

subatomic particle in physics, a particle that is smaller than an atom. Such particles may be indivisible ◊elementary particles, such as the ◊electron and ◊quark, or they may be composites, such as the ◊proton, ◊neutron, and ◊alpha particle. See also ◊particle physics.

subduction zone region where two plates of the Earth's rigid lithosphere collide, and one plate descends below the other into the semiliquid asthenosphere. Subduction occurs along ocean trenches, most of which encircle the Pacific Ocean; portions of the ocean plate slide beneath other plates carrying continents.

Ocean trenches are usually associated with volcanic ◊island arcs and deep-focus earthquakes (more than 185 mi/300 km below the surface), both the result of disturbances caused by the plate subduction. The Aleutian Trench bordering Alaska is an example of an active subduction zone, which has produced the Aleutian Island arc.

sublimation in chemistry, the conversion of a solid to vapour without passing through the liquid phase.

Sublimation depends on the fact that the boiling-point of the solid substance is lower than its melting-point at atmospheric pressure. Thus by increasing pressure, a substance which sublimes can be made to go through a liquid stage before passing into the vapour state.

Some substances that do not sublime at atmospheric pressure can be made to do so at low pressures. This is the principle of freeze-drying, during which ice sublimes at low pressure.

subliminal message any message delivered beneath the human conscious threshold of perception. It may be visual (words or images flashed between the frames of a cinema or TV film), or aural (a radio message broadcast constantly at very low volume).

The aim may be commercial (to sell a product) or psychological (to wean a patient from alcohol or smoking). Subliminal advertising is illegal in many countries, including Britain. It has been claimed, without evidence, that subliminal messages have also been included in pop music.

submarine underwater warship. The first underwater boat was constructed in 1620 for James I of England by the Dutch scientist Cornelius van Drebbel (1572–1633). A naval submarine, or submersible torpedo boat, the *Gymnote*, was launched by France 1888. The conventional submarine of World War I was driven by diesel engine on the surface and by battery-powered electric motors underwater.
history In the 1760s, the American David Bushnell (1742–1824) designed a submarine called *Turtle* for attacking British ships, and in 1800 Robert Fulton designed a submarine called *Nautilus* for Napoleon for the same purpose. John P Holland, an Irish emigrant to the USA, designed a submarine about 1875, which was used by both the US and the British navies at the turn of the century. Submarine warfare was really established as a distinct form of naval tactics during World War I and submarines, from the ocean-going to the midget type, played a vital role in both world wars. In particular, German U-boats caused great difficulty to Allied merchant shipping, until the radio codes were broken 1942.
nuclear submarines In 1954 the USA launched the first nuclear-powered submarine, the *Nautilus*. The US nuclear submarine *Ohio*, in service from 1981, is 170 m/560 ft long and carries 24 Trident missiles, each with 12 independently targetable nuclear warheads. The nuclear warheads on US submarines have a range that is being extended to 11,000 km/6,750 mi. Operating depth is usually up to 300 m/1,000 ft, and nuclear-powered speeds of 30 knots (55 kph/34 mph) are reached. As in all nuclear submarines, propulsion is by steam turbine driving a propeller. The steam is raised using the heat given off by the nuclear reactor (see ◊nuclear energy). In oceanography, salvage, and pipe-laying, smaller submarines called submersibles are used.

subpoena (Latin 'under penalty') in law, an order requiring someone who might not otherwise come forward of his or her own volition to give evidence before a court or judicial official at a specific time and place. A witness who fails to comply with a subpoena is in ◊contempt of court.

subsistence farming farming when the produce is enough to feed only the farmer and family and there is no surplus to sell.

substitution reaction in chemistry, the replacement of one atom or ◊functional group in an organic molecule by another.

substrate in biochemistry, a compound or mixture of compounds acted on by an enzyme. The term also refers to a substance such as ◊agar that provides the nutrients for the metabolism of microorganisms. Since the enzyme systems of microorganisms regulate their metabolism, the essential meaning is the same.

succession in ecology, a series of changes that occur in the structure and composition of the vegetation in a given area from the time it is first colonized by plants (primary succession), or after it has been disturbed by fire, flood, or clearing (secondary succession).

If allowed to proceed undisturbed, succession leads naturally to a stable climax community (a community that is relatively stable in its environment, for example, oak and hickory forest or savannah grassland) that is determined by the climate and soil characteristics of the area.

Succot or ***Sukkoth*** in Judaism, a harvest festival celebrated in Oct, also known as the Feast of Booths, which commemorates the time when the Israelites lived in the wilderness during the ◊Exodus from Egypt. As a reminder of the shelters used in the wilderness, huts are built and used for eating and sleeping during the seven days of the festival.

succubus a female spirit; see ◊incubus.

succulent plant thick, fleshy plant that stores water in its tissues; for example, cacti and stonecrops *Sedum*. Succulents live either in areas where water is very scarce, such as deserts, or in places where it is not easily obtainable because of the high concentrations of salts in the soil, as in salt marshes. Many desert plants are ◊xerophytes.

Suchocka Hanna 1946– . Polish politician, prime minister 1992–93. She was chosen by President Walesa because her unaligned background won her the support of seven of the eight parties that agreed to join a coalition government. In 1993 she lost a vote of confidence prior to her centrist coalition being ousted in a general election.

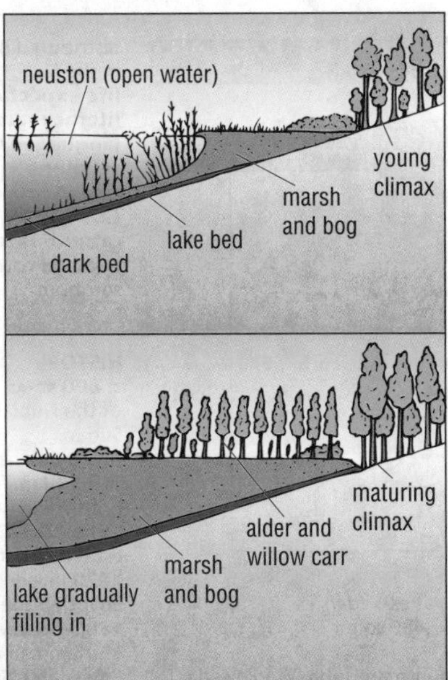

succession The succession of plant types along a lake. As the lake gradually fills in, a mature climax community of trees forms inland from the shore. Extending out from the shore, a series of plant communities can be discerned with small, rapidly growing species closest to the shore.

sucker fish another name for ◊remora.

suckering in plants, reproduction by new shoots (suckers) arising from an existing root system rather than from seed. Plants that produce suckers include elm, dandelion, and members of the rose family.

Sucre legal capital and judicial seat of Bolivia; population (1992) 131,000. It stands on the central plateau at an altitude of 2,840 m/9,320 ft.

The city was founded 1538, its cathedral dates from 1553, and the University of San Francisco Xavier (1624) is probably the oldest in South America. The first revolt against Spanish rule in South America began here 25 May 1809. It is the commercial centre for the agricultural area.

Sucre Antonio José de 1795–1830. South American revolutionary leader. As chief lieutenant of Simón ◊Bolívar, he won several battles in freeing the colonies of Ecuador and Bolivia from Spanish rule, and in 1826 became president of Bolivia. After a mutiny by the army and invasion by Peru, he resigned in 1828 and was assassinated in 1830 on his way to join Bolívar.

sucrose or ***cane sugar*** or ***beet sugar*** $C_{12}H_{22}O_{11}$ a sugar found in the pith of sugar cane and in sugar beets. It is popularly known as ◊sugar.

Sucrose is a disaccharide sugar, each of its molecules being made up of two simple sugar (monosaccharide) units: glucose and fructose.

Sudan country in NE Africa, bounded N by Egypt, NE by the Red Sea, E by Ethiopia and Eritrea, S by Kenya, Uganda, and the Democratic Republic of

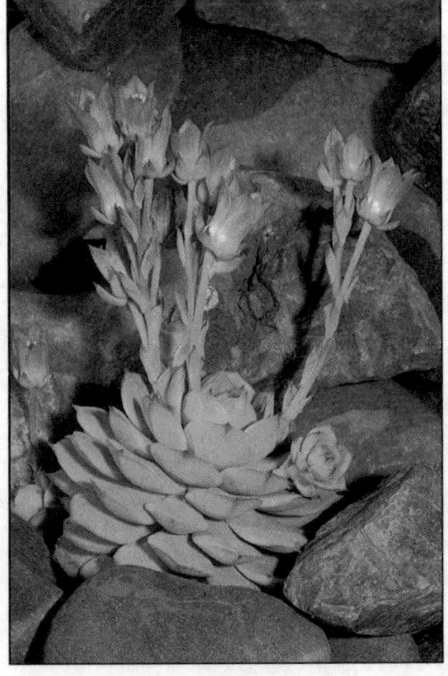

succulent plant In *Echeveria derenbergii* from Mexico, a member of the stonecrop family Crassulaceae, it is the leaves which are succulent rather than the stems as in most cacti and many other succulents. Succulent plants from many families are widely grown for their ornamental appearance. *Premaphotos Wildlife*

SUDAN
Democratic Republic of

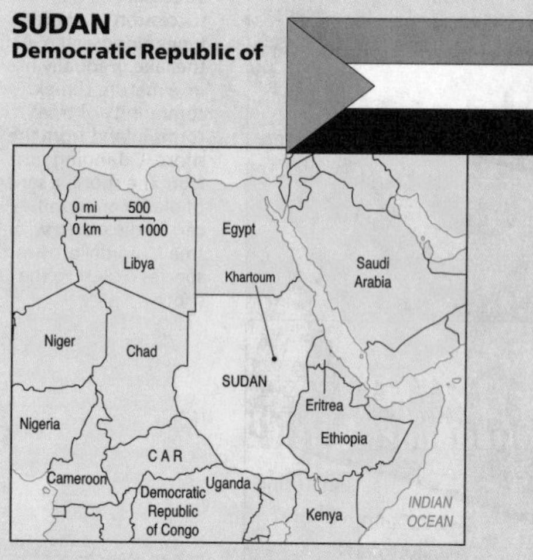

national name *Jamhuryat es-Sudan*
area 2,505,800 sq km/967,489 sq mi
capital Khartoum
major towns/cities Omdurman, Juba, Wadi Medani, al-Obeid, Kassala, Atbara, al-Qadarif, Kosti
major ports Port Sudan
physical features fertile valley of river Nile separates Libyan Desert in W from high rocky Nubian Desert in E; largest country in Africa
head of state and government General Omar Hassan Ahmed al-Bashir from 1989
political system military republic
administrative divisions 26 states
political parties officially banned from 1989, but an influential grouping is the fundamentalist National Islamic Front
population 28,098,000 (1995 est)
population growth rate 2.7% (1990–95); 2.6% (2000–05)
ethnic distribution over 50 ethnic groups and almost 600 subgroups; the population is broadly distributed between Arabs in the N and black Africans in the S
life expectancy 51 (men), 53 (women)
literacy rate men 43%, women 12%
languages Arabic 51% (official), local languages
religions Sunni Muslim; also animist and Christian
currency Sudanese dinar
GDP (US $) 17.2 billion (1994)
growth rate 2.0% (1994)
exports cotton, gum arabic, sesame seed, peanuts, sorghum

HISTORY
c. 600 BC–AD 350 Meroë, near Khartoum, was capital of the Nubian Empire, which covered S Egypt and N Sudan.
6th C Converted to Coptic Christianity.
7th C Islam first introduced by Arab invaders, but did not spread widely until the 15th century.
16th–18th Cs Arab-African Fur and Fung Empires established in central and northern Sudan.
1820 Invaded by Muhammad Ali and brought under Egyptian control.
1881–85 Revolt led to capture of Khartoum by Sheik Muhammad Ahmed, a self-proclaimed Mahdi ('messiah'), and the killing of British general Charles Gordon.
1898 Anglo-Egyptian offensive led by Lord Kitchener subdued Mahdi revolt at the battle of Omdurman in which 20,000 Sudanese died.
1899 Sudan administered as an Anglo-Egyptian condominium.
1923 White Flag League formed by Sudanese nationalists in the N; the British instituted a policy of reducing contact between northern and southern Sudan, with the aim that the S would become part of a federation of eastern African states.
1955 Civil war between the dominant Arab Muslim N and black African Christian and animist S broke out.
1956 Sudan achieved independence from Britain and Egypt as a republic.
1958 Military coup replaced civilian government with Supreme Council of the Armed Forces.
1964 Civilian rule reinstated after the October Revolution of student demonstrations.
1969 Coup led by Col Gaafar Mohammed al-Nimeri abolished political institutions and concentrated power in a leftist Revolutionary Command Council.
1971 Nimeri confirmed as president and the Sudanese Socialist Union (SSU) declared the only legal party by a new constitution.
1972 Plans to form a Federation of Arab Republics, comprising Sudan, Egypt, and Syria, abandoned due to internal opposition. To end the 17-year-long civil war, Nimeri agreed to give the S greater autonomy.
1974 National assembly established.
1980 Country reorganized into six regions, each with own assembly and effective autonomy.
1983 Shari'a (Islamic law) imposed. Sudan People's Liberation Movement (SPLM) formed in the S as civil war broke out again.
1985 Nimeri deposed in a bloodless coup led by General Swar al-Dahab following industrial unrest in the N. State of emergency declared.
1986 Coalition government formed after general election, with Sadiq al-Mahdi, great-grandson of the Mahdi, as prime minister.
1987 Virtual civil war with Sudan People's Liberation Army (SPLA), military wing of SPLM; drought and famine in the S and refugee influx from Ethiopa and Chad.
1988 Peace pact signed with SPLA, but fighting continued.
1989 Al-Mahdi overthrown in coup led by Islamic fundamentalist General Omar Hassan Ahmed el-Bashir. All political activity suspended.
1991 Federal system introduced, with division of country into nine states as civil war continued.
1995 SPLA faction leaders agreed to cease-fire, but fighting continued.
1996 First presidential and parliamentary elections held since coup of 1989.
1997 Treaty signed between Sudan's Islamic government and four southern rebel groups.

SEE ALSO Khartoum; Nubia

Congo, W by the Central African Republic and Chad, and NW by Libya. It is the largest country in Africa.

'So many men, so many opinions.'
SUETONIUS
Phormio

sudden infant death syndrome (SIDS) in medicine, the technical term for ◊cot death.

Sudetenland mountainous region in NE Bohemia, Czech Republic, extending eastwards along the border with Poland. Sudetenland was annexed by Germany under the ◊Munich Agreement 1938; it was returned to Czechoslovakia 1945.

Suetonius (Gaius Suetonius Tranquillus) c. AD 69–c. 140. Roman historian. He was the author of *Lives of the Caesars* (Julius Caesar to Domitian).

Suez (Arabic ***El Suweis***) port at the Red Sea terminus of the Suez Canal; population (1994) 458,000. Industries include oil refining and the manufacture of fertilizers. It was reconstructed 1979, after the ◊Arab-Israeli Wars.

Suez Canal artificial waterway, 160 km/100 mi long, from Port Said to Suez, linking the Mediterranean and Red seas, separating Africa from Asia, and providing the shortest eastwards sea route from Europe. It was opened 1869, nationalized 1956, blocked by Egypt during the Arab-Israeli War 1967, and not reopened until 1975.

The French Suez Canal Company was formed 1858 to execute the scheme of Ferdinand de Lesseps. The canal was opened 1869, and in 1875 British prime minister ◊Disraeli acquired a major shareholding for Britain from the khedive of Egypt. The 1888 Convention of Constantinople opened it to all nations. The Suez Canal was administered by a company with offices in Paris controlled by a council of 33 (10 of them British) until 1956 when it was forcibly nationalized by President ◊Nasser of Egypt. The new Damietta port complex on the Mediterranean at the mouth of the canal was inaugurated 1986. The port is designed to handle 16 million tonnes of cargo.

'I have always found Suffolk farmers great boasters of their superiority over others; and I must say that it is not without reason.'
On SUFFOLK
William Cobbett
Rural Rides – Eastern Tour 22 March 1830

Suez Crisis military confrontation Oct–Dec 1956 following the nationalization of the Suez Canal by President Nasser of Egypt. In an attempt to reassert international control of the canal, Israel launched an attack, after which British and French troops landed. Widespread international censure forced the withdrawal of the British and French. The crisis resulted in the resignation of British prime minister Eden.

At a London conference of maritime powers the Australian prime minister, Robert Menzies, was appointed to negotiate a settlement in Cairo. His mission was unsuccessful. The military intervention met Soviet protest and considerable domestic opposition, and the USA did not support it. British, French, and Australian relations with the USA were greatly strained during this period.

Suffolk county of E England
area 3,800 sq km/1,467 sq mi (*see United Kingdom map*)
towns Ipswich (administrative headquarters), Bury St Edmunds, Lowestoft, Felixstowe
features undulating lowlands and flat coastline; rivers: Waveney, Alde, Deben, Orwell, Stour, Little Ouse; part of the Norfolk Broads; Minsmere marshland bird reserve, near Aldeburgh; the Sandlings (heathlands and birds); ◊Sutton Hoo (7th-century ship burial); Sizewell B, Britain's first pressurized-water nuclear reactor plant, in operation 1995 (an application to build a second reactor, Sizewell C, was made 1993)
industries cereals, sugar beet, working horses (Suffolk punches), fertilizers, agricultural machinery, fishing
population (1991) 636,300
famous people Thomas Gainsborough, George Crabbe, John Constable, Elizabeth Garrett Anderson, Benjamin Britten.

suffragette or ***suffragist*** woman fighting for the right to vote. In the UK, women's suffrage bills were repeatedly introduced and defeated in Parliament between 1886 and 1911, and a militant campaign was launched 1906 by Emmeline ◊Pankhurst and her daughters. In 1918 women were granted limited franchise; in 1928 it was extended to all women over 21. In the USA the 19th amendment to the constitution 1920 gave women the vote in federal and state elections.

Suffragettes (the term was coined by a *Daily Mail* reporter) chained themselves to railings, heckled political meetings, refused to pay taxes, and in 1913 bombed the home of Lloyd George, then chancellor of the Exchequer. One woman, Emily ◊Davison, threw herself under the king's horse at the Derby horse race in 1913 and was killed. Many suffragettes were imprisoned and were force-fed when they went on hunger strike; under the notorious 'Cat and Mouse Act' of 1913 they could be repeatedly released to regain their health and then rearrested. The struggle was called off on the outbreak of World War I. ▷ *See feature on pp. 1152–1153.*

Sufism mystical movement of ◊Islam that originated in the 8th century. Sufis believe that deep intuition is the only real guide to knowledge. The movement has a strong strain of asceticism. The name derives from Arabic *suf*, a rough woollen robe worn as an indication of disregard for material things. There are a number of groups or brotherhoods within Sufism, each with its own method of meditative practice, one of which is the whirling dance of the ◊dervishes.

Sufism was originally influenced by the ascetics of the early Christian church, but later developed within the structure of orthodox Islam.

sugar or ***sucrose*** sweet, soluble crystalline carbohydrate found in the pith of sugar cane and in sugar beet. It is a disaccharide sugar, each of its molecules being made up of two simple-sugar (monosaccharide) units: glucose and fructose. Sugar is easily digested and forms a major source of energy in humans, being used in cooking and in the food industry as a sweetener and, in high concentrations, as a preservative. A high consumption is associated with obesity and tooth decay. In the UK, sucrose may not be used in baby foods.

The main sources of sucrose sugar are tropical sugar cane *Saccharum officinarum*, which accounts for two-thirds of production, and temperate sugar beet *Beta vulgaris*. Minor quantities are produced from the sap of maple trees, and from sorghum and date palms. Raw sugar crystals obtained by heating the juice of sugar canes are processed to form brown sugars, such as Muscovado and Demerara, or refined and sifted to produce white sugars, such as granulated, caster, and icing sugar. The syrup that is drained away from the raw sugar is molasses; it may be processed to form golden syrup or treacle, or fermented to form rum. Molasses obtained from sugar beet juice is too bitter for human consumption. The fibrous residue of sugar cane, called bagasse, is used in the manufacture of paper, cattle feed, and fuel; and new types of cane are being bred for low sugar and high fuel production.

sugar maple E North American ◊maple tree *Acer saccharum*.

Suharto Thojib I 1921– . Indonesian politician and general, president from 1967. Formerly Chief of Staff under ◊Sukarno, he dealt harshly with a left-wing attempt to unseat his predecessor and then assumed power himself. He ended confrontation with Malaysia, invaded East Timor 1975, and reached a cooperation agreement with Papua New Guinea 1979. His authoritarian rule has met with domestic opposition from the left, but the Indonesian economy has enjoyed significant growth. He was re-elected 1973, 1978, 1983, 1988, and 1993.

suicide the act of killing oneself intentionally; also someone who does this. Around four times as many young men kill themselves as women. Although often considered a crime (in English law, it was a criminal offence, if committed while of sound mind, until 1961), some cultures consider suicide honourable behaviour, for example in ancient Rome, historic hara-kiri in Japan, and ◊suttee in India.

In English law, to aid and abet another's suicide is an offence, and euthanasia or mercy killing may amount to aiding in this context. Where there is a suicide pact and one survives, he or she may be charged with ◊manslaughter.

Sui dynasty Chinese ruling family 581–618 which reunited China after the strife of the ◊Three Kingdoms era. There were two Sui emperors: Yang Qien (Yang Chien, 541–604), and Yangdi (Yang-ti, ruled 605–17). Though short-lived, the Sui re-established strong centralized government, rebuilding the ◊Great Wall and digging canals which later formed part of the Grand Canal system. The Sui capital was Chang'an.

suite in Baroque music, a set of contrasting instrumental pieces based on dance forms, known by their French names as allemande, bourrée, courante, gavotte, gigue, minuet, musette, passepied,

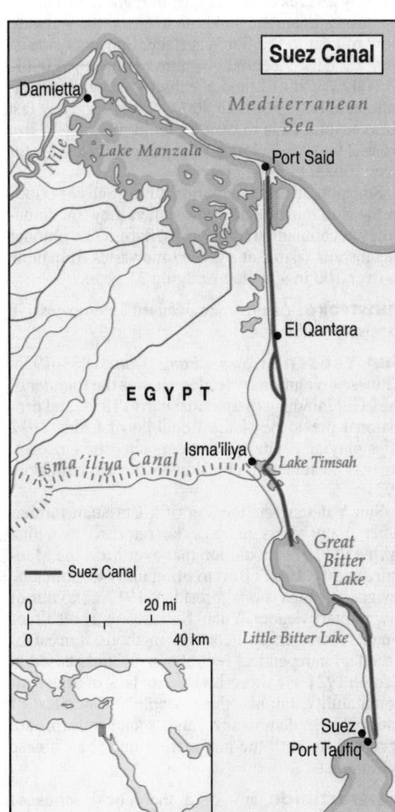

rigaudon, sarabande, and so on. The term refers in more recent usage to a concert arrangement of set pieces from an extended ballet or stage composition, such as Tchaikovsky's *Nutcracker Suite* 1891–92. Stravinsky's suite from *The Soldier's Tale* 1920 incorporates a tango, waltz, and ragtime.

Sukarno Achmed 1901–1970. Indonesian nationalist, president 1945–67. During World War II he cooperated in the local administration set up by the Japanese, replacing Dutch rule. After the war he became the first president of the new Indonesian republic, becoming president-for-life in 1966; he was ousted by ◊Suharto.

Sulawesi formerly ***Celebes*** island in E Indonesia, one of the Sunda Islands; area (with dependent islands) 190,000 sq km/73,000 sq mi; population (1990) 12,520,700. It is mountainous and forested and produces copra and nickel.

Suleiman or ***Solyman*** c. 1494–1566. Ottoman sultan from 1520, known as ***the Magnificent*** and ***the Lawgiver***. Under his rule, the Ottoman Empire flourished and reached its largest extent. He made conquests in the Balkans, the Mediterranean, Persia, and N Africa, but was defeated at Vienna in 1529 and Valletta (on Malta) in 1565. He was a patron of the arts, a poet, and an administrator.

Suleiman captured Belgrade in 1521, the Mediterranean island of Rhodes in 1522, defeated the Hungarians at Mohács in 1526, and was halted in his advance into Europe only by his failure to take Vienna, capital of the Austro-Hungarian Empire, after a siege Sept–Oct 1529. In 1534 he turned more successfully against Persia, and then in campaigns against the Arab world took almost all of N Africa and the Red Sea port of Aden. Only the ◊Knights of Malta inflicted severe defeat on both his army and fleet when he tried to take Valletta in 1565.

Sulla Lucius Cornelius 138–78 BC. Roman general and politician, a leader of the senatorial party. He was nicknamed Felix ('Lucky'). Forcibly suppressing the democrats by marching on Rome in 88 BC, he departed for a successful campaign against ◊Mithridates VI of Pontus. The democrats seized power in his absence, but on his return in 82 Sulla captured Rome and massacred all opponents. The reforms he introduced as dictator, which strengthened the Senate, were conservative and short-lived. He retired 79 BC.

Sullivan Arthur Seymour 1842–1900. English composer. He wrote operettas in collaboration with William Gilbert, including *HMS Pinafore* 1878, *The Pirates of Penzance* 1879, and *The Mikado* 1885. Their partnership broke down 1896. Sullivan also composed serious instrumental, choral, and operatic works – for example, the opera *Ivanhoe* 1890 – which he valued more highly than the operettas.

Other Gilbert and Sullivan operettas include *Patience* (which ridiculed the Aesthetic Movement) 1881, *The Yeomen of the Guard* 1888, and *The Gondoliers* 1889.

Sullivan Louis Henry 1856–1924. US architect. He was a leader of the ◊Chicago School and an early developer of the ◊skyscraper. His skyscrapers include the Wainwright Building, St Louis, 1890, the Guaranty Building, Buffalo, 1894, and the Carson, Pirie and Scott Store, Chicago, 1899. He was the teacher of Frank Lloyd ◊Wright.

Sully Maximilien de Béthune, Duc de Sully 1560–1641. French politician, who served with the Protestant ◊Huguenots in the Wars of Religion, and, as Henry IV's superintendent of finances 1598–1611, aided French recovery.

sulphate SO_4^{2-} salt or ester derived from sulphuric acid. Most sulphates are water soluble (the exceptions are lead, calcium, strontium, and barium sulphates), and require a very high temperature to decompose them.

The commonest sulphates seen in the laboratory are copper(II) sulphate ($CuSO_4$), iron(II) sulphate ($FeSO_4$), and aluminium sulphate ($Al_2(SO_4)_3$). The ion is detected in solution by using barium chloride or barium nitrate to precipitate the insoluble sulphate.

sulphide compound of sulphur and another element in which sulphur is the more electronegative element (see ◊electronegativity). Sulphides occur in a number of minerals. Some of the more

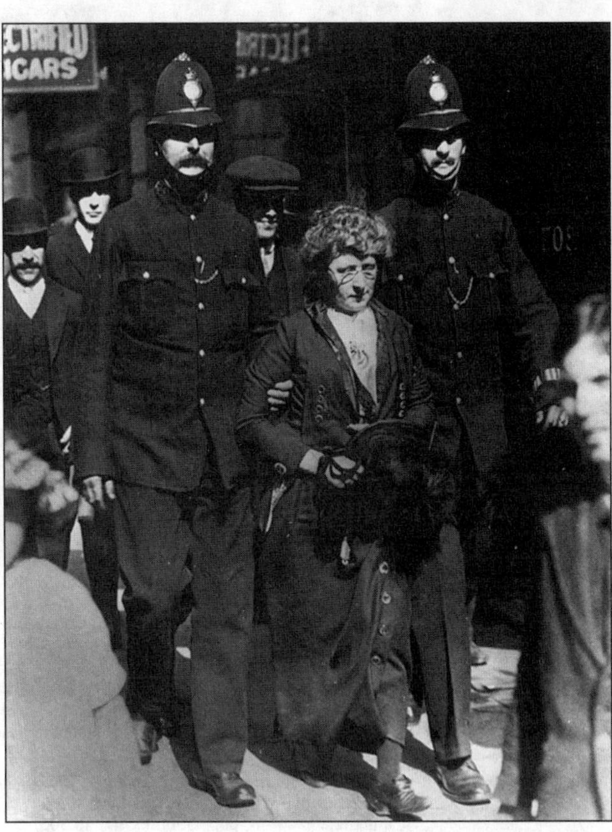

suffragette The arrest of a suffragette by two policemen in London in about 1905. In the UK, the vote was granted to women over 30 in 1918, and to all women over 21 in 1928. *Corbis*

volatile sulphides have extremely unpleasant odours (hydrogen sulphide smells of bad eggs).

sulphite SO_3^{2-} salt or ester derived from sulphurous acid.

sulphonamide any of a group of compounds containing the chemical group sulphonamide (SO_2NH_2) or its derivatives, which were, and still are in some cases, used to treat bacterial diseases. Sulphadiazine ($C_{10}H_{10}N_4O_2S$) is an example.

Sulphonamide was the first commercially available antibacterial drug, the forerunner of a range of similar drugs. Toxicity and increasing resistance have limited their use chiefly to the treatment of urinary-tract infection.

sulphur brittle, pale-yellow, nonmetallic element, symbol S, atomic number 16, relative atomic mass 32.064. It occurs in three allotropic forms: two crystalline (called rhombic and monoclinic, following the arrangements of the atoms within the crystals) and one amorphous. It burns in air with a blue flame and a stifling odour. Insoluble in water but soluble in carbon disulphide, it is a good electrical insulator. Sulphur is widely used in the manufacture of sulphuric acid (used to treat phosphate rock to make fertilizers) and in making paper, matches, gunpowder and fireworks, in vulcanizing rubber, and in medicines and insecticides.

It is found abundantly in nature in volcanic regions combined with both metals and nonmetals, and also in its elemental form as a crystalline solid. It is a constituent of proteins, and has been known since ancient times.

sulphur dioxide SO_2 pungent gas produced by burning sulphur in air or oxygen. It is widely used for disinfecting food vessels and equipment, and as a preservative in some food products. It occurs in industrial flue gases and is a major cause of ◊acid rain.

sulphuric acid or ***oil of vitriol*** H_2SO_4 a dense, viscous, colourless liquid that is extremely corrosive. It gives out heat when added to water and can cause severe burns. Sulphuric acid is used extensively in the chemical industry, in the refining of petrol, and in the manufacture of fertilizers, detergents, explosives, and dyes. It forms the acid component of car batteries.

sulphurous acid H_2SO_3 solution of sulphur dioxide (SO_2) in water. It is a weak acid.

Sulu Archipelago group of about 870 islands off SW Mindanao in the Philippines, between the Sulawesi and Sulu seas; area 2,700 sq km/1,042 sq

❝I am a sundial, and I make a botch / Of what is done much better by a watch.❞

On SUNDIALS
Hilaire Belloc 'On a Sundial'

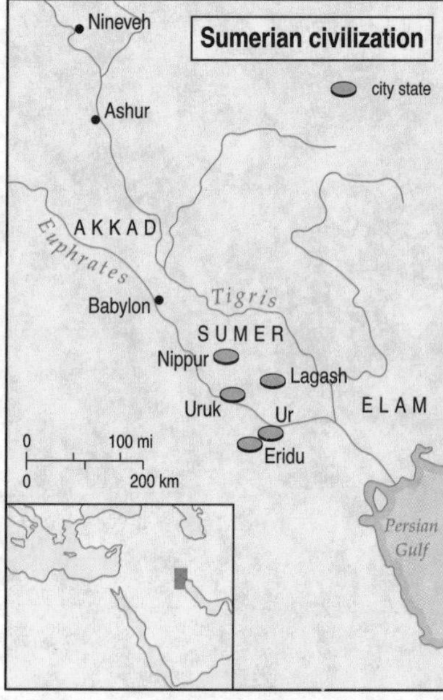

mi; population (1989) 12,507,700. The capital is Jolo, on the island (the largest) of the same name. Until 1940 the islands were an autonomous sultanate.

Sumatra or ***Sumatera*** second-largest island of Indonesia, one of the Sunda Islands; area 473,600 sq km/182,800 sq mi; population (1990) 36,505,700. East of a longitudinal volcanic mountain range is a wide plain; both are heavily forested. Products include rubber, rice, tobacco, tea, timber, tin, and petroleum.

Northern Sumatra is rapidly being industrialized, and the Asakan River (rising in Lake Toba) was dammed for power 1974. The main towns are Palembang, Padang, and Benkuelen.

A Hindu empire was founded in the 8th century, but Islam was introduced by Arab traders from the 13th century and by the 16th century was adopted throughout the island.

Sumerian civilization the world's earliest civilization, dating from about 3500 BC and located at the confluence of the Tigris and Euphrates rivers in lower Mesopotamia (present-day Iraq). It was a city-state with priests as secular rulers. After 2300 BC, Sumer declined.

Sumerian culture was based on the taxation of the surplus produced by agricultural villagers to support the urban ruling class and its public-works programme, which included state-controlled irrigation. Cities included ◊Lagash, ◊Eridu, and ◊Ur. Centralized control over the region (an empire) was first asserted by neighbouring Akkad, about 2300 BC. Trade with Egypt and the Indus valley may have influenced the formation of the ancient civilizations there.

Sumerian civilization A Sumerian clay tablet with incised cuneiform characters tallying sheep and goats. Sumer, in the southern part of ancient Babylonia (now part of Iraq), was the site of a civilization that was the first to develop written language, in the 3rd millennium BC. *Corbis*

summer time practice introduced in the UK 1916 whereby legal time from spring to autumn is an hour in advance of Greenwich mean time.

Continental Europe 'puts the clock back' a month earlier than the UK in autumn. British summer time was permanently in force Feb 1940–Oct 1945 and Feb 1968–Oct 1971. Double summer time (2 hours in advance) was in force during the summers of 1941–45 and 1947.

In North America the practice is known as daylight saving time.

summit or ***summit conference*** in international diplomacy, a personal meeting between heads of state to settle international crises and other matters of general concern. 'Summit' was first used in this sense by Winston Churchill in 1950, although it could be applied to the meetings between himself, Roosevelt, and Stalin at Tehran and Yalta during World War II. During the ◊Cold War, the term 'superpower summit' was applied to meetings between the Soviet Union's Communist party leader and the US president.

sumo wrestling national sport of Japan. Fighters of larger than average size (rarely less than 130 kg/21 st or 285 lb) try to push, pull, or throw each other out of a circular ring.

Fighters follow a traditional diet and eat a great deal to build up body weight. In the ring, they try to get their centre of gravity as low to the ground as possible. Championships, lasting up to 15 days each, are held six times a year in Japan; millions of fans watch the contests live and on television. Sumo wrestling originated as a religious ritual performed at Shinto shrines. In the 17th and 18th centuries it evolved into a popular spectator sport.

Sun the ◊star at the centre of the Solar System. Its diameter is 1,392,000 km/865,000 mi; its temperature at the surface is about 5,800K (5,500°C/9,900°F), and at the centre 15,000,000K (about 15,000,000°C/27,000,000°F). It is composed of about 70% hydrogen and 30% helium, with other elements making up less than 1%. The Sun's energy is generated by nuclear fusion reactions that turn hydrogen into helium at its centre. The gas core is far denser than mercury or lead on Earth. The Sun is about 4.7 billion years old, with a predicted lifetime of 10 billion years.

At the end of its life, it will expand to become a ◊red giant the size of Mars's orbit, then shrink to become a ◊white dwarf. The Sun spins on its axis every 25 days near its equator, but more slowly towards its poles. Its rotation can be followed by watching the passage of dark ◊sunspots across its disc. Sometimes bright eruptions called ◊flares occur near sunspots. Above the Sun's ◊photosphere lies a layer of thinner gas called the chromosphere, visible only by means of special instruments or at eclipses. Tongues of gas called ◊prominences extend from the chromosphere into the corona, a halo of hot, tenuous gas surrounding the Sun. Gas boiling from the corona streams outwards through the Solar System, forming the ◊solar wind. Activity on the Sun, including sunspots, flares, and prominences, waxes and wanes during the solar cycle, which peaks every 11 years or so, and seems to be connected with the solar magnetic field.

Sunda Islands islands W of Maluku (Moluccas), in the Malay Archipelago, the greater number belonging to Indonesia. They are so named because they lie largely on the Indonesian extension of the Sunda continental shelf. The ***Greater Sundas*** include Borneo, Java (including the small island of Madura), Sumatra, Sulawesi, and Belitung. The ***Lesser Sundas*** (Indonesian *Nusa Tenggara*) are all Indonesian and include Bali, Lombok, Flores, Sumba, Sumbawa, and Timor.

Sundanese the second-largest ethnic group in the Republic of Indonesia. There are more than 20 million speakers of Sundanese, a member of the western branch of the Austronesian family. Like their neighbours, the Javanese, the Sundanese are predominantly Muslim.

They are known for their performing arts, especially *jaipongan* dance traditions, and distinctive batik fabrics.

Sunday trading buying and selling on Sunday; this was banned in the UK by the Shops Act 1950, but the ban may have been in breach of Article 30 of the Treaty of Rome as amounting to an unlawful restraint on the free movement of goods. Following the defeat of a bill to enable widespread Sunday trading April 1986, compromise legislation was introduced 1994 in Britain which allowed shops to open but restricted larger stores (over 280 sq m) to a maximum of six hours. Shops in Scotland, where Sunday trading is fully deregulated, retained the right to open at any time.

Legislation against Sunday trading in the USA has long been very laxly enforced, and in some cases repealed. The conflict is between the free market on the one hand and, on the other, the trade unions' fear of longer working hours and the Christian lobby's traditional opposition to secular activity on the Sabbath.

Sunderland city and port in Tyne and Wear, NE England, at the mouth of the river Wear; population (1991) 289,000.

Industries were formerly only coal mining (exported from the 14th century onwards, but all pits have closed) and shipbuilding but have now diversified to electronics, glass, pottery, chemicals, paper manufacture, furniture, and cars (Nissan). There is a civic theatre, the Sunderland Empire. Sunderland was granted city status by Royal Charter 1992.

sundew any insectivorous plant of the genus *Drosera*, family Droseraceae, with viscid hairs on the leaves for catching prey.

sundial instrument measuring time by means of a shadow cast by the Sun. Almost completely superseded by the proliferation of clocks, it survives ornamentally in gardens. The dial is marked with the hours at graduated distances, and a style or gnomon (parallel to Earth's axis and pointing to the north) casts the shadow.

sunfish marine fish *Mola mola* with disc-shaped body 3 m/10 ft long found in all temperate and tropical oceans. The term also applies to fish of the North American freshwater Centrarchidae family, which have compressed, almost circular bodies, up to 80 cm/30 in long, and are nestbuilders and avid predators.

sunflower tall plant of the genus *Helianthus*, family Compositae. The common sunflower *H. annuus*, probably native to Mexico, grows to 4.5 m/15 ft in favourable conditions. It is commercially cultivated in central Europe, the USA, Russia, Ukraine, and Australia for the oil-bearing seeds that follow the yellow-petalled flowers.

Sunni member of the larger of the two main sects of ◊Islam, with about 680 million adherents. Sunni Muslims believe that the first three caliphs were all legitimate successors of the prophet Muhammad, and that guidance on belief and life should come from the Koran and the Hadith, and from the Shari'a, not from a human authority or spiritual leader. Imams in Sunni Islam are educated lay teachers of the faith and prayer leaders.

The name derives from the *Sunna*, Arabic 'code of behaviour', the body of traditional law evolved from the teaching and acts of Muhammad.

sunspot dark patch on the surface of the Sun, actually an area of cooler gas, thought to be caused by strong magnetic fields that block the outward flow of heat to the Sun's surface. Sunspots consist of a dark central umbra, about 4,000K (3,700°C/6,700°F), and a lighter surrounding penumbra, about 5,500K (5,200°C/9,400°F). They last from several days to over a month, ranging in size from 2,000 km/1,250 mi to groups stretching for over 100,000 km/62,000 mi.

Sunspots are more common during active periods in the Sun's magnetic cycle, when they are sometimes accompanied by nearby ◊flares. The number of sunspots visible at a given time varies from none to over 100 in a cycle averaging 11 years.

sunstroke ◊heatstroke caused by excessive exposure to the Sun.

Sun Yat-sen or ***Sun Zhong Shan*** 1867–1925. Chinese revolutionary leader. He was the founder of the ◊Guomindang (nationalist party) 1894, and provisional president of the Republic of China 1912 after playing a vital part in deposing the emperor. He was president of a breakaway government from 1921.

Sun Yat-sen was the son of a Christian farmer. After many years in exile he returned to China during the 1911 revolution that overthrew the Manchu dynasty. In an effort to bring unity to China, he resigned as provisional president 1912 in favour of the military leader Yuan Shikai. As a result of Yuan's increasingly dictatorial methods, Sun established an independent republic in S China based in Canton 1921. He was criticized for lack of organizational ability, but his 'three people's principles' of nationalism, democracy, and social reform are accepted by both the nationalists and the Chinese communists.

superactinide any of a theoretical series of superheavy, radioactive elements, starting with atomic number 113, that extend beyond the ◊transactinide series in the periodic table. They do not occur in nature and none has yet been synthesized.

It is postulated that this series has a group of elements that have half-lives longer than those of the transactinide series.

This group, centred on element 114, is referred to as the 'island of stability', based on the nucleon arrangement. The longer half-lives will, it is hoped, allow enough time for their chemical and physical properties to be studied when they have been synthesized.

Super Bowl US professional football championship, inaugurated 1966. It is the annual end-of-season contest between the American Football Conference (AFC) and the National Football Conference (NFC) champions. See ◊football, American.

superbug popular name for an infectious bacterium that has developed resistance to most or all known antibiotics. Methicillin-resistant ◊*Staphylococcus aureus* (MRSA) is a superbug that causes problems in many hospitals. So far outbreaks of MRSA, which can cause temporary closure of operating rooms and intensive care units, have been met with vancomycin, a 'last resort' antibiotic normally reserved for life-threatening infections.

In 1998 US researchers successfully synthesized vancomycin, thus making it possible to also synthesize slightly altered versions of the drug with which to treat vancomycin-resistant bacteria.

supercomputer the fastest, most powerful type of computer, capable of performing its basic operations in picoseconds (thousand-billionths of a second), rather than nanoseconds (billionths of a second), like most other computers. Of the world's 500 most powerful supercomputers 232 are in the USA, 109 in Japan, and 140 in Europe, with 23 in the UK.

superconductivity in physics, increase in electrical conductivity at low temperatures. The resistance of some metals and metallic compounds decreases uniformly with decreasing temperature until at a critical temperature (the superconducting point), within a few degrees of absolute zero (0K/−273.15°C/−459.67°F), the resistance suddenly falls to zero. The phenomenon was discovered by Dutch scientist Heike Kamerlingh Onnes in 1911.

Some metals, such as platinum and copper, do not become superconductive; as the temperature decreases, their resistance decreases to a certain point but then rises again. Superconductivity can be nullified by the application of a large magnetic field.

In the superconducting state, an electric current will continue indefinitely once started, provided that the material remains below the superconducting point. In 1986 IBM researchers achieved superconductivity with some ceramics at −243°C/−405°F), opening up the possibility of 'high-temperature' superconductivity; Paul Chu at the University of Houston, Texas, achieved superconductivity at −179°C/−290°F, a temperature that can be sustained using liquid nitrogen. In 1992, two Japanese researchers developed a material which becomes superconducting at around −103°C/−153°F.

The Los Alamos National Laboratory, New Mexico, produced a flexible superconducting film 1995. The film, which can carry enough current for practical applications such as electromagnets, works at the relatively high temperature of 77K (−196°C/−320°F). It is made of yttrium barium copper oxide with a backing of nickel tape coated with zirconia.

supercooling the cooling of a liquid below its freezing point without freezing taking place; or the cooling of a ◊saturated solution without crystallization taking place, to form a supersaturated solution. In both cases supercooling is possible because of the lack of solid particles around which crystals can form. Crystallization rapidly follows the introduction of a small crystal (seed) or agitation of the supercooled solution.

superego in Freudian psychology, the element of the human mind concerned with the ideal, responsible for ethics and self-imposed standards of behaviour. It is characterized as a form of conscience, restraining the ◊ego, and responsible for feelings of guilt when the moral code is broken.

superfluid fluid that flows without viscosity or friction and has a very high thermal conductivity. Liquid helium at temperatures below 2K (−271°C/−456°F) is a superfluid: it shows unexpected behaviour; for instance, it flows uphill in apparent defiance of gravity and, if placed in a container, will flow up the sides and escape.

supergiant the largest and most luminous type of star known, with a diameter of up to 1,000 times that of the Sun and absolute magnitudes of between −5 and −9. Supergiants are likely to become ◊supernovae.

superheterodyne receiver the most widely used type of radio receiver, in which the incoming signal is mixed with a signal of fixed frequency generated within the receiver circuits. The resulting signal, called the intermediate-frequency (i.f.) signal, has a frequency between that of the incoming signal and the internal signal. The intermediate frequency is near the optimum frequency of the amplifier to which the i.f. signal is passed.

This arrangement ensures greater gain and selectivity. The superheterodyne system is also used in basic television receivers.

Superior, Lake largest and deepest of the ◊Great Lakes of North America, and the second largest lake in the world; area 83,300 sq km/32,200 sq mi.

supernova the explosive death of a star, which temporarily attains a brightness of 100 million Suns or more, so that it can shine as brilliantly as a small galaxy for a few days or weeks. Very approximately, it is thought that a supernova explodes in a large galaxy about once every 100 years. Many supernovae remain undetected because of obscuring by interstellar dust – astronomers estimate some 50%.

The name 'supernova' was coined by US astronomers Fritz Zwicky and Walter Baade 1934. Zwicky was also responsible for the division into types I and II. Type I supernovae are thought to occur in ◊binary star systems, in which gas from one star falls on to a ◊white dwarf, causing it to explode.

Type II supernovae occur in stars ten or more times as massive as the Sun, which suffer runaway internal nuclear reactions at the ends of their lives, leading to explosions. These are thought to leave behind ◊neutron stars and ◊black holes. Gas ejected by such an explosion causes an expanding radio source, such as the ◊Crab nebula. Supernovae are thought to be the main source of elements heavier than hydrogen and helium.

superphosphate phosphate fertilizer made by treating apatite with sulphuric or phosphoric acid. The commercial mixture contains largely monocalcium phosphate. Single-superphosphate obtained from apatite and sulphuric acid contains 16–20% available phosphorus, as P_2O_5; triple-superphosphate, which contains 45–50% phosphorus, is made by treating apatite with phosphoric acid.

superpower state that through disproportionate military or economic strength can dominate smaller nations. The term was used to describe the USA and the USSR from the end of World War II, when they emerged as significantly stronger than all other countries. With the collapse of the Soviet Union in 1991, the USA is, arguably, now the world's sole superpower.

supersaturation in chemistry, the state of a solution that has a higher concentration of solute (dissolved substance) than would normally be obtained in a ◊saturated solution.

Many solutes have a higher ◊solubility at high temperatures. If a hot saturated solution is cooled slowly, sometimes the excess solute does not come out of solution. This is an unstable situation and the introduction of a small solid particle will encourage the release of excess solute.

supersonic speed speed greater than that at which sound travels, measured in ◊Mach numbers. In dry air at 0°C/32°F, sound travels at about 1,170 kph/727 mph, but decreases its speed with altitude until, at 12,000 m/39,000 ft, it is only 1,060 kph/658 mph.

When an aircraft passes the ◊sound barrier, shock waves are built up that give rise to ◊sonic boom, often heard at ground level. US pilot Captain Charles Yeager was the first to achieve supersonic flight, in a Bell VS-1 rocket plane on 14 Oct 1947.

superstring theory in physics, a mathematical theory developed in the 1980s to explain the properties of ◊elementary particles and the forces between them (in particular, gravity and the nuclear forces) in a way that combines ◊relativity and ◊quantum theory.

In string theory, the fundamental objects in the universe are not pointlike particles but extremely small stringlike objects. These objects exist in a universe of ten dimensions, although, for reasons not yet understood, only three space dimensions and one dimension of time are discernible.

There are many unresolved difficulties with superstring theory, but some physicists think it may be the ultimate 'theory of everything' that explains all aspects of the universe within one framework.

supersymmetry in physics, a theory that relates the two classes of elementary particle, the ◊fermions and the ◊bosons. According to supersymmetry, each fermion particle has a boson partner particle, and vice versa. It has not been possible to marry up all the known fermions with the known bosons, and so the theory postulates the existence of other, as yet undiscovered fermions, such as the photinos (partners of the photons), gluinos (partners of the gluons), and gravitinos (partners of the gravitons). Using these ideas, it has become possible to develop a theory of gravity – called supergravity – that extends Einstein's work and considers the gravitational, nuclear, and electromagnetic forces to be manifestations of an underlying superforce. Supersymmetry has been incorporated into the ◊superstring theory, and appears to be a crucial ingredient in the 'theory of everything' sought by scientists.

supply and demand one of the fundamental approaches to economics, which examines and compares the supply of a good with its demand (usually in the form of a graph of supply and demand curves plotted against price). For a typical good, the supply curve is upward-sloping (the higher the price, the more the manufacturer is

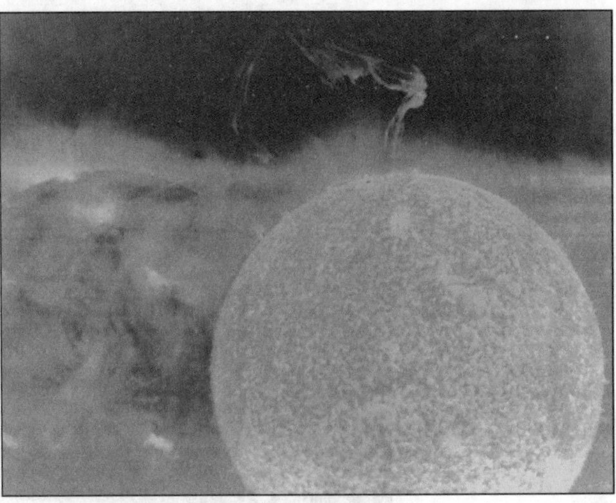

Sun The Sun photographed during the Skylab 3 mission 1973. The granular appearance of the Sun's surface, or photosphere, shows where cells of hot gas are constantly welling up from below. The solar eruption seen in this picture is a cloud of escaping helium reaching a height of over 800,000 km/500,000 mi. *National Aeronautical Space Agency*

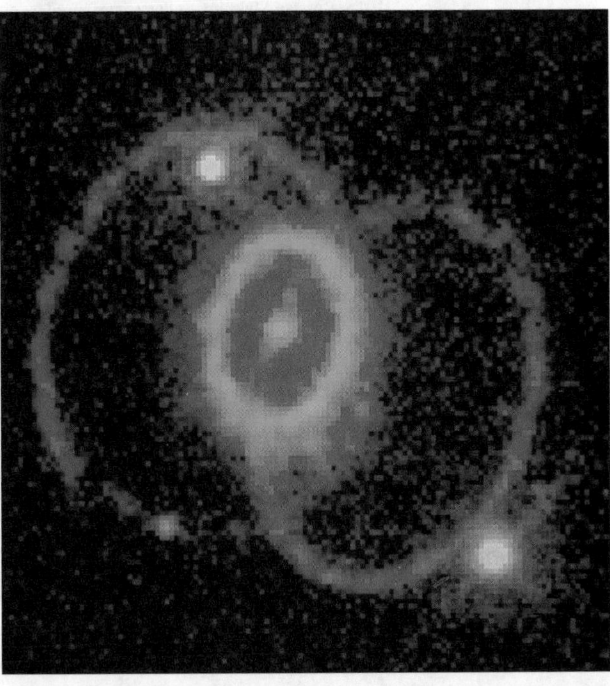

supernova A supernova pictured by the Hubble Space Telescope in 1987, and subsequently named 1987A. Massive waves of energy can be seen being emitted by the nuclear explosion that marks the death of a star. *NASA/Image Select (UK) Ltd*

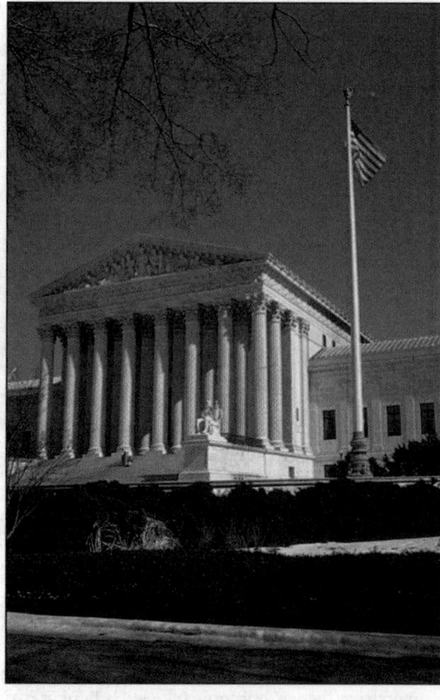

Supreme Court The Supreme Court Building, Washington DC, home of the highest law court in the USA. The court reviews the actions of the government, the judiciary, and the president and can declare them unconstitutional. *David Pratt*

willing to sell), while the demand curve is downward-sloping (the cheaper the good, the more demand there is for it). The point where the curves intersect is the equilibrium price at which supply equals demand.

supply-side economics school of economic thought advocating government policies that allow market forces to operate freely, such as privatization, cuts in public spending and income tax, reductions in trade-union power, and cuts in the ratio of unemployment benefits to wages. Supply-side economics developed as part of the monetarist (see ◊monetarism) critique of ◊Keynesian economics.

suprarenal gland alternative name for the ◊adrenal gland.

Supremacy, Acts of two UK acts of Parliament 1534 and 1559, which established Henry VIII and Elizabeth I respectively as head of the English church in place of the pope.

Suprematism Russian abstract-art movement developed about 1913 by Kasimir ◊Malevich. Suprematist painting gradually became more severe, until in 1918 it reached a climax with Malevich's *White on White* series showing white geometrical shapes on a white ground.

Suprematism was inspired in part by Futurist and Cubist ideas.

Early paintings such as Malevich's *Black Square* 1915 (Russian Museum, St Petersburg) used purely geometrical shapes in bold dynamic compositions. The aims of the movement were expressed by Malevich as 'the supremacy of pure feeling or perception in the pictorial arts – the expression of non-objectivity'. Suprematism greatly influenced the painter Wassily ◊Kandinsky and the ◊Bauhaus school of design.

Supreme Court highest US judicial tribunal, composed since 1869 of a chief justice (William Rehnquist from 1986) and eight associate justices. Appointments are made for life by the president, with the advice and consent of the Senate, and justices can be removed only by impeachment.

In Britain, the Supreme Court of Judicature is made up of the Court of Appeal and the High Court.

'Surrealism is destructive, but it destroys only what it considers to be shackles limiting our vision.'

On SURREALISM Salvador Dali, declaration

Supremes, the US vocal group, pioneers of the Motown sound, formed 1959 in Detroit. Beginning 1962, the group was a trio comprising, initially, Diana Ross (1944–), Mary Wilson (1944–), and Florence Ballard (1943–1976). The most successful female group of the 1960s, they had a string of pop hits beginning with 'Where Did Our Love Go?' 1964 and 'Baby Love' 1964. Diana Ross left to pursue a solo career 1969.

Surabaya port on the island of Java, Indonesia; population (1990) 2,421,000. It has oil refineries and shipyards and is a naval base.

Surat city in Gujarat, W India, at the mouth of the Tapti River; population (1991) 1,499,000. The chief industry is textiles. The first East India Company trading post in India was established here 1612.

surface tension in physics, the property that causes the surface of a liquid to behave as if it were covered with a weak elastic skin; this is why a needle can float on water. It is caused by the exposed surface's tendency to contract to the smallest possible area because of cohesive forces between ◊molecules at the surface. Allied phenomena include the formation of droplets, the concave profile of a meniscus, and the ◊capillary action by which water soaks into a sponge.

surfactant (contraction of ***surface-active agent***) substance added to a liquid in order to increase its wetting or spreading properties. Detergents are examples.

surfing in computing, exploring the ◊Internet. The term is rather misleading: the glitches, delays, and complexities of the system mean the experience is more like wading through mud.

surge abnormally high tide; see ◊storm surge.

surgeon fish any fish of the tropical marine family Acanthuridae. It has a flat body up to 50 cm/20 in long, is brightly coloured, and has a movable spine on each side of the tail that can be used as a weapon.

surgery branch of medicine concerned with the treatment of disease, abnormality, or injury by operation. Traditionally it has been performed by means of cutting instruments, but today a number of technologies are used to treat or remove lesions, including ultrasonic waves and laser surgery. Surgery is carried out under sterile conditions using an ◊anaesthetic. There are many specialized fields, including cardiac (heart), orthopaedic (bones and joints), ophthalmic (eye), neuro (brain and nerves), thoracic (chest), and renal (kidney) surgery; other specialities include plastic and reconstructive surgery, and ◊transplant surgery. ▷*See feature on pp. 1024–1025.*

surgical spirit ◊ethanol to which has been added a small amount of methanol to render it unfit to drink. It is used to sterilize surfaces and to cleanse skin abrasions and sores.

Suriname country on the N coast of South America, bounded W by French Guiana, S by Brazil, E by Guyana, and N by the Atlantic Ocean. *See country box opposite.*

Surrealism movement in art, literature, and film that developed out of ◊Dada around 1922. Led by André ◊Breton, who produced the *Surrealist Manifesto* 1924, the Surrealists were inspired by the thoughts and visions of the subconscious mind.

They explored varied styles and techniques, and the movement became the dominant force in Western art between World Wars I and II.

Surrealism followed Sigmund Freud's theory of the unconscious and his 'free association' technique for bypassing the conscious mind. In art it encompassed the automatic drawings of André Masson (1896–1987); paintings based on emotive semi-abstract forms (Max Ernst, Joan Miró, Yves Tanguy); and dreamlike images painted in a realistic style (Salvador Dali, René Magritte). Pablo Picasso worked along Surrealist lines for a time in the early 1920s. The poets Louis Aragon and Paul Eluard and the filmmaker Luis Buñuel were also part of the movement.

Surrey county of S England
area 1,660 sq km/641 sq mi (*see United Kingdom map*)
towns Kingston upon Thames (administrative headquarters), Guildford, Woking, Reigate, Leatherhead
features rivers: Thames, Mole, Wey; hills: Box and Leith; North Downs; Runnymede, Thameside site of the signing of Magna Carta; Yehudi Menuhin School; Kew Palace and Royal Botanic Gardens
industries vegetables, agricultural products, service industries
population (1991) 1,018,000
famous people John Galsworthy, Aldous Huxley, Laurence Olivier, Eric Clapton.

Surrey Henry Howard, Earl of Surrey c. 1517–1547. English courtier and poet. With Thomas ◊Wyatt, he introduced the sonnet to England and was a pioneer of ◊blank verse. He was executed on a poorly based charge of high treason.

surrogacy practice whereby a woman is sought, and usually paid, to bear a child for an infertile couple or a single parent.

Such commercial surrogacy is practised in some European countries and in the USA. In the UK, the Warnock Report 1984 on ◊embryo research condemned surrogacy. Under the Surrogacy Arrangements Act 1985 it became illegal for third parties to negotiate or facilitate any surrogacy for payment. The act did not affect non-commercial surrogacy agencies nor did it regulate negotiations directly made between the mother and the commissioning parents. Under the Human Fertilization and Embryo Bill 1989 a statutory licensing authority was established to regulate research and treatment in human infertility and embryology. The act enabled any established surrogacy services to be brought within the control of the authority.

Surtees John 1934– . British racing driver and motorcyclist, the only person to win world titles on two and four wheels.

After winning seven world motorcycling titles 1956–60, he turned to motor racing and won the world title in 1964. He later produced his own racing cars.

surveying the accurate measuring of the Earth's crust, or of land features or buildings. It is used to establish boundaries, and to evaluate the topography for engineering work. The measurements used are both linear and angular, and geometry and trigonometry are applied in the calculations.

Sūrya in Hindu mythology, the sun god, son of the sky god Indra. His daughter, also named Sūrya, is a female personification of the Sun.

suslik small Eurasian ground ◊squirrel *Citellus citellus.*

suspension mixture consisting of small solid particles dispersed in a liquid or gas, which will settle on standing. An example is milk of magnesia, which is a suspension of magnesium hydroxide in water.

Sussex former county of England, on the south coast, now divided into ◊East Sussex and ◊West Sussex.

Sutherland Graham Vivian 1903–1980. English painter, graphic artist, and designer. He executed portraits, landscapes, and religious subjects, often using a semi-abstract style. In the late 1940s he turned increasingly to portraiture. His portrait of Winston Churchill 1954 was disliked by its subject and eventually burned on the instructions of Lady Churchill (studies survive).

Sutherland Joan 1926– . Australian soprano. She is noted for her commanding range and impeccable technique. She made her debut England 1952,

Sutherland The soprano Joan Sutherland. Her highly flexible voice is well-suited to a variety of roles, but her greatest success was in Italian bel canto opera of the 18th and 19th centuries. She has a huge range and is one of the foremost coloratura sopranos of the century. *Polygram*

SURINAME

Republic of (formerly *Dutch Guiana*)

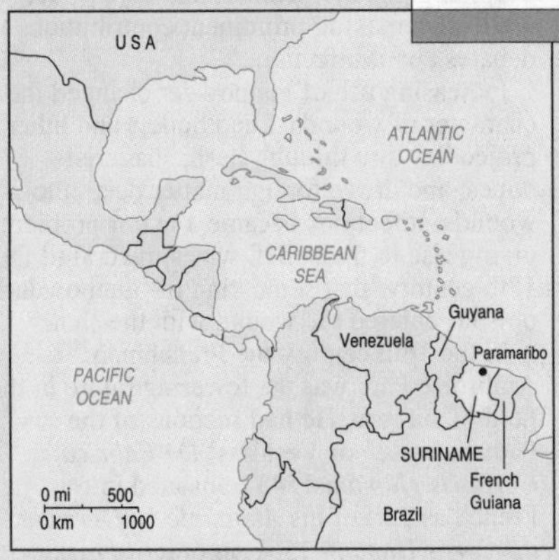

USA
ATLANTIC OCEAN
CARIBBEAN SEA
Guyana
Venezuela
Paramaribo
PACIFIC OCEAN
SURINAME
French Guiana
Brazil
0 mi 500
0 km 1000

national name *Republiek Suriname*
area 163,820 sq km/63,243 sq mi
capital Paramaribo
major towns/cities Nieuw Nickerie, Brokopondo, Nieuw Amsterdam
physical features hilly and forested, with flat and narrow coastal plain; Suriname River
head of state and government Jules Wijdenbosch from 1996
political system emergent democratic republic
administrative divisions nine districts
political parties New Front (NF), alliance of four left-of-centre parties: Party for National Unity and Solidarity (KTPI), Suriname National Party (NPS), Progressive Reform Party (VHP), Suriname Labour Party (SPA); National Democratic Party (NDP), left of centre; Democratic Alternative 1991 (DA '91), alliance of three left-of-centre parties
population 432,900 (1996 est)
population growth rate 1.1% (1990–95)
ethnic distribution a wide ethnic composition, including Creoles, East Indians, Indonesians, Africans, Amerindians, Europeans, and Chinese
life expectancy 68 (men), 73 (women)
literacy rate men 95%, women 95%
languages Dutch (official), Sranan (creole), English, Hindi, Javanese, Chinese. Spanish is the main working language
religions Christian, Hindu, Muslim
currency Surinam guilder
GDP (US $) 1.3 billion (1995)
growth rate 4.5% (1992)
exports alumina, aluminium, bauxite, rice, timber, shrimps, bananas

HISTORY
AD **1593** Visited and claimed by Spanish explorers; the name Suriname derived from the country's earliest inhabitants, the Surinen, who were driven out by other Amerindians in the 16th century.
1602 Dutch settlements were established.
1651 British colony founded by settlers sent from Barbados.
1667 Became a Dutch colony, received in exchange for New Amsterdam (New York) by the Treaty of Breda.
1682 Coffee and sugar-cane plantations introduced, worked by imported African slaves.
1795–1802 and 1804–16 Under British rule.
1863 Slavery abolished and indentured labourers were then brought in from China, India, and Java.
1915 Bauxite was discovered and gradually became the main export.
1954 Achieved internal self-government as Dutch Guiana.
1958–69 Politics dominated by Johan Pengel, charismatic leader of the mainly Creole Suriname National Party (NPS).
1975 Independence achieved, with Dr Johan Ferrier as president and Henck Arron (NPS) as prime minister; 40% of the population emigrated to the Netherlands.
1980 Arron's government overthrown in army coup; Ferrier refused to recognize military regime; appointed Dr Henk Chin A Sen of the Nationalist Republican Party (PNR) to lead civilian administration. Army replaced Ferrier with Dr Chin A Sen.
1982 Army, led by Lt Col Desi Bouterse, seized power, setting up a Revolutionary People's Front; economic aid from Netherlands and US cut off after opposition leaders, charged with plotting a coup, were executed.
1985 Ban on political activities lifted.
1986 Antigovernment rebels brought economic chaos to Suriname.
1988 Ramsewak Shankar of the combined opposition parties elected president under new constitution.
1989 Bouterse rejected peace accord reached by President Shankar with guerrilla insurgents, the Bush Negro (descendents of escaped slaves) maroons, and vowed to continue fighting.
1990 Shankar deposed in army coup engineered by Bouterse.
1991 Johan Kraag (NPS) became interim president. New Front opposition alliance won assembly majority. Ronald Venetiaan elected civilian president.
1992 Peace accord reached with guerrilla groups.
1996 General election result inconclusive.

in *The Magic Flute*; later roles included *Lucia di Lammermoor*, Donna Anna in *Don Giovanni*, and Desdemona in *Otello*. She retired from the stage 1990.

sūtra in Buddhism, discourse attributed to the historical Buddha. In Hinduism, the term generally describes any sayings that contain moral instruction.

suttee Hindu custom whereby a widow committed suicide by joining her husband's funeral pyre, often under public and family pressure. Banned in the 17th century by the Mogul emperors, the custom continued even after it was made illegal under British rule 1829. There continue to be sporadic revivals.

Sutton outer borough of S Greater London
features probably a Saxon settlement in 6th and 7th centuries; site of Nonsuch Palace, built by Henry VIII, demolished in the 17th century; parish church of St Nicholas, rebuilt 1862; All Saints Church (1865); one of the first nursery schools in England, founded 1909; central library, opened 1975, one of the finest local libraries in Europe; large shopping mall, St Nicholas Centre, 1991
population (1991) 164,300
history Sutton expanded in the mid-19th century, after construction of a railway line, and became an early commuter town. It has remained a residential area.

Sutton Hoo archaeological site in Suffolk, England, where in 1939 a Saxon ship burial was excavated. It may be the funeral monument of Raedwald, King of the East Angles, who died about 624 or 625. The jewellery, armour, and weapons discovered were placed in the British Museum, London. ▷ *See feature on pp. 200–201.*

Suu Kyi Aung San 1945– . Myanmar (Burmese) politician and human-rights campaigner, leader of the National League for Democracy (NLD), the main opposition to the military junta. Despite Suu Kyi being placed under house arrest 1989, the NLD won the 1990 elections, although the junta refused to surrender power. She was awarded the Nobel Prize for Peace 1991. Finally released from house arrest 1995, she was banned from resuming any leadership post within the NLD by the junta. She is the daughter of former Burmese premier ◊Aung San.

Suva capital and industrial port of Fiji Islands, on Viti Levu; population (1986) 69,700. It produces soap and coconut oil.

Suzhou or ***Soochow*** (formerly 1912–49 ***Wuhsien***) city S of the Yangtze river delta and E of the ◊Grand Canal, in Jiangsu province, China; population (1990) 706,000. It has embroidery and jade-carving traditions and Shizilin and Zhuozheng gardens. The city dates from about 1000 BC, and the name Suzhou from the 7th century AD; it was reputedly visited by the Venetian Marco ◊Polo.

Suzman Helen Gavronsky 1917– . South African politician and human-rights activist. A university lecturer concerned about the inhumanity of the apartheid system, she joined the white opposition to the ruling National Party and became a strong advocate of racial equality, respected by black communities inside and outside South Africa. In 1978 she received the United Nations Human Rights Award.

Svalbard Norwegian archipelago in the Arctic Ocean. The main island is Spitsbergen; other islands include North East Land, Edge Island, Barents Island, and Prince Charles Foreland.
area 62,000 sq km/23,938 sq mi
towns Longyearbyen on Spitsbergen
features weather and research stations; wildlife includes walrus and polar bear; fossil palms show that it was in the tropics 40 million years ago
industries coal, phosphates, asbestos, iron ore, and galena – all mined by Russia, Kazakhstan, and Norway
population (1995 est) 3,000; 62% Russian, 36% Norwegian
history under the Svalbard Treaty 1925, Norway has sovereignty, but allows free scientific and economic access to others.

Svedberg Theodor 1884–1971. Swedish chemist. In 1924 he constructed the first ultracentrifuge, a machine that allowed the rapid separation of particles by mass. This can reveal the presence of contaminants in a sample of a new protein, or distinguish between various long-chain polymers. Nobel Prize for Chemistry 1926.

Sverdlovsk former name (1924–91) of the Russian town of Ekaterinburg.

Svetambara ('white-clad') sect of Jain monks (see ◊Jainism) who wear white loincloths, as opposed to the Digambaras sect, which believes that total nudity is correct for the Jain monk.

Svevo Italo. Pen name of Ettore Schmitz 1861–1928. Italian novelist, encouraged by James Joyce. His work includes *As a Man Grows Older* 1898 and his comic masterpiece *Confessions of Zeno* 1923, one of the first novels to be based on Freudian analysis.

Swabia (German ***Schwaben***) historic region of SW Germany, an independent duchy in the Middle Ages. It includes Augsburg and Ulm and forms part of the *Länder* (states) of Baden-Württemberg, Bavaria, and Hessen.

Swahili (Arabic *sawahil* 'coasts') language belonging to the Bantu branch of the Niger-Congo family, widely used in east and central Africa. Swahili originated on the E African coast as a *lingua franca* used among traders, and contains many Arabic loan words. It is an official language in Kenya and Tanzania.

The name Swahili is also used for the group of African people using the language, especially those living in Zanzibar and adjoining coastal areas of Kenya and Tanzania. The Swahili are not an isolated people, but are part of a mixed coastal society engaged in fishing and trading.

swallow any bird of the family Hirundinidae of small, insect-eating birds in the order Passeriformes, with long, narrow wings, and deeply forked tails. Swallows feed while flying, capturing winged insects in the mouth, which is lined with bristles made viscid (sticky) by a salivary secretion.
species The common swallow *Hirundo rustica* has a dark blue back, brown head and throat, and pinkish breast. It winters in Africa and tropical Asia, and visits Europe April–Sept. It feeds in flight. Two broods a year are reared in nests of mud, hair, feathers, and straw, shaped like a half-saucer and built on ledges or the rafters of barns. Other species include the red-rumped swallow *Cecropsis daurica* of the eastern Mediterranean, and the ◊martins.

swamp region of low-lying land that is permanently saturated with water and usually overgrown with vegetation; for example, the everglades of Florida, USA. A swamp often occurs where a lake has filled up with sediment and plant material. The flat surface so formed means that runoff is slow, and the water table is always close to the surface. The high humus content of swamp soil means that good agricultural soil can be obtained by draining.

Surgery: from Trepanning to Transplant

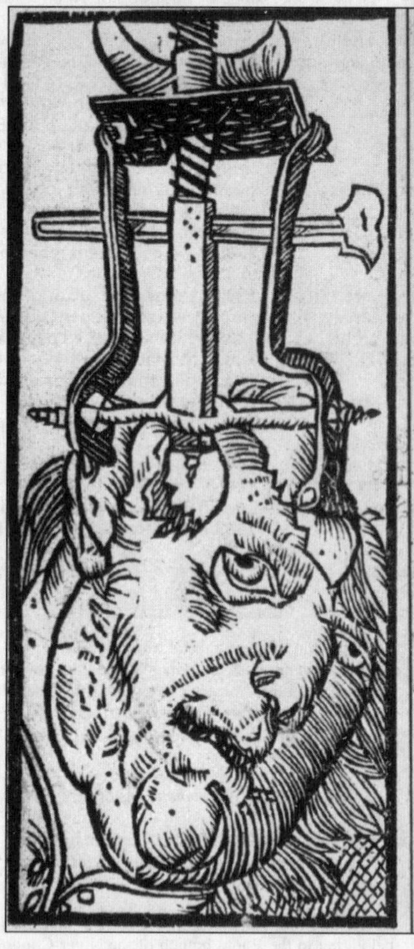
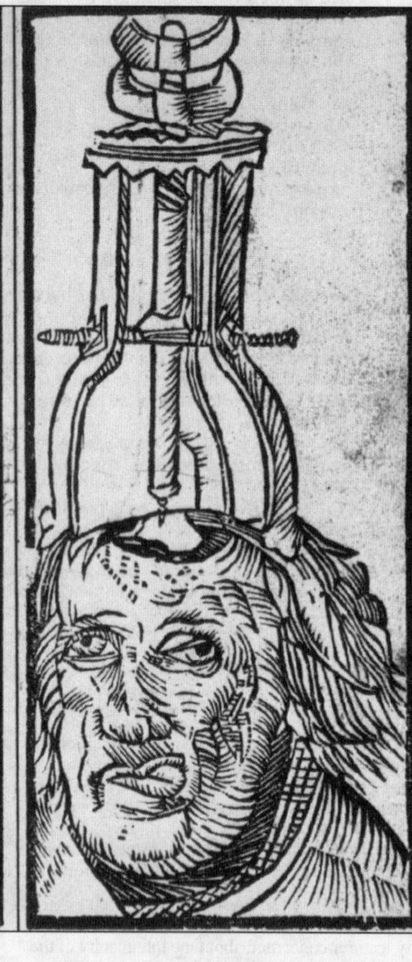

The cutting or drilling of a hole in the skull, known as trepanning, is a form of surgery that dates from Neolithic times – long before this 16th-century woodcut showing apparatus for the operation. *Corbis*

Surgery is one of the most ancient forms of healing. Archaeologists have found Palaeolithic trepanned skulls – the holes were presumably bored to let evil spirits escape – and many preliterate peoples developed fine skills in sewing wounds or setting fractured limbs. From Babylonian, Egyptian, and Greek times onwards, a repertoire of surgical interventions developed. These included bloodletting, lancing boils, dressing skin infections, pulling teeth, delivering babies in difficult labours, managing broken limbs, trussing ruptures, treating leg ulcers, patching up battle-wounds, and medicating venereal infections. Other medical traditions developed their own invasive procedures, notably acupuncture, used in China for a wide variety of therapeutic purposes and also to induce anaesthesia.

Surgeons vs. physicians

From Greek times traditional surgeons had to minister to a vast range of external conditions requiring routine maintenance through cleansing, pus removal, ointments, and bandaging. The conditions treated were mostly not life-threatening, and surgeons knew their limits. Nevertheless, surgeons were regarded as subordinate medical practitioners. Physicians were believed to be men of learning, employing their intellect to diagnose the causes of disease. Surgeons by contrast used their hands, not their heads; and the fact that their work involved the shedding of blood allowed them to be likened disdainfully to butchers.

Over the centuries surgery gradually acquired a higher reputation. In the 13th and 14th centuries distinguished treatises were written by two major figures in French surgery: Henri de Mondeville (born 1260), who was surgeon to the king of France, and Guy de Chauliac, whose *Grande Chirurgie* 1363 dominated the field for two centuries. Chauliac's work emphasized the importance of anatomical dissection in training surgeons, and he invented several surgical instruments.

Nevertheless the lower status of surgery was confirmed from medieval times when it became normal for physicians to acquire an academic education and a university degree. Surgeons, on the other hand, acquired their skills by mere apprenticeship, and often practised barbering as well as surgery. In England barbers and surgeons were linked in the same guild until the mid-18th century.

The battlefield as a school for surgeons

From the late Middle Ages, many surgeons learned or developed their skill in the army or the navy. Because warfare presented a vast number of different injuries, which often led to amputations, the battlefield was known as the 'school for surgery'. Not surprisingly, it was army surgeons who wrote the most influential accounts of such complications as hospital gangrene, tetanus, and erysipelas, while also making prominent contributions to debates about infection.

Increasing use of gunpowder changed the character of wounds. Lead bullets and other projectiles tore through flesh, shattered bones, and drove foreign matter deep into wounds. Infections became a major problem, giving rise to the belief, widespread until the 18th century, that some kind of 'gunpowder poison' entered the wound with the shot.

In the 16th century the Frenchman Ambroise Paré was the towering figure in the field of surgery. He had sections of the Paduan professor Vesalius' *De Fabrica Corporis Humani* 1543 translated into French as part of his *Anatomie Universelle du Corps Humain* 1561, in order to make anatomical study available to barber-surgeons who knew no Latin.

Paré was apprenticed to a barber-surgeon before seeing extensive military service. Many of the treatments described in his *Oeuvres* 1585 were developed as a result of his experience with battlefield wounds. The most important of these were the Paré ligature for tying off blood vessels, and his development of a substitute for the traditional hot-oil cauterization of open wounds. As related in his *Method of Treating Wounds* 1545, Paré concocted an ointment (or 'digestive') from egg yolk, rose-oil, and turpentine, which he applied to wounds. The mixture proved successful – wounds treated with Paré's digestive were less painful and generally remained uninflamed. Concluding that gunshot wounds did not automatically require cauterization – this should be reserved for gangrenous wounds or employed as a means of stopping bleeding in infected wounds – Paré abandoned the hot-oil treatment.

Later surgeons who gained their eminence from military experience included the Scotsman John Hunter (1728–1793) and Napoleon's chief surgeon, Dominique Jean Larrey (1776–1842).

Anaesthetics and antiseptics

The growing study of anatomy and dissection and the new importance of hospitals assisted the rise of surgery.

The English surgeon Joseph Lister. He developed antiseptic surgery by pioneering the use of carbolic spray to prevent sepsis. *Corbis*

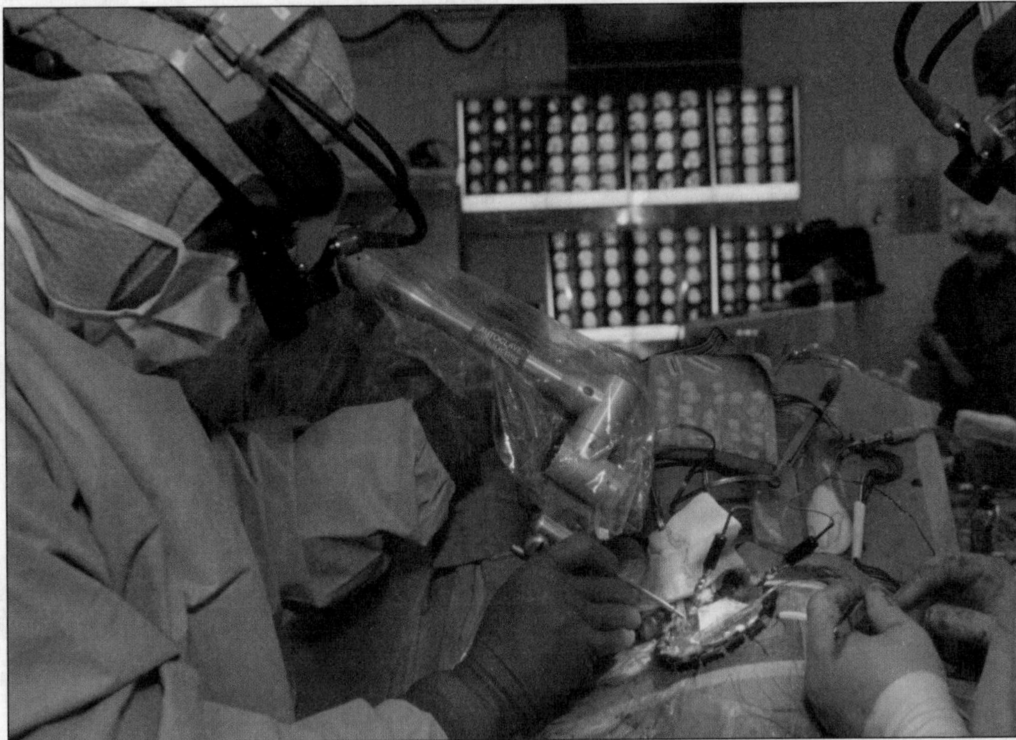

Instrument-guided brain surgery. The surgeons are using microscope viewers to carry out the operation. Monitors along the wall display images produced by the viewers. *Corbis*

However, genuine advances in surgical achievements stemmed from two 19th-century innovations: anaesthesia and antisepsis.

The anaesthetics ether and chloroform were introduced in the 1840s, and from then it became possible to perform what would otherwise have been unbearably painful internal operations. Within 20 years antiseptic techniques had been pioneered by Joseph Lister in Glasgow. Until this time, the second overwhelming obstacle to internal surgery had been infection. Operative wounds had generally led to septicaemia or gangrene, and certain death. Drawing on Louis Pasteur's demonstration that micro-organisms caused disease, Lister showed that rigorous cleanliness, combined with the use of antiseptic chemicals like carbolic acid, prevented infection. For the first time the operating theatre could be made safe.

Major internal surgery and transplants

As a consequence, surgery made more progress during the next half-century than it had during the previous 2,000 years. Operations became possible for the first time on the internal organs – the stomach, liver, kidneys, and later the lungs and heart. The celebrated German surgeon Theodor Billroth (1829–94) was a pioneer, performing the first total larynx removal for cancer, pioneering abdominal surgery, and developing surgery for many forms of cancer, especially cancer of the breast. In the United States, William Halsted devised the operation known as radical mastectomy, in which the breast, all the lymph glands in the nearest armpit, and the muscles of the chest wall were removed – it remained the most frequently used treatment for breast cancer for many years.

Appendectomies became more common from the 1880s; in 1901, the British king Edward VII was operated on when his appendix caused trouble just before his coronation. Removal of gallstones became common, and cholecystectomy, the removal of the gall bladder itself, was introduced in 1882. Urological surgery developed, especially prostate operations. In such advances diagnosis was helped by the introduction of X-rays in 1896.

The use of lasers for surgery is increasing, since they enable surgeons to operate without making incisions. They also reduce blood loss during and after surgery, since they seal blood vessels. *Corbis*

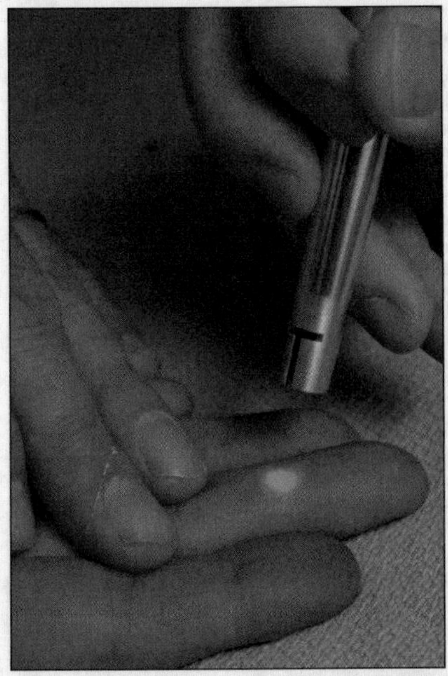

Open-heart surgery became practicable from around 1950, and more spectacular still was the pioneering of transplants. The first kidney transplant was accomplished in 1954 and, thanks to the introduction of immunosuppressives, success rates improved, permitting the first heart transplant, performed by Christiaan Barnard (1922–   ) in Cape Town, South Africa, in December 1967. Nowadays, tens of thousands of organ transplants are performed every year, and multiple organ transplants are becoming more common.

Ethics and technological wonders

From 1978 scientific breakthroughs and surgical skills combined to make test-tube babies possible, leading to various forms of surrogate pregnancy. Such developments have also, however, prompted ethical debate on issues such as the buying and selling of organs, and philosophico-legal questions of identity and personality (for example if it became possible to perform a brain transplant).

Despite these issues, surgery continues to advance in countless uncontroversial ways, aided by new diagnostic technology such as CAT scanners, developed in 1972 by Godfrey Newbold Hounsfield, which can provide detailed images of internal organs without the need for exploratory surgery. Lasers, or 'optical knives', have proved valuable in eye surgery and also in internal surgery, where they can be aimed from within the body, thanks to endoscopy, which permits the examination of internal organs via a tube equipped with lenses and a light. Keyhole surgery, which does not require the body to be cut open as in conventional surgery, results in more rapid recovery rates; hip-replacement operations spare elderly people pain and disability. After many years as a lesser department of medicine, at the end of the 20th century surgery can claim to be on the leading-edge of medical advance.

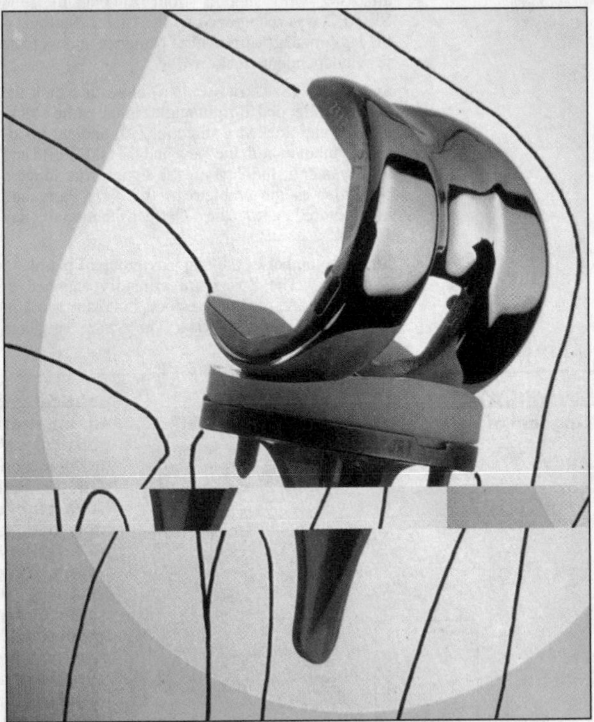

Prosthetic-artificial knee joint. The most common prosthetic implant surgery performed is hip replacement in post-menopausal women. However, a major problem with artificial joints is that over a long period they can become loosened, and must be replaced by further surgery. This is due to inflammation and consequent slow destruction of the bone around the implanted joint. *Image Select (UK) Ltd*

Roy Porter

SEE ALSO
anaesthetic; keyhole surgery; laser surgery; Paré, Ambroise; transplant

swan any of several large, long-necked, aquatic, web-footed birds, genus *Cygnus*, family Anatidae, order Anseriformes, which also includes ducks and geese. Swans are either white or black in colour, and are among the largest birds that can fly. The base of the bill is fleshy and naked, and the sexes are similar in plumage. Pairing is generally for life, and the young (cygnets) are at first grey, later brownish.

The mute swan *Cygnus olor* is up to 150 cm/5 ft long, has white plumage, an orange bill with a black knob surmounting it, and black legs; the voice is a harsh hiss. The young of the smaller Polish swan, a subspecies, are white.

It is wild in eastern Europe, and semi-domesticated in the west. Other species include the whooper *C. cygnus* of N Europe and Asia, and Bewick's swan *C. bewicki*, both rare in Britain. The North American trumpeter swan *C. buccinator* is the largest, with a wingspan of 2.4 m/8 ft. This species was nearly extinct by 1900, and although numbers have recovered, it is still endangered.

In England the swan is a royal bird, since it was once highly valued as food.

Swansea (Welsh ***Abertawe***) port at the mouth of the river Tawe where it meets the Bristol Channel, created a unitary authority of Wales 1996 (*see United Kingdom map*); population (1991) 181,900. It is the second-largest city in Wales. It has oil refineries, chemicals, metallurgical industries, tin plate manufacturing, and produces stained glass (since 1936). It is the vehicle-licensing centre of the UK.

SWAPO (***South West Africa People's Organization***) organization formed 1959 in South West Africa (now ◊Namibia) to oppose South African rule. SWAPO guerrillas, led by Sam Nujoma, began attacking with support from Angola. In 1966 SWAPO was recognized by the United Nations as the legitimate government of Namibia, and won the first independent election 1989.

swastika (Sanskrit *svastika*) cross in which the bars are extended at right angles in the same clockwise or anticlockwise direction. An ancient good-luck symbol in both the New and the Old World and an Aryan and Buddhist mystic sign, it was adopted by Hitler as the emblem of the Nazi Party and incorporated into the German national flag 1935–45.

Swazi member of the majority group of people in Swaziland. The Swazi are primarily engaged in cultivating and raising livestock, but many work in industries in South Africa. The Swazi language belongs to the Bantu branch of the Niger-Congo family.

Swazi kingdom S African kingdom, established by Sobhuza I (died 1839), and named after his successor Mswati (ruled 1840–75). The kingdom was established by Sobhuza as a result of the ◊Mfecane disturbances.

Swaziland country in SE Africa, bounded E by Mozambique and SE, S, W, and N by South Africa. *See country box below.*

sweat gland ◊gland within the skin of mammals that produces surface perspiration. In primates, sweat glands are distributed over the whole body, but in most other mammals they are more localized; for example, in cats and dogs, they are restricted to the feet and around the face.

In humans, sweat glands occur in larger numbers in the male than the female and the odours produced are thought to be used in communicating sexual and social messages.

sweatshop workshop or factory where employees work long hours under substandard conditions for low wages. Exploitation of labour in this way is associated with unscrupulous employers, who often employ illegal immigrants or children in their labour force.

swede annual or biennial plant *Brassica napus*, widely cultivated for its edible root, which is purple, white, or yellow. It is similar in taste to the turnip *B. rapa* but is of greater food value, firmer fleshed, and longer keeping. The yellow variety is commonly known as rutabaga.

Sweden country in N Europe, bounded W by Norway, NE by Finland and the Gulf of Bothnia, SE by the Baltic Sea, and SW by the Kattegat. *See country box opposite.*

Swedenborg Emanuel, (born Svedberg) 1688–1772. Swedish mystic and scientist. In *Divine Love and Wisdom* 1763, he concluded that the Last Judgement had taken place in 1757, and that the New Church, of which he was the prophet, had now been inaugurated. His writings are the scriptures of the sect popularly known as Swedenborgians, and his works are kept in circulation by the Swedenborg Society, London.

As assessor to the Swedish Royal College of Mines, Swedenborg carried out research that anticipated many later discoveries in the fields of engineering, navigation, and astronomy. In *Opera Philosophica et Mineralia/Philosophical and Logical Works* 1734, he attempted to explain the natural world as having a spiritual foundation. From 1744 he devoted himself exclusively to religious speculation, claiming access to God via the angels, and formulating a 'doctrine of correspondence' whereby all things in the material world have spiritual counterparts. This doctrine resembled neo-Platonism and influenced the Romantics, notably William Blake, and the French theorists of Symbolism.

Swedish architecture style of building in Sweden.

medieval The Romanesque cathedrals of Uppsala (brick) and Lund (stone) are from the 11th century. Gothic churches include Riddarholms church in Stockholm and the cathedral in Linköping.

The former Hanseatic city of Visby, Gotland, has three Gothic churches and the ruins of 12 more; some medieval domestic buildings have also survived there within the old city wall.

16th century This was a time for building and rebuilding castles under German Renaissance influence. Examples are Gripsholm, Vadstena, and Kalmar.

17th century Three architects emerged who had studied Baroque in Rome: Jean de la Vallée (1620–1696), Nicodemus Tessin the Elder (1615–1681), and his son Nicodemus Tessin the Younger (1654–1728). Together or separately they created several important buildings in Stockholm and elsewhere; for example, Drottningholm Palace, begun 1662.

18th century Rococo prevailed in the midcentury and left its traces mostly in interiors; for example, the Royal Palace in Stockholm by the younger Tessin.

early 19th century Neo-Classical architecture includes what is now the State Historical Museum, Stockholm.

late 19th–early 20th century The Jugend style, exemplified by the Royal Dramatic Theatre, Stockholm, gave way to a domestic nationalist style with simple lines, built in brick and granite, used in many public and residential buildings.

mid–late 20th century Modernism took off in Sweden in the 1930s.

Swedish language member of the Germanic branch of the Indo-European language family, spoken in Sweden and Finland and closely related to Danish and Norwegian.

sweet cicely plant *Myrrhis odorata* of the carrot family Umbelliferae, native to S Europe; the root is eaten as a vegetable, and the aniseed-flavoured leaves are used in salads.

SWAZILAND
Kingdom of

Mbabane
SWAZILAND
INDIAN OCEAN
ATLANTIC OCEAN
Mozambique
South Africa
0 mi 500
0 km 1000

national name *Umbuso weSwatini*
area 17,400 sq km/6,716 sq mi
capital Mbabane
major towns/cities Manzini, Big Bend, Mhlume
physical features central valley; mountains in W (Highveld); plateau in E (Lowveld and Lubombo plateau)
head of state King Mswati III from 1986
head of government Barnabas Sibusiso Dlamini from 1997
political system transitional absolute monarchy
administrative divisions four regions
political parties Imbokodvo National Movement (INM), nationalist monarchist; Swaziland United Front (SUF), left of centre; Swaziland Progresssive Party (SPP), left of centre; People's United Democratic Movement, left of centre
population 881,000 (1996 est)
population growth rate 2.8% (1990–95); 2.6% (2000–05)
ethnic distribution about 90% indigenous African, comprising the Swazi, Zulu, Tonga, and Shangaan peoples; there are European and Afro-European (Eurafrican) minorities numbering around 22,000
life expectancy 53 (men), 60 (women)
literacy rate 72%
languages Swazi, English (both official)
religions Christian, animist
currency lilangeni
GDP (US $) 1.2 billion (1997 est)
growth rate −3.0% (1994)
exports sugar, canned fruit, wood pulp, asbestos

HISTORY
late 16th C King Ngwane II crossed Lubombo mountains from the E and settled in SE Swaziland; his successors established a strong centralized Swazi kingdom, dominating the long-settled Nguni and Sothi peoples.
mid-19th C Swazi nation was ruled by the warrior King Mswati who, at the height of his power, controlled an area three times the size of the present-day state.
1882 Gold was discovered in the NW, attracting European fortune hunters, who coerced Swazi rulers into granting land concessions.
1894 Came under joint rule of Britain and the Boer republic of Transvaal.
1903 Following the South African War, Swaziland became a special British protectorate, or High Commission territory, against South Africa's wishes.
1922 King Sobhuza II succeeded to the Swazi throne.
1968 Independence achieved within the Commonwealth, as the Kingdom of Swaziland, with King (or Ngwenyama) Sobhuza II as head of state.
1973 The king suspended the constitution, banned political activity, and assumed absolute powers after the opposition deputies had been elected to parliament.
1977 King announced substitution of traditional tribal communities (*tinkhundla*) for the parliamentary system, arguing it was more suited to Swazi values.
1982 King Sobhuza died; his place was taken by one of his wives, Queen Dzeliwe, until his son, Prince Makhosetive, reached the age of 21.
1983 Queen Dzeliwe ousted by a younger wife, Queen Ntombi, as real power passed to the prime minister, Prince Bhekimpi Dlamini.
1984 After royal power struggle, it was announced that the crown prince would become king at 18.
1986 Crown prince formally invested as King Mswati III.
1993 Direct elections of *tinkhundla* candidates held for the first time; Prince Jameson Mbilini Dlamini appointed premier.
1996 Dlamini dismissed without a successor being named.
1997 Barnabas Sibusiso Dlamini appointed prime minister.

SWEDEN
Kingdom of

national name *Konungariket Sverige*
area 450,000 sq km/173,745 sq mi
capital and port Stockholm
major towns/cities Uppsala, Norrköping, Västeraòs, Linköping, Orebro
major ports Helsingborg, Malmö, Göteborg
physical features mountains in W; plains in S; thickly forested; more than 20,000 islands off the Stockholm coast; lakes, including Vänern, Vättern, Mälaren, and Hjälmaren
head of state King Carl XVI Gustaf from 1973
head of government Goran Persson from 1996
political system constitutional monarchy
administrative divisions 24 counties
political parties Christian Democratic Community Party (KdS), Christian, centrist; Left Party (Vp), European, Marxist; Social Democratic Labour Party (SAP), moderate, left of centre; Moderate Party (M), right of centre; Liberal Party (Fp), centre-left; Centre Party (C), centrist; Ecology Party (MpG), ecological; New Democracy (NG), right-wing, populist
armed forces 64,000 (1995)
conscription 7–15 months (army and navy); 8–12 months (air force)
defence spend (% GDP) 2.5 (1994)
education spend (% GNP) 8.3 (1992)
health spend (% GDP) 6.2 (1993)
death penalty abolished 1972
population 8,780,000 (1995 est)
population growth rate 0.5% (1990–95); 0.3% (2000–05)
age distribution (% of total population) <15 19.0%, 15–65 63.7%, >65 17.3% (1995)
ethnic distribution predominantly of Teutonic descent, with small minories of Saami (Lapps), Finns, and Germans
population density (per sq km) 19 (1994)
urban population (% of total) 83 (1995)
labour force 54% of population: 4% agriculture, 30% industry, 66% services (1990)
unemployment 7.7% (1995)
child mortality rate (under 5, per 1,000 live births) 6 (1993)
life expectancy 75 (men), 81 (women)
education (compulsory years) 9
literacy rate 99%
languages Swedish; there are Finnish-and Saami-speaking minorities
religion Evangelical Lutheran (established national church)
TV sets (per 1,000 people) 469 (1992)
currency Swedish krona
GDP (US $) 229.1 billion (1995)
GDP per capita (PPP) (US $) 18,201 (1995)
growth rate 3.0% (1994/95)
average annual inflation 3.6% (1995)
major trading partners Germany, UK, Norway, USA, Denmark, France
resources iron ore, uranium, copper, lead, zinc, silver, hydroelectric power, forests
industries motor vehicles, foodstuffs, machinery, precision equipment, iron and steel, metal products, wood products, chemicals, shipbuilding, electrical goods
exports forestry products (wood, pulp, and paper), machinery, motor vehicles, power-generating non-electrical machinery, chemicals, iron and steel. Principal market: Germany 14.4% (1993)
imports machinery and transport equipment, chemicals, mineral fuels and lubricants, textiles, clothing, footwear, food and live animals. Principal source: Germany 17.9% (1993)
arable land 6.2% (1993)
agricultural products barley, wheat, oats, potatoes, sugar beet, tame hay, oil seed; livestock and dairy products

HISTORY

8th C Kingdom of the Svear, based near Uppsala, extended its rule across much of southern Sweden.
9th–11th Cs Swedish Vikings raided and settled along the rivers of Russia.
c. 1000 Olaf Skötkonung, king of the Svear, adopted Christianity and united much of Sweden (except the S and W coasts, which remained Danish until the 17th century).
11th–13th Cs Sweden existed as an isolated kingdom under the Stenkil, Sverker, and Folkung dynasties; a series of crusades incorporated Finland.
1397 Union of Kalmar: Sweden, Denmark, and Norway united under a single monarch; Sweden effectively ruled by a succession of regents.
1448 Breach with Denmark: Sweden alone elected Charles VIII as king.
1523 Gustavus Vasa, leader of insurgents, became king of fully independent Sweden.
1527 Swedish Reformation: Gustavus confiscated church property and encouraged Lutherans.
1544 Swedish crown became hereditary in House of Vasa.
1592–1604 Sigismund Vasa, a Catholic, was king of both Sweden and Poland until ousted from the Swedish throne by his Lutheran uncle Charles IX.
17th C Sweden, a great military power under Gustavus Adolphus 1611–32, Charles X 1654–60, and Charles XI 1660–97, fought lengthy wars with Denmark, Russia, Poland, and the Holy Roman Empire.
1709 Battle of Poltava: Russians inflicted major defeat on Swedes under Charles XII.
1720 Limited monarchy established; political power passed to *Riksdag* (parliament) dominated by nobles.
1721 Great Northern War ended with Sweden losing nearly all its conquests of the previous century.
1741–43 Sweden defeated in disastrous war with Russia; further conflict 1788–90.
1771–92 Gustavus III increased royal power and introduced wide-ranging reforms; assassinated at a masked ball.
1809 Russian invaders annexed Finland; Swedish nobles staged coup and restored powers of Riksdag.
1810 Napoleonic marshal, Jean-Baptiste Bernadotte, elected crown prince of Sweden, as Charles XIII had no heir.
1812 Bernadotte allied Sweden with Russia against France.
1814 Treaty of Kiel: Sweden obtained Norway from Denmark.
1818–44 Bernadotte reigned in Sweden as Charles XIV John.
1846 Free enterprise established by abolition of trade guilds and monopolies.
1866 Series of liberal reforms culminated in new two-chambered *Riksdag* dominated by bureaucrats and farmers.
late 19th C Development of large-scale forestry and iron-ore industry; neutrality adopted in foreign affairs.
1905 Union with Norway dissolved.
1907 Adoption of proportional representation and universal suffrage.
1920s Economic boom transformed Sweden from an agricultural to an industrial economy.
1932 Social Democrat government of Per Halbin Hansson introduced radical public works programme to combat trade slump.
1940–43 Under duress, neutral Sweden permitted limited transit of German forces through its territory.
1946–69 Social Democrat government of Tage Erlander developed comprehensive welfare state.
1959 Sweden joined the European Free Trade Association.
1969–76 Olaf Palme, head of Social Democratic Party, prime minister.
1971 Constitution amended to create single-chamber Riksdag.
1975 Remaining constitutional powers of monarch removed.
1976–82 Centre-right government of Thorbjörn Fälldin ended 44 years of Social Democrat dominance.
1982 Palme regained premiership; assassinated 1986.
1995 Sweden became a member of the European Union.
1996 Goran Persson replaced Ingvar Carlsson as prime minister.

SEE ALSO Denmark; Finland; Norway; Viking

sweetener any chemical that gives sweetness to food. Caloric sweeteners are various forms of ◊sugar; noncaloric, or artificial, sweeteners are used by dieters and diabetics and provide neither energy nor bulk. Questions have been raised about the long-term health effects from several artificial sweeteners.

Sweeteners are used to make highly processed foods attractive, whether sweet or savoury. Most of the noncaloric sweeteners do not have E numbers. Some are banned for baby foods and for young children: thaumatin, aspartame, acesulfame-K, sorbitol, and mannitol. Cyclamate is banned in the UK and the USA; acesulfame-K is banned in the USA.

sweet pea plant of the ◊pea family.

sweet potato tropical American plant *Ipomoea batatas* of the morning-glory family Convolvulaceae; the white-orange tuberous root is used as a source of starch and alcohol and eaten as a vegetable.

sweet william biennial to perennial plant *Dianthus barbatus* of the pink family Caryophyllaceae, native to S Europe. It is grown for its fragrant red, white, and pink flowers. *See illustration on following page.*

Sweyn I King of Denmark from about 986, nicknamed 'Forkbeard'. He raided England, finally conquered it in 1013, and styled himself king, but his early death led to the return of ◊Ethelred II.

swift fast-flying, short-legged bird of the family Apodidae, order Apodiformes, of which there are about 75 species, found largely in the tropics. They are 9–23 cm/4–11 in long, with brown or grey plumage, long, pointed wings, and usually a forked tail. They are capable of flying 110 kph/70 mph.

The nests of the grey-rumped swiftlet *Collocalia francica* of Borneo consist almost entirely of solidified saliva, and are harvested for bird's-nest soup. The increasing removal of nests for commercial purposes is endangering the birds.

The common swift. *Apus apus* is about 16.5 cm/6.5 in long, dark brown with a small greyish white patch under the chin, long swept-back wings, and migrates to Europe in summer from Africa. It catches insects on the wing, and rarely perches except at the nest, even sleeping on the wing high in the air. Swifts often make colonies of nests on buildings, sticking the nest material together with saliva. They lay two or three large white eggs.

Swift Jonathan 1667–1745. Irish satirist and Anglican cleric. He wrote ◊*Gulliver's Travels* 1726, an allegory describing travel to lands inhabited by giants, miniature people, and intelligent horses. Other works include *The Tale of a Tub* 1704, attacking corruption in religion and learning; contributions to the Tory paper *The Examiner*, of which he was editor 1710–11; the satirical pamphlet *A Modest Proposal* 1729, which suggested that children of the poor should be eaten; and many essays and pamphlets.

Swift, born in Dublin, became secretary to the diplomat William Temple (1628–1699) at Moor Park, Surrey, where his friendship with the child 'Stella' (Hester Johnson 1681–1728) began 1689. Returning to Ireland, he was ordained in the Church of England 1694, and in 1699 was made a prebendary of St Patrick's, Dublin. In 1710 he became a Tory pamphleteer, and obtained the deanery of St Patrick 1713.

> *'Few are qualified to shine in company; but it is in most men's power to be agreeable.'*
>
> **JONATHAN SWIFT**
> *Thoughts on Various Subjects*

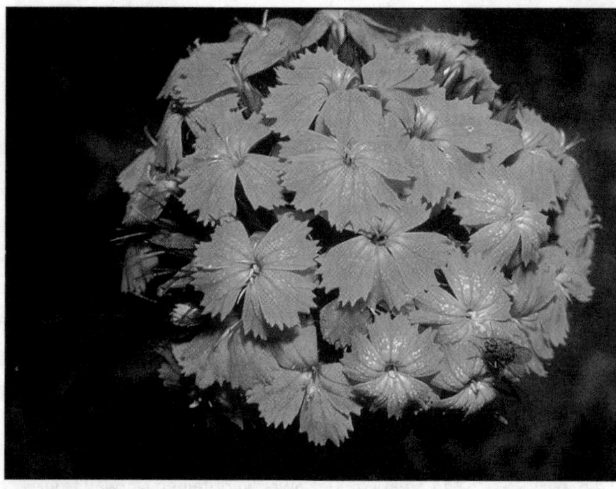

sweet william The crowded heads of bright pink flowers are typical of the wild sweet william, although cultivated varieties are often red, purple, or white. The long-tubed flowers are visited by butterflies and hawk moths. *Premaphotos Wildlife*

His *Journal to Stella* is a series of letters, 1710–13, in which he described his life in London. 'Stella' remained the love of his life, but 'Vanessa' (Esther Vanhomrigh 1690–1723), a Dublin woman who had fallen in love with him, jealously wrote to her rival 1723 and so shattered his relationship with both women. From about 1738 his mind began to fail.

swim bladder thin-walled, air-filled sac found between the gut and the spine in bony fishes. Air enters the bladder from the gut or from surrounding capillaries (see ◊capillary), and changes of air pressure within the bladder maintain buoyancy whatever the water depth.

In evolutionary terms, the swim bladder of higher fishes is a derivative of the lungs present in all primitive fishes (not just lungfishes).

❝We thank with brief thanksgiving / Whatever gods may be / That no man lives forever, / That dead men rise up never; / That even the weariest river / Winds somewhere safe to sea.❞

ALGERNON CHARLES SWINBURNE
Garden of Proserpine

swimming self-propulsion of the body through water. There are four strokes in competitive swimming: freestyle, breaststroke, backstroke, and butterfly. Distances of races vary between 50 and 1,500 m. Olympic-size pools are 50 m/55 yd long and have eight lanes. Swimming has been included in the Olympic Games since 1896 for men and 1912 for women. The world championships were introduced in 1973, later held in 1975 and 1978 and every four years since.

Swimming has been known since ancient times, in the training of Greek and Roman warriors. Competitive swimming is known to have taken place in Japan 36 BC, and became compulsory in schools there in 1603. Fear of infection prevented Europeans from swimming during the Middle Ages.

The freestyle stroke (also known as front crawl) is the fastest stroke. It was developed by Australians from a South Sea island technique in the early 20th century. The breaststroke is the slowest of the four strokes and was developed in the 16th century. The backstroke was developed in the 1920s and, because the swimmer's head is out of the water, makes breathing easier. The newest and second fastest of the strokes is the butterfly, developed in the USA in the 1930s from the breaststroke. In races the swimmers enter the water with a 'racing plunge' (a form of dive) with the exception of the backstroke, when competitors start in the water.

Swift Despite the cynical tone of much of his writing, Jonathan Swift had a genuine concern for humanity, and wrote pamphlets campaigning for the rights of the Irish people under English rule. With Alexander Pope and others, he formed the Scriblerus Club, which produced satirical writings intended to combat pedantry. *Corbis*

Synchronized swimming is a form of 'ballet' performed in and under water. Underwater swimming developed with the invention of such equipment as flippers, snorkel, and self-contained underwater breathing apparatus (scuba). It was introduced into the Olympic swimming programme in 1984. See also ◊diving.

Swinburne Algernon Charles 1837–1909. English poet. He attracted attention with the choruses of his Greek-style tragedy *Atalanta in Calydon* 1865, but he and ◊Rossetti were attacked 1871 as leaders of 'the fleshly school of poetry', and the revolutionary politics of *Songs before Sunrise* 1871 alienated others.

Swindon town 124 km/77 mi W of London, created a unitary authority of England 1997 (*see United Kingdom map*); population (1995) 152,600. The site of a major railway engineering works 1841–1986 on the Great Western Railway, the town has diversified since 1950 into heavy engineering, electronics, electrical manufacture, and cars (Honda). Swindon Rail Works Ltd specializes in repair work for steam railway preservation societies. There is a railway museum. The White Horse of Uffington is nearby.

swine vesicular disease virus disease (porcine enterovirus) closely resembling foot and mouth disease, and communicable to humans. It may have originated in the infection of pigs by a virus that causes flulike symptoms in people.

Known in Italy and Hong Kong, swine vesicular disease first occurred in Britain in 1972, and a slaughter policy was pursued.

swing music jazz style popular in the 1930s–40s, a big-band dance music with a simple harmonic base of varying tempo from the rhythm section (percussion, guitar, piano), harmonic brass and woodwind sections (sometimes strings), and superimposed solo melodic line from, for example, trumpet, clarinet, or saxophone. Exponents included Benny Goodman, Duke Ellington, and Glenn Miller, who introduced jazz to a mass white audience.

swing wing correctly ***variable-geometry wing*** aircraft wing that can be moved during flight to provide a suitable configuration for either low-speed or high-speed flight. The British engineer Barnes Wallis (1887–1979) developed the idea of the swing wing, first used on the US-built Northrop X-4, and since used in several aircraft, including the US F-111, F-114, and the B-1, the European Tornado, and several Soviet-built aircraft.

These craft have their wings projecting nearly at right angles for takeoff and landing and low-speed flight, and swung back for high-speed flight.

Swiss cheese plant common name for ◊monstera, a plant of the arum family.

Swithun, St or ***Swithin*** c. 800–c. 862. English priest, chancellor of King Ethelwolf and bishop of Winchester from 852. According to legend, the weather on his feast day (15 July) is said to continue as either wet or fine for 40 days.

Switzerland landlocked country in W Europe, bounded N by Germany, E by Austria and Liechtenstein, S by Italy, and W by France. *See country box on p. 1030.*

swordfish marine bony fish *Xiphias gladius*, the only member of its family (Xiphiidae), characterized by a long swordlike beak protruding from the upper jaw. It may reach 4.5 m/15 ft in length and weigh 450 kg/1,000 lb.

sycamore tree *Acer pseudoplatanus* native to Europe. The leaves are five-lobed, and the hanging racemes of flowers are followed by winged fruits. The timber is used for furniture making.

The sycamore was introduced to Britain by the 16th century. It is a rapidly growing and tenacious tree that displaces other trees in woodland. In the USA, plane trees are called sycamores.

Sydenham Thomas 1624–1689. English physician, the first person to describe measles and to recommend the use of quinine for relieving symptoms of malaria. His original reputation as the 'English Hippocrates' rested upon his belief that careful observation is more useful than speculation. His *Observationes medicae* was published in 1676.

sycamore The sycamore is a maple native to S Europe but widely distributed elsewhere. The leaves are five-lobed and the fruits have wings.

Sydney capital and port of New South Wales, Australia; population (1993) 3,713,500. Industries include engineering, oil refining, electronics, scientific equipment, chemicals, clothing, and furniture. It is a financial centre, and has three universities. The 19th-century Museum of Applied Arts and Sciences is the most popular museum in Australia. It has been chosen as the site of the 2000 Olympic Games.

Originally a British penal colony 1788, Sydney developed rapidly following the discovery of gold in the surrounding area. The main streets still follow the lines of the original wagon tracks, and the Regency Bligh House survives. Modern landmarks are the harbor bridge (single span 503.5 m/1,652 ft) 1932, Opera House 1973, and Centre Point Tower 1980.

syenite grey, crystalline, plutonic (intrusive) ◊igneous rock, consisting of feldspar and hornblende; other minerals may also be present, including small amounts of quartz.

Syktyvkar capital of the autonomous republic of Komi, N central Russia; population (1994) 227,000. Industries include timber, paper, and tanning. It was founded 1740 as a Russian colony.

syllogism set of philosophical statements devised by Aristotle in his work on logic. It establishes the conditions under which a valid conclusion follows or does not follow by deduction from given premises. The following is an example of a valid syllogism: 'All men are mortal, Socrates is a man, therefore Socrates is mortal.'

symbiosis any close relationship between two organisms of different species, and one where both partners benefit from the association. A well-known example is the pollination relationship between insects and flowers, where the insects feed on nectar and carry pollen from one flower to another. This is sometimes known as ◊mutualism.

Symbiosis in a broader sense includes ◊commensalism, ◊parasitism, and inquilinism (one animal living in the home of another and sharing its food).

symbol in general, something that stands for something else. A symbol may be an aesthetic device or a sign used to convey information visually, thus saving time, eliminating language barriers, or overcoming illiteracy.

Symbols are used in art, mathematics, music, and literature; for practical use in science and medicine; for road signs; and as warnings – for example, a skull and crossbones to indicate dangerous contents.

symbolic interactionism sociological method, founded by the US pragmatist George Mead, that studies the behaviour of individuals and small groups through observation and description, viewing people's appearance, gestures, and language as symbols they use to interact with others in social situations. In contrast to theories such as Marxism or functionalism that attempt to analyse society as a whole through economic or political systems, it takes a perspective of society from within, as created by people themselves.

Symbolism in the arts, the use of symbols as a device for concentrating or intensifying meaning. In particular, the term is used for a late 19th-century movement in French poetry, associated with Paul Verlaine, Stéphane Mallarmé, and Arthur Rimbaud, who used words for their symbolic rather than concrete meaning.

Symbolism late 19th-century movement in French poetry, which inspired a similar trend in French painting. The Symbolist poets used words for their symbolic rather than concrete meaning. Leading exponents were Paul Verlaine, Stéphane Mallarmé, and Arthur Rimbaud. The Symbolist painters rejected realism and Impressionism, seeking to express moods and psychological states through colour, line, and form. Their subjects were often mythological, mystical, or fantastic. Gustave Moreau was a leading Symbolist painter. Others included Puvis de Chavannes and Odilon Redon in France, Arnold Böcklin in Switzerland, and Edward Burne-Jones in Britain.

Gauguin and his disciples of Pont-Aven give the clearest pictorial interpretation of what was described as an 'ideational, synthetic, subjective, decorative' aim. Thus local colour was once more emphasized, given an emotional value of suggestion, and substituted for the Impressionist effects of light. Decided black outlines stressed the decorative and symbolic character of such a work as Gauguin's *Le Christ Jaune*.

symmetry exact likeness in shape about a given line (axis), point, or plane. A figure has symmetry if one half can be rotated and/or reflected onto the other. (Symmetry preserves length, angle, but not necessarily orientation.) In a wider sense, symmetry exits if a change in the system leaves the essential features of the system unchanged; for example, reversing the sign of electric charges does not change the electrical behaviour of an arrangement of charges.

symphony abstract musical composition for orchestra, traditionally in four separate but closely related movements. It developed from the smaller ◊sonata form, the Italian ◊overture, and the concerto grosso (a composition for a small ensemble featuring a solo instrumental group playing in opposition to an accompanying group).

Haydn established the mature form of the symphony, written in slow, minuet, and allegro movements. Mozart and Beethoven (who replaced the ◊minuet with the ◊scherzo) expanded the form, which has since been modified and dramatized as quasi programme music by Brahms, Tchaikovsky, Bruckner, Dvořák, Mahler, Sibelius, Vaughan Williams, Walter Piston, Prokofiev, Carl Nielsen, Shostakovich, Stravinsky, and Aaron Copland.

synagogue in Judaism, a place of worship, also (in the USA) called a temple. As an institution it dates from the destruction of the Temple in Jerusalem AD 70, though it had been developing from the time of the Babylonian exile as a substitute for the Temple. In antiquity it was a public meeting hall where the Torah was also read, but today it is used primarily for prayer and services. A service requires a quorum (*minyan*) of ten adult Jewish men.

In addition to the ark (the sacred ornamented enclosure that holds the Torah scrolls), the synagogue contains a raised platform (*bimah*) from which the service is conducted, with pews or seats for the high priests. The rest of the congregation sits or stands facing it. Two tablets above the ark are inscribed with the Ten Commandments. In Orthodox synagogues women sit apart from the men.

synapse junction between two ◊nerve cells, or between a nerve cell and a muscle (a neuromuscular junction), across which a nerve impulse is transmitted. The two cells are separated by a narrow gap called the synaptic cleft. The gap is bridged by a chemical ◊neurotransmitter, released by the nerve impulse.

The threadlike extension, or ◊axon, of the transmitting nerve cell has a slightly swollen terminal point, the synaptic knob. This forms one half of the synaptic junction and houses membrane-bound vesicles, which contain a chemical neurotransmitter. When nerve impulses reach the knob, the vesicles release the transmitter and this flows across the gap and binds itself to special receptors on the receiving cell's membrane. If the receiving cell is a nerve cell, the other half of the synaptic junction will be one or more extensions called ◊dendrites; these will be stimulated by the neurotransmitter to set up an impulse, which will then be conducted along the length of the nerve cell and on to its own axons. If the receiving cell is a muscle cell, it will be stimulated by the neurotransmitter to contract.

Synapsida group of mammal-like reptiles living 315–195 million years ago, whose fossil record is largely complete, and who were for a while the dominant land animals, before being replaced by the dinosaurs. The true mammals are their descendants.

synchrotron particle ◊accelerator in which particles move, at increasing speed, around a hollow ring. The particles are guided around the ring by electromagnets, and accelerated by electric fields at points around the ring. Synchrotrons come in a wide range of sizes, the smallest being about a metre across while the largest is 27 km across. The Tevatron synchrotron at ◊Fermilab is some 6 km in circumference and accelerates protons and antiprotons to 1 TeV.

syncline geological term for a fold in the rocks of the Earth's crust in which the layers or beds dip inwards, thus forming a trough-like structure with a sag in the middle. The opposite structure, with the beds arching upwards, is an ◊anticline.

syndicalism (French *syndicat* 'trade union') political movement in 19th-century Europe that rejected parliamentary activity in favour of direct action, culminating in a revolutionary general strike to secure worker ownership and control of industry. After 1918 syndicalism was absorbed in communism, although it continued to have an independent existence in Spain until the late 1930s.

The idea originated under Robert ◊Owen's influence in the 1830s, acquired its name and its more violent aspects in France from the philosopher Georges Sorel (1847–1922), and also reached the USA (see ◊Industrial Workers of the World).

Synge J(ohn) M(illington) 1871–1909. Irish dramatist. He was a leading figure in the Irish dramatic revival of the early 20th century. His six plays reflect the speech patterns of the Aran Islands and W Ireland. They include *In the Shadow of the Glen* 1903, *Riders to the Sea* 1904, and *The Playboy of the Western World* 1907, which caused riots at the Abbey Theatre, Dublin, when first performed.

Synge Richard Laurence Millington 1914–1994. British biochemist who improved paper ◊chromatography (a means of separating mixtures) to the point where individual amino acids could be identified. He developed the technique, known as partition chromatography, with his colleague Archer Martin (1910–) 1944. They shared the 1952 Nobel Prize for Chemistry.

swing wing USAF 509th Bomber wing FB-111A Bomber aircraft with swing wings. Swing wings allow an aircraft to take off with wings extended at right angles to the fuselage providing the necessary lift. Once airborne the pilot can swing the wings so that they are parallel to the aircraft permitting ballistic flight. *US Airforce/ Image Select (UK) Ltd*

synodic period the time taken for a planet or moon to return to the same position in its orbit as seen from the Earth; that is, from one ◊opposition to the next. It differs from the ◊sidereal period because the Earth is moving in orbit around the Sun.

synovial fluid viscous colourless fluid that bathes movable joints between the bones of vertebrates. It nourishes and lubricates the ◊cartilage at the end of each bone.

Synovial fluid is secreted by a membrane, the synovium, that links movably jointed bones. The same kind of fluid is found in bursae, the membranous sacs that buffer some joints, such as in the shoulder and hip region.

synovitis inflammation of the membranous lining of a joint, or of a tendon sheath, caused by injury or infection.

syntax the structure of language; the ways in which words are ordered and combined to convey meaning. Syntax applies principally to grammar, and a grammatically correct sentence is also syntactically correct, but syntax has a wider significance.

synthetic any material made from chemicals. Since the 1900s, more and more of the materials used in everyday life are synthetics, including plastics (polythene, polystyrene), synthetic fibres (nylon, acrylics, polyesters), synthetic resins, and synthetic rubber. Most naturally occurring organic substances are now made synthetically, especially pharmaceuticals.

symbiosis These green tree ants *Oecophylla smaragdina* in Australia will fiercely defend the *Narathura* species butterfly larva, of the Lycaenidae family. In return, the ants feed on a sugary secretion exuded from a gland on the caterpillar's back. *Premaphotos Wildlife*

SWITZERLAND
Swiss Confederation

national name German *Schweiz*, French *Suisse*, Romansch *Svizra*
area 41,300 sq km/15,946 sq mi
capital Bern (Berne)
major towns/cities Zürich, Geneva, Lausanne
major ports river port Basel (on the Rhine)
physical features most mountainous country in Europe (Alps and Jura mountains); highest peak Dufourspitze 4,634 m/15,203 ft in Apennines
head of state and government Ruth Dreifuss from 1999
government federal democratic republic
administrative divisions 20 cantons and six demi-cantons
political parties Radical Democratic Party (FDP/PRD), radical, centre-left; Social Democratic Party (SP/PS), moderate, left of centre; Christian Democratic People's Party (CVP/PDC), Christian, moderate, centrist; Swiss People's Party (SVP/UDC), centre-left; Liberal Party (LPS/PLS), federalist, right of centre; Green Party (GPS/PES), ecological
armed forces 625,000 (on mobilization; 1994)
conscription 17 weeks' recruit training, followed by refresher training of varying length according to age
defence spend (% GDP) 1.6 (1994)
education spend (% GNP) 5.2 (1992)
health spend (% GDP) 6.8 (1993)
death penalty abolished 1992
population 7,202,000 (1995 est)
population growth rate 1.1% (1990–95); 0.5% (2000–05)
age distribution (% of total population) <15 17.7%, 15–65 68.1%, >65 14.2% (1995)
ethnic distribution majority of Alpine descent; sizeable Nordic element
population density (per sq km) 173 (1994)
urban population (% of total) 61 (1995)
labour force 53% of population: 6% agriculture, 35% industry, 60% services (1990)
unemployment 4.2% (1995)
child mortality rate (under 5, per 1,000 live births) 8 (1993)
life expectancy 75 (men), 81 (women)
education (compulsory years) 8–9 (depending on canton)
literacy rate 99%
languages German 64%, French 19%, Italian 8%, Romansch 0.6% (all official)
religions Roman Catholic 50%, Protestant 48%
TV sets (per 1,000 people) 407 (1992)
currency Swiss franc
GDP (US $) 303.9 billion (1995)
GDP per capita (PPP) (US $) 24,432 (1995)
growth rate 0.7% (1994/95)
average annual inflation 0.9% (1994); 3.7% (1984–94)
major trading partners EU (principally Germany, France, Italy, and UK), USA, Japan
resources salt, hydroelectric power, forest
industries heavy engineering, machinery, precision engineering (clocks and watches), jewellery, textiles, chocolate, dairy products, cigarettes, footwear, wine, international finance and insurance services, tourism
exports machinery and equipment, pharmaceutical and chemical products, foodstuffs, precision instruments, clocks and watches, metal products. Principal market: Germany 22.9% (1993)
imports machinery, motor vehicles, agricultural and forestry products, construction material, fuels and lubricants, chemicals, textiles and clothing. Principal source: Germany 32.6% (1993)
arable land 9.6% (1993)
agricultural products sugar beet, potatoes, wheat, apples, pears, tobacco, grapes; livestock and dairy products, notably cheese

HISTORY
58 BC Celtic Helvetii tribe submitted to Roman authority after defeat by Julius Caesar.
4th C AD Region overrun by Germanic tribes, Burgundians, and Alemannians.
7th C Formed part of Frankish kingdom and embraced Christianity.
9th C Included in Charlemagne's Holy Roman Empire.
12th C Many autonomous feudal holdings developed as power of Holy Roman Empire declined.
13th C Habsburgs became dominant as overlords of eastern Switzerland.
1291 Cantons of Schwyz, Uri, and Lower Unterwalden formed Everlasting League, a loose confederation to resist Habsburg control.
1315 Battle of Morgarten: Swiss Confederation defeated Habsburgs.
14th C Luzern, Zürich, Basel, and other cantons joined Swiss Confederation, which became independent of Habsburgs.
1523–29 Zürich, Bern, and Basel accepted the Reformation but rural cantons remained Roman Catholic.
1648 Treaty of Westphalia recognized Swiss independence from Holy Roman Empire.
1798 French invasion established Helvetic Republic, a puppet state with centralized government.
1803 Napoleon's Act of Mediation restored considerable autonomy to cantons.
1814 End of French domination; Switzerland reverted to loose confederation of sovereign cantons with a weak federal parliament.
1815 Great Powers recognized 'Perpetual Neutrality' of Switzerland.
1845 Seven Catholic cantons founded Sonderbund league to resist any strengthening of central government by Liberals.
1847 Federal troops defeated Sonderbund in brief civil war.
1848 New constitution introduced greater centralization; Bern chosen as capital.
1874 Powers of federal government increased; principle of referendum introduced.
late 19th C Development of industry, railways, and tourism led to growing prosperity.
1920 League of Nations selected Geneva as its headquarters.
1923 Switzerland formed customs union with Liechtenstein.
1960 Joined European Free Trade Association (EFTA).
1971 Women gained right to vote in federal elections.
1986 Referendum rejected proposal for membership of United Nations (UN).
1992 Closer ties with European Community (EC) rejected in national referendum.
1999 Ruth Dreifuss elected as president, the first woman to hold this office.

'There is a feeling of incredible age here, an easy country over which armies have marched since the first days of mankind.'

On SYRIA
Freya Stark, letter
31 May 1937

Plastics are made mainly from petroleum chemicals by ◊polymerization, in which small molecules are joined to make very large ones.

syphilis sexually transmitted disease caused by the spiral-shaped bacterium (spirochete) *Treponema pallidum*. Untreated, it runs its course in three stages over many years, often starting with a painless hard sore, or chancre, developing within a month on the area of infection (usually the genitals). The second stage, months later, is a rash with arthritis, hepatitis, and/or meningitis. The third stage, years later, leads eventually to paralysis, blindness, insanity, and death. The Wassermann test is a diagnostic blood test for syphilis.

With widespread availability of antibiotics, syphilis is now increasingly cured in the industrialized world, at least to the extent that the final stage of the disease is rare. The risk remains that the disease may go undiagnosed or that it may be transmitted by a pregnant woman to her fetus.

Syracuse (Italian ***Siracusa***) industrial port (chemicals, salt) in E Sicily; population (1992) 126,800. It has a cathedral and remains of temples, aqueducts, catacombs, and an amphitheatre. Founded 734 BC by the Corinthians, it became a centre of Greek culture under the elder and younger ◊Dionysius. After a three-year siege it was taken by Rome 212 BC. In AD 878 it was destroyed by the Arabs, and the rebuilt town came under Norman rule in the 11th century.

Syria country in W Asia, on the Mediterranean Sea, bounded N by Turkey, E by Iraq, S by Jordan, and SW by Israel and Lebanon. *See country box opposite.*

Syriac language ancient Semitic language, originally the Aramaic dialect spoken in and around Edessa (now in Turkey) and widely used in W Asia from about 700 BC to AD 700. From the 3rd to 7th centuries it was a Christian liturgical and literary language.

syringa common, but incorrect, name for the ◊mock orange *Philadelphus*. The genus *Syringa* includes ◊lilac *S. vulgaris*, and is not related to mock orange.

syrinx the voice-producing organ of a bird. It is situated where the trachea divides in two and consists of vibrating membranes, a reverberating capsule, and numerous controlling muscles.

systems analysis in computing, the investigation of a business activity or clerical procedure, with a view to deciding if and how it can be computerized. The analyst discusses the existing procedures with the people involved, observes the flow of data through the business, and draws up an outline specification of the required computer system. The next step is systems design.

Szechwan alternative spelling for the central Chinese province of ◊Sichuan.

Szent-Györgyi Albert von Nagyrapolt 1893–1986. Hungarian-born US biochemist who isolated vitamin C and B_2, and studied the chemistry of muscular activity. He was awarded the Nobel Prize for Physiology or Medicine 1937.

In 1928 Szent-Györgyi isolated a substance from the adrenal glands that he named hexuronic acid; he also found it in oranges and paprika, and in 1932 proved it to be vitamin C.

SYRIA
Syrian Arab Republic

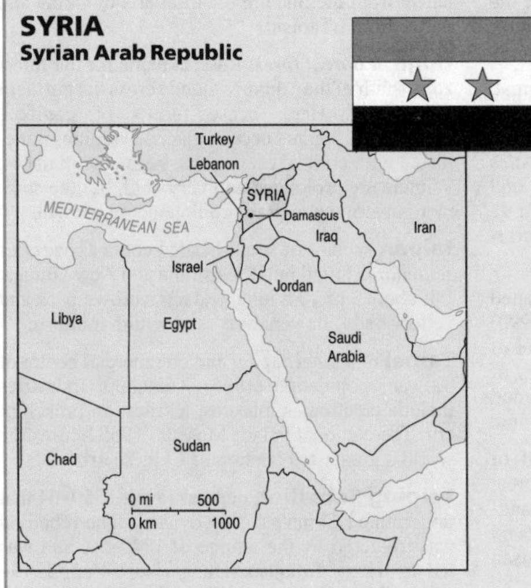

national name *al-Jamhuriya al-Arabya as-Suriya*
area 185,200 sq km/71,506 sq mi
capital Damascus
major towns/cities Aleppo, Homs, Hama
major ports Latakia
physical features mountains alternate with fertile plains and desert areas; Euphrates River
head of state Hafez al-Assad from 1971
head of government Hafez al-Assad from 1971
political system socialist republic
administrative divisions 14 administrative districts
political parties National Progressive Front (NPF), pro-Arab, socialist coalition, including the Communist Party of Syria, the Arab Socialist Party, the Arab Socialist Unionist Party, the Syrian Arab Socialist Union Party, the Ba'ath Arab Socialist Party
armed forces 363,000; reserve forces 400,000; paramiltary forces 8,000 (1995)
conscription 30 months
defence spend (% GDP) 8.6 (1994)
education spend (% GNP) 4.2 (1992)
health spend (% GDP) 0.4 (1990)
death penalty retained and used for ordinary crimes
population 14,661,000 (1995 est)
population growth rate 3.4% (1990–95); 3.2% (2000–05)
age distribution (% of total population) <15 47.3%, 15–65 49.9%, >65 2.8% (1995)
ethnic distribution predominantly Arab, with many differences in language and regional affiliations
population density (per sq km) 77 (1994)
urban population (% of total) 52 (1995)
labour force 28% of population: 33% agriculture, 24% industry, 43% services (1990)
unemployment n.a.
child mortality rate (under 5, per 1,000 live births) 38 (1994)
life expectancy 65 (men), 69 (women)
education (compulsory years) 6
literacy rate 78% (men), 51% (women)
languages Arabic 89% (official), Kurdish 6%, Armenian 3%
religions Sunni Muslim 90%; other Islamic sects, Christian
TV sets (per 1,000 people) 61 (1992)
currency Syrian pound
GDP (US $) 21.93 billion (1994)
GDP per capita (PPP) (US $) 1,496 (1994)
growth rate 5.5% (1994)
average annual inflation 20% (1994); 18.8% (1980–93)
major trading partners Germany, Italy, France, Lebanon, Japan, UK, Romania, Belgium
resources petroleum, natural gas, iron ore, phosphates, salt, gypsum, sodium chloride, bitumen
industries petroleum and petroleum products, coal, rubber and plastic products, textiles, clothing, leather products, tobacco, processed food
exports crude petroleum, textiles, vegetables, fruit, raw cotton, natural phosphate. Principal market: Italy 30.8% (1993)
imports crude petroleum, wheat, base metals, metal products, foodstuffs, machinery, motor vehicles. Principal source: Germany 10.2% (1993)
arable land 27.6% (1993)
agricultural products cotton, wheat, barley, maize, olives, lentils, sugar beet, fruit, vegetables; livestock, principally sheep and goats

HISTORY
c.1750 BC Syria became part of the Babylonian Empire; during the next millennium it was successively conquered by Hittites, Assyrians, Chaldeans, and Persians.
333 BC Alexander the Great of Macedonia conquered Persia and Syria.
301 BC Seleucus I, one of the generals of Alexander the Great, founded kingdom of Syria, which the Seleucid dynasty ruled for over 200 years.
64 BC Syria became part of Roman Empire.
4th C AD After division of Roman Empire, Syria came under Byzantine rule.
634 Arabs conquered most of Syria and introduced Islam.
661–750 Damascus was capital of Muslim Empire.
1055 Seljuk Turks overran Syria.
1095–99 First Crusade established Latin states on Syrian coast.
13th C Mameluke sultans of Egypt took control.
1516 Ottoman Turks conquered Syria.
1831 Egyptians led by Mehemet Ali drove out Turks.
1840 Turkish rule restored; Syria opened up to European trade.
late 19th C French firms built ports, roads, and railways in Syria.
1916 Sykes-Picot Agreement: secret Anglo-French deal to partition Turkish Empire allotted Syria to France.
1918 British expelled Turks with help of Arab revolt.
1919 Syrian national congress called for independence under Emir Faisal and opposed transfer to French rule.
1920 Syria became a League of Nations protectorate, administered by France.
1925 People's Party founded to campaign for independence and national unity; insurrection by Druse religious sect against French control.
1936 France promised independence within three years, but martial law imposed 1939.
1941 British forces ousted Vichy French regime in Damascus and occupied Syria in conjunction with Free French.
1944 Syrian independence proclaimed but French military resisted transfer of power.
1946 Syria achieved effective independence when French forces withdrew.
1948–49 Arab-Israeli War: Syria joined unsuccessful invasion of newly independent Israel.
1958 Syria and Egypt merged to form United Arab Republic (UAR).
1959 USSR agreed to give financial and technical aid to Syria.
1961 Syria seceded from UAR.
1964 Ba'ath Socialist Party established military dictatorship.
1967 Six-Day War: Syria lost Golan Heights to Israel.
1970–71 Syria invaded Jordan in support of Palestinian guerrillas.
1970 Hafez al-Assad staged coup; elected president 1971.
1973 Yom Kippur War: Syrian attack on Israel repulsed.
1976 Start of Syrian military intervention in Lebanese civil war.
1978 Syria opposed peace deal between Egypt and Israel.
1986 Britain broke off diplomatic relations, accusing Syria of involvement in international terrorism.
1990 Diplomatic links with Britain restored.
1991 Syria contributed troops to US-led coalition in Gulf War against Iraq. US Middle East peace plan approved by Assad.
1994 Israel offered partial withdrawal from Golan Heights in return for peace, but Syria remained sceptical.
1995 Security framework agreement with Israel.

SEE ALSO Assad, Hafez-al; Ba'ath Party; Druse

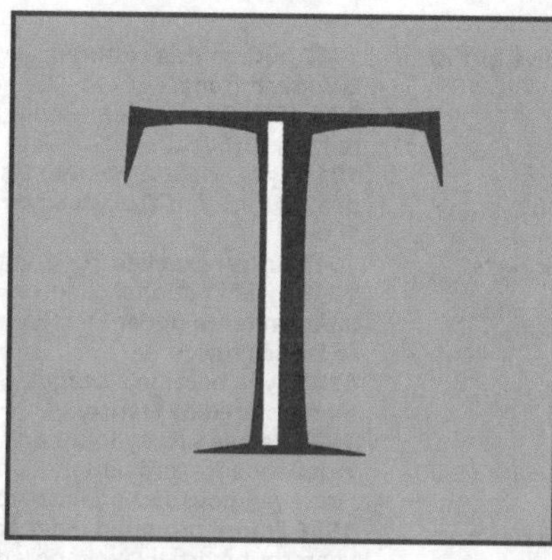

Table Bay wide bay on the north coast of the Cape of Good Hope, South Africa, on which Cape Town stands. It is overlooked by Table Mountain (highest point Maclear's Beacon 1,087 m/3,568 ft); the cloud that often hangs above it being known as the 'tablecloth'.

It is human nature to hate the man whom you have hurt.

TACITUS
Agricola

table tennis or ***ping pong*** indoor game played on a rectangular table by two or four players. It was developed in Britain about 1880 and derived from lawn tennis. World championships were first held 1926.

Play takes place on a table measuring 2.74 m/9 ft long by 1.52 m/5 ft wide. Across the middle is a 15.25-cm/6-in-high net over which the ball must be hit. The players use small, wooden paddles covered in sponge or rubber. A feature of the game is the amount of spin put on the small plastic ball. Volleying is not allowed. Points are scored by forcing the opponent(s) into an error. The first to score 21 wins the game. A match may consist of three or five games. In doubles play, the players must hit the ball in strict rotation.

taboo (Polynesian *tabu*, 'that contact would profane') prohibition applied to magical and religious objects. In psychology and the social sciences the term refers to practices that are generally prohibited because of religious or social pressures; for example, ◊incest is forbidden in most societies.

tabula rasa (Latin 'scraped tablet', from the Romans' use of wax-covered tablets which could be written on with a pointed stick and cleared by smoothing over the surface) a mind without any preconceived ideas.

Tachisme (French 'blotting, staining') French style of abstract painting current in the 1940s and 1950s, the European equivalent to ◊Abstract Expressionism. Breaking free from the restraints of ◊Cubism, the Tachistes adopted a novel, spontaneous approach to brushwork, typified by all-over blotches of impastoed colour and dribbled paint, or swirling calligraphy applied straight from the tube, as in the work of Georges Mathieu (1921–). The terms *L'Art Informel*, meaning gestural or ◊action painting, and *abstraction lyrique* ('lyrical abstraction') are also used to describe the style. Other prominent Tachistes were the German-born painters Hans Hartung (1904–1989) and A O Wolfgang Schulze Wols (1913–1951).

tachograph combined speedometer and clock that records a vehicle's speed (on a small card disc, magnetic disc, or tape) and the length of time the vehicle is moving or stationary. It is used to monitor a lorry driver's working hours.

takahe The takahe is a flightless member of the rail family, native to New Zealand. It lives in remote tussock grassland in mountain regions of SW South Island. Once thought to be extinct, the takahe's habitat is protected and numbers are gradually increasing – in 1995 there were approximately 180 birds.

Tacitus Publius Cornelius c. AD 56–c. 120. Roman historian. A public orator in Rome, he was consul under Nerva 97–98 and proconsul of Asia 112–113. He wrote histories of the Roman Empire, *Annales* and *Historiae*, covering the years AD 14–68 and 69–97 respectively. He wrote a *Life of Agricola* 97 (he married Agricola's daughter 77) and a description of the Germanic tribes, *Germania* 98.

Taegu third-largest city in South Korea, situated between Seoul and Pusan; population (1990) 2,228,800. Nearby is the Haeinsa Temple, one of the country's largest monasteries and repository of the *Triptaka Koreana*, a collection of 80,000 wood blocks on which the Buddhist scriptures are carved.

Taejon (Korean 'large rice paddy') capital of South Chungchong province, central South Korea; population (1990) 1,062,100. Korea's tallest standing Buddha and oldest wooden building are found NE of the city at Popchusa in the Mount Songnisan National Park.

tae kwon do Korean ◊martial art similar to ◊karate, which includes punching and kicking. It was included in the 1988 Olympic Games as a demonstration sport.

taffeta (Persian 'spun') light, plain-weave fabric with a high lustre, originally silk but today also manufactured from artificial fibres.

Taft William Howard 1857–1930. 27th president of the USA 1909–13, a Republican. He was secretary of war 1904–08 in Theodore Roosevelt's administration, but as president his conservatism provoked Roosevelt to stand against him in the 1912 election. Taft served as chief justice of the Supreme Court 1921–30.

Tagalog the majority ethnic group living around Manila on the island of Luzon, in the Philippines, who number about 10 million (1988). The Tagalog live by fishing and trading. In its standardized form, known as Pilipino, Tagalog is the official language of the Philippines, and belongs to the Western branch of the Austronesian family. The Tagalog religion is a mixture of animism, Christianity, and Islam.

tagging, electronic long-distance monitoring of the movements of people charged with or convicted of a crime, thus enabling them to be detained in their homes rather than in prison. They are fitted with a tamper-proof anklet, or tag, and their home with a special receiver-dialling unit. If the person moves out of the range of the unit, a signal is transmitted to a central computer. In the UK, legislation passed 1991 allowed for the use of electronic tagging as an aid to bail and as a means of enforcing punishment, for example a curfew.

Tagore Rabindranath 1861–1941. Bengali Indian writer. He translated into English his own verse *Gitanjali* ('song offerings') 1912 and his verse play *Chitra* 1896. An ardent nationalist and advocate of social reform, he resigned his knighthood as a gesture of protest against British repression in India. Nobel Prize for Literature 1913.

Tagus (Spanish ***Tajo***, Portuguese ***Tejo***) river rising in Aragon, Spain, and reaching the Atlantic Ocean at Lisbon, Portugal; length 1,007 km/626 mi.

Tahiti largest of the Society Islands, in ◊French Polynesia; area 1,042 sq km/402 sq mi; population (1988) 115,800. Its capital is Papeete. Tahiti was visited by Capt James ◊Cook 1769 and by Admiral ◊Bligh of the *Bounty* 1788. It came under French control 1843 and became a colony 1880. ▷*See feature on pp. 806–807.*

Tai member of any of the groups of SE Asian peoples who speak Tai languages, all of which belong to the Sino-Tibetan language family. There are over 60 million speakers, the majority of whom live in Thailand. Tai peoples are also found in SW China, NW Myanmar (Burma), Laos, and N Vietnam.

t'ai chi series of 108 complex, slow-motion movements, each named (for example, the White Crane Spreads Its Wings) and designed to ensure effective circulation of the *chi*, or intrinsic energy of the universe, through the mind and body. It derives partly from the Shaolin ◊martial arts of China and partly from ◊Taoism.

taiga or ***boreal forest*** Russian name for the forest zone south of the ◊tundra, found across the northern hemisphere. Here, dense forests of conifers, birches, and poplars occupy glaciated regions punctuated with cold lakes, streams, bogs, and marshes. Winters are prolonged and very cold, but the summer is warm enough to promote dense growth.

taipan species of small-headed cobra *Oxyuranus scutellatus* found in NE Australia and New Guinea. It is about 3 m/10 ft long, and has a brown back and yellow belly. Its venom is fatal within minutes.

Taipei or ***Taibei*** capital and commercial centre of Taiwan; population (1995) 2,639,300. Industries include electronics, plastics, textiles, and machinery. The National Palace Museum 1965 houses the world's greatest collection of Chinese art.

Taiping Rebellion popular revolt 1850–64 that undermined China's ◊Qing dynasty. The rebellion was triggered by the famine of 1849–50, and was led by Hong Xiuquan (Hung Hsui-ch'an, 1813–1864). By 1853 the rebels had secured control over much of the central and lower Chang Jiang valley region, taking Nanjing as their capital and instituting radical, populist land reforms. Civil war continued until 1864, when the Taipings, weakened by internal dissension, were overcome by the provincial Hunan army of ◊Zeng Guofan and the Ever-Victorious Army, led by American F T Ward and British soldier Charles ◊Gordon.

Taira or ***Heike*** in Japanese history, a military clan prominent in the 10th–12th centuries and dominant at court 1159–85. Their destruction by their rivals, the ◊Minamoto, 1185 is the subject of the 13th-century literary classic *Heike Monogatari/The Tale of the Heike*.

Taiwan country in E Asia, officially the Republic of China, occupying the island of Taiwan between the E China Sea and the S China Sea, separated from the coast of China by the Formosa Strait. *See country box opposite.*

Taiyuan capital of Shanxi province, on the river Fen He, NE China; population (1993) 1,680,000. Industries include iron, steel, agricultural machinery, and textiles. It is a walled city, founded in the 5th century AD, and is the seat of Shanxi University.

Taizé ecumenical Christian community based in the village of that name in SE France. Founded 1940 by Swiss theologian Roger Schutz (1915–), it has been a communal centre for young Christians since the 1960s.

Tajik or ***Tadzhik*** the majority ethnic group living in Tajikistan. Tajiks also live in Afghanistan and parts of Pakistan and W China. The Tajiki language belongs to the West Iranian subbranch of the Indo-European family, and is similar to Farsi; it is written in the Cyrillic script. The Tajiks have long been associated with neighbouring Turkic peoples and their language contains Altaic loan words. The majority of the Tajik people are Sunni Muslims.

Tajikistan formerly (to 1991) ***Tadzhikistan*** country in central Asia, bounded N by Kyrgyzstan and Uzbekistan, E by China, and S by Afghanistan and Pakistan. *See country box on p. 1034.*

Taj Mahal white marble mausoleum built 1630–53 on the river Jumna near Agra, India. Erected by Shah Jahan to the memory of his favourite wife, it is a celebrated example of Indo-Islamic architecture, the fusion of Muslim and Hindu styles. It took 20,000 workers to build the Taj Mahal, which has a central dome and minarets on each corner. Every façade is inlaid with semiprecious stones. Ransacked in the 18th century, it was restored in the early 20th century and is a symbol of India to the world.

takahe rare flightless bird *Porphyrio mantelli* of the rail family, order Gruiformes, native to New Zealand. It is about 60 cm/2 ft tall and weighs just over 2 kg/4.4 lb, with blue and green plumage and a red bill.

Talbot William Henry Fox 1800–1877. English pioneer of photography. He invented the paper-based ◊calotype process 1841, the first negative/positive method. Talbot made photograms (pictures produced on photographic material by exposing it to

TAIWAN
Republic of China

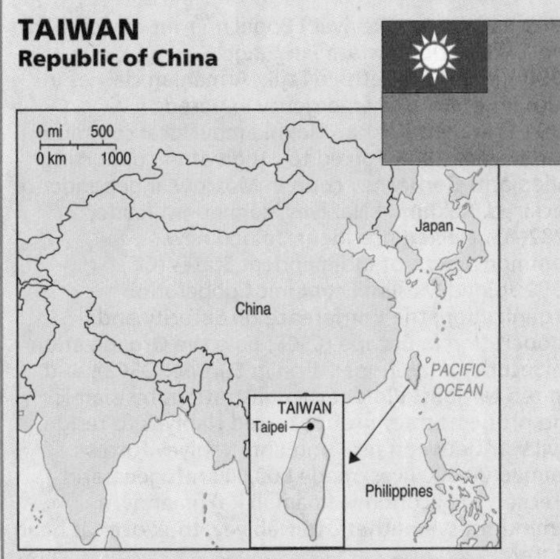

national name *Chung Hua Min Kuo*
area 36,179 sq km/13,965 sq mi
capital Taipei
major ports Kaohsiung, Keelung
physical features island (formerly Formosa) off People's Republic of China; mountainous, with lowlands in W; Penghu (Pescadores), Jinmen (Quemoy), Mazu (Matsu) islands
head of state Lee Teng-hui from 1988
head of government Vincent Siew from 1997
political system emergent democracy
administrative divisions two special municipalities, five municipalities, and 16 counties
political parties Nationalist Party of China (Kuomintang: KMT), anticommunist, Chinese nationalist; Democratic Progressive Party (DPP), centrist-pluralist, proself-determination grouping; Workers' Party (Kuntang), left of centre
population 21,465,900 (1996 est)
population growth rate 0.9% (1994)
ethnic distribution 98% Han Chinese and 2% aboriginal by descent; around 87% are Taiwan-born and 13% are 'mainlanders'
life expectancy 72 men, 77 women
literacy rate 91%
languages Mandarin Chinese (official); Taiwan, Hakka dialects
religions officially atheist; Taoist, Confucian, Buddhist, Christian
currency New Taiwan dollar
GDP (US $) 241.9 billion (1994)
growth rate 6.5% (1994)
exports textiles, steel, plastics, electronics, foodstuffs, metal goods, machinery, footwear, headwear, umbrellas, toys, games, sports equipment

HISTORY
7th C AD Island occupied by an aboriginal community of Malayan descent; the immigration of Chinese from the mainland began, but remained limited before the 15th century.
1517 Sighted by Portuguese vessels en route to Japan and named Ilha Formosa ('beautiful island').
1624 Occupied and controlled by Dutch.
1662 Dutch defeated by a Chinese Ming general, Cheng Ch'eng-kung (Koxinga), whose family came to rule Formosa for a short period.
1683 Annexed by China's rulers, the Manchu Qing.
1786 Major rebellion against Chinese rule.
1860 Ports opened to Western trade.
1895 Ceded 'in perpetuity' to Japan under Treaty of Shominoseki at end of Sino-Japanese war.
1945 Recovered by China's Kuomintang (spelt Guomindang in Thailand; Nationalist) government at the end of World War II.
1947 Rebellion against Chinese rule brutally suppressed.
1949 Flight of Nationalist government, led by Generalissimo Chiang Kai-shek, to Taiwan after Chinese communist revolution. They retained the designation of Republic of China (ROC), claiming to be the legitimate government for all China, and were recognized by the USA and United Nations (UN).
1950s onwards Rapid economic growth as Taiwan became a successful export-orientated Newly Industrializing Country (NIC) and land was redistributed from the gentry 'to-the-tiller'.
1954 US–Taiwanese mutual defence treaty.
1971 Expulsion from UN as USA adopted new policy of détente towards communist China.
1972 Commencement of legislature elections as programme of gradual democratization and Taiwanization launched by the mainlander-dominated Kuomintang.
1975 President Chiang Kai-shek died; replaced as Kuomintang leader by his son, Chiang Ching-kuo.
1979 USA severed diplomatic relations and annulled 1954 security pact.
1986 Centrist Democratic Progressive Party (DPP) formed as opposition to the nationalist Kuomintang.
1987 Martial law lifted; opposition parties legalized; press restrictions lifted.
1988 President Chiang Ching-kuo died; replaced by Taiwanese-born Lee Teng-hui.
1990 Chinese-born Kuomintang members became minority in parliament.
1991 President Lee Teng-hui declared end to civil war with China. Constitution amended. Kuomintang won landslide victory in elections to new National Assembly, the 'superparliament'.
1993 Cooperation pact with China signed.
1995 Ruling Kuomintang retained its majority in working assembly (Legislative Yuan) by a slim margin.
1996 Lee Teng-hui elected president in first-ever Chinese democratic election.
1997 Government narrowly survived no-confidence motion. Vincent Siew became prime minister.

SEE ALSO China; Guomindang; Sino-Japanese Wars

light, but without using a camera) several years before Louis Daguerre's invention was announced. In 1851 he made instantaneous photographs by electric light and in 1852 photo engravings. *The Pencil of Nature* 1844–46 by Talbot was the first book illustrated with photographs to be published.

talc $Mg_3Si_4O_{10}(OH)_2$, mineral, hydrous magnesium silicate. It occurs in tabular crystals, but the massive impure form, known as steatite or soapstone, is more common. It is formed by the alteration of magnesium compounds and is usually found in metamorphic rocks. Talc is very soft, ranked 1 on the Mohs' scale of hardness. It is used in powdered form in cosmetics, lubricants, and as an additive in paper manufacture.

Talibaan 'the Seekers', Afghan political and religious military force which seized control of southern and central Afghanistan, including the country's capital, Kabul, in September 1996. An Islamic regime was imposed, and by the end of 1996 the Talibaan controlled two-thirds of the country. In 1997 the Talibaan changed the country's official name to the Islamic Emirate of Afghanistan. The Talibaan receives financial support from Saudi Arabia, but the regime was, as of mid-1998, recognized by only three states: Saudi Arabia, the United Arab Emirates, and Pakistan.

The Talibaan was founded in 1994 by around 2,000 Pathan Sunni Muslim theology students based in madrassas (religious schools) near the Pakistan border. The force pledged to end the internecine conflict between the divergent Mujaheddin elements that had continued after the overthrow of communist leader Najibullah Ahmadzai in April 1992. The group also pledged to establish a united and patriarchal Islamic state and to eradicate the booming drugs trade. In April 1998 a temporary cease-fire was agreed and a promise was made of peace talks with the opposition United Islamic Front for Salvation of Afghanistan (UIPSA).

Afghanistan was the third country since 1979, after Iran and Sudan, to pass into the hands of an Islamic revivalist government.

Taliesin lived c. 550. Legendary Welsh poet, a bard at the court of the king of Rheged in Scotland. Taliesin allegedly died at Taliesin (named after him) in Dyfed, Wales.

Talking Heads US New Wave rock group formed 1975 in New York; disbanded 1991. Their nervy Minimalist music was inspired by African rhythms; albums include *More Songs About Buildings and Food* 1978, *Fear of Music* 1979, and *Naked* 1988. All band members also recorded separately.

Tallahassee (Cree Indian 'old town') capital of Florida, USA; an agricultural and lumbering centre; population (1992) 130,400. The Spanish explorer Hernando ◊de Soto founded an Indian settlement here 1539, and the site was chosen as the Florida territorial capital 1821. During the Civil War, Tallahassee was the only Confederate capital E of the Mississippi River not captured by Union troops.

Talleyrand-Périgord Charles Maurice de 1754–1838. French politician and diplomat. As bishop of Autun 1789–91 he supported moderate reform during the ◊French Revolution, was excommunicated by the pope, and fled to the USA during the Terror (persecution of anti-revolutionaries). He returned and became foreign minister under the Directory 1797–99 and under Napoleon 1799–1807. He represented France at the Congress of ◊Vienna 1814–15.

Tallinn (German ***Reval***) naval port and capital of Estonia; population (1995) 435,000. Industries include electrical and oil-drilling machinery,

Talbot 'A fruit piece', calotype by William Henry Fox Talbot, published in *The Pencil of Nature* 1844. An illustration from the first book with photographic illustrations ever published. *Corbis*

'He who has not lived during the years around 1789 does not know what is meant by the joy of living.'

Charles-Maurice de Talleyrand-Périgord
On the French Revolution, in M Guizot *Mémoires pour servir à l'histoire de mon temps*

TAJIKISTAN
Republic of

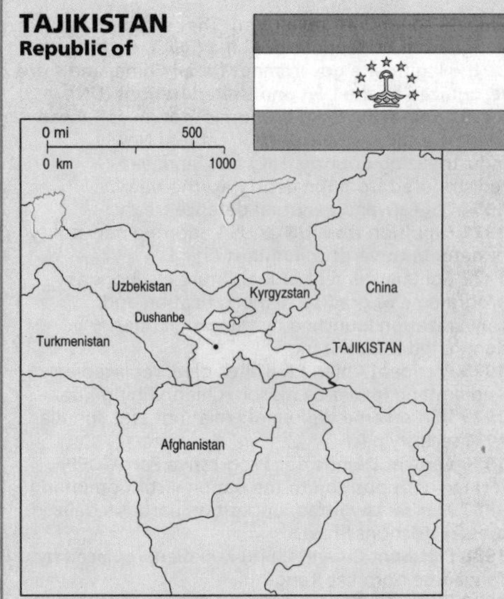

national name *Respublika i Tojikiston*
area 143,100 sq km/55,251 sq mi
capital Dushanbe
major towns/cities Khodzhent (formerly Leninabad), Kurgan-Tyube, Kulyab
physical features mountainous, more than half of its territory lying above 3,000 m/10,000 ft; huge mountain glaciers, which are the source of many rapid rivers
head of state Imamali Rakhmanov from 1994
head of government Yahya Azimov from 1996
political system authoritarian nationalist
administrative divisions 19 regions and the municipality of Dushanbe
political parties Communist Party of Tajikistan (CPT), pro-Rakhmanov; Democratic Party of Tajikistan (DP), anticommunist (banned from 1993); Party of Popular Unity and Justice, anticommunist
population 5,935,000 (1996 est)
population growth rate 2.9% (1990–95); 2.5% (2000–05)
ethnic distribution 62% ethnic Tajik, 24% Uzbek, 8% ethnic Russian, 1% Tatar, 1% Kyrgyz, and 1% Ukrainian
life expectancy 67 (men), 72 (women)
literacy rate 97%
language Tajik (official), similar to Farsi (Persian)
religion Sunni Muslim
currencies Tajik and Russian rouble
GDP (US $) 2.0 billion (1994)
growth rate −21.4% (1994)
exports fruit, cereals, cotton, cattle, sheep, silks, carpets, coal, lead, zinc, chemicals, oil, gas

HISTORY
c. 330 Formed an eastern part of the empire of Alexander the Great of Macedonia.
8th C Tajiks established as distinct ethnic group, with semi-independent territories under the tutelage of the Uzbeks, to the W; spread of Islam.
13th C Conquered by Genghis Khan and became part of Mongol Empire.
1860–1900 Northern Tajikistan came under tsarist Russian rule, while the S was annexed by Emirate of Bukhara, to the W.
1917–18 Attempts to establish Soviet control after the Bolshevik revolution in Russia resisted initially by armed guerrillas (basmachi).
1921 Became part of Turkestan Soviet Socialist Autonomous Republic.
1924 Tajik Autonomous Soviet Socialist Republic formed.
1929 Became a constituent republic of Soviet Union (USSR).
1930s Stalinist era of collectivization led to widespread repression of Tajiks.
1978 13,000 participated in anti-Russian riots.
late 1980s Resurgence in Tajik consciousness, stimulated by the *glasnost* initiative of Soviet leader Mikhail Gorbachev.
1989 Rastokhez ('Revival') Popular Front established and Tajik declared state language.
1990 Violent interethnic Tajik–Armenian clashes in Dushanbe; state of emergency imposed.
1991 President Kakhar Makhkamov, local communist leader since 1985, forced to resign after supporting failed anti-Gorbachev coup in Moscow. Independence declared. Rakhman Nabiyev, communist leader 1982–85, elected president. Joined new Commonwealth of Independent States (CIS).
1992 Joined Muslim Economic Cooperation Organization, the Conference on Security and Cooperation in Europe (CSCE; now the Organization on Security and Cooperation in Europe, OSCE), and United Nations. Violent demonstrations by Islamic and prodemocracy groups forced Nabiyev to resign. Civil war between pro- and anti-Nabiyev forces claimed 20,000 lives, made 600,000 refugees, and wrecked the economy. Imamali Rakhmanov, a communist sympathetic to Nabiyev, took over as head of state.
1993 Nabiyev and his militia ally, Sangak Safarov, died. Government forces regained control of most of the country. CIS peacekeeping forces drafted in to patrol border with Afghanistan, the base of pro-Islamic rebels.
1994 Cease-fire agreed. Rakhmanov popularly elected president under new constitution.
1995 Parliamentary elections won by Rakhmanov's supporters. Renewed fighting on Afghan border.
1996 Pro-Islamic rebels captured towns in SW. UN-sponsored ceasefire between government and rebels.
1997 Four-stage peace plan signed. President Rakhmanov seriously injured by grenade. Peace accord with Islamic rebel group, the United Tajik Opposition (UTO).
1998 Members of Islamic UTO appointed to government, as part of peace plan. Opposition fighters moved from mountains into UN-monitored camps.

SEE ALSO Russian Federation; Union of Soviet Socialist Republics

textiles, and paper. Founded 1219, it was a member of the ◊Hanseatic League; it passed to Sweden 1561 and to Russia 1750. Vyshgorod Castle (13th century) and other medieval buildings remain.

Tallis Thomas c. 1505–1585. English composer. He was a master of ◊counterpoint. His works include *Tallis's Canon* ('Glory to thee my God this night') 1567, the antiphonal *Spem in alium non habui* (about 1573) for 40 voices in various groupings, and a collection of 34 motets, *Cantiones sacrae*, 1575 (of which 16 are by Tallis and 18 by Byrd). In 1575 Elizabeth I granted Tallis and Byrd the monopoly for printing music and music paper in England.

Talmud the two most important works of post-Biblical Jewish literature. The Babylonian and the Palestinian (or Jerusalem) Talmud provide a compilation of ancient Jewish law and tradition. The Babylonian Talmud was edited at the end of the 5th century AD and is the more authoritative version for later Judaism; both Talmuds are written in a mix of Hebrew and Aramaic. They contain the commentary (*gemara*) on the ◊*Mishnah* (early rabbinical commentaries compiled about AD 200), and the material can be generally divided into *halakhah*, consisting of legal and ritual matters, and *aggadah* (or *haggadah*), concerned with ethical, theological, and folklorist matters.

Tamar river rising in N Cornwall, England, and flowing to Plymouth Sound; for most of its 97 km/60 mi length it forms the Devon–Cornwall border.

tamarind evergreen tropical tree *Tamarindus indica*, family Leguminosae, native to the Old World, with pinnate leaves and reddish-yellow flowers, followed by pods. The pulp surrounding the seeds is used medicinally and as a flavouring.

tamarisk any small tree or shrub of the genus *Tamarix*, flourishing in warm, salty, desert regions of Europe and Asia. The common tamarisk *T. gallica* has scalelike leaves and spikes of very small, pink flowers.

Tamayo Rufino 1899–1991. Mexican painter and printmaker. His work, nurtured by both European Modernism and pre-Columbian indigenous art, demonstrates a clear break with the rhetoric and pictoralism of the preceding generation of Mexican muralists. His mainly easel-sized paintings, with their vibrant colours and cryptic, semi-abstract figures, display strong Cubist, Expressionist, and Surrealist elements, as in *Women Reaching for the Moon* 1946 (Cleveland Museum of Art, Cleveland, Ohio).

Tambo Oliver 1917–1993. South African nationalist politician, in exile 1960–90, president of the African National Congress (ANC) 1977–91. Because of poor health, he was given the honorary post of national chair July 1991, and Nelson ◊Mandela resumed the ANC presidency.

tambourine musical percussion instrument of ancient origin, almost unchanged since Roman times, consisting of a shallow drum with a single skin and loosely set jingles in the rim that accentuate the beat.

Tamerlane or ***Tamburlaine*** or ***Timur i Leng*** ('Timur the Lame') 1336–1405. Mongol ruler of Samarkand, in Uzbekistan, from 1369 who conquered Persia, Azerbaijan, Armenia, and Georgia. He defeated the ◊Golden Horde 1395, sacked Delhi 1398, invaded Syria and Anatolia, and captured the Ottoman sultan in Ankara 1402; he died invading China. He was a descendant of the Mongol leader Genghis Khan and the great-grandfather of Babur, founder of the Mogul Empire.

Tamil the majority ethnic group living in the Indian state of Tamil Nadu (formerly Madras). Tamils also live in S India, N Sri Lanka, Malaysia, Singapore, and South Africa, totalling 35–55 million worldwide. Tamil belongs to the Dravidian family of languages; written records in Tamil date from the 3rd century BC. The 3 million Tamils in Sri Lanka are predominantly Hindu, unlike the Sinhalese, the majority group there, who are mainly Buddhist. The ◊Tamil Tigers, most prominent of the various Tamil groupings, want to create a separate homeland in N Sri Lanka through both political and military means.

Tamil Hinduism traditional form of Hinduism found in S India, particularly in Tamil Nadu, where the invasions and political upheavals of N India had little influence. The important centres of Tamil Hinduism are Rameshvaram, dedicated to Shiva; Shrirangam, dedicated to Vishnu; and Madurai, dedicated to Meenakshi, the wife of Shiva. Tamil temple architecture is characterized by towering *gopurams*, or temple gateways.

Tamil Nadu formerly (until 1968) ***Madras State*** state of SE India
area 130,100 sq km/50,219 sq mi
capital Madras
industries mainly industrial: cotton, textiles, silk, electrical machinery, tractors, rubber, sugar refining, tea, coffee, spices
population (1994 est) 58,840,000
language Tamil
history the present state was formed 1956. Tamil Nadu comprises part of the former British Madras presidency (later province) formed from areas taken from France and Tipu Sahib, the sultan of Mysore, in the 18th century, which became a state of the Republic of India 1950. The NE was detached to form Andhra Pradesh 1953; in 1956 other areas went to Kerala and Mysore (now Karnataka), and the Laccadive Islands (now Lakshadweep) became a separate union territory.

Tamil Tigers Tamil separatist guerrilla movement. Known as the Liberation Tigers of Tamil Eelam (LTTE), based in N Sri Lanka, it has been fighting a civil war against the country's Sinhalese majority community and governments since the late 1970s. The aim of the LTTE is to establish an autonomous Tamil state in N and E Sri Lanka,

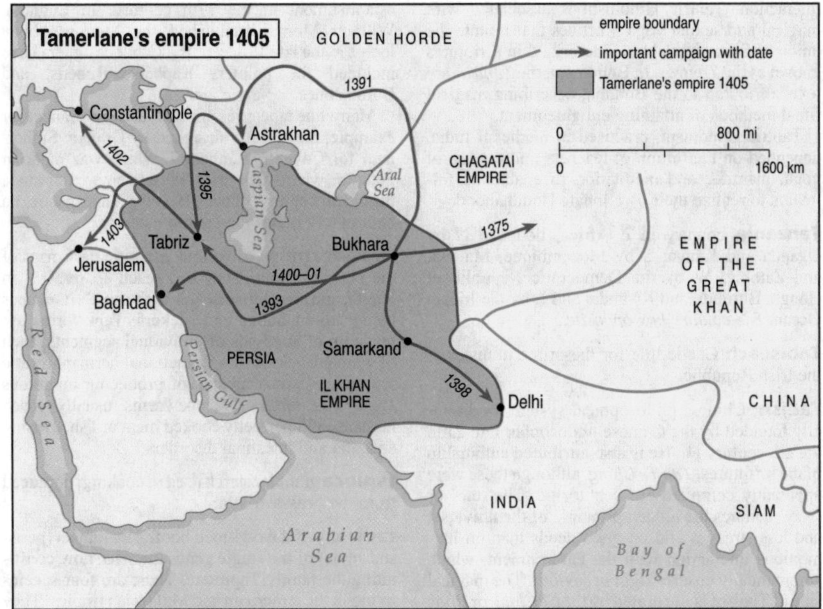

known as Eelam (the Tamil name for the island formerly called Ceylon). Separatist violence by the LTTE, whose stronghold is in the Jaffna peninsula in the far north, escalated particularly from 1983.

After a ceasefire in 1989–90, fighting resumed; in 1991 and 1993 LTTE terrorists were implicated in the assassinations of both the former Indian prime minister Rajiv Gandhi and the Sri Lankan president Ranasinghe Premadasa. At the outset of 1995, a brief ceasefire was maintained by the LTTE, but from mid-1995 a major new government military offensive was launched to drive them from the Jaffna Peninsula.

They were officially outlawed after bombing Sri Lanka's holiest Buddhist site 1998.

Tammany Hall Democratic Party organization in New York. It originated 1789 as the Society of St Tammany, named after an Native American chief. It was dominant from 1800 until the 1930s and gained a reputation for corruption and rule by bosses; its domination was broken by Mayor ◊La Guardia in the 1930s and Mayor Koch in the 1970s.

Tammuz in Sumerian mythology, a vegetation god, who died at midsummer and was brought back from the underworld in spring by his lover Ishtar. His cult spread over Babylonia, Syria, Phoenicia, and Palestine. In Greek mythology Tammuz appears as ◊Adonis.

tamoxifen oestrogen-blocking drug used to treat breast cancer and also infertility. It kills cancer cells by preventing formation of the tiny blood vessels that supply the tumour. Without a blood supply the tumour shrinks as its cells die.

Tampere (Swedish ***Tammerfors***) city in SW Finland; population (1994) 179,000, metropolitan area 258,000. Industries include textiles, paper, footwear, and turbines. It is the second-largest city in Finland.

Tamworth town in Staffordshire, England, on the river Tame, NE of Birmingham; population (1991) 70,100. Industries include engineering, paper, clothing, and brick and tile manufacturing.

Tana lake in Ethiopia, 1,800 m/5,900 ft above sea level; area 3,600 sq km/1,390 sq mi. It is the source of the Blue Nile.

Tanabata (Japanese 'star festival') festival celebrated annually on 7 July, introduced to Japan from China in the 8th century. It is dedicated to Altair and Vega, two stars in the constellations Aquila and Lyra respectively, separated by the Milky Way. According to legend they represent two star-crossed lovers allowed by the gods to meet on that night.

tanager New World bird of the family Emberizidae, order Passeriformes. There are about 230 species in forests of Central and South America, all brilliantly coloured. They are 10–20 cm/4–8 in long, with plump bodies and conical beaks. *See illustration on following page.*

Tanagra ancient city in ◊Boeotia, central Greece. Sparta defeated Athens there 457 BC. Terracotta statuettes called tanagras were excavated 1874.

Tanaka Kakuei 1918–1993. Japanese right-wing politician, leader of the dominant Liberal Democratic Party (LDP) and prime minister 1972–74. In 1976 he was charged with corruption and resigned from the LDP but remained a powerful faction leader.

Tanganyika, Lake lake 772 m/2,534 ft above sea level in the Great Rift Valley, E Africa, with the Democratic Republic of Congo to the W, Zambia to the S, and Tanzania and Burundi to the E. It is about 645 km/400 mi long, with an area of about 31,000 sq km/12,000 sq mi, and is the deepest lake (1,435 m/4,710 ft) in Africa. The chief ports on the lake are Bujumbura (Burundi), Kigoma (Tanzania), and Kalémié (Democratic Republic of Congo).

Tang dynasty the greatest of China's imperial dynasties, which ruled 618–907. Founded by the ◊Sui official Li Yuan (566–635), it extended Chinese authority into central Asia, Tibet, Korea, and Annam, establishing what was then the world's largest empire. The dynasty's peak was reached during the reign (712–56) of Emperor Minghuang (Hsuan-tsung).

The Tang dynasty set up a centralized administrative system based on the ◊Han examination model. Buddhism continued to spread and the arts and science flourished. Printing was invented, gunpowder first used, and seaborne and overland trade and cultural contacts were widened.

Tange Kenzo 1913– . Japanese Modernist architect. His works include the National Gymnasium, Tokyo, for the 1964 Olympics with its vast catenary steel roof, and the crescent-shaped city of Abuja, which replaced Lagos as the capital of Nigeria 1992. In 1991 he completed the 70-storey City Hall, Tokyo – Japan's tallest building.

tangent in geometry, a straight line that touches a curve and gives the ◊gradient of the curve at the point of contact. At a maximum, minimum, or point of inflection, the tangent to a curve has zero gradient. Also, in trigonometry, a function of an acute angle in a right-angled triangle, defined as the ratio of the length of the side opposite the angle to the length of the side adjacent to it; a way of expressing the gradient of a line. *See illustration on following page.*

tangerine small ◊orange *Citrus reticulata*.

Tangier or ***Tangiers*** or ***Tanger*** port in N Morocco, on the Strait of Gibraltar; population (urban area, 1990) 420,000. It was a Phoenician trading centre in the 15th century BC. Captured by the Portuguese 1471, it passed to England 1662 as part of the dowry of Catherine of Braganza, but was abandoned 1684, and later became a lair of ◊Barbary Coast pirates. From 1923 Tangier and a small surrounding enclave became an international zone, administered by Spain 1940–45. In 1956 it was transferred to independent Morocco and became a free port 1962.

tango dance for couples, developed in Argentina during the early 20th century, or the music for it. The dance consists of two long steps followed by two short steps then one long step, using stylized body positions. The music is in moderately slow duple time (2/4) and employs syncopated rhythms.

Tanguy Yves 1900–1955. French painter. He lived in the USA from 1939. A leading Surrealist, he created dreamlike desert landscapes peopled by metallic, semi-abstract forms casting long shadows. Tanguy was first inspired to paint by the works of de ◊Chirico and in 1925 he joined the Surrealist movement. He soon developed his characteristic style with bizarre, slender forms in a typically Surrealist wasteland.

Tanizaki Jun-ichirō 1886–1965. Japanese novelist. His works include a version of ◊Murasaki's *The Tale of Genji* 1939–41, *The Makioka Sisters* in three volumes 1943–48, and *The Key* 1956.

Tammany Hall A cartoon satirizing Tammany Hall, the Democratic Party organization in New York, in the 1870s. The cartoon, which appeared in *Harper's Weekly* Sept 1871, accuses Tammany Hall of sacrificing children's education in order to win Catholic votes. *Corbis*

tanager The male scarlet tanager is distinguished by its bright red plumage and black wings and tail. It lives in the canopy of deciduous woodland in central and eastern US.

tank armoured fighting vehicle fitted with weapons systems capable of defeating other tanks and destroying life and property. The term was originally a code name for the first effective tracked and armoured fighting vehicle, invented by the British soldier and scholar Ernest Swinton, and first used in the Battle of the Somme 1916. A tank consists of a body or hull of thick steel, on which are mounted machine guns and a larger gun. The hull contains the crew (usually consisting of a commander, driver, and one or two soldiers), engine, radio, fuel tanks, and ammunition. The tank travels on caterpillar tracks that enable it to cross rough ground and debris. It is known today as an MBT (main battle tank).

Tannenberg, Battle of victory of a combined Polish and Lithuanian army over the Knights of the Teutonic Order 1410, at Tannenberg, a village in northern Poland (now Grünwald). The battle broke the Knights' hold over Old Prussia (approximately modern Poland); their defeat led to the Treaty of Thorn and to an independent Polish state.

Tannenberg, Battle of in World War I, victory of German forces led by ◊Hindenburg over Russian forces under General Alexander Samsonov Aug 1914 at a village in East Prussia (now Grünwald, Poland) 145 km/90 mi northeast of Warsaw.

tannic acid or ***tannin*** $C_{14}H_{10}O_9$ yellow astringent substance, composed of several ◊phenol rings, occurring in the bark, wood, roots, fruits, and galls (growths) of certain trees, such as the oak. It precipitates gelatin to give an insoluble compound used in the manufacture of leather from hides (tanning).

tanning treating animal skins to preserve them and make them into leather. In vegetable tanning, the prepared skins are soaked in tannic acid. Chrome tanning, which is much quicker, uses solutions of chromium salts.

Tannu-Tuva former independent republic in NE Asia; see ◊Tuva.

tantalum hard, ductile, lustrous, grey-white, metallic element, symbol Ta, atomic number 73, relative atomic mass 180.948. It occurs with niobium in tantalite and other minerals. It can be drawn into wire with a very high melting point and great tenacity, useful for lamp filaments subject to vibration. It is also used in alloys, for corrosion-resistant laboratory apparatus and chemical equipment, as a catalyst in manufacturing synthetic rubber, in tools and instruments, and in rectifiers and capacitors.

Tantalus in Greek mythology, a king who deceived the gods by serving them human flesh at a banquet. His crimes were punished in ◊Tartarus (a part of the underworld) by the provision of food and drink he could not reach.

Tantrism forms of Hinduism and Buddhism that emphasize the division of the universe into male and female forces which maintain its unity by their interaction. Tantric Hinduism is associated with magical and sexual yoga practices that imitate the union of Siva and Sakti, as described in scriptures known as the *Tantras*. In Buddhism, the *Tantras* are texts attributed to the Buddha, describing magical ritual methods of attaining enlightenment.

Tantric Buddhism, practised in medieval India, depended on the tuition of teachers and the use of yoga, mantras, and meditation to enable its followers to realize their own innate Buddhahood.

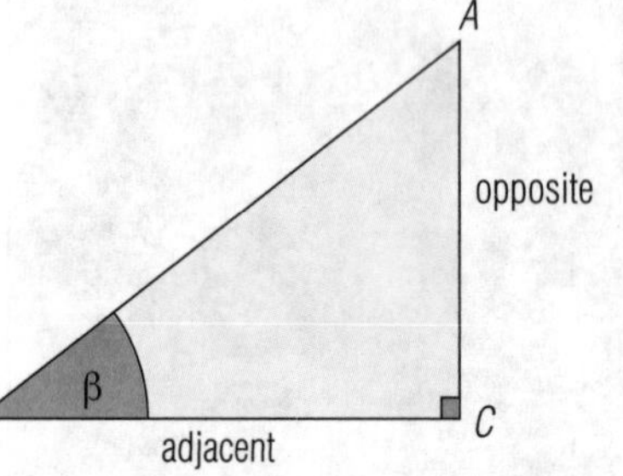

$$\text{tangent } \beta = \frac{\sin \beta}{\cos \beta} = \frac{\text{opposite}}{\text{adjacent}} = \frac{AC}{BC}$$

tangent The tangent of an angle is a mathematical function used in the study of right-angled triangles. If the tangent of an angle β is known, then the length of the opposite side can be found given the length of the adjacent side, or vice versa.

Tanzania country in E Africa, bounded N by Uganda and Kenya; S by Mozambique, Malawi, and Zambia; W by the Democratic Republic of Congo, Burundi, and Rwanda; and E by the Indian Ocean. *See country box opposite.*

Taoiseach Gaelic title for the prime minister of the Irish Republic.

Taoism Chinese philosophical system, traditionally founded by the Chinese philosopher Lao Zi in the 6th century BC. He is also attributed authorship of the scriptures, *Tao Te Ching*, although these were apparently compiled 3rd century BC. The 'tao' or 'way' denotes the hidden principle of the universe, and less stress is laid on good deeds than on harmonious interaction with the environment, which automatically ensures right behaviour. The magical side of Taoism is illustrated by the ◊*I Ching* or *Book of Changes*, a book of divination.

beliefs The universe is believed to be kept in balance by the opposing forces of yin and yang that operate in dynamic tension between themselves. Yin is female and watery: the force in the Moon and rain which reaches its peak in the winter; yang is masculine and solid: the force in the Sun and earth which reaches its peak in the summer. The interaction of yin and yang is believed to shape all life.

This magical, ritualistic aspect of Taoism developed from the 2nd century AD and was largely responsible for its popular growth; it stresses physical immortality, which was attempted by means ranging from dietary regulation and fasting to alchemy. By the 3rd century, worship of gods had begun to appear, including that of the stove god Tsao Chun. From the 4th century, rivalry between Taoists and Mahāyāna Buddhists was strong in China, leading to persecution of one religion by the other; this was resolved by mutual assimilation, and Taoism developed monastic communities similar to those of the Buddhists.

Taormina coastal resort in E Sicily, at the foot of Mount Etna; population (1985) 9,000. It has an ancient Greek theatre.

tap dancing rapid step dance, derived from clog dancing. Its main characteristic is the tapping of toes and heels accentuated by steel taps affixed to the shoes. It was popularized in vaudeville and in 1930s films by such dancers as Fred Astaire and Bill 'Bojangles' Robinson (1878–1949).

tape recording, magnetic method of recording electric signals on a layer of iron oxide, or other magnetic material, coating a thin plastic tape. The electrical signals from the microphone are fed to the electromagnetic recording head, which magnetizes the tape in accordance with the frequency and amplitude of the original signal. The impulses may be audio (for sound recording), video (for television), or data (for computer). For playback, the tape is passed over the same, or another, head to convert magnetic into electrical signals, which are then amplified for reproduction. Tapes are easily demagnetized (erased) for reuse, and come in cassette, cartridge, or reel form.

Taperinha archaeological site on the Amazon River, E of Santarem, Brazil. Its discovery 1991 provided evidence that an ancient New World civilization, predating Mexican and Andean cultures, existed 6,000–8,000 years ago.

tapestry ornamental woven textile used for wall hangings, furniture, and curtains. The tapestry design is threaded into the warp with various shades of yarn. The great European centres of tapestry weaving were in Belgium, France, and England.

Tapestries have been woven for centuries in many countries, and during the Middle Ages the art was practised in monasteries. European tapestries of the 13th century frequently featured oriental designs brought back by the Crusaders. The ◊Gobelins tapestry factory of Paris was made a royal establishment in the 17th century. In England, William Morris established the Merton Abbey looms in the late 19th century. Other designers have included the painters Raphael, Rubens, and Burne-Jones.

Many fine tapestries are still made in France; for example, the tapestry designed by Graham Sutherland for Coventry Cathedral, which was made at Felletin, where tapestries have been woven since the 15th century. The ◊Bayeux Tapestry is an embroidery rather than a true tapestry.

tapeworm any of various parasitic flatworms of the class Cestoda. They can reach 15 m/50 ft in length, and attach themselves to the host's intestines by means of hooks and suckers. Tapeworms are made up of hundreds of individual segments, each of which develops into a functional hermaphroditic reproductive unit capable of producing numerous eggs. The larvae of tapeworms usually reach humans in imperfectly cooked meat or fish, causing anaemia and intestinal disorders.

tapioca granular starch used in cooking, produced from the ◊cassava root.

tapir any of the odd-toed hoofed mammals (perissodactyls) of the single genus *Tapirus*, now constituting the family Tapiridae. There are four species living in the American and Malaysian tropics. They reach 1 m/3 ft at the shoulder and weigh up to 350 kg/770 lb. Tapirs have thick, hairy, black skin, short tails, and short trunks. They are vegetarian, harmless, and shy. They are related to the ◊rhinoceros, and slightly more distantly to the horse. Their survival is in danger because of destruction of the forests.

taproot in botany, a single, robust, main ◊root that is derived from the embryonic root, or ◊radicle, and grows vertically downwards, often to considerable depth. Taproots are often modified for food storage and are common in biennial plants such as the carrot *Daucus carota*, where they act as ◊perennating organs.

tar dark brown or black viscous liquid obtained by the destructive distillation of coal, shale, and wood. Tars consist of a mixture of hydrocarbons, acids, and bases. ◊Creosote and ◊paraffin are produced from wood tar. See also ◊coal tar.

Tara Hill ancient religious and political centre in County Meath, S Ireland. It was the site of a palace and coronation place of many Irish kings, abandoned in the 6th century. St ◊Patrick, patron saint of Ireland, preached here.

tarantella S Italian dance in very fast compound time (6/8); also a piece of music composed for, or in the rhythm of, this dance. It is commonly believed to be named after the tarantula spider which was (incorrectly) thought to cause tarantism (hysterical ailment), at one time epidemic in the S Italian town of Taranto, and whose cure was thought to involve wild dancing.

Tarantino Quentin 1963– . US film director and screenwriter whose films are characterized by a fragmented structure and often explicit violence. His first feature, *Reservoir Dogs* 1992, deals with the aftermath of an unsuccessful jewel heist. His second, *Pulp Fiction* 1994, was more humorous and intertwined several storylines. Tarantino also wrote the screen story of *Natural Born Killers* 1994, though he disowned Oliver Stone's completed film.

Taranto naval base and port in Puglia region, SE Italy; population (1992) 230,200. It is an important commercial centre, and its steelworks are part of the new industrial complex of S Italy. It was the site of the ancient Greek *Tarentum*, founded in the 8th century BC by ◊Sparta, and was captured by the Romans 272 BC.

tarantula wolf spider *Lycosa tarantula* (family Lycosidae) with a 2.5 cm/1 in body. It spins no web, relying on its speed in hunting to catch its prey. The name 'tarantula' is also used for any of the numerous large, hairy spiders of the family Theraphosidae, with large poison fangs, native to the southwestern USA and tropical America.

In the Middle Ages, the wolf spider's bite was thought to cause hysterical ailments or tarantism for which dancing was the cure, hence the name 'tarantula' and its popular association with the dance 'tarantella'. *See illustration on p. 1038.*

TANZANIA
United Republic of

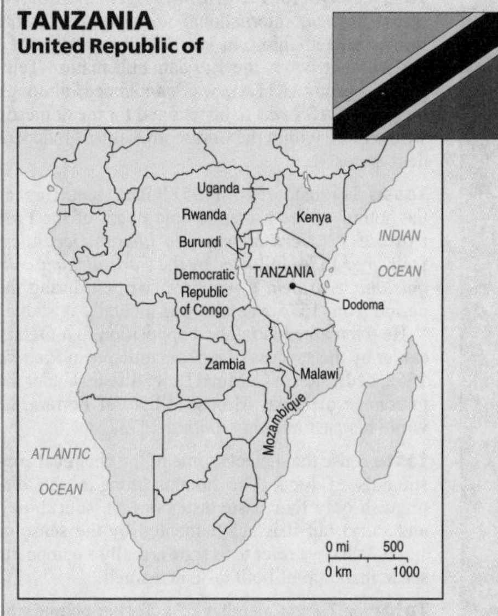

national name *Jamhuri ya Muungano wa Tanzania*
area 945,000 sq km/364,865 sq mi
capital Dodoma (since 1983)
major towns/cities Zanzibar Town, Mwanza
major ports (former capital) Dar es Salaam
physical features central plateau; lakes in N and W; coastal plains; lakes Victoria, Tanganyika, and Nyasa; half the country is forested; comprises islands of Zanzibar and Pemba; Mount Kilimanjaro, 5,895 m/19,340 ft, the highest peak in Africa; Olduvai Gorge; Ngorongoro Crater, 14.5 km/9 mi across, 762 m/2,500 ft deep
head of state Benjamin Mkapa from 1995
head of government Cleoopa Msuya from 1994
political system emergent democracy
administrative divisions 25 administrative regions
political parties Revolutionary Party of Tanzania (CCM), African, socialist; Civic Party (Chama Cha Wananchi), left of centre; Tanzania People's Party (TPP), left of centre; Democratic Party (DP), left of centre; Zanzibar United Front (Kamahuru), Zanzibar-based, centrist
armed forces 34,600; citizen's militia of 80,000 (1995)
conscription two years
defence spend (% GDP) 3.5 (1994)
education spend (% GNP) 5.0 (1992)
health spend (% GDP) 3.2 (1990)
death penalty retained and used for ordinary crimes
population 29,685,000 (1995 est)
population growth rate 3.0% (1990–95); 2.6% (2000–05)
age distribution (% of total population) <15 45.9%, 15–65 51.6%, >65 2.6% (1995)
ethnic distribution 99% of the population are Africans, ethnically classified as Bantus, and distributed among over 130 tribes; main tribes are Bantu, Vilotic, Nilo-Hamitic, Khoisan, and Iraqwi
population density (per sq km) 31 (1994)
urban population (% of total) 24% (1995)
labour force 52% of population: 84% agriculture, 5% industry, 11% services (1990)
unemployment n.a.
child mortality rate (under 5, per 1,000 live births) 159 (1994)
life expectancy 49 (men), 54 (women)
education (compulsory years) 7
literacy rate 65%
languages Kiswahili, English (both official)
religions Muslim, Christian, traditional religions
TV sets (per 1,000 people) 2 (1992)
currency Tanzanian shilling
GDP (US $) 2.44 billion (1994)
GDP per capita (PPP) (US $) 630 (1993)
growth rate 3.5% (1994)
average annual inflation 35% (1994); 25.8 (1985–93)
major trading partners UK, Germany, Japan, India, the Netherlands, Belgium, Italy, Oman
resources diamonds, other gemstones, gold, salt, phosphates, coal, gypsum, tin, kaolin (exploration for petroleum in progress)
industries food processing, textiles, cigarette production, pulp and paper, petroleum refinery, diamonds, cement, brewing, fertilizers, clothing, footwear, pharmaceuticals, electrical goods, metalworking, vehicle assembly
exports coffee beans, raw cotton, tobacco, tea, cloves, cashew nuts, minerals, petroleum products. Principal market: Germany 15.6% (1992)
imports machinery and transport equipment, crude petroleum and petroleum products, construction materials, foodstuffs, consumer goods. Principal source: UK 9.8% (1992)
arable land 3.2% (1993)
agricultural products coffee, cotton, tobacco, cloves, tea, cashew nuts, sisal, pyrethrum, sugar cane, coconuts, cardamom

HISTORY
8th C Growth of city states along coast after settlement by Arabs from Oman.
1499 Portuguese navigator Vasco da Gama visited island of Zanzibar.
16th C Portuguese occupied Zanzibar, defeated coastal states, and exerted spasmodic control over them.
1699 Portuguese ousted from Zanzibar by Arabs of Oman.
18th C Sultan of Oman reasserted Arab overlordship of E African coast, which became subordinate to Zanzibar.
1744–1837 Revolt of ruler of Mombasa against Oman spanned 93 years until final victory of Oman.
1822 Moresby Treaty: Britain recognized regional dominance of Zanzibar, but protested against slave trade.
1840 Sultan Seyyid bin Sultan moved his capital from Oman to Zanzibar; trade in slaves and ivory flourished.
1861 Sultanates of Zanzibar and Oman separated on death of Seyyid.
19th C Europeans started to explore inland, closely followed by Christian missionaries.
1884 German Colonization Society began to acquire territory on mainland in defiance of Zanzibar.
1890 Britain obtained protectorate over Zanzibar, abolished slave trade, and recognized German claims to mainland.
1897 German East Africa formally established as colony.
1905–06 Maji Maji revolt suppressed by German troops.
1916 Conquest of German East Africa by British and South African forces, led by General Jan Smuts.
1919 Most of German East Africa became British League of Nations mandate of Tanganyika.
1946 Britain continued to govern Tanganyika as United Nations (UN) trusteeship.
1954 Julius Nyerere organized the Tanganyikan African National Union (TANU) to campaign for independence.
1961 Tanganyika achieved independence from Britain with Nyerere as prime minister.
1962 Tanganyika became republic under President Nyerere.
1963 Zanzibar achieved independence.
1964 Arab-dominated sultanate of Zanzibar overthrown by Afro-Shirazi Party in violent revolution; Zanzibar merged with Tanganyika to form United Republic of Tanzania.
1967 East African Community (EAC) formed by Tanzania, Kenya, and Uganda to retain customs union formed in colonial period; Arusha Declaration by Nyerere pledged to build socialist state.
1977 Revolutionary Party of Tanzania (CCM) proclaimed as only legal party; EAC dissolved.
1979 Tanzanian troops intervened in Uganda to help overthrow President Idi Amin.
1985 Nyerere retired as president; succeeded by Ali Hassan Mwinyi.
1990 Nyerere surrendered leadership of CCM to Mwinyi.
1992 Multiparty politics permitted.
1995 Benjamin Mkapa of CCM elected president.

SEE ALSO Nyerere, Julius; Zanzibar

Tarawa port and capital of Kiribati; population (1990) 28,800. Mother-of-pearl and copra are exported.

Tarbell Ida Minerva 1857–1944. US journalist whose exposés of corruption in high places made her one of the most prominent 'muckrakers' in the USA. She was an editor and contributor to *McClure's Magazine* 1894–1906. Her book *The History of the Standard Oil Company* 1904 sparked antitrust reform.

tare alternative common name for ◊vetch.

tariff tax or duty placed on goods when they are imported into a country or trading bloc (such as the European Union) from outside. The aim of tariffs is to reduce imports by making them more expensive. Organizations such as the EU, the European Free Trade Association (EFTA), and the World Trade Organization (WTO) have worked towards mutual lowering of tariffs among countries. Tariffs have generally been used by governments to protect home industries from lower-priced foreign goods, and have been opposed by supporters of free trade.

Tariff Reform League organization set up 1903 as a vehicle for the ideas of the Liberal politician Joseph ◊Chamberlain on protective tariffs. It aimed to unify the British Empire by promoting imperial preference in trade. This policy was unacceptable to dominion governments as it would constrict their economic policies and put a tax on foodstuffs imported into Britain. Consequently, the league's objective became the introduction of protection for British goods against competition from Germany and the USA.

Tarkington (Newton) Booth 1869–1946. US novelist. His novels for young people, which include *Penrod* 1914, are classics. He was among the best-selling authors of the early 20th century with works such as *Monsieur Beaucaire* 1900 and novels of the Midwest, including *The Magnificent Ambersons* 1918 (filmed 1942 by Orson Welles).

Tarkovsky Andrei Arsenyevich 1932–1986. Soviet film director. His work is characterized by an epic style combined with intense personal spirituality. His films include *Solaris* 1972, *Zerkalo/Mirror* 1975, *Stalker* 1979, and *Offret/The Sacrifice* 1986.

taro or *eddo* plant *Colocasia esculenta* of the arum family Araceae, native to tropical Asia; the tubers are edible and are the source of Polynesian poi (a fermented food).

tarot cards fortune-telling aid consisting of 78 cards: the minor arcana in four suits (resembling playing cards) and the major arcana, 22 cards with densely symbolic illustrations that have links with astrology and the ◊kabbala.

The earliest known reference to tarot cards is from 1392. The pack is of unknown (probably medieval) origin and may have been designed in Europe in the early 14th century as a repository of Gnostic ideas then being suppressed by the Christian church. Since the 18th century the tarot has interested occult scholars.

Tarquinius Superbus (Tarquin the Proud) lived 6th century BC. Last king of Rome 534–510 BC. He abolished certain rights of Romans, and made the city powerful. According to legend, he was deposed when his son Sextus raped ◊Lucretia.

tarragon perennial bushy herb *Artemisia dracunculus* of the daisy family Compositae, native to the Old World, growing to 1.5 m/5 ft, with narrow leaves and small green-white flower heads arranged in groups. Tarragon contains an aromatic oil; its leaves are used to flavour salads, pickles, and tartar sauce.

Tarragona port in Catalonia, Spain; population (1994) 115,000. Industries include petrochemicals, pharmaceuticals, and electrical goods. It has a cathedral and Roman remains, including an aqueduct and amphitheatre.

tarsier any of three species of the prosimian primates, genus *Tarsius*, of the East Indies and the Philippines. These survivors of early primates are about the size of a rat with thick, light-brown fur, very large eyes, and long feet and hands. They are nocturnal, arboreal, and eat insects and lizards.

tarantula The mygalomorph bird-eating spider *Stichoplastus incei* and related species are generally described as tarantulas. Native to tropical America, they are largely nocturnal and feed mainly on insects, but will also attack larger prey such as mice and birds. Their bite is painful but not fatal. *Premaphotos Wildlife*

‘None merits the name of Creator but God and the poet.’

TORQUATO TASSO
Discorsi del Poema Eroico

tartan woollen cloth woven in specific chequered patterns individual to Scottish clans, with stripes of different widths and colours crisscrossing on a coloured background; it is used in making skirts, kilts, trousers, and other articles of clothing. Developed in the 17th century, tartan was banned after the 1745 ◊Jacobite rebellion, and not legalized again until 1782.

Tartar variant spelling of ◊Tatar.

tartaric acid $HCOO(CHOH)_2COOH$ organic acid present in vegetable tissues and fruit juices in the form of salts of potassium, calcium, and magnesium. It is used in carbonated drinks and baking powders.

Tartarus in Greek mythology, a part of ◊Hades, the underworld, where the wicked were punished.

tartrazine (E102) yellow food colouring produced synthetically from petroleum. Many people are allergic to foods containing it. Typical effects are skin disorders and respiratory problems. It has been shown to have an adverse effect on hyperactive children.

Tarzan fictitious hero inhabiting the African rainforest, created by US writer Edgar Rice ◊Burroughs in *Tarzan of the Apes* 1914, with numerous sequels. He and his partner Jane have featured in films, comic strips, and television series.

Tasaday an indigenous people of the rainforests of Mindanao in the ◊Philippines, contacted in the 1960s. Some anthropologists doubt their claim to leading a hunter-gatherer way of life.

Tashkent capital of Uzbekistan; population (1994) 2,100,000. Industries include the manufacture of mining machinery, chemicals, textiles, and leather goods. Founded in the 7th century, it was taken by the Turks in the 12th century and captured by Tamerlane 1361. In 1865 it was taken by the Russians.

A temporary truce between Pakistan and India over ◊Kashmir was established at the Declaration of Tashkent 1966.

TASM abbreviation for ***tactical air-to-surface missile***, ◊missile with a range of under 500 km/300 mi and a nuclear warhead. TASMs were developed independently by the USA and France to replace the surface-to-surface missiles being phased out by NATO from 1990.

Tasman Abel Janszoon 1603–1659. Dutch navigator. In 1642, he was the first European to see Tasmania. He also made the first European sightings of New Zealand, Tonga, and Fiji Islands.

Tasmania formerly (1642–1856) ***Van Diemen's Land*** island off the south coast of Australia; a state of the Commonwealth of Australia
area 67,800 sq km/26,171 sq mi
capital Hobart
towns and cities Launceston (chief port)
features an island state (including small islands in the Bass Strait, and Macquarie Island); Franklin River, a wilderness area saved from a hydroelectric scheme 1983, which also has a prehistoric site; unique fauna including the Tasmanian devil
industries wool, dairy products, apples and other fruit, timber, iron, tin, coal, copper, silver
population (1994 est) 471,450
history the first European to visit here was Abel Tasman 1642; the last of the Tasmanian Aboriginals died 1876. Tasmania joined the Australian Commonwealth as a state 1901.

Tasmanian devil carnivorous marsupial *Sarcophilus harrisii*, in the same family (Dasyuridae) as native 'cats'. It is about 65 cm/2.1 ft long with a 25 cm/10 in bushy tail. It has a large head, strong teeth, and is blackish with white patches on the chest and hind parts. It is nocturnal, carnivorous, and can be ferocious when cornered. It survives only in remote parts of Tasmania.

Tasmanian wolf or ***thylacine*** carnivorous marsupial *Thylacinus cynocephalus*, in the family Dasyuridae, doglike in appearance with a long tail, characteristic dark stripes on back and hindquarters, and measuring nearly 2 m/6 ft from nose to tail tip. It was hunted to probable extinction in the 1930s, but there are still occasional unconfirmed reports of sightings, both on the Australian mainland and in the Tasmanian mountains.

Tasman Sea part of the ◊Pacific Ocean between SE Australia and NW New Zealand. It is named after the Dutch explorer Abel Tasman.

Tasmania

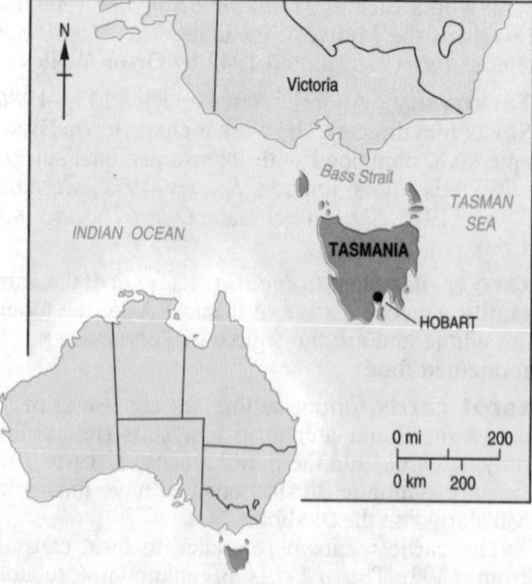

Tass acronym for ***Telegrafnoye Agentstvo Sovyetskovo Soyuza***, international news agency of the former Soviet Union. In Jan 1992 the creation of a replacement body, the Russian Information Telegraph Agency (RITA), was announced, although the name TASS was to be retained for the domestic wire service within the Commonwealth of Independent States.

Tasso Torquato 1544–1595. Italian poet. He was the author of the romantic epic poem of the First Crusade *Gerusalemme liberata/Jerusalem Delivered* 1574, followed by the *Gerusalemme conquistata/Jerusalem Conquered*, written during the period from 1576 when he was mentally unstable.

He overcame his father's opposition to a literary career by the success of his romantic poem *Rinaldo* 1562, dedicated to Cardinal Luigi d'Este. Under the patronage of Duke Alfonso d'Este of Ferrara, he wrote his pastoral play *Aminta* 1573.

taste sense that detects some of the chemical constituents of food. The human ◊tongue can distinguish only four basic tastes (sweet, sour, bitter, and salty) but it is supplemented by the sense of smell. What we refer to as taste is really a composite sense made up of both taste and smell.

Tatar or ***Tartar*** member of a Turkic people, the descendants of the mixed Mongol and Turkic followers of ◊Genghis Khan, called the Golden Horde because of the wealth they gained by plunder.

The vast Tatar state was conquered by Russia 1552. The Tatars now live mainly in the Russian autonomous republic of Tatarstan, W Siberia, Turkmenistan, and Uzbekistan (where they were deported from the Crimea 1944). There are over 5 million speakers of the Tatar language, which belongs to the Turkic branch of the Altaic family. The Tatar people are mainly Muslim.

In 1988 a federal ruling confirmed the right of deported Tatars to residency in the Crimea.

Tatarstan formerly ***Tatar Autonomous Republic*** autonomous republic of E Russian Federation
area 68,000 sq km/26,250 sq mi
capital Kazan
physical in Volga River basin
industries oil, chemicals, textiles, timber
population (1992) 3,696,000 (48% Tatar, 43% Russian)
history a territory of Volga-Kama Bulgar state from the 10th century when Islam was introduced; conquered by the Mongols 1236; the capital of the powerful Khanate of Kazan until conquered by Russia 1552; an autonomous republic from 1920; independent republic in the Russian Federation from 1992.

Tate Nahum 1652–1715. Irish poet. He wrote an adaptation of Shakespeare's *King Lear* with a happy ending. He also produced a version of the psalms and hymns; among his poems is 'While shepherds watched'. He became British poet laureate 1692.

Tate Phyllis Margaret Duncan 1911–1987. British composer. Her works include *Concerto for Saxophone and Strings* 1944, the opera *The Lodger* 1960, based on the story of Jack the Ripper, and *Serenade to Christmas* for soprano, chorus, and orchestra 1972.

Tate Gallery art gallery in London, housing British art from the late 16th century and international art from 1810. Endowed by the sugar merchant Henry Tate (1819–1899), it was opened 1897.

The Tate Gallery has unique collections of the work of J M W Turner and William Blake, also one of the best collections of Pre-Raphaelite painting. More recently the Tate Gallery has begun to form a major collection of modern British prints and an archive of modern British art. The Clore Gallery extension for Turner paintings was opened 1987. A Liverpool branch of the Tate Gallery opened 1988 and the St Ives extension 1993.

Tati Jacques. Stage name of Jacques Tatischeff 1908–1982. French comic actor, director, and writer. He portrayed Monsieur Hulot, the embodiment of polite opposition to modern mechanization, in a series of films beginning with *Les Vacances de M Hulot/Monsieur Hulot's Holiday* 1953, and including *Mon Oncle/My Uncle* 1959 and *Playtime* 1968.

Tatlin Vladimir (Yevgrapovich) 1885–1953. Russian artist. He was a cofounder of ◊Constructivism. After encountering Cubism in Paris 1913, he evolved his first Constructivist works, using such

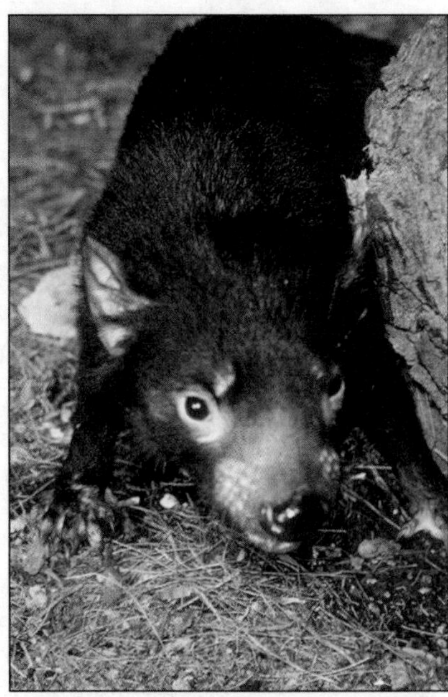

Tasmanian devil The Tasmanian devil, despite its name, is not particularly aggressive – it is more likely to scavenge for dead animals than to attack living ones. Nevertheless, its powerful jaws, capable of crushing large bones, are to be respected.

materials as glass, metal, plaster, and wood to create totally abstract sculptures, some of which were meant to be suspended in the air. He worked as a stage designer 1933–52.

Tatra Mountains range in central Europe, extending for about 65 km/40 mi along the Polish-Slovakian border; the highest part of the central ◊Carpathian Mountains.

tatting lacework in cotton, made since medieval times by knotting and looping a single thread with a small shuttle.

tattoo a permanent mark or design under the top layer of skin made by the injection of coloured pigments. The art of tattooing is widespread and cave paintings and statuettes with tattoolike marks from archaeological sites indicate that the art is thousands of years old.

Tattoos have been used for a variety of reasons: to identify slaves or criminals; to signify marital availability, skill as a warrior, or social class, clan, or group affiliation; or for beauty. In religious ceremonies receiving a tattoo is believed to have ritual significance and magical powers. Tattooing is increasing in popularity among both men and women. Today most tattoos are applied by an electric needle in special studios or parlours.

Tatum Art(hur) 1910–1956. US jazz pianist. He is considered among the most technically brilliant of jazz pianists and his technique and chromatic harmonies influenced many musicians, such as Oscar Peterson (1925–). He worked mainly as a soloist in the 1930s and improvised with the guitarist Tiny Grimes (1916–) in a trio from 1943.

tau ◊elementary particle with the same electric charge as the electron but a mass nearly double that of a proton. It has a lifetime of around 3×10^{-13} seconds and belongs to the ◊lepton family of particles – those that interact via the electromagnetic, weak nuclear, and gravitational forces, but not the strong nuclear force.

Tau Ceti one of the nearest stars visible to the naked eye, 11.9 light years from Earth in the constellation Cetus. It has a diameter slightly less than that of the Sun, and an actual luminosity of about 45% of the Sun's.

Taunton market town and administrative headquarters of Somerset, England; population (1991) 55,900. Industries include cider, leather, optical instruments, computer software, aeronautical instruments, precast concrete, and light engineering; there is a weekly cattle market. The Elizabethan hall survives, in which Judge ◊Jeffreys held the Bloody Assizes 1685 after the Duke of Monmouth's rebellion.

Taunus Mountains mountain range in Hessen, Germany; the Grosser Feldberg, 881 m/2,887 ft, is the highest peak in the Rhenish uplands. There are several mineral spas, including Wiesbaden, Bad Nauheim, and Bad Soden.

Taupo largest lake in New Zealand, in a volcanic area of hot springs; area 620 sq km/239 sq mi. It is the source of the Waikato River.

Taurus conspicuous zodiacal constellation in the northern hemisphere near ◊Orion, represented as a bull. The Sun passes through Taurus from mid-May to late June. In astrology, the dates for Taurus are between about 20 April and 20 May (see ◊precession).

The V-shaped Hyades open ◊star cluster forms the bull's head, with ◊Aldebaran as the red eye. The ◊Pleiades open cluster is in the shoulder. Taurus also contains the ◊Crab nebula.

tautology repetition of the same thing in different words. For example, it is tautologous to say that something is *most unique*, since something unique cannot, by definition, be comparative.

tautomerism form of isomerism in which two interconvertible ◊isomers are in equilibrium. It is often specifically applied to an equilibrium between the keto (–C–C=O) and enol (–C=C–OH) forms of carbonyl compounds.

Tavener John Kenneth 1944– . English composer. He has written austere vocal works including the dramatic cantata *The Whale* 1968 and the opera *Thérèse* 1979. *The Protecting Veil*, composed 1987 for cello and strings alone, became a best-selling classical recording. Tavener draws on Eastern European idioms and Orthodox Christian traditions; he described his chamber opera *Mary of Egypt* 1991 as 'a moving icon'.

Taverner John c.1495–1545. English organist and composer. He wrote masses and motets in polyphonic style, showing great contrapuntal skill, but as a Protestant renounced his art. He was imprisoned 1528 for heresy, and, as an agent of Thomas Cromwell, assisted in the dissolution of the monasteries.

taxation raising of money from individuals and organizations by the state in order to pay for the goods and services it provides. Taxation can be ***direct*** (a deduction from income) or ***indirect*** (added to the purchase price of goods or services, that is, a tax on consumption). The standard form of indirect taxation in Europe is ***value-added tax (VAT)***. ***Income tax*** is the most common form of direct taxation.

The proportions of direct and indirect taxation in the total tax revenue vary widely from country to country. By varying the effect of a tax on the richer and poorer members of society, a government can attempt to redistribute wealth from the richer to the poorer, both by taxing the rich more severely and by returning some of the collected wealth in the form of benefits. A ***progressive*** tax is one that falls proportionally more on the rich; most income taxes, for example, have higher rates for those with higher incomes. A ***regressive*** tax, on the other hand, affects the poor proportionally more than the rich.

In Britain, income tax is collected by the Inland Revenue, as are the other direct taxes, namely ***corporation tax*** on company profits; ***capital gains tax***, introduced to prevent the use of capital as untaxed income 1961; and ***inheritance tax*** (which replaced capital transfer tax). Levels of taxation on land and inherited wealth in Britain were in 1994 among the lowest in the world. The UK has a high proportion of direct taxation compared, for example, with the USA which has a higher proportion of indirect taxation.

VAT was introduced in the UK 1973. It is paid on the value added to any goods or services at each particular stage of the process of production or distribution and, although collected from traders at each stage, it is in effect a tax on consumer expenditure. In some states of the USA a similar result is achieved by a ***sales tax*** deducted by the retailer at the point of sale. In the UK, a ◊council tax, based on property values, is the form of taxation that pays for local government spending. It replaced the unpopular ***poll tax*** or community charge of 1989–93, levied on each person of voting age. In other countries, including the USA, there are local property taxes or a local income tax. In Britain taxes are also levied on tobacco, wine, beer, and petrol, in the form of excise duties.

The UK tax system has been criticized in many respects; alternatives include an expenditure tax, which would be imposed only on income spent, and the tax-credit system under which all are guaranteed an income bolstered as necessary by social-security benefits, taxation beginning only above that level, hence eliminating the 'poverty trap', by which the unemployed receiving state benefits may have a net loss in income if they take employment at a low wage.

'All taxes must, at last, fall upon agriculture.'

On TAXATION
Edward Gibbon
Decline and Fall of the Roman Empire
1776–88

tax avoidance conducting of financial affairs in such a way as to keep tax liability to a minimum within the law.

tax evasion failure to meet tax liabilities by illegal action, such as not declaring income. Tax evasion is a criminal offence.

tax haven country or state where taxes are much lower than elsewhere. It is often used by companies of another country that register in the tax haven to avoid tax. Any business transacted is treated as completely confidential. Tax havens include the Channel Islands, Switzerland, Bermuda, the Bahamas, and Liberia.

taxis (plural *taxes*) or ***tactic movement*** in botany, the movement of a single cell, such as a bacterium, protozoan, single-celled alga, or gamete, in response to an external stimulus. A movement directed towards the stimulus is described as positive taxis, and away from it as negative taxis. The alga *Chlamydomonas*, for example, demonstrates positive ***phototaxis*** by swimming towards a light source to increase the rate of photosynthesis.

taxonomy another name for the ◊classification of living organisms.

tax year twelve-month period over which an individual or company calculates its income and liability to pay tax. The British tax year runs from 6 April of one year to 5 April in the following year.

Tay longest river in Scotland; length 189 km/118 mi. Rising in NW Central region, it flows northeast through Loch Tay, then east and southeast past Perth to the Firth of Tay, crossed at Dundee by the Tay Bridge, before joining the North Sea. Its main tributaries are the Tummel, Isla, and Earn.

Taylor Elizabeth Rosemond 1932– . English-born US actress. She graduated from juvenile leads to dramatic roles, becoming one of the most glamorous stars of the 1950s and 1960s. Her films include *National Velvet* 1944, *Cat on a Hot Tin Roof* 1958, *Butterfield 8* 1960 (Academy Award), *Cleopatra* 1963, and *Who's Afraid of Virginia Woolf?* 1966 (Academy Award).

Taylor Frederick Winslow 1856–1915. US engineer and management consultant, the founder of scientific management. His ideas, published in *Principles of Scientific Management* 1911, were based on the breakdown of work to the simplest

Taylor Elizabeth Taylor in the title role of the 1963 film *Cleopatra*.

‘Is there no Latin word for Tea? Upon my soul, if I had known that I would have left the vulgar stuff alone.’

On TEA
Hilaire Belloc
On Nothing 1908

tasks, the separation of planning from execution of tasks, and the introduction of time-and-motion studies.

Taylor Robert 1714–1788. English Neo-Palladian architect and sculptor. He was immensely successful during his lifetime, although little of his work has survived. Stone Building in Lincoln's Inn Fields, London 1775, is the finest extant example.

Taylor Zachary 1784–1850. 12th president of the USA 1849–50. A veteran of the War of 1812 and a hero of the Mexican War (1846–48), he was nominated for the presidency by the Whigs in 1848 and was elected, but died less than one and a half years into his term.

Tay-Sachs disease inherited disorder, due to a defective gene, causing an enzyme deficiency that leads to blindness, retardation, and death in infancy. It is most common in people of E European Jewish descent.

Tayside former region of Scotland, created 1975, abolished 1996.

TB abbreviation for the infectious disease ◊***tuberculosis***.

Tbilisi formerly ***Tiflis*** capital of Georgia; industries include textiles, machinery, ceramics, and tobacco; population (1994 est) 1,300,000. Dating from the 5th century, it is a centre of Georgian culture, with fine medieval churches.

Anti-Russian demonstrations were quashed here by troops 1981 and 1989. In 1991 at least 50 people were killed as well-armed opposition forces attempted to overthrow President Gamsakhurdia, eventually forcing him to flee.

T cell or ***T lymphocyte*** immune cell (see ◊immunity and ◊lymphocyte) that plays several roles in the body's defences. T cells are so called because they mature in the ◊thymus.

There are three main types of T cells: T helper cells (Th cells), which allow other immune cells to go into action; T suppressor cells (Ts cells), which stop specific immune reactions from occurring; and T cytotoxic cells (Tc cells), which kill cells that are cancerous or infected with viruses. Like ◊B cells, to which they are related, T cells have surface receptors that make them specific for particular antigens.

Tchaikovsky Pyotr Il'yich 1840–1893. Russian composer. His strong sense of melody, personal expression, and brilliant orchestration are clear throughout his many Romantic works, which include six symphonies, three piano concertos, a violin concerto, operas (for example, *Eugene Onegin* 1879), ballets (for example, *The Nutcracker* 1891–92), orchestral fantasies (for example, *Romeo and Juliet* 1870), and chamber and vocal music.

Professor of harmony at Moscow 1865, he later met Mily ◊Balakirev, becoming involved with the nationalist movement in music. He was the first Russian composer to establish a reputation with Western audiences.

Tchaikovsky The composer Pyotr Tchaikovsky in a drawing by W I Bruckman. Although he distanced himself from Balakirev's circle of nationalist composers, Tchaikovsky's love of his country and its folk song ensured that a Russian flavour remained. *Image Select (UK) Ltd*

tea evergreen shrub *Camellia sinensis*, family Theaceae, of which the fermented, dried leaves are infused to make a beverage of the same name. Known in China as early as 2737 BC, tea was first brought to Europe AD 1610 and rapidly became a popular drink. In 1823 it was found growing wild in N India, and plantations were later established in Assam and Sri Lanka; producers today include Africa, South America, Georgia, Azerbaijan, Indonesia, and Iran.

Growing naturally to 12 m/40 ft, the tea plant is restricted in cultivation to bushes 1.5 m/4 ft high. The young shoots and leaves are picked every five years. Once plucked, the young leaves are spread out on shelves in withering lofts and allowed to wither in a current of air for 4 to 18 hours. They are then broken up by rolling machines to release the essential oils, and left to ferment. Green teas (from China, Taiwan, and Japan) are steamed or heated and then rolled, dried, and finally graded. They are partly green in colour. Black teas (from Ceylon and India) are macerated in rolling machines, allowed to ferment, and then dried and graded. They are a blackish-brown colour.

Grading is carried out according to the size of leaf. For example, some Ceylon tea grades are orange pekoe, flowery pekoe, broken orange pekoe, broken pekoe, and fannings. The latter grades dominate the black teas sold in tea bags. Black teas make up 75% of the world's trade in tea. Some teas are scented with plant oils: Earl Grey, for example, is flavoured with oil of ◊bergamot. Methods of consumption in different countries vary: in Japan special teahouses and an elaborate tea ceremony have evolved and in Tibet hard slabs of compressed tea are used as money before being finally brewed.

teacher training in the UK, teachers are trained either by means of the four-year Bachelor of Education degree, which integrates professional training and the study of academic subjects, or by means of the postgraduate Certificate of Education, which offers one year of professional training to follow a degree course in a specialist subject. The majority of BEd students train to teach in primary schools; two-thirds of PGCE students to teach specialist subjects in secondary schools.

Teague Walter Dorwin 1883–1960. US industrial designer. Active in New York, he was a pioneer of industrial design in the 1930s. His first client was Eastman Kodak and he is best known for his redesign of Kodak's 'Box Brownie' camera 1934 and his remodelling of Texaco's gas stations at the end of the decade, both in the popular 'streamline' style of the day. He is often called the 'dean of industrial design', implying his leadership in the field. He chaired the Board of Design for the New York World's Fair 1939.

teak tropical Asian timber tree *Tectona grandis*, family Verbenaceae, with yellowish wood used in furniture and shipbuilding.

teal any of various small, short-necked dabbling ducks of the genus *Anas*, order Anseriformes, but particularly *A. crecca*. The male is dusky grey; its tail-feathers ashy grey; the crown of its head deep cinnamon or chestnut; its eye is surrounded by a black band, glossed with green or purple, which unites on the nape; its wing markings are black and white; and its bill is black. The female is mottled brown. The total length is about 35cm/14 in.

Teapot Dome Scandal US political scandal that revealed the corruption of President ◊Harding's administration. It centred on the leasing of naval oil reserves 1921 at Teapot Dome, Wyoming, without competitive bidding, as a result of bribing the secretary of the interior, Albert B Fall (1861–1944). Fall was tried and imprisoned 1929.

tear gas any of various volatile gases that produce irritation and watering of the eyes, used by police against crowds and used in chemical warfare. The gas is delivered in pressurized, liquid-filled canisters or grenades, thrown by hand or launched from a specially adapted rifle. Gases (such as Mace) cause violent coughing and blinding tears, which pass when the victim breathes fresh air.

tears salty fluid exuded by lacrimal glands in the eyes. The fluid contains proteins that are antibacterial, and also absorbs oils and mucus. Apart from cleaning and disinfecting the surface of the eye, the fluid supplies nutrients to the cornea, which does not have a blood supply.

teasel erect, prickly, biennial herb *Dipsacus fullonum*, family Dipsacaceae, native to Eurasia. The dry, spiny seed heads were once used industrially to tease, or raise the nap of, cloth.

Tebbit Norman Beresford. Baron Tebbit 1931– . British Conservative politician. He was minister for employment 1981–83, minister for trade and industry 1983–85, chancellor of the Duchy of Lancaster 1985–87, and chair of the party 1985–87.

technetium (Greek *technetos* 'artificial') silver-grey, radioactive, metallic element, symbol Tc, atomic number 43, relative atomic mass 98.906. It occurs in nature only in extremely minute amounts, produced as a fission product from uranium in ◊pitchblende and other uranium ores. Its longest-lived isotope, Tc-99, has a half-life of 216,000 years. It is a superconductor and is used as a hardener in steel alloys and as a medical tracer.

Technicolor trade name for a film colour process using three separate negatives of blue, green, and red images. It was invented by Daniel F Comstock and Herbert T Kalmus in the USA 1922. Originally, Technicolor was a two-colour process in which superimposed red and green images were projected on to the screen by a special projector. When the three-colour process was introduced 1932, the system was widely adopted, culminating in its use in *The Wizard of Oz* and *Gone With the Wind*, both 1939.

techno dance music in Minimalist style played on electronic instruments, created with extensive use of studio technology for a futuristic, machine-made sound, sometimes with sampled soul vocals. The German band Kraftwerk (formed 1970) is an early example, and Germany continued to produce some of the best techno records in the 1990s.

technology the use of tools, power, and materials, generally for the purposes of production. Almost every human process for getting food and shelter depends on complex technological systems, which have been developed over a 3-million-year period. Significant milestones include the advent of the ◊steam engine 1712, the introduction of ◊electricity and the ◊internal combustion engine in the mid-1870s, and recent developments in communications, ◊electronics, and the nuclear and space industries. The advanced technology (highly automated and specialized) on which modern industrialized society depends is frequently contrasted with the low technology (labour-intensive and unspecialized) that characterizes some developing countries. ◊Intermediate technology is an attempt to adapt scientifically advanced inventions to less developed areas by using local materials and methods of manufacture. Appropriate technology refers to simple and small-scale tools and machinery of use to developing countries.

power In human prehistory, the only power available was muscle power, augmented by primitive tools, such as the wedge or lever. The domestication of animals about 8500 BC and invention of the wheel about 2000 BC paved the way for the water mill (1st century BC) and later the windmill (12th century AD). Not until 1712 did an alternative source of power appear in the form of the first working steam engine, constructed by English inventor Thomas Newcomen; subsequent modifications improved its design. English chemist and physicist Michael Faraday's demonstration of the dynamo 1831 revealed the potential of the electrical motor, and in 1876 the German scientist Nikolaus Otto introduced the four-stroke cycle used in the modern internal-combustion engine. The 1940s saw the explosion of the first atomic bomb and the subsequent development of the nuclear power industry. Latterly concern over the use of nonrenewable power sources and the ◊pollution caused by the burning of fossil fuels has caused technologists to turn increasingly to exploring renewable sources of energy, in particular ◊solar energy, wind energy, and ◊wave power.

materials The earliest materials used by humans were wood, bone, horn, shell, and stone. Metals were rare and/or difficult to obtain, although forms of bronze and iron were in use from 6000 BC and 1000 BC respectively. The introduction of the blast furnace in the 15th century enabled cast iron to be extracted, but this process remained expensive until English ironmaker Abraham Darby substituted coke for charcoal 1709, thus ensuring a plentiful supply of cheap iron at the start of the Industrial Revolution. Rubber, glass, leather, paper, bricks, and porcelain underwent similar processes of trial and error before becoming readily available. From the mid-1800s, entirely new materials, synthetics, appeared. First dyes, then plastic and the more versatile celluloid, and later drugs were synthesized, a process continuing into the 1980s with the growth of ◊genetic engineering, which enabled the production of synthetic insulin and growth hormones.

production The utilization of power sources and materials for production frequently lagged behind their initial discovery. The ◊lathe, known in antiquity in the form of a pole powered by a foot treadle, was not fully developed until the 18th century when it was used to produce objects of great precision, ranging from astronomical instruments to mass-produced screws. The realization that gears, cranks, cams, and wheels could operate in harmony to perform complex motion made ◊mechanization possible.

Early attempts at ◊automation include Scottish engineer James Watt's introduction of the fly-ball governor into the steam engine 1769 to regulate the machine's steam supply automatically, and French textile maker Joseph Marie Jacquard's demonstration 1804 of how looms could be controlled automatically by punched cards. The first moving assembly line appeared 1870 in meat-packing factories in Chicago, USA, transferring to the motor industry 1913. With the perfection of the programmable electronic computer in the 1960s, the way lay open for fully automatic plants.

The 1960s–90s saw extensive developments in the electronic and microelectronic industries (initially in the West, later overtaken by Japan and the Pacific region) and in the field of communications.

tectonics in geology, the study of the movements of rocks on the Earth's surface. On a small scale tectonics involves the formation of ◊folds and ◊faults, but on a large scale ◊plate tectonics deals with the movement of the Earth's surface as a whole.

Tecumseh 1768–1813. Native American chief of the Shawnee. He attempted to unite the Indian peoples from Canada to Florida against the encroachment of white settlers, but the defeat of his brother Tenskwatawa, 'the Prophet', at the battle of Tippecanoe in Nov 1811 by W H Harrison, governor of the Indiana Territory, largely destroyed the confederacy built up by Tecumseh.

Tedder Arthur William, 1st Baron Tedder 1890–1967. UK marshal of the Royal Air Force in World War II. As deputy supreme commander under US general Eisenhower 1943–45, he was largely responsible for the initial success of the 1944 Normandy landings. He was air officer commanding RAF Middle East 1941–43, where his method of pattern bombing became known as 'Tedder's carpet'.

Tees river flowing from the Pennines in Cumbria, England, to the North Sea via Tees Bay in ◊Cleveland; length 130 km/80 mi.

Teesside industrial area at the mouth of the river Tees, Cleveland, NE England; population (1981) 382,700. Industries include high technology, plastics, petrochemicals, electronics, capital-intensive steelmaking, chemicals, an oil-fuel terminal, and the main North Sea natural-gas terminal. A gas-fired power station opened 1993, the largest combined heat and power plant in the world.

tefillin or ***phylacteries*** in Judaism, two small leather boxes containing scrolls from the Torah, that are strapped to the left arm and the forehead by Jewish men for daily prayer.

Teflon trade name for polytetrafluoroethene (PTFE), a tough, waxlike, heat-resistant plastic used for coating nonstick cookware and in gaskets and bearings.

Tegucigalpa capital of Honduras; population (1991 est) 670,100. Industries include textiles and food-processing. It was founded 1524 as a gold- and silver-mining centre.

Tehran capital of Iran; population (1991) 6,476,000. Industries include textiles, chemicals, engineering, and tobacco. It was founded in the 12th century and made the capital 1788 by Muhammad Shah. Much of the city was rebuilt in the 1920s and 1930s. Tehran is the site of the Gulistan Palace (the former royal residence). There are three universities; the Shahyad Tower is a symbol of modern Iran.

Tehran Conference conference held 1943 in Tehran, Iran, the first meeting of World War II Allied leaders Churchill, Roosevelt, and Stalin. The chief subject discussed was coordination of Allied strategy in W and E Europe.

Teilhard de Chardin Pierre 1881–1955. French Jesuit theologian, palaeontologist, and philosopher. He developed a creative synthesis of nature and religion, based on his fieldwork and fossil studies. Publication of his *Le Phénomène humain/The Phenomenon of Man*, written 1938–40, was delayed (owing to his unorthodox views) until after his death by the embargo of his superiors. He saw humanity as being in a constant process of evolution, moving towards a perfect spiritual state.

Tej Bahadur 1621–1675. Indian religious leader, ninth guru (teacher) of Sikhism 1664–75, executed for refusing to renounce his faith.

Te Kanawa Kiri Janette 1944– . New Zealand soprano. Te Kanawa's first major role was the Countess in Mozart's *The Marriage of Figaro* at Covent Garden, London, 1971. Her voice combines the purity and intensity of the upper range with an extended lower range of great richness and resonance. She has also featured popular music in her repertoire, such as the 1984 recording of Leonard Bernstein's *West Side Story*.

tektite (from Greek *tektos* 'molten') small, rounded glassy stone, found in certain regions of the Earth, such as Australasia. Tektites are probably the scattered drops of molten rock thrown out by the impact of a large ◊meteorite.

Tel Aviv officially ***Tel Aviv-Jaffa*** city in Israel, on the Mediterranean coast; population (1994) 355,200. Industries include textiles, chemicals, sugar, printing, and publishing. Tel Aviv was founded 1909 as a Jewish residential area in the Arab town of Jaffa, with which it was combined 1949; their ports were superseded 1965 by Ashdod to the south. It is regarded by the UN as the capital of Israel.

telecommunications communications over a distance, generally by electronic means. Long-distance voice communication was pioneered 1876 by Alexander Graham Bell when he invented the telephone. Today it is possible to communicate internationally by telephone cable or by satellite or microwave link, with over 100,000 simultaneous conversations and several television channels being carried by the latest satellites.

history The first mechanical telecommunications systems were the ◊semaphore and heliograph (using flashes of sunlight), invented in the mid-19th century, but the forerunner of the present telecommunications age was the electric telegraph. The earliest practicable telegraph instrument was invented by William Cooke and Charles Wheatstone (1802–1875) in Britain 1837 and used by railway companies. In the USA, Samuel Morse invented a signalling code, ◊Morse code, which is still used, and a recording telegraph, first used commercially between England and France 1851.

Following German physicist Heinrich ◊Hertz's discoveries using electromagnetic waves, Italian inventor Guglielmo ◊Marconi pioneered a 'wireless' telegraph, ancestor of the radio. He established wireless communication between England and France 1899 and across the Atlantic 1901.

The modern telegraph uses teleprinters to send coded messages along telecommunications lines. Telegraphs are keyboard-operated machines that transmit a five-unit Baudot code (see ◊baud). The receiving teleprinter automatically prints the received message.

communications satellites The drawback to long-distance voice communication via microwave radio transmission is that the transmissions follow a straight line from tower to tower, so that over the sea the system becomes impracticable. A solution was put forward 1945 by the science-fiction writer Arthur C Clarke, when he proposed a system of communications satellites in an orbit 35,900 km/22,300 mi above the equator, where they would circle the Earth in exactly 24 hours, and thus appear fixed in the sky. Such a system is now in operation internationally. The satellites are called geostationary satellites (syncoms). The first to be successfully launched, by Delta rocket from Cape Canaveral, was *Syncom 2* in July 1963. Many such satellites are now in use, concentrated over heavy traffic areas such as the Atlantic, Indian, and Pacific oceans. Telegraphy, telephony, and television transmissions are carried simultaneously by high-frequency radio waves. They are beamed to the satellites from large dish antennae or Earth stations, which connect with international networks.

◊Integrated-Services Digital Network (ISDN) makes videophones and high-quality fax possible; the world's first large-scale centre of ISDN began operating in Japan 1988. ISDN is a system that transmits voice and image data on a single transmission line by changing them into digital signals. The chief method of relaying long-distance calls on land is microwave radio transmission.

Fibre-optic cables consisting of fine glass fibres present an alternative to the usual copper cables for telephone lines. The telecommunications signals are transmitted along the fibres as pulses of laser light.

In the UK, the first public telegraph line was laid between Paddington and Slough 1843. In 1980 the Post Office opened its first System X (all-electronic, digital) telephone exchange in London, a method already adopted in North America. In the UK Goonhilly and Madley are the main Earth stations for satellite transmissions. *See timeline on following page.*

Te Kanawa The soprano Kiri Te Kanawa. She left her native New Zealand and made her debut at Covent Garden in 1971 as Mozart's Countess Almaviva. Her warm voice is matched by a magnetic stage presence. *Polygram*

TELECOMMUNICATIONS: TIMELINE

1794	Claude Chappe in France built a long-distance signalling system using semaphore.
1839	Charles Wheatstone and William Cooke devised an electric telegraph in England.
1843	Samuel Morse transmitted the first message along a telegraph line in the USA, using his Morse code of signals – short (dots) and long (dashes).
1858	The first transatlantic telegraph cable was laid.
1876	Alexander Graham Bell invented the telephone.
1877	Thomas Edison invented the carbon transmitter for the telephone.
1878	The first telephone exchange was opened at New Haven, Connecticut.
1884	The first long-distance telephone line was installed, between Boston and New York, USA.
1891	A telephone cable was laid between England and France.
1892	The first automatic telephone exchange was opened, at La Porte, Indiana, USA.
1894	Guglielmo Marconi pioneered wireless telegraphy in Italy, later moving to England.
1900	Reginald Fessenden in the USA first broadcast voice by radio.
1901	Marconi transmitted the first radio signals across the Atlantic.
1904	John Ambrose Fleming invented the thermionic valve.
1907	Charles Krumm introduced the forerunner of the teleprinter.
1920	Stations in Detroit and Pittsburgh, USA began regular radio broadcasts.
1922	The BBC began its first radio transmissions, for the London station 2LO.
1932	The Telex was introduced in the UK.
1956	The first transatlantic telephone cable was laid.
1962	Telstar pioneered transatlantic satellite communications, transmitting live TV pictures.
1966	Charles Kao in England advanced the idea of using optical fibres for telecommunications transmissions.
1969	Live TV pictures were sent from astronauts on the Moon back to Earth.
1975	Prestel, the world's first viewdata system, using the telephone lines to link a computer data bank with the TV screen, was introduced in the UK.
1977	The first optical fibre cable was installed in California, USA.
1984	First commercial cellphone service started in Chicago, USA.
1988	International Services Digital Network (ISDN), an international system for sending signals in digital format along optical fibres and coaxial cables, launched in Japan.
1989	The first transoceanic optical fibre cable, capable of carrying 40,000 simultaneous telephone conversations, was laid between Europe and the USA.
1991	ISDN introduced in the UK.
1992	Videophones, made possible by advances in image compression and the development of ISDN, introduced in the UK.
1993	Electronic version of the *Guardian* newspaper, for those with impaired vision, launched in the UK. It enabled the newspaper to be transmitted to the user's home and printed out in braille or spoken by a speech synthesizer.
1995	The USA's main carrier of long-distance telecommunications, AT&T, processed 160 million calls daily, an increase of 50% since 1990.
1996	Researchers in Tokyo and California used lasers to communicate with an orbiting satellite – the first time lasers had been used in two-way communication with space. Work began on laying the world's longest optical fibre cable, on a 17,000-mile route around the globe.
1997	Plans announced in the USA for Internet2.

telegraphy transmission of coded messages along wires by means of electrical signals. The first modern form of telecommunication, it now uses printers for the transmission and receipt of messages. Telex is an international telegraphy network.

Overland cables were developed in the 1830s, but early attempts at underwater telegraphy were largely unsuccessful until the discovery of the insulating gum gutta-percha 1843 enabled a cable to be laid across the English Channel 1851. Duplex telegraph was invented in the 1870s, enabling messages to be sent in both directions simultaneously. Early telegraphs were mainly owned by the UK: 72% of all submarine cables were British-owned in 1900.

Telemachus in Greek mythology, son of ◊Odysseus and ◊Penelope. He attempted to control the conduct of his mother's suitors in Homer's *Odyssey* while his father was believed dead, but on Odysseus' return helped him to kill them, with the support of the goddess ◊Athena.

Telemann Georg Philipp 1681–1767. German Baroque composer, organist, and conductor. His prolific output of concertos for both new and old instruments, including violin, viola da gamba, recorder, flute, oboe, trumpet, horn, and bassoon, represent a methodical and fastidious investigation into the tonal resonances and structure of the new Baroque orchestra, research noted by J S Bach. Other works include 25 operas, numerous sacred cantatas, and instrumental fantasias.

telepathy 'the communication of impressions of any kind from one mind to another, independently of the recognized channels of sense', as defined by F W H Myers (1843–1901), cofounder 1882 of the Psychical Research Society, who coined the term.

telephone instrument for communicating by voice over long distances, developed by Alexander Graham ◊Bell 1876. The transmitter (mouthpiece) consists of a carbon microphone, with a diaphragm that vibrates when a person speaks into it. The diaphragm vibrations compress grains of carbon to a greater or lesser extent, altering their resistance to an electric current passing through them. This sets up variable electrical signals, which travel along the telephone lines to the receiver of the person being called. There they cause the magnetism of an electromagnet to vary, making a diaphragm above the electromagnet vibrate and give out sound waves, which mirror those that entered the mouthpiece originally.

The standard instrument has a handset, which houses the transmitter (mouthpiece), and receiver (earpiece), resting on a base, which has a dial or push-button mechanism for dialling a telephone number. Some telephones combine a push-button mechanism and mouthpiece and earpiece in one unit. A cordless telephone is of this kind, connected to a base unit not by wires but by radio. It can be used at distances up to about 100 m/330 ft from the base unit. In 1988 Japan and in 1991 Britain introduced an ◊Integrated Services Digital Network (see ◊telecommunications), providing fast transfer of computerized information.

See also ◊cellular phone, ◊mobile phone.

telephone tapping or ***telephone bugging*** listening in on a telephone conversation, without the knowledge of the participants; in the UK and the USA this is a criminal offence if done without a warrant or the consent of the person concerned.

teleprinter or ***teletypewriter*** transmitting and receiving device used in telecommunications to handle coded messages. Teleprinters are automatic typewriters keyed telegraphically to convert typed words into electrical signals (using a five-unit Baudot code, see ◊baud) at the transmitting end, and signals into typed words at the receiving end.

telescope optical instrument that magnifies images of faint and distant objects; any device for collecting and focusing light and other forms of electromagnetic radiation. It is a major research tool in astronomy and is used to sight over land and sea; small telescopes can be attached to cameras and rifles. A telescope with a large aperture, or opening, can distinguish finer detail and fainter objects than one with a small aperture. The ***refracting telescope*** uses lenses, and the ***reflecting telescope*** uses mirrors. A third type, the ***catadioptric telescope***, is a combination of lenses and mirrors. See also ◊radio telescope.

refractor In a refractor, light is collected by a ◊lens called the object glass or objective, which focuses light down a tube, forming an image magnified by an eyepiece. Invention of the refractor is attributed to a Dutch optician, Hans ◊Lippershey 1608. Hearing of the invention 1609, ◊Galileo quickly constructed one for himself and went on to produce a succession of such instruments which he used from 1610 onwards for astronomical observations. The largest refracting telescope in the world, at ◊Yerkes Observatory, Wisconsin, USA, has an aperture of 102 cm/40 in.

reflector In a reflector, light is collected and focused by a concave mirror. The first reflector was built about 1670 by Isaac ◊Newton. Large mirrors are cheaper to make and easier to mount than large lenses, so all the largest telescopes are reflectors. The largest reflector with a single mirror, 6 m/236 in, is at ◊Zelenchukskaya, Russia. Telescopes with larger apertures composed of numerous smaller segments have been built, such as the ◊Keck Telescope on ◊Mauna Kea. A ***multiple-mirror telescope*** was installed on Mount Hopkins, Arizona, USA, 1979. It consists of six mirrors of 1.8 m/72 in aperture, which perform like a single 4.5 m/176 in mirror. ◊***Schmidt telescopes*** are used for taking wide-field photographs of the sky. They have a main mirror plus a thin lens at the front of the tube to increase the field of view.

The ***liquid-mirror telescope*** is a reflecting telescope constructed with a rotating mercury mirror. In 1995 NASA completed a 3-m/9.8-ft liquid mirror telescope at its Orbital Debris Observatory in New Mexico, USA.

telescopes in space Large telescopes can now be placed in orbit above the distorting effects of the Earth's atmosphere. Telescopes in space have been used to study infrared, ultraviolet, and X-ray radiation that does not penetrate the atmosphere but carries much information about the births, lives, and deaths of stars and galaxies. The 2.4-m/94-in ◊Hubble Space Telescope, launched 1990, can see the sky more clearly than can any telescope on Earth.

In 1996 an X-ray telescope was under development by UK, US, and Australian astronomers, based on the structure of a lobster's eye, which has thousands of square tubes reflecting light onto the retina. The £4 million Lobster Eye telescope will contain millions of tubes 10–20 micrometres across and is intended for use on a satellite. ▷ *See feature on pp. 70–71.*

teletext broadcast system of displaying information on a television screen. The information – typically about news items, entertainment, sport, and finance – is constantly updated. Teletext is a form of ◊videotext, pioneered in Britain by the British Broadcasting Corporation (BBC) with Ceefax and by Independent Television with Teletext.

televangelist in North America, a fundamentalist Christian minister, often of a Pentecostal church, who hosts a television show and solicits donations from viewers. Well-known televangelists include Jim Bakker, convicted 1989 of fraudulent misuse of donations, and Jimmy Swaggart.

television (TV) reproduction at a distance by radio waves of visual images. For transmission, a television camera converts the pattern of light it takes in into a pattern of electrical charges. This is scanned line by line by a beam of electrons from an electron gun, resulting in variable electrical signals that represent the picture. These signals are combined with a radio carrier wave and broadcast as electromagnetic waves. The TV aerial picks up the wave and feeds it to the receiver (TV set). This separates out the vision signals, which pass to a cathode-ray tube where a beam of electrons is made to scan across the screen line by line, mirroring the action of the electron gun in the TV camera. The result is a recreation of the pattern of light that entered the camera. Twenty-five pictures are built up each second with interlaced scanning in Europe (30 in North America), with a total of 625 lines in Europe (525 lines in North America and Japan).

receiving aerials Because the wavelength of any television station is short a resonant ◊aerial becomes possible, and this usually consists of a half-wave aerial made of light alloy or steel tube, and fed at the centre with low-impedance coaxial or balanced cable. Greater gain is obtained if a reflector element is added, and quite complicated arrays are used in areas of weak signal strength.

These aerials are mounted either vertically or horizontally to conform with the polarization of the transmitting aerials. Tubing is used for the elements, since an aerial made of wire would be too sharply resonant, with resulting loss of bandwidth, and therefore poor picture definition.

television channels In addition to transmissions received by all viewers, the 1970s and 1980s saw the growth of pay-television cable networks, which are received only by subscribers, and of devices, such as those used in the Qube system (USA), which allow the viewers' opinions to be transmitted instantaneously to the studio via a response button, so that, for example, a home viewing audience can vote in a talent competition. The number of programme channels continues to increase, following the introduction of satellite-beamed TV signals.

Further use of TV sets has been brought about by ◊videotext and the use of video recorders to tape programmes for playback later or to play prerecorded video cassettes, and by their use as computer screens and for security systems. Extended-definition television gives a clear enlargement from

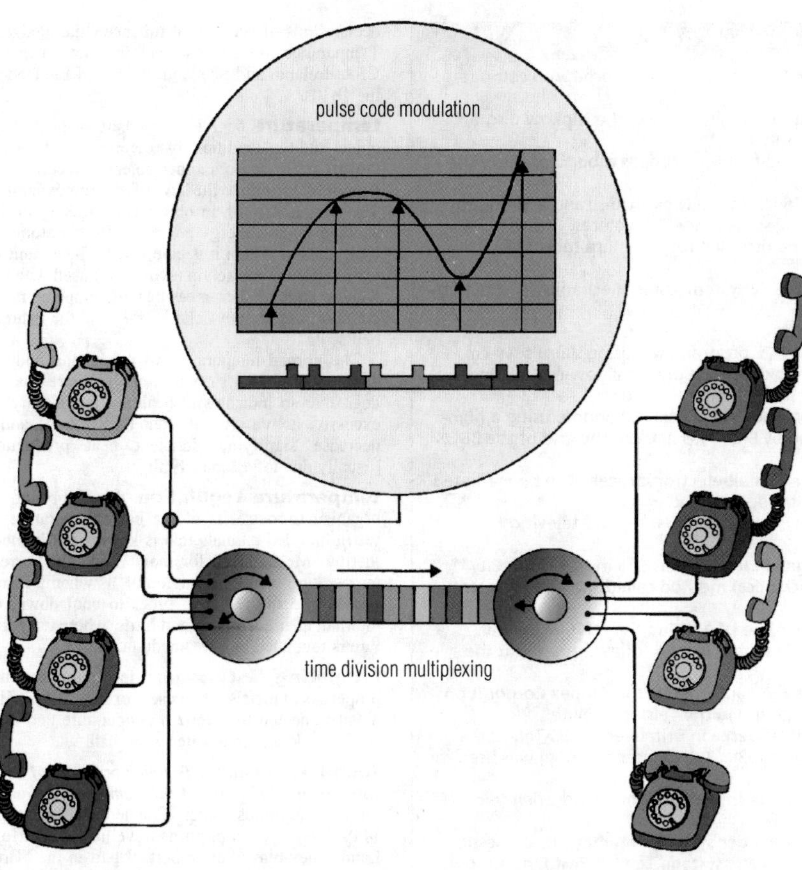

telephone In the telephone sound vibrations are converted to an electric signal and back again. The mouthpiece contains a carbon microphone that produces an electrical signal which varies in step with the spoken sounds. The signal is routed to the receiver via local or national exchanges. The earpiece contains an electromagnetic loudspeaker which reproduces the sounds by vibrating a diaphragm.

a microscopic camera and was first used 1989 in neurosurgery to enable medical students to watch brain operations.

history In 1873 it was realized that, since the electrical properties of the nonmetallic chemical element selenium vary according to the amount of light to which it is exposed, light could be converted into electrical impulses, making it possible to transmit such impulses over a distance and then reconvert them into light. The chief difficulty was seen to be the 'splitting of the picture' so that the infinite variety of light and shade values might be transmitted and reproduced. In 1908 it was found that cathode-ray tubes would best effect transmission and reception. Mechanical devices were used at the first practical demonstration of television, given by Scottish electrical engineer John Logie ◊Baird in London 27 Jan 1926, and cathode-ray tubes were used experimentally in the UK from 1934. The first high-definition television service in the world began Nov 1936 with the opening of the BBC's station at Alexandra Palace, London.

colour television Baird was an early pioneer in this area, and one of the first techniques developed employed a system whereby the normal frame frequency was increased by a factor of three, each successive frame containing the material for one primary colour. The receiver used revolving colour discs in front of the viewing screen, synchronized with the correct frame colours at the camera. A similar system replaced the colour discs by three superimposed projected pictures corresponding to the three primary colours. Baird demonstrated colour TV in London 1928, but it was not until Dec 1953 that the first successful system was adopted for broadcasting, in the USA. This is called the NTSC system, since it was developed by the National Television System Committee, and variations of it have been developed in Europe; for example, SECAM (sequential and memory) in France and Eastern Europe, and PAL (phase alternation by line) in most of Western Europe. The three differ only in the way colour signals are prepared for transmission, the scanning rate, and the number of lines used. When there was no agreement on a universal European system 1964, in 1967 the UK, West Germany, the Netherlands, and Switzerland adopted PAL while France and the USSR adopted SECAM. In 1989 the European Community (now the European Union) agreed to harmonize TV channels from 1991, allowing any station to show programmes anywhere in the EC.

The method of colour reproduction is related to that used in colour photography and printing. It uses the principle that any colours can be made by mixing the primary colours red, green, and blue in appropriate proportions. (This is different from the mixing of paints, where the primary colours are red, yellow, and blue.) In colour television the receiver reproduces only three basic colours: red, green, and blue. The effect of yellow, for example, is produced by combining equal amounts of red and green light, while white is formed by a mixture of all three basic colours.

Signals indicate the amounts of red, green, and blue light to be generated at the receiver. To transmit each of these three signals in the same way as the single brightness signal in black and white television would need three times the normal band width and reduce the number of possible stations and programmes to one-third of that possible with monochrome television. The three signals are therefore coded into one complex signal, which is transmitted as a more or less normal black and white signal and produces a satisfactory – or compatible – picture on black and white receivers. A fraction of each primary red, green, and blue signal is added together to produce the normal brightness, or luminance, signal. The minimum of extra colouring information is then sent by a special subcarrier signal, which is superimposed on the brightness signal. This extra colouring information corresponds to the hue and saturation of the transmitted colour, but without any of the fine detail of the picture. The impression of sharpness is conveyed only by the brightness signal, the colouring being added as a broad colour wash. The various colour systems differ only in the way in which the colouring information is sent on the subcarrier signal. The colour receiver has to amplify the complex signal and decode it back to the basic red, green, and blue signals; these primary signals are then applied to a colour cathode-ray tube.

The colour display tube is the heart of any colour receiver. Many designs of colour picture tubes have been invented; the most successful of these is known as the 'shadow mask tube'. It operates on similar electronic principles to the black and white television picture tube, but the screen is composed of a fine mosaic of over 1 million dots arranged in an orderly fashion. The glowing dots are so small that from a normal viewing distance the red, green, and blue merge into one another and a picture with a full range of colours is seen. **Digital television** (DTV) is a system of transmitting television programmes in digital codes. A common world standard for DTV, the ◊MPEG-2, was agreed in April 1993 at a meeting of engineers representing manufacturers and broadcasters from 18 countries. It is expected that DTV will have superseded the analogue television system by 2006. *See timeline on p. 1044.*

Already we Viewers, when not viewing, have begun to whisper to one another that the more we elaborate our means of communication, the less we communicate.

On TELEVISION
J B Priestley
Thoughts in the Wilderness 1957

telescope Three kinds of telescope. The refracting telescope uses a large objective lens to gather light and form an image which the smaller eyepiece lens magnifies. A reflecting telescope uses a mirror to gather light. The Schmidt telescope uses a corrective lens to achieve a wide field of view. It is one of the most widely used tools of astronomy.

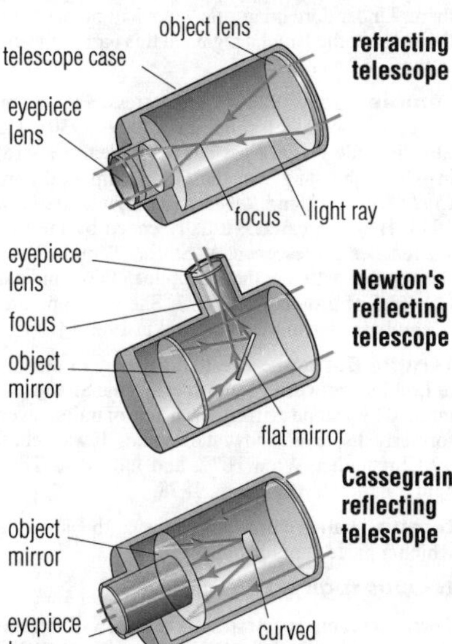

telex (acronym for *tel*eprinter *ex*change) international telecommunications network that handles telegraph messages in the form of coded signals. It uses ◊teleprinters for transmitting and receiving, and makes use of land lines (cables) and radio and satellite links to make connections between subscribers.

Telford Thomas 1757–1834. Scottish civil engineer. He opened up N Scotland by building roads and waterways. He constructed many aqueducts and canals, including the Caledonian Canal 1802–23, and erected the Menai road suspension bridge between Wales and Anglesey 1819–26, a type of structure scarcely tried previously in the UK. In Scotland he constructed over 1,600 km/1,000 mi of road and 1,200 bridges, churches, and harbours. In 1963 the new town of Telford, Shropshire, 32 km/20 mi NW of Birmingham, was named after him.

Tell Wilhelm (William) legendary 14th-century Swiss archer, said to have refused to salute the Habsburg badge at Altdorf on Lake Lucerne. Sentenced to shoot an apple from his son's head, he did so, then shot the tyrannical Austrian ruler Gessler, symbolizing his people's refusal to submit to external authority. The first written account of the legend dates from 1474, the period of the wars of the Swiss against Charles the Bold of Burgundy; but the story of a man showing his skill with the crossbow in such a way is much earlier.

Tell el Amarna site of the ancient Egyptian capital ◊Akhetaton. The Amarna tablets (a

TELEVISION: TIMELINE

1878	William Crookes in England invented the Crookes tube, which produced cathode rays.
1884	Paul Nipkow in Germany built a mechanical scanning device, the Nipkow disc, a rotating disc with a spiral pattern of holes in it.
1897	Karl Ferdinand Braun, also in Germany, modified the Crookes tube to produce the ancestor of the TV receiver picture tube.
1906	Boris Rosing in Russia began experimenting with the Nipkow disc and cathode-ray tube, eventually succeeding in transmitting some crude TV pictures.
1923	Vladimir Zworykin in the USA invented the first electronic camera tube, the iconoscope.
1926	John Logie Baird demonstrated a workable TV system, using mechanical scanning by Nipkow disc.
1928	Baird demonstrated colour TV.
1929	The BBC began broadcasting experimental TV programmes, using Baird's system.
1931	US physicist Allen Balcom Du Mont perfected the first practical, low-cost cathode-ray tube.
1936	The BBC began regular broadcasting from Alexandra Palace, London, using a high-definition all-electronic system developed by EMI. This marked the end of the BBC's usage of Baird's system.
1938	Allen Balcom Du Mont manufactured the first all-electronic receiver to be marketed in the USA. It used a huge 35 cm/14 in cathode-ray tube.
1939	The NBC (National Broadcasting Company) began the first regular television broadcasting service in the USA.
1940	Experimental colour TV transmission began in the USA, as CBS in New York City made colour broadcasts using a semi-mechanical method called the 'field sequential system'.
1953	Successful colour TV transmissions began in the USA, using the NTSC (National Television Systems Committee) system. This system is used today throughout the American continents and Japan.
1956	The first videotape recorder was produced in California by the Ampex Corporation.
1962	TV signals were transmitted across the Atlantic via the Telstar satellite.
1970	The first videodisc system was announced by Decca in Britain and AEG-Telefunken in Germany, but it was not perfected until the 1980s, when laser scanning was used for playback.
1973	The BBC and Independent Television in the UK introduced the world's first teletext systems, Ceefax and Oracle, respectively.
1975	Sony introduced their videocassette tape-recorder system, Betamax, for domestic viewers, six years after their professional U-Matic system. The UK Post Office (now British Telecom) announced their Prestel viewdata system.
1979	Matsushita in Japan developed a pocket-sized, flat-screen TV set, using a liquid-crystal display.
1986	Data broadcasting using digital techniques was developed; an enhancement of teletext was produced.
1989	The Japanese began broadcasting high-definition television; satellite television was introduced in the UK.
1990	The BBC introduced a digital stereo sound system (NICAM); MAC, a European system allowing greater picture definition, more data, and sound tracks, was introduced.
1992	All-digital high-definition television demonstrated in the USA.
1993	A worldwide standard for digital television agreed at meeting of manufacturers and broadcasters in Sydney, Australia. The Japanese electronics company NEC announced the development of a flat thin screen that produces full-colour high resolution pictures, without a cathode-ray tube. Television in the form of wraparound 'Sport' television glasses went on sale in the USA, enabling the wearer to watch television whilst walking.
1995	US House of Representatives voted in favour of including a chip in all TV sets that will allow parents to censor and block out certain categories of programmes that they consider unsuitable for their children's viewing.
1996	Agreement between television and computer industries heralded the development of next-generation TVs, high-definition televisions that incorporate digital receivers, modems, and other interactive services.

collection of Egyptian clay tablets with cuneiform inscriptions) were found there.

Teller Edward 1908– . Hungarian-born US physicist known as the father of the ◊hydrogen bomb. He worked on the fission bomb – the first atomic bomb – 1942–46 (the Manhattan Project) and on the fusion bomb, or H-bomb, 1946–52. In the 1980s he was one of the leading supporters of the Star Wars programme (◊Strategic Defense Initiative).

tellurium (Latin *Tellus* 'Earth') silver-white, semi-metallic (◊metalloid) element, symbol Te, atomic number 52, relative atomic mass 127.60. Chemically it is similar to sulphur and selenium, and it is considered one of the sulphur group. It occurs naturally in telluride minerals, and is used in colouring glass blue-brown, in the electrolytic refining of zinc, in electronics, and as a catalyst in refining petroleum. Its strength and hardness are greatly increased by addition of 0.1% lead; in this form it is used for pipes and cable sheaths.

Tellus in Roman mythology, the goddess of the Earth, identified with a number of other agricultural gods and celebrations.

Telstar US communications satellite, launched 10 July 1962, which relayed the first live television transmissions between the USA and Europe. *Telstar* orbited the Earth in 158 minutes, and so had to be tracked by ground stations, unlike the geostationary satellites of today.

Telugu language spoken in SE India. It is the official language of Andhra Pradesh, and is also spoken in Malaysia, giving a total number of speakers of around 50 million. Written records in Telugu date from the 7th century AD. Telugu belongs to the Dravidian family.

tempera painting medium in which powdered pigments are mixed with a water-soluble binding agent such as egg yolk. Tempera is noted for its strong, translucent colours. A form of tempera was used in ancient Egypt, and egg tempera was the foremost medium for panel painting in late medieval and early Renaissance Europe. It was gradually superseded by oils from the late 15th century.

temperament in music, a system of tuning ('tempering') the ◊pitches of a mode (a scale of five or more pitches to the octave) or ◊scale whereby ◊intervals are lessened or enlarged, away from the 'natural'. In folk music this is done to preserve its emotional or ritual meaning; in Western music to allow a measure of freedom in changing key.

temperance movement societies dedicated to curtailing the consumption of alcohol by total prohibition, local restriction, or encouragement of declarations of personal abstinence ('the pledge'). Temperance movements were first set up in the USA, Ireland, and Scotland, then in N England in the 1830s.

temperature degree or intensity of heat of an object and the condition that determines whether it will transfer heat to another object or receive heat from it, according to the laws of ◊thermodynamics. The temperature of an object is a measure of the average kinetic energy possessed by the atoms or molecules of which it is composed. The SI unit of temperature is the kelvin (symbol K) used with the Kelvin scale. Other measures of temperature in common use are the Celsius scale and the Fahrenheit scale.

The normal temperature of the human body is about 36.9°C/98.4°F. Variation by more than a degree or so indicates ill health, a rise signifying excessive activity (usually due to infection), and a decrease signifying deficient heat production (usually due to lessened vitality).

temperature regulation the ability of an organism to control its internal body temperature; in warm-blooded animals this is known as ◊homeothermy. Mechanisms for maintaining the correct temperature may be behavioural, as when a lizard moves into the shade in order to cool down, or internal, as in mammals and birds, where temperature is regulated by the ◊medulla.

tempering heat treatment for improving the properties of metals, often used for steel alloys. The metal is heated to a certain temperature and then cooled suddenly in a water or oil bath.

Templars or ***Knights Templar*** or ***Order of Poor Knights of Christ and of the Temple of Solomon*** military religious order founded in Jerusalem 1119–20 to protect pilgrims travelling to the Holy Land. They played an important part in the ◊Crusades of the 12th and 13th centuries. Innocent II placed them under direct papal authority 1139, and their international links allowed them to adapt to the 13th-century decline of the Crusader states by becoming Europe's bankers. The Templars' independence, power, and wealth, rather than their alleged heresy, probably motivated ◊Philip IV of France, helped by the Avignon pope Clement V, to suppress the order 1307–14. ▷*See feature on pp. 280–281.*

temple place of religious worship.

Temple site of Jewish national worship in Jerusalem in both ancient and modern days. The Western or Wailing Wall is the surviving part of the western wall of the enclosure of Herod's Temple. Since the destruction of the Temple AD 70, Jews have gone there to pray and to mourn their dispersion and the loss of their homeland.

Three temples have occupied the site: Solomon's Temple, built about 950 BC, which was destroyed by the Babylonian king Nebuchadnezzar 586 BC; Zerubbabel's Temple, built after the return of the Jews from Babylonian captivity 536 BC; and Herod's Temple, which was destroyed by the Romans. The Mosque of Omar currently stands there. Under Jordanian rule Jews had no access to the site, but the Israelis regained this part of the city in the 1967 war.

Temple Shirley 1928– . US actress. She became the most successful child star of the 1930s. Her films include *Bright Eyes* 1934 (Academy Award), in which she sang 'On the Good Ship Lollipop', *Curly Top* 1935, and *Rebecca of Sunnybrook Farm* 1938. Her film career virtually ended by the time she reached adolescence. As Shirley Temple Black, she became active in the Republican Party and was US chief of protocol 1976–77. She was appointed US ambassador to Czechoslovakia 1989.

Temple Bar former western gateway of the City of London, between Fleet Street and the Strand (site marked by a stone griffin); the heads of traitors were formerly displayed above it on spikes. It was rebuilt by Christopher Wren 1672, and moved to Theobald's Park, Hertfordshire, 1878.

tempo (Italian 'time') in music, the speed at which a piece should sound.

tempus fugit (Latin) time flies.

Temuco capital of Araucanía region, S Chile, situated to the N of the Lake District; population (1992) 240,900. Founded 1881, it is a market town for the

Mapuche Indians and a centre for coal, steel, and textile production.

tench European freshwater bony fish *Tinca tinca*, a member of the carp family, now established in North America. It is about 45 cm/18 in long, weighing 2 kg/4.5 lb, coloured olive green above and grey beneath. The scales are small and there is a barbel at each side of the mouth.

Ten Commandments in the Old Testament, the laws given by God to the Hebrew leader Moses on Mount Sinai, engraved on two tablets of stone. They are: to have no other gods besides Jehovah; to make no idols; not to misuse the name of God; to keep the sabbath holy; to honour one's parents; not to commit murder, adultery, or theft; not to give false evidence; and not to be covetous. They form the basis of Jewish and Christian moral codes; the 'tablets of the Law' given to Moses are also mentioned in the Koran. The giving of the Ten Commandments is celebrated in the Jewish festival of *Shavuot* (see ◊Pentecost).

tendon or ***sinew*** in vertebrates, a cord of very strong, fibrous connective tissue that joins muscle to bone. Tendons are largely composed of bundles of fibres made of the protein collagen, and because of their inelasticity are very efficient at transforming muscle power into movement.

tendril in botany, a slender, threadlike structure that supports a climbing plant by coiling around suitable supports, such as the stems and branches of other plants.

Tenerife largest of the ◊Canary Islands, Spain; area 2,060 sq km/795 sq mi; population (1986) 759,400. Santa Cruz is the main town, and Pico de Teide is an active volcano.

Teng Hsiao-ping alternative spelling of ◊Deng Xiaoping, Chinese politician.

Teniers David, ***the Younger*** 1610–1690. Flemish painter. He is best known for his scenes of peasant life, full of vitality, inspired by Adriaen Brouwer (1605–1638). His works were immensely popular and he became court painter to Archduke Leopold Wilhelm, governor of the Netherlands, in Brussels.

He was the son of David Teniers the Elder (1582–1649), from whom he received his principal instruction. Among his finest works are *Meeting of the Civic Guards* 1642 (Hermitage, St Petersburg) and *Village Fête* 1643 (National Gallery, London). As curator of the archduke's art collection, he made many copies of the pictures and a collection of engravings, *Theatrum Pictorium/Picture Theatre* 1660. He also painted portraits.

tendril Tendrils are specially modifed leaves, shoots, or stems. They support the plant by twining around the stems of other plants nearby, as in the pea, or they may attach themselves to suitable surfaces by means of suckers, as in the virginia creeper.

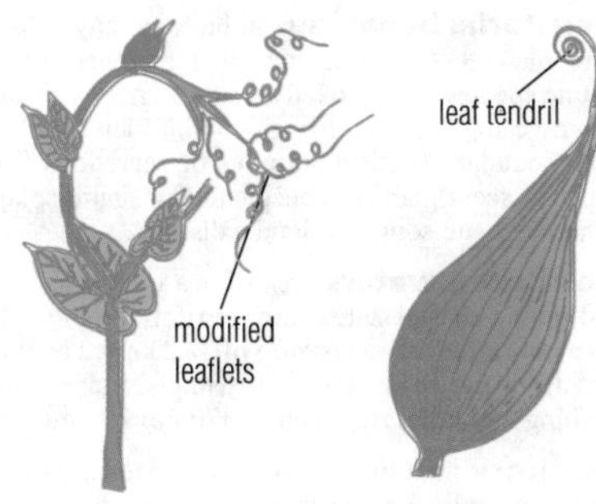

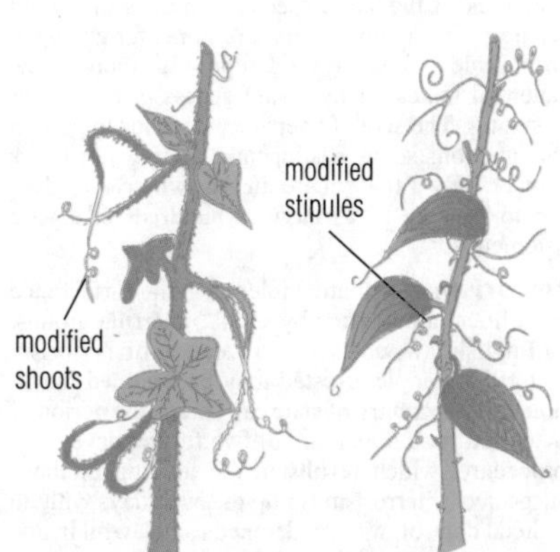

Tennessee state in E central USA; nicknamed Volunteer State
area 109,200 sq km/42,151 sq mi
capital Nashville
towns and cities Memphis, Knoxville, Chattanooga, Clarksville
features Great Smoky Mountains national park; Cumberland River; Newfoundland Gap, with Clingmans Dome (2,024 m/6,643 ft), the highest point in the state; Nashville, the capital of country music, with Opryland USA (*Grand Ole Opry*, the oldest radio show in the USA, started 1925, is broadcast from here); Memphis, home of the blues, with Sun Studio (the birthplace of rock and roll); the National Civil Rights Museum, site of the assassination of Martin Luther King Jr 1968; Civil War battlefield at Chattanooga; the headquarters of the Tennessee Valley Authority (TVA), established 1933, the largest electricity-generating station in the USA, at Knoxville; Oak Ridge National Laboratory, founded 1943 as part of the Manhattan Project to develop an atomic bomb; Fisk University, Vanderbilt University, and Belmont College, in Nashville; Graceland, the estate of Elvis Presley

Tennessee

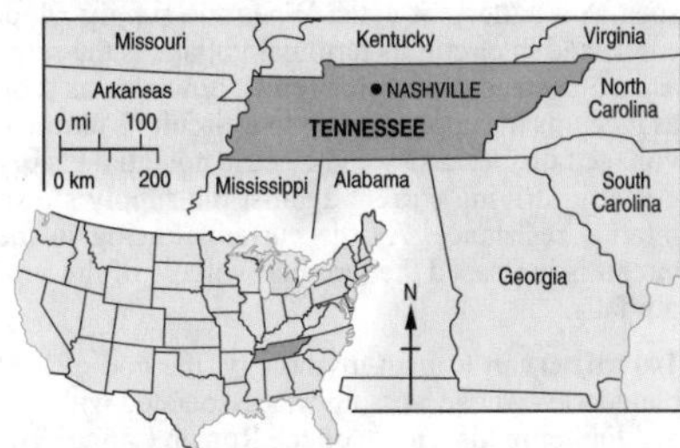

industries cereals, cotton, tobacco, soya beans, livestock, timber, coal, zinc, copper, chemicals
population (1990) 4,877,200
famous people Davy Crockett, David Farragut, W C Handy, Cordell Hull, Andrew Jackson, Andrew Johnson, Dolly Parton, John Crowe Ransom, Bessie Smith
history settled by Europeans 1757; became a state 1796. Tennessee was deeply divided in the Civil War; the battles of Shiloh, Murfreesboro, Chattanooga, and Nashville were fought here.

Tenniel John 1820–1914. English illustrator and cartoonist. He is known for his cartoons for *Punch* magazine and for his illustrations for Lewis Carroll's *Alice's Adventures in Wonderland* 1865 and *Through the Looking-Glass* 1872.

tennis or ***lawn tennis*** racket-and-ball game invented towards the end of the 19th century, derived from ◊real tennis. Although played on different surfaces (grass, wood, shale, clay, concrete), it is also called 'lawn tennis'. The aim of the two or four players is to strike the ball into the prescribed area of the court, with oval-headed rackets (strung with gut or nylon), in such a way that it cannot be returned. The game is won by those first winning four points (called 15, 30, 40, game), unless both sides reach 40 (deuce), when two consecutive points are needed to win. A set is won by winning six games with a margin of two over opponents, though a tie-break system operates, that is at six games to each side (or in some cases eight) except in the final set. A match lasts a maximum of five sets for men, three for women.

Major events include the ◊Davis Cup first contested 1900 for international men's competition, and the annual All England Tennis Club championships (originating 1877), an open event for players of both sexes at ◊Wimbledon. Wimbledon is one of the four Grand Slam events; the others are the US Open, first held 1881 as the US Championships, becoming the US Open 1968; the French Championships; and the Australian Championships. *See list of tables on p. 1177.*

Tennstedt Klaus 1926–1998. German conductor. A noted interpreter of Mozart, Beethoven, Bruckner, and Mahler, he was musical director of the London Philharmonic Orchestra 1983–87.

Tennyson A portrait of English poet Alfred, Lord Tennyson by the Swedish photographer Oscar Gustav Rejlander. Tennyson became poet laureate in 1850 and is admired for the lyrical quality of his work. His preference for narrative and epic form is demonstrated in such works as 'The Lotus Eaters' and 'Morte d'Arthur'. *Corbis*

Tennyson Alfred, 1st Baron Tennyson 1809–1892. English poet. He was poet laureate 1850–92. His verse has a majestic, musical quality, and few poets have surpassed his precision and delicacy of language. His works include 'The Lady of Shalott' 1833, 'The Lotus Eaters' 1833, 'Ulysses' 1842, 'Break, Break, Break' 1842, and 'The Charge of the Light Brigade' 1854; the longer narratives *Locksley Hall* 1832 and *Maud* 1855; and a long series of poems on the Arthurian legends, *The Idylls of the King* 1859–89.

The death of English writer Arthur Hallam (a close friend) 1833 prompted the elegiac sequence *In Memoriam*, which grew over the years into a record of spiritual conflict and a confession of faith; it was finally published (anonymously) 1850, the year in which he succeeded Wordsworth as poet laureate and married Emily Sellwood (1811–1889).

Tenochtitlán capital of the Mexican ◊Aztecs. It was founded c. 1325 on an island among the lakes that occupied much of the Valley of Mexico, on the site of modern Mexico City. Its population reached about 150,000. Spanish conquistador Hernán ◊Cortés met Aztec ruler ◊Montezuma here Nov 1519. Welcomed as guests, the Spaniards captured Montezuma and forced him to recognize the sovereignty of ◊Charles V. Cortés destroyed Tenochtitlán 1521 and rebuilt it as a Spanish colonial city.

tenor in music, the highest range of adult male voice when not using ◊falsetto, approximately C3–A5. It is the preferred voice for operatic heroic roles.

tenpin bowling indoor sport popular in North America and, since the 1960s, in Britain. As in skittles, the object is to bowl a ball down an alley at ten pins. The game is usually between two players or teams. A game of tenpins is made up of ten 'frames'. The frame is the bowler's turn to play and in each frame he or she may bowl twice. One point is scored for each pin knocked down, with bonus points for knocking all ten pins down in either one ball or two. The player or team making the greater score wins.

The game of ninepins was introduced to America by Dutch immigrants in the 17th century. By the end of the 19th century it was very popular as a gambling game on the streets of New York. Consequently it was outlawed; the extra pin was added to get round the law.

tension reaction force set up in a body that is subjected to stress. In a stretched string or wire it exerts a pull that is equal in magnitude but opposite in direction to the stress being applied at its ends. Tension originates in the net attractive intermolecular force created when a stress causes the mean distance separating a material's molecules to become greater than the equilibrium distance. It is measured in newtons.

tenure employment terms and conditions. Security of tenure is often granted to the judiciary,

'For men may come and men may go, / But I go on for ever.'

ALFRED TENNYSON
'The Brook'

I am a man, I count nothing human indifferent to me.

TERENCE
Heauton Timoroumenos

civil servants, educators, and others in public office, where impartiality and freedom from political control are considered necessary. The length of tenure depends on the service involved, and termination of it would only occur in exceptional cases, such as serious misconduct.

Tenzing Norgay known as *Sherpa Tenzing* 1914–1986. Nepalese mountaineer. In 1953 he was the first, with Edmund Hillary, to reach the summit of Mount Everest. He had previously made 19 Himalayan expeditions as a porter. He subsequently became a director of the Himalayan Mountaineering Institute, Darjeeling.

Teotihuacán huge ancient city in central Mexico, founded about 300 BC, about 32 km/20 mi N of modern Mexico City. Known as the 'metropolis of the gods', it reached its zenith in the 5th–6th centuries AD. As a religious centre of Mesoamerica, it contained two great pyramids and the temple of ◊Quetzalcoatl. It is one of the best-excavated archaeological sites in Mexico.

tequila Mexican alcoholic drink distilled from the ◊agave plant. It is named after the place, near Guadalajara, where the conquistadors first developed it from Aztec *pulque*, which would keep for only a day.

terbium soft, silver-grey, metallic element of the ◊lanthanide series, symbol Tb, atomic number 81, relative atomic mass 158.925. It occurs in gadolinite and other ores, with yttrium and ytterbium, and is used in lasers, semiconductors, and television tubes.

Terence (Publius Terentius Afer) c. 190–c. 159 BC. Roman dramatist. Born in Carthage, he was taken as a slave to Rome where he was freed and came under the patronage of the Roman general Scipio Africanus Minor. His surviving six comedies (including *The Eunuch* 161 BC) are subtly characterized and based on Greek models.

To keep a lamp going we have to keep putting oil in it.

MOTHER TERESA
Quoted in *Time* 29 Dec 1975

Teresa Mother (born Agnes Gonxha Bojaxhiu) 1910–1997. Roman Catholic nun. She was born in Skopje, Macedonia, and at 18 entered a Calcutta convent and became a teacher. In 1948 she became an Indian citizen and founded the Missionaries of Charity, an order for men and women based in Calcutta that helps abandoned children and the dying. Nobel Peace Prize 1979.

Teresa, St 1515–1582. Spanish mystic who founded an order of nuns 1562. She was subject to fainting fits, during which she saw visions. She wrote *The Way to Perfection* 1583 and an autobiography, *Life of the Mother Teresa of Jesus*, 1611. In 1622 she was canonized, and in 1970 was made the first female Doctor of the Church.

Tereshkova Valentina Vladimirovna 1937– . Soviet cosmonaut, the first woman to fly in space. In June 1963 she made a three-day flight in *Vostok 6*, orbiting the Earth 48 times.

term in architecture, a pillar in the form of a pedestal supporting the bust of a human or animal figure. Such objects derive from Roman boundary marks sacred to Terminus, the god of boundaries.

terminal in computing, a device consisting of a keyboard and display screen (◊VDU) to enable the operator to communicate with the computer. The terminal may be physically attached to the computer or linked to it by a telephone line (remote terminal).

terminal moraine linear, slightly curved ridge of rocky debris deposited at the front end, or snout, of a glacier. It represents the furthest point of advance of a glacier, being formed when deposited material (till), which was pushed ahead of the snout as it advanced, became left behind as the glacier retreated.

terminal velocity or ***terminal speed*** the maximum velocity that can be reached by a given object moving through a fluid (gas or liquid). As the speed of the object increases so does the total magnitude of the forces resisting its motion. Terminal velocity is reached when the resistive forces exactly balance the applied force that has caused the object to accelerate; because there is now no resultant force, there can be no further acceleration. For example, an object falling through air will reach a terminal velocity and cease to accelerate under the influence of gravity when the air resistance equals the object's weight.

terminal voltage the potential difference (pd) or voltage across the terminals of a power supply, such as a battery of cells. When the supply is not connected in circuit its terminal voltage is the same as its ◊electromotive force (emf); however, as soon as it begins to supply current to a circuit its terminal voltage falls because some electric potential energy is lost in driving current against the supply's own internal resistance. As the current flowing in the circuit is increased the terminal voltage of the supply falls.

Terminus in Roman mythology, the god of land boundaries whose worship was associated with that of ◊Jupiter in his temple on the Roman Capitol. His feast day was Feb 23.

termite any member of the insect order Isoptera. Termites are soft-bodied social insects living in large colonies which include one or more queens (of relatively enormous size and producing an egg every two seconds), much smaller kings, and still smaller soldiers, workers, and immature forms. Termites build galleried nests of soil particles that may be 6 m/20 ft high.

tern any of various lightly built seabirds in the gull family Laridae, order Charadriiformes, with pointed wings and bill, and usually a forked tail. Terns plunge-dive after aquatic prey. They are 20–50 cm/8–20 in long, and usually coloured in combinations of white and black. They are extensively distributed, especially in temperate climates. The common tern *Sterna hirundo* has white underparts, grey upper wings, and a black crown on its head. ▷ *See feature on pp. 704–705.*

terracotta (Italian 'baked earth') brownish-red baked clay, usually unglazed, used in building, sculpture, and pottery. The term is specifically applied to small figures or figurines, such as those found at ◊Tanagra in central Greece. Excavations at Xian, China, have revealed life-size terracotta figures of the army of the Emperor Shi Huangdi dating from the 3rd century BC.

terra firma (Latin) dry land; solid ground.

Terragni Giuseppe 1904–1942. Italian architect. He was largely responsible for introducing the ◊Modern Movement to Italy. As a leading member of Gruppo 7, he advocated a return to the principles of ◊Rationalism, inciting widespread opposition from the orthodox architectural establishment. Notable among his designs are the Novecomum block of flats, Como, 1927, and his masterpiece, the Casa del Fascio, Como, 1932–36, a crystalline white cube, devoid of ornament but clearly exhibiting its structure.

terra incognita (Latin) an unknown region.

terrane in geology, a tract of land with a distinct geological character. The term exotic terrane is commonly used to describe a rock mass that has a very different history from others near by.

terrapin member of some species of the order Chelonia (◊turtles and ◊tortoises). Terrapins are small to medium-sized, aquatic or semi-aquatic, and are found widely in temperate zones. They are omnivorous, but generally eat aquatic animals. Some species are in danger of extinction owing to collection for the pet trade; most of the animals collected die in transit.

terrier any of various breeds of highly intelligent, active dogs. They are usually small. Types include the bull, cairn, fox, Irish, Scottish, Sealyham, Skye, and Yorkshire terriers. They were originally bred for hunting rabbits and following quarry such as foxes down into burrows.

Territorial Army British force of volunteer soldiers, created from volunteer regiments (incorporated 1872) as the Territorial Force 1908. It was raised and administered by county associations, and intended primarily for home defence. It was renamed Territorial Army 1922. Merged with the Regular Army in World War II, it was revived 1947, and replaced by a smaller, more highly trained Territorial and Army Volunteer Reserve, again renamed Territorial Army 1979.

territorial behaviour in biology, any behaviour that serves to exclude other members of the same species from a fixed area or ◊territory. It may involve aggressively driving out intruders, marking the boundary (with dung piles or secretions from special scent glands), conspicuous visual displays, characteristic songs, or loud calls.

territorial waters area of sea over which the adjoining coastal state claims territorial rights. This is most commonly a distance of 22.2 km/12 nautical mi from the coast, but, increasingly, states claim fishing and other rights up to 370 km/200 mi.

territory in animal behaviour, a fixed area from which an animal or group of animals excludes other members of the same species. Animals may hold territories for many different reasons; for example, to provide a constant food supply, to monopolize potential mates, or to ensure access to refuges or nest sites. The size of a territory depends in part on its function: some nesting and mating territories may be only a few square metres, whereas feeding territories may be as large as hundreds of square kilometres.

terrorism systematic violence in the furtherance of political aims, often by small ◊guerrilla groups. In English law, under the Prevention of Terrorism Act 1984, people arrested may be detained for 48 hours; the secretary of state can extend the period of detention for a maximum of five further days. This procedure, which results in the holding of those suspected of terrorism for up to seven days with no judicial control, was condemned as unlawful by the European Court of Human Rights 1988.

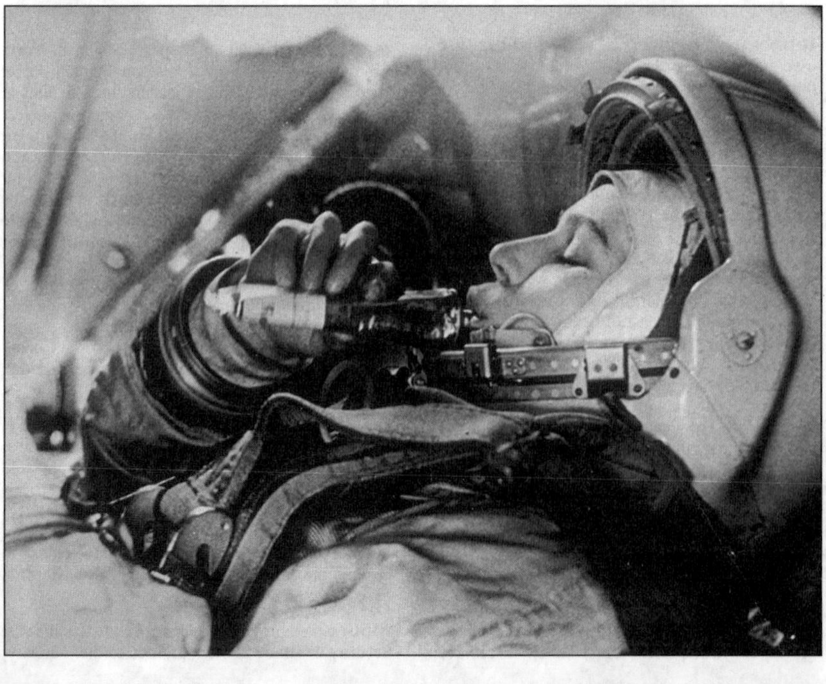

Tereshkova Russian cosmonaut and first woman in space Valentina Tereshkova, shown in the command module of *Vostok 6*. During her historic flight she made 48 orbits of the Earth with a total duration of nearly 71 hours. *Ann Ronan/Image Select (UK) Ltd*

territory Territorial activity of males of the small European bee *Lasioglossum calceatum*. They are seen here forming leks on vegetation – closely spaced sets of very small territories, each the preserve of a single male. Lekking behaviour has been observed among antelopes, birds, and insects – in particular butterflies, moths, flies, wasps, and bees. *K G Preston-Mafham/Premaphotos Wildlife*

Terror, Reign of period of the ◊French Revolution when the Jacobins were in power (Oct 1793–July 1794) under ◊Robespierre and instituted mass persecution of their opponents. About 1,400 were executed, mainly by guillotine, until public indignation rose and Robespierre was overthrown July 1794.

Terry (Alice) Ellen 1847–1928. English actress. She was leading lady to Henry ◊Irving from 1878. She excelled in Shakespearean roles, such as Ophelia in *Hamlet*. She corresponded with the dramatist G B Shaw.

Terry (John) Quinlan 1937– . English Post-Modernist architect. He works in a Neo-Classical idiom. His projects include country houses, for example Merks Hall, Great Dunmow, Essex, 1982, and the larger-scale riverside project at Richmond, London, commissioned 1984.

tertiary in the Roman Catholic Church, a member of a 'third order' (see under ◊holy orders); a lay person who, while marrying and following a normal employment, attempts to live in accordance with a modified version of the rule of one of the religious orders. The first such order was founded by St ◊Francis 1221.

Tertiary period of geological time 65–1.64 million years ago, divided into five epochs: Palaeocene, Eocene, Oligocene, Miocene, and Pliocene. During the Tertiary, mammals took over all the ecological niches left vacant by the extinction of the dinosaurs, and became the prevalent land animals. The continents took on their present positions, and climatic and vegetation zones as we know them became established. Within the geological time column the Tertiary follows the Cretaceous period and is succeeded by the Quaternary period.

Tertullian Quintus Septimius Florens c. AD 155–c. 222. Carthaginian theologian, one of the so-called Fathers of the Church and the first major Christian writer in Latin. He became a leading exponent of ◊Montanism.

Teruel province of northeastern Spain in Aragón autonomous community; area 14,802 sq km/5,715 sq mi; population (1991) 143,300. The province is mountainous – the highest point is the Jabalambre (2,020 m/6,627 ft) – and several rivers flow through it, including the Guadalaviar, the Guadalope, and the Turia. The economy is based mainly on sheep-rearing; other products include cereal, fruit, olive oil, and wine, and there are iron and lignite deposits. The capital is Teruel.

Terylene trade name for a polyester synthetic fibre produced by the chemicals company ICI. It is made by polymerizing ethylene glycol and terephthalic acid. Cloth made from Terylene keeps its shape after washing and is hard-wearing. Since 1970 it has been the most widely produced synthetic fibre, often under the generic name polyester.

terza rima poetical metre used in Dante's *Divine Comedy*, consisting of three-line stanzas in which the second line rhymes with the first and third of the following stanza.

tesla SI unit (symbol T) of ◊magnetic flux density. One tesla represents a flux density of one ◊weber per square metre, or 10^4 ◊gauss. It is named after Nikola Tesla.

Tesla Nikola 1856–1943. Croatian-born US physicist and electrical engineer who invented fluorescent lighting, the Tesla induction motor 1882–87, and the Tesla coil, and developed the ◊alternating current (AC) electrical supply system.

The Tesla coil is an air core transformer with the primary and secondary windings tuned in resonance to produce high-frequency, high-voltage electricity. Using this device, Tesla produced an electric spark 40 m/135 ft long in 1899. He also lit more than 200 lamps over a distance of 40 km/25 mi without the use of intervening wires. Gas-filled tubes are readily energized by high-frequency currents and so lights of this type were easily operated within the field of a large Tesla coil. Tesla soon developed all manner of coils which have since found numerous applications in electrical and electronic devices.

testa the outer coat of a seed, formed after fertilization of the ovule. It has a protective function and is usually hard and dry. In some cases the coat is adapted to aid dispersal, for example by being hairy.

Test Act act of Parliament passed in England 1673, more than 100 years after similar legislation in Scotland, requiring holders of public office to renounce the doctrine of ◊transubstantiation and take the sacrament in an Anglican church, thus excluding Catholics, Nonconformists, and non-Christians from office. Its clauses were repealed 1828–29. Scottish tests were abolished 1889. In Ireland the Test Act was introduced 1704 and English legislation on oaths of allegiance and religious declarations were made valid there 1782. All these provisions were abolished 1871.

Test Ban Treaty agreement signed by the USA, the USSR, and the UK 5 Aug 1963 contracting to test nuclear weapons only underground. In the following two years 90 other nations signed the treaty, the only major nonsignatories being France and China, which continued underwater and ground-level tests. In 1996 France announced the ending of its test programme, and supported the implementation of a universal test ban.

test cross in genetics, breeding experiment used to discover the genotype of an individual organism. By crossing with a double recessive of the same species, the offspring will indicate whether the test individual is homozygous or heterozygous for the characteristic in question. In peas, a tall plant under investigation would be crossed with a double recessive short plant with known genotype tt. The results of the cross will be all tall plants if the test plant is TT. If the individual is in fact Tt then there will be some short plants (genotype tt) among the offspring.

testis (plural *testes*) the organ that produces ◊sperm in male (and hermaphrodite) animals. In vertebrates it is one of a pair of oval structures that are usually internal, but in mammals (other than elephants and marine mammals), the paired testes (or testicles) descend from the body cavity during development, to hang outside the abdomen in a scrotal sac. The testes also secrete the male sex hormone ◊androgen.

Test match sporting contest between two nations, the most familiar being those played between the eight nations that play Test cricket (England, Australia, West Indies, India, New Zealand, Pakistan, South Africa, and Sri Lanka). Test matches can also be found in Rugby League and Rugby Union. A cricket Test match lasts a maximum of five days and a Test series usually consists of four to six matches. The first cricket Test match was between Australia and England in Melbourne, Australia, 1877.

testosterone in vertebrates, hormone secreted chiefly by the testes, but also by the ovaries and the cortex of the adrenal glands. It promotes the development of secondary sexual characteristics in males. In animals with a breeding season, the onset of breeding behaviour is accompanied by a rise in the level of testosterone in the blood.

Synthetic or animal testosterone is used to treat inadequate development of male characteristics or (illegally) to aid athletes' muscular development. Like other sex hormones, testosterone is a ◊steroid.

tetanus or ***lockjaw*** acute disease caused by the toxin of the bacillus *Clostridium tetani*, which usually enters the body through a wound. The bacterium is chiefly found in richly manured soil. Untreated, in seven to ten days tetanus produces muscular spasm and rigidity of the jaw spreading to other parts of the body, convulsions, and death. There is a vaccine, and the disease may be treatable with tetanus antitoxin and antibiotics.

tetany in medicine, muscle spasm caused by reduction in the concentration of calcium circulating in the blood. In the absence of calcium, the muscles become hyperexcitable and will go into spasm on the slightest stimulus. It is treated with calcium salts and vitamin D.

Tethys Sea sea that once separated ◊Laurasia from ◊Gondwanaland. It has now closed up to become the Mediterranean, the Black, the Caspian, and the Aral seas.

Tetley Glen 1926– . US choreographer and dancer. He was the first choreographer to attempt the

'It is certain because it is impossible.'

TERTULLIAN
De Carne Christi

Terry, Ellen British actress Ellen Terry, who played Mamilius in *The Winter's Tale* at the age of eight. She went on to become the leading Shakespearean actress of her time and had roles written for her by both George Bernard Shaw and James Barrie. *Private collection*

❛If a man's character is to be abused, say what you will, there's nobody like a relation to do the business.❜

William Makepeace Thackeray *Vanity Fair*

blending of ballet with modern dance idioms without strict adherence to the conventions of either, as in his first major work, *Pierrot lunaire* 1962, set to music by Schoenberg. Closely associated with the Netherlands Dance Theatre in the 1960s, he became director of the Stuttgart Ballet 1974–76, and often worked with the Ballet Rambert, as with his *The Tempest* 1979. In 1986, he staged *Alice*, based on Lewis Carroll's Wonderland stories, for the National Ballet of Canada, subsequently becoming the company's associate artistic adviser 1987.

Tet Offensive in the Vietnam War, a prolonged attack mounted by the ◊Vietcong against Saigon (now Ho Chi Minh City) and other South Vietnamese cities and hamlets (including the US Marine base at ◊Khe Sanh), which began 30 Jan 1968. Although the Vietcong were finally forced to withdraw, the Tet Offensive brought into question the ability of the South Vietnamese army and their US allies to win the war and added fuel to the antiwar movement in both the USA and Australia.

tetra any of various brightly coloured tropical freshwater bony fishes of the family Characidae, formerly placed in the genus *Tetragonopterus*. Tetras are found mainly in tropical South America, and also in Africa.

tetrachloromethane CCl_4 or ***carbon tetrachloride*** chlorinated organic compound that is a very efficient solvent for fats and greases, and was at one time the main constituent of household dry-cleaning fluids and of fire extinguishers used with electrical and petrol fires. Its use became restricted after it was discovered to be carcinogenic.

tetracycline one of a group of antibiotic compounds having in common the four-ring structure of chlortetracycline, the first member of the group to be isolated. They are prepared synthetically or obtained from certain bacteria of the genus *Streptomyces*. They are broad-spectrum antibiotics, effective against a wide range of disease-causing bacteria.

tetraethyl lead $Pb(C_2H_5)_4$ compound added to leaded petrol as a component of ◊antiknock to increase the efficiency of combustion in car engines. It is a colourless liquid that is insoluble in water but soluble in organic solvents such as benzene, ethanol, and petrol.

tetrahedron (plural ***tetrahedra***) in geometry, a solid figure (◊polyhedron) with four triangular faces; that is, a ◊pyramid on a triangular base. A regular tetrahedron has equilateral triangles as its faces. In chemistry and crystallography, tetrahedra describe the shapes of some molecules and crystals.

tetrapod (Greek 'four-legged') type of ◊vertebrate. The group includes mammals, birds, reptiles, and amphibians. Birds are included because they evolved from four-legged ancestors, the forelimbs having become modified to form wings. Even snakes are tetrapods, because they are descended from four-legged reptiles.

Teutonic Knight member of a German Christian military order, the ***Knights of the Teutonic Order***, founded 1190 by Hermann of Salza in Palestine. They crusaded against the pagan Prussians and Lithuanians from 1228 and controlled Prussia until the 16th century. They wore white robes with black crosses. Their capital was Marienburg (now Malbork, Poland).

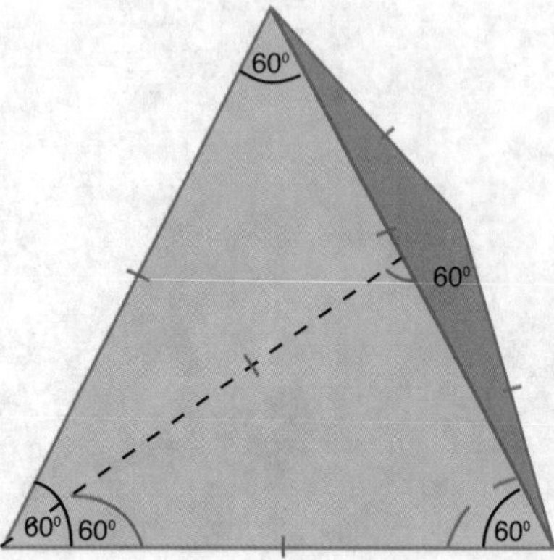

tetrahedron A regular tetrahedron is a pyramid on a triangular base with all its sides equal in length.

Texas state in southwestern USA; nicknamed Lone Star State
area 691,200 sq km/266,803 sq mi
capital Austin
towns and cities Houston, Dallas-Fort Worth, San Antonio, El Paso, Corpus Christi, Lubbock
features Rio Grande; Red River; arid *Llano Estacado* (Staked Plains); Big Bend national park in the Guadalupe Mountains, with canyons, the Chihuahuan Desert, and the Chisos Mountains; large pine forests in the east; Mission Ysleta, the oldest Spanish mission in the southwest; the Alamo, San Antonio, a monument to those who died 1836 while being besieged by the Mexican army; Lyndon B Johnson Space Center, Houston; Kimbell Art Museum, Fort Worth; buildings designed by I M Pei, including the First Interstate Bank Building, Dallas (1986), the Texas Commerce Tower, Houston, and the Morton H Meyerson Symphony Center, Dallas (1989); Rice University; Texas Medical Center; Lyndon B Johnson library and museum, Austin; Dallas, the site of the assassination of President J F Kennedy 1963
industries rice, cotton, sorghum, wheat, hay, livestock, shrimps, meat products, lumber, wood and paper products, petroleum (nearly one-third of US production), natural gas, sulphur, salt, uranium, chemicals, petrochemicals, nonelectrical machinery, fabricated metal products, transportation equipment, electric and electronic equipment
population (1990) 16,986,500
famous people James Bowie, George Bush, Buddy Holly, Sam Houston, Howard Hughes, Lyndon Johnson, Janis Joplin, Katherine Anne Porter, Patrick Swayze, Tina Turner
history settled by the Spanish 1682; part of Mexico 1821–36; Santa Anna massacred the Alamo garrison 1836, but was defeated by Sam Houston at San Jacinto the same year; Texas became an independent republic 1836–45, with Houston as president; in 1845 it became a state of the USA. Texas is the only state in the USA previously to have been an independent republic.

Texas

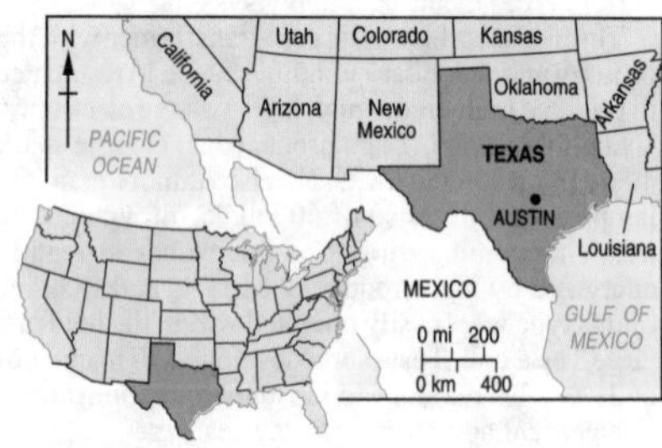

Texel or ***Tessel*** largest and southernmost of the ◊Frisian Islands, in North Holland province, the Netherlands; area 190 sq km/73 sq mi; population (1991) 12,700. Texel sheep are kept for their wool and cheese. The island is a good breeding ground for birds. Den Burg is the chief settlement.

textile (Latin *texere* 'to weave') woven fabric; formerly a material woven from natural spun thread, now loosely extended to machine knits and spun-bonded fabrics (in which a web of fibre is created and then fuse-bonded by passing it through controlled heat).
natural textiles These are made from natural fibres and include cotton, linen, silk, and wool (including angora, llama, and many others). For particular qualities, such as flame resistance or water and stain repellence, these may be combined with synthetic fibres or treated with various chemicals.
synthetics The first commercial synthetic thread was 'artificial silk', or rayon, with filaments made from modified cellulose (wood pulp) and known according to later methods of manufacture as viscose (using caustic soda and carbon disulphide) or acetate (using acetic acid); the first fully synthetic textile fibre was ◊nylon 1937. These, with acrylics, such as Orlon, used in knitwear, polyesters, such as Terylene, and spandex or elastomeric fibres, for example Lycra, form the basis of most of today's industry.
geotextiles These are made from plastic and synthetic fibres; either felted for use as filters or stabilizing grids, or woven for strength. They form part of drainage systems, road foundations, and barriers to sea and river defences against erosion.

The oldest known textile in the world, discovered in SE Turkey, is a fragment of woven linen which was carbon-dated 1993 as being 9,000 years old.

A fabric woven from flax, found in the Orkney Islands, was dated as being from around 2000 BC and is the oldest known British textile.

textured vegetable protein manufactured meat substitute; it is commonly known as TVP.

Teyte Maggie (Margaret) 1888–1976. English lyric soprano. She brought a French intimacy of style to her Mozartian roles, such as Cherubino in *The Marriage of Figaro*, and was coached as Mélisande in *Pelléas et Mélisande* by the opera's composer, Debussy.

TGV (abbreviation for ***train à grande vitesse***) (French 'high-speed train') French electrically powered train that provides the world's fastest rail service. Since it began operating 1981, it has carried more than 100 million passengers between Paris and Lyon, at average speeds of 214 kph/133 mph. In 1990, a TGV broke the world speed record, reaching a speed of 515.3 kph/320.2 mph on a stretch of line near Tours.

In 1990 a second service, the Atlantique, was launched, running from Paris to Le Mans and Tours. A third linking Paris with the Channel Tunnel, Brussels, and Cologne opened 1993. The TGV network now extends to the Mediterranean, Switzerland, and Brittany.

Thackeray William Makepeace 1811–1863. English novelist and essayist. He was a regular contributor to *Fraser's Magazine* and *Punch*. His first novel was *Vanity Fair* 1847–48, followed by *Pendennis* 1848, *Henry Esmond* 1852 (and its sequel *The Virginians* 1857–59), and *The Newcomes* 1853–55, in which Thackeray's tendency to sentimentality is most marked.

He studied law, and then art in Paris, before becoming a journalist in London. Other works include *The Book of Snobs* 1848 and the fairy tale *The Rose and the Ring* 1855.

Thai the majority ethnic group living in Thailand and N Myanmar (Burma). Thai peoples also live in SW China, Laos, and N Vietnam. They speak Tai languages, all of which belong to the Sino-Tibetan language family. There are over 60 million speakers, the majority of whom live in Thailand. Most Thais are Buddhists, but the traditional belief in spirits, *phi*, remains.

Thailand former name (to 1939 and 1945–49) ***Siam*** country in SE Asia on the Gulf of Siam, bounded E by Laos and Cambodia, S by Malaysia, and W by Myanmar (Burma). *See country box opposite and illustration on p. 1050.*

Thaïs lived 4th century BC. Greek courtesan, mistress of ◊Alexander the Great and later wife of ◊Ptolemy I, King of Egypt. She allegedly instigated the burning of ◊Persepolis.

thalassaemia or ***Cooley's anaemia*** any of a group of chronic hereditary blood disorders that are widespread in the Mediterranean countries, Africa, the Far East, and the Middle East. They are characterized by an abnormality of the red blood cells and bone marrow, with enlargement of the spleen.

Thalberg Irving Grant 1899–1936. US film-production executive. Aged 20 he was head of production at Universal Pictures, and in 1924 he became production supervisor of the newly formed Metro-Goldwyn-Mayer (MGM). He was responsible for such prestige films as *Ben Hur* 1926 and *Mutiny on the Bounty* 1935. With Louis B Mayer, he built up MGM into one of the biggest Hollywood studios of the 1930s.

Thales c. 624–c. 547 BC. Greek philosopher and scientist. He made advances in geometry, predicted an eclipse of the Sun 585 BC, and, as a philosophical materialist, theorized that water was the first principle of all things. He speculated that the Earth floated on water, and so proposed an explanation for earthquakes.

thalidomide ◊hypnotic drug developed in the 1950s for use as a sedative. When taken in early pregnancy, it caused malformation of the fetus (such as abnormalities in the limbs) in over 5,000 recognized cases, and the drug was withdrawn.

THAILAND
Kingdom of

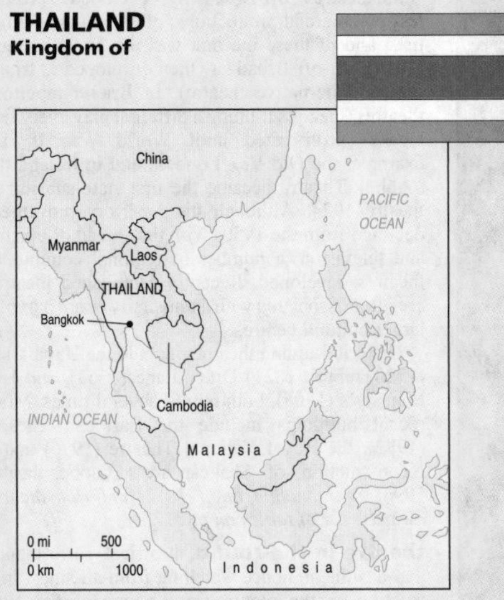

national name *Prathet Thai* or *Muang Thai*
area 513,115 sq km/198,108 sq mi
capital and chief port Bangkok
major towns/cities Chiangmai, Hat Yai, Khon Kaen
major ports Nakhon Sawan
physical features mountainous, semi-arid plateau in NE, fertile central region, tropical isthmus in S; rivers Chao Phraya, Mekong, and Salween
head of state King Bhumibol Adulyadej from 1946
head of government Chuan Leekpai from 1997
political system military-controlled emergent democracy
administrative divisions 76 provinces
political parties Democrat Party (DP), centre-left; Thai Nation (Chart Thai), right-wing, pro-private enterprise; New Aspiration Party (NAP), centrist; Palang Dharma Party (PDP), anti-corruption, Buddhist; Social Action Party (SAP), moderate, conservative; Chart Pattana (National Development), conservative
armed forces 258,000 (1995)
conscription two years
defence spend (% GDP) 2.6 (1994)
education spend (% GNP) 4.0 (1992)
health spend (% GDP) 1.1 (1990)
death penalty retained and used for ordinary crimes
population 58,703,000 (1996 est)
population growth rate 1.1% (1990–95); 0.9% (2000–05)
age distribution (% of total population) <15 28.3%, 15–65 66.7%, >65 5.0% (1995)
ethnic distribution 75% of the population is of Thai descent; 14% ethnic Chinese, one-third of whom live in Bangkok; Thai Malays constitute the next largest minority, followed by hill tribes; a substantial Kampuchean (Khmer) refugee community resides in border camps
population density (per sq km) 113 (1994)
urban population (% of total) 20% (1995)
labour force 57% of population: 64% agriculture, 14% industry, 22% services (1990)
unemployment 3.2% (1993)
child mortality rate (under 5, per 1,000 live births) 32 (1994)
life expectancy 65 (men), 69 (women)
education (compulsory years) 6
literacy rate 96% (men), 90% (women)
languages Thai and Chinese (both official); Lao, Chinese, Malay, Khmer
religion Buddhist
TV sets (per 1,000 people) 114 (1992)
currency baht
GDP (US $) 143.2 billion (1994)
GDP per capita (PPP) (US $) 6,350 (1993)
growth rate 8.5% (1994)
average annual inflation 5.1% (1994); 4.1% (1985–93)
major trading partners Japan, USA, Singapore, Germany, Taiwan, Hong Kong
resources tin ore, lignite, gypsum, antimony, manganese, copper, tungsten, lead, gold, zinc, silver, rubies, sapphires, natural gas, petroleum, fish
industries textiles and clothing, electronics, electrical goods, cement, petroleum refinery, sugar refinery, motor vehicles, agricultural products, beverages, tobacco, metals and metal products, plastics, furniture, tourism
exports textiles and clothing, electronic goods, rice, rubber, gemstones, sugar, cassava (tapioca), fish (especially prawns), machinery and manufactures, chemicals. Principal market: USA 21.5% (1993)
imports petroleum and petroleum products, machinery, chemicals, iron and steel, consumer goods. Principal source: Japan 30.2% (1993)
arable land 34.3% (1993)
agricultural products rice, cassava, rubber, sugar cane, maize, kenat (a jute-like fibre), tobacco, coconuts; fishing (especially prawns) and livestock (mainly buffaloes, cattle, pigs, and poultry)

HISTORY
13th C Siamese (Thai) people migrated south and settled in valley of Chao Phraya river in Khmer Empire.
1238 Siamese ousted Khmer governors and formed new kingdom based at Sukhothai.
14th and 15th Cs Siamese expanded at expense of declining Khmer Empire.
1350 Siamese capital moved to Ayatthaya (which also became name of kingdom).
1511 Portuguese traders first reached Siam.
1569 Conquest of Ayatthaya by Burmese ended years of rivalry and conflict.
1589 Siamese regained independence under King Naresuan.
17th C Foreign trade under royal monopoly developed with Chinese, Japanese, and Europeans.
1690s Siam expelled European military advisers and missionaries and adopted policy of isolation.
1767 Burmese invaders destroyed city of Ayatthaya, massacred ruling families and withdrew, leaving Siam in a state of anarchy.
1782 Reunification of Siam after civil war under General Phraya Chakri, who founded new capital at Bangkok and proclaimed himself King Rama I.
1824–51 King Rama III reopened Siam to European diplomats and missionaries.
1851–68 King Mongkut helped by European advisers modernized government, legal system, and army.
1856 Royal monopoly on foreign trade ended.
1868–1910 King Chulalongkorn continued modernization and developed railway network using Chinese immigrant labour; Siam became major exporter of rice.
1896 Anglo-French agreement recognized Siam as independent buffer state between British Burma and French Indo-China.
1932 Bloodless coup forced King Rama VII to grant a constitution with mixed civilian-military government.
1939 Siam changed its name to Thailand (briefly reverting to Siam 1945–49).
1941 Japanese invaded; Thailand became puppet ally of Japan under Field Marshal Phibun Songkhram.
1945 Japanese withdrawal; Thailand compelled to return territory taken from Laos, Cambodia, and Malaya.
1946 King Ananda Mahidol assassinated.
1947 Phibun regained power in military coup, reducing monarch to figurehead; Thailand adopted strongly pro-American foreign policy.
1955 Political parties and free speech introduced.
1957 State of emergency declared; Phibun deposed in bloodless coup; military dictatorship continued under General Sarit Thanarat (1957–63) and General Thanom Kittikachorn (1963–73).
1967–72 Thai troops fought with USA in Vietnam War.
1973 Military government overthrown by student riots.
1974 Adoption of democratic constitution, followed by civilian coalition government.
1976 Military reassumed control in response to mounting strikes and political violence.
1978 General Kriangsak Chomanan introduced constitution with mixed civilian-military government.
1980 General Prem Tinsulanonda assumed power.
1983 Prem relinquished army office to head civilian government; martial law maintained.
1988 Chatichai Choonhavan succeeded Prem as prime minister.
1991 Military coup imposed new military-oriented constitution despite mass protests.
1992 General election produced five-party coalition; riots forced Prime Minister Suchinda Kraprayoon to flee; Chuan Leekpai formed new coalition government.
1995 Ruling coalition collapsed; Banharn Silpa-archa appointed premier.
1996 Banharn resigned; general election resulted in new six-party coalition led by Chavalit Yongchaiyudh.
1997 Major financial crisis led to floating of currency. Austerity rescue plan agreed with International Monetary Fund (IMF).

SEE ALSO Buddhism; Bhumibol Adulyadej

In 1995 US researchers announced trials using thalidomide derivatives for a variety of immune disorders, including AIDS, cancer, and graft-versus-host disease (a complication of bone marrow transplants). It is already used routinely in the treatment of leprosy.

thallium soft, bluish-white, malleable, metallic element, symbol Tl, atomic number 81, relative atomic mass 204.38. It is a poor conductor of electricity. Its compounds are poisonous and are used as insecticides and rodent poisons; some are used in the optical-glass and infrared-glass industries and in photocells.

thallus any plant body that is not divided into true leaves, stems, and roots. It is often thin and flattened, as in the body of a seaweed, lichen, or liverwort, and the gametophyte generation (◊prothallus) of a fern.

Thames river in S England; length 338 km/210 mi. The longest river in England, it rises in the Cotswold Hills above Cirencester and is tidal as far as Teddington. Below London there is protection from flooding by means of the Thames Barrier (completed 1982). The headstreams unite at Lechlade.

Tributaries from the north are the Windrush, Evenlode, Cherwell, Thame, Colne, Lea, and Roding; and from the south, the Kennet, Loddon, Wey, Mole, Darent, and Medway. Around Oxford the river is sometimes called the Isis. *See illustration on following page.*

thane or ***thegn*** Anglo-Saxon hereditary nobleman rewarded by the granting of land for service to the monarch or a lord.

Thanet, Isle of northeast corner of Kent, England, bounded by the North Sea and the river Stour. It was an island until the 16th century, and includes the coastal resorts of Broadstairs, Margate, and Ramsgate.

Thanksgiving (Day) national holiday in the USA (fourth Thursday in Nov) and Canada (second Monday in Oct), first celebrated by the Pilgrim settlers in Massachusetts after their first harvest 1621.

Thant, U 1909–1974. Burmese diplomat, secretary general of the United Nations 1962–71. He helped to resolve the US-Soviet crisis over the Soviet installation of missiles in Cuba, and he made the controversial decision to withdraw the UN peacekeeping force from the Egypt–Israel border 1967 (see ◊Arab-Israeli Wars).

Tharp Twyla 1941– . US modern-dance choreographer and dancer. Tharp's work both entertains and challenges audiences with her ability to create serious and beautifully constructed ballets with an often amusing or flippant veneer. Reflecting her eclectic training, she has fused many dance styles including ballet, jazz, modern, tap, and avant-garde dance. Her works, frequently to set to popular music, include *Eight Jelly Rolls* 1971, *Deuce Coupe* 1973 (music by the Beach Boys), and *Push Comes to Shove* 1976 with Mikhail Baryshnikov, which was one of the most popular works of the decade.

In the 1980s Tharp focused on integrating emotional content into dance, as in *The Catherine Wheel* 1983. She has been instrumental in preserving the classical technique within the framework of modern dance.

‘I have known only too late ... the absolutely literal truth of Turner's saying, that the most beautiful skies in the world known to him were those of the Isle of Thanet.’

On the ISLE OF THANET
John Ruskin
Praeterita

Thailand An aerial view of Sukhothai, the capital of the Thai empire in the 13th–15th centuries, although the city is much older than this. Situated 450 km/280 mi NW of Bangkok, Sukhothai, or 'the dawn of happiness', was the cradle of Thai civilization. In the centre of the picture is a *chedi*, a Buddhist shrine. Despite the modern road which runs straight through the site, the area is now a historical park. *UNESCO*

Thatcher Margaret Hilda (born Roberts), Baroness Thatcher 1925– . British Conservative politician, prime minister 1979–90. She was education minister 1970–74 and Conservative Party leader 1975–90. In 1982 she sent British troops to recapture the Falkland Islands from Argentina. She confronted trade-union power during the miners' strike 1984–85, sold off majority stakes in many public utilities to the private sector, and reduced the influence of local government through such measures as the abolition of metropolitan councils, the control of expenditure through 'rate-capping', and the introduction of the community charge, or ◊poll tax, 1989. In 1990, splits in the cabinet over the issues of Europe and consensus government forced her resignation. An astute Parliamentary tactician, she tolerated little disagreement, either from the opposition or from within her own party.

Thatcher was the most influential peacetime Conservative prime minister of the 20th century. She claimed to have 'rolled back the frontiers of the state' by reducing income-tax rates, selling off council houses, and allowing for greater individual choice in areas such as education. However, such initiatives often resulted paradoxically in greater central government control. She left the opposition Labour Party in disarray, and forced it to a fundamental review of its policies. Her vindictiveness against the left was revealed in her crusade against local councils, which she pursued at the cost of a concern for social equity. In 1991 she made it evident that she intended to remain an active voice in domestic and international politics.

After leaving public office, in 1990, she has devoted herself to the development of her individual philosophy through the 'Thatcher Foundation'.

'I am extraordinarily patient, provided I get my own way in the end.'

MARGARET THATCHER Quoted in the *Observer* 4 April 1989

Thatcherism political outlook comprising a belief in the efficacy of market forces, the need for strong central government, and a conviction that self-help is preferable to reliance on the state, combined with a strong element of ◊nationalism. The ideology is associated with Margaret Thatcher but stems from an individualist view found in Britain's 19th-century Liberal and 20th-century Conservative parties, and is no longer confined to Britain.

theatre a place or building in which dramatic performances for an audience take place; these include ◊drama, dancing, music, ◊mime, ◊opera, ◊ballet, and ◊puppets. Theatre history can be traced to Egyptian religious ritualistic drama as long ago as 3200 BC. The first known European theatres were in Greece from about 600 BC.

The earliest theatres were natural amphitheatres. By the Hellenistic period came the development of the stage, a raised platform on which the action took place. In medieval times, temporary stages of wood and canvas, one for every scene, were set up in churches and market squares for the performance of mimes and ◊miracle plays. With the Renaissance came the creation of scenic illusion, with the actors appearing within a proscenium arch; in the 19th century the introduction of the curtain and interior lighting further heightened this illusion. In the 20th century, alternative types of theatre have been developed, including open stage, thrust stage, theatre in the round, and studio theatre.

Famous theatre companies include the ◊Comédie Française in Paris (founded by Louis XIV 1690 and given a permanent home 1792), the first national theatre. The Living Theater experimental group was founded in New York 1947 by Julian Beck and Judith Malina. In Britain the ◊National Theatre company was established 1963; other national theatres exist in Stockholm, Moscow, Athens, Copenhagen, Vienna, Warsaw, and elsewhere.

For traditional Japanese theatre, see ◊Nō and ◊kabuki.

centres of world theatre In the USA the centre of commercial theatre is New York City, with numerous theatres on or near ◊Broadway, although Williamsburg, Virginia (1716), and Philadelphia (1766) had the first known American theatres. The 'little theatres', off-Broadway, developed to present less commercial productions, often by new dramatists, and of these the first was the Theater Guild (1919); off-off-Broadway then developed as fringe theatre (alternative theatre). In Britain repertory theatres (theatres running a different play every few weeks) proliferated until World War II, for example, the Old Vic, London; and in Ireland the ◊Abbey Theatre became the first state-subsidized theatre 1924. Although the repertory movement declined from the 1950s with the spread of cinema and television, a number of regional community theatres developed. Recently established theatres are often associated with a university or are part of a larger cultural centre.

Historic London theatres include the Haymarket (1720, rebuilt 1821) Drury Lane (1663), and Her Majesty's (1705), both rebuilt several times. More recent buildings include the Barbican Theatre (1982), the Royal National Theatre (1976) and a reconstruction of Shakespeare's Globe theatre 1996. *See timeline on p. 1052 and (for theatre awards) list of tables on p. 1177.*

theatre-in-the-round theatrical performance that has the audience watching from all sides. In a reaction to the picture-frame stage of the 19th century, a movement began in the mid-20th century to design theatres with the performing area placed centrally in the auditorium. Notable examples are The Arena Stage in Washington, DC, USA, 1961 and the Royal Exchange in Manchester, England, 1976.

Thebes Greek name of an ancient city (***Niut-Amen***) in Upper Egypt, on the Nile. Probably founded under the first dynasty, it was the centre of the worship of Amen, and the Egyptian capital under the New Kingdom from about 1550 BC. Temple ruins survive near the villages of Karnak and Luxor, and in the nearby Valley of the Kings are buried the 18th–20th dynasty kings, including Tutankhamen and Amenhotep III.

Thebes capital of Boeotia in ancient Greece. In the Peloponnesian War it was allied with Sparta against Athens. For a short time after 371 BC when Thebes defeated Sparta at Leuctra, it was the most powerful state in Greece. Alexander the Great destroyed it 336 BC and although it was restored, it never regained its former power.

theft dishonest appropriation of another's property with the intention of depriving him or her of it permanently. In Britain, under the Theft Act 1968, the maximum penalty is ten years' imprisonment. The act placed under a single heading forms of theft that had formerly been dealt with individually; for example, burglary and larceny.

theism belief in the existence of gods, but more specifically in that of a single personal God, at once immanent (active) in the created world and transcendent (separate) from it.

theme park amusement park devised around a central theme or themes. The first theme park, Disneyland, opened 1955 in Anaheim, California, USA, and features Walt Disney's cartoon characters; other Disney parks exist in Florida, Japan, and France.

Disneyland covers 30 hectares/74 acres. Walt Disney World (approximately 11,000 hectares/27,000 acres) opened 1971 near Orlando, Florida; it was later enhanced by the creation of an adjacent Experimental Prototype Community of Tomorrow (EPCOT) centre (1982), featuring displays of advanced technology and re-creations of historical landmarks. Other ventures continuing the Disney theme include the Tokyo Disneyland (1983) and Euro Disney, near Paris (1992), which covers an area one-fifth the size of Paris. Features to be found in most theme parks include animatronics, robots which look like animals and people, all of which are programmed to perform lifelike movements and gestures to the accompaniment of a soundtrack.

There are some 15 theme parks in the UK. The three largest, all multi-themed, are Alton Towers in Staffordshire (1979), which attracts over 2 million visitors annually, and Thorpe Park (1980) and Chessington World of Adventure (1987), both in Surrey.

Themis in Greek mythology, one of the ◊Titans, the daughter of Uranus and Gaia. She was the personification of law and order.

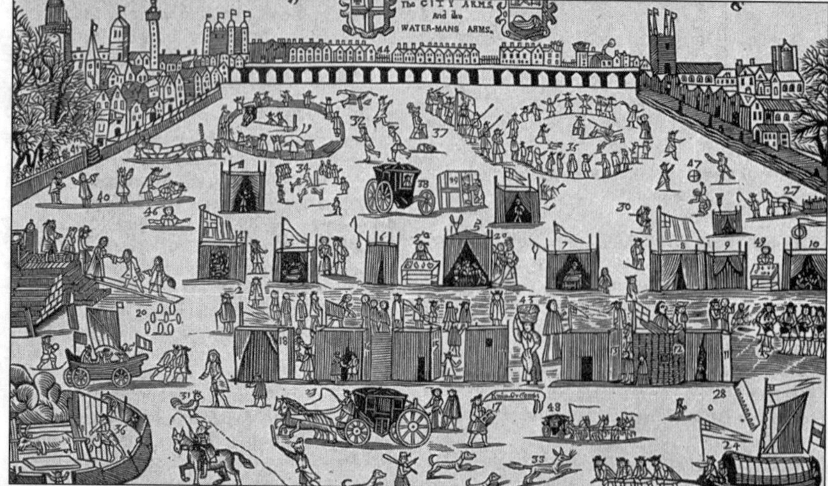

Thames A so-called frost fair, held on the frozen river Thames in the winter of 1683–84. *Philip Sauvain*

Thebes Ancient Egyptian wall paintings in a tomb at Thebes from about 1380 BC. *Philip Sauvain*

Themistocles c. 528–c. 462 BC. Athenian soldier and politician. Largely through his success in persuading the Athenians to build a navy, Greece was saved from Persian conquest. He fought with distinction in the Battle of ◊Salamis 480 BC during the Persian War. About 470 he was accused of embezzlement and conspiracy against Athens, banished, and fled to Asia, where Artaxerxes, the Persian king, received him with favour.

theocracy political system run by priests, as was once found in Tibet. In practical terms it means a system where religious values determine political decisions. The closest modern example was Iran during the period when Ayatollah Khomeini was its religious leader, 1979–89.

Theocritus c. 310–c. 250 BC. Greek poet. His *Idylls* became models for later pastoral poetry. Probably born in Syracuse, he spent much of his life in Alexandria under the Greek dynasty of the Ptolemies.

theodolite instrument for the measurement of horizontal and vertical angles, used in surveying. It consists of a small telescope mounted so as to move on two graduated circles, one horizontal and the other vertical, while its axes pass through the centre of the circles. See also ◊triangulation.

Theodora c. 508–548. Byzantine empress from 527. She was originally the mistress of Emperor Justinian before marrying him 525. She earned a reputation for charity, courage, and championing the rights of women. Justinian consulted her on all affairs of state.

Theodorakis Mikis 1925– . Greek composer. He was imprisoned 1967–70 for attempting to overthrow the military regime of Greece.

Theodoric the Great c. 455–526. King of the Ostrogoths from 474 in succession to his father. He invaded Italy 488, overthrew King Odoacer, and established his own Ostrogothic kingdom there, with its capital in Ravenna. He had no strong successor, and his kingdom eventually became part of the Byzantine Empire of Justinian.

Theodosius (I) the Great c. AD 346–395. Roman emperor. Appointed emperor of the East 379, he fought against the ◊Goths successfully, and established Christianity throughout the region. He invaded Italy 393, restoring unity to the empire, and died in Milan. He was buried in Constantinople.

Theodosius II 401–450. Byzantine emperor from 408 who defeated the Persians 421 and 441, and from 441 bought off ◊Attila's Huns with tribute.

theology study of God or gods, either by reasoned deduction from the natural world (natural theology) or through divine revelation (revealed theology), as in the scriptures of Christianity, Islam, or other religions. Other branches of theology include comparative theology (the study of the similarities and differences between faiths) and eschatology (the study of the hypothetical end of the world and afterlife).

Theophrastus c. 372–c. 287 BC. Greek philosopher, regarded as the founder of botany. A pupil of Aristotle, Theophrastus took over the leadership of his school 323 BC, consolidating its reputation. Of his extensive writings, surviving work is mainly on scientific topics, but includes the *Characters*, a series of caricatures which may have influenced the comic dramatist ◊Menander.

Theophrastus covered most aspects of botany: descriptions of plants, classification, plant distribution, propagation, germination, and cultivation. He distinguished between two main groups of flowering plants – dicotyledons and monocotyledons in modern terms – and between flowering plants and cone-bearing trees (angiosperms and gymnosperms).

theorbo bass ◊lute or archlute developed around 1500 and incorporating dual sets of strings, a set of freely vibrating bass strings for plucking with the thumb in addition to five to seven courses over a fretted fingerboard. It survived to form part of the Italian Baroque orchestra about 1700.

theorem mathematical proposition that can be deduced by logic from a set of axioms (basic facts that are taken to be true without proof). Advanced mathematics consists almost entirely of theorems and proofs, but even at a simple level theorems are important.

theory in science, a set of ideas, concepts, principles, or methods used to explain a wide set of observed facts. Among the major theories of science are ◊relativity, ◊quantum theory, ◊evolution, and ◊plate tectonics.

theosophy any religious or philosophical system based on intuitive insight into the nature of the divine, but especially that of the Theosophical Society, founded in New York 1875 by Madame Blavatsky and H S Olcott. It was based on Hindu ideas of ◊karma and ◊reincarnation, with ◊nirvana as the eventual aim.

Theravāda one of the two major forms of ◊Buddhism, common in SE Asia (Sri Lanka, Thailand, Cambodia, and Myanmar); the other is the later Mahāyāna. ▷ *See feature on pp. 162–163.*

Thérèse of Lisieux, St (originally Thérèse Martin) 1873–1897. French saint. She was born in Alençon, and entered a Carmelite convent in Lisieux at 15, where her holy life induced her superior to ask her to write her spiritual autobiography. She advocated the 'Little Way of Goodness' in small things in everyday life, and became known as the 'Little Flower of Jesus'. She died of tuberculosis and was canonized 1925.

therm unit of energy defined as 10^5 British thermal units; equivalent to 1.055 x 10^8 joules. It is no longer in scientific use.

thermal capacity another name for ◊heat capacity

thermal conductivity in physics, the ability of a substance to conduct heat. Good thermal conductors, like good electrical conductors, are generally materials with many free electrons (such as metals). Thermal conductivity is expressed in units of joules per second per metre per kelvin ($J s^{-1} m^{-1} K^{-1}$). For a block of material of cross-sectional area a and length l, with temperatures T_1 and T_2 at its end faces, the thermal conductivity λ equals $Hl/at(T_2 - T_1)$, where H is the amount of heat transferred in time t.

thermal expansion in physics, expansion that is due to a rise in temperature. It can be expressed in terms of linear, area, or volume expansion. The coefficient of linear expansion α is the fractional increase in length per degree temperature rise; area, or superficial, expansion β is the fractional increase in area per degree; and volume, or cubic, expansion γ is the fractional increase in volume per degree. To a close approximation, $\beta = 2\alpha$ and $\gamma = 3\alpha$.

thermal reactor nuclear reactor in which the neutrons released by fission of uranium-235 nuclei are slowed down in order to increase their chances of being captured by other uranium-235 nuclei, and so induce further fission. The material (commonly graphite or heavy water) responsible for doing so is called a moderator. When the fast newly-emitted neutrons collide with the nuclei of the moderator's atoms, some of their kinetic energy is lost and their speed is reduced. Those that have been slowed down to a speed that matches the thermal (heat) energy of the surrounding material are called thermal neutrons, and it is these that are most likely to induce fission and ensure the continuation of the chain reaction. See ◊nuclear reactor and ◊nuclear energy.

thermic lance cutting tool consisting of a tube of mild steel, enclosing tightly packed small steel rods and fed with oxygen. On ignition temperatures above 3,000°C/5,400°F are produced and the thermic lance becomes its own sustaining fuel. It rapidly penetrates walls and a 23-cm/9-in steel door can be cut through in less than 30 seconds.

Thermidor 11th month of the French Revolutionary calendar, which gave its name to the period after the fall of the Jacobins and the proscription of Robespierre by the National Convention 9 Thermidor 1794.

thermionics branch of electronics dealing with the emission of electrons from matter under the influence of heat. The thermionic valve (electron tube), used in radio and radar, is a device using space conduction by thermionically emitted electrons from an electrically heated cathode. In most applications valves have been replaced by ◊transistors.

thermistor semiconductor device whose electrical ◊resistance falls as temperature rises. The current passing through a thermistor increases rapidly as its temperature rises, and so they are used in electrical thermometers.

thermite process method used in incendiary devices and welding operations. It uses a powdered mixture of aluminium and (usually) iron oxide, which, when ignited, gives out enormous heat. The oxide is reduced to iron, which is molten at the high temperatures produced. This can be used to make a weld.

thermocouple electric temperature-measuring device consisting of a circuit having two wires made of different metals welded together at their ends. A current flows in the circuit when the two junctions are maintained at different temperatures (◊Seebeck effect). The electromotive force generated – measured by a millivoltmeter – is proportional to the temperature difference.

thermodynamics branch of physics dealing with the transformation of heat into and from other forms of energy. It is the basis of the study of the efficient working of engines, such as the steam and internal-combustion engines. The three laws of thermodynamics are (1) energy can be neither created nor destroyed, heat and mechanical work being mutually convertible; (2) it is impossible for an unaided self-acting machine to convey heat from one body to another at a higher temperature; and (3) it is impossible by any procedure, no matter how idealized, to reduce any system to the ◊absolute zero of temperature (0 K/−273°C/−459°F) in a finite number of operations. Put into mathematical form, these laws have widespread applications in physics and chemistry.

‘The stage is not merely the meeting place of all the arts, but is also the return of art to life.’

On the THEATRE
Oscar Wilde
Nineteenth Century
1885

THEATRE: TIMELINE

c. 3200 BC	Beginnings of Egyptian religious drama, essentially ritualistic.
c. 600	Choral performances (dithyrambs) in honour of Dionysus formed the beginnings of Greek tragedy, according to Aristotle.
500–300	Great age of Greek drama, which included tragedy, comedy, and satyr plays (grotesque farce).
468	Sophocles' first victory at the Athens festival. His use of a third actor altered the course of the tragic form.
458	Aeschylus' *Oresteia* first performed.
c. 425–388	Comedies of Aristophanes including *The Birds* 414, *Lysistrata* 411, and *The Frogs* 405. In tragedy the importance of the chorus diminished under Euripides, author of *The Bacchae* c. 405.
c. 320	Menander's 'New Comedy' of social manners developed.
c. 240 BC–AD 100	Emergence of Roman drama, adapted from Greek originals. Plautus, Terence, and Seneca were the main dramatists.
c. AD 400	Kālidāsa's *Sakuntalā* marked the height of Sanskrit drama in India.
c. 1250–1500	European mystery (or miracle) plays flourished, first in the churches, later in marketplaces, and were performed in England by town guilds.
c. 1375	Nō (or Noh) drama developed in Japan.
c. 1495	*Everyman*, the best known of all the morality plays, was first performed.
1525–1750	Italian commedia dell'arte troupes performed popular, improvised comedies; they were to have a large influence on Molière and on English harlequinade and pantomime.
c. 1540	Nicholas Udall wrote *Ralph Roister Doister*, the first English comedy.
c. 1576	The first English playhouse, The Theatre, was built by James Burbage in London.
c. 1587	Christopher Marlowe's play *Tamburlaine the Great* marked the beginning of the great age of Elizabethan and Jacobean drama in England.
c. 1588	Thomas Kyd's play *The Spanish Tragedy* was the first of the 'revenge' tragedies.
c. 1590–1612	Shakespeare's greatest plays, including *Hamlet* and *King Lear*, were written.
1604	Inigo Jones designed *The Masque of Blackness* for James I, written by Ben Jonson.
c. 1614	Lope de Vega's *Fuenteovejuna* marked the Spanish renaissance in drama. Other writers included Calderón de la Barca.
1636	Pierre Corneille's *Le Cid* established classical tragedy in France.
1642	An act of Parliament closed all English theatres.
1660	With the restoration of Charles II to the English throne, dramatic performances recommenced. The first professional actress appeared as Desdemona in Shakespeare's *Othello*.
1664	Molière's *Tartuffe* was banned for five years by religious factions.
1667	Jean Racine's first success, *Andromaque*, was staged.
1680	The Comédie Française was formed by Louis XIV.
1700	William Congreve, the greatest exponent of Restoration comedy, wrote *The Way of the World*.
1716	The first known American theatre was built in Williamsburg, Virginia.
1728	John Gay's *The Beggar's Opera* was first performed.
1737	The Stage Licensing Act in England required all plays to be approved by the Lord Chamberlain before performance.
1747	The actor David Garrick became manager of the Drury Lane Theatre, London.
1773	In England, Oliver Goldsmith's *She Stoops to Conquer* and Richard Sheridan's *The Rivals* 1775 established the 'comedy of manners'. Goethe's *Götz von Berlichingen* was the first *Sturm und Drang* play (literally, storm and stress).
1781	Friedrich Schiller's *Die Räuber/The Robbers*.
1784	Beaumarchais' *Le Mariage de Figaro/The Marriage of Figaro* (written 1778) was first performed.
1830	Victor Hugo's *Hernani* caused riots in Paris. His work marked the beginning of a new Romantic drama, changing the course of French theatre.
1878	Henry Irving became actor-manager of the Lyceum with Ellen Terry as leading lady.
1879	Henrik Ibsen's *A Doll's House*, an early example of realism in European theatre.
1888	August Strindberg wrote *Miss Julie*.
1893	George Bernard Shaw wrote *Mrs Warren's Profession* (banned until 1902 because it deals with prostitution). Shaw's works brought the new realistic drama to Britain and introduced social and political issues as subjects for the theatre.
1895	Oscar Wilde's comedy *The Importance of Being Earnest*.
1896	The first performance of Anton Chekhov's *The Seagull* failed. Alfred Jarry's *Ubu Roi*, a forerunner of Surrealism, produced in Paris.
1904	Chekhov's *The Cherry Orchard*. The Academy of Dramatic Art (Royal Academy of Dramatic Art 1920) was founded in London to train young actors. The Abbey Theatre, Dublin, opened by W B Yeats and Lady Gregory, marked the beginning of an Irish dramatic revival.
1919	The Theater Guild was founded in the USA to perform less commercial new plays.
1920	*Beyond the Horizon*, Eugene O'Neill's first play, marked the beginning of serious theatre in the USA.
1921	Luigi Pirandello's *Six Characters in Search of an Author* introduced themes of the individual and exploration of reality and appearance.
1927	*Show Boat*, composed by Jerome Kern with libretto by Oscar Hammerstein II, laid the foundations of the US musical.
1928	Bertolt Brecht's *Die Dreigroschenoper/The Threepenny Opera* with score by Kurt Weill; other political satires by Karel Čapek and Elmer Rice. In the USA musical comedies by Cole Porter, Irving Berlin, and George Gershwin were popular.
1930s	US social-protest plays of Clifford Odets, Lillian Hellman, Thornton Wilder, and William Saroyan.
1935	T S Eliot's *Murder in the Cathedral*.
1935–39	WPA Federal Theater Project in the USA.
1938	Publication of Antonin Artaud's *Theatre and Its Double*.
1943	The first of the Rodgers and Hammerstein musicals, *Oklahoma!*, opened.
1944	Jean-Paul Sartre's *Huis Clos/In Camera*; Jean Anouilh's *Antigone*.
post-1945	Resurgence of German-language theatre, including Wolfgang Borchert, Max Frisch, Friedrich Dürrenmatt, and Peter Weiss.
1947	Tennessee Williams' *A Streetcar Named Desire*. First Edinburgh Festival, Scotland, with fringe theatre events.
1949	Bertolt Brecht and Helene Weigel founded the Berliner Ensemble in East Germany.
1953	Arthur Miller's *The Crucible* opened in the USA; *En attendant Godot/Waiting for Godot* by Samuel Beckett exemplified the Theatre of the Absurd.
1956	The English Stage Company was formed at the Royal Court Theatre, London to provide a platform for new dramatists. John Osborne's *Look Back in Anger* was included in its first season.
1957	Leonard Bernstein's *West Side Story* opened in New York.
1960	Harold Pinter's *The Caretaker* was produced in London.
1960s	Off-off-Broadway theatre, a more daring and experimental type of drama, began to develop in New York. Fringe theatre developed in Britain.
1961	The Royal Shakespeare Company was formed in the UK under the directorship of Peter Hall.
1963–64	The UK National Theatre Company was formed at the Old Vic under the directorship of Laurence Olivier.
1964	Théâtre du Soleil, directed by Ariane Mnouchkine, founded in Paris.
1967	Athol Fugard founded the Serpent Players as an integrated company in Port Elizabeth, South Africa; success in the USA of *Hair*, the first of the 'rock' musicals; Tom Stoppard's *Rosencrantz and Guildenstern are Dead* was produced in London.
1968	Abolition of pre-censorship theatre in the UK.
1970	Peter Brook founded his international company, the International Centre for Theatre Research, in Paris; first festival of Chicano theatre in the USA.
1970s	Women's theatre movement developed in the USA and Europe.
1972	Sam Shepherd's *The Tooth of Crime* performed in London.
1974	Athol Fugard's *Statements After an Arrest under the Immorality Act* performed in London.
1975	*A Chorus Line* opened in New York; Tadeusz Kantor's *Dead Class* produced in Poland.
1980	Howard Brenton's *The Romans in Britain* led in the UK to a private prosecution of the director for obscenity; David Edgar's *The Life and Times of Nicholas Nickleby* performed in London.
1985	Peter Brook's first production of *The Mahabharata* produced at the Avignon Festival.
1987	The Japanese Ninagawa Company performed Shakespeare's *Macbeth* in London.
1989	Discovery of the remains of the 16th-century Rose and Globe theatres, London.
1990	The Royal Shakespeare Company suspended its work at the Barbican Centre, London, for six months, pleading lack of funds.
1992	Ariane Mnouchkine's production of *Les Atrides* performed in Paris and the UK; Robert Wilson's production of *Alice* performed in Germany.
1993	Construction of the new Globe Theatre, a replica of the Elizabethan Globe Playhouse, began in London, approximately 183 m/600 ft from the site of the original Globe.
1994	The Abbey Theatre in Dublin produced Frank McGuinness's *Observe the Sons of Ulster Marching Towards the Somme* as a gesture of peace and reconciliation following the declaration of the Northern Ireland cease-fire.
1995	The National Lottery in the UK began to distribute millions of pounds to the theatre. However, most was allocated to the large prestigious concerns, and many small and medium-scale touring companies were left disappointed.
1996	Trevor Nunn was appointed director of the Royal National Theatre in London. The Prologue Season at the new Globe Theatre in London opened with *The Two Gentlemen of Verona*.

thermography photographic recording of heat patterns. It is used medically as an imaging technique to identify 'hot spots' in the body – for example, tumours, where cells are more active than usual. Thermography was developed in the 1970s and 1980s by the military to assist night vision by detecting the body heat of an enemy or the hot engine of a tank. It uses a photographic method (using infrared radiation) employing infrared-sensitive films.

thermoluminescence release in the form of light of stored energy from a substance heated by irradiation. It occurs with most crystalline substances to some extent. It is used in archaeology to date pottery, and by geologists in studying terrestrial rocks and meteorites.

thermometer instrument for measuring temperature. There are many types, designed to measure different temperature ranges to varying degrees of accuracy. Each makes use of a different physical effect of temperature. Expansion of a liquid is employed in common ***liquid-in-glass thermometers***, such as those containing mercury or alcohol. The more accurate ***gas thermometer*** uses the effect of temperature on the pressure of a gas held at constant volume. A ***resistance thermometer*** takes advantage of the change in resistance of a conductor (such as a platinum wire) with variation in temperature. Another electrical thermometer is the ◊thermocouple. Mechanically, temperature change can be indicated by the change in curvature of a bimetallic strip (as commonly used in a ◊thermostat).

thermoplastic or ***thermosoftening plastic*** type of ◊plastic that always softens on repeated heating. Thermoplastics include polyethylene (polyethene), polystyrene, nylon, and polyester.

Thermopylae, Battle of battle during the ◊Persian Wars 480 BC when Leonidas, King of Sparta, and 300 men defended the pass of Thermopylae against a much greater force of Persians. The pass led from Thessaly to Phocis in central Greece.

thermoset type of ◊plastic that remains rigid when set, and does not soften with heating. Examples include Bakelite, resins, melamine, and urea-formaldehyde resins.

thermosphere layer in the Earth's ◊atmosphere above the mesosphere and below the exosphere. Its lower level is about 80 km/50 mi above the ground, but its upper level is undefined. The ionosphere is located in the thermosphere. In the thermosphere the temperature rises with increasing height to several thousand degrees Celsius. However, because of the thinness of the air, very little heat is actually present.

thermometer **Maximum and minimum thermometers are universally used in weather-reporting stations. The maximum thermometer, shown here, includes a magnet that fits tightly inside a capillary tube and is moved up it by the rising mercury. When the temperature falls, the magnet remains in position, thus enabling the maximum temperature to be recorded.**

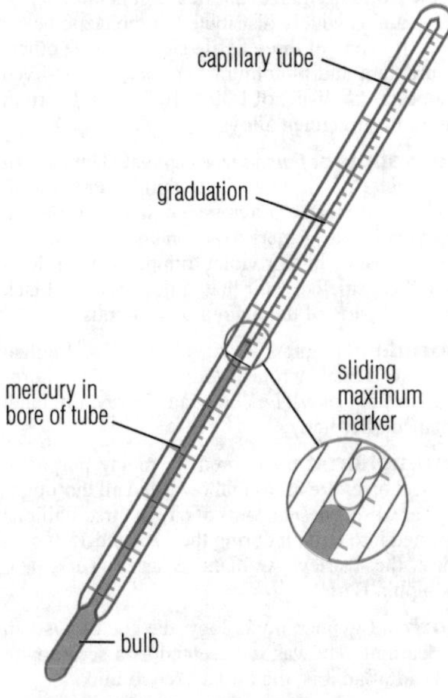

thermostat temperature-controlling device that makes use of feedback. It employs a temperature sensor (often a bimetallic strip) to operate a switch or valve to control electricity or fuel supply. Thermostats are used in central heating, ovens, and car engines.

Theroux Paul Edward 1941– . US novelist and travel writer. His works include the novels *Saint Jack* 1973, *The Mosquito Coast* 1981, *Doctor Slaughter* 1984, and *Chicago Loop* 1990. His accounts of his travels by train, notable for their sharp depiction of the socio-economic divides, include *The Great Railway Bazaar* 1975, *The Old Patagonian Express* 1979, *The Kingdom by the Sea* 1983, and *Riding the Iron Rooster* 1988.

thesaurus (Greek 'treasure') extensive collection of synonyms or words with related meaning. Thesaurus compilers include Francis ◊Bacon, Comenius (1592–1670), and Peter Mark ◊Roget, whose work was published 1852.

Theseus in Greek mythology, a hero of ◊Attica, supposed to have united the states of the area under a constitutional government in Athens. Ariadne, whom he later abandoned on Naxos, helped him find his way through the Labyrinth to kill the ◊Minotaur. He also fought the Amazons and was one of the ◊Argonauts.

Thespis lived 6th century BC. Greek poet. He is said to have introduced the first actor into dramatic performances (previously presented by choruses only), hence the word thespian for an actor. He is also said to have invented tragedy and to have introduced the wearing of linen masks.

Thessaloníki (English ***Salonika***) port in Macedonia, NE Greece, at the head of the Gulf of Thessaloníki; the second-largest city in Greece; population (1991) 378,000. Industries include textiles, shipbuilding, chemicals, brewing, and tanning. It was founded from Corinth by the Romans 315 BC as ***Thessalonica***, captured by the Saracens AD 904 and by the Turks 1430, and restored to Greece 1912.

Thessaly (Greek ***Thessalia***) region of E central Greece, on the Aegean; area 13,904 sq km/5,367 sq mi; population (1991) 731,200. It is a major area of cereal production. It was an independent state in ancient Greece and later formed part of the Roman province of ◊Macedonia. It was Turkish from the 14th century until incorporated in Greece 1881.

Thetford market town in Norfolk, England; population (1991) 20,100. There is light industry and printing.

Thetis in Greek mythology, daughter of Nereus, and mother of ◊Achilles, to whom she brings armour forged by Hephaestus in Homer's *Iliad*. Fated to have a son more powerful than his father, she was married by the gods to a mortal, Peleus.

thiamine or ***vitamin*** B_1 a water-soluble vitamin of the B complex. It is found in seeds and grain. Its absence from the diet causes the disease ◊beriberi.

Thimbu or ***Thimphu*** capital since 1962 of the Himalayan state of Bhutan; population (1993) 30,300. There is a 13th-century fortified monastery, Tashichoedzong, and the Memorial Charter to the Third King (1974).

Third Age in education, late middle age and older. A Université du Troisième Age was established in France 1972 to offer people over 50 the opportunity to continue their education. In the UK, the University of the Third Age established 1982 has no teachers and no qualifications for entry, but aims to help its 120 local groups to pursue any topics that interest them.

third estate or *tiers état* in pre-revolutionary France, the order of society comprising the common people as distinct from members of the first (noble) or the second (clerical) estates. All three met collectively as the States General.

Third Reich (Third Empire) Germany during the years of Hitler's dictatorship after 1933. The idea of the Third Reich was based on the existence of two previous German empires, the medieval Holy Roman Empire and the second empire 1871–1918.

Third World another name for ◊***developing world*** those countries that are less developed than the industrialized free-market countries of the West (First World) and the industrialized former Communist countries (Second World). Third World countries are the poorest, as measured by their income per head of population, and are concentrated in Asia, Africa, and Latin America.

Thirteen Colonies 13 American colonies that signed the ◊Declaration of Independence from Britain 1776. Led by George Washington, the Continental Army defeated the British army in the ◊American Revolution 1776–81 to become the original 13 United States of America: Connecticut, Delaware, Georgia, Maryland, Massachusetts, New Hampshire, New Jersey, New York, North Carolina, Pennsylvania, Rhode Island, South Carolina, and Virginia. They were united first under the Articles of ◊Confederation and from 1789, the US ◊constitution. ▷ *See feature on pp. 32–33.*

38th parallel demarcation line between North (People's Democratic Republic of) and South (Republic of) Korea, agreed at the Yalta Conference 1945 and largely unaltered by the Korean War 1950–53.

35 mm width of photographic film, the most popular format for the camera today. The 35-mm camera falls into two categories, the ◊SLR and the ◊rangefinder.

Thirty-Nine Articles set of articles of faith defining the doctrine of the Anglican Church; see under ◊Anglican Communion.

Thirty Years' War major war 1618–48 in central Europe. Beginning as a German conflict between Protestants and Catholics, it was gradually transformed into a struggle to determine whether the ruling Austrian Habsburg family could gain control of all Germany. Under the Peace of Westphalia the German states were granted their sovereignty and the emperor retained only nominal control.

1618–20 A Bohemian revolt against Austrian rule was defeated. Some Protestant princes continued the struggle against Austria.

1625–27 Denmark entered the war on the Protestant side.

1630 Gustavus Adolphus of Sweden intervened on the Protestant side, overrunning N Germany.

1631 The Catholic commander Tilly stormed Magdeburg.

1632 Tilly was defeated at Breitenfeld and the river Lech, and was killed. The German general Wallenstein was defeated at the Battle of Lützen; Gustavus Adolphus was killed.

1634 When the Swedes were defeated at Nördlingen, ◊Richelieu brought France into the war to

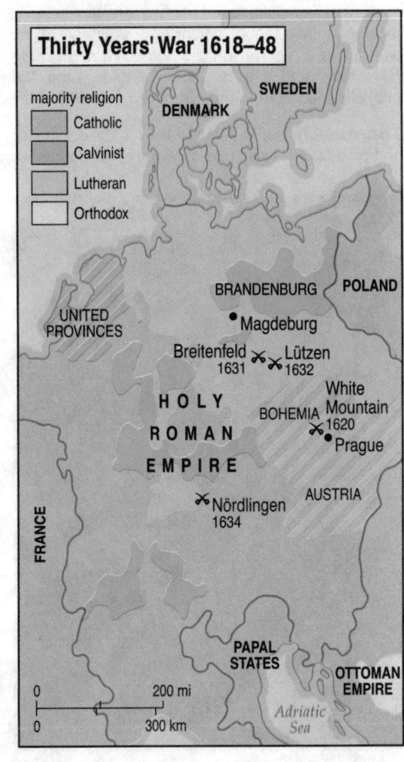

Extensive travelling induces a feeling of encapsulation, and travel, so broadening at first, contracts the mind.

PAUL THEROUX
The Great Railway Bazaar

Thirty Years' War The siege of Jülich in the Thirty Years' War. *Philip Sauvain*

inflict several defeats on Austria's Spanish allies. Wallenstein was assassinated.

1648 The Peace of Westphalia gave France S Alsace, and Sweden certain Baltic provinces, the emperor's authority in Germany becoming only nominal. The mercenary armies of Wallenstein, Tilly, and Mansfeld devastated Germany.

thistle prickly plant of several genera, such as *Carduus*, *Carlina*, *Onopordum*, and *Cirsium*, in the family Compositae. The stems are spiny, the flower heads purple, white, or yellow and cottony, and the leaves deeply indented with prickly margins. The thistle is the Scottish national emblem.

Thistle, Order of the Scottish order of ◊knighthood.

Thomas Dylan Marlais 1914–1953. Welsh poet. His poems, characterized by complex imagery and a strong musicality, include the celebration of his 30th birthday 'Poem in October' and the evocation of his youth 'Fern Hill' 1946. His 'play for voices' *Under Milk Wood* 1954 describes with humour and compassion a day in the life of the residents of a small Welsh fishing village, Llareggub. The short stories of *Portrait of the Artist as a Young Dog* 1940 are autobiographical.

Born in Swansea, son of the English teacher at the local grammar school where he was educated, he worked as a reporter on the *South Wales Evening Post*, then settled as a journalist in London and published his first volume *Eighteen Poems* 1934.

Do not go gentle into that good night, / Old age should burn and rave at close of day; / Rage, rage, against the dying of the light.

DYLAN THOMAS
'Do Not Go Gentle Into That Good Night'

Thomas Michael Tilson 1944– . US conductor and pianist. He was appointed principal conductor of the London Symphony Orchestra 1988. An enthusiastic proponent of 'authentic' restorations of modern repertoire, he has championed US composers. He has made first recordings of Steve Reich's *The Desert Music* 1983, the complete symphonies of Charles Ives, and a reconstruction of George Gershwin's original *Rhapsody in Blue*.

Thomas Welsh poet Dylan Thomas. Thomas had a fine speaking voice and his BBC broadcasts of his poems and short stories, particularly the warm and intimate recollections of his childhood in Wales, were very popular and made him one of the best known British poets of the 1940s and 1950s. *Topham*

Thomas à Kempis adopted name of Thomas Hämmerken c. 1380–1471. German Augustinian monk. His *De Imitatio Christi/Imitation of Christ* is probably the most widely known Christian devotional work ever written.

Thomas Aquinas medieval philosopher; see ◊Aquinas, St Thomas.

Thomas, St died AD 53. in the New Testament, one of the 12 Apostles, said to have preached in S India, hence the ancient churches there were referred to as the 'Christians of St Thomas'. He is not the author of the Gospel of St Thomas, the Gnostic collection of Jesus' sayings.

Thomism in philosophy, the method and approach of Thomas ◊Aquinas. Neo-Thomists apply this philosophical method to contemporary problems. It is a form of scholasticism.

Thompson Daley Francis Morgan 1958– . English decathlete who broke the world record four times since winning the Commonwealth Games decathlon title 1978. He won two more Commonwealth titles (1982, 1986), two Olympic gold medals (1980, 1984), three European medals (silver 1978; gold 1982, 1986), and a world title (1983). He retired in 1992.

Thompson Emma 1959– . English actress. She has worked in cinema, theatre, and television, ranging from song-and-dance to Shakespeare, often playing variations on the independent woman. In 1989 she married actor-director Kenneth ◊Branagh, and appeared in his films, including *Henry V* 1989, *Dead Again* 1991, and *Much Ado About Nothing* 1993; the couple separated 1995. Away from Branagh, she won an Academy Award for her performance in *Howards End* 1992 and appeared in *The Remains of the Day* 1993. Her adaptation 1995 of Jane Austen's novel *Sense and Sensibility*, in which she also played the role of Elinor, secured a second Academy Award (Best Adapted Screenplay).

Thompson Hunter Stockton 1939– . US writer and journalist. A proponent of the New Journalism school of reporting, which made the writer an essential component of the story, Thompson mythologized himself as the outrageous Doctor Gonzo in his political journalism of the 1960s. An acute observer of the decadence and depravity in American life, he wrote such books as *Hell's Angels* 1966, *Fear and Loathing on the Campaign Trail '72* 1973, and the reportage novel *Fear and Loathing in Las Vegas* 1971. He also wrote the collections *Generation of Swine* 1988 and *Songs of the Doomed* 1990.

Thompson Richard 1949– . English virtuoso guitarist, songwriter, and singer. His work spans rock, folk, and avant-garde. He was a member of pioneering folk-rock group Fairport Convention 1966–71, contributing to albums like *What We Did on Our Holidays* 1968. With his wife Linda Thompson he made several albums, among them *Shoot Out the Lights* 1982. Later solo work includes *Rumor and Sigh* 1991.

Thomson George Paget 1892–1975. English physicist whose work on ◊interference phenomena in the scattering of electrons by crystals helped to confirm the wavelike nature of particles. He shared a Nobel prize 1937.

Thomson J(oseph) J(ohn) 1856–1940. English physicist. He discovered the ◊electron 1897. His work inaugurated the electrical theory of the atom, and his elucidation of positive rays and their application to an analysis of neon led to the discovery of ◊isotopes. Nobel prize 1906.

Using magnetic and electric fields to deflect positive rays, Thomson found 1912 that ions of neon gas are deflected by different amounts, indicating that they consist of a mixture of ions with different charge-to-mass ratios. English chemist Frederick ◊Soddy had earlier proposed the existence of isotopes and Thomson proved this idea correct when he identified, also 1912, the isotope neon-22.

Thomson Virgil 1896–1989. US composer and critic. He is best known for his opera *Four Saints in Three Acts* 1927–33 to a libretto by Stein, and the film scores *The Plow That Broke the Plains* 1936 and *Louisiana Story* 1948. His music is notable for a refined absence of expression, his criticism for trenchant matter-of-factness, both at odds with the prevailing US musical culture.

Thor in Norse mythology, the god of thunder (his hammer), and represented as a man of enormous strength defending humanity against demons. He was the son of Odin and Freya, and Thursday is named after him.

thorax in four-limbed vertebrates, the part of the body containing the heart and lungs, and protected by the ribcage; in arthropods, the middle part of the body, between the head and abdomen. In mammals the thorax is separated from the abdomen by the muscular diaphragm. In insects the thorax bears the legs and wings. The thorax of spiders and crustaceans, such as lobsters, is fused with the head, to form the cephalothorax.

Thoreau Henry David 1817–1862. US author. One of the most influential figures of 19th-century US literature, he is best known for his vigorous defence of individualism and the simple life. His work *Walden, or Life in the Woods* 1854 stimulated the back-to-nature movement, and he completed some 30 volumes based on his daily nature walks. His essay 'Civil Disobedience' 1849, prompted by his refusal to pay taxes, advocated peaceful resistance to unjust laws and had a wide impact, even in the 20th century.

It takes two to speak the truth, – one to speak, and another to hear.

HENRY THOREAU
A Week on the Concord and Merrimack Rivers

thorium dark-grey, radioactive, metallic element of the ◊actinide series, symbol Th, atomic number 90, relative atomic mass 232.038. It occurs throughout the world in small quantities in minerals such as thorite and is widely distributed in monazite beach sands. It is one of three fissile elements (the others are uranium and plutonium), and its longest-lived isotope has a half-life of 1.39×10^{10} years. Thorium is used to strengthen alloys.

thorn apple or ***jimson weed*** annual plant *Datura stramonium* of the nightshade family, growing to 2 m/6 ft in northern temperate and subtropical areas; native to America and naturalized worldwide. It bears white or violet trumpet-shaped flowers and capsulelike fruit that split to release black seeds. All parts of the plant are poisonous.

Thorndike (Agnes) Sybil 1882–1976. English actress. G B Shaw wrote *St Joan* for her. The Thorndike Theatre (1969), Leatherhead, Surrey, England, is named after her.

thoroughbred horse bred for racing purposes. All racehorses are thoroughbreds, and all thoroughbreds are direct descendants of one of three stallions imported into Britain during the 17th and 18th centuries: the Darley Arabian, Byerley Turk, and Godolphin Barb.

Thoth in Egyptian mythology, the god of wisdom and learning. He was represented as a scribe with the head of an ibis, the bird sacred to him.

Thothmes four kings (pharaohs) of ancient Egypt of the 18th dynasty, including:

Thothmes I king (pharaoh) of ancient Egypt, reigned c. 1504–c. 1492 BC. He campaigned in Syria.

Thothmes III king (pharaoh) of ancient Egypt, reigned c. 1479–c. 1425 BC. He extended the empire to the river Euphrates, and conquered Nubia. He was a grandson of Thothmes I.

Thousand Islands group of about 1,700 islands in the upper St Lawrence River, on the border between Canada and the USA. Most of them are in Ontario, Canada; the rest are in the US state of New York. Some are in Canada's St Lawrence Islands National Park; many of the others are privately owned. The largest is Wolfe Island in Ontario, 49 sq mi/127 sq km.

Thrace (Greek ***Thráki***) ancient region of the Balkans, SE Europe, formed by parts of modern Greece and Bulgaria. It was held successively by the Greeks, Persians, Macedonians, and Romans. The heart of the ancient Thracian Empire was Bulgaria. The area was conquered by Persia mid-5th century BC and by Macedonia 4th–2nd centuries BC. From AD 46 it was a Roman province, then part of the Byzantine Empire, and Turkish from the 15th century until 1878; it was then subject to constant dispute until after World War I, when it was divided (1923) into western Thrace (the Greek province of Thráki) and eastern Thrace (European Turkey).

threadworm kind of ◊nematode.

Three Age System the division of prehistory into the Stone Age, Bronze Age, and Iron Age, proposed by Danish archaeologist Christian Thomsen between 1816 and 1819. Subsequently, the Stone Age was subdivided into the Old and the New (the Palaeolithic and Neolithic); the Middle (Mesolithic) Stone Age was added later, as well as the Copper (Chalcolithic) Age (inserted between the New Stone Age and Bronze Age). Although providing a valid classification system for prehistoric material, the Three Age System did not provide dates but only a sequence of developmental stages, which, furthermore, were not necessarily followed in that order by different societies.

Three Kingdoms period in Chinese history 220–581, an era of disruptive, intermittent warfare between three powers. Sometimes the term is used to cover only the period 220–280 following the end of the ◊Han dynasty when the Wei, Shu, and Wu fought for supremacy.

From 265 the Wei established their pre-eminence and united the country under the Western Jin (Chin) dynasty until 316. N China fell under the control of the Sixteen Dynasties 317–386, before the rise of the Northern Wei 386–535, founded by the barbarian Xianbi (Hsien-pi), a proto-Mongol people who established their capital at Luoyang (Lo-yang). The period 317–581, known as the era of the Northern and Southern Dynasties, was characterized by political decentralization and the growing influence of Buddhism.

Three Mile Island island in the Shenandoah River near Harrisburg, Pennsylvania, USA, site of a nuclear power station which was put out of action following a major accident March 1979. Opposition to nuclear power in the USA was reinforced after this accident and safety standards reassessed.

threshing agricultural process of separating cereal grains from the plant. Traditionally, the work was carried out by hand in winter months using the flail, a jointed beating stick. Today, threshing is done automatically inside the combine harvester at the time of cutting.

thrift or ***sea pink*** any plant of the genus *Armeria*, family Plumbaginaceae. *A. maritima* occurs on seashores and cliffs in Europe. The leaves are small and linear; the dense round heads of pink flowers rise on straight stems.

thrips any of a number of tiny insects of the order Thysanoptera. Many of the 3,000 species live in flowers and suck their juices, causing damage and spreading disease. Others eat fungi, decaying matter, or smaller insects.

throat in human anatomy, the passage that leads from the back of the nose and mouth to the ◊trachea and ◊oesophagus. It includes the ◊pharynx and the ◊larynx, the latter being at the top of the trachea. The word 'throat' is also used to mean the front part of the neck. In engineering, it is any narrowing entry, such as the throat of a carburettor.

thrombosis condition in which a blood clot forms in a vein or artery, causing loss of circulation to the area served by the vessel. If it breaks away, it often travels to the lungs, causing pulmonary embolism. Thrombosis in veins of the legs is often seen in association with ◊phlebitis, and in arteries with ◊atheroma. Thrombosis increases the risk of heart attack and stroke. It is treated by surgery and/or anticoagulant drugs.

throwing event field competition in athletics. There are four at most major international track and field meetings: ◊discus, ◊hammer, ◊javelin, and ◊shot put. ◊Caber tossing is also a throwing event but is found only at ◊Highland Games.

thrush any bird of the large family Turdidae, order Passeriformes, found worldwide and known for their song. Thrushes are usually brown with speckles of other colours. They are 12–30 cm/5–12 in long. The song thrush *Turdus philomelos* is 23 cm/ long, brown above and with a paler throat and breast speckled with dark brown. Slightly larger is the mistle thrush *T. viscivorus*, so-called because of its habit of defending a clump of mistletoe during the winter to use as a food store.

thrush infection usually of the mouth (particularly in infants), but also sometimes of the vagina, caused by a yeastlike fungus (◊*Candida*). It is seen as white patches on the mucous membranes. Thrush, also known as ***candidiasis***, may be caused by antibiotics removing natural antifungal agents from the body. It is treated with a further antibiotic.

Thrust SSC jet-propelled car in which British driver Andy Green set a new supersonic world-land speed record in the Black Rock Desert of Nevada, USA, 15 October 1997. The record speed was Mach 1.020/763.035 mph/1227.983kph

Thucydides c. 455–c. 400 BC. Athenian historian. He exercised military command in the ◊Peloponnesian War with Sparta, but was banished from Athens 424. In his *History of the Peloponnesian War*, he gave a detailed account of the conflict down to 411.

thug originally a member of a Hindu sect who strangled travellers as sacrifices to ◊Kali, the goddess of destruction. The sect was suppressed about 1830.

Thule Greek and Roman name for the most northernly land known, originally used by the explorer Pytheas to refer to land he discovered six days after leaving the northern coast of Britain. It has been identified with the Shetlands, the Orkneys, Iceland, and Scandinavia.

thulium soft, silver-white, malleable and ductile, metallic element, of the ◊lanthanide series, symbol Tm, atomic number 69, relative atomic mass 168.94. It is the least abundant of the rare-earth metals, and was first found in gadolinite and various other minerals. It is used in arc lighting.

thorn apple Although generally thought of as the fruit of the jimson weed, the typical thorn apple is also produced by other species of *Datura*, such as this *D. discolor* from California. *Premaphotos Wildlife*

Thunderbird legendary bird of the North American Indians, the creator of storms. It is said to produce thunder by flapping its wings and lightning by opening and closing its eyes.

thunderstorm severe storm of very heavy rain, thunder, and lightning. Thunderstorms are usually caused by the intense heating of the ground surface during summer. The warm air rises rapidly to form tall cumulonimbus clouds with a characteristic anvil-shaped top. Electrical charges accumulate in the clouds and are discharged to the ground as flashes of lightning. Air in the path of lightning becomes heated and expands rapidly, creating shock waves that are heard as a crash or rumble of thunder.

The rough distance between an observer and a lightning flash can be calculated by timing the number of seconds between the flash and the thunder. A gap of 3 seconds represents about a kilometre; 5 seconds represents about a mile.

Thurber James Grover 1894–1961. US humorist. His short stories, written mainly for the *New Yorker* magazine, include 'The Secret Life of Walter Mitty' 1932. His doodle drawings include fanciful impressions of dogs.

‘Well, if I called the wrong number, why did you answer the phone?’

JAMES THURBER
Cartoon caption in the *New Yorker*
5 June 1937

Thuringia administrative *Land* (state) of Germany;
area 15,482 sq km/5,980 sq mi
capital Erfurt
towns and cities Weimar, Gera, Jena, Eisenach
industries machine tools, optical instruments, steel, vehicles, ceramics, electronics, glassware, timber
population (1994 est) 2,533,000

thrush The mistle thrush *Turdus viscivorus*. A common garden bird, it is found throughout Asia, Europe, and North America. It feeds mainly on worms and berries (especially mistletoe berries, hence its name). The smaller song thrush *Turdus philomelos* is declining in numbers, though it is not yet clear why. *Premaphotos Wildlife*

'A great soaring place ... where the depths of the valleys were higher than the summits of the Alps.'

On TIBET
James Cameron
Point of Departure

history a province 1918 and a region of East Germany 1946. It was split into the districts of Erfurt, Gera, and Suhl 1952 but reconstituted as a state following German reunification 1990.

Thurso port in Highland Region, Scotland; population (1991) 8,500. It is the mainland terminus of the steamer service to the Orkney Islands. The experimental nuclear reactor site of Dounreay to the west was closed down 1994, and replaced by a nuclear waste reprocessing plant.

Thyestes in Greek mythology, the son of Pelops and brother of ◊Atreus. His rivalry with Atreus for the kingship of Mycenae was continued by their sons, Aegisthus and Agamemnon.

thylacine another name for the ◊Tasmanian wolf.

thyme herb, genus *Thymus*, of the mint family Labiatae. Garden thyme *T. vulgaris*, native to the Mediterranean, grows to 30 cm/1 ft high, and has pinkish flowers. Its aromatic leaves are used for seasoning.

thymus organ in vertebrates, situated in the upper chest cavity in humans. The thymus processes ◊lymphocyte cells to produce T-lymphocytes (T denotes 'thymus-derived'), which are responsible for binding to specific invading organisms and killing them or rendering them harmless. The stock of T-lymphocytes is built up early in life, so this function diminishes in adults, but the thymus continues to produce the hormone thymosin, which stimulates the activity of the T-lymphocytes.

thyristor type of ◊rectifier, an electronic device that conducts electricity in one direction only. The thyristor is composed of layers of ◊semiconductor material sandwiched between two electrodes called the anode and cathode. The current can be switched on by using a third electrode called the gate. Thyristors are used to control mains-driven motors and in lighting dimmer controls.

thyroid ◊endocrine gland of vertebrates, situated in the neck in front of the trachea. It secretes several hormones, principally thyroxine, an iodine-containing hormone that stimulates growth, metabolism, and other functions of the body. The thyroid gland may be thought of as the regulator gland of the body's metabolic rate. If it is overactive, as in ◊hyperthyroidism, the sufferer feels hot and sweaty, has an increased heart rate, diarrhoea, and weight loss. Conversely, an underactive thyroid leads to myxoedema, a condition characterized by sensitivity to the cold, constipation, and weight gain. In infants, an underactive thyroid leads to cretinism, a form of mental retardation.

Tiahuanaco site of a city in Bolivia 24 km/15 mi S of Lake Titicaca in the Andes. Dating from c. 600, Tiahuanaco was situated 4,000 m/13,000 ft above sea level. It gave its name to the 8th–14th-century civilizations found in Peru and Bolivia that preceded the Inca.

Tiananmen Square (Chinese 'Square of Heavenly Peace') paved open space in central Beijing (Peking), China, the largest public square in the world (area 0.4 sq km/0.14 sq mi). On 3–4 June 1989 more than 1,000 unarmed protesters were killed by government troops in a massacre that crushed China's emerging prodemocracy movement.

Hundreds of thousands of demonstrators had occupied the square from early May, calling for political reform and the resignation of the communist leadership. They were led by students, 3,000 of whom staged a hunger strike in the square. The massacre that followed was sanctioned by the old guard of leaders, including Deng Xiaoping.

thyme The wild thyme *Thymus drucei* is widespread in W Europe and the British Isles, often forming a dense fragrant mat on downs, heaths, and coastal dunes. It produces masses of tiny pink flowers from May to Aug. *Premaphotos Wildlife*

Tianjin or ***Tientsin*** port and industrial and commercial city in Hubei province, central China; population (1993) 4,970,000. The special municipality of Tianjin has an area of 4,000 sq km/1,544 sq mi and a population (1994) of 10,400,000. Its handmade silk and wool carpets are renowned. Dagan oilfield is nearby. Tianjin was opened to foreign trade 1860 and occupied by the Japanese 1937.

Tianjin, Treaty of agreement 1858 between China and Western powers, signed at the end of the Second Opium (Arrow) War. It was one of the unequal treaties forced on China by the West, through which Western powers won diplomatic privileges and territorial concessions in China and Japan. A further ten treaty ports, mainly along the Chang Jiang, were opened to Britain, France, Russia, and the USA.

Tiber (Italian ***Tevere***) river in Italy on which Rome is built; length from its source in the Apennines to the Tyrrhenian Sea 400 km/250 mi.

Tiberias, Lake or ***Sea of Galilee*** lake in N Israel, 210 m/689 ft below sea level, into which the river ◊Jordan flows; area 170 sq km/66 sq mi.

Tiberius (Tiberius Claudius Nero) 42 BC–AD 37. Roman emperor, the stepson, adopted son, and successor of Augustus from AD 14. He was a cautious ruler whose reign was marred by the heavy incident of trials for treason or conspiracy. Tiberius fell under the influence of Sejanus, who encouraged the emperor's fear of assassination and was instrumental in Tiberius' departure from Rome to Caprae (Capri).

Tibet autonomous region of SW China (Pinyin form ***Xizang***)
area 1,221,600 sq km/471,538 sq mi
capital Lhasa
features Tibet occupies a barren plateau bounded S and SW by the Himalayas and N by the Kunlun Mountains, traversed W to E by the Bukamagna, Karakoram, and other mountain ranges, and having an average elevation of 4,000–4,500 m/13,000–15,000 ft. The Sutlej, Brahmaputra, and Indus rivers rise in Tibet, which has numerous lakes, many of which are salty. The ◊yak is the main domestic animal
government Tibet is an autonomous region of China, with its own People's Government and People's Congress. The controlling force in Tibet is the Communist Party of China, represented locally by First Secretary Wu Jinghua from 1985. Tibetan nationalists regard the province as being under colonial rule. There is a government-in-exile in Dharmsala, Himachel Pradesh, India, where the ◊Dalai Lama lives
industries wool, borax, salt, horn, musk, herbs, furs, gold, iron pyrites, lapis lazuli, mercury, textiles, chemicals, agricultural machinery. Tibet has the largest uranium reserves in the world
population (1993) 2,290,000; many Chinese have settled in Tibet; 2 million Tibetans live in China outside Tibet
religion traditionally Lamaist (a form of Mahāyāna Buddhism)
history Tibet was an independent kingdom from the 5th century AD. It came under nominal Chinese rule about 1700. From 1910–13 the capital, Lhasa, was occupied by Chinese troops, after which independence was re-established. China regained control 1951 when the historic ruler and religious leader, the ◊Dalai Lama, was driven from the country and the monks were forced out of the monasteries. The Chinese People's Liberation Army (PLA) controlled Tibet 1951–59, although the Dalai Lama returned as nominal spiritual and temporal head of state. In 1959 a Tibetan uprising spread from bordering regions to Lhasa and was supported by Tibet's local government. The rebellion was suppressed by the PLA, prompting the Dalai Lama and 9,000 Tibetans to flee to India. The Chinese proceeded to dissolve the Tibet local government, abolish serfdom, collectivize agriculture, and suppress ◊Lamaism. In 1965 Tibet became an autonomous region of China. Chinese rule continued to be resented, however, and the economy languished.

From 1979, the leadership in Beijing adopted a more liberal and pragmatic policy towards Tibet. Traditional agriculture, livestock, and trading practices were restored, a number of older political leaders and rebels were rehabilitated or pardoned, and the promotion of local Tibetan cadres was encouraged. In addition, a somewhat more tolerant attitude towards Lamaism has been adopted and attempts have been made to persuade the Dalai Lama to return from exile.

Pro-independence demonstrations erupted in Lhasa 1987, repeatedly throughout 1988, and in 1989. These were forcibly suppressed by Chinese troops and in 1989 all foreigners were expelled. Lhasa became a special economic zone 1992, attracting thousands more Han Chinese and continuing the move towards a consumer-led culture.

The country is of immense strategic importance to China, being the site of 50,000–100,000 troops and a major nuclear missile base at Nagchuka. ▷ *See feature on pp. 162–163.*

Tibetan a Mongolian people inhabiting Tibet who practise a form of Mahāyāna Buddhism, introduced in the 7th century. Since China's Cultural Revolution 1966–68, refugee communities have formed in India and Nepal. The Tibetan language belongs to the Sino-Tibetan language family.

tibia the anterior of the pair of bones in the leg between the ankle and the knee. In humans, the tibia is the shinbone. It articulates with the ◊femur above to form the knee joint, the ◊fibula externally at its upper and lower ends, and with the talus below, forming the ankle joint.

tick any of an arachnid family Ixodoidae, order Acarina, of large bloodsucking mites. They have flat bodies protected by horny shields. Many carry and transmit diseases to mammals (including humans) and birds. During part of their existence they are parasites. Their eggs are laid on rough herbage and hatch into white six-legged larvae, which climb up the legs of passing animals and in some species complete their life history on the animal's skin, but in others return to the grass for a period, dropping from the host when engorged with blood.

tidal energy energy derived from the tides. The tides mainly gain their potential energy from the gravitational forces acting between the Earth and the Moon. If water is trapped at a high level during high tide, perhaps by means of a barrage across an estuary, it may then be gradually released and its associated gravitational potential energy (energy possessed by an object when placed in a position from which, if it were free to do so, it would fall under the influence of gravity) exploited to drive turbines and generate electricity. Several schemes have been proposed for the Bristol Channel, in SW England, but environmental concerns as well as construction costs have so far prevented any decision from being taken. ▷ *See feature on pp. 360–361.*

tidal power station ◊hydroelectric power plant that uses the 'head' of water created by the rise and fall of the ocean tides to spin the water turbines. The world's only large tidal power station is located on the estuary of the river Rance in the Gulf of St Malo, Brittany, France, which has been in use since 1966. It produces 240 megawatts and can generate electricity on both the ebb and flow of the tide.

tidal wave common name for a ◊tsunami.

tide the rhythmic rise and fall of sea level in the Earth's oceans and their inlets and estuaries due to the gravitational attraction of the Moon and, to a lesser extent, the Sun, affecting regions of the Earth unequally as it rotates. Water on the side of the Earth nearest the Moon feels the Moon's pull and accumulates directly below it producing high tide.

High tide occurs at an interval of 12 hr 24 min 30 sec. The maximum high tides, or spring tides, occur at or near new and full Moon when the Moon and Sun are in line and exert the greatest combined gravitational pull. Lower high tides, or neap tides, occur when the Moon is in its first or third quarter and the Moon and Sun are at right angles to each other.

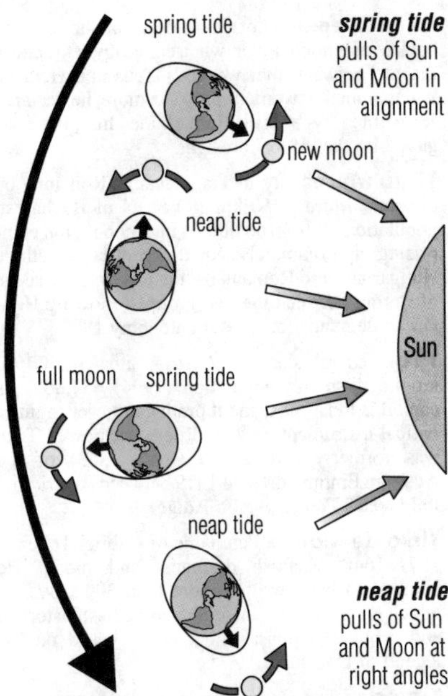

tide The gravitational pull of the Moon is the main cause of the tides. Water on the side of the Earth nearest the Moon feels the Moon's pull and accumulates directly under the Moon. When the Sun and the Moon are in line, at new and full Moon, the gravitational pull of Sun and Moon are in line and produce a high spring tide. When the Sun and Moon are at right angles, lower neap tides occur.

Tiepolo Giovanni Battista (Giambattista) 1696–1770. Italian painter. He was one of the first exponents of Italian Rococo and created monumental decorative schemes in palaces and churches in NE Italy, SW Germany, and Madrid. His style is light-hearted, his colours light and warm, and he made great play with illusion.

He painted religious and, above all, historical or allegorical pictures. With immense virtuosity and a quality of colour entirely his own, he covered the walls and ceilings of many villas and palaces in Venice and elsewhere in N Italy, the series of *Antony and Cleopatra* (Palazzo Labia) being the high point. The decoration of the Villa S Sebastiano at Malmarana, near Vicenza, 1737, with scenes from the *Iliad*, *Orlando furioso*, and *Gerusalemme liberata*, is another of his many works in Italy.

In 1751 he went to Würzburg, Germany, to decorate the Prince Archbishop's Palace, being assisted by his sons, Giovanni Domenico (1727–1802) and Lorenzo (1736–before 1776). The finest examples of his work there include scenes from the life of Frederick Barbarossa. In 1755 he was elected president of the Venetian Academy and in 1762 was invited to Spain by Charles III. He worked there until 1770, carrying out a scheme of decoration for the Palacio Real, and painting altarpieces for S Pasquale in Aranjuez. These were later replaced by pictures by the Neo-Classicist Anton Mengs (1728–1779), his competitor and opponent in style.

Tierra del Fuego island group divided between Chile and Argentina. It is separated from the mainland of South America by the Strait of Magellan, and Cape Horn is at the southernmost point. The chief town, Ushuaia, Argentina, is the world's most southerly town. Industries include oil and sheep farming.

Tiffany Louis Comfort 1848–1933. US artist and glassmaker. He was the son of Charles Louis Tiffany, who founded Tiffany and Company, the New York City jewellers. He produced stained-glass windows, iridescent Favrile (from Latin *faber* 'craftsman') glass, and lampshades in the Art Nouveau style. He used glass that contained oxides of iron and other elements to produce rich colours.

tiger largest of the great cats, *Panthera tigris* (family Felidae, order Carnivora), formerly found in much of central and S Asia, from Siberia south to Sumatra, but nearing extinction because of hunting and the high prices paid for the pelt, as well as the destruction of its natural habitat.

The tiger can grow to 3.6 m/12 ft long, while the female averages about 2.6 m/8.5 ft. It weighs up to 300 kg/660 lbs, and has a yellow-orange coat with black stripes. Tigers are solitary, and largely nocturnal. They will eat carrion, but generally kill for themselves. Their food consists mainly of deer, antelopes, and smaller animals, but they sometimes kill wild boar. Human-eating tigers are rare and are the result of weakened powers or shortage of game.

Tigré a people of N Ethiopia. The Tigré language is spoken by about 2.5 million people; it belongs to the SE Semitic branch of the Afro-Asiatic (Hamito-Semitic) family. Tigrinya is a closely related languagespoken slightly to the south.

Tigré or ***Tigray*** region in the northern highlands of Ethiopia; area 65,900 sq km/25,444 sq mi. The chief town is Mekele. The region had an estimated population of 2.4 million in 1984, at a time when drought and famine were driving large numbers of people to fertile land in the south or into neighbouring Sudan. Since 1978 a guerrilla group known as the Tigré People's Liberation Front (TPLF) has been fighting for regional autonomy.

Tigris (Arabic ***Shatt Dijla***) river flowing through Turkey and Iraq (see also ◊Mesopotamia), joining the ◊Euphrates above Basra, where it forms the ◊Shatt-al-Arab; length 1,600 km/1,000 mi.

Tihuanaco alternative spelling of ◊Tiahuanaco, an ancient Bolivian city.

Tijuana city and resort in NW Mexico; population (1990) 742,700. It is known for horse races and casinos. ◊San Diego adjoins it across the US border.

Tilbury port in Essex, England, on the north bank of the Thames; population (1991) 11,700. Greatly extended 1976, it became London's largest container port. It dates from Roman times.

till or ***boulder clay*** deposit of clay, mud, gravel, and boulders left by a ◊glacier. It is unsorted, with all sizes of fragments mixed up together, and shows no stratification.

Tillich Paul Johannes 1886–1965. Prussian-born US theologian, best remembered for his *Systematic Theology* 1951–63.

Tilly Jan Tserklaes, Count von Tilly 1559–1632. Flemish commander of the army of the Catholic League and imperial forces in the ◊Thirty Years' War. Notorious for his storming of Magdeburg, E Germany, 1631, he was defeated by the Swedish king Gustavus Adolphus at Breitenfeld and at the river Lech in SW Germany, where he was mortally wounded.

tiger The tiger's stripes give it a highly effective camouflage in its native habitat. In recent times poaching for bones and internal organs, used in traditional Chinese medicine, has severely reduced the surviving wild stocks of the tiger, particularly in India. *Premaphotos Wildlife*

Tilson Thomas see ◊Thomas, Michael Tilson, US conductor.

tilt-rotor aircraft type of vertical takeoff aircraft, also called a ◊convertiplane.

timber wood used in construction, furniture, and paper pulp. ***Hardwoods*** include tropical mahogany, teak, ebony, rosewood, temperate oak, elm, beech, and eucalyptus. All except eucalyptus are slow-growing, and world supplies are almost exhausted. ***Softwoods*** comprise the ◊conifers (pine, fir, spruce, and larch), which are quick to grow and easy to work but inferior in quality of grain. ***White woods*** include ash, birch, and sycamore; all have light-coloured timber, are fast-growing, and can be used as veneers on cheaper timber.

timbre in music, the tone colour, or quality of tone, characteristic of a particular instrument or voice.

Timbuktu or ***Tombouctou*** town in Mali; population about 20,500. A camel caravan centre on the fringe of the Sahara from the 11th century, it was taken over 1433 by the Tuareg, nomads of the region, replacing the rule of the Mali. Since 1960 it has been surrounded by the southward movement of the desert, and the former canal link with the river Niger is dry. Products include salt.

time continuous passage of existence, recorded by division into hours, minutes, and seconds. Formerly the measurement of time was based on the Earth's rotation on its axis, but this was found to be irregular. Therefore the second, the standard ◊SI unit of time, was redefined 1956 in terms of the Earth's annual orbit of the Sun, and 1967 in terms of a radiation pattern of the element caesium.

Universal time (UT), based on the Earth's actual rotation, was replaced by coordinated universal time (UTC) 1972, the difference between the two involving the addition (or subtraction) of leap seconds on the last day of June or December. National observatories (in the UK until 1990 the Royal Greenwich Observatory) make standard time available, and the BBC broadcasts six pips at certain hours (five short, from second 55 to second 59, and one long, the start of which indicates the precise minute). Its computerized clock has an accuracy greater than 1 second in 4,000 years. From 1986 the term Greenwich Mean Time was replaced by UTC. However, the Greenwich meridian, adopted 1884, remains that from which all longitudes are measured, and the world's standard time zones are calculated from it.

time and motion study process of analysis applied to a job or number of jobs to check the efficiency of the work method, equipment used, and the worker. Its findings are used to improve performance.

Timişoara capital of Timiş county, W Romania; population (1993) 325,000. Industries include electrical engineering, chemicals, pharmaceuticals, textiles, food processing, metal, and footwear. The revolt against the Ceauşescu regime began here 1989 when demonstrators prevented the arrest and deportation of a popular Protestant minister who was promoting the rights of ethnic Hungarians. This soon led to large prodemocracy rallies.

Timon Athenian of the age of ◊Pericles notorious for his misanthropy, which was reported and elaborated by classical authors.

Timor largest and most easterly of the Lesser Sunda Islands, part of Indonesia; area 33,610 sq km/12,973 sq mi. Its indigenous people were the Atoni; successive migrants have included the Malay, Melanesian, Chinese, Arab, and Gujerati. Timor was divided into ***West Timor*** and ◊***East Timor*** by treaties of 1859 and 1913 and subjected to Dutch and Portuguese control respectively; during World War II both parts were occupied by Japan. West Timor (capital Kupang) became part of Indonesia 1949. East Timor (capital Dili) comprises the enclave on the northwest coast, and the islands of Atauro and Jaco. It was seized by Indonesia 1975, and became an Indonesian province 1976 (East Timor is the English name for the Indonesian province of Timor Timur). The annexation is not recognized by the United Nations, and guerrilla warfare by local people seeking independence continues.

‘The atmosphere … in this climate, where gale succeeds gale, with rain, hail, and sleet, seems blacker than anywhere else.’

On Tierra del Fuego
Charles Darwin
Voyage of the HMS Beagle 1839

❝Tiryns, where Art seems to have rivalled Nature in the eternity of her existence.❞

On **Tiryns**
E D Clarke *Travels in Various Countries*

Timothy died AD c. 97. in the New Testament, companion to St ◊Paul, both on his missionary journeys and in prison. Two of Paul's epistles are addressed to him.

Timur i Leng alternative spelling of ◊Tamerlane, Mongol ruler.

tin soft, silver-white, malleable and somewhat ductile, metallic element, symbol Sn (from Latin *stannum*), atomic number 50, relative atomic mass 118.69. Tin exhibits ◊allotropy, having three forms: the familiar lustrous metallic form above 13.2°C/55.8°F; a brittle form above 161°C/321.8°F; and a grey powder form below 13.2°C/55.8°F (commonly called tin pest or tin disease). The metal is quite soft and can be rolled, pressed, or hammered into extremely thin sheets; it has a low melting point. In nature it occurs rarely as a free metal. It resists corrosion and is therefore used for coating and plating other metals.

Tin and copper smelted together form the oldest desired alloy, bronze; since the Bronze Age (3500 BC) that alloy has been the basis of both useful and decorative materials. The mines of Cornwall were the principal western source from then until the 19th century, when rich deposits were found in South America, Africa, and SE Asia. Tin is also alloyed with metals other than copper to make solder and pewter.

tinamou fowl-like bird of the family Tinamidae, in the South American order Tinamiformes, of which there are some 45 species. They are up to 40 cm/16 in long, and their drab colour provides good camouflage. They are excellent runners but poor flyers and are thought to be related to the ◊ratites (flightless birds).

Tinbergen Jan 1903– . Dutch economist. He shared a Nobel prize 1969 with Ragnar Frisch for his work on econometrics (the mathematical-statistical expression of economic theory).

Tinbergen Niko(laas) 1907–1988. Dutch-born British zoologist. He specialized in the study of instinctive behaviour in animals. One of the founders of ◊ethology, the scientific study of animal behaviour in natural surroundings, he shared a Nobel prize 1973 with Konrad ◊Lorenz (with whom he worked on several projects) and Karl von Frisch.

Tinbergen investigated other aspects of animal behaviour, such as learning, and also studied human behaviour, particularly aggression, which he believed to be an inherited instinct that developed when humans changed from being predominantly herbivorous to being hunting carnivores.

tinnitus in medicine, constant buzzing or ringing in the ears. The phenomenon may originate from prolonged exposure to noisy conditions (drilling, machinery, or loud music) or from damage to or disease of the middle or inner ear. The victim may become overwhelmed by the relentless noise in the head. Devices can be worn that create pleasant, soothing sounds to override the noise.

tin ore mineral from which tin is extracted, principally cassiterite, SnO_2. The world's chief producers are Malaysia, Thailand, and Bolivia. The UK was a major producer in the 19th century but today only a few working mines remain.

tinplate milled steel coated with tin, the metal used for most 'tin' cans. The steel provides the strength, and the tin provides the corrosion resistance, ensuring that the food inside is not contaminated.

Tintagel village resort on the coast of N Cornwall, England. There are castle ruins, and legend has it that King ◊Arthur was born and held court here.

Tintoretto adopted name of Jacopo Robusti 1518–1594. Italian painter. The leading Mannerist of Venice, he painted portraits and religious works of great intensity. Outstanding among his many works is a series of religious works in the Scuola di S Rocco in Venice 1564–88, the dramatic figures lit by a flickering, unearthly light, the space around them distorted into long perspectives. Among his best-known works is *St George and the Dragon* about 1570 (National Gallery, London).

He was born in Venice, studied under ◊Titian, and was strongly influenced by ◊Michelangelo. His works are characterized by broad and dramatic composition, fine draughtsmanship, and a superb use of colour, the scenes spectacularly lit and full of movement. They include the *Miracle of St Mark Rescuing a Slave* 1548 (Accademia, Venice); his lives of Christ and the Virgin for the Scuola di S Rocco (including the vast *Christ before Pilate* and *The Last Supper*); his *Paradise* 1588, for the Doge's Palace; his *St George and the Dragon*, which demonstrates his characteristic originality in depicting figures in rushing movement; and *The Origin of the Milky Way* after 1570 (National Gallery, London), one of the finest of his allegories.

He also painted a large number of portraits, such as the *Doge Mocenigo* (Accademia, Venice), *Self-Portrait* (Louvre, Paris), and *Vincenzo Morosini* (National Gallery, London). Other works, apart from his religious works on a decorative scale, include *Susanna and the Elders* (Accademia, Vienna).

Tiomkin Dimitri 1899–1979. Russian composer. He lived in the USA from 1925 and from 1930 wrote Hollywood film scores, including music for *Duel in the Sun* 1946, *The Thing* 1951, and *Rio Bravo* 1959. His score for *High Noon* 1952 won him an Academy Award.

Tipperary county of the Republic of Ireland, in the province of Munster, divided into North and South Ridings; county town Clonmel; area 4,255 sq km/1,643 sq mi; population (1991) 132,600. It includes part of the Golden Vale, a dairy-farming region. There is horse and greyhound breeding.

Tippett Michael Kemp 1905–1998. English composer. His works include the operas *The Midsummer Marriage* 1952, *The Knot Garden* 1970, and *New Year* 1989; four symphonies; *Songs for Ariel* 1962; and choral music including *The Mask of Time* 1982. His work ranges from the dissonant and dense to the lyrical and expansive.

Tipu Sultan c. 1750–1799. Sultan of Mysore (now Karnataka) in SW India from the death of his father, ◊Hyder Ali, 1782. He died of wounds when his capital, Seringapatam, was captured by the British. His rocket brigade led Sir William Congreve (1772–1828) to develop the weapon for use in the ◊Napoleonic Wars.

Tirana or *Tiranë* capital (since 1920) of Albania; population (1991) 251,000. Industries include metallurgy, cotton textiles, soap, and cigarettes. It was founded in the early 17th century by Turks when part of the Ottoman Empire.

Tiresias or *Teiresias* in Greek mythology, a man blinded by the gods and given the ability to predict the future. According to the Roman poet Ovid, Tiresias once saw two snakes mating, struck at them, and was changed into a woman. Seven years later, in a repetition of the same scene, he reverted back to manhood. Later, when called upon to settle a dispute between the two gods Zeus and Hera on whether men or women enjoy sex more, he declared for women. As a result Hera blinded him, but Zeus gave him the gift of foresight.

Tipu Sultan The mausoleum of Tipu Sultan. He was the ruler of Mysore (now Karnataka) from 1782, and was killed when the British captured his capital 1799. *Corbis*

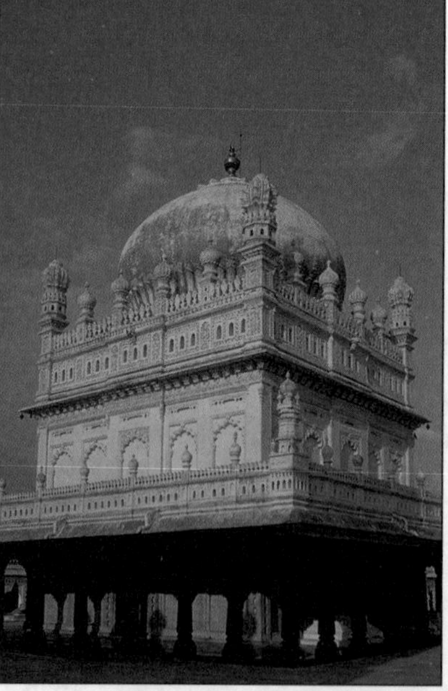

Tîrgu Mureş city in Transylvania, Romania, on the river Mureş, 450 km/280 mi N of Bucharest; population (1993) 166,000. With a population comprising approximately equal numbers of ethnic Hungarians and Romanians, the city was the scene of rioting between the two groups following Hungarian demands for greater autonomy 1990.

Tirol federal state of Austria; area 12,600 sq km/4,864 sq mi; population (1994) 654,800. Its capital is Innsbruck, and it produces diesel engines, optical instruments, and hydroelectric power. Tirol was formerly a province (from 1363) of the Austrian Empire, divided 1919 between Austria and Italy (see ◊Trentino–Alto Adige).

Tirso de Molina Pen name of Gabriel Téllez c. 1571–1648. Spanish dramatist and monk. He claimed to have written more than 300 plays, of which 80 are extant, including comedies, historical and biblical dramas, and a series based on the legend of Don Juan.

Tiryns ancient Greek city in the Peloponnese on the plain of Argos, with remains of the ◊Mycenaean civilization.

Tissot James (Joseph Jacques) 1836–1902. French painter. He is best known for detailed depictions of Victorian high society during a ten-year stay in England, as in *Ball on Shipboard* 1874 (Tate Gallery, London). Initially he was influenced by ◊Degas and shared his interest in Japanese prints. He settled in England after 1870 where he contributed illustrations to London journals. He also illustrated the life of Christ, spending ten years in Palestine, though his fame was established by his scenes of contemporary life, including *The Picnic* (Tate Gallery, London). He was also an accomplished etcher.

tissue in biology, any kind of cellular fabric that occurs in an organism's body. Several kinds of tissue can usually be distinguished, each consisting of cells of a particular kind bound together by cell walls (in plants) or extracellular matrix (in animals). Thus, nerve and muscle are different kinds of tissue in animals, as are parenchyma (tissue composed of loosely packed, more or less spherical cells, with thin cellulose walls) and sclerenchyma (tissue composed of tough, thick-walled cells) in plants.

tissue culture process by which cells from a plant or animal are removed from the organism and grown under controlled conditions in a sterile medium containing all the necessary nutrients. Tissue culture can provide information on cell growth and differentiation, and is also used in plant propagation and drug production.

tissue plasminogen activator (tPA) naturally occurring substance in the body tissues that activates the enzyme plasmin that is able to dissolve blood clots. Human tPA, produced in bacteria by genetic engineering, has been used to dissolve blood clots in the coronary arteries of heart-attack victims.

tit or ***titmouse*** any of 65 species of insectivorous, acrobatic bird of the family Paridae, order Passeriformes. Tits are 8–20 cm/3–8 in long and have grey or black plumage, often with blue or yellow markings. They are found in Eurasia and Africa, and also in North America.

British species include the bluetit *Parus caeruleus*, often seen in gardens. Its prevailing colour is blue, with green above, and a black throat. The coal tit *P. ater* has a black head, with a white patch on the nape. The great tit *P. major* is about 15 cm/6 in long and is yellow on the back, breast, and sides, with grey wings and tail, and black head and throat. The marsh tit *P. palustris* and the willow tit *P. montanus* resemble the coal tit except for the latter's white nape and white spots on the wings. The long-tailed tit *Aegithalos caudatus* is about 13 cm/5 in long, and has prolonged, graduated black tail feathers.

Titan in astronomy, largest moon of the planet Saturn, with a diameter of 5,150 km/3,200 mi and a mean distance from Saturn of 1,222,000 km/759,000 mi. It was discovered 1655 by Dutch

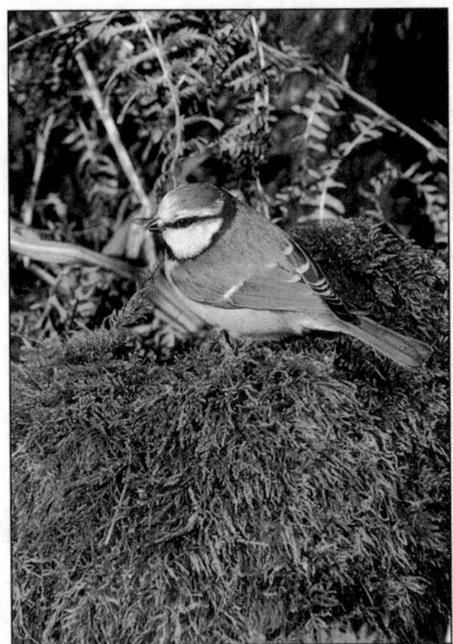

tit The blue tit is common in gardens throughout the year in the British Isles and across Europe as far eastwards as Iran. A woodland bird, it can be attracted to gardens by nest boxes that mimic the tree holes used by most tits for nesting. *Premaphotos Wildlife*

mathematician and astronomer Christiaan ◊Huygens, and is the second largest moon in the Solar System (Ganymede, of Jupiter, is larger).

Titan is the only moon in the Solar System with a substantial atmosphere (mostly nitrogen), topped with smoggy orange clouds that obscure the surface, which may be covered with liquid ethane lakes.

Titan in Greek mythology, any of the giant children of Uranus and Gaia, who included Kronos, Rhea, Themis, and Oceanus. Kronos and Rhea were in turn the parents of Zeus, who ousted Kronos as the ruler of the world.

Titanic British passenger liner, supposedly unsinkable, that struck an iceberg and sank off the Grand Banks of Newfoundland on its first voyage 14–15 April 1912; estimates of the number of lives lost vary from between 1,503 and 1,517. In 1985 it was located by robot submarine 4 km/2.5 mi down in an ocean canyon, preserved by the cold environment. In 1996 it was revealed that a series of short slits, rather than a gaping gash, was the damage caused by the iceberg.

titanium strong, lightweight, silver-grey, metallic element, symbol Ti, atomic number 22, relative atomic mass 47.90. The ninth-most abundant element in the Earth's crust, its compounds occur in practically all igneous rocks and their sedimentary deposits. It is very strong and resistant to corrosion, so it is used in building high-speed aircraft and spacecraft; it is also widely used in making alloys, as it unites with almost every metal except copper and aluminium.

titanium ore any mineral from which titanium is extracted, principally ilmenite ($FeTiO_3$) and rutile (TiO_2). Brazil, India, and Canada are major producers. Both these ore minerals are found either in rock formations or concentrated in heavy mineral sands.

Titan rocket family of US space rockets, developed from the Titan intercontinental missile. Two-stage Titan rockets launched the ◊Gemini crewed missions. More powerful Titans, with additional stages and strap-on boosters, were used to launch spy satellites and space probes, including the ◊Viking and ◊Voyager probes and ◊*Mars Observer*.

tithe formerly, payment exacted from the inhabitants of a parish for the maintenance of the church and its incumbent; some religious groups continue the practice by giving 10% of members' incomes to charity.

It was originally the grant of a tenth of all agricultural produce made to priests in Hebrew society. In the Middle Ages the tithe was adopted as a tax in kind paid to the local parish church, usually for the support of the incumbent, and stored in a special tithe ◊barn; as such, it survived into contemporary times in Europe and Britain. In Protestant countries, these payments were often appropriated by lay landlords.

Titian anglicized form of Tiziano Vecellio c. 1487–1576. Italian painter. He was one of the greatest artists of the High Renaissance. During his long career he was court painter to Charles V, Holy Roman Emperor, and to his son, Philip II of Spain. He produced a vast number of portraits, religious paintings, and mythological scenes, including *Bacchus and Ariadne* 1520–23 (National Gallery, London) and *Venus and Adonis* 1554 (Prado, Madrid).

The most famous of his early works are *Flora* about 1515 (Uffizi, Florence), the so-called *Sacred and Profane Love* about 1516 (Borghese, Rome), *Man with a Glove* about 1520 (Louvre, Paris), and *Christ and the Tribute Money* (Gemäldegalerie Alter Meister, Dresden). After about 1518 his reputation rose rapidly, and the great religious works *The Assumption of the Virgin* (Church of the Frari, Venice) and *The Entombment* (Louvre, Paris) belong to this period.

In 1533 he was introduced to the emperor Charles V, who sat for his portrait. Titian was by now internationally famous and worked in a number of centres: in Venice, where in 1537 he painted his *Battle of Cadore* (destroyed by fire 1577); in Milan, where in 1541 he was with the emperor; in Rome, 1545, at the invitation of the pope; and in Augsburg, 1548, where he painted Philip of Spain. From this time onwards he painted mainly in Venice, producing late works profound in feeling and characterized by remarkable developments in technique.

Titicaca lake in the Andes, 3,810 m/12,500 ft above sea level and 1,220 m/4,000 ft above the tree line; area 8,300 sq km/3,200 sq mi, the largest lake in South America, and the world's highest navigable body of water. It is divided between Bolivia (port at Guaqui) and Peru (ports at Puno and Huancane). It has enormous edible frogs, and is one of the few places in the world where reed boats are still made.

Tito adopted name of Josip Broz 1892–1980. Yugoslav communist politician, in effective control of Yugoslavia from 1943. In World War II he organized the National Liberation Army to carry on guerrilla warfare against the German invasion 1941, and was created marshal 1943. As prime minister 1945–53 and president from 1953, he followed a foreign policy of 'positive neutralism'.

Born in Croatia, Tito served in the Austrian army during World War I, was captured by the Russians, and fought in the Red Army during the civil wars. Returning to Yugoslavia 1923, he became prominent as a communist and during World War II as ◊partisan leader against the Nazis. In 1943 he established a provisional government and gained Allied recognition (previously given to the ◊Chetniks) 1944, and with Soviet help proclaimed the federal republic 1945. As prime minister, he settled the Yugoslav minorities question on a federal basis, and in 1953 took the newly created post of president (for life from 1974). In 1948 he was criticized by the USSR and other communist countries for his successful system of decentralized profit-sharing workers' councils, and became a leader of the ◊non-aligned movement.

titration in analytical chemistry, a technique to find the concentration of one compound in a solution by determining how much of it will react with a known amount of another compound in solution. One of the solutions is measured by pipette into the reaction vessel. The other is added a little at a time from a burette. The end-point of the reaction is determined with an ◊indicator or an electrochemical device.

Titus (Titus Flavius Vespasianus) AD 39–81. Roman emperor from AD 79. Eldest son of ◊Vespasian, he captured Jerusalem 70 to end the Jewish revolt in Roman Palestine. He completed the Colosseum, and helped to mitigate the suffering from the eruption of Vesuvius in 79, which destroyed Pompeii and Herculaneum.

Tivoli town NE of Rome, Italy; population (1990) 52,000. It has remains of Hadrian's villa, with gardens; and the Villa d'Este, with Renaissance gardens laid out 1549 for Cardinal Ippolito d'Este.

Titian *Noli me Tangere* c. 1510 by Titian (National Gallery, London). With a career spanning a remarkable 70 years, Titian dominated Venetian painting during the 16th century, his work exploiting to the full the two major characteristics of art in Venice – brilliant colour and an expressive handling of paint. *Corbis*

Tlatelolco, Treaty of international agreement signed 1967 in Tlatelolco, Mexico, prohibiting nuclear weapons in Latin America.

Tlingit a Native American people of the NW coast, living in S Alaska and N British Columbia. They used to carve wooden poles representing their family crests, showing such animals as the raven, whale, octopus, beaver, bear, wolf, and the mythical ◊Thunderbird. Their language is related to the Athabaskan languages.

TLR camera twin-lens reflex camera that has a viewing lens of the same angle of view and focal length mounted above and parallel to the taking lens.

TNT (abbreviation for ***trinitrotoluene***) $CH_3C_6H_2(NO_2)_3$, a powerful high explosive. It is a yellow solid, prepared in several isomeric forms from ◊toluene by using sulphuric and nitric acids.

toad any of the more terrestrial warty-skinned members of the tailless amphibians (order Anura). The name commonly refers to members of the genus *Bufo*, family Bufonidae, which are found worldwide, except for Australia (where the marine or ◊cane toad *B. marinus* has been introduced), Madagascar, and Antarctica. They differ from ◊frogs chiefly by the total absence of teeth.

Toads may grow up to 25 cm/10 in long. They live in cool, moist places and lay their eggs in water. The eggs are laid not in a mass as with frogs, but in long strings. The common toad *B. bufo* of Europe

Titicaca

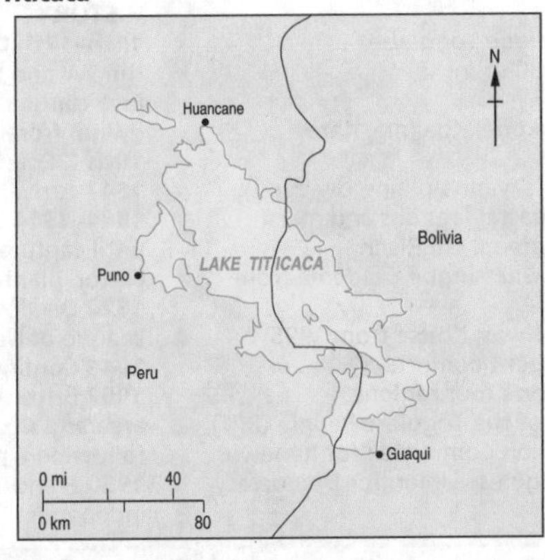

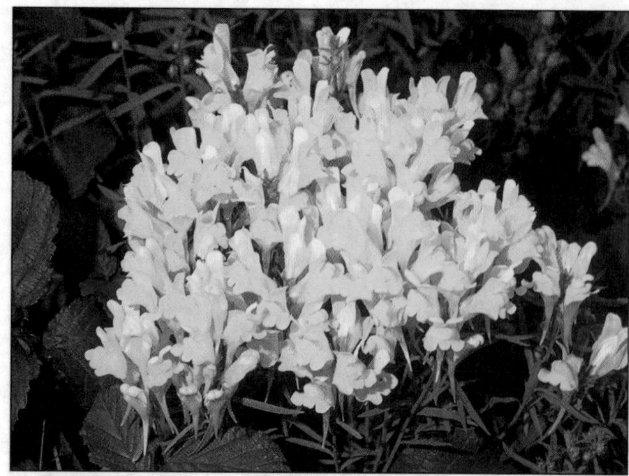

toadflax Common toadflax *Linaria vulgaris* is frequent on grassy riverbanks, roadsides, and waste ground almost throughout the British Isles and across Europe eastwards to the Altai Mountains. It is naturalized in the USA. Pollination is only by large bumblebees powerful enough to force open the hinge on the two-lipped flowers. *Premaphotos Wildlife*

and Asia has a rough, usually dark-brown skin in which there are glands secreting a poisonous fluid that makes it unattractive as food for other animals; it needs this protection because its usual progress is a slow, ungainly crawl.

toadflax any small W Eurasian plant of the genus *Linaria* of the snapdragon family Scrophulariaceae. Toadflaxes have spurred, two-lipped flowers, commonly purple or yellow, and grow to 20–80 cm/ 8–32 in tall.

toadstool common name for many umbrella-shaped fruiting bodies of fungi. The term is normally applied to those that are inedible or poisonous.

tobacco any large-leaved plant of the genus *Nicotiana* of the nightshade family Solanaceae, native to tropical parts of the Americas. *N. tabacum* is widely cultivated in warm, dry climates for use in cigars and cigarettes, and in powdered form as snuff.

The leaves are cured, or dried, and matured in storage for two to three years before use. Introduced to Europe as a medicine in the 16th century, tobacco was recognized from the 1950s as a major health hazard; see ◊cancer. The leaves also yield the alkaloid nicotine, a colourless oil, one of the most powerful poisons known, and addictive in humans. It is used in insecticides.

Worldwide, the tobacco conglomerations reap $6 billion net each year in profit. In the USA, a Supreme Court decision 1992 ruled that tobacco companies can be held legally responsible for the hazardous effects of smoking on health; conglomerations spend $50 million a year on legal advice to avoid paying out compensation to victims. However, in 1996 the Liggett Group became the first tobacco company to agree to settle smoking-related claims.

Tobago island in the West Indies; part of the republic of ◊Trinidad and Tobago.

toboggan flat-bottomed sledge, curved upwards and backwards at the front, used on snow or ice slopes or banked artificial courses. An example of such a course is the Cresta run in Switzerland. Olympic toboggans are either luge type seating one or two, without brakes or steering; or bobsleighs seating two or four, with streamlined 'cowls' at the front, steering, and brakes.

toccata in music, a display piece for keyboard instruments, such as the organ. The word 'toccata' refers to the finger technique being emphasized.

Toc H interdenominational organization for Christian fellowship, founded 1915 in Belgium as a welfare society with a Christian basis for troops in World War I by Neville Talbot and P T B Clayton (1885–1972).

tocopherol or ***vitamin E*** fat-soluble chemical found in vegetable oils. Deficiency of tocopherol leads to multiple adverse effects on health. In rats, vitamin E deficiency has been shown to cause sterility.

Tocqueville Alexis Charles Henri Clérel de 1805–1859. French politician, sociologist, and historian. He was the author of the first analytical study of the strengths and weaknesses of US society, *De la Démocratie en Amérique/Democracy in America* 1835. He also wrote a penetrating description of France before the Revolution, *L'Ancien Régime et la Révolution/The Old Regime and the Revolution* 1856. Elected to the Chamber of Deputies 1839, Tocqueville became vice president of the Constituent Assembly and minister of foreign affairs 1849. He retired after Napoleon III's coup 1851.

tofu or ***dofu*** or ***doufu*** pressed ◊soya bean curd derived from soya milk. It is a good source of protein and naturally low in fat. The flavour is bland, but it combines readily with other ingredients.

tog unit of measure of thermal insulation used in the textile trade; a light summer suit provides 1.0 tog. The tog-value of an object is equal to ten times the temperature difference (in °C) between its two surfaces when the flow of heat is equal to one watt per square metre; one tog equals 0.645 ◊clo.

toga loosely draped outer garment worn by the citizens of ancient Rome, later the exclusive dress of the upper-class Romans, consisting of a piece of cloth draped around the body.

Togliatti Palmiro 1893–1964. Italian politician who was a founding member of the Italian Communist Party 1921 and effectively its leader for almost 40 years from 1926 until his death. In exile 1926–44, he returned after the fall of the Fascist dictator Mussolini to become a member of Badoglio's government and held office until 1946.

Togo country in W Africa, on the Atlantic Ocean, bounded N by Burkina Faso, E by Benin, and W by Ghana. *See country box below.*

toilet place where waste products from the body are excreted. Simple latrines, with sewers to carry away waste, have been found in the Indus Valley and ancient Babylon; the medieval garderobe is essentially the same, although flushing lavatories had been known to Roman civilizations.

The valve cistern, with a base that could be opened or closed, was invented by John Harington, godson of Queen Elizabeth I of England. He described it 1596, although, following the introduction of the ball valve 1748, it was independently reinvented and patented by Alexander Cummings 1775. Cummings's design included a U-bend to keep smells out. This design was then improved in 1778 by Joseph Bramah (1748–1814), establishing the basic action that has largely continued to the present day. The present style of toilet dates from Davis Bostel's invention of 1889, which featured a ballcock valve system to refill the flushing cistern.

Tōjō Hideki 1884–1948. Japanese general and premier 1941–44 during World War II. Promoted to

TOGO
Republic of (formerly *Togoland*)

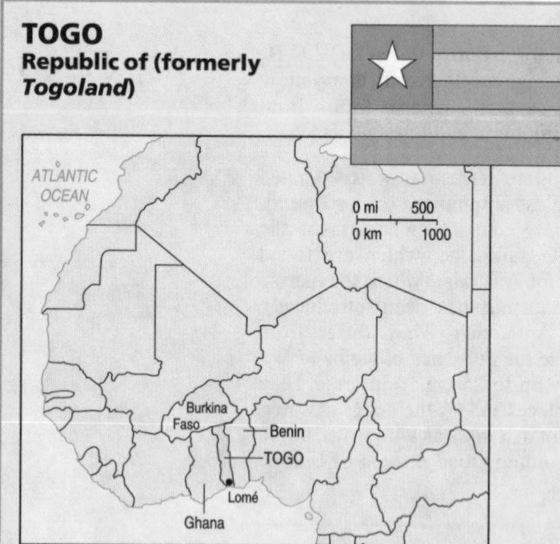

national name *République Togolaise*
area 56,800 sq km/21,930 sq mi
capital Lomé
major towns/cities Sokodé, Kpalimé, Kara, Atakpamé
physical features two savanna plains, divided by range of hills NE–SW; coastal lagoons and marsh; Mono Tableland, Oti Plateau, Oti River
head of state Etienne Gnassingbé Eyadéma from 1967
head of government Kwasi Klutse from 1996
political system emergent democracy
administrative divisions four regions
political parties Rally of the Togolese People (RPT), nationalist, centrist; Action Committee for Renewal (CAR), left of centre; Togolese Union for Democracy (UTD), left of centre
population 4,138,000 (1995 est)
population growth rate 3.2% (1990–95); 2.9% (2000–05)
ethnic distribution predominantly of Sudanese Hamitic origin in the N, and black African in the S; they are distributed among 37 different ethnic group. There are also European, Syrian, and Lebanese minorities.
life expectancy 53 (men), 57 (women)
literacy rate men 56%, women 31%
languages French (official), Ewe, Kabre, Gurma
religions animist, Catholic, Muslim, Protestant
currency franc CFA
GDP (US $) 1.01 billion (1994)
growth rate 16.3% (1994)
exports phosphates, cocoa, coffee, coconuts, cotton, palm kernels

HISTORY
15th–17th Cs Formerly dominated by Kwa peoples in the SW and Gur-speaking Votaic peoples in the N, Ewe clans immigrated from Nigeria and the Ane (Mina) from Ghana and the Ivory Coast.
18th C Coastal area held by Danes.
1847 Arrival of German missionaries.
1884–1914 Togoland was a German protectorate until captured by Anglo-French forces; cocoa and cotton plantations developed, using forced labour.
1922 Divided between Britain and France under League of Nations mandate.
1946 Continued under United Nations trusteeship.
1957 British Togoland, comprising one-third of the area and situated in the W, integrated with Ghana, following a plebiscite.
1960 French Togoland, situated in the E, achieved independence from France as the Republic of Togo with Sylvanus Olympio, the leader of the United Togolese (UP) party, as head of state.
1963 Olympio killed in a military coup. His brother-in-law, Nicolas Grunitzky, became president.
1967 Grunitzky replaced by Lt-Gen Etienne Gnassingbé Eyadéma in bloodless coup; political parties banned.
1969 Assembly of the Togolese People (RPT) formed by Eyadéma as sole legal political party.
1975 EEC Lomé convention signed in Lomé, establishing trade links with developing countries.
1977 Assassination plot against Eyadéma, allegedly involving Olympio family, thwarted.
1979 Eyadéma returned in election. Further EEC Lomé convention signed.
1986 Attempted coup failed and situation stabilized with the help of French troops.
1990 Violent antigovernment demonstrations in Lomé suppressed with casualties; Eyadéma re-legalized political parties.
1991 Gilchrist Olympio returned from exile. Eyadéma was forced to call a national conference which limited the president's powers, and elected Joseph Kokou Koffigoh head of interim government. Three attempts by Eyadéma's troops to unseat government failed.
1992 Strikes in S Togo; Olympio was attacked by soldiers and fled to France. Overwhelming referendum support for multiparty politics. New constitution adopted.
1993 Eyadéma won first multiparty presidential elections amid widespread opposition.
1994 Antigovernment coup foiled. Opposition CAR polled strongly in assembly elections. Eyadéma appointed Edem Kodjo of the minority UTD as prime minister.
1996 Kwasi Klutse appointed prime minister.

Tokugawa Triptych depicting the shoguns who ruled Japan during the Tokugawa shogunate 1603–1868. Tsunayoshi, the infamous 'Dog Shogun' whose laws placed dogs on a higher level than humans, sits in the foreground with one of his pets. Under the Tokugawa regime Japan enjoyed a period of pre-industrial stability and prosperity. *Corbis*

'Faithless is he that says farewell when the road darkens.'

J R R TOLKIEN *The Fellowship of the Ring*

Chief of Staff of Japan's Guangdong army in Manchuria 1937, he served as minister for war 1940–41 where he was responsible for negotiating the tripartite Axis alliance with Germany and Italy 1940. He was held responsible for defeats in the Pacific 1944 and forced to resign. After Japan's defeat, he was hanged as a war criminal.

tokamak acronym for ***toroidal magnetic chamber***, an experimental machine conceived by Soviet physicist Andrei ◊Sakharov and developed in the Soviet Union to investigate controlled nuclear fusion. It consists of a doughnut-shaped chamber surrounded by electromagnets capable of exerting very powerful magnetic fields. The fields are generated to confine a very hot (millions of degrees) ◊plasma of ions and electrons, keeping it away from the chamber walls. See also ◊JET.

Tokay sweet white wine made near the Hungarian town of Tokaj; also the grape from which it is made.

Tokugawa military family that controlled Japan as ◊shoguns 1603–1868. ***Tokugawa Ieyasu*** (1542–1616) was the Japanese general and politician who established the Tokugawa shogunate. The Tokugawa were feudal lords who ruled about one-quarter of Japan. Undermined by increasing foreign incursions, they were overthrown by an attack of provincial forces from Chōshū, Satsuma, and Tosa, who restored the ◊Meiji emperor to power.

Tokyo capital of Japan, on Honshu Island; population (1994) 7,874,000. It is Japan's main cultural and industrial centre (engineering, chemicals, textiles, electrical goods). Founded in the 16th century as ***Yedo*** (or ***Edo***), it was renamed when the emperor moved his court here from Kyoto 1868. An earthquake 1923 killed 58,000 people and destroyed much of the city, which was again severely damaged by Allied bombing in World War II when 60% of Tokyo's housing was destroyed; US firebomb raids of 1945 were particularly destructive with over 100,000 people killed in just one night of bombing 9 March. The subsequent rebuilding has made it into one of the world's most modern cities.

Features include the Imperial Palace, National Diet (parliament), Asakusa Kannon Temple (7th century, rebuilt after World War II), National Theatre, National Museum and other art collections, Tokyo University 1877, Tokyo Disneyland, and the National Athletic Stadium. The Sumida River delta separates the city from its suburb of Honjo.

Tokyo trials war-crimes trials 1946–48 of Japan's wartime leaders, held during the Allied occupation after World War II. Former prime minister Tōjō was among the seven sentenced to death by an international tribunal, while 16 were given life imprisonment. Political considerations allowed Emperor ◊Showa (Hirohito) to escape trial.

Toledo city on the river Tagus, Castilla–La Mancha, central Spain; population (1982) 62,000. It was the capital of the Visigoth kingdom 534–711 (see ◊Goth), then became a Moorish city, and was the Castilian capital 1085–1560.

In the 12th century Toledo had a flourishing steel industry and a school of translators, run by Archbishop Raymond (1125–1151), writing Latin versions of Arabic philosophical works.

Toledo port on Lake Erie, Ohio, USA, at the mouth of the Maumee River; population (1992) 329,300. Industries include food processing and the manufacture of vehicles, electrical goods, and glass. A French fort was built 1700, but permanent settlement did not begin until after the War of 1812.

Tolkien J(ohn) R(onald) R(euel) 1892–1973. English writer. He created the fictional world of Middle Earth in *The Hobbit* 1937 and the trilogy *The Lord of the Rings* 1954–55, fantasy novels peopled with hobbits, dwarves, and strange magical creatures. His work developed a cult following in the 1960s and had many imitators. At Oxford University he was professor of Anglo-Saxon 1925–45 and Merton professor of English 1945–59.

Tolpuddle Martyrs six farm labourers of Tolpuddle, a village in Dorset, SW England, who were transported to Australia 1834 after being sentenced for 'administering unlawful oaths' – as a 'union', they had threatened to withdraw their labour unless their pay was guaranteed, and had been prepared to put this in writing. They were pardoned two years later, after nationwide agitation. They returned to England and all but one migrated to Canada.

Tolstoy Leo Nikolaievich 1828–1910. Russian novelist. He wrote *War and Peace* 1863–69 and *Anna Karenina* 1873–77. He was offended by the materialism of western Europe and in the 1860s and 1870s he became a pioneer of 'free education'. From 1880 he underwent a profound spiritual crisis and took up various moral positions, including passive resistance to evil, rejection of authority (religious or civil) and private ownership, and a return to basic mystical Christianity. He was excommunicated by the Orthodox Church, and his later works were banned.

His first published work was *Childhood* 1852, the first part of the trilogy that was completed with *Boyhood* 1854 and *Youth* 1857. *Tales from Sevastopol* was published 1856; later books illustrating and disseminating the personal philosophy he developed after his crisis include *What I Believe* 1883, *The Kreutzer Sonata* 1889, and the novel *Resurrection* 1900. His desire to give up his property and live as a peasant disrupted his family and he finally fled his home and died of pneumonia at the railway station in Astapovo. As a writer he has had considerable influence on subsequent literature, but as a thinker he has proved much less influential; his only great disciple in his philosophy of nonresistance to evil was Mahatma ◊Gandhi.

Toltec member of an ancient Native American people who ruled much of Mexico in the 10th–12th centuries, with their capital and religious centre at Tula, NE of Mexico City. They also constructed a similar city at Chichén Itzá in Yucatán. After the Toltecs' fall the Aztecs took over much of their former territory, except for the regions regained by the Maya.

toluene or ***methyl benzene*** $C_6H_5CH_3$ colourless, inflammable liquid, insoluble in water, derived from petroleum. It is used as a solvent, in aircraft fuels, in preparing phenol (carbolic acid, used in making resins for adhesives, pharmaceuticals, and as a disinfectant), and the powerful high explosive ◊TNT.

Tomasi Giuseppe. Prince of Lampedusa Italian writer; see ◊Lampedusa.

tomato annual plant *Lycopersicon esculentum* of the nightshade family Solanaceae, native to South America. It is widely cultivated for the many-seeded red fruit (technically a berry), used in salads and cooking.

Tomba Alberto 1964– . Italian skier who became the Olympic and World Cup slalom and giant-slalom champion in 1988. He won the World Cup giant-slalom championships again in 1991. Tomba's gold medal in the giant slalom at the 1992 Albertville Winter Olympics enabled him to become the first skier to retain his Olympic gold medal.

Tombaugh Clyde William 1906–1997. US astronomer who discovered the planet ◊Pluto 1930.

Tombstone former silver-mining town in the desert of SE Arizona, USA. The gunfight at the OK Corral, with deputy marshal Wyatt Earp, his brothers, and 'Doc' Holliday against the Clanton gang, took place here 26 Oct 1881.

Tommy gun popular name for Thompson submachine-gun; see ◊machine gun.

tomography the technique of using X-rays or ultrasound waves to procure images of structures

Toledo Nestling into a curve of the Rio Tajo and dominated by the 16th-century Alcázar and 13th-century cathedral, the city of Toledo in central Spain has been an important centre of trade and culture since Roman times. It was the Spanish capital until 1561. The Alcázar (top right), originally an Arab fortress, has been destroyed many times and was rebuilt in 16th-century style after the Spanish Civil War. *Spanish Tourist Office*

deep within the body for diagnostic purposes. In modern medical imaging there are several techniques, such as the ◊CAT scan (computerized axial tomography).

Tom Thumb tiny hero of English folk tale. An old, childless couple wish for a son and are granted a thumb-sized boy. After many adventures he becomes a brave, miniature knight at the court of King Arthur. His name has often been given to those of small stature, including Charles Sherwood Stratton 1838–1883, nicknamed General Tom Thumb by the circus proprietor P T Barnum.

ton imperial unit of mass. The long ton, used in the UK, is 1,016 kg/2,240 lb; the short ton, used in the USA, is 907 kg/2,000 lb. The metric ton or tonne is 1,000 kg/2,205 lb.

ton in shipping, unit of volume equal to 2.83 cubic metres/100 cubic feet. Gross tonnage is the total internal volume of a ship in tons; net register tonnage is the volume used for carrying cargo or passengers. Displacement tonnage is the weight of the vessel, in terms of the number of imperial tons of seawater displaced when the ship is loaded to its load line; it is used to describe warships.

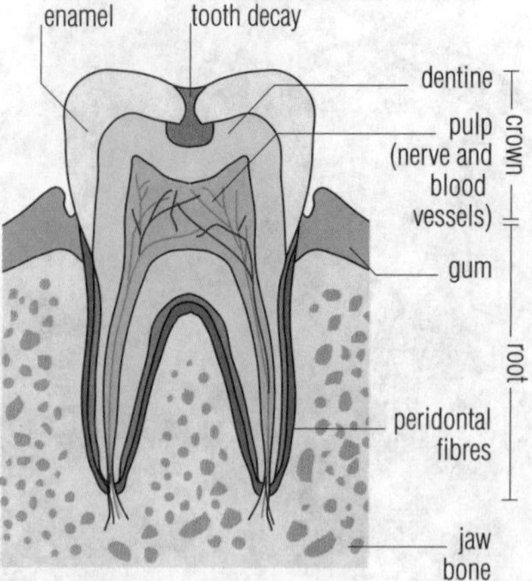

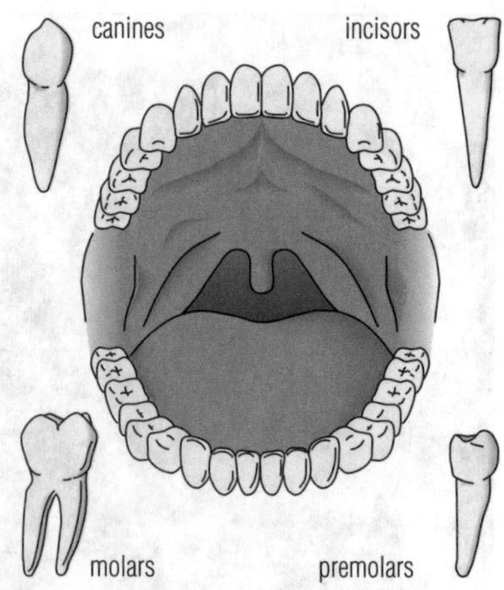

tooth Adults have 32 teeth: two incisors, one canine, two premolars, and three molars on each side of each jaw. Each tooth has three parts: crown, neck, and root. The crown consists of a dense layer of mineral, the enamel, surrounding hard dentine with a soft centre, the pulp.

tonality in music, a sense of key orientation in relation to form, for example the step pattern of a dance as expressed by corresponding changes of direction from a tonic or 'home' key to a related key. Most popular and folk music worldwide recognizes an underlying tonality or reference pitch against which the movement of a melody can be clearly heard. The opposite of tonality is atonality.

Tone (Theobald) Wolfe 1763–1798. Irish nationalist, prominent in the revolutionary society of the United Irishmen. In 1798 he accompanied the French invasion of Ireland, was captured and condemned to death, but slit his own throat in prison.

Tonga country in the SW Pacific Ocean, in ◊Polynesia. *See country box below.*

Tongariro volcanic peak at the centre of North Island, New Zealand. Considered sacred by the Maori, the mountain was presented to the government by chief Te Heuheu Tukino IV 1887. It was New Zealand's first national park and the fourth to be designated in the world.

tongue in tetrapod vertebrates, a muscular organ usually attached to the floor of the mouth. It has a thick root attached to a U-shaped bone (hyoid), and is covered with a mucous membrane (thin mucus-secreting skin) containing nerves and taste buds. It is the main organ of taste. The tongue directs food to the teeth and into the throat for chewing and swallowing. In humans, it is crucial for speech; in other animals, for lapping up water and for grooming, among other functions.

tongues the gift of speaking in tongues; see ◊glossolalia.

tonic in music, the key note of a scale (for example, the note C in the scale of C major), or the 'home key' in a composition (for example, the chord of C major in a composition in the same key).

Tonkin Gulf Incident clash that triggered US entry into the Vietnam War in Aug 1964. Two US destroyers (USS *C Turner Joy* and USS *Maddox*) reported that they were fired on by North Vietnamese torpedo boats. It is unclear whether hostile shots were actually fired, but the reported attack was taken as a pretext for making air raids against North Vietnam. On 7 Aug the US Congress passed the Tonkin Gulf Resolution, which formed the basis for the considerable increase in US military involvement in the Vietnam War.

tonne the metric ton of 1,000 kg/2,204.6 lb; equivalent to 0.9842 of an imperial ◊ton.

Tönnies Ferdinand Julius 1855–1936. German social theorist and philosopher, one of the founders of the sociological tradition of community studies and urban sociology through his key work, ◊*Gemeinschaft – Gesellschaft* 1887.

Tönnies contrasted the nature of social relationships in traditional societies and small organizations (*Gemeinschaft*, 'community') with those in industrial societies and large organizations (*Gesellschaft*, 'association'). He was pessimistic about the effect of industrialization and urbanization on the social and moral order, seeing them as a threat to traditional society's sense of community.

tonsillitis inflammation of the ◊tonsils.

tonsils in higher vertebrates, masses of lymphoid tissue situated at the back of the mouth and throat (palatine tonsils), and on the rear surface of the tongue (lingual tonsils). The tonsils contain many ◊lymphocytes and are part of the body's defence system against infection.

Tonton Macoute member of a private army of death squads on Haiti. The Tontons Macoutes were initially organized by François ◊Duvalier, president of Haiti 1957–71, and continued to terrorize the population under his successor J C Duvalier.

Tony award annual award by the League of New York Theaters to dramatists, performers, and technicians in ◊Broadway plays. It is named after the US actress and producer Antoinette Perry (1888–1946). *See list of tables on p. 1177.*

tooth in vertebrates, one of a set of hard, bonelike structures in the mouth, used for biting and chewing food, and in defence and aggression. In humans, the first set (20 milk teeth) appear from age six months to two and a half years. The permanent ◊dentition replaces these from the sixth year onwards, the wisdom teeth (third molars) sometimes not appearing until the age of 25 or 30. Adults have 32 teeth: two incisors, one canine (eye tooth), two premolars, and three molars on each side of each jaw. Each

TONGA

Kingdom of (or *Friendly Islands*)

PACIFIC OCEAN
Papua New Guinea
Solomon Islands
Samoa
Fiji Islands
TONGA
Australia
Nuku'alofa
PACIFIC OCEAN

national name *Pule'anga Fakatu'i 'o Tonga*
area 750 sq km/290 sq mi
capital Nuku'alofa (on Tongatapu island)
major towns/cities Pangai, Neiafu
physical features three groups of islands in SW Pacific, mostly coral formations, but actively volcanic in W; of the 170 islands in the Tonga group, 36 are inhabited
head of state King Taufa'ahau Tupou IV from 1965
head of government Baron Vaea from 1991
political system constitutional monarchy
administrative divisions three districts
political parties legally none, but one prodemocracy grouping, the People's Party
population 98,000 (1996 est)
population growth rate 0.4% (1990–95)
ethnic distribution 98% of Tongan ethnic origin, a Polynesian group with a small mixture of Melanesian; the remainder is European and part-European
life expectancy 69 (men), 74 (women)
literacy rate 99%
languages Tongan (official), English
religions Free Wesleyan Church
currency Tongan dollar or pa'anga
GDP (US $) 228 million (1995)
growth rate 2.5% (1994)
exports coconut oil, vanilla beans, coconut, watermelons, knitted clothes, cassava, yams, footwear, tapa cloth, mato, fibreglass boats

HISTORY
c. 1000 BC Settled by Polynesian immigrants from Fiji.
c. AD 950 The legendary Aho'eitu became the first hereditary Tongan king (Tu'i Tonga).
13th–14th Cs Tu'i Tonga kingdom at the height of its power.
1643 Visited by the Dutch navigator, Abel Tasman.
1773 Visited by the British navigator Capt James Cook, who named them the 'Friendly Islands'.
1826 Methodist mission established.
1831 Tongan dynasty founded by a Christian convert and chief of Ha'apai, Prince Taufa'ahau Tupou, who became king 14 years later.
1845–93 Reign of King George Tupou I, during which the country was reunited after half a century of civil war; Christianity was spread and a modern constitution adopted in 1875.
1900 Friendship ('Protectorate') treaty signed between King George Tupou II and Britain, establishing a British control over defence and foreign affairs, but leaving internal political affairs under Tongan control.
1918 Queen Salote Tupou III ascended the throne.
1965 Queen Salote died; succeeded by her son, King Taufa'ahau Tupou IV, who had been prime minister since 1949.
1970 Independence from Britain, but remained within the Commonwealth.
1993 Six prodemocracy candidates elected. Calls for reform of absolutist power.
1996 Prodemocracy movement led by People's Party won a majority of the 'commoner' seats in legislative assembly.

SEE ALSO: Australasia and Oceania

tooth consists of an enamel coat (hardened calcium deposits), dentine (a thick, bonelike layer), and an inner pulp cavity, housing nerves and blood vessels. Mammalian teeth have roots surrounded by cementum, which fuses them into their sockets in the jawbones. The neck of the tooth is covered by the gum.

Toowoomba town and commercial and industrial centre (coal mining, iron working, engineering, clothing) in the Darling Downs, SE Queensland, Australia; population (1994) 89,500.

topaz mineral, aluminium fluorosilicate, $Al_2(F_2SiO_4)$. It is usually yellow, but pink if it has been heated, and is used as a gemstone when transparent. It ranks 8 on the Mohs' scale of hardness.

tope tumulus found in India and SE Asia; a Buddhist monument usually built over a relic of Buddha or his disciples. Topes date from 400–300 BC including ones at Sanchi, near Bhilsa, central India.

tope slender shark *Galeorhinus galeus* ranging through temperate and tropical seas. Dark grey above and white beneath, it reaches 2 m/6 ft in length.

Topeka capital of Kansas, USA; population (1992) 120,300. It is a centre for agricultural trade, and its products include processed food, printed materials, and rubber and metal products.

topiary clipping of trees and shrubs into ornamental shapes, originated by the Romans in the 1st century and revived in the 16th–17th centuries in formal European and American gardens.

topography the surface shape and composition of the landscape, comprising both natural and artificial features, and its study. Topographical features include the relief and contours of the land; the distribution of mountains, valleys, and human settlements; and the patterns of rivers, roads, and railways.

topology branch of geometry that deals with those properties of a figure that remain unchanged even when the figure is transformed (bent, stretched) – for example, when a square painted on a rubber sheet is deformed by distorting the sheet. Topology has scientific applications, as in the study of turbulence in flowing fluids.

The map of the London Underground system is an example of the topological representation of a network; connectivity (the way the lines join together) is preserved, but shape and size are not.

topsoil the upper, cultivated layer of soil, which may vary in depth from 8 to 45 cm/3 to 18 in. It contains organic matter – the decayed remains of vegetation, which plants need for active growth – along with a variety of soil organisms, including earthworms.

topology A topological oddity, the Klein bottle is a bottle in name only because it has only one surface and no outside or inside.

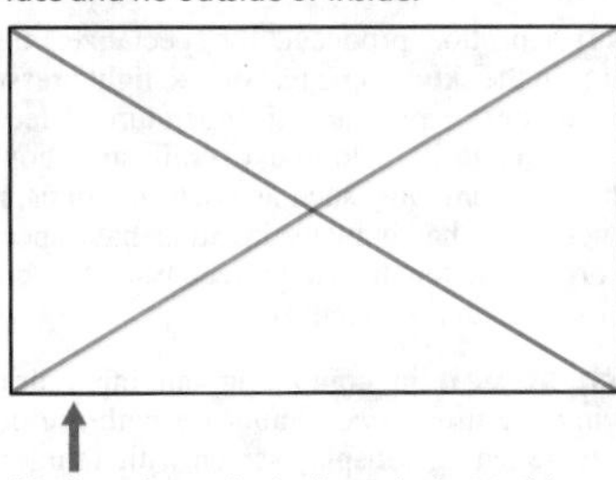

this figure is topologically equivalent to this one

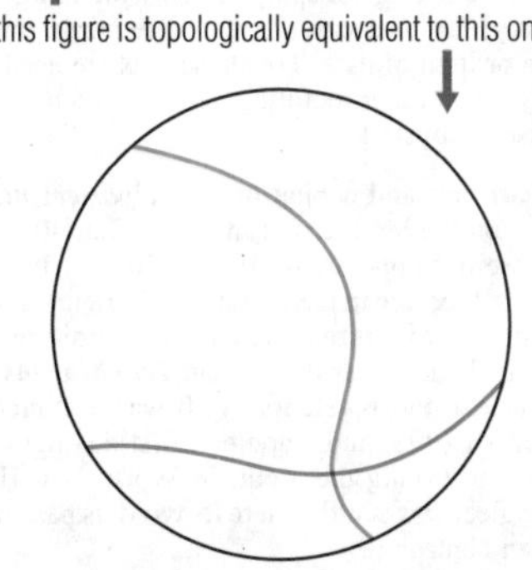

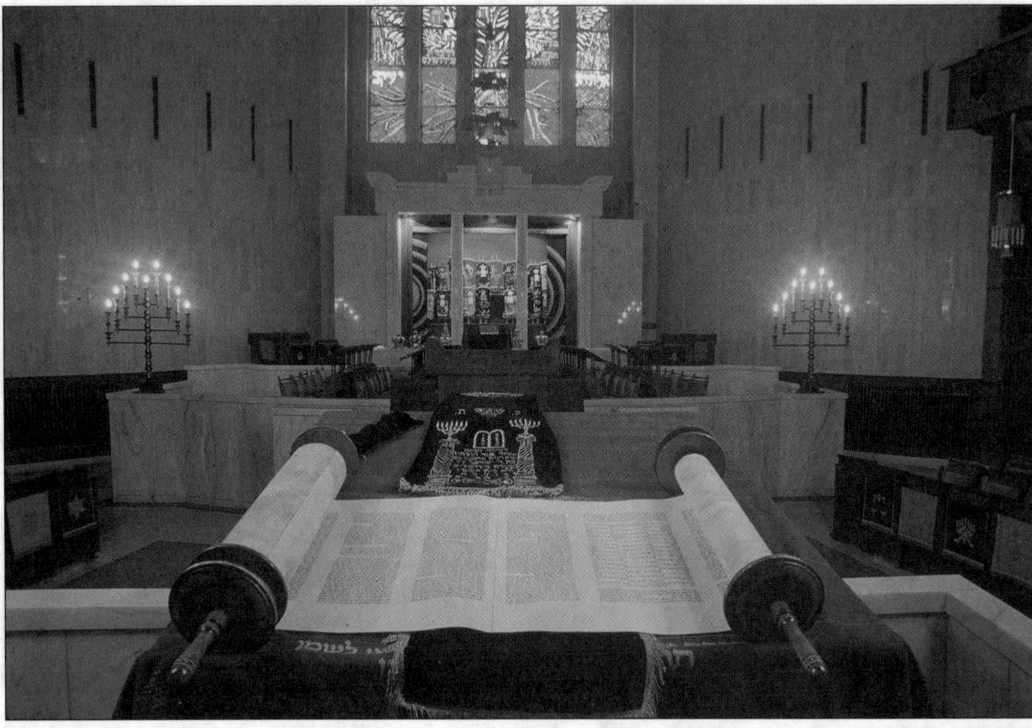

Torah A Torah lies open on the altar of the Great Synagogue, Jerusalem, Israel. The word Torah comes from the Hebrew for 'law'. *Corbis*

tor isolated mass of rock, often granite, left upstanding on a hilltop after the surrounding rock has been broken down. Weathering takes place along the joints in the rock, reducing the outcrop into a mass of rounded blocks.

Torah in ◊Judaism, the first five books of the Hebrew Bible (Christian Old Testament). It contains a traditional history of the world from the Creation to the death of Moses; it also includes the Hebrew people's covenant with their one God, rules for religious observance, and guidelines for social conduct, including the Ten Commandments.

Scrolls on which the Torah is handwritten in the original Hebrew are housed in a sacred enclosure, the ark, in every synagogue, and are treated with great respect. Jews believe that by observing the guidelines laid down in the Torah, they fulfil their part of their covenant with God.

Torbay district in S Devon, England; population (1981) 116,000. It was created 1968 by the union of the seaside resorts of Paignton, Torquay, and Brixham.

Tordesillas, Treaty of agreement reached 1494 when Spain and Portugal divided the uncharted world between themselves. An imaginary line was drawn 370 leagues W of the Azores and the Cape Verde Islands, with Spain receiving all lands discovered to the W, and Portugal those to the E.

Torfaen unitary authority of Wales created 1996 *(see United Kingdom map).*

tornado extremely violent revolving storm with swirling, funnel-shaped clouds, caused by a rising column of warm air propelled by strong wind. A tornado can rise to a great height, but with a diameter of only a few hundred metres or less. Tornadoes move with wind speeds of 160–480 kph/100–300 mph, destroying everything in their path. They are common in central USA and Australia.

Toronto (Native American 'place of meeting'; known until 1834 as ***York***) port and capital of Ontario, Canada, on Lake Ontario; metropolitan population (1991) 2,275,800. It is Canada's main industrial and commercial centre (banking, shipbuilding, cars, farm machinery, food processing, publishing) and also a cultural centre, with theatres and a film industry. A French fort was established 1749, and the site became the provincial capital 1793.

torpedo or ***electric ray*** any species of the order Torpediniformes of mainly tropical rays (cartilaginous fishes), whose electric organs between the pectoral fin and the head can give a powerful shock. They can grow to 180 cm/6 ft in length.

torpedo self-propelled underwater missile, invented 1866 by British engineer Robert Whitehead (1823–1905). Modern torpedoes are homing missiles; some resemble mines in that they lie on the seabed until activated by the acoustic signal of a passing ship. A television camera enables them to be remotely controlled, and in the final stage of attack they lock on to the radar or sonar signals of the target ship.

Torquay resort in S Devon, England, part of the district of ◊Torbay. It is a sailing centre and has an annual regatta in August.

torque the turning effect of force on an object. A turbine produces a torque that turns an electricity generator in a power station. Torque is measured by multiplying the force by its perpendicular distance from the turning point.

Torquemada Tomás de 1420–1498. Spanish Dominican monk, confessor to Queen Isabella I. In 1483 he revived the ◊Inquisition on her behalf, and at least 2,000 'heretics' were burned; Torquemada also expelled the Jews from Spain 1492, with a resultant decline of the economy.

torr unit of pressure equal to 1/760 of an ◊atmosphere, used mainly in high-vacuum technology. One torr is equivalent to 133.322 pascals, and for practical purposes is the same as the millimetre of mercury. It is named after Evangelista ◊Torricelli.

Torremolinos tourist resort on the Costa del Sol between Málaga and Algeciras in Andalucia, S Spain; population (1991) 31,700. There is a wine museum and a modern congress and exhibition centre.

Torres Strait channel separating New Guinea from Australia, with scattered reefs; width 130 km/80 mi. The first European to sail through it was the Spanish navigator Luis Vaez de Torres 1606.

Torricelli Evangelista 1608–1647. Italian physicist who established the existence of atmospheric pressure and devised the mercury ◊barometer 1644. In 1643 Torricelli filled a long glass tube, closed at one end, with mercury and inverted it in a dish of mercury. Atmospheric pressure supported a column of mercury about 76 cm/30 in long; the space above the mercury was a vacuum. Noticing that the height of the mercury column varied slightly from day to day, he came to the conclusion that this was a reflection of variations in atmospheric pressure.

torsion in physics, the state of strain set up in a twisted material; for example, when a thread, wire, or rod is twisted, the torsion set up in the material tends to return the material to its original state. The torsion balance, a sensitive device for measuring

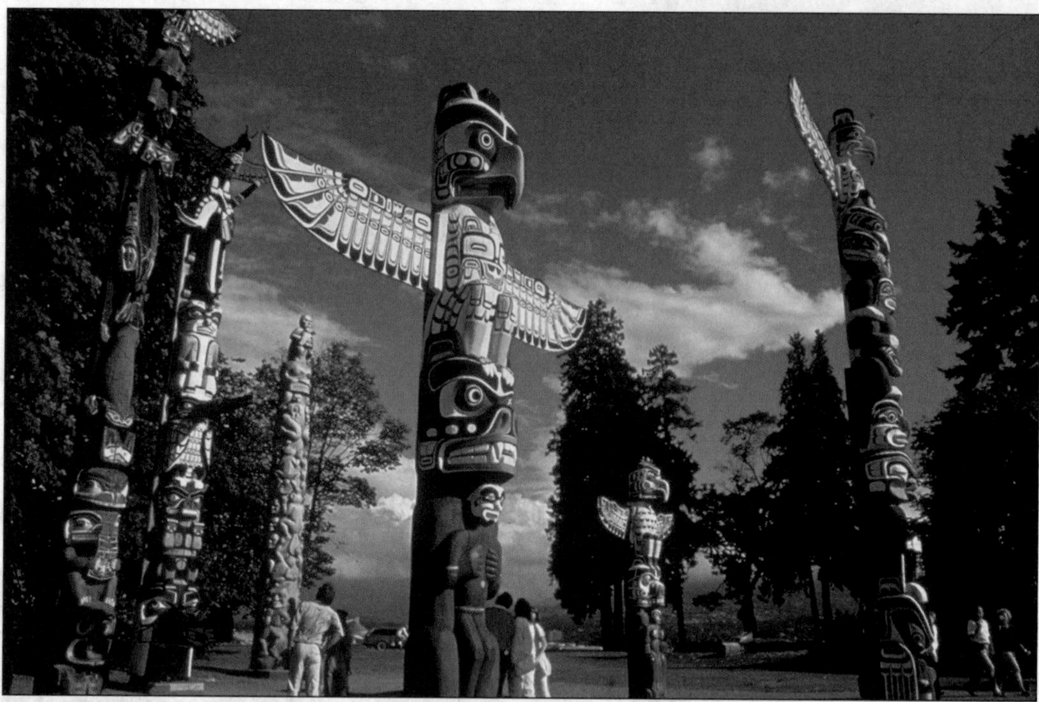

totemism Totem poles in Stanley Park, Vancouver, Canada. Among the Amerindians of the NW coast of America, images of totems – the animals with which a tribe or group within a tribe felt a special affinity – were often carved out of tall trees. In declaring the totem animal, totem poles often also announced the status, wealth, and family history of the owners. *Canadian Tourist Office*

small gravitational or magnetic forces, or electric charges, balances these against the restoring force set up by them in a torsion suspension.

tort in law, a wrongful act for which someone can be sued for damages in a civil court. It includes such acts as libel, trespass, injury done to someone (whether intentionally or by negligence), and inducement to break a contract (although breach of contract itself is not a tort). In general a tort is distinguished from a crime in that it affects the interests of an individual rather than of society at large, but some crimes can also be torts (for example assault).

Tortelier Paul 1914–1990. French cellist. His powerfully intuitive style brought him widespread fame as a soloist from 1947. Romantic in temperament, he specialized in the standard 19th-century repertoire, from Bach's solo suites to Elgar, Walton, and Kodály. From 1956 he taught at the Paris Conservatoire, where his pupils included English cellist Jacqueline du Pré.

tortoise reptile of the order Chelonia, family Testudinidae, with the body enclosed in a hard shell. Tortoises are related to the ◊terrapins and ◊turtles, and range in length from 10 cm/4 in to 150 cm/5 ft. The shell consists of a curved upper carapace and flattened lower plastron joined at the sides. The head and limbs is withdrawn into it when the tortoise is in danger. Most land tortoises are herbivorous, feeding on plant material, and have no teeth. The mouth forms a sharp-edged beak. Tortoises have been known to live for 150 years.

The giant tortoises of the Galápagos in the Pacific and the Seychelles in the Indian Ocean may reach a length of 150 cm/5 ft and weigh over 225 kg/500 lbs.

Tortoiseshell is the semi-transparent shell of the hawksbill turtle.

Tortuga (French ***La Tortue*** 'turtle') island off the north coast of ◊Haiti; area 180 sq km/69 sq mi. It was a pirate lair during the 17th century.

torture infliction of bodily pain to extort evidence or confession. In the 20th century torture is widely (though, in most countries, unofficially) used. The human-rights organization ◊Amnesty International investigates and publicizes the use of torture on prisoners of conscience. Torture was legally abolished in England about 1640, but allowed in Scotland until 1708 and in France until 1789.

physical torture In the Middle Ages physical torture employed devices such as the rack (to stretch the victim's joints to breaking point), the thumbscrew, the boot (which crushed the foot), heavy weights that crushed the whole body, the iron maiden (cage shaped like a human being with interior spikes to spear the occupant), and so on. While similar methods survive today, electric shocks and sexual assault are also common.

brainwashing This was developed in both the communist and Western blocs in the 1950s, often using drugs. From the early 1960s a method used in the West replaced isolation by severe sensory deprivation; for example, IRA guerrillas were prevented from seeing by a hood, from feeling by being swathed in a loose-fitting garment, and from hearing by a continuous loud noise at about 85 decibels, while being forced to maintain themselves in a 'search' position against a wall by their fingertips.

❛One leader, one people, signifies one master and millions of slaves.❜

On TOTALITARIANISM
Albert Camus
The Rebel 1951

torus ring with a D-shaped cross-section used to contain ◊plasma in nuclear fusion reactors such as the Joint European Torus (◊JET) reactor.

Torvill and Dean Jayne Torvill (1957–) and Christopher Dean (1959–) British ice-dance champions. They won the world title four times 1981–84 and were the 1984 Olympic champions. They turned professional shortly thereafter, but returned to international competition 1994 and immediately won the European Championship. They retired again from competitive ice dance after a bronze medal in the same year at the Olympic Games in Lillehammer, Norway.

Tory Party the forerunner of the British ◊Conservative Party about 1680–1830. It was the party of the squire and parson, as opposed to the Whigs (supported by the trading classes and Nonconformists). The name is still applied colloquially to the Conservative Party. In the USA a Tory was an opponent of the break with Britain in the American Revolution 1775–83.

The original Tories were Irish guerrillas who attacked the English, and the name was applied (at first insultingly) to royalists who opposed the Exclusion Bill (see under Duke of ◊Monmouth). Although largely supporting the 1688 revolution, the Tories were suspected of ◊Jacobite sympathies, and were kept from power 1714–60, but then held office almost continuously until 1830.

Toscanini Arturo 1867–1957. Italian conductor. He made his mark in opera as three-times musical director of La Scala, Milan, 1898–1903, 1906–08, and 1921–29, and subsequently as conductor 1937–54 of the NBC Symphony Orchestra which was established for him by NBC (National Broadcasting Company) Radio. His wide-ranging repertoire included Debussy and Respighi, and he imparted an Italianate simplicity to Mozart and Beethoven when exaggerated solemnity was the trend in Germany.

totalitarianism government control of all activities within a country, overtly political or otherwise, as in fascist or communist dictatorships. Examples of totalitarian regimes are Italy under Benito ◊Mussolini 1922–45; Germany under Adolf ◊Hitler 1933–45; the USSR under Joseph ◊Stalin from the 1930s until his death 1953; and more recently Romania under Nicolae ◊Ceaușescu 1974–89.

totalizator or ***Tote*** system of betting on racehorses or greyhounds. All money received is divided in equal shares among winning ticket owners, less expenses. It was first introduced 1928.

totemism (Algonquin Indian 'mark of my family') the belief in individual or clan kinship with an animal, plant, or object. This totem is sacred to those concerned, and they are forbidden to eat or desecrate it; marriage within the clan is usually forbidden. Totemism occurs among Pacific Islanders and Australian Aborigines, and was formerly prevalent throughout Europe, Africa, and Asia. Most Native American societies had totems as well.

Totem poles are carved by indigenous peoples of the NW coast of North America and incorporate totem objects (carved and painted) as a symbol of the people or to commemorate the dead.

Tottenham district of the Greater London borough of ◊Haringey.

toucan any South and Central American forest-dwelling bird of the genus *Ramphastos*, family Ramphastidae, order Piciformes. Toucans have very large, brilliantly coloured beaks and handsome plumage: the groundcolour is generally black and the throat, breast and rump are adorned with yellow, red and white. They live in small flocks and eat fruits, seeds, and insects. They nest in holes in trees; both parents care for the eggs and young. There are 37 species, ranging from 30 cm/1 ft to 60 cm/2 ft in size.

toucan The toucan has a large, brightly coloured bill, which accounts for almost half its body length. The bill is very light and strong, being constructed of honeycomb material. The plumage is usually dark with patches of bright colours on the head and neck.

touch sensation produced by specialized nerve endings in the skin. Some respond to light pressure, others to heavy pressure. Temperature detection may also contribute to the overall sensation of touch. Many animals, such as nocturnal ones, rely on touch more than humans do. Some have specialized organs of touch that project from the body, such as whiskers or antennae.

touch screen in computing, an input device allowing the user to communicate with the computer by touching a display screen with a finger. In this way, the user can point to a required ◊menu option or item of data. Touch screens are used less widely than other pointing devices such as the ◊mouse or joystick.

Toulon port and capital of Var *département*, SE France, on the Mediterranean Sea, 48 km/30 mi SE of Marseille; population (1990) 170,200. It is the chief Mediterranean naval station of France. Industries include oil refining, chemicals, furniture, and clothing. Toulon was the Roman ***Telo Martius*** and was made a port by Henry IV. It was occupied by the British 1793, and Napoleon first distinguished himself in driving them out. In World War II the French fleet was scuttled here to avoid its passing to German control.

Toulouse capital of Haute-Garonne *département*, SW France, on the river Garonne, SE of Bordeaux; population (1990) 365,900. The chief industries are textiles and aircraft construction (Concorde was built here). It was the capital of the Visigoths (see ◊Goth) and later of Aquitaine 781–843.
features Toulouse is known as *la ville rose* ('the red city') because most of the buildings are made from red brick. It has a fine 12th–13th-century Romanesque church (St Sernin), the church of the Jacobins (belonging to a monastery founded 1216), and the 11th–17th-century cathedral of St Etienne. The main square is the Place du Capitole. The university was founded 1229.
history Founded by the Romans, Toulouse was the Visigoth capital in the 5th century, then capital of Aquitaine 781–843, and later of Languedoc. The cultural centre of medieval France in the 12th–13th centuries, it was captured 1218 by Simon de Montfort in the pope's crusade against the Albigensian heretics (the Count of Toulouse had been accused of complicity in the murder of a papal legate). The Duke of Wellington repulsed the French marshal Soult here 1814 in the ◊Peninsular War. During the 20th century the city expanded as a major European centre of scientific research (aerospace, electronics, data processing, agriculture).

Toulouse-Lautrec Henri Marie Raymond de 1864–1901. French artist. He was active in Paris, where he painted entertainers and prostitutes in a style characterized by strong colours, bold design, and brilliant technical skill. From 1891 his lithographic posters were a great success, skilfully executed and yet retaining the spontaneous character of sketches. His later work was to prove vital to the development of ◊poster art.

Toulouse-Lautrec was born in Albi in SW France, a descendant of the ancient counts of Toulouse. He broke both legs in boyhood, as a result of which he was stunted in growth. His main activity as an artist belongs to the decade 1885–95, when his life revolved round Montmartre, Paris. At home in society of every kind, he drew and observed in the cafés, cabarets, and *maisons closes* (brothels), giving a wonderful picture of what has been called 'midnight civilization'. Among his cast of characters are Yvette Guilbert, La Goulue, Valentin, Chocolate the Negro dancer, and Jane Avril.

touraco or ***turaco*** any fruit-eating African bird of the family Musophagidae, order Cuculiformes. They have a small high bill, notched and serrated mandibles, a long tail, erectile crest, and short, rounded wings. The largest are 70 cm/28 in long. Many of them are brilliantly coloured with glossy blue, red, violet, and green plumage.

Toulouse-Lautrec *Jane Avril* 1899, a poster by the French artist Toulouse-Lautrec. With their strong colours and bold designs, his posters – many of them, like this one, for famous music hall performers – made a huge impact on commercial art. *Corbis*

Tour de France French road race for professional cyclists held annually over approximately 4,800 km/3,000 mi of primarily French roads. The race takes about three weeks to complete and the route varies each year, often taking in adjoining countries, but always ending in Paris. A separate stage is held every day, and the overall leader at the end of each stage wears the coveted 'yellow jersey' (French *maillot jaune*).

First held 1903, it is now the most watched sporting event in the world, with more than 10 million spectators. Although it is a race for individuals, sponsored teams of 12 riders take part, each with its own 'star' rider whom team members support.

The Tour of Britain is the English equivalent of the Tour de France but on a smaller scale, and involves amateur and professional teams. *See list of tables on p. 1177.*

Tourette's syndrome or ***Gilles de la Tourette syndrome*** rare neurological condition characterized by multiple tics and vocal phenomena such as grunting, snarling, and obscene speech, named after French physician Georges Gilles de la Tourette (1859–1904). It affects one to five people per 10,000, with males outnumbering females by four to one, and the onset is usually around the age of six. There are no convincing explanations of its cause, and it is usually resistant to treatment.

tourism travel and visiting places for pleasure, often involving sightseeing and staying in overnight accommodation. Regarded as an industry, tourism can increase the wealth and job opportunities in an area, although the work is often seasonal and low paid. Among the negative effects of tourism are traffic and people congestion as well as damage to the environment.

Tourism is the world's largest industry. It sustained 120 million jobs in 1995 accounting for 7% of the global workforce. It is estimated that the number of international travellers will reach 1 billion by 2010. In the UK, tourism generates £8 billion a year in foreign exchange and accounts for 4% of ◊GDP. It provides jobs for about 1.5 million people.

tourmaline hard, brittle mineral, a complex silicate of various metals, but mainly sodium aluminium borosilicate. Small tourmalines are found in granites and gneisses. The common varieties range from black (schorl) to pink, and the transparent gemstones may be colourless (achromatic), rose pink (rubellite), green (Brazilian emerald), blue (indicolite, verdelite, Brazilian sapphire), or brown (dravite).

Tournai (Flemish ***Doornik***) town in Hainaut province, Belgium, on the river Scheldt; population (1995 est) 68,100. Industries include carpets, cement, and leather. It stands on the site of a Roman relay post and has an 11th-century Romanesque cathedral.

Tourneur Cyril 1575–1626. English dramatist. Little is known about his life, but *The Atheist's Tragedy* 1611 and *The Revenger's Tragedy* 1607 (thought by some scholars to be by Thomas ◊Middleton) are among the most powerful of Jacobean dramas.

Tours industrial city (chemicals, textiles, machinery) and capital of the Indre-et-Loire *département*, W central France, on the river Loire; population (1990) 133,400. It has a 13th–15th-century cathedral. An ancient city and capital of the former province of Touraine, it was the site of the French defeat of the Arabs 732 under ◊Charles Martel. Tours became the French capital for four days during World War II.

Toussaint L'Ouverture Pierre Dominique c. 1743–1803. Haitian revolutionary leader, born a slave. He joined the insurrection of 1791 against the French colonizers and was made governor by the revolutionary French government. He expelled the Spanish and British, but when the French emperor Napoleon reimposed slavery he revolted, was captured, and died in prison in France. In 1983 his remains were returned to Haiti. ▷ *See feature on pp. 982–983.*

Tower Hamlets inner borough of E Greater London. It includes the districts of Limehouse, Spitalfields, Bethnal Green, ◊Wapping, Poplar, Stepney, and the Isle of Dogs
features Tower of London; the Isle of Dogs bounded on three sides by the Thames; ◊Docklands redevelopment area (including ◊Canary Wharf); site of Billingsgate fish market; Limehouse, the main centre of 18th- and 19th-century shipbuilding; Spitalfields, which derives its name from the priory and hospital of St Mary's Spital (1197); Bethnal Green Museum of Childhood (1872); Victoria Park (1840s)
population (1991) 161,100
history Richard II met the Essex rebels at Mile End Green (now Stepney Green) during the Peasant's Revolt 1381. In the 17th century, the name Tower Hamlets referred to the E London military district of 21 hamlets from which the Lieutenant of the Tower of London had the right to muster militia.

Tower of London fortress on the bank of the river Thames to the east of the City of London, England. The keep, or White Tower, was built about 1078 by Bishop Gundulf on the site of British and Roman fortifications. It is surrounded by two strong walls and a moat (now dry), and was for centuries a royal residence and the principal state prison. Today it is a barracks, an armoury, and a museum. In 1994 the crown jewels, traditionally kept in a bunker in the tower, were moved to a specially designed showcase, the Jewel House, situated above ground level.

Townes Charles Hard 1915– . US physicist who in 1953 designed and constructed the first ◊maser. For this work, he shared the 1964 Nobel prize.

Townshend Charles, 2nd Viscount Townshend (known as 'Turnip' Townshend) 1674–1738. English politician and agriculturalist. He was secretary of state under George I 1714–17, when dismissed for opposing the king's foreign policy, and again 1721–30, after which he retired to his farm and did valuable work in developing crop rotation and cultivating winter feeds for cattle (hence his nickname).

Townshend Charles 1725–1767. British politician, chancellor of the Exchequer 1766–67. The Townshend Acts, designed to assert Britain's traditional authority over its colonies, resulted in widespread resistance. Among other things they levied taxes on imports (such as tea, glass, and paper) into the North American colonies. Opposition in the colonies to taxation without representation (see ◊Stamp Act) precipitated the American Revolution.

Townswomen's Guilds, National Union of in the UK, an urban version of the ◊Women's Institute. It was founded 1929.

toxaemia another term for ◊blood poisoning; toxaemia of pregnancy is another term for ◊pre-eclampsia.

toxicity tests tests carried out on new drugs, cosmetics, food additives, pesticides, and other synthetic chemicals to see whether they are safe for humans to use. They aim to identify potential toxins, carcinogens, teratogens, and mutagens. Traditionally such tests use live animals such as rats,

Toussaint L'Ouverture The Haitian revolutionary leader was given the name *L'Ouverture* ('the Opening') in 1793, after leading an uprising that freed the slaves. In 1795 the French revolutionary government recognized him as governor of their part of the island; but when Napoleon came to power and restored slavery, Toussaint L'Ouverture was captured and taken to France, where he died in prison. *Corbis*

'Were't not for gold and women, there would be no damnation.'

CYRIL TOURNEUR
The Revenger's Tragedy

rabbits, and mice. Animal tests have become a target for criticism by antivivisection groups, and alternatives have been sought. These include tests on human cells cultured in a test tube and on bacteria.

toxic shock syndrome rare condition marked by rapid onset of fever, vomiting, and low blood pressure, sometimes leading to death. It is caused by a toxin of the bacterium *Staphylococcus aureus*, normally harmlessly present in the body. It is seen most often in young women using tampons during menstruation.

toxic syndrome fatal disease for which the causes are not confirmed. In an outbreak in Spain in the early 1980s, more than 20,000 people became ill and 600–700 died. Studies have pointed to the use of a 'plaguicide' product, Nemacur (produced by Bayer), which contains organophosphates, and can be dangerous if fruit and vegetables treated with it are eaten too soon after its application.

toxic waste dumped ◊hazardous waste.

toxin any poison produced by another living organism (usually a bacterium) that can damage the living body. In vertebrates, toxins are broken down by ◊enzyme action, mainly in the liver.

toxocariasis human infestation with the larvae of roundworms, sometimes present in dogs and cats. Symptoms include fever, rash, aching joints and muscles, vomiting and convulsions; there may be enlargement of the liver and damage to the lungs. Small children are most at risk.

toxoplasmosis disease transmitted to humans by animals, often in pigeon or cat excrement, or in undercooked meat. It causes flulike symptoms and damages the central nervous system, eyes, and visceral organs. It is caused by a protozoan, *Toxoplasma gondii*.

Toynbee Arnold 1852–1883. English economic historian who coined the term 'industrial revolution' in his 'Lectures on the Industrial Revolution', published 1884.

Toyota Japan's top industrial company, formed 1937, manufacturing motor vehicles. It was founded by Sakichi Toyoda (1894–1952), the inventor of an automatic loom.

Toyotomi Hideyoshi. Adopted name of Kinoshita Tōkichirō 1537–1598. Japanese warlord, one of the three military leaders who unified Japan in the 16th century (◊Momoyama period). Successful military campaigns and alliances gave him control of central and SW Japan by 1587 and E Japan by 1590. His invasion of Korea 1592–98 was, however, defeated. He was an able administrator, introducing new land and tax systems and ordering the disarmament of all but the samurai class. He instigated land surveys and in 1590 a population census.

trace element chemical element necessary in minute quantities for the health of a plant or animal. For example, magnesium, which occurs in chlorophyll, is essential to photosynthesis, and iodine is needed by the thyroid gland of mammals for making hormones that control growth and body chemistry.

tracer in science, a small quantity of a radioactive ◊isotope (form of an element) used to follow the path of a chemical reaction or a physical or biological process. The location (and possibly concentration) of the tracer is usually detected by using a Geiger-Muller counter. For example, the activity of the thyroid gland can be monitored by giving the patient an injection containing a small dose of a radioactive isotope of iodine, which is selectively absorbed from the bloodstream by the gland.

trachea tube that forms an airway in air-breathing animals. In land-living ◊vertebrates, including humans, it is also known as the windpipe and runs from the larynx to the upper part of the chest. Its diameter is about 1.5 cm/0.6 in and its length 10 cm/4 in. It is strong and flexible, and reinforced by rings of ◊cartilage.

In the upper chest, the trachea branches into two tubes: the left and right bronchi, which enter the lungs. Insects have a branching network of tubes called tracheae, which conduct air from holes (◊spiracles) in the body surface to all the body tissues. The finest branches of the tracheae are called tracheoles.

With all their faults, trade-unions have done more for humanity than any other organization.

On TRADE UNIONS Clarence Darrow *The Railroad Trainman* 1909

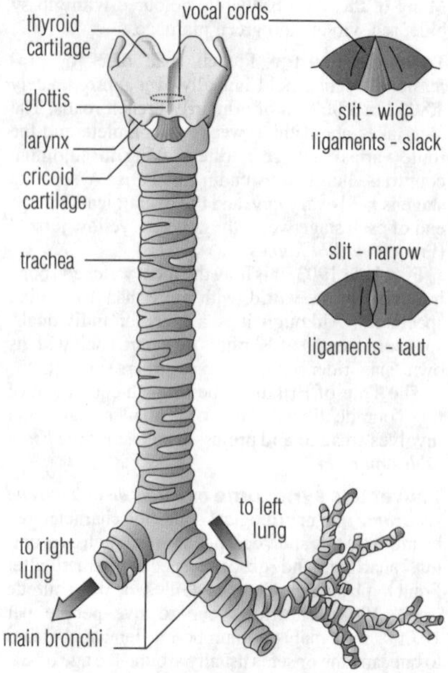

trachea The human trachea, or windpipe. The larynx, or voice box, lies at the entrance to the trachea. The two vocal cords are membranes that normally remain open and still. When they are drawn together, the passage of air makes them vibrate and produce sounds.

tracheid cell found in the water-conducting tissue (◊xylem) of many plants, including gymnosperms (conifers) and pteridophytes (ferns). It is long and thin with pointed ends.

tracheotomy or ***tracheostomy*** surgical opening in the windpipe (trachea), usually created for the insertion of a tube to enable the patient to breathe. It is done either to bypass an airway impaired by disease or injury, or to safeguard it during surgery or a prolonged period of mechanical ventilation.

trachoma chronic eye infection, resembling severe ◊conjunctivitis. The conjunctiva becomes inflamed, with scarring and formation of pus, and there may be damage to the cornea. It is caused by a viruslike organism (◊chlamydia), and is a disease of dry tropical regions. Although it responds well to antibiotics, it remains the biggest single cause of blindness worldwide.

Tractarianism another name for the ◊Oxford Movement, 19th-century movement for Catholic revival within the Church of England.

Tracy Spencer 1900–1967. US actor. He was distinguished for his understated, seemingly effortless, natural performances. His films include *Captains Courageous* 1937 and *Boys' Town* 1938 (for both of which he won Academy Awards), and he starred with Katharine Hepburn in nine films, including *Adam's Rib* 1949 and *Guess Who's Coming to Dinner* 1967, his final appearance. His other films include *Bad Day at Black Rock* 1955, *The Last Hurrah* 1958, *The Old Man and the Sea* 1958, and *Inherit the Wind* 1960.

trade exchange of commodities between groups or individuals. Direct trade is usually known as barter, whereas indirect trade is carried out through a medium such as money. In the 17th and 18th centuries, for example, barter between Europeans and West Africans was based on units of value called sortings. A sorting might consist of a quantity of cloth or oil. The amount of goods in each sorting varied according to supply and demand.

Trade and Industry, Department of (DTI) UK government department established 1970, bringing together the Board of Trade, founded in 1786, and the Ministry of Technology, formed in 1964; it took over the responsibilities of the Department of Energy in 1992. It is responsible for administration of policies on international trade, industry, competition, industrial research and assistance to exporters.

trade cycle or ***business cycle*** period of time that includes a peak and trough of economic activity, as measured by a country's national income. In Keynesian economics, one of the main roles of the government is to smooth out the peaks and troughs of the trade cycle by intervening in the economy, thus minimizing 'overheating' and 'stagnation'. This is accomplished by regulating interest rates and government spending.

trade description description of the characteristics of goods, including their quality, quantity, and fitness for the purpose for which they are required. Under the Trade Descriptions Acts 1968 and 1972, making a false trade description is a criminal offence in English law. The offence may be committed by applying a false trade description directly, such as on a label attached to goods; indirectly, such as by deliberately concealing faults in goods; or in an advertisement. Misleading statements are also illegal.

trademark name of a company or brand that identifies it in the minds of consumers. Examples are Persil, St Michael (Marks & Spencer), Hoover, and Nintendo. Trademarks can be registered so that only the individual or company registering the trademark is legally entitled to use it.

Tradescant John 1570–c. 1638. English gardener and botanist who travelled widely in Europe. He was appointed gardener to Charles I and was succeeded by his son, John Tradescant the Younger (1608–1662). The younger Tradescant undertook three plant-collecting trips to Virginia in North America. The Tradescants introduced many new plants to Britain, including the acacia, lilac, and occidental plane. Tradescant senior is generally considered the earliest collector of plants and other natural-history objects.

tradescantia any plant of the genus *Tradescantia* of the family Commelinaceae, native to North and Central America. The spiderwort *T. virginiana* is a cultivated garden plant; the wandering jew *T. albiflora* is a common house plant, with green oval leaves tinged with pink or purple or silver-striped.

Trades Union Congress (TUC) voluntary organization of trade unions, founded in the UK 1868, in which delegates of affiliated unions meet annually to consider matters affecting their members. In 1996 there were 73 affiliated unions, with an aggregate membership of 6.8 million (in 1991, membership was10.4 million).

trade union organization of workers that exists to promote and defend the interests of its members. Trade unions are particularly concerned with pay,

tradescantia *Tradescantia occidentalis* from Arizona is one of a number of blue- or mauve-flowered members of the genus which inhabit the deserts of the SW USA and Mexico. *Premaphotos Wildlife*

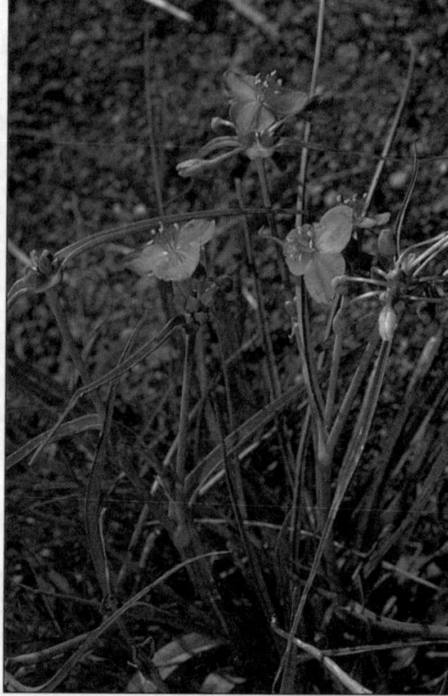

working conditions, job security, and redundancy. Four types of trade union are often distinguished: general unions, craft unions, industrial unions, and white-collar unions. Trade-union members in a place of work elect a ◊shop steward to represent them and their concerns to the management. Trade unions also employ full-time trade-union officers who tend to cover a geographical area. Top trade-union officials must be elected by a secret ballot of members.

Unions negotiate with employers over any differences they may have. Both parties may invite an outside body such as the ◊Advisory, Conciliation and Arbitration Service (ACAS) to conciliate or arbitrate in an industrial dispute. Alternatively, trade-union members may take industrial action: going on strike or working to rule, for example.

history Trade unions of a kind existed in the Middle Ages as artisans' guilds, and combinations of wage earners were formed at the time of industrialization in the 18th century; but trade unions did not formally (or legally) come into existence in Britain until the Industrial Revolution in the 19th century. The early history of trade unions is one of illegality and of legislation to prevent their existence. Five centuries of repressive legislation in Britain culminated in the passing of the ◊Combination Laws 1799 and 1800 which made unions illegal. The repeal of these 1824–25 enabled organizations of workers to engage in collective bargaining, although still subject to legal restrictions and with no legal protection for their funds until the enactment of a series of Trade Union Acts 1871–76. In 1868, 34 delegates representing 118,000 trade unionists met at a 'congress' in Manchester; the Trades Union Congress (TUC) gradually became accepted as the central organization for trade unions.

Under the Trade Union Act of 1871 unions became full legal organizations and union funds were protected from dishonest officials. Successive acts of Parliament enabled the unions to broaden their field of action; for example, the Trade Disputes Act of 1906 protected the unions against claims for damages by their employers, and the 1913 Trade Union Act allowed the unions to raise a political levy. The TUC was for many years representative mainly of unions of skilled workers, but in the 1890s the organization of unskilled labour spread rapidly. Industrial unionism (the organization of all workers in one industry or trade) began about this time, but characteristic of the so-called New Unionism at the time of the 1889 dock strike was the rise of general labour unions (for example, the Dock Workers and General Labourers in the gas industry).

During World War I the leading trade unions cooperated with the employers and the government, and by 1918 were stronger than ever before with a membership of 8 million. In 1926, following a protracted series of disputes in the coal industry, the TUC called a general strike in support of the miners; this collapsed and after nine days it was called off, leaving the miners' union to continue the strike alone for a further six months. Under the Trade Disputes and Trade Union Act of 1927 general strikes or strikes called in sympathy with other workers were made illegal.

During World War II a number of trade-union leaders served in the coalition government and membership of trade unions had again risen to 8 million by 1944. The restrictive 1927 Act was repealed under the Labour government in 1946. The postwar period was marked by increased unionism among white-collar workers. From the 1960s onwards there were confrontations between the government and the trade unions, and unofficial, or wildcat, strikes set public opinion against the trade-union movement. The Labour governments' (1964–70) attempts to introduce legislative reform of the unions was strongly opposed and eventually abandoned in 1969. The Conservative government's Industrial Relations Act 1971 (including registration of trade unions, legal enforcement of collective agreements, compulsory cooling-off periods, and strike ballots) was repealed by the succeeding Labour government 1974, and voluntary wage restraint attempted under a ◊social contract. The Employment Protection Act 1975 and the Trade Union Act 1976 increased the involvement of the government in industrial relations. ACAS was set up 1975 to arbitrate in industrial disputes. Trade union membership peaked 1979 in the UK, with 13.5 million members (representing 54 % of the workforce).

The Thatcher government, in the Employment Acts of 1980 and 1982, restricted the closed shop, picketing, secondary action against anyone other than the employer in dispute, immunity of trade unions in respect of unlawful activity by their officials, and the definition of a trade dispute, which must be between workers and employers, not between groups of workers. The Trade Union Act 1984 made it compulsory to have secret ballots for elections and before strikes. Picketing was limited to the establishment at which strikes were taking place. The Employment Act 1988 further regulated union affairs, including additional requirements for ballots; rights for members not to be unfairly disciplined (for example, for failing to support a strike); and prohibiting the use of union funds to indemnify union officers fined for contempt of court or other offences.

trade unionism, international worldwide cooperation between unions. In 1973 a European Trade Union Confederation was established, membership 29 million, and there is an International Labour Organization, established 1919 and affiliated to the United Nations from 1945, which formulates standards for labour and social conditions. Other organizations are the International Confederation of Free Trade Unions (1949) – which includes the American Federation of Labor and Congress of Industrial Organizations and the UK Trades Union Congress – and the World Federation of Trade Unions (1945).

trade wind prevailing wind that blows towards the equator from the northeast and southeast. Trade winds are caused by hot air rising at the equator and the consequent movement of air from north and south to take its place. The winds are deflected towards the west because of the Earth's west-to-east rotation. The unpredictable calms known as the ◊doldrums lie at their convergence.

trading standards department local authority department responsible for enforcing consumer legislation. Trading standards departments are responsible for checking garages to ensure that, under the ◊Weights and Measures Act 1963, the right amount of petrol is given from the pumps. They check any premises preparing or serving food because under the Food and Drugs Act 1955 food sold must be fit for human consumption. They also enforce the Trade Descriptions Act 1968, which makes it a legal offence to give false or misleading descriptions of goods or services for sale.

Trafalgar, Battle of during the ◊Napoleonic Wars, victory of the British fleet, commanded by Admiral Horatio Nelson, over a combined French and Spanish fleet 21 Oct 1805; Nelson was mortally wounded during the action. The victory laid the foundation for British naval supremacy throughout the 19th century. It is named after Cape Trafalgar, a low headland in SW Spain, near the western entrance to the Straits of Gibraltar.

The British fleet consisted of 27 ships of the line mounting 2,138 guns; the Franco-Spanish fleet consisted of 33 ships with 2,640 guns under Admiral Pierre de Villeneuve. The French were sailing in a loose line formation and Nelson divided his force into two parts which he intended to drive through the French line at different points. The manoeuvre was successful, Nelson's flagship *Victory* passing the stern of the French flagship *Bucentaure* and discharging its broadside at a range of 11 m/12 yd, causing 400 casualties, and other British ships used similar tactics of close-quarter gunnery. The battle commenced at about 12 noon, and at 1.30 p.m. Nelson was mortally wounded by a musket-shot. By 3 p.m. the battle was over, and the surviving French and Spanish ships were concentrating on escape. Of their number, 15 had been sunk, and of the 18 which escaped 2 were wrecked 24 Oct and 4 taken by a British squadron 3 Nov. The British lost no ships and sustained casualties of 449 killed and 1,242 wounded; French and Spanish casualties amounted to about 14,000. ▷ *See feature on pp. 748–749.*

tragedy in the ◊theatre, a play dealing with a serious theme, traditionally one in which a character meets disaster as a result either of personal failings or circumstances beyond his or her control. Historically the classical view of tragedy, as expressed by the Greek tragedians Aeschylus, Euripides, and Sophocles, and the Roman tragedian Seneca, has been predominant in the Western tradition. In the 20th century tragedies dealing with exalted or heroic figures in an elevated manner have virtually died out. Tragedy has been replaced by dramas with 'tragic' implications or overtones, as in the work of Ibsen, O'Neill, Tennessee Williams, and Osborne, for example, or by the problem plays of Pirandello, Brecht, and Beckett.

The Greek view of tragedy was developed by the philosopher Aristotle, but it was the Roman Seneca (whose works were probably intended to be read rather than acted) who influenced the Elizabethan tragedies of Marlowe and Shakespeare. French classical tragedy developed under the influence of both Seneca and an interpretation of Aristotle which gave rise to the theory of unities of time, place, and action, as observed by Racine, one of its greatest exponents. In Germany the tragedies of Goethe and Schiller led to the exaggerated ◊melodrama, which replaced pure tragedy. In the 18th century attempts were made to 'domesticate' tragedy, notably by Lessing, but it was the realistic dramas of Ibsen that confirmed the transformation of serious drama.

> *'A perfect Tragedy is the noblest Production of human Nature.'*
>
> On TRAGEDY
> Joseph Addison
> *Spectator* 39

tragicomedy drama that contains elements of tragedy and comedy; for example, Shakespeare's 'reconciliation' plays, such as *The Winter's Tale*, which reach a tragic climax but then lighten to a happy conclusion. A tragicomedy is the usual form for plays in the tradition of the Theatre of the ◊Absurd, such as Samuel ◊Beckett's *En attendant Godot/Waiting for Godot* 1952 and Tom ◊Stoppard's *Rosencrantz and Guildenstern are Dead* 1967.

tragopan any of several species of bird of the genus *Tragopan*, a short-tailed pheasant living in wet forests along the S Himalayas. Tragopans are brilliantly coloured with arrays of spots, long crown feathers and two blue erectile crests. Males inflate coloured wattles and throat pouches in their spring courtship displays.

Traherne Thomas c. 1637–1674. English Christian mystic. His moving lyric poetry and his prose *Centuries of Meditations* were unpublished until 1903.

trahison des clercs (French 'the treason of the intellectuals') the involvement of intellectuals in active politics.

training process of acquiring new work-related skills. Training can be on-the-job or off-the-job or a combination of both, as in an apprenticeship scheme. Induction is the term used to describe the training given to a worker when he or she first starts a new job.

Poor levels of training in the UK are seen as one of the reasons why the UK has had a poor economic growth performance relative to its industrial competitors overseas over the past 40 years. The government supports training through Training and Enterprise Councils (TECs). These are based locally and made up primarily of local business people. TECs are given grants by government but are also expected to find money from local businesses to support training in the area. They are now responsible for financing Youth Training, the scheme whereby the government has guaranteed to provide training for up to 12 months for all unemployed 16–18 year olds.

Training Agency UK government-sponsored organization responsible for retraining of unemployed workers. Founded as the Manpower Services Commission 1974, the organization operated such schemes as the Training Opportunities Scheme (TOPS), the Youth Opportunities Programme (YOP) 1978, the Youth Training Scheme (YTS) 1983, and the Technical and Vocational Initiative (TVEI).

Trajan (Marcus Ulpius Trajanus) AD 52–117. Roman emperor and soldier. He was adopted as heir by ◊Nerva, whom he succeeded AD 98, and proved a just and conscientious ruler. He conquered Dacia (Romania) 101–07 and much of ◊Parthia (113–17), bringing the empire to its greatest extent. Trajan's Column, erected in the Forum he had constructed, commemorates his Dacian victories.

trampolining gymnastics performed on a sprung canvas sheet which allows the performer to reach great heights before landing again. Marks are gained for carrying out difficult manoeuvres. Synchronized trampolining and tumbling are also popular forms of the sport. Used as a circus or show-business act in the early part of the 20th century, trampolining developed as a sport from 1936 when George Nissen of the USA invented a prototype trampoline.

tramway transport system for use in cities, where wheeled vehicles run along parallel rails. Trams are powered either by electric conductor rails below ground or by conductor arms connected to overhead wires. Greater manoeuvrability is achieved with the ◊trolley bus, similarly powered by conductor arms overhead but without tracks.

Trams originated in collieries in the 18th century, and the earliest passenger system was in use in New York 1832. Tramways were widespread in Europe and the USA from the late 19th to the mid-20th century after which they were phased out, especially in the UK and the USA, under pressure from the motor-transport lobby. In the 1990s both trams and trolley buses were being revived in some areas and are still found in many cities on the Continent; in the Netherlands several neighbouring towns share an extensive tram network.

Trams returned to the UK in 1992 after an absence of 40 years, when the Metrolink scheme in Manchester, connecting two commuter railways by 3 km/1.8 mi of track through the centre of the city, was completed.

trance mental state in which the subject loses the ordinary perceptions of time and space, and even of his or her own body. In this highly aroused state, often induced by rhythmic music, 'speaking in tongues' (glossolalia) may occur (see ◊Pentecostal movement). It is also practised by Native American and Australian Aboriginal healers, Afro-Brazilian spirit mediums, and Siberian shamans.

tranquillizer common name for any drug for reducing anxiety or tension, such as ◊benzodiazepines, barbiturates, antidepressants, and beta-blockers.

transactinide element any of a series of eight radioactive, metallic elements with atomic numbers that extend beyond the ◊actinide series, those from 104 (dubnium) to 111 (unununium). They are grouped because of their expected chemical similarities (they are all bivalent), the properties differing only slightly with atomic number. All have ◊half-lives that measure less than two minutes.

Trans-Alaskan Pipeline one of the world's greatest civil engineering projects, the construction of a pipeline to carry petroleum (crude oil) 1,285 km/800 mi from N Alaska to the ice-free port of Valdez. It was completed 1977 after three years' work and much criticism by ecologists.

Trans-Amazonian Highway or ***Transamazonica*** road in Brazil, linking Recife in the east with the provinces of Rondonia, Amazonas, and Acre in the west.

Transcaucasia geographical region S of the Caucasus Mountains, which includes Armenia, Azerbaijan, and Georgia. It formed the Transcaucasian Republic 1922, but was broken up 1936 into three separate Soviet republics. All three republics became independent 1991.

transcendentalism philosophy inaugurated in the 18th century by the German philosopher Immanuel Kant. As opposed to metaphysics in the traditional sense, transcendental philosophy is concerned with the conditions of possibility of experience, rather than the nature of being. It seeks to show the necessary structure of our 'point of view' on the world.

transcendental meditation (TM) technique of focusing the mind, based in part on Hindu meditation. Meditators are given a mantra (a special word or phrase) to repeat over and over in the mind; such meditation is believed to benefit the practitioner by relieving stress and inducing a feeling of wellbeing and relaxation. It was introduced to the West by Maharishi Mahesh Yogi and popularized by the Beatles in the late 1960s.

transcription in living cells, the process by which the information for the synthesis of a protein is transferred from the ◊DNA strand on which it is carried to the messenger ◊RNA strand involved in the actual synthesis. It occurs by the formation of ◊base pairs when a single strand of unwound DNA serves as a template for assembling the complementary nucleotides that make up the new RNA strand.

Trans-Dniester region of NE Moldova, lying between the river Dniester and the Ukraine, largely inhabited by ethnic Slavs (Russians and Ukrainians). In Oct 1990, Slav separatists unilaterally declared a breakaway republic, fearing a resurgence of ethnic Romanian nationalism as Moldova moved towards independence. A state of emergency was declared Nov 1990. The violence escalated May 1992 and by July 1992 hundreds had died in the fighting. By Aug a ceasefire was in place and a Russian peacekeeping force reportedly deployed in the region.

transducer device that converts one form of energy into another. For example, a thermistor is a transducer that converts heat into an electrical voltage, and an electric motor is a transducer that converts an electrical voltage into mechanical energy.

transfer orbit elliptical path followed by a spacecraft moving from one orbit to another, designed to save fuel although at the expense of a longer journey time. Space probes travel to the planets on transfer orbits. A probe aimed at Venus has to be 'slowed down' relative to the Earth, so that it enters an elliptical transfer orbit with its perigee (point of closest approach to the Sun) at the same distance as the orbit of Venus; towards Mars, the vehicle has to be 'speeded up' relative to the Earth, so that it reaches its apogee (furthest point from the Sun) at the same distance as the orbit of Mars.

Geostationary transfer orbit is the highly elliptical path followed by satellites to be placed in ◊geostationary orbit around the Earth (an orbit coincident with Earth's rotation). A small rocket is fired at the transfer orbit's apogee to place the satellite in geostationary orbit.

transformation in mathematics, a mapping or ◊function, especially one which causes a change of shape or position in a geometric figure. Reflection, rotation, enlargement, and translation are the main geometrical transformations.

transformational grammar theory of language structure initiated by the US linguist Noam ◊Chomsky, which proposes that below the actual phrases and sentences of a language (its surface structure) there lies a more basic layer (its deep structure), which is processed by various transformational rules when we speak and write.

Below the surface structure 'the girl opened the door' would lie the deep structure 'the girl open + (past tense) the door'. Note that there is usually more than one way in which a deep structure can be realized; in this case, 'the door was opened by the girl'.

transformer device in which, by electromagnetic induction, an alternating current (AC) of one voltage is transformed to another voltage, without change of ◊frequency. Transformers are widely used in electrical apparatus of all kinds, and in particular in power transmission where high voltages and low currents are utilized.

A transformer has two coils, a primary for the input and a secondary for the output, wound on a common iron core. The ratio of the primary to the secondary voltages (and currents) is directly (and inversely) proportional to the number of turns in the primary and secondary coils.

transfusion intravenous delivery of blood or blood products (plasma, red cells) into a patient's circulation to make up for deficiencies due to disease, injury, or surgical intervention. Cross-matching is carried out to ensure the patient receives the right blood group. Because of worries about blood-borne disease, there is a growing interest in autologous transfusion with units of the patient's own blood 'donated' over the weeks before an operation.

Blood transfusion, first successfully pioneered in humans 1818, remained highly risky until the discovery of blood groups, by Austrian-born immunologist Karl ◊Landsteiner 1900, indicated the need for compatibility of donated blood.

transgenic organism plant, animal, bacterium, or other living organism, which has had a foreign gene added to it by means of ◊genetic engineering.

transhumance seasonal movement by pastoral farmers of their livestock between areas of different climate. There are three main forms: in Alpine regions, such as Switzerland, cattle are moved to high-level pastures in summer and returned to milder valley pastures in winter; in Mediterranean lands, summer heat and drought make it necessary to move cattle to cooler mountain slopes; in W Africa, the nomadic herders of the ◊Fulani peoples move cattle south in search of grass and water in the dry season and north in the wet season to avoid the ◊tsetse fly.

transistor solid-state electronic component, made of ◊semiconductor material, with three or more ◊electrodes, that can regulate a current passing through it. A transistor can act as an amplifier, ◊oscillator, ◊photocell, or switch, and (unlike earlier thermionic valves) usually operates on a very small amount of power. Transistors commonly consist of a tiny sandwich of ◊germanium or ◊silicon, alternate layers having different electrical properties because they are impregnated with minute amounts of different impurities.

A crystal of pure germanium or silicon would act as an insulator (nonconductor). By introducing impurities in the form of atoms of other materials (for example, boron, arsenic, or indium) in minute amounts, the layers may be made either n-type, having an excess of electrons, or p-type, having a deficiency of electrons. This enables electrons to flow from one layer to another in one direction only.

Transistors have had a great impact on the electronics industry, and thousands of millions are now made each year. They perform many of the functions of the thermionic valve, but have the advantages of greater reliability, long life, compactness, and instantaneous action, no warming-up period being necessary. They are widely used in most electronic equipment, including portable radios and televisions, computers, and satellites, and are the basis of the ◊integrated circuit (silicon chip). They were invented at Bell Telephone Laboratories in the USA 1948 by John ◊Bardeen and Walter Brattain (1902–1987), developing the work of William Shockley (1910–1989).

transit in astronomy, the passage of a smaller object across the visible disc of a larger one. Transits of the inferior planets occur when they pass directly between the Earth and the Sun, and are seen as tiny dark spots against the Sun's disc. The passage of an object in the sky across the observer's meridian is also known as a transit.

transition metal any of a group of metallic elements that have incomplete inner electron shells and exhibit variable valency – for example, cobalt, copper, iron, and molybdenum. They are excellent conductors of electricity, and generally form highly coloured compounds.

Transkei former independent homeland ◊Black National State within South Africa, part of Eastern Cape Province from 1994. It became self-governing 1963, and achieved full independence 1976. The region covers an area of 43,808 sq km/16,910 sq mi. Industries include livestock, coffee, tea, sugar, maize, and sorghum.

translation in living cells, the process by which proteins are synthesized. During translation, the information coded as a sequence of nucleotides in messenger ◊RNA is transformed into a sequence of amino acids in a peptide chain. The process involves the 'translation' of the ◊genetic code. See also ◊transcription.

transmigration of souls another name for ◊reincarnation.

transmission electron microscope (TEM) the most powerful type of ◊electron microscope, with a resolving power ten times better than that of a ◊scanning electron microscope and a thousand times better than that of an optical microscope. A fine electron beam passes through the specimen, which must therefore be sliced extremely thinly – typically to about one-thousandth of the thickness of a sheet of paper (100 nanometres). The TEM can resolve objects 0.001 micrometres (0.04 millionth of an inch) apart, a gap that is 100,000 times smaller than the unaided eye can see.

The high voltage transmission electron microscope (HVEM) uses voltages of up to 3 million volts to accelerate the electron beam. The largest of these instruments is as tall as a three-storey building.

The first experimental TEM was built in 1931 by German scientists Max Knoll and Ernest Ruska of

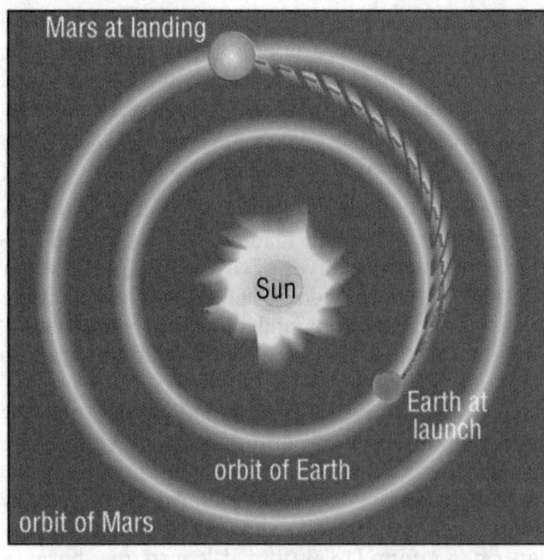

transfer orbit The transfer orbit used by a spacecraft when travelling from Earth to Mars. The orbit is chosen to minimize the fuel needed by the spacecraft; the craft is in free fall for most of the journey.

the Technische Hochschule, Berlin, Germany. They produced a picture of a platinum grid magnified 117 times.

transparency in photography, a picture on slide film. This captures the original in a positive image (direct reversal) and can be used for projection or printing on positive-to-positive print material, for example by the Cibachrome or Kodak R-type process. Slide film is usually colour.

transpiration the loss of water from a plant by evaporation. Most water is lost from the leaves through pores known as ◊stomata, whose primary function is to allow ◊gas exchange between the plant's internal tissues and the atmosphere. Transpiration from the leaf surfaces causes a continuous upward flow of water from the roots via the ◊xylem, which is known as the transpiration stream.

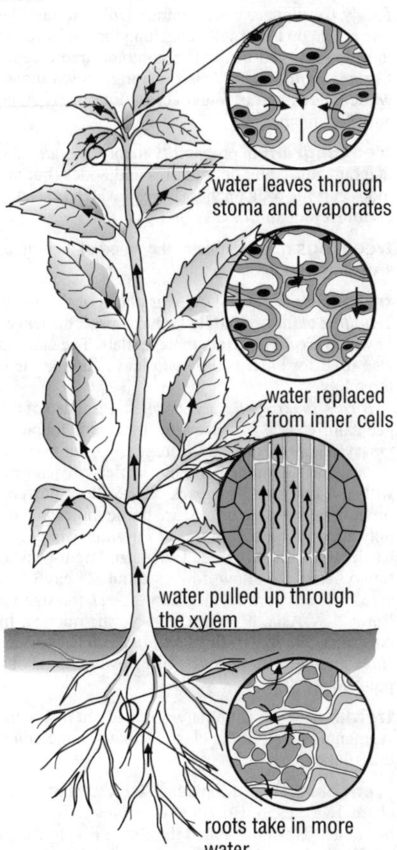

transpiration The loss of water from a plant by evaporation is known as transpiration. Most of the water is lost through the surface openings, or stomata, on the leaves. The evaporation produces what is known as the transpiration stream, a tension that draws water up from the roots through the xylem, water-carrying vessels in the stem.

transplant in medicine, the transfer of a tissue or organ from one human being to another or from one part of the body to another (skin grafting). In most organ transplants, the operation is for life-saving purposes, though the immune system tends to reject foreign tissue. Careful matching and immunosuppressive drugs must be used, but these are not always successful.

Corneal grafting, which may restore sight to a diseased or damaged eye, was pioneered 1905, and is the oldest successful human transplant procedure. Of the internal organs, kidneys were first transplanted successfully in the early 1950s and remain most in demand. Modern transplantation also encompasses the heart, lungs, liver, pancreatic tissue, bone, and bone-marrow.

Most transplant material is taken from cadaver donors, usually those suffering death of the ◊brainstem, or from frozen tissue banks. In rare cases, kidneys, corneas, and part of the liver may be obtained from living donors. The first experiments to use genetically altered animal organs in humans were given US government approval 1995. However, in 1997 US researchers called for a ban on transplants from pigs, after discovering that pigs can carry a virus that can be passed on to humans. ▷ *See feature on pp. 1024–1025.*

Transport and General Workers' Union (TGWU) UK trade union founded 1921 by the amalgamation of a number of dockers' and road-transport workers' unions, previously associated in the Transport Workers' Federation. It is the largest trade union in Britain.

transportation punishment of sending convicted persons to overseas territories to serve their sentences. It was introduced in England towards the end of the 17th century and although it was abolished 1857 after many thousands had been transported, mostly to Australia, sentences of penal servitude continued to be partly carried out in Western Australia up until 1867. Transportation was used for punishment of criminals by France until 1938.

The first British convict ship to reach Australia arrived at Sydney Cove, New South Wales, Jan 1788 with 736 convicts surviving the journey. The last convict ship to arrive in Australia was the *Hougoumont* which brought 279 prisoners to Fremantle, Western Australia, 1868. In all, about 137,000 male and 25,000 female convicts were transported to Australia.

Most convicts went into private service; under the assignment system, convicts were assigned to settlers as servants and labourers. Misbehaviour was punished by flogging, working in government chain gangs, usually on road building, or by confinement in a special penal settlement such as was set up at Newcastle, later moved to Moreton Bay, Norfolk Island, and Port Arthur. Many convicts managed to escape to the bush, some becoming bushrangers.

Trans-Siberian Railway the world's longest railway line, connecting the cities of European Russia with Omsk, Novosibirsk, Irkutsk, and Khabarovsk, and terminating at Vladivostok on the Pacific coast. It was built 1891–1905; from St Petersburg to Vladivostok is about 8,700 km/5,400 mi. A northern line, 3,102 km/1,928 mi long, was completed 1984 after ten years' work.

transubstantiation in Christian theology, the doctrine that the whole substance of the bread and wine changes into the substance of the body and blood of Jesus when consecrated in the ◊Eucharist.

transuranic element or ***transuranium element*** chemical element with an atomic number of 93 or more – that is, with a greater number of protons in the nucleus than has uranium. All transuranic elements are radioactive. Neptunium and plutonium are found in nature; the others are synthesized in nuclear reactions.

Transvaal former province of NE South Africa to 1994, bordering Zimbabwe to the N. It was settled by *Voortrekkers*, Boers who left Cape Colony in the Great Trek from 1831. Independence was recognized by Britain 1852, until the settlers' difficulties with the conquered Zulus led to British annexation 1877. It was made a British colony after the South African War 1899–1902, and in 1910 became a province of the Union of South Africa.

transverse wave ◊wave in which the displacement of the medium's particles is at right-angles to the direction of travel of the wave motion.

Transylvania mountainous area of central and NW Romania, bounded to the S by the Transylvanian Alps (an extension of the ◊Carpathian Mountains). Formerly a principality, with its capital at Cluj, it was part of Hungary from about 1000 until its people voted to unite with Romania 1918. It is the home of the vampire legends. In a 1996 treaty Hungary renounced its claims on Transylvania. *See illustrations on following page.*

trapezium in geometry, a four-sided plane figure (quadrilateral) with two of its sides parallel. If the parallel sides have lengths a and b and the perpendicular distance between them is h (the height of the trapezium), its area $A = \frac{1}{2}h(a + b)$. An isosceles trapezium has its sloping sides equal, and is symmetrical about a line drawn through the midpoints of its parallel sides.

Trappist member of a Roman Catholic order of monks and nuns, renowned for the strictness of their rule, which includes the maintenance of silence, manual labour, and a vegetarian diet. The order was

trajan

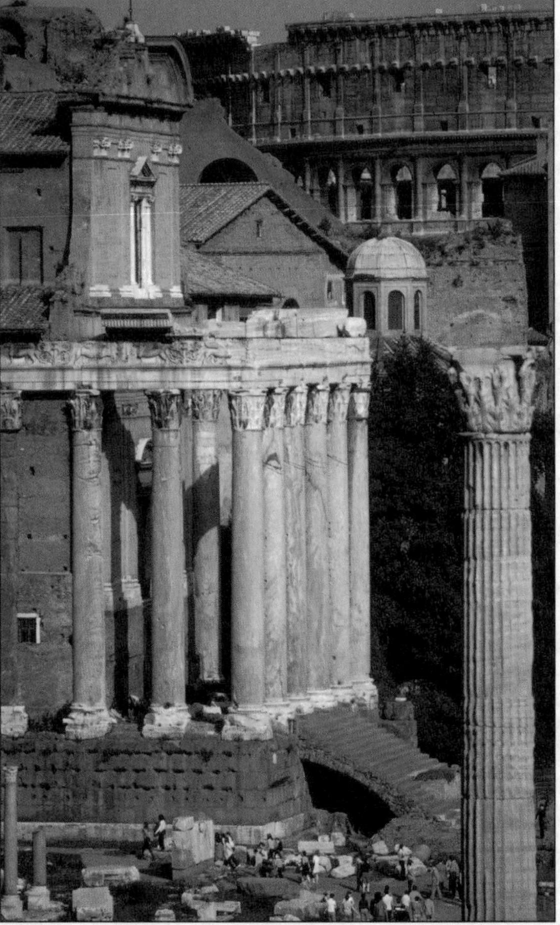

Trajan A view of Trajan's Forum in Rome. The forum (literally 'market-place') was a large, flat, central area found in every Roman town. Rome itself had several, of which Trajan's Forum, begun by the emperor Trajan in AD 113, was the latest and most magnificent. It contains Trajan's Column, a huge monument commemorating his campaigns. *Corbis*

founded 1664 at La Trappe, in Normandy, France, by Armand de Rancé (1626–1700) as a reformed version of the ◊Cistercian order.

trauma in psychiatry, a painful emotional experience or shock with lasting psychic consequences; in medicine, any physical damage or injury. In psychiatric terms a trauma may have long-lasting effects, during which an insignificant event triggers the original distress. A person then may have difficulties in normal life, such as in establishing relationships or sleeping. In psychological terms this is known as post-traumatic stress disorder. It can be treated by ◊psychotherapy.

‘The national sport of England is obstacle-racing. People fill their rooms with useless and cumbersome furniture, and spend the rest of their lives trying to dodge it.’

HERBERT BEERBOHM TREE
Quoted in Hesketh Pearson *Beerbohm Tree*

travel sickness nausea and vomiting caused by the motion of cars, boats, or other forms of transport. Constant vibration and movement may stimulate changes in the fluid of the semicircular canals (responsible for balance) of the inner ear, to which the individual fails to adapt, and to which are added visual and psychological factors. Some proprietary remedies contain ◊antihistamine drugs.

Space sickness is a special case: in weightless conditions normal body movements result in unexpected and unfamiliar signals to the brain. Astronauts achieve some control of symptoms by wedging themselves in their bunks.

Traven B(en). Pen name of Albert Otto Max Feige c. 1882–1969. German-born US novelist. His true identity was not revealed until 1979. His books include the bestseller *The Death Ship* 1926 and *The Treasure of the Sierra Madre* 1934, which was made into a film starring Humphrey Bogart 1948.

Travers Ben(jamin) 1886–1980. English dramatist. He wrote (for actors Tom Walls, Ralph Lynn, and Robertson Hare) the ‘Aldwych farces’ of the 1920s, so named from the London theatre in which they were played. They include *A Cuckoo in the Nest* 1925 and *Rookery Nook* 1926.

Transylvania A demonstration at Odorheiu Secuiesc, in the Hungarian-speaking area of Transylvania, against an education law proposing that all school lessons be conducted in Hungarian. Transylvania, which is now in Romania, was formerly part of Hungary. The Hungarian language, a member of the Finno-Ugric family, is spoken in parts of Romania, the Slovak Republic, and Yugoslavia, as well as in Hungary. *Corbis*

treadmill wheel turned by foot power (often by a domesticated animal) and used, for instance, to raise water from a well or grind grain. The human treadmill was used as a form of labour discipline in British prisons during the 19th century.

treason act of betrayal, in particular against the sovereign or the state to which the offender owes allegiance. Treason is punishable in Britain by death. It includes: plotting the wounding or death of the sovereign or his or her spouse or heir; levying war against the sovereign in his or her realm; and giving aid or comfort to the sovereign's enemies in wartime. During World War II, treachery (aiding enemy forces or impeding the crown) was punishable by death, whether or not the offender owed allegiance to the crown.

treasure trove in England, any gold or silver, plate or bullion, found concealed in a house or the ground, the owner being unknown. Normally, treasure originally hidden, and not abandoned, belongs to the crown, but if the treasure was casually lost or intentionally abandoned, the first finder is entitled to it against all but the true owner. Objects buried with no intention of recovering them, for example in a burial mound, do not rank as treasure trove, and belong to the owner of the ground.

Treasury UK government department established 1612 to collect and manage the public revenue and coordinate national economic policy. Technically, the prime minister is the first lord of the Treasury, but the chancellor of the Exchequer is the acting financial head.

Treasury bill in Britain, borrowing by the government in the form of a promissory note to repay the bearer 91 days from the date of issue; such bills represent a flexible and relatively cheap way for the government to borrow money for immediate needs.

treasury counsel in the UK, a group of barristers who receive briefs from the ◊Director of Public Prosecutions to appear for the prosecution in criminal trials at the Central Criminal Court (◊Old Bailey).

treaty written agreement between two or more states. Treaties take effect either immediately on signature or, more often, on ratification. Ratification involves a further exchange of documents and usually takes place after the internal governments have approved the terms of the treaty. Treaties are binding in international law, the rules being laid down in the Vienna Convention on the Law of Treaties 1969.

treaty port port in Asia where the Western powers had special commercial privileges in the 19th century. As a result of the enforced unequal treaties forced on China by the West, through which Western powers won diplomatic privileges and territorial concessions in China and Japan, treaty ports were established in China from 1842, and Japan 1854–99. Foreigners living in ‘concessions’ in the ports were not subject to local taxes or laws.

Treblinka German extermination camp 80 km/50 mi NW of Warsaw. About 800,000 prisoners were killed here before a mass escape took place April 1943 in which many of the SS guards were killed by the inmates. After severe reprisals the camp was closed down and dismantled in Nov 1943.

tree perennial plant with a woody stem, usually a single stem or ‘trunk’, made up of ◊wood and protected by an outer layer of ◊bark. It absorbs water through a ◊root system. There is no clear dividing line between ◊shrubs and trees, but sometimes a minimum achievable height of 6 m/20 ft is used to define a tree.

A treelike form has evolved independently many times in different groups of plants. Among the ◊angiosperms, or flowering plants, most trees are ◊dicotyledons. This group includes trees such as oak, beech, ash, chestnut, lime, and maple, and they are often referred to as ◊broad-leaved trees because their leaves are broader than those of conifers, such as pine and spruce. In temperate regions angiosperm trees are mostly ◊deciduous (that is, they lose their leaves in winter), but in the tropics most angiosperm trees are evergreen. There are fewer trees among the ◊monocotyledons, but the palms and bamboos (some of which are treelike) belong to this group. The ◊gymnosperms include many trees and they are classified into four orders: Cycadales (including cycads and sago palms), Coniferales (the conifers), Ginkgoales (including only one living species, the ginkgo, or maidenhair tree), and Taxales (including yews). Apart from the ginkgo and the larches (conifers), most gymnosperm trees are evergreen. There are also a few living trees in the ◊pteridophyte group, known as tree ferns. In the swamp forests of the Carboniferous era, 300 million years ago, there were giant treelike horsetails and club mosses in addition to the tree ferns. The world's oldest trees are found in the Pacific forest of North America, some more than 2,000 years old.

The great storm Oct 1987 destroyed some 15 million trees in Britain, and showed that large roots are less significant than those of 10 cm/4 in diameter or less. If enough of these are cut, the tree dies or falls.

Tree Herbert Draper Beerbohm 1853–1917. English actor and theatre manager. Noted for his lavish Shakespeare productions, he was founder of the Royal Academy of Dramatic Art (RADA). He was the half-brother of Max ◊Beerbohm.

tree creeper small, short-legged bird of the family Certhiidae, which spirals with a mouselike movement up tree trunks searching for food with its thin downcurved beak. The common tree creeper *Certhia familiaris* is 12 cm/5 in long, brown above, white below, and is found across Europe, N Asia, and North America.

tree diagram in probability theory, a branching diagram consisting only of arcs and nodes (but not loops curving back on themselves), which is used to establish probabilities.

tree rings rings visible in the wood of a cut tree; see ◊annual rings.

trefoil any of several ◊clover plants of the genus *Trifolium* of the pea family Leguminosae, the leaves of which are divided into three leaflets. The name is also used for other plants with leaves divided into three lobes.

Bird's-foot trefoil *Lotus corniculatus*, also of the pea family, is a low-growing perennial found in grassy places throughout Europe, N Asia, parts of Africa, and Australia. It has five leaflets to each leaf, with the first two bent back. The yellow flowers, often tinged orange or red, are borne in heads with only a few blooms. ***Hop trefoil*** *Trifolium campestre* has leaves with only three leaflets and tight-packed round heads of yellow flowers about 1.5 cm/0.6 in across. It also grows in grassy places throughout Europe, W Asia, N Africa, and North America. In Australia, ***Austral trefoil*** *Lotus australis* is a widespread native with pink or white flowers. It may be poisonous.

trematode parasitic flatworm with an oval non-segmented body, of the class Trematoda, including the ◊fluke.

Trenchard Hugh Montague, 1st Viscount Trenchard 1873–1956. British aviator and police commissioner. He commanded the Royal Flying Corps in World War I 1915–17, and 1918–29 organized the Royal Air Force, becoming its first marshal 1927. As commissioner of the Metropolitan Police 1931–35, he established the Police College at Hendon and carried out the Trenchard Reforms, which introduced more scientific methods of detection.

Trent third longest river of England; length 275 km/170 mi. Rising in the S Pennines, it flows first S and then NE through the Midlands to the Humber estuary and out into the North Sea.

Trent Bridge Test-cricket ground in Nottingham, home of the Nottinghamshire county side. One of the oldest cricket grounds in Britain, it was opened 1838. The ground covers approximately 2.5 hectares and the present-day capacity is around 30,000.

Trent, Council of conference held 1545–63 by the Roman Catholic Church at Trento, N Italy, initiating the ◊Counter-Reformation; see also ◊Reformation.

Trentino–Alto Adige autonomous region of N Italy, comprising the provinces of Bolzano and Trento; capital Trento; chief towns Trento in the Italian-speaking southern area, and Bolzano-Bozen in the northern German-speaking area of South Tirol (the region was Austrian until ceded to Italy in the settlement following World War I 1919); area 13,600 sq km/5,250 sq mi; population (1992 est) 896,700.

Trento capital of Trentino–Alto Adige region, Italy, on the Adige River; population (1992) 101,500. Industries include the manufacture of electrical goods and chemicals. The Council of ◊Trent was held here 1545–63.

Trenton capital and industrial city (metalworking, ceramics) of New Jersey, USA, on the Delaware River; population (1992) 87,800. It was first settled by Quakers 1679; George Washington defeated the British here 1776. It became the state capital 1790.

trespass going on to the land of another without authority. In law, a landowner has the right to eject a trespasser by the use of reasonable force and can sue for any damage caused. A trespasser who refuses to leave when requested may, in certain circumstances, be committing a criminal offence under the ◊Public Order Act 1986 (designed to combat convoys of caravans trespassing on farm land).

Treurnicht Andries Petrus 1921–1993. South African Conservative Party politician. He was elected to the South African parliament as a National Party member 1971 but left it 1982 to form a new right-wing Conservative Party, opposed to any dilution of the ◊apartheid system. Towards the end of his life Treurnicht softened the party's approach and participated in multiparty constitutional talks.

Trevelyan George Macaulay 1876–1962. British historian. Regius professor of history at Cambridge 1927–40, he pioneered the study of social history, as in his *English Social History* 1942.

Trevino Lee Buck 1939– . US golfer who won his first major title, the 1968 US Open, as a virtual unknown, and won it again in 1971. He also won the British Open and US PGA titles twice, and is one of only five players to have won the US Open and British Open in the same year. He played in six Ryder Cup matches.

Trevithick Richard 1771–1833. English engineer, constructor of a steam road locomotive 1801, the first to carry passengers, and probably the first steam engine to run on rails 1804. Trevithick also built steamboats, river dredgers, and threshing machines.

Trevor William (pseudonym of William Trevor Cox) 1928– . Irish writer. He came to prominence with his second novel, *The Old Boys* 1964; subsequent novels include *The Children of Dynmouth* 1976 and *Fools of Fortune* 1983. Widely regarded as one of Ireland's finest contemporary short-story writers, he has published the collections *The Day We Got Drunk On Cake* 1967 and *The News from Ireland* 1986. His novels, stories, and plays are noted for their gentle irony, humour, and subtle characterization.

Triad secret society, founded in China as a Buddhist cult AD 36. It became known as the Triad because the triangle played a significant part in the initiation ceremony. Today it is reputed to be involved in organized crime (drugs, gambling, prostitution) among overseas Chinese. Its headquarters are alleged to be in Hong Kong.

In the 18th century the Triad became political, aiming at the overthrow of the Manchu dynasty, and backed the Taiping Rebellion 1851 and Sun Yatsen's establishment of a republic 1912.

trial in law, the determination of an accused person's innocence or guilt by means of the judicial examination of the issues of the case in accordance with the law of the land. The two parties in a trial, the defendant and plaintiff, or their counsels, put forward their cases and question the witnesses; on the basis of this evidence the jury or other tribunal body decides on the innocence or guilt of the defendant.

trial by ordeal see ◊ordeal, trial by.

triangle in geometry, a three-sided plane figure, the sum of whose interior angles is 180°. Triangles can be classified by the relative lengths of their sides. A ***scalene triangle*** has three sides of unequal length; an ***isosceles triangle*** has at least two equal sides; an ***equilateral triangle*** has three equal sides (and three equal angles of 60°).

A ***right-angled triangle*** has one angle of 90°. If the length of one side of a triangle is l and the perpendicular distance from that side to the opposite corner is h (the height or altitude of the triangle), its area $A = \frac{1}{2} lh$.

triangle of forces method of calculating the force (the resultant) produced by two other forces. It is based on the fact that if three forces acting at a point can be represented by the sides of a triangle, the forces are in equilibrium. See ◊parallelogram of forces.

triangulation technique used in surveying and navigation to determine distances, using the properties of the triangle. To begin, surveyors measure a certain length exactly to provide a base line. From each end of this line they then measure the angle to a distant point, using a ◊theodolite. They now have a triangle in which they know the length of one side and the two adjacent angles. By simple trigonometry they can work out the lengths of the other two sides. To make a complete survey of the region, they repeat the process, building on the first triangle.

Triassic period of geological time 245–208 million years ago, the first period of the Mesozoic era. The continents were fused together to form the world continent ◊Pangaea. Triassic sediments contain remains of early dinosaurs and other reptiles now extinct. By late Triassic times, the first mammals had evolved.

triathlon test of stamina involving three sports: swimming 3.8 km/2.4 mi, cycling 180 km/112 mi, and running a marathon 42.195 km/26 mi 385 yd, each one immediately following the last. It was first established as a sport in the USA 1974. The most celebrated event is the Hawaii Ironman.

tribal society way of life in which people govern their own affairs as independent local communities of families and clans without central government organizations or states. They are found in parts of SE Asia, New Guinea, South America, and Africa. As the world economy expands, natural resources belonging to tribal peoples are coveted and exploited for farming or industrial use and the people are frequently dispossessed. Pressure groups have been established in some Western countries to support the struggle of tribal peoples for property rights as well as civil rights within the borders of the countries of which they are technically a part.

tribunal strictly, a court of justice, but used in English law for a body appointed by the government to arbitrate in disputes, or investigate certain matters. Tribunals usually consist of a lawyer as chair, sitting with two lay assessors.

In English law, there are various kinds of tribunal. ***Administrative tribunals*** deal with claims and disputes about rights and duties under statutory schemes; for example, industrial tribunals (dealing with employment rights, such as unfair dismissal claims) and rent tribunals (fixing fair rents for protected tenants). ***Mental health review tribunals*** make decisions about patients detained in mental hospitals. ***Domestic tribunals*** are the internal disciplinary bodies of organizations such as professional bodies and trade unions. ***Tribunals of inquiry*** are

Education ... has produced a vast population able to read but unable to distinguish what is worth reading.

GEORGE MACAULAY TREVELYAN
English Social History

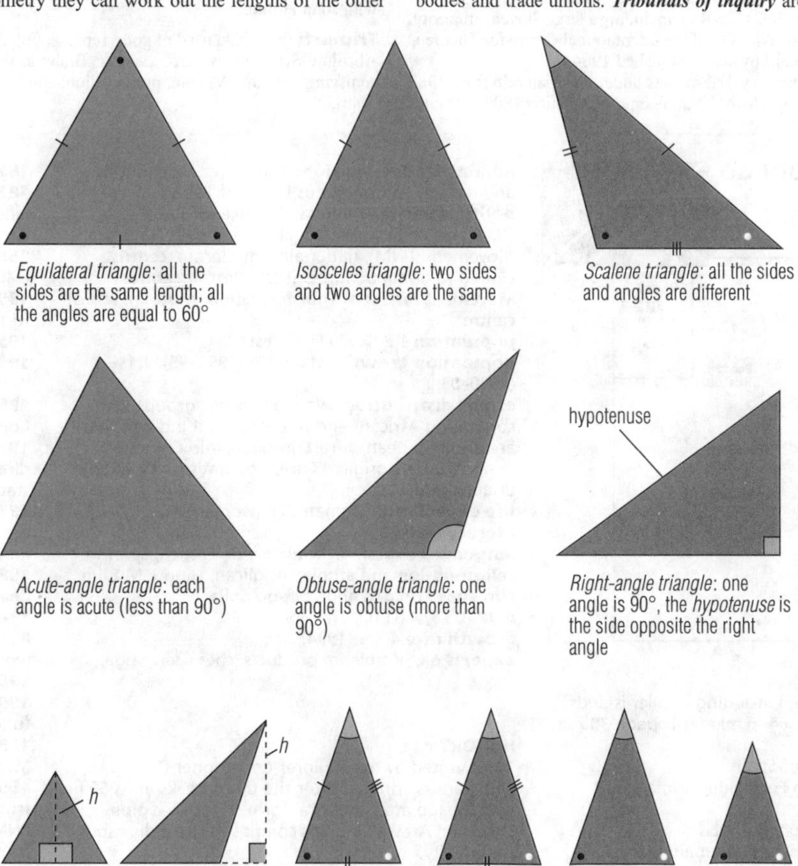
Equilateral triangle: all the sides are the same length; all the angles are equal to 60°
Isosceles triangle: two sides and two angles are the same
Scalene triangle: all the sides and angles are different
hypotenuse
Acute-angle triangle: each angle is acute (less than 90°)
Obtuse-angle triangle: one angle is obtuse (more than 90°)
Right-angle triangle: one angle is 90°, the *hypotenuse* is the side opposite the right angle
h
l
Area of triangle = $\frac{1}{2}lh$
Triangles are *congruent* if corresponding sides and corresponding angles are equal
Similar triangles have corresponding angles that are equal; they therefore have the same shape

triangle Types of triangles.

set up by the government to investigate matters of public concern.

tribune Roman magistrate of ◊plebeian family, elected annually to defend the interests of the common people; only two were originally chosen in the early 5th century BC, but there were later ten. They could veto the decisions of any other magistrate.

triceratops any of a genus *Triceratops* of massive, horned dinosaurs of the order Ornithischia. They had three horns and a neck frill and were up to 8 m/25 ft long; they lived in the Cretaceous period.

trichloromethane technical name for ◊chloroform.

tricolour (French ***tricolore***) any flag or similar made up of three colours. The French national flag has three vertical bands of red, white, and blue. The red and blue were the colours of Paris and the white represented the royal house of Bourbon. The flag was first adopted on 17 July 1789, three days after the storming of the Bastille during the French Revolution. The Russian tricolour, introduced 1991, is also red, white, and blue.

tricuspid valve flap of tissue situated on the right side of the ◊heart between the atrium and the ventricle. It prevents blood flowing backwards when the ventricle contracts.

Trident nuclear missile deployed on certain US nuclear-powered submarines and in the 1990s also being installed on four UK submarines. Each missile has eight warheads (◊MIRVs) and each of the four submarines will have 16 Trident D-5 missiles. The Trident replaced the earlier Polaris and Poseidon missiles.

Trier (French ***Trèves***) city in Rhineland-Palatinate, Germany; population (1991) 98,800. It is a centre for the wine trade. Once the capital of the Treveri, a Celto-Germanic tribe, it became known as Augusta Treverorum under the Roman emperor Augustus about 15 BC and was the capital of an ecclesiastical principality during the 14th–18th centuries.

Trieste port on the Adriatic coast, opposite Venice, in Friuli-Venezia-Giulia, Italy; population (1992) 228,400, including a large Slovene minority. It is the site of the International Centre for Theoretical Physics, established 1964.
history Trieste was under Austrian rule from 1382 (apart from Napoleonic occupation 1809–14) until transferred to Italy 1918. It was claimed after World War II by Yugoslavia; established as a Free Post 1947; the city and surrounding territory were divided 1954 between Italy and Yugoslavia. The territory is now part of Slovenia.

triggerfish any marine bony fish of the family Balistidae, with a laterally compressed body, up to 60 cm/2 ft long, and deep belly. The first spine on the dorsal fin locks into an erect position, allowing them to fasten themselves securely in crevices for protection; it can only be moved by depressing the smaller third ('trigger') spine. There are many species, found mainly in warm waters, and some are very colourful.

triglyceride chemical name for ◊fat comprising three fatty acids reacted with a glycerol.

trigonometry branch of mathematics that solves problems relating to plane and spherical triangles. Its principles are based on the fixed proportions of sides for a particular angle in a right-angled triangle, the simplest of which are known as the ◊sine, ◊cosine, and ◊tangent (so-called trigonometrical ratios). It is of practical importance in navigation, surveying, and simple harmonic motion in physics.

Invented by ◊Hipparchus, trigonometry was developed by ◊Ptolemy of Alexandria and was known to early Hindu and Arab mathematicians.

trilobite any of a large class (Trilobita) of extinct, marine, invertebrate arthropods of the Palaeozoic era, with a flattened, oval body, 1–65 cm/0.4–26 in long. The hard-shelled body was divided by two deep furrows into three lobes. Some were burrowers, others were swimming and floating forms. Their worldwide distribution, many species, and the immense quantities of their remains make them useful in geological dating.

Trimble David 1944– . Northern Ireland politician, leader of the ◊Ulster Unionist party (UUP) from 1995. Representing the Upper Bann constituency in the House of Commons from 1990, he won the leadership of the UUP in Aug 1995, when James ◊Molyneaux decided to retire at the age of 75. He was awarded the Nobel Peace Prize 1998, jointly with John Hume.

Trimurti the Hindu triad of gods, representing the Absolute Spirit in its three aspects: Brahma, personifying creation; Vishnu, preservation; and Siva, destruction.

Trinidad and Tobago country in the West Indies, off the coast of Venezuela. *See country box below.*

Trinitarianism belief in the Christian Trinity.

Trinity in Christianity, the union of three persons – Father, Son, and Holy Ghost/Spirit – in one godhead. The precise meaning of the doctrine has been the cause of unending dispute, and was the chief cause of the split between the Eastern Orthodox and Roman Catholic churches.

Tripitaka (Sanskrit 'three baskets') the canonical texts of Theravāda Buddhism, divided into three parts: the Vinaya-pitaka, containing the rules governing the monastic community; the Sūtra-pitaka, a collection of scriptures recording the teachings of the Buddha; and Abhidharma-pitaka, a collection of Buddhist philosophical writings.

Triple Alliance pact from 1882 between Germany, Austria-Hungary, and Italy to offset the power of Russia and France. It was last renewed 1912, but during World War I Italy's initial neutrality gradually changed and it denounced the alliance 1915. The term also refers to other alliances: 1668 – England, Holland, and Sweden; 1717 – Britain, Holland, and France (joined 1718 by Austria); 1788 – Britain, Prussia, and Holland; 1795 – Britain, Russia, and Austria.

triple bond three covalent bonds between adjacent atoms, as in the ◊alkynes (–C≡C–).

Triple Entente alliance of Britain, France, and Russia 1907–17. In 1911 this became a military alliance and formed the basis of the Allied powers in World War I against the Central Powers, Germany and Austria-Hungary.

triple jump track and field event in athletics comprising a hop, step, and jump sequence from a take-off board into a sandpit landing area measuring 8 m/26.25 ft (minimum) in length. The take-off board is usually 13 m/42.65 ft from the landing area. Each competitor has six trials and the winner is the one who covers the longest distance.

Tripoli (Arabic ***Tarabolus al-Gharb***) capital and chief port of Libya, on the Mediterranean coast; population (1991 est) 1,000,000. Products include olive oil, fruit, fish, and textiles.
history Tripoli was founded about the 7th century BC by Phoenicians from Oea (now Tripoli in

TRINIDAD AND TOBAGO
Republic of

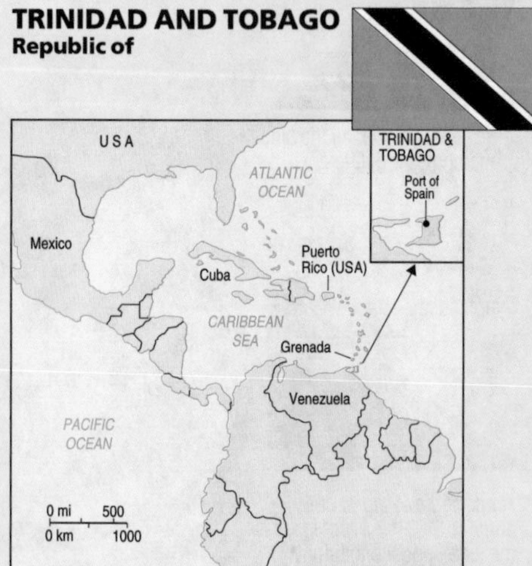

area 5,130 sq km/1,981 mi including smaller islands (Trinidad 4,828 sq km/1,864 sq mi and Tobago 300 sq km/116 sq mi)
capital (and port) Port-of-Spain
major towns/cities San Fernando, Arima, Point Fortin
major ports Scarborough, Point Lisas
physical features comprises two main islands and some smaller ones in Caribbean Sea; coastal swamps and hills E–W
head of state Noor Hassanali from 1987
head of government Basdeo Panday from 1995
political system democratic republic
administrative divisions four cities, six counties, and the semi-autonomous island of Tobago
political parties National Alliance for Reconstruction (NAR), nationalist, left of centre; People's National Movement (PNM), nationalist, moderate, centrist; United National Congress (UNC), left of centre; Movement for Social Transformation (Motion), left of centre
population 1,297,000 (1996 est)
population growth rate 1.1% (1990–95); 1.1% (2000–05)
ethnic distribution two main ethnic groups, one comprising Africans and the other East Indians; there are also European, Afro-European, and Chinese minorities. The original Carib population has largely disappeared
life expectancy 68 (men), 72 (women)
literacy rate 96%
languages English (official), Hindi, French, Spanish
religions Roman Catholic, Anglican, Hindu, Muslim
currency Trinidad and Tobago dollar
GDP (US $) 4.81 billion (1994)
growth rate 4.7% (1994)
exports oil, petroleum products, chemicals, sugar, cocoa

HISTORY
1498 Visited by the explorer Christopher Columbus, who named Trinidad after the three peaks at its SE tip and Tobago after the local form of tobacco pipe. Carib and Arawak Indians comprised the indigenous community.
1532 Trinidad was colonized by Spain.
1630s Tobago was settled by the Dutch, who introduced sugar-cane growing.
1797 Trinidad was captured by Britain and ceded by Spain five years later under Treaty of Amiens.
1814 Tobago was ceded to Britain by France.
1834 Slavery abolished, resulting in indentured labourers being brought in from India, rather than Africa, to work the sugar plantations.
1889 Trinidad and Tobago amalgamated as a British colony.
1956 The People's National Movement (PNM) founded by Eric Williams, a moderate nationalist.
1958–62 Part of West Indies Federation.
1959 Achieved internal self-government, with Williams as chief minister.
1962 Independence achieved within the Commonwealth, with Williams as prime minister.
1970 Army mutiny and violent Black Power riots directed against the minority East Indian population; state of emergency imposed for two years.
1976 Became a republic, with the former governor general Ellis Clarke as president and Williams as prime minister.
1981 Williams died and was succeeded by George Chambers.
1986 The Tobago-based National Alliance for Reconstruction (NAR), headed by Arthur Robinson, won general election.
1987 Noor Hassanali became president.
1990 Attempted antigovernment coup by Islamic fundamentalists foiled.
1991 General election victory for PNM, with Patrick Manning as prime minister.
1995 United National Congress (UNC), a breakaway from the NAR rooted in the Indian community, and PNM tied in general election; UNC–NAR coalition formed, led by Basdeo Panday.

SEE ALSO Arawak; Carib

Lebanon). It was a base for Axis powers during World War II.

triptych painting consisting of three panels, usually hinged together with the central panel being twice the width of the wings, which may fold inwards. The triptych developed from the diptych (consisting of two panels) and was used both as a portable altar and, on a larger scale, as an ◊altarpiece.

Tripura state of NE India since 1972, formerly a princely state, between Bangladesh and Assam
area 10,500 sq km/4,053 sq mi
capital Agartala
features agriculture on a rotation system in the rainforest, now being superseded by modern methods
industries rice, cotton, tea, sugar cane; steel, jute
population (1994 est) 3,055,000
language Bengali, Kokbarak
religion Hindu.

trireme ancient Greek warship with three banks of oars as well as sails, 38 m/115 ft long. Triremes were used at the Battle of ◊Salamis and by the Romans until the 4th century AD.

Tristan legendary Celtic hero. He fell in love with Isolde, the bride he was sent to win for his uncle King Mark of Cornwall. The story became part of the Arthurian cycle.

Tristan da Cunha group of islands in the S Atlantic, part of the British dependency of ◊St Helena
area 110 sq km/42 sq mi
features comprises four islands: Tristan, Gough, Inaccessible, and Nightingale. Tristan consists of a single volcano 2,060 m/6,761 ft; it is an important meteorological and radio station
government administrator and island council
industries crayfish
currency pound sterling
population (1992) 295
language English
history the first European to visit the then uninhabited islands was the Portuguese admiral after whom they are named, 1506; they were annexed by Britain 1816. The Tristan volcano erupted 1961 and the population was evacuated; in 1963 they chose to return.

tritium radioactive isotope of hydrogen, three times as heavy as ordinary hydrogen, consisting of one proton and two neutrons. It has a half-life of 12.5 years.

Triton in astronomy, the largest of Neptune's moons. It has a diameter of 2,700 km/1,680 mi, and orbits Neptune every 5.88 days in a retrograde (east to west) direction. It is slightly larger than the planet Pluto, which it is thought to resemble in composition and appearance. Triton's surface, as revealed by the *Voyager 2* space probe, has a temperature of 38K (−235°C/−391°F), making it the coldest known place in the solar system. It is covered with frozen nitrogen and methane, some of which evaporates to form a tenuous atmosphere with a pressure only 0.00001 that of the Earth at sea level. Triton has a pink south polar cap, probably coloured by the effects of solar radiation on methane ice. Dark streaks on Triton are thought to be formed by geysers of liquid nitrogen.

troglodyte For many thousands of years people have sought shelter and safety in caves. Some cave-dwellers – like those who lived at this site in Myra, S Turkey – were part of a highly sophisticated urban culture. *Edith Harkness*

Triton in Greek mythology, a merman sea god, the son of ◊Poseidon and the sea goddess Amphitrite. Traditionally, he is shown blowing on a conch shell.

triumvir one of a group of three administrators sharing power in ancient Rome, as in the First Triumvirate 60 BC: Caesar, Pompey, Crassus; and Second Triumvirate 43 BC: Augustus, Antony, and Lepidus.

Trobriand Islands group of coral islands in the Solomon Sea, forming part of the province of Milne Bay, Papua New Guinea; chief town Losuia; area 440 sq km/170 sq mi.

troglodyte Greek term for a cave dweller, designating certain peoples in the ancient world. The troglodytes of S Egypt and Ethiopia were a pastoral people.

trogon any species of the family Trogonidae, order Trogoniformes, of tropical birds, up to 50 cm/1.7 ft long, with resplendent plumage, living in the Americas, Africa, and Asia. They are primarily birds of forest or woodland. Most striking is the ◊quetzal.

Trojan horse seemingly innocuous but treacherous gift from an enemy. In Greek mythology, during the siege of Troy, an enormous wooden horse left by the Greek army outside the gates of the city. When the Greeks had retreated, the Trojans, believing it to be a religious offering, brought the horse in. Greek soldiers then emerged from within the hollow horse and opened the city gates to enable Troy to be captured.

trolley bus bus driven by electric power collected from overhead wires. It has greater manoeuvrability than a tram (see ◊tramway). Its obstructiveness in present-day traffic conditions led to its withdrawal in the UK.

Trollope Anthony 1815–1882. English novelist. He delineated provincial English middle-class society in a series of novels set in or around the imaginary cathedral city of Barchester. *The Warden* 1855 began the series, which includes *Barchester Towers* 1857, *Doctor Thorne* 1858, and *The Last Chronicle of Barset* 1867. His political novels include *Can You Forgive Her?* 1864, *Phineas Finn* 1867–69, and *The Prime Minister* 1875–76.

He went to Ireland at the age of 26 as a junior Post Office official and his first two novels had Irish themes.

trombone brass wind instrument of mainly cylindrical bore, incorporating a movable slide which allows a continuous glissando (slide) in pitch over a span of half an octave. A descendant of the Renaissance sackbut, the Baroque trombone has a shallow cup mouthpiece and modestly flared bell giving a firm, noble tone, to which the modern wide bell adds a brassy sheen. The tenor and bass trombones are staple instruments of the orchestra and brass band, also of Dixieland and jazz bands, either separately or as a tenor-bass hybrid.

Tromp Maarten Harpertszoon 1597–1653. Dutch admiral. He twice defeated the occupying Spaniards 1639. He was defeated by English admiral Blake May 1652, but in Nov triumphed over Blake in the Strait of Dover. In Feb–June 1653 he was defeated by Blake and Monk, and was killed off the Dutch coast. His son, Cornelius Tromp (1629–1691), also an admiral, fought a battle against the English and French fleets in 1673.

trompe l'oeil (French 'deceives the eye') painting that gives a convincing illusion of three-dimensional reality. As an artistic technique, it has been in common use in most stylistic periods in the West, originating in Classical Greek art.

Tromsø fishing port and the largest town in NW Norway, on Tromsø Island; population (1991) 51,300. A church was founded here in the 13th century and the town grew up around it. It is used as a base for Arctic expeditions.

Trondheim fishing port in Norway; population (1994) 134,000. It has canning, textile, margarine, and soap industries. It was the medieval capital of Norway, and Norwegian kings are crowned in the cathedral (1066–93). Trondheim was occupied by the Germans 1940–45.

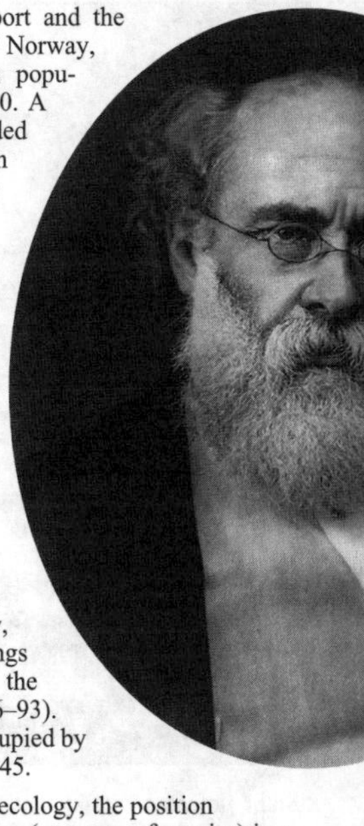

Trollope English novelist Anthony Trollope, who produced a remarkable quantity of fine novels, biographies, and travel books while pursuing a successful career as a civil servant in the Post Office. Trollope introduced the pillar box for letters to Britain and stood unsuccessfully for Parliament in 1868. *Corbis*

trophic level in ecology, the position occupied by a species (or group of species) in a ◊food chain. The main levels are primary producers (photosynthetic plants), primary consumers (herbivores), secondary consumers (carnivores), and decomposers (bacteria and fungi).

tropical disease any illness found mainly in hot climates. The most important tropical diseases worldwide are ◊malaria, ◊leishmaniasis, ◊sleeping sickness, lymphatic filiarasis, and ◊schistosomiasis. Other major scourges are ◊Chagas's disease, ◊leprosy, and ◊river blindness. All the main tropical diseases are potentially curable, but the facilities for diagnosis and treatment are rarely adequate in the countries where they occur.

tropics the area between the tropics of Cancer and Capricorn, defined by the parallels of latitude approximately 23°30′ N and S of the equator. They are the limits of the area of Earth's surface in which the Sun can be directly overhead. The mean monthly temperature is over 20°C/68°F.

Climates within the tropics lie in parallel bands. Along the equator is the intertropical convergence zone (where trade winds converge and rise to form cloud and rain), characterized by high temperatures and year-round heavy rainfall. Tropical rainforests are found here. Along the tropics themselves lie the tropical high-pressure zones, characterized by descending dry air and desert conditions. Between these, the conditions vary seasonally between wet and dry, producing the tropical grasslands.

Three hours a day will produce as much as a man ought to write.

Anthony Trollope
Autobiography

tropism or ***tropic movement*** the directional growth of a plant, or part of a plant, in response to an external stimulus such as gravity or light. If the movement is directed towards the stimulus it is described as positive; if away from it, it is negative. Geotropism for example, the response of plants to gravity, causes the root (positively geotropic) to grow downwards, and the stem (negatively geotropic) to grow upwards. Phototropism occurs in response to light, hydrotropism to water, chemotropism to a chemical stimulus, and thigmotropism, or haptotropism, to physical contact, as in the tendrils of climbing plants when they touch a support and then grow around it.

troposphere lower part of the Earth's ◊atmosphere extending about 10.5 km/6.5 mi from the Earth's surface, in which temperature decreases with height to about −60°C/−76°F except in local layers of temperature inversion. The tropopause is the upper boundary of the troposphere, above which the temperature increases slowly with height within the atmosphere. All of the Earth's weather takes place within the troposphere.

Trossachs woodland glen between lochs Katrine and Achray in Central Region, Scotland, 3 km/2 mi long.

Trotsky Leon. Adopted name of Lev Davidovitch Bronstein 1879–1940. Russian revolutionary. He joined the Bolshevik party and took a leading part in the seizure of power 1917 and raising the Red Army that fought the Civil War 1918–20. In the struggle for power that followed ◊Lenin's death 1924,

Old age is the most unexpected of all things that happen to a man.

Leon Trotsky
Diary in Exile

Trotsky Russian revolutionary Leon Trotsky in Aug 1940, a few weeks before his assassination. Trotsky had been one of the leaders of the Bolshevik revolution but was forced into exile 1929 by Stalin, who was systematically ridding himself of real or imagined threats to his position. When Trotsky continued to condemn Stalin's policies and methods, Stalin ordered his assassination. *Topham*

'When humour can be made to alternate with melancholy, one has a success, but when the same things are funny and melancholic at the same time, it's just wonderful.'

FRANÇOIS TRUFFAUT
Letter 15 Jan 1980

◊Stalin defeated Trotsky, and this and other differences with the Communist Party led to his exile 1929. He settled in Mexico, where he was assassinated at Stalin's instigation. Trotsky believed in world revolution and in permanent revolution (see ◊Trotskyism), and was an uncompromising, if liberal, idealist.

Trotsky became a Marxist in the 1890s and was imprisoned and exiled for opposition to the tsarist regime. He lived in W Europe from 1902 until the 1905 revolution, when he was again imprisoned but escaped to live in exile until 1917, when he returned to Russia and joined the Bolsheviks. Although as a young man Trotsky admired Lenin, when he worked with him organizing the revolution of 1917, he objected to Lenin's dictatorial ways. He was second in command until Lenin's death, and was minister for foreign affairs 1917–18 and minister for war 1918–Jan 1925. In exile in Mexico, he was killed with an ice pick. Official Soviet recognition of responsibility for his assassination through the secret service came in 1989.

Trotsky's later works are critical of the Soviet regime; for example, *The Revolution Betrayed* 1937. His greatest work is his magisterial *History of the Russian Revolution* 1932–33.

Trotskyism form of Marxism advocated by Leon Trotsky. Its central concept is that of permanent revolution. In his view a proletarian revolution, leading to a socialist society, could not be achieved in isolation, so it would be necessary to spark off further revolutions throughout Europe and ultimately worldwide. This was in direct opposition to the Stalinist view that socialism should be built and consolidated within individual countries.

Trotskyism developed in an attempt to reconcile Marxist theory with actual conditions in Russia in the early 20th century, but it was never officially accepted within the USSR. Instead it found much support worldwide, primarily in Third World countries, and the Fourth ◊International, which Trotsky founded 1938, has sections in over 60 countries.

Truman Harry S Truman was US president during the Allied victory in World War II and US involvement in the Korean War. *Topham*

trotting another name for the sport of ◊harness racing.

troubadour class of poet musicians in Provence and S France in the 12th–13th centuries, which included both nobles and wandering minstrels. The troubadours originated a type of lyric poetry devoted to themes of courtly love (the medieval code of amorous conduct between noblemen and women) and the idealization of women, and to glorifying the deeds of their patrons, reflecting the chivalric ideals of the period. Little is known of their music, which was passed down orally.

Among the troubadours were Bertran de Born (1140–c. 1215), Arnaut Daniel, and Bernard de Ventadour. The troubadour tradition spread to other parts of Europe, including northern France (the *trouvères*) and Germany (the Minnesingers).

trout any of various bony fishes in the salmon family, popular for sport and food, usually speckled and found mainly in fresh water. They are native to the northern hemisphere. The common trout *Salmo trutta* is widely distributed in Europe, occurring in British fresh and coastal waters. Sea trout are generally silvery and river trout olive-brown, both with spotted fins and sides.

Troy (Latin ***Ilium***) ancient city (now Hissarlik or Hisarlih in Turkey) of Asia Minor, just S of the Dardanelles, besieged in the legendary ten-year Trojan War (mid-13th century BC), as described in Homer's *Iliad*. According to the legend, the city fell to the Greeks, who first used the stratagem of leaving behind, in a feigned retreat, a large wooden horse containing armed infiltrators to open the city's gates. Believing it to be a religious offering, the Trojans took it within the walls.

Nine cities found one beneath another were originally excavated by Heinrich ◊Schliemann 1874–90. Recent research suggests that the seventh, sacked and burned about 1250 BC, is probably the Homeric Troy. The later city of Ilium was built on the same site in the 7th century BC, and survived to the Roman period. It has been suggested that Homer's tale of war might have a basis in fact, for example, a conflict arising from trade rivalry (Troy was on a tin trade route), which might have been triggered by such an incident as Paris running off with ◊Helen. The wooden horse may have been a votive offering for ◊Poseidon (whose emblem was a horse) left behind by the Greeks after an earthquake had opened breaches in the city walls.

Troyes industrial city (textiles and food processing) in Champagne-Ardenne, NE France; population (1990) 60,800. It was the capital of the medieval province of Champagne. The Treaty of Troyes 1420 made Henry V of England heir to the French crown.

troy system system of units used for precious metals and gems. The pound troy (0.37 kg) consists of 12 ounces (each of 120 carats) or 5,760 grains (each equal to 65 mg).

Trudeau Pierre Elliott 1919– . Canadian Liberal politician. He was prime minister 1968–79 and 1980–84. In 1980, having won again by a landslide on a platform opposing Quebec separatism, he helped to defeat the Quebec independence movement in a referendum. He repatriated the constitution from Britain 1982, but by 1984 had so lost support that he resigned.

Truffaut François 1932–1984. French ◊New Wave film director and actor. He was formerly a critic. A romantic and intensely humane filmmaker, he wrote and directed a series of semi-autobiographical films starring Jean-Pierre Léaud, beginning with *Les Quatre Cent Coups/The 400 Blows* 1959. His other films include *Jules et Jim* 1961, *Fahrenheit 451* 1966, *L'Enfant sauvage/The Wild Child* 1970, and *La Nuit américaine/Day for Night* 1973 (Academy Award). His later work includes *The Story of Adèle H* 1975 and *Le Dernier Métro/The Last Metro* 1980. He played one of the leading roles in Steven Spielberg's *Close Encounters of the Third Kind* 1977.

truffle subterranean fungus of the order Tuberales. Certain species are valued as edible delicacies; in particular, *Tuber melanosporum*, generally found growing under oak trees. It is native to the Périgord region of France but cultivated in other areas as well. It is rounded, blackish brown, externally covered with warts, and with blackish flesh. Dogs and pigs are traditionally used to discover truffles, but in 1990 an artificial 'nose' developed at the University of Manchester Institute of Science and Technology, England, proved more effective in tests in Bordeaux.

Trujillo city in NW Peru, with its port at Salaverry; population (1993) 509,300. Industries include engineering, copper, sugar milling, vehicle assembly, and trade in agricultural produce.

Truk group of about 55 volcanic islands surrounded by a coral reef in the E Caroline islands of the W Pacific, forming one of the four states of the Federated States of Micronesia. Fish and copra are the main products.

Truman Harry S 1884–1972. 33rd president of the USA 1945–53, a Democrat. In Jan 1945 he became vice president to F D Roosevelt, and president when Roosevelt died in April that year. He used the atom bomb against Japan, launched the ◊Marshall Plan to restore W Europe's economy, and nurtured the European Community (now the European Union) and NATO (including the rearmament of West Germany).

As president Truman took part in the ◊Potsdam Conference July 1945. In 1947 he initiated the Truman Doctrine, a policy for helping countries threatened by, or anxious to resist, communism. In 1948 he was elected as president for a second term in a surprise victory over Thomas Dewey (1902–1971), governor of New York. At home, he had difficulty converting the economy back to peacetime conditions, and failed to prevent witch-hunts on suspected communists such as Alger ◊Hiss. In Korea, he intervened when the South was invaded, but sacked General ◊MacArthur when the general's policy threatened to start World War III. Truman's decision not to enter Chinese territory, betrayed by the double agent Kim Philby, led to China's entry into the Korean War.

Truman Doctrine US president Harry Truman's 1947 dictum that the USA would 'support free peoples who are resisting attempted subjugation by armed minorities or by outside pressures'. It was used to justify sending a counterinsurgency military mission to Greece after World War II and sending US troops abroad (for example, to Korea).

trumpet member of an ancient family of lip-reed instruments existing worldwide in a variety of forms and materials, and forming part of the brass section in a modern orchestra. Its distinguishing features are a generally cylindrical bore and straight or coiled shape, producing a penetrating tone of stable pitch for signalling and ceremonial use. Valve trumpets were introduced around 1820, giving access to the full range of chromatic pitches.

Today's orchestral trumpet is valued for its clearly focused, brilliant tone, and variants of the normal C4 trumpet in current use include the soprano in D, piccolo (clarino) trumpet in C5, and bass trumpet in C3. In brass bands the B flat soprano instrument is normally used. The trumpet is a traditional solo jazz instrument, and players demonstrate particular skill in high harmonics.

trumpeter any South American bird of the genus *Psophia*, family Psophiidae, order Gruiformes, up to 50 cm/20 in tall, related to the cranes. Trumpeters have long legs, a short bill, and dark plumage. There are three species. The trumpeter ◊swan is unrelated.

Truro market town in Cornwall, England, and administrative headquarters of the county; population (1994 est) 17,200. Truro was the traditional meeting place of the Stannary (local parliament; see ◊Cornwall), and was formerly a centre for the tin-mining industry. The cathedral, designed by J L Pearson (1817–1897) dates from 1880–1910, and the museum and art gallery has works by John Opie. Present industries include pottery, biscuit manufacturing, and seaweed fertilizer.

trust arrangement whereby a person or group of people (the trustee or trustees) hold property for others (the beneficiaries) entitled to the beneficial interest. A trust can be a legal arrangement under which A is empowered to administer property belonging to B for the benefit of C. A and B may be the same person; B and C may not.

A ◊*unit trust* holds and manages a number of marketable securities; by buying a 'unit' in such a trust, the purchaser has a proportionate interest in each of the securities so that his or her risk is spread. Nowadays, an *investment trust* is not a trust, but a public company investing in marketable securities money subscribed by its shareholders who receive dividends from the income earned.

A *charitable trust*, such as the UK ◊National Trust or Oxfam, administers funds for charitable purposes.

A *business trust* is formed by linking several companies by transferring shares in them to trustees; or by the creation of a holding company, whose shares are exchanged for those of the separate companies. Competition is thus eliminated, and in the USA both types were outlawed by the Sherman Antitrust Act 1890.

Trustee, Public in England, an official empowered to act as executor and trustee, either alone or with others, of the estate of anyone who appoints him or her. In 1986 powers were extended to cover, among other things, the affairs of mentally ill patients.

Trusthouse Forte (THF) British hotel and catering group, formed 1970 in a merger between Trust Houses (founded 1903 to restore hotels) and Forte Holdings (founded 1935 as a catering interest). By the end of the 1980s, THF were operating 800 hotels worldwide, including 250 in the UK, as well as more than 300 Little Chef and 85 Happy Eater motorway restaurants. The company was bought by leisure and media group Granada plc 1996.

trust territory country or area placed within the United Nations trusteeship system and, as such, administered by a UN member state on the UN's behalf. A trust territory could be one of three types: one administered under a mandate given by the UN, or its predecessor, the League of Nations; a territory which was removed from an enemy state, namely Germany, Italy, or Japan, at the end of World War II; or a territory which had been placed voluntarily within the trusteeship system by a member state responsible for its administration. The last territory remaining under the UN trusteeship system, the Republic of Palau, became independent 1994.

Truth Sojourner. Adopted name of Isabella Baumfree, later Isabella Van Wagener c. 1797–1883. US antislavery and women's-suffrage campaigner. Born a slave, she ran away and became involved with religious groups. In 1843 she was 'commanded in a vision' to adopt the name Sojourner Truth. She published an autobiography, *The Narrative of Sojourner Truth*, in 1850.

trypanosomiasis any of several debilitating long-term diseases caused by a trypanosome (protozoan of the genus *Trypanosoma*). They include sleeping sickness (nagana) in Africa, transmitted by the bites of ◊tsetse flies, and ◊Chagas's disease in Central and South America, spread by assassin bugs.

trypsin an enzyme in the vertebrate gut responsible for the digestion of protein molecules. It is secreted by the pancreas but in an inactive form known as trypsinogen. Activation into working trypsin occurs only in the small intestine, owing to the action of another enzyme enterokinase, secreted by the wall of the duodenum.

tsar the Russian imperial title 1547–1721 (although it continued in popular use to 1917), derived from Latin *caesar*.

tsetse fly any of a number of blood-feeding African flies of the genus *Glossina*, some of which transmit the disease nagana to cattle and sleeping sickness to human beings. Tsetse flies may grow up to 1.5 cm/0.6 in long.

Tsiolkovsky Konstantin Eduardovich 1857–1935. Russian scientist who developed the theory of space flight. He published the first practical paper on astronautics 1903, dealing with space travel by rockets using liquid propellants, such as liquid oxygen.

tsunami (Japanese 'harbour wave') ocean wave generated by vertical movements of the sea floor resulting from ◊earthquakes or volcanic activity. Unlike waves generated by surface winds, the entire depth of water is involved in the wave motion. In the open ocean the tsunami takes the form of several successive waves, rarely in excess of 1 m/3 ft in height but travelling at speeds of 650-800 kph/400-500 mph. In the coastal shallows tsunamis slow down and build up producing huge swells over 15 m/45 ft high in some cases and over 30 m/90 ft in rare instances. The waves sweep inland causing great loss of life and property.

Tswana majority ethnic group living in Botswana. The Tswana are divided into four subgroups: the Bakwena, the Bamangwato, the Bangwaketse, and the Batawana. Traditionally they are rural-dwelling farmers, though many now leave their homes to work as migrant labourers. The Tswana language belongs to the Bantu branch of the Niger-Congo family.

Tuamotu Archipelago two parallel ranges of 78 atolls, part of ◊French Polynesia; area 690 sq km/266 sq mi; population (1988) 12,400, including the Gambier Islands to the east. The atolls stretch 2,100 km/1,300 mi N and E of the Society Islands. The administrative headquarters is Apataki. The largest atoll is Rangiroa, the most significant is Hao; they produce pearl shell and copra.

Tuareg Arabic name given to nomadic stockbreeders from west and central Sahara and Sahel (Algeria, Libya, Mali, Niger, and Burkina Faso). The eight Tuareg groups refer to themselves by their own names. Their language, Tamashek, belongs to the Berber branch of the Hamito-Semitic family and is spoken by 500,000–850,000 people. Tuareg men wear dark-blue robes, turbans, and veils. Some still live in tents and herd goats and camels, though many Tuareg have settled in urban areas. Their society was extremely hierarchical, with noblemen, craftsmen, vassals, and slaves.

tuatara lizardlike reptile of the genus *Sphenodon*, found on islands off New Zealand. It grows up to 70 cm/2.3 ft long, is greenish black, and has a spiny crest down its back. On the top of its head is the ◊pineal body, or so-called 'third eye', linked to the brain, which probably acts as a kind of light meter. It is the sole survivor of the reptilian order Rhynchocephalia. It lays eggs in burrows that it shares with seabirds.

tuba member of a family of valved lip-reed brass instruments of conical bore and deep, mellow tone, introduced around 1830 as bass members of the orchestra brass section and the brass band. The tuba is surprisingly agile and delicate for its size and pitch. Different shapes exist, including oval, upright with forward-facing bell, and the circular or helicon sousaphone which wraps around the player. The Wagner tuba is a horn variant.

tuber swollen region of an underground stem or root, usually modified for storing food. The potato is a *stem tuber*, as shown by the presence of terminal and lateral buds, the 'eyes' of the potato. ***Root tubers***, for example dahlias, developed from adventitious roots (growing from the stem, not from other roots) lack these. Both types of tuber can give rise to new individuals and so provide a means of ◊vegetative reproduction. Unlike a bulb, a tuber persists for one season only; new tubers developing on a plant in the following year are formed in different places. See also ◊rhizome.

tuatara The lizardlike tuatara is found on some of the islands and rocky stacks off New Zealand. It is the sole remaining representative of a family of reptiles which first evolved before the dinosaurs. It has a third 'eye' on the top of its head which is sensitive to light, although is unable actually to 'see'.

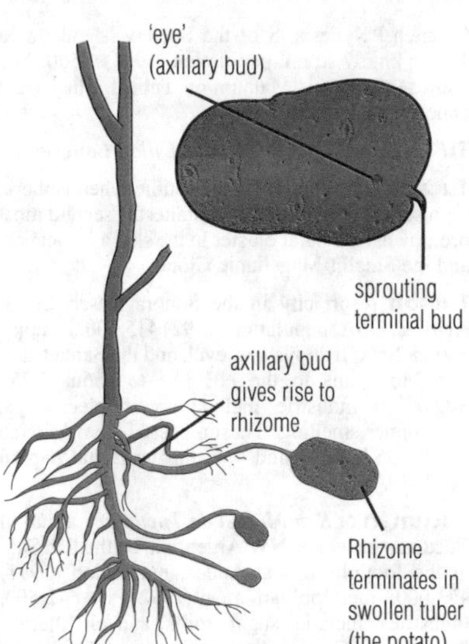

tuber Tubers are produced underground from stems, as in the potato, or from roots, as in the dahlia. Tubers can grow into new plants.

tuberculosis (TB) formerly known as ***consumption*** or ***phthisis*** infectious disease caused by the bacillus *Mycobacterium tuberculosis*. It takes several forms, of which pulmonary tuberculosis is by far the most common. A vaccine, ◊BCG, was developed around 1920 and the first antituberculosis drug, streptomycin, 1944. The bacterium is mostly kept in check by the body's immune system; about 5% of those infected develop the disease. Treatment of patients with a combination of anti-TB medicines for 6–8 months produces a cure rate of 80%.

In pulmonary TB, a patch of inflammation develops in the lung, with formation of an abscess. Often, this heals spontaneously, leaving only scar tissue. The dangers are of rapid spread through both lungs (what used to be called 'galloping consumption') or the development of miliary tuberculosis (spreading in the bloodstream to other sites) or tuberculous ◊meningitis.

From the mid-1980s there was a sharp resurgence in countries where the disease was in decline. The increase has been most marked in deprived inner city areas, particularly in the USA, and here there is a clear link between TB and HIV, the virus which causes AIDS. TB is the main cause of death in HIV positive individuals.

According to a World Health Organization report 1995, TB is responsible for more than a quarter of all adult deaths in developing countries; worldwide there are 20 million with the disease and approximately 1.9 billion infected with the TB bacterium but not displaying symptoms. TB caused around 3.1 million deaths during 1995.

Tübingen town in Baden-Württemberg, Germany, on the river Neckar, 30 km/19 m S of Stuttgart; population (1985) 75,000. Industries include paper, textiles, and surgical instruments. The town dates from the 11th century; the university was established 1477. It was capital of the French zone of occupation after World War II.

Tubman Harriet Ross 1821–1913. US abolitionist. Born a slave in Maryland, she escaped to Philadelphia (where slavery was outlawed) 1849. She set up the ***Underground Railroad***, a secret network of sympathizers, to help slaves escape to the North and Canada. During the American ◊Civil War she spied for the Union army. She spoke against slavery and for women's rights, and founded schools for emancipated slaves after the Civil War.

Tubman William Vacanarat Shadrach 1895–1971. Liberian politician, president 1944–71. He concentrated on uniting the various ethnic groups, and survived several assassination attempts.

'The buck stops here.'

Harry S Truman
Sign on his presidential desk

Tubuai Islands or *Austral Islands* chain of volcanic islands and reefs 1,300 km/800 mi long in

◊French Polynesia, S of the Society Islands; area 148 sq km/57 sq mi; population (1988) 6,500. The main settlement is Mataura on Tubuai. They were annexed by France 1880.

TUC abbreviation for ◊***Trades Union Congress***.

Tucana constellation of the southern hemisphere, represented as a toucan. It contains the second most prominent ◊globular cluster in the sky, 47 Tucanae, and the Small ◊Magellanic Cloud.

Tucson resort city in the Sonora Desert in SE Arizona, USA; population (1992) 415,100. It stands 760 m/2,500 ft above sea level, and the Santa Catalina Mountains to the NE rise to about 2,750 m/9,000 ft. Industries include aircraft, electronics, and copper smelting. Tucson passed from Mexico to the USA 1853 and was the territorial capital 1867–77.

Tucumán or ***San Miguel de Tucumán*** capital of Tucumán province, NW Argentina, on the Rio Sali, in the foothills of the Andes; population (1991) 473,000; metropolitan area (1992 est) 642,500. Industries include sugar mills and distilleries. Founded 1565, Tucumán was the site of the signing of the Argentine declaration of independence from Spain 1816.

Tudjman Franjo 1922– . Croatian nationalist leader and historian, president from 1990. As leader of the centre-right Croatian Democratic Union (CDU), he led the fight for Croatian independence. During the 1991–92 civil war, his troops were hampered by lack of arms and the military superiority of the Serb-dominated federal army, but Croatia's independence was recognized following a successful United Nations-negotiated ceasefire Jan 1992. Tudjman was re-elected 1992 and again 1995.

Tudor architecture see ◊English architecture.

Tudor dynasty English dynasty 1485–1603, descended from the Welsh Owen Tudor (c. 1400–1461), second husband of Catherine of Valois (widow of Henry V of England). Their son Edmund married Margaret Beaufort (1443–1509), the great-granddaughter of ◊John of Gaunt, and was the father of Henry VII, who became king by overthrowing Richard III 1485. The dynasty ended with the death of Elizabeth I 1603.

Tu Fu or ***Du Fu*** 712–770. Chinese poet of the Tang dynasty. With Li Po, he was one of the two greatest Chinese poets. He wrote about the social injustices of his time, peasant suffering, and war, as in *The Army Carts* on conscription, and *The Beauties*, comparing the emperor's wealth with the lot of the poor.

Tula ancient Toltec city in Mexico, 65 km/40 mi NW of Mexico City, which flourished c. 750–1168. It had a population of about 40,000. The modern town of Tula de Allende is nearby.

Tula Remains of the Temple of Quetzalcoatl in Tula, Mexico, ancient city and capital of the Toltecs. Several temples to Quetzalcoatl, the feathered serpent god of air and water, were built by the Toltecs and their successors, the Aztecs. *Corbis*

Tula city in the Russian Federation, on the river Upa, 193 km/121 mi S of Moscow; population (1994) 535,000. Industries include engineering and metallurgy. It was the site of the government ordnance factory, founded 1712 by Peter the Great.

tulip plant of the genus *Tulipa*, family Liliaceae, usually with single goblet-shaped flowers on the end of an upright stem and leaves of a narrow oval shape with pointed ends. It is widely cultivated as a garden flower. *T. gesnerana*, from which most of the garden cultivars have been derived, probably originated in Asia Minor. Quickly adopted in Europe from Turkey during the 16th century, it became a craze in 17th-century Holland, and was the subject of a novel, *The Black Tulip*, by Alexandre Dumas (*père*) 1850. Today it is commercially cultivated on a large scale in the Netherlands and East Anglia, England.

Tull Jethro 1674–1741. English agriculturist who about 1701 developed a drill that enabled seeds to be sown mechanically and spaced so that cultivation between rows was possible in the growth period. His chief work, *Horse-Hoeing Husbandry*, was published 1733. Tull also developed a plough with blades set in such as way that grass and roots were pulled up and left on the surface to dry.

tumour overproduction of cells in a specific area of the body, often leading to a swelling or lump. Tumours are classified as benign or malignant (see ◊cancer). Benign tumours grow more slowly, do not invade surrounding tissues, do not spread to other parts of the body, and do not usually recur after removal. However, benign tumours can be dangerous in areas such as the brain.

tuna any of various large marine bony fishes of the mackerel family, especially the genus *Thunnus*, popular as food and game. Tuna may grow up to 2.5 m/8 ft long and weigh 200 kg/440 lbs. The ***Skipjack*** or ***bonito tuna*** *Euthynnus pelamis* is one of the most commercially important species, and is the species most commonly sold in tins in the UK. It is a small tuna, growing up to 1 m/3 ft long. ***Albacore*** *T. alalunga*, ***bluefin tuna*** *T. thynnus*, and ***yellowfin tuna*** *T. albacares* are also important.

Tuna fish gather in shoals and migrate inshore to breed, where they are caught in large numbers. The increasing use by Pacific tuna fishers of enormous driftnets, which kill dolphins, turtles, and other marine creatures as well as catching the fish, has caused protests by environmentalists; tins labelled 'dolphin-friendly' contain tuna not caught by driftnets. Thailand is a major tuna-importing and canning country.

Tunbridge Wells, Royal spa town in Kent, SE England, with iron-rich springs discovered 1606; population (1991) 60,300. There is an expanding light industrial estate. The Pantiles or shopping parade (paved with tiles in the reign of Queen Anne), was a fashionable resort; the town was named 'Royal' after visits by Queen Victoria.

tundra region of high latitude almost devoid of trees, resulting from the presence of ◊permafrost. The vegetation consists mostly of grasses, sedges, heather, mosses, and lichens. Tundra stretches in a continuous belt across N North America and Eurasia. Tundra is also used to describe similar conditions at high altitudes.

tungsten (Swedish *tung sten* 'heavy stone') hard, heavy, grey-white, metallic element, symbol W (from German *Wolfram*), atomic number 74, relative atomic mass 183.85. It occurs in the minerals wolframite, scheelite, and hubertite. It has the highest melting point of any metal (3,410°C/6,170°F) and is added to steel to make it harder, stronger, and more elastic; its other uses include high-speed cutting tools, electrical elements, and thermionic couplings. Its salts are used in the paint and tanning industries.

tungsten ore either of the two main minerals, wolframite $(FeMn)WO_4$ and scheelite, $CaWO_4$, from which tungsten is extracted. Most of the world's tungsten reserves are in China, but the main suppliers are Bolivia, Australia, Canada, and the USA.

Tunguska Event explosion at Tunguska, central Siberia, Russia, in June 1908, which devastated around 6,500 sq km/2,500 sq mi of forest. It is thought to have been caused by either a cometary nucleus or a fragment of ◊Encke's comet about 200 m/220 yards across, or possibly an asteroid. The magnitude of the explosion was equivalent to an atom bomb (10–20 megatons) and produced a colossal shock wave; a bright falling object was seen 600 km/375 mi away and was heard up to 1,000 km/625 mi away.

tunicate any marine ◊chordate of the subphylum Tunicata (Urochordata), for example the ◊sea squirt. Tunicates have transparent or translucent tunics made of cellulose. They vary in size from a few millimetres to 30 cm/1 ft in length, and are cylindrical, circular, or irregular in shape. There are more than 1,000 species.

tuning fork in music, a device for providing a reference pitch, invented in England 1711. It is made from hardened metal and consists of parallel bars about 10 cm/3–4 in long joined at one end and terminating in a blunt point. When the fork is struck and the point placed on a wooden surface, a pure tone is heard. There are tuning forks for each musical pitch.

Tunis capital and chief port of Tunisia; population (1994) 674,100. Industries include chemicals and textiles. Founded by the Arabs, it was captured by the Turks 1533, then occupied by the French 1881 and by the Axis powers 1942–43. The ruins of ancient ◊Carthage are to the NE.

Tunisia country in N Africa, on the Mediterranean Sea, bounded SE by Libya and W by Algeria. *See country box opposite.*

Tunja capital of the Andean department of Boyacá, E central Colombia; population (1992) 112,000. Formerly the seat of the Chibcha Indian kings, the Spanish built a city here 1539. Industries include agriculture and mining.

tunnel passageway through a mountain, under a body of water, or underground. Tunnelling is a significant branch of civil engineering in both mining and transport. The difficulties naturally increase with the size, length, and depth of tunnel, but with the mechanical appliances now available no serious limitations are imposed. Granite or other hard rock presents little difficulty to modern power drills. In recent years there have been notable developments in linings (for example, concrete segments and steel liner plates), and in the use of rotary diggers and cutters and explosives.

Major tunnels include:

Orange–Fish River (South Africa) 1975. Longest irrigation tunnel, 82 km/51 mi;

Chesapeake Bay Bridge-Tunnel (USA) 1963. Combined bridge, causeway, and tunnel structure, 28 km/17.5 mi;

St Gotthard (Switzerland–Italy) 1980. Longest road tunnel, 16.3 km/10.1 mi;

Tunisia An open air forum and a columned building at Sbeitla, Tunisia. *Corbis*

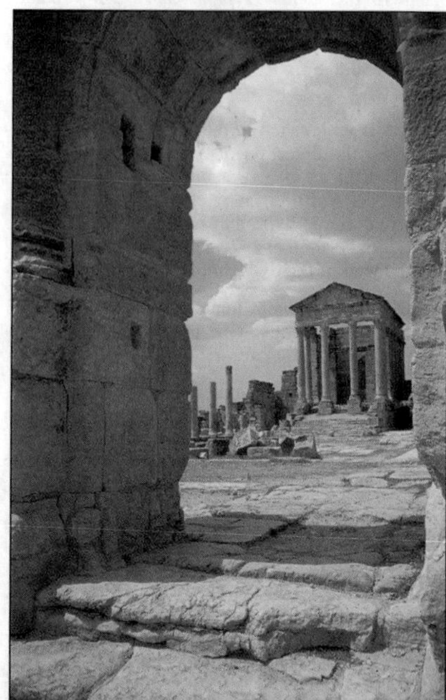

TUNISIA
Tunisian Republic

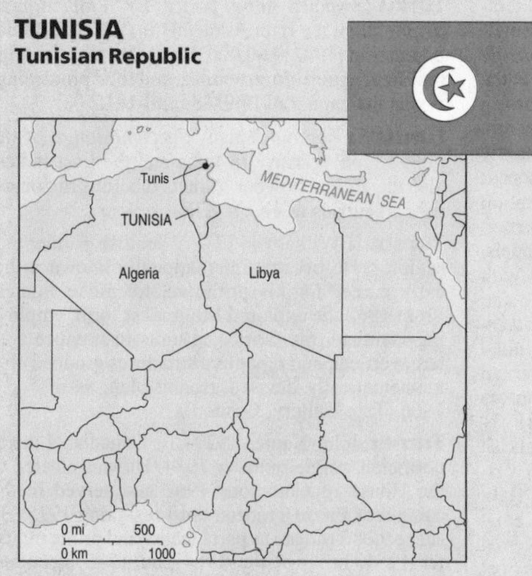

national name *al-Jumhuriya at-Tunisiya*
area 164,150 sq km/63,378 sq mi
capital and chief port Tunis
major ports Sfax, Sousse, Bizerta
physical features arable and forested land in N graduates towards desert in S; fertile island of Jerba, linked to mainland by causeway (identified with island of lotus-eaters); Shott el Jerid salt lakes
head of state Zine el-Abidine Ben Ali from 1987
head of government Hamed Karoui from 1989
political system emergent democratic republic
administrative divisions 23 governorates
political parties Constitutional Democratic Rally (RCD), nationalist, moderate, socialist; Popular Unity Movement (MUP), radical, left of centre; Democratic Socialists Movement (MDS), left of centre; Renovation Movement (MR), reformed communists
population 8,896,000 (1995 est)
population growth rate 1.9% (1990–95); 1.5% (2000–05)
ethnic distribution about 10% of the population is Arab; the remainder are of Berber-Arab descent. There are small Jewish and French communities
life expectancy 68 (men), 71 (women)
literacy rate men 74%, women 56%
languages Arabic (official), French
religions Sunni Muslim; Jewish, Christian
currency Tunisian dinar
GDP (US $) 15.73 billion (1994)
growth rate 3.4% (1994)
exports oil, phosphates, chemicals, textiles, food, olive oil, dates, fertilizers, fruit, leather and shoes, fishery products, electrical appliances

HISTORY
814 BC Phoenician emigrants from Tyre, in Lebanon, founded Carthage, near modern Tunis, as a trading post. By the 6th century BC the Carthaginian kingdom dominated the western Mediterranean.
146 BC Carthage was destroyed by the Punic Wars with Rome, which began in 264 BC; Carthage became part of Rome's African province.
AD 533 Came under control of the Byzantine Empire.
7th C Invaded by Arabs and Islam was introduced. A succession of Islamic dynasties followed, including the Aghlabids (9th century), Fatimids (10th century), and Almohads (12th century).
1574 Became part of the Islamic Turk Ottoman Empire and a base for 'Barbary Pirates' who operated against European shipping until the 19th century.
1705 Husayn Bey founded a local dynasty, which held power under the rule of the Ottomans.
early 19th C Ahmad Bey launched a programme of economic modernization, which was to nearly bankrupt the country.
1881 Became a French protectorate, with the bey retaining local power.
1920 Destour (Constitution) Party, named after the original Tunisian constitution of 1861, founded to campaign for equal Tunisian participation in the French dominated government.
1934 Habib Bourguiba founded a radical splinter party, the Neo-Destour Party, to spearhead the nationalist movement.
1942–43 Brief German occupation during World War II.
1956 Independence achieved as a monarchy under the bey, with Bourguiba as prime minister.
1957 Bey deposed; became a one-party republic with Bourguiba as president.
1975 Bourguiba made president for life.
1979 Headquarters for Arab League moved to Tunis after Egypt signed the Camp David Accords with Israel.
1981 Multiparty elections held, as a sign of political liberalization, but were won by Bourguiba's Destourian Socialist Party (DSP).
1982 Allowed the Palestine Liberation Organization (PLO) to use Tunis for its headquarters.
1985 Diplomatic relations with Libya severed; Israel attacked the PLO headquarters.
1987 Zine el-Abidine Ben Ali, the new prime minister, declared Bourguiba (now aged 84) incompetent for government and seized power as president.
1988 2,000 political prisoners freed; privatization initiative. Diplomatic relations with Libya restored. DSP renamed RCD.
1990 Arab League's headquarters returned to Cairo, Egypt.
1991 Opposition to US actions during the Gulf War. Crackdown on religious fundamentalists; Renaissance Party banned.
1992 Western criticism of human-rights transgressions.
1994 Ben Ali and RCD re-elected. PLO transferred its headquarters to Gaza City in Palestine.

SEE ALSO Bourguiba, Habib; Carthage

Seikan (Japan) 1964–85. Longest rail tunnel, Honshu–Hokkaido, under Tsugaru Strait, 53.9 km/33.5 mi, 23.3 km/14.5 mi undersea (however, a bullet-train service is no longer economical);
Simplon (Switzerland–Italy) 1906. Longest rail tunnel on land, 19.8 km/12.3 mi;
Rogers Pass (Canada) 1989. Longest tunnel in the western hemisphere, 35 km/22 mi long, through the Selkirk Mountains, British Columbia;
Channel Tunnel linking England and France (begun by the French and British governments 1986, and opened 1994), 50 km/31 mi.
See list of tables on p. 1177.

Tunney Gene James Joseph 1898–1978. US boxer. As a professional he won the US light-heavyweight title 1922. He began to fight as a heavyweight in 1924 and was the upset winner over heavyweight champion Jack Dempsey 1926. Tunney retained the title against Dempsey in the famous 'Long Count' bout 1927 and retired undefeated 1928. After his retirement, he became successful in business.

tunny another name for ◊tuna.

Tupamaros urban guerrilla movement operating in Uruguay, aimed at creating a Marxist revolution, largely active in the 1960s and 1970s, named after 18th-century revolutionary Túpac Amarú. It was founded by Raul Sendic (died 1989).

turbine engine in which steam, water, gas, or air (see ◊windmill) is made to spin a rotating shaft by pushing on angled blades. Turbines are among the most powerful machines. Steam turbines are used to drive generators in power stations and ships' propellers; water turbines spin the generators in hydroelectric power plants; and gas turbines (as jet engines; see ◊jet propulsion) power most aircraft and drive machines in industry.

The high-temperature, high-pressure steam for ***steam turbines*** is raised in boilers heated by furnaces burning coal, oil, or gas, or by nuclear energy. A steam turbine consists of a shaft, or rotor, which rotates inside a fixed casing (stator). The rotor carries 'wheels' consisting of blades, or vanes. The stator has vanes set between the vanes of the rotor, which direct the steam through the rotor vanes at the optimum angle. When steam expands through the turbine, it spins the rotor by ◊reaction.

Water turbines look much like propellers and are fully immersed in the water. In a ***gas turbine*** a compressed mixture of air and gas, or vaporized fuel, is ignited, and the hot gases produced expand through the turbine blades, spinning the rotor. In the industrial gas turbine, the rotor shaft drives machines. In the jet engine, the turbine drives the compressor, which supplies the compressed air to the engine, but most of the power developed comes from the jet exhaust in the form of propulsive thrust.

turbocharger turbine-driven device fitted to engines to force more air into the cylinders, producing extra power. The turbocharger consists of a 'blower', or ◊compressor, driven by a turbine, which in most units is driven by the exhaust gases leaving the engine.

turbofan jet engine of the type used by most airliners, so called because of its huge front fan. The fan sends air not only into the engine for combustion but also around the engine for additional thrust. This results in a faster and more fuel-efficient propulsive jet (see ◊jet propulsion).

turbojet jet engine that derives its thrust from a jet of hot exhaust gases. Pure turbojets can be very powerful but use a lot of fuel. A single-shaft turbojet consists of a shaft (rotor) rotating in a casing. At the front is a multiblade ◊compressor, which takes in and compresses air and delivers it to one or more combustion chambers. Fuel (kerosene) is then sprayed in and ignited. The hot gases expand through a nozzle at the rear of the engine after spinning a ◊turbine. The turbine drives the compressor. Reaction to the backward stream of gases produces a forward propulsive thrust.

turboprop jet engine that derives its thrust partly from a jet of exhaust gases, but mainly from a propeller powered by a turbine in the jet exhaust. Turboprops are more economical than turbojets but can be used only at relatively low speeds. A turboprop typically has a twin-shaft rotor. One shaft carries the compressor and is spun by one turbine, while the other shaft carries a propeller and is spun by a second turbine.

turbot any of various flatfishes of the flounder group prized as food, especially *Scophthalmus maximus* found in European shallow coastal waters. It grows up to 1 m/3 ft long and weighs up to 14 kg/30 lb. It is brownish above and whitish underneath.

turbulence irregular fluid (gas or liquid) flow, in which vortices and unpredictable fluctuations and motions occur. ◊Streamlining reduces the turbulence of flow around an object, such as an aircraft, and reduces drag. Turbulent flow of a fluid occurs when the ◊Reynolds number is high.

Turgenev Ivan Sergeievich 1818–1883. Russian writer. He is notable for poetic realism, pessimism, and skill in characterization. His works include the play *A Month in the Country* 1849, and the novels *A Nest of Gentlefolk* 1858, *Fathers and Sons* 1862, and *Virgin Soil* 1877. His series *A Sportsman's Sketches* 1852 criticized serfdom.

> *Go and try to disprove death. Death will disprove you, and that's all there is to it!*
>
> IVAN TURGENEV, *Fathers and Sons*

turgor the rigid condition of a plant caused by the fluid contents of a plant cell exerting a mechanical pressure against the cell wall. Turgor supports plants that do not have woody stems.

Turin (Italian ***Torino***) capital of Piedmont, NW Italy, on the river Po; population (1992) 952,700. Industries include iron, steel, cars, silk and other textiles, fashion goods, chocolate, and wine. There is a university, established 1404, and a 15th-century cathedral. Features include the Palazzo Reale (Royal Palace) 1646–58 and several gates to the city. It was the first capital of united Italy 1861–64.

Turin became important after the union of Savoy and Piedmont 1416. Its growth as a major city dates from 1559 when Emanuele Filiberto chose it as the capital of the House of Savoy, with Italian as the official language. In 1706 Prince ◊Eugène defeated a French army besieging the city, thus ensuring the survival of the Savoy duchy.

> *My arrival at Turin was the first and only moment of intoxication I have found in Italy. It is a city of palaces.*
>
> On TURIN, William Hazlitt *Notes of a Journey through France and Italy* 1826

Turing Alan Mathison 1912–1954. English mathematician and logician. In 1936 he described a 'universal computing machine' that could theoretically be programmed to solve any problem capable of solution by a specially designed machine. This concept, now called the Turing machine, foreshadowed the digital computer.

Turin shroud ancient piece of linen bearing the image of a body, claimed to be that of Jesus. Independent tests carried out 1988 by scientists in Switzerland, the USA, and the UK showed that the cloth of the shroud dated from between 1260 and 1390. The shroud, property of the pope, is kept in Turin Cathedral, Italy.

Turk any of the Turkic-speaking peoples of Asia and Europe, especially the principal ethnic group of Turkey. Turkic languages belong to the Altaic family and include Uzbek, Ottoman, Turkish, Azeri, Turkoman, Tatar, Kirghiz, and Yakut.

Turkana, Lake formerly (until 1979) ***Lake Rudolf*** lake in the Great Rift Valley, 375 m/1,230 ft above sea level, with its northernmost end in Ethiopia and the rest in Kenya; area 9,000 sq km/3,475 sq mi. It is saline, and shrinking by evaporation. Its shores were an early human hunting ground, and valuable remains have been found.

Turkestan area of central Asia divided among Kazakhstan, Kyrgyzstan, Tajikistan, Turkmenistan, Uzbekistan, Afghanistan, and China (part of Xinjiang Uygur). Stretching from Turkey to W China in the Middle Ages, Turkestan was from the 19th century administered by Russia as a single colony of smaller extent. After the Russian Revolution, the Turkestanis applied for autonomy, and in 1918 declared a Turkestan Independent Islamic Republic, and in 1921 the Turkestan Autonomous Soviet Socialist Republic which were forcibly put down 1918–24. Stalin subsequently carved up the area into separate republics to prevent a resurgence of separatist sentiment.

turkey any of several large game birds of the pheasant family, Meleagrididae, order Galliformes, native to the Americas. The wild turkey *Meleagris galloparvo* reaches a length of 1.3 m/4.3 ft, and is native to North and Central American woodlands. The domesticated turkey derives from the wild species. It was introduced to Europe in the 16th century and since World War II it has been intensively bred, in the same way as the chicken.

Turkey country between the Black Sea to the N and the Mediterranean Sea to the S, bounded E by Armenia, Georgia, and Iran, SE by Iraq and Syria, W by Greece and the Aegean Sea, and NW by Bulgaria. *See country box opposite.*

turkish bath bathing that involves exposure to warm air and steam, followed by massage and cold-water immersion. Originating from Roman and East Indian traditions, the concept was introduced to Western Europe by the Crusaders but only became popular when hot water could be supplied in sufficient quantities.

Turkish language language of central and W Asia, the national language of Turkey. It belongs to the Altaic language family. Varieties of Turkish are spoken in NW Iran and several of the Central Asian Republics, and all have been influenced by Arabic and Persian. Originally written in Arabic script, it has been written within Turkey in a variant of the Roman alphabet since 1928.

Turkish literature for centuries Turkish literature was based on Persian models, but under ◊Suleiman the Magnificent (1494–1566) the Golden Age began, of which the poet Fuzuli (died 1563) is the great exemplar, and continued in the following century with the great poet satirist Nef'i of Erzerum (died 1635) and others. In the 19th century, mainly under French influence, Turkish writers adopted Western literary forms such as the novel. Ibrahim Shinasi Effendi (1826–1871), poet and prose writer, was one of those who made use of French models. Effendi was co-founder of the New School with Mehmed Namik Kemal (1840–1880), poet and author of the revolutionary play *Vatan/The Fatherland,* which led to his exile by the sultan. Unlike these, the poet Tevfik Fikret (1867–1915) turned rather to Persian and Arabic than to native sources for his vocabulary. The poet Mehmed Akif (1873–1936) was the author of the words of the Turkish national anthem; other distinguished modern writers include the novelist and satirist Refik Halit (1888–1965), the traditionalist poet Yahya Kemal (1884–1958), and the realist novelist Orhan Kemal (1914–1970). The work of the contemporary poet and novelist Yashar Kemal (1923–) describes the hard life of the peasant (*Memed, My Hawk* 1955 and *The Wind from the Plain* 1961).

Turkmenistan country in central Asia, bounded N by Kazakhstan and Uzbekistan, W by the Caspian Sea, and S by Iran and Afghanistan. *See country box on p. 1080.*

Turkoman or ***Turkman*** the majority ethnic group in Turkmenistan. They live to the E of the Caspian Sea, around the Kara Kum Desert, and along the borders of Afghanistan and Iran. Their language belongs to the Turkic branch of the Altaic family.

Turks and Caicos Islands British crown colony in the West Indies, the southeastern archipelago of the Bahamas
area 430 sq km/166 sq mi
capital Cockburn Town on Grand Turk
features a group of 30 islands, of which six are inhabited. The largest is the uninhabited Grand Caicos; others include Grand Turk (1990 population 3,761), South Caicos (1,220), Middle Caicos (275), North Caicos (1,305), Providenciales (5,586), and Salt Cay (213); since 1982 the Turks and Caicos have developed as a tax haven
government governor, with executive and legislative councils (chief minister from 1993 Charles W Misick)
exports crayfish and conch; tourism is important
currency US dollar
population (1990 est) 12,400, 90% of African descent
language English, French Creole
religion Christian
history uninhabited islands discovered by the Spanish 1512; they remained unoccupied until British settlers established a salt panning industry 1678. Secured by Britain 1766 against French and Spanish claims, the islands were a Jamaican dependency 1873–1962, and became a separate colony 1962.

Turkey Mount Ararat, in E Turkey, where Noah's ark was said to have landed. According to tradition, the olives growing on the nearby plain were the source of the olive branch brought to Noah by a dove. *Turkish Tourist Board*

Turku (Swedish ***Åbo***) port in SW Finland, near the mouth of the river Aura, on the Gulf of Bothnia; population (1992) 160,000. Industries include shipbuilding, engineering, textiles, and food processing. It was the capital of Finland until 1812.

turmeric perennial plant *Curcuma longa* of the ginger family, native to India and the East Indies; also the ground powder from its tuberous rhizomes, used in curries to give a yellow colour.

Turnbull William 1922– . Scottish painter and sculptor. He became internationally known in his early career for his primitive, totemlike figures. From 1962, he explored Minimalist form, employing identical, pre-fabricated units to produce austere, vertical, and repetitive structures grouped on a mathematically devised ground plan, as in *5 x 1* 1966 (Tate Gallery, London).

Turner John Napier 1929– . Canadian Liberal politician, prime minister 1984. He was elected to the House of Commons 1962 and served in the cabinet of Pierre Trudeau until resigning 1975. He succeeded Trudeau as party leader and prime minister 1984, but lost the 1984 and 1988 elections. Turner resigned as leader 1989, and returned to his law practice.

Turner Joseph Mallord William 1775–1851. English painter. He was the most original landscape artist of his day and remains one of England's greatest painters. His landscapes became increasingly Romantic, with the subject often transformed in scale and flooded with brilliant, hazy light. Many later works anticipate Impressionism, for example *Rain, Steam and Speed* 1844 (National Gallery, London).

Turner travelled extensively in France, Switzerland, Italy, and the Rhineland as well as in Britain, constantly recording the effects of sea, sky, mountain, and plain in watercolour. He continued to produce series of watercolour studies, which were issued as engravings, throughout his life (for example *Rivers of France* 1833–35 and *Rivers of England* 1823–27).

His early oil paintings show Dutch influence (such as that of van de Velde), but by the 1800s he had begun to paint landscapes in the 'Grand Manner', reflecting the Italianate influences of ◊Claude Lorrain and Richard ◊Wilson. Having mastered a range of styles, Turner evolved one distinctively his own in which his highly individual use of colour and his increasingly free brushwork allow him to capture both the subtlest effects of light and atmosphere and also the most violent forces of nature.

Examples of his major works include *Shipwreck* 1805, *Snowstorm: Hannibal Crossing the Alps* 1812, and *Destruction of Sodom* 1805 (all Tate Gallery, London); *Rain, Steam and Speed*; and *The Slave Ship* 1839 (Museum of Fine Arts, Boston, Massachusetts).

Turner Robert Edward III ('Ted') 1938– . US media magnate, founder of the Cable News Network (CNN) and vice-head of the Times-Warner media empire. He began his career in the 1960s in advertising, in Georgia. In 1980 he formed CNN to provide round-the-clock and round-the-globe cable television news coverage. CNN merged with Times-Warner in 1996. In September 1997 Turner announced his intention to donate $1 billion to the United Nations to support the organization's humanitarian initiatives. He is married to actress Jane Fonda.

Turner Tina. Adopted name of Annie Mae Bullock 1940– . US rhythm-and-blues singer. She recorded 1960–76 with her husband Ike Turner (1931–), including *River Deep, Mountain High* 1966, produced by Phil Spector (1940–). In the 1980s she achieved success as a solo artist, recording such albums as *Private Dancer* 1984, and as a live performer. *See illustration on p. 1080.*

Turner Prize British art prize. *See list of tables on p. 1177.*

turnip biennial plant *Brassica rapa* cultivated in temperate regions for its edible white- or yellow-fleshed root and the young leaves, which are used as a green vegetable. Closely allied to it is the ◊swede *Brassica napus.*

turnover in finance, the value of sales of a business organization over a period of time. For example, if a shop sells 10,000 items in a week at an average price of £2 each, then its weekly turnover is £20,000.

turnpike road road with a gate or barrier preventing access until a toll had been paid, common

TURKEY
Republic of

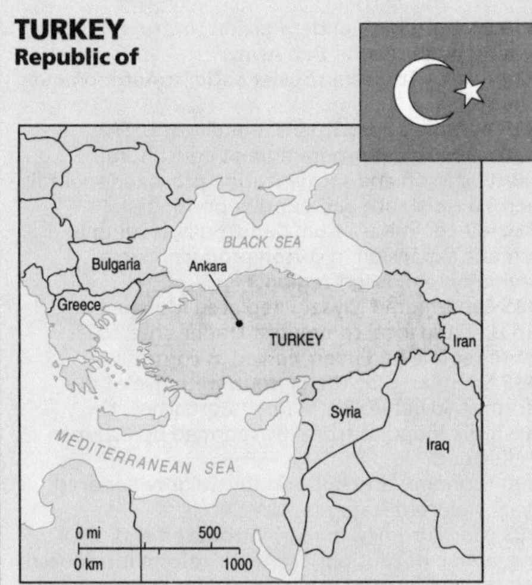

national name *Türkiye Cumhuriyeti*
area 779,500 sq km/300,965 sq mi
capital Ankara
major towns/cities Adana, Antakya, Konya, Edirne
major ports Istanbul and Izmir
physical features central plateau surrounded by mountains, partly in Europe (Thrace) and partly in Asia (Anatolia); Bosporus and Dardanelles; Mount Ararat (highest peak Great Ararat, 5,137 m/16,854 ft); Taurus Mountains in SW (highest peak Kaldi Dag, 3,734 m/12,255 ft); sources of rivers Euphrates and Tigris in E
head of state Suleiman Demirel from 1993
head of government Bulent Ecevit from 1999
political system democratic republic
administrative divisions 73 provinces
political parties Motherland Party (ANAP), Islamic, nationalist, right of centre; Republican People's Party (CHP), centre-left; True Path Party (DYP), centre-right, pro-Western; Welfare Party (Refah), Islamic fundamentalist
armed forces 503,800 (1995)
conscription 18 months
defence spend (% GDP) 3.2 (1994)
education spend (% GNP) 2.8 (1980)
health spend (% GDP) 1.5 (1990)
death penalty retained for ordinary crimes, but considered abolitionist in practice; last execution 1984
population 61,797,000 (1996 est)
population growth rate 2.0% (1990–95); 1.5% (2000–05)
age distribution (% of total population) <15 33.9%, 15–65 61.1%, >65 5.0% (1995)
ethnic distribution over 90% of the population are Turks, although only about 5% are of Turki or Western Mongoloid descent; most are descended from earlier conquerors, such as the Greeks
population density (per sq km) 78 (1994)
urban population (% of total) 69 (1995)
labour force 45% of population: 53% agriculture, 18% industry, 29% services (1990)
unemployment 7.9% (1995)
child mortality rate (under 5, per 1,000 live births) 55 (1994)
life expectancy 65 (men), 68 (women)
education (compulsory years) 5
literacy rate 90% (men), 71% (women)
languages Turkish (official), Kurdish, Arabic
religions Sunni Muslim; Orthodox, Armenian churches
TV sets (per 1,000 people) 176 (1992)
currency Turkish lira
GDP (US $) 182.6 billion (1996)
GDP per capita (PPP) (US $) 5,619 (1995)
growth rate 7.3% (1994/95)
average annual inflation 106.4% (1994); 65.8% (1984–94)
major trading partners Germany, USA, Italy, France, Saudi Arabia, UK
resources chromium, copper, mercury, antimony, borax, coal, petroleum, natural gas, iron ore, salt
industries textiles, food processing, petroleum refinery, coal, iron and steel, industrial chemicals, tourism
exports textiles and clothing, agricultural products and foodstuffs (including figs, nuts, and dried fruit), tobacco, leather, glass, refined petroleum and petroleum products. Principal market: Germany 21.7% (1994)
imports machinery, construction material, motor vehicles, consumer goods, crude petroleum, iron and steel, chemical products, fertilizer, livestock. Principal source: Germany 15.7% (1994)
arable land 31.4% (1993)
agricultural products barley, wheat, maize, sunflower and other oilseeds, sugar beet, potatoes, tea (world's 5th largest producer), olives, fruits, tobacco

HISTORY
1st C BC Asia Minor became part of the Roman Empire, later passing to Byzantine Empire.
6th C AD Turkic peoples spread from Mongolia into Turkestan, where they adopted Islam.
13th C Ottoman Turks, driven west by the Mongols, became vassals of the Seljuk Turks.
c. 1299 Osman I founded a small Ottoman kingdom, which displaced the Seljuks to include all Asia Minor.
1354 Ottoman Turks captured Gallipoli and began their conquests in Europe.
1389 Battle of Kossovo: Turks defeated the Serbs to take control of most of the Balkan peninsula.
1453 Constantinople, capital of the Byzantine Empire, fell to the Turks; became capital of Ottoman Empire as Istanbul.
16th C Ottoman Empire reached its zenith under Suleiman the Magnificent 1520–66; Turks conquered Egypt, Syria, Arabia, Mesopotamia, Tripoli, Cyprus, and most of Hungary.
1683 Failure of the Siege of Vienna marked the start of the decline of the Ottoman Empire.
1699 Treaty of Karlowitz: Turks forced out of Hungary by Austrians.
1774 Treaty of Kuchuk Kainarji: Russia drove Turks from Crimea and won the right to intervene on behalf of Christian subjects of the sultan.
19th C 'The Eastern Question': Ottoman weakness caused intense rivalry between the great Powers to shape the future of the Near East.
1821–29 Greek war of independence: Greeks defeated the Turks with help of Russia, Britain, and France.
1854–56 Crimean War: Britain and France fought to defend the Ottoman Empire from further pressure by the Russians.
1877–78 Russo-Turkish War ended with the Treaty of Berlin and the withdrawal of Turks from Bulgaria.
1908 Young Turk revolution forced sultan to grant a constitution; start of political modernization.
1911–12 Italo-Turkish War: Turkey lost Tripoli (Libya).
1912–13 Balkan War: Greece, Serbia, and Bulgaria expelled the Turks from Macedonia and Albania.
1914 Ottoman Empire entered World War I on German side.
1919 Following Turkish defeat, Mustapha Kemal launched nationalist revolt to resist foreign encroachments.
1920 Treaty of Sèvres partitioned the Ottoman Empire, leaving no part of Turkey fully independent.
1922 Kemal, having defied the Allies, expelled Greeks, French, and Italians from Asia Minor; sultanate abolished.
1923 Treaty of Lausanne recognized Turkish independence; secular republic established by Kemal, who imposed rapid Westernization.
1935 Kemal adopted the surname Atatürk ('Father of the Turks').
1938 Death of Kemal Atatürk; succeeded as president by Ismet Inönü.
1950 First free elections won by opposition Democratic Party; Adnan Menderes became prime minister.
1952 Turkey became a member of NATO.
1960 Military coup led by General Cemal Gürsel deposed Menderes, who was executed 1961.
1961 Inönü returned as prime minister; politics dominated by the issue of Cyprus.
1965 Justice Party came to power under Suleyman Demirel.
1971–73 Prompted by strikes and student unrest, the army imposed military rule.
1974 Turkey invaded northern Cyprus.
1980–83 Political violence led to further military rule.
1984 Kurds began guerrilla war in quest for greater autonomy.
1989 Application to join European Community rejected.
1990–91 Turkey joined UN coalition against Iraq in Gulf War.
1995 Turkish offensives against Kurdish bases in N Iraq; Islamicist Welfare Party won largest number of seats in general election.
1997 Plans agreed for curbing of Muslim fundamentalism. Mesut Yilmaz appointed prime minister. Agreement with Greece on peaceful resolution of disputes.
1998 Islamic Welfare Party (RP) banned by Constitutional Court, and regrouped as Virtue Party (FP).
1999 Coalition government formed in Jan, headed by Bulent Ecevit.

SEE ALSO Atatürk, Kemal; Balkan Wars; Cyprus; Istanbul; Ottoman Empire

from the mid-16th–19th centuries. In 1991, a plan for the first turnpike road to be built in the UK since the 18th century was announced: the privately funded Birmingham northern relief road, 50 km/31 mi long.

turpentine solution of resins distilled from the sap of conifers, used in varnish and as a paint solvent but now largely replaced by ◊white spirit.

Turpin Ben 1874–1940. US comedian. A star of silent films, his hallmarks were his cross-eyed grimace and a taste for parodying his fellow actors. His work includes *The Shriek of Araby* 1923, *A Harem Knight* 1926, and *Broke in China* 1927.

Turpin Dick (Richard) 1705–1739. English highwayman. The son of an innkeeper, he turned to highway robbery, cattle-thieving, and smuggling, and was hanged at York, England. His legendary ride from London to York on his mare Black Bess is probably based on one of about 305 km/190 mi from Gad's Hill to York completed in 15 hours 1676 by highwayman John Nevison (1639–1684).

turquoise mineral, hydrous basic copper aluminium phosphate, $CuAl_6(PO_4)_4(OH)_8.5H_2O$. Blue-green, blue, or green, it is a gemstone. Turquoise is found in Australia, Egypt, Ethiopia, France, Germany, Iran, Turkestan, Mexico, and southwestern USA.

turtle freshwater or marine reptile whose body is protected by a shell. Turtles are related to tortoises, and some species can grow to a length of up to 2.5 m/8 ft. Turtles often travel long distances to lay their eggs on the beaches where they were born. Many species have suffered through destruction of their breeding sites as well as being hunted for food and their shell.

Marine turtles are generally herbivores, feeding mainly on sea grasses. Freshwater turtles eat a range of animals including worms, frogs, and fish. They are excellent swimmers, having legs that are modified to oarlike flippers but which make them awkward on land. The shell is more streamlined and lighter than that of the tortoise. Species include the green turtle *Chelonia mydas*; the loggerhead *Caretta caretta*; the giant leathery or leatherback turtle *Dermochelys coriacea*; and the hawksbill *Eretmochelys imbricata*, which is hunted for its shell which provides tortoiseshell, used in jewellery and ornaments, and is now endangered. Other turtles suffer because their eggs are taken by collectors and their breeding sites are regularly destroyed, often for tourist developments.

The use of radiotransmitters has shown that migrating leatherback turtles navigate by following the contours of the Earth's crust along existing pathways. The identification and protection of these pathways could substantially reduce the numbers of leatherback turtles drowned in driftnets or caught on fishing lines. *See illustration on following page.*

Tuscan in classical architecture, one of the five ◊orders (types of ◊column).

Tuscany (Italian *Toscana*) region of N central Italy, on the west coast; area 23,000 sq km/8,878 sq

TURKMENISTAN
Republic of

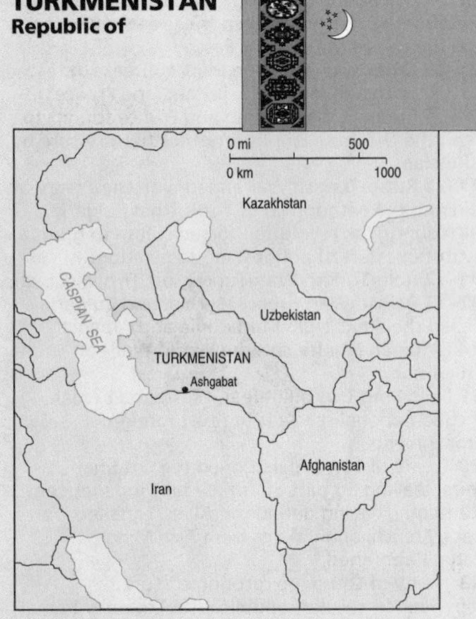

area 488,100 sq km/188,406 sq mi
capital Ashgabat
major towns/cities Chardzhov, Mary, Nebit-Dag
major ports Turkmenbashi
physical about 90% of land is desert including the Kara Kum 'Black Sands' desert (area 310,800 sq km/120,000 sq mi)
head of state and government Saparmurad Niyazov from 1991
political system authoritarian nationalist
administrative divisions five regions
political parties Democratic Party of Turkmenistan, ex-communist, pro-Niyazov; Turkmen Popular Front (Agzybirlik), nationalist
population 4,099,000 (1995 est)
population growth rate 2.3% (1990–95); 1.9% (2000–05)
ethnic distribution 72% ethnic Turkmen, 10% ethnic Russian, 9% Uzbek, 3% Kazakh, and 1% Ukrainian
life expectancy 63 (men), 70 (women)
literacy rate 98%
language West Turkic, closely related to Turkish
religion Sunni Muslim
currency manat
GDP (US $) 5.15 billion (1994 est)
growth rate −20.0% (1994)
exports silk, karakul, sheep, astrakhan fur, carpets, chemicals, natural gas

HISTORY
6th C BC Part of the Persian Empire of Cyrus the Great.
4th C BC Part of the empire of Alexander the Great of Macedonia.
7th C Spread of Islam into the Transcaspian region, followed by Arab rule from 8th century.
10th–13th Cs Immigration from the NE by nomadic Oghuz Seljuk and Mongol tribes, whose Turkic-speaking descendants now dominate the country; conquest by Genghis Khan.
16th C Came under the dominance of Persia, to the S.
1869–81 Fell under the control of tsarist Russia after 150,000 Turkmen were killed in the battle of Gok Tepe 1881; became part of Russia's Turkestan Governor-Generalship.
1916 Turkmen revolted violently against Russian rule; autonomous Transcaspian government formed after Russian Revolution of 1917.
1919 Brought back under Russian control following invasion by the Soviet Red Army.
1921 Part of Turkestan Soviet Socialist Autonomous Republic.
1925 Became a constituent republic of USSR.
1920s–30s Soviet programme of agricultural collectivization and secularization provoked sporadic guerrilla resistance and popular uprisings.
1960–67 Lenin Kara-Kum Canal built, leading to a dramatic expansion in cotton production in a previously semidesert region.
1985 Saparmurad Niyazov replaced Muhammad Gapusov, the local communist leader since 1971, whose regime had been viewed as corrupt.
1989 Stimulated by the *glasnost* initiative of the reformist Soviet leader Mikhail Gorbachev, the Agzybirlik 'popular front' was formed by Turkmen intellectuals.
1990 Economic and political sovereignty declared. Niyazov elected state president.
1993 New currency, manat, introduced and programme of cautious economic reform introduced, with foreign investment in the country's huge oil and gas reserves encouraged; but the economy contracted to 1995.
1991 Niyazov initially supported attempted anti-Gorbachev coup in Moscow. Independence was later declared; joined new Commonwealth of Independent States (CIS).
1992 Joined the Muslim Economic Cooperation Organization and United Nations; new constitution adopted.
1994 Nationwide referendum overwhelmingly backed Niyazov's presidency. Ex-communists won most seats in parliamentary elections.
1997 Private land ownership legalized.

SEE ALSO Russian Federation; Union of Soviet Socialist Republics

mi; population (1992 est) 3,528,700. Its capital is Florence, and cities include Pisa, Livorno, and Siena. The area is mainly agricultural, with many vineyards, such as in the Chianti hills; it also has lignite and iron mines and marble quarries (Carrara marble is from here). The Tuscan dialect has been adopted as the standard form of Italian. Tuscany was formerly the Roman ***Etruria***, and was inhabited by Etruscans around 500 BC. In medieval times the area was divided into small states, united under Florentine rule during the 15th–16th centuries. It became part of united Italy 1861.

‘For the Church in any country to retreat from politics is nothing short of heresy. Christianity is political or it is not Christianity.’

DESMOND TUTU
Quoted in the *Observer* 1994

Tussaud Madame (Anne Marie Grosholtz) 1761–1850. French wax-modeller. In 1802 she established an exhibition of wax models of celebrities in London. It was destroyed by fire 1925, but reopened 1928. During the French Revolution, she and her wax-modeller uncle, Philippe Curtius, were forced to take death masks of many victims and leaders (some still exist in the Chamber of Horrors).

Turner Singer Tina Turner who blends rhythm and blues, soul, and rock in her music. She first attracted attention outside the USA with the song 'River Deep, Mountain High' 1966 (with her husband Ike Turner), and later built up a highly successful solo career, her stage act noted for its energy and assertive sexuality. *Topham*

Tutankhamen King (pharaoh) of ancient Egypt of the 18th dynasty, about 1333–1323 BC. A son of Akhenaton (also called Amenhotep IV), he was about 11 at his accession. In 1922 his tomb was discovered by the British archaeologists Lord Carnarvon and Howard Carter in the Valley of the Kings at Luxor, almost untouched by tomb robbers. The contents included many works of art and his solid-gold coffin, which are now displayed in a Cairo museum.

Tutin Dorothy 1931– . English actress. Her roles include most of Shakespeare's leading heroines for the Royal Shakespeare Company, and Lady Macbeth for the National Theatre Company. She has also acted in the first productions of plays by John Osborne and Harold Pinter.

Tutsi minority ethnic group living in Rwanda and Burundi. Although fewer in number, they have traditionally been politically dominant over the Hutu majority and the Twa (or Pygmies). In Burundi, positions of power were monopolized by the Tutsis, who carried out massacres in response to Hutu rebellions, notably 1972 and 1988. In Rwanda, where the balance of power is more even, bloody intertribal violence erupted 1994, after the presidents of both Rwanda and Burundi were killed in an air crash, and Tutsis were massacred in their thousands by Hutu militia.

Tutu Desmond Mpilo 1931– . South African priest, Anglican archbishop of Cape Town 1986–96 and general secretary of the South African Council of Churches 1979–84. One of the leading figures in the struggle against ◊apartheid in the Republic of South Africa, he was awarded the 1984 Nobel Peace Prize.

In 1995 Tutu was named as the head of the Truth and Reconciliation Commission, a commission set up by Nelson Mandela to investigate abuses by both government and opposition groups during the apartheid era.

Tuva autonomous republic (administrative unit) of the Russian Federation, in Siberia
area 170,500 sq km/65,813 sq mi
capital Kyzyl
physical basin of the Yenisey River
industries mining of gold, asbestos and cobalt; cattle farming
population (1992) 306,000
history part of Mongolia until 1911 and declared a Russian protectorate 1914; after the 1917 revolution it became the independent Tannu-Tuva republic 1920, until incorporated in the USSR as an autonomous region 1944. It was made the Tuva Autonomous Republic 1961. In 1993 the republic's parliament claimed the rights of self-determination and of secession from the Russian federation, following constitutional amendments.

Tuvalu country in the SW Pacific Ocean; formerly (until 1976) the Ellice Islands; part of ◊Polynesia. *See country box opposite.*

TVP (abbreviation for ***texturized vegetable protein***) meat substitute usually made from soya beans.

Twa ethnic group comprising 1% of the populations of Burundi and Rwanda. The Twa are the aboriginal inhabitants of the region. They are a pygmoid people, and live as nomadic hunter-gatherers in the forests.

Twain Mark. Pen name of Samuel Langhorne Clemens 1835–1910. US writer. He established his reputation with the comic masterpiece *The Innocents Abroad* 1869 and two classic American novels, in dialect, *The Adventures of Tom Sawyer* 1876 and *The Adventures of Huckleberry Finn* 1885. He also wrote satire, as in *A Connecticut Yankee at King Arthur's Court* 1889. He is recognized as one of America's finest and most characteristic writers.

turtle The common musk turtle lives in the slow, shallow, muddy streams of the US. Also known as the stinkpot, this turtle gives off an offensive-smelling fluid when disturbed.

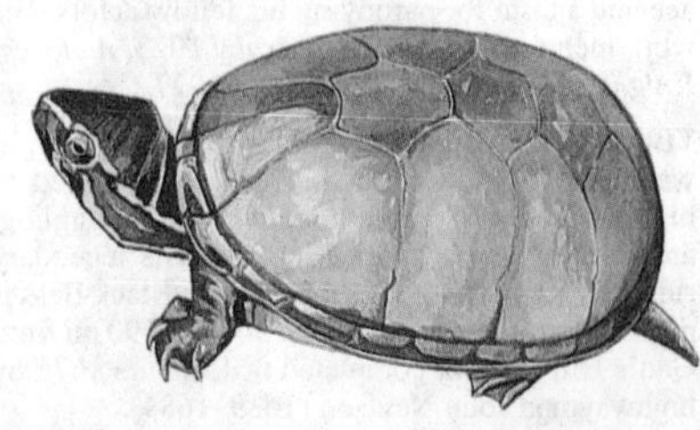

Born in Florida, Missouri, Twain grew up along the Mississippi River in Hannibal, Missouri, the setting for many of his major works. He was apprenticed to a printer, writing articles for the *Missouri Courier*, and from 1857 was employed as a riverboat pilot until the river boats stopped running on the outbreak of the Civil War. He then moved west, taking a job as city editor of a Nevada newspaper. There he began to write under the pseudonym 'Mark Twain'. As his writing career blossomed, he also became successful as a lecturer. In 1884 he invested in a publishing house; it went bankrupt a decade later, leaving Twain penniless. In 1895 he embarked on a world lecture tour and cleared his debts.

Huckleberry Finn is Twain's masterpiece, for its use of the vernacular, vivid characterization and descriptions, and its theme, underlying the humour, of man's inhumanity to man. He also wrote *Roughing It* 1872, *The Gilded Age* 1873, *Old Times on the Mississippi* 1875, *A Tramp Abroad* 1880, *The Prince and the Pauper* 1882, *Life on the Mississippi* 1883, *Pudd'nhead Wilson* 1894, and *Personal Recollections of Joan of Arc* 1896. His later works, such as *The Mysterious Stranger*, unpublished until 1916, are less humorous and more pessimistic. *See illustration on following page.*

tweed cloth made of woollen yarn, usually of several shades, but in its original form without a regular pattern and woven on a hand loom in the more remote parts of Ireland, Wales, and Scotland, UK. Harris tweed is made on the island of Harris in the Outer Hebrides; it is highly durable and largely weatherproof. Nowadays, tweed is often machine-woven, patterned, and processed.

Tweed river rising in SW Borders Region, Scotland, and entering the North Sea at Berwick-upon-Tweed, Northumberland; length 156 km/97 mi. From Coldstream until near Berwick-upon-Tweed it forms the border between England and Scotland.

Twelfth Day the 12th and final day of the Christmas celebrations, 6 January; the feast of the ◊Epiphany.

twelve-tone system or ***twelve-note system*** method of musical composition invented by Arnold ◊Schoenberg about 1921 in which all 12 notes of the ◊chromatic scale are arranged in a particular order of the composer's choice, without repeating any of the notes. Such an arrangement is called a 'series' or 'tone row'. The initial series may be transposed, divided, and otherwise mutated to provide a complete resource for all melodic and harmonic material in a work.

Twentieth Century Fox US film-production company, formed 1935 when the Fox Company merged with Twentieth Century. Its president was Joseph Schenck (1878–1961), with Darryl F Zanuck (1902–1979) vice president in charge of production. The company made high-quality films and, despite a financial crisis in the early 1960s, is still a major studio. Recent successes include the *Star Wars* trilogy (1977–1983).

Twickenham stadium in SW London, the ground at which England play home rugby-union internationals. The first international was held there in 1910. The Rugby Football Union has its headquarters at Twickenham, and the Harlequins club plays some of its home matches there.

twill one of the basic cloth structures, characterized by a diagonal line on the face of the fabric. Variations in structure include herringbone weaves. Denim, gabardine, serge, and some flannels and tweeds are examples of twill fabrics.

twin one of two young produced from a single pregnancy. Human twins may be genetically identical (monozygotic), having been formed from a single fertilized egg that splits into two cells, both of which became implanted. Nonidentical (fraternal or dizygotic) twins are formed when two eggs are fertilized at the same time. *See illustration on following page.*

two-stroke cycle operating cycle for internal combustion piston engines. The engine cycle is completed after just two strokes (up or down) of the piston, which distinguishes it from the more common ◊four-stroke cycle. Power mowers and lightweight motorcycles use two-stroke petrol engines, which are cheaper and simpler than four-strokes.

Most marine diesel engines are also two-stroke. In a typical two-stroke motorcycle engine, fuel mixture is drawn into the crankcase as the piston moves up on its first stroke to compress the mixture above it. Then the compressed mixture is ignited, and hot gases are produced, which drive the piston down on its second stroke. As it moves down, it uncovers an opening (port) that allows the fresh fuel mixture in the crankcase to flow into the combustion space above the piston. At the same time, the exhaust gases leave through another port.

Tyburn stream in London, England, near which (at the junction of Oxford Street and Edgware Road) Tyburn gallows stood from the 12th century until 1783. The Tyburn now flows underground.

Tuscany A small farm in Tuscany, central Italy. Largely mountainous, Tuscany is an important agricultural area, producing grain, tobacco, and grapes (used for Chianti wine). It also has important mineral deposits, which are being increasingly exploited. *Sally Jenkins*

TUVALU

South West Pacific State of (formerly *Ellice Islands*)

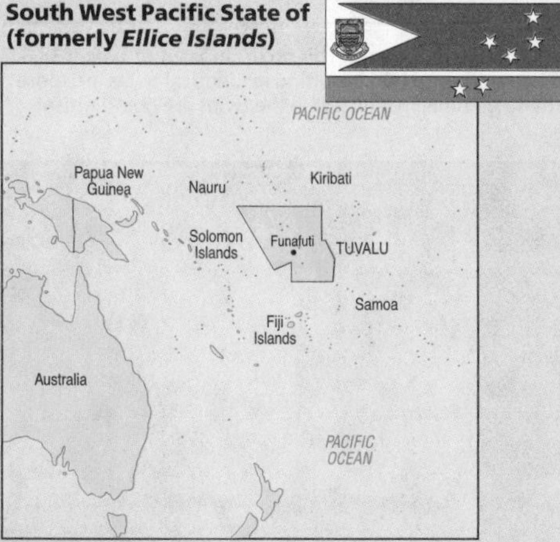

area 25 sq km/10 sq mi
capital Fongafale (on Funafuti atoll)
physical features nine low coral atolls forming a chain of 579 km/650 mi in the SW Pacific
head of state Elizabeth II from 1978, represented by governor general Tulaga Manuella from 1994
head of government Bikenibeu Paeniu from 1996
political system liberal democracy
administrative divisions each of the nine inhabited atolls has its own council
political parties none; members are elected to parliament as independents
population 10,000 (1996 est)
population growth rate 1.4% (1990–95)
ethnic distribution almost entirely of Polynesian origin, maintaining close ties with the Samoans and Tokelauans to the S and E
life expectancy 60 (men), 63 (women)
literacy rate 95%
languages Tuvaluan, English
religions Christian (mainly Protestant)
currency Australian dollar
GDP (US $) 8 million (1995)
growth rate 1.0% (1992)
exports copra, handicrafts, stamps

HISTORY

c. 300 BC First settled by Polynesian peoples.
16th C Invaded and occupied by Samoans.
1765 Islands were first reached by Europeans.
1850–75 Population decimated by European slave traders capturing Tuvaluans to work in South America and by exposure to European diseases.
1856 The four southern islands, including Funafuti, claimed by the USA.
1865 Christian mission established.
1877 Came under the control of the British Western Pacific High Commission (WPHC), with its headquarters in Fiji.
1892 Known as the Ellice Islands, they were joined with the Gilbert Islands (now Kiribati) to form a British protectorate.
1916 Gilbert and Ellice Islands colony formed.
1942–43 Became a base for US airforce operations when Japan occupied the Gilbert Islands during World War II.
1975 Following a referendum, the predominantly Melanesian-peopled Ellice Islands, fearing domination by the Micronesian-peopled Gilbert Islands in an independent state, were granted separate status.
1978 Independence achieved within the Commonwealth, with Toaripi Lauti as prime minister; reverted to former name Tuvalu ('eight standing together').
1979 The USA signed a friendship treaty, relinquishing its claim to the four southern atolls in return for continued access to military bases.
1981 Dr Tomasi Puapua became premier after Louti was implicated in an alleged investment scandal.
1986 Islanders rejected proposal for republican status.
1989 Bikenibeu Paeniu became prime minister.
1993 Kamuta Laatasi became prime minister.
1995 Union Jack removed from national flag, presaging a move towards republican status.
1996 Bikenibeu Paeniu became prime minister.

SEE ALSO Australasia and Oceania; Kiribati

Tyche personification of Chance in classical Greek thought, whose cult developed in the Hellenistic and Roman periods, when it was identified with that of the Roman ◊Fortuna.

Tyler John 1790–1862. 10th president of the USA 1841–45, succeeding William H ◊Harrison, who died after only a month in office. Tyler's government annexed Texas 1845.

Tyler Wat died 1381. English leader of the ◊Peasants' Revolt of 1381. He was probably born in Kent or Essex, and may have served in the French wars. After taking Canterbury, he led the peasant army to Blackheath, outside London, and went on to invade the city. King Richard II met the rebels at Mile End and promised to redress their grievances, which included the imposition of a poll tax. At a further conference at Smithfield, London, Tyler was murdered.

Tyndale William c. 1492–1536. English translator of the Bible. The printing of his New Testament (the basis of the Authorized Version) was begun in Cologne 1525 and, after he had been forced to flee, completed in Worms. He was strangled and burned as a heretic at Vilvorde in Belgium.

Tyne river of NE England formed by the union of the North Tyne (rising in the Cheviot Hills) and South Tyne (rising in Cumbria) near Hexham, Northumberland, and reaching the North Sea at Tynemouth; length 72 km/45 mi. Kielder Water (1980) in the North Tyne Valley is Europe's largest artificial lake, 12 km/7.5 mi long and 0.8 km/0.5 mi wide, and supplies the industries of Tyneside, Wearside, and Teesside.

Tyne and Wear metropolitan county of NE England, created 1974; in 1986, most of the functions of the former county council were transferred to the metropolitan district councils
area 540 sq km/208 sq mi *(see United Kingdom map)*
towns and cities Newcastle upon Tyne, South Shields, North Shields, Gateshead, Sunderland
features bisected by the rivers Tyne and Wear; includes part of ◊Hadrian's Wall; Newcastle and Gateshead, linked with each other and with the coast on both sides by the Tyne and Wear Metro (a light railway using existing suburban lines, extending 54 km/34 mi); Tyneside International Film Festival
industries once a centre of heavy industry, it is now being redeveloped and diversified; car manufacturing on Wearside, electronics, offshore technology (floating production vessels), automobile components, pharmaceuticals, computer science
population (1991) 1,095,200
famous people Thomas Bewick, Robert Stephenson, Harry Patterson ('Jack Higgins').

Tynwald parliament of the Isle of ◊Man.

typeface style of printed lettering. Books, newspapers, and other printed matter display different styles of lettering; each style is named, common examples being Times and ◊Baskerville. These different 'families' of alphabets have been designed over the centuries since printing was first introduced to Europe in the 15th century, and each has distinguishing characteristics. See also ◊typography and ◊font.

typesetting means by which text, or copy, is prepared for ◊printing, now usually carried out by computer. Text is keyed on a typesetting machine in a similar way to typing. Laser or light impulses are projected on to light-sensitive film that, when developed, can be used to make plates for printing.

typewriter keyboard machine that produces characters on paper. The earliest known typewriter design was patented by Henry Mills in England 1714. However, the first practical typewriter was built 1867 in Milwaukee, Wisconsin, USA, by Christopher Sholes, Carlos Glidden, and Samuel Soulé. By 1873 Remington and Sons, US gunmakers, produced under contract the first typing machines for sale and in 1878 patented the first with lower-case as well as upper-case (capital) letters.

The first typewriter patented by Sholes included an alphabetical layout of keys, but Remington's first commercial typewriter had the QWERTY keyboard (the now standard arrangement of keys on a UK or US keyboard, in which q, w, e, r, t, and y are the first six keys on the top alphabetic line), designed by Sholes to slow down typists who were too fast for their mechanical keyboards. Other layouts include the Dvorak keyboard developed by John Dvorak 1932, in which the most commonly used letters are evenly distributed between left and right, and are positioned under the strongest fingers. Later developments included tabulators from about 1898, portable machines about 1907, the gradual introduction of electrical operation (allowing increased speed, since the keys are touched, not depressed), proportional spacing 1940, and the rotating typehead with stationary plates 1962. More recent typewriters work electronically, are equipped with a memory, and can be given an interface that enables them to be connected to a computer. The word processor has largely replaced the typewriter for typing letters and text (see ◊word processing).

typhoid fever acute infectious disease of the digestive tract, caused by the bacterium *Salmonella typhi*, and usually contracted through a contaminated water supply. It is characterized by bowel haemorrhage and damage to the spleen. The symptoms begin 10–14 days after ingestion and include fever, headache, cough, constipation, and rash. Treatment is with antibiotics. The combined TAB vaccine protects both against typhoid and the milder related condition known as paratyphoid fever.

typhoon violent revolving storm, a ◊hurricane in the W Pacific Ocean.

Tyrone

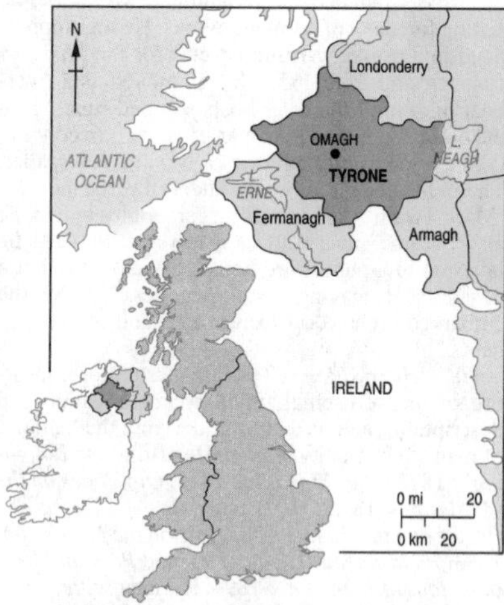

typhus any one of a group of infectious diseases caused by bacteria of the genus *Rickettsia*, especially *R. pronazekii*, transmitted by lice, fleas, mites, and ticks. Symptoms include fever, headache, and rash. The most serious form is epidemic typhus, which also affects the brain heart, lungs, and kidneys and is associated with insanitary overcrowded conditions. Treatment is by antibiotics. A preventive vaccine exists.

typography design and layout of the printed word. Typography began with the invention of writing and developed as printing spread throughout Europe after the invention of metal moveable type by Johann ◊Gutenberg about 1440. Hundreds of variations have followed since, but the basic design of the Frenchman Nicholas Jensen (about 1420–1480), with a few modifications, is still the ordinary ('roman') type used in printing.

Typography, for centuries the domain of engravers and printers, is now a highly computerized process, and can be carried out on a PC using specialist software.

Type sizes are measured in points (there are approximately 2.8 points to the millimetre); the length of a typeset line, called the measure, is measured in pica ems (1 pica em has a width of a little over 4 mm/0.15 in). The space between lines (known as leading) is also measured in points, although new photosetting and computer-assisted setting systems also work in metric sizes.

Tyr in Norse mythology, the god of battles, whom the Anglo-Saxons called Týw, hence 'Tuesday'.

tyrannosaurus any of a genus *Tyrannosaurus* of gigantic flesh-eating ◊dinosaurs, order Saurischia, that lived in North America and Asia about

Twain US writer Mark Twain, whose *Huckleberry Finn* 1885 confirmed his power as an innovative and challenging writer. Although Twain made his name writing humorous pieces of journalism, the death of his wife in 1904 and of two of his three daughters, along with the financial difficulties which clouded the last years of his life are likely to have contributed to the pessimism of his last works. *Corbis*

twin A pair of twins, two children resulting from a single pregnancy. This occurs in 1 out of every 83 human pregnancies, either because a fertilized egg splits into two, resulting in identical twins, or, more commonly, because two eggs are fertilized at the same time, in which case the twins are nonidentical. *Image Select (UK) Ltd*

70 million years ago. They had two feet, were up to 15 m/50 ft long, 6.5 m/20 ft tall, weighed 10 tonnes, and had teeth 15 cm/6 in long.

tyre inflatable rubber hoop fitted round the rims of bicycle, car, and other road-vehicle wheels. The first pneumatic rubber tyre was patented in 1845 by the Scottish engineer Robert William Thomson (1822–73), but it was Scottish inventor John Boyd Dunlop of Belfast who independently reinvented pneumatic tyres for use with bicycles 1888–89. The rubber for car tyres is hardened by ◊vulcanization.

Tyre (Arabic ***Sur*** or ***Soûr***) town in SW Lebanon, about 80 km/50 mi S of Beirut, formerly a port until its harbour silted up; population (1991 est) 70,000. It stands on the site of the ancient city of the same name, a seaport of ◊Phoenicia.
history Built on the mainland and two small islands, the city was a commercial centre, known for its purple dye. Besieged and captured by Alexander the Great 333–332 BC, it came under Roman rule 64 BC and was taken by Arab forces AD 638. The Crusaders captured it 1124, and it never recovered from the destruction it suffered when retaken by the Arabs 1291. In the 1970s it became a Palestinian guerrilla stronghold.

Tyrol variant spelling of ◊Tirol, a state of Austria.

Tyrone county of Northern Ireland
area 3,160 sq km/1,220 sq mi
towns and cities Omagh (county town), Dungannon, Strabane, Cookstown
features rivers: Derg, Blackwater, Foyle; Lough Neagh; Sperrin Mountains
industries mainly agricultural: barley, flax, potatoes, turnips, cattle, sheep
population (1991) 158,500.

Tyrrell British motor-racing team founded by Ken Tyrrell 1970. He formed a partnership with Jackie Stewart and the celebrated driver won all three of his world titles in Tyrrell-run teams. The team won the world constructors' title 1971.

Tyrrhenian Sea arm of the Mediterranean Sea surrounded by mainland Italy, Sicily, Sardinia, Corsica, and the Ligurian Sea. It is connected to the Ionian Sea through the Straits of Messina. Islands include Elba, Ustica, Capri, Stromboli, and the Lipari Islands.

Tyson Mike (Michael Gerald) 1966– . US heavyweight boxer, undisputed world champion from Aug 1987 to Feb 1990. He won the World Boxing Council heavyweight title 1986 when he beat Trevor Berbick to become the youngest world heavyweight champion.

He was undefeated until 1990, when he lost the championship in an upset to James 'Buster' Douglas. Tyson was scheduled to fight again for the championship, but was convicted of rape and imprisoned 1992–95. He regained the World Boxing Council title 1996 when he defeated Frank Bruno in Las Vegas, but later lost it to Evander Holyfield.

Tyuratam site of the ◊Baikonur Cosmodrome in Kazakhstan.

Tywi or ***Towy*** river in SW Wales; length 108 km/68 mi. It rises in the Cambrian Mountains of central Wales, flowing SW to enter Carmarthen Bay.

Tzu-Hsi alternative transliteration of ◊Zi Xi, dowager empress of China.

Tyre A monumental arch and paved street in the Roman city of Tyre, SW Lebanon. Founded by the Phoenicians, and for many centuries a prosperous and strategically important city, Tyre shows evidence of many civilizations – Egyptian, Greek, Roman, Byzantine, Arab, and European. *UNESCO*

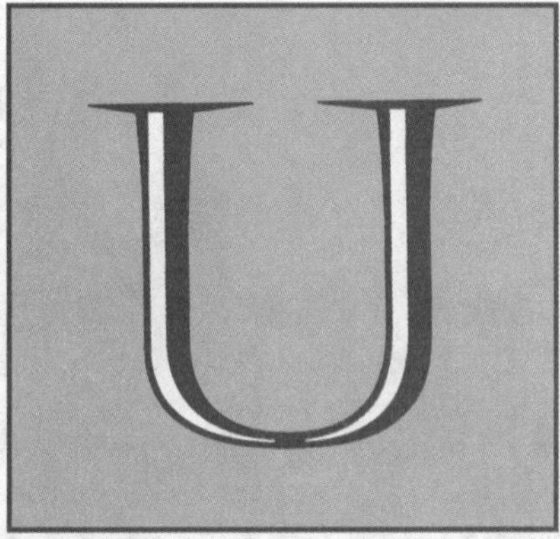

U-2 US military reconnaissance aeroplane, used in secret flights over the USSR from 1956 to photograph military installations. Designed by Richard Bissell, the U-2 flew higher (21,000 m/70,000 ft) and further (3,500 km/2,200 mi) than any previous plane. In 1960 a U-2 was shot down over the USSR and the pilot, Gary Powers, was captured and imprisoned. He was exchanged for a US-held Soviet agent two years later.

The U-2 affair led to the cancellation of a proposed meeting in Moscow between President Eisenhower and Soviet leader Khrushchev, precipitating a greatly increased Soviet arms spending in the 1960s and 1970s. In 1962 U-2 flights revealed the construction of Soviet missile bases in Cuba.

U2 Irish rock group formed 1977 by singer Bono Vox (born Paul Hewson, 1960–), guitarist Dave 'The Edge' Evans (1961–), bassist Adam Clayton (1960–), and drummer Larry Mullen (1961–). The band's albums include *The Unforgettable Fire* 1984, *The Joshua Tree* 1987, and *Achtung Baby* 1992.

uakari any of several rare South American monkeys of the genus *Cacajao*. There are three species. They have bald faces and long fur. About 55 cm/1.8 ft long in head and body, and with a comparatively short 15 cm/6 in tail, they rarely leap, but are good climbers, remaining in the tops of the trees in swampy forests and feeding largely on fruit. The black uakari is in danger of extinction because it is found in such small numbers already, and the forests where it lives are fast being destroyed.

Uccello Paolo. Adopted name of Paolo di Dono 1397–1475. Italian painter. Active in Florence, he was one of the first to experiment with the new Renaissance science of perspective, though his love of detail, decorative colour, and graceful line remains Gothic. His works include *St George and the Dragon* about 1460 (National Gallery, London) and *A Hunt* about 1460 (Ashmolean, Oxford).

Uccello is famous for his study of perspective, though he used it imaginatively rather than with scientific accuracy or consistency. His works in fresco include his painting (in imitation of an equestrian statue) of the English *condottiere* (hired soldier) Sir John Hawkwood (known as *Giovanni Acuto*) 1436 in Florence Cathedral, and a series in the Chiostro Verde (Green Cloister) of Santa Maria Novella, Florence, the principal composition being the *Deluge* of about 1445. He is, however, more celebrated for his panel pictures, notably the *Battle of San Romano* c. 1455, three pictures of the battle between the Florentines and the Sienese in 1432 painted for the Medici (Uffizi, Florence; Louvre, Paris; and National Gallery, London).

Udmurt (Russian ***Udmurtskaya***) autonomous republic in central Russian Federation
area 42,100 sq km/16,200 sq mi
capital Izhevsk
physical in the foothills of the W Ural Mountains
industries timber, flax, potatoes, peat, quartz
population (1992) 1,637,000 (59% Russian, 31% Udmurt, 7% Tatar)
history conquered in the 15th–16th centuries; constituted the Votyak Autonomous Region 1920; name changed to Udmurt 1932; Autonomous Republic 1934; part of the independent republic of Russia from 1991.

Ufa industrial city (engineering, oil refining, petrochemicals, distilling, timber) and capital of the Bashkir autonomous republic, central Russian Federation, on the river Bielaia, in the W Urals; population (1994) 1,092,000.

Uffizi art gallery in Florence, Italy. Built by ◊Vasari in the 16th century as government offices, it was opened as a gallery 1765. Its collection, based on that of the Medici family, is one of the finest in Europe. The collection illustrates the whole development of the Florentine School from Cimabue and Giotto onwards, and the schools of Siena, Ferrara, Bologna, and Emilia, and also contains a number of works by Flemish, Dutch, and German artists.

Among the best-known works housed in the Uffizi are *The Holy Family* by Michelangelo, the unfinished *Adoration of the Magi* by Leonardo, the *Madonna of the Goldfinch* by Raphael, Botticelli's masterpieces *Primavera*, *The Birth of Venus*, and *The Calummy of Apelles*, and Bellini's *Sacra Conversazione*.

UFO abbreviation for ◊***unidentified flying object***.

Uganda landlocked country in E Africa, bounded N by Sudan, E by Kenya, S by Tanzania and Rwanda, and W by the Democratic Republic of Congo. *See country box opposite.*

Uganda Martyrs 22 Africans, of whom 12 were boy pages, put to death 1885–87 by King Mwanga of Uganda for refusing to renounce Christianity. They were canonized as the first African saints of the Roman Catholic Church 1964.

Ugarit ancient trading-city kingdom (modern ***Ras Shamra***) on the Syrian coast. It was excavated by the French archaeologist Claude Schaeffer (1898–1982) from 1929, with finds dating from about 7000 to about 1300 BC, including the earliest known alphabet.

ugli fruit trademark for a cultivated Jamaican citrus fruit, a three-way cross between a grapefruit, a tangerine, and an orange. Sweeter than a grapefruit but sharper than a tangerine, with rough skin, it is eaten fresh or used in jams and preserves for a sweet-sour flavour. It is native to the East Indies and its name comes from its misshapen appearance.

UHF (abbreviation for ***ultra high frequency***) referring to radio waves of very short wavelength, used, for example, for television broadcasting.

UHT abbreviation for ***ultra-heat treated*** or ◊***ultra-heat treatment***.

Uigur a Turkic people living in NW China and Kazakhstan; they form about 80% of the population of the Chinese province of Xinjiang Uygur. There are about 5 million speakers of Uigur, a language belonging to the Turkic branch of the Altaic family; it is the official language of the province. The Uigur are known to have lived in the region since the 3rd century AD, and converted to Islam in the 14th century. They have been under Chinese rule since the 17th century. A small number fled to Kazakhstan at that time, and it is from them that the present minority is descended.

Ujung Pandang formerly (until 1973) ***Macassar*** or ***Makassar*** chief port (trading in coffee, rubber, copra, and spices) on Sulawesi, Indonesia, with fishing and food-processing industries; population (1990) 913,200. It was established by Dutch traders 1607.

ukiyo-e (Japanese 'pictures of the floating world') Japanese colour print depicting scenes from everyday life, the dominant art form in 18th- and 19th-century Japan. Aiming to satisfy the tastes of the increasingly affluent merchant classes, ukiyo-e artists employed bright colours and strong designs, made possible by improvements in block printing, and featured actors, prostitutes, and landscapes among their favoured subjects; over a quarter of all the illustrated ukiyo-e works produced were erotic works. ◊Hiroshige, ◊Utamaro, ◊Hokusai, and Suzuki (1725–1770) were leading exponents. The flat decorative colour and lively designs of ukiyo-e prints were later to influence many prominent French avant-garde artists.

Ukraine country in E central Europe, bounded E by Russia, N by Belarus, S by Moldova, Romania, and the Black Sea, and W by Poland, the Slovak Republic, and Hungary. *See country box on p. 1086.*

Ukrainian the majority ethnic group living in Ukraine; there are minorities in Siberian Russia, Kazakhstan, Poland, Slovakia, and Romania. There are 40–45 million speakers of Ukrainian, a member of the East Slavonic branch of the Indo-European family, closely related to Russian. Ukrainian-speaking communities are also found in Canada and the USA.

The word 'Ukraine' is derived from a Slav word meaning 'borderland', and historically the region was ruled by Russians and Poles. It is sometimes referred to by Russians as Little Russia, although this is a description that Ukrainians generally do not find appropriate. In the Ukraine there are distinct Ukrainian communities in the west (Lemky), east (Verkhovyntsi), north (Volhynians), and southwest (Hutsuls).

ukulele small four-stringed Hawaiian guitar, of Portuguese origin; it is easy to play. Music for ukulele is written in a form of tablature showing finger positions on a chart of the fingerboard.

Ulaanbaatar or *Ulan Bator* (formerly until 1924 ***Urga***) capital of the Mongolian Republic; a trading centre producing carpets, textiles, and vodka; population (1992) 601,000.

Ulbricht Walter 1893–1973. East German communist politician, in power 1960–71. He lived in exile in the USSR during Hitler's rule 1933–45. A

Uccello *Saint George and the Dragon* c. 1460 by Uccello (National Gallery, London). Though the horse in this picture clearly illustrates Uccello's fascination with the new science of perspective, the picture as a whole still has the decorative elegance of late Medieval painting. *Corbis*

UGANDA
Republic of

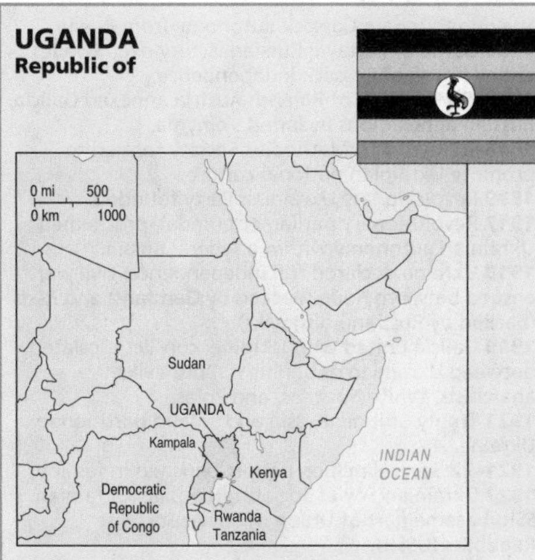

area 236,600 sq km/91,351 sq mi
capital Kampala
major towns/cities Jinja, Mbale, Entebbe, Masaka
physical features plateau with mountains in W (Ruwenzori Range, with Mount Margherita, 5,110 m/16,765 ft); forest and grassland; 18% is lakes, rivers, and wetlands (Owen Falls on White Nile where it leaves Lake Victoria; Lake Albert in W); arid in NE
head of state Yoweri Museveni from 1986
head of government Kinti Musoke from 1994
political system emergent democratic republic
administrative divisions ten provinces subdivided into 38 districts
political parties National Resistance Movement (NRM), left of centre; Democratic Party (DP), centre-left; Conservative Party (CP), centre-right; Uganda People's Congress (UPC), left of centre; Uganda Freedom Movement (UFM), left of centre. From 1986, political parties were forced to suspend activities
population 22,167,000 (1998 est)
population growth rate 3.4% (1990–95); 2.7% (2000–05)
ethnic distribution about 40 different peoples concentrated into four main groups; the Bantu (the most numerous), Eastern Nilotic, Western Nilotic, and Central Sudanic; there are also Rwandan, Sudanese, Zairean, and Kenyan minorities
life expectancy 42 (men), 44 (women)
literacy rate 48% (1995)
languages English (official), Kiswahili, Bantu and Nilotic languages
religions Christian 50%, animist 40%, Muslim 10%
currency Uganda new shilling
GDP (US $) 6.5 billion (1997)
growth rate 10.0% (1994)
exports coffee, cotton, tea, copper, tobacco

HISTORY
16th C Bunyoro kingdom founded by Lwo-speaking immigrants from SE Sudan.
17th C Rise of kingdom of Buganda people, which became particularly powerful from 17th century.
mid-19th C Arabs, trading ivory and slaves, reached Uganda; first visits by European explorers and Christian missionaries.
1885–87 Uganda Martyrs: Christians persecuted by the Buganda ruler, Mwanga.
1890 Royal Charter granted to British East African Company, a trading company whose agent, Frederick Lugard, concluded treaties with local rulers, including the Buganda and the western states of Ankole and Toro.
1894 British protectorate established, with Buganda retaining some autonomy under its traditional prince (Kabaka) and other resistance being crushed.
1904 Cotton growing introduced by Buganda peasants.
1958 Internal self-government granted.
1962 Independence achieved from Britain, within the Commonwealth, with Milton Obote of the Uganda People's Congress (UPC) as prime minister.
1963 Proclaimed a federal republic with King Mutesa II (of Buganda) as president and Obote as prime minister.
1966 King Mutesa, who opposed the creation of a one-party state, ousted in coup led by Obote, who ended the federal status and became executive president.
1969 All opposition parties banned after assassination attempt on Obote; key enterprises nationalized.
1971 Obote overthrown in army coup led by Maj-Gen Idi Amin Dada; constitution suspended and ruthlessly dictatorial regime established; nearly 49,000 Ugandan Asians expelled; over 300,000 opponents of regime killed.
1976 Relations with Kenya strained by Amin's claims to parts of Kenya.
1979 After annexing part of Tanzania, Amin forced to leave country by opponents backed by Tanzanian troops. Provisional government set up with Yusuf Lule as initial president and then Godfrey Binaisa.
1978–79 Fighting broke out against Tanzanian troops.
1980 Binaisa overthrown by army. Elections held and Milton Obote returned to power.
1985 After opposition by pro-Lule National Resistance Army (NRA), and indiscipline in army, Obote ousted by General Tito Okello; constitution suspended; power-sharing agreement entered into with NRA leader Yoweri Museveni.
1986 Museveni became president, heading broad-based coalition government.
1993 King of Buganda reinstated as formal monarch, in the person of Ronald Muwenda Mutebi II.
1996 Landslide victory won by Museveni in the first direct presidential elections.
1997 Uprisings by rebel forces.

SEE ALSO Amin, Idi; Buganda; Uganda Martyrs

Stalinist, he became first secretary of the Socialist Unity Party in East Germany 1950 and (as chair of the Council of State from 1960) was instrumental in the building of the Berlin Wall 1961. He established East Germany's economy and recognition outside the Eastern European bloc.

ulcer any persistent breach in a body surface (skin or mucous membrane). It may be caused by infection, irritation, or tumour and is often inflamed. Common ulcers include aphthous (mouth), gastric (stomach), duodenal, decubitus ulcers (pressure sores), and those complicating varicose veins. Treatment depends on the site. Drugs are the first line of attack against peptic ulcers (those in the digestive tract), though surgery may be necessary. Bleeding stomach ulcers can be repaired without an operation by the use of endoscopy: a flexible fibre-optic tube is passed into the stomach and under direct vision fine instruments are used to repair the tissues. Stomach ulcers are linked to the bacteria *Helicobacter pylori* found in the stomachs of 60% of adults in the West by the time they are 60.

***ukiyo-e** Two Women Admiring a Houseplant*, a ukiyo-e print by Utamaro. Concentrating on everyday subjects, and developing a delicacy of colour and line seldom surpassed, Utamaro was one of the very finest of the ukiyo-e artists. *Corbis*

ulna one of the two bones found in the lower limb of the tetrapod (four-limbed) vertebrate. It articulates with the shorter radius and ◊humerus (upper arm bone) at one end and with the radius and wrist bones at the other.

Ulster former kingdom in Northern Ireland, annexed by England 1461, from Jacobean times a centre of English, and later Scottish, settlement on land confiscated from its owners; divided 1921 into Northern Ireland (counties Antrim, Armagh, Down, Fermanagh, Londonderry (now Derry), and Tyrone) and the Republic of Ireland (counties Cavan, Donegal, and Monaghan).

Ulster Defence Association (UDA) Northern Ireland Protestant paramilitary organization responsible for a number of sectarian killings. Fanatically loyalist, it established a paramilitary wing (the Ulster Freedom Fighters) to combat the ◊Irish Republican Army (IRA) on its own terms and by its own methods. No political party has acknowledged any links with the UDA. In 1994, following a cessation of military activities by the IRA, the UDA, along with other Protestant paramilitary organisations, declared a cease-fire.

Ulster Freedom Fighters (UFF) paramilitary wing of the Ulster Defence Association.

Ulster Unionist Party (UUP) also known as the ***Official Unionist Party (OUP)*** the largest political party in ◊Northern Ireland. Right-of-centre in orientation, it advocates equality for Northern Ireland within the UK and opposes union with the Republic of Ireland. The party has the broadest support of any Ulster party, and has consistently won a large proportion of parliamentary and local seats. Its central organization, dating from 1905, is formally called the Ulster Unionist Council. Its leader from 1995 is David ◊Trimble.

The party advocates equal local-government rights for the people of Ulster compared with the rest of the UK. The party has been generally hostile to the terms of the UK's membership of the European Union (EU). Within Westminster the Ulster Unionist members of Parliament have generally voted with the Conservative Party.

Under Trimble's leadership the UUP accepted the 1998 Good Friday Agreement on power-sharing. It secured 28 of the 108 seats in the new Northern Ireland Assembly, elected in June 1998, and Trimble was elected Northern Ireland's first minister at the Assembly's first meeting on 1 July.

ultrafiltration process by which substances in solution are separated on the basis of their molecular size. A solution is forced through a membrane with pores large enough to permit the passage of small solute molecules but not large ones. Ultrafiltration is a vital mechanism in the vertebrate kidney: the cell membranes lining the Bowman's capsule act as semipermeable membranes allowing water and low-molecular-weight substances such as urea and salts to pass through into the urinary tubules but preventing the larger proteins from being lost from the blood.

ultra-heat treatment (UHT) preservation of milk by raising its temperature to 132°C/269°F or more. It uses higher temperatures than pasteurization, and kills all bacteria present, giving the milk a long shelf life but altering the flavour.

ultrasonics branch of physics dealing with the theory and application of ultrasound: sound waves occurring at frequencies too high to be heard by the human ear (about 20 kHz). The earliest practical application of ultrasonics was the detection of submarines during World War I by reflecting pulses of sound from them (see ◊sonar). Similar principles are now used in industry for nondestructive testing of materials and in medicine to produce images of internal organs and developing fetuses (◊ultrasound scanning). High-power ultrasound can be used for

‘My experience in the Cape Colony leads me to believe that the Ulster question is one which would soon settle itself.’

On **Ulster**
Cecil Rhodes, letter to Charles Stewart Parnell 19 June 1888

UKRAINE

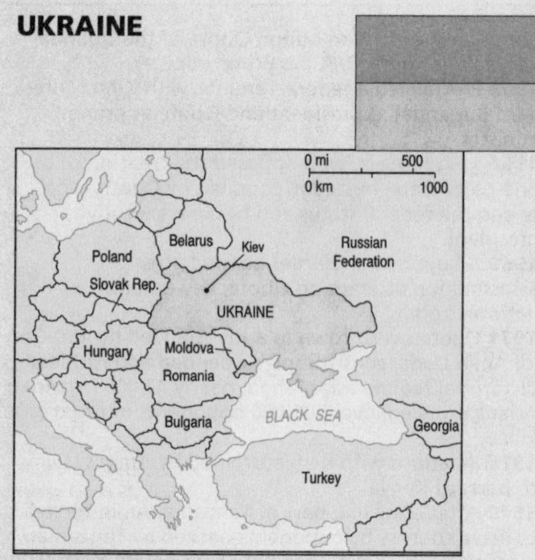

area 603,700 sq km/233,089 sq mi
capital Kiev
major towns/cities Kharkov, Donetsk, Dnepropetrovsk, Lugansk (Voroshilovgrad), Lviv (Lvov), Mariupol (Zhdanov), Krivoi Rog, Zaporozhye
physical features Russian plain; Carpathian and Crimean Mountains; rivers: Dnieper (with the Dnieper dam 1932), Donetz, Bug
head of state Leonid Kuchma from 1994
head of government Valery Pustovoitenko from 1997
political system emergent democracy
administrative divisions 24 provinces and one semi-autonomous region (Crimea)
political parties Ukrainian Communist Party (UCP), left-wing, anti-nationalist (banned 1991–93); Peasants' Party of the Ukraine (PPU), conservative agrarian; Ukrainian Socialist Party (SPU), left-wing, anti-nationalist; Ukrainian People's Movement (Rukh), Ukrainian Republican Party (URP), Congress of Ukrainian Nationalists (CUN), and Democratic Party of Ukraine (DPU) – all moderate nationalist; Social Democratic Party of Ukraine (SDPU), federalist
armed forces 517,000 (1994)
conscription 18 months (males over 18)
defence spend (% GDP) 2.1 (1994)
education spend (% GNP) 7.8 (1992)
health spend (% GDP) 3.3 (1991)
death penalty moratorium placed on executions since 1991 as condition for application to join Council of Europe (joined 1995). Despite continued demands by Council to uphold moratorium, executions have continued
population 51,380,000 (1995 est)
population growth rate −0.1% (1990–95); −0.2% (1993–2000)
age distribution (% of total population) <15 20.1%, 15–65 65.9%, >65 14.0% (1995)
ethnic distribution 73% of the population is of Ukrainian descent; 22% ethnic Russian; 1% Jewish; 1% Belarussian
population density (per sq km) 86 (1994)
urban population (% of total) 70 (1995)
labour force 50% of population: 20% agriculture, 40% industry, 40% services (1990)
unemployment 0.6% (1995)
child mortality rate (under 5, per 1,000 live births) 25 (1993)
life expectancy 66 (men), 75 (women)
education (compulsory years) 8 (7–15 age limit)
literacy rate n/a
language Ukrainian (a Slavonic language)
religions traditionally Ukrainian Orthodox; also Ukrainian Catholic
TV sets (per 1,000 people) 339 (1993)
currency hryvna
GDP (US $) 109.1 billion (1993)
GDP per capita (PPP) (US $) 3,250 (1993)
growth rate −24.3% (1994)
average annual inflation 891.0% (1994); 37.2% (1980–93)
trading partners Russia, Belarus, China, Moldova, Turkmenistan, USA, Switzerland, Germany
resources coal, iron ore (world's fifth-largest producer), crude oil, natural gas, salt, chemicals, brown coal, alabaster, gypsum
industries metallurgy, mechanical engineering, chemicals, machinery products
exports grain, coal, oil, various minerals. Principal market: Russia 39% (1994)
imports mineral fuels, machine-building components, chemicals and chemical products. Principal source: Russia 59% (1994)
arable land 55.2% (1993)
agricultural products wheat, buckwheat, sugar beet, potatoes, fruit and vegetables, sunflowers, cotton, flax, tobacco, hops; animal husbandry accounts for more than 50% of agricultural activity

HISTORY

9th C Rus' people established state centred on Kiev and adopted Eastern Orthodox Christianity 988.
1199 Reunification of southern Rus' lands, after period of fragmentation, under Prince Daniel of Galicia-Volhynia.
13th C Mongol-Tatar Golden Horde sacked Kiev and destroyed Rus' state.
14th C Poland annexed Galicia; Lithuania absorbed Volhynia and expelled Tatars; Ukraine peasants became serfs of Polish and Lithuanian nobles.
1569 Poland and Lithuania formed single state; clergy of Ukraine formed Uniate Church, which recognized papal authority but retained Orthodox rites, to avoid Catholic persecution.
16th and 17th Cs Runaway serfs known as Cossacks ('outlaws') formed autonomous community in eastern borderlands.
1648 Cossack revolt led by General Bogdan Khmelnitsky drove out Poles from central Ukraine.
1654 Khmelnitsky accepted Russian protectorate.
1660–90 'Epoch of Ruins': Ukraine devastated by civil war and invasions by Russians, Poles, and Turks; Poland regained W Ukraine.
1687 General Ivan Mazepa entered into alliance with Sweden to regain Cossack autonomy from Russia.
1709 Battle of Poltava: Russian victory over Swedes ended hopes of Cossack independence.
1772–95 Partition of Poland: Austria annexed Galicia, Russian annexations included Volhynia.
1846–47 Cyril and Methodius Society formed to promote Ukrainian national culture.
1899 Revolutionary Ukrainian Party founded.
1917 Revolutionary parliament (Rada), proclaimed Ukrainian autonomy within a federal Russia.
1918 Ukraine declared full independence; civil war ensued between Rada (backed by Germans) and Reds (backed by Russian Bolsheviks).
1919 Galicia united with Ukraine; conflict escalated between Ukrainian nationalists, Bolsheviks, anarchists, White Russians, and Poles.
1921 Treaty of Riga: Russia and Poland partitioned Ukraine.
1921–22 Several million people perished in famine.
1922 Ukrainian Soviet Socialist Republic (Ukrainian SSR) became part of Union of Soviet Socialist Republics (USSR).
1932–33 Enforced collectivization of agriculture caused another catastrophic famine with more than 7.5 million deaths.
1939 USSR annexed E Poland and added Galicia-Volhynia to Ukrainian SSR.
1940 USSR seized N Bukhovina from Romania and added it to Ukrainian SSR.
1941–44 Germany occupied Ukraine; many Ukrainians collaborated; millions of Ukrainians and Ukrainian Jews enslaved and exterminated by Nazis.
1945 USSR annexed Ruthenia from Czechoslovakia and added it to Ukrainian SSR, which became a nominal member of United Nations (UN).
1946 Uniate Church forcibly merged with Russian Orthodox Church.
1954 Crimea transferred from Russian Federation to Ukrainian SSR.
1986 Nuclear reactor explosion at Chernobyl, N of Kiev.
1989 Rukh (nationalist movement) established as political party; ban on Uniate Church lifted.
1990 Ukraine declared sovereignty under President Leonid Kravchuk, leader of the CP.
1991 Ukraine declared independence from USSR; President Kravchuk left CP; Ukraine joined newly formed Commonwealth of Independent States (CIS).
1992 Crimean sovereignty declared but rescinded.
1994 Election gains for radical nationalists in W Ukraine and Russian unionists in E Ukraine; Leonid Kuchma succeeded Kravchuk as president.
1996 New constitution replaced Soviet system; remaining nuclear warheads returned for destruction to Russia; new currency introduced.
1997 New government appointments made to speed economic reform. Treaty of friendship with Russia signed, solving issue of Russian Black Sea fleet. Prime Minister Lazarenko replaced by Valery Pustovoitenko. Loan of $750 million from International Monetary Fund (IMF) approved.

SEE ALSO Chernobyl; Commonwealth of Independent States; Crimea; Union of Soviet Socialist Republics

cleaning, welding plastics, and destroying kidney stones without surgery.

ultrasound scanning or ***ultrasonography*** in medicine, the use of ultrasonic pressure waves to create a diagnostic image. It is a safe, noninvasive technique that often eliminates the need for exploratory surgery. The sound waves transmitted through the body are absorbed and reflected to different degrees by different body tissues.

ultraviolet astronomy study of cosmic ultraviolet emissions using artificial satellites. The USA has launched a series of satellites for this purpose, receiving the first useful data 1968. Only a tiny percentage of solar ultraviolet radiation penetrates the atmosphere, this being the less dangerous longer-wavelength ultraviolet. The dangerous shorter-wavelength radiation is absorbed by gases in the ozone layer high in the Earth's upper atmosphere.

The US Orbiting Astronomical Observatory (OAO) satellites provided scientists with a great deal of information regarding cosmic ultraviolet emissions. *OAO-1*, launched 1966, failed after only three days, although *OAO-2*, put into orbit 1968, operated for four years, and carried out the first ultraviolet observations of a supernova and also of Uranus. *OAO-3* (*Copernicus*), launched 1972, continued transmissions into the 1980s and discovered many new ultraviolet sources. The *International Ultraviolet Explorer (IUE)*, launched Jan 1978 and still operating 1995, observed all the main objects in the Solar System (including Halley's comet), stars, galaxies, and the interstellar medium.

ultraviolet radiation electromagnetic radiation invisible to the human eye, of wavelengths from about 400 to 4 nm (where the ◊X-ray range begins). Physiologically, ultraviolet radiation is extremely powerful, producing sunburn and causing the formation of vitamin D in the skin. Ultraviolet rays are strongly germicidal and may be produced artificially by mercury vapour and arc lamps for therapeutic use. The radiation may be detected with ordinary photographic plates or films. It can also be studied by its fluorescent effect on certain materials.

ultra vires (Latin 'beyond the powers') any act by a public authority, company, or other agency that goes beyond the limits of its powers. In ◊administrative law, the doctrine of ultra vires governs all delegated legislation. Where an act is found to be ultra vires, it will have no legal effect.

Ulysses Roman name for ◊Odysseus, the Greek mythological hero.

Ulysses novel by James ◊Joyce, published 1922. It was first published in Paris but, because of obscenity prosecutions, was not published in the UK until 1936. It was later acknowledged as one of the most significant novels of the 20th century. Using the basic plot of the ◊*Odyssey*, Joyce matches equivalent episodes to a day in the life of characters in Dublin in 1904. The use of ◊stream of consciousness techniques and linguistic mastery transforms the smallest details of everyday life.

Ulysses space probe to study the Sun's poles, launched 1990 by a US space shuttle. It is a joint project by NASA and the European Space Agency. In Feb 1992, the gravity of Jupiter swung *Ulysses* on to a path that looped it first under the Sun's south pole in 1994 and then over the north pole in 1995 to study the Sun and solar wind at latitudes not observable from the Earth.

Umar c. 581–644. Adviser of the prophet Muhammad. In 634 he succeeded Abu Bakr as caliph (civic and religious leader of Islam), and conquered Syria, Palestine, Egypt, and Persia. He was assassinated by a slave. The Mosque of Omar in Jerusalem is attributed to him.

Umayyad dynasty Arabian dynasty of the Islamic Empire who reigned as caliphs (civic and religious leaders of Islam) 661–750, when they were overthrown by Abbasids. A member of the family, Abd al-Rahmam, escaped to Spain and in 756 assumed the title of emir of Córdoba. His dynasty, which took the title of caliph 929, ruled in Córdoba until the early 11th century.

Umberto I 1844–1900. King of Italy from 1878, who joined the Triple Alliance 1882 with Germany and Austria-Hungary; his colonial ventures included the defeat at Aduwa, Abyssinia, 1896. He was assassinated by an anarchist.

Umberto II 1904–1983. Last king of Italy 1946. On the abdication of his father, Victor Emmanuel III, he ruled 9 May–13 June 1946, when he had to abdicate since a referendum established a republic. He retired to Portugal.

umbilical cord connection between the ◊embryo and the ◊placenta of placental mammals. It has one vein and two arteries, transporting oxygen and nutrients to the developing young, and removing waste products. At birth, the connection between the young and the placenta is no longer necessary. The umbilical cord drops off or is severed, leaving a scar called the navel.

umbrella bird any of three species of bird of tropical South and Central America, family Cotingidae, order Passeriformes, about 45 cm/18 in long. The Amazonian species *Cephalopterus ornatus*, the ornate umbrella bird, has an inflatable wattle at the neck to amplify its humming call, and in display elevates a long crest (12 cm/4 in) lying above the bill so that it rises umbrella-like above the head. These features are less noticeable in the female, which is brownish, whereas the male is blue-black.

umbrella tree tree *Schefflera actinophylla* of Queensland and the Northern Territory, Australia, with large digitately compound shining leaves and small raspberrylike clusters of red flowers, which are borne at the ends of branches in long radiating spikelike compound umbels. It is common as an indoor plant in many countries.

Umbria mountainous region of Italy in the central Apennines, including the provinces of Perugia and Terni; area 8,500 sq km/3,281 sq mi; population (1992 est) 815,000. Its capital is Perugia, and the river Tiber rises in the region. Industries include wine, grain, olives, tobacco, textiles, chemicals, and metalworking. This is the home of the Umbrian school of artists, including Raphael.

UN abbreviation for ◊***United Nations***.

uncertainty principle or ***indeterminacy principle*** in quantum mechanics, the principle that it is meaningless to speak of a particle's position, momentum, or other parameters, except as results of measurements; measuring, however, involves an interaction (such as a ◊photon of light bouncing off the particle under scrutiny), which must disturb the particle. The principle implies that one cannot, even in theory, predict the moment-to-moment behaviour of such a system. It was established by German physicist Werner ◊Heisenberg, and gave a theoretical limit to the precision with which a particle's momentum and position can be measured simultaneously: the more accurately the one is determined, the more uncertainty there is in the other.

Uncle Sam nickname for the US government. It was coined during the War of 1812 by opponents of US policy. It was probably derived from the initials 'US' placed on government property.

Uncle Tom's Cabin best-selling US novel by Harriet Beecher ◊Stowe, published 1851–52. A sentimental but powerful portrayal of the cruelties of slave life on Southern plantations, it promoted the call for abolition. The heroically loyal slave Uncle Tom has in the 20th century become a byword for black subservience. Abraham Lincoln acknowledged that it had stirred Northern sentiments and helped precipitate the American Civil War.

unconformity surface of erosion or nondeposition eventually overlain by younger ◊sedimentary rock strata and preserved in the geologic record. A surface where the beds above and below lie at different angles is called an angular unconformity. The boundary between older igneous or metamorphic rocks that are truncated by erosion and later covered by younger sedimentary rocks is called a nonconformity.

Umbria An isolated *casa colònica* (farmhouse) near Norcia in the landlocked, almost entirely mountainous region of Umbria, central Italy. Little changed over the centuries, the landscape supports many small farms, producing in particular cereals, grapes, and olives, and now attracts a large number of tourists. *Sally Jenkins*

unconscious in psychoanalysis, a part of the personality of which the individual is unaware, and which contains impulses or urges that are held back, or repressed, from conscious awareness.

underground (North American ***subway***) rail service that runs underground. The first underground line in the world was in London, opened 1863; it was essentially a roofed-in trench. The London Underground is still the longest, with over 400 km/250 mi of routes. Many large cities throughout the world have similar systems.

Underground Railroad in US history, a network established in the North before the ◊American Civil War to provide sanctuary and assistance for escaped black slaves. Safe houses, transport facilities, and 'conductors' existed to lead the slaves to safety in the North and Canada, although the number of fugitives who secured their freedom by these means may have been exaggerated.

undernourishment condition that results from consuming too little food over a period of time. Like malnutrition – the result of a diet that is lacking in certain nutrients (such as protein or vitamins) – undernourishment is common in poor countries. Both lead to a reduction in mental and physical efficiency, a lowering of resistance to disease in general, and often to deficiency diseases such as beriberi or anaemia. In the developing world, lack of adequate food is a common cause of death.

In 1996, an estimated 195 million children under the age of five were undernourished in the world. Undernourishment is not just a problem of the developing world: there were an estimated 12 million children eating inadequately in the USA 1992. According to UN figures there were 200 million Africans suffering from undernourishment 1996.

unemployment lack of paid employment. The unemployed are usually defined as those out of work who are available for and actively seeking work. Unemployment is measured either as a total or as a percentage of those who are available for work, known as the working population, or labour force. Periods of widespread unemployment in Europe and the USA in the 20th century include 1929–1930s, and the years since the mid-1970s. In 1993, more than 820 million people – 30% of the world's labour force – were unemployed or working for less than a subsistence wage. Unemployment in industrialized countries (the members of the ◊Organization for Economic Cooperation and Development (OECD)) in 1995 averaged 7.5%, and in the European Union (EU) 11.1%. Within the OECD group the country with the lowest percentage of unemployed in 1995 was Japan (3%) and the highest was Spain (22.6%).

Many developing world countries suffer from severe unemployment and underemployment; the problem is exacerbated by rapid growth of population and lack of skills. In industrialized countries, the rise in world oil prices in the mid-1970s caused a downturn in economic activity, and greater use of high technology has improved output without the need for more jobs. There continues to be a great deal of youth unemployment despite government training and job creation schemes. In the USA the official unemployment rate was 5.3% in 1989, but it is estimated that 20% to 25% of those who want employment cannot find any, and have never had a job or are out of work longer than unemployment compensation is paid, so are not counted by labour statisticians. In China, nearly a quarter of the urban labour force is unemployed.

In Britain, for at least 150 years before 1939, the supply of labour always exceeded demand except in wartime, and economic crises accompanied by mass unemployment were recurrent from 1785. The percentage of unemployed in trade unions averaged 6% during 1883–1913 and 14.2% (of those covered by the old Unemployment Insurance Acts) 1921–38. World War II and the rebuilding and expansion that followed meant shortage of labour rather than unemployment in the Western world, and in Britain in the 1950s the unemployment rate fell to 1.5%. Fluctuation in employment returned in the 1960s, and was a worldwide problem in the recession of the mid-1970s to 1980s.

In Britain deflationary economic measures tended to exacerbate the trend, and in the mid-1980s the rate had risen to 14%, although the basis on which it is calculated has in recent years been changed several times and many commentators argue that the real rate is higher. Since Sept 1988 it has been measured as the total or percentage of the working population unemployed and claiming benefit. This only includes people aged 18 or over, since the under-18s are assumed to be in full-time education or training, which is not always the case. As the British economy experienced significant economic growth between 1986 and 1989, the rate of unemployment fell to a low of 5.6% in April 1990 (using the post-1988 definition) but rose again during the subsequent recession, reaching a peak of 10.5% in April 1993. The average number of unemployed people in 1995 was 2.3 million.

Most present-day governments attempt to prevent unemployment. The ideas of economist John Maynard ◊Keynes influenced British government unemployment policies during the 1950s and 1960s. The existence of a clear link between unemployment and inflation (that high unemployment can be dealt with by governments only at the cost of higher inflation) is now disputed.

UNESCO (acronym for ***United Nations Educational, Scientific, and Cultural Organization***) agency of the UN, established 1946, with its headquarters in Paris. The USA, contributor of 25% of its budget, withdrew 1984 on grounds of its 'over-politicization and mismanagement'. In Feb 1995 the US State Department recommended that it should rejoin not later than 1997.

unfair dismissal sacking of an employee unfairly. Under the terms of the UK Employment Acts, this means the unreasonable dismissal of someone who has been in continuous employment for a period of two years; that is, dismissal on grounds not in accordance with the codes of disciplinary practice and procedures prepared by ◊the Advisory, Conciliation, and Arbitration Service. Dismissed employees may take their case to an industrial tribunal for adjudication.

ungulate general name for any hoofed mammal. Included are the odd-toed ungulates (perissodactyls) and the even-toed ungulates (artiodactyls), along with subungulates such as elephants.

Uniate Church any of the ◊Orthodox Churches that accept the Catholic faith and the supremacy of the pope and are in full communion with the Roman Catholic Church, but retain their own liturgy and separate organization. In Ukraine, despite being proscribed 1946–89, the Uniate Church claimed some 4.5 million adherents when it was once again officially recognized. Its rehabilitation was marked by the return of its spiritual leader, Cardinal Miroslav Lubachivsky, to take up residence in Lvi'v in W Ukraine after 52 years' exile in Rome.

unicellular organism animal or plant consisting of a single cell. Most are invisible without a microscope but a few, such as the giant ◊amoeba, may be visible to the naked eye. The main groups of unicellular organisms are bacteria, protozoa, unicellular algae, and unicellular fungi or yeasts. Some become disease-causing agents, ◊pathogens.

unicorn mythical animal referred to by classical writers, said to live in India and resembling a horse, but with one spiralled horn growing from the forehead.

unidentified flying object or ***UFO*** any light or object seen in the sky whose immediate identity is not apparent. Despite unsubstantiated claims, there is no evidence that UFOs are alien spacecraft. On investigation, the vast majority of sightings turn out to have been of natural or identifiable objects, notably bright stars and planets, meteors, aircraft, and satellites, or to have been perpetrated by pranksters. The term flying saucer was coined 1947 and has been in use since.

Unification Church or ***Moonies*** church founded in Korea 1954 by the Reverend Sun Myung ◊Moon. The number of members (often called 'moonies') is about 200,000 worldwide. In the 1970s, the Unification Church was criticized for its methods of recruitment and alleged 'brainwashing', as well as for its business, far-right political, and journalistic activities.

The theology unites Christian and Taoist ideas and is based on Moon's book *Divine Principle*, which teaches that the original purpose of creation was to set up a perfect family, in a perfect relationship with God. This was thwarted by the Fall of Man, and history is seen as a continuous attempt to restore the original plan, now said to have found its fulfilment in Reverend and Mrs Moon. The Unification Church teaches that marriage is essential for spiritual fulfilment, and marriage partners are sometimes chosen for members by Reverend Moon, although individuals are free to reject a chosen partner. Marriage, which takes the form of mass blessings by Reverend and Mrs Moon, is the most important ritual of the church; it is preceded by the wine or engagement ceremony.

unified field theory in physics, the theory that attempts to explain the four fundamental forces (strong nuclear, weak nuclear, electromagnetic, and gravity) in terms of a single unified force (see ◊particle physics). Research was begun by Albert Einstein and, by 1971, a theory developed by US physicists Steven Weinberg and Sheldon Glashow, Pakistani physicist Abdus Salam, and others, had demonstrated the link between the weak and electromagnetic forces. The next stage is to develop a theory (called the ◊grand unified theory) that combines the strong nuclear force with the electroweak force. The final stage will be to incorporate gravity into the scheme. Work on the ◊superstring theory indicates that this may be the ultimate 'theory of everything'.

uniformitarianism in geology, the principle that processes that can be seen to occur on the Earth's surface today are the same as those that have occurred throughout geological time. For example, desert sandstones containing sand-dune structures must have been formed under conditions similar to those present in deserts today. The principle was formulated by James ◊Hutton and expounded by Charles ◊Lyell.

Uniformity, Acts of two acts of Parliament in England. The first in 1559 imposed the Prayer Book on the whole English kingdom; the second in 1662 required the Prayer Book to be used in all churches, and some 2,000 ministers who refused to comply were ejected.

Unilateral Declaration of Independence (UDI) unnegotiated severing of relations with a colonial power; especially, the declaration made by Ian Smith's Rhodesian Front government 11 Nov 1965, announcing the independence of Rhodesia (now Zimbabwe) from Britain.

Smith unilaterally declared Rhodesia an independent state, to resist sharing power with the black African majority. It was a move condemned by the United Nations and by the UK, who imposed trade restrictions and an oil embargo. With the support of the UN, Britain also imposed a naval blockade, but this was countered by the South African government breaking sanctions. Negotiations between British prime minister Harold Wilson and Smith foundered. It was not until April 1980 that the Republic of Zimbabwe was proclaimed.

unilateralism in politics, support for unilateral nuclear disarmament: scrapping a country's nuclear weapons without waiting for other countries to agree to do so at the same time. In the UK this principle was Labour Party policy in the 1980s but was abandoned 1989.

Unilever multinational food, drink, and detergent company formed 1930 in a merger between British and Dutch companies. The merger took in Lever Brothers, founded 1885 by William Hesketh Lever (1851–1935) and James Darcy Lever (who built Port Sunlight, a model village built near Liverpool for workers at the Lever Brothers soap factory). By 1990 Unilever employed more than 300,000 people across the world, with 53,000 in the UK. Its headquarters are in Rotterdam, the Netherlands.

Union, Act of 1707 act of Parliament that brought about the union of England and Scotland; that of 1801 united England and Ireland. The latter was revoked when the Irish Free State was constituted 1922.

union flag British national ◊flag. It is popularly called the ***Union Jack***, although, strictly speaking, this applies only when it is flown on the jackstaff of a warship.

Union Movement British political group. Founded as the New Party by Oswald ◊Mosley and a number of Labour members of Parliament 1931, it developed into the British Union of Fascists 1932. In 1940 the organization was declared illegal and its leaders interned, but it was revived as the Union Movement 1948, characterized by racist doctrines including anti-Semitism.

Union of Soviet Socialist Republics (USSR) former country in N Asia and E Europe that reverted to independent states 1991; see ◊Armenia, ◊Azerbaijan, ◊Belarus, ◊Estonia, ◊Georgia, ◊Kazakhstan, ◊Kyrgyzstan, ◊Latvia, ◊Lithuania, ◊Moldova, ◊Russian Federation, ◊Tajikistan, ◊Turkmenistan, ◊Ukraine, and ◊Uzbekistan.

history The Union of Soviet Socialist Republics was formed 1922, and a constitution adopted 1923. Lenin, who had led the new regime, died 1924, and an internal party controversy broke out between the communist leaders Stalin and Trotsky over the future of socialism and the necessity of world revolution.

Stalin's socialism Trotsky was expelled 1927, and Stalin's policy of socialism in one country adopted. During the first two five-year plans 1928–39, heavy and light industries were developed, and agriculture collectivized. The country was transformed as industry grew rapidly, with, as a consequence, the size of the manual workforce quadrupling and the urban population doubling. However, the social cost was enormous, with millions dying in the Ukraine and Kazakhstan famine of 1932–34, as well as in the political purges and liquidations launched during the 1920s and 1930s. Leading party figures, including Nikolai Bulkharin, Lev Kamenev, and Grigory Zinoviev were victims of these 'show trial' purges. In the process, the Soviet political system was deformed, as inner-party democracy gave way to autocracy based around a Stalinist personality cult.

In 1939 the USSR concluded a nonaggression pact with Germany, and Poland was invaded and divided between them. The USSR invaded Finland 1939 but signed a brief peace 1940. Some 25 million Russians perished during this 'Great Patriotic War'.

Cold War During the immediate postwar years the USSR concentrated on consolidating its empire in Eastern Europe and on providing indirect support to anticolonial movements in the Far East. Relations with the West, particularly the USA, sharply deteriorated. On the death of Stalin in March 1953, a collective leadership, including Nikita Khrushchev (CPSU first or general secretary 1953–64), Georgi Malenkov (prime minister 1953–55), Nikolai Bulganin (prime minister 1955–58), Vyacheslav Molotov (foreign minister 1953–56), and Lazar Kaganovich, assumed power. They combined to remove the secret-police chief Lavrenti Beria in Dec 1953, and introduced a new legal code that regularized the political system. Strong differences emerged within the collective leadership over future political and economic reform, and a fierce succession struggle developed.

Khrushchev's 'liberalization policy' Khrushchev emerged dominant from this contest, ousting Malenkov, Molotov, and Kaganovich June 1957 and Bulganin June 1958 to combine the posts of prime minister and party first secretary. At the 1961 Party Congress, Khrushchev introduced a new programme for rapid agricultural, industrial, and technological development, aiming to move the USSR ahead of the USA in economic terms by 1980 and attain full communism. He launched a 'virgin lands' cultivation campaign in Kazakhstan, increased rural incentives, and decentralized industrial management.

In addition, Khrushchev introduced radical party rule changes, sanctioned a cultural thaw, and devised the principle of 'peaceful coexistence' with the West to divert resources from the military sector. These reforms enjoyed initial success; having exploded its first hydrogen bomb 1953 and launched a space satellite (Sputnik I) 1957, the USSR emerged as a serious technological rival to the USA. But Khrushchev's liberalization policy and his denunciation of the errors and crimes of the Stalin era at the Feb 1956 Party Congress had serious repercussions among the USSR's satellites – a nationalist revolt in Hungary and a breach in relations with Yugoslavia and China – while his administrative reforms were opposed by senior bureaucrats. After a series of poor harvests in over-cropped Kazakhstan and the ◊Cuban missile crisis 1962, these opponents succeeded in ousting Khrushchev at the Central Committee meeting Oct 1964.

A new and conservative collective leadership, based around the figures of Leonid Brezhnev (CPSU general secretary 1964–82), Alexei Kosygin (prime minister 1964–80), Nikolai Podgorny (state president 1965–77), and Mikhail Suslov (ideology secretary 1964–82), assumed power and immediately abandoned Khrushchev's industrial and party reforms and reimposed strict censorship in the cultural sphere. Priority was now given to the expansion and modernization of the Soviet armed forces, including the creation of a naval force with global reach. This, coupled with the Warsaw Pact invasion of Czechoslovakia 1968, resulted in a renewal of the ◊Cold War 1964–70.

the Brezhnev doctrine During the later 1960s, Leonid Brezhnev emerged as the dominant figure. He governed in a cautious and consensual manner and brought into the Politburo leaders from all the significant centres of power, including the ◊KGB (Yuri Andropov), the army (Marshal Andrei Grechko), and the diplomatic service (Andrei Gromyko). Priority was now given to agricultural and consumer-goods production. A new constitution 1977 set out the limits for internal dissent; the

USSR: POSTWAR TIMELINE

1947	Cominform created by the USSR to direct international communism.
1949	The Council for Mutual Economic Assistance (Comecon) economic bloc established in Central and Eastern Europe.
1953	General strike and demonstrations in East Germany against 'Sovietization'.
1955	Warsaw Pact defence alliance formed by Central and Eastern European communist states.
1956	USSR suppressed Hungarian reform initiative with troops and tanks.
1961	Berlin Wall built to prevent the mass exodus of East Germans to the West.
1962	Cuban missile crisis.
1968	Warsaw Pact forces intervened in Czechoslovakia to prevent liberalization.
1975	Helsinki CSCE conference (Conference on Security and Cooperation in Europe) confirmed the postwar division of Europe.
1979	USSR invaded Afghanistan in support of a communist puppet regime.
1980–81	Solidarity reform movement in Poland; martial law imposed.
1983	Star Wars plan for militarization of space unveiled by US president Ronald Reagan.
1985	Mikhail Gorbachev, the new Soviet leader, embarked on ambitious reform programme.
1987	USSR–US agreement to scrap intermediate range nuclear forces in Europe; Boris Yeltsin, Moscow communist party chief, dismissed for criticizing slow pace of reform.
1988	Nationalist demonstrations in Baltic republics, Armenia, Azerbaijan, and Kazakhstan.
1989	Massacre of pro-independence demonstrators in Tbilisi, Georgia; USSR troops withdrawn from Afghanistan; communist regimes collapsed in Bulgaria, Czechoslovakia, East Germany, and Romania; transition to democracy agreed in Hungary and Poland.
1990	Troops sent to Azerbaijan during civil war with Armenia; end of Cold War declared at CSCE conference in Paris; Yeltsin became president of Russian Federation; East and West Germany unified; sanctions imposed against Lithuania after declaration of independence.
1991	USSR–US Strategic Arms Reduction Treaty signed; coup attempt against Gorbachev thwarted; Baltic republics broke away; USSR dissolved and replaced by Commonwealth of Independent States, with Yeltsin president of the Russian Federation.

'Brezhnev doctrine' was also promulgated 1968, establishing the power of the USSR to intervene to 'preserve socialism' in E Europe as it did in Czechoslovakia.

era of détente Brezhnev, who became the new state president May 1977, emerged as an international figure during the 1970s, frequently meeting Western leaders during a new era of détente. The landmarks of this period were the SALT I and SALT II Soviet–US arms-limitation agreements of 1972 and 1979 (see ◊Strategic Arms Limitation Talks) and the Helsinki Accord 1975, which brought Western recognition of the postwar division of Eastern Europe. Another cultural thaw resulted in the emergence of a vocal dissident movement. The political and military influence of the USSR was extended into Africa with the establishment of new communist governments in Mozambique 1974, Angola and Ethiopia 1975, and South Yemen 1978.

The détente era was brought to an end by the Soviet invasion of Afghanistan in Dec 1979 and the Polish crisis 1980–81. The final years of the Brezhnev administration were ones of mounting corruption and economic stagnation.

Andropov and Chernenko Yuri Andropov, the former KGB chief, was elected CPSU leader on Brezhnev's death Nov 1982 and began energetically to introduce a series of radical economic reforms aimed at decentralizing the planning system, inculcating greater labour discipline, and attacking official corruption. When Andropov died Feb 1984 he was succeeded by the cautious and elderly Konstantin Chernenko (a Brezhnev supporter).

Gorbachev's 'market socialism' On Chernenko's death in March 1985, power was transferred to a new generation led by Mikhail Gorbachev, at 54 the CPSU's youngest leader since Stalin, although Andrei Gromyko was actually president of the USSR 1985–88. Gorbachev introduced a number of reforms. He began to free farmers and factory managers from bureaucratic interference and to increase material incentives in a 'market socialist' manner. He replaced cautious Brezhnevites with ambitious technocrats and promoted *glasnost* ('openness').

détente initiative Working with Foreign Secretary Edvard Shevardnadze, Gorbachev made skilful use of the foreign media to put the case against space weapons and nuclear testing. He met US president Reagan in Geneva and Reykjavik in Nov 1985 and Oct 1986, and, at the Washington summit of Dec 1987, he concluded a treaty designed to eliminate medium-range Intermediate Nuclear Forces (INF) from European soil, ratified in Moscow in June 1988. As part of the new détente initiative, the USSR also withdrew all its troops from Afghanistan in Feb 1989 and made broad cutbacks in the size of its conventional forces 1989–90.

glasnost and perestroika Gorbachev pressed for an acceleration of his domestic, economic, and political programme of restructuring (*perestroika*) from 1987, but faced growing opposition both from conservatives grouped around Yegor Ligachev and radicals led by Boris Yeltsin. Gorbachev's *glasnost* policy helped fan growing nationalist demands for secession among the republics of the Baltic and Transcaucasia. To add momentum to the reform process, in June 1988 Gorbachev convened a special All-Union Party Conference, the first since 1941, to approve a radical constitutional overhaul. A new competitively elected 'super-legislature', the Congress of the USSR People's Deputies (CUPD), was created, from which a full-time working parliament was subsequently to be elected, headed by a state president with increased powers.

It was also agreed to reintroduce private leasehold farming, reform the price system, and allow part-time private enterprise in the service and small-scale industry sectors.

'socialist pluralism' The June 1988 reforms constituted the most fundamental reordering of the Soviet policy since the 'Stalinist departure' of 1928, entailing the creation of a new type of 'socialist democracy', as well as a new mixed economic system. In May 1989, the CUPD elected Gorbachev as state president. During 1989 this movement towards 'socialist pluralism' was furthered by Gorbachev's abandonment of the ◊Brezhnev Doctrine and his

cont. on p. 1092

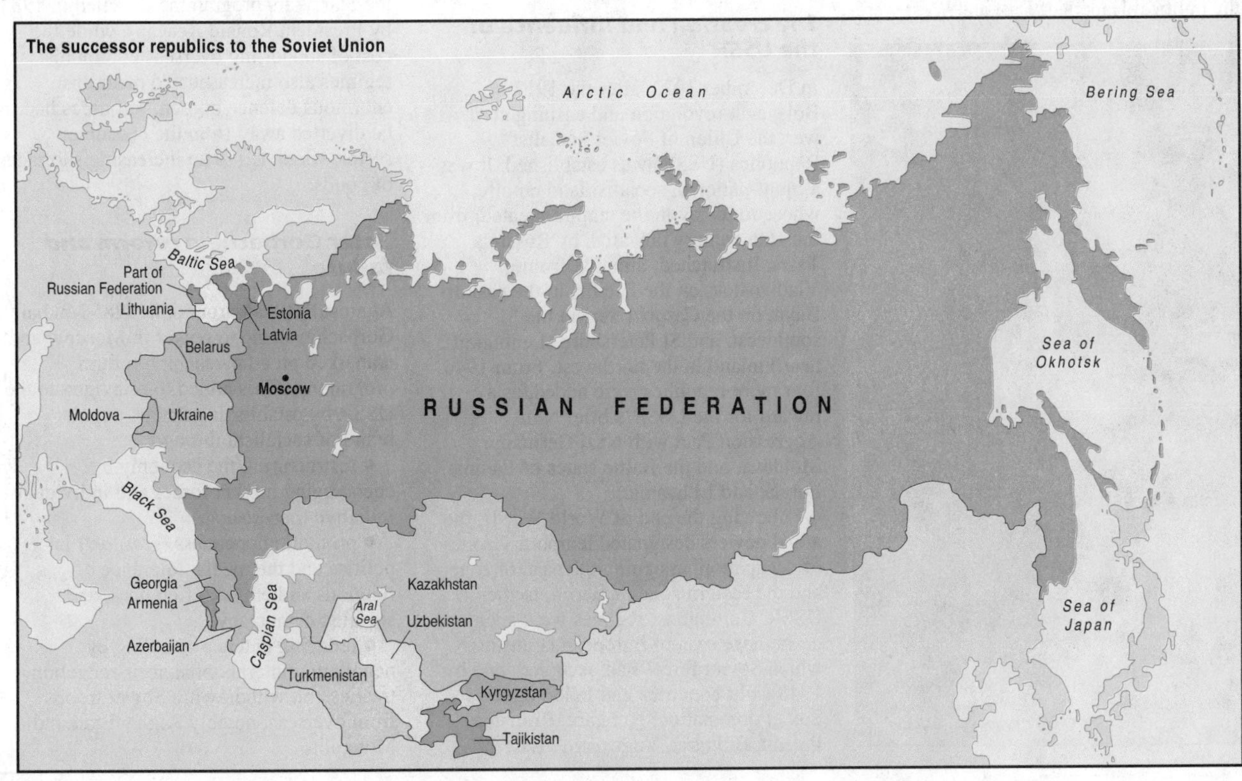

The Break-up of the USSR

A man throws himself under a Soviet Army tank driving towards the Russian Federation building in Moscow, 19 Aug 1991, following an attempted coup against President Gorbachev. The man was pulled away unharmed, the coup was unsuccessful, and political reform in the USSR went ahead. *Popper*

At the end of World War II, the seeds of another conflict were sown – one that was to span five decades and bring the world to the brink of nuclear war. Between the 1950s and the end of the 1980s, the Cold War divided the world into two ideological camps: the communist, led by the Soviet Union, where all aspects of life were subject to state control; and the liberal democratic capitalist, spearheaded by the United States and its allies in Western Europe and Japan. It was an era of nuclear confrontation and state-sponsored espionage, a time when contacts between the political leaders of East and West were so limited that each was termed a 'superpower summit'.

In 22 months, between 9 November 1989, when the Berlin Wall was opened, allowing free movement from formerly communist East Germany to the West, and 22 August 1991, when a last-ditch attempted coup by communist reactionaries in Moscow was thwarted, this world order was shattered. Communism was overthrown in central and eastern Europe and on 8 December 1991, with the USSR disbanded, a new world order was left to be constructed.

Burning pictures of Stalin after his death, when his repressive regime and purges were denounced by the Soviet authorities. Khrushchev was the first official to denounce Stalin for crimes against the Party and a programme of de-Stalinization was instigated. Many of the victims of Stalin's purges were rehabilitated. *Corbis*

The creation and influence of the USSR

In December 1922, after the 1917 Bolshevik revolution and ensuing civil war, the Union of Soviet Socialist Republics (USSR) was established. It was a multi-national, socialist land empire, whose roots lay in the empire created, from the 16th century onwards, by Russia's Tsars. It stretched, initially, from Vladivostok, on the Pacific, in the east, to Baku, on the Caspian Sea, in the southwest, and St Petersburg (Leningrad), near Finland in the northwest. From 1940, four more republics were added, as a reward for the USSR's brief Non-Aggression Pact with Nazi Germany: Moldova, and the Baltic states of Estonia, Latvia, and Lithuania.

Following the end of World War II, the allied powers designated temporary zones of occupation, assigning the eastern zone, and the eastern zone of Berlin, to the USSR. Communist regimes were soon set up in those eastern European countries which Soviet forces had occupied, and by 1948 eight countries had fallen under Soviet domination: Hungary, Romania, Poland, Bulgaria, Yugoslavia, East Germany, Czechoslovakia, and Albania. Further afield, by the 1980s allied 'puppet regimes' had been established in most regions of the world, including Cuba in the Caribbean, Angola in southern Africa, and Vietnam in SE Asia.

The size and its expansionary character partly explained the fear the USSR generated in the West during the postwar era. The other reason was its military strength. By the mid-1970s, the USSR produced one-fifth of the world's industrial output and, by annually diverting one-seventh of this national wealth into the defence sector, had a huge standing army, the world's second largest navy, and an intimidating arsenal of nuclear weapons.

An uneasy union: tensions within

Moscow maintained control over its new Central European satellites through establishing the Warsaw Pact defence alliance (1955), the Comecon economic bloc (1949), and by carefully vetting and training, at the Moscow Party School, their communist leaders. Within the USSR, a new atheistic and patriotic 'soviet' identity was promoted, through the education system and propaganda, and opponents of the regime were 'purged' or imprisoned.

While the USSR was perhaps at its most powerful in 1979, with its invasion of Afghanistan, it was during this decade that the seeds of later decline were sown. Its centrally-planned 'command economy' had led to inefficient use of resources and had failed to provide incentives for entrepreneurial innovation. Consequently, the pace of Soviet and Central European economic growth more than halved between the 1960s and early 1980s. Yet during this period the arms race with the United States intensified (particularly with the Star Wars programme unveiled in 1983 by President Ronald Reagan), while the cost of supporting overseas communist regimes also increased. To meet this enormous defence burden, resources had to be diverted away from the consumer sector, which led to an increasing shortages of goods.

Enter Gorbachev: reform and failure

Against this background, in 1985 Mikhail Gorbachev came to power in Moscow and embarked on a far-reaching reform programme. This aimed to reinvigorate the USSR by establishing a new, popular brand of socialism through:

- restructuring the economy by encouraging market forces and individual initiative (*perestroika*)
- promoting openness (*glasnost*) in politics and the media, tolerance of religious and ethnic differences, and socialist democracy
- reducing defence spending by negotiating international arms-reduction treaties and withdrawing Soviet troops from overseas, notably Afghanistan and Mongolia.

Despite some successes, this programme failed in its goal and, instead, resulted in undermining the Soviet empire, starting at its weakest link – its Central European satellites. There, reforms were also being implemented, with very differing degrees of enthusiasm. The collapse was inadvertently triggered by the 'reform-communist' leaders of Hungary who, in May 1989, opened the country's border with Austria. This provided an exit route to the West for tens of thousands of East Germans, and in November 1989, following large pro-democracy demonstrations in Dresden, Leipzig, and East Berlin, East Germany's communist rulers reluctantly conceded sweeping reforms which ended their monopoly of power. The Berlin Wall came down.

On previous such occasions, in Hungary in 1956 and Czechoslovakia in 1968, the USSR had sent in tanks and troops to prevent the overthrow of communism (as China's leaders had done in Tiananmen Square in June 1989). But this time, Gorbachev refused to sanction the use of force, and by 1990 popular revolutions had also toppled the communist regimes of Bulgaria, Czechoslovakia, and Romania, while in Hungary and Poland a peaceful transition to democracy was underway.

Unbottled by glasnost, ethnic regional unrest also surfaced from 1988 within the USSR, in the fiercely nationalist Baltic republics and in the Caucasus region, which included Armenia, Azerbaijan, and Georgia. Meanwhile, perestroika, combined with declarations of autonomy by individual republics, had brought a mounting economic crisis, as the supply links of the planned economy unravelled. On 19 August 1991 – one day before a new, more truly federal, Union Treaty was due to be signed – a desperate coup was carried out by an alliance of Communist Party conservatives, the KGB, and the military, whose aim was to turn back the clock and re-establish central authority. However, the coup was poorly planned and failed to gain the support of Boris Yeltsin, the reform-communist president of the Russian republic and of the Red Army. After three days the plotters were arrested. Gorbachev was returned to power, but was a diminished figure: real power within the USSR now lay with Yeltsin. In December 1991, after the Baltic republics had already broken away, the dissolution of the Soviet Union was negotiated.

Defiant Czechs carry their nation's flag past a burning Soviet tank in Prague, Czechoslovakia, on 21 Aug 1968, after troops from the USSR and four of its Warsaw Pact partners invaded Czechoslovakia to snuff out the liberal reform movement. *Corbis*

The consequences of dissolution

Created in December 1991 as a much less influential successor to the USSR, the Commonwealth of Independent States (CIS) was joined eventually by 12 former republics (the Baltic states remained outside). The Warsaw Pact and Comecon had already collapsed with the break-away of the Central European satellites in 1989, and the succeeding new world order was thus dominated by the one remaining superpower, the United States, and by the ideologies of liberal democracy and capitalism. China, Cuba, North Korea, and Vietnam were left as isolated communist outposts. The former satellite states of Central Europe edged ever closer to the West, with aspirations to join NATO and, eventually, the European Union.

Meanwhile, the political future remained uncertain in the successor states of the former USSR. In the Caucasus region, Central Asia, and southern Russia, ethnic disputes flared up and the transition towards a market economy proved uneasy, characterized by increasing economic inequalities, rocketing crime levels, and political instability.

Ian Derbyshire

Boris Yeltsin waves to supporters from the balcony of the Russian parliament on 19 Aug 1991 – the day of the attempted Communist Party coup. He led the reform-communist opposition to the reactionaries, defeated them, and went on to become president and prime minister of the Commonwealth of Independent States. *Popper*

SEE ALSO

Cold War; glasnost; Gorbachev, Mikhail; perestroika; Russian Federation; Union of Soviet Socialist Republics sanctioning of the establishment of noncommunist and 'reform communist' governments elsewhere in Eastern Europe. This led to the ruling regimes of Poland, Czechoslovakia, and Romania being overthrown in a wave of 'people's power'.

Responding to these developments, in March 1990 the Soviet Parliament authorized private ownership of the means of production, forbidden since the 1920s. Further constitutional amendments made 1990 supported the right of self-determination, including secession of republics, and ended the CPSU's monopoly of power.

popular discontent The Gorbachev reform programme showed signs of running out of control 1989–90 as a result both of growing nationalist tensions (which in April 1989 and Jan 1990 had prompted the despatch of troops to the Caucasus region, first to break up demonstrations in Tbilisi, Georgia, and then to attempt to quell a civil war between Armenia and Azerbaijan over the disputed enclave of Nagorno-Karabakh) and mounting popular discontent over the failure of *perestroika* to improve living standards.

end of Cold War In their Dec 1989 summit meeting in Malta, Gorbachev and US president Bush declared an end to the Cold War, opening the possibility of membership of General Agreement on Tariffs and Trade (GATT), and an influx of Western investment.

moves towards independence in the republics Throughout 1990 the political and economic situation deteriorated. In pluralist elections, anticommunist, nationalist, and radical deputies polled strongly, particularly in the Baltic republics and cities. Their new governments issued declarations of republican sovereignty and, in the case of the Baltics, independence. These Moscow refused to recognize, and imposed a temporary economic blockade on Lithuania. As the year progressed, a 'war of laws' developed between the centre and the republics, who kept back funds (leading to a worsening federal budget deficit), and the system of central economic planning and resource distribution began to break down. As a consequence, with crime and labour unrest also increasing, the USSR's national income fell by 20% during 1990 and 1991. Mounting food shortages led to rationing.

break-up of the CPSU The CPSU also began to fracture during 1990 as a result of nationalist challenges within the republics and policy divisions among conservatives, liberals, and radicals. A split was formalized at the 28th CPSU Congress July 1990, when Boris Yeltsin, the new indirectly elected president of the Russian Federation (RSFR), Gavriil Popov, and Anatoly Sobchak (radical mayors of Moscow and Leningrad), resigned their party membership. Earlier, in the RSFR, a new Russian Communist Party had been formed.

Gorbachev's swing to the right In Dec 1990, concerned at the gathering pace of economic and political disintegration and ethnic strife, Gorbachev persuaded the Soviet parliament to vote him increased emergency presidential powers. Under pressure from the right, a clear rightward shift in policy became apparent – this was seen in the appointment of the conservative Valentin Pavlov as prime minister; the resignation of foreign minister Shevardnadze (who warned of an impending dictatorship); the dispatch of paratroopers to Vilnius and Rega to seize political and communications buildings; and the retightening of press and television censorship. In protest, striking miners called for Gorbachev's resignation.

proposed new union treaty From the spring of 1991, after his proposal to preserve the USSR as a 'renewed federation of equal sovereign republics' secured public approval in a unionwide referendum, Gorbachev again attempted to reconstruct a centre-left reform alliance with liberals and radicals. In June 1991 the draft of a new Union Treaty was approved by nine republics; this treaty entailed a much greater devolution of authority and the establishment of a new two-chamber federal legislature and a directly elected executive president.

In July 1991 Gorbachev's standing was further enhanced by the signing of a Strategic Arms Reduction Treaty (START), to reduce the number of US and Soviet long-range nuclear missiles. At home, however, Boris Yeltsin, who was popularly elected as the RSFR's president June 1991, pressed for even greater reform and in July 1991 Communist Party cells were banned from operating in factories, farms, and government offices in the Russian Republic.

abortive anti-Gorbachev coup These liberal-radical initiatives raised disquiet among CPSU conservatives and on 19 Aug 1991, a day before the new union treaty was to be signed, an attempted coup was launched by a reactionary alliance of leaders of the Communist Party *apparatchiki*, the military-industrial complex, the KGB, and the armed forces. It was declared that President Gorbachev was ill and that Vice President Gennady Yanayev would take over as president as part of an eight-person emergency committee.

The committee assumed control over radio and television, banned demonstrations and most newspapers, imposed a curfew, and sent tanks into Moscow. They failed, however, to arrest the Russian president Boris Yeltsin, who defiantly stood out as head of a democratic 'opposition state' based at the Russian Parliament, the so-called 'White House'. Yeltsin called for a general strike and the reinstatement of President Gorbachev. Two days later, having failed to wrest control of the 'White House' and win either international or unionwide acknowledgement of the change of regime, and in the face of large public demonstrations, the coup disintegrated. The junta's leaders were arrested and in the early hours of Thursday 22 Aug President Gorbachev, fully reinstated, arrived back in Moscow.

aftermath of the coup In the wake of the failed coup, established communist structures, as well as the union itself, rapidly disintegrated, faced by a popular backlash which resulted in icons of communism being toppled and the Red Flag burned, being replaced by traditional, in some cases tsarist, symbols. President Gorbachev initially misjudged the changed mood, intimating his continued faith in the popularly discredited Communist Party and seeking to keep to a minimum of changes in personnel and institutions. However, forced by pressure exerted by the public and by Boris Yeltsin, whose stature both at home and abroad had been hugely enhanced, a succession of far-reaching reforms were instituted which effectively sounded the death knell of Soviet communism and resulted in the fracturing of the union and its subsequent refounding on a much changed and truncated basis.

The new union cabinet was effectively selected by Yeltsin and staffed largely with radical democrats from the Russian Republic. Yeltsin also declared himself to have assumed charge of the armed forces within the Russian Republic and, at a heated session of the Russian Parliament, pressurized President Gorbachev into signing a decree suspending the activities of the Russian Communist Party. In addition, a new Russian national guard was established and control assumed over all economic assets in the republic.

Recognizing the changed realities, on 24 Aug 1991 Gorbachev resigned as general secretary of the Communist Party of the Soviet Union and ordered its Central Committee to dissolve itself.

republics declare independence The attempted

UNITED ARAB EMIRATES

(UAE) federation of the emirates of Abu Dhabi, Ajman, Dubai, Fujairah, Ras al Khaimah, Sharjah, Umm al Qaiwain

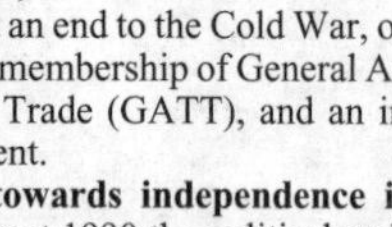

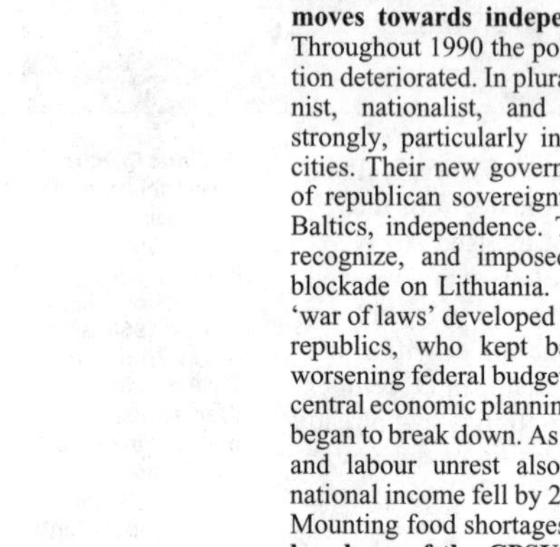

national name *Ittihad al-Imarat al-Arabiyah*
area 83,657 sq km/32,292 sq mi
capital Abu Dhabi
major towns/cities Sharjah, Ras al-Khaimah
major ports Dubai
physical features desert and flat coastal plain; mountains in E
head of state and government Sheik Zayed bin Sultan al-Nahayan of Abu Dhabi from 1971
supreme council of rulers *Abu Dhabi* Sheik Sultan Zayed bin al-Nahayan, president (1966); *Ajman* Sheik Humaid bin Rashid al-Nuami (1981); *Dubai* Sheik Maktoum bin Rashid al-Maktoum (1990); *Fujairah* Sheik Hamad bin Muhammad al-Sharqi (1974); *Ras al Khaimah* Sheik Saqr bin Muhammad al-Quasimi (1948); *Sharjah* Sheik Sultan bin Muhammad al-Quasimi (1972); *Umm al Qaiwain* Sheik Rashid bin Ahmad al-Mu'alla (1981)
political system absolutism
administrative divisions federation of seven self-governing emirates
political parties none
population 2,260,000 (1996 est)
population growth rate 2.6% (1990–95); 1.8% (2000–05)
ethnic distribution 75% Iranians, Indians, and Pakistanis; about 25% Arabs
life expectancy 70 (men), 74 (women)
literacy rate 55%
languages Arabic (official), Farsi, Hindi, Urdu, English
religions Muslim 96%, Christian, Hindu
currency UAE dirham
GDP (US $) 45.1 billion (1997)
growth rate −0.6% (1994)
exports oil, natural gas, fish, dates

HISTORY

7th C AD Islam introduced.
early 16th C Portuguese established trading contacts with the Persian Gulf states.
18th C Rise of trade and seafaring among the Qawasim and Bani Yas, respectively in Ras al-Khaimah and Sharjah in the N and Abu Dhabi and Dubai in the desert of the S. The Emirates' current ruling families are descended from these peoples.
early 19th C Britain signed treaties ('truces') with local rulers, ensuring that British shipping through the Gulf was free from 'pirate' attacks and bringing the Emirates under British protection.
1892 The Trucial Sheiks signed Exclusive Agreements with Britain, agreeing not to cede, sell, or mortgage territory to another power.
1952 Trucial Council established by the seven sheikdoms of Abu Dhabi, Ajman, Dubai, Fujairah, Ras al Khaimah, Sharjah, and Umm al Qawain, with a view to later forming a federation.
1958 Large-scale exploitation of oil reserves, which led to rapid economic progress.
1968 Britain's announcement that it would remove its forces from the Persian Gulf by 1971 led to an abortive attempt to arrange a federation between the seven Trucial States and Bahrain and Qatar.
1971 Bahrain and Qatar ceded from the Federation of Arab Emirates, which was dissolved. Six Trucial States formed United Arab Emirates, with ruler of Abu Dhabi, Sheik Zayed, as president. Provisional constitution adopted.
1972 The seventh state, Ras al Khaimah, joined the federation.
1976 Sheik Zayed threatened to relinquish presidency unless progress towards centralization became more rapid.
1985 Diplomatic and economic links with Soviet Union and China established.
1987 Diplomatic relations with Egypt restored.
1990–91 Iraqi invasion of Kuwait opposed; UAE troops fought as part of United Nations coalition.
1991 Bank of Commerce and Credit International (BCCI), controlled by Abu Dhabi's ruler, collapsed at a cost to the UAE of $10 billion.
1992 Border dispute with Iran.
1994 Abu Dhabi agreed to pay BCCI creditors $1.8 billion.

SEE ALSO Abu Dhabi; Arabia

coup speeded up the movement towards dissolution of the Soviet Union. During the coup, when Red Army tanks were sent into their capitals with orders to seize radio and television stations, the Estonian and Latvian parliaments followed the earlier example of Lithuania and declared independence. After the coup the largely conservative-communist controlled republics of Azerbaijan, Belarus, and Uzbekistan, as well as the key republic of Ukraine, also joined the Baltics, Georgia, Moldova, and Armenia in declaring their independence.

new union treaty signed At an emergency session of the Congress of People's Deputies, ten republics – the three Baltics, Georgia, and Moldova being the exceptions – declared a willingness to join a new loose confederation, or 'Union of Sovereign States', and acknowledged the rights of republics to secede. This opened the way 6 Sept 1991 for President Gorbachev to formally recognize the independence of the Baltic states by decree.

decentralization and new realities However, concerned at the accumulation of political and economic authority by Russia, several of the republics began to seek full independence so as to escape Russian domination, refusing to sign new economic and political agreements. As a consequence, President Gorbachev occupied the position of a figurehead leader, possessing little real authority, although his position was slightly strengthened by the return of Shevardnadze to head the foreign relations ministry Nov 1991. Instead, the pre-eminent leader in the new USSR, governing significantly from the former office of the CPSU Politburo, was Russia's president, Boris Yeltsin. In Nov 1991 the Russian Republic took over control of the Soviet money supply and exchange rate, and began implementing a market-centred economic reform programme.

On 8 Dec 1991 the most powerful of the republics – Russia, Belarus, and Ukraine – agreed to form the ◊Commonwealth of Independent States (CIS), a development denounced by Gorbachev. By mid-Dec, the five Central Asian republics (Kazakhstan, Kyrgyzstan, Tajikistan, Turkmenistan, and Uzbekistan) had announced that they would join the CIS, and Gorbachev had agreed on a transfer of power from the centralized government to the CIS. The remaining republics (Armenia, Azerbaijan, and Moldova) except Georgia, torn by civil war, joined the others in signing agreements on 21 Dec to establish the commonwealth, formally designated an alliance of independent states. The formal dissolution of the USSR came on 25 Dec when Gorbachev resigned as president. ▷ *See feature on pp. 1090–1091.*

UNITA acronym for ***União Nacional para a Independencia Total de Angola*** (National Union for the Total Independence of Angola), Angolan nationalist movement founded by Jonas ◊Savimbi 1966. Backed by South Africa, UNITA continued to wage guerrilla warfare against the ruling People's Movement for the Liberation of Angola (MPLA) after the latter gained control of the country 1976. A peace agreement was signed May 1991, but fighting recommenced Sept 1992, after Savimbi disputed an election victory for the ruling party, and escalated into a bloody civil war 1993. A peace agreement was signed 1994. President José Dos Santos offered Savimbi the vice presidency in a coalition government 1996, but Savimbi rejected the proposal. An agreement was made 1998 for the demilitarization of UNITA, and its transformation into a political party.

Unitarianism a Christian denomination that rejects the orthodox doctrine of the Trinity, asserts the fatherhood of God and the brotherhood of humanity, and gives a pre-eminent position to Jesus as a religious teacher, while denying his divinity. Unitarians believe in individual conscience and reason as a guide to right action, rejecting the doctrines of original sin, the atonement, and eternal punishment. Unitarianism is widespread in England and North America. See also ◊Arianism.

unitary authority administrative unit of Great Britain. From 1996 the two-tier structure of local government ceased to exist in Scotland and Wales, and in some parts of England, and was replaced by unitary authorities, responsible for all local government services.

Following the review of the structure of local government by the Local Government Commission, the Scottish regions and districts were replaced by 32 unitary authorities, and the Welsh counties and districts by 22 unitary authorities. 46 unitary authorities were created in England, in addition to the existing London and Metropolitan Boroughs, which already had unitary powers. In some counties the two-tier structure has been retained.

United Arab Emirates federation in SW Asia, on the Arabian Gulf, bounded NW by Qatar, SW by Saudi Arabia, and SE by Oman. *See country box opposite.*

United Arab Republic union formed 1958, broken 1961, between ◊Egypt and ◊Syria. Egypt continued to use the name after the breach up until 1971.

United Artists (UA) Hollywood film production, releasing, and distribution company formed 1919 by silent-screen stars Charles Chaplin, Mary Pickford, and Douglas Fairbanks, and director D W Griffith, in order to take control of their artistic and financial affairs. The company nearly collapsed after the box-office disaster of Michael Cimino's *Heaven's Gate* 1980, and UA was subsequently bought by Metro-Goldwyn-Mayer.

United Democratic Front moderate multiracial political organization in South Africa, founded 1983. It was an important focus of anti-apartheid action in South Africa until 1989, when the African National Congress and Pan-Africanist Congress were unbanned.

United Kingdom (UK) country in NW Europe off the coast of France, consisting of England, Scotland, Wales, and Northern Ireland. *See country box on page 1094.*

United Nations (UN) association of states for international peace, security, and cooperation, with its headquarters in New York. The UN was

UNITED KINGDOM
of Great Britain and Northern Ireland (UK)

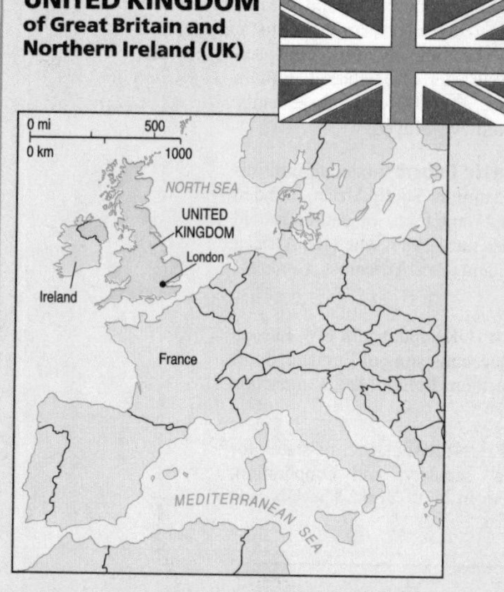

area 244,100 sq km/94,247 sq mi
capital London
major towns/cities Birmingham, Glasgow, Leeds, Sheffield, Liverpool, Manchester, Edinburgh, Bradford, Bristol, Belfast, Newcastle, Cardiff
major ports London, Grimsby, Southampton, Liverpool
physical features became separated from European continent about 6000 BC; rolling landscape, increasingly mountainous towards the N, with Grampian Mountains in Scotland, Pennines in N England, Cambrian Mountains in Wales; rivers include Thames, Severn, and Spey
territories Anguilla, Bermuda, British Antarctic Territory, British Indian Ocean Territory, British Virgin Islands, Cayman Islands, Falkland Islands, Gibraltar, Hong Kong (until 1997), Montserrat, Pitcairn Islands, St Helena and Dependencies (Ascension, Tristan da Cunha), Turks and Caicos Islands. The Channel Islands and the Isle of Man are not part of the UK but are direct dependencies of the crown
head of state Queen Elizabeth II from 1952
head of government Tony Blair from 1997
political system liberal democracy
administrative divisions England: 35 counties, 27 unitary authorities, 6 metropolitan counties; Scotland: 32 unitary authorities; Wales: 22 unitary authorities; Northern Ireland: 26 districts within 6 geographical counties
political parties Conservative and Unionist Party, right of centre; Labour Party, moderate left of centre; Social and Liberal Democrats, centre-left; Scottish National Party (SNP), Scottish nationalist; Plaid Cymru (Welsh Nationalist Party), Welsh nationalist; Official Ulster Unionist Party (OUP), Democratic Unionist Party (DUP), Ulster People's Unionist Party (UPUP), all Northern Ireland right of centre, in favour of remaining part of United Kingdom; Social Democratic Labour Party (SDLP), Northern Ireland, moderate left of centre; Green Party, ecological
armed forces 254,300 (1994)
conscription none
defence spend (% GDP) 3.4 (1994)
education spend (% GNP) 5.2 (1992)
health spend (% GDP) 5.9 (1993)
death penalty abolished for ordinary crimes only 1973; laws provide for the death penalty for exceptional crimes only; last execution 1964
population 58,970,000 (1998 est)
population growth rate 0.1% (2000–05)
age distribution (% of total population) <15 19.6%, 15–65 65.0%, >65 15.5% (1995)
ethnic distribution 81.5% English; 9.6% Scots; 2.4% Irish; 1.9% Welsh; 2% West Indians, Asians, Africans
population density (per sq km) 238 (1994)
urban population (% of total) 89 (1995)
labour force 50% of population: 2% agriculture, 29% industry, 69% services (1990)
unemployment 8.3% (1995)
child mortality rate (under 5, per 1,000 live births) 7 (1998)
life expectancy 75 (men), 79 (women)
education (compulsory years) 11
literacy rate 99%
languages English, Welsh, Gaelic
religions Church of England (established church); other Protestant denominations, Roman Catholic, Muslim, Jewish, Hindu, Sikh
TV sets (per 1,000 people) 612 (1996)
currency pound sterling (£)
GDP (US $) 1,278.4 billion (1997)
GDP per capita (PPP) (US $) 18,360 (1995)
growth rate 2.4% (1994/95)
average annual inflation 2.9% (1995)
major trading partners Germany, USA, France, the Netherlands, Japan
resources coal, limestone, crude petroleum, natural gas, tin, iron, salt, sand and gravel
industries machinery and transport equipment, steel, metals and metal products, food processing, shipbuilding, aircraft, petroleum and gas extraction, electronics and communications, chemicals and chemical products, business and financial services, tourism
exports industrial and electrical machinery, automatic data processing equipment, motor vehicles, petroleum, chemicals, finished and semi-finished manufactured products, agricultural products and foodstuffs. Principal market: Germany 14.0% (1993)
imports industrial and electrical machinery, motor vehicles, food and live animals, petroleum, computing equipment, consumer goods, textiles, paper, paper board. Principal source: Germany 15.1% (1993)
arable land 24.8% (1993)
agricultural products wheat, barley, potatoes, sugar beet, fruit, vegetables; livestock rearing (chiefly poultry and cattle), animal products, and fishing

HISTORY

c. 400–200 BC British Isles conquered by the Celts.
55–54 BC Romans led by Julius Caesar raided Britain.
AD 43–60 Romans conquered England and Wales, which formed the province of Britannia; Picts stopped them penetrating further N.
5th–7th Cs After Romans withdrew, Anglo-Saxons overran most of England and formed kingdoms, including Wessex, Northumbria, and Mercia; Wales was stronghold of Celts.
500 The Scots, a Gaelic-speaking tribe from Ireland, settled in the kingdom of Dalriada (Argyll).
5th–6th Cs British Isles converted to Christianity.
829 King Egbert of Wessex overlord of all England.
c. 843 Kenneth McAlpin unified Scots and Picts to become first king of Scotland.
9th–11th Cs Vikings raided British Isles, conquering N and E England and N Scotland.
1066 Normans led by William I defeated Anglo-Saxons at Battle of Hastings and conquered England.
12th–13th Cs Anglo-Norman adventurers conquered much of Ireland, but effective English rule remained limited to area around Dublin.
1215 King John of England forced to sign Magna Carta, which placed limits on royal powers.
1265 Simon de Montfort summoned the first English parliament in which the towns were represented.
1284 Edward I of England invaded Scotland; Scots defeated English at Battle of Stirling Bridge 1297.
1314 Robert the Bruce led Scots to victory over English at Battle of Bannockburn; England recognized Scottish independence 1328.
1455–85 Wars of the Roses: House of York and House of Lancaster disputed the English throne.
1513 Battle of Flodden: Scots defeated by English; James IV of Scotland killed.
1529 Henry VIII founded Church of England after break with Rome; Reformation effective in England and Wales, but not in Ireland.
1536–43 Acts of Union united Wales with England.
1541 Irish parliament recognized Henry VIII of England as king of Ireland.
1603 Union of crowns: James VI of Scotland became James I of England also.
1607 First successful English colony in Virginia marked start of three centuries of overseas expansion.
1610 James I established plantation of Ulster in Northern Ireland with Protestant settlers from England and Scotland.
1642–52 English Civil War between king and Parliament, with Scottish intervention and Irish rebellion, resulted in victory for Parliament.
1649 Execution of Charles I; Oliver Cromwell appointed Lord Protector 1653; monarchy restored 1660.
1689 'Glorious Revolution' confirmed power of Parliament; replacement of James II by William III resisted by Scottish Highlanders and Catholic Irish.
1707 Act of Union between England and Scotland created United Kingdom of Great Britain, governed by a single parliament.
1721–42 Cabinet government developed under Robert Walpole, in effect the first prime minister.
1745 'The Forty-Five': rebellion of Scottish Highlanders in support of Jacobite pretender to throne; defeated 1746.
c. 1760–1850 Industrial Revolution: Britain became the first industrial nation in the world.
1775–83 American Revolution: Britain lost 13 American colonies; empire continued to expand in Canada, India, and Australia.
1793–1815 Britain at war with revolutionary France, except for 1802–03.
1800 Act of Union created United Kingdom of Great Britain and Ireland, governed by a single parliament; effective 1801.
1832 Great Reform Act extended the franchise; further extensions 1867, 1884, 1918, and 1928.
1846 Repeal of the Corn Laws reflected shift of power from landowners to industrialists.
1870 Home Rule Party formed to campaign for restoration of a separate Irish parliament.
1880–90s Rapid expansion of British Empire in Africa.
1906–14 Liberal governments introduced social reforms and curbed power of House of Lords.
1914–18 United Kingdom played a leading part in World War I; Empire expanded in the Middle-East.
1919–21 Anglo-Irish war ended with secession of S Ireland as Irish Free State; Ulster remained within United Kingdom of Great Britain and Northern Ireland with some powers devolved to a Northern Irish parliament.
1924 First Labour government led by Ramsay MacDonald.
1926 General Strike arose from coal dispute. Equality of status recognized between United Kingdom and Dominions of British Commonwealth.
1931 National Government coalition formed to face economic crisis; unemployment reached 3 million.
1939–45 United Kingdom played a leading part in World War II.
1945 First Scottish Nationalist MP elected; first Welsh Nationalist MP 1966.
1945–51 Labour government of Clement Attlee created welfare state and nationalized major industries.
1947–71 Decolonization and end of British Empire.
1969 Start of the Troubles in Northern Ireland; Northern Irish Parliament suspended 1972.
1973 UK joined European Economic Community.
1979 Referenda failed to approve devolution of power to Scottish and Welsh assemblies.
1979–90 Conservative government of Margaret Thatcher pursued radical free-market economic policies.
1982 Unemployment over 3 million. Falklands War.
1991 British troops took part in US-led war against Iraq under United Nations umbrella. Severe economic recession and unemployment.
1993 Peace proposal for Northern Ireland, the Downing Street Declaration, issued jointly with Irish government.
1994 Irish Republican Army and Protestant paramilitary declared cease-fire in Northern Ireland.
1996 IRA renewed bombing campaign in London.
1997 Labour Party won landslide victory in general election. Tony Blair became prime minister. Blair launched new Anglo-Irish peace initiative; IRA declared a cease-fire. Princess Diana killed in car crash. Meeting between Blair and Sinn Fein leader Gerry Adams; all-party peace talks began in Northern Ireland. Scotland and Wales voted in favour of devolution.
1998 Historic multiparty agreement (known as the Good Friday Agreement) was reached on the future of Northern Ireland. Peace plan approved by referenda in both Northern Ireland and the Irish Republic. UUP leader, David Trimble, elected first minister. 'Real IRA' exploded large bomb in Omagh, Northern Ireland. Strong anti-terrorist legislation passed. Nobel Peace Prize jointly awarded to John Hume and David Trimble.

SEE ALSO Britain, ancient; British Empire; England; Industrial Revolution; Ireland, Northern; Roman Britain; Scotland; Wales established 1945 by 51 states as a successor to the ◊League of Nations, and has played a role in many areas, such as refugees, development assistance, disaster relief, cultural cooperation, and peacekeeping. Its membership in 1996 stood at 185 states, and the total proposed budget for 1995–96 (raised by the member states) was $2,600 million supporting more than 50,000 staff. Boutros ◊Boutros-Ghali was succeeded as secretary general in 1996 by Kofi ◊Annan. There are six official working languages: English, French, Russian, Spanish, Chinese, and Arabic. The name 'United Nations' was coined by the US president Franklin D Roosevelt.

The principal institutions are the General Assembly, the Security Council, the Economic and Social Council, the Trusteeship Council, all based in New York; and the International Court of Justice in The Hague, Netherlands. There are many specialized agencies, involved either in promoting communication between states (such as the International Telecommunication Union, ITU), or concerned with welfare of states, such as the World Health Organization (WHO), the UN Educational, Scientific and Cultural Organization (UNESCO), and the International Bank for Reconstruction and Development (World Bank). The work of the specialized welfare agencies consists mainly of research and field work in the developing countries.

In its peacekeeping role, acting in pursuance of Security Council resolutions, the UN has had mixed success. The number of peacekeeping operations increased from 1 between 1975–85 to 25 between 1985–95; in 1995 its 65,000 peacekeepers cost a total of $2 billion. The UN has always suffered from a lack of adequate and independent funds and forces. In 1996, owed $3 billion by its members (two-thirds by the USA and Russia), it was forced to slash many programmes and cut staff by 10%; in the same year, UN forces were largely replaced by NATO units. The USA regularly (often alone or nearly so) votes against General Assembly resolutions on aggression, international law, human-rights abuses, and disarmament, and has exercised its veto on the Security Council more times than any other member (the UK is second, France a distant third). *See list of tables on p.1177.*

United Provinces federation of states in N Netherlands 1579–1795, comprising Holland, Zeeland, Friesland, Gelderland, Utrecht, Overijssel, and Groningen. Established by the Union of ◊Utrecht, its aim was to assert independence from the Spanish crown. See ◊Netherlands.

United Provinces of Agra and Oudh former province of British India, which formed the major part of the state of ◊Uttar Pradesh; see also ◊Agra, ◊Oudh.

United States architecture little survives of early indigenous American architecture, although the early settlers in each region recorded the house and village styles of the local Indians. The most notable prehistoric remains are the cliff dwellings in the Southwest. Archaeologists have also discovered traces of structures associated with the moundbuilding peoples in the Mississippi river valley. Subsequent architectural forms are those that came with colonizers from European cultures and were adapted to American conditions and social development.

16th and 17th centuries The earliest European architectural influences were those of the Spanish colonizers, coming north from their Mexican colony or from early settlements in Florida; most were small or transitory. The dominant American colonial architecture came to the east coast from 17th-century English immigrants, but also from Dutch, Swedish, and German settlers. Generally, new arrivals attempted to reconstruct the architecture they had known in their home countries, making adaptations to available materials and craftsmanship. Houses most often were small, had massive chimney stacks, and were timber-framed with brick, clapboard, or wattle-and-daub walls. By the end of the century, more elegant and elaborate examples of Jacobean and Queen Anne styles were built, and imposing public architecture was constructed, such as William and Mary College in Williamsburg, Virginia.

18th century The Neo-Classical style dominated and was referred to as Georgian architecture, although designs lagged behind English sources, and the scale of projects was generally modest. Itinerant master craftsmen with plan-and-model books, working for educated colonial sponsors, diffused European-style developments along the eastern seaboard. Many fine homes were built, with distinct variations preferred in each of the colonial regions. Churches and public buildings were influenced by Christopher Wren. As settlement moved inland, the rough-hewn timber or log cabin became an American architectural mainstay. Other, finer, buildings from this period include numerous plantation houses; Dutch patroon mansions along the Hudson River in New York or in E Pennsylvania; the then Virginia capital of Williamsburg; churches with steeples, such as Christ Church in Philadelphia; and public buildings, such as Independence Hall in Philadelphia.

19th century Early in the century, Neo-Classicism was introduced by Thomas Jefferson (Jefferson's house at Monticello, the Federal Capitol at Washington by William Thornton (1759–1828), and the ◊White House by James Hoban). Other structures from the first half of the century include the Greek-revival work of Charles Bulfinch and Benjamin Latrobe (1764–1820), notably in their work on the US Capitol. After the Civil War, Romanesque forms in stone and brick were promoted by Henry Hobson Richardson. An appreciation for and adaptation of French Renaissance design emerged, as well as a Romantic revival of Gothic architecture in both domestic and public buildings.

20th century Most dramatically, this was the century of the modern architect, and America became a centre for innovative and creative design; the ◊skyscraper became the fundamental US contribution to world architecture. Spare, functional Modernist form predominated by the mid-century, but by the 1980s a reinterpretation of earlier styles was promoted by Post-Modernists. Notable 20th-century architects working in the USA include Frank Lloyd Wright, Louis Henry Sullivan, Walter Gropius, Ludwig Mies van der Rohe, Eliel and Eero Saarinen, I M Pei, Philip Johnson, Robert Venturi, and Michael Graves.

United States art painting and sculpture in the USA from colonial times to the present. The unspoiled landscapes romantically depicted in the 18th and 19th centuries gave way to realistic city scenes in the 20th. Modern movements have flourished in the USA, among them Abstract Expressionism and Pop art.

colonial Painting in colonial America begins with the work of artist-explorers and naturalists, of whom the 16th-century watercolourist, John White, is a notable example. A provincial form of portrait painting, Dutch and English, next developed as the colonies were settled, exemplified by the work of the 'Freake Limner' (painter of the Freake family), c. 1670–5, in New England.

18th century The early 18th century saw a more elaborate reflection of European portraiture in John Smibert (1688–1751, a Scot from Edinburgh who painted in the style of Kneller), Robert Feke, and others. In the later 18th century, London called to American-born painters, for example Benjamin West and J S Copley, but both artists had much influence in America, for example on Charles Willson Peale and John Trumbull. A native development in the 18th and 19th centuries was that of a 'primitive' or folk art practised by sign painters and other craftspeople and amateurs, Edward Hicks being of note.

19th century Romanticism, more particularly in landscape, was a growth of the 19th century, first marked by the imaginative paintings of Washington Allston, then by, for example Thomas Cole, Albert Bierstadt, and Caleb Bingham, Cole being one of a number of artists painting along the Hudson River and loosely grouped under the title of the 'Hudson River School'. The explorations of landscape painters were complemented by those of the artist-naturalist Audubon. The later 19th century saw many artists again turning back to Rome, Paris or London for training, inspiration, or a sympathetic environment. James McNeill Whistler and John Singer Sargent were the outstanding examples, while a host of others studied in the academic *ateliers* of Munich and Paris. The high regard in which Winslow Homer and Thomas Eakins are held stems in part from their sturdy independence of this trend, and their portrayal of US life.

early 20th century The early 20th century saw determined and courageous efforts to look at the USA in an American way. 'The Eight', a group of 1908 (Henri, Glackens, Luks, Prendergast, Lawson, Shinn, Sloan, and Davies), though varied in their individual styles, combined to make a gesture towards this end. They were dubbed the 'Ashcan School' in reference to the liking that appeared for city squalor. It has its continuance in the work of Bellows, Hopper, Marsh, and others. The realism first applied to New York expanded into the 'regionalism' of the 1930s, as in the work of Benton, Curry, and Grant Wood. Enthusiasm for a modern art of international validity was quickened, however, by the celebrated Armory Show of 1913, and by acquaintance with the School of Paris in the expatriate 1920s (see John Marin and Marsden Hartley). The influence of modern European art was intensified by World War II, which brought many artists to the USA from Europe, such as Chagall, Léger, Grosz, and Feininger.

mid-20th century Abstract Expressionism was exemplified by the inventor of action painting, Jackson Pollock, and the spiritual Mark Rothko. The more politically concerned Ben Shahn created influential graphics. The sculptor Alexander Calder invented mobiles.

late 20th century The Pop-art movement, led by artists such as Andy Warhol and Roy Lichtenstein, dominated the 1960s and fostered multimedia works and performance art in the following decades. US sculptors of the 20th century include Carl Andre, David Smith, Louise Nevelson, and George Segal.

United States literature early US literature falls into two distinct periods: colonial writing of the 1600s–1770s, largely dominated by the Puritans, and post-Revolutionary literature from the 1780s, when the ideal of US literature developed, and poetry, fiction, and drama began to evolve on national principles. Early 19th-century Romanticism contrasted sharply with the social realism of subsequent post-Civil War writing. 20th-century US writers have continued the trend towards realism, as well as developing various forms of modernist experimentation.

colonial (1607–1770s) Literature of this period includes travel books and religious verse, but is mainly theological: Roger Williams (1603–1683), Cotton Mather, and Jonathan Edwards (1703–1758) were typical Puritan writers. The *Autobiography* of Benjamin Franklin (1706–1790) is the first work of more than historical interest.

post-Revolutionary (1780s–1820s) This period produced much political writing, by Thomas Paine, Thomas Jefferson (1743–1826), and Alexander Hamilton (1755–1804), and one noteworthy poet, Philip Freneau (1752–1832).

early 19th century The influence of English Romantics became evident, notably on the poems of William Cullen Bryant, Washington Irving's tales, Charles Brockden Brown's Gothic fiction, and James Fenimore Cooper's novels of frontier life. During 1830–60 intellectual life was centred in New England, which produced the essayists Ralph Waldo Emerson, Henry Thoreau, and Oliver Wendell Holmes; the poets Henry Wadsworth Longfellow, James Lowell, and John Whittier; and the novelists Nathaniel Hawthorne and Louisa May Alcott. Outside the New England circle were the novelists Edgar Allan Poe and Herman Melville.

post-Civil War period (1865–1900) The disillusionment of this period found expression in the realistic or psychological novel. Ambrose Bierce and Stephen Crane wrote realistic war stories; Mark Twain and Bret Harte dealt with Western life; the growth of industrialism led to novels of social realism, notably the works of William Howells and Frank Norris; and Henry James and his disciple Edith Wharton developed the novel of psychological analysis among the well-to-do. The dominant poets were Walt Whitman and Emily Dickinson. The short story flourished, its leading practitioners being Hawthorne, Poe, James, Harte, and O Henry.

20th century Writers specializing in the short story have included Ring Lardner, Katherine Anne Porter, Flannery O'Connor, William Saroyan, Eudora Welty, Grace Paley, and Raymond Carver.

drama The USA produced a powerful group of dramatist between the wars, including Eugene O'Neill, Maxwell Anderson, Lillian Hellman, Elmer Rice, Thornton Wilder, and Clifford Odets.

'The United States is a country unique in the world because it was populated not merely by people who live in it by the accident of birth, but by those who willed to come here.'

On the **United States**
John Gunther
Inside USA

They were followed by Arthur Miller and Tennessee Williams. A later generation now includes Edward Albee, Neil Simon, David Mamet, John Guare, and Sam Shepard.

poetry Poets like Edwin Arlington Robinson, Carl Sandburg, Vachel Lindsay, Robert Frost, and Edna St Vincent Millay extended the poetic tradition of the 19th century, but after the Imagist movement (see ◊Imagism) of 1912–14 an experimental modern tradition arose with Ezra Pound, T S Eliot, William Carlos Williams, Marianne Moore, 'HD' (Hilda Doolittle), and Wallace Stevens. Attempts at writing the modern US epic include Pound's *Cantos*, Hart Crane's *The Bridge*, and William Carlos Williams' *Paterson*. Among the most striking post-World War II poets are Karl Shapiro, Theodore Roethke, Robert Lowell, Charles Ulson, Sylvia Plath, Gwendolyn Brooks (1917–), Denise Levertov, John Ashbery, A R Ammons (1926–), and Allen Ginsberg.

literary criticism Irving Babbitt (1865–1933), George Santayana (1863–1953), H L Mencken, and Edmund Wilson were dominant figures, followed by Lionel Trilling, Van Wyck Brooks, Yvor Winters (1900–1968), and John Crowe Ransom, author of *The New Criticism* 1941, which stressed structural and linguistic factors. More recently, US criticism has been influenced by French literary theory and the journalistic criticism of Gore Vidal, Tom Wolfe, George Plimpton, and Susan Sontag.

novel The main trends have been realism, as exemplified in the work of Jack London, Upton Sinclair, and Theodore Dreiser, and modernist experimentation. After World War I, Sherwood Anderson, Sinclair Lewis, Ernest Hemingway, William Faulkner, Thomas Wolfe, F Scott Fitzgerald, John Dos Passos, Henry Miller, and Richard Wright established the main literary directions. Among the internationally known novelists since World War II have been John O'Hara, James Michener, Eudora Welty, Truman Capote, J D Salinger, Saul Bellow, John Updike, Norman Mailer, Vladimir Nabokov, Bernard Malamud, Philip Roth, Ralph Ellison, Thomas Pynchon, and James Baldwin. Recent US literature increasingly expresses the cultural pluralism, regional variety, and historical and ethnic range of US life. Feminism and minority consciousness have been brought to the fore by authors such as Alice Walker, Toni Morrison (Nobel Prize 1993), and Maya Angelou.

United States of America (USA) country in North America, extending from the Atlantic Ocean in the east to the Pacific Ocean in the west, bounded north by Canada and south by Mexico, and including the outlying states of Alaska and Hawaii. *See country box on p. 1098 and table on p. 1099.*

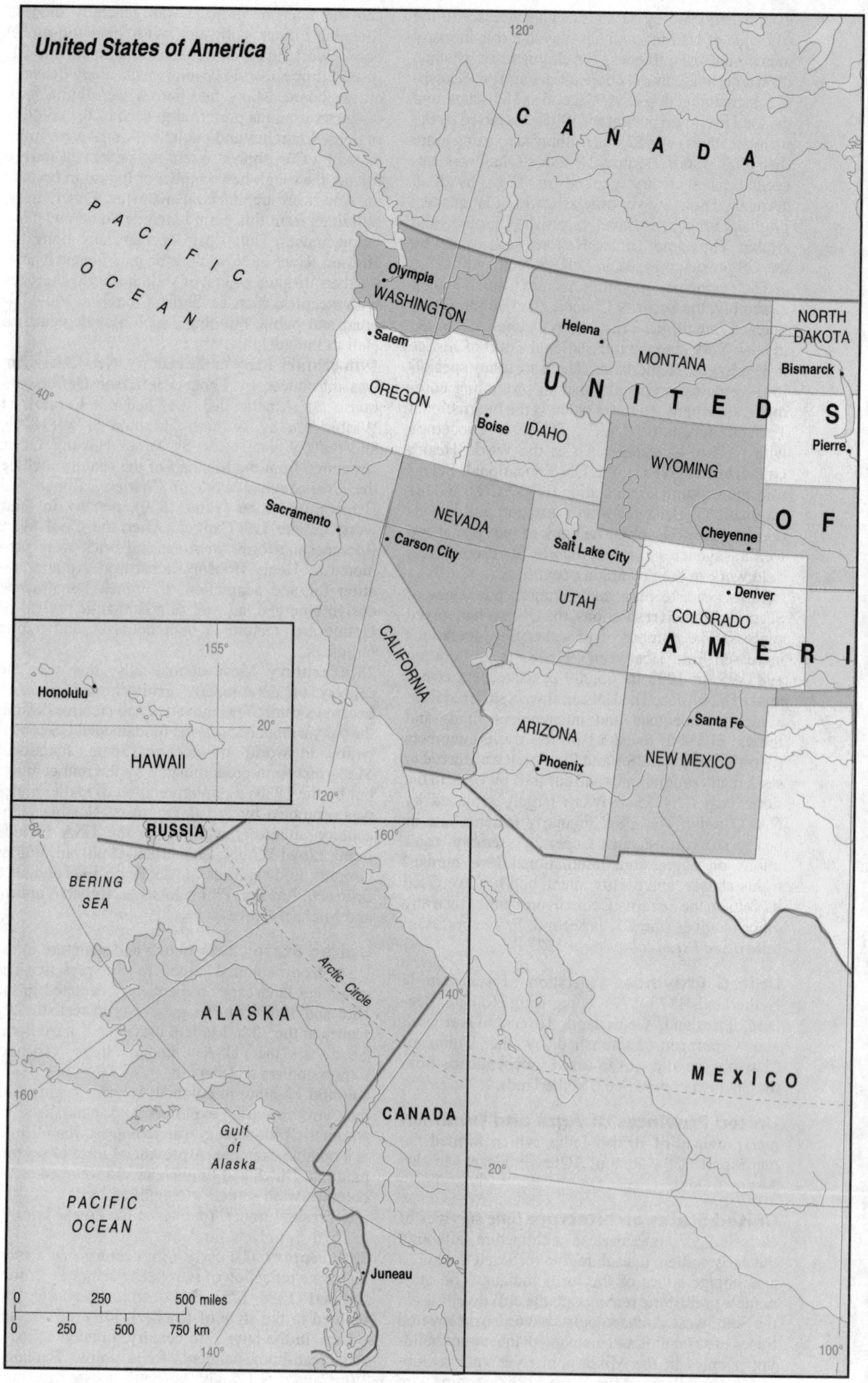

unit trust company that invests its clients' funds in other companies. The units it issues represent holdings of shares, which means unit shareholders have a wider spread of capital than if they bought shares on the stock market. Unit trusts appeal to the small investor, and in recent years, business generated by them has increased rapidly. Many unit trusts specialize in a geographical region or particular type of industry, using their expertise more effectively than if they were to make random investments.

universal in philosophy, a property that is instantiated by all the individual things of a specific class: for example, all red things instantiate 'redness'. Many philosophical debates have centred on the status of universals, including the medieval debate between ◊nominalism and ◊realism.

Universal Hollywood film studio founded 1915 by Carl Laemmle. Despite the immense success of *All Quiet on the Western Front* 1930, the changeover to sound caused a decline in the studio's fortunes, apart from a cycle of horror classics such as *Frankenstein* 1931. In the 1950s the studio re-emerged (as Universal International) with a series of successful romantic comedies with such stars as Rock Hudson and Doris Day. In the 1970s and 1980s Universal became one of the industry's leaders with box-office hits from the producer and director Steven Spielberg such as *ET* 1982 and *Back to the Future* 1985.

universal indicator in chemistry, a mixture of ◊pH indicators, used to gauge the acidity or alkalinity of a solution. Each component changes colour at a different pH value, and so the indicator is capable of displaying a range of colours, according to the pH of the test solution, from red (at pH 1) to purple (at pH 13).

universal joint flexible coupling used to join rotating shafts; for example, the drive shaft in a car. In a typical universal joint the ends of the shafts to be joined end in U-shaped yokes. They dovetail into each other and pivot flexibly about an X-shaped spider. This construction allows side-to-side and up-and-down movement, while still transmitting rotary motion.

universe all of space and its contents, the study of which is called ◊cosmology. The universe is thought to be between 10 billion and 20 billion years old, and is mostly empty space, dotted with ◊galaxies for as far as telescopes can see. The most distant detected galaxies and ◊quasars lie 10 billion light years or more from Earth, and are moving farther apart as the universe expands. Several theories attempt to explain how the universe came into being and evolved; for example, the ◊Big Bang theory of an expanding universe originating in a single explosive event, and the ◊steady-state theory.

Apart from those galaxies within the ◊Local Group, all the galaxies we see display ◊red shifts in their spectra, indicating that they are moving away from us. The farther we look into space, the greater are the observed red shifts, which implies that the more distant galaxies are receding at ever greater speeds. This observation led to the theory of an expanding universe, first proposed by Edwin ◊Hubble 1929, and to Hubble's law, which states that the speed with which one galaxy moves away from another is proportional to its distance from it. Current data suggest that the galaxies are moving apart at a rate of 50–100 kps/30–60 mps for every million ◊parsecs of distance. ▷*See feature on pp. 70–71.*

university institution of higher learning for those who have completed primary and secondary education. The first European university was Salerno in Italy, established in the 9th century, followed by Bologna, Paris, Oxford, and Cambridge, and Montpellier in the 12th century and Toulouse in the 13th century. The universities of Prague, Vienna, Heidelberg, and Cologne were established in the 14th

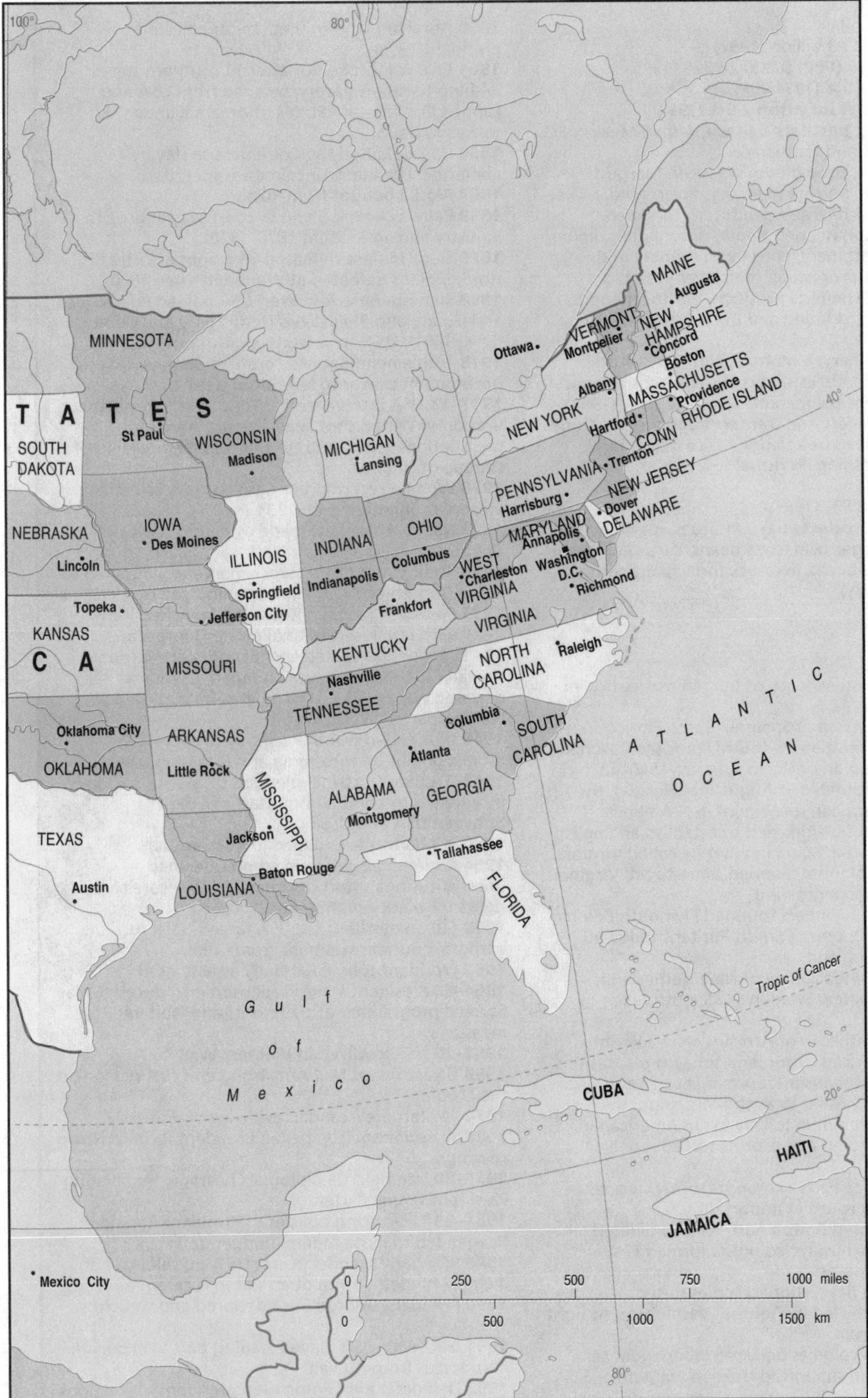

century as well as many French universities, including those at Avignon, Orléans, Cahors, Grenoble, Angers, and Orange. The universities of Aix, Dole, Poitiers, Caen, Nantes, Besançon, Bourges, and Bordeaux were established in the 15th century. St Andrew's, the first Scottish university, was founded in 1411, and Trinity College, Dublin, in 1591. In the UK, a number of universities were founded in the 19th and earlier 20th centuries mainly in the large cities (London 1836, Manchester 1851, Wales 1893, Liverpool 1903, Bristol 1909, and Reading 1926). These became known as the 'redbrick' universities. After World War II, many more universities were founded, among them Nottingham 1948 and Exeter 1955 and were nicknamed, from their Modernist buildings, the 'plate-glass' universities. In the 1960s seven new universities were established on greenfield sites, including Sussex and York. Seven colleges of advanced technology were given university status. In 1992 the polytechnics and some colleges of higher education already awarding degrees also became universities.

The number of university students in the UK almost doubled after the major expansion of the 1960s to stand at 303,000 in 1991. There was an even greater increase in degree-level students in the public-sector colleges, which educated more graduates than the universities. The more generous funding of traditional universities was phased out and a joint funding council established. Research is funded separately from teaching, and the new universities have gained access to research funds for the first time.

The USA has both state universities (funded by the individual states) and private universities. The oldest universities in the USA are all private: Harvard 1636, William and Mary 1693, Yale 1701, Pennsylvania 1741, and Princeton 1746. Recent innovations include universities serving international areas; for example, the Middle East Technical University 1961 in Ankara, Turkey, supported by the United Nations; the United Nations University in Tokyo 1974; and the British ◊Open University 1969. The Open University has been widely copied; for example, in the National University Consortium set up in the USA 1980.

UNIX multiuser ◊operating system designed for minicomputers but becoming increasingly popular on large microcomputers, workstations, mainframes, and supercomputers. It was developed by AT&T's Bell Laboratories in the USA during the late 1960s, using the programming language ◊C. It could therefore run on any machine with a C compiler, so ensuring its wide portability. Its wide range of functions and flexibility, in addition to the fact that it was available free 1976–1983, have made it widely used by universities and in commercial software.

unleaded petrol petrol manufactured without the addition of ◊antiknock. It has a slightly lower octane rating than leaded petrol, but has the advantage of not polluting the atmosphere with lead compounds. Many cars can be converted to running on unleaded petrol by altering the timing of the engine, and most new cars are designed to do so. Cars fitted with a ◊catalytic converter must use unleaded fuel.

Aromatic hydrocarbons and alkenes are added to unleaded petrol instead of lead compounds to increase the octane rating. After combustion the hydrocarbons produce volatile organic compounds. These have been linked to cancer, and are involved in the formation of phytochemical smog. A low-lead fuel is less toxic than unleaded petrol for use in cars that are not fitted with a catalytic converter.

The use of unleaded petrol has been standard in the USA for some years. Its use is increasing in the UK (encouraged by a lower rate of tax than that levied on leaded petrol). In 1987 only 5% of petrol sold in the UK was unleaded; by 1992 this had risen to 45%. Between 1988 and 1990 UK lead emission fell by 30%.

unnilennium synthesized radioactive element of the ◊transactinide series, symbol Une, atomic number 109, relative atomic mass 266. It was first produced 1982 at the Laboratory for Heavy Ion Research in Darmstadt, Germany, by fusing bismuth and iron nuclei; it took a week to obtain a single new, fused nucleus. The element is (like unniloctium, unnilpentium, unnilseptium, ununnilium, and unununium) as yet unnamed; temporary identification was assigned until a name is approved by the International Union of Pure and Applied Chemistry.

unnilhexium temporary identification assigned to the element ◊rutherfordium 1974–94.

unniloctium synthesized, radioactive element of the ◊transactinide series, symbol Uno, atomic number 108, relative atomic mass 265. It was first synthesized 1984 by the Laboratory for Heavy Ion Research in Darmstadt, Germany.

unnilpentium synthesized, radioactive, metallic element of the ◊transactinide series, symbol Unp, atomic number 105, relative atomic mass 261. Six isotopes have been synthesized, each with very short (fractions of a second) half-lives. Two institutions claim to have been the first to produce it: the Joint Institute for Nuclear Research in Dubna, Russia, 1967 (proposed name nielsbohrium); and the University of California at Berkeley, USA, who disputed the Soviet claim, 1970 (proposed name hahnium).

unnilquadium temporary identification assigned to the element ◊dubnium 1964–95.

unnilseptium synthesized, radioactive element of the ◊transactinide series, symbol Uns, atomic number 107, relative atomic mass 262. It was first synthesized by the Joint Institute for Nuclear Research in Dubna, Russia, 1976; in 1981 the Laboratory for Heavy Ion Research in Darmstadt, Germany, confirmed its existence.

Unrepresented Nations' and Peoples' Organization (UNPO) international association founded 1991 to represent ethnic and minority groups unrecognized by the United Nations and to defend the right to self-determination of oppressed peoples around the world. The founding charter was signed by representatives of Tibet, the Kurds, Turkestan, Armenia, Estonia, Georgia, the Volga region, the Crimea, the Greek minority in Albania, North American Indians, Australian Aborigines, West Irians, West Papuans, the minorities of the Cordillera in the Philippines, and the non-Chinese in Taiwan.

unsaturated compound chemical compound in which two adjacent atoms are bonded by a double or triple covalent bond. Examples are ◊alkenes and

UNITED STATES OF AMERICA

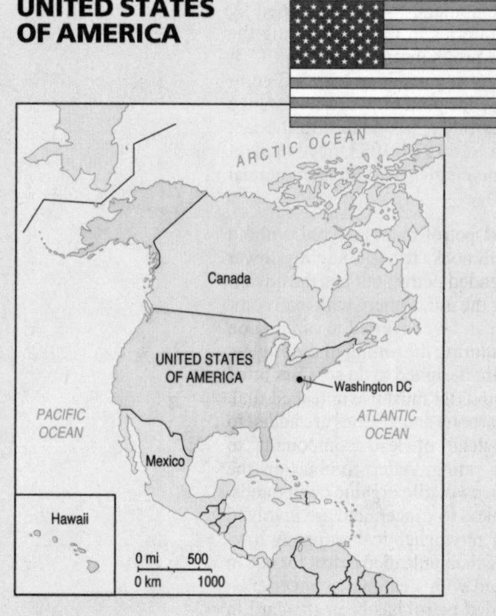

area 9,372,610 km/3,618,764 mi
capital Washington DC
major towns/cities New York, Los Angeles, Chicago, Philadelphia, Detroit, San Francisco, Washington, Dallas, San Diego, San Antonio, Houston, Boston, Baltimore, Phoenix, Indianapolis, Memphis, Honolulu, San José
physical features topography and vegetation from tropical (Hawaii) to arctic (Alaska); mountain ranges parallel with E and W coasts; the Rocky Mountains separate rivers emptying into the Pacific from those flowing into the Gulf of Mexico; Great Lakes in N; rivers include Hudson, Mississippi, Missouri, Colorado, Columbia, Snake, Rio Grande, Ohio
territories the commonwealths of Puerto Rico and Northern Marianas; Guam, the US Virgin Islands, American Samoa, Wake Island, Midway Islands, and Johnston and Sand Islands
head of state Bill Clinton from 1993
head of government Bill Clinton from 1993
political system liberal democracy
administrative divisions 50 states
political parties Democratic Party, liberal centre; Republican Party, centre-right
armed forces 1,650,500 (1994)
conscription none
defence spend (% GDP) 4.3 (1994)
education spend (% GNP) 5.3 (1992)
health spend (% GDP) 6.2 (1993)
death penalty retained and used for ordinary crimes
population 270,312,000 (1998 est)
population growth rate 0.8% (2000–05)
age distribution (% of total population) <15 22.0%, 15–65 65.3%, >65 12.6% (1995)
ethnic distribution approximately three-quarters of the population are of European origin, including 29% who trace their descent from Britain and Ireland, 8% from Germany, 5% from Italy, and 3% each from Scandinavia and Poland; 12% are African-Americans, 8% Hispanic, and 3% Asian and Pacific islander; African-Americans form 30% of the population of the states of the 'Deep South', namely Alabama, Georgia, Louisiana, Mississippi, and South Carolina; Asians are most concentrated in California
population density (per sq km) 28 (1994)
urban population (% of total) 76 (1995)
labour force 50% of population: 3% agriculture, 26% industry, 71% services (1990)
unemployment 5.6% (1995)
child mortality rate (under 5, per 1,000 live births) 9 (1997)
life expectancy men 73, women 80
education (compulsory years) 10
literacy rate 99%
languages English, Spanish
religions Christian 86.5% (Roman Catholic 26%, Baptist 19%, Methodist 8%, Lutheran 5%); Jewish 1.8%; Muslim 0.5%; Buddhist and Hindu less than 0.5%
TV sets (per 1,000 people) 806 (1996)
currency US dollar
GDP (US $) 7,819.3 billion (1997)
GDP per capita (PPP) (US $) 26,525 (1995)
growth rate 2.0% (1994/95)
average annual inflation 2.6% (1994)
major trading partners Canada, Japan, Mexico, EU (principally UK and Germany)
resources coal, copper (world's second-largest producer), iron, bauxite, mercury, silver, gold, nickel, zinc (world's fifth-largest producer), tungsten, uranium, phosphate, petroleum, natural gas, timber
industries machinery, petroleum refinery and products, food processing, motor vehicles, pig iron and steel, chemical products, electrical goods, metal products, printing and publishing, fertilizers, cement
exports machinery, motor vehicles, agricultural products and foodstuffs, aircraft, weapons, chemicals, electronics. Principal market: Canada 20.2% (1993)
imports machinery and transport equipment, crude and partly refined petroleum, office machinery, textiles and clothing. Principal source: Canada 18.5% (1993)
arable land 18.9% (1993)
agricultural products hay, potatoes, maize, wheat, barley, oats, sugar beet, soya beans, citrus and other fruit, cotton, tobacco; livestock (principally cattle, pigs, and poultry)

HISTORY

c. 15,000 BC First evidence of human occupation in North America.
1513 Ponce de Léon of Spain explored Florida in search of the Fountain of Youth; Francisco Coronado explored SW region of North America 1540–42.
1565 Spanish founded St Augustine (Florida), the first permanent European settlement in N America.
1585 Sir Walter Raleigh tried to establish an English colony on Roanoke Island in what he called Virginia.
1607 English colonists founded Jamestown, Virginia, and began tobacco growing.
1620 The Pilgrim Fathers founded Plymouth Colony (near Cape Cod); other English Puritans followed them to New England.
1624 Dutch formed colony of New Netherland; Swedes formed New Sweden 1638; both taken by England 1664.
17th–18th Cs Millions of Africans were sold into slavery on American cotton and tobacco plantations.
1763 British victory over France in Seven Years' War secured territory as far W as the Mississippi river.
1765 British attempted to levy tax in American colonies with Stamp Act; protest forced repeal in 1767.
1773 'Boston Tea Party': colonists threw cargoes of tea into sea in protest at import duty.
1774 British closed Boston harbour and billeted troops in Massachusetts; colonists formed First Continental Congress.
1775 American Revolution: colonies raised Continental Army led by George Washington to fight against British rule.
1776 American colonies declared independence; France and Spain supported them in war with Britain.
1781 Americans defeated British at Battle of Yorktown; rebel states formed loose confederation, codified in the Articles of Confederation.
1783 Treaty of Paris: Britain accepted loss of colonies.
1787 'Founding Fathers' devised new constitution for the United States of America.
1789 Washington elected first president of the USA.
1791 Bill of Rights guaranteed individual freedom.
1803 Louisiana Purchase: France sold former Spanish lands between Mississippi River and Rocky Mountains to USA.
1812–14 War with Britain arose from dispute over blockade rights during Napoleonic Wars.
1819 USA bought Florida from Spain.
19th Cs Mass immigration from Europe; settlers moved westwards, crushing Indian resistance and claiming 'manifest destiny' of USA to control North America. By end of century, number of states in the Union had increased from 17 to 45.
1846–48 Mexican War: Mexico ceded vast territory to USA.
1854 Kansas–Nebraska Act heightened controversy over slavery in southern states; abolitionists formed Republican Party.
1860 Abraham Lincoln (Republican) elected president.
1861 Civil war broke out after 11 southern states, wishing to retain slavery, seceded from USA and formed Confederate States of America under Jefferson Davis.
1865 USA defeated the Confederacy; slavery abolished; President Lincoln assassinated.
1867 Alaska bought from Russia.
1869 Railway linked E and W coasts; rapid growth of industry and agriculture 1870–1920.
1876 Sioux Indians defeated US troops at Little Big Horn; Indians defeated at Wounded Knee 1890.
1898 Spanish–American War: USA gained Puerto Rico and Guam; also Philippines (until 1946) and Cuba (until 1901); USA annexed Hawaii.
1913 16th amendment to constitution gave federal government power to levy income tax.
1917–18 USA intervened in World War I; President Woodrow Wilson took leading part in peace negotiations 1919, but USA rejected membership of League of Nations.
1920 Women received the right to vote; sale of alcohol prohibited, until 1933.
1924 Native Americans made citizens of USA by Congress.
1929 'Wall Street Crash': stock market collapse led to Great Depression; 13 million unemployed by 1933.
1933 President Franklin Roosevelt launched 'New Deal' with public works to alleviate Depression.
1941 Japanese attacked US fleet at Pearl Harbor, Hawaii; USA declared war on Japan; Germany declared war on USA, which henceforth played a leading part in World War II.
1945 USA ended war in Pacific by dropping two atomic bombs on Hiroshima and Nagasaki, Japan.
1947 'Truman Doctrine' pledged US aid for nations threatened by communism; start of Cold War between USA and USSR.
1950–53 US forces engaged in Korean War.
1954 Racial segregation in schools deemed unconstitutional; start of campaign to secure civil rights for black Americans.
1962 Cuban missile crisis: USA forced USSR to withdraw nuclear weapons from Cuba.
1963 President John F Kennedy assassinated.
1964–68 President Lyndon Johnson introduced 'Great Society' programme of civil-rights and welfare measures.
1961–75 USA involved in Vietnam War.
1969 US astronaut Neil Armstrong was first person on the Moon.
1974 'Watergate' scandal: evidence of domestic political espionage compelled President Richard Nixon to resign.
1979–80 Iran held US diplomats hostage, humiliating President Jimmy Carter.
1981–89 Tax-cutting policies of President Ronald Reagan led to large federal budget deficit.
1986 'Irangate' scandal: secret US arms sales to Iran illegally funded Contra guerrillas in Nicaragua.
1990 President George Bush declared end to Cold War.
1991 Gulf War: USA played leading part in expelling Iraqi forces from Kuwait.
1992 Democrat Bill Clinton won presidential elections and his running mate Al Gore became vice president.
1996 Clinton re-elected. US missile attacks on Iraq in response to Saddam Hussein's incursions into Kurdish safe havens.
1997 Budget deal agreed between President and Congress. Reform in welfare law brought substantial drop in number of welfare recipients. President used increased veto powers to block military construction projects. Democratic Party's 1996 election fund-raising investigated.
1998 In Aug President Clinton testified before a grand jury that he had misled the public for seven months about his 'inappropriate' relationship with the White House intern, Monica Lewinsky. In response to bombings of US embassies in Tanzania and Kenya by an Islamic group, the USA bombed sites in Afghanistan and Sudan.
1999 Clinton cleared of perjury and obstruction of justice in an impeachment trial.

SEE ALSO American Indian; American Revolution; Civil War, American; Vietnam War

UNITED STATES OF AMERICA: STATES

State	Nickname(s)	Abbreviation(s)	Capital	area in sq km/sq mi	Population (1991)	Joined the union
Alabama	Heart of Dixie/Camellia State	AL, Ala	Montgomery	134,700/51,994	4,089,000	1819
Alaska	Mainland State/The Last Frontier	AK, Alas	Juneau	1,531,100/ 591,005	570,000	1959
Arizona	Grand Canyon State/Apache State	AZ, Ariz	Phoenix	294,100/113,523	3,750,000	1912
Arkansas	Wonder State/Bear State/Land of Opportunity	AR, Ark	Little Rock	137,800/53,191	2,372,000	1836
California	Golden State	CA, Cal, Calif	Sacramento	411,100/158,685	30,380,000	1850
Colorado	Centennial State	CO, Colo	Denver	269,700/104,104	3,377,000	1876
Connecticut	Constitution State/Nutmeg State	CT, Conn	Hartford	13,000/5018	3,291,000	1788
Delaware	First State/Diamond State	DE/Del	Dover	5,300/2,046	680,000	1787
Florida	Sunshine State/Everglade State	FL, Fla	Tallahassee	152,000/58,672	13,277,000	1845
Georgia	Empire State of the South/Peach State	GA, Ga	Atlanta	152,600/58,904	6,623,000	1788
Hawaii	Aloha State	HI	Honolulu	16,800/6,485	1,135,000	1959
Idaho	Gem State	ID, Id, Ida	Boise	216,500/83,569	1,039,000	1890
Illinois	Inland Empire/Prairie State/Land of Lincoln	IL, Ill	Springfield	146,100/56,395	11,543,000	1818
Indiana	Hoosier State	IN, In, Ind	Indianapolis	93,700/36,168	5,610,000	1816
Iowa	Hawkeye State/Corn State	IA, Ia	Des Moines	145,800/56,279	2,795,000	1846
Kansas	Sunflower State/Jayhawker State	KS, Kans	Topeka	213,200/82,295	2,495,000	1861
Kentucky	Bluegrass State	KY, Ky	Frankfort	104,700/40,414	3,713,000	1792
Louisiana	Pelican State/Sugar State/Creole State	LA, La	Baton Rouge	135,900/52,457	4,252,000	1792
Maine	Pine Tree State	ME, Me	Augusta	86,200/33,273	1,235,000	1820
Maryland	Old Line State/Free State	MD, Md	Annapolis	31,600/12,198	4,860,000	1788
Massachusetts	Bay State/Old Colony	MA, Mass	Boston	21,500/8,299	5,996,000	1788
Michigan	Great Lake State/Wolverine State	MI, Mich	Lansing	151,600/58,518	9,368,000	1837
Minnesota	North Star State/Gopher State	MN, Minn	St Paul	218,700/84,418	4,432,000	1858
Mississippi	Magnolia State	MS, Miss	Jackson	123,600/47,710	2,592,000	1817
Missouri	Show Me State/Bullion State	MO, Mo	Jefferson City	180,600/69,712	5,158,000	1821
Montana	Treasure State/Big Sky Country	MT, Mont	Helena	381,200/147,143	808,000	1889
Nebraska	Cornhusker State/Beef State	NE, Neb, Nebr	Lincoln	200,400/77,354	1,593,000	1867
Nevada	Sagebrush State/Silver State/Battleborn State	NV, Nev	Carson City	286,400/110,550	1,284,000	1864
New Hampshire	Granite State	NH	Concord	24,000/9,264	1,105,000	1788
New Jersey	Garden State	NJ	Trenton	20,200/7,797	7,760,000	1787
New Mexico	Land of Enchantment/Sunshine State	NM, N Mex	Santa Fé	315,000/121,590	1,548,000	1912
New York	Empire State	NY	Albany	127,200/49,099	18,058,000	1788
North Carolina	Tar Heel State/Old North State	NC	Raleigh	136,400/52,650	6,737,000	1789
North Dakota	Sioux State/Flickertail State	ND, N Dak	Bismarck	183,100/70,677	635,000	1889
Ohio	Buckeye State	OH, O	Columbus	107,100/41,341	10,939,000	1803
Oklahoma	Sooner State	OK, Okla	Oklahoma City	181,100/69,905	3,175,000	1907
Oregon	Beaver State/Sunset State	OR, Oreg	Salem	251,500/97,079	2,922,000	1859
Pennsylvania	Keystone State	PA, Pa, Penn, Penna	Harrisburg	117,400/45,316	11,961,000	1787
Rhode Island	Little Rhody/Ocean State/Plantation State	RI	Providence	3,100/1,197	1,004,000	1790
South Carolina	Palmetto State	SC	Columbia	80,600/31,112	3,560,000	1788
South Dakota	Coyote State/Sunshine State	SD, S Dak	Pierre	199,800/77,123	703,000	1889
Tennessee	Volunteer State	TN, Tenn	Nashville	109,200/42,151	4,953,000	1796
Texas	Lone Star State	TX, Tex	Austin	691,200/266,803	17,349,000	1845
Utah	Beehive State/Mormon State	UT, Ut	Salt Lake City	219,900/84,881	1,770,000	1896
Vermont	Green Mountain State	VT, Vt	Montpelier	24,900/9,611	567,000	1791
Virginia	Old Dominion State/Mother of Presidents	VA, Va	Richmond	105,600/40,762	6,286,000	1788
Washington	Evergreen State/Chinook State	WA, Wash, Wa	Olympia	176,700/68,206	5,018,000	1889
West Virginia	Mountain State/Panhandle State	WV, W Va	Charleston	62,900/24,279	1,801,000	1863
Wisconsin	Badger State/America's Dairyland	WI, Wis, Wisc	Madison	145,500/56,163	4,955,000	1848
Wyoming	Equality State	WY, Wyo	Cheyenne	253,400/97,812	460,000	1890
District of Columbia (Federal District)	–	DC	Washington	180/69	598,000	established by Act of Congress 1790–91

◊alkynes, where the two adjacent atoms are both carbon, and ◊ketones, where the unsaturation exists between atoms of different elements. The laboratory test for unsaturated compounds is the addition of bromine water; if the test substance is unsaturated, the bromine water will be decolorized.

unsaturated solution solution that is capable of dissolving more solute than it already contains at the same temperature.

untouchable or ***harijan*** member of the lowest Indian ◊caste, formerly forbidden to be touched by members of the other castes.

ununnilium synthesized radioactive element of the ◊transactinide series, symbol Uun, atomic number 110, relative atomic mass 269. It was discovered Oct 1994, detected for a millisecond, at the GSI heavy-ion cyclotron, Darmstadt, Germany, while lead atoms were bombarded with nickel atoms.

unununium synthesized radioactive element of the ◊transactinide series, symbol Uuu, atomic number 111, relative atomic mass 272. It was detected at GSI heavy-ion cyclotron, Darmstadt, Germany, in Dec 1994, when they bombarded bismuth-209 with nickel.

Unzen active volcano on the Shimbara peninsula, Kyushu Island, Japan, opposite the city of Kumamoto. Its eruption June 1991 led to the evacuation of 10,000 people.

Upanishad one of a collection of Hindu sacred treatises, written in Sanskrit, connected with the ◊Vedas but composed later, about 800–200 BC. Metaphysical and ethical, their doctrine equated the atman (self) with the Brahman (supreme spirit) – *'Tat tvam asi'* ('Thou art that') – and developed the theory of the transmigration of souls.

Updike John Hoyer 1932– . US writer. Associated with the *New Yorker* magazine from 1955, he soon established a reputation for polished prose, poetry, and criticism. His novels include *The Poorhouse Fair* 1959, *The Centaur* 1963, *Couples* 1968, *The Witches of Eastwick* 1984, *Roger's Version* 1986, and *S.* 1988, and deal with the tensions and frustrations of contemporary US middle-class life and their effects on love and marriage.

Updike was born in Shillington, Pennsylvania, and graduated from Harvard University. Two characters recur in his novels: the former basketball player 'Rabbit' Angstrom, who matures in the series *Rabbit, Run* 1960, *Rabbit Redux* 1971, *Rabbit is Rich* 1981 (Pulitzer prize), and *Rabbit at Rest* 1990 (Pulitzer prize); and the novelist Henry Bech, who appears in *Bech: A Book* 1970 and *Bech is Back* 1982. Other novels by Updike include *Of the Farm* 1965, *A Month of Sundays* 1972, *Marry Me* 1976, *The Coup* 1978, and *Memories of the Ford Administration* 1992. His short-story collections include *The Same Door* 1959, *Pigeon Feathers* 1962, *Museums and Women* 1972, and *Problems* 1979. His body of work includes essay collections, such as *Hugging the Shore* 1983, and the play *Buchanan Dying* 1974.

Upper Austria (German ***Oberösterreich***) mountainous federal province of Austria, drained by the river Danube; area 12,000 sq km/4,632 sq mi; population (1994) 1,383,600. Its capital is Linz. In addition to wine, sugar beet, and grain, there are

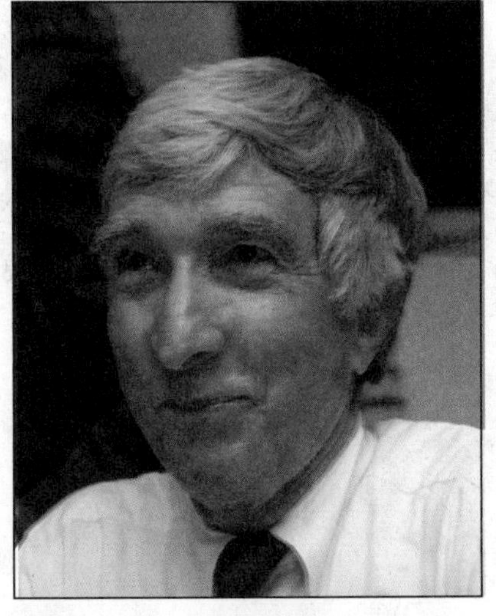

Updike US novelist John Updike. A prolific and stylish author, Updike writes poignant, closely observed novels about the moral and emotional perplexities of the suburban middle classes, particularly those brought about by changes in sexual morality. *The Witches of Eastwick* was filmed 1987. *Topham*

Urban II A 16th-century drawing showing Pope Urban II urging Christian knights to join the First Crusade at the Council of Clermont 1095. The First Crusade succeeded in recapturing Jerusalem, resulting in a massacre of the Muslims. *Philip Sauvain*

reserves of oil. Manufactured products include textiles, chemicals, and metal goods.

Upper Volta former name (to 1984) of ◊Burkina Faso.

Uppsala city in Sweden, NW of Stockholm; population (1994) 181,200. Industries include engineering and pharmaceuticals. The university was founded 1477; there are Viking relics and a Gothic cathedral. The botanist Carolus Linnaeus lived here.

Ur ancient city of the ◊Sumerian civilization, in modern Iraq. Excavations by the British archaeologist Leonard Woolley show that it was inhabited from about 3500 BC. He discovered evidence of a flood that may have inspired the *Epic of ◊Gilgamesh* as well as the biblical account, and remains of ziggurats, or step pyramids.

Ural Mountains (Russian ***Ural'skiy Khrebet***) mountain system running from the Arctic Ocean to the Caspian Sea, traditionally separating Europe from Asia. The highest peak is Naradnaya, 1,894 m/6,214 ft. It has vast mineral wealth. The middle Urals is one of the most industrialized regions of Russia. Perm, Chelyabinsk, Ekaterinburg (Sverdlovsk), Magnitogorsk, and Zlatoust are major industrial centres.

uraninite uranium oxide, UO_2, an ore mineral of uranium, also known as pitchblende when occurring in massive form. It is black or brownish black, very dense, and radioactive. It occurs in veins and as massive crusts, usually associated with granite rocks.

uranium hard, lustrous, silver-white, malleable and ductile, radioactive, metallic element of the ◊actinide series, symbol U, atomic number 92, relative atomic mass 238.029. It is the most abundant radioactive element in the Earth's crust, its decay giving rise to essentially all radioactive elements in nature; its final decay product is the stable element lead. Uranium combines readily with most elements to form compounds that are extremely poisonous. The chief ore is ◊pitchblende, in which the element was discovered by German chemist Martin Klaproth 1789; he named it after the planet Uranus, which had been discovered 1781. Many countries mine uranium; large deposits are found in Canada, the USA, Australia, and South Africa.

Uranium is one of three fissile elements (the others are thorium and plutonium). It was long considered to be the element with the highest atomic number to occur in nature. The isotopes U-238 and U-235 have been used to help determine the age of the Earth. Uranium-238, which comprises about 99% of all naturally occurring uranium, has a half-life of 4.51×10^9 years. Because of its abundance, it is the isotope from which fissile plutonium is produced in breeder ◊nuclear reactors. The fissile isotope U-235 has a half-life of 7.13×10^8 years and comprises about 0.7% of naturally occurring uranium; it is used directly as a fuel for nuclear reactors and in the manufacture of nuclear weapons.

Uranus the seventh planet from the Sun, discovered by William ◊Herschel 1781. It is twice as far out as the sixth planet, Saturn. Uranus has a mass 14.5 times that of Earth. The spin axis of Uranus is tilted at 98°, so that one pole points towards the Sun, giving extreme seasons.
mean distance from the Sun 2.9 billion km/1.8 billion mi
equatorial diameter 50,800 km/31,600 mi
rotation period 17.2 hr
year 84 Earth years
atmosphere deep atmosphere composed mainly of hydrogen and helium
surface composed primarily of hydrogen and helium but may also contain heavier elements, which might account for Uranus's mean density being higher than Saturn's
satellites 15 moons; 11 thin rings around the planet's equator were discovered 1977.

Uranus has a peculiar magnetic field, whose axis is tilted at 60° to its axis of spin, and is displaced about one-third of the way from the planet's centre to its surface. Uranus spins from east to west, the opposite of the other planets, with the exception of Venus and possibly Pluto. The rotation rate of the atmosphere varies with latitude, from about 16 hours in mid-southern latitudes to longer than 17 hours at the equator.

Uranus's equatorial ring system comprises 11 rings. The ring furthest from the planet centre (51,000 km/31,800 mi), Epsilon, is 100 km/62 mi at its widest point. In 1995, US astronomers determined the ring particles contained long-chain hydrocarbons. Looking at the brightest region of Epsilon, they were also able to calculate the ◊precession of Uranus as 264 days, the fastest known precession in the Solar System.

The space probe *Voyager 2* detected ten small moons in addition to the five visible from Earth. Titania, the largest moon, has a diameter of 1,580 km/980 mi. The rings are charcoal black, and may be debris of former 'moonlets' that have broken up.

Uranus in Greek mythology, the primeval sky god, whose name means 'Heaven'. He was responsible for both the sunshine and the rain, and was the son and husband of ◊Gaia, the goddess of the Earth. Uranus and Gaia were the parents of ◊Kronos and the ◊Titans.

Urban six popes, including:

Urban II c. 1042–1099. Pope 1088–99. He launched the First ◊Crusade at the Council of Clermont in France 1095. ▷*See feature on pp. 280–281.*

Urban VIII Maffeo Barberini 1568–1644. Pope 1623–44. His policies during the ◊Thirty Years' War were designed more to maintain the balance of forces in Europe and prevent one side from dominating the papacy than to further the ◊Counter-Reformation. He extended the papal dominions and improved their defences. During his papacy, ◊Galileo was summoned 1633 to recant the theories that the Vatican condemned as heretical.

urbanization process by which the proportion of a population living in or around towns and cities increases through migration and natural increase as the agricultural population decreases. The growth of urban concentrations in the USA and Europe is a relatively recent phenomenon, dating back only about 150 years to the beginning of the Industrial Revolution (although the world's first cities were built more than 5,000 years ago). The UN Population Fund reported 1996 that within ten years the majority of the world's population would be living in urban conglomerations. Almost all urban growth will occur in the developing world, spawning ten large cities a year. In England, about 705 sq km/705,000 hectares of former agricultural land was lost to housing, industrial development, and road building 1945–92.

Urdu language member of the Indo-Iranian branch of the Indo-European language family, related to Hindi and written not in Devanagari but in Arabic script. Urdu is strongly influenced by Farsi (Persian) and Arabic. It is the official language of Pakistan and is used by Muslims in India.

urea $CO(NH_2)_2$ waste product formed in the mammalian liver when nitrogen compounds are broken down. It is filtered from the blood by the kidneys, and stored in the bladder as urine prior to release. When purified, it is a white, crystalline solid. In industry it is used to make urea-formaldehyde plastics (or resins), pharmaceuticals, and fertilizers.

ureter tube connecting the kidney to the bladder. Its wall contains fibres of smooth muscle whose contractions aid the movement of urine out of the kidney.

urethra in mammals, a tube connecting the bladder to the exterior. It carries urine and, in males, semen.

kidney
not drawn to scale
glomerulus
vena cava
renal vein
arteriole
tubule
renal artery
cortex (outer layer)
medulla (inner layer)
calyx and renal
aorta
urine
ureter
urine flow in collection tube
heart
renal veins and arteries
ureter
aorta
kidney
bladder
urethra
bladder

urinary system The human urinary system. At the bottom right, the complete system in outline; on the left, the arrangement of blood vessels connected to the kidney; at the top right, a detail of the network of vessels within a kidney.

Urey Harold Clayton 1893–1981. US chemist. In 1932 he isolated ◊heavy water and discovered ◊deuterium, for which he was awarded the 1934 Nobel Prize for Chemistry. During World War II he was a member of the Manhattan Project, which produced the atomic bomb, and after the war he worked on tritium (another isotope of hydrogen, of mass 3) for use in the hydrogen bomb, but later he advocated nuclear disarmament and world government.

uric acid $C_5H_4N_4O_3$ nitrogen-containing waste substance, formed from the breakdown of food and body protein. It is only slightly soluble in water. Uric acid is the normal means by which most land animals that develop in a shell (birds, reptiles, insects, and land gastropods) deposit their waste products. The young are unable to get rid of their excretory products while in the shell and therefore store them in this form. Humans and other primates produce some uric acid as well as urea, the normal nitrogenous waste product of mammals, adult amphibians, and many marine fishes. If formed in excess and not excreted, uric acid may be deposited in sharp crystals in the joints and other tissues, causing gout; or it may form stones (calculi) in the kidneys or bladder.

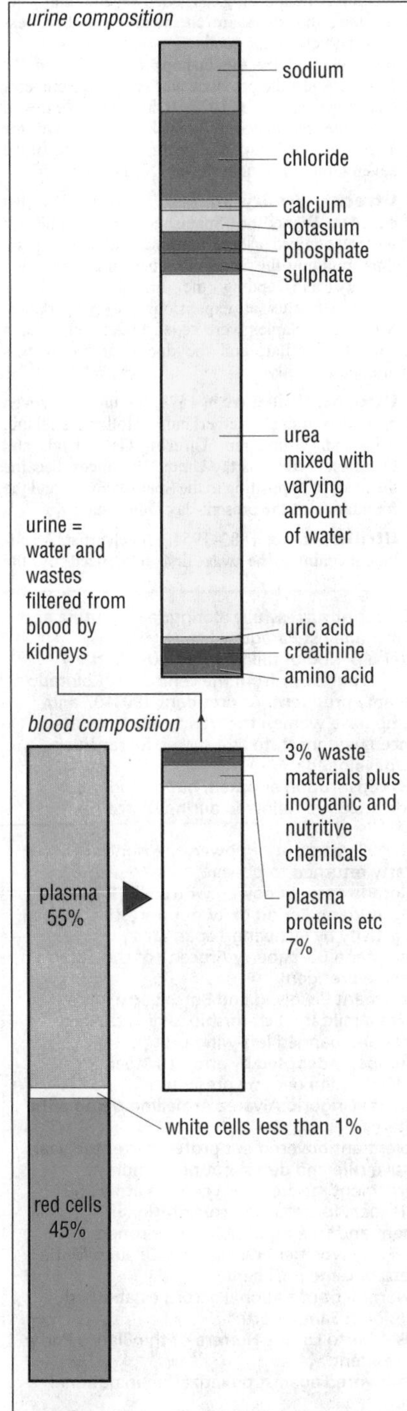

urine Urine consists of excess water and waste products that have been filtered from the blood by the kidneys; it is stored in the bladder until it can be expelled from the body via the urethra. Analysing the composition of an individual's urine can reveal a number of medical conditions, such as poorly functioning kidneys, kidney stones, and diabetes.

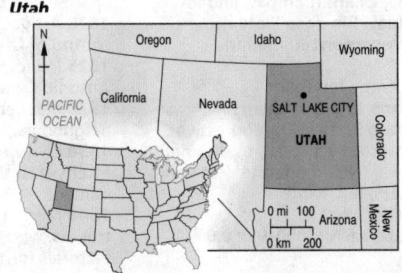

urinary system system of organs that removes nitrogenous waste products and excess water from the bodies of animals. In vertebrates, it consists of a pair of kidneys, which produce urine; ureters, which drain the kidneys; and (in bony fishes, amphibians, some reptiles, and mammals) a bladder that stores the urine before its discharge. In mammals, the urine is expelled through the urethra; in other vertebrates, the urine drains into a common excretory chamber called a ◊cloaca, and the urine is not discharged separately.

urine amber-coloured fluid filtered out by the kidneys from the blood. It contains excess water, salts, proteins, waste products in the form of urea, a pigment, and some acid. The kidneys pass it through two fine tubes (ureters) to the bladder, which may act as a reservoir for up to 0.7 l/1.5 pt at a time. In mammals, it then passes into the urethra, which opens to the outside by a sphincter (constricting muscle) under voluntary control. In reptiles and birds, nitrogenous wastes are discharged as an almost solid substance made mostly of ◊uric acid, rather than urea.

URL (abbreviation for ***Uniform Resource Locator***) series of letters and/or numbers specifying the location of a document on the ◊World Wide Web. Every URL consists of a domain name, a description of the document's location within the host computer and the name of the document itself, separated by full stops and backslashes. Thus *The Times* web site can be found at http://www.the-times.co.uk/news/pages/home.html, and a tribute to Elvis Presley is at http://www.mit.edu:8001/activities/41West/elvis.html. The complexity of URLs explains why bookmarks and links, which save the user from the chore of typing them in, are so popular.

Urquiza Justo José de 1801–1870. Argentine president 1854–60, regarded as the organizer of the Argentine nation. Governor of Entre Ríos from 1841, he set up a progressive administration. Supported by Brazil and Uruguay, he defeated the unpopular dictator Juan Manuel de ◊Rosas in the Battle of Caseros 1852. As president he fostered internal economic development and created the Argentine Confederation 1853 which united the country's provinces, but he failed to bring Buenos Aires into it.

Ursa Major (Latin 'Great Bear') the third largest constellation in the sky, in the north polar region. Its seven brightest stars make up the familiar shape of the Big Dipper or Plough. The second star of the handle of the dipper, called Mizar, has a companion star, Alcor. Two stars forming the far side of the bowl act as pointers to the north pole star, ◊Polaris. Dubhe, one of them, is the constellation's brightest star.

Ursa Minor (Latin 'Little Bear') small constellation of the northern hemisphere. It is shaped like a dipper, with the bright north pole star ◊Polaris at the end of the handle. Two other bright stars in this group, Beta and Gamma Ursae Minoris, are called 'the Guards' or 'the Guardians of the Pole'. The constellation also contains the orange subgiant Kochab, about 95 light years from Earth.

urticaria or ***nettle rash*** or ***hives*** irritant skin condition characterized by itching, burning, stinging, and the spontaneous appearance of raised patches of skin. Treatment is usually by ◊antihistamines or steroids taken orally or applied as lotions. Its causes are varied and include allergy and stress.

Uruguay country in South America, on the Atlantic coast, bounded N by Brazil and W by Argentina. *See country box on following page.*

Urumqi or ***Urumchi*** industrial city and capital of Xinjiang Uygur autonomous region, China, at the northern foot of the Tian Shan Mountains; population (1993) 1,110,000. It produces cotton textiles, cement, chemicals, iron, and steel.

USA official abbreviation for ◊***United States of America***; ***US Army***.

user interface in computing, the procedures and methods through which the user operates a program. These might include ◊menus, input forms, error messages, and keyboard procedures. A ◊graphical user interface (GUI or WIMP) is one that makes use of icons (small pictures) and allows the user to make menu selections with a mouse.

Ushuaia southernmost town in the world, at the tip of Tierra del Fuego, Argentina, less than 1,000 km/620 mi from Antarctica; population (1991) 29,700. It is a free port and naval base. Industries include lumbering, sheeprearing, and fishing.

US Naval Observatory US government observatory in Washington DC, which provides the nation's time service and publishes almanacs for navigators, surveyors, and astronomers. It contains a 66-cm/26-in refracting telescope opened 1873. A 1.55-m/61-in reflector for measuring positions of celestial objects was opened 1964 at Flagstaff, Arizona.

Uštaše Croatian nationalist terrorist organization founded 1929 and led by Ante Pavelić against the Yugoslav state. During World War II, it collaborated with the Nazis and killed thousands of Serbs, Romanies, and Jews. It also carried out deportations and forced conversions to Roman Catholicism in its attempt to create a 'unified' Croatian state. It was responsible for the murder of King Alexander of Yugoslavia in France 1934 but first came to prominence during World War II through collaboration with the Italian and German forces occupying Yugoslavia. It achieved some success in establishing a puppet Croatian state led by Pavelić, but carried out widespread atrocities against ethnic minorities in its territories. It is thought some 80,000 people died in Uštaše death camps during World War II, about half of them Serbs. The state was destroyed by the Axis defeat 1945 and Pavelić fled to South America where he died. The organization persisted underground during the communist period and some of its members re-emerged to play a role in the formation of a separate Croatian state after the collapse of Yugoslavia 1990–92.

Ustinov Peter Alexander 1921– . English stage and film actor, writer, and director. He won an Academy Award for *Spartacus* 1960. He wrote, produced, directed, and acted in several films, including *Romanoff and Juliet* 1961, *Billy Budd* 1962, and *Lady L* 1965. Other film appearances include *Topkapi* 1964, *Death on the Nile* 1978, and *Evil under the Sun* 1981. He published his autobiography *Dear Me* 1983.

usury former term for charging interest on a loan of money. In medieval times, usury was held to be a sin, and Christians were forbidden to lend (although not to borrow). The practice of charging interest is still regarded as usury in some Muslim countries. Under English law, usury remained forbidden until the 13th century, when trade and the need for credit was increased; for example, Jews were absolved from the ban on usury by the Fourth Lateran Council of 1215.

Utah state in western USA; nicknamed Beehive State/Mormon State
area 219,900 sq km/84,881 sq mi
capital Salt Lake City
towns and cities Provo, Ogden
physical Colorado Plateau to the E, mountains in centre, Great Basin to the W, Great Salt Lake

Utah

Oregon
Idaho
Wyoming
PACIFIC OCEAN
California
Nevada
SALT LAKE CITY
UTAH
Colorado
Arizona
New Mexico
0 mi 100
0 km 200

Contrary to general belief, I do not believe that friends are necessarily the people you like best, they are merely the people who got there first.

PETER USTINOV
Dear Me

That inland briny sea, which apparently has no business there.

On the Great Salt Lake, UTAH
Richard Burton
The City of the Saints

features Great American Desert; Colorado river system; five national parks: the Arches, Bryce Canyon, Canyonlands, Capitol Reef, and Zion; the Uinta Mountains, Utah's tallest mountains (highest peak 4,123 m/13,528 ft); the Wasatch Mountains (over 3,300 m/11,000 ft); Great Salt Lake; Dinosaur national monument, with Dinosaur Quarry; Rainbow Bridge national monument; Natural Bridges national monument; Great Basin desert region; Green River; Nine Mile Canyon, with rock carvings by the Fremont American Indians; Hovenweep national monument, with tower structures that may have been used by the Anasazi American Indians for making astronomical observations; Golden Spike national historic site, where the Union Pacific and Central Pacific railroads met 1869, completing the first transcontinental route; Bingham Canyon Copper Mine; Salt Lake City, based on Brigham Young's grid plan, with Temole Square, the Tabernacle (home of the Mormon Tabernacle Choir), the Family History Library (the largest collection of genealogical data in the world), the Beehive House (1854, Brigham Young's home), the Union Pacific Railroad Depot (1909), and the Utah state capitol (1915, a fine example of Renaissance Revival architecture); Brigham Young University; Monument Valley Tribal Park, a Navajo centre; Anasazi Indian village state park; Fremont Indian state park; Utah Shakespearean Festival, in an open-air replica of the Globe Theatre, at Cedar City; Intermountain Power Project, the world's largest coal-fired generating station; auto racing at Bonneville Salt Flats; 70% of the population are members of the Mormon church; Utah has the highest proportion of high-school graduates of any state
industries wool, gold, silver, copper, coal, salt, steel
population (1991) 1,770,000
famous people Brigham Young
history explored first by Franciscan friars for Spain 1776; Great Salt Lake discovered by US frontier scout Jim Bridger 1824; part of the area ceded by Mexico 1848; developed by Mormons, still by far the largest religious group in the state; territory 1850, but not admitted to statehood until 1896 because of Mormon reluctance to relinquish plural marriage. The world's largest open-pit copper mine began 1906 at Bingham Canyon.

Utamaro Kitagawa 1753–1806. Japanese colour-print artist of the ◊ukiyo-e school. He is known for his muted colour prints of women engaged in everyday activities, including informal studies of prostitutes.

Utamaro was the first Japanese artist to become well known in Europe, many of his prints being sent there during his lifetime by Dutch merchants resident in Nagasaki. His style is distinctive: his subject is often seen close up, sometimes from unusual angles or viewpoints, and he made use of sensuous lines and highly decorative textiles. *See illustration on p. 1085.*

uterus hollow muscular organ of female mammals, located between the bladder and rectum, and connected to the Fallopian tubes above and the vagina below. The embryo develops within the uterus, and in placental mammals is attached to it after implantation via the ◊placenta and umbilical cord. The outer wall of the uterus is composed of smooth muscle, capable of powerful contractions (induced by hormones) during childbirth.

The lining of the uterus changes during the ◊menstrual cycle. In humans and other higher primates, it is a single structure, but in other mammals it is paired.

U Thant Burmese diplomat; see ◊Thant, U.

Uthman c. 574–656. Third caliph (leader of the Islamic Empire) from 644, a son-in-law of the prophet Muhammad. Under his rule the Arabs became a naval power and extended their rule to N Africa and Cyprus, but Uthman's personal weaknesses led to his assassination. He was responsible for the compilation of the authoritative version of the Koran, the sacred book of Islam.

Uthman I another name for the Turkish sultan ◊Osman I.

utilitarianism philosophical theory of ethics outlined by the philosopher Jeremy ◊Bentham and developed by John Stuart Mill. According to utilitarianism, an action is morally right if it has consequences that lead to happiness, and wrong if it brings about the reverse. Thus society should aim for the greatest happiness of the greatest number.

Utopia (Greek 'no place') any ideal state in literature, named after philosopher Thomas More's ideal commonwealth in his book *Utopia* 1516. Other versions include Plato's *Republic*, Francis Bacon's *New Atlantis*, and *City of the Sun* by the Italian Tommaso Campanella (1568–1639). Utopias are a common subject in ◊science fiction. See also ◊dystopia.

Utrecht province of the Netherlands lying SE of Amsterdam, on the Kromme Rijn (Crooked Rhine); area 1,330 sq km/513 sq mi; capital Utrecht; population (1995) 1,063,500. Other towns and cities include Amersfoort, Zeist, Nieuwegeun, and Veenendaal. Industries are chemicals, livestock, textiles, and electrical goods
history ruled by the bishops of Utrecht in the Middle Ages, the province was sold to the emperor Charles V of Spain 1527. It became a centre of Protestant resistance to Spanish rule and, with the signing of the Treaty of Utrecht, became one of the seven United Provinces of the Netherlands 1579.

Utrecht, Treaty of treaty signed 1713 that ended the War of the ◊Spanish Succession. Philip V was recognized as the legitimate king of Spain, thus founding the Spanish branch of the Bourbon dynasty and ending the French king Louis XIV's attempts at expansion; the Netherlands, Milan, and Naples were ceded to Austria; Britain gained Gibraltar; and the duchy of Savoy was granted to Sicily.

Utrecht, Union of in 1579, the union of seven provinces of the N Netherlands – Holland, Zeeland, Friesland, Groningen, Utrecht, Gelderland, and Overijssel – that, as the United Provinces, became the basis of opposition to the Spanish crown and the foundation of the present-day Dutch state.

Utrillo Maurice 1883–1955. French artist. A self-taught painter, he was first influenced by the

URUGUAY
Oriental Republic of

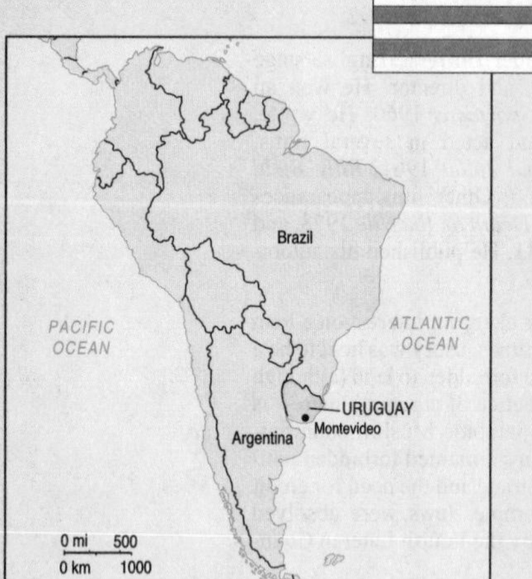

national name *República Oriental del Uruguay*
area 176,200 sq km/68,031 sq mi
capital Montevideo
major towns/cities Salto, Paysandú
physical features grassy plains (pampas) and low hills; rivers Negro, Uruguay, Río de la Plata
head of state and government Julio Maria Sanguinetti from 1994
political system democratic republic
administrative divisions 19 departments
political parties Colorado Party (PC), progressive, centre-left; National (Blanco) Party (PN), traditionalist, right of centre; New Space (NE), moderate, left-wing; Progressive Encounter (EP), left-wing
population 3,186,000 (1995 est)
population growth rate 0.6% (1990–95); 0.6% (2000–05)
ethnic distribution predominantly of European descent: about 54% Spanish, 22% Italian, with minorities from other European countries
life expectancy 69 (men), 76 (women)
literacy rate men 97%, women 96%
language Spanish (official)
religions mainly Roman Catholic
currency Uruguayan peso
GDP (US $) 15.54 billion (1994)
growth rate 5.1% (1994)
exports meat and meat products, leather, wool, textiles, fish and seafood

HISTORY
1516 The Rio de la Plata was visited by the Spanish navigator Juan Diaz de Solis, who was killed by native Charrua Amerindians. This discouraged European settlement for more than a century.
1680 Portuguese from Brazil founded Nova Colonia do Sacramento on the Rio de la Plata estuary.
1726 The Spanish established a fortress at Montevideo and wrested control over Uruguay from Portugal, with much of the Amerindian population being killed.
1776 Became part of the Viceroyalty of La Plata, with its capital at Buenos Aires.
1808 With the Spanish monarchy overthrown by Napoleon Bonaparte, the La Plata Viceroyalty became autonomous, but Montevideo remained loyal to the Spanish Crown and rebelled against Buenos Aires control.
1815 The dictator José Gervasio Artigas overthrew Spanish and Buenos Aires control.
1820 Artigas was ousted by Brazil, which disputed control of Uruguay with Argentina.
1825 Independence declared after fight led by Juan Antonio Lavalleja.
1828 Independence recognized by the country's neighbours.
1836 Civil war between the Reds and the Whites, after which the Colorado and Blanco parties were named.
1840 Merino sheep were introduced by British traders, who later established meat-processing factories for the export trade.
1865–70 Fought successfully alongside Argentina and Brazil in war against Paraguay.
1903 After a period of military rule, José Battle y Ordonez, a progressive from the centre-left Colorado Party, became president. As president 1903–07 and 1911–15, he gave women the franchise and created an advanced welfare state as a successful ranching economy developed.
1930 First constitution adopted, but period of military dictatorship followed during Depression period.
1958 After 93 years out of power, the right-of-centre Blanco Party returned to power.
1967 Colorado Party in power, with Jorge Pacheco Areco as president. Period of labour unrest and urban guerrilla activity by left-wing Tupamaros.
1972 Juan María Bordaberry Arocena of the Colorado Party became president.
1973 Parliament dissolved and Bordaberry shared power with a military dictatorship, which crushed the Tupamaros and banned left-wing groups.
1976 Bordaberry deposed by army; Dr Aparicio Méndez Manfredini became president.
1981 General Grigorio Alvárez Armellino became the new military ruler.
1984 Violent antigovernment protests after ten years of repressive rule and deteriorating economy.
1985 Agreement reached between the army and political leaders for return to constitutional government and freeing of political prisoners. Colorado Party won general election; Dr Julio María Sanguinetti became president.
1986 Government of national accord established under President Sanguinetti.
1989 Luis Alberto Lacalle Herrera of the Blanco Party elected president.
1992 Public voted against privatization in national referendum.
1994 Colorado candidate Julio Maria Sanguinetti elected president.

SEE ALSO Buenos Aires; Tupamaros

UZBEKISTAN
Republic of

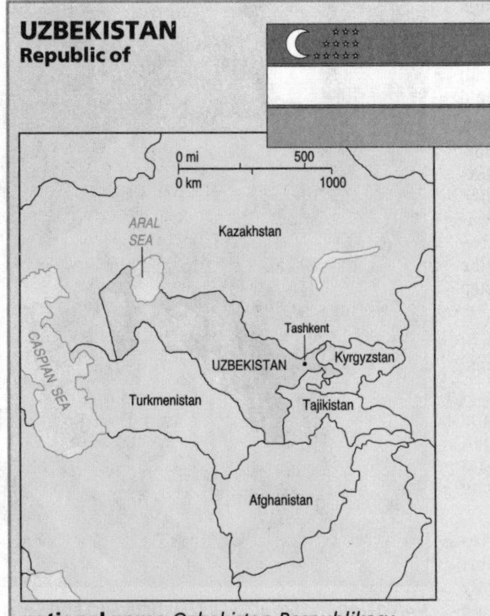

national name *Ozbekistan Respublikasy*
area 447,400 sq km/172,741 sq mi
capital Tashkent
major towns/cities Samarkand, Bukhara, Namangan, Andizhan
physical features oases in the deserts; rivers: Amu Darya, Syr Darya; Fergana Valley; rich in mineral deposits
head of state Islam Karimov from 1990
head of government Otkir Sultonov from 1995
political system authoritarian nationalist
administrative divisions 12 regions
political parties People's Democratic Party of Uzbekistan (PDP), reform socialist (ex-communist); Fatherland Progress Party (FP; Vatan Taraqioti), pro-private enterprise; Erk (Freedom Democratic Party), mixed economy; Social Democratic Party of Uzbekistan, pro-Islamic; National Revival Democratic Party, centrist, intelligentsia-led
population 22,843,000 (1995 est)
population growth rate 2.2% (1990–95); 1.9% (2000–05)
life expectancy 66 (men), 73 (women)
literacy rate 85%
language Uzbek, a Turkic language
religion Sunni Muslim
currency som
GDP (US $) 36.2 billion (1994)
growth rate −2.6% (1994)
exports rice, dried fruit, vine fruits (all grown by irrigation); cotton, silk

HISTORY
6th C BC Part of the Persian Empire of Cyrus the Great.
4th C BC Part of the empire of Alexander the Great of Macedonia.
1st C BC Samarkand (Maracanda) developed as a transit point on the strategic Silk Road trading route between China and Europe.
7th C City of Tashkent founded; spread of Islam.
12th C Tashkent taken by the Turks; Khorezem (Khiva), in the NW, became the centre of a large Central Asian polity, stretching from the Caspian Sea to Samarkand in the E.
13th–14th Cs Conquered by Genghis Khan and became part of the Mongol Empire, with Samarkand serving as the capital for Tamerlane.
18th–19th Cs Dominated by the independent emirates and khanates (chiefdoms) of Bukhara in the SW, Kokand in the E, and Samarkand in the centre.
1865–67 Tashkent was taken by Russia and made capital of the Governor-Generalship of Turkestan.
1868–76 Tsarist Russia annexed the emirate of Bukhara (1868); and the khanates of Samarkand (1868), Khiva (1873), and Kokand (1876).
1917 Following the Bolshevik revolution in Russia, a Tashkent soviet ('people's council') was established, which deposed the emir of Bukhara and the other khans 1920.
1918–22 Mosques were closed and Muslim clergy persecuted as part of a secularization drive by the new communist rulers, despite nationalist guerrilla (basmachi) resistance.
1921 Part of Turkestan Soviet Socialist Autonomous Republic.
1925 Became constituent republic of the USSR.
1930s Skilled ethnic Russians immigrated into urban centres as industries developed.
1944 About 160,000 Meskhetian Turks forcibly transported from their native Georgia to Uzbekistan by Soviet dictator Joseph Stalin.
1950s–80s Major irrigation projects stimulated cotton production, but led to the desiccation of the Aral Sea.
late 1980s Upsurge in Islamic consciousness stimulated by the *glasnost* initiative of the Soviet Union's reformist leader Mikhail Gorbachev.
1989 Birlik ('Unity'), a nationalist movement, formed. Violent attacks on Meskhetian and other minority communities in Ferghana Valley.
1990 Economic and political sovereignty declared by increasingly nationalist UCP, led by Islam Karimov, who became president.
1991 Attempted anti-Gorbachev coup by conservatives in Moscow initially supported by President Karimov. Independence declared. Joined new Commonwealth of Independent States (CIS); Karimov directly elected president.
1992 Violent food riots in Tashkent. Joined Economic Cooperation Organization and United Nations. New constitution adopted.
1993 Crackdown on Islamic fundamentalists as economy deteriorated.
1994 Economic, military, and social union formed with Kazakhstan and Kyrgyzstan. Economic integration treaty signed with Russia. Links with Turkey strengthened and foreign inward investment encouraged.
1995 Ruling PDP (formerly the UCP) won general election, from which opposition was banned from participating. Karimov's tenure extended for further five-year term by national plebiscite.
1996 Agreement with Kazakhstan and Kyrgyzstan to create single economic market.

SEE ALSO Bukhara; Genghis Khan; Samarkand; Union of Soviet Socialist Republics

Impressionists, but soon developed a distinctive, almost naive style characterized by his subtle use of pale tones and muted colours. After his Impressionist phase he arrived at his characteristic 'white period' about 1909–16, painting in pictures of great beauty the streets and the peeling plaster of white walls in his native Montmartre. His style changed from about 1917, with brighter colours and a more rudimentary kind of drawing appearing, though this in turn gradually gave way to a return to his earlier style. Often based on postcards, his views perpetuated the romantic view of Paris, though at their best they possess a touching poignancy and display a subtle use of space. Typical is *La Place du Tertre* about 1911 (Tate Gallery, London).

Uttar Pradesh state of N India
area 294,400 sq km/113,638 sq mi
capital Lucknow
towns and cities Kanpur, Varanasi, Agra, Allahabad, Meerut
features most populous state; Himalayan peak Nanda Devi 7,817 m/25,655 ft
industries India's largest producer of grains; sugar, oil refining, textiles, leatherwork
population (1994 est) 150,695,000
famous people Indira Gandhi, Ravi Shankar
language Hindi
religion 80% Hindu, 15% Muslim
history formerly the heart of the Mogul Empire and generating point of the ◊Indian Mutiny 1857 and subsequent opposition to British rule; see also ◊Agra and ◊Oudh. There are secessionist demands for a new hill state carved out of Uttar Pradesh.

Uzbek the majority ethnic group (almost 70%) living in Uzbekistan; minorities live in Turkmenistan, Tajikistan, Kazakhstan, and Afghanistan. There are 10–14 million speakers of the Uzbek language, which belongs to the Turkic branch of the Altaic family. Uzbeks are predominantly Sunni Muslims. Uzbeks were part of the 13th-century ◊Golden Horde and were traditionally tent-dwelling pastoralists. Collectivization of the land was introduced under the Soviet government of the 1930s, though some groups in N Afghanistan remained partly nomadic.

Uzbekistan country in central Asia, bounded N by Kazakhstan and the Aral Sea, E by Kyrgyzstan and Tajikistan, S by Afghanistan, and W by Turkmenistan. *See country box above.*

Utrillo, Maurice *Church at Stains*, Minneapolis Institute of Arts, Minnesota, USA. Utrillo began painting in 1902 as a therapeutic distraction between his many bouts of hospitalization for alcohol and drug abuse. By the 1920s he had become famous, and his paintings, mostly Parisian street scenes, were widely imitated. *Corbis*

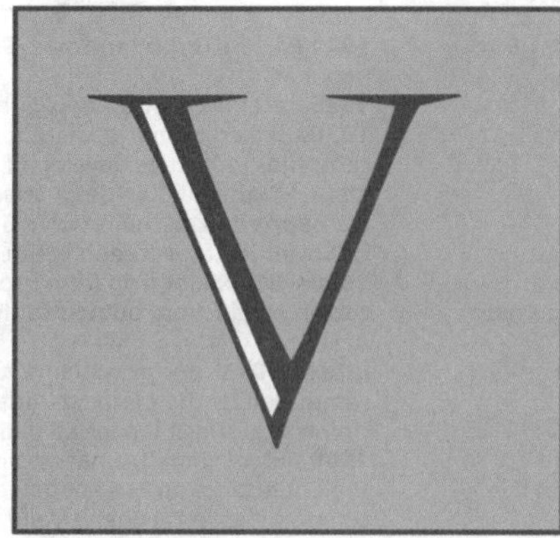

V1, V2 (German *Vergeltungswaffe* 'revenge weapons') German flying bombs of World War II, launched against Britain in 1944 and 1945. Many thousands were killed in air raids on London using these weapons. The V1, also called the doodlebug and buzz bomb, was an uncrewed monoplane carrying a bomb, powered by a simple kind of jet engine called a pulse jet. The V2, a rocket bomb with a preset guidance system, was the first long-range ballistic ◊missile. It was developed by the rocket engineer Wernher ◊von Braun. After the war captured V2 material became the basis of the space race in both the USSR and the USA.

Vaal river in South Africa, the chief tributary of the Orange River. It rises in the Drakensberg mountain range and is 1,200 km/750 mi long.

vaccine any preparation of modified pathogens (viruses or bacteria) that is introduced into the body, usually either orally or by a hypodermic syringe, to induce the specific ◊antibody reaction that produces ◊immunity against a particular disease. In 1796, Edward ◊Jenner was the first to inoculate a child successfully with cowpox virus to produce immunity to smallpox. His method, the application of an infective agent to an abraded skin surface, is still used in smallpox inoculation.

In the UK, children are routinely vaccinated against diphtheria, tetanus, whooping cough, polio, measles, mumps, German measles, and tuberculosis (see ◊BCG).

'What has always been believed by everyone, everywhere, will most likely turn out to be false.'

PAUL VALÉRY
Moralities

vacuole in biology, a fluid-filled, membrane-bound cavity inside a cell. It may be a reservoir for fluids that the cell will secrete to the outside, or may be filled with excretory products or essential nutrients that the cell needs to store. In amoebae (single-cell animals), vacuoles are the sites of digestion of engulfed food particles. Plant cells usually have a large central vacuole for storage.

vacuum in general, a region completely empty of matter; in physics, any enclosure in which the gas pressure is considerably less than atmospheric pressure (101,325 pascals).

vacuum cleaner cleaning device invented 1901 by the Scot Hubert Cecil Booth 1871–1955. Having seen an ineffective dust-blowing machine, he reversed the process so that his machine (originally on wheels, and operated from the street by means of tubes running into the house) operated by suction.

vacuum flask or ***Dewar flask*** or ***Thermos flask*** container for keeping things either hot or cold. It has two silvered glass walls with a vacuum between them, in a metal or plastic outer case. This design reduces the three forms of heat transfer: radiation (prevented by the silvering), conduction, and convection (both prevented by the vacuum). A vacuum flask is therefore equally efficient at keeping cold liquids cold or hot liquids hot.

vacuum flask The vacuum flask allows no heat to escape from or enter its contents. It has double walls with a vacuum between to prevent heat loss by conduction. Radiation is prevented by silvering the walls. The vacuum flask was invented by Scottish chemist James Dewar about 1872.

Vadodara formerly (until 1976) ***Baroda*** industrial city (metal goods, chemicals, jewellery, textiles) and rail junction in Gujarat, W India; population (1991) 1,115,000. Until 1947 it was capital of the princely state of Baroda. It has Lakshmi Vilas Palace, Pratap Vilas Palace (now the Railway Staff College), and several multi-level step wells (baoli).

Vaduz capital of the European principality of Liechtenstein; industries include engineering and agricultural trade; population (1994 est) 5,067.

vagina the lower part of the reproductive tract in female mammals, linking the uterus to the exterior. It admits the penis during sexual intercourse, and is the birth canal down which the baby passes during delivery.

vagrancy homelessness. English law classifies as vagrants tramps who do not make use of available shelter, but also prostitutes who behave indecently in public, pedlars who trade without a licence, those who collect for charity under false pretences, and those armed with offensive weapons. The Vagrancy Act 1824 was introduced in the depression after the Napoleonic Wars to push destitute soldiers off the streets. It made it an offence for any person to be 'wandering abroad and lodging in the open air'; it also made begging an offence. Although repealed in Scotland, the act has been increasingly used in England in the 1980s and 1990s against the homeless.

Valdivia Pedro de c. 1497–1554. Spanish explorer who travelled to Venezuela about 1530 and accompanied Francisco ◊Pizarro on his second expedition to Peru. He then went south into Chile, where he founded the cities of Santiago 1541 and Valdivia 1544. In 1552 he crossed the Andes to explore the Negro River. He was killed by Araucanian Indians.

valence electron in chemistry, an electron in the outermost shell of an ◊atom. It is the valence electrons that are involved in the formation of ionic and covalent bonds (see ◊molecule). The number of electrons in this outermost shell represents the maximum possible valence for many elements and matches the number of the group that the element occupies in the ◊periodic table of the elements.

Valencia industrial city (wine, fruit, chemicals, textiles, ship repair) in Valencia region, E Spain; population (1994) 764,000. The Community of Valencia, consisting of Alicante, Castellón, and Valencia, has an area of 23,300 sq km/8,994 sq mi and a population of 3,772,000. Valencia was ruled by El ◊Cid 1094–99, after he recaptured it from the Moors. There is a cathedral of the 13th–15th centuries and a university founded 1500.

valency in chemistry, the measure of an element's ability to combine with other elements, expressed as the number of atoms of hydrogen (or any other standard univalent element) capable of uniting with (or replacing) its atoms. The number of electrons in the outermost shell of the atom dictates the combining ability of an element. The elements are described as uni-, di-, tri-, and tetravalent when they unite with one, two, three, and four univalent atoms respectively. Some elements have variable valency: for example, nitrogen and phosphorus have a valency of both three and five. The valency of oxygen is two: hence the formula for water, H_2O (hydrogen being univalent).

Valentine, St according to tradition, a bishop of Terni martyred in Rome, now omitted from the calendar of saints' days as probably nonexistent. His festival was 14 Feb, but the custom of sending 'valentines' to a loved one on that day seems to have arisen because the day accidentally coincided with the Roman mid-February festival of ◊Lupercalia.

Valentino Rudolph. Adopted name of Rodolfo Alfonso Guglielmi di Valentina d'Antonguolla 1895–1926. Italian-born US film actor and dancer. He was the archetypal romantic lover of the Hollywood silent era. Valentino came to the USA 1913 and worked as a gardener and a dancer in New York City before appearing as a dancer in a 1918 Hollywood film. His screen debut was 1919, but his first starring role was in *The Four Horsemen of the Apocalypse* 1921. His subsequent films include *The Sheik* 1921 and *Blood and Sand* 1922. He became the screen idol of his day, in such films as *Monsieur Beaucaire* 1924, *The Eagle* 1925, and *Son of the Sheik* 1926.

Valentino US film actor and archetypal 'Latin lover' Rudolph Valentino. He had emigrated from his native Italy to the USA 1913, but did not achieve stardom until his role in *The Four Horsemen of the Apocalypse* 1921. His death from a perforated ulcer provoked near riots and suicides from distraught female fans. *British Film Institute*

Vale of Glamorgan unitary authority of Wales created 1996 (*see United Kingdom map*).

Valera Éamon de. Irish politician; see ◊de Valera.

valerian perennial plant of either of two genera, *Valeriana* and *Centranthus*, family Valerianaceae, native to the northern hemisphere, with clustered heads of fragrant tubular flowers in red, white, or pink. The root of the common valerian or garden heliotrope *Valeriana officinalis* is used medicinally to relieve flatulence and as a sedative.

Valéry Paul Amboise 1871–1945. French poet and mathematician. His poetry, which combines delicate lyricism with intellectual rigour, includes *La Jeune Parque/The Young Fate* 1917 and *Charmes/Enchantments* 1922, which contains 'Le Cimetière marin/The Graveyard by the Sea', one of the major poems of 20th-century French literature.

Valéry French symbolist poet and philosopher Paul Valéry, photographed around 1925. In addition to his work for a news agency, he wrote prolifically on a wide range of subjects. He was elected to the Académie Française 1925. *Corbis*

He also wrote critical essays and many volumes of journals, which he regarded as among his most important work.

Valhalla in Norse mythology, the hall in ◊Odin's palace where he feasted with the souls of those heroes killed in battle that went to join him after death.

validation in computing, the process of checking input data to ensure that it is complete, accurate, and reasonable. Although it would be impossible to guarantee that only valid data are entered into a computer, a suitable combination of validation checks should ensure that most errors are detected.

Valkyrie in Norse mythology, any of the female attendants of ◊Odin. They selected the most valiant warriors to die in battle and escorted them either to Valhalla or to the abode of Freya.

Valladolid industrial city (food processing, vehicles, textiles, engineering), and capital of Valladolid province, Spain; population (1994) 337,000. It was the capital of Castile and León in the 14th–15th centuries, then of Spain until 1560. The Catholic monarchs Ferdinand and Isabella were married at Valladolid 1469. The explorer Christopher Columbus died here, and the home of the writer Miguel de Cervantes is preserved. It has a university founded 1346 and a cathedral 1595.

Valle d'Aosta autonomous region of NW Italy; area 3,300 sq km/1,274 sq mi; population (1992 est) 117,200, many of whom are French-speaking. It produces wine and livestock. Its capital is Aosta.

Valletta capital and port of Malta; population (1995) 9,129 (inner harbour area 102,600). It was founded 1566 by the Knights of ◊St John of Jerusalem and named after their grand master Jean de la Valette (1494–1568), who fended off a Turkish siege May–Sept 1565. The 16th-century palace of the grand masters survives. Malta was formerly a British naval base and came under heavy attack in World War II.

Valley Forge site in Pennsylvania 32 km/20 mi NW of Philadelphia, USA, where George Washington's army spent the winter of 1777–78 in great hardship during the ◊American Revolution. Of the 10,000 men there, 2,500 died of disease and the rest suffered from lack of rations and other supplies; many deserted.

Valley of Ten Thousand Smokes valley in SW Alaska, on the Alaska Peninsula, where in 1912 Mount Katmai erupted in one of the largest volcanic explosions ever known, though without loss of human life since the area was uninhabited. The valley was filled with ash to a depth of 200 m/660 ft. It was dedicated as the Katmai National Monument 1918. Thousands of fissures on the valley floor continue to emit steam and gases.

Valley of the Kings burial place of ancient kings opposite ◊Thebes, Egypt, on the left bank of the Nile. It was established as a royal cemetery during the reign of Thotmes I (c. 1500 BC) and abandoned during the reign of Ramses XI (c. 1100 BC). A vast underground tomb believed to be the burial site of 50 of the sons of Ramses II was discovered by archaeologists May 1995; it was the largest yet found in the Valley of the Kings.

Valmy, Battle of during the French ◊Revolutionary Wars, comprehensive French victory over the Prussians 20 Sept 1792, near Valmy, a French village about 55 km/35 mi southwest of Reims. This forthright defeat of a powerful army by the previously despised revolutionary forces set the seal upon the authority of the revolutionary French government.

Valois branch of the Capetian dynasty, originally counts of Valois (see Hugh ◊Capet) in France, members of which occupied the French throne from Philip VI 1328 to Henry III 1589.

Valparaíso industrial port (sugar refining, textiles, chemicals) in Chile, on the Pacific Ocean; capital of Valparaíso province; population (1992) 276,700. Founded 1536, it was occupied 1595 by the English naval adventurers Francis ◊Drake 1578 and John Hawkins (1532–1595), pillaged by the Dutch 1600, and bombarded by Spain 1866; it has also suffered from earthquakes.

value-added tax (VAT) tax on goods and services. VAT is imposed by the European Union on member states. The tax varies from state to state. An agreed proportion of the tax money is used to fund the EU. VAT is applied at each stage of the production of a commodity, and it is charged only on the value added at that stage. It is not levied, unlike sales tax, on the sale of the commodity itself, but at this stage the VAT paid at earlier stages of the commodity's manufacture cannot be reclaimed.

valve in animals, a structure for controlling the direction of the blood flow. In humans and other vertebrates, the contractions of the beating heart cause the correct blood flow into the arteries because a series of valves prevent back flow. Diseased valves, detected as 'heart murmurs', have decreased efficiency. The tendency for low-pressure venous blood to collect at the base of limbs under the influence of gravity is counteracted by a series of small valves within the veins. It was the existence of these valves that prompted the 17th-century physician William Harvey to suggest that the blood circulated around the body.

valve or ***electron tube*** in electronics, a glass tube containing gas at low pressure, which is used to control the flow of electricity in a circuit. Three or more metal electrodes are inset into the tube. By varying the voltage on one of them, called the grid electrode, the current through the valve can be controlled, and the valve can act as an amplifier. Valves have been replaced for most applications by ◊transistors. However, they are still used in high-power transmitters and amplifiers, and in some hi-fi systems.

valve device that controls the flow of a fluid. Inside a valve, a plug moves to widen or close the opening through which the fluid passes. The valve was invented by US radio engineer Lee de Forest (1873–1961). Common valves include the cone or needle valve, the globe valve, and butterfly valve, all named after the shape of the plug. Specialized valves include the one-way valve, which permits fluid flow in one direction only, and the safety valve, which cuts off flow under certain conditions.

valvular heart disease damage to the heart valves, leading to either narrowing of the valve orifice when it is open (stenosis) or leaking through the valve when it is closed (regurgitation). Worldwide, rheumatic fever is the commonest cause of damage to the heart valves, but in industrialized countries it is being replaced by bacterial infection of the valves themselves (infective endocarditis) and ischaemic heart disease as the main causes. Valvular heart disease is diagnosed by hearing heart murmurs with a stethoscope, or by cardiac ◊ultrasound.

vampire (Hungarian *vampir* (and similar forms in other Slavonic languages)) in Hungarian and Slavonic folklore, an 'undead' corpse that sleeps by day in its native earth, and by night, often in the form of a bat, sucks the blood of the living. ◊Dracula is a vampire in popular fiction.

vampire bat South and Central American bat of the family Desmodontidae, of which there are three species. The ***common vampire*** *Desmodus rotundus* is found from N Mexico to central Argentina; its head and body grow to 9 cm/3.5 in. Vampire bats feed on the blood of birds, and of mammals including horses, cattle, and occasionally humans. They slice a piece of skin from a sleeping animal with their sharp incisor teeth and lap up the flowing blood. They chiefly approach their prey flying low then crawling and leaping. The bite is painless and the loss of blood is small (about 1 cubic cm/0.06 cubic in); the victim seldom comes to any harm. Vampire bats are intelligent and among the few mammals to show altruistic behaviour (they adopt orphans and help other bats in need).

Van city in Turkey on a site on ***Lake Van*** that has been inhabited for more than 3,000 years; population (1990) 153,100. It is a commercial centre for a fruit- and grain-producing area.

vanadium silver-white, malleable and ductile, metallic element, symbol V, atomic number 23, relative atomic mass 50.942. It occurs in certain iron, lead, and uranium ores and is widely distributed in small quantities in igneous and sedimentary rocks. It is used to make steel alloys, to which it adds tensile strength.

Spanish mineralogist Andrés del Rio (1764–1849) and Swedish chemist Nils Sefström (1787–1845) discovered vanadium independently, the former 1801 and the latter 1831. Del Rio named it 'erythronium', but was persuaded by other chemists that he had not in fact discovered a new element; Sefström gave it its present name, after the Norse goddess of love and beauty, Vanadis (or Freya).

Van Allen James Alfred 1914– . US physicist whose instruments aboard the first US satellite *Explorer 1* 1958 led to the discovery of the Van Allen belts, two zones of intense radiation around the Earth. He pioneered high-altitude research with rockets after World War II.

Van Allen radiation belts two zones of charged particles around the Earth's magnetosphere, discovered 1958 by US physicist James Van Allen. The atomic particles come from the Earth's upper atmosphere and the ◊solar wind, and are trapped by the Earth's magnetic field. The inner belt lies 1,000–5,000 km/620–3,100 mi above the equator, and contains ◊protons and ◊electrons. The outer belt lies 15,000–25,000 km/9,300–15,500 mi above the equator, but is lower around the magnetic poles. It contains mostly electrons from the solar wind. The Van Allen belts are hazardous to astronauts, and interfere with electronic equipment on satellites.

Vanbrugh John 1664–1726. English Baroque architect and dramatist. He designed Blenheim Palace, Oxfordshire, and Castle Howard, Yorkshire, and wrote the comic dramas *The Relapse* 1696 and *The Provok'd Wife* 1697. He was imprisoned in France 1688–93 as a political hostage during the war between France and the Grand Alliance (including Britain). *See illustration on following page.*

Van Buren Martin 1782–1862. 8th president of the US 1837–41, a Democrat, who had helped establish the ◊Democratic Party. He was secretary of state 1829–31, minister to Britain 1831–33, vice president 1833–37, and president during the Panic of 1837, the worst US economic crisis until that time, caused by land speculation in the West. Refusing to intervene, he advocated the establishment of an independent treasury, one not linked to the

'The want of a thing is perplexing enough, but the possession of it is intolerable.'

JOHN VANBRUGH
The Confederacy

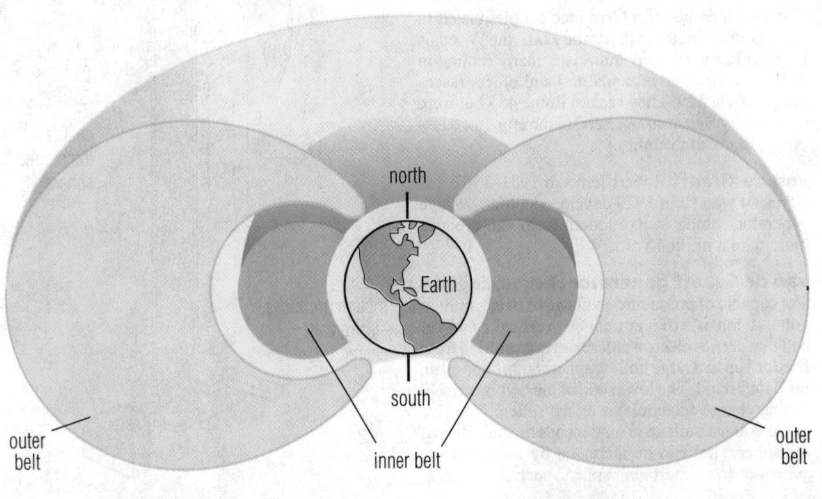

Van Allen radiation belts The Van Allen belts of trapped charged particles are a hazard to spacecraft, affecting on-board electronics and computer systems. Similar belts have been discovered around the planets Mercury, Jupiter, Saturn, Uranus, and Neptune.

Vanbrugh Castle Howard, North Yorkshire, England. It was designed by John Vanbrugh and Nicholas Hawksmoor for the Earl of Carlisle 1699. *Corbis*

federal government, worsening the depression and losing the 1840 election.

Vance Cyrus Roberts 1917– . US Democratic politician, secretary of state 1977–80. He was United Nations negotiator in the peace talks on ◊Bosnia-Herzegovina 1992–93; together with European Community negotiator Lord Owen, he devised the Vance–Owen peace plan for dividing the republic into ten semi-autonomous provinces. The plan was rejected by the Bosnian Serbs.

Vancouver industrial city (oil refining, engineering, shipbuilding, aircraft, timber, pulp and paper, textiles, fisheries) in Canada, its chief Pacific seaport, on the mainland of British Columbia; population (1991) 1,602,500.

Vancouver is situated on Burrard Inlet, at the mouth of the Fraser River. George Vancouver took possession of the site for Britain 1792. It was settled by 1875, under the name of Granville, and was renamed when it became a city 1886, having been reached by the Canadian Pacific Railroad. In 1989 it had an ethnic Chinese population of 140,000, and this was rapidly augmented by thousands of immigrants from Hong Kong.

Vancouver Island island off the west coast of Canada, part of British Columbia
area 32,136 sq km/12,404 sq mi
towns and cities Victoria, Nanaimo, Esquimalt (naval base)
industries coal, timber, fish
history visited by British explorer Capt Cook 1778; surveyed 1792 by Capt George Vancouver.

Vandal member of a Germanic people related to the ◊Goths. In the 5th century AD the Vandals invaded Roman ◊Gaul and Spain, many settling in Andalusia (formerly Vandalitia) and others reaching N Africa 429. They sacked Rome 455 but were defeated by Belisarius, general of the emperor ◊Justinian, in the 6th century.

van de Graaff Robert Jemison 1901–1967. US physicist who from 1929 developed a high-voltage generator, which in its modern form can produce more than a million volts.

van de Graaff generator electrostatic generator capable of producing a voltage of over a million volts. It consists of a continuous vertical conveyor belt that carries electrostatic charges (resulting from friction) up to a large hollow sphere supported on an insulated stand. The lower end of the belt is earthed, so that charge accumulates on the sphere. The size of the voltage built up in air depends on the radius of the sphere, but can be increased by enclosing the generator in an inert atmosphere, such as nitrogen.

Organized religion is making Christianity political, rather than making politics Christian.

LAURENS VAN DER POST Quoted in the *Observer* 9 Nov 1986

van der Post Laurens Jan 1906–1996. South African writer. His books, many of them autobiographical, reflect his openness to diverse cultures and his belief in the importance of intuition, individualism, and myth in human experience. His best-known works, which record the disappearing culture of the Bushmen of the Kalahari, are *The Lost World of the Kalahari* 1958, *The Heart of the Hunter* 1961, and *Testament to the Bushmen* 1984.

His first novel, *In a Province* 1934, was an indictment of racism in South Africa; later works include *Flamingo Feather* 1955, *The Hunter and the Whale* 1967, *A Story like the Wind* 1972, and *A Far-off Place* 1974. He wrote about Japanese prisoner-of-war camps in *The Seed and the Sower* 1963 (filmed as *Merry Christmas Mr Lawrence*).

van der Waals' law modified form of the ◊gas laws that includes corrections for the non-ideal behaviour of real gases (the molecules of ideal gases occupy no space and exert no forces on each other).

van de Graaff generator US physicist Robert Jemison van de Graaff developed this high-powered generator that can produce more than a million volts. Experiments involving charged particles make use of van de Graaff generators as particle accelerators.

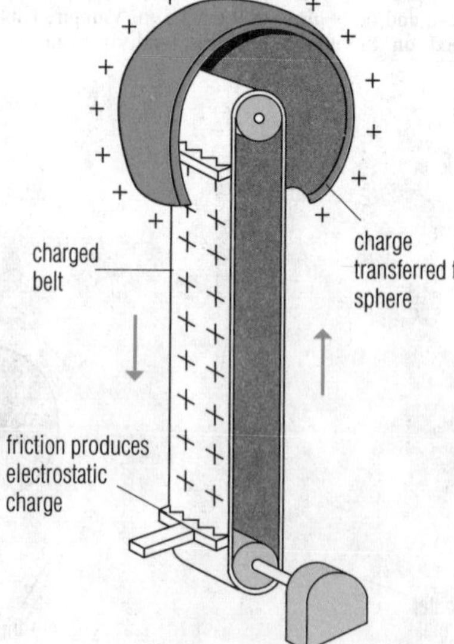

It is named after Dutch physicist J D van der Waals (1837–1923). The equation derived from the law states that:

$$(P + a/V^2)(V - b) = RT$$

where P, V, and T are the pressure, volume, and temperature (in kelvin) of the gas, respectively; R is the ◊gas constant; and a and b are constants for that particular gas.

van Diemen Anthony 1593–1645. Dutch admiral, see ◊Diemen, Anthony van.

van Dyck Anthony. Flemish painter; see ◊Dyck, Anthony van.

Vane Henry 1613–1662. English politician. In 1640 elected a member of the ◊Long Parliament, he was knighted in the same year. He was prominent in the impeachment of Archbishop ◊Laud and in 1643–53 was in effect the civilian head of the Parliamentary government. At the Restoration of the monarchy he was executed.

Vänern, Lake largest lake in Sweden, area 5,550 sq km/2,140 sq mi. Karlstad, Vänersborg, Lidköping, and Mariestad are on its banks.

van Eyck Jan. Flemish painter; see ◊Eyck, Jan van.

van Gogh Vincent. Dutch painter; see ◊Gogh, Vincent van.

Vanguard early series of US Earth-orbiting satellites together with their associated rocket launcher. Vanguard 1 was the second US satellite, launched 17 March 1958 by the three-stage Vanguard rocket. Tracking of its orbit revealed that Earth is slightly pear-shaped. The series ended Sept 1959 with Vanguard 3.

vanilla any climbing orchid of the genus *Vanilla*, native to tropical America but cultivated elsewhere, with fragrant, large, white or yellow flowers. The dried and fermented fruit, or podlike capsules, of *V. planifolia* are the source of the vanilla flavouring used in cookery and baking. Annual world production of vanilla pods is estimated at 1,500 tonnes. Vanilla flavouring (vanillin) can now be produced artificially from waste sulphite liquor, a by-product of paper pulp-making.

Vanuatu group of islands in the SW Pacific Ocean, part of ◊Melanesia. *See country box opposite.*

vapour one of the three states of matter (see also ◊solid and ◊liquid). The molecules in a vapour move randomly and are far apart, the distance between them, and therefore the volume of the vapour, being limited only by the walls of any vessel in which they might be contained. A vapour differs from a ◊gas only in that a vapour can be liquefied by increased pressure, whereas a gas cannot unless its temperature is lowered below its critical temperature (the temperature above which a particular gas cannot be converted into a liquid by pressure alone); it then becomes a vapour and may be liquefied.

vapour density density of a gas, expressed as the ◊mass of a given volume of the gas divided by the mass of an equal volume of a reference gas (such as hydrogen or air) at the same temperature and pressure. It is equal approximately to half the relative molecular weight (mass) of the gas.

vapour pressure pressure of a vapour given off by (evaporated from) a liquid or solid, caused by vibrating atoms or molecules continuously escaping from its surface. In an enclosed space, a maximum value is reached when the number of particles leaving the surface is in equilibrium with those returning to it; this is known as the ***saturated vapour pressure*** or ***equilibrium vapour pressure***.

Var river in S France, rising in the Maritime Alps and flowing generally SSE for 134 km/84 mi into the Mediterranean near Nice. It gives its name to a *département* in the Provence-Alpes-Côte d'Azur region.

Varanasi or ***Benares*** or ***Banaras*** holy city of the Hindus in Uttar Pradesh, India, on the river Ganges; population (1991) 932,000. There are 1,500 golden shrines, and a 5 km/3 mi frontage to the Ganges with sacred stairways (ghats) for purification by bathing. At the burning ghats, the ashes of the dead are scattered on the river to ensure a favourable reincarnation.

VANUATU
Republic of

national name *Ripablik blong Vanuatu*
area 14,800 sq km/5,714 sq mi
capital Port-Vila (on Efate)
major towns/cities Luganville (on Espíritu Santo)
major ports Santo, Port-Vila
physical features comprises around 70 inhabited islands, including Espíritu Santo, Malekula, and Efate; densely forested, mountainous; three active volcanoes; cyclones on average twice a year
head of state Jean Marie Leye from 1994
head of government Donald Kalpokas from 1998
political system democratic republic
administrative divisions four regions
political parties Union of Moderate Parties (UMP), Francophone centrist; National United Party (NUP), formed by Walter Lini; Vanua'aku Pati (VP), Anglophone centrist; Melanesian Progressive Party (MPP), Melanesian centrist; Fren Melanesian Party
population 174,000 (1996 est)
population growth rate 2.5% (1990–95)
ethnic distribution 95% Melanesian, 3% European or mixed European, and 2% Vietnamese, Chinese, or other Pacific islands
life expectancy 67 (men), 71 (women)
literacy rate 67%
languages Bislama 82%, English, French (all official)
religions Christian 80%, animist
currency vatu
GDP (US $) 198.9 million (1994 est)
growth rate 3.0% (1994)
exports copra, coffee, cocoa, tuna, beef, timber, kava

HISTORY
1606 Visited by Portuguese navigator Pedro Fernandez de Queiras, who named the islands Espirítu Santo.
1774 Visited by the British navigator Capt James Cook, who named them the New Hebrides, after the Scottish islands.
1830s European merchants attracted to the islands by the sandalwood trade; Christian missionaries arrived, but many were attacked by the indigenous Melanesians who, in turn, were ravaged by exposure to European diseases.
later 19th C Britain and France disputed control; islanders were shipped to Australia, Fiji, Samoa, and New Caledonia to work as plantation labourers.
1906 Islands jointly administered by France and Britain as the Condominium of the New Hebrides.
1963 Na-Griamel (NG) political grouping formed on Espíritu Santo to campaign against European acquisition of more than a third of the land area.
1975 Representative assembly established following pressure from the VP, formed 1972 by English-speaking Melanesian Protestants.
1978 Government of national unity formed, with Father Gerard Leymang as chief minister.
1980 Revolt on the island of Espíritu Santo by French settlers and pro-NG plantation workers delayed independence but it was achieved within the Commonwealth, with George Kalkoa (adopted name Sokomanu) as president and left-of-centre Father Walter Lini (VP) as prime minister.
1988 Dismissal of Lini by Sokomanu led to Sokomanu's arrest for treason. Lini reinstated.
1989 Sokomanu succeeded as president by Fred Timakata.
1991 Lini voted out by party members; replaced by Donald Kalpokas. General election produced coalition government of the Francophone Union of Moderate Parties (UMP) and Lini's new National United Party (NUP) under Maxime Carlot Korman.
1993 Cyclone caused extensive damage.
1994 Timakata succeeded as president by Jean Marie Leye.
1995 Governing UMP–NUP coalition won general election, but Serge Vohor, of the VP-dominated Unity Front, became prime minister.
1996 Vohor replaced by Maxime Carlot Korman, then returned to power after Carlot government implicated in financial scandal.
1997 Prime Minister Vohor formed new coalition. Legislature dissolved and new elections called after no-confidence motion against Vohor.
1998 Two-week state of emergency after rioting in capital. Donald Kalpokas elected prime minister after early election, heading VP-NUP coalition.

SEE ALSO Australasia and Oceania; Pacific peoples

Varangian (Old Norse, *varan* 'to swear') member of the Byzantine imperial guard founded 988 by Vladimir of Kiev (955–1015), which lasted until the fall of Constantinople 1453. The name came to be used for a widespread Swedish Viking people in E Europe and the Balkans. From the late 11th century, the Byzantine guard included English and Norman mercenaries, as well as Scandinavians. Feared and respected as an elite military force, it occasionally dabbled in politics.

Varda Agnès 1928– . French film director. Favouring a documentary form throughout her career, she explored feminist themes in such films as *Cleó de Cinq à Sept/Cleo from Five to Seven* 1961 and *L'Une Chante, L'Autre Pas/One Sings the Other Doesn't* 1977. She has also made short films on political topics, and the film *Jacquot de Nantes* 1991, on her husband, the director Jacques Demy (1931–1990).

Varèse Edgard Victor Achille Charles 1883–1965. French composer. He left Paris for New York 1916 where he cofounded the New Symphony Orchestra 1919 with the French-born US harpist Carlos Salzédo (1885–1961) to promote modern and pre-classical music. Renouncing the values of tonality, he discovered new resources of musical expression in the percussion sonorities of *Ionisation* 1929–31, the swooping sound of two theremins (an early electronic musical instrument) in *Hyperprism* 1933–34, and the combination of taped and live instrumental sounds in *Déserts* 1950–54.

Vargas Getúlio Dorneles 1883–1954. President of Brazil 1930–45 and 1951–54. He overthrew the republic 1930 and in 1937 set up a totalitarian, profascist state known as the *Estado Novo*. Ousted by a military coup 1945, he returned as president 1951 but, amid mounting opposition and political scandal, committed suicide 1954.

Varanasi Standing on the banks of the river Ganges, Varanasi (Benares) is a major pilgrimage centre for Hindus. Pilgrims worship at the many shrines that crowd its streets and use *ghats* (stone stairways) to bathe in the holy river, on whose waters the ashes of the dead are scattered. *Sally Jenkins*

Vargas Llosa (Jorge) Mario (Pedro) 1936– . Peruvian novelist and politician. Belonging to the magic realist school, his works include *La ciudad y los perros/The Time of the Hero* 1963, *La tía Julia y el escribidor/Aunt Julia and the Scriptwriter* 1977, a humorously autobiographical novel, *La guerra del fin del mundo/The War at the End of the World* 1982, and *The Storyteller* 1990.

variable in computing, a quantity that can take different values. Variables can be used to represent different items of data in the course of a program. A computer programmer will choose a symbol to represent each variable used in a program. The computer will then automatically assign a memory location to store the current value of each variable, and use the chosen symbol to identify this location. For example, the letter *P* might be chosen by a programmer to represent the price of an article. The computer would automatically reserve a memory location with the symbolic address *P* to store the price being currently processed.

variable in mathematics, a changing quantity (one that can take various values), as opposed to a ◊constant. For example, in the algebraic expression $y = 4x^3 + 2$, the variables are x and y, whereas 4 and 2 are constants. A variable may be dependent or independent. Thus if y is a ◊function of x, written $y = f(x)$, such that $y = 4x^3 + 2$, the domain of the function includes all values of the ***independent variable*** x while the range (or co-domain) of the function is defined by the values of the ***dependent variable*** y.

variable star in astronomy, a star whose brightness changes, either regularly or irregularly, over a period ranging from a few hours to months or years. The ◊Cepheid variables regularly expand and contract in size every few days or weeks. Stars that change in size and brightness at less precise intervals include ***long-period variables***, such as the red giant ◊Mira in the constellation ◊Cetus (period about 330 days), and ***irregular variables***, such as some red supergiants. ***Eruptive variables*** emit sudden outbursts of light. Some suffer flares on their surfaces, while others, such as a ◊nova, result from transfer of gas between a close pair of stars. A ◊supernova is the explosive death of a star. In an

◊*eclipsing binary*, the variation is due not to any change in the star itself, but to the periodic eclipse of a star by a close companion. The different types of variability are closely related to different stages of stellar evolution.

variance in statistics, the square of the standard deviation, the measure of spread of data. Population and sample variance are denoted by σ^2 or s^2, respectively. Variance provides a measure of the dispersion of a set of statistical results about the mean or average value.

variation in music, a form based on constant repetition of a simple theme, each new version being elaborated or treated in a different manner. The theme is easily recognizable; it may be a popular tune or – as a gesture of respect – the work of a fellow composer; for example, Brahms' *Variations on a Theme by Haydn* 1873, based on a theme known as the *St Antony Chorale*, although it may also be an original composition. The principle of variations has been adopted in larger-scale and orchestral works by modern composers, for example Elgar's *Enigma Variations* 1899.

varicose veins or ***varicosis*** condition where the veins become swollen and twisted. The veins of the legs are most often affected; other vulnerable sites include the rectum (◊haemorrhoids) and testes. Some people have an inherited tendency to varicose veins, and the condition often appears in pregnant women, but obstructed blood flow is the direct cause. They may cause a dull ache or may be the site for ◊thrombosis, infection, or ulcers. The affected veins can be injected with a substance that causes them to shrink, or surgery may be needed.

variegation description of plant leaves or stems that exhibit patches of different colours. The term is usually applied to plants that show white, cream, or yellow on their leaves, caused by areas of tissue that lack the green pigment ◊chlorophyll. Variegated plants are bred for their decorative value, but they are often considerably weaker than the normal, uniformly green plant. Many will not breed true and require ◊vegetative reproduction.

The term is sometimes applied to abnormal patchy colouring of petals, as in the variegated petals of certain tulips, caused by a virus infection. A mineral deficiency in the soil may also be the cause of variegation.

Varuna in early Hindu mythology, the sky god and king of the universe.Varuna may be equated with the Graeco-Roman sky god Ouranos/Uranus and with Orion.

varve in geology, a pair of thin sedimentary beds, one coarse and one fine, representing a cycle of thaw followed by an interval of freezing, in lakes of glacial regions. Each couplet thus constitutes the sedimentary record of a year, and by counting varves in glacial lakes a record of absolute time elapsed can be determined. Summer and winter layers often are distinguished also by colour, with lighter layers representing summer deposition, and darker layers the result of dark clay settling from water while the lake was frozen.

variegation This elder tree *Sambucus nigra* exhibits clumps of variegated leaves among a majority of normal leaves. Usually an accident in nature, variegation is encouraged in some ornamentals. *Premaphotos Wildlife*

Vasa dynasty Swedish royal house founded by ◊Gustavus Vasa. He liberated his country from Danish rule 1520–23 and put down local uprisings of nobles and peasants. By 1544 he was secure enough to make his title hereditary. His grandson, ◊Gustavus Adolphus, became king 1611 and led the armies of the Protestant princes in the ◊Thirty Years' War until his death. The dynasty ended 1809 when Gustavus IV was deposed by a revolution and replaced by his uncle Charles XIII. With no heir to the throne, the crown was offered 1810 to one of Napoleon's generals, Bernadotte, who became King Charles John until his death in 1844.

Vasarély Victor 1908–1997. Hungarian-born French artist. He was one of the leading exponents of ◊Op art. After studying medicine in Budapest, he went to Paris 1930. He initially worked as a graphic artist, concentrating on black-and-white artwork. In the 1940s he developed precise geometric compositions, full of visual puzzles and effects of movement, which he created with complex arrangements of hard-edged geometric shapes and subtle variations in colours.

Vasari Giorgio 1511–1574. Italian art historian, architect, and painter. He is best known for *Le vite de' più eccelenti architetti, pittori, et sculteri italiani/The Lives of the Most Excellent Italian Architects, Painters, and Sculptors* 1550 (enlarged 1568), which provides an invaluable source of information on Italian Renaissance artists. His most important architectural work was the Uffizi Palace, Florence (now an art gallery).

During his lifetime he was famous as a painter and architect, his Mannerist style showing the strong influence of Michelangelo. As well as the Uffizi, he designed the Palazzo Vecchio, Florence, and its frescoes 1555. His painting can also be studied in his own house in Arezzo 1547, which he decorated lavishly (it is now a museum). He also designed palaces and churches in Pisa and Arezzo. As a painter he has never been highly rated, though he is of interest as an example of the Mannerist exaggeration which the devotion to Michelangelo produced. His *Lives*, however, is a classic, and, though corrected in a number of particulars by modern research, remains of the greatest value as an account of the progress of Italian art from the Middle Ages to the Renaissance. It was partly rewritten and enlarged 1568, and contains his autobiography.

Vasco da Gama Portuguese navigator; see ◊Gama.

vascular bundle in botany, strand of primary conducting tissue (a 'vein') in vascular plants, consisting mainly of water-conducting tissues, metaxylem and protoxylem, which together make up the primary ◊xylem, and nutrient-conducting tissue, ◊phloem. It extends from the roots to the stems and leaves. Typically the phloem is situated nearest to the epidermis and the xylem towards the centre of the bundle. In plants exhibiting ◊secondary growth, the xylem and phloem are separated by a thin layer of vascular ◊cambium, which gives rise to new conducting tissues.

vascular plant plant containing vascular bundles. ◊Pteridophytes (ferns, horsetails, and club mosses), ◊gymnosperms (conifers and cycads), and ◊angiosperms (flowering plants) are all vascular plants.

vas deferens in male vertebrates, a tube conducting sperm from the testis to the urethra. The sperm is carried in a fluid secreted by various glands, and can be transported very rapidly when the smooth muscle in the wall of the vas deferens undergoes rhythmic contraction, as in sexual intercourse.

vasectomy male sterilization; an operation to cut and tie the ducts (see ◊vas deferens) that carry sperm from the testes to the penis. Vasectomy does not affect sexual performance, but the semen produced at ejaculation no longer contains sperm. Some surgical attempts to reopen the duct have been successful, and some have opened spontaneously, thus making conception possible.

vassal in medieval Europe, a person who paid feudal homage to a superior lord (see ◊feudalism), and who promised military service and advice in return for a grant of land. The term was used from the 9th century. The relationship of vassalage was the mainstay of the feudal system and declined along with it during the transition to bastard feudalism, the system in which grants of land were replaced by money as rewards for service.

Vassar Matthew 1792–1868. British-born US entrepreneur and educational philanthropist. A proponent of higher education for women, he endowed Vassar Female College in Poughkeepsie, New York, 1861. The school opened 1865 with a full college curriculum and became one of the finest women's educational institutions in the USA.

Born in England, Vassar came to the USA with his family 1796. He worked in his father's brewery in Poughkeepsie before establishing his own firm 1811, and successfully expanded his business interests and real-estate investments.

Vassiliou Georgios Vassos 1931– . Greek-Cypriot politician and entrepreneur, president of Cyprus 1988–93. A self-made millionaire, he entered politics as an independent and in 1988 won the presidency, with Communist Party support. He subsequently, with United Nations help, tried to heal the rift between the Greek and Turkish communities, but was unsuccessful. In the Feb 1993 presidential elections he was narrowly defeated by Glafkos Clerides.

VAT abbreviation for ◊***value-added tax***.

Vatican City State sovereign area within the city of Rome, Italy. *See country box opposite.*

Vatican Council either of two Roman Catholic ecumenical councils called by Pope Pius IX 1869 (which met 1870) and by Pope John XXIII 1959 (which met 1962). These councils deliberated over elements of church policy.

Vauban Sébastien le Prestre de 1633–1707. French marshal and military engineer. In Louis XIV's wars he conducted many sieges and rebuilt many of the fortresses on France's east frontier.

Vaucluse mountain range in SE France, part of the Provence Alps, E of Avignon, rising to 1,242 m/ 4,075 ft. It gives its name to a *département*. The Italian poet Petrarch lived in the Vale of Vaucluse 1337–53.

Vaughan Sarah Lois 1924–1990. US jazz singer. She began by singing bebop with such musicians as Dizzy Gillespie and later moved effortlessly between jazz and romantic ballads, her voice having a range of nearly three octaves. She toured very widely and had several hit singles, including 'Make Yourself Comfortable' 1954, 'Mr Wonderful' 1956, and 'Broken-Hearted Melody' 1959.

Vaughan Williams Ralph 1872–1958. English composer. His style was tonal and often evocative of the English countryside through the use of folk themes. Among his works are the orchestral *Fantasia on a Theme by Thomas Tallis* 1910; the opera *Sir John in Love* 1929, featuring the Elizabethan song 'Greensleeves'; and nine symphonies 1909–57.

He studied at Cambridge, the Royal College of Music, with Max Bruch (1838–1920) in Berlin, and Maurice ◊Ravel in Paris. His choral poems include *Toward the Unknown Region* (Whitman) 1907 and *On Wenlock Edge* (Housman) 1909, *A Sea Symphony* 1910, and *A London Symphony* 1914. Later works include *Sinfonia Antartica* 1953, developed from his film score for *Scott of the Antarctic* 1948, and Symphony no 9 1957. He also wrote *A Pastoral Symphony* 1922, sacred music for unaccompanied choir, the ballad opera *Hugh the Drover* 1924, and the operatic morality play *The Pilgrim's Progress* 1951.

vault arched ceiling or roof built mainly of stone or bricks. Of the many different types of vault, the ***barrel vault*** or ***tunnel vault*** is the simplest form of semi-cylindrical ceiling, consisting of a continuous line of semicircular or pointed vaults. Supporting walls usually require ◊buttresses to contain the thrust of the vault. The ***fan vault***, characteristic of Gothic architecture, is composed of a number of intersecting sections of cones, which are often highly decorated. The ***groin vault*** is formed by the intersection of barrel vaults running at right angles to each other.

VDU abbreviation for ◊***visual display unit***.

vector graphics computer graphics that are stored in the computer memory by using geometric formulas. Vector graphics can be transformed (enlarged, rotated, stretched, and so on) without loss

VATICAN CITY STATE

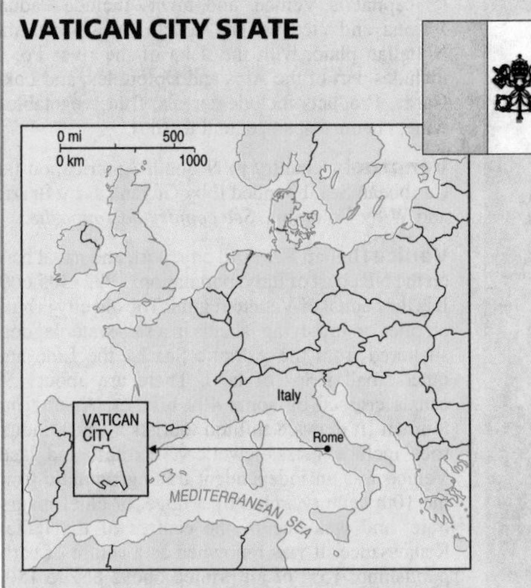

national name *Stato della Città del Vaticano*
area 0.4 sq km/109 acres
physical features forms an enclave in the heart of Rome, Italy
head of state John Paul II from 1978
head of government Cardinal Sebastiano Baggio
political system absolute Catholicism
population 1,000 (1994 est)
languages Latin (official), Italian
religions Roman Catholic
currency Vatican City lira; Italian lira

HISTORY

AD 64 Death of St Peter, a Christian martyr who, by legend, was killed in Rome and became regarded as the first bishop of Rome. The Pope, as head of the Roman Catholic Church, is viewed as the spiritual descendent of St Peter.
756 The Pope became temporal ruler of the Papal States, which stretched across central Italy, centred around Rome.
11th–13th Cs Under Gregory VII and Innocent III the papacy enjoyed its greatest temporal power.
1377 After seven decades in which the papacy was based in Avignon (France), Rome once again became the headquarters for the Pope, with the Vatican Palace becoming the official residence.
1860 Umbria, Marche, and much of Emilia Romagna which, along with Lazio formed the Papal States, were annexed by the new unified Italian state.
1870 First Vatican Council defined as a matter of faith the absolute primacy of the Pope and the infallibility of his pronouncements on 'matters of faith and morals'.
1870–71 French forces, which had been protecting the Pope, were withdrawn, allowing Italian nationalist forces to capture Rome, which became the capital of Italy; Pope Pius IX retreated into the Vatican Palace, from which no Pope was to emerge until 1929.
1929 Lateran Agreement, signed by the Italian fascist leader Benito Mussolini and Pope Pius XI, restored full sovereign jurisdiction over the Vatican City State to the bishopric of Rome (Holy See) and declared the new state to be a neutral and inviolable territory.
1947 New Italian constitution confirmed the sovereignty of the Vatican City State.
1962 Second Vatican Council called by Pope John XXIII.
1978 John Paul II became the first non-Italian pope for more than 400 years.
1985 New concordat signed under which Roman Catholicism ceased to be Italy's state religion.
1992 Relations with East European states restored.

SEE ALSO John Paul II; Lateran Treaties; Roman Catholicism

of picture resolution. It is also possible to select and transform any of the components of a vector-graphics display because each is separately defined in the computer memory. In these respects vector graphics are superior to ◊raster graphics. Vector graphics are typically used for drawing applications, allowing the user to create and modify technical diagrams.

vector quantity any physical quantity that has both magnitude and direction (such as the velocity or acceleration of an object) as distinct from ◊scalar quantity (such as speed, density, or mass), which has magnitude but no direction. A vector is represented either geometrically by an arrow whose length corresponds to its magnitude and points in an appropriate direction, or by two or three numbers representing the magnitude of its components.

Vectors can be added graphically by constructing a parallelogram of vectors (such as the ◊parallelogram of forces commonly employed in physics and engineering).

If two forces *p* and *q* are acting on a body at *A*, then the parallelogram of forces is drawn to determine the resultant force and direction *r*. *p*, *q*, and *r* are vectors. In technical writing, a vector is denoted by bold type, underlined AB, or overlined AB.

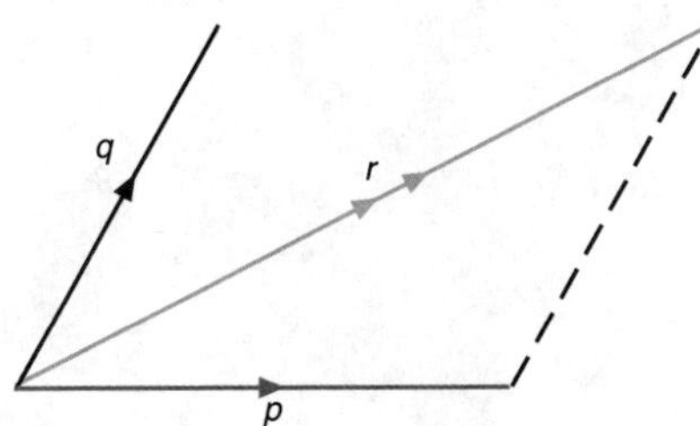

vector quantity A parallelogram of vectors. Vectors can be added graphically using the parallelogram rule. According to the rule, the sum of vectors *p* and *q* is the vector *r* which is the diagonal of the parallelogram with sides *p* and *q*.

Veda (Sanskrit 'divine knowledge') the most sacred of the Hindu scriptures, hymns written in an old form of Sanskrit; the oldest may date from 1500 or 2000 BC. The four main collections are: the *Rig-veda* (hymns and praises); *Yajur-Veda* (prayers and sacrificial formulae); *Sâma-Veda* (tunes and chants); and *Atharva-Veda*, or Veda of the Atharvans, the officiating priests at the sacrifices.

Vedānta Sanskrit, 'knowledge's end' school of Hindu philosophy that developed the teachings of the *Upanishads*. One of its teachers was Samkara, who lived in S India in the 8th century AD and is generally regarded as a manifestation of Siva. He taught that there is only one reality, Brahman, and that knowledge of Brahman leads finally to *moksha*, or liberation from reincarnation.

Vedda (Sinhalese 'hunter') the aboriginal peoples of Sri Lanka, who occupied the island before the arrival of the Aryans about 550 BC. Formerly cave-dwelling hunter-gatherers, they have now almost died out or merged with the rest of the population. They speak a Sinhalese language, belonging to the Indo-European family. They live mainly in the central highlands, and many practise shifting cultivation.

Vega or ***Alpha Lyrae*** brightest star in the constellation ◊Lyra and the fifth brightest star in the night sky. It is a blue-white star, 25 light years from Earth, with a luminosity 50 times that of the Sun. In 1983 the Infrared Astronomy Satellite (IRAS) discovered a ring of dust around Vega, possibly a disc from which a planetary system is forming.

Vega Lope Felix de (Carpio) 1562–1635. Spanish poet and dramatist. He was one of the founders of modern Spanish drama. He wrote epics, pastorals, odes, sonnets, novels, and, reputedly, over 1,500 plays (of which 426 are still in existence), mostly tragicomedies. He set out his views on drama in *Arte nuevo de hacer comedias/The New Art of Writing Plays* 1609, in which he defended his innovations while reaffirming the classical forms. *Fuenteovejuna* about 1614 has been acclaimed as the first proletarian drama.

He was born in Madrid, served with the Armada 1588, and in 1613 took holy orders.

vegan vegetarian who eats no foods of animal origin whatever, including fish, eggs, and milk. Theoretically vegans are at risk of a deficiency of vitamin B_{12}, which is needed by the body for blood cell and nerve formation (see ◊vitamin); it can be absorbed from fortified soya products and yeast extracts. Vegans ensure an adequate supply of calcium (commonly obtained from dairy products) from greens, seeds, nuts, and soya products, and vitamin D from sunshine.

vegetable any food plant, especially leafy plants (cabbage and lettuce), roots and tubers (carrots, parsnips, and potatoes), legumes (peas, lentils, and beans), and even flowers (cauliflower, broccoli, and artichoke). Tomatoes, peppers, aubergines, and cucumbers are generally regarded as vegetables but are technically fruits. Green leafy vegetables and potatoes are good sources of vitamin C, though much is lost in cooking, and legumes are a main source of protein. Cooking softens vegetables by dissolving pectins and hemicellulose and gelatinizing starch.

vegetarian person who eats only foods obtained without slaughter, for humanitarian, aesthetic, political, or health reasons. ◊Vegans abstain from all foods of animal origin.

vegetative reproduction type of ◊asexual reproduction in plants that relies not on spores, but on multicellular structures formed by the parent plant. Some of the main types are ◊stolons and runners, ◊bulbils, sucker shoots produced from roots (such as in the creeping thistle *Cirsium arvense*), ◊tubers, ◊bulbs, ◊corms, and ◊rhizomes. Vegetative reproduction has long been exploited in horticulture and agriculture, with various methods employed to multiply stocks of plants. See also ◊plant propagation. *See illustration on following page.*

vein in animals with a circulatory system, any vessel that carries blood from the body to the heart. Veins contain valves that prevent the blood from running back when moving against gravity. They always carry deoxygenated blood, with the exception of the veins leading from the lungs to the heart in birds and mammals, which carry newly oxygenated blood. The term is also used more loosely for any system of channels that strengthens living tissues and supplies them with nutrients – for example, leaf veins (see ◊vascular bundle), and the veins in insects' wings.

Vela bright constellation of the southern hemisphere near Carina, represented as the sails of a ship. It contains large wisps of gas – called the Gum nebula after its discoverer, the Australian astronomer Colin Gum (1924–1960) – believed to be the remains of one or more ◊supernovae. Vela also contains the second optical ◊pulsar (a pulsar that flashes at a visible wavelength) to be discovered. Vela was originally regarded as part of the constellation Argo. Its four brightest stars are second-magnitude, one of them being Suhail, about 490 light years from Earth.

Velázquez Diego Rodríguez de Silva y 1599–1660. Spanish painter. One of the outstanding artists of the 17th century, he was court painter to Philip IV in Madrid, where he produced many portraits of the royal family as well as occasional religious paintings, genre scenes, and other works. Notable among his portraits is *Las Meninas/The Maids of Honour* 1656 (Prado, Madrid), while *Women Frying Eggs* 1618 (National Gallery of Scotland, Edinburgh) is a typical genre scene.

Throughout his career realism was the basis of Velázquez's art, but his colour became cooler and his brushwork freer, and in his late works the brushstrokes appear meaningless when viewed closely, but at the right distance coalesce to form shapes and spaces rendered with an astonishingly convincing tone and atmosphere, culminating in *Las Meninas*.

With his technical development went an increasing psychological penetration, and whether he was painting the king of Spain, then the most powerful man in the world, or the court dwarfs, Velázquez approached his work with the same complete honesty, conviction, and respect for the humanity of his sitters. His portrait of *Pope*

vegetative reproduction In the *Kalanchoe tubiflora* from Madagascar numerous tiny plantlets with roots develop along the leaf edges. These are easily detached and root where they fall. *Premaphotos Wildlife*

'It seems like being both in town and at sea, at one and the same time.'

On VENICE
J P Cobbett *Journal of a Tour in Italy*

Innocent X 1650 (Doria Pamphili Gallery, Rome) is among his most important achievements in portraiture.

Among his other major works are *The Surrender of Breda* 1634–35 (Prado), one of the greatest contemporary history paintings; *The Rokeby Venus* about 1648 (National Gallery, London), the first Spanish nude; and the portraits *Philip IV* (National Gallery, London) and *Juan de Pareja* 1650 (Metropolitan Museum of Art, New York).

Velcro (from French *velours* 'velvet' and *crochet* 'hook') system of very small hooks and eyes for fastening clothing, developed by Swiss inventor Georges de Mestral (1902–1990) after studying why burrs stuck to his trousers and noting that they were made of thousands of tiny hooks.

veldt subtropical grassland in South Africa, equivalent to the ◊Pampas of South America.

vellum type of parchment, often rolled in scrolls, made from the skin of a calf, kid, or lamb. It was used from the late Roman Empire and Middle Ages for exceptionally important documents and the finest manuscripts. For example, Torahs (the five books of Moses) are always written in Hebrew on vellum. The modern term now describes thick, high-quality paper that resembles fine vellum parchment.

Velázquez A portrait of his servant, Ivan de Pareja, by the Spanish painter Velázquez. Velázquez was the most prominent artist in 17th-century Spain, and was court painter to Philip IV. He produced religious scenes and depictions of everyday life as well as portraits of the royal family. *Image Select (UK) Ltd*

velocity speed of an object in a given direction. Velocity is a ◊vector quantity, since its direction is important as well as its magnitude (or speed). The velocity at any instant of a particle travelling in a curved path is in the direction of the tangent to the path at the instant considered. The velocity v of an object travelling in a fixed direction may be calculated by dividing the distance s it has travelled by the time t taken to do so, and may be expressed as:

$$v = s/t$$

velvet fabric of silk, cotton, nylon, or other textile, with a short, thick pile. Utrecht in the Netherlands and Genoa, Italy, are traditional centres of manufacture. It is woven on a double loom, then cut between the centre pile to form velvet nap.

vena cava either of the two great veins of the trunk, returning deoxygenated blood to the right atrium of the ◊heart. The ***superior vena cava***, beginning where the arches of the two innominate veins join high in the chest, receives blood from the head, neck, chest, and arms; the ***inferior vena cava***, arising from the junction of the right and left common iliac veins, receives blood from all parts of the body below the diaphragm.

Venda former Republic of; former independent homeland ◊Black National State within South Africa, independent from 1979 (but not recognized by the United Nations) until 1994 when it was re-integrated into South Africa, in Northern Transvaal. The region covers an area of 6,500 sq km/2,510 sq mi. Towns and cities include Makwarela, Makhade, and Sibasa; its main industries are coal, copper, graphite, and construction stone. Luvenda and English are spoken here.

Vendée river in W France that rises near the village of La Châtaigneraie and flows 72 km/45 mi to join the Sèvre Niortaise 11 km/7 mi E of the Bay of Biscay.

Vendôme Louis Joseph, Duc de Vendôme 1654–1712. Marshal of France under Louis XIV, he lost his command after defeat by the British commander Marlborough at Oudenaarde, Belgium, 1708, but achieved successes in the 1710 Spanish campaign during the War of the ◊Spanish Succession.

veneer thin layers of fine wood applied to the surface of furniture made with a coarser or cheaper wood. Veneer has been widely used from the second half of the 17th century.

venereal disease (VD) any disease mainly transmitted by sexual contact, although commonly the term is used specifically for gonorrhoea and syphilis, both occurring worldwide, and chancroid ('soft sore') and lymphogranuloma venerum, seen mostly in the tropics. The term ◊sexually transmitted disease (STD) is more often used to encompass a growing list of conditions passed on primarily, but not exclusively, by sexual contact.

Veneto region of NE Italy, comprising the provinces of Belluno, Padova (Padua), Treviso, Rovigo, Venezia (Venice), and Vicenza; area 18,400 sq km/7,102 sq mi; population (1992 est) 4,395,300. Its capital is Venice, and towns include Padua, Verona, and Vicenza. The Veneto forms part of the N Italian plain, with the delta of the river Po; it includes part of the Alps and Dolomites, and Lake Garda. Products include cereals, fruit, vegetables, wine, chemicals, ships, and textiles.

Venezuela country in N South America, on the Caribbean Sea, bounded E by Guyana, S by Brazil, and W by Colombia. *See country box opposite.*

Venice (Italian ***Venezia***) city, port, and naval base on the NE coast of Italy; population (1992) 305,600. It is the capital of Veneto region. The old city is built on piles on low-lying islands in a salt-water lagoon, sheltered from the Adriatic Sea by the Lido and other small strips of land. There are about 150 canals crossed by some 400 bridges. Apart from tourism (it draws 8 million tourists a year), industries include glass, jewellery, textiles, and lace. Venice was an independent trading republic from the 10th century, ruled by a doge, or chief magistrate, and was one of the centres of the Italian Renaissance. It was renowned as a centre of early publishing; 15% of all printed books before 1500 were printed in Venice.

features It is now connected with the mainland and its industrial suburb, Mestre, by road and rail viaduct. The Grand Canal divides the city and is crossed by the Rialto Bridge; transport is by traditional gondola or *vaporetto* (water bus). St Mark's Square has the 11th-century Byzantine cathedral of San Marco, the 9th–16th-century campanile (rebuilt 1902), and the 14th–15th-century Gothic Doge's Palace (linked to the former state prison by the 17th-century Bridge of Sighs). The nearby Lido is a bathing resort.

The Venetian School of artists includes the Bellinis, Carpaccio, Giorgione, Titian, Tintoretto, and Veronese. The Venetian Carnival is held annually at the end of February, with spectacular costumes and masks. Venice's opera house, La Fenice, considered to be one of the city's most beautiful monuments, was destroyed by fire Jan 1996.

history In 1991 archaeologist Ernesto Canal established that the city was founded by the Romans in the 1st century AD; it was previously thought to have been founded by mainlanders fleeing from the Barbarians in AD 421. Venice became a wealthy independent trading republic in the 10th century, stretching by the mid-15th century to the Alps and

Venn diagram Venn diagram. (a) a Venn diagram of two intersecting sets; (b) a Venn diagram showing the set of whole numbers from 1 to 20 and the subsets P and O of prime and odd numbers, respectively. The intersection of P and O contains all the prime numbers that are also odd.

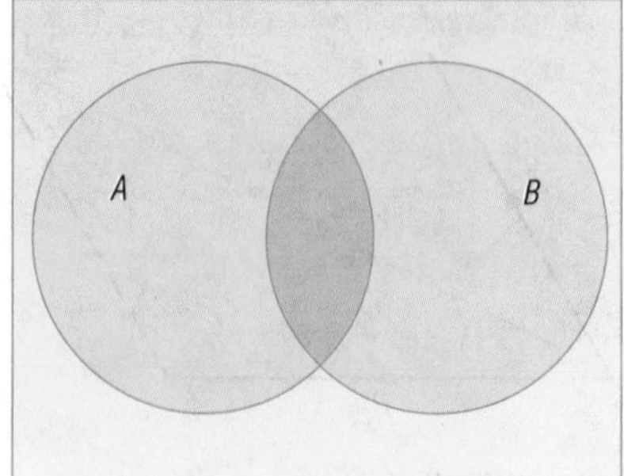

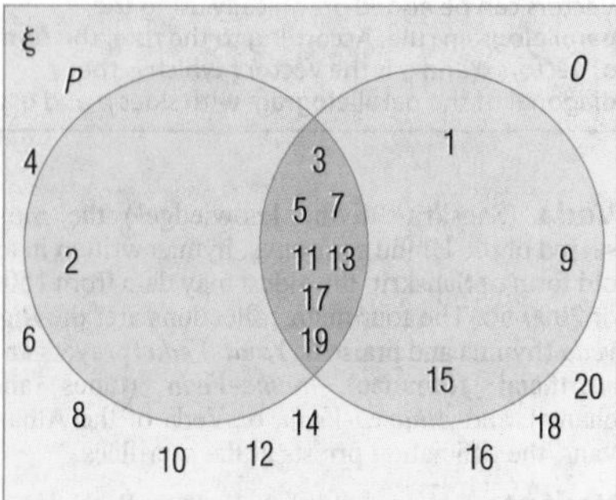

VENEZUELA
Republic of

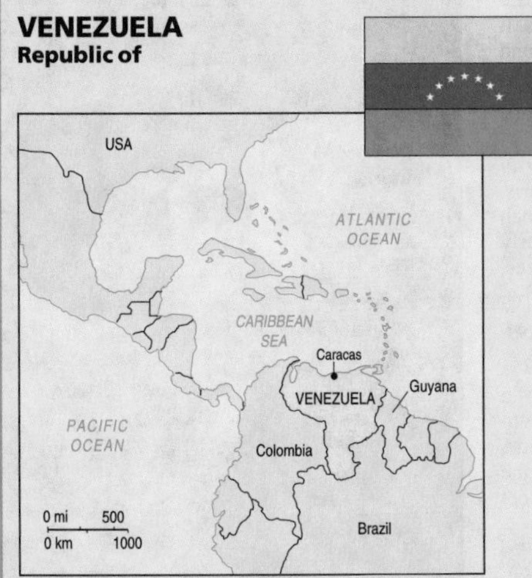

national name *República de Venezuela*
area 912,100 sq km/352,162 sq mi
capital Caracas
major towns/cities Barquisimeto, Valencia
major ports Maracaibo
physical features Andes Mountains and Lake Maracaibo in NW; central plains (llanos); delta of river Orinoco in E; Guiana Highlands in SE
head of state and government Rafael Caldera Rodriguez from 1993
political system federal democratic republic
administrative divisions 20 states, two federal territories, 72 federal dependencies, and one federal district
political parties Democratic Action Party (AD), moderate left of centre; Christian Social Party (COPEI), Christian, centre-right; National Convergence (CN), broad coalition grouping; Movement towards Socialism (MAS), left of centre; Radical Cause (LCR), left-wing
population 21,844,000 (1995 est)
population growth rate 2.3% (1990–95); 1.8% (2000–05)
ethnic distribution 67% mestizos (of Spanish-American and American-Indian descent), 21% Europeans, 10% Africans, and 2% Indians
life expectancy 67 (men), 74 (women)
literacy rate men 87%, women 90%
languages Spanish (official), Indian languages 2%
religions Roman Catholic
currency bolívar
GDP (US $) 55.03 billion (1994)
growth rate −3.3% (1994)
exports coffee, timber, oil, aluminium, iron ore, petrochemicals, bauxite

HISTORY
1st millenium BC Beginnings of settled agriculture.
AD 1498–99 Visited by Christopher Columbus and Alonso de Ojeda, at which time the principal indigenous Indian communities were the Caribs, Arawaks, and Chibchas; it was named Venezuela ('little Venice') since the coastal Indians lived in stilted thatched houses.
1521 Spanish settlement established on the NE coast and was ruled by Spain from Santo Domingo (Dominanican Republic).
1567 Caracas founded by Diego de Losada.
1739 Became part of the newly created Spanish Viceroyalty of New Granada, with a capital at Bogotá (Colombia), but, lacking gold mines, retained great autonomy.
1749 First rebellion against Spanish colonial rule.
1806 Rebellion against Spain began, led by Francisco Miranda.
1811–12 First Venezuelan Republic declared by patriots, taking advantage of invasion of Spain by Napoleon Bonaparte, but Spanish Royalist forces re-established their authority.
1813–14 The Venezuelan, Simón Bolívar, 'El Libertador' (the Liberator), created another briefly independent republic, before being forced to withdraw to Colombia.
1821 After battle of Carabobo, Venezuelan independence achieved within Republic of Gran Colombia (which also comprised Colombia, Ecuador, and Panama).
1829 Became separate state of Venezuela after leaving Republic of Gran Colombia.
1830–48 Gen José Antonio Páez, the first of a series of caudillos (military leaders), established political stability.
1870–88 Antonio Guzmán Blanco ruled as benevolent liberal-conservative dictator, modernizing the infrastructure and developing agriculture, notably coffee, and education.
1899 International arbitration tribunal found in favour of British Guiana (Guyana) in long-running dispute over border with Venezuela.
1902 Ports blockaded by British, Italian, and German navies as a result of Venezuela's failure to repay loans.
1908–35 Harsh rule of the dictator Juan Vicente Gómez, during which period Venezuela became world's largest exporter of oil, which had been discovered in 1910.
1947 First truly democratic elections held, but the new president, Rómulo Gallegos, was removed within eight months by the military in the person of Col Marcos Pérez Jimenez.
1958 Overthrow of Perez and establishment of an enduring civilian democracy, headed by the left-wing Romulo Betancourt of the Democratic Action Party (AD).
1964 Dr Raúl Leoni (AD) became president in first-ever constitutional handover of civilian power.
1969 Dr Rafael Caldera Rodríguez, of the centre-right Christian Social Party (COPEI), became president.
1974 Carlos Andrés Pérez (AD) became president, with the economy remaining buoyant through oil revenues. Oil and iron industries nationalized.
1979 Dr Luis Herrera (COPEI) became president.
1984 Dr Jaime Lusinchi (AD) became president; social pact established between government, trade unions, and business; national debt rescheduled as oil revenues plummeted.
1987 Widespread social unrest triggered by inflation; student demonstrators shot by police.
1989 Carlos Andrés Pérez (AD) elected president. Economic austerity programme enforced by a loan of $4.3 billion from International Monetary Fund. Price increases triggered riots known as 'Caracazo'; 300 people killed. Martial law declared. General strike followed. Elections boycotted by opposition groups.
1992 Attempted antigovernment coups failed, at a cost of 120 lives.
1993 Pérez resigned, accused of corruption; Ramon José Velasquez succeeded him as interim head of state. Former president Dr Rafael Caldera (COMEI) re-elected.
1996 Pérez found guilty on corruption charges and imprisoned.

SEE ALSO Arawak; Bolívar, Simón; Carib

including Crete. It was governed by an aristocratic oligarchy, the Council of Ten, and a senate, which appointed the doge 697–1797. Venice helped defeat the Ottoman Empire in the naval battle of Lepanto 1571 but the republic was overthrown by Napoleon 1797. It passed to Austria 1815 but finally became part of the kingdom of Italy 1866.

veni, vidi, vici (Latin 'I came, I saw, I conquered') Julius ◊Caesar's description of his victory over King Pharnaces II (63–47 BC) at Zela in 47 BC.

Venn diagram in mathematics, a diagram representing a ◊set or sets and the logical relationships between them. The sets are drawn as circles. An area of overlap between two circles (sets) contains elements that are common to both sets, and thus represents a third set. Circles that do not overlap represent sets with no elements in common (disjoint sets). The method is named after the British logician John Venn (1834–1923).

ventral surface the front of an animal. In vertebrates, the side furthest from the backbone; in invertebrates, the side closest to the ground. The positioning of the main nerve pathways on the ventral side is a characteristic of invertebrates.

ventricle in zoology, either of the two lower chambers of the heart that force blood into the circulation by contraction of their muscular walls. The term also refers to any of four cavities within the brain in which cerebrospinal fluid is produced.

Ventris Michael George Francis 1922–1956. English architect. Deciphering Minoan Linear B, the language of the tablets found at Knossos and Pylos, he showed that it was a very early form of Greek, thus revising existing views on early Greek history. *Documents in Mycenaean Greek*, written with John Chadwick (1920–), was published shortly after he died.

Venturi Robert Charles 1925– . US architect. He pioneered ◊Post-Modernism through his books *Complexity and Contradiction in Architecture* 1967 (Pulitzer prize 1991) and *Learning from Las Vegas* 1972. In 1986 he was commissioned to design the Sainsbury Wing extension to the National Gallery, London, opened 1991. He is famous for his slogan 'Less is a bore', countering German architect Ludwig Mies van der Rohe's 'Less is more'.

Venturi tube device for measuring the rate of fluid flow through a pipe. It consists of a tube with a constriction (narrowing) in the middle of its length. The constriction causes a drop in pressure in the fluid flowing in the pipe. A pressure gauge attached to the constriction measures the pressure drop and this is used to find the rate of fluid flow. Venturi tubes are also used in the carburettor of a motor car to draw petrol into the engine.

Venus in Roman mythology, the goddess of love and beauty, equivalent to the Greek ◊Aphrodite. The patrician Romans believed that they were descended from Aeneas, who was the son of the goddess and Anchises, a Trojan noble. She was therefore venerated as the guardian of the Roman people, as well as goddess of military victory and patroness of spring.

Venus second planet from the Sun. It can approach Earth to within 38 million km/24 million mi, closer than any other planet. Its mass is 0.82 that of Earth. Venus rotates on its axis more slowly than any other planet, from east to west, the opposite direction to the other planets (except Uranus and possibly Pluto)
mean distance from the Sun 108.2 million km/67.2 million mi
equatorial diameter 12,100 km/7,500 mi
rotation period 243 Earth days
year 225 Earth days
atmosphere Venus is shrouded by clouds of sulphuric acid droplets that sweep across the planet from east to west every four days. The atmosphere is almost entirely carbon dioxide, which traps the Sun's heat by the ◊greenhouse effect and raises the planet's surface temperature to 480°C/900°F, with an atmospheric pressure of 90 times that at the surface of the Earth
surface consists mainly of silicate rock and may have an interior structure similar to that of Earth: an iron nickel core, a ◊mantle composed of more mafic rocks (rocks made of one or more ferromagnesian, dark-coloured minerals), and a thin siliceous outer ◊crust. The surface is dotted with deep impact craters. Some of Venus's volcanoes may still be active.
satellites no moons

The first artificial object to hit another planet was the Soviet probe *Venera 3*, which crashed on Venus 1 March 1966. Later Venera probes parachuted down through the atmosphere and landed successfully on its surface, analysing surface material and sending back information and pictures. In Dec 1978 a US ◊Pioneer Venus probe went into orbit around the planet and mapped most of its surface by radar, which penetrates clouds. In 1992 the US space probe *Magellan* mapped 99% of the planet's surface to a resolution of 100 m/ 330 ft.

The largest highland area is Aphrodite Terra near the equator, half the size of Africa. The highest mountains are on the northern highland region of Ishtar Terra, where the massif of Maxwell Montes rises to 10,600 m/35,000 ft above the average surface level. The highland areas on Venus were formed by volcanoes. *See illustration on following page.*

Venus flytrap insectivorous plant *Dionaea muscipula* of the sundew family, native to the SE USA; its leaves have two hinged blades that close and entrap insects.

Veracruz port (trading in coffee, tobacco, and vanilla) in E Mexico, on the Gulf of Mexico;

Venus View of the surface of Venus, showing the northern hemisphere. Venus is often described as Earth's twin planet because it is the closest planet to Earth and has a similar size, with a diameter of 12,100 km/7,500 mi to Earth's 12,756 km/7,923 mi. The atmosphere of Venus, however, is carbon dioxide, and temperatures reach 480°C/900°F. *Image Select (UK) Ltd*

population (1990) 328,600. Products include chemicals, sisal, and textiles. It was founded by the Spanish conquistador Hernando Cortés as Villa Nueva de la Vera Cruz ('new town of the true cross') on a nearby site 1519 and transferred to its present site 1599.

verbena any plant of the genus *Verbena*, family Verbenaceae, of about 100 species, mostly found in the American tropics. The leaves are fragrant and the tubular flowers arranged in close spikes in colours ranging from white to rose, violet, and purple. The garden verbena is a hybrid annual.

Vercingetorix died 46 BC. Gallic chieftain. Leader of a revolt of all the tribes of Gaul against the Romans 52 BC; he lost, was captured, displayed in Julius Caesar's triumph 46 BC, and later executed. This ended the Gallic resistance to Roman rule.

Verdi Giuseppe Fortunino Francesco 1813–1901. Italian opera composer of the Romantic period. He took his native operatic style to new heights of dramatic expression. In 1842 he wrote the opera *Nabucco*, followed by *Ernani* 1844 and *Rigoletto* 1851. Other works include *Il trovatore* and *La traviata* both 1853, *Aïda* 1871, and the masterpieces of his old age, *Otello* 1887 and *Falstaff* 1893. His *Requiem* 1874 commemorates Alessandro ◊Manzoni.

During the mid-1800s, Verdi became a symbol of Italy's fight for independence from Austria, frequently finding himself in conflict with the Austrian authorities, who felt that his operas encouraged Italian nationalism.

verbena *Verbena elegans* is one of numerous verbenas which occur in the deserts of the SW USA and Mexico. They flower in profusion after heavy rains. *Premaphotos Wildlife*

verdigris green-blue coating of copper ethanoate that forms naturally on copper, bronze, and brass. It is an irritating, greenish, poisonous compound made by treating copper with ethanoic acid, and was formerly used in wood preservatives, antifouling compositions, and green paints.

Verdun fortress town in NE France in the *département* of the Meuse, 280 km/174 mi east of Paris. During World War I it became a symbol of French resistance and was the centre of a series of bitterly fought actions between French and German forces, finally being recaptured Sept 1918.

Vergil alternative spelling of ◊Virgil, Roman poet.

Verginia in Roman mythology, a girl who was killed by her father to protect her from the lust of a Roman magistrate. Her death prompted a revolution, concluded by the publication of a law code, the Twelve Tables. Her story was told by both the Italian poet ◊Petrarch and the English poet ◊Chaucer in the Middle Ages.

verification in computing, the process of checking that data being input to a computer have been accurately copied from a source document. This may be done visually, by checking the original copy of the data against the copy shown on the VDU screen. A more thorough method is to enter the data twice, using two different keyboard operators, and then to check the two sets of input copies against each other. The checking is normally carried out by the computer itself, any differences between the two copies being reported for correction by one of the the keyboard operators.

vérité (French 'realism'), as in ◊*cinéma vérité*, used to describe a realistic or documentary style.

Verlaine Paul Marie 1844–1896. French lyric poet. He was acknowledged as the leader of the Symbolist poets (see ◊Symbolism). His volumes of verse, strongly influenced by the poets Charles ◊Baudelaire and Arthur ◊Rimbaud, include *Poèmes saturniens/Saturnine Poems* 1866, *Fêtes galantes/Amorous Entertainments* 1869, and *Romances sans paroles/Songs without Words* 1874. In 1873 he was imprisoned for shooting and wounding Rimbaud. His later works reflect his attempts to lead a reformed life.

Vermeer Jan 1632–1675. Dutch painter, active in Delft. He painted quiet, everyday scenes that are characterized by an almost abstract simplicity, subtle colour harmonies, and a remarkable ability to suggest the fall of light on objects. Examples are *The Lacemaker* about 1655 (Louvre, Paris) and *Maidservant Pouring Milk* about 1658 (Rijksmuseum, Amsterdam).

Vermeer is remarkable among Dutch painters for the stress he places not on the subject of a picture but its formal qualities: the balance and simplicity of design, colour harmonies, and the subtleties of texture, tone, and light. Italian influence can be seen in his early work, for example *Diana and her Nymphs* about 1655 (Mauritshuis, The Hague) and *The Courtesan* 1656 (Gemäldegalerie Alter Meister, Dresden), but a totally independent – totally Dutch – vision appears in such landscapes as the *View of Delft* 1658–60 (Mauritshuis, The Hague) and *The Little Street* (Rijksmuseum, Amsterdam), works which convey an astonishing sense of physical immediacy (Vermeer may well have used a ◊camera obscura).

The interiors for which he is best known – transcending the delicacy and brilliance of Pieter de Hooch, Gerard Terborch, and Gabriel Metsu – include *Lady Standing at the Virginals* (National Gallery, London), *The Painter's Studio* (Kunsthistorisches Museum, Vienna), *Girl with a Turban* (Mauritshuis, The Hague), and *A Woman Weighing Pearls* (National Gallery of Art, Washington DC).

Verdi The composer Giuseppe Verdi (1813–1901) in a print published in 1886, the year before his *Otello* appeared. He was one of the greatest opera composers of all time, but his music was once devalued by scholars for following predictable formulae until, ironically, German critics of the 1920s recognized his genius. *Image Select (UK) Ltd*

vermilion HgS red form of mercuric sulphide; a scarlet that occurs naturally as the crystalline mineral ◊cinnabar.

Vermont state in NE USA; nicknamed Green Mountain State
area 24,900 sq km/9,611 sq mi
capital Montpelier
towns and cities Burlington, Rutland, Barre
features Green Mountain national forest, with brilliant autumn foliage; Mount Mansfield (1,339 m/4,393 ft), the highest peak in the state; Lake Champlain; no large cities or industrial areas; covered bridges; Bennington, site of the Battle of Bennington 1777, with the Bennington Battle Monument and Bennington Museum, with paintings by Grandma Moses; Newfane, with Greek Revival courthouse; birthplace and family home of Calvin Coolidge at Plymouth; Woodstock (settled 1761), site of America's first ski tow (1934); Middlebury College (1800); Shelburne museum of the history of American life; State House, Montpelier; Marlboro Music Festival; Barre, the site of the world's largest granite quarry; Trapp Family Lodge, Stowe; winter sports
industries apples, maple syrup, dairy products, china clay, granite, marble, slate, business machines, paper and allied products; tourism is important
population (1991) 567,000
famous people Chester A Arthur, Calvin Coolidge, John Dewey
history explored by the Frenchman Samuel de Champlain from 1609; settled by the French 1666 and the English 1724; became a state 1791.

vermouth sweet or dry white wine flavoured with bitter herbs and fortified with alcohol. It is made in France, Italy and the USA.

vernal equinox see spring ◊equinox.

vernalization the stimulation of flowering by exposure to cold. Certain plants will not flower

Vermont

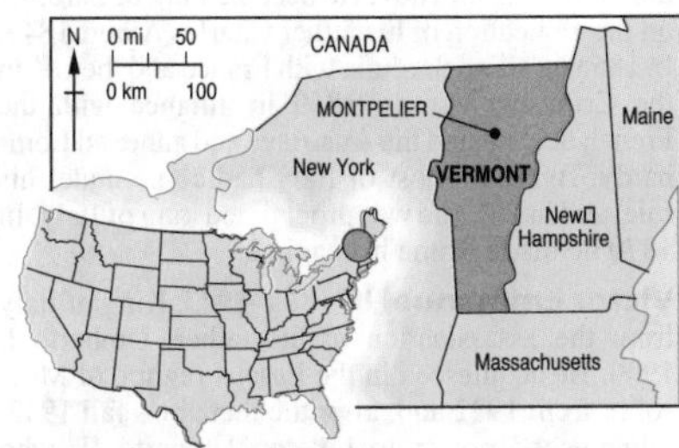

unless subjected to low temperatures during their development. For example, winter wheat will flower in summer only if planted in the previous autumn. However, by placing partially germinated seeds in low temperatures for several days, the cold requirement can be supplied artificially, allowing the wheat to be sown in the spring.

Verne Jules 1828–1905. French author. He wrote tales of adventure that anticipated future scientific developments: *Five Weeks in a Balloon* 1862, *Journey to the Centre of the Earth* 1864, *Twenty Thousand Leagues under the Sea* 1870, and *Around the World in Eighty Days* 1873.

Verona industrial city (printing, paper, plastics, furniture, pasta) in Veneto, Italy, on the Adige River; population (1992) 255,500. It also trades in fruit and vegetables. Its historical sights include one of the largest Roman amphitheatres in the world; Castelvecchio, the 14th-century residence of the Scaligers, lords of Verona; the tomb of Juliet; and a 12th-century cathedral.

Veronese Paolo (Paolo Caliari) c. 1528–1588. Italian painter. He was active mainly in Venice. He specialized in grand decorative schemes, such as his ceilings in the Doge's Palace, noted for their rich colouring, broad composition, *trompe l'oeil* effects, and inventive detail. Religious, mythological, historical, or allegorical, his paintings – usually of banquets and scenes of pageantry – celebrated the power and splendour of Venice.

Many of his finest paintings and frescoes are in Venice – in the Doge's Palace, the church of San Sebastiano, the Accademia, and the Villa Masiera – but masterpieces elsewhere are the great *Marriage at Cana* 1562–63 (Louvre, Paris), the *Family of Darius before Alexander* about 1570 (National Gallery, London), and the *Finding of Moses* (Mellon Collection, Washington DC).

The *Marriage at Cana* is typical in its pomp and luxury, containing more than 130 figures, including portraits of many celebrities of the time – Charles V, Francis I, Sultan Suleiman II, the painters Titian, Bassano, and Tintoretto, and the writer Pietro Aretino – together with an assortment of fools, dwarfs, pages, and dogs, in a grandiose architectural setting.

Veronica, St lived 1st century AD. Woman of Jerusalem who, according to tradition, lent her veil to Jesus to wipe the sweat from his brow on the road to Calvary, whereupon the image of his face was printed upon it. A relic alleged to be the actual veil is preserved in St Peter's Basilica, Rome.

Verrocchio Andrea del (Andrea di Cione) c. 1435–1488. Italian sculptor, painter, and goldsmith. He ran a large workshop in Florence and received commissions from the Medici family. His works include the vigorous equestrian statue of *Bartolomeo Colleoni* begun about 1480 (Campo SS Giovanni e Paolo, Venice) and the painting *The Baptism of Christ* about 1470 (Uffizi, Florence).

He studied as a goldsmith under Giuliano Verrocchi and was probably also a pupil of Donatello. He is famous principally as a sculptor, his bronze equestrian statue of Colleoni being one of the great masterpieces of Renaissance sculpture. As a painter he is less eminent; the only painting that can be attributed to him with certainty is *The Baptism of Christ*. However, his studio-workshop, in which painting was only one of many activities, was an important Florentine training ground, and Verrocchio has a secondary reputation as the master of Leonardo da Vinci, Perugino, and Lorenzo di Credi. A well-grounded tradition has it that Leonardo painted the angel (on the left) in *The Baptism of Christ*. ▷ *See feature on pp. 626–627.*

verruca growth on the skin; see ◊wart.

Versace Gianni 1946–1997. Italian fashion designer. He opened his own business and presented a menswear collection 1978. He diversified into women's wear, accessories, perfumes, furs, and costumes for opera, theatre, and ballet. He used simple shapes and strong colours to create provocative clothing. He was shot dead in 1997.

Versailles city in N France, capital of Les Yvelines *département*, on the outskirts of Paris; population (1990) 91,000. It grew up around the palace of Louis XIV, built 1661–87 on the site of Louis XIII's hunting lodge. Within the palace park are two small châteaux, Le Grand Trianon and Le Petit Trianon, built for Louis XIV (by Jules-Hardouin ◊Mansart (1646–1708)) and Louis XV (by Jacques Gabriel (1698–1782) respectively. Versailles was France's seat of government 1682–1789.

Versailles, Treaty of peace treaty after World War I between the Allies and Germany, signed 28 June 1919. It established the League of Nations. Germany surrendered Alsace-Lorraine to France, and large areas in the east to Poland, and made smaller cessions to Czechoslovakia, Lithuania, Belgium, and Denmark. The Rhineland was demilitarized, German rearmament was restricted, and Germany agreed to pay reparations for war damage. The treaty was never ratified by the USA, which made a separate peace with Germany and Austria 1921.

verse arrangement of words in a rhythmic pattern, which may depend on the length of syllables (as in Greek or Latin verse), or on stress, as in English. Classical Greek verse depended upon quantity, a long syllable being regarded as occupying twice the time taken up by a short syllable.

In English verse syllables are either stressed (strong) or unstressed (weak), and are combined in feet, examples of which are: iamb (unstressed/stressed); trochee (stressed/unstressed); spondee (stressed/stressed); pyrrhic (unstressed/unstressed); anapaest (unstressed/unstressed/stressed); and dactyl (stressed/unstressed/unstressed).

Rhyme (repetition of sounds in the endings of words) was introduced to W European verse in late Latin poetry, and alliteration (repetition of the same initial letter in successive words) was the dominant feature of Anglo-Saxon poetry. Both these elements helped to make verse easily remembered in the days when it was spoken rather than written.

The Spenserian stanza (in which ◊Spenser wrote *The Faerie Queene*) has nine iambic lines rhyming ababbcbcc. In English, the ◊sonnet has 14 lines, generally of ten syllables each; it has several rhyme schemes.

Blank verse, consisting of unrhymed five-stress lines, as used by Marlowe, Shakespeare, and Milton, develops an inner cohesion that replaces the props provided by rhyme and stanza. It became the standard metre for English dramatic and epic poetry.

◊***Free verse***, or *vers libre*, avoids rhyme, stanza form, and any obvious rhythmical basis.

versus (abbreviation v. or vs; Latin) against.

vertebral column the backbone, giving support to an animal and protecting its spinal cord. It is made up of a series of bones or vertebrae running from the skull to the tail, with a central canal containing the nerve fibres of the spinal cord. In tetrapods the vertebrae show some specialization with the shape of the bones varying according to position. In the chest region the upper or thoracic vertebrae are shaped to form connections to the ribs. The backbone is only slightly flexible to give adequate rigidity to the animal structure.

vertebrate any animal with a backbone. The 41,000 species of vertebrates include mammals, birds, reptiles, amphibians, and fishes. They include most of the larger animals, but in terms of numbers of species are only a tiny proportion of the world's animals. The zoological taxonomic group Vertebrata is a subgroup of the ◊phylum Chordata.

A giant conodont (an eel-like organism from the Cambrian period) was discovered in South Africa 1995, and is believed to be one of the first vertebrates. Conodonts evolved 520 million years ago, predating the earliest fish by about 50 million years.

vertex (plural ***vertices***) in geometry, a point shared by three or more sides of a solid figure; the point farthest from a figure's base; or the point of

Vermeer *The Lacemaker* c. 1655 by Jan Vermeer (Louvre, Paris). Vermeer's astonishing realism is based on his understanding of visual perception. For example, in this picture – a humble, everyday scene typical of Vermeer – there is a subtle but very effective contrast between those objects which are clearly defined and those which are slightly out of focus. *Corbis*

intersection of two sides of a plane figure or the two rays of an angle.

vertical takeoff and landing craft (VTOL) aircraft that can take off and land vertically. ◊Helicopters, airships, and balloons can do this, as can a few fixed-wing aeroplanes, like the ◊convertiplane.

vertigo dizziness; a whirling sensation accompanied by a loss of any feeling of contact with the ground. It may be due to temporary disturbance of the sense of balance (as in spinning for too long on one spot), psychological reasons, disease such as ◊labyrinthitis, or intoxication.

Verulamium Roman-British town whose remains have been excavated close to St Albans, Hertfordshire. Alban was martyred here, perhaps during the reign of Septimus ◊Severus. A fragmentary inscription from the forum records the name of the Roman governor ◊Agricola.

Verwoerd Hendrik (Frensch) 1901–1966. South African right-wing Nationalist Party politician, prime minister 1958–66. As minister of native affairs 1950–58, he was the chief promoter of apartheid legislation (segregation by race). He made the country a republic 1961. He was assassinated 1966.

Very Large Array (VLA) largest and most complex single-site radio telescope in the world. It is located on the Plains of San Augustine, 80 km/50 mi west of Socorro, New Mexico. It consists of 27 dish antennae, each 25 m/82 ft in diameter, arranged along three equally spaced arms forming a Y-shaped array. Two of the arms are 21 km/13 mi long, and the third, to the north, is 19 km/11.8 mi long. The dishes are mounted on railway tracks enabling the configuration and size of the array to be altered as required.

Pairs of dishes can also be used as separate interferometers (see ◊radio telescope), each dish having its own individual receivers that are remotely controlled, enabling many different frequencies to be studied. There are four standard configurations of antennae ranging from A (the most extended) through B and C to D. In the A configuration the antennae are spread out along the full extent of the arms and the VLA can map small, intense radio sources with high resolution. The smallest configuration, D, uses arms that are just 0.6 km/0.4 mi long for mapping larger sources. Here the resolution is lower, although there is greater sensitivity to fainter, extended fields of radio emission. ▷ *See feature on pp. 70–71.*

Vesalius Andreas 1514–1564. Belgian physician. He revolutionized anatomy by performing

> *‘It is wonderfully beautiful! You gaze, and stare, and try to understand that it is real ... The scene thrills one like military music!’*
>
> On VERSAILLES
> Mark Twain
> *The Innocents Abroad*

Vesalius *The title page of Andreas Vesalius's 1543 masterpiece on human anatomy De Humani Corporis Fabrica. It contained magnificent illustrations of a quality never before seen in a medical book, and described and depicted several organs, such as the thalamus, for the first time. Vesalius's book met with bitter controversy and criticism and led him to abandon anatomy altogether. Ann Ronan/ Image Select (UK) Ltd*

postmortem dissections and making use of illustrations to teach anatomy. The dissections (then illegal) enabled him to discover that ◊Galen's system of medicine was based on fundamental anatomical errors. Vesalius's book *De humani corporis fabrica/On the Structure of the Human Body* 1543, together with the main work of astronomer ◊Copernicus, published in the same year, marked the dawn of modern science. ▷ *See feature on pp. 1024–1025.*

Vespasian (Titus Flavius Vespasianus) AD 9–79. Roman emperor from AD 69. Proclaimed emperor by his soldiers while he was campaigning in Palestine, he reorganized the eastern provinces, and was a capable administrator. He was responsible for the construction of the Colosseum in Rome, which was completed by his son ◊Titus. He was commander of the Second Legion during the invasion of Britain AD 42–43.

vespers the seventh of the eight canonical hours in the Catholic church; the seventh Roman Catholic office (or non-Eucharistic service) of the day. It is also used by the Anglican Church to refer to evensong, an evening service in which most of the liturgy is sung in Anglican chant. Claudio Monteverdi and W A Mozart composed notable settings for this service.

The phrase ***Sicilian Vespers*** refers to the massacre of the French rulers in Sicily 1282, signalled by vesper bells on Easter Monday.

Vespucci Amerigo 1454–1512. Florentine merchant. The Americas were named after him as a result of the widespread circulation of his accounts of his explorations. His accounts of the voyage 1499–1501 include descriptions of places he could not possibly have reached (the Pacific Ocean, British Columbia, Antarctica).

vest sleeveless top, usually made of stretch cotton, jersey, or silk, which is worn as underwear or as part of a summer or sports outfit.

Vesta in Roman mythology, the goddess of the hearth, equivalent to the Greek ◊Hestia. In Rome, the sacred flame in her shrine in the Forum represented the spirit of the community, and was kept constantly lit by the six Vestal Virgins.

vestigial organ in biology, an organ that remains in diminished form after it has ceased to have any significant function in the adult organism. In humans, the appendix is vestigial, having once had a digestive function in our ancestors.

Vesuvius (Italian ***Vesuvio***) active volcano SE of Naples, Italy; height 1,277 m/4,190 ft. In AD 79 it destroyed the cities of Pompeii, Herculaneum, and Stabiae.

vetch trailing or climbing plant of any of several genera, family Leguminosae, usually having seed pods and purple, yellow, or white flowers, including the fodder crop alfalfa *Medicago sativa*.

Veterans Day in the USA, the name adopted 1954 for ◊Armistice Day and from 1971 observed by most states on the fourth Monday in Oct. The equivalent in the UK and Canada is ◊Remembrance Sunday.

❛Uniform ideas originating among entire peoples unknown to each other must have a common ground of truth.❜

Giambattista Vico
The New Science

veto (Latin 'I forbid') exercise by a sovereign, branch of legislature, or other political power, of the right to prevent the enactment or operation of a law, or the taking of some course of action. In the UK the sovereign has a right to refuse assent to any measure passed by Parliament, but this has not been exercised since the 18th century; the House of Lords also has a suspensory veto on all legislation except finance measures, but this is comparatively seldom exercised.

In the USA, the president may veto legislation, but this can be overruled by a two-thirds majority in Congress. At the United Nations, members of the Security Council can exercise a veto on resolutions.

VHF (abbreviation for ***very high frequency***) referring to radio waves that have very short wavelengths (10 m–1 m). They are used for interference-free FM transmissions (see ◊frequency modulation). VHF transmitters have a relatively short range because the waves cannot be reflected over the horizon like longer radio waves.

Viagra drug used to treat impotence, approved by the US Food and Drug Administration (FDA) in March 1998. Viagra works by dilating the blood vessels of the penis and must be taken about an hour before intercourse. Side effects include headaches and fainting (due to dilation of blood vessels), and blue tinted vision.

Viborg industrial town (brewing, engineering, textiles, tobacco) in Jutland, Denmark; population (1990) 39,400. It is also the Swedish name for ◊Vyborg, a port and naval base in Russia.

vibraphone musical percussion instrument resembling a ◊xylophone but with metal keys. Electrically driven discs spin within resonating tubes under each key to add a tremulant effect that can be controlled in length with a foot pedal.

vibrato in music, a rapid fluctuation of pitch for dynamic and expressive effect. It is distinct from a tremolo, which is a fluctuation in intensity of the same note.

viburnum any small tree or shrub of the genus *Viburnum* of the honeysuckle family Caprifoliaceae, found in temperate and subtropical regions, including the ◊wayfaring tree, the laurustinus, and the guelder rose of Europe and Asia, and the North American blackhaws and arrowwoods.

vicar Church of England priest, originally one who acted as deputy to a ◊rector, but now also a parish priest.

Vicenza city in Veneto region, NE Italy, capital of Veneto province, manufacturing textiles and musical instruments; population (1992) 107,500. It has a 13th-century cathedral and many buildings by ◊Palladio, including the Teatro Olimpico 1583.

Vichy government in World War II, the right-wing government of unoccupied France after the country's defeat by the Germans June 1940, named after the spa town of Vichy, France, where the national assembly was based under Prime Minister Pétain until the liberation 1944. Vichy France was that part of France not occupied by German troops until Nov 1942. Authoritarian and collaborationist, the Vichy regime cooperated with the Germans even after they had moved to the unoccupied zone Nov 1942. It imprisoned some 135,000 people, interned another 70,000, deported some 76,000 Jews, and sent 650,000 French workers to Germany.

Vico Giambattista (Giovanni Battista) 1668–1744. Italian philosopher, considered the founder of the modern philosophy of history. He argued that we can understand history more adequately than nature, since it is we who have made it. He believed that the study of language, ritual, and myth was a way of understanding earlier societies. His cyclical theory of history (the birth, development, and decline of human societies) was put forward in *New Science* 1725.

Vico postulated that society passes through a cycle of four phases: the divine, or theocratic, when people are governed by their awe of the supernatural; the aristocratic, or 'heroic' (Homer, *Beowulf*); the democratic and individualistic; and chaos, a fall into confusion that startles people back into supernatural reverence. This is expressed in his dictum *verum et factum convertuntur* ('the true and the made are convertible').

Victor Emmanuel three kings of Italy, including:

Victor Emmanuel II 1820–1878. First king of united Italy from 1861. He became king of Sardinia on the abdication of his father Charles Albert 1849. In 1855 he allied Sardinia with France and the UK in the Crimean War. In 1859 in alliance with the French he defeated the Austrians and annexed Lombardy. By 1860 most of Italy had come under his rule, and in 1861 he was proclaimed king of Italy. In 1870 he made Rome his capital.

Victor Emmanuel III 1869–1947. King of Italy from the assassination of his father, Umberto I, 1900. He acquiesced in the Fascist regime of Mussolini from 1922 and, after the dictator's fall 1943, relinquished power to his son Umberto II, who cooperated with the Allies. Victor Emmanuel formally abdicated 1946.

Victoria state of SE Australia
area 227,600 sq km/87,854 sq mi
capital Melbourne
towns and cities Geelong, Ballarat, Bendigo
physical part of the Great Dividing Range, running E–W and including the larger part of the Australian Alps; Gippsland lakes; shallow lagoons on the coast; the ◊mallee shrub region
industries sheep, beef cattle, dairy products, tobacco, wheat, vines for wine and dried fruit, orchard fruits, vegetables, gold, brown coal (Latrobe Valley), oil and natural gas (Bass Strait)
population (1993 est) 4,468,300; 70% in the Melbourne area
history annexed for Britain by Capt Cook 1770; settled in the 1830s; after being part of New South Wales became a separate colony 1851, named after the queen; became a state 1901.

Victoria

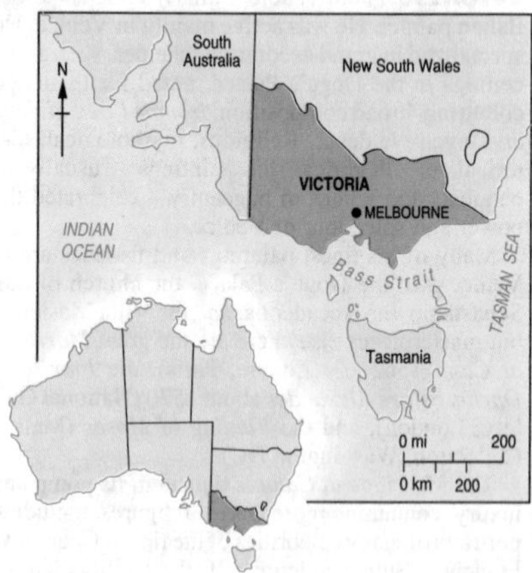

Victoria industrial port (shipbuilding, chemicals, clothing, furniture) on Vancouver Island, capital of British Columbia, Canada; population (1986) 66,303. It was founded as Fort Victoria 1843 by the Hudson's Bay Company. Its university was founded 1964.

Victoria 1819–1901. Queen of the UK from 1837, when she succeeded her uncle William IV, and empress of India from 1877. In 1840 she married Prince ◊Albert of Saxe-Coburg and Gotha. Her relations with her prime ministers ranged from the affectionate (Melbourne and Disraeli) to the stormy (Peel, Palmerston, and Gladstone). Her golden jubilee 1887 and diamond jubilee 1897 marked a waning of republican sentiment, which had developed with her withdrawal from public life on Albert's death 1861.

Only child of Edward, Duke of Kent, fourth son of George III, she was born 24 May 1819 at Kensington Palace, London. She and Albert had four sons and five daughters. After Albert's death 1861 she lived mainly in retirement. Nevertheless, she kept control of affairs, refusing the Prince of Wales (Edward VII) any active role. From 1848 she regularly visited the Scottish Highlands, where she had a house at Balmoral built to Prince Albert's designs. She died at Osborne House, her home in the Isle of Wight, 22 Jan 1901, and was buried at Windsor.

Victoria and Albert Museum museum of decorative arts in South Kensington, London, founded 1852. It houses prints, paintings, and temporary exhibitions, as well as one of the largest collections of decorative arts in the world.

Originally called the Museum of Ornamental Art, it had developed from the Museum of Manufacturers at Marlborough House, which had been founded in the aftermath of the Great Exhibition of 1851. In 1857 it became part of the South Kensington Museum, and was renamed the Victoria and Albert Museum 1899. The museum was inspired by Prince ◊Albert and Henry Cole (1808–1882), English industrial designer and writer on decorative arts. He selected the museum's first acquisitions and became its first director. In 1990 the Nehru Indian Gallery was opened, displaying a selection of the museum's Indian collection. This derives ultimately from the East India Company's Museum, acquired 1858.

Victoria Cross British decoration for conspicuous bravery in wartime, instituted by Queen Victoria 1856. It is bronze, with a 4 cm/1.5 in diameter, and has a crimson ribbon. Victoria Crosses are struck from the metal of guns captured from the Russians at Sevastopol during the Crimean War.

Victoria Falls or ***Mosi-oa-tunya*** waterfall on the river Zambezi, on the Zambia–Zimbabwe border. The river is 1,700 m/5,580 ft wide and drops 120 m/400 ft to flow through a 30-m/100-ft wide gorge. The falls were named after Queen Victoria by the Scottish explorer David Livingstone 1855.

Victoria, Lake or ***Victoria Nyanza*** largest lake in Africa; area over 69,400 sq km/26,800 sq mi; length 410 km/255 mi. It lies on the equator at an altitude of 1,136 m/3,728 ft, bounded by Uganda, Kenya, and Tanzania. It is a source of the river Nile. The British explorer John Speke named it after Queen Victoria 1858.

Victoria, Lake

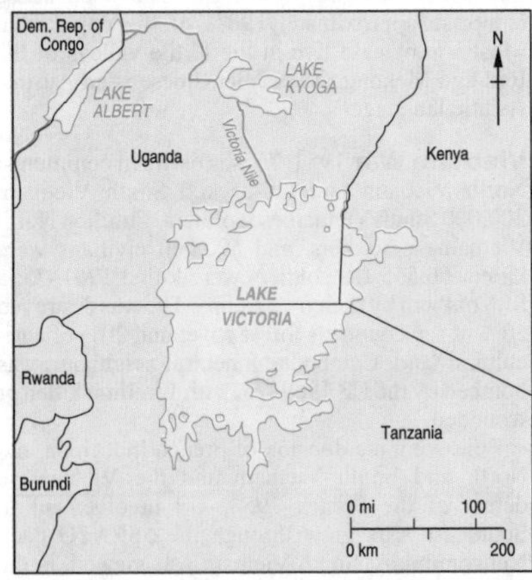

Victorian the mid- and late-19th century in England, covering the reign of Queen Victoria 1837–1901. Victorian style was often very ornate, markedly so in architecture, and Victorian Gothic drew on the original Gothic architecture of medieval times. It was also an era when increasing mass production by machines threatened the existence of crafts and craft skills. Despite the popularity of extravagant decoration, Renaissance styles were also favoured and many people, such as John ◊Ruskin, believed in designing objects and architecture primarily for their function, and not for mere appearance.

Victory British battleship, 2,198 tonnes/2,164 tons, launched 1765, and now in dry dock in Portsmouth harbour, England. It was the flagship of Admiral Nelson at Trafalgar.

vicuna ◊ruminant mammal *Lama vicugna* of the camel family that lives in herds on the Andean plateau. It can run at speeds of 50 kph/30 mph. It has good eyesight, fair hearing, and a poor sense of smell. Hunted close to extinction for its meat and soft brown fur, which was used in textile manufacture, the vicuna is now a protected species. Its populations are increasing thanks to strict conservation measures; by 1996 they had reached 100,000–200,000. The vicuna is listed on ◊CITES Appendix 2 (vulnerable). It is related to the ◊alpaca, the ◊guanaco, and the ◊llama.

Vidal Gore (originally Eugene Luther Vidal) 1925– . US writer and critic. Much of his fiction deals satirically with history and politics and includes the novels *Myra Breckinridge* 1968, *Burr* 1973, and *Empire* 1987, plays and screenplays, including *Suddenly Last Summer* 1958, and essays, such as 'Armageddon?' 1987. His autobiography *Palimpsest* appeared 1995.

Victoria Queen Victoria with family. *Image Select (UK) Ltd*

Videnov Zhan (Jan) Vassilev 1959– . Bulgarian politician, prime minister 1995–96. He played a key role in the remodelling of the Bulgarian Communist Party (BKP) as the reformed Bulgarian Socialist Party (BSP), becoming its leader from 1991. He took the party back to power in the 1994 general election, but resigned Dec 1996 after a BSP-backed candidate was defeated in the presidential election.

video camera or ***camcorder*** portable television camera that takes moving pictures electronically on magnetic tape. It produces an electrical output signal corresponding to rapid line-by-line scanning of the field of view. The output is recorded on video cassette and is played back on a television screen via a video cassette recorder. *See illustration on following page.*

video cassette recorder (VCR) device for recording on and playing back video cassettes; see ◊videotape recorder.

videoconferencing in computing, system which allows people in different locations to interact via video and audio. It is essentially multi-party telephone conferencing with pictures. Older videoconferencing systems required expensive equipment set up in a special-purpose room. By the mid 1990s, newer systems became available for desktop videoconferencing using much cheaper equipment so that videoconferencing facilities could be deployed to individual users' desks.

video disc disc with pictures and sounds recorded on it, played back by laser. The video disc is a type of ◊compact disc and was originated by Scottish inventor John Logie Baird 1928; commercially available from 1978. It is chiefly used to provide commercial films for private viewing. Most systems use a 30 cm/12 in rotating vinyl disc coated with a reflective material. Laser scanning recovers picture and sound signals from the surface where they are recorded as a spiral of microscopic pits.

vicuna The vicuna is a species of llama found in the high Andes. It lives in small herds of 6–12 females with a lone male. The male keeps watch, uttering a shrill whistle at the least sign of danger, and acts to protect the retreating herd.

video game electronic game played on a visual-display screen or, by means of special additional or built-in components, on the screen of a television set. The first commercially sold was a simple bat-and-ball game developed in the USA 1972, but complex variants are now available in colour and with special sound effects.

videotape recorder (VTR) device for recording pictures and sound on cassettes or spools of magnetic tape. The first commercial VTR was launched 1956 for the television broadcasting industry, but from the late 1970s cheaper models developed for home use, to record broadcast programmes for future viewing and to view rented or owned video cassettes of commercial films.

Video recording works in the same way as audio ◊tape recording: the picture information is stored as a line of varying magnetism, or track, on a plastic tape covered with magnetic material. The main difficulty – the huge amount of information needed to reproduce a picture – is overcome by arranging the video track diagonally across the tape. During recording, the tape is wrapped around a drum in a spiral fashion. The recording head rotates inside the drum. The combination of the forward motion of the tape and the rotation of the head produces a diagonal track. The audio signal accompanying the video signal is recorded as a separate track along the edge of the tape.

Two video cassette systems were introduced to the mass market by Japanese firms in the 1970s, but the Betamax standard was first introduced 1965. The Sony Betamax was technically superior, but Matsushita's VHS had larger marketing resources behind it and after some years became the sole system on the market. Super-VHS is an improved version of the VHS system, launched 1989, with higher picture definition and colour quality. *See illustration on following page.*

videotext system in which information (text and simple pictures) is displayed on a television (video) screen. There are two basic systems, known as ◊teletext and ◊viewdata. In the teletext system information is broadcast with the ordinary television signals, whereas in the viewdata system information is relayed to the screen from a central data bank via the telephone network. Both systems require the use of a television receiver (or a connected VTR) with special decoder.

Vidor King Wallis 1896–1982. US film director. He made such epics as *The Big Parade* 1925 and *Duel in the Sun* 1946. He has been praised for his stylistic experimentation and socially concerned themes. His other films include *The Crowd* 1928 and *Guerra e Pace/War and Peace* 1956. He was instrumental in setting up the Screen Directors' Guild 1936 and was a crucial figure in 1930s Hollywood. Honorary Academy Award 1979.

'There is something about a bureaucrat that does not like a poem.'

GORE VIDAL
Sex, Death and Money, preface

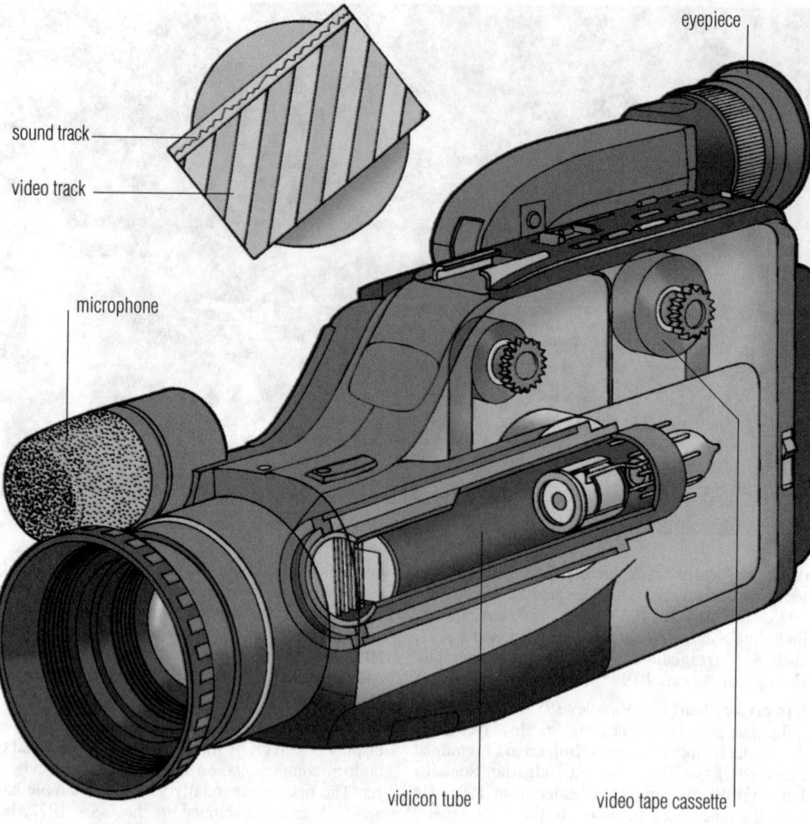

video camera The heart of the video camera is the vidicon tube which converts light entering the front lens to an electrical signal. An image is formed on a light-sensitive surface at the front of the tube. The image is then scanned by an electron beam, to give an output signal corresponding to the image brightness. The signal is recorded as a magnetic track traversing the tape diagonally. The sound track, which records the sounds picked up by the microphone, runs along the edge of the tape.

Vienna (German ***Wien***) capital of Austria, on the river Danube at the foot of the Wiener Wald (Vienna Woods); population (1991) 1,539,800. Industries include engineering and the production of electrical goods and precision instruments. The United Nations city (1979) houses the United Nations Industrial Development Organization (UNIDO) and the International Atomic Energy Agency (IAEA)
features Renaissance and Baroque architecture; the Hofburg (former imperial palace), which was severely damaged by fire 1992; the 18th-century royal palaces of Schönbrunn and Belvedere, with formal gardens; the Steiner House (1910) by Adolf Loos; and several notable collections of paintings. Vienna is known for its theatre and opera. Sigmund Freud's home is a museum, and there is a university, built 1365
history Vienna was the capital of the Austro-Hungarian Empire 1278–1918 and the commercial centre of E Europe. The old city walls were replaced by a wide street, the Ringstrasse, 1860. After much destruction in World War II the city was divided into US, British, French, and Soviet occupation zones 1945–55. Vienna is associated with J Strauss waltzes, as well as the music of Haydn, Mozart, Beethoven, and Schubert and the development of atonal music. Also figuring in Vienna's cultural history were the Vienna Sezession group of painters and the philosophical Vienna Circle; psychoanalysis originated here.

Vienna, Congress of international conference held 1814–15 that agreed the settlement of Europe after the Napoleonic Wars. National representatives included the Austrian foreign minister Metternich, Alexander I of Russia, the British foreign secretary Castlereagh and military commander Wellington, and the French politician Talleyrand.

Its final act created a kingdom of the Netherlands, a German confederation of 39 states, Lombardy-Venetia subject to Austria, and the kingdom of Poland. Monarchs were restored in Spain, Naples, Piedmont, Tuscany, and Modena; Louis XVIII was confirmed king of France.

Vientiane (Lao ***Vieng Chan***) capital and chief port of Laos on the Mekong River; population (1992) 449,000. Noted for its pagodas, canals, and houses on stilts, it is a trading centre for forest products and textiles. The Temple of the Heavy Buddha, the Pratuxai triumphal arch, and the Black Stupa are here. The Great Sacred Stupa to the north-east of the city is the most important national monument in Laos.

Vietcong (Vietnamese 'Vietnamese communists') in the Vietnam War 1954–75, the members of the National Front for the Liberation of South Vietnam, founded 1960, who fought the South Vietnamese and US forces. The name was coined by the South Vietnamese government to differentiate these communist guerrillas from the Vietminh.

Vietminh the Vietnam Independence League, founded 1941 to oppose the Japanese occupation of Indochina and later directed against the French colonial power. The Vietminh were instrumental in achieving Vietnamese independence through military victory at Dien Bien Phu 1954.

Vietnam country in SE Asia, on the South China Sea, bounded N by China and W by Cambodia and Laos. *See country box on p. 1118.*

Vietnamese inhabitants of Vietnam; people of Vietnamese culture or descent. The Vietnamese comprise approximately 90% of the population. Most Vietnamese live in the fertile valleys of the Red and Mekong rivers. Vietnamese is an Austro-Asiatic language.

Vietnam War 1954–75 war between communist North Vietnam and US-backed South Vietnam. 200,000 South Vietnamese soldiers, 1 million North Vietnamese soldiers, and 500,000 civilians were killed. 56,555 US soldiers were killed 1961–75, a fifth of them by their own troops. The war destroyed 50% of the country's forest cover and 20% of agricultural land. Cambodia, a neutral neighbour, was bombed by the US 1969–75, with 1 million killed or wounded.

Following the division of French Indochina into North and South Vietnam and the Vietnamese defeat of the French 1954, US involvement in Southeast Asia grew through the ◊SEATO pact. Noncommunist South Vietnam was viewed, in the context of the 1950s and the ◊Cold War, as a bulwark against the spread of communism throughout SE Asia. The USA spent $141 bn in aid to the South Vietnamese government, but corruption and inefficiency led the US to assume ever greater responsibility for the war effort, until 1 million US combat troops were engaged.

In the US, the draft, the high war casualties, and the undeclared nature of the war resulted in growing domestic resistance, which caused social unrest and forced President Johnson to abandon re-election plans. President Nixon first expanded the war to Laos and Cambodia but finally phased out US involvement; his national security adviser Henry Kissinger negotiated a peace treaty 1973 with North Vietnam, which soon conquered the South and united the nation. Although US forces were never militarily defeated, Vietnam was considered a most humiliating political defeat for the US.

viewdata system of displaying information on a television screen in which the information is extracted from a computer data bank and transmitted via the telephone lines. It is one form of ◊videotext. The British Post Office (now British Telecom) developed the first viewdata system, Prestel, 1975. Similar systems are now in widespread use in other countries. Users have access to a large store of information, presented on the screen in the form of 'pages'.

Prestel has hundreds of thousands of pages, presenting all kinds of information, from local weather and restaurant menus to share prices and airport timetables. Since viewdata uses telephone lines, it

videotape recorder Home video recorders use 12.65-mm/0.5-in wide tape. A series of rollers guides the tape past the recording and erase heads in the recorder. The sloping video head records the picture as a diagonal pattern across the tape. This enables more information to be held on the tape. If the signal was recorded in a straight line down the tape, it would take 33 km/20 mi of tape to make a one-hour recording. The sound track runs along the edge of the tape.

Vienna, Congress of The Congress of Vienna 1814–15. The purpose of the congress was to redefine territorial borders in Europe and create a balance of power after Napoleon's attempted conquests. It was attended by delegates from all over Europe, but real power was wielded by Britain, Prussia, Austria, and Russia. Delegates included most of the distinguished statesmen of the day – Castlereagh and Wellington from Britain, Prince Metternich from Austria, and Alexander I of Russia. Surprisingly, the French delegate, Talleyrand, also had much influence. *Corbis*

can become a two-way interactive information system, making possible, for example, home banking and shopping. In contrast, the only user input allowed by the ◊teletext system is to select the information to be displayed.

vigilante in US history, originally a member of a 'vigilance committee', a self-appointed group to maintain public order in the absence of organized authority, especially in Western frontier communities. Early vigilante groups included the 'Regulators' in South Carolina in the 1760s and in Pennsylvania 1794 during the Whiskey Rebellion. Many more appeared in the 19th century in frontier towns. Once authorized police forces existed, certain vigilante groups, such as the post-Civil War racist ◊Ku Klux Klan, operated outside the law, often as perpetrators of mob violence such as lynching.

The vigilante tradition continues with present-day urban groups patrolling streets and subways to deter muggers and rapists; for example, the Guardian Angels in New York.

Vignola Giacomo Barozzi da 1507–1573. Italian Mannerist architect. He is largely remembered for his architectural textbook *Regole delle cinque ordini/On the Five Orders* 1562. He appears to have designed much of the complex plan for the Villa Giulia, Rome 1551–55, a building whose idiosyncratic Classicism influenced the development of contemporary ◊Post-Modernism. From 1559 Vignola worked on the completion of the design for the Villa Caprarola by Peruzzi (1481–1536), and later succeeded Michelangelo as architect to St Peter's, Rome. The Gesù church in Rome, another of Vignola's highly influential designs, was built 1568–75 for the Jesuits.

Vijayanagar the capital of the last extensive Hindu empire in India between the 14th and 17th centuries, situated on the river Tungabhadra, S India. The empire attained its peak under the warrior Krishna Deva Raya (reigned 1509–65), when the city had an estimated population of 500,000. Thereafter it came under repeated attack by the Deccani Muslim kingdoms of Ahmadnagar, Bijapur, and Golconda.

The empire was established by Harihara I (reigned 1336–57), a warrior chief from the Sangama dynasty, and was extended to the S and NE by his brother Bukka (reigned 1344–77) and by Devaraya II (reigned 1422–46). The Sangama dynasty was overthrown 1485 by provincial governor Saluva Narasimha (reigned 1486–91), and the Saluvas were replaced by the Tiluvas (c. 1505–65). The city was destroyed after defeat at the Battle of Talikota 1565.

Viking or ***Norseman*** the inhabitants of Scandinavia in the period 800–1100. They traded with, and raided, much of Europe, and often settled there. In their narrow, shallow-draught, highly manoeuvrable longships, the Vikings penetrated far inland along rivers. They plundered for gold and land, and were equally energetic as colonists – with colonies stretching from North America to central Russia – and as traders, with main trading posts at Birka (near Stockholm) and Hedeby (near Schleswig). The Vikings had a sophisticated literary culture, with ◊sagas and runic inscriptions, and an organized system of government with an assembly ('thing'). Their kings and chieftains were buried with their ships, together with their possessions.

In France the Vikings were given ◊Normandy. Under Sweyn I they conquered England (where they were known as 'Danes') 1013, and his son Canute was king of England as well as Denmark and Norway. In the east they established the first Russian state and founded ◊Novgorod. They reached the Byzantine Empire in the south, and in the west sailed to Ireland, Iceland, Greenland, visited by ◊Eric the Red, and North America, by his son Leif ◊Ericsson who named it 'Vinland'. As ◊'Normans' they achieved a second conquest of England 1066.

Viking art sculpture and design of the Vikings, dating from the 8th to 11th century. Viking artists are known for woodcarving and finely wrought personal ornaments in gold and silver, and for an intricate interlacing decorative style similar to that found in ◊Celtic art. A dragonlike creature, known as the 'Great Beast', is a recurring motif.

In England Viking art did not in any sense replace that of the Celts and Saxons (see ◊Anglo-Saxon art), and it is not until the latter part of the 10th century that its influence becomes at all marked. In many parts of Europe Viking art was gradually absorbed into the Romanesque style.

There are three styles of Viking art:

Jellinge style Named from a Danish royal grave in Jutland, this is based on heavy animal designs, of which the Great Beast, to be seen on the famous Jellinge rune-stone itself, is one variety. The style also has affinities with the patterns of Irish manuscript illumination. In Britain it is well represented on the 2-m/6.5-ft-high standing cross in a churchyard in Gosforth, Cumberland, N England.

Ringerike style Characterized by elaborate foliage ornament and interlacing, this style is named after the district in Norway where it is represented in local sandstone. However, one origin of the style can be found in the Winchester school of illuminated manuscripts. A particularly interesting example of it is an early 11th-century sculpture of a Great Beast and serpent, originally coloured and rune-inscribed, which is part of a tomb found in the churchyard of St Paul's Cathedral, London, 1852 and now in the Guildhall (City of London) Museum. Another noteworthy relic of the same style and date is a bronze plate, part of a weather vane, found in Winchester and now in the Cathedral Library. The influence of the Ringerike style is well represented in English manuscripts, and there are also a few exceedingly competent carvings in ivory.

Urnes style The carving on the wooden doors of Urnes Church on the Sognefjord, Norway, gives its name to the third style, though the distribution in Scandinavia is wider than this name might suggest. It found brilliant exposition in Irish metalwork, for example the 12th-century Cross of Cong, and it had an equally important place in English Christian art.

***Viking* probes** two US space probes to Mars, each one consisting of an orbiter and a lander. They were launched 20 Aug and 9 Sept 1975. They transmitted colour pictures and analysed the soil. *Viking 1* carried life detection labs and landed in the Chryse lowland area on 20 July 1976 for detailed research and photos. Designed to work for 90 days, it operated for six and a half years, going silent Nov 1982. *Viking 2* was similar in set-up to *Viking 1*; it landed in Utopia 3 Sept 1976 and functioned for three and a half years.

Vila or ***Port-Vila*** port and capital of Vanuatu, on the southwest of Efate Island; population (1989) 19,400.

Villa-Lobos Heitor 1887–1959. Brazilian composer and conductor. He absorbed Russian and French influences in the 1920s to create Neo-Baroque works in Brazilian style, using native colours and rhythms. His gift for melody is displayed in the 'Chôros' (serenades) series 1920–29 for various ensembles, and the series of nine

'I regard the war in Indochina as the greatest military, political, economic, and moral blunder in our national history.'

On the **Vietnam War**
George McGovern
The Congressional Record 22 June 1970

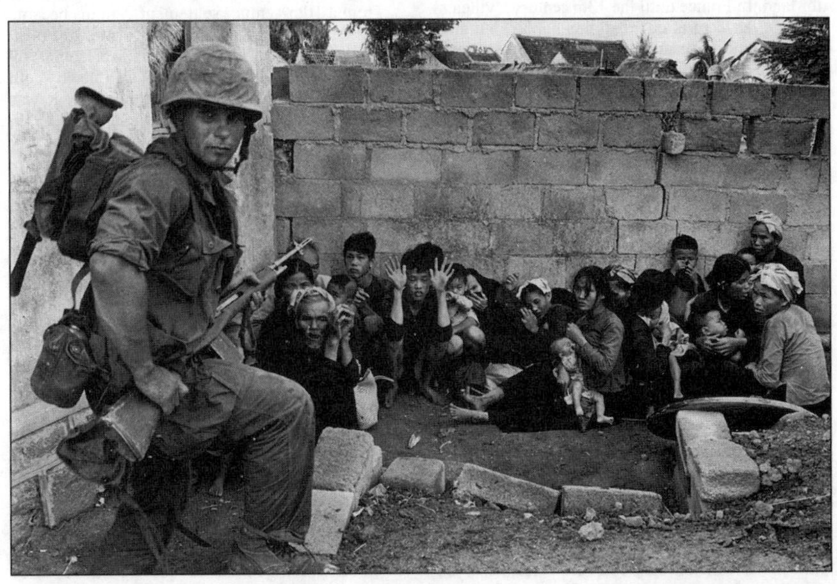

Vietnam War Women, children, and old men from the South Vietnamese village of Qui Nhon under armed US guard, 1965. The villagers had been rounded up by US marines suspecting sniper attacks after the younger men had all fled the area. *Corbis*

VIETNAM
Socialist Republic of

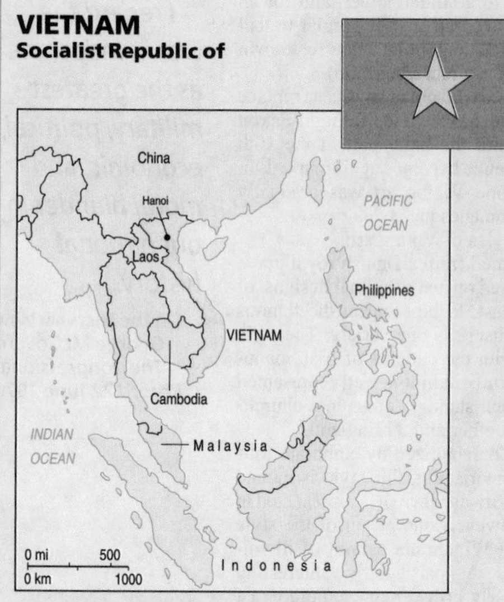

national name *Công Hòa Xã Hôi Chu Nghĩa Viêt Nam*
area 329,600 sq km/127,259 sq mi
capital Hanoi
major ports Ho Chi Minh City (formerly Saigon), Da Nang, Haiphong
physical features Red River and Mekong deltas, centre of cultivation and population; tropical rainforest; mountainous in N and NW
head of state Tran Duc Luong from 1997
head of government Phan Van Khai from 1997
political system communism
administrative divisions 36 provinces, three municipalities, and one special zone
political party Communist Party
population 74,545,000 (1995 est)
population growth rate 2.2% (1990–95); 1.9% (2000–05)
ethnic distribution 88% Viet (also known as Kinh), 2% Chinese, 2% Khmer, 8% consists of more than 50 minority nationalities, including the Hmong, Meo, Muong, Nung, Tay, Thai, and Tho tribals groups
life expectancy 62 (men), 66 (women)
literacy rate men 90%, women 84%
languages Vietnamese (official), French, English, Khmer, Chinese, local languages
religions Taoist, Buddhist, Roman Catholic
currency dong
GDP (US $) 16.26 billion (1994)
growth rate 8.8% (1994)
exports rice, rubber, coal, iron, apatite, farm produce, livestock, fish

HISTORY
300 BC Rise of Dong Son culture.
111 BC Came under Chinese rule.
1st–6th C AD Southern Mekong delta region controlled by independent Indianized Funan kingdom.
939 Chinese overthrown by Ngo Quyen at battle of Bach Dang River, and first Vietnamese dynasty founded.
11th C Theravāda Buddhism promoted.
15th C North and South Vietnam united, as kingdom of Champa in the S was destroyed in 1471.
16th C Contacts with French missionaries and European traders as political power became decentralized.
early 19th C Under Emperor Nguyen Anh authority was briefly recentralized.
1858–84 Conquered by France and divided into protectorates of Tonkin (North Vietnam) and Annam (South Vietnam).
1887 Became part of French Indo-China Union, which included Cambodia and Laos.
late 19th–early 20th C Development of colonial economy based in the S on rubber and rice, drawing migrant labourers from the N.
1930 Indochinese Communist Party (ICP) formed by Ho Chi Minh to fight for independence.
1941 Occupied by Japanese during World War II; ICP formed the Vietminh as a guerrilla resistance force designed to overthrow the Japanese-installed puppet regime headed by Bao Dai, the Emperor of Annam.
1945 Japanese removed from Vietnam at end of World War II and the Vietminh, led by Ho Chi Minh, in control of much of the country, declared independence.
1946 Vietminh war began against French, who tried to re-assert colonial control and set up a non-communist state in the S 1949.
1954 France decisively defeated at Dien Bien Phu. Vietnam divided along 17th parallel between the communist-controlled N and the US-backed S.
1963 Ngo Dinh Diem, leader of South Vietnam, overthrown in a military coup by Lt-Gen Nguyen Van Thieu.
1964 US combat troops entered Vietnam War as N Vietnamese army began to attack the S and allegedly attacked US destroyers in the Tonkin Gulf.
1969 Death of Ho Chi Minh, who was succeeded as Communist Party leader by Le Duan; US forces, which numbered 545,000 at their peak, gradually began to be withdrawn from Vietnam as a result of domestic opposition to the rising casualty toll.
1973 Paris cease-fire agreement provided for withdrawal of US troops and release of US prisoners of war.
1975 Saigon captured by North Vietnam, violating the Paris Agreements.
1976 Socialist Republic of Vietnam proclaimed. Hundreds of thousands of southerners became political prisoners; many more fled abroad. Collectivization extended to the S.
1978 Diplomatic relations severed with China. Admission into Comecon. Vietnamese invasion of Cambodia.
1979 Sino-Vietnamese 17-day border war; 700,000 Chinese and middle-class Vietnamese fled abroad as 'boat people' refugees.
1986 Death of Le Duan and retirement of 'old guard' leaders; pragmatic Nguyen Van Linh became Communist Party leader and encouraged the private sector through a *doi moi* ('renovation') initiative.
1987–88 Over 10,000 political prisoners released.
1989 Troops fully withdrawn from Cambodia.
1991 Economic reformer Vo Van Kiet replaced Do Muoi as prime minister. Cambodia peace agreement signed. Relations with China normalized.
1992 New constitution adopted, guaranteeing economic freedoms. Conservative Le Duc Anh elected president. Relations with South Korea normalized.
1994 US 30-year-old trade embargo removed.
1995 Full diplomatic relations re-established with USA. Became full member of ASEAN.
1996 Economic upturn gained pace.
1997 Diplomatic relations with USA restored. Tran Duc Luong elected president, Phan Van Khai as prime minister.

SEE ALSO boat people; Cambodia; Vietminh; Vietnam War

Bachianas Brasileiras 1930–45, treated in the manner of Bach. His other works include guitar and piano solos, chamber music, choral works, film scores, operas, and 12 symphonies.

Villehardouin Geoffroy de c. 1160–c. 1213. French historian. He was the first to write in the French language. He was a leader of the Fourth ◊Crusade, of which his *Conquest of Constantinople* (about 1209) is an account.

villeinage system of serfdom that prevailed in Europe in the Middle Ages. A villein was a peasant who gave dues and services to his lord in exchange for land. In France until the 13th century, 'villeins' could refer to rural or urban non-nobles, but after this, it came to mean exclusively rural non-noble freemen. In Norman England, it referred to free peasants of relatively high status. At the time of the Domesday Book, the villeins were the most numerous element in the English population, providing the labour force for the manors. By the 15th century villeinage had been supplanted by a system of free tenure and labour in England, but it continued in France until 1789.

Villeneuve Jacques 1971– . Canadian racing driver. The son of the Formula 1 driver Gilles Villeneuve, he rose to prominence in 1995 when he won the Indy-Car World Series and the Indianapolis 500. Two years later he became the first Canadian to win the Formula 1 World Drivers' Championship.

Villiers de l'Isle Adam (Jean Marie Philippe) Auguste, Comte de 1838–1889. French poet. He was the inaugurator of the Symbolist movement. His work includes the drama *Axel* 1890; *Isis* 1862, a romance of the supernatural; verse; and short stories.

Villon François 1431–c. 1465. French poet. He used satiric humour, pathos, and lyric power in works written in the slang of the time. Among the little of his work that survives, *Petit Testament* 1456 and *Grand Testament* 1461 are prominent (the latter includes the 'Ballade des dames du temps jadis/ Ballad of the Ladies of Former Times').

villus plural ***villi*** small fingerlike projection extending into the interior of the small intestine and increasing the absorptive area of the intestinal wall. Digested nutrients, including sugars and amino acids, pass into the villi and are carried away by the circulating blood.

Vilnius capital of Lithuania; population (1995) 576,000. Industries include engineering and the manufacture of textiles, chemicals, and foodstuffs.

From a 10th-century settlement, Vilnius became the Lithuanian capital 1323 and a centre of Polish and Jewish culture. It was then Polish from 1569 until the Russian annexation 1795. Claimed by both Poland and Lithuania after World War I, it was given to Poland 1920, occupied by the USSR 1939, and immediately transferred to Lithuania. The city was the focal point of Lithuania's agitation for independence from the USSR 1989–91, and became the country's capital when independence was achieved 1991.

Vimy Ridge hill in N France, taken in World War I by Canadian troops during the battle of Arras, April 1917, at the cost of 11,285 lives. It is a spur of the ridge of Notre Dame de Lorette, 8 km/5 mi NE of Arras.

Vincennes the University of Paris VIII, usually known as Vincennes after the suburb of E Paris where it was founded 1970 (following the 1968 student rebellion) for blue-collar workers. By 1980, it had 32,000 students. In June 1980, it was moved to the industrial suburb of St-Denis.

Vincent de Paul, St c. 1580–1660. French Roman Catholic priest and founder of the two charitable orders of Dazarists 1625 and Sisters of Charity 1634. After being ordained 1600, he was captured by Barbary pirates and held as a slave in Tunis until he escaped 1607. He was canonized 1737; feast day 19 July.

vincristine ◊alkaloid extracted from the blue periwinkle plant (*Vinca rosea*). Developed as an anticancer agent, it has revolutionized the treatment of childhood acute leukaemias; it is also included in ◊chemotherapy regimens for some lymphomas (cancers arising in the lymph tissues) and lung and breast cancers. Side effects, such as nerve damage and loss of hair, are severe but usually reversible.

vine or ***grapevine*** any of various climbing woody plants of the genus *Vitis*, family Vitaceae, especially *V. vinifera*, native to Asia Minor and cultivated from antiquity. Its fruit is eaten or made into wine or other fermented drinks; dried fruits of certain varieties are known as raisins and currants. Many other species of climbing plant are also termed vines.

vinegar sour liquid consisting of a 4% solution of acetic acid produced by the oxidation of alcohol, used to flavour food and as a preservative in pickling. Malt vinegar is brown and made from malted cereals; white vinegar is distilled from it. Other sources of vinegar include cider, wine, and honey. Balsamic vinegar is wine vinegar aged in wooden barrels.

Vinland Norse name for the area of North America, probably the coast of Nova Scotia or New England, which the Norse adventurer and explorer Leif ◊Ericsson visited about 1000. It was named after the wild grapes that grew there and is celebrated in an important Norse saga.

Vinson Massif highest point in ◊Antarctica, rising to 5,140 m/16,863 ft in the Ellsworth Mountains.

viol member of a Renaissance family of bowed six-stringed musical instruments with flat backs and narrow shoulders that flourished particularly in England about 1540–1700, before their role was taken by the violins. Normally performing as an ensemble or consort, their repertoire is a development of ◊madrigal style with idiomatic decoration.

The three principal instruments, treble, tenor, and bass, are played upright, resting on the leg (da gamba), and produce a transparent, harmonious sound. The smaller instruments are rested on the knee, not held under the chin. Tuning is largely in fourths, like a guitar. The bass viol or violone, used in Baroque orchestras as bass-line support to the harpsichord or organ, became the model for the present-day ◊double bass.

viola bowed, stringed musical instrument, the alto member of the ◊violin family. With its dark, vibrant tone, it is suitable for music of reflective character, as in Stravinsky's *Elegy* 1944. Its principal function is supportive in string quartets and orchestras.

violet any plant of the genus *Viola*, family Violaceae, with toothed leaves and mauve, blue, or white flowers, such as the heath dog violet *V. canina* and sweet violet *V. odorata*. A ◊pansy is a kind of violet.

violin bowed, four-stringed musical instrument, the smallest and highest pitched (treble) of the violin family. The strings are tuned in fifths (G3, D4, A4, and E5).

Developed gradually during the 16th century from a variety of fiddle types, the violin was perfected in Italy by a group of makers including Nicolò Amati, Antonio Stradivari, and Guarneri del Gesù working in Cremona around 1670–1710. Designed without frets and with a complex body curvature to radiate sound, its voicelike tone and extended range established a new humanistic aesthetic of solo instrumental expression and, together with the viola and cello, laid the foundation of the modern orchestra. Today's violin has not changed in form since that time, but in the late 18th century aspects of the design were modified to produce a bigger sound and greater projection for the concert hall and to allow for evolving virtuoso expression. These include a lengthened fingerboard, an angled neck, and larger-sized basebar and soundpost.

The repertoire for solo violin exceeds that for most other instruments. Composers include Vivaldi, Tartini, J S Bach, Mozart, Beethoven, Brahms, Mendelssohn, Paganini, Elgar, Berg, Bartók, and Carter.

violin family family of bowed stringed instruments developed in 17th-century Italy, which eventually superseded the viols and formed the basis of the modern orchestra. There are four instruments: violin, viola, cello (or violoncello), and the double bass which is descended from the bass viol (or violone).

violoncello full name of the ◊*cello*, tenor member of the ◊violin family.

Vionnet Madeleine 1876–1975. French fashion designer. During the 1920s and 1930s she achieved critical acclaim when she developed the bias cut (cutting the fabric at an angle of 45 degrees from the selvage across the thread that runs lengthways through the fabric). This enabled her to create simple fluid shapes in crêpe de chine, satin, and gaberdine.

viper any front-fanged venomous snake of the family Viperidae. Vipers range in size from 30 cm/1 ft to 3 m/10 ft, and often have diamond or jagged markings. Most give birth to live young. There are 150 species of viper. The true vipers, subfamily Viperinae, abundant in Africa and SW Asia, include the ◊adder *Vipera berus*, the African puff adder *Bitis arietans*, and the horned viper of North Africa *Cerastes cornutus*. The second subfamily Crotalinae includes the mostly New World pit vipers, such as ◊rattlesnakes and copperheads of the Americas, which have a heat-sensitive pit between each eye and nostril.

Virchow Rudolf Ludwig Carl 1821–1902. German pathologist, the founder of cellular pathology. Virchow was the first to describe leukaemia (cancer of the blood). In his book *Die cellulare Pathologie/Cellular Pathology* 1858, he proposed that disease is not due to sudden invasions or changes, but to slow processes in which normal cells give rise to abnormal ones.

viper The common viper, or adder, is widely distributed in Europe as far east as Siberia. It is a short, sturdy snake that lives on the ground. Being slow-moving, adders do not chase prey, but wait in a concealed position to ambush lizards, mice, voles, shrews, and frogs.

Virgil (Publius Vergilius Maro) 70–19 BC. Roman poet. He wrote the *Eclogues* 37 BC, a series of pastoral poems; the *Georgics* 30 BC, four books on the art of farming; and his epic masterpiece, the *Aeneid* 30–19 BC. He was patronized by Maecenas on behalf of Octavian (later the emperor Augustus).

Born near Mantua, Virgil was educated in Cremona and Mediolanum (Milan), and later studied philosophy and rhetoric at Rome. He wrote his second work, the *Georgics*, in honour of his new patron, Maecenas, to whom he introduced ◊Horace. He passed much of his later life at Naples and devoted the last decade of it to the composition of the *Aeneid*, often considered the most important poem in Latin literature. In 19 BC Virgil went to Greece and caught a fever while visiting the ruins of Megara. Returning to Italy, he died soon after landing at Brundisium. The *Aeneid*, which he had wanted destroyed, was published by his executors on the order of the emperor Augustus. Later Christian adaptations of his work, in particular of the prophetic *Fourth Eclogue*, greatly enhanced his mystical status in the Middle Ages, resulting in his adoption by ◊Dante as his guide to the underworld in the *Divine Comedy*.

virginal in music, a small type of ◊harpsichord.

Virginia state in E USA; nicknamed Old Dominion
area 105,600 sq km/40,762 sq mi
capital Richmond
towns and cities Norfolk, Virginia Beach, Newport News, Hampton, Chesapeake, Portsmouth
features Blue Ridge Mountains, with the Shenandoah national park; Luray Caverns; George Washington and Jefferson national forests; Jamestown Island, the site of the first permanent English settlement in North America (1607); Colonial Williamsburg, with craft workers and costumed guides, and buildings including the capitol and the governor's palace (1720), and the DeWitt Wallace Decorative Arts Gallery; Alexandria Old Town (established 1749), with the Torpedo Factory Art Center; Fredericksburg, with a national historic district; old Richmond, with the Virginia state capitol (designed by Thomas Jefferson 1785); Mount Vernon (1754), home of George Washington; Monticello, Thomas Jefferson's house at Charlottesville; Civil War battlefields, including Manassas (or Bull Ring) national battlefield park, Fredericksburg, and Spotsylvania national military park, and Petersburg national battlefield; Appomattox Court House, the site of General Robert E Lee's surrender to General Ulysses S Grant 1865; Arlington national cemetery, the burial place of many US presidents, and veterans of 20th-century wars; Booker T Washington national monument (his birthplace, and a museum of life under slavery). More US presidents have come from Virginia than from any other state
industries sweet potatoes, maize, tobacco, apples, peanuts, coal, ships, lorries, paper, chemicals, processed food, textiles
population (1991) 6,286,000.

Virginia

Virginia creeper or ***woodbine*** E North American climbing vine *Parthenocissus quinquefolia* of the grape family, having tendrils, palmately compound leaves, green flower clusters, and blue berries consumed by numerous birds but inedible to humans.

Virgin Islands group of about 100 small islands, northernmost of the Leeward Islands in the Antilles, West Indies. Tourism is the main industry. They comprise the ***US Virgin Islands*** St Thomas (with the capital, Charlotte Amalie), St Croix, St John, and about 50 small islets; area 350 sq km/135 sq mi; population (1990) 101,800; and the ***British Virgin Islands*** Tortola (with the capital, Road Town), Virgin Gorda, Anegada, and Jost van Dykes, and about 40 islets (11 islands are inhabited); area 150 sq km/58 sq mi; population (1991) 16,100.

The US Virgin Islands were purchased from Denmark 1917, and form an 'unincorporated territory'. The British Virgin Islands were taken over from the Dutch by British settlers 1666, and have partial internal self-government.

Virgin Islands

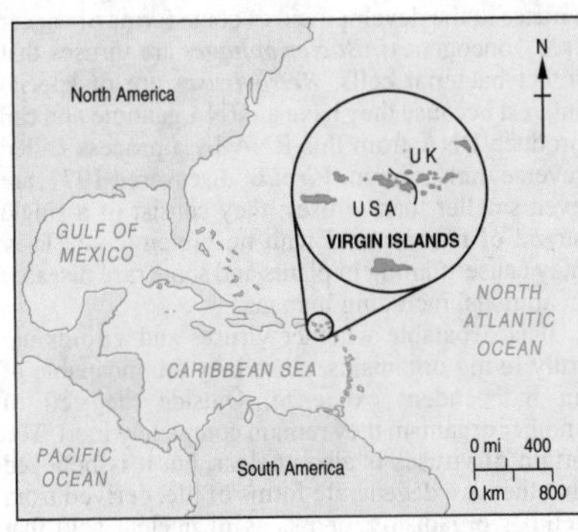

Virgo zodiacal constellation of the northern hemisphere, the second largest in the sky. It is represented as a maiden holding an ear of wheat, marked by first-magnitude ◊Spica, Virgo's brightest star. The Sun passes through Virgo from late Sept to the end of Oct. In astrology, the dates for Virgo are between about 23 Aug and 22 Sept (see ◊precession).

Virgo contains the nearest large cluster of galaxies to us, 50 million light years away, consisting of about 3,000 galaxies centred on the giant elliptical galaxy M87. Also in Virgo is the nearest ◊quasar, 3C 273, an estimated 3 billion light years away.

virtual in computing, without physical existence. Some computers have virtual memory, making their immediate-access memory seem larger than it is. Virtual reality is a computer simulation of a whole physical environment.

virtual reality advanced form of computer simulation, in which a participant has the illusion of being part of an artificial environment. The participant views the environment through two tiny television screens (one for each eye) built into a visor. Sensors detect movements of the participant's head or body, causing the apparent viewing position to change. Gloves (datagloves) fitted with sensors may be worn, which allow the participant seemingly to pick up and move objects in the environment. The technology is still under development but is expected to have widespread applications; for example, in military and surgical training, architecture, and home entertainment.

virus in computing, a piece of ◊software that can replicate and transfer itself from one computer to another, without the user being aware of it. Some viruses are relatively harmless, but others can damage or destroy data. They are written by anonymous programmers, and are spread on floppy discs, on local networks, and more recently on the ◊Internet. Antivirus software can be used to detect and destroy

'Meanwhile, Time is flying – flying, never to return.'

VIRGIL
Georgics III

well-known viruses, but new viruses continually appear and these may bypass existing antivirus programs. Viruses may be programmed to operate on a particular date, such as the Michelangelo Virus, which was triggered on 6 March 1992 (the anniversary of the birthday of Italian artist Michelangelo) and erased hard discs.

In the UK, the Computer Misuse Act of 1990 made the release of computer viruses an offence. In Nov 1995 Christopher Pile (known as the Black Baron) was sentenced to 18 months in prison for writing a virus, becoming the first person to be imprisoned for this offence.

virus infectious particle consisting of a core of nucleic acid (DNA or RNA) enclosed in a protein shell. Viruses are acellular and able to function and reproduce only if they can invade a living cell to use the cell's system to replicate themselves. In the process they may disrupt or alter the host cell's own DNA. The healthy human body reacts by producing an antiviral protein, ◊interferon, which prevents the infection spreading to adjacent cells. Many viruses mutate continuously so that the host's body has little chance of developing permanent resistance; others transfer between species, with the new host similarly unable to develop resistance. The viruses that cause ◊AIDS and ◊Lassa fever are both thought to have 'jumped' to humans from other mammalian hosts.

Among diseases caused by viruses are canine distemper, chickenpox, common cold, herpes, influenza, rabies, smallpox, yellow fever, AIDS, and many plant diseases. Recent evidence implicates viruses in the development of some forms of cancer (see ◊oncogenes). ***Bacteriophages*** are viruses that infect bacterial cells. ***Retroviruses*** are of special interest because they have an RNA genome and can produce DNA from this RNA by a process called reverse transcription. ***Viroids***, discovered 1971, are even smaller than viruses; they consist of a single strand of nucleic acid with no protein coat. They may cause stunting in plants and some rare diseases in animals, including humans.

It is debatable whether viruses and viroids are truly living organisms, since they are incapable of an independent existence. Outside the cell of another organism they remain completely inert. The origin of viruses is also unclear, but it is believed that they are degenerate forms of life, derived from cellular organisms, or pieces of nucleic acid that have broken away from the genome of some higher organism and taken up a parasitic existence.

Antiviral drugs are difficult to develop because viruses replicate by using the genetic machinery of host cells, so that drugs tend to affect the host cell as well as the virus. Acyclovir (used against the herpes group of diseases) is one of the few drugs so far developed that is successfully selective in its action. It is converted to its active form by an enzyme that is specific to the virus, and it then specifically inhibits viral replication. Some viruses have shown developing resistance to the few antiviral drugs available.

Viruses have recently been found to be very abundant in seas and lakes, with between 5 and 10 million per millilitre of water at most sites tested, but up to 250 million per millilitre in one polluted lake. These viruses infect bacteria and, possibly, single-celled algae. They may play a crucial role in controlling the survival of bacteria and algae in the plankton.

viscacha Argentinian Pampas and scrubland-dwelling rodent *Lagostomus maximus* of the chinchilla family. It is up to 70 cm/2.2 ft long with a 20 cm/8 in tail, and weighs 7 kg/15 lb. It is grey and black and has a large head and small ears. Viscachas live in warrens of up to 30 individuals. They are usually nocturnal and feed on grasses, roots, and seeds. Four species of ***Mountain viscachas*** genus *Lagidium*, also called Peruvian hares, are smaller and have long ears and tails and are found in rocky places feeding by day on sparse vegetation.

viscacha Unlike the nocturnal viscacha, the mountain viscacha *Lagidium viscacia* comes out during the day and is therefore easily observed in its habitat among rocks in the Andean altiplano. With its large ears it looks more like a rabbit than a rodent. Its alarm call is a high-pitched whistle. *Premaphotos Wildlife*

viscera general term for the organs contained in the chest and abdominal cavities.

Visconti dukes and rulers of Milan 1277–1447. They originated as north Italian feudal lords who attained dominance over the city as a result of alliance with the Holy Roman emperors. Despite papal opposition, by the mid-14th century they ruled 15 other major towns in northern Italy. The duchy was inherited by the ◊Sforzas 1447. They had no formal title until Gian Galeazzo (1351–1402) bought the title of duke from Emperor Wenceslas IV (1361–1419). On the death of the last male Visconti, Filippo Maria, 1447, the duchy was passed to the Sforzas 1450 after a short-lived republic.

Visconti Luchino 1906–1976. Italian film, opera, and theatre director. The film *Ossessione* 1942 pioneered Neo-Realist cinema despite being subject to censorship problems from the fascist government. His later works include *Rocco and His Brothers* 1960, *The Leopard* 1963, *The Damned* 1969, and *Death in Venice* 1971. His powerful social commentary led to clashes with the Italian government and Roman Catholic Church.

viscose yellowish, syrupy solution made by treating cellulose with sodium hydroxide and carbon disulphide. The solution is then regenerated as continuous filament for the making of ◊rayon and as cellophane.

viscosity in physics, the resistance of a fluid to flow, caused by its internal friction, which makes it resist flowing past a solid surface or other layers of the fluid. It applies to the motion of an object moving through a fluid as well as the motion of a fluid passing by an object. Fluids such as pitch, treacle, and heavy oils are highly viscous; for the purposes of calculation, many fluids in physics are considered to be perfect, or nonviscous.

viscount in the UK peerage, the fourth degree of nobility, between earl and baron.

Visegrad Group association of the four neighbouring central European states of the Czech Republic, Hungary, Poland, and the Slovak Republic. Originally the 'Visegrad Three', the group was formed in 1991 when Czechoslovakia, Hungary, and Poland signed the Visegrad cooperation treaty in the wake of their recent democratization. The treaty was extended in 1992 by a Central European Free Trade Agreement (CEFTA). With the division of Czechoslovakia into the Czech Republic and the Slovak Republic in 1994, the 'Visegrad Four' was created. Close ties were also developed with Slovenia in 1995.

Vishnu in Hinduism, the second in the triad of gods (with Brahma and Siva) representing three aspects of the supreme spirit. He is the Preserver, and is believed to have assumed human appearance in nine *avatāras*, or incarnations, in such forms as Rama and Krishna. His worshippers are the Vaishnavas.

Visigoth member of the western branch of the ◊Goths, an E Germanic people.

vision defect any abnormality of the eye that causes less-than-perfect sight. Common defects are ◊short-sightedness or myopia; ◊long-sightedness or hypermetropia; lack of ◊accommodation or presbyopia; and ◊astigmatism. Other eye defects include colour blindness.

visitation in the Christian church, a formal visit by a bishop or church official to examine the churches or abbeys within his jurisdiction. In medieval visitations, records were kept of the *detecta*, matters disclosed to the visitor, and *comperta*, what the visitor found for himself.

In Christian art, a Visitation depicts the meeting of the Virgin Mary with her pregnant older relative Elizabeth (Luke 1:39–56). On this occasion Mary gives voice to the ◊Magnificat.

Vistula (Polish ***Wisła***) river in Poland that rises in the Carpathian Mountains and runs NW to the Baltic Sea at Gdańsk; length 1,090 km/677 mi. It is heavily polluted, carrying into the Baltic every year large quantities of industrial and agricultural waste, including phosphorus, oil, nitrogen, mercury, cadmium, and zinc.

visual display unit (VDU) computer terminal consisting of a keyboard for input data and a screen for displaying output. The oldest and the most popular type of VDU screen is the ◊cathode-ray tube (CRT), which uses essentially the same technology as a television screen. Other types use plasma display technology and ◊liquid-crystal displays.

vitamin any of various chemically unrelated organic compounds that are necessary in small quantities for the normal functioning of the human body. Many act as coenzymes, small molecules that enable ◊enzymes to function effectively. Vitamins must be supplied by the diet because the body cannot make them. They are normally present in adequate amounts in a balanced diet. Deficiency of a vitamin may lead to a metabolic disorder ('deficiency disease'), which can be remedied by sufficient intake of the vitamin. They are generally classified as water-soluble (B and C) or fat-soluble (A, D, E, and K). See separate entries for individual vitamins, also ◊nicotinic acid, ◊folic acid, and ◊pantothenic acid.

Scurvy (the result of vitamin C deficiency) was observed at least 3,500 years ago, and sailors from the 1600s were given fresh sprouting cereals or citrus-fruit juice to prevent or cure it. The concept of scurvy as a deficiency disease, however, caused by the absence of a specific substance, emerged later. In the 1890s a Dutch doctor, Christiaan ◊Eijkman, discovered that he could cure hens suffering from a condition like beriberi by feeding them on wholegrain, rather than polished, rice. In 1912 Casimir ◊Funk, a Polish-born biochemist, had proposed the existence of what he called 'vitamines' (vital amines), but it was not fully established until about 1915 that several deficiency diseases were preventable and curable by extracts from certain foods. By then it was known that two groups of factors were involved, one being water-soluble and present, for example, in yeast, rice-polishings, and wheat germ, and the other being fat-soluble and present in egg yolk, butter, and fish-liver oils. The water-soluble substance, known to be effective against beriberi, was named vitamin B. The fat-soluble vitamin complex was at first called vitamin A. As a result of analytical techniques these have been subsequently separated into their various components, and others have been discovered.

Megavitamin therapy has yielded at best unproven effects; some vitamins (A, for example) are extremely toxic in high doses.

Other animals may also need vitamins, but not necessarily the same ones. For example, choline, which humans can synthesize, is essential to rats and some birds, which cannot produce sufficient for themselves.

vitamin A another name for ◊retinol.

vitamin B_1 another name for ◊thiamine.

vitamin B_{12} another name for ◊cyanocobalamin.

vitamin B_2 another name for ◊riboflavin.

vitamin B_6 another name for ◊pyridoxine.

vitamin C another name for ◊ascorbic acid.

vitamin D another name for ◊cholecalciferol.

vitamin E another name for ◊tocopherol.

vitamin H another name for ◊biotin.

vitamin K another name for ◊phytomenadione.

vitreous humour transparent jellylike substance behind the lens of the vertebrate ◊eye. It gives rigidity to the spherical form of the eye and allows light to pass through to the retina.

vitriol any of a number of sulphate salts. Blue, green, and white vitriols are copper, ferrous, and zinc sulphate, respectively. ***Oil of vitriol*** is sulphuric acid.

Vitruvius (Marcus Vitruvius Pollio) lived 1st century BC. Roman architect. His ten-volume interpretation of Roman architecture, *De architectura*, provided an impetus for the Renaissance; it was first printed in Rome 1486. Although often obscure, his writings have had a lasting influence on Western perceptions of Classical architecture, mainly through the work of Leon Battista Alberti, and later Raphael and Palladio.

Vitus, St lived early 4th century. Christian saint, perhaps Sicilian, who was martyred in Rome early in the 4th century. Feast day 15 June.

Vivaldi Antonio Lucio 1678–1741. Italian Baroque composer, violinist, and conductor. He wrote 23 symphonies; 75 sonatas; over 400 concertos, including *The Four Seasons* 1725 for violin and orchestra; over 40 operas; and much sacred music. His work was largely neglected until the 1930s.

viva voce (Latin 'with living voice') an oral examination.

viviparous in animals, a method of reproduction in which the embryo develops inside the body of the female from which it gains nourishment (in contrast to ◊oviparous and ◊ovoviviparous). Vivipary is best developed in placental mammals, but also occurs in some arthropods, fishes, amphibians, and reptiles that have placentalike structures. In plants, it is the formation of young plantlets or bulbils instead of flowers. The term also describes seeds that germinate prematurely, before falling from the parent plant. Premature germination is common in mangrove trees, where the seedlings develop sizable spearlike roots before dropping into the swamp below; this prevents their being washed away by the tide.

vivisection literally, cutting into a living animal. Used originally to mean experimental surgery or dissection practised on a live subject, the term is often used by antivivisection campaigners to include any experiment on animals, surgical or otherwise. Britain's 1876 Cruelty to Animals Act was the world's first legislation specifically to protect laboratory animals.

Vladikavkaz (formerly (1954–91) ***Ordzhonikidze***) capital of the autonomous republic of Alania (formerly North Ossetia), in the Russian Federation, on the river Terek in the Caucasus Mountains; population (1994) 311,000. Metal products, vehicles, and textiles are produced. Vladikavkaz was founded 1784 as a frontier fortress.

Vladimir I (St Vladimir of Kiev) 956–1015. Russian saint, prince of Novgorod, and grand duke of Kiev. Converted to Christianity 988, he married Anna, Christian sister of the Byzantine emperor ◊Basil II, and established the Byzantine rite of Orthodox Christianity as the Russian national faith. Feast day 15 July.

Vladivostok port (naval and commercial) in the Russian Federation, in E Siberia, at the Amur Bay on the Pacific coast; population (1994) 637,000. It is kept open by icebreakers during winter. Industries include shipbuilding and the manufacture of precision instruments. There is a large Chinese population.

It was established 1860 as a military port, and was the eastern capital of the 19th-century Russian Empire. It is the administrative centre of the Far East Science Centre 1969, with subsidiaries at Petropavlovsk, Khabarovsk, and Magadan. The eastern terminal of the Trans–Siberian Railway is here; it was one of the busiest railway terminals in the former Soviet Union.

VLF in physics, abbreviation for ***very low ◊frequency***. VLF radio waves have frequencies in the range 3–30 kHz.

vocal cords the paired folds, ridges, or cords of tissue within a mammal's larynx, and a bird's syrinx. Air constricted between the folds or membranes makes them vibrate, producing sounds. Muscles in the larynx change the pitch of the sounds produced, by adjusting the tension of the vocal cords.

vodka strong colourless alcoholic beverage distilled from rye, potatoes, or barley.

First produced in the 15th century, vodka was originally 40% pure spirit by weight, made from rye malt and rye grain without other ingredients.

voice in music, the human singing voice. The voice is driven by air in the lungs pressurized by contraction of the diaphragm, and uses the vocal folds, flanges of tissue in the larynx, as a flexible valve controlling the escape of air as a series of pulses. The larynx can be relaxed or tensed at will to vary the pitch. The timbre of the voice is created by the resonances of the mouth and nasal cavities.

The art of singing consists largely of training the voice to develop a pure and powerful tone. Formerly, theorists divided the voice into different registers, known as the chest voice and head voice, based on what was believed to be the physiological source of voice production. Modern vocal registers are concerned primarily with the vocal range: soprano, mezzo-soprano, and contralto (or simply alto) for women; tenor, baritone, and bass for men; and treble and alto for boys.

The term 'voice' is also used to refer to the independent parts of a contrapuntal work, whether played or sung.

voice mail ◊electronic mail including spoken messages and audio. Messages can also be generated electronically using speech synthesis. In offices, voice mail systems are often included in computerized telephone switchboards.

voiceprint graph produced by a sound spectograph showing frequency and intensity changes in the human voice when visually recorded. It enables individual speech characteristics to be determined. First used as evidence in criminal trials in the USA 1966, voiceprints were banned 1974 by the US Court of Appeal as 'not yet sufficiently accepted by scientists'.

Vojvodina autonomous province in N Serbia, Yugoslavia, 1945–1990; area 21,500 sq km/8,299 sq mi; population (1991) 2,012,500, including 1,110,000 Serbs and 390,000 Hungarians, as well as Croat, Slovak, Romanian, and Ukrainian minorities. Its capital is Novi Sad. In Sept 1990 Serbia effectively stripped Vojvodina of its autonomous status, causing antigovernment and anticommunist riots in early 1991.

volatile in chemistry, term describing a substance that readily passes from the liquid to the vapour phase. Volatile substances have a high ◊vapour pressure.

volcanic rock another name for ◊extrusive rock, igneous rock formed on the Earth's surface.

volcano crack in the Earth's crust through which hot magma (molten rock) and gases well up. The magma is termed lava when it reaches the surface. A volcanic mountain, usually cone shaped with a crater on top, is formed around the opening, or vent, by the build-up of solidified lava and ashes (rock fragments). Most volcanoes arise on plate margins (see ◊plate tectonics), where the movements of plates generate magma or allow it to rise from the mantle beneath. However, a number are found far from plate-margin activity, on 'hot spots' where the Earth's crust is thin.

There are two main types of volcano:

Composite volcanoes, such as Stromboli and Vesuvius in Italy, are found at destructive plate margins (areas where plates are being pushed together), usually in association with island arcs and

volcano The Mount Mayon volcano of the Philippines with incandescent lava cascading down its gully at dawn on 26 March 1993. It had been erupting for several days. In the foreground is the city of Legazpi, more than 10 km/6 mi away from the volcano. *Corbis* coastal mountain chains. The magma is mostly derived from plate material and is rich in silica. This makes a very stiff lava such as andesite, which solidifies rapidly to form a high, steep-sided volcanic mountain. The magma often clogs the volcanic vent, causing violent eruptions as the blockage is blasted free, as in the eruption of Mount St Helens, USA, 1980. The crater may collapse to form a ◊caldera.

Shield volcanoes, such as Mauna Loa in Hawaii, are found along the rift valleys and ocean ridges of constructive plate margins (areas where plates are moving apart), and also over hot spots. The magma is derived from the Earth's mantle and is quite free-flowing. The lava formed from this magma – usually basalt – flows for some distance over the surface before it sets and so forms broad low volcanoes. The lava of a shield volcano is not ejected violently but simply flows over the crater rim.

The type of volcanic activity is also governed by the age of the volcano. The first stages of an eruption are usually vigorous as the magma forces its way to the surface. As the pressure drops and the vents become established, the main phase of activity begins, composite volcanoes giving ◊pyroclastic debris and shield volcanoes giving lava flows. When the pressure from below ceases, due to exhaustion of the magma chamber, activity wanes and is confined to the emission of gases and in time this also ceases. The volcano then enters a period of quiescence, after which activity may resume after a period of days, years, or even thousands of years. Only when the root zones of a volcano have been exposed by erosion can a volcano be said to be truly extinct.

Many volcanoes are submarine and occur along mid-ocean ridges. The chief terrestrial volcanic regions are around the Pacific rim (Cape Horn to Alaska); the central Andes of Chile (with the world's highest volcano, Guallatiri, 6,060 m/19,900 ft); North Island, New Zealand; Hawaii; Japan; and Antarctica. There are more than 1,300 potentially active volcanoes on Earth. Volcanism has helped shape other members of the Solar System, including the Moon, Mars, Venus, and Jupiter's moon Io.

An undersea volcano erupted June 1995, adding an island of about one hectare in size and 15 m/49 ft above sea level to the kingdom of Tonga.

vole any of various rodents of the family Cricetidae, subfamily Microtinae, distributed over Europe, Asia, and North America, and related to hamsters and lemmings. They are characterized by stout bodies and short tails. They have brown or grey fur, and blunt noses, and some species reach a length of 30 cm/12 in. They feed on grasses, seeds, aquatic plants, and insects. Many show remarkable fluctuations in numbers over 3–4 year cycles.

The most common genus is *Microtus*, which includes 45 species distributed across North America and Eurasia. British species include the ***water vole*** or ***water 'rat'*** *Arvicola terrestris*, brownish above and grey-white below, which makes a burrow in riverbanks; and the ***field*** or ***short-tailed vole*** *Microtus agrestis*. In Dec 1995 the water vole was listed on the UK's Biodiversity Action Plan, signalling increased investment in its conservation.

Volga longest river in Europe; 3,685 km/2,290 mi, 3,540 km/2,200 mi of which are navigable. It drains most of the central and eastern parts of European Russia, rises in the Valdai plateau, and flows into the Caspian Sea 88 km/55 mi below the city of Astrakhan.

Volgograd formerly (until 1925) ***Tsaritsyn*** and (1925–61) ***Stalingrad*** industrial city (metal goods, machinery, sawmills, oil refining) in SW Russian Federation, on the river Volga; population (1994) 1,000,000. Its successful defence 1942–43 against Germany was a turning point in World War II.

'If we do not find anything very pleasant, at least we shall find something new.'

VOLTAIRE
Candide

volleyball indoor and outdoor team game played on a court between two teams of six players each. A net is placed across the centre of the court, and players hit the ball with their hands over it, the aim being to ground it in the opponents' court.

Originally called Mintonette, the game was invented 1895 by William G Morgan in Massachusetts, USA, as a rival to the newly developed basketball. The playing area measures 18 m/59 ft by 9 m/29 ft 5 in. The ball, slightly smaller than a basketball, may not be hit more than three times on one team's side of the net. The world championships were first held 1949 for men, and 1952 for women and are held every four years (Olympic winners automatically become world champions).

volt SI unit of electromotive force or electric potential, symbol V. A small battery has a potential of 1.5 volts, whilst a high-tension transmission line may carry up to 765,000 volts. The domestic electricity supply in the UK is 230 volts (lowered from 240 volts 1995); it is 110 volts in the USA.

The absolute volt is defined as the potential difference necessary to produce a current of one ampere through an electric circuit with a resistance of one ohm. It can also be defined as the potential difference that requires one joule of work to move a positive charge of one coulomb from the lower to the higher potential. It is named after the Italian scientist Alessandro Volta.

Volta main river in Ghana, about 1,600 km/1,000 mi long, with two main upper branches, the Black and White Volta. It has been dammed to provide power.

Volta Alessandro Giuseppe Antonio Anastasio, Count 1745–1827. Italian physicist who invented the first electric cell (the voltaic pile, 1800), the electrophorus (an early electrostatic generator, 1775), and an ◊electroscope.

In 1776 Volta discovered methane by examining marsh gas found in Lago Maggiore. He then made the first accurate estimate of the proportion of oxygen in the air by exploding air with hydrogen to remove the oxygen. In about 1795, Volta recognized that the vapour pressure of a liquid is independent of the pressure of the atmosphere and depends only on temperature.

voltage commonly used term for ◊potential difference (pd) or ◊electromotive force (emf).

voltage amplifier electronic device that increases an input signal in the form of a voltage or ◊potential difference, delivering an output signal that is larger than the input by a specified ratio.

Voltaire pen name of François-Marie Arouet 1694–1778. French writer. He is the embodiment of the 18th-century ◊Enlightenment. He wrote histories, books of political analysis and philosophy, essays on science and literature, plays, poetry, and the satirical fable *Candide* 1759, his best-known work. A trenchant satirist of social and political evils, he was often forced to flee from his enemies and was twice imprisoned. His works include *Lettres philosophiques sur les Anglais/Philosophical Letters on the English* 1733 (essays in favour of English ways, thought, and political practice), *Le Siècle de Louis XIV/The Age of Louis XIV* 1751, and *Dictionnaire philosophique/Philosophical Dictionary* 1764.

Voltaire was born in Paris, the son of a notary, and used his pen name from 1718. He was twice imprisoned in the Bastille and exiled from Paris 1716–26 for libellous political verse. *Oedipe/Oedipus*, his first essay in tragedy, was staged 1718. While in England 1726–29 he dedicated an epic poem on Henry IV, *La Henriade/The Henriade*, to Queen Caroline, and on returning to France published the successful *Histoire de Charles XII/History of Charles XII* 1731, and produced the play *Zaïre* 1732.

He took refuge with his lover, the Marquise de Châtelet (1706–1749), at Cirey in Champagne, where he wrote the play *Mérope* 1743 and much of *Le Siècle de Louis XIV*. Among his other works are histories of Peter the Great, Louis XV, and India; the satirical tale *Zadig* 1748; *La Pucelle/The Maid* 1755, on Joan of Arc; and the tragedy *Irène* 1778. From 1751 to 1753 he stayed at the court of Frederick II (the Great) of Prussia, who had long been an admirer, but the association ended in deep enmity. From 1754 he established himself near Geneva, and after 1758 at Ferney, just across the French border.

voltmeter instrument for measuring potential difference (voltage). It has a high internal resistance (so that it passes only a small current), and is connected in parallel with the component across which potential difference is to be measured. A common type is constructed from a sensitive current-detecting moving-coil ◊galvanometer placed in series with a high-value resistor (multiplier). To measure an AC (◊alternating current) voltage, the circuit must usually include a rectifier; however, a moving-iron instrument can be used to measure alternating voltages without the need for such a device.

volume in geometry, the space occupied by a three-dimensional solid object. A prism (such as a cube) or a cylinder has a volume equal to the area of the base multiplied by the height. For a pyramid or cone, the volume is equal to one-third of the area of the base multiplied by the perpendicular height. The volume of a sphere is equal to $\frac{4}{3} \times \pi r^3$, where r is the radius. Volumes of irregular solids may be calculated by the technique of integration.

volumetric analysis procedure used for determining the concentration of a solution. A known volume of a solution of unknown concentration is reacted with a solution of known concentration (standard). The standard solution is delivered from a burette, which can deliver measured quantities of a liquid, so the volume added is known. This technique is known as ◊titration. Often an indicator is used to show when the correct proportions have reacted. This procedure is used for acid–base, ◊redox, and certain other reactions involving solutions.

voluntary in music, a generic term for a quasi-improvisatory composition of the 16th century, but more specifically a piece for solo organ played at the beginning or end of a church service. As the name suggests, the organ voluntary is often free in style, and may be improvised. During the 16th century voluntaries were usually short contrapuntal pieces, without a cantus firmus ('fixed melody'). In the 17th and 18th centuries they developed a more secular style, incorporating elements of the suite, sonata, toccata, and even the operatic aria. Composers of voluntaries include Purcell, John Blow, and Samuel Wesley.

Volvo (Latin 'I roll') Swedish motor vehicle manufacturer founded 1925 by Gustaf Larson and Assar Gabrielsson; in the mid-1970s Volvo acquired the Dutch DAF concern.

von Braun Wernher Magnus Maximilian 1912–1977. German rocket engineer who developed military rockets (◊V1 and V2) during World War II and later worked for the space agency ◊NASA in the USA. During the 1940s his research team at Peenemünde on the Baltic coast produced the V1 (flying bomb) and supersonic V2 rockets. In the 1950s he was part of the team that produced rockets for US satellites (the first, *Explorer 1*, was launched early 1958) and early space flights by astronauts.

von Karajan Herbert, Austrian conductor. See ◊Karajan, Herbert von.

Vonnegut Kurt, Jr 1922– . US writer. His early works, *Player Piano* 1952 and *The Sirens of Titan* 1959, used the science-fiction genre to explore issues of technological and historical control. He turned to more experimental methods with his highly acclaimed, popular success *Slaughterhouse-Five* 1969, a novel that mixed a world of fantasy with the author's experience of the fire-bombing of Dresden during World War II. His later novels, marked by a bittersweet spirit of absurdist anarchy and folksy fatalism, include *Breakfast of Champions* 1973, *Slapstick* 1976, *Jailbird* 1979, *Deadeye Dick* 1982, *Galapagos* 1985, *Hocus Pocus* 1990, and *The Face* 1992. His short stories are collected in *Welcome to the Monkey House* 1968, and he has written two volumes of autobiography, *Palm Sunday* 1981 and *Fates Worse Than Death: An Autobiographical Collage of the 1980s* 1992.

Von Neumann John, (originally Johann) 1903–1957. Hungarian-born US scientist and mathematician, a pioneer of computer design. He invented his 'rings of operators' (called Von Neumann algebras) in the late 1930s, and also contributed to set theory, game theory, quantum mechanics, cybernetics (with his theory of self-reproducing automata, called Von Neumann machines), and the development of the atomic and hydrogen bombs. He designed and supervised the construction of the first computer able to use a flexible stored program (named MANIAC-1) at the Institute for Advanced Study at Princeton 1940–1952. This work laid the foundations for the design of all subsequent programmable computers.

voodoo set of magical beliefs and practices, followed in some parts of Africa, South America, and the West Indies, especially Haiti. It arose in the 17th century on slave plantations as a combination of Roman Catholicism and W African religious traditions; believers retain membership in the Roman Catholic church. Beliefs include the existence of *loa*, spirits who closely involve themselves in human affairs, and some of whose identities mesh with those of Christian saints. The loa are invoked by the priest (*houngan*) or priestess (*manbo*) at ceremonies, during which members of the congregation become possessed by the spirits and go into a trance.

A voodoo temple (*houmfort*) has a central post from which the loa supposedly descend to 'mount' the worshipper. The loa can be identified by the characteristic behaviour of the possessed person. Loa include Baron Samedi, who watches over the land of the dead; Erzulie, the black Virgin or Earth goddess; Ogu, a warrior, corresponding to St James the Great; and Legba, the lord of the road and interpreter between humans and spirits, who corresponds to St Anthony the hermit.

Vorarlberg ('in front of the Arlberg') Alpine federal state of W Austria draining into the river Rhine and Lake Constance; area 2,600 sq km/1,004 sq mi; population (1994) 342,500. Its capital is Bregenz. Industries include forestry and dairy farming.

Voronezh industrial city (chemicals, construction machinery, electrical equipment) and capital of the Voronezh region of the Russian Federation, S of Moscow on the Voronezh River; population (1994) 905,000. There has been a town on the site since the 11th century.

Vorster John, (originally Balthazar Johannes) 1915–1983. South African Nationalist politician, prime minister 1966–78, and president 1978–79. During his term as prime minister some elements of apartheid were allowed to lapse, and attempts were made to improve relations with the outside world. He resigned the presidency because of a financial scandal.

Vorticism short-lived British literary and artistic movement 1912–15, influenced by Cubism and Futurism and led by Wyndham ◊Lewis. Lewis believed that painting should reflect the complexity and rapid change of the modern world; he painted in a harsh, angular, semi-abstract style. The last Vorticist exhibition was held 1915.

The aim was to build up 'a visual language as abstract as music' and also to make use of machine forms, which constituted as real a world to the artist as the forms of nature. Its manifesto appeared in the publication *Blast*, June 1914, of which only one other issue came out, 1915. A number of distinguished artists had some association with the movement, including Henri Gaudier Brzeska, William Roberts, Edward Wadsworth, and David Bomberg. World War I halted the Vorticist activity, but a number of Lewis's associates were later prominent in the London Group.

Vosges mountain range in E France, rising in the Ballon de Guebwiller to 1,422 m/4,667 ft and forming the western edge of the Rhine rift valley. It gives its name to a *département*.

Voskhod (Russian 'ascent') Soviet spacecraft used in the mid-1960s; it was modified from the single-seat Vostok, and was the first spacecraft capable of carrying two or three cosmonauts. During *Voskhod 2*'s flight 1965, Aleksi Leonov made the first space walk.

Vostok (Russian 'east') first Soviet spacecraft, used 1961–63. Vostok was a metal sphere 2.3 m/7.5 ft in diameter, capable of carrying one cosmonaut. It made flights lasting up to five days. *Vostok 1* carried the first person into space, Yuri ◊Gagarin.

vote expression of opinion by ◊ballot, show of hands, or other means. In systems that employ direct vote, the ◊plebiscite and ◊referendum are fundamental mechanisms. In parliamentary elections the results can be calculated in a number of ways. The main electoral systems are:

simple plurality or ***first past the post***, with single-member constituencies (USA, UK, India, Canada);

absolute majority, achieved for example by the alternative vote, where the voter, in single-member constituencies, chooses a candidate by marking preferences (Australia), or by the second ballot, where, if a clear decision is not reached immediately, a second ballot is held (France, Egypt);

◊proportional representation, achieved for example by the party list system (Israel, most countries of Western Europe, and several in South America);

additional member system or ***AMS*** (Germany);

single transferable vote (Ireland and Malta);

limited vote (Japan's upper house and Liechtenstein).

Revised voting systems were adopted by Italy and New Zealand 1993, in which both houses were elected by a combination of simple majority voting and proportional representation on the AMS model. In Japan AMS was adopted for the lower house in 1994.

In one-party states some degree of choice may be exercised by voting for particular candidates within the party list. In some countries where there are problems of literacy or differing local languages, pictorial party emblems may be printed on the ballot paper instead of the names of candidates. The absence of accurate registers in some countries can encourage plural voting, so electors may be marked on the hand with temporarily indelible ink after they have voted.

The qualifications for voting have been liberalized during the present century. New Zealand was the first country to give women the vote 1893, and, among economically advanced states, Switzerland was one of the last 1971, with Liechtenstein 1984. The minimum age for voting has also been reduced over the years. The age of 18 has now been adopted by most countries, but a few have adopted an even lower figure. The age qualification in Iran for presidential elections is 15.

All British subjects over 18, except peers, the insane, and felons, are entitled to vote in UK local government and parliamentary elections. A register is prepared annually, and since 1872 voting has been by secret ballot. Under the Corrupt and Illegal Practices Act 1883, any candidate attempting to influence voters by gifts, loans or promises, or by intimidation, is liable to a fine or imprisonment. The voting system is by a simple majority in single-member constituencies. Critics point out that under this system many electors have no say, since votes for a defeated candidate are wasted, and governments may take office with a minority of the total vote. When there are two main parties, divided along class lines, the one in power often undoes the legislation of its predecessor. Supporters of the system argue the danger of increasing party fragmentation, and they believe continual coalition governments would be ineffective.

In the USA the voting age is 18. Conditions of residence vary from state to state and registration is required before election day. Until declared illegal 1965, literacy tests or a ◊poll tax were often used to prevent black people from voting in the South. Voter registration and turnout in the USA remains the lowest in the industrialized world. In 1988, 37% of potential voters failed to register and barely 50% voted in the presidential election, so that George Bush became president with the support of only 27% of the people. In 1996 turnout fell further to a record low of 49%. The two major parties are the only effective political organizations, and the candidate receiving the greater number of votes wins. Critics contend that this deprives the losing side of a voice, although calls for proportional voting have never gained much support.

Voyager two US space probes. *Voyager 1*, launched 5 Sept 1977, passed Jupiter March 1979, and reached Saturn Nov 1980. *Voyager 2* was launched earlier, 20 Aug 1977, on a slower trajectory that took it past Jupiter July 1979, Saturn Aug 1981, Uranus Jan 1986, and Neptune Aug 1989. Like the ◊*Pioneer* probes, the *Voyagers* are on their way out of the Solar System; at the start of 1995, *Voyager 1* was 8.8 billion km/5.5 billion mi from Earth, and *Voyager 2* was 6.8 billion km/4.3 billion mi from Earth. Their tasks now include helping scientists to locate the position of the heliopause, the boundary at which the influence of the Sun gives way to the forces exerted by other stars. Both *Voyagers* carry specially coded long-playing records called *Sounds of Earth* for the enlightenment of any other civilizations that might find them.

Voysey Charles Francis Annesley 1857–1941. English architect and designer. He designed country houses which are characteristically asymmetrical with massive buttresses, long sloping roofs, and roughcast walls, for example The Cottage, Bishop's Itchington, Warwickshire, 1888–89. He also designed textiles and wallpaper in the ◊Arts and Crafts tradition.

Voznesensky Andrey Andreyevich 1933– . Russian poet. Coming to prominence in the early 1960s, he was (along with ◊Yevtushenko) one of the most original Soviet poets to emerge during the cultural and intellectual thaw that followed the death of Stalin. He gave many popular readings, both in Russia and the West; poems such as 'Goya' and 'Antiworlds' have reached an international audience.

Vranitzky Franz 1937– . Austrian socialist politician, federal chancellor from 1986. A banker, he entered the political arena through the moderate, left-of-centre Socialist Party of Austria (SPÖ), and became minister of finance 1984. He succeeded Fred Sinowatz as federal chancellor 1986, heading an SPÖ-ÖVP (Austrian People's Party) coalition, which was returned in the Oct 1994 and Dec 1995 general elections.

V-shaped valley river valley with a V-shaped cross-section. Such valleys are usually found near the source of a river, where the steeper gradient means that there is a great deal of ◊corrasion (grinding away by rock particles) along the stream bed and erosion cuts downwards more than it does sideways. However, a V-shaped valley may also be formed in the lower course of a river when its powers of downward erosion become renewed by a fall in sea level, a rise in land level, or the capture of another river.

VSTOL abbreviation for ***vertical/short takeoff and landing***, aircraft capable of taking off and landing either vertically or using a very short length of runway (see ◊STOL). Vertical takeoff requires a vector-control system that permits the thrust of the aircraft engine to be changed from horizontal to vertical for takeoff and back again to horizontal to permit forward flight. An alternative VSTOL technology developed in the USA involves tilting the wings of the aircraft from vertical to horizontal and along with them the aircraft propellers, thus changing from vertical lift to horizontal thrust.

'Suffrage is the pivotal right.'

On the right to VOTE Susan B Anthony in *Arena* 1897

vulture The vulture is a heavily built bird. There are 15 species in Africa, Asia, and Europe, with a further seven species in America. Most have dark plumage, bare head and neck, strongly curved beak, and powerful talons.

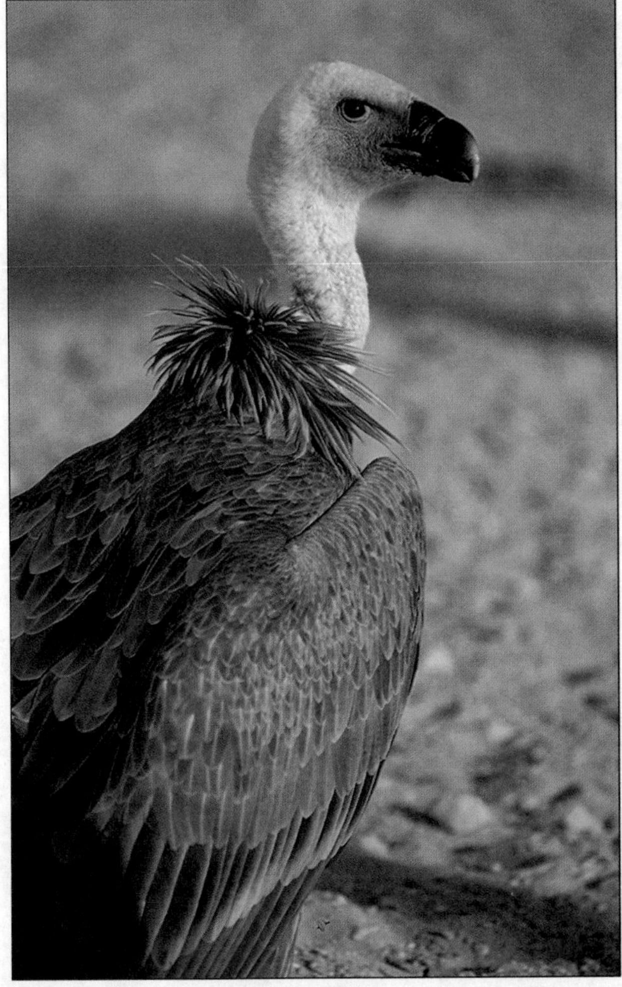

The British ◊Harrier fighter bomber was the first VSTOL aircraft. It is now manufactured under licence in the USA and provides integral air support for the US Marines. In addition to the UK's Royal Air Force and Royal Navy, the Indian, Spanish, and Italian navies are equipped with the Harrier. It was used in the 1982 Falklands conflict and the 1991 Gulf War.

Vuillard (Jean) Edouard 1868–1940. French painter and printmaker. He was a founding member of *les ◊Nabis*, and is noted for his decorative paintings of intimate domestic interiors with figures and for his brilliantly coloured lithographs.

He was closely linked with Pierre ◊Bonnard, his friend from youth, and took a parallel direction in art. As Vuillard himself said, there was 'nothing of the revolutionary' about him. The term *Intimiste*, applied both to him and to Bonnard, refers particularly aptly to the gentle and seclusive spirit in which Vuillard painted lamplit domestic interiors. He was less venturesome and more academic in tendency than Bonnard, though in colour lithography, inspired by Japanese prints, he developed some brilliant and unconventional designs.

Vukovar river port in Croatia at the junction of the rivers Vuka and Danube, 32 km/20 mi SE of Osijek; population (1991) 44,600. Industries include foodstuffs manufacture, fishing, and agricultural trade. In 1991 the town resisted three months of siege by the Serb-dominated Yugoslav army before capitulating. It suffered the severest damage inflicted to any European city since the bombing of Dresden during World War II.

Vulcan in Roman mythology, the god of fire and destruction, later identified with the Greek god ◊Hephaestus.

vulcanization technique for hardening rubber by heating and chemically combining it with sulphur. The process also makes the rubber stronger and more elastic. If the sulphur content is increased to as much as 30%, the product is the inelastic solid known as ebonite. More expensive alternatives to sulphur, such as selenium and tellurium, are used to vulcanize rubber for specialized products such as vehicle tyres. The process was discovered accidentally by US inventor Charles ◊Goodyear 1839 and patented 1844.

Accelerators can be added to speed the vulcanization process, which takes from a few minutes for small objects to an hour or more for vehicle tyres. Moulded objects are often shaped and vulcanized simultaneously in heated moulds; other objects may be vulcanized in hot water, hot air, or steam.

Vulgate (Latin 'common') the Latin translation of the Bible produced by St Jerome in the 4th century. It became the most popular Latin version from the 7th century (hence its name), and in 1546 was adopted by the Council of Trent as the official Roman Catholic Bible.

Vulpecula small constellation in the northern hemisphere just south of ◊Cygnus, represented as a fox. It contains a major planetary ◊nebula, the Dumbbell, and the first ◊pulsar (pulsating radio source) to be discovered.

vulture any of various carrion-eating birds of prey in the order Falconiformes, with naked heads and necks, strong hooked bills, and keen senses of sight and smell. Vultures are up to 1 m/3.3 ft long, with wingspans of up to 3.7 m/12 ft. The plumage is usually dark, and the head brightly coloured. Its eyes are adapted to give an overall view with a magnifying area in the centre, enabling it to locate possible food sources and see the exact site in detail. *See illustration on previous page.*

Vyborg (Finnish ***Viipuri***) port (trading in timber and wood products) and naval base in E Karelia, NW Russian Federation, on the Gulf of Finland, 112 km/70 mi NW of St Petersburg; population (1973) 51,000. Products include electrical equipment and agricultural machinery. Founded by the Swedes 1293, it was part of Finland until 1940.

Vyshinsky Andrei Yanuaryevich 1883–1954. Soviet politician. As commissar for justice, he acted as prosecutor at Stalin's treason trials 1936–38. He was foreign minister 1949–53 and often represented the USSR at the United Nations.

Waddenzee European estuarine area (tidal flats, salt marshes, islands, and inlets) N of the Netherlands and Germany, and W of Denmark; area 10,000 sq km/4,000 sq mi.

Wade (Sarah) Virginia 1945– . English tennis player. She won the Wimbledon singles title in 1977; she also won the US Open in 1968 and the Australian Open 1972. She holds a record number of appearances for the Wightman and Federation Cup teams and her total of eight Grand Slam titles is a post-war British record equalled only by Ann Jones.

wadi in arid regions of the Middle East, a steep-sided valley containing an intermittent stream that flows in the wet season.

Wafd (Arabic 'deputation') the main Egyptian nationalist party between World Wars I and II. Under Nahas Pasha it formed a number of governments in the 1920s and 1930s. Dismissed by King Farouk in 1938, it was reinstated by the British 1941. The party's pro-British stance weakened its claim to lead the nationalist movement, and the party was again dismissed by Farouk 1952; it was banned 1953.

Wagenfeld Wilhelm 1900–1990. German architect and industrial designer. A graduate of the ◊Bauhaus design school, Wagenfeld went on to become one of the country's leading proponents of the machine style (a geometric, undecorated style deemed appropriate for industrial products) in the areas of metal and glass goods.

Wagga Wagga agricultural town in SE New South Wales, Australia; population (1994 est) 56,700.

Wagner Otto 1841–1918. Viennese architect. Initially working in the Art Nouveau style, for example the Vienna Stadtbahn 1894–97, he later rejected ornament for ◊Rationalism, as in the Post Office Savings Bank, Vienna, 1904–06. He influenced such Viennese architects as Josef Hoffmann, Adolf Loos, and Joseph Olbrich.

Wagner (Wilhelm) Richard 1813–1883. German opera composer. He revolutionized the 19th-century conception of opera, envisaging it as a wholly new art form in which musical, poetic, and scenic elements should be unified through such devices as the ◊leitmotif. His operas include *Tannhäuser* 1845, *Lohengrin* 1848, and *Tristan und Isolde* 1865. In 1872 he founded the Festival Theatre in Bayreuth; his masterpiece *Der Ring des Nibelungen/The Ring of the Nibelung*, a sequence of four operas, was first performed there 1876. His last work, *Parsifal*, was produced 1882.

Wagner's early career was as director of the Magdeburg Theatre, where he unsuccessfully produced his first opera *Das Liebesverbot/Forbidden Love* 1836. He lived in Paris 1839–42 and conducted the Dresden Opera House 1842–48. He fled Germany to escape arrest for his part in the 1848 revolution, but in 1861 he was allowed to return. He won the favour of Ludwig II of Bavaria 1864 and was thus able to set up the Festival Theatre in Bayreuth. The Bayreuth tradition was continued by his wife Cosima (Liszt's daughter, whom he married after her divorce from Hans von Bülow (1830–1894)); by his son Siegfried Wagner (1869–1930), a composer of operas such as *Der Bärenhäuter*; and by later descendants.

Wagner Robert F(erdinand) 1877–1953. US Democratic senator 1927–49, a leading figure in the development of welfare provision in the USA, especially in the ◊New Deal era. He helped draft much new legislation, including the National Industrial Recovery Act 1933, the Social Security Act 1936, and the National Labor Relations Act 1935, known as the Wagner Act.

Wagram, Battle of during the Napoleonic Wars, decisive French victory 6 July 1809 over the Austrians led by the Archduke Charles near Wagram, an Austrian village 18 km/11 mi northeast of Vienna. Austria was forced to concede general defeat to Napoleon. ▷ *See feature on pp. 748–749.*

wagtail slim, narrow-billed bird of the genus *Motacilla*, in the family Motacillidae, order Passeriformes, about 18 cm/7 in long, with a characteristic flicking movement of the tail. There are about 30 species, found mostly in Eurasia and Africa. British species include the ***pied wagtail*** *M. alba* with black, grey, and white plumage, the ***grey wagtail*** *M. cinerae*, and, a summer visitor, the ***yellow wagtail*** *M. flava*.

Wahabi puritanical Saudi Islamic sect founded by Muhammad ibn-Abd-al-Wahab (1703–1792), which regards all other sects as heretical. By the early 20th century it had spread throughout the Arabian peninsula; it still remains the official ideology of the Saudi Arabian kingdom.

Waikato river on North Island, New Zealand, 355 km/220 mi long; Waikato is also the name of the dairy area the river traverses; chief town Hamilton.

Wailing Wall or (in Judaism) ***Western Wall*** the remaining part of the ◊Temple in Jerusalem, a sacred site of pilgrimage and prayer for Jews. They offer prayers either aloud ('wailing') or on pieces of paper placed between the stones of the wall.

Wain John Barrington 1925–1994. English poet and novelist. His first novel, *Hurry on Down* 1953, expresses the radical political views of the ◊'Angry Young Men' of the 1950s. He published several volumes of verse, collected in *Poems 1949–79*, and was professor of poetry at Oxford 1973–80.

Wainwright Alfred 1907–1991. English walker and author of guidebooks. His first articles appeared 1955 in a local paper, and he eventually produced over 40 meticulously detailed books, including volumes on the Lake District, Pennine Way, and other areas of N England.

Wairarapa area of North Island, New Zealand, round ***Lake Wairarapa***, specializing in lamb and dairy farming; population (1986) 39,600. The chief market centre is Masterton.

Wairau river in N South Island, New Zealand, flowing 170 km/105 mi NE to Cook Strait.

Waitaki river in SE South Island, New Zealand, that flows 215 km/135 mi to the Pacific Ocean.

Waitangi Day the national day of New Zealand: 6 Feb.

Waitangi, Treaty of treaty negotiated in New Zealand 1840 between the British government and the indigenous Maori. The treaty guaranteed the Maori their own territory and gave them British citizenship. The British claimed sovereignty over the territory and the treaty is seen as the establishment of modern New Zealand.

Waite Terry (Terence Hardy) 1939– . British religious adviser to the archbishop of Canterbury (then Dr Robert ◊Runcie) 1980–87. As the archbishop's special envoy, Waite disappeared 20 Jan 1987 while engaged in secret negotiations to free European hostages in Beirut, Lebanon. He was taken hostage by an Islamic group and released 18 Nov 1991.

Waits Tom 1949– . US singer, songwriter, musician, and actor, with a characteristic gravelly voice. His songs typically deal with urban street life and have jazz-tinged arrangements, as on *Rain Dogs* 1985. He has written music for and acted in several films, including Jim Jarmusch's *Down by Law* 1986.

Wajda Andrzej 1926– . Polish film and theatre director, a major figure in postwar European cinema. His films have great intensity and are frequently concerned with the predicament and disillusion of individuals caught up in political events. His works include *Ashes and Diamonds* 1958, *Man of Marble* 1977, *Man of Iron* 1981, *Danton* 1982, and *Korczak* 1990.

Wakefield industrial city (chemicals, machine tools, wool textiles), administrative headquarters of West Yorkshire, England, on the river Calder, S of Leeds; population (1991) 306,300.

Waksman Selman Abraham 1888–1973. US biochemist, born in Ukraine. He coined the word 'antibiotic' for bacteria-killing chemicals derived from microorganisms. He was awarded a Nobel prize in 1952 for the discovery of streptomycin, an antibiotic used against tuberculosis.

Walachia alternative spelling of ◊Wallachia, part of Romania.

Walcheren island in Zeeland province, the Netherlands, in the estuary of the river Scheldt
area 200 sq km/80 sq mi
capital Middelburg
towns and cities Vlissingen (Flushing)
features flat and for the most part below sea level
industries dairy, sugar beet, and other root vegetables
history a British force seized Walcheren 1809; after 7,000 of the garrison of 15,000 had died of malaria, the remainder were withdrawn. It was flooded by deliberate breaching of the dykes to drive out the Germans 1944–45, and in 1953 by abnormally high tides.

Walcott Derek Walton 1930– . St Lucian poet and playwright. His work fuses Caribbean and European, classical and contemporary elements, and deals with the divisions within colonial society and his own search for cultural identity. His works include the long poem *Omeros* 1990, and his adaptation for the stage of Homer's *Odyssey* 1992; his *Collected Poems* were published 1986. Nobel Prize for Literature 1992.

Wald George 1906–1997. US biochemist who explored the chemistry of vision. He discovered the role played in night vision by the retinal pigment rhodopsin, and later identified the three primary-colour pigments. Nobel Prize for Physiology or Medicine 1967.

Waldemar or ***Valdemar*** four kings of Denmark, including:

Waldemar (I) the Great 1131–1182. King of Denmark from 1157, who defeated rival claimants to the throne and overcame the ◊Wends on the Baltic island of Rügen 1169.

Waldemar (II) the Conqueror 1170–1241. King of Denmark from 1202. He was the second son of Waldemar the Great and succeeded his brother Canute VI. He gained control of land north of the river Elbe (which he later lost), as well as much of Estonia, and he completed the codification of Danish law.

Waldemar IV 1320–1375. King of Denmark from 1340, responsible for reuniting his country by capturing Skaône (S Sweden) and the island of Gotland 1361. However, the resulting conflict with the ◊Hanseatic League led to defeat by them, and in 1370 he was forced to submit to the Peace of Stralsund.

Waldenses also known as ***Waldensians*** or ***Vaudois*** Protestant religious sect, founded c. 1170 by Peter Waldo, a merchant of Lyons. They were allied to the ◊Albigenses. They lived in voluntary poverty, refused to take oaths or take part in war, and later rejected the doctrines of transubstantiation, purgatory, and the invocation of saints. Although subjected to persecution until the 17th century, they spread in France, Germany, and Italy, and still survive in Piedmont.

Waldheim Kurt 1918– . Austrian politician and diplomat, president 1986–92. He was secretary general of the United Nations 1972–81, having been Austria's representative there 1964–68 and 1970–71.

He was elected president of Austria despite revelations that during World War II he had been an intelligence officer in an army unit responsible for transporting Jews to death camps. His election therefore led to some diplomatic isolation of Austria, and in 1991 he announced that he would not run for re-election.

'Where the speech of men stops short, then the art of music begins.'

RICHARD WAGNER
A Happy Evening

Wałesa Lech Wałesa won a landslide victory in his country's 1990 presidential election. Poland's most prominent opposition figure in the 1980s, as chair of the Polish Solidarity labour union, Wałesa played a vital role in talks between the government and Solidarity leaders in 1989, paving the way for the dismantling of the communist regime. He was awarded the Nobel Peace Prize in 1983. *Topham*

Waldsterben (German 'forest death') tree decline related to air pollution, common throughout the industrialized world. It appears to be caused by a mixture of pollutants; the precise chemical mix varies between locations, but it includes acid rain, ozone, sulphur dioxide, and nitrogen oxides. *Waldsterben* was first noticed in the Black Forest of Germany during the late 1970s, and is spreading to many developing world countries, such as China. Research has shown Britain's trees to be among the most badly affected in Europe. ▷*See feature on pp. 858–859.*

Wales (Welsh ***Cymru***) Principality of; constituent part of the UK, in the west between the British Channel and the Irish Sea
area 20,780 sq km/8,021 sq mi
capital Cardiff
towns and cities Swansea, Wrexham, Newport, Carmarthen
features Snowdonia Mountains (Snowdon 1,085 m/3,561 ft, the highest point in England and Wales) in the northwest and in the southeast the Black Mountains, Brecon Beacons, and Black Forest ranges; rivers Severn, Wye, Usk, and Dee
industries traditional industries have declined, but varied modern and high-technology ventures are being developed. There are oil refineries and open-cast coal mining. Wales has the largest concentration of Japanese-owned plants in the UK. It also has the highest density of sheep in the world and a dairy industry; tourism is important
currency pound sterling
population (1993 est) 2,906,000
language English, 19% Welsh-speaking
religion Nonconformist Protestant denominations; Roman Catholic minority
government Wales returns 38 members to the UK Parliament. In 1996, the eight counties established in 1974 were replaced by 22 unitary authorities (*see list of tables on p. 1177 and United Kingdom map*).

Wałesa Lech 1943– . Polish trade-union leader, president of Poland 1990–95. He founded ◊Solidarity (Solidarność) 1980, an organization, independent of the Communist Party, which forced substantial political and economic concessions from the Polish government 1980–81 until being outlawed. Nobel Peace Prize 1983.

As an electrician at the Lenin shipyard in Gdańsk, Wałesa became a trade-union organizer and led a series of strikes that drew wide public support. The coalition government elected 1989 was dominated by Solidarity; Wałesa went on to be elected president 1990. In 1991 Wałesa left Solidarity and in 1993 publicly disassociated himself from the party. He was narrowly defeated in the 1995 presidential elections by his communist challenger, Alexander ◊Kwasniewski.

Wales, Church in the Welsh Anglican Church, independent from the ◊Church of England. The Welsh church became strongly Protestant in the 16th century, but in the 17th and 18th centuries declined from being led by a succession of English-appointed bishops. Disestablished by an act of Parliament 1920, with its endowments appropriated, the Church in Wales today comprises six dioceses (with bishops elected by an electoral college of clergy and lay people) with an archbishop elected from among the six bishops.

WALES: TIMELINE

For ancient history, see also ◊Britain, ancient and ◊United Kingdom.

c. 400 BC	Wales occupied by Celts from central Europe.
AD 50–60	Wales became part of the Roman Empire.
c. 200	Christianity adopted.
c. 450–600	Wales became the chief Celtic stronghold in the west since the Saxons invaded and settled in S Britain. The Celtic tribes united against England.
8th C	Frontier pushed back to Offa's Dyke.
9th–11th Cs	Vikings raided the coasts. At this time Wales was divided into small states organized on a clan basis, although princes such as Rhodri (844–878), Howel the Good (c. 904–949), and Griffith ap Llewelyn (1039–1063) temporarily united the country.
11th–12th Cs	Continual pressure on Wales from the Normans across the English border was resisted, notably by Llewelyn I and II.
1277	Edward I of England accepted as overlord by the Welsh.
1284	Edward I completed the conquest of Wales begun by the Normans.
1294	Revolt against English rule put down by Edward I.
1350–1500	Welsh nationalist uprisings against the English; the most notable was that led by Owen Glendower.
1485	Henry Tudor, a Welshman, became Henry VII of England.
1536–43	Acts of Union united England and Wales after conquest under Henry VIII. Wales sent representatives to the English Parliament; English law was established in Wales; English became the official language.
18th C	Evangelical revival made Nonconformism a powerful factor in Welsh life. A strong coal and iron industry developed in the south.
19th C	The miners and ironworkers were militant supporters of Chartism, and Wales became a stronghold of trade unionism and socialism.
1893	University of Wales founded.
1920s–30s	Wales suffered from industrial depression; unemployment reached 21% 1937, and a considerable exodus of population took place.
post-1945	Growing nationalist movement and a revival of the Welsh language, earlier suppressed or discouraged.
1966	Plaid Cymru, the Welsh National Party, returned its first member to Westminster.
1979	Referendum rejected a proposal for limited home rule.
1988	Bombing campaign against estate agents selling Welsh properties to English buyers.
1996	Local government reform: unitary authorities replaced county and district councils.
1997	Referendum approved devolution.

WALES: SOVEREIGNS AND PRINCES 844–1282

844–78	Rhodri the Great
878–916	Anarawd
915–50	Hywel Dda (Hywel the Good)
950–79	Iago ab Idwal
979–85	Hywel ab Ieuaf (Hywel the Bad)
985–86	Cadwallon
986–99	Maredudd ab Owain ap Hywel Dda
999–1008	Cynan ap Hywel ab Ieuaf
1018–23	Llywelyn ap Seisyll
1023–39	Iago ab Idwal ap Meurig
1039–63	Gruffydd ap Llywelyn ap Seisyll
1063–75	Bleddyn ap Cynfyn
1075–81	Trahaern ap Caradog
1081–1137	Gruffydd ap Cynan ab Iago
1137–70	Owain Gwynedd
1170–94	Dafydd ab Owain Gwynedd
1194–1240	Llywelyn Fawr (Llywelyn the Great)
1240–46	Dafydd ap Llywellyn
1246–82	Llywellyn ap Gruffydd ap Llywellyn

Wales, Prince of title conferred on the eldest son of the UK's sovereign. Prince ◊Charles was invested as 21st prince of Wales at Caernarvon 1969 by his mother, Elizabeth II.

walkabout Australian Aboriginal term for a nomadic ritual return into the bush by an urbanized Aboriginal; also used more casually for any similar excursion.

Walker Alice Malsenior 1944– . US poet, novelist, critic, and essay writer. She has been active in the US civil-rights movement since the 1960s and, as a black woman, wrote about the double burden of racist and sexist oppression, about colonialism, and the quest for political and spiritual recovery. Her novel *The Color Purple* 1982 (filmed 1985), told in the form of letters, won a Pulitzer prize. Her other works include *Possessing the Secret of Joy* 1992, which deals passionately with female circumcision.

Walker Horatio 1858–1938. Canadian artist. His subjects were chiefly Canadian landscapes and farm scenes, composed in a broad and simple manner showing the influence of the French painter ◊Millet.

Walker T-Bone (Aaron Thibeaux) 1910–1975. US blues guitarist, singer, and songwriter. His sophisticated guitar technique incorporated jazz idioms and he was one of the first to use an electrically amplified guitar, from the mid-1930s. He was active mainly in California, and often worked with jazz musicians. His recordings include 'Call It Stormy Monday' 1946 and the album *T-Bone Blues* 1960.

Walker William 1824–1860. US adventurer who for a short time established himself as president of a republic in NW Mexico, and was briefly president of Nicaragua 1856–57. He was eventually executed and is now regarded as a symbol of US imperialism in Central America.

Wall Max. Stage name of Maxwell George Lorimer 1908–1990. English music-hall comedian. Towards the end of his career he appeared in starring roles as a serious actor, in John Osborne's *The Entertainer* 1974, in Harold Pinter's *The Caretaker* 1977, and in Samuel Beckett's *Waiting for Godot* 1980. In his solo comedy performances his trademark was an eccentric walk.

wallaby any of various small and medium-sized members of the ◊kangaroo family.

Wallace Alfred Russel 1823–1913. Welsh naturalist who collected animal and plant specimens in South America and SE Asia, and independently arrived at a theory of evolution by natural selection similar to that proposed by Charles ◊Darwin.

In 1858, Wallace wrote an essay outlining his ideas on evolution and sent it to Darwin, who had not yet published his. Together they presented a paper to the Linnaean Society that year. Wallace's section, entitled 'On the Tendency of Varieties to Depart Indefinitely from the Original Type', described the survival of the fittest. Although both thought that the human race had evolved to its present physical form by natural selection, Wallace was of the opinion that humans' higher mental capabilities had arisen from some 'metabiological' agency.

Wallace Irving 1916–1990. US novelist. He was one of the most popular writers of the 20th century. He wrote 17 works of nonfiction and 16 novels; they include *The Chapman Report* 1960, a novel inspired by the Kinsey Report on sexual behaviour, and *The Prize* 1962.

Wallace Richard 1818–1890. English art collector. He inherited a valuable art collection from his father, the Marquess of Hertford, which was given 1897 by his widow to the UK as the Wallace Collection, containing many 18th-century French paintings.

Wallace William 1272–1305. Scottish nationalist who led a revolt against English rule 1297, won a victory at Stirling, and assumed the title 'governor of Scotland'. Edward I defeated him at Falkirk 1298, and Wallace was captured and executed.

Wallace line imaginary line running down the Lombok Strait in SE Asia, between the island of Bali and the islands of Lombok and Sulawesi. It was identified by English naturalist Alfred Russel Wallace as separating the S Asian (Oriental) and Australian biogeographical regions, each of which has its own distinctive animals.

Wallachia independent medieval principality, founded 1290, with allegiance to Hungary until 1330 and under Turkish rule 1387–1861, when it was united with the neighbouring principality of Moldavia to form Romania.

wallaby Wallaby is the name given to generally small to medium-sized kangaroos. This is the agile wallaby *Macropus agilis*, a graceful species from E Australia. Like most kangaroos, it grazes on grass. *Premaphotos Wildlife*

Wallenberg Raoul 1912–c. 1947. Swedish business executive who attempted to rescue several thousand Jews from German-occupied Budapest 1944, during World War II. He was taken prisoner by the Soviet army 1945 and was never heard from again.

Wallenstein Albrecht Eusebius Wenzel von 1583–1634. German general who, until his defeat at Lützen 1632, led the Habsburg armies in the Thirty Years' War. He was assassinated.

Waller Fats (Thomas Wright) 1904–1943. US jazz pianist and composer. He had a forceful ◊stride piano style. His songs, many of which have become jazz standards, include 'Ain't Misbehavin' 1929, 'Honeysuckle Rose' 1929, and 'Viper's Drag' 1934. An exuberant, humorous performer, Waller toured extensively and appeared in several musical films, including *Stormy Weather* 1943. In the 1930s he worked with a small group (as Fats Waller and his Rhythm Boys), before leading a big band 1939–42.

Wallenberg Raoul Wallenberg, who was a Swedish business executive working in Hungary during World War II. He saved the lives of thousands of Jews when the Germans occupied Budapest 1944 by hiding them or supplying them with false papers. He was arrested by the Russians when they entered Budapest in 1945 and was never seen again. *Corbis*

wallflower European perennial garden plant *Cheiranthus cheiri*, family Cruciferae, with fragrant red or yellow flowers in spring.

Wallis and Futuna two island groups in the SW Pacific Ocean, an overseas territory of France; area 367 sq km/143 sq mi; population (1990) 13,700. They produce copra, yams, and bananas. Discovered by European sailors in the 18th century, the islands became a French protectorate 1842 and an overseas territory 1961.

Walloon a French-speaking people of SE Belgium and adjacent areas of France.

Wall Street street in Manhattan, New York, on which the stock exchange is situated, and a synonym for stock dealing in the USA.

Wall Street crash 1929 panic selling on the New York Stock Exchange following an artificial boom 1927–29 fed by speculation. On 24 Oct 1929, 13 million shares changed hands, with further heavy selling on 28 Oct and the disposal of 16 million shares on 29 Oct. Many shareholders were ruined, banks and businesses failed, and in the Depression that followed, unemployment rose to approximately 17 million.

The repercussions of the Wall Street crash, experienced throughout the USA, were also felt in Europe, worsened by the reduction of US loans. A world economic crisis followed the crash, bringing an era of depression and unemployment.

walnut tree *Juglans regia*, probably originating in SE Europe. It can reach 30 m/100 ft, and produces a full crop of edible nuts about a dozen years from planting; the timber is used in furniture and the oil is used in cooking.

Walpole Horace, 4th Earl of Orford 1717–1797. English novelist, letter writer and politician, the son of Robert Walpole. He was a Whig member of Parliament 1741–67. He converted his house at Strawberry Hill, Twickenham, into a Gothic castle; his work *The Castle of Otranto* 1764 established the genre of the Gothic novel.

Walpole Hugh Seymour 1884–1941. English novelist, born in New Zealand. His books include *The Cathedral* 1922 and *The Old Ladies* 1924. He also wrote the historical 'Lakeland Saga' of the *Herries Chronicle* 1930–33.

Walpole Robert, 1st Earl of Orford 1676–1745. British Whig politician, the first 'prime minister' as First Lord of the Treasury and chancellor of the Exchequer 1715–17 and 1721–42. He encouraged trade and tried to avoid foreign disputes (until forced into the War of Jenkins' Ear with Spain 1739).

Opponents thought his foreign policies worked to the advantage of France. He held favour with George I and George II, struggling against ◊Jacobite intrigues, and received an earldom when he retired.

Walpurga, St c. 710–c. 779. English abbess who preached Christianity in Germany. ***Walpurgis Night***, the eve of 1 May (one of her feast days), became associated with witches' sabbaths and other superstitions. Her feast day is 25 Feb.

walrus Arctic marine carnivorous mammal *Odobenus rosmarus* of the same family (Otaridae) as the eared ◊seals. It can reach 4 m/13 ft in length, and weigh up to 1,400 kg/3,000 lb. It has webbed flippers, a bristly moustache, and large tusks, and feeds mainly on molluscs. It has been hunted for its ivory tusks, hide, and blubber.

Walsh Raoul 1887–1980. US film director. He was originally an actor. A specialist in tough action stories, he made a number of outstanding films, including *The Thief of Bagdad* 1924, *The Roaring Twenties* 1939, *Objective Burma* 1945, *White Heat* 1949, and *The Tall Men* 1955.

'This world is a comedy to those that think, a tragedy to those that feel.'

HORACE WALPOLE
Letter to the Countess of Upper Ossory 1776

Walsingham Francis c. 1530–1590. English politician who, as secretary of state from 1573, both advocated a strong anti-Spanish policy and ran the efficient government spy system that made it work.

Walter Hubert died 1205. Archbishop of Canterbury 1193–1205. As justiciar (chief political and legal officer) 1193–98, he ruled England during

walnut The walnut is a tall, deciduous tree prized for its dark timber. The wrinkled nut is contained in a hard shell which is in turn surrounded by a fleshy green layer.

Look to your health; and if you have it, praise God, and value it next to a good conscience.

IZAAK WALTON
The Compleat Angler

In the future everyone will be famous for 15 minutes.

ANDY WARHOL
Exposures

Richard I's absence and introduced the offices of coroner and justice of the peace.

Walter John 1739–1812. British newspaper editor, founder of *The Times* (originally the *Daily Universal Register* 1785, but renamed 1788).

Walter Lucy c. 1630–1658. Mistress of ◊Charles II, whom she met while a Royalist refugee in The Hague, Netherlands, 1648; the Duke of ◊Monmouth was their son.

Waltham Forest outer borough of N Greater London. It includes the suburbs of Chingford, Leyton, and Walthamstow
features takes its name from former name for Epping Forest, referring to forest around Waltham Abbey; Lea Valley Regional Park (1967), including Walthamstow Marshes; Water House, Walthamstow, home of William Morris, now the William Morris Gallery
population (1991) 212,000
famous people Martin Frobisher. Cardinal Wiseman lived in Leyton.

Walther von der Vogelweide c. 1170–1230. German poet. The greatest of the ◊Minnesingers, his songs dealt mainly with courtly love, but also with religion and politics. Of noble birth, he lived in his youth at the Austrian ducal court in Vienna, adopting a wandering life after the death of his patron in 1198.

Walton Izaak 1593–1683. English author. He is known for his classic fishing compendium *The Compleat Angler* 1653. He also wrote short biographies of the poets George Herbert and John Donne and the theologian Richard Hooker.

Walton William Turner 1902–1983. English composer. Among his works are *Façade* 1923, a series of instrumental pieces designed to be played in conjunction with the recitation of surrealist poems by Edith Sitwell; the oratorio *Belshazzar's Feast* 1931; and *Variations on a Theme by Hindemith* 1963. He also composed a viola concerto 1929, two symphonies 1935, a violin concerto 1939, and a sonata for violin and pianoforte 1950.

waltz ballroom dance in moderate triple time (3/4) that developed in Germany and Austria during the late 18th century from the Austrian *Ländler* (traditional peasants' country dance). Associated particularly with Vienna and the ◊Strauss family, the waltz has remained popular up to the present day.

Walvis Bay chief port serving Namibia, situated on the Atlantic Ocean, 275 km/171 mi WSW of Windhoek; population about 26,000. It is the only deep water harbour on the Namibian coast and has a fishing industry with allied trades. It was a detached part (area 1,100 sq km/425 sq mi) of Cape Province, South Africa, 1884–1993 (administered solely by South Africa 1922–92; from 1992 jointly by South Africa and Namibia). In 1993 South Africa waived its claim to sovereignty and control was passed to Namibia 1994.

wampum cylindrical beads ground from sea shells, of white and purple, for ceremony, currency, and decoration by North American Indians of the northeastern woodlands.

Wandering Jew in medieval legend, a Jew named Ahasuerus, said to have insulted Jesus on his way to Calvary and to have been condemned to wander the world until the Second Coming.

Warhol US Pop artist and filmmaker Andy Warhol. *Topham*

Wandsworth inner borough of SW central Greater London
features made famous for hats in the 18th century by influx of Huguenot refugees who were skilled hatters (Roman cardinals ordered their hats from here); mills on river Wandle; Wandsworth Prison (1857); brewing industry (important since the 16th century); Battersea Park and Putney Heath are both in the borough.
population (1991) 252,400.

Wang An 1920–1990. Chinese-born US engineer, founder of Wang Laboratories 1951, one of the world's largest computer companies in the 1970s. In 1948 he invented the computer memory core, the most common device used for storing computer data before the invention of the integrated circuit (chip).

Wanganui port (textiles, clothing) in SW North Island, New Zealand, at the mouth of the Wanganui River; population (1993) 44,600.

Wankel engine rotary petrol engine developed by the German engineer Felix Wankel (1902–1988) in the 1950s. It operates according to the same stages as the ◊four-stroke petrol engine cycle, but these stages take place in different sectors of a figure-eight chamber in the space between the chamber walls and a triangular rotor. Power is produced once on every turn of the rotor. The Wankel engine is simpler in construction than the four-stroke piston petrol engine, and produces rotary power directly (instead of via a crankshaft). Problems with rotor seals have prevented its widespread use.

wapiti or *elk* species of deer *Cervus canadensis*, native to North America, Europe, and Asia, including New Zealand. It is reddish brown in colour, about 1.5 m/5 ft at the shoulder, weighs up to 450 kg/1,000 lb, and has antlers up to 1.2 m/4 ft long. It is becoming increasingly rare.

Wapping district of the Greater London borough of ◊Tower Hamlets. The redevelopment of the London ◊Docklands began here 1969 with work on St Katherine Dock. From the mid-1980s it has been a centre of the newspaper industry.

war act of force, usually on behalf of the state, intended to compel a declared enemy to obey the will of the other. The aim is to render the opponent incapable of further resistance by destroying its capability and will to bear arms in pursuit of its own aims. War is therefore a continuation of politics carried on with violent and destructive means, as an instrument of policy. War is generally divided into strategy, the planning and conduct of a war, and tactics, the deployment of forces in battle.

In the wars of the late 20th century, 90% of casualties have been civilian (in World War II, the figure was 50%; in World War I only 5%). According to the Stockholm International Peace Research Institute (SIPRI), there were fewer wars in 1995 than at any time since the end of the Cold War in 1989. All 30 of the wars in 1995 were civil wars fought within nations, apparently signalling a further shift from the pattern of inter-state wars which had characterized the modern era. More of these internal conflicts were fought over territory than over government control.

The estimated figure for loss of life in wars in the developing world since 1945 is 17 million.

Warbeck Perkin c. 1474–1499. Flemish pretender to the English throne. Claiming to be Richard, brother of Edward V, he led a rising against Henry VII 1497, and was hanged after attempting to escape from the Tower of London.

warbler any of two families of songbirds, order Passeriformes. The Old World warblers are in the family Muscicapidae, while the New World warblers are members of the Parulidae. Old World species, which grow up to 25 cm/10 in long, and feed on berries and insects, include the chiffchaff, blackcap, goldcrest, ◊willow warbler, and the tropical long-tailed tailorbird *Orthotomus sutorius*. The Dartford warbler *Sylvia undata* is one of Britain's rarest birds.

Warburg Otto Heinrich 1883–1970. German biochemist who in 1923 devised a manometer (pressure gauge) sensitive enough to measure oxygen uptake of respiring tissue. By measuring the rate at which cells absorb oxygen under differing conditions, he was able to show that enzymes called ◊cytochromes enable cells to process oxygen. Nobel Prize for Physiology or Medicine 1931.

war crime offence (such as murder of a civilian or a prisoner of war) that contravenes the internationally accepted laws governing the conduct of wars, particularly The Hague Convention 1907 and the Geneva Convention 1949. A key principle of the law relating to such crimes is that obedience to the orders of a superior is no defence. In practice, prosecutions are generally brought by the victorious side.

ward of court in the UK, a child whose guardian is the High Court. Any person may, by issuing proceedings, make the High Court guardian of any child within its jurisdiction. No important step in the child's life can then be taken without the court's leave.

warfarin poison that induces fatal internal bleeding in rats; neutralized with sodium hydroxide, it is used in medicine as an anticoagulant in the treatment of ◊thrombosis: it prevents blood clotting by inhibiting the action of vitamin K. It can be taken orally and begins to act several days after the initial dose. ◊Heparin may be given in treatment at the same time and discontinued when warfarin takes effect. It is often given as a preventive measure, to reduce the risk of ◊thrombosis or ◊embolism after major surgery.

Warhol Andy. Adopted name of Andrew Warhola 1928–1987. US Pop artist and filmmaker. He made his name 1962 with paintings of Campbell's soup cans, Coca-Cola bottles, and film stars. In his New York studio, The Factory, he and his assistants produced series of garish silk-screen prints dealing with car crashes and suicides, Marilyn Monroe, Elvis Presley, and flowers. His films, beginning with *Sleep* 1963, include *Chelsea Girls* 1966, *Trash* 1970, and *Bad* 1977, and have a strong improvisational element.

Warhol was born in Pittsburgh, Pennsylvania, where he studied art. In the 1950s he became a leading commercial artist in New York. With the breakthrough of Pop art, his bizarre personality and flair for self-publicity made him a household name. He was a pioneer of multimedia events with the 'Exploding Plastic Inevitable' touring show 1966 featuring the Velvet Underground rock group. In 1968 he was shot and nearly killed by a radical feminist, Valerie Solanas.

In the 1970s and 1980s Warhol was primarily a society portraitist, although his activities included a magazine (*Interview*) and a cable TV show. His books include *The Philosophy of Andy Warhol (From A to B and Back Again)* 1975 and *Popism* 1980.

Warlock Peter. Pen name of Philip Arnold Heseltine 1894–1930. English composer. His style was influenced by the music of the Elizabethan age and by that of Delius. His works include the orchestral suite *Capriol* 1926 based on 16th-century dances, and the song cycle *The Curlew* 1920–22. His works of musical theory and criticism were published under his real name.

warlord in China, any of the provincial leaders who took advantage of central government weakness, after the death of the first president of republican China 1912, to organize their own private armies and fiefdoms. They engaged in civil wars until the nationalist leader Chiang Kai-shek's Northern Expedition against them 1926, and they exerted power until the communists seized control under Mao Zedong 1949.

Warner Bros US film production company, founded 1923 by Harry, Albert, Sam, and Jack Warner. It became one of the major Hollywood studios after releasing the first talking film, *The Jazz Singer* 1927. During the 1930s and 1950s, company stars included Humphrey Bogart, Errol Flynn, and Bette Davis. It suffered in the 1960s through competition with television and was taken over by Seven Art Productions. In 1969 there was another takeover by Kinney National Service, and the whole company became known as Warner Communications.

Warner Brothers Records (now WEA) was

formed in the late 1950s. It became one of the six major record companies in the 1970s, with artists like Joni Mitchell, Randy Newman, and Prince. Warner Communications subsidiaries include Sire, which in 1983 signed Madonna.

War of 1812 war between the USA and Britain caused by British interference with US trade (shipping) as part of the economic warfare against Napoleonic France. Tensions with the British in Canada led to plans for a US invasion but these were never realized and success was limited to the capture of Detroit and a few notable naval victories. In 1814, British forces occupied Washington DC, and burned the White House and the Capitol. A treaty signed in Ghent, Belgium, Dec 1814 ended the conflict.

War on Want international organization established 1952 to support development work in the Third World and to campaign in Europe on world poverty. Projects have included urban and community development programmes, peasant cooperatives, clinics, and literacy programmes.

Warren Robert Penn 1905–1989. US poet and novelist. His work explored the moral problems of the South. His most important novel, *All the King's Men* 1946 (Pulitzer prize 1947), depicts the rise and fall of a back-country demagogue modelled on the career of US politician Huey Long (1893–1935). He also won Pulitzer prizes for *Promises* 1968 and *Now and Then: Poems* 1976–78. He was a senior figure of the ◊New Criticism, and the first official US poet laureate 1986–88.

Warrington industrial town (metal goods, chemicals, brewing, iron foundry, tanning, engineering, high technology industries) in Cheshire, NW England, on the river Mersey; population (1989 est) 188,000. A trading centre since Roman times, it was designated a new town 1968.

Warsaw (Polish ***Warszawa***) capital of Poland, on the river Vistula; population (1993) 1,653,300. Industries include engineering, food processing, printing, clothing, and pharmaceuticals.
history Founded in the 13th century, it replaced Kraków as capital 1595. Its university was founded 1818. It was taken by the Germans after heavy fighting during World War I and following the war became capital of independent Poland. Between the mid-19th century and 1940, a third of the population were Jews. It was taken by the Germans 27 Sept 1939 and its Jews were forced to live in the city's ghetto. In 1943 there was an uprising by those who had survived; this was put down and the survivors killed. In 1944 the Polish resistance attempted to gain control of the city before the arrival of the Russian army. The Warsaw Rising, as it became known, was crushed by the Germans after nine weeks. Warsaw was finally liberated 17 Jan 1945.

Warsaw ghetto area in the centre of Warsaw, Poland, established by the Nazis 1939 into which some 433,000 Jews were crowded. In July 1942 shipments of Jews to the extermination camp at ◊Treblinka began. On 19 April 1943 a detachment of SS were sent into the ghetto to round up the remaining inhabitants and destroy the buildings. Rather than submit, the Jews fought back with small arms and grenades they had managed to acquire. Resistance ended 16 May when the main synagogue was blown up. Many Jews escaped via the sewers and joined the Polish Home Army, a clandestine Polish resistance force.

Warsaw Pact or ***Eastern European Mutual Assistance Pact*** military alliance 1955–91 between the USSR and East European communist states, originally established as a response to the admission of West Germany into NATO. Its military structures and agreements were dismantled early in 1991; a political organization remained until the alliance was officially dissolved July 1991.

warship fighting ship armed and crewed for war. The supremacy of the battleship at the beginning of the 20th century was rivalled during World War I by the development of ◊submarine attack, and was rendered obsolescent in World War II with the advent of long-range air attack. Today the largest and most important surface warships are the ◊aircraft carriers.

wart protuberance composed of a local overgrowth of skin. The common wart (*verruca vulgaris*) is due to a virus infection. It usually disappears spontaneously within two years, but can be treated with peeling applications, burning away (cautery), or freezing (cryosurgery).

wart hog African wild ◊pig *Phacochoerus aethiopicus*, which has a large head with a bristly mane, fleshy pads beneath the eyes, and four large tusks. It has short legs and can grow to 80 cm/2.5 ft at the shoulder.

Warton Thomas Wain 1728–1790. English critic. He was professor of poetry at Oxford 1757–67 and published the first *History of English Poetry* 1774–81. He was poet laureate from 1785.

Warwick market town, administrative headquarters of Warwickshire, England; population (1991) 22,500. Industries include carpets and engineering. Founded 914, it has many fine medieval buildings, including a 14th-century castle.

Warwick Richard Neville, 1st or 16th Earl of Warwick 1428–1471. English politician, called the Kingmaker. During the Wars of the ◊Roses he fought at first on the Yorkist side against the Lancastrians, and was largely responsible for placing Edward IV on the throne. Having quarrelled with him, he restored Henry VI 1470, but was defeated and killed by Edward at Barnet, Hertfordshire.

Warwickshire county of central England
area 1,980 sq km/764 sq mi (*see United Kingdom map*)
towns and cities Warwick (administrative headquarters), Royal Leamington Spa, Nuneaton, Rugby, Stratford-upon-Avon
features river Avon; Kenilworth and Warwick castles; remains of the 'Forest of Arden'; site of the Battle of Edgehill; annual Royal Agricultural Show held at Stoneleigh
industries mainly agricultural, engineering, textiles
population (1991) 484,200
famous people William Shakespeare, George Eliot, Rupert Brooke.

Wash, the bay of the North Sea between Norfolk and Lincolnshire, England. The rivers Nene, Ouse, Welland, and Witham drain into the Wash. In 1992, 10,120 ha/25,000 acres of mudflats, marshes, and sand banks were designated a national nature reserve.

washing soda $Na_2CO_3.10H_2O$ (chemical name ***sodium carbonate decahydrate***) substance added to washing water to 'soften' it (see ◊hard water).

Washington town on the river Wear, Tyne and Wear, NE England, designated a new town 1964; population (1991) 56,800. Industries include textiles, electronics, car assembly, chemicals, and electrical goods. Beamish Open-Air Museum is nearby.

Washington state in northwestern USA; nicknamed Evergreen State/Chinook State
area 176,700 sq km/68,206 sq mi
capital Olympia
towns and cities Seattle, Spokane, Tacoma
features Columbia River; Cascade Range, with volcanic peaks in Mount Rainier national park (Mount Rainier 4,392 m/14,410 ft), North Cascades national park, and Mount St Helens national volcanic monument; Olympic Peninsula, with Olympic national forest and Dungeness national wildlife refuge; Mount Adams (3,867 m/12,688 ft); Whidbey Island; Long Beach Peninsula; Seattle, with the Seattle Art Museum (1991, designed by Robert Venturi), the Klondike gold rush national historic park, the Seattle Center (built for the 1992 World Fair), the Space Needle, Pioneer Square, and the International District, including the Nippon Kan Theater; vineyards in the Yakima Valley; 90 dams
industries apples and other fruits, potatoes, livestock, fish, timber, processed food, wood products, paper and allied products, aircraft and aerospace equipment, aluminium
population (1991) 5,018,000 (including 1.4% Indians, mainly of the Yakima people)
famous people Bing Crosby, Jimi Hendrix, Mary McCarthy, Theodore Roethke
history explored by Spanish, British, and Americans in the 18th century; settled from 1811; became a territory 1853 and a state 1889.

Washington

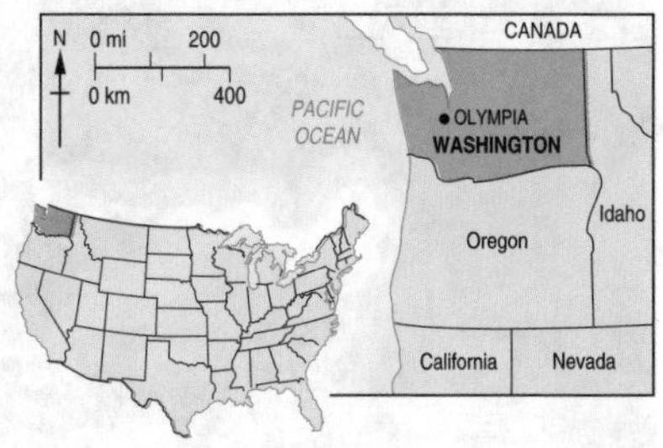

Washington Booker T(aliaferro) 1856–1915. US educationist, pioneer in higher education for black people in the South. He was the founder and first principal of Tuskegee Institute, Alabama, in 1881, originally a training college for blacks, and now an academic institution. He maintained that economic independence was the way to achieve social equality.

Washington George 1732–1799. Commander of the American forces during the American Revolutionary War and 1st president of the United States 1789–97; known as 'the father of his country'. An experienced soldier, he had fought in campaigns against the French during the French and Indian War of 1756–63. He was elected to the Virginia House of Burgesses 1759 and was a leader of the Virginia militia, gaining valuable exposure to wilderness fighting. As a strong opponent of the British government's policy, he sat in the Continental Congresses of 1774 and 1775, and on the outbreak of the ◊American Revolution was chosen commander in chief of the Continental army. After many setbacks, he accepted the surrender of British general Cornwallis at Yorktown 1781.

After the war Washington retired to his Virginia estate, Mount Vernon, but in 1787 he re-entered politics as president of the Constitutional Convention in Philadelphia, and was elected US president 1789. He attempted to draw his ministers from all factions, but his aristocratic outlook and acceptance of the fiscal policy championed by Alexander ◊Hamilton alienated his secretary of state, Thomas Jefferson, who resigned 1793, thus creating the two-party system. Washington was re-elected president 1793 but refused to serve a third term. He was buried at Mount Vernon.

'Associate yourself with men of good quality if you esteem your own reputation; for 'tis better to be alone than in bad company.'

George Washington
Rules of Civility and Decent Behaviour

Washington Convention alternative name for ◊CITES, the international agreement that regulates trade in endangered species.

Washington DC (District of Columbia) capital city of the United States of America, on the Potomac River; the world's first planned national capital. It was named Washington DC to distinguish it from the state of Washington and because it is situated in, and coextensive with, the District of

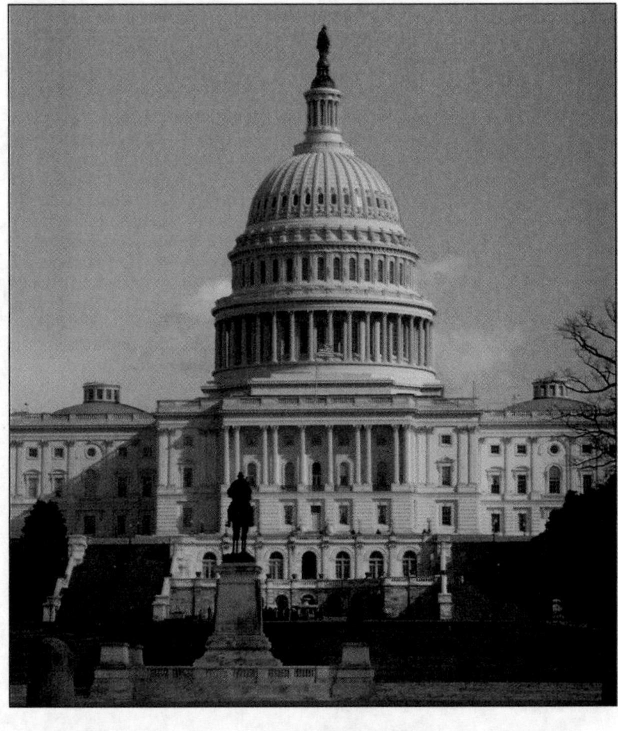

Washington DC The Capitol building, Washington DC, USA, seat of the US Congress. Its neo-classical style and name (after the Capitoline Hill, one of the seven hills of ancient Rome) are deliberately intended to recall the virtues of the great classical civilizations. It was first built 1793 but was not completed in its final form until 1863. *Image Select (UK) Ltd*

wasp Wasps can be social or solitary in behaviour. The social wasp will feed the young on masticated prey directly while the solitary wasp will drag paralysed caterpillars or larva to the nest.

Columbia, an area of 174 sq km/69 sq mi within the city; Washington DC has a population of 585,200 (1992); metropolitan area, extending outside the District of Columbia 3,923,600 (1990)

design and foundation the location of the District of Columbia was selected by George Washington himself and established by an act of Congress 1790–91; Congress first convened in the Capitol 1 Dec 1800. The first structures date from 1793.

Washington is distinctive as a city in being planned from the first as a capital worthy of a great nation. The city was the master plan of the young French engineer Pierre L'Enfant (1754–1825) and completed by Andrew Ellicott and Benjamin Banneker. The L'Enfant plan concentrated on spaciousness and long vistas rather than on convenience of access or the provision of services. The most prominent feature of the plan was the setting of the Congress building (the present structure was begun 1818, but not completed until the 1860s) on an eminence overlooking the 3.5 km/2 mi Mall, a grass-covered vista stretching west to the Potomac, with government buildings flanking it. A secondary feature of the plan was the imposition upon a basic grid-iron of streets of a large number of diagonal avenues, intersecting with each other at 'circles'.

features buildings include the Capitol, the Pentagon, the White House, the Supreme Court 1935, the Jefferson Memorial 1943, the Lincoln Memorial 1927, the J Edgar Hoover Federal Bureau of Investigation Building 1974, the Washington Monument 1884, and the Vietnam Veterans Memorial 1982. Washington DC has a famous football team, the Washington Redskins. The National Zoo is here

arts and institutions Washington houses much of the nation's historical and cultural wealth: it has one of the leading art galleries in the world, the National Gallery of Art 1941, with the East Building designed by I M Pei; the National Collection of Fine Arts; and the Smithsonian Institution (founded 1846), the largest complex of museums in the world, which includes the National Air and Space Museum 1976, the Hirshhorn Museum and Sculpture Garden 1974, the National Museum of American History, and the Smithsonian Quadrangle 1987 with the National Museum of African Art and the Arthur M Sackler Gallery (Asian art). Other outstanding museums include the Corcoran Gallery of Art 1871 (mainly American art) and the Phillips Collection 1921 (19th- and 20th-century art). The Folger Shakespeare Library has the largest collection of works by and about Shakespeare in the world. Dumbarton Oaks has outstanding collections of Byzantine and pre-Columbian art, and formal gardens. The John F Kennedy Center for the Performing Arts opened 1971.

Universities include Georgetown University 1789, the oldest Jesuit college in the USA, George Washington University, and Howard University, which opened in the 1860s for black students.

Wasim Akram 1966– . Pakistan cricketer. A left-arm fast bowler and hard-hitting batsman who made his Test debut in 1985 at the age of 18. He has taken more wickets in one day internationals than any other player, and is the only player to have taken 300 wickets or more in both Test and one-day international cricket.

The awful daring of a moment's surrender / Which an age of prudence can never retract.

From THE WASTE LAND
T S Eliot, 1922

wasp any of several families of winged stinging insects of the order Hymenoptera, characterized by a thin stalk between the thorax and the abdomen. Wasps can be social or solitary. Among social wasps, the queens devote themselves to egg laying, the fertilized eggs producing female workers; the males come from unfertilized eggs and have no sting. The larvae are fed on insects, but the mature wasps feed mainly on fruit and sugar. In winter, the fertilized queens hibernate, but the other wasps die.

WASP acronym for ***white Anglo-Saxon Protestant***, common (frequently derogatory) term to describe the white elite in American society, specifically those educated at Ivy League universities and belonging to the Episcopalian Church.

waste materials that are no longer needed and are discarded. Examples are household waste, industrial waste (which often contains toxic chemicals), medical waste (which may contain organisms that cause disease), and ◊nuclear waste (which is radioactive). By ◊recycling, some materials in waste can be reclaimed for further use. In 1990 the industrialized nations generated 2 billion tonnes of waste. In the USA, 40 tonnes of solid waste are generated annually per person, roughly twice as much as in Europe or Japan.

There has been a tendency to increase the amount of waste generated per person in industrialized countries, particularly through the growth in packaging and disposable products, creating a 'throw-away society'. In Britain, the average person throws away about ten times their own body weight in household refuse each year. Collectively the country generates about 50 million tonnes of waste per year.

waste disposal depositing waste. Methods of waste disposal vary according to the materials in the waste and include incineration, burial at designated sites, and dumping at sea. Organic waste can be treated and reused as fertilizer (see ◊sewage disposal). ◊Nuclear waste and ◊toxic waste is usually buried or dumped at sea, although this does not negate the danger.

Waste disposal is an increasing problem in the late 20th century. Environmental groups, such as Greenpeace and Friends of the Earth, are campaigning for more recycling, a change in lifestyle so that less waste (from packaging and containers to nuclear materials) is produced, and safer methods of disposal.

The industrial waste dumped every year by the UK in the North Sea includes 550,000 tonnes of fly ash from coal-fired power stations. The British government agreed 1989 to stop North Sea dumping from 1993, but dumping in the heavily polluted Irish Sea continues. Industrial pollution is suspected of causing ecological problems, including an epidemic that killed hundreds of seals 1989. ▷*See feature on pp. 858–859.*

Waste Land, The poem by T S ◊Eliot, first published 1922. A long, complex, and innovative poem, it expressed the prevalent mood of disillusionment after World War I and is a key work of Modernism in literature.

watch portable timepiece. In the early 20th century increasing miniaturization, mass production, and, in World War I, the advantages of the wristband led to the watch moving from the pocket to the wrist. Watches were also subsequently made waterproof, antimagnetic, self-winding, and shock-resistant. In 1957 the electric watch was developed, and in the 1970s came the digital watch, which dispensed with all moving parts.

history Traditional mechanical watches with analogue dials (hands) are based on the invention by Peter Henlein (1480–1542) of the mainspring as the energy store. By 1675 the invention of the balance spring allowed watches to be made small enough to move from waist to pocket. By the 18th century pocket-watches were accurate, and by the 20th century wristwatches were introduced. In the 1950s battery-run electromagnetic watches were developed; in the 1960s electronic watches were marketed, which use the ◊piezoelectric oscillations of a quartz crystal to mark time and an electronic circuit to drive the hands. In the 1970s quartz watches without moving parts were developed – the solid-state watch with a display of digits. Some include a tiny calculator and such functions as date, alarm, stopwatch, and reminder beeps.

water cycle About one-third of the solar energy reaching the Earth is used in evaporating water. About 380,000 cubic km/95,000 cubic mi is evaporated each year. The entire contents of the oceans would take about one million years to pass through the water cycle.

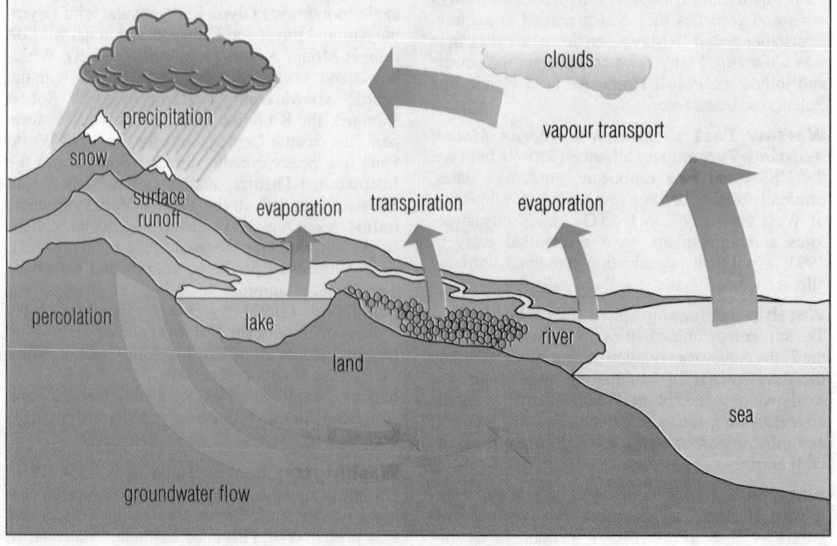

An electric watch has no mainspring, the mechanism being kept in motion by the mutual attraction of a permanent magnet and an electromagnet, which pushes the balance wheel. In a digital watch the time is usually indicated by a ◊liquid crystal display.

water H_2O liquid without colour, taste, or odour. It is an oxide of hydrogen with a relative molecular mass of 18. Water begins to freeze at 0°C or 32°F, and to boil at 100°C or 212°F. When liquid, it is virtually incompressible; frozen, it expands by 1/11 of its volume. At 4°C/39.2°F, one cubic centimetre of water has a mass of one gram; this is its maximum density, forming the unit of specific gravity. It has the highest known specific heat, and acts as an efficient solvent, particularly when hot.

Water covers 70% of the Earth's surface and occurs as standing (oceans, lakes) and running (rivers, streams) water, rain, and vapour and supports all forms of life on Earth. Most of the world's water is in the sea; less than 0.01% is fresh water.

Water makes up 60–70% of the human body. About 1.5 l/2.6 pt a day are lost through breathing, perspiration, and faeces, and the additional amount lost in urine is the amount needed to keep the balance between input and output. People cannot survive more than five or six days without water or two or three days in a hot environment.

water boatman any water ◊bug of the family Corixidae that feeds on plant debris and algae. It has a flattened body 1.5 cm/0.6 in long, with oarlike legs. The name is sometimes also used for the backswimmers, genus *Notonecta*, which are superficially similar, but which can fly and which belong to a different family (Notonectidae) of bugs.

water-borne disease disease associated with poor water supply. In the Third World four-fifths of all illness is caused by water-borne diseases, with diarrhoea being the leading cause of childhood death. Malaria, carried by mosquitoes dependent on stagnant water for breeding, affects 400 million people every year and kills 5 million. Polluted water is also a problem in industrialized nations, where industrial dumping of chemical, hazardous, and radioactive wastes causes a range of diseases from headache to cancer.

waterbuck any of several African ◊antelopes of the genus *Kobus* which usually inhabit swampy tracts and reedbeds. They vary in size from about 1.8m/6 ft to 2.1 m/7.25 ft long, are up to 1.4 m/4.5 ft tall at the shoulder, and have long brown fur. The large curved horns, normally carried only by the males, have corrugated surfaces. Some species have white patches on the buttocks.

watercolour painting method of painting with pigments mixed with water, known in China as early as the 3rd century. The art as practised today began in England in the 18th century with the work of Paul Sandby and was developed by Thomas Girtin, John Sell Cotman, and J M W Turner. Other outstanding watercolourists were Raoul Dufy, Paul Cézanne, and John Marin. The technique of watercolour painting requires great skill since its transparency rules out overpainting.

Western artists excelling in watercolour painting include J R Cozens, Peter de Wint, John Constable, David Cox, John Singer Sargent, Philip Wilson Steer, Paul Signac, Emil Nolde, Paul Klee, and Paul Nash.

watercress perennial aquatic plant *Nasturtium officinale* of the crucifer family, found in Europe and Asia, and cultivated as a salad crop. It requires 4.5 million litres/1 million gallons of running water daily per hectare/2.5 acres in cultivation.

water cycle or ***hydrological cycle*** in ecology, the natural circulation of water through the ◊biosphere. Water is lost from the Earth's surface to the atmosphere either by evaporation caused by the Sun's heat on the surface of lakes, rivers, and oceans, or through the transpiration of plants. This atmospheric water is carried by the air moving across the Earth, and condenses as the air cools to form clouds, which in turn deposit moisture on the land and sea as rain or snow. The water that collects on land flows to the ocean in streams and rivers.

waterfall cascade of water in a river or stream. It occurs when a river flows over a bed of rock that resists erosion; weaker rocks downstream are worn away, creating a steep, vertical drop and a plunge pool into which the water falls. Over time, continuing erosion causes the waterfall to retreat upstream forming a deep valley, or ◊gorge.

water flea any aquatic crustacean in the order Cladocera, of which there are over 400 species. The commonest species is *Daphnia pulex*, used in the pet trade to feed tropical fish.

Waterford county of the Republic of Ireland, in the province of Munster; county town Waterford; area 1,840 sq km/710 sq mi; population (1991) 91,600. It includes the rivers Suir and Blackwater, and the Comeragh and Monavallagh mountain ranges in the north and centre. Products include cattle, beer, whiskey, and glassware.

Waterford port and county town of County Waterford, SE Republic of Ireland, on the river Suir; population (1991) 40,300. Handmade Waterford crystal glass (34% lead content instead of the normal 24%) was made here until 1851 and again from 1951.

water gas fuel gas consisting of a mixture of carbon monoxide and hydrogen, made by passing steam over red-hot coke. The gas was once the chief source of hydrogen for chemical syntheses such as the Haber process for making ammonia, but has been largely superseded in this and other reactions by hydrogen obtained from natural gas.

Watergate US political scandal, named after the building in Washington DC that housed the headquarters of the Democratic National Committee in the 1972 presidential election. Five men, hired by the Republican Committee for the Re-election of the President (popularly known as CREEP), were caught after breaking into the Watergate with complex electronic surveillance equipment. Investigations revealed that the White House was implicated in the break-in, and that there was a 'slush fund', used to finance unethical activities, including using the CIA and the Internal Revenue Service for political ends, setting up paramilitary operations against opponents, altering and destroying evidence, and bribing defendants to lie or remain silent. In Aug 1974, President ◊Nixon was forced by the Supreme Court to surrender to Congress tape recordings of conversations he had held with administration officials, which indicated his complicity in a cover-up. Nixon resigned rather than face impeachment for obstruction of justice and other crimes.

water glass common name for sodium metasilicate (Na_2SiO_3). It is a colourless, jellylike substance that dissolves readily in water to give a solution used for preserving eggs and fireproofing porous materials such as cloth, paper, and wood. It is also used as an adhesive for paper and cardboard and in the manufacture of soap and silica gel, a substance that absorbs moisture.

Waterhouse Alfred 1830–1905. English architect. He was a leading exponent of Victorian Neo-Gothic, typically using multicoloured tiles and bricks. His works include the Natural History Museum, London, 1868.

water hyacinth tropical aquatic plant *Eichhornia crassipes* of the pickerelweed family Pontederiaceae. In one growing season 25 plants can produce 2 million new plants. It is liable to choke waterways, depleting the water of nutrients and blocking the sunlight, but can be used as a purifier of sewage-polluted water as well as in making methane gas, compost, concentrated protein, paper, and baskets. Originating in South America, it now grows in more than 50 countries.

water lily aquatic plant of the family Nymphaeaceae. The fleshy roots are embedded in mud and the large round leaves float on the water. The cup-shaped flowers may be white, pink, yellow, or blue. The white *Nymphaea alba* and yellow *Nuphar lutea* are common in Europe, and *Victoria regia*, with leaves about 2 m/6 ft in diameter, occurs in the Amazon, South America.

Waterloo, Battle of final battle of the Napoleonic Wars 18 June 1815 in which a coalition force of British, Prussian, and Dutch troops under the Duke of Wellington defeated Napoleon near the village of Waterloo, 13 km/8 mi south of Brussels, Belgium. Napoleon found Wellington's army isolated from his allies and began a direct offensive to smash them, but the British held on until joined by the Prussians under Marshal Gebhard von Blücher. Four days later Napoleon abdicated for the second and final time.

Wellington had 67,000 soldiers (of whom 24,000 were British, the remainder being German, Dutch, and Belgian) and Napoleon had 74,000. The French casualties numbered about 37,000; coalition casualties were similar including some 13,000 British troops. ▷ *See feature on pp. 748–749.*

water meadow irrigated meadow. By flooding the land for part of each year, increased yields of hay are obtained. Water meadows were common in Italy, Switzerland, and England (from 1523) but have now largely disappeared.

watermelon large ◊melon *Citrullus vulgaris* of the gourd family, native to tropical Africa, with pink, white, or yellow flesh studded with black seeds and a green rind. It is widely cultivated in subtropical regions.

water mill machine that harnesses the energy in flowing water to produce mechanical power,

WATERFALLS

Name and location	Total drop (m/ft)
Angel Falls (Venezuela)	979/3,212
Yosemite Falls (USA)	739/2,425
Mardalsfossen – South (Norway)	655/2,149
Tugela Falls (South Africa)	614/2,014
Cuquenan (Venezuela)	610/2,000
Sutherland (South Island, New Zealand)	580/1,903
Takkakaw Falls (Canada)	503/1,650
Ribbon Fall, Yosemite (USA)	491/1,612
Great Karamang River Falls (Guyana)	488/1,600
Mardalsfossen – North (Norway)	468/1,535
Della Falls (Canada)	440/1,443
Gavarnie (France)	422/1,385
Skjeggedal (Norway)	420/1,378
Glass Falls (Brazil)	404/1,325
Krimml (Austria)	400/1,312
Trummelbach (Switzerland)	400/1,312
Silver Strand Falls, Yosemite (USA)	357/1,170
Wallaman, Stony Creek (Australia)	346/1,137
Wollomombi (Australia)	335/1,100
Cusiana River Falls (Colombia)	300/984
Giessbach (Switzerland)	300/984
Skykkjedalsfossen (Norway)	300/984
Staubbach (Switzerland)	300/984

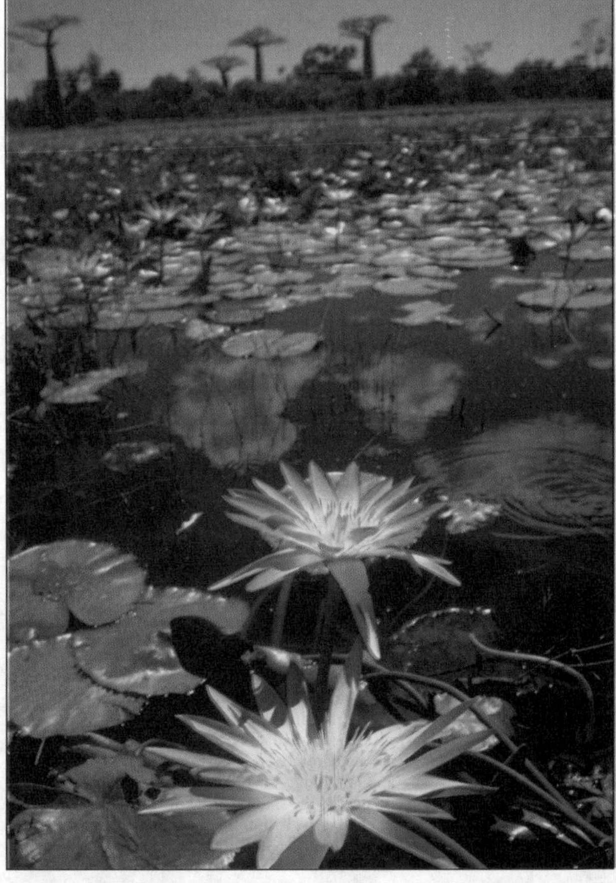

water lily Blue- or mauve-flowered water lilies, such as this *Nymphaea stellata* from Madagascar, are common in lakes and swamps in the Old World tropics. *Premaphotos Wildlife*

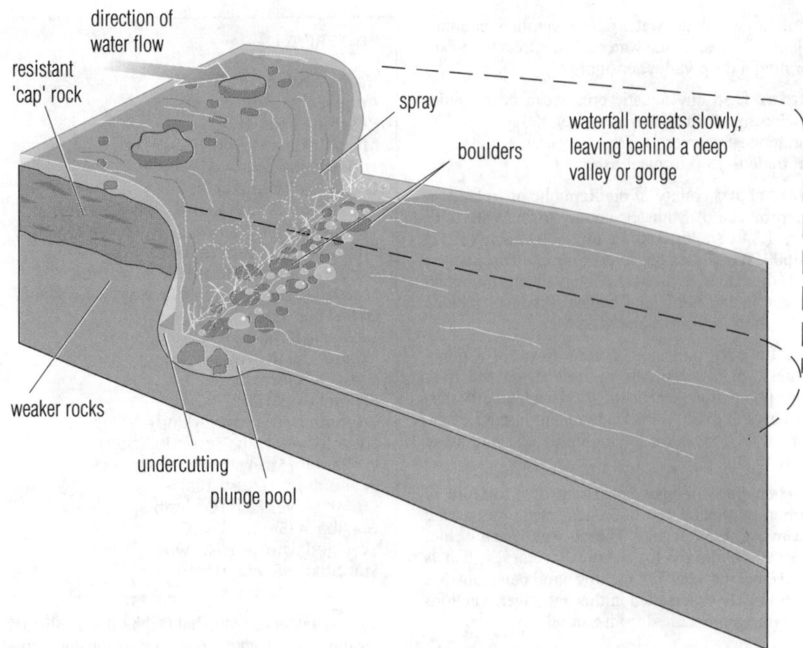

waterfall When water flows over hard rock and soft rock, the soft rocks erode creating waterfalls. As the erosion processes continue, the falls move backwards, in the opposite direction of the water.

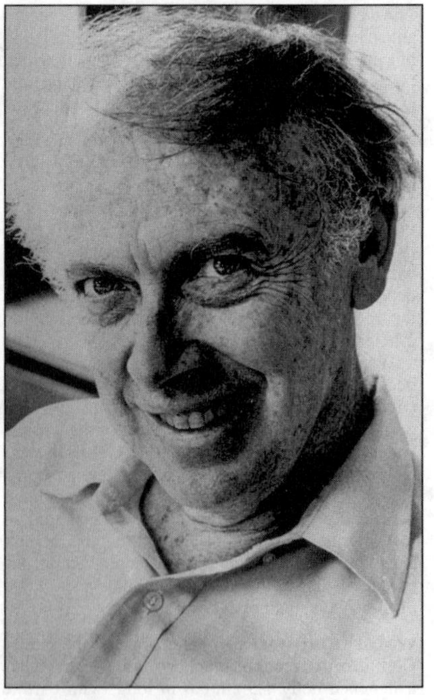

Watson American biologist James Dewey Watson who with Francis Crick determined the structure of DNA at the Cavendish Laboratory in Cambridge, England. *Image Select (UK) Ltd*

typically for milling (grinding) grain. Water from a stream is directed against the paddles of a water wheel to make it turn. Simple gearing transfers this motion to the millstones. The modern equivalent of the water wheel is the water turbine, used in ◊hydro-electric power plants.

The familiar vertical water wheel came into widespread use in Roman times. There were two types: ***undershot***, in which the wheel simply dipped into the stream, and the more powerful ***overshot***, in which the water was directed at the top of the wheel. The Domesday Book records over 7,000 water mills in Britain. Water wheels remained a prime source of mechanical power until the development of a reliable steam engine in the 1700s, not only for milling, but also for metalworking, crushing and grinding, and driving machines in the early factories.

water of crystallization water chemically bonded to a salt in its crystalline state. For example, in copper(II) sulphate, there are five moles of water per mole of copper sulphate: hence its formula is $CuSO_4.5H_2O$. This water is responsible for the colour and shape of the crystalline form. When the crystals are heated gently, the water is driven off as steam and a white powder is formed.

$$CuSO_4.5H_2O_{(s)} \rightarrow CuSO_{4\,(s)} + 5H_2O_{(g)}$$

water pollution any addition to fresh or sea water that disrupts biological processes or causes a health hazard. Common pollutants include nitrates, pesticides, and sewage (see ◊sewage disposal), though a huge range of industrial contaminants, such as chemical byproducts and residues created in the manufacture of various goods, also enter water – legally, accidentally, and through illegal dumping. ▷ *See feature on pp. 858–859.*

water polo water sport developed in England 1869, originally called 'soccer-in-water'. The aim is to score goals, as in soccer, at each end of a swimming pool. It is played by teams of seven on each side (from squads of 13). An inflated ball is passed among the players, who must swim around the pool without touching the bottom. A goal is scored when the ball is thrown past the goalkeeper and into a net. The Swimming Association of Great Britain recognized the game 1885. World championships were first held 1973; they are held during the world swimming championships.

water skiing water sport in which a person is towed across water on a ski or skis, wider than those used for skiing on snow, by means of a rope (23 m/75 ft long) attached to a speedboat. Competitions are held for overall performances, slalom, tricks, and jumping. In 1922, Ralph Samuelson (USA) pioneered the sport as it is known today. Its governing body, the Union Internationale de Ski Nautique, was founded 1946. World championships were first held 1949.

water softener any substance or unit that removes the hardness from water. Hardness is caused by the presence of calcium and magnesium ions, which combine with soap to form an insoluble scum, prevent lathering, and cause deposits to build up in pipes and cookware (kettle fur). A water softener replaces these ions with sodium ions, which are fully soluble and cause no scum.

water supply distribution of water for domestic, municipal, or industrial consumption. Water supply in sparsely populated regions usually comes from underground water rising to the surface in natural springs, supplemented by pumps and wells. Urban sources are deep artesian wells, rivers, and reservoirs, usually formed from enlarged lakes or dammed and flooded valleys, from which water is conveyed by pipes, conduits, and aqueducts to filter beds. As water seeps through layers of shingle, gravel, and sand, harmful organisms are removed and the water is then distributed by pumping or gravitation through mains and pipes.

water treatment Often other substances are added to the water, such as chlorine and fluoride; aluminium sulphate, a clarifying agent, is the most widely used chemical in water treatment. In coastal desert areas, such as the Arabian peninsula, desalination plants remove salt from sea water.

drought A period of prolonged dry weather can disrupt water supply and lead to drought. The area of the world subject to serious droughts, such as the Sahara, is increasing because of destruction of forests, overgrazing, and poor agricultural practices. According to the United Nations in 1997, large areas of the globe will start running critically short of water in the next 30 years unless there is a radical change in the way people use this resource.

Total worldwide water consumption has been growing roughly twice as fast as population growth. It has risen sixfold during the 20th century. With some 300 major river basins crossing national boundaries, growing demands for this resource could lead to future conflicts. Among the most likely flashpoints are the river Jordan, which is shared between Israel and Arab neighbours; the Nile which flows through Egypt, Ethiopia, and Sudan; and the headwaters of the Euphrates and Tigris shared between Turkey, Syria, and Iraq.

water table the upper level of ground water (water collected underground in porous rocks). Water that is above the water table will drain downwards; a spring forms where the water table cuts the surface of the ground. The water table rises and falls in response to rainfall and the rate at which water is extracted, for example, for irrigation and industry.

Watford industrial town (printing, engineering, and electronics) in Hertfordshire, SE England; population (1991) 74,600; dormitory town for London.

Watson James Dewey 1928– . US biologist. His research on the molecular structure of ◊DNA and the genetic code, in collaboration with Francis ◊Crick, earned him a shared Nobel prize 1962. Based on earlier works, they were able to show that DNA formed a double helix of two spiral strands held together by base pairs.

Crick and Watson published their work on the proposed structure of DNA 1953, and explained how genetic information could be coded.

Watson John Broadus 1878–1958. US psychologist, founder of behaviourism. He rejected introspection (observation by an individual of his or her own mental processes) and regarded psychology as the study of observable behaviour, within the scientific tradition.

Watson Tom (Thomas Sturges) 1949– . US golfer who won the British Open five times (1975, 1977, 1980, 1982, 1983) and by 1990 was ranked third in career earnings in professional golf.

Watson, born in Kansas City, turned professional

Watt James Watt's steam engines, dating from 1769, were an improvement on that of Thomas Newcomen in that they had a separate condenser and permitted steam to be admitted alternately on either side of the piston.

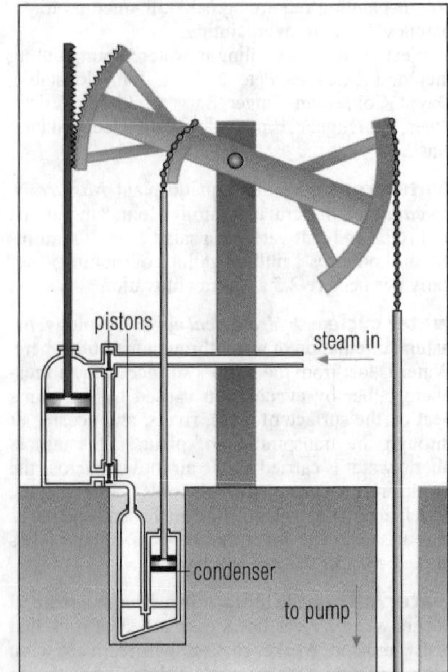

1971 and has won more than 30 tournaments on the US Tour, including the Masters and US Open. In 1988 he succeeded Jack ◊Nicklaus as the game's biggest money winner, but was overtaken by Tom Kite 1989.

watt SI unit (symbol W) of power (the rate of expenditure or consumption of energy) defined as one joule per second. A light bulb, for example, may use 40, 60, 100, or 150 watts of power; an electric heater will use several kilowatts (thousands of watts). The watt is named after the Scottish engineer James Watt.

The absolute watt is defined as the power used when one joule of work is done in one second. In electrical terms, the flow of one ampere of current through a conductor whose ends are at a potential difference of one volt uses one watt of power (watts = volts × amperes).

Watt James 1736–1819. Scottish engineer. He developed the steam engine in the 1760s, making Thomas ◊Newcomen's engine vastly more efficient by cooling the used steam in a condenser separate from the main cylinder.

Steam engines incorporating governors, sun-and-planet gears, and other devices of his invention were successfully built by him in partnership with Matthew Boulton (1728–1809) and were vital to the ◊Industrial Revolution. Watt also devised the horsepower as a description of an engine's rate of working.

Watteau (Jean-)Antoine 1684–1721. French Rococo painter. He developed a new category of genre painting known as the *fête galante* – fanciful scenes depicting elegantly dressed young people engaged in outdoor entertainment. One of the best-known examples is *The Embarkation for Cythera* 1717 (Louvre, Paris).

He studied with Claude Gillot (1673–1722) and painted scenes from the commedia dell'arte (Italian comedy), which was then in vogue in Paris. Among the finest is *Gilles* (Louvre, Paris), its subtle characterization showing his typical blend of gaiety and sadness. Inspired by various old masters, in particular ◊Rubens, Watteau began to develop his own distinctive style for painting elegant party groups, such as those hosted by his patron, Crozat. In 1717 he was made a member of the French Royal Academy.

wattle certain species of ◊acacia in Australia, where their fluffy golden flowers are the national emblem.

wave Waves crashing on the shore. Waves are ridges of water usually caused by the action of wind on the open water, and cause coastal erosion and deposition. *Image Select (UK) Ltd*

wattle and daub method of constructing walls consisting of upright stakes bound together with withes (strong flexible shoots or twigs, usually of willow), and covered in mud or plaster. This was the usual way of building houses in medieval Europe; it was also the traditional method used in Australia, Africa, the Middle East, and the Far East.

Watts Alan Witson 1915–1973. British-born US philosopher. He was a longtime student of Eastern religions and published *The Spirit of Zen* 1936. As a popular lecturer and author, he became a spiritual leader of the 'beat generation' of the 1950s. His books include *The Way of Zen* 1957.

Watts George Frederick 1817–1904. English painter and sculptor. His fame was based largely on his moralizing allegories, such as *Hope* 1886 (Tate Gallery, London). He was also a portrait painter, his works including *Gladstone* and *Tennyson* (National Portrait Gallery, London).

Waugh Evelyn Arthur St John 1903–1966. English novelist. His social satires include *Decline and Fall* 1928, *Vile Bodies* 1930, and *The Loved One* 1948. A Roman Catholic convert from 1930, he developed a serious concern with religious issues in *Brideshead Revisited* 1945. *The Ordeal of Gilbert Pinfold* 1957 is largely autobiographical.

Watteau *The Scale of Love* c. 1715 by Watteau (National Gallery, London). Meant for aristocratic patrons, Watteau's depictions of amorous dalliance are gentle, elegant, and playful, the nuances of gesture and pose suggesting a subtle choreography. *Corbis*

wave in the oceans, a ridge or swell formed by wind or other causes. The power of a wave is determined by the strength of the wind and the distance of open water over which the wind blows (the fetch). Waves are the main agents of ◊coastal erosion and deposition: sweeping away or building up beaches, creating ◊spits and berms (ridges of sand or pebbles running parallel to the water's edge), and wearing down cliffs by their hydraulic action and by the corrasion of the sand and shingle that they carry. A ◊tsunami (misleadingly called a 'tidal wave') is formed after a submarine earthquake.

Atmospheric instability caused by the ◊greenhouse effect appears to be increasing the severity of Atlantic storms and the heights of the ocean waves. An increase of 20% in the heights of Atlantic waves has been recorded since the 1960s.

wave in physics, a disturbance travelling through a medium (or space). There are two types: in a ◊longitudinal wave, such as a sound wave, the disturbance is parallel to the wave's direction of travel; in a ◊transverse wave, such as an electromagnetic wave, it is perpendicular. The medium (for example the Earth, for seismic waves) is not permanently displaced by the passage of a wave. See also ◊standing wave.

wavelength the distance between successive crests of a ◊wave. The wavelength of a light wave determines its colour; red light has a wavelength of about 700 nanometres, for example. The complete range of wavelengths of electromagnetic waves is called the electromagnetic ◊spectrum.

Wavell Archibald Percival, 1st Earl Wavell 1883–1950. British field marshal in World War II. As commander in chief in the Middle East, he successfully defended Egypt against Italy July 1939 and successfully conducted the North African war against Italy 1940–41. He was transferred as commander in chief in India in July 1941, and became Allied Supreme Commander after Japan entered the war. He was unable to prevent Japanese advances in Malaya and Burma. He was made viceroy of India 1943–47.

wave power power obtained by harnessing the energy of water waves. Various schemes have been advanced since 1973, when oil prices rose dramatically and an energy shortage threatened. In 1974 the British engineer Stephen Salter developed the duck – a floating boom whose segments nod up and down with the waves. The nodding motion can be used to drive pumps and spin generators. Another device, developed in Japan, uses an oscillating water column to harness wave power. A major breakthrough will be required if wave power is ever to contribute significantly to the world's energy needs, although several ideas have reached prototype stage. ▷ *See feature on pp. 360–361.*

'Manners are especially the need of the plain. The pretty can get away with anything.'

EVELYN WAUGH
Quoted in the *Observer* 15 April 1962

Waverley John Anderson, 1st Viscount Waverley 1882–1958. British administrator. He organized civil defence for World War II, becoming home

Wayne US film actor John Wayne in *The Man Who Shot Liberty Valance* 1961. Wayne started his film career 1927, using the name Duke Morrison. He went on to make over 175 films.

secretary and minister for home security in 1939. Anderson shelters, home outdoor air-raid shelters, were named after him. He was chancellor of the Exchequer 1943–45.

wax solid fatty substance of animal, vegetable, or mineral origin. Waxes are composed variously of ◊esters, ◊fatty acids, free ◊alcohols, and solid hydrocarbons.

Mineral waxes are obtained from petroleum and vary in hardness from the soft petroleum jelly (or petrolatum) used in ointments to the hard paraffin wax employed for making candles and waxed paper for drinks cartons.

Animal waxes include beeswax, the wool wax lanolin, and spermaceti from sperm-whale oil; they are used mainly in cosmetics, ointments, and polishes. Another animal wax is tallow, a form of suet obtained from cattle and sheep's fat, once widely used to make candles and soap. Sealing wax is made from lac or shellac, a resinous substance obtained from secretions of ◊scale insects.

Vegetable waxes, which usually occur as a waterproof coating on plants that grow in hot, arid regions, include carnauba wax (from the leaves of the carnauba palm) and candelilla wax, both of which are components of hard polishes such as car waxes.

waxbill any of a group of small, mainly African, seed-eating birds in the family Estrildidae, order Passeriformes, which also includes the grass finches of Australia. Waxbills grow to 15 cm/6 in long, are brown and grey with yellow, red, or brown markings, and have waxy-looking red or pink beaks.

waxwing any of several fruit-eating birds of the family Bombycillidae, order Passeriformes. They are found in the northern hemisphere. The Bohemian waxwing *Bombycilla garrulus* of North America and Eurasia is about 18 cm/7 in long, and is greyish brown above with a reddish-chestnut crest, black streak at the eye, and variegated wings.

wayfaring tree European shrub *Viburnum lantana* of the honeysuckle family, with clusters of fragrant white flowers, found on limy soils; naturalized in the northeastern USA.

Wayne John ('Duke'). Stage name of Marion Michael Morrison 1907–1979. US actor. He played the archetypal Western hero: plain-speaking, brave, and solitary. His films include *Stagecoach* 1939, *Red River* 1948, *She Wore a Yellow Ribbon* 1949, *The Searchers* 1956, *Rio Bravo* 1959, *The Man Who Shot Liberty Valance* 1962, and *True Grit* 1969 (Academy Award). He was active in conservative politics.

Wayne also appeared in many war films, such as *The Sands of Iwo Jima* 1945, *In Harm's Way* 1965, and *The Green Berets* 1968. His other films include *The Quiet Man* 1952, *The High and the Mighty* 1954, and *The Shootist* 1976, his last.

WCC abbreviation for ◊***World Council of Churches***, international Christian body.

weak acid acid that only partially ionizes in aqueous solution. Weak acids include ethanoic acid and carbonic acid. The pH of such acids lies between pH 3 and pH 6.

weak base base that only partially ionizes in aqueous solution; for example, ammonia. The pH of such bases lies between pH 8 and pH 10.

weak nuclear force or ***weak interaction*** one of the four fundamental forces of nature, the other three being gravity, the electromagnetic force, and the strong force. It causes radioactive decay and other subatomic reactions. The particles that carry the weak force are called ◊weakons.

weakon or ***intermediate vector boson*** in physics, a ◊gauge boson that carries the weak nuclear force, one of the fundamental forces of nature. There are three types of weakon, the positive and negative W particle and the neutral Z particle.

Weald, the (Old English 'forest') area between the North and South Downs, England, once thickly wooded, and forming part of Kent, Sussex, Surrey, and Hampshire. Now an agricultural area, it produces fruit, hops, and vegetables. In the Middle Ages its timber and iron ore made it the industrial heart of England. The name often refers only to the area of Kent SW of the greensand ridge running from Hythe to Westerham.

wealth in economics, the wealth of a nation is its stock of physical capital, human capital, and net financial capital owned overseas. Physical capital is the stock of buildings, factories, offices, machines, roads, and so on. Human capital is the workforce; not just the number of workers, but also their stock of education and training which makes them productive. Net financial capital is the difference between the money value of assets owned by foreigners in the domestic economy and the assets owned by the country abroad.

For individuals, the most significant wealth they have is their ability to generate an income by working. After that, the largest item of wealth is likely to be their house. Possessions, money, and insurance policies are other examples of individual wealth.

weapon any implement used for attack and defence, from simple clubs, spears, and bows and arrows in prehistoric times to machine guns and nuclear bombs in modern times. The first revolution in warfare came with the invention of ◊gunpowder and the development of cannons and shoulder-held guns. Many other weapons now exist, such as grenades, shells, torpedoes, rockets, and guided missiles. The ultimate in explosive weapons are the atomic (fission) and hydrogen (fusion) bombs. They release the enormous energy produced when atoms split or fuse together (see ◊nuclear warfare). There are also chemical and bacteriological weapons, which release poisons or disease.

Wear river in NE England; length 107 km/67 mi. From its source in the Pennines it flows eastwards, past Durham to meet the North Sea at Sunderland.

weasel any of various small, short-legged carnivorous mammals with bushy tails, especially the genus *Mustela*, found worldwide except Australia. They feed mainly on small rodents although some, like the mink *M. vison*, hunt aquatic prey. Most are 12–25 cm/5–10 in long, excluding tail. In cold regions the coat colour of several species changes to white during the winter.

weather day-to-day variation of climatic and atmospheric conditions at any one place, or the state of these conditions at a place at any one time. Such conditions include humidity, precipitation, temperature, cloud cover, visibility, and wind. To a meteorologist the term 'weather' is limited to the state of the sky, precipitation, and visibility as affected by fog or mist. A region's ◊climate is derived from the average weather conditions over a long period of time. See also ◊meteorology.

Weather forecasts, in which the likely weather is predicted for a particular area, based on meteorological readings, may be short-range (covering a period of one or two days), medium-range (five to seven days), or long-range (a month or so). Readings from a series of scattered recording stations are collected and compiled on a weather map, using conventional symbols to show the state of the sky, the wind speed and direction, the kind of precipitation, and other details at each gathering station. Points of equal atmospheric pressure are joined by lines called isobars. The trends shown on such a map can be extrapolated to predict what weather is coming.

weathering process by which exposed rocks are broken down on the spot by the action of rain, frost, wind, and other elements of the weather. It differs from ◊erosion in that no movement or transportion of the broken-down material takes place. Two types of weathering are recognized: physical (or mechanical) and chemical. They usually occur together.

physical weathering This includes such effects as freeze–thaw (the splitting of rocks by the alternate freezing and thawing of water trapped in cracks) and exfoliation, or onion-skin weathering (flaking caused by the alternate expansion and contraction of rocks in response to extreme changes in temperature).

chemical weathering Involving a chemical change in the rocks affected, the most common form is caused by rainwater that has absorbed carbon dioxide from the atmosphere and formed a weak carbonic acid. This then reacts with certain minerals in the rocks and breaks them down. Examples are the solution of caverns in limestone terrains, and the breakdown of feldspars in granite to form china clay or kaolin.

weaver any small bird of the family Ploceidae, order Passeriformes; they are mostly about 15 cm/6 in long. The majority of weavers are African, a few Asian. The males use grasses to weave elaborate globular nests in bushes and trees. The nests are entered from beneath, and the male hangs from it calling and flapping his wings to attract a female. Males are often more brightly coloured than females.

waxbill Male blue waxbill *Uraeginthus angolensis* in South African savannah. Waxbills are extemely popular as pets. *K G Preston-Mafham/Premaphotos Wildlife*

'The weather is like the government, always in the wrong.'

On the WEATHER
Jerome K Jerome
Idle Thoughts of an Idle Fellow 1889

weaving the production of ◊textile fabric by means of a loom. The basic process is the interlacing at right angles of longitudinal threads (the warp) and horizontal threads (the weft), the latter being carried across from one side of the loom to the other by a type of bobbin called a shuttle.

The technique of weaving has been used all over the world since ancient times and has only fairly recently been mechanized. Hand looms are still used, in many societies. They may be horizontal or vertical; industrial looms are generally vertical. In the hand-loom era the ◊Jacquard machine, the last in a series of inventions for producing complicated designs, was perfected in the early 19th century.

The power loom 1786 was essentially the invention of an English cleric, Edmund ◊Cartwright. The speed limitations caused by the slow passage of the shuttle have been partly overcome by the use of water- and air-jet insertion methods, and by the development in the 1970s of 'multiphase' looms in which the weft is inserted in continuous waves across the machine, rather than one weft at a time.

Webb Aston 1849–1930. English architect. He was responsible for numerous public buildings at the turn of the century. His work in London includes the main section of the Victoria and Albert Museum 1891–1909, Admiralty Arch 1908–09, and the façade of Buckingham Palace 1912–13.

Webb (Martha) Beatrice (born Potter) (1858–1943) and Sidney James, 1st Baron Passfield (1859–1947). English social reformers, writers, and founders of the London School of Economics (LSE) 1895. They were early members of the socialist ◊Fabian Society, and were married in 1892. They argued for social insurance in their minority report (1909) of the Poor Law Commission, and wrote many influential books, including *The History of Trade Unionism* 1894, *English Local Government* 1906–29, and *Soviet Communism* 1935.

Sidney Webb was professor of public administration at the LSE 1912–27. He was a member of the Labour Party executive 1915–25, entered Parliament 1922, and was president of the Board of Trade 1924, dominions secretary 1929–30, and colonial secretary 1929–31.

Webb Philip Speakman 1831–1915. English architect. He was a leading figure (along with Richard Norman Shaw (1831–1912) and Charles ◊Voysey) of the Arts and Crafts movement, which was instrumental in the revival of English domestic architecture in the late 19th century. He mostly designed private houses, notably the Red House, Bexleyheath, Kent, 1859, for William ◊Morris. Other houses include Joldwyns, Surrey, 1873, Clouds, East Knoyle, Wiltshire, 1876–91, and Standen, East Grinstead, 1891–94.

Webber Andrew Lloyd. English composer of musicals: see ◊Lloyd Webber.

weber SI unit (symbol Wb) of ◊magnetic flux (the magnetic field strength multiplied by the area through which the field passes). One weber equals 10^8 ◊maxwells. A change of flux at a uniform rate of one weber per second in an electrical coil with one turn produces an electromotive force of one volt in the coil.

Weber Carl Maria Friedrich Ernst von 1786–1826. German composer. He established the Romantic school of opera with *Der Freischütz/The Marksman* 1821 and *Euryanthe* 1823. He was kapellmeister (chief conductor) at Breslau 1804–06, Prague 1813–16, and Dresden 1816. He died during a visit to London where he produced his opera *Oberon* 1826, written for the Covent Garden Theatre.

Weber Max 1864–1920. German sociologist, one of the founders of modern sociology. He emphasized cultural and political factors as key influences on economic development and individual behaviour. Weber argued for a scientific and value-free approach to research, yet highlighted the importance of meaning and consciousness in understanding social action. Key works include *The Protestant Ethic and the Spirit of Capitalism* 1902, *Economy and Society* 1922, *The Methodology of the Social Sciences* 1949, and *The Sociology of Religion* 1920.

Webern Anton (Friedrich Wilhelm von) 1883–1945. Austrian composer. He wrote spare, enigmatic miniatures combining a pastoral poetic with severe structural rigour. He became a pupil of

Webern The composer Anton Webern (1883–1945). One of the three composers of the Second Viennese School, Webern was artistically the most strict and concise of the group. Although he received very little recognition during his lifetime, he is acknowledged as having had an enormous impact on future composers. *Image Select (UK) Ltd*

Arnold ◊Schoenberg, whose twelve-tone system he reinterpreted as abstract design in works such as the Concerto for nine Instruments 1931–34 and the Cantata no. 2 1941–43. His constructivist aesthetic influenced the postwar generation of advanced composers.

Webster John c. 1580–c. 1625. English dramatist. He ranks after Shakespeare as the greatest tragedian of his time, and is the Jacobean whose plays are most frequently performed today. His two great plays *The White Devil* 1612 and *The Duchess of Malfi* 1614 are dark, violent tragedies obsessed with death and decay.

Webster Noah 1758–1843. US lexicographer whose books on grammar and spelling and *American Dictionary of the English Language* 1828 standardized US English.

Weddell Sea arm of the S Atlantic Ocean that cuts into the Antarctic continent SE of Cape Horn; area 8,000,000 sq km/3,000,000 sq mi. Much of it is covered with thick pack ice for most of the year. It is named after the British explorer James Weddell (1787–1834).

Wedekind Frank 1864–1918. German dramatist. He was a forerunner of Expressionism with *Frühlings Erwachen/The Awakening of Spring* 1891, and *Der Erdgeist/The Earth Spirit* 1895 and its sequel *Der Marquis von Keith. Die Büchse der Pandora/Pandora's Box* 1904 was the source for Berg's opera *Lulu*.

Wedgwood Josiah 1730–1795. English pottery manufacturer. He set up business in Staffordshire in the early 1760s to produce his agateware as well as unglazed blue or green stoneware (jasper) decorated with white neo-Classical designs, using pigments of his own invention.

weedkiller or ***herbicide*** chemical that kills some or all plants. Selective herbicides are effective with cereal crops because they kill all broad-leaved plants without affecting grasslike leaves. Those that kill all plants include sodium chlorate and paraquat; see also ◊Agent Orange. The widespread use of weedkillers in agriculture has led to an increase in crop yield but also to pollution of soil and water supplies and killing of birds and small animals, as well as creating a health hazard for humans. ▷*See feature on pp. 858–859.*

weevil any of a superfamily (Curculionoidea) of ◊beetles, usually less than 6 mm/0.25 in long, and with a head prolonged into a downward beak, which is used for boring into plant stems and trees for feeding. The larvae are usually white and the adults green, black, or brown. The grain weevil *Sitophilus granarius* is a serious pest of stored grain and the boll weevil *Anthonomus grandis* damages cotton crops.

Wegener Alfred Lothar 1880–1930. German meteorologist and geophysicist whose theory of ◊continental drift, expounded in *Origin of Continents and Oceans* 1915, was originally known as 'Wegener's hypothesis'. His ideas can now be explained in terms of ◊plate tectonics, the idea that the Earth's crust consists of a number of plates, all moving with respect to one another.

Wei Jingsheng 1951– . Chinese prodemocracy activist and essayist, imprisoned 1979–93 for attacking the Chinese communist system. He was re-arrested twice 1993–94 and again 1995 on the capital charge of trying to overthrow the government. He is regarded as one of China's most important political dissidents.

Weigel Helene 1900–1971. Austrian actress and director. She co-founded the Berliner Ensemble with her husband Berthold ◊Brecht 1949 and took leading roles in productions of his plays, visiting

'The idea of duty in one's calling prowls about in our life like the ghost of dead religious beliefs.'

MAX WEBER
The Protestant Ethic

'We think caged birds sing, when indeed they cry.'

JOHN WEBSTER
The White Devil

weevil The long down-turned snout or beak typical of the weevil is clearly seen on this *Rhinastus latesternus* from the rainforests of Peru. This is a giant of its kind; most European weevils would fit comfortably on the tip of its snout. The larvae develop inside tree branches. *Premaphotos Wildlife*

weightlifting A weightlifter at the Women's Weightlifting World Championships. Weightlifting was included in the Ancient Olympic Games, and was a popular attraction at fairgrounds and circuses in the 19th century. The first world championship was held 1891. *Image Select (UK) Ltd*

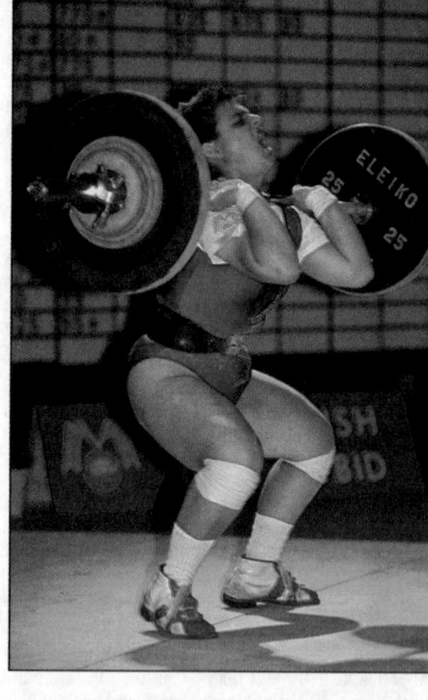

London 1956 and 1965. She took over direction of the Ensemble after Brecht's death 1956.

I hate television. I hate it as much as peanuts. But I can't stop eating peanuts.

ORSON WELLES
Quoted in the *New York Herald Tribune* 12 Oct 1956

weight the force exerted on an object by ◊gravity. The weight of an object depends on its mass – the amount of material in it – and the strength of the Earth's gravitational pull, which decreases with height. Consequently, an object weighs less at the top of a mountain than at sea level. On the Moon, an object has only one-sixth of its weight on Earth, because the pull of the Moon's gravity is one-sixth that of the Earth.

If the mass of a body is m kilograms and the gravitational field strength is g newtons per kilogram, its weight W in newtons is given by:

$$W = mg$$

weightlessness the apparent loss in weight of a body in ◊free fall. Astronauts in an orbiting spacecraft do not feel any weight because they are falling freely in the Earth's gravitational field. The same phenomenon can be experienced in a falling lift or in an aircraft deliberately imitating the path of a freely falling object.

weightlifting sport of lifting the heaviest possible weight above one's head to the satisfaction of judges. In international competitions there are two standard lifts: ***snatch*** and ***jerk***. In the ***snatch***, the bar and weights are lifted from the floor to a position with the arms outstretched and above the head in one continuous movement. The arms must be locked for two seconds for the lift to be good. The ***jerk*** is a two-movement lift: from the floor to the chest, and from the chest to the outstretched position. The aggregate weight of the two lifts counts. The International Weightlifting Federation was formed 1920, although a world championship was first held 1891. The first women's world championship was held 1987 in Florida, USA.

Welles Orson Welles as Harry Lime in *The Third Man* 1949. By his mid-twenties Welles had established himself as an outstanding director, writer, and actor with his first film *Citizen Kane*, an influential film widely accepted as a classic. As an actor he appeared most memorably – though briefly – in Carol Reed's *The Third Man*. *British Film Institute*

Weights and Measures Act 1963 act of Parliament which makes it illegal for businesses to give short weights or short measures to consumers. ◊Trading standards departments are responsible for enforcing the Weights and Measures Act.

Weil Simone 1909–1943. French writer who became a practising Catholic after a mystical experience in 1938. Apart from essays, her works (advocating political passivity) were posthumously published, including *Waiting for God* 1951, *The Need for Roots* 1952, and *Notebooks* 1956.

Weill Kurt Julian 1900–1950. German composer. He was a US citizen from 1943. He wrote chamber and orchestral music and collaborated with Bertolt ◊Brecht on operas such as *Die Dreigroschenoper/The Threepenny Opera* 1928 and *Aufsteig und Fall der Stadt Mahagonny/The Rise and Fall of the City of Mahagonny* 1930, all attacking social corruption. He tried to evolve a new form of ◊music theatre, using subjects with a contemporary relevance and the simplest musical means.

In 1935 he left Germany for the USA where he wrote a number of successful scores for Broadway, among them the antiwar musical *Johnny Johnson* 1936 and *Street Scene* 1947 based on an Elmer Rice play set in the Depression. His musical *Love Life* 1948, with lyrics by Alan Jay Lerner, describes a typical US couple over a period of 150 years of US history, and expresses Weill's mixture of fascination and repulsion towards the 'American Dream'.

Weil's disease or ***leptospirosis*** infectious disease of animals that is occasionally transmitted to human beings, usually by contact with water contaminated with rat urine. It is characterized by acute fever, and infection may spread to the brain, liver, kidneys, and heart. The condition responds poorly to antibiotics, and death may result.

Weimar Republic the constitutional republic in Germany 1919–33, which was crippled by the election of antidemocratic parties to the Reichstag (parliament), and then subverted by the Nazi leader Hitler after his appointment as chancellor 1933.

weir low wall built across a river to raise the water level. The oldest surviving weir in England is at Chester, across the river Dee, dating from around 1100.

Weir Peter Lindsay 1944– . Australian film director who has also worked in the USA. His films ranged from melodramas to comedies, but frequently are marked by an an atmospheric quality and often contain a strong spiritual element. His Australian films include *Picnic at Hanging Rock* 1975 and *Gallipoli* 1981. Among his American films are *Witness* 1985, *Dead Poets Society* 1989, the comedy *Green Card* 1990, and *Fearless* 1993.

Weismann August Friedrich Leopold 1834–1914. German biologist, one of the founders of ◊genetics. He postulated that every living organism contains a special hereditary substance, the 'germ plasm', and in 1892 he proposed that changes to the body do not in turn cause an alteration of the genetic material.

Weissmuller Johnny (Peter John) 1904–1984. US film actor. Formerly an Olympic swimmer, he played Tarzan in a long-running series of films for MGM and RKO including *Tarzan the Ape Man* 1932, *Tarzan and His Mate* 1934, and *Tarzan and the Mermaids* 1948. He later starred in the *Jungle Jim* series of B-movies.

Weizmann Chaim Azriel 1874–1952. Zionist leader, the first president of Israel (1948–52), and a chemist. He conducted the negotiations leading up to the Balfour Declaration, by which Britain declared its support for an independent Jewish state.

Born in Russia, he became a naturalized British subject, and as director of the Admiralty laboratories 1916–19 discovered a process for manufacturing acetone, a solvent. He became head of the Hebrew University in Jerusalem, then in 1948 became the first president of the new republic of Israel.

Weizsäcker Richard, Baron von 1920– . German Christian Democrat politician, president 1984–94. A lawyer, he was also active in the German Protestant church and in Christian Democratic Union party politics. He was elected to the West German Bundestag (parliament) 1969 and served as mayor of West Berlin from 1981, before being elected federal president 1984.

Welch Raquel. Stage name of Raquel Tejada 1940– . US actress. She was a sex symbol of the 1960s in such films as *One Million Years BC* 1966, *Myra Breckinridge* 1970, and *The Three Musketeers* 1973.

welding joining pieces of metal (or nonmetal) at faces rendered plastic or liquid by heat or pressure (or both). The principal processes today are gas and arc welding, in which the heat from a gas flame or an electric arc melts the faces to be joined. Additional 'filler metal' is usually added to the joint.

Weldon Fay 1931– . English novelist and dramatist. Her work deals with feminist themes, often in an ironic or comic manner. Novels include *The Fat Woman's Joke* 1967, *Female Friends* 1975, *Remember Me* 1976, *Puffball* 1980, *The Life and Loves of a She-Devil* 1984 (film 1990), *The Hearts and Lives of Men* 1987, and *Splitting* 1995. She has also written plays for the stage, radio, and television.

Welensky Roy (originally Roland) 1907–1991. Rhodesian politician. He was instrumental in the creation 1953 of the Central African Federation, comprising Northern Rhodesia (now Zambia), Southern Rhodesia (now Zimbabwe), and Nyasaland (now Malawi), and was prime minister 1956–63, when the federation was disbanded. His Southern Rhodesian Federal Party was defeated by Ian Smith's Rhodesian Front in 1964. In 1965, following Smith's Rhodesian unilateral declaration of Southern Rhodesian independence from Britain, Welensky left politics.

welfare state political system under which the state (rather than the individual or the private sector) has responsibility for the welfare of its citizens. Services such as unemployment and sickness benefits, family allowances and income supplements, pensions, medical care, and education may be provided and financed through state insurance schemes and taxation.

In Britain, David Lloyd George, as chancellor, introduced a National Insurance Act 1911. The idea of a welfare state developed in the UK from the 1942 Beveridge Report on social security, which committed the government after World War II to the provision of full employment, a free national health service, and a social-security system. The wartime coalition government accepted its main provisions and they were largely put into effect by the Labour government 1945–51. Since then, economic stringencies and changes in political attitudes have done something to erode the original schemes but the concept remains as an ideal. In 1994 a Commission on Social Justice, established by the Labour Party, recommended a radical review of the welfare state.

Internationally, the aim of creating a welfare state has been adopted in several countries, particularly in Scandinavia, but, again, often more as an ideal than a reality. The welfare-state concept was built into the political structures of communist states, led by the USSR, but even here economic realities tempered its practical implementation.

Welland Ship Canal Canadian waterway, part of the ◊St Lawrence Seaway, linking Lake Erie to Lake Ontario.

Welles (George) Orson 1915–1985. US actor and film and theatre director. His first film was *Citizen Kane* 1941, which he produced, directed, and starred in. He subsequently directed very few films in Hollywood, and worked mainly in Europe. His performances as an actor include the character of Harry Lime in *The Third Man* 1949.

In 1937 he founded the Mercury Theater, New York, with John Houseman. Welles's realistic radio broadcast of H G Wells's *The War of the Worlds* 1938 caused panic and fear of Martian invasion in the USA. His films include *The Magnificent Ambersons* 1942, *The Lady from Shanghai* 1948 with his wife Rita Hayworth, *Touch of Evil* 1958, and *Chimes at Midnight* 1966, a Shakespeare adaptation.

Wellesley Richard Colley, Marquess Wellesley 1760–1842. British administrator; brother of the 1st

Duke of Wellington. He was governor general of India 1798–1805, and by his victories over the Marathas of W India greatly extended the territory under British rule. He was foreign secretary 1809–12, and lord lieutenant of Ireland 1821–28 and 1833–34.

Wellesz Egon Joseph 1885–1974. Austrian-born British composer and musicologist. He taught at Vienna University 1913–38, specializing in the history of Byzantine, Renaissance, and modern music. He moved to England 1938 and lectured at Oxford from 1943. His compositions include operas such as *Alkestis* 1924; symphonies, notably the Fifth 1957; ballet music; and a series of string quartets.

Wellington capital and industrial port (woollen textiles, chemicals, soap, footwear, bricks) of New Zealand on North Island on the Cook Strait; population (1993) 326,900 (urban area). The harbour was sighted by Capt James Cook 1773. Founded 1840 by Edward Gibbon Wakefield as the first settlement of the New Zealand Company, it has been the seat of government since 1865, when it replaced Auckland. Victoria University was founded 1897. A new assembly hall (popularly called 'the beehive') was opened 1977 alongside the original parliament building.

Wellington Arthur Wellesley, 1st Duke of Wellington 1769–1852. British soldier and Tory politician. As commander in the ◊Peninsular War, he expelled the French from Spain 1814. He defeated Napoleon Bonaparte at Quatre-Bras and Waterloo 1815, and was a member of the Congress of Vienna. As prime minister 1828–30, he was forced to concede Roman Catholic emancipation.

Wellington was born in Ireland, the son of an Irish peer, and sat for a time in the Irish parliament. He was knighted for his army service in India and became a national hero with his victories of 1808–14 in the Peninsular War and as general of the allies against Napoleon. At the Congress of Vienna he opposed the dismemberment of France and supported restoration of the Bourbons. As prime minister he modified the Corn Laws but became unpopular for his opposition to parliamentary reform and his lack of opposition to Catholic emancipation. He was foreign secretary 1834–35 and a member of the cabinet 1841–46. He held the office of commander in chief of the forces at various times from 1827 and for life from 1842. His home was Apsley House in London. ▷*See feature on pp. 748–749.*

Wellington Portrait of Arthur Wellesley, British soldier and statesman. He was created Duke of Wellington as part of the honours for his victory over Napoleon in the Peninsular Wars. He was nicknamed the 'Iron Duke' by his troops for his notoriously harsh discipline. *Image Select (UK) Ltd*

Wells market and cathedral city in Somerset, SW England; population (1991) 9,800. Industries include printing, paper, cheese, electronics, textiles, and the manufacture of animal foodstuffs. The cathedral, built near the site of a Saxon church in the 12th and 13th centuries, has a west front with 386 carved figures. Wells was made the seat of a bishopric about 900 (Bath and Wells from 1244).

Wells H(erbert) G(eorge) 1866–1946. English writer. He is best remembered for his 'scientific romances' such as *The Time Machine* 1895 and *The War of the Worlds* 1898. His later novels had an anti-establishment, anti-conventional humour remarkable in its day, for example *Kipps* 1905 and *Tono-Bungay* 1909. His many other books include *Outline of History* 1920 and *The Shape of Things to Come* 1933, a number of his prophecies from which have since been fulfilled. He also wrote many short stories.

Welsh people of ◊Wales; see also ◊Celts. The term is thought to be derived from an old Germanic term for 'foreigner', and so linked to Walloon (Belgium) and Wallachian (Romania). It may also derive from the Latin *Volcae*, the name of a Celtic people of France.

Welsh corgi breed of dog with a foxlike head and pricked ears, originally bred for cattle herding. Corgis are about 30 cm/12 in at the shoulder, and weigh up to 12 kg/27 lb. The Pembrokeshire corgi has a finely textured coat, yellowish or reddish brown, or sometimes black and tan, and has almost no tail. The Cardiganshire corgi has a short, rough coat, usually red and white, and a long furry tail.

Welsh language (in Welsh, ***Cymraeg***) member of the Celtic branch of the Indo-European language family, spoken chiefly in the rural north and west of Wales. Spoken by 18.7% of the Welsh population, it is the strongest of the surviving Celtic languages. Welsh has been in retreat in the face of English expansion since the accession of the Welsh Henry Tudor (as Henry VII) to the throne of England 1485. Modern Welsh, like English, is not a highly inflected language, but British, the Celtic ancestor of Welsh, was, like Latin and Anglo-Saxon, highly inflected. The continuous literature of the Welsh, from the 6th century onwards, contains the whole range of change from British to present-day Welsh. Nowadays, few Welsh people speak only Welsh; they are either bilingual or speak only English.

During the 20th century the decline of Welsh has been slowed: from about 900,000 speakers at the turn of the century, the number had shrunk to half a million 1995. However, due to vigorous campaigning the numbers speaking Welsh has stabilized. According to a survey, in 1995 21% of the population spoke the national tongue; of that number, it was the mother tongue of 55%. Use of the language among young people increased as a result of its inclusion in the national curriculum; in 1993–94, 78.4% of pupils learnt it as either first or second language.

Welsh literature the prose and poetry of Wales, written predominantly in Welsh but also, more recently, in English. The chief remains of early Welsh literature are contained in the Four Ancient Books of Wales – the *Black Book of Carmarthen*, the *Book of Taliesin*, the *Book of Aneirin*, and the *Red Book of Hergest* – anthologies of prose and verse of the 6th–14th centuries. Characteristic of Welsh poetry is the bardic system, which ensured the continuance of traditional conventions; most celebrated of the 12th-century bards was Cynddelw Brydydd Mawr (active 1155–1200).

The English conquest of 1282 involved the fall of the princes who supported these bards, but after a period of decline a new school arose in South Wales with a new freedom in form and sentiment, the most celebrated poet in the 14th-century being Dafydd ap Gwilym, and in the next century the classical metrist Dafydd ap Edmwnd (active 1450–1459). With the Reformation biblical translations were undertaken, and Morgan Llwyd (1619–1659) and Ellis Wynne (1671–1734) wrote religious prose. Popular metres resembling those of England developed – for example, the poems of Huw Morys (1622–1709).

In the 18th century the classical poetic forms revived with Goronwy Owen, and the ◊eisteddfod (literary festival) movement began: popular measures were used by the hymn-writer William Williams Pantycelyn (1717–1791).

The 19th century saw few notable figures save the novelist Daniel Owen (1836–1895), but the foundation of a Welsh university and the work there of John Morris Jones (1864–1929) produced a 20th-century revival, including T Gwynn Jones (1871–1949), W J Gruffydd (1881–1954), and R Williams Parry (1884–1956). Later writers included the poet J Kitchener Davies (1902–1952), the dramatist and poet Saunders Lewis (1893–1985), and the novelist and short-story writer Kate Roberts (1891–1985). Among writers of the postwar period are the poets Waldo Williams (1904–1971), Euros Bowen (1904–), and Bobi Jones (1929–), and the novelists Islwyn Ffowc Elis (1924–) and Jane Edwards (1938–). Those who have expressed the Welsh spirit in English include the poets Edward Thomas, Vernon Watkins (1906–67), Dylan Thomas, R S Thomas, and Dannie Abse (1923–), and the novelist Emyr Humphreys (1919–).

Wells English journalist and novelist H G Wells, who became known for his science fiction and popular accounts of history and science. He was a passionate advocate of socialism, feminism, and evolutionism, and believed that the advancement of science would bring huge material, social, and political benefits. *Corbis*

Welsh Office UK government department established 1951 to administer policies on agriculture, education, health and social services, local government, planning, sport, and tourism. Replaced 1999 by ◊National Assembly for Wales.

Weltanschauung (German 'worldview') a philosophy of life.

Weltpolitik (German 'world politics') term applied to German foreign policy after about 1890, which represented Emperor Wilhelm II's attempt to make Germany into a world power through an aggressive foreign policy on colonies and naval building combined with an increase in nationalism at home.

Welty Eudora Alice 1909– . US novelist and short-story writer. Her works reflect life in the American South and are notable for their creation of character and accurate rendition of local dialect. Her novels include *Delta Wedding* 1946, *Losing Battles* 1970, and *The Optimist's Daughter* 1972. Her *Collected Stories* appeared 1982.

welwitschia woody plant *Welwitschia mirabilis* of the order Gnetales, found in the deserts of SW Africa. It has a long, water-absorbent taproot and can live for a hundred years.

Welwyn Garden City industrial town (chemicals, electrical engineering, plastics, clothing, food) in Hertfordshire, England, 32 km/20 mi N of London; population (1991) 42,100. It was founded as a ◊garden city 1919–20 by Ebenezer Howard, and designated a new town 1948.

Wembley district of the Greater London borough of Brent, site of Wembley Stadium.

Wembley Stadium sports ground in N London, England, completed 1923, since when it has been

'I always say that, next to a battle lost, the greatest misery is a battle gained.'

ARTHUR WELLESLEY, DUKE OF WELLINGTON
Quoted in S Rogers *Recollections*

'In England we have come to rely upon a comfortable time-lag of fifty years or a century intervening between the perception that something ought to be done and a serious attempt to do it.'

H G WELLS
Work, Wealth and Happiness of Mankind

> I look upon all the world as my parish.
>
> JOHN WESLEY *Journal* 1739

the scene of the annual Football Association (FA) Cup final. The 1948 Olympic Games and many concerts, including the Live Aid concert 1985, were held here. Adjacent to the main stadium, which holds 78,000 people, are the Wembley indoor arena (which holds about 10,000) and conference centre. The largest recorded crowd at Wembley is 126,047 for its first FA Cup final.

Wenceslas, St c. 907–929. Duke of Bohemia. He attempted to Christianize his people and was murdered by his brother. He is patron saint of the Czech Republic and the 'good King Wenceslas' of a popular carol. Feast day 28 Sept.

Wenders Wim (Wilhelm) 1945– . German film director, screenwriter, and producer. He has worked in both Germany and the USA, and many of his films explore the relationship between the two cultures. They include *Paris, Texas* 1984 and *Der Himmel über Berlin/Wings of Desire* 1987. With Werner ◊Herzog and Rainer Werner ◊Fassbinder, Wenders was one of the most prominent figures to emerge from the New German Cinema movement of the 1970s. Other films include *The State of Things* 1982, *Bis ans Ende der Welte/Until the End of the World* 1991, and *In weiter Ferne, so nah!/Far Away, So Close!* 1993.

Wends NW Slavonic peoples who settled east of the rivers Elbe and Saale in the 6th–8th centuries. By the 12th century most had been forcibly Christianized and absorbed by invading Germans; a few preserved their identity and survive as the Sorbs of Lusatia (E Germany/Poland).

werewolf in folk belief, a human being either turned by spell into a wolf or having the ability to assume a wolf form. The symptoms of ◊porphyria may have fostered the legends.

Werfel Franz 1890–1945. Austrian poet, dramatist, and novelist. He was a leading Expressionist. His works include the poem 'Der Weltfreund der Gerichtstag'/'The Day of Judgement' 1919; the plays *Juarez und Maximilian* 1924 and *Das Reich Gottes in Böhmen/The Kingdom of God in Bohemia* 1930; and the novels *Verdi* 1924 and *Das Lied von Bernadette/The Song of Bernadette* 1941.

Werner Alfred 1866–1919. French-born Swiss chemist. He was awarded a Nobel prize in 1913 for his work on valency theory, which gave rise to the concept of coordinate bonds and coordination compounds.

Wesker Arnold 1932– . English dramatist. His socialist beliefs were reflected in the trilogy *Chicken Soup with Barley*, *Roots*, and *I'm Talking About Jerusalem* 1958–60. He established a catchphrase with *Chips with Everything* 1962. Later plays include *The Merchant* 1978 and *Lady Othello* 1987.

Wesley John 1703–1791. English founder of ◊Methodism. When the pulpits of the Church of England were closed to him and his followers, he took the gospel to the people. For 50 years he rode about the country on horseback, preaching daily, largely in the open air. His sermons became the doctrinal standard of the Wesleyan Methodist Church.

He was born in Epworth, Lincolnshire, where his father was the rector, and went to Oxford University together with his brother Charles, where their circle was nicknamed Methodists because of their religious observances. He was ordained in the Church of England 1728 and returned to his Oxford college 1729 as a tutor. In 1735 he went to Georgia, USA, as a missionary. On his return he experienced 'conversion' 1738, and from being rigidly High Church developed into an ardent Evangelical. His *Journal* gives an intimate picture of the man and his work.

> When choosing between two evils, I always like to pick the one I never tried before.
>
> MAE WEST in *Klondike Annie* 1936

Wesley Samuel 1776–1837. English organist and composer. Son of the well known composer of hymns, Charles Wesley (1707–1788), he was regarded as the best organist of his day. He wrote many masses, motets, anthems (including *In exitu Israel*), and also secular music.

Wessex the kingdom of the West Saxons in Britain, said to have been founded by Cerdic about AD 500, covering present-day Hampshire, Dorset, Wiltshire, Berkshire, Somerset, and Devon. In 829 Egbert established West Saxon supremacy over all England.

Thomas ◊Hardy used the term Wessex in his novels for the SW counties of England.

West Benjamin 1738–1820. American Neo-Classical painter. A noted history painter, he was active in London from 1763 and enjoyed the patronage of George III for many years. *The Death of General Wolfe* 1770 (National Gallery of Canada, Ottawa) began a vogue for depicting recent events as they might realistically have happened, rather than presenting them through Classical allusion.

West Mae 1892–1980. US vaudeville, stage, and film actress. She wrote her own dialogue, setting herself up as a provocative sex symbol and the mistress of verbal innuendo. She appeared on Broadway in *Sex* 1926, *Drag* 1927, and *Diamond Lil* 1928, which was the basis of the film (with Cary Grant) *She Done Him Wrong* 1933. Her other films include *I'm No Angel* 1933, *My Little Chickadee* 1940 (with W C Fields), *Myra Breckinridge* 1969, and *Sextette* 1977. Both her plays and her films led to legal battles over censorship.

West US film and vaudeville actress Mae West who wrote and delivered some of the most often quoted lines in film history. She specialized in glamorous roles, made memorable by her languid and suggestive delivery of the dialogue.

West Nathanael. Pen name of Nathan Wallenstein Weinstein 1903–1940. US writer. He is noted as an idiosyncratic black-humour parodist. His surrealist-influenced novels capture the absurdity and extremity of American life and the dark side of the American Dream. His most powerful novel, *The Day of the Locust* 1939, is a vivid exploration of the apocalyptic violence given release by the fantasies created by Hollywood, where West had been a screenwriter. His other work consisted of *The Dream Life of Balso Snell* 1931, *Miss Lonelyhearts* 1933, and *A Cool Million* 1934.

West Rebecca. Pen name of Cicily Isabel Fairfield 1892–1983. Irish journalist and novelist, an active feminist from 1911. *The Meaning of Treason* 1959 deals with the spies Burgess and Maclean. Her novels have political themes and include *The Fountain Overflows* 1956 and *The Birds Fall Down* 1966.

West African Economic Community international organization established 1975 to end barriers in trade and to achieve cooperation in development. Members include Burkina Faso, Ivory Coast, Mali, Mauritania, Niger, and Senegal; Benin and Togo have observer status.

West, American generally, the region of the USA to the west of the Mississippi River from Canada to Mexico.

West Bank area (5,879 sq km/2,270 sq mi) on the west bank of the river Jordan; population (1994) 1,070,000. The West Bank was taken by the Jordanian army 1948 at the end of the Arab-Israeli war that followed the creation of the state of Israel, and was captured by Israel during the Six-Day War 5–10 June 1967. The continuing Israeli occupation and settlement of the area created tensions with the Arab population and after 1987, as the ◊Intifada (uprising) gained strength in the occupied territories, Israeli-military presence increased significantly. In Sept 1993 Israel signed a historic accord with the ◊Palestine Liberation Organization, under which a phased withdrawal of Israeli troops was undertaken from the West Bank town of Jericho and responsibility for its administration transferred to the PLO May 1994; self-rule arrangements for remaining Palestinian areas in the West Bank were agreed Sept 1995. Israeli troops began their withdrawal from West Bank cities on schedule during 1995, but the town of ◊Hebron was still occupied by late 1996, straining relations between Israel and Palestine. In June 1997 riots erupted in the West Bank and Gaza as an Egyptian mediation attempt failed.

West Bengal state of NE India
area 88,700 sq km/34,247 sq mi
capital Calcutta
towns and cities Asansol, Durgarpur
physical occupies the west part of the vast alluvial plain created by the rivers Ganges and Brahmaputra, with the Hooghly River; annual rainfall in excess of 250 cm/100 in
industries rice, jute, tea, coal, iron, steel, cars, locomotives, aluminium, fertilizers
population (1994 est) 73,600,000
history created 1947 from the former British province of Bengal, with later territories added: Cooch Behar 1950, Chandernagore 1954, and part of Bihar 1956.

West Dunbartonshire local authority of Scotland created 1996 (*see United Kingdom map*).

Westerlies prevailing winds from the west that occur in both hemispheres between latitudes of about 35° and 60°. Unlike the ◊trade winds, they are very variable and produce stormy weather. The Westerlies blow mainly from the SW in the northern hemisphere and the NW in the southern hemisphere, bringing moist weather to the W coast of the landmasses in these latitudes.

Western genre of popular fiction and film based on the landscape and settlement of the American West, with emphasis on the conquest of Indian territory. It developed in American ◊dime novels and frontier literature (writing reflecting the experience of US frontier life). The Western became established in written form with such novels as Owen Wister's *The Virginian* 1902 and Zane Grey's *Riders of the Purple Sage* 1912. From the earliest silent films, movies extended the Western mythology and, with Italian 'spaghetti' Westerns and Japanese Westerns, established it as an international form.

Westerns go back to J F Cooper's *Leatherstocking Tales* 1823–41, and the hunter stories of the German writer Karl May (1842–1912). In stylized form, they became frontier stories of cowboy rangers and Indian villains, set vaguely in the post-Civil War era. *The Virginian* is the 'serious' version of the form, but prolific writers like Zane Grey and Frederick Faust (1892–1944) developed its place in universal fantasy.

A memorable early Western film is *The Great Train Robbery* 1903. The silent era produced such epics as *The Iron Horse* 1924, and the genre remained popular into the coming of sound. The 1930s saw many epics, such as *Union Pacific* 1939, whereas the 1940s often dwelt on specific historical events (including Custer's last stand in *They Died With Their Boots On* 1941). The 1950s brought more realism and serious issues, such as the treatment of the Indians. The Westerns of the 1960s contained an increased amount of violence, partly owing to the influence of the 'spaghetti Westerns' (often directed by Sergio ◊Leone). The genre became less popular in the 1970s.

Western Australia state of Australia
area 2,525,500 sq km/974,843 sq mi
capital Perth
towns and cities main port Fremantle, Bunbury, Geraldton, Kalgoorlie-Boulder, Albany, Broome
features largest state in Australia; Monte Bello Islands; rivers Fitzroy, Fortescue, Gascoyne, Murchison, Swan; northwest coast subject to hurricanes (willy-willies); Nullarbor Plain; Gibson, Sandy, and Great Victoria deserts; old goldfields and ghost towns; karri and jarrah forests, and the Darling Range, in the southwest; the Kimberleys in the north
industries wheat, fresh and dried fruit, meat and dairy products, natural gas (northwest shelf) and oil (Canning Basin), iron (the Pilbara), copper, nickel, uranium, gold, diamonds, wine growing (in southwest), lumbering, bauxite

Western Australia

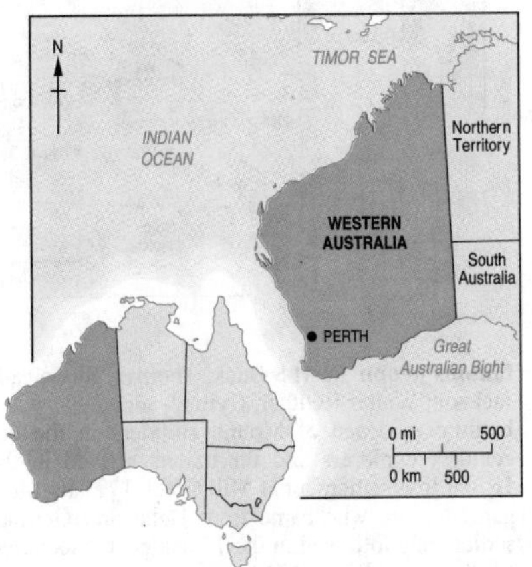

population (1993) 1,667,300
history a short-lived convict settlement at King George Sound 1826; first non-convict settlement founded at Perth 1829 by Capt James Stirling (1791–1865); self-government 1890; became a state 1901.

Western Cape province of the Republic of South Africa from 1994, formerly part of Cape Province
area 129,386 sq km/49,956 sq mi
capital Cape Town
towns and cities Simonstown, Stellenbosch
features Table Mountain (highest point McClear's Beacon 1,087 m/3,567 ft)
industries copper, fruit, wine, wheat, tobacco
population (1995 est) 3,721,200
languages Afrikaans 63%, English 20%, Xhosa 16%.

Western European Union (WEU) organization established 1955 as a consultative forum for military issues among the W European governments: Belgium, France, the Netherlands, Italy, Luxembourg, the UK, Germany, Spain and Portugal (from 1988), and Greece (from 1992). The WEU is charged under its charter with ensuring close cooperation with NATO. In the early 1990s attempts were made to transform the WEU into a body to coordinate W European security policy either within NATO or within the European Community (now the European Union) if the latter were to adopt a common security policy. In 1992 it was announced that a joint force, called the European Corps or Eurocorps, was to be created to work with NATO forces for the defence of Europe. In November 1995 the Eurocorps, comprising troops from Belgium, France, Luxembourg and Spain, was declared operational.

Western Front battle zone in World War I between Germany and its enemies France and Britain, extending as lines of trenches from Nieuport on the Belgian coast through Ypres, Arras, Albert, Soissons, and Rheims to Verdun, constructed by both Germany and the Allies.

During the period of trench warfare, poison gas was used by Germany at Ypres, Belgium, April 1915 and tanks were employed by Britain on the River Somme in Sept 1916. A German offensive in the spring of 1918 enabled the troops to reach the Marne River. By summer the Allies were advancing all along the front and the Germans were driven back into Belgium.

Western Isles island area of Scotland, comprising the Outer Hebrides (Lewis, Harris, North and South Uist, Benbecula, and Barra); also local authority of Scotland, created 1975, retained in the reorganization of local government 1996 (*see United Kingdom map*)
area 2,900 sq km/1,120 sq mi
towns and cities Stornoway on Lewis (administrative headquarters)
features divided from the mainland by the Minch channel; Callanish monolithic circles of the Stone Age on Lewis
industries Harris tweed, sheep, fish, cattle
population (1991) 29,100
famous people Flora MacDonald.

Western Jin or ***Western Chin*** in Chinese history, the period 265–316 when the Wei dynasty established its pre-eminence and united the country. The Western Jin falls in the ◊Three Kingdoms era.

Western Sahara (formerly ***Spanish Sahara***) disputed territory in NW Africa bounded to the north by Morocco, to the east and south by Mauritania, and to the west by the Atlantic Ocean
area 266,800 sq km/103,011 sq mi
capital Laâyoune (Arabic *El Aaiún*)
towns and cities Dhakla
features electrically monitored fortified wall enclosing the phosphate area
exports phosphates
currency dirham
population (1993 est) 214,000; another estimated 196,000 live in refugee camps near Tindouf, SW Algeria. Ethnic composition: Sawrawis (traditionally nomadic herders)
language Arabic
religion Sunni Muslim
government administered by Morocco
history this Saharan coastal region (1,000 km/625 mi long) was designated a Spanish 'sphere of influence' 1884 because it lies opposite the Spanish-ruled Canary Islands. On securing its independence 1956, Morocco laid claim to and invaded the 'Spanish Sahara' territory, but was repulsed. Spanish Sahara became a Spanish province 1958. Moroccan interest was rekindled from 1965, following the discovery of rich phosphate resources at Bou-Craa, and within Spanish Sahara a pro-independence nationalist movement developed, spearheaded by the Popular Front for the Liberation of Saguia al Hamra and Rio de Oro (Polisario), established 1973
partition after the death of the Spanish ruler General Franco, Spain withdrew and the territory was partitioned between Morocco and Mauritania 1976. Polisario rejected this partition, declared their own independent Saharan Arab Democratic Republic (SADR), and proceeded to wage a guerrilla war, securing indirect support from Algeria and, later, Libya. By 1979 they had succeeded in their struggle against Mauritania, which withdrew from their southern sector and concluded a peace agreement with Polisario, and in 1982 the SADR was accepted as a full member of the ◊Organization of African Unity
defensive wall Morocco, which occupied the Mauritanian-evacuated zone, still retained control over the bulk of the territory, including the key towns and phosphate mines, which they protected with an 'electronic defensive wall' 2,500 km/1,550 mi long, completed 1987. From the mid-1980s this wall was gradually extended outwards as Libya and Algeria reduced their support for Polisario and drew closer to Morocco. In 1988, Morocco and the Polisario Front agreed to United Nations-sponsored plans for a cease-fire and a referendum in Western Sahara to decide the territory's future. However, subsequent divisions over the terms of the referendum resulted in continued fighting and the breakdown of UN-sponsored peace talks between Morocco and the Polisario.

Western Samoa see ◊Samoa, Western.

Western swing big-band, jazz-influenced country music that originated in Texas in the 1930s. A swinging, inventive dance music, with the fiddle a predominant instrument, it was developed by Bob ◊Wills and his Texas Playboys and remained a strong influence on popular music into the 1950s, with a revival of interest beginning in the early 1970s and still continuing.

West Germany see ◊Germany, West.

West Glamorgan (Welsh ***Gorllewin Morgannwg***) former county of SW Wales, established 1974, abolished 1996.

West Indian inhabitant of or native to the West Indies, or person of West Indian descent. The West Indies are culturally heterogeneous; in addition to the indigenous Carib and Arawak Indians, there are peoples of African, European, and Asian descent, as well as peoples of mixed descent.

West Indies archipelago of about 1,200 islands, dividing the Atlantic Ocean from the Gulf of Mexico and the Caribbean Sea. The islands are divided into:

◊***Bahamas***; ***Greater Antilles*** Cuba, Hispaniola (Haiti, Dominican Republic), Jamaica, and Puerto Rico; ***Lesser Antilles*** Aruba, Netherlands Antilles, Trinidad and Tobago, the Windward Islands (Grenada, Barbados, St Vincent, St Lucia, Martinique, Dominica, Guadeloupe), the Leeward Islands (Montserrat, Antigua, St Christopher (St Kitts)–Nevis, Barbuda, Anguilla, St Martin, British and US Virgin Islands), and many smaller islands.

West Indies, Federation of the federal union 1958–62 comprising Antigua, Barbados, Dominica, Grenada, Jamaica, Montserrat, St Christopher (St Kitts)–Nevis and Anguilla, St Lucia, St Vincent, and Trinidad and Tobago. This federation came to an end when Jamaica and then Trinidad and Tobago withdrew.

West Irian former name of ◊Irian Jaya, a province of Indonesia.

West Lothian local authority of Scotland created 1996 (*see United Kingdom map*).

Westman Islands small group of islands off the south coast of Iceland. In 1973 volcanic eruption caused the population of 5,200 to be temporarily evacuated, and added 2.5 sq km/1 sq mi to the islands' area. Heimaey, the largest of the islands, is one of Iceland's chief fishing ports.

'God forbid that any book should be banned. The practice is as indefensible as infanticide.'
Rebecca West
The Strange Necessity

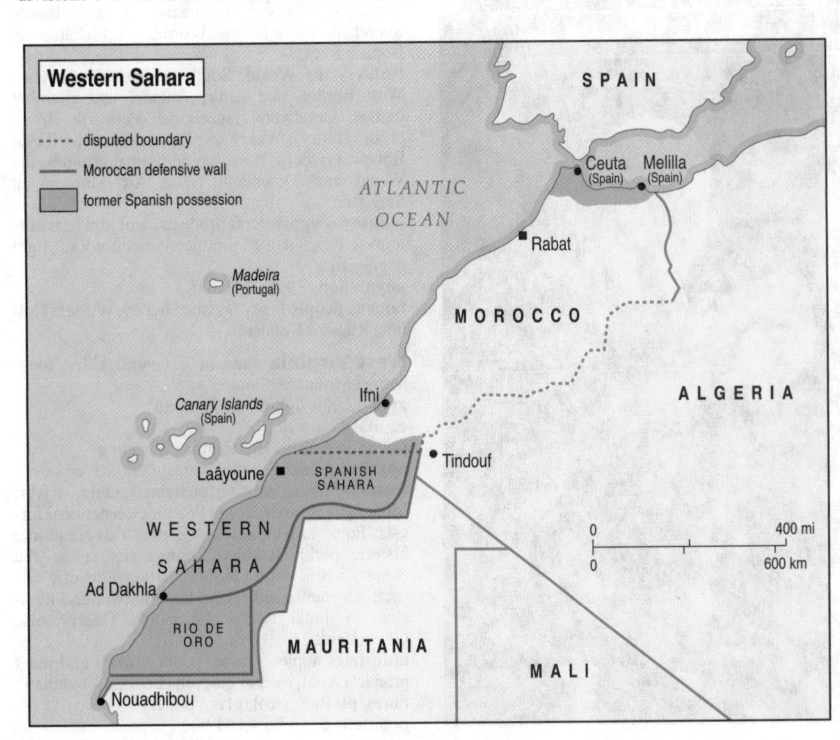

Westmeath county of the Republic of Ireland, in the province of Leinster; county town Mullingar; area 1,760 sq km/679 sq mi; population (1991) 61,900. There are the rivers Shannon, Inny, and Brosna, and the lakes Ree, Sheelin, and Ennell. It is low-lying, with much pasture. Agricultural and dairy products, limestone, and textiles are produced.

West Midlands metropolitan county of central England, created 1974; in 1986, most of the functions of the former county council were transferred to the metropolitan district councils
area 900 sq km/347 sq mi
towns and cities Birmingham, Wolverhampton, Coventry, Walsall, Dudley
industries industrial goods; coal mining; chemicals; machine tools; engineering; motor vehicles; aircraft components; electrical equipment
population (1991) 2,551,700
famous people Edward Burne-Jones, Neville Chamberlain, Philip Larkin.

Westminster, City of inner borough of central Greater London, on the N bank of the river Thames between Kensington and the City of London. It encompasses Bayswater, Belgravia, Mayfair, Paddington, Pimlico, Soho, St John's Wood, and Westminster
population (1991) 174,800
features includes the following well-known areas:

Bayswater a residential and hotel area N of Kensington Gardens; Tyburn, near Marble Arch, site of public executions until 1783

Belgravia bounded to the N by Knightsbridge, has squares laid out 1825–30 by Thomas Cubitt; Grosvenor estate

Mayfair between Oxford Street and Piccadilly, includes Park Lane and Grosvenor Square (with the US embassy)

Paddington includes Little Venice on the Grand Union Canal

Pimlico has the Tate Gallery (Turner collection, British, and modern art); developed by Thomas Cubitt in 1830s

Soho has many restaurants and a Chinese community around Gerrard Street. It was formerly known for strip clubs and sex shops

St John's Wood has Lord's cricket ground and the studios at 3 Abbey Road where the Beatles recorded their music

Westminster encompasses Buckingham Palace, Green Park, St James's Park and St James's Palace (16th century), Marlborough House, Westminster Abbey, Westminster Hall (1097–1401), the Houses of Parliament with Big Ben, Whitehall (government offices), Downing Street (homes of the prime minister at number 10 and the chancellor of the Exchequer at number 11), Hyde Park with the Albert Memorial (1876) opposite the Royal Albert Hall (1871), Trafalgar Square with the National Gallery, the National Portrait Gallery, and the church of St Martin in the Fields (1722–24).

Weyden *Mary Magdalen Reading* c. 1435 by Rogier van der Weyden (National Gallery, London). As in all early Netherlandish painting, the artist has used symbols to identify the figures depicted. Here, a small jar identifies Mary Magdalen, who used ointment to anoint Christ. *Corbis*

Westminster Abbey Gothic church in central London, officially the Collegiate Church of St Peter. It was built 1050–1745 and consecrated under Edward the Confessor 1065. The west towers are by Nicholas ◊Hawksmoor, completed after his death 1745. Since William I nearly all English monarchs have been crowned in the abbey, and several are buried there; many poets are buried or commemorated there, at Poets' Corner; and some 30 scientists, including Isaac Newton, Lord Kelvin, and James Prescott, are either buried or commemorated there.

Weston Edward 1886–1958. US photographer. A founding member of the 'f/64' group (after the smallest lens opening), a school of photography advocating sharp definition. He is noted for the technical mastery, composition, and clarity in his California landscapes, clouds, gourds, cacti, and nude studies.

Weston-super-Mare seaside resort and administrative headquarters of North Somerset, SW England, on the Bristol Channel; population (1991) 69,400. Industries include plastics and engineering.

West Pakistan a province of ◊Pakistan.

Westphalia independent medieval duchy, incorporated in Prussia by the Congress of Vienna 1815, and made a province 1816 with Münster as its capital. Since 1946 it has been part of the German *Land* (region) of ◊North Rhine–Westphalia.

The kingdom of Westphalia, created by the French emperor Napoleon 1807–13, did not include the duchy, but was made up of Prussian lands W of the Elbe, Hessen, Brunswick, and Hanover.

Westphalia, Treaty of agreement 1648 ending the ◊Thirty Years' War. The peace marked the end of the supremacy of the Holy Roman Empire and the emergence of France as a dominant power. It recognized the sovereignty of the German states, Switzerland, and the Netherlands; Lutherans, Calvinists, and Roman Catholics were given equal rights.

West Point former fort in New York State, on the Hudson River, 80 km/50 mi N of New York City, site of the US Military Academy (commonly referred to as West Point), established 1802.

West Sussex county of S England, created 1974, formerly part of Sussex
area 2,020 sq km/780 sq mi (*see United Kingdom map*)
towns and cities Chichester (administrative headquarters), Crawley, Horsham, Haywards Heath, Shoreham (port); resorts: Worthing, Littlehampton, Bognor Regis
features the Weald, South Downs; rivers Arun, West Rother, and Adur; Arundel and Bramber castles; Goodwood racecourse; Petworth House (17th century); Wakehurst Place, where the Royal Botanic Gardens, Kew, has additional grounds; the Weald and Downland Open Air Museum at Singleton
industries agricultural products, including cereals, root crops, dairy produce; electronics, light engineering
population (1991) 702,300
famous people Percy Bysshe Shelley, William Collins, Richard Cobden.

West Virginia state in E central USA; nicknamed Mountain State
area 62,900 sq km/24,279 sq mi
capital Charleston
towns and cities Huntington, Wheeling
physical Allegheny Mountains; Ohio River
features Allegheny Mountains; Ohio River; Monongahela and George Washington national forests; Potomac Highlands; Harpers Ferry national historic park; Berkeley Springs state park, the country's first spa; Lewisburg national historic district; Blennerhassett Island historic park and mansion; National Radio Astronomy Observatory, Green Bank
industries apples, maize, poultry, dairy and meat products, coal, natural gas, oil, chemicals, synthetic fibres, plastics, steel, glass, pottery
population (1991) 1,801,000

West Virginia

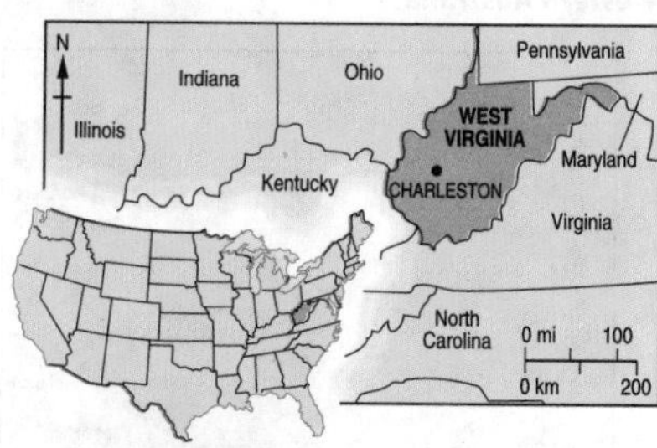

famous people Pearl S Buck, Thomas 'Stonewall' Jackson, Walter Reuther, Cyrus Vance
history evidence of Mound Builders in the 6th century; explorers and fur traders arrived in the 1670s; first settlement at Mill Creek 1731 by Morgan Morgan, who came from Delaware; German settlements followed in the 1730s; coal discovered on the Coal River 1742; industrial development began in the early 19th century. On the secession of Virginia from the Union 1861, west Virginians dissented and formed a new state 1863. Industrial expansion was accompanied by labour strife in the early 20th century.

Westwood Vivienne 1941– . English fashion designer. She first attracted attention in the mid-1970s as co-owner of a shop with the rock-music entrepreneur Malcolm McLaren (1946–), which became a focus for the punk movement in London. Early in the 1980s her 'Pirate' and 'New Romantics' looks gained her international recognition. Later she also designed clothes and accessories for mail-order companies and young people's high-street fashion stores.

West Yorkshire metropolitan county of NE England, created 1974; in 1986, most of the functions of the former county council were transferred to the metropolitan district councils
area 2,040 sq km/787 sq mi
towns and cities Wakefield, Leeds, Bradford, Halifax, Huddersfield
features Ilkley Moor, Haworth Moor, Haworth Parsonage; part of the Peak District National Park; British Library, Boston Spa (scientific, technical, and business documents)
industries woollen textiles. Coal mining is in decline
population (1991) 2,013,700
famous people the Brontës, J B Priestley, Henry Moore, David Hockney.

wet in UK politics, a derogatory term used to describe a moderate or left-wing supporter of the Conservative Party, especially those who opposed the monetary or other hardline policies of its former leader Margaret Thatcher.

wetland permanently wet land area or habitat. Wetlands include areas of ◊marsh, fen, ◊bog, flood plain, and shallow coastal areas. They provide warm, sheltered waters for fisheries, lush vegetation for grazing livestock, and an abundance of wildlife.

The term is often more specifically applied to a naturally flooding area that is managed for agriculture or wildlife. A water meadow, where a river is expected to flood grazing land at least once a year thereby replenishing the soil, is a traditional example.

Wexford county of the Republic of Ireland, in the province of Leinster; county town Wexford; 2,350 sq km/907 sq mi; population (1991) 102,000. The port of Rosslare has ferry links to England. Industries include fish, livestock, oats, barley, potatoes, cattle, agricultural machinery, and food processing. It was the first Irish county to be colonized from England 1169.

Wexford seaport and county town of Wexford, Republic of Ireland, on the estuary of the river Slaney; population (1991) 9,500. Products include textiles, cheese, agricultural machinery, food processing, and motor vehicles. There is an annual opera festival in October. Wexford was founded by the Danes in the 9th century and devastated by Oliver Cromwell 1649.

Weyden Rogier van der c. 1399–1464. Netherlandish artist. He was the official painter to the city of Brussels from 1436. One of the major figures of early Netherlandish painting, he produced portraits and religious subjects in a refined and elegant realist style. *The Last Judgement* about 1450 (Hôtel-Dieu, Beaune) is typical.

He visited Italy 1450, and had a busy workshop in Brussels until his death. Though he signed no paintings, his work is as distinct as that of Jan van ◊Eyck, and the products of his studio exerted an important influence not only in N Europe, but also in Spain and, to some extent, in Italy. Lucid and graceful composition, a feeling for relief (suggesting that he made use of effects observed in Gothic sculpture), and a warm humanity and mastery of emotional expression characterize his work and account for his eminent position. These qualities can be seen in his *Deposition* before 1443 (Prado, Madrid).

Among his religious works are the *Pietà* (Mauritshuis, The Hague), the polyptych of the *Last Judgement*, the *Seven Sacraments* (Musée Royal des Beaux-Arts, Antwerp), and the *Adoration of the Magi* (Gemäldegalerie, Berlin). His portraits include the *Portrait of a Lady* (National Gallery, Washington).

Weymouth seaport and resort in Dorset, S England; population (1991 est) 46,100. It is linked by ferry to France and the Channel Islands. Weymouth dates from the 10th century, and was popularized as a bathing resort by George III.

whale any marine mammal of the order Cetacea, The only mammals to have adapted to living entirely in water, they have front limbs modified into flippers and no externally visible traces of hind limbs. They have horizontal tail flukes. When they surface to breathe, the hot air they breathe out condenses to form a 'spout' through the blowhole (single or double nostrils) in the top of the head. Whales are intelligent and have a complex communication system, known as 'songs'. They occur in all seas of the world.

The order is divided into two groups: the toothed whales (Odontoceti) and the baleen whales (Mysticeti). Toothed whales are predators, feeding on fish and squid. They include ◊dolphins and ◊porpoises, along with large forms such as sperm whales. The largest whales are the baleen whales, with plates of modified mucous membrane called baleen (whalebone) in the mouth; these strain the food from the water, mainly microscopic plankton. Baleen whales include the finback and right whales, and the blue whale, the largest animal that has ever lived, of length up to 30 m/100 ft.

Whale James 1886–1957. English film director. He went to Hollywood to film his stage success *Journey's End* 1930, and then directed four horror films: *Frankenstein* 1931, *The Old Dark House* 1932, *The Invisible Man* 1933, and *Bride of Frankenstein* 1935. He also directed the musical *Show Boat* 1936.

whaling the hunting of whales. Whales have been killed by humans at least since the Middle Ages. There were hundreds of thousands of whales at the beginning of the 20th century, but the invention of the harpoon 1870 and improvements in ships and mechanization have led to the near-extinction of several species of whale. Commercial whaling was largely discontinued 1986, although Norway and Japan have continued commercial whaling.

Traditional whaling areas include the coasts of Greenland and Newfoundland, but the Antarctic, in the summer months, supplied the bulk of the catch.

Practically the whole of the animal can be utilized in one form or another: whales are killed for whale oil (made from the thick layer of fat under the skin called 'blubber'), used as a lubricant, or for making soap, candles, and margarine; for the large reserve of oil in the head of the sperm whale, used in the leather industry; and for ambergris, a waxlike substance from the intestines of the sperm whale, used in making perfumes. Whalebone was used by corset manufacturers and in the brush trade; there are now synthetic substitutes for all these products. Whales have also been killed for use in petfood manufacture in the USA and Europe, and as a food in Japan. The flesh and ground bones are used as soil fertilizers.

Wharton Edith Newbold (born Jones) 1862–1937. US novelist. Her work, known for its subtlety and form and influenced by her friend Henry James, was mostly set in New York society. It includes *The House of Mirth* 1905, which made her reputation; the grim, uncharacteristic novel of New England *Ethan Frome* 1911; and *The Age of Innocence* 1920 (Pulitzer prize).

wheat cereal plant derived from the wild *Triticum*, a grass native to the Middle East. It is the chief cereal used in breadmaking and is widely cultivated in temperate climates suited to its growth. The main wheat-producing areas of the world are the Ukraine, the prairie states of the USA, the Punjab in India, the prairie provinces of Canada, parts of France, Poland, S Germany, Italy, Argentina, and SE Australia. Flour is milled from the ◊endosperm; the coatings of the grain produce bran. Semolina is also prepared from wheat.

wheatear small (15 cm/6 in long) migratory bird *Oenanthe oenanthe* of the family Muscicapidae, order Passeriformes. Wheatears are found throughout the Old World and also breed in far northern parts of North America. The plumage is light grey above and white below with a buff tinge on the breast, a black face-patch, and black and white wings and tail.

Wheatley Dennis Yates 1897–1977. English thriller and adventure novelist. His works include a series dealing with black magic and occultism, but he also wrote crime novels in which the reader was invited to play the detective, as in *Murder off Miami* 1936, with real clues such as ticket stubs.

wheel and axle simple machine with a rope wound round an axle connected to a larger wheel with another rope attached to its rim. Pulling on the wheel rope (applying an effort) lifts a load attached to the axle rope. The velocity ratio of the machine (distance moved by load divided by distance moved by effort) is equal to the ratio of the wheel radius to the axle radius.

Wheeler (Robert Eric) Mortimer 1890–1976. English archaeologist. As director-general of archaeology in India in the 1940s he excavated two major cities of the ◊Indus valley civilization, ◊Mohenjo Daro and ◊Harappa. He helped to popularize archaeology by his television appearances.

whelk any of various families of large marine snails with a thick spiral shell, especially the family Buccinidae. Whelks are scavengers, and also eat other shellfish. The largest grow to 40 cm/16 in long. Tropical species, such as the conches, can be very colourful. The common whelk *Buccinum undatum* is widely distributed around the North Sea and Atlantic.

whey watery by-product of the cheesemaking process, which is drained off after the milk has been heated and ◊rennet (a curdling agent) added to induce its coagulation. In Scandinavia, especially Norway, whey is turned into cheese, *mysost* and

‘Mrs Ballinger is one of the ladies who pursue Culture in bands, as though it were dangerous to meet it alone.’

Edith Wharton
Xingu

whale A white whale, or 'beluga', photographed in an aquarium, Vancouver, British Columbia, Canada. This species of whale is grey when young and becomes almost pure white when adult. Found mainly in Arctic waters, they live in groups of ten or so individuals, gathering in much larger herds to migrate south in the winter. They feed on crustacens and fish and can swim under the pack ice. White whales were known as 'sea canaries' by 19th-century whalers because of their intricate songs. *Corbis*

"Never expected to hear a coxcomb ask two hundred guineas for flinging a pot of paint in the public's face."

John Ruskin's comment on J M WHISTLER'S *Nocturne in Black and Gold*

(from goat's whey) *gjetost*. The flavour of whey cheese is sweet from added brown sugar and is an acquired taste.

Whig Party in the UK, predecessor of the Liberal Party. The name was first used of rebel ◊Covenanters and then of those who wished to exclude James II from the English succession (as a Roman Catholic). They were in power continuously 1714–60 and pressed for industrial and commercial development, a vigorous foreign policy, and religious toleration. During the French Revolution, the Whigs demanded parliamentary reform in Britain, and from the passing of the Reform Bill 1832 became known as Liberals.

Whig Party in the USA, political party opposed to the autocratic presidency of Andrew Jackson from 1834. The Whig presidents were W H Harrison, Taylor, and Fillmore. The party diverged over the issue of slavery: the Northern Whigs joined the Republican party and the Southern or 'Cotton' Whigs joined the Democrats. The title was taken from the British Whig Party which supported Parliament against the king. During the American Revolution, colonial patriots described themselves as Whigs, while those remaining loyal to Britain were known as Tories.

whimbrel wading bird *Numenius phaeopus*, order Charadriiformes, with a medium-sized downcurved bill, streaked brown plumage, and striped head. About 40 cm/1.3 ft long, it breeds in the Arctic, and winters in Africa, S North America, South America, and S Asia.

whip (the whipper-in of hounds at a foxhunt) in UK politics, the member of Parliament who ensures the presence of colleagues in the party when there is to be a vote in Parliament at the end of a debate. The written appeal sent by the whips to MPs is also called a whip; this letter is underlined once, twice, or three times to indicate its importance. A ***three-line whip*** is the most urgent, and every MP is expected to attend and vote with their party. An MP who fails to attend may be temporarily suspended from the party, a penalty known as 'having the whip withdrawn'.

"Democracy is the recurrent suspicion that more than half of the people are right more than half of the time."

E B WHITE *New Yorker* 3 July 1944

whiplash injury damage to the neck vertebrae and their attachments caused by a sudden backward jerk of the head and neck. It is most often seen in vehicle occupants as a result of the rapid deceleration experienced in a crash.

whippet breed of dog resembling a small greyhound. It grows to 56 cm/22 in at the shoulder, and 9 kg/20 lb in weight. The whippet was developed by northern English coalminers for racing. It was probably produced by crossing a terrier and a greyhound.

Whipple George Hoyt 1878–1976. US physiologist whose research interest concerned the formation of haemoglobin in the blood. He showed that anaemic dogs, kept under restricted diets, responded well to a liver regime, and that their haemoglobin quickly regenerated. This work led to a cure for pernicious anaemia. He shared the 1934 Nobel Prize for Physiology or Medicine with George Minot (1885–1950) and William Murphy (1892–1987).

whippoorwill North American ◊nightjar *Caprimulgus vociferus*, order Caprimulgiformes, so called from its cry during the nights of its breeding season. It is about 25 cm/10 in long, mottled tawny brown in colour, with a white collar on the throat, and long, stiff bristles at the base of the bill.

whip snake or ***coachwhip*** any of the various species of nonpoisonous slender-bodied tree-dwelling snakes of the New World genus *Masticophis*, family Colubridae. They are closely allied to members of the genus *Coluber* of SW North America, Eurasia, Australasia, and N Africa, some of which are called whip snakes in the Old World, but racers in North America. Whip snakes grow to about 1.5 m/5 ft in length, move very quickly, and are partially tree-dwelling.

"Virtue is, anyway, frequently in the nature of an iceberg, the other parts of it submerged."

PATRICK WHITE *The Tree of Man*

whirlwind rapidly rotating column of air, often synonymous with a ◊tornado. On a smaller scale it produces the dust-devils seen in deserts.

whisky or ***whiskey*** (Gaelic *uisge beatha* 'water of life') distilled spirit made from cereals: Scotch whisky from malted barley, Irish whiskey usually from barley, and North American whiskey and bourbon from maize and rye. Scotch is usually blended; pure malt whisky is more expensive. Whisky is generally aged in wooden casks for 4–12 years.

The spelling 'whisky' usually refers to Scotch or Canadian drink and 'whiskey' to Irish or American. The earliest written record of whisky comes from Scotland 1494 but the art of distillation is thought to have been known before this time.

whist card game for four, predecessor of ◊bridge, in which the partners try to win a majority of the 13 tricks (the highest card played being the winner of the trick).

Whistler James Abbott McNeill 1834–1903. US painter and etcher. Active in London from 1859, he was a leading figure in the ◊Aesthetic Movement. Influenced by Japanese prints, he painted riverscapes and portraits that show subtle composition and colour harmonies, for example *Arrangement in Grey and Black: Portrait of the Painter's Mother* 1871 (Musée d'Orsay, Paris). The delicacy of his work is best seen in his etchings, lithographs, pastels, and watercolours. His 'Peacock Room' 1876–77 for the London home of a Liverpool shipping magnate was an original departure in interior decoration (reconstruction in Freer Gallery, Washington DC).

Whitbread Literary Award literary prize open to writers in the UK and Ireland. *See list of tables on p. 1177.*

Whitby port and resort in North Yorkshire, England, on the North Sea coast; population (1991) 13,600. Industries include boat building, fishing, and plastics. The town is known for its jet, and has potash reserves which run under the sea. Remains of a Benedictine abbey built 1078 survive on the site of the original foundation by St Hilda 657, which was destroyed by the Danes 867. Capt Cook's ship *Resolution* was built in Whitby, where he had served his apprenticeship, and he sailed from here on his voyage to the Pacific Ocean 1768; there is a Capt Cook Memorial Museum. Bram Stoker's *Dracula* (1897) was set here.

Whitby, Synod of council summoned by King Oswy of Northumbria 664, which decided to adopt the Roman rather than the Celtic form of Christianity for Britain.

White counter-revolutionary, especially during the Russian civil wars 1917–21. Originally the term described the party opposing the French Revolution, when the royalists used the white lily of the French monarchy as their badge.

White E(lwyn) B(rooks) 1899–1985. US writer. He was long associated with the *New Yorker* magazine and renowned for his satire, such as *Is Sex Necessary?* 1929 (with the humorist James Thurber). White also wrote two children's classics, *Stuart Little* 1945 and *Charlotte's Web* 1952.

White Gilbert 1720–1793. English naturalist and cleric. He was the author of *The Natural History and Antiquities of Selborne* 1789, which records the flora and fauna of an area of Hampshire.

White Patrick Victor Martindale 1912–1990. Australian writer. His partly allegorical novels explore the lives of early settlers in Australia and often deal with misfits or inarticulate people. They include *The Aunt's Story* 1948, *The Tree of Man* 1955, and *Voss* 1957 (based on the ill-fated 19th-century explorer Friedrich Leichhardt (1813–1848)). Nobel Prize for Literature 1973.

White Australia Policy Australian government policy of immigration restriction, mainly aimed at non-Europeans, which began in the 1850s in an attempt to limit the number of Chinese entering the Australian goldfields and was official until 1945.

whitebait any of the fry (young) of various silvery fishes, especially ◊herring. It is also the name for a Pacific smelt *Osmerus mordax*.

whitebeam tree *Sorbus aria*, native to S Europe, usually found growing on chalk or limestone. It can reach 20 m/60 ft. It takes its name from the pinnately compound leaves, which have a dense coat of short white hairs on the underside.

white blood cell or ***leucocyte*** one of a number of different cells that play a part in the body's defences and give immunity against disease. Some (◊phagocytes and ◊macrophages) engulf invading microorganisms, others kill infected cells, while ◊lymphocytes produce more specific immune responses. White blood cells are colourless, with clear or granulated cytoplasm, and are capable of independent amoeboid movement. They occur in the blood, ◊lymph, and elsewhere in the body's tissues. Unlike mammalian red blood cells, they possess a nucleus. Human blood contains about 11,000 leucocytes to the cubic millimetre – about one to every 500 red cells.

white-collar worker non-manual employee, such as an office worker or manager. With more mechanized production methods, the distinction between white- and blue-collar (manual) workers is becoming increasingly blurred.

white dwarf small, hot ◊star, the last stage in the life of a star such as the Sun. White dwarfs make up 10% of the stars in the Galaxy; most have a mass 60% of that of the Sun, but only 1% of the Sun's diameter, similar in size to the Earth. Most have surface temperatures of 8,000°C/14,400°F or more, hotter than the Sun. Yet, being so small, their overall luminosities may be less than 1% of that of the Sun. The Milky Way contains an estimated 50 billion white dwarfs.

White dwarfs consist of degenerate matter in which gravity has packed the protons and electrons together as tightly as is physically possible, so that a spoonful of it weighs several tonnes. They slowly cool and fade over billions of years.

whitefish any of various freshwater fishes, genera *Coregonus* and *Prosopium* of the salmon family, found in lakes and rivers of North America and Eurasia. They include the whitefish *C. clupeaformis* and cisco *C. artedi*. The three species found in Britain are the gwyniad *C. pennantii*, found in Bala Lake, Wales; powan *C. lavaretus*, and vendace *C. gracilior*, found in lakes in NW England.

Whitehall street in central London, England, between Trafalgar Square and the Houses of Parliament, with many government offices and the Cenotaph war memorial.

Whitehaven town and port in Cumbria, NW England, on the Irish Sea coast; population (1991) 26,500. Industries include chemicals, printing, textiles, and food processing. Britain's first nuclear power station was sited at Calder Hall to the SE, where there is also a plant for reprocessing spent nuclear fuel at ◊Sellafield.

Whitehead Alfred North 1861–1947. English philosopher and mathematician. In his 'theory of organism', he attempted a synthesis of metaphysics

Whitman US poet Walt Whitman, whose breaking away from conventional form made him one of the most influential writers of his generation. The main themes in his poetry include the sacredness of the self, the beauty of death, the equality of all people, brotherly love, and the immortality of the soul. *Sachem*

and science. His works include *Principia Mathematica* 1910–13 (with Bertrand ◊Russell), *The Concept of Nature* 1920, and *Adventures of Ideas* 1933.

Whitehorse capital of Yukon Territory, Canada; population (1986) 15,199. Whitehorse is on the NW Highway. It replaced Dawson as capital 1953.

White Horse any of several hill figures in England, including the one on Bratton Hill, Wiltshire, said to commemorate Alfred the Great's victory over the Danes at Ethandun 878; and the one at Uffington, Berkshire, 110 m/360 ft long, and probably a tribal totem of the late Bronze Age.

White House official residence of the president of the USA, in Washington DC. It is a plain edifice of sandstone, built in Italian Renaissance style 1792–99 to the designs of James Hoban, who also restored it after it was burned by the British 1814; it was then painted white to hide the scars.

Whitehouse Mary 1910– . British media activist. A founder of the National Viewers' and Listeners' Association, she has campaigned to censor radio and television for their treatment of sex and violence.

Whitelaw William Stephen Ian, 1st Viscount Whitelaw 1918– . British Conservative politician. As secretary of state for Northern Ireland he introduced the concept of power sharing. He was chief Conservative whip 1964–70, and leader of the House of Commons 1970–72. He became secretary of state for employment 1973–74, but failed to conciliate the trade unions. He was chair of the Conservative Party 1974 and home secretary 1979–83, when he was made a peer. He resigned 1988.

Whiteman Paul 1890–1967. US dance-band and swing-orchestra leader. He specialized in 'symphonic jazz'. He commissioned George Gershwin's *Rhapsody in Blue*, conducting its premiere 1924.

whiteout 'fog' of grains of dry snow caused by strong winds in temperatures of between −18°C/0°F and −1°C/30°F. The uniform whiteness of the ground and air causes disorientation in humans.

White Paper in the UK and some other countries, an official document that expresses government policy on an issue. It is usually preparatory to the introduction of a parliamentary bill (a proposed act of Parliament).

Whiteread Rachel 1963– . British sculptor. Her most characteristic works are casts of empty spaces, such as the inside of a wardrobe, or the space under a chair. In 1993 she won the Turner Prize for art with a piece called *House*, the cast made of the inside of an entire house. She has also designed a monument to Austrian Jews who died in the Holocaust, to be set up in the Judenplatz, Vienna.

White Sea (Russian ***Beloye More***) gulf of the Arctic Ocean, on which the port of Archangel stands. There is a warship construction base, including nuclear submarines, at Severodvinsk. The North Dvina and Onega rivers flow into it, and there are canal links with the Baltic, Black, and Caspian seas.

white spirit colourless liquid derived from petrol; it is used as a solvent and in paints and varnishes.

whitethroat any of several Old World warblers of the genus *Sylvia* in the family Muscicapidae, order Passeriformes. They are found in scrub, hedges, and wood clearings of Eurasia in summer, migrating to Africa in winter. They are about 14 cm/5.5 in long.

whiting predatory fish *Merlangius merlangus* common in shallow sandy N European waters. It grows to 70 cm/2.3 ft.

Whitlam (Edward) Gough 1916– . Australian politician, leader of the Labor Party 1967–78 and prime minister 1972–75. He cultivated closer relations with Asia, attempted redistribution of wealth, and raised loans to increase national ownership of industry and resources.

When the opposition blocked finance bills in the Senate, following a crisis of confidence, Whitlam refused to call a general election, and was dismissed by the governor general (Sir John Kerr). He was defeated in the subsequent general election by Malcolm ◊Fraser.

Who, the English rock group the Who. Originally a London mod band of the 1960s, the Who established themselves worldwide with songs of teenage rebellion and defiance, such as 'My Generation' 1966, and a wild and destructive stage act. *Topham*

Whitman Walt(er) 1819–1892. US poet. He published *Leaves of Grass* 1855, which contains the symbolic 'Song of Myself'. It used unconventional free verse (with no rhyme or regular rhythm) and scandalized the public by its frank celebration of sexuality. In 1865 he published *Drum-Taps*, a volume inspired by his work as an army nurse during the Civil War. *Democratic Vistas* 1871 is a collection of his prose pieces. He also wrote an elegy for Abraham Lincoln, 'When Lilacs Last in the Dooryard Bloom'd'. He preached a particularly American vision of individual freedom and human brotherhood. Such poets as Ezra Pound, Wallace Stevens, and Allen Ginsberg show his influence in their work.

Whitney Eli 1765–1825. US inventor who in 1794 patented the cotton gin, a device for separating cotton fibre from its seeds. Also a manufacturer of firearms, he created a standardization system that was the precursor of the assembly line.

Whitstable resort in Kent, SE England, at the mouth of the river Swale, noted for its oysters; population (1991) 28,900.

Whit Sunday Christian church festival held seven weeks after Easter, commemorating the descent of the Holy Spirit on the Apostles. The name is probably derived from the white garments worn by candidates for baptism at the festival. Whit Sunday corresponds to the Jewish festival of Shavuot (Pentecost).

Whittier John Greenleaf 1807–1892. US poet. He was a powerful opponent of slavery, as shown in the verse *Voices of Freedom* 1846. Among his other works are *Legends of New England in Prose and Verse, Songs of Labor* 1850, and the New England nature poem 'Snow-Bound' 1866.

Whittington Dick (Richard) c. 1358–1423. English cloth merchant who was mayor of London 1397–98, 1406–07, and 1419–20. According to legend, he came to London as a poor boy with his cat when he heard that the streets were paved with gold and silver. His cat first appears in a play from 1605.

Whittle Frank 1907–1996. British engineer. He patented the basic design for the turbojet engine 1930. In the Royal Air Force he worked on jet propulsion 1937–46. In May 1941 the Gloster E 28/39 aircraft first flew with the Whittle jet engine. Both the German (first operational jet planes) and the US jet aircraft were built using his principles. Knighted 1948.

WHO acronym for ◊***World Health Organization***.

Who, the English rock group, formed 1964, with a hard, aggressive sound, high harmonies, and a propensity for destroying their instruments on stage. Their albums include *Tommy* 1969, *Who's Next* 1971, and *Quadrophenia* 1973.

whooping cough or ***pertussis*** acute infectious disease, seen mainly in children, caused by colonization of the air passages by the bacterium *Bordetella pertussis*. There may be catarrh, mild fever, and loss of appetite, but the main symptom is violent coughing, associated with the sharp intake of breath that is the characteristic 'whoop', and often followed by vomiting and severe nose bleeds. The cough may persist for weeks. Immunization lessens the incidence and severity of the disease.

whortleberry a form of ◊bilberry.

Whyalla port and industrial city (iron and steel) in South Australia; population (1994) 24,650.

whydah any of various African birds of the genus *Vidua*, order Passeriformes, of the weaver family. They lay their eggs in the nests of waxbills, which rear the young. Males have long tail feathers used in courtship displays.

Whymper Edward 1840–1911. English mountaineer. He made the first ascent of many Alpine peaks, including the Matterhorn 1865, and in the Andes scaled Chimborazo and other mountains.

Wick fishing port and industrial town (shipping, distilleries, knitwear, North Sea oil) in NE Scotland, in Highland Region; population about 8,000. Air services to the Orkney and Shetland islands operate from here. An opera house at 15th-century Ackergill Tower opened 1994.

wickerwork furniture or other objects made from flexible rods or shoots, usually willow, as developed from stake-frame basketry. It is made by weaving strands in and out of a wicker frame.

Wickerwork stools were made in ancient Rome and Egypt. Examples dating from the 3rd millennium BC have been found in Egyptian tombs. The

'I believe a leaf of grass is no less than the journey-work of the stars.'

WALT WHITMAN
'Song of Myself'

'Walt Whitman who laid end to end words never seen in each other's company before outside of a dictionary.'

On WALT WHITMAN
David Lodge
Changing Places

whydah During the breeding season the male paradise whydah has elongated black tail feathers 28 cm/11 in long. The paradise whydah lives in dry bush country in central Africa.

Once you bring life into the world, you must protect it. We must protect it by changing the world.

ELIE WIESEL
In *Writers at Work* ed G Plimpton

form of basket tub chair popular today may date from before the Middle Ages, and a circular wickerwork screen is shown in a painting c. 1420–30 of the Virgin and Child by the Netherlandish painter Robert Campin (National Gallery, London). Wills dating from the 16th and 17th centuries refer to wickerwork chairs in the houses of the nobility. The craft was revived in Leicester, England, 1910.

Wicklow county of the Republic of Ireland, in the province of Leinster; county town Wicklow; area 2,030 sq km/784 sq mi; population (1991) 97,300. It has the Wicklow Mountains, the rivers Slaney and Liffey, and the coastal resort Bray. The village of Shillelagh gave its name to rough cudgels of oak or blackthorn made there. The main occupation is agriculture.

Wicklow port and county town of County Wicklow, Republic of Ireland; population (1991) 5,800.

wide-angle lens photographic lens of shorter focal length than normal, taking in a wider angle of view.

wide area network in computing, a ◊network that connects computers distributed over a wide geographical area.

Wieland Christoph Martin 1733–1813. German poet and novelist. After attempts at religious poetry, he came under the influence of Voltaire and Rousseau, and wrote novels such as *Die Geschichte des Agathon/The History of Agathon* 1766–67 and the satirical *Die Abderiten* 1774 (translated as *The Republic of Fools* 1861); and tales in verse such as *Musarion oder Die Philosophie der Grazien* 1768, *Oberon* 1780, and others. He translated Shakespeare into German 1762–66.

Wiene Robert 1881–1938. German film director. His reputation rests solely on a single film, the exceptional psychological horror film *Das Kabinett des Dr Caligari/The Cabinet of Dr Caligari* 1919. Its stylized Expressionist design suggests a disturbed world in which the story of murder and madness takes place.

If you are not too long, I will wait here for you all my life.

OSCAR WILDE
The Importance of Being Earnest

Wiener Norbert 1894–1964. US mathematician, credited with the establishment of the science of cybernetics in his book *Cybernetics* 1948. In mathematics, he laid the foundation of the study of stochastic processes (those dependent on random events), particularly Brownian motion (the continuous random motion of particles in a fluid medium).

Wiener Werkstätte (German *'Vienna Workshops'*) group of artisans and artists, founded in Vienna 1903 by Josef Hoffmann and Kolo Moser, who were both members of the Vienna ◊Sezession. They designed objects, ranging from furniture and jewellery to metal and books, in a rectilinear Art Nouveau style influenced by Charles Rennie ◊Mackintosh. The workshop, financed by Fritz Wärndorfer, closed 1932.

Wien's displacement law in physics, a law of radiation stating that the wavelength carrying the maximum energy is inversely proportional to the absolute temperature of a black body (a hypothetical object that completely absorbs all electromagnetic radiation striking it): the hotter a body is, the shorter the wavelength. It has the form $\lambda_{max}T$ = constant, where λ_{max} is the wavelength of maximum intensity and T is the temperature. The law is named after German physicist Wilhelm Wien.

Wiesel Elie (Eliezer) 1928– . US academic and human-rights campaigner, born in Romania. He was held in Buchenwald concentration camp during World War II, and has assiduously documented wartime atrocities against the Jews in an effort to alert the world to the dangers of racism and violence. Nobel Peace Prize 1986.

Marriage is a bribe to make a housekeeper think she's a householder.

THORNTON WILDER
The Matchmaker

Wigan industrial town (food processing, engineering, paper) in Greater Manchester, NW England; population (1988 est) 307,600. The Wigan Alps are a recreation area with ski slopes and water sports created from industrial dereliction including colliery spoil heaps. Wigan Pier was made famous by the writer George Orwell in *The Road to Wigan Pier* 1932.

wigeon either of two species of dabbling duck of genus *Anas*, order Anseriformes. The Eurasian wigeon *A. penelope* is about 45 cm/18 in long. The male has a red-brown head with a cream crown, greyish-pink breast and white beneath. The bill is blue-grey. The female is brown with a white belly and shoulders. The wigeon breeds in N Eurasia, and winters in Africa or S Asia.

Wight, Isle of island and unitary authority of S England

area 380 sq km/147 sq mi (*see United Kingdom map*)

towns and cities Newport (administrative headquarters), resorts: Ryde, Sandown, Shanklin, Ventnor

features the Needles, a group of pointed chalk rocks up to 30 m/100 ft high in the sea to the west; the Solent, the sea channel between Hampshire and the island (including the anchorage of Spithead opposite Portsmouth, used for naval reviews); Cowes, venue of Regatta Week and headquarters of the Royal Yacht Squadron; Osborne House (1845), near Cowes, a home of Queen Victoria; Farringford, home of the poet Alfred Tennyson, near Freshwater

industries chiefly agricultural; shipbuilding; tourism

population (1991) 124,600

famous people Robert Hooke, Thomas Arnold

history called *Vectis* ('separate division') by the Romans, who conquered it AD 43. Charles I was imprisoned 1647–48 in Carisbrooke Castle, now ruined.

Wightman Cup annual tennis competition between international women's teams from the USA and the UK. The trophy, first contested 1923, was donated by Hazel Hotchkiss Wightman (1886–1974), a former US tennis player who won singles, doubles, and mixed-doubles titles in the US Championships 1909–1911. Because of US domination of the contest it was abandoned 1990, but was reinstated 1991 with the UK side assisted by European players.

Wilander Mats 1964– . Swedish lawn-tennis player. He won his first Grand Slam event 1982 when he beat Guillermo Vilas to win the French Open, and had won eight Grand Slam titles by 1990. He played a prominent role in Sweden's rise to the forefront of men's tennis in the 1980s, including Davis Cup successes.

Wilberforce William 1759–1833. English reformer. He was instrumental in abolishing slavery in the British Empire. He entered Parliament 1780; in 1807 his bill for the abolition of the slave trade was passed, and in 1833, largely through his efforts, slavery was abolished throughout the empire. ▷ *See feature on pp. 982–983.*

Wilbur Richard Purdy 1921– . US poet. He is noted for his cultural conservatism, urbane wit, and the elegance of his verse in such volumes as *The Beautiful Changes* 1947 and *Things of This World* 1956. He also published children's verse, as in *Loudmouse* 1963 and *Opposites* 1973.

Wilde Cornel(ius Louis) 1915–1989. Austrian-born US actor and film director. He worked in the USA from 1932. He starred as the composer and pianist Chopin in *A Song to Remember* 1945, and directed *The Naked Prey* 1966, *Beach Red* 1967, and *No Blade of Grass* 1970, among other films.

Wilde Oscar (Fingal O'Flahertie Wills) 1854–1900. Irish writer. With his flamboyant style and quotable conversation, he dazzled London society and, on his lecture tour 1882, the USA. He published his only novel, *The Picture of Dorian Gray*, 1891, followed by a series of sharp comedies, including *A Woman of No Importance* 1893 and *The Importance of Being Earnest* 1895. In 1895 he was imprisoned for two years for homosexual offences; he died in exile.

Wilde was born in Dublin and studied at Dublin and Oxford, where he became known as a supporter of the Aesthetic movement ('art for art's sake'). He published *Poems* 1881, and also wrote fairy tales and other stories, criticism, and a long, anarchic political essay, 'The Soul of Man Under Socialism' 1891. His elegant social comedies include *Lady Windermere's Fan* 1892 and *An Ideal Husband* 1895. The drama *Salome* 1893, based on the biblical character, was written in French; considered scandalous by the British censor, it was first performed in Paris 1896 with the actress Sarah Bernhardt in the title role.

Among his lovers was Lord Alfred ◊Douglas, whose father provoked Wilde into a lawsuit that led to his social and financial ruin and imprisonment. The long poem *Ballad of Reading Gaol* 1898 and a letter published as *De Profundis* 1905 were written in jail to explain his side of the relationship. After his release from prison 1897, he lived in France; he was buried in Père Lachaise cemetery, Paris.

Wilde Irish writer Oscar Wilde, who was a leading figure of the Aesthetic movement – 'art for art's sake'. His only novel *The Picture of Dorian Gray* scandalized readers when it first appeared, but Wilde claimed, 'There is no such thing as a moral or an immoral book. Books are well written or badly written. That is all'. *Corbis*

wildebeest another name for ◊gnu.

Wilder Billy (Samuel) 1906– . Austrian-born accomplished US screenwriter and film director. He directed and co-scripted the cynical *Double Indemnity* 1944, *The Lost Weekend* (Academy Award for best director) 1945, *Sunset Boulevard* 1950, *Some Like It Hot* 1959, and *The Apartment* (Academy Award) 1960.

Wilder Thornton Niven 1897–1975. US dramatist and novelist. He won Pulitzer prizes for the novel *The Bridge of San Luis Rey* 1927 and for the plays *Our Town* 1938 and *The Skin of Our Teeth* 1942. His farce *The Matchmaker* 1954 was filmed 1958. In 1964 it was adapted into the hit stage musical *Hello, Dolly!*, also made into a film. His plays are overtly philosophical, they generally employ no props or scenery, and the characters often directly address the audience.

wilderness area of uninhabited land that has never been disturbed by humans, usually located some distance from towns and cities. According to estimates by US group Conservation International, 52% (90 million sq km/35 million sq mi) of the Earth's total land area was still undisturbed 1994.

wildlife trade international trade in live plants and animals, and in wildlife products such as skins, horns, shells, and feathers. The trade has made some species virtually extinct, and whole ecosystems (for example, coral reefs) are threatened. Wildlife trade is to some extent regulated by ◊CITES (Convention on International Trade in Endangered Species).

Species almost eradicated by trade in their products include many of the largest whales, crocodiles, marine turtles, and some wild cats. Until recently, some 2 million snake skins were exported from India every year. Populations of black rhino and African elephant have collapsed because of hunting for their horns and tusks (◊ivory), and poaching remains a problem in cases where trade is prohibited.

wild type in genetics, the naturally occurring gene for a particular character that is typical of most individuals of a given species, as distinct from new genes that arise by mutation.

Wilfrid, St 634–709. Northumbrian-born bishop of York from 665. He defended the cause of the Roman Church at the Synod of ◊Whitby 664 against that of Celtic Christianity. Feast day 12 Oct.

Wilkes John 1727–1797. British Radical politician, imprisoned for his political views; member of Parliament 1757–64 and from 1774. He championed parliamentary reform, religious toleration, and US independence.

His attacks on the Tory prime minister Bute in his paper *The North Briton* led to his being outlawed 1764; he fled to France, and on his return 1768 was imprisoned. In 1774 he was allowed to take his seat in Parliament.

Wilkins George Hubert 1888–1958. Australian polar explorer, a pioneer in the use of surveys by both aircraft and submarines. In 1928 he flew from Barrow (Alaska) to Green Harbour (Spitsbergen), and in 1928–29 made an Antarctic flight that proved that Graham Land is an island. He also planned to reach the North Pole by submarine.

Wilkins Maurice Hugh Frederick 1916– . New Zealand-born British molecular biologist. In 1962 he shared the Nobel Prize for Physiology or Medicine with Francis ◊Crick and James ◊Watson for his work on the molecular structure of nucleic acids, particularly ◊DNA, using X-ray diffraction.

Wilkins William 1778–1839. English architect. He pioneered the Greek Revival in England with his design for Downing College, Cambridge, 1807–20. Other works include the main block of University College London 1827–28, and the National Gallery, London, 1834–38.

will in law, declaration of how a person wishes his or her property to be disposed of after death. It also appoints administrators of the estate (◊executors) and may contain wishes on other matters, such as place of burial or use of organs for transplant. Wills must comply with formal legal requirements of the local jurisdiction. Some US states permit people, usually the terminally ill, to specify at what stage they should be allowed to die, in a living will (a written declaration of a person's wishes regarding medical treatment if in the future he or she should become too ill to communicate).

In English law wills must be in writing, signed by the testator (the person making the will) in the presence of two witnesses who must also sign, and who may not be beneficiaries under the will. Wills cannot be made by minors or the mentally incapable. There are exceptions in formalities for members of the armed forces on active service, who can make a will in any clear form and when under 18. Additions or changes can be made to a will by a codicil, which is a document supplementary to an existing will.

William (full name William Arthur Philip Louis) 1982– . Prince of the UK, first child of the Prince and Princess of Wales.

William (I) the Conqueror c. 1027–1087. King of England from 1066. He was the illegitimate son of Duke Robert the Devil and succeeded his father as duke of Normandy 1035. Claiming that his relative King Edward the Confessor had bequeathed him the English throne, William invaded the country 1066, defeating ◊Harold II at Hastings, Sussex, and was crowned king of England on Christmas Day. He completed the establishment of feudalism in England, compiling detailed records of land and property in the Domesday Book, and kept the barons firmly under control. He died in Rouen after a fall from his horse and is buried in Caen, France. He was succeeded by his son William II.

William (II) Rufus ('the Red') c. 1056–1100. King of England from 1087, the third son of William the Conqueror. He spent most of his reign attempting to capture Normandy from his brother ◊Robert II, Duke of Normandy. His extortion of money led his barons to revolt and caused confrontation with Bishop Anselm. He was killed while hunting in the New Forest, Hampshire, and was succeeded by his brother Henry I.

William (III) of Orange 1650–1702. King of Great Britain and Ireland from 1688, the son of William II of Orange and Mary, daughter of Charles I. He was offered the English crown by the parliamentary opposition to James II. He invaded England 1688 and in 1689 became joint sovereign with his wife, ◊Mary II. He spent much of his reign campaigning, first in Ireland, where he defeated James II at the battle of the Boyne 1690, and later against the French in Flanders. He was succeeded by Mary's sister, Anne.

Born in the Netherlands, William was made *stadtholder* (chief magistrate) 1672 to resist the French invasion. He forced Louis XIV to make peace 1678 and then concentrated on building up a European alliance against France. In 1677 he married his cousin Mary, daughter of the future James II. When invited by both Whig and Tory leaders to take the crown from James, he landed with a large force at Torbay, Devon. James fled to France, and his Scottish and Irish supporters were defeated at the battles of Dunkeld 1689 and the Boyne 1690.

William IV 1765–1837. King of Great Britain and Ireland from 1830, when he succeeded his brother George IV; third son of George III. He was created duke of Clarence 1789, and married Adelaide of Saxe-Meiningen (1792–1849) 1818. During the Reform Bill crisis he secured its passage by agreeing to create new peers to overcome the hostile majority in the House of Lords. He was succeeded by Victoria.

William I 1797–1888. King of Prussia from 1861 and emperor of Germany from 1871; the son of Friedrich Wilhelm III. He served in the Napoleonic Wars 1814–15 and helped to crush the 1848 revolution. After he succeeded his brother Friedrich Wilhelm IV to the throne of Prussia, his policy was largely dictated by his chancellor ◊Bismarck, who secured his proclamation as emperor.

William II (German ***Wilhelm II***) 1859–1941. Emperor of Germany from 1888, the son of Frederick III and Victoria, daughter of Queen Victoria of Britain. In 1890 he forced Chancellor Bismarck to resign and began to direct foreign policy himself, which proved disastrous. He encouraged warlike policies and built up the German navy. In 1914 he first approved Austria's ultimatum to Serbia and then, when he realized war was inevitable, tried in vain to prevent it. In 1918 he fled to Holland, after Germany's defeat and his abdication.

William I 1772–1844. King of the Netherlands 1815–40. He lived in exile during the French occupation 1795–1813 and fought against the emperor Napoleon at Jena and Wagram. The Austrian Netherlands were added to his kingdom by the Allies 1815, but secured independence (recognized by the major European states 1839) by the revolution of 1830. William's unpopularity led to his abdication 1840.

William II 1792–1849. King of the Netherlands 1840–49, son of William I. He served with the British army in the Peninsular War and at Waterloo. In 1848 he averted revolution by conceding a liberal constitution.

William III 1817–1890. King of the Netherlands 1849–90, the son of William II. In 1862 he abolished slavery in the Dutch East Indies.

William the Lion 1143–1214. King of Scotland from 1165. He was captured by Henry II while invading England 1174, and forced to do homage, but Richard I abandoned the English claim to suzerainty for a money payment 1189. In 1209 William was forced by King John to renounce his claim to Northumberland.

William the Silent 1533–1584. Prince of Orange from 1544. Leading a revolt against Spanish rule in the Netherlands from 1573, he briefly succeeded in uniting the Catholic south and Protestant northern provinces, but the former provinces submitted to Spain while the latter formed a federation 1579 (Union of Utrecht) which repudiated Spanish suzerainty 1581.

William, brought up at the court of Charles V, was appointed governor of Holland by Philip II of Spain 1559, but joined the revolt of 1572 against Spain's oppressive rule and, as a Protestant from 1573, became the national leader and first *stadtholder* (the title of the chief magistrate of the United Provinces of the Netherlands). He was known as 'the Silent' because of his absolute discretion. He was assassinated by a Spanish agent.

William of Malmesbury c. 1080–c. 1143. English historian and monk. He compiled the *Gesta regum/Deeds of the Kings* c.1120–40 and *Historia novella*, which together formed a history of England to 1142.

William of Wykeham c. 1323–1404. English politician, bishop of Winchester from 1367, Lord Chancellor 1367–72 and 1389–91, and founder of Winchester College (public school) 1378 and New College, Oxford 1379.

Williams British racing-car manufacturing company started by Frank Williams 1969 when he modified a Brabham BT26A. The first Williams Grand Prix car was designed by Patrick Head 1978 and since then the team has been one of the most successful in Grand Prix racing.

Australian driver Alan Jones won the World Drivers Championship in a Williams 1979; other champions have been Keke Rosberg 1981 and Nelson Piquet 1987. The team won the drivers' championship 1980, 1982, 1987, 1992 and 1993, and the constructors' championship 1980–81, 1986–87, 1992–94, and 1996.

Williams (George) Emlyn 1905–1987. Welsh actor and dramatist. His plays, in which he appeared, include *Night Must Fall* 1935 and *The Corn Is Green* 1938. He was also acclaimed for his solo performance as the author Charles Dickens.

Williams (Hiram) Hank 1923–1953. US country singer, songwriter, and guitarist. He was the author of dozens of country standards and one of the originators of modern country music. His songs are characteristically mournful and blues-influenced, like 'Your Cheatin' Heart' 1953, but also include the uptempo 'Jambalaya' 1952 and the proto-rockabilly 'Hey, Good-Lookin'' 1951.

Williams John Christopher 1942– . Australian guitarist, resident in London since 1952. After studying with Segovia, he made his formal debut 1958.

Williams J(ohn) P(eter) R(hys) 1949– . Welsh rugby union player. With 55 appearances for his country, he is Wales's most capped player. He played in three Grand Slam winning teams and twice toured with winning British Lions teams.

Williams Robbie (Robert Peter Maximilian) 1974– . English musician. He joined Take That at the age of 16 and stayed with the band 1990–1995. In 1996 he released his first solo single, 'Freedom '96'. He won six nominations for the 1999 Brit Awards.

Williams Roger c. 1603–1683. American colonist, founder of the Rhode Island colony 1636, based on democracy and complete religious freedom. He tried to maintain good relations with the Indians of the region, although he fought against them in the Pequot War and King Philip's War.

Williams Shirley Vivien Teresa Brittain, Baroness Williams of Crosby 1930– . British Liberal Democrat Party politician. She was Labour minister for prices and consumer protection 1974–76, and education and science 1976–79. She became a founder member of the SDP (Social Democrat Party) 1981, its president 1982, but lost her parliamentary seat 1983. In 1988 she joined the newly-merged Social and Liberal Democratic Party (SLDP).

Williams Tennessee (Thomas Lanier) 1911–1983. US dramatist. His work is characterized by fluent dialogue and searching analysis of the psychological deficiencies of his characters. His plays are usually set in the Deep South against a background of decadence and degradation, and include *The Glass Menagerie* 1945, *A Streetcar Named Desire* 1947, and *Cat on a Hot Tin Roof* 1955, the last two of which earned Pulitzer prizes.

Williams William Carlos 1883–1963. US poet, essayist, and

The chapter of accidents is the longest chapter in the book.

John Wilkes
Attributed remark

We're all of us guinea pigs in the laboratory of God. Humanity is just a work in progress.

Tennessee Williams
Camino Real

William (I) the Conqueror The Great Seal of William I, the Norman king who mounted the last successful conquest of England. He successfully subdued the country and imposed a new system of government dominated by an aristocratic Norman elite. *Philip Sauvain*

"Hence the practised performances of latter-day politicians in the game of musical daggers: never be left holding the dagger when the music stops."

HAROLD WILSON
The Governance of Britain

theoretician. He was associated with ◊Imagism and Objectivism (a loose association of US poets), and is noted for advancing poetics of visual images and colloquial American rhythms. His epic poem *Paterson* 1946–58 is written in a form of free verse that combines historical documents, newspaper material, and letters, to celebrate his home town in New Jersey. *Pictures from Brueghel* 1963 won him, posthumously, a Pulitzer prize. His vast body of prose work includes novels, short stories, essays, and the play *A Dream of Love* 1948.

Williamson David Keith 1942– . Australian dramatist and scriptwriter. He is noted for his witty fast-moving dialogue and realistic plots and settings. His plays include *The Removalists* 1971, which won awards in both Australia and in the UK, *Don's Party* 1971, *The Department* 1975, *The Club* 1977, *Travelling North* 1979, *The Perfectionist* 1981, and *Siren* 1990. Screenplays include *Stork* 1971, *Eliza Fraser* 1976, *Gallipoli* 1981, and *The Year of Living Dangerously* 1982 (co-writer).

Williamson Henry 1895–1977. English author. His stories of animal life include *Tarka the Otter* 1927. He described his experiences in restoring an old farm in *The Story of a Norfolk Farm* 1941 and wrote the fictional, 15-volume sequence *Chronicles of Ancient Sunlight*.

Williamson Malcolm Benjamin Graham Christopher 1931– . Australian composer, pianist, and organist. He settled in Britain 1953. His works include operas such as *Our Man in Havana* 1963, symphonies, and chamber music. He became Master of the Queen's Musick 1975.

Willis Norman David 1933– . British trade-union leader. A trade-union official since leaving school, he was the general secretary of the Trades Union Congress (TUC) 1984–93. He presided over the TUC at a time of falling union membership, hostile legislation from the Conservative government, and a major review of the role and policies of the Labour Party.

"No one can worship God or love his neighbour on an empty stomach."

WOODROW WILSON
Speech 1912

will-o'-the-wisp light sometimes seen over marshy ground, believed to be burning gas containing methane from decaying organic matter.

willow any tree or shrub of the genus *Salix*, family Salicaceae. There are over 350 species, mostly in the northern hemisphere, and they flourish in damp places. The leaves are often lance-shaped, and the male and female catkins are found on separate trees. Species include the ***crack willow*** *S. fragilis*, the ***white willow*** *S. alba*, the ***goat willow*** *S. caprea*, the ***weeping willow*** *S. babylonica*, native to China but cultivated worldwide, and the common ***osier*** *S. viminalis*.

willowherb any plant of either of two genera *Epilobium* and *Chamaenerion* of perennial weeds. The ***rosebay willowherb*** or ***fireweed*** *C. angustifolium* is common in woods and wasteland. It grows to 1.2 m/4 ft with long terminal racemes of red or purplish flowers.

willow warbler bird *Phylloscopus trochilus*, family Muscicapidae, order Passeriformes. It is about 11 cm/4 in long, similar in appearance to the chiffchaff, but with a distinctive song. It is found in woods and shrubberies, and migrates from N Eurasia to Africa.

Wills Bob (James Robert) 1905–1975. US country fiddle player and composer. As leader of the band known from 1934 as Bob Wills and his Texas Playboys, Wills became a pioneer of ◊Western swing and a big influence on US popular music. His songs include 'San Antonio Rose' 1938.

willow The willow tree is deciduous with simple leaves and small erect catkins. Willows are found throughout the world, except Australasia.

Wilson Angus Frank Johnstone 1913–1991. English novelist, short-story writer, and biographer. His acidly humorous books include *Anglo-Saxon Attitudes* 1956 and *The Old Men at the Zoo* 1961. In his detailed portrayal of English society he extracted high comedy from its social and moral grotesqueries.

Wilson Edward Osborne 1929– . US zoologist whose books have stimulated interest in biogeography, the study of the distribution of species, and sociobiology, the evolution of behaviour. He is a world authority on ants.

Wilson (James) Harold, Baron Wilson of Rievaulx 1916–1995. British Labour politician, party leader from 1963, prime minister 1964–70 and 1974–76. His premiership was dominated by the issue of UK admission to membership of the European Community (now the European Union), the social contract (unofficial agreement with the trade unions), and economic difficulties.

Wilson, born in Huddersfield, West Yorkshire, studied at Oxford, where he gained a first-class degree in philosophy, politics, and economics. During World War II he worked as a civil servant, and in 1945 stood for Parliament and won the marginal seat of Ormskirk. Assigned by Prime Minister Clement Attlee to a junior post in the Ministry of Works, he progressed to become president of the Board of Trade 1947–51 (when he resigned because of social-service cuts). In 1963 he succeeded Hugh Gaitskell as Labour leader and became prime minister the following year, increasing his majority 1966. He formed a minority government Feb 1974 and achieved a majority of three Oct 1974. He resigned 1976 and was succeeded by James Callaghan.

Wilson Henry Maitland ('Jumbo'), 1st Baron Wilson 1881–1964. British field marshal in World War II. He was commander in chief in Egypt 1939, led the unsuccessful Greek campaign of 1941, was commander in chief in the Middle East 1943, and in 1944 was supreme Allied commander in the Mediterranean.

Wilson Richard 1714–1782. Welsh painter. His landscapes, infused with an Italianate atmosphere, are painted in a Classical manner reminiscent of ◊Claude Lorrain. His work influenced the development of English landscape painting, and J M W ◊Turner in particular.

Wilson Teddy (Theodore Shaw) 1912–1986. US bandleader and jazz pianist. He toured with Benny Goodman 1935–39 and during that period recorded in small groups with many of the best musicians of the time; some of his 1930s recordings feature the singer Billie Holiday. Wilson led a big band 1939–40 and a sextet 1940–46.

Wilson (Thomas) Woodrow 1856–1924. 28th president of the USA 1913–21, a Democrat. He kept the USA out of World War I until 1917, and in Jan 1918 issued his 'Fourteen Points' as a basis for a just peace settlement. At the peace conference in Paris he secured the inclusion of the ◊League of Nations in individual peace treaties, but these were not ratified by Congress, so the USA did not join the League. Nobel Peace Prize 1919.

Wilson, born in Virginia, became president of Princeton University 1902. In 1910 he became governor of New Jersey. Elected president 1912 against Theodore Roosevelt and William Taft, he initiated anti-trust legislation and secured valuable social reforms in his progressive 'New Freedom' programme. He strove to keep the USA neutral during World War I but the German U-boat campaign forced him to declare war 1917. In 1919 he suffered a stroke from which he never fully recovered.

wilting the loss of rigidity (◊turgor) in plants, caused by a decreasing wall pressure within the cells making up the supportive tissues. Wilting is most obvious in plants that have little or no wood.

Wilton market town in Wiltshire, S England, outside Salisbury; population (1991) 3,700. It manufactured carpets from the 16th century until 1995, when the Wilton Royal Carpet Factory closed. Wilton House, the seat of the earls of Pembroke, was built from designs by Holbein and Inigo Jones, and is associated with Sir Philip Sidney and Shakespeare.

Wilson The 28th president of the USA, Democrat Woodrow Wilson. He won the presidential election on his neutrality in the face of World War I, but public sentiment kindled by U-boat attacks on the Allies forced him to enter the hostilities. *Image Select (UK) Ltd*

Wiltshire county of SW England (*see United Kingdom map*)
towns and cities Trowbridge (administrative headquarters), Salisbury, Wilton
features Marlborough Downs; Savernake Forest; rivers: Kennet, Wylye, Salisbury and Bristol Avons; Salisbury Plain, a military training area used since Napoleonic times; Longleat House (Marquess of Bath); Wilton House (Earl of Pembroke); Stourhead, with 18th-century gardens; Neolithic Stonehenge, Avebury stone circle, Silbury Hill, West Kennet Long Barrow, dating from the 3rd millennium BC
industries wheat, cattle, pig and sheep farming, rubber, engineering, clothing, brewing
famous people Christopher Wren, William Talbot, Isaac Pitman.

Wimbledon district of the Greater London borough of ◊Merton. The headquarters of the All-England Lawn Tennis and Croquet Club are here, and the Wimbledon Championships are played in June. On Wimbledon Common there is an Iron Age fort, Caesar's Camp, and a windmill where Robert ◊Baden-Powell wrote *Scouting for Boys*. Among its buildings are the Old Rectory (about 1500), Eagle House (1613), and the mid-17th century Rose and Crown public house.

Wimbledon English lawn-tennis centre used for international championship matches, situated in south London. There are currently 18 courts. The first centre was at Worple Road when it was the home of the All England Croquet Club. Tennis was first played there 1875, and in 1877 the club was renamed the All England Lawn Tennis and Croquet Club. The first all England championship was held in the same year. The club and championship moved to their present site in Church Road in 1922.

Martina ◊Navratilova won six successive women's titles at Wimbledon 1982–87; of the men Björn ◊Borg won five successive titles 1976–80, and William Renshaw won six 1881–86. The youngest winners are Boris ◊Becker 1985 and Martina Hingis 1997, both aged 17. The Wimbledon championship is one of the sport's four Grand Slam events; the others are the US Open, French Championships, and Australian Championships.

WIMP (acronym for ***windows, icons, menus, pointing device***) in computing, another name for ◊graphical user interface (GUI).

Winchester cathedral city and administrative headquarters of Hampshire, on the river Itchen; population (1991) 36,100. Tourism is important, and there is also light industry. Originally a Roman town, Winchester was capital of the Anglo-Saxon kingdom of Wessex, and later of England. The cathedral is the longest medieval church in Europe and was remodelled from Norman-Romanesque to Perpendicular Gothic under the patronage of William of Wykeham (founder of Winchester College), who is buried there, as are Saxon kings, St ◊Swithun, and the writers Izaac Walton and Jane Austen.

A tribal centre of the Britons under the name ***Caer Gwent*** and later one of the largest Roman settlements in Britain as ***Venta Belgarum***, the town become capital of Wessex 519 and under Alfred the Great and Canute was the seat of government. In 827 Egbert was crowned first king of all England here. Under William the Conqueror, Winchester was declared dual capital of England with London.

wind the lateral movement of the Earth's atmosphere from high-pressure areas (anticyclones) to low-pressure areas (depression). Its speed is measured using an ◊anemometer or by studying its effects on, for example, trees by using the ◊Beaufort scale. Although modified by features such as land and water, there is a basic worldwide system of ◊trade winds, ◊Westerlies, and polar easterlies.

A belt of low pressure (the ◊doldrums) lies along the equator. The ***trade winds*** blow towards this from the horse latitudes (areas of high pressure at about 30° N and 30° S of the equator), blowing from the NE in the northern hemisphere, and from the SE in the southern. The ***Westerlies*** (also from the horse latitudes) blow north of the equator from the SW and south of the equator from the NW.

Cold winds blow outwards from high-pressure areas at the poles. More local effects result from landmasses heating and cooling faster than the adjacent sea, producing onshore winds in the daytime and offshore winds at night.

The ◊monsoon is a seasonal wind of S Asia, blowing from the SW in summer and bringing the rain on which crops depend. It blows from the NE in winter.

Famous or notorious warm winds include the chinook of the eastern Rocky Mountains, North America; the *föhn* of Europe's Alpine valleys; the *sirocco* (Italy), *khamsin* (Egypt), *sharav* (Israel), spring winds that bring warm air from the Sahara and Arabian deserts across the Mediterranean; and the Santa Ana, a periodic warm wind from the inland deserts that strikes the California coast. The dry northerly bise (Switzerland) and the mistral, which strikes the Mediterranean area of France, are unpleasantly cold winds.

wind-chill factor or ***wind-chill index*** estimate of how much colder it feels when a wind is blowing. It is the sum of the temperature (in °F below zero) and the wind speed (in miles per hour). So for a wind of 15 mph at an air temperature of −5°F, the wind-chill factor is 20.

Windermere largest lake in England, in Cumbria, 17 km/10.5 mi long and 1.6 km/1 mi wide.

wind farm array of windmills or ◊wind turbines used for generating electrical power. A wind farm at Altamont Pass, California, USA, consists of 300 wind turbines, the smallest producing 60 kW and the largest 750 kW of electricity. Wind farms supply about 1.5% of California's electricity needs. To produce 1,200 megawatts of electricity (an output comparable with that of a nuclear power station), a wind farm would need to occupy around 370 sq km/140 sq mi. Denmark built the world's first offshore wind farm, off Vindeby on Lolland Island in the North Sea.

Windhoek capital of Namibia; population (1992) 126,000. It is just north of the Tropic of Capricorn, 290 km/180 mi from the west coast.

wind instrument musical instrument that is sounded by an airflow (the performer's breath) to make a column of air vibrate within a vented tubular resonator, sometimes activating a reed or reeds. The pitch of the note is controlled by the length of the column. Major types of wind instrument are the ◊voice; whistles, including the recorder and flute; reed instruments, including most other woodwinds; ◊brass instruments, including horns; and free-reed instruments, such as the mouth organ.

windmill mill with sails or vanes that, by the action of wind upon them, drive machinery for grinding corn or pumping water, for example. ◊Wind turbines, designed to use wind power on a large scale, usually have a propeller-type rotor mounted on a tall shell tower. The turbine drives a generator for producing electricity.

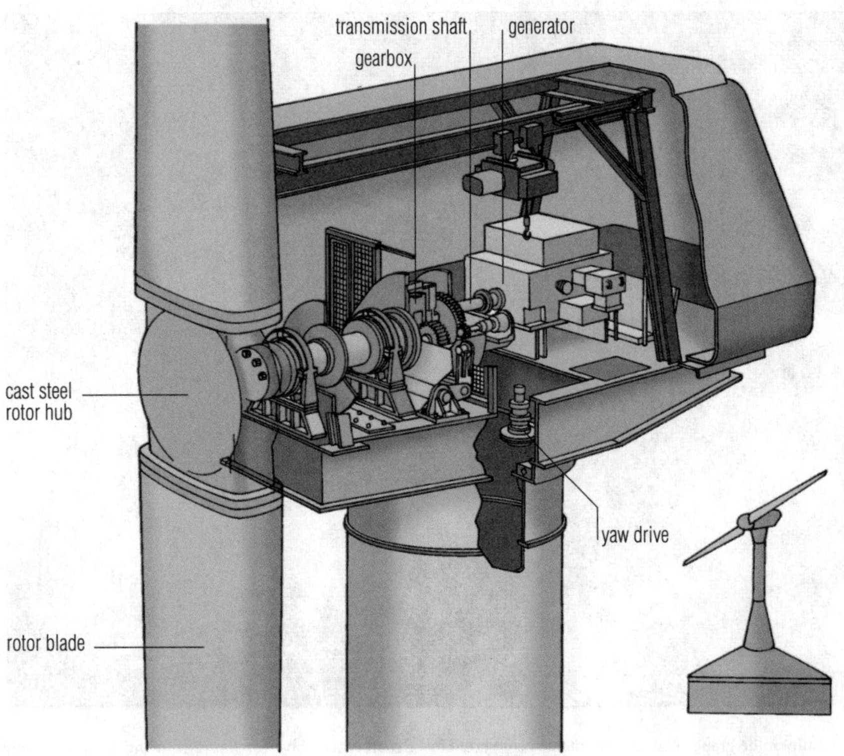

wind power The wind turbine is the modern counterpart of the windmill. The rotor blades are huge – up to 100 m/330 ft across – in order to extract as much energy as possible from the wind. Inside the turbine head, gears are used to increase the speed of the turning shaft so that the electricity generation is as efficient as possible.

Windmills were used in the East in ancient times, and in Europe they were first used in Germany and the Netherlands in the 12th century. The main types of traditional windmill are the ***post mill***, which is turned around a post when the direction of the wind changes, and the ***tower mill***, which has a revolving turret on top. It usually has a device (fantail) that keeps the sails pointing into the wind. In the USA windmills were used by the colonists and later a light type, with steel sails supported on a long steel girder shaft, was introduced for use on farms.

window in computing, a rectangular area on the screen of a ◊graphical user interface. A window is used to display data and can be manipulated in various ways by the computer user.

Windows ◊graphical user interface (GUI) from Microsoft that has become the standard for IBM PCs and clones. There are two versions of Windows: Windows 95, designed for homes and offices uses the ◊MS-DOS operating system; Windows NT is a 32-bit multiuser and ◊multitasking operating system, used by engineers, scientists, and other professions that require a high-processing capacity. Windows NT is seen as a rival to ◊UNIX.

wind power the harnessing of wind energy to produce power. The wind has long been used as a source of energy: sailing ships and windmills are ancient inventions. After the energy crisis of the 1970s ◊wind turbines began to be used to produce electricity on a large scale. ▷*See feature on pp. 360–361.*

Windscale former name of ◊Sellafield, a nuclear power station in Cumbria, England.

Windsor town in Berkshire, S England, on the river Thames; population (1991) 30,100. It is the site of Windsor Castle and Eton College (public school, 1540), and has a 17th-century guildhall designed by Christopher Wren.

Windsor Duchess of, title of Wallis Warfield ◊Simpson.

Windsor Duke of, title of ◊Edward VIII.

Windsor Castle British royal residence in Windsor, Berkshire, founded by William the Conqueror on the site of an earlier fortress. It includes the Perpendicular Gothic St George's Chapel and the Albert Memorial Chapel, beneath which George III, George IV, and William IV are buried. In the Home Park adjoining the castle is the Royal Mausoleum where Queen Victoria and Prince Albert are buried.

St George's is the chapel of the Order of the Garter. Beyond the Round Tower or Keep are the state apartments and the sovereign's private apartments. Windsor Great Park lies to the south. In 1990 the royal residence Frogmore House, near Windsor Castle, as well as the Royal Mausoleum, were opened to the public.

On 20 Nov 1992 the castle was heavily damaged by a fire in its 14th century St George's Hall. In April 1993 the Queen decided to open Buckingham Palace to the public to raise money for the necessary repair work.

Windsor, House of official name of the British royal family since 1917, adopted in place of Saxe-Coburg-Gotha. Since 1960 those descendants of Elizabeth II not entitled to the prefix HRH (His/Her Royal Highness) have borne the surname Mountbatten-Windsor.

windsurfing or ***boardsailing*** or ***sailboarding*** water sport combining elements of surfing and sailing, first developed in the USA 1968. The windsurfer stands on a board that is propelled and steered by means of a sail attached to a mast that is articulated at the foot. Since 1984 the sport has been included in the Olympic Games as part of the yachting events. From 1992 men and women have to compete in separate categories. There are also annual boardsailing world championships. *See illustration on following page.*

wind tunnel test tunnel in which air is blown over, for example, a stationary model aircraft, motor vehicle, or locomotive to simulate the effects of movement. Lift, drag, and airflow patterns are observed by the use of special cameras and sensitive instruments. Wind-tunnel testing assesses aerodynamic design, preparatory to full-scale construction.

wind turbine windmill of advanced aerodynamic design connected to an electricity generator and used in wind-power installations. Wind turbines can be either large propeller-type rotors mounted on a tall tower, or flexible metal strips fixed to a vertical axle at top and bottom. The world's largest wind turbine is on Hawaii, in the Pacific Ocean.

Worldwide, wind turbines on land produce only the energy equivalent of a single nuclear power station.

Windward Islands islands in the path of the prevailing wind, notably: West Indies (see ◊Antilles); ◊Cape Verde Islands; and ◊French Polynesia (Tahiti, Moorea, Makatea).

wine alcoholic beverage, usually made from fermented grape pulp, although wines have also traditionally been made from many other fruits such as damsons and elderberries. ***Red wine*** is the product of the grape with the skin; ***white wine*** of the inner

‘A good general rule is to state that the bouquet is better than the taste, and vice versa.’

On **WINE**
Stephen Potter
One-Upmanship

windsurfing A windsurfer. Windsurfing was developed in the USA 1968, and has been an Olympic sport since 1984. The sport combines elements of surfing and sailing. *Image Select (UK) Ltd*

pulp of the grape. The sugar content is converted to ethyl alcohol by the yeast *Saccharomyces ellipsoideus*, which lives on the skin of the grape. The largest wine-producing countries are Italy, France, Russia, Georgia, Moldova, Armenia, and Spain; others include almost all European countries, Australia, South Africa, the USA, and Chile.

types of wine For ***dry wine*** the fermentation is allowed to go on longer than for ***sweet*** or ***medium***; ◊champagne (sparkling wine from the Champagne region of France) is bottled while still fermenting, but other sparkling wines are artificially carbonated. Some wines are fortified with additional alcohol obtained from various sources, and with preservatives. Some of the latter may cause dangerous side effects (see ◊additive). For this reason, organic wines with no preservatives have become popular.

vintage wines A vintage wine is produced during a good year (as regards quality of wine, produced by favourable weather conditions) in recognized vineyards of a particular area; France has a guarantee of origin (*appellation controlée*), as do Italy (*Denominazione di Origine Controllata*), Spain (*Denominación Controlata*), and Germany (a series of graded qualities running from *Qualitätswein* to *Beerenauslese*).

alcohol content The greatest alcohol concentration that yeasts can tolerate is 16%; most wines have an alcohol content of 10–12%. ***Fortified wine*** has had alcohol added to bring the content up to about 20%. Such wines keep well because the alcohol kills microorganisms that spoil natural wines. Port, sherry, vermouth, madeira, and Marsala are fortified after fermentation and madeira is then heated gradually.

colouring The yellowish tinge of white wine is caused by tannin contained in the wood of the cask, oxidized while the wine matures. Red wine is mainly made from black grapes, which have a blue-black pigment under the skin that turns red in the presence of acids in the grape juice during pressing. The alcohol in the fermentation dissolves the pigment, which is carried into the wine. Tannin in the skin imparts a bitter taste to the wine.

Vins rosés, pink, pale-red wines are produced in one of two ways. The grape juice, after a very brief fermentation with the skins to give it colour, may be drawn off from them to ferment apart, or the grapes may be pressed as for white wine, and the must poured back on the *marc* (the solid matter) to ferment with it long enough to gain colour.

British wines Winemaking in England and Wales developed throughout the 1980s, mainly in Lincolnshire, East Anglia, the south, and Wales. White grapes grow best in the British climate. English vineyards existed by 703, and in Norman times produced nearly all the wine consumed in England, but as imports grew in the 14th century, the vineyards declined, and wine cultivation was merely a hobby for the rich in the 18th and 19th centuries, before the 20th-century revival.

wing in biology, the modified forelimb of birds and bats, or the membranous outgrowths of the ◊exoskeleton of insects, which give the power of flight. Birds and bats have two wings. Bird wings have feathers attached to the fused digits ('fingers') and forearm bones, while bat wings consist of skin stretched between the digits. Most insects have four wings, which are strengthened by wing veins.

Wingate Orde Charles 1903–1944. British soldier. In 1936 he established a reputation for unorthodox tactics in Palestine. In World War II he served in the Middle East and organized guerilla forces in Ethiopia, and later led the Chindits, the 3rd Indian Division, in guerrilla operations against the Japanese army in Burma (now Myanmar).

Winnipeg capital and industrial city (processed foods, textiles, transportation, and transportation equipment) in Manitoba, Canada, on the Red River, S of Lake Winnipeg; population (1986) 623,000. Established as Winnipeg 1870 on the site of earlier forts, the city expanded with the arrival of the Canadian Pacific Railroad 1881.

Winnipeg, Lake lake in S Manitoba, Canada, draining much of the Canadian prairies; area 24,500 sq km/9,460 sq mi.

Winslet Kate 1975– . English screen actress. She made her film debut in the New Zealand period piece *Heavenly Creatures* (1994) based on the real-life stories of two school girls whose obsessive friendship drives them to commit murder. This was followed by her performance in the adaptation of Jane Austen's *Sense and Sensibility* (1995) and a star role in the blockbuster *Titanic* (1997).

wintergreen any of several plants of the genus *Gaultheria* of the heath family Ericaceae, especially *G. procumbens* of NE North America, creeping underground and sending up tiny shoots. Oil of wintergreen, used in treating rheumatism, is extracted from its leaves. Wintergreen is also the name for various plants of the family Pyrolaceae.

Winter Olympics a four yearly series of sports competitions on snow and ice, first held in 1924, and organized like the summer ◊Olympics under the auspices of the International Olympic Committee.

Winterson Jeanette 1959– . English novelist. Her autobiographical first novel, *Oranges Are Not the Only Fruit* 1985, humorously describes her upbringing as an Evangelical Pentecostalist in Lancashire, and her subsequent realization of her homosexuality. Later novels include *The Passion* 1987, *Sexing the Cherry* 1989, *Written On the Body* 1992, and *Art and Lies* 1994.

Winter War the USSR's invasion of Finland 30 Nov 1939–12 March 1940, also called the Russo-Finnish War.

wire thread of metal, made by drawing a rod through progressively smaller-diameter dies. Fine-gauge wire is used for electrical power transmission; heavier-gauge wire is used to make load-bearing cables. Galvanized wire (coated with zinc) does not rust; barbed wire and wire mesh are used for fencing. Needles, pins, nails, and rivets are made from wire.

wireless original name for a radio receiver. In early experiments with transmission by radio waves, notably by Italian inventor Guglielmo ◊Marconi in Britain, signals were sent in Morse code, as in telegraphy. Radio, unlike the telegraph, used no wires for transmission, and the means of communication was termed 'wireless telegraphy'.

Wisconsin state in N central USA; nicknamed Badger State

area 145,500 sq km/56,163 sq mi

capital Madison

cities Milwaukee, Green Bay, Racine

features Lakes Superior and Michigan, with Apostles Islands national lakeshore; Mississippi and Wisconsin rivers; Door Peninsula, with cherry trees; Wisconsin Dells; Milwaukee, with the Milwaukee Art Museum, Kilbourntown House (1844)

Winnipeg The Legislative Building at Winnipeg, Manitoba, Canada. Established 1873 on the site of a trading post going back to the 1730s, Winnipeg owes its importance to the arrival of the Canadian Pacific Railway 1881. It is now a centre of transportation and commerce, and one of the biggest grain markets in the world. *Canadian Tourist Office*

Wisconsin

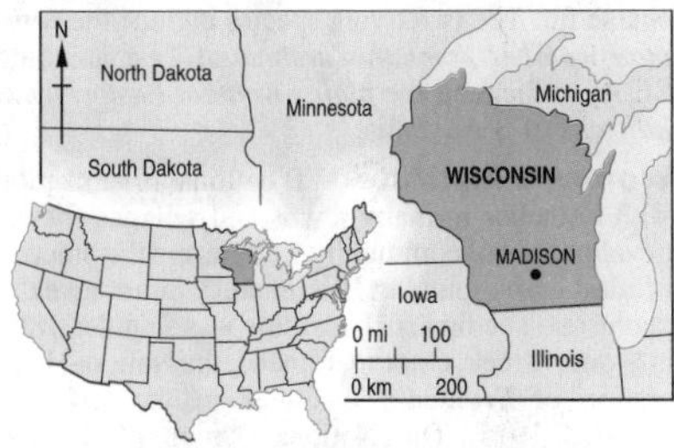

and the Allen-Bradley Company clock (the largest four-faced clock in the world); Prairie du Chien (1673); Old World Wisconsin in Southern Kettle Moraine State Forest; Spring Green, with Taliesin, the home of Frank Lloyd Wright, and the school of architecture started by him; Kohler, a planned village surrounding the factories of the plumbing fixtures manufacturer Kohler Company; Circus World Museum, Baraboo (where the Ringling Brothers Circus spent the winters); University of Wisconsin (1849), including the Golda Meir Library, with the map collection of the American Geographical Society
industries leading US dairy state; maize, hay, industrial and agricultural machinery, engines and turbines, precision instruments, paper products, cars and lorries, plumbing equipment
population (1991) 4,955,000
famous people Edna Ferber, Harry Houdini, Joseph McCarthy, Spencer Tracy, Orson Welles, Thornton Wilder, Frank Lloyd Wright
history explored by Jean Nicolet for France 1634; originally settled near Ashland by the French; passed to Britain 1763; included in the USA 1783. Wisconsin became a territory 1836 and a state 1848.

wisent another name for the European ◊bison.

Wishart George c. 1513–1546. Scottish Protestant reformer burned for heresy, who probably converted John ◊Knox.

Wister Owen 1860–1938. US novelist. He created the ◊Western genre. He became known for stories of cowboys, including *The Virginian* 1902. He also wrote *Roosevelt: The Story of a Friendship 1880–1919* 1930, about his relationship with US president Theodore Roosevelt.

wisteria any climbing shrub of the genus *Wisteria*, including *W. sinensis*, of the family Leguminosae, native to the eastern USA and E Asia. Wisterias have racemes of bluish, white, or pale mauve flowers, and pinnate leaves (leaves on either side of the stem).

Witan or ***Witenagemot*** council of the Anglo-Saxon kings, the forerunner of Parliament, but including only royal household officials, great landowners, and top churchmen.

witchcraft the alleged possession and exercise of magical powers – ***black magic*** if used with evil intent, and ***white magic*** if benign. Its origins lie in traditional beliefs and religions. Practitioners of witchcraft have often had considerable skill in, for example, herbal medicine and traditional remedies.

The Christian church persecuted witches in Europe between the 15th and 17th centuries and in North America. The last official execution of a witch in Europe was that of Anna Goddi, hanged in Switzerland in 1782. ***Obi*** is the witchcraft of black Africa imported to the West Indies, and includes Christian elements; ◊***voodoo*** is a similar cult.

wisteria This leguminous climbing shrub is named after US anatomist Caspar Wistar (1761–1818). The clusters of pealike, often purple flowers make this a handsome ornamental and it is often grown to cover walls, conservatories, and verandas.

witch doctor alternative name for a ◊shaman.

witch hazel any flowering shrub or small tree of the genus *Hamamelis* of the witch-hazel family, native to North America and E Asia, especially *H. virginiana*. An astringent extract prepared from the bark or leaves is used in medicine as an eye lotion and a liniment.

witch-hunt persecution of minority political opponents or socially nonconformist groups without any regard for their guilt or innocence. Witch-hunts are often accompanied by a degree of public hysteria; for example, the ◊McCarthy anticommunist hearings during the 1950s in the USA.

Witt Johann de 1625–1672. Dutch politician, grand pensionary of Holland and virtual prime minister from 1653. His skilful diplomacy ended the Dutch Wars of 1652–54 and 1665–67, and in 1668 he formed a triple alliance with England and Sweden against Louis XIV of France. He was murdered by a rioting mob.

Witt Katarina 1965– . German ice-skater. She was 1984 Olympic champion (representing East Germany) and by 1990 had won four world titles (1984–85, 1987–88) and six consecutive European titles (1983–88). After four years as a professional she returned to competitive skating in 1993.

Wittenberg town in the state of Saxony-Anhalt, Germany, on the river Elbe, SW of Berlin; population (1989 est) 53,600. Wittenberg university was founded 1502, but transferred to Halle 1815. Luther preached in the Stadtkirche (in which he is buried), nailed his 95 theses to the door of the Schlosskirche 1517, and taught philosophy at the university.

Wittgenstein Ludwig Josef Johann 1889–1951. Austrian philosopher. In his *Tractatus Logico-Philosophicus* 1922 he postulated the 'picture theory' of language: that words represent things according to social agreement. He subsequently rejected this idea, and developed the idea that usage was more important than convention.

Witwatersrand (Afrikaans 'ridge of white water') or ***the Rand*** economic heartland of Gauteng Province, South Africa. Its reef, which stretches nearly 100 km/60 mi, produces over half the world's gold. Gold was first found here 1854. The chief city of the region is Johannesburg. Forming a watershed between the Vaal and the Olifant rivers, the Rand comprises a series of parallel ranges which extend 100 km/60 mi E–W and rise to 1,525–1,830 m/5,000–6,000 ft above sea level.

woad biennial plant *Isatis tinctoria*, family Cruciferae, native to Europe, with arrow-shaped leaves and clusters of yellow flowers. It was formerly cultivated for a blue dye extracted from its leaves. Ancient Britons used the blue dye as a body paint in battle.

Wodehouse P(elham) G(renville) 1881–1975. English novelist. He became a US citizen 1955. His humorous novels portray the accident-prone world of such characters as the socialite Bertie Wooster and his invaluable and impeccable manservant Jeeves, and Lord Emsworth of Blandings Castle with his prize pig, the Empress of Blandings.

From 1906, Wodehouse also collaborated on the lyrics of Broadway musicals by Jerome Kern, Gershwin, and others. Staying in France 1941, during World War II, he was interned by the Germans; he made some humorous broadcasts from Berlin, which were taken amiss in Britain at the time, but he was later exonerated. His work is admired for its style and geniality, and includes *Indiscretions of Archie* 1921, *Uncle Fred in the Springtime* 1939, and *Aunts Aren't Gentlemen* 1974.

Woden or ***Wodan*** the foremost Anglo-Saxon god, whose Norse counterpart is ◊Odin.

Wittgenstein Austrian-born philosopher Ludwig Wittgenstein who had a profound influence on the development of 20th-century British and American philosophy. Though his early and late philosophies differ radically, they are both based on a concern with the relationship between language, thought, and reality. *Topham*

Woffington Peg (Margaret) c. 1714–1760. Irish actress. She played in Dublin as a child and made her debut at Covent Garden, London, 1740. She acted in many Restoration comedies, often taking male roles, such as Lothario in Rowe's *The Fair Penitent*.

Wöhler Friedrich 1800–1882. German chemist who in 1828 became the first person to synthesize an organic compound (◊urea) from an inorganic compound (ammonium cyanate). He also devised a method 1827 that isolated the metals aluminium, beryllium, yttrium, and titanium from their ores.

wolf any of two species of large wild dogs of the genus *Canis*. The ***grey*** or ***timber wolf*** *C. lupus*, of North America and Eurasia, is highly social, measures up to 90 cm/3 ft at the shoulder, and weighs up to 45 kg/100 lb. It has been greatly reduced in numbers except for isolated wilderness regions. The ***red wolf*** *C. rufus*, generally more slender and smaller (average weight about 15 kg/35 lb) and tawnier in colour, may not be a separate species, but a grey wolf–coyote hybrid. It is now thought to be extinct in the wild. Wolves disappeared from England at the end of the 13th century, and from Scotland by the 17th century.

Wolf Hugo (Filipp Jakob) 1860–1903. Austrian composer. He brought a new concentration and tragic eloquence to the art of *lieder* (songs) and composed more than 250 *lieder*, including the *Mörike-Lieder/Mörike Songs* 1888 and the two-volume *Italienisches Liederbuch/Italian Songbook* 1891, 1896. Among his other works are the opera *Der Corregidor/The Magistrate* 1895 and orchestral works, such as *Italian Serenade* 1892.

Wolfe Gene 1931– . US writer. He is known for the science-fiction series *The Book of the New Sun* 1980–83, with a Surrealist treatment of stock

'The Right Hon. was a tubby little chap who looked as if he had been poured into his clothes and had forgotten to say 'When!''

P G Wodehouse
'Jeeves and the Impending Doom'

Wodehouse English comic novelist P G Wodehouse in 1971. A fine stylist with an exquisite sense of the absurd, he used the English upper classes of an untroubled Edwardian era as his subject material, filling novel after novel with feckless young men and their eccentric relatives, debutante flappers, American millionaires, and resourceful manservants. *Topham*

'Taught from their infancy that beauty is woman's sceptre, the mind shapes itself to the body, and roaming round its gilt cage, only seeks to adorn its prison.'

Mary Wollstonecraft
A Vindication of the Rights of Woman

themes, and for the urban fantasy *Free, Live Free* 1985.

Wolfe James 1727–1759. British soldier. With the outbreak of the Seven Years' War (the French and Indian War in North America), he was posted to Canada and played a conspicuous part in the siege of the French stronghold of Louisburg 1758. He was promoted to major general 1759. In the same year he commanded a victorious expedition against the French general Montcalm in Quebec on the Plains of Abraham, during which both commanders were killed. The British victory established their supremacy over Canada.

Wolfe Thomas Clayton 1900–1938. US novelist. He is noted for the unrestrained rhetoric and emotion of his prose style. He wrote four hauntingly powerful autobiographical novels, mostly of the South: *Look Homeward, Angel* 1929, *Of Time and the River* 1935, *The Web and the Rock* 1939, and *You Can't Go Home Again* 1940 (the last two published posthumously).

Wolfe Tom. Pen name of Thomas Kennerly, Jr 1931– . US journalist and novelist. In the 1960s he was a founder of the 'New Journalism', which brought fiction's methods to reportage. Wolfe recorded US mores and fashions in pop-style essays in, for example, *The Kandy-Kolored Tangerine-Flake Streamline Baby* 1965. His sharp social eye is applied to the New York of the 1980s in his novel *The Bonfire of the Vanities* 1988. He also wrote *The Electric Kool-Aid Acid Test* 1968, *Radical Chic and Mau-Mauing the Flak Catchers* 1970, and *The Right Stuff* 1979.

Wolfenden Report the findings, published 1957, of a British royal commission on homosexuality and prostitution. The report recommended legalizing homosexual acts between consenting adults of 21 and over, in private. This became law 1967.

Wolfit Donald 1902–1968. English actor and manager. He formed his own theatre company 1937, and excelled in the Shakespearean roles of Shylock and Lear, and Volpone (in Ben Jonson's play).

wolfram alternative name for ◊tungsten

wolframite iron manganese tungstate, (Fe,Mn)WO_4, an ore mineral of tungsten. It is dark grey with a submetallic surface lustre, and often occurs in hydrothermal veins in association with ores of tin.

Wolsey Cardinal Thomas Wolsey, an oil painting by an unknown artist. Lord chancellor 1515–29, Wolsey was the last major figure in the long history of clerical domination of the English administration. He died, accused of treason after his failure to obtain papal dispensation for Henry VIII's divorce from Catherine of Aragon, on the eve of the English Reformation. *Image Select (UK) Ltd*

Wollstonecraft English author and proto-feminist Mary Wollstonecraft. Her best-known work is *A Vindication of the Rights of Woman*, written in 1792. She was also the mother of Mary Shelley. *Corbis*

Wolfsburg town NE of Brunswick in Lower Saxony, Germany, chosen 1938 as the Volkswagen factory site; population (1993) 128,500.

Wollaston William Hyde 1766–1828. English chemist and physicist who discovered in 1804 how to make malleable platinum. He went on to discover the new elements palladium 1804 and rhodium 1805. He also contributed to optics through the invention of a number of ingenious and still useful measuring instruments.

Wollongong industrial city (iron, steel) in New South Wales, Australia, 65 km/40 mi S of Sydney; population (1985, with Port Kembla) 238,000.

Wollstonecraft Mary 1759–1797. British feminist. She was a member of a group of radical intellectuals called the English Jacobins. Her book *A Vindication of the Rights of Women* 1792 demanded equal educational opportunities for women. She married William Godwin and died giving birth to a daughter, Mary (later Mary ◊Shelley).

Wolof the majority ethnic group living in Senegal. There is also a Wolof minority in Gambia. There are about 2 million speakers of Wolof, a language belonging to the Niger-Congo family. The Wolof are predominantly arable farmers, and some also raise cattle; they are Muslims.

Wolseley Garnet Joseph, 1st Viscount Wolseley 1833–1913. British army officer. He fought in the Crimean War 1853–56 and then commanded in both the Ashanti War 1873–74 and last part of the Zulu War 1879–80. He campaigned in Egypt, but was too late to relieve General ◊Gordon at Khartoum.

Wolsey Thomas c. 1475–1530. English cleric and politician. In Henry VIII's service from 1509, he became archbishop of York 1514, cardinal and lord chancellor 1515, and began the dissolution of the monasteries. His reluctance to further Henry's divorce from Catherine of Aragon led to his downfall 1529. He was charged with high treason 1530 but died before being tried.

Wolverhampton industrial town (metalworking, chemicals, tyres, aircraft, bicycles, locks and keys, engineering, commercial vehicles) in West Midlands, England, 20 km/12 mi NW of Birmingham; population (1991) 242,200.

wolverine largest land member *Gulo gulo* of the weasel family (Mustelidae), found in Europe, Asia, and North America. It is stocky in build, about 1 m/3.3 ft long. Its long, thick fur is dark brown on the back and belly and lighter on the sides.

womb common name for the ◊uterus.

wombat any of a family (Vombatidae) of burrowing, herbivorous marsupials, native to Tasmania and S Australia. They are about 1 m/3.3 ft long, heavy, with a big head, short legs and tail, and coarse fur. The two living species include the ***common wombat*** *Vombatus ursinus* of Tasmania and SE Australia, and the ***plains wombat*** *Lasiorhirnus latifrons* of S Australia.

Women's Institute (WI) national organization with branches in many towns and villages for the development of community welfare and the practice of rural crafts found in Britain and Commonwealth countries. The first such institute was founded 1897 at Stoney Creek, Ontario, Canada; the National Federation of Women's Institutes in the UK was founded 1915. The National Union of Townswomen's Guilds, founded 1929, is the urban equivalent.

Women's Land Army in Britain, organization founded 1916 for the recruitment of women to work on farms during World War I. At its peak Sept 1918 it had 16,000 members. It re-formed June 1939, before the outbreak of World War II. Many 'Land Girls' joined up to help the war effort and, by Aug 1943, 87,000 were employed in farm work.

women's movement campaign for the rights of women, including social, political, and economic equality with men. Early European campaigners of the 17th–19th centuries fought for women's right to own property, to have access to higher education, and to vote (see ◊suffragette). Once women's suffrage was achieved in the 20th century, the emphasis of the movement shifted to the goals of equal social and economic opportunities for women, including employment. A continuing area of concern in industrialized countries is the contradiction between the now generally accepted principle of equality and the demonstrable inequalities that remain between the sexes in state policies and in everyday life.

history Pioneer 19th-century feminists, considered radical for their belief in the equality of the sexes, include Mary ◊Wollstonecraft and Emmeline ◊Pankhurst in the UK, and Susan B ◊Anthony and Elizabeth Cady ◊Stanton in the USA. The women's movement gained worldwide impetus after World War II with such theorists as Simone de ◊Beauvoir, Betty ◊Friedan, Kate ◊Millett, Gloria ◊Steinem, and Germaine ◊Greer, and the founding of the National Organization for Women (NOW) in New York 1966. From the late 1960s the movement argued that women were oppressed by the male-dominated social structure as a whole, which they saw as pervaded by ◊sexism, despite legal concessions towards equality of the sexes.

US legislation In the USA the Equal Employment Opportunity Commission, a government agency, was formed 1964 to end discrimination (including sex discrimination) in hiring workers. The Equal Rights Amendment (ERA), a proposed constitutional amendment prohibiting sex discrimination, was passed by Congress 1972 but failed to be ratified by the necessary majority of 38 states. In 1993 Canada changed its immigration rules to grant refugee status to women facing persecution in their homeland because of their sex. Following a US circuit-court decision 1992, women may be granted asylum in the USA if they are persecuted because of their sex or feminist views.

UK legislation In Britain the denial of a woman's right to own property was eventually overcome by the Married Women's Property Act 1882. Legislation for giving the vote to women was passed several times by the House of Commons from 1886 until 1911, but was always vetoed by the House of

wombat The wombat is a powerfully built marsupial. There are three species found in Australia and one in Tasmania. In some ways, they resemble badgers, being large burrowing animals, building burrows up to 30 m/100 ft long with a nest chamber at the end.

WOMEN'S MOVEMENT: UK TIMELINE

1562	The Statute of Artificers made it illegal to employ men or women in a trade before they had served seven years' apprenticeship. (It was never strictly enforced for women, as many guilds still allowed members to employ their wives and daughters in workshops.)
1753	Lord Hardwick's Marriage Act brought marriage under state control and created a firmer distinction between the married and unmarried.
1792	Mary Wollstonecraft published *A Vindication of the Rights of Woman*.
1803	Abortion was made illegal.
1839	Custody of Infants Act allowed mothers to have custody of their children under seven years old.
1840s	Factory Acts limited the working day of women and children.
1857	Marriage and Divorce Act enabled a man to obtain a divorce if his wife committed adultery. (Women could obtain a divorce only if husband's adultery was combined with incest, sodomy, cruelty, etc.)
1860s	Fathers could be named and required to pay maintenance for illegitimate children.
1862–70	Contagious Diseases Acts introduced compulsory inspection of prostitutes for venereal disease (suspended 1883; repealed 1886).
1864	Schools Enquiry Commission encouraged establishment of high schools for girls.
1867	The first women's suffrage committee was formed in Manchester.
1869	Women ratepayers were allowed to vote in municipal (local) elections.
1871	Newnham College, Cambridge, was founded for women.
1872	The Elizabeth Garrett Anderson Hospital for women opened in London.
1876	Medical Act permitted registration of women doctors.
1882	Married Women's Property Act gave married women the right of separate ownership of property of all kinds.
1887	The National Union of Women's Suffrage Societies became a nationwide group under Millicent Fawcett.
1894	Women permitted to serve as parish and district councillors.
1903	Emmeline Pankhurst founded the Women's Social and Political Union (WSPU).
1905–10	Militant suffragette campaigns split the WSPU.
1916	Women's employment increased by 2 million in a year due to war.
1918	Parliament (Qualification of Women) Act gave the vote to women householders over 30.
1919	Nancy Astor was the first woman to take her seat in Parliament.
1920	Oxford University permitted women to be awarded degrees.
1923	Wives were given equal rights to sue for divorce on grounds of adultery.
1925	Equal rights of guardianship of children established.
1927	Church of England approved equal marriage vows for women.
1928	The 'flapper' vote: all women over 21 given the vote.
1929	Margaret Bondfield became the first woman Cabinet minister.
1941	Women conscripted for auxiliary armed services.
1948	Cambridge University permitted women to be awarded degrees.
1967	Abortion made legal under medical supervision under certain criteria.
1970	Equal Pay Act established the principle of equal pay for equal work (effective from 1975).
1971	Biggest-ever women's liberation march staged in London.
1975	Sex Discrimination Act outlawed discrimination on grounds of sex or marital status and established the Equal Opportunities Commission.
1979	Margaret Thatcher became the first woman prime minister.
1984	Matrimonial and Family Proceedings Act made it less likely for a woman to be granted maintenance on divorce.
1990	Legal limit for abortion reduced to 24 weeks.
1991	Rape within marriage became a prosecutable offence.
1992–4	Women's armed services merged with mainstream army, navy, and air force.
1994	Church of England ordained its first women priests.
1996	Alex Greaves on Portuguese Lil becomes the first woman to ride in the Derby at Epsom, Surrey, England.
1998	Plans by Royal Family to remove gender bias from British succession rules.

Lords. In 1918 a bill granting limited franchise was passed, and ten years later full equality in this respect was attained. In the UK since 1975 discrimination against women in employment, education, housing, and provision of goods, facilities, and services to the public has been illegal under the Sex Discrimination and Equal Pay Acts.

world statistics Women own 1% of the world's property, and earn 10% of the world's income. When housework and childcare are included, women work longer hours than men in both the industrialized world (by about 20%) and the developing world (by about 30%). They are under-represented in the parliaments of virtually all nations: Sweden had the highest proportion 1995, with 42%; the average for the Middle East was 3%; the UK had 9% and the USA 11%. The world average was 9% 1995, down from 15% 1988. In Bahrain, Kuwait, and the United Arab Emirates, women can neither stand for election nor vote. Under Finnish law, public authorities must employ at least 40% women. ▷*See feature on pp. 1152–1153.*

women's services the organized military use of women on a large scale, a 20th-century development. First, women replaced men in factories, on farms, and in noncombat tasks during wartime; they are now found in combat units in many countries, including the USA, Cuba, the UK, and Israel. In Britain there are separate corps for all three services: ***Women's Royal Army Corps*** (WRAC) created 1949 to take over the functions of the Auxiliary Territorial Service, established 1938 – its World War I equivalent was the Women's Army Auxiliary Corps (WAAC); ***Women's Royal Naval Service*** (WRNS) 1917–19 and 1939 onwards, allowed in combat roles on surface ships from 1990; and the ***Women's Royal Air Force*** (WRAF) established 1918 but known 1939–48 as the Women's Auxiliary Air Force (WAAF).

Women's Social and Political Union (WSPU) British political movement founded 1903 by Emmeline ◊Pankhurst to organize a militant crusade for female suffrage. In 1909, faced with government indifference, the WSPU embarked on a campaign of window smashing, telephone-wire cutting, and arson of public buildings. This civil disobedience had little result and was overtaken by the outbreak of World War I. In 1917 the WSPU became the ***Women's Party***, led by Christabel Pankhurst.

Wonder Stevie. Stage name of Steveland Judkins Morris 1950– . US pop musician, singer, and songwriter. He is associated with Motown Records, and had his first hit, 'Fingertips', at the age of 12. Later hits, most of which he composed and sang, and on which he also played several instruments, include 'My Cherie Amour' 1973, 'Master Blaster (Jammin')' 1980, and the album *Innervisions* 1973.

wood the hard tissue beneath the bark of many perennial plants; it is composed of water-conducting cells, or secondary ◊xylem, and gains its hardness and strength from deposits of ◊lignin. ***Hardwoods***, such as oak, and ***softwoods***, such as pine, have commercial value as structural material and for furniture.

The central wood in a branch or stem is known as ***heartwood*** and is generally darker and harder than the outer wood; it consists only of dead cells. As well as providing structural support, it often contains gums, tannins, or pigments which may impart a characteristic colour and increased durability. The surrounding ***sapwood*** is the functional part of the xylem that conducts water. The ***secondary xylem*** is laid down by the vascular ◊cambium which forms a new layer of wood annually, on the outside of the existing wood and visible as an ◊annual ring when the tree is felled; see ◊dendrochronology.

Wood Haydn 1882–1959. British composer. A violinist, he wrote a violin concerto among other works, and is known for his songs, which include 'Roses of Picardy', associated with World War I.

Wood Henry Joseph 1869–1944. English conductor. From 1895 until his death, he conducted the London Promenade Concerts, now named after him. He promoted a national interest in music and encouraged many young composers. As a composer he is remembered for the *Fantasia on British Sea Songs* 1905, which ends each Promenade season.

Wood John, ***the Elder*** c. 1705–1754. English architect. He was known as 'Wood of Bath' because of his many works in that city. His plan to restore the Roman character of Bath in strict Palladian style was only partially realized. His designs include Queen Square 1729–36 and the Circus 1754, a circular space with streets radiating out from it, which was not yet built by the time he died. His son ***John Wood, the Younger*** (1728–1782) carried on his work, and himself designed the Royal Crescent 1767–75 and Assembly Rooms 1769–71.

Wood Natalie. Stage name of Natasha Gurdin 1938–1981. US film actress. She started out as a child star. Her films include *Miracle on 34th Street* 1947, *Rebel Without a Cause* 1955, *The Searchers* 1956, and *Bob and Carol and Ted and Alice* 1969.

woodcarving art form practised in many parts of the world since prehistoric times: for example, the NW Pacific coast of North America, in the form of totem poles, and W Africa, where there is a long tradition of woodcarving, notably in Nigeria. Woodcarvings survive less often than sculpture in stone or metal because of the comparative fragility of the material. European wood carvers include Veit Stoss (c. 1450–1533) and Grinling ◊Gibbons.

woodcock either of two species of wading birds, genus *Scolopax*, of the family Scolopacidae, which have barred plumage and long bills, and live in wet woodland areas. They belong to the long-billed section of the snipes, order Charadriiformes.

Woodcraft Folk British name for the youth organization founded in the USA as the Woodcraft League by Ernest Thompson Seton 1902, with branches in many countries. Inspired by the ◊Scouts, it differs in that it is for mixed groups and is socialist in outlook.

woodcut print made by a woodblock in which a picture or design has been cut in relief along the grain of the wood. The woodcut is the oldest method of ◊printing, invented in China in the 5th century AD. In the Middle Ages woodcuts became popular in Europe, illustrating early printed books and broadsides.

The German artist Albrecht Dürer was an early exponent of the technique. Multicoloured woodblock prints were developed in Japan in the mid-18th century. ***Wood engraving*** is an allied but finer technique, the cuts being made across the end-grain of a block. The English artist Thomas Bewick was one of the first exponents of wood engraving. *See illustration on p. 1154.*

woodland area in which trees grow more or less thickly; generally smaller than a forest. Temperate climates, with four distinct seasons a year, tend to support a mixed woodland habitat, with some conifers but mostly broad-leaved and deciduous trees, shedding their leaves in autumn and regrowing them in spring. In the Mediterranean region and

'It is a subject which makes the Queen so furious that she cannot contain herself. God created men and women different – let them remain each in their own position.'

On the WOMEN'S MOVEMENT
Queen Victoria, letter to Theodore Martin 1870

cont. on p. 1154

Women and the Workplace

Emmeline Pankhurst, the militant campaigner for women's right to vote in the UK, being arrested outside Buckingham Palace, London, in May 1914. She had only recently been released from prison after serving less than a year of a three-year sentence for a series of arson attacks in 1913. *Corbis*

The prime workplace for women has always been the home. From time immemorial, women have borne the brunt of all child care, cleaning, and cooking in the household, though this is rarely seen as comparable to paid employment outside the home. Today, women in industrialized societies perform around 80% of domestic labour, even when they are working full time outside the home.

It is often believed that working women are a modern urban phenomenon. But women worked on the pyramids in Egypt, dug canals in Burma, and carried huge loads of wood and water, as well as goods for trading over long distances. Ancient records show that women of all cultures have been doctors and midwives, priestesses, artists and teachers, farmers and fisherwomen, gravediggers and layers out of the dead.

The Industrial Revolution

The great change for women workers came in the early 19th century, with the advent of factory production. Previously, no matter how hard a woman weaver had laboured at her loom as a cottage industry, she at least controlled her own hours and conditions of work, and could care for her family at the same time.

But women lost even this degree of independence when they went to work in factories. Even worse was the fate of women who worked in the mines: in the course of a 14-hour day, they might crawl for up to 20 miles through low passages, harnessed to heavy trucks of coal. Many miscarried, or gave birth to deformed children because of the pressure of the harness on the baby's head. Others were so exhausted that they fell to their deaths from the basket drawing them up to the surface at the end of the day.

World War II exploded the myth that women were only suited to domestic work. When the men went away to fight, women like this welder proved themselves to be adept and competent at jobs previously only done by men. *Hulton Getty*

By the end of the 19th century, the British government was forced to legislate against subhuman conditions such as these. Other legislation from the 1840s onwards reformed conditions in factories and mills, and, by allowing married women to own property, permitted them to keep their own wages for the first time.

A changing world

The two world wars increased the demand for women to work in factories. As men went away to fight, women were left to staff the munitions factories and work in aircraft manufacture. They also worked as doctors and nurses, front-line ambulance and military drivers, flight controllers and intelligence and espionage operatives, and in the armed services. The contribution of women workers during World War I helped to weaken traditions which had decreed idleness for the rich, and a lifetime 'in service' for the less well off. Legal and social developments affecting their status and health were also helping women to escape from menial drudgery and to approach work as an opportunity rather than a chore. The spread of education from the start of the 20th century led to the first women doctors, barristers, and university lecturers.

The granting of the vote by 1920 in the USA and by 1928 in Britain meant that women became full citizens and were liable to taxes, which in turn affected their attitude to employment. Most crucial of all, the advent of reliable female contraception freed women from the tyranny of uncontrolled reproduction for the first time in history.

A cult of domesticity in the 1950s tried to restore the view that a woman's place was in the home, where she could be mistress of a new range of household tools. *Corbis*

Back to the home

After the disruptions of World War II, a strong social impetus to rebuild the family unit drove women back to the home. Women who in wartime had been driving buses and running businesses were now expected to hand back these responsibilities and return to the kitchen. Women were excluded or deterred from outside employment by a raft of new restrictions: many employers required women to resign when they married, and regulations introduced by tax legislation and the new welfare state enshrined husbands' control over their wives' incomes and employment. This inequality was not debated publicly until the American housewife Betty Friedan, author of *The Feminine Mystique* 1963, described the average woman's domestic routine, and asked 'Is this all?'.

A woman's place is in the world

In 1960, the world's first woman prime minister, Sirimavo Bandaranaike, was elected in Ceylon (now Sri Lanka). In the following years Israel, Britain, the Philippines, India, Norway, Canada, France, Ireland, and Iceland were all to have women prime ministers or heads of state. As women were seen as capable of the highest occupations, it became harder to maintain the restrictive practices that kept them out of many jobs or to pay them less than men for the work they performed. From the 1970s, many countries introduced legislation to end discrimination against women in the workplace, and to ensure that their pay was equal to men's.

Some still more equal than others

Equality for women at work has proved hard to achieve. In the UK, nearly 30 years after the Equal Pay Act 1970, women manual workers still receive on average only 73% of a man's pay, while professional women fare even worse at 68%. Even at board level a woman is typically paid only two-thirds of what her male colleagues receive. The hourly earnings of a female secondary-school teacher are only 89% of her male colleagues' hourly earnings.

Discrimination against women is also evident in the low female representation in senior posts. In the UK women make up half the workforce, yet only 5% of High Court judges, and 5 and 7% of professors at Oxford and Cambridge Universities respectively. While the 1997 general election increased the number of women MPs significantly, they still make up only 18% of the House of Commons. Women form 30% of all professional workers and 33% of all managers in industry and commerce, and are less well represented on boards of directors than men.

Progress towards equality is not encouraging. Most women remain in low-paid, low-status jobs with no prospect of promotion – 85% of part-time workers in Great Britain are women. On average, the earnings of a woman who works part time are only 58% pro rata of those of a man who works full time, a disparity that has hardly changed since the mid-1970s. The belief that women do not need to be taken as seriously as men can be found at all levels of employment, regardless of the women's level of education, achievement, and ability. At the present rate of promoting women judges in Britain, for example, it will be over 200 years before women achieve parity on the Bench. By contrast, other European Union (EU) countries have full nursery support for working women, and parental leave. The rights of part-time women workers receive more protection throughout the EU, and in the USA women have benefited from programmes of affirmative action.

Meanwhile, women continue to perform two-thirds of the world's work hours for one-tenth of its income. The value of their unpaid domestic work has been estimated at £2 trillion annually. By performing around 80% of all domestic work, women workers are supporting their husbands' careers at the expense of their own. Young women today enjoy work opportunities that their grandmothers could not have imagined; but as long as they continue to shoulder an unfair share of the domestic burden, they will not realize their career potential on a level with men.

Future issues

Achieving equal pay and genuine equality of opportunity remain paramount problems in a world that has remained largely hostile to women's presence except at the lowest levels. Men are also finding that working long hours, 5–7 days a week, often with prolonged commuting, is not compatible with family life. For men and women to participate fully and equally in the world of work, attitudes to work and to social relations must continue to change, to the benefit of all.

Rosalind Miles

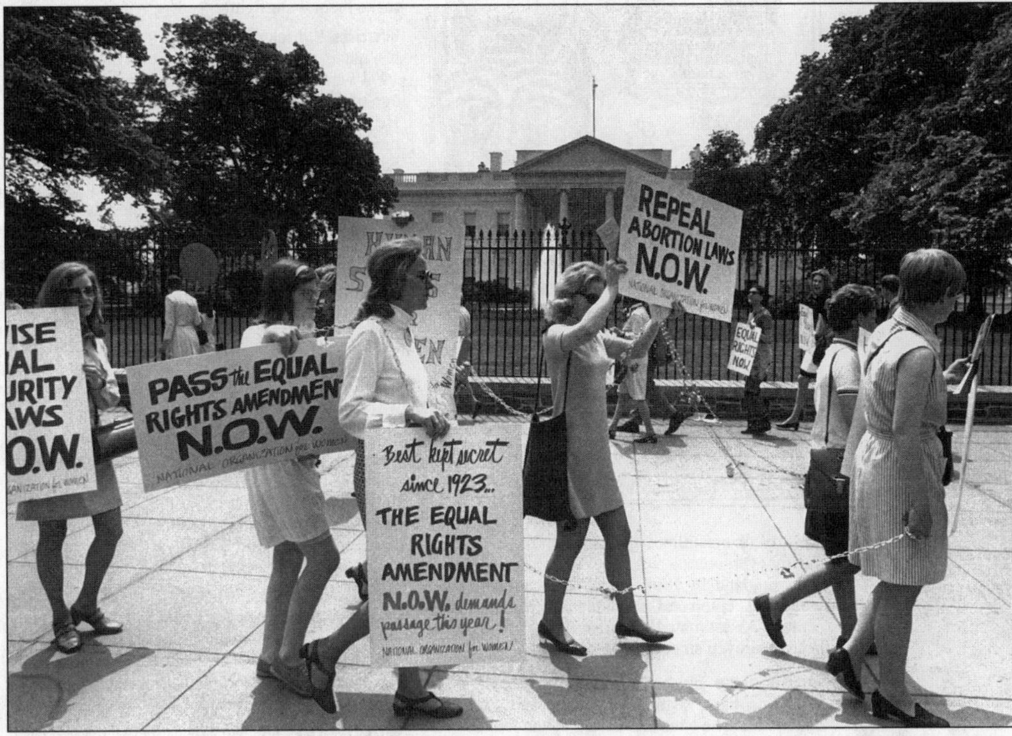

Women demanding equal rights with men were among the many groups who staged demonstrations in the streets of Western cities in the late 1960s. These supporters of the National Organization for Women (NOW) – symbolically linked by chains, decorated with flowers – picketed the White House, Washington, USA in 1969. *Corbis*

Equal but still unequal. Women may be breaking new ground in getting the same jobs as men, but only rarely do they get the same pay. *Tony Stone*

SEE ALSO
equal opportunities; family planning; Friedan, Betty; women's movement

woodcut *The Kazan Cat*, 18th-century Russian woodcut. Before the advent of engraving in the 16th century, woodcuts were a popular and convenient means of illustrating books, broadsides, and playing-cards. Woodcuts survived alongside the more sophisticated engravings, and were revived in the 19th century by William Morris. *Corbis*

parts of the southern hemisphere, the trees are mostly evergreen.

In England in 1900, about 2.5% of land was woodland, compared to about 3.4% in the 11th century. An estimated 33% of ancient woodland has been destroyed since 1945.

woodlouse crustacean of the order Isopoda. Woodlice have segmented bodies and flattened undersides. The eggs are carried by the female in a pouch beneath the thorax.

'Women have served all these centuries as looking-glasses possessing the magic and delicious power of reflecting the figure of man at twice its natural size.'

VIRGINIA WOOLF
A Room of One's Own

woodmouse or ***long-tailed field mouse*** nocturnal rodent *Apodemus sylvaticus* that lives in woodlands, hedgerows, and sometimes open fields in Britain and Europe. About 9 cm/3.5 in long, with a similar length of tail, it is yellow-brown above, white below, and has long oval ears.

woodpecker bird of the family Picidae, the order Piciformes. They are adapted for climbing up the bark of trees, and picking out insects to eat from the crevices. There are about 200 species worldwide. The European ***green woodpecker*** or ***yaffle*** *Picus viridis* is green with a red crown and yellow rump, and about the size of a jay. The ***greater*** and ***lesser spotted woodpeckers*** *Dendrocopos major* and *D. minor*, also British species, have black, red, and white plumage. The ***wryneck*** *Jynx torquilla* is a slightly aberrant form.

wood pitch by-product of charcoal manufacture, made from ***wood tar***, the condensed liquid produced from burning charcoal gases. The wood tar is boiled to produce the correct consistency. It has been used since ancient times for caulking wooden ships (filling in the spaces between the hull planks to make them watertight).

woodpecker The green woodpecker is, in some areas, called the yaffle, a name supposedly resembling its call. Like other woodpeckers, it feeds on the larvae of wood-boring insects which it digs from tree trunks, but it also feeds on the ground, hopping along as it searches for ants and seeds.

Woods Eldrick 'Tiger' 1976– . US golfer. He has made a phenomenal impact on the game since 1994 when he became the youngest player, at the age of 18, to win the US Amateur Championship. He turned professional in 1996, and in his first six months as a professional he won four tournaments on the US PGA circuit. In the 1997 Masters at Augusta, Georgia, he won by the largest ever margin, and achieved the best ever four-round score at that tournament.

Woodstock the first free rock festival, held near Bethel, New York State, USA, over three days in Aug 1969. It was attended by 400,000 people, and performers included the Band, Country Joe and the Fish, the Grateful Dead, Jimi Hendrix, Jefferson Airplane, and the Who. The festival was a landmark in the youth culture of the 1960s (see ◊hippie) and was recorded in the film *Woodstock* 1970.

Woodward Joanne Gignilliat 1930– . US actress. She is active in film, television, and theatre. She was directed by her husband Paul Newman in the film *Rachel Rachel* 1968, and also starred in *The Three Faces of Eve* 1957, *They Might Be Giants* 1971, and *Harry and Son* 1984. She has appeared with Newman in several films, including *Mr and Mrs Bridge* 1990.

Woodward Robert Burns 1917–1979. US chemist who worked on synthesizing a large number of complex molecules. These included quinine 1944, cholesterol 1951, chlorophyll 1960, and vitamin B_{12} 1971. Nobel prize 1965.

woodwind musical instrument from which sound is produced by blowing into a tube, causing the air within to vibrate. Woodwind instruments include those, like the flute, originally made of wood but now more commonly of metal. The saxophone, made of metal, is an honorary woodwind because it is related to the clarinet. The oboe, bassoon, flute, and clarinet make up the normal woodwind section of an orchestra.

Woodwind instruments fall into two categories: reed instruments, in which air passes via an aperture controlled by a vibrating flexible reed or pair of reeds; and those without a reed where air is simply blown into or across a tube. In both cases, different notes are obtained by changing the length of the tube by covering holes along it. Reed instruments include clarinet, oboe, cor anglais, saxophone, and bassoon. In the recorder, flute, and piccolo, the function of a reed is achieved by design of the mouthpiece.

woodworm common name for the larval stage of certain wood-boring beetles. Dead or injured trees are their natural target, but they also attack structural timber and furniture. Included are the furniture beetle *Anobium punctatum*, which attacks older timber; the powder-post beetle genus *Lyctus*, which attacks newer timber; the ◊deathwatch beetle, whose presence always coincides with fungal decay; and wood-boring ◊weevils. Special wood preservatives have been developed to combat woodworm infestation.

wool the natural hair covering of the sheep, and also of the llama, angora goat, and some other ◊mammals. The domestic sheep *Ovis aries* provides the great bulk of the fibres used in (textile) commerce. Lanolin is a by-product.

Sheep have been bred for their wool since ancient times. Hundreds of breeds were developed in the Middle East, Europe, and Britain over the centuries, several dozen of which are still raised for their wool today. Most of the world's finest wool comes from the merino sheep, originally from Spain. In 1797 it was introduced into Australia, which has become the world's largest producer of merino wool; South Africa and South America are also large producers. Wools from crossbred sheep (usually a cross of one of the British breeds with a merino) are produced in New Zealand. Since the 1940s, blendings of wool with synthetic fibres have been developed for textiles.

In Britain there are some 40 breeds of sheep, and the wool is classified as lustre (including Lincoln, Leicester, S Devon, Cotswold, Dartmoor), demi-lustre (Cheviot, Exmoor Horn, Romney Marsh), down (Dorset, Oxford, Suffolk, Hampshire, Southdown), and mountain (Blackface, Swaledale, Welsh White, Welsh Black).

Woolcott Marion Post 1910–1990. US documentary photographer. She is best known for her work for the Farm Security Administration (with Walker ◊Evans and Dorothea ◊Lange), showing the conditions of poor farmers in the late 1930s in Kentucky and the deep South.

Woolf (Adeline) Virginia (born Stephen) 1882–1941. English novelist and critic. In novels such as *Mrs Dalloway* 1925, *To the Lighthouse* 1927, and *The Waves* 1931, she used a 'stream of consciousness' technique to render inner experience. In *A Room of One's Own* 1929, *Orlando* 1928, and *The Years* 1937, she examines the importance of economic independence for women and other feminist principles.

Her first novel, *The Voyage Out* 1915, explored the tensions experienced by women who want marriage and a career. After the death of her father, she and her siblings moved to Bloomsbury, forming the nucleus of the ◊Bloomsbury Group. She produced a succession of novels, short stories, and critical essays, which include *The Common Reader* 1925, 1932. She was plagued by bouts of depression and committed suicide 1941.

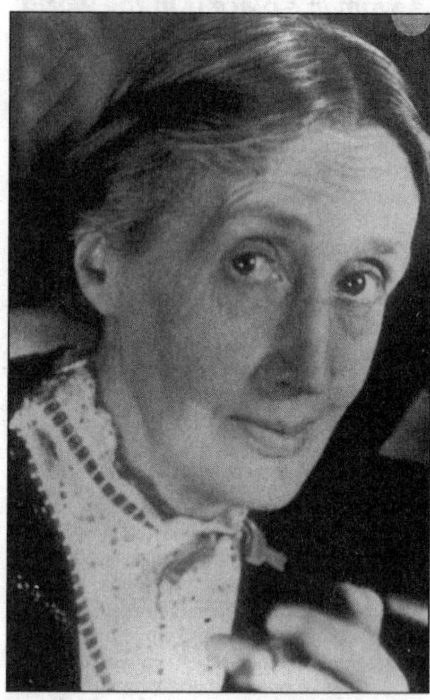

Woolf Novelist and essayist Virginia Woolf, one of the major English writers of the 20th century. She developed an experimental fiction, using her 'stream of consciousness' technique to capture the subtle, ceaseless flow of everyday experience. In several influential essays she argued that women had to develop their own form of fiction. *Topham*

Woollcott Alexander Humphreys 1887–1943. US theatre critic and literary figure. He was *The New York Times*' theatre critic 1914–22, a regular contributor to *The New Yorker* from its inception 1925, and hosted the radio interview programme *Town Crier* 1929–42. He appeared on stage in *The Man Who Came to Dinner* 1939 as a character based on himself.

Woolley (Charles) Leonard 1880–1960. British archaeologist. He excavated at Carchemish in Syria, Tell el Amarna in Egypt, Atchana (the ancient Alalakh) on the Turkish-Syrian border, and Ur in Iraq. He is best remembered for the work on Ur, which he carried out for the British Museum and Pennsylvania University Museum 1922–29.

woolsack in the UK, the seat of the Lord High Chancellor in the House of Lords: it is a large square bag of wool and is a reminder of the principal source of English wealth in the Middle Ages.

Woolwich district in London, England, cut through by the river Thames, the N part being in the borough of ◊Newham and the S part in the borough of Greenwich. The Thames Barrier (a flood barrier, constructed 1982) is here. The Woolwich Royal Arsenal, an ordnance depot from 1518 and centre for the manufacture and testing of arms, is still partly in use. The Royal Military Academy and the Royal Artillery Institution Museum are located here. Eltham Palace dates from the 13th century, with a 15th-century great hall and 16th-century chapel. The Town Hall (1905) is the centre of local government for the borough of Greenwich.

Woolworth Frank Winfield 1852–1919. US entrepreneur. He opened his first successful 'five and ten cent' store in Lancaster, Pennsylvania, in 1879, and, together with his brother C S Woolworth (1856–1947), built up a chain of similar stores throughout the USA, Canada, the UK, and Europe.

Woosnam Ian 1958– . Welsh golfer who, in 1987, became the first UK player to win the World Match-Play Championship. He has since won many tournaments, including the World Cup 1987, World Match-Play 1990, and US Masters 1991. Woosnam was Europe's leading moneywinner in 1987 (as a result of winning the $1 million Sun City Open in South Africa) and again in 1990. He was ranked Number One in the world for 50 weeks in 1991–92.

Wootton Barbara Frances. Baroness Wootton of Abinger 1897–1988. British educationist and economist. She taught at London University, and worked in the fields of politics, media, social welfare, and penal reform. Her books include *Freedom under Planning* 1945 and *Social Science and Social Pathology* 1959.

Worcester cathedral city with industries (shoes, Worcester sauce; Royal Worcester porcelain) in Hereford and Worcester, W central England, administrative headquarters of the county, on the river Severn; population (1991) 81,700. The cathedral dates from the 13th and 14th centuries. At the Battle of Worcester 1651 Oliver Cromwell defeated Charles II.

Worcester Porcelain Factory English porcelain factory, since 1862 the Royal Worcester Porcelain Factory. The factory was founded 1751 and produced a hard-wearing type of softpaste porcelain, mainly as tableware and decorative china. It employed advanced transfer printing techniques on a variety of shapes often based on Chinese porcelain.

word processing storage and retrieval of written text by computer. Word-processing software packages enable the writer to key in text and amend it in a number of ways. A print-out can be obtained or the text could be sent to another person or organization on disc or via ◊electronic mail. Word processing has revolutionized the task of a typing secretary. Word-processing packages can be used with databases or graphics packages, and desktop publishing packages are available too.

Wordsworth Dorothy 1771–1855. English writer. She was the only sister of William ◊Wordsworth and lived with him (and later his wife) as a companion and support from 1795 until his death. Her journals describe their life in Alfoxden, Somerset, and at Grasmere in the Lake District, and their travels.

Wordsworth William 1770–1850. English Romantic poet. In 1797 he moved with his sister Dorothy ◊Wordsworth to Somerset, where he lived near Samuel Taylor ◊Coleridge and collaborated with him on *Lyrical Ballads* 1798 (which included 'Tintern Abbey', a meditation on his response to nature). From 1799 he lived in the Lake District. His most notable individual poems were published in *Poems* 1807 (including 'Intimations of Immortality'). At intervals between then and 1839 he revised *The Prelude* (posthumously published 1850), the first part of his uncompleted philosophical, creative, and spiritual autobiography in verse. He was appointed poet laureate 1843.

Wordsworth was born in Cockermouth, Cumberland, and studied at Cambridge. In 1792 he returned to England from a visit to France, having fallen in love with Annette Vallon (1766–1841), with whom he had an illegitimate daughter. In 1802 he married Mary Hutchinson (1770–1859). *The Prelude* and *The Excursion* 1814 were written to form part of the longer autobiographical work *The Recluse*, which was never completed.

A leader of the Romantic movement, Wordsworth is best known as the poet who reawakened his readers to the beauty of nature, describing the emotions and perceptive insights which natural beauty arouses in the sensitive observer. At a deeper level, he saw himself as a philosophical poet and his nature mysticism had a strong, though diffuse, effect on his successors.

work in physics, a measure of the result of transferring energy from one system to another to cause an object to move. Work should not be confused with ◊energy (the capacity to do work, which is also measured in joules) or with ◊power (the rate of doing work, measured in joules per second).

Work is equal to the product of the force used and the distance moved by the object in the direction of that force. If the force is F newtons and the distance moved is d metres, then the work W is given by:

$$W=Fd$$

For example, the work done when a force of 10 newtons moves an object 5 metres against some sort of resistance is 50 joules (50 newton-metres).

worker cooperative business owned and controlled by its workers rather than outside shareholders. In some worker cooperatives each member worker has one vote at meetings, however many shares he or she owns. There are relatively few worker cooperatives in the UK; they are far more popular in Europe and Japan.

Workers' Educational Association (WEA) British institution that aims to provide democratically controlled education for working people. It was founded 1903 and first received grant aid for its classes 1907. Since then it has been funded partly by the government, although jealously guarding its independence. Its activities are split between traditional liberal education and training for trade unionists.

Workers' Party of Kurdistan (PKK) Kurdish guerrilla organization, active in Turkey from 1974. Initially it aimed to secure an independent Kurdish state, ◊Kurdistan, but has since modified its demands, indicating a preparedness to accept autonomy within a federal system. Responsible for many civilian deaths and bombings of private as well as government buildings, the PKK has been the subject of a prolonged and unrelenting campaign of suppression by the Turkish authorities.

workhouse in the UK, a former institution to house and maintain people unable to earn their own living. Groups of parishes in England combined to build workhouses for the poor, the aged, the disabled, and orphaned children from about 1815 until about 1930. They were made redundant by new welfare legislation in the early 20th century.

working conditions the physical environment in which a worker has to work, as well as the way workers are expected to complete their tasks. The Health and Safety Inspectorate is responsible for ensuring that working conditions conform to the Health and Safety at Work Act 1974.

working men's club social ◊club set up in the 19th century to cater for the education and re-creation of working men. Today the clubs have few limitations on membership and are entirely social.

Educational institutes for working men were a feature of most industrial towns in Britain by the early 19th century. In 1852 the Collonade Working-men's Club in London became the first to provide purely recreational facilities. The Reverend Henry Solley established the Working Men's Club and Institute Union in 1862, a forerunner of the national organization to which today's clubs belong.

Worksop market and industrial town (coal, glass, chemicals, light engineering, food processing) in Nottinghamshire, central England, on the river Ryton; population (1991) 37,200. Mary Queen of Scots was imprisoned at Worksop Manor (burned 1761).

workstation high-performance desktop computer with strong graphics capabilities, traditionally used for engineering (◊CAD and ◊CAM), scientific research, and desktop publishing. Frequently based on fast RISC (reduced instruction-set computer) chips, workstations generally offer more processing power than microcomputers (although the distinction between workstations and the more powerful microcomputer models is becoming increasingly blurred). Most workstations use UNIX as their operating system, and have good networking facilities.

World Bank popular name for the ***International Bank for Reconstruction and Development*** specialized agency of the United Nations that borrows in the commercial market and lends on commercial terms. It was established 1945 under the 1944 Bretton Woods agreement, which also created the International Monetary Fund. The ***International Development Association*** is an arm of the World Bank.

The World Bank now earns almost as much money from interest and loan repayments as it hands out in new loans every year. Over 60% of the bank's loans go to suppliers outside the borrower countries for such things as consultancy services, oil, and machinery. Control of the bank is vested in a board of executives representing national governments, whose votes are apportioned according to the amount they have funded the bank.

World Council of Churches (WCC) international organization aiming to bring together diverse movements within the Christian church. Established 1945, it has a membership of more than 100 countries and more than 300 churches; its headquarters are in Geneva, Switzerland. The supreme governing body, the assembly, meets every seven or eight years to frame policy. A 150-member central committee meets once a year and a 22-member executive committee twice a year.

World Cup the most prestigious competition in international soccer; World Cup events are also held in rugby union, cricket, and other sports. Most World Cup events are held every four years but the skiing World Cup is an annual event.

World Health Organization (WHO) agency of the United Nations established 1946 to prevent the spread of diseases and to eradicate them. To improve disease monitoring, the WHO operates a worldwide computer network, WHONET. Its headquarters are in Geneva, Switzerland.

World Intellectual Property Organization (WIPO) specialist agency of the United Nations established 1974 to coordinate the international protection (initiated by the Paris convention 1883) of inventions, trademarks, and industrial designs, and also literary and artistic works (as initiated by the Berne convention 1886).

World Meteorological Organization agency, part of the United Nations since 1950, that promotes the international exchange of weather information through the establishment of a worldwide network of meteorological stations. It was founded as the International Meteorological Organization 1873, and its headquarters are now in Geneva, Switzerland.

world music or ***roots music*** any music whose regional character has not been lost in the melting pot of the pop industry. Examples are W African mbalax, E African soukous, S African mbaqanga, French Antillean zouk, Javanese gamelan, Latin American salsa and lambada, Cajun music, European folk music, and rural blues, as well as combinations of these (flamenco guitar and kora; dub polka).

World Series annual ◊baseball competition between the winning teams of the National League (NL) and American League (AL). It is a best-of-seven series played each Oct. The first World Series was played 1903.

World Trade Organization (WTO) world trade monitoring body established Jan 1995, on approval of the Final Act of the Uruguay round of the ◊General Agreement on Tariffs and Trade (GATT). Under the Final Act, the WTO, a permanent trading body with a status commensurate with that of the International Monetary Fund or the World Bank, effectively replaced GATT. The WTO monitors agreements to reduce barriers to trade, such as tariffs, subsidies, quotas, and regulations which discriminate against imported products. Its headquarters are in Geneva, Switzerland.

World War I (1914–18) war between the Central European Powers (Germany, Austria-Hungary, and allies) on one side and the Triple Entente (Britain and the British Empire, France, and Russia) and their allies, including the USA (which entered 1917), on the other side. An estimated 10 million lives were lost and twice that number were

'A broker is a man who takes your fortune and runs it into a shoestring.'

ALEXANDER WOOLLCOTT
Quoted in S H Adams *Alexander Woollcott*

'That best portion of a good man's life; / His little, nameless, unremembered acts / Of kindness and of love.'

WILLIAM WORDSWORTH
Lines Written a Few Miles Above Tintern Abbey

World War I British soldiers firing 20-cm/8-in howitzers during the Battle of the Somme. Artillery was used to soften up the enemy lines before the infantry advanced. Ensconced in their trenches, however, German forces were able to withstand the bombardment and little ground was made during the four-month campaign. *Corbis*

wounded. It was fought on the eastern and western fronts, in the Middle East, in Africa, and at sea.

causes By the early 20th century, competition for trade markets and imperial possessions worldwide had led to a growth of nationalistic sentiment. This nationalism created great political tension between the single-nation states such as France and Germany, and threatened the stability of multi-nation states such as Austria-Hungary. These tensions were reflected in jingoistic propaganda, an arms race between the major powers, and trade barriers and tariffs which exacerbated tensions further. At the same time, German diplomatic efforts to recover the stability of Bismarck's day in Europe by combining Central Europe into a formidable *bloc* increased fears of German expansionism in France and Russia.

outbreak of war Widespread nationalistic unrest in the Balkan provinces of the Austro-Hungarian Empire had resulted in strained relations between Austria-Hungary and Serbia, regarded as sponsor of the nationalist movements. While visiting Sarajevo, capital of the Austro-Hungarian province of Bosnia-Herzegovina, 28 June 1914 Archduke Franz Ferdinand, heir of the Austro-Hungarian emperor, was assassinated by a Bosnian student, Gavrilo Prinzip, backed by the Serbian nationalist Black Hand organization.

The Austro-Hungarian government sought to punish Serbia for the crime and Germany promised support, despite the danger of involving Russia, ultimate patron of the Balkan nationalist movements. Austria-Hungary presented Serbia with an ultimatum 23 July, requesting a reply within 48 hours. Serbia, on Russian advice, agreed to all the demands except two which conflicted with its authority as a sovereign state. Austro-Hungarian armies near the Serbian border were mobilized.

Russia mobilized its forces against Austria-Hungary 29 July. On the same day Austrian artillery bombarded the Serbian capital, Belgrade. News of the Russian mobilization reached Berlin 31 July; Germany demanded that Russian mobilization should cease, and asked France for a notification by the following day that it would remain neutral in the event of a Russo-German war, despite treaty obligations to Russia.

Britain asked for renewed assurances that Belgian neutrality (guaranteed by a treaty of 1839) would be respected. France gave these guarantees, but Germany's answer was evasive and Britain formally notified Germany 1 Aug that it could not ignore a threat to Belgian neutrality. The following day German troops entered Luxembourg, and shortly after there were skirmishes between French and German troops in Alsace.

Meanwhile, Germany demanded the right of passage through Belgium to counter possible French moves. Asquith, the British prime minister, issued orders for mobilization 2 Aug and the

WORLD WAR I: TIMELINE

1914 June	Assassination of Archduke Franz Ferdinand of Austria 28 June.
July	German government issued 'blank cheque' to Austria, offering support in war against Serbia. Austrian ultimatum to Serbia; Serbs accepted all but two points. Austria refused to accept compromise and declared war. Russia began mobilization to defend Serbian ally. Germany demanded Russian demobilization.
Aug	Germany declared war on Russia. France mobilized to assist Russian ally. Germans occupied Luxembourg and demanded access to Belgian territory, which was refused. Germany declared war on France and invaded Belgium. Britain declared war on Germany, then on Austria. Dominions within the British Empire, including Australia, automatically involved. Battle of Tannenburg between Central Powers and Russians. Russian army encircled.
Sept	British and French troops halted German advance just short of Paris, and drove them back. First Battle of the Marne, and of the Aisne. Beginning of trench warfare.
Oct–Nov	First Battle of Ypres. Britain declared war on Turkey.
1915 April–May	Gallipoli offensive launched by British and dominion troops against Turkish forces. Second Battle of Ypres. First use of poison gas by Germans. Italy joined war against Austria. German sumbarine sank ocean liner *Lusitania* 7 May, later helping to bring USA into the war.
Aug–Sept	Warsaw evacuated by the Russians. Battle of Tarnopol. Vilna taken by the Germans. Tsar Nicholas II took supreme control of Russian forces.
1916 Jan	Final evacuation of British and dominion troops from Gallipoli.
Feb	German offensive against Verdun began, with huge losses for little territorial gain.
May	Naval battle of Jutland between British and German imperial fleets ended inconclusively, but put a stop to further German naval participation in the war.
June	Russian (Brusilov) offensive against the Ukraine began.
July–Nov	First Battle of the Somme, a sustained Anglo-French offensive which won little territory and lost a huge number of lives.
Aug	Hindenburg and Ludendorff took command of the German armed forces. Romania entered the war against Austria but was rapidly overrun.
Sept	Early tanks used by British on Western Front.
Nov	Nivelle replaced Joffre as commander of French forces. Battle of the Ancre on the Western Front.
Dec	French completed recapture of Verdun fortifications. Austrians occupied Bucharest.
1917 Feb	Germany declared unrestricted submarine warfare. Russian Revolution began and tsarist rule overthrown.
March	British seizure of Baghdad and occupation of Persia.
March–April	Germans retreated to Siegfried Line (Arras-Soissons) on Western Front.
April–May	USA entered the war against Germany. Unsuccessful British and French offensives. Mutinies among French troops. Nivelle replaced by Pétain.
July–Nov	Third Ypres offensive including Battle of Passchendaele.
Sept	Germans occupied Riga.
Oct–Nov	Battle of Caporetto saw Italian troops defeated by Austrians.
Dec	Jerusalem taken by British forces under Allenby.
1918 Jan	US President Woodrow Wilson proclaimed 'Fourteen Points' as a basis for peace settlement.
March	Treaty of Brest-Litovsk with Central Powers ended Russian participation in the war, with substantial concessions of territory and reparations. Second Battle of the Somme began with German spring offensive.
July–Aug	Allied counter-offensive, including tank attack at Amiens, drove Germans back to the Siegfried Line.
Sept	Hindenburg and Ludendorff called for an armistice.
Oct	Armistice offered on the basis of the 'Fourteen Points'. German naval and military mutinies at Kiel and Wilhelmshaven.
Nov	Austria-Hungary signed armistice with Allies. Kaiser Wilhelm II of Germany went into exile. Provisional government under social democrat Friedrich Ebert formed. Germany agreed armistice. Fighting on Western Front stopped.
1919 Jan	Peace conference opened at Versailles.
May	Demands presented to Germany.
June	Germany signed peace treaty at Versailles, followed by other Central Powers: Austria (Treaty of St Germain-en-Laye, Sept), Bulgaria (Neuilly, Nov), Hungary (Trianon, June 1920), and Turkey (Sèvres, Aug 1920).

'The lamps are going out all over Europe; we shall not see them lit again in our lifetime.'

On World War I
Lord Grey of Falloden
3 Aug 1914
(the eve of Britain's declaration of war)

following day Belgium rejected the German demand and Germany declared war on France. Germany invaded Belgium 4 Aug. Britain demanded German withdrawal: there was no formal reply, and so from midnight on Tuesday 4 Aug 1914 Britain and Germany were at war.

consequences World War I was a watershed for both Europe and the USA and had far-reaching consequences on both sides of the Atlantic. The Treaty of Versailles, mostly at the insistence of France, sought to disarm and punish Germany, and to weaken it with reparations. Industrial assets were stripped from the Ruhr by the French, the Rhineland was demilitarized, and limits were set on the strength of the German Army. These factors, combined with weak government in the form of the Weimar Republic, made Germany even more vulnerable to the ravages of the Depression than other European nations. These circumstances combined to form a breeding ground for German resentment and resurgent nationalism. Hitler and National Socialism was the inevitable consequence.

The events of World War I accelerated the collapse of the Russian monarchy, the 1917 revolution, and the rise of Bolshevism. They also led directly to the collapse of the Austro-Hungarian Empire and the creation of new nation states in Central Europe. The war also engaged the USA in Europe's affairs; after the sinking of US shipping by German submarines in 1917, the US navy underwent major expansion in 1917–18, confirming the USA as a global naval power. US intervention in 1917 created a precedent for its involvement in 1942 in World War II.

The 1914–18 war bled Europe economically. While Europe struggled to recover, the USA, relatively untouched by war, prospered. But the disparity between the European and US economies meant that there were no export markets for the USA. The US economy overheated, resulting in the Wall Street Crash of 1929 and the Great Depression.

Though the Great War was thought to be 'the war to end all wars', it can be said to have led directly to the policies of appeasement of Hitler in the 1930s, and hence to have contributed to the causes of World War II.

World War II (1939–45) war between Germany, Italy, and Japan (the Axis powers) on one side, and Britain, the Commonwealth, France, the USA, the USSR, and China (the Allied powers) on the other. An estimated 55 million lives were lost (20 million of them citizens of the USSR), and 60 million people in Europe were displaced because of bombing raids. The war was fought in the Atlantic and Pacific theatres.

In May 1945, Germany surrendered but Japan fought on until the USA dropped atomic bombs on Hiroshima and Nagasaki in August of that year.

causes Tension had been rising in Europe throughout the 1930s as Nazi Germany first broke virtually all the treaty obligations imposed upon it following World War I, and then embarked on a programme of aggressive expansionism. The process was made worse by the prevarication of the Western powers in the face of flagrant breaches of international law by Germany, so that finally each side reached a position from which it could not withdraw.

invasion of Poland On 1 Sept 1939, five German armies invaded Poland. The Poles had placed their armies on the borders, so that once the initial blow had pierced their lines they were rapidly rolled up and destroyed in Europe's first experience of Blitzkrieg warfare.

As agreed in a secret clause in the Ribbentrop–Molotov pact, two Soviet armies marched into Poland from the east 17 Sept and the country was divided between the two invaders. West Poland was divided: part was absorbed into Germany and part administered as the government of occupation. East Poland became Soviet territory and remained so until the end of the Cold War. With the invasion of Poland, Britain and France declared war on Germany.

consequences The main consequence of World War II was the division of Europe by what Winston Churchill called an Iron Curtain, stretching from the Baltic to the Mediterranean. This frontier between those countries occupied by the Soviet Union in 1945 and those nations liberated by the Western allies dominated postwar politics until the collapse of the Soviet Union in 1989. It resulted in the absence of democratic government in central Europe for 40 years, but also in the creation of a democratic West Germany – which in turn became the driving force for a unified Germany.

The war also spawned a host of international institutions, notably the United Nations (UN), the North Atlantic Treaty Organization (NATO), and the European Economic Community (EEC), now the European Union (EU), all of which continue to play a vital role in world politics and economy.

World War II 1939–45

Another major consequence of the war was the process of decolonization it set in motion, including the end of the British Empire, and the start of decades of adjustment for former imperial powers. In the UK, the welfare state was very much a consequence of the war. And, while nuclear fission would have been discovered eventually, World War II brought about an Anglo–American accelerated programme of development which led directly to Hiroshima in 1945. This heralded the age of Mutual Assured Destruction (MAD) for the next 45 years, underpinned by the ideological conflicts of the Cold War. *See timeline on p. 1158.*

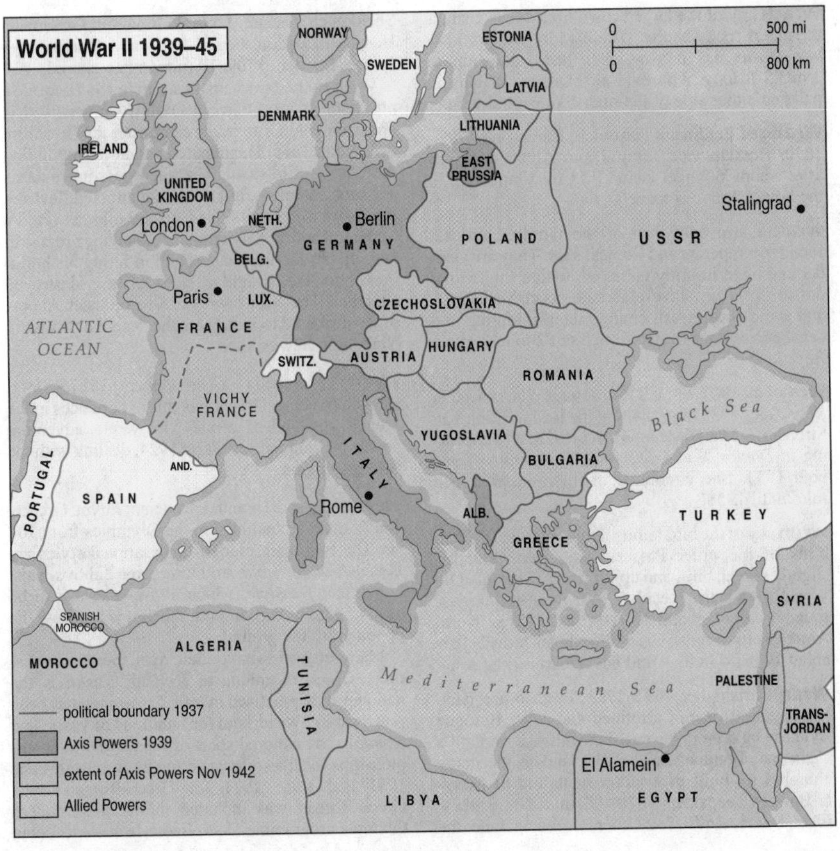

World Wide Fund for Nature (WWF, formerly the ***World Wildlife Fund***) international organization established 1961 to raise funds for conservation by public appeal. Projects include conservation of particular species, for example, the tiger and giant panda, and special areas, such as the Simen Mountains, Ethiopia. Its headquarters are in Gland, Switzerland.

World Wide Web (WWW) ◊hypertext system for publishing information on the ◊Internet. World Wide Web documents ('web pages') are text files coded using ◊HTML to include text and graphics, stored on a special computer (a web server) connected to the Internet. Web pages may also contain ◊Java applets for enhanced animation, video, sound, and interactivity.

Every web page has a ◊URL (Uniform Resource Locator) – a unique address (usually starting with http://www), which tells a ◊browser program (such as Netscape or Microsoft Explorer) where to find it. An important feature of the World Wide Web is that most documents contain links enabling readers to follow whatever aspects of a subject that interest them most. These links may connect to different computers all over the world. Interlinked or nested web pages belonging to a single organization are known as a 'web site'.

World Wildlife Fund former and US name of the ***World Wide Fund for Nature***.

worm any of various elongated limbless invertebrates belonging to several phyla. Worms include the ◊flatworms, such as ◊flukes and ◊tapeworms; the roundworms or ◊nematodes, such as the eelworm and the hookworm; the marine ribbon worms or nemerteans; and the segmented worms or ◊annelids.

WORM (acronym for ***write once read many times***) in computing, a storage device, similar to ◊CD-ROM. The computer can write to the disc directly, but cannot later erase or overwrite the same area. WORMs are mainly used for archiving and backup copies.

Worms industrial town in Rhineland-Palatinate, Germany, on the river Rhine; population (1991) 77,400. The vineyards of the Liebfrauenkirche produced the original Liebfraumilch wine; it is now produced by many growers around Worms. The Protestant reformer Martin Luther appeared before the Diet (Assembly) of Worms 1521 and was declared an outlaw by the Roman Catholic church.

wormwood any plant of the genus *Artemisia*, family Compositae, especially the aromatic herb *A. absinthium*, the leaves of which are used in ◊absinthe.

Worner Manfred 1934–1994. German politician, NATO secretary-general 1988–94. As a specialist in strategic affairs, he served as defence minister under Chancellor Kohl 1982–88. He was a proponent of closer European military collaboration, and succeeded the British politician Peter Carrington as secretary-general of NATO.

worsted (from Worstead, Norfolk, where it was first made) stiff, smooth woollen fabric.

Worthing seaside resort in West Sussex, England, at the foot of the South Downs; population (1991) 96,200. Industries include electronics, engineering, plastics, furniture, and horticulture. There are traces of prehistoric and Roman occupation in the vicinity.

Wounded Knee site on the Oglala Sioux Reservation, South Dakota, USA, of a confrontation between the US Army and Native Americans. Chief Sitting Bull was killed, supposedly resisting arrest, on 15 Dec 1890, and on 29 Dec a group of Indians

If you would see his monument, look around.

On **Christopher Wren** Inscription in St Paul's Cathedral, London, attributed to Wren's son

WORLD WAR II: TIMELINE

1939 Sept	German invasion of Poland; Britain and France declared war on Germany; USSR invaded Poland; fall of Warsaw (Poland divided between Germany and USSR).
Nov	USSR invaded Finland.
1940 March	Soviet peace treaty with Finland.
April	Germany occupied Denmark, Norway, the Netherlands, Belgium, and Luxembourg. In Britain, a coalition government was formed under Churchill.
May	Germany outflanked the defensive French Maginot Line.
May–June	Evacuation of 337,131 Allied troops from Dunkirk, France, across the Channel to England.
June	Italy declared war on Britain and France; the Germans entered Paris; French prime minister Pétain signed an armistice with Germany and moved the seat of government to Vichy.
July–Oct	Battle of Britain between British and German air forces.
Sept	Japanese invasion of French Indochina.
Oct	Abortive Italian invasion of Greece.
1941 April	Germany occupied Greece and Yugoslavia.
June	Germany invaded USSR; Finland declared war on USSR.
July	German troops entered Smolensk, USSR.
Dec	German troops came within 40 km/25 mi of Moscow, with Leningrad (now St Petersburg) under siege. First Soviet counteroffensive. Japan bombed Pearl Harbor, Hawaii, and declared war on USA and Britain. Germany and Italy declared war on USA.
1942 Jan	Japanese conquest of the Philippines.
June	Naval battle of Midway, the turning point of the Pacific War.
Aug	German attack on Stalingrad (now Volgograd), USSR.
Oct–Nov	Battle of El Alamein in N Africa, turn of the tide for the Western Allies.
Nov	Soviet counteroffensive on Stalingrad.
1943 Jan	The Casablanca Conference issued the Allied demand of unconditional surrender; German troops retreated from Stalingrad.
March	USSR drove Germans back to the river Donetz.
May	End of Axis resistance in N Africa.
July	A coup by King Victor Emmanuel and Marshal Badoglio forced Mussolini to resign.
Aug	Beginning of the campaign against the Japanese in Burma (now Myanmar); US Marines landed on Guadalcanal, Solomon Islands.
Sept	Italy surrendered to the Allies; Mussolini was rescued by the Germans, who set up a Republican Fascist government in N Italy; Allied landings at Salerno; USSR retook Smolensk.
Oct	Italy declared war on Germany.
Nov	US Navy defeated the Japanese in the Battle of Guadalcanal.
Nov–Dec	Allied leaders met at the Tehran Conference.
1944 Jan	Allied landing in Nazi-occupied Italy: Battle of Anzio.
March	End of German U-boat campaign in the Atlantic.
May	Fall of Monte Cassino, S Italy.
6 June	D-day: Allied landings in Nazi-occupied and heavily defended Normandy.
July	Bomb plot by German generals against Hitler failed.
Aug	Romania joined the Allies.
Sept	Battle of Arnhem on the Rhine; Soviet armistice with Finland.
Oct	The Yugoslav guerrilla leader Tito and Soviet troops entered Belgrade.
Dec	German counteroffensive, Battle of the Bulge.
1945 Feb	Soviet troops reached German border; Yalta conference; Allied bombing campaign over Germany (Dresden destroyed); US reconquest of the Philippines was completed; US troops landed on Iwo Jima, S of Japan.
April	Hitler committed suicide; Mussolini was captured by Italian partisans and shot.
May	German surrender to the Allies.
June	US troops completed the conquest of Okinawa (one of the Japanese Ryukyu Islands).
July	Potsdam Conference issued an Allied ultimatum to Japan.
Aug	Atom bombs dropped by USA on Hiroshima and Nagasaki; Japan surrendered.

Wright The Guggenheim Museum, New York, designed by Frank Lloyd Wright to house the superb collection of modern art made by the industrialist Solomon R Guggenheim. The building was commissioned 1943 and opened 1959, ten years after Guggenheim's death. In a radical departure from traditional museum design, the works of art are displayed on a continual spiral ramp, which is clearly expressed in the exterior of the building. *Corbis*

involved in the Ghost Dance Movement (aimed at resumption of Indian control of North America with the aid of the spirits of dead braves) were surrounded and 153 killed.

W particle in physics, an ◊elementary particle, one of the weakons responsible for transmitting the ◊weak nuclear force.

wrack any of the large brown ◊seaweeds characteristic of rocky shores. The bladder wrack *Fucus vesiculosus* has narrow, branched fronds up to 1 m/3.3 ft long, with oval air bladders, usually in pairs on either side of the midrib or central vein.

Wrangel Ferdinand Petrovich, Baron von 1797–1870. Russian vice admiral and Arctic explorer, after whom Wrangel Island (Ostrov Vrangelya) in the Soviet Arctic is named.

wrasse any bony fish of the family Labridae, found in temperate and tropical seas. They are slender and often brightly coloured, with a single long dorsal fin. They have elaborate courtship rituals, and some species can change their colouring and sex. Species vary in size from 5 cm/2 in to 2 m/6.5 ft.

Wray Fay 1907– . US film actress. She starred in *King Kong* 1933 after playing the lead in Erich von Stroheim's *The Wedding March* 1928, and appearing in *Doctor X* and *The Most Dangerous Game* both 1932. She continued in intermittent screen roles until 1958.

wren any of the bird family Troglodytidae of small birds of the order Passeriformes, with slender, slightly curved bills, and uptilted tails. The only Old World wren is the species *Troglodytes troglodytes*, found in Europe and N Asia, as well as North America. Its plumage is rich reddish brown. It is about 10 cm/4 in long and has a loud trilling song.

Wren Christopher 1632–1723. English architect. His ingenious use of a refined and sober Baroque style can be seen in his best-known work, St Paul's Cathedral, London, 1675–1710, and in the many churches he built in London including St Mary-le-Bow, Cheapside, 1670–77 and St Bride's, Fleet Street, 1671–78. Other works include the Sheldonian Theatre, Oxford, 1664–69; Greenwich Hospital, London, begun 1694; and Marlborough House, London, 1709–10 (now much altered).

Wren studied mathematics, and in 1660 became a professor of astronomy at Oxford University. His opportunity as an architect came after the Great Fire of London 1666. He prepared a plan for rebuilding the city on Classical lines, incorporating piazzas and broad avenues, but it was not adopted. Instead, Wren was commissioned to rebuild St Paul's Cathedral and 51 City churches, showing great skill both in varying the designs and in fitting his buildings into the irregular sites of the destroyed churches. The west towers of Westminster Abbey, often attributed to him, were the design of his pupil Nicholas ◊Hawksmoor.

Wren P(ercival) C(hristopher) 1875–1941. English novelist. Drawing on his experiences in the French and Indian armies, he wrote adventure novels including *Beau Geste* 1924, dealing with the Foreign Legion.

wrestling sport popular in ancient Egypt, Greece, and Rome, and included in the Olympics from 704 BC. The two main modern international styles are ***Greco-Roman***, concentrating on above-waist holds, and ***freestyle***, which allows the legs to be used to hold or trip; in both the aim is to throw the opponent to the ground.

Many countries have their own forms of wrestling. *Glima* is unique to Iceland; *Kushti* is the national style practised in Iran; *Schwingen* has been practised in Switzerland for hundreds of years; and ◊*sumo* is the national sport of Japan. World championships for freestyle wrestling have existed since 1951 and since 1921 for Greco-Roman style. Greco-Roman was included in the first modern Olympic programme 1896; freestyle made its debut

1904. Competitors are categorized according to weight: there are ten weight divisions in each style of wrestling.

Wrexham (Welsh ***Wrecsam***) town in NE Wales, 19 km/12 mi SW of Chester, and from 1996 a unitary authority (*see United Kingdom map*); population (1991) 40,600. Industries include coal, electronics, pharmaceuticals, chemicals, cables, and metal goods. It is the seat of the Roman Catholic bishopric of Menevia (Wales). Elihu Yale, founder of Yale University, is buried in the 15th-century church of St Giles.

Wright Frank Lloyd 1869–1959. US architect. He is known for 'organic architecture', in which buildings reflect their natural surroundings. From the 1890s, he developed his celebrated 'prairie-house' style, a series of low, spreading houses with projecting roofs. He later diversified, employing reinforced concrete to explore a variety of geometric forms. Among his buildings are his Wisconsin home, Taliesin East, 1925, in prairie-house style; Falling Water, near Pittsburgh, Pennsylvania, 1936, a house of cantilevered terraces straddling a waterfall; and the Guggenheim Museum, New York, 1959, a spiral ramp rising from a circular plan.

Wright also designed buildings in Japan 1915–22, most notably the Imperial Hotel in Tokyo 1916. In 1938 he built his winter home in the Arizona Desert, Taliesin West, and established an architectural community there. He always designed the interiors and furnishings for his projects, to create a total environment for his patrons.

Wright Joseph 1734–1797. English painter. He was known as ***Wright of Derby***, from his birthplace. He painted portraits, landscapes, and groups performing scientific experiments. His work is often dramatically lit – by fire, candlelight, or even volcanic explosion. Several of his subjects are highly original, for example *The Experiment on a Bird in the Air Pump* 1768 (National Gallery, London). His portraits include the reclining figure of *Sir Brooke Boothby* 1781 (Tate Gallery, London).

Wright Peter 1916–1995. English intelligence agent. His book *Spycatcher* 1987, written after his retirement, caused an international stir when the British government tried unsuccessfully to block its publication anywhere in the world because of its damaging revelations about the secret service. In *Spycatcher* he claimed, among other things, that Roger Hollis (1905–1973), head of MI5 1955–65, had been a Soviet double agent; this was later denied by the KGB.

Wright Richard 1908–1960. US novelist. He was one of the first to depict the condition of black people in 20th-century US society with his powerful tragic novel *Native Son* 1940 and the autobiography *Black Boy* 1945. His other works include *White Man, Listen!* 1957, originally a series of lectures.

Wright brothers Orville (1871–1948) and Wilbur (1867–1912) US inventors; brothers who pioneered piloted, powered flight. Inspired by Otto ◊Lilienthal's gliding, they perfected their piloted glider 1902. In 1903 they built a powered machine, a 12-hp 341-kg/750-lb plane, and became the first to make a successful powered flight, near Kitty Hawk, North Carolina. Orville flew 36.6 m/120 ft in 12 seconds; Wilbur, 260 m/852 ft in 59 seconds.

Wright brothers US aviator Orville Wright (wearing the hat) with Lt Selfridge in 1908. During their flight, which was to test new propellers, the craft fell and Selfridge was killed. In 1903, Orville and his brother Wilbur, self-taught aviators, had become the first to fly a heavier-than-air machine at Kitty Hawk, North Carolina, USA. *Topham*

writ in law, a document issued by a court requiring performance of certain actions. These include a writ of delivery (for the seizure of goods), writ of execution (enforcement of a judgement), writ of summons (commencing proceedings in the High Court), or writ of ◊habeas corpus.

writing any written form of communication using a set of symbols: see ◊alphabet, ◊cuneiform, ◊hieroglyphic. The last two used ideographs (picture writing) and phonetic word symbols side by side, as does modern Chinese. Syllabic writing, as in Japanese, develops from the continued use of a symbol to represent the sound of a short word. Some 8,000-year-old inscriptions, thought to be pictographs, were found on animal bones and tortoise shells in Henan province, China, at a Neolithic site at Jiahu. They are thought to predate by 2,500 years the oldest known writing (Mesopotamian cuneiform of 3,500 BC).

Wroclaw (formerly ***Breslau***) industrial river port in Poland, on the river Oder; population (1993) 643,600. Industries include shipbuilding, engineering, textiles, and electronics. It was the capital of the German province of Lower Silesia until 1945.

wrought iron fairly pure iron containing some beads of slag, widely used for construction work before the days of cheap steel. It is strong, tough, and easy to machine. It is made in a puddling furnace, invented by Henry Colt in England 1784. Pig iron is remelted and heated strongly in air with iron ore, burning out the carbon in the metal, leaving relatively pure iron and a slag containing impurities. The resulting pasty metal is then hammered to remove as much of the remaining slag as possible. It is still used in fences and grating.

Wuhan river port and capital of Hubei province, China, at the confluence of the Han and Chang Jiang rivers, formed 1950 as one of China's greatest industrial areas by the amalgamation of Hankou, Hanyang, and Wuchang; population (1993) 3,860,000. It produces iron, steel, machine tools, textiles, and fertilizer. A centre of revolt in both the Taiping Rebellion 1851–65 and the 1911 revolution, it had an anti-Mao revolt 1967 during the Cultural Revolution.

Wundt Wilhelm Max 1832–1920. German physiologist who regarded psychology as the study of internal experience or consciousness. His main psychological method was introspection; he also studied sensation, perception of space and time, and reaction times.

Würzburg industrial city (engineering, printing, wine, brewing) in NW Bavaria, Germany; population (1993) 129,200. The bishop's palace was decorated by the Italian Rococo painter Tiepolo.

WWF abbreviation for ◊***World Wide Fund for Nature*** (formerly World Wildlife Fund).

Wyatt James 1746–1813. English architect. A contemporary of the Adam brothers, he designed in the Neo-Gothic style. His overenthusiastic 'restorations' of medieval cathedrals earned him the nickname 'Wyatt the Destroyer'.

Wyatt Thomas c. 1503–1542. English poet. He was employed on diplomatic missions by Henry VIII, and in 1536 was imprisoned for a time in the Tower of London, suspected of having been the lover of Henry's second wife, Anne Boleyn. In 1541 Wyatt was again imprisoned on charges of treason. With the Earl of Surrey, he introduced the sonnet to England.

Wycherley William 1640–c. 1716. English Restoration dramatist. His first comedy, *Love in a Wood*, won him court favour 1671, and later bawdy works include *The Country Wife* 1675 and *The Plain Dealer* 1676.

Wycliffe John c. 1320–1384. English religious reformer. Allying himself with the party of John of Gaunt, which was opposed to ecclesiastical influence at court, he attacked abuses in the church, maintaining that the Bible rather than the church was the supreme authority. He criticized such fundamental doctrines as priestly absolution, confession, and indulgences, and set disciples to work on translating the Bible into English. He was denounced as a heretic, but died peacefully at Lutterworth, Leicestershire.

Wye (Welsh ***Gwy***) river in Wales and England; length 208 km/130 mi. It rises on Plynlimmon, NE Dyfed, flows SE and E through Powys, and Hereford and Worcester, then follows the Monmouthshire–Gloucestershire border before joining the river Severn S of Chepstow. Other rivers of the same name in the UK are found in Buckinghamshire (15 km/9 mi) and Derbyshire (32 km/20 mi).

Wyeth Andrew Newell 1917– . US painter. His portraits and landscapes, usually in watercolour or tempera, are naturalistic, minutely detailed, and often convey a strong sense of the isolation of the countryside; for example, *Christina's World* 1948 (Museum of Modern Art, New York).

Wyler William 1902–1981. German-born film director. He lived in the USA from 1922. Noted for his adroit, painstaking style, he directed *Wuthering Heights* 1939, *Mrs Miniver* 1942, *Ben Hur* 1959, and *Funny Girl* 1968, among others.

Wyndham John. Pen name of John Wyndham Parkes Lucas Beynon Harris 1903–1969. English science-fiction writer. He wrote *The Day of the Triffids* 1951, *The Chrysalids* 1955, and *The Midwich Cuckoos* 1957. A recurrent theme in his work is people's response to disaster, whether caused by nature, aliens, or human error.

Wyoming state in western USA; nicknamed Equality State
area 253,400 sq km/97,812 sq mi
capital Cheyenne
cities Casper, Laramie
features Rocky Mountains; Yellowstone national park, the first national park in the USA (1872), with geysers (including Old Faithful), hot springs, and mud pots; Grand Teton national park; Bighorn Mountains; Gannett Peak (4,207 m/13,804 ft) in the Wind River Range, the highest peak in the state; Flaming George national park; Devils Tower national monument; Jackson; Buffalo Bill Historical Center, Cody; state capitol, Cheyenne (1886); Wyoming Territorial Prison Park, Laramie; University of Wyoming
industries oil, natural gas, sodium salts, coal, uranium, sheep, beef

Wyoming

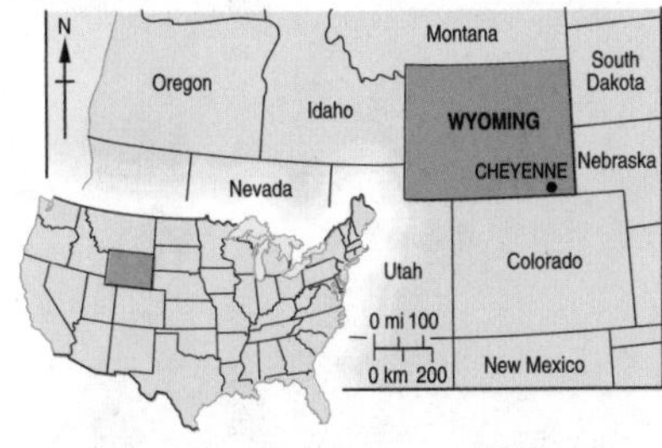

The physician can bury his mistakes, but the architect can only advise his client to plant vines.

Frank Lloyd Wright
New York Times Magazine 4 Oct 1953

population (1991) 460,000
famous people Buffalo Bill, Jackson Pollock
history acquired by the USA from France as part of the ◊Louisiana Purchase 1803; Fort Laramie, a trading post, was settled 1834; women achieved the vote 1869; became a state 1890. Despite the development of its energy resources, Wyoming remains sparsely settled, with large ranches dotting the arid landscape.

WYSIWYG (acronym for ***what you see is what you get***) in computing, a program that attempts to display on the screen a faithful representation of the final printed output. For example, a WYSIWYG word processor would show actual page layout – line widths, page breaks, and the sizes and styles of type.

Wyss Johann David 1743–1818. Swiss author. He is remembered for the children's classic *Swiss Family Robinson* 1812–13.

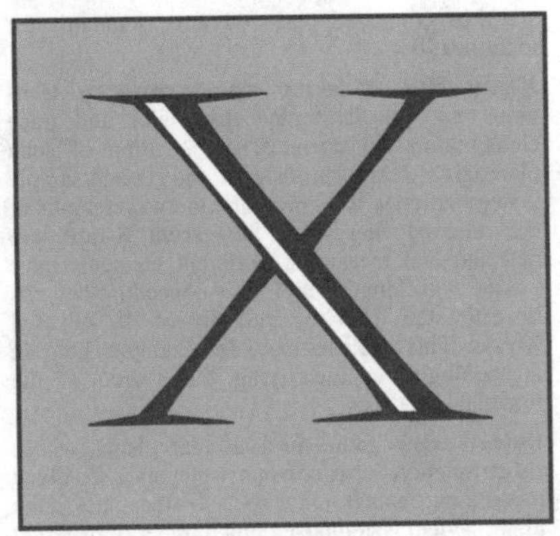

X Roman numeral *ten*; a person or thing unknown.

xanthophyll yellow pigment in plants that, like ◊chlorophyll, is responsible for the production of carbohydrates by photosynthesis.

Xavier, St Francis 1506–1552. Spanish Jesuit missionary. He went to the Portuguese colonies in the East Indies, arriving at Goa 1542. He was in Japan 1549–51, establishing a Christian mission that lasted for 100 years. He returned to Goa 1552, and sailed for China, but died of fever there. He was canonized 1622.

X chromosome larger of the two sex chromosomes, the smaller being the ◊Y chromosome. These two chromosomes are involved in sex determination. Females have two X chromosomes, males have an X and a Y. Genes carried on the X chromosome produce the phenomenon of ◊sex linkage.

Xenakis Iannis 1922– . Romanian-born Greek composer. He studied music in Paris 1947–51 while practising as an engineering draughtsman for French architect Le Corbusier. Compositions such as *Metastaseis/After Change* 1953–54 for 61 players apply stochastic principles (for example, describing particle motion in fluids) to the composition of densely-textured effects in which change is perceived globally. Later works, including a setting of the *Oresteia* 1965–66 for choir and ensemble, draw on Greek mythology.

xenon (Greek *xenos* 'stranger') colourless, odourless, gaseous, non-metallic element, symbol Xe, atomic number 54, relative atomic mass 131.30. It is grouped with the ◊inert gases and was long believed not to enter into reactions, but is now known to form some compounds, mostly with fluorine. It is a heavy gas present in very small quantities in the air (about one part in 20 million).

Xenon is used in bubble chambers, light bulbs, vacuum tubes, and lasers. It was discovered 1898 in a residue from liquid air by Scottish chemists William Ramsay and Morris Travers.

Xenophanes Greek poet and philosopher. He attacked the immoral and humanlike gods depicted by the poet Homer, holding that there is only one deity, 'in no way like men in body or in thought'. He speculated that stars were ignited clouds, and that everything was mud since fossils of sea creatures were found inland.

Born in Colophon, he left Ionia at the age of 25 and travelled around the Greek world reciting his philosophical and other poems. His outlook was generally undogmatic, because 'seeming is wrought over all things'. Considerable fragments of his elegies and of his poem *On Nature* have survived.

xenophobia fear (◊phobia) or strong dislike of strangers or anybody foreign or different.

Xenophon c. 430–354 BC. Greek historian, philosopher, and soldier. He was a disciple of ◊Socrates (described in Xenophon's *Symposium*). In 401 he joined a Greek mercenary army aiding the Persian prince Cyrus, and on the latter's death took command. His *Anabasis* describes how he led 10,000 Greeks on a 1,600-km/1,000-mile march home across enemy territory. His other works include *Memorabilia*, *Apology*, and *Hellenica/A History of My Times*.

xenotransplant animal to human transplant. Animals used as organ and tissue sources include pigs and primates. Transplants carried out (with varying degrees of success) include heart, kidney, liver, bone marrow, fetal neural tissue (to treat Parkinson's disease), and fetal islet tissue (for diabetes). The first xenotransplants took place in 1964 (pig heart valves in the UK; chimpanzee kidneys in the USA).

Clinical trials were halted in the USA 1995 because of fears that diseases could be spread from animals to humans. In 1996 an advisory panel concluded that the benefits were such that this risk was justified. However, US researchers called for a ban on transplants from pigs in 1997, following the discovery that pigs can carry a virus that can be passed to humans. The use of primates as donors was ruled unethical in the UK 1996.

xerography dry, electrostatic method of producing images, without the use of negatives or sensitized paper, invented in the USA by Chester Carlson 1938 and applied in the Xerox photocopier.

An image of the document to be copied is projected on to an electrostatically charged photo-conductive plate. The charge remains only in the areas corresponding to its image. The latent image on the plate is then developed by contact with ink powder, which adheres only to the image, and is then usually transferred to ordinary paper or some other flat surface, and quickly heated to form a permanent print.

xerophyte plant adapted to live in dry conditions. Common adaptations to reduce the rate of ◊transpiration include a reduction of leaf size, sometimes to spines or scales; a dense covering of hairs over the leaf to trap a layer of moist air (as in edelweiss); water storage cells; sunken stomata; and permanently rolled leaves or leaves that roll up in dry weather (as in marram grass). Many desert cacti are xerophytes.

Xerxes c. 519–465 BC. King of Persia from 486 BC when he succeeded his father Darius. In 480, at the head of a great army which was supported by the Phoenician navy, he crossed the Dardanelles over a bridge of boats. He captured and burned Athens, but the Persian fleet was defeated at Salamis and Xerxes was forced to retreat. His general Mardonius remained behind in Greece, but was defeated by the Greeks at Plataea 479. Xerxes was eventually murdered in a court intrigue.

XGA (abbreviation for ***extended graphics array***) in computing, colour display system which provides either 256 colours on screen and a resolution of 1,024 × 768 pixels or 25,536 colours with a resolution of 640 × 480. This gives a much sharper image than, for example, VGA, which can display only 16 colours at 480 lines of 640 pixels.

Xhosa a Bantu people of southern Africa, living mainly in Eastern Cape Province. Traditionally, the Xhosa were farmers and pastoralists, with a social structure based on a monarchy. Many are now town-dwellers, and provide much of the unskilled labour in South African mines and factories. Their Bantu language belongs to the Niger-Congo family.

Xia dynasty or ***Hsia dynasty*** China's first legendary ruling family, c. 2200–c. 1500 BC, reputedly founded by the model emperor Yu the Great. He is believed to have controlled floods by constructing dykes. Archaeological evidence suggests that the Xia dynasty really did exist, as a Bronze Age civilization where writing was being developed, with its capital at Erlidou (Erh-li-t'ou) in Henan (Honan).

Xian industrial city and capital of Shaanxi province, China; population (1993) 2,360,000. It produces chemicals, electrical equipment, and fertilizers.

It was the capital of China under the Zhou dynasty (1066–221 BC); under the Han dynasty (206 BC–AD 220), when it was called ***Changan*** ('long peace'); and under the Tang dynasty (618–907), as ***Siking*** ('western capital'). The Manchus called it ***Sian*** ('western peace'), now spelled Xian. It reverted to Changan 1913–32, was Siking 1932–43, and again Sian from 1943. It was here that the imperial court retired after the Boxer Rebellion 1900.

Its treasures include the 600-year-old Ming wall; the terracotta army, consisting of pottery soldiers buried to protect the tomb of the first Qin emperor, Shi Huangdi; Big Wild Goose Pagoda, one of the oldest in China; and the Great Mosque 742.

Xian Incident kidnapping of the Chinese generalissimo and politician ◊Chiang Kai-shek in Xian 12 Dec 1936, by one of his own generals, to force his cooperation with the communists against the Japanese invaders.

Xi Jiang or ***Si-Kiang*** river in China, that rises in Yunnan province and flows into the South China Sea; length 1,900 km/1,200 mi. Guangzhou lies on the northern arm of its delta, and Hong Kong island at its mouth. The name means 'west river'.

Xining or ***Sining*** industrial city (chemicals, textiles, machinery, processed foods) and capital of Qinghai province, China, on the Xining River; population (1990) 552,000. For centuries it was a major trading centre on the caravan route to Tibet.

Xinjiang Uygur or ***Sinkiang Uighur*** autonomous region of NW China
area 1,646,800 sq km/635,665 sq mi
capital Urumqi
features largest of Chinese administrative areas; Junggar Pendi (Dzungarian Basin) and Tarim Pendi (Tarim Basin, which includes Lop Nor, China's

The whole of human life is so short – not one of this great number will be alive a hundred years from now.

XERXES
On his army, quoted in Herodotus *Histories*

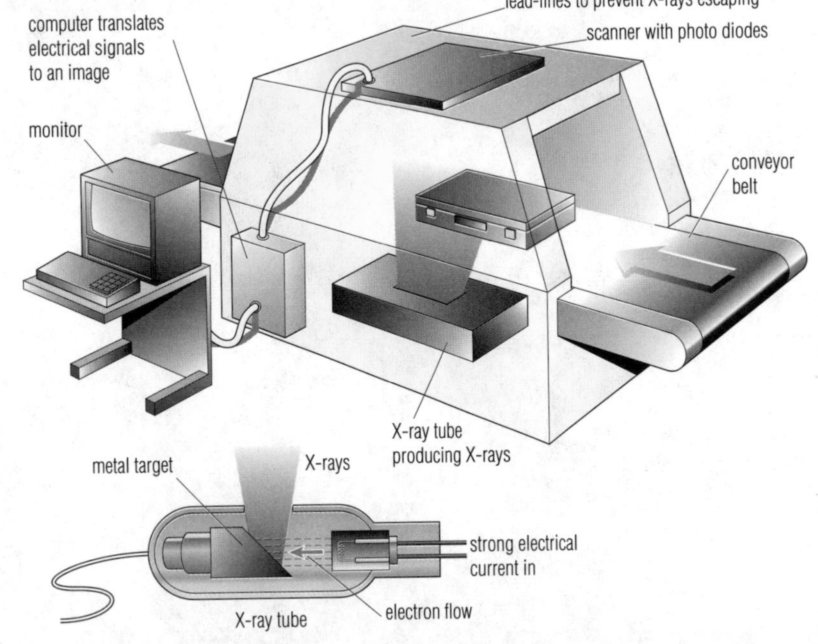

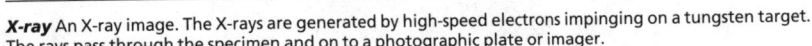

X-ray An X-ray image. The X-rays are generated by high-speed electrons impinging on a tungsten target. The rays pass through the specimen and on to a photographic plate or imager.

nuclear testing ground, although the research centres were moved to the central province of Sichuan 1972) separated by the Tian Shan Mountains
industries cereals, cotton, fruit in valleys and oases; uranium, coal, iron, copper, tin, oil
population (1990) 15,370,000; the region has 13 recognized ethnic minorities, the largest being 6 million Uigurs (Muslim descendants of Turks)
religion 50% Muslim
history under Manchu rule from the 18th century. Large sections were ceded to Russia 1864 and 1881; China has raised the question of their return and regards the frontier between Xinjiang Uygur and Tajikistan, which runs for 480 km/300 mi, as undemarcated.

Xiongnu or ***Hsiung-nu*** Turkish-speaking nomad horseriding peoples from central Asia, who founded an extensive Chinese steppe empire and harried N Chinese states in the 3rd century BC. Originating in Mongolia and S Siberia, they were forced back to the Gobi Desert 119 BC by China's Han-dynasty emperor Wudi (Wu-ti, reigned 141–87 BC) through a bloody war of attrition. The ◊Great Wall of China was then extended to strengthen defences against them. The Xiongnu later became vassals of China, being employed as frontier troops.

X-ray band of electromagnetic radiation in the wavelength range 10^{-11} to 10^{-9} m (between gamma rays and ultraviolet radiation; see ◊electromagnetic waves). Applications of X-rays make use of their short wavelength (as in ◊X-ray diffraction) or their penetrating power (as in medical X-rays of internal body tissues). X-rays are dangerous and can cause cancer.

X-rays with short wavelengths pass through most body tissues, although dense areas such as bone prevent their passage, showing up as white areas on X-ray photographs. The X-rays used in ◊radiotherapy have very short wavelengths that penetrate tissues deeply and destroy them.

X-rays were discovered by German experimental physicist Wilhelm Röntgen 1895 and formerly called roentgen rays. They are produced when high-energy electrons from a heated filament cathode strike the surface of a target (usually made of tungsten) on the face of a massive heat-conducting anode, between which a high alternating voltage (about 100 kV) is applied.

X-ray astronomy detection of X-rays from intensely hot gas in the universe. Such X-rays are prevented from reaching the Earth's surface by the atmosphere, so detectors must be placed in rockets and satellites. The first celestial X-ray source, Scorpius X-1, was discovered by a rocket flight 1962. Many X-ray sources are believed to be gas falling on to ◊neutron stars and ◊black holes.

X-ray diffraction method of studying the atomic and molecular structure of crystalline substances by using ◊X-rays. X-rays directed at such substances spread out as they pass through the crystals owing to ◊diffraction (the slight spreading of waves around the edge of an opaque object) of the rays around the atoms. By using measurements of the position and intensity of the diffracted waves, it is possible to calculate the shape and size of the atoms in the crystal. The method has been used to study substances such as ◊DNA that are found in living material.

X-ray diffraction analysis the use of X-rays to study the atomic and molecular structure of crystalline substances such as ceramics, stone, sediments, and weathering products on metals. The sample is ground to powder, and exposed to X-rays at various angles; the diffraction patterns produced are then compared with reference standards for identification.

X-ray fluorescence spectrometry technique used to determine the major and trace elements in the chemical composition of such materials as ceramics, obsidian, and glass. A sample is bombarded with X-rays, and the wavelengths of the released energy, or fluorescent X-rays, are detected and measured. Different elements have unique wavelengths, and their concentrations can be estimated from the intensity of the released X-rays. This analysis may, for example, help an archaeologist in identifying the source of the material.

xylem tissue found in ◊vascular plants, whose main function is to conduct water and dissolved mineral nutrients from the roots to other parts of the plant. Xylem is composed of a number of different types of cell, and may include long, thin, usually dead cells known as ◊tracheids; fibres (schlerenchyma); parenchyma cells (loosely packed, more or less spherical cells with thin cellulose walls); and conducting vessels.

Non-woody plants contain only primary xylem, derived from the procambium, whereas in trees and shrubs this is replaced for the most part by secondary xylem, formed by ◊secondary growth from the actively dividing vascular ◊cambium. The cell walls of the secondary xylem are thickened by a deposit of ◊lignin, providing mechanical support to the plant; see ◊wood.

xylophone musical ◊percussion instrument of African and Indonesian origin, consisting of a series of resonant hardwood bars of varying lengths, each with its own distinct pitch, arranged in sequence and played with hard sticks. It first appeared as an orchestral instrument in Saint-Saëns's *Danse macabre* 1874, illustrating dancing skeletons.

yak Domesticated yaks like these pack animals in Tibet are found throughout Central Asia and the Himalayas. Yaks have been domesticated for hundreds of years for their milk, meat, hides, and wool. Wild yaks, on the other hand, have been so extensively hunted that they are now an endangered species. *Corbis*

yachting pleasure cruising or racing a small and light vessel, whether sailing or power-driven. At the Olympic Games, seven sail-driven categories exist: Soling, Flying Dutchman, Star, Finn, Tornado, 470, and Windglider or ◊windsurfing (boardsailing). The Finn and Windglider are solo events; the Soling class is for three-person crews; all other classes are for crews of two.

Yahya Khan Agha Muhammad 1917–1980. Pakistani president 1969–71. His mishandling of the Bangladesh separatist issue led to civil war, and he was forced to resign.

Yahya Khan fought with the British army in the Middle East during World War II. He supported General Ayub Khan's 1958 coup and in 1969 became military ruler. Following defeat by India 1971, he resigned and was under house arrest 1972–75.

yak species of cattle *Bos grunniens*, family Bovidae, which lives in wild herds at high altitudes in Tibet. It stands about 2 m/6 ft at the shoulder and has long shaggy hair on the underparts. It has large, upward-curving horns and humped shoulders. It is in danger of becoming extinct.

In the wild, the yak is brown or black, but the domesticated variety, which is half the size of the wild form, may be white. It is used for milk, meat, leather, and as a beast of burden. The yak is protected from extremes of cold by its thick coat and by the heat produced from the fermentation in progress in its stomach.

Yakutia (Russian ***Yakutskaya***) former name of ◊Sakha, an autonomous republic in the Russian Federation.

Yakutsk capital of Sakha autonomous republic, Russian Federation (formerly Yakutia), on the river Lena; population (1994) 187,000. Industries include timber, tanning, and brick-making. It is the coldest point of the Arctic in NE Siberia, average winter temperature −50° C/-68° F, and has an institute for studying the permanently frozen soil area (permafrost). The lowest temperature ever recorded was in Yakutia, −70° C/−126° F.

yakuza (Japanese 'good for nothing') Japanese gangster. Organized crime in Japan is highly structured, and the various syndicates between them employed some 110,000 people 1989, with a turnover of an estimated 1.5 trillion yen. The *yakuza* have been unofficially tolerated and are very powerful.

Their main areas of activity are prostitution, pornography, sports, entertainment, and moneylending; they have close links with the construction industry and with some politicians. There is considerable rivalry between gangs. Many *yakuza* have one or more missing fingertips, a self-inflicted ritual injury in atonement for an error.

Yale University US university, founded 1701 in New Haven, Connecticut. It was named after Elihu Yale (1648–1721), born in Boston, Massachusetts, one-time governor of Fort St George, Madras, India.

Yalta Conference in 1945, a meeting at which the Allied leaders Churchill (UK), Roosevelt (USA), and Stalin (USSR) completed plans for the defeat of Germany in World War II and the foundation of the United Nations. It took place in Yalta, a Soviet holiday resort in the Crimea. *See illustration on following page.*

yam any climbing plant of the genus *Dioscorea*, family Dioscoreaceae, cultivated in tropical regions; its starchy tubers are eaten as a vegetable. The Mexican yam *D. composita* contains a chemical used in the manufacture of the contraceptive pill.

Yamamoto Gombei 1852–1933. Japanese admiral and politician. As prime minister 1913–14, he began Japanese expansion into China and initiated political reforms. He became premier again 1923 but resigned the following year.

Yamamoto Kansai 1944– . Japanese fashion designer. He opened his own house 1971. The presentation of his catwalk shows made him famous, with dramatic clothes in an exciting atmosphere. He blends the powerful and exotic designs of traditional Japanese dress with Western sportswear to create a unique, abstract style.

Yamamoto Yohji 1943– . Japanese fashion designer. He formed his own company 1972 and showed his first collection 1976. He is an uncompromising, nontraditionalist designer who swathes and wraps the body in unstructured, loose, voluminous garments.

Yamato ancient name of Japan and particularly the province of W Honshu where Japanese civilization began and where the early capitals were located; also the clan from which all emperors of Japan are descended, claiming the sun-goddess as ancestor. The Yamato period is often taken as AD 539–710 (followed by the Nara period).

According to legend, the Japanese empire dates from the conquest of the Yamato region by Emperor Jimmu 660 BC. Two chronicles, the *Kojiki/Record of Ancient Matters* 7th century and the *Nihon shoki/Chronicles of Japan* 720, give creation myths and annals of legendary and early historical reigns. The 29th emperor, Kimmei (reigned 539–71), is regarded as the first fully historical emperor. In the era of Prince Shōtoku Taishi (574–622) and the Taika reform period 645–50, the Yamato rulers became greatly influenced by the culture of ◊Tang dynasty China, notably Buddhism, Confucianism, and China's bureaucratic system. In the mid-9th century the emperors ceded effective control of government to the ◊Fujiwara clan and hardly ever ruled in their own right until the Meiji restoration 1868.

Yamoussoukro capital of ◊Côte d'Ivoire; population (1990 est) 120,000. The economy is based on tourism and agricultural trade.

A Roman Catholic basilica (said to be the largest church in the world) was completed 1989.

Yanamamo or ***Yanomamo*** (plural ***Yanamami***) a semi-nomadic Native South American people, numbering approximately 15,000, who live in S Venezuela and N Brazil. The Yanamamo language belongs to the Macro-Chibcha family. In Nov 1991 Brazil granted the Yanamami possession of their original land, 58,395 km/36,293 sq mi on its northern border.

Yanayev Gennady 1937– . Soviet communist politician, leader of the Aug 1991 anti-Gorbachev attempted coup, after which he was arrested and charged with treason. He was released 1994 under an amnesty. He was vice president of the USSR 1990–91.

Yangon formerly (until 1989) ***Rangoon*** capital and chief port of Myanmar (Burma) on the Yangon River, 32 km/20 mi from the Indian Ocean; population (1983) 2,459,000. Products include timber, oil, and rice. The city Dagon was founded on the site AD 746; it was given the name Rangoon (meaning 'end of conflict') by King Alaungpaya 1755.

Yang Shangkun 1907–1998. Chinese communist politician. He held a senior position in the party 1956–66 but was demoted during the Cultural Revolution. He was rehabilitated 1978, elected to the Politburo 1982, and served as state president 1988–93.

The son of a wealthy Sichuan landlord and a veteran of the ◊Long March 1934–35 and the war against Japan 1937–45, Yang rose in the ranks of the Chinese Communist Party before being purged for alleged revisionism in the Cultural Revolution. He was a trusted supporter of Deng Xiaoping.

Yankee colloquial (often disparaging) term for an American. Outside the USA the term is applied to any American.

During the American Civil War, the term was applied by Southerners to any Northerner or member of the Union Army and is still used today to refer to Northerners. A 'real yankee' is a person from the New England states, especially someone descended from a colonial founding family. The word has come to connote craftiness and business acumen, as in 'yankee ingenuity'.

Yao a people living in S China, N Vietnam, N Laos, Thailand, and Myanmar (Burma), and numbering about 4 million (1984). The Yao language may belong to either the Sino-Tibetan or the Thai language family. The Yao incorporate elements of ancestor worship in their animist religion.

The Yao are generally hill-dwelling farmers practising shifting cultivation, growing rice, vegetables, and also opium poppies. Some are nomadic.

Yaoundé capital of Cameroon, 210 km/130 mi E of the port of Douala; population (1991) 750,000. Industries include tourism, oil refining, and cigarette manufacturing. Established by the Germans as a military port 1899, it became capital of French Cameroon 1921.

Yalta Conference Winston Churchill, Franklin D Roosevelt, and Joseph Stalin at the Yalta Conference in Yalta in the Crimea, Feb 1945. They met not only to make final plans for the defeat of Germany, but also to make decisions on the subsequent division of Europe – decisions that were to have a profound effect on history in the second half of the 20th century. *Image Select (UK) Ltd*

yapok nocturnal ◊opossum *Chironectes minimus* found in tropical South and Central America. It is about 33 cm/1.1 ft long, with a 40 cm/1.3 ft tail. It has webbed hind feet and thick fur, and is the only aquatic marsupial. The female has a watertight pouch.

yard unit (symbol yd) of length, equivalent to three feet (0.9144 m).

In the USA, it is sometimes used to denote a cubic yard (0.7646 cubic meters) as of topsoil.

Yarkand or ***Shache*** walled city in the Xinjiang Uygur region of China, in an oasis of the Tarim Basin, on the caravan route to India and W Russia; population (1985) 100,000. It is a centre of Islamic culture.

Yarmouth or ***Great Yarmouth*** holiday resort and port in Norfolk, England, at the mouth of the river Yare; population (1991) 56,200. Formerly a herring-fishing port, it is now a base for North Sea oil and gas.

yarmulke or ***kippa*** skullcap worn by Jewish men.

yarrow or ***milfoil*** perennial herb *Achillea millefolium* of the family Compositae, with feathery, scented leaves and flat-topped clusters of white or pink flowers.

yashmak traditional Muslim face veil, worn by devout Muslim women in the presence of men.

yaws contagious tropical disease common in the West Indies, W Africa, and some Pacific islands, characterized by red, raspberrylike eruptions on the face, toes, and other parts of the body, sometimes followed by lesions of the bones; these may progress to cause gross disfigurement. It is caused by a spirochete (*Treponema pertenue*), a bacterium related to the one that causes ◊syphilis. Treatment is by antibiotics.

‘Hearts are not had as a gift but hearts are earned / By those that are not entirely beautiful.’

W B Yeats
'Prayer for my Daughter'

Y chromosome smaller of the two sex chromosomes. In male mammals it occurs paired with the other type of sex chromosome (X), which carries far more genes. The Y chromosome is the smallest of all the mammalian chromosomes and is considered to be largely inert (that is, without direct effect on the physical body). See also ◊sex determination.

In humans, about one in 300 males inherits two Y chromosomes at conception, making him an XYY triploid. Few if any differences from normal XY males exist in these individuals, although at one time they were thought to be emotionally unstable and abnormally aggressive. In 1989 the gene determining that a human being is male was found to occur on the X as well as on the Y chromosome; however, it is not activated in the female.

year unit of time measurement, based on the orbital period of the Earth around the Sun. The ***tropical year***, from one spring ◊equinox to the next, lasts 365.2422 days. It governs the occurrence of the seasons, and is the period on which the calendar year is based. The ***sidereal year*** is the time taken for the Earth to complete one orbit relative to the fixed stars, and lasts 365.2564 days (about 20 minutes longer than a tropical year). The difference is due to the effect of ◊precession, which slowly moves the position of the equinoxes. The ***calendar year*** consists of 365 days, with an extra day added at the end of Feb each leap year. ***Leap years*** occur in every year that is divisible by four, except that a century year is not a leap year unless it is divisible by 400. Hence 1900 was not a leap year, but 2000 will be.

A ***historical year*** begins on 1 Jan, although up to 1752, when the Gregorian ◊calendar was adopted in England, the civil or legal year began on 25 March. The English ***fiscal/financial year*** still ends on 5 April, which is 25 March plus the 11 days added under the reform of the calendar in 1752. The ***regnal year*** begins on the anniversary of the sovereign's accession; it is used in the dating of acts of Parliament.

The ***anomalistic year*** is the time taken by any planet in making one complete revolution from perihelion to perihelion; for the Earth this period is about 5 minutes longer than the sidereal year due to the gravitational pull of the other planets.

yeast one of various single-celled fungi (especially the genus *Saccharomyces*) that form masses of minute circular or oval cells by budding. When placed in a sugar solution the cells multiply and convert the sugar into alcohol and carbon dioxide. Yeasts are used as fermenting agents in baking, brewing, and the making of wine and spirits. Brewer's yeast *S. cerevisiae* is a rich source of vitamin B.

yeast artificial chromosome (YAC) fragment of ◊DNA from the human genome inserted into a yeast cell. The yeast replicates the fragment along with its own DNA. In this way the fragments are copied to be preserved in a gene library. YACs are characteristically between 250,000 and 1 million base pairs in length. A cosmid (a fragment of DNA from the human genome inserted into a bacterial cell) works in the same way.

Yeats W(illiam) B(utler) 1865–1939. Irish poet. He was a leader of the Celtic revival and a founder of the ◊Abbey Theatre in Dublin. His early work was romantic and lyrical, as in the poem 'The Lake Isle of Innisfree' and the plays *The Countess Cathleen* 1892 and *The Land of Heart's Desire* 1894. His later books of poetry include *The Wild Swans at Coole* 1917 and *The Winding Stair* 1929. He was a senator of the Irish Free State 1922–28. Nobel Prize for Literature 1923.

Yeats was born in Dublin. His early poetry includes *The Wind Among the Reeds* 1899, and he drew on Irish legend for his poetic plays, including *Deirdre* 1907, but broke through to a new sharply resilient style with *Responsibilities* 1914. In his personal life there was also a break: the beautiful Maude Gonne, to whom many of his poems had been addressed, refused to marry him, and in 1917 he married Georgie Hyde-Lees, whose work as a medium reinforced his leanings towards mystic symbolism, as in the prose work *A Vision* 1925 and 1937. Among his later volumes of verse are *The Tower* 1928 and *Last Poems and Two Plays* 1939. His other prose works include *Autobiographies* 1926 and *Dramatis Personae* 1936.

Yedo or ***Edo*** former name of ◊Tokyo, Japan, until 1868.

yeheb nut small tree *Cordeauxia adulis* found in Ethiopia and Somalia and formerly much valued as a food source for its nuts. Although cultivated as a food crop in Kenya and Sudan, it is now critically endangered in the wild and has at most three known sites remaining. Overgrazing by cattle and goats has prevented regeneration, and nuts are taken for consumption thus preventing reseeding.

yellow archangel flowering plant *Lamiastrum galeobdolon* of the mint family Labiatae, found over much of Europe. It grows up to 60 cm/2 ft tall and has nettlelike leaves and whorls of yellow flowers, the lower lips streaked with red in early summer.

Yeats Irish poet and dramatist, W B Yeats, who developed an interest in the supernatural as a student at Dublin School of Art. *A Vision* 1925 is an occult-based, esoteric text inspired by Blake, whose poems he edited in 1893. In Yeats's own early writings, Irish legend provided a major source, and later his marriage to Georgie Hyde-Lees, a spiritualist medium, reinforced his mystical leanings. *Corbis*

yellow fever or ***yellow jack*** acute tropical viral disease, prevalent in the Caribbean area, Brazil, and on the west coast of Africa. The yellow fever virus is an arbovirus transmitted by mosquitoes. Its symptoms include a high fever, headache, joint and muscle pains, vomiting, and yellowish skin (jaundice, possibly leading to liver failure); the heart and kidneys may also be affected. Mortality is high in serious cases.

Before the arrival of Europeans, yellow fever was not a problem because indigenous people had built up an immunity. The disease was brought under control after the discovery that it is carried by the mosquito *Aëdes aegypti*. The first effective vaccines were produced by Max Theiler (1899–1972) of South Africa, for which he was awarded the 1951 Nobel Prize for Medicine. The World Health Organization estimates there are about 200,000 cases of yellow fever each year in Africa, with 30,000 deaths (1993).

yellowhammer Eurasian bird *Emberiza citrinella* of the bunting family Emberizidae, order Passeriformes. About 16.5 cm/6.5 in long, the male has a yellow head and underside, a chestnut rump, and a brown-streaked back. The female is duller.

yellowhammer A pair of yellowhammers, or yellow buntings, *Emberiza citrinella*. The male has a bright yellow head and underparts; the female's plumage is less colourful.

Yellowknife capital of Northwest Territories, Canada, on the northern shore of Great Slave Lake; population (1986) 11,753. It was founded 1935 when gold was discovered in the area and became the capital 1967.

Yellow River English name for the ◊Huang He River, China.

Yellow Sea gulf of the Pacific Ocean between China and Korea; area 466,200 sq km/180,000 sq mi. It receives the Huang He (Yellow River) and Chang Jiang.

yellow star-of-Bethlehem rare flowering plant *Gagea lutea*. It has clusters of stalked yellow flowers that appear in very early spring, and is found in damp ◊loam, usually by woodland streams, mainly in N England.

Yellowstone National Park largest US nature reserve, established 1872, on a broad plateau in the Rocky Mountains, chiefly in NW Wyoming, but also in SW Montana and E Idaho; area 8,983 sq km/3,469 sq mi. The park contains more than 3,000 geysers and hot springs, including periodically erupting Old Faithful. It is one of the world's greatest wildlife refuges. Much of the park was ravaged by forest fires 1988.

Yeltsin Boris Nikolayevich 1931– . Russian politician, president of the Russian Soviet Federative Socialist Republic (RSFSR) 1990–91, and president of the newly independent Russian Federation from 1991. He played a prominent role in securing the reinstatement of President Mikhail Gorbachev in the coup staged by the Communist Party of the Soviet Union (CPSU) Aug 1991. The failed coup precipitated the dissolution of the Soviet Union and in the aftermath, Yeltsin directed the Federation's secession from the USSR and the formation of a new, decentralized confederation, the ◊Commonwealth of Independent States (CIS), with himself as the most powerful leader. In early 1995 Yeltsin directed a full-scale military offensive in the breakaway republic of Chechnya; a peace agreement was negotiated with the rebels May 1996. He was re-elected in the June 1996 presidential elections, defeating Communist Party leader Gennady Zyuganov.

▷ *See feature on pp. 1090–1091.*

Yemen country in SW Asia, bounded N by Saudi Arabia, E by Oman, S by the Gulf of Aden, and W by the Red Sea. *See country box below.*

yen the standard currency of Japan.

Yenisei river in Asian Russia, rising in the Tuva region and flowing across the Siberian plain into the Arctic Ocean; length 4,100 km/2,550 mi.

yeoman in England, a small landowner who farmed his own fields – a system that formed a bridge between the break-up of feudalism and the agricultural revolution of the 18th–19th centuries.

Yeomen of the Guard English military corps, popularly known as ***Beefeaters***, the sovereign's bodyguard since the corps was founded by Henry VII 1485. Its duties are now purely ceremonial.

Yerevan industrial city (tractor parts, machine tools, chemicals, bricks, bicycles, wine, fruit canning) and capital of Armenia, a few miles north of the Turkish border; population (1994) 1,200,000. It was founded in the 7th century and was alternately Turkish and Persian from the 15th century until ceded to Russia 1828. Armenia became an independent republic 1991.

The city has seen mounting inter-ethnic violence and Armenian nationalist demonstrations since 1988, fanned by the ◊Nagorno-Karabakh dispute.

Yerkes Observatory astronomical centre in Wisconsin, USA, founded by George Hale 1897. It houses the world's largest refracting optical ◊telescope, with a lens of diameter 102 cm/40 in.

Yersin Alexandre Emile Jean 1863–1943. Swiss bacteriologist who discovered the bubonic plague bacillus in Hong Kong 1894 and prepared a serum against it. The bacillus was discovered independently, in the same epidemic, by Japanese bacteriologist Shibasaburō ◊Kitasato, who published his results before Yersin did.

Yesenin Sergei Aleksandrovich, alternative form of ◊Esenin, Russian poet.

yeti Tibetan for the ◊abominable snowman.

Yevtushenko Yevgeny Aleksandrovich 1933– . Soviet poet. He aroused controversy with his anti-Stalinist 'Stalin's Heirs' 1956, published with Khrushchev's support, and 'Babi Yar' 1961, which attacked Russian as well as Nazi anti-Semitism. His other works include the long poem *Zima Junction* 1956, the novel *Berries* 1981, and *Precocious Autobiography* 1963.

yew any evergreen coniferous tree of the genus *Taxus* of the family Taxaceae, native to the northern hemisphere. The leaves and bright red berrylike seeds are poisonous; the wood is hard and close-grained.

The western or Pacific yew *T. brevifolia* is native to North America. English yew *T. baccata* is widely cultivated as an ornamental. The wood was used to make longbows. The anticancer drug taxol is synthesized from the bark of the Pacific yew.

Yezidi Islamic sect originating as disciples of the Sufi saint Sheik Adi ibn Musafir (12th century). The beliefs of its adherents mingle folk traditions with Islam, also incorporating features of Judaism and Christianity (they practise circumcision and baptism), and include a cult of the Fallen Angel who has been reconciled with God. Their chief centre is near Mosul, Iraq.

'Truth is truth, and the truth will overcome the left, the right and the centre.'

Boris Yeltsin Interview in *Newsweek* 1994

YEMEN
Republic of

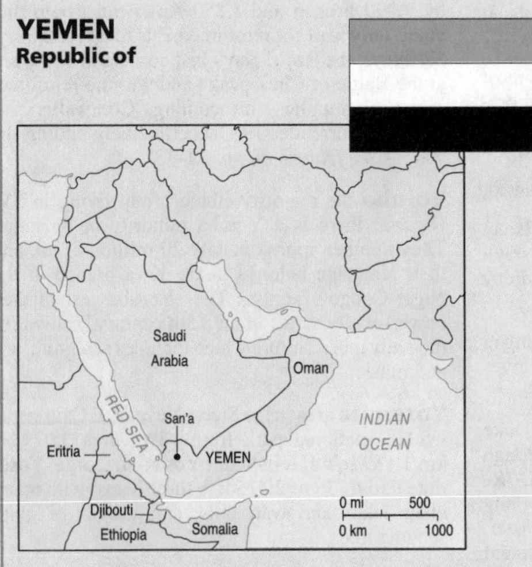

national name *Jamhuriya al Yamaniya*
area 531,900 sq km/205,367 sq mi
capital San'a
major towns/cities Ta'iz, Mukalla
major ports Aden
physical features hot moist coastal plain, rising to plateau and desert
head of state Ali Abdullah Saleh from 1990
head of government Farag Said Ben Ghanem from 1997
political system emergent democratic republic
administrative divisions 38 provinces
political parties General People's Congress (GPC), left of centre; Yemen Socialist Party (YSP), left-wing; Yemen Reform Group (al-Islah), Islamic, right of centre; National Opposition Front, left of centre
population 14,501,000 (1995 est)
population growth rate 5.0% (1990–95); 3.1% (2000–05)
ethnic distribution predominantly Arabs
life expectancy 52 (men), 52 (women)
literacy rate men 53%, women 26%
language Arabic
religions Sunni Muslim 63%, Shi'ite Muslim 37%
currency riyal in the N, dinar in the S (both legal currency throughout the country)
GDP (US $) 18.17 billion (1994 est)
growth rate 5.7% (1994)
exports cotton, coffee, grapes, vegetables, fish, petroleum

HISTORY
1st millenium BC South Yemen (Aden) was divided between the economically advanced Qataban and Hadramawt kingdoms.
c. 5th C BC Qataban fell to the Sabaeans (Shebans) of North Yemen (Sana).
c. 100 BC–AD 525 All of Yemen became part of Himyarite kingdom.
AD 628 Islam introduced.
1174–1229 Under the control of the Egyptian Ayyubids.
1229–1451 'Golden age' for arts and sciences under the Rasulids, who had served as governors of Yemen under the Ayyubids.
1538 North Yemen came under the control of the Turkish Ottoman Empire.
1636 Ottomans left North Yemen and power fell into the hands of the Yemeni Imams, based on local Zaydi tribes, who also held South Yemen until 1735.
1839 Aden became a British territory. The port was developed into an important ship refuelling station after the opening of the Suez Canal in 1869, and a protectorate established gradually over the 23 Sultanates inland.
1870s The Ottomans re-established control over North Yemen.
1918 North Yemen became independent, with the Imam Yahya from the Hamid al-Din family as king.
1937 Aden became a British crown colony.
1948 Imam Yahya was assassinated by the exiled Free Yemenis nationalist movement, but the uprising was crushed by his son, Imam Ahmad.
1959 Federation of South Arabia formed by Britain between the city of Aden and the feudal Sultanates (Aden Protectorate).
1962 Military coup on the death of Imam Ahmad, and North Yemen declared the Yemen Arab Republic (YAR), with Abdullah al-Sallal as president. Civil war broke out between royalists (supported by Saudi Arabia) and republicans (supported by Egypt).
1963 Armed rebellion, by National Liberation Front (NLF), began against British rule in Aden.
1967 Civil war ended with the republicans victorious. Sallal deposed and replaced by Republican Council. The Independent People's Republic of South Yemen was formed after British withdrawal from Aden. Many fled to the N as repressive communist NLF regime took over in the S.
1970 People's Republic of South Yemen renamed People's Democratic Republic of Yemen.
1971–72 War between South Yemen and the YAR; union agreement brokered by the Arab League signed but not kept.
1974 The pro-Saudi Col Ibrahim al-Hamadi seized power in North Yemen and Military Command Council set up.
1977 Hamadi assassinated and replaced by Col Ahmed ibn Hussein al-Ghashmi.
1978 Constituent people's assembly appointed in North Yemen and Military Command Council dissolved. Ghashmi killed by envoy from South Yemen; succeeded by Ali Abdullah Saleh. War broke out again between the two Yemens. South Yemen president deposed and executed; Yemen Socialist Party (YSP) formed in the S by communists.
1979 Cease-fire agreed with commitment to future union.
1980 YSP leader Ali Nasser Muhammad became head of state in South Yemen.
1986 Civil war in South Yemen; autocratic Ali Nasser dismissed. New administration formed under the more moderate Haydar Abu Bakr al-Attas, who was committed to negotiating union with the N as a result of a deteriorating economy in the S.
1989 Draft multiparty constitution for single Yemen state published.
1990 Border between two Yemens opened; countries formally united 22 May as Republic of Yemen.
1991 New constitution approved; Yemen opposed the US-led operations against Iraq in the Gulf War.
1992 Anti-government riots.
1993 Saleh's General People's Congress (GPC) won most seats in general election but no overall majority; five-member presidential council elected, including Saleh as president, YSP leader Ali Salim al-Baidh as vice president, and Bakr al-Attas as prime minister.
1994 Fighting erupted between northern forces, led by President Saleh, and southern forces, led by Vice President al-Baidh as southern Yemen announced its secession. Saleh inflicted crushing defeat on al-Baidh and new GPC coalition appointed.
1997 GPC election victory. Farag Said Ben Ghanem appointed prime minister.
1998 Diplomatic relations between Yemen and Britain grow tense following hostage-taking by Yemeni Islamic fighters and tribesmen.

SEE ALSO Arabia; Ottoman Empire; South Arabia, Federation of

yew The yew is a slow-growing evergreen, the longest living of all European trees, probably reaching ages of 1,000 years. The seeds are enclosed in a fleshy covering called an aril which is eaten by birds; the seed itself is poisonous, like the rest of the tree.

Yggdrasil in Scandinavian mythology, the world tree, a sacred ash that spans heaven and hell. It is evergreen and tended by the Norns, goddesses of past, present, and future.

Yggdrasil has three roots with a spring under each one. One root covers Nifelheim, the realm of the dead; another runs under Jotunheim, where the giants live; the third under Asgard, home of the gods. By the Norns' well at the third root, the gods regularly gather to confer. Various animals inhabit and feed off the tree.

Yi a people living in S China, Laos, Thailand, and Vietnam, population totalling about 5.5 million (1987). The Yi are farmers, producing both crops and livestock. Their language belongs to the Sino-Tibetan family; their religion is animist.

Yichang port at the head of navigation of the Chang Jiang River, Hubei province, China; population (1990) 372,000.

Yiddish language member of the west Germanic branch of the Indo-European language family, deriving from 13th–14th-century Rhineland German and spoken by northern, central, and eastern European Jews, who have carried it to Israel, the USA, and many other parts of the world. It is written in the Hebrew alphabet and has many dialects reflecting European areas of residence, as well as many borrowed words from Polish, Russian, Lithuanian, and other languages encountered.

In the USA, Yiddish has had a powerful impact on English. Such words as *bagel*, *chutzpah*, *kibbitz*, *mench*, *nosh*, *schlemiel*, *schmaltz*, and *schmuck* have entered the American language. The novelist and short-story writer Isaac Bashevis ◊Singer wrote in Yiddish.

Yilmaz A Mesut 1947– . Turkish politician, prime minister 1991, 1996, and from 1997. He rose to power through a number of ministerial posts 1986–1990 and became leader of the Motherland Party (ANAP) 1991, and was appointed prime minister by President Ozal. His premiership involved various coalitions and in June 1996 he was briefly replaced by Necmettin Erbakan.

yin and yang (Chinese 'dark' and 'bright') the passive (characterized as feminine, negative, intuitive) and active (characterized as masculine, positive, intellectual) principles of nature. Their interaction is believed to maintain equilibrium and harmony in the universe and to be present in all things. In Taoism and Confucianism they are represented by two interlocked curved shapes within a circle, one white, one black, with a spot of the contrasting colour within the head of each.

Yinchuan capital of Ningxia autonomous region, NW China, on the Huang He River; population (1993) 430,000. It is a trading centre for the Ningxia plain, producing textiles and coal.

YMCA abbreviation for ***Young Men's Christian Association***.

Ymir in Scandinavian mythology, the first living being, a giant who grew from melting frost. Of his descendants, the god Odin and his two brothers, Vili and Ve, killed Ymir and created heaven and earth from parts of his body.

yoga (Sanskrit 'union') Hindu philosophical system attributed to Patanjali, who lived about 150 BC at Gonda, Uttar Pradesh, India. He preached mystical union with a personal deity through the practice of self-hypnosis and a rising above the senses by abstract meditation, adoption of special postures, and ascetic practices. As practised in the West, yoga is more a system of mental and physical exercise, and of induced relaxation as a means of relieving stress.

yoghurt or ***yogurt*** or ***yoghourt*** semisolid curdlike dairy product made from milk fermented with bacteria. It was originally made by nomadic tribes of Central Asia from mare's milk in leather pouches attached to their saddles. It is drunk plain throughout the Asian and Mediterranean region, to which it spread, but honey, sugar, and fruit were added in Europe and the USA, and the product made solid and creamy, to be eaten by spoon.

Heat-treated, homogenized milk is inoculated with a culture of *Streptococcus lactis* and *Lactobacillus bulgaricus* in equal amounts, which change the lactose in the milk to lactic acid. Acetaldehyde gives yoghurt its characteristic flavour. Commercially, fruit, flavourings, and colouring and thickening agents are added to the fermented yoghurt.

Yogyakarta city in Java, Indonesia, capital 1945–1949; population (1990) 412,400. The Buddhist pyramid shrine to the NW at Borobudur (122 m/400 ft square) was built AD 750–850.

Yokohama Japanese port on Tokyo Bay; population (1994) 3,265,000. Industries include shipbuilding, oil refining, engineering, textiles, glass, and clothing.

In 1859 it was the first Japanese port opened to foreign trade. From then it grew rapidly from a small fishing village to become the chief centre of trade with Europe and the USA. Almost destroyed in an earthquake 1923, it was again rebuilt after World War II.

yolk store of food, mostly in the form of fats and proteins, found in the ◊eggs of many animals. It provides nourishment for the growing embryo.

yolk sac sac containing the yolk in the egg of most vertebrates. The term is also used for the membranous sac formed below the developing mammalian embryo and connected with the umbilical cord.

Yom Kippur the Jewish Day of ◊Atonement.

Yom Kippur War the surprise attack on Israel Oct 1973 by Egypt and Syria; see ◊Arab-Israeli Wars. It is named after the Jewish national holiday on which it began, the holiest day of the Jewish year.

Yonne French river, 290 km/180 mi long, rising in central France and flowing N into the Seine; it gives its name to a *département* in Burgundy region.

York English dynasty founded by Richard, Duke of York (1411–60). He claimed the throne through his descent from Lionel, Duke of Clarence (1338–1368), third son of Edward III, whereas the reigning monarch, Henry VI of the rival house of Lancaster, was descended from the fourth son. The argument was fought out in the Wars of the ◊Roses. York was killed at the Battle of Wakefield 1460, but next year his son became King Edward IV, in turn succeeded by his son Edward V and then by his brother Richard III, with whose death at Bosworth the line ended. The Lancastrian victor in that battle was crowned Henry VII and consolidated his claim by marrying Edward IV's eldest daughter, Elizabeth.

York cathedral and industrial city (scientific instruments, sugar, chocolate, and glass) in N England, and from 1996 a unitary authority (*see United Kingdom map*); population (1991) 105,500. Britain's last train-building factory closed Oct 1995. The city is visited by 3 million tourists a year

features the Gothic York Minster contains medieval stained glass; the south transept was severely damaged by fire 1984, but has been restored. Much of the 14th-century city wall survives, with four gates or 'bars', as well as the medieval streets collectively known as the Shambles (after the slaughterhouse). The Jorvik Viking Centre, opened 1984 after excavation of a site at Coppergate, contains wooden remains of Viking houses. There are fine examples of 17th- to 18th-century domestic architecture; the Theatre Royal, site of a theatre since 1765; the Castle Museum; the National Railway Museum; and the university 1963

history traditionally the capital of the north of England, the city became from AD 71 the Roman fortress of Eboracum. Recent excavations of the Roman city have revealed the fortress, baths, and temples to Serapis and Mithras. The first bishop of York (Paulinus) was consecrated 627 in the wooden church that preceded York Minster. Paulinus baptized King Edwin there 627, and York was created an archbishopric 732. In the 10th century it was a Viking settlement. During the Middle Ages its commercial prosperity depended on the wool trade. An active Quaker element in the 18th and 19th centuries included the Rowntree family, which founded the chocolate factory.

York Frederick Augustus, duke of York 1763–1827. Second son of George III. He was an unsuccessful commander in the Netherlands 1793–99 and British commander in chief 1798–1809.

The nursery rhyme about the 'grand old duke of York' who marched his troops up the hill and down again commemorates him, as does the Duke of York's column in Waterloo Place, London.

Yorkshire former county in NE England on the North Sea, traditionally divided administratively into North, East, and West Ridings, but reorganized 1974 to form a number of new counties including North, South, and West Yorkshire. The 1996 local government reorganization restored the East Riding of Yorkshire and made York a unitary authority.

Yorkshire terrier breed of toy dog from N England. Its long, straight coat is blue-black on the body and red or tan on the head, chest, and legs. It weighs just 3 kg/6.5 lb, and its body is long in proportion to its short legs.

Yorktown, Battle of decisive British defeat in the American Revolution Sept–Oct 1781 at Yorktown, Virginia, 105 km/65 mi southeast of Richmond. The British commander Lord Cornwallis had withdrawn into Yorktown where he was besieged by 7,000 French and 8,850 American troops and could only wait for reinforcements to arrive by sea. However, the Royal Navy lost command of the sea at the Battle of Chesapeake and with no reinforcements or supplies forthcoming, Cornwallis was forced to surrender 19 Oct, effectively ending the war. ▷ *See feature on pp. 32–33.*

Yoruba the majority ethnic group living in SW Nigeria; there is a Yoruba minority in E Benin. They number approximately 20 million in all, and their language belongs to the Kwa branch of the Niger-Congo family. The Yoruba established powerful city states in the 15th century, known for their advanced culture which includes sculpture, art, and music.

Yosemite area in the Sierra Nevada, E California, USA, a national park from 1890; area 3,079 sq km/1,189 sq mi. It includes Yosemite Gorge, Yosemite Falls (739 m/2,425 ft in three leaps) with many other lakes and waterfalls, and groves of giant sequoia trees.

Yoshida Shigeru 1878–1967. Japanese conservative (Liberal Party) politician who served as prime minister of US-occupied Japan for most of the post–World War II period 1946–54. He was foreign minister 1945–46.

Young Arthur 1741–1820. English writer and publicizer of the new farm practices associated with the ◊agricultural revolution. When the Board of Agriculture was established 1792, Young was appointed secretary, and was the guiding force behind the production of a county-by-county survey of British agriculture.

His early works, such as *Farmer's Tour through the East of England* and *A Six Months' Tour through the North of England*, contained extensive comment and observations gathered during the course of a series of journeys around the country. He published the *Farmers' Calendar* 1771, and in 1784 began the *Annals of Agriculture*, which ran for 45 volumes, and contained contributions from many eminent farmers of the day.

Young Brigham 1801–1877. US ◊Mormon religious leader, born in Vermont. He joined the Mormon Church, or Church of Jesus Christ of Latter-day Saints, 1832, and three years later was appointed an apostle. After a successful recruiting mission in Liverpool, England, he returned to the USA and, as successor of Joseph Smith (who had been murdered), led the Mormon migration to the

Great Salt Lake in Utah 1846, founded Salt Lake City, and headed the colony until his death.

Young David Ivor. Baron Young of Graffham 1932– . British Conservative politician, chair of the Manpower Services Commission (MSC) 1982–84, secretary for employment from 1985, trade and industry secretary 1987–89, when he retired from politics for a new career in business. He was subsequently criticized by a House of Commons select committee over aspects of the privatization of the Rover car company.

Young John Watts 1930– . US astronaut. His first flight was on *Gemini 3* 1965. He landed on the Moon with *Apollo 16* 1972, and was commander of the first flight of the space shuttle *Columbia* 1981.

Young Lester Willis 1909–1959. US tenor saxophonist and jazz composer. He was a major figure in the development of his instrument for jazz music from the 1930s and was an accompanist for the singer Billie Holiday, who gave him the nickname 'President', later shortened to 'Pres'.

Young Neil 1945– . Canadian rock guitarist, singer, and songwriter. He lived in the USA from 1966. His high, plaintive voice and loud, abrasive guitar make his work instantly recognizable, despite abrupt changes of style throughout his career. *Rust Never Sleeps* 1979 and *Arc Weld* 1991 (both with the group Crazy Horse) are among his best work.

Young Thomas 1773–1829. British physicist, physician, and Egyptologist who revived the wave theory of light and identified the phenomenon of ◊interference in 1801. He also established many important concepts in mechanics.

In 1793, Young recognized that focusing of the eye (◊accommodation) is achieved by a change of shape in the lens of the eye, the lens being composed of muscle fibres. He also showed that ◊astigmatism is due to irregular curvature of the cornea. In 1801, he became the first to recognize that colour sensation is due to the presence in the retina of structures that respond to the three colours red, green, and violet.

Young Ireland Irish nationalist organization, founded 1840 by William Smith O'Brien (1803–1864), who attempted an abortive insurrection of the peasants against the British in Tipperary 1848. O'Brien was sentenced to death, but later pardoned.

Young Italy Italian nationalist organization founded 1831 by Giuseppe ◊Mazzini while in exile in Marseille. The movement, which was immediately popular, was followed the next year by Young Germany, Young Poland, and similar organizations. All the groups were linked by Mazzini in his Young Europe movement, but none achieved much practical success; attempted uprisings by Young Italy 1834 and 1844 failed miserably. It was superseded in Italy by the ◊Risorgimento.

Young Men's Christian Association (YMCA) international organization founded 1844 by George Williams (1821–1905) in London and 1851 in the USA. It aims at self-improvement – spiritual, intellectual, and physical. From 1971 women were accepted as members.

young offender institution in the UK, establishment of detention for lawbreakers under 17 (juveniles) and 17–21 (young adults). The period of detention depends on the seriousness of the offence and on the age and sex of the offender. The institution was introduced by the Criminal Justice Act 1988.

Young Pretender nickname of ◊Charles Edward Stuart, claimant to the Scottish and English thrones.

Young Turk member of a reformist movement of young army officers in the Ottoman Empire founded 1889. The movement was instrumental in the constitutional changes of 1908 and the abdication of Sultan Abd al-Hamid II 1909. It gained prestige during the Balkan Wars 1912–13 and encouraged Turkish links with the German empire. Its influence diminished after 1918. The term is now used for a member of any radical or rebellious faction within a party or organization.

Young Women's Christian Association (YWCA) organization for women and girls, formed 1887 when two organizations, both founded 1855 – one by Emma Robarts and the other by Lady Kinnaird – combined their work.

Yourcenar Marguerite. Pen name of Marguerite de Crayencour 1903–1987. French writer. She first gained recognition as a novelist in France in the 1930s with books such as *La Nouvelle Euridyce/The New Euridyce* 1931. Her evocation of past eras and characters, exemplified in *Les Mémoires d'Hadrien/The Memoirs of Hadrian* 1951, brought her acclaim as a historical novelist. In 1939 she settled in the USA. In 1980 she became the first woman to be elected to the French Academy.

Youth Hostels Association (YHA) registered charity founded in Britain 1930 to promote knowledge and care of the countryside by providing cheap overnight accommodation for young people on active holidays (such as walking or cycling). Types of accommodation range from castles to log cabins.

YHA is a member of the ***International Youth Hostel Federation***, with over 5,000 youth hostels in countries all over the world. YHA membership is open to individuals of 14 or over (or 5 if accompanied by an adult). In addition to basic accommodation, YHA provides sporting activities including climbing, windsurfing, hang-gliding, and horse riding.

Youth Training Scheme (YTS) in the UK, a one- or two-year course of training and work experience for unemployed school leavers aged 16 and 17, from 1989 provided by employer-led Training and Enterprise Councils at local levels and renamed Youth Training.

Ypres, Battles of (Flemish ***Ieper***) in World War I, three major battles 1914–17 between German and Allied forces near Ypres, a Belgian town in W Flanders, 40 km/25 mi S of Ostend. Neither side made much progress in any of the battles, despite heavy casualties, but the third battle in particular (also known as Passchendaele) July–Nov 1917 stands out as an enormous waste of life for little return. The Menin Gate 1927 is a memorial to British soldiers lost in these battles.

Ypres, 1st Earl of title of Sir John French (1852–1925), British field marshal.

ytterbium soft, lustrous, silvery, malleable, and ductile element of the ◊lanthanide series, symbol Yb, atomic number 70, relative atomic mass 173.04. It occurs with (and resembles) yttrium in gadolinite and other minerals, and is used in making steel and other alloys.

In 1878 Swiss chemist Jean-Charles de Marignac gave the name ytterbium (after the Swedish town of Ytterby, near where it was found) to what he believed to be a new element. French chemist Georges Urbain (1872–1938) discovered 1907 that this was in fact a mixture of two elements: ytterbium and lutetium.

yttrium silver-grey, metallic element, symbol Y, atomic number 39, relative atomic mass 88.905. It is associated with and resembles the rare earth elements (◊lanthanides), occurring in gadolinite, xenotime, and other minerals. It is used in colour-television tubes and to reduce steel corrosion.

The name derives from the Swedish town of Ytterby, near where it was first discovered 1788. Swedish chemist Carl Mosander (1797–1858) isolated the element 1843.

Yuan dynasty ◊Mongol rulers of China 1279–1368 after ◊Kublai Khan defeated the Song dynasty. Much of Song China's administrative infrastructure survived and internal and foreign trade expanded. The Silk Road to the west was re-established and the Grand Canal extended north to Beijing to supply the court with grain.

The Mongol conquest was particularly brutal, and relations with the Chinese were never easy, resulting in the recruitment of foreigners such as central Asian Muslims to act as officials. The Venetian traveller Marco ◊Polo also served at the court. After the death of Temur (ruled 1294–1307), there was increasing internal disorder and economic discontent. This was the first dynasty to control territories S of the Chang Jiang.

Yuan Shikai 1859–1916. Chinese soldier and politician, leader of Republican China 1911–16. He assumed dictatorial powers 1912, dissolving parliament and suppressing Sun Yat-sen's ◊Guomindang. He died soon after proclaiming himself emperor.

Although committed to military reform, Yuan betrayed the modernizing emperor Guangxu and sided with the Empress Dowager ◊Zi Xi during the Hundred Days' Reform 1898. With a power base in N China, he was appointed prime minister and commander in chief after the 1911 revolution against the Manchu Qings and was made president 1912. He lost credibility after submitting to Japan's Twenty-one demands 1915, ceding territory to Japan.

Yucatán peninsula in Central America, divided among Mexico, Belize, and Guatemala; area 180,000 sq km/70,000 sq mi. Tropical crops are grown. It is inhabited by Maya Indians and contains the remains of their civilization.

There are ruins at Chichén Itzá and Uxmal. The Mexican state of Yucatán has an area of 39,340 sq km/15,189 sq mi, and a population (1990) of 1,362,900. Its capital is Mérida.

yucca plant of the genus *Yucca*, family Liliaceae, with over 40 species found in Latin America and southwest USA. The leaves are stiff and sword-shaped and the flowers white and bell-shaped.

Yuccas grow in dry soils where nitrate salts, required for protein manufacture, are in short supply. They have therefore evolved the ability to use ammonia, absorbed from animal urine, instead.

Ypres, Battles of The ruins of Ypres, Belgium, devastated in three fierce battles during World War I. The battles were among the worst of the war, causing massive loss of life for little gain, especially the third battle, often known as Passchendaele. The second battle of Ypres saw the first use of poison gas (chlorine) in war. *Corbis*

Feeding extracts of yucca to livestock has been shown to reduce the emission of unpleasant ammoniacal smells from factory farms.

Yugoslavia country in SE Europe, with a SW coastline on the Adriatic Sea, bounded W by Bosnia-Herzegovina, NW by Croatia, N by Hungary, E by Romania and Bulgaria, and S by the Former Yugoslav Republic of Macedonia and Albania. *See country box below.*

Yü-huang in Taoism and Chinese folk religion, the 'Jade Emperor', supreme amongst the gods, and the lord of creation.

Yukawa Hideki 1907–1981. Japanese physicist. In 1935 he discovered the ◊strong nuclear force that binds protons and neutrons together in the atomic nucleus, and predicted the existence of the subatomic particle called the ◊meson. He was awarded a Nobel prize in 1949.

Yukawa was born and educated in Kyoto and spent his career at Kyoto University, becoming professor 1939 and director of the university's newly created Research Institute for Fundamental Physics from 1953.

Yukawa's theory of nuclear forces postulated the existence of a nuclear 'exchange force' that counteracted the mutual repulsion of the protons and therefore held the nucleus together. He predicted that this exchange force would involve the transfer of a particle (the existence of which was then unknown), and calculated the range of the force and the mass of the hypothetical particle,

YUGOSLAVIA
Federal Republic of

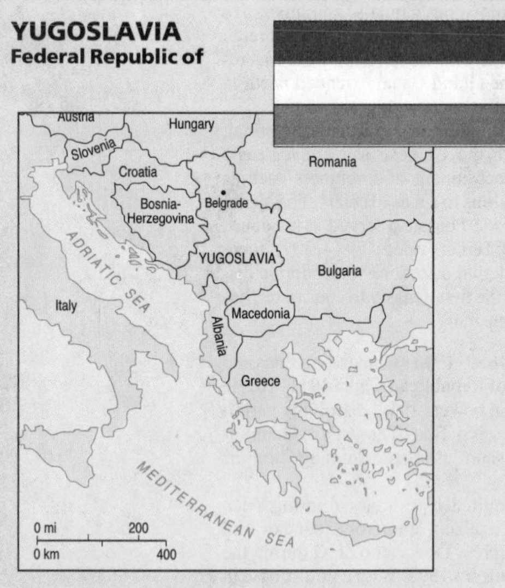

national name *Federativna Republika Jugoslavija*
area 58,300 sq km/22,503 sq mi
capital Belgrade
major towns/cities Novi Sad, Niš, Kragujevac, Podgorica (formerly Titograd), Subotica
physical features federation of republics of Serbia and Montenegro and two former autonomous provinces, Kosovo and Vojvodina
head of state Slobodan Milošević from 1997
head of government Momir Bulatović from 1998
political system socialist pluralist republic
administrative divisions federal republic consists of the two republics of Montenegro and Serbia. Within Serbia are the autonomous provinces of Vojvodina and Kosovo-Metohija
political parties Socialist Party of Serbia (SPS), Serb nationalist, reform socialist (ex-communist); Montenegrin Social Democratic Party (SDPCG), federalist, reform socialist (ex-communist); Serbian Radical Party (SRS), Serb nationalist, extreme right-wing; People's Assembly Party, Christian democrat, centrist; Democratic Party (DS), moderate nationalist; Democratic Party of Serbia (DSS), moderate nationalist; Democratic Community of Vojvodina Hungarians (DZVM), ethnic Hungarian; Democratic Party of Albanians/Party of Democratic Action (DPA/PDA), ethnic Albanian; New Socialist Party of Montenegro (NSPM), left of centre
population 10,294,000 (1996 est)
population growth rate 1.3% (1990–95); 0.4% (2000–05)
ethnic distribution according to the 1991 census, 62% of the population of the rump federal republic is ethnic Serb, 17% Albanian, 5% Montenegrin, 3% 'Yugoslav', and 3% Muslim. Serbs predominate in the republic of Serbia, where they form (excluding the autonomous areas of Kosovo and Vojvodina) 85% of the population; in Vojvodina they comprise 55% of the population. Albanians constitute 77% of the population of Kosovo; Montenegrins comprise 69% of the population of the republic of Montenegro; and Muslims predominate in the Sandzak region, which straddles the Serbian and Montenegrin borders. Since 1992 an influx of Serb refugees from Bosnia and Kosovo has increased the proportion of Serbs in Serbia, while many ethnic Hungarians have left Vojvodina, and an estimated 500,000 Albanians have left Kosovo
life expectancy 70 (men), 76 (women)
literacy rate 93%
languages Serbo-Croatian; Albanian (in Kosovo)
religions Serbian and Montenegrin Orthodox; Muslim in S Serbia
currency new Yugoslav dinar
GDP (US $) 15.9 billion (1995 est)
growth rate 6.5% (1994)
exports machinery, electrical goods, chemicals, clothing, tobacco, agricultural produce

HISTORY
3rd C BC Serbia (then known as Moesia Superior) was conquered by the Romans, with the empire being extended to Belgrade centuries later by Emperor Augustus.
6th C AD Slavic tribes, including Serbs, Croats, and Slovenes, crossed Danube river and settled in Balkan Peninsula.
879 Serbs converted to Orthodox Church by St Cyril and St Methodius.
mid-10th–11th Cs Serbia broke free briefly from Byzantine Empire to establish independent state.
1217 Independent Serbian kingdom re-established, reaching its height in the mid-14th century under Stefan Dushan, when it controlled much of Albania and northern Greece.
1389 Serbian army defeated by Ottoman Turks at Battle of Kosovo and the area became a Turkish *pashalik* (province). Montenegro in the SW survived as sovereign principality. Croatia and Slovenia in the NW became part of the Habsburg Empire.
18th C Vojvodina enjoyed protection by the Austrian Habsburgs.
1815 Uprisings against Turkish rule secured autonomy for Serbia.
1878 Indepedence achieved as Kingdom of Serbia, after Turks defeated by Russians in a war over Bulgaria.
1912–13 During Balkan Wars, Serbia expanded its territory at expense of Turkey and Bulgaria.
1918 Joined Croatia and Slovenia, formerly under Austrian Habsburg control, to form Kingdom of Serbs, Croats, and Slovenes under Serbian Peter Karageorgevic (Peter I); Montenegro's citizens voted to depose their ruler, King Nicholas, and join the union.
1929 New name of Yugoslavia ('Land of the Southern Slavs') adopted, and Serbian-dominated military dictatorship established by King Alexander I as opposition mounted from Croatian federalists.
1934 Alexander I assassinated by a Macedonian with Croatian terrorist links; his young son Peter II succeeded, with Paul, his uncle, as regent; Nazi Germany and fascist Italy increased their influence.
1941 Following coup by pro-Allied air-force officers, Nazi Germany invaded and Peter II fled to England. Armed resistance to German rule began, spearheaded by pro-royalist, Serbian-based Chetniks ('Army of the Fatherland'), led by Gen Draza Mihailović, and communist Partisans ('National Liberation Army'), led by Marshal Tito. An estimated 900,000 Yugoslavs were killed during the war.
1943 Provisional government formed by Tito at liberated Jajce in Bosnia.
1945 Yugoslav Federal People's Republic formed under leadership of Tito; communist constitution introduced.
1948 Split with Soviet Union after Tito objected to Soviet 'hegemonism'; expelled from Cominform.
1953 Workers' self-management principle enshrined in constitution and private farming supported; Tito became president.
1961 Nonaligned movement formed under Yugoslavia's leadership.
1971 In response to mounting separatist demands in Croatia, a new system of collective and rotating leadership introduced.
1980 Tito died; collective leadership assumed power.
1981–82 Demonstrations by Albanians in Kosovo province, S Serbia, for full republic status suppressed by armed force.
1986 Slobodan Milošević became leader of communist party in the Serbian republic.
1988 Economic difficulties: 1,800 strikes, 250% inflation, 20% unemployment. Ethnic unrest in Montenegro and Vojvodina, and separatist demands in rich NW republics of Croatia and Slovenia; 'market socialist' reform package, and austerity wage freeze.
1989 Reformist Croatian Ante Marković became prime minister. Ethnic riots in Kosovo province against Serbian attempt to end autonomous status of Kosovo and Vojvodina; at least 30 were killed and a state of emergency imposed.
1990 Multiparty systems established in the republics; Kosovo and Vojvodina stripped of their autonomy. In Croatia, Slovenia, Bosnia, and Macedonia elections bought to power new non-communist governments seeking a looser confederation.
1991 Demonstrations against Serbian president Slobodon Milošević in Belgrade. Slovenia and Croatia declared independence, resulting in clashes between federal and republican armies; Slovenia accepted peace pact sponsored by European Community (EC), but fighting intensified in Croatia, where Serb militias controlled over one-third of the republic; Federal President Stipe Mesic and Prime Minister Markovic resigned.
1992 EC-brokered cease-fire in Croatia; EC and USA recognized Slovenia's and Croatia's independence. Bosnia-Herzegovina and Macedonia declared independence. Bosnia-Herzegovina recognized as independent by EC and USA. New Federal Republic of Yugoslavia (FRY) proclaimed by Serbia and Montenegro but not recognized externally. International sanctions imposed. UN membership suspended. Ethnic Albanians proclaimed new 'Republic of Kosovo', but it was not recognized.
1993 Pro-Milošević Zoran Lilic became Yugoslav president. Antigovernment rioting in Belgrade. Macedonia recognized as independent under name of Former Yugoslav Republic of Macedonia. Economy severely damaged by international sanctions.
1994 Border blockade imposed by Yugoslavia against Bosnian Serbs; sanctions eased as a result.
1995 Serbia played key role in US-brokered Dayton peace accord for Bosnia-Herzegovina and accepted separate existence of Bosnia and Croatia. US economic sanctions against Serbia lifted.
1996 Diplomatic relations restored between Serbia and Croatia. UN sanctions against Serbia lifted. Allies of Milošević successful in parliamentary elections. Full diplomatic relations established with Bosnia-Herzegovina. Ruling party won assembly elections. Mounting opposition to Milošević's government, following its refusal to accept opposition victories in municipal elections.
1997 Serbian parliament passed legislation recognizing the elections, thus ending opposition demonstrations. Slobodan Milošević elected president.
1998 Unrest in republic of Montenegro as Milo Djukanović, a reformist opponent of President Milošević, became its president. Escalating violence in predominantly Albanian Muslim southern province of Kosovo, as Serb security forces cracked down on activities of Kosovo Liberation Army (UCK), a paramilitary separatist force. Serb Socialist Party formed controversial coalition in Serbia with extreme nationalist Serbian Radical Party. Currency devalued by 45% in March. Moderate Radoje Kontić replaced as prime minister in May by Momir Bulatović.
1999 NATO forces launched air strikes against Serbia in response to abuses by Serbian authorities against ethnic Albanians in Kosovo. Hundreds of thousands of ethnic Albanians were expelled from Kosovo.

SEE ALSO Bosnia-Herzegovina; Croatia; Serbia; Tito

which would be radioactive, with an extremely short half-life. The muon, or μ meson, discovered 1936, fitted part of the description, and the pion, or π meson, discovered 1947, fitted all of it.

In 1936 Yukawa predicted that a nucleus could absorb one of the innermost orbiting electrons and that this would be equivalent to emitting a positron. These innermost electrons belong to the K electron shell, and this process of electron absorption by the Nucleus is known as K capture.

Yukon territory of NW Canada
area 483,500 sq km/186,631 sq mi
capital Whitehorse
towns and cities Dawson, Mayo
features named after its chief river, the Yukon; includes the highest point in Canada, Mount Logan, 6,050 m/19,850 ft; Klondike Gold Rush International Historical Park, which extends into Alaska
industries gold, silver, lead, zinc, oil, natural gas, coal
population (1991) 26,500
history settlement dates from the gold rush 1896–1910, when 30,000 people moved to the ◊Klondike river valley (silver is now worked there). It became separate from the Northwest Territories 1898, with Dawson as the capital 1898–1951. Construction of the Alcan Highway during World War II helped provide the basis for further development.

Yukon River river in North America, 3,185 km/1,979 mi long, flowing from Lake Tagish in Yukon Territory into Alaska, where it empties into the Bering Sea.

Yunnan province of SW China, adjoining Myanmar (Burma), Laos, and Vietnam
area 436,200 sq km/168,373 sq mi
capital Kunming
physical rivers: Chang Jiang, Salween, Mekong; crossed by the Burma Road; mountainous and well forested
industries rice, tea, timber, wheat, cotton, rubber, tin, copper, lead, zinc, coal, salt
population (1990) 36,750,000.

Yuppie acronym for **young urban professional**, a term used – sometimes pejoratively – to describe a social group that emerged in the 1970s. Yuppies are characterized by their ambition and by their conspicuously affluent lifestyle.

Yuzovka former name (1872–1924) for the town of ◊Donetsk, Ukraine, named after the Welshman John Hughes who established a metallurgical factory here in the 1870s.

YWCA abbreviation for ***Young Women's Christian Association***.

Yukon Territory

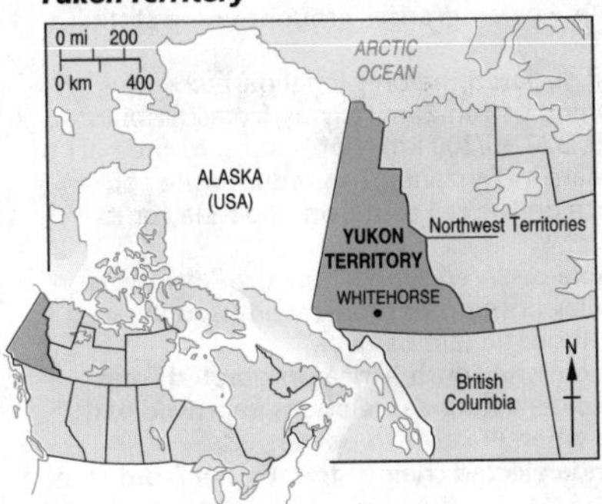

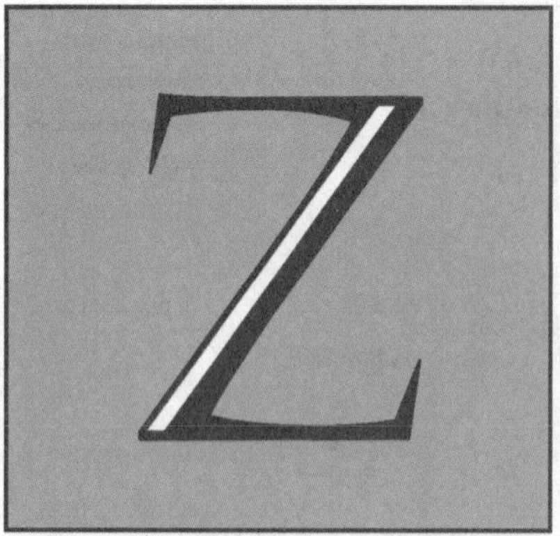

Z in physics, the symbol for ***impedance*** (electricity and magnetism).

Zaandam industrial port (timber, paper) in North Holland province, the Netherlands, on the river Zaan, NW of Amsterdam, since 1974 included in the municipality of Zaanstad.

Zaanstad industrial town in W Netherlands which includes the port of Zaandam; population (1994) 132,500.

Zagreb industrial city (leather, linen, carpets, paper, and electrical goods) and capital of Croatia, on the Sava River; population (1991) 726,800. The site of Zagreb was occupied by a settlement in Roman times; in 1093 it became a bishop's see, and in 1242 a free royal city. Zagreb became the capital of Croatia and Slavonia in 1867 and became part of the Kingdom of the Serbs, Croats, and Slovenes (which became Yugoslavia in 1918). It has a Gothic cathedral. Its university was founded 1874. The city was damaged by bombing Oct 1991 during the Croatian civil war.

Zaharias Babe (Mildred Ella), (born Didrikson) 1914–1956. US sportswoman. One of the most talented and versatile figures in the history of sport, in 1932 she became the first athlete to win individual Olympic medals in running, jumping, and throwing events. She later became the world's leading female golfer, winning the US Women's Open 1948, 1950, and 1954.

She was born at Port Arthur, Texas. She was a high school basketball star and made the All-American team 1930–32. In the same period she won or shared ten titles in six different events at the National Amateur Athletic Union track and field championships. At the 1932 meeting she single-handedly won the team event, entering eight of the ten events and coming first in five of them. Shortly afterwards at the Los Angeles Olympics she won gold medals in the 80 metre hurdles and javelin, and a silver in the high jump, events at which she was already the world record holder. In the high jump she actually cleared the same height as the winner, but her western roll style was ruled unacceptable by the judges and she had to make do with second place. She took up golf competitively 1935 and went on to win 55 amateur and professional tournaments including the British and US Amateur Championships and three US Women's Opens. She was diagnosed with cancer 1953 but made a remarkable comeback the following year to win the US Open by a record margin. However, she eventually lost her fight against the disease and died 1956 at the age of 42.

Zahir Shah Muhammad 1914– . King of Afghanistan 1933–73. Zahir, educated in Kabul and Paris, served in the government 1932–33 before being crowned king. He was overthrown 1973 by a republican coup and went into exile. He became a symbol of national unity for the ◊Mujaheddin Islamic fundamentalist resistance groups. In 1991 the Afghan government restored Zahir's citizenship.

Zahir ud-Din Muhammad first Mogul emperor of India; see ◊Babur.

zaibatsu (Japanese 'financial clique') Japanese industrial conglomerate (see ◊cartel).

The old, family-owned Japanese *zaibatsu* had been involved in the military buildup preceding World War II, and in 1945, after the country's defeat, were broken up by the authorities of the US occupation. Similar conglomerates soon formed in the course of Japan's industrial revival. By the late 1980s there were six *zaibatsu* with 650-member companies between them, employing 6% of the country's workforce and controlling more than 2% of the world economy.

Zaire former name (to 1997) of ◊Democratic Republic of Congo.

Zaïre River formerly (until 1971) ***Congo*** second-longest river in Africa, rising near the Zambia–Democratic Republic of Congo border (and known as the ***Lualaba River*** in the upper reaches) and flowing 4,500 km/2,800 mi to the Atlantic Ocean, running in a great curve that crosses the equator twice, and discharging a volume of water second only to the Amazon. The chief tributaries are the Ubangi, Sangha, and Kasai.

Navigation is interrupted by dangerous rapids up to 160 km/100 mi long, notably from the Zambian border to Bukama; below Kongolo, where the gorge known as the Gates of Hell is located; above Kisangani, where the Stanley Falls are situated; and between Kinshasa and Matadi.

Boma is a large port on the estuary; Matadi is a port 80 km/50 mi from the Atlantic, for ocean-going ships; and at Pool Malebo (formerly Stanley Pool) are Brazzaville on the western shore and Kinshasa on the southwestern. The Inga Dam supplies Matadi and Kinshasa with electricity.

history The mouth of the Zaïre was seen by the Portuguese navigator Diego Cão 1482, but the vast extent of its system became known to Europeans only with the explorations of David Livingstone and Henry Stanley.

Zama, Battle of battle fought 202 BC in Numidia (now Algeria), in which the Carthaginians under Hannibal were defeated by the Romans under the younger Scipio, so ending the Second Punic War. The Carthaginians were forced to give up Spain and were also subject to harsh peace terms.

Zambia landlocked country in S central Africa, bounded N by Zaire and Tanzania, E by Malawi, S by Mozambique, Zimbabwe, Botswana, and Namibia, and W by Angola. *See country box opposite.*

Zambezi river in central and SE Africa; length 2,650 km/1,650 mi from NW Zambia through Mozambique to the Indian Ocean, with a wide delta

ZAMBIA

Republic of (formerly *Northern Rhodesia*)

Democratic Republic of Congo
Tanzania
INDIAN OCEAN
Angola
ZAMBIA
Lusaka
Malawi
Mozambique
Zimbabwe
Namibia
Botswana
ATLANTIC OCEAN
0 mi 500
0 km 1000

area 752,600 sq km/290,579 sq mi
capital Lusaka
major towns/cities Kitwe, Ndola, Kabwe, Mufulira, Chingola
physical features forested plateau cut through by rivers; Zambezi River, Victoria Falls, Kariba Dam
head of state and government Frederick Chiluba from 1991
political system emergent democratic republic
administrative divisions eight provinces
political parties United National Independence Party (UNIP), African socialist; Movement for Multiparty Democracy (MMD), moderate, left of centre; Multiracial Party (MRP), moderate, left of centre, multiracial; National Democratic Alliance (NADA), left of centre; Democratic Party (DP), left of centre
population 8,275,000 (1996 est)
population growth rate 3.0% (1990–95); 2.4% (2000–05)
ethnic distribution over 95% indigenous Africans, belonging tomore than 70 different ethnic groups, including the Bantu-Botatwe and the Bemba
life expectancy 54 (men), 57 (women)
literacy rate men 81%, women 65%
languages English (official); Bantu languages
religions Christian, animist, Hindu, Muslim
currency Zambian kwacha
GDP (US $) 3.46 billion (1994)
growth rate −5.4% (1994)
exports copper, cobalt, zinc, emeralds, tobacco

HISTORY

16th C Immigration of peoples from the Luba and Lunda Empires of Zaire, to the NW, who set up small kingdoms.
late 18th C Visited by Portuguese explorers.
19th C Instability with immigration of Ngoni from the E, Kololo from the W, the establishment of Bemba kingdom in the N, and the slave-trading activities of Portuguese and Arabs from E Africa.
1851 Visited by the British missionary and explorer David Livingstone.
1889 As Northern Rhodesia, came under administration of the British South Africa Company of Cecil Rhodes, and became involved in copper mining, especially from the 1920s.
1924 Became a British protectorate.
1948 Northern Rhodesia African Congress (NRAC) formed by black Africans to campaign for self-rule.
1953 Became part of Central African Federation, which included South Rhodesia (Zimbabwe) and Nyasaland (Malawi).
1960 UNIP formed by Kenneth Kaunda as breakaway from NRAC, as African socialist body to campaign for independence and dissolution of the Federation which was dominated by the white minority of South Rhodesia.
1963 Federation dissolved and internal self-government achieved.
1964 Independence achieved within the Commonwealth as the Republic of Zambia with Kaunda of the UNIP as president.
later 1960s Key enterprises brought under state control.
1972 UNIP declared the only legal party.
1975 Opening of Tan-Zam railway from Zambian copperbelt, 322 mi/200 km N of Lusaka, to the port of Dar es Salaam in Tanzania. This reduced the country's dependence on the rail route via Rhodesia for its exports.
1976 Zambia declared support for the Patriotic Front (PF) guerrillas fighting to topple whites-dominated regime in Rhodesia (Zimbabwe).
1980 Unsuccessful South African-promoted coup against President Kaunda; relations improved with Zimbabwe when PF came to power.
1985 Kaunda elected chair of the African Front Line States.
1991 New multiparty constitution adopted. MMD won landslide election victory, and its leader Frederick Chiluba became president in what was the first democratic change of government in English-speaking black Africa.
1993 State of emergency declared after rumours of planned anti-government coup, privatization programme launched.
1996 Kaunda barred from future elections; President Chiluba re-elected.
1997 Abortive anti-government coup.
1998 Former president Kaunda placed under house arrest after alleged involvement in anti-government coup. Kaunda formally charged.

SEE ALSO Kaunda, Kenneth

near Chinde. Major tributaries include the Kafue in Zambia. It is interrupted by rapids, and includes on the Zimbabwe–Zambia border the Victoria Falls (Mosi-oa-tunya) and Kariba Dam, which forms the reservoir of Lake Kariba with large fisheries.

Zamenhof Lazarus Ludovik 1859–1917. Polish inventor of the international language ◊Esperanto 1887.

ZANU (acronym for ***Zimbabwe African National Union***) political organization founded in 1963 by the Reverend Ndabaningi Sithole and later led by Robert Mugabe. It was banned 1964 by Ian Smith's Rhodesian Front government, against which it conducted a guerrilla war from Zambia until the free elections of 1980, when the ZANU Patriotic Front party, led by Mugabe, won 63% of the vote. In 1987 it merged with ◊ZAPU in preparation for making Zimbabwe a one-party state.

Zanzibar island region of Tanzania
area 1,658 sq km/640 sq mi (80 km/50 mi long)
towns and cities Zanzibar
industries cloves, copra
population (1988) 375,500
history settled by Arab traders in the 7th century; occupied by the Portuguese in the 16th century; became a sultanate in the 17th century; under British protection 1890–1963. Together with the island of Pemba, some nearby islets, and a strip of mainland territory, it became a republic 1963. It merged with Tanganyika as Tanzania 1964.

Zapata Emiliano 1879–1919. Mexican Indian revolutionary leader. He led a revolt against dictator Porfirio Díaz (1830–1915) from 1911 under the slogan 'Land and Liberty', to repossess for the indigenous Mexicans the land taken by the Spanish. By 1915 he was driven into retreat, and was assassinated.

Zapotec a Native American people of S Mexico, now numbering approximately 250,000, living mainly in Oaxaca. The Zapotec language, which belongs to the Oto-Mangean family, has nine dialects. The ancient Zapotec built the ceremonial centre of Monte Albán 1000–500 BC. They developed one of the classic Mesoamerican civilizations by AD 300, but declined under pressure from the Mixtecs from 900 until the Spanish Conquest 1530s.

Zappa Frank (Francis Vincent) 1940–1993. US rock musician, bandleader, and composer. His crudely satirical songs (*Joe's Garage* 1980), deliberately bad taste, and complex orchestral and electronic compositions (*Hot Rats* 1969, *Jazz from Hell* 1986) make his work hard to categorize. His group the Mothers of Invention 1965–73 was part of the 1960s avant-garde, and the Mothers' hippie parody *We're Only in It for the Money* 1967 was popular with its target.

ZAPU (acronym for ***Zimbabwe African People's Union***) political organization founded by Joshua Nkomo 1961 and banned 1962 by the Rhodesian government. It engaged in a guerrilla war in alliance with ◊ZANU against the Rhodesian regime until late 1979. In the 1980 elections ZAPU was defeated and was then persecuted by the ruling ZANU Patriotic Front party. In 1987 the two parties merged.

Zaragoza (English ***Saragossa***) industrial city (iron, steel, chemicals, plastics, canned food, electrical goods) in Aragon, Spain; population (1994) 607,000. The medieval city walls and bridges over the river Ebro survive, and there is a 15th-century university.
history A Celtic settlement known as *Salduba* was captured by the Romans in the 1st century BC; they named it *Caesarea Augusta*, after their leader; later it was captured by Visigoths and Moors and was taken 1118 by Alfonso the Warrior, King of Navarre and Aragon, after a nine-month siege. It remained the capital of Aragon until the end of the 15th century. From June 1808 to Feb 1809, in the Peninsular War, it resisted a French siege. Maria Augustin (died 1859), known as the 'Maid of Zaragoza', became a national hero for her part in the defence; her story is told in Byron's *Childe Harold* 1812–18.

zebra The Cape mountain zebra *Equus zebra zebra*. It now survives mainly in the Mountain Zebra National Park near Cradock in South Africa, having been saved from near extinction (numbers had been reduced to about 40 individuals). Hartmann's mountain zebra is more widely distributed in the semi-deserts of Namibia. *Premaphotos Wildlife*

Zebu carts are widely used in Madagascar for carrying all kinds of loads. Zebu represent wealth for many farmers in Africa and Madagascar, but cause far more damage to fragile habitats than the equivalent native animals of the area, such as (in Africa) antelope.

zazen formal seated meditation in Zen Buddhism. Correct posture and breathing are necessary.

zebra black and white striped member of the horse genus *Equus* found in Africa; the stripes serve as camouflage or dazzle and confuse predators. It is about 1.5 m/5 ft high at the shoulder, with a stout body and a short, thick mane. Zebras live in family groups and herds on mountains and plains, and can run at up to 60 kph/40 mph.

The ***mountain zebra*** *E. zebra* was once common in Cape Colony and Natal and still survives in parts of South Africa and Angola. It has long ears and is silvery-white with black or dark brown markings. ***Grevy's zebra*** *E. grevyi* is much larger, with finer and clearer markings; it inhabits Ethiopia and Somalia. ***Burchell's*** or the ***common zebra*** *E. burchelli* is intermediate in size, has white ears, a long mane, and full tail; it roams the plains north of the Orange River in South Africa.

zebu any of a species of ◊cattle *Bos indicus* found domesticated in E Asia, India, and Africa. It is usually light-coloured, with large horns and a large fatty hump near the shoulders. It is used for pulling loads, and is held by some Hindus to be sacred. There are about 30 breeds.

Zebus have been crossbred with other species of cattle in hot countries to pass on their qualities of heat tolerance and insect resistance. In the USA, they are called Brahman cattle.

Zedekiah lived early 6th century. Last king of Judah 597–586 BC. Placed on the throne by Nebuchadnezzar, he rebelled, was forced to witness his sons' execution, then was blinded and sent to Babylon. The witness to these events was the prophet Jeremiah, who describes them in the Old Testament.

Zeebrugge small Belgian ferry port on the North Sea, linked to Bruges by a canal (built 1896–1907), 14 km/9 mi long. It was occupied by the Germans in World War I and developed as a major naval base. In March 1987 it was the scene of a disaster in which over 180 passengers lost their lives when the car ferry *Herald of Free Enterprise* put to sea from Zeebrugge with its car-loading doors still open.

Zen ... does not confuse spirituality with thinking about God while one is peeling potatoes. Zen spirituality is just to peel the potatoes.

On **Zen**
Alan Watts *The Way of Zen*

Zeeland province of the SW Netherlands, mostly below sea level; it is protected by a system of dykes; area 1,790 sq km/691 sq mi; capital Middelburg; population (1995) 365,800. Industries include cereals and potatoes.
history disputed by the counts of Flanders and Holland during the Middle Ages, Zeeland was annexed to Holland 1323 by Count William III.

Zeffirelli Franco (Corsi) 1923– . Italian theatre, opera and film director, and stage designer. He is acclaimed for his stylish designs and lavish productions. His films include *Romeo and Juliet* 1968, *La Traviata* 1983, *Otello* 1986, and *Hamlet* 1990.

Zeiss Carl 1816–1888. German optician. He opened his first workshop in Jena 1846, and in 1866 joined forces with Ernst Abbe (1840–1905) producing cameras, microscopes, and binoculars.

Zeitgeist (German 'time spirit') spirit of the age. The term was used as the title of an exhibition of Neo-Expressionist paintings held in Berlin 1982.

Zelenchukskaya site of the world's largest single-mirror optical telescope, with a mirror of 6 m/236 in diameter, in the Caucasus Mountains of Russia. At the same site is the RATAN 600 radio telescope, consisting of radio reflectors in a circle of 600 m/2,000 ft diameter. Both instruments are operated by the Academy of Sciences in St Petersburg.

Zelenograd city on the Skhodnia River, 37 km/23 mi NW of Moscow, in the Russian Federation; population (1992) 170,000. Construction began 1960 and it achieved city status 1963. It is a centre for the microelectronics industry; construction materials and fruit and vegetables are also produced.

Zemin Jiang 1926– . Chinese political leader, state president from 1993. He succeeded ◊Zhao Ziyang as Communist Party leader after the Tiananmen Square massacre of 1989. Jiang is a cautious proponent of economic reform who has held with unswerving adherence to the party's 'political line'.

The son-in-law of ◊Li Xiannian and a graduate in engineering, Jiang joined the Chinese Communist Party's politburo 1967 after serving in the Moscow embassy and as mayor of Shanghai. During the 1989 student protests, he secured a peaceful end to the demonstrations in Shanghai and was rewarded by being appointed Communist Party leader. He subsequently succeeded his patron ◊Deng Xiaoping as head of the influential central military commission and replaced Yang Shangkun as state president March 1993.

Zen (abbreviation of Japanese *zenna* 'quiet mind concentration') form of ◊Buddhism introduced from India to Japan via China in the 12th century. *Kōan* (paradoxical questions), intense meditation, and sudden enlightenment are elements of Zen practice. Soto Zen was spread by the priest Dōgen (1200–1253), who emphasized work, practice, discipline, and philosophical questions to discover one's Buddha-nature in the 'realization of self'. ▷*See feature on pp. 162–163.*

Zend-Avesta sacred scriptures of ◊Zoroastrianism, today practised by the Parsees. They comprise the ***Avesta*** (liturgical books for the priests); the ***Gathas*** (the discourses and revelations of Zoroaster); and the ***Zend*** (commentary upon them).

Zeng Guofan or ***Tseng Kuo-fan*** 1811–1872. Chinese imperial official who played a crucial role in crushing the ◊Taiping Rebellion. He raised the Hunan army 1852 to organize resistance to this revolt, eventually capturing Nanjing 1864. The regional influence he acquired made him in some ways a forerunner of the 20th-century Chinese warlords.

zenith uppermost point of the celestial horizon, immediately above the observer; the ◊nadir is below, diametrically opposite. See ◊celestial sphere.

Zenobia lived 3rd century. Queen of Palmyra AD 266–272. She assumed the crown as regent for her sons, after the death of her husband Odaenathus, and in 272 was defeated at Emesa (now Homs) by Aurelian and taken captive to Rome.

Zeno of Citium c. 335–262 BC. Greek founder of the ◊stoic school of philosophy in Athens, about 300 BC.

Zeno of Elea c. 490–c. 430 BC. Greek philosopher. He pointed out several paradoxes that raised 'modern' problems of space and time. For example, motion is an illusion, since an arrow in flight must occupy a determinate space at each instant, and therefore must be at rest.

Communists should be the first to be concerned about other people and country and the last to enjoy themselves.

Zhao Ziyang
Quoted in the *Financial Times* 21 March 1988

zeolite any of the hydrous aluminium silicates, also containing sodium, calcium, barium, strontium, or potassium, chiefly found in igneous rocks and characterized by a ready loss or gain of water. Zeolites are used as 'molecular sieves' to separate mixtures because they are capable of selective absorption. They have a high ion-exchange capacity and can be used to make petrol, benzene, and toluene from low-grade raw materials, such as coal and methanol.

Permutit is a synthetic zeolite used to soften hard water.

Zephyrus in Greek mythology, the god of the west wind, husband of Iris, and father of the horses of ◊Achilles in Homer's *Iliad*.

Zeppelin Ferdinand Adolf August Heinrich, Count von Zeppelin 1838–1917. German ◊airship pioneer. His first airship was built and tested 1900. During World War I a number of ***zeppelins*** bombed England. They were also used for luxury passenger transport but the construction of hydrogen-filled airships with rigid keels was abandoned after several disasters in the 1920s and 1930s. Zeppelin also helped to pioneer large multi-engine bomber planes.

Zermatt ski resort in the Valais canton, Switzerland, at the foot of the Matterhorn; population (1985) 3,700.

Zeroual Lamine 1941– . Algerian politican and soldier, president from 1994. He was brought into government 1993 as defence minister, and the following year became commander-in-chief of the armed forces. Appointed president at a time of increasing civil strife, he initially attempted dialogue and reconciliation with imprisoned Islamic fundamentalist leaders. After this failed, Zeroual increasingly resorted to military tactics to counter the unrest. His victory in a direct presidential election Nov 1995 was followed Sept 1996 by an announcement of plans for constitutional changes, allowing for multiparty politics.

Zeus in Greek mythology, the chief of the gods (Roman Jupiter). He was the son of Kronos, whom he overthrew; his brothers included Pluto and Poseidon, his sisters Demeter and Hera. As the supreme god he dispensed good and evil and was the father and ruler of all humankind. His emblems are the thunderbolt and aegis (shield), representing the thundercloud. The colossal ivory and gold statue of the seated god, made by Phidias for the temple of Zeus in the Peloponnese, was one of the ◊Seven Wonders of the World.

Zhangjiakou or ***Changchiakow*** historic city and trade centre in Hebei province, China, 160 km/100 mi NW of Beijing, on the Great Wall; population (1990) 670,000. Zhangjiakou is on the border of Inner Mongolia (its Mongolian name is ***Kalgan***, 'gate') and on the road and railway to Ulaanbaatar in Mongolia. It developed under the Manchu dynasty, and was the centre of the tea trade from China to Russia.

Zhao Ziyang 1919– . Chinese politician, prime minister 1980–87 and secretary of the Chinese Communist Party 1987–89. His reforms included self-management and incentives for workers and factories. He lost his secretaryship and other posts after the Tiananmen Square massacre in Beijing June 1989.

Zhejiang or ***Chekiang*** province of SE China
area 101,800 sq km/39,295 sq mi
capital Hangzhou
features smallest of the Chinese provinces; the base of the Song dynasty 12th–13th centuries; densely populated
industries rice, cotton, sugar, jute, maize; timber on the uplands
population (1990) 40,840,000.

Zhelev Zhelyu 1935– . Bulgarian politician, president 1990–96. In 1989 he became head of the opposition Democratic Forces coalition. He was made president of Bulgaria 1990 after the demise of the 'reform communist' regime, and was directly elected to the post 1992. In June 1996 he was defeated in the presidential primary election by Peter Stoyanov.

Zhengzhou or ***Chengchow*** industrial city (light engineering, cotton textiles, foods) and capital (from 1954) of Henan province, China, on the Huang He River; population (1993) 1,530,000.

In the 1970s the earliest city found in China, from 1500 BC, was excavated near the walls of Zhengzhou. The Shaolin temple, where the martial art of kung fu originated, is nearby.

Zhirinovsky Vladimir 1946– . Russian politician, leader of the far-right Liberal Democratic Party of Russia (LDPR) from 1991. He advocates the use of nuclear weapons and the restoration of the Russian empire. He won third place out of six candidates in Russia's first free presidential elections 1991; in the June 1996 presidential elections his support fell.

Zhitomir capital of Zhitomir region in W Ukraine, W of Kiev; population (1992) 299,000. It is a timber and grain centre and has furniture factories. Zhitomir dates from the 13th century.

Zhivkov Todor 1911–1998. Bulgarian Communist Party (BCP) leader 1954–89, prime minister 1962–71, president 1971–89. His period in office was one of caution and conservatism. In 1990 he was charged with embezzlement during his time in office. His trial began Feb 1991 but was subsequently postponed indefinitely on health grounds.

Zhou dynasty or ***Chou dynasty*** Chinese succession of rulers c. 1122–256 BC, during which cities emerged and philosophy flourished. The dynasty was established by the Zhou, a semi-nomadic people from the Wei Valley region, west of the great bend in the Huang He (Yellow River). Zhou influence waned from 403 BC, as the Warring States era began.

The founder was Wu Wang, 'the Martial', who claimed that ◊Shang dynasty misrule justified the transfer of the 'mandate of heaven'. Under the Zhou, agriculture and commerce developed further, iron implements and metal coins came into use, cities grew up, and the philosophies of Confucius, Lao Zi, Mencius, and Taoism flowered. The Western Zhou controlled feudal vassal states in the Wei Valley, basing their capital at Hao, near Xian, until 771 BC. A new capital was later set up at Luoyang, to serve the Eastern Zhou. Zhou society had a very similar structure to later feudal European and Japanese periods, with strict divisions and hereditary classes.

Zhou Enlai or ***Chou En-lai*** 1898–1976. Chinese politician. Zhou, a member of the Chinese Communist Party (CCP) from the 1920s, was prime minister 1949–76 and foreign minister 1949–58. He was a moderate Maoist and weathered the Cultural Revolution. He played a key role in foreign affairs.

Born into a declining mandarin gentry family near Shanghai, Zhou studied in Japan and Paris, where he became a founder member of the overseas branch of the CCP. He adhered to the Moscow line of urban-based revolution in China, organizing communist cells in Shanghai and an abortive uprising in Nanchang 1927. In 1935 Zhou supported the election of Mao Zedong as CCP leader and remained a loyal ally during the next 40 years. He served as liaison officer 1937–46 between the CCP and Chiang Kai-shek's nationalist Guomindang government. In 1949 he became prime minister, an office he held until his death Jan 1976.

Zhou, a moderator between the opposing camps of Liu Shaoqi and Mao Zedong, restored orderly progress after the Great Leap Forward (1958–60) and the Cultural Revolution (1966–69), and was the architect of the Four Modernizations programme 1975.

Zhu De or ***Chu Teh*** 1886–1976. Chinese Red Army leader from 1931. He devised the tactic of mobile guerrilla warfare and organized the ◊Long March to Shaanxi 1934–36. He was made a marshal 1955.

Zhukov Georgi Konstantinovich 1896–1974. Marshal of the USSR in World War II and minister of defence 1955–57. As chief of staff from 1941, he defended Moscow 1941, counterattacked at Stalingrad (now Volgograd) 1942, organized the relief of Leningrad (now St Petersburg) 1943, and led the offensive from the Ukraine March 1944 which ended in the fall of Berlin.

Zhukov joined the Bolsheviks and the Red Army 1918 and led a cavalry regiment in the Civil War 1918–20. His army defeated the Japanese forces in Mongolia 1939. At the end of World War II, he headed the Allied delegation that received the German surrender, and subsequently commanded the Soviet occupation forces in Germany. Under the Khrushchev regime he was denounced 1957 for obstructing party work and encouraging a Zhukov cult, but was restored 1965.

Zhu Rongji 1928– . Chinese communist politician, vice-premier from 1991 and prime minister from 1998. He became a vice-premier in 1991, with a particular interest in economic affairs, and entered the Chinese Communist Party (CCP) Politburo in 1992. The 1997 party congress designated Zhu the third-ranking figure in the CCP, behind President Jiang Zemin and Li Peng whom he replaced as prime minister in March 1998. He immediately announced a radical 'downsizing' of the government to meet the needs of a market economy.

Zia Begum Khaleda 1945– . Bangladeshi conservative politician, prime minister 1991–96. As leader of the Bangladesh Nationalist Party (BNP) from 1984, she successfully oversaw the transition from presidential to democratic parliamentary government, but faced mounting opposition from 1994.

In 1958 she married Captain Zia ur Rahman who assumed power in a military coup 1976. He became president 1977, and was assassinated 1981. Begum Khaleda Zia then entered opposition politics, becoming leader of the BNP 1984. In 1990 she helped form a seven-party alliance, whose pressure for a more democratic regime resulted in the toppling of General ◊Ershad, a long-standing military ruler, during whose regime she had been detained seven times. The opposition boycotted the Feb 1996 general elections; in the general election that followed in June 1996, the BNP was defeated by its chief rival, the Awami League.

Zia ul-Haq Muhammad 1924–1988. Pakistani general, in power from 1977 until his death, probably an assassination, in an aircraft explosion. He became army chief of staff 1976, led the military coup against Zulfikar Ali ◊Bhutto 1977, and became president 1978. Zia introduced a fundamentalist Islamic regime and restricted political activity.

zidovudine (formerly *AZT*) antiviral drug used in the treatment of ◊AIDS. It is not a cure for AIDS but is effective in prolonging life; it does not, however, delay the onset of AIDS in people carrying the virus.

Zidovudine was developed in the mid-1980s and approved for use by 1987. It reduces the risk of opportunistic infection and relieves many neurological complications; however, frequent blood monitoring is required to control anaemia, a potentially life-threatening side effect of zidovudine. Blood transfusions are often necessary, and the drug must be withdrawn if bone-marrow function is severely affected.

A US trial 1994 showed that the drug does provide some protection to babies born to HIV-positive mothers. The number of babies infected was reduced by two-thirds where mothers received zidovudine during pregnancy. Long-term affects of zidovudine on the babies' health remain to be determined.

Ziegler Karl 1898–1973. German organic chemist. In 1963 he shared the Nobel Prize for Chemistry with Giulio Natta (1903–1979) of Italy for his work on the chemistry and technology of large polymers. He combined simple molecules of the gas ethylene (ethene) into the long-chain plastic ◊polyethylene (polyethene).

Ziegler and Natta discovered 1953 a family of stereo-specific catalysts capable of introducing an exact and regular structure to various polymers. This discovery formed the basis of nearly all later developments in synthetic plastics, fibres, rubbers, and films derived from such olefins as ethylene (ethene) and butadiene (but-1,2:3,4-diene).

ziggurat in ancient Babylonia and Assyria, a step pyramid of sun-baked brick faced with glazed bricks or tiles on which stood a shrine. The Tower of Babel as described in the Bible may have been a ziggurat.

Zimbabwe landlocked country in S central Africa, bounded N by Zambia, E by Mozambique, S by South Africa, and W by Botswana. *See country box on p. 1174.*

Zimbabwe or ***Great Zimbabwe*** extensive stone architectural ruins near Victoria in Mashonaland, Zimbabwe. The structure was probably the work of the Shona people who established their rule about AD 1000 and who mined minerals for trading. The word *zimbabwe* means 'house of stone' in the Shona language.

zinc (Germanic *zint* 'point') hard, brittle, bluish-white, metallic element, symbol Zn, atomic number 30, relative atomic mass 65.37. The principal ore is sphalerite or zinc blende (zinc sulphide, ZnS). Zinc is little affected by air or moisture at ordinary temperatures; its chief uses are in alloys such as brass and in coating metals (for example, galvanized iron). Its compounds include zinc oxide, used in ointments (as an astringent) and cosmetics, paints, glass, and printing ink.

Zinc is an essential trace element in most animals; adult humans have 2–3 g/0.07–0.1 oz zinc in their bodies. There are more than 300 known enzymes that contain zinc.

Zinc has been used as a component of brass since the Bronze Age, but it was not recognized as a separate metal until 1746, when it was described by German chemist Andreas Sigismund Marggraf (1709–1782).

zinc ore mineral from which zinc is extracted, principally sphalerite (Zn,Fe)S, but also zincite, ZnO_2, and smithsonite, $ZnCO_3$, all of which occur in mineralized veins. Ores of lead and zinc often occur together, and are common worldwide; Canada, the USA, and Australia are major producers.

zinc oxide ZnO white powder, yellow when hot, that occurs in nature as the mineral zincite. It is used in paints and as an antiseptic in zinc ointment; it is the main ingredient of calamine lotion.

zinc sulphide ZnS yellow-white solid that occurs in nature as the mineral sphalerite (also called zinc blende). It is the principal ore of zinc, and is used in the manufacture of fluorescent paints.

Zinnemann Fred(erick) 1907–1997. Austrian film director. He lived in the USA from 1921, and latterly in the UK. His films include *High Noon* 1952, *From Here to Eternity* 1953 (Academy Award), *A Man For All Seasons* 1966 (Academy Award), *The Day of the Jackal* 1973, and *Five Days One Summer* 1982.

zinnia any annual plant of the genus *Zinnia*, family Compositae, native to Mexico and South America, notably the cultivated hybrids of *Z. elegans*, with brightly coloured, daisylike flowers.

Zinoviev Grigory Yevseyevich 1883–1936. Russian communist politician whose name was attached to a forgery, the ***Zinoviev letter***, inciting Britain's communists to rise, which helped to topple the Labour government 1924.

A prominent Bolshevik, Zinoviev returned to Russia 1917 with Lenin and played a leading part in the Revolution. He became head of the Communist ◊International 1919. As one of the 'Old Bolsheviks', he was seen by Stalin as a threat. He was accused of complicity in the murder of the Bolshevik leader Sergei Kirov 1934, and was tried and shot.

zinnia Zinnias belong to the sunflower family. *Zinnia elegans*, a species with plentiful natural variation, has been used to produce a wide range of colourful garden varieties.

ziggurat This ziggurat, at Choqa Zanbil in Iran, was built by the Elamites in about 1250 BC. The ziggurat form derived from stepped platforms built for temples by the Sumerian people of Mesopotamia 1,000 years earlier. The last examples in the region date from about 450 BC, though similar structures were built in the Americas. *Corbis*

Zinovyev Alexander Aleksandrovich 1922– . Russian satirical writer and mathematician. He now lives in Munich, Germany. His first book *Ziyayushchie vysoty/Yawning Heights* 1976, a surreal, chaotic narrative, represents a formal negation of the socialist realist novel and the promised 'great Future' of Soviet ideology. He complicates the quasi-scientific stance of his writing by deliberate disorganization, even in his treatise *Kommunizm kak realnost/The Reality of Communism* 1981.

Zion Jebusite (Amorites of Canaan) stronghold in Jerusalem captured by King David, and the hill on which he built the Temple, symbol of Jerusalem and of Jewish national life.

Zionism political movement advocating the re-establishment of a Jewish homeland in Palestine, the 'promised land' of the Bible, with its capital Jerusalem, the 'city of Zion'.

1896 As a response to European ◊anti-Semitism, Theodor Herzl published his *Jewish State*, outlining a scheme for setting up an autonomous Jewish commonwealth under Ottoman suzerainty.

1897 The World Zionist Congress was established in Basel, Switzerland, with Herzl as its first president. 'Hatikva' (The Hope) was adopted as the Zionist anthem, which was the unofficial anthem of Palestine until 1948 when it was sung at the proclamation of the State of Israel on 14 May.

1917 The ◊Balfour Declaration was secured from Britain by Chaim Weizmann. It promised the Jews a homeland in Palestine.

1940–48 Jewish settlement in the British mandate of Palestine led to armed conflict between militant Zionists (see ◊Irgun) and both Palestinian Arabs and the British.

1947 In Nov the United Nations (UN) divided Palestine into Jewish and Arab states, with Jerusalem as an international city.

1948 The Jews in Palestine proclaimed the State of Israel on 14 May, but the Arab states rejected both the partition of Palestine and the existence of Israel. The armies of Iraq, Syria, Lebanon, Trans-Jordan, Saudi Arabia, Yemen, and Egypt crossed Israel's borders and attacked en masse but were defeated by the Israeli army (*Haganah*).

1948–73 In addition to constant border sniping and clashes, one or more Arab nations attacked Israel in the on-going ◊Arab-Israeli wars of 1956, 1967, and 1973.

1975 The General Assembly of the UN condemned Zionism as 'a form of racism and racial discrimination'; among those voting against the resolution were the USA and the members of the European Community (now the European Union).

1991 Attacked during the ◊Gulf War by Iraqi missiles and criticized for its adamant attitude against Palestinian aspirations, Israel met with Arab nations for the first time in a historic Middle East peace conference held in Spain. The UN General Assembly repealed its 1975 resolution condemning Zionism.

ZIMBABWE
Republic of (formerly *Southern Rhodesia*)

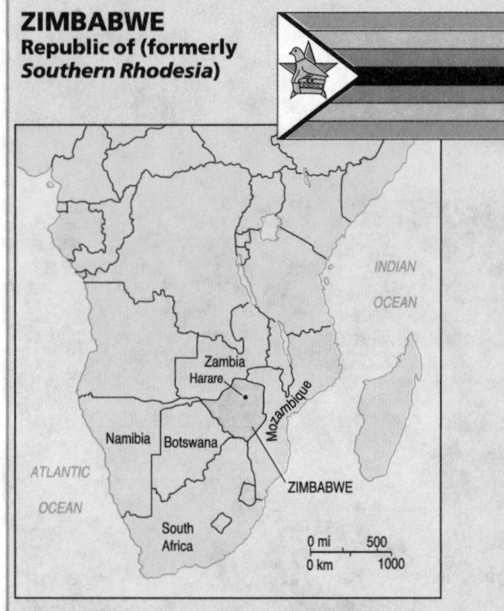

area 390,300 sq km/150,695 sq mi
capital Harare
major towns/cities Bulawayo, Gweru, Kwekwe, Mutare, Hwange, Chitungwiza
physical features high plateau with central high veld and mountains in E; rivers Zambezi, Limpopo; Victoria Falls
head of state Robert Mugabe from 1987
head of government Robert Mugabe from 1987
political system effectively one-party socialist republic
administrative divisions eight provinces and two cities with provincial status
political parties Zimbabwe African National Union–Patriotic Front (ZANU–PF), African socialist; opposition parties exist but none have mounted serious challenge to ruling party
armed forces 45,000; paramilitary police force 19,500; national militia 1,000 (1995)
conscription none
defence spend (% GDP) 3.5 (1994)
education spend (% GNP) 9.1 (1992)
health spend (% GDP) 3.2 (1990)
death penalty retained and used for ordinary crimes
population 11,439,000 (1996 est)
population growth rate 2.6% (1990–95); 2.0% (2000–05)
age distribution (% of total population) <15 44.1%, 15–65 53.1%, >65 2.8% (1995)
ethnic distribution four distinct ethnic groups: indigenous Africans, who account for about 95% of the population, Europeans (mainly British), who account for about 3.5%, and Afro-Europeans and Asians, who each comprise about 0.5%
population density (per sq km) 28 (1994)
urban population (% of total) 32 (1995)
labour force 46% of population: 68% agriculture, 8% industry, 24% services (1990)
unemployment 44% (1993)
child mortality rate (under 5, per 1,000 live births) 81 (1994)
life expectancy 59 (men), 63 (women)
education (compulsory years) 8
literacy rate 74% (men), 60% (women)
languages English (official), Shona, Sindebele
religions Christian, Muslim, Hindu, animist
TV sets (per 1,000 people) 27 (1992)
currency Zimbabwe dollar
GDP (US $) 5.43 billion (1994)
GDP per capita (PPP) (US $) 2,100 (1993)
growth rate 7.4% (1994)
average annual inflation 22.2% (1994); 18.7% (1985–92)
trading partners South Africa, UK, Germany, Japan, USA
resources gold, nickel, asbestos, coal, chromium, copper, silver, emeralds, lithium, tin, iron ore, cobalt
industries metal products, food processing, textiles, furniture and other wood products, chemicals, fertilizers
exports tobacco, metals and metal alloys, textiles and clothing, cotton lint. Principal market: South Africa 12.9% (1993)
imports machinery and transport equipment, basic manufactures, mineral fuels, chemicals, foodstuffs. Principal source: South Africa 40% (1993)
arable land 7.0% (1993)
agricultural products tobacco, maize, cotton, coffee, sugar cane, wheat, soya beans, groundnuts, horticulture; livestock (chiefly cattle)

HISTORY
13th C Shona people settled Mashonaland (E Zimbabwe), erecting stone buildings (hence name Zimbabwe, 'stone house').
15th C Shona Empire reached its greatest extent.
16th–17th Cs Portuguese settlers developed trade with Shona states and achieved influence over kingdom of Mwanamutapa in N Zimbabwe 1629.
1837 Ndebele (or Matabele) people settled in SW Zimbabwe after being driven north from Transvaal by Boers; Shona defeated by Ndebele led by King Mzilikazi who formed military empire based at Bulawayo.
1870 King Lobengula succeeded King Mzilikazi.
1889 British South Africa Company (BSA Co) of Cecil Rhodes obtained exclusive rights to exploit mineral resources in Lobengula's domains.
1890 Creation of white colony in Mashonaland and founding of Salisbury (Harare) by Leander Starr Jameson, associate of Rhodes.
1893 Matabele War: Jameson defeated Lobengula; white settlers took control of country.
1895 Matabeleland, Mashonaland, and Zambia named Rhodesia after Cecil Rhodes.
1896 Matabele revolt suppressed.
1898 Southern Rhodesia (Zimbabwe) became British protectorate administered by BSA Co; farming, mining, and railways developed.
1922 Union with South Africa rejected by referendum among white settlers.
1923 Southern Rhodesia became a self-governing colony; Africans progressively disenfranchised.
1933–53 Prime Minister Godfrey Huggins (later Lord Malvern) pursued 'White Rhodesia' policy of racial segregation.
1950s Immigration doubled white population to around 250,000, while indigenous African population stood at around 6 million.
1953 Southern Rhodesia formed part of Federation of Rhodesia and Nyasaland.
1961 Zimbabwe African People's Union (ZAPU) formed with Joshua Nkomo as leader; declared illegal a year later.
1962 Rhodesia Front party of Winston Field took power in Southern Rhodesia, pledging to preserve white rule.
1963 Federation of Rhodesia and Nyasaland dissolved as Zambia and Malawi moved towards independence; Zimbabwe African National Union (ZANU) formed, with Robert Mugabe as secretary; declared illegal a year later.
1964 Ian Smith became prime minister; he rejected British terms for independence which required moves towards black majority rule; Nkomo and Mugabe imprisoned.
1965 Smith made unilateral declaration of independence (UDI); Britain broke off all relations.
1966–68 United Nations (UN) imposed economic sanctions on Rhodesia, which still received help from South Africa and Portugal.
1969 Rhodesia declared itself a republic.
1972 Britain rejected draft independence agreement as unacceptable to African population.
1974 Nkomo and Mugabe released and jointly formed Patriotic Front to fight Smith regime in mounting civil war.
1975 Geneva Conference between British, Smith regime, and African nationalists failed to reach agreement.
1978 At height of civil war, whites were leaving Rhodesia at rate of 1,000 per month.
1979 Rhodesia became Zimbabwe-Rhodesia with new 'majority' constitution which nevertheless retained special rights for whites; Bishop Abel Muzorewa became premier; Mugabe and Nkomo rejected settlement; Lancaster House Agreement temporarily restored Rhodesia to British rule.
1980 Zimbabwe achieved independence from Britain with full transition to African majority rule; Mugabe became prime minister with Rev Canaan Banana as president.
1981 Rift between Mugabe (ZANU-PF) and Nkomo (ZAPU); Nkomo dismissed from cabinet 1982.
1984 ZANU-PF party congress agreed to principle of one-party state.
1987 Mugabe combined posts of head of state and prime minister as executive president; Nkomo became vice president.
1989 ZANU-PF and ZAPU formally merged; Zimbabwe Unity Movement founded by Edgar Tekere to oppose one-party state.
1992 United Party formed to oppose ZANU-PF. Mugabe declared drought and famine a national disaster.
1996 Mugabe re-elected president.
1998 Anti-government protests launched by students.

SEE ALSO Matabeleland; Mugabe, Robert; Smith, Ian

'We need not feel ashamed of flirting with the zodiac. The zodiac is well worth flirting with.'

On the ZODIAC
D H Lawrence
introduction to Frederick Carter's *The Dragon of the Apocalypse* 1930

zip fastener fastening device used in clothing, invented in the USA by Whitcomb Judson 1891, originally for doing up shoes. It has two sets of interlocking teeth, meshed by means of a slide that moves up and down. It did not become widely used in the clothing industry till the 1930s.

Zircon codename for a British signals-intelligence satellite originally intended to be launched 1988. The revelation of the existence of the Zircon project (which had been concealed by the government), and the government's subsequent efforts to suppress a programme about it on BBC television, caused much controversy 1987. Its intended function was to intercept radio and other signals from the USSR, Europe, and the Middle East and transmit them to the Government Communications Headquarters (GCHQ) in Cheltenham, England.

zircon zirconium silicate, $ZrSiO_4$, a mineral that occurs in small quantities in a wide range of igneous, sedimentary, and metamorphic rocks. It is very durable and is resistant to erosion and weathering. It is usually coloured brown, but can be other colours, and when transparent may be used as a gemstone.

Zircons contain abundant radioactive isotopes of uranium and so are useful for uranium–lead dating to determine the ages of rocks.

zirconium (Germanic *zircon*, from Persian *zargun* 'golden') lustrous, greyish-white, strong, ductile, metallic element, symbol Zr, atomic number 40, relative atomic mass 91.22. It occurs in nature as the mineral zircon (zirconium silicate), from which it is obtained commercially. It is used in some ceramics, alloys for wire and filaments, steel manufacture, and nuclear reactors, where its low neutron absorption is advantageous.

It was isolated 1824 by Swedish chemist Jöns Berzelius. The name was proposed by English chemist Humphry Davy 1808.

zither member of a family of musical instruments consisting of one or more strings stretched over a resonating frame. The modern concert zither has up to 45 strings of which five, passing over frets, are plucked with a plectrum for melody, and the remainder are plucked with the fingers for harmonic accompaniment.

Simple stick and board zithers are widespread in Africa; in India the vina represents a developed form of stick zither, while in Indonesia and the Far East versions of the ***long zither*** prevail. Tuning is by movable bridges and the long zither is played with a plectrum, producing an intense tone of sharp attack.

Zi Xi or ***Tz'u-hsi*** c. 1834–1908. Empress dowager of China. She was presented as a concubine to the emperor Xianfeng. On his death 1861 she became regent for her young son Tongzhi (1856–1875) until 1873 and, after his death, for her nephew Guangxu (1871–1908) until 1889. A ruthless conservative, she blocked the Hundred Days' Reform launched 1898 and assumed power again, having Guangxu imprisoned. Her policies helped deny China a peaceful transition to political and economic reform.

zodiac zone of the heavens containing the paths of the Sun, Moon, and planets. When this was devised by the ancient Greeks, only five planets were known, making the zodiac about 16° wide. In astrology, the zodiac is divided into 12 signs, each 30° in extent: Aries, Taurus, Gemini, Cancer, Leo, Virgo, Libra, Scorpio, Sagittarius, Capricorn, Aquarius, and Pisces. These do not cover the same areas of sky as the astronomical constellations.

The 12 astronomical constellations are uneven in size and do not between them cover the whole zodiac, or even the line of the ecliptic, much of which lies in Ophiuchus.

zodiacal light cone-shaped light sometimes seen extending from the Sun along the ◊ecliptic, visible after sunset or before sunrise. It is due to thinly spread dust particles in the central plane of the Solar System. It is very faint, and requires a dark, clear sky to be seen.

Zoë c. 978–1050. Byzantine empress who ruled from 1028 until 1050. She gained the title by marriage to the heir apparent Romanus III Argyrus, but was reputed to have poisoned him (1034) in order to marry her lover Michael. He died 1041 and Zoë and her sister Theodora were proclaimed joint empresses. Rivalry led to Zoë marrying Constantine IX Monomachus with whom she reigned until her death.

Zog Ahmed Bey Zogu 1895–1961. King of Albania 1928–39. He became prime minister of Albania 1922, president of the republic 1925, and proclaimed himself king 1928. He was driven out by the Italians 1939 and settled in England.

zoidogamy type of plant reproduction in which male gametes (antherozoids) swim in a film of water to the female gametes. Zoidogamy is found in algae, bryophytes, pteridophytes, and some gymnosperms (others use siphonogamy, in which a pollen tube grows to enable male gametes to pass to the ovary without leaving the protection of the plant).

Zola Émile Edouard Charles Antoine 1840–1902. French novelist and social reformer. He made his name with *Thérèse Raquin* 1867, a grim, powerful story of remorse. With *La Fortune des Rougon/The Fortune of the Rougons* 1867 he began a series of some 20 naturalistic novels collectively known as *Le Rougon-Macquart*, portraying the fortunes of a French family under the Second Empire. They include *Le Ventre de Paris/The Underbelly of Paris* 1873, *Nana* 1880, and *La Débâcle/The Debacle* 1892. In 1898 he published *J'accuse/I Accuse*, a pamphlet indicting the persecutors of Alfred ◊Dreyfus, for which he was prosecuted for libel but later pardoned.

Zola was born in Paris. He became a journalist and a clerk in the publishing house of Hachette. He wrote literary and art criticisms and published several collections of short stories, beginning with *Contes à Ninon/Stories for Ninon* 1864. Having discovered his real talent as a novelist, he produced the volumes of *Le Rougon-Macquart* steadily over a quarter of a century, proving himself a master of realism. Other titles in the series are *La Faute de l'Abbé Mouret/The Simple Priest* 1875, *L'Assommoir/Drunkard* 1878, *Germinal* 1885, *La Terre/Earth* 1888, *La Bête humaine/The Human Beast* 1890, and *L'Argent/Money* 1891. Among later novels are the trilogy *Trois Villes/Three Cities* 1894–98 (*Lourdes* 1894, *Rome* 1896, *Paris* 1898), and *Les Quatre Evangiles/The Four Gospels* 1899–1903 (*Fécondité/Fecundity* 1899, *Travail/Work* 1902, *Vérité/Truth* 1903, and the unfinished *Justice*).

The truth is on the move and nothing can stop her now.

EMILE ZOLA
on the Dreyfus affair

Zola French novelist and social reformer Émile Zola. Zola's reforming zeal took him from naturalistic novels to the defence of Capt Dreyfus in *J'accuse/I Accuse* 1898, the famous open letter to the president. *Topham*

L'AURORE

Littéraire, Artistique, Sociale

J'Accuse...!

TTRE AU PRÉSIDENT DE LA RÉPUBLIQ

Par ÉMILE ZOLA

Zola Gianfranco 1966– . Italian footballer. A skilful attacking player, he has made a major impact on English football since his £4.5 million transfer to Chelsea from Parma in 1996. He was born in Sardinia, and played for Nuorese and Torres before making his debut in the Italian first division with Napoli in 1989. Understudying and then replacing Diego ◊Maradona, he emerged as one of Italy's most promising young players. He made his full Italian debut in 1991, but it was not until his £5.5 million transfer to Parma in 1993 that his talent fully blossomed. In 102 appearances for the club he scored 49 goals, including 19 in the 1994–95 season when Parma won the UEFA Cup. In 1997 he played in the FA Cup final, and was voted the English Football Writers' Association Player of the Year.

Zollverein 19th-century German customs union, begun under Prussian auspices 1828; the union included most German-speaking states except Austria by 1834.

Although designed to remove tariff barriers and facilitate trade within the German confederation, the Zollverein also had a political effect in isolating Austria. The Austrians were committed to trade tariffs to protect their agriculture and industry; thus their inability to join the Zollverein served to increase Prussian power in the confederation.

zombie corpse believed to be reanimated by a spirit and enslaved. The idea, widespread in Haiti, possibly arose from voodoo priests using the nerve poison tetrodotoxin (from the puffer fish) to produce a semblance of death from which the victim afterwards physically recovers. Those eating incorrectly prepared puffer fish in Japan have been similarly affected.

zone system in photography, a system of exposure estimation invented by Ansel ◊Adams that groups infinite tonal gradations into ten zones, zone 0 being black and zone 10 white.

zone therapy alternative name for ◊reflexology.

zoo (abbreviation for ***zoological gardens***) place where animals are kept in captivity. Originally created purely for visitor entertainment and education, zoos have become major centres for the breeding of endangered species of animals; a 1984 report identified 2,000 vertebrate species in need of such maintenance. The Arabian oryx has already been preserved in this way; it was captured 1962, bred in captivity, and released again in the desert 1972, where it has flourished.

Notable zoos exist in New York, San Diego, Toronto, Chicago, London, Paris, Berlin, Moscow, and Beijing (Peking). Many groups object to zoos because they keep animals in unnatural conditions alien to their habitat.

Henry I started a royal menagerie at Woodstock, Oxfordshire, later transferred to the Tower of London. The Zoological Society of London was founded 1826 by Stamford Raffles in Regent's Park, London, and in 1827 the gardens were opened to members. In 1831 William IV presented the royal menagerie to the Zoological Society; the public were admitted from 1848. The name 'zoo' dates from 1867. London Zoo currently houses some 8,000 animals of over 900 species. A threat of closure 1991, because of falling income, was reversed Sept 1992 and the zoo was to be transformed into a conservation park, with Whipsnade as the national collection of animals. In 1991 the number of animals in Britain's zoos totalled approximately 35,000.

zoology branch of biology concerned with the study of animals. It includes any aspect of the study of animal form and function – description of present-day animals, the study of evolution of animal forms, ◊anatomy, ◊physiology, ◊embryology, behaviour, and geographical distribution.

zoom lens photographic lens that, by variation of focal length, allows speedy transition from long shots to close-ups.

zoonosis any infectious disease that can be transmitted to humans by other vertebrate animals. Probably the most feared example is ◊rabies. The transmitted microorganism sometimes causes disease only in the human host, leaving the animal host unaffected.

Zoroaster or ***Zarathustra*** c. 638–c. 553 BC. Persian prophet and religious teacher, founder of Zoroastrianism. Zoroaster believed that he had seen God, Ahura Mazda, in a vision. His first vision came at the age of 30 and, after initial rejection and violent attack, he converted King Vishtaspa. Subsequently, his teachings spread rapidly, becoming the official religion of the kingdom.

Zoroastrianism pre-Islamic Persian religion founded by the Persian prophet Zoroaster in the 6th century BC, and still practised by the ◊Parsees in India. The ◊Zend-Avesta are the sacred scriptures of the faith. The theology is dualistic, Ahura Mazda or Ormuzd (the good God) being perpetually in conflict with Ahriman (the evil God), but the former is assured of eventual victory. There are approximately 100,000 (1991) Zoroastrians worldwide; membership is restricted to those with both parents belonging to the faith.

beliefs Humanity has been given free will to choose between the two powers, thus rendering believers responsible for their fate after death in heaven or hell. Moral and physical purity is central to all aspects of Zoroastrian *yasna* or worship: since life and work are part of worship, there should be purity of action. Fire is considered sacred, and Ahura Mazda believed to be present when the ritual flame is worshipped at home or in the temple. It is believed that there will be a second universal judgement at *Frashokereti*, a time when the dead will be raised and the world cleansed of unnatural impurity. The Parsee community in Bombay is now the main centre of Zoroastrianism, but since conversion is generally considered impossible, the numbers in India have been steadily decreasing at the rate of 10% per decade since 1947. Parsee groups, mainly in Delhi and outside India, have been pushing for the acceptance of converts, but the concern of the majority in Bombay is that their religious and cultural heritage will be lost.

zouk (Creole 'to party') Caribbean dance music originally created in France by musicians from the Antilles. It draws on Latin American, Haitian, and African rhythms and employs electronic synthesizers as well as ethnic drums. Zouk was developed from 1978 and is popular in Paris and parts of the West Indies.

Z particle in physics, an ◊elementary particle, one of the weakons responsible for carrying the ◊weak nuclear force.

Zsigmondy Richard Adolf 1865–1929. Austrian-born German chemist who devised and built an ultramicroscope in 1903. The microscope's illumination was placed at right angles to the axis. (In a conventional microscope the light source is placed parallel to the instrument's axis.) Zsigmondy's arrangement made it possible to observe particles with a diameter of 10-millionth of a millimetre. Nobel Prize for Chemistry 1925.

zucchini alternative name for the courgette, a type of ◊marrow.

Zugzwang (German) a position in chess from which it is impossible to move without worsening one's situation.

Zuider Zee former sea inlet in the NW Netherlands, closed off from the North Sea by a 32-km/20-mi dyke 1932; much of it has been reclaimed as land. The remaining lake is called the ◊Ijsselmeer.

Zukofsky Louis 1904–1978. US poet. He combined poetry, prose, criticism, musical notation, and drama in his complex epic *A* (complete publication 1979). He was a major theorist and practitioner of Objectivism. Zukofsky also published fiction, translations, and works of criticism and aesthetics

In Zürich there was a lot besides Zürich – the roofs up-led the eyes to tinkling cow-pastures, which in turn modified hilltops further up.

On **Zürich**
F Scott Fitzgerald
Tender is the Night

including *Bottom: On Shakespeare* 1963 and *Prepositions* 1967. His short lyric poems were collected in two volumes 1965 and 1966.

Zulu member of a group of southern African peoples mainly from Kwa Zulu Natal, South Africa. Today many Zulus work in the industrial centres around Johannesburg and Durban. The Zulu language, closely related to Xhosa, belongs to the Bantu branch of the Niger-Congo family. Many Zulus are supporters of the political organization ◊Inkatha.

Zululand region in KwaZulu Natal, South Africa, largely corresponding to the former Black National State ◊KwaZulu. The Zulus formed a powerful kingdom in the early 19th century under Shaka (died 1828) and built up an empire in Natal, displacing other peoples of southern Africa. They were defeated by the British army at Ulundi 1879. Zululand became part of the British colony of Natal 1897.

Zürich financial centre and industrial city (machinery, electrical goods, textiles) on Lake Zürich; population (1994) 353,400. Situated at the foot of the Alps, it is the capital of Zürich canton and the largest city in Switzerland.

The university was founded 1833, and the Federal Institute of Technology (the Polytechnicum) was founded 1855.

Zweig Stefan 1881–1942. Austrian writer. He was the author of plays, poems, and many biographies of writers (including Balzac and Dickens) and historical figures (including Marie Antoinette and Mary Stuart). He and his wife, exiles from the Nazis from 1934, despaired at what they saw as the end of civilization and culture and committed suicide in Brazil.

Zwicky Fritz 1898–1974. Swiss astronomer. He predicted the existence of ◊neutron stars 1934. He discovered 18 supernovae and determined that cosmic rays originate in them.

Zwicky observed that most galaxies occur in clusters, each of which contains several thousand galaxies. He made spectroscopic studies of the ◊Virgo and Coma Berenices clusters and calculated that the distribution of galaxies in the Coma Berenices cluster was statistically similar to the distribution of molecules in a gas when its temperature is at equilibrium. Beginning 1936, he compiled a catalogue of galaxies and galaxy clusters in which he listed 10,000 clusters.

Zwingli Ulrich 1484–1531. Swiss Protestant reformer. He was ordained a Roman Catholic priest 1506, but by 1519 was a Reformer and led the Reformation in Switzerland with his insistence on the sole authority of the Scriptures. He was killed in a skirmish at Kappel during a war against the cantons that had not accepted the Reformation.

zwitterion ion that has both a positive and a negative charge, such as an ◊amino acid in neutral solution. For example, glycine contains both a basic amino group (NH^2) and an acidic carboxyl group (-COOH); when both these are ionized in aqueous solution, the acid group loses a proton to the amino group, and the molecule is positively charged at one end and negatively charged at the other.

Zwolle capital of Overijssel province, the Netherlands; a market town with brewing, distilling, butter-making, and other industries; population (1994) 99,100.

Zworykin Vladimir Kosma 1889–1982. Russian-born US electronics engineer who invented a television camera tube and developed the ◊electron microscope.

zydeco dance music originating in Louisiana, USA, similar to ◊Cajun but more heavily influenced by blues and West Indian music.

Zydeco is fast and bouncy, using instruments like the accordion, saxophone, and washboard. It was widely popularized by singer and accordion player Clifton Chenier (1925–1987).

zygote ◊ovum (egg) after ◊fertilization but before it undergoes cleavage to begin embryonic development.

Zyuganov Gennadi Andreyevich 1944– . Russian politician, leader of the Communist Party of the Russian Federation (CPRF) from 1992. During President Mikhail Gorbachev's ◊*glasnost* programme 1988–91, he served as deputy director of the party's ideology department. Zyuganov failed in his challenge for the presidency against Boris Yeltsin 1996.

Zyuganov was born near Orel, Russia, and joined the Soviet Communist Party during his 20s. In Dec 1992, after the break-up of the Soviet Union, he assumed leadership of the (then-banned) reform-socialist CPRF and oversaw the resurrection of the party's fortunes. In the Dec 1995 Russian parliamentary elections, the CPRF finished in first place with 22% of the vote. In the July 1996 Russian presidential election Zyuganov attracted 40% of the national vote.

List of Tables

AWARDS AND PRIZES

Film Awards

ACADEMY AWARDS

Annual film award in many categories, given since 1927 by the American Academy of Motion Picture Arts and Sciences (AMPAS), founded by Louis B Mayer of Metro-Goldwyn-Mayer 1927. Arguably the film community's most prestigious accolade, the award is a gold-plated statuette, which has been nicknamed 'Oscar' since 1931.

Recent winners

	Best picture	Best director	Best actor	Best actress	Best supporting actor	Best supporting actress
1977	*Annie Hall*	Woody Allen *Annie Hall*	Richard Dreyfuss *The Goodbye Girl*	Diane Keaton *Annie Hall*	Jason Robards *Julia*	Vanessa Redgrave *Julia*
1978	*The Deer Hunter*	Michael Cimino *The Deer Hunter*	Jon Voight *Coming Home*	Jane Fonda *Coming Home*	Christopher Walken *The Deer Hunter*	Maggie Smith *California Suite*
1979	*Kramer vs Kramer*	Robert Benton *Kramer vs Kramer*	Dustin Hoffman *Kramer vs Kramer*	Sally Field *Norma Rae*	Melvyn Douglas *Being There*	Meryl Streep *Kramer vs Kramer*
1980	*Ordinary People*	Robert Redford *Ordinary People*	Robert De Niro *Raging Bull*	Sissy Spacek *Coal Miner's Daughter*	Timothy Hutton *Ordinary People*	Mary Steenburgen *Melvin and Howard*
1981	*Chariots of Fire*	Warren Beatty *Reds*	Henry Fonda *On Golden Pond*	Katharine Hepburn *On Golden Pond*	John Gielgud *Arthur*	Maureen Stapleton *Reds*
1982	*Gandhi*	Richard Attenborough *Gandhi*	Ben Kingsley *Gandhi*	Meryl Streep *Sophie's Choice*	Louis Gossett Jr *An Officer and a Gentleman*	Jessica Lange *Tootsie*
1983	*Terms of Endearment*	James L Brooks *Terms of Endearment*	Robert Duvall *Tender Mercies*	Shirley Maclaine *Terms of Endearment*	Jack Nicholson *Terms of Endearment*	Linda Hunt *The Year of Living Dangerously*
1984	*Amadeus*	Milos Forman *Amadeus*	F Murray Abraham *Amadeus*	Sally Field *Places in the Heart*	Haing S Ngor *The Killing Fields*	Dame Peggy Ashcroft *A Passage to India*
1985	*Out of Africa*	Sydney Pollack *Out of Africa*	William Hurt *Kiss of the Spider Woman*	Geraldine Page *The Trip to Bountiful*	Don Ameche *Cocoon*	Anjelica Huston *Prizzi's Honor*
1986	*Platoon*	Oliver Stone *Platoon*	Paul Newman *The Color of Money*	Marlee Matlin *Children of a Lesser God*	Michael Caine *Hannah and Her Sisters*	Dianne Wiest *Hannah and Her Sisters*
1987	*The Last Emperor*	Bernardo Bertolucci *The Last Emperor*	Michael Douglas *Wall Street*	Cher *Moonstruck*	Sean Connery *The Untouchables*	Olympia Dukakis *Moonstruck*
1988	*Rain Man*	Barry Levington *Rain Man*	Dustin Hoffman *Rain Man*	Jodie Foster *The Accused*	Kevin Kline *A Fish Called Wanda*	Geena Davis *The Accidental Tourist*
1989	*Driving Miss Daisy*	Oliver Stone *Born on the Fourth of July*	Daniel Day-Lewis *My Left Foot*	Jessica Tandy *Driving Miss Daisy*	Denzel Washington *Glory*	Brenda Fricker *My Left Foot*
1990	*Dances with Wolves*	Kevin Costner *Dances with Wolves*	Jeremy Irons *Reversal of Fortune*	Kathy Bates *Misery*	Joe Pesci *Goodfellas*	Whoopi Goldberg *Ghost*
1991	*The Silence of the Lambs*	Jonathan Demme *The Silence of the Lambs*	Anthony Hopkins *The Silence of the Lambs*	Jodie Foster *The Silence of the Lambs*	Jack Palance *City Slickers*	Mercedes Ruehl *The Fisher King*
1992	*Unforgiven*	Clint Eastwood *Unforgiven*	Al Pacino *Scent of a Woman*	Emma Thompson *Howard's End*	Gene Hackman *Unforgiven*	Marisa Tomei *My Cousin Vinny*
1993	*Schindler's List*	Steven Spielberg *Schindler's List*	Tom Hanks *Philadelphia*	Holly Hunter *The Piano*	Tommy Lee Jones *The Fugitive*	Anna Paquin *The Piano*
1994	*Forrest Gump*	Robert Zemeckis *Forrest Gump*	Tom Hanks *Forrest Gump*	Jessica Lange *Blue Sky*	Martin Landau *Ed Wood*	Dianne Wiest *Bullets Over Broadway*
1995	*Braveheart*	Mel Gibson *Braveheart*	Nicolas Cage *Leaving Las Vegas*	Susan Sarandon *Dead Man Walking*	Kevin Spacey *The Usual Suspects*	Mira Sorvino *Mighty Aphrodite*
1996	*The English Patient*	Anthony Minghella *The English Patient*	Geoffrey Rush *Shine*	Frances McDormand *Fargo*	Cuba Gooding Jr *Jerry Maguire*	Juliette Binoche *The English Patient*
1997	*Titanic*	James Cameron *Titanic*	Jack Nicholson *As Good As It Gets*	Helen Hunt *As Good As It Gets*	Robin Williams *Good Will Hunting*	Kim Basinger *LA Confidential*
1998	*Shakespeare in Love*	Steven Spielberg *Saving Private Ryan*	Roberto Benigni *Life is Beautiful*	Gwyneth Paltrow *Shakespeare in Love*	James Coburn *Affliction*	Judi Dench *Shakespeare in Love*

BAFTA AWARDS

British film awards given by the British Academy of Film and Television Arts, formed 1959 as a result of the amalgamation of the British Film Academy (founded 1948) and the Guild of Television Producers (founded 1954).

Recent winners

Best Film

- **1988** *Jean de Florette* (France)
- **1989** *The Last Emperor* (USA)
- **1990** *Dead Poets Society* (USA)
- **1991** *Goodfellas* (USA)
- **1992** *The Commitments* (UK)
- **1993** *Howard's End* (UK)
- **1994** *Schindler's List* (USA)
- **1995** *Four Weddings and a Funeral* (UK)
- **1996** *Sense and Sensibility* (UK)
- **1997** *The English Patient* (UK)
- **1998** *The Full Monty* (UK)
- **1999** *Shakespeare in Love* (UK)

CANNES FILM FESTIVAL

International film festival held annually in Cannes, France. The first festival was held in 1947. The main award is the Palme d'Or (known as the Grand Prix prior to 1955) for best film.

Recent winners

Palme d'Or for Best Film

- **1988** *Pelle the Conqueror* (Denmark)
- **1989** *Sex, Lies and Videotape* (USA)
- **1990** *Wild at Heart* (USA)
- **1991** *Barton Fink* (USA)
- **1992** *The Best Intentions* (Sweden)
- **1993** *The Piano* (NZ/Australia); *Farewell to my Concubine* (Hong Kong/China)
- **1994** *Pulp Fiction* (USA)
- **1995** *Underground* (Bosnia-Herzegovina)
- **1996** *Secrets and Lies* (UK)
- **1997** *Unagi/The Eel* (Japan); *The Taste of Cherries* (Iran)
- **1998** *Mia Eoniotita Ke Mia Mera/Eternity and a Day* (Greece)

VENICE FILM FESTIVAL

International film festival held annually in Venice, Italy.

Recent winners

Golden Lion (Grand Prix) for Best Film

- **1988** *La Leggenda del santo Bevitore (The Legend of the Holy Drinker)* (Italy)
- **1989** *Beiqing Chengshi (City of Sadness)* (Taiwan)
- **1990** *Rosencrantz and Guildenstern are Dead* (UK)
- **1991** *Urga* (Russia)
- **1992** *Story of Qiu Ju* (China)
- **1993** *Short Cuts* (USA); *Three Colors Blue* (Poland)
- **1994** *Vive l'Amour* (Taiwan); *Before the Rain* (Macedonia)
- **1995** *Cyclo* (France)
- **1996** *Michael Collins* (USA)
- **1997** *Hana-bi* (Japan)
- **1998** *Cosi Ridevano* (Italy)

Literary Awards

BOOKER PRIZE

British literary prize of £20,000 awarded annually (from 1969) to a Commonwealth writer by the Booker company (formerly Booker McConnell) for a novel published in the UK during the previous year.

Recent winners

1978 Iris Murdoch *The Sea, The Sea*
1979 Penelope Fitzgerald *Offshore*
1980 William Golding *Rites of Passage*
1981 Salman Rushdie *Midnight's Children*
1982 Thomas Keneally *Schindler's Ark*
1983 J M Coetzee *The Life and Times of Michael K*
1984 Anita Brookner *Hotel du Lac*
1985 Keri Hulme *The Bone People*
1986 Kingsley Amis *The Old Devils*
1987 Penelope Lively *Moon Tiger*
1988 Peter Carey *Oscar and Lucinda*
1989 Kazuo Ishiguro *The Remains of the Day*
1990 A S Byatt *Possession*
1991 Ben Okri *The Famished Road*
1992 Barry Unsworth *Sacred Hunger*; Michael Ondaatje *The English Patient*
1993 Roddy Doyle *Paddy Clarke Ha Ha Ha*
1994 James Kelman *How Late It Was, How Late*
1995 Pat Barker *The Ghost Road*
1996 Graham Swift *Last Orders*
1997 Arundhati Roy *The God of Small Things*
1998 Ian McEwan *Amsterdam*

PRIX GONCOURT

French literary award, founded in 1903; awarded annually in November by the Académie Goncourt for the best French novel of the year. The prize is a nominal 50 FF plus a lifelong annuity of 250 FF per year.

Recent winners

1982	Dominique Fernandez	*Dans la main de l'Ange*
1983	Frederick Tristan	*Les Egares*
1984	Marguerite Duras	*The Lover*
1985	Yann Queffelect	*Les Noces barbares*
1986	Michel Host	*Valet de nuit*
1987	Tahar Ben Jelloun	*La Nuit sacrée*
1988	Erik Orsenna	*L'Exposition coloniale*
1989	Jean Vautrin	*Un Grand Pas vers le bon Dieu Grasset*
1990	Jean Rouault	*Les Champs d'honneur*
1991	Pierre Combescot	*Les Filles du Calvaire*
1992	Patrick Chamoisean	*Texaco*
1993	Amin Maalouf	*Le Rocher de Tanios*
1994	Didier van Cauwelaert	*Un Aller simple*
1995	Andréï Makine	*Le Testament français*
1996	Pascale Roze	*Le Chasseur Zéro*
1997	Patrick Rambeau	*La Bataille*
1998	Paule Constant	*Confidence pour confidence*

POETS LAUREATE OF THE UNITED KINGDOM

The Poet of the British royal household is so called because of the laurel wreath awarded to eminent poets in the Greco-Roman world. There is a stipend of £70 a year, plus £27 in lieu of the traditional butt of sack (cask of wine).

Appointed Poet Laureate

1668 John Dryden (1631–1700)
1689 Thomas Shadwell (c 1642–92)
1692 Nahum Tate (1652–1715)
1715 Nicholas Rowe (1674–1718)
1718 Laurence Eusden (1688–1730)
1730 Colley Cibber (1671–1757)
1757 William Whitehead (1715–85)
1785 Thomas Warton (1728–90)
1790 Henry James Pye (1745–1813)
1813 Robert Southey (1774–1843)
1843 William Wordsworth (1770–1850)
1850 Alfred, Lord Tennyson (1809–92)
1896 Alfred Austin (1835–1913)
1913 Robert Bridges (1844–1930)
1930 John Masefield (1878–1967)
1968 Cecil Day Lewis (1904–72)
1972 Sir John Betjeman (1906–84)
1984 Ted Hughes (1930–98)

PULITZER PRIZES IN LETTERS: FICTION

The Pulitzer Prizes were endowed by Joseph Pulitzer (1847–1911), the Hungarian-born US newspaper publisher. The prizes have been awarded since 1917 by Columbia University on the recommendation of the Pulitzer Prize Board; they are awarded in the fields of fiction, drama, history, biography or autobiography, poetry, and general non-fiction. A gold medal is awarded for Meritorious Public Service; all other prizes are $3,000.

Recent winners

1978 James Alan McPherson *Elbow Room*
1979 John Cheever *The Stories of John Cheever*
1980 Norman Mailer *The Executioner's Song*
1981 John Kennedy Toole *A Confederacy of Dunces*
1982 John Updike *Rabbit is Rich*
1983 Alice Walker *The Color Purple*
1984 William Kennedy *Ironweed*
1985 Alison Lurie *Foreign Affairs*
1986 Larry McMurtry *Lonesome Dove*
1987 Peter Taylor *A Summons to Memphis*
1988 Toni Morrison *Beloved*
1989 Anne Tyler *Breathing Lessons*
1990 Oscar Hijuelos *The Mambo Kings Play Songs of Love*
1991 John Updike *Rabbit at Rest*
1992 Jane Smiley *A Thousand Acres*
1993 Robert Olen Butler *A Good Scent From a Strange Mountain*
1994 E Annie Proulx *The Shipping News*
1995 Carol Shields *The Stone Diaries*
1996 Richard A Ford *Independence Day*
1997 Steven Millhauser *Martin Dressler: The Tale of an American Dreamer*
1998 Philip Roth *American Pastoral*

WHITBREAD LITERARY AWARD: NOVEL

British literary prize of £23,000 open to writers in the UK and Ireland. Nominations are in five categories: novel, first novel, children's novel, autobiography/biography, and poetry, each receiving £2,000. The overall winner receives a further £21,000. The award, which is administered by the Booksellers Association, was founded 1971 by Whitbread, a brewery; it is awarded annually in January.

Recent winners

1977 Beryl Bainbridge *Injury Time*
1978 Paul Theroux *Picture Palace*
1979 Jennifer Johnston *The Old Jest*
1980 David Lodge *How Far Can You Go?*
1981 Maurice Leitch *Silver's City*
1982 John Wain *Young Shoulders*
1983 William Trevor *Fools of Fortune*
1984 Christopher Hope *Kruger's Alp*
1985 Peter Ackroyd *Hawksmoor*
1986 Kazuo Ishiguro *An Artist of the Floating World*
1987 Ian McEwan *The Child in Time*
1988 Salman Rushdie *The Satanic Verses*
1989 Lindsay Clarke *The Chymical Wedding*
1990 Nicholas Mosley *Hopeful Monsters*
1991 Jane Gardam *The Queen of the Tambourine*
1992 Alasdair Gray *Poor Things*
1993 Joan Brady *Theory of War*
1994 William Trevor *Felicia's Journey*
1995 Salman Rushdie *The Moor's Last Sigh*
1996 Beryl Bainbridge *Every Man for Himself*
1997 Jim Crace *Quarantine*
1998 Justin Cartwright *Leading the Cheers*

W H SMITH LITERARY AWARD

The W H Smith Literary Award is given to a Commonwealth or UK Citizen for a UK-published book. The award was established in 1959 and is presented each March with a cash prize of £10,000.

Year	Winner	Awarded for
1990	V S Pritchett	*A Careless Widow, and Other Stories*
1991	Derek Walcott	*Omeros*
1992	Thomas Pakenham	*The Scramble for Africa*
1993	Michèle Roberts	*Daughters of the House*
1994	Vikram Seth	*A Suitable Boy*
1995	Alice Monro	*Open Secrets*
1996	Simon Schama	*Landscape and Memory*
1997	Orlando Figes	*A People's Tragedy*
1998	Ted Hughes	*Tales for Ovid*
1999	Beryl Bainbridge	*Master George*

Nobel Prizes

The Nobel Prizes were first awarded 1901 under the will of Swedish chemist Alfred B Nobel (1833–96). The interest on the Nobel endowment fund is divided annually among the persons who have made the greatest contributions in the fields of physics, chemistry, medicine, literature, and world peace. The first four are awarded by academic committees based in Sweden, while the peace prize is awarded by a committee of the Norwegian parliament. A sixth prize, for economics, financed by the Swedish National Bank, was first awarded 1969. The prizes have a large cash award and are given to organizations (such as the United Nations peacekeeping forces) as well as individuals.

NOBEL PRIZE FOR CHEMISTRY	
1988	Johann Deisenhofer (West Germany), Robert Huber (West Germany), and Hartmut Michel (West Germany): three-dimensional structure of the reaction centre of photosynthesis
1989	Sidney Altman (USA) and Thomas Cech (USA): discovery of catalytic function of RNA
1990	Elias James Corey (USA): new methods of synthesizing chemical compounds
1991	Richard R Ernst (Switzerland): improvements in the technology of nuclear magnetic resonance (NMR) imaging
1992	Rudolph A Marcus (USA): theoretical discoveries relating to reduction and oxidation reactions
1993	Kary Mullis (USA): invention of the polymerase chain reaction technique for amplifying DNA; Michael Smith (Canada): development of techniques for splicing foreign genetic segments into an organism's DNA in order to modify the proteins produced
1994	George A Olah (USA): development of technique for examining hydrocarbon molecules
1995	F Sherwood Roland (USA), Mario Molina (Mexico), and Paul Crutzen (Netherlands): explaining the chemical process of the ozone layer
1996	Robert F Curl (USA), Harold W Kroto (UK), and Richard E Smalley (USA): discovery of fullerenes
1997	John Walker (UK), Paul Boyer (USA), and Jens Skou (Denmark): study of the enzymes involved in the production of adenosine triphosphate (ATP), which acts as a store of energy in bodies called mitochondria inside cells
1998	John Pople (UK) and Walter Kohn (Austria): work in quantum chemistry

NOBEL PRIZE FOR ECONOMICS	
1988	Maurice Allais (France): contributions to the theory of markets and efficient use of resources
1989	Trygve Haavelmo (Norway): testing fundamental econometric theories
1990	Harry Markowitz, Merton Miller, and William Sharpe (USA): pioneering theories on managing investment portfolios and corporate finances
1991	Ronald H Coase (USA): work on value and social problems of companies
1992	Gary S Becker (USA): work linking economic theory to aspects of human behaviour, drawing on other social sciences
1993	Robert Fogel and Douglass North (USA): creating a new method of studying economic history (cliometrics)
1994	John F Nash and John C Harsanyi (USA), and Reinhard Selten (Germany): work on 'game theory', which investigates decision-making in a competitive environment
1995	Robert E Lucas Jr (USA): developing the 'rational expectations' school, which questions a government's ability to steer the economy
1996	James A Mirrlees (UK) and William Vickrey (USA): fundamental contributions to the economic theory of incentives under asymmetric information
1997	Robert Merton (USA) and Myron Scholes (USA): pioneering contribution to economic sciences by developing a new method of determining the value of derivatives
1998	Amartya Sen (India): research into the social and economic causes of famine

NOBEL PRIZE FOR LITERATURE	
1988	Naguib Mahfouz (Egypt)
1989	Camilo José Cela (Spain)
1990	Octavio Paz (Mexico)
1991	Nadine Gordimer (South Africa)
1992	Derek Walcott (St Lucia)
1993	Toni Morrison (USA)
1994	Kenzaburo Oe (Japan)
1995	Seamus Heaney (Ireland)
1996	Wislawa Szymborska (Poland)
1997	Dario Fo (Italy)
1998	José Saramgo (Portugal)

NOBEL PEACE PRIZE	
1988	United Nations peacekeeping forces
1989	The Dalai Lama (Tibet): spiritual and exiled temporal leader of Tibet
1990	Mikhail Gorbachev (Russia): promoting greater openness in the USSR and helping to end the Cold War
1991	Aung San Suu Kyi (Burma): nonviolent campaign for democracy
1992	Rigoberta Menchu (Guatemala): campaign for indigenous people
1993	Nelson Mandela and Frederik Willem de Klerk (South Africa): work towards dismantling apartheid and negotiating transition to nonracial democracy
1994	Yassir Arafat (Palestine), Yitzhak Rabin (Israel), and Shimon Peres (Israel): agreement of an accord on Palestinian self-rule
1995	Joseph Rotblat (UK) and the Pugwash Conferences on Science and World Affairs: campaign against nuclear weapons
1996	Carlos Filipe Ximenes Belo and José Ramos-Horta (East Timor): work towards a just and peaceful solution to the conflict in East Timor
1997	Jody Williams (USA) and the International Campaign to Ban Landmines (ICBL): campaign for global ban of antipersonnel mines
1998	John Hume (UK) and David Trimble (UK): work towards finding a peaceful solution to conflict in Northern Ireland

NOBEL PRIZE FOR PHYSICS	
1988	Leon M Lederman (USA), Melvin Schwartz (USA), and Jack Steinberger (Germany): neutrino-beam method, and demonstration of the doublet structure of leptons through discovery of muon neutrino
1989	Norman Ramsey (USA): measurement techniques leading to discovery of caesium atomic clock; Hans Dehmelt (USA) and Wolfgang Paul (Germany): ion-trap method for isolating single atoms
1990	Jerome Friedman (USA), Henry Kendall (USA), and Richard Taylor (Canada): experiments demonstrating that protons and neutrons are made up of quarks
1991	Pierre-Gilles de Gennes (France): work on disordered systems including polymers and liquid crystals; development of mathematical methods for studying the behaviour of molecules in a liquid on the verge of solidifying
1992	Georges Charpak (Poland): invention and development of detectors used in high-energy physics
1993	Joseph Taylor (USA) and Russell Hulse (USA): discovery of first binary pulsar (confirming the existence of gravitational waves)
1994	Clifford G Shull (USA) and Bertram N Brockhouse (Canada): development of technique known as 'neutron scattering' which led to advances in semiconductor technology
1995	Frederick Reines (USA): discovery of the neutrino; Martin L Perl (USA): discovery of the tau lepton
1996	David M Lee, Douglas D Osheroff, and Robert C Richardson (USA): discovery of superfluidity in helium-3
1997	Claude Cohen-Tannoudji (France), William Phillips (USA), and Steven Chu (USA): discovery of a way to slow down individual atoms using lasers for study in a near-vacuum
1998	Robert B Laughlin (USA), Horst L Störmer (Germany), and Daniel C Tsui (USA): discovery of a new form of quantum fluid with fractionally charged excitations

NOBEL PRIZE FOR PHYSIOLOGY OR MEDICINE	
1988	James Black (UK), Gertrude Elion (USA), and George Hitchings (USA): principles governing the design of new drug treatment
1989	Michael Bishop (USA) and Harold Varmus (USA): discovery of oncogenes, genes carried by viruses that can trigger cancerous growth in normal cells
1990	Joseph Murray (USA) and Donnall Thomas (USA): pioneering work in organ and cell transplants
1991	Erwin Neher (Germany) and Bert Sakmann (Germany): discovery of how gatelike structures (ion channels) regulate the flow of ions into and out of cells
1992	Edmund Fisher (USA) and Erwin Krebs (USA): isolating and describing the action of the enzyme responsible for reversible protein phosphorylation, a major biological control mechanism
1993	Phillip Sharp (USA) and Richard Roberts (UK): discovery of split genes (genes interrupted by nonsense segments of DNA)
1994	Alfred Gilman (USA) and Martin Rodbell (USA): discovery of a family of proteins (G proteins) that translate messages – in the form of hormones or other chemical signals – into action inside cells
1995	Edward B Lewis and Eric F Wieschaus (USA), and Christiane Nüsslein-Volhard (Germany): discovery of genes which control the early stages of the body's development
1996	Peter C Doherty (Australia), and Rolf M Zinkernagel (Switzerland): discovery of how the immune system recognizes virus-infected cells
1997	Stanley Prusiner (USA): discoveries, including the 'prion' theory, that could lead to new treatments of dementia-related diseases, including Alzheimer's and Parkinson's diseases
1998	Robert Furchgott (USA), Ferid Murad (USA), and Louis Ignarro (USA): discovery that nitric oxide acts as a key chemical messenger in the body

Theatre, Art, and Music Awards

EVENING STANDARD DRAMA AWARDS

UK annual drama awards, sponsored by the *Evening Standard* newspaper.

Recent winners

	Best play	Best musical	Best comedy
1987	*A Small Family Business*	*Follies*	*Serious Money*
1988	*Aristocrats*	no award	*Lettice and Lovage*
1989	*Ghetto*	*Miss Saigon*	*Henceforward*
1990	*Shadowlands*	*Into the Woods*	*Man of the Moment*; *Jeffrey Bernard is Unwell* (joint award)
1991	*Dancing at Lughnasa*	*Carmen Jones*	*Kvetch*
1992	*Angels in America*	*Kiss of the Spider Woman*	*The Rise and Fall of Little Voice*
1993	*Arcadia*	*City of Angels*	*Jamais Vu*
1994	*Three Tall Women*	no award	*My Night With Reg*
1995	*Pentecost*	*Dealer's Choice*	*Mack and Mabel*
1996	*Stanley*	*Passion*	*Art*
1997	*The Invention of Love*	*Lady in the Dark*	*Closer*
1998	*Copenhagen*	*Oklahoma!*	*No award*

LAURENCE OLIVIER AWARDS

UK annual theatre awards, presented by the Society of West End Theatre.

Recent winners

	Best play	Best musical	Best comedy
1987	*Serious Money*	*Follies*	*Three Men on a Horse*
1988	*Our Country's Good*	*Candide*	*Shirley Valentine*
1989/90	*Racing Demon*	*Return to the Forbidden Planet*	*Single Spies*
1991	*Dancing at Lughnasa*	*Sunday in the Park with George*	*Out of Order*
1992	*Death and the Maiden*	*Carmen Jones*	*La Bête*
1993	*Six Degrees of Separation*	*Crazy for You*	*The Rise and Fall of Little Voice*
1994	*Arcadia*	*City of Angels*	*Hysteria*
1995	*Broken Glass*	*Once on this Island*	*My Night with Reg*
1996	*Skylight*	*Jolson*	*Mojo*
1997	*Stanley*	*Martin Guerre*	*Art*
1998	*Closer*	*Beauty and the Beast*	*Popcorn*
1999	*The Weir*	*Kat and the Kings*	*Cleo, Camping, Emmanuelle and Dick*

TONY AWARDS

US annual theatre awards, awarded by the League of New York Theaters for Broadway plays.

Recent winners

	Best play	Best musical
1988	*M. Butterfly*	*The Phantom of the Opera*
1989	*The Heidi Chronicles*	*Jerome Robbins' Broadway*
1990	*The Grapes of Wrath*	*City of Angels*
1991	*Lost in Yonkers*	*The Will Rogers Follies*
1992	*Dancing at Lughnasa*	*Crazy for You*
1993	*Angels in America: Millennium Approaches*	*Kiss of the Spider Woman*
1994	*Angels in America: Perestroika*	*Passion*
1995	*Love! Valour! Compassion!*	*Sunset Boulevard*
1996	*Master Class*	*Rent*
1997	*The Last Night of Ballyhoo*	*Titanic*
1998	*Art*	*The Lion King*

TURNER PRIZE

British art prize, established in 1984. Open to any British artist under 50, the prize is intended to encourage discussion about new developments in contemporary British art. The prize is £20,000 and is awarded annually in November by the Tate Gallery in London.

1986	Gilbert and George
1987	Richard Deacon
1988	Tony Cragg
1989	Richard Long
1990	no award
1991	Anish Kapoor
1992	Grenville Davey
1993	Rachel Whiteread
1994	Antony Gormley
1995	Damien Hirst
1996	Douglas Gordon
1997	Gillian Wearing
1998	Chris Ofili

GRAMMY AWARDS

US annual music awards which are for outstanding achievement in the record industry for the previous year. The gold-plated discs are presented by the National Academy of Recording Arts and Sciences. The first Grammy Awards were for records released in 1958.

1999

Category	Awarded to
Record of the Year	Celine Dion *My Heart Will Go On*
Album of the Year	Lauryn Hill *The Miseducation of Lauryn Hill*
Song of the Year	James Horner & Will Jennings, songwriters (Celine Dion) 'My Heart Will Go On'
New Artist	Lauryn Hill
Female Pop Vocal Performance	Celine Dion 'My Heart Will Go On'
Male Pop Vocal Performance	Eric Clapton 'My Father's Eyes'
Pop Duo or Group Performance	Brian Setzer Orchestra 'Jump, Jive An' Wail'
Pop Album	Madonna *Ray of Light*
Female Rock Vocal Performance	Alanis Morissette 'Uninvited'
Male Rock Vocal Performance	Lenny Kravitz 'Fly Away'
Rock Vocal Duo or Group Performance	Aerosmith 'Pink'
Rock Song	Alanis Morissette, songwriter (Alanis Morissette) 'Uninvited'
Rock Album	Sheryl Crow *The Globe Sessions*
Hard Rock Performance	Jimmy Page & Robert Plant 'Most High'
Metal Performance	Metallica 'Better Than You'
Female R&B Performance	Lauryn Hill 'Doo Wop (That Thing)'
Male R&B Vocal Performancce	Stevie Wonder 'St Louis Blues'
R&B Duo or Group Performance	Brandy and Monica 'The Boy Is Mine'
R&B Song	Lauryn Hill, songwriter (Lauryn Hill) 'Doo Wop (That Thing)'
R&B Album	Lauryn Hill *The Miseducation of Lauryn Hill*

MAJOR RELIGIOUS FESTIVALS

Festival	Description	Normally held	2000	2001
Buddhism				
Theravada (Southern Buddhism) Predominant mainly in Sri Lanka and Southeast Asia.				
New Year Festival	Images of the Buddha are bathed in scented water and stupas of sand are built on river banks or in temple grounds to be washed away at New Year, symbolizing the clearing away of negative deeds	beginning of Citta	April 2000[1]	April 2001[1]
Vesakha	Celebrates the Buddha's birth, enlightenment, and passing into nirvana; processions take place in the temple, bodhi trees are sprinkled with scented water, lanterns are lit, and street stalls are erected	full moon of Vesakha	18 May 2000	7 May 2001
Asalha	Commemorates the Buddha's first sermon and marks the beginning of the three-month rainy season, a period of temple retreat known as Vassa	full moon of Asalha	16 July 2000	5 July 2001
Assayuja	Celebrates the return of the Buddha from heaven after passing on the teachings to his mother; Assayuja marks the end of Vassa	third full moon of Vassa	October 2000[1]	October 2001[1]
Kattika	Commemorates the first Buddhist missionaries who went out to spread the Buddha's teachings; this is also the date for the end of Vassa if the rains continue longer than usual	full moon of Kattika	November 2000[1]	November 2001[1]
Kathina	Offerings, especially robes, are presented to the monasteries in elaborate ceremonies	end of Vassa	October/November 2000[1]	October/November 2001[1]
Mahayana/East (Eastern Buddhism) Predominant mainly in China, Taiwan, Korea and Japan.				
Birth of Buddha	Images of the Buddha as a child are bathed in scented water or tea, and offerings are made at temples and shrines	eighth day of the fourth lunar month	8 April 2000 (Japan)	8 April 2001 (Japan)
Birth of Kuan Yin	The Bodhisattva of Mercy; offerings and prayers are made to her by those who seek help in times of need	19th day of second lunar month	February/March 2000[1]	February/March 2001[1]
Enlightenment of Kuan Yin		19th day of sixth lunar month	June/July 2000[1]	June/July 2001[1]
Death of Kuan Yin		19th day of ninth lunar month	September/October 2000[1]	September/October 2001[1]
Hungry Ghost Festival	Unsettled spirits of the dead are calmed with chanting and offerings to enable them to pass peacefully into the next world	8–15th days of the Chinese seventh lunar month	July/August 2000[1]	July/August 2001[1]
O-Bon	Families reunite to remember and honour their ancestors; offerings are made to the Buddha and monks visit home shrines to read Buddhist scriptures	13–15 July (Japan)	13–15 July 2000 (Japan)	13–15 July 2001 (Japan)
Mahayana/North (Northern Buddhism) Predominant mainly in Tibet, Nepal, Bhutan, Mongolia, parts of western China, southern Siberia, and northern India.				
Tibetan New Year	Houses are cleaned to sweep away any negative aspects from the last year; costumed monks perform new year rituals and chants; people light firecrackers or torches to chase away the spirits	new moon of February	6 February 2000	25 January 2001
Modlam Chenmo	The Great Prayer Festival is celebrated with traditional stories, puppet shows, and butter sculptures in the monasteries	8–15th of the first lunar month	February 2000[1]	February 2001[1]
The Buddha's Enlightenment and Passing into Nirvana	Pilgrims visit monasteries to make offerings; traditional Chan dancing is performed	15th day of the fourth lunar month	May 2000[1]	May 2001[1]
Guru Rinpoche's Birthday	Commemorates the Indian teacher who helped establish Buddhist teachings in Tibet towards the end of the 8th century AD	tenth day of sixth lunar month	July 2000[1]	July 2001[1]
Chokhor Duchen	Celebrates the Buddha's first sermon after his enlightenment	fourth day of the sixth lunar month	July 2000[1]	July 2001[1]
Lhabab Duchen	Commemorates the descent of the Buddha from heaven after giving the teachings to his mother	22nd day of the ninth lunar month	October 2000[1]	October 2001[1]

Festival	Description	Normally held	2000	2001
		Christianity[2]		
Christmas Day	Celebration of the birth of Jesus in Bethlehem; Christians meet for worship, often at midnight, when the events are retold through words, music, drama, and pictures		25 December 2000	25 December 2001
Epiphany	Celebrates the arrival of the three wise men from the east who came looking for a newborn king and were led by a bright star to Bethlehem; they brought Jesus gifts of gold, frankincense, and myrrh		6 January 2000	6 January 2001
Ash Wednesday	In many churches, people come forward to be marked with ashes, an ancient symbol of sorrow and repentance; Lent is a time of reflection and fasting which recalls the 40 days Jesus spent fasting and praying in the desert	start of Lent (six weeks before Easter)	8 March 2000	28 February 2001
Palm Sunday	Christians recall Jesus's entry into Jerusalem during the last week of his life, when he was welcomed by people waving palm fronds; other important days of Holy week are Maundy Thursday, when Jesus shared the last supper with his disciples, and Good Friday, when he was crucified	start of Holy Week (one week before Easter)	16 April 2000	8 April 2001
Easter Sunday	Time of rejoicing that recalls the disciples' discovery that Jesus was alive, and that he had been resurrected; many churches keep a vigil throughout Saturday night so that they can greet Easter Day with services, family meals, and the exchange of flowers and eggs	between 23 March and 24 April in the Roman Catholic and Protestant churches	23 April 2000	15 April 2001
Ascension Day	This day commemorates the disciples witnessing Jesus being lifted up to heaven 40 days after Easter Day	40 days after Easter	1 June 2000	24 May 2001
Pentecost or Whitsun	When Jesus left his disciples for the last time after his resurrection, he promised them a 'comforter' who would be with them forever; Pentecost celebrates the coming of the Holy Spirit upon the disciples	seventh Sunday after Easter	11 June 2000	3 June 2001
		Hinduism		
Mahashivaratri	'Great Night of Shiva' when Shiva, his wife Parvati, and their child Ganesh are honoured; offerings are made to Shiva between midnight and sunrise and the 24-hour fast is broke at dawn	13th or 14th day of dark half of Magh	4 March 2000	21 February 2001
Sarasvati Puja	Sarasvati, the patron of the arts and learning, is celebrated with music and by wearing yellow clothes, symbolizing the warmth of spring	first day of spring season (Phalgun)	February/March 2000[1]	February/March 2001[1]
Holi	The pranks that Krishna played as a child are celebrated, and the story of Prahalad, a prince who was willing to sacrifice himself for Vishnu, is remembered; offerings are made around bonfires and coloured water or powder is sprayed in high-spirited games	full moon day of Phalgun	21 March 2000	10 March 2001
Rama Naumi	Celebrates the birthday of the god Rama, hero of the epic Ramayana that is recited during the festival; offerings are also made in temples to a statue of the baby Rama	ninth day of the bright half of Caitra	12 April 2000[3]	2 April 2001[3]
Ratha Yatra	A statute of Vishnu, also called Jagganath, Lord of the Universe, is placed on a large wooden chariot and pulled through the streets where lamps, flowers, and other offerings are laid in his path	16th day of Asadha	June/July 20001	June/July 2001[1]
Raksha Bandhan	Sisters tie rakhis, silk threads decorated with flowers, onto their brothers' wrists as symbol of protection	full moon day of Sravana	15 August 2000	4 August 2001
Janmashtarni	The birth of Krishna is celebrated as an image of the child Krishna is washed with yoghurt, ghee, honey, and milk, and then placed on a swing	eighth day of Bhadrapada	22 August 2000	12 August 2001

Festival	Description	Normally held	2000	2001
Navaratri Dusshera	The festival of Dusshera follows immediately after Navaratri; over nine nights different manifestations of the goddess Durga are honoured; in the form of Durga she is the destroyer of evil, as Kali she is the destroyer of time, and as Parvati she is the faithful wife of Shiva; at Dusshera, an effigy of the demon Ravana is burnt to celebrate Durga's power over demons	first ten days of the bright half of Aswin	7 October 2000	26 October 2001
Diwali	Accounts are settled at this time and worship is given to Lakshmi, goddess of wealth and good fortune; coloured patterns are made on the ground; windows are illuminated with lamps and candles; this festival also celebrates the return of Rama and Sita from exile, a story told in the Ramayana	13th day of the dark half of Aswin	26 October 2000	14 November 2001
		Islam		
Islamic years (AH)				
AH = Anno Hegirae, the Muslim era. The Islamic calendar is entirely lunar, and unlike most other lunar calendars, is not adjusted to keep in step with the solar year.[4]				
Festival of Ashura	Festival commemorating both the escape of the Israelites from Egypt, and also the day Noah's ark touched ground after the flood; in Shi'a Islam, Ashurra also celebrates the martyrdom of Ali	10 Muharram	*1421* 15 April 2000	*1422* 4 April 2001[3]
Ramadan	This month of fasting is one of the Five Pillars of Islam, when adult Muslims refrain from drinking, eating, smoking, and conjugal relations from dawn until dusk	ninth month of the year	27 November 2000	17 November 2001[3]
The Night of Power – Lailat ul Qadr	During the last ten days of Ramadan many Muslims spend time praying in the mosque since prayers made on the Night of Power are said to be 'better than a thousand months'	around 27 Ramadan	3 January 2000	3 December 2001[3]
Eid ul-Fitr	Important time of communal prayer and celebration when families and friends gather to share special foods and exchange gifts	end of Ramadan, heralded by the sight of a new moon	8 January 2000	16 December 2001[3]
Pilgrimage to Mecca	In the Five Pillars of Islam, this is the most important time, but only those who have sufficient finances and are physically able are expected to make the journey	8–13 Dhu al-Hijjah	14–19 March 2000	April 2001[1]
Eid-ul-Adha	The willingness of the prophet Ibrahim to sacrifice his son Ishmael is remembered; at God's command a lamb was sacrificed instead, an act commemorated at this time in the sacrifice of a lamb or goat	10 Dhu al-Hijjah	16 March 2000[3]	6 March 2001[3]
Birthday of the Prophet Mohammed (Milad-un-Nabi)	The scale of celebrations varies according to country; for example, thousands of pilgrims gather on Lamu island off the coast of Kenya for processions, speeches, and prayers	month Rabi I	15 June 2000	4 June 2001
		Judaism		
Jewish years (AM)				
Jewish year AM = Anno Mundi; runs from September to August				
Rosh Hashanah	Jewish New Year, a ten-day period of repentance leading up to Yom Kippur	1 Tishri	*5759* 30 September–1 October 2000	*5762* 18–19 September 2001
Yom Kippur	Day of Atonement, a time when Jews seek forgiveness of those who have been wronged; also the major fast of the year	10 Tishri	9 October 2000	27 September 2001
Succoth	Feast of Tabernacles, a time when families build and eat in open-air shelters in commemoration of the temporary desert shelters built by the Israelites during their journey to the Promised Land	15–23 Tishri	14–22 October 2000	2–10 October 2001
Simhat Torah	End of Succoth and the end of the annual reading of the Torah, which is processed around the synagogue on this day	24 Tishri	22 October 2000	10 October 2001

Festival	Description	Normally held	2000	2001
Hanukkah	Dedication of the Temple, a time when the eight-branched Hanukkah candle is lit commemorating the rededication of the Temple in Jerusalem in the 2nd century BC, when the Temple lamp miraculously stayed alight for ten days, even though there was only enough oil to last one day	25 Kislev–3 Tebet	22 December 2000	30 November 2001
Purim	Celebration of the story of Esther who saved her people from destruction at the hands of Haman; the congregation dress in unusual clothes for the synagogue service and boo when Haman's name is read out from the scrolls of Esther	14 Adar	21 March 2000	9 March 2001
Pesach	Passover, celebrating God's deliverance of the Israelites from captivity in Egypt; families gather for the first evening of the festival to share the Seder meal, which recalls in words and symbols the departure of the Isrealites from Egypt	15–22 Nisan	20–27 April 2000	8–15 April 2001
Shavuot	Also known as the Pentecost or the Feast of Weeks, this is both a harvest festival and a thanksgiving for the gift of Torah to Moses on Mount Sinai	6–7 Sivan	9–10 June 2000	28–29 May 2001
Tishah B'Av	This date recalls the disasters that have befallen the Jewish people, including the destruction of the first and second temples in Jerusalem; it is also a time to mourn the events of the Holocaust	9 Av	10 August 2000	29 July 2001
		Sikhism		
Baisakhi	Commemorates the founding of the Order of the Khalsa in 1699, the community of committed Sikhs who undertake to uphold their faith and defend the weak; it is the usual time for Sikhs to join the Khalsa	13 April (occasionally on the 14 April), first day of the solar month of Baisakh (Sanskrit Vaisakha)	13 April 2000	April 2001[1]
Martyrdom of the Guru Arjan Dev	Time of celebration and sorrow when Sikhs remember those who have suffered for their faith; there is a continuous reading of the Guru Granth Sahib in the gurdwara	fourth Jaistha	5 June 2000	June 2001[1]
Diwali	Divali lamps are lit at home, and the release from prison of Guru Hargobind is commemorated	second day of Kartik	26 October 2000	October 2001[1]
Guru Nanak's Birthday	Colourful street processions are held and hymns honouring Guru Gobind Singh (1469–1539), the founder of the Khalsa, are sung in the gurdwara	full moon day of Kartik	11 November 2000[5]	November 2001[1,5]
Hola Mohalla	Falls at the same time as the Hindu festival of Holi; celebrated with games and pranks; sporting contests take place as well as religious congregations, political conferences, pilgrimages, and administration of baptism	starting a day earlier and finishing a day later than Holi; full moon day of Phalgun	20–22 March 2000	9–11 March 2001

[1] Date unknown.
[2] The calendar reform by pope Gregory XIII in 1582 was rejected by the Orthodox Church. Since 1923, the Orthodox Church has been divided over the calendar. The Greek Church adopted the new calendar except the days that depend on Easter. Others (mostly Slavic) have retained the Julian calendar and therefore remain 13 days behind in their dating (Christmas: 7 January, New Year: 14 January).
[3] Unconfirmed.
[4] Some dates are therefore approximate and some are not yet known by the relevant authorities; this applies particularly to moveable feasts, based on lunar reckonings.
[5] Date AD varies from year to year in accordance with traditional dates of the Indian Calendar (Bikrami Sambat); often falls in November.

MEASUREMENTS AND NUMBERS

BEAUFORT SCALE

Number and description	Features	Air speed mi per hr	Air speed m per sec
0 calm	smoke rises vertically; water smooth	less than 1	less than 0.3
1 light air	smoke shows wind direction; water ruffled	1–3	0.3–1.5
2 slight breeze	leaves rustle; wind felt on face	4–7	1.6–3.3
3 gentle breeze	loose paper blows around	8–12	3.4–5.4
4 moderate breeze	branches sway	13–18	5.5–7.9
5 fresh breeze	small trees sway, leaves blown off	19–24	8.0–10.7
6 strong breeze	whistling in telephone wires; sea spray from waves	25–31	10.8–13.8
7 moderate gale	large trees sway	32–38	13.9–17.1
8 fresh gale	twigs break from trees	39–46	17.2–20.7
9 strong gale	branches break from trees	47–54	20.8–24.4
10 whole gale	trees uprooted, weak buildings collapse	55–63	24.5–28.4
11 storm	widespread damage	64–72	28.5–32.6
12 hurricane	widespread structural damage	73–82	above 32.7
13		83–92	
14		93–103	
15		104–114	
16		115–125	
17		126–136	

CONVERSION TABLES

To convert from imperial to metric	*Multiply by*	*To convert from metric to imperial*	*Multiply by*
Length			
inches	25.4	millimetres	0.03937
feet	0.3048	metres	3.2808
yards	0.9144	metres	1.0936
furlongs	0.201	kilometres	4.971
miles	1.6093	kilometres	0.6214
Area			
square inches	6.4516	square centimetres	0.1550
square feet	0.0929	square metres	10.7639
square yards	0.8361	square metres	1.1960
square miles	2.5900	square kilometres	0.3861
acres	4046.86	square metres	0.000247
acres	0.4047	hectares	2.47105
hectares	0.001	square kilometres	1,000
Volume, capacity			
cubic inches	16.3871	cubic centimetres	0.0610
cubic feet	0.02832	cubic metres	35.3134
cubic yards	0.7646	cubic metres	1.3079
fluid ounces	28.4131	millilitres	0.0352
pints	0.5683	litres	1.760
quarts	1.1365	litres	0.88
imperial gallons	4.54609	litres	0.21997
US gallons	3.7854	litres	0.2642
Mass			
ounces	28.3495	grams	0.03527
pounds	0.4536	kilograms	2.2046
stone (14 lb)	6.3503	kilograms	0.1575
tons (imperial)	1016.05	kilograms	0.00098
tons (US)	907.2	kilograms	0.001
tons (imperial)	0.9842	tonnes	1.0161
tons (US)	0.9072	tonnes	1.102
Speed			
miles per hour	1.6093	kilometres per hour	0.6214
feet per second	0.3048	metres per second	3.2808
Force			
pound force	4.448	newton	0.2248
kilogram force	9.8096	newton	0.1019
Pressure			
pounds per square inch	6.89476	kilopascals	0.1450
tons per square inch	15.4443	megapascals	0.0647
atmospheres	101,325	newtons per square metre	0.00000986
atmospheres	14.69	pounds per square inch	0.068
Energy			
calorie	4.186	joule	0.238
kilowatt hour	3,600,000	joule	0.000000277
Power			
horsepower	0.7457	kilowatts	1.341
Fuel consumption			
miles per gallon	0.3540	kilometres per litre	2.825
miles per US gallon	0.4251	kilometres per litre	2.3521
gallons per mile	2.8248	litres per kilometre	0.3540
US gallons per mile	2.3521	litres per kilometre	0.4251

DECIBEL SCALE

Decibels	Typical sound
0	threshold of hearing
10	rustle of leaves in gentle breeze
10	quiet whisper
20	average whisper
20–50	quiet conversation
40–45	hotel; theatre (between performances)
50–65	loud conversation
65–70	traffic on busy street
65–90	train
75–80	factory (light/medium work)
90	heavy traffic
90–100	thunder
110–140	jet aircraft on take off
130	threshold of pain
140–190	space rocket at take-off

IMPERIAL SYSTEM: UNITS

Length	
1 foot	= 12 inches
1 yard	= 3 feet
1 rod	= 5½ yards
1 chain	= 4 rods (= 22 yards)
1 furlong	= 10 chain (= 220 yards)
1 mile	= 5,280 feet
1 mile	= 1,760 yards
1 mile	= 8 furlongs
Nautical	
1 fathom	= 6 feet
1 cable length	= 100 fathoms
1 nautical mile	= 6,080 feet
Area	
1 square foot	= 144 square inches
1 square yard	= 9 square feet
1 square rod	= 30¼ square yards
1 rood	= 40 square rods
1 acre	= 4 roods
1 acre	= 4,840 square yards
1 square mile	= 640 acres
Volume	
1 cubic foot	= 1,728 cubic inches
1 cubic yard	= 27 cubic feet
1 bulk barrel	= 5.8 cubic feet
Shipping	
1 register ton	= 100 cubic feet
Capacity	
1 fluid ounce	= 8 fluid drahms
1 gill	= 5 fluid ounces
1 pint	= 4 gills
1 quart	= 2 pints
1 gallon	= 4 quarts
1 peck	= 2 gallons
1 bushel	= 4 pecks
1 quarter	= 8 bushels
1 bulk barrel	= 36 gallons
Mass (avoirdupois)	
1 ounce	= 437½ grains
1 ounce	= 16 drams
1 pound	= 16 ounces
1 stone	= 14 pounds
1 quarter	= 28 pounds
1 hundredweight	= 4 quarters
1 ton	= 20 hundredweight

MERCALLI SCALE

Intensity value	Description
I	only detected by instrument
II	felt by people resting
III	felt indoors; hanging objects swing; feels like passing traffic
IV	feels like passing heavy traffic; standing cars rock; windows, dishes, and doors rattle; wooden frames creak
V	felt outdoors; sleepers are woken; liquids spill; doors swing open
VI	felt by everybody; people stagger; windows break; trees and bushes rustle; weak plaster cracks
VII	difficult to stand upright; noticed by vehicle drivers; plaster, loose bricks, tiles, and chimneys fall; bells ring
VIII	car steering affected; some collapse of masonry; chimney stacks and towers fall; branches break from trees; cracks in wet ground
IX	general panic; serious damage to buildings; underground pipes break; cracks and subsidence in ground
X	most buildings destroyed; landslides; water thrown out of canals
XI	rails bent; underground pipes totally destroyed
XII	damage nearly total; rocks displaced; objects thrown into the air

MOHS' SCALE

Number	Defining mineral	Other substances compared
1	talc	
2	gypsum	2½ fingernail
3	calcite	3½ copper coin
4	fluorite	
5	apatite	5½ steel blade
6	orthoclase	5¾ glass
7	quartz	7 steel file
8	topaz	
9	corundum	
10	diamond	

Note that the scale is not regular; diamond, at number 10 the hardest natural substance, is 90 times harder in absolute terms than corundum, number 9

NUMBER SYSTEMS

Decimal Number System (base 10)

In the decimal number system numbers can be seen as written under columns based on the number 10, as with number 2,567 below.

1000s	100s	10s	1s
(10^3)	*(10^2)*	*(10^1)*	*(10^0)*
2	5	6	7

Binary Number System (base 2)

In the binary number system numbers can be seen as written under columns based on the number 2. The binary number 1101 corresponds to the decimal number 13.

8s	4s	2s	1s
(2^3)	*(2^2)*	*(2^1)*	*(2^0)*
1	1	0	1

Octal Number System (base 8)

In the octal number system numbers can be seen as written under columns based on the number 8. The octal number 2164 corresponds to the decimal number 1,140.

512s	64s	8s	1s
(8^3)	*(8^2)*	*(8^1)*	*(8^0)*
2	1	6	4

Hexadecimal Number System (base 16)

In the hexadecimal number system numbers can be seen as written under columns based on the number 16. Since digits up to a value of decimal 15 are permitted, the letters A to F are used to represent digits corresponding to decimal 10 to 15. The hexadecimal number 23BF corresponds to the decimal number 9151.

4096s	256s	16s	1s
(16^3)	*(16^2)*	*(16^1)*	*(16^0)*
2	3	B	F

METRIC SYSTEM: UNITS

Length		
1 centimetre (cm)	= 10 millimetres (mm)	
1 decimetre (dm)	= 10 centimetres	= 100 millimetres
1 metre (m)	= 10 decimetres	= 1,000 millimetres
1 decametre (dam)	= 10 metres	
1 hectometre (hm)	= 10 decametres	= 100 metres
1 kilometre (km)	= 10 hectometres	= 1,000 metres
Area		
1 square centimetre (cm^2)	= 100 square millimetres (mm^2)	
1 square metre (m^2)	= 10,000 square centimetres	= 1,000,000 square millimetres
1 acre (a)	= 100 square metres	
1 hectare (ha)	= 100 acres	= 10,000 square metres
1 square kilometre (km^2)	= 100 hectares	= 1,000,000 square metres
Mass (avoirdupois)		
1 centigram (cg)	= 10 milligrams (mg)	
1 decigram (dg)	= 10 centigram	= 100 milligrams
1 gram (g)	= 10 decigrams	= 1,000 milligrams
1 decagram (dag)	= 10 grams	
1 hectogram (hg)	= 10 decagrams	= 100 grams
1 kilogram (kg)	= 10 hectograms	= 1,000 grams
1 tonne or metric ton (t)	= 1,000 kilograms	
Volume		
1 cubic centimetre (cm^3)	= 1,000 cubic millimetres (mm^3)	
1 cubic decimetre (dm^3)	= 1,000 cubic centimetres	= 1,000,000 cubic millimetres
1 cubic metre (m^3)	= 1,000 cubic decimetres	= 1,000,000,000 cubic millimetres
Capacity		
1 centilitre (cl)	= 10 millilitres (ml)	
1 decilitre (dl)	= 10 centilitres	= 100 millilitres
1 litre (l)	= 10 decilitres	= 1,000 millilitres
1 decalitre (dal)	= 10 litres	
1 hectolitre (hl)	= 10 decalitres	= 100 litres
1 kilolitre (kl)	= 10 hectolitres	= 1,000 litres

RICHTER SCALE

Magnitude	Relative amount of energy released	Examples	Year
1			
2			
3			
4	1	Carlisle, England	1979
5	30	San Francisco, USA	1979
		Wrexham, Wales	1990
6	1,000	San Fernando, California	1971
7	30,000	Santa Cruz, California	1989
		Armenia, USSR	1988
		Kobe, Japan	1995
8	1,000,000	Tangshan, China	1976
		San Francisco	1906
		Lisbon, Portugal	1755
		Alaska	1964
		Gansu, China	1920

SI UNITS

Quantity	SI unit	Symbol
absorbed radiation dose	gray	Gy
amount of substance	mole*	mol
electric capacitance	farad	F
electric charge	coulomb	C
electric conductance	siemens	S
electric current	ampere*	A
energy or work	joule	J
force	newton	N
frequency	hertz	Hz
illuminance	lux	lx
inductance	henry	H
length	metre*	m
luminous flux	lumen	lm
luminous intensity	candela*	cd
magnetic flux	weber	Wb
magnetic flux density	tesla	T
mass	kilogram*	kg
plane angle	radian	rad
potential difference	volt	V
power	watt	W
pressure	pascal	Pa
radiation dose equivalent	sievert	Sv
radiation exposure	roentgen	r
radioactivity	becquerel	Bq
resistance	ohm	Ω
solid angle	steradian	sr
sound intensity	decibel	dB
temperature	°Celsius	°C
temperature, thermodynamic	kelvin*	K
time	second*	s

*SI base unit

SI prefixes

multiple	Prefix	Symbol	Example
1,000,000,000,000,000,000 (10^{18})	exa-	E	Eg (exagram)
1,000,000,000,000,000 (10^{15})	peta-	P	PJ (petajoule)
1,000,000,000,000 (10^{12})	tera-	T	TV (teravolt)
1,000,000,000 (10^{9})	giga-	G	GW (gigawatt)
1,000,000 (10^{6})	mega-	M	MHz (megahertz)
1,000 (10^{3})	kilo-	k	kg (kilogram)
100 (10^{2})	hecto-	h	hm (hectometre)
10	deca-	da	daN (decanewton)
1/10 (10^{-1})	deci-	d	dC (decicoulomb)
1/100 (10^{-2})	centi-	c	cm (centimetre)
1/1,000 (10^{-3})	milli-	m	mA (milliampere)
1/1,000,000 (10^{-6})	micro-	μ	μF (microfarad)
1/1,000,000,000 (10^{-9})	nano-	n	nm (nanometre)
1/1,000,000,000,000 (10^{-12})	pico-	p	ps (picosecond)
1/1,000,000,000,000,000 (10^{-15})	femto-	f	frad (femtoradian)
1/1,000,000,000,000,000,000 (10^{-18})	atto-	a	aT (attotesla)

TEMPERATURE SCALES

Celsius and Fahrenheit temperatures can be converted as follows:
$C = (F - 32) \times {}^5/_9$ $F = (C \times {}^9/_5) + 32$

Table of equivalent temperatures

°C	°F	°C	°F	°C	°F	°C	°F
100	212.0	70	158.0	40	104.0	10	50.0
99	210.2	69	156.2	39	102.2	9	48.2
98	208.4	68	154.4	38	100.4	8	46.4
97	206.6	67	152.6	37	98.6	7	44.6
96	204.8	66	150.8	36	96.8	6	42.8
95	203.0	65	149.0	35	95.0	5	41.0
94	201.2	64	147.2	34	93.2	4	39.2
93	199.4	63	145.4	33	91.4	3	37.4
92	197.6	62	143.6	32	89.6	2	35.6
91	195.8	61	141.8	31	87.8	1	33.8
90	194.0	60	140.0	30	86.0	0	32.0
89	192.2	59	138.2	29	84.2	−1	30.2
88	190.4	58	136.4	28	82.4	−2	28.4
87	188.6	57	134.6	27	80.6	−3	26.6
86	186.8	56	132.8	26	78.8	−4	24.8
85	185.0	55	131.0	25	77.0	−5	23.0
84	183.2	54	129.2	24	75.2	−6	21.2
83	181.4	53	127.4	23	73.4	−7	19.4
82	179.6	52	125.6	22	71.6	−8	17.6
81	177.8	51	123.8	21	69.8	−9	15.8
80	176.0	50	122.0	20	68.0	−10	14.0
79	174.2	49	120.2	19	66.2	−11	12.2
78	172.4	48	118.4	18	64.4	−12	10.4
77	170.6	47	116.6	17	62.6	−13	8.6
76	168.8	46	114.8	16	60.8	−14	6.8
75	167.0	45	113.0	15	59.0	−15	5.0
74	165.2	44	111.2	14	57.2	−16	3.2
73	163.4	43	109.4	13	55.4	−17	1.4
72	161.6	42	107.6	12	53.6	−18	−0.4
71	159.8	41	105.8	11	51.8	−19	−2.2

SPORTS

ATHLETICS: OLYMPIC CHAMPIONS

Atlanta Olympics 1996 (26th Olympic Games)

Event	Men	Women
100 metres	Donovan Bailey *(Canada)*	Gail Devers *(USA)*
200 metres	Michael Johnson *(USA)*	Marie-Jose Perec *(France)*
400 metres	Michael Johnson *(USA)*	Marie-Jose Perec *(France)*
800 metres	Verbjoern Rodal *(Norway)*	Svetlana Masterkova *(Russia)*
1,500 metres	Noureddine Morceli *(Algeria)*	Svetlana Masterkova *(Russia)*
5,000 metres	Venuste Niyongabo *(Burundi)*	Wang Junxia *(China)*
10,000 metres	Haile Gebrselassie *(Ethiopia)*	Fernanda Ribeiro *(Portugal)*
marathon	Josia Thugwane *(South Africa)*	Fatuma Roba *(Ethiopia)*
100-metre hurdles	–	Ludmila Engquist *(Sweden)*
110-metre hurdles	Allen Johnson *(USA)*	–
400-metre hurdles	Derrick Adkins *(USA)*	Deon Hemmings *(Jamaica)*
3,000-metre steeplechase	Joseph Keter *(Kenya)*	–
10,000-metre walk	–	Yelena Nikolayeva *(Russia)*
20,000-metre walk	Jefferson Perez *(Ecuador)*	–
50,000-metre walk	Robert Korzeniowski *(Poland)*	–
4 × 100-metre relay	Canada	USA
4 × 400-metre relay	USA	USA
high jump	Charles Austin *(USA)*	Stefka Kostadinova *(Bulgaria)*
long jump	Carl Lewis *(USA)*	Chioma Ajunwa *(Nigeria)*
triple jump	Kenny Harrison *(USA)*	Inessa Kravets *(Ukraine)*
pole vault	Jean Galfione *(France)*	–
javelin	Jan Zelezny *(Czech Republic)*	Heli Ratenen *(Finland)*
hammer	Balazs Kiss *(Hungary)*	–
discus	Lars Riedel *(Germany)*	Ilke Wyludda *(Germany)*
shot put	Randy Barnes *(USA)*	Astrid Kumbernuss *(Germany)*
decathlon	Dan O'Brien *(USA)*	–
heptathlon	–	Ghada Shouaa *(Syria)*

BASEBALL: RECENT WORLD SERIES CHAMPIONS

NL = National League; AL = American League

1982	St Louis Cardinals (NL)
1983	Baltimore Orioles (AL)
1984	Detroit Tigers (AL)
1985	Kansas City Royals (AL)
1986	New York Mets (NL)
1987	Minnesota Twins (AL)
1988	Los Angeles Dodgers (NL)
1989	Oakland Athletics (AL)
1990	Cincinnati Reds (NL)
1991	Minnesota Twins (AL)
1992	Toronto Blue Jays (AL)
1993	Toronto Blue Jays (AL)
1994	World Series cancelled (pay dispute)
1995	Atlanta Braves (NL)
1996	New York Yankees (AL)
1997	Florida Marlins (NL)
1998	New York Yankees (AL)

ATHLETICS: OUTDOOR WORLD RECORDS

at 1 November 1998

Men

Event	Record	Record holder
100 metres	9.84 sec	Donovan Bailey *(Canada)*
200 metres	19.32 sec	Michael Johnson *(USA)*
400 metres	43.29 sec	Butch Reynolds *(USA)*
800 metres	1 min 41.11 sec	Wilson Kipketer *(Denmark)*
1,000 metres	2 min 12.18 sec	Sebastian Coe *(Great Britain)*
1,500 metres	3 min 26.00 sec	Hicham El Guerrouj *(Morocco)*
mile	3 min 44.39 sec	Noureddine Morceli *(Algeria)*
2,000 metres	4 min 47.88 sec	Noureddine Morceli *(Algeria)*
3,000 metres	7 min 20.67 sec	Daniel Komen *(Kenya)*
5,000 metres	12 min 39.36 sec	Haile Gebrselassie *(Ethiopia)*
10,000 metres	26 min 22.75 sec	Haile Gebrselassie *(Ethiopia)*
20,000 metres	56 min 55.6 sec	Arturo Barrios *(Mexico)*
21,101 metres	1 hr	Arturo Barrios *(Mexico)*
25,000 metres	1 hr 13 min 55.8 sec	Toshihiko Seko *(Japan)*
30,000 metres	1 hr 29 min 18.8 sec	Toshihiko Seko *(Japan)*
110-metre hurdles	12.91 sec	Colin Jackson *(Great Britain)*
400-metre hurdles	46.78 sec	Kevin Young *(USA)*
3,000-metre steeplechase	7 min 55.72 sec	Bernard Barmasai *(Kenya)*
4 × 100-metre relay	37.40 sec	USA
4 × 400-metre relay	2 min 54.20 sec	USA
4 × 800-metre relay	7 min 03.89 sec	Great Britain
4 × 1,500-metre relay	14 min 38.8 sec	West Germany
high jump	2.45 metres	Javier Sotomayor *(Cuba)*
pole vault	6.14 metres	Sergey Bubka *(Ukraine)*
long jump	8.95 metres	Mike Powell *(USA)*
triple jump	18.29 metres	Jonathan Edwards *(Great Britain)*
shot	23.12 metres	Randy Barnes *(USA)*
discus	74.08 metres	Jürgen Schult *(East Germany)*
hammer	86.74 metres	Yuriy Sedykh *(USSR)*
javelin	98.48 metres	Jan Železny *(Czech Republic)*
decathlon	8,891 points	Dan O'Brien *(USA)*
marathon	2 hr 6 min 05 sec	Ronaldo da Costa *(Brazil)*

Women

Event	Record	Record holder
100 metres	10.49 sec	Florence Griffith-Joyner *(USA)*
200 metres	21.34 sec	Florence Griffith-Joyner *(USA)*
400 metres	47.60 sec	Marita Koch *(East Germany)*
800 metres	1 min 53.28 sec	Jarmila Kratochvilova *(Czechoslovakia)*
1,500 metres	3 min 50.46 sec	Qu Yunxia *(China)*
mile	4 min 12.56 sec	Svetlana Masterkova *(Russia)*
1,000 metres	2 min 28.98 sec	Svetlana Masterkova *(Russia)*
2,000 metres	5 min 25.36 sec	Sonia O'Sullivan *(Ireland)*
3,000 metres	8 min 06.11 sec	Wang Junxia *(China)*
5,000 metres	14 min 28.09 sec	Jiang Bo *(China)*
10,000 metres	29 min 31.78 sec	Wang Junxia *(China)*
25,000 metres	1 hr 29 min 29.2 sec	Karolina Szabo *(Hungary)*
30,000 metres	1 hr 49 min 5.6 sec	Karolina Szabo *(Hungary)*
100-metre hurdles	12.21 sec	Yordanka Donkova *(Bulgaria)*
400-metre hurdles	52.61 sec	Kim Batten *(USA)*
4 × 100-metre relay	41.37 sec	East Germany
4 × 200-metre relay	1 min 28.15 sec	East Germany
4 × 400-metre relay	3 min 15.17 sec	USSR
high jump	2.09 metres	Stefka Kostadinova *(Bulgaria)*
pole vault	4.60 metres	Emma George *(Australia)*
long jump	7.52 metres	Galina Chistiakova *(Russia)*
triple jump	15.5 metres	Inessa Kravets *(Ukraine)*
shot	22.63 metres	Natalya Lisovskaya *(Russia)*
discus	76.80 metres	Gaby Reinsch *(Germany)*
hammer	73.14 metres	Michaela Melinte *(Romania)*
javelin	80.00 metres	Petra Felke *(Germany)*
heptathlon	7,291 points	Jackie Joyner-Kersee *(USA)*
marathon	2 hr 20 min 47 sec	Tegla Laroupe *(Kenya)*

BASKETBALL: RECENT WINNERS

World Championship

first held 1950 for men, 1953 for women; contested every four years

Men

1990	Yugoslavia
1994	USA
1998	Yugoslavia

Women

1990	USA
1994	Brazil
1998	USA

NBA (US National Basketball Association) Championship

US end-of-season contest, first held 1947, between the top teams of the two professional leagues, the Western Conference and the Eastern Conference

1988	Los Angeles Lakers
1989	Detroit Pistons
1990	Detroit Pistons
1991	Chicago Bulls
1992	Chicago Bulls
1993	Chicago Bulls
1994	Houston Rockets
1995	Houston Rockets
1996	Chicago Bulls
1997	Chicago Bulls
1998	Chicago Bulls

BOXING: RECENT WINNERS

World heavyweight champions

WBC = World Boxing Council; WBA = World Boxing Association; IBF = International Boxing Federation; WBO = World Boxing Organization

1986	Mike Tyson *USA* (WBC)
1986	James Smith *USA* (WBA)
1987	Mike Tyson *USA* (WBA)
1987	Tony Tucker *USA* (IBF)
1987	Mike Tyson *USA* (undisputed)
1989	Francesco Damiani *Italy* (WBO)
1990	James Douglas *USA* (undisputed)
1990	Evander Holyfield *USA* (undisputed)
1992	Riddick Bowe *USA* (WBA, IBF)
1992	Lennox Lewis *UK* (WBC)
1992	Michael Moorer *USA* (WBO)
1993	Tommy Morrison *USA* (WBO)
1993	Michael Bentt *USA* (WBO)
1993	Evander Holyfield *USA* (WBA, IBF)
1994	Herbie Hide *UK* (WBO)
1994	Michael Moorer *USA* (WBA, IBF)
1994	Oliver McCall *USA* (WBC)
1994	George Foreman *USA* (WBA, IBF)
1995	Riddick Bowe *USA* (WBO)
1995	Frank Bruno *UK* (WBC)
1996	Mike Tyson *USA* (WBC)
1996	Michael Moorer *USA* (IBF)
1996	Henry Akinwande *UK* (WBO)
1996	Evander Holyfield *USA* (WBA)
1997	Lennox Lewis *UK* (WBC)
1997	Evander Holyfield *USA* (WBA, IBF)
1997	Herbie Hide *UK* (WBO)

CHESS: RECENT WINNERS

World champions (FIDt)

Men

1963	Tigran Petrosian *(USSR)*
1969	Boris Spassky *(USSR)*
1972	Bobby Fischer *(USA)*
1975	Anatoly Karpov *(USSR)*
1985	Gary Kasparov *(USSR/Azerbaijan)*
1993	Anatoly Karpov *(Russia)*

Women

1962	Nona Gaprindashvili *(USSR)*
1978	Maya Chiburdanidze *(USSR)*
1991	Xie Jun *(China)*
1996	Zsuzsu Polgar *(Hungary)*
1997	Harriet Hunt *(UK)*
1998	Zsuzsa Polgar *(Hungary)*

World champions (PCA)

1993	Gary Kasparov *(Russia/Azerbaijan)*

CYCLING: RECENT WINNERS

Tour de France
first held 1903

1988	Pedro Delgado *(Spain)*
1989	Greg LeMond *(USA)*
1990	Greg LeMond *(USA)*
1991	Miguel Indurain *(Spain)*
1992	Miguel Indurain *(Spain)*
1993	Miguel Indurain *(Spain)*
1994	Miguel Indurain *(Spain)*
1995	Miguel Indurain *(Spain)*
1996	Bjarne Riis *(Denmark)*
1997	Jan Ullrich *(Germany)*
1998	Marco Pantani *(Italy)*

World Professional Road Race Champions
first held 1927

1988	Maurizio Fondriest *(Italy)*
1989	Greg LeMond *(USA)*
1990	Rudy Dhaenens *(Belgium)*
1991	Gianni Bugno *(Italy)*
1992	Gianni Bugno *(Italy)*
1993	Lance Armstrong *(USA)*
1994	Luc Leblanc *(France)*
1995	Abraham Olano *(Spain)*
1996	Johan Museeuw *(Belgium)*
1997	Laurent Brochard *(France)*
1998	Oscar Camenzind *(Switzerland)*

Tour of Britain
formerly the Milk Race; first held 1951 revived in 1998 as the Pru Tour of Britain

1987	Malcolm Elliott *(UK)*
1988	Vasily Zhdanov *(USSR)*
1989	Brian Walton *(Canada)*
1990	Shane Sutton *(Australia)*
1991	Chris Walker *(UK)*
1993	Chris Lillywhite *(UK)*
1994	Maurizio Fondriest *(Italy)*
1995	no race
1996	no race
1997	no race
1998	Stuart O'Grady *(Australia)*

CRICKET: RECENT WINNERS

English County Championship
first held officially 1890

1985	Middlesex	**1992**	Essex
1986	Essex	**1993**	Middlesex
1987	Nottinghamshire	**1994**	Warwickshire
1988	Worcestershire	**1995**	Warwickshire
1989	Worcestershire	**1996**	Leicestershire
1990	Middlesex	**1997**	Glamorgan
1991	Essex	**1998**	Leicestershire

AXA Equity and Law League
formerly Refuge Assurance League; first held 1969

1985	Essex	**1992**	Middlesex
1986	Hampshire	**1993**	Glamorgan
1987	Worcestershire	**1994**	Warwickshire
1988	Worcestershire	**1995**	Kent
1989	Lancashire	**1996**	Surrey
1990	Derbyshire	**1997**	Warwickshire
1991	Nottinghamshire	**1998**	Lancashire

NatWest Trophy
formerly the Gillette Cup; first held 1963

1985	Essex	**1992**	Northamptonshire
1986	Sussex	**1993**	Warwickshire
1987	Nottinghamshire	**1994**	Worcestershire
1988	Middlesex	**1995**	Warwickshire
1989	Warwickshire	**1996**	Lancashire
1990	Lancashire	**1997**	Essex
1991	Hampshire	**1998**	Lancashire

Benson and Hedges Cup
first held 1972

1985	Leicestershire	**1992**	Hampshire
1986	Middlesex	**1993**	Derbyshire
1987	Yorkshire	**1994**	Warwickshire
1988	Hampshire	**1995**	Lancashire
1989	Nottinghamshire	**1996**	Lancashire
1990	Lancashire	**1997**	Surrey
1991	Worcestershire	**1998**	Essex

Sheffield Shield
first held 1891/2

1982–83	New South Wales	**1990–91**	Victoria
1983–84	Western Australia	**1991–92**	Western Australia
1984–85	New South Wales	**1992–93**	New South Wales
1985–86	New South Wales	**1993–94**	New South Wales
1986–87	Western Australia	**1994–95**	Queensland
1987–88	Western Australia	**1995–96**	South Australia
1988–89	Western Australia	**1996–97**	Queensland
1989–90	New South Wales	**1997–98**	Western Australia

CRICKET: TEST CRICKET

Test Match Statistics

at 1 November 1998

	Tests	Won	Lost	Drawn	Tied
Australia	584	245	164	173	2
England	752	254	215	283	–
South Africa	225	58	90	77	–
West Indies	343	132	84	126	1
New Zealand	262	39	108	115	–
India	319	59	104	155	1
Pakistan	251	71	57	123	–
Sri Lanka	87	14	37	36	–
Zimbabwe	31	2	15	14	–

One Day International World Cup
first held 1975, contested every four years

1975	West Indies	**1987**	Australia
1979	West Indies	**1992**	Pakistan
1983	India	**1996**	Sri Lanka

SQUASH: RECENT WINNERS

World Open championship
first held 1975

	men	women
1988	Jansher Khan *(Pakistan)*	(not held)
1989	Jansher Khan *(Pakistan)*	Martine Le Moignan *(Great Britain)*
1990	Jansher Khan *(Pakistan)*	Sue Devoy *(New Zealand)*
1991	Rodney Martin *(Australia)*	Sue Devoy *(New Zealand)*
1992	Jansher Khan *(Pakistan)*	Sue Devoy *(New Zealand)*
1993	Jansher Khan *(Pakistan)*	Michelle Martin *(Australia)*
1994	Jansher Khan *(Pakistan)*	Michelle Martin *(Australia)*
1995	Jansher Khan *(Pakistan)*	Michelle Martin *(Australia)*
1996	Jansher Khan *(Pakistan)*	Sarah Fitz-Gerald *(Australia)*
1997	Rodney Eyles *(Australia)*	Sarah Fitz-Gerald *(Australia)*
1998	Jonathon Power *(Canada)*	Sarah Fitz-Gerald *(Australia)*

FOOTBALL, ASSOCIATION: RECENT WINNERS

World Cup
first held 1930; contested every four years

1978 Argentina
1982 Italy
1986 Argentina
1990 West Germany
1994 Brazil
1998 France

European Championship
instituted 1958, first final 1960; contested every four years

1960 USSR
1964 Spain
1968 Italy
1972 West Germany
1976 Czechoslovakia
1980 West Germany
1984 France
1988 Holland
1992 Denmark
1996 Germany

European Champions' Cup

1987 FC Porto *(Portugal)*
1988 PSV Eindhoven *(Holland)*
1989 AC Milan *(Italy)*
1990 AC Milan *(Italy)*
1991 Red Star Belgrade *(Yugoslavia)*
1992 Barcelona *(Spain)*
1993 Marseille *(France)* (later disqualified)
1994 AC Milan *(Italy)*
1995 Ajax *(Holland)*
1996 Juventus *(Italy)*
1997 Borussia Dortmund *(Germany)*
1998 Real Madrid *(Spain)*

European Cup Winners' Cup
first held 1960

1987 Ajax *(Holland)*
1988 Mechelen *(Belgium)*
1989 Barcelona *(Spain)*
1990 Sampdoria *(Italy)*
1991 Manchester United *(England)*
1992 Werder Bremen *(Germany)*
1993 Parma *(Italy)*
1994 Arsenal *(England)*
1995 Real Zaragoza *(Spain)*
1996 Paris St Germain *(France)*
1997 Barcelona *(Spain)*
1998 Chelsea *(England)*

UEFA Cup
formerly Inter Cities Fairs Cup; first held 1955

1987 IFK Gothenburg *(Sweden)*
1988 Bayer Leverkusen *(West Germany)*
1989 Napoli *(Italy)*
1990 Juventus *(Italy)*
1991 Internazionale Milan *(Italy)*
1992 Ajax *(Holland)*
1993 Juventus *(Italy)*
1994 Inter Milan *(Italy)*
1995 Parma *(Italy)*
1996 Bayern Munich *(Germany)*
1997 Schalke *(Germany)*
1998 Inter Milan *(Italy)*

English Premier League Champions
formerly Division One Champions; Football League founded 1888–89

1986–87 Everton
1987–88 Liverpool
1988–89 Arsenal
1989–90 Liverpool
1990–91 Arsenal
1991–92 Leeds United
1992–93 Manchester United
1993–94 Manchester United
1994–95 Blackburn Rovers
1995–96 Manchester United
1996–97 Manchester United
1997–98 Arsenal

English FA Cup
knockout club competition, first held 1872

1987 Coventry City
1988 Wimbledon
1989 Liverpool
1990 Manchester United
1991 Tottenham Hotspur
1992 Liverpool
1993 Arsenal
1994 Manchester United
1995 Everton
1996 Manchester United
1997 Chelsea
1998 Arsenal

English Football League Cup
currently known as the Worthington Cup, formerly the Coca Cola Cup, the Rumbelows Cup, the Milk Cup, and the Littlewoods Cup; first final 1961 in two stages, since 1967 a single game

1987 Arsenal
1988 Luton Town
1989 Nottingham Forest
1990 Nottingham Forest
1991 Sheffield Wednesday
1992 Manchester United
1993 Arsenal
1994 Aston Villa
1995 Liverpool
1996 Aston Villa
1997 Leicester City
1998 Chelsea

Scottish Premier Division Champions
Scottish League formed 1899–91, reformed into three divisions 1975–76

1987–88 Celtic
1988–89 Rangers
1989–90 Rangers
1990–91 Rangers
1991–92 Rangers
1992–93 Rangers
1993–94 Rangers
1994–95 Rangers
1995–96 Rangers
1995–96 Rangers
1996–97 Rangers
1997–98 Celtic

Scottish FA Cup
first final held 1874

1987 St Mirren
1988 Celtic
1989 Celtic
1990 Aberdeen
1991 Motherwell
1992 Rangers
1993 Rangers
1994 Dundee United
1995 Celtic
1996 Rangers
1997 Kilmarnock
1998 Hearts

FOOTBALL, AMERICAN: RECENT WINNERS

Super Bowl

1988 Washington Redskins
1989 San Francisco 49ers
1990 San Francisco 49ers
1991 New York Giants
1992 Washington Redskins
1993 Dallas Cowboys
1994 Dallas Cowboys
1995 San Francisco 49ers
1996 Dallas Cowboys
1997 Green Bay Packers
1998 Denver Broncos
1999 Denver Broncos

FOOTBALL, ASSOCIATION: WOMEN'S WORLD CUP

first held 1991

1991 USA
1995 Norway

GOLF: RECENT WINNERS

British Open
first held 1860

Year	Winner
1981	Bill Rogers *(USA)*
1982	Tom Watson *(USA)*
1983	Tom Watson *(USA)*
1984	Severiano Ballesteros *(Spain)*
1985	Sandy Lyle *(UK)*
1986	Greg Norman *(Australia)*
1987	Nick Faldo *(UK)*
1988	Severiano Ballesteros *(Spain)*
1989	Mark Calcavecchia *(USA)*
1990	Nick Faldo *(UK)*
1991	Ian Baker-Finch *(Australia)*
1992	Nick Faldo *(UK)*
1993	Greg Norman *(Australia)*
1994	Nick Price *(Zimbabwe)*
1995	John Daly *(USA)*
1996	Tom Lehman *(USA)*
1997	Justin Leonard *(USA)*
1998	Mark O'Meara *(USA)*

US Open
first held 1895

Year	Winner
1981	David Graham *(Australia)*
1982	Tom Watson *(USA)*
1983	Larry Nelson *(USA)*
1984	Fuzzy Zoeller *(USA)*
1985	Andy North *(USA)*
1986	Ray Floyd *(USA)*
1987	Scott Simpson *(USA)*
1988	Curtis Strange *(USA)*
1989	Curtis Strange *(USA)*
1990	Hale Irwin *(USA)*
1991	Payne Stewart *(USA)*
1992	Tom Kite *(USA)*
1993	Lee Janzen *(USA)*
1994	Ernie Els *(South Africa)*
1995	Corey Pavin *(USA)*
1996	Steve Jones *(USA)*
1997	Ernie Els *(South Africa)*
1998	Lee Janzen *(USA)*

US Masters
first held 1934

Year	Winner
1982	Craig Stadler *(USA)*
1983	Severiano Ballesteros *(Spain)*
1984	Ben Crenshaw *(USA)*
1985	Bernhard Langer *(West Germany)*
1986	Jack Nicklaus *(USA)*
1987	Larry Mize *(USA)*
1988	Sandy Lyle *(UK)*
1989	Nick Faldo *(UK)*
1990	Nick Faldo *(UK)*
1991	Ian Woosnam *(UK)*
1992	Fred Couples *(USA)*
1993	Bernard Langer *(Germany)*
1994	Jose Maria Olazabal *(Spain)*
1995	Ben Crenshaw *(USA)*
1996	Nick Faldo *(UK)*
1997	Tiger Woods *(USA)*
1998	Mark O'Meara *(USA)*
1999	Jose Maria Olazabal *(Spain)*

US PGA Championship
first held 1916

Year	Winner
1981	Larry Nelson *(USA)*
1982	Raymond Floyd *(USA)*
1983	Hal Sutton *(USA)*
1984	Lee Trevino *(USA)*
1985	Hubert Green *(USA)*
1986	Bob Tway *(USA)*
1987	Larry Nelson *(USA)*
1988	Jeff Sluman *(USA)*
1989	Payne Stewart *(USA)*
1990	Wayne Grady *(Australia)*
1991	John Daly *(USA)*
1992	Nick Price *(Zimbabwe)*
1993	Paul Azinger *(USA)*
1994	Nick Price *(Zimbabwe)*
1995	Steve Elkington *(Australia)*
1996	Mark Brooks *(USA)*
1997	Davis Love III *(USA)*
1998	Vijay Singh *(Fiji)*

HORSE RACING: RECENT WINNERS

Derby
first held 1780; 1 mi 4 furlongs long

	Horse/Jockey
1987	Reference Point/Steve Cauthen
1988	Kahyasi/Ray Cochrane
1989	Nashwan/Willie Carson
1990	Quest for Fame/Pat Eddery
1991	Generous/Alan Munroe
1992	Dr Devious/John Reid
1993	Commander In Chief/Michael Kinane
1994	Erhaab/Willie Carson
1995	Lammtarra/Walter Swinburn
1996	Shaamit/Michael Hills
1997	Benny the Dip/Willie Ryan
1998	High-Rise/Olivier Peslier

Oaks
first held 1779; 1 mi 4 furlongs long

	Horse/Jockey
1987	Unite/Walter Swinburn
1988	Diminuendo/Steve Cauthen
1989	Snow Bride/Steve Cauthen
1990	Salsabil/Willie Carson
1991	Jet Ski Lady/Christy Roche
1992	User Friendly/George Duffield
1993	Intrepidity/Michael Roberts
1994	Balanchine/Frankie Dettori
1995	Moonshell/Frankie Dettori
1996	Lady Carla/Pat Eddery
1997	Reams of Verse/Kieren Fallon
1998	Shahtoush/Michael Kinane

1,000 Guineas
first held 1814; 1 mi long

	Horse/Jockey
1987	Miesque/Freddy Head
1988	Ravinella/Gary Moore
1989	Musical Bliss/Walter Swinburn
1990	Salsabil/Willie Carson
1991	Shadayid/Willie Carson
1992	Hatoof/Walter Swinburn
1993	Sayyedati/Walter Swinburn
1994	Las Meninas/John Reid
1995	Harayir/Richard Hills
1996	Bosra Sham/Pat Eddery
1997	Sleepytime/Kieren Fallon
1998	Cape Verdi/Frankie Dettori

2,000 Guineas
first held 1809; 1 mi long

	Horse/Jockey
1987	Don't Forget Me/Willie Carson
1988	Doyoun/Walter Swinburn
1989	Nashwan/Willie Carson
1990	Tirol/Michael Kinane
1991	Mystiko/Michael Roberts
1992	Rodrigo de Triano/Lester Piggott
1993	Zafonic/Pat Eddery
1994	Mister Baileys/Jason Weaver
1995	Pennekamp/Thierry Jarnet
1996	Mark of Esteem/Frankie Dettori
1997	Entrepreneur/Michael Kinane
1998	King of Kings/Michael Kinane

St Leger
the oldest English classic, first held 1776; 1 mi 6 furlongs 127 yd long

	Horse/Jockey
1988	Minster Son/Willie Carson
1989	Michelozza/Steve Cauthen
1990	Snurge/Richard Quinn
1991	Toulon/Pat Eddery
1992	User Friendly/George Duffield
1993	Bob's Return/Philip Robinson
1994	Moonax/Pat Eddery
1995	Classic Cliché/Frankie Dettori
1996	Shantou/Frankie Dettori
1997	Silver Patriarch/Pat Eddery
1998	Nedawi/John Reid

Grand National
steeplechase; first held 1847; 4 mi 4 furlongs long

	Horse/Jockey
1987	Maori Venture/Steve Knight
1988	Rhyme N'Reason/Brendan Powell
1989	Little Polveir/Jimmy Frost
1990	Mr Frisk/Marcus Armytage
1991	Seagram/Nigel Hawke
1992	Party Politics/Carl Llewellyn
1993	void
1994	Miinnehoma/Richard Dunwoody
1995	Royal Athlete/Jason Titley
1996	Rough Quest/Mick Fitzgerald
1997	Lord Gyllene/Tony Dobbin
1998	Earth Summit/Carl Llewellyn
1999	Bobbyjo/Paul Carberry

Prix de l'Arc de Triomphe
first held 1920; 2,400 m long

	Horse/Jockey
1987	Trempolino/Pat Eddery
1988	Tony Bin/John Reid
1989	Caroll House/Michael Kinane
1990	Saumarez/Gerald Mosse
1991	Suave Dancer/Cash Asmussen
1992	Subotica/Thierry Jarnet
1993	Urban Sea/Eric St Martin
1994	Carnegie/Thierry Jarnet
1995	Lammtarra/Frankie Dettori
1996	Helissio/Olivier Peslier
1997	Peintre Celebre/Olivier Peslier
1998	Segamix/Olivier Peslier

Melbourne Cup
first held 1861; 3,200 m long

	Horse/Jockey
1987	Kensei/Larry Olsen
1988	Empire Rose/Tony Allan
1989	Tawriffic/Shane Dye
1990	Kingston Rule/Darren Beadman
1991	Let's Elope/Stephen King
1992	Subzero/Greg Hall
1993	Vintage Crop/Michael Kinane
1994	Jeune/Wayne Harris
1995	Doriemus/Damien Oliver
1996	Saintly/Darren Beadman
1997	Might and Power/Jim Cassidy
1998	Jezabeel/Chris Munie

MOTOR RACING: RECENT WINNERS

World Drivers' Championship
Formula One Grand Prix racing; instituted 1950

Driver/Manufacturer

1987 Nelson Piquet/Williams *(Brazil)*
1988 Ayrton Senna/McLaren *(Brazil)*
1989 Alain Prost/McLaren *(France)*
1990 Ayrton Senna/McLaren *(Brazil)*
1991 Ayrton Senna/McLaren *(Brazil)*
1992 Nigel Mansell/Williams *(UK)*
1993 Alain Prost/Williams *(France)*
1994 Michael Schumacher/Benetton *(Germany)*
1995 Michael Schumacher/Benetton *(Germany)*
1996 Damon Hill/Williams *(UK)*
1997 Jacques Villeneuve/Williams *(Canada)*
1998 Mika Hakkinen/McLaren *(Finland)*

Formula 1 Constructors' Championship
Formula One Grand Prix racing: instituted 1958

1987 Williams-Honda
1988 McClaren-Honda
1989 McClaren-Honda
1990 McClaren-Honda
1991 McClaren-Honda
1992 Williams-Renault
1993 Williams-Renault
1994 Williams-Renault
1995 Williams-Renault
1996 Williams-Renault
1997 Williams-Renault
1998 McLaren-Mercedes

Le Mans Grand Prix d'Endurance
Le Mans 24-Hour Race; first held 1923

1987 Hans Stuck *(West Germany)*/Derek Bell *(UK)*/Al Holbert *(USA)*
1988 Jan Lammers *(Netherlands)*/Johnny Dumfries *(UK)*/Andy Wallace *(UK)*
1989 Jochen Mass *(West Germany)*/Manuel Reuter *(West Germany)*/Stanley Dickens *(Sweden)*
1990 John Nielsen *(Denmark)*/Price Cobb *(USA)*/Martin Brundle *(UK)*
1991 Volker Weidler *(Germany)*/John Herbert *(Great Britain)*/Bertrand Gachot *(Belgium)*
1992 Derek Warwick *(UK)*/Yannick Dalmas *(France)*/Mark Blundell *(UK)*
1993 Geoff Brabham *(Australia)*/Christophe Bouchut *(France)*/Eric Helary *(France)*
1994 Yannick Dalmas *(France)*/Hurley Haywood *(USA)*/ Mauro Baldi *(Italy)*
1995 Yannick Dalmas *(France)*/J J Lehto *(Finland)*/Masanori Sekiya *(Japan)*
1996 Davy Jones *(USA)*/Manuel Reuter *(Germany)*/Alexander Würz *(Austria)*
1997 Michele Alboreto *(Italy)*/Stefan Johansson *(Sweden)*/Tom Kristensen *(Denmark)*
1998 Allan McNish/Stephane Ortelli *(France)*/Laurent Aiello *(France)*

Monte Carlo Rally
first held 1911

1987 Mikki Biasion *(Italy)*
1988 Bruno Saby *(France)*
1989 Mikki Biasion *(Italy)*
1990 Didier Auriol *(France)*
1991 Carlos Sainz *(Spain)*
1992 Didier Auriol *(France)*
1993 Didier Auriol *(France)*
1994 François Delecour *(France)*
1995 Carlos Sainz *(Spain)*
1996 Patrick Bernardini *(France)*
1997 Piero Liatti *(Italy)*
1998 Carlos Sainz *(Spain)*
1999 Tommi Mäkinen *(Finland)*

RAC Rally
formerly RAC International Rally of Great Britain; first held 1927

1987 Juha Kankkunen *(Finland)*
1988 Markku Alén *(Finland)*
1989 Pentti Arikkala *(Finland)*
1990 Carlos Sainz *(Spain)*
1991 Juha Kankkunen *(Finland)*
1992 Carlos Sainz *(Spain)*
1993 Juha Kankkunen *(Finland)*
1994 Colin McRae *(UK)*
1995 Colin McRae *(UK)*
1996 Armin Schwarz *(Germany)*
1997 Colin McRae *(UK)*
1998 Richard Burns *(UK)*

Indianapolis 500
first held 1911

Driver/Manufacturer

1987 Al Unser, Jr/March–Cosworth *(USA)*
1988 Rick Mears/Penske–Chevrolet *(USA)*
1989 Emerson Fittipaldi/Penske–Chevrolet *(Brazil)*
1990 Arie Luyendyk/Lola–Chevrolet *(Holland)*
1991 Rick Mears/Penske–Chevrolet *(USA)*
1992 Al Unser, Jr/Galmer–Chevy A *(USA)*
1993 Emerson Fittipaldi/Penske–Chevrolet *(Brazil)*
1994 Al Unser, Jr/Penske–Mercedes *(USA)*
1995 Jacques Villeneuve/Reynard–Ford *(Canada)*
1996 Buddy Lazier/Reynard–Ford *(USA)*
1997 Arie Luyendyk/G-Force-Aurora *(Holland)*
1998 Eddie Cheever Jr/Dallara-Aurora *(USA)*

RUGBY UNION: RECENT WINNERS

World Cup
William Webb Ellis Trophy; first held 1987

1987 New Zealand
1991 Australia
1995 South Africa

Super 12
tournament for clubs in the southern hemisphere; first held 1996

1996 Auckland Blues (*New Zealand*)
1997 Auckland Blues (*New Zealand*)
1998 Canterbury Crusaders (*New Zealand*)

European Cup
European club competition; first held 1995–96

1996 Toulouse (*France*)
1997 Brive (*France*)
1998 Bath (*England*)
1999 Ulster (*Ireland*)

International Championship (Five Nations)
instituted 1884, now a tournament between England, France, Ireland, Scotland, and Wales

1988 France and Wales
1989 France
1990 Scotland
1991 England
1992 England
1993 France
1994 Wales
1995 England
1996 England
1997 France
1998 France
1999 Scotland

County Championship
first held 1889

1987 Yorkshire
1988 Lancashire
1989 Durham
1990 Lancashire
1991 Cornwall
1992 Lancashire
1993 Lancashire
1994 Yorkshire
1995 Warwickshire
1996 Gloucestershire
1997 Cumbria
1998 Cheshire

English Club Championship
first held 1987–88

1989 Bath
1990 Wasps
1991 Bath
1992 Bath
1993 Bath
1994 Bath
1995 Leicester
1996 Bath
1997 Wasps
1998 Newcastle

Irish Club Championship
first held 1990–91

1992 Garryowen
1993 Young Munster
1994 Garryowen
1995 Shannon
1996 Shannon
1997 Shannon
1998 Shannon

Welsh Club Championship
first held 1990–91

1992 Swansea
1993 Llanelli
1994 Swansea
1995 Cardiff
1996 Neath
1997 Pontypridd
1998 Swansea

Scottish Club Championship
first held 1974
division one

1987 Hawick
1988 Kelso
1989 Kelso
1990 Melrose
1991 Boroughmuir
1992 Melrose
1993 Melrose
1994 Melrose
1995 Stirling County
1996 Melrose
1997 Melrose
1998 Watsonians

Tetley Bitter Cup Final
formerly the John Player Special Cup and the Pilkington Cup; the English club knockout tournament, first held 1971–72

1987 Bath
1988 Harlequins
1989 Bath
1990 Bath
1991 Harlequins
1992 Bath
1993 Leicester
1994 Bath
1995 Bath
1996 Bath
1997 Leicester
1998 Saracens

Swalec Welsh Cup
formerly the Schweppes Welsh Cup; the Welsh club knockout tournament, first held 1971–72

1986 Cardiff
1987 Cardiff
1988 Llanelli
1989 Neath
1990 Neath
1991 Llanelli
1992 Llanelli
1993 Llanelli
1994 Cardiff
1995 Swansea
1996 Pontypridd
1997 Cardiff
1998 Llanelli

Scottish Rugby Union Tennent's 1556 Cup
Scottish knockout tournament; first held 1996

1996 Hawick
1997 Melrose
1998 Glasgow Hawks

Tri-Nations Series
tournament between Australia, New Zealand, and South Africa, first held 1996

1996 New Zealand
1997 New Zealand
1998 South Africa

TENNIS: RECENT WINNERS

Wimbledon championships
All-England Lawn Tennis Club championships; first held 1877; grass surface

Men's singles

1987 Pat Cash *(Australia)*
1988 Stefan Edberg *(Sweden)*
1989 Boris Becker *(West Germany)*
1990 Stefan Edberg *(Sweden)*
1991 Michael Stich *(Germany)*
1992 Andre Agassi *(USA)*
1993 Pete Sampras *(USA)*
1994 Pete Sampras *(USA)*
1995 Pete Sampras *(USA)*
1996 Richard Krajicek *(Netherlands)*
1997 Pete Sampras *(USA)*
1998 Pete Sampras *(USA)*

Women's singles

1987 Martina Navratilova *(USA)*
1988 Steffi Graf *(West Germany)*
1989 Steffi Graf *(West Germany)*
1990 Martina Navratilova *(USA)*
1991 Steffi Graf *(Germany)*
1992 Steffi Graf *(Germany)*
1993 Steffi Graf *(Germany)*
1994 Conchita Martinez *(Spain)*
1995 Steffi Graf *(Germany)*
1996 Steffi Graf *(Germany)*
1997 Martina Hingis *(Switzerland)*
1998 Jana Novotna *(Czech Republic)*

US Open
first held 1881 as the United States Championship; became the United States Open 1968; concrete surface

Men's singles

1987 Ivan Lendl *(Czechoslovakia)*
1988 Mats Wilander *(Sweden)*
1989 Boris Becker *(West Germany)*
1990 Pete Sampras *(USA)*
1991 Stefan Edberg *(Sweden)*
1992 Stefan Edberg *(Sweden)*
1993 Pete Sampras *(USA)*
1994 Andre Agassi *(USA)*
1995 Pete Sampras *(USA)*
1996 Pete Sampras *(USA)*
1997 Patrick Rafter *(Australia)*
1998 Patrick Rafter *(Australia)*

Women's singles

1987 Martina Navratilova *(USA)*
1988 Steffi Graf *(West Germany)*
1989 Steffi Graf *(West Germany)*
1990 Gabriela Sabatini *(Argentina)*
1991 Monica Seles *(Yugoslavia)*
1992 Monica Seles *(Yugoslavia)*
1993 Steffi Graf *(Germany)*
1994 Arantxa Sanchez Vicario *(Spain)*
1995 Steffi Graf *(Germany)*
1996 Steffi Graf *(Germany)*
1997 Martina Hingis *(Switzerland)*
1998 Lindsay Davenport *(USA)*

Fed Cup
first held 1963 as the Federation Cup; an international women's team competition

1988 Czechoslovakia
1989 USA
1990 USA
1991 Spain
1992 Germany
1993 Spain
1994 Spain
1995 Spain
1996 USA
1997 France
1998 Spain

French Open
first held 1891, a national championship until 1924; clay surface

Men's singles

1987 Ivan Lendl *(Czechoslovakia)*
1988 Mats Wilander *(Sweden)*
1989 Michael Chang *(USA)*
1990 Andres Gomez *(Ecuador)*
1991 Jim Courier *(USA)*
1992 Jim Courier *(USA)*
1993 Sergi Bruguera *(Spain)*
1994 Sergi Bruguera *(Spain)*
1995 Thomas Muster *(Austria)*
1996 Yevgeny Kafelnikov *(Russia)*
1997 Gustavo Kuerten *(Brazil)*
1998 Carlos Moya *(Spain)*

Women's singles

1987 Steffi Graf *(West Germany)*
1988 Steffi Graf *(West Germany)*
1989 Arantxa Sanchez Vicario *(Spain)*
1990 Monica Seles *(Yugoslavia)*
1991 Monica Seles *(Yugoslavia)*
1992 Monica Seles *(Yugoslavia)*
1993 Steffi Graf *(Germany)*
1994 Arantxa Sanchez Vicario *(Spain)*
1995 Steffi Graf *(Germany)*
1996 Steffi Graf *(Germany)*
1997 Iva Majoli *(Croatia)*
1998 Arantxa Sanchez Vicario *(Spain)*

Australian Open
first held 1905, a national championship until 1925; hard court

Men's singles

1989 Ivan Lendl *(Czechoslovakia)*
1990 Ivan Lendl *(Czechoslovakia)*
1991 Boris Becker *(Germany)*
1992 Jim Courier *(USA)*
1993 Jim Courier *(USA)*
1994 Pete Sampras *(USA)*
1995 Andre Agassi *(USA)*
1996 Boris Becker *(Germany)*
1997 Pete Sampras *(USA)*
1998 Petr Korda *(Czech Republic)*
1999 Yevgeny Kafelnikov *(Russia)*

Women's singles

1989 Steffi Graf *(West Germany)*
1990 Steffi Graf *(West Germany)*
1991 Monica Seles *(Yugoslavia)*
1992 Monica Seles *(Yugoslavia)*
1993 Monica Seles *(Yugoslavia)*
1994 Steffi Graf *(Germany)*
1995 Mary Pierce *(France)*
1996 Monica Seles *(USA)*
1997 Martina Hingis *(Switzerland)*
1998 Martina Hingis *(Switzerland)*
1999 Martina Hingis *(Switzerland)*

Davis Cup
first held 1900; lawn tennis tournament for men's international teams

1987 Sweden
1988 West Germany
1989 West Germany
1990 USA
1991 France
1992 USA
1993 Germany
1994 Sweden
1995 USA
1996 France
1997 Sweden
1998 Sweden

OLYMPIC GAMES: VENUES

1984 Los Angeles, USA (summer games)
1984 Sarajevo, Yugoslavia (winter games)
1988 Seoul, South Korea (summer games)
1988 Calgary, Canada (winter games)
1992 Barcelona, Spain (summer games)
1992 Albertville, France (winter games)
1994 Lillehammer, Norway (winter games)
1996 Atlanta, USA (summer games)
1998 Nagano, Japan (winter games)
2000 Sydney, Australia (summer games)
2002 Salt Lake City, USA (winter games)
2004 Athens, Greece (summer games)

COMMONWEALTH GAMES: VENUES

1974 Christchurch, New Zealand
1978 Edmonton, Canada
1982 Brisbane, Australia
1986 Edinburgh, Scotland
1990 Auckland, New Zealand
1994 Victoria, Canada
1998 Kuala Lumpur, Malaysia
2002 Manchester, England

SKIING: RECENT WINNERS

Alpine World Cup
first held 1967

	Men – overall	Women – overall
1988	Pirmin Zurbriggen *(Switzerland)*	Michela Figini *(Switzerland)*
1989	Marc Girardelli *(Luxembourg)*	Vreni Schneider *(Switzerland)*
1990	Pirmin Zurbriggen *(Switzerland)*	Petra Krönberger *(Austria)*
1991	Marc Girardelli *(Luxembourg)*	Petra Krönberger *(Austria)*
1992	Paul Accola *(Switzerland)*	Petra Krönberger *(Austria)*
1993	Marc Girardelli *(Luxembourg)*	Anita Wachter *(Austria)*
1994	Kjetil-Andre Aamodt *(Norway)*	Vreni Schneider *(Switzerland)*
1995	Alberto Tomba *(Italy)*	Vreni Schneider *(Switzerland)*
1996	Lasse Kjus *(Norway)*	Katja Seizinger *(Germany)*
1997	Luc Alphand *(France)*	Pernilla Wiberg *(Sweden)*
1998	Hermann Maier *(Austria)*	Katja Seizinger *(Germany)*

Olympic Games
events introduced 1936

	Men – downhill	Women – downhill
1972	Bernhard Russi *(Switzerland)*	Marie-Therese Nadig *(Switzerland)*
1976	Franz Klammer *(Austria)*	Rosi Mittermaier *(West Germany)*
1980	Leonhard Stock *(Austria)*	Annemarie Moser-Proll *(Austria)*
1984	William Johnson *(USA)*	Michela Figini *(Switzerland)*
1988	Pirmin Zurbriggen *(Switzerland)*	Marina Kiehl *(West Germany)*
1992	Patrick Ortleib *(Austria)*	Kerrin Lee-Gartner *(Canada)*
1994	Tommy Moe *(USA)*	Katja Seizinger *(Germany)*
1998	Jean-Luc Crétier *(France)*	Katja Seizinger *(Germany)*
	Men – slalom	**Women – slalom**
1972	Francisco Fernandez Ochoa *(Spain)*	Barbara Cochran *(USA)*
1976	Piero Gros *(Italy)*	Rosi Mittermaier *(West Germany)*
1980	Ingemar Stenmark *(Sweden)*	Hanni Wenzel *(Liechtenstein)*
1984	Phil Mahre *(USA)*	Paoletta Magoni *(Italy)*
1988	Alberto Tomba *(Italy)*	Vreni Schneider *(Switzerland)*
1992	Christian Jagge *(Norway)*	Petra Krönberger *(Austria)*
1994	Thomas Stangassinger *(Austria)*	Vreni Schneider *(Switzerland)*
1998	Hans-Peter Buraas *(Norway)*	Hilde Gerg *(Germany)*

SWIMMING: RECENT WINNERS

Olympic Games
Atlanta Olympics 1996 (26th Olympic Games)

Event	Men/Women
100 metres backstroke	Jeff Rouse *(USA)*/Beth Botsford *(USA)*
200 metres backstroke	Brad Bridgewater *(USA)*/Kristina Egerszegi *(Hungary)*
100 metres breaststroke	Fred Deburghgraeve *(Belgium)*/Penny Heyns *(South Africa)*
200 metres breaststroke	Norbert Rozsa *(Hungary)*/Penny Heyns *(South Africa)*
100 metres butterfly	Denis Pankratov *(Russia)*/Amy van Dyken *(USA)*
200 metres butterfly	Denis Pankratov *(Russia)*/Susan O'Neill *(Australia)*
50 metres freestyle	Aleksandr Popov *(Russia)*/Amy van Dyken *(USA)*
100 metres freestyle	Aleksandr Popov *(Russia)*/Jingyi Le *(China)*
200 metres freestyle	Danyon Loader *(New Zealand)*/Claudia Poll *(Costa Rica)*
400 metres freestyle	Danyon Loader *(New Zealand)*/Michelle Smith *(Ireland)*
800 metres freestyle	- /Brooke Bennett *(USA)*
1,500 metres freestyle	Kieren Perkins *(Australia)*/ -
200 metres individual medley	Attila Czene *(Hungary)*/Michelle Smith *(Ireland)*
400 metres individual medley	Tom Dolan *(USA)*/Michelle Smith *(Ireland)*
4 x 100 metres freestyle relay	USA/USA
4 x 200 metres freestyle relay	USA/USA
4 x 100 metres medley relay	USA/USA
synchronized swimming (team)	USA

Most gold medals

9	Mark Spitz *(USA)*	1968, 1972
8	Matt Biondi *(USA)*	1984, 1988, 1992
6	Kristin Otto *(East Germany)*	1988
5	Charles Daniels *(USA)*	1904, 1908
5	Johnny Weissmuller *(USA)*	1924, 1928
5	Don Schollander *(USA)*	1964, 1968
5	Kristina Egerszegi *(Hungary)*	1988, 1992, 1996
4	Henry Taylor *(UK)*	1906, 1908
4	Murray Rose *(Australia)*	1956, 1960
4	Dawn Fraser *(Australia)*	1956, 1960, 1964
4	Roland Matthes *(East Germany)*	1968, 1972
4	John Naber *(USA)*	1976
4	Kornelia Ender *(East Germany)*	1976
4	Vladimir Salnikov *(USSR)*	1980, 1988
4	Tamás Darnyi *(Hungary)*	1988, 1992
4	Janet Evans *(USA)*	1988, 1992
4	Aleksandr Popov *(Russia)*	1992, 1996
4	Amy van Dyken *(USA)*	1996

Most medals

11	Mark Spitz *(USA)*	1968, 1972
11	Matt Biondi *(USA)*	1984, 1988, 1992
8	Charles Daniels *(USA)*	1904, 1908
8	Roland Matthes *(East Germany)*	1968, 1972
8	Henry Taylor *(UK)*	1906, 1908, 1912, 1920
8	Dawn Fraser *(Australia)*	1956, 1960, 1964
8	Kornelia Ender *(East Germany)*	1972, 1976
8	Shirley Babashoff *(USA)*	1972, 1976

ROWING: RECENT WINNERS

World championship
first held 1962 for men, 1974 for women; Olympic winners automatically become world champions

Single Sculls

	Men
1987	Thomas Lange *(East Germany)*
1988	Thomas Lange *(East Germany)*
1989	Thomas Lange *(East Germany)*
1990	Uri Janson *(USSR)*
1991	Thomas Lange *(Germany)*
1992	Thomas Lange *(Germany)*
1993	Derek Porter *(Canada)*
1994	Andre Wilms *(Germany)*
1995	Iztok Cop *(Slovenia)*
1996	Xeno Mueller *(Switzerland)*
1997	Jamie Koven *(USA)*
1998	Rob Waddell *(New Zealand)*
	Women
1987	Magdalena Georgeyeva *(Bulgaria)*
1988	Jutta Behrendt *(East Germany)*
1989	Elisabeta Lipa *(Romania)*
1990	Birgit Peter *(East Germany)*
1991	Silke Laumann *(Canada)*
1992	Elisabeta Lipa *(Romania)*
1993	Jana Thieme *(Germany)*
1994	Trine Hansen *(Denmark)*
1995	Maria Brandin *(Sweden)*
1996	Yekaterina Khodotovich *(Belarus)*
1997	Yekaterina Khodotovich *(Belarus)*
1998	Irina Fedotova *(Russia)*

The Boat Race
first held 1829; rowed annually by crews from Oxford and Cambridge Universities, between Putney and Mortlake on the river Thames

1988	Oxford
1989	Oxford
1990	Oxford
1991	Oxford
1992	Oxford
1993	Cambridge
1994	Cambridge
1995	Cambridge
1996	Cambridge
1997	Cambridge
1998	Cambridge
1999	Cambridge

wins

Cambridge	76
Oxford	68

SNOOKER: RECENT WINNERS

World Professional Championship
first held 1927

1998	Steve Davis *(England)*
1989	Steve Davis *(England)*
1990	Stephen Hendry *(Scotland)*
1991	John Parrott *(England)*
1992	Stephen Hendry *(Scotland)*
1993	Stephen Hendry *(Scotland)*
1994	Stephen Hendry *(Scotland)*
1995	Stephen Hendry *(Scotland)*
1996	Stephen Hendry *(Scotland)*
1997	Ken Doherty *(Republic of Ireland)*
1998	John Higgins *(Scotland)*

World Amateur Championship
first held 1963

1988	James Wattana *(Thailand)*
1989	Ken Doherty *(Republic of Ireland)*
1990	Stephen O'Connor *(Republic of Ireland)*
1991	Noppadon Noppachom *(Thailand)*
1992	Neil Mosley *(England)*
1993	Chuchat Triratanapradit *(Thailand)*
1994	Mohammed Yusuf *(Pakistan)*
1995	Mohammed Yusuf *(Pakistan)*
1996	Stuart Bingham *(England)*
1997	Marco Fu *(Hong Kong)*
1998	Luke Simmonds *(England)*

LEADERS AND GOVERNMENT

AUSTRALIA: PRIME MINISTERS FROM 1901

Term	Name	Party
1901–03	Edmund Barton	Protectionist
1903–04	Alfred Deakin	Protectionist
1904	John Watson	Labor
1904–05	G Reid	Free Trade–Protectionist coalition
1905–08	Alfred Deakin	Protectionist
1908–09	Andrew Fisher	Labor
1909–10	Alfred Deakin	Fusion
1910–13	Andrew Fisher	Labor
1913–14	J Cook	Liberal
1914–15	Andrew Fisher	Labor
1915–23	William Morris Hughes	Labor (National Labor from 1917)
1923–29	Stanley Bruce	National–Country Coalition
1929–32	J H Scullin	Labor
1932–39	Joseph Aloysius Lyons	United Australia–Country coalition
1939	Earle Page	United Australia–Country Coalition
1939–41	R G Menzies	United Australia
1941–41	A W Fadden	Country–United Australia coalition
1941–45	John Curtin	Labor
1945	F M Forde	Labor
1945–49	J B Chifley	Labor
1949–66	R G Menzies	Liberal–Country coalition
1966–67	Harold Holt	Liberal–Country coalition
1967–68	John McEwen	Liberal–Country coalition
1968–71	J G Gorton	Liberal–Country coalition
1971–72	William McMahon	Liberal–Country coalition
1972–75	Gough Whitlam	Labor
1975–83	Malcolm Fraser	Liberal–National coalition
1983–91	Robert Hawke	Labor
1991–96	Paul Keating	Labor
1996–	John Howard	Liberal–National coalition

FRANCE: LEADERS FROM 1959

Term	Name	Party
Presidents		
1959–69	General Charles de Gaulle	Gaullist
1969–74	Georges Pompidou	Gaullist
1974–81	Valéry Giscard d'Estaing	Republican/Union of French Democracy
1981–95	François Mitterand	Socialist
1995–	Jacques Chirac	Neo-Gaullist RPR
Prime ministers		
1959–62	Michel Debré	Gaullist
1962–68	Georges Pompidou	Gaullist
1968–69	Maurice Couve de Murville	Gaullist
1969–72	Jacques Chaban-Delmas	Gaullist
1972–74	Pierre Messmer	Gaullist
1974–76	Jacques Chirac	Gaullist
1976–81	Raymond Barre	Union of French Democracy
1981–84	Pierre Mauroy	Socialist
1984–86	Laurent Fabius	Socialist
1986–88	Jacques Chirac	Neo-Gaullist RPR
1988–91	Michel Rocard	Socialist
1991–92	Edith Cresson	Socialist
1992–93	Pierre Bérégovovoy	Socialist
1993–95	Edouard Balladur	Neo-Gaullist RPR
1995–97	Alain Juppé	Neo-Gaullist RPR
1997–	Lionel Jospin	Socialist

IRELAND: PRIME MINISTERS FROM 1922

Term	Name	Party
1922	Michael Collins	Sinn Féin
1922–32	William T Cosgrave	Fine Gael
1932–48	Eamon de Valera	Fianna Fáil
1948–51	John A Costello	Fine Gael
1951–54	Eamon de Valera	Fianna Fáil
1954–57	John A Costello	Fine Gael
1957–59	Eamon de Valera	Fianna Fáil
1959–66	Sean Lemass	Fianna Fáil
1966–73	Jack Lynch	Fianna Fáil
1973–77	Liam Cosgrave	Fine Gael
1977–79	Jack Lynch	Fianna Fáil
1979–81	Charles Haughey	Fianna Fáil
1981–82	Garrett Fitzgerald	Fine Gael
1982	Charles Haughey	Fianna Fáil
1982–87	Garrett Fitzgerald	Fine Gael
1987–92	Charles Haughey	Fianna Fáil
1992–94	Albert Reynolds	Fianna Fáil
1994–97	John Bruton	Fine Gael
1997–	Bertie Ahern	Fianna Fáil

CANADA: PRIME MINISTERS FROM 1867

Term	Name	Party
1867–73	John A Macdonald	Conservative
1873–78	Alexander Mackenzie	Liberal
1878–91	John A Macdonald	Conservative
1891–92	John J Abbott	Conservative
1892–94	John S D Thompson	Conservative
1894–96	Mackenzie Bowell	Conservative
1896	Charles Tupper	Conservative
1896–1911	Wilfred Laurier	Liberal
1911–20	Robert L Borden	Conservative
1920–21	Arthur Meighen	Conservative
1921–26	William L M King	Liberal
1926–26	Arthur Meighen	Conservative
1926–30	William L M King	Liberal
1930–35	Richard B Bennett	Conservative
1935–48	William L M King	Liberal
1948–57	Louis S St Laurent	Liberal
1957–63	John G Diefenbaker	Conservative
1963–68	Lester B Pearson	Liberal
1968–79	Pierre E Trudeau	Liberal
1979–80	Joseph Clark	Progressive Conservative
1980–84	Pierre E Trudeau	Liberal
1984	John Turner	Liberal
1984–93	Brian Mulroney	Progressive Conservative
1993	Kim Campbell	Progressive Conservative
1993–	Jean Chretien	Liberal

GERMANY: LEADERS FROM 1949

Federal Republic

Term	Chancellor	Party
1949–63	Konrad Adenauer	Christian Democrat
1963–66	Ludwig Erhard	Christian Democrat
1966–69	Kurt Kiesinger	Christian Democrat
1969–74	Willy Brandt	Social Democrat
1974–82	Helmut Schmidt	Social Democrat
1982–98[1]	Helmut Kohl	Christian Democrat
1998–	Gerhard Schröder	Social Democrat

Democratic Republic

Term	Communist Party leader
1949–50	Wilhelm Pieck
1950–71	Walter Ulbricht
1971–89	Erich Honecker
1989	Egon Krenz

[1] The official reunification of the two countries, with Kohl as chancellor, took place in 1990.

JAPAN: PRIME MINISTERS FROM 1945

Term	Name	Party
1945–46	Kijurō Shidehara	coalition
1946–47	Shigeru Yoshida	Liberal
1947–48	Tetsu Katayama	coalition
1948–48	Hitoshi Ashida	Democratic
1948–54	Shigeru Yoshida	Liberal
1954–56	Ichirō Hatoyama	Liberal*
1956–57	Tanzan Ishibashi	LDP
1957–60	Nobusuke Kishi	LDP
1960–64	Hayato Ikeda	LDP
1964–72	Eisaku Satō	LDP
1972–74	Kakuei Tanaka	LDP
1974–76	Takeo Miki	LDP
1976–78	Takeo Fukuda	LDP
1978–80	Masayoshi Ohira	LDP
1980–82	Zenkō Suzuki	LDP
1982–87	Yasuhiro Nakasone	LDP
1987–89	Noboru Takeshita	LDP
1989–89	Sōsuke Uno	LDP
1989–91	Toshiki Kaifu	LDP
1991–93	Kiichi Miyazawa	LDP
1993–94	Morohiro Hosokawa	JNP-led coalition
1994–94	Tsutoma Hata	Shinseito-led coalition
1994–96	Tomiichi Murayama	SDPJ-led coalition
1996–	Ryutaro Hashimoto	LDP

* The conservative parties merged 1955 to form the Liberal Democratic Party (LDP, Jiyū-Minshūtō).

NEW ZEALAND: PRIME MINISTERS

Term	Name	Party	Term	Name	Party
1891–93	J Ballance	Liberal	**1957**	K J Holyoake	National
1893–1906	R J Seddon	Liberal	**1957–60**	Walter Nash	Labour
1906	W Hall-Jones	Liberal	**1960–72**	K J Holyoake	National
1906–12	Joseph Ward	Liberal	**1972**	J Marshall	National
1912	T MacKenzie	Liberal	**1972–74**	N Kirk	Labour
1912–25	W F Massey	Reform	**1974–75**	W Rowling	Labour
1925–28	J G Coates	Reform	**1975–84**	R Muldoon	National
1928–30	Joseph Ward	United	**1984–89**	D Lange	Labour
1930–35	G W Forbes	United	**1989–90**	G Palmer	Labour
1935–40	M J Savage	Labour	**1990–97**	J Bolger	National
1940–49	P Fraser	Labour	**1997–**	J Shipley	National
1949–57	S G Holland	National			

UNITED KINGDOM: PRIME MINISTERS FROM 1721

Term	Name	Party	Term	Name	Party
1721–42	Sir Robert Walpole	Whig	**1868**	Benjamin Disraeli	Conservative
1742–43	Earl of Wilmington	Whig	**1868–74**	W E Gladstone	Liberal
1743–54	Henry Pelham	Whig	**1874–80**	Benjamin Disraeli	Conservative
1754–56	Duke of Newcastle	Whig	**1880–85**	W E Gladstone	Liberal
1756–57	Duke of Devonshire	Whig	**1885–86**	Marquess of Salisbury	Conservative
1757–62	Duke of Newcastle	Whig	**1886**	W E Gladstone	Liberal
1762–63	Earl of Bute	Tory	**1886–92**	Marquess of Salisbury	Conservative
1763–65	George Grenville	Whig	**1892–94**	W E Gladstone	Liberal
1765–66	Marquess of Rockingham	Whig	**1894–95**	Earl of Rosebery	Liberal
1767–70	Duke of Grafton	Whig	**1895–1902**	Marquess of Salisbury	Conservative
1770–82	Lord North	Tory	**1902–05**	Arthur James Balfour	Conservative
1782	Marquess of Rockingham	Whig	**1905–08**	Sir H Campbell-Bannerman	Liberal
1782–83	Earl of Shelburne	Whig	**1908–15**	H H Asquith	Liberal
1783	Duke of Portland	coalition	**1915–16**	H H Asquith	coalition
1783–1801	William Pitt the Younger	Tory	**1916–22**	David Lloyd George	coalition
1801–04	Henry Addington	Tory	**1922–23**	Andrew Bonar Law	Conservative
1804–06	William Pitt the Younger	Tory	**1923–24**	Stanley Baldwin	Conservative
1806–07	Lord Grenville	coalition	**1924**	Ramsay MacDonald	Labour
1807–09	Duke of Portland	Tory	**1924–29**	Stanley Baldwin	Conservative
1809–12	Spencer Perceval	Tory	**1929–31**	Ramsay MacDonald	Labour
1812–27	Earl of Liverpool	Tory	**1931–35**	Ramsay MacDonald	national coalition
1827	George Canning	coalition	**1935–37**	Stanley Baldwin	national coalition
1827–28	Viscount Goderich	Tory	**1937–40**	Neville Chamberlain	national coalition
1828–30	Duke of Wellington	Tory	**1940–45**	Sir Winston Churchill	coalition
1830–34	Earl Grey	Tory	**1945–51**	Clement Attlee	Labour
1834	Viscount Melbourne	Whig	**1951–55**	Sir Winston Churchill	Conservative
1834–35	Sir Robert Peel	Whig	**1955–57**	Sir Anthony Eden	Conservative
1835–41	Viscount Melbourne	Whig	**1957–63**	Harold Macmillan	Conservative
1841–46	Sir Robert Peel	Conservative	**1963–64**	Sir Alec Douglas-Home	Conservative
1846–52	Lord Russell	Liberal	**1964–70**	Harold Wilson	Labour
1852	Earl of Derby	Conservative	**1970–74**	Edward Heath	Conservative
1852–55	Lord Aberdeen	Peelite	**1974–76**	Harold Wilson	Labour
1855–58	Viscount Palmerston	Liberal	**1976–79**	James Callaghan	Labour
1858–59	Earl of Derby	Conservative	**1979–90**	Margaret Thatcher	Conservative
1859–65	Viscount Palmerston	Liberal	**1990–97**	John Major	Conservative
1865–66	Lord Russell	Liberal	**1997–**	Tony Blair	Labour
1866–68	Earl of Derby	Conservative			

UNITED KINGDOM: CABINET MINISTERS

Cabinet ministers	Position
Beckett; The Right Honourable Margaret Beckett MP	President of the Council and Leader of the House of Commons
Blair; The Right Honourable Tony Blair MP	Prime Minister, First Lord of the Treasury and Minister for the Civil Service
Blunkett; The Right Honourable David Blunkett MP	Secretary of State for Education and Employment
Brown; The Right Honourable Gordon Brown MP	Chancellor of the Exchequer
Brown; The Right Honourable Nick Brown MP	Minister of Agriculture, Fisheries, and Food
Byers; The Right Honourable Stephen Byers MP	Secretary of State for Trade and Industry
Carter; The Right Honourable The Lord Carter	Captain of the Gentleman-At-Arms (Government Chief Whip, House of Lords)
Cook; The Right Honourable Robin Cook MP	Secretary of State for Foreign and Commonwealth Affairs
Cunningham; The Right Honourable Dr Jack Cunningham MP	Minister for the Cabinet Office
Darling; The Right Honourable Alistair Darling MP	Secretary of State for Social Security
Dewar; The Right Honourable Donald Dewar MP	Secretary of State for Scotland
Dobson; The Right Honourable Frank Dobson MP	Secretary of State for Health
Irvine; The Right Honourable The Lord Irvine of Lairg QC	Lord Chancellor
Jay; The Right Honourable The Baroness Jay of Paddington	Leader of the Lords and Minister for Women
Michael; The Right Honourable Alun Michael MP	Secretary of State for Wales
Milburn; The Right Honourable Alan Milburn MP	Chief Secretary to the Treasury
Mowlam; The Right Honourable Dr Marjorie Mowlam MP	Secretary of State for Northern Ireland
Prescott; The Right Honourable John Prescott MP	Deputy Prime Minister and Secretary of State for the Environment, Transport, and the Regions
Reid; The Right Honourable Dr John Reid MP	Minister of State, Department of the Environment, Transport and the Regions, with responsibility for Transport (non-Cabinet member invited to Cabinet)
Robertson; The Right Honourable George Robertson MP	Secretary of State for Defence
Short; The Right Honourable Clare Short MP	Secretary of State for International Development
Smith; The Right Honourable Chris Smith MP	Secretary of State for Culture, Media, and Sport
Straw; The Right Honourable Jack Straw MP	Secretary of State for the Home Department
Taylor; The Right Honourable Ann Taylor MP	Chief Whip

UNITED STATES: PRESIDENTS AND ELECTIONS

Year elected/ took office	President	Party
1789	1. George Washington	Federalist
1792	re-elected	
1796	2. John Adams	Federalist
1800	3. Thomas Jefferson	Democrat–Republican
1804	re-elected	
1808	4. James Madison	Democrat–Republican
1812	re-elected	
1816	5. James Monroe	Democrat–Republican
1820	re-elected	
1824	6. John Quincy Adams	Democrat–Republican
1828	7. Andrew Jackson	Democrat
1832	re-elected	
1836	8. Martin Van Buren	Democrat
1840	9. William Henry Harrison	Whig
1841	10. John Tyler[1]	Whig
1844	11. James K Polk	Democrat
1848	12. Zachary Taylor	Whig
1850	13. Millard Fillmore[2]	Whig
1852	14. Franklin Pierce	Democrat
1856	15. James Buchanan	Democrat
1860	16. Abraham Lincoln	Republican
1864	re-elected	
1865	17. Andrew Johnson[3]	Democrat
1868	18. Ulysses S Grant	Republican
1872	re-elected	
1876	19. Rutherford B Hayes	Republican
1880	20. James A Garfield	Republican
1881	21. Chester A Arthur[4]	Republican
1884	22. Grover Cleveland	Democrat
1888	23. Benjamin Harrison	Republican
1892	24. Grover Cleveland	Democrat
1896	25. William McKinley	Republican
1900	re-elected	
1901	26. Theodore Roosevelt[5]	Republican
1904	re-elected	
1908	27. William H Taft	Republican
1912	28. Woodrow Wilson	Democrat
1916	re-elected	
1920	29. Warren G Harding	Republican
1923	30. Calvin Coolidge[6]	Republican
1924	re-elected	
1928	31. Herbert Hoover	Republican
1932	32. Franklin D Roosevelt	Democrat
1936	re-elected	
1940	re-elected	
1944	re-elected	
1945	33. Harry S Truman[7]	Democrat
1948	re-elected	
1952	34. Dwight D Eisenhower	Republican
1956	re-elected	
1960	35. John F Kennedy	Democrat
1963	36. Lyndon B Johnson[8]	Democrat
1964	re-elected	
1968	37. Richard M Nixon	Republican
1972	re-elected	
1974	38. Gerald R Ford[9]	Republican
1976	39. Jimmy Carter	Democrat
1980	40. Ronald Reagan	Republican
1984	re-elected	
1988	41. George Bush	Republican
1992	42. Bill Clinton	Democrat
1996	re-elected	

[1]*Became president on death of Harrison*
[2]*Became president on death of Taylor*
[3]*Became president on assassination of Lincoln*
[4]*Became president on assassination of Garfield*
[5]*Became president on assassination of McKinley*
[6]*Became president on death of Harding*
[7]*Became president on death of F D Roosevelt*
[8]*Became president on assassination of Kennedy*
[9]*Became president on resignation of Nixon*

THE WORLD – *Engineering*

BRIDGES: LONGEST BY SPAN

Name	Location	Date	Length (m/ft)
Suspension spans			
Akashi-Kaikyo	Honshu-Awaji Islands, Japan	1998	1,990/6,527
Store Baelt	Zealand-Funen, Denmark	1997	1,600/5,248
Humber Estuary	Hull, England	1973–81	1,410/4,626
Verrazono Narrows	Brooklyn-Staten Island, New York Harbor, USA	1959–64	1,298/4,260
Golden Gate	San Francisco, California, USA	1937	1,280/4,200
Mackinac Straits	Michigan, USA	1957	1,158/3,800
Bosporus	Golden Horn, Istanbul, Turkey	1973	1,074/3,524
George Washington	Hudson River, New York, USA	1927–31	1,067/3,500
Ponte 25 Abril (Salazar)	Tagus River, Lisbon, Portugal	1966	1,013/3,323
Firth of Forth (road)	South Queensferry, Scotland	1958–64	1,006/3,300
Severn River	Beachley, England	1961–66	988/3,240
Cable-stayed spans			
Pont de Normandie	Seine Estuary, France	1995	2,200/7,216
Skarnsundet	Near Trondheim, Norway	1991	530/1,740
Cantilever spans			
Pont de Quebec (railroad)	St Lawrence, Canada	1918	549/1,800
Ravenswood	West Virginia, USA	1981	525/1,723
Firth of Forth (rail)	South Queensferry, Scotland	1882–90	521/1,710
Commodore Barry	Chester, Pennsylvania, USA	1974	494/1,622
Greater New Orleans	Mississippi River, Louisiana, USA	1958	480/1,575
Howrah (railroad)	Hooghly River, Calcutta, India	1936–43	457/1,500
Steel arch spans			
New River Gorge	Fayetteville, West Virginia, USA	1977	518.2/1,700
Bayonne (Killvan Kull)	New Jersey–Staten Island, USA	1932	504/1,652
Sydney Harbour	Sydney, Australia	1923–32	503/1,500

BUILDINGS: TALLEST

Building and location	Year completed	Height m	Height ft	Storeys
Tallest inhabited buildings				
Chongqing Tower, Chongqing, China	1997	460	1,509*	114
Petronas Tower, Kuala Lumpur, Malaysia	1996	452	1,483*	113
Sears Tower, Chicago	1974	443	1,454*	110
World Trade Center, New York	1972–73	417	1,368*	110
Empire State Building, New York	1931	381	1,250*	102
Bank of China, Hong Kong	1989	368	1,209	72
Amoco Building, Chicago	1971	346	1,136	80
John Hancock Center, Chicago	1967	344	1,127	100
Chrysler Building, New York	1930	319	1,046	77
First Interstate World Center, Los Angeles	1989	310	1,017	73
Texas Commerce Tower, Houston	1981	305	1,002	75
Allied Bank Plaza, Houston	1983	302	992	71
Messe Turm Building, Frankfurt	1991	256	841	70
Canary Wharf Tower, London	1990	244	800	56
Tallest structures				
Warszawa Radio Mast**, Konstantynow, Poland	1974	646	2,120	
KTHI-TV Mast, Fargo, North Dakota	1963	629	2,063	
CN Tower, Metro Center, Toronto	1976	555	1,822	

* excluding TV antennas
** collapsed during renovation, Aug 1991

DAMS: HIGHEST

Name	Country	Height above lowest formation m	ft
Rogun*	Tajikistan	335	1,099
Nurek	Tajikistan	300	984
Grand Dixence	Switzerland	285	935
Inguri	Georgia	272	892
Boruca*	Costa Rica	267	875
Chicoasen	Mexico	261	856
Tehri*	India	261	856
Kambaratinsk*	Kyrgyzstan	255	836
Kishau*	India	253	830
Sayano-Shushensk*	Russian Federation	245	804
Guavio	Colombia	243	797
Mica	Canada	242	794
Ertan*	China	240	787
Mauvoisin	Switzerland	237	778
Chivor	Colombia	237	778
Contra	Switzerland	235	772
Mratinje	Yugoslavia	235	772
El Cajon	Honduras	234	768
Chirkey	Russian Federation	233	765
Oroville	USA	230	754
Bekhme*	Iraq	230	754
Bhakra	India	226	741
Hoover	USA	225	738

* under construction

RAILWAY TUNNELS: LONGEST

Tunnel	Location	Date	Length km	mi
Seikan*	Japan	1985	54	33.5
Channel Tunnel	UK–France	1994	50	31
Dai-shimizu	Japan	1979	23	14
Simplon No 1 and 2	Switzerland–Italy	1906, 1922	19	12
Kanmon	Japan	1975	19	12
Apennine	Italy	1934	18	11
Rokko	Japan	1972	16	10
Mt MacDonald	Canada	1989	15	9.1
Gotthard	Switzerland	1882	14	9
Lotschberg	Switzerland	1913	14	9
Hokuriku	Japan	1962	14	9
Mont Canis (Frejus)	France–Italy	1871	13	8
Shin-Shimizu	Japan	1961	13	8
Aki	Japan	1975	13	8
Cascade	USA	1929	13	8
Flathead	USA	1970	13	8
Keijo	Japan	1970	11	7
Lierasen	Norway	1973	11	7
Santa Lucia	Italy	1977	10	6
Arlberg	Austria	1884	10	6
Moffat	USA	1928	10	6
Shimizu	Japan	1931	10	6

* longest sub-aqueous rail

CANALS: LONGEST SHIP CANALS

Canal	Year opened	Route	Length (km/mi)
Baltic to White Sea (formerly Stalin)	1933	canalized river	235/146
Suez*	1869	Red Sea to Mediterranean Sea	166/103
V I Lenin Volga Don	1952	Black Sea to Caspian Sea	100/62.2
Kiel (or North Sea)	1895	North Sea to Baltic Sea	98/61
Houston Ship*	1940	Houston to Gulf of Mexico	91/56.7
Alfonso XIII	1926	Seville to Gulf of Cadiz	85/53
Panama	1914	Pacific Ocean to Caribbean Sea	81/50.5
Manchester Ship	1894	Manchester to Mersey estuary	57/35.5
Welland	1929	Lake Ontario to Lake Erie	45/28
Brussels (Willebroeck)	1922	Brussels to North Sea	32/19.8

*Has no locks.

Natural Features

DESERTS: LARGEST

Desert	Location	Area* sq km	sq mi
Sahara	northern Africa	9,065,000	3,500,000
Gobi	Mongolia/northeastern China	1,295,000	500,000
Patagonian	Argentina	673,000	260,000
Rub al-Khali	southern Arabian peninsula	647,500	250,000
Chihuahuan	Mexico/southwestern USA	362,600	140,000
Taklimakan	northern China	362,600	140,000
Great Sandy	northwestern Australia	338,500	130,000
Great Victoria	southwestern Australia	338,500	130,000
Kalahari	southwestern Africa	260,000	100,000
Kyzyl Kum	Uzbekistan	259,000	100,000
Thar	India/Pakistan	259,000	100,000
Sonoran	Mexico/southwestern USA	181,300	70,000
Simpson	Australia	103,600	40,000
Mojave	southwestern USA	51,800	20,000

*Desert areas are very approximate, because clear physical boundaries may not occur.

MOUNTAINS: HIGHEST (HEIGHTS ARE GIVEN TO THE NEAREST 10M)

Name	Height (m/ft)	Location
Everest	8,850/29,030	China–Nepal
K2	8,610–28,250	Kashmir–Jammu
Kangchenjunga	8,590/28,170	India–Nepal
Lhotse	8,500/27,890	China–Nepal
Kangchenjunga South Peak	8,470/27,800	India–Nepal
Makalu I	8,470/27,800	China–Nepal
Kangchenjunga West Peak	8,420/27,620	India–Nepal
Llotse East Peak	8,380/27,500	China–Nepal
Dhaulagiri	8,170/26,810	Nepal
Cho Oyu	8,150/26,750	China–Nepal
Manaslu	8,130/26,660	Nepal
Nanga Parbat	8,130/26,660	Kashmir–Jammu
Annapurna I	8,080/26,500	Nepal
Gasherbrum I	8,070/26,470	Kashmir–Jammu
Broad-highest	8,050/26,400	Kashmir–Jammu
Gasherbrum II	8,030/26,360	Kashmir–Jammu
Gosainthan	8,010/26,290	China
Broad-middle	8,000/26,250	Kashmir–Jammu
Gasherbrum III	7,950/26,090	Kashmir–Jammu
Annapurna II	7,940/26,040	Nepal
Nanda Devi	7,820/25,660	India
Rakaposhi	7,790/25,560	Kashmir
Kamet	7,760/25,450	India
Ulugh Muztagh	7,720/25,340	Tibet
Tirich Mir	7,690/25,230	Pakistan

RIVERS: LONGEST

River	Location	Approximate length km	mi
Nile	Africa	6,695	4,160
Amazon	South America	6,570	4,083
Chang Jiang (Yangtze)	China	6,300	3,915
Mississipi–Missouri–Red Rock	USA	6,020	3,741
Huang He (Yellow River)	China	5,464	3,395
Ob–Irtysh	China/Kazakhstan/Russia	5,410	3,362
Amur–Shilka	Asia	4,416	2,774
Lena	Russia	4,400	2,734
Congo–Zaïre	Africa	4,374	2,718
Mackenzie–Peace–Finlay	Canada	4,241	2,635
Mekong	Asia	4,180	2,597
Niger	Africa	4,100	2,548
Yenisei	Russia	4,100	2,548
Parana	Brazil	3,943	2,450
Mississippi	USA	3,779	2,348
Murray–Darling	Australia	3,751	2,331
Missouri	USA	3,726	2,315
Volga	Russia	3,685	2,290
Madeira	Brazil	3,241	2,014
Purus	Brazil	3,211	1,995
São Francisco	Brazil	3,199	1,988
Yukon	USA/Canada	3,185	1,979
Rio Grande	USA/Mexico	3,058	1,900
Indus	Tibet/Pakistan	2,897	1,800
Danube	eastern Europe	2,858	1,776
Japura	Brazil	2,816	1,750
Salween	Myanmar/China	2,800	1,740
Brahmaputra	Asia	2,736	1,700
Euphrates	Iraq	2,736	1,700
Tocantins	Brazil	2,699	1,677
Zambezi	Africa	2,650	1,647
Orinoco	Venzuela	2,559	1,590
Paraguay	Paraguay	2,549	1,584
Amu Darya	Tajikistan/Turkmenistan/Uzbekistan	2,540	1,578
Ural	Russia/Kazakhstan	2,535	1,575
Kolyma	Russia	2,513	1,562
Ganges	India/Bangladesh	2,510	1,560
Arkansas	USA	2,344	1,459
Colorado	USA	2,333	1,450
Dnieper	eastern Europe	2,285	1,420
Syr Darya	Asia	2,205	1,370

LAKES: LARGEST

Lake	Location	Area* sq km	sq mi
Caspian Sea	Azerbaijan/Russia/Kazakhstan/Turkmenistan/Iran	370,990	143,239
Superior	USA/Canada	82,071	31,688
Victoria	Tanzania/Kenya/Uganda	69,463	26,820
Aral Sea	Kazakhstan/Uzbekistan	64,500	24,903
Huron	USA/Canada	59,547	22,991
Michigan	USA	57,735	22,291
Tanganyika	Tanzania/Democratic Republic of Congo/Zambia/Burundi	32,880	12,695
Baikal	Russia	31,499	12,162
Great Bear	Canada	31,316	12,091
Malawi	Malawi/Tanzania/Mozambique	28,867	11,146
Great Slave	Canada	28,560	11,027
Erie	USA/Canada	25,657	9,906
Winnipeg	Canada	25,380	9,799
Ontario	USA/Canada	19,010	7,340
Balkhash	Kazakhstan	18,421	7,112
Ladoga	Russia	17,695	6,832
Chad	Chad/Cameroon/Nigeria	16,310	6,297
Maracaibo	Venezuela	13,507	5,215

MAJOR VOLCANOES ACTIVE IN THE 20TH CENTURY, BY REGION

Volcano	Height m	Height ft	Location	Date of last eruption or activity
Africa				
Cameroon	4,096	13,353	isolated mountain, Cameroon	1986
Nyiragongo	3,470	11,385	Virungu, Democratic Republic of Congo	1994
Nyamuragira	3,056	10,028	Democratic Republic of Congo	1994
Ol Doinyo Lengai	2,886	9,469	Tanzania	1993
Lake Nyos	918	3,011	Cameroon	1986
Erta-Ale	503	1,650	Ethiopia	1995
Antarctica				
Erebus	4,023	13,200	Ross Island, McMurdo Sound	1995
Deception Island	576	1,890	South Shetland Isalnd	1970
Asia				
Kerinci	3,800	12,487	Sumatra, Indonesia	1987
Rindjani	3,726	12,224	Lombok, Indonesia	1966
Semeru	3,676	12,060	Java, Indonesia	1995
Slamet	3,428	11,247	Java, Indonesia	1989
Raung	3,322	10,932	Java, Indonesia	1993
Agung	3,142	10,308	Bali, Indonesia	1964
On-Taka	3,063	10,049	Honshu, Japan	1991
Merapi	2,911	9,551	Java, Indonesia	1998
Marapi	2,891	9,485	Sumatra, Indonesia	1993
Asama	2,530	8,300	Honshu, Japan	1990
Nigata Yake-yama	2,475	8,111	Honshu, Japan	1989
Mayon	2,462	8,084	Luzon, Philippines	1993
Canlaon	2,459	8,070	Negros, Philippines	1993
Chokai	2,225	7,300	Honshu, Japan	1974
Galunggung	2,168	7,113	Java, Indonesia	1984
Azuma	2,042	6,700	Honshu, Japan	1977
Sangeang Api	1,935	6,351	Lesser Sunda Island, Indonesia	1988
Pinatubo	1,759	5,770	Luzon, Philippines	1995
Kelut	1,730	5,679	Java, Indonesia	1990
Unzen	1,360	4,462	Japan	1996
Krakatoa	818	2,685	Sumatra, Indonesia	1996
Taal	300	984	Philippines	1977
Atlantic Ocean				
Pico de Teide	3,716	12,192	Tenerife, Canary Islands, Spain	1909
Fogo	2,835	9,300	Cape Verde Islands	1995
Beerenberg	2,277	7,470	Jan Mayen Island, Norway	1985
Hekla	1,491	4,920	Iceland	1991
Krafla	654	2,145	Iceland	1984
Helgafell	215	706	Iceland	1973
Surtsey	174	570	Iceland	1967
Caribbean				
La Grande Soufrière	1,467	4,813	Basse-Terre, Guadeloupe	1977
Pelée	1,397	4,584	Martinique	1932
La Soufrière St Vincent	1,234	4,048	St Vincent and the Grenadines	1979
Soufriere Hills/Chances Peak	968	3,176	Montserrat	1997
Central America				
Acatenango	3,960	12,922	Sierra Madre, Guatemala	1972
Fuego	3,835	12,582	Sierra Madre, Guatemala	1991
Tacana	3,780	12,400	Sierra Madre, Guatemala	1988
Santa Maria	3,768	12,362	Sierra Madre, Guatemala	1993
Irazú	3,452	11,325	Cordillera Central, Costa Rica	1992
Turrialba	3,246	10,650	Cordillera Central, Costa Rica	1992
Póas	2,721	8,930	Cordillera Central, Costa Rica	1994
Pacaya	2,543	8,346	Sierra Madre, Guatemala	1996
San Miguel	2,131	6,994	El Salvador	1986
Arenal	1,552	5,092	Costa Rica	1996
Europe				
Kliuchevskoi	4,750	15,584	Kamchatka Peninsula, Russia	1997
Koryakskaya	3,456	11,339	Kamchatka Peninsula, Russia	1957
Sheveluch	3,283	10,771	Kamchatka Peninsula, Russia	1997
Etna	3,236	10,625	Sicily, Italy	1998
Bezymianny	2,882	9,455	Kamchatka Peninsula, Russia	1997
Alaid	2,335	7,662	Kurile Islands, Russia	1986
Tiatia	1,833	6,013	Kurile Islands, Russia	1981
Sarychev Peak	1,512	4,960	Kurile Islands, Russia	1989
Vesuvius	1,289	4,203	Italy	1944
Stromboli	931	3,055	Lipari Islands, Italy	1996
Santorini (Thera)	584	1,960	Cyclades, Greece	1950
Indian Ocean				
Karthala	2,440	8,000	Comoros	1991
Piton de la Fournaise (Le Volcan)	1,823	5,981	Réunion Island, France	1998
Mid-Pacific				
Mauna Loa	4,170	13,681	Hawaii, USA	1984
Kilauea	1,247	4,100	Hawaii, USA	1998
North America				
Popocatépetl	5,452	17,887	Altiplano de México, Mexico	1997
Colima	4,268	14,003	Altiplano de México, Mexico	1994
Spurr	3,374	11,070	Alaska Range (AK), USA	1953
Lassen Peak	3,186	10,453	California, USA	1921
Redoubt	3,108	10,197	Alaska Range (AK), USA	1991
Iliamna	3,052	10,016	Alaska Range (AK), USA	1978
Shishaldin	2,861	9,387	Aleutian Islands (AK), USA	1997
St Helens	2,549	8,364	Washington, USA	1995
Pavlof	2,517	8,261	Alaska Range (AK), ISA	1997
Veniaminof	2,507	8,225	Alaska Range (AK), USA	1995
Novarupta (Katmai)	2,298	7,540	Alaska Range (AK), USA	1931
El Chichon	2,225	7,300	Altiplano de México, Mexico	1982
Makushin	2,036	6,680	Aleutian Islands (AK), USA	1987
Oceania				
Ruapehu	2,796	9,175	New Zealand	1997
Ulawun	2,296	7,532	Papua New Guinea	1993
Ngauruhoe	2,290	7,515	New Zealand	1977
Bagana	1,998	6,558	Papua New Guinea	1993
Manam	1,829	6,000	Papua New Guinea	1997
Lamington	1,780	5,844	Papua New Guinea	1956
Karkar	1,499	4,920	Papua New Guinea	1979
Lopevi	1,450	4,755	Vanuatu	1982
Ambrym	1,340	4,376	Vanuatu	1991
Tarawera	1,149	3,770	New Zealand	1973
Langila	1,093	3,586	Papua New Guinea	1996
Rabaul	688	2,257	Papua New Guinea	1997
Pagan	570	1,870	Mariana Islands	1993
White Island	328	1,075	New Zealand	1995
South America				
San Pedro	6,199	20,325	Andes, Chile	1960
Guallatiri	6,060	19,882	Andes, Chile	1993
Lascar	5,990	19,652	Andes, Chile	1995
San José	5,919	19,405	Andes, Chile	1931
Cotopaxi	5,897	19,347	Andes, Ecuador	1975
Tutupaca	5,844	19,160	Andes, Ecuador	1902
Ubinas	5,710	18,720	Andes, Peru	1969
Tupungatito	5,640	18,504	Andes, Chile	1986
Islunga	5,566	18,250	Andes, Chile	1960
Nevado del Ruiz	5,435	17,820	Andes, Colombia	1992
Tolima	5,249	17,210	Andes, Colombia	1943
Sangay	5,230	17,179	Andes, Ecuador	1996

Population

WORLD'S LARGEST COUNTRIES BY POPULATION

Rank	Country	Population (millions)	% of world population
1996			
1	China	1,232	21.4
2	India	945	16.4
3	USA	269	4.7
4	Indonesia	200	3.5
5	Brazil	161	2.8
6	Russia	148	2.6
7	Pakistan	140	2.4
8	Japan	125	2.2
9	Bangladesh	120	2.1
10	Nigeria	115	2.0
2015			
1	China	1,409	19.3
2	India	1,212	16.6
3	USA	311	4.2
4	Indonesia	252	3.5
5	Pakistan	224	3.1
6	Brazil	200	2.7
7	Nigeria	191	2.6
8	Bangladesh	163	2.2
9	Russia	138	1.9
10	Japan	126	1.7
2050			
1	India	1,533	16.4
2	China	1,516	16.2
3	Pakistan	357	3.8
4	USA	348	3.7
5	Nigeria	338	3.6
6	Indonesia	318	3.4
7	Brazil	243	2.6
8	Bangladesh	218	2.3
9	Ethiopia	213	2.3
10	Iran	170	1.8

HIGHEST AND LOWEST LIFE EXPECTANCIES

Nation	Men	Women	Average
Highest			
Liechtenstein	78	83	81
Japan	76	82	79
Switzerland	74	82	78
Australia	75	80	78
Netherlands	74	81	78
Sweden	74	81	78
Iceland	74	80	77
Spain	74	80	77
Italy	73	80	77
Jamaica	75	78	77
Norway	73	80	77
Canada	72	79	76
USA	72	79	76
Lowest			
Ethiopia	38	38	38
Guinea	39	42	41
Afghanistan	43	41	42
Gambia	42	42	42
Guinea-Bissau	42	42	42
Angola	40	44	42
Central African Republic	41	45	43
Bhutan	44	43	44
Cambodia	42	45	44
Chad	42	45	44
Sierra Leone	41	47	44
Benin	42	46	44
Burkina Faso	44	47	46
Mali	44	47	46
Mauritania	43	48	46
Equatorial Guinea	44	48	46

Where separate figures are given for male and female life expectancy, the ranking is based on a simple average of the two.

WORLD'S LARGEST CITIES 1950–2015

Rank	City	Population (millions)	Rank	City	Population (millions)	Rank	City	Population (millions)
1995			**2000**			**2015**		
1	Tokyo, Japan	26.84	1	Tokyo, Japan	27.90	1	Tokyo, Japan	28.70
2	Saõ Paulo, Brazil	16.42	2	Bombay, India	18.10	2	Bombay, India	27.40
3	New York (NY), USA	16.33	3	Saõ Paulo, Brazil	17.80	3	Lagos, Nigeria	24.40
4	Mexico City, Mexico	15.64	4	Shanghai, China	17.20	4	Shanghai, China	23.40
5	Bombay, India	15.09	5	New York (NY), USA	16.60	5	Jakarta, Indonesia	21.20
6	Shanghai, China	15.08	6	Mexico City, Mexico	16.40	6	Saõ Paulo, Brazil	20.80
7	Los Angeles (CA), USA	12.41	7	Beijing, China	14.20	7	Karachi, Pakistan	20.60
8	Beijing, China	12.36	8	Jakarta, Indonesia	14.10	8	Beijing, China	19.40
9	Calcutta, India	11.67	9	Lagos, Nigeria	13.50	9	Dhaka, Bangladesh	19.00
10	Seoul, South Korea	11.64	10	Los Angeles (CA), USA	13.10	10	Mexico City, Mexico	18.80

HIGHEST AND LOWEST POPULATION DENSITIES

Country	Population per sq km
Highest Density	
Monaco	32,097
Singapore	5,476
Vatican City State	2,273
Malta	1,168
Maldives	884
Bahrain	840
Bangladesh	834
Barbados	608
Taiwan	589
Mauritius	553
Lowest Density	
Namibia	2
Mongolia	2
Mauritania	2
Australia	2
Suriname	3
Libya	3
Iceland	3
Canada	3
Botswana	3
Guyana	4
Gabon	4

WORLD'S LARGEST COUNTRIES BY AREA

Country	Area sq km	sq mi
Russia	17,075,400	6,592,811
Canada	9,970,610	3,849,652
China	9,572,900	3,695,942
United States	9,372,615	3,618,766
Brazil	8,511,965	3,286,469
Australia	7,682,300	2,966,136
India	3,166,829	1,222,713
Argentina	2,780,092	1,073,393
Kazakhstan	2,717,300	1,049,150
Sudan	2,505,800	967,489
Algeria	2,381,741	919,590
Congo, Democratic Republic of	2,344,900	905,366
Saudi Arabia	2,200,518	849,620
Mexico	1,958,201	756,061
Indonesia	1,904,569	735,354
Libya	1,759,540	679,358
Iran	1,648,000	636,292
Mongolia	1,565,000	604,246
Peru	1,285,200	496,216
Chad	1,284,000	495,752

Money: WORLD CURRENCIES

Country	Currency
Afghanistan	afgháni
Albania	lek
Algeria	dinar
Andorra	French franc Spanish peseta
Angola	kwanza
Antigua	East Caribbean dollar
Argentina	peso
Aruba	florin
Australia	Australian dollar
Austria	schilling
Azores	port escudo
Bahamas	Bahamian dollar
Bahrain	dinar
Balearic Islands	Spanish peseta
Bangladesh	taka
Barbados	Barbados dollar
Belgium	Belgian franc
Belize	Belize dollar
Benin	CFA franc
Bermuda	Bermudian dollar
Bhutan	ngultrum
Bolivia	boliviano
Botswana	pula
Bouvet Island	Norwegian krone
Brazil	real
Brunei	Brunei dollar
Bulgaria	lev
Burkina Faso	CFA franc
Burundi	Burundi franc
Cambodia	riel
Cameroon	CFA franc
Canada	Canadian dollar
Canary Islands	Spanish peseta
Cape Verde	Cape Verde escudo
Cayman Islands	Cayman Island dollar
Central African Republic	CFA franc
Chad	CFA franc
Chile	Chilean peso
China	Renminbi yuan
Colombia	Colombian peso
Commonwealth of	rouble
Independent States	rouble
Comoros	CFA franc
Congo, Democratic Republic of	zaire
Congo, Republic of	CFA franc
Costa Rica	colón
Côte d'Ivoire	CFA franc
Cuba	Cuban peso
Cyprus	Cyprus pound
Czech Republic	koruna
Denmark	Danish krone
Djibouti Republic	Djibouti franc
Dominica	East Caribbean dollar
Dominican Republic	Dominican peso
Ecuador	sucre
Egypt	Egyptian pound
El Salvador	colón
Equatorial Guinea	CFA franc
Estonia	kroon
Ethiopia	birr
Falkland Islands	Falkland pound
Faroe Islands	Danish krone
Fiji Islands	Fiji dollar
Finland	markka
France	French franc
French Guiana	French franc
French Pacific Islands	CFP franc
Gabon	CFA franc
Gambia	dalasi
Germany	Deutschmark
Ghana	cedi
Gibraltar	Gibraltar pound
Greece	drachma
Greenland	Danish krone
Grenada	East Caribbean dollar
Guadaloupe	local franc
Guam	US dollar
Guatemala	quetzal
Guinea	Guinea franc
Guinea-Bissau	Guinea-Bissau peso
Guyana	Guyanese dollar
Haiti	goude
Honduras	lempira
Hong Kong	Hong Kong dollar
Hungary	forint
Iceland	Icelandic krona
India	Indian rupee
Indonesia	rupiah
Iran	Iranian rial
Iraq	Iraqi dinar
Irish Republic	punt
Israel	shekel
Italy	Italian lira
Jamaica	Jamaican dollar
Japan	yen
Jordan	Jordanian dinar
Kenya	Kenyan shilling
Kiribati	Australian dollar
Korea, North	won
Korea, South	won
Kuwait	Kuwaiti dinar
Laos	new kip
Latvia	latis
Lebanon	Lebanese pound
Lesotho	maluti
Liberia	Liberian dollar
Libya	Libyan dinar
Liechtenstein	Swiss franc
Lithuania	Lita
Luxembourg	Luxembourg franc
Macao	pataca
Madagascar	Malagasy franc
Madeira	Portuguese escudo
Malawi	kwacha
Malaysia	ringgit
Maldive Islands	rufiya
Mali Republic	CFA franc
Malta	Maltese lira
Martinique	local franc
Mauritania	ouguiya
Mauritius	Mauritian rupee
Mexico	Mexican peso
Monaco	French franc
Mongolia	tugrik
Montserrat	East Caribbean dollar
Morocco	dirham
Mozambique	metical
Myanmar	kyat
Namibia	South African Rand
Nauru Island	Australian dollar
Nepal	Nepalese rupee
Netherlands	guilder
Netherland Antilles	Antillian guilder
New Zealand	New Zealand dollar
Nicaragua	gold cordoba
Niger Republic	CFA franc
Nigeria	naira
Norway	Norwegian krone
Oman	Omani rial
Pakistan	Pakistani rupee
Panama	balboa
Papua New Guinea	kina
Paraguay	guaraní
Peru	new sol
Philippines	peso
Pitcairn Islands	New Zealand dollar
Poland	zloty
Portugal	escudo
Puerto Rico	US dollar
Qatar	riyal
Réunion Islands	French franc
Romania	leu
Rwanda	Rwandan franc
St Christopher	East Caribbean dollar
St Helena	pound sterling
St Lucia	East Caribbean dollar
St Pierre	French franc
St Vincent	East Caribbean dollar
Samoa	tala
San Marino	Italian lira
São Tomé e Principe	dobra
Saudi Arabia	riyal
Senegal	CFA franc
Seychelles	Seychelles rupee
Sierra Leone	leone
Singapore	Singapore dollar
Slovak Republic	koruna
Slovenia	tolar
Solomon Islands	Solomon Island dollar
Somali Republic	Somali shilling
South Africa	rand
Spain	peseta
Sri Lanka	Srin Lankan rupee
Sudan Republic	Sudanese dinar
Surinam	Surinam guilder
Swaziland	lilangeni
Sweden	krona
Switzerland	Swiss franc
Syria	Syrian pound
Taiwan	New Taiwan dollar
Tanzania	Tanzanian shilling
Thailand	baht
Togo Republic	CFA franc
Tonga Islands	pa'anga
Trinidad and Tobago	Trinidad and Tobago dollar
Tunisia	Tunisian dinar
Turkey	Turkish lira
Turks and Caicos Islands	US dollar
Tuvalu	Australian dollar
Uganda	new shilling
Ukraine	karbovanets
United Arab Emirates	UAE dirham
United Kingdom	pound sterling
United States	US dollar
Uruguay	nuevo peso
Vanuatu	vatu
Vatican City State	lira
Venezuela	bolivar
Vietnam	dong
Virgin Islands, British	US dollar
Virgin Islands, US	US dollar
Yemen, Republic of	rial
Zambia	kwacha
Zimbabwe	Zimbabwe dollar

TIME ZONES AND RELATIVE TIMES IN CITIES THROUGHOUT THE WORLD

The surface of the Earth is divided into 24 time zones. Each zone represents 15° of longitude or 1 hour of time. Countries to the east of London and the Greenwich meridian are ahead of Greenwich Mean Time (GMT) and countries to the west are behind. The time indicated in the table below is fixed by law and is called standard time. Use of daylight saving time (such as British Summer Time) varies widely. At 12.00 noon, GMT, the standard time elsewhere around the world is as follows:

City	Time	City	Time
Abu Dhabi, United Arab Emirates	16:00	Lagos, Nigeria	13:00
Accra, Ghana	12:00	Le Havre, France	13:00
Addis Ababa, Ethiopia	15:00	Lima, Peru	07:00
Adelaide, Australia	21:30	Lisbon, Portugal	12:00
Alexandria, Egypt	14:00	London, England	12:00
Algiers, Algeria	13:00	Luanda, Angola	13:00
Al Manamah (also called Bahrain), Bahrain	15:00	Luxembourg, Luxembourg	13:00
Amman, Jordan	14:00	Lyon, France	13:00
Amsterdam, The Netherlands	13:00	Madras, India	17:30
Anchorage (AK), USA	02:00	Madrid, Spain	13:00
Ankara, Turkey	14:00	Manila, Philippines	20:00
Athens, Greece	14:00	Marseilles, France	13:00
Auckland, New Zealand	24:00	Mecca, Saudi Arabia	15:00
Baghdad, Iraq	15:00	Melbourne, Australia	22:00
Bahrain	15:00	Mexico City, Mexico	06:00
Bangkok, Thailand	19:00	Milan, Italy	13:00
Barcelona, Spain	13:00	Minsk, Belarus	15:00
Beijing, China	20:00	Monrovia, Liberia	11:00
Beirut, Lebanon	14:00	Montevideo, Uruguay	09:00
Belgrade, Yugoslavia	13:00	Montreal, Canada	07:00
Berlin, Germany	13:00	Moscow, Russia	15:00
Berne, Switzerland	13:00	Munich, Germany	13:00
Bogota, Colombia	07:00	Nairobi, Kenya	15:00
Bombay, India	17:30	New Orleans (LA), USA	06:00
Bonn, Switzerland	13:00	New York (NY), USA	07:00
Brazzaville, Republic of the Congo	13:00	Nicosia, Cyprus	14:00
Brisbane, Australia	22:00	Oslo, Norway	13:00
Brussels, Belgium	13:00	Ottawa, Canada	07:00
Bucharest, Romania	14:00	Panama City, Panama	07:00
Budapest, Hungary	13:00	Paris, France	13:00
Buenos Aires, Argentina	09:00	Perth, Australia	20:00
Cairo, Egypt	14:00	Port Said, Egypt	14:00
Calcutta, India	17:30	Prague, Czech Republic	13:00
Canberra, Australia	22:00	Rangoon, Myanmar	18:30
Cape Town, South Africa	14:00	Rawalpindi, Pakistan	17:00
Caracas, Venezuela	08:00	Reykjavik, Iceland	12:00
Casablanca, Morocco	12:00	Rio de Janeiro, Brazil	09:00
Chicago (IL), USA	06:00	Riyadh, Saudi Arabia	15:00
Cologne, Germany	13:00	Rome, Italy	13:00
Colombo, Sri Lanka	17:30	San Francisco (CA), USA	04:00
Copenhagen, Denmark	13:00	Santiago, Chile	08:00
Damascus, Syria	14:00	Seoul, South Korea	21:00
Dar es Salaam, Tanzania	15:00	Shanghai, China	20:00
Darwin, Australia	21:30	Singapore City, Singapore	20:00
Delhi, India	17:30	Sofia, Bulgaria	14:00
Denver (CO), USA	05:00	St Petersburg, Russia	15:00
Dhaka, Bangladesh	18:00	Stockholm, Sweden	13:00
Dubai, United Arab Emirates	16:00	Sydney, Australia	22:00
Dublin, Republic of Ireland	12:00	Taipei, China	20:00
Florence, Italy	13:00	Tashkent, Uzbekistan	18:00
Frankfurt, Germany	13:00	Tehran, Iran	15:30
Gdansk, Poland	13:00	Tel Aviv, Israel	14:00
Geneva, Switzerland	13:00	Tenerife, Canary Islands	12:00
Gibraltar	13:00	Tokyo, Japan	21:00
Hague, the, The Netherlands	13:00	Toronto, Canada	07:00
Harare, Zimbabwe	14:00	Tripoli, Libya	13:00
Havana, Cuba	07:00	Tunis, Tunisia	13:00
Helsinki, Finland	14:00	Valparaiso, Chile	08:00
Hobart, Australia	22:00	Vancouver, Canada	04:00
Ho Chi Minh City, Vietnam	19:00	Vatican City	13:00
Hong Kong, China	20:00	Venice, Italy	13:00
Istanbul, Turkey	14:00	Vienna, Austria	13:00
Jakarta, Indonesia	19:00	Vladivostok, Russia	22:00
Jerusalem, Israel	14:00	Volgograd, Russia	16:00
Johannesburg, South Africa	14:00	Warsaw, Poland	13:00
Karachi, Pakistan	17:00	Wellington, New Zealand	24:00
Kiev, Ukraine	15:00	Yokohama, Japan	06:00
Kuala Lumpur, Malaysia	20:00	Zagreb, Yugoslavia	13:00
Kuwait City, Kuwait	15:00	Zurich, Switzerland	13:00
Kyoto, Japan	21:00		

THE WORLD: PHYSICAL

NORTH AMERICA
SOUTH AMERICA
PACIFIC OCEAN
ATLANTIC OCEAN
ROCKY MOUNTAINS
ANDES
Beaufort Sea
Victoria Island
Baffin Island
Baffin Bay
Greenland
Iceland
British Isles
Arctic Circle
Bering Strait
Yukon
Mt McKinley 6194
Bering Sea
Gulf of Alaska
Aleutian Islands
Queen Charlotte Islands
Vancouver Island
Coast Mts
Great Bear Lake
Great Slave Lake
Hudson Bay
Davis Strait
Denmark Strait
Labrador
Canadian Shield
Newfoundland
L. Winnipeg
Missouri
Great Plains
L. Superior
L. Michigan
L. Huron
L. Ontario
L. Erie
St Lawrence
Cascade Range
Mt Elbert 4399
Arkansas
Colorado
Ohio
Appalachian Mts
Mississippi
Mt Whitney 4418
Rio Grande
Azores
Madeira
Canary Islands
Bermuda
Hawaiian Islands
Tropic of Cancer
Sierra Madre
Gulf of Mexico
Bahamas
Citlaltépetl 5896
Popocatépetl 5340
Yucatán
Cuba
Hispaniola
Greater Antilles
Caribbean Sea
Lesser Antilles
Cape Verde Islands
Panama Canal
L. Maracaibo
Orinoco
Trinidad
Llanos
Guiana Highlands
Mt Roraima 2810
Equator
Polynesia
Line Islands
Galapagos Is.
Cotopaxi 5896
Chimborazo 6310
Amazon
Amazon Basin
Phoenix Islands
Marquesas Is.
Huascarán 6768
Mato Grosso Plateau
Tocantins
Samoan Is.
Tuamotu Is.
Cook Islands
Atacama Desert
Titicaca
Gran Chaco
Paraguay
Paraná
Brazilian Highlands
St Helena
Tropic of Capricorn
Pitcairn Is.
Easter Island
Juan Fernández Is.
Aconcagua 6960
Pampas
Rio de la Plata
Patagonia
Falkland Is.
Tierra del Fuego
Cape Horn
South Georgia
Drake Passage
Antarctic Circle
Antarctic Peninsula
Weddell Sea
120°W
60°W